GW00670119

The Form Book ®

Flat Annual for 2010

Including all the 2009 returns

The BHA's Official Record

Complete record of Flat Racing
from 1 January to 31 December 2009

Associated Raceform products

The Form Book, is updated weekly. Subscribers receive a binder, together with all the early racing. Weekly sections and a new index are threaded into the binder to keep it up to date.

The data contained in The Form Book Flat Annual for 2010 is available in paper form or on computer disk. The disk service, Raceform Interactive, contains the same data as Raceform, The Form Book, and operates on any PC within a 'Windows' environment. The database is designed to allow access to the information in a number of different ways, and is extremely quick and easy to use.

Published in 2010 by Raceform Ltd
Compton, Newbury, Berkshire, RG20 6NL

A catalogue record for this book is available from the British Library,

ISBN 978-1-906820-22-0

Printed in the UK by CPI William Clowes Beccles NR34 7TL

Full details of all Raceform services and publications are available from:

Raceform Ltd, Compton, Newbury, Berkshire RG20 6NL
Tel: 01635 578080 • Fax: 01635 578101
Email: rfsubscription@racingpost.co.uk
www.racingpost.com

Cover photo: Sea The Stars (Mick Kinane) winning the Coral-Eclipse Stakes at Sandown from Rip Van Winkle (Johnny Murtagh).
© Edward Whitaker/Racing Post

CONTENTS

Editor: Graham Dench

Head of Analysis Team: Ashley Rumney

Race Analysts & Notebook Writers:
Gavin Beech, Dave Bellingham, Mark Brown, Steffan Edwards, Walter Glynn, Jeremy Grayson, Niall Hannity, David Lawrence, Richard Lowther, Lee McKenzie, Simon Milham, Dave Moon, Graeme North. Sandra Noble, David Orton, Ashley Rumney, Anthony Rushmer, Desmond Stoneham, David Toft, Ron Wood, Richard Young.

Production: Ashley Rumney & Richard Lowther

The Official Scale of Weight, Age & Distance (Flat)

The following scale should only be used in conjunction with the Official ratings published in this book. Use of any other scale will introduce errors into calculations. The allowances are expressed as the number of pounds that is deemed the average horse in each group falls short of maturity at different dates and distances.

Dist		Jan		Feb		Mar		Apr		May		Jun		Jul		Aug		Sep		Oct		Nov		Dec	
(fur)	Age	1-15	16-31	1-14	15-28	1-15	16-31	1-15	16-30	1-15	16-31	1-15	16-30	1-15	16-31	1-15	16-31	1-15	16-30	1-15	16-31	1-15	16-30	1-15	16-31
5	2	-	-	-	-	-	47	44	41	38	36	34	32	30	28	26	24	22	20	19	18	17	17	16	16
	3	15	15	14	14	13	12	11	10	9	8	7	6	5	4	3	2	1	1	-	-	-	-	-	-
6	2	-	-	-	-	-	-	-	-	44	41	38	36	33	31	28	26	24	22	21	20	19	18	17	17
	3	16	16	15	15	14	13	12	11	10	9	8	7	6	5	4	3	2	2	1	1	-	-	-	-
7	2	-	-	-	-	-	-	-	-	-	-	-	-	38	35	32	30	27	25	23	22	21	20	19	19
	3	18	18	17	17	16	15	14	13	12	11	10	9	8	7	6	5	4	3	2	2	1	1	-	-
8	2	-	-	-	-	-	-	-	-	-	-	-	-	-	-	37	34	31	28	26	24	23	22	21	20
	3	20	20	19	19	18	17	15	14	13	12	11	10	9	8	7	6	5	4	3	3	2	2	1	1
9	3	22	22	21	21	20	19	17	15	14	13	12	11	10	9	8	7	6	5	4	4	3	3	2	2
	4	1	1	-	-	-	-	-	-	-	-	-	-	-	-	-	-	-	-	-	-	-	-	-	-
10	3	23	23	22	22	21	20	19	17	15	14	13	12	11	10	9	8	7	6	5	5	4	4	3	3
	4	2	2	1	1	-	-	-	-	-	-	-	-	-	-	-	-	-	-	-	-	-	-	-	-
11	3	24	24	23	23	22	21	20	19	17	15	14	13	12	11	10	9	8	7	6	6	5	5	4	4
	4	3	3	2	2	1	1	-	-	-	-	-	-	-	-	-	-	-	-	-	-	-	-	-	-
12	3	25	25	24	24	23	22	21	20	19	17	15	14	13	12	11	10	9	8	7	7	6	6	5	5
	4	4	4	3	3	2	2	1	1	-	-	-	-	-	-	-	-	-	-	-	-	-	-	-	-
13	3	26	26	25	25	24	23	22	21	20	19	17	15	14	13	12	11	10	9	8	8	7	7	6	6
	4	5	5	4	4	3	3	2	1	-	-	-	-	-	-	-	-	-	-	-	-	-	-	-	-
14	3	27	27	26	26	25	24	23	22	21	20	19	17	15	14	13	12	11	10	9	9	8	8	7	7
	4	6	6	5	5	4	4	3	2	1	-	-	-	-	-	-	-	-	-	-	-	-	-	-	-
15	3	28	28	27	27	26	25	24	23	22	21	20	19	17	15	14	13	12	11	10	9	8	8	7	7
	4	6	6	5	5	4	4	3	3	2	1	-	-	-	-	-	-	-	-	-	-	-	-	-	-
16	3	29	29	28	28	27	26	25	24	23	22	21	20	19	17	15	14	13	12	11	10	9	9	8	8
	4	7	7	6	6	5	5	4	4	3	2	1	-	-	-	-	-	-	-	-	-	-	-	-	-
18	3	31	31	30	30	29	28	27	26	25	24	23	22	21	20	18	16	14	13	12	11	10	10	9	9
	4	8	8	7	7	6	6	5	5	4	3	2	1	-	-	-	-	-	-	-	-	-	-	-	-
20	3	33	33	32	32	31	30	29	28	27	26	25	24	23	22	20	18	16	14	13	12	11	11	10	10
	4	9	9	8	8	7	7	6	6	5	4	3	2	1	-	-	-	-	-	-	-	-	-	-	-

The Form Book

Flat Racing Annual for 2010

Welcome to the 2010 edition of *The Form Book,* comprising the complete year's results from 2009.

Race details contain Racing Post Ratings assessing the merit of each individual performance, speed figures for every horse that clocks a worthwhile time, weight-for-age allowances, stall positions for every race and the starting price percentage, in addition to the traditional features.

Race Focus comments are printed below each race along with official explanations and notebook comments for all British races of Class 3 and above, all two-year-old races and foreign races. The comments provide an analysis of the winning performance and, where applicable, explain possible reasons for improvement or attempt to explain why any horse failed to run to its best. More importantly, our team will also indicate the conditions under which horses are likely to be seen to best advantage.

The official record

THE FORM BOOK records comprehensive race details of every domestic race, every major European Group race and every foreign event in which a British-trained runner participated. In the **NOTEBOOK** section, extended interpretation is provided for all runners worthy of a mention, including all placed horses and all favourites. Generally speaking, the higher the class of race, the greater the number of runners noted.

MEETING BACK REFERENCE NUMBER is the Raceform number of the last meeting run at the track and is shown to the left of the course name. Abandoned meetings are signified by a dagger.

THE GOING, The Official going, shown at the head of each meeting, is recorded as follows: Turf: Hard; Firm; Good to firm; Good; Good to soft; Soft; Heavy. All-Weather: Fast; Standard to fast; Standard; Standard to slow; Slow. There may be variations for non-British meetings

Where appropriate, a note is included indicating track bias and any differences to the official going indicated by race times.

THE WEATHER is shown below to th e date for selected meetings.

THE WIND is given as a strength and direction at the Winning Post, classified as follows:
Strength: gale; v.str; str; fresh; mod; slt; almost nil; nil.
Direction: (half) against; (half) bhd; (half) across from or towards stands.

VISIBILITY is good unless otherwise stated.

RACE NUMBERS for Foreign races carry the suffix 'a' in the race header and in the index.

RACE TITLE is the name of the race as shown in the Racing Calendar.

COMPETITIVE RACING CLASSIFICATIONS are shown on a scale from Class 1 to Class 7. All Pattern races are Class 1.

THE RACE DISTANCE is given for all races, and is accompanied by (s) for races run on straight courses and (r) for courses where there is a round track of comparable distance. On All-Weather courses (F) for Fibresand or (P) for Polytrack indicates the nature of the artificial surface on which the race is run.

OFFICIAL RACE TIME as published in the Racing Calendar is followed in parentheses by the time when the race actually started. This is followed by the race class, age restrictions, handicap restrictions and the official rating of the top weight.

PRIZE MONEY shows penalty values down to sixth place (where applicable).

THE POSITION OF THE STARTING STALLS is shown against each race, in the form of: High (H), Centre (C) or Low (L). If one stands at the start facing towards the finish, the stalls are numbered from left to right. If the stalls are placed adjacent to the left rail they are described as low, if against the right rail they are described as high. Otherwise they are central.

IN THE RACE RESULT, the figures to the far left of each horse (under FORM) show the most recent form figures. The figure in bold is the finishing position in this race as detailed below.

1...40 - finishing positions first to fortieth; **b** - brought down; **c** - carried out; **f** - fell; **p** - pulled up; **r** - refused; **ro** - ran out; **s** - slipped up; **u** - unseated rider; **v** - void race.

THE OFFICIAL DISTANCES between the horses are shown on the left-hand side immediately after their position at the finish.

NUMBER OF DAYS SINCE PREVIOUS RUN is the superscript figure immediately following the horse name and suffix.

PREVIOUS RACEFORM RACE NUMBER is the boxed figure to the right of the horse's name.

THE HORSE'S AGE is shown immediately before the weight carried.

WEIGHTS shown are actual weights carried.

OFFICIAL RATING is the figure in bold type directly after the horse's name in the race result. This figure indicates the Official BHB rating, at entry, after the following adjustments had been made:
(i) Overweight carried by the rider.
(ii) The number of pounds out of the handicap (if applicable).
(iii) Penalties incurred after the publication of the weights.
However, no adjustments have been made for:
(i) Weight-for-age.
(ii) Riders' claims.

HEADGEAR is shown immediately befoe the jockey's name and in parentheses and expressed as: **b** (blinkers); **v** (visor); **h** (hood); **e** (eyeshield); **c** (eyecover); **p** (sheepskin cheekpieces).

THE JOCKEY is shown for every runner followed, in superscript, by apprentice allowances in parentheses.

APPRENTICE ALLOWANCES The holders of apprentice jockeys' licences under the provisions of Rule 60(iii) are permitted to claim the following allowances in Flat races:
7lb until they have won 20 Flat races run under the Rules of any recognised Turf Authority; thereafter 5lb until they have won 50 such Flat races; thereafter 3lb until they have won 95 such Flat races. These allowances can be claimed in the Flat races set out below, with the exception of races confined to apprentice jockeys:
(a) All handicap handicaps other than those Rated stakes which are classified as listed races.
(b) All selling and claiming races.
(b) All weight-for-age races classified 3, 4, 5, 6 and 7.

THE DRAW for places at the start is shown after each jockey's name.

RACING POST RATINGS, which record the level of performance attained in this race for each horse, appear in the end column after each horse. These are the work of handicappers Simon Turner, Sam Walker and Paul Curtis, who head a dedicated team dealing with Flat races for Raceform and sister publication, the *Racing Post*.

THE TRAINER is shown for every runner.

COMMENT-IN-RUNNING is shown for each horse in an abbreviated form. Details of abbreviations appear later in this section.

STARTING PRICES appear below the jockey in the race result. The favourite indicator appears to the right of the Starting Price; 1 for the favourite, 2 for the second-favourite and 3 for third-favourite. Joint favourites share the same number.

RACE TIMES in Great Britain are official times which are electronically recorded and shown to 100th of a second. Figures in parentheses following the time show the number of seconds faster or slower than the Raceform Median Time for the course and distance.

RACEFORM MEDIAN TIMES are compiled from all races run over the course and distance in the preceding five years. Times equal to the median are shown as (0.00). Times under the median are preceded by minus, for instance, 1.8 seconds under the median would be shown (-1.8). Record times are displayed either referring to the juvenile record (1.2 under 2y best) or to the overall record (1.2 under best).

GOING CORRECTION appears against each race to allow for changing conditions of the ground. It is shown to a hundredth of a second and indicates the adjustment per furlong against the median time. The going based on the going correction is shown in parentheses and is recorded in the following stages:
Turf: HD (Hard); F (Firm); GF (Good to firm); G (Good); GS (Good to soft); S (Soft); HVY (Heavy). All-Weather: FST (Fast); SF (Standard to fast); STD (Standard); SS (Standard to slow); SLW (Slow)

WEIGHT-FOR-AGE allowances are given where applicable for mixed-age races.

STARTING PRICE PERCENTAGE follows the going correction and weight-for-age details, and gives the total SP percentage of all runners that competed. It precedes the number of runners taking part in the race.

SELLING DETAILS (where applicable) and details of any claim are given. Friendly claims are not detailed.

SPEED RATINGS appear below the race time and going correction. They are the work of time expert Dave Bellingham and differ from conventional ratings systems in that they are an expression of a horse's ability in terms of lengths-per-mile, as opposed to pounds in weight. They are not directly comparable with BHB and Racing Post ratings.

The ratings take no account of the effect of weight, either historically or on the day, and this component is left completely to the user's discretion. What is shown is a speed rating represented in its purest form, rather than one that has been altered for weight using a mathematical formula that treats all types of horses as if they were the same.

A comparison of the rating achieved with the 'par' figure for the grade of race - the rating that should be achievable by an average winner in that class of race- will both provide an at-a-glance indication of whether or not a race was truly run and also highlight the value of the form from a time perspective.

In theory, if a horse has a best speed figure five points superior to another and both run to their best form in a race over a mile, the first horse should beat the second by five lengths. In a race run over two miles, the margin should be ten lengths and so on.

Before the speed figures can be calculated, it is necessary to establish a set of standard or median times for every distance at every track, and this is done by averaging the times of all winners over a particular trip going back several years. No speed ratings are produced when insufficient races have been run over a distance for a reliable median time to be calculated.

Once a meeting has taken place, a raw unadjusted speed rating is calculated for each winner by calculating how many lengths per mile the winning time was faster or slower than the median for the trip. A difference of 0.2 of a second equals one length. The raw speed ratings of all winners on the card are then compared to the 'par' figure for the class of race. The difference between the 'raw' speed rating and the 'par' figure for each race is then noted, and both the fastest and slowest races are discarded before the rest are averaged to produce the going allowance or track variant. This figure gives an idea as to how much the elements, of which the going is one, have affected the final times of each race.

The figure representing the going allowance is then used to adjust the raw speed figures and produce the final ratings, which represent how fast the winners would have run on a perfectly good surface with no external influences, including the weather. The ratings for beaten horses are worked out by taking the number of lengths they were behind the winner, adjusting that to take into account the distance of the race, and deducting that figure from the winner's rating. The reader is left with a rating which provides an instant impression of the value of a time performance.

The speed 'pars' below act as benchmark with which to compare the speed figures earned by each horse in each race. A horse that has already exceeded the 'par' for the class he is about to run in, is of special interest, especially if he has done it more than once, as are horses that have consistently earned higher figures than their rivals.

Class 1 Group One	117
Class 1 Group Two	115
Class 1 Group Three	113
Class 1 Listed	111
Class 2	109
Class 3	107
Class 4	105
Class 5	103
Class 6	101
Class 7	97

Allowances need to be made for younger horses and for fillies. These allowances are as follows.

MONTH	2yo	3yo
Jan / Feb	n/a	-6
Mar / Apr	-11	-5
May / Jun	-10	-4
Jul / Aug	-9	-3
Sep / Oct	-8	-2
Nov / Dec	-7	-1
Races contested by fillies only		-3

Allowances are cumulative. For example, using a combination of the above pars and allowances, the par figure for the Epsom Oaks would be 110. The Group One par is 117, then deduct 4 because the race is confined to three year olds and run in June, then subtract another 3 because the race is confined to fillies.

TOTE prices include £1 stake. Exacta dividends are shown in parentheses. The Computer Straight Forecast dividend is preceded by the letters CSF, Computer Tricast is preceded by CT and Tote Trio dividend is preceded by the word Trio. Jackpot, Placepot and Quadpot details appear at the end of the meeting to which they refer.

OWNER is followed by the breeder's name and the trainer's location.

STEWARDS' ENQUIRIES are included with the result, and any suspensions and/or fines incurred. Objections by jockeys and officials are included, where relevant.

HISTORICAL FOCUS details occasional points of historical significance.

FOCUS The Focus section has been enhanced to help readers distinguish good races from bad races and reliable form from unreliable form, by drawing together the opinions of handicapper, time expert and paddock watcher and interpreting their views in a punter-friendly manner.

NOTEBOOK horses marked with the diamond symbol are those deemed by our racereaders especially worthy of note in future races.

OFFICIAL EXPLANATIONS, where the horse is deemed to have run well above or below expectations

Abbreviations and their meanings

Paddock comments

gd sort - well made, above average on looks
h.d.w - has done well, improved in looks
wl grwn - well grown, has filled to its frame
lengthy - longer than average for its height
tall - tall
rangy - lengthy and tall but in proportion.
cl cpld - close coupled
scope - scope for physical development
str - strong, powerful looking
w'like - workmanlike, ordinary in looks
lt-f - light-framed, not much substance
cmpt - compact
neat - smallish, well put together
leggy - long legs compared with body
angular - unfurnished behind the saddle, not filled to frame
unf - unfurnished in the midriff, not filled to frame
narrow - not as wide as side appearance would suggest
small - lacks any physical scope
nt grwn - not grown
lw - looked fit and well
bkwd - backward in condition
t - tubed
swtg - sweating
b (off fore or nr fore) - bandaged in front
b.hind (off or nr) - bandaged behind

At the start

stdd s - jockey purposely reins back the horse
dwlt - missed the break and left for a short time
s.s - slow to start, left longer than a horse that dwelt
s.v.s - started very slowly
s.i.s - started on terms but took time to get going
ref to r - either does not jump off, or travels a few yards and then stops
rel to r - tries to pull itself up in mid-race
w.r.s - whipped round start

Position in the race

led - in lead on its own
disp ld - upsides the leader

w ldr - almost upsides the leader
w ldrs - in a line of three or more disputing the lead
prom - on the heels of the leaders, in the front third of the field
trckd ldr(s) - just in behind the leaders giving impression that it could lead if asked
chsd ldr - horse in second place
chsd clr ldrs - horse heads main body of field behind two clear leaders
chsd ldrs - horse is in the first four or five but making more of an effort to stay close to the pace than if it were tracking the leaders.
clsd - closed
in tch - close enough to have a chance
hdwy - making ground on the leader
gd hdwy - making ground quickly on the leader, could be a deliberate move
sme hdwy - making some ground but no real impact on the race
w.w - waited with
stdy hdwy - gradually making ground
ev ch - upsides the leaders when the race starts in earnest
rr - at the back of main group but not detached
bhd - detached from the main body of runners
hld up - restrained as a deliberate tactical move
nt rcvr - lost all chance after interference, mistake etc.
wknd - stride shortened as it began to tire
lost tch - had been in the main body but a gap appeared as it tired
lost pl - remains in main body of runners but lost several positions quickly

Riding

effrt - short-lived effort
pushed along - received urgings with hands only, jockey not using legs
rdn - received urgings from saddle, including use of whip
hrd rdn - received maximum assistance from the saddle including use of whip
drvn - received forceful urgings, jockey putting in a lot of effort and using whip
hrd drvn - jockey very animated, plenty of kicking, pushing and reminders

Finishing comments

jst failed - closing rapidly on the winner and probably would have led a stride after the line
r.o - jockey's efforts usually involved to produce an increase in pace without finding an appreciable turn of speed
r.o wl - jockey's efforts usually involved to produce an obvious increase in pace without finding an appreciable turn of speed
unable qckn - not visibly tiring but does not possess a sufficient change of pace
one pce - not tiring but does not find a turn of speed, from a position further out than unable qckn
nt r.o. - did not consent to respond to pressure
styd on - going on well towards the end, utilising stamina
nvr able to chal - unable to produce sufficient to reach a challenging position
nvr nr to chal - in the opinion of the racereader, the horse was never in a suitable position to challenge.
nrst fin - nearer to the winner in distance beaten than at any time since the race had begun in earnest
nvr nrr - nearer to the winner position-wise than at any time since the race had begun in earnest
rallied - responded to pressure to come back with a chance having lost its place
no ex - unable to sustain its run
bttr for r - likely to improve for the run and experience
rn green - inclined to wander and falter through inexperience
too much to do - left with too much leeway to make up

Winning comments

v.easily - a great deal in hand
easily - plenty in hand
comf - something in hand, always holding the others
pushed out - kept up to its work with hands and heels without jockey resorting to whip or kicking along and wins fairly comfortably
rdn out - pushed and kicked out to the line, with the whip employed
drvn out - pushed and kicked out to the line, with considerable effort and the whip employed
all out - nothing to spare, could not have found any more
jst hld on - holding on to a rapidly diminishing lead, could not have found any more if passed
unchal - must either make all or a majority of the running and not be challenged from an early stage

Complete list of abbreviations

a - always
gng - going
qckn - quicken
a.p - always prominent
gp - group
r - race
abt - about
grad - gradually
racd - raced
appr - approaching
grnd - ground
rch - reach
awrdd - awarded
hd - head
rcvr - recover
b.b.v - broke blood-vessel
hdd - headed
rdn - ridden
b.d - brought down
hdwy - headway
rdr - rider
bdly - badly
hld - held
reard - reared
bef - before
hmpd - hampered
ref - refused
bhd - behind
imp - impression
rn - ran
bk - back
ins - inside
rnd - round
blkd - baulked
j.b - jumped badly
r.o - ran on
blnd - blundered
j.w - jumped well
rr - rear
bmpd - bumped

jnd - joined
rspnse - response
bnd - bend
jst - just
rt - right
btn- beaten
kpt - kept
s - start
bttr - better
l - length
sddle - saddle
c - came
ld - lead
shkn - shaken
ch - chance
ldr - leader
slt - slight
chal - challenged
lft - left
sme - some
chse - chase
m - mile
sn - soon
chsd - chased
m.n.s - made no show
spd- speed
chsng - chasing
mde - made

st - straight
circ - circuit
mod - moderate
stmbld - stumbled
cl - close
mid div - mid division
stdd - steadied
clr - clear
mstke - mistake
stdy - steady
clsd - closed
n.d - never dangerous
strly - strongly
comf - comfortably
n.g.t - not go through
styd - stayed
cpld - coupled
n.m.r - not much room
styng - staying
crse - course
nk - neck
s.u - slipped up
ct - caught
no ex - no extra
swtchd - switched
def - definite
nr - near
swvd - swerved

dismntd - dismounted
nrr - nearer
tk - took
disp - disputed
nrst fin - nearest finish
t.k.h - took keen hold
dist - distance
nt - not
t.o - tailed off
div - division
nvr - never
tch - touch
drvn - driven
one pce - one pace
thrght - throughout
dwlt - dwelt
out - from finish
trbld - troubled
edgd - edged
outpcd - outpaced
trckd - tracked
effrt - effort
p.u - pulled up
u.p - under pressure
ent - entering
pce - pace
u.str.p- under strong pressure

ev ch - every chance
pckd - pecked
w - with
ex - extra
pl - place
w.r.s - whipped round start
f - furlong
plcd - placed
wd - wide
fin - finished
plld - pulled
whn - when
fnd - found
press - pressure
wknd - weakened
fnl - final
prog - progress
wl - well
fr - from
prom - prominent
wnr - winner
gd - good
qckly - quickly
wnt - went
w.w - waited with
1/2-wy - halfway

Racing Post Ratings

Racing Post Ratings for each horse are shown in the right hand column, headed RPR, and indicate the actual level of performance attained in that race. The figure in the back index represents the BEST public form that Raceform's Handicappers still believe the horse capable of reproducing.

To use the ratings constructively in determining those horses best-in in future events, the following procedure should be followed:

(i) In races where all runners are the same age and are set to carry the same weight, no calculations are necessary. The horse with the highest rating is best-in.

(ii) In races where all runners are the same age but are set to carry different weights, add one point to the Raceform Rating for every pound less than 10 stone to be carried; deduct one point for every pound more than 10 stone.

For example,

Horse	Age & wt	Adjustment from 10st	Base rating	Adjusted rating
Treclare	3-10-1	-1	78	77
Buchan	3-9-13	+1	80	81
Paper Money	3-9-7	+7	71	78
Archaic	3-8-11	+17	60	77

Therefore Buchan is top-rated (best-in)

(iii) In races concerning horses of different ages the procedure in (ii) should again be followed, but reference must also be made to the Official Scale of Weight-For-Age.

For example,

12 furlongs, July 20th

Horse	Age & wt	Adjustment from 10st	Base rating	Adjusted rating	W-F-A deduct	Final rating
Orpheus	5-10-0	0	90	90	Nil	90
Lemonora	4-9-9	+5	88	88	Nil	88
Tamar	3-9-4	+10	85	95	-12	83
Craigangower	4-8-7	+21	73	94	Nil	94

Therefore Craigangower is top-rated (best-in)

(A 3-y-o is deemed 12lb less mature than a 4-y-o or older horse on 20th July over 12f. Therefore, the deduction of 12 points is necessary.)

The following symbols are used in conjunction with the ratings:

++: almost certain to prove better

+: likely to prove better

d: disappointing (has run well below best recently)

?: form hard to evaluate

t: tentative rating based on race-time rating may prove unreliable

Weight adjusted ratings for every race are published daily in Raceform Private Handicap and our new service Raceform Private handicap ONLINE (www.raceform.co.uk).

For subscription terms please contact the Subscription Department on (01635) 578080.

Effect of the draw

(R.H.) denotes right-hand and (L.H.) left-hand courses.

* Draw biases shown below apply to straight-course races unless otherwise stipulated.

** Most races, outside Festival meetings, are now restricted to 20 runners, which means it's now particularly worth looking at the stalls position, as many courses can accommodate more than that number.

ASCOT (R-H) - Following extensive redevelopment there have been some pretty exaggerated draw biases. Watering often seems to be the deciding factor and far too much has been applied on more than one occasion.

STALLS: Usually go up the stands' side (low).

BIASES: One side or other was often favoured last season but the middle can also ride best, and biases remain very hard to predict.

SPLITS: Are common in big-field handicaps and occasionally will occur on soft ground in round-course races, when some head for the outside rail (covered by trees).

AYR (L-H) - Throughout the 90s high numbers were massively favoured in the Gold and Silver Cups but things have become less clear-cut since. Traditionally the centre of the course has ridden slower here but the strip is nothing like the disadvantage it once was.

STALLS: Usually go up the stands' side (high) in sprints, but occasionally go on the other side. It isn't uncommon for jockeys to switch from the far side to race down the centre or even come right across to the stands' rail.

BIASES: There's ultimately not a lot between the two sides in big fields now.

SPLITS: Are becoming more common, having only usually occurred in the Silver and Gold Cups in the past.

BATH (L-H) - The draw is of less importance than the pace at which races are run. In big fields, runners drawn low are often inclined to go off too fast to hold a rail position (the course turns left most of the way, including one major kink) and this can see hold-up horses drawn wide coming through late. Conversely, in smaller fields containing little pace, up front and on the inside is often the place to be.

STALLS: Always go on the inside (low).

SPLITS: Fields almost always stick together, but soft ground can see a split, with the outside rail (high) then favoured.

BEVERLEY (R-H) - A high draw used to be essential on good to soft or faster ground over 5f and also on the round course, particularly in races of 7f100y and 1m100y. However, things were far less clear cut last year, presumably down to watering. The course management experimented with moving stalls to the stands' side over 5f in 2002 (unsuccessfully, as it led to a huge low bias) and haven't done so since.

STALLS: Go on the inside (high) at all distances.

BIASES: High numbers are traditionally best on good to soft or faster ground but watering looked to play a big part last year.

SPLITS: Splits are rare and only likely over 5f on soft ground.

BRIGHTON (L-H) - Much depends on the going and time of year. On good to soft or slower ground runners often head for the outside rail, while in late season it's usually just a case of whichever jockey finds the least cut-up strip of ground. Otherwise, low-drawn prominent-racers tend to hold sway in fast-ground sprints, with double figures always facing an uphill task over 5f59y.

STALLS: Always go on the inside (low) in sprints.

SPLITS: These occur frequently, as jockeys look for a fresh strip on ground that seems to churn up easily.

CARLISLE (R-H) - Runners racing with the pace and hardest against the inside rail (high) do well in big fields on decent ground. This is largely down to the fact that the Flat course and NH course are one and the same, and that those racing nearest the fence are running where the hurdle wings were positioned, while those wider out are on the raced-on surface. On soft ground, the bias swings completely, with runners racing widest (low) and grabbing the stands' rail in the straight favoured at all distances.

STALLS: Normally go on the inside (high) but can go down the middle in sprints (usually on slow ground).

BIASES: High numbers are best in fast-ground sprints, but look to back low numbers on soft/heavy ground.

SPLITS: Rarely will two groups form but, on easy ground, runners often spread out.

CATTERICK (L-H) - When the ground is testing, the stands' rail is definitely the place to be, which suits high numbers in 5f races and high-drawn prominent-racers at all other distances. However, when the ground is good to firm or faster, horses drawn on the inside (low) often hold the edge, and there have been several meetings over the last few seasons in which those racing prominently hardest against the inside rail have dominated (over all distances).

STALLS: Go on the inside (low) at all distances these days (they often used to go on the outer over 5f212y).

BIASES: Low numbers are best in sprints on fast ground (particularly watered firm going) but the stands' rail (high) rides faster under slower conditions.

SPLITS: Are common over 5f on easy ground.

CHEPSTOW (L-H) - High numbers enjoyed a massive advantage in straight-course races in 2000 and the course management duly took steps to eradicate the faster strip, using the same 'earthquake' machine as had been employed at Goodwood in the late 90s. This has led to little in the way of a draw bias since.

STALLS: Always go stands' side (high) on the straight course.

BIASES: Have become hard to predict in recent times.

SPLITS: Are common and jockeys drawn low often head far side.

CHESTER (L-H) - It's well known that low numbers are favoured at all distances here, even in the 2m2f Chester Cup, and the bias is factored into the prices these days. That said sprints (and in particular handicaps) are still playable, as it often pays to stick to a runner drawn 1-3.

STALLS: Go on the inside (low) at all distances bar 1m2f75y and 2m2f117y (same starting point) when they go on the outside. Certain starters ask for the stalls to come off the inside rail slightly in sprints.

BIASES: Low numbers are favoured at all distances. Soft ground seems to accentuate the bias until a few races have been staged, when a higher draw becomes less of a disadvantage as the ground on the inside becomes chewed up.

DONCASTER (L-H) - There's been very little between the two sides since the course reopened. Jockeys now tend to swerve the stands' rail (high) on good or slower ground, instead preferring to head for the centre.

STALLS: Can go either side but tend to go up the stands' side (high) when possible.

BIASES: Runners down the centre are usually worst off. The longer the trip on the straight course the better chance the far side (low) has against the stands' side in big fields.

EPSOM (L-H) - When the going is on the soft side, jockeys tack over to the stands' side for the better ground (this strip rides quicker in such conditions as the course cambers away from the stands' rail). In 5f races, the stalls are invariably placed on the stands' side, so when the going is soft the majority of the runners are on the best ground from the outset. Prominent-racers drawn low in round-course races are able to take the shortest route around Tattenham Corner, and on faster ground have a decisive edge over 6f, 7f and 1m114y. Over 5f, high numbers used to hold quite an advantage, but the bias is not so great on fast going these days.

STALLS: Always go on the outside (high) over 5f and 6f (races over the latter trip start on a chute) and inside (low) at other distances, bar 1m4f10y (centre).

BIASES: Low-drawn prominent racers are favoured at between 6f and 1m114y.

SPLITS: Good to soft ground often leads to a few trying the stands'-side route.

FOLKESTONE (R-H) - Prior to 1998, Folkestone was never thought to have much in the way of a bias, but nowadays the draw is often crucial on the straight course (up to 7f). On very soft ground, the far rail (high) rides faster than the stands' rail. However, on good to soft or faster ground runners tend to stay up the near side now (the ambulance used to go this side of the far rail but now goes the other side of the fence) and those racing on the pace hardest against the fence often enjoy a major advantage.

STALLS: Usually go up the stands' side (low) on the straight track, but occasionally down the centre.

BIASES: High numbers are favoured over 6f and 7f, and also over the minimum trip when 14 or more line up. However, very low numbers have a good record in smaller fields over 5f. Front-runners are well worth considering at all distances.

SPLITS: Often occur.

GOODWOOD (R-H) & (L-H) - The course management took steps to end the major high bias seen in the Stewards' Cup throughout the late 90s by breaking up the ground by machine in 1998. This led to the stands' side (low) dominating the race in 1999 before the far side gradually took over again.

STALLS: Invariably go on the stands' side (low).

BIASES: High numbers are best at between 7f-1m1f and the faster the ground the more pronounced the bias (keep an eye out for the rail on the home turn being moved during Glorious week, usually after the Thursday).

SPLITS: Although fields tend not to break into groups in most sprints, runners often spread out to about two-thirds of the way across in fields of around 20.

HAMILTON (R-H) - Extensive drainage work was carried out in the winter of 2002 in a bid to level up the two sides of the track but, after encouraging early results, the natural bias in favour of high numbers (far side) kicked in again. This can be altered by watering on faster going, though, and low numbers were definitely favoured under such conditions in 2008. Things were less clear cut last year, however, and jockeys more often than not headed for the centre. High numbers are best over 1m65y, thanks to runners encountering a tight right-handed loop soon after the start.

STALLS: It's not uncommon for the ground to become too soft for the use of stalls, but otherwise they go either side.

BIASES: High draws are best in soft/heavy-ground sprints, but the bias becomes middle to high otherwise (often switching to low on watered fast ground). Front-runners do particularly well at all distances.

SPLITS: Rarely happen now.

HAYDOCK (L-H) - High numbers used to enjoy a major advantage in soft-ground sprints and there were signs last year that this bias has returned. Otherwise, runners usually head for the centre these days, the draw rarely making much of a difference.

STALLS: Usually go down the centre in the straight.

KEMPTON All-Weather (R-H) - High numbers are best over 5f and preferable over 6f, while those drawn very low over 7f often have a bit to do. Otherwise, pace of races counts for a lot and this is one of the fairest courses around in that respect.

LEICESTER (R-H) - There was a four-year spell between 1998 and 2001 when the centre-to-far-side strip (middle to high) enjoyed a decisive advantage over the stands' rail, jockeys eventually choosing to avoid the near side. However, that's changed recently, with very low numbers more than holding their own.

STALLS: Invariably go up the stands' side (low).

SPLITS: Still occur occasionally.

LINGFIELD Turf (L-H) - Following a less predictable spell, the stands' rail (high) has taken over again in the past couple of years. The one factor that can have a massive effect on the draw is heavy rainfall on to firm ground. Presumably because of the undulating nature of the track and the fact that the far rail on the straight course is towards the bottom of a slope where it joins the round course, rainfall seems to make the middle and far side ride a deal slower. In these conditions, the top three or four stalls have a massive edge.

STALLS: Go up the stands' side (high) at between 5f and 7f and down the middle over 7f140y.

BIASES: High numbers favoured unless ground is genuinely soft.

SPLITS: It's unusual to see two distinct groups, but runners often fan out centre to stands' side in big fields.

LINGFIELD All-Weather (L-H) - There is little bias over most trips, but it is an advantage to be drawn low over 6f and 1m2f, with both starts being situated very close to the first bend. A low to middle draw is preferable over 5f, even with a safety limit of just ten, though the very inside stall has a poor recent record. No horse managed to win from stall 1 over that trip in 2004, which suggests the ground right against the inside rail is slower than elsewhere.

STALLS: Go against the outside rail (high) over 5f and 1m, but against the inside rail (low) for all other distances.

SPLITS: Fields never split but runners usually come wide off the home turn.

MUSSELBURGH (R-H) - The bias in favour of low numbers over 5f isn't as pronounced as many believe, apart from on soft ground, while the bias in favour of high numbers at 7f and 1m isn't that big.

STALLS: Usually go up the stands' side (low) over 5f nowadays, but they can be rotated.

SPLITS: Look out for runners drawn very high in big-field 5f races on fast ground, as they occasionally go right to the far rail.

NEWBURY (L-H) - There's basically little between the two sides these days, apart from on soft ground, in which case the stands' rail (high) is definitely the place to be. When the ground is testing it's not uncommon to see runners race wide down the back straight and down the side at between 1m3f56y and 2m (particularly over 1m5f61y). In such circumstances, a high draw becomes an advantage.

STALLS: Can go anywhere for straight-course races.

SPLITS: Are pretty rare.

NEWCASTLE (L-H) - It used to be a case of high numbers best at up to and including 7f on good or firmer, and low numbers having the advantage when the ground is good to soft or softer. However, now things depend largely on the positioning of the stands' rail. If the course is at its widest high numbers are almost always best off, while if the rail is further in things are less clear cut.

STALLS: Invariably go on the stands' side (high) and are only switched to the inside under exceptional circumstances.

SPLITS: Two groups are usually formed when 14+ go to post, and often when 8-13 line up.

NEWMARKET July Course (R-H) - The major draw biases seen under the former Clerk of the Course have become a thing of the past and now only the occasional meeting will be affected. The course is permanently divided into two halves by a rail (the Racing Post now carry information regarding which side is to be used) and, as a rule of thumb, the two outside rails (stands' rail when they're on the stands'-side half, far rail when they're on the far-side half) ride faster than the dividing rail.

Stands'-side half - On fast ground (particularly watered) very high numbers are often favoured at up to 1m, when there's a narrow strip hard against the fence that rides quicker. However, on good to soft or slower ground, runners racing in the centre are favoured.

Far-side half - There's rarely much in the draw, apart from on slow ground, when the far side (low) rides faster.

STALLS: Can go either side on either half of the track.

SPLITS: Runners just about tend to form two groups in capacity fields, but are more likely to run to their draw here than at tracks such as Newcastle.

NEWMARKET Rowley Mile (R-H) - Similarly to the July Course, the draw seems to have been evened out since the Clerk of the Course change, although it's still generally a case of the further away from the stands' rail (low) the better.

STALLS: Can go anywhere and are rotated.

BIASES: High numbers have dominated the 2m2f Cesarewitch in recent years, the logic being that those on the inside can be switched off early, while low numbers have to work to get into position before the sole right-handed turn.

SPLIT: It's not unusual for jockeys to come stands' side on slow ground in round-course races.

NOTTINGHAM (L-H) - Biases are far harder to predict now on the both the inner (spring/autumn) and outer (summer) course.

STALLS: Tend to go on the stands' side (high) unless the ground is very soft.

SPLITS: Fields usually split in sprints when 14+ line up.

PONTEFRACT (L-H) - Low numbers have always been considered best here for the same reason as at Chester, in that the course has several distinct left-hand turns with a short home straight, and it's always worth considering low-drawn front-runners on fast going. Drainage work was carried out in the late 90s to try and eradicate the outside-rail bias on slow ground, and this worked immediately afterwards, but during the last few seasons there have been definite signs that it's now riding much faster when it's bottomless.

STALLS: Go on the inside (low) unless the ground is very soft, when they're switched to the outside rail.

SPLITS: Although it's uncommon to see distinct groups, high numbers usually race wide these days on soft/heavy ground.

REDCAR (L-H) - It's not unusual to see big fields throughout the season but the draw rarely makes a difference.

STALLS: Go towards the stands' side (high).

SPLITS: Splits are unusual.

RIPON (R-H) - The draw is often the sole deciding factor in big-field sprints and watering plays a major part. As a general rule, low numbers are best when the ground is good to firm or faster, while the far side is always best on softer going but, ultimately, the best guide these days is the most recent meeting.

STALLS: Go on the stands' side (low) apart from under exceptional circumstances.

BIASES: Front-runners (particularly from high draws over 1m) have an excellent record and any horse trying to make ground from behind and out wide is always facing a tough task.

SPLITS: Fields tend to stay together in races of 12 or fewer, but a split is near guaranteed when 15 or more line up. Look for 'draw' jockeys who might chance going far side in fields of 13-14.

SALISBURY (R-H) - For most of last year those racing against the inside rail (high) on fast ground looked worst off if anything (centre often best), which is the opposite of how things have been in the past. Presumably this was down to watering. On slower ground jockeys invariably head towards the stands' rail (good to soft seems to be the cut-off point) and whoever grabs the fence in front can prove hard to pass.

STALLS: Go on the far side (high) unless the ground is soft, when they're often moved to the near side.

BIASES: Low numbers are always best on soft/heavy ground.

SPLITS: Fields only tend to divide on good to soft ground; otherwise they converge towards either rail, dependent on going.

SANDOWN (R-H) - On the 5f chute, when the going is on the soft side and the stalls are on the far side (high), high numbers enjoy a decisive advantage. On the rare occasions that the stalls are placed on the stands' side, low numbers enjoy a slight advantage when all the runners stay towards the stands' rail, but when a few break off and go to the far side high numbers comfortably hold the upper hand again. High numbers enjoy a decent advantage in double-figure fields over 7f and 1m on good going or faster, but jockeys invariably head for the stands' side on slow ground.

STALLS: Usually go far side (high) over 5f, as the course is more level that side.

SPLITS: It's unusual for runners to split over 5f, with capacity fields rare and jockeys all inclined to head for the far rail.

SOUTHWELL All-Weather (L-H) - Over most trips on the round track it is preferable to be drawn away from the extreme inside or outside. The exceptions are over 6f and 1m3f, which both start close to the first bend (better to be drawn low to middle). At most meetings the centre of the track rides faster than either rail, although that can change in extreme weather when power-harrowing can even out the bias. A low to middle draw is preferable over 5f.

STALLS: Are placed next to the inside rail (low), except over 5f when they go next to the stands' rail (high).

SPLITS: Fields don't split into groups as such, but can fan out and take varied routes once into the home straight. Even in big fields over the straight 5f, the runners basically stick to their draw and race straight from start to finish.

THIRSK (L-H) - This used to be the biggest draw course in the country, back in the days of the old watering system (which was badly affected by the wind) but, while biases still often show up, they're not as predictable as used to be the case. Field sizes, watering and going always have to be taken into account when 12 or more line up (11 or fewer runners and it's rare to see anything bar one group up the stands' rail, with high numbers best). Otherwise, either rail can enjoy the edge on watered fast ground (the one place not to be under any circumstances is down the middle). Low-drawn prominent-racers are well worth considering whatever the distance on the round course.

STALLS: Always go up the stands' side (high).

BIASES: High numbers are best in sprints when 11 or fewer line up, but it's hard to know which side is likely to do best in bigger fields on fast ground. The far (inside) rail is always best on slow going (the softer the ground, the greater the advantage).

SPLITS: Runners invariably stay towards the stands' side in sprints containing 12 or fewer runners (unless the ground is soft) and frequently when 13-14 line up. Any more and it becomes long odds-on two groups.

WARWICK (L-H) - Low numbers are no longer favoured, whatever the ground, and jockeys rarely if ever stick to the inside rail now. Presumably this is down to watering (hold-up runners are not as badly off as they used to be).

STALLS: Always go on the inside (low).

WINDSOR (Fig. 8) - The bias in favour of high numbers on fast ground is nothing like as predictable as it used to be, presumably because of watering. On slower ground, jockeys head centre to far side, and right over to the far rail (low) on genuine soft/heavy.

STALLS: Can be positioned anywhere for sprints.

BIASES: High-drawn prominent-racers are often favoured in fast-ground sprints, and also over 1m67y. On good to soft going, there's rarely much between the two sides, but it's a case of nearer to the far rail (low) the better on bad ground.

SPLITS: Splits only tend to occur on good to soft ground, and even then it's rare to see two defined groups.

WOLVERHAMPTON All-Weather (L-H) - A low draw is a big advantage over 5f20y and 5f216y, and low to middle is preferable over 7f32y. Beyond that it doesn't seem to matter, although it's never a good idea to race too wide on the home bend, as those that do rarely seem to make up the lost ground.

STALLS: Are placed against the outside rail (high) over 7f32y and against the inside (low) at all other distances.

YARMOUTH (L-H) - High numbers enjoyed a major advantage for much of the 90s, but this was put an end to by the course switching from pop-up sprinklers (which were affected by the off-shore breeze) to a Briggs Boom in '99. These days a bias will appear occasionally but it's hard to predict, and runners often head for the centre whatever the going.

STALLS: Go one side or the other.

SPLITS: It's common to see groups form, often including one down the centre, in big fields.

YORK (L-H) - The draw is nothing like as unpredictable in sprints as many believe, although things are never quite as clear cut in September/October as earlier in the season. Essentially, on good or faster ground, the faster strip is to be found centre to far side, which means in capacity fields, the place to be is stall 6-12, while in fields of 12-14 runners drawn low are favoured (the course is only wide enough to house 20 runners). On soft/heavy ground, the stands' side (high) becomes the place to be.

STALLS: Can go anywhere.

BIASES: Prominent-racers drawn down the centre are favoured in fast-ground sprints, but high numbers take over on genuine soft/heavy ground.

SPLITS: Defined groups are rare.

Key to racereaders' initials

WG ....Walter Glynn
KH ....Keith Hewitt
RL ....Richard Lowther
LM...................Lee McKenzie
TM ....Tim Mitchell
JN.............Jonathan Neesom
DO ....Darren Owen
SP ....Steve Payne
CR ....Colin Roberts
JR ....Joe Rowntree
JS.........................John Santer
ST ....Steve Taylor
RY ....Richard Young

SOUTHWELL (L-H)

Thursday, January 1

OFFICIAL GOING: Standard to slow

Wind: Nil Weather: Cold and overcast

1 HAPPY NEW YEAR APPRENTICE MEDIAN AUCTION MAIDEN STKS 1m 3f (F)

12:25 (12:25) (Class 6) 4-6-Y-0 **£2,047** (£604; £302) **Stalls** Low

Form RPR

352- **1** **Red Tarn**[22] 7632 4-8-13 57 TravisBlock 8 64
(B Smart) *in tch: carried sltly wd and pushed along bnd after 3f: hdwy 1/2-way: chsd ldrs 4f out: sn niggled along: rdn to chse ldr over 2f out: drvn to chal ent fnl f: styd on u.p to ld fnl 100yds* **11/8**[1]

424- **2** *nk* **Orpenella**[22] 7634 4-8-8 61 (b) AndrewMullen 5 58
(K A Ryan) *cl up: led 3f out: rdn over 1f out: drvn and edgd rt ins fnl f: hdd and no ex fnl 100yds* **2/1**[2]

23P- **3** *12* **Jordi Roper (IRE)**[5] 7799 4-8-8 51 (b[1]) AshleyMorgan(5) 1 43
(S Parr) *trckd ldrs: effrt 3f out: rdn 2f out and grad wknd* **10/1**

50- **4** *2 1/4* **A Valley Away (IRE)**[14] 7713 5-8-6 0 RossAtkinson(5) 3 34
(Jane Chapple-Hyam) *trckd ldrs: pushed along over 4f out: rdn over 3f out and sn outpcd* **17/2**[3]

0- **5** *14* **Grange Corner**[22] 7632 4-8-1 0 AndrewHeffernan(7) 6 10
(Garry Moss) *in rr: rdn along 1/2-way: nvr a factor* **100/1**

6 *1 3/4* **Tuxsumdoin**[16] 5-8-8 0 WilliamCarson(3) 7 7
(J R Weymes) *a in rr* **11/1**

466- **7** *2* **Martingrange Lass (IRE)**[3] 7815 4-8-8 40 (v[1]) TolleyDean 4 4
(S Parr) *led: rdn along and hdd 3f out: sn wknd* **40/1**

305- **8** *14* **Fifth Zak**[296] 843 5-9-2 50 LukeMorris 2 —
(S R Bowring) *towards rr: pushed along after 4f: rdn 1/2-way: bhd fnl 3f* **16/1**

2m 30.95s (2.95) **Going Correction** +0.275s/f (Slow)
WFA 4 from 5yo 3lb **8** Ran SP% **112.7**
Speed ratings: **100,99,91,89,79 77,76,66**
toteswinger: 1&2 £1.20, 1&3 £3.80, 2&3 £4.40. CSF £4.08 TOTE £3.50: £1.10, £1.30, £2.00; EX 4.10 Trifecta £13.90 Pool: £302.17 - 16.02 winning units..
Owner Alan Zheng **Bred** N E and Mrs Poole and Trickledown Stud **Trained** Hambleton, N Yorks

FOCUS
This was a very poor and uncompetitive older-horse apprentice maiden with which to start the new year and two dominated the market. Ultimately it was they who dominated the race as well.
Martingrange Lass(IRE) Official explanation: jockey said filly ran too free and had no more to give in the closing stages

2 WILLIAM HILL JANUARY SALE NOW ON! H'CAP 5f (F)

1:00 (1:01) (Class 2) 4-Y-0+ **£11,656** (£3,468; £1,733; £865) **Stalls** High

Form RPR

034- **1** **Pawan (IRE)**[16] 7697 9-8-4 91 oh3 ow5 (b) AnnStokell(5) 1 99
(Miss A Stokell) *sn rdn along to chse ldrs: swtchd rt and hdwy over 1f out: styd on u.p ins fnl f to ld fnl 50yds* **6/1**[3]

603- **2** *1/2* **Rebel Duke (IRE)**[16] 7697 5-7-11 86 oh6 RossAtkinson(7) 5 92
(D W Barker) *cl up: effrt 2f out: rdn to ld over 1f out: drvn ins fnl f: hdd and nt qckn fnl 50yds* **9/2**[2]

014- **3** *2 1/4* **How's She Cuttin' (IRE)**[40] 7421 6-8-9 91 (v) TomEaves 9 89
(T D Barron) *led: rdn along and hdd over 1f out: drvn and one pce ins fnl f* **7/2**[1]

103- **4** *3 3/4* **Harry Up**[14] 7716 8-8-5 87 (p) CatherineGannon 6 71
(K A Ryan) *cl up: rdn along 2f out: grad wknd* **11/1**

050- **5** *3/4* **Excusez Moi (USA)**[96] 6285 7-9-3 104 DanielleMcCreery(5) 2 86
(Mrs R A Carr) *s.i.s: outpcd and bhd tl hdwy over 1f out: styd on ins fnl f: nrst fin* **18/1**

140- **6** *hd* **Irish Pearl (IRE)**[23] 7614 4-8-13 95 FergusSweeney 3 76
(K R Burke) *cl up: rdn along 2f out: sn edgd lft and wknd over 1f out* **8/1**

520- **7** *3/4* **Sands Crooner (IRE)**[2] 7826 6-8-4 86 oh8 (v) JimmyQuinn 4 64
(J G Given) *in tch: rdn along 2f out: drvn over 1f out: sn no imp* **9/1**

006- **8** *3 1/2* **Tartatartufata**[23] 7614 7-8-4 86 oh9 (v) ChrisCatlin 7 52
(J G Given) *sn rdn along in rr and a outpcd* **20/1**

213- **9** *1 1/2* **Matsunosuke**[4] 7805 7-9-2 98 6ex TPQueally 8 58
(A B Coogan) *sn pushed along: a in rr* **7/2**[1]

59.80 secs (0.10) **Going Correction** +0.25s/f (Slow) **9** Ran SP% **116.4**
Speed ratings (Par 109): **109,108,104,98,97 97,95,90,87**
toteswinger: 1&2 £7.60, 1&3 £4.30, 2&3 £6.00. CSF £33.43 CT £110.14 TOTE £8.00: £2.30, £2.00, £1.20; EX 40.30 Trifecta £100.70 Pool: £449.14 - 3.30 winning units..
Owner Ms Caron Stokell **Bred** Hadi Al Tajir **Trained** Brompton-on-Swale, N Yorks

FOCUS
A decent sprint handicap despite four of the nine runners being out of the handicap. They went a good pace as they always do over this straight 5f, with four in a line across the track battling for the early lead. It has been rated around the winner to his best turf form over the previous 12 months.

NOTEBOOK
Pawan(IRE) does not win the number of races his ability entitles him to, but he got it right this time and he had the plum draw, which was a big help. Not for the first time (and almost certainly not for the last) he had overweight to carry, this time 5lb, which negated his rider's claim and meant that he was effectively 8lb wrong, but he was always in a good position to attack when the pacesetters faltered and this time he put himself in front where it mattered, with his delighted trainer/jockey waving to the crowd. He will no doubt be back in a similar event before long, but in view of his record he is probably one to take on next time. (op 11-1)
Rebel Duke(IRE) is proven over this course and distance and his rider's claim helped negate being 6lb wrong. He did best of the quartet that set the early pace and he looked the most likely winner until Pawan pounced. He should continue to go well, but the Handicapper may put him up a bit for this. (op 5-1)
How's She Cuttin'(IRE), far from disgraced in Listed company last time but 9lb higher than when bolting up over course and distance prior to that, had the stands' rail draw to overcome, but her rider did his best to offset that by steering her more towards the centre of the track in the early stages. She showed good early speed and had every chance, but did not quite get home this time. (op 9-4)
Harry Up, a confirmed trailblazer, also showed plenty of early pace, but he could not dominate and was eventually left behind by the front three. He has never shown his best form here and will be happier back on Polytrack. (op 9-1 tchd 17-2 and 12-1)
Excusez Moi(USA), a smart sprinter for Clive Brittain making his debut for his new yard after a three-month absence, gave himself a mountain to climb after fluffing the start, but he did make up quite a bit of late ground and is not a lost cause, especially back on Polytrack. (op 22-1)
Irish Pearl(IRE), a dual winner over 6f here in the autumn but very disappointing over this trip back here last time, was the other to help share the early advantage but she stopped very quickly inside the last furlong and now has questions to answer. (tchd 15-2 and 9-1)
Sands Crooner(IRE), 8lb wrong and reappearing just two days after a modest effort at Wolverhampton, likes to come from off the pace so this track was never going to play to his strengths. (op 14-1 tchd 16-1)

3 WILLIAM HILL JANUARY SALE - BETTER ODDS! H'CAP 1m 6f (F)

1:35 (1:35) (Class 5) (0-75,72) 4-Y-0+ **£2,590** (£770; £385; £192) **Stalls** Low

Form RPR

143- **1** **My Friend Fritz**[19] 7664 9-9-8 66 ChrisCatlin 1 73
(P W Hiatt) *t.k.h: cl up: led 4f out: rdn over 2f out: drvn ent fnl f: hld on wl towards fin* **7/1**

164- **2** *1 1/4* **Dart**[23] 7617 5-9-9 67 AdamKirby 2 72
(J R Fanshawe) *hld up in tch: stdy hdwy over 3f out: rdn to chal over 1f out: sn drvn and ev ch tl no ex wl ins fnl f* **9/4**[1]

631- **3** *2 3/4* **Victory Quest (IRE)**[16] 7696 9-10-0 72 (v) JimmyQuinn 7 73
(Mrs S Lamyman) *prom: led 1/2-way: pushed along and hdd 4f out: rdn 3f out: drvn wl over 1f out and kpt on same pce* **4/1**[2]

524- **4** *5* **Swords**[14] 7722 7-9-6 64 PaulMulrennan 3 58
(R E Peacock) *trckd ldrs: hdwy over 4f out: rdn along to chse ldng pair over 3f out: drvn 2f out and sn wknd* **5/1**[3]

100- **5** *5* **Hill Billy Rock (IRE)**[5] 7797 6-9-12 70 TomEaves 5 57
(G A Swinbank) *in tch: effrt to chse ldrs over 4f out: rdn along 3f out and sn outpcd* **9/1**

000- **6** *6* **Mikado**[31] 7515 8-9-7 65 (v[1]) MickyFenton 4 44
(Jonjo O'Neill) *led: rdn along and hdd 1/2-way: sn wknd* **12/1**

200- **7** *11* **They All Laughed**[159] 4432 6-9-12 70 TGMcLaughlin 6 33
(P W Hiatt) *hld up: rdn along over 4f out: a in rr* **8/1**

606- **8** *20* **Red Wine**[5] 7797 10-9-5 70 KarenKenny(7) 8 5
(A J McCabe) *hld up towards rr: rdn along 4f out and sn bhd* **16/1**

3m 11.99s (3.69) **Going Correction** +0.275s/f (Slow) **8** Ran SP% **114.6**
Speed ratings (Par 103): **100,99,97,94,92 88,82,70**
toteswinger: 1&2 £4.00, 1&3 £5.00, 2&3 £2.40. CSF £23.24 CT £72.09 TOTE £6.90: £1.50, £1.40, £1.90; EX 18.20 Trifecta £37.80 Pool: £409.02 - 7.99 winning units..
Owner P W Hiatt **Bred** Butts Enterprises Limited **Trained** Hook Norton, Oxon

FOCUS
The staying races around here are usually a test of stamina and this was even more the case with the overnight frost resulting in going which the jockeys described as 'holding'. The form looks sound enough rated around the third.
Mikado Official explanation: vet said gelding was lame post-race

4 BARRY ARNOLD 70TH BIRTHDAY H'CAP 6f (F)

2:05 (2:05) (Class 5) (0-75,70) 3-Y-0 **£2,729** (£806; £403) **Stalls** Low

Form RPR

610- **1** **Takeover Bid (USA)**[34] 7475 3-9-4 70 GregFairley 4 82
(M Johnston) *cl up: rdn to ld 2f out: drvn over 1f out: kpt on wl u.p ins fnl f* **5/2**[1]

21- **2** *1 1/4* **Hellbender (IRE)**[5] 7794 3-9-2 68 6ex RichardKingscote 3 76
(S Kirk) *cl up: rdn and ev ch whn hung bdly lft 2f out: drvn and hdwy whn hung rt over 1f out: chal and ev ch ins fnl f: no ex fnl 100yds* **5/2**[1]

622- **3** *2 3/4* **Abu Derby (IRE)**[5] 7794 3-9-4 70 TPQueally 5 69
(J G Given) *cl up on outer: effrt to chal 2f out: sn rdn and ev ch tl drvn and one pce appr fnl f* **5/2**[1]

204- **4** *4* **Hawkspring (IRE)**[5] 7789 3-8-8 60 (t) ChrisCatlin 1 46
(S Parr) *led: rdn along and hdd 2f out: sn drvn and wknd* **7/2**[2]

010- **5** *1* **Ridgeway Silver**[15] 7700 3-8-10 67 GabrielHannon(5) 2 50
(M D I Usher) *prom: rdn along wl over 2f out: drvn and grad wknd fr wl over 1f out* **25/1**[3]

1m 18.43s (1.93) **Going Correction** +0.275s/f (Slow) **5** Ran SP% **111.8**
Speed ratings (Par 97): **98,96,92,87,86**
CSF £9.20 TOTE £4.20: £2.60, £2.10; EX 11.80.
Owner Sheikh Hamdan Bin Mohammed Al Maktoum **Bred** Darley **Trained** Middleham Moor, N Yorks

FOCUS
A very ordinary sprint handicap for three-year-olds and sound form with the winner rated as having improved a length on his Wolverhampton maiden win.
Ridgeway Silver Official explanation: jockey said filly moved poorly

5 WILLIAM HILL JANUARY SALE - WHY BET ELSEWHERE? (S) STKS 1m (F)

2:40 (2:41) (Class 6) 3-Y-0 **£2,047** (£604; £302) **Stalls** Low

Form RPR

006- **1** **Cause For Applause (IRE)**[13] 7735 3-8-7 45 (v) ChrisCatlin 3 56
(B Smart) *sn cl up on outer: effrt 3f out: led over 2f out: rdn clr wl over 1f out: easily* **3/1**[2]

00- **2** *13* **Captain Bradz (USA)**[199] 3078 3-8-12 0 LeeEnstone 5 31
(P T Midgley) *cl up: led after 2f: rdn along 3f out: hdd over 2f out: sn drvn and kpt on same pce* **7/2**[3]

510- **3** *nk* **Miss Xu Xia**[30] 7531 3-8-10 54 (p) DuranFentiman(3) 2 31
(G R Oldroyd) *dwlt and sn pushed along: hdwy 1/2-way: rdn to chse wnr over 2f out: sn drvn and no imp: lost 2nd nr fin* **1/1**[1]

00- **4** *11* **Betsy The Best**[19] 7660 3-8-11 0 ow4 (tp) PaulMulrennan 4 4
(R Bastiman) *led 2f: cl up tl rdn along 1/2-way and sn wknd* **14/1**

464- **5** *1/2* **Talulah Bells**[211] 2720 3-8-4 35 LukeMorris(3) 1 —
(A W Carroll) *chsd ldrs on inner: rdn along 1/2-way: sn outpcd and bhd* **10/1**

1m 47.0s (3.30) **Going Correction** +0.275s/f (Slow) **5** Ran SP% **113.0**
Speed ratings (Par 95): **94,81,80,69,69**
CSF £13.97 TOTE £4.60: £1.50, £1.70; EX 15.70.There was no bid for the winner.
Owner Gerry Slater & Allen Evans **Bred** Castlefarm Stud **Trained** Hambleton, N Yorks

FOCUS
Sellers do not come much worse than this and the form is not to be trusted.
Miss Xu Xia Official explanation: jokcey said filly was never travelling

6 KINGSCLERE RACING CLUB H'CAP 1m (F)

3:15 (3:15) (Class 2) (0-100,89) 4-Y-0+ **£11,656** (£3,468; £1,733; £865) **Stalls** Low

Form RPR

031- **1** **Councellor (FR)**[13] 7737 7-9-2 87 (t) MickyFenton 3 97
(Stef Liddiard) *in tch: pushed along 1/2-way: gd hdwy on outer 3f out: rdn to ld 2f out: drvn ent fnl f: edgd lft and kpt on wl* **6/1**[2]

013- **2** *1* **Majuro (IRE)**[40] 7418 5-9-4 89 NCallan 1 97
(K A Ryan) *trckd ldng pair: hdwy on inner 3f out: rdn to chse wnr over 1f out: drvn and ev ch ent fnl f: sn one pce* **2/1**[1]

604- **3** *2* **Lady Jane Digby**[12] 7740 4-9-1 86 GregFairley 5 89
(M Johnston) *led: rdn along 3f out: hdd 2f out: sn drvn and one pce ent fnl f* **8/1**[3]

111- **4** *3 3/4* **Mozayada (USA)**[14] 7724 5-8-6 **77** ChrisCatlin 7 71
(M Brittain) *cl up: effrt 3f out: rdn over 2f out: sn drvn and btn over 1f out* **2/1**[1]

244- **5** *3/4* **Just Bond (IRE)**[19] 7670 7-8-12 **83** PaulMulrennan 6 76
(G R Oldroyd) *t.k.h: hld up in tch: effrt 3f out: sn rdn along and no imp fnl 2f* **9/1**

113- **6** *1 1/2* **Spinning**[12] 7750 6-8-10 **81** (b) TomEaves 2 70
(T D Barron) *s.i.s and towards rr: sme hdwy 1/2-way: rdn along over 2f out: sn hung lft and n.d* **10/1**

045- **7** *2* **New Beginning (IRE)**[19] 7580 5-8-4 **75** oh7 (p) JimmyQuinn 4 60
(Mrs S Lamyman) *dwlt: a towards rr* **33/1**

1m 44.28s (0.58) **Going Correction** +0.275s/f (Slow) **7** Ran SP% **114.1**
Speed ratings (Par 109): **108,107,105,101,100 99,97**
toteswinger: 1&2 £2.60, 1&3 £7.60, 2&3 £3.20. CSF £18.38 TOTE £7.50: £3.50, £1.70; EX 21.80.

Owner ownaracehorse.co.uk **Bred** Janus Bloodstock & Pontchartrain Stud **Trained** Great Shefford, Berks

FOCUS
Not many runners, but a decent and competitive handicap nonetheless. The pace looked solid without being anything out of the ordinary, but the form looks sound enough rated around the runner-up.

NOTEBOOK
Councellor(FR) was raised 3lb for beating a subsequent winner at Wolverhampton last time and is effective around here too. He travelled very comfortably in the middle of the field towards the outside early and, when produced with his effort towards the nearside in the straight, battled on very gamely to score. A versatile sort, this was the highest mark he has ever won off and he looks better than ever. (op 13-2 tchd 7-1)

Majuro(IRE) ◆, third in a hot Lingfield handicap on his debut for the yard last time and a convincing winner over this course and distance prior to that, had the inside stall, which probably was not ideal, and he was also forced to make his effort tight against the inside rail starting up the home straight, but he still had every chance and could not quite match the winner's finishing pace. He should be winning again soon. (op 11-4 tchd 3-1)

Lady Jane Digby, highly tried in her career so far and 9lb lower than for her only previous start in a handicap, was on Fibresand for the first time and she ran a solid race from the front, but may need to drop a few pounds more. (tchd 15-2 and 9-1)

Mozayada(USA), bidding for a course five-timer off a 5lb higher mark, raced up with the pace for most of the way, but it became obvious from the two-furlong pole that her winning run was coming to an end. She does look most effective when able to dominate from the start, but these much better rivals were a bigger problem and a lot now depends on how quickly she comes down the weights again. (op 15-8 tchd 6-4)

Just Bond(IRE), a multiple winner on the Wolverhampton Polytrack, was trying Fibresand for the first time. He never looked that happy and could never make much impression from off the pace, but he should still be capable of finding races back at his beloved Dunstall Park. He was reported to have hung right. Official explanation: jockey said gelding hung right (tchd 12-1)

Spinning, 2lb higher than when narrowly failing to complete a Polytrack hat-trick last month, gave himself plenty to do after missing the break and could never get involved. His rider reported that he had hung left. Official explanation: jockey said gelding hung left (op 7-1)

7 SOUTHWELL-RACECOURSE.CO.UK H'CAP — 1m (F)
3:45 (3:46) (Class 6) (0-55,55) 4-Y-0+ — **£2,047** (£604; £302) — **Stalls** Low

Form RPR

103- **1** **Mrs Bun**[19] 7658 4-9-0 **55** (b) NCallan 9 69+
(K A Ryan) *trckd ldrs: gd hdwy 3f out: led over 2f out: rdn wl over 1f out: drvn ins fnl f and kpt on wl* **7/1**

244- **2** *3/4* **Betteras Bertie**[19] 7658 6-8-10 **51** JimmyQuinn 1 63
(M Brittain) *hld up towards rr: gd hdwy on inner over 2f out: rdn to chse wnr over 1f out: drvn and styd on ins fnl f* **13/2**[3]

532- **3** *4* **Thornaby Green**[17] 7692 8-8-9 **55** DeanHeslop(5) 6 58
(T D Barron) *midfield: gd hdwy 3f out: rdn to chse ldrs 2f out: drvn and one pce appr fnl f* **7/2**[1]

055- **4** *1 3/4* **General Tufto**[5] 7799 4-7-12 **46** (b) AndrewHeffernan(7) 4 45
(C Smith) *in tch: hdwy 3f out: rdn to chse ldng pair over 2f out: sn drvn and kpt on same pce fr over 1f out* **18/1**

050- **5** *4* **Penel (IRE)**[141] 4961 8-8-2 **50** (p) PaulPickard(7) 10 40
(P T Midgley) *towards rr and sn rdn along: hdwy on outer 2f out: sn drvn and kpt on appr fnl f: nt rch ldrs* **20/1**

300- **6** *3 3/4* **Capped For Victory (USA)**[9] 7772 8-8-9 **50** TomEaves 14 31
(G A Swinbank) *chsd ldrs on outer: effrt 3f out: rdn over 2f out and sn one pce* **9/1**

240- **7** *2 1/4* **Very Well Red**[9] 7772 6-8-9 **50** (b) ChrisCatlin 11 26
(P W Hiatt) *led 1f: cl up tl rdn along over 2f out and grad wknd* **8/1**

060- **8** *1* **Anduril**[4] 6912 8-8-7 **48** (b) PatrickMathers 13 22
(I W McInnes) *s.i.s and bhd: wd st: sme hdwy on outer 2f out: nvr a factor* **12/1**

050- **9** *3 1/4* **Government (IRE)**[6] 7779 8-7-12 **46** oh1 AlexEdwards(7) 12 12
(M C Chapman) *prom on inner: led after 1f: rdn along 3f out: sn hdd & wknd* **50/1**

500- **10** *3 1/4* **Komreyev Star**[93] 6353 7-9-0 **55** (t) PaulMulrennan 2 14
(R E Peacock) *towards rr on inner: rdn along 1/2-way: nvr a factor* **33/1**

043- **11** *6* **Louisiade (IRE)**[9] 7772 8-9-0 **55** (b) GregFairley 5 —
(M C Chapman) *cl up: rdn along 3f out: sn drvn and wknd over 2f out* **9/2**[2]

226- **12** *1 1/4* **Dark Planet**[24] 7177 6-8-9 **50** (v) AndrewElliott 7 —
(D W Thompson) *a towards rr* **14/1**

500- **13** *6* **Only A Grand**[148] 4748 5-8-3 **47** (b) DuranFentiman(3) 8 —
(R Bastiman) *cl up on inner: rdn along over 3f out and sn wknd* **16/1**

1m 45.3s (1.60) **Going Correction** +0.275s/f (Slow) **13** Ran SP% **122.5**
Speed ratings (Par 101): **103,102,98,96,92 88,86,85,82,79 73,71,65**
toteswinger: 1&2 £10.30, 1&3 £5.70, 2&3 £5.30. CSF £52.51 CT £196.96 TOTE £7.80: £2.50, £2.50, £1.30; EX 43.10 Trifecta £80.20 Pool: £448.94 - 4.14 winning units. Place 6: £15.60, Place 5: £12.98..

Owner Guy Reed **Bred** Guy Reed **Trained** Hambleton, N Yorks

FOCUS
A moderate contest and very few came into it in the best of form. It has been rated around the third. The winning time was over a second slower than the preceding 86-100 handicap.

Very Well Red Official explanation: trainer said, regarding the poor performance shown, that the mare ran yesterday and today's race came too soon

Anduril Official explanation: jockey said gelding missed the break

Komreyev Star Official explanation: jockey said gelding was never travelling

T/Plt: £31.50 to a £1 stake. Pool: £39,181.16. 906.65 winning tickets. T/Qpdt: £13.40 to a £1 stake. Pool: £2,976.40. 163.60 winning tickets. JR

[1]SOUTHWELL (L-H)
Friday, January 2

OFFICIAL GOING: Standard to slow
Wind: Light across Weather: Bright and dry

8 SOUTHWELL-RACECOURSE.CO.UK AMATEUR RIDERS' H'CAP — 2m (F)
12:10 (12:17) (Class 6) (0-65,63) 4-Y-0+ — **£1,977** (£608; £304) — **Stalls** Low

Form RPR

200- **1** **Hi Dancer**[62] 6786 6-10-6 **55** MissEStead(7) 7 72
(P C Haslam) *trckd ldrs: hdwy 4f out: chsd ldr 3f out: led over 2f out and sn clr: easily* **16/1**

110- **2** *11* **Zaffeu**[24] 7617 8-11-7 **63** MrSDobson 11 66
(A G Juckes) *trckd ldrs: hdwy over 5f out: led over 4f out: rdn and hdd over 2f out: sn drvn and kpt on same pce* **9/1**[3]

000- **3** *12* **Que Beauty (IRE)**[10] 7776 4-9-8 **50** oh4 ow1 (p) MrJohnWilley(7) 3 39
(R C Guest) *s.i.s and in rr: hdwy 4f out: rdn along 3f out: styd on fnl 2f: edgd lft ins fnl f: tk 3rd towards fin* **150/1**

/00- **4** *3/4* **Goblin**[6] 7787 8-10-12 **54** MrSWalker 5 42
(D E Cantillon) *chsd ldrs: pushed along over 6f out: rdn to chse ldng pair 3f out: sn drvn and plugged on same pce: lost 3rd towards fin* **3/1**[1]

501- **5** *nk* **Stravita**[10] 7776 5-10-11 **58** 6ex (p) MrStephenHarrison(5) 12 46
(R Hollinshead) *hld up towards rr: hdwy on inner 4f out: rdn 3f out: sn drvn and kpt on same pce fnl 2f* **3/1**[1]

045- **6** *9* **Restart (IRE)**[27] 7587 8-10-2 **49** oh4 (p) MrJPFeatherstone(5) 2 26
(Lucinda Featherstone) *prom on inner: rdn along 5f out: wknd over 3f out* **12/1**

/30- **7** *6* **Optimum (IRE)**[316] 374 7-10-2 **49** oh4 PeterToole(5) 8 19
(J T Stimpson) *led 5f: cl up tl rdn along 4f out and grad wknd* **14/1**

404- **8** *3 3/4* **Reminiscent (IRE)**[21] 7647 10-10-2 **49** oh4 (p) MissAWallace(5) 6 14
(B P J Baugh) *in tch: hdwy to chse ldrs 4f out: rdn along 3f out: sn wknd* **40/1**

600/ **9** *21* **Eforetta (GER)**[540] 3467 7-11-1 **60** MrMJJSmith(3) 10 —
(A W Carroll) *cl up: led after 5f: rdn along and hdd over 4f out: sn wknd* **16/1**

000- **10** *2 3/4* **Spiritonthemount (USA)**[46] 7366 4-11-0 **63** (b) MrsMarieKing 9 —
(P W Hiatt) *prom: rdn along over 4f out: sn wknd* **12/1**

300- **11** *3* **Sovietta (IRE)**[182] 3698 8-10-0 **49** oh2 (t) MrOJMurphy(7) 4 —
(Ian Williams) *hld up towards rr: effrt over 6f out: sn rdn along and wknd: bhd whn v wd home bnd* **25/1**

010- **12** *7* **Cumbrian Knight (IRE)**[17] 7512 11-11-2 **61** MissRJefferson(3) 14 —
(J M Jefferson) *wnt lft s: hld up and bhd: effrt and pushed along 1/2-way: rdn over 6f out and a in rr* **7/1**[2]

206- **13** *4* **York Cliff**[25] 7608 11-10-8 **53** (e) MrBenBrisbourne(3) 1 —
(W M Brisbourne) *chsd ldrs: rdn along after 6f: sn wknd and bhd fnl 6f* **20/1**

000- **14** *hd* **Charlie Bear**[10] 7776 8-10-7 **49** oh4 GemmaGracey-Davison 13 —
(Miss Z C Davison) *dwlt: a in rr* **100/1**

3m 52.26s (6.76) **Going Correction** +0.325s/f (Slow)
WFA 4 from 5yo+ 7lb **14** Ran SP% **119.0**
Speed ratings (Par 101): **96,90,84,84,83 79,76,74,64,62 61,57,55,55**
toteswinger: 1&2 £18.80, 1&3 £317.40, 2&3 £134.40. CSF £146.13 CT £19078.10 TOTE £23.50: £4.90, £3.00, £26.20; EX 178.60 TRIFECTA Not won..

Owner Middleham Park Racing & R Tocher **Bred** Mrs E Roberts **Trained** Middleham Moor, N Yorks

FOCUS
A moderate amateurs' event and a severe test of stamina on this slow surface. It has not been rated that positively.

Cumbrian Knight(IRE) Official explanation: trainer's representative said said the gelding was never travelling

9 WILLIAM HILL JANUARY SALE NOW ON! H'CAP — 7f (F)
12:40 (12:45) (Class 4) (0-85,81) 4-Y-0+ — **£4,857** (£1,445; £722; £360) — **Stalls** Low

Form RPR

012- **1** **Nightjar (USA)**[20] 7668 4-9-2 **79** GregFairley 8 95
(M Johnston) *cl up: led over 2f out: rdn over 1f out: kpt on wl fnl f* **2/1**[1]

246- **2** *1 1/4* **Blue Charm**[7] 7782 5-8-6 **69** JamesDoyle 3 82
(S Kirk) *trckd ldrs: hdwy 3f out: rdn to chse wnr 2f out: drvn ent fnl f: kpt on same pce* **14/1**

120- **3** *1 3/4* **Resplendent Nova**[12] 7755 7-9-4 **81** JimmyQuinn 7 89
(P Howling) *hld up in tch: hdwy 3f out: swtchd lft and rdn wl over 1f out: drvn and chsd ldng pair ent fnl f: one pce towards fin* **9/2**[3]

012- **4** *8* **Captain Macarry (IRE)**[6] 7796 4-8-11 **74** (v) TomEaves 4 61
(B Smart) *chsd ldrs: rdn along and outpcd after 3f: hdwy to chse ldrs 2f: sn drvn and no imp* **9/4**[2]

040- **5** *3 1/2* **Xpres Maite**[23] 7633 6-8-10 **80** (v) AndrewYoxall(7) 1 57
(S R Bowring) *led: rdn along and hdd 3f out: sn wknd* **25/1**

506- **6** *6* **Kabeer**[10] 7777 11-8-10 **80** (t) KarenKenny(7) 2 41
(A J McCabe) *cl up: led 3f out: rdn and hdd over 2f out: sn wknd* **33/1**

/56- **7** *26* **Eau Good**[249] 1683 5-8-13 **79** KevinGhunowa(3) 6 —
(G J Smith) *in tch: rdn along 3f out: sn wknd* **33/1**

214- **8** *3* **Yes One (IRE)**[227] 2271 5-9-3 **80** ChrisCatlin 5 —
(K A Ryan) *n.m.r sn after s: hld up in rr: effrt on inner 1/2-way: sn rdn and nvr a factor* **5/1**

1m 30.74s (0.44) **Going Correction** +0.325s/f (Slow) **8** Ran SP% **115.3**
Speed ratings (Par 105): **110,108,106,97,93 86,56,53**
toteswinger: 1&2 £5.40, 1&3 £3.60, 2&3 £5.40. CSF £30.01 CT £113.37 TOTE £2.80: £1.20, £3.30, £1.20; EX 29.90 Trifecta £73.70 Pool: £724.73 - 7.27 winning units..

Owner Crone Stud Farms Ltd **Bred** Derry Meeting Farm & London Thoroughbred Services **Trained** Middleham Moor, N Yorks

FOCUS
A fair handicap run in a good time and rated around the winner and third.

10 ALISON GREEN'S BIG BIRTHDAY TODAY CLAIMING STKS — 6f (F)
1:15 (1:20) (Class 6) 3-Y-0 — **£2,047** (£604; £302) — **Stalls** Low

Form RPR

046- **1** **Dancing Wave**[6] 7795 3-8-2 45 AmyBaker(5) 3 55
(M C Chapman) *mde all: rdn 2f out: edgd rt ins fnl f: kpt on* **25/1**

015- **2** *nk* **Glan Lady (IRE)**[14] 7728 3-8-2 60 (p) LiamJones 1 49
(J L Spearing) *rrd s: sn chsng ldrs: rdn over 2f out: drvn over 1f out: kpt on u.p ins fnl f* **4/1**[3]

465- **3** *hd* **Swiss Art (IRE)**[21] 7645 3-8-9 62 (b1) KevinGhunowa(3) 4 58
(R A Harris) *t.k.h: cl up on outer: swtchd wd and effrt 2f out: sn rdn: drvn to chse wnr over 1f out: hrd drvn and edgd lft ins fnl f: nt run on towards fin* **15/8**[1]

034- **4** *6* **Officer Mor (USA)**[3] 7825 3-8-5 61........................(e[1]) DeclanCannon(7) 6 39
(K R Burke) *t.k.h: cl up: rdn along and outpcd 1/2-way: drvn and kpt on fnl 2f: no imp* **3/1**[2]

030- **5** *5* **Sally's Dilemma**[11] 7760 3-8-6 65..................................(t) TolleyDean(3) 2 20
(W G M Turner) *cl up on inner: rdn along wl over 2f out: sn wknd* **4/1**[3]

400- **6** *16* **Jaslyn (IRE)**[21] 7652 3-8-2 46.. JimmyQuinn 5 —
(J R Weymes) *a in rr* **12/1**

1m 19.98s (3.48) **Going Correction** +0.325s/f (Slow) **6** Ran SP% **111.3**
Speed ratings (Par 95): **89,88,88,80,73 52**
toteswinger: 1&2 £7.80, 1&3 £6.90, 2&3 £2.00. CSF £117.26 TOTE £23.70: £5.50, £1.90; EX 112.30.Glan Lady was claimed by Graham Smith for £3,000.
Owner Mrs M Chapman **Bred** B J Goldsmith **Trained** Market Rasen, Lincs

FOCUS
A moderate three-year-old claimer and a very unsatisfactory result. The form is dubious, although the third has been used as the guide for now.

11 WILLIAM HILL JANUARY SALE - BETTER ODDS! MAIDEN STKS 1m 4f (F)
1:45 (1:50) (Class 5) 4-Y-O+ **£2,729** (£806; £403) **Stalls** Low

Form RPR

65- **1** **El Diego (IRE)**[24] 7617 5-9-7 72... ChrisCatlin 9 71
(J R Gask) *cl up: led over 4f out: rdn over 2f out: drvn and edgd rt over 1f out: kpt on u.p ins fnl f* **4/7**[1]

000- **2** *3/4* **Our Nations**[92] 6421 4-9-3 42.. DNolan 7 70
(D Carroll) *trckd ldrs: hdwy and cl up 1/2-way: rdn along 3f out: drvn 2f out: edgd lft over 1f out: rallied u.p ins fnl f: no ex towards fin* **50/1**

454- **3** *10* **Euroceleb (IRE)**[29] 7545 4-8-12 68.. SteveDrowne 2 49
(H Morrison) *trckd ldrs: effrt to chse ldng pair over 3f out: sn rdn and one pce fnl 2f* **11/4**[2]

56- **4** *4* **Tampa Boy (IRE)**[15] 7721 7-9-7 0.. GregFairley 5 47
(M F Harris) *towards rr: sme hdwy over 3f out: sn rdn and kpt on same pce fnl 2f* **25/1**

5- **5** *3 3/4* **Auction Belle**[121] 5117 4-8-12 0.................................... GrahamGibbons 1 36
(R Curtis) *chsd ldrs: rdn along 1/2-way: plugged on same pce fnl 3f* **25/1**

0- **6** *1* **Whiston Pat**[23] 7631 4-9-3 0... PaulEddery 6 40
(S R Bowring) *a in rr* **66/1**

7 *30* **Wing Stealth (IRE)**[126] 5484 4-8-12 0.................................(b) TPQueally 3 —
(M G Quinlan) *led: rdn along and hdd over 4f out: sn wknd* **14/1**[3]

0- **8** *nk* **Stockman**[15] 7721 5-9-7 0.. TravisBlock 8 —
(H Morrison) *rdn along sn after s: a in rr* **16/1**

004/ **9** *30* **Tivers Song (USA)**[463] 5754 5-9-7 55........................ StephenDonohoe 4 —
(John A Harris) *in tch: rdn along and wknd 1/2-way: sn bhd* **16/1**

2m 44.59s (3.59) **Going Correction** +0.325s/f (Slow)
WFA 4 from 5yo+ 4lb **9** Ran SP% **119.9**
Speed ratings (Par 103): **101,100,93,91,88 88,68,67,47**
toteswinger: 1&2 £11.60, 1&3 £1.80, 2&3 £13.60. CSF £57.78 TOTE £1.70: £1.02, £10.80, £1.10; EX 68.60 Trifecta £131.00 Pool: £1003.98 - 5.67 winning units..
Owner Horses First Racing Limited **Bred** Tower Bloodstock **Trained** Sutton Veny, Wilts

FOCUS
This was a very weak maiden, run at a solid early gallop and the first pair pulled clear. Tricky form to pin down but it has been rated at face value for the time being.

12 MEMBERSHIP AT SOUTHWELL GOLF CLUB CLAIMING STKS 1m (F)
2:15 (2:20) (Class 6) 4-Y-O+ **£2,047** (£604; £302) **Stalls** Low

Form RPR

634- **1** **Transmission (IRE)**[6] 7799 4-9-5 60.................................... TomEaves 4 73
(B Smart) *trckd ldrs: hdwy over 3f out: pushed along to chse ldr over 2f out: rdn to ld 1 1/2f out: drvn ins fnl f: kpt on* **9/2**[3]

451- **2** *nk* **Clear Sailing**[15] 7723 6-8-13 74..................................(p) PaulMulrennan 8 66
(Ollie Pears) *sn led: rdn and hung lft 2f out: sn hdd: drvn and rallied ins fnl f: kpt on towards fin* **13/8**[1]

213- **3** *5* **Boundless Prospect (USA)**[15] 7723 10-8-2 70..... PatrickDonaghy(5) 3 49
(P D Evans) *dwlt: sn rdn along and outpcd in rr: hdwy over 2f out: kpt on u.p appr last: nrst fin* **5/2**[2]

000- **4** *11* **Pembo**[35] 7469 4-8-8 48... KevinGhunowa(3) 6 28
(R A Harris) *sn rdn along and outpcd in rr: hdwy over 2f out: styd on u.p appr last: nvr nr ldrs* **40/1**

04- **5** *1/2* **Shortwall Lady (IRE)**[18] 7690 4-8-4 0.................................(b[1]) LiamJones 2 19
(J L Spearing) *in tch: rdn along 3f out: no hdwy* **66/1**

006- **6** *1* **High Five Society**[23] 7634 5-8-9 48 ow2.............(bt) StephenDonohoe 11 22
(S R Bowring) *cl up: rdn along 1/2-way: drvn 3f out and sn wknd* **18/1**

000- **7** *7* **Shadow Jumper (IRE)**[187] 1550 8-8-10 40 ow1.....(v) GrahamGibbons 5 —
(J T Stimpson) *chsd ldrs: rdn along over 3f out and sn wknd* **80/1**

006- **8** *1 3/4* **Redeemed**[14] 7727 4-8-6 58.. JimmyQuinn 1 —
(M Brittain) *midfield: effrt and sme hdwy over 3f out: sn rdn along and wknd* **33/1**

/00- **9** *12* **I'm Agenius**[25] 7608 6-8-4 37.................................... FrankieMcDonald 10 —
(R Curtis) *chsd ldng pair: rdn along 1/2-way: sn wknd* **66/1**

/14- **10** *6* **Blue Sky Thinking (IRE)**[281] 1041 10-9-1 72............ DarrenWilliams 7 —
(K R Burke) *chsd ldrs: rdn along 3f out and sn wknd* **11/2**

/60- **11** *12* **Mays Louise**[344] 289 5-8-8 30.. AndrewElliott 9 —
(B P J Baugh) *chsd ldrs on wd outside: rdn along over 3f out and sn wknd* **100/1**

1m 45.3s (1.60) **Going Correction** +0.325s/f (Slow) **11** Ran SP% **116.1**
Speed ratings (Par 101): **105,104,99,88,88 87,80,78,66,60 48**
toteswinger: 1&2 £3.00, 1&3 £3.40, 2&3 £2.60. CSF £11.86 TOTE £5.40: £1.60, £1.40, £1.20; EX 14.50 Trifecta £52.90 Pool: £946.77 - 13.22 winning units.Transmission was the subject of a friendly claim.
Owner M Barber **Bred** M J Halligan **Trained** Hambleton, N Yorks

FOCUS
A modest claimer in which they went a decent pace and the field finished very well spread out. On the face of it this is an improved effort from the winner, but it is more likely that the runner-up and third ran below form.
Blue Sky Thinking(IRE) Official explanation: jockey said gelding was never travelling

13 WILLIAM HILL JANUARY SALE - WHY BET ELSEWHERE? H'CAP 6f (F)
2:50 (2:56) (Class 5) (0-70,70) 4-Y-O+ **£2,729** (£806; £403) **Stalls** Low

Form RPR

004- **1** **Realt Na Mara (IRE)**[15] 7724 6-9-4 70.............................. TravisBlock 10 79
(H Morrison) *in tch: hdwy 2f out: rdn over 1f out: styd on ins fnl f to ld last 50yds* **13/2**[3]

000- **2** *nk* **Jack Rackham**[55] 7239 5-9-4 70..(v[1]) TomEaves 6 78
(B Smart) *towards rr: hdwy on wd outside over 2f out: rdn to chse ldrs over 1f out: styd on wl fnl f* **13/2**[3]

230- **3** *3/4* **Whitbarrow (IRE)**[33] 7510 10-8-13 68....................(b) JamesMillman(3) 7 73
(B R Millman) *cl up: led 1/2-way: rdn wl over 1f out: drvn and edgd lft appr last: hdd and no ex last 50yds* **5/1**[1]

563- **4** *1 1/4* **Replicator**[13] 7743 4-9-1 67...(v[1]) PaulEddery 11 68
(Pat Eddery) *cl up on outer: hdwy over 2f out: rdn to chal over 1f out and ev ch tl drvn: edgd lft and one pce ent fnl f* **10/1**

120- **5** *1 1/2* **Bold Diva**[11] 7762 4-7-13 56..(v) AmyBaker(5) 5 53
(A W Carroll) *hld up in rr: hdwy 2f out: sn rdn and styd on ins fnl f: nrst fin* **14/1**

000- **6** *1/2* **Cape Of Storms**[56] 7228 6-8-1 56.............................. AndrewMullen(3) 4 51
(R Brotherton) *chsd ldrs: rdn along over 2f out: drvn and one pce fr over 1f out* **12/1**

050- **7** *1* **Fulford**[154] 4609 4-8-5 57.. JimmyQuinn 8 49
(M Brittain) *midfield: hdwy over 2f out: sn rdn and no imp appr fnl f* **13/2**[3]

164- **8** *1* **River Thames**[14] 7730 6-9-1 67..(p) ChrisCatlin 9 56
(K A Ryan) *chsd ldrs: rdn along 2f out: sn drvn and wknd over 1f out* **6/1**[2]

600- **9** *3/4* **Tag Team (IRE)**[178] 3819 8-8-8 60 ow1..................... StephenDonohoe 3 46
(John A Harris) *led: hdd 1/2-way: sn rdn and grad wknd fnl 2f* **22/1**

000- **10** *5* **Loose Caboose (IRE)**[14] 7730 4-8-11 70................(p) KarenKenny(7) 1 40
(A J McCabe) *chsd ldrs on inner: rdn along 3f out: sn wknd* **50/1**

240- **11** *1 1/2* **Cool Sands (IRE)**[23] 7633 7-9-4 70....................................(v) TPQueally 2 35
(J G Given) *dwlt: a in rr* **5/1**[1]

1m 18.31s (1.81) **Going Correction** +0.325s/f (Slow) **11** Ran SP% **117.4**
Speed ratings (Par 103): **100,99,98,96,94 94,92,91,90,83 81**
toteswinger: 1&2 £12.00, 1&3 £5.50, 2&3 £8.40. CSF £48.33 CT £231.00 TOTE £8.40: £2.60, £3.30, £2.10; EX 58.00 Trifecta £685.20 Part won. Pool: £926.50 - 0.97 winning units..
Owner H Morrison **Bred** J C Condon **Trained** East Ilsley, Berks
■ Stewards' Enquiry : Tom Eaves caution: used whip with excessive frequency

FOCUS
A wide-open sprint handicap and there were many in with a chance down the home straight. Solid form rated around the third.
Whitbarrow(IRE) Official explanation: jockey said gelding hung badly left

14 PLAY GOLF AT SOUTHWELL GOLF CLUB H'CAP 7f (F)
3:20 (3:26) (Class 6) (0-60,62) 4-Y-O+ **£2,047** (£604; £302) **Stalls** Low

Form RPR

501- **1** **Norcroft**[10] 7779 7-9-6 62 6ex..(p) VinceSlattery 12 73
(Mrs C A Dunnett) *a.p: effrt to chal 2f out: sn rdn and styd on to ld ent fnl f: drvn: edgd lft and kpt on gamely towards fin* **10/1**

032- **2** *1/2* **Hamaasy**[14] 7727 8-9-0 59.. KevinGhunowa(3) 5 68
(R A Harris) *prom: hdwy to chal over 2f out: rdn and led briefly over 1f out: drvn and hdd ent fnl f: kpt on* **9/2**[2]

066- **3** *1/2* **Mister Benji**[10] 7772 10-8-4 46 oh1..........................(p) AndrewElliott 13 54
(B P J Baugh) *sn led: rdn over 2f out: drvn and hdd over 1f out: kpt on gamely u.p ins fnl f* **33/1**

050- **4** *shd* **Nabeeda**[75] 6840 4-8-13 55.. JimmyQuinn 10 63
(M Brittain) *prom: effrt 3f out: rdn to chal 2f out and ev ch tl drvn and no ex ins fnl f* **9/1**

502- **5** *2* **The City Kid (IRE)**[10] 7779 6-9-1 57................................ DaneO'Neill 11 59
(Miss Gay Kelleway) *towards rr: hdwy over 2f out: rdn wl over 1f out: edgd lft and kpt on insdie last: nrst fin* **4/1**[1]

323- **6** *3/4* **Solicitude**[31] 7533 6-9-2 58..(p) TPQueally 7 58
(D Haydn Jones) *chsd ldrs on outer: hdwy over 2f out: rdn to chal wl over 1f out and ev ch tl drvn and wknd ent fnl f* **13/2**[3]

510- **7** *1 3/4* **Isabella's Fancy**[31] 7533 4-8-3 52........................... DeclanCannon(7) 14 48
(A G Newcombe) *hld up in rr: hdwy 2f out: styd on ins fnl f: nrst fin* **16/1**

606- **8** *3/4* **Magical Song**[6] 7799 4-8-6 53 ow3.......................(p) GabrielHannon(5) 4 47
(R Curtis) *in tch on inner: rdn along 4f out: drvn 3f out and kpt on one pce* **12/1**

050- **9** *1* **Ronnie Howe**[10] 7778 5-9-1 57.................................(t) StephenDonohoe 8 48
(S R Bowring) *chsd ldrs: rdn along over 2f out: sn wknd* **25/1**

424- **10** *shd* **Jojesse**[20] 7663 5-8-7 49.. PaulQuinn 2 40
(G A Swinbank) *bhd tl sme late hdwy* **9/1**

005- **11** *8* **Shava**[22] 7636 9-8-3 48.. DuranFentiman(3) 6 17
(H J Evans) *in tch: rdn along 3f out: sn wknd* **16/1**

000- **12** *1 1/4* **To Bubbles**[31] 7534 4-9-4 60.. SimonWhitworth 1 26
(A G Newcombe) *dwlt: a in rr* **33/1**

205- **13** *nk* **Avoca Dancer (IRE)**[14] 7727 6-9-4 60................................(e) ChrisCatlin 9 25
(Miss Gay Kelleway) *a towards rr* **25/1**

000- **14** *5* **Rabbit Fighter (IRE)**[21] 7653 5-9-4 60......................(v) DarrenWilliams 3 11
(D Shaw) *dwlt: a in rr* **8/1**

1m 31.78s (1.48) **Going Correction** +0.325s/f (Slow) **14** Ran SP% **124.7**
Speed ratings (Par 101): **104,103,102,102,100 99,97,96,95,95 86,84,84,78**
toteswinger: 1&2 £8.60, 1&3 £61.20, 2&3 £33.90. CSF £54.53 CT £1500.75 TOTE £13.20: £3.30, £1.70, £8.60; EX 67.50 TRIFECTA Not won. Place 6: £238.30 Place 5: £18.99.
Owner The Star Seekers **Bred** Norcroft Park Stud **Trained** Hingham, Norfolk

FOCUS
A moderate if competitive handicap and there were five in a line across the track passing the furlong pole. It paid to be handy though, as the first four home were all up with the pace throughout. The form looks solid despite the surprisingly good run from the third.
T/Jkpt: Not won. T/Plt: £177.40 to a £1 stake. Pool: £76,494.03. 314.63 winning tickets. T/Qpdt: £5.60 to a £1 stake. Pool: £8,596.33. 1,117.75 winning tickets. JR

WOLVERHAMPTON (A.W) (L-H)
Friday, January 2

OFFICIAL GOING: Standard
Wind: Nil Weather: Clear and cold

15 STAY AT THE WOLVERHAMPTON HOLIDAY INN H'CAP 5f 20y(P)
6:50 (6:50) (Class 6) (0-65,65) 4-Y-O+ **£2,047** (£604; £302) **Stalls** Low

Form RPR

604- **1** **Nickel Silver**[14] 7733 4-8-13 60..(b[1]) TomEaves 1 79+
(B Smart) *mde all: edgd rt and rdn over 1f out: r.o wl* **13/2**[3]

201- **2** *3 1/4* **Admiral Bond (IRE)**[31] 7528 4-9-1 62....................(p) PaulMulrennan 9 69
(G R Oldroyd) *hld up in mid-div: rdn and edgd lft over 1f out: hdwy fnl f: tk 2nd towards fin: nt trble wnr* **15/2**

425- **3** *1* **Liberty Ship**[25] 7611 4-9-2 63..(tp) JimmyQuinn 7 66
(J D Bethell) *hld up in tch: swtchd lft wl over 1f out: wnt 2nd wl ins fnl f: no ex* **5/1**[1]

210- **4** *nk* **Grand Palace (IRE)**[39] 7435 6-9-4 65........................(v) DarrenWilliams 10 67
(D Shaw) *s.i.s: towards rr: rdn wl over 1f out: hdwy fnl f: r.o* **18/1**

263- **5** *nk* **Ryedane (IRE)**[14] 7733 7-8-12 62..............................(b) DuranFentiman(3) 2 63
(T D Easterby) *hld up in tch: rdn and chsd wnr over 1f out: lost 2nd and no ex wl ins fnl f* **11/2**[2]

106- **6** *1* **Royal Manor**[11] 7762 4-9-3 64.. FergusSweeney 13 62
(N J Vaughan) *wnt sltly rt s: t.k.h in rr: swtchd lft after 1f: swtchd rt over 1f out: late prog: nvr nrr* **16/1**

000- **7** *nse* **Decider (USA)**[11] 7762 6-8-12 62 KevinGhunowa(3) 4 59
(R A Harris) *w wnr 3f: rdn over 1f out: hld whn n.m.r towards fin* **14/1**

403- **8** *3/4* **Punching**[23] 7629 5-9-4 65 LPKeniry 12 60+
(C R Dore) *hld up in rr: swtchd lft after 1f: nt clr run wl over 1f out tl r.o ins fnl f: nt clr run towards fin* **16/1**

244- **9** *nk* **Bluebok**[13] 7743 8-8-11 63 (bt) MCGeran(5) 11 57
(J M Bradley) *s.i.s: t.k.h early towards rr: n.d* **22/1**

205- **10** *2 1/2* **Metal Guru**[32] 7517 5-8-13 63 (p) RussellKennemore(3) 8 48
(R Hollinshead) *hld up in tch: c wd st: rdn and wknd wl over 1f out* **10/1**

005- **11** *1/2* **Ten Down**[13] 7743 4-9-3 64 ShaneKelly 3 47
(M Quinn) *hld up in tch: rdn wl over 1f out: sn wknd* **7/1**

200- **12** *nk* **Gwilym (GER)**[30] 7540 6-9-2 63 (b) TPQueally 5 45
(D Haydn Jones) *prom tl rdn and wknd wl over 1f out* **11/1**

/R0- **13** *2 1/2* **Fitolini**[214] 2660 4-9-0 61 GrahamGibbons 6 34
(Mrs G S Rees) *hld up in mid-div: short-lived effrt on ins over 1f out: wknd ins fnl f* **50/1**

61.62 secs (-0.68) **Going Correction** +0.10s/f (Slow) **13** Ran SP% **117.1**
Speed ratings (Par 101): **109,103,102,101,101 99,99,98,97,93 93,92,88**
toteswinger: 1&2 £14.00, 1&3 £6.60, 2&3 £9.70. CSF £53.49 CT £274.66 TOTE £5.90: £4.40, £2.90, £2.00; EX 97.50.
Owner M Barber **Bred** Mrs Sheila White **Trained** Hambleton, N Yorks

FOCUS
A wide-open handicap featuring a number of horses who like to be up with the pace. The form looks sound rated around the runner-up and third.
Punching Official explanation: jockey said gelding was denied a clear run
Fitolini Official explanation: jockey said filly lost its action

16 DINE IN THE HORIZONS RESTAURANT CLAIMING STKS 1m 141y(P)
7:20 (7:21) (Class 5) 3-Y-O £2,729 (£806; £403) **Stalls** Low

Form RPR

114- **1** **Hold The Bucks (USA)**[15] 7718 3-8-9 67 LukeMorris 2 64
(J S Moore) *led over 1f: a.p: hrd rdn to ld towards fin* **2/5**[1]

440- **2** *1/2* **Turn To Dreams**[2] 7832 3-8-0 47 JimmyQuinn 3 54
(P D Evans) *led 7f out: hrd rdn wl over 1f out: sn edgd rt: hdd towards fin* **10/1**[3]

160- **3** *3/4* **Madison Belle**[21] 7645 3-8-9 68 DarrenWilliams 5 61
(K R Burke) *carried lft s: t.k.h in tch: wnt 2nd over 2f out: rdn and ev ch ins fnl f: nt qckn cl home* **13/2**[2]

000- **4** *3/4* **Sicilian Warrior (USA)**[11] 7760 3-8-7 0 (t) LPKeniry 7 58
(P F I Cole) *s.i.s: stdd after 1f: hld up and bhd: rdn 3f out: hdwy 1f out: sn edgd lft: kpt on one pce* **10/1**[3]

000- **5** *1* **Talsarnau (IRE)**[152] 4658 3-8-5 48 LiamJones 6 53?
(W M Brisbourne) *wnt lft s: t.k.h: chsd ldr after 6f tl over 2f out: one pce* **50/1**

606- **6** *nk* **Give (IRE)**[25] 7607 3-8-0 49 (p) FrankieMcDonald 4 48
(R A Harris) *hmpd s: hld up: n.m.r over 2f out: rdn over 1f out: nvr able to chal* **18/1**

1m 53.65s (3.15) **Going Correction** +0.10s/f (Slow) **6** Ran SP% **110.2**
Speed ratings (Par 97): **90,89,88,88,87 87**
toteswinger: 1&2 £1.10, 1&3 £4.90, 2&3 £18.80. CSF £5.10 TOTE £1.30: £1.02, £3.90; EX 4.30.
Owner E Moore & J S Moore **Bred** David E Hager II **Trained** Upper Lambourn, Berks

FOCUS
A moderate claimer and the winner did not have to be at his best to score. The runner-up and fourth are the best guide to the level.

17 WILLIAM HILL JANUARY SALE NOW ON! H'CAP 1m 141y(P)
7:50 (7:50) (Class 4) (0-85,85) 4-Y-O+ £5,180 (£1,541; £770; £384) **Stalls** Low

Form RPR

110- **1** **Harald Bluetooth (IRE)**[153] 4641 4-9-3 83 FergusSweeney 4 94+
(D M Simcock) *hld up and bhd: swtchd lft and hdwy on ins wl over 1f out: led ins fnl f: pushed clr* **3/1**[1]

166- **2** *2 3/4* **Randama Bay (IRE)**[13] 7740 4-8-9 75 CatherineGannon 10 80
(I A Wood) *led 7f out: rdn over 1f out: hdd and nt qckn ins fnl f* **25/1**

44-5 **3** *nk* **Just Bond (IRE)**[1] 6 7-9-4 83 PaulMulrennan 9 87
(G R Oldroyd) *t.k.h towards rr: hdwy on outside over 3f out: rdn and kpt on ins fnl f* **4/1**[2]

164- **4** *1/2* **Mister New York (USA)**[12] 7755 4-9-5 85 GeorgeBaker 8 88
(Noel T Chance) *hld up and bhd: c wd st: rdn wl over 1f out: sn hung lft: kpt on ins fnl f* **3/1**[1]

420- **5** *3/4* **Wisdom's Kiss**[53] 7278 5-8-11 76 (b) JimmyQuinn 2 77
(J D Bethell) *t.k.h in tch: rdn wl over 1f out: one pce ins fnl f* **15/2**

5/1- **6** *nk* **January**[18] 7690 6-9-3 82 (t) ShaneKelly 5 83
(T M Walsh, Ire) *s.i.s: t.k.h: sn in tch: rdn and btn 1f out* **6/1**[3]

416- **7** *nk* **Direct Debit (IRE)**[28] 7564 6-8-13 78 LukeMorris 6 78
(M Wellings) *led over 1f: chsd ldr: ev ch over 2f out: rdn over 1f out: wknd wl ins fnl f* **10/1**

100/ **8** *8* **Lets Get Cracking (FR)**[293] 3058 5-8-5 70 oh5 NeilChalmers 1 51
(A E Jones) *prom tl wknd over 2f out* **100/1**

5/3- **P** **Fifty Cents**[274] 1174 5-9-3 82 SteveDrowne 3 —
(M F Harris) *hld up in mid-div: lost pl over 4f out: lost action and p.u over 2f out: dismntd* **20/1**

1m 52.39s (1.89) **Going Correction** +0.10s/f (Slow)
WFA 4 from 5yo+ 1lb **9** Ran SP% **114.7**
Speed ratings (Par 105): **95,92,92,91,91 90,90,83,—**
toteswinger: 1&2 £39.60, 1&3 £10.50, 2&3 £26.40. CSF £81.36 CT £306.36 TOTE £5.30: £1.70, £6.10, £2.20; EX 148.20.
Owner Ahmad Al Shaikh **Bred** Airlie Stud And Sir Thomas Pilkington **Trained** Newmarket, Suffolk

FOCUS
A decent handicap and a clear-cut winner. The bare form is ordinary, though, rated around the runner-up and fourth to their recent best off stiffish marks.
Just Bond(IRE) Official explanation: jockey said gelding hung right
Fifty Cents Official explanation: jockey said gelding had lost its action

18 WILLIAM HILL JANUARY SALE - BETTER ODDS! H'CAP 1m 4f 50y(P)
8:20 (8:20) (Class 6) (0-55,55) 4-Y-O+ £2,047 (£604; £302) **Stalls** Low

Form RPR

01- **1** **Blockley (USA)**[23] 7626 5-9-2 54 StephenDonohoe 9 64
(Ian Williams) *hld up in mid-div: pushed along over 6f out: rdn and hdwy 3f out: led ins fnl f: r.o* **6/1**

650- **2** *1/2* **Dansilver**[46] 4704 5-9-2 54 ShaneKelly 4 64
(A W Carroll) *hld up towards rr: c wd st: rdn and hdwy over 1f out: r.o to take 2nd wl ins fnl f* **33/1**

334- **3** *2 1/4* **Compton Falcon**[16] 7702 5-9-0 52 TPQueally 6 58
(G A Butler) *hld up in rr: hdwy over 2f out: n.m.r ent st: sn edgd lft: kpt on to take 3rd towards fin* **4/1**[2]

040- **4** *1* **Fenners (USA)**[23] 7626 6-8-13 51 (v[1]) DaleGibson 1 55
(M W Easterby) *hld up towards rr: rdn and hdwy over 2f out: edgd lft over 1f out: kpt on u.p ins fnl f* **15/2**

112/ **5** *nse* **Bernabeu (IRE)**[89] 6513 7-9-1 53 JamesDoyle 8 57
(S Curran) *chsd ldr: led jst over 3f out: hrd rdn and hdd ins fnl f: fdd* **12/1**

005- **6** *nk* **Snow Dancer (IRE)**[21] 7656 5-8-11 54 (p) SladeO'Hara(5) 7 58
(H A McWilliams) *a.p: rdn 3f out: chal 2f out tl no ex ins fnl f* **16/1**

063- **7** *3 1/4* **Desert Hawk**[20] 7667 8-8-13 51 LukeMorris 11 50
(W M Brisbourne) *hld up in rr: c wd st: rdn over 1f out: n.d* **16/1**

330- **8** *1/2* **Ready To Crown (USA)**[58] 6255 5-9-1 53 ChrisCatlin 3 51
(Andrew Turnell) *prom: rdn over 2f out: wknd fnl f* **9/1**

/30- **9** *3/4* **Daggerman**[31] 7532 4-8-13 55 GrahamGibbons 2 52
(R Curtis) *hld up in mid-div: rdn and flashed tail wl over 1f out: sn btn* **66/1**

210- **10** *11* **Sagunt (GER)**[5] 7806 6-8-10 55 (p) RossAtkinson(7) 5 34
(S Curran) *s.i.s: in rr: no ch fnl 2f* **5/1**[3]

452- **11** *7* **Sir Liam (USA)**[16] 7702 5-9-2 54 RichardKingscote 10 22
(Tom Dascombe) *led: hdd jst over 3f out: rdn and wknd over 2f out* **3/1**[1]

2m 40.7s (-0.40) **Going Correction** +0.10s/f (Slow)
WFA 4 from 5yo+ 4lb **11** Ran SP% **121.6**
Speed ratings (Par 101): **105,104,103,102,102 102,100,99,99,91 87**
toteswinger: 1&2 £4.20, 1&3 £11.60, 2&3 £29.30. CSF £187.92 CT £898.02 TOTE £7.80: £3.20, £4.60, £1.40; EX 260.40.
Owner Ian Williams **Bred** Payson Stud Inc **Trained** Portway, Worcs

FOCUS
An ordinary handicap but solid enough form rated through the fairly reliable third and fourth.

19 WOLVERHAMPTON-RACECOURSE.CO.UK MAIDEN STKS 5f 216y(P)
8:50 (8:52) (Class 5) 3-Y-O £3,070 (£906; £453) **Stalls** Low

Form RPR

222- **1** **Romantic Queen**[22] 7640 3-8-12 67 DaneO'Neill 4 68
(E A L Dunlop) *hld up: hdwy 2f out: swtchd lft wl over 1f out: rdn to ld ins fnl f: drvn clr* **9/2**[2]

220- **2** *2* **Minotaurious (IRE)**[104] 6102 3-8-12 79 FergusSweeney 8 62
(K R Burke) *t.k.h: led early: chsd ldr: led over 2f out: hdd and edgd rt ins fnl f: nt qckn* **5/4**[1]

04- **3** *3/4* **Gurteen Diamond**[14] 7735 3-8-12 0 LukeMorris 2 59
(N J Vaughan) *s.i.s: hld up: nt clr run wl over 1f out: sn swtchd rt: r.o ins fnl f: tk 3rd post* **12/1**

04- **4** *nse* **Giant Strides**[7] 7783 3-8-12 0 JamesDoyle 7 59
(P D Evans) *in rr: r.o ins fnl f: nvr nr to chal* **40/1**

400- **5** *3/4* **My Best Man**[74] 6865 3-9-3 65 TGMcLaughlin 1 62
(B R Millman) *a.p: rdn over 1f out: one pce* **5/1**[3]

5- **6** *2* **Keep Icy Calm (IRE)**[36] 7458 3-8-12 0 MichaelHills 3 50
(W J Haggas) *hld up in tch: wnt 2nd briefly wl over 1f out: rdn and wknd ins fnl f* **11/2**

056- **7** *2 3/4* **Jhinga Palak (IRE)**[20] 7660 3-8-12 0 StephenDonohoe 6 41
(P D Evans) *prom 2f: sn pushed along and struggling* **22/1**

564- **8** *4 1/2* **Swiss Lake Sweetie (USA)**[14] 7734 3-8-12 61 ChrisCatlin 5 27
(George Baker) *t.k.h: sn led: hdd over 2f out: wknd over 1f out* **14/1**

1m 16.15s (1.15) **Going Correction** +0.10s/f (Slow) **8** Ran SP% **115.8**
Speed ratings (Par 97): **96,93,92,92,91 88,84,78**
toteswinger: 1&2 £1.10, 1&3 £6.00, 2&3 £11.50. CSF £10.67 TOTE £5.80: £1.20, £1.10, £3.40; EX 14.80.
Owner Mohammed Jaber **Bred** G B Turnbull Ltd **Trained** Newmarket, Suffolk

FOCUS
No more than a modest maiden. It has been rated around the winner, fourth and fifth.

20 WILLIAM HILL JANUARY SALE - WHY BET ELSEWHERE? H'CAP 5f 216y(P)
9:20 (9:22) (Class 4) (0-80,85) 4-Y-O+ £5,180 (£1,541; £770; £384) **Stalls** Low

Form RPR

123- **1** **Princess Valerina**[20] 7671 5-8-11 72 TPQueally 5 83
(D Haydn Jones) *t.k.h in tch: led over 1f out: edgd lft ins fnl f: r.o wl* **4/1**[2]

321- **2** *2 1/4* **Dvinsky (USA)**[3] 7828 8-9-10 85 6ex (b) PaulDoe 7 89
(P Howling) *chsd ldr: ev ch 1f out: nt qckn* **5/1**[3]

0/ **3** *1* **Collingwood (IRE)**[28] 7572 7-8-9 70 (b) ShaneKelly 1 71
(T M Walsh, Ire) *hld up: swtchd rt over 1f out: kpt on to take 3rd wl ins fnl f* **4/1**[2]

000- **4** *hd* **Count Ceprano (IRE)**[26] 7592 5-9-3 78 LiamJones 6 78
(C R Dore) *hld up: rdn 1f out: kpt on: nvr able to chal* **6/1**

304- **5** *1 3/4* **Distinctly Game**[44] 7384 7-9-2 77 ChrisCatlin 3 72
(K A Ryan) *led: rdn and hdd over 1f out: wknd wl ins fnl f* **11/4**[1]

016- **6** *1/2* **Trimlestown (IRE)**[13] 7748 6-8-11 72 (p) DaneO'Neill 2 65
(P D Evans) *anticipated s: prom: ev ch over 1f out: sn rdn: wknd wl ins fnl f* **6/1**

1m 14.41s (-0.59) **Going Correction** +0.10s/f (Slow) **6** Ran SP% **111.9**
Speed ratings (Par 105): **107,104,102,102,100 99**
toteswinger: 1&2 £1.10, 1&3 £2.30, 2&3 £15.00. CSF £23.52 TOTE £4.20: £1.80, £2.90; EX 19.30 Place 6: £55.36 Place 5: £26.30.
Owner G J Hicks **Bred** George Joseph Hicks **Trained** Efail Isaf, Rhondda C Taff

FOCUS
A fair handicap but ordinary form.
T/Plt: £104.00 to a £1 stake. Pool: £133,275.25. 934.90 winning tickets. T/Qpdt: £30.30 to a £1 stake. Pool: £8,045.79. 196.35 winning tickets. KH

KEMPTON (A.W) (R-H)
Saturday, January 3

OFFICIAL GOING: Standard
Wind: Light, half against Weather: Bright

21 WILLIAM HILL TELEBETTING SALE - 0800 44 40 40 H'CAP 1m 3f (P)
2:05 (2:05) (Class 5) (0-75,74) 4-Y-O+ £2,590 (£770; £385; £192) **Stalls** High

Form RPR

441- **1** **Sky Quest (IRE)**[17] 7702 11-8-5 62 NathanAlison(7) 5 68
(J R Boyle) *trckd ldrs: effrt over 1f out: led ins fnl f: edgd lft: hld on wl* **11/2**

662- **2** *nk* **Will He Wish**[12] 7758 13-9-10 74 (v[1]) TPQueally 6 79
(S Gollings) *chsd ldr: led 2f out out to ins fnl f: r.o u.p* **15/2**

613- **3** *1/2* **Tropical Tradition (IRE)**[26] 7604 4-8-7 60 RichardKingscote 7 65
(D W P Arbuthnot) *set modest pce to 2f out: rallied: one pce ins fnl f* **3/1**[1]

311- **4** *hd* **Can Can Star**[27] 7590 6-9-6 70 JimCrowley 3 74
(A W Carroll) *t.k.h: hld up in tch: effrt 2f out: kpt on same pce u.p fnl f* **7/2**[2]

056- 5 hd **Epidaurian King (IRE)**[12] 7758 6-8-11 61.................. DarrenWilliams 4 65
(D Shaw) *plld hrd: hld up: effrt over 1f out: rdn and no ex fnl f* 16/1

053- 6 ½ **Mr Napoleon (IRE)**[28] 7580 7-9-5 69.................................. AdamKirby 1 72
(G L Moore) *prom: outpcd 2f out: kpt on u.p fnl f: no imp* 5/1[3]

125- 7 1¼ **Ryedale Ovation (IRE)**[43] 7405 6-9-2 66.................. SimonWhitworth 2 67
(M Hill) *dwlt: hld up: rdn over 2f out: no imp fr over 1f out* 7/2[2]

2m 28.5s (6.60) **Going Correction** +0.20s/f (Slow)
WFA 4 from 6yo+ 3lb 7 Ran SP% **119.1**
Speed ratings (Par 103): **84,83,83,83,83 82,81**
toteswinger: 1&2 £6.70, 1&3 £4.60, 2&3 £7.40. CSF £47.56 TOTE £7.30: £2.60, £3.70; EX 39.30.
Owner M C Cook **Bred** Pendley Farm **Trained** Epsom, Surrey

FOCUS
A steady pace to this modest handicap resulted in a bunch finish and the form looks somewhat suspect.

22 WILLIAMHILL.COM SALE - BETTER ODDS! H'CAP (DIV I) 6f (P)
2:35 (2:38) (Class 6) (0-60,59) 4-Y-0+ **£1,706** (£503; £252) **Stalls** High

Form RPR

004- 1 **Namu**[12] 7762 6-9-3 58...(p) AdamKirby 9 70
(Miss T Spearing) *hld up: qcknd to ld appr fnl f: kpt on wl fnl f* 7/1

420- 2 1 **Duke Of Milan (IRE)**[5] 7808 6-8-13 54.............................. TPQueally 4 63
(G C Bravery) *stdd rr: hdwy whn nt clr run and swtchd rt over 1f out: chsd wnr ins fnl f: r.o* 6/1[3]

022- 3 2 **Welsh Opera**[5] 7809 4-8-9 55..................................(t) WilliamCarson(5) 7 58
(S C Williams) *trckd ldrs: rdn and edgd lft 2f out: kpt on same pce fnl f* 9/4[1]

250- 4 nk **Muktasb (USA)**[14] 7745 8-9-2 57....................................(v) JimCrowley 10 59
(D Shaw) *hld up in tch: hdwy and ev ch over 1f out: one pce fnl f* 4/1[2]

033- 5 1 **Green Lagonda (AUS)**[187] 3559 7-9-3 58..................... MickyFenton 5 56
(Stef Liddiard) *led to appr fnl f: no ex ins fnl f* 8/1

603- 6 nk **Sherjawy (IRE)**[11] 7774 5-8-4 45..........................(b) SimonWhitworth 3 42
(Miss Z C Davison) *trckd ldrs: rdn and outpcd wl over 1f out: kpt on fnl f: no imp* 16/1

660- 7 1 **Wiltshire (IRE)**[154] 4653 7-8-12 53.................................(v) TonyCulhane 8 47
(P T Midgley) *hld up in tch: hdwy 2f out: rdn appr fnl f: sn no ex* 15/2

050- 8 1¾ **Tyrannosaurus Rex (IRE)**[11] 7778 5-9-1 56...........(v) DarrenWilliams 6 45
(D Shaw) *hld up: effrt on outside over 1f out: wknd ins fnl f* 10/1

550- 9 8 **King Of Charm (IRE)**[4] 2097 6-8-1 47.........................(b) AmyBaker(5) 1 10
(M Hill) *w ldr tl wknd fr 2f out* 25/1

1m 13.5s (0.40) **Going Correction** +0.20s/f (Slow) 9 Ran SP% **119.3**
Speed ratings (Par 101): **105,103,101,100,99 98,97,95,84**
toteswinger: 1&2 £7.30, 1&3 £3.30, 2&3 £5.70. CSF £50.18 CT £127.16 TOTE £7.30: £2.20, £2.00, £1.40; EX 56.20 Trifecta £177.80 Pool: £528.83 - 2.20 winning units..
Owner Advantage Chemicals Holdings Ltd **Bred** Philip Graham Harvey **Trained** Alcester, Warwicks

FOCUS
A moderate sprint.
Duke Of Milan(IRE) Official explanation: jockey said gelding was denied a clear run

23 WILLIAMHILL.COM SALE - BONUSES GALORE! H'CAP 7f (P)
3:10 (3:10) (Class 6) (0-50,50) 4-Y-0+ **£2,047** (£604; £302) **Stalls** High

Form RPR

000- 1 **Too Grand**[17] 7707 4-9-0 50..(v) NeilChalmers 13 61
(J J Bridger) *dwlt: sn midfield: hdwy over 2f out: led ins fnl f: drvn out* 14/1

000- 2 2½ **Balerno**[4] 7817 10-8-10 46..(b) PaulDoe 12 50
(Mrs L J Mongan) *prom: rdn over 2f out: edgd lft wl over 1f out: chsd wnr ins fnl f: r.o* 16/1

000- 3 ¾ **Chalentina**[4] 7818 6-8-3 46 oh1.................................. PNolan(7) 11 48
(J E Long) *s.i.s: bhd tl styd on fr 2f out: nrst fin* 33/1

012- 4 shd **Cavalry Guard (USA)**[4] 7818 5-8-9 50..........................(v) AmyBaker(5) 8 52
(T D McCarthy) *chsd ldrs: outpcd over 3f out: hdwy over 1f out: kpt on wl fnl f* 10/3[1]

/32- 5 nse **Mocha Java**[15] 7736 6-8-11 47.. JimmyQuinn 2 49
(M Salaman) *hld up: pushed along 1/2-way: kpt on wl fnl f: nrst fin* 11/2[3]

000- 6 ½ **Briannsta (IRE)**[4] 7817 7-8-12 48..............................(b[1]) RichardThomas 9 48
(J E Long) *t.k.h: led: clr 1/2-way: rdn and hung lft over 1f out: edgd rt and hdd ins fnl f: sn btn* 20/1

066- 7 ½ **Prix Masque (IRE)**[4] 7818 5-9-0 50.............................. DarrenWilliams 6 49
(Christian Wroe) *stdd and swtchd rt s: hld up: hdwy 2f out: no imp fnl f* 9/1

000- 8 ¾ **Beckenham's Secret**[20] 7678 5-8-11 47 oh1 ow1........... AdamKirby 14 44
(A W Carroll) *chsd ldr: rdn over 2f out: wknd ins fnl f* 14/1

060- 9 2½ **Nordic Light (USA)**[22] 7644 5-8-10 46 oh1......................... LukeMorris 10 36
(J M Bradley) *in tch: rdn 3f out: wknd over 1f out* 28/1

603- 10 1¼ **Franksalot (IRE)**[4] 7817 9-8-13 49..........................(b) PatrickMathers 4 36
(I W McInnes) *bhd and sn pushed along: sme late hdwy: nvr on terms* 5/1[2]

024- 11 7 **Rosie Cross (IRE)**[20] 7678 5-8-3 46 oh1...............(p) DanielBlackett(7) 1 14
(Eve Johnson Houghton) *racd wd in midfield: lost pl 1/2-way: n.d after* 10/1

050- 12 1¼ **Stargazy**[73] 6913 5-8-5 46 oh1............................ WilliamCarson(5) 3 10
(W G M Turner) *bhd: drvn along 1/2-way: nvr on terms* 22/1

000- 13 4½ **Mr Rev**[17] 7706 6-8-11 47...(p) SteveDrowne 5 —
(J M Bradley) *midfield on outside: lost pl after 3f: n.d after* 16/1

040- 14 3¼ **Tuning Fork**[4] 7818 9-8-10 46 oh1..................................(e) JimCrowley 7 —
(M J Attwater) *in tch: drvn 3f out: btn over 1f out* 9/1

1m 27.21s (1.21) **Going Correction** +0.20s/f (Slow) 14 Ran SP% **124.8**
Speed ratings (Par 101): **101,98,97,97,97 96,95,95,92,90 82,81,76,72**
toteswinger: 1&2 £66.90, 1&3 £123.00, 2&3 £125.60. CSF £217.93 CT £4000.46 TOTE £18.50: £3.50, £6.90, £13.10; EX 201.90 Trifecta £300.90 Pool: £813.50 - 2.00 winning units..
Owner J J Bridger **Bred** Miss J Chaplin **Trained** Liphook, Hants

FOCUS
A very moderate handicap which was run at a strong pace and the form looks suspect.
Cavalry Guard(USA) Official explanation: trainer said that the race may have come too soon for the gelding

24 WILLIAMHILL.COM SALE - DAILY DOUBLES! H'CAP 6f (P)
3:40 (3:40) (Class 4) (0-85,83) 4-Y-0+ **£4,857** (£1,445; £722; £360) **Stalls** High

Form RPR

241- 1 **River Kirov (IRE)**[3] 7834 6-8-8 70 6ex ow2..................... SteveDrowne 5 86+
(M Wigham) *trckd ldrs: smooth hdwy 2f out: shkn up to ld ent fnl f: pushed clr: readily* 11/10[1]

340- 2 3 **Restless Genius (IRE)**[7] 7796 4-8-5 67.................................. PaulDoe 7 73
(B Ellison) *chsd ldr: rdn and ev ch 1f out: kpt on: nt pce of wnr* 14/1

351- 3 nse **Musical Script (USA)**[12] 7762 6-8-11 73..................(b) TGMcLaughlin 3 79
(Mouse Hamilton-Fairley) *bhd: effrt and swtchd rt 2f out: kpt on u.p fnl f* 7/1

005- 4 1 **Fromsong (IRE)**[13] 7756 11-9-2 83.......................... JamesO'Reilly(5) 4 86
(D K Ivory) *led to ent fnl f: kpt on same pce* 14/1

032- 5 1 **Forest Dane**[12] 7762 9-8-9 71.. JimCrowley 2 71
(Mrs N Smith) *hld up: rdn over 2f out: no imp fnl f* 11/2[3]

143- 6 ½ **Resplendent Alpha**[15] 7730 5-9-2 78................................ JimmyQuinn 6 76
(P Howling) *hld up: effrt 2f out: no ex ins fnl f* 7/2[2]

520- 7 6 **Red Rudy**[215] 2667 7-8-7 69.. LukeMorris 1 48
(A W Carroll) *t.k.h: in tch tl rdn and wknd over 1f out* 20/1

1m 12.4s (-0.70) **Going Correction** +0.20s/f (Slow) 11 Ran SP% **115.8**
Speed ratings (Par 105): **112,108,107,106,105 104,96**
toteswinger: 1&2 £4.90, 1&3 £1.90, 2&3 £9.90. CSF £19.59 TOTE £1.80: £1.40, £5.80; EX 19.40.
Owner A Darke T Matthews M Wigham **Bred** Kildaragh Stud **Trained** Newmarket, Suffolk

FOCUS
A fair handicap.
River Kirov(IRE) Official explanation: jockey said gelding was denied a clear run

25 WILLIAM HILL TELEBETTING SALE - ENHANCED FAVOURITES! H'CAP 1m (P)
4:10 (4:11) (Class 6) (0-65,63) 4-Y-0+ **£2,047** (£604; £302) **Stalls** High

Form RPR

000- 1 **Lopinot (IRE)**[7] 7790 6-8-12 57...(v) JimCrowley 5 69
(M R Bosley) *hld up in tch: effrt and rdn over 1f out: led wl ins fnl f: r.o* 14/1

006/ 2 nk **Kilburn**[483] 5218 5-9-1 60.. SteveDrowne 10 71
(A J Lidderdale) *led: rdn and qcknd 2f out: hdd wl ins fnl f: kpt on* 6/1

510- 3 2¼ **Fine Ruler (IRE)**[8] 7786 5-9-3 62..................................... VinceSlattery 8 68
(M R Bosley) *hld up: hdwy 2f out: rdn and r.o fnl f* 6/1

304/ 4 1 **Bollywood Style**[411] 6865 4-8-6 51.. LiamJones 9 55
(J R Best) *prom: effrt 2f out: kpt on same pce fnl f* 8/1

513- 5 nk **Baileborough (IRE)**[15] 7732 10-8-11 56........................... JimmyQuinn 2 59+
(B Ellison) *midfield: rdn over 3f out: nt clr run and outpcd wl over 1f out: kpt on wl fnl f* 9/2[2]

354- 6 1¾ **Charming Escort**[12] 7763 5-8-12 57...................................... TPQueally 3 56
(T T Clement) *hld up: rdn 2f out: kpt on fnl f: nvr rchd ldrs* 6/1

305- 7 1¾ **Spinning Ridge (IRE)**[15] 7729 4-9-1 63.................. KevinGhunowa(3) 6 58
(R A Harris) *cl up: rdn 2f out: wknd ent fnl f* 40/1

405- 8 1¾ **Jessica Wigmo**[147] 4863 6-8-10 55....................................... LukeMorris 7 46+
(A W Carroll) *s.i.s: bhd: rdn whn nt clr run wl over 1f out: n.d* 12/1

400- 9 5 **Inquisitress**[6] 7800 5-8-5 50...................................... FrankieMcDonald 4 29
(J J Bridger) *cl up tl wknd wl over 1f out* 11/2[3]

011- 10 8 **Tuxedo**[12] 7763 4-9-2 61.. TGMcLaughlin 1 22
(P W Hiatt) *bhd on outside: drvn 1/2-way: wknd over 2f out: eased whn no ch fnl f* 4/1[1]

1m 41.38s (1.58) **Going Correction** +0.20s/f (Slow) 10 Ran SP% **124.3**
Speed ratings (Par 101): **100,99,97,96,96 94,92,90,85,77**
toteswinger: 1&2 £30.00, 1&3 £22.10, 2&3 £13.80. CSF £101.94 CT £585.60 TOTE £20.80: £4.80, £3.10, £2.40; EX 150.70.
Owner Mrs Jean M O'Connor **Bred** G And Mrs Middlebrook **Trained** Chalfont St Giles, Bucks

FOCUS
A modest handicap in which the early pace was not strong.
Spinning Ridge(IRE) Official explanation: jockey said colt hung left
Inquisitress Official explanation: jockey said mare was denied a clear run
Tuxedo Official explanation: jockey said gelding lost its action

26 WILLIAM HILL SALE - WHY BET ELSEWHERE? CLAIMING STKS 1m (P)
4:40 (4:40) (Class 6) 4-Y-0+ **£2,047** (£604; £302) **Stalls** High

Form RPR

023- 1 **Jake The Snake (IRE)**[4] 7821 8-8-10 73............................. AmyBaker(5) 1 82
(A W Carroll) *t.k.h: hld up in tch: effrt 2f out: led wl ins fnl f: r.o* 4/1[3]

563- 2 nk **Formation (USA)**[82] 6704 4-9-5 85................................... MartinDwyer 5 85
(J R Boyle) *set slow pce: pushed along 2f out: rdn: flashed tail and hdd wl ins fnl f: no ex* 6/5[1]

204- 3 hd **Murfreesboro**[8] 7780 6-8-12 80.......................................(v) AdamKirby 4 78
(D Shaw) *trckd ldrs: effrt and rdn over 1f out: kpt on u.p fnl f* 11/4[2]

101- 4 4½ **Smokey Rye**[6] 7801 4-8-5 70...................................... FrankieMcDonald 2 61
(George Baker) *pressed ldr tl rdn and wknd over 1f out* 9/2

1m 42.16s (2.36) **Going Correction** +0.20s/f (Slow) 4 Ran SP% **110.3**
Speed ratings (Par 101): **96,95,95,91**
CSF £9.48 TOTE £3.30; EX 11.50.
Owner D Morgan & Mrs E M Clarke **Bred** J F Tuthill **Trained** Cropthorne, Worcs

FOCUS
A good claimer, but it was steadily run.

27 WILLIAM HILL TELEBETTING SALE - NOW ON! H'CAP (DIV II) 6f (P)
5:10 (5:10) (Class 6) (0-60,60) 4-Y-0+ **£1,706** (£503; £252) **Stalls** High

Form RPR

344- 1 **What Katie Did (IRE)**[14] 7745 4-9-3 59.......................(p) SteveDrowne 7 68
(J M Bradley) *sn midfield: hdwy over 2f out: rdn to ld ins fnl f: all out* 7/1

041- 2 shd **Kaystar Ridge**[34] 7508 4-8-10 57........................(bt) JamesO'Reilly(5) 1 65
(D K Ivory) *hld up: effrt wl over 1f out: kpt on wl fnl f: jst failed* 12/1

053- 3 ¾ **Ishibee (IRE)**[4] 7818 5-8-4 46 oh1.....................................(p) NeilChalmers 2 52
(J J Bridger) *bhd tl hdwy over 1f out: kpt on fnl f: nrst fin* 20/1

423- 4 1 **Mind Alert**[5] 7808 8-8-13 55..(v) DarrenWilliams 3 58
(D Shaw) *stdd and swtchd rt s: stdy hdwy over 2f out: effrt over 1f out: kpt on ins fnl f* 9/1

215- 5 ½ **Whiskey Creek**[14] 7746 4-9-0 56.......................................(b) TGMcLaughlin 4 57
(C A Dwyer) *racd keenly: set decent gallop: qcknd clr 2f out: hdd & wknd ins fnl f* 11/2[3]

320- 6 3¾ **Joss Stick**[20] 7679 4-9-1 60..(p) KevinGhunowa(3) 11 49
(R A Harris) *t.k.h early: cl up tl wknd appr fnl f* 16/1

000- 7 hd **Desert Light (IRE)**[5] 7809 8-8-4 46 oh1.......................(v) PatrickMathers 9 35
(D Shaw) *towards rr: drvn and outpcd 1/2-way: kpt on fnl f: no imp* 16/1

22- 8 1½ **Compton Classic**[30] 7544 7-9-2 58......................... RichardKingscote 10 42
(Tom Dascombe) *plld hrd: chsd ldrs tl wknd wl over 1f out* 2/1[1]

263- 9 ¾ **Tamino (IRE)**[5] 7809 6-8-13 55..(t) JimmyQuinn 6 36
(P Howling) *trckd ldr tl rdn and wknd wl over 1f out* 5/1[2]

666- 10 2 **Reigning Monarch (USA)**[5] 7809 6-8-8 50............... SimonWhitworth 8 25
(Miss Z C Davison) *prom: drvn along 1/2-way: wknd 2f out* 14/1

460- 11 8 **Night Prospector**[17] 7710 9-8-11 53......................(p) FrankieMcDonald 5 2
(R A Harris) *racd wd: hld up: struggling 1/2-way: sn btn* **33/1**
1m 13.74s (0.64) **Going Correction** +0.20s/f (Slow) 11 Ran SP% **121.7**
Speed ratings (Par 101): **103,102,101,100,99 94,94,92,91,88 78**
toteswinger: 1&2 £9.40, 1&3 £29.00, 2&3 £25.00. CSF £91.12 CT £1648.23 TOTE £7.30: £2.10, £4.10, £5.10; EX 94.10 Place 6: £12,304.96 Place 5: £979.10.
Owner Mr & Mrs M B Carver **Bred** Brian Williamson **Trained** Sedbury, Gloucs
■ Stewards' Enquiry : James O'Reilly two-day ban: use of whip (Jan 17-18)
T G McLaughlin one-day ban: used whip in incorrect place (Jan 17th)
FOCUS
This second division of the sprint handicap was another ordinary heat.
T/Plt: £6,336.20 to a £1 stake. Pool: £135,837.88. 15.65 winning tickets. T/Qpdt: £1,317.80 to a £1 stake. Pool: £9,972.95. 5.60 winning tickets. RY

LINGFIELD (L-H)
Saturday, January 3

OFFICIAL GOING: Standard
Wind: nil Weather: bright

28 WEATHERBYS ALL WEATHER "HANDS AND HEELS" APPRENTICE SERIES H'CAP 1m (P)
12:40 (12:40) (Class 5) (0-75,75) 4-Y-0+ **£2,900** (£856; £428) **Stalls** High

Form RPR
562- 1 **Bavarica**[6] 7800 7-8-2 61 oh4................ TobyAtkinson(3) 8 67
(Miss J Feilden) *stdd s: t.k.h: hld up in last pl: hdwy over 1f out: led ins fnl f: r.o strly* **3/1**[1]
050- 2 2 **Hucking Hero (IRE)**[12] 7758 4-9-3 73...................... PNolan 1 74+
(J R Best) *hld up in last pair: rdn over 2f out: hdwy and nt clr run over 1f out: swtchd rt ent fnl f: r.o wl fnl 100yds: wnt 2nd last strides* **7/1**
/26- 3 hd **Ede's Dot Com (IRE)**[35] 7490 5-8-3 62................ AndrewHeffernan(3) 5 63
(P M Phelan) *plld hrd: hld up in tch: effrt and rdn jst over 2f out: pressed ldrs ins fnl f: no ex fnl 100yds* **7/2**[2]
003- 4 shd **Wavertree Warrior (IRE)**[32] 7525 7-8-11 72...............(b) AlexOwen(5) 2 72
(N P Littmoden) *t.k.h: chsd ldrs: wnt 2nd 3f out: led over 1f out: hdd ins fnl f: no ex: lost 2 pls cl home* **5/1**[3]
103- 5 1 **Salt Of The Earth (IRE)**[12] 7763 4-8-11 67.................. DebraEngland 7 65
(T G Mills) *chsd ldr tl 3f out: rdn and wd bnd 2f out: kpt on same pce* **7/2**[2]
210- 6 ½ **Master Mahogany**[113] 5863 8-8-10 66........................ CharlesEddery 4 63
(R J Hodges) *led: rdn and hdd over 1f out: wknd ins fnl f: eased nr fin* **13/2**
1m 38.84s (0.64) **Going Correction** +0.025s/f (Slow) 6 Ran SP% **111.9**
Speed ratings (Par 103): **97,95,94,94,93 93**
toteswinger: 1&2 £4.30, 1&3 £2.50, 2&3 £6.10. CSF £23.55 CT £74.25 TOTE £3.10: £1.80, £2.70; EX 26.40 Trifecta £138.60 Pool: £417.69 - 2.23 winning units..
Owner Miss J Feilden **Bred** Juddmonte Farms **Trained** Exning, Suffolk
FOCUS
Mainly exposed and unreliable performers on show in this modest heat and there was not much pace on early so the form is not anything to get carried away with.

29 WILLIAM HILL JANUARY SALE NOW ON! CLAIMING STKS 1m 2f (P)
1:10 (1:10) (Class 6) 4-Y-0+ **£2,047** (£604; £302) **Stalls** Low

Form RPR
425- 1 **Slip**[16] 7717 4-9-5 84.. MartinDwyer 6 75
(J R Boyle) *chsd ldr: chal over 2f out: led wl over 1f out: edgd lft ent fnl f: hrd pressed ins fnl f: fnd ex nr fin* **9/4**[1]
425- 2 nk **Teasing**[8] 7786 5-8-10 70..(v) RobertHavlin 1 63
(J Pearce) *disp 2nd: rdn and effrt on inner jst over 2f out: str chal ins fnl f: no ex nr fin* **17/2**
005- 3 1 ¾ **Blacktoft (USA)**[42] 7423 6-8-13 73.............................(e) ChrisCatlin 2 65+
(S C Williams) *t.k.h: led: stdd pce 7f out: rdn 2f out: hdd wl over 1f out: stl ev ch whn short of room and snatched up 1f out: sn swtchd rt: one pce after* **7/1**
323- 4 ¾ **Zero Cool (USA)**[17] 7707 5-8-9 75...................... FergusSweeney 3 57
(G L Moore) *t.k.h early: hld up in last trio: rdn over 2f out: kpt on same pce u.p fnl f* **11/4**[2]
046- 5 ½ **Tenement (IRE)**[4] 7816 5-8-4 52.............................. MCGeran(5) 5 56
(Jamie Poulton) *in tch in last trio: effrt and rdn jst over 2f out: kpt on same pce u.p fnl f* **33/1**
413- 6 38 **Rapid City**[6] 7800 6-8-11 67....................................(p) JamesDoyle 4 —
(A J McCabe) *taken down early: t.k.h: hld up in last trio: rdn over 3f out: lost tch qckly over 2f out: eased over 1f out: t.o* **3/1**[3]
2m 5.95s (-0.65) **Going Correction** +0.025s/f (Slow)
WFA 4 from 5yo+ 2lb 6 Ran SP% **108.4**
Speed ratings (Par 101): **103,102,101,100,100 69**
toteswinger: 1&2 £3.60, 1&3 £2.70, 2&3 £4.90. CSF £19.79 TOTE £2.80: £2.00, £2.80; EX 13.40.
Owner M Khan X2 **Bred** Mrs H T Jones **Trained** Epsom, Surrey
■ Stewards' Enquiry : Martin Dwyer two-day ban: careless riding (Jan 17-18)
FOCUS
A fair claimer.

30 WILLIAM HILL JANUARY SALE - 0800 44 40 40 CONDITIONS STKS 1m (P)
1:45 (1:45) (Class 3) 4-Y-0+ **£7,771** (£2,312; £1,155; £577) **Stalls** High

Form RPR
116- 1 **Premio Loco (USA)**[91] 6476 5-9-0 109...................... GeorgeBaker 3 94+
(C F Wall) *taken down early: hld up in tch: hdwy to chse ldr 2f out: hanging lft after: led 1f out: pushed out* **4/9**[1]
121- 2 ½ **Red Somerset (USA)**[5] 7813 6-8-9 89........................ MCGeran(5) 1 93
(R J Hodges) *led: qcknd over 2f out: rdn 2f out: hdd 1f out: kpt on but a readily hld* **14/1**[3]
000- 3 ¾ **Capricorn Run (USA)**[27] 7594 6-9-4 90...................... JamesDoyle 2 95
(A J McCabe) *dwlt: trckd ldrs: rdn over 2f out: sltly outpcd over 1f out: rallied u.p ins fnl f: styd on* **33/1**
003- 4 1 ½ **Whistledownwind**[27] 7594 4-9-0 99............................ ShaneKelly 5 88
(J Noseda) *hld up in tch: effrt on outer 2f out: kpt on same pce fr over 1f out* **3/1**[2]
100/ 5 3 ¾ **Swiss Act**[562] 2790 5-9-0 85...................................... GregFairley 4 79
(M Johnston) *dwlt: sn chsng ldr: rdn 3f out: lost pl 2f out: wknd ent fnl f* **16/1**
1m 38.54s (0.34) **Going Correction** +0.025s/f (Slow) 5 Ran SP% **109.7**
Speed ratings (Par 107): **99,98,97,96,92**
CSF £8.08 TOTE £1.50: £1.10, £3.50; EX 6.20.
Owner Bernard Westley **Bred** Kidder, Cole & Griggs **Trained** Newmarket, Suffolk

FOCUS
A good race but the early pace was steady.
NOTEBOOK
Premio Loco(USA) was a bit keen through the early stages, but he had 10lb and more in hand of all of his rivals and, although he had to work hard in the straight, his class advantage got him through. Even so, he ought to have beaten the runner-up by much further. He was most progressive on the Polytrack at Kempton last year, and he did not run at all badly in the Cambridgeshire (although connections feel he did not get the trip), given where he was drawn and forced to race. We did not learn a great deal more about him here, although he would obviously need a stronger pace to be seen at his best, and a step up in class is on the cards. A Listed race at Kempton in February is his next target and he will apparently strip much fitter for this. (op 4-7 tchd 4-6 in places)
Red Somerset(USA) is officially rated 20lb inferior to the winner, so he ran a terrific race to go down by such a narrow margin off level weights less the rider's allowance. A literal reading of this makes him a well-handicapped horse, but we know enough about him to assume that is unlikely to be the case. More likely is that the winner did not need to be at his best. (op 12-1)
Capricorn Run(USA) broke almost on terms for a change then stayed on well and ran his best race for some time. There will be easier opportunities for him but he has become hard to trust, given his propensity to miss the break. (tchd 28-1)
Whistledownwind was a touch disappointing. He was on the winner's quarters turning for home but could not pick up with the same gusto and it may be he needs a stronger pace. (op 5-2)

31 WILLIAM HILL JANUARY SALE - BONUSES GALORE! H'CAP 7f (P)
2:15 (2:17) (Class 5) (0-70,70) 4-Y-0+ **£2,900** (£856; £428) **Stalls** Low

Form RPR
004- 1 **Pegasus Again (USA)**[26] 7603 4-9-4 70......................(p) RobertHavlin 7 79
(T G Mills) *sn rdn up to ld: mde virtually all: rdn 2f out: drvn and styd on wl fnl f* **7/1**[3]
506- 2 ½ **Lend A Grand (IRE)**[14] 7742 5-8-11 63.................. FergusSweeney 1 71
(Miss Jo Crowley) *dwlt: hld up in last: c v wd bnd 2f out: edging lft over 1f out: str run fnl f: wnt 2nd towards fin: nt quite rch wnr: burst blood vessel* **16/1**
46-2 3 nk **Blue Charm**[1] 9 5-9-1 67.. LPKeniry 4 74
(S Kirk) *trckd ldrs: pushed along 4f out: rdn jst over 2f out: chsd wnr ins fnl f: kpt on same pce: lost 2nd towards fin* **10/3**[2]
644- 4 1 ½ **Divertimenti (IRE)**[20] 7677 5-9-0 66...........................(p) LiamJones 5 69
(C R Dore) *in tch in midfield: rdn over 1f out: kpt on but nvr pce to rch ldrs* **15/2**
500- 5 nse **Princess Rose Anne (IRE)**[39] 7448 4-9-4 70................ GeorgeBaker 3 73
(J R Best) *plld hrd: hld up in midfield: effrt wl over 1f out: kpt on fnl f: nt pce to rch ldrs* **8/1**
025- 6 shd **Napoletano (GER)**[12] 7771 8-9-3 69..............................(p) NCallan 8 72
(S Dow) *plld hrd: hld up towards rr: rdn over 2f out: styd on same pce fr over 1f out* **8/1**
122- 7 nk **Sendreni (FR)**[28] 7586 5-9-4 70................................ ChrisCatlin 2 72
(M Wigham) *plld hrd: trckd ldrs: wnt 2nd jst over 2f out: hrd drvn ent fnl f: wknd fnl 100yds* **2/1**[1]
516- 8 2 ½ **Motivated Choice**[40] 7435 4-9-1 67........................ DaneO'Neill 6 62
(Miss Amy Weaver) *chsd ldr: rdn 3f out: lost 2nd jst over 2f out: wknd over 1f out* **18/1**
1m 24.27s (-0.53) **Going Correction** +0.025s/f (Slow) 8 Ran SP% **114.0**
Speed ratings (Par 103): **104,103,103,101,101 101,100,98**
toteswinger: 1&2 £16.50, 1&3 £5.20, 2&3 £10.20. CSF £106.86 CT £443.31 TOTE £7.50: £2.10, £3.50, £1.40; EX 109.60 Trifecta £638.50 Part won. Pool: £862.87 - 0.10 winning units..
Owner T G Mills **Bred** Stonestreet Mares Llc **Trained** Headley, Surrey
FOCUS
A modest handicap and another race that was run at a steady early gallop.
Lend A Grand(IRE) Official explanation: trainer said gelding bled from the nose
Princess Rose Anne(IRE) Official explanation: jockey said filly ran too free

32 WILLIAM HILL JANUARY SALE - BETTER ODDS! MAIDEN STKS 1m 2f (P)
2:50 (2:50) (Class 5) 3-Y-O **£2,729** (£806; £403) **Stalls** Low

Form RPR
342- 1 **Lord Chancellor (IRE)**[21] 7660 3-9-3 84........................ GregFairley 1 83+
(M Johnston) *mde all: clr and rdn wl over 1f out: r.o wl and in command fnl f* **5/6**[1]
625- 2 2 ¼ **Mellow Mixture**[17] 7699 3-9-3 72............................ DaneO'Neill 6 78
(R Hannon) *chsd wnr after 1f: rdn and nt pce of wnr 2f out: readily hld fnl f* **11/2**[3]
002- 3 2 ¼ **Mile High Lad (USA)**[24] 7622 3-9-3 75........................ ChrisCatlin 3 74
(George Baker) *chsd wnr for 1f: chsd ldng pair after: rdn over 2f out: 3rd and wl hld fr over 1f out* **9/4**[2]
0- 4 6 **Tropical Duke (IRE)**[50] 7312 3-9-3 0.............................. MartinDwyer 4 62
(D W P Arbuthnot) *hld up in tch: pushed along 5f out: rdn and outpcd wl over 2f out: no ch w ldrs after* **20/1**
5 12 **Spirit Of The Glen** 3-8-12 0.. RobertHavlin 2 33
(Jamie Poulton) *s.i.s: rn green in rr: reminder 9f out: pushed along 8f out: rdn and lost tch over 3f out* **33/1**
000- 6 7 **Prima Fonteyn**[40] 7438 3-8-12 40.......................... EdwardCreighton 5 19
(Miss Sheena West) *led to post: s.i.s: in tch in rr: rdn 4f out: lost tch wl over 2f out* **100/1**
2m 8.05s (1.45) **Going Correction** +0.025s/f (Slow) 6 Ran SP% **109.4**
Speed ratings (Par 97): **95,93,91,86,77 71**
toteswinger: 1&2 £2.00, 1&3 £1.50, 2&3 £1.40. CSF £5.61 TOTE £1.70: £1.10, £2.30; EX 4.60.
Owner Sheikh Hamdan Bin Mohammed Al Maktoum **Bred** Darley **Trained** Middleham Moor, N Yorks
FOCUS
No strength in depth to this maiden. It only concerned three in the betting and they finished clear of the stragglers.

33 WILLIAM HILL JANUARY SALE - ENHANCED FAVOURITES! H'CAP 1m 4f (P)
3:25 (3:25) (Class 2) (0-100,111) 4-Y-0+ **£11,656** (£3,468; £1,733; £865) **Stalls** Low

Form RPR
040- 1 **Evident Pride (USA)**[29] 7556 6-8-10 88 ow1.................. IanMongan 9 93
(B R Johnson) *stdd and dropped in bhd after s: t.k.h: hld up in rr: hdwy and nt clr run briefly 2f out: str run ins fnl f: led nr fin* **16/1**
511- 2 ½ **Grande Caiman (IRE)**[16] 7717 5-9-12 104....................(b) DaneO'Neill 4 108
(R Hannon) *led at stdy gallop: clr over 4f out: rdn 2f out: kpt on and looked wnr tl collared cl home* **9/2**[2]
361- 3 nk **Millville**[43] 7404 9-10-5 111.. NCallan 7 115
(M A Jarvis) *chsd ldr over 9f out: rdn over 2f out: kpt on steadily u.p fnl f: lost 2nd nr fin* **4/1**[1]
442- 4 shd **Pevensey (IRE)**[84] 6646 7-8-12 90..........................(p) LPKeniry 3 94
(J J Quinn) *chsd ldr tl over 9f out: 3rd and rdn over 2f out: outpcd wl over 1f out: kpt on again u.p fnl f* **8/1**

002- **5** *1 1/4* **Celtic Spirit (IRE)**[16] 7717 6-9-3 **95** GeorgeBaker 2 97
(G L Moore) *stdd s: hld up in last trio: effrt and nt clr run briefly over 2f out: sn rdn: no real hdwy tl styd on ins fnl f: nvr rchd ldrs* **5/1**[3]

401- **6** *1/2* **Paktolos (FR)**[35] 7493 6-9-0 **92** (b) EddieAhern 5 93
(A King) *in tch: rdn and effrt to chse ldng trio jst over 2f out: plugged on same pce fnl f* **9/2**[2]

000- **7** *16* **Group Captain**[14] 7244 7-9-2 **94** RobertHavlin 6 69
(H J Collingridge) *t.k.h: chsd ldrs: rdn over 3f out: lost pl over 3f out: wl bhd and eased fnl f* **8/1**

010- **8** *11* **Young Mick**[35] 7491 7-9-8 **100** (v) RobertWinston 10 58
(G G Margarson) *t.k.h: chsd ldrs on outer tl stdd into last trio over 8f out: rdn and struggling 3f out: wl btn and eased fnl f: t.o* **8/1**

2m 30.18s (-2.82) **Going Correction** +0.025s/f (Slow)
WFA 4 from 5yo+ 4lb **8** Ran SP% **112.2**
Speed ratings (Par 109): **110,109,109,109,108 108,97,90**
toteswinger: 1&2 £11.70, 1&3 £10.20, 2&3 £3.50. CSF £83.09 CT £347.61 TOTE £17.30: £4.70, £1.90, £1.60; EX 162.50 Trifecta £1034.60 Part won. Pool: £1398.16 - 0.50 winning units..
Owner Dempsey, Fitzpatrick, Nash **Bred** Juddmonte Farms Inc **Trained** Ashtead, Surrey
■ Stewards' Enquiry : Eddie Ahern two-day ban: careless riding (Jan 17-18)

FOCUS
By far the most competitive race on the card, and a cracking good handicap that produced an exciting finish.

NOTEBOOK
Evident Pride(USA), the outsider of the field, had been most progressive on this surface until struggling throughout 2008. However, a drop in the weights (although just out of the handicap) enabled him to bounce back to form and he also almost certainly posted a career-best performance and relished the step up to 1m4f. (op 14-1)
Grande Caiman(IRE) ◆ was the pacesetter and had poached a couple of lengths advantage entering the final half-mile. Halfway up the straight, it looked as though he had done enough to hold on, but he was mugged in the final 20 yards by the fast-finishing winner. Having been hiked up another 5lb for his latest Great Leighs win, he ran a blinder from the front. He has yet to finish worse than second in seven visits to Lingfield and is not done with yet, despite this career-high mark. (tchd 5-1)
Millville won this race last year off an 8lb lower mark and, coming here in excellent shape, he ran another big race, closing on the leader turning for home and sticking to his task all the way up the straight. (op 5-1)
Pevensey(IRE) stayed on well after coming under pressure some way out. He would have been better suited by a more even gallop and this was a creditable effort. (op 5-1)
Celtic Spirit(IRE) was squeezed out by the weakening Group Captain as the field came to the end of the back straight, costing him momentum just as he was beginning to make a move. He stuck on well once he got going again and remains of interest in this sort of race. (op 9-2 tchd 11-2)
Paktolos(FR) did not get the strong pace he needs but still kept on stoutly to complete the group of six that finished a long way clear. (op 5-1 tchd 4-1)

34 WILLIAM HILL JANUARY SALE - WHY BET ELSEWHERE? H'CAP 5f (P)
3:55 (3:55) (Class 5) (0-70,69) 3-Y-O **£2,900** (£856; £428) **Stalls** High

Form RPR

233- **1** **Barnezet (GR)**[20] 7673 3-9-1 **68** PatrickHills(3) 6 76
(R Hannon) *in tch in midfield: swtchd lft to rail over 1f out: led ins fnl f: r.o wl* **6/1**

032- **2** *1 1/4* **Fangfoss Girls**[7] 7788 3-9-1 **65** EddieAhern 5 68
(L Wells) *broke wl and led: sn hdd: mostly chsd ldr after: drvn 2f out: kpt on same pce fnl f* **4/1**[3]

602- **3** *1/2* **Edith's Boy (IRE)**[6] 7802 3-8-10 **60** IanMongan 7 61
(S Dow) *sn led: rdn and edgd rt wl over 1f out: hdd ins fnl f: no ex: lost 2nd wl ins fnl f* **5/2**[1]

051- **4** *1 1/2* **Trick Or Two**[7] 7795 3-9-4 **68** LPKeniry 2 64
(Mrs R A Carr) *hld up in last trio: hdwy over 1f out: rdn 1f out: kpt on but nvr pce to rch ldrs* **7/1**

604- **5** *1/2* **Sills Vincero**[7] 7795 3-8-10 **60** RobertWinston 1 54
(D Shaw) *hld up in pair: rdn and effrt wl over 1f out: nt pce to rch ldrs* **16/1**

025- **6** *1 3/4* **Dedante**[35] 7501 3-8-12 **62** (b) DaneO'Neill 3 50
(D K Ivory) *t.k.h: chsd ldrs: wnt 2nd over 2f out tl 2f out: sn drvn and unable qck: one pce fnl f* **10/1**

211- **7** *2 1/2* **Imaginary Diva**[4] 7825 3-9-5 **69** 6ex ChrisCatlin 4 48
(G G Margarson) *a in last pl: c wd over 3f out: nvr a factor* **7/2**[2]

58.40 secs (-0.40) **Going Correction** +0.025s/f (Slow) **7** Ran SP% **112.6**
Speed ratings (Par 97): **104,102,101,98,98 95,91**
toteswinger: 1&2 £3.50, 1&3 £4.90, 2&3 £3.10. CSF £29.04 TOTE £8.00: £3.80, £2.80; EX 30.00 Place 6: £47.46 Place 5: £15.97.
Owner Robin Blunt **Bred** Stavloi Th Nanou S A **Trained** East Everleigh, Wilts

FOCUS
Just an ordinary sprint handicap, but the pace was honest enough.
Trick Or Two Official explanation: jockey said gelding hung right
Imaginary Diva Official explanation: jockey said filly was hampered at the start
T/Plt: £75.60 to a £1 stake. Pool: £115,224.24. 1,111.31 winning tickets. T/Qpdt: £11.90 to a £1 stake. Pool: £7,378.65. 455.60 winning tickets. SP

[8]SOUTHWELL (L-H)
Sunday, January 4

OFFICIAL GOING: Standard to slow
Wind: Light across Weather: Overcast

35 WILLIAM HILL JANUARY SALE NOW ON! CLAIMING STKS 6f (F)
12:40 (12:40) (Class 6) 4-Y-0+ **£2,047** (£604; £302) **Stalls** Low

Form RPR

220- **1** **Don Pele (IRE)**[6] 7811 7-9-0 **71** (p) KevinGhunowa(3) 2 78
(R A Harris) *chsd ldrs: edgd lft fr over 1f out: rdn to ld ins fnl f: styd on wl* **11/4**[2]

010- **2** *1 1/4* **Crocodile Bay (IRE)**[9] 7780 6-8-10 **68** ow2 (b) JamesO'Reilly(5) 3 72
(John A Harris) *led: rdn and hung lft over 1f out: hdd and unable qck ins fnl f* **7/2**[3]

405- **3** *3 1/2* **Hurricane Coast**[12] 7774 10-8-6 **55** MarieLequarre(7) 1 59+
(D Flood) *hld up: r.o ins fnl f: nvr nrr* **16/1**

500- **4** *nk* **Kinout (IRE)**[48] 7359 4-8-13 **60** RobertWinston 4 58
(K A Ryan) *chsd ldr: rdn over 2f out: sn edgd lft: no ins fnl f* **7/1**

000- **5** *nse* **Majestic Cheer**[12] 7779 5-8-8 **47** ow1 (p) StephenDonohoe 8 53
(John A Harris) *in tch: rdn over 2f out: styd on same pce* **50/1**

100- **6** *1/2* **Soba Jones**[16] 7727 12-8-6 **55** TolleyDean(3) 7 52
(J Balding) *trckd ldrs: racd keenly: rdn over 2f out: styd on same pce* **25/1**

204- **7** *10* **Swinbrook (USA)**[120] 5708 8-8-11 **70** (v) TonyHamilton 6 22
(R A Fahey) *s.i.s: sn drvn along in rr: sme hdwy 1/2-way: wknd 2f out* **7/4**[1]

1m 18.14s (1.64) **Going Correction** +0.325s/f (Slow) **7** Ran SP% **109.4**
Speed ratings (Par 101): **102,100,95,95,95 94,81**
toteswinger: 1&2 £1.60, 1&3 £5.40, 2&3 £7.50. CSF £11.63 TOTE £3.80: £1.50, £2.50; EX 12.90 Trifecta £145.00 Pool: £478.39 - 2.44 winning units..
Owner Robert & Nina Bailey **Bred** John J Cosgrave **Trained** Earlswood, Monmouths
■ Stewards' Enquiry : James O'Reilly one-day ban: used whip in incorrect way and place (Jan 19)

FOCUS
This was a typically moderate claimer that took little winning. The form is not solid.
Hurricane Coast Official explanation: jockey said, regarding the running and riding, that her instructions were to jump out and make the running but the horses on the right were away more quickly and her horse resented the kickback, thus had to switch the gelding and produce the gelding later than required. Trainer confirmed the instuctions adding that the gelding is quirky and does not respond well to the whip
Swinbrook(USA) Official explanation: trainer was unable to offer any explanation for the poor form shown

36 WILLIAM HILL JANUARY SALE - BETTER ODDS! MAIDEN FILLIES' STKS 6f (F)
1:10 (1:11) (Class 5) 3-Y-0+ **£2,729** (£806; £403) **Stalls** Low

Form RPR

/02- **1** **Lemon N Sugar (USA)**[69] 7026 4-9-10 **69** ShaneKelly 10 78+
(J Noseda) *trckd ldrs: led on bit over 2f out: clr over 1f out: eased ins fnl f* **1/3**[1]

/03- **2** *4 1/2* **Silk Gallery (USA)**[33] 7527 4-9-10 **48** (t) JimmyQuinn 6 58
(E J Alston) *a.p: wnt 2nd 2f out: no ch w wnr* **12/1**[3]

000- **3** *3 1/4* **Lady Dunhill (IRE)**[79] 6785 3-8-8 **49** TonyHamilton 4 44
(E W Tuer) *sn pushed along in rr: hdwy u.p over 1f out: nvr trbld ldrs* **50/1**

4 *3* **Singapore Girl** 3-8-5 **0** DuranFentiman(3) 9 34
(G R Oldroyd) *prom: rdn over 3f out: wknd over 1f out* **20/1**

0- **5** *3/4* **Beaux Yeux**[23] 7649 3-8-9 **0** ow1 RobertWinston 5 33
(P T Midgley) *s.i.s: sn pushed along in rr: mod late prog: n.d* **100/1**

0- **6** *1* **Flirty (IRE)**[28] 7593 3-8-8 **0** SteveDrowne 8 29
(Rae Guest) *sn pushed along in rr: n.d* **33/1**

7 *1 1/2* **April Lady (IRE)** 3-8-3 **0** DanielleMcCreery(5) 2 24
(A Berry) *chsd ldrs tl wknd over 2f out* **100/1**

0- **8** *2* **Always Engaged**[25] 7631 4-9-10 **0** PaulMulrennan 3 22
(J R Norton) *led: rdn and hdd over 2f out: wknd over 1f out* **150/1**

03- **9** *3/4* **Nizhoni (USA)**[8] 7798 4-9-10 **0** TomEaves 7 19
(B Smart) *s.i.s: hld up: racd keenly: hdwy over 3f out: rdn over 2f out: sn wknd* **9/2**[2]

1m 18.25s (1.75) **Going Correction** +0.325s/f (Slow)
WFA 3 from 4yo 16lb **9** Ran SP% **113.2**
Speed ratings (Par 100): **101,95,90,86,85 84,82,79,78**
toteswinger: 1&2 £2.20, 1&3 £9.90, 2&3 £21.20. CSF £4.96 TOTE £1.40: £1.02, £2.00, £8.90; EX 6.80 Trifecta £68.30 Pool: £401.06 - 4.34 winning units..
Owner The Searchers **Bred** Establo Madoca Corp **Trained** Newmarket, Suffolk

FOCUS
A very weak maiden and plating-class form behind the easy winner.
Nizhoni(USA) Official explanation: the trainer was unable to offer any explanation for the poor form shown other than the filly may have been run too soon

37 SOUTHWELL-RACECOURSE.CO.UK (S) STKS 7f (F)
1:40 (1:40) (Class 6) 3-Y-0+ **£2,047** (£604; £302) **Stalls** Low

Form RPR

100- **1** **Vogarth**[8] 7799 5-9-11 **59** (v[1]) JamesMillman(3) 5 69
(B R Millman) *s.i.s: hdwy over 4f out: rdn to ld wl over 1f out: edgd lft towards fin: jst hld on* **5/1**[2]

030- **2** *hd* **Cap St Jean (IRE)**[8] 7799 5-9-2 **57** (p) DavidKenny(7) 2 63
(R Hollinshead) *s.i.s: hld up: nt clr run 3f out: hdwy over 1f out: edgd lft ins fnl f: r.o u.p* **6/1**[3]

524- **3** *2 3/4* **Elusive Warrior (USA)**[17] 7723 6-10-0 **66** (p) JamesDoyle 1 61
(A J McCabe) *chsd ldrs: led over 4f out: rdn and hdd wl over 1f out: styd on same pce fnl f* **5/4**[1]

555- **4** *nse* **Tender Process (IRE)**[21] 7675 6-10-0 **66** (b) TonyHamilton 7 60
(R A Fahey) *sn pushed along and prom: rdn and ev ch wl over 1f out: styd on same pce fnl f* **5/1**[2]

50-0 **5** *5* **Government (IRE)**[3] 7 8-9-9 **41** RobertWinston 8 42
(M C Chapman) *chsd ldrs: rdn over 3f out: wknd 2f out* **16/1**

503- **6** *nk* **Sion Hill (IRE)**[20] 7692 8-9-9 **54** (p) StephenDonohoe 3 41
(John A Harris) *sn led: hdd over 4f out: rdn over 2f out: wknd over 1f out* **8/1**

000- **7** *3/4* **Swallow Senora (IRE)**[16] 7727 7-9-4 **35** TomEaves 10 34
(M C Chapman) *s.i.s: sn mid-div: lost pl over 4f out: n.d after* **100/1**

500- **8** *1 3/4* **Fish Called Johnny**[15] 7745 5-9-4 **46** SladeO'Hara(5) 6 34
(A Berry) *sn pushed along in rr: rdn over 2f out: n.d* **40/1**

000- **9** *8* **Arrabiata**[22] 7663 4-9-4 **38** (b) FrankieMcDonald 9 8
(C N Kellett) *chsd ldrs: rdn 1/2-way: sn wknd* **100/1**

000- **10** *2* **Lonsdale Lad**[12] 7773 3-8-5 **31** (p) JimmyQuinn 4 7
(R C Guest) *prom: lost pl over 4f out: sn rdn: bhd fnl 3f* **125/1**

1m 32.42s (2.12) **Going Correction** +0.325s/f (Slow)
WFA 3 from 4yo+ 18lb **10** Ran SP% **114.3**
Speed ratings (Par 101): **100,99,96,96,90 90,89,87,78,76**
toteswinger: 1&2 £6.90, 1&3 £2.80, 2&3 £3.00. CSF £34.09 TOTE £6.60: £1.50, £2.20, £1.30; EX 34.20 Trifecta £116.20 Pool: £546.88 - 3.48 winning units..The winner was sold to Mike Chapman for £3,000 guineas.
Owner P Millman **Bred** Rosyground Stud **Trained** Kentisbeare, Devon

FOCUS
This seller was run at a sound pace and the first pair came clear. The winner is probably the best guide to the value of the form.

38 PLAY GOLF AT SOUTHWELL GOLF CLUB H'CAP 1m 6f (F)
2:10 (2:10) (Class 6) (0-60,57) 4-Y-0+ **£2,047** (£604; £302) **Stalls** Low

Form RPR

446- **1** **Sabancaya**[13] 7761 4-8-13 **52** LPKeniry 11 66
(Mrs P Sly) *hld up: hdwy over 4f out: shkn up to ld over 1f out: rdn clr: eased nr fin* **5/1**[2]

233- **2** *5* **Fortunella**[12] 7775 4-9-2 **55** (v[1]) AdamKirby 10 60
(Miss Gay Kelleway) *hld up: hdwy 9f out: rdn over 4f out: chsd wnr over 1f out: no ex ins fnl f* **9/2**[1]

012- **3** *nk* **Gayanula (USA)**[16] 7729 4-8-11 **57** BMcHugh(7) 7 62
(Miss J A Camacho) *hld up: hdwy over 4f out: nt clr run and lost pl sn after: styd on fr over 1f out: nvr able to chal* **6/1**[3]

505- **4** ¾ **Pick Of The Day (IRE)**[25] 7632 4-8-8 **47**.................... PaulMulrennan 8 51
(J G Given) *chsd ldrs: rdn 5 out: led 3f out: edgd lft and hdd over 1f out: no ex fnl f* **10/1**

400- **5** 2 **Blue Hills**[29] 7587 8-9-10 **57**.......................(b) DarrenWilliams 2 58
(P W Hiatt) *sn chsng ldr: led over 4f out: rdn and hdd 3f out: wknd and eased ins fnl f* **17/2**

006- **6** 6 **Niqaab**[20] 7688 5-8-12 **45**.................... TonyCulhane 5 37
(W J Musson) *prom: rdn over 3f out: wknd over 2f out* **14/1**

023- **7** 1 **Corking (IRE)**[74] 6897 4-8-13 **55**.................... KevinGhunowa(3) 13 46
(J L Flint) *chsd ldrs: rdn 8f out: wknd over 2f out* **17/2**

040- **8** 11 **Matinee Idol**[9] 5396 6-8-12 **45**.......................(b) RobertWinston 12 21
(Mrs S Lamyman) *s.i.s: pushed along 10f out: a in rr* **40/1**

606- **9** 4 ½ **Muntami (IRE)**[22] 4490 8-8-13 **46**.......................(p) StephenDonohoe 1 15
(John A Harris) *s.i.s: sn pushed along: a in rr* **20/1**

036- **10** *nse* **Bond Casino**[12] 7776 5-8-9 **45**.......................(v) DuranFentiman(3) 3 14
(G R Oldroyd) *led: rdn and hdd over 4f out: wknd over 3f out* **25/1**

002- **11** 13 **Oberlin (USA)**[12] 7775 4-9-3 **56**.................... NickyMackay 14 7
(T Keddy) *prom: rdn over 8f out: wknd 5f out* **9/2**[1]

3m 15.06s (6.76) **Going Correction** +0.325s/f (Slow)
WFA 4 from 5yo+ 6lb **11** Ran SP% **115.2**
Speed ratings (Par 101): **93,90,89,89,88 84,84,78,75,75 68**
toteswinger: 1&2 £4.90, 1&3 £6.70, 2&3 £3.90. CSF £26.47 CT £137.73 TOTE £5.70: £2.00, £1.70, £2.10; EX 26.80 Trifecta £84.40 Pool: £528.22 - 4.63 winning units..
Owner David L Bayliss **Bred** Mrs M Slack **Trained** Thorney, Cambs

FOCUS
This weak staying handicap was run at a fair pace and the form looks straightforward rated through the placed horses.
Oberlin(USA) Official explanation: jockey said gelding was never travelling

39 WILLIAM HILL JANUARY SALE - WHY BET ELSEWHERE? H'CAP 1m (F)
2:40 (2:41) (Class 5) (0-70,70) 4-Y-0+ **£2,729** (£806; £403) **Stalls** Low

Form RPR

001- **1** **United Nations**[8] 7799 8-8-13 **65**.......................(b) LeeEnstone 7 76
(N Wilson) *s.i.s: hdwy 6f out: jnd ldr over 2f out: styd on u.p to ld post* **7/2**[2]

002- **2** *nse* **Rock Anthem (IRE)**[23] 7650 5-8-12 **64**.................... LPKeniry 8 75
(Mike Murphy) *led early: w ldr tl led 3f out: rdn fr over 1f out: hdd post* **7/2**[2]

432- **3** 3 ½ **Davenport (IRE)**[12] 7777 7-9-1 **70**.......................(p) JamesMillman(3) 3 73
(B R Millman) *s.i.s: hdwy over 4f out: rdn over 2f out: styd on same pce appr fnl f* **10/3**[1]

002- **4** 1 ¼ **Elk Trail (IRE)**[16] 7731 4-9-2 **68**.................... AdamKirby 5 68+
(Mrs P Sly) *trckd ldrs: racd keenly: n.m.r and lost pl 6f out: swtchd lft over 1f out: r.o ins fnl f* **7/2**[2]

45-0 **5** 3 ½ **New Beginning (IRE)**[3] 6 5-9-2 **68**.......................(p) JimmyQuinn 2 60
(Mrs S Lamyman) *chsd ldrs: rdn over 3f out: wknd 2f out* **15/2**[3]

003- **6** 5 **Dancing Duo**[65] 7112 5-7-11 **56** oh9.......................(v) MatthewLawson(7) 1 36
(D Shaw) *sn led: hdd 3f out: rdn and wknd over 1f out* **33/1**

300- **7** 3 **Alucica**[41] 7433 6-8-1 **56** oh1.......................(v) DuranFentiman(3) 6 30
(D Shaw) *hld up: rdn and wknd over 2f out* **25/1**

000- **8** 40 **Centenerola (USA)**[81] 6734 4-8-13 **65**.......................(v[1]) DarrenWilliams 4 —
(D Shaw) *prom: rdn and lost pl over 4f out: sn bhd: t.o* **40/1**

1m 45.16s (1.46) **Going Correction** +0.325s/f (Slow) **8** Ran SP% **110.7**
Speed ratings (Par 103): **105,104,101,100,96 91,88,48**
toteswinger: 1&2 £3.40, 1&3 £3.50, 2&3 £3.00. CSF £14.98 CT £40.87 TOTE £4.80: £1.60, £1.60, £1.40; EX 21.30 Trifecta £37.00 Pool: £853.39 - 17.04 winning units..
Owner Beverley Embassy Syndicate **Bred** Cyril Humphris **Trained** Flaxton, N Yorks

FOCUS
An open handicap, run at an average pace and the first pair came clear in a tight finish. The form looks sound enough rated through the second and third.

40 HOSPITALITY AT SOUTHWELL RACECOURSE H'CAP 1m 4f (F)
3:10 (3:10) (Class 6) (0-65,65) 4-Y-0+ **£2,047** (£604; £302) **Stalls** Low

Form RPR

000- **1** **Raquel White**[22] 7667 5-8-11 **58**.................... KevinGhunowa(3) 2 63
(J L Flint) *chsd ldr 2f: remained handy: rdn over 3f out: styd on u.p to ld wl ins fnl f* **12/1**

045- **2** ½ **Trans Sonic**[23] 7650 6-9-7 **65**.................... TonyHamilton 4 69
(A J Lockwood) *led: rdn and hdd 2f out: ev ch ins fnl f: styd on* **7/1**

056- **3** *nk* **Black Falcon (IRE)**[17] 7723 9-8-12 **56**.................... RobertWinston 7 60
(John A Harris) *hld up in tch: lost pl 8f out: rdn over 3f out: led and hung lft fr 2f out: hdd wl ins fnl f* **11/2**[3]

023- **4** 2 **Colourful Move**[22] 7661 4-8-12 **60**.................... SteveDrowne 8 61
(P G Murphy) *chsd ldr 10f out: led over 2f out: sn rdn and hdd: styng on same pce whn n.m.r ins fnl f* **15/8**[1]

4- **5** 5 **Savaronola (USA)**[22] 7661 4-9-3 **65**.................... TPQueally 6 58
(A P Stringer) *hld up: rdn over 4f out: n.d* **9/2**[2]

410- **6** ½ **Three Strings (USA)**[25] 7630 6-9-2 **60**.......................(p) PaulMulrennan 1 52
(P D Niven) *prom: rdn over 2f out: sn wknd* **9/2**[2]

000- **7** 76 **Kames Park (IRE)**[15] 7744 7-9-7 **65**.......................(b) TomEaves 3 —
(I W McInnes) *s.i.s: hld up: rdn and wknd over 3f out: t.o* **25/1**

2m 43.35s (2.35) **Going Correction** +0.325s/f (Slow)
WFA 4 from 5yo+ 4lb **7** Ran SP% **110.6**
Speed ratings (Par 101): **105,104,104,103,99 99,48**
toteswinger: 1&2 £11.70, 1&3 £8.60, 2&3 £7.90. CSF £84.70 CT £493.74 TOTE £12.00: £3.50, £3.40; EX 65.10 Trifecta £770.30 Part won..
Owner N Poacher **Bred** C And Mrs Wilson **Trained** Kenfig Hill, Bridgend
■ Stewards' Enquiry : Kevin Ghunowa one-day ban: used whip with excessive frequency

FOCUS
The first four came clear in this poor handicap and the form has been rated around the second and third to their recent best.

41 SOUTHWELL GOLF CLUB H'CAP 6f (F)
3:40 (3:40) (Class 6) (0-60,60) 3-Y-0 **£2,047** (£604; £302) **Stalls** Low

Form RPR

022- **1** **La Capriosa**[8] 7795 3-9-3 **59**.................... RobertWinston 8 66
(A J McCabe) *racd keenly: w ldrs: led 1/2-way: hdd over 2f out: rallied to ld over 1f out: styd on* **7/2**[2]

061- **2** 1 **Halaak (USA)**[16] 7728 3-8-12 **54**.......................(b) GregFairley 9 57
(D M Simcock) *s.i.s: hdwy over 4f out: led over 2f out: rdn: hung lft and hdd over 1f out: sn hung rt: nt qckn towards fin* **2/1**[1]

302- **3** ¾ **Bulella**[16] 7728 3-8-11 **60**.................... AndrewHeffernan(7) 3 61
(Garry Moss) *s.i.s: hdwy over 3f out: rdn over 1f out: styd on* **4/1**[3]

433- **4** 1 ½ **Lois Darlin (IRE)**[6] 7810 3-8-9 **54**.......................(p) KevinGhunowa(3) 6 50
(R A Harris) *hld up: rdn 1/2-way: hdwy u.p over 1f out: nt trble ldrs* **5/1**

664- **5** 2 **Wee Bizzom**[20] 7689 3-8-3 **50**.................... DanielleMcCreery(5) 4 40
(A Berry) *hld up: hdwy u.p 2f out: no imp fnl f* **25/1**

000- **6** 1 ¾ **Sunshine Ellie**[4] 7833 3-8-12 **54**.................... DarrenWilliams 7 38
(D Shaw) *sn pushed along in rr: rdn 1/2-way: n.d* **10/1**

630- **7** 8 **Senora Verde**[16] 7728 3-8-4 **46** oh1.......................(p) FrankieMcDonald 5 —
(P T Midgley) *led: rdn and hdd 1/2-way: sn wknd* **11/1**

000- **8** 4 **Angelsbemine**[22] 7659 3-7-11 **46** oh1.................... MatthewLawson(7) 1 —
(J R Norton) *chsd ldr: rdn and wknd over 2f out* **100/1**

1m 19.19s (2.69) **Going Correction** +0.325s/f (Slow) **8** Ran SP% **114.5**
Speed ratings (Par 95): **95,93,92,90,88 85,75,69**
toteswinger: 1&2 £3.50, 1&3 £3.20, 2&3 £2.80. CSF £10.94 CT £28.21 TOTE £4.80: £1.30, £1.20, £1.80; EX 17.00 Trifecta £47.80 Pool: £1078.72 - 16.77 winning units. Place 6: £113.70, Place 5: £41.52.
Owner Paul J Dixon **Bred** Slatch Farm Stud **Trained** Averham Park, Notts

FOCUS
A very ordinary sprint that was run at a sound pace. The placed horses are the guide to the level of the form.
T/Plt: £89.00 to a £1 stake. Pool: £108,731.80. 891.69 winning tickets. T/Qpdt: £24.80 to a £1 stake. Pool: £9,152.80. 273.00 winning tickets. CR

[28]LINGFIELD (L-H)
Monday, January 5

OFFICIAL GOING: Standard
This meeting was organised at late notice due to bad weather causing abandonments.
Wind: fresh, half against Weather: cloudy, cold

42 FELBRIDGE (S) STKS 1m (P)
1:15 (1:16) (Class 6) 4-Y-0+ **£1,978** (£584; £292) **Stalls** High

Form RPR

203- **1** **Surwaki (USA)**[8] 7803 7-8-13 60.................... JimCrowley 5 67
(R M H Cowell) *chsd ldr tl rdn to ld 2f out: styd on wl and in command fnl f* **1/1**[1]

050- **2** 1 ¾ **Red Current**[19] 7707 5-8-8 49.................... SimonWhitworth 7 58
(R A Harris) *chsd ldng pair: rdn to chse wnr over 1f out: readily hld fnl f* **16/1**

040- **3** 2 ¾ **Putra Laju (IRE)**[19] 7702 5-8-13 57.................... MartinDwyer 1 57
(J W Hills) *dwlt: in tch: rdn to chse ldng pair 1f out: no imp* **9/1**[3]

503- **4** 2 ½ **Artreju (GER)**[8] 7807 6-8-13 63.................... FergusSweeney 3 51
(G L Moore) *stdd s: t.k.h: hld up in rr: hdwy over 3f out: chsd ldrs and rdn 2f out: carried hd awkwardly and nt qckn wl over 1f out: no ch fnl f* **2/1**[2]

00-0 **5** 3 ¼ **Beckenham's Secret**[2] 23 5-8-13 42.......................(b) TPQueally 6 43
(A W Carroll) *racd keenly: led tl rdn and hdd 2f out: wknd qckly jst over 1f out* **25/1**

0- **6** 1 ¼ **Special Chapter (IRE)**[42] 7436 4-8-2 0 ow1.................... PNolan(7) 2 37
(A B Haynes) *dwlt: towards rr: rdn along 5f out: outpcd over 2f out: n.d after* **50/1**

566- **7** 1 ¼ **Looter (FR)**[43] 5086 4-8-6 50.......................(tp) AndrewHeffernan(7) 9 38
(P Butler) *t.k.h: racd in midfield: lost pl and rdn 3f out: no ch after* **33/1**

000- **8** 5 **King Bathwick (IRE)**[39] 3206 4-8-13 65.............(b[1]) RichardKingscote 8 26
(A B Haynes) *a in rr: rdn over 4f out: wl bhd fnl 2f* **11/1**

1m 38.69s (0.49) **Going Correction** +0.125s/f (Slow) **8** Ran SP% **116.3**
Speed ratings (Par 101): **102,100,97,95,91 90,89,84**
toteswinger: 1&2 £3.60, 1&3 £3.40, 2&3 £33.70. CSF £19.89 TOTE £1.90: £1.10, £5.70, £4.30; EX 17.60.There was no bid for the winner.
Owner T W Morley **Bred** Airlie Stud **Trained** Six Mile Bottom, Cambs

FOCUS
Not a bad race of its type with several of the runners rated in the low 60s but the betting suggested this was a two-horse contest, although it did not quite work out that way.

43 FOREST ROW CLASSIFIED STKS 1m (P)
1:45 (1:47) (Class 7) 4-Y-0+ **£1,706** (£503; £252) **Stalls** High

Form RPR

006- **1** **Samson Quest**[22] 7678 7-9-0 45.................... JimCrowley 12 53
(B Smart) *in tch in midfield: hdwy to chse ldng pair over 2f out: rdn to ld ent fnl f: styd on wl u.p* **5/2**[1]

000- **2** 1 **I Certainly May**[6] 7817 4-9-0 43.......................(p) PatDobbs 9 51
(S Dow) *hld up towards rr: hdwy over 2f out: rdn 2f out: chsd wnr ins fnl f: styd on but unable to rch wnr* **8/1**

000- **3** ½ **Dynamo Dave (USA)**[16] 7746 4-9-0 43.................... FergusSweeney 6 50
(M D I Usher) *hld up in rr: rdn and hdwy 2f out: c wd wl over 1f out: r.o wl fnl f: wnt 3rd wl ins fnl f: nt rch ldng pair* **40/1**

000- **4** 1 **Halsion Challenge**[6] 7817 4-8-7 42.......................(tp) PNolan(7) 10 47
(J R Best) *chsd ldrs: wnt 2nd wl over 2f out: rdn to ld wl over 1f out: hdd ent fnl f: one pce after: lost 2 pls fnl f* **11/2**[2]

005- **5** *hd* **Ma Ridge**[22] 7678 5-9-0 45.................... EdwardCreighton 2 47
(T D McCarthy) *chsd ldrs: rdn and unable qck over 1f out: kpt on same pce fnl f* **8/1**

300- **6** 1 ¼ **Kinsman (IRE)**[22] 7678 12-9-0 44.......................(p) JamesDoyle 11 44
(T D McCarthy) *in tch in midfield: rdn and effrt jst over 2f out: drvn over 1f out: kpt on same pce fnl f* **20/1**

600- **7** *hd* **Abbeygate**[17] 7736 8-9-0 45.......................(p) TPQueally 1 44
(T Keddy) *chsd ldrs: rdn and hung rt fr over 1f out: nvr pce to chal ldrs* **9/1**

060- **8** 7 **Hawkstar Express (IRE)**[9] 6753 4-9-0 45....................(t) MartinDwyer 5 28
(J R Boyle) *rdn along thrght: bhd over 4f out: lost tch 2f out* **10/1**

000- **9** 1 **Mythical Charm**[8] 7801 10-9-0 45.......................(t) NeilChalmers 8 25
(J J Bridger) *stdd and dropped in bhd after s: rdn and no rspnse over 2f out: nvr a factor* **10/1**

000- **10** *nse* **Golden Square**[32] 3360 7-8-7 42.................... BMcHugh(7) 7 25
(A W Carroll) *led tl rdn and hdd wl over 1f out: wknd qckly over 1f out* **13/2**[3]

600- **11** 4 ½ **Tagula Sands (IRE)**[8] 7801 5-9-0 43.................... RichardSmith 3 15
(J C Fox) *hld up in midfield on inner: rdn and struggling 2f out: sn wl btn* **66/1**

550- **12** 10 **Bobal Girl**[14] 7759 4-9-0 45.......................(t) IanMongan 4 —
(M D Squance) *sn pushed up to press ldr: rdn wl over 2f out: wknd qckly 2f out: eased whn wl bhd fnl f* **12/1**

1m 38.51s (0.31) **Going Correction** +0.125s/f (Slow) **12** Ran SP% **124.1**
Speed ratings (Par 97): **103,102,101,100,100 99,98,91,90,90 86,76**
toteswinger: 1&2 £25.10, 1&3 £25.10, 2&3 Not won. CSF £23.82 TOTE £5.00: £1.40, £5.90, £11.40; EX 41.90.
Owner John McMahon **Bred** A W J Perry **Trained** Hambleton, N Yorks

FOCUS
A typical classified event but fairly competitive with the whole field rated within 3lb of each other and the time fractionally faster than the earlier seller.

44 WILLIAMHILL.COM SALE - NOW ON! H'CAP 6f (P)
2:15 (2:16) (Class 6) (0-58,57) 4-Y-0+ £1,978 (£584; £292) Stalls Low

Form RPR
15-5 1 **Whiskey Creek**[2] 27 4-9-1 56....(b) MartinDwyer 4 65
(C A Dwyer) *racd keenly: mde all: nudged clr wl over 1f out: 3l clr 1f out: eased nr fin* 9/4[2]

006- 2 1 1/2 **Arfinnit (IRE)**[5] 7835 8-8-6 47....(v) NeilChalmers 5 51
(Mrs A L M King) *a chsng wnr: rdn and unable qckn wl over 1f out: plugged on fnl f: unable to chal wnr* 14/1

112- 3 1 **Fantasy Fighter (IRE)**[7] 7808 4-8-5 53.... BMcHugh(7) 3 54
(J J Quinn) *plld hrd: hld up in tch: chsd ldng pair jst over 2f out: nt qckn wl over 1f out: kpt on ins fnl f: nvr chal wnr* 5/4[1]

304- 4 1/2 **Simpsons Gamble (IRE)**[34] 7521 6-9-2 57....(p) JimCrowley 9 56
(R A Teal) *hld up towards rr: effrt on outer jst over 2f out: edgd lft fr over 1f out: kpt on but nvr chal wnr* 11/2[3]

20-5 5 shd **Bold Diva**[3] 13 4-9-1 56....(v) TPQueally 6 55+
(A W Carroll) *stdd s: t.k.h: hld up in rr: rdn and little rspnse over 2f out: styd on fnl f: nvr rchd ldrs* 8/1

053- 6 1 1/4 **Magic Glade**[22] 7672 10-9-2 57....(b) PatrickMathers 8 52
(Peter Grayson) *plld hrd: hld up in midfield: drvn and unable qck jst over 2f out: kpt on same pce fnl 2f* 16/1

000- 7 1 1/4 **Szaba**[14] 7759 4-8-7 48 ow3.... EdwardCreighton 7 39
(J Akehurst) *chsd ldrs: rdn over 3f out: struggling jst over 2f out: no ch w wnr fr over 1f out* 33/1

063- 8 3/4 **Elusive Dreams (USA)**[16] 7745 5-9-0 55.... IanMongan 2 44
(P Howling) *s.i.s: a bhd: rdn over 2f out: swtchd off rail over 1f out: kpt on but nvr nr ldrs* 11/2[3]

204- 9 4 1/2 **Stoneacre Pat (IRE)**[5] 7835 4-8-5 53....(b) AndrewHeffernan(7) 1 27
(Peter Grayson) *plld hrd: in tch tl lost pl and rdn over 2f out: wl btn fnl f* 25/1

1m 12.47s (0.57) **Going Correction** +0.125s/f (Slow) 9 Ran SP% **136.4**
Speed ratings (Par 101): **101,99,97,97,96 95,93,92,86**
toteswinger: 1&2 £11.90, 1&3 £2.80, 2&3 £5.50. CSF £39.94 CT £60.30 TOTE £4.00: £2.30, £2.80, £1.10; EX 46.40.
Owner Mrs L Wheeler **Bred** R J H West **Trained** Burrough Green, Cambs

FOCUS
A moderate sprint handicap and the time was nearly a second faster than the following three-year-old contest.
Elusive Dreams(USA) Official explanation: vet said gelding was lame

45 WILLIAMHILL.COM SALE - WHY BET ELSEWHERE? H'CAP 6f (P)
2:45 (2:45) (Class 5) (0-70,73) 3-Y-O £2,590 (£770; £385; £192) Stalls Low

Form RPR
21-2 1 **Hellbender (IRE)**[4] 4 3-9-2 65.... JamesDoyle 1 70
(S Kirk) *led for 1f: chsd ldr after: rdn 2f out: drvn over 1f out: led wl ins fnl f: r.o wl* 11/4[3]

054- 2 1 1/4 **Mandhooma**[9] 7788 3-8-4 53 ow1.... PaulDoe 5 54
(P W Hiatt) *sltly hmpd s: led after 1f: drvn over 1f out: hdd and no ex wl ins fnl f* 16/1

315- 3 1 **My Best Bet**[19] 7700 3-9-7 70.... EdwardCreighton 2 68
(M R Channon) *hld up in tch: hdwy on inner 2f out: disp 2nd and drvn jst over 1f out: no ex ins fnl f* 7/4[1]

22-1 4 1 1/2 **Romantic Queen**[3] 19 3-9-10 73 6ex.... DaneO'Neill 3 66
(E A L Dunlop) *t.k.h: hld up in tch: rdn and unable qck jst over 2f out: sn hanging lft and one pce* 9/4[2]

224- 5 3 3/4 **Bold Rose**[18] 7719 3-8-12 61.... MartinDwyer 4 42
(M D I Usher) *wnt rt s: chsd ldrs: hung bdly rt and lost pl bnd jst over 2f out: no ch after* 8/1

1m 13.41s (1.51) **Going Correction** +0.125s/f (Slow) 5 Ran SP% **110.8**
Speed ratings (Par 97): **94,92,91,89,84**
CSF £35.98 TOTE £2.80: £1.10, £6.30; EX 29.00.
Owner Norman Ormiston **Bred** James Lombard **Trained** Upper Lambourn, Berks

FOCUS
A fair sprint for horses just out of their juvenile year and run 0.94secs slower than the preceding Class 6 event for older horses, which in comparison is about right for the grade.
Bold Rose Official explanation: jockey said filly hung right

46 WILLIAM HILL TELEBETTING SALE 0800 444040 H'CAP 5f (P)
3:15 (3:19) (Class 6) (0-52,52) 4-Y-0+ £1,978 (£584; £292) Stalls High

Form RPR
500- 1 **The Magic Blanket (IRE)**[152] 4725 4-8-12 50.... TPQueally 6 63
(Stef Liddiard) *chsd ldrs: led wl over 1f out: clr ins fnl f: readily* 8/1[3]

404- 2 2 1/4 **Taboor (IRE)**[5] 7836 11-8-10 48.... JimCrowley 2 52
(R M H Cowell) *in tch: rdn to chse wnr ent fnl f: drvn and no imp fnl f* 5/1[2]

066- 3 1 1/2 **Rightcar Lewis**[5] 7836 4-8-9 47....(b) PatrickMathers 8 46
(Peter Grayson) *s.i.s: bhd: rdn and n.m.r wl over 1f out: stl last over 1f out: r.o wl ins fnl f: wnt 3rd wl ins fnl f: nt rch ldrs* 28/1

035- 4 2 **Green Velvet**[19] 7710 4-9-0 52.... TravisBlock 9 44
(P J Makin) *racd in midfield on outer: rdn 1/2-way: outpcd 2f out: plugged on fnl f but nvr pce to rch ldrs* 10/1

022- 5 1/2 **Bollin Franny**[19] 7710 5-9-0 52.... RichardThomas 3 42
(J E Long) *t.k.h: hld up in tch: effrt and rdn over 1f out: fnd nil and no imp after* 4/6[1]

635- 6 hd **Lady Bahia (IRE)**[5] 7835 8-8-5 50....(b) AndrewHeffernan(7) 4 39
(Peter Grayson) *s.i.s: bhd: rdn jst over 2f out: nvr trbld ldrs* 8/1[3]

330- 7 2 1/2 **Fastrac Boy**[5] 7836 6-8-5 50....(t) PNolan(7) 5 30
(J R Best) *led: rdn and hdd wl over 1f out: drvn and wknd ent fnl f* 12/1

6/0- 8 4 1/2 **Stoneacre Baby (USA)**[346] 298 4-8-8 46 oh1.... JamesDoyle 1 10
(Peter Grayson) *chsd ldr tl over 2f out: sn drvn: wknd over 1f out* 66/1

59.40 secs (0.60) **Going Correction** +0.125s/f (Slow) 8 Ran SP% **120.6**
Speed ratings (Par 101): **100,96,94,90,90 89,85,78**
toteswinger: 1&2 £4.00, 1&3 Not won, 2&3 £27.20. CSF £50.21 CT £1097.49 TOTE £9.80: £3.10, £1.90, £6.90; EX 49.30.
Owner David Gilbert **Bred** Mrs M Shenkin **Trained** Great Shefford, Berks

FOCUS
A moderate sprint but a clear-cut winner.
Lady Bahia(IRE) Official explanation: jockey said the mare's saddle slipped

47 HARTFIELD H'CAP 1m 2f (P)
3:45 (3:45) (Class 5) (0-70,69) 4-Y-0+ £2,590 (£770; £385; £192) Stalls Low

Form RPR
032- 1 **Majehar**[8] 7807 7-8-10 59.... TPQueally 2 66+
(A G Newcombe) *t.k.h: trckd ldng pair tl pressed ldr 7f out: led narrowly over 2f out: pushed along and definate advantage over 1f out: pushed out* 8/13[1]

005- 2 1 1/2 **Kings Topic (USA)**[21] 7686 9-8-9 65....(p) PNolan(7) 6 69
(A B Haynes) *led after 1f: chsd ldrs after: dropped to last and rdn over 2f out: hdwy over 1f out: kpt on to go 2nd wl ins fnl f: nt trble wnr* 8/1[3]

425- 3 hd **Magic Warrior**[8] 7801 9-8-3 59.... CharlesEddery(7) 3 63
(J C Fox) *hld up in tch: hdwy on outer over 3f out: rdn over 2f out: chsd wnr 1f out: no imp: lost 2nd wl ins fnl f* 12/1

140- 4 1/2 **Play Up Pompey**[16] 7742 7-8-6 55.... NeilChalmers 7 58
(J J Bridger) *stdd s: t.k.h: hld up in tch: effrt and rdn jst over 2f out: kpt on same pce fnl f* 8/1[3]

040- 5 5 **Master Pegasus**[19] 7610 6-8-13 62.... JimCrowley 4 55
(J R Boyle) *led for 1f: led again 7f out tl over 2f out: rdn ent fnl 2f: lost 2nd 1f out: eased whn btn ins fnl f* 7/2[2]

2m 8.93s (2.33) **Going Correction** +0.125s/f (Slow) 5 Ran SP% **114.1**
Speed ratings (Par 103): **95,93,93,93,89**
toteswinger: 1&2 £26.10. CSF £6.77 TOTE £1.50: £1.10, £2.50; EX 5.50 Place 6 £100.17, Place 5 £61.69.
Owner J R Salter **Bred** Darley **Trained** Yarnscombe, Devon

FOCUS
Another small field for this modest race and a comfortable win for the odds-on favourite.
T/Plt: £143.90 to a £1 stake. Pool: £129,365.72. 656.26 winning tickets. T/Qpdt: £30.20 to a £1 stake. Pool: £10,925.06. 266.90 winning tickets. SP

[15] WOLVERHAMPTON (A.W) (L-H)
Monday, January 5

48 Meeting Abandoned - Frost and Snow

[21] KEMPTON (A.W) (R-H)
Tuesday, January 6

OFFICIAL GOING: Standard
Wind: Light, across Weather: Sunny, bitterly cold

56 WILLIAM HILL TELEBETTING SALE 0800 44 40 40 CLASSIFIED STKS 6f (P)
2:20 (2:28) (Class 7) 4-Y-0+ £1,706 (£503; £252) Stalls High

Form RPR
03-6 1 **Sherjawy (IRE)**[3] 22 5-9-0 45....(b) SimonWhitworth 5 50
(Miss Z C Davison) *sn trckd ldr: rdn to ld wl over 1f out: asserted ins fnl f: hld on* 9/2[2]

500- 2 1/2 **Flamestone**[149] 4891 5-9-0 45.... StephenDonohoe 2 48
(A E Price) *dwlt: hld up in last: stl there wl over 1f out: gd prog after: r.o to take 2nd and cl on wnr nr fin* 66/1

006- 3 nk **Baba Ghanoush**[20] 7705 7-9-0 39....(b) PaulDoe 10 47
(M J Attwater) *dwlt and n.m.r sn after s: rchd midfield after 2f: prog to chse ldng pair wl over 1f out: tk ins route and styd on fnl f* 28/1

000- 4 1/2 **Ignition**[8] 7809 7-9-0 42.... MartinDwyer 11 46
(A Kirtley) *led: drvn and hdd wl over 1f out: kpt on tl lost 2 pls wl ins fnl f* 16/1

24-0 5 1/2 **Rosie Cross (IRE)**[3] 23 5-9-0 45....(p) StephenCarson 7 47+
(Eve Johnson Houghton) *trckd ldrs: cl up whn squeezed out over 2f out: renewed effrt over 1f out: kpt on same pce* 5/1[3]

056/ 6 nse **Ames Souer (IRE)**[45] 6-9-0 40.... TGMcLaughlin 3 44
(P D Evans) *racd on outer in midfield: rdn 2f out: prog 1f out: styd on but nvr quite pce to chal* 25/1

53-3 7 1/2 **Ishibee (IRE)**[3] 27 5-9-0 45....(p) NeilChalmers 6 42
(J J Bridger) *hld up towards rr: prog over 1f out: tried to cl on ldrs ins fnl f: one pce* 5/2[1]

640- 8 1 1/2 **Lady Fas (IRE)**[23] 7678 6-9-0 44.... AdamKirby 8 38
(A W Carroll) *hld up towards rr: effrt on inner 2f out: clsd over 1f out: wknd ins fnl f* 9/1

00-0 9 1 1/4 **Desert Light (IRE)**[3] 27 8-9-0 45....(v) JimCrowley 4 34
(D Shaw) *prom: rdn to chse ldng pair on outer over 2f out to wl over 1f out: wknd fnl f* 9/2[2]

600- 10 1 1/4 **Gone'N'Dunnett (IRE)**[8] 7808 10-9-0 43....(v) VinceSlattery 12 30
(Mrs C A Dunnett) *pressed ldng pair tl jst after 1/2-way: sn rdn: wknd over 1f out* 12/1

650- 11 1 **Heavenly Encounter**[130] 5457 4-9-0 40.... TPQueally 9 26
(K R Burke) *stdd s: t.k.h and hld up in last pair: shkn up and no rspnse wl over 1f out* 33/1

004- 12 1 1/4 **Where's Dids**[194] 3406 4-9-0 45.... JamesDoyle 1 22
(P D Evans) *a towards rr on outer: rdn and struggling over 2f out* 16/1

1m 14.53s (1.43) **Going Correction** +0.15s/f (Slow) 12 Ran SP% **122.8**
Speed ratings (Par 97): **96,95,94,94,93 93,92,90,89,87 86,84**
toteswinger: 1&2 £51.30, 1&3 £26.60, 2&3 £80.00. CSF £294.89 TOTE £6.20: £2.00, £13.10, £6.50; EX 268.40.
Owner Andy Irvine **Bred** Darley **Trained** Hammerwood, E Sussex

FOCUS
A desperate contest. They only went an ordinary pace early and the front seven finished in a heap.

57 WILLIAM HILL TELEBETTING SALE - BONUSES GALORE! CLAIMING STKS 6f (P)
2:50 (2:58) (Class 6) 4-Y-0+ £1,978 (£584; £292) Stalls High

Form RPR
131- 1 **Mutamared (USA)**[15] 7768 9-9-5 84.... JimCrowley 5 81+
(K A Ryan) *trckd ldr: effrt to ld over 1f out: rdn and fnd enough fnl f to hold on* 2/7[1]

006- 2 1/2 **Angel Voices (IRE)**[7] 7819 6-8-5 65....(v[1]) MartinDwyer 4 65
(K R Burke) *led: rdn and hdd over 1f out: kpt on wl enough fnl f but a hld* 7/1[2]

054- 3 1 **Obe Royal**[11] 7782 5-8-10 58....(b) StephenDonohoe 3 67
(P D Evans) *hld up in 4th: rdn 2f out: plugged on at one pce fr over 1f out* 14/1

20-0 **4** *1 ½* **Red Rudy**[3] 24 7-8-12 69........ ShaneKelly 2 64
(A W Carroll) *trckd ldr: rdn 2f out: hanging and fnd nil over 1f out: btn after* **8/1**[3]

000- **5** *11* **Stoneacre Donny (IRE)**[26] 7636 5-8-1 42........ AndrewHeffernan(7) 1 25
(Peter Grayson) *stdd s: hld up in last: lost tch bef 1/2-way: shkn up over 2f out: t.o* **66/1**

1m 13.52s (0.42) **Going Correction** +0.15s/f (Slow) **5** Ran SP% **109.5**
Speed ratings (Par 101): **103,102,101,99,84**
CSF £2.84 TOTE £1.40: £1.10, £2.40; EX 3.20.
Owner Errigal Racing **Bred** E J Hudson Jr, Irrevocable Trust & Kilroy T'Bred **Trained** Hambleton, N Yorks

FOCUS
An ordinary and uncompetitive claimer. The winning time was just over a second quicker than the opener.

58 WILLIAM HILL TELEBETTING SALE - ENHANCED FAVOURITES MEDIAN AUCTION MAIDEN STKS 1m 3f (P)
3:20 (3:25) (Class 6) 4-6-Y-0 **£1,978** (£584; £292) **Stalls** High

Form RPR

3/- **1** **American Spin**[801] 6214 5-9-6 0........ AdamKirby 4 71+
(L A Dace) *stdd s: hld up in 4th: sauntered into the ld wl over 1f out: v easily* **7/2**[2]

643- **2** *4 ½* **Dontpaytheferryman (USA)**[15] 7761 4-9-3 52.....(t) StephenDonohoe 2 57
(P D Evans) *hld up in 5th: rdn over 2f out: plugged on to take 2nd last 100yds* **4/1**[3]

24-2 **3** *1* **Orpenella**[5] 1 4-8-12 61........(b) JimCrowley 3 51
(K A Ryan) *trckd ldr: shkn up over 2f out: nt qckn whn carried lft fnl 2f: one pce* **5/4**[1]

43- **4** *nk* **Russian Angel**[20] 7701 5-9-1 0........ LPKeniry 7 50
(Jean-Rene Auvray) *led: hung bdly lft u.p fr 2f out and hdd sn after: lost 2nd ins fnl f* **11/1**

02- **5** *½* **Sestet**[37] 7504 4-8-12 0........ TonyCulhane 6 49
(S Dow) *hld up in last: shuffled along fr 2f out: cl enough to plcd horses ent fnl f: no ex* **9/2**

356- **6** *23* **Coco L'Escargot**[19] 7713 5-9-1 48........(v) TPQueally 1 10
(J R Jenkins) *chsd ldng pair tl wknd wl over 3f out: t.o* **20/1**

2m 23.97s (2.07) **Going Correction** +0.15s/f (Slow)
WFA 4 from 5yo+ 3lb **6** Ran SP% **117.9**
Speed ratings: **98,94,94,93,93 76**
toteswinger: 1&2 £2.40, 1&3 £1.70, 2&3 £1.40. CSF £18.81 TOTE £3.90: £1.90, £2.60; EX 21.50.
Owner The Tuesday Syndicate **Bred** Cheveley Park Stud Ltd **Trained** Five Oaks, W Sussex

FOCUS
A very uncompetitive older-horse maiden in which the pace was modest.
Russian Angel Official explanation: jockey said mare hung left

59 WILLIAMHILL.COM SALE - WHY BET ELSEWHERE? H'CAP 1m 4f (P)
3:50 (3:56) (Class 6) (0-60,55) 4-Y-0+ **£1,978** (£584; £292) **Stalls** Centre

Form RPR

643- **1** **Imperium**[20] 7702 8-9-8 55........ JimCrowley 11 65
(Jean-Rene Auvray) *stdd s: hld up in midfield: smooth prog to ld wl over 1f out: drvn and styd on wl fnl f: won gng away* **10/1**

053- **2** *2* **Terminate (GER)**[9] 7806 7-9-3 50........ StephenDonohoe 3 57
(Ian Williams) *stdd s: t.k.h 1st 2f: hld up in last: gd prog to chal wl over 1f out: chsd wnr after: lft bhd fnl f* **2/1**[1]

50-2 **3** *nk* **Dansilver**[4] 18 5-9-7 54........ ShaneKelly 2 61
(A W Carroll) *hld up in last trio: prog over 2f out: chsd ldrs and drvn over 1f out: styd on same pce* **4/1**[2]

154- **4** *1* **Ministerofinterior**[17] 7742 4-9-4 55........(be) GeorgeBaker 10 60
(G L Moore) *trckd ldng trio: carried lft but led over 2f out: hdd and nt qckn wl over 1f out: one pce after* **4/1**[2]

0/0- **5** *6* **Tecktal (FR)**[61] 7217 6-9-5 52........ IanMongan 1 47
(P M Phelan) *stdd s: hld up in last trio: nt clr run briefly 3f out: prog over 2f out: pressed ldrs over 1f out: wknd rapidly fnl f* **33/1**

000- **6** *2 ¼* **Always Certain (USA)**[20] 7702 4-9-3 54........ RobertHavlin 5 46
(P G Murphy) *led: hung bdly lft and hdd over 2f out: wknd over 1f out* **25/1**

556- **7** *2 ½* **Foreign King (USA)**[31] 7587 5-9-8 55........ LPKeniry 9 43
(J W Mullins) *chsd ldr to 5f out: sn u.p: 2nd again 4f out to wl over 2f out: wknd* **15/2**[3]

050- **8** *½* **Sir Haydn**[20] 7702 9-9-1 48........ TPQueally 6 35
(J R Jenkins) *trckd ldrs: hrd rdn on outer over 2f out: sn wknd* **25/1**

650- **9** *24* **Cover Drive (USA)**[43] 7440 6-9-8 55........ EdwardCreighton 7 4
(Christian Wroe) *stdd s: t.k.h and hld up bhd ldrs: disp 2nd 4f out: hanging and wknd over 2f out: eased: t.o* **15/2**[3]

000- **10** *38* **Lord Laing (USA)**[39] 7473 6-8-12 45........(v) MickyFenton 8 —
(H J Collingridge) *prom: wnt 2nd 5f out to 4f out: sn wknd rapidly: t.o* **40/1**

2m 36.24s (1.74) **Going Correction** +0.15s/f (Slow)
WFA 4 from 5yo+ 4lb **10** Ran SP% **119.0**
Speed ratings (Par 101): **100,98,98,97,93 92,90,90,74,48**
toteswinger: 1&2 £5.20, 1&3 £4.50, 2&3 £3.60. CSF £30.08 CT £98.05 TOTE £8.30: £2.30, £1.40, £2.00; EX 31.40.
Owner Lambourn Racing **Bred** Mrs H B Raw **Trained** Maiden Bradley, Wilts

FOCUS
A modest handicap in which the early pace was moderate. As a result it developed into something of a 2f sprint, and despite the modest early tempo the principals all came from well off the pace.
Cover Drive(USA) Official explanation: jockey said gelding hung right

60 WILLIAMHILL.COM SALE - BETTER ODDS! FILLIES' H'CAP 1m (P)
4:20 (4:27) (Class 5) (0-70,67) 4-Y-0+ **£2,590** (£770; £385; £192) **Stalls** High

Form RPR

043- **1** **Aphrodisia**[38] 7494 5-9-6 66........ StephenDonohoe 6 73+
(Ian Williams) *stdd s: hld up last in slowly run r: brought to outer and effrt over 1f out: r.o ins fnl f: led last stride* **7/4**[1]

/02- **2** *shd* **Lady Aspen (IRE)**[10] 7790 6-8-6 52........(t) PaulDoe 4 57
(Ian Williams) *trckd ldrs: prog to ld sn after 1/2-way: drvn over 2f out: kpt on u.p: hdd last stride* **7/1**

00-0 **3** *1 ½* **Alucica**[2] 39 6-8-9 55........(v) JimCrowley 5 57
(D Shaw) *t.k.h early: hld up bhd ldrs: effrt over 2f out: drvn to dispute 2nd over 1f out: nt qckn and hld after* **14/1**

202- **4** *shd* **Moon Crystal**[15] 7771 4-9-7 67........(t) TGMcLaughlin 8 68
(E A L Dunlop) *dwlt: t.k.h and sn trckd ldng pair: lost pl sn after 1/2-way: renewed effrt 2f out: disp 2nd 1f out: nt qckn* **5/2**[2]

056- **5** *hd* **Debdene Bank (IRE)**[95] 6446 6-9-3 63........ GeorgeBaker 1 64
(Mrs Mary Hambro) *hld up in last pair: quick move to press ldr sn after 1/2-way: nt qckn over 1f out: one pce fnl f* **11/1**

041- **6** *3* **Bookiebasher Babe (IRE)**[24] 7662 4-9-5 65........ ShaneKelly 3 59
(M Quinn) *led: hdd and dropped to 3rd sn after 1/2-way: styd cl up tl wknd jst over 1f out* **11/2**[3]

630- **7** *3* **Onenightinlisbon (IRE)**[15] 7771 5-9-5 65........ MartinDwyer 2 52
(J R Boyle) *trckd ldr to sn after 1/2-way: squeezed out and snatched up after: wknd over 1f out* **11/1**

1m 44.75s (4.95) **Going Correction** +0.15s/f (Slow) **7** Ran SP% **116.2**
Speed ratings (Par 100): **81,80,79,79,79 76,73**
toteswinger: 1&2 £3.80, 1&3 £6.20, 2&3 £9.80. CSF £15.28 CT £131.27 TOTE £3.00: £2.10, £3.70; EX 21.40.
Owner bellhouseracing.com **Bred** Theobalds Stud **Trained** Portway, Worcs
■ Stewards' Enquiry : Paul Doe two day ban: careless riding (Jan 20-21)

FOCUS
A modest fillies' handicap, but still the classiest race on the card. They went a dawdle until the runner-up took the race by the scruff of the neck just after halfway.

61 WILLIAMHILL.COM SALE - DAILY DOUBLES! H'CAP 1m (P)
4:50 (4:56) (Class 6) (0-50,56) 4-Y-0+ **£1,978** (£584; £292) **Stalls** High

Form RPR

000- **1** **Highly Regal (IRE)**[20] 7707 4-8-8 46........(b[1]) LPKeniry 8 67
(R A Teal) *trckd ldng pair: wnt 2nd over 3f out: led 2f out: drew rt away fr over 1f out* **12/1**

054- **2** *9* **Just Jimmy (IRE)**[8] 7809 4-8-12 50........ JamesDoyle 11 49
(P D Evans) *hld up in rr and off the pce: prog wl over 2f out: chsd clr ldng pair over 1f out: kpt on to take 2nd last 100yds: wnr already home* **4/1**[1]

535- **3** *1* **Glamoroso (IRE)**[8] 7815 4-8-8 46 oh1........ MartinDwyer 10 43
(A Kirtley) *settled midfield: rdn 3f out: kpt on fnl 2f to take 3rd nr fin: no ch* **8/1**

003- **4** *hd* **Waterloo Dock**[15] 7759 4-8-12 50........ ShaneKelly 6 47
(M Quinn) *led at str pce: hdd 2f out but clr of rest: wknd and lost 2 pls fnl f* **5/1**[3]

00-1 **5** *1 ¼* **Too Grand**[3] 23 4-9-4 56 6ex........(v) NeilChalmers 4 50
(J J Bridger) *hld up in last and sn wl off the pce: rdn over 2f out: r.o fr over 1f out on wd outside: no ch* **4/1**[1]

300- **6** *3 ½* **Frosty's Gift**[34] 7535 5-8-10 48........ RichardSmith 12 33
(J C Fox) *a in midfield: lft bhd by ldrs fr 3f out: one pce and no imp after* **16/1**

/00- **7** *1 ¼* **Lady Charlemagne**[69] 7072 4-8-11 49........(v) LukeMorris 13 31
(N P Littmoden) *t.k.h: hld up in last trio and wl off the pce: no prog 3f out: plugged on* **25/1**

464- **8** *nk* **Amwell House**[20] 7701 4-8-8 46 oh1........ SimonWhitworth 3 27
(J R Jenkins) *chsd ldng trio: rdn to go 3rd over 2f out to over 1f out: wknd rapidly* **9/1**

060- **9** *2* **Buck Cannon (IRE)**[23] 7676 4-8-11 49........ IanMongan 1 26
(P M Phelan) *a in rr: u.p and struggling 3f out: bhd after* **9/2**[2]

0/5- **10** *5* **Alloro**[25] 1587 5-8-1 46 oh1........ MatthewDavies(7) 7 11
(A Kirtley) *drvn fr s to chse ldr: lost 2nd and wknd over 3f out* **66/1**

500- **11** *9* **Caught In Paradise (IRE)**[36] 5399 4-8-8 46 oh1... StephenDonohoe 14 —
(D W Thompson) *drvn to try to hold prom pl on inner but sn dropped to rr: a toiling after: t.o* **33/1**

600- **12** *3 ¼* **Actress Annie**[68] 7088 4-8-9 47 oh1 ow1........ JimCrowley 2 —
(Mike Murphy) *hld up: effrt into midfield over 3f out: sn wknd u.p: t.o* **33/1**

1m 39.76s (-0.04) **Going Correction** +0.15s/f (Slow) **12** Ran SP% **120.8**
Speed ratings (Par 101): **106,97,96,95,94 91,89,89,87,82 73,70**
toteswinger: 1&2 £12.50, 1&3 £12.90, 2&3 £7.30. CSF £59.16 CT £421.40 TOTE £14.70: £4.80, £2.40, £3.10; EX 114.10 Place 6: £95.89, Place 5: £14.72.
Owner J Morton **Bred** Mervyn Stewkesbury **Trained** Ashtead, Surrey

FOCUS
Another moderate handicap and only three of these had tasted success before. They went a decent pace though, and the winning time was nearly five seconds quicker than the preceding fillies' handicap. Very few ever got into it.
T/Jkpt: Not won. T/Plt: £191.20 to a £1 stake. Pool: £96,343.65. 367.81 winning tickets. T/Qpdt: £41.70 to a £1 stake. Pool: £7,665.05. 135.90 winning tickets. JN

[35]SOUTHWELL (L-H)
Tuesday, January 6

OFFICIAL GOING: Standard to slow
Wind: Nil Weather: Cold and dry

62 WILLIAM HILL JANUARY SALE - NOW ON! H'CAP 6f (F)
12:40 (12:41) (Class 6) (0-52,52) 4-Y-0+ **£2,047** (£604; £302) **Stalls** Low

Form RPR

355- **1** **Charlotte Grey**[31] 7582 5-8-9 48........ ChrisCatlin 9 60
(P J McBride) *mde virtually all: jnd 2f out and sn rdn: drvn clr ent fnl f: kpt on* **8/1**

000- **2** *3 ¾* **Nautical**[28] 7618 11-8-10 49 ow1........ JerryO'Dwyer 3 49
(J R Holt) *hld up in rr: stdy hdwy on inner 2f out: rdn over 1f out: kpt on ins fnl f: nrst fin* **40/1**

540- **3** *nk* **Head To Head (IRE)**[10] 7793 5-8-3 49........(p) TerenceFury(7) 12 48
(A D Brown) *dwlt: sn chsng ldrs: hdwy to chal 2f out and ev ch tl rdn: edgd lft and one pce ent fnl f* **12/1**

000- **4** *hd* **Phinerine**[162] 4476 6-8-6 52 ow2........(be) KrishGundowry(7) 6 50
(A Berry) *s.i.s and rr: hdwy 1/2-way: chsd ldrs 2f out: sn rdn and edgd lft appr fnl f: kpt on same pce*

450- **5** *nk* **Vanatina (IRE)**[17] 7746 5-8-6 45........ LiamJones 7 42
(W M Brisbourne) *chsd ldrs: rdn along over 2f out: drvn and kpt on same pce appr fnl f* **13/2**[3]

252- **6** *1 ½* **Mister Incredible**[14] 7774 6-8-7 51........(v) MCGeran(5) 2 44
(J M Bradley) *hld up in rr: effrt whn nt clr run 2f out: sn rdn and kpt on appr fnl f: nvr nr ldrs* **9/4**[1]

026- **7** *1 ¼* **Tadlil**[17] 7746 7-8-8 50........(v) TolleyDean(3) 8 39
(J M Bradley) *hld up towards rr: hdwy on outer wl over 2f out: sn rdn and no imp fr over 1f out* **3/1**[2]

/04- **8** *shd* **Rapid Flow**[269] 1338 7-7-13 45........ AlexEdwards(7) 5 33
(J W Unett) *cl up on inner: rdn along wl over 2f out and sn wknd* **12/1**

050- **9** *2 ¼* **Bahamian Bay**[24] 7663 7-8-6 45........ JimmyQuinn 1 26
(M Brittain) *midfield on inner: effrt over 2f out: sn rdn and nvr a factor* **12/1**

065- **10** *2 ½* **Berrymead**[8] 7808 4-8-6 50 ow3........ AnnStokell(5) 11 23
(Miss A Stokell) *chsd ldrs: rdn along wl over 2f out and sn wknd* **14/1**

600- **11** 7 **Fan Club**[14] 7779 5-8-6 **45**..........(b) AndrewElliott 14 —
(Mrs R A Carr) *cl up on outer: rdn along wl over 2f out: sn wknd* **50/1**

1m 18.93s (2.43) **Going Correction** +0.375s/f (Slow) **11** Ran SP% **117.3**
Speed ratings (Par 101): **98,93,92,92,91 89,88,88,85,81 72**
toteswinger: 1&2 £38.70, 1&3 £17.30, 2&3 £54.30. CSF £287.86 CT £3844.83 TOTE £9.90: £2.60, £7.70, £3.50; EX 272.60 TRIFECTA Not won..
Owner N Davies **Bred** Finbar Kent **Trained** Newmarket, Suffolk

FOCUS
A very moderate sprint handicap.

63 SOUTHWELL-RACECOURSE.CO.UK H'CAP 1m (F)
1:10 (1:10) (Class 6) (0-60,65) 4-Y-0+ **£2,047** (£604; £302) **Stalls** Low

Form RPR
323- **1** **Mambo Sun**[10] 7799 6-9-4 **60**.......... RobertWinston 5 70
(R Curtis) *trckd ldrs: hdwy over 2f out: rdn to chal and edgd lft over 1f out: drvn to ld ent fnl f: sn hung lft and kpt on* **8/1**

34-1 **2** 1 ½ **Transmission (IRE)**[4] 12 4-9-9 **65** 6ex.......... TomEaves 10 72
(B Smart) *always prom: led 3f out: rdn wl over 1f out: drvn and hdd ent fnl f: kpt on same pce* **15/8**[1]

44-2 **3** ½ **Betteras Bertie**[5] 7 6-8-9 **51**.......... JimmyQuinn 6 56
(M Brittain) *dwlt and towards rr: hdwy 3f out: chsd ldrs 2f out: sn rdn and styd on ins fnl f: nrst fin* **3/1**[2]

152- **4** hd **Rub Of The Relic (IRE)**[10] 7799 4-9-1 **57**..........(v) FrankieMcDonald 3 62
(P T Midgley) *sn led: pushed along and hdd 3f out: cl up and rdn 2f out: drvn and wknd ent fnl f* **8/1**

43-0 **5** 7 **Louisiade (IRE)**[5] 7 8-8-8 **55**.......... AnnStokell(5) 11 44
(M C Chapman) *in rr: rdn along and hdwy over 2f out: kpt on u.p ins fnl f: nvr nr ldrs* **20/1**

211- **6** 5 **Run Free**[14] 7772 5-9-2 **58**.......... LeeEnstone 4 35
(N Wilson) *trckd ldrs on inner: hdwy over 2f out: rdn wl over 1f out and grad wknd* **5/1**[3]

030- **7** 9 **Naughty Girl (IRE)**[119] 5776 9-8-4 **46** oh1.......... ChrisCatlin 9 3
(John A Harris) *in tch on outer: rdn along 3f out: sn wknd* **66/1**

046/ **8** 7 **Final Bid (IRE)**[253] 1026 6-8-5 **54**..........(b) KrishGundowry(7) 2 —
(A Berry) *dwlt: a towards rr* **66/1**

003- **9** 15 **Sir Billy Nick**[19] 7725 4-9-1 **57**.......... DarrenWilliams 1 —
(S Wynne) *in tch: rdn along 3f out and sn wknd* **33/1**

0-05 **10** 7 **Government (IRE)**[2] 37 8-8-4 **46** oh1.......... AndrewElliott 7 —
(M C Chapman) *prom: rdn along over 3f out and sn wknd* **33/1**

1m 45.94s (2.24) **Going Correction** +0.375s/f (Slow) **10** Ran SP% **112.3**
Speed ratings (Par 101): **103,101,101,100,93 88,79,72,57,50**
toteswinger: 1&2 £3.80, 1&3 £4.10, 2&3 £2.30. CSF £21.68 CT £55.02 TOTE £7.70: £2.20, £1.80, £1.20; EX 31.00 Trifecta £106.90 Pool: £394.58 - 2.73 winning units..
Owner Market Avenue Racing Club Ltd **Bred** Michael John Williamson **Trained** Lambourn, Berks

FOCUS
A moderate handicap run at a noticeably ordinary pace early on.
Run Free Official explanation: jockey said gelding felt wrong in its action late on
Government(IRE) Official explanation: vet said gelding bled

64 HOSPITALITY AT SOUTHWELL RACECOURSE CLAIMING STKS 7f (F)
1:40 (1:40) (Class 6) 3-Y-0 **£2,047** (£604; £302) **Stalls** Low

Form RPR
60-3 **1** **Madison Belle**[4] 16 3-9-0 68.......... DarrenWilliams 3 69
(K R Burke) *cl up: led 3f out: rdn clr over 2f out: easily* **3/1**[2]

00- **2** 5 **Art Discovery (IRE)**[8] 7812 3-8-11 0.......... PaulMulrennan 4 53
(M H Tompkins) *chsd ldng pair: rdn along 3f out: styd on fr over 1f out: tk 2nd ins fnl f: no ch w wnr* **50/1**

231- **3** ¾ **Smalljohn**[25] 7652 3-9-1 74..........(v) TomEaves 2 54
(B Smart) *led: rdn along and hdd 3f out: swtchd wd over 2f out: sn drvn: hung rt and wknd* **1/3**[1]

30-5 **4** 17 **Sally's Dilemma**[4] 10 3-8-6 63 ow1..........(p) TolleyDean(3) 1 3
(W G M Turner) *hld up in tch: effrt 3f out: sn rdn along and outpcd fnl 2f* **22/1**[3]

1m 33.37s (3.07) **Going Correction** +0.375s/f (Slow) **4** Ran SP% **106.3**
Speed ratings (Par 95): **97,91,90,71**
CSF £43.17 TOTE £2.70; EX 44.50.
Owner Paul Sweeting & Mrs L Wright **Bred** Paul Sweeting **Trained** Middleham Moor, N Yorks

FOCUS
An uncompetitive claimer.
Smalljohn Official explanation: trainer was unable to offer any explanation for poor showing

65 MEMBERSHIP AT SOUTHWELL GOLF CLUB APPRENTICE H'CAP 1m 4f (F)
2:10 (2:10) (Class 5) (0-70,72) 4-Y-0+ **£2,729** (£806; £403) **Stalls** Low

Form RPR
401- **1** **Benedict Spirit (IRE)**[18] 7729 4-9-2 **70**.......... AshleyMorgan(3) 1 74
(M H Tompkins) *chsd clr ldr: hdwy over 4f out: rdn to ld wl over 1f out: drvn ent fnl f and kpt on* **7/4**[1]

136- **2** 1 ½ **Chookie Hamilton**[60] 7230 5-9-9 **70**.......... PatrickDonaghy 3 72
(I Semple) *trckd ldrs: rdn along and sltly outpcd over 2f out: drvn wl over 1f out: styd on ins fnl f* **6/1**[2]

056- **3** nk **Bienheureux**[10] 7787 8-8-4 **56** oh7..........(t) MatthewLawson(5) 4 58
(Miss Gay Kelleway) *dwlt: hld up in rr: swtchd wd and hdwy wl over 1f out: styd on strly ins fnl f: nrst fin* **16/1**

43-1 **4** ½ **My Friend Fritz**[5] 3 9-9-11 **72** 6ex.......... WilliamCarson 5 73
(P W Hiatt) *chsd clr ldr: hdwy 4f out: rdn over 2f out and ev ch tl drvn and wknd ins fnl f* **7/4**[1]

213- **5** ½ **Prince Golan (IRE)**[11] 7786 5-9-0 **66**..........(p) AlexEdwards(5) 6 66+
(J W Unett) *t.k.h: sn led and clr whn sddle slipped sltly after 4f: pushed along over 3f out: hdd wl over 1f out and grad wknd* **8/1**[3]

0/6- **6** 2 ¼ **Head To Kerry (IRE)**[28] 5653 9-8-6 **56** oh11..........(t) BillyCray(3) 2 52
(D J S Ffrench Davis) *hld up: a towards rr* **28/1**

2m 46.96s (5.96) **Going Correction** +0.375s/f (Slow)
WFA 4 from 5yo+ 4lb **6** Ran SP% **107.5**
Speed ratings (Par 103): **95,94,93,93,93 91**
toteswinger: 1&2 £1.70, 1&3 £4.50, 2&3 £3.90. CSF £11.83 TOTE £2.30: £1.40, £2.90; EX 10.10.
Owner Mrs S Ashby **Bred** Allevamento Pian Di Neve Srl **Trained** Newmarket, Suffolk

FOCUS
A modest handicap restricted to apprentices who had not ridden more than 50 winners. The pace was steady through the first couple of furlongs or so, but Prince Golan raced very freely down the back straight and pulled himself into a clear lead.

66 WILLIAM HILL JANUARY SALE - BETTER ODDS! CLAIMING STKS 1m 4f (F)
2:40 (2:40) (Class 6) 4-Y-0+ **£2,047** (£604; £302) **Stalls** Low

Form RPR
111- **1** **La Estrella (USA)**[21] 7695 6-9-10 88.......... DaneO'Neill 3 87+
(D E Cantillon) *hld up: smooth hdwy over 4f out: shkn up to ld 2f out and sn clr: easily* **1/3**[1]

556- **2** 6 **St Savarin (FR)**[19] 7717 8-9-1 86.......... FergusSweeney 5 62
(B R Johnson) *trckd ldrs: hdwy to ld 4f out: rdn and hdd 2f out: sn drvn and one pce* **10/3**[2]

240- **3** 4 **My Mirasol**[21] 7695 5-8-10 60.......... ChrisCatlin 2 51
(D E Cantillon) *led: rdn along and hdd 4f out: drvn over 2f out and grad wknd* **16/1**[3]

000- **4** 6 **Force Tradition (IRE)**[75] 6934 4-8-8 58.......... PaulMulrennan 1 43
(M H Tompkins) *chsd ldrs: rdn along over 4f out and sn outpcd* **33/1**

105- **5** 10 **Ricci De Mare**[24] 7662 4-8-1 52.......... FrankieMcDonald 6 20
(G J Smith) *hld up in rr: hdwy 1/2-way: chsd ldrs 4f out: sn rdn along and wknd 3f out* **50/1**

0/0- **6** 16 **Siegfrieds Night (IRE)**[19] 7723 8-8-2 40.......... AlexEdwards(7) 4 —
(M C Chapman) *chsd ldr: rdn along 7f out: sn lost pl and bhd: t.o fnl 3f* **150/1**

2m 45.8s (4.80) **Going Correction** +0.375s/f (Slow)
WFA 4 from 5yo+ 4lb **6** Ran SP% **109.5**
Speed ratings (Par 101): **99,95,92,88,81 71**
toteswinger: 1&2 £1.70, 1&3 £1.60, 2&3 £2.30. CSF £1.59 TOTE £1.70: £1.02, £1.80; EX 1.80.
Owner Mrs J Hart C Lynas & M Freedman **Bred** Five Horses Ltd And Theatrical Syndicate **Trained** Newmarket, Suffolk

FOCUS
A reasonable claimer.

67 WILLIAM HILL JANUARY SALE - WHY BET ELSEWHERE? H'CAP 5f (F)
3:10 (3:10) (Class 4) (0-85,83) 4-Y-0+ **£4,857** (£1,445; £722; £360) **Stalls** High

Form RPR
03-2 **1** **Rebel Duke (IRE)**[5] 2 5-9-1 **80**.......... TonyHamilton 5 92
(D W Barker) *cl up: led 1/2-way: rdn over 1f out: drvn and edgd lft ins fnl f: kpt on* **11/8**[1]

150- **2** ½ **First Order**[19] 7716 8-8-10 **80**..........(v) AnnStokell(5) 1 90
(Miss A Stokell) *chsd ldrs on outer: hdwy wl over 1f out: rdn to chal ent fnl f and ev ch tl no ex towards fin* **16/1**

154- **3** 2 **Canadian Danehill (IRE)**[7] 7826 7-9-0 **79**..........(p) RobertWinston 6 82
(R M H Cowell) *cl up: rdn along wl over 1f out and kpt on same pce ent fnl f* **6/1**[3]

415- **4** 3 ¼ **The Tatling (IRE)**[7] 7826 12-8-13 **83**.......... MCGeran(5) 4 74
(J M Bradley) *chsd ldrs: swtchd rt and hdwy 2f out: sn rdn and no imp appr fnl f* **7/1**

213- **5** 1 ¼ **Northern Empire (IRE)**[7] 7826 6-8-9 **74**.......... ChrisCatlin 2 61
(K A Ryan) *sn cl up: effrt 1/2-way and ev ch tl rdn and wknd wl over 1f out* **3/1**[2]

020- **6** 2 **Bo McGinty (IRE)**[16] 7756 8-8-8 **80**..........(b) BMcHugh(7) 3 59
(R A Fahey) *sn pushed along and outpcd in rr: bhd fr 1/2-way* **14/1**

310- **7** 23 **Dodaa (USA)**[210] 2906 6-8-1 **69**.......... DuranFentiman(3) 7 —
(N Wilson) *led: hdd 1/2-way: sn rdn and cl up tl wknd qckly wl over 1f out* **20/1**

60.89 secs (1.19) **Going Correction** +0.375s/f (Slow) **7** Ran SP% **111.2**
Speed ratings (Par 105): **105,104,101,95,93 90,53**
toteswinger: 1&2 £4.80, 1&3 £2.90, 2&3 £8.70. CSF £24.07 TOTE £2.10: £1.30, £6.30; EX 21.20.
Owner Ian Bishop **Bred** Rathbarry Stud **Trained** Scorton, N Yorks
■ Stewards' Enquiry : Tony Hamilton two day ban: excessive use of the whip (Jan 20-21)

FOCUS
A good sprint handicap.
Canadian Danehill(IRE) Official explanation: jockey said gelding hung right

68 ARENALEISUREPLC.COM H'CAP 6f (F)
3:40 (3:40) (Class 4) (0-85,85) 4-Y-0+ **£4,857** (£1,445; £722; £360) **Stalls** Low

Form RPR
40-5 **1** **Xpres Maite**[4] 9 6-8-13 **80**..........(b) DaneO'Neill 4 93
(S R Bowring) *towards rr: rdn along and hdwy on outer 2f out: drvn to chse ldng pair over 1f out: styd on u.p to ld ins fnl f* **5/1**[3]

211- **2** 1 ¾ **Charles Parnell (IRE)**[18] 7730 6-9-1 **82**.......... DaleGibson 6 89
(M Dods) *chsd ldrs: hdwy 2f out: rdn and ev ch over 1f out tl drvn and nt qckn ins fnl f* **7/2**[2]

146- **3** 6 **Lethal**[132] 5400 6-8-4 **71** oh2.......... FrankieMcDonald 7 59
(R A Fahey) *in tch: effrt 2f out: sn rdn and kpt on ins fnl f: nrst fin* **14/1**

045- **4** nk **Red Cape (FR)**[11] 7782 6-8-4 **71** oh1..........(b) AndrewElliott 1 58
(Mrs R A Carr) *sn led and clr: rdn along over 2f out: drvn over 1f out: hdd ent fnl f and wknd* **20/1**

00-2 **5** 1 ¾ **Jack Rackham**[4] 13 5-8-4 **71** oh1..........(v) ChrisCatlin 2 52
(B Smart) *sltly hmpd s and sn rdn along in rr: nvr a factor* **7/4**[1]

411- **6** nse **Came Back (IRE)**[18] 7727 6-8-13 **85**.......... AnnStokell(5) 5 66
(Miss A Stokell) *chsd ldr: rdn along over 2f out: sn drvn and wknd* **6/1**

250- **7** 2 ½ **Luscivious**[28] 7614 5-9-2 **83**..........(b) RobertWinston 3 56
(A J McCabe) *wnt lft s: sn chsng ldrs: rdn along over 2f out and sn wknd* **6/1**

1m 16.87s (0.37) **Going Correction** +0.375s/f (Slow) **7** Ran SP% **115.3**
Speed ratings (Par 105): **112,109,101,101,98 98,95**
toteswinger: 1&2 £4.90, 1&3 £12.60, 2&3 £7.30. CSF £23.16 TOTE £6.70: £3.40, £2.40; EX 31.60 Place £146.46, Place 5: £14.32.
Owner Charterhouse Holdings Plc **Bred** S R Bowring **Trained** Edwinstowe, Notts

FOCUS
A fair sprint handicap, but the pace was very strong and the winning time was smart.
Jack Rackham Official explanation: jockey said gelding was unsuited by the kick-back
Came Back(IRE) Official explanation: trainer said gelding was unsuited by the slow ground
T/Plt: £192.50 to a £1 stake. Pool: £76,735.49. 290.93 winning tickets. T/Qpdt: £19.60 to a £1 stake. Pool: £6,867.86. 258.78 winning tickets. JR

[56]KEMPTON (A.W) (R-H)

Wednesday, January 7

OFFICIAL GOING: Standard

Wind: Nil

69 WILLIAM HILL TELEBETTING SALE 0800 44 40 40 MEDIAN AUCTION MAIDEN STKS 6f (P)

1:55 (2:05) (Class 6) 3-5-Y-O £2,047 (£604; £302) Stalls High

Form RPR

243- 1 **Five Star Junior (USA)**[21] 7700 3-8-10 72 EddieAhern 8 79+
(Mrs L Stubbs) *trckd ldrs: swtchd lft and qcknd to ld appr fnl f: comf* **7/4**[1]

544- 2 1 3/4 **Princess Cagliari**[21] 7708 3-8-5 64 HayleyTurner 2 69
(R Hannon) *chsd ldrs: drvn along 3f out: styd on fr over 1f to chse wnr ins fnl f but a wl hld* **8/1**

236- 3 1 3/4 **Diamond Twister (USA)**[21] 7700 3-8-10 70 LPKeniry 5 68
(J R Best) *trckd ldr: chal gng wl appr fnl 2f: rdn over 1f out and sn outpcd* **7/2**[3]

02- 4 nk **Towy Valley**[70] 7074 4-9-7 0 AdamKirby 7 66
(C G Cox) *led: kpt slt advantage whn strly chal fr 2f out: shkn up and hdd appr fnl f: styd on same pce* **2/1**[2]

5 12 **Royal Mischief (IRE)**[80] 6844 3-8-5 50 CatherineGannon 1 24
(P D Evans) *s.i.s: a in rr* **100/1**

000- 6 6 **Valid Point (IRE)**[16] 7769 3-8-10 0 StephenDonohoe 3 9
(Sir Mark Prescott) *a in rr* **33/1**

- 7 3 3/4 **Lilleput** 4-9-7 0 TGMcLaughlin 4 —
(Ms J S Doyle) *in rr but in tch tl wknd qckly 1/2-way* **66/1**

1m 12.91s (-0.19) **Going Correction** +0.10s/f (Slow)
WFA 3 from 4yo 16lb 7 Ran SP% **108.5**
Speed ratings (Par 101): **105,102,100,99,83 75,70**
toteswinger: 1&2 £3.00, 1&3 £1.60, 2&3 £2.70. CSF £14.33 TOTE £2.60: £1.20, £3.10; EX 12.40.
Owner Moyns Park Stud **Bred** Robert W Sanford **Trained** Norton, N Yorks

FOCUS
A weak sprint maiden.
Royal Mischief(IRE) Official explanation: jockey said filly hung left

70 WILLIAM HILL TELEBETTING SALE - BONUSES GALORE! CLAIMING STKS 7f (P)

2:25 (2:35) (Class 5) 4-Y-O+ £2,590 (£770; £385; £192) Stalls High

Form RPR

322- 1 **Desert Dreamer (IRE)**[16] 7768 8-8-11 77 RichardKingscote 4 80
(Tom Dascombe) *t.k.h: trckd ldrs in cl 3rd: qcknd to ld wl over 1f out: readily* **15/8**[1]

314- 2 2 1/4 **Electric Warrior (IRE)**[10] 7804 6-9-2 82 DarrenWilliams 6 79
(K R Burke) *sn trcking ldr: pushed along and ev ch ins fnl 2f: outpcd fnl f: jst hld 2nd* **2/1**[2]

512- 3 shd **Sofia's Star**[20] 7724 4-9-3 76 (p) JimCrowley 2 80
(S Dow) *stdd s and rr: hdwy on ins whn nt clr run over 2f out: rdn and one pce over 1f out: styd on ins fnl f and clsng for 2nd nr fin but no ch w wnr* **13/2**

034- 4 nk **Dressed To Dance (IRE)**[74] 6981 5-9-2 79 (v) StephenDonohoe 1 78
(P D Evans) *in rr but in tch: rdn ins fnl 2f: styd on fnl f and gng on nr fin but nvr any ch w wnr* **14/1**

200- 5 2 1/4 **Jewelled Dagger (IRE)**[60] 7245 5-9-12 74 (b) LeeEnstone 3 82
(I Semple) *led: rdn over 2f out: hdd wl over 1f out: wknd ins fnl f* **7/2**[3]

1m 25.81s (-0.19) **Going Correction** +0.10s/f (Slow) 5 Ran SP% **110.3**
Speed ratings (Par 103): **105,102,102,101,99**
toteswinger: 1&2 £3.70. CSF £5.99 TOTE £2.40: £1.60, £1.90; EX 5.60.
Owner ONEWAY Partners **Bred** Gainsborough Stud Management Ltd **Trained** Lambourn, Berks

FOCUS
This claimer was always going to be a tricky, tactical affair.

71 WILLIAM HILL TELEBETTING SALE - ENHANCED FAVOURITES H'CAP 7f (P)

2:55 (3:06) (Class 6) (0-55,61) 4-Y-O+ £2,047 (£604; £302) Stalls High

Form RPR

/00- 1 **Street Power (USA)**[111] 6047 4-9-0 55 GregFairley 5 63
(J R Gask) *t.k.h: chsd ldrs: led jst ins fnl 2f: pushed along ins fnl f: jst hld on* **8/1**

401- 2 nk **Mr Chocolate Drop (IRE)**[23] 7691 5-8-13 54 AdamKirby 2 62
(Miss M E Rowland) *in rr tl hdwy ins fnl 2f: n.m.r whn styng on ins fnl f: fin strly: nt quite get up* **12/1**

302- 3 hd **Sarah's Art (IRE)**[18] 7746 6-9-0 55 MickyFenton 1 62
(Stef Liddiard) *wnt lft s: sn mid-div: hdwy over 2f out: styd on wl fnl f: gng on cl home* **12/1**

235- 4 1/2 **Thabaat**[16] 7766 5-9-0 55 (b) DaneO'Neill 14 61
(J M Bradley) *chsd ldrs: wnt 2nd and rdn over 1f out and sn ev ch: one pce fnl 100yds* **5/1**[1]

151- 5 1/2 **Marmooq**[10] 7803 6-9-6 61 6ex JimCrowley 11 65
(M J Attwater) *mid-div tl outpcd and lost position 3f out: styd on fr over 1f out: mde hdwy ins fnl f: fin wl* **11/2**[2]

144- 6 nse **Guildenstern (IRE)**[15] 7772 7-9-0 55 TGMcLaughlin 10 59
(P Howling) *in rr tl rdn and hdwy 2f out: styd on wl fnl f gng on cl home* **15/2**

142- 7 nk **Shaded Edge**[10] 7803 5-8-13 54 (p) MartinDwyer 6 57
(D W P Arbuthnot) *in tch tl outpcd and lost position 3f out: sn pushed along: hdwy again fnl f: kpt on cl home* **11/2**[2]

050- 8 1 1/2 **Mr Skipiton (IRE)**[25] 7669 4-9-0 55 StephenCarson 7 54
(B J McMath) *led 2f: styd chsng ldr and rdn 2f out: wknd fnl 100yds* **100/1**

23-4 9 1/2 **Mind Alert**[4] 27 8-9-0 55 (v) DarrenWilliams 12 53
(D Shaw) *plld hrd: sn prom: chsd ldrs and rdn over 2f out: wknd fnl f* **13/2**[3]

010- 10 2 3/4 **Copper King**[16] 7763 5-9-0 55 StephenDonohoe 8 46
(Miss Tor Sturgis) *towards rr and outpcd most of way* **20/1**

225- 11 1 1/4 **Palais Polaire**[54] 7320 7-9-0 55 (p) RobertHavlin 9 42
(J A Geake) *chsd ldrs: rdn 2f out: wknd appr fnl f* **14/1**

000- 12 3/4 **Farsighted**[20] 5161 4-8-13 54 LukeMorris 3 39
(J M P Eustace) *slowly in to stride: a in rr* **100/1**

000- 13 7 **Sharps Gold**[28] 7620 4-8-13 54 (vt[1]) HayleyTurner 13 20
(D Morris) *led after 2f: hdd jst ins fnl 2f: wknd fnl f* **20/1**

1m 26.85s (0.85) **Going Correction** +0.10s/f (Slow) 13 Ran SP% **117.2**
Speed ratings (Par 101): **99,98,98,97,97 97,96,95,94,91 90,89,81**
toteswinger: 1&2 £22.30, 1&3 £26.50, 2&3 £15.60. CSF £95.02 CT £778.12 TOTE £9.80: £3.10, £3.10, £3.00; EX 257.40.
Owner Horses First Racing Limited **Bred** John Hawkins **Trained** Sutton Veny, Wilts

FOCUS
A moderate but very competitive handicap. The early pace was ordinary, resulting in a rather messy race, and unusually for Kempton, the low draws dominated.
Street Power(USA) Official explanation: trainer said regarding the improvement in form that the gelding had been gelded and rested since its previous run

72 WILLIAMHILL.COM SALE - WHY BET ELSEWHERE? H'CAP 2m (P)

3:25 (3:36) (Class 4) (0-85,85) 4-Y-O+ £4,727 (£1,406; £702; £351) Stalls High

Form RPR

221- 1 **Wine 'n Dine**[21] 7704 4-9-3 81 EddieAhern 7 91+
(G L Moore) *trckd ldrs: tk slt ld jst ins fnl 2f: edgd rt appr fnl f: kpt on under hand driving ins fnl f* **6/4**[1]

424- 2 3/4 **Salute (IRE)**[18] 7747 10-9-2 73 RobertHavlin 6 82
(P G Murphy) *chsd ldrs: led 4f out: narrowly hdd jst ins fnl 2f: styd upsides ins fnl f: nt pce of wnr nr fin* **5/1**[3]

604- 3 2 **Greenwich Meantime**[16] 7770 9-10-0 85 DaneO'Neill 5 92
(A King) *in tch: hdwy 3f out: disp 2nd 2f out but nvr quite gng pce to chal: one pce fnl f* **11/2**

42/ 4 8 **Kavaloti (IRE)**[318] 4951 5-9-4 75 GeorgeBaker 1 72
(G L Moore) *slowly away: in rr tl sme prog ins fnl 3f: nvr in contention* **16/1**

5 3 1/4 **Aldiruos (IRE)**[171] 9-8-9 66 oh1 LukeMorris 4 59
(A W Carroll) *in rr: rdn along 5f out: hdwy on ins 3f out and briefly chsd ldrs over 2f out: sn wknd* **66/1**

023- 6 2 3/4 **Calculating (IRE)**[22] 7696 5-8-12 69 HayleyTurner 2 59
(M D I Usher) *chsd ldr after 5f: upsides 7f out to 4f out: wknd 3f out* **6/1**

1- 7 28 **Anfield Road**[20] 7713 4-8-13 77 RobertWinston 8 33
(L Corcoran) *led tl hdd 4f out: wknd qckly over 2f out* **9/2**[2]

3m 32.78s (2.68) **Going Correction** +0.10s/f (Slow)
WFA 4 from 5yo+ 7lb 7 Ran SP% **111.9**
Speed ratings (Par 105): **97,96,95,91,90 88,74**
toteswinger: 1&2 £3.20, 1&3 £2.60, 2&3 £3.70. CSF £8.92 CT £30.83 TOTE £2.60: £1.70, £3.00; EX 11.10.
Owner Mrs Charles Cyzer **Bred** C A Cyzer **Trained** Lower Beeding, W Sussex

FOCUS
This was a fair staying handicap for the class. It was run at an average pace and the first three came clear.
Anfield Road Official explanation: jockey said gelding was unsuited by the right handed track

73 WILLIAMHILL.COM SALE - BETTER ODDS! H'CAP 7f (P)

3:55 (4:07) (Class 2) (0-100,107) 4-Y-O+

£11,215 (£3,358; £1,679; £840; £419; £210) Stalls High

Form RPR

321- 1 **Aeroplane**[10] 7804 6-9-2 98 6ex HayleyTurner 2 108+
(S A Callaghan) *hld up in rr: stdy hdwy fr 2f out: qcknd to ld and edgd lft fnl 100yds: readily* **2/1**[1]

302- 2 1 1/4 **Bonus (IRE)**[21] 7703 9-9-11 107 (b) EddieAhern 5 114
(G A Butler) *hld up in rr but in tch: hdwy 2f out: kpt on to chal ins fnl f: one pce whn n.m.r fnl 100yds* **9/4**[2]

562- 3 1 1/4 **Nezami (IRE)**[10] 7804 4-8-5 87 ow1 MartinDwyer 1 90
(J Akehurst) *hld up in tch: hdwy over 2f out: drvn to ld appr fnl f: hdd and one pce fnl 100yds* **11/2**

313- 4 1 1/4 **Abbondanza (IRE)**[18] 7740 6-8-11 93 (p) PaulMulrennan 3 93
(I Semple) *sn led: rdn and styd on whn chal fr over 2f out: hdd appr fnl f: wknd and no ch whn n.m.r fnl 100yds* **6/1**

506- 5 2 **My Gacho (IRE)**[17] 7755 7-8-7 89 (b) GregFairley 6 84
(M Johnston) *t.k.h: chsd ldrs: rdn 2f out: wknd over 1f out* **5/1**[3]

3/0- 6 nse **Count Trevisio (IRE)**[18] 7740 6-8-8 90 RichardKingscote 4 85
(J R Gask) *chsd ldrs: rdn and ev ch 2f out: wknd over 1f out* **25/1**

1m 25.36s (-0.64) **Going Correction** +0.10s/f (Slow) 6 Ran SP% **114.3**
Speed ratings (Par 109): **107,105,104,102,100 100**
toteswinger: 1&2 £1.80, 1&3 £3.20, 2&3 £3.70. CSF £7.02 TOTE £2.60: £1.40, £2.20; EX 5.80.
Owner Saleh Al Homaizi & Imad Al Sagar **Bred** C R Mason **Trained** Newmarket, Suffolk

FOCUS
Only six runners, but this was a decent handicap. The winning time, although quicker than the two previous 7f races on the card, suggests the pace was just fair, and that was how it looked.

NOTEBOOK
Aeroplane has a particularly high cruising speed and is at his best when held up off a strong gallop, so he deserves credit for coming from last to first off what was seemingly no more than an ordinary tempo. It is fair to say that he has been something of an underachiever for most of his career, but Hayley Turner got a great tune out of him when he landed a similar race over this trip at Lingfield last time, and this was another peach of a ride, this time off a 6lb higher mark. Having followed Bonus (similarly held up) through at the cutaway in the straight, he got a lovely gap against the inside rail and was kidded into the lead with just hands-and-heels riding. He edged slightly left near the line, again hinting at waywardness, but the race was in safe-keeping by that point. He is surely high on confidence now and gives the impression he will improve again when dropped back to 6f, where he will be well suited by a quicker all-round gallop. It remains to be seen where he will go next, but he is equally effective on turf and looks an ideal type for the Dubai Carnival. (op 7-4)
Bonus(IRE), runner-up in a course-and-distance Listed race on his previous start, travelled well under restraint as usual, but he ultimately found the concession of 9lb to the talented winner too much. (op 5-2 tchd 11-4)
Nezami(IRE) had his chance but could not reverse recent Lingfield placings with Aeroplane on 6lb better terms. (op 15-2)
Abbondanza(IRE) set an even pace in front and can have no excuses. (op 13-2)
My Gacho(IRE) did not pick up after racing a little keenly. (op 9-2 tchd 11-2)
Count Trevisio(IRE) was not beaten all that far and this was only his second start for his current connections.

74 WILLIAMHILL.COM SALE - DAILY DOUBLES! H'CAP 1m (P)

4:25 (4:37) (Class 5) (0-75,75) 3-Y-O £2,590 (£770; £385; £192) Stalls High

Form RPR

041- 1 **Blaise Tower**[20] 7720 3-9-4 75 GeorgeBaker 8 78+
(G L Moore) *trckd ldrs: wnt 2nd and drvn ins fnl f: qcknd u.p to ld cl home* **2/1**[1]

012- 2 hd **Andean Margin (IRE)**[11] 7789 3-8-13 70 (b) HayleyTurner 6 72
(S A Callaghan) *led: rdn and stl 1 l ahd ins fnl f: ct cl home* **13/2**[3]

14-1 **3** 2 1/4 **Hold The Bucks (USA)**[5] 16 3-9-2 73 6ex.................... LukeMorris 5 70
(J S Moore) *in tch whn rdn along over 3f out: outpcd over 1f out: styd on again ins fnl f* **13/2**[3]
654- **4** 1/2 **It's A Mans World**[21] 7709 3-8-13 70.............................. DaneO'Neill 2 66
(P J McBride) *sn chsng ldr: rdn over 2f out: wknd ins fnl f* **11/4**[2]
462- **5** 8 **Cognac Boy (USA)**[16] 7760 3-8-8 65........................... EddieAhern 7 43
(R Hannon) *hld up in rr but in tch: hdwy on ins to chse ldrs 2f out: wknd fnl f* **10/1**
606- **6** 3 3/4 **Rocoppelia (USA)**[7] 7833 3-8-5 62 oh1 ow1.................. MartinDwyer 4 30
(Mrs A J Perrett) *slowly away: a in rr* **9/1**
465- **7** 2 3/4 **Ymir**[30] 7602 3-8-13 70... PaulDoe 1 33
(M J Attwater) *t.k.h: chsd ldrs: rdn 3f out: wknd over 2f out* **12/1**
1m 40.93s (1.13) **Going Correction** +0.10s/f (Slow) **7** Ran SP% **113.4**
Speed ratings (Par 97): **98,97,95,95,87 83,80**
toteswinger: 1&2 £2.70, 1&3 £3.40, 2&3 £4.20. CSF £15.30 CT £70.14 TOTE £3.20: £1.80, £1.90; EX 10.30 Place 6: £38.49, Place 5: £19.16.
Owner D J Deer **Bred** D J And Mrs Deer **Trained** Lower Beeding, W Sussex
FOCUS
A modest, but competitive handicap for three-year-olds. It was run at a routine pace and the form is rated through the third.
T/Plt: £69.90 to a £1 stake. Pool: £97,989.18. 1,022.15 winning tickets. T/Qpdt: £28.20 to a £1 stake. Pool: £5,921.84. 155.28 winning tickets. ST

15 WOLVERHAMPTON (A.W) (L-H)
Wednesday, January 7

OFFICIAL GOING: Standard
Wind: Nil Weather: Fine and cold

75 PARADE RESTAURANT APPRENTICE (S) STKS 5f 216y(P)
2:20 (2:20) (Class 6) 3-Y-O £2,047 (£604; £302) **Stalls** Low

Form RPR
533- **1** **Kheley (IRE)**[23] 7687 3-8-4 53.............................. DeanHeslop(3) 9 51
(W M Brisbourne) *t.k.h: a.p: led over 4f out tl over 3f out: led over 2f out: rdn and edgd lft over 1f out: r.o* **4/1**[3]
300- **2** hd **Weet In Nerja**[91] 6579 3-8-7 58...............................(p) DavidKenny(5) 4 55
(R Hollinshead) *a.p: rdn and hung lft over 1f out: r.o ins fnl f: tk 2nd cl home* **7/1**
3 1 **Villaruz (IRE)**[87] 6686 3-8-7 0............................ MatthewLawson(5) 2 52
(Karen George) *w ldrs: led over 3f out tl over 2f out: sn rdn: nt qckn and lost 2nd cl home* **17/2**
566- **4** hd **Raimond Ridge (IRE)**[20] 7719 3-8-12 60........................ MCGeran 5 51
(M R Channon) *s.i.s: hld up: hdwy over 3f out: rdn wl over 1f out: kpt on ins fnl f* **3/1**[1]
005- **5** 1 1/4 **Sorrel Ridge (IRE)**[11] 7788 3-8-12 46...........................(p) NicolPolli 1 47+
(M G Quinlan) *hld up: hdwy over 3f out: n.m.r on ins over 2f out: swtchd rt jst over 1f out: kpt on towards fin* **12/1**
404- **6** 4 **River Rye (IRE)**[24] 7673 3-8-11 68.......................... WilliamCarson 6 33
(J S Moore) *broke wl: prom: lost pl after 2f: n.d after* **10/3**[2]
500- **7** 7 **Tartan Turban (IRE)**[30] 7600 3-8-11 52...................... CharlesEddery(5) 7 16
(R Hannon) *a bhd* **17/2**
000- **8** 5 **Yes She Can Can**[23] 7689 3-8-2 42...................... AndrewHeffernan(5) 3 —
(Peter Grayson) *led over 1f: rdn and wknd 2f out* **66/1**
500- **9** 3/4 **Inn Swinger (IRE)**[36] 7530 3-8-4 40...................... AshleyMorgan(5) 8 —
(W G M Turner) *s.i.s: a bhd* **100/1**
1m 16.49s (1.49) **Going Correction** +0.10s/f (Slow) **9** Ran SP% **111.8**
Speed ratings (Par 95): **94,93,92,92,90 85,75,69,68**
toteswinger: 1&2 £6.80, 1&3 £8.60, 2&3 £15.10. CSF £30.61 TOTE £4.30: £1.60, £2.30, £3.20; EX 37.00 Trifecta £332.80 Part won. Pool: £449.83 - 0.77 winning units..There was no bid for the winner. Villaruz was claimed by D. J. Flood for £6,000.
Owner W M Clare **Bred** Matt Gilsenan **Trained** Great Ness, Shropshire
FOCUS
The snow meant track preparation had been disrupted and the surface was riding a shade slower than usual. This was an open seller.

76 WILLIAM HILL JANUARY SALE - NOW ON! H'CAP 5f 216y(P)
2:50 (2:50) (Class 5) (0-75,74) 4-Y-O+ £2,729 (£806; £403) **Stalls** Low

Form RPR
41-1 **1** **River Kirov (IRE)**[4] 24 6-9-4 74 12ex........................ SteveDrowne 1 83+
(M Wigham) *a.p: swtchd rt jst over 1f out: qcknd to ld towards fin: readily* **8/13**[1]
003- **2** 3/4 **War And Peace (IRE)**[9] 7811 5-9-2 72.................. FrankieMcDonald 8 79
(Jane Chapple-Hyam) *broke wl: led early: chsd ldr: rdn to ld 1f out: hdd towards fin* **8/1**[3]
026- **3** 1 1/2 **Peter's Storm (USA)**[43] 7448 4-9-4 74........................ JimmyQuinn 2 76
(K A Ryan) *sn led: hdd 1f out: rdn and nt qckn wl ins fnl f* **14/1**
600- **4** 3/4 **Maybe I Wont**[9] 7811 4-8-7 63...................................... LiamJones 3 63
(Lucinda Featherstone) *hld up and bhd: rdn and r.o ins fnl f: tk 4th cl home* **40/1**
120- **5** hd **Gainshare**[8] 7829 4-8-2 63.................................. DeanHeslop(5) 6 62
(Mrs R A Carr) *hld up and bhd: hdwy on outside over 1f out: rdn and kpt on ins fnl f* **20/1**
426- **6** 3/4 **Incomparable**[25] 7671 4-9-0 70..................................(p) ShaneKelly 5 67
(A J McCabe) *s.i.s: t.k.h in tch: rdn and one pce fnl f* **11/1**
032- **7** 1 1/4 **Figaro Flyer (IRE)**[19] 7733 6-9-0 70........................ IanMongan 7 63
(P Howling) *hld up: hdwy 3f out: rdn and wknd ins fnl f* **13/2**[2]
6/0- **8** 2 3/4 **Dark Tara**[122] 5714 4-8-9 65................................ TonyHamilton 4 49
(R A Fahey) *hld up in tch: wknd over 2f out* **33/1**
1m 16.29s (1.29) **Going Correction** +0.10s/f (Slow) **8** Ran SP% **111.5**
Speed ratings (Par 103): **95,94,92,91,90 89,88,84**
toteswinger: 1&2 £3.30, 1&3 £3.00, 2&3 £10.10. CSF £5.61 CT £33.23 TOTE £1.40: £1.02, £2.00, £2.60; EX 6.50 Trifecta £39.40 Pool: £341.09 - 6.40 winning units..
Owner A Darke T Matthews M Wigham **Bred** Kildaragh Stud **Trained** Newmarket, Suffolk
FOCUS
A fair sprint handicap, but a steady pace.
War And Peace(IRE) Official explanation: jockey said gelding hung left
Incomparable Official explanation: jockey said gelding fly-leapt leaving the stalls and as a result was slowly away
Figaro Flyer(IRE) Official explanation: jockey said gelding lost a front shoe

77 RINGSIDE SUITE 700 THEATRE STYLE CONFERENCE H'CAP 1m 141y(P)
3:20 (3:20) (Class 6) (0-60,60) 3-Y-O £2,047 (£604; £302) **Stalls** Low

Form RPR
010- **1** **Thewaytosanjose (IRE)**[11] 7789 3-8-13 55..................... JamesDoyle 7 56
(S Kirk) *hld up and bhd: hdwy on outside over 3f out: led over 2f out: rdn and hung lft over 1f out: drvn out* **7/1**[3]
503- **2** hd **Barcode**[37] 7519 3-8-11 53.. SteveDrowne 4 53
(R Hannon) *hld up and bhd: hdwy on ins over 2f out: n.m.r and bmpd jst over 1f out: r.o ins fnl f* **6/1**[2]
000- **3** 1 **Royal Salsa (IRE)**[105] 6214 3-8-6 48........................ JimmyQuinn 5 46+
(R A Fahey) *hld up in mid-div: lost pl 4f out: hrd rdn wl over 1f out: hdwy and bmpd ent fnl f: r.o* **15/2**
40-2 **4** nk **Turn To Dreams**[5] 16 3-8-13 55.................................. ShaneKelly 1 52
(P D Evans) *a.p: nt clr run and swtchd rt jst over 1f out: kpt on ins fnl f* **11/1**
513- **5** 1/2 **Autumn Morning (IRE)**[11] 7789 3-9-3 59........................ TomEaves 3 58+
(P D Evans) *s.i.s: t.k.h in rr: hdwy on ins wl over 1f out: nt clr run ins fnl f: kpt on* **9/2**[1]
304- **6** nse **Inca Slew (IRE)**[201] 3225 3-8-8 55.................(p) PatrickDonaghy(5) 9 51
(P C Haslam) *hld up and bhd: hdwy over 4f out: pushed along over 3f out: lost pl over 2f out: c wd st: kpt on on outside towards fin* **16/1**
502- **6** dht **Betws Y Coed (IRE)**[8] 7824 3-8-9 51........................(p) NickyMackay 13 47
(A Bailey) *hdwy to ld over 6f out: hdd over 5f out: chsd ldr tl over 2f out: edgd lft and bmpd jst over 1f out: no ex ins fnl f* **6/1**[2]
062- **8** nk **King's Chorister**[12] 7781 3-9-4 60............................(b[1]) LiamJones 12 55
(Miss Gay Kelleway) *prom: rdn and outpcd wl over 1f out: kpt on towards fin* **22/1**
050- **9** nk **Vien (IRE)**[37] 7514 3-8-12 54...................................... PatDobbs 2 49+
(R Hannon) *led: hdd over 6f out: led over 5f out tl over 2f out: rdn whn hmpd on ins jst over 1f out: nt rcvr* **9/1**
005- **10** 2 1/4 **Spring Quartet**[22] 7693 3-9-1 57................................ PaulEddery 8 46
(Pat Eddery) *prom: lost pl wl over 3f out: n.d after* **20/1**
500- **11** 1 **Vodka Shot (USA)**[21] 7699 3-8-11 53............................ TPQueally 11 40
(M L W Bell) *hld up in mid-div: hdwy over 5f out: wknd over 2f out* **12/1**
1m 54.89s (4.39) **Going Correction** +0.10s/f (Slow) **11** Ran SP% **112.0**
Speed ratings (Par 95): **84,83,82,82,82 82,82,81,81,79 78**
toteswinger: 1&2 £7.30, 1&3 £12.90, 2&3 £5.80. CSF £46.22 CT £321.41 TOTE £7.50: £2.50, £2.40, £3.00; EX 49.50 Trifecta £349.20 Part won. Pool: £472.01 - 0.20 winning units..
Owner Andy J Smith **Bred** Baronrath Stud **Trained** Upper Lambourn, Berks
■ Stewards' Enquiry : James Doyle three day ban: careless riding (Jan 21-23)
Shane Kelly two day ban: careless riding (Jan 21-22)
FOCUS
This was a really competitive handicap and the front nine were covered by around two lengths as they crossed the line.

78 WOLVERHAMPTON-RACECOURSE.CO.UK H'CAP 1m 141y(P)
3:50 (3:50) (Class 6) (0-50,51) 4-Y-O+ £2,047 (£604; £302) **Stalls** Low

Form RPR
033- **1** **Joe Jo Star**[24] 6570 7-8-10 49.................................. TonyHamilton 8 58+
(R A Fahey) *hld up in tch: led ins fnl f: pushed out* **4/6**[1]
500- **2** 1 **The Graig**[86] 6693 5-8-10 49...................................... JerryO'Dwyer 10 56
(J R Holt) *hld up in tch: rdn to ld over 2f out: hdd ins fnl f: nt qckn* **50/1**
32-5 **3** 3/4 **Mocha Java**[4] 23 6-8-8 47.. JimmyQuinn 2 52+
(M Salaman) *led early: a.p: ev ch 1f out: rdn and nt qckn wl ins fnl f* **9/2**[2]
/00- **4** nk **Ridgeway Jazz**[25] 7665 4-8-8 48.............................. FergusSweeney 5 53
(M D I Usher) *hld up in rr: hdwy 2f out: r.o towards fin* **50/1**
60-0 **5** 1/2 **Anduril**[6] 7 8-8-9 48..(b) TomEaves 6 51
(I W McInnes) *hld up towards rr: rdn and hdwy over 1f out: r.o one pce fnl f* **22/1**
040- **6** 1 1/2 **Casablanca Minx (IRE)**[23] 7692 6-8-11 50.................(b) SteveDrowne 4 50
(Miss Gay Kelleway) *hld up in mid-div: lost pl over 3f out: rdn wl over 1f out: styd on ins fnl f: n.d* **16/1**[3]
200- **7** nk **Dushstorm (IRE)**[51] 7368 8-8-11 50.............................. TPQueally 11 49
(R J Price) *hld up in mid-div: hdwy over 2f out: rdn over 1f out: wknd ins fnl f* **18/1**
501- **8** 3/4 **Hi Spec (IRE)**[19] 7736 6-8-6 48.........................(p) DuranFentiman(3) 13 46
(Miss M E Rowland) *hld up in rr: hdwy on wd outside 3f out: c v wd st: wknd over 1f out* **22/1**
026- **9** 3/4 **Maddy**[11] 7792 4-8-8 48...(p) FrankieMcDonald 9 44
(George Baker) *hld up towards rr: short-lived effrt on outside 3f out* **20/1**
000- **10** 2 **Gifted Heir (IRE)**[11] 7792 5-8-7 46...........................(v[1]) NickyMackay 7 37
(A Bailey) *a in rr* **16/1**[3]
004- **11** 1 3/4 **King Of Cadeaux (IRE)**[8] 7818 4-8-6 51 ow2.....(p) GabrielHannon(5) 12 38
(M A Magnusson) *sn led: hdd over 2f out: rdn and wknd over 1f out* **20/1**
030- **12** 7 **Moorside Diamond**[20] 7723 5-8-11 50.....................(b) GrahamGibbons 3 21
(A D Brown) *t.k.h: sn chsng ldr: lost 2nd over 2f out: wknd wl over 1f out: eased ins fnl f* **28/1**
1m 52.27s (1.77) **Going Correction** +0.10s/f (Slow)
WFA 4 from 5yo+ 1lb **12** Ran SP% **120.8**
Speed ratings (Par 101): **96,95,94,94,93 92,92,91,90,89 87,81**
toteswinger: 1&2 £15.10, 1&3 £2.60, 2&3 £26.10. CSF £65.04 CT £112.88 TOTE £1.90: £1.10, £11.30, £1.60; EX 43.50 Trifecta £188.70 Pool: £461.63 - 1.81 winning units..
Owner The Ipso Facto Syndicate **Bred** B J And Mrs Crangle **Trained** Musley Bank, N Yorks
FOCUS
This was a very moderate handicap and the winner had to only run to his old Flat form to score.
Gifted Heir(IRE) Official explanation: jockey said horse hung right
Moorside Diamond Official explanation: jockey said mare hung right-handed

79 WILLIAM HILL JANUARY SALE - BETTER ODDS! H'CAP 1m 1f 103y(P)
4:20 (4:20) (Class 4) (0-85,84) 4-Y-O+ £4,857 (£1,445; £541; £541) **Stalls** Low

Form RPR
045- **1** **Spectait**[28] 7633 7-8-13 78.. ShaneKelly 8 88
(Jonjo O'Neill) *hld up in tch: led wl over 2f out: sn clr: pushed out* **15/2**
143- **2** 2 **Stand Guard**[17] 7753 5-8-13 78.................................. IanMongan 6 84+
(P Howling) *hld up in rr: hdwy on outside wl over 1f out: r.o to take 2nd wl ins fnl f: nt trble wnr* **11/2**[2]
010- **3** 1/2 **Faithful Ruler (USA)**[61] 7224 5-8-6 71........................ DaleGibson 3 76
(R A Fahey) *hld up in tch: rdn over 1f out: kpt on same pce fnl f* **8/1**
201- **3** dht **Dream Of Fortune (IRE)**[11] 7791 5-8-12 77...............(t) JerryO'Dwyer 2 82+
(M G Quinlan) *hld up in rr: nt clr run on ins over 2f out: hdwy over 1f out: r.o ins fnl f: nrst fin* **9/1**
000- **5** 2 1/4 **Scamperdale**[39] 7496 7-9-4 83.................................. TPQueally 12 83
(B P J Baugh) *hld up in rr: hdwy on outside over 2f out: rdn over 1f out: one pce fnl f* **14/1**

123- **6** *1* **Hucking Heat (IRE)**[12] 7785 5-8-13 **78**....................(p) GrahamGibbons 7 76
(R Hollinshead) *hld up in mid-div: hdwy over 2f out: rdn over 1f out: wknd ins fnl f* **13/2**[3]

441- **7** *1 1/4* **Silver Hotspur**[11] 7796 5-9-5 **84**.. LiamJones 10 80
(C R Dore) *hld up and bhd: sme hdwy over 1f out: no further prog fnl f* **14/1**

216- **8** *1/2* **Royal Amnesty**[26] 7657 6-8-13 **78**....................................(b) TomEaves 4 73
(I Semple) *hld up in mid-div: no hdwy fnl 2f* **12/1**

504- **9** *2* **Rebellious Spirit**[18] 7750 6-9-0 **79**................................ JamesDoyle 11 69
(S Curran) *prom: rdn over 3f out: wknd wl over 1f out* **12/1**

000- **10** *1* **Bee Stinger**[18] 7740 7-8-12 **77**...(v) JoeFanning 9 65
(I A Wood) *hld up in tch: pushed along over 3f out: sn wknd* **33/1**

3/6- **11** *hd* **Noubian (USA)**[18] 7747 7-8-10 **75**................................ FergusSweeney 5 63
(C R Dore) *a bhd* **22/1**

405- **12** *18* **Kildare Sun (IRE)**[39] 7502 7-8-7 **72**....................... NickyMackay 13 22
(J Mackie) *sn chsng ldr: led over 3f out tl wl over 2f out: wknd wl over 1f out: eased fnl f* **33/1**

302- **13** *2 3/4* **Emperor Court (IRE)**[36] 7526 5-9-1 **80**........................... SteveDrowne 1 24
(P J Makin) *led: hdd over 3f out: wknd over 2f out: eased over 1f out* **5/1**[1]

2m 0.05s (-1.65) **Going Correction** +0.10s/f (Slow) **13** Ran SP% **117.2**
Speed ratings (Par 105): **111,109,108,108,106 105,104,104,102,101 101,85,83**PL: Dream Of Fortune: £1.30, Faithful Ruler: £1.50, Tricast: S-SG-DOF: £188.66, S-SG-FR: £169.82. toteswinger: 1&2 £14.80, 1&3 S-DOF £7.70, S-FR £12.60, 2&3 SG-DOF £4.40, SG-FR £7.00. CSF £46.47 TOTE £10.90: £3.80, £1.90; EX 76.10 Trifecta £105.20 with DOF Pool: £27 Owner.

FOCUS
This had the look of a fair handicap and the form is probably sound rated through the third.
Emperor Court(IRE) Official explanation: trainer was unable to offer any explanation for the poor performance

80 HOTEL & CONFERENCING AT WOLVERHAMPTON MAIDEN STKS 1m 141y(P)
4:50 (4:51) (Class 5) 4-Y-0+ **£2,729** (£806; £403) **Stalls** Low

Form RPR

646- **1** **Watson's Bay**[39] 7494 4-9-3 66.................................... FergusSweeney 10 73
(Miss Tor Sturgis) *hld up in mid-div: hdwy 3f out: led over 1f out: edgd rt ins fnl f: drvn out* **11/4**[2]

020- **2** *2 3/4* **Focail Eile**[12] 7786 4-9-3 60... GrahamGibbons 8 67
(E S McMahon) *a.p: led over 2f out: rdn and hdd over 1f out: edgd lft ins fnl f: no ex* **9/2**[3]

0- **3** *12* **Coill Glas (IRE)**[25] 7669 4-9-3 0.. LiamJones 4 39
(W J Haggas) *hld up in mid-div: rdn and hdwy over 2f out: wnt modest 3rd ins fnl f* **5/2**[1]

0- **4** *3/4* **Waldorf (IRE)**[17] 7757 4-9-3 0.. SteveDrowne 7 38
(W R Muir) *chsd ldr: led over 5f out tl over 2f out: rdn and wknd wl over 1f out* **5/2**[1]

6/0- **5** *1* **Princess Zhukova (IRE)**[360] 146 4-8-12 0........................ TPQueally 3 30
(R J Price) *hld up and bhd: sme prog on ins over 2f out: nvr nr ldrs* **66/1**

000- **6** *nk* **Beresford Lady**[15] 7772 5-8-13 41...................................(p) AndrewElliott 6 30
(A D Brown) *prom tl wknd over 2f out* **66/1**

7 *6* **Aegean Rose** 4-8-12 0.. JimmyQuinn 9 16
(M Blanshard) *dwlt: a in rr* **20/1**

600/ **8** *42* **Wizzy Izzy (IRE)**[498] 4924 4-8-5 35....................................... BMcHugh(7) 2 —
(N Wilson) *led: hdd over 5f out: wknd 3f out: t.o* **40/1**

1m 50.42s (-0.08) **Going Correction** +0.10s/f (Slow)
WFA 4 from 5yo 1lb **8** Ran SP% **112.2**
Speed ratings (Par 103): **104,101,90,90,89 89,83,46**
toteswinger: 1&2 £3.60, 1&3 £4.80, 2&3 £4.80. CSF £14.60 TOTE £4.00: £1.40, £1.90, £1.10; EX 17.30 Trifecta £69.50 Pool: £558.82 - 5.95 winning units..
Owner Miss Tor Sturgis **Bred** De Burgh Equine **Trained** Lambourn, Berks

FOCUS
An uncompetitive maiden that saw two draw clear with the winner rated to previous form.
Waldorf(IRE) Official explanation: trainer had no explanation for the colt's poor run

81 SPONSOR A RACE BY CALLING 01902 390009 H'CAP 1m 1f 103y(P)
5:20 (5:20) (Class 6) (0-52,52) 4-Y-0+ **£2,047** (£604; £302) **Stalls** Low

Form RPR

455- **1** **Giddywell**[70] 7085 5-8-9 **50**...............................(p) RussellKennemore(3) 10 62
(R Hollinshead) *hld up towards rr: hdwy wl over 1f out: carried rt ins fnl f: sn led: r.o wl* **11/1**

000- **2** *1 3/4* **Scutch Mill (IRE)**[68] 7112 7-8-7 **50**........................(t) PatrickDonaghy(5) 4 58
(P C Haslam) *hld up towards rr: hdwy on ins wl over 1f out: led ins fnl f: edgd rt and sn hdd: nt qckn* **7/1**[3]

013- **3** *2 1/4* **Tarkamara (IRE)**[11] 7792 5-8-12 **50**................................ JoeFanning 2 53
(P F I Cole) *a.p: led over 2f out: rdn and hdd ins fnl f: no ex* **5/1**[1]

260- **4** *1 1/4* **Moyoko (IRE)**[19] 7732 6-9-0 **52**...................................... JimmyQuinn 3 55+
(M Salaman) *hld up in mid-div: hdwy on ins over 2f out: rdn whn hmpd ins fnl f: one pce* **8/1**

660- **5** *2 3/4* **Semah Harold**[11] 7799 4-8-13 **52**..............................(v) GrahamGibbons 1 47
(E S McMahon) *hld up in mid-div: rdn and hdwy wl over 1f out: no imp fnl f* **9/1**

035- **6** *hd* **Jarvo**[11] 7792 8-8-11 **49**..(v) PatrickMathers 5 43
(I W McInnes) *hld up in rr: hrd rdn and hdwy over 1f out: nvr trbld ldrs* **16/1**

033- **7** *nk* **Turkish Sultan (IRE)**[23] 7691 6-8-7 **50**.........................(p) MCGeran(5) 9 44
(J M Bradley) *wnt lft s: hld up in mid-div: no hdwy fnl 2f* **15/2**

026- **8** *1/2* **Tapas Lad (IRE)**[25] 7663 4-8-10 **52**..........................(v) KevinGhunowa(3) 8 45
(G J Smith) *hld up in tch: rdn over 2f out: wknd over 1f out* **16/1**

010- **9** *7* **Whodunit (UAE)**[21] 7702 5-8-13 **51**..............................(b) ShaneKelly 6 29
(P W Hiatt) *led: hdd over 2f out: wknd over 1f out* **10/1**

024- **10** *1* **Victory Spirit**[16] 7765 5-9-0 **52**... TomEaves 7 28
(I Semple) *n.m.r s: a in rr* **6/1**[2]

605- **11** *3/4* **Atlantic Gamble (IRE)**[30] 7608 9-8-11 **49**....................(p) AndrewElliott 12 23
(K R Burke) *hld up in tch: wknd over 2f out* **8/1**

000- **12** *6* **Zabeel House**[23] 7691 6-9-0 **52**................................(p) FergusSweeney 11 14
(John A Harris) *s.i.s: hld up towards rr: short-lived effrt over 3f out* **40/1**

300- **13** *4* **Kansas Gold**[37] 7516 6-8-13 **51**....................................(p) NickyMackay 13 4
(J Mackie) *sn chsng ldr: reminder wl over 3f out: sn lost 2nd: wknd over 2f out* **25/1**

2m 1.14s (-0.56) **Going Correction** +0.10s/f (Slow)
WFA 4 from 5yo+ 1lb **13** Ran SP% **122.9**
Speed ratings (Par 101): **106,104,102,101,98 98,98,98,91,90 90,84,81**
toteswinger: 1&2 £24.70, 1&3 £17.10, 2&3 £11.60. CSF £88.54 CT £445.09 TOTE £12.10: £4.30, £3.20, £1.80; EX 75.00 Trifecta £107.70 Pool: £378.65 - 2.60 winning units..
Owner The Giddy Gang **Bred** R Hollinshead **Trained** Upper Longdon, Staffs
■ Stewards' Enquiry : Patrick Donaghy two-day ban: careless riding (Jan 21-22)

FOCUS
They went a fair pace in this moderate contest and the form looks sound with the third the best guide.

82 WILLIAM HILL JANUARY SALE - WHY BET ELSEWHERE? H'CAP 1m 4f 50y(P)
5:50 (5:50) (Class 4) (0-85,85) 4-Y-0+ **£4,857** (£1,445; £722; £360) **Stalls** Low

Form RPR

51- **1** **Cape Express (IRE)**[32] 7583 4-9-0 **83**................................ ShaneKelly 6 101+
(M A Jarvis) *led 3f: chsd ldr: led 3f out: rdn and edgd lft 2f out: edgd lft jst ins fnl f: drvn clr* **11/8**[1]

531- **2** *6* **Heathyards Pride**[18] 7744 9-9-1 **80**............................. GrahamGibbons 5 87
(R Hollinshead) *hld up in tch: wnt 2nd and sltly impeded 2f out: rdn over 1f out: no ex ins fnl f* **4/1**[2]

530- **3** *1 3/4* **Aureate**[88] 3045 5-9-6 **85**.. TomEaves 7 90
(B Ellison) *s.i.s: hld up and bhd: rdn and hdwy over 2f out: styd on same pce fnl f* **10/1**

164- **4** *2 1/2* **Aypeeyes (IRE)**[31] 7595 5-9-2 **81**....................................(v) TPQueally 8 82
(A King) *hld up and bhd: swtchd rt over 2f out: rdn and sme hdwy over 1f out: n.d* **15/2**

153- **5** *4* **Bentley Brook (IRE)**[20] 7717 7-8-13 **83**................... GabrielHannon(5) 2 77
(R Curtis) *hld up in tch: rdn over 3f out: wknd over 2f out* **16/1**

351- **6** *2 3/4* **Clear Reef**[12] 7785 5-9-3 **82**... IanMongan 9 72
(Jane Chapple-Hyam) *w ldr: led after 3f: hdd 3f out: sn rdn: wknd wl over 1f out* **9/2**[3]

030- **7** *59* **Indicible (FR)**[39] 7493 5-9-0 **79**................................ FergusSweeney 8/1 —
(A King) *prom tl rdn and wknd over 3f out: t.o* **8/1**

2m 38.92s (-2.18) **Going Correction** +0.10s/f (Slow)
WFA 4 from 5yo+ 4lb **7** Ran SP% **118.1**
Speed ratings (Par 105): **111,107,105,104,101 99,60**
toteswinger: 1&2 £2.40, 1&3 £6.80, 2&3 £6.30. CSF £7.52 CT £39.87 TOTE £1.90: £1.40, £2.00; EX 9.30 Trifecta £84.70 Pool: 733.73 - 6.41 winning units. Place 6: £30.76, Place 5: £10.92.
Owner A D Spence **Bred** March Thoroughbreds **Trained** Newmarket, Suffolk

FOCUS
They went no pace early here and the race developed into a bit of a sprint. The runner-up ran close to previous course and distance form.
T/Jkpt: £5,637.00 to a £1 stake. Pool: £106,468.21. 13.41 winning tickets. T/Plt: £24.60 to a £1 stake. Pool: £96,533.55. 2,854.76 winning tickets. T/Qpdt: £6.80 to a £1 stake. Pool: £7,573.38. 817.73 winning tickets. KH

GREAT LEIGHS (A.W) (L-H)
Thursday, January 8

OFFICIAL GOING: Standard
Last race abandoned due to fog.
Wind: nil Weather: foggy, cold

83 BLACKWATER H'CAP 5f (P)
1:55 (2:10) (Class 5) (0-75,74) 4-Y-0+ **£2,590** (£770; £385; £192) **Stalls** Low

Form RPR

61P- **1** **Godfrey Street**[37] 7529 6-8-7 **70**..............................(p) DeclanCannon(7) 3 81
(A G Newcombe) *chsd ldrs: led over 1f out: hld on wl fnl 100yds* **11/1**

342- **2** *1/2* **Silvanus (IRE)**[9] 7828 4-9-2 **72**.. DaneO'Neill 1 81
(I Semple) *dwlt: midfield: hdwy over 2f out: ev ch ins fnl f: no ex nr fin* **10/11**[1]

500- **3** *4* **Caribbean Coral**[29] 7621 10-9-3 **73**................................ GeorgeBaker 5 68
(A B Haynes) *dwlt: bhd: hdwy fnl f: wnt 3rd nr fin: nvr trbld ldrs* **16/1**

450- **4** *hd* **Steel City Boy (IRE)**[20] 7730 6-8-12 **68**.......................... JimCrowley 4 62
(D Shaw) *midfield: rdn 1/2-way: no ch w ldrs fnl 100yds* **11/2**[2]

016- **5** *1* **Bookiesindex Boy**[19] 7743 5-9-3 **73**........................(v) StephenDonohoe 6 63
(J R Jenkins) *led: hdd over 1f out: 3rd and btn fnl 100yds: lost 2 pls nr fin* **12/1**

100- **6** *2 3/4* **Desert Opal**[19] 7743 9-8-10 **66**..(b) LiamJones 2 46
(C R Dore) *a bhd* **12/1**

604- **7** *1/2* **Woodcote (IRE)**[17] 7768 7-9-4 **74**.................................(tp) LPKeniry 7 53
(P R Chamings) *chsd ldr early: rdn 1/2-way: wl btn ins fnl f* **7/1**[3]

360- **8** *1/2* **Jane's Payoff (IRE)**[10] 7811 4-8-11 **67**..................... RichardThomas 8 44
(Mrs L C Jewell) *chsd ldrs: rdn and struggling 1/2-way:* **25/1**

60.45 secs (0.25) **Going Correction** +0.125s/f (Slow) **8** Ran SP% **113.7**
Speed ratings (Par 103): **103,102,95,95,93 89,88,87**
toteswinger: 1&2 £3.70, 1&3 £11.20, 2&3 £6.70. CSF £21.29 CT £169.44 TOTE £12.50: £3.60, £1.10, £3.60; EX 25.40.
Owner M K F Seymour **Bred** Miss S N Ralphs **Trained** Yarnscombe, Devon

FOCUS
Visibility was poor due to the fog and the race was made even trickier as there was a false start, and the field had to be quickly pulled up, but few looked to get much further than the first bend. Obviously this is form to treat with caution, although the time was good for the grade. The form is rated around the first two.

84 BOYNE CLAIMING STKS 1m 5f 66y(P)
2:25 (2:37) (Class 6) 4-Y-0+ **£1,942** (£578; £288; £144) **Stalls** Low

Form RPR

11-1 **1** **La Estrella (USA)**[2] 66 6-9-13 88.................................... DaneO'Neill 3 91
(D E Cantillon) *t.k.h: hld up in 3rd pl: rdn and effrt over 2f out: swtchd ins wl over 1f out: led over 1f out: rdn out* **2/7**[1]

121- **2** *1/2* **Bridgewater Boys**[9] 7816 8-8-11 70.......................(b) StephenDonohoe 5 74
(P D Evans) *hld up in last pl: effrt over 2f out: ev ch ins fnl f: unable qck fnl 100yds* **9/2**[2]

/66- **3** *4* **Ebert**[46] 7083 6-9-4 80... TonyHamilton 2 75?
(R A Fahey) *chsd ldr: rdn wl over 2f out: 3rd and outpcd fnl f* **16/1**[3]

440- **4** *4 1/2* **Barawin (IRE)**[36] 7539 4-8-5 78.......................................(b[1]) LiamJones 1 60?
(K R Burke) *led at stdy gallop: rdn 3f out: hdd over 1f out: sn wknd* **16/1**[3]

3m 0.32s (6.72) **Going Correction** +0.125s/f (Slow)
WFA 4 from 6yo+ 5lb **4** Ran SP% **107.7**
Speed ratings (Par 101): **84,83,81,78**
CSF £1.89 TOTE £1.30; EX 1.60.
Owner Mrs J Hart C Lynas & M Freedman **Bred** Five Horses Ltd And Theatrical Syndicate **Trained** Newmarket, Suffolk

The Form Book, Raceform Ltd, Compton, RG20 6NL

FOCUS
Visibility was once again poor and the runners did not come back into view until the final 100 yards. The front pair are the best guide and are rated close to their previous best.

85 FOYLE MAIDEN STKS 5f (P)
2:55 (3:07) (Class 5) 3-Y-0+ £2,590 (£770; £385; £192) Stalls Low

Form RPR

1 **Changing The Guard** 3-8-12 0 TonyHamilton 1 69+
(R A Fahey) *hld up in rr: hdwy on inner over 2f out: qcknd to ld wl ins fnl f: comf* 12/1

4- 2 1 1/4 **Circle Dance (IRE)**[12] 7798 4-9-13 65 (v) JimCrowley 6 71
(D Shaw) *led: rdn 1/2-way: hdd and no ex wl ins fnl f* 15/2[3]

20-2 3 1/2 **Minotaurious (IRE)**[6] 19 3-8-7 79 FergusSweeney 8 58
(K R Burke) *pressed ldr: ev ch and rdn over 2f out: kpt on same pce* 8/13[1]

040- 4 3 **Kingsgate Storm (IRE)**[9] 7820 3-8-12 80 SteveDrowne 3 52
(J R Best) *chsd ldng pair: rdn over 3f out: outpcd over 2f out: kpt on same pce after* 10/3[2]

0- 5 3 3/4 **Countrywide Jaime (IRE)**[11] 7802 3-8-7 0 StephenDonohoe 7 33
(S A Callaghan) *in tch in midfield: rdn and outpcd over 2f out: no ch w ldrs fnl f* 33/1

0- 6 1 1/2 **Field Fantasy**[35] 7546 3-8-7 0 PatrickMathers 5 28
(Garry Moss) *chsd ldng trio: rdn and outpcd over 2f out: no ch w ldrs fnl f* 66/1

7 2 3/4 **Petrenko** 3-8-5 0 BMcHugh(7) 2 23
(R A Fahey) *sn detached in last pl* 25/1

61.62 secs (1.42) **Going Correction** +0.125s/f (Slow)
WFA 3 from 4yo 15lb 7 Ran SP% 112.7
Speed ratings (Par 103): **93,91,90,85,79 77,72**
toteswinger: 1&2 £4.10, 1&3 £2.90, 2&3 £1.90. CSF £89.72 TOTE £10.80: £3.30, £1.90; EX 45.90.
Owner I L Davies **Bred** R A Bonnycastle And Marston Stud **Trained** Musley Bank, N Yorks

FOCUS
Once again vision was very limited for this weak maiden, despite the course turning on the floodlights to help. The winner did it nicely and his handicap mark depends on whether the form the third and fourth showed is taken literally.

86 LIFFEY H'CAP 6f (P)
3:25 (3:35) (Class 3) (0-95,95) 4-Y-0+
£7,352 (£2,201; £1,100; £551; £274; £138) Stalls Low

Form RPR

13-0 1 **Matsunosuke**[7] 2 7-9-3 **94** TPQueally 2 109
(A B Coogan) *stdd s: hld up in last pl: hdwy on bit over 2f out: in ld and clr fnl 100yds: easily* 4/1[3]

624- 2 4 **Epic Odyssey**[11] 7805 4-8-6 **83** MartinDwyer 5 85
(J R Boyle) *led: rdn over 2f out: 2nd and no ch w wnr fnl 100yds* 11/2

405- 3 3/4 **Soopacal (IRE)**[30] 7614 4-8-9 **86** JimCrowley 1 86
(B Smart) *racd in last trio: hdwy on inner and rdn jst over 2f out: 3rd and no ch w wnr fnl 100yds* 7/2[2]

11-6 4 2 1/4 **Came Back (IRE)**[2] 68 6-8-5 **87** ow2 AnnStokell(5) 3 80
(Miss A Stokell) *w ldrs: rdn jst over 2f out: 4th and no ch w wnr fnl 100yds* 7/1

444- 5 nk **Beat The Bell**[32] 7594 4-8-13 **90** NeilChalmers 8 82
(A Bailey) *chsd ldrs: effrt u.p over 2f out: no ch w wnr fnl 100yds* 5/2[1]

600- 6 5 **Mr Lambros**[20] 7737 8-8-13 **90** (vt) SteveDrowne 4 66
(Miss Gay Kelleway) *racd in rr: rdn 3f out: wl btn fnl f* 16/1

40-6 7 10 **Irish Pearl (IRE)**[7] 2 4-8-11 **95** DeclanCannon(7) 6 39
(K R Burke) *dwlt: chsd ldr 4f out tl over 2f out: sn wknd: t.o* 14/1

1m 12.48s (-1.22) **Going Correction** +0.125s/f (Slow) 7 Ran SP% 111.2
Speed ratings (Par 107): **113,107,106,103,103 96,83**
toteswinger: 1&2 £4.00, 1&3 £3.40, 2&3 £4.30. CSF £24.47 CT £80.09 TOTE £4.50: £1.70, £3.10; EX 24.20.
Owner A B Coogan **Bred** R Coogan **Trained** Soham, Cambs

FOCUS
The visibility remained poor. This had the look of a relatively competitive sprint on paper and the smart winner put up a slight personal best in a race run at a good pace.

NOTEBOOK
Matsunosuke emerged from the gloom a clear best. Now 4lb higher than when winning over course and distance last month, he was held up in rear early on, but started to make strong headway and won with tons in hand. He will need to pull out more if he is to win again, but is clearly in top form. (tchd 7-2 and 9-2)
Epic Odyssey, second off this mark over course and distance last month, finished last of four at Lingfield last time, but he came back to something like his best here, despite proving no match for the winner. (op 5-1 tchd 6-1)
Soopacal(IRE) is beginning to slip back down to a decent mark, but he was seemingly unable to quicken in the straight. (tchd 4-1)
Came Back(IRE) won twice at a lower level towards the end of last year, but he struggled back in handicap company last time, and again came up well short. (op 8-1 tchd 9-1)
Beat The Bell managed to get a decent position from his wide draw, but was under pressure entering the straight, and could find no extra. (tchd 9-4)

87 SUIR (S) STKS 6f (P)
3:55 (4:06) (Class 5) 3-Y-0+ £2,590 (£770; £385; £192) Stalls Low

Form RPR

305- 1 **Mafaheem**[9] 7819 7-9-7 68 GeorgeBaker 5 70
(A B Haynes) *hld up in rr: hdwy over 2f out: chsd ldrs fnl 100yds: r.o wl to ld on post* 7/2[3]

003- 2 shd **One More Round (USA)**[9] 7819 11-9-13 74 (b) JamesDoyle 9 76
(P D Evans) *racd on outer: hdwy 3f out: rdn and pressed ldrs 2f out: in ld fnl 100yds: hdd on post* 3/1[2]

060/ 3 3/4 **Stonecrabstomorrow (IRE)**[447] 6313 6-9-7 0 TonyHamilton 6 67
(R A Fahey) *in tch: rdn and hdwy over 2f out: chsd ldrs 2f out: pressed ldr fnl 100yds: no ex towards fin* 2/1[1]

0- 4 1/2 **Hint Of Honey**[59] 7275 3-8-0 0 CatherineGannon 1 57
(A G Newcombe) *s.i.s: bhd: hdwy over 2f out: chsd ldrs fnl 100yds: kpt on same pce fnl 100yds* 40/1

400- 5 1 1/4 **Chookie Heiton (IRE)**[9] 7829 11-9-0 62 BMcHugh(7) 3 62
(I Semple) *hld up in tch towards rr: hdwy over 2f out: 5th and one pce fnl 100yds* 14/1

000- 6 1 **Whistleupthewind**[40] 7497 6-9-2 50 (b) LukeMorris 4 53
(J M P Eustace) *chsd ldrs: rdn over 2f out: 6th and wl hld fnl 100yds* 33/1

/06- 7 3 3/4 **Running Buck (USA)**[16] 7779 4-9-7 47 (v[1]) NeilChalmers 7 46
(A Bailey) *sn pushed up to ld: rdn over 2f out: 7th and wl btn fnl 100yds* 28/1

220- 8 1 1/2 **Dubai To Barnsley**[12] 7793 4-9-0 48 AndrewHeffernan(7) 2 42
(Garry Moss) *hld up in tch: swtchd to outer and effrt jst over 2f out: no ch fnl 100yds* 7/1

0/0- 9 3 1/4 **Mumaathel (IRE)**[12] 7793 6-9-7 57 MartinDwyer 8 31
(W R Muir) *restless in stalls: w ldr: rdn and wkng over 2f out: wl bhd fnl f* 12/1

1m 14.32s (0.62) **Going Correction** +0.125s/f (Slow)
WFA 3 from 4yo+ 16lb 9 Ran SP% **116.2**
Speed ratings (Par 103): **100,99,98,98,96 95,90,88,83**
toteswinger: 1&2 £3.40, 1&3 £2.80, 2&3 £2.90. CSF £14.32 TOTE £4.50: £1.40, £1.30, £1.30; EX 11.10 Place 6: £77.36, Place 5: £48.12.There was no bid for the winner.
Owner WCR V - The Conkwell Connection **Bred** J H And J M Wall **Trained** Limpley Stoke, Bath

FOCUS
The visibility was yet again very poor for this seller, but the field appeared to go off at a decent clip. Not a bad race for the grade, and the form is rated around the runner-up.

88 SLANEY H'CAP 1m 2f (P)
() (Class 5) (0-70,) 3-Y-O £

T/Plt: £107.40 to a £1 stake. Pool: £101,309.03. 688.40 winning tickets. T/Qpdt: 25.60 to a £1 stake. Pool: £5,552.70. 160.00 winning tickets. SP

[62]SOUTHWELL (L-H)
Thursday, January 8

OFFICIAL GOING: Standard
Wind: Nil Weather: Cloudy and dry

89 HOSPITALITY AT SOUTHWELL RACECOURSE APPRENTICE CLAIMING STKS 5f (F)
12:50 (12:50) (Class 6) 4-Y-0+ £2,047 (£604; £302) Stalls High

Form RPR

215- 1 **Calmdownmate (IRE)**[12] 7793 4-8-13 63 LukeMorris 3 75
(Mrs R A Carr) *dwlt: sn trcking ldrs: smooth hdwy 1/2-way: led wl over 1f out: rdn ent fnl f and kpt on* 4/1[3]

20-1 2 1 1/4 **Don Pele (IRE)**[4] 35 7-8-9 71 (p) MatthewDavies(5) 1 71
(R A Harris) *trckd ldrs: hdwy 2f out: rdn to chse wnr over 1f out: drvn and kpt on ins fnl f* 3/1[1]

534- 3 3/4 **Monte Major (IRE)**[12] 7793 8-8-3 56 (v) LeeTopliss(7) 9 64
(D Shaw) *chsd ldrs: hdwy 2f out: sn rdn and edgd lft ent fnl f: kpt on u.p towards fin* 18/1

223- 4 1 3/4 **Grimes Faith**[20] 7727 6-9-2 65 (p) AndrewMullen 7 64
(K A Ryan) *in tch: rdn along 1/2-way: styd on u.p ins fnl f: nrst fin* 7/2[2]

050- 5 2 **Mr Rooney (IRE)**[62] 7231 6-8-13 53 SladeO'Hara(3) 4 57
(A Berry) *cl up: rdn along 1/2-way: grad wknd fr wl over 1f out* 33/1

100- 6 hd **She's Our Beauty (IRE)**[12] 7793 6-8-5 45 (v) DuranFentiman 2 45
(S T Mason) *sn led: rdn along over 2f out: hdd wl over 1f out and grad wknd* 33/1

00-0 7 shd **Loose Caboose (IRE)**[6] 13 4-9-3 70 (v[1]) TolleyDean 8 57
(A J McCabe) *chsd ldrs: rdn along over 2f out: grad wknd* 25/1

042- 8 hd **Colorus (IRE)**[12] 7793 6-8-13 63 (p) AmyBaker(3) 6 55
(W J H Ratcliffe) *n.m.r s and sn in rr: pushed along and hung lft 1/2-way: rdn to chse ldrs wl over 1f out: wknd appr fnl f* 9/2

233- 9 nse **Savile's Delight (IRE)**[234] 2255 10-8-11 75 CharlesEddery(5) 5 55
(Tom Dascombe) *awkward s: sn towards rr and swtchd lft to far rail 1/2-way: rdn wl over 1f out and nvr a factor* 7/1

000- 10 14 **Flying Indian**[16] 7774 4-8-10 56 ow1 (p) RussellKennemore 10 —
(J Balding) *dwlt: sn chsng ldrs on outer: rdn along over 2f out and sn wknd* 100/1

59.79 secs (0.09) **Going Correction** +0.075s/f (Slow) 10 Ran SP% **113.9**
Speed ratings (Par 101): **102,100,98,96,92 92,92,92,91,69**
toteswinger: 1&2 £3.40, 1&3 £13.40, 2&3 £10.80. CSF £15.52 TOTE £5.50: £1.80, £1.10, £3.70; EX 22.80 Trifecta £303.80 Part won. Pool: £410.66 - 0.10 winning units..
Owner David W Chapman **Bred** J Costello **Trained** Huby, N Yorks
■ Stewards' Enquiry : Lee Topliss two-day ban: careless riding (Jan 22-23)

FOCUS
On paper this looked a competitive sprint, as most of these had been in some sort of form in recent weeks on this surface. In fact, four of these had clashed in a similar contest at the end of December and it was one of those that proved victorious. It is likely the second and fourth were below par and the form is rated around the third.
Savile's Delight(IRE) Official explanation: jockey said gelding hung left in the closing stages

90 WILLIAM HILL JANUARY SALE - NOW ON! MAIDEN STKS 1m 3f (F)
1:20 (1:24) (Class 5) 4-Y-0+ £2,729 (£806; £403) Stalls Low

Form RPR

404- 1 **Onemoreandstay**[112] 6055 4-8-12 67 RobertWinston 9 69+
(R W Price) *trckd ldrs: hdwy 3f out: swtchd rt wl over 1f out: rdn to ld 1f out: kpt on* 11/2

/36- 2 1 1/4 **Ibrox (IRE)**[94] 6529 4-9-3 63 GrahamGibbons 2 72
(A D Brown) *trckd ldrs: hdwy over 2f out: rdn to ld wl over 1f out: drvn and hdd 1f out: kpt on u.p ins fnl f* 4/1[3]

332- 3 1 1/4 **Augustus John (IRE)**[12] 7798 6-9-6 67 AdamKirby 7 70
(S Parr) *trckd ldrs: rdn along and sltly outpcd 3f out: drvn and styd on appr fnl f: nrst fin* 4/1[3]

42- 4 2 1/4 **Wing Diva (IRE)**[21] 7721 4-8-12 0 TomEaves 5 61
(B Smart) *trckd ldr: hdwy to ld 3f out: rdn along 2f out: sn hdd and drvn: wknd appr fnl f* 7/2[2]

623- 5 11 **Musashi (IRE)**[18] 7752 4-9-3 68 MickyFenton 4 47
(Jane Chapple-Hyam) *led: rdn along and hdd 3f out: sn drvn and wknd fnl 2f* 11/4[1]

55-4 6 21 **General Tufto**[7] 7 4-9-0 45 (b) TolleyDean(3) 3 12
(C Smith) *midfield: rdn along and outpcd over 4f out* 40/1

5-5 7 2 **Auction Belle**[6] 11 4-8-7 0 GabrielHannon(5) 1 —
(R Curtis) *prom: rdn along after 3f: sn lost pl and bhd fnl 4f* 66/1

000- 8 24 **Aura**[31] 7599 4-8-12 42 (bt) JimmyQuinn 6 —
(H J L Dunlop) *a in rr: t.o fnl 4f* 100/1

P6- 9 2 1/4 **Redlynch**[12] 7798 4-9-3 0 DaleGibson 8 —
(S Parr) *sn outpcd and a bhd: t.o fnl 4f* 100/1

2m 28.61s (0.61) **Going Correction** +0.15s/f (Slow)
WFA 4 from 6yo 3lb 9 Ran SP% **110.2**
Speed ratings (Par 103): **103,102,101,99,91 76,74,57,55**
toteswinger: 1&2 £4.90, 1&3 £5.10, 2&3 £3.60. CSF £25.52 TOTE £7.00: £2.00, £1.40, £2.00; EX 32.30 Trifecta £199.40 Pool: £730.54 - 2.71 winning units..
Owner Mrs Elizabeth Macdonald **Bred** The Duke Of Devonshire **Trained** Newmarket, Suffolk

The Form Book, Raceform Ltd, Compton, RG20 6NL

FOCUS
A weak maiden in which Musashi looked to go off too quickly, which helped set this up for those ridden with a little more restraint. The form looks sound enough rated around the third and fourth, with the winner close to her turf maiden form.

91 SOUTHWELL RACECOURSE FOR CONFERENCES H'CAP 5f (F)
1:50 (1:50) (Class 6) (0-60,65) 3-Y-O £2,047 (£604; £302) **Stalls** High

Form RPR

61-2 **1** **Halaak (USA)**[4] 41 3-8-12 **54** ....(b) ChrisCatlin 1 66+
(D M Simcock) *chsd ldrs: hdwy on outer 1/2-way: rdn to ld appr fnl f: sn clr and rdn out* **13/8**[1]

64-5 **2** *3 1/4* **Wee Bizzom**[4] 41 3-8-3 **50** .... DanielleMcCreery(5) 7 50
(A Berry) *sn rdn along towards rr: hdwy 2f out: swtchd lft over 1f out: styd on u.p ins fnl f: no ch w wnr* **20/1**

22-1 **3** *1 1/4* **La Capriosa**[4] 41 3-9-9 **65** 6ex .... RobertWinston 8 61
(A J McCabe) *cl up: led 1/2-way: rdn and hdd wl over 1f out: sn drvn and kpt on underpress ins fnl f* **7/2**[3]

423- **4** *3/4* **Readily**[12] 7795 3-8-9 **51** .... RichardKingscote 4 44
(J G Portman) *led: rdn along and hdd 1/2-way: sn drvn and kpt on same pce fr over 1f out* **11/4**[2]

04-5 **5** *1/2* **Sills Vincero**[5] 34 3-9-4 **60** .... DarrenWilliams 9 51
(D Shaw) *cl up: rdn along over 2f out and grad wknd* **12/1**

000- **6** *1/2* **You'relikemefrank**[24] 7689 3-8-4 **46** oh1 ....(p) AndrewElliott 2 35
(J Balding) *prom: rdn 2f out and sn led: drvn and hdd appr fnl f: 2nd and hld whn stmbld ins fnl f and wknd after* **50/1**

060- **7** *3* **Valdemar**[51] 7372 3-8-3 **52** ....(p) TerenceFury(7) 3 30
(A D Brown) *sn outpcd and a in rr* **28/1**

003- **8** *10* **Cafe Fiore (IRE)**[9] 7825 3-8-1 **50** ....(b) MatthewLawson(7) 6 —
(T J Pitt) *a in rr* **16/1**

60.76 secs (1.06) **Going Correction** +0.075s/f (Slow) 8 Ran SP% **110.7**
Speed ratings (Par 95): **94,88,86,85,84 84,79,63**
toteswinger: 1&2 £6.00, 1&3 £2.10, 2&3 £5.40. CSF £36.29 CT £97.23 TOTE £2.90: £1.30, £3.20, £1.50; EX 27.50 Trifecta £128.40 Pool: £574.33 - 3.31 winning units..
Owner Saeed Misleh **Bred** Brereton C Jones **Trained** Newmarket, Suffolk

FOCUS
Most of these had clashed recently in similar contests, so the form is probably reliable for the class although the runner-up sounds a note of caution. The winner improved over this shorter trip.

92 WILLIAM HILL JANUARY SALE - BETTER ODDS! (S) STKS 7f (F)
2:20 (2:20) (Class 6) 3-Y-O £2,047 (£604; £302) **Stalls** Low

Form RPR

04-4 **1** **Hawkspring (IRE)**[7] 4 3-9-4 59 ....(t) AdamKirby 5 67
(S Parr) *trckd ldrs: hdwy over 2f out: rdn to ld wl over 1f out: clr ins fnl f* **15/8**[2]

0- **2** *4 1/2* **Yellow River (USA)**[35] 7546 3-8-7 72 .... JimmyQuinn 9 44
(S A Callaghan) *dwlt: sn in tch: hdwy on outer 3f out: rdn to chse wnr over 1f out: sn drvn and no imp* **5/4**[1]

005- **3** *nk* **Jack's House (IRE)**[10] 7810 3-8-12 51 ....(t) FrankieMcDonald 8 48
(Jane Chapple-Hyam) *cl up: led 3f out: rdn over 2f out: drvn and hdd wl over 1f out: kpt on same pce* **8/1**[3]

250- **4** *3* **That Boy Ronaldo**[23] 7694 3-8-2 50 .... DanielleMcCreery(5) 3 35
(A Berry) *chsd ldrs: rdn along 2f out: drvn and wknd appr fnl f* **25/1**

5 *7* **Snoozing** 3-8-2 0 ow2 .... AshleyMorgan(7) 6 18
(M H Tompkins) *dwlt: sn rdn along and outpcd in rr tl styd on fnl 2f* **14/1**

00-2 **6** *6* **Captain Bradz (USA)**[7] 5 3-8-12 0 .... LeeEnstone 1 5
(P T Midgley) *led: rdn along and hdd 3f out: sn wknd* **20/1**

00- **7** *2 1/4* **Northern Shore (IRE)**[152] 4873 3-8-12 0 ....(b[1]) ChrisCatlin 7 —
(K A Ryan) *a in rr: bhd fr 1/2-way* **22/1**

050- **8** *38* **Colin Staite**[66] 7165 3-8-12 40 ....(b[1]) PaulMulrennan 2 —
(R Brotherton) *cl up: rdn along over 3f out and sn wknd: bhd and eased fnl f* **100/1**

1m 33.11s (2.81) **Going Correction** +0.15s/f (Slow) 8 Ran SP% **111.0**
Speed ratings (Par 95): **89,83,83,80,72 65,62,19**
toteswinger: 1&2 £1.90, 1&3 £3.00, 2&3 £2.90. CSF £4.14 TOTE £2.50: £1.10, £1.10, £1.80; EX 5.80 Trifecta £20.70 Pool: £440.54 - 15.68 winning units..There was no bid for the winner. Yellow River was claimed for £5,500 by E.J. Creighton.
Owner Willie McKay **Bred** Mrs S M Roy **Trained**

FOCUS
An uncompetitive seller. The winner appeared to show improved form but the time does not back that up.

93 PLAY GOLF AT SOUTHWELL GOLF CLUB H'CAP 1m (F)
2:50 (2:50) (Class 5) (0-70,71) 4-Y-O+ £2,729 (£806; £403) **Stalls** Low

Form RPR

01-1 **1** **United Nations**[4] 39 8-9-7 **71** 6ex ....(b) LeeEnstone 6 81
(N Wilson) *dwlt: sn chsng ldrs: hdwy on outer to ld over 3f out: sn rdn clr: easily* **11/4**[2]

4-12 **2** *8* **Transmission (IRE)**[2] 63 4-9-1 **65** 6ex .... TomEaves 2 57
(B Smart) *led: rdn along and hdd over 3f out: sn drvn and kpt on same pce* **11/8**[1]

455- **3** *3 3/4* **Tiger's Rocket (IRE)**[18] 7752 4-9-2 **66** ....(b[1]) ChrisCatlin 3 49
(S Gollings) *cl up: rdn along over 3f out: drvn over 2f out sn one pce* **33/1**

02-4 **4** *3 1/2* **Elk Trail (IRE)**[4] 39 4-9-4 **68** .... MickyFenton 4 43
(Mrs P Sly) *in tch: rdn along 3f out: drvn and no imp fnl 2f* **10/3**[3]

- **5** *5* **Redwater River**[69] 7123 5-9-0 **64** .... PaulMulrennan 5 27
(Mrs R A Carr) *cl up: rdn along 1/2-way: sn wknd* **15/2**

1m 44.29s (0.59) **Going Correction** +0.15s/f (Slow) 5 Ran SP% **106.6**
Speed ratings (Par 103): **103,95,91,87,82**
toteswinger: 1&2 £3.00. CSF £6.48 TOTE £3.80: £1.60, £1.60; EX 6.40.
Owner Beverley Embassy Syndicate **Bred** Cyril Humphris **Trained** Flaxton, N Yorks

FOCUS
A modest handicap and the in-form winner was in a league of his own, although he was almost certainly the only one to run their rae. This was his best form since he was a 3yo.

94 WILLIAM HILL JANUARY SALE - WHY BET ELSEWHERE? H'CAP 7f (F)
3:20 (3:20) (Class 5) (0-75,73) 4-Y-O+ £2,729 (£806; £403) **Stalls** Low

Form RPR

120- **1** **Tri Chara (IRE)**[9] 7829 5-8-9 **64** ....(p) GrahamGibbons 8 73
(R Hollinshead) *prom: led 3f out: rdn wl over 1f out: drvn ins fnl f and kpt on wl* **4/1**[1]

054- **2** *1 1/2* **Caprio (IRE)**[19] 7748 4-9-3 **72** .... RichardKingscote 5 77
(Tom Dascombe) *stdd s: hld up towards rr: hdwy on outer over 2f out: rdn to chse ldrs and hung lft over 1f out: drvn and kpt on ins fnl f* **9/2**[2]

30-3 **3** *hd* **Whitbarrow (IRE)**[6] 13 10-8-11 **69** ow1 ....(b) JamesMillman(3) 1 73
(B R Millman) *led: rdn along and hdd wl over 2f out: drvn over 1f out: kpt on* **5/1**[3]

24-3 **4** *2* **Elusive Warrior (USA)**[4] 37 6-8-11 **66** ....(p) RobertWinston 9 65
(A J McCabe) *chsd ldrs: rdn over 2f out: drvn wl over 1f out and sn one pce* **11/2**

045- **5** *2 1/2* **Haroldini (IRE)**[12] 7796 7-8-9 **64** ....(p) PaulMulrennan 6 56
(J Balding) *in rr tl styd on fnl 2f: nrst fin* **8/1**

1/0- **6** *7* **Pharaohs Justice (USA)**[49] 7398 4-9-3 **72** .... AdamKirby 7 45
(N P Littmoden) *chsd ldrs: rdn along wl over 2f out: sn one pce* **25/1**

336- **7** *1/2* **Montiboli (IRE)**[124] 5713 4-9-3 **72** .... ChrisCatlin 2 44
(K A Ryan) *blindfold removed late: chsd ldrs: rdn along over 2f out: sn drvn and wknd* **9/1**

300- **8** *hd* **Certain Justice (USA)**[31] 7603 11-8-9 **64** .... MickyFenton 4 35
(Stef Liddiard) *in tch: rdn along 1/2-way: sn wknd* **10/1**

205- **9** *13* **Prince Noel**[66] 7167 5-9-4 **73** ....(p) LeeEnstone 3 9
(N Wilson) *dwlt: sn rdn along and a in rr: bhd fnl 2f* **8/1**

1m 30.79s (0.49) **Going Correction** +0.15s/f (Slow) 9 Ran SP% **115.4**
Speed ratings (Par 103): **103,101,101,98,95 87,87,87,72**
toteswinger: 1&2 £4.40, 1&3 £5.00, 2&3 £4.30. CSF £21.94 CT £91.77 TOTE £5.20: £2.10, £1.90, £1.60; EX 24.30 Trifecta £149.20 Pool: £594.95 - 2.95 winning units..
Owner The Tri Chara Partnership **Bred** High Bramley Grange Stud **Trained** Upper Longdon, Staffs

FOCUS
A modest handicap. Straightforward form rated through the runner-up, with a step up from the winner back on this surface.
Tri Chara(IRE) Official explanation: trainer's representative said gelding benefitted fom being able to dominate the racc

95 SOUTHWELL-RACECOURSE.CO.UK H'CAP 6f (F)
3:50 (3:50) (Class 6) (0-65,65) 4-Y-O+ £2,047 (£604; £302) **Stalls** Low

Form RPR

3P-3 **1** **Jordi Roper (IRE)**[7] 1 4-8-4 **51** .... DaleGibson 8 64
(S Parr) *towards rr: hdwy on outer over 2f out: rdn wl over 1f out: styd on to chal ins fnl f and sn edgd lft: led fnl 50yds* **20/1**

32-2 **2** *3/4* **Hamaasy**[6] 14 8-8-9 **59** .... KevinGhunowa(3) 9 69
(R A Harris) *trckd ldrs: hdwy over 2f out: rdn to ld over 1f out: drvn and edgd lft ins fnl f: hdd and no ex last 50yds* **15/8**[1]

50-4 **3** *3/4* **Nabeeda**[6] 14 4-8-3 **55** .... JimmyQuinn 7 63
(M Brittain) *cl up: hdwy to ld over 2f out and sn rdn: drvn and hdd over 1f out: ev ch tl no ex wl ins fnl f* **5/2**[2]

00-6 **4** *1* **Cape Of Storms**[6] 13 6-8-6 **56** .... AndrewMullen(3) 2 61
(R Brotherton) *chsd ldrs: hdwy over 2f out: rdn over 1f out: drvn and one pce ent fnl f* **12/1**

00-4 **5** *3 1/4* **Phinerine**[2] 62 6-7-13 **51** oh1 ....(be) DanielleMcCreery(5) 3 45
(A Berry) *dwlt and in rr: gd hdwy on inner over 2f out: rdn to chse ldrs over 1f out: wknd ent fnl f* **20/1**

505- **6** *3* **Everything**[30] 7615 4-8-10 **57** .... FrankieMcDonald 4 42
(P T Midgley) *trckd ldrs: effrt over 2f out: sn rdn and grad wknd fr over 1f out* **17/2**[3]

10-4 **7** *1 3/4* **Grand Palace (IRE)**[6] 15 6-9-4 **65** ....(v) DarrenWilliams 10 44
(D Shaw) *towards rr: sme hdwy on outer over 2f out: sn rdn and no imp* **17/2**[3]

460- **8** *12* **Blakeshall Quest**[30] 7618 9-8-9 **56** ow1 ....(b) PaulMulrennan 5 —
(R Brotherton) *led 2f: cl up tl rdn over 2f out and sn wknd* **20/1**

00-4 **9** *2 1/4* **Kinout (IRE)**[4] 35 4-8-13 **60** ....(b) ChrisCatlin 1 —
(K A Ryan) *cl up on inner: led after 2f: rdn and hdd over 2f out: sn wknd* **10/1**

1m 16.76s (0.26) **Going Correction** +0.15s/f (Slow) 9 Ran SP% **115.5**
Speed ratings (Par 101): **104,103,102,100,96 92,90,74,71**
toteswinger: 1&2 £5.80, 1&3 £8.80, 2&3 £2.00. CSF £56.35 CT £130.85 TOTE £21.70: £4.90, £1.10, £1.40; EX 106.60 Trifecta £118.10 Pool: £710.62 - 4.45 winning units. Place 6: £7.54, Place 5: £4.07..
Owner Chris Roper & Jordan Lund **Bred** Olive O'Connor **Trained**

FOCUS
The pace appeared sound throughout and the form looks solid and should be reliable in the short term.
T/Jkpt: Not won. T/Plt: £27.90 to a £1 stake. Pool: £84,301.64. 2,201.32 winning tickets. T/Qpdt: £2.40 to a £1 stake. Pool: £7,853.90. 2,345.45 winning tickets. JR

[42]LINGFIELD (L-H)
Friday, January 9

OFFICIAL GOING: Standard
Wind: nil Weather: misty,cold

96 SPELDHURST H'CAP (DIV I) 5f (P)
12:30 (12:31) (Class 6) (0-65,66) 4-Y-O+ £1,706 (£503; £252) **Stalls** High

Form RPR

04-1 **1** **Nickel Silver**[7] 15 4-9-5 **66** 6ex ....(b) TomEaves 1 81
(B Smart) *sn bustled up to ld: mde rest: rdn clr over 1f out: styd on strly* **5/2**[2]

402- **2** *2 1/4* **Ridley Didley (IRE)**[9] 7836 4-8-4 **51** oh1 .... JimmyQuinn 2 58
(N Wilson) *racd keenly: chsd wnr: rdn wl over 1f out: kpt on same pce fnl f* **9/2**[3]

052- **3** *1 3/4* **Bertie Southstreet**[9] 7834 6-9-3 **64** ....(b) GeorgeBaker 6 65+
(J R Boyle) *t.k.h: hld up towards rr: effrt on outer 2f out: drvn over 1f out: r.o to go 3rd last strides: nvr nr ldng pair* **15/8**[1]

03-0 **4** *hd* **Punching**[7] 15 5-9-4 **65** .... LPKeniry 9 65
(C R Dore) *t.k.h: chsd ldrs: rdn and unable qckn 2f out: no imp on ldng pair fnl f: lost 3rd last strides* **10/1**

020- **5** *1* **Scarlet Oak**[18] 7762 5-8-12 **59** ....(p) AndrewElliott 5 55
(A M Hales) *hld up in rr: rdn and effrt 2f out: nvr trbld ldrs* **10/1**

44-0 **6** *1/2* **Bluebok**[7] 15 8-9-2 **63** ....(bt) DaneO'Neill 8 57
(J M Bradley) *racd on outer: stdd s: hdwy to chse ldrs 1/2-way: rdn and outpcd 2f out: wknd over 1f out* **14/1**

000- **7** *2 1/4* **Daddy Cool**[23] 7706 5-8-4 **51** oh6 ....(b) CatherineGannon 4 37
(W G M Turner) *in tch: rdn and struggling jst over 2f out: no ch fnl f* **100/1**

205- **8** *1* **Lake Sabina**[98] 6448 4-8-13 **60** .... JimCrowley 7 43
(M R Hoad) *chsd ldrs tl lost pl after 2f out: bhd fnl 2f* **20/1**

58.40 secs (-0.40) **Going Correction** 0.0s/f (Stan) 8 Ran SP% **112.1**
Speed ratings (Par 101): **103,99,96,96,94 93,90,88**
toteswinger: 1&2 £2.30, 1&3 £1.70, 2&3 £2.20. CSF £13.64 CT £24.31 TOTE £3.30: £1.10, £1.50, £1.10; EX 11.50 Trifecta £24.80 Pool: £277.25 - 8.25 winning units..
Owner M Barber **Bred** Mrs Sheila White **Trained** Hambleton, N Yorks

FOCUS
This moderate handicap was run at a sound pace, and it paid to race handily. The form looks straightforward rated around the placed horses.

97 ASHDOWN FOREST (S) STKS 7f (P)
1:00 (1:02) (Class 6) 4-Y-0+ **£2,047** (£604; £302) **Stalls** Low

Form RPR

104- **1** **Northern Desert (IRE)**[12] 7801 10-8-10 65 (p) PaulDoe 3 68
(S Curran) *hld up in tch in midfield: hdwy jst over 2f out: nt clr run and swtchd lft wl over 1f out: led ins fnl f: r.o wl* **9/2[2]**

401- **2** ¾ **C'Mon You Irons (IRE)**[10] 7819 4-9-1 65 JimCrowley 1 71
(M R Hoad) *chsd ldng pair: rdn and effrt to chse ldr 2f out: led ent fnl f: hdd ins fnl f: kpt on same pce* **6/1[3]**

23-6 **3** *shd* **Solicitude**[7] 14 6-8-5 58 (p) HayleyTurner 8 61
(D Haydn Jones) *in tch in midfield: rdn 3f out: hdwy u.p fnl f: clsng on ldrs towards fin* **9/2[2]**

430- **4** 2½ **Nikki Bea (IRE)**[18] 7765 6-8-0 52 MCGeran(5) 5 54
(Jamie Poulton) *hld up in midfield: hdwy over 2f out: nt clr run briefly 2f out: styng on whn nt clr run and swtchd lft ins fnl f: wnt 4th last stride: nt rch ldrs* **11/1**

060- **5** *nse* **Bridge Of Fermoy (IRE)**[12] 7801 4-8-10 72 (tp) SteveDrowne 6 59
(Miss Gay Kelleway) *chsd ldrs: rdn over 2f out: kpt on same pce u.p fr over 1f out* **8/1**

005- **6** ½ **Landucci**[18] 7764 8-8-10 68 JamieSpencer 12 58+
(J W Hills) *stdd after s: hld up towards rr: hdwy and in tch whn nt clr run over 1f out: swtchd rt ent fnl f: r.o but nvr able to chal* **7/2[1]**

052- **7** 2 **Kabis Amigos**[10] 7817 7-8-10 45 (b) TomEaves 9 52
(S T Mason) *led: rdn 2f out: hdd ent fnl f: wknd qckly fnl f* **10/1**

305- **8** *shd* **Mountain Pass (USA)**[39] 7513 7-8-10 55 (p) LPKeniry 4 52
(B J Llewellyn) *hld up towards rr on inner: rdn and effrt ent fnl 2f: nvr trbld ldrs* **14/1**

650- **9** 2½ **Faintly Hopeful**[37] 7541 4-8-10 47 (p) DaneO'Neill 7 45
(R A Teal) *chsd ldr tl 2f out: wknd u.p over 1f out* **66/1**

000- **10** 1½ **Usetheforce (IRE)**[80] 6878 4-8-10 53 ShaneKelly 10 41
(M Quinn) *bhd: swtchd wd over 3f out: rdn and struggling 3f out: wl btn whn carried wd bnd 2f out* **66/1**

664- **11** 1¼ **Countrywide Comet (IRE)**[286] 1081 4-8-11 54 ow1 IanMongan 2 39
(P Howling) *stdd s: hld up bhd: nvr a factor* **66/1**

000- **12** 4 **Silidan**[18] 7765 6-8-10 53 (be[1]) FergusSweeney 11 27
(G L Moore) *stdd s: racd wd: hld up towards rr: sme hdwy over 4f out: struggling 3f out: bhd whn hung rt bnd 2f out: wl btn after* **20/1**

1m 23.84s (-0.96) **Going Correction** 0.0s/f (Stan) **12** Ran SP% **117.3**
Speed ratings (Par 101): **105,104,104,101,101 100,98,98,95,93 92,87**
toteswinger: 1&2 £5.80, 1&3 £6.70, 2&3 £6.40. CSF £30.65 TOTE £5.80: £2.10, £2.60, £1.70; EX 35.30 Trifecta £255.80 Part won. Pool: £345.70 - 0.20 winning units..There was no bid for the winner. Landucci was claimed by Sean Curran for £6,000.
Owner L Power & Miss N Henton **Bred** J P Hardiman **Trained** Hatford, Oxon

FOCUS
A routine Polytrack seller. They went a decent pace and the form looks sound rated around the placed horses and seventh.

98 THREE BRIDGES MAIDEN STKS 7f (P)
1:30 (1:30) (Class 5) 3-Y-0+ **£2,729** (£806; £403) **Stalls** Low

Form RPR

1 **St Moritz (IRE)** 3-8-9 0 JoeFanning 3 80+
(M Johnston) *s.i.s: sn in tch: effrt on outer 2f out: led jst ins fnl f: drew clr fnl 100yds: readily* **6/4[1]**

633- **2** 2¾ **Rebel City**[23] 7709 3-8-9 70 ShaneKelly 5 72
(S A Callaghan) *s.i.s: sn handy: chsd ldr over 5f out: rdn to ld jst over 2f out: edgd rt over 1f out: hdd jst ins fnl f: nt pce of wnr fnl 100yds* **10/3[3]**

032- **3** 2 **Head Down**[28] 7655 3-8-9 76 DaneO'Neill 4 67
(R Hannon) *chsd ldr tl over 5f out: chsd ldrs after: drvn and effrt 2f out: pressed ldrs ent fnl f: outpcd ins fnl f* **15/2**

5- **4** 2 **Kamanja (UAE)**[23] 7708 3-8-5 0 ow1 MartinDwyer 7 57
(M A Jarvis) *led: rdn and hdd jst over 2f out: styd pressing ldrs tl wknd ins fnl f* **3/1[2]**

5 2¼ **Bromhead (USA)** 3-8-9 0 JamieSpencer 1 55
(B J Meehan) *taken down early: s.i.s: t.k.h: hld up in last trio: rdn and effrt 2f out: wknd over 1f out* **16/1**

43- **6** 1½ **Light The Light (IRE)**[19] 7757 4-9-8 0 JimCrowley 6 50
(Rae Guest) *stdd after s: t.k.h: hld up in last trio: rdn and unable qck over 2f out: wl hld over 1f out* **25/1**

7 1½ **General Sam (USA)** 3-8-9 0 RichardSmith 2 47
(R Hannon) *s.i.s: a bhd: rdn and struggling over 2f out: n.d* **66/1**

1m 25.23s (0.43) **Going Correction** 0.0s/f (Stan)
WFA 3 from 4yo 18lb **7** Ran SP% **111.1**
Speed ratings (Par 103): **97,93,91,89,86 85,83**
toteswinger: 1&2 £3.00, 1&3 £3.30, 2&3 £4.10. CSF £6.29 TOTE £2.20: £1.50, £2.70; EX 7.50.
Owner Mrs R J Jacobs **Bred** Newsells Park Stud Limited **Trained** Middleham Moor, N Yorks

FOCUS
An ordinary maiden and doubts about the form but a decent performance from the winner.
General Sam(USA) Official explanation: jockey said colt ran green

99 SPELDHURST H'CAP (DIV II) 5f (P)
2:00 (2:01) (Class 6) (0-65,65) 4-Y-0+ **£1,706** (£503; £252) **Stalls** High

Form RPR

05-0 **1** **Ten Down**[7] 15 4-9-3 64 MartinDwyer 3 70
(M Quinn) *dwlt: sn bustled up to ld: rdn over 1f out: kpt on wl fnl f: jst hld on* **3/1[1]**

00-0 **2** *shd* **Gwilym (GER)**[7] 15 6-9-2 63 HayleyTurner 9 69
(D Haydn Jones) *hld up in rr: rdn and effrt 2f out: no real hdwy tl swtchd lft ins fnl f: str burst fnl 150yds: jst failed* **8/1**

006- **3** *shd* **Drifting Gold**[21] 7733 5-9-4 65 (v) AdamKirby 7 71
(C G Cox) *stdd s: hld up in rr hdwy u.p over 1f out: str chal wl ins fnl f: lost 2nd last stride* **8/1**

452- **4** ½ **Night Premiere (IRE)**[26] 7672 4-8-6 53 (b) JimmyQuinn 6 57
(R Hannon) *chsd ldrs: rdn to press wnr over 1f out: ev ch but edgd rt jst ins fnl f: no ex fnl 50yds* **7/2[2]**

665- **5** *nk* **Spoof Master (IRE)**[26] 7679 5-8-13 60 (p) JoeFanning 8 63
(C R Dore) *w wnr: rdn over 2f out: unable qckn u.p jst over 1f out: kpt on again towards fin* **13/2**

440- **6** 1¾ **Pegasus Dancer (FR)**[37] 7540 5-8-13 60 (b) VinceSlattery 10 56
(R H York) *in tch: rdn and nt qckn jst over 2f out: kpt on same pce fnl f* **16/1**

/01- **7** 2¾ **Sir Don (IRE)**[344] 372 10-8-11 58 (p) ShaneKelly 4 45
(E S McMahon) *t.k.h: hld up in midfield: short of room and lost pl over 2f out: rdn and no hdwy 2f out* **5/1[3]**

004- **8** 3 **Ben**[33] 7589 4-8-10 57 (v) SteveDrowne 1 33
(P G Murphy) *in tch in midfield: rdn and effrt ent fnl 2f: wknd u.p over 1f out* **12/1**

58.88 secs (0.08) **Going Correction** 0.0s/f (Stan) **8** Ran SP% **113.0**
Speed ratings (Par 101): **99,98,98,97,97 94,90,85**
toteswinger: 1&2 £7.00, 1&3 £5.90, 2&3 £11.50. CSF £26.72 CT £173.10 TOTE £3.40: £1.10, £2.50, £3.70; EX 25.70 Trifecta £96.80 Pool: £301.16 - 2.30 winning units..
Owner A G MacLennan **Bred** Baydon House Stud **Trained** Newmarket, Suffolk

FOCUS
A moderate handicap, but no shortage of established front-runners. Despite what looked a solid pace, the winning time was almost half a second slower than the first division and the form looks very ordinary rated around the fourth and fifth.
Ten Down Official explanation: trainer said regarding apparent improvement in form that on its previous outing the gelding missed the break, was hampered early and therefore was unable to dominate.
Sir Don(IRE) Official explanation: jockey said gelding was squeezed out at 3f mark

100 WILLIAM HILL JANUARY SALE - NOW ON! H'CAP 1m 2f (P)
2:30 (2:30) (Class 6) (0-55,60) 4-Y-0+ **£2,047** (£604; £302) **Stalls** Low

Form RPR

422- **1** **Colonel Sherman (USA)**[12] 7806 4-8-13 54 AdamKirby 8 71
(L A Dace) *mde all: 5l clr 2f out: unchal* **7/2[1]**

30-0 **2** 4½ **Ready To Crown (USA)**[7] 18 5-9-0 53 (b[1]) DaneO'Neill 11 60
(Andrew Turnell) *s.i.s: hld up towards rr: hdwy over 2f out: chsd wnr 2f out: nvr able to chal* **6/1[3]**

006- **3** *hd* **Mix N Match**[26] 7676 5-8-10 49 FrankieMcDonald 6 56
(R M Stronge) *racd in midfield: 5th and u.p 2f out: 3rd and no ch w wnr wl ins fnl f* **11/1**

00-0 **4** 2¾ **Inquisitress**[6] 25 5-8-11 50 NeilChalmers 3 51
(J J Bridger) *hld up towards rr: hdwy and 6th 2f out: nvr able to chal wnr* **12/1**

434- **5** ¾ **Apache Dawn**[37] 7541 5-8-10 49 FergusSweeney 14 49
(G L Moore) *stdd s: hld up in rr: effrt u.p and 8th 2f out: nvr nr wnr* **11/2[2]**

656- **6** ¾ **Tabulate**[30] 7626 6-8-13 52 IanMongan 12 50
(P Howling) *hld up towards rr: 7th and u.p 2f out: nvr nr wnr* **13/2**

33-0 **7** 1 **Turkish Sultan (IRE)**[2] 81 6-8-6 50 (p) MCGeran(5) 4 46
(J M Bradley) *hld up towards rr: 10th and rdn 2f out: n.d* **12/1**

000- **8** *nk* **Space Pirate**[25] 7688 4-8-5 46 (v) JimmyQuinn 9 42
(J Pearce) *chsd wnr: clr of remainder 5f out: rdn and outpcd by wnr over 2f out: lost 2nd 2f out: wknd* **12/1**

531- **9** 1¼ **Royal Choir**[12] 7807 5-8-10 56 6ex SPRyan(7) 13 49
(H E Haynes) *chsd ldrs: 4th and drvn 2f out: wknd* **12/1**

006- **10** 8 **King's Alchemist**[167] 4428 4-8-6 47 MartinDwyer 5 24
(M D I Usher) *chsd ldrs: 9th and wkng 2f out* **28/1**

066- **11** 10 **Silver Spruce**[18] 7765 4-8-7 48 ow1 (be) JamieSpencer 10 5
(D Flood) *hld up in rr: 11th and no prog u.p 2f out* **7/1**

000- **12** 5 **Indiana Fox**[14] 6896 6-8-8 52 GabrielHannon(5) 7 —
(B G Powell) *in tch: pushed along and losing pl over 4f out: t.o last 2f* **50/1**

2m 3.88s (-2.72) **Going Correction** 0.0s/f (Stan)
WFA 4 from 5yo+ 2lb **12** Ran SP% **122.2**
Speed ratings (Par 101): **110,106,106,104,103 102,102,101,100,94 86,82**
toteswinger: 1&2 £8.90, 1&3 £16.20, 2&3 £18.00. CSF £24.65 CT £216.73 TOTE £3.10: £1.50, £2.70, £4.80; EX 26.50 Trifecta £137.60 Part won. Pool: £185.95 - 0.30 winning units..
Owner Gayler William Chambers **Bred** Fred M Allor **Trained** Five Oaks, W Sussex

FOCUS
Visibilty was poor due to fog. This was a very open handicap and the form looks fairly solid.

101 WILLIAM HILL JANUARY SALE - BETTER ODDS! H'CAP 1m 2f (P)
3:00 (3:01) (Class 4) (0-85,83) 3-Y-0 **£4,857** (£1,445; £722; £360) **Stalls** Low

Form RPR

226- **1** **State General (IRE)**[22] 7718 3-8-13 75 JimCrowley 3 81
(Miss J Feilden) *t.k.h: hld up in tch: effrt 2f out: rdn to ld jst ins fnl f: r.o wl* **6/1**

253- **2** ¾ **Barwell Bridge**[14] 7784 3-9-1 77 JamieSpencer 2 83+
(S Kirk) *t.k.h: hld up in tch: trckd ldrs and nt clr run over 1f out: dropped bk and swtchd rt 1f out: r.o to go 2nd towards fin: unable to chal wnr* **5/1[3]**

151- **3** ¾ **Doncosaque (IRE)**[14] 7784 3-9-7 83 ShaneKelly 5 86
(P Howling) *chsd ldr: upsides ldr over 2f out: rdn to ld narrowly over 1f out: hdd jst ins fnl f: wknd towards fin* **5/2[2]**

414- **4** 1¼ **Neuchatel (GER)**[51] 7391 3-9-3 79 JoeFanning 4 80
(M Johnston) *sn bustled up to ld: jnd and rdn over 2f out: hdd over 1f out: wknd ins fnl f* **1/1[1]**

005- **5** 3 **Innactualfact**[22] 7718 3-8-2 64 oh7 FrankieMcDonald 1 59
(L A Dace) *a last: in tch tl rdn and outpcd 2f out* **50/1**

2m 5.54s (-1.06) **Going Correction** 0.0s/f (Stan) **5** Ran SP% **111.5**
Speed ratings (Par 99): **104,103,102,101,99**
CSF £33.91 TOTE £7.60: £2.50, £2.40; EX 25.30.
Owner Ocean Trailers & Partners **Bred** Don Commins **Trained** Exning, Suffolk

FOCUS
A tight little three-year-old handicap and the pace was just a fair one with the winning time 1.66 seconds slower than the preceding contest.. All bar the complete outsider were still in with every chance entering the last furlong with the placed horses close to previous Wolverhampton form.

102 EDENBRIDGE MAIDEN STKS 1m 4f (P)
3:30 (3:32) (Class 5) 4-Y-0+ **£2,729** (£806; £403) **Stalls** Low

Form RPR

63- **1** **Celtic Gold (USA)**[32] 7609 5-9-7 0 DaneO'Neill 2 64
(Andrew Turnell) *s.i.s: in tch: chsd ldr 5f out: rdn to ld over 1f out: hrd drvn ent fnl f: hld on gamely* **6/1**

245- **2** *nk* **Hammer**[23] 7704 4-9-3 68 HayleyTurner 7 64
(R T Phillips) *t.k.h: hld up towards rr: hdwy on inner 2f out: chal ent fnl f: rdn and nt qckn fnl 100yds* **6/4[1]**

3 1¼ **Regal Angel**[571] 6-9-2 0 JimCrowley 5 57
(Jean-Rene Auvray) *hld up in tch: 5th and rdn whn rn wd bnd 2f out: styd on fnl f: wnt 3rd wl ins fnl f: nt rch ldng pair* **9/2[3]**

040- **4** ¾ **Shayera**[18] 7761 4-8-12 59 (t) AdamKirby 6 56?
(B R Johnson) *hld up towards rr: 6th and rdn jst over 2f out: kpt on fnl f: nt rch ldrs* **7/1**

050- **5** 1 **Romantic Retreat**[10] 7822 4-8-12 0 SteveDrowne 4 54
(G L Moore) *chsd ldr: in ld 5f out: rdn and hdd over 1f over: wknd ins fnl f: lost 2 pls fnl 100yds* **14/1**

000- **6** *hd* **Rock Peak (IRE)**[84] 6775 4-9-3 65 LPKeniry 1 59
(B J Llewellyn) *chsd ldrs: 4th and rdn jst over 2f out: kpt on same pce* 7/2[2]

0- **7** *11* **Jolies Dee**[10] 7822 4-8-12 0 SimonWhitworth 3 36
(J R Jenkins) *t.k.h: led at slow pce: lost pl and 4th 5f out: bhd and rdn 2f out: wl btn fnl f* 80/1

2m 44.72s (11.72) **Going Correction** 0.0s/f (Stan)
WFA 4 from 5yo+ 4lb 7 Ran SP% **115.1**
Speed ratings (Par 103): **60,59,58,58,57 57,50**
toteswinger: 1&2 £3.10, 1&3 £2.40, 2&3 £2.90. CSF £15.70 TOTE £5.90: £2.80, £1.30; EX 12.00.
Owner L G Kimber **Bred** Darley **Trained** Broad Hinton, Wilts

FOCUS
A poor maiden, run at a very slow early pace and the form looks messy. The runners went out of sight down the back straight as the fog refused to lift.
Jolies Dee Official explanation: jockey said saddle slipped

103 WILLIAM HILL JANUARY SALE - WHY BET ELSEWHERE? H'CAP 1m 4f (P)
4:00 (4:02) (Class 5) (0-70,69) 4-Y-0+ £2,900 (£856; £428) Stalls Low

Form RPR
433- **1** **Night Orbit**[30] 7630 5-8-13 **65** (v) AmyBaker(5) 6 71
(Miss J Feilden) *hld up in midfield: chsd ldrs wl ins fnl f: burst between horses to ld nr fin* 6/1[2]

320- **2** *½* **Star Choice**[38] 7526 4-8-13 **64** JimmyQuinn 4 69
(J Pearce) *chsd ldr: rdn to ld 2f out: hdd nr fin* 5/2[1]

301- **3** *nse* **Little Richard (IRE)**[27] 7667 10-9-0 **61** (p) AdamKirby 7 66
(M Wellings) *hld up in midfield: rdn and hdwy 2f out: ev ch wl ins fnl f: no ex nr fin* 14/1

104- **4** *hd* **Drum Major (IRE)**[23] 7704 4-9-4 **69** GeorgeBaker 5 74
(G L Moore) *in tch: ev ch ins fnl f: no ex nr fin* 7/1[3]

325- **5** *1* **Parnassian**[22] 7722 9-8-7 **54** (v) RichardThomas 12 57
(J A Geake) *hld up in rr: hdwy and rdn 2f out: chsd ldrs wl ins fnl f: nt rch ldrs* 25/1

/55- **6** *hd* **Sunset Boulevard (IRE)**[23] 7711 6-9-2 **63** DaneO'Neill 8 66
(Miss Tor Sturgis) *hld up towards rr: hdwy and rdn 2f out: nt rch ldrs* 7/1[3]

144- **7** *¾* **Bluebell Ridge (IRE)**[18] 7761 4-8-12 **63** MartinDwyer 11 64
(D W P Arbuthnot) *in tch: u.p 2f out: one pce after* 12/1

200- **8** *½* **Dubai Petal (IRE)**[95] 6529 4-8-12 **63** LPKeniry 10 64
(J S Moore) *in tch: kpt on same pce fnl 2f* 8/1

430- **9** *1* **William's Way**[23] 7711 7-9-2 **63** CatherineGannon 9 62
(I A Wood) *hld up in last pl early: nvr trbld ldrs* 18/1

2/0- **10** *4* **Up In Arms (IRE)**[212] 2952 5-9-6 **67** JimCrowley 1 60
(P Winkworth) *t.k.h: chsd ldrs: struggling u.p 2f out* 11/1

304- **11** *3 ¼* **Flam**[12] 7807 4-8-13 **64** JamieSpencer 2 51
(A M Hales) *led tl 2f out: sn wknd* 14/1

2m 33.16s (0.16) **Going Correction** 0.0s/f (Stan)
WFA 4 from 5yo+ 4lb 11 Ran SP% **117.4**
Speed ratings (Par 103): **99,98,98,98,97 97,97,96,96,93 91**
toteswinger: 1&2 £5.30, 1&3 £7.80, 2&3 £8.90. CSF £21.26 CT £204.85 TOTE £7.90: £2.20, £1.60, £4.20; EX 25.60 Trifecta £384.30 Pool: £571.30 - 1.10 winning units. Place 6 £89.38, Place 5 £75.45..
Owner Stowstowquickquickstow Partnership **Bred** Juddmonte Farms Ltd **Trained** Exning, Suffolk

FOCUS
An ordinary middle-distance handicap, but still quite competitive. Unfortunately, the fog had become so dense that visibility was very poor. The principals finished in a bit of a heap which suggests that the form is nothing to write home about, and although the winning time was a massive 11.56 seconds faster than the preceding maiden, that race was so slowly run that comparisons are probably meaningless.
T/Plt: £112.50 to a £1 stake. Pool: £87,852.16. 569.95 winning tickets. T/Qpdt: £93.80 to a £1 stake. Pool: £5,619.40. 44.30 winning tickets. SP

[75]WOLVERHAMPTON (A.W) (L-H)
Friday, January 9

OFFICIAL GOING: Standard
Wind: Nil Weather: Sunny

104 BOOK TICKETS ONLINE APPRENTICE CLASSIFIED STKS 7f 32y(P)
2:05 (2:17) (Class 7) 4-Y-0+ £1,364 (£403; £201) Stalls Low

Form RPR
50-0 **1** **Stargazy**[6] 23 5-8-7 45 HollyHall(7) 1 55
(W G M Turner) *dwlt: hld up in rr: hdwy wl over 1f out: led ins fnl f: edgd rt: r.o* 12/1

064- **2** *nk* **Amber Moon**[21] 7736 4-8-11 45 (b) PNolan(3) 11 54
(J A Osborne) *hld up: sn in tch: rdn 3f out: r.o ins fnl f: nt rch wnr* 8/1

006- **3** *4* **Convince (USA)**[176] 4102 8-9-0 45 BMcHugh 8 43
(K M Prendergast) *a.p: rdn over 1f out: one pce fnl f* 12/1

045- **4** *shd* **Elkhart Lake (IRE)**[21] 7736 4-9-0 45 (bt[1]) BACurtis 10 43
(Adrian McGuinness, Ire) *sn prom: rdn and one pce fnl f* 4/1[2]

50-5 **5** *¾* **Vanatina (IRE)**[3] 62 5-9-0 45 DeanHeslop 4 41
(W M Brisbourne) *prom early: lost pl and settled in mid-div over 5f out: sme hdwy on ins over 2f out: no real prog fnl f* 10/3[1]

000- **6** *shd* **Spanish Ace**[18] 7765 8-9-0 45 (b) MatthewDavies 6 41
(J M Bradley) *t.k.h: chsd ldr: led over 2f out: hdd ins fnl f: fdd towards fin* 12/1

006- **7** *½* **Stormburst (IRE)**[180] 5-8-9 45 RyanClark(5) 5 39
(A J Chamberlain) *hld up and bhd: c wd st: sme late prog: n.d* 9/1

025- **8** *1 ¼* **Desert Lover (IRE)**[194] 808 7-9-0 45 AshleyMorgan 2 36
(R J Price) *hld up: sn towards rr: short-lived effrt on ins over 1f out* 7/1[3]

60-0 **9** *1 ¼* **Nordic Light (USA)**[6] 23 5-9-0 45 (b) BillyCray 7 33
(J M Bradley) *hld up towards rr: short-lived effrt over 2f out* 7/1[3]

600- **10** *3 ¾* **So Sublime**[17] 7776 4-8-9 45 (b) AlexEdwards(5) 3 23
(M C Chapman) *bolted bef s: led: hdd over 2f out: rdn and wknd wl over 1f out* 33/1

04-0 **11** *hd* **Where's Dids**[3] 56 4-8-9 45 (p) DavidKenny(5) 9 22
(P D Evans) *s.i.s: a in rr* 40/1

0/0- **12** *3* **Avery**[29] 7637 5-9-0 44 JemmaMarshall 12 14
(R J Hodges) *a in rr* 100/1

1m 30.25s (0.65) **Going Correction** 0.0s/f (Stan) 12 Ran SP% **118.6**
Speed ratings (Par 97): **96,95,91,90,90 90,89,88,86,82 82,78**
toteswinger: 1&2 £20.20, 1&3 £37.90, 2&3 £20.10. CSF £103.95 TOTE £18.80: £4.70, £2.40, £4.30; EX 125.80.
Owner Kachina Racing **Bred** Bearstone Stud **Trained** Sigwells, Somerset
■ Holly Hall's first winner.

FOCUS
The entire field were separated by just 1lb on official ratings in this 0-45 apprentice classified stakes. The early gallop was strong although the overall time was ordinary, but the form looks sound.
Stargazy Official explanation: trainer said, regarding apparent improvement in form, that the gelding may have benefited from the drop in class.

105 WOLVERHAMPTON-RACECOURSE.CO.UK (S) STKS 1m 1f 103y(P)
2:35 (2:46) (Class 6) 4-Y-0+ £2,047 (£604; £302) Stalls Low

Form RPR
323- **1** **Ahlawy (IRE)**[81] 6862 6-9-0 68 (bt) FBranca 12 64
(F Sheridan) *hld up in mid-div: swtchd rt and n.m.r over 3f out: hdwy whn bmpd wl over 1f out: led ins fnl f: r.o wl* 11/10[1]

510- **2** *3 ¼* **Buscador (USA)**[20] 7744 10-9-0 62 RichardKingscote 5 57
(W M Brisbourne) *sn chsng ldr: led over 2f out: edgd rt and rdn over 1f out: hdd ins fnl f: no ex* 16/1

000- **3** *½* **Ten Spot (IRE)**[20] 7744 4-8-10 51 ow2 (t) MickyFenton 10 53
(Stef Liddiard) *in rr: plld out ent st: rdn and hdwy over 1f out: swtchd lft ins fnl f: r.o to take 3rd cl home* 100/1

/12- **4** *nk* **Alf Tupper**[25] 7691 6-9-6 55 RobertWinston 6 61
(Adrian McGuinness, Ire) *hld up towards rr: hdwy on outside over 2f out: rdn and hung lft 1f out: kpt on one pce* 11/1[3]

/00- **5** *½* **Barodine**[14] 7606 6-8-9 62 (bt[1]) WilliamCarson(5) 1 54
(R J Hodges) *hld up in mid-div: hdwy 2f out: rdn and one pce ins fnl f* 33/1

300- **6** *2 ¼* **Ten Pole Tudor**[39] 7513 4-8-10 62 KevinGhunowa(3) 2 50
(R A Harris) *hld up in mid-div: c wd st: rdn over 1f out: kpt on fnl f: n.d* 25/1

050- **7** *¾* **Wusuul**[101] 6363 4-8-8 63 JerryO'Dwyer 8 43
(R A Harris) *s.i.s: bhd: hdwy on ins 2f out: btn whn nt clr run jst over 1f out* 40/1

053- **8** *1 ½* **Climate (IRE)**[10] 7816 10-9-6 58 (p) StephenDonohoe 7 51
(P D Evans) *hld up towards rr: rdn and sme prog 1f out: wknd ins fnl f* 25/1

050- **9** *3* **Ardent Prince**[25] 7691 6-8-11 53 (p) TolleyDean(3) 9 39
(A J McCabe) *sn led: hdd over 2f out: rdn and wknd jst over 1f out* 50/1

14-0 **10** *2 ¾* **Blue Sky Thinking (IRE)**[7] 12 10-9-0 72 DarrenWilliams 13 33
(K R Burke) *hld up in mid-div: hdwy on outside over 3f out: rdn and wknd over 1f out* 16/1

355- **11** *2 ¼* **Piermarini**[27] 7661 4-8-13 65 (v[1]) LeeEnstone 3 28
(P T Midgley) *prom: rdn over 2f out: wknd jst over 1f out* 50/1

400- **12** *18* **Zach's Harmoney (USA)**[38] 7532 5-8-11 62 (t) DuranFentiman(3) 11 —
(Miss M E Rowland) *prom tl rdn and wknd over 3f out: eased ins fnl f* 40/1

133- **13** *20* **Golden Bishop**[43] 7461 4-8-13 68 TonyHamilton 4 —
(R A Fahey) *led early: prom tl wknd wl over 1f out: virtually p.u ins fnl f: b.b.v* 5/2[2]

2m 1.24s (-0.46) **Going Correction** 0.0s/f (Stan)
WFA 4 from 5yo+ 1lb 13 Ran SP% **116.7**
Speed ratings (Par 101): **102,99,98,98,97 95,95,93,91,88 86,70,53**
toteswinger: 1&2 £5.90, 1&3 £27.90, 2&3 £59.90. CSF £19.84 TOTE £2.10: £1.10, £3.20, £19.50; EX 27.50.The winner was bought in for 10,500gns.
Owner A Zanoboni **Bred** Castlemartin Stud And Skymarc Farm **Trained** Stoke Heath, Shropshire
■ A first winner in Britain for Irish-based Italian rider Fabio Branca.

FOCUS
Very few had a realistic chance in this on official ratings and the betting suggested it was a match between Ahlawy and Golden Bishop. The form is not bad for the grade.
Golden Bishop Official explanation: vet said gelding bled from the nose

106 WILLIAM HILL JANUARY SALE - NOW ON! H'CAP 7f 32y(P)
3:05 (3:15) (Class 4) (0-85,85) 4-Y-0+ £5,180 (£1,541; £770; £384) Stalls Low

Form RPR
231- **1** **Southandwest (IRE)**[9] 7837 5-9-4 **82** 6ex LukeMorris 2 94
(J S Moore) *hld up: hdwy over 1f out: rdn to ld ins fnl f: r.o wl* 4/1[3]

226- **2** *1 ¼* **Ravi River (IRE)**[10] 7828 5-8-9 **73** RichardKingscote 5 82
(Tom Dascombe) *a.p: led jst over 1f out: rdn and hdd ins fnl f: nt qckn* 12/1

6-23 **3** *1* **Blue Charm**[6] 31 5-8-4 **68** oh1 DaleGibson 3 74
(S Kirk) *hld up: hdwy over 2f out: ev ch 1f out: nt qckn* 4/1[3]

454- **4** *nk* **Silver Wind**[42] 7470 4-9-0 **78** (v) RobertWinston 1 83
(P D Evans) *hld up in rr: rdn over 2f out: c wd st: rdn and hdwy over 1f out: sn edgd lft: no ex ins fnl f* 9/1

12-1 **5** *2* **Nightjar (USA)**[7] 9 4-9-7 **85** 6ex GregFairley 7 85
(M Johnston) *prom: chsd ldr over 5f out tl wl over 1f out: sn rdn: fdd ins fnl f* 9/4[1]

533- **6** *3 ½* **Willkandoo (USA)**[21] 7737 4-9-4 **82** StephenDonohoe 6 73
(D M Simcock) *led after 1f: rdn and hdd jst over 1f out: wknd fnl f* 3/1[2]

200- **7** *12* **Only A Game (IRE)**[21] 7730 4-8-10 **77** DuranFentiman(3) 4 35
(Miss M E Rowland) *led 1f: prom tl wknd over 2f out* 66/1

1m 28.76s (-0.84) **Going Correction** 0.0s/f (Stan) 7 Ran SP% **115.0**
Speed ratings (Par 105): **104,102,101,101,98 94,81**
toteswinger: 1&2 £7.00, 1&3 £3.30, 2&3 £7.80. CSF £48.99 TOTE £5.10: £2.70, £4.70; EX 43.70.
Owner Wall To Wall Partnership **Bred** Paul Hardy **Trained** Upper Lambourn, Berks

FOCUS
They went off very strong in this decent handicap and the form looks sound rated around the runner-up and fourth.

107 WILLIAM HILL JANUARY SALE - BETTER ODDS! H'CAP 1m 4f 50y(P)
3:35 (3:45) (Class 6) (0-55,61) 4-Y-0+ £2,388 (£705; £352) Stalls Low

Form RPR
000/ **1** **Safin (GER)**[93] 6803 9-8-9 **48** GrahamGibbons 9 55
(R Curtis) *hld up in mid-div: hdwy on outside 2f out: rdn to ld last stride* 66/1

040/ **2** *hd* **Slew Charm (FR)**[468] 5531 7-9-2 **55** TravisBlock 7 62
(Noel T Chance) *hld up and bhd: hdwy on ins over 2f out: led ins fnl f: rdn and hdd last stride* 8/1

43-2 **3** *1 ¼* **Dontpaytheferryman (USA)**[3] 58 4-8-9 **52** (t) StephenDonohoe 6 57
(P D Evans) *hld up towards rr: hdwy on ins over 3f out: led over 2f out: sn rdn: hdd ins fnl f: nt qckn* 5/2[1]

032- **4** *½* **Dazzling Begum**[17] 7776 4-8-9 **52** (v[1]) JerryO'Dwyer 2 56
(J Pearce) *chsd ldr 2f: prom: rdn over 2f out: hung lft wl over 1f out: styd on one pce fnl f* 4/1[2]

63-0 **5** *shd* **Desert Hawk**[7] 18 8-8-11 **50** LukeMorris 1 54
(W M Brisbourne) *hld up in mid-div: rdn and hdwy over 1f out: styd on towards fin* 13/2[3]

665- **6** *13* **Semi Detached (IRE)**[27] 7667 6-8-11 **50** MickyFenton 10 33
(J W Unett) *chsd ldr after 2f: led 3f out: sn hdd: wkng whn carried lft wl over 1f out* **18/1**

000/ **7** *nk* **Akash (IRE)**[601] 685 9-8-7 **53** BMcHugh(7) 12 36
(K M Prendergast) *a in rr* **66/1**

00-1 **8** *hd* **Hi Dancer**[7] 8 6-9-3 **61** 6ex PatrickDonaghy(5) 11 43
(P C Haslam) *hld up in mid-div: stdy prog on outside over 5f out: wknd wl over 1f out* **4/1**[2]

360- **9** *7* **Bourbon Highball (IRE)**[22] 7723 4-8-10 **53** (tp) LeeEnstone 8 24
(P C Haslam) *prom: wkng whn hmpd jst over 2f out* **33/1**

040- **10** *6* **Sceilin (IRE)**[12] 7800 5-8-9 **48** (t) PaulMulrennan 5 10
(J Mackie) *led: rdn and hdd 3f out: wknd 2f out* **22/1**

600/ **11** *9* **Jamaahir (USA)**[512] 4544 6-8-11 **50** RobertWinston 3 —
(George Baker) *dwlt: a in rr* **17/2**

2m 40.72s (-0.38) **Going Correction** 0.0s/f (Stan)
WFA 4 from 5yo+ 4lb **11** Ran SP% **119.1**
Speed ratings (Par 101): **101,100,100,99,99 90,90,90,85,81 75**
toteswinger: 1&2 £56.40, 1&3 £24.00, 2&3 £7.20. CSF £530.33 CT £1847.24 TOTE £65.30: £14.30, £3.20, £1.10; EX 639.40.

Owner Mrs Joanna Hughes **Bred** German American Bloodstock 1 **Trained** Lambourn, Berks

FOCUS
They went a steady gallop to halfway in this modeate contest but the overall time was not bad. The third, fourth and fifth are the best guides to the level.

Dazzling Begum Official explanation: jockey said filly lost a front shoe

108 HOTEL & CONFERENCING AT WOLVERHAMPTON H'CAP 5f 216y(P)
4:05 (4:15) (Class 6) (0-55,58) 4-Y-0+ **£2,388** (£705; £352) **Stalls** Low

Form RPR

02-3 **1** **Sarah's Art (IRE)**[2] 71 6-9-1 **55** MickyFenton 3 67
(Stef Liddiard) *hld up and bhd: hdwy on outside over 1f out: rdn to ld nr fin* **7/4**[1]

60-0 **2** *½* **Wiltshire (IRE)**[6] 22 7-8-13 **53** (v) LeeEnstone 6 63
(P T Midgley) *hld up: hdwy over 1f out: led ins fnl f: rdn and hdd nr fin* **10/1**

05-3 **3** *1 ¼* **Hurricane Coast**[5] 35 10-9-1 **55** FBranca 1 61
(D Flood) *hld up and bhd: hdwy 1f out: kpt on ins fnl f* **10/1**

52-6 **4** *¾* **Mister Incredible**[3] 62 6-8-11 **51** (v) LukeMorris 7 55
(J M Bradley) *a.p: rdn over 1f out: no ex wl ins fnl f* **8/1**[3]

320- **5** *1 ¼* **Westwood Dawn**[11] 7808 4-9-1 **55** (v) DarrenWilliams 8 57+
(D Shaw) *s.i.s: hld up in rr: rdn and hdwy on ins over 1f out: nt clr run and swtchd rt ins fnl f: one pce* **20/1**

22-3 **6** *2* **Welsh Opera**[6] 22 4-9-1 **55** (v[1]) RichardKingscote 11 49
(S C Williams) *led 1f: w ldr tl rdn over 2f out: wknd ins fnl f* **11/2**[2]

000- **7** *nk* **Dasheena**[12] 7801 6-8-3 **50** (p) KarenKenny(7) 10 43
(A J McCabe) *in rr: rdn and hdwy over 1f out: n.d* **33/1**

000- **8** *¾* **Royal Acclamation (IRE)**[42] 7471 4-9-1 **55** PaulMulrennan 4 48+
(G A Harker) *prom: nt clr run jst ins fnl f: n.d after* **16/1**

561- **9** *hd* **Helping Hand (IRE)**[11] 7808 4-8-11 **58** 6ex DavidKenny(7) 2 48
(R Hollinshead) *led after 1f: rdn over 1f out: hdd & wknd ins fnl f* **11/2**[2]

000- **10** *1 ¾* **Danzig Fox**[49] 7399 4-8-5 **52** PNolan(7) 12 36
(M Mullineaux) *mid-div: pushed along over 3f out: wknd over 2f out* **25/1**

000- **11** *2 ¼* **A Wish For You**[33] 7589 4-8-11 **56** ow2 (p) JamesO'Reilly(5) 5 33
(D K Ivory) *s.i.s: hld up and bhd: sme prog on ins whn hmpd over 1f out: n.d after* **25/1**

400- **12** *1 ½* **Weetfromthechaff**[312] 780 4-9-1 **55** (p) TGMcLaughlin 13 27
(R Hollinshead) *c wd st: a in rr* **50/1**

1m 14.92s (-0.08) **Going Correction** 0.0s/f (Stan) **12** Ran SP% **119.7**
Speed ratings (Par 101): **100,99,97,96,95 92,91,90,90,88 85,83**
toteswinger: 1&2 £6.90, 1&3 £2.90, 2&3 £21.80. CSF £19.26 CT £145.25 TOTE £2.80: £1.10, £2.70, £3.60; EX 21.90.

Owner ownaracehorse.co.uk (Shefford) **Bred** Newtownbarry House Stud **Trained** Great Shefford, Berks

FOCUS
A moderate contest run at a strong early pace and the form looks solid with the third and fourth closer to their recent best.

Royal Acclamation(IRE) Official explanation: jockey said gelding had to ease slightly final furlong

109 WILLIAM HILL JANUARY SALE - WHY BET ELSEWHERE? H'CAP 5f 216y(P)
4:35 (4:45) (Class 4) (0-85,85) 3-Y-0 **£5,180** (£1,541; £770; £384) **Stalls** Low

Form RPR

111- **1** **Smokey Ryder**[26] 7673 3-8-6 **76** KevinGhunowa(3) 5 82
(R A Harris) *chsd ldr: led wl over 1f out: rdn ins fnl f: r.o* **11/4**[1]

521- **2** *¾* **Bobs Dreamflight**[18] 7769 3-8-7 **77** DuranFentiman(3) 1 81
(D K Ivory) *hld up and bhd: hdwy over 1f out: rdn and ev ch ins fnl f: nt qckn* **9/2**[3]

01- **3** *3 ¾* **Cecily**[207] 3085 3-9-4 **85** StephenDonohoe 6 77
(Sir Mark Prescott) *s.i.s: hld up: hdwy over 2f out: one pce fnl f* **4/1**[2]

212- **4** *2 ¼* **Satwa Street (IRE)**[38] 7523 3-8-8 **82** ChrisHough(7) 3 67
(D M Simcock) *plld hrd: prom tl wknd wl over 1f out* **11/4**[1]

103- **5** *hd* **Lesley's Choice**[22] 7714 3-8-12 **79** GrahamGibbons 4 63
(R Curtis) *led: hdd wl over 1f out: sn rdn: wknd ins fnl f* **17/2**

151- **6** *6* **Sir Geoffrey (IRE)**[84] 6769 3-8-13 **83** TolleyDean(3) 2 48
(A J McCabe) *t.k.h in tch: wknd wl over 1f out* **8/1**

1m 15.2s (0.20) **Going Correction** 0.0s/f (Stan) **6** Ran SP% **113.2**
Speed ratings (Par 99): **98,97,92,89,88 80**
toteswinger: 1&2 £2.60, 1&3 £2.70, 2&3 £2.40. CSF £15.61 TOTE £3.70: £2.00, £3.00; EX 14.20 Place 6 £431.49, Place 5 £50.57..

Owner The Govin Partnership **Bred** Jeremy Hinds **Trained** Earlswood, Monmouths

FOCUS
A fair handicap but, despite the presence of a couple of confirmed front-runners, Lesley's Choice set a steady pace. Only the front pair appeared to show their form.

T/Jkpt: Not won. T/Plt: £342.80 to a £1 stake. Pool: £109,445.99. 233.04 winning tickets. T/Qpdt: £41.80 to a £1 stake. Pool: £10,696.93. 189.10 winning tickets. KH

[69]KEMPTON (A.W) (R-H)
Saturday, January 10

OFFICIAL GOING: Standard
This meeting was a replacement for Kempton's scheduled jumps card which was frozen off.
Wind: Light, across Weather: Misty, very cold

111 PLAY BINGO @ WILLIAMHILL.COM H'CAP 6f (P)
2:15 (2:20) (Class 6) (0-54,54) 4-Y-0+ **£2,047** (£604; £302) **Stalls** High

Form RPR

036- **1** **Hollow Jo**[12] 7808 9-9-0 **50** FergusSweeney 5 60
(J R Jenkins) *hld up in abt 7th: pushed along and stdy prog fr 2f out: sustained effrt and cajoled into ld fnl 75yds* **6/1**[3]

26-0 **2** *¾* **Tadlil**[4] 62 7-9-0 **50** (v) RobertWinston 9 58
(J M Bradley) *t.k.h early: prom: trckd ldr over 2f out: rdn to ld over 1f out: hdd and outpcd last 75yds* **9/2**[1]

63-0 **3** *1* **Tamino (IRE)**[7] 27 6-9-4 **54** (t) JimmyQuinn 10 59
(P Howling) *led: drvn and hdd over 1f out: kpt on same pce* **5/1**[2]

3-61 **4** *½* **Sherjawy (IRE)**[4] 56 5-9-1 **51** 6ex (b) SimonWhitworth 8 54
(Miss Z C Davison) *t.k.h: trckd ldng pair: tried to chal up ins over 1f out: nt qckn ent fnl f: one pce* **6/1**[3]

045- **5** *2 ½* **Davids Mark**[12] 7809 9-9-0 **50** StephenDonohoe 1 45
(J R Jenkins) *hld up in abt 8th: outpcd over 2f out: drvn and kpt on fr over 1f out: nt pce to threaten* **12/1**

3-30 **6** *1* **Ishibee (IRE)**[4] 56 5-8-12 **48** (p) NeilChalmers 6 40
(J J Bridger) *chsd ldrs: cl enough 2f out: sn nt qckn and btn* **10/1**

334- **7** *¾* **Grizedale (IRE)**[11] 7817 10-9-4 **54** (tp) IanMongan 2 44
(M J Attwater) *hld up in last pair: urged along and fnd nil over 2f out: mde modest and reluctant late hdwy* **6/1**[3]

06-2 **8** *2* **Arfinnit (IRE)**[5] 44 8-8-11 **47** (v) ChrisCatlin 7 30
(Mrs A L M King) *settled in abt 6th: rdn over 2f out: sn outpcd: wknd fnl f* **5/1**[2]

000- **9** *½* **Mr Loire**[64] 7225 5-8-12 **48** (b) TGMcLaughlin 4 30
(K G Wingrove) *rel to r: mostly in last and nvr a factor* **50/1**

060- **10** *1 ¾* **Affirmatively**[49] 7416 4-8-9 **50** MCGeran(5) 3 26
(A W Carroll) *chsd ldr to over 2f out: sn btn: wknd fnl f* **20/1**

1m 13.63s (0.53) **Going Correction** +0.125s/f (Slow) **10** Ran SP% **117.9**
Speed ratings (Par 101): **101,100,98,98,94 93,92,89,89,86**
toteswinger: 1&2 £8.70, 1&3 £8.80, 2&3 £4.90. CSF £33.58 CT £150.27 TOTE £8.50: £2.40, £2.00, £2.00; EX 49.30 Trifecta £282.60 Part won. Pool £381.98 - 0.60 winning units..

Owner Jim McCarthy **Bred** K J Reddington **Trained** Royston, Herts

FOCUS
The race was delayed due to frozen stalls mechanism. A moderate sprint handicap.

112 PLAY POKER @ WILLIAMHILL.COM H'CAP 2m (P)
2:45 (2:47) (Class 5) (0-70,70) 4-Y-0+ **£2,590** (£770; £385; £192) **Stalls** High

Form RPR

011- **1** **Zuwaar**[11] 7827 4-9-2 **67** (t) StephenDonohoe 7 78+
(Ian Williams) *hld up in last trio: pushed along and prog on inner fr 4f out: wnt 2nd over 2f out: rdn to ld wl over 1f out: styd on wl: eased nr fin* **2/1**[1]

016- **2** *1 ¾* **Snowberry Hill (USA)**[11] 7827 6-8-12 **56** LiamJones 4 63
(Lucinda Featherstone) *led: set slow pce to 1/2-way: rdn over 2f out: hdd wl over 1f out: kpt on but no ch w wnr* **15/2**

600/ **3** *4* **Tutor (IRE)**[23] 4491 5-9-9 **70** (b) KevinGhunowa(3) 9 72
(Mrs A M Thorpe) *plld hrd: hld up bhd ldrs: plld out and effrt to dispute 2nd over 2f out: nt qckn and sn lft bhd by ldng pair* **66/1**

000/ **4** *¾* **Nothing Is Forever (IRE)**[11] 5120 5-8-11 **55** VinceSlattery 8 56
(L Corcoran) *trckd ldr for 6f and again 3f out to over 2f out: sn outpcd* **11/1**

502- **5** *½* **Squirtle (IRE)**[11] 7827 6-8-8 **59** MatthewLawson(7) 5 60
(W M Brisbourne) *settled in last rdn over 5f out: sn struggling: wl bhd 3f out: plugged on fnl 2f* **9/1**

124- **6** *1 ¼* **Irish Ballad**[13] 7806 7-8-11 **55** NickyMackay 2 54
(S Dow) *chsd ldr after 6f to 3f out: wknd 2f out* **11/2**[3]

606- **7** *¾* **Peas 'n Beans (IRE)**[42] 7489 6-8-7 **51** oh4 JimmyQuinn 3 49?
(T Keddy) *hld up in rr: effrt 4f out: chsd ldrs and in tch over 2f out: steadily fdd* **66/1**

615- **8** *2* **Coda Agency**[18] 7775 6-9-6 **64** ChrisCatlin 6 60
(D W P Arbuthnot) *t.k.h: trckd ldrs: rdn and wknd 4f out: wl bhd over 2f out* **10/3**[2]

111- **9** *54* **Mujamead**[13] 461 5-9-0 **63** (p) MCGeran(5) 1 —
(A W Carroll) *in tch: rdn 5f out: sn wknd: eased whn no ch 2f out: t.o* **10/1**

3m 32.28s (2.18) **Going Correction** +0.125s/f (Slow)
WFA 4 from 5yo+ 7lb **9** Ran SP% **114.0**
Speed ratings (Par 103): **99,98,96,95,95 94,94,93,66**
toteswinger: 1&2 £3.90, 1&3 £18.40, 2&3 £40.20. CSF £17.60 CT £718.45 TOTE £3.00: £1.50, £2.30, £5.80; EX 17.00 Trifecta £209.70 Part won. Pool £283.40 - 0.10 winning units..

Owner Dr Marwan Koukash **Bred** Shadwell Estate Company Limited **Trained** Portway, Worcs

FOCUS
Probably only a modest staying handicap.
Coda Agency Official explanation: trainer's rep said gelding ran flat
Mujamead Official explanation: jockey said gelding lost its action

113 LIVE CASINO GAMES @ WILLIAMHILL.COM H'CAP 7f (P)
3:15 (3:16) (Class 4) (0-85,89) 4-Y-0+ **£4,857** (£1,445; £722; £360) **Stalls** High

Form RPR

20-3 **1** **Resplendent Nova**[8] 9 7-9-0 **81** JimmyQuinn 6 90
(P Howling) *settled off the pce in midfield: rdn and prog over 2f out: wnt 2nd 1f out: styd on wl to ld last 75yds* **4/1**[3]

634- **2** *½* **Totally Focussed (IRE)**[11] 7821 4-8-11 **78** IanMongan 3 86
(S Dow) *trckd ldng pair gng wl: led over 2f out: rdn 2 l clr over 1f out: unable to sustain gallop and hdd last 75yds* **7/2**[2]

31-1 **3** *1 ¼* **Southandwest (IRE)**[1] 106 5-9-8 **89** 6ex ChrisCatlin 1 93
(J S Moore) *t.k.h early and trapped out wd first 2f: hld up in last: effrt over 2f out: trying to cl but making hrd work of it whn n.m.r over 1f out: kpt on to snatch 3rd post* **11/4**[1]

021- **4** *shd* **The Cayterers**[27] 7677 7-8-3 **75** MCGeran(5) 5 79
(A W Carroll) *t.k.h early: hld up off the pce: rdn over 2f out: kpt on fr over 1f out to press for 3rd nr fin* **10/1**

04-1 **5** *nse* **Pegasus Again (USA)**[7] 31 4-8-9 **76** (p) StephenDonohoe 7 80
(T G Mills) *trckd ldr: chal and upsides over 2f out: sn nt qckn: one pce fr over 1f out* **6/1**

060- **6** *1* **Dudley Docker (IRE)**[10] 7837 7-8-12 **79**.........................(b) LiamJones 2 80
(C R Dore) *stdd s: t.k.h and hld up in last pair: effrt on inner over 2f out: tried to cl over 1f out: one pce fnl f* **20/1**

132- **7** *4* **Monkey Glas (IRE)**[15] 7780 5-9-4 **85**.........................(b[1]) AndrewElliott 4 75
(J R Gask) *led at decent pce: rdn and hdd over 2f out: hld whn squeezed out 1f out and snatched up* **15/2**

1m 25.84s (-0.16) **Going Correction** +0.125s/f (Slow) **7** Ran SP% **108.8**
Speed ratings (Par 105): **105,104,103,102,102 101,97**
toteswinger: 1&2 £3.60, 1&3 £2.00, 2&3 £1.90. CSF £16.50 TOTE £4.80: £2.50, £2.70; EX 22.80.
Owner The Oh So Sharp Racing Partnership **Bred** A Turner **Trained** Newmarket, Suffolk
■ Stewards' Enquiry : Stephen Donohoe two-day ban: careless riding (Jan 24-25)

FOCUS
A really good handicap, that was run at a good pace.

114 WILLIAM HILL TELEBETTING SALE - 0800 44 40 40 H'CAP 7f (P)
3:45 (3:45) (Class 6) (0-54,54) 4-Y-O+ **£2,047** (£604; £302) **Stalls** High

Form RPR

030- **1** **Takitwo**[29] 7653 6-9-4 **54**.........................(v) SimonWhitworth 8 62
(P D Cundell) *settled in midfield: rdn and prog jst over 2f out: chsd ldr ent fnl f: styd on wl to ld last 50yds* **12/1**

04/4 **2** *hd* **Bollywood Style**[7] 25 4-9-1 **51**......................... LiamJones 1 58+
(J R Best) *dropped in fr wdst draw: hld up in last trio: prog wl over 2f out: chsd ldng gp over 1f out: styd on strly fnl f: jst failed* **20/1**

000- **3** *hd* **Patavium Prince (IRE)**[49] 7416 6-9-3 **53**................. FergusSweeney 11 59
(Miss Jo Crowley) *hld up in midfield: smooth prog over 2f out: got through to ld jst over 1f out and looked likely wnr: worn down last 50yds* **8/1[3]**

000- **4** *2 1/4* **First In Show**[11] 7818 4-8-11 **47**.........................(bt[1]) NeilChalmers 14 47
(A M Balding) *trckd ldrs: effrt on inner over 2f out: led briefly over 1f out: one pce ins fnl f* **16/1**

002- **5** *1 1/2* **Torquemada (IRE)**[19] 7766 8-9-3 **53**.........................(t) PaulDoe 12 49
(M J Attwater) *hld up bhd ldrs: gng easily 2f out: rdn and fnd nil over 1f out* **8/1[3]**

200- **6** *3/4* **Batchworth Blaise**[13] 7803 6-9-3 **53**......................... StephenCarson 5 60+
(E A Wheeler) *dropped in fr wd draw and hld up in rr: prog on inner over 2f out: cl up bhd ldrs whn nowhere to go over 1f out: nt rcvr* **33/1**

623- **7** *1 1/2* **Eleanor Eloise (USA)**[30] 7637 5-9-2 **52**......................... ChrisCatlin 13 42
(J R Gask) *mde most: drvn over 2f out: hdd & wknd over 1f out* **5/1[2]**

02-2 **8** *2* **Lady Aspen (IRE)**[4] 60 6-9-2 **52**.........................(t) StephenDonohoe 10 37
(Ian Williams) *w ldr: u.str.p wl over 2f out: sn lost pl: wl btn over 1f out* **9/4[1]**

05-0 **9** *1* **Jessica Wigmo**[7] 25 6-8-11 **52**......................... AmyBaker(5) 3 34
(A W Carroll) *restrained s and dropped in fr wd draw: effrt over 2f out: sn no real prog and btn* **16/1**

030- **10** *3 1/4* **Charmel's Lad**[24] 7710 4-9-2 **52**.........................(t) IanMongan 6 25
(W R Swinburn) *dropped in after s: t.k.h towards rr: u.p 3f out: struggling after* **11/1**

400- **11** *1* **Landikhaya (IRE)**[13] 7807 4-8-12 **53** ow1.............(v[1]) JamesO'Reilly(5) 7 24
(D K Ivory) *racd on outer: trckd ldrs: rdn over 3f out: losing pl whn hmpd over 2f out* **20/1**

025- **12** *6* **Harrison's Flyer (IRE)**[29] 7653 8-8-12 **53**.........................(p) MCGeran(5) 4 7
(J M Bradley) *wl in rr whn hung lft bnd 4f out and dropped to last: no ch after* **22/1**

200- **13** *7* **Straight Face (IRE)**[19] 7766 5-8-9 **52**.........................(b) KylieManser(7) 9 —
(Miss Gay Kelleway) *w ldng pair and racd on outer: wknd 3f out: t.o* **14/1**

1m 26.46s (0.46) **Going Correction** +0.125s/f (Slow) **13** Ran SP% **120.9**
Speed ratings (Par 101): **102,101,101,98,97 96,94,92,91,87 86,79,71**
toteswinger: 1&2 £34.50, 1&3 £15.20, 2&3 £23.50. CSF £237.53 CT £2102.19 TOTE £16.90: £4.20, £3.90, £2.60; EX 247.60 TRIFECTA Not won..
Owner Miss M C Fraser **Bred** Roden House Stud **Trained** Compton, Berks

FOCUS
A moderate handicap.
Takitwo Official explanation: trainer's rep said, regarding apparent improvement in form, that the gelding benefited from re-application of the visor, a stronger rider and its favourite track.
Batchworth Blaise Official explanation: jockey said gelding was denied a clear run
Harrison's Flyer(IRE) Official explanation: jockey said gelding failed to handle the bend

115 WILLIAMHILL.COM SALE - ENHANCED PRICES! MAIDEN STKS 1m (P)
4:15 (4:17) (Class 5) 3-Y-O+ **£2,590** (£770; £385; £192) **Stalls** High

Form RPR

04- **1** **Cool Hand Jake**[24] 7699 3-8-8 0......................... FergusSweeney 5 69
(P J Makin) *trckd ldrs: wnt 2nd over 4f out: clr of rest over 3f out: rdn and hanging over 2f out but steadily clsd to ld jst over 1f out: kpt on* **2/1[2]**

4- **2** *1 3/4* **Avoir Choisi (IRE)**[74] 7051 3-8-9 0 ow1......................... IanMongan 6 66+
(P W Chapple-Hyam) *sn led: drew at least 3 l clr over 3f out: drvn 2f out: hdd jst over 1f out: nt qckn* **6/4[1]**

0- **3** *hd* **More Time Tim (IRE)**[162] 4613 4-10-0 66................. TGMcLaughlin 10 69
(J R Boyle) *hld up: prog to go 3rd 3f out but ldng pair already clr: kpt on steadily u.p fnl 2f: nrly grabbed 2nd* **5/1[3]**

00- **4** *1* **Crazy Colours**[12] 7812 3-8-8 0.........................(b[1]) FrankieMcDonald 3 63
(Jane Chapple-Hyam) *broke on terms but sn heavily restrained in last then early reminders: slapped along and styd on wl fnl 2f: nrst fin* **25/1**

00- **5** *1/2* **Witch Of The Wave (IRE)**[24] 7699 3-8-3 0......................... JimmyQuinn 9 57
(Miss J S Davis) *chsd ldrs: wl outpcd sn after 1/2-way and trapped bhd wkng rivals: plld out and effrt to go 4th over 2f out: plugged on but nvr pce to threaten* **66/1**

5- **6** *4* **Toll Road**[12] 7812 3-8-3 0......................... ChrisCatlin 2 47
(E A L Dunlop) *outpcd and rdn in rr 1/2-way: no ch after: plugged on slowly fnl 2f* **8/1**

0/4- **7** *24* **Boogie Dancer**[85] 53 5-9-9 58......................... StephenDonohoe 7 —
(H S Howe) *chsd ldr to over 4f out: wknd over 3f out: t.o* **14/1**

8 *1 1/2* **Would I Lie To You**[30] 5-10-0 0......................... SimonWhitworth 4 —
(J R Jenkins) *chsd ldrs: outpcd sn after 1/2-way: sn wknd: t.o* **50/1**

40-0 **P** **Lady Fas (IRE)**[4] 56 6-9-4 44......................... MCGeran(5) 8 —
(A W Carroll) *broke down and p.u after 1f* **25/1**

1m 39.93s (0.13) **Going Correction** +0.125s/f (Slow)
WFA 3 from 4yo+ 20lb **9** Ran SP% **118.9**
Speed ratings (Par 103): **104,102,102,101,100 96,72,71,—**
toteswinger: 1&2 £1.90, 1&3 £3.10, 2&3 £2.00. CSF £5.41 TOTE £2.80: £1.10, £1.50, £1.80; EX 7.80.
Owner Wedgewood Estates **Bred** Wedgewood Estates **Trained** Ogbourne Maisey, Wilts

FOCUS
A race to rate around More Time Tim, who has had plenty of chances and looks a modest yardstick.
Crazy Colours ◆ Official explanation: jockey said colt hung left

116 WILLIAMHILL.COM H'CAP (DIV I) 1m 3f (P)
4:45 (4:48) (Class 6) (0-52,52) 4-Y-O+ **£1,706** (£503; £252) **Stalls** High

Form RPR

/05- **1** **Lytham (IRE)**[27] 7676 8-8-12 **46**......................... VinceSlattery 2 57
(A W Carroll) *hld up in rr: pushed along and prog to chse clr ldng pair over 1f out: inclined to hang but encouraged along and r.o to ld last 50yds* **7/2[1]**

044- **2** *1/2* **Vanquisher (IRE)**[14] 7787 5-8-12 **46**.....................(t) StephenDonohoe 11 56
(Ian Williams) *trckd ldng trio: quick move to ld over 2f out: drvn over 1f out: collared last 50yds* **7/2[1]**

030- **3** *1 3/4* **Amwell Brave**[13] 7806 8-8-11 **45**......................... SimonWhitworth 8 52
(J R Jenkins) *settled in midfield: stdy prog fr 3f out: chsd ldr 2f out and sn chal: nt qckn and hld 1f out: lost 2nd ins fnl f* **13/2[2]**

260- **4** *2 3/4* **Rockjumper**[48] 6746 4-9-1 **52**......................... FergusSweeney 5 54
(Mrs T J Hill) *hld up wl in rr: rdn over 2f out: styd on at one pce fr over 1f out: nvr able to rch ldrs* **10/1[3]**

/00- **5** *3/4* **Festival Dreams**[39] 7520 4-8-13 **50**......................... JimmyQuinn 6 51
(Miss J S Davis) *mostly in midfield: rdn over 3f out: prog u.p to chse clr ldng pair briefly over 1f out: sn no hdwy* **20/1**

506- **6** *2 1/2* **Hatch A Plan (IRE)**[86] 6753 8-9-0 **48**......................... NeilChalmers 4 45
(Mouse Hamilton-Fairley) *trckd ldrs: lost pl in general bunching over 2f out: renewed effrt over 1f out: no imp on ldrs* **13/2[2]**

004- **7** *3* **Autumn Charm**[12] 7815 4-8-8 **45**......................... LiamJones 3 37+
(Lucinda Featherstone) *hld up in rr: effrt on inner over 2f out: tried to make hdwy whn short of room and snatched up over 1f out: no ch after* **16/1**

50-4 **8** *nk* **A Valley Away (IRE)**[9] 1 5-8-13 **47**......................... FrankieMcDonald 7 38
(Jane Chapple-Hyam) *travelled keenly in ldng trio: disputing 2nd over 2f out: wknd over 1f out* **12/1**

000- **9** *2 3/4* **Titfer (IRE)**[15] 6757 4-8-5 **47**......................... AmyBaker(5) 1 34
(A W Carroll) *chsd ldr after 3f: rdn wl over 3f out: wknd over 2f out* **16/1**

000- **10** *3/4* **Tiegs (IRE)**[31] 7626 7-8-11 **45**......................... ChrisCatlin 9 30
(P W Hiatt) *led at gd pce to over 2f out: sn wknd* **16/1**

11 *9* **Pomander (IRE)**[8] 1556 6-9-2 **50**......................... IanMongan 10 20
(C Gordon) *awkward s: a last and nvr gng wl: detached 3f out: t.o* **14/1**

2m 21.51s (-0.39) **Going Correction** +0.125s/f (Slow)
WFA 4 from 5yo+ 3lb **11** Ran SP% **117.0**
Speed ratings (Par 101): **106,105,104,102,101 100,97,97,95,95 88**
toteswinger: 1&2 £3.90, 1&3 £5.30, 2&3 £6.20. CSF £14.24 CT £76.26 TOTE £5.00: £2.10, £1.80, £2.40; EX 15.40.
Owner Patrick McGee **Bred** Mrs A S O'Brien And Lars Pearson **Trained** Cropthorne, Worcs

FOCUS
A very moderate event.
Autumn Charm Official explanation: jockey said filly was denied a clear run

117 WILLIAMHILL.COM H'CAP (DIV II) 1m 3f (P)
5:15 (5:18) (Class 6) (0-52,49) 4-Y-O+ **£1,706** (£503; £252) **Stalls** High

Form RPR

054- **1** **Carlton Scroop (FR)**[327] 606 6-9-2 **49**.........................(b) LukeMorris 9 55
(J Jay) *reluctant ldr 1f: styd prom: wnt 2nd 3f out: clsd u.p to ld jst over 1f out: waved tail but sn in command* **10/3[1]**

300- **2** *1 1/2* **Prince Of Medina**[39] 7520 6-8-12 **45**.........................(t) RobertWinston 6 48
(J R Best) *trckd ldrs: hrd rdn to go 3rd 2f out: styd on w limited enthusiasm fnl f to take 2nd nr fin* **9/2[3]**

340- **3** *1/2* **Magic Amigo**[69] 5631 8-8-13 **46**.........................(b) SimonWhitworth 1 49
(J R Jenkins) *plld way to ld after 1f: j. path 1/2-way: over 2 l clr 3f out and most of rest in trble: hdd jst over 1f out: lost 2nd nr fin* **7/1**

000- **4** *2* **Satindra (IRE)**[14] 7787 5-9-0 **47**.........................(tp) LiamJones 5 46
(C R Dore) *trckd ldr after 1f to 3f out: steadily fdd u.p* **7/1**

055- **5** *nk* **Backlash**[53] 3901 8-8-12 **45**.........................(p) ChrisCatlin 7 44
(A W Carroll) *hld up in 5th: rdn over 2f out: one pce and nvr able to trble ldrs* **8/1**

540- **6** *2* **Norwegian**[35] 7585 8-8-13 **46**......................... StephenDonohoe 10 41
(Ian Williams) *hld up in last trio: shkn up over 2f out: v modest late prog and no threat* **9/1**

605- **7** *1/2* **Aston Boy**[33] 7599 4-8-10 **46**......................... JimmyQuinn 4 40
(M Blanshard) *trckd ldrs: rdn over 3f out: struggling over 2f out: no real prog after* **4/1[2]**

000- **8** *9* **Oakbridge (IRE)**[52] 1064 7-9-1 **48**.........................(t) VinceSlattery 2 27
(R Brotherton) *a wl in rr: u.p in last 3f out: t.o* **25/1**

40-0 **9** *5* **Tuning Fork**[7] 23 9-8-5 **45**.........................(e) KierenFox(7) 8 16
(M J Attwater) *hld up in last pair: effrt on outer over 3f out: bmpd along and no prog 2f out: wknd: t.o* **20/1**

2m 26.5s (4.60) **Going Correction** +0.125s/f (Slow)
WFA 4 from 5yo+ 3lb **9** Ran SP% **116.0**
Speed ratings (Par 101): **88,86,86,85,84 83,83,76,72**
toteswinger: 1&2 £3.80, 1&3 £4.40, 2&3 £6.30. CSF £18.46 CT £98.37 TOTE £3.90: £1.70, £1.70, £2.20; EX 16.10.
Owner David Fremel **Bred** Jonathan Jay **Trained** Newmarket, Suffolk

FOCUS
A poor gallop, so a horse needing a true test was at a significant disadvantage.

118 WILLIAMHILL.COM SALE - SPECIAL OFFERS! H'CAP 7f (P)
5:45 (5:47) (Class 6) (0-60,60) 4-Y-O+ **£2,047** (£604; £302) **Stalls** High

Form RPR

0- **1** **Downhill Skier (IRE)**[29] 7656 5-9-0 **56**......................... TGMcLaughlin 9 66
(W M Brisbourne) *t.k.h early: a ldng trio: chsd ldr over 2f out: looked hld ent fnl f: styd on to ld last 100yds* **12/1**

20-2 **2** *1/2* **Duke Of Milan (IRE)**[7] 22 6-9-2 **58**......................... SimonWhitworth 10 67
(G C Bravery) *hld up in last trio: styd prog on inner 2f out: got through ins fnl f to take 2nd and press wnr nr fin: shade too much to do* **6/1[2]**

001- **3** *3/4* **Langham House**[19] 7759 4-9-0 **56**......................... NickyMackay 8 63
(J R Jenkins) *t.k.h early: led: set modest pce to 1/2-way: kicked on sn after: 2 l up ent fnl f: hdd and hdd last 100yds* **20/1**

020- **4** *1/2* **Valentino Swing (IRE)**[32] 7619 6-8-13 **58**......................... TolleyDean(3) 5 64
(Miss T Spearing) *hld up in last pair: urged along wl over 2f out: prog on outer over 1f out: styd on fnl f: nrst fin* **14/1**

000- **5** *1/2* **Liberty Valance (IRE)**[11] 7829 4-9-0 **56**.........................(t) IanMongan 4 60
(S Kirk) *hld up in midfield on outer: effrt over 2f out: rdn to dispute 3rd over 1f out: kpt on same pce* **8/1[3]**

35-4 **6** *nk* **Thabaat**[3] 71 5-8-8 **55**.........................(b) MCGeran(5) 7 58
(J M Bradley) *stdd s: t.k.h early and sn trckd ldrs: rdn to dispute 3rd over 1f out: nt qckn: wl hld whn no room nr fin* **7/2[1]**

54-6 **7** *¾* **Charming Escort**[7] 25 5-8-13 **55**..........................(v[1]) RobertWinston 11 56
(T T Clement) *t.k.h early: hld up bhd ldrs: effrt over 2f out: disp 3rd over 1f out but fnd little: hld whn rn out of room ins fnl f* **7/2**[1]

0-55 **8** *hd* **Bold Diva**[5] 44 4-8-8 **55**..........................(v) AmyBaker(5) 6 56+
(A W Carroll) *settled in rr: effrt and making prog whn rn into wall of rivals over 1f out and snatched up: nt rcvr* **12/1**

044- **9** *4* **Mistress Cooper**[10] 7834 4-9-4 **60**.......................... ChrisCatlin 3 50
(W J Musson) *t.k.h: mostly chsd ldr to over 2f out: sn wknd* **8/1**[3]

104- **10** *3 ¾* **Billy Hot Rocks (IRE)**[11] 7819 4-9-4 **60**..........................(p) JimmyQuinn 2 40
(Miss Gay Kelleway) *stdd s: hld up in rr: effrt on inner whn rdr dropped whip 2f out: sn wknd* **16/1**

225- **11** *11* **Hennessy Island (USA)**[18] 7779 4-9-2 **58**..........................(p) StephenDonohoe 1 8
(T G Mills) *chsd ldrs 4f: sn wknd: t.o* **12/1**

1m 26.6s (0.60) **Going Correction** +0.125s/f (Slow) **11** Ran SP% **121.3**
Speed ratings (Par 101): **101,100,99,99,98 98,97,97,92,88 75**
toteswinger: 1&2 £20.40, 1&3 £51.20, 2&3 £10.60. CSF £85.03 CT £1010.18 TOTE £20.30: £3.50, £2.50, £7.10; EX 124.30 Place 6 £58.23, Place 5 £34.56..
Owner Miss P D Insull **Bred** Swettenham Stud **Trained** Great Ness, Shropshire
■ Stewards' Enquiry : M C Geran one-day ban: careless riding (Jan 24)

FOCUS
A modest handicap.
T/Plt: £216.30 to a £1 stake. Pool: £126,810.00. 427.86 winning tickets. T/Qpdt: £33.80 to a £1 stake. Pool: £6,818.00. 148.90 winning tickets. JN

96 LINGFIELD (L-H)
Saturday, January 10

OFFICIAL GOING: Standard
Wind: Nil. Weather: cold, dry

119 BANGORERRIS CLAIMING STKS 1m 2f (P)
12:40 (12:42) (Class 6) 4-Y-0+ **£2,047** (£604; £302) **Stalls** Low

Form RPR

115- **1** **Sabre Light**[24] 7707 4-9-7 77..........................(v[1]) JerryO'Dwyer 4 85
(J Pearce) *chsd ldng pair: chsd ldr jst over 2f out: led wl over 1f out: clr 1f out: comf* **9/4**[2]

0- **2** *3* **Gasat (IRE)**[77] 6985 8-8-6 82 ow1..........................(t) FBranca 1 62
(F Sheridan) *led: clr 1/2-way: rn wd bnd 2f out: sn hdd: kpt on but no ch w wnr fnl f* **3/1**[3]

0/3- **3** *1 ¾* **Corriolanus (GER)**[21] 7744 9-8-13 79.......................... FrancisNorton 6 65
(A M Balding) *hld up in last pair: hdwy over 2f out: rdn 2f out: chsd ldng pair over 1f out: no imp* **5/4**[1]

000- **4** *1 ¼* **Royal Straight**[36] 7553 4-9-1 62.......................... JimCrowley 3 67
(B N Pollock) *chsd ldr tl jst over 2f out: wknd u.p over 1f out* **16/1**

46-5 **5** *5* **Tenement (IRE)**[7] 29 5-8-0 52.......................... MCGeran(5) 5 45
(Jamie Poulton) *in tch in midfield: rdn and struggling over 2f out: no ch fnl 2f* **16/1**

6 *22* **Chef De Camp (FR)**[208] 6-9-11 0.......................... IanMongan 2 21
(M R Hoad) *t.k.h: hld up in last pl: rdn and wknd over 2f out: t.o* **100/1**

2m 5.22s (-1.38) **Going Correction** -0.025s/f (Stan)
WFA 4 from 5yo+ 2lb **6** Ran SP% **113.0**
Speed ratings (Par 101): **104,101,100,99,95 77**
toteswinger: 1&2 £1.50, 1&3 £1.10, 2&3 £7.90. CSF £9.57 TOTE £3.00: £1.10, £2.20; EX 9.60.Gasat was claimed by A B Haynes for £5,000.
Owner Jeff Pearce **Bred** D J And Mrs Deer **Trained** Newmarket, Suffolk

FOCUS
A fair claimer.

120 CHRIS BROWN 40TH BIRTHDAY MAIDEN STKS 1m 2f (P)
1:10 (1:12) (Class 5) 4-Y-0+ **£2,729** (£806; £403) **Stalls** Low

Form RPR

35- **1** **Annabelle's Charm (IRE)**[33] 7609 4-8-12 0.......................... JamieSpencer 1 77+
(L M Cumani) *hld up in 3rd pl: chsd ldr jst over 2f out: swtchd rt over 1f out: led 1f out: hrd hld* **1/4**[1]

00- **2** *1 ¼* **Middle Of Nowhere (USA)**[58] 7304 4-9-3 0..........................(t) EddieAhern 3 64
(M A Magnusson) *led: rdn jst over 2f out: hdd 1f out: kpt on same pce* **8/1**[2]

0- **3** *6* **Oxus (IRE)**[20] 7757 4-9-3 0.......................... IanMongan 4 52
(B R Johnson) *chsd ldr tl hung lft and lost 2nd bnd jst over 2f out: wl btn over 1f out* **20/1**[3]

060- **4** *3 ½* **Ray Diamond**[48] 5537 4-9-3 42.......................... MickyFenton 5 45
(M Madgwick) *a bhd: rdn 5f out: lost tch over 2f out* **8/1**[2]

2m 6.42s (-0.18) **Going Correction** -0.025s/f (Stan) **4** Ran SP% **107.0**
Speed ratings (Par 103): **99,98,93,90**
CSF £2.72 TOTE £1.10; EX 2.40.
Owner Merry Fox Stud Limited **Bred** Swordlestown Stud **Trained** Newmarket, Suffolk

FOCUS
An uncompetitive maiden.

121 WILLIAM HILL JANUARY SALE - NOW ON! MEDIAN AUCTION MAIDEN STKS 1m (P)
1:45 (1:48) (Class 5) 3-Y-0 **£2,729** (£806; £403) **Stalls** High

Form RPR

0- **1** **The Mumbo**[27] 7674 3-8-12 0.......................... JoeFanning 9 66
(W Jarvis) *pressed ldr: rdn and ev ch fr over 2f out: battled on gamely: led on post* **40/1**

6- **2** *nse* **Best In Class**[30] 7638 3-9-3 0.......................... RichardKingscote 1 71
(Tom Dascombe) *led at stdy gallop: rdn over 2f out: battled on wl tl hdd last stride* **25/1**

03- **3** *nk* **Haljaferia (UAE)**[24] 7699 3-9-3 0.......................... HayleyTurner 2 70
(D R C Elsworth) *dwlt: t.k.h: sn wl in tch: swtchd rt jst ins fnl f: r.o wl fnl 100yds: nt quite rch ldng pair* **9/2**[3]

4 *½* **Lady's Art (FR)** 3-8-12 0.......................... TPQueally 5 64+
(E F Vaughan) *w.w towards rr: nt clr run 2f out: swtchd rt and hdwy over 1f out: chsng ldrs and swtchd rt ins fnl f: r.o wl: nt quite rch ldrs* **14/1**

00- **5** *1* **Pyrus Time (IRE)**[42] 7498 3-9-3 0.......................... LukeMorris 6 67+
(J S Moore) *stdd s: t.k.h: hld up in rr: stl plenty to do over 1f out: r.o strly fnl f: nt rch ldrs* **66/1**

6 *¾* **Silca Meydan** 3-9-3 0.......................... TonyCulhane 8 65+
(M R Channon) *stdd s: hld up towards rr: hdwy and edging lft over 1f out: styd on fnl f: nt rch ldrs* **25/1**

2- **7** *¾* **Commandingpresence (USA)**[22] 7735 3-8-12 0...... JamieSpencer 11 58
(B J Meehan) *trckd ldrs: rdn jst over 2f out: hung lft and nt qckn over 1f out: wknd ins fnl f* **4/5**[1]

8 *1* **Red Suede Shoes** 3-9-0 0.......................... JamesMillman(3) 3 61
(B R Millman) *v s.i.s: rn v green in rr: rdn over 4f out: hdwy on inner 2f out: kpt on same pce fnl f* **66/1**

2- **9** *nk* **Premier Angel (USA)**[19] 7767 3-8-12 0.......................... ShaneKelly 12 55
(Jane Chapple-Hyam) *hld up in tch in midfield: rdn and nt qckn over 1f out: no imp after* **5/2**[2]

0- **10** *2 ½* **Esteem Lord**[19] 7767 3-9-3 0.......................... FrancisNorton 7 54
(Jamie Poulton) *hld up in tch in midfield: lost pl and bhd over 2f out* **50/1**

06- **11** *½* **Screaming Brave**[24] 7699 3-9-3 0.......................... EdwardCreighton 4 53
(M R Channon) *chsd ldrs tl wknd u.p over 2f out* **50/1**

64- **12** *1* **Maison D'Or**[12] 7812 3-9-3 0.......................... MickyFenton 10 51
(R Ingram) *rrd s: t.k.h: hld up bhd: lost tch wl over 2f out* **33/1**

1m 40.31s (2.11) **Going Correction** -0.025s/f (Stan) **12** Ran SP% **129.0**
Speed ratings (Par 97): **88,87,87,87,86 85,84,83,83,80 80,79**
toteswinger: 1&2 £52.50, 1&3 £35.80, 2&3 £6.20. CSF £792.06 TOTE £35.00: £7.50, £5.00, £1.80; EX 435.90 TRIFECTA Not won..
Owner Willie W Robertson **Bred** Mount Coote Partnership **Trained** Newmarket, Suffolk

FOCUS
An ordinary maiden and something of a shock result.
Commandingpresence(USA) Official explanation: jockey said filly was upset in preliminaries and hung left
Red Suede Shoes Official explanation: jockey said gelding ran green
Maison D'Or Official explanation: jockey said gelding hung right

122 WILLIAM HILL JANUARY SALE - BETTER ODDS! H'CAP 7f (P)
2:20 (2:20) (Class 4) (0-85,81) 3-Y-0 **£4,857** (£1,445; £722; £360) **Stalls** Low

Form RPR

022- **1** **Dream Date (IRE)**[15] 7783 3-8-2 **68**..........................(t) GilmarPereira(3) 5 76
(W J Haggas) *chsd ldr tl led after 1f: mde rest: shkn up and qcknd clr over 1f out: r.o strly* **3/1**[2]

12-2 **2** *2 ¼* **Andean Margin (IRE)**[3] 74 3-8-7 **70**..........................(b) HayleyTurner 2 72
(S A Callaghan) *led at slow pce for 1f: chsd wnr after: rdn and nt pce of wnr over 1f out: no ch w wnr fnl f* **4/6**[1]

233- **3** *2 ½* **Sign Of Approval**[21] 7739 3-9-0 **77**.......................... JimCrowley 3 72
(K R Burke) *stdd s: t.k.h: hld up in last: rdn 2f out: wnt 3rd over 1f out: nvr trbld ldrs* **5/1**[3]

034- **4** *2 ½* **Joannadarc (USA)**[18] 7773 3-8-7 **70**.......................... FrancisNorton 1 58
(S A Callaghan) *hld up in 3rd pl: rdn and nt pce of ldrs over 1f out: wl btn after* **9/1**

1m 26.54s (1.74) **Going Correction** -0.025s/f (Stan) **4** Ran SP% **111.7**
Speed ratings (Par 99): **89,86,83,80**
CSF £5.71 TOTE £3.90; EX 6.00.
Owner Exors of the Late F C T Wilson **Bred** J Hanly, A Stroud And T Stewart **Trained** Newmarket, Suffolk
■ The first winner in Britain for Brazilian jockey Gilmar Pereira.

FOCUS
With only four runners going to post, this was always likely to prove a tactical affair, and so it proved. The pace in the early stages was very moderate and the winner was in exactly the right place to benefit.

123 WILLIAM HILL JANUARY SALE - WHY BET ELSEWHERE? CONDITIONS STKS 6f (P)
2:50 (2:51) (Class 3) 3-Y-0+ **£7,771** (£2,312; £1,155; £577) **Stalls** Low

Form RPR

000- **1** **Contest (IRE)**[119] 5922 5-9-12 104.......................... JimCrowley 5 115
(D M Simcock) *chsd ldng pair: wl clr of remainder: rdn to chal on inner ent fnl f: led fnl 75yds: r.o wl* **9/1**

011- **2** *1 ¼* **Turn On The Style**[13] 7805 7-9-5 101..........................(b) PaulMulrennan 2 104
(J Balding) *led: rdn over 1f out: hdd and no ex fnl 75yds* **4/1**[3]

02-2 **3** *3 ¼* **Bonus (IRE)**[3] 73 9-9-10 107..........................(v) EddieAhern 1 99+
(G A Butler) *stdd s: hld up wl out of tch in last pair: hanging lft over 1f out: r.o fnl f: nvr nr enough to chal* **10/3**[2]

21-1 **4** *½* **Aeroplane**[3] 73 6-9-5 92.......................... HayleyTurner 6 92+
(S A Callaghan) *stdd s and dropped in bhd: sn wl off the pce in last pair: wnt modest 4th wl over 1f out: r.o but nvr nr enough to chal* **5/4**[1]

122- **5** *6* **Medicea Sidera**[85] 6782 5-9-0 96.......................... JamieSpencer 7 68
(E F Vaughan) *stdd and dropped in after s: sn wl off the pce in 4th: rdn 3f out: n.d* **8/1**

313- **6** *3 ½* **Lone Wolfe**[20] 7756 5-9-5 91.......................... MickyFenton 3 62+
(Jane Chapple-Hyam) *chsd ldr: rdn and ev ch over 1f out: cl 3rd whn lost action ins fnl f: virtually p.u after* **16/1**

69.99 secs (-1.91) **Going Correction** -0.025s/f (Stan) course record **6** Ran SP% **114.5**
Speed ratings (Par 107): **111,109,105,104,96 91**
toteswinger: 1&2 £20.80, 1&3 £8.00, 2&3 £2.90. CSF £45.12 TOTE £12.00: £2.60, £2.30; EX 69.30.
Owner Tick Tock Partnership **Bred** Mrs D Nagle **Trained** Newmarket, Suffolk

FOCUS
A decent contest but an unsatisfactory result in as much the first two in the betting were given far too much to do and were never in a position to throw down a challenge. Turn On The Style and Lone Wolfe broke sharply out of the stalls and set a proper gallop out in front, while the winner got the run of things just in behind.

NOTEBOOK
Contest(IRE) ◆, the subject of support from as big as 33-1 in the morning, was making his debut for his new stable having left David Wachman last autumn. He looked an up-and-coming sprinter early last year but did not progress as one might have hoped, but this was a drop in class for him from the Group 3 contest he ran in last time and he took full advantage, picking up well to see off course specialist Turn On The Style inside the last. He is entitled to have needed this run, so there could be more to come, and he is now booked on a plane for the Dubai Carnival, where it would not be a surprise to see him pick up a valuable handicap. (op 25-1)
Turn On The Style loves it around here, and once again he took up his favoured front-running role. He went down fighting and remains at the top of his game. (op 7-2 tchd 3-1)
Bonus(IRE), like Aeroplane, is a tricky ride who needs to be held up for a late challenge, but Turner and Ahern were so concerned about marking each other that they allowed the first three far too much rope and could never get into the race despite a good gallop. Bonus tracked Aeroplane throughout, edging ahead of that rival close home, but it was all for nothing. Official explanation: jockey said gelding hung left (op 4-1 tchd 9-2)
Aeroplane, whose rider was clearly most concerned about Bonus, let the first three gain far too big an advantage early on in the race, and when Medicea Sidera failed to close the gap for him running down the hill the game was up. He did eventually run on late in the straight, dragging Bonus, who edged past close home, with him, but this is a race both Hayley Turner and Eddie Ahern will want to forget. (op 11-10)
Medicea Sidera was returning from a break and is more of a 7f mare.

Lone Wolfe was challenging and had every chance a furlong out when he went wrong, and was immediately eased right down. Official explanation: vet said gelding was lame in front

124 WILLIAM HILL JANUARY SALE - BONUSES GALORE! H'CAP 1m 2f (P)
3:20 (3:22) (Class 2) (0-100,101) 4-Y-0+ **£11,656** (£3,468; £1,733; £865) **Stalls** Low

Form RPR
04-3 **1** **Lady Jane Digby**[9] 6 4-8-4 **86** GregFairley 7 96
(M Johnston) *chsd ldng pair: chsd ldr over 1f out: drvn to ld ins fnl f: r.o strly* **7/1**
005- **2** *1 1/4* **Baylini**[12] 7814 5-8-7 **87** EdwardCreighton 3 94
(Ms J S Doyle) *stdd s: hld up in rr: hdwy on outer jst over 2f out: rdn over 1f out: r.o ins fnl f: wnt 2nd on post* **16/1**
601- **3** *nse* **Sgt Schultz (IRE)**[12] 7814 6-9-1 **95** LukeMorris 5 102
(J S Moore) *hld up in last trio: hdwy over 2f out: chsd ldrs and rdn whn carried rt over 1f out: styd on u.p fnl f: chsd wnr wl ins fnl f: lost 2nd on post* **5/1**[3]
305- **4** *1* **Philatelist (USA)**[42] 7491 5-9-7 **101** ShaneKelly 8 106
(M A Jarvis) *hld up in tch: hdwy to chse ldr 2f out: rdn and ev ch whn wnt rt over 1f out: drvn and kpt on same pce ins fnl f* **9/4**[1]
003- **5** *1/2* **John Terry (IRE)**[85] 6784 6-8-11 **91** JimCrowley 6 95
(Mrs A J Perrett) *chsd ldr tl led over 2f out: rdn over 1f out: hdd ins fnl f: fdd and lost 3 pls wl ins fnl f* **11/2**
003- **6** *1* **Art Man**[12] 7813 6-8-6 **86** oh1 HayleyTurner 1 88
(G L Moore) *hld up in tch: rdn and nt qckn over 1f out: kpt on same pce fnl f* **11/4**[2]
4/0- **7** *9* **Aviso (GER)**[20] 7756 5-8-9 **89** ow1 TPQueally 4 73
(A P Stringer) *racd keenly: led: rdn and hdd over 2f out: wknd wl over 1f out* **40/1**
4/5- **8** *37* **Naomh Geileis (USA)**[13] 7804 4-8-12 **94** JoeFanning 2 4
(M Johnston) *hld up in rr: rdn and struggling 3f out: lost tch 2f out: t.o* **16/1**

2m 2.32s (-4.28) **Going Correction** -0.025s/f (Stan) course record
WFA 4 from 5yo+ 2lb **8** Ran SP% **116.2**
Speed ratings (Par 109): **116,115,114,114,113 112,105,76**
toteswinger: 1&2 £12.70, 1&3 £5.70, 2&3 £8.20. CSF £109.13 CT £611.48 TOTE £9.20: £2.30, £3.70, £1.50; EX 105.80 Trifecta £481.80 Part won. Pool: £651.13 - 0.94 winning units..
Owner Miss K Rausing **Bred** Miss K Rausing **Trained** Middleham Moor, N Yorks

FOCUS
This looked a strong handicap despite a few of them having questions to answer. The pace looked mostly even throughout, but a sprint to the line did seem to start at about the three-furlong pole.

NOTEBOOK
Lady Jane Digby ◆ was once touted as a Classic aspirant, but she rather lost her way until showing some promise of her last two outings. Always well positioned here, she quickened nicely when asked to, and won most impressively after gaining an advantage. (op 13-2 tchd 11-2)
Baylini, who was behind Sgt Schultz last time, has not been running well in her past few runs and has come down the weights a bit as a result. She had all of her rivals to pass rounding the home bend and was never going to get on terms. (op 14-1 tchd 12-1)
Sgt Schultz(IRE) bounced right back to form last time at Great Leighs when winning by a clear margin over a trip he had never won over (all of his previous success had come over 1m4f). He became outpaced when the race started in earnest and will be better suited by further in this sort of company in the future. Official explanation: jockey said gelding hung right (op 4-1)
Philatelist(USA), who was drawn widest, was dropping back into handicap company after three runs at a higher grade. He had his chance, but the Handicapper appears to have his measure for now. (op 7-2)
John Terry(IRE) was not beaten that far by Philatelist in the Rosebery Handicap at Kempton last March and continued to show good form, without winning, after that. Having his first run since October, he tried to make his stamina count from the three-furlong pole but was made to look very one-paced in the final furlong. This sort of trip is too short for him. (op 5-1)
Art Man, racing from 1lb out of the handicap, has won plenty of times on the all-weather at this trip and looked on a handy mark. Back up to 1m2f after running well over 1m last time, he was settled in midfield but could not quicken significantly when asked to. (op 3-1 tchd 10-3 and 7-2 in a place)

125 WILLIAM HILL JANUARY SALE - ENHANCED FAVOURITES! H'CAP 1m 2f (P)
3:50 (3:50) (Class 5) (0-70,70) 4-Y-0+ **£2,900** (£856; £428) **Stalls** Low

Form RPR
154- **1** **Millie's Rock (IRE)**[175] 4183 4-9-0 **66** JamieSpencer 10 74+
(K A Ryan) *mde all: rdn over 1f out: styd on wl fnl f* **3/1**[2]
136- **2** *3/4* **General Feeling (IRE)**[13] 7807 8-8-10 **60** HayleyTurner 6 66
(S T Mason) *hld up in tch in midfield: hdwy and rdn jst over 2f out: r.o to 2nd ins fnl f: nt rch wnr* **10/1**
012- **3** *1 1/2* **Saucy**[21] 7742 8-9-1 **65** RichardKingscote 1 68
(Tom Dascombe) *chsd wnr tl over 5f out: chsd wnr again 2f out: rdn and no imp jst ins fnl f: lost 2nd ins fnl f* **5/2**[1]
25-2 **4** *1/2* **Teasing**[7] 29 5-9-6 **70** (v) JerryO'Dwyer 7 72
(J Pearce) *hld up in rr: rdn and effrt on outer bnd 2f out: r.o to go 4th ins fnl f: nvr trbld ldrs* **7/1**
620- **5** *1 1/2* **It's My Day (IRE)**[218] 2785 4-9-1 **67** JimCrowley 9 66
(C Gordon) *stdd s: hld up in rr: hdwy wl over 1f out: chsd ldrs and carried hd awkwardly u.p jst over 1f out: no imp fnl f* **25/1**
325- **6** *hd* **Siena Star (IRE)**[13] 7807 11-8-11 **61** MickyFenton 8 60
(Stef Liddiard) *chsd ldrs: hdwy to chse wnr over 5f out tl 2f out: unable qck u.p over 1f out: kpt on same pce fnl f* **4/1**[3]
000- **7** *2 1/4* **Paradise Dancer (IRE)**[33] 7603 5-9-6 **70** EddieAhern 4 64
(J A R Toller) *hld up towards rr: rdn and effrt jst over 2f out: drvn and wknd ent fnl f* **16/1**
060- **8** *2 1/2* **Stark Contrast (USA)**[21] 7750 5-8-8 **63** GabrielHannon(5) 2 52
(M D I Usher) *in tch: rdn and effrt on inner wl over 1f out: wknd ent fnl f* **20/1**
200- **9** *1 1/2* **Hilbre Court (USA)**[19] 7758 4-9-1 **67** (p) TonyCulhane 3 53
(B P J Baugh) *t.k.h: chsd ldrs: rdn over 2f out: wknd qckly over 1f out* **10/1**
/ **10** *31* **Ocarito (GER)**[60] 8-9-1 **65** PaulMulrennan 5 —
(G F Bridgwater) *stdd s: a bhd: detached last fr 5f out: t.o fnl 2f* **33/1**

2m 4.48s (-2.12) **Going Correction** -0.025s/f (Stan)
WFA 4 from 5yo+ 2lb **10** Ran SP% **121.7**
Speed ratings (Par 103): **107,106,105,104,103 103,101,99,98,73**
toteswinger: 1&2 £6.80, 1&3 £3.40, 2&3 £3.90. CSF £33.92 CT £88.06 TOTE £5.00: £1.50, £2.50, £1.90; EX 53.70 Trifecta £191.10 Pool: £284.15 - 1.10 winning units. Place 6 £1,432.82, Place 5 £672.96..
Owner Mike & Denise Dawes **Bred** Mrs U Schwarzenbach **Trained** Hambleton, N Yorks

FOCUS
A modest handicap but a fine front-running performance from Millie's Rock.
T/Plt: £569.40 to a £1 stake. Pool: £81,172.33. 104.05 winning tickets. T/Qpdt: £110.10 to a £1 stake. Pool: £5,197.00. 34.90 winning tickets. SP

[83]GREAT LEIGHS (A.W) (L-H)
Sunday, January 11

OFFICIAL GOING: Standard
Wind: fresh, behind Weather: bright spells

126 DERG H'CAP 1m 5f 66y(P)
1:25 (1:32) (Class 6) (0-65,65) 4-Y-0+ **£1,942** (£578; £288; £144) **Stalls** Low

Form RPR
625/ **1** **Dishdasha (IRE)**[30] 7187 7-8-11 **55** (t) JamieSpencer 9 62+
(Mrs A M Thorpe) *confidently rdn: stdd and dropped in bhd s: t.k.h: swtchd rt wl over 1f out: edgd lft but str run to ld ins fnl f: readily* **10/3**[1]
216- **2** *1 1/2* **Lapina (IRE)**[29] 7667 5-9-7 **65** (b) IanMongan 5 70
(A Middleton) *t.k.h: hld up wl in tch: effrt and rdn over 1f out: ev ch briefly jst ins fnl f: chsd wnr and one pce after* **10/1**
322- **3** *1* **Generous Star**[15] 7787 6-8-13 **57** JimmyQuinn 8 61
(J Pearce) *mostly chsd ldr: rdn 3f out: drvn to ld over 1f out: hdd ins fnl f: one pce after* **6/1**
315- **4** *2* **Eureka Moment**[15] 7797 4-9-2 **65** EddieAhern 2 66
(E A L Dunlop) *hld up in tch: hdwy to chse ldng trio over 2f out: rdn and unable qck over 1f out: edgd lft and plugged on same pce fnl f* **14/1**
000- **5** *nse* **John Dillon (IRE)**[71] 4299 5-8-11 **60** (v) PatrickDonaghy(5) 3 60
(P C Haslam) *dwlt: bustled along early: towards rr: bmpd and lost pl wl over 3f out: bhd and rdn over 2f out: styd on fnl f: nvr trbld ldrs* **20/1**
044- **6** *nse* **Sarando**[24] 7721 4-9-2 **65** ChrisCatlin 1 65
(R Charlton) *led at stdy pce tl hdd over 6f out: chsd ldrs after: rdn wl over 3f out: kpt on same pce u.p fr over 1f out* **15/2**
01-1 **7** *1/2* **Blockley (USA)**[9] 18 5-9-1 **59** StephenDonohoe 4 59
(Ian Williams) *hld up in midfield: bmpd and lost pl over 3f out: swtchd rt and rdn over 1f out: kpt on but nvr able to chal ldrs* **5/1**[3]
664- **8** *2 1/4* **Shanafarahan (IRE)**[154] 4902 4-8-7 **56** NickyMackay 7 52
(K A Morgan) *stdd s: t.k.h: hld up towards rr: hdwy 8f out: led over 6f out: rdn over 2f out: hdd over 1f out: wknd fnl f* **50/1**
013- **9** *nse* **Spume (IRE)**[12] 7827 5-8-9 **53** (t) LiamJones 10 49
(S Parr) *t.k.h: hld up towards rr: hdwy 3f out: rdn 2f out: wknd jst over 1f out* **7/2**[2]
410- **10** *1* **Capitalise (IRE)**[225] 2628 6-8-10 **61** KylieManser(7) 6 56
(Miss Gay Kelleway) *t.k.h: hld up towards rr: hdwy on outer over 3f out: rdn wl over 1f out: edgd lft and wknd ent fnl f* **16/1**
00-0 **11** *22* **Spiritonthemount (USA)**[9] 8 4-8-12 **61** (b) TGMcLaughlin 11 23
(P W Hiatt) *chsd ldrs tl rdn and lost pl over 5f out: t.o and eased fr over 1f out* **25/1**

2m 55.86s (2.26) **Going Correction** +0.15s/f (Slow)
WFA 4 from 5yo+ 5lb **11** Ran SP% **120.2**
Speed ratings (Par 101): **99,98,97,96,96 96,95,94,94,93 80**
toteswinger: 1&2 £8.60, 1&3 £3.90, 2&3 £10.70. CSF £37.35 CT £197.34 TOTE £3.40: £1.20, £3.80, £2.30; EX 39.80 Trifecta £153.10 Pool: £351.83 - 1.70 winning units..
Owner Tristar **Bred** Locsot S R L **Trained** Bronwydd Arms, Carmarthens
■ Stewards' Enquiry : Eddie Ahern caution: used whip down shoulder in forehand position.

FOCUS
A modest contest in which they went a fairly steady gallop until Shanafarahan took over at the front around seven furlongs out and picked up the pace.

127 SHANNON MAIDEN STKS 6f (P)
1:55 (2:01) (Class 5) 3-Y-0 **£2,590** (£770; £385; £192) **Stalls** Low

Form RPR
635- **1** **Green Onions**[14] 7802 3-8-12 68 GabrielHannon(5) 6 69
(D J S Ffrench Davis) *racd keenly: led after 1f: mde rest: rdn over 1f out: styd on wl* **14/1**
622- **2** *3/4* **Auld Arty (FR)**[25] 7700 3-9-3 77 ShaneKelly 1 67
(T G Mills) *led for 1f: chsd wnr: rdn over 2f out: drvn ent fnl f: nt qckn and hld by wnr fnl f* **8/13**[1]
6- **3** *1 1/4* **Dance And Dance (IRE)**[20] 7769 3-9-3 0 JamieSpencer 4 63
(E F Vaughan) *s.i.s: wl bhd: hdwy into modest 4th 2f out: clsd steadily after: wnt 3rd nr fin: nt rch ldng pair* **4/1**[2]
0- **4** *nk* **Theta Wave (USA)**[43] 7501 3-9-3 0 ChrisCatlin 7 62
(J R Gask) *chsd ldng pair: wl clr of remainder: rdn over 2f out: drvn and kpt on same pce fr over 1f out: lost 3rd nr line* **33/1**
400- **5** *3 1/4* **Quick Single (USA)**[44] 7472 3-9-3 67 StephenDonohoe 5 52
(D R C Elsworth) *sn outpcd in rr gp: rdn 4f out: kpt on fnl f but nvr trbld ldrs* **5/1**[3]
- **6** *1/2* **Chase End** 3-8-12 0 LukeMorris 2 45
(J M P Eustace) *s.i.s: rn green in rr: hung lft but sme hdwy fr over 1f out: nvr nr ldrs* **20/1**
0- **7** *24* **Cool Madam**[35] 7593 3-8-12 0 TonyCulhane 3 —
(D Flood) *a outpcd in rr gp: t.o fr wl over 1f out* **100/1**

1m 14.67s (0.97) **Going Correction** +0.15s/f (Slow) **7** Ran SP% **113.9**
Speed ratings (Par 97): **99,98,96,95,91 90,58**
toteswinger: 1&2 £2.50, 1&3 £3.10, 2&3 £1.20. CSF £23.43 TOTE £9.90: £2.50, £1.20; EX 30.80.
Owner Smart Racing Ltd **Bred** Lady Bland **Trained** Lambourn, Berks

FOCUS
A modest maiden run at a good gallop.
Cool Madam Official explanation: jockey said filly hung left throughout

128 REE H'CAP 6f (P)
2:30 (2:36) (Class 4) (0-85,84) 4-Y-0+ **£5,051** (£1,503; £751; £375) **Stalls** Low

Form RPR
21-2 **1** **Dvinsky (USA)**[9] 20 8-9-4 **84** (b) JimmyQuinn 5 92
(P Howling) *mde all: crossed to rail after 1f: rdn clr over 2f out: rdn out* **4/1**[2]
00-4 **2** *3/4* **Count Ceprano (IRE)**[9] 20 5-8-11 **77** LiamJones 1 83
(C R Dore) *chsd wnr for 1f: wnt 2nd again over 2f out: drvn and hung rt over 1f out: kpt on u.p fnl f* **14/1**
34-4 **3** *4 1/2* **Dressed To Dance (IRE)**[4] 70 5-8-13 **79** (v) StephenDonohoe 2 71
(P D Evans) *hld up wl in tch: stmbld wl over 3f out: outpcd over 2f out: drvn 2f out: kpt on to go 3rd ins fnl f: nvr threatened ldng pair* **18/1**
50-2 **4** *1/2* **First Order**[5] 67 8-8-9 **80** (v) AnnStokell(5) 8 70
(Miss A Stokell) *t.k.h: hld up in tch in rr: hdwy and rdn 3f out: chsd ldng pair u.p over 1f out: no imp: lost 3rd ins fnl f* **4/1**[2]
443- **5** *1 3/4* **Mogok Ruby**[44] 7466 5-8-9 **75** TGMcLaughlin 3 59
(L Montague Hall) *v.s.a: bhd: stl last whn hmpd over 3f out: sn rdn: swtchd ins wl over 1f out: nvr trbld ldrs* **10/1**

006- **6** 6 **Geoffdaw**13 7811 4-8-7 73 LukeMorris 4 38
(P D Evans) *chsd ldrs early: steadily lost pl: bhd fr 1/2-way* **8/1**3
000- **7** 1 **Falcolnry (IRE)**116 6027 4-8-11 77 JamieSpencer 6 39
(E F Vaughan) *chsd wnr after 1f tl over 2f out: rdn and c centre st: sn wknd* **11/8**1
1m 13.39s (-0.31) **Going Correction** +0.15s/f (Slow) 7 Ran SP% **114.2**
Speed ratings (Par 105): **108,107,101,100,98 90,88**
toteswinger: 1&2 £6.30, 1&3 £4.30, 2&3 £10.90. CSF £54.70 CT £897.78 TOTE £4.90: £1.90, £4.60; EX 36.80 Trifecta £125.00 Pool: £699.53 - 4.14 winning units..
Owner Richard Berenson **Bred** Eclipse Bloodstock & Tipperary Bloodstock **Trained** Newmarket, Suffolk
FOCUS
This had the look of a decent sprint handicap, though the pace was only steady. The huge gamble on Falconry went awry in a major way.

129 CORRIB (S) STKS 1m (P)
3:05 (3:10) (Class 5) 4-Y-0+ **£2,590** (£770; £385; £192) **Stalls** Centre

Form RPR
313- **1** **Singleb (IRE)**16 7780 5-9-3 65 (p) JamieSpencer 6 70
(Miss Gay Kelleway) *chsd ldr tl over 6f out: hld up in tch after: trcking ldrs but nt clr run wl over 1f out: gap opened ins fnl f and rdn to ld towards fin* **9/4**2
106- **2** ½ **Sotik Star (IRE)**12 7821 6-8-12 75 TonyCulhane 3 64
(K A Morgan) *s.i.s: t.k.h: hld up in rr: hdwy to chse ldng pair over 5f out: rdn to ld 1f out: drvn and hdd towards fin* **5/6**1
203- **3** 1¾ **Rowan Lodge (IRE)**36 7585 7-8-12 58 (b) ChrisCatlin 5 60
(Ollie Pears) *t.k.h: chsd ldr over 6f out: rdn to ld over 1f out: hdd 1f out: outpcd by ldng pair fnl 100yds* **12/1**
00-1 **4** ½ **Vogarth**7 37 5-9-3 59 (v) JimCrowley 4 64
(M C Chapman) *t.k.h: hld up in tch: rdn 2f out: kpt on same pce fnl f* **7/1**3
53-0 **5** ½ **Climate (IRE)**2 105 10-9-3 58 (p) StephenDonohoe 2 63
(P D Evans) *t.k.h: hld up in rr: swtchd rt and rdn wl over 1f out: no imp fnl f* **20/1**
/00- **6** 2½ **Simplified**32 7631 6-8-0 40 (t) AlexEdwards(7) 1 47?
(M C Chapman) *led: pushed along 3f out: rdn and hdd over 1f out: wknd ins fnl f* **100/1**
1m 42.0s (2.10) **Going Correction** +0.15s/f (Slow) 6 Ran SP% **111.3**
Speed ratings (Par 103): **95,94,92,92,91 89**
toteswinger: 1&2 £1.20, 1&3 £2.10, 2&3 £2.60. CSF £4.37 TOTE £3.30: £1.60, £1.50; EX 5.70.There was no bid for the winner.
Owner Mrs Donna Joslyn **Bred** Spratstown Stud Gm **Trained** Exning, Suffolk
FOCUS
An interesting claimer, featuring the class-dropping Sotik Star, who had 15lb in hand of his nearest rival on adjusted official ratings.

130 ALEEN H'CAP 1m (P)
3:35 (3:40) (Class 6) (0-52,52) 4-Y-0+ **£2,047** (£604; £302) **Stalls** Centre

Form RPR
560- **1** **Safebreaker**88 6729 4-8-9 **47** JamieSpencer 3 56
(K A Ryan) *trckd ldrs: rdn and ev ch over 1f out: drvn and hung rt after: led ins fnl f: hld on* **5/6**1
13-3 **2** hd **Tarkamara (IRE)**4 81 5-8-12 **50** JoeFanning 2 58
(P F I Cole) *t.k.h: hld up in midfield on inner: swtchd rt and effrt 2f out: drvn 1f out: str chal ins fnl f: hld nr fin* **9/4**2
40-0 **3** 1 **Very Well Red**10 7 6-8-9 **47** ChrisCatlin 7 53
(P W Hiatt) *chsd ldr: rdn to ld 2f out: drvn over 1f out: hdd ins fnl f: 3rd and hld whn short of room and snatched up nr fin* **11/1**
000- **4** 3½ **Takaamul**25 7706 6-9-0 **52** TonyCulhane 8 50
(K A Morgan) *t.k.h: trckd ldrs: rdn 2f out: keeping on same pce whn sltly hmpd ent fnl f: one pce after* **33/1**
005- **5** ½ **Aggbag**29 7663 5-8-6 **51** BillyCray(7) 4 48
(B P J Baugh) *t.k.h: hld up towards rr: rdn over 2f out: drvn and effrt wl over 1f out: no imp fnl f* **8/1**3
000- **6** 2½ **Asmodea**89 6716 4-8-11 **49** RichardKingscote 1 40
(B G Powell) *stdd s: t.k.h: hld up in last pl: rdn and effrt wl over 1f out: nvr pce to threaten ldrs* **20/1**
00-0 **7** 1 **Golden Square**6 43 7-8-9 **47** oh1 ow1 ShaneKelly 6 36
(A W Carroll) *sn pushed up to ld: rdn and hdd 2f out: wknd ent fnl f* **25/1**
200- **8** 8 **Hollywood George**22 7746 5-8-8 **49** (p) DuranFentiman(3) 5 19
(Miss M E Rowland) *hld up towards rr: rdn and short lived effrt on outer jst over 2f out: sn wl btn* **25/1**
1m 41.42s (1.52) **Going Correction** +0.15s/f (Slow) 8 Ran SP% **120.2**
Speed ratings (Par 101): **98,97,96,93,92 90,89,81**
toteswinger: 1&2 £1.50, 1&3 £3.40, 2&3 £2.70. CSF £2.88 CT £11.43 TOTE £1.80: £1.10, £1.20, £2.00; EX 4.50 Trifecta £37.50 Pool: £668.04 - 13.16 winning units..
Owner Hambleton Racing Ltd X **Bred** Gainsborough Stud Management Ltd **Trained** Hambleton, N Yorks
FOCUS
This was not much of a race.

131 GARA CLASSIFIED STKS 1m (P)
4:05 (4:10) (Class 7) 3-Y-0+ **£1,706** (£503; £252) **Stalls** Centre

Form RPR
00-6 **1** **Kinsman (IRE)**6 43 12-9-1 44 (p) AmyBaker(5) 2 51
(T D McCarthy) *stdd s: t.k.h: hld up in rr: rdn and prog over 2f out: gd hdwy over 1f out: drvn to ld ins fnl f: r.o wl* **16/1**
000- **2** 1¼ **Bad Moon Rising**20 7765 4-9-6 45 (p) JoeFanning 9 48
(J Akehurst) *t.k.h: chsd ldrs: rdn and ev ch over 1f out: led ent fnl f: hdd and no ex ins fnl f* **16/1**
0-05 **3** 1 **Beckenham's Secret**6 42 5-9-6 42 ShaneKelly 8 46
(A W Carroll) *t.k.h: chsd ldrs: swtchd rt and drvn wl over 1f out: sn ev ch: no ex fnl 100yds* **11/1**
06-1 **4** ½ **Samson Quest**6 43 7-9-12 45 JimCrowley 12 51
(B Smart) *hld up in tch in midfield: hdwy over 2f out: hrd rdn and ev ch ent fnl f: wknd fnl 100yds* **9/4**2
030- **5** ¾ **The Power Of Phil**245 930 5-9-6 42 RichardKingscote 6 43
(Tom Dascombe) *dwlt: hld up in rr: hdwy on outer wl over 2f out: edgd lft u.p fr over 1f out: r.o but nvr rchd ldrs* **15/8**1
00-3 **6** 1 **Dynamo Dave (USA)**6 43 4-9-6 43 IanMongan 7 41
(M D I Usher) *hld up bhd: rdn 3f out: carried lft fr over 1f out: r.o u.str.p: nvr rchd ldrs* **9/1**3
/30- **7** ¾ **Riviera Red (IRE)**352 299 9-9-6 45 (b1) TGMcLaughlin 1 39
(L Montague Hall) *stdd s: t.k.h: hld up in rr: rdn over 2f out: styd on fnl f: nvr trbld ldrs* **20/1**
600- **8** nk **Veronicas Way**13 7815 4-9-1 39 (v1) GabrielHannon(5) 3 38
(G J Smith) *t.k.h: in tch: rdn wl over 1f out: wknd fnl f* **80/1**

05-5 **9** ½ **Ma Ridge**6 43 5-9-6 45 LiamJones 10 37
(T D McCarthy) *t.k.h: chsd ldr: rdn to ld wl over 1f out: hrd rdn and hdd ent fnl f: wknd fnl f* **16/1**
/00- **10** 1 **Sahara Prince (IRE)**13 7815 9-9-6 39 (p) TonyCulhane 11 35
(K A Morgan) *racd keenly: sn led: rdn and hdd wl over 1f out: stil ev ch ent fnl f: wknd fnl f* **20/1**
000- **11** 3½ **Finished Article (IRE)**40 7520 12-9-6 42 JimmyQuinn 4 27
(Mrs D Thomas) *racd in midfield: rdn wl over 3f out: struggling over 2f out: no ch fnl 2f* **20/1**
050/ **12** 25 **Bayberry King (USA)**52 3375 6-9-6 44 ChrisCatlin 5 —
(Mrs A M Thorpe) *stdd after s: hld up towards rr: rdn and struggling 3f out: t.o and eased fnl f* **16/1**
1m 42.32s (2.42) **Going Correction** +0.15s/f (Slow) 12 Ran SP% **122.9**
Speed ratings (Par 97): **93,91,90,90,89 88,87,87,86,85 82,57**
toteswinger: 1&2 £33.70, 1&3 £25.40, 2&3 £29.80. CSF £243.37 TOTE £21.20: £3.80, £5.10, £3.00; EX 217.90 TRIFECTA Not won..
Owner Exors of the late W Weeding **Bred** Elsdon Farms **Trained** Godstone, Surrey
FOCUS
A poor race but a pleasing return to winning form for old favourite Kinsman.

132 DERRAVARAGH APPRENTICE H'CAP 1m 2f (P)
4:35 (4:40) (Class 6) (0-60,65) 4-Y-0+ **£1,942** (£578; £288; £144) **Stalls** Low

Form RPR
003- **1** **Samurai Warrior**14 7801 4-9-0 **55** DeanHeslop 10 63
(P D Evans) *chsd clr ldrs 8f out: clsd over 4f out: wnt 2nd over 3f out: ev ch and drvn over 1f out: led 1f out: kpt on wl* **7/1**
004- **2** ½ **Broughtons Flight (IRE)**24 7725 4-8-11 **55** DebraEngland(3) 6 62
(W J Musson) *racd off the pce in midfield: hdwy 5f out: wnt 3rd over 2f out: ev ch and drvn ent fnl f: unable qck fnl 100yds* **16/1**
62-1 **3** 1¾ **Bavarica**8 28 7-9-7 **65** TobyAtkinson(5) 8 69+
(Miss J Feilden) *stdd s: hld up in rr: hdwy over 2f out: 7th and rdn wl over 1f out: r.o to go 3rd wl ins fnl f: nt rch ldrs* **11/4**2
060- **4** 1½ **Bespoke Boy**14 7276 4-9-5 **60** (t) DeclanCannon 7 61
(P C Haslam) *t.k.h: hld up off the pce in midfield: hdwy over 4f out: chsd ldrs and drvn over 1f out: kpt on same pce fnl f* **20/1**
000/ **5** 2¼ **Rough Sketch (USA)**457 6139 4-9-0 **55** RosieJessop 9 51+
(Sir Mark Prescott) *led tl hdd 8f out: sn clr w ldr: led again over 5f out: rdn jst over 2f out: hdd 1f out: wknd fnl f* **15/8**1
/04- **6** 4 **Gizmondo**14 7800 6-9-6 **59** (b1) JemmaMarshall 4 47
(G L Moore) *stdd s: hld up bhd: hdwy 4f out: rdn over 2f out: drvn and no prog wl over 1f out* **9/2**3
000- **7** 3¼ **Bobering**33 7613 9-8-7 **46** oh1 BillyCray 3 28
(B P J Baugh) *hld up wl in rr: rdn 5f out: nvr trbld ldrs* **33/1**
66-0 **8** 1¾ **Silver Spruce**2 100 4-7-13 **47** (be) MarieLequarre(7) 5 25
(D Flood) *chsd ldr tl led 8f out: sn clr w rival: hdd over 5f out: lost 2nd over 3f out: wknd over 2f out* **25/1**
600- **9** 1 **Galley Slave (IRE)**41 3551 4-8-1 **47** AlexEdwards(5) 2 23
(M C Chapman) *prom in main gp tl 5f out: wl bhd fnl 2f* **33/1**
00-0 **10** 10 **Space Pirate**2 100 4-8-5 **46** (v) BMcHugh 1 2
(J Pearce) *a wl bhd: rdn and no rspnse 3f out* **10/1**
2m 7.90s (-0.70) **Going Correction** +0.15s/f (Slow)
WFA 4 from 6yo+ 2lb 10 Ran SP% **121.6**
Speed ratings (Par 101): **108,107,106,105,103 100,97,96,95,87**
toteswinger: 1&2 £8.10, 1&3 £4.70, 2&3 £8.50. CSF £107.88 CT £385.04 TOTE £9.10: £2.50, £5.60, £1.30; EX 69.40 Trifecta £598.90 Part won. Place 6: £107.38 Place 5: £44.16..
Owner Mrs I M Folkes **Bred** Lady Lonsdale **Trained** Pandy, Monmouths
FOCUS
This was not much of a contest, but fairly competitive all the same.
Bobering Official explanation: jockey said gelding was denied a clear run
Space Pirate Official explanation: jockey said colt never travelled
T/Jkpt: Not won. T/Plt: £218.20 to a £1 stake. Pool: £108,703.13. 363.55 winning tickets. T/Qpdt: £100.70 to a £1 stake. Pool: £7,731.13. 56.80 winning tickets. SP

104WOLVERHAMPTON (A.W) (L-H)
Monday, January 12

OFFICIAL GOING: Standard
Wind: Almost nil Weather: Raining

133 WOLVERHAMPTON-RACECOURSE.CO.UK CLAIMING STKS 7f 32y(P)
2:10 (2:10) (Class 6) 4-Y-0+ **£2,047** (£604; £302) **Stalls** Low

Form RPR
54-4 **1** **Silver Wind**3 106 4-9-7 78 (v) RobertWinston 4 75
(P D Evans) *a.p: rdn over 1f out: led ins fnl f: r.o* **11/4**2
52-0 **2** nse **Kabis Amigos**3 97 7-8-9 49 (b) GregFairley 6 63
(S T Mason) *s.i.s: hld up towards rr: hdwy whn nt clr run over 2f out: nt clr run and swtchd lft 1f out: ev ch wl ins fnl f: r.o* **22/1**
22-1 **3** hd **Desert Dreamer (IRE)**5 70 8-8-13 77 RichardKingscote 5 66
(Tom Dascombe) *hld up in mid-div: hdwy 2f out: rdn over 1f out: ev ch wl ins fnl f: r.o* **4/5**1
066- **4** 1¾ **Imprimis Tagula (IRE)**33 7633 5-8-13 75 BACurtis(5) 8 66
(A Bailey) *hld up in mid-div: hdwy on outside 2f out: c wd st: rdn ins fnl f: kpt on to take 4th last strides* **16/1**
341- **5** hd **Dancing Deano (IRE)**17 7780 7-8-8 65 RussellKennemore(3) 7 59
(R Hollinshead) *sn chsng ldr: led over 2f out: rdn wl over 1f out: hdd ins fnl f: no ex towards fin* **8/1**3
00-0 **6** 2½ **Dasheena**3 108 6-8-4 48 (p) LukeMorris 1 45
(A J McCabe) *prom: pushed along over 3f out: nt clr run briefly on ins jst over 2f out: rdn over 1f out: wknd ins fnl f* **33/1**
300- **7** 9 **Flagstone (USA)**56 7368 5-8-13 53 StephenDonohoe 2 30
(Ian Williams) *a in rr* **66/1**
300- **8** nk **Bungie**17 7782 5-8-9 44 (b) JimmyQuinn 9 25
(Jennie Candlish) *rdr slow to remove blindfold and s.s: a in rr* **300/1**
006- **9** 1¼ **Jimmy Dean**17 7780 4-8-11 44 (tp) PaulFitzsimons 3 24
(M Wellings) *led: rdn and hdd over 2f out: wknd over 1f out* **250/1**
1m 29.39s (-0.21) **Going Correction** 0.0s/f (Stan) 9 Ran SP% **108.7**
Speed ratings (Par 101): **101,100,100,98,98 95,85,85,83**
toteswinger: 1&2 £6.30, 1&3 £1.80, 2&3 £4.40. CSF £53.79 TOTE £2.90: £1.30, £4.50, £1.02; EX 52.20 Trifecta £162.60 Pool: £718.54 - 3.27 winning units..
Owner Silver Wind Partnership **Bred** W H R John And Partners **Trained** Pandy, Monmouths
FOCUS
A reasonable claimer on paper, but an ordinary early pace resulted in a bunch finish. Tricky form to pin down and probably not that strong.

Bungie Official explanation: jockey said he was unable to remove the blinds quickly

134 WILLIAM HILL JANUARY SALE - NOW ON! H'CAP 1m 1f 103y(P)
2:40 (2:40) (Class 6) (0-60,60) 3-Y-O £2,047 (£604; £302) Stalls Low

Form RPR
00-4 1 **Sicilian Warrior (USA)**[10] 16 3-9-4 60.....(t) JoeFanning 4 66+
(P F I Cole) hld up and bhd: hdwy on outside over 3f out: carried rt wl over 1f out: led ins fnl f: r.o wl 7/1[3]
325- 2 2 ½ **Precocious Air (IRE)**[21] 7760 3-9-4 60..... ShaneKelly 7 61
(J A Osborne) sn led: clr over 2f out: hung rt wl over 1f out: hdd and no ex ins fnl f 7/1[3]
003- 3 ¾ **Miss Cameo (USA)**[27] 7693 3-7-13 48..... DeclanCannon(7) 3 47
(R M Whitaker) t.k.h in tch: n.m.r wl over 2f out: edgd rt fr wl over 1f out: sn rdn: kpt on one pce ins fnl f 17/2
060- 4 1 **In Step**[30] 7659 3-8-12 54..... LiamJones 6 51
(W J Haggas) hld up towards rr: carried rt over 2f out: hdwy on ins wl over 1f out: sn hung rt: hung bdly rt ins fnl f: nvr able to chal 9/1
13-5 5 2 ¾ **Autumn Morning (IRE)**[5] 77 3-9-3 59..... StephenDonohoe 1 51
(P D Evans) t.k.h in mid-div: hdwy wl over 1f out: wknd ins fnl f 2/1[1]
50-0 6 ½ **Vien (IRE)**[5] 77 3-8-12 54..... PatDobbs 8 45
(R Hannon) prom: rdn over 2f out: wknd wl over 1f out 7/1[3]
000- 7 hd **Rebelwithoutacause (IRE)**[24] 7728 3-8-8 50.....(p) ChrisCatlin 9 40
(George Baker) sn chsng ldr: lost 2nd over 2f out: wknd wl over 1f out 50/1
04-6 8 1 ¼ **Inca Slew (IRE)**[5] 77 3-8-8 55.....(v[1]) PatrickDonaghy(5) 11 42
(P C Haslam) s.i.s: pushed along over 3f out: a bhd 14/1
00-5 9 1 ½ **Talsarnau (IRE)**[10] 16 3-8-12 54..... PatCosgrave 10 38
(W M Brisbourne) hld up in mid-div: rdn over 3f out: wknd over 2f out 33/1
000- 10 41 **Red Eric**[13] 7824 3-8-4 46 oh1..... PaulQuinn 2 —
(W M Brisbourne) prom: pushed along over 3f out: wkng whn bdly hmpd wl over 2f out: eased wl over 1f out 100/1
330- 11 48 **Josiah Bartlett (IRE)**[30] 7666 3-9-2 58..... JamieSpencer 5 —
(J W Hills) hld up and bhd: sme prog on ins whn bdly hmpd over 3f out: sn eased: virtually p.u over 2f out 5/1[2]

2m 3.88s (2.18) **Going Correction** 0.0s/f (Stan) 11 Ran SP% 120.6
Speed ratings (Par 95): **90,87,87,86,83 83,83,82,80,44 1**
toteswinger: 1&2 £7.00, 1&3 £10.70, 2&3 £5.90. CSF £56.44 CT £431.20 TOTE £6.80: £2.60, £2.10, £2.30; EX 42.50 Trifecta £336.50 Part won. Pool: £454.86 - 0.45 winning units..
Owner C Shiacolas **Bred** Claude Schoch **Trained** Whatcombe, Oxon
■ Stewards' Enquiry : Declan Cannon ten-day ban: careless riding (Jan 26-Feb 4)

FOCUS
A very moderate three-year-old handicap. The runner-up is the best guide and the winner showed improvement. They went a pretty steady pace.

135 HOTEL & CONFERENCING AT WOLVERHAMPTON H'CAP 5f 216y(P)
3:10 (3:11) (Class 6) (0-55,55) 3-Y-O £2,047 (£604; £302) Stalls Low

Form RPR
025- 1 **Forever's Girl**[16] 7794 3-8-9 53..... DuranFentiman(3) 9 66
(G R Oldroyd) mde all: clr over 2f out: rdn fnl f: r.o 9/2[2]
33-1 2 2 ¼ **Kheley (IRE)**[5] 75 3-8-7 53..... DeanHeslop(5) 3 59
(W M Brisbourne) hld up in tch: rdn wl over 1f out: wnt 2nd ins fnl f: nt trble wnr 5/1[3]
040- 3 7 **Mean Mr Mustard (IRE)**[158] 4768 3-8-13 54..... ShaneKelly 7 38
(J A Osborne) in tch: lost pl over 4f out: hdwy over 1f out: lft 3rd ins fnl f 14/1
005- 4 ½ **Kina Jazz**[32] 7638 3-8-11 52..... TonyCulhane 6 34
(M E Rimmer) hld up in rr: c wd st: hdwy over 1f out: no real prog fnl f 20/1
043- 5 2 ¼ **Itsher**[12] 7832 3-9-0 55..... JamieSpencer 1 54+
(S C Williams) chsd wnr 1f and again over 3f out: hung bdly lft fr over 2f out: sn btn: eased and lost 3 pls ins fnl f 13/8[1]
056- 6 1 ½ **Lady Norlela**[81] 6923 3-8-7 48..... ChrisCatlin 5 18
(R Hannon) a bhd 10/1
000- 7 1 ½ **Multi Tasker**[51] 7415 3-9-0 55..... PaulFitzsimons 8 20
(Miss J R Tooth) chsd wnr after 1f tl reminders over 3f out: rdn and wknd over 2f out 18/1
600- 8 9 **Downstream**[39] 7546 3-8-13 54.....(t) StephenDonohoe 2 —
(D M Simcock) a bhd 7/1
5 9 16 **Royal Mischief (IRE)**[5] 69 3-8-9 50..... RobertWinston 4 —
(P D Evans) prom tl wknd over 3f out 40/1

1m 15.61s (0.61) **Going Correction** 0.0s/f (Stan) 9 Ran SP% 113.7
Speed ratings (Par 95): **95,92,82,82,79 77,75,63,41**
toteswinger: 1&2 £3.40, 1&3 £7.80, 2&3 £6.40. CSF £26.80 CT £289.20 TOTE £5.30: £1.60, £1.60, £3.40; EX 24.80 Trifecta £249.30 Pool: £619.95 - 1.84 winning units..
Owner R C Bond **Bred** R C Bond **Trained** Brawby, N Yorks
■ Stewards' Enquiry : Paul Fitzsimons one-day ban: careless riding (Jan 26)

FOCUS
Little better than a seller and the race was over by around halfway as Forever's Girl had built up a clear advantage and never looked like being caught. Only the first two showed their form.
Itsher Official explanation: jockey said filly hung badly left and he was unable to ride it out
Royal Mischief(IRE) Official explanation: jockey said filly moved poorly throughout

136 SPONSOR A RACE BY CALLING 01902 390009 CLAIMING STKS 1m 141y(P)
3:40 (3:40) (Class 6) 3-Y-O £2,047 (£604; £302) Stalls Low

Form RPR
162- 1 **Double Act**[17] 7784 3-9-9 79.....(t) ShaneKelly 5 78
(J Noseda) hld up in rr: hdwy on outside wl over 1f out: sn rdn: edgd lft wl ins fnl f: r.o to ld last strides 11/10[1]
501- 2 shd **Mullitovermaurice**[13] 7824 3-8-7 61..... ChrisCatlin 3 62
(J G Given) a.p: led 1f out: rdn and hdd last strides 17/2
004- 3 ½ **Common Diva**[13] 7824 3-8-6 63..... JimmyQuinn 4 60
(A J McCabe) wnt rt s: hld up: hdwy over 2f out: rdn and r.o ins fnl f 18/1
4-13 4 ½ **Hold The Bucks (USA)**[5] 74 3-9-3 67..... LukeMorris 2 70
(J S Moore) hld up and bhd: rdn over 3f out: hdwy over 1f out: nt qckn cl home 3/1[2]
0-24 5 6 **Turn To Dreams**[5] 77 3-8-4 57 ow2..... LiamJones 7 43
(P D Evans) wnt lft s: sn led: rdn and hdd 1f out: wknd ins fnl f 20/1
03- 6 ¾ **Mytivil (IRE)**[13] 7823 3-8-12 0..... RichardKingscote 1 49
(Tom Dascombe) led early: hld up in tch: rdn wl over 1f out: wknd fnl f 7/1[3]
02-6 7 13 **Betws Y Coed (IRE)**[5] 77 3-7-12 55.....(p) NickyMackay 6 5
(A Bailey) hmpd s: hdwy to chse ldr over 6f out: rdn and lost 2nd wl over 2f out: sn wknd 11/1

1m 51.01s (0.51) **Going Correction** 0.0s/f (Stan) 7 Ran SP% 114.0
Speed ratings (Par 95): **97,96,96,96,90 90,78**
toteswinger: 1&2 £2.80, 1&3 £5.50, 2&3 £9.00. CSF £11.56 TOTE £2.10: £1.10, £3.70; EX 12.30.Mullitovermaurice was subject to a friendly claim.
Owner Highclere Thoroughbred Racing (VC2) **Bred** Cheveley Park Stud Ltd **Trained** Newmarket, Suffolk

FOCUS
An ordinary three-year-old claimer and, despite the pace appearing sound, the first four finished in a heap. The form is sound enough.

137 WILLIAM HILL JANUARY SALE - BETTER ODDS! H'CAP 1m 141y(P)
4:10 (4:10) (Class 5) (0-75,75) 3-Y-O £2,729 (£806; £403) Stalls Low

Form RPR
351- 1 **Petrovsky**[26] 7699 3-9-4 75..... GregFairley 2 78+
(M Johnston) led after 1f: edgd rt wl over 1f out: sn hdd: rdn to ld ins fnl f: r.o 2/5[1]
021- 2 ¾ **Luckier (IRE)**[26] 7708 3-9-3 74..... JamieSpencer 3 75
(S Kirk) led 1f: a.p: edgd lft and led over 1f out: rdn and hdd ins fnl f: nt qckn 5/2[2]
440- 3 8 **Helpmeronda**[76] 7052 3-8-5 62..... ChrisCatlin 4 45
(S A Callaghan) chsd ldr: lost 2nd 2f out: sn wknd 33/1
346- 4 1 **Inthawain**[86] 6809 3-8-8 65..... DuranFentiman(3) 1 46
(N Wilson) hld up in last: pushed along and hdwy over 2f out: wknd over 1f out 28/1[3]

1m 53.79s (3.29) **Going Correction** 0.0s/f (Stan) 4 Ran SP% 106.4
Speed ratings (Par 97): **85,84,77,76**
CSF £1.57 TOTE £1.50; EX 1.50.
Owner Sheikh Hamdan Bin Mohammed Al Maktoum **Bred** Gainsborough Stud Management Ltd **Trained** Middleham Moor, N Yorks

FOCUS
Basically a two-horse race, run at a slow pace. Petrovsky is better than he showed and is sure to rate higher.

138 WOLVERHAMPTON-RACECOURSE.CO.UK MAIDEN STKS 1m 1f 103y(P)
4:40 (4:40) (Class 5) 3-Y-O £2,729 (£806; £403) Stalls Low

Form RPR
05- 1 **Tinshu (IRE)**[20] 7773 3-8-12 0..... PatCosgrave 9 71
(D Haydn Jones) t.k.h: w ldrs: led 3f out: rdn clr wl over 1f out: drvn out 33/1
53-2 2 1 **Barwell Bridge**[3] 101 3-9-3 77..... JamieSpencer 5 74+
(S Kirk) led over 1f: prom: swtchd rt over 2f out: sn rdn: pushed wd ent st: wnt 2nd 1f out: edgd lft ins fnl f: nt rch wnr 4/6[1]
0- 3 5 **Green Passion (USA)**[170] 4415 3-9-3 0..... JoeFanning 7 63
(M Johnston) awkward s: sn prom: rdn and one pce fnl 2f 8/1[3]
5- 4 ¾ **Spartan Prince (USA)**[31] 7649 3-9-3 0..... RobertWinston 1 62+
(T D Barron) prom early: stdd into mid-div 7f out: rn green over 1f out: edgd lft ins fnl f: tk 4th towards fin 28/1
4- 5 ½ **Key Of Fortune (IRE)**[17] 7781 3-8-12 0..... JimmyQuinn 2 56
(Jennie Candlish) hld up towards rr: short-lived effrt wl over 1f out 150/1
3- 6 1 **Misyaar (IRE)**[26] 7708 3-8-12 0..... ShaneKelly 6 54
(M A Jarvis) prom: chsd wnr wl over 1f out: wknd ins fnl f 2/1[2]
00- 7 6 **Spruzzo**[69] 7172 3-9-3 0..... FergusSweeney 3 46
(C W Thornton) hld up and bhd: rdn over 2f out: sn struggling 200/1
3- 8 2 ½ **Fire Me Gun**[17] 7781 3-8-12 0..... LiamJones 10 36
(M Mullineaux) reminders over 7f out: a in rr 50/1
0- 9 2 ½ **Tiffany Lady**[26] 7699 3-8-7 0..... GabrielHannon(5) 4 31
(M D I Usher) t.k.h in mid-div: wknd over 2f out 200/1
4- 10 nk **Aliybee (IRE)**[24] 7726 3-8-12 0..... ChrisCatlin 8 30
(E J O'Neill) led 7f out to 3f out: wknd 2f out 33/1

2m 1.95s (0.25) **Going Correction** 0.0s/f (Stan) 10 Ran SP% 117.4
Speed ratings (Par 97): **98,97,92,92,91 90,85,83,80,80**
toteswinger: 1&2 £6.20,1&3 £13.20, 2&3 £3.90. CSF £56.86 TOTE £22.70: £4.70, £1.02, £2.40; EX 103.00 Trifecta £623.10 Part won. Pool: £842.09 - 0.65 winning units..
Owner Llewelyn, Runeckles **Bred** Mrs M L Parry & P Steele-Mortimer **Trained** Efail Isaf, Rhondda C Taff

FOCUS
An ordinary maiden run at a modest pace. Not easy form to pin down, with the fifth perhaps the best long-term guide.
Fire Me Gun Official explanation: jockey said filly never travelled

139 WILLIAM HILL JANUARY SALE - WHY BET ELSEWHERE? H'CAP 1m 4f 50y(P)
5:10 (5:10) (Class 5) (0-75,74) 4-Y-O+ £2,729 (£806; £403) Stalls Low

Form RPR
65-1 1 **El Diego (IRE)**[10] 11 5-9-4 72..... ChrisCatlin 3 79
(J R Gask) a.p: rdn to ld ins fnl f: r.o 11/2
103- 2 nk **Long Distance (FR)**[26] 7711 4-9-1 73.....(v[1]) JamieSpencer 1 79
(J R Fanshawe) hld up in mid-div: hdwy on ins over 2f out: sn rdn: ev ch ins fnl f: r.o 4/1[2]
500- 3 nk **River Ardeche**[15] 4682 4-9-0 72..... LeeEnstone 7 78
(P C Haslam) led 1f: chsd ldr: led over 3f out: rdn 2f out: hdd ins fnl f: nt qckn towards fin 66/1
0/2- 4 1 ¾ **Mr Aitch (IRE)**[25] 7722 7-9-5 73.....(t) JoeFanning 6 76
(R T Phillips) hld up in rr: hdwy on outside over 3f out: rdn over 1f out: kpt on same pce 16/1
/05- 5 ½ **Leslingtaylor (IRE)**[30] 5199 7-9-3 71..... GrahamGibbons 8 73
(J J Quinn) a.p: rdn over 1f out: one pce 5/1[3]
441- 6 nse **Mission Control (IRE)**[21] 7761 4-8-13 71..... PatCosgrave 10 73+
(J R Boyle) hld up in mid-div: rdn over 2f out: styd on towards fin: nt rch ldrs 3/1[1]
365- 7 4 ½ **Josh You Are**[190] 3756 6-9-2 70..... StephenDonohoe 9 65
(Ian Williams) hld up in rr: short-lived effrt on ins wl over 1f out 20/1
134- 8 ½ **Karmest**[16] 7797 5-8-12 71..... PatrickDonaghy(5) 11 65
(A D Brown) s.i.s: sn swtchd lft: a towards rr 33/1
512- 9 19 **Man Of Gwent (UAE)**[17] 7786 5-9-4 72..... RobertWinston 12 36
(P D Evans) led after 1f: hdd over 3f out: wknd 2f out 7/1
330- 10 4 ½ **Graylyn Ruby (FR)**[25] 7715 4-9-2 74..... LukeMorris 5 31
(J Jay) prom: rdn over 3f out: wknd over 2f out 15/2
206/ 11 1 ½ **Five A Side**[95] 5623 5-9-6 74..... FergusSweeney 4 28
(Evan Williams) hld up in mid-div: bhd fnl 3f 20/1

2m 39.64s (-1.46) **Going Correction** 0.0s/f (Stan)
WFA 4 from 5yo+ 4lb 11 Ran SP% 121.2
Speed ratings (Par 103): **104,103,103,102,102 102,99,98,86,83 82**
toteswinger: 1&2 £5.30, 1&3 £78.80, 2&3 £38.00. CSF £27.54 CT £1338.21 TOTE £7.40: £3.00, £1.20, £16.40; EX 37.60 TRIFECTA Not won..

Owner Horses First Racing Limited **Bred** Tower Bloodstock **Trained** Sutton Veny, Wilts

FOCUS
A modest but competitive handicap which was steadily run. The form makes sense rated around the first two and the fourth and fifth.

T/Jkpt: Not won. T/Plt: £25.50 to a £1 stake. Pool: £84,708.97. 2,417.20 winning tickets. T/Qpdt: £9.40 to a £1 stake. Pool: £4,763.00. 374.50 winning tickets. KH

126 GREAT LEIGHS (A.W) (L-H)

Tuesday, January 13

OFFICIAL GOING: Standard
Wind: modest, behind Weather: dry, partly cloudy

140 ROSE H'CAP — 5f (P)
2:10 (2:10) (Class 5) (0-75,74) 3-Y-O — **£1,680** (£1,680; £385; £192) **Stalls** Low

Form — RPR
063- **1** **Lady Vivien**[16] [7802] 3-8-4 **60** .... ChrisCatlin 3 — 62
(D H Brown) *chsd ldr: rdn over 2f out: ev ch fr over 1f out: drvn to ld ins fnl f: jnd on line* **9/2**[3]
214- **1** *dht* **Desert Strike**[14] [7820] 3-9-4 **74** .... JamieSpencer 1 — 79+
(P F I Cole) *stdd s: t.k.h: sn trcking ldrs: nt clr run fr wl over 1f out tl ins fnl f: rdn and str chal fnl 100yds: jnd rival on post* **11/10**[1]
123- **3** *1 3/4* **Deckchair**[13] [7833] 3-7-13 **60** oh3 ....(v) AmyBaker(5) 4 — 56
(H J Collingridge) *s.i.s: racd in last pl: nt clr run on rail and grad swtchd rt fr over 1f out: r.o ins fnl f: wnt 3rd nr fin* **9/1**
000- **4** *hd* **Ruby Tallulah**[38] [7575] 3-9-1 **71** .... IanMongan 6 — 66
(C R Dore) *dropped in bhd after s: hld up in last pair: effrt and rdn 2f out: hrd drvn and ev ch ins fnl f: wknd fnl 75yds* **16/1**
105- **5** *3 1/4* **The Cuckoo**[14] [7825] 3-9-1 **71** .... PatCosgrave 2 — 55
(M Quinn) *led: rdn over 1f out: drvn and hdd ins fnl f: sn wknd* **9/1**
22-3 **6** *2 1/2* **Abu Derby (IRE)**[12] [4] 3-9-2 **72** .... TPQueally 5 — 47
(J G Given) *chsd ldrs: rdn jst over 2f out: wknd fnl f* **7/2**[2]

60.68 secs (0.48) **Going Correction** +0.075s/f (Slow) **6 Ran SP% 113.9**
Speed ratings (Par 97): **99,99,97,97,91 87**
Win: Desert Strike: £1.10; Lady Viven: £2.40; Places: DS £1.60, LV £1.90; Exacta: DS & LV £4.90, LV & DS £3.20; CSF DS & LV £3.31 LV & DS £5.09; toteswinger: DS&LV £2.20, DS&3 £2.30, LV&3 £5.00..
Owner P F I Cole Ltd **Bred** Mrs Mary Rowlands **Trained** Whatcombe, Oxon
Owner Ron Hull **Bred** Wheelers Land Stud **Trained** Maltby, S Yorks
■ Stewards' Enquiry : Chris Catlin caution: using his whip down the shoulder in the forehand position

FOCUS
A modest handicap which produced a dead-heat. Desert Strike looked unlucky not to win outright and Lady Vivien is rated up 7lb, but this is not strong form.

141 WELLS H'CAP — 6f (P)
2:40 (2:40) (Class 5) (0-75,75) 4-Y-O+ — **£2,590** (£770; £385; £192) **Stalls** Low

Form — RPR
611- **1** **Milne Bay (IRE)**[32] [7653] 4-8-5 **62** ....(t) JimmyQuinn 1 — 79
(D M Simcock) *mde all: rdn and clr wnt clr over 1f out: in n.d fnl f: eased towards fin* **10/11**[1]
065- **2** *5* **Elusive Hawk (IRE)**[49] [7448] 5-9-0 **71** .... TPQueally 3 — 73
(A P Stringer) *awkward s and s.i.s: sn in tch: rdn over 2f out: outpcd by wnr over 1f out: chsd wnr vainly ent fnl f* **14/1**
22-0 **3** *1 1/2* **Sendreni (FR)**[10] [31] 5-8-13 **70** .... FrancisNorton 2 — 67
(M Wigham) *chsd wnr: rdn and outpcd over 1f out: no ch w wnr after and lost 2nd ent fnl f* **2/1**[2]
04-5 **4** *1 3/4* **Distinctly Game**[11] [20] 7-9-4 **75** .... JamieSpencer 5 — 67
(K A Ryan) *t.k.h: hld up in tch: c centre and rdn 2f out: sn wl outpcd: no ch after* **13/2**[3]
065- **5** *3/4* **Memphis Man**[14] [7828] 6-8-12 **74** .... PatrickDonaghy(5) 4 — 63
(P D Evans) *awkward leaving stalls and slowly away: sn in tch in rr: swtchd rt 5f out: rdn and struggling 2f out: wl btn after* **16/1**

1m 13.12s (-0.58) **Going Correction** +0.075s/f (Slow) **5 Ran SP% 111.6**
Speed ratings (Par 103): **106,99,97,95,94**
CSF £14.46 TOTE £1.90: £1.10, £4.90; EX 15.60.
Owner DXB Bloodstock Ltd **Bred** Michael Boland **Trained** Newmarket, Suffolk

FOCUS
An uncompetitive sprint handicap. The winner is progressive but the main danger clearly did not run his race. The form has been rated at something like face value.

142 WALSHAM LE WILLOWS H'CAP — 1m 6f (P)
3:10 (3:10) (Class 4) (0-85,85) 4-Y-O+ — **£5,051** (£1,503; £751; £375) **Stalls** Low

Form — RPR
014- **1** **Nobelix (IRE)**[32] [7657] 7-9-7 **78** .... TPQueally 5 — 85
(J R Gask) *racd keenly: mostly chsd ldr: led on bit wl over 1f out: rdn and kpt on wl fnl f* **7/1**
51-6 **2** *3/4* **Clear Reef**[6] [82] 5-9-11 **82** .... JamieSpencer 3 — 88
(Jane Chapple-Hyam) *stdd s: hld up in last pl: hdwy over 2f out: c centre and rdn 2f out: edging lft after: r.o to snatch 2nd on line: nvr gng to rch wnr* **7/2**[2]
233- **3** *shd* **Baan (USA)**[26] [7715] 6-8-7 **64** .... JimmyQuinn 1 — 70
(H J Collingridge) *hld up in last trio: hdwy to chse ldng pair over 2f out: rdn 2f out: chsd wnr ent fnl f: no imp: lost 2nd on post* **4/1**[3]
541- **4** *2 1/4* **Taikoo**[31] [7664] 4-9-8 **85** .... ChrisCatlin 6 — 88
(H Morrison) *chsd ldrs tl hdwy to ld after 2f: rdn over 2f out: hdd over 1f out: drvn ent fnl f: one pce fnl 100yds* **7/2**[2]
01-1 **5** *6* **Benedict Spirit (IRE)**[7] [65] 4-8-0 **70** .... AshleyMorgan(7) 7 — 64
(M H Tompkins) *stdd s: hld up in midfield: rdn and unable qck over 2f out: no ch fnl f* **3/1**[1]
300/ **6** *1 3/4* **Arctic Wings (IRE)**[18] [6145] 5-8-6 **63** oh2 .... LukeMorris 2 — 55
(A W Carroll) *stdd s: hld up in last pair: clsd over 4f out: rdn over 2f out: wl btn wl over 1f out* **7/1**
516- **7** *3/4* **Mistress Eva**[27] [6898] 4-8-8 **71** .... StephenCarson 4 — 62
(L Corcoran) *set stdy pce for 2f: chsd ldng pair after tl drvn and struggling over 2f out: no ch wl over 1f out* **25/1**

3m 4.43s (1.23) **Going Correction** +0.075s/f (Slow) **7 Ran SP% 118.3**
WFA 4 from 5yo+ 6lb
Speed ratings (Par 105): **99,98,98,97,93 92,92**
toteswinger: 1&2 £4.30, 1&3 £4.80, 2&3 £3.80. CSF £33.16 TOTE £8.40: £3.60, £2.40; EX 37.40.
Owner Resurrection Partners **Bred** Horst Rapp And Dieter Burkle **Trained** Sutton Veny, Wilts

FOCUS
A fair staying handicap. The pace was steady early on, but increased noticeably after a couple of furlongs or so. Muddling form, with the market principals all having shown their best form previously at Southwell.

143 ISIS H'CAP — 1m (P)
3:40 (3:41) (Class 5) (0-75,74) 4-Y-O+ — **£2,590** (£770; £385; £192) **Stalls** Centre

Form — RPR
006- **1** **Murrin (IRE)**[22] [7771] 5-8-11 **67** .... StephenDonohoe 1 — 74
(T G Mills) *hld up in midfield: hdwy on inner over 2f out: rdn to chse ldr over 1f out: led ins fnl f: edgd rt after: drvn out* **11/4**[1]
03-4 **2** *3/4* **Wavertree Warrior (IRE)**[10] [28] 7-9-2 **72** ....(b) LukeMorris 6 — 77
(N P Littmoden) *chsd ldr: rdn over 2f out: drvn and lost 2nd over 1f out: kpt on u.p to regain 2nd wl ins fnl f* **12/1**
003- **3** *1/2* **Pension Policy (USA)**[22] [7771] 4-9-0 **70** ....(v) JimmyQuinn 2 — 74
(R Charlton) *chsd ldrs: rdn and effrt jst over 2f out: drvn ent fnl f: swtchd slty rt ins fnl f: kpt on: wnt 3rd nr fin* **11/4**[1]
05-3 **4** *hd* **Blacktoft (USA)**[10] [29] 6-9-2 **72** ....(e) ChrisCatlin 5 — 76
(S C Williams) *led: clr 5f out: rdn wl over 2f out: hrd drvn ent fnl f: edgd rt and hdd ins fnl f: lost 2 pls fnl 75yds* **6/1**[3]
302- **5** *1* **Kensington (IRE)**[14] [7829] 8-8-13 **74** .... PatrickDonaghy(5) 7 — 75
(P D Evans) *stdd after s: hld up in midfield: rdn and unable qck over 2f out: kpt on u.p fnl f: nt pce to chal ldrs* **9/1**
001- **6** *3* **Millfield (IRE)**[45] [7495] 6-9-3 **73** .... TonyCulhane 4 — 67
(P R Chamings) *stdd s: t.k.h: hld up in rr: effrt and rdn wl over 1f out: no imp* **10/1**
530- **7** *6* **Networker**[31] [7668] 6-8-13 **69** .... JamieSpencer 3 — 50
(P J McBride) *hld up in last pair: swtchd rt and rdn over 1f out: sn hanging lft and no hdwy: eased ins fnl f* **3/1**[2]

1m 39.44s (-0.46) **Going Correction** +0.075s/f (Slow) **7 Ran SP% 119.4**
Speed ratings (Par 103): **105,104,103,103,102 99,93**
toteswinger: 1&2 £9.70, 1&3 £2.00, 2&3 £6.80. CSF £37.48 TOTE £4.40: £1.90, £5.30; EX 41.00.
Owner Miss J A Leighs **Bred** E Campion **Trained** Headley, Surrey
■ Stewards' Enquiry : Luke Morris one-day ban: using whip down the shoulder in the forehand position (Jan 27)

FOCUS
A modest handicap but it was the only truly run race on the card. The bare form is ordinary and the winner should still be on a fair mark after this.
Networker Official explanation: jockey said gelding was never travelling and hung left throughout

144 HEDGE END ISLAND MEDIAN AUCTION MAIDEN STKS — 1m 1f 46y(P)
4:10 (4:14) (Class 6) 3-Y-O — **£1,942** (£578; £288; £144) **Stalls** Low

Form — RPR
1 **Open Sesame (IRE)** 3-9-3 0 .... TPQueally 7 — 73+
(P W Chapple-Hyam) *stdd s: hld up in tch: hdwy to trck ldrs over 2f out: rdn to ld ins fnl f: sn rdn clr: readily* **8/13**[1]
53- **2** *1 1/2* **Solo Choice**[21] [7773] 3-9-3 0 .... TonyCulhane 6 — 65
(D Flood) *disp 2nd tl led over 2f out: drvn and pressed over 1f out: hdd ins fnl f: no ch w wnr* **12/1**
00- **3** *1* **Derringbay (IRE)**[90] [6737] 3-8-10 0 .... AshleyMorgan(7) 2 — 63
(M H Tompkins) *chsd ldr: rdn and effrt on inner 2f out: ev ch over 1f out: outpcd by wnr ins fnl f* **66/1**
4 *1 1/4* **Gaselee (USA)** 3-8-12 0 .... ChrisCatlin 3 — 55
(Rae Guest) *dwlt: hld up in tch in rr: hdwy on outer jst over 2f out: rdn wl over 1f out: edgd lft and one pce ent fnl f* **16/1**
04-4 **5** *4 1/2* **Giant Strides**[11] [19] 3-8-12 62 .... StephenDonohoe 1 — 46
(P D Evans) *hld up in tch: rdn and unable qck wl over 1f out: wknd over 1f out* **8/1**[3]
42- **6** *46* **Dante Deo (USA)**[32] [7646] 3-8-12 0 .... JamieSpencer 4 — —
(T D Barron) *led: rn green fr 6f out: rdn and hdd over 2f out: sn bhd: virtually p.u fnl f: t.o* **11/4**[2]

2m 4.57s (124.57) **6 Ran SP% 114.8**
toteswinger: 1&2 £2.40, 1&3 £9.90, 2&3 £12.80. CSF £10.29 TOTE £1.80: £1.60, £2.90; EX 10.10.
Owner Joy And Valentine Feerick **Bred** Glending Bloodstock **Trained** Newmarket, Suffolk

FOCUS
A weak juvenile maiden which was slowly run. The winner had little to beat with his market rival running poorly, and although he did it well the bare form is probably very modest.
Dante Deo(USA) Official explanation: vet said filly finished distressed

145 FYFIELD H'CAP — 1m 2f (P)
4:40 (4:41) (Class 6) (0-50,55) 4-Y-O+ — **£1,942** (£578; £288; £144) **Stalls** Low

Form — RPR
604- **1** **Ruwain**[142] [5321] 5-8-3 **48** .... AshleyMorgan(7) 6 — 54
(P J McBride) *mde all: rdn over 1f out: styd on wl fnl f* **12/1**
33-1 **2** *1 1/4* **Joe Jo Star**[6] [78] 7-9-3 **55** 6ex .... JamieSpencer 1 — 58
(R A Fahey) *hld up in tch: hdwy to trck ldrs gng wl over 2f out: drvn to chse wnr ent fnl f: nt qckn and a hld fnl f* **8/11**[1]
452- **3** *1* **Miss Understanding**[75] [7088] 4-8-6 **46** ....(b) ChrisCatlin 7 — 47
(J R Weymes) *chsd ldrs: lft 2nd and hmpd over 7f out: rdn and tried to chal over 1f out: one pce u.p fnl f* **10/1**[3]
00-2 **4** *3* **Scutch Mill (IRE)**[6] [81] 7-8-7 **50** ....(t) PatrickDonaghy(5) 4 — 45
(P C Haslam) *stdd s: hld up in last pair: hdwy jst over 2f out: chsd ldng trio and drvn over 1f out: no imp* **9/4**[2]
6-00 **5** *2 3/4* **Silver Spruce**[2] [132] 4-8-0 **47** ....(b) MarieLequarre(7) 2 — 37
(D Flood) *hld up in last pl: rdn and no hdwy 2f out* **40/1**
662- **6** *5* **Jiminor Mack**[15] [7815] 6-8-5 **46** oh1 ....(p) DominicFox(3) 5 — 26
(W J H Ratcliffe) *chsd ldrs: rdn and struggling over 2f out: wl bhd fnl f* **25/1**
0/4- **P** **Kentavr's Dream**[61] [7300] 6-8-11 **49** .... JimmyQuinn 3 — —
(P Howling) *chsd wnr tl lost action and eased over 7f out: eventually p.u and dismntd over 4f out* **40/1**

2m 12.23s (3.63) **Going Correction** +0.075s/f (Slow) **7 Ran SP% 114.2**
WFA 4 from 5yo+ 2lb
Speed ratings (Par 101): **88,87,86,83,81 77,—**
toteswinger: 1&2 £2.20, 1&3 £5.40, 2&3 £2.10. CSF £21.53 TOTE £12.40: £3.80, £1.10; EX 27.90 Place 6: £36.29, Place 5: £23.77.
Owner P J McBride **Bred** W J Musson **Trained** Newmarket, Suffolk

FOCUS
A very moderate handicap, and a bit of turn up. The winner was allowed an easy lead, and this is weak form.
Kentavr's Dream Official explanation: jockey said mare lost her action

T/Plt: £129.30 to a £1 stake. Pool: £50,174.32. 283.25 winning tickets. T/Qpdt: £65.10 to a £1 stake. Pool: £4,058.67. 46.10 winning tickets. SP

[89]SOUTHWELL (L-H)

Tuesday, January 13

OFFICIAL GOING: Standard

Wind: Light half-behind Weather: Overcast

146 WILLIAM HILL JANUARY SALE - NOW ON! (S) STKS 5f (F)

1:00 (1:00) (Class 6) 4-Y-O+ **£2,047** (£604; £302) **Stalls** High

Form RPR

312- **1** **Back In The Red (IRE)**[14] [7819] 5-9-5 65..............(b) FrankieMcDonald 3 76
(R A Harris) *mde virtually all: rdn 2f out: hung lft ins fnl f: styd on u.p* **4/1[3]**

23-4 **2** *hd* **Grimes Faith**[5] [89] 6-9-0 65..............................(p) TomEaves 7 70
(K A Ryan) *hmpd s: sn prom: chsd wnr over 1f out: sn rdn and ev ch: edgd lft ins fnl f: styd on* **7/4[1]**

34-3 **3** *2 1/4* **Monte Major (IRE)**[5] [89] 8-8-7 56..............................(v) LeeTopliss(7) 2 62
(D Shaw) *chsd ldrs: rdn 1/2-way: no ex ins fnl f* **11/4[2]**

50-0 **4** *3 1/2* **Ronnie Howe**[11] [14] 5-9-0 54..............................(vt[1]) LeeEnstone 6 50
(S R Bowring) *wnt rt s: prom: rdn 1/2-way: wknd fnl f* **8/1**

00-0 **5** *4 1/2* **Tag Team (IRE)**[11] [13] 8-9-0 57.............................. RobertWinston 9 33
(John A Harris) *chsd ldrs: rdn over 3f out: wkng whn hmpd wl over 1f out* **20/1**

00-0 **6** *3/4* **Flying Indian**[5] [89] 4-8-9 56..............................(v[1]) PaulMulrennan 1 26
(J Balding) *chsd ldrs: rdn 1/2-way: wknd wl over 1f out* **50/1**

100- **7** *3 1/4* **Mac Dalia**[133] [5592] 4-8-6 65..............................(p) TolleyDean(3) 4 14
(A J McCabe) *chsd ldrs: rdn 1/2-way: edgd rt and wknd wl over 1f out* **12/1**

000- **8** *1/2* **Diminuto**[24] [7746] 5-8-9 56.............................. CatherineGannon 8 12
(M D I Usher) *sn outpcd* **33/1**

57.99 secs (-1.71) **Going Correction** -0.30s/f (Stan) **8** Ran SP% **111.5**

Speed ratings (Par 101): **101,100,97,91,84 83,77,77**

toteswinger: 1&2 £1.90, 1&3 £2.30, 2&3 £1.80. CSF £10.78 TOTE £4.00: £1.30, £1.10, £1.20; EX 10.70 Trifecta £26.40 Pool: £414.82 - 11.62 winning units..The winner was bought in for 5,000 guineas.

Owner Mrs Ruth M Serrell **Bred** Mrs Rachanee Butler **Trained** Earlswood, Monmouths

FOCUS

The surface had quickened up appreciably since last week and the time was inside the Racing Post's standard. The winner and third are the best guides to the form.

147 WILLIAM HILL JANUARY SALE - BETTER ODDS! H'CAP 1m 4f (F)

1:30 (1:31) (Class 6) (0-60,60) 4-Y-O+ **£2,047** (£604; £302) **Stalls** Low

Form RPR

304- **1** **Merrion Tiger (IRE)**[46] [7340] 4-9-0 56.............................. GregFairley 7 72+
(A G Foster) *chsd ldr tl led over 4f out: clr 3f out: sn rdn: styd on wl: eased nr fin* **8/1**

12-3 **2** *3 1/2* **Gayanula (USA)**[9] [38] 4-8-8 57.............................. BMcHugh(7) 4 63
(Miss J A Camacho) *sn pushed along in rr: hdwy over 4f out: rdn to chse wnr over 1f out: sn edgd lft: no imp fnl f* **12/1**

56-3 **3** *3 3/4* **Bienheureux**[7] [65] 8-8-4 49..............................(e[1]) MatthewLawson(7) 6 49
(Miss Gay Kelleway) *dwlt: sn pushed along in rr: styd on fnl 2f: nvr nrr* **17/2**

56-3 **4** *3 3/4* **Black Falcon (IRE)**[9] [40] 9-9-4 56.............................. RobertWinston 13 50
(John A Harris) *sn pushed along in rr: hdwy and hung lft fr over 3f out: sn rdn: wknd fnl f* **6/1[2]**

506- **5** *2 1/4* **Blushing Heart**[73] [7128] 5-9-8 60.............................. MickyFenton 10 50
(G M Moore) *prom: rdn over 3f out: wknd over 1f out* **20/1**

05-4 **6** *5* **Pick Of The Day (IRE)**[9] [38] 4-8-5 47..............................(v[1]) DaleGibson 8 29
(J G Given) *mid-div: hdwy 1/2-way: rdn to chse wnr over 3f out: wknd 2f out* **11/1**

00-4 **7** *1/2* **Satindra (IRE)**[3] [117] 5-8-9 47..............................(tp) LiamJones 5 29
(C R Dore) *chsd ldrs: rdn over 4f out: wkng whn hmpd over 3f out* **10/1**

52-1 **8** *7* **Red Tarn**[12] [1] 4-9-4 60.............................. TomEaves 14 30
(B Smart) *mid-div: sn drvn along: lost pl over 9f out: hdwy 1/2-way: rdn and wknd over 2f out* **5/1[1]**

32-4 **9** *4 1/2* **Dazzling Begum**[4] [107] 4-8-10 52..............................(v) JerryO'Dwyer 1 15
(J Pearce) *sn pushed along and prom: rdn over 5f out: wknd 4f out* **5/1[1]**

05-0 **10** *5* **Fifth Zak**[12] [1] 5-8-9 47.............................. PaulEddery 11 2
(S R Bowring) *chsd ldrs: rdn over 4f out: hmpd and wknd over 3f out* **66/1**

0/0- **11** *3 1/4* **Menkaura**[31] [7667] 6-8-8 46.............................. NeilChalmers 12 —
(John R Upson) *mid-div: rdn 1/2-way: wknd over 4f out* **100/1**

5/4- **12** *1* **Jocheski (IRE)**[31] [7085] 5-9-8 60.............................. FergusSweeney 2 8
(A G Newcombe) *hld up: rdn over 5f out: sn wknd* **7/1[3]**

304- **13** *13* **Mill Beattie**[98] [6562] 4-8-4 49.............................. DuranFentiman(3) 3 —
(J Mackie) *led at sound pce: hdd over 4f out: wkng whn hmpd over 3f out* **40/1**

14 *7* **Seven Sky (FR)**[419] 6-9-3 55.............................. PaulMulrennan 9 —
(P F I Cole) *mid-div: rdn and lost pl over 5f out: sn bhd* **40/1**

2m 39.12s (-1.88) **Going Correction** -0.15s/f (Stan)

WFA 4 from 5yo+ 4lb **14** Ran SP% **119.0**

Speed ratings (Par 101): **100,97,95,92,91 87,87,82,79,76 74,73,65,60**

toteswinger: 1&2 £16.00, 1&3 £15.70, 2&3 £10.90. CSF £95.52 CT £845.26 TOTE £10.30: £3.10, £1.80, £2.30; EX 84.70 Trifecta £284.00 Part won. Pool: £383.83 - 0.95 winning units..

Owner S C B Limited **Bred** Denis Fehan **Trained** Haddington, East Lothian

FOCUS

A low-grade stayers' handicap run at a very strong pace for the first half-mile. Much-improved form from the winner, with the race rated around the runner-up.

Black Falcon(IRE) Official explanation: jockey said gelding hung left

Pick Of The Day(IRE) Official explanation: jockey said gelding was hampered on first bend

Satindra(IRE) Official explanation: jockey said gelding was denied a clear run

Dazzling Begum Official explanation: jockey said filly ran flat

148 WILLIAM HILL JANUARY SALE - WHY BET ELSEWHERE? H'CAP 2m (F)

2:00 (2:00) (Class 6) (0-60,58) 4-Y-O+ **£2,047** (£604; £302) **Stalls** Low

Form RPR

46- **1** **Sea Cliff (IRE)**[36] [7605] 5-9-2 46.............................. ShaneKelly 6 56
(Jonjo O'Neill) *hld up: hdwy over 3f out: n.m.r sn after out: rdn to ld 2f out: edgd rt over 1f out: styd on wl* **15/2**

2 *2 3/4* **Roisin's Prince (IRE)**[16] [4713] 7-9-5 49..............................(t) LiamJones 8 56
(M Sheppard) *mid-div: hdwy 5f out: chsd ldr 3f out: rdn and ev ch over 1f out: no ex ins fnl f* **14/1**

010- **3** *3 3/4* **Amron Hill**[14] [7827] 6-9-6 50.............................. FergusSweeney 7 52
(R Hollinshead) *led: rdn and hdd 2f out: styd on same pce appr fnl f* **6/1[3]**

46-1 **4** *3/4* **Sabancaya**[9] [38] 4-9-7 58 6ex.............................. MickyFenton 12 59
(Mrs P Sly) *dwlt: hld up: hdwy over 4f out: sn rdn: edgd lft over 1f out: styd on same pce* **5/4[1]**

325- **5** *6* **Kangrina**[21] [7776] 7-9-4 55.............................. MatthewDavies(7) 1 49
(George Baker) *chsd ldrs: rdn over 3f out: wknd 2f out* **14/1**

30-0 **6** *3 1/2* **Optimum (IRE)**[11] [8] 7-9-1 45.............................. DaleGibson 13 35
(J T Stimpson) *chsd ldrs: rdn over 5f out: wknd 3f out* **20/1**

400- **7** *3 3/4* **Archimboldo (USA)**[27] [5367] 6-8-12 49..............................(b) JoshWall(7) 5 34
(T Wall) *s.s: bhd tl hdwy 1/2-way: rdn whn hmpd over 3f out: sn wknd* **14/1**

00- **8** *1 1/2* **Dasher Reilly (USA)**[16] [7744] 8-9-7 51..............................(b) TomEaves 9 34
(A Sadik) *sn pushed along in rr: hdwy 1/2-way: rdn over 4f out: sn wknd* **125/1**

/0-6 **9** *3 1/2* **Siegfrieds Night (IRE)**[7] [66] 8-8-8 45..............................(t) AlexEdwards(7) 2 24
(M C Chapman) *mid-div: hdwy 1/2-way: wknd over 6f out* **125/1**

33-2 **10** *1 3/4* **Fortunella**[9] [38] 4-9-4 55..............................(v) PaulMulrennan 3 32
(Miss Gay Kelleway) *chsd ldr tl rdn over 3f out: wknd over 2f out* **11/2[2]**

02-0 **11** *6* **Oberlin (USA)**[9] [38] 4-9-5 56..............................(p) NickyMackay 11 26
(T Keddy) *sn drvn along and prom: wknd over 6f out* **20/1**

40-0 **12** *1 1/2* **Matinee Idol**[9] [38] 6-9-1 45..............................(b) RobertWinston 4 13
(Mrs S Lamyman) *s.s: hdwy after 2f: rdn 1/2-way: wknd 6f out* **50/1**

3m 43.29s (-2.21) **Going Correction** -0.15s/f (Stan)

WFA 4 from 5yo+ 7lb **12** Ran SP% **119.0**

Speed ratings (Par 101): **99,97,95,95,92 90,88,88,86,85 82,81**

toteswinger: 1&2 £22.20, 1&3 £9.80, 2&3 £21.90. CSF £101.88 CT £676.32 TOTE £10.40: £2.60, £3.70, £2.00; EX 116.90 Trifecta £238.40 Part won. Pool: £322.20 - 0.30 winning units..

Owner John P McManus **Bred** G W Robinson **Trained** Cheltenham, Gloucs

FOCUS

A 46-60 handicap with the actual top-weight 5lb below the race ceiling, run at a sensible pace. The first two were both entitled to rate this high on their jumps form.

Oberlin(USA) Official explanation: vet said gelding scoped unsatisfactarily post-race

149 PLAY GOLF AT SOUTHWELL GOLF CLUB H'CAP 6f (F)

2:30 (2:30) (Class 5) (0-70,68) 3-Y-O **£2,729** (£806; £403) **Stalls** Low

Form RPR

500- **1** **My Sweet Georgia (IRE)**[27] [7700] 3-9-1 65..............(b[1]) MickyFenton 6 73
(S A Callaghan) *dwlt: hdwy over 4f out: rdn 2f out: led ins fnl f: r.o* **10/3[1]**

053- **2** *1* **Diamond Surprise**[17] [7794] 3-8-7 62.............................. GabrielHannon(5) 4 67
(R Curtis) *chsd ldrs: rdn to ld 1f out: sn hdd and edgd lft: styd on same pce* **9/2[3]**

00-5 **3** *4 1/2* **My Best Man**[11] [19] 3-9-1 65.............................. TGMcLaughlin 1 56
(B R Millman) *hld up: rdn 1/2-way: wnt 3rd post: n.d* **7/2[2]**

51-4 **4** *nk* **Trick Or Two**[10] [34] 3-9-4 68.............................. PaulMulrennan 5 58
(Mrs R A Carr) *led: rdn and hdd 1f out: sn wknd* **7/2[2]**

2-13 **5** *2 1/4* **La Capriosa**[5] [91] 3-8-8 65 6ex.............................. KarenKenny(7) 2 47
(A J McCabe) *chsd ldr: rdn and ev ch over 1f out: wknd ins fnl f* **8/1**

400- **6** *hd* **Paymaster In Chief**[120] [5960] 3-8-6 56.............................. CatherineGannon 3 38
(M D I Usher) *broke wl: lost pl 5f out: rdn over 3f out: n.d after* **13/2**

1m 15.8s (-0.70) **Going Correction** -0.15s/f (Stan) **6** Ran SP% **110.1**

Speed ratings (Par 97): **98,96,90,90,87 87**

toteswinger: 1&2 £3.60, 1&3 £3.00, 2&3 £3.60. CSF £17.66 TOTE £3.40: £1.40, £3.40; EX 19.20.

Owner Hinge, Searchfield & Tamburro **Bred** Epona Bloodstock Ltd **Trained** Newmarket, Suffolk

FOCUS

A modest handicap run at a sound pace and won by something of a gamble. There is a bit of a doubt over how much improvement the first two showed.

150 SOUTHWELL-RACECOURSE.CO.UK H'CAP 7f (F)

3:00 (3:00) (Class 6) (0-52,54) 4-Y-O+ **£2,047** (£604; £302) **Stalls** Low

Form RPR

55-1 **1** **Charlotte Grey**[7] [62] 5-8-12 54 6ex.............................. DuranFentiman(3) 1 63
(P J McBride) *chsd ldr tl led 4f out: rdn over 1f out: styd on* **11/1**

06-0 **2** *1* **Magical Song**[11] [14] 4-8-11 50..............................(p) ShaneKelly 3 56
(R Curtis) *s.i.s: sn drvn along to ld: hdd 4f out: sn rdn: r.o* **9/2[3]**

10-0 **3** *1/2* **Isabella's Fancy**[11] [14] 4-8-5 51.............................. DeclanCannon(7) 12 56
(A G Newcombe) *hld up: hdwy over 1f out: r.o: nt rch ldrs* **8/1**

00-2 **4** *2 1/2* **Nautical**[7] [62] 11-8-9 48.............................. JerryO'Dwyer 6 46
(J R Holt) *hld up: hdwy over 1f out: nt trble ldrs* **10/1**

50-5 **5** *2* **Penel (IRE)**[12] [7] 8-8-2 48..............................(p) PaulPickard(7) 5 41
(P T Midgley) *dwlt: sn pushed along in rr: styd on fnl f: nvr nrr* **9/1**

00-5 **6** *1 1/2* **Majestic Cheer**[9] [35] 5-8-8 47..............................(p) RobertWinston 13 35
(John A Harris) *prom: rdn over 2f out: wknd fnl f* **11/1**

66-3 **7** *3/4* **Mister Benji**[11] [14] 10-8-7 46..............................(p) AndrewElliott 7 32
(B P J Baugh) *chsd ldrs: rdn over 2f out: wknd fnl f* **7/2[1]**

/00- **8** *nse* **Actuality**[14] [7817] 7-8-9 48 ow1..............................(tp) PaulMulrennan 11 34
(J Balding) *prom: rdn 1/2-way: wknd fnl f* **4/1[2]**

00-0 **9** *3/4* **Only A Grand**[12] [7] 5-8-6 45..............................(b) LiamJones 4 29
(R Bastiman) *mid-div: rdn 1/2-way: wknd over 1f out* **28/1**

500- **10** *2 1/2* **Bewdley**[29] [7692] 4-8-6 45.............................. GregFairley 9 23
(R E Peacock) *chsd ldrs: rdn 1/2-way: wknd over 2f out* **28/1**

500- **11** *shd* **Spy Gun (USA)**[162] [4683] 9-8-3 49 ow4.............................. JoshWall(7) 8 26
(T Wall) *in rr: sme hdwy 4f out: sn wknd* **40/1**

000- **12** *14* **Tycoon's Buddy**[110] [6224] 4-8-1 45.............................. DeanHeslop(5) 2 —
(S Wynne) *s.s: outpcd* **66/1**

1m 29.34s (-0.96) **Going Correction** -0.15s/f (Stan) **12** Ran SP% **118.1**

Speed ratings (Par 101): **99,97,97,94,92 90,89,89,88,85 85,69**

toteswinger: 1&2 £4.90, 1&3 £7.90, 2&3 £7.30. CSF £58.22 CT £433.54 TOTE £7.90: £2.00, £1.70, £3.40; EX 38.80 Trifecta £87.60 Pool: £343.42 - 2.90 winning units..

Owner N Davies **Bred** Finbar Kent **Trained** Newmarket, Suffolk

FOCUS

In effect a low-grade 46-54 handicap. The form looks sound enough with a bit more improvement from the winner.

Bewdley Official explanation: trainer said filly bled from the nose post-race

151 ARENALEISUREPLC.COM MAIDEN STKS 1m (F)

3:30 (3:35) (Class 5) 3-Y-O+ **£2,729** (£806; £403) **Stalls** Low

Form RPR

063- **1** **Ultimate**[31] [7660] 3-8-8 76.............................. RobertWinston 2 69+
(H Morrison) *mde all: shkn up and clr over 1f out: comf* **2/5[1]**

0- **2** *4 1/2* **Miss Christophene (IRE)**[38] [7578] 3-8-0 0.............................. AndrewMullen(3) 1 51
(Mrs S Lamyman) *s.i.s: hld up: hdwy to chse wnr 3f out: rdn over 1f out: styd on same pce* **40/1**

3 *2 3/4* **Antipodean (UAE)** 3-8-1 0.............................. PaulPickard(7) 6 50
(P T Midgley) *s.i.s: hld up: hdwy 3f out: rdn and hung lft over 1f out: sn wknd* **33/1**

6- 4 *shd* **Kochanski (IRE)**[156] 4897 3-8-3 0 .... GregFairley 4 44
(M Johnston) *chsd wnr tl rdn over 3f out: sn outpcd* **10/3**[2]

0- 5 *12* **First Hand**[49] 7443 3-8-3 0 .... DaleGibson 5 17
(M W Easterby) *chsd ldrs: rdn 3f out: sn wknd* **66/1**

6 *shd* **Benozzo Gozzoli** 3-8-8 0 .... MickyFenton 3 22
(H Morrison) *s.s: outpcd* **12/1**[3]

1m 42.82s (-0.88) **Going Correction** -0.15s/f (Stan) 6 Ran SP% **109.1**
Speed ratings (Par 103): **98,93,90,90,78 78**
toteswinger: 1&2 £4.90, 1&3 £3.70, 2&3 £10.40. CSF £22.45 TOTE £1.40: £1.02, £10.80; EX 23.40.
Owner Gillian, Lady Howard De Walden **Bred** Avington Manor Stud **Trained** East Ilsley, Berks

FOCUS
An uncompetitive and modest maiden in which it is doubtful if the winner had to match his previous form.

152 SOUTHWELL RACECOURSE FOR CONFERENCES H'CAP 7f (F)
4:00 (4:01) (Class 5) (0-70,70) 4-Y-O+ **£2,729** (£806; £403) **Stalls** Low

Form RPR

03-1 1 **Mrs Bun**[12] 7 4-8-11 **61** ....(b) TomEaves 3 71
(K A Ryan) *sn chsng ldr: rdn over 2f out: styd on u.p to ld wl ins fnl f* **4/1**[3]

10-2 2 *nk* **Crocodile Bay (IRE)**[9] 35 6-9-4 **68** ....(b) MickyFenton 2 77
(John A Harris) *sn led: rdn over 1f out: hdd wl ins fnl f* **6/1**

1- 3 *4* **Triple Axel (IRE)**[17] 7798 5-9-3 **67** .... ShaneKelly 5 65
(J Noseda) *hld up: rdn over 2f out: hung lft fr 1f out: nt trble ldrs* **7/2**[2]

20-1 4 *2 ¾* **Tri Chara (IRE)**[5] 94 5-9-6 **70** 6ex ....(p) FergusSweeney 7 61
(R Hollinshead) *chsd ldrs: rdn over 2f out: wknd ins fnl f* **15/8**[1]

005- 5 *½* **World Of Choice (USA)**[31] 7665 4-8-4 **54** oh1 .... DaleGibson 4 43
(M W Easterby) *chsd ldrs: lost pl over 5f out: sn rdn: n.d after* **10/1**

00-0 6 *6* **To Bubbles**[11] 14 4-8-6 **56** .... FrankieMcDonald 6 29
(A G Newcombe) *hld up: rdn 1/2-way: sn lost tch* **28/1**

/00- 7 *nk* **Sarwin (USA)**[291] 1048 6-8-12 **62** .... RobertWinston 1 34
(G A Swinbank) *prom: rdn and wknd over 2f out* **9/1**

1m 28.17s (-2.13) **Going Correction** -0.15s/f (Stan) 7 Ran SP% **113.8**
Speed ratings (Par 103): **106,105,101,97,97 90,90**
toteswinger: 1&2 £3.10, 1&3 £2.80, 2&3 £3.80. CSF £27.53 TOTE £5.10: £2.40, £4.40; EX 26.10 Place 6: £186.35, Place 5: £161.55.
Owner Guy Reed **Bred** Guy Reed **Trained** Hambleton, N Yorks

FOCUS
Not a bad race for the grade with three last-time-out winners. The form is sound with Mrs Bun continuing her modest progress.
Sarwin(USA) Official explanation: jockey said gelding had no more to give
T/Plt: £119.80 to a £1 stake. Pool: £51,779.34. 315.48 winning tickets. T/Qpdt: £42.50 to a £1 stake. Pool: £3,601.87. 62.60 winning tickets. CR

[111] KEMPTON (A.W) (R-H)
Wednesday, January 14

OFFICIAL GOING: Standard
Wind: Almost Nil Weather: Dark

153 BLUE SQUARE CLASSIFIED STKS 6f (P)
6:50 (6:51) (Class 7) 4-Y-O+ **£1,364** (£403; £201) **Stalls** High

Form RPR

00-2 1 **Flamestone**[8] 56 5-9-0 45 .... StephenDonohoe 8 56
(A E Price) *stdd s: hld up in last pair: prog on inner 2f out: got through to ld jst ins fnl f: drvn and hld on wl* **6/1**[3]

00-0 2 *hd* **Mr Rev**[11] 23 6-9-0 45 ....(b) RobertWinston 11 55
(J M Bradley) *towards rr: prog wl over 2f out: rdn to ld briefly jst over 1f out: pressed wnr fnl f: kpt on* **10/1**

-614 3 *1 ½* **Sherjawy (IRE)**[4] 111 5-9-6 45 ....(b) SimonWhitworth 12 57
(Miss Z C Davison) *trckd ldrs: prog on outer to chal and upsides over 1f out: no ex ins fnl f* **9/4**[1]

0-00 4 *2 ¼* **Nordic Light (USA)**[5] 104 5-9-0 44 ....(bt) ChrisCatlin 9 43
(J M Bradley) *t.k.h early and restrained bhd ldng pair: effrt to ld briefly over 1f out: sn nt qckn: one pce u.p* **11/2**[2]

00-0 5 *¾* **Gone'N'Dunnett (IRE)**[8] 56 10-9-0 43 ....(p) VinceSlattery 2 41
(Mrs C A Dunnett) *disp ld: narrow advantage over 2f out to over 1f out: fdd ins fnl f* **18/1**

0-00 6 *1 ¼* **Desert Light (IRE)**[8] 56 8-8-7 44 ....(v) LeeTopliss(7) 3 37
(D Shaw) *trckd ldrs: gng wl 1/2-way: rdn and nt qckn 2f out: one pce after* **12/1**

06-0 7 *¾* **Stormburst (IRE)**[5] 104 5-9-0 45 .... NeilChalmers 1 35
(A J Chamberlain) *hld up in midfield: shkn up and no rspnse 2f out: btn after* **11/1**

06-3 8 *hd* **Baba Ghanoush**[8] 56 7-9-0 39 ....(b) PaulDoe 7 34
(M J Attwater) *racd wd: rdn in midfield 1/2-way: no prog: wl btn fnl f* **8/1**

255- 9 *nse* **Lady Hopeful (IRE)**[247] 2050 7-9-0 45 ....(b) PatrickMathers 5 34
(Peter Grayson) *v awkward s: mostly last: effrt 2f out: no real prog 1f out: wl btn after* **25/1**

00-5 10 *5* **Stoneacre Donny (IRE)**[8] 57 5-8-7 42 .... AndrewHeffernan(7) 10 18
(Peter Grayson) *chsd ldrs: u.p wl over 2f out: sn wknd* **33/1**

00-0 11 *3 ¾* **Tagula Sands (IRE)**[9] 43 5-9-0 43 ....(p) RichardSmith 6 6
(J C Fox) *disp ld to over 2f out: wknd rapidly* **66/1**

205- 12 *½* **Naias (IRE)**[18] 7798 4-9-0 45 .... TonyHamilton 4 4
(R A Fahey) *drvn on outer bef 1/2-way: sn btn* **10/1**

1m 13.5s (0.40) **Going Correction** +0.275s/f (Slow) 12 Ran SP% **119.3**
Speed ratings (Par 97): **108,107,105,102,101 100,99,98,98,92 87,86**
toteswinger 1&2 £5.50, 1&3 £3.50, 2&3 £6.40. CSF £64.24 TOTE £8.40: £2.50, £4.00, £1.60; EX 78.40.
Owner Mrs H L Price **Bred** J Hamilton **Trained** Leominster, H'fords

FOCUS
A very ordinary event run at a decent pace. The form looks slightly above average for the grade.

154 BLUE SQUARE CASINO MAIDEN STKS 7f (P)
7:20 (7:35) (Class 5) 3-Y-O+ **£2,590** (£770; £385; £192) **Stalls** High

Form RPR

534- 1 **Syrinx (IRE)**[127] 5788 3-8-2 73 .... ChrisCatlin 7 70
(J Noseda) *trckd ldng pair: prog to ld over 1f out: edgd lft fnl f: hld on* **7/4**[1]

2 *hd* **Thief Of Time (IRE)** 3-8-8 0 ow1 .... JamieSpencer 8 75+
(P W Chapple-Hyam) *s.s: sn midfield: effrt and nt clr run briefly over 2f out: prog over 1f out to chse wnr ins fnl f: rn green but clsng at fin* **8/1**

- 3 *4* **Know By Now** 3-8-8 0 ow1 .... MickyFenton 4 65+
(T P Tate) *trckd ldng pair: nt qckn over 2f out: kpt on again to take 3rd nr fin* **11/2**[3]

00- 4 *¾* **Duke Of Normandy (IRE)**[91] 6737 3-8-7 0 .... GregFairley 9 62
(M Johnston) *racd freely and disp ld: nt qckn and hdd over 1f out: folded tamely fnl f* **3/1**[2]

5 *1 ¾* **Destinationunknown (USA)** 3-8-2 0 .... LiamJones 1 52+
(W J Haggas) *s.s: settled in rr: pushed along and kpt on fnl 2f: nvr on terms* **8/1**

30- 6 *nk* **Ziggy Lee**[145] 5213 3-8-7 0 .... DaleGibson 6 56
(S C Williams) *awkward s: tk furious hold and disp ld to over 1f out: emptied rapidly fnl f* **50/1**

634- 7 *2 ¼* **Eagle Nebula**[126] 5802 5-9-11 60 .... IanMongan 10 54
(B R Johnson) *chsd ldrs: outpcd 1/2-way: tried to cl over 1f out: sn wknd* **13/2**

8 *8* **Patience Rewarded** 3-8-2 0 .... LukeMorris 5 23
(J S Moore) *s.s: a in last pair: pushed along 1/2-way: sn bhd* **33/1**

9 *3 ¼* **Dontriskit** 3-8-2 0 .... CatherineGannon 3 15
(J L Spearing) *s.s: racd wd and t.k.h: lost tch 3f out* **100/1**

1m 28.93s (2.93) **Going Correction** +0.275s/f (Slow)
WFA 3 from 4yo+ 18lb 9 Ran SP% **118.2**
Speed ratings (Par 103): **94,93,89,88,86 86,83,74,70**
toteswinger 1&2 £4.20, 1&3 £2.60, 2&3 £10.10. CSF £17.39 TOTE £2.80: £1.20, £2.10, £2.00; EX 17.40.
Owner Michael Tabor **Bred** Oak Lodge Bloodstock **Trained** Newmarket, Suffolk

FOCUS
A modest maiden involving a majority of newcomers. The winner did not have to improve on his previous form, and the next two shaped with promise. There was an horrific incident at the start when newcomer Blue Warrior (25/1, withdrawn) broke through the stalls with the blindfold on, crashed through the rail and fell in the lake. Fortunately he swam to the other side and eventually climbed out of the water and was taken to safety by the stalls handlers.

155 BLUE SQUARE MOBILE H'CAP 7f (P)
7:50 (8:03) (Class 6) (0-65,65) 4-Y-O+ **£2,047** (£604; £302) **Stalls** High

Form RPR

51-5 1 **Marmooq**[7] 71 6-8-12 **59** .... IanMongan 9 68
(M J Attwater) *hld up in midfield: rdn 3f out: no prog tl swtchd out wd wl over 1f out: r.o fnl f to ld nr fin* **4/1**[2]

00-5 2 *¾* **Liberty Valance (IRE)**[4] 118 4-8-9 **56** ....(t) SimonWhitworth 1 63
(S Kirk) *trckd ldng pair: wnt 2nd 2f out: sustained chal after: fnlly wore down ldr nr fin as wnr shot past* **16/1**

421- 3 *nk* **King's Colour**[18] 7790 4-9-4 **65** .... FergusSweeney 3 71
(B R Johnson) *trckd ldr: led over 2f out: hrd pressed fnl f: hdd nr fin* **3/1**[1]

050- 4 *¾* **Inside Story (IRE)**[14] 7834 7-9-3 **64** ....(b) FrankieMcDonald 4 68
(C R Dore) *s.i.s: sn chsd ldrs on outer: struggling u.p over 2f out: kpt on at one pce fr over 1f out* **14/1**

01-1 5 *nse* **Norcroft**[12] 14 7-9-4 **65** ....(p) VinceSlattery 12 69
(Mrs C A Dunnett) *hld up in midfield: rdn over 2f out: kpt on at one pce fnl 2f: nvr able to chal* **8/1**

04-1 6 *1 ¼* **Namu**[11] 22 6-9-3 **64** ....(p) ChrisCatlin 6 65
(Miss T Spearing) *s.i.s: hld up in last: effrt on inner 2f out: plugged on: nt pce to threaten* **14/1**

635- 7 *½* **Haasem (USA)**[17] 7803 6-9-2 **63** ....(v) StephenDonohoe 8 62
(J R Jenkins) *hld up in rr: rdn over 2f out: one pce and no real imp on ldrs* **7/1**

200- 8 *½* **Dawson Creek (IRE)**[25] 7742 5-9-3 **64** .... JamieSpencer 7 62
(B Gubby) *led to over 2f out: nt qckn u.p: wknd fnl f* **16/1**

305- 9 *1 ¼* **Mr Garston**[23] 7763 6-9-2 **63** ....(b[1]) TGMcLaughlin 11 58
(J R Boyle) *t.k.h early: hld up in rr: rdn over 2f out: no real prog* **9/1**

600- 10 *nk* **Cheap Street**[14] 7834 5-8-8 **58** .... TolleyDean(3) 13 52
(J G Portman) *trckd ldrs on inner: rdn over 2f out: nt qckn and sn btn* **16/1**

000- 11 *1* **Ike Quebec (FR)**[23] 7763 4-9-2 **63** ....(b) PatCosgrave 5 54
(J R Boyle) *t.k.h early: hld up in rr: no prog over 2f out: sn btn* **33/1**

3-63 12 *2 ¼* **Solicitude**[5] 97 6-8-10 **57** ....(p) TPQueally 10 42
(D Haydn Jones) *t.k.h early: hld up in rr: nt keen and btn over 2f out* **6/1**[3]

1m 26.84s (0.84) **Going Correction** +0.275s/f (Slow) 12 Ran SP% **126.8**
Speed ratings (Par 101): **106,105,104,103,103 102,101,101,99,99 98,95**
toteswinger 1&2 £24.00, 1&3 £3.60, 2&3 £20.40. CSF £71.99 CT £230.73 TOTE £6.00: £2.30, £4.70, £2.00; EX 82.40.
Owner The Attwater Partnership **Bred** Matthews Breeding And Racing Ltd **Trained** Epsom, Surrey

FOCUS
A moderate but fairly competitive handicap which produced a thrilling finish. It was the clear pick of the three course-and-distance races on time and the form is solid.

156 BLUE SQUARE SP GUARANTEE H'CAP 1m 4f (P)
8:20 (8:32) (Class 4) (0-85,84) 4-Y-O+ **£4,727** (£1,406; £702; £351) **Stalls** Centre

Form RPR

232- 1 **Scarab (IRE)**[19] 7785 4-8-11 **77** .... GregFairley 3 85
(M Johnston) *trckd ldng pair: rdn to ld wl over 1f out: edgd lft fnl f but styd on wl* **7/4**[1]

301- 2 *1 ½* **Spirit Of Adjisa (IRE)**[84] 6898 5-9-2 **78** ....(b) PatDobbs 4 84
(Pat Eddery) *trckd ldng pair: pushed along and nt qckn over 2f out and lost pl: rdn and styd on fr over 1f out: tk 2nd fnl 100yds: unable to chal* **8/1**

604- 3 *½* **Profit's Reality (IRE)**[24] 7753 7-9-6 **82** .... IanMongan 9 87
(M J Attwater) *settled in last pair: rdn 3f out: styd on u.p on outer fnl 2f: nrst fin* **6/1**[3]

156- 4 *2* **Remember Ramon (USA)**[28] 7712 6-9-0 **76** .... ChrisCatlin 1 78
(J R Gask) *led after 1f: restrained and hdd after 2f: keen after: effrt to ld over 2f out: hdd wl over 1f out: wknd ins fnl f* **5/1**[2]

030- 5 *hd* **Bassinet (USA)**[48] 7459 5-9-0 **76** .... JamieSpencer 8 78
(J A R Toller) *hld up in 5th: effrt over 2f out: one pce and no imp over 1f out* **15/2**

254- 6 *3 ¼* **Mafeking (UAE)**[16] 7814 5-9-8 **84** .... AndrewElliott 5 80
(M R Hoad) *reluctant to enter stalls: led 1f and again after 2f: hdd over 2f out: grad wknd* **5/1**[2]

000- 7 *14* **Allanit (GER)**[46] 7496 5-9-8 **84** .... TPQueally 2 58
(A P Stringer) *taken down early: t.k.h: hld up last: brief effrt 4f out: moving bdly and wknd fnl 2f: t.o* **14/1**

2m 35.72s (1.22) **Going Correction** +0.275s/f (Slow)
WFA 4 from 5yo+ 4lb 7 Ran SP% **113.5**
Speed ratings (Par 105): **106,105,104,103,103 101,91**
toteswinger 1&2 £3.40, 1&3 £2.70, 2&3 £10.10. CSF £16.39 CT £68.50 TOTE £2.90: £1.30, £3.10; EX 13.70.
Owner Sheikh Hamdan Bin Mohammed Al Maktoum **Bred** Gainsborough Stud Management Ltd **Trained** Middleham Moor, N Yorks

FOCUS
The most valuable race on the card. It was run at a stop-start gallop and the bare form looks ordinary with the second and third close to their marks. The winner ran only to previous course-and-distance form in success.

157 BLUE SQUARE POKER H'CAP 1m (P)
8:50 (9:02) (Class 5) (0-70,70) 4-Y-0+ £2,590 (£770; £385; £192) Stalls High

Form RPR
023- 1 **Fancy Footsteps (IRE)**[33] 7653 4-8-11 63 .... IanMongan 10 74
(C G Cox) *trckd ldrs: effrt to ld over 1f out: rdn clr fnl f* 7/2[1]
02-2 2 2 1/4 **Rock Anthem (IRE)**[10] 39 5-8-12 64 .... PatDobbs 9 70
(Mike Murphy) *sn led: drvn and hdd over 1f out: kpt on to hold on for 2nd but no ch w wnr* 9/2[3]
121- 3 nk **Balata**[15] 7829 4-9-4 70 .... TGMcLaughlin 5 75
(B R Millman) *t.k.h: hld up in midfield: nt qckn over 2f out: styd on fr over 1f out to take 3rd nr fin* 4/1[2]
615- 4 nk **Dinner Date**[34] 7642 7-9-2 68 .... ShaneKelly 3 72
(T Keddy) *hld up in last pair: promising hdwy over 2f out to cl on ldrs over 1f out: effrt petered out fnl f* 6/1
25-3 5 1 **Magic Warrior**[9] 47 9-8-6 58 .... PaulFitzsimons 8 60
(J C Fox) *s.i.s: sn rcvrd and hld up in midfield: effrt on inner 2f out: sn nt qckn and hld* 11/1
520- 6 nk **Diego Rivera**[58] 7360 4-8-13 65 .... FergusSweeney 2 66
(P J Makin) *t.k.h on outer: mostly chsd ldr to 2f out: fdd* 14/1
44-4 7 nk **Divertimenti (IRE)**[11] 31 5-9-0 66 ....(p) LiamJones 6 67
(C R Dore) *t.k.h: trckd ldrs: lost pl over 2f out: n.d after: plugged on fnl f* 9/1
000- 8 1 **Pha Mai Blue**[23] 7764 4-8-13 65 .... PatCosgrave 7 63
(J R Boyle) *awkward s: a in last pair: shkn up and no prog over 2f out* 25/1
015- 9 1/2 **Tobar Suil Lady (IRE)**[41] 7548 4-9-0 66 .... StephenDonohoe 4 63
(J L Spearing) *t.k.h: hld up and racd wd: rapid prog to chal 3f out: sn rdn: grad wknd over 2f out* 8/1

1m 43.09s (3.29) **Going Correction** +0.275s/f (Slow) 9 Ran SP% 114.6
Speed ratings (Par 103): **94,91,91,91,90 89,89,88,88**
toteswinger 1&2 £2.00, 1&3 £4.00, 2&3 £3.40. CSF £19.13 CT £64.94 TOTE £4.70: £1.50, £2.40, £1.60; EX 14.00.
Owner John And Anne Soul **Bred** Brian Dolan **Trained** Lambourn, Berks

FOCUS
A fair handicap. The early pace was steady but the form reads sound enough, and the winner has a progressive profile.

158 BLUE SQUARE H'CAP 7f (P)
9:20 (9:23) (Class 5) (0-75,73) 3-Y-0 £2,590 (£770; £385; £192) Stalls High

Form RPR
351- 1 **Cut And Thrust (IRE)**[14] 7832 3-8-13 68 ....(p) ShaneKelly 2 78+
(M A Jarvis) *trckd ldr: rdn to ld 2f out: asserted over 1f out: drvn out fnl f* 6/5[2]
121- 2 1 1/4 **Lexlenos (IRE)**[28] 7700 3-9-4 73 .... JamieSpencer 5 80+
(D R C Elsworth) *hld up in last pair: rdn over 2f out: chsd wnr over 1f out: kpt on but nvr able to chal* 8/11[1]
004- 3 6 **Lucky Fortune (IRE)**[23] 7767 3-8-12 67 ....(b[1]) MickyFenton 4 58
(Miss Amy Weaver) *t.k.h early: led: rdn 1/2-way: hdd 2f out: wknd jst over 1f out* 16/1[3]
06- 4 15 **Mrs Slocombe (IRE)**[14] 7830 3-9-1 70 .... IanMongan 6 20
(J Akehurst) *rdn and dropped to last sn after 1/2-way: wknd over 2f out: t.o* 18/1

1m 28.03s (2.03) **Going Correction** +0.275s/f (Slow) 4 Ran SP% 114.5
Speed ratings (Par 97): **99,97,90,73**
CSF £2.60 TOTE £4.30; EX 3.30 Place 6: £25.37 Place 5: £14.67.
Owner A D Spence **Bred** Bloomsbury Stud **Trained** Newmarket, Suffolk

FOCUS
Not many runners but this was an interesting tactical event, involving a couple of progressive types in what was effectively a match. A fairly positive view has been taken of the form.
T/Plt: £13.10 to a £1 stake. Pool: £102,007.75. 5,670.61 winning tickets. T/Qpdt: £8.40 to a £1 stake. Pool: £6,873.07. 600.24 winning tickets. JN

119 LINGFIELD (L-H)
Wednesday, January 14

OFFICIAL GOING: Standard
Racing was put back an hour due to fog.
Wind: nil Weather: very foggy

159 JOSEPH LOSEY CLAIMING STKS 7f (P)
12:10 (1:12) (Class 6) 3-Y-0 £2,047 (£604; £302) Stalls Low

Form RPR
62-5 1 **Cognac Boy (USA)**[7] 74 3-8-3 64 ....(b[1]) JimmyQuinn 2 63
(R Hannon) *in tch: effrt and chsd ldrs over 1f out: in ld fnl 100yds: rdn out* 7/1
664- 2 2 **Flawless Diamond (IRE)**[14] 7832 3-8-0 52 ....(p) LukeMorris 1 54
(J S Moore) *chsd ldr: rdn to ld wl over 1f out: 2nd and one pce fnl 100yds* 14/1
313- 3 2 **Gone Hunting**[15] 7820 3-9-6 88 ....(t) TolleyDean(3) 5 72
(W G M Turner) *towards rr: pushed along over 3f out: hdwy to chse ldrs 2f out: 3rd and btn fnl 100yds* 11/8[1]
04-6 4 1 **River Rye (IRE)**[7] 75 3-8-0 68 ....(p) CatherineGannon 9 46
(J S Moore) *hld up bhd: hdwy and nt clr run jst over 2f out: c wd wl over 1f out: kpt on to go 4th fnl 100yds: nvr chal ldrs* 16/1
65-3 5 2 **Swiss Art (IRE)**[12] 10 3-8-5 62 .... JoeFanning 8 46
(R A Harris) *in tch in midfield: effrt over 2f out: pressed ldrs over 1f out: wknd and wl hld fnl 100yds* 11/2[3]
501- 6 1 1/2 **Art Fund (USA)**[25] 7738 3-8-9 63 .... FergusSweeney 7 46
(G L Moore) *chsd ldrs: effrt and rdn 2f out: wknd fnl f* 3/1[2]
7 1/2 **Whotsit (IRE)** 3-8-3 0 .... ChrisCatlin 4 39
(Miss Amy Weaver) *towards rr: pushed along over 3f out: no hdwy 2f out* 25/1
000- 8 1 3/4 **Ruby Best**[107] 6342 3-8-7 44 .... JamesO'Reilly(5) 6 43
(D K Ivory) *a towards rr: rdn and no hdwy over 2f out* 66/1
000- 9 nse **Buddy Marvellous (IRE)**[30] 7687 3-8-3 48 ....(p) FrankieMcDonald 3 34
(R A Harris) *led: drvn and hdd wl over 1f out: wknd* 66/1

1m 24.74s (-0.06) **Going Correction** +0.075s/f (Slow) 9 Ran SP% 114.4
Speed ratings (Par 95): **103,100,98,97,95 93,92,90,90**
toteswinger 1&2 £7.70, 1&3 £2.80, 2&3 £5.30. CSF £94.77 TOTE £8.30: £1.90, £2.90, £1.10; EX 75.70 Trifecta £283.60 Pool: £383.26 - 1.00 winning units..The winner was claimed by A. B. Haynes for £5000.
Owner Patrick J Fahey **Bred** J Kirk & Judy Robison **Trained** East Everleigh, Wilts

FOCUS
The usual wide range of abilities in this claimer, which was run at a steady pace in foggy conditions. The two favourites were below par.
Buddy Marvellous(IRE) Official explanation: jockey said colt hung right

160 CECIL BEATON MEDIAN AUCTION MAIDEN STKS 7f (P)
12:40 (1:37) (Class 6) 3-Y-0 £2,047 (£604; £302) Stalls Low

Form RPR
003- 1 **Royal Collection (IRE)**[75] 7104 3-9-3 72 .... PatCosgrave 10 78
(J Pearce) *chsd ldr: rdn jst over 2f out: led ins fnl f: styd on wl* 11/4[2]
33-2 2 2 **Rebel City**[5] 98 3-9-3 70 .... JamieSpencer 1 73
(S A Callaghan) *led: rdn and hung rt fr over 1f out: hdd and no ex ins fnl f* 8/11[1]
0- 3 4 1/2 **Kiss A Prince**[86] 6863 3-8-12 0 .... JamesO'Reilly(5) 4 61
(D K Ivory) *hld up towards rr on inner: 6th and outpcd over 2f out: r.o fnl f: snatched 3rd nr fin: nvr nr ldrs* 100/1
024- 4 nk **Why Nee Amy**[15] 7823 3-8-12 65 .... ChrisCatlin 9 55
(Miss Gay Kelleway) *s.i.s: towards rr: rdn along over 4f out: chsd clr ldng trio 2f out: no imp* 25/1
5 nk **Divine Force** 3-9-3 0 .... ShaneKelly 6 59
(J A Osborne) *in tch: hdwy to chse ldng pair over 2f out: rdn and unable qck 2f out: wknd fnl f: lost 2 pls towards fin* 33/1
6 nk **Dollar Express (USA)** 3-9-3 0 .... TPQueally 7 58+
(J Noseda) *s.i.s: bhd: 9th and rdn over 2f out: styd on steadily fnl f: nvr trbld ldrs* 7/1[3]
0 7 4 1/2 **General Sam (USA)**[5] 98 3-9-3 0 .... PatDobbs 8 46
(R Hannon) *in tch in midfield: rdn and struggling over 2f out: no ch fr wl over 1f out* 66/1
003- 8 1/2 **Cousin Charlie**[19] 7783 3-9-3 67 .... IanMongan 5 45
(S Kirk) *chsd ldrs tl rdn over 2f out: sn wknd* 20/1
0- 9 1 **Fleuron**[125] 5835 3-8-12 0 .... JimmyQuinn 2 37
(P Howling) *in tch in midfield: rdn and struggling over 2f out: n.d after* 50/1
10 5 **Soho Secrets** 3-8-12 0 .... JoeFanning 3 24
(M Johnston) *rn green in rr thrght* 20/1

1m 24.78s (-0.02) **Going Correction** +0.075s/f (Slow) 10 Ran SP% 117.8
Speed ratings (Par 95): **103,100,95,95,94 94,89,88,87,81**
toteswinger 1&2 £1.90, 1&3 £55.10, 2&3 £32.10. CSF £4.80 TOTE £6.20: £1.30, £1.10, £37.60; EX 6.80 Trifecta £272.60 Part won.
Owner Matthew Green **Bred** Lawn View Stud **Trained** Newmarket, Suffolk

FOCUS
A fair maiden which the betting market suggested was a two-horse race, and that was how it panned out as they finished clear.
Dollar Express(USA) ◆ Official explanation: jockey said colt missed break

161 JOYCE DOBIE MEMORIAL CLAIMING STKS 2m (P)
1:10 (2:01) (Class 6) 4-Y-0+ £2,047 (£604; £302) Stalls Low

Form RPR
161- 1 **Wind Flow**[14] 7831 5-9-7 68 ....(b) CatherineGannon 4 66
(C A Dwyer) *mde all: rdn wl over 1f out: drvn and forged clr 1f out: styd on wl* 13/8[1]
600/ 2 1 1/4 **Alrafid (IRE)**[68] 3195 10-9-5 70 ....(b) FergusSweeney 8 63
(G L Moore) *t.k.h: hld up in last pair: rdn and hdwy over 2f out: disp 2nd and rdn wl over 1f out: kpt on same pce fnl f* 13/2[3]
302- 3 hd **Acropolis (IRE)**[15] 7816 8-9-12 89 .... VinceSlattery 6 69
(A W Carroll) *stdd s: t.k.h: hld up in last pair: hdwy to trck ldrs 2f out: swtchd rt over 1f out: rdn ent fnl f: kpt on fnl 100yds to go 3rd towards fin: nvr rchd ldr* 7/4[2]
120- 4 nk **Mayadeen (IRE)**[29] 7696 7-9-0 56 ....(v) TonyHamilton 7 57
(R A Fahey) *in tch: effrt on inner over 2f out: disp 2nd wl over 1f out: one pce u.p fnl f* 9/1
00-6 5 4 **Always Certain (USA)**[8] 59 4-8-11 54 .... ChrisCatlin 5 56
(P G Murphy) *chsd wnr tl wl over 1f out: wknd u.p over 1f out: eased towards fin* 10/1
060- 6 30 **Smetana**[27] 7713 4-8-10 47 .... EdwardCreighton 3 19
(E J Creighton) *stdd s: t.k.h: chsd ldrs: rdn over 3f out: sn lost pl: t.o last 2f* 33/1

3m 30.45s (4.75) **Going Correction** +0.075s/f (Slow)
WFA 4 from 5yo+ 7lb 6 Ran SP% 109.8
Speed ratings (Par 101): **91,90,90,90,88 73**
toteswinger 1&2 £2.40, 1&3 £1.30, 2&3 £3.00. CSF £12.00 TOTE £2.30: £1.40, £2.60; EX 12.30 Trifecta £36.60 Pool: £230.74 - 4.66 winning units..
Owner Super Six Partnership **Bred** Lord Halifax **Trained** Burrough Green, Cambs

FOCUS
The winner set a steady gallop in this staying event.

162 HAL ROACH MEDIAN AUCTION MAIDEN STKS 6f (P)
1:45 (2:26) (Class 6) 3-5-Y-0 £2,217 (£654; £327) Stalls Low

Form RPR
03- 1 **Cheap Thrills**[165] 4634 3-8-5 0 .... ChrisCatlin 7 66
(J A Osborne) *stdd and dropped in after s: hld up in midfield: rdn over 3f out: hdwy on inner over 1f out: drvn and ev ch 1f out: led fnl 100yds: hld on gamely* 5/2[1]
44-2 2 hd **Princess Cagliari**[7] 69 3-8-5 64 .... JimmyQuinn 8 65
(R Hannon) *chsd ldrs rdn 2f out: ev ch u.p jst ins fnl f: kpt on wl: hld nr fin* 5/2[1]
5- 3 nk **Flamsteed (IRE)**[34] 7640 3-8-10 0 .... FrancisNorton 6 69
(M Quinn) *chsd ldr tl 2f out: sn rdn: drvn to ld 1f out: hdd fnl 100yds: no ex* 7/1[3]
036- 4 1 1/2 **Amosite**[30] 7689 3-8-5 65 ....(v) NickyMackay 3 59
(J R Jenkins) *led: hung rt and rdn bnd 2f out: hdd ent fnl f: one pce after* 20/1
532- 5 1/2 **Dark Camellia**[23] 7759 4-9-7 62 ....(t) TPQueally 2 62
(H J L Dunlop) *stdd s: sn wl in tch: rdn to chse ldr 2f out: led ent fnl f: sn hdd and btn* 4/1[2]
6 8 **Stylish Mover** 4-9-12 0 .... MickyFenton 5 41
(R Ingram) *awkward s and v.s.a: a bhd: lost tch wl over 2f out* 33/1
430- 7 2 3/4 **Rich Red (IRE)**[154] 4975 3-8-10 65 .... PatDobbs 4 28
(R Hannon) *dwlt: a in rr: lost tch wl over 2f out* 8/1

The Form Book, Raceform Ltd, Compton, RG20 6NL

8 4 1/2 **Uncle Brit** 3-8-10 0 StephenDonohoe 1 14
(Sir Mark Prescott) *dwlt: sn pushed along in last trio: lost tch wl over 2f out* **16/1**

1m 12.23s (0.33) **Going Correction** +0.075s/f (Slow)
WFA 3 from 4yo 16lb **8** Ran SP% **114.3**
Speed ratings (Par 101): **100,99,99,97,96 86,82,76**
toteswinger 1&2 £2.40, 1&3 £4.50, 2&3 £3.30. CSF £8.63 TOTE £3.00: £1.40, £1.40, £2.10; EX 6.10 Trifecta £43.10 Pool: £365.67 -6.27 winning units..
Owner Mr And Mrs Christopher Wright **Bred** Stratford Place Stud **Trained** Upper Lambourn, Berks

FOCUS
A modest maiden run at just a steady pace.
Rich Red(IRE) Official explanation: jockey said gelding was never travelling

163 WILLIAM HILL JANUARY SALE - BETTER ODDS! H'CAP 1m 2f (P)
2:20 (2:51) (Class 4) (0-80,80) 4-Y-O+ **£4,857** (£1,445; £722; £360) **Stalls** Low

Form RPR
005- **1** **Basra (IRE)**38 7595 6-9-6 **80** JamieSpencer 3 87
(Miss Jo Crowley) *hld up in tch: hdwy 2f out: short of room over 1f out: squeezed through jst ins fnl f: drvn to ld fnl 100yds: r.o wl* **4/1**3

032- **2** *nk* **Summer Winds**24 7752 4-8-13 **75** ShaneKelly 1 81
(T G Mills) *led at v slow pce for 1f: chsd ldr after tl rdn to ld 2f out: drvn ent fnl f: hdd fnl 100yds: kpt on same pce* **7/2**2

004- **3** 1/2 **Halsion Chancer**28 7712 5-9-5 **79** RobertWinston 2 84
(J R Best) *trckd ldng pair: rdn and effrt jst over 2f out: drvn: ev ch ins fnl f: unable qck fnl 100yds* **5/1**

10-3 **4** *hd* **Faithful Ruler (USA)**7 79 5-8-11 **71** TonyHamilton 4 76
(R A Fahey) *in tch: rdn and unable qck bnd jst over 2f out: drvn and kpt on fnl f: nt quite pce to chal ldrs* **7/2**2

000- **5** 3/4 **Kestrel Cross (IRE)**13 6035 7-9-0 **74** (t) LukeMorris 6 77
(A W Carroll) *s.i.s: sn in tch in rr: rdn and no imp jst over 2f out: kpt on fnl f: nt pce to rch ldrs2* **33/1**

041- **6** 1 3/4 **Phoenix Flight (IRE)**77 7070 4-9-4 **80** StephenDonohoe 7 80
(Sir Mark Prescott) *led after 1f: rdn and hdd 2f out: sn edgd rt u.p: stl ev ch 1f out: sn wknd* **11/4**1

430- **7** 5 **Mcconnell (USA)**28 7712 4-9-2 **78** FergusSweeney 5 68
(G L Moore) *stdd after s: t.k.h: hld up in last pair: rdn and no rspnse over 2f out* **16/1**

2m 9.09s (2.49) **Going Correction** +0.075s/f (Slow)
WFA 4 from 5yo+ 2lb **7** Ran SP% **116.6**
Speed ratings (Par 105): **93,92,92,92,91 90,86**
toteswinger 1&2 £1.70, 1&3 £2.20, 2&3 £2.70. CSF £19.03 TOTE £6.30: £1.90, £2.00; EX 22.10.
Owner Mrs Liz Nelson **Bred** Redmondstown Stud **Trained** Whitcombe, Dorset

FOCUS
This was a fair handicap, but they went just a slow gallop and it turned into something of a sprint.

164 WILLIAM HILL JANUARY SALE - NOW ON! H'CAP 1m 2f (P)
2:50 (3:16) (Class 5) (0-75,72) 3-Y-O **£2,900** (£856; £428) **Stalls** Low

Form RPR
613- **1** **True Britannia**15 7824 3-8-4 **58** (v) AndrewElliott 3 59
(A M Hales) *hld up in last pl: effrt and rdn 2f out: drvn and str chal wl ins fnl f: led on post* **8/1**

334- **2** *nse* **Black N Brew (USA)**35 7623 3-9-1 **69** RobertWinston 2 70
(J R Best) *chsd ldng trio tl wnt 2nd over 2f out: rdn 2f out: drvn over 1f out: led wl ins fnl f: hdd on post* **6/4**2

436- **3** 2 **Special Bond**15 7824 3-8-11 **65** (b1) ShaneKelly 1 62
(J A Osborne) *led: rdn wl over 1f out: hdd wl ins fnl f: wknd towards fin* **7/1**3

412- **4** 4 **Supernoverre (IRE)**45 7505 3-9-4 **72** PatDobbs 4 61
(Mrs A J Perrett) *chsd ldr tl over 2f out: rdn and dropped to last 2f out: eased whn btn ins fnl f* **11/8**1

2m 8.61s (2.01) **Going Correction** +0.075s/f (Slow) **4** Ran SP% **105.7**
Speed ratings (Par 97): **94,93,92,89**
CSF £19.54 TOTE £5.60; EX 13.30.
Owner Brick Farm Racing **Bred** Cleaboy Farms Co **Trained** Wardington, Oxon

FOCUS
An interesting little handicap despite the small field, and a good finish with the lead changing hands twice inside the last furlong. The pace was fairly steady before it was stepped up in the final half-mile.

165 WILLIAM HILL JANUARY SALE - WHY BET ELSEWHERE? H'CAP 5f (P)
3:25 (3:40) (Class 5) (0-75,75) 4-Y-O+ **£2,900** (£856; £428) **Stalls** High

Form RPR
4-11 **1** **Nickel Silver**5 96 4-9-4 **75** 6ex (b) TomEaves 5 88
(B Smart) *mde all: rdn clr over 1f out: in n.d fnl f: rdn out* **7/4**1

052- **2** 2 1/2 **After The Show**25 7743 8-8-8 **65** ChrisCatlin 6 69+
(Rae Guest) *stdd after s: hld up in rr: hdwy over 1f out: swtchd rt ins fnl f: r.o to go 2nd nr fin: nvr able to chal wnr* **5/2**2

4-06 **3** 1/2 **Bluebok**5 96 8-8-5 **62** (bt) LukeMorris 4 64
(J M Bradley) *racd keenly: chsd ldrs: wnt 2nd over 2f out: rdn and nt pce of wnr over 1f out: lost 2nd nr fin* **9/1**

00-3 **4** 1/2 **Caribbean Coral**6 83 10-9-2 **73** TPQueally 2 73
(A B Haynes) *s.i.s: hld up towards rr: hdwy over 2f out: wnt 3rd and drvn over 1f out: wl hld fnl f* **15/2**3

33-0 **5** 1 1/4 **Savile's Delight (IRE)**6 89 10-9-4 **75** FergusSweeney 7 71
(Tom Dascombe) *hld up bhd: rdn and effrt on outer wl over 1f out: edgd lft ent fnl f: nvr nr wnr* **12/1**

53-6 **6** 3/4 **Magic Glade**9 44 10-8-4 **61** oh4 (b) PatrickMathers 1 54
(Peter Grayson) *hld up in rr: brief effrt on inner over 1f out: n.d* **16/1**

16-5 **7** 1 1/2 **Bookiesindex Boy**6 83 5-9-2 **73** (v) StephenDonohoe 3 61
(J R Jenkins) *chsd ldr tl over 2f out: rdn over 1f out: wknd ent fnl f* **10/1**

04-0 **8** 6 **Stoneacre Pat (IRE)**9 44 4-7-11 **61** oh9 (b) AndrewHeffernan(7) 8 27
(Peter Grayson) *chsd ldrs: rdn 2f out: wknd qckly over 1f out* **40/1**

58.46 secs (-0.34) **Going Correction** +0.075s/f (Slow) **8** Ran SP% **111.8**
Speed ratings (Par 103): **105,101,100,99,97 96,93,84**
toteswinger 1&2 £1.40, 1&3 £4.50, 2&3 £5.00. CSF £5.84 CT £27.08 TOTE £2.30: £1.10, £1.30, £2.50; EX 6.60 Trifecta £31.20 Pool: £463.02 - 10.98 winning units..
Owner M Barber **Bred** Mrs Sheila White **Trained** Hambleton, N Yorks

FOCUS
A fair handicap.

Savile's Delight(IRE) ◆ Official explanation: jockey said gelding hung left

166 BENEDICT ARNOLD APPRENTICE H'CAP 6f (P)
3:55 (4:06) (Class 6) (0-60,60) 4-Y-O+ **£2,047** (£604; £302) **Stalls** Low

Form RPR
20-6 **1** **Joss Stick**11 27 4-8-12 **60** SPRyan(7) 10 68
(R A Harris) *taken down early: chsd ldrs: wnt 2nd 2f out: sn ev ch: in ld ins fnl f: hld on wl* **12/1**

22-0 **2** *nk* **Compton Classic**11 27 7-8-12 **58** (t) NathanAlison(5) 2 65
(Tom Dascombe) *towards rr: c wd and hdwy bnd 2f out: pressed wnr ins fnl f: no ex towards fin* **13/2**

04-4 **3** 1/2 **Simpsons Gamble (IRE)**9 44 6-9-2 **57** (p) MatthewDavies 6 62
(R A Teal) *hld up in midfield: rdn and hdwy towards inner 2f out: chsd ldng pair ins fnl f: kpt on* **9/2**2

331- **4** 3/4 **Loyal Royal (IRE)**15 7818 6-9-2 **57** (b) BillyCray 3 60
(J M Bradley) *towards rr on inner: hdwy over 2f out: chsd ldrs ins fnl f: kpt on same pce cl home* **5/1**3

220- **5** 1 1/4 **Morse (IRE)**66 7255 8-8-13 **57** (p) PNolan(3) 5 56
(J A Osborne) *led: rdn over 2f out: hrd pressed wl over 1f out: 5th and btn ins fnl f* **9/2**2

500- **6** 1/2 **Mansii**85 6889 4-9-5 **60** AshleyMorgan 1 57
(P J McBride) *s.i.s: detached last 4f out: hdwy over 2f out: styd on but nvr rchd ldrs* **4/1**1

05-0 **7** 1 1/2 **Avoca Dancer (IRE)**12 14 6-9-3 **58** (v) KylieManser 9 51
(Miss Gay Kelleway) *in tch on outer: pushed along 4f out: rdn and chsd ldrs 2f out: wknd fnl f* **17/2**

004- **8** 3 3/4 **One Way Ticket**28 7710 9-8-5 **46** oh1 (p) DeanHeslop 8 27
(J M Bradley) *chsd ldrs: rdn ent fnl 2f: wl btn ins fnl f* **16/1**

400- **9** 4 1/2 **Orphan Boy**22 7774 4-8-5 **46** oh1 JemmaMarshall 4 12
(H J Collingridge) *towards rr: effrt and wd bnd 2f out: nvr nr ldrs* **50/1**

006- **10** *hd* **Rightcar Dominic**31 7679 4-8-4 **50** AndrewHeffernan(5) 7 16
(Peter Grayson) *chsd ldr tl 2f out: sn wknd* **12/1**

1m 12.14s (0.24) **Going Correction** +0.075s/f (Slow) **10** Ran SP% **120.1**
Speed ratings (Par 101): **101,100,99,98,97 96,94,89,83,83**
toteswinger 1&2 £17.40, 1&3 £12.20, 2&3 £5.50. CSF £90.51 CT £424.00 TOTE £14.00: £3.30, £2.60, £1.30; EX 128.40 TRIFECTA Not won. Place 6: £140.90 Place 5: £78.69 .
Owner Mrs Ruth M Serrell **Bred** K W Green **Trained** Earlswood, Monmouths
■ The first winner for Shane Ryan.

FOCUS
The fog had come down again before this low-grade apprentice event.
Mansii Official explanation: jockey said gelding missed break
T/Plt: £122.30 to a £1 stake. Pool: £46,464.55. 277.24 winning tickets. T/Qpdt: £77.90 to a £1 stake. Pool: £3,108.70. 29.50 winning tickets. SP

140 GREAT LEIGHS (A.W) (L-H)
Thursday, January 15

OFFICIAL GOING: Standard
Wind: Light, across Weather: Fine **The last meeting before the track was shut down**

167 RED KITE H'CAP 6f (P)
6:50 (6:50) (Class 5) (0-70,70) 4-Y-O+ **£3,238** (£963; £481; £240) **Stalls** Low

Form RPR
403- **1** **Billy Red**15 7834 5-8-8 **60** (b) FergusSweeney 12 75
(J R Jenkins) *broke wl: sn crossed to rails' and mde all: rdn and drew clr over 1f out: styd on wl* **15/2**

031- **2** 2 3/4 **Leading Edge (IRE)**17 7811 4-9-4 **70** TonyCulhane 10 76
(M R Channon) *towards rr: rdn and hdwy wl over 1f out: styd on to chse wnr fnl 100yds: nvr able to chal* **12/1**

2/0- **3** 1 1/4 **Capefly**261 1699 4-9-3 **69** (t) TPQueally 1 71
(P W Chapple-Hyam) *sn pushed up to chse ldrs: rdn to chse wnr wl over 1f out: sn outpcd by wnr: lost 2nd fnl 100yds* **25/1**

160- **4** 1 1/4 **Step It Up (IRE)**26 7743 5-9-0 **66** PatCosgrave 11 64
(J R Boyle) *towards rr: styd on u.p fr over 1f out: nvr nr wnr* **16/1**

54-3 **5** 3/4 **Obe Royal**9 57 5-8-6 **58** (b) StephenDonohoe 6 54+
(P D Evans) *s.i.s: sn pushed along in rr: drvn over 2f out: keeping on whn nt clr run and swtchd rt 1f out: kpt on but nvr nr wnr* **6/1**3

52-3 **6** 3/4 **Bertie Southstreet**6 96 6-8-13 **65** JimCrowley 7 59
(J R Boyle) *hld up in tch: rdn and nt qckn 2f out: kpt on same pce and no ch after* **3/1**1

4-16 **7** 3/4 **Namu**1 155 6-8-12 **64** (p) ChrisCatlin 8 55
(Miss T Spearing) *stdd s: t.k.h: hld up in rr: rdn and sme hdwy fr 2f out: n.d* **8/1**

00-4 **8** *hd* **Maybe I Wont**8 76 4-8-9 **61** LiamJones 3 52+
(Lucinda Featherstone) *s.i.s: bhd: rdn and effrt on inner wl over 1f out: keeping on but no ch whn nt clr run and swtchd lft ins fnl f* **20/1**

463- **9** *nk* **Asian Power (IRE)**24 7762 4-9-2 **68** ShaneKelly 5 58
(P J O'Gorman) *racd in midfield: rdn and fnd little wl over 1f out: wknd ent fnl f* **9/2**2

020- **10** 3 1/4 **Splash The Cash**54 7428 4-8-12 **64** JamieSpencer 2 43
(K A Ryan) *chsd wnr tl wl over 1f out: sn wknd u.p: eased whn no ch insde fnl f* **9/1**

63-4 **11** 2 1/4 **Replicator**13 13 4-9-0 **66** (v) PaulEddery 9 38
(Pat Eddery) *chsd ldrs tl rdn over 3f out: wknd wl over 1f out* **10/1**

1m 12.34s (-1.36) **Going Correction** +0.075s/f (Slow) **11** Ran SP% **121.6**
Speed ratings (Par 103): **112,108,106,105,104 103,102,101,101,97 94**
toteswinger 1&2 £28.80, 1&3 Not won, 2&3 £28.80. CSF £97.25 CT £2201.20 TOTE £12.50: £4.40, £3.60, £8.50; EX 143.90.
Owner Mrs Irene Hampson **Bred** D R Tucker **Trained** Royston, Herts
■ Stewards' Enquiry : Shane Kelly 13-day ban (takes into account previous offences; two days deferred): careless riding (Jan 30-Feb 9)

FOCUS
A modest if competitive sprint handicap, but the winning time was very decent for a race of its type. The form looks sound, with a personal best from the winner.
Obe Royal Official explanation: jockey said gelding was denied a clear run
Maybe I Wont Official explanation: jockey said gelding was denied a clear run

168 GOSHAWK H'CAP 1m 6f (P)
7:20 (7:20) (Class 6) (0-65,63) 4-Y-O+ **£2,590** (£770; £385; £192) **Stalls** Low

Form RPR
126- **1** **Little Carmela**28 7715 5-10-0 **63** ChrisCatlin 7 69
(S C Williams) *dwlt: t.k.h: chsd ldr after 2f: rdn to ld over 2f out: drvn and hrd pressed 1f out: edgd lft but hld on gamely fnl f* **13/8**1

130- **2** *hd* **Ice Bellini**[58] 7376 4-9-6 **61**..(b[1]) JamieSpencer 1 67
(Miss Gay Kelleway) *chsd ldng pair: reminders 5f out: sn rdn: hrd drvn and str chal ins fnl f: jst hld* **13/2**

000- **3** *1 1/4* **Double Spectre (IRE)**[98] 6607 7-9-11 **60**.......................... JimCrowley 6 65+
(Jean-Rene Auvray) *stdd s: hld up in rr: hdwy on bit 2f out: chal and rdn ent fnl f: nt qckn after: 3rd and hld whn nt clr run and snatched up towards fin* **9/2[2]**

600- **4** *1/2* **Champagne Shadow (IRE)**[15] 7831 8-8-12 **47**.........(p) JerryO'Dwyer 2 50
(J Pearce) *in tch in midfield: rdn 4f out: chsd ldng trio ent fnl f: kpt on same pce u.p* **20/1**

403/ **5** *4 1/2* **Enthusius**[49] 7012 6-9-3 **52**.................................(b[1]) FergusSweeney 8 49
(G L Moore) *led: rdn 3f out: hdd over 2f out: wknd ent fnl f* **6/1[3]**

06-0 **6** *4* **Peas 'n Beans (IRE)**[5] 112 6-8-12 **47**.............................. JimmyQuinn 4 38
(T Keddy) *hld up in last trio: rdn and effrt on outer over 2f out: wknd over 1f out* **17/2**

050- **7** *3* **Three Boars**[50] 7455 7-9-11 **60**................................(b) RobertWinston 5 47
(S Gollings) *t.k.h: chsd ldr for 2f: in tch in midfield after: rdn and wknd over 2f out* **7/1**

060/ **8** *9* **Charleston**[408] 7012 8-8-3 **45**.. RichardRowe(7) 3 20
(R Rowe) *prom early: lost pl and last 10f out: lost tch 7f out* **33/1**

3m 4.50s (1.30) **Going Correction** +0.075s/f (Slow)
WFA 4 from 5yo+ 6lb **8** Ran SP% **114.6**
Speed ratings (Par 101): **99,98,98,97,95 93,91,86**
toteswinger 1&2 £5.40, 1&3 £2.20, 2&3 £15.60. CSF £12.79 CT £39.85 TOTE £2.90: £1.10, £1.90, £2.30; EX 15.30.
Owner O Pointing **Bred** O Pointing **Trained** Newmarket, Suffolk
■ Stewards' Enquiry : Chris Catlin three-day ban: careless riding (Jan 29-31)

FOCUS
A modest staying handicap in which Enthusius was allowed an easy time of things in front and he set just modest fractions. The winner probably didn't have to improve and the second was a shade off her Southwell form.

169 GOLDEN EAGLE CLASSIFIED STKS 1m 5f 66y(P)
7:50 (7:51) (Class 7) 4-Y-O+ **£1,706** (£503; £252) **Stalls** Low

Form RPR

30-3 **1** **Amwell Brave**[5] 116 8-9-3 45.................................... SimonWhitworth 14 57
(J R Jenkins) *stdd and dropped in bhd after s: hld up wl bhd: nt clr run on inner over 2f out: stl plenty to do and swtchd rt wl over 1f out: gd hdwy but edging lft fr over 1f out: led ins fnl f: sn clr* **6/1[3]**

550- **2** *2 1/2* **Limelight (USA)**[91] 6753 4-8-12 45........................... StephenDonohoe 3 53
(Sir Mark Prescott) *chsd ldr tl 8f out: chsd ldrs after: rdn wl over 3f out: drvn to ld over 1f out: hung lft u.p: hdd ins fnl f: no ch w wnr* **15/2**

00-2 **3** *2 3/4* **Prince Of Medina**[5] 117 6-9-3 41................................(t) RobertWinston 5 49
(J R Best) *t.k.h: hld up towards rr: hdwy 3f out: drvn ent fnl 2f: chsd ldrs and edgd lft ent fnl f: outpcd by ldng pair after: plugged on to go 3rd fnl 75yds* **9/2[1]**

60-0 **4** *3/4* **Hawkstar Express (IRE)**[10] 43 4-8-12 45...............(b[1]) PatCosgrave 7 48
(J R Boyle) *in tch: rdn 4f out: effrt u.p to chse ldrs over 1f out: edgd lft and one pce fnl f* **33/1**

660- **5** *nk* **Viscount Rossini**[20] 5869 7-9-3 45..............................(b) JamieSpencer 1 48
(S Gollings) *t.k.h: in tch: chsd ldr 5f out: drvn wl over 1f out: outpcd jst ins fnl f* **11/2[2]**

040/ **6** *1 1/4* **Green Day Packer (IRE)**[59] 5626 5-8-12 45......... PatrickDonaghy(5) 13 46
(P C Haslam) *chsd ldrs: wnt 2nd 8f out tl led 5f out: rdn 2f out: hdd over 1f out: wknd jst ins fnl f* **10/1**

163- **7** *hd* **Itsawindup**[17] 7815 5-9-3 44..................................(t) EdwardCreighton 6 45
(Miss Sheena West) *in tch in midfield: rdn and effrt 3f out: keeping on same pce whn slty hmpd over 1f out: no imp fnl f* **9/1**

04-0 **8** *3/4* **Autumn Charm**[5] 116 4-8-12 43.. LiamJones 2 46+
(Lucinda Featherstone) *plld hrd: hld up towards rr: hdwy and n.m.r on inner 3f out tl 2f out: chsng ldrs whn nt clr run and snatched up ent fnl f: swtchd rt ins fnl f: nvr able to chal* **16/1**

540- **9** *shd* **Summer Bounty**[31] 7688 13-9-3 43................................ JerryO'Dwyer 4 44
(F Jordan) *t.k.h: hld up in midfield: n.m.r on inner 3f out: drvn and effrt 2f out: chsng ldrs and keeping on same pce whn hmpd ent fnl f: no imp after* **28/1**

06-6 **10** *1 1/2* **Niqaab**[11] 38 5-9-3 45.. ChrisCatlin 10 42
(W J Musson) *t.k.h: hld up in rr: hmpd over 1f out: nvr nr ldrs* **7/1**

000/ **11** *1 1/4* **Strident (USA)**[39] 8-8-12 43.. AmyBaker(5) 11 40
(N P Moore) *led: hdd 5f out: rdn 4f out: styd chsng ldrs untl wknd qckly ent fnl f* **20/1**

050- **12** *7* **Bonzo**[19] 7787 4-8-12 45..(b[1]) JimmyQuinn 9 29
(P Howling) *dwlt: hld up towards rr: effrt and rdn whn bmpd wl over 1f out: sn no prog and wl btn* **16/1**

U60- **13** *3* **Sir Joey**[30] 7695 4-8-9 44....................................(v[1]) RussellKennemore(3) 8 25
(B D Leavy) *hld up bhd: hmpd after 1f: rdn 5f out: wl bhd fnl 2f* **66/1**

0- **14** *18* **Treetops Hotel (IRE)**[109] 6309 10-9-3 44..................... VinceSlattery 12 —
(L R James) *s.i.s: t.k.h: sn in tch: rdn over 4f out: wknd qckly over 3f: t.o* **33/1**

2m 56.1s (2.50) **Going Correction** +0.075s/f (Slow)
WFA 4 from 5yo+ 5lb **14** Ran SP% **118.6**
Speed ratings (Par 97): **95,93,91,91,91 90,90,89,89,88 88,83,81,70**
toteswinger 1&2 £10.70, 1&3 £3.40, 2&3 £8.90. CSF £46.93 TOTE £5.70: £1.40, £3.10, £2.20; EX 55.20.
Owner Amwell Racing **Bred** Wayland Stud **Trained** Royston, Herts
■ Stewards' Enquiry : Robert Winston two-day ban: careless riding (Jan 29-30)

FOCUS
Not a bad race for the grade, and an impressive performance from the winner who is rated back to the form of this time last year. The pace was only steady.
Autumn Charm Official explanation: jockey said filly was denied a clear run
Niqaab Official explanation: jockey said mare was hampered on the first bend

170 HEN HARRIER H'CAP 5f (P)
8:20 (8:21) (Class 4) (0-85,84) 4-Y-O+ **£5,180** (£1,541; £770; £384) **Stalls** Low

Form RPR

342- **1** **Wotashirtfull (IRE)**[17] 7811 4-8-11 **77**..........................(p) JamieSpencer 6 86
(K A Ryan) *mde all: hrd pressed and drvn over 1f out: styd on gamely fnl f: jst hld on* **3/1[2]**

11- **2** *shd* **Ivory Silk**[16] 7826 4-9-4 **84**...(b) ChrisCatlin 4 93
(J R Gask) *squeezed s: towards rr: hdwy and c wd off bnd 2f out: drvn ent fnl f: str run fnl 100yds: jst failed* **11/10[1]**

05-4 **3** *3/4* **Fromsong (IRE)**[12] 24 11-8-11 **82**.............................. JamesO'Reilly(5) 3 88
(D K Ivory) *sn pushed up to chse ldrs: clipped heels and stmbld over 2f out: drvn and upsides wnr over 1f out: no ex towards fin* **7/1[3]**

140- **4** *1 1/4* **Know No Fear**[127] 5796 4-8-11 **77**.................................. DarrenWilliams 7 79
(D Shaw) *stdd and dropped in bhd after s: hdwy on inner over 1f out: no imp fnl 100yds* **20/1**

060- **5** *1* **Almaty Express**[16] 7826 7-8-1 **74**..........................(b) DeclanCannon(7) 2 72
(J R Weymes) *awkward s and slowly away: sn pushed along towards rr: hmpd over 2f out: effrt on inner over 1f out: nvr nr ldrs* **16/1**

606- **6** *1/2* **Silver Prelude**[25] 7756 8-8-11 **77**.. JimCrowley 8 73
(S C Williams) *chsd ldrs: swtchd rt over 1f out: drvn ent fnl f: wknd ins fnl f* **12/1**

104- **7** *2* **Storey Hill (USA)**[225] 2732 4-8-9 **75**............................... RobertWinston 1 64
(D Shaw) *pressed ldr: rdn 2f out: wknd ent fnl f* **16/1**

59.84 secs (-0.36) **Going Correction** +0.075s/f (Slow) **7** Ran SP% **109.3**
Speed ratings (Par 105): **105,104,103,101,100 99,96**
toteswinger 1&2 £1.50, 1&3 £2.70, 2&3 £1.10. CSF £6.03 CT £16.20 TOTE £3.90: £1.70, £1.10; EX 6.80.
Owner Sporting Gunners Syndicate Two **Bred** Luke O'Reilly **Trained** Hambleton, N Yorks

FOCUS
There was no hiding place here as the pace was strong throughout. The winner is rated to last year's turf best, with the second continuing her recent progress.
Storey Hill(USA) Official explanation: jockey said gelding had no more to give

171 OSPREY (S) STKS 1m 2f (P)
8:50 (8:50) (Class 5) 4-Y-O+ **£2,590** (£770; £385; £192) **Stalls** Low

Form RPR

51-2 **1** **Clear Sailing**[13] 12 6-9-6 72.......................................(p) ChrisCatlin 10 75
(Ollie Pears) *mde virtually all: clr 8f out: 6 l clr over 2f out: rdn over 1f out: kpt on gamely fnl f: jst lasted* **3/1[2]**

2-13 **2** *nse* **Bavarica**[4] 132 7-8-4 65.. AmyBaker(5) 3 64+
(Miss J Feilden) *stdd s: t.k.h: hld up in last pl: hdwy over 2f out: modest 5th ent st: rdn over 1f out: r.o wl: jst failed* **2/1[1]**

04-3 **3** *1 3/4* **Murfreesboro**[12] 26 6-9-0 75......................................(v) DarrenWilliams 1 66
(D Shaw) *t.k.h: hld up in midfield: hdwy over 4f out: chsd clr ldr over 2f out: rdn and clsd over 1f out: drvn to chal and hld hd awkwardly 1f out: btn fnl 100yds: fdd towards fin* **7/2[3]**

530- **4** *1* **Sheer Fantastic**[110] 3555 4-8-12 68.................................(v) TonyCulhane 8 64
(P C Haslam) *w.w in midfield: swtchd rt 5f out: lost pl and rdn over 3f out: hdwy over 1f out: chsd ldrs 1f out: kpt on but nt pce to rch ldrs* **14/1**

5 *4 1/2* **Tigerbythetale (IRE)**[41] 4-8-12 0.................................(t) HayleyTurner 6 55
(D R C Elsworth) *v awkward and propped leaving stalls: bhd in last pair: styd on and edgd lft fr over 1f out: nvr nr ldrs* **8/1**

606- **6** *3/4* **Competitor**[15] 7831 8-9-0 48...(b) IanMongan 4 53
(J Akehurst) *chsd ldr: hung lft and lost 2nd over 2f out: wl btn fr over 1f out* **33/1**

/50- **7** *1 1/4* **Dancing Lyra**[285] 1217 8-9-0 70.. TonyHamilton 5 51
(R A Fahey) *hld up bhd: drvn 2f out: n.d* **10/1**

506- **8** *1 1/4* **Bury Treasure (IRE)**[19] 7790 4-8-5 63........................... KylieManser(7) 9 48
(Miss Gay Kelleway) *t.k.h: chsd ldrs: rdn and struggling over 2f out: wl btn over 1f out* **33/1**

55-0 **9** *6* **Piermarini**[6] 105 4-8-5 65... PaulPickard(7) 2 36
(P T Midgley) *hld up towards rr: hdwy on outer over 4f out: rdn and struggling 3f out: wl bhd over 1f out* **66/1**

000- **10** *1 1/4* **The Slider**[30] 5787 5-8-9 29...............................(p) FrankieMcDonald 7 29
(Mrs L C Jewell) *chsd ldrs tl lost pl 4f out: wl bhd fr over 2f out* **100/1**

2m 7.69s (-0.91) **Going Correction** +0.075s/f (Slow)
WFA 4 from 5yo+ 2lb **10** Ran SP% **115.8**
Speed ratings (Par 103): **106,105,104,103,100 99,98,97,92,91**
toteswinger 1&2 £1.30, 1&3 £1.50, 2&3 £1.40. CSF £9.17 TOTE £4.50: £2.00, £1.10, £1.10; EX 7.80.There was no bid for the winner. Murfreesboro was claimed by Alan Edward Jones for £8,000.
Owner We-Know Partnership **Bred** Juddmonte Farms Ltd **Trained** Norton, N Yorks

FOCUS
Although this was a much lesser contest, the finish was very similar to the previous event as the winner hung on gamely from the fast-finishing favourite. The sixth is perhaps the best guide to the form and the winner is rated 5lb off his recent Southwell win.
Bury Treasure(IRE) Official explanation: jockey said gelding hung left

172 PEREGRINE H'CAP 1m 2f (P)
9:20 (9:20) (Class 5) (0-75,75) 4-Y-O+ **£3,238** (£963; £481; £240) **Stalls** Low

Form RPR

231- **1** **Folio (IRE)**[25] 7753 9-9-4 **73**.. ChrisCatlin 3 78
(W J Musson) *hld up in midfield: hdwy to chse ldrs and n.m.r wl over 1f out: swtchd sltly rt jst ins fnl f: r.o wl to ld nr fin* **3/1[1]**

464/ **2** *hd* **Just Observing**[524] 4365 6-9-1 **70**.............................(p) MickyFenton 8 74
(P T Midgley) *sn led and set stdy gallop: rdn over 1f out: kpt on wl tl hdd nr fin* **28/1**

002- **3** *1/2* **Fandango Boy**[27] 7732 8-8-2 **64**.. JPFahy(7) 4 67
(D Carroll) *plld hrd: hld up towards rr: hdwy 2f out: drvn and ev ch ins fnl f: no ex towards fin* **8/1**

50-2 **4** *3/4* **Hucking Hero (IRE)**[12] 28 4-9-2 **73**................................... JimCrowley 2 75
(J R Best) *stdd s: hld up towards rr: swtchd rt and effrt over 1f out: kpt on u.p fnl f: nt rch ldrs* **13/2[3]**

12-0 **5** *nk* **Man Of Gwent (UAE)**[3] 139 5-9-3 **72**......................... RobertWinston 1 77+
(P D Evans) *puled hrd: chsd ldrs: hanging lft bnd over 2f out: nt clr run fr over 1f out: eased towards fin* **5/1[2]**

130- **6** *1 1/2* **Metal Madness (IRE)**[17] 6188 4-8-12 **69**......................... TonyCulhane 9 67
(M G Quinlan) *chsd ldr: rdn jst over 2f out: drvn and ev ch ent fnl f: struggling whn hmpd jst ins fnl f: btn after* **13/2[3]**

/32- **7** *2 1/2* **Rawdon (IRE)**[19] 7797 8-9-6 **75**..................................(vt) HayleyTurner 7 68
(M L W Bell) *stdd s: hld up in rr: rdn and no rspnse over 2f out: nvr trbld ldrs* **3/1[1]**

015- **8** *3* **What's Up Doc (IRE)**[83] 6663 8-9-6 **75**......................... FergusSweeney 6 68
(Mrs T J Hill) *stdd after s: t.k.h: hld up in rr: effrt and sltly hmpd over 1f out: hanging lft and eased ent fnl f* **12/1**

2m 11.72s (3.12) **Going Correction** +0.075s/f (Slow)
WFA 4 from 5yo+ 2lb **8** Ran SP% **115.6**
Speed ratings (Par 103): **90,89,89,88,88 87,85,83**
toteswinger 1&2 £23.30, 1&3 £4.70, 2&3 £23.30. CSF £89.60 CT £615.37 TOTE £3.80: £1.20, £3.20, £2.90; EX 51.80 Place 6 £54.71, Place 5 £4.80..
Owner Goodey and Broughton **Bred** Lord Rothschild **Trained** Newmarket, Suffolk

FOCUS
A very slow time for the grade and the front five finished in a heap. Messy form, rated around the third and fourth. The winner is rated as finishing upsides the winner.
Man Of Gwent(UAE) Official explanation: jockey said, regarding easing his mount approaching the final furlong, fearing his gap on the rails was about to close and he was to suffer interference he felt it prudent to ease his mount as a precaution.
What's Up Doc(IRE) Official explanation: jockey reported gelding hung left

T/Plt: £22.10 to a £1 stake. Pool: £97,603.42. 3,210.98 winning tickets. T/Qpdt: £4.10 to a £1 stake. Pool: £9,903.00. 1,760.40 winning tickets. SP

[146]SOUTHWELL (L-H)

Thursday, January 15

OFFICIAL GOING: Standard

Wind: Light across Weather: Overcast and light rain showers

173 WILLIAM HILL JANUARY SALE - WHY BET ELSEWHERE? H'CAP (DIV I) 5f (F)

1:00 (1:00) (Class 6) (0-60,62) 4-Y-0+ **£2,729** (£806; £403) **Stalls** High

Form RPR

5-51 **1** **Whiskey Creek**[10] 44 4-8-13 **62** 6ex.............................(b) BMcHugh(7) 8 77
(C A Dwyer) *dwlt: sn chsng ldrs: cl up 1/2-way: sn led: rdn ent fnl f and kpt on wl* **11/2**[3]

140- **2** *2 1/2* **The Geester**[26] 7746 5-9-0 **56**.............................(b) PaulEddery 1 62
(S R Bowring) *bmpd s: cl up: effrt over 2f out: sn rdn and ev ch: drvn over 1f out and kpt on same pce* **2/1**[1]

00-0 **3** *hd* **Decider (USA)**[13] 15 6-9-4 **60**............................. JoeFanning 7 65
(R A Harris) *led: rdn along 1/2-way and sn hdd: drvn over 1f out and kpt on same pce u.p ins fnl f* **4/1**[2]

50-5 **4** *1 1/4* **Mr Rooney (IRE)**[7] 89 6-8-8 **55** ow2............................. SladeO'Hara(5) 2 56
(A Berry) *in tch: hdwy over 2f out: swtchd lft and rdn over 1f out: kpt on ins fnl f: nrst fin* **7/1**

024- **5** *1 1/2* **Mystickhill (IRE)**[23] 7778 4-9-2 **58**............................. PaulMulrennan 4 53
(J Balding) *cl up: rdn along 1/2-way and grad wknd* **8/1**

000- **6** *3 1/4* **Piccolo Diamante (USA)**[23] 7778 5-8-13 **55**.....................(t) JohnEgan 3 39
(S Parr) *dwlt: sn chsng ldrs on outer: rdn along over 2f out and sn wknd* **10/1**

004- **7** *1 3/4* **Briery Lane (IRE)**[218] 2934 8-8-8 **50**............................. LukeMorris 6 27
(J M Bradley) *sn outpcd and rdn along in rr: bhd fr 1/2-way* **25/1**

004- **8** *4 1/2* **Twinned (IRE)**[23] 7774 6-8-5 **47**.............................(p) FrankieMcDonald 9 8
(Mike Murphy) *chsd ldrs: rdn along 1/2-way: sn wknd* **14/1**

59.96 secs (0.26) **Going Correction** +0.05s/f (Slow) **8** Ran SP% **111.9**

Speed ratings (Par 101): **99,95,94,92,90 85,82,75**

toteswinger 1&2 £3.50, 1&3 £5.00, 2&3 £3.00. CSF £16.18 CT £47.64 TOTE £8.70: £2.90, £1.20, £1.70; EX 20.80 Trifecta £60.10 Pool: £224.41 - 2.76 winning units..

Owner Mrs L Wheeler **Bred** R J H West **Trained** Burrough Green, Cambs

FOCUS

A moderate sprint handicap. The winner confirmed his latest improvement on Polytrack with a fair step forward on his first try here.

Decider(USA) Official explanation: jockey reported gelding hung left

174 WEATHERBYS AWT "HANDS AND HEELS" APPRENTICE SERIES H'CAP 1m (F)

1:30 (1:30) (Class 6) (0-55,55) 4-Y-0+ **£2,388** (£705; £352) **Stalls** Low

Form RPR

5-33 **1** **Hurricane Coast**[6] 108 10-8-9 **55**............................. HollyHall(5) 4 63
(D Flood) *trckd ldrs: hdwy over 2f out: rdn to chal ent fnl f: led fnl 100yds: jst hld on* **9/1**[3]

P-31 **2** *nse* **Jordi Roper (IRE)**[7] 95 4-8-9 **53** 6ex................. AndrewHeffernan(3) 7 61
(S Parr) *cl up: led after 3f: rdn wl over 1f out: hdd fnl 100yds: rallied wl nr line: jst hld* **11/10**[1]

5-46 **3** *2* **General Tufto**[7] 90 4-8-2 **46** oh1.............................(b) RichardRowe(3) 8 49
(C Smith) *cl up: effrt over 2f out: sn chal and ev ch tl rdn and hld whn ntmuch room wl ins fnl f* **10/1**

000- **4** *5* **Doctor Delta**[72] 7180 4-8-5 **49** ow1............................. JohnCavanagh(3) 2 41
(M Brittain) *chsd ldrs: rdn along over 3f out: kpt on same pce fnl 2f* **25/1**

050- **5** *shd* **Afton View (IRE)**[17] 7809 4-8-6 **52**............................. RyanClark(5) 6 43
(S Parr) *v s.i.s and lost several l s: hdwy and in tch 5f out: rdn along 3f out: kpt on same pce fnl 2f* **9/2**[2]

000- **6** *5* **Top Jaro (FR)**[19] 7799 6-8-9 **55**.............................(b[1]) PaulPickard(5) 1 35
(Mrs R A Carr) *led 3f: rdn along 1/2-way: wknd over 2f out* **20/1**

/5-0 **7** *1* **Alloro**[9] 61 5-8-5 **46** oh1............................. PNolan 10 23
(A Kirtley) *chsd ldrs: rdn along 3f out: sn wknd* **80/1**

06-6 **8** *1* **High Five Society**[13] 12 5-8-1 **47**.............................(bt) AlexEdwards(5) 5 22
(S R Bowring) *a towards rr* **9/2**[2]

0/0- **9** *1 1/4* **Super King**[199] 3557 8-7-12 **46** oh1............................. TerenceFury(7) 9 18
(A D Brown) *a towards rr* **40/1**

46/0 **10** *4* **Final Bid (IRE)**[9] 63 6-8-10 **54**.............................(b) KrishGundowry(3) 3 17
(A Berry) *a in rr* **33/1**

1m 43.94s (0.24) **Going Correction** -0.025s/f (Stan) **10** Ran SP% **118.3**

Speed ratings (Par 101): **97,96,94,89,89 84,83,82,81,77**

toteswinger 1&2 £2.50, 1&3 £6.40, 2&3 £3.60. CSF £18.91 CT £108.44 TOTE £9.90: £2.80, £1.10, £2.50; EX 15.00 Trifecta £81.30 Pool: £258.31 - 2.35 winning units..

Owner Barrie Kirby **Bred** Ian H Wills **Trained**

■ Stewards' Enquiry : Krish Gundowry seven-day ban: improper riding - used whip in hands and heels race (Jan 29, 31, Feb 5, 6, 9, 12, 13)

FOCUS

A moderate apprentice handicap and very few ever got into it. The form seems sound enough for the grade.

175 WILLIAM HILL JANUARY SALE - NOW ON! CLASSIFIED STKS 7f (F)

2:00 (2:01) (Class 7) 4-Y-0+ **£1,364** (£403; £201) **Stalls** Low

Form RPR

0-55 **1** **Vanatina (IRE)**[6] 104 5-8-11 45............................. DuranFentiman(3) 8 51
(W M Brisbourne) *mde all: rdn 2f out: drvn ins fnl f and styd on gamely towards fin* **4/1**[3]

64-2 **2** *shd* **Amber Moon**[6] 104 4-9-0 45.............................(b) ShaneKelly 12 51
(J A Osborne) *prom: rdn along over 2f out: drvn and hung rt over 1f out: styd on strly ins fnl f: jst failed* **2/1**[1]

50-0 **3** *1 1/2* **Bahamian Bay**[9] 62 7-8-7 45.............................(v[1]) JohnCavanagh(7) 4 47
(M Brittain) *trckd ldrs: rdn along and sltly outpcd 3f out: hdwy 2f out: chal ent fnl f and ev ch tl drvn and no ex fnl 100yds* **14/1**

/40- **4** *1/2* **Buds Dilemma**[18] 1968 5-9-0 40.............................(b) HayleyTurner 7 45
(S Gollings) *towards rr: hdwy 2f out: sn rdn and styd on ins fnl f: nrst fin* **14/1**

550- **5** *nse* **Big Boom**[266] 1581 4-9-0 43............................. PatCosgrave 11 45
(M Quinn) *chsd ldrs: rdn along over 2f out: drvn over 1f out: sn edgd lft and one pce ent fnl f* **3/1**[2]

/06- **6** *2* **Fortuitous (IRE)**[20] 823 5-9-0 45.............................(v[1]) RobertWinston 6 40
(S Gollings) *s.i.s and bhd tl styd on fnl 2f: nrst fin* **33/1**

00-0 **7** *1/2* **Spy Gun (USA)**[2] 150 9-8-7 43............................. JoshWall(7) 13 38
(T Wall) *in midfield: hdwy on outer to chse ldrs 3f out: sn rdn and one pce fnl 2f* **28/1**

00-0 **8** *3/4* **So Sublime**[6] 104 4-9-0 45.............................(bt) GrahamGibbons 1 36
(M C Chapman) *midfield: effrt and sme hdwy 3f out: sn rdn and no imp fnl 2f* **14/1**

600- **9** *4* **Welcome Releaf**[35] 7637 6-9-0 45.............................(b[1]) StephenDonohoe 3 26
(P Leech) *s.i.s: a in rr* **17/2**

000- **10** *2 1/2* **Nabra**[58] 7369 5-9-0 44............................. JimmyQuinn 14 19
(M Brittain) *a towards rr* **33/1**

000- **11** *1/2* **Naledi**[18] 5779 5-9-0 42............................. PaulMulrennan 9 18
(J R Norton) *a bhd* **40/1**

66-0 **12** *1/2* **Martingrange Lass (IRE)**[14] 1 4-9-0 39.....................(b) JohnEgan 2 16
(S Parr) *cl up on inner: rdn along 3f out and sn wknd* **22/1**

1m 30.64s (0.34) **Going Correction** -0.025s/f (Stan) **12** Ran SP% **125.0**

Speed ratings (Par 97): **97,96,95,94,94 92,91,90,86,83 82,82**

toteswinger 1&2 £2.50, 1&3 £6.20, 2&3 £5.30. CSF £12.44 TOTE £5.30: £1.80, £1.20, £3.30; EX 15.00 Trifecta £121.70 Pool: £329.04 - 2.00 winning units..

Owner Black Diamond Racing **Bred** Rathbarry Stud **Trained** Great Ness, Shropshire

FOCUS

A dire contest and another race where it paid to race handily. The form looks sound with the winner rated to the level she was showing in slightly better races last month.

Martingrange Lass(IRE) Official explanation: jockey said gelding hung left

176 WILLIAM HILL JANUARY SALE - BETTER ODDS! FILLIES' H'CAP 1m (F)

2:30 (2:31) (Class 4) (0-80,77) 4-Y-0+ **£5,118** (£1,511; £756) **Stalls** Low

Form RPR

11-4 **1** **Mozayada (USA)**[14] 6 5-9-4 **77**............................. FrancisNorton 2 85
(M Brittain) *mde all: rdn clr wl over 1f out: kpt on ins fnl f* **13/8**[1]

351- **2** *1 1/4* **Quick Off The Mark**[20] 7786 4-8-6 **65**............................. HayleyTurner 1 70
(J G Given) *trckd ldrs on inner: effrt to chse wnr over 1f out: sn rdn and edgd rt ins fnl f: drvn and kpt on towards fin* **7/1**

02-4 **3** *2 1/4* **Moon Crystal**[9] 60 4-8-8 **67**.............................(t) JimmyQuinn 4 67
(E A L Dunlop) *hld up in tch: hdwy over 2f out: sn rdn and kpt on same pce appr fnl f* **10/3**[2]

41-6 **4** *nk* **Bookiebasher Babe (IRE)**[9] 60 4-8-6 **65**............................. LiamJones 6 64
(M Quinn) *cl up: rdn along over 2f out and grad wknd* **7/2**[3]

406- **5** *nse* **Friends Hope**[151] 5118 8-9-4 **77**............................. GrahamGibbons 3 76
(R Curtis) *dwlt: sn cl up: rdn along 3f out: sn drvn and wknd* **14/1**

350- **6** *nse* **Coral Shores**[36] 7620 4-8-4 **63**.............................(v) LukeMorris 5 62
(P W Hiatt) *in rr: rdn along and outpcd 3f out: kpt on u.p appr fnl f* **9/1**

1m 42.65s (-1.05) **Going Correction** -0.025s/f (Stan) **6** Ran SP% **112.6**

Speed ratings (Par 102): **104,102,100,100,100 100**

toteswinger 1&2 £1.60, 1&3 £1.30, 2&3 £1.70. CSF £13.75 TOTE £2.30: £1.80, £2.90; EX 7.90.

Owner Mel Brittain **Bred** Shadwell Farm LLC **Trained** Warthill, N Yorks

FOCUS

A decent little fillies' handicap and a solid pace despite the small field. The winner was back to form with another slight personal best and the second also produced a slight step up.

177 WILLIAM HILL JANUARY SALE - WHY BET ELSEWHERE? H'CAP (DIV II) 5f (F)

3:00 (3:01) (Class 6) (0-60,60) 4-Y-0+ **£2,729** (£806; £403) **Stalls** High

Form RPR

105- **1** **Spic 'n Span**[32] 7672 4-9-2 **58**.............................(b) JoeFanning 1 69
(R A Harris) *mde all: shkn up over 1f out: rdn: edgd lft and kpt on ins fnl f* **7/2**[1]

02-2 **2** *1 1/2* **Ridley Didley (IRE)**[6] 96 4-8-8 **53**............................. DuranFentiman(3) 5 58
(N Wilson) *in tch: hdwy 2f out: rdn to chse wnr over 1f out: drvn and hung lft ins fnl f: one pce* **7/2**[1]

65-5 **3** *2* **Spoof Master (IRE)**[6] 99 5-9-4 **60**.............................(p) LiamJones 3 58
(C R Dore) *chsd ldrs: rdn 2f out: drvn and edgd lft over 1f out: swtchd rt and styd on ins fnl f* **5/1**[3]

0-45 **4** *1 1/4* **Phinerine**[7] 95 6-8-3 **50**.............................(be) DanielleMcCreery(5) 9 44
(A Berry) *rdn along and outpcd towards rr: hdwy over 2f out: styd on ins fnl f: nrst fin* **25/1**

50-4 **5** *3/4* **Muktasb (USA)**[12] 22 8-8-7 **56**.............................(v) LeeTopliss(7) 6 47
(D Shaw) *towards rr and sn rdn along: hdwy 2f out: styd on ins fnl f: nrst fin* **14/1**

121- **6** *shd* **Lithaam (IRE)**[15] 7836 5-9-1 **57**.............................(p) RobertWinston 7 47
(J M Bradley) *prom: rdn along over 2f out: sn drvn and wknd over 1f out* **4/1**[2]

61-0 **7** *2 3/4* **Helping Hand (IRE)**[6] 108 4-9-2 **58**............................. HayleyTurner 10 39
(R Hollinshead) *chsd ldrs on wd outside: rdn along 2f out and sn wknd* **9/1**

35-6 **8** *nk* **Lady Bahia (IRE)**[10] 46 8-8-0 **49**.....................(b) AndrewHeffernan(7) 2 28
(Peter Grayson) *dwlt and towards rr: rdn and sme hdwy 1/2-way: sn wknd* **12/1**

00-0 **9** *3/4* **Fan Club**[9] 62 5-8-4 **46** oh1.............................(b) AndrewElliott 4 23
(Mrs R A Carr) *s.i.s: a in rr* **66/1**

66-3 **10** *1 1/4* **Rightcar Lewis**[10] 46 4-8-4 **46** oh1.............................(b) PatrickMathers 8 18
(Peter Grayson) *a in rr* **33/1**

59.57 secs (-0.13) **Going Correction** +0.05s/f (Slow) **10** Ran SP% **113.7**

Speed ratings (Par 101): **103,100,97,95,94 94,89,89,87,85**

toteswinger 1&2 £3.10, 1&3 £5.10, 2&3 £4.40. CSF £15.02 CT £59.56 TOTE £4.30: £1.10, £1.70, £2.10; EX 17.70 Trifecta £42.40 Pool: £596.86 - 10.40 winning units..

Owner Mrs Ruth M Serrell **Bred** C A Cyzer **Trained** Earlswood, Monmouths

FOCUS

Another modest sprint handicap in which the winning time was 0.39 seconds faster than the first division. The winner ran to a similar level to his maiden win here.

Spic 'n Span Official explanation: trainer said, regarding the apparent improvement in form, that he ran the gelding too quickly following its previous race two days earlier.

178 SOUTHWELL-RACECOURSE.CO.UK MAIDEN STKS 1m 4f (F)

3:30 (3:30) (Class 5) 4-Y-0+ **£3,070** (£906; £453) **Stalls** Low

Form RPR

36-2 **1** **Ibrox (IRE)**[7] 90 4-9-3 63............................. JimmyQuinn 4 71
(A D Brown) *trckd ldrs: hdwy over 4f out: chsd ldr over 2f out: rdn to ld over 1f out: styd on wl* **6/4**[1]

4- **2** *5* **If You Knew Suzy**[49] 7463 4-8-12 0.............................(t) RobertWinston 1 58
(G A Swinbank) *plld hrd: cl up: led over 3f out: rdn 2f out: drvn and hdd over 1f out: kpt on same pce* **12/1**

32-3 **3** *4 1/2* **Augustus John (IRE)**[7] 90 6-9-7 67.............................(b[1]) JohnEgan 6 56
(S Parr) *led: rdn along and hdd over 3f out: sn drvn and plugged on same pce* **85/40**[2]

002- **4** 2 1/4 **Monaadi (IRE)**[33] 7661 4-9-3 64 .... GrahamGibbons 3 52
(R Hollinshead) *sn rdn along in rr: hdwy 1/2-way: rdn along to chse ldrs 3f out: sn drvn and no imp* 5/1[3]
0-6 **5** 4 1/2 **Whiston Pat**[13] 11 4-9-3 0 .... PaulEddery 7 45
(S R Bowring) *chsd ldrs: rdn along over 4f out and sn wknd* 40/1
333/ **6** 6 **Almamia**[434] 6737 4-8-12 70 .... StephenDonohoe 5 30
(Sir Mark Prescott) *pushed along in rr after 4f: rdn along over 4f out: nvr a factor* 6/1
P6-0 **7** 30 **Redlynch**[7] 90 4-8-10 0 .... (p) AndrewHeffernan(7) 2 —
(S Parr) *chsd ldrs to 1/2-way: sn lost pl and bhd* 66/1

2m 39.22s (-1.78) **Going Correction** -0.025s/f (Stan)
WFA 4 from 6yo 4lb 7 Ran SP% **114.6**
Speed ratings (Par 103): **104,100,97,96,93 89,69**
toteswinger 1&2 £3.70, 1&3 £1.80, 2&3 £3.40. CSF £21.11 TOTE £2.70: £1.30, £3.80; EX 17.30.

Owner sportaracing.com **Bred** Hellwood Stud Farm **Trained** Yedingham, N Yorks

FOCUS
A weak and very uncompetitive maiden and they finished well spread out. The winner might have improved but this form does not look too solid.

179 TREAT THE KIDS AT HALF TERM FILLIES' H'CAP 7f (F)
4:00 (4:00) (Class 5) (0-75,75) 4-Y-0+ **£3,070** (£906; £453) **Stalls** Low

Form RPR
066- **1** **Indian Diva (IRE)**[44] 7525 4-9-4 **75** .... (t) GrahamGibbons 4 86
(R Curtis) *cl up: led over 2f out and sn rdn: drvn over 1f out: kpt on wl fnl f* 17/2
411- **2** 3 1/2 **To Be Or Not To Be**[26] 7748 4-8-12 **69** .... LukeMorris 1 71
(John Berry) *trckd ldrs: effrt over 2f out: rdn to chse wnr over 1f out: drvn and no imp ins fnl f* 15/8[1]
000- **3** 2 1/2 **Sweet Gale (IRE)**[92] 6734 5-8-8 **65** .... FrankieMcDonald 5 60
(Mike Murphy) *in tch: hdwy on outer 1/2-way: rdn to chal 2f out: sn drvn and one pce appr last* 7/2[3]
453- **4** 1/2 **Another Genepi (USA)**[20] 7782 6-8-6 **63** .... (b) EdwardCreighton 3 56
(E J Creighton) *chsd ldrs: rdn along over 2f out: sn drvn and wknd appr last* 5/1
05- **5** 6 **Milton Of Campsie**[44] 7534 4-8-12 **69** .... JohnEgan 6 46
(S Parr) *cl up: rdn over 2f out: drvn wl over 1f out and sn wknd* 11/4[2]
046- **6** 6 **Aegean Pride**[39] 7591 4-7-13 **61** oh5 .... DanielleMcCreery(5) 2 22
(A Berry) *led: rdn along 3f out: sn hdd & wknd* 18/1

1m 28.65s (-1.65) **Going Correction** -0.025s/f (Stan) 6 Ran SP% **116.1**
Speed ratings (Par 100): **108,104,101,100,93 86**
toteswinger 1&2 £4.00, 1&3 £7.20, 2&3 £3.30. CSF £26.01 TOTE £9.90: £4.60, £1.50; EX 31.90 Place 6: £9.30 Place 5: £7.28 .
Owner H Downs **Bred** Mountarmstrong Stud **Trained** Lambourn, Berks

FOCUS
A modest handicap and all six fillies were still within a length or so of each other approaching the last two furlongs. The form looks sound.
Milton Of Campsie Official explanation: trainer had no explanation for the poor form shown
T/Plt: £8.30 to a £1 stake. Pool: £46,677.04. 4,095.43 winning tickets. T/Qpdt: £4.70 to a £1 stake. Pool: £3,149.30. 489.80 winning tickets. JR

NAD AL SHEBA (L-H)
Thursday, January 15
OFFICIAL GOING: Dirt course - standard; turf course - good to soft

180a MUHTATHIR (H'CAP) (F&M) (TURF) 7f 110y(D)
3:45 (3:47) (90-110,106) 3-Y-0+
£45,833 (£15,277; £7,638; £3,819; £2,291; £1,527)

RPR
1 **Miss Gorica (IRE)**[41] 7565 5-9-2 **101** .... TedDurcan 4 105+
(Ms Joanna Morgan, Ire) *broke awkwardly: mid-div: smooth prog to ld 1 1/2f out: r.o wl* 25/1
2 1 1/4 **Lessing (FR)**[154] 5038 4-9-1 **100** .... C-PLemaire 5 101
(X Nakkachdji, France) *trckd ldrs: t.k.h: ev ch 2f out: outpcd by wnr 1 1/2f out: r.o wl* 12/1
3 1/2 **Clifton Dancer**[133] 5644 4-8-9 **95** .... RichardKingscote 3 94
(Tom Dascombe) *set stdy pce for 2f: trckd ldrs tl 3f out: one pce fnl 2f* **8/1**
4 1/4 **Happy Spirit (SAF)**[222] 5-9-0 **99** .... RyanMoore 1 98
(H J Brown, South Africa) *in rr of mid-div: rdn 2 1/2f out: r.o fnl 1 1/2f: nrst fin* 10/3[2]
5 1 **Jalmira (IRE)**[62] 7328 8-9-6 **106** .... TPO'Shea 2 102
(E Charpy, UAE) *trckd ldrs: led 5f out: clr 2 1/2f out: hdd 1 1/2f out: wknd* 10/1
6 2 **Estrela Boa (BRZ)**[235] 4-8-2 **95** .... WilliamBuick 6 79+
(P Bary, France) *settled in rr: rdn 3f out: nvr nr to chal* 7/2[3]
7 1/2 **Inca Noble (ARG)**[565] 5-9-1 **100** .... KShea 7 90+
(M F De Kock, South Africa) *slowly away: restrained in last: t.k.h: rdn 3f out: n.d* 7/4[1]

1m 35.61s (4.01) **Going Correction** +0.60s/f (Yiel) 7 Ran SP% **113.4**
Speed ratings: **103,101,101,101,100 98,97**
CSF 271.10.
Owner G Tierney **Bred** Miss A R Byrne **Trained** Ballivor, Co Meath

FOCUS
An ordinary fillies and mares handicap for the class, made up mainly of exposed sorts, and they went a very steady pace early, resulting in most of these racing keenly. The form is rated around the first two.

NOTEBOOK
Miss Gorica(IRE) was dismissed in the betting following a couple of below-par efforts on the Polytrack at Dundalk last backend, but she was weighted to get much closer to Jalmira on their running at the same course in October, and she readily reversed form. She took a bit of a grip early, but was not as keen as some of her rivals, and picked up well off the modest gallop, with her natural speed (6f winner) a real asset considering how the race unfolded. Things are likely to get tougher from now on, but she has clearly acclimatised well, and her connections believe she is even better over shorter.
Lessing(FR) has lacked consistency, but she has bits and pieces of smart form to her name in France. She did well to take second considering she raced keenly with no cover early on, but it remains to be seen what the form is worth.
Clifton Dancer was a little keen through the first couple of furlongs after being restrained in front, and eventually got a lead. However, considering she had pretty much made the running for her three wins, she would surely have been better served by bowling along in front, especially considering there was no pace on, and the way she stayed on to snatch third supports that view.
Happy Spirit(SAF) ◆ is a Grade 1 filly in her native South Africa, but her best form has been at around 1m2f and she had been off since last June. She was not given an overly hard time by Ryan Moore in the straight, with it obvious she was always held, and a significantly improved effort can be expected if she steps back up in trip next time. (op 3-1)
Jalmira(IRE) raced freely and took the lead after a couple of furlongs. Unsurprisingly she failed to see her race out, and she can do better when there is more pace on. (op 9-1)
Estrela Boa(BRZ) was keen early and did not run on for pressure in the straight.
Inca Noble(ARG), who had been off the track since showing smart form in Brazil in 2007, was sent off favourite, but it's interesting to note Mike De Kock reported beforehand that, having thought the filly was "something special" last year, she then got injured and had not been showing much zest in her work. (op 13-8)

181a NAYEF FILLIES 1400 (CONDITIONS RACE) (F&M) (DIRT) 7f (D)
4:20 (4:20) 3-Y-0+
£20,833 (£6,944; £3,472; £1,736; £1,041; £694)

RPR
1 **Sos Brillante (CHI)**[292] 4-9-4 100 .... LDettori 6 102+
(Saeed Bin Suroor) *trckd ldng duo: chsd ldrs 2 1/2f out: led last 110yds: comf* 7/2[2]
2 2 **India Tiberina (CHI)**[299] 4-9-4 100 .... KShea 1 97+
(M F De Kock, South Africa) *slowly away: trckd ldr: led 2 1/2f out: hdd 110yds out* 1/2[1]
3 3 **Purple Sage (IRE)**[82] 6982 3-8-9 89 .... RichardMullen 2 88
(E Martins, Bahrain) *mid-div on rail: rdn to chse ldrs 3f out: r.o same pce* 33/1
4 2 1/2 **Jargelle (IRE)**[104] 6441 3-8-9 101 .... MJKinane 5 81
(E Martins, Bahrain) *racd in rr: r.o one pce: nvr able to chal* 14/1
5 2 1/4 **Esta Bailando (CHI)**[208] 4-9-11 96 .... JVerenzuela 3 83
(J Barton, Saudi Arabia) *sn led: hdd 2 1/2f out: sn wknd* 6/1[3]
6 1 1/4 **Ever Loved (USA)**[135] 5590 3-8-9 78 .... TedDurcan 4 72
(S Seemar, UAE) *in rr of main gp: rdn 4f out: n.d* 66/1

1m 26.32s (1.52) **Going Correction** +0.325s/f (Slow)
WFA 3 from 4yo 18lb 6 Ran SP% **114.3**
Speed ratings: **104,101,98,95,92 91**
CSF 5.78.
Owner Sheikh Ahmed Bin Mohammed Al Maktoum **Bred** Haras Carioca **Trained** Newmarket, Suffolk

FOCUS
Basically a trial for the UAE 1000 Guineas and this promised to be a cracker, with both Saeed Bin Suroor and Mike De Kock sending out potential classic contenders who shared almost identical profiles. However, the race itself was slightly disappointing, with the De Kock runner failing to live up to expectations after being backed off the boards, some less likely candidates finishing plenty close enough for comfort, and the winner hinting at a suspect attitude. The third and sixth set the standard.

NOTEBOOK
Sos Brillante(CHI), the wide-margin winner of a maiden in Chile last March, travelled like a smart filly, but once under pressure she continually flashed her tail and carried her head at an awkward angle. She eventually found enough to get by the favourite, but she made hard work of it, especially considering the De Kock runner appeared to have little left to give, and her attitude has to be called into question. However, it would probably be unwise to get carried away with her apparent wayward tendencies, as her trainer hinted beforehand that this race might come a little soon for her, and she is obviously still immature. Whatever the case, she possesses a fair amount of ability and has the size and scope to make up into a high-class filly, provided of course her talents can be harnessed in the right direction. She ought to be good enough to win the UAE 1000 Guineas, which will surely be her next target. (op 11-4)
India Tiberina(CHI), like the winner successful in a 6f maiden in Chile on her only previous start last March, was probably beaten by a very decent filly, but this was still disappointing. She did not convince with her attitude before the start, hinting she might be a little moody, and she was ultimately well held in second. She recovered from a sluggish start to race close up towards the inside rail, and she found a length when first challenged by the winner in the straight, but she had little left inside the final furlong. Her connections can take heart from the fact last year's UAE 1000 Guineas and Oaks winner, Cocoa Beach, was only second in this race last year, but India Tiberina is not that big and lacks the scope of the winner. (op 4-6)
Purple Sage(IRE) was rated only 89 when with Barry Hills, and did not look an obvious contender beforehand, so her proximity does little for the form.
Jargelle(IRE), who won the Super Sprint for William Haggas last year and had yet to race beyond 6f, didn't run at all badly under vastly different conditions on her first start since October. However, she was still some way below her official mark of 101, and was apparently reluctant to go to post.
Esta Bailando(CHI), off the track since gamely landing a Grade 1 in Chile in June, set off in front but was readily outpaced in the straight. She looks in need of a step up in trip.
Ever Loved(USA) had been off since winning a Fibresand maiden for Godolphin in September and looked out of her depth.

182a MUJAHID (H'CAP) (TURF) 7f 110y(D)
4:55 (4:55) (95-110,110) 3-Y-0+
£50,000 (£16,666; £8,333; £4,166; £2,500; £1,666)

RPR
1 **Silver Mist (SAF)**[173] 7-9-2 **106** .... KShea 12 111+
(M F De Kock, South Africa) *settled in rr: 10th 3f out: smooth prog 2f out: led 1f out: comf* 9/2[2]
2 1 1/4 **Fateh Field (USA)**[181] 4153 4-9-0 **104** .... (v) TedDurcan 1 104
(Saeed Bin Suroor) *led main gp: led 3f out: hdd 1f out* 7/1[3]
3 5 1/4 **Seihali (IRE)**[627] 10-9-6 **110** .... WilliamBuick 7 97
(D Selvaratnam, UAE) *settled in rr: 11th 3f out: smooth prog on rail 2 1/2f out: r.o same pce* 25/1
4 2 1/4 **King Jock (USA)**[25] 8-9-4 **108** .... MJKinane 4 89
(A Manuel, UAE) *mid-div: gng wl 3f out: r.o: nt qckn fnl 1 1/2f* 12/1
5 1 1/2 **Emirates Gold (IRE)**[32] 6-9-0 **104** .... (t) TPO'Shea 5 82
(E Charpy, UAE) *racd in 3rd: chsd ldrs 3f out: wknd fnl 1 1/2f* 12/1
6 1/4 **Yaddree**[14] 4-9-1 **105** .... JRosales 8 82
(M bin Shafya, UAE) *in rr of mid-div: rdn 3f out: n.d* 10/1
7 5 1/4 **Masaalek**[147] 5208 4-9-1 **105** .... RHills 2 69
(Doug Watson, UAE) *slowly away: racd in rr: nvr able to chal* 4/1[1]
8 1/4 **Boston Lodge**[315] 815 9-8-13 **102** .... (vt) EddieAhern 10 66
(F Nass, Bahrain) *nvr able to chal: r.o fnl 2f* 33/1
9 4 3/4 **Emirates Skyline (USA)**[14] 6-9-0 **104** .... WJSupple 9 55
(A bin Huzaim, UAE) *nvr bttr than mid-div* 20/1
10 2 1/4 **Grand Vista**[25] 5-8-13 **102** .... (t) KLatham 3 49
(H J Brown, South Africa) *v.s.a: racd in last: nvr nr to chal* 14/1
11 1/2 **Dijeerr (USA)**[75] 7147 5-9-5 **109** .... (v) AhmedAjtebi 11 53
(M bin Shafya, UAE) *mid-div: rdn to chse ldrs 2 1/2f out: wknd* 14/1
12 3/4 **Iguazu Falls (USA)**[118] 6073 4-8-13 **102** .... (v) LDettori 6 46+
(Saeed Bin Suroor) *sn led: clr after 1 1/2f: rn wd 3f out: sn btn* 4/1[1]

1m 32.57s (0.97) **Going Correction** +0.60s/f (Yiel) 12 Ran SP% **120.0**
Speed ratings: **119,117,112,110,108 108,103,103,98,96 95,94**
CSF 35.71; Tricast 720.38.

Owner Sheikh Rashid bin Humaid Al Nuaimi **Bred** Midlands Equine Entreprises Ltd **Trained** South Africa

FOCUS

All of these are thoroughly exposed and a strong pace, provided by Iguazu Falls, sorted them out. The form, although not particularly strong, at least looks reliable. The form is rated around the second, fourth and sixth.

NOTEBOOK

Silver Mist(SAF), who has some reasonable Graded form to his name in South Africa, made a winning debut for the Mike De Kock yard. He was held up well out the back early, so the strong pace suited, and he showed a smart turn of foot when taken wide with his challenge in the straight. However, this looked a soft race for the class and things are likely to be tougher next time. (op 5-1\n\x\x)

Fateh Field(USA), tried in a visor for the first time, emerges with plenty of credit as he led the pack chasing his stablemate, and kept on all the way to the line. His running style suggests he has got to be worth a try on dirt. (op 13-2)

Seihali(IRE), a Group 2 winner over slightly further at this track in 2007, made a very pleasing return after 627 days off, staying on well after getting a dream run against the inside rail. Things are unlikely to get any easier for this ten-year-old, but he clearly remains competitive.

King Jock(USA) is one of the regulars here, but he got going too late to pose any kind of threat.

Emirates Gold(IRE) had won his last two starts at Abu Dhabi, including a Listed race, but he was well held this time, and has yet to win at the Carnival.

Yaddree should benefit from a return to further.

Masaalek ran nowhere near his British form on his debut for a new trainer.

Iguazu Falls(USA) was upwards of six lengths clear at one stage, but he proved impossible to steer around the turn into the straight and ended up extremely wide, which obviously cost him any chance he might have had.

183a GREEN DESERT (H'CAP) (TURF) 1m 194y(T)

5:30 (5:30) (100-115,115) 3-Y-0+

£72,916 (£24,305; £12,152; £6,076; £3,645; £2,430)

RPR

1 **Third Set (IRE)**^{90} 6780 6-8-13 **107**.....(t) AhmedAjtebi 7 108+
(M bin Shafya, UAE) *settled in rr: smooth prog and rn wd 2 1/2f out: led last 55yds* **11/1**

2 1½ **Brave Tin Soldier (USA)**^{14} 5-8-13 **107**..... KShea 4 104
(M F De Kock, South Africa) *trckd ldr on rail: led 2 1/2f out: r.o wl: hdd cl home* **9/2**^{2}

3 1 **Yasoodd**^{25} 6-8-9 **104**.....(e) WilliamBuick 2 98
(D Selvaratnam, UAE) *mid-div: rdn 2 1/2f out: r.o one pce* **14/1**

4 ¾ **With Interest**^{14} 6-9-1 **109**..... JRosales 8 102
(M bin Shafya, UAE) *trckd ldrs: rdn 2 1/2f out: wknd fnl f* **10/1**

5 ¼ **Hearthstead Maison (IRE)**^{113} 6201 5-9-6 **115**..... RyanMoore 6 107
(M Johnston) *settled in rr: r.o fnl 2 1/2f: nvr nr to chal* **14/1**

6 3¼ **Glen Nevis (USA)**^{14} 5-8-8 **102**.....(v) RoystonFfrench 9 88
(A Al Raihe, UAE) *a in mid-div* **12/1**

7 4½ **Igor Protti**^{14} 7-8-8 **102**.....(b) WJSupple 12 79
(A bin Huzaim, UAE) *sn led: hdd 2 1/2f out: one pce fnl 1 1/2f* **20/1**

8 1¾ **Charlie Cool**^{14} 6-8-6 **100**..... DO'Donohoe 1 73
(D Selvaratnam, UAE) *s.i.s: settled in rr: n.m.r after 3f: nvr nr to chal* **22/1**

9 hd **Estrela Do Oriente (BRZ)**^{200} 4-8-3 **103** ow3..... C-PLemaire 5 70
(P Bary, France) *mid-div: hrd rdn 3f out: sn btn* **15/8**^{1}

10 dist **Fathayer (USA)**^{14} 4-8-7 **102**..... RichardMullen 10 —
(A Al Raihe, UAE) *trckd ldrs tl wknd qckly 3 1/2f out* **33/1**

11 dist **Irish Mayhem (USA)**^{124} 5907 4-8-7 **102**..... TedDurcan 11 —
(Saeed Bin Suroor) *racd in rr: hrd rdn 4f out: nvr able to chal* **5/1**^{3}

1m 52.91s (2.91) **Going Correction** +0.60s/f (Yiel)

WFA 4 from 5yo+ 1lb **11** Ran SP% **120.1**

Speed ratings: **111,109,108,108,107 105,101,99,99,— —**

CSF 59.87; Tricast 715.74.

Owner Sultan Ali **Bred** A Stroud & J Hanly **Trained** United Arab Emirates

FOCUS

A high-class handicap. The pace seemed pretty ordinary early on, but looked to increase after three furlongs or so. The form is rated around the runner-up.

NOTEBOOK

Third Set(IRE), a dual winner (handicap off 102, then a Listed contest) over the bare 1m for Godolphin at last year's Carnival, is now back in the ownership of Sultan Ali, who had him when he was with Roger Charlton at the beginning of his career, having gone 0-3 in Britain this year. He's a horse who has nearly always carried his head high, and he did so once again, but that little quirk was nowhere near as pronounced as it has been in the past, and he seems to have benefited from the fitting of a tongue-tie for the first time, suggesting he may have had breathing issues. Although now six, he is very smart on his day, and if the tongue strap continues to work he is one to keep on side. (op 10-1)

Brave Tin Soldier(USA), a winner on the dirt here in a non-Carnival handicap at the beginning of the year, ran right up to his best off a 7lb higher mark back on turf. He is clearly versatile and should pick up plenty of prize money in the coming months.

Yasoodd is now 0-12 since switching to the UAE, but this was a respectable showing.

With Interest would have appreciated the return to turf after unsurprisingly appearing to resent the dirt last time, and this was not a bad effort.

Hearthstead Maison(IRE) ran a massive race considering he was racing over a trip shorter than ideal, off a handicap mark of 115, and conceding upwards of 5lb all round. He stuck on gamely in the straight, and there should be more to come when he returns to a more suitable distance. However, there is a suspicion he might not be the easiest to place.

Charlie Cool was far too keen for his own good.

Estrela Do Oriente(BRZ) was well-backed, but he looked in trouble before the straight and was a major disappointment. He was successful in both Grade 2 and Grade 1 company when trained in Brazil, and was apparently a possible for the first round of the Al Maktoum challenge. It was disappointing he did not put up more of a show, but it's interesting to note his trainer's two other runners on the night both ran below form. (tchd 7-4)

Irish Mayhem(USA) had been progressing well for Brian Meehan on Polytrack when last seen, but he ran as though something was amiss on his debut for new connections.

184a AL MAKTOUM CHALLENGE R1 (GROUP 3) (DIRT) 1m (D)

6:05 (6:05) 3-Y-0+

£83,333 (£27,777; £13,888; £6,944; £4,166; £2,777)

RPR

1 **My Indy (ARG)**^{292} 1088 5-9-0 106..... LDettori 10 116
(Saeed Bin Suroor) *wl away: trckd ldrs: led 2f out: drew clr: easily* **4/1**^{2}

2 5¾ **Green Coast (IRE)**^{35} 6-9-0 107..... FJara 7 104+
(Doug Watson, UAE) *in rr of mid-div: prog to chse wnr 2 1/2f: r.o wl* **10/1**

3 3¾ **Don Renato (CHI)**^{292} 1087 6-9-0 109.....(vt) JVerenzuela 3 95
(J Barton, Saudi Arabia) *slowly away: settled in rr: nvr nr to chal: r.o fnl 3f: nrst fin* **6/1**^{3}

4 hd **Frosty Secret (USA)**^{7} 5-9-0 106..... KLatham 8 95
(M F De Kock, South Africa) *trckd ldr: led briefly 2 1/f out: outpcd fnl 2f* **12/1**

5 2½ **Gloria De Campeao (BRZ)**^{103} 6499 6-9-0 111..... C-PLemaire 12 90
(P Bary, France) *settled in rr: rdn 3f out: nvr able to chal* **7/1**

6 nse **Royal Vintage (SAF)**^{110} 6287 5-9-0 113..... KShea 2 89
(M F De Kock, South Africa) *mid-div on rail: trckd ldrs 4f out: rdn 3f out: one pce fnl 2 1/2f* **3/1**^{1}

7 1¾ **Jet Express (SAF)**^{14} 7-9-0 102.....(t) RoystonFfrench 1 86
(A Al Raihe, UAE) *sn led: hdd 2 1/2f out: kpt on one pce* **25/1**

8 2¾ **Art Of War (SAF)**^{175} 5-9-0 101.....(b) TedDurcan 11 79
(M F De Kock, South Africa) *trckd ldrs: rn wd: ev ch 3 1/2f out: rdn 2 1/2f out: wknd* **16/1**

9 ½ **Golden Arrow (IRE)**^{28} 6-9-0 108.....(bt) TPO'Shea 4 78
(E Charpy, UAE) *mid-div: rdn 2 1/2f out: nt qckn* **12/1**

10 5¾ **Etihaad**^{14} 7-9-0 90.....(t) WayneSmith 6 66
(R Bouresly, Kuwait) *mid-div: n.d* **100/1**

11 1½ **Happy Boy (BRZ)**^{110} 6287 6-9-0 110..... AhmedAjtebi 9 62
(M bin Shafya, UAE) *in rr of mid-div: nvr nr to chal* **8/1**

12 19 **Trinity College (USA)**^{145} 5-9-0 105.....(b) RyanMoore 5 21
(M F De Kock, South Africa) *trckd ldrs tl 4f out: wknd qckly* **20/1**

1m 36.52s (-0.18) **Going Correction** +0.325s/f (Slow) **12** Ran SP% **122.9**

Speed ratings: **113,107,103,103,100 100,99,96,95,90 88,69**

CSF 44.87.

Owner Godolphin **Bred** Haras La Quebrada **Trained** Newmarket, Suffolk

FOCUS

The first round of the Al Maktoum challenge is rarely that strong a race and this looked just an ordinary Group 3 contest. The fourth sets the standard.

NOTEBOOK

My Indy(ARG) showed himself to be a cut above this lot with a stylish success. Formerly trained in Argentina, he had plenty to find on the form he showed during his Classic campaign at last year's Carnival, having finished behind Royal Vintage on all three of his starts, but his connections had reported he had thrived since, and they were proved right in no uncertain terms. Always nicely placed, close up out wide, away from the kickback, he travelled strongly throughout and quickly opened up a healthy advantage in the straight, although it has to be said he did flash his tail under pressure. There's no doubt he's a much better horse this year than last, but things are about to get a whole lot tougher. At this stage he has a long way to go in order to develop into a genuine World Cup contender, but we will learn more should he contest either of the remaining rounds of this series.

Green Coast(IRE) doesn't look a genuine Group horse, but he helps set the standard having won a 7f handicap here off a mark of 102 on his latest start. (op 9-1)

Don Renato(CHI) ◆, off the track since finishing third after not enjoying the best of trips in the Godolphin Mile last March, is again a fair bit better than he was able to show. A low draw did him no favours and, after starting a little slowly, he had to battle his way through towards the inside. He could be one for the second round of this series, with the extra furlong almost sure to suit.

Frosty Secret(USA) managed third in this race last year, but his latest win was gained over 6f, and he ran as though this trip stretched him.

Gloria De Campeao(BRZ), last year's runner-up, was a fair way below form, just like his trainer's other two runners on the night.

Royal Vintage(SAF) has been gelded having run below expectations in a couple of runs in Britain. He again failed to run up to his best, but was not helped by an inside draw and can be given another chance.

Happy Boy(BRZ) was the runaway winner of this race last year, but he now looks a shadow of the horse he once was. (op 9-1)

185a HAAFHD (H'CAP) (TURF) 1m 4f (T)

6:40 (6:40) (95-110,109) 3-Y-0+

£50,000 (£16,666; £8,333; £4,166; £2,500; £1,666)

RPR

1 **Crime Scene (IRE)**^{14} 6-9-1 **104**..... JRosales 8 112
(M bin Shafya, UAE) *mid-div and rn wd: smooth prog to chse ldrs 2 1/2f out: led last 110yds* **16/1**

2 1¼ **Engrupido (ARG)**^{322} 742 6-9-2 **105**..... KShea 11 111
(M F De Kock, South Africa) *trckd ldr: led 1 1/2f out to 110yds out* **11/2**^{3}

3 3 **Age Of Reason (UAE)**^{159} 4856 4-8-10 **102**..... TedDurcan 7 104
(Saeed Bin Suroor) *mid-div: rdn to chse ldrs 2 1/2f out: one pce* **12/1**

4 1¼ **Far From Old (IRE)**^{35} 7643 6-8-13 **101**..... FJara 10 101
(J E Hammond, France) *settled last: r.o fnl 2 1/2f: nvr nr to chal* **5/1**^{2}

5 ¼ **Sugar Ray (IRE)**^{109} 6303 5-9-2 **105**.....(vt) LDettori 1 104
(Saeed Bin Suroor) *sn led: rdn 3f out: hdd 1 1/2f out: one pce* **7/2**^{1}

6 ½ **Rohaani (USA)**^{27} 7-8-13 **101**..... RHills 5 100
(Doug Watson, UAE) *v.s.a: settled in rr: nvr able to chal* **7/1**

7 hd **Varsity**^{69} 7235 6-9-0 **102**.....(tp) KLatham 6 101
(C F Swan, Ire) *s.i.s: in rr of mid-div: nvr nr to chal* **12/1**

8 4¼ **Lion Sands**^{109} 6303 5-9-6 **109**..... WJSupple 3 100
(A bin Huzaim, UAE) *trckd ldr tl rdn and wknd 2 1/2f out* **14/1**

9 1½ **Book Of Music (IRE)**^{145} 5288 6-9-3 **106**.....(vt) RichardMullen 2 94
(S Seemar, UAE) *nvr bttr than mid-div* **12/1**

10 ¼ **Gravitas**^{71} 7193 6-9-2 **105**..... AhmedAjtebi 4 93
(M bin Shafya, UAE) *in rr of mid-div: nvr able to chal* **12/1**

11 ¼ **Detonator (IRE)**^{115} 6171 4-8-10 **102**..... MJKinane 9 91
(M bin Shafya, UAE) *racd in rr: tk v t.k.h: nvr able to chal* **14/1**

12 19 **Before You Go (IRE)**^{328} 673 6-8-13 **101**..... TPO'Shea 12 59
(E Charpy, UAE) *mid-div: nvr able to chal* **16/1**

2m 35.82s (4.82) **Going Correction** +0.60s/f (Yiel)

WFA 4 from 5yo+ 4lb **12** Ran SP% **122.6**

Speed ratings: **107,106,104,103,103 102,102,99,98,98 98,85**

CSF 105.20; Tricast 1,124.49. PLACEPOT Part won. £8,394.40. Pool £12,238.93. 0.55 winning tickets. Pool of £5,507.51 carried forward. QUADPOT £144.90. Pool £1,528.02. 7.80 winning tickets..

Owner H R H Princess Haya Of Jordan **Bred** Gainsborough Stud Management Ltd **Trained** United Arab Emirates

FOCUS

A high-class handicap, and quite competitive, but as is the case with a lot of these Carnival races, the field was made up of mainly exposed sorts. The winner is rated to his course best.

NOTEBOOK

Crime Scene(IRE) was just about as exposed as any of these, but this was only his second start for a new yard (who struck with Third Set earlier on the card) and he was a determined winner. A recent run over 1m2f on dirt clearly put him spot on.

Engrupido(ARG), 3lb higher than when winning over 1m2f at last year's Carnival, was always close up and had every chance.

Age Of Reason(UAE) does not seem to have much in hand of the handicapper, but this was a respectable first run for Godolphin.

Far From Old(IRE) ◆ is one no doubt many will take from this race, as although he didn't look particularly unlucky, there can be little doubt he is a fair bit better than he was able to show. Given an awful lot to do, he did not enjoy the best of runs towards the inside in the straight and it was a case of 'nearest finish'. He looks handicapped to win a similar race in the coming weeks. (op 11-2)

Sugar Ray(IRE), an expensive purchase out of Sir Michael Stoute's yard, gave himself little chance of getting home by refusing to settle in front.

Rohaani(USA) was not the best away and was never involved.

Varsity is probably better than she showed, as a steadily-run race did not really suit. She might be worth dropping in trip, as they rarely go that quick over 1m4f here. (op 14-1)
Detonator(IRE) was unlikely to be suited by a hold-up ride considering his last success came over 1m6f.

[159]LINGFIELD (L-H)

Friday, January 16

OFFICIAL GOING: Standard
Wind: Moderate, behind Weather: Overcast

186 COLEMANS HATCH H'CAP (DIV I) 1m 2f (P)
12:20 (12:21) (Class 6) (0-55,55) 4-Y-0+ **£1,706** (£503; £252) **Stalls** Low

Form RPR
06-3 **1** **Mix N Match**[7] 100 5-8-9 **48** FrankieMcDonald 9 56
(R M Stronge) *taken down early: hld up in last pair: hmpd 4f out: gd prog on wd outside over 2f out: drvn to chse ldrs over 1f out: styd on wl fnl f to ld nr fin* **7/2**[2]
03-1 **2** ½ **Samurai Warrior**[5] 132 4-8-9 **55** DeanHeslop(5) 10 62
(P D Evans) *dwlt but sn prom: led over 7f out: rdn over 2f out: kpt on tl hdd and no ex nr fin* **13/8**[1]
256- **3** 1½ **King Of The Beers (USA)**[32] 7691 5-8-12 **54**......(p) KevinGhunowa(3) 8 58
(R A Harris) *wl in tch: rdn and effrt over 2f out: nt qckn over 1f out: styd on fnl f to take 3rd nr fin* **15/2**[3]
/00- **4** ½ **Lunar Limelight**[39] 7599 4-8-9 **50** FergusSweeney 11 53
(P J Makin) *stdd s: hld up in last: rapid prog on outer 4f out to chse ldr over 2f out: nt qckn 1f out: fdd ins fnl f* **25/1**
000- **5** ½ **Touch Of Style (IRE)**[19] 7807 5-9-2 **55**......(v) PatCosgrave 3 57
(J R Boyle) *trckd ldrs on inner: cl up and rdn over 2f out: nt qckn over 1f out: one pce after* **9/1**
300- **6** 3 **Fairly Honest**[85] 6927 5-8-5 **49** WilliamCarson(5) 1 45
(P W Hiatt) *led to over 7f out: chsd ldr to over 2f out: wknd fnl f* **25/1**
6-55 **7** ½ **Tenement (IRE)**[6] 119 5-8-8 **52** MCGeran(5) 4 47
(Jamie Poulton) *settled in midfield: pushed along and lost pl on inner 3f out: no prog fnl 2f* **16/1**
00-2 **8** 1½ **I Certainly May**[11] 43 4-8-5 **46** oh1......(p) NickyMackay 5 38
(S Dow) *towards rr: rdn wl over 3f out: struggling after: no imp on ldrs fnl 2f* **12/1**
00-0 **9** 2 **Farsighted**[9] 71 4-8-13 **54** ChrisCatlin 2 42
(J M P Eustace) *dropped to last trio u.p bef 1/2-way: detached in last pair over 2f out* **50/1**
050- **10** 8 **Rampant Ronnie (USA)**[138] 5537 4-9-0 **55** JimCrowley 6 27
(P W D'Arcy) *t.k.h early: prom 6f: wknd: detached over 2f out: t.o* **11/1**

2m 7.24s (0.64) **Going Correction** +0.20s/f (Slow)
WFA 4 from 5yo 2lb **10** Ran SP% **113.6**
Speed ratings (Par 101): **105,104,103,103,102 100,99,98,97,90**
toteswinger: 1&2 £2.40, 1&3 £5.40, 2&3 £4.10. CSF £9.06 CT £37.90 TOTE £4.30: £1.50, £1.50, £1.70; EX 10.50 Trifecta £14.60 Pool: £131.06, 6.60 winning units..
Owner Tim Whiting **Bred** Mrs K E Collie **Trained** Beedon Common, Berks
■ Stewards' Enquiry : Nicky Mackay three-day ban: careless riding (Jan 30-Feb 1)
Dean Heslop three-day ban: excessive use of the whip (Jan 30-Feb 1)

FOCUS
A very moderate handicap, but it was at least competitive. The pace seemed reasonable and the form looks sound enough at face value.

187 COPTHORNE (S) STKS 1m 4f (P)
12:50 (12:50) (Class 6) 4-6-Y-0 **£2,047** (£604; £302) **Stalls** Low

Form RPR
13-6 **1** **Rapid City**[13] 29 6-9-8 66......(p) PatCosgrave 4 63
(A J McCabe) *t.k.h: hld up in last pair: smooth prog 3f out to chse ldr on inner over 1f out: urged along wout recrse to whip and styd on to ld last strides* **11/4**[2]
002- **2** *hd* **Poppy Red**[16] 7831 4-8-1 46......(p) AndrewHeffernan(7) 3 53
(C J Gray) *led: hrd pressed over 1f out: kpt on fnl f: hdd last strides* **16/1**
66-3 **3** ½ **Ebert**[8] 84 6-9-3 80 TonyHamilton 1 57
(R A Fahey) *prom: chsd ldr over 3f out to over 1f out: styd pressing but nt qckn ins fnl f* **11/10**[1]
00-5 **4** 4 **Barodine**[7] 105 6-8-12 62......(bt) WilliamCarson(5) 2 51
(R J Hodges) *dwlt: in tch: outpcd by ldrs over 2f out: n.d after: plugged on* **13/2**[3]
005- **5** 2½ **Roundthetwist (IRE)**[17] 7818 4-8-13 47 DarrenWilliams 7 47
(K R Burke) *stdd s: hld up in last pair: prog on inner over 2f out: chsd ldng trio over 1f out: sn wknd* **16/1**
504- **6** 4 **Shouldntbethere (IRE)**[16] 7831 5-8-10 51 NBazeley(7) 5 40
(Mrs P N Dutfield) *chsd ldr to over 3f out: sn wknd u.p* **12/1**
00-0 **7** 13 **Indiana Fox**[7] 100 6-8-7 52......(b[1]) GabrielHannon(5) 6 15
(B G Powell) *chsd ldrs tl wknd over 3f out: t.o fnl 2f* **66/1**
000- **8** 9 **Flying Goose (IRE)**[33] 7677 5-9-0 65 KevinGhunowa(3) 8 5
(R A Harris) *rel to r: tk furious hold and hld up in last: plld way through to go prom 5f out: wknd rapidly over 2f out: t.o* **8/1**

2m 35.81s (2.81) **Going Correction** +0.20s/f (Slow)
WFA 4 from 5yo+ 4lb **8** Ran SP% **119.7**
Speed ratings: **98,97,97,94,93 90,81,75**
toteswinger: 1&2 £6.50, 1&3 £2.30, 2&3 £3.30. CSF £47.21 TOTE £4.50: £1.20, £3.00, £1.10; EX 38.60 Trifecta £57.90 Pool: £221.52, 2.83 winning units..There was no bid for the winner.
Owner Mrs M J McCabe **Bred** Juddmonte Farms Ltd **Trained** Averham Park, Notts

FOCUS
This looked a reasonable seller beforehand, but the proximity of the 46-rated runner-up does little for the form. They crawled early on, as is so often the case at Lingfield and this does not look form to take at face value.
Rapid City Official explanation: trainer's rep said, regarding apparent improvement in form, that the gelding had pulled a muscle in its previous race.
Flying Goose(IRE) Official explanation: jockey said gelding ran too free

188 FELBRIDGE MAIDEN STKS 5f (P)
1:20 (1:20) (Class 5) 3-Y-0 **£2,729** (£806; £403) **Stalls** High

Form RPR
323- **1** **Comadoir (IRE)**[25] 7769 3-9-3 80 FergusSweeney 2 79
(Miss Jo Crowley) *mde all: set v stdy pce to 1/2-way: pressed over 1f out: pushed out firmly and a holding runner-up* **9/4**[2]
2- **2** ¾ **Theatre Street (IRE)**[25] 7769 3-8-12 0 ShaneKelly 6 71
(J Noseda) *hld up in 4th: effrt to chse wnr over 1f out but carried hd high: r.o fnl f but a readily hld* **4/6**[1]
4- **3** 3¼ **Acrosstheuniverse (USA)**[19] 7802 3-8-12 0 ChrisCatlin 5 60
(J R Gask) *t.k.h: chsd wnr to over 1f out: outpcd after* **10/1**[3]
5-6 **4** 1 **Keep Icy Calm (IRE)**[14] 19 3-8-12 0......(b[1]) JamieSpencer 4 56
(W J Haggas) *chsd ldng pair to over 1f out: sn outpcd* **16/1**
06- **5** ¾ **Lana's Charm**[86] 6894 3-8-12 0 CatherineGannon 1 53
(P J Makin) *stdd s: t.k.h and hld up in detached last pair: outpcd 2f out: shuffled along and kpt on fnl f: nvr nr ldrs* **66/1**
66- **6** 3¼ **Menhir Bay**[19] 7802 3-9-3 0 JimCrowley 7 47
(D K Ivory) *t.k.h: hld up in detached last pair: outpcd 2f out: no ch after* **66/1**

61.55 secs (2.75) **Going Correction** +0.20s/f (Slow) **6** Ran SP% **108.7**
Speed ratings (Par 97): **86,84,79,78,76 71**
toteswinger: 1&2 £1.10, 1&3 £1.30, 2&3 £1.60. CSF £3.77 TOTE £2.20: £1.20, £1.20; EX 4.30.
Owner Mrs Liz Nelson **Bred** J S Bolger **Trained** Whitcombe, Dorset

FOCUS
A more interesting maiden than appeared the case at first glance and a race to keep an eye on, although the bare form must be treated with caution, as the winner made all at a steady pace and is the best guide.

189 BLINDLEY HEATH CLAIMING STKS 6f (P)
1:50 (1:50) (Class 6) 4-Y-0+ **£2,047** (£604; £151; £151) **Stalls** Low

Form RPR
31-1 **1** **Mutamared (USA)**[10] 57 9-9-5 84......(t) JamieSpencer 9 83+
(K A Ryan) *hld up in midfield: swift prog over 2f out to ld wl over 1f out: 2l clr fnl f: idled and drvn out* **8/11**[1]
03-2 **2** ½ **One More Round (USA)**[8] 87 11-8-5 72......(b) PatrickDonaghy(5) 2 72
(P D Evans) *stdd s: hld up in last pair: nt clr run briefly over 2f out: prog on wd outside over 1f out: r.o to take 2nd and cl on wnr ins fnl f: nvr gng to get there* **5/1**[2]
55-4 **3** ¾ **Tender Process (IRE)**[12] 37 6-8-8 66......(v) TonyHamilton 3 68
(R A Fahey) *trckd ldng pair: outpcd and lost pl over 2f out: hanging lft over 1f out and nt clr run briefly sn after: styd on again last 150yds* **14/1**
26P- **3** *dht* **Parisian Gift (IRE)**[40] 7592 4-8-11 79 ChrisCatlin 5 71
(J R Gask) *disp ld tl def advantage over 2f out: hdd and outpcd wl over 1f: kpt on last 75yds* **10/1**
050- **5** 1½ **Interactive (IRE)**[44] 7540 6-8-10 64 HayleyTurner 7 65
(Andrew Turnell) *trckd ldng pair: nt qckn 2f out: one pce fnl f* **10/1**
0-12 **6** 2¼ **Don Pele (IRE)**[8] 89 7-8-9 71......(b) KevinGhunowa(3) 1 60
(R A Harris) *t.k.h: disp ld to over 2f out: nt qckn: wknd fnl f* **8/1**[3]
50-0 **7** 1½ **Faintly Hopeful**[7] 97 4-8-8 47......(p) JoeFanning 4 51
(R A Teal) *dwlt: hld up in midfield: outpcd fr 2f out* **50/1**
560- **8** 3 **Teen Ager (FR)**[216] 3033 5-8-12 60 TGMcLaughlin 6 46
(P Burgoyne) *awkward s: t.k.h and hld up in last pair: effrt over 2f out but sn wknd* **33/1**

1m 12.69s (0.79) **Going Correction** +0.20s/f (Slow) **8** Ran SP% **115.4**
Speed ratings (Par 101): **102,101,100,100,98 95,93,89**PL: M £1.10, OMR £2.00, PG £0.80, TP £1.40. toteswinger: M&OMR £2.00, M&PG £1.20, M&TP £1.70, OMR&PG £2.50, OMR&TP £3.80. CSF £4.75 TOTE £1.70; EX 5.20 TRIFECTA Pool: £547.71. With Parisian Gift £8.90, 22.63 winning units; with Tender Proc27 Owner.

FOCUS
A reasonable claimer rated around the dead-heating third and seventh.
Parisian Gift(IRE) Official explanation: jockey said he took evasive action to avoid another horse

190 WILLIAM HILL JANUARY SALE - BETTER ODDS! H'CAP 2m (P)
2:20 (2:20) (Class 6) (0-65,65) 4-Y-0+ **£2,047** (£604; £302) **Stalls** Low

Form RPR
555- **1** **Dramatic Solo**[17] 7827 4-9-8 **65**......(b) AndrewElliott 9 74
(K R Burke) *trckd ldng trio: prog to ld 3f out: drvn and styd on strly fnl 2f* **9/2**
240- **2** 3¾ **Pseudonym (IRE)**[17] 7827 7-10-0 **64**......(vt[1]) FergusSweeney 8 69
(M F Harris) *settled midfield: rdn and prog 3f out: chsd wnr jst over 2f out: hanging over 1f out: styd on but no imp fnl f* **12/1**
23-4 **3** 3 **Colourful Move**[12] 40 4-9-3 **60** JamieSpencer 5 61
(P G Murphy) *settled midfield: hrd rdn wl over 2f out: sn outpcd by ldrs: styd on to take 3rd fnl f* **7/2**[3]
24-6 **4** 3½ **Irish Ballad**[6] 112 7-9-5 **55** NickyMackay 3 52
(S Dow) *trckd ldng pair: effrt 3f out: chsd wnr briefly over 2f out: sn btn: wknd fnl f* **10/3**[2]
46-1 **5** *nse* **Sea Cliff (IRE)**[3] 148 5-9-2 **52** 6ex ShaneKelly 1 49
(Jonjo O'Neill) *hld up towards rr: outpcd whn ldrs kicked on over 2f out: hrd rdn and nt qckn wl over 1f out: plugged on* **5/2**[1]
560- **6** 4½ **Fateful Attraction**[16] 7831 6-8-12 **48**......(t) PaulDoe 2 39
(I A Wood) *hld up in last trio: rdn wl over 3f out: sn struggling* **22/1**
45-6 **7** 3¾ **Restart (IRE)**[14] 8 8-8-9 **45** LiamJones 6 32
(Lucinda Featherstone) *pushed up to ld: sn t.k.h and set decent pce: hdd & wknd rapidly 3f out* **14/1**
000- **8** ½ **Drombeg Pride (IRE)**[70] 3780 5-8-9 **45** ChrisCatlin 7 31
(G P Enright) *mostly chsd ldr to 3f out: sn wknd rapidly* **100/1**
0/0- **9** 88 **Cellarmaster (IRE)**[165] 2832 8-9-5 **58** TolleyDean(3) 4 —
(Mark Gillard) *hld up in last: rdn and wknd 6f out: sn hopelessly t.o* **66/1**

3m 25.78s (0.08) **Going Correction** +0.20s/f (Slow)
WFA 4 from 5yo+ 7lb **9** Ran SP% **113.2**
Speed ratings (Par 101): **107,105,103,101,101 99,97,97,53**
toteswinger: 1&2 £5.80, 1&3 £2.50, 2&3 £4.90. CSF £54.16 CT £208.24 TOTE £5.20: £1.80, £4.20, £1.80; EX 47.80 Trifecta £251.90 Part won. Pool: £340.42, 0.20 winning units..
Owner Malih L Al Basti **Bred** Matthews Breeding And Racing Ltd **Trained** Middleham Moor, N Yorks

FOCUS
A modest staying handicap run at a steady early pace but the overall time was reasonable and the form is rated around the first two.

191 WILLLIAM HILL JANUARY SALE - NOW ON! H'CAP 7f (P)
2:55 (2:57) (Class 5) (0-75,75) 4-Y-0+ **£2,900** (£856; £428) **Stalls** Low

Form RPR
215- **1** **Trafalgar Square**[18] 7813 7-9-3 **74** JimCrowley 11 86
(M J Attwater) *hld up in midfield on inner: gd run through over 2f out to press ldrs over 1f out: led last 100yds: r.o wl* **13/2**[3]
124- **2** 1 **Everybody Knows**[20] 7796 4-9-4 **75** IanMongan 4 84
(Miss Jo Crowley) *taken down early: pressed ldr: led 1/2-way: drvn over 1f out: hdd and one pce last 100yds* **9/1**
003- **3** ¾ **Strabinios King**[17] 7829 5-8-13 **70** FrancisNorton 5 77
(M Wigham) *t.k.h: prom: rdn 2f out: chsd ldng pair ins fnl f: nt qckn last 100yds* **9/2**[1]
504- **4** 1 **Miss Mujanna**[16] 7837 4-9-2 **73** ChrisCatlin 7 77
(J Akehurst) *chsd ldrs: rdn wl over 2f out: nt qckn sn after: renewed effrt over 1f out: kpt on same pce* **16/1**
050- **5** ½ **Super Frank (IRE)**[16] 7837 6-9-0 **71** JoeFanning 13 74
(J Akehurst) *wl plcd: chsd ldr 2f out to over 1f out: fdd ins fnl f* **16/1**

21-4 **6** ½ **The Cayterers**[6] 113 7-8-13 **75** .... MCGeran(5) 2 77
(A W Carroll) *stdd s: t.k.h: hld up towards rr on inner: stl there over 1f out: shuffled along and kpt on* **8/1**

102- **7** *shd* **Tous Les Deux**[17] 7821 6-9-1 **72** .... FergusSweeney 10 73+
(G L Moore) *t.k.h: hld up in last pair: effrt on wd outside over 2f out: kpt on fnl f: nvr on terms* **13/2[3]**

056- **8** ½ **Royal Envoy (IRE)**[25] 7763 6-8-8 **68** .... TolleyDean(3) 3 70+
(P Howling) *hld up wl in rr: effrt 2f out: styng on but no ch of rching ldrs whn short of room ins fnl f* **33/1**

212- **9** *shd* **I Confess**[16] 7837 4-8-13 **75** ....(b) PatrickDonaghy(5) 9 75
(P D Evans) *fast away: led to 1/2-way: sn rdn: chsd ldr to 2f out: wknd fnl f* **5/1[2]**

265- **10** *nse* **Cornus**[16] 7837 7-9-2 **73** ....(be) PatCosgrave 12 73
(A J McCabe) *mounted on crse and taken down early: hld up towards rr: prog 2f out: cl up bhd ldrs over 1f out: sn nt qckn and btn: plugged on* **20/1**

330- **11** 1¾ **Shakespeare's Son**[25] 7762 4-8-9 **69** .... DuranFentiman(3) 6 64
(H J Evans) *t.k.h: hld up wl in rr: pushed along and no prog fnl 2f* **12/1**

00-5 **12** *hd* **Princess Rose Anne (IRE)**[13] 31 4-8-13 **70** .... RobertWinston 8 64
(J R Best) *plld hrd: restrained bhd ldrs but wd: effrt over 2f out: wknd over 1f out* **16/1**

051- **13** *nk* **Royal Island (IRE)**[41] 7585 7-8-10 **67** .... VinceSlattery 1 60
(M G Quinlan) *t.k.h: hld up in last pair: pushed along 2f out: nvr a factor* **16/1**

1m 24.37s (-0.43) **Going Correction** +0.20s/f (Slow) **13** Ran SP% **121.6**
Speed ratings (Par 103): **110,108,108,106,106 105,105,105,104,104 102,102,102**
toteswinger: 1&2 £10.20, 1&3 £11.40, 2&3 £12.80. CSF £65.18 CT £304.93 TOTE £7.00: £2.20, £3.70, £2.30; EX 87.80 Trifecta £254.40 Part won. Pool: £343.86, 0.10 winning units..
Owner Canisbay Bloodstock **Bred** Matthews Breeding And Racing Ltd **Trained** Epsom, Surrey

FOCUS
A modest but competitive handicap. The pace set by course specialist I Confess was solid and the time was decent, suggesting the form is straightforward.
Princess Rose Anne(IRE) Official explanation: jockey said filly ran too free early on

192 WILLIAM HILL JANUARY SALE - WHY BET ELSEWHERE? H'CAP 1m (P)
3:30 (3:31) (Class 6) (0-60,60) 4-Y-O+ **£2,047** (£604; £302) **Stalls** High

Form RPR

36-2 **1** **General Feeling (IRE)**[6] 125 8-9-4 **60** .... HayleyTurner 7 70
(S T Mason) *hld up in last pair: gd prog and dream run through on inner fr 2f out: pushed into ld ins fnl f: in command after* **11/4[1]**

30-4 **2** *1* **Nikki Bea (IRE)**[7] 97 6-8-10 **52** .... PaulDoe 5 60
(Jamie Poulton) *trckd ldrs: produced to chal 1f out and sn upsides: outpcd by wnr fnl 100yds* **7/1**

005- **3** 1¾ **Copperwood**[17] 7817 4-8-8 **50** .... FergusSweeney 3 54+
(M Blanshard) *hld up in last: tk wd route to make prog 2f out: pushed along and hdwy over 1f out: r.o fnl f: no ch of rching ldng pair* **13/2**

50-2 **4** *1* **Red Current**[11] 42 5-8-4 **49** .... KevinGhunowa(3) 12 51
(R A Harris) *t.k.h: pressed ldr: led 2f out: hdd and fdd ins fnl f* **11/2[3]**

051- **5** 1¼ **Upstairs**[25] 7766 5-8-13 **60** .... AmyBaker(5) 2 59
(D R C Elsworth) *t.k.h: hld up in midfield: gng easily 2f out but racd awkwardly whn asked for effrt over 1f out: outpcd* **3/1[2]**

160- **6** *nk* **Siryena**[105] 6436 4-9-0 **56** ....(tp) ShaneKelly 9 54
(B I Case) *trckd ldrs: rdn and cl up 2f out: outpcd fr over 1f out* **33/1**

0-36 **7** *nk* **Dynamo Dave (USA)**[5] 131 4-7-11 **46** oh1 .... SeanPalmer(7) 8 43
(M D I Usher) *hld up in rr: effrt and wd bnd 2f out: bmpd along and kpt on: no ch* **16/1**

000- **8** 2¾ **Minwir (IRE)**[68] 7255 4-8-13 **55** .... PatCosgrave 6 46
(M Quinn) *hld up towards rr: rdn over 2f out: wd bnd after: no prog over 1f out* **25/1**

000- **9** *nk* **Titus Gent**[44] 7536 4-9-1 **57** .... MickyFenton 10 47
(J Ryan) *led: rdn over 3f out: hdd 2f out: sn wknd* **33/1**

00-0 **10** *shd* **Szaba**[11] 44 4-8-4 **46** oh1 .... NickyMackay 4 36
(J Akehurst) *t.k.h: pressed ldrs tl wknd wl over 1f out* **33/1**

0-15 **11** 1¼ **Too Grand**[10] 61 4-9-1 **57** ....(v) NeilChalmers 11 44
(J J Bridger) *hld up towards rr and racd wdst of all: no prog after wd bnd 2f out* **20/1**

1m 39.65s (1.45) **Going Correction** +0.20s/f (Slow) **11** Ran SP% **116.2**
Speed ratings (Par 101): **100,99,97,96,95 94,94,91,91,91 90**
toteswinger: 1&2 £4.00, 1&3 £6.40, 2&3 £5.60. CSF £20.49 CT £111.44 TOTE £3.90: £1.10, £2.10, £2.40; EX 13.10 Trifecta £87.20 Pool: £440.01, 3.73 winning units..
Owner Middleham Park Racing LX **Bred** John Graham And Leslie Laverty **Trained**

FOCUS
A moderate handicap run at an ordinary pace with the runner-up the best guide to the level.
Upstairs Official explanation: trainer said gelding did not stay

193 COLEMANS HATCH H'CAP (DIV II) 1m 2f (P)
4:05 (4:05) (Class 6) (0-55,55) 4-Y-O+ **£1,706** (£503; £252) **Stalls** Low

Form RPR

/01- **1** **Chalice Welcome**[15] 7815 6-8-12 **51** .... HayleyTurner 3 59+
(N B King) *hld up in rr: prog on inner over 2f out: waited for gap and threaded through over 1f out: led jst ins fnl f: rdn clr* **8/1**

40-4 **2** 1½ **Play Up Pompey**[11] 47 7-9-0 **53** .... JimCrowley 9 58
(J J Bridger) *hld up towards rr: prog on outer whn forced v wd bnd 2f out: hdwy over 1f out: chsd wnr wl ins fnl f: no imp* **7/1**

04-2 **3** *nk* **Broughtons Flight (IRE)**[5] 132 4-9-0 **55** .... TonyCulhane 1 59
(W J Musson) *trckd ldrs: gng easily 2f out: hanging and nt keen whn asked to go through gap over 1f out: kpt on again to take 3rd nr fin* **10/3[2]**

003- **4** *nk* **Alberts Story (USA)**[19] 6955 5-8-9 **48** .... TonyHamilton 6 51
(R A Fahey) *trckd ldr: rdn wl over 2f out: fnlly got upsides ent fnl f: sn outpcd* **6/1[3]**

56-6 **5** ¾ **Tabulate**[7] 100 6-8-13 **52** .... IanMongan 5 54
(P Howling) *hld up in midfield: prog to press ldrs 2f out: looked dangerous over 1f out: fdd fnl f* **8/1**

100- **6** *nk* **Darley Star**[37] 7626 4-8-7 **51** ....(p) KevinGhunowa(3) 2 52
(R A Harris) *led: set slow pce for 4f out: drvn over 2f out: hdd & wknd jst ins fnl f* **20/1**

600- **7** 1¾ **Historical Giant (USA)**[81] 7010 4-8-9 **50** ....(p) JamieSpencer 10 48
(E F Vaughan) *hld up in midfield: prog to chse ldng pair over 3f out: sn drvn: wnt wd bnd 2f out: no prog after: wknd fnl f* **3/1[1]**

8 1½ **Huck Finn (NZ)**[14] 9-9-2 **55** .... MickyFenton 7 50
(M Madgwick) *chsd ldrs: pushed along bef 1/2-way: dropped to last 2f out and sn detached: plugged on fnl f* **66/1**

046- **9** ½ **Pajada**[28] 7736 5-8-8 **47** oh1 ow1 .... FergusSweeney 4 41
(M D I Usher) *hld up in last trio: no prog fnl 2f* **33/1**

302- **10** *2* **The Little Master (IRE)**[30] 7701 5-8-10 **54** ....(t) AmyBaker(5) 8 44
(D R C Elsworth) *lft at least 20 l s: ct up after 3f due to v slow pce: bmpd along and no rspnse 2f out* **10/1**

2m 11.02s (4.42) **Going Correction** +0.20s/f (Slow)
WFA 4 from 5yo+ 2lb **10** Ran SP% **115.4**
Speed ratings (Par 101): **90,88,88,88,87 87,86,84,84,82**
toteswinger: 1&2 £6.10, 1&3 £5.30, 2&3 £5.10. CSF £61.01 CT £224.08 TOTE £8.60: £2.50, £2.30, £1.20; EX 50.60 Trifecta £240.40 Pool: £324.99 - 0.99 winning units. Place 6: £7.08, Place 5: £5.91..
Owner The Dyball Partnership **Bred** The Dyball Partnership **Trained** Newmarket, Suffolk

FOCUS
They went very steady, even by Lingfield standards, resulting in a winning time over 3secs slower than the first division. The form looks shaky and weak.
The Little Master(IRE) Official explanation: jockey said gelding missed the break
T/Plt: £14.20 to a £1 stake. Pool: £42,312.80. 2,174.60 winning tickets. T/Qpdt: £13.40 to a £1 stake. Pool: £3,296.50. 180.80 winning tickets. JN

133 WOLVERHAMPTON (A.W) (L-H)
Friday, January 16

OFFICIAL GOING: Standard
Wind: Fresh, half behind Weather: Overcast, turning to rain after race 1

194 WILLIAM HILL JANUARY SALE - NOW ON! H'CAP 1m 1f 103y(P)
6:50 (6:50) (Class 6) (0-65,65) 4-Y-O+ **£2,388** (£705; £352) **Stalls** Low

Form RPR

216- **1** **Templetuohy Max (IRE)**[21] 7786 4-9-1 **62** ....(v) JimmyQuinn 6 71
(J D Bethell) *hld up in tch: nt clr run over 2f out: rdn: n.m.r and hung lft over 1f out: styd on to ld nr fin* **8/1**

461- **2** ½ **Formidable Guest**[19] 7800 5-8-12 **58** .... TGMcLaughlin 9 66
(J Pearce) *hld up: hdwy over 3f out: led 2f out: sn rdn and edgd rt: hdd nr fin* **17/2**

3 2¼ **Oddshoes (IRE)**[365] 6789 7-8-6 **59** .... BMcHugh(7) 8 62
(K M Prendergast) *half-rrd s: hld up: hdwy over 2f out: rdn over 1f out: edgd lft: styd on u.p* **14/1**

1- **4** *shd* **Rambling Dancer (IRE)**[27] 7749 5-9-0 **60** .... WJLee 3 63
(Mrs Valerie Keatley, Ire) *chsd ldrs: rdn and ev ch ins fnl f: styd on same pce* **7/1[3]**

310- **5** 1¾ **Moment Of Clarity**[28] 7732 7-8-12 **58** ....(p) PaulEddery 11 57
(R C Guest) *hld up in tch: n.m.r and lost pl 3f out: rallied over 1f out: no ex ins fnl f* **16/1**

56-5 **6** 2¾ **Epidaurian King (IRE)**[13] 21 6-9-1 **61** .... DarrenWilliams 7 54
(D Shaw) *hld up: hmpd 3f out: styd on u.p fr over 1f out: n.d* **20/1**

204- **7** 1½ **Manchestermaverick (USA)**[41] 7581 4-8-12 **59** .... ChrisCatlin 4 49
(H Morrison) *prom: chsd ldr 6f out tl led over 2f out: sn hdd: wknd ins fnl f* **9/2[2]**

456- **8** *shd* **Drawn Gold**[60] 7364 5-9-3 **63** .... GrahamGibbons 5 53+
(R Hollinshead) *s.i.s: hld up: n.m.r and dropped to rr 6f out: rdn over 3f out: nvr nrr* **7/2[1]**

9 ½ **Vinorine (FR)**[27] 4574 5-8-9 **60** .... BACurtis(5) 13 49
(R P Burns, Ire) *hld up: rdn over 2f out: n.d* **100/1**

10-2 **10** 1½ **Buscador (USA)**[7] 105 10-9-2 **62** .... LiamJones 10 48
(W M Brisbourne) *awkward leaving stalls: pushed along to ld after 1f: rdn and hdd over 2f out: wknd over 1f out* **12/1**

10-6 **11** *3* **Master Mahogany**[13] 28 8-9-0 **65** .... WilliamCarson(5) 1 44
(R J Hodges) *led 1f: chsd ldrs: rdn and wknd over 2f out* **16/1**

03-3 **12** 4½ **Rowan Lodge (IRE)**[5] 129 7-8-12 **58** ....(b) JamieMoriarty 2 28
(Ollie Pears) *prom: rdn over 3f out: sn wknd* **12/1**

504- **13** *38* **Pearl Dealer (IRE)**[34] 7665 4-8-13 **60** ....(tp) LukeMorris 12 —
(N J Vaughan) *trckd ldrs: racd keenly: rdn over 3f out: sn wknd* **12/1**

2m 1.31s (-0.39) **Going Correction** +0.10s/f (Slow)
WFA 4 from 5yo+ 1lb **13** Ran SP% **121.8**
Speed ratings (Par 101): **105,104,102,102,100 98,97,97,96,95 92,88,54**
toteswinger: 1&2 £7.50, 1&3 not won, 2&3 not won. CSF £75.97 CT £954.19 TOTE £10.00: £3.60, £4.30, £6.70; EX 145.90.
Owner Craig Monty **Bred** Jim Shanahan **Trained** Middleham Moor, N Yorks
■ Stewards' Enquiry : Graham Gibbons one-day ban: used whip with excessive force (Jan 30)

FOCUS
A run-of-the-mill handicap in which the two market leaders disappointed and the form looks ordinary. The pace was only fair and the action unfolded towards the inside rail in the straight.
Drawn Gold Official explanation: jockey said gelding never travelled

195 STAY AT THE WOLVERHAMPTON HOLIDAY INN CLAIMING STKS 1m 141y(P)
7:20 (7:20) (Class 6) 4-Y-O+ **£2,729** (£806; £403) **Stalls** Low

Form RPR

445- **1** **Dichoh**[17] 7821 6-9-9 80 ....(p) ChrisCatlin 4 86
(M A Jarvis) *hld up: hdwy over 2f out: rdn to ld and hung lft ins fnl f: jst hld on* **6/4[1]**

400- **2** *hd* **Mataram (USA)**[17] 7821 6-9-1 79 .... JoeFanning 7 77
(W Jarvis) *trckd ldrs: racd keenly: led over 2f out: rdn: hdd and carried lft ins fnl f: r.o* **4/1[2]**

5-24 **3** ½ **Teasing**[6] 125 5-8-13 70 ....(v) TGMcLaughlin 5 74
(J Pearce) *s.s: hld up: hdwy over 1f out: nt clr run and swtchd lft ins fnl f: r.o: nt rch ldrs* **13/2[3]**

66-2 **4** 3½ **Randama Bay (IRE)**[14] 17 4-9-3 75 .... CatherineGannon 6 71
(I A Wood) *trckd ldr: rdn and hdd over 2f out: no ex fnl f* **9/1**

41-0 **5** *nk* **Silver Hotspur**[9] 79 5-9-9 84 .... LiamJones 8 75
(C R Dore) *prom: chsd ldr over 5f out: ev ch over 2f out: styng on same pce whn nt clr run ins fnl f* **4/1[2]**

14-0 **6** 4½ **Yes One (IRE)**[14] 9 5-9-2 78 .... BMcHugh(7) 3 65
(K A Ryan) *chsd ldrs: rdn over 2f out: wknd fnl f* **8/1**

200- **7** *19* **The London Gang**[162] 4797 6-8-3 41 ....(b) DeanHeslop(5) 2 6
(S Wynne) *chsd ldr 3f: rdn over 3f out: sn wknd* **66/1**

1m 50.56s (0.06) **Going Correction** +0.10s/f (Slow)
WFA 4 from 5yo+ 1lb **7** Ran SP% **115.9**
Speed ratings (Par 101): **103,102,102,99,99 95,78**
toteswinger: 1&2 £3.50, 1&3 £1.10, 2&3 £10.20. CSF £8.00 TOTE £2.20: £1.10, £3.40; EX 11.90.
Owner T G Warner **Bred** Red House Stud **Trained** Newmarket, Suffolk
■ Stewards' Enquiry : Chris Catlin caution: careless riding. Two-day ban: used whip without giving gelding time to respond down shoulder in forehand position (Feb 1-2)

FOCUS
A couple of fair sorts in a reasonable claimer but not a strong gallop. Things again unfolded centre to far side in the straight and the winner and third are rated to recent marks.

196 SPONSOR A RACE BY CALLING 01902 390009 H'CAP — 1m 141y(P)
7:50 (7:51) (Class 6) (0-55,54) 3-Y-O — **£2,388** (£705; £352) **Stalls** Low

Form — RPR

006- **1** **Fantastic Fred (IRE)**[135] 5599 3-8-13 **53** .... TPQueally 9 — 56
(J A Osborne) *hld up in tch: rdn and hung lft fr over 1f out: styd on u.p to ld wl ins fnl f* — **12/1**

045- **2** ½ **Honorable Endeavor**[43] 7543 3-8-13 **53** .... JamieSpencer 11 — 55
(E F Vaughan) *stdd and swtchd lft sn after s: hld up: pushed along and hdwy over 2f out: rdn and hung lft over 1f out: swtchd rt: hung lft and r.o u.p ins fnl f* — **11/4**[1]

400- **3** 1¼ **Rigged**[129] 5784 3-8-10 **50** .... HayleyTurner 10 — 49
(J A Osborne) *chsd ldr: rdn to ld over 1f out: hdd and hung lft wl ins fnl f* — **20/1**

065- **4** 1½ **Ed's Pride (IRE)**[34] 7659 3-8-5 **45** ....(b) FrancisNorton 4 — 40
(K A Ryan) *chsd ldrs: rdn over 2f out: n.m.r and no ex wl ins fnl f* — **8/1**

004- **5** nk **Dark Desert**[34] 7659 3-8-6 **46** .... ChrisCatlin 5 — 41
(A G Newcombe) *hld up: hdwy u.p fr over 1f out: hung lft ins fnl f: nt trble ldrs* — **5/1**

005- **6** ¾ **Fleur De'Lion (IRE)**[20] 7789 3-8-10 **50** .... JimmyQuinn 8 — 43
(S Kirk) *chsd ldrs: rdn over 2f out: no ex ins fnl f* — **4/1**[3]

00-3 **7** 3 **Royal Salsa (IRE)**[9] 77 3-8-8 **48** .... TonyHamilton 2 — 34
(R A Fahey) *prom: rdn over 2f out: wknd fnl f* — **7/2**[2]

50 **8** ¾ **Royal Mischief (IRE)**[4] 135 3-8-10 **50** .... CatherineGannon 7 — 34
(P D Evans) *led: rdn and hdd over 1f out: wknd ins fnl f* — **66/1**

600- **9** 4½ **Refuse To Decline**[55] 7422 3-8-10 **50** .... StephenDonohoe 6 — 24
(D M Simcock) *hld up: rdn over 5f out: wknd 3f out* — **25/1**

0-50 **10** 16 **Talsarnau (IRE)**[4] 134 3-9-0 **54** .... LiamJones 3 — —
(W M Brisbourne) *hld up: rdn 1/2-way: wknd 3f out* — **14/1**

1m 53.94s (3.44) **Going Correction** +0.10s/f (Slow) — **10** Ran SP% **121.1**
Speed ratings (Par 95): **88,87,86,85,84 84,81,80,76,62**
toteswinger: 1&2 £20.00, 1&3 £9.60, 2&3 £23.20. CSF £46.19 CT £556.16 TOTE £10.40: £4.00, £1.60, £3.80; EX 76.20.
Owner H R H Prince of Saxe-Weimar **Bred** Gainsborough Stud Management Ltd **Trained** Upper Lambourn, Berks
■ Stewards' Enquiry : Hayley Turner 15-day ban (takes into account previous offences; three days deferred): careless riding (Jan 30-Feb 10)

FOCUS
A modest handicap run at an ordinary gallop, in which the winner and second raced in the centre in the straight. The form looks weak.
Fantastic Fred(IRE) Official explanation: trainer said, regarding running, that the gelding had possibly benefited from a 135 day break.
Royal Mischief(IRE) Official explanation: jockey said filly hung badly right-handed

197 WILLIAM HILL JANUARY SALE - BETTER ODDS! H'CAP — 5f 216y(P)
8:20 (8:20) (Class 4) (0-80,80) 4-Y-O+ — **£5,180** (£1,541; £770; £384) **Stalls** Low

Form — RPR

4- **1** **Mrs Penny (AUS)**[17] 7828 5-9-4 **80** .... ChrisCatlin 4 — 91
(J R Gask) *hld up: hdwy over 1f out: shkn up to ld ins fnl f: r.o wl* — **3/1**[2]

0-42 **2** 2¼ **Count Ceprano (IRE)**[5] 128 5-9-1 **77** .... LiamJones 1 — 80
(C R Dore) *chsd ldrs: rdn 1/2-way: ev ch ins fnl f: unable qckn* — **4/1**[3]

26-3 **3** ¾ **Peter's Storm (USA)**[9] 76 4-8-12 **74** .... JamieSpencer 2 — 75
(K A Ryan) *led: rdn over 1f out: hdd and no ex ins fnl f* — **6/1**

23-1 **4** 1 **Princess Valerina**[14] 20 5-9-1 **77** .... TPQueally 3 — 75
(D Haydn Jones) *trckd ldr 5f out: racd keenly: chal on bit over 1f out: rdn and hung lft ins fnl f: fnd nil* — **11/8**[1]

604- **5** 3½ **Qadar (IRE)**[290] 1134 7-9-1 **77** ....(b) LukeMorris 5 — 64
(N P Littmoden) *awkward leaving stalls: hld up: hdwy 1/2-way: rdn over 1f out: wknd fnl f* — **11/1**

1m 15.26s (0.26) **Going Correction** +0.10s/f (Slow) — **5** Ran SP% **109.7**
Speed ratings (Par 105): **102,99,98,96,92**
toteswinger: 1&2 £4.80. CSF £14.77 TOTE £3.70: £1.70, £1.60; EX 19.90.
Owner Horses First Racing Limited **Bred** L J Fleming **Trained** Sutton Veny, Wilts

FOCUS
A reasonable handicap, despite the lack of runners, but a moderate gallop saw the majority pulling for their heads in the first half and the market leader proved disappointing. The winner, a progressive type, raced centre to far side in the straight and the placed horses give the form a fairly sound look.

198 NAME A RACE TO ENHANCE YOUR BRAND H'CAP — 5f 216y(P)
8:50 (8:51) (Class 6) (0-55,61) 4-Y-O+ — **£2,388** (£705; £352) **Stalls** Low

Form — RPR

2-31 **1** **Sarah's Art (IRE)**[7] 108 6-9-6 **61** 6ex .... MickyFenton 11 — 75
(Stef Liddiard) *mid-div: hdwy over 2f out: led ins fnl f: rdn out* — **7/4**[1]

000- **2** ¾ **Inca Soldier (FR)**[159] 4903 6-8-13 **54** .... PaulEddery 12 — 66
(R C Guest) *hld up: hdwy over 2f out: rdn and ev ch ins fnl f: nt qckn towards fin* — **33/1**

6-02 **3** 4½ **Tadlil**[6] 111 7-8-9 **50** ....(v) RobertWinston 13 — 47
(J M Bradley) *chsd ldrs: led and hung lft over 1f out: sn rdn: hdd and no ex ins fnl f* — **5/1**[3]

303- **4** 3½ **Argentine (IRE)**[65] 7288 5-8-11 **52** ....(t) PaulMulrennan 1 — 38
(L Lungo) *sn pushed along and prom: nt clr run over 2f out: rdn over 1f out: styd on same pce* — **4/1**[2]

2-64 **5** 1 **Mister Incredible**[7] 108 6-8-10 **51** ....(v) LukeMorris 6 — 34
(J M Bradley) *chsd ldrs: rdn over 1f out: wknd fnl f* — **7/1**

0- **6** 2 **Donard Lodge (IRE)**[18] 7809 4-8-11 **52** .... AndrewElliott 7 — 28
(J Balding) *hld up: n.d* — **22/1**

600- **7** 1 **Just Joey**[64] 7295 5-8-13 **54** ....(b) ChrisCatlin 4 — 27
(J R Weymes) *mid-div: rdn over 2f out: sn wknd* — **14/1**

601- **8** 1½ **Marvin Gardens**[51] 7453 6-8-11 **52** ....(b) JerryO'Dwyer 10 — 20
(P S McEntee) *led: rdn: hung lft and hdd over 1f out: wknd fnl f* — **8/1**

000/ **9** 1 **Cate Washington**[743] 33 6-8-0 **46** oh1 .... DeanHeslop(5) 8 — 11
(Mrs L Williamson) *mid-div: rdn and wknd over 2f out* — **100/1**

50-0 **10** ¾ **Mr Skipiton (IRE)**[9] 71 4-9-0 **55** .... StephenCarson 2 — 18
(B J McMath) *chsd ldrs: rdn over 2f out: wknd over 1f out* — **12/1**

R0-0 **11** 1½ **Fitolini**[14] 15 4-9-0 **55** .... GrahamGibbons 5 — 13
(Mrs G S Rees) *s.s: a in rr* — **40/1**

00-0 **12** 1¼ **Mr Loire**[6] 111 5-8-7 **48** ....(t) HayleyTurner 3 — —
(K G Wingrove) *s.i.s: a in rr* — **16/1**

000/ **13** 13 **Magical Mimi**[956] 2288 8-8-5 **46** oh1 ....(t) JimmyQuinn 9 — —
(K G Wingrove) *s.i.s: a in rr* — **40/1**

1m 14.93s (-0.07) **Going Correction** +0.10s/f (Slow) — **13** Ran SP% **130.0**
Speed ratings (Par 101): **104,103,97,92,91 88,87,85,83,82 80,79,61**
toteswinger: 1&2 £14.30, 1&3 £1.90, 2&3 not won. CSF £87.19 CT £270.79 TOTE £3.10: £1.70, £8.00, £1.80; EX 39.90.
Owner ownaracehorse.co.uk (Shefford) **Bred** Newtownbarry House Stud **Trained** Great Shefford, Berks

FOCUS
A modest handicap in which the pace was sound throughout. Winner and second, who pulled clear, came down the centre in the straight with the former rated back to his best.
Magical Mimi Official explanation: jockey said mare fly-leaped leaving stalls

199 WILLIAM HILL JANUARY SALE - WHY BET ELSEWHERE? H'CAP — 1m 141y(P)
9:20 (9:20) (Class 4) (0-85,84) 4-Y-O+ — **£5,180** (£1,541; £770; £384) **Stalls** Low

Form — RPR

45-1 **1** **Spectait**[9] 79 7-9-5 **84** 6ex .... JamieMoriarty 5 — 95
(Jonjo O'Neill) *hld up in tch: rdn to ld and hung lft ins fnl f: r.o* — **11/4**[1]

211- **2** ½ **Hyde Lea Flyer**[27] 7750 4-8-8 **74** .... GrahamGibbons 6 — 84
(E S McMahon) *trckd ldrs: led over 1f out: rdn and hdd ins fnl f: styd on* — **11/4**[1]

4-53 **3** 2¼ **Just Bond (IRE)**[14] 17 7-9-3 **82** .... PaulMulrennan 7 — 87
(G R Oldroyd) *led: rdn and hdd over 1f out: n.m.r and no ex ins fnl f* — **13/2**[3]

542- **4** 3½ **Saltagioo (ITY)**[26] 7753 5-9-5 **84** ....(t) TPQueally 9 — 81
(M Botti) *prom: chsd ldr 7f out: rdn over 1f out: wknd fnl f* — **7/1**

130- **5** 7 **Marning Star**[119] 6070 4-8-12 **78** .... StephenDonohoe 2 — 59
(Ian Williams) *s.i.s: hld up: hdwy over 2f out: wknd sn after* — **14/1**

001- **6** 17 **Theonebox (USA)**[39] 7610 4-8-12 **78** .... LukeMorris 1 — 20+
(N J Vaughan) *hld up: hmpd 3f out: nt rcvr* — **9/2**[2]

312- **P** **Bluejain**[18] 7813 4-9-2 **82** .... JamieSpencer 3 — —
(Miss Gay Kelleway) *chsd ldrs tl broke down and p.u 3f out* — **13/2**[3]

1m 50.61s (0.11) **Going Correction** +0.10s/f (Slow)
WFA 4 from 5yo+ 1lb — **7** Ran SP% **117.3**
Speed ratings (Par 105): **103,102,100,97,91 76,—**
toteswinger: 1&2 £3.40, 1&3 £2.50, 2&3 £3.90. CSF £10.75 CT £44.46 TOTE £3.60: £1.70, £1.90; EX 16.60 Place 6: £124.92, Place 5: £18.57..
Owner John P McManus **Bred** Blyth Tait **Trained** Cheltenham, Gloucs
■ Stewards' Enquiry : Jamie Moriarty one-day ban: careless riding (Jan 30)

FOCUS
Several in-form sorts in this decent handicap with the third setting the standard. The gallop was a moderate one and the first two ended up towards the inside rail in the closing stages.
Theonebox(USA) Official explanation: jockey said gelding suffered interference in running
T/Plt: £218.10 to a £1 stake. Pool: £118,296.93. 395.87 winning tickets. T/Qpdt: £18.90 to a £1 stake. Pool: £10,280.20. 400.60 winning tickets. CR

[186] LINGFIELD (L-H)
Saturday, January 17

OFFICIAL GOING: Standard
Wind: Blustery, half behind Weather: Fine

200 WILLIAM HILL JANUARY SALE - NOW ON! (S) STKS — 6f (P)
12:45 (12:45) (Class 6) 3-Y-O — **£2,047** (£604; £302) **Stalls** Low

Form — RPR

66-4 **1** **Raimond Ridge (IRE)**[10] 75 3-8-12 57 .... TonyCulhane 3 — 62
(M R Channon) *dwlt: t.k.h early and hld up: rdn and prog towards inner wl over 1f out: drvn ahd ins fnl f: kpt on wl* — **10/1**

54-4 **2** nk **It's A Mans World**[10] 74 3-8-12 69 .... JimmyQuinn 7 — 61
(P J McBride) *stdd s: hld up in last: smooth prog on inner over 1f out: pushed along to chal ins fnl f: drvn last 100yds: hld* — **11/8**[1]

00-5 **3** ¾ **Quick Single (USA)**[6] 127 3-8-12 67 ....(b[1]) HayleyTurner 5 — 59
(D R C Elsworth) *trckd ldr: hrd rdn to chal over 1f out: outpcd ins fnl f: kpt on* — **9/1**

4-64 **4** nk **River Rye (IRE)**[3] 159 3-8-12 62 ....(p) LukeMorris 4 — 58
(J S Moore) *trckd ldrs: gng wl 2f out: rdn and nt qckn over 1f out: kpt on fnl f: a readily hld* — **17/2**[3]

512- **5** hd **Elusive Ronnie (IRE)**[28] 7738 3-9-3 58 ....(p) JimCrowley 2 — 62
(R A Teal) *led: c quite wd bnd 2f out: drvn and hdd ins fnl f: fdd nr fin* — **10/1**

01-6 **6** ½ **Art Fund (USA)**[3] 159 3-9-3 63 .... FergusSweeney 6 — 60
(G L Moore) *towards rr and wd: rdn wl over 2f out: wd bnd 2f out and then hung rt in st: styd on fnl f: n.d* — **3/1**[2]

23-4 **7** 1 **Readily**[9] 91 3-8-7 51 .... RichardKingscote 9 — 47
(J G Portman) *racd wd: pressed ldng pair: niggled along fr 1/2-way: wd bnd 2f out: grad fdd* — **14/1**

00-0 **8** 2½ **Inn Swinger (IRE)**[10] 75 3-8-7 36 .... LiamJones 1 — 39
(W G M Turner) *chsd ldrs: rdn over 2f out: fdd over 1f out* — **100/1**

0-2 **9** 1½ **Yellow River (USA)**[9] 92 3-8-7 65 .... EdwardCreighton 10 — 34
(E J Creighton) *awkward s: a in rr: struggling wl over 2f out* — **33/1**

1m 12.64s (0.74) **Going Correction** -0.025s/f (Stan) — **9** Ran SP% **116.4**
Speed ratings (Par 95): **94,93,92,92,91 91,89,86,84**
toteswinger: 1&2 £5.00, 1&3 £16.30, 2&3 £4.40. CSF £24.38 TOTE £12.70: £4.10, £1.10, £3.10; EX 34.20 Trifecta £143.00 Part won. Pool: £193.29 - 0.55 winning units..There was no bid for the winner. It's a Man World was claimed by Mrs S Dow for £6,000.
Owner M Channon **Bred** Myles And Mrs Joan Doyle **Trained** West Ilsley, Berks

FOCUS
A weak race even for the grade and there was only a couple of lengths or so separating the first six home but the pace was honest.

201 WILLIAM HILL JANUARY SALE - BETTER ODDS! MAIDEN STKS — 1m (P)
1:15 (1:17) (Class 5) 3-Y-O — **£2,729** (£806; £403) **Stalls** High

Form — RPR

0- **1** **Strong Storm (USA)**[107] 6425 3-9-3 0 .... ShaneKelly 5 — 71+
(J Noseda) *cl up: effrt over 2f out: hrd rdn to chse ldr over 1f out: styd on ins fnl f to ld last strides* — **4/1**[3]

0- **2** nk **Badge Of Honour**[25] 7773 3-9-3 0 .... GregFairley 11 — 70+
(M Johnston) *t.k.h: w ldr: led over 2f out: urged along and stl looked green over 1f out: kpt on but worn down last strides* — **8/1**

3 ¾ **Carbon Hoofprint** 3-9-3 0 .... FergusSweeney 3 — 68+
(P J Makin) *s.i.s: t.k.h early and hld up towards rr: gng strly over 2f out: eased out and prog over 1f out: shkn up and styd on encouragingly fnl f* — **20/1**

6- **4** 2 **Divinatore**[22] 7783 3-9-3 0 .... PatCosgrave 1 — 64
(D Haydn Jones) *s.i.s: sn pushed up to trck ldrs: rdn and nt qckn 2f out: kpt on fnl f* — **14/1**

03- **5** *nse* **Longboat Key**[87] 6892 3-9-3 0 JoeFanning 2 64
(M Johnston) *mde most to over 2f out: grad outpcd u.p fr over 1f out* **9/4**[1]

06- **6** *2 3/4* **Philmack Dot Com**[19] 7812 3-9-3 0 MickyFenton 10 57
(Miss Amy Weaver) *restrained fr wd draw and hld up in rr: rchd midfield over 2f out: shuffled along and grad lost grnd on ldrs fnl f* **28/1**

7 *shd* **Bomber Brown (IRE)** 3-9-3 0 JamieSpencer 4 57+
(P W Chapple-Hyam) *s.i.s: hld up in last and rn green: detached over 2f out and wd bnd sn after: penny dropped and styd on fnl f* **7/2**[2]

0- **8** *nk* **Arabian Silk (IRE)**[42] 7578 3-8-12 0 JimmyQuinn 6 51
(D M Simcock) *s.i.s: a in rr: pushed along and struggling over 2f out* **66/1**

60- **9** *1 1/4* **Clinging Vine (USA)**[63] 7332 3-8-12 0 PatDobbs 7 48
(R Hannon) *trckd ldrs and racd wd: lost grnd fr wl over 2f out: no ch over 1f out* **6/1**

0- **10** *1/2* **Flying River (IRE)**[28] 7738 3-8-12 0 RichardKingscote 8 47
(Tom Dascombe) *a in rr: struggling fr 1/2-way* **50/1**

05- **11** *2 3/4* **Lovely Steps (USA)**[29] 7735 3-8-12 0 StephenDonohoe 9 41
(D M Simcock) *trckd ldng pair tl wknd rapidly over 2f out* **40/1**

1m 39.35s (1.15) **Going Correction** -0.025s/f (Stan) **11** Ran SP% **119.2**
Speed ratings (Par 97): **93,92,91,89,89 87,87,86,85,85 82**
toteswinger: 1&2 £24.70, 1&3 £39.30, 2&3 £35.50. CSF £34.52 TOTE £3.20: £1.50, £2.20, £7.10; EX 26.30 Trifecta £75.50 Part won. Pool: £102.20 - 0.45 winning units..
Owner Tom Ludt **Bred** Mckee Stables Inc **Trained** Newmarket, Suffolk

FOCUS
By no means a strong maiden and form pick Longboat Key weakened away pretty tamely in the straight so the form is modest.
Bomber Brown(IRE) Official explanation: jockey said he suffered a bloodied nose and was unable to ride out

202 WILLIAM HILL JANUARY SALE - WHY BET ELSEWHERE? H'CAP 1m 4f (P)
1:50 (1:50) (Class 5) (0-70,70) 4-Y-0+ £2,900 (£856; £428) **Stalls** Low

Form RPR

55-6 **1** **Sunset Boulevard (IRE)**[8] 103 6-8-13 **61** ChrisCatlin 6 68
(Miss Tor Sturgis) *t.k.h early: hld up towards rr: cruising over 2f out: prog on outer and rdn over 1f out: narrow ld ins fnl f: hld on wl* **9/1**

25/1 **2** *hd* **Dishdasha (IRE)**[6] 126 7-8-13 **61** 6ex (t) JamieSpencer 3 68
(Mrs A M Thorpe) *stdd s: hld up in rr: cruising over 2f out: prog on outer over 1f out: drvn to press wnr ins fnl f: r.o but jst hld* **7/4**[1]

11-4 **3** *nk* **Can Can Star**[14] 21 6-9-8 **70** ShaneKelly 11 76
(A W Carroll) *stdd s: hld up in last trio: cruising over 2f out: prog after: rdn to ld jst over 1f out: hdd ins fnl f: r.o but a jst hld* **10/1**

01-3 **4** *3/4* **Little Richard (IRE)**[8] 103 10-8-13 **61** (p) NeilChalmers 5 66
(M Wellings) *hld up in rr: rdn 3f out: wdst of all bnd 2f out: prog over 1f out: styd on wl fnl f but a hld* **18/1**

061- **5** *3/4* **Zalkani (IRE)**[20] 7806 9-8-13 **61** JerryO'Dwyer 1 65
(J Pearce) *hld up in midfield: rdn and effrt on inner over 2f out: styd on fr over 1f out but nt pce of ldrs* **16/1**

063- **6** *nk* **Mustajed**[21] 7797 8-9-3 **68** (v) JamesMillman[(3)] 8 71
(B R Millman) *t.k.h early: wl plcd: pressed ldrs and rdn over 2f out: nt qckn over 1f out: kpt on ins fnl f* **16/1**

023/ **7** *2* **Imperial Harry**[282] 4630 6-9-3 **65** HayleyTurner 12 65
(D E Pipe) *plld hrd: hld up but tugged way through to go prom after 4f: wnt 2nd 5f out: rdn over 3f out: stl upsides over 1f out: fdd* **25/1**

06-0 **8** *1/2* **Red Wine**[16] 3 10-9-1 **63** RobertWinston 9 62
(A J McCabe) *stdd s: t.k.h early and hld up in last trio: rdn at bk of main gp wl over 2f out: no prog tl r.o last 150yds* **40/1**

13-3 **9** *hd* **Tropical Tradition (IRE)**[14] 21 4-8-8 **60** RichardKingscote 10 59
(D W P Arbuthnot) *trckd ldr to 5f out: styd cl up on inner: upsides over 1f out: wknd ins fnl f* **6/1**[3]

321- **10** *1/2* **Cossack Prince**[50] 7078 4-9-4 **70** IanMongan 4 68
(Mrs L J Mongan) *led: slow pce for 3f: rdn over 3f out: hdd & wknd jst over 1f out* **16/1**

060- **11** *2 1/4* **Resplendent Ace (IRE)**[31] 7711 5-9-6 **68** JimmyQuinn 2 63
(P Howling) *trckd ldrs: stl cl up wl over 1f out: wknd fnl f* **11/2**[2]

130- **12** *6* **Days Of Pleasure (IRE)**[58] 1487 4-9-1 **67** JimCrowley 7 52
(C Gordon) *prom to 1/2-way: sn lost pl u.p: detached in last 3f out* **100/1**

2m 31.94s (-1.06) **Going Correction** -0.025s/f (Stan)
WFA 4 from 5yo+ 4lb **12** Ran SP% **115.3**
Speed ratings (Par 103): **102,101,101,101,100 100,99,98,98,98 96,92**
toteswinger: 1&2 £3.50, 1&3 £27.50, 2&3 £6.70. CSF £23.99 CT £165.10 TOTE £12.60: £2.70, £1.30, £2.90; EX 37.40 Trifecta £172.30 Part won. Pool: £232.86 - 0.50 winning units..
Owner Miss Tor Sturgis **Bred** A J Martin **Trained** Lambourn, Berks

FOCUS
The field fanned right across the track entering the final furlong as the closers made their move and the pace collapsed.

203 WILLIAM HILL JANUARY SALE - 0800 44 40 40 H'CAP 6f (P)
2:20 (2:20) (Class 4) (0-85,83) 3-Y-0 £4,857 (£1,445; £722; £360) **Stalls** Low

Form RPR

43-1 **1** **Five Star Junior (USA)**[10] 69 3-8-10 **75** ShaneKelly 3 84
(Mrs L Stubbs) *hld up in last pair: gd prog wl over 1f out and swtchd rt sn after: led 1f and sn in command: idled and drvn out last 100yds* **5/2**[2]

1-21 **2** *3/4* **Hellbender (IRE)**[12] 45 3-8-7 **72** RichardKingscote 2 79
(S Kirk) *hld up in 5th: effrt 2f out: outpcd over 1f out: styd on wl fnl f to take 2nd last strides* **6/1**

12-4 **3** *shd* **Satwa Street (IRE)**[8] 109 3-9-3 **82** HayleyTurner 5 89
(D M Simcock) *pressed ldr: led 2f out gng wl: drvn and hdd 1f out: sn wl hld by wnr: kpt on but lost 2nd last strides* **5/1**[3]

11-1 **4** *2* **Smokey Ryder**[8] 109 3-8-13 **81** KevinGhunowa[(3)] 1 82
(R A Harris) *trckd ldng pair on inner: effrt 2f out: outpcd over 1f out: kpt on again ins fnl f* **2/1**[1]

014- **5** *3 3/4* **Sharpener (IRE)**[42] 7575 3-8-6 **71** ChrisCatlin 6 60
(R Hannon) *stdd s: hld up in last pair: pushed along and no prog wl over 1f out* **16/1**

632- **6** *1 1/2* **Love You Louis**[18] 7820 3-8-13 **78** (p) SimonWhitworth 7 62
(J R Jenkins) *pressed ldng pair on outer to 2f out: sn btn* **9/1**

51-6 **7** *1 1/2* **Sir Geoffrey (IRE)**[8] 109 3-9-1 **83** TolleyDean[(3)] 4 62
(A J McCabe) *taken down early: led: drvn and hdd 2f out: sn wknd* **25/1**

1m 11.3s (-0.60) **Going Correction** -0.025s/f (Stan) **7** Ran SP% **112.6**
Speed ratings (Par 99): **103,102,101,99,94 92,90**
toteswinger: 1&2 £2.00, 1&3 £2.40, 2&3 £6.20. CSF £17.22 TOTE £3.20: £1.50, £3.80; EX 16.20.
Owner Moyns Park Stud **Bred** Robert W Sanford **Trained** Norton, N Yorks

FOCUS
A strongly run race, but the small field were tightly grouped turning for home.

204 WILLIAM HILL JANUARY SALE - ENHANCED FAVOURITES! H'CAP 6f (P)
2:55 (2:55) (Class 2) (0-100,102) 4-Y-0+ **£11,656** (£3,468; £1,733; £865) **Stalls** Low

Form RPR

115- **1** **Doubtful Sound (USA)**[30] 7716 5-8-6 **88** (p) JimCrowley 3 101
(R Hollinshead) *trckd ldng pair and clr of rest: wnt 2nd 2f out: effrt to ld 1f out: drvn clr* **12/1**

142- **2** *2 1/4* **Little Edward**[18] 7826 11-8-0 **87** MCGeran[(5)] 6 93
(R J Hodges) *hld up in midfield and off the pce: rdn and prog wl over 1f out: styd on to take 2nd wl ins fnl f: no ch w wnr* **9/1**

3-01 **3** *nk* **Matsunosuke**[9] 86 7-9-6 **102** LukeMorris 1 107+
(A B Coogan) *stdd s: hld up in last pair: gng wl but stl last of main gp over 2f out: nt clr run wl over 1f out: gd prog ent fnl f: r.o and nrly snatched 2nd* **15/2**[3]

211- **4** *1 1/4* **The Game**[30] 7716 4-8-10 **92** RichardKingscote 4 93
(Tom Dascombe) *blasted off at str pce and clr w two rivals: hdd & wknd 1f out* **4/1**[2]

000- **5** *1 3/4* **Tamagin (USA)**[112] 6269 6-9-1 **97** JamieSpencer 8 92
(K A Ryan) *pressed ldr at str pce to 2f out: wknd over 1f out* **4/1**[2]

500- **6** *1 1/4* **El Dececy (USA)**[91] 6810 5-8-4 **86** oh8 LiamJones 5 77
(S Parr) *chsd clr ldng trio: rdn wl over 2f out: tried to cl over 1f out but no real imp* **33/1**

542- **7** *nk* **Ebraam (USA)**[20] 7805 6-8-11 **96** TolleyDean[(3)] 9 86
(P Howling) *stdd s: wl in rr and wl off the pce: rdn over 2f out: no prog tl kpt on fnl f* **9/1**

00-6 **8** *hd* **Mr Lambros**[9] 86 8-7-11 **86** oh1 (vt) MatthewLawson[(7)] 7 76
(Miss Gay Kelleway) *dwlt: wl in rr: struggling sn after 1/2-way: last of main gp over 1f out: plugged on* **28/1**

111- **9** *1/2* **Internationaldebut (IRE)**[43] 7556 4-9-1 **97** JohnEgan 11 85
(S Parr) *out of tch in midfield: u.p 3f out: nvr on terms* **3/1**[1]

631- **10** *2* **Fyodor (IRE)**[21] 7793 8-9-3 **99** IanMongan 2 81
(C R Dore) *chsd clr ldng trio: no real imp 2f out: wknd fnl f* **25/1**

0/0- **11** *33* **Wotavadun (IRE)**[331] 642 6-8-4 **86** oh41 (b) ChrisCatlin 10 —
(D Flood) *t.o after 2f* **100/1**

69.72 secs (-2.18) **Going Correction** -0.025s/f (Stan) course record **11** Ran SP% **115.7**
Speed ratings (Par 109): **113,110,109,107,105 103,103,103,102,99 55**
toteswinger: 1&2 £10.30, 1&3 £11.20, 2&3 £5.40. CSF £109.57 CT £882.74 TOTE £17.10: £4.00, £2.20, £2.00; EX 112.10 TRIFECTA Not won..
Owner Phil Pye **Bred** Millsec, Ltd **Trained** Upper Longdon, Staffs

FOCUS
A cracking good handicap featuring several bang in-form performers, but the pace was blistering as The Game and Tamagin went off far too quick, stretching out the field like washing. The hold-up performers got themselves too far back and couldn't make up the ground, but the winner was positioned perfectly just off the pace.

NOTEBOOK
Doubtful Sound(USA) was settled behind the tearaway leaders, but clear of the main group, and that enabled him to get first run on the rest of the closers. He travelled smoothly and when the front two came under strong driving turning for home, it was obvious he was going to pick them off. Credit must go to Crowley, a jockey riding at the very top of his game, who was alert to the way the race was being run and he executed perfect tactics. He was clearly not right when disappointing at Great Leighs last time, and he had never run here, but he resumed his progressive profile since joining Reg Hollinshead to defy a career-high mark. (op 10-1 tchd 9-1)
Little Edward finished well, but was never going to reel in the winner and in any case he's vulnerable from a handicapping point of view now. (op 14-1 tchd 8-1)
Matsunosuke arguably produced a career-best last time, but he would have needed a pair of wings to land this given how far off the pace he was and, although he finished with his customary charge, he was never going to trouble the judge. Official explanation: jockey said gelding was denied a clear run (tchd 10-1)
The Game went off far too quick so probably did well to hang on for fourth. (op 7-2)
Tamagin(USA), back on sand following a break, has only the one way of running so probably did as well as could be expected as he couldn't dominate thanks to the presence of The Game and the pair rather lit each other up. (tchd 7-2)
Internationaldebut(IRE) didn't look the same horse as he had done in rattling up a hat-trick before the turn of the year. (op 10-3)

205 WILLIAM HILL JANUARY SALE - BONUSES GALORE! H'CAP 1m 2f (P)
3:30 (3:34) (Class 6) (0-65,67) 3-Y-0 £2,047 (£604; £302) **Stalls** Low

Form RPR

05-5 **1** **Innactualfact**[8] 101 3-8-10 **57** JimCrowley 7 66+
(L A Dace) *hld up towards rr: stdy prog over 2f out gng easily: led jst over 1f out: rdn wl clr* **10/1**

222- **2** *5* **Svindal (IRE)**[35] 7659 3-9-4 **65** (b) ChrisCatlin 5 64
(K A Ryan) *sn led: reminders and hanging over 3f out: hdd jst over 1f out: immediately outpcd and btn* **5/1**[1]

550- **3** *hd* **Liberty Beau (IRE)**[27] 7754 3-8-11 **58** HayleyTurner 6 57+
(D R C Elsworth) *stmbld s: settled last: urged along and looked like losing tch 1/2-way: prog 3f out: drvn and styd on to take 3rd fnl f: gaining on runner-up fin* **10/1**

500- **4** *1 1/4* **Good Buy Dubai (USA)**[163] 4776 3-8-9 **56** RobertWinston 10 53+
(J R Best) *s.s: rn in snatches towards rr: lost tch over 2f out and looked like being t.o: r.o fnl f and passed 4 rivals nr fin* **11/2**[2]

435- **5** *1/2* **Captain Walcot**[17] 7832 3-8-12 **59** (b) PatDobbs 11 55
(R Hannon) *hld up in last trio: rdn 3f out: no prog tl kpt on u.p fr over 1f out: no ch* **7/1**

13-1 **6** *1/2* **True Britannia**[3] 164 3-9-3 **64** 6ex (v) AndrewElliott 9 59
(A M Hales) *prom: effrt to dispute 2nd 3f out to over 1f out: wknd* **13/2**[3]

4-41 **7** *nk* **Hawkspring (IRE)**[9] 92 3-9-6 **67** (t) JohnEgan 3 61
(S Parr) *trckd ldrs: rdn wl over 2f out on outer: steadily wknd fr over 1f out* **10/1**

041- **8** *hd* **Dream Huntress**[47] 7514 3-9-1 **62** JamieSpencer 1 56
(B J Meehan) *pressed ldr 3f: restrained: effrt to dispute 2nd again 3f out to over 1f out: wknd* **11/2**[2]

60-4 **9** *8* **In Step**[5] 134 3-8-7 **54** (b[1]) LiamJones 8 32
(W J Haggas) *t.k.h early: trckd ldr after 3f to 3f out: sn btn* **11/2**[2]

004- **10** *23* **Ringo Zaar**[56] 7415 3-8-10 **57** (b) FergusSweeney 4 —
(A B Haynes) *in tch tl wknd 4f out: t.o* **33/1**

2m 7.05s (0.45) **Going Correction** -0.025s/f (Stan) **10** Ran SP% **118.9**
Speed ratings (Par 95): **97,93,92,91,91 91,90,90,84,65**
toteswinger: 1&2 £8.60, 1&3 £7.70, 2&3 £9.20. CSF £60.61 CT £524.03 TOTE £12.50: £3.00, £2.20, £2.70; EX 63.60 TRIFECTA Not won..
Owner Let's Have Fun Syndicate **Bred** Hedsor Stud **Trained** Five Oaks, W Sussex
■ Stewards' Enquiry : Chris Catlin caution: used whip down shoulder in forehand position.

FOCUS
A moderate handicap with a nine-raced maiden and inconsistent performer absolutely sluicing up.

Svindal(IRE) Official explanation: jockey said gelding hung badly right

206 WILLIAM HILL JANUARY SALE - BET NOW! H'CAP 1m (P)
4:00 (4:01) (Class 2) (0-100,108) 4-Y-O+ £11,656 (£3,468; £1,733; £865) Stalls High

Form RPR
21-2 1 **Red Somerset (USA)**14 30 6-8-2 89 MCGeran(5) 5 97
(R J Hodges) *trckd ldr in steadily run r: effrt to ld over 2f out: jnd fnl f: jst hld on* 13/2
111- 2 nse **Titan Triumph**18 7821 5-8-6 88 (t) JimCrowley 2 96
(W J Knight) *hld up in 7th and t.k.h: prog on outer over 2f out: drvn to join wnr ins fnl f: jst pipped* 3/1[2]
163- 3 1 1/4 **Samarinda (USA)**27 7755 6-8-13 95 MickyFenton 4 100
(Mrs P Sly) *t.k.h: hld up in 5th: nt clr run briefly wl over 1f out and hanging: r.o to take 3rd nr fin* 6/1[3]
014- 4 1 1/4 **Atlantic Story (USA)**31 7703 7-9-12 108 (t) JamieSpencer 7 110
(M W Easterby) *trckd ldng trio: effrt over 1f out to chal ent fnl f: nt qckn sn after: wknd nr fin* 11/4[1]
242- 5 hd **Ace Of Hearts**107 6431 10-9-1 97 IanMongan 1 99
(C F Wall) *trckd ldng pair: lost pl on inner whn pce lifted over 2f out: renewed effrt over 1f out: nt pce to threaten* 14/1
00-3 6 shd **Capricorn Run (USA)**14 30 6-8-8 90 ChrisCatlin 3 92
(A J McCabe) *racd wd in 6th: prog to chal over 2f out: nt qckn wl over 1f out: one pce after* 10/1
536- 7 1/2 **Kayak (SAF)**42 7579 7-8-4 86 oh1 (b) HayleyTurner 6 86
(D M Simcock) *led at stdy pce: hdd over 2f out: grad outpcd* 15/2
00/5 8 3/4 **Swiss Act**14 30 5-8-4 86 oh1 GregFairley 8 85+
(M Johnston) *settled in 8th: rdn 3f out: dropped to last and struggling 2f out: kpt on again fnl 150yds* 16/1
000- 9 1 **Fajr (IRE)**56 7418 7-9-7 103 (v1) JimmyQuinn 9 99
(Miss Gay Kelleway) *dropped in fr wd draw and hld up in last: no prog whn shkn up over 1f out* 33/1

1m 38.75s (0.55) **Going Correction** -0.025s/f (Stan) 9 Ran SP% 115.6
Speed ratings (Par 109): **96,95,94,93,93 93,92,91,90**
toteswinger: 1&2 £4.40, 1&3 £4.20, 2&3 £4.40. CSF £26.37 CT £124.15 TOTE £8.70: £2.10, £1.70, £2.30; EX 32.10 Trifecta £176.50 Pool: £329.32 - 1.38 winning units. Place 6: £417.27 Place 5: 235.30.
Owner R J Hodges **Bred** Haras D'Etreham **Trained** Charlton Mackrell, Somerset

FOCUS
A good race on paper, but the early pace was very steady and it turned into a sprint off the home turn. As a result the winning time was very slow.

NOTEBOOK
Red Somerset(USA) took over off the home turn and battled on gamely to hold off the strong finish of Titan Triumph in a desperately tight finish. He had run such a big race on unfavoured terms in a conditions race here last time and has been in peak form this winter. He was given an excellent ride by his young apprentice, who bagged a good position on the heels of the pace before kicking on at just the right time. (tchd 6-1)
Titan Triumph has been a revelation this winter but this was by far his toughest test to date, up in the weights again and up significantly in class. In the circumstances he ran a blinder and the handicapper is having trouble nailing him.
Samarinda(USA), supported in the market, stayed on well up the inside despite not helping his rider late on. (op 8-1 tchd 11-2)
Atlantic Story(USA) looked a big danger early in the straight, but his effort petered out in the final furlong. (op 5-2)
Ace Of Hearts was a bit too keen early, but he finished well enough on his first run on the all-weather in seven years. (op 12-1 tchd 16-1)
Capricorn Run(USA) kept on well having come under pressure before the home turn. (op 8-1)
T/Plt: £305.50 to a £1 stake. Pool: £65,716.21. 157.03 winning tickets. T/Qpdt: £30.70 to a £1 stake. Pool: £4,066.61. 97.90 winning tickets. JN

153 KEMPTON (A.W) (R-H)
Sunday, January 18

OFFICIAL GOING: Standard
Wind: Fresh, across

207 BLUE SQUARE CLAIMING STKS 5f (P)
2:20 (2:20) (Class 6) 3-Y-O £2,047 (£604; £302) Stalls High

Form RPR
130- 1 **Just The Lady**93 6769 3-8-7 73 StephenDonohoe 3 49+
(D Nicholls) *wnt rt s: mde all: clr 1/2-way: unchal* 13/8[2]
60-0 2 1 3/4 **Valdemar**10 91 3-8-9 49 (p) JimmyQuinn 4 45
(A D Brown) *chsd wnr after 1f: one pce and jst hld on for 2nd cl home* 8/1[3]
60- 3 nse **Dancing Welcome**253 2011 3-8-5 0 LukeMorris 5 41
(J M Bradley) *wnt lft s: in rr tl styd on to go 3rd appr fnl f: jst failed to snatch 2nd* 12/1
00-0 4 9 **Yes She Can Can**11 75 3-7-12 36 ow1 (b1) AndrewHeffernan(7) 1 8
(Peter Grayson) *sltly bmpd leaving stalls: racd 3rd tl wknd appr fnl f* 33/1
413- P **The Magic Of Rio**22 7788 3-8-12 87 LPKeniry 2 —
(Peter Grayson) *chsd wnr for 1f: sn eased and p.u over 1f out: lame* 1/1[1]

61.77 secs (1.27) **Going Correction** +0.25s/f (Slow) 5 Ran SP% 109.8
Speed ratings (Par 95): **99,96,96,81,—**
CSF £13.94 TOTE £2.50: £1.50, £3.20; EX 15.90.
Owner Dr Marwan Koukash **Bred** Mrs Monica Teversham **Trained** Sessay, N Yorks

FOCUS
This looked a two-horse race beforehand, but with the favourite failing to finish the winner was left with a simple task. She still performed well below her mark in winning.
The Magic Of Rio Official explanation: jockey said, regarding running and riding, that he felt the filly lose its action and felt it prudent to pull up; vet said, filly was lame on left fore

208 BLUE SQUARE CASINO MAIDEN STKS 5f (P)
2:50 (2:50) (Class 4) 3-Y-O+ £4,727 (£1,406; £702; £351) Stalls High

Form RPR
02-4 1 **Towy Valley**11 69 4-9-7 66 AdamKirby 5 71
(C G Cox) *mde all: rdn over 1f out: kpt on wl* 9/4[2]
03-2 2 1 1/4 **War And Peace (IRE)**11 76 5-9-12 74 PatCosgrave 8 72
(Jane Chapple-Hyam) *trckd ldrs: rdn 2f out: styd on to go 2nd ins fnl f: kpt on but no imp towards fin* 6/5[1]
4-2 3 1 **Circle Dance (IRE)**10 85 4-9-12 70 (v) DarrenWilliams 3 68
(D Shaw) *in tch: styd on to go 3rd ins fnl f* 9/1
02-3 4 nk **Edith's Boy (IRE)**15 34 3-8-11 65 IanMongan 6 61
(S Dow) *sn trckd wnr: lost 2nd and no ex ins fnl f* 7/1[3]
5- 5 3/4 **Captain Flasheart (IRE)**51 7465 3-8-11 0 LukeMorris 2 58
(S C Williams) *hld up in rr: styd on fnl f: nvr nrr* 25/1
0- 6 1 1/4 **Here Comes Danny**79 7104 3-8-11 0 FrancisNorton 7 54
(M Wigham) *slowly away: in rr: mde sme late hdwy* 16/1
225- 7 6 **North South Divide (IRE)**39 7624 5-9-12 55 (b1) DaneO'Neill 4 38
(Peter Grayson) *plld hrd in tch: u.p 2f out: sn wknd* 14/1

61.36 secs (0.86) **Going Correction** +0.25s/f (Slow)
WFA 3 from 4yo+ 15lb 7 Ran SP% 115.1
Speed ratings (Par 105): **103,101,99,98,97 95,86**
toteswinger: 1&2 £1.60, 1&3 £3.40, 2&3 £1.80. CSF £5.39 TOTE £4.20: £2.40, £1.30; EX 6.80.
Owner The Godparents **Bred** G J Hamer **Trained** Lambourn, Berks

FOCUS
A modest sprint maiden run at a steady pace for the trip with the winner rated to his previous best and the third and fourth looking the best guides.

209 BLUE SQUARE MOBILE H'CAP 1m 2f (P)
3:20 (3:22) (Class 4) (0-85,83) 3-Y-O £4,727 (£1,406; £702; £351) Stalls High

Form RPR
3-22 1 **Barwell Bridge**6 138 3-9-3 79 JamesDoyle 3 84
(S Kirk) *led tl hdd 2f out: rallied ins fnl f to ld again cl home* 4/1[3]
041- 2 nk **Bushveld (IRE)**57 7424 3-9-4 80 JoeFanning 4 85
(M Johnston) *trckd ldr: led 2f out: rdn and hdd cl home* 3/1[2]
51-3 3 2 **Doncosaque (IRE)**9 101 3-9-7 83 IanMongan 1 84
(P Howling) *hld up in last pl: rdn and hdwy to go 3rd 1f out* 5/1
41-1 4 2 1/4 **Blaise Tower**11 74 3-9-3 79 FergusSweeney 5 75
(G L Moore) *t.k.h early: racd in 3rd pl: rdn over 2f out: one pce and lost 3rd 1f out* 7/4[1]
12-4 5 3 1/2 **Supernoverre (IRE)**4 164 3-8-10 72 JimCrowley 2 61
(Mrs A J Perrett) *racd in 4th pl: pushed along over 3f out: no hdwy ins fnl 2f* 8/1

2m 8.03s (0.03) **Going Correction** +0.25s/f (Slow) 5 Ran SP% 109.1
Speed ratings (Par 99): **109,108,107,105,102**
CSF £15.78 TOTE £5.00: £2.10, £2.00; EX 15.90.
Owner N Pickett **Bred** Dominic J Burke **Trained** Upper Lambourn, Berks
■ Stewards' Enquiry : James Doyle three-day ban: used whip with excessive frequency without giving colt time to respond (Feb 1-3)

FOCUS
The pace seemed reasonable enough considering the small field, but the first two were in the first two throughout. The winner came back well at the stronger travelling second.
Blaise Tower Official explanation: jockey said colt ran flat

210 BLUE SQUARE SP GUARANTEE H'CAP (DIV I) 1m (P)
3:50 (3:51) (Class 6) (0-50,58) 4-Y-O+ £1,706 (£503; £252) Stalls High

Form RPR
00-1 1 **Highly Regal (IRE)**12 61 4-9-6 58 (b) LPKeniry 3 65
(R A Teal) *trckd ldrs: tk narrow ld 2f out: edgd rt u.p ins fnl f: hld on* 9/4[1]
03-6 2 hd **Dancing Duo**14 39 5-8-10 48 ow1 (v) DarrenWilliams 7 55
(D Shaw) *hld up: hdwy over 2f out: rdn whn carried sltly rt ins fnl f: jst hld* 12/1
300- 3 1 **Ten To The Dozen**54 7441 6-8-10 48 JamesDoyle 5 53
(S T Mason) *mid-div: hdwy over 3f out: ev ch 2f out tl nt qckn towards fin* 5/1[3]
2-53 4 nk **Mocha Java**11 78 6-8-10 48 JimmyQuinn 4 52
(M Salaman) *mid-div: rdn and hdwy to hold ev ch 2f out tl no ex towards fin* 4/1[2]
0-04 5 nk **Inquisitress**9 100 5-8-10 48 NeilChalmers 2 51
(J J Bridger) *in rr: hdwy 2f out: kpt on one pce fnl f* 8/1
12-4 6 1 3/4 **Cavalry Guard (USA)**15 23 5-8-7 50 (b) AmyBaker(5) 8 49
(T D McCarthy) *led tl hdd 2f out: wknd ins fnl f* 15/2
01-0 7 2 1/4 **Hi Spec (IRE)**11 78 6-8-11 49 ow1 (p) AdamKirby 10 43
(Miss M E Rowland) *towards rr tl hdwy over 2f out: wknd ins fnl f* 16/1
00-2 8 8 **Balerno**15 23 10-8-9 47 (b) PaulDoe 9 23
(Mrs L J Mongan) *in tch: rdn and hdwy over 2f out: wknd over 1f out* 20/1
0/0- 9 4 1/2 **Desert Lark**270 1556 4-8-12 50 ChrisCatlin 1 15
(K A Ryan) *t.k.h: trckd ldr: chal over 2f out: rdn and sn wknd* 12/1
04-5 10 19 **Shortwall Lady (IRE)**16 12 4-8-6 47 oh1 ow1 (b) TolleyDean(3) 6 —
(J L Spearing) *stdd s: a last: rdn 1/2-way and lost tch 2f out: t.o* 66/1

1m 42.28s (2.48) **Going Correction** +0.25s/f (Slow) 10 Ran SP% 117.8
Speed ratings (Par 101): **97,96,95,95,95 93,91,83,78,59**
toteswinger: 1&2 £9.00, 1&3 £7.10, 2&3 £16.90. CSF £32.10 CT £126.12 TOTE £2.70: £1.60, £4.40, £2.30; EX 42.60.
Owner J Morton **Bred** Mervyn Stewkesbury **Trained** Ashtead, Surrey
■ Stewards' Enquiry : L P Keniry 14-day ban (takes into account previous offences; two days deferred): careless riding (Jan 30-Feb 10)

FOCUS
A very moderate handicap, run at just an ordinary pace. The winning time was 0.63 seconds slower than the second division and the form looks muddling.

211 BLUE SQUARE SP GUARANTEE H'CAP (DIV II) 1m (P)
4:20 (4:20) (Class 6) (0-50,51) 4-Y-O+ £1,706 (£503; £252) Stalls High

Form RPR
00-2 1 **The Graig**11 78 5-8-13 51 JerryO'Dwyer 9 59
(J R Holt) *trckd ldrs: rdn to ld over 1f out: jst hld on* 7/1[3]
000- 2 hd **Gun For Sale (USA)**41 7605 4-8-9 47 TravisBlock 6 55
(P J Makin) *plld hrd: hld up in rr: hdwy 2f out: swtchd rt and chal ins fnl f: jst failed* 25/1
54-2 3 3/4 **Just Jimmy (IRE)**12 61 4-8-11 49 CatherineGannon 3 55
(P D Evans) *mid-div: rdn 3f out: hdwy over 1f out: styd on wl: nvr nrr* 6/1[2]
3-32 4 1 **Tarkamara (IRE)**7 130 5-8-12 50 JoeFanning 8 54
(P F I Cole) *t.k.h: prom: ev ch appr fnl f: kpt on one pce* 5/4[1]
0-03 5 2 **Very Well Red**7 130 6-8-9 47 (b) ChrisCatlin 5 46
(P W Hiatt) *led tl hdd over 1f out: wknd ins fnl f* 6/1[2]
3-00 6 1/2 **Turkish Sultan (IRE)**9 100 6-8-5 48 (p) MCGeran(5) 4 46
(J M Bradley) *in rr: mde sme late hdwy: n.d* 12/1
005- 7 4 1/2 **Battling Lil (IRE)**51 7469 5-8-11 49 ow1 (b1) AdamKirby 10 37
(J L Spearing) *mid-div: rdn and wknd over 1f out* 10/1
400- 8 12 **Certifiable**27 7764 8-8-10 48 PaulDoe 2 8
(Miss Z C Davison) *trckd ldr tl rdn and wknd over 2f out* 16/1
30-0 9 10 **Moorside Diamond**11 78 5-8-10 48 (p) JimmyQuinn 1 —
(A D Brown) *mid-div tl lost pl over 2f out* 16/1

1m 41.55s (1.75) **Going Correction** +0.25s/f (Slow) 9 Ran SP% 117.9
Speed ratings (Par 101): **101,100,100,99,97 96,92,80,70**
toteswinger: 1&2 £18.50, 1&3 £5.10, 2&3 £14.40. CSF £162.27 CT £1120.86 TOTE £9.30: £2.20, £4.60, £1.40; EX 130.60.
Owner J R Holt **Bred** Hedsor Stud **Trained** Peckleton, Leics

FOCUS
They went steady, but the winning time was 0.63 seconds quicker than the first division, which was also run at a modest pace. the form is rather muddling with the third to his recent best the most reliable guide.

212 BLUE SQUARE POKER H'CAP 6f (P)
4:50 (4:51) (Class 4) (0-85,90) 4-Y-0+ **£4,727** (£1,406; £702; £351) **Stalls** High

Form RPR

43-5 **1** **Mogok Ruby**[7] 128 5-8-9 **75**........ LukeMorris 4 83
(L Montague Hall) *stdd s: t.k.h in mid-div: hdwy over 1f out: hrd rdn to ld ins fnl f: hld on* **16/1**

51-3 **2** *nk* **Musical Script (USA)**[15] 24 6-8-7 **73**........(b) ChrisCatlin 7 80
(Mouse Hamilton-Fairley) *hld up in rr: hdwy 2f out: rdn to go 2nd ins fnl f: kpt on* **9/2**

13-5 **3** *½* **Northern Empire (IRE)**[12] 67 6-8-9 **75**........ FrancisNorton 3 80
(K A Ryan) *mid-div: swtchd lft over 1f out: r.o strly fnl f: nvr nrr* **14/1**

000- **4** *1* **Vhujon (IRE)**[19] 7826 4-9-2 **82**........ TGMcLaughlin 6 84
(P D Evans) *racd in 3rd pl: led wl over 1f out tl hdd and lost 2nd ins fnl f* **7/2**[2]

1-21 **5** *½* **Dvinsky (USA)**[7] 128 8-9-10 **90** 6ex........(b) JimmyQuinn 5 91
(P Howling) *led tl hdd 2f out: kpt on one pce after* **6/1**

-422 **6** *nk* **Count Ceprano (IRE)**[2] 197 5-8-11 **77**........ LiamJones 8 77
(C R Dore) *trckd ldr: led briefly 2f out: one pce fnl f* **4/1**[3]

1-11 **7** *¾* **River Kirov (IRE)**[11] 76 6-9-1 **81**........ SteveDrowne 2 78
(M Wigham) *trckd ldrs: effrt over 2f out: sn u.p and wknd* **5/2**[1]

044- **8** *8* **Brandywell Boy (IRE)**[20] 7811 6-7-13 **72**........ BillyCray(7) 1 44
(D J S Ffrench Davis) *v.s.a: rdn over 3f out: nvr got into r* **33/1**

1m 13.68s (0.58) **Going Correction** +0.25s/f (Slow) 8 Ran SP% **118.8**
Speed ratings (Par 105): **106,105,104,103,102 102,101,90**
toteswinger: 1&2 £12.70, 1&3 £13.90, 2&3 £9.20. CSF £89.48 CT £1062.91 TOTE £27.90: £3.70, £1.60, £2.40; EX 147.10.
Owner The Ruby Partnership **Bred** R Pain **Trained** Epsom, Surrey

FOCUS
A fair sprint handicap rated around the runner-up.
Brandywell Boy(IRE) Official explanation: jockey said gelding missed the break

213 BLUE SQUARE AMATEUR JOCKEYS ASSOCIATION H'CAP (FOR AMATEUR RIDERS) 1m 4f (P)
5:20 (5:20) (Class 6) (0-60,56) 4-Y-0+ **£1,977** (£608; £304) **Stalls** Centre

Form RPR

050- **1** **Corlough Mountain**[21] 7806 5-10-5 **46**........ MissMBryant(7) 6 54
(P Butler) *broke wl: sn mid-div: hdwy over 1f out: rdn to ld nr fin: all out* **16/1**

00/1 **2** *nk* **Safin (GER)**[9] 107 9-11-4 **52**........ MissEJJones 12 60
(R Curtis) *mid-div: hdwy over 1f out: led wl over 1f out: rdn and hdd nr fin* **10/1**

100- **3** *1 ¼* **Ardmaddy (IRE)**[32] 7711 5-11-3 **56**........(b) MissHayleyMoore(5) 2 62
(G L Moore) *a in tch: gd hdwy over 2f out: ev ch ins fnl f: no ex nr fin* **8/1**

06-0 **4** *1* **York Cliff**[16] 8 11-10-13 **50**........ MrBenBrisbourne(3) 7 54
(W M Brisbourne) *in rr: hdwy over 2f out: chsd ldrs fr over 1f out* **12/1**

6/4- **5** *1* **Inn For The Dancer**[32] 330 7-10-10 **49**.... MissSarah-JaneDurman(5) 3 52
(J C Fox) *slowly away: rdn and hdwy on outside over 1f out: nvr nrr* **20/1**

03/- **6** *1 ½* **Sue Princesse (IRE)**[679] 5931 6-10-10 **49**........ MrJohnEnnis(5) 5 49
(Ruaidhri Joseph Tierney, Ire) *led tl hdd 7f out: led again briefly 2f out: wknd 1f out* **14/1**

00-0 **7** *1 ¾* **Landikhaya (IRE)**[8] 114 4-10-5 **50**........ MissECrossman(7) 14 48
(D K Ivory) *nvr bttr than mid-div* **16/1**

224- **8** *nk* **Ba Dreamflight**[26] 7776 4-10-12 **55**........ MissVCartmel(5) 10 52
(H Morrison) *towards rr: rdn and hdwy on outside 2f out: sn one pce* **4/1**[1]

0-23 **9** *1 ½* **Prince Of Medina**[3] 169 6-10-5 **46**........(t) KathrynFerguson(7) 11 41
(J R Best) *s.i.s: a in rr* **4/1**[1]

006- **10** *6* **Schinken Otto (IRE)**[53] 7385 8-11-1 **52**........ MissRJefferson(3) 9 37
(J M Jefferson) *slowly away: sn mid-div: hdwy to ld 7f out: hdd 2f out: sn wknd* **5/1**[2]

000/ **11** *9* **Cartoonist (IRE)**[29] 3017 6-10-8 **47**........(p) MissMMullineaux(5) 4 18
(M Mullineaux) *trckd ldr to 7f out: rdn 3f out: wknd over 2f out* **66/1**

000- **12** *2 ½* **Karky Schultz (GER)**[44] 6004 4-10-9 **54**........ MrDJEustace(7) 1 21
(J M P Eustace) *plld hrd: trckd ldr after 7f: wknd 2f out* **7/1**[3]

2m 40.63s (6.13) **Going Correction** +0.25s/f (Slow)
WFA 4 from 5yo+ 4lb 12 Ran SP% **121.7**
Speed ratings (Par 101): **89,88,87,87,86 85,84,84,83,79 73,71**
toteswinger: 1&2 £17.40, 1&3 £31.90, 2&3 £13.30. CSF £171.59 CT £1395.32 TOTE £19.70: £4.80, £4.30, £2.70; EX 146.70 Place 6: £206.75, Place 5: £93.41.
Owner Miss M Bryant **Bred** Bottisham Heath Stud **Trained** East Chiltington, E Sussex

FOCUS
A really messy amateur riders' handicap and not a race to dwell on. It was quite steadily run and the form looks moderate.
T/Plt: £294.60 to a £1 stake. Pool: £76,581.57. 189.74 winning tickets. T/Qpdt: £96.00 to a £1 stake. Pool: £5,450.25. 42.00 winning tickets. JS

194 WOLVERHAMPTON (A.W) (L-H)
Monday, January 19

OFFICIAL GOING: Standard
Wind: Cloudy with sunny spells Weather: Fresh behind

214 WOLVERHAMPTON-RACECOURSE.CO.UK H'CAP 7f 32y(P)
2:00 (2:05) (Class 6) (0-60,60) 3-Y-0 **£2,047** (£604; £302) **Stalls** High

Form RPR

1 **Alexander Family (IRE)**[92] 6844 3-9-4 **60**........ JamieSpencer 10 66
(E F Vaughan) *s.i.s: hld up: swtchd wd 5f out: hdwy to chse ldr over 3f out: hrd rdn fnl 2f: hung lft over 1f out: r.o to ld post* **10/1**

060- **2** *shd* **Miss Mojito (IRE)**[114] 6273 3-9-0 **56**........ ChrisCatlin 8 61
(J W Hills) *hld up in tch: rdn over 2f out: hung lft over 1f out: led wl ins fnl f: hdd post* **22/1**

462- **3** *½* **Imperial Skylight**[19] 7832 3-9-3 **59**........ TonyCulhane 4 63
(M R Channon) *led 6f out: rdn over 1f out: hdd wl ins fnl f* **7/2**[1]

016- **4** *¾* **Tillers Satisfied (IRE)**[23] 7794 3-9-4 **60**........ GrahamGibbons 5 62
(R Hollinshead) *hld up: hdwy over 1f out: sn rdn: r.o: nt rch ldrs* **7/1**[3]

64-2 **5** *½* **Flawless Diamond (IRE)**[5] 159 3-8-10 **52**........(p) LukeMorris 2 53+
(J S Moore) *prom: racd keenly: rdn 1/2-way: nt clr run and lost pl over 2f out: rallied over 1f out: r.o* **4/1**[2]

056- **6** *¾* **Tricky Trev (USA)**[19] 7832 3-9-1 **57**........ PaulDoe 9 56
(S Curran) *s.i.s: hld up: hdwy over 1f out: nt trble ldrs* **8/1**

33-4 **7** *2 ½* **Lois Darlin (IRE)**[15] 41 3-8-11 **56**........(p) KevinGhunowa(3) 3 48
(R A Harris) *led 1f: chsd ldr to over 3f out: sn rdn: wknd fnl f* **12/1**

8 *2* **Northern Champ (IRE)**[93] 6834 3-8-5 **47**........ RPCleary 1 33
(Patrick G Kelly, Ire) *prom: lost pl 4f out: n.d after* **7/1**[3]

064- **9** *2 ¼* **Nun Today (USA)**[19] 7833 3-8-8 **50** ow1........(p) LPKeniry 12 30
(J S Moore) *prom: rdn 1/2-way: wknd over 1f out* **11/1**

250- **10** *7* **Kitty Allen**[54] 7451 3-9-0 **56**........ JimmyQuinn 6 18
(C N Kellett) *s.i.s: hld up: rdn over 2f out: a in rr* **33/1**

000- **11** *3 ½* **Calypso Prince**[19] 7833 3-8-4 **46** oh1........ HayleyTurner 7 —
(M D I Usher) *chsd ldrs: rdn 1/2-way: wknd over 2f out* **40/1**

1m 31.0s (1.40) **Going Correction** 0.0s/f (Stan) 11 Ran SP% **113.2**
Speed ratings (Par 95): **92,91,91,90,89 89,86,83,81,73 69**
toteswinger: 1&2 £15.00, 1&3 £5.40, 2&3 £12.30. CSF £204.23 CT £933.23 TOTE £11.40: £3.20, £7.10, £1.40; EX 153.50 TRIFECTA Not won..
Owner Noel O'Callaghan **Bred** Tally-Ho Stud **Trained** Newmarket, Suffolk

FOCUS
A moderate three-year-old handicap run at an ordinary pace. The form looks sound enough with the front pair unexposed and the next two pretty solid on recent form.
Alexander Family(IRE) Official explanation: trainer's rep said, regarding apparent improvement in form, he had no explanation but added that he did note that the filly had been running on soft ground in Ireland.

215 WOLVERHAMPTON RACECOURSE - ALL CONFERENCING NEEDS MET (S) STKS 1m 141y(P)
2:30 (2:35) (Class 6) 4-Y-0+ **£2,047** (£604; £302) **Stalls** Low

Form RPR

13-1 **1** **Singleb (IRE)**[8] 129 5-9-5 65........(p) JamieSpencer 4 71
(Miss Gay Kelleway) *hld up in tch: swtchd rt over 2f out: rdn and hung lft over 1f out: styd on to ld nr fin* **5/2**[1]

000- **2** *nk* **Garden Party**[112] 6336 5-9-0 66........ FrankieMcDonald 6 65
(R A Harris) *hld up in tch: rdn over 1f out: led wl ins fnl f: hdd nr fin* **7/1**[3]

/23- **3** *shd* **Forbidden (IRE)**[59] 7412 6-9-0 58........(t) RPCleary 12 65
(Daniel Mark Loughnane, Ire) *hld up: hdwy over 3f out: rdn to ld over 1f out: hdd wl ins fnl f* **16/1**

05-0 **4** *1 ¾* **Prince Noel**[11] 94 5-9-0 72........ LeeEnstone 2 61
(N Wilson) *chsd ldrs: led over 2f out: hdd over 1f out: no ex wl ins fnl f* **5/2**[1]

300- **5** *2* **Bold Indian (IRE)**[93] 6827 5-9-0 55........ TomEaves 10 56+
(I Semple) *hld up: nt clr run over 2f out: hdwy over 1f out: nt rch ldrs* **10/1**

063- **6** *1 ¾* **Redarsene**[77] 7166 4-8-13 67........ GrahamGibbons 5 52
(S Wynne) *prom: nt clr run and swtchd lft over 2f out: sn rdn: styd on same pce appr fnl f* **7/2**[2]

00-0 **7** *4* **The London Gang**[3] 195 6-8-9 41........(b) DeanHeslop(5) 11 43
(S Wynne) *dwlt: hld up: bmpd 2f out: nvr nrr* **66/1**

00-0 **8** *3 ¼* **Shadow Jumper (IRE)**[17] 12 8-8-11 38.....(p) RussellKennemore(3) 7 36
(J T Stimpson) *chsd ldrs: rdn over 2f out: sn wknd* **100/1**

/20- **9** *2 ¼* **Viscaya (IRE)**[146] 5380 4-8-8 51........(p) RichardKingscote 9 26
(N J Vaughan) *s.s: hld up: a in rr* **20/1**

64-0 **10** *½* **Countrywide Comet (IRE)**[10] 97 4-8-13 50........ IanMongan 13 29
(P Howling) *hld up: rdn and wknd over 2f out: bmpd sn after* **66/1**

/00- **11** *6* **Grand Court (IRE)**[28] 7766 6-8-9 41........(p) ChrisCatlin 8 11
(George Baker) *sn pushed along in rr: wknd 3f out* **40/1**

00- **12** *4 ½* **Mickys Mate**[48] 7527 4-8-13 0........ PaulMulrennan 1 5
(A Crook) *plld hrd: disp ld tl rdn and hdd over 2f out: sn wknd* **100/1**

000- **13** *1 ¾* **Herrbee (IRE)**[42] 7605 4-8-13 35........ AdamKirby 3 1
(J L Spearing) *disp ld tl rdn over 2f out: sn wknd* **80/1**

1m 50.84s (0.34) **Going Correction** 0.0s/f (Stan)
WFA 4 from 5yo+ 1lb 13 Ran SP% **120.2**
Speed ratings (Par 101): **98,97,97,96,94 92,89,86,84,83 78,74,72**
toteswinger: 1&2 £6.60, 1&3 £10.10, 2&3 £18.50. CSF £20.74 TOTE £4.40: £1.60, £2.30, £3.70; EX 30.70 Trifecta £313.70 Part won. Pool: £423.92 - 0.45 winning units..The winner was bought in for 6,500 guineas.
Owner Mrs Donna Joslyn **Bred** Spratstown Stud Gm **Trained** Exning, Suffolk
■ Stewards' Enquiry : Graham Gibbons one-day ban: careless riding (Feb 2)

FOCUS
A good, competitive seller, and sound form. The winner has a good record in this grade and is rated to form.
Viscaya(IRE) Official explanation: jockey said filly was slowly away

216 PLAY BINGO @ WILLIAMHILL.COM H'CAP (DIV I) 1m 141y(P)
3:00 (3:06) (Class 6) (0-55,55) 4-Y-0+ **£1,577** (£354; £354; £118; £58) **Stalls** Low

Form RPR

005- **1** **King Of Legend (IRE)**[160] 4949 5-9-0 **55**........ GregFairley 4 62
(A G Foster) *chsd ldr: rdn to ld over 1f out: edgd lft: r.o* **4/1**[1]

03-6 **2** *nk* **Sion Hill (IRE)**[15] 37 8-8-13 **54**........(p) ChrisCatlin 1 60
(John A Harris) *led: racd keenly: rdn and hdd over 1f out: r.o gamely* **8/1**

60-4 **2** *dht* **Moyoko (IRE)**[12] 81 6-8-11 **52**........(b[1]) JimmyQuinn 5 58+
(M Salaman) *s.i.s: hld up: hdwy over 1f out: r.o* **5/1**[2]

05-0 **4** *½* **Mountain Pass (USA)**[10] 97 7-9-0 **55**........(p) LPKeniry 10 60
(B J Llewellyn) *hld up in tch: rdn over 1f out: r.o* **10/1**

00-4 **5** *1* **Ridgeway Jazz**[12] 78 4-8-7 **49**........ HayleyTurner 8 52+
(M D I Usher) *hld up: hdwy over 1f out: r.o: nt rch ldrs* **10/1**

40-3 **6** *½* **Putra Laju (IRE)**[14] 42 5-9-0 **55**........ MartinDwyer 2 57
(J W Hills) *a.p: rdn over 1f out: styd on same pce fnl f* **9/1**

0- **7** *¾* **Dobravany (IRE)**[45] 7569 5-8-5 **46** oh1........ RPCleary 12 46+
(Adrian McGuinness, Ire) *hld up: rdn over 2f out: r.o ins fnl f: nt rch ldrs* **15/2**

006- **8** *½* **Bidable**[35] 7692 5-8-9 **50**........ CatherineGannon 11 49
(B Palling) *mid-div: hdwy 1/2-way: rdn over 2f out: styd on same pce appr fnl f* **12/1**

303- **9** *nk* **Sarraaf (IRE)**[68] 7287 13-8-12 **53**........ TomEaves 7 51
(I Semple) *hld up: rdn over 2f out: n.d* **16/1**

06-0 **10** *1* **Redeemed**[17] 12 4-8-6 **48**........ FrancisNorton 3 44
(M Brittain) *trckd ldrs: racd freely: rdn over 1f out: wknd fnl f* **33/1**

11 *1 ¼* **Theteasthaticy (IRE)**[85] 4262 5-8-0 **46** oh1........ AmyBaker(5) 9 39
(A E Jones) *s.i.s: hld up: rdn over 2f out: bhd whn hung lft over 1f out* **33/1**

-331 **12** *3* **Hurricane Coast**[4] 174 10-9-0 **55**........ TonyCulhane 13 41
(D Flood) *hld up: hdwy 5f out: rdn over 3f out: wknd over 2f out* **7/1**[3]

1m 51.3s (0.80) **Going Correction** 0.0s/f (Stan)
WFA 4 from 5yo+ 1lb 12 Ran SP% **119.7**
Speed ratings (Par 101): **96,95,95,95,94 93,93,92,92,91 90,87**Place 2: SH: £2.10, M: £2.40; Exacta: KL & SH: £23.80, KL & M: £13.20; CSF: KL & SH: £18.14, KL & M: £11.72; Tricast: KL, SH, M: £82.01, KL, M, KL: £76.69; toteswinger: 1&SH £8.50, 1&M £5.90, SH&M £10.40. TOTE £4.60: £2.20 TRI27 Owner.

FOCUS
A weak handicap and the slowest of the three course-and-distance races. It paid to race handy with the first two nearly always 1-2, and the form is a bit muddling.

217 NAME A RACE TO ENHANCE YOUR BRAND MAIDEN STKS 1m 1f 103y(P)
3:30 (3:37) (Class 5) 4-Y-0+ £2,729 (£806; £403) Stalls Low

Form RPR
240- 1 **Brouhaha**[157] 5069 5-9-4 56 RichardKingscote 4 68
(Tom Dascombe) *led 1f: chsd ldrs: rdn to ld ins fnl f: r.o* 11/4[2]
2- 2 ¾ **Lady Longcroft**[281] 1344 4-8-12 0 JimmyQuinn 6 61
(J Pearce) *trckd ldr: plld hrd: wnt 2nd 3f out: led 2f out: rdn: edgd lft and hdd ins fnl f: styd on* 7/2[3]
522- 3 1 ¾ **Royal Encore**[49] 7516 5-8-13 56 RobertWinston 11 58
(J R Fanshawe) *a.p: rdn over 2f out: edgd lft over 1f out: styd on same pce fnl f* 5/2[1]
6/ 4 shd **Emerald Rock (CAN)**[439] 6723 4-9-3 0 LukeMorris 10 63
(N J Vaughan) *mid-div: rdn over 3f out: hdwy u.p over 1f out: nt rch ldrs* 4/1
00- 5 3 **Japura (USA)**[59] 7403 5-9-4 62 GregFairley 5 56
(T J Pitt) *chsd ldr tl led over 8f out: rdn and hdd 2f out: wknd ins fnl f* 33/1
/30- 6 7 **Spares And Repairs**[361] 283 6-9-4 57 MickyFenton 9 42
(Mrs S Lamyman) *hld up: pushed along over 3f out: wknd over 2f out* 33/1
7 3 ½ **Kenai**[106] 6513 4-9-3 57 (p) ChrisCatlin 7 34
(W K Goldsworthy) *chsd ldr over 6f out: rdn 3f out: sn wknd* 14/1
8 8 **Sugar State** 4-9-3 0 AdamKirby 1 17
(J L Spearing) *hld up: hdwy over 5f out: rdn and wknd over 2f out* 66/1
9 22 **Fine The World** 5-8-13 0 FrankieMcDonald 3 —
(G A Ham) *s.s: a in rr: wknd 3f out* 66/1

2m 1.93s (0.23) **Going Correction** 0.0s/f (Stan)
WFA 4 from 5yo+ 1lb 9 Ran SP% **113.0**
Speed ratings (Par 103): **98,97,95,95,93 86,83,76,57**
toteswinger: 1&2 £2.60, 1&3 £1.60, 2&3 £3.00. CSF £12.24 TOTE £2.80: £1.10, £2.70, £1.10; EX 12.50 Trifecta £22.20 Pool: £463.50 - 14.09 winning units..
Owner G D Newton **Bred** Mrs Rosamund Furlong **Trained** Lambourn, Berks

FOCUS
A very modest older-horse maiden. The winner ran a slight personal best at face value. Once again it proved difficult to make up significant amounts of ground.

218 WILLIAM HILL TELEBETTING ON 0800 44 40 40 H'CAP 7f 32y(P)
4:00 (4:05) (Class 4) (0-80,78) 4-Y-0+ £4,857 (£1,445; £722; £360) Stalls High

Form RPR
03-3 1 **Strabinios King**[3] 191 5-8-10 70 FrancisNorton 1 84
(M Wigham) *trckd ldr: led ins fnl f: rdn clr* 13/8[1]
45-4 2 2 ¾ **Red Cape (FR)**[13] 68 6-8-7 67 (b) AndrewElliott 6 74
(Mrs R A Carr) *sn led: rdn and hdd ins fnl f: styd on same pce* 12/1
02-5 3 1 ¼ **Kensington (IRE)**[6] 143 8-8-9 74 (b) PatrickDonaghy[(5)] 9 78
(P D Evans) *s.i.s: hld up: styd on fr over 1f out: nvr nr to chal* 12/1
60-6 4 4 ½ **Dudley Docker (IRE)**[9] 113 7-9-4 78 (b) LiamJones 3 69
(C R Dore) *s.i.s: hld up: plld hrd: styd on appr fnl f: nvr nr ldrs* 14/1
16-0 5 1 ¾ **Direct Debit (IRE)**[17] 17 6-9-2 76 AdamKirby 5 63
(M Wellings) *hld up in tch: rdn over 2f out: wknd fnl f* 6/1[3]
55- 6 ¾ **Secret Dubai (IRE)**[21] 7811 4-9-0 74 JohnEgan 4 59
(M Botti) *chsd ldrs: rdn over 1f out: sn wknd* 7/2[2]
110- 7 1 ¾ **Willie Ever**[154] 5156 5-8-11 71 RoystonFfrench 2 51
(I W McInnes) *hld up: hdwy 3f out: sn rdn: wknd 2f out* 12/1
601- 8 6 **Carnivore**[37] 7668 7-9-4 78 TomEaves 7 42
(T D Barron) *prom: shkn up 3f out: wkng whn n.m.r 2f out* 8/1
00-0 9 5 **Only A Game (IRE)**[10] 106 4-9-0 74 (p) ChrisCatlin 8 24
(Miss M E Rowland) *hld up: rdn over 2f out: sn wknd* 50/1

1m 28.17s (-1.43) **Going Correction** 0.0s/f (Stan) 9 Ran SP% **117.4**
Speed ratings (Par 105): **108,104,103,98,96 95,93,86,80**
toteswinger: 1&2 £6.60, 1&3 £4.90, 2&3 £12.90. CSF £23.99 CT £183.88 TOTE £2.90: £1.40, £3.40, £2.20; EX 30.60 Trifecta £236.50 Pool: £463.50 - 1.45 winning units..
Owner Val Kelly **Bred** Newsells Park Stud Limited **Trained** Newmarket, Suffolk

FOCUS
An ordinary handicap for the grade. Overall this looks a race to be fairly positively about, with the winner rated up 10lb.

219 DINE IN THE HORIZONS RESTAURANT H'CAP 1m 5f 194y(P)
4:30 (4:35) (Class 5) (0-70,71) 4-Y-0+ £2,729 (£806; £403) Stalls Low

Form RPR
000- 1 **Riguez Dancer**[30] 6054 5-9-0 67 (t) PatrickDonaghy[(5)] 13 76+
(P C Haslam) *a.p: led 5f out: rdn 2f out: styd on wl: eased nr fin* 10/1
00-0 2 1 ¾ **They All Laughed**[18] 3 6-9-5 67 ChrisCatlin 6 73
(P W Hiatt) *hld up: hdwy over 3f out: sn rdn: styd on: no ch w wnr* 33/1
21-2 3 hd **Bridgewater Boys**[11] 84 8-9-8 70 (b) JohnEgan 2 76+
(P D Evans) *dwlt: hld up: nt clr run over 2f out: hdwy u.p over 1f out: styd on* 16/1
36-2 4 ½ **Chookie Hamilton**[13] 65 5-9-8 70 PaulMulrennan 3 75
(I Semple) *hld up: hdwy over 3f out: rdn to chse wnr over 2f out: hung lft over 1f out: styd on same pce* 20/1
30-4 5 2 **Sheer Fantastic**[4] 171 4-9-0 68 (v) LeeEnstone 4 71
(P C Haslam) *broke wl: sn lost pl: hdwy 6f out: rdn over 2f out: no ex fnl f* 28/1
55-1 6 19 **Dramatic Solo**[3] 190 4-9-3 71 6ex (b) AndrewElliott 8 47
(K R Burke) *hld up: hdwy over 5f out: chsd wnr over 3f out: sn rdn: wknd 2f out* 4/1[2]
204- 7 2 ¼ **Nero West (FR)**[79] 7128 8-9-6 68 (b) TomEaves 1 41
(I Semple) *prom: chsd ldr 7f out to 5f out: sn rdn: wknd over 2f out* 12/1
04- 8 9 **Captain Hook**[82] 7036 5-9-4 66 (p) RPCleary 9 26
(Daniel Mark Loughnane, Ire) *chsd ldrs: rdn 5f out: wknd over 3f out* 6/1[3]
24-4 9 2 **Swords**[18] 3 7-8-7 62 BMcHugh[(7)] 7 19
(R E Peacock) *hld up: hdwy 6f out: rdn and wknd over 3f out* 14/1
54-3 10 5 **Euroceleb (IRE)**[17] 11 4-8-12 66 (p) SteveDrowne 5 16
(H Morrison) *sn led: rdn and hdd 5f out: wknd over 3f out* 14/1
541- 11 109 **Antillia**[42] 7604 4-8-13 67 IanMongan 12 —
(C F Wall) *racd keenly: w ldr to over 7f out: sn lost pl: bhd fnl 5f: eased: t.o* 5/4[1]

3m 2.07s (-3.93) **Going Correction** 0.0s/f (Stan)
WFA 4 from 5yo+ 6lb 11 Ran SP% **125.9**
Speed ratings (Par 103): **111,110,109,109,108 97,96,91,90,87 —**
toteswinger: 1&2 £36.60, 1&3 £21.20, 2&3 £22.70. CSF £316.66 CT £5185.66 TOTE £10.30: £4.10, £6.50, £3.20; EX 185.00 TRIFECTA Not won..
Owner Middleham Park Racing Xii **Bred** Plantation Stud **Trained** Middleham Moor, N Yorks

FOCUS
A modest staying handicap. The favourite flopped but this is still sound form with the winner only having to match his old Flat form here.
Antillia Official explanation: jockey said filly ran too freely early; vet said filly trotted up lame near-fore

220 PLAY POKER @ WILLIAMHILL.COM H'CAP 1m 1f 103y(P)
5:00 (5:05) (Class 5) (0-75,75) 4-Y-0+ £2,590 (£770; £385; £192) Stalls Low

Form RPR
23-1 1 **Ahlawy (IRE)**[10] 105 6-8-12 68 (bt) FBranca 6 84
(F Sheridan) *hld up in tch: led over 1f out: edgd lft and rdn clr ins fnl f* 11/4[1]
62-2 2 4 ½ **Will He Wish**[16] 21 13-9-5 75 (b) PatCosgrave 10 81
(S Gollings) *chsd ldrs: rdn over 2f out: wnt 2nd ins fnl f: styd on same pce* 16/1
136- 3 ¾ **Ours (IRE)**[23] 7796 6-9-0 70 (p) ChrisCatlin 4 75
(John A Harris) *hld up: hdwy u.p over 1f out: edgd lft ins fnl f: nt rch ldrs* 16/1
405- 4 ½ **New Star (UAE)**[42] 7606 5-9-3 73 GrahamGibbons 5 77
(W M Brisbourne) *chsd ldr tl led over 2f out: rdn and hdd over 1f out: no ex ins fnl f* 13/2[3]
5-05 5 nk **New Beginning (IRE)**[15] 39 5-8-9 65 RobertWinston 7 68+
(Mrs S Lamyman) *hld up: hdwy over 1f out: r.o: nrst fin* 14/1
120- 6 ¾ **Top Seed (IRE)**[24] 7786 8-8-10 66 StephenDonohoe 1 67+
(Ian Williams) *sn bhd: styd on ins fnl f: nvr nrr* 33/1
461- 7 shd **Bourse (IRE)**[21] 7224 4-8-10 67 GregFairley 9 68
(A G Foster) *hld up: rdn over 3f out: n.d* 7/1
033- 8 ¾ **Morbick**[38] 7657 5-9-2 72 TGMcLaughlin 2 72
(W M Brisbourne) *prom: rdn over 2f out: wknd ins fnl f* 6/1[2]
32-3 9 hd **Davenport (IRE)**[15] 39 7-9-0 70 (p) DaneO'Neill 11 69
(B R Millman) *hld up: hdwy u.p over 2f out: wknd over 1f out* 11/1
13-5 10 1 **Prince Golan (IRE)**[13] 65 5-8-10 66 (p) HayleyTurner 3 63
(J W Unett) *chsd ldrs: rdn over 3f out: wknd over 1f out: n.m.r ins fnl f* 10/1
613- 11 ½ **Supercast (IRE)**[28] 7758 6-9-5 75 LukeMorris 8 71
(N J Vaughan) *led: rdn and hdd over 2f out: edgd rt over 1f out: wkng whn nt clr run ins fnl f* 13/2[3]

1m 59.35s (-2.35) **Going Correction** 0.0s/f (Stan)
WFA 4 from 5yo+ 1lb 11 Ran SP% **118.9**
Speed ratings (Par 103): **110,106,105,104,104 103,103,103,103,102 101**
toteswinger: 1&2 £8.70, 1&3 £10.90, 2&3 £16.80. CSF £52.59 CT £609.11 TOTE £3.80: £1.30, £3.90, £5.30; EX 55.40 Trifecta £347.70 Part won. Pool: £469.91 - 0.55 winning units..
Owner A Zanoboni **Bred** Castlemartin Stud And Skymarc Farm **Trained** Stoke Heath, Shropshire
■ Stewards' Enquiry : Luke Morris one-day ban: failed to keep straight from stalls (Feb 2)

FOCUS
A modest handicap, but an open race and sound form. The winner looks back to his best for his new yard.
New Star(UAE) Official explanation: jockey said gelding was struck into

221 PLAY BINGO @ WILLIAMHILL.COM H'CAP (DIV II) 1m 141y(P)
5:30 (5:36) (Class 6) (0-55,55) 4-Y-0+ £1,577 (£472; £236; £118; £58) Stalls Low

Form RPR
50-0 1 **Ardent Prince**[10] 105 6-8-9 50 RobertWinston 1 59
(A J McCabe) *hld up: hdwy over 2f out: rdn to ld ins fnl f: r.o* 17/2
13-5 2 hd **Baileborough (IRE)**[16] 25 10-9-0 55 JimmyQuinn 13 64
(B Ellison) *mid-div: hdwy over 2f out: rdn: edgd lft and ev ch ins fnl f: r.o* 7/2[1]
0-24 3 2 ¾ **Red Current**[3] 192 5-8-9 53 KevinGhunowa[(3)] 4 56
(R A Harris) *chsd ldrs: led 2f out: sn rdn: hdd and unable qck ins fnl f* 10/1
340- 4 1 ¼ **Winged Farasi**[55] 7442 5-8-6 47 (p) ChrisCatlin 9 47
(Miss J E Foster) *s.i.s: hld up: hdwy over 1f out: nt rch ldrs* 11/1
054- 5 nk **Machinate (USA)**[35] 7692 7-9-0 55 LiamJones 2 54
(W M Brisbourne) *hld up: hdwy over 1f out: sn rdn: styd on same pce ins fnl f* 9/2[2]
00-6 6 1 **Top Jaro (FR)**[4] 174 6-9-0 55 (b) PaulMulrennan 10 52
(Mrs R A Carr) *sn led: rdn and hdd over 2f out: hung lft over 1f out: no ex fnl f* 33/1
25-0 7 ½ **Desert Lover (IRE)**[10] 104 7-8-5 46 oh1 HayleyTurner 11 42
(R J Price) *chsd ldrs: led over 2f out: sn rdn and hdd: wknd ins fnl f* 25/1
00-4 8 nk **Doctor Delta**[4] 174 4-8-6 48 (v[1]) FrancisNorton 5 43+
(M Brittain) *hld up: rdn over 1f out: n.d* 14/1
123/ 9 ¾ **Almahaza (IRE)**[413] 7009 5-8-11 52 (b) NeilChalmers 3 45
(A J Chamberlain) *hld up: sme hdwy over 1f out: wknd ins fnl f* 12/1
0-05 10 1 **Anduril**[3] 78 8-8-7 48 (b) RoystonFfrench 8 39
(I W McInnes) *mid-div: n.m.r over 5f out: sn rdn: wknd over 2f out* 14/1
24-0 11 ½ **Victory Spirit**[12] 81 5-8-11 52 (p) TomEaves 7 42
(I Semple) *led early: chsd ldrs: rdn whn nt clr run 2f out: sn wknd* 10/1
32-3 12 5 **Thornaby Green**[18] 7 8-8-9 55 DeanHeslop[(5)] 12 33
(T D Barron) *prom: rdn over 3f out: wknd over 2f out* 7/1[3]
650- 13 28 **Crosby Jemma**[38] 3360 5-8-2 48 oh1 ow2 PatrickDonaghy[(5)] 6 —
(M E Sowersby) *s.s: a bhd* 16/1

1m 50.11s (-0.39) **Going Correction** 0.0s/f (Stan)
WFA 4 from 5yo+ 1lb 13 Ran SP% **123.6**
Speed ratings (Par 101): **101,100,98,97,97 96,95,95,94,93 93,88,64**
toteswinger: 1&2 £9.80, 1&3 £22.40, 2&3 £8.00. CSF £39.59 CT £324.95 TOTE £10.70: £3.40, £1.70, £4.20; EX 52.50 Trifecta £208.60 Pool: £408.84 - 1.45 winning units. Place 6: £210.70, Place 5: £74.76.
Owner Barry M Fletcher **Bred** Anthem Flight Partnership **Trained** Averham Park, Notts

FOCUS
A moderate handicap, but the winning time was 1.19 seconds quicker than the first division, and also faster than the earlier seller. Sound form, with the winner rated to his best.
Ardent Prince Official explanation: trainer's rep said, regarding apparent improvement in form, that the gelding settled better with a stronger pace.

T/Jkpt: Not won. T/Plt: £103.10 to a £1 stake. Pool: £92,801.47. 656.92 winning tickets. T/Qpdt: £25.70 to a £1 stake. Pool: £6,729.20. 193.30 winning tickets. CR

[173]SOUTHWELL (L-H)

Tuesday, January 20

OFFICIAL GOING: Standard
Wind: Fresh behind Weather: Bright and dry

222 PLAY BINGO @ WILLIAMHILL.COM H'CAP 6f (F)
1:00 (1:06) (Class 6) (0-55,55) 4-Y-O+ **£2,047** (£604; £302) **Stalls Low**

Form RPR

40-3 **1** **Head To Head (IRE)**[14] 62 5-8-8 **49**....................(p) GrahamGibbons 3 56
(A D Brown) *dwlt and towards rr: stdy hdwy 1/2-way: cl up 2f out: sn led and rdn over 1f out: drvn ins fnl f and kpt on wl* **8/1**

-312 **2** *nk* **Jordi Roper (IRE)**[5] 174 4-9-0 **55**.......................... AdamKirby 6 61
(S Parr) *towards rr: pushed along and hdwy over 2f out: rdn to chse ldrs over 1f out: drvn ins fnl f: styd on wl towards fin* **5/2**[1]

0-43 **3** *nk* **Nabeeda**[12] 95 4-8-7 **55**.......................... JohnCavanagh(7) 11 60
(M Brittain) *cl up: effrt 2f out: sn rdn and ev ch tl drvn and kpt on same pce wl ins fnl f* **4/1**[2]

0-64 **4** *3/4* **Cape Of Storms**[12] 95 6-8-10 **54**.......................... AndrewMullen(3) 12 57
(R Brotherton) *prom: hdwy on outer to chal 2f out: sn rdn and ev ch tl drvn and one pce ins fnl f* **17/2**

00-0 **5** *nk* **Straight Face (IRE)**[10] 114 5-8-9 **50**..........................(e[1]) HayleyTurner 7 52
(Miss Gay Kelleway) *in rr: pushed along 1/2-way: hdwy on inner 2f out: sn rdn and kpt on wl fnl f: nrst fin* **20/1**

50-5 **6** *1/2* **Afton View (IRE)**[5] 174 4-8-11 **52**.......................... LiamJones 2 52
(S Parr) *led: hdd 1/2-way and cl up: rdn along and ev ch 2f out: drvn and wknd appr fnl f* **9/1**

65-0 **7** *2 1/4* **Berrymead**[14] 62 4-8-8 **54** oh1 ow8.......................... AnnStokell(5) 8 47
(Miss A Stokell) *midfield: rdn along over 2f out and sn no imp* **40/1**

3-40 **8** *3/4* **Mind Alert**[13] 71 8-8-13 **54**..........................(v) DarrenWilliams 5 44
(D Shaw) *hld up in rr: stdy hdwy on inner 1/2-way: rdn to chal and ev ch wl over 1f out: drvn and wknd appr fnl f* **12/1**

043- **9** *2 3/4* **Cabopino (IRE)**[48] 7536 4-8-12 **53**.......................... JamieSpencer 13 35
(K R Burke) *in tch on outer: rdn along over 2f out and sn wknd* **5/1**[3]

00-6 **10** *1/2* **Soba Jones**[16] 35 12-8-10 **54**.......................... TolleyDean(3) 1 34
(J Balding) *cl up: led 1/2-way: rdn 2f out and sn hdd: grad wknd* **33/1**

-050 **11** *4* **Government (IRE)**[14] 63 8-8-0 **46** oh1.......................... AmyBaker(5) 14 13
(M C Chapman) *a towards rr* **80/1**

000- **12** *11* **George The Best (IRE)**[332] 684 8-8-5 **46** oh1............. PaulHanagan 4 —
(Micky Hammond) *a in rr* **100/1**

1m 16.22s (-0.28) **Going Correction** -0.175s/f (Stan) **12** Ran SP% **116.9**
Speed ratings (Par 101): **94,93,93,92,91 91,88,87,83,82 77,62**
toteswinger: 1&2 £6.60, 1&3 £8.00, 2&3 £2.90. CSF £26.96 CT £95.51 TOTE £10.50: £2.80, £1.40, £1.70; EX 43.00 Trifecta £106.70 Pool: £302.90 - 2.10 winning units..
Owner A D Brown **Bred** Sean Connolly **Trained** Yedingham, N Yorks
■ Stewards' Enquiry : John Cavanagh two-day ban: carless riding; two-day ban: excessive use of the whip (Feb 3-6.)

FOCUS
A moderate but competitive sprint handicap. The second, third and fourth were close to their running here earlier in the month, but the time was modest and this form does not look to solid.
Cabopino(IRE) Official explanation: jockey said filly moved poorly throughout
George The Best(IRE) Official explanation: jockey said gelding hung left-handed throughout

223 WILLIAM HILL TELEBETTING ON 0800 44 40 40 (S) STKS 7f (F)
1:30 (1:35) (Class 6) 4-Y-O+ **£2,047** (£604; £302) **Stalls Low**

Form RPR

46-3 **1** **Lethal**[14] 68 6-9-0 68.......................... PaulHanagan 4 64
(R A Fahey) *mde all: rdn 2f out: drvn over 1f out: styd on gamely ins fnl f* **11/2**

30-2 **2** *hd* **Cap St Jean (IRE)**[16] 37 5-8-7 56..........................(p) DavidKenny(7) 5 64
(R Hollinshead) *towards rr: hdwy over 2f out: swtchd lft and rdn over 1f out: styd on strly ins fnl f: edgd rt and nt qckn towards fin* **11/1**

432- **3** *1/2* **Kingsmaite**[28] 7772 8-9-0 57..........................(b) DaneO'Neill 7 63
(S R Bowring) *cl up: effrt 2f out: sn rdn and ev ch tl drvn and one pce ins fnl f* **9/2**[3]

6-02 **4** *1 3/4* **Magical Song**[7] 150 4-9-0 50..........................(b) GrahamGibbons 10 58
(R Curtis) *cl up: effrt 2f out: sn rdn and ev ch tl drvn and one pce ins fnl f* **16/1**

2-22 **5** *1 1/4* **Hamaasy**[12] 95 8-8-11 60.......................... KevinGhunowa(3) 1 55
(R A Harris) *trckd ldrs: hdwy on inner 1/2-way: rdn and ch 2f out: sn drvn and wknd over 1f out* **5/2**[1]

600- **6** *6* **Bobski (IRE)**[120] 6177 7-9-0 78..........................(p) JamieSpencer 2 39
(Miss Gay Kelleway) *dwlt: a towards rr* **10/3**[2]

0-00 **7** *3/4* **So Sublime**[5] 175 4-8-9 42..........................(b) AmyBaker(5) 8 37
(M C Chapman) *a towards rr* **100/1**

11-6 **8** *4 1/2* **Run Free**[14] 63 5-9-5 58.......................... LeeEnstone 11 31
(N Wilson) *chsd ldrs on outer: rdn along over 3f out and sn wknd* **9/1**

0-55 **9** *3/4* **Penel (IRE)**[7] 150 8-8-7 48..........................(p) PaulPickard(7) 6 24
(P T Midgley) *s.i.s: a bhd* **50/1**

1m 28.73s (-1.57) **Going Correction** -0.175s/f (Stan) **9** Ran SP% **112.4**
Speed ratings (Par 101): **101,100,100,98,96 89,89,83,83**
toteswinger: 1&2 £11.20, 1&3 £4.90, 2&3 £9.10. CSF £61.64 TOTE £6.10: £1.60, £2.80, £1.70; EX 61.70 Trifecta £138.10 Pool: £363.99 - 1.95 winning units..The winner was bought in for 4,000gns.
Owner The Matthewman One Partnership **Bred** A S Reid **Trained** Musley Bank, N Yorks

FOCUS
A reasonable seller and quite competitive. Sound form despite the market leaders running poorly.
Bobski(IRE) Official explanation: trainer said gelding was unsuited by the fibresand.

224 PLAY POKER @ WILLIAMHILL.COM H'CAP 1m (F)
2:00 (2:10) (Class 6) (0-65,65) 4-Y-O+ **£2,047** (£604; £302) **Stalls Low**

Form RPR

323- **1** **West End Lad**[49] 7532 6-9-2 **63**..........................(b) DaneO'Neill 6 74
(S R Bowring) *cl up: led 3f out: rdn along and hdd 2f out: drvn to ld appr fnl f: kpt on wl* **9/2**[2]

0-14 **2** *1 3/4* **Vogarth**[9] 129 5-8-8 **60**..........................(b[1]) AmyBaker(5) 7 67
(M C Chapman) *cl up: rdn to ld 2f out: hdd appr fnl f and kpt on same pce* **22/1**

00-0 **3** *2 1/4* **Hilbre Court (USA)**[10] 125 4-9-2 **63**.......................... GrahamGibbons 2 65
(B P J Baugh) *towards rr and pushed along 1/2-way: hdwy over 2f out: rdn to chse ldrs and edgd lft over 1f out: kpt on ins fnl f* **16/1**

23-1 **4** *3 3/4* **Mambo Sun**[14] 63 6-9-4 **65**.......................... RobertWinston 4 58
(R Curtis) *trckd ldrs: hdwy over 2f out: rdn wl over 1f out and kpt on same pce* **9/2**[2]

45-5 **5** *1 1/2* **Haroldini (IRE)**[12] 94 7-9-1 **62**..........................(p) PaulMulrennan 11 52
(J Balding) *chsd ldrs: rdn along over 2f out: drvn and one pce over 1f out* **10/1**

060- **6** *1/2* **Tevez**[29] 7771 4-9-1 **62**.......................... JimmyQuinn 5 50
(Miss Amy Weaver) *chsd ldrs: rdn along over 2f out: snd drvn and btn* **7/2**[1]

3-05 **7** *3 1/4* **Louisiade (IRE)**[14] 63 8-8-5 **52**.......................... HayleyTurner 14 33
(M C Chapman) *in tch on outer: hdwy over 2f out: sn rdn and no imp* **14/1**

440- **8** *1* **Sularno**[39] 7650 5-9-4 **65**.......................... TravisBlock 13 44
(H Morrison) *midfield: rdn along wl over 2f out: nvr a factor* **8/1**[3]

60-5 **9** *3/4* **Bridge Of Fermoy (IRE)**[11] 97 4-8-11 **65**...........(b) KylieManser(7) 10 42
(Miss Gay Kelleway) *a towards rr* **25/1**

00-0 **10** *1 1/4* **Komreyev Star**[19] 7 7-8-3 **53**..........................(p) DuranFentiman(3) 12 27
(R E Peacock) *led 2f: prom tl rdn along over 3f out and sn wknd* **66/1**

52-4 **11** *2 1/2* **Rub Of The Relic (IRE)**[14] 63 4-8-11 **58**................(v) JamieMoriarty 8 26
(P T Midgley) *a towards rr* **9/1**

000- **12** *2 3/4* **Mont Cervin**[92] 6868 4-8-13 **60**.......................... StephenDonohoe 3 22
(Mrs R A Carr) *cl up: led after 2f: rdn along and hdd 3f out: sn wknd* **66/1**

/00- **13** *19* **Petroglyph**[7] 4709 5-8-9 **56** ow1.......................... JamieSpencer 9 —
(P Bowen) *a bhd* **16/1**

55-3 **14** *1 1/4* **Tiger's Rocket (IRE)**[12] 93 4-9-2 **63**..........................(b) ChrisCatlin 1 —
(S Gollings) *a bhd* **40/1**

1m 41.32s (-2.38) **Going Correction** -0.175s/f (Stan) **14** Ran SP% **120.8**
Speed ratings (Par 101): **104,102,100,96,94 94,91,90,89,88 85,82,63,62**
toteswinger: 1&2 £22.50, 1&3 £20.20, 2&3 £74.40. CSF £108.95 CT £1468.88 TOTE £6.10: £2.30, £6.40, £7.10; EX 87.80 TRIFECTA Not won..
Owner K Nicholls **Bred** Keith Nicholls **Trained** Edwinstowe, Notts
■ Stewards' Enquiry : Kylie Manser caution: used whip when out of contention.

FOCUS
A moderate handicap and it paid to race handy. Ordinary form for the grade.

225 PLAY GOLF AT SOUTHWELL GOLF CLUB H'CAP 7f (F)
2:30 (2:37) (Class 2) (0-100,104) 4-Y-O+ **£11,656** (£3,468; £1,733; £865) **Stalls Low**

Form RPR

2-15 **1** **Nightjar (USA)**[11] 106 4-8-4 **86** oh1.......................... HayleyTurner 5 98
(M Johnston) *trckd ldng pair: smooth hdwy on inner over 2f out: rdn to chal over 1f out: qckd to ld appr fnl f: kpt on strly* **7/2**[2]

13-2 **2** *1 1/4* **Majuro (IRE)**[19] 6 5-8-10 **92**.......................... JamieSpencer 7 101
(K A Ryan) *cl up: rdn to ld 2f out: drvn and hdd appr fnl f: kpt on same pce* **6/5**[1]

1-41 **3** *5* **Mozayada (USA)**[5] 176 5-8-4 **83** 6ex.......................... JimmyQuinn 3 82
(M Brittain) *led: rdn along and hdd 2f out: drvn and wknd over 1f out* **7/1**[3]

64-4 **4** *2 1/4* **Mister New York (USA)**[18] 17 4-8-4 **86** oh2.......................... ChrisCatlin 1 75
(Noel T Chance) *chsd ldrs: rdn along on inner wl over 2f out: sn one pce* **14/1**

11-0 **5** *2* **Internationaldebut (IRE)**[3] 204 4-9-1 **97**.......................(t) AdamKirby 4 81
(S Parr) *chsd ldrs: rdn along over 2f out: grad wknd* **7/2**[2]

50-5 **6** *1/2* **Excusez Moi (USA)**[19] 2 7-9-3 **104**................ DanielleMcCreery(5) 2 87
(Mrs R A Carr) *dwlt and in rr: rdn and sme hdwy over 2f out: nvr nr ldrs* **28/1**

400- **7** *11* **Haajes**[73] 7245 5-8-11 **93**..........................(t) LiamJones 6 46
(S Parr) *in tch: rdn along 3f out: sn wknd* **28/1**

1m 27.01s (-3.29) **Going Correction** -0.175s/f (Stan) **7** Ran SP% **116.0**
Speed ratings (Par 109): **111,109,103,101,99 98,85**
toteswinger: 1&2 £1.90, 1&3 £2.70, 2&3 £2.00. CSF £8.35 TOTE £5.20: £2.50, £1.20; EX 10.40.
Owner Crone Stud Farms Ltd **Bred** Derry Meeting Farm & London Thoroughbred Services **Trained** Middleham Moor, N Yorks

FOCUS
A decent handicap run at an even pace. Perhaps not the strongest race for the grade though, as only the first three have form here, although there are positives to take from the race.

NOTEBOOK
Nightjar(USA) was not at his best in a similarly decent race on the Polytrack at Wolverhampton last time, but he proved well suited by the return to Southwell and is now 3-3 on Fibresand. It obviously remains to be seen whether he will be as effective elsewhere, but whatever the case he looks to be improving. (tchd 3-1 and 4-1)
Majuro(IRE) was a well-backed favourite, but his supporters are entitled to feel disappointed with this effort. A bit too keen early, he basically seemed to race awkwardly throughout and looked ungainly under pressure in the straight. He has load of ability, but looks best watched for the time being. (op 5-4 tchd 11-8)
Mozayada(USA) had won five of her last six starts at this track, but it was a weak race for the class she landed last time and she was held by Majuro on their running here at the beginning of the month. (op 8-1 tchd 9-1)
Mister New York(USA) looked to handle the surface okay on his first try on Fibresand, but he seemed to find the company a bit hot. (op 12-1)
Internationaldebut(IRE) is a multiple Polytrack winner, but he was not at his best on that surface just three days earlier and he failed to run to form on this first try on Fibresand, his rider reporting that he had no more to give. It's interesting to note he had a tongue-tie fitted for the first time since May last year. Official explanation: jockey said gelding had no more to give (op 4-1 tchd 9-2)
Excusez Moi(USA) looks the type to do well for his new yard in time, but he is probably too high in the weights at the moment. (op 25-1)

226 THANK YOU CHRISTINE H'CAP 1m 4f (F)
3:00 (3:06) (Class 4) (0-85,83) 4-Y-O+ **£5,180** (£1,541; £770; £384) **Stalls Low**

Form RPR

00-3 **1** **River Ardeche**[8] 139 4-8-2 **72**.......................... PatrickDonaghy(5) 5 83
(P C Haslam) *mde all: pushed along 3f out and sn qcknd clr: rdn wl over 1f out and rdr dropped reins: drvn ins fnl f and hld on wl* **14/1**

1- **2** *1/2* **Take Me There**[33] 7721 6-8-11 **72**.......................... JimCrowley 6 82
(John Berry) *trckd wnr: rdn along 3f out: drvn 2f out: styd on u.p ent fnl f* **11/4**[2]

23-6 **3** *7* **Hucking Heat (IRE)**[13] 79 5-9-2 **77**..........................(p) HayleyTurner 8 76
(R Hollinshead) *chsd ldrs: hdwy 4f out: rdn wl over 2f out: kpt on same pce* **12/1**

616- **4** *hd* **Puy D'Arnac (FR)**[38] 7459 6-9-2 **77**.......................... RobertWinston 3 76
(G A Swinbank) *in tch: hdwy over 4f out: rdn along 3f out: drvn 2f out and no imp* **11/1**

1-62 **5** *nse* **Clear Reef**[7] 142 5-9-6 **81**.......................... JamieSpencer 9 80
(Jane Chapple-Hyam) *hld up and bhd: hdwy 4f out: rdn over 2f out: kpt on: nt rch ldrs* **5/2**[1]

112- **6** *6* **Red Fama**[126] 5992 5-9-1 **76**.......................... JimmyQuinn 10 65
(N Bycroft) *a towards rr* **15/2**

322- **7** *nk* **Persian Peril**[84] 7046 5-9-3 **78**.......................... TomEaves 1 67
(G A Swinbank) *chsd ldng pair: rdn along 4f out: drvn and wknd over 2f out* **12/1**

21- **8** *8* **Il Grande Ardone**[24] 7797 4-9-1 **80**..........................(tp) FBranca 2 56
(F Sheridan) *trckd ldrs: rdn along over 4f out and sn wknd* **11/2**[3]

40-4 9 10 **Barawin (IRE)**[12] 84 4-8-9 74 ....(b) LiamJones 11 34
(K R Burke) *a in rr* **80/1**

/06- 10 1 **Sommersturm (GER)**[34] 7704 5-9-8 83 .... MickyFenton 7 41
(A P Stringer) *in tch: rdn along over 4f out and sn wknd* **40/1**

2m 35.98s (-5.02) **Going Correction** -0.175s/f (Stan)
WFA 4 from 5yo+ 4lb **10** Ran SP% **116.4**
Speed ratings (Par 105): **109,108,104,103,103 99,99,94,87,86**
toteswinger: 1&2 £9.20, 1&3 £20.20, 2&3 £6.60. CSF £52.47 CT £491.13 TOTE £13.40: £2.80, £1.50, £2.50; EX 51.70 Trifecta £305.30 Part won. Pool: £412.57 - 0.10 winning units..
Owner Mark James & Mrs C Barclay **Bred** D R Tucker **Trained** Middleham Moor, N Yorks
■ Stewards' Enquiry : Jim Crowley two-day ban: used whip in incorrect place (Feb 3-4)

FOCUS
A fair middle-distance handicap won gamely by River Ardeche, but front runners did well through the card and this form is not rated too positively.
Clear Reef Official explanation: jockey said horse ran too free
Il Grande Ardone Official explanation: trainer said colt would not face the kickback.

227 MEMBERSHIP OF SOUTHWELL GOLF CLUB MAIDEN STKS 6f (F)
3:30 (3:37) (Class 5) 3-Y-0+ **£2,729** (£806; £403) **Stalls** Low

Form RPR
1 **Angel Song** 3-8-6 0 .... StephenDonohoe 3 70+
(Sir Mark Prescott) *cl up: led over 3f out: rdn 2f out: styd on strly u.p fnl f* **9/2**[2]

6-3 2 4 ½ **Dance And Dance (IRE)**[9] 127 3-8-11 0 .... JamieSpencer 1 64
(E F Vaughan) *wnt rt s: sn trcking ldrs: hdwy to chse wnr over 2f out: rdn wl over 1f out and sn no imp* **5/6**[1]

0-5 3 3 ¾ **Beaux Yeux**[16] 36 3-8-9 0 ow3 .... RobertWinston 10 47
(P T Midgley) *chsd ldrs on outer: rdn along over 2f out: sn drvn and one pce* **33/1**

000- 4 ¾ **Only Hope**[41] 7624 5-9-8 41 ....(be) JerryO'Dwyer 9 45
(P S McEntee) *chsd ldrs: rdn along over 2f out: drvn over 1f out: sn one pce* **40/1**

5 ¾ **Lively Blade** 3-8-11 0 .... GrahamGibbons 2 44+
(E S McMahon) *dwlt and hmpd s: sn rn green and rdn along in rr: bhd 1/2-way: hdwy on inner 2f out: sn rdn and styd on wl fnl f: nrst fin* **7/1**

0 6 10 **Petrenko**[12] 85 3-8-11 0 .... PaulHanagan 5 12
(R A Fahey) *chsd ldrs: rdn along 1/2-way and sn wknd* **25/1**

- 7 ½ **Unbelievable Jeff** 3-8-12 0 ow1 .... AdamKirby 6 11
(S Parr) *a towards rr* **6/1**[3]

00/0 8 1 **Wizzy Izzy (IRE)**[13] 80 4-9-8 34 .... LeeEnstone 7 —
(N Wilson) *led tl hdd over 3f out: sn rdn along and wknd* **66/1**

9 15 **Croy (IRE)** 4-9-8 0 .... LPKeniry 4 —
(S Parr) *dwlt: a in rr* **16/1**

1m 16.29s (-0.21) **Going Correction** -0.175s/f (Stan)
WFA 3 from 4yo+ 16lb **9** Ran SP% **116.1**
Speed ratings (Par 103): **94,88,83,82,81 67,67,65,45**
toteswinger: 1&2 £2.60, 1&3 £8.50, 2&3 £6.00. CSF £8.48 TOTE £5.20: £1.40, £1.02, £5.20; EX 10.60 Trifecta £146.20 Pool: £427.01 - 2.16 winning units..
Owner Plantation Stud **Bred** R T And Mrs Watson **Trained** Newmarket, Suffolk
■ Stewards' Enquiry : Stephen Donohoe caution: careless riding.

FOCUS
These 3yo-plus sprint maidens are always uncompetitive affairs and this was no different. Plenty of doubts over the form and the winner might not have achieved too much.
Beaux Yeux Official explanation: jockey said filly hung right-handed on home turn

228 MORE JUMP RACING AT SOUTHWELL IN 2009 H'CAP 1m (F)
4:00 (4:05) (Class 6) (0-60,60) 3-Y-0 **£2,047** (£604; £302) **Stalls** Low

Form RPR
016- 1 **Shifting Gold (IRE)**[71] 7266 3-9-2 58 ....(b) JamieSpencer 7 67
(K A Ryan) *mde all: rdn over 2f out: drvn over 1f out: kpt on wl u.p fnl f* **10/3**[2]

501- 2 1 ½ **Kingaroo (IRE)**[49] 7531 3-8-8 57 .... AndrewHeffernan(7) 4 63
(Garry Moss) *trckd ldrs: hdwy to chse wnr 3f out: rdn over 2f out: drvn over 1f out: kpt on ins fnl f* **5/2**[1]

00-3 3 nk **Lady Dunhill (IRE)**[16] 36 3-8-7 49 .... PaulHanagan 8 54
(E W Tuer) *midfield: hdwy over 3f out: rdn to chse ldng pair 2f out: drvn and kpt on same pce fnl f* **9/1**

320- 4 4 **Le Petit Vigier**[49] 7531 3-8-8 50 ....(t) AndrewElliott 6 46
(P Beaumont) *in tch: hdwy on outer to chse ldrs 2f out: sn rdn and no imp appr fnl f* **7/1**[3]

400- 5 9 **Chantilly Dancer (IRE)**[24] 7789 3-8-12 54 .... LiamJones 11 29
(M Quinn) *towards rr: rdn along 1/2-way: nvr a factor* **16/1**

526- 6 nk **Kneesy Earsy Nosey**[24] 7789 3-8-8 55 ow1 .... AnnStokell(5) 9 29
(Miss A Stokell) *nvr nr ldrs* **14/1**

06-1 7 2 ½ **Cause For Applause (IRE)**[19] 5 3-9-4 60 ....(v) TomEaves 2 29
(B Smart) *dwlt and a in rr* **15/2**

040- 8 1 ¼ **Lomica**[109] 6451 3-9-2 58 .... PaulMulrennan 1 24
(Miss J A Camacho) *chsd ldrs on inner: rdn along 1/2-way and sn wknd* **16/1**

030- 9 4 ½ **Cool Sonata (IRE)**[50] 7514 3-8-4 46 oh1 .... JimmyQuinn 10 —
(M Brittain) *a in rr* **18/1**

62-0 10 4 ½ **King's Chorister**[13] 77 3-9-3 59 ....(b) HayleyTurner 3 —
(Miss Gay Kelleway) *chsd wnr: rdn along over 3f out and sn wknd* **11/1**

1m 42.74s (-0.96) **Going Correction** -0.175s/f (Stan) **10** Ran SP% **117.9**
Speed ratings (Par 95): **97,95,95,91,82 81,79,78,73,69**
toteswinger: 1&2 £3.70, 1&3 £8.20, 2&3 £7.10. CSF £12.25 CT £68.56 TOTE £3.90: £1.50, £1.60, £2.10; EX 13.40 Trifecta £47.90 Pool: £434.47 - 6.70 winning units. Place 6: £81.87, Place 5: £54.99.
Owner Hambleton Racing Ltd VIII **Bred** Watership Down Stud **Trained** Hambleton, N Yorks
■ Stewards' Enquiry : Jamie Spencer caution: careless riding; caution: used whip down shoulder in forehand position.

FOCUS
This was a moderate handicap but the time was respectable and this was probably a reasonable race for the grade. The winner was in the best place up front and this is sound if limited form.
T/Jkpt: Not won. T/Plt: £69.50 to a £1 stake. Pool: £90,195.68. 946.30 winning tickets. T/Qpdt: £12.80 to a £1 stake. Pool: £6,671.30. 385.30 winning tickets. JR

207 KEMPTON (A.W) (R-H)
Wednesday, January 21

OFFICIAL GOING: Standard
Wind: modest, behind Weather: dry

229 BLUE SQUARE CASINO H'CAP 6f (P)
6:50 (6:50) (Class 5) (0-70,74) 3-Y-0 **£2,590** (£770; £385; £192) **Stalls** High

Form RPR
500- 1 **Perfect Class**[82] 7113 3-8-6 58 .... LukeMorris 11 64
(C G Cox) *racd in midfield: effrt and rdn 2f out: ev ch ent fnl f: led wl ins fnl f: r.o wl* **12/1**

4-22 2 hd **Princess Cagliari**[7] 162 3-8-12 64 .... JamieSpencer 1 70
(R Hannon) *stdd and dropped in bhd after s: wl bhd: pushed along 4f out: hdwy over 2f out: swtchd rt and gd hdwy over 1f out: ev ch fnl f: unable qck towards fin* **7/2**[1]

15-3 3 nk **My Best Bet**[16] 45 3-8-13 70 .... MCGeran(5) 3 75
(M R Channon) *s.i.s: towards rr: hdwy on outer and jostled 2f out: ev ch fnl f: unable qck fnl 50yds* **6/1**[3]

1-21 4 nse **Halaak (USA)**[13] 91 3-8-10 62 ....(b) ChrisCatlin 5 66
(D M Simcock) *stdd s: hld up in midfield: swtchd lft and jostled 2f out: rdn to ld 1f out: hdd and no ex wl ins fnl f* **14/1**

23-3 5 2 **Deckchair**[8] 140 3-8-0 57 ....(v) AmyBaker(5) 9 55
(H J Collingridge) *s.i.s: hld up in last trio: nt clr run on inner over 2f out tl jst over 2f out: hdwy jst over 1f out: chsd ldrs ins fnl f: no imp fnl 100yds* **9/1**

32-2 6 4 **Fangfoss Girls**[18] 34 3-8-11 66 .... KevinGhunowa(3) 10 51
(L Wells) *stdd after s: in tch: effrt jst over 2f out: hrd drvn and ev ch over 1f out: wknd fnl f* **7/1**

35-1 7 ½ **Green Onions**[10] 127 3-9-3 74 6ex .... GabrielHannon(5) 6 58
(D J S Ffrench Davis) *racd keenly: sn led: rdn 2f out: hdd 1f out: sn wknd: eased towards fin* **9/1**

24-5 8 shd **Bold Rose**[16] 45 3-8-7 59 .... MartinDwyer 2 42
(M D I Usher) *swtchd rt and dropped in bhd after s: rdn and effrt wl over 2f out: nvr nr ldrs* **33/1**

445- 9 nse **Hand Painted**[93] 6863 3-9-2 68 .... TravisBlock 4 51
(P J Makin) *chsd ldrs: rdn wl over 2f out: drvn and wknd over 1f out* **4/1**[2]

405- 10 hd **Old Sarum (IRE)**[54] 7464 3-8-7 59 .... LiamJones 7 41
(D R C Elsworth) *t.k.h: chsd ldr tl wknd qckly wl over 1f out* **14/1**

432- 11 22 **Bold Account (IRE)**[42] 7628 3-8-13 65 .... AndrewElliott 8 —
(Garry Moss) *chsd ldrs tl wknd 2f out: eased fnl f: t.o* **20/1**

1m 13.27s (0.17) **Going Correction** +0.10s/f (Slow) **11** Ran SP% **117.7**
Speed ratings (Par 97): **102,101,101,101,98 93,92,92,92,92 62**
toteswinger: 1&2 £9.00, 1&3 £20.20, 2&3 £7.60. CSF £53.84 CT £289.54 TOTE £15.10: £4.50, £1.40, £3.30; EX 49.60.
Owner The Perfect Partnership **Bred** Cheveley Park Stud Ltd **Trained** Lambourn, Berks

FOCUS
A competitive handicap for three-year-olds, that appeared to be run at a good pace, although it must be said that most of the field looked to hold a chance about two furlongs out. The form looks pretty sound, rated around the runner-up.
Perfect Class Official explanation: trainer said, regarding the improved form shown, filly was suited by the step up to 6f

230 BLUE SQUARE MEDIAN AUCTION MAIDEN STKS 7f (P)
7:20 (7:20) (Class 5) 3-5-Y-0 **£2,590** (£770; £385; £192) **Stalls** High

Form RPR
4-2 1 **Avoir Choisi (IRE)**[11] 115 3-8-8 0 .... JamieSpencer 4 74+
(P W Chapple-Hyam) *trckd ldng pair: wnt 2nd over 2f out: rdn to ld over 1f out: clr ins fnl f: eased fnl 75yds: v easily* **4/9**[1]

052- 2 3 **Elisiario (IRE)**[31] 7757 4-9-12 70 .... PatCosgrave 2 67
(J R Boyle) *t.k.h: led: drvn and hdd over 1f out: no ch w wnr ins fnl f: eased towards fin* **4/1**[2]

3 ½ **Saints Bay (IRE)** 3-8-3 0 .... FrankieMcDonald 5 56+
(R Hannon) *stdd and wnt rt s: bhd: rdn wl over 2f out: hdwy to go modest 3rd wl over 1f out: r.o: nvr threatened ldrs* **16/1**

0- 4 9 **Esteem Dancer**[22] 7823 3-8-8 0 .... HayleyTurner 7 36
(J G Given) *in tch in midfield tl pushed along and outpcd over 3f out: rallied briefly over 2f out: wknd wl over 1f out* **10/1**[3]

5 1 ½ **Lyrical Intent** 3-8-8 0 .... LiamJones 3 32
(P Howling) *s.i.s: bhd: hdwy to chse ldrs 4f out: rdn and wknd over 2f out* **40/1**

00-6 6 ¾ **Valid Point (IRE)**[14] 69 3-8-8 0 .... StephenDonohoe 6 30
(Sir Mark Prescott) *wnt lft s: a bhd: lost tch 3f out* **33/1**

7 29 **Hidden Horse**[26] 5-9-7 0 .... EdwardCreighton 1 —
(M R Channon) *t.k.h: chsd ldr tl hung bdly lft over 2f out: sn bhd: eased fnl f: t.o* **20/1**

1m 28.56s (2.56) **Going Correction** +0.10s/f (Slow)
WFA 3 from 4yo+ 18lb **7** Ran SP% **114.4**
Speed ratings (Par 103): **89,85,85,74,73 72,39**
toteswinger: 1&2 £1.40, 1&3 £2.70, 2&3 £6.00. CSF £2.48 TOTE £1.50: £1.20, £2.10; EX 2.80.
Owner Joy And Valentine Feerick **Bred** Patrick Cummins **Trained** Newmarket, Suffolk

FOCUS
This maiden looked very weak and probably took little winning, despite the official rating of the runner-up.
Hidden Horse Official explanation: jockey said mare lost her action

231 BLUE SQUARE MOBILE CLAIMING STKS 1m (P)
7:50 (7:50) (Class 6) 3-Y-0 **£2,047** (£604; £302) **Stalls** High

Form RPR
62-1 1 **Double Act**[9] 136 3-9-4 79 ....(t) JamieSpencer 1 76
(J Noseda) *stdd after s: hld up wl bhd: stl plenty to do 3f out: hdwy on inner wl over 2f out: swtchd lft to outer jst over 2f out: chsd ldr and rdn over 1f out: led fnl 100yds: rdn out* **5/6**[1]

-134 2 hd **Hold The Bucks (USA)**[9] 136 3-9-1 72 .... LukeMorris 7 73
(J S Moore) *racd in midfield: hanging lft bnd over 3f out: hdwy to ld 2f out: rdn over 1f out: hdd and no ex fnl 100yds* **13/2**[3]

024- 3 2 ½ **Jonnie Skull (IRE)**[32] 7738 3-8-10 59 ....(b) HayleyTurner 9 62
(D R C Elsworth) *chsd ldrs: rdn and effrt 2f out: chsd ldng pair over 1f out: kpt on same pce* **18/1**

-245 4 11 **Turn To Dreams**[9] 136 3-8-2 57 .... CatherineGannon 8 29
(P D Evans) *led: jnd wl over 2f out: hdd 2f out: wknd qckly over 1f out* **33/1**

240- 5 1 ½ **Celtic Commitment**[34] 7718 3-8-13 66 .... PatDobbs 3 36
(R Hannon) *chsd ldrs: rdn and ev ch over 2f out: wknd qckly 2f out* **5/1**[2]

25-2 **6** 3¼ **Precocious Air (IRE)**[9] [134] 3-8-4 60 ChrisCatlin 4 20
(J A Osborne) *chsd ldr: upsides ldr wl over 2f out: wknd qckly over 1f out* **8/1**

5 **7** 11 **Snoozing**[13] [92] 3-8-2 0 ow3 AshleyMorgan(7) 6 —
(M H Tompkins) *stdd s: a bhd: rdn over 3f out: wl bhd fnl 2f: t.o* **66/1**

36-3 **8** ¾ **Special Bond**[7] [164] 3-8-6 65 (b) MartinDwyer 2 —
(J A Osborne) *dwlt: sn pushed up and in tch: rdn over 3f out: wl bhd fnl 2f: t.o* **9/1**

00-0 **9** 29 **Tartan Turban (IRE)**[14] [75] 3-8-8 50 FergusSweeney 5 —
(R Hannon) *a in rr: lost tch over 2f out: t.o* **40/1**

1m 40.52s (0.72) **Going Correction** +0.10s/f (Slow) **9** Ran SP% **117.8**
Speed ratings (Par 95): **100,99,97,86,84 81,70,69,40**
toteswinger: 1&2 £2.20, 1&3 £6.50, 2&3 £14.80. CSF £6.98 TOTE £1.90: £1.20, £1.80, £3.00; EX 6.80.Double Act was claimed by R. E. R. Williams for £15000.
Owner Highclere Thoroughbred Racing (VC2) **Bred** Cheveley Park Stud Ltd **Trained** Newmarket, Suffolk

FOCUS
At least half of these appeared to have little chance of getting involved on previous form, so it would be unwise to get too carried away with the bare result, even in this grade, although the first three did pull clear. There looked to be around half a furlong between first and last.

232 BLUE SQUARE SP GUARANTEE H'CAP — 1m (P)
8:20 (8:22) (Class 3) (0-90,90) 4-Y-O+
£7,477 (£2,239; £1,119; £560; £279; £140) **Stalls** High

Form RPR

10-1 **1** **Harald Bluetooth (IRE)**[19] [17] 4-9-4 **90** JamieSpencer 7 97+
(D M Simcock) *stdd s: hld up in rr: niggled along over 3f out: stl plenty to do and plld out wd over 2f out: rdn and hdwy over 1f out: edgd rt but r.o wl to ld towards fin: dismntd after fin: lame* **4/5**[1]

354- **2** nk **Ocean Legend (IRE)**[23] [7813] 4-8-5 **77** LiamJones 1 83
(Miss J Feilden) *in tch: rdn over 3f out: hdwy u.p over 2f out: led wl ins fnl f: hdd and no ex towards fin* **14/1**

R15- **3** 1 **L'Hirondelle (IRE)**[35] [7712] 5-8-5 **77** LukeMorris 8 81
(M J Attwater) *chsd ldrs: rdn and effrt 2f out: drvn to ld ent fnl f: hdd ins fnl f: kpt on same pce fnl 100yds* **9/2**[2]

34-2 **4** ½ **Totally Focussed (IRE)**[11] [113] 4-8-9 **81** IanMongan 3 86+
(S Dow) *t.k.h: hld up in last pair: hdwy over 3f out: hanging rt and rdn over 2f out: hdwy u.p over 1f out: pressing ldrs but keeping on same pce and hld whn short of room and snatched up nr fin* **7/1**[3]

0-31 **5** 2¼ **Resplendent Nova**[11] [113] 7-9-0 **86** JimmyQuinn 6 83
(P Howling) *hld up in midfield: effrt on inner 2f out: drvn and no imp fr jst over 1f out* **10/1**

343- **6** ½ **Gallantry**[24] [7804] 7-8-10 **85** TolleyDean(3) 4 81
(P Howling) *led: rdn wl over 2f out: hdd ent fnl f: wknd* **14/1**

005- **7** 2¼ **The Jostler**[33] [7737] 4-8-11 **83** ChrisCatlin 5 74
(B W Hills) *hld up in last trio: rdn and carried hd awkwardly over 2f out: nvr nr ldrs* **12/1**

/0-6 **8** 9 **Count Trevisio (IRE)**[14] [73] 6-9-0 **86** GregFairley 2 56
(J R Gask) *chsd ldr tl over 2f out: sn wknd: wl bhd fnl f* **25/1**

1m 39.15s (-0.65) **Going Correction** +0.10s/f (Slow) **8** Ran SP% **120.2**
Speed ratings (Par 107): **107,106,105,105,102 102,100,91**
toteswinger: 1&2 £5.10, 1&3 £1.60, 2&3 £17.60. CSF £15.71 CT £38.83 TOTE £1.90: £1.10, £3.10, £2.00; EX 18.80.
Owner Ahmad Al Shaikh **Bred** Airlie Stud And Sir Thomas Pilkington **Trained** Newmarket, Suffolk
■ Stewards' Enquiry : Jamie Spencer seven-day ban: careless riding (Feb 4-10)
Liam Jones two-day ban: used whip with excessive frequency (Feb 4-5)

FOCUS
This was by far the most competitive race on the card, despite the fact that the favourite went off a fairly short price. The form ought to be very solid, if ordinary for the grade, but unfortunately the winner looked to be injured and may not be seen for a while.

NOTEBOOK
Harald Bluetooth(IRE) always looked to have plenty of ability when with James Fanshawe but was well beaten on his last start for him. Picked up by David Simcock at the sales last October, he made the perfect start for that trainer when winning at Wolverhampton at the start of the month. Raised 7lb for that easy success, he took a long time to get going but was comfortably on top passing the line. However, he was quickly dismounted by Jamie Spencer after the line and was taken away in a horse ambulance. (op 11-10 tchd 5-4)

Ocean Legend(IRE) is a consistent sort and battled on very bravely for pressure. He still awaits his first victory in handicap company. (op 10-1)

L'Hirondelle(IRE), so impressive when landing a maiden two outings ago, ran nicely on his handicap debut at Lingfield last time and did nothing wrong again, but was slightly fortunate to nab third. (op 6-1 tchd 13-2 in a place)

Totally Focussed(IRE) was only just denied by Resplendent Nova when they clashed last time but comprehensively reversed that form in this. However, luck deserted him again, as he would have finished third had he not been tightened up close to the line. (op 6-1 tchd 11-2)

Resplendent Nova, stepped up to a mile again, had every chance but could not pick up. (op 8-1)

Gallantry probably went off too quickly and weakened about a furlong out. (op 9-1)

233 BLUE SQUARE POKER H'CAP — 2m (P)
8:50 (8:52) (Class 4) (0-85,77) 4-Y-O+ **£4,727** (£1,406; £702; £351) **Stalls** High

Form RPR

101- **1** **Greenwich Village**[30] [7770] 6-9-13 **77** JimCrowley 7 88+
(W J Knight) *trckd ldng pair: chal over 2f out: led 2f out: drvn and styd on wl fnl f* **11/4**[1]

42/4 **2** 2 **Kavaloti (IRE)**[14] [72] 5-9-9 **73** (b) FergusSweeney 6 80
(G L Moore) *in tch: rdn and nt qckn over 2f out: hdwy over 1f out: chsd ldng pair 1f out: kpt on to go 2nd nr fin: nvr pce to chal wnr* **11/2**

141- **3** nk **Alnwick**[186] [4193] 5-9-9 **73** DaneO'Neill 3 80
(P D Cundell) *led: rdn over 2f out: hdd 2f out: kpt on same pce fnl f: lost 2nd nr fin* **9/2**[3]

23-6 **4** 1½ **Calculating (IRE)**[14] [72] 5-9-4 **68** HayleyTurner 8 73
(M D I Usher) *stdd s: hld up in rr: effrt on outer over 2f out: hung rt after: modest 6th over 1f out: r.o wl fnl f: nvr nr ldrs* **12/1**

11-1 **5** 2¾ **Zuwaar**[11] [112] 4-9-4 **75** (t) StephenDonohoe 4 77
(Ian Williams) *in tch in midfield: rdn 3f out: chsd ldrs over 2f out: no imp after* **3/1**[2]

24-2 **6** 1 **Salute (IRE)**[14] [72] 10-9-11 **75** RobertHavlin 2 76
(P G Murphy) *chsd ldr: rdn over 3f out: drvn and wknd ent fnl 2f* **6/1**

- **7** 29 **Jeczmien (POL)**[458] 6-9-9 **73** (t) ChrisCatlin 5 39
(N J Gifford) *t.k.h: hld up in last pair: pushed along over 8f out: wknd qckly wl over 2f out: eased fnl f: t.o* **25/1**

8 shd **Sahara Sunshine**[58] 4-9-2 **73** IanMongan 1 39
(Mrs L J Mongan) *stdd s: t.k.h: hld up in last trio: rdn 3f out: wknd over 2f out: t.o and eased fnl f* **25/1**

3m 31.82s (1.72) **Going Correction** +0.10s/f (Slow)
WFA 4 from 5yo+ 7lb **8** Ran SP% **114.9**
Speed ratings (Par 105): **99,98,97,97,95 95,80,80**
toteswinger: 1&2 £5.80, 1&3 £3.20, 2&3 £5.20. CSF £18.44 CT £63.78 TOTE £4.00: £1.60, £2.90, £2.40; EX 24.50.
Owner Ecurie Franglaise **Bred** Cotswold Stud **Trained** Patching, W Sussex
■ Stewards' Enquiry : Fergus Sweeney caution: used whip with excessive frequency

FOCUS
A fair staying handicap for the class and, as one would expect, the early gallop was nothing out of the ordinary. Another step forward from the progressive winner.

234 BLUE SQUARE H'CAP — 7f (P)
9:20 (9:21) (Class 6) (0-55,55) 4-Y-O+ **£2,047** (£604; £302) **Stalls** High

Form RPR

44-6 **1** **Guildenstern (IRE)**[14] [71] 7-9-0 **55** JimmyQuinn 1 67
(P Howling) *stdd and dropped in bhd after s: hdwy and nt clr run 2f out: gd hdwy over 1f out: led ins fnl f: drvn and r.o wl* **10/1**

320- **2** 1½ **Fun In The Sun**[63] [7382] 5-8-12 **53** StephenDonohoe 4 61
(A B Haynes) *hld up in midfield: hdwy and rdn 2f out: chsd wnr ins fnl f: r.o but no imp on wnr* **12/1**

0-52 **3** 3¾ **Liberty Valance (IRE)**[7] [155] 4-9-0 **55** (t) SimonWhitworth 13 53
(S Kirk) *chsd ldrs: rdn to chal over 2f out: led over 1f out: hdd ins fnl f: sn outpcd by ldng pair* **9/4**[1]

330- **4** shd **Outer Hebrides**[29] [7779] 8-8-6 **52** (v) AmyBaker(5) 12 50
(J M Bradley) *pressed ldr tl led narrowly 4f out: rdn over 2f out: hdd over 1f out: nt pce of ldrs fnl f* **11/1**

5-46 **5** ½ **Thabaat**[11] [118] 5-9-0 **55** (b) RobertWinston 11 51
(J M Bradley) *hld up in midfield: effrt and rdn 2f out: drvn and plugged on same pce fnl f* **5/1**[2]

010- **6** ½ **Greek Secret**[23] [7809] 6-8-9 **55** ow3 JamesO'Reilly(5) 5 50
(J O'Reilly) *rrd s: t.k.h: hld up towards rr: effrt on inner over 2f out: chsd ldrs and drvn over 1f out: outpcd fnl f* **25/1**

00-6 **7** 1½ **Batchworth Blaise**[11] [114] 6-8-12 **53** StephenCarson 2 44
(E A Wheeler) *stdd s: hld up in last pl: rdn and effrt over 2f out: kpt on but hung rt after: nvr nr ldrs* **14/1**

000- **8** 2¼ **Over To You Bert**[24] [7803] 10-8-9 **55** MCGeran(5) 14 40
(R J Hodges) *led tl 4f out: styd pressing ldr: rdn over 2f out: wknd qckly over 1f out* **7/1**[3]

36-1 **9** 4½ **Hollow Jo**[11] [111] 9-9-0 **55** MickyFenton 6 28
(J R Jenkins) *chsd ldrs: rdn over 2f out: wknd wl over 1f out: wl btn fnl f* **17/2**

34-0 **10** 3¾ **Grizedale (IRE)**[11] [111] 10-8-13 **54** (tp) IanMongan 10 16
(M J Attwater) *t.k.h: hld up wl in tch: rdn and fnd nil over 2f out: wknd 2f out: wl btn fnl f* **11/1**

400- **11** 8 **Metropolitan Chief**[221] [3034] 5-8-9 **50** LPKeniry 7 —
(P Burgoyne) *stdd s: t.k.h: sn in midfield: rdn over 3f out: bhd fnl 2f: eased ins fnl f* **40/1**

25-0 **12** 4 **Palais Polaire**[14] [71] 7-8-13 **54** (tp) MartinDwyer 3 —
(J A Geake) *in tch in midfield on outer tl lost pl and bhd over 3f out: rdn and no rspnse 3f out: eased ins fnl f* **25/1**

1m 26.86s (0.86) **Going Correction** +0.10s/f (Slow) **12** Ran SP% **120.7**
Speed ratings (Par 101): **99,97,93,92,92 91,90,87,82,78 68,64**
toteswinger: 1&2 £21.70, 1&3 £4.80, 2&3 £15.00. CSF £123.85 CT £373.49 TOTE £9.70: £2.50, £3.60, £1.60; EX 108.20 Place 6: £ 6.70 Place 5: £3.29.
Owner David Andrew Brown **Bred** Peter E Daly **Trained** Newmarket, Suffolk

FOCUS
Most of this lot are unreliable and/or out of form horses, so while it was a competitive event, the form looks decidedly dodgy.
Batchworth Blaise Official explanation: jockey said gelding hung right
T/Plt: £11.50 to a £1 stake. Pool: £118,723.54. 7,515.11 winning tickets. T/Qpdt: £5.70 to a £1 stake. Pool: £6,696.72. 858.32 winning tickets. SP

[214]WOLVERHAMPTON (A.W) (L-H)
Wednesday, January 21

OFFICIAL GOING: Standard
Wind: Light half behind Weather: Light rain 4.20 onwards

235 RINGSIDE SUITE - 700 THEATRE STYLE H'CAP — 5f 216y(P)
2:20 (2:21) (Class 6) (0-65,66) 4-Y-O+ **£2,047** (£604; £302) **Stalls** Low

Form RPR

0-40 **1** **Grand Palace (IRE)**[13] [95] 6-9-3 **64** (v) DaneO'Neill 7 74
(D Shaw) *a.p: edgd lft fnl f: r.o to ld nr fin* **20/1**

2 hd **Under Warranty (ITY)**[172] 5-8-13 **60** (t) FBranca 5 69
(F Sheridan) *led over 2f: led wl over 1f out: rdn and hdd nr fin* **4/1**[2]

404- **3** ½ **Strathmore (IRE)**[232] [2703] 5-9-2 **63** PaulHanagan 9 71
(R A Fahey) *a.p: rdn and ev ch whn edgd lft fnl f: nt qckn cl home* **12/1**

-311 **4** 1 **Sarah's Art (IRE)**[5] [198] 6-9-5 **66** 6ex MickyFenton 6 73+
(Stef Liddiard) *hld up towards rr: hdwy on ins wl over 1f out: styng on whn nt clr run towards fin* **11/8**[1]

3-04 **5** ½ **Punching**[12] [96] 5-9-2 **63** LPKeniry 10 66+
(C R Dore) *t.k.h in mid-div: hdwy over 1f out: styng on whn nt clr run wl ins fnl f* **12/1**

4-35 **6** hd **Obe Royal**[6] [167] 5-9-3 **64** (b) StephenDonohoe 1 66
(P D Evans) *s.i.s: hld up and bhd: hdwy fnl f: nrst fin* **9/1**[3]

614- **7** 1¾ **Littledodayno (IRE)**[30] [7762] 6-9-3 **64** SteveDrowne 11 61
(M Wigham) *hld up in mid-div: no real prog fnl 2f* **12/1**

200- **8** ½ **Trinculo (IRE)**[75] [7225] 12-8-11 **61** (b) KevinGhunowa(3) 8 56
(R A Harris) *w ldr: led over 3f out tl wl over 1f out: wknd ins fnl f* **50/1**

456- **9** 3¾ **Bishopbriggs (USA)**[22] [7826] 4-9-4 **65** AdamKirby 12 48
(S Parr) *a in rr* **14/1**

020/ **10** 1½ **Gower**[189] [4094] 5-9-2 **63** JimmyQuinn 13 41
(R J Price) *a bhd* **33/1**

41-2 **11** 3½ **Kaystar Ridge**[18] [27] 4-8-9 **61** (bt) JamesO'Reilly(5) 4 28
(D K Ivory) *s.i.s: a bhd* **11/1**

041- **12** ½ **Brazilian Brush (IRE)**[101] [6680] 4-9-4 **65** (t) RobertWinston 3 31
(J M Bradley) *prom 4f* **14/1**

1m 15.41s (0.41) **Going Correction** +0.125s/f (Slow) **12** Ran SP% **126.5**
Speed ratings (Par 101): **102,101,101,99,99 98,96,95,90,88 84,83**
toteswinger: 1&2 £55.80, 1&3 £40.40, 2&3 £18.60. CSF £103.57 CT £1051.29 TOTE £18.10: £6.30, £1.40, £3.70; EX 240.10 TRIFECTA Not won..
Owner ownaracehorse.co.uk (Shakespeare) **Bred** D McDonnell And Tower Bloodstock **Trained** Danethorpe, Notts

FOCUS
This was a wide-open handicap. The time was reasonable and the form is sound.
Grand Palace(IRE) Official explanation: trainer's rep said, regarding the improved form shown, gelding was probably better suited to the polytrack
Sarah's Art(IRE) Official explanation: jockey said gelding was denied a clear run
Bishopbriggs(USA) Official explanation: jockey said, regarding the running and riding, his orders were to get across from a wide draw and then ride the race to the best of his ability to achieve the most favourable placing, adding that the horse hung right from 5f out rendering it difficult to ride the horse in a vigorous manner to the line
Brazilian Brush(IRE) Official explanation: jockey said the gelding hung left

236 HOTEL & CONFERENCING AT WOLVERHAMPTON MAIDEN STKS 5f 216y(P)
2:50 (2:50) (Class 5) 3-Y-O **£2,729** (£806; £403) **Stalls** Low

Form RPR
03- **1** **Pearl Of Manacor (IRE)**[159] 5053 3-9-3 0 TonyCulhane 1 78+
(M R Channon) *hld up in mid-div: bmpd over 3f out: hdwy on ins over 2f out: led ins fnl f: pushed out* **3/1**[2]
04-3 **2** 2 1/2 **Gurteen Diamond**[19] 19 3-8-12 62 LukeMorris 10 61
(N J Vaughan) *prom: jnd ldr 4f out: rdn to ld 1f out: hdd and nt qckn ins fnl f* **12/1**
50- **3** 3 1/2 **One Cool Mission (IRE)**[35] 7708 3-8-12 0 (t) RichardKingscote 3 50
(Tom Dascombe) *hld up: sn mid-div: bmpd over 3f out: rdn and hdwy over 1f out: r.o to take 3rd cl home* **6/1**[3]
4 nk **Foreign Investment (IRE)** 3-8-12 0 JimmyQuinn 2 49+
(P D Evans) *s.s: in rr: hdwy fnl f: nrst fin* **28/1**
056- **5** 1 1/4 **Fashion Icon (USA)**[161] 4965 3-8-7 62 DeanHeslop(5) 11 45
(T D Barron) *led: hdd 1f out: wknd ins fnl f* **40/1**
0- **6** 3/4 **Cruise Control**[22] 7823 3-9-3 0 GregFairley 7 47
(R J Price) *s.i.s: bhd: hdwy on ins wl over 1f out: no further prog fnl f* **66/1**
260- **7** 1 1/2 **Aahaygirl (IRE)**[115] 6319 3-8-12 82 FergusSweeney 6 38
(K R Burke) *prom: rdn over 1f out: wknd fnl f* **1/1**[1]
8 nk **Chief Wild Cat (IRE)**[146] 5434 3-8-10 73 GFCarroll(7) 8 42
(C Moore, Ire) *prom tl rdn and wknd 2f out* **28/1**
-6 **9** 7 **Chase End**[10] 127 3-8-12 0 DaleGibson 5 14
(J M P Eustace) *a bhd* **50/1**
050- **10** hd **Pedregal**[201] 3669 3-9-3 58 PaulHanagan 9 19
(R A Fahey) *hld up in tch: lost pl over 3f out: bhd fnl 2f* **40/1**
11 4 1/2 **Brett Vale (IRE)** 3-9-3 0 StephenDonohoe 12 4
(Sir Mark Prescott) *s.i.s: a in rr* **20/1**
00- **12** 2 3/4 **Minibuzz**[37] 7689 3-9-3 0 (v[1]) GrahamGibbons 4 —
(Mrs G S Rees) *prom: n.m.r on ins over 3f out: wknd over 2f out* **200/1**

1m 16.24s (1.24) **Going Correction** +0.125s/f (Slow) **12 Ran SP% 117.5**
Speed ratings (Par 97): **96,92,88,87,85 84,82,82,73,72 66,63**
toteswinger: 1&2 £5.00, 1&3 £5.00, 2&3 £7.50. CSF £34.28 TOTE £6.00: £1.70, £1.50, £1.60; EX 25.20 Trifecta £88.50 Pool: £290.48 - 2.43 winning units..
Owner Findlay Bloom & Channon **Bred** Budget Stable **Trained** West Ilsley, Berks
■ Stewards' Enquiry : G F Carroll caution: careless riding

FOCUS
This was an uncompetitive maiden, weakened by the favourite's poor show, and there is a bit of doubt about the worth of the form. The winner should rate higher.
Aahaygirl(IRE) Official explanation: jockey said filly moved poorly throughout
Pedregal Official explanation: jockey said gelding hung right
Brett Vale(IRE) Official explanation: jockey said gelding missed the break

237 STAY AT THE WOLVERHAMPTON HOLIDAY INN CLAIMING STKS 1m 4f 50y(P)
3:20 (3:20) (Class 6) 4-Y-O+ **£2,047** (£604; £302) **Stalls** Low

Form RPR
13-3 **1** **Boundless Prospect (USA)**[19] 12 10-8-4 68 DeanHeslop(5) 5 52
(P D Evans) *hld up in rr: rdn over 2f out: hdwy over 1f out: r.o wl u.p to ld nr fin* **7/1**
525- **2** 1/2 **Quince (IRE)**[26] 7785 6-9-13 78 (v) JimmyQuinn 1 69
(J Pearce) *hld up in tch: led jst ins fnl f: rdn and hdd nr fin* **7/4**[1]
13-0 **3** 1/2 **Spume (IRE)**[10] 126 5-9-5 53 (t) AdamKirby 6 60
(S Parr) *hld up in mid-div: stdy prog over 3f out: rdn over 1f out: styd on towards fin* **10/1**
053- **4** 1 1/4 **Nawamees (IRE)**[21] 7831 11-8-13 70 (p) StephenDonohoe 8 52
(P D Evans) *chsd ldr: led over 3f out: rdn and hdd over 2f out: ev ch ins fnl f: no ex towards fin* **5/2**[2]
520- **5** 1 **Calzaghe (IRE)**[96] 6775 5-8-12 67 (v) NSLawes(7) 9 56
(D Nicholls) *t.k.h early: sn prom: led over 2f out: rdn wl over 1f out: hdd jst ins fnl f: fdd towards fin* **4/1**[3]
600- **6** 12 **Mister Maq**[42] 7634 6-8-9 35 (b) AndrewElliott 7 27
(A Crook) *hld up and bhd: pushed along 3f out: sn struggling* **200/1**
000- **7** 7 **Still Dreaming**[61] 7400 5-8-3 40 (b) DeclanCannon(7) 4 17
(R J Price) *led: hdd over 3f out: wknd wl over 2f out* **33/1**

2m 43.23s (2.13) **Going Correction** +0.125s/f (Slow) **7 Ran SP% 110.0**
Speed ratings (Par 101): **97,96,96,95,94 86,82**
toteswinger: 1&2 £3.00, 1&3 £3.30, 2&3 £3.20. CSF £18.20 TOTE £7.90: £2.50, £1.70; EX 24.00 Trifecta £53.50 Pool: £513.79 - 7.10 winning units..
Owner Diamond Racing Ltd **Bred** Mrs Edgar Scott Jr & Mrs Lawrence Macelree **Trained** Pandy, Monmouths
■ Stewards' Enquiry : Stephen Donohoe one-day ban: failed to ride to draw (Feb 4); two-day ban: careless riding (Feb 5-6)

FOCUS
A modest claimer which was slowly run, and the form is a bit dubious. The third seems the best guide.

238 PLAY BINGO @ WILLIAMHILL.COM H'CAP 1m 141y(P)
3:50 (3:50) (Class 5) (0-75,74) 4-Y-O+ **£2,729** (£806; £403) **Stalls** Low

Form RPR
612- **1** **Plush**[32] 7750 6-8-13 68 RichardKingscote 4 87+
(Tom Dascombe) *s.i.s: hld up and bhd: c wd st: hdwy to ld 1f out: easily* **15/8**[1]
120- **2** 3 3/4 **Star Strider**[22] 7821 5-9-4 73 SteveDrowne 5 80
(Miss Gay Kelleway) *hld up: hdwy on outside over 2f out: chal over 1f out: no ch w wnr ins fnl f* **9/1**
060- **3** 2 1/4 **Bull Market (IRE)**[171] 4662 6-9-5 74 StephenDonohoe 1 76
(Ian Williams) *hld up and bhd: hdwy wl over 1f out: rdn and kpt on same pce ins fnl f* **16/1**
61-0 **4** 2 **Bourse (IRE)**[2] 220 4-8-11 67 GregFairley 9 64
(A G Foster) *a.p: rdn and ev ch over 1f out: wknd ins fnl f* **9/1**
46-1 **5** 3/4 **Watson's Bay**[14] 80 4-8-12 68 FergusSweeney 2 64
(Miss Tor Sturgis) *hld up in tch: rdn and wknd ins fnl f* **7/2**[2]
60-0 **6** 1 1/4 **Stark Contrast (USA)**[11] 125 5-8-6 61 HayleyTurner 3 54
(M D I Usher) *led over 1f: chsd ldr: led wl over 1f out: sn edgd rt: hdd 1f out: wknd ins fnl f* **10/1**
044- **7** 2 **Ninth House (USA)**[26] 7786 7-8-11 66 (b) PaulMulrennan 8 54
(Mrs R A Carr) *s.i.s: sn prom: led 7f out: hdd wl over 1f out: sn rdn and wknd* **8/1**[3]
10-0 **8** 2 3/4 **Willie Ever**[2] 218 5-9-2 71 DarrenWilliams 7 53
(I W McInnes) *hld up in tch: wknd wl over 1f out* **16/1**
313- **9** 31 **Kingsholm**[25] 7796 7-8-13 68 LeeEnstone 6 —
(N Wilson) *hld up: hdwy over 6f out: rdn over 3f out: wknd over 2f out* **12/1**

1m 50.47s (-0.03) **Going Correction** +0.125s/f (Slow)
WFA 4 from 5yo+ 1lb **9 Ran SP% 116.7**
Speed ratings (Par 103): **105,101,99,97,97 96,94,91,64**
toteswinger: 1&2 £2.90, 1&3 £9.80, 2&3 £22.30. CSF £20.12 CT £212.80 TOTE £2.60: £1.50, £2.40, £4.50; EX 23.50 Trifecta £219.20 Pool: £432.65 - 1.46 winning units..
Owner John Reed **Bred** Cheveley Park Stud Ltd **Trained** Lambourn, Berks

FOCUS
A modest handicap that saw virtually all of them in with a chance as they straightened for home. Hold-up horses dominated and the winner continues to progress.
Ninth House(USA) Official explanation: jockey said gelding was reluctant to race in the early stages
Kingsholm Official explanation: jockey said gelding ran flat

239 WILLIAM HILL TELEBETTING ON 0800 44 40 40 H'CAP 1m 141y(P)
4:20 (4:20) (Class 5) (0-70,71) 3-Y-O **£2,729** (£806; £403) **Stalls** Low

Form RPR
04-3 **1** **Common Diva**[9] 136 3-8-12 63 RobertWinston 3 70
(A J McCabe) *chsd ldr: led wl over 1f out: rdn ins fnl f: r.o wl* **11/2**[3]
220- **2** 1 3/4 **Captainrisk (IRE)**[42] 7622 3-9-4 69 JimmyQuinn 1 72
(M Botti) *hld up in tch: rdn over 1f out: chsd wnr fnl f: no imp* **11/8**[1]
-410 **3** 1 1/2 **Hawkspring (IRE)**[4] 205 3-9-2 67 (t[1]) AdamKirby 7 67
(S Parr) *a.p: rdn and one pce fnl f* **6/1**
06-0 **4** 2 3/4 **Screaming Brave**[11] 121 3-8-9 60 TonyCulhane 5 53
(M R Channon) *hld up in rr: kpt on to take 4th nr fin: nvr trbld ldrs* **10/1**
00-1 **5** hd **My Sweet Georgia (IRE)**[8] 149 3-9-6 71 6ex MickyFenton 6 64
(S A Callaghan) *hld up: rdn over 1f out: no rspnse* **7/2**[2]
00-3 **6** 1 **Rigged**[5] 196 3-8-4 55 oh5 (b[1]) RichardThomas 4 45
(J A Osborne) *led: pushed along over 2f out: hdd wl over 1f out: wknd ins fnl f* **10/1**

1m 53.73s (3.23) **Going Correction** +0.125s/f (Slow) **6 Ran SP% 112.2**
Speed ratings (Par 97): **90,88,87,84,84 83**
toteswinger: 1&2 £2.50, 1&3 £3.00, 2&3 £2.50. CSF £13.57 TOTE £6.10: £2.20, £1.20; EX 15.40.
Owner Alotincommon Partnership **Bred** Llety Stud **Trained** Averham Park, Notts

FOCUS
There was not much pace on in this moderate handicap. The form is messy and pretty weak.

240 DINE IN THE HORIZONS RESTAURANT MEDIAN AUCTION MAIDEN STKS 1m 4f 50y(P)
4:50 (4:51) (Class 5) 4-6-Y-O **£2,729** (£806; £403) **Stalls** Low

Form RPR
3- **1** **Castaneous (IRE)**[46] 7583 5-9-7 0 (b) DaneO'Neill 2 66+
(P J Rothwell, Ire) *a.p: led wl over 2f out: sn clr: eased ins fnl f* **4/6**[1]
430- **2** 8 **Valentine Blue**[90] 6929 4-9-3 48 (p) JimmyQuinn 5 50
(A B Haynes) *a.p: wnt 2nd over 4f out: ev ch wl over 2f out: sn btn* **6/1**[3]
-463 **3** 5 **General Tufto**[6] 174 4-8-10 42 (b) RichardRowe(7) 6 42
(C Smith) *led after 1f: hdd wl over 2f out: wknd wl over 1f out* **10/1**
0-6 **4** 5 **Special Chapter (IRE)**[16] 42 4-8-5 0 PNolan(7) 3 29
(A B Haynes) *bhd: reminders after 3f: rdn over 5f out: struggling over 3f out* **33/1**
0- **5** 25 **Hurforharmony (IRE)**[37] 7688 6-9-2 45 RobertWinston 1 —
(Adrian McGuinness, Ire) *prom tl wknd over 2f out* **10/3**[2]
500/ **6** 4 1/2 **Taran Tregarth**[24] 6835 5-8-13 38 DuranFentiman(3) 7 —
(W M Brisbourne) *led 1f: w ldr tl over 4f out: wknd over 3f out* **25/1**
7 134 **Listen Carefully (IRE)**[61] 7410 5-9-2 0 AdamKirby 4 —
(P J Rothwell, Ire) *a in rr: lost tch over 3f out: virtually p.u fnl f* **16/1**

2m 41.48s (0.38) **Going Correction** +0.125s/f (Slow)
WFA 4 from 5yo+ 4lb **7 Ran SP% 119.1**
Speed ratings: **103,97,94,91,74 71,—**
toteswinger: 1&2 £1.70, 1&3 £2.80, 2&3 £3.50. CSF £5.94 TOTE £1.70: £1.10, £3.00; EX 7.60.
Owner Celtic Dragon Syndicate **Bred** S Donohoe **Trained** Tinahely, Co. Wicklow

FOCUS
A very weak, uncompetitive maiden. Easy for Castaneous, who didn't need to improve.
Hurforharmony(IRE) Official explanation: jockey said mare lost her action
Listen Carefully(IRE) Official explanation: jockey said mare moved poorly throughout

241 PLAY POKER @ WILLIAMHILL.COM H'CAP 7f 32y(P)
5:20 (5:22) (Class 5) (0-70,70) 4-Y-O+ **£3,070** (£906; £453) **Stalls** High

Form RPR
/0-0 **1** **Dark Tara**[14] 76 4-8-8 60 PaulHanagan 7 70
(R A Fahey) *hld up and bhd: hdwy over 2f out: led jst over 1f out: drvn out* **66/1**
015- **2** 1/2 **A Big Sky Brewing (USA)**[22] 7829 5-8-12 69 (b) DeanHeslop(5) 5 78
(T D Barron) *hld up in tch: rdn over 2f out: ev ch over 1f out: kpt on u.str.p ins fnl f* **7/1**[2]
03-5 **3** 2 **Salt Of The Earth (IRE)**[18] 28 4-9-0 66 RobertHavlin 6 70
(T G Mills) *hld up and bhd: swtchd rt and hdwy over 1f out: kpt on ins fnl f* **16/1**
50-4 **4** 1/2 **Inside Story (IRE)**[7] 155 7-8-12 64 (b) AdamKirby 9 66
(C R Dore) *s.i.s: hld up in rr: pushed wd ent st: styd on fnl f: nvr able to chal* **20/1**
0-33 **5** 4 **Whitbarrow (IRE)**[13] 94 10-9-0 69 (b) JamesMillman(3) 3 60
(B R Millman) *sn chsng ldr: led over 3f out: rdn over 2f out: hdd jst over 1f out: wknd ins fnl f* **14/1**[3]
11-1 **6** 1 1/2 **Milne Bay (IRE)**[8] 141 4-9-2 68 6ex (t) JimmyQuinn 2 55
(D M Simcock) *hld up in tch: swtchd rt and n.m.r over 3f out: n.m.r over 1f out: wknd ins fnl f* **4/6**[1]
106- **7** 3 1/2 **Romantic Verse**[22] 7829 4-9-1 67 GrahamGibbons 4 45
(E S McMahon) *prom: nt clr run briefly over 1f out: sn rdn and wknd* **16/1**
200- **8** 38 **Orpen's Art (IRE)**[91] 6915 4-9-3 69 DaneO'Neill 1 —
(George Baker) *led: hdd over 3f out: hmpd on ins wl over 2f out: wknd qckly* **33/1**

1m 28.96s (-0.64) **Going Correction** +0.125s/f (Slow) **8 Ran SP% 100.1**
Speed ratings (Par 103): **108,107,105,104,100 98,94,50**
toteswinger: 1&2 £27.40, 1&3 £35.70, 2&3 £3.90. CSF £336.66 CT £4571.93 TOTE £47.80: £18.90, £1.40, £3.60; EX 341.70 TRIFECTA Not won..
Owner J E M Hawkins Ltd **Bred** J E M Hawkins Ltd **Trained** Musley Bank, N Yorks
■ Stewards' Enquiry : Jimmy Quinn three-day ban: careless riding (Feb 4-6)

FOCUS
A modest handicap but it was run at a good gallop and the winner's victory was no fluke despite the big price.

242 WOLVERHAMPTON CORPORATE HOSPITALITY - A PLEASURE APPRENTICE H'CAP 7f 32y(P)
5:50 (5:51) (Class 6) (0-60,60) 4-Y-0+ £2,047 (£604; £302) Stalls High

Form RPR
0-1 1 **Downhill Skier (IRE)**[11] 118 5-9-0 60 PaulPickard(5) 6 68
(W M Brisbourne) *hld up in mid-div: hdwy over 3f out: led wl over 1f out: rdn fnl f: r.o* 3/1[1]
00-6 2 nk **Ten Pole Tudor**[12] 105 4-8-13 59 SPRyan(5) 4 66
(R A Harris) *s.i.s: in rr: c v wd st: rdn and hdwy over 1f out: edgd lft and r.o ins fnl f: nt rch wnr* 4/1[2]
440- 3 2 **Fraizer (IRE)**[37] 7692 5-8-0 46 oh1 AlexEdwards(5) 11 48
(Adrian McGuinness, Ire) *hld up and bhd: hdwy over 2f out: chsd wnr fnl f: sn edgd lft: one pce* 8/1
31-4 4 2 **Loyal Royal (IRE)**[7] 166 6-8-11 57 (b) NathanAlison(5) 2 53+
(J M Bradley) *plld hrd: prom: chsd wnr wl over 1f out tl no ex fnl f* 13/2
00-0 5 ½ **Weetfromthechaff**[12] 108 4-8-7 53 (p) DavidKenny(5) 5 48
(R Hollinshead) *hld up and bhd: hdwy over 2f out: no imp fnl f* 33/1
0-01 6 hd **Stargazy**[12] 104 5-8-5 51 HollyHall(5) 9 45
(W G M Turner) *hld up and bhd: hdwy on outside 3f out: c wd st: rdn over 1f out: no imp fnl f* 11/1
0-06 7 2¾ **Dasheena**[9] 133 6-8-4 48 (p) KarenKenny(3) 12 35
(A J McCabe) *chsd ldrs: rdn over 1f out: wknd ins fnl f* 18/1
3-62 8 nse **Dancing Duo**[3] 210 5-8-2 50 ow3 (v) LeeTopliss(7) 8 37
(D Shaw) *in rr: struggling 4f out: nvr nr ldrs* 5/1[3]
00-0 9 4 **Diminuto**[8] 146 5-8-8 56 SeanPalmer(7) 10 32
(M D I Usher) *mid-div: lost pl over 3f out: n.d after* 50/1
060- 10 2¼ **Imperial Djay (IRE)**[29] 7772 4-8-13 57 (p) JohnCavanagh(3) 3 27
(G J Smith) *chsd ldr tl rdn over 2f out: wknd wl over 1f out* 12/1
25-0 11 7 **Harrison's Flyer (IRE)**[11] 114 8-8-11 52 (b) PNolan 1 3
(J M Bradley) *led: rdn over 2f out: hdd wl over 1f out: sn wknd* 16/1

1m 30.36s (0.76) **Going Correction** +0.125s/f (Slow) 11 Ran SP% 118.2
Speed ratings (Par 101): **100,99,97,95,94 94,91,91,86,83 75**
toteswinger: 1&2 £4.70, 1&3 £10.10, 2&3 £9.70. CSF £14.69 CT £89.62 TOTE £4.80: £1.70, £2.00, £3.30; EX 19.30 Trifecta £249.50 Part won. Place 6: £60.27 Place 5: £12.53.
Owner Miss P D Insull **Bred** Swettenham Stud **Trained** Great Ness, Shropshire
■ Stewards' Enquiry : Sean Palmer one-day ban: failed to ride to draw (Feb 4)

FOCUS
An ordinary apprentices' handicap run at a good gallop. The form is sound.
Imperial Djay(IRE) Official explanation: trainer said gelding had a breathing problem
T/Plt: £75.70 to a £1 stake. Pool: £82,351.75. 793.75 winning tickets. T/Qpdt: £5.60 to a £1 stake. Pool: £7,135.60. 928.06 winning tickets. KH

229 KEMPTON (A.W) (R-H)
Thursday, January 22

OFFICIAL GOING: Standard
Wind: Moderate, across Weather: Dry 1st 4 races, heavy rain remainder

243 BLUE SQUARE CASINO H'CAP 5f (P)
6:50 (6:50) (Class 5) (0-70,70) 4-Y-0+ £5,051 (£1,503; £751; £375) Stalls High

Form RPR
06-3 1 **Drifting Gold**[13] 99 5-9-0 66 (v) AdamKirby 10 77
(C G Cox) *settled in midfield: prog 2f out: clsd 1f out: led ins fnl f: kpt on* 8/1
26-6 2 ½ **Incomparable**[15] 76 4-9-3 69 (p) MickyFenton 9 78
(A J McCabe) *dwlt but rousted up to press ldr and led after 1f: drvn over 1f out: hdd ins fnl f: kpt on but a hld* 5/1[2]
44-1 3 1¼ **What Katie Did (IRE)**[19] 27 4-8-12 64 (p) SteveDrowne 7 69
(J M Bradley) *a chsng ldrs: kpt on same pce u.p fr over 1f out* 11/1
50-4 4 ½ **Steel City Boy (IRE)**[14] 83 6-9-1 67 JimCrowley 1 70
(D Shaw) *towards rr: rdn 2f out: prog on inner over 1f out: kpt on but nvr able to chal* 12/1
63-0 5 1½ **Asian Power (IRE)**[7] 167 4-9-2 68 RobertHavlin 11 65+
(P J O'Gorman) *stdd s: hld up in last trio: nvr remotely on terms: nudged along fr over 1f out: running on fin and appeared to fin w plenty lft* 9/2[1]
100- 6 shd **Fizzlephut (IRE)**[30] 7774 7-8-6 58 WandersonD'Avila 6 55
(Miss J R Tooth) *chsd ldrs: u.p 2f out: struggling after: plugged on* 33/1
2-02 7 ½ **Compton Classic**[8] 166 7-8-6 58 (vt) PaulDoe 5 53
(Tom Dascombe) *dwlt: t.k.h: hld up in 8th: shuffled along over 1f out: kpt on but nvr remotely nr ldrs* 7/1
42-0 8 shd **Colorus (IRE)**[14] 89 6-8-11 63 (p) JoeFanning 8 58
(W J H Ratcliffe) *led 1f: chsd ldr to jst ins fnl f: wknd rapidly* 15/2
0-02 9 nk **Gwilym (GER)**[13] 99 6-8-12 64 HayleyTurner 12 58+
(D Haydn Jones) *sn stdd and hld up in last trio: stl last on inner over 1f out: nt clr run sn after: appeared to fin w plenty lft* 11/2[3]
041- 10 1 **Cosmic Destiny (IRE)**[52] 7517 7-9-4 70 LPKeniry 3 60+
(E F Vaughan) *stdd s: hld up in last trio: nvr remotely on terms: shuffled along and no prog fnl f* 12/1
5-01 11 1½ **Ten Down**[13] 99 4-9-0 66 MartinDwyer 4 51
(M Quinn) *awkward s: sn chsd ldrs on outer: lost pl 2f out: sn wknd* 12/1

59.43 secs (-1.07) **Going Correction** -0.075s/f (Stan) 11 Ran SP% 120.0
Speed ratings (Par 103): **105,104,102,101,99 98,98,97,97,95 93**
toteswinger: 1&2 £14.70, 1&3 £15.40, 2&3 £16.30. CSF £48.78 CT £450.97 TOTE £11.00: £4.70, £2.40, £1.90; EX 62.10.
Owner Martin C Oliver **Bred** Witney And Warren Enterprises Ltd **Trained** Lambourn, Berks

FOCUS
A modest handicap. The time was decent and the form among the principals is sound, although nothing got into the race form the rear.
Colorus(IRE) Official explanation: jockey said gelding hung left
Gwilym(GER) Official explanation: jockey said gelding was denied a clear run
Cosmic Destiny(IRE) Official explanation: jockey said mare was denied a clear run

244 BLUE SQUARE CLAIMING STKS 1m 2f (P)
7:20 (7:28) (Class 5) 4-Y-0+ £3,561 (£1,059; £529; £264) Stalls High

Form RPR
15-1 1 **Sabre Light**[12] 119 4-9-0 77 (v) LiamJones 2 83
(J Pearce) *hld up in last pair: pushed along over 2f out: prog on wd outside to ld over 1f out: sn drew rt away* 1/1[1]
005- 2 7 **Wahoo Sam (USA)**[26] 7790 9-8-5 56 CatherineGannon 3 58
(P D Evans) *pressed ldr: rdn to ld jst over 2f out: hdd over 1f out: no ch w wnr after* 66/1
230- 3 1¼ **Inquest**[74] 7260 4-8-9 69 JimCrowley 5 62
(Mrs A J Perrett) *in tch: cl enough wl over 1f out: sn nt qckn u.p and btn* 10/1
010- 4 5 **Don Pietro**[47] 7580 6-8-9 71 (p) HayleyTurner 1 50
(R Curtis) *led to jst over 2f out: wknd over 1f out* 13/2[3]
25-1 5 10 **Slip**[19] 29 4-9-3 84 MartinDwyer 4 40
(J R Boyle) *trckd ldng pair 6f out: hrd rdn over 2f out: sn btn: wknd bdly fnl f* 13/8[2]
50-0 6 25 **Cover Drive (USA)**[16] 59 6-8-9 53 (b) EdwardCreighton 6 —
(Christian Wroe) *dwlt: t.k.h and hanging bdly thrght: lost tch over 3f out: virtually p.u* 50/1

2m 6.92s (-1.08) **Going Correction** -0.075s/f (Stan)
WFA 4 from 6yo+ 2lb 6 Ran SP% 114.0
Speed ratings (Par 103): **101,95,94,90,82 62**
toteswinger: 1&2 £6.80, 1&3 £2.50, 2&3 £13.60. CSF £54.47 TOTE £1.80: £1.10, £11.70; EX 46.00.
Owner Jeff Pearce **Bred** D J And Mrs Deer **Trained** Newmarket, Suffolk
■ Blacktoft (7/2) was withdrawn (bolted on way to s). R4 applies, deduct 20p in the £. New market formed.

FOCUS
With his main rival not running up to form, the favourite did not have much to beat. He still produced another slightly improved effort.
Cover Drive(USA) Official explanation: jockey said gelding hung badly throughout

245 BLUE SQUARE MOBILE (S) STKS 6f (P)
7:50 (7:56) (Class 5) 4-Y-0+ £3,070 (£906; £453) Stalls High

Form RPR
50-5 1 **Interactive (IRE)**[6] 189 6-8-12 64 HayleyTurner 4 71
(Andrew Turnell) *chsd ldng pair: clsd 2f out: rdn to ld over 1f out: pushed out firmly and kpt on fnl f* 8/1
60/3 2 1½ **Stonecrabstomorrow (IRE)**[14] 87 6-8-12 64 (p) PaulHanagan 9 67
(R A Fahey) *chsd ldrs: drvn and effrt over 2f out: wnt 2nd jst over 1f out: kpt on but no real imp on wnr* 3/1[2]
0-02 3 1¾ **Wiltshire (IRE)**[13] 108 7-8-12 56 (v) MickyFenton 5 61
(P T Midgley) *chsd ldrs: effrt over 2f out: cl enough bhd ldng pair over 1f out: drvn and fin v weakly* 7/1
3-22 4 ¾ **One More Round (USA)**[6] 189 11-9-4 72 (b) JimCrowley 7 65
(P D Evans) *hld up in 7th: smooth prog over 2f out to chse ldrs: rdn and no rspnse over 1f out: one pce after* 2/1[1]
-356 5 ¾ **Obe Royal**[1] 235 5-8-12 64 (b) PaulDoe 8 56
(P D Evans) *awkward s: drvn hrd to ld: hdd 2f out: steadily fdd* 4/1[3]
05-1 6 2½ **Mafaheem**[14] 87 7-9-4 67 RobertHavlin 1 54
(A B Haynes) *dropped in fr wd draw and hld up in 8th: rdn and struggling over 2f out: modest late prog* 14/1
0-04 7 nk **Red Rudy**[16] 57 7-8-12 65 AdamKirby 2 47
(A W Carroll) *v restless in stalls: pressed ldr: led 2f out: hdd and fnd nil over 1f out: wknd tamely fnl f* 16/1
04-0 8 4 **Ben**[13] 99 4-8-12 54 (v) SteveDrowne 6 34
(P G Murphy) *mostly in midfield: effrt on inner over 2f out: wknd rapidly over 1f out* 50/1
0-00 9 17 **Tagula Sands (IRE)**[8] 153 5-8-5 40 (p) GemmaElford(7) 3 —
(J C Fox) *dropped in fr wd draw and hld up last: drifted towards nr side in st and sn t.o* 100/1

1m 13.01s (-0.09) **Going Correction** +0.20s/f (Slow) 9 Ran SP% 117.4
Speed ratings (Par 103): **108,106,103,102,101 98,97,92,69**
toteswinger: 1&2 £6.20, 1&3 £10.40, 2&3 £5.20. CSF £32.85 TOTE £9.00: £2.40, £1.20, £2.70; EX 40.10.There was no bid for the winner.
Owner Griffiths Gifts Limited **Bred** J Cullinan **Trained** Broad Hinton, Wilts

FOCUS
A reasonable and competitive seller. The winner is rated back towards somewhere near his form of last winter.
Tagula Sands(IRE) Official explanation: jockey said gelding hung badly left throughout

246 BLUE SQUARE SP GUARANTEE H'CAP 6f (P)
8:20 (8:22) (Class 6) (0-55,55) 3-Y-O £3,043 (£905; £452; £226) Stalls High

Form RPR
3-12 1 **Kheley (IRE)**[10] 135 3-9-1 54 LiamJones 4 57
(W M Brisbourne) *t.k.h early: hld up in last pair: rdn over 2f out: gd prog on wd outside fr ins fnl 2f to ld jst over 1f out: idled and drvn out* 5/2[1]
05-5 2 ¾ **Sorrel Ridge (IRE)**[15] 75 3-8-13 52 (p) AdamKirby 6 56+
(M G Quinlan) *trckd ldrs on inner: gng strly whn chopped off wl over 1f out and swtchd lft: styd on fnl f to take 2nd last strides* 9/2[3]
40-3 3 hd **Mean Mr Mustard (IRE)**[10] 135 3-9-1 54 (b) JimCrowley 1 54
(J A Osborne) *led and allowed easy ld: drvn 2f out: sn hung rt: hdd jst over 1f out: nt qckn: lost 2nd last strides* 11/2
4-55 4 2½ **Sills Vincero**[14] 91 3-9-2 55 SteveDrowne 5 47
(D Shaw) *chsd ldr: effrt and cl up whn hmpd on inner over 1f out: brief rally 1f out: wknd last 100yds* 4/1[2]
504- 5 4 **Silver Salsa**[49] 7543 3-9-0 53 FergusSweeney 2 32
(J R Jenkins) *t.k.h: hld up in tch: rdn over 2f out: wknd over 1f out* 16/1
330- 6 ½ **Lady Gem**[34] 7728 3-8-10 49 (p) PaulHanagan 3 27
(D H Brown) *t.k.h: disp 2nd pl: drvn 2f out: wknd tamely jst over 1f out* 11/2
000- 7 2½ **Pepin (IRE)**[55] 7465 3-8-10 49 HayleyTurner 7 19
(D Haydn Jones) *settled in last: shkn up over 2f out: no prog* 9/1

1m 14.66s (1.56) **Going Correction** +0.20s/f (Slow) 7 Ran SP% 113.4
Speed ratings (Par 95): **97,96,95,92,87 86,83**
toteswinger: 1&2 £2.90, 1&3 £3.40, 2&3 £7.40. CSF £13.70 TOTE £3.80: £1.50, £2.10; EX 15.00.
Owner W M Clare **Bred** Matt Gilsenan **Trained** Great Ness, Shropshire

FOCUS
The time compared well to the previous seller and the winner posted a personal best. The form is rated through the third.

247 BLUE SQUARE POKER CLASSIFIED STKS 1m (P)
8:50 (8:54) (Class 7) 3-Y-O+ £2,047 (£604; £302) Stalls High

Form RPR
060- 1 **Prince Rossi (IRE)**[232] 2731 5-9-6 44 (v[1]) JimCrowley 8 49
(A E Price) *quick move to ld after 1f: mde rest: kpt on steadily u.p whn chal fnl 2f: fnlly asserted last 75yds: hld on* 15/2[3]
400- 2 ½ **Your Golf Travel**[181] 4381 4-9-6 42 SteveDrowne 12 48
(M Wigham) *trckd ldrs: wnt 3rd jst over 2f out but sn u.str.p: no imp tl kpt on ins fnl f to take 2nd nr fin* 7/2[2]
0-02 3 ¾ **Mr Rev**[8] 153 6-9-6 45 (b) FergusSweeney 9 46
(J M Bradley) *trckd wnr after 1f: persistent chal fr over 2f out: stl upsides ins fnl f: wknd last 75yds* 8/1

64-0 **4** *nk* **Amwell House**[16] 61 4-9-6 42................................ SimonWhitworth 10 46+
(J R Jenkins) *s.s: settled wl in rr: prog u.p on outer fr 2f out: clsd on ldrs ent fnl f: nt qckn after* **14/1**

30-5 **5** *shd* **The Power Of Phil**[11] 131 5-9-6 42...................... RichardKingscote 11 46
(Tom Dascombe) *dwlt: rousted up to rch midfield: hrd rdn over 2f out: tried to cl on ldrs 1f out: one pce fnl 100yds* **5/2**[1]

0-61 **6** *1 ½* **Kinsman (IRE)**[11] 131 12-9-7 42.................................(p) AmyBaker(5) 7 48
(T D McCarthy) *hld up in midfield on inner: rdn over 2f out: plugged on but nvr rchd ldrs* **12/1**

-005 **7** *nse* **Silver Spruce**[9] 145 4-8-13 45...(p) HollyHall(7) 6 42
(D Flood) *t.k.h: hld up wl in rr: prog u.p on wd outside fr 2f out: no ex fnl f* **16/1**

5-50 **8** *3* **Ma Ridge**[11] 131 5-9-6 44.. RobertHavlin 4 35
(T D McCarthy) *t.k.h: snatched up after 1f: hld up in midfield: drvn and no prog 2f out* **33/1**

/00- **9** *1* **Almora Guru**[157] 5157 5-9-6 45... LiamJones 2 33
(W M Brisbourne) *a in rr: last and struggling wl over 2f out: modest late prog* **33/1**

-053 **10** *2 ½* **Beckenham's Secret**[11] 131 5-9-6 42........................... AdamKirby 14 27
(A W Carroll) *led at dawdle for 1f: prom tl wknd 2f out* **17/2**

00-0 **11** *2 ¾* **Lady Charlemagne**[16] 61 4-9-6 45............................(b[1]) LukeMorris 5 21
(N P Littmoden) *t.k.h: hld up in midfield: no prog over 2f out: sn wknd* **40/1**

6-30 **12** *1 ¼* **Baba Ghanoush**[8] 153 7-9-6 44....................................(b) PaulDoe 1 18
(M J Attwater) *racd wd: in tch: lost pl u.p over 2f out: sn no ch* **40/1**

0-20 **13** *2* **I Certainly May**[6] 186 4-9-6 45..................................(p) NickyMackay 3 13
(S Dow) *chsd ldrs on outer: u.p fr 1/2-way: wknd 3f out* **8/1**

1m 42.7s (2.90) **Going Correction** +0.20s/f (Slow) 13 Ran SP% **126.3**
Speed ratings (Par 97): **93,92,91,91,91 89,89,86,85,83 80,79,77**
toteswinger: 1&2 £9.30, 1&3 £13.70, 2&3 £8.60. CSF £35.08 TOTE £10.10: £3.30, £2.40, £1.90; EX 51.50.
Owner Business Development Consultants Limited **Bred** Sir Eric Parker **Trained** Leominster, H'fords
■ Stewards' Enquiry : Richard Kingscote one-day ban: careless riding (Feb 6)

FOCUS
This was slowly run and looks weak form, even for this grade.
Lady Charlemagne Official explanation: jockey said filly ran too free

248 BLUE SQUARE APPRENTICE H'CAP — 1m 4f (P)
9:20 (9:20) (Class 6) (0-55,55) 4-Y-0+ **£3,043** (£905; £452; £226) **Stalls** Centre

Form RPR

403- **1** **Ben Bacchus (IRE)**[26] 7787 7-8-6 49..................................... KierenFox(7) 3 57
(P W Hiatt) *prom: pushed along 5f out: prog over 2f out: narrow ld over 1f out: kpt on wl and jst hld on* **11/1**

12/5 **2** *nk* **Bernabeu (IRE)**[20] 18 7-8-12 53...................................... RyanClark(5) 13 61
(S Curran) *prom: effrt over 2f out: chal over 1f out: pressed wnr after: urged along and jst hld* **10/3**[1]

52-0 **3** *2 ½* **Sir Liam (USA)**[20] 18 5-9-3 53... PNolan 9 57
(Tom Dascombe) *wl plcd: nt qckn over 2f out: wnt 3rd over 1f out: kpt on but no imp on ldng pair* **7/1**

3-05 **4** *4* **Desert Hawk**[13] 107 8-8-10 49............................... MatthewLawson(3) 5 46
(W M Brisbourne) *restless stalls: s.s: hit rail after 3f: wl in rr tl prog on wd outside over 3f out: styd on fnl 2f: nt rch ldrs* **11/1**

460/ **5** *shd* **King Gabriel (IRE)**[44] 976 7-8-10 51........................ ThomasBubb(5) 12 48
(Andrew Turnell) *hld up in midfield: in rr of main gp over 2f out: kpt on fr over 1f out: n.d* **5/1**[2]

00-5 **6** *nse* **Touch Of Style (IRE)**[6] 186 5-9-0 55........................(v) NathanAlison(5) 2 52
(J R Boyle) *plld hrd on outer and hld up bhd ldrs: swtchd to inner 1/2-way but stl t.k.h: bmpd along 2f out: no imp* **8/1**

04-1 **7** *7* **Ruwain**[9] 145 5-9-1 54 6ex.............................. AndrewHeffernan(3) 10 40
(P J McBride) *led: drew 4 l clr over 3f out w rest being pushed along: wknd and hdd over 1f out* **13/2**[3]

500- **8** *½* **Blushing Hilary (IRE)**[27] 7520 6-8-8 49.................(p) TobyAtkinson(5) 6 34
(Mrs S J Humphrey) *a bhd: t.o 4f out: kpt on fnl 2f* **33/1**

3/-6 **9** *1 ¼* **Sue Princesse (IRE)**[4] 213 6-8-6 49...................... BryanJCooper(7) 8 32
(Ruaidhri Joseph Tierney, Ire) *chsd ldr 4f: prom tl wknd rapidly over 2f out* **12/1**

55-5 **10** *1* **Backlash**[12] 117 8-8-7 46 oh1...................................... KarenKenny(3) 1 27
(A W Carroll) *hld up on outer: prog to chse ldrs 4f out: wknd rapidly jst over 2f out* **33/1**

0/4- **11** *2 ¼* **Lady Llanover**[189] 4123 9-8-5 46 oh1.............................. HollyHall(5) 11 24
(P D Evans) *a bhd: lost tch over 3f out* **16/1**

02-2 **12** *7* **Poppy Red**[6] 187 4-8-1 46.......................................(p) PaulPickard(5) 4 12
(C J Gray) *chsd ldr after 4f to 3f out: wknd rapidly: t.o* **10/1**

060- **13** *8* **Malt Empress (IRE)**[35] 2719 4-8-8 48.................................... AmyScott 7 2
(B W Duke) *a bhd: lost tch over 3f out: t.o* **66/1**

2m 37.12s (2.62) **Going Correction** +0.20s/f (Slow)
WFA 4 from 5yo+ 4lb 13 Ran SP% **123.4**
Speed ratings (Par 101): **99,98,97,94,94 94,89,89,88,87 86,81,76**
toteswinger: 1&2 £11.20, 1&3 £7.40, 2&3 £8.30. CSF £48.62 CT £288.83 TOTE £11.70: £2.30, £1.90, £2.50; EX 73.10 Place 6 £134.79, Place 5 £41.10..
Owner Exors of the Late John Hedges **Bred** Elisabeth And Neil Draper **Trained** Hook Norton, Oxon
■ Kieren Fox's first winner.

FOCUS
A modest race run at an ordinary pace. The form is sound, rated around the first three.
T/Plt: £144.40 to a £1 stake. Pool: £106,898.11. 540.17 winning tickets. T/Qpdt: £30.20 to a £1 stake. Pool: £7,822.24. 191.30 winning tickets. JN

235 WOLVERHAMPTON (A.W) (L-H)
Thursday, January 22

OFFICIAL GOING: Standard
Wind: Fresh behind Weather: Cloudy with sunny spells

249 PLAY BINGO @ WILLIAMHILL.COM H'CAP (DIV I) — 2m 119y(P)
2:00 (2:00) (Class 6) (0-65,65) 4-Y-0+ **£1,706** (£503; £252) **Stalls** Low

Form RPR

/04- **1** **Market Watcher (USA)**[21] 7293 8-8-11 53..................... ShaneFoley(5) 10 60
(Seamus Fahey, Ire) *a.p: chsd ldr 11f out: led 5f out: drvn out* **7/1**[3]

44-2 **2** *½* **Vanquisher (IRE)**[12] 116 5-8-12 49........................(t) StephenDonohoe 2 56
(Ian Williams) *hld up: hdwy over 4f out: rdn to chse wnr over 1f out: styd on* **11/4**[1]

3 *1 ¼* **Winged Arrow (IRE)**[61] 7062 7-9-12 63........................ JamieMoriarty 9 68
(Jonjo O'Neill) *hld up: hdwy u.p over 2f out: styd on: nt rch ldrs* **10/1**

56-4 **4** *nk* **Tampa Boy (IRE)**[20] 11 7-10-0 65............................ FergusSweeney 6 70
(M F Harris) *a.p: chsd wnr over 4f out: rdn over 1f out: sn hung lft: no ex ins fnl f* **12/1**

02-5 **5** *7* **Squirtle (IRE)**[12] 112 6-9-7 58.. LukeMorris 3 54
(W M Brisbourne) *prom: rdn over 3f out: wknd fnl f* **11/4**[1]

5-50 **6** *14* **Auction Belle**[14] 90 4-8-4 48.................................. FrankieMcDonald 1 27
(R Curtis) *chsd ldrs: rdn over 5f out: wknd over 3f out* **33/1**

00-0 **7** *1 ¾* **Archimboldo (USA)**[9] 148 6-8-5 49...........................(b) JoshWall(7) 11 26
(T Wall) *s.s: hdwy to latch onto main gp after 3f: wknd 4f out* **14/1**

00-0 **8** *10* **Dasher Reilly (USA)**[7] 148 8-9-0 51................................... ChrisCatlin 8 16
(A Sadik) *in rr: hdwy after 3f: rdn and wknd over 3f out* **66/1**

000/ **9** *11* **Michaels Dream (IRE)**[75] 3300 10-8-6 46 oh1.....(b) DuranFentiman(3) 4 —
(N Wilson) *led: rdn and hdd 5f out: wknd 4f out* **20/1**

00-2 **P** **Our Nations**[20] 11 4-9-7 65.. DNolan 5 —
(D Carroll) *hld up: hdwy 6f out: p.u and dismntd sn after* **4/1**[2]

3m 42.81s (1.01) **Going Correction** +0.05s/f (Slow)
WFA 4 from 5yo+ 7lb 10 Ran SP% **118.5**
Speed ratings (Par 101): **99,98,98,98,94 88,87,82,77,—**
toteswinger: 1&2 £4.20, 1&3 £10.10, 2&3 £6.50. CSF £26.63 CT £197.47 TOTE £7.60: £2.20, £1.40, £3.60; EX 31.00 TRIFECTA Not won..
Owner J J Bailey **Bred** Phipps Stable **Trained** Monestereven, Co. Kildare

FOCUS
A moderate staying handicap and they went a modest pace until the tempo picked up around half a mile from home. The form is modest, with the runner-up the best guide.

250 ENJOY THE LUCKY 7 GROUP OFFER CLAIMING STKS — 5f 20y(P)
2:30 (2:30) (Class 6) 4-Y-0+ **£2,047** (£604; £302) **Stalls** Low

Form RPR

03-4 **1** **Harry Up**[21] 2 8-9-1 87...(p) JamieSpencer 1 93
(K A Ryan) *mde all: rdn clr over 1f out: r.o* **4/7**[1]

1P-1 **2** *3 ¼* **Godfrey Street**[14] 83 6-8-6 75.............................(p) DeclanCannon(7) 6 79
(A G Newcombe) *chsd ldrs: sn pushed along: rdn to chse wnr over 1f out: no imp* **4/1**[2]

230- **3** *5* **Desperate Dan**[93] 6881 8-8-5 71...................................(b) PNolan(7) 2 60
(A B Haynes) *s.i.s: hdwy over 3f out: wnt 2nd briefly 2f out: wknd fnl f* **17/2**[3]

-000 **4** *1 ½* **So Sublime**[2] 223 4-8-3 42......................................(b) AmyBaker(5) 5 51
(M C Chapman) *sn outpcd* **150/1**

10-0 **5** *8* **Dodaa (USA)**[16] 67 6-8-13 65... LeeEnstone 3 27
(N Wilson) *chsd wnr: rdn 1/2-way: wknd over 1f out* **14/1**

004- **6** *1 ¾* **First Trim (IRE)**[48] 7565 4-8-13 75................................ ShaneFoley(5) 7 26
(Seamus Fahey, Ire) *s.s: outpcd* **10/1**

61.05 secs (-1.25) **Going Correction** +0.05s/f (Slow) 6 Ran SP% **110.6**
Speed ratings (Par 101): **112,106,98,96,83 80**
toteswinger: 1&2 £1.30, 1&3 £1.50, 2&3 £2.60. CSF £3.04 TOTE £1.50: £1.10, £1.90; EX 3.30.
Owner The Fishermen **Bred** J E Rose **Trained** Hambleton, N Yorks

FOCUS
Plenty of front-runners in opposition for this 5f claimer, but nothing could match Harry Up, who arguably returned to his best but more likely matched his recent handicap form. The time was decent.

251 WOLVERHAMPTON CORPORATE HOSPITALITY - A PLEASURE MAIDEN FILLIES' STKS — 7f 32y(P)
3:00 (3:00) (Class 5) 3-Y-0+ **£2,590** (£770; £385; £192) **Stalls** High

Form RPR

42- **1** **Desert Bump**[38] 7689 3-8-8 0....................................... JamieSpencer 8 68+
(E F Vaughan) *sn led: hdd over 5f out: trckd ldrs: wnt 2nd over 1f out: led on bit ins fnl f: comf* **8/11**[1]

2 *¾* **Air Maze** 3-8-8 0.. StephenDonohoe 11 57+
(Sir Mark Prescott) *chsd ldrs: led over 5f out: rdn over 1f out: hdd and unable qck ins fnl f* **4/1**[2]

60- **3** *3* **Jaq's Sister**[27] 7830 3-8-8 0... JimmyQuinn 10 49
(M Blanshard) *chsd ldrs: rdn over 2f out: styd on same pce fnl f* **66/1**

0P- **4** *hd* **Crown Affair (IRE)**[175] 4562 3-8-8 0......................... SimonWhitworth 4 48
(J W Hills) *hld up: hdwy over 2f out: rdn over 1f out: nt rch ldrs* **40/1**

4 **5** *hd* **Singapore Girl**[18] 36 3-8-5 0.................................. DuranFentiman(3) 12 48
(G R Oldroyd) *chsd ldrs: rdn over 2f out: no ex fnl f* **25/1**

0- **6** *1* **Happy And Glorious (IRE)**[159] 5097 3-8-6 0 ow3.. GabrielHannon(5) 1 48+
(J W Hills) *hld up: hdwy and hung lft over 1f out: nt rch ldrs* **18/1**

0- **7** *1 ¼* **Buail Isteach (IRE)**[32] 7757 4-9-7 0......................... ShaneCreighton(5) 9 42
(E J Creighton) *s.i.s: hld up: hdwy over 1f out: no ex fnl f* **66/1**

25- **8** *2* **Twenty Score**[46] 7593 3-8-8 0.. PaulFitzsimons 3 36+
(Miss J R Tooth) *s.s: plld hrd: hdwy on outside over 4f out: rdn and wknd over 1f out* **9/2**[3]

9 *12* **Sampower Sarge (IRE)** 3-8-8 0.................................... AndrewElliott 6 4
(D Carroll) *hld up: rdn and wknd 1/2-way* **50/1**

10 *nse* **Sampower Shamrock (IRE)** 3-8-9 0 ow1.................. RobertWinston 7 5
(D Carroll) *a in rr: bhd fr 1/2-way* **14/1**

11 *8* **Miss Sampower (IRE)** 3-8-10 0 ow2.................................... DNolan 5 —
(D Carroll) *chsd ldrs: rdn 1/2-way: sn wknd* **40/1**

1m 31.51s (1.91) **Going Correction** +0.05s/f (Slow)
WFA 3 from 4yo+ 18lb 11 Ran SP% **121.7**
Speed ratings (Par 100): **91,90,86,86,86 85,83,81,67,67 58**
toteswinger: 1&2 £2.60, 1&3 £8.00, 2&3 £20.60. CSF £3.85 TOTE £1.80: £1.10, £1.20, £6.60; EX 5.30 Trifecta £80.70 Pool: £309.79 - 2.84 winning units..
Owner Mrs Emma Kennedy **Bred** Biddestone Stud **Trained** Newmarket, Suffolk

FOCUS
Not many could be seriously fancied in this maiden, but the pace was solid enough. A very weak race and the easy winner is rated value for 4l. The form behind the firfst two is likely to prove no better than plating class.
Twenty Score Official explanation: jockey said filly was reluctant to jump out of the stalls

252 PLAY BINGO @ WILLIAMHILL.COM H'CAP (DIV II) — 2m 119y(P)
3:30 (3:31) (Class 6) (0-65,64) 4-Y-0+ **£1,706** (£503; £252) **Stalls** Low

Form RPR

0-23 **1** **Dansilver**[16] 59 5-9-7 57.. LukeMorris 8 67
(A W Carroll) *hld up in tch: rdn over 1f out: led ins fnl f: styd on wl* **9/2**[2]

502- **2** *1* **Taxman (IRE)**[38] 7688 7-8-8 51................................. DeclanCannon(7) 1 60+
(A G Newcombe) *hld up: hdwy over 2f out: rdn and ev ch ins fnl f: no ex nr fin* **7/1**

40-2 **3** *5* **Pseudonym (IRE)**[6] 190 7-10-0 64..........................(vt) FergusSweeney 9 67
(M F Harris) *chsd ldrs: led 6f out: sn clr: rdn over 1f out: hdd and hung lft ins fnl f: wknd towards fin* **11/2**[3]

22-3 **4** *2 ¼* **Generous Star**[11] 126 6-9-8 58.. JimmyQuinn 5 58
(J Pearce) *hld up: pushed along over 4f out: hdwy over 3f out: sn rdn: wknd ins fnl f* **7/2**[1]

304- 5 3/4 **Daraiym (IRE)**[23] 7827 4-8-5 48 ChrisCatlin 7 47
(Paul Green) *chsd ldrs: rdn over 3f out: wknd fnl f* 6/1
00-3 6 nk **Que Beauty (IRE)**[20] 8 4-7-12 48 ow3 (p) AndrewHeffernan(7) 3 46
(R C Guest) *s.i.s: hld up: hdwy and hung lft over 1f out: nt trble ldrs* 40/1
600/ 7 10 **Flying Doctor**[38] 4096 6-8-13 49 PaulMulrennan 2 36
(N G Richards) *prom: rdn over 4f out: wknd 3f out* 17/2
25-5 8 3 3/4 **Kangrina**[9] 148 7-8-12 55 MatthewDavies(7) 11 37
(George Baker) *led over 10f: rdn over 4f out: wknd over 3f out* 20/1
0-60 9 7 **Siegfrieds Night (IRE)**[9] 148 8-8-4 45 (t) AmyBaker(5) 10 19
(M C Chapman) *chsd ldr 10f: wknd 4f out* 100/1
0/12 10 1 1/4 **Safin (GER)**[4] 213 9-9-2 52 JamieSpencer 4 24
(R Curtis) *hld up: effrt over 2f out: sn wknd and eased* 9/2[2]

3m 42.89s (1.09) **Going Correction** +0.05s/f (Slow)
WFA 4 from 5yo+ 7lb 10 Ran SP% **119.5**
Speed ratings (Par 101): **99,98,96,95,94 94,89,88,84,84**
toteswinger: 1&2 £6.40, 1&3 £4.90, 2&3 £8.10. CSF £36.46 CT £180.09 TOTE £6.40: £2.00, £2.70, £1.90; EX 36.60 Trifecta £204.10 Pool: £286.86 - 1.04 winning units..
Owner John W Egan **Bred** Mrs J L Egan **Trained** Cropthorne, Worcs

FOCUS
Another modest staying handicap, but unlike the first division the first two home came from well off the pace. The winning time was fractionally slower. The form is rated through the winner to last year's turf form.
Safin(GER) Official explanation: jockey said gelding hung right

253 WILLIAM HILL TELEBETTING ON 0800 44 40 40 H'CAP 1m 1f 103y(P)
4:00 (4:00) (Class 6) (0-65,65) 4-Y-0+ £2,047 (£604; £302) Stalls Low

Form RPR
61-2 1 **Formidable Guest**[6] 194 5-8-12 58 JimmyQuinn 8 65
(J Pearce) *hld up: hdwy over 2f out: rdn to ld wl ins fnl f: edgd lft: r.o* 10/3[1]
000- 2 hd **Watchmaker**[140] 5630 6-9-5 65 ChrisCatlin 11 71
(Miss Tor Sturgis) *chsd ldr tl led over 2f out: rdn over 1f out: hdd wl ins fnl f: r.o* 25/1
3-14 3 nse **Mambo Sun**[2] 224 6-9-5 65 RobertWinston 3 71
(R Curtis) *chsd ldrs: rdn over 2f out: r.o* 5/1[3]
303- 4 hd **Pelham Crescent (IRE)**[41] 7656 6-8-12 58 CatherineGannon 9 64
(B Palling) *s.i.s: hld up: swtchd lft and hdwy u.p over 1f out: r.o* 8/1
0-20 5 3/4 **Buscador (USA)**[6] 194 10-9-2 62 RichardKingscote 10 66
(W M Brisbourne) *sn led: rdn over 3f out: hdd over 2f out: unable qck nr fin* 25/1
56-5 6 3/4 **Debdene Bank (IRE)**[16] 60 6-9-2 62 DaleGibson 1 64
(Mrs Mary Hambro) *chsd ldrs: rdn over 2f out: styd on same pce ins fnl f* 20/1
5-35 7 nse **Magic Warrior**[8] 157 9-8-12 58 PaulFitzsimons 2 60
(J C Fox) *hld up in tch: racd keenly: rdn over 1f out: styd on same pce ins fnl f* 16/1
405- 8 3 1/4 **Alexander Guru**[66] 7367 5-8-11 57 DaneO'Neill 5 53
(M Blanshard) *hld up: hdwy over 2f out: rdn over 1f out: wknd ins fnl f* 8/1
31-0 9 6 **Royal Choir**[13] 100 5-8-9 55 LukeMorris 12 38
(H E Haynes) *chsd ldrs: rdn over 3f out: wknd over 2f out* 12/1
02-3 10 2 1/2 **Fandango Boy**[7] 172 8-8-11 64 JPFahy(7) 6 42
(D Carroll) *hld up: hdwy over 5f out: rdn over 2f out: wknd over 1f out* 7/2[2]
05-2 11 3 1/2 **Kings Topic (USA)**[17] 47 9-9-5 65 (p) StephenDonohoe 13 35
(A B Haynes) *sn pushed along and prom: rdn over 3f out: wknd over 2f out* 14/1
100/ 12 1 1/2 **Maidanni (USA)**[409] 7099 7-9-5 65 GregFairley 4 32
(J R Gask) *hld up: plld hrd: wknd over 2f out* 12/1

2m 2.51s (0.81) **Going Correction** +0.05s/f (Slow)
WFA 4 from 5yo+ 1lb 12 Ran SP% **124.6**
Speed ratings (Par 101): **98,97,97,97,96 96,96,93,88,85 82,81**
toteswinger: 1&2 £24.10, 1&3 £6.60, 2&3 £49.10. CSF £95.98 CT £424.16 TOTE £4.60: £1.40, £6.10, £2.70; EX 114.80 TRIFECTA Not won..
Owner Macniler Racing Partnership **Bred** Kingwood Bloodstock **Trained** Newmarket, Suffolk
■ Stewards' Enquiry : Richard Kingscote one-day ban: failed to ride to draw (Feb 5)
Chris Catlin one-day ban: failed to ride to draw (Feb 5)

FOCUS
This looked competitive and it certainly played out that way, the front seven being separated by under two lengths. The pace was ordinary though, and the form only modest.

254 RINGSIDE SUITE - 700 THEATRE STYLE CONFERENCE CLASSIFIED STKS 1m 1f 103y(P)
4:30 (4:30) (Class 7) 4-Y-0+ £1,364 (£403; £201) Stalls Low

Form RPR
334/ 1 **Agilete**[510] 4994 7-9-0 45 JerryO'Dwyer 7 63
(J Pearce) *trckd ldrs: led over 1f out: sn rdn clr: eased ins fnl f* 8/1[3]
0-00 2 7 **Spy Gun (USA)**[7] 175 9-8-7 43 (p) JoshWall(7) 2 48
(T Wall) *chsd ldrs: rdn and ev ch over 1f out: sn outpcd* 33/1
40-6 3 nse **Norwegian**[12] 117 8-9-0 43 (p) StephenDonohoe 13 48
(Ian Williams) *hld up: hdwy over 1f out: nrst fin* 9/2[2]
40-0 4 1/2 **Summer Bounty**[7] 169 13-9-0 43 JimmyQuinn 6 47
(F Jordan) *s.s: hld up: hdwy over 1f out: sn rdn: no ex fnl f* 8/1[3]
000- 5 1/2 **Rain Stops Play (IRE)**[140] 5631 7-9-0 45 PaulMulrennan 5 46
(N G Richards) *hld up: hdwy over 3f out: n.m.r and lost pl over 2f styd on ins fnl f* 9/2[2]
0-00 6 1 1/4 **The London Gang**[3] 215 6-8-9 41 (b) DeanHeslop(5) 3 43
(S Wynne) *s.i.s: hld up: rdn over 3f out: styd on fnl f: n.d* 20/1
00-6 7 1/2 **Frosty's Gift**[16] 61 5-9-0 45 PaulFitzsimons 4 42
(J C Fox) *hld up: hdwy over 2f out: wknd fnl f* 16/1
00-0 8 1 1/4 **Abbeygate**[17] 43 8-8-7 42 (b) KylieManser(7) 12 39
(T Keddy) *chsd ldrs: led over 2f out: hdd over 1f out: sn hung lft and wknd* 16/1
00-0 9 hd **Bobering**[11] 132 9-9-0 44 AndrewElliott 9 39
(B P J Baugh) *led: rdn and hdd over 2f out: wknd fnl f* 14/1
0-0 10 1 1/2 **Dobravany (IRE)**[3] 216 5-9-0 42 (p) RPCleary 1 43+
(Adrian McGuinness, Ire) *hld up in tch: nt clr run over 2f out: btn whn hmpd 1f out: eased* 3/1[1]
05-5 11 10 **Ricci De Mare**[16] 66 4-8-10 45 (b[1]) KevinGhunowa(3) 10 15
(G J Smith) *chsd ldr: rdn over 3f out: wknd over 2f out* 28/1
06-6 12 3/4 **Fortuitous (IRE)**[7] 175 5-9-0 45 (v) RobertWinston 11 39+
(S Gollings) *reminders after s: sn mid-div: hdwy over 5f out: rdn over 2f out: wkng whn hung lft over 1f out: hmpd and eased sn after* 11/1

2m 1.73s (0.03) **Going Correction** +0.05s/f (Slow)
WFA 4 from 5yo+ 1lb 12 Ran SP% **121.5**
Speed ratings (Par 97): **101,94,94,94,93 92,92,91,91,89 80,80**
toteswinger: 1&2 £39.90, 1&3 £7.40, 2&3 £25.50. CSF £255.68 TOTE £6.40: £2.60, £7.90, £1.50; EX 178.10 TRIFECTA Not won..
Owner Mrs M Miller **Bred** J W Parker And Lavington Stud **Trained** Newmarket, Suffolk

FOCUS
A very poor race, with the winner at least, but the winning time was 0.78 seconds faster than the preceding Class 6 handicap. The winner was better than this grade when last seen.
Dobravany(IRE) Official explanation: jockey said gelding was denied a clear run

255 SPONSOR A RACE AT WOLVERHAMPTON MEDIAN AUCTION MAIDEN STKS 1m 141y(P)
5:00 (5:00) (Class 6) 4-6-Y-0 £2,047 (£604; £302) Stalls Low

Form RPR
20-2 1 **Focail Eile**[15] 80 4-9-3 63 StephenDonohoe 2 74
(Miss Gay Kelleway) *a.p: racd keenly: chsd ldr over 2f out: rdn over 1f out: edgd lft and r.o to ld wl ins fnl f* 6/1
0-3 2 3/4 **More Time Tim (IRE)**[12] 115 4-9-3 66 PatCosgrave 5 72
(J R Boyle) *chsd ldrs tl led over 3f out: rdn over 1f out: hdd wl ins fnl f* 13/8[1]
2- 3 3 **Magners Hill (IRE)**[41] 7654 5-9-4 0 RPCleary 3 65
(Gerard Keane, Ire) *hld up: hdwy over 2f out: rdn and edgd lft over 1f out: styd on same pce* 3/1[3]
4 2 **Seeu Central (IRE)**[21] 5-9-4 0 (p) DaneO'Neill 4 61
(P J Rothwell, Ire) *s.s: hld up: hdwy u.p over 1f out: nt trble ldrs* 16/1
24- 5 2 1/4 **Keepsgettingbetter (IRE)**[32] 7757 4-9-3 0 ChrisCatlin 8 55
(J R Gask) *trckd ldrs: racd keenly: rdn over 2f out: wknd over 1f out* 5/2[2]
0-5 6 2 3/4 **Hurforharmony (IRE)**[1] 240 6-8-13 45 RobertWinston 1 44
(Adrian McGuinness, Ire) *hld up: hdwy over 2f out: sn rdn: wknd over 1f out* 22/1
00-0 7 26 **Tycoon's Buddy**[9] 150 4-9-3 40 LeeEnstone 7 —
(S Wynne) *led: rdn and hdd over 3f out: wknd over 2f out* 66/1

1m 50.11s (-0.39) **Going Correction** +0.05s/f (Slow)
WFA 4 from 5yo+ 1lb 7 Ran SP% **117.7**
Speed ratings: **103,102,99,97,95 93,70**
toteswinger: 1&2 £2.80, 1&3 £2.50, 2&3 £2.40. CSF £16.98 TOTE £6.70: £2.70, £1.30; EX 22.60 Trifecta £37.90 Pool: £352.78 -6.88 winning units..
Owner Cathal Fegan **Bred** D Robb **Trained** Exning, Suffolk

FOCUS
A weak and uncompetitive maiden though the pace was reasonable. The runner-up is the best guide to this modeest form.

256 PLAY POKER @ WILLIAMHILL.COM H'CAP 1m 141y(P)
5:30 (5:30) (Class 6) (0-60,60) 4-Y-0+ £2,047 (£604; £302) Stalls Low

Form RPR
12-4 1 **Alf Tupper**[13] 105 6-9-5 60 RobertWinston 2 73+
(Adrian McGuinness, Ire) *a.p: rdn and hung lft over 1f out: r.o to ld towards fin* 7/1
041- 2 1 **Pab Special (IRE)**[52] 7516 6-9-3 58 IanMongan 13 66
(B R Johnson) *chsd ldrs: led over 2f out: rdn over 1f out: hdd towards fin* 4/1[2]
002- 3 1 **Kargan (IRE)**[55] 6951 4-9-0 56 GregFairley 10 62
(A G Foster) *a.p: rdn and ev ch ins fnl f: nt run on* 13/2[3]
54-5 4 1 1/2 **Machinate (USA)**[3] 221 7-8-11 55 DuranFentiman(3) 9 57
(W M Brisbourne) *chsd ldr 5f: rdn over 1f out: nt clr run ins fnl f: styd on same pce* 7/1
036- 5 3/4 **Kannon**[43] 7631 4-9-0 56 DarrenWilliams 4 57
(I W McInnes) *chsd ldrs: rdn over 2f out: one pce fnl f* 11/1
055- 6 1 **Media Stars**[187] 4182 4-9-4 60 PatCosgrave 3 58
(J A Osborne) *s.i.s: hld up: hdwy over 3f out: rdn over 1f out: styd on* 17/2
01-2 7 1 1/2 **Mr Chocolate Drop (IRE)**[15] 71 5-9-1 56 (v) ChrisCatlin 8 51
(Miss M E Rowland) *hld up: hdwy over 2f out: sn rdn: no imp fnl f* 7/2[1]
562- 8 2 **That'll Do Nicely (IRE)**[33] 7749 6-9-2 57 PaulMulrennan 12 47
(N G Richards) *hld up: rdn over 2f out: n.d* 14/1
300- 9 hd **Time To Regret**[43] 7634 9-9-4 59 (p) DanielTudhope 6 49
(I W McInnes) *led: rdn and hdd over 2f out: wknd fnl f* 28/1
050- 10 10 **Alseraaj (USA)**[154] 5198 4-9-1 57 StephenDonohoe 1 24
(Ian Williams) *s.i.s: hld up: a in rr: wknd 3f out* 33/1
/0 11 10 **Ocarito (GER)**[12] 125 8-9-5 60 VinceSlattery 7 4
(G F Bridgwater) *mid-div: lost pl over 5f out: wknd over 3f out* 66/1
12 1/2 **Vanilla Bally (ISR)**[216] 4-9-4 60 DaneO'Neill 11 3
(George Baker) *s.s: hld up: a in rr: rdn and wknd 3f out* 16/1

1m 51.3s (0.80) **Going Correction** +0.05s/f (Slow)
WFA 4 from 5yo+ 1lb 12 Ran SP% **119.8**
Speed ratings (Par 101): **98,97,96,94,94 93,92,90,90,81 72,71**
toteswinger: 1&2 £6.10, 1&3 £11.30, 2&3 £8.20. CSF £35.07 CT £198.32 TOTE £9.10: £2.40, £1.90, £3.20; EX 38.10 Trifecta £133.20 Part won. Place 6: £59.13 Place 5: £25.74 .
Owner Curb Your Enthusiasm Syndicate **Bred** L A C Ashby Newhall Estate Farm **Trained** Lusk, Co Dublin

FOCUS
Another modest handicap, but still quite competitive. They only went a modest pace early and the winning time was 1.19 seconds slower than the maiden. Those that raced handily were at an advantage as a result. The form makes sense around the placed horses.
Alseraaj(USA) Official explanation: jockey said filly had a breathing problem
T/Jkpt: £3,832.10 to a £1 stake. Pool: £215,517.80. 39.93 winning tickets. T/Plt: £53.10 to a £1 stake. Pool: £97,497.66. 1,338.99 winning tickets. T/Qpdt: £19.30 to a £1 stake. Pool: £5,679.70. 216.70 winning tickets. CR

[180] NAD AL SHEBA (L-H)
Thursday, January 22
OFFICIAL GOING: Turf course - good; dirt course - fast

257a JAGUAR XK TROPHY (H'CAP) (TURF) 6f 110y(T)
2:55 (2:57) (95-110,110) 3-Y-0+
£50,000 (£16,666; £8,333; £4,166; £2,500; £1,666)

RPR
1 **Hunting Tower (SAF)**[180] 7-9-4 108 KShea 4 110+
(M F De Kock, South Africa) *trckd ldng pair: gng wl 2 1/2f out: swtchd 1f out: led 55yds out: comf* 5/1[2]
2 1 1/4 **Instant Recall (IRE)**[14] 8-9-1 105 (v) WayneSmith 10 103
(M Al Muhairi, UAE) *wl away: led: drew clr 2 1/2f out: hdd cl home* 20/1
3 1/4 **Grantley Adams**[32] 6-8-13 102 TPO'Shea 5 100
(E Charpy, UAE) *in rr of mid-div: gng wl whn n.m.r 2 1/2f out: r.o fnl 1 1/2f* 10/1
4 hd **So Will I**[350] 472 8-9-2 106 (t) RHills 12 103
(Doug Watson, UAE) *trckd ldrs: rdn to cl 2 1/2f out: nt qckn* 16/1

5 2 1/4 **Prince Tamino**[322] 814 6-9-3 **107** RoystonFfrench 6 97
(A Al Raihe, UAE) *mid-div: rdn 2 1/2f out: one pce fnl 1 1/2f* **9/1**
6 *nse* **Hatta Fort**[89] 4-9-4 **108** (t) LDettori 1 98
(Saeed Bin Suroor) *in rr of mid-div: n.m.r 3f out or 2f out: r.o wl once clr* **11/4**[1]
7 *1* **Lion's Blood (SAF)**[201] 5-9-0 **104** JohnEgan 9 91
(H J Brown, South Africa) *broke awkwardly: racd in rr: nvr able to chal* **14/1**
8 *shd* **Confuchias (IRE)**[36] 7703 5-8-13 **102** EddieAhern 8 90
(K R Burke) *mid-div: wd 3f out: nvr able to chal* **16/1**
9 1 1/4 **Balthazaar's Gift (IRE)**[96] 6814 6-9-6 **110** DO'Donohoe 2 93
(R Simpson, UAE) *racd in last: nvr able to chal* **14/1**
10 *hd* **Mandobi (IRE)**[34] 8-8-13 **102** (vt) WilliamBuick 11 86
(D Selvaratnam, UAE) *s.i.s: racd in mid-div: r.o fnl 2f: n.d* **12/1**
11 *2* **Santiago Atitlan**[110] 7-9-0 **104** (b) MJKinane 7 81
(A Wohler, Germany) *in rr of mid-div: rdn to cl 3f out: sn btn* **10/1**
12 1 1/4 **Valery Borzov (IRE)**[124] 6104 5-8-11 **101** AdrianTNicholls 3 74
(D Nicholls) *mid-div on rail: hmpd 3f out: n.d after* **8/1**[3]

1m 18.35s (0.85) **Going Correction** +0.20s/f (Good) **12** Ran SP% **120.2**
Speed ratings: **103,101,101,101,98 98,97,97,95,95 93,91**
CSF 101.98; Tricast 976.63.
Owner Sheikh Mohammed Bin Khalifa Al Maktoum **Bred** Mrs B D Oppenheimer **Trained** South Africa

FOCUS
This was a decent sprint handicap, but it did feature largely exposed horses. The race was run at an uneven pace and it looked an advantage to race prominently. The winning time was 0.27 seconds slower than the second division.

NOTEBOOK
Hunting Tower(SAF) ◆, who landed South Africa's most prestigious race in 2007, the Grade 1 Durban July, made a ready winning debut for his new high-profile connections over a trip short of his best. He took time to settle, but had the box seat throughout and showed a very likable attitude to settle the race inside the final furlong. He obviously has a touch of class about him and should come on nicely for the run, so looks one to follow through the Carnival, with the promise of more to come as he steps back up in trip. (op 9-2)
Instant Recall(IRE) had tailed off on his comeback at the track a fortnight earlier. That race was on dirt, however, and while he has won on that surface at Jebel Ali his improvement last year at this track came on turf. He set off in front and got an easy lead, but showed battling qualities to hold off the finishers for second. This was obviously a big improvement, but he still looks weighted to his best and has to rate a little flattered as he had the run of things.
Grantley Adams had taken a Listed event over 7f at Abu Dhabi on his debut for this stable 32 days previously and that was his first success since winning over course and distance for Mick Channon back in 2007. He ran a solid race in defeat, faring best of those to be held up, and helps to set the level of the form. (tchd 11-1)
So Will I was having his first run since winning over course and distance last year. He was never far away and again showed he goes well after a break, but one will have to be a little wary of the bounce factor next time.
Prince Tamino, a dual winner over course and distance, had won first time up last year yet that was off a 9lb lower mark. He ran his race and is another who helps to set the level of the form, but does look handicapped to the hilt on a mark of 107. (op 8-1)
Hatta Fort, who returned to his best when sent to the US last autumn, was restrained from his inside draw and was full of running at the two-furlong pole. He endured a nightmare passage when trying to make his challenge, however, and should be rated a good deal better than the bare form. It would not be a surprise to see him go in next time. (op 3-1)
Lion's Blood(SAF) was another who shaped a little better than the bare form as he lacked the pace to go the early gallop and ran on encouragingly down the home straight. He was placed in Grade 1 company in his native South Africa and looks an improver when reverting to a suitably longer trip.
Confuchias(IRE) did not seem to have too many excuses.
Balthazaar's Gift(IRE) was making his debut for an in-form stable. He has yet to win a handicap, however, and was never in contention after being settled out last for most of the race.
Valery Borzov(IRE) raced handily and met some trouble on the rail after turning in, but eventually faded to finish last of all on this first run for 124 days. He would have likely found the ground faster than he cares for and a drop back in trip will help.

258a FORD FLEX TROPHY (CONDITIONS RACE) (DIRT) 7f (D)
3:25 (3:30) 3-Y-O

£20,833 (£6,944; £3,472; £1,736; £1,041; £694)

RPR
1 **Desert Party (USA)**[143] 3-9-0 108 (t) LDettori 6 114
(Saeed Bin Suroor) *trckd ldng pair: swtchd to rail: led 1f out: r.o wl* **15/8**[1]
2 1/2 **Regal Ransom (USA)**[116] 3-8-9 95 (t) TedDurcan 14 107
(Saeed Bin Suroor) *trckd ldr: led briefly 1 1/2f out: r.o wl: clsng at fin* **14/1**
3 3 3/4 **Redding Colliery (USA)**[92] 6910 3-8-9 85 (b) JohnEgan 12 97
(H J Brown, South Africa) *sn led: hdd 1 1/2f out: r.o wl* **16/1**
4 2 1/2 **Blues And Rock (ARG)**[285] 4-9-4 100 RyanMoore 16 98+
(M F De Kock, South Africa) *mid-div: rdn 3 1/2f out: r.o wl fnl 1 1/2f* **8/1**[3]
5 2 3/4 **Rocks Off (ARG)**[180] 4-9-11 107 KShea 11 92
(M F De Kock, South Africa) *trckd ldng pair: rdn to chse ldrs 2 1/2f out: kpt on same pce: tired fnl 1/2f* **9/4**[2]
6 *nse* **Absent Pleasure (USA)**[89] 6972 3-8-9 97 RichardMullen 10 83
(E Martins, Bahrain) *mid-div: rdn to chse ldrs 2 1/2f out: nt qckn* **20/1**
7 3 1/4 **Fullback (IRE)**[117] 6284 3-8-9 97 TPO'Shea 2 74
(J S Moore) *nvr bttr than mid-div* **20/1**
8 1 1/4 **Felix (PER)**[14] 4-9-4 100 AhmedAjtebi 8 73
(M bin Shafya, UAE) *nvr bttr than mid-div* **14/1**
9 1/2 **Classic Blade (IRE)**[111] 6442 3-9-0 108 FJara 15 74
(Doug Watson, UAE) *mid-div: rdn 3f out: one pce* **12/1**
10 3/4 **Indiscutible (CHI)**[313] 4-9-6 95 KLatham 13 71
(M F De Kock, South Africa) *sn pushed along in rr: nvr able to chal* **20/1**
11 5 1/4 **Dr Smart (IRE)**[14] 3-8-2 65 SophieDoyle(7) 1 53
(M Al Muhairi, UAE) *in rr of main gp: nvr involved* **100/1**
12 *4* **Molnaya (IRE)**[64] 7388 3-8-9 55 (t) RMBurke 3 42
(A Manuel, UAE) *mid-div on rail: rdn 4f out: sn btn* **200/1**
13 3 1/2 **Keeptheboatafloat (USA)**[122] 6176 3-8-9 91 EddieAhern 4 33
(K R Burke) *nvr able to chal* **33/1**
14 1 1/2 **Versaki (IRE)**[100] 6717 3-8-9 88 AdrianTNicholls 7 29
(D Nicholls) *settled in rr: nvr involved* **40/1**
15 6 3/4 **Ab Include (USA)** 3-8-9 (b) RoystonFfrench 9 —
(A Al Raihe, UAE) *s.i.s: a in rr* **100/1**
16 *5* **Ard Na Greine (IRE)**[97] 6797 3-8-9 90 KJManning 5 —
(J S Bolger, Ire) *mid-div: rdn to chse ldrs 2 1/2f out: wknd* **18/1**

1m 24.43s (-0.37) **Going Correction** +0.35s/f (Slow)
WFA 3 from 4yo 18lb **16** Ran SP% **131.0**
Speed ratings: **116,115,111,108,105 105,101,99,99,98 92,87,83,82,74 68**
CSF: 30.79.
Owner Godolphin **Bred** David Smith & Steven Sinatra **Trained** Newmarket, Suffolk

FOCUS
A race won by three of the last four UAE 2000 Guineas winners, and the latest two, Mike De Kock's pair, Honour Devil and Asiatic Boy, both went on to land the Derby as well. De Kock was well represented once again, but it was Godolphin who dominated. At this stage it's hard to be sure how this compares with some of the previous runnings, but it looked a good race and they went a strong pace, so the form should be reliable.

NOTEBOOK
Desert Party(USA) was well backed throughout the day and justified the support with a workmanlike success. Having landed a Grade 2 in the States last year, he fluffed his lines in a decent Grade 1 contest when last seen, but he confirmed himself pretty smart by defying a penalty on his debut in the UAE. Having chased the pace towards the inside early on, he stuck to the rail in the straight and gradually wore down his stablemate, Regal Ransom, who was in receipt of 5lb. He looked as though he will stay 1m and is obviously a leading contender for UAE 2000 Guineas, where he won't have to carry a penalty.
Regal Ransom(USA), who like the winner started off in the US, winning a maiden before finishing down the field in a Grade 1 (subsequent Breeders' Cup Juvenile winner second) after racing too keenly, ran well in defeat. He was given a really positive ride and found plenty in the straight, but was simply beaten by a better rival on the day.
Redding Colliery(USA) was well regarded when with Jane Chapple-Hyam and won a Kempton maiden by five lengths when last seen three months previously. He went off quick, but kept on really well and ran just into a couple of smart colts. This was his first try on dirt, but he's bred to be suited by the surface and there should be a lot more to come.
Blues And Rock(ARG), a 5f winner in Argentina, could not quite lay up with the strong pace, but he saw his race out well and will be suited by a step up in trip.
Rocks Off(ARG) was the champion juvenile in South Africa and, although he had yet to race on dirt, he's a half-brother to UAE 2000 Guineas winner Gold For Sale. However, a 7lb penalty meant he had to concede weight all round and he simply wasn't good enough on the day. He had his chance, but could not sustain his challenge. He should be suited by the return to 1m, and won't have a penalty in the Guineas, but it remains to be seen whether he's quite up to that class.
Absent Pleasure(USA), Listed placed over 6f on turf for Brian Meehan last year, ran a respectable race under this very different conditions, keeping on against the inside rail in the straight.
Fullback(IRE) had something to find at this level and was never competitive.
Classic Blade(IRE), surprisingly for a July Stakes winner, lacked the pace to get a handy position on this first try on dirt.
Keeptheboatafloat(USA) was never really going.
Versaki(IRE) did not seem to take to the surface, but he had something in find in this company in any case.
Ard Na Greine(IRE) should be suited by a return to turf.

259a LAND ROVER TROPHY (H'CAP) (TURF) 6f 110y(T)
3:55 (3:58) (95-110,110) 3-Y-O+

£50,000 (£16,666; £8,333; £4,166; £2,500; £1,666)

RPR
1 **Munaddam (USA)**[32] 7-9-3 **107** RHills 2 113
(E Charpy, UAE) *slowly away: settled in rr: prog on rail 2 1/2f out: swtchd 1 1/2f out: led 110yds out: jst hld on* **14/1**
2 1/2 **Leandros (FR)**[90] 6961 4-8-13 **102** (b) KLatham 9 107+
(G M Lyons, Ire) *settled in rr: prog 2 1/2f out: hung rt 1 1/2f out: r.o wl: jst failed* **9/1**
3 1 1/2 **Miss Gorica (IRE)**[7] 180 5-9-1 **105** TedDurcan 5 105
(Ms Joanna Morgan, Ire) *mid-div: smooth prog 3f out: led 1 1/2f out: outpcd fnl 110yds* **12/1**
4 *2* **Asset (IRE)**[117] 6285 6-9-2 **106** (v) LDettori 6 100
(Saeed Bin Suroor) *mid-div: rdn to chse ldrs 2 1/2f out: r.o same pce* **9/4**[1]
5 *1* **Remarque (IRE)**[62] 4-8-11 **101** (bt) GMarcelli 11 92
(L Riccardi, Italy) *sn led: hdd 1 1/2f out: wknd* **25/1**
6 1 3/4 **Drift Ice (SAF)**[21] 8-9-1 **105** (be) KShea 1 91
(M F De Kock, South Africa) *mid-div: ev ch whn n.m.r 2f out: one pce* **13/2**[2]
7 1/2 **Conquest (IRE)**[14] 5-9-6 **110** AhmedAjtebi 3 95
(M bin Shafya, UAE) *trckd ldr: hrd rdn 2 1/2f out: wknd* **10/1**
8 3/4 **Buachaill Dona (IRE)**[131] 5890 6-8-13 **102** AdrianTNicholls 4 86
(D Nicholls) *chsd ldrs: hrd rdn 2 1/2f out: one pce* **14/1**
9 3 1/4 **Flying Blue (FR)**[49] 7550 4-8-13 **102** (t) JMartinez 12 76
(R Martin Sanchez, Spain) *nvr able to chal* **33/1**
10 3 1/2 **Contest (IRE)**[12] 123 5-9-4 **108** (tp) RichardMullen 7 71
(C Theodorakis, Greece) *in rr of mid-div: gng wl 2 1/2f out: n.m.r 2f out: one pce* **7/1**[3]
11 1 3/4 **Easy Target (FR)**[78] 7201 4-8-10 **100** FJara 8 58
(X Nakkachdji, France) *mid-div: rn wd 3f out: one pce fnl 2 1/2* **16/1**
12 1/2 **Golden Riviera (SAF)**[291] 5-8-10 **100** RyanMoore 10 57
(H J Brown, South Africa) *mid-div: rn wd: nvr able to chal* **8/1**

1m 18.08s (0.58) **Going Correction** +0.20s/f (Good) **12** Ran SP% **120.5**
Speed ratings: **104,103,101,99,98 96,95,94,91,87 85,84**
CSF 136.62; Tricast 1,575.31..
Owner Hamdan Al Maktoum **Bred** Shadwell Farm LLC **Trained** United Arab Emirates

FOCUS
Another decent sprint handicap, run at a solid pace. The winning time was 0.27 seconds quicker than the opener, which was basically the first division.

NOTEBOOK
Munaddam(USA) came through from off the pace under a fine ride and scored with something left in the tank. He had won this race back in 2007 and finished second in it last year, before failing to fire when tried on the dirt. This was his highest winning mark to date and he obviously retains his ability, so while a rise in the weights will make things tougher he may still have some more to offer.
Leandros(FR) has done all of his winning on Dundalk's Polytrack and was last seen recording a personal-best at that venue 90 days earlier. He posted a very encouraging effort in defeat, responding gamely for pressure at the furlong pole and ultimately did his best work towards the finish. A return to 7f should prove spot-on and he looks side with next time.
Miss Gorica(IRE) was 4lb higher than when winning here against her own sex a week earlier. She put up an improved effort in defeat and rates the benchmark, but really looks to want a stiffer test.
Asset(IRE) had been given a chance by the Handicapper for this UAE debut. He got a patient ride and made his move nearing the final furlong, but not for the first time he looked unco-operative when push really came to shove. He was held prior to the runner-up coming across him late on and for all his talent, he is one to avoid for betting purposes at present.
Remarque(IRE) has made the running in the past and was soon at the head of affairs. He was cooked shortly after passing the furlong marker though and his previous best efforts suggest this ground would have been plenty fast enough. In the circumstances this was not a bad effort from his wide stall and a slight drop back in trip will suit.
Drift Ice(SAF), who landed the first division of this contest last year, was done no favours as the long-time leader came across him on the rail and he has to be rated better than his finishing position indicates. (tchd 7-1)
Conquest(IRE), who not that surprisingly failed to cope with the dirt on debut for connections a fortnight previously, raced far too prominently for his liking and will surely revert to more patient tactics in the future.
Buachaill Dona(IRE) was well below the pick of his British form.

Golden Riviera(SAF), making his debut for new connections, was taken very wide into the home straight and shaped as though the run was needed. He should better this when stepping back up in distance.

260a JAGUAR XF TROPHY (H'CAP) (TURF) 7f 110y(D)

4:25 (4:26) (100-129,120) 3-Y-O+

£72,916 (£24,305; £12,152; £6,076; £3,645; £2,430)

RPR

1 **Gladiatorus (USA)**[466] 6222 4-8-8 **108** AhmedAjtebi 2 112
(M bin Shafya, UAE) *led after 1 1/2f: drew clr 3f out: r.o wl: game* **12/1**

2 2 ½ **Calming Influence (IRE)**[82] 7147 4-8-5 **105** (t) TedDurcan 3 105+
(Saeed Bin Suroor) *settled in rr: rdn to cl 3f out: hung rt 1 1/2f out: one pce* **6/5**[1]

3 4 ½ **Biarritz (SAF)**[362] 6-9-0 **113** (b) KShea 9 101+
(M F De Kock, South Africa) *settled in rr: rdn 3f out: nvr nr to chal: r.o* **10/3**[2]

4 8 ¼ **Jay Peg (SAF)**[249] 2234 6-9-6 **120** (b) RyanMoore 7 86
(H J Brown, South Africa) *wl away: led for 1 1/2f: trckd ldr tl 3f out: one pce* **7/2**[3]

5 ¾ **Montpellier (IRE)**[32] 6-8-5 **101** (t) RoystonFfrench 8 69
(A Al Raihe, UAE) *racd in last: nvr able to chal* **18/1**

6 7 **Tasdeer (USA)**[35] 4-8-5 **102** RHills 6 52
(Doug Watson, UAE) *mid-div: rdn to cl 2 1/2f out: nt qckn* **16/1**

7 6 **Bruges (IRE)**[167] 4832 4-8-5 **100** (t) RichardMullen 1 37
(A Al Raihe, UAE) *nvr bttr than mid-div* **33/1**

8 5 ¾ **Jack Junior (USA)**[117] 6287 5-8-5 **100** AdrianTNicholls 5 22
(D Nicholls) *in rr of mid-div: wd 3f out: nvr nr to chal* **20/1**

1m 29.35s (-2.25) **Going Correction** +0.20s/f (Good) **8** Ran SP% **117.3**
Speed ratings: **119,116,112,103,103 96,90,84**
CSF 27.70; Tricast 63.33..
Owner Sheikh Mansoor bin Mohammed al Maktoum **Bred** Az Agr Le Ferriere Di Raponi Giampaolo **Trained** United Arab Emirates

FOCUS
A high-class handicap, although not that competitive as a few of these were returning from long lay-offs, and all the money was for Calming Influence.

NOTEBOOK
Gladiatorus(USA) was returning from a longer break than any of these (466 days), but he was obviously straighter than the likes of Biarritz and Jay Peg and received a fine front-running ride from Ahmed Ajtebi, particularly considering it's rare a horse makes most at this track. He was around four lengths clear at the top of the straight and was always doing enough to keep the awkward-looking runner-up well at bay. He was a very smart juvenile in Italy, winning six of his nine starts in 2007 as well as placing in a Group 1, and he clearly retains plenty of ability, but it has to be said everything went his way this time. There's obviously the chance he'll strip even fitter for this, but he could just as easily bounce and he might be best watched if a short price to follow up.
Calming Influence(IRE), despite settling better in the early part of the race than is often the case, proved a most awkward ride under pressure, continually hanging left against the inside rail in the straight, and he looked a horse with issues. Had he consented to run on there can be little doubt he would have won, and there's no denying his talent, but he looks best avoided on this evidence. (op 11-8)
Biarritz(SAF) ◆, returning from a year off, was given a hold-up ride and never got competitive, but he ought to be a lot sharper next time. The Jebel Hatta could be his next target and his trainer was hopeful at the start of the Carnival that he could progress into a Duty Free horse.
Jay Peg(SAF) ◆ needed his first few runs last year before landing the Duty Free at odds of 50/1 and his trainer warned he would again come on for this first outing, and maybe even his second, having been off since winning the Singapore International Cup last May. He had no easy task first-time up off a mark of 120 and never threatened. (tchd 100-30)
Montpellier(IRE) was well held. (op 16-1)
Tasdeer(USA) was a touch keen through the first furlong or so and ended up well held.
Jack Junior(USA) did not handle the bend into the straight and ran a stinker.

261a FORD MUSTANG TROPHY (H'CAP) (DIRT) 1m 110y(D)

4:55 (4:55) (90-105,105) 3-Y-O+

£45,833 (£15,277; £7,638; £3,819; £2,291; £1,527)

RPR

1 **Glen Nevis (USA)**[7] 183 5-9-1 **100** (v) RoystonFfrench 6 105
(A Al Raihe, UAE) *racd in rr: r.o wl fnl 3f: led last 55yds: comf* **14/1**

2 2 ¼ **Aamaaq**[35] 6-8-6 **91** RHills 4 91
(A Al Raihe, UAE) *mid-div: trckd ldr 3f out: led 1 1/2f out: hdd cl home* **12/1**

3 7 ¼ **Quicksand (SAF)**[224] 5-8-11 **97** KShea 5 80+
(M F De Kock, South Africa) *trckd ldrs: led 5 1/2f out: hdd 1 1/2f out: one pce* **2/1**[1]

4 1 ¼ **Fares (IRE)**[497] 5355 5-8-11 **97** (v) DO'Donohoe 8 77
(Doug Watson, UAE) *trckd ldrs: ev ch 3f out: nt qckn fnl 2 1/2f* **33/1**

5 9 ½ **Etihaad**[7] 184 7-8-5 **90** (t) FJara 2 50
(R Bouresly, Kuwait) *led for 3f: sn rdn: wknd fnl 2 1/2* **40/1**

6 2 ¼ **Bucked Off (SAF)**[222] 5-8-10 **96** JohnEgan 9 50
(H J Brown, South Africa) *nvr bttr than mid-div* **14/1**

7 1 ¼ **Bright Halo (BRZ)**[235] 5-8-9 **95** (t) RyanMoore 1 47
(J De Roualle, France) *mid-div: hrd rdn 4f out: n.d* **3/1**[2]

8 19 **Without A Prayer (IRE)**[42] 7643 4-9-4 **105** WilliamBuick 3 15
(R M Beckett) *mid-div: rdn 4f out: n.d* **10/3**[3]

9 dist **Rock Ascot (URU)**[382] 5-9-4 **104** (t) KLatham 7 —
(H J Brown, South Africa) *sn rdn in rr: nvr involved* **10/1**

1m 45.03s (1.03) **Going Correction** +0.35s/f (Slow) **9** Ran SP% **116.9**
Speed ratings: **109,107,100,99,91 89,87,71,—**
CSF 169.89; Tricast 483.08.
Owner Sh Zayed Bin Almur Al Maktoum **Bred** Nutbush Farm **Trained** UAE

FOCUS
A weak handicap by Carnival standards and not form to dwell on. There was a battle for the early lead, resulting in a strong end-to-end gallop.

NOTEBOOK
Glen Nevis(USA) stayed on best having been out the back early. Successful over 1m2f on the turf here off a mark of 98 last year, he had shown little on his two previous tries on dirt, but he handled the surface okay this time, even if he was unable to lay up early. However, this rather fell in his lap and his best chance of following up may come back on the grass.
Aamaaq, successful in lesser company on the dirt here on his last couple of starts, looked all over the winner when still going easily after taking over the lead from Quicksand halfway up the straight, but he had sat closer to the strong gallop than Glen Nevis and ran out of energy late on. (op 10-1\n\x\x)
Quicksand(SAF), a multiple winner in South Africa who was returning from a 224-day break, used up plenty of energy early on in getting the lead outright and didn't seem to get a breather in. Unsurprisingly he failed to see his race out. (op 9-4)
Fares(IRE) was a triple Polytrack winner for Clive Brittain, but this was his first try on dirt after 16 months off. He raced close up early, but found little for pressure. (op 28-1)
Bucked Off(SAF) carried his head very high for much of the way and seemingly hated the kickback.
Bright Halo(BRZ), a multiple Group winner on dirt in Uruguay, offered absolutely nothing on her UAE debut. (op 10/3)
Without A Prayer(IRE), a recent Listed winner on Polytrack in France, could not hold his position early and did not seem to take to the dirt. (op 3-1)

262a RANGE ROVER TROPHY (H'CAP) (TURF) 1m 4f (T)

5:25 (5:26) (95-110,109) 3-Y-O+

£50,000 (£16,666; £8,333; £4,166; £2,500; £1,666)

RPR

1 **Gravitas**[7] 185 6-9-2 **105** AhmedAjtebi 2 107+
(M bin Shafya, UAE) *mid-div: trckd ldrs 2 1/2f out: led 1f out: jst hld on* **20/1**

2 ½ **Captain Webb**[201] 3719 4-8-5 **95** (t) TedDurcan 11 99
(Saeed Bin Suroor) *in rr of mid-div: rdn to cl 3f out: ev ch fnl 2f: one pce fnl f* **7/2**[1]

3 ¼ **Big Robert**[47] 7579 5-8-6 **95** EddieAhern 9 96
(K R Burke) *mid-div on rail: smooth prog 2f out: ev ch fnl 1 1/2f: nt qckn fnl 110yds* **12/1**

4 hd **Sanbuch**[116] 6306 5-8-10 **109** AntiocoMurgia[(10)] 12 109+
(M bin Shafya, UAE) *settled in rr: nvr nr to chal: r.o v wl fnl 2f: nrst fin* **12/1**

5 ½ **Sunday Symphony**[34] 7-8-8 **97** (vt) RichardMullen 10 96
(S Seemar, UAE) *mid-div: r.o wl fnl 2f* **33/1**

6 1 ¼ **Bennie Blue (SAF)**[21] 7-8-9 **98** ow1 (b) KShea 4 95
(M F De Kock, South Africa) *trckd ldng pair: led 2f out: one pce fnl f* **14/1**

7 1 ½ **Colony (IRE)**[176] 4519 4-8-5 **96** DO'Donohoe 15 93
(Saeed Bin Suroor) *settled in last: nvr able to chal: r.o fnl 1 1/2f* **5/1**[2]

8 1 ¼ **Love Galore (IRE)**[111] 6444 4-8-8 **100** RyanMoore 1 94
(M Johnston) *mid-div on rail: rdn 3f out: nt qckn* **12/1**

9 ¼ **Detonator (IRE)**[7] 185 4-8-10 **102** JRosales 6 96
(M bin Shafya, UAE) *sn led: hdd 2f out: wknd* **33/1**

10 shd **Leitmotiv (IRE)**[14] 6-8-8 **97** (v) WilliamBuick 8 90
(M Al Muhairi, UAE) *settled in rr: nvr able to chal* **14/1**

11 hd **Hawks Home (USA)**[11] 6-8-8 **97** (v) WayneSmith 7 89
(M Al Muhairi, UAE) *nvr bttr than mid-div* **13/2**[3]

12 hd **Craigstown**[14] 4-8-5 **95** TPO'Shea 5 90
(E Charpy, UAE) *nvr bttr than mid-div* **20/1**

13 5 ½ **Pearly King (USA)**[35] 6-8-7 **96** RoystonFfrench 3 79
(M Al Muhairi, UAE) *trckd ldrs: rdn 2 1/2f out: wknd* **20/1**

14 6 ¼ **Noble Bedouin (IRE)**[14] 5-8-11 **100** (t) JVerenzuela 14 73
(J Barton, Saudi Arabia) *mid-div: rdn 3f out: sn btn* **12/1**

15 1 ½ **Polan (FR)**[95] 4-8-5 **95** JMartinez 13 69
(R Martin Sanchez, Spain) *mid-div: nvr nr to chal* **16/1**

16 6 ½ **Tricien (FR)**[42] 7643 5-8-6 **95** FJara 16 55
(L A Urbano-Grajales, France) *mid-div: wknd 3f out: eased* **33/1**

2m 31.6s (0.60) **Going Correction** +0.20s/f (Good)
WFA 4 from 5yo+ 4lb **16** Ran SP% **125.3**
Speed ratings: **106,105,105,105,105 104,103,102,102,102 102,101,98,94,93 88**
CSF 84.87;. Tricast 909.51..
Owner Sheikh Hamdan Bin Mohammed Al Maktoum **Bred** Exors Of The Late Gerald W Leigh **Trained** United Arab Emirates

FOCUS
A good, competitive handicap and the pace seemed reasonable. There could be more to come from the winner on his old figures.

NOTEBOOK
Gravitas seemed to race plenty keen enough for much of the way but he picked up well in the straight and found plenty when strongly challenged to provide his in-form trainer/jockey combination with another Carnival success. He was well beaten in a similar event over course and distance the previous week (first start since leaving Godolphin), but it's becoming apparent many of the Bin Shafya runners improve significantly for a run and he benefited from a more positive ride this time. He might be capable of even better if he is more settled in future.
Captain Webb won a Listed race for Mark Johnston in May, but he had not been seen since July. He didn't seem to do much wrong on his debut for new connections and should be up to winning a similar race.
Big Robert did not enjoy the best of runs in the straight and had to switch a couple of times, but he seemed to have his chance inside the final 200m.
Sanbuch, a winner over 1m6f at Glorious Goodwood for Luca Cumani last year, was given an awful lot to but fairly motored home under his 10lb claimer and would have been in front in another 50 yards or so. This was a pleasing debut for new connections and he should do even better under a more positive ride.
Sunday Symphony was another who finished quite well.
Bennie Blue(SAF) was beautifully placed throughout and had his chance.
Colony(IRE), off since last July, was quite well backed on his first start since leaving Sir Michael Stoute, but he was another who going too late.
Love Galore(IRE) never featured on his return from nearly four months off.

263a AL TAYER MOTORS TROPHY (H'CAP) (TURF) 1m 2f (T)

5:55 (5:57) (95-110,110) 3-Y-O+

£50,000 (£16,666; £8,333; £4,166; £2,500; £1,666)

RPR

1 **Presvis**[124] 6120 5-9-2 **106** RyanMoore 5 115+
(L M Cumani) *mid-div: gng v wl 3f out: r.o wl fnl 2f: led 1 1/2f out: comf* **10/11**[1]

2 3 ½ **Yaddree**[7] 182 4-9-0 **105** AhmedAjtebi 4 108
(M bin Shafya, UAE) *settled in rr: nvr nr to chal: r.o wl fnl 2f* **16/1**

3 ½ **Al Shemali**[138] 5694 5-9-4 **108** (t) JRosales 6 109
(M bin Shafya, UAE) *trckd ldrs: ev ch 2 1/2f out: one pce fnl 1 1/2f* **10/1**[3]

4 1 ¼ **Great Plains**[13] 7-8-10 **100** RHills 2 99
(E Charpy, UAE) *mid-div: smooth prog 2 1/2f out: nt qckn fnl f* **33/1**

5 1 **Military Power**[14] 4-8-5 **95** CSanchez 11 94
(M bin Shafya, UAE) *sn led: hdd 2f out: wknd fnl 110yds* **14/1**

6 1 ¾ **Meydan City (USA)**[21] 4-8-9 **100** CSandoval 1 94
(M bin Shafya, UAE) *mid-div: rn wd 2 1/2f out: one pce fnl 1 1/2f* **16/1**

7 1 ¼ **Royal Prince**[14] 8-8-7 **97** DO'Donohoe 9 88
(Doug Watson, UAE) *mid-div: rdn 3f out: nt qckn* **20/1**

8 ½ **Fenice (IRE)**[39] 6-8-10 **100** (t) RichardMullen 13 90
(S Seemar, UAE) *settled in rr: nvr nr to chal* **33/1**

9 ½ **Via Galilei (IRE)**[95] 6850 4-8-10 **101** KJManning 3 91
(J S Bolger, Ire) *trckd ldrs: ev ch 2f out: wknd fnl f* **12/1**

10 3 ½ **Naipe Marcado (URU)**[14] 6-8-5 **95** (t) TPO'Shea 8 77
(E Charpy, UAE) *nvr bttr than mid-div* **25/1**

11 1 **Grand Hombre (USA)**[21] 9-8-5 **95** RMBurke 12 75
(R Bouresly, Kuwait) *mid-div: rdn 4f out: sn btn* **33/1**

12 ½ **Munsef**[140] 5646 7-8-13 **102**.......... AdrianTNicholls 7 82
(D Nicholls) *nvr able to chal* **25/1**
13 *nse* **Basaltico (IRE)**[74] 7263 5-9-6 **110**.......... KLatham 10 88
(H J Brown, South Africa) *slowly away: nvr nr to chal* **14/1**
14 1 ¾ **Varsity**[7] 185 6-8-13 **102**..........(tp) TedDurcan 14 78
(C F Swan, Ire) *settled in rr: nvr nr to chal* **20/1**
15 9 ½ **Drill Sergeant**[92] 6921 4-9-0 **105**.......... LDettori 15 62
(M Johnston) *trckd ldrs tl wknd 2 1/2f out* **9/1**[2]
16 6 **Dr Faustus (IRE)**[131] 5894 4-8-7 **98**.......... FJara 16 43
(Doug Watson, UAE) *mid-div: rn wd: nvr able to chal* **25/1**

2m 5.50s (1.00) **Going Correction** +0.20s/f (Good)
WFA 4 from 5yo+ 2lb **16** Ran SP% **134.2**
Speed ratings: **104,101,100,99,99 97,96,96,95,93 92,91,91,90,82 77**
CSF 17.54;. Tricast 115.23..
Owner L Marinopoulos **Bred** Mrs M Campbell-Andenaes **Trained** Newmarket, Suffolk

FOCUS
A good handicap and a very smart winner in the form of the extremely well-backed Presvis.

NOTEBOOK
Presvis ◆ readily defied a 14lb rise for his seven-length success at Newbury in September. The pace was just ordinary, but Luca Cumani's gelding had overcame even slower fractions when so impressive last time, and his potent turn of foot was evident once again. That said, there will surely be even more to come when he gets a stronger end-to-end gallop, and it's just an indication of how good he is that he has been able to pick up so well off a steady tempo the last twice. It's fair to say the runner-up would have been closer had he enjoyed a better trip, but Cumani has probably left plenty to work on with Presvis and there should be better to come again. His trainer regards him as a 1m4f horse in the making and he may have options in the coming weeks. He'll take another hefty rise in the weights for this, and it looks just a matter of time before he's contesting Group races, but he might still be able to contest a handicap next time if connections so choose. There is a race for horses rated 95 and above back over this course and distance on February 12, as well as a handicap with identical conditions over 1m4f the following week, and victory in either of those would surely earn him a place in the Group 2 Dubai City of Gold Stakes on Super Thursday (March 5). (op 6-5)
Yaddree ◆ found an extended 7f too short the previous week and appreciated the step up to his furthest trip to date. He was denied a clear run when trying to make a move towards the inside in the straight and was forced to switch, so he should have finished closer to the well-handicapped winner. He's a smart horse in his own right and very much appeals as one to very much keep in mind for a similar event.
Al Shemali, 4lb higher than when winning over course and distance at this meeting last year, had his chance and ran well.
Great Plains seemed to have every chance and ran well at a big price.
Military Power did not get home ridden from the front, confirming yet again that is tough to make all over this sort of trip at this track.
Meydan City(USA) ◆ showed signs of a revival for his in-form team. (op 14-1)
Fenice(IRE) ◆ finished in eye-catching style.
Via Galilei(IRE) was too keen and did not get home.
Munsef offered little for a yard that rarely make much impression in Dubai. (op 20-1)
Varsity never got in a blow on this drop in trip.
Drill Sergeant ran abysmally.

264a AL SHINDAGHA SPRINT (SPONSORED BY AL TAYER MOTORS) (GROUP 3) (DIRT) 6f (D)
6:25 (6:28) 3-Y-0+

£83,333 (£27,777; £13,888; £6,944; £4,166; £2,777)

RPR
1 **Big City Man (USA)**[14] 4-9-2 111.......... JVerenzuela 6 113+
(J Barton, Saudi Arabia) *trckd ldrs: led 2 1/2f out: r.o wl* **7/4**[1]
2 ¾ **Star Crowned (USA)**[48] 6-9-2 110..........(t) MJKinane 9 110
(R Bouresly, Kuwait) *trckd ldrs: rdn to chal 3f out: r.o wl fnl 2 1/2f* **15/2**
3 6 ¼ **Diana's Choice (SAF)**[257] 5-8-11 102.......... KShea 4 88+
(M F De Kock, South Africa) *chsd ldrs: outpcd 3f out: r.o wl* **5/1**[3]
4 3 ¾ **League Champion (USA)**[21] 6-9-2 98.......... KJohn 7 80
(R Bouresly, Kuwait) *nvr nr to chal* **66/1**
5 ¾ **Force Freeze (USA)**[21] 4-9-2 106..........(t) FJara 10 78
(Doug Watson, UAE) *mid-div: rdn 2 1/2f out: one pce* **4/1**[2]
6 *shd* **Sea Hunter**[21] 7-9-2 96..........(vt) RoystonFfrench 3 77
(A Al Raihe, UAE) *s.i.s: sn rdn in rr: nvr involved* **50/1**
7 7 ¼ **Salaam Dubai (AUS)**[21] 8-9-2 100.......... RichardMullen 5 56
(A Selvaratnam, UAE) *mid-div: wknd 2 1/2f out* **20/1**
8 6 **Strike Up The Band**[109] 6518 6-9-2 108.......... AdrianTNicholls 1 38
(D Nicholls) *wl away: sn led: hdd 3f out: wknd* **25/1**
9 *nse* **Barbecue Eddie (USA)**[151] 5-9-2 108..........(bt) RHills 12 38
(Doug Watson, UAE) *racd nr side: a struggling* **5/1**[3]
10 7 **Northern Fling**[124] 6104 5-9-2 98.......... MHarley 8 17
(D Nicholls) *nvr able to chal* **66/1**
11 ¼ **Ekhtiaar**[21] 5-9-2 98.......... AhmedAjtebi 11 16
(A Al Raihe, UAE) *nvr able to chal* **33/1**
12 2 ½ **Terrific Challenge (USA)**[42] 7-9-2 107..........(vt) TedDurcan 2 8
(S Seemar, UAE) *nvr bttr than mid-div* **10/1**

1m 10.31s (0.11) **Going Correction** +0.35s/f (Slow) **12** Ran SP% **127.0**
Speed ratings: **113,112,103,98,97 97,87,79,79,70 70,66**
CSF 16.23..
Owner Prince Sultan Mohammed Saud Al Kabeer **Bred** Four Horsemen's Ranch **Trained** Saudi Arabia

FOCUS
The sprints on the dirt in Dubai are traditionally quite weak until the Americans arrive for the Golden Shaheen on World Cup night, but the winner of this one was formerly trained in the States and to be fair this looked a decent race.

NOTEBOOK
Big City Man(USA), a triple winner in the US as a juvenile in 2007, won very nicely in a conditions contest over this course and distance on his return from an absence/debut for these connections two weeks previously and confirmed that promise on this step up to Group 3 company. He was pushed all the way to the line by the runner-up, but his rider gave the impression he was always confident and he probably won with something to spare. There is a handicap over this course and distance on February 20, but the Group 3 Mahab Al Shimaal on Super Thursday (March 5) is the obvious target. (op 2-1)
Star Crowned(USA) ran a big race in second and finished well clear of the remainder. He progressed into a smart performer at last year's Carnival and is evidently still going the right way. (op 7-1)
Diana's Choice(SAF), the only filly in the line up, ran her race but was no match for the front two. This was her first start since landing a Listed race in South Africa last May, should she is entitled to come on for the run.
League Champion(USA) ran about as well as could have been expected.
Force Freeze(USA) found this tougher than the handicap he won over course and distance on new year's day.
Strike Up The Band showed loads of speed but did not get home.
Barbecue Eddie(USA) was only a length behind Star Crowned when fourth in his last year's Golden Shaheen, but he ran no sort of race on his return from a spell in the US. (op 11-2)
Northern Fling never featured.

265a AL TAYER MOTORS 1600 (H'CAP) (TURF) 1m (T)
6:55 (6:57) (95-110,109) 3-Y-0+

£50,000 (£16,666; £8,333; £4,166; £2,500; £1,666)

RPR
1 **Alexandros**[82] 7147 4-9-4 **108**.......... LDettori 11 114
(Saeed Bin Suroor) *trckd ldng gp: led 1f out: comf* **13/2**[3]
2 1 ¼ **Kal Barg**[21] 4-8-6 **96**.......... AhmedAjtebi 1 99
(M bin Shafya, UAE) *mid-div: trckd ldrs 2 1/2f out: nt qckn fnl 110yds* **14/1**
3 1 ¼ **Prince Shaun (IRE)**[96] 6831 4-9-3 **107**..........(t) DO'Donohoe 3 107
(Doug Watson, UAE) *trckd ldr: led 2 1/2f out: hdd 1f out: one pce* **20/1**
4 3 **Bound By Honour (SAF)**[201] 6-9-3 **107**.......... RyanMoore 2 100
(H J Brown, South Africa) *in rr of mid-div: rdn 3f out: r.o fnl 1 1/2f: nvr nr to chal* **6/1**[2]
5 1 ¾ **Stepping Up (IRE)**[34] 6-8-10 **100**..........(t) TPO'Shea 4 89
(E Charpy, UAE) *in rr of mid-div: r.o fnl 2f: nrst fin* **25/1**
6 *shd* **Perfect Season (SAF)**[271] 5-8-8 **98**.......... EddieAhern 9 87
(H J Brown, South Africa) *mid-div on rail: nvr nr to chal* **25/1**
7 ½ **King Jock (USA)**[7] 182 8-9-2 **106**.......... KJManning 15 94
(A Manuel, UAE) *mid-div: r.o one pce fnl 2f* **16/1**
8 ½ **Noble Citizen (USA)**[64] 7381 4-8-5 **95**.......... RichardMullen 14 82
(D M Simcock) *nvr nr to chal* **25/1**
9 1 **Ragheed (USA)**[39] 5-8-10 **100**..........(vt) RHills 5 84
(E Charpy, UAE) *mid-div: chsd ldrs 2 1/2f out: one pce fnl 1 1/2f* **25/1**
10 1 **Swop (IRE)**[110] 6476 6-8-10 **100**.......... TedDurcan 10 82
(L M Cumani) *mid-div: rdn to chse ldrs 2 1/2f out: n.m.r 1 1/2f out: nt rcvr* **15/8**[1]
11 *hd* **Kachgai (IRE)**[35] 6-8-5 **95**.......... WilliamBuick 13 77
(L A Urbano-Grajales, France) *trckd ldrs: rn wd 3f out: sn struggling* **20/1**
12 ¾ **T-Bird (SAF)**[14] 8-8-7 **97**..........(t) FJara 8 77
(Doug Watson, UAE) *racd in last: nvr nr to chal* **16/1**
13 1 **Royal Power (IRE)**[154] 5208 6-8-9 **99**.......... AdrianTNicholls 7 77
(D Nicholls) *sn led: hdd 1 1/2f out: wknd qckly* **14/1**
14 4 ¼ **Gold Sovereign (IRE)**[82] 7146 5-8-10 **100**.......... RoystonFfrench 16 68
(I Mohammed, UAE) *nvr nr to chal* **33/1**
15 2 ¼ **Desert Links (SAF)**[173] 6-9-4 **108**..........(b) KLatham 12 71
(H J Brown, South Africa) *racd in rr: nvr able to chal* **12/1**
16 4 ¼ **Dijeerr (USA)**[7] 182 5-8-9 **109**..........(v) AntiocoMurgia[(10)] 6 62
(M bin Shafya, UAE) *trckd ldrs tl 2 1/2f out: wknd* **33/1**

1m 38.06s (-0.24) **Going Correction** +0.20s/f (Good) **16** Ran SP% **126.0**
Speed ratings: **109,107,106,103,101 101,101,100,99,98 98,97,96,92,90 85**
CSF 85.36; Tricast 1,748.93. PLACEPOT £621.90. Pool £25,730.51. 30.20 winning tickets. QUADPOT £51.80. Pool £679.89. 9.70 winning tickets..
Owner Godolphin **Bred** Darley **Trained** Newmarket, Suffolk

FOCUS
A decent, competitive big-field handicap.

NOTEBOOK
Alexandros underachieved in Britain last year, but he was a smart juvenile when with Andre Fabre and returned to something like his best on this first start in Dubai with a convincing success. He carried his head at a slight angle under pressure, and also edged left, but he certainly found plenty off the bridle having travelled well early.
Kal Barg got a run against the inside rail but simply found one too good. This was a significant improvement on the form he showed on the dirt first-time up for this stable.
Prince Shaun(IRE), a dual winner when trained in Ireland, had a tongue-tie fitted for the first time on his UAE debut, and he ran well under a positive ride, back from a three-month break.
Bound By Honour(SAF) ◆ was returning from nearly seven months off. He was never competitive having raced well off the pace, but he finished nicely and will be suited by a step up in trip now he has had a run.
Stepping Up(IRE) was another who got going too late.
Perfect Season(SAF) ◆ had been off for nearly nine months and should be suited by further.
Noble Citizen(USA) might be suited by a drop in trip, but it remains to be seen whether he is up to this class.
Swop(IRE) was beaten when short of room in the closing stages and was very disappointing. He had previously looked most progressive, and this was only his seventh start, so it's far too early to give up on him. (op 2-1)
Royal Power(IRE) was too free in front.

200 LINGFIELD (L-H)
Friday, January 23

OFFICIAL GOING: Standard
Wind: Strong, half against Weather: Overcast becoming brighter, heavy rain before racing

266 EDENBRIDGE CLAIMING STKS 7f (P)
12:40 (12:42) (Class 6) 4-Y-0+ **£2,047** (£604; £302) **Stalls** Low

Form RPR
1-11 1 **Mutamared (USA)**[7] 189 9-9-4 84..........(t) JamieSpencer 1 84+
(K A Ryan) *t.k.h early: hld up bhd ldrs: swtchd to outer 2f out: tending to hang but prog to ld fnl 150yds: cajoled along and sn in command* **2/1**[1]
0-56 2 ¾ **Excusez Moi (USA)**[3] 225 7-9-7 104..........(b) LiamJones 4 85
(Mrs R A Carr) *dwlt: t.k.h early: hld up in last pair: prog on inner 2f out: rdn to chal ent fnl f: readily hld by wnr* **11/4**[2]
2-13 3 *shd* **Desert Dreamer (IRE)**[11] 133 8-8-11 77.......... RichardKingscote 7 75
(Tom Dascombe) *t.k.h early: pressed ldr: narrow advantage 2f out tl last 150yds: one pce* **2/1**[1]
01-2 4 2 ¼ **C'Mon You Irons (IRE)**[14] 97 4-8-10 67.......... JimCrowley 3 68
(M R Hoad) *led: set stdy pce to 3f out: narrowly hdd 2f out: stl upsides ent fnl f: wknd* **8/1**[3]
000- 5 1 **Cactus King**[37] 7712 6-9-4 77.......... IanMongan 9 73
(P M Phelan) *t.k.h early: trckd ldng pair: urged along and nt qckn wl over 1f out: fdd fnl f* **20/1**
036- 6 ¾ **Sir Ike (IRE)**[46] 7609 4-8-11 60..........(tp) ShaneKelly 8 64
(W S Kittow) *hld up in last pair: nt qckn over 2f out: sn lft bhd by rest: kpt on fnl 100yds* **50/1**

1m 26.81s (2.01) **Going Correction** +0.10s/f (Slow) **6** Ran SP% **111.2**
Speed ratings (Par 101): **92,91,91,88,87 86**
toteswinger: 1&2 £1.60, 1&3 £1.30, 2&3 £2.40. CSF £7.67 TOTE £2.40: £1.60, £1.30; EX 8.00 Trifecta £16.50 Pool: £458.55 - 16.50 winning units..
Owner Errigal Racing **Bred** E J Hudson Jr, Irrevocable Trust & Kilroy T'Bred **Trained** Hambleton, N Yorks

FOCUS
Despite the small field, this was a very interesting claimer. The principals fought out a blanket finish.

267 DANIEL CHUMLEY 21ST BIRTHDAY H'CAP 7f (P)
1:10 (1:10) (Class 6) (0-60,60) 3-Y-O **£2,047** (£604; £302) **Stalls** Low

Form RPR
400- 1 **Ain't Talkin'**[23] 7833 3-8-5 46 oh1 PaulDoe 6 53
(M J Attwater) *t.k.h: w ldr: led 3f out: kicked 2 l clr over 2f out: drvn and kpt on wl fr over 1f out* **12/1**
62-3 2 1 1/4 **Imperial Skylight**[4] 214 3-9-4 59 TonyCulhane 2 63
(M R Channon) *hld up bhd ldrs: rdn to chse wnr 2f out: cl enough after and kpt on but no imp fnl f* **15/8**[1]
4-25 3 3 **Flawless Diamond (IRE)**[4] 214 3-8-11 52 (b) LukeMorris 7 48
(J S Moore) *hld up in last pair: outpcd whn effrt on outer and wd bnd 2f out: nt qckn after: plugged on fnl f to snatch 3rd on line* **5/2**[2]
64-0 4 nse **Nun Today (USA)**[4] 214 3-8-8 49 (b) LPKeniry 5 45
(J S Moore) *pressed ldng pair on outer: nt qckn 2f out and sn outpcd: n.d after: lost 3rd post* **12/1**
05-6 5 nse **Fleur De'Lion (IRE)**[7] 196 3-8-9 50 MartinDwyer 3 46
(S Kirk) *settled in last: pushed along 3f out: outpcd and nt clr run over 2f out: effrt on outer over 1f out: styd on wl fnl f: nrly snatched 3rd* **10/1**
601- 6 8 **Trusted Venture (USA)**[27] 7789 3-9-5 60 SteveDrowne 1 34
(J R Best) *t.k.h: hld up bhd ldrs: rdn 3f out: sn wknd and bhd* **7/2**[3]
050- 7 5 **Spiritual Bond**[66] 7370 3-8-8 52 KevinGhunowa(3) 4 13
(R A Harris) *narrow ld to 3f out: wknd rapidly 2f out: t.o* **50/1**

1m 25.33s (0.53) **Going Correction** +0.10s/f (Slow) 7 Ran SP% **112.0**
Speed ratings (Par 95): **100,98,95,95,95 85,80**
toteswinger: 1&2 £6.00, 1&3 £5.80, 2&3 £1.30. CSF £33.57 TOTE £26.00: £6.20, £1.10; EX 78.90.
Owner Canisbay Bloodstock **Bred** Canisbay Bloodstock Ltd **Trained** Epsom, Surrey

FOCUS
A modest three-year-old handicap run at no more than an ordinary pace and the fact that the winning time was 1.48 seconds faster than the claimer demonstrates just how slowly run that race was. There was no fluke about the winner's effort and the next two ran close to their form here last month.
Trusted Venture(USA) Official explanation: trainer had no explanation for the poor form shown

268 ASHURST WOOD (S) STKS 5f (P)
1:40 (1:41) (Class 6) 3-Y-O **£2,047** (£604; £302) **Stalls** High

Form RPR
400- 1 **Red Cell (IRE)**[36] 7719 3-9-5 62 (b) TomEaves 2 61
(I W McInnes) *blindfold late off and last away: trckd ldng pair over 3f out: cl up 2f out: drvn to chal on inner 1f out: led fnl 75yds: hld on* **9/1**
3-40 2 nse **Lois Darlin (IRE)**[4] 214 3-8-6 56 (b) KevinGhunowa(3) 3 51
(R A Harris) *pushed along to chse ldr: cl up 2f out: rdn and nt qckn over 1f out: hrd drvn and anther effrt on outer ins fnl f: jst hld* **11/2**[3]
30-1 3 1/2 **Just The Lady**[5] 207 3-9-0 73 StephenDonohoe 4 54
(D Nicholls) *fast away: led and sn 2 l clr: drvn over 1f out: hdd and fdd fnl 75yds* **1/1**[1]
0-53 4 3 1/4 **Quick Single (USA)**[6] 200 3-9-0 67 (b) HayleyTurner 1 42
(D R C Elsworth) *sn rdn: dropped to last over 3f out and outpcd: nvr on terms after* **15/8**[2]

60.18 secs (1.38) **Going Correction** +0.10s/f (Slow) 4 Ran SP% **110.2**
Speed ratings (Par 95): **92,91,91,85**
CSF £47.05 TOTE £10.70; EX 29.30.There was no bid for the winner.
Owner R E Hall & Son, I Woolfitt **Bred** Holborn Trust Co **Trained** Catwick, E Yorks

FOCUS
There was no hanging about in this typically moderate little seller and the first three came home in a blanket finish. The time was slow and the form is rated around the first two.

269 PLAY BINGO @ WILLIAMHILL.COM H'CAP 5f (P)
2:15 (2:16) (Class 6) (0-62,68) 4-Y-0+ **£2,047** (£604; £302) **Stalls** High

Form RPR
-511 1 **Whiskey Creek**[8] 173 4-8-13 68 6ex (b) BMcHugh(7) 10 79
(C A Dwyer) *trckd ldrs on outer: gng wl 1/2-way: effrt to ld over 1f out: drvn clr fnl f: decisively* **11/4**[2]
013- 2 1 1/2 **Now You See Me**[23] 7835 5-8-13 61 TonyCulhane 1 67
(D Flood) *hld up at rr of main gp: effrt on outer over 1f out: styd on fnl f to take 2nd last strides* **7/1**[3]
0-61 3 hd **Joss Stick**[9] 166 4-8-9 64 ow4 (p) SPRyan(7) 5 69
(R A Harris) *hld up bhd ldrs: stdy prog 2f out: effrt to chal on inner 1f out: sn brushed aside by wnr: lost 2nd last strides* **7/1**[3]
60-0 4 1 **Teen Ager (FR)**[7] 189 5-8-12 60 LPKeniry 7 62
(P Burgoyne) *led 100yds: styd chsng ldrs: effrt over 1f out: kpt on same pce* **33/1**
01-2 5 1 **Admiral Bond (IRE)**[21] 15 4-9-0 62 (p) ChrisCatlin 2 60+
(G R Oldroyd) *sn bdly outpcd in last pair and wl adrift: wd bnd 2f out: styd on fr over 1f out: nrst fin* **2/1**[1]
05-1 6 2 1/4 **Spic 'n Span**[8] 177 4-8-13 64 6ex (b) KevinGhunowa(3) 9 54
(R A Harris) *trckd ldr after 1f: led over 2f out: drvn and hdd over 1f out: wknd ins fnl f* **15/2**
40-6 7 1 1/2 **Pegasus Dancer (FR)**[14] 99 5-8-10 58 (v[1]) VinceSlattery 4 43
(R H York) *chsd ldrs: lost pl on inner 2f out: struggling over 1f out* **14/1**
000- 8 hd **Babel**[35] 7727 4-8-12 60 SimonWhitworth 8 44
(M Wigham) *led after 100yds to over 2f out: wknd over 1f out* **16/1**
05-0 9 3/4 **Lake Sabina**[14] 96 4-8-9 57 JimCrowley 6 38
(M R Hoad) *settled in last: sn bdly outpcd and wl adrift: shuffled along over 1f out: gaining on wkng rivals fin* **25/1**

58.60 secs (-0.20) **Going Correction** +0.10s/f (Slow) 9 Ran SP% **116.1**
Speed ratings (Par 101): **105,102,102,100,99 95,93,92,91**
toteswinger: 1&2 £5.20, 1&3 £4.20, 2&3 £6.10. CSF £22.64 CT £122.84 TOTE £3.50: £1.30, £2.40, £1.50; EX 24.20 Trifecta £412.90 Pool: £803.63 - 1.44 winning units.
Owner Mrs L Wheeler **Bred** R J H West **Trained** Burrough Green, Cambs

FOCUS
A modest sprint handicap, but quite a competitive event of its type run in a good time for the grade. Sound form.

270 LORD SWALE BIRTHDAY H'CAP 5f (P)
2:50 (2:50) (Class 4) (0-85,82) 4-Y-0+ **£4,857** (£1,445; £722; £360) **Stalls** High

Form RPR
051- 1 **Chjimes (IRE)**[60] 7435 5-8-10 74 LPKeniry 4 83
(C R Dore) *t.k.h: hld up in last pair: eased to outer and prog over 1f out: tending to hang but r.o wl fnl f to ld last strides* **14/1**
3-53 2 hd **Northern Empire (IRE)**[5] 212 6-8-11 75 (p) JamieSpencer 8 83
(K A Ryan) *chsd ldr after 1f: drvn over 1f out: clsd grad fnl f: got there as wnr flew past on line* **7/2**[2]
-111 3 nse **Nickel Silver**[9] 165 4-9-2 80 6ex (b) TomEaves 9 88
(B Smart) *led and racd keenly: rdn over 1f out: looked like holding on but collared last strides* **9/4**[1]
20-6 4 2 **Bo McGinty (IRE)**[17] 67 8-8-13 77 (b) PaulHanagan 5 78
(R A Fahey) *hld up towards rr: rdn and effrt 2f out: kpt on same pce and no threat to ldrs* **22/1**
211- 5 1 **Thoughtsofstardom**[34] 7743 6-8-12 76 LukeMorris 6 73
(P S McEntee) *prom: chsd ldng pair 2f out: no imp: lost pl fnl f* **8/1**
5-43 6 nk **Fromsong (IRE)**[8] 170 11-8-13 82 JamesO'Reilly(5) 3 78
(D K Ivory) *hld up in midfield: effrt 2f out: chsd ldrs but no imp over 1f out: fdd* **6/1**[3]
41-0 7 1/2 **Cosmic Destiny (IRE)**[1] 243 7-8-6 70 ChrisCatlin 7 64
(E F Vaughan) *racd wd: hld up in last pair: effrt over 1f out: sme prog ent fnl f: pushed along and no hdwy after* **12/1**
54-3 8 2 1/4 **Canadian Danehill (IRE)**[17] 67 7-9-1 79 (p) ShaneKelly 2 65
(R M H Cowell) *chsd ldr 1f: styd prom tl wknd over 1f out* **6/1**[3]
40-4 9 3 3/4 **Know No Fear**[8] 170 4-8-13 77 DarrenWilliams 1 50
(D Shaw) *dwlt: t.k.h: snatched up on inner after 1f: nvr really a factor: wknd over 1f out* **12/1**

57.96 secs (-0.84) **Going Correction** +0.10s/f (Slow) 9 Ran SP% **119.1**
Speed ratings (Par 105): **110,109,109,106,104 104,103,99,93**
toteswinger: 1&2 £12.60, 1&3 £9.40, 2&3 £2.90. CSF £64.64 CT £157.28 TOTE £20.30: £4.20, £1.60, £1.30; EX 86.50 Trifecta £584.70 Part won. Pool: £790.23 - 0.94 Winning units..
Owner Sean J Murphy **Bred** Morgan O'Flaherty **Trained** Cowbit, Lincs

FOCUS
A decent sprint and there was no hanging about, which probably helped the winner no end. The winning time was 0.64 seconds faster than the preceding Class 6 handicap. Sound form.

271 WILLIAM HILL TELEBETTING ON 0800 44 40 40 H'CAP 1m 2f (P)
3:25 (3:25) (Class 4) (0-85,85) 4-Y-0+ **£4,857** (£1,445; £722; £360) **Stalls** Low

Form RPR
324- 1 **Confidentiality (IRE)**[149] 5410 5-9-4 83 NickyMackay 10 91
(M Wigham) *trckd ldrs: wnt 3rd 2f out: rdn to ld 1f out: sn wl in command* **33/1**
2 1 1/2 **Horseshoe Reef (AUS)**[170] 6-8-11 76 ChrisCatlin 13 81
(J R Gask) *racd keenly: led after 2f: jnd wl over 1f out: hdd 1f out: kpt on same pce* **33/1**
01-3 3 3/4 **Dream Of Fortune (IRE)**[16] 79 5-8-12 77 (t) JamieSpencer 4 80
(M G Quinlan) *prom: wnt 2nd 1/2-way: chal and upsides wl over 1f out: hung rt and fnd nil: folded up ins fnl f* **9/2**[2]
43-2 4 nse **Stand Guard**[16] 79 5-9-1 80 IanMongan 1 83
(P Howling) *trckd ldrs: rdn and nt qckn wl over 1f out: styd on again ins fnl f* **11/4**[1]
160/ 5 hd **Sharpazmax (IRE)**[596] 2400 5-9-0 79 SteveDrowne 6 82
(P J Makin) *settled in midfield: effrt towards outer over 2f out: nt qckn over 1f out: styd on again ins fnl f* **20/1**
555- 6 1 1/4 **Kidlat**[46] 7603 4-8-7 74 (t) HayleyTurner 9 74
(B G Powell) *v awkward s: t.k.h and hld up in last pair: sme prog towards inner fr 2f out: kpt on but nt pce to threaten* **12/1**
00-5 7 1 1/2 **Scamperdale**[16] 79 7-9-3 82 JimCrowley 14 79
(B P J Baugh) *hld up towards rr on inner: sme prog wl over 1f out: no imp after* **11/1**
265- 8 nk **Princess Cocoa (IRE)**[186] 4244 6-8-10 75 PaulHanagan 2 72
(R A Fahey) *led 2f: chsd ldr to 1/2-way: styd cl up tl wknd jst over 1f out* **28/1**
41-6 9 1/2 **Phoenix Flight (IRE)**[9] 163 4-8-13 80 StephenDonohoe 11 76
(Sir Mark Prescott) *s.s: hld up in last: pushed along on inner over 2f out: no ch whn drvn over 1f out* **8/1**
000- 10 1/2 **Alpes Maritimes**[24] 7821 5-9-1 80 FergusSweeney 7 75
(G L Moore) *hld up in midfield: gng wl enough 3f out: rdn on outer 2f out: hanging and fnd nil* **11/2**[3]
11 10 **Sufad**[45] 3464 4-8-11 78 DaneO'Neill 5 53
(G L Moore) *a wl in rr: u.p and struggling 3f out: sn bhd* **50/1**
010- 12 1/2 **Cold Turkey**[329] 757 9-8-13 85 JemmaMarshall(7) 3 59
(G L Moore) *hld up towards rr: no prog over 2f out: sn wl bhd* **33/1**
510- 13 2 3/4 **Ellmau**[55] 7493 4-9-4 85 RobertWinston 8 53
(A J McCabe) *v awkward s: hld up in last pair: sme prog on wd outside over 2f out: v wd and hanging bnd sn after: wknd rapidly* **10/1**
004- 14 2 3/4 **Polish Power (GER)**[82] 7150 9-9-3 82 LPKeniry 12 45
(J S Moore) *pressed ldng pair: u.p 4f out: wknd rapidly over 2f out* **25/1**

2m 5.89s (-0.71) **Going Correction** +0.10s/f (Slow)
WFA 4 from 5yo+ 2lb 14 Ran SP% **119.3**
Speed ratings (Par 105): **106,104,104,104,104 103,101,101,101,100 92,92,90,87**
toteswinger: 1&2 £175.20, 1&3 £27.00, 2&3 £21.00. CSF £819.68 CT £5734.50 TOTE £51.10: £11.30, £8.50, £1.70; EX 456.80 TRIFECTA Not won..
Owner J M Cullinan **Bred** Kevin Foley **Trained** Newmarket, Suffolk

FOCUS
A decent and competitive handicap, but despite what seemed a fair pace the first four home were handy from the outset. The form looks ordinary for the grade but the winner produced a personal best on her return to Polytrack.
Sharpazmax(IRE) Official explanation: jockey said gelding cocked its jaw and ducked right in back straight
Ellmau Official explanation: jockey said he lost an iron leaving stalls

272 PLAY POKER @ WILLIAMHILL.COM MAIDEN STKS 1m 2f (P)
4:00 (4:03) (Class 5) 3-Y-O **£2,729** (£806; £403) **Stalls** Low

Form RPR
0- 1 **Signella**[85] 7097 3-8-12 0 ChrisCatlin 12 66
(P W Chapple-Hyam) *mde virtually all: drvn 2f out: hung rt fnl f: hld on wl* **22/1**
0 2 nk **Red Suede Shoes**[13] 121 3-9-0 0 JamesMillman(3) 5 71
(B R Millman) *reluctant to enter stalls: trckd ldrs: effrt 2f out: wnt 2nd 1f out and sn chalng: carried rt and nt qckn: jst hld after* **25/1**
03-3 3 nk **Haljaferia (UAE)**[13] 121 3-9-3 72 JamieSpencer 1 70
(D R C Elsworth) *trckd ldrs: squeezed though to get clsr wl over 2f out: effrt over 1f out but nt qckn: styd on last 100yds: a hld* **5/6**[1]
4 1 1/4 **Lacrosse** 3-9-3 0 ShaneKelly 10 68+
(M A Jarvis) *dwlt: hld up in midfield: outpcd over 2f out: shkn up and styd on quite promisingly fnl f* **10/3**[2]
0- 5 hd **Dubai Storming**[170] 4728 3-9-3 0 SteveDrowne 6 69+
(E A L Dunlop) *hld up in 8th: effrt on outer 2f out: hanging and stmbld wl over 1f out: styd on ins fnl f* **33/1**

0-3 **6** 3/4 **Green Passion (USA)**[11] 138 3-9-3 0 JimCrowley 7 69+
(M Johnston) *trckd wnr: asked to chal over 1f out but hanging and fnd nil: wl hld whn squeezed out last 75yds* **4/1**[3]

0-4 **7** 2 **Tropical Duke (IRE)**[20] 32 3-9-3 0 MartinDwyer 9 62
(D W P Arbuthnot) *prom: losing pl whn c wd bnd 2f out: pushed along and nt on terms after* **33/1**

06-6 **8** 4 1/2 **Give (IRE)**[21] 16 3-8-12 49 (p) FrankieMcDonald 2 48
(R A Harris) *hld up in midfield: gng wl enough on inner over 2f out: pushed along and steadily wknd* **50/1**

4- **9** 10 **Rebel Prince (IRE)**[120] 6234 3-9-3 0 EdwardCreighton 8 33
(M G Quinlan) *t.k.h: hld up in last pair: lost tch 3f out: bhd after* **33/1**

0- **10** 31 **Risque Belle**[69] 7341 3-8-12 0 StephenDonohoe 3 —
(E J Creighton) *t.k.h: hld up in last: wknd rapidly over 3f out: t.o* **100/1**

2m 10.27s (3.67) **Going Correction** +0.10s/f (Slow) **10** Ran SP% **117.6**
Speed ratings (Par 97): **89,88,88,87,87 86,85,81,73,48**
toteswinger: 1&2 £18.60, 1&3 £5.90, 2&3 £6.10. CSF £414.61 TOTE £21.20: £3.60, £3.60, £1.10; EX 282.30 TRIFECTA Not won. Place 6: £563.02 Place 5: £310.18.
Owner Woodcote Stud Ltd **Bred** Ridgecourt Stud **Trained** Newmarket, Suffolk
■ Stewards' Enquiry : Jamie Spencer three-day ban: careless riding (Feb 11-13)

FOCUS
A modest maiden and a rather messy contest having been steadily run. The favourite set the standard and was probably below his best.
Risque Belle Official explanation: jockey said filly moved poorly
T/Plt: £446.90 to a £1 stake. Pool: £64,775.55. 105.79 winning tickets. T/Qpdt: £58.00 to a £1 stake. Pool: £6,207.83. 79.20 winning tickets. JN

249 WOLVERHAMPTON (A.W) (L-H)

Friday, January 23

OFFICIAL GOING: Standard
Wind: Almost nil Weather: Fine

273 PLAY BINGO @ WILLIAMHILL.COM H'CAP 5f 20y(P)
6:50 (6:51) (Class 6) (0-55,60) 3-Y-O **£2,729** (£806; £403) **Stalls** Low

Form RPR

-121 **1** **Kheley (IRE)**[1] 246 3-9-6 60 6ex LiamJones 2 67
(W M Brisbourne) *chsd ldr: edgd lft wl over 1f out: sn rdn: r.o to ld towards fin* **9/2**[3]

5-52 **2** 1/2 **Sorrel Ridge (IRE)**[1] 246 3-8-12 52 (p) AdamKirby 1 57
(M G Quinlan) *hmpd s: hld up in mid-div: hdwy over 2f out: led over 1f out: edgd rt and hdd towards fin* **7/2**[2]

00-6 **3** 1 1/2 **You'relikemefrank**[15] 91 3-8-5 45 (p) AndrewElliott 8 45
(J Balding) *led: hdd over 1f out: sn rdn: no ex towards fin* **33/1**

25-1 **4** 1/2 **Forever's Girl**[11] 135 3-9-2 59 6ex DuranFentiman(3) 4 57
(G R Oldroyd) *wnt lft s: hld up in tch: rdn over 1f out: kpt on same pce ins fnl f* **7/4**[1]

503- **5** 2 1/4 **Rocket Ruby**[36] 7719 3-8-9 49 ow1 DarrenWilliams 6 46+
(D Shaw) *hld up in mid-div: lost pl 3f out: rdn and hdwy over 1f out: styng on whn eased towards fin: sddle slipped* **16/1**

000- **6** 2 **Flaming Ruby**[99] 6764 3-8-5 45 JimmyQuinn 3 28
(N Tinkler) *hld up and bhd: hdwy 2f out: wknd 1f out* **12/1**

050- **7** 3 3/4 **Fasliyanne (IRE)**[45] 7612 3-9-0 54 (p) TomEaves 10 23
(K A Ryan) *hld up in tch: lost pl over 3f out: n.d after* **15/2**

505- **8** nk **Meg Jicaro**[83] 7130 3-8-5 45 LukeMorris 9 13
(Mrs L Williamson) *prom tl rdn and wknd over 2f out* **40/1**

0-26 **9** 1 1/4 **Captain Bradz (USA)**[15] 92 3-7-13 46 ow1 PaulPickard(7) 5 9
(P T Midgley) *s.i.s: a in rr* **50/1**

460- **10** 1 **Usual Suspects**[144] 5567 3-8-1 48 AndrewHeffernan(7) 11 8
(Peter Grayson) *s.i.s: hld up and bhd: short-lived effrt on ins over 2f out* **100/1**

62.24 secs (-0.06) **Going Correction** -0.125s/f (Stan) **10** Ran SP% **110.4**
Speed ratings (Par 95): **95,94,91,91,87 84,78,77,75,74**
toteswinger: 1&2 £4.40, 1&3 £26.70, 2&3 £17.80. CSF £19.05 CT £436.26 TOTE £6.10: £1.10, £1.90, £4.10; EX 17.80.
Owner W M Clare **Bred** Matt Gilsenan **Trained** Great Ness, Shropshire

FOCUS
A very moderate handicap but it was run at a decent pace and two horses who fought out the finish at Kempton the previous night dominated once again. Kheley improved in defying a 6lb penalty, but the form is not entirely convincing.
Rocket Ruby Official explanation: jockey said saddle slipped
Meg Jicaro Official explanation: jockey said filly hung right

274 VAUXHALL INSIGNIA CAR OF THE YEAR 2009 CLAIMING STKS 1m 141y(P)
7:20 (7:21) (Class 6) 4-Y-O+ **£2,047** (£604; £302) **Stalls** Low

Form RPR

-243 **1** **Teasing**[7] 195 5-8-13 69 (v) RobertHavlin 3 73
(J Pearce) *s.i.s: hld up in rr: rdn and hdwy over 1f out: led wl ins fnl f: drvn out* **11/4**[2]

41-5 **2** 1 3/4 **Dancing Deano (IRE)**[11] 133 7-8-8 65 ow1 RussellKennemore(3) 1 67
(R Hollinshead) *led early: a.p: rdn to ld 1f out: hdd and no ex wl ins fnl f* **9/1**[3]

1-11 **3** 2 3/4 **United Nations**[15] 93 8-8-10 84 (b) LeeEnstone 2 60
(N Wilson) *prom: wnt 2nd 2f out: rdn to chal 2f out: wknd ins fnl f* **8/15**[1]

023- **4** nk **Kipchak (IRE)**[41] 7662 4-8-13 60 HayleyTurner 4 63
(C E Brittain) *sn led: rdn and hdd 1f out: wknd wl ins fnl f* **16/1**

1m 48.67s (-1.83) **Going Correction** -0.125s/f (Stan) **4** Ran SP% **107.8**
WFA 4 from 5yo+ 1lb
Speed ratings (Par 101): **103,101,99,98**
CSF £20.62 TOTE £4.20; EX 15.60.
Owner D Leech **Bred** Chippenham Lodge Stud Ltd **Trained** Newmarket, Suffolk

FOCUS
On paper this was an easy task for the market leader, but events did not unfold as expected. The early pace was fair then slowed mid-race, giving all four runners some sort of chance and they were all in a line a furlong from home. Dancing Deano did not need to match her recent best, with United Nations way below his recent Fibresand form.

275 DANCE 'TIL LATE IN THE RINGSIDE H'CAP 1m 1f 103y(P)
7:50 (7:50) (Class 6) (0-52,57) 4-Y-O+ **£2,047** (£604; £302) **Stalls** Low

Form RPR

0-45 **1** **Ridgeway Jazz**[4] 216 4-8-8 49 LukeMorris 8 60
(M D I Usher) *hld up in rr: hdwy on outside over 2f out: rdn to ld wl ins fnl f: r.o* **5/1**[2]

01-1 **2** 1 3/4 **Chalice Welcome**[7] 193 6-9-3 57 6ex HayleyTurner 7 64
(N B King) *hld up and bhd: hdwy on outside over 2f out: rdn to ld 1f out: hdd and nt qckn wl ins fnl f* **7/4**[1]

005- **3** 1 3/4 **John Potts**[74] 7274 4-8-9 50 (p) AndrewElliott 13 53
(B P J Baugh) *hld up in mid-div: hdwy on ins over 2f out: rdn and ev ch ins fnl f: one pce* **80/1**

0-40 **4** 1 1/2 **Doctor Delta**[4] 221 4-8-7 48 JimmyQuinn 10 48
(M Brittain) *hld up in tch: chsd ldr 3f out tl over 1f out: wknd ins fnl f* **5/1**[2]

00-6 **5** 1/2 **Fairly Honest**[7] 186 5-8-4 49 WilliamCarson(5) 2 48
(P W Hiatt) *led: clr over 3f out: rdn and hdd 1f out: wknd ins fnl f* **16/1**

00-3 **6** 9 **Ten Spot (IRE)**[14] 105 4-8-10 51 (t) MickyFenton 11 31
(Stef Liddiard) *stdd s: hld up in rr: rdn wl over 1f out: nvr nr ldrs* **7/1**[3]

050- **7** 1 1/4 **Carry On Cleo**[104] 6654 4-8-0 46 (v) DanielleMcCreery(5) 5 24
(A Berry) *a bhd* **25/1**

502/ **8** shd **Dictation**[70] 7330 7-8-5 45 (b) RPCleary 6 22
(Mrs Valerie Keatley, Ire) *hld up in tch: rdn over 2f out: wknd wl over 1f out* **14/1**

600- **9** 12 **Jonquille (IRE)**[53] 7518 4-8-11 52 LiamJones 9 4
(R Ford) *chsd ldr tl rdn 3f out: sn wknd* **50/1**

35-6 **10** 47 **Jarvo**[16] 81 8-8-9 49 (v) TomEaves 4 —
(I W McInnes) *prom: rdn over 4f out: wknd over 3f out: t.o* **10/1**

2m 0.36s (-1.34) **Going Correction** -0.125s/f (Stan)
WFA 4 from 5yo+ 1lb **10** Ran SP% **110.9**
Speed ratings (Par 101): **100,98,96,95,95 87,86,85,75,33**
toteswinger: 1&2 £13.40, 1&3 £13.40, 2&3 £12.20. CSF £13.19 CT £573.92 TOTE £7.30: £1.70, £1.20, £14.30; EX 18.40.
Owner The Ridgeway Bloodstock Company Ltd **Bred** Templeton Stud And Bricklow Ltd **Trained** Upper Lambourn, Berks

FOCUS
The pace did not look that strong, but the field was strung out early, which perhaps said more about the overall quality of the competition. The first and second came from off the pace and the first five finished close up.
Jarvo Official explanation: jockey said gelding lost its action

276 WILLIAM HILL TELEBETTING ON 0800 44 40 40 H'CAP 7f 32y(P)
8:20 (8:20) (Class 4) (0-85,79) 3-Y-O **£5,180** (£1,541; £770; £384) **Stalls** High

Form RPR

22-1 **1** **Dream Date (IRE)**[13] 122 3-8-9 73 (t) GilmarPereira(3) 4 80
(W J Haggas) *sn led: rdn over 1f out: r.o* **8/1**

003- **2** 3/4 **Shaws Diamond (USA)**[42] 7646 3-8-13 74 AdamKirby 1 79
(D Shaw) *t.k.h: hdwy over 5f out: chsd wnr over 1f out: sn rdn: kpt on ins fnl f* **7/1**

-212 **3** 3 3/4 **Hellbender (IRE)**[6] 203 3-8-11 72 RichardKingscote 6 67
(S Kirk) *hld up in tch: rdn and hung lft fr over 1f out: one pce* **15/8**[1]

1- **4** 1 1/2 **Trueblue Wizard (IRE)**[31] 7773 3-9-0 75 MartinDwyer 5 66
(W R Muir) *sn chsng wnr: rdn wl over 2f out: lost 2nd over 1f out: wknd ins fnl f* **7/2**[2]

325- **5** nk **Grand Honour (IRE)**[24] 7820 3-9-4 79 JimmyQuinn 7 69
(P Howling) *hld up and bhd: hdwy on ins over 2f out: rdn and no imp fnl f* **8/1**

060- **6** 3/4 **Citizenship**[111] 6481 3-8-12 73 StephenDonohoe 3 61
(Ian Williams) *a in rr* **40/1**

41- **7** 7 **Ajara (IRE)**[49] 7561 3-8-10 71 LukeMorris 2 40
(N J Vaughan) *led early: prom tl wknd over 3f out* **5/1**[3]

1m 28.88s (-0.72) **Going Correction** -0.125s/f (Stan) **7** Ran SP% **110.8**
Speed ratings (Par 99): **99,98,93,92,91 90,82**
toteswinger: 1&2 £10.50, 1&3 £1.90, 2&3 £19.10. CSF £57.41 TOTE £5.30: £2.20, £4.90; EX 30.50.
Owner Exors of the Late F C T Wilson **Bred** J Hanly, A Stroud And T Stewart **Trained** Newmarket, Suffolk

FOCUS
An enterprising ride dictating the pace paid dividends as the winner kicked on from the home turn and left everything else toiling behind. She is rated up another 4lb on her revised Lingfield mark.
Hellbender(IRE) Official explanation: jockey said colt hung badly right

277 FRANKSALOT'S 100TH RACE TONIGHT H'CAP 7f 32y(P)
8:50 (8:50) (Class 6) (0-55,61) 4-Y-O+ **£1,942** (£578; £288; £144) **Stalls** High

Form RPR

4-61 **1** **Guildenstern (IRE)**[2] 234 7-9-5 61 6ex JimmyQuinn 4 72
(P Howling) *hld up in mid-div: hdwy on ins to ld jst over 1f out: drvn out* **11/2**[3]

0-01 **2** 2 **Ardent Prince**[4] 221 6-9-0 56 6ex RobertWinston 5 62
(A J McCabe) *hld up in tch: ev ch jst over 1f out: sn rdn: nt qckn* **9/2**[2]

-016 **3** nk **Stargazy**[2] 242 5-8-2 51 HollyHall(7) 1 56
(W G M Turner) *s.i.s: hld up in rr: hdwy wl over 1f out: r.o ins fnl f* **20/1**

05-5 **4** 1/2 **Aggbag**[12] 130 5-8-9 51 (p) AndrewElliott 2 54
(B P J Baugh) *led early: a.p: rdn over 1f out: kpt on same pce fnl f* **11/1**

-433 **5** 1/2 **Nabeeda**[3] 222 4-8-13 55 DanielTudhope 10 57
(M Brittain) *sn led: rdn over 2f out: hdd jst over 1f out: one pce* **11/2**[3]

60-5 **6** 2 3/4 **Semah Harold**[16] 81 4-8-8 50 (v) GrahamGibbons 6 45
(E S McMahon) *prom tl rdn and wknd over 1f out* **14/1**

45-4 **7** hd **Elkhart Lake (IRE)**[14] 104 4-8-1 46 oh1 (bt) DuranFentiman(3) 3 40
(Adrian McGuinness, Ire) *hld up in rr: sme hdwy wl over 1f out: n.d* **25/1**

005- **8** 1 3/4 **All You Need (IRE)**[39] 7692 5-8-8 50 (p) HayleyTurner 12 39
(R Hollinshead) *hld up in rr: swtchd lft sn after s: c v wd st: hung lft jst ins fnl f: n.d* **17/2**

00-0 **9** 5 **Fish Called Johnny**[19] 37 5-7-13 46 oh1 (b) DanielleMcCreery(5) 7 22
(A Berry) *hld up in mid-div: c wd st: wknd over 1f out* **66/1**

2-02 **10** 2 1/4 **Kabis Amigos**[11] 133 7-8-8 50 (b) GregFairley 9 20
(S T Mason) *t.k.h: hdwy after 1f: wknd wl over 1f out* **11/4**[1]

03-0 **11** 1 **Franksalot (IRE)**[20] 23 9-8-11 53 (b) PatrickMathers 11 20
(I W McInnes) *prom tl rdn wl over 1f out: rdn and bhd fnl 3f* **33/1**

4-00 **12** 22 **Victory Spirit**[4] 221 5-8-10 52 (b) TomEaves 8 —
(I Semple) *prom tl wknd wl over 2f out: eased over 1f out* **20/1**

1m 28.82s (-0.78) **Going Correction** -0.125s/f (Stan) **12** Ran SP% **118.9**
Speed ratings (Par 101): **99,96,96,95,95 92,91,89,84,81 80,55**
toteswinger: 1&2 £6.50, 1&3 £30.30, 2&3 £27.50. CSF £28.51 CT £468.31 TOTE £6.20: £2.50, £3.30, £8.80; EX 22.50.
Owner David Andrew Brown **Bred** Peter E Daly **Trained** Newmarket, Suffolk
■ Franksalot finished eleventh in his 'own' race.

FOCUS
There was a battle for the early lead, and the final time was almost identical to the class 4 handicap earlier on the card. There is a little doubt over the form with both the front pair regularly beaten off lower marks before winning ordinary races latest, and the favourite disappointing.

278 PLAY POKER @ WILLIAMHILL.COM CONDITIONS STKS 1m 141y(P)
9:20 (9:20) (Class 2) 4-Y-0+
£12,462 (£3,732; £1,866; £934; £466; £234) Stalls Low

Form RPR
410- 1 Mahadee (IRE)[55] 7492 4-8-13 90.....(b) JamieSpencer 4 101
(C E Brittain) *a gng wl: shkn up to ld ins fnl f: readily* 5/2[2]
13-4 2 3 Abbondanza (IRE)[16] 73 6-9-3 93.....(p) TomEaves 3 97
(I Semple) *sn led: rdn and hung bdly rt over 1f out: hdd ins fnl f: sn btn* 4/1[3]
520- 3 ½ Docofthebay (IRE)[111] 6476 5-9-0 104..... ShaneKelly 1 93
(J A Osborne) *hld up: hdwy wl over 1f out: rdn and one pce fnl f* 6/4[1]
410- 4 3¼ Tourist[209] 3494 4-9-2 79..... DarrenWilliams 7 88?
(D Shaw) *hld up in rr: rdn and hdwy over 1f out: no imp fnl f* 14/1
66-1 5 2 Indian Diva (IRE)[8] 179 4-8-8 75.....(t) GrahamGibbons 2 76
(R Curtis) *led early: chsd ldr tl rdn over 1f out: wknd fnl f* 16/1
00-0 6 ¾ Fajr (IRE)[6] 206 7-9-0 103.....(v) JimmyQuinn 5 79
(Miss Gay Kelleway) *hld up: short-lived effrt on outside over 2f out* 11/1
/5-0 7 9 Naomh Geileis (USA)[13] 124 4-8-8 90..... GregFairley 6 53
(M Johnston) *hld up in tch: wknd over 2f out* 25/1

1m 48.37s (-2.13) **Going Correction** -0.125s/f (Stan)
WFA 4 from 5yo+ 1lb 7 Ran SP% 113.3
Speed ratings (Par 109): **104,101,100,98,96 95,87**
CSF £12.71 TOTE £2.30: £2.50, £2.10; EX 6.80 Place 6: £549.73 Place 5: £245.74.
Owner Saeed Manana **Bred** Darley **Trained** Newmarket, Suffolk

FOCUS
A competitive conditions race with several in-form horses lining up. The pace was only ordinary and the form is rated around the runner-up, with the progressive Mahadee taking another step forward.

NOTEBOOK
Mahadee(IRE), under a typically cool ride from Jamie Spencer, having his only ride of the meeting, tracked the early pace and, when sent to challenge in the home straight, comfortably pulled clear. Having been outclassed in Listed company on his last run back in November, he appreciated this easier test and won like a progressive horse. It was probably an easier win than expected, for the jockey was alert to the danger of the market leader, but that challenge never materialised, and he had previously defeated the second comprehensively in a handicap at Great Leighs. (op 9-4)
Abbondanza(IRE) loves to dominate over this course and distance. A winner of four from six previous starts here, he is remarkably consistent, which has earned him a career-high mark, from which he was a one-paced fourth in a better race last time. Setting the pace once again, he looked tired when drifting right in the final furlong, then drifted left but kept on. (op 7-2)
Docofthebay(IRE) Getting away slowly, \bDocofthebay\p was soon tracking the winner on the rail, but looked awkward with nothing left to give in the straight. The market leader was well treated on the pick of his handicap form, though he seems best in the hurly-burly of a big field, so facing just six runners on his first run since October was probably not ideal. He was sweating beforehand and will come on for this run.\n (op 2-1)
Tourist, sold out of Barry Hills's yard for just 5,000gns in October, plugged on from the rear but was outclassed. However, this was a decent enough all-weather debut, considering he has not raced since June. (op 33-1)
Indian Diva(IRE), stepping up in trip after winning a fillies' handicap at Southwell last time, had a lot to find on official ratings but ran creditably in the circumstances, tracking the leader until the home turn before fading. (op 14-1)
Fajr(IRE) looked to be travelling well in the back straight but soon came under pressure. He is rated 103 but has not run to that level since winning over a mile at Lingfield a year ago and may be better over shorter. (op 14-1)
Naomh Geileis(USA) was highly tried as a juvenile, but after more than a year off she has struggled for form this winter, and again faded out of contention. (op 18-1)
T/Plt: £242.30 to a £1 stake. Pool: £122,557.16. 369.23 winning tickets. T/Qpdt: £14.60 to a £1 stake. Pool: £11,381.14. 576.10 winning tickets. KH

266 LINGFIELD (L-H)
Saturday, January 24

OFFICIAL GOING: Standard
Wind: modest, across Weather: cloudy, chilly

279 LIVE CASINO GAMES @ WILLIAMHILL.COM MAIDEN STKS 1m 4f (P)
12:50 (12:50) (Class 5) 4-Y-0+
£2,729 (£806; £403) Stalls Low

Form RPR
1 Quite A Fella (USA)[50] 4-9-3 0..... ChrisCatlin 4 69+
(Andrew Turnell) *stdd s and s.i.s: bhd: rdn and hdwy on outer over 2f out: led ent fnl f: r.o wl* 9/2[2]
3 2 1½ Regal Angel[15] 102 6-9-2 0..... JimCrowley 3 62+
(Jean-Rene Auvray) *s.i.s: sn in tch: chsd ldr 9f out tl over 5f out: rdn and unable qck over 2f out: styd on u.p to go 2nd wl ins fnl f: nt threaten wnr* 4/1[1]
354- 3 1¼ Dusk[32] 7775 4-9-3 67.....(b) DaneO'Neill 2 65
(Mrs S J Humphrey) *stdd s: t.k.h: hld up in last pair: hdwy to chse ldrs over 2f out: ev ch and drvn ent fnl f: nt qckn and fdd fnl 5yds* 5/1[3]
45-2 4 ½ Hammer[15] 102 4-9-3 68..... SteveDrowne 7 64
(R T Phillips) *led at stdy gallop tl hdd over 3f out: rdn to ld again wl over 1f out: hdd ent fnl f: one pce* 9/2[2]
5 ¾ One Zero (USA)[148] 5483 4-8-12 0..... PatCosgrave 9 58
(M G Quinlan) *mounted on crse: t.k.h: in tch: hdwy to chse ldr over 5f out: led over 3f out tl hrd drvn and hdd wl over 1f out: btn ent fnl f* 11/2
56- 6 3 Lucky Dancer[25] 7822 4-9-3 0..... HayleyTurner 5 58
(D R C Elsworth) *wnt lft s: t.k.h: chsd ldrs: rdn and effrt over 2f out: one pce and no imp* 11/2
0- 7 43 Lukatara (USA)[34] 7757 4-8-10 0..... JemmaMarshall[(7)] 6 —
(Miss Sheena West) *t.k.h: hld up in tch: rdn and wknd qckly over 2f out: t.o* 100/1
8 22 Flanders Fields[243] 4-9-3 0..... FergusSweeney 8 —
(G L Moore) *t.k.h: hld up towards rr: lost tch qckly over 3f out: t.o* 12/1

2m 33.6s (0.60) **Going Correction** 0.0s/f (Stan)
WFA 4 from 6yo 4lb 8 Ran SP% 112.5
Speed ratings (Par 103): **98,97,96,95,95 93,64,50**
toteswinger: 1&2 £9.10, 1&3 £24.00, 2&3 £21.30. CSF £22.05 TOTE £6.50: £2.10, £2.10, £1.70; EX 30.90 Trifecta £134.30 Part won. Pool: £181.55 - 0.57 winning units..
Owner The Chosen Few **Bred** Lincoln Collins & Luke Lillingston **Trained** Broad Hinton, Wilts

FOCUS
An interesting maiden, with first and second places going to ex-bumper performers. The pace was modest until stepping up significantly at halfway. The race has been rated around the third and fourth.

280 PLAY ROULETTE @ WILLIAMHILL.COM MAIDEN STKS 1m (P)
1:25 (1:28) (Class 5) 3-Y-0+
£2,729 (£806; £403) Stalls High

Form RPR
2 1 Thief Of Time (IRE)[10] 154 3-8-8 0 ow1..... JamieSpencer 9 75+
(P W Chapple-Hyam) *s.i.s: t.k.h: hld up towards rr: hdwy over 2f out: drvn and qcknd over 1f out: led wl ins fnl f: r.o wl* 4/5[1]
06- 2 nk Capeability (IRE)[154] 5271 3-8-7 0..... EdwardCreighton 4 70+
(M R Channon) *t.k.h: hld up in tch: rdn to chse ldng pair 2f out: led ins fnl f: hdd and no ex wl ins fnl f* 11/4[2]
00-5 3 1¼ Pyrus Time (IRE)[14] 121 3-8-7 68..... LukeMorris 5 67
(J S Moore) *taken down early: stdd s: t.k.h: hld up towards rr: hdwy 2f out: edging lft fr over 1f out: wnt 3rd ins fnl f: nt rch ldng pair* 20/1
4 3¼ Crag Path 3-7-11 0..... AmyBaker[(5)] 7 55+
(D R C Elsworth) *v.s.a: hld up bhd: hdwy on outer over 2f out: edging lft fr over 1f out: styd on steadily fnl f: nvr trbld ldrs* 50/1
3-6 5 nk Misyaar (IRE)[12] 138 3-8-2 0..... ChrisCatlin 12 54
(M A Jarvis) *in tch: hdwy to join ldrs wl over 2f out: led jst over 2f out: rdn and clr wl over 1f out: hdd ins fnl f: wknd qckly* 11/1
4- 6 ¾ Green Dynasty (IRE)[50] 7554 3-8-7 0..... JoeFanning 8 57
(M Johnston) *chsd ldr: led wl over 2f out: hdd jst over 2f out: sn drvn and outpcd: wknd ent fnl f* 6/1[3]
4- 7 ½ Dead Cat Bounce (IRE)[82] 7164 3-8-7 0..... HayleyTurner 2 56+
(J Pearce) *chsd ldrs: nt clr run and swtchd rt 2f out: kpt on fnl f: nt pce to trble ldrs* 25/1
040- 8 ½ Squad[122] 6198 3-8-7 63..... NickyMackay 3 55+
(S Dow) *s.i.s: a towards rr* 66/1
9 2¾ Ensnare 4-9-13 0..... DaneO'Neill 1 52
(A M Hales) *v.s.a: sn in tch in midfield: shuffled bk bnd and lost pl jst over 2f out: swtchd rt ent fnl f: nvr trbld ldrs* 66/1
33/ 10 ¾ Strategic Knight (USA)[406] 7152 4-9-13 0..... PaulEddery 11 52
(R C Guest) *led and grad crossed to rail: hdd wl over 2f out: wknd u.p 2f out* 33/1
66-0 11 nk Prix Masque (IRE)[21] 23 5-9-10 47..... AlanCreighton[(3)] 10 51?
(Christian Wroe) *tk keen hold: hld up in tch: rdn and struggling over 2f out: no ch fr over 1f out* 50/1

1m 39.06s (0.86) **Going Correction** 0.0s/f (Stan)
WFA 3 from 4yo+ 20lb 11 Ran SP% 123.3
Speed ratings (Par 103): **95,94,93,90,89 89,88,88,85,84 84**
toteswinger: 1&2 £2.40, 1&3 £7.20, 2&3 £16.30. CSF £3.07 TOTE £2.00: £1.10, £1.10, £5.10; EX 4.30 Trifecta £41.50 Pool: £430.53 - 7.66 winning units..
Owner Michael Daffey & Robert Markwick **Bred** J Crowe **Trained** Newmarket, Suffolk

FOCUS
The pace was pedestrian but the winner and third both came from off the pace. The form looks unreliable, with the seventh having been well held in a seller previously.

281 SECOND "SHAREN BLAQUIERE CELEBRATE A LIFE" H'CAP 6f (P)
2:00 (2:00) (Class 5) (0-75,74) 4-Y-0+
£2,900 (£856; £428) Stalls Low

Form RPR
4-54 1 Distinctly Game[11] 141 7-9-3 73.....(t) JoeFanning 5 84
(K A Ryan) *chsd ldr: rdn jst over 2f out: led jst over 1f out: styd on gamely u.p fnl f* 6/1
2 1 Catalan Bay (AUS)[294] 5-9-4 74..... ChrisCatlin 2 82+
(J R Gask) *racd in midfield: swtchd rt and chsd ldng pair over 3f out: rdn over 2f out: pressed wnr ins fnl f: kpt on same pce* 7/2[1]
32-5 3 hd Forest Dane[21] 24 9-9-1 71..... HayleyTurner 3 78
(Mrs N Smith) *hld up in last pair: hdwy on inner over 2f out: ev ch ins fnl f: no ex fnl 100yds* 11/2
51-5 4 2¼ Upstairs[8] 192 5-7-13 60..... AmyBaker[(5)] 4 60
(D R C Elsworth) *stdd s: niggled along in last pl over 4f out: hdwy and rdn wl over 1f out kpt on: nvr nr ldrs* 4/1[2]
31-2 5 hd Leading Edge (IRE)[9] 167 4-9-0 70..... TonyCulhane 7 69
(M R Channon) *chsd ldrs: rdn 3f out: lost pl bnd 2f out: styd on again fnl f: nt pce to chal ldrs* 6/1
03-1 6 1½ Billy Red[9] 167 5-8-11 67.....(b) FergusSweeney 8 61
(J R Jenkins) *led: clr over 4f out: rdn wl over 1f out: hdd jst over 1f out: wknd ins fnl f* 11/2
05-5 7 ½ Milton Of Campsie[9] 179 4-8-11 67..... AdamKirby 1 60
(S Parr) *racd in midfield: rdn and unable to qckn jst over 2f out: nt trble ldrs* 18/1
/0-3 8 3¾ Capefly[9] 167 4-8-12 68.....(t) JamieSpencer 6 49
(P W Chapple-Hyam) *hld up in rr: rdn and effrt on outer over 2f out: wl btn over 1f out: eased ins fnl f* 5/1[3]

1m 10.55s (-1.35) **Going Correction** 0.0s/f (Stan) course record 8 Ran SP% 123.5
Speed ratings (Par 103): **109,107,107,104,104 102,101,96**
toteswinger: 1&2 £8.30, 1&3 £8.20, 2&3 £8.90. CSF £29.67 CT £127.48 TOTE £9.10: £2.60, £1.70, £2.50; EX 39.60 TRIFECTA Not won..
Owner Mr & Mrs Julian And Rosie Richer **Bred** J A Forsyth **Trained** Hambleton, N Yorks

FOCUS
A strong gallop even for this trip, and the race has been rated around the third to his recent best.

282 24HR TELEPHONE BETTING @ WILLIAM HILL 0800 44 40 40 H'CAP 7f (P)
2:30 (2:30) (Class 4) (0-85,80) 4-Y-0+
£4,857 (£1,445; £722; £360) Stalls Low

Form RPR
15-1 1 Trafalgar Square[8] 191 7-9-3 79..... JimCrowley 2 89+
(M J Attwater) *t.k.h: hld up in last pair: edgd out off rail and rdn wl over 1f out: chsd ldr over 1f out: hrd drvn and r.o ins fnl f to ld towards fin* 11/10[1]
0-60 2 nk Mr Lambros[7] 204 8-8-11 80.....(vt) KylieManser[(7)] 4 89
(Miss Gay Kelleway) *sn led: clr over 4f out: reduced advantage over 2f out: rdn clr again over 1f out: hdd and no ex towards fin* 4/1[2]
6-24 3 1 Randama Bay (IRE)[8] 195 4-8-12 74..... CatherineGannon 1 80
(I A Wood) *chsd ldr: pushed long over 3f out: drvn and sltly outpcd over 1f out: kpt on same pce fnl f* 10/1
024- 4 nk Autumn Blades (IRE)[48] 7592 4-9-0 76..... HayleyTurner 5 81
(A Bailey) *stdd s: hld up in last pl: stl gng wl 2f out: shkn up and effrt jst over 1f out: hdd and no imp ins fnl f* 4/1[2]
300- 5 2½ Compton's Eleven[66] 7386 8-9-2 78..... EdwardCreighton 6 77
(M R Channon) *chsd ldng pair: pushed along over 3f out: rdn jst over 2f out: wknd fnl f* 6/1[3]

1m 25.23s (0.43) **Going Correction** 0.0s/f (Stan) 5 Ran SP% 111.0
Speed ratings (Par 105): **97,96,95,95,92**
toteswinger: 1&2 £5.10 CSF £5.87 TOTE £1.90: £1.20, £2.80; EX 7.40.

Owner Canisbay Bloodstock **Bred** Matthews Breeding And Racing Ltd **Trained** Epsom, Surrey
■ Stewards' Enquiry : Jim Crowley caution: used whip in incorrect place.
FOCUS
A small field in which the runner-up was allowed an easy lead and set a stop-start gallop.

283 BETLIVE & IN-RUNNING @ WILLIAMHILL.COM H'CAP 1m (P)
3:05 (3:05) (Class 4) (0-85,84) 4-Y-O+ **£4,857** (£1,445; £722; £360) **Stalls** High

Form RPR
206- **1** **Den's Gift (IRE)**[61] 7439 5-9-0 **80**.....................(b) AdamKirby 1 87
(C G Cox) *chsd ldr: rdn to ld jst over 2f out: drvn over 1f out: hld on wl towards fin* **7/2**[1]
04-3 **2** *hd* **Halsion Chancer**[10] 163 5-8-13 **79**..................... RobertWinston 6 86
(J R Best) *w.w in tch: rdn and effrt wl over 1f out: chsd wnr ins fnl f: r.o and clsng towards fin* **15/2**
4-44 **3** *½* **Mister New York (USA)**[4] 225 4-9-4 **84**..................(b[1]) HayleyTurner 9 89
(Noel T Chance) *stdd after s: hld up in last pl: rdn and gd hdwy jst over 1f out: r.o wl: nt quite rch ldng pair* **5/1**
600- **4** *2 ¼* **Solent Ridge (IRE)**[94] 6900 4-8-9 **75**..................... LPKeniry 2 75
(J S Moore) *chsd ldng pair: rdn and unable qck wl over 1f out: kpt on same pce after* **9/2**[3]
12-3 **5** *½* **Sofia's Star**[17] 70 4-8-10 **76**..................... JimCrowley 3 75
(S Dow) *hld up in midfield: lost pl 3f out: rdn and effrt on inner over 1f out: no imp ins fnl f* **12/1**
03-6 **6** *½* **Art Man**[14] 124 6-9-4 **84**..................... FergusSweeney 5 82
(G L Moore) *stdd s: hld up in last trio: hdwy int midfield jst over 2f out: rdn and nt qckn wl over 1f out: nvr trbld ldrs* **4/1**[2]
250- **7** *½* **Glencalvie (IRE)**[24] 7837 8-8-10 **76**.....................(p) DaneO'Neill 4 73
(J Akehurst) *led: rdn and hdd jst over 2f out: wknd ent fnl f* **20/1**
-533 **8** *2 ¼* **Just Bond (IRE)**[8] 199 7-9-0 **80**..................... ChrisCatlin 8 72
(G R Oldroyd) *stdd after s: hld up in rr on outer: effrt and hanging rt bnd jst over 2f out: nvr trbld ldrs* **15/2**
00-0 **9** *3 ¾* **Bee Stinger**[17] 79 7-8-7 **73**..................... CatherineGannon 7 56
(I A Wood) *racd in midfield: rdn and lost pl over 2f out: bhd fnl 2f* **20/1**

1m 36.86s (-1.34) **Going Correction** 0.0s/f (Stan) **9** Ran SP% **117.8**
Speed ratings (Par 105): **106,105,105,103,102 102,101,99,95**
toteswinger: 1&2 £6.20, 1&3 £8.20, 2&3 £7.20. CSF £30.91 CT £129.58 TOTE £4.80: £1.70, £2.00, £2.60; EX 29.40 Trifecta £170.50 Pool: £361.94 - 1.57 winning units..
Owner Mrs Olive Shaw **Bred** Mrs J A Dene **Trained** Lambourn, Berks
■ Stewards' Enquiry : Adam Kirby caution: used whip with excessive frequency.
FOCUS
A game effort from the winner, who helped set a fair pace and kept finding more when challenged. Solid from rated around the placed horses.
Just Bond(IRE) Official explanation: jockey said gelding hung right
Bee Stinger Official explanation: jockey said gelding stopped quickly

284 LIVE CASINO GAMES @ WILLIAMHILL.COM H'CAP 1m 2f (P)
3:40 (3:40) (Class 2) (0-100,103) 4-Y-O+ **£11,656** (£3,468; £1,733; £865) **Stalls** Low

Form RPR
63-2 **1** **Formation (USA)**[21] 26 4-8-4 **86** oh1..................... HayleyTurner 7 93
(J R Boyle) *hld up in rr: hdwy to chse ldrs jst over 2f out: hung lft over 1f out: pressed ldrs ins fnl f: led nr fin* **11/1**
4-31 **2** *hd* **Lady Jane Digby**[14] 124 4-8-8 **90**..................... GregFairley 3 97
(M Johnston) *chsd ldrs: wnt 2nd 8f out: led narrowly over 2f out: rdn 2f out: battled on gamely tl hdd nr fin* **5/2**[2]
05-2 **3** *nk* **Baylini**[14] 124 5-8-7 **87**..................... JamesDoyle 1 93
(Ms J S Doyle) *hld up in midfield: hdwy over 3f out: pressed ldr fr 2f out: drvn and unable qck fnl f* **13/2**
1-05 **4** *1 ½* **Internationaldebut (IRE)**[4] 225 4-9-1 **97**..................... AdamKirby 4 100
(S Parr) *stdd s: hld up in rr: hdwy on inner jst over 2f out: chsd ldrs and drvn ent fnl f: one pce fnl 100yds* **7/1**
022- **5** *9* **Australia Day (IRE)**[26] 7814 6-8-12 **92**..................... MartinDwyer 6 77
(P R Webber) *prom: led after 1f: rdn and hdd over 2f out: sn struggling: wl btn fnl 2f* **9/2**[3]
306- **6** *19* **Kandidate**[152] 5348 7-9-9 **103**.....................(t) JamieSpencer 2 50
(C E Brittain) *chsd ldr tl 8f out: styd chsng ldrs tl wknd qckly jst over 2f out: eased ins fnl f* **9/4**[1]

2m 3.18s (-3.42) **Going Correction** 0.0s/f (Stan)
WFA 4 from 5yo+ 2lb **6** Ran SP% **111.7**
Speed ratings (Par 109): **113,112,112,111,104 89**
toteswinger: 1&2 £5.80, 1&3 £7.10, 2&3 £3.30. CSF £38.21 TOTE £13.50: £4.10, £2.30; EX 44.20.
Owner M Khan X2 **Bred** Loch Lea Farm **Trained** Epsom, Surrey
■ Stewards' Enquiry : James Doyle caution: used whip with excessive frequency.
FOCUS
A remarkable result, with some classy types being beaten by a disappointing horse who had been turned over in a claimer last time. It has been rated around the runner-up and third.
NOTEBOOK
Formation(USA), though something of a character and a major underachiever, has been a handy sort in the past and it might be that his new connections - for whom this was only his second race - have begun to work him out. In addition, Turner deserves credit for coaxing him forwards when he was hanging off the turn, and then putting his head in front on the line. (op 12-1)
Lady Jane Digby, who has rediscovered her form since being raised in trip, came to complete a two-week course-and-distance double only to be run out of it near the line. This 4lb higher mark looks about right, but it was hard to take into account the improvement shown by the winner. (tchd 3-1, tchd 7-2 in a place)
Baylini, ridden more positively this time, continues to look capable of finding a decent race over this course and distance. (op 11-2)
Internationaldebut(IRE) looked effective enough at this return to 1m2f, if not quite good enough off this higher mark against smart opponents. (op 14-1)
Australia Day(IRE) faded disappointingly after setting just a fair, even gallop. (op 11-4)
Kandidate, capable of much better, trailed in a long way last with Spencer sitting up in the straight. Official explanation: trainer said regarding running that the horse never travelled and hung left (op 3-1 tchd 10-3 and 15-8)

285 PLAY ROULETTE @ WILLIAMHILL.COM H'CAP 1m 2f (P)
4:15 (4:15) (Class 5) (0-70,71) 4-Y-O+ **£2,900** (£856; £428) **Stalls** Low

Form RPR
1-43 **1** **Can Can Star**[7] 202 6-9-7 **71**..................... ShaneKelly 12 79
(A W Carroll) *hld up in midfield: hdwy over 2f out: chsd ldrs and drvn over 1f out: r.o wl to ld nr fin* **7/2**[2]
22-1 **2** *nk* **Colonel Sherman (USA)**[15] 100 4-8-12 **64**..................... AdamKirby 4 72+
(L A Dace) *led: rdn 2f out: edgd rt fr over 1f out: kpt on wl tl hdd and no ex nr fin* **2/1**[1]
-132 **3** *nk* **Bavarica**[9] 171 7-8-9 **64**..................... AmyBaker[(5)] 3 71
(Miss J Feilden) *stdd s: hld up in rr: swtchd to outer over 2f out: stl plenty to do do wl over 1f out: r.o wl and clsng towards fin: nt quite rch ldng pair* **6/1**[3]
210- **4** *1 ¾* **Solo River**[143] 5602 4-8-9 **61**..................... FergusSweeney 13 65
(P J Makin) *chsd ldrs: wnt 2nd 3f out: rdn and carried rt over 1f out: one pce fnl f* **33/1**
30-0 **5** *1 ¼* **William's Way**[15] 103 7-8-10 **60**..................... CatherineGannon 11 61
(I A Wood) *hld up in rr: swtchd to outer and hdwy over 2f out: rdn and no imp wl over 1f out: styd on ins fnl f: nvr rchd ldrs* **12/1**
63-1 **6** *hd* **Celtic Gold (USA)**[15] 102 5-9-6 **70**..................... DaneO'Neill 5 71
(Andrew Turnell) *racd in midfield: rdn and effrt on inner jst over 2f out: no imp ins fnl f* **16/1**
660- **7** *nse* **Inch Lodge**[60] 7447 7-8-12 **62**..................... MartinDwyer 14 63
(Miss D Mountain) *in tch: chsd ldng trio and rdn jst over 2f out: kpt on same pce fnl f* **20/1**
50-6 **8** *1* **Coral Shores**[9] 176 4-8-9 **61**.....................(v) LukeMorris 1 60
(P W Hiatt) *pushed along early: t.k.h and hld up towards rr after 2f: rdn and effrt over 1f out: kpt on ins fnl f: nvr nr ldrs* **25/1**
30-6 **9** *shd* **Metal Madness (IRE)**[9] 172 4-9-0 **66**.....................(p) TonyCulhane 7 64
(M G Quinlan) *in tch: rdn and unable qck jst over 2f out: plugged on fnl f: nvr pce to rch ldrs* **16/1**
/3-3 **10** *nk* **Corriolanus (GER)**[14] 119 9-8-12 **69**..................... RichardRowe[(7)] 8 67
(A M Balding) *chsd ldrs: rdn 2f out: wknd jst ins fnl f* **9/1**
51-0 **11** *1 ¼* **Royal Island (IRE)**[8] 191 7-9-3 **67**..................... VinceSlattery 6 62
(M G Quinlan) *hld up in midfield: shuffled bk and lost pl over 3f out: rdn and smo hdwy over 1f out: nvr trbld ldrs* **20/1**
463- **12** *¾* **Krugerrand (USA)**[89] 7009 10-9-3 **67**..................... ChrisCatlin 9 61
(W J Musson) *hld up towards rr on outer: effrt 2f out: nvr pce to rch ldrs* **14/1**
10-5 **13** *4 ½* **Moment Of Clarity**[8] 194 7-8-6 **56**.....................(p) PaulEddery 10 41
(R C Guest) *chsd ldr untl 3f out: rdn over 2f out: wknd qckly ent fnl f* **25/1**
006- **14** *3 ¾* **Bid Art (IRE)**[76] 2244 4-8-7 **59**..................... FrankieMcDonald 2 36
(Jamie Snowden) *stdd s: a bhd: rdn and struggling 3f out: no ch after* **80/1**

2m 4.41s (-2.19) **Going Correction** 0.0s/f (Stan)
WFA 4 from 5yo+ 2lb **14** Ran SP% **127.4**
Speed ratings (Par 103): **108,107,107,106,105 104,104,104,104,103 102,102,98,95**
toteswinger: 1&2 £2.50, 1&3 £6.10, 2&3 £4.30. CSF £10.55 CT £43.98 TOTE £5.60: £1.80, £1.50, £1.90; EX 11.60 Trifecta £34.60 Pool: £340.82 - 7.28 winning units. Place 6: £26.30 Place 5: £15.18.
Owner K F Coleman **Bred** A W And I Robinson **Trained** Cropthorne, Worcs
FOCUS
A solid gallop set by the runner-up, whose attempt to make all only just failed. The form looks sound rated through the third to last year's best.
T/Plt: £82.50 to a £1 stake. Pool: £55,409.10. 489.94 winning tickets. T/Qpdt: £37.90 to a £1 stake. Pool: £3,633.34. 70.90 winning tickets. SP

[273]WOLVERHAMPTON (A.W) (L-H)
Sunday, January 25
OFFICIAL GOING: Standard
Wind: Almost nil Weather: Fine

286 BETLIVE & IN-RUNNING @ WILLIAMHILL.COM MEDIAN AUCTION MAIDEN STKS 5f 20y(P)
2:25 (2:25) (Class 6) 3-5-Y-O **£2,388** (£705; £352) **Stalls** Low

Form RPR
63- **1** **Jolly Ranch**[41] 7689 3-8-5 0..................... SimonWhitworth 3 53
(A G Newcombe) *wnt sltly rt s: mde all: rdn ins fnl f: r.o* **16/1**[3]
023- **2** *¾* **Piazza San Pietro**[90] 7020 3-8-10 84..................... ChrisCatlin 1 55
(J R Gask) *wnt rt s: a.p: chsd wnr over 1f out: rdn and nt qckn ins fnl f* **4/11**[1]
4-23 **3** *1* **Circle Dance (IRE)**[7] 208 4-9-11 70.....................(v) DarrenWilliams 8 58
(D Shaw) *a.p: rdn and edgd lft over 1f out: kpt on ins fnl f* **9/2**[2]
005- **4** *1* **Firewalker**[33] 7778 4-9-6 45.....................(b) FrankieMcDonald 9 49
(P T Dalton) *w wnr tl rdn and hung rt 2f out: kpt on same pce fnl f* **50/1**
0-6 **4** *dht* **Field Fantasy**[17] 85 3-8-5 0..................... PatrickMathers 2 43+
(Garry Moss) *hmpd s: outpcd: bhd tl hdwy fr over 1f out: nrst fin* **100/1**
556- **6** *nk* **Cindy Incidentally**[37] 7734 3-8-5 48..................... JimmyQuinn 6 42
(Miss Gay Kelleway) *prom: nt clr run wl over 1f out: rdn and wknd ins fnl f* **25/1**
0 **7** *4 ½* **April Lady (IRE)**[21] 36 3-8-0 0..................... DanielleMcCreery[(5)] 7 26
(A Berry) *outpcd* **100/1**
\- **8** *8* **Little Miss Ginger** 5-9-6 0..................... BrianReilly 4 3
(P S McEntee) *sltly bmpd s: outpcd* **33/1**
\- **9** *7* **Thoosa** 3-8-5 0..................... HayleyTurner 5 —
(P S McEntee) *s.i.s: outpcd* **33/1**

63.01 secs (0.71) **Going Correction** +0.075s/f (Slow)
WFA 3 from 4yo+ 15lb **9** Ran SP% **111.0**
Speed ratings (Par 101): **97,95,94,92,92 92,84,72,60**
toteswinger: 1&2 £2.10, 1&3 £2.20, 2&3 £1.60. CSF £21.79 TOTE £10.80: £2.10, £1.02, £1.20; EX 29.20 Trifecta £48.80 Pool £246.35 - 3.73 winning units..
Owner David Bramhill **Bred** C G Reid **Trained** Yarnscombe, Devon
FOCUS
A very modest maiden judged by the proximity of the platers in fourth and sixth. The favourite was way below his juvenile form.
Circle Dance(IRE) Official explanation: jockey said gelding hung left
April Lady(IRE) Official explanation: jockey said, regarding the running and riding, her orders were to have the filly handy but if this was not possible then not to knock her about. She added the filly was slowly away and felt weak throughout the race. Also, in her opinion, she may have been better suited to the slower surface at Southwell on her first run.

287 PLAY ROULETTE @ WILLIAMHILL.COM H'CAP 1m 141y(P)
2:55 (2:56) (Class 6) (0-60,59) 3-Y-O **£2,388** (£705; £352) **Stalls** Low

Form RPR
06-1 **1** **Fantastic Fred (IRE)**[9] 196 3-9-2 **57**..................... ShaneKelly 7 61+
(J A Osborne) *hld up in rr: hdwy on ins whn hmpd wl over 1f out: sn plld out: rdn and str run to ld cl home* **7/1**
2454 **2** *½* **Turn To Dreams**[4] 231 3-8-13 **54**..................... CatherineGannon 2 55
(P D Evans) *led: rdn wl over 1f out: edgd lft ins fnl f: hdd cl home* **16/1**
640- **3** *½* **Tarawa Atoll**[64] 7415 3-8-13 **54**..................... TonyCulhane 1 54
(M R Channon) *hld up in tch: wnt 2nd wl over 1f out: sn rdn: kpt on ins fnl f* **14/1**

01-2 **4** *shd* **Kingaroo (IRE)**[5] 228 3-9-2 **57** .... HayleyTurner 5 56
(Garry Moss) *hld up and bhd: c wd st: rdn and edgd lft over 1f out: styd on wl towards fin: nvr nrr* **6/4**[1]

30-0 **5** *1* **Josiah Bartlett (IRE)**[13] 134 3-9-1 **56** .... LiamJones 4 53
(J W Hills) *hld up and bhd: hdwy over 2f out: rdn over 1f out: kpt on same pce ins fnl f* **14/1**

35-5 **6** *½* **Captain Walcot**[8] 205 3-9-3 **58** ....(b) DaneO'Neill 6 54
(R Hannon) *chsd ldr: rdn over 2f out: lost 2nd wl over 1f out: fdd towards fin* **6/1**[3]

3-55 **7** *1½* **Autumn Morning (IRE)**[13] 134 3-9-4 **59** .... JamieSpencer 3 60+
(P D Evans) *stdd s: hld up in rr: hdwy whn swtchd lft wl over 1f out: cl 2nd whn bdly hmpd on ins fnl f: nt rcvr and eased* **7/2**[2]

006- **8** *24* **Sweet Virginia (USA)**[58] 7467 3-8-4 **45** .... AndrewElliott 8 —
(K R Burke) *prom: reminders sn after s: wknd wl over 2f out* **33/1**

1m 51.2s (0.70) **Going Correction** +0.075s/f (Slow) **8** Ran SP% **111.2**
Speed ratings (Par 95): **99,98,98,98,97 96,95,74**
toteswinger: 1&2 £8.60, 1&3 £10.60, 2&3 £14.10. CSF £101.67 CT £1485.83 TOTE £7.40: £1.70, £3.60, £3.50; EX 52.30 TRIFECTA Not won..
Owner H R H Prince of Saxe-Weimar **Bred** Gainsborough Stud Management Ltd **Trained** Upper Lambourn, Berks
■ Stewards' Enquiry : Jamie Spencer two-day ban: careless riding (Feb 14-15)
Catherine Gannon two-day ban: careless riding (Feb 8-9)

FOCUS
Turn To Dreams ensured this was run at a decent clip and the field were fairly strung out early. A modest race on balance but the form could rate a little higher.
Captain Walcot Official explanation: jockey said gelding hung left

288 LIVE CASINO GAMES @ WILLIAMHILL.COM H'CAP 5f 216y(P)
3:25 (3:25) (Class 4) (0-85,84) 3-Y-O **£5,180** (£1,541; £770; £384) **Stalls** Low

Form RPR

3-11 **1** **Five Star Junior (USA)**[8] 203 3-8-13 **79** .... ShaneKelly 2 90+
(Mrs L Stubbs) *hld up: hdwy over 2f out: swtchd rt over 1f out: edgd lft and led wl ins fnl f: r.o* **2/1**[1]

1 **2** *¾* **Changing The Guard**[17] 85 3-8-9 **75** .... PaulHanagan 3 80
(R A Fahey) *hld up: rdn and hdwy on ins over 2f out: led jst ins fnl f: sn hdd: nt qckn* **9/2**[3]

1- **3** *2¼* **Stash**[57] 7501 3-9-0 **80** .... GrahamGibbons 4 78
(R Hollinshead) *led early: chsd ldr: led wl over 1f out: hdd jst ins fnl f: one pce* **15/2**

213- **4** *½* **Woolston Ferry (IRE)**[67] 7389 3-9-4 **84** .... CatherineGannon 1 80
(M R Channon) *outpcd: rdn wl over 1f out: late hdwy: nt rch ldrs* **10/1**

01-3 **5** *nse* **Cecily**[16] 109 3-8-10 **83** .... RosieJessop(7) 6 79
(Sir Mark Prescott) *a.p: one pce fnl f* **15/2**

10-1 **6** *¾* **Takeover Bid (USA)**[24] 4 3-8-11 **77** .... GregFairley 5 71
(M Johnston) *bhd: rdn and edgd lft over 1f out: nvr trbld ldrs* **4/1**[2]

32-6 **7** *7* **Love You Louis**[8] 203 3-8-12 **78** ....(v) SimonWhitworth 7 49
(J R Jenkins) *t.k.h: sn led: hdd wl over 1f out: sn wknd* **22/1**

1m 14.61s (-0.39) **Going Correction** +0.075s/f (Slow) **7** Ran SP% **108.5**
Speed ratings (Par 99): **105,104,101,100,100 99,89**
toteswinger: 1&2 £2.40, 1&3 £3.30, 2&3 £2.90. CSF £9.86 TOTE £2.70: £1.50, £2.60; EX 9.90.
Owner Moyns Park Stud **Bred** Robert W Sanford **Trained** Norton, N Yorks

FOCUS
A strong pace here and they were quite well strung out early, but the picture had changed by the time the field straightened up for home. The third and fourth give a good guide to the level of the form and the winner was value for a bit extra.

289 24HR TELEPHONE BETTING @ WILLIAM HILL 0800 44 40 40 H'CAP 7f 32y(P)
3:55 (3:55) (Class 6) (0-65,65) 4-Y-O+ **£2,388** (£705; £352) **Stalls** High

Form RPR

5-43 **1** **Tender Process (IRE)**[9] 189 6-9-4 **65** ....(v) PaulHanagan 3 74
(R A Fahey) *a.p: led and hung lft ins fnl f: r.o* **8/1**

222- **2** *1¾* **Boss Hog**[43] 7665 4-9-4 **65** .... GrahamGibbons 1 73+
(R Curtis) *led: rdn over 1f out: hdd and carried lft ins fnl f: hld whn nt clr run on ins cl home* **10/3**[1]

-020 **3** *½* **Kabis Amigos**[2] 277 7-8-13 **60** ....(b) GregFairley 2 63
(S T Mason) *hld up in mid-div: hdwy on ins 2f out: kpt on ins fnl f* **12/1**

1-51 **4** *nse* **Marmooq**[11] 155 6-9-3 **64** .... IanMongan 4 67+
(M J Attwater) *hld up in tch: rdn whn nt clr run and lost pl over 2f out: swtchd rt over 1f out: rallied ins fnl f: fin wl* **7/1**

16-0 **5** *nse* **Motivated Choice**[22] 31 4-9-4 **65** .... DaneO'Neill 7 68
(Miss Amy Weaver) *hld up in mid-div: hdwy over 2f out: swtchd lft wl over 1f out: hrd rdn: kpt on ins fnl f* **28/1**

0-11 **6** *1* **Downhill Skier (IRE)**[4] 242 5-8-13 **60** .... ShaneKelly 10 60
(W M Brisbourne) *hld up and bhd: c wd st: hdwy on outside over 1f out: rdn and one pce fnl f* **7/2**[2]

0-44 **7** *½* **Inside Story (IRE)**[4] 241 7-9-3 **64** ....(b) ChrisCatlin 12 63
(C R Dore) *dwlt: hld up in rr: hdwy whn swtchd lft over 1f out: sn hung lft: no further prog* **11/2**[3]

1-15 **8** *shd* **Norcroft**[11] 155 7-9-4 **65** ....(p) VinceSlattery 8 64
(Mrs C A Dunnett) *a.p: chsd ldr over 2f out tl rdn over 1f out: wknd ins fnl f* **10/1**

-160 **9** *1½* **Namu**[10] 167 6-9-3 **64** ....(p) AdamKirby 5 59
(Miss T Spearing) *hld up and bhd: sme hdwy whn sltly hmpd jst over 1f out: n.d* **20/1**

100- **10** *1½* **Party In The Park**[107] 6628 4-9-1 **62** .... HayleyTurner 11 53
(Miss J A Camacho) *hld up and bhd: short-lived effrt on ins wl over 1f out* **33/1**

0/0- **11** *3* **Professor Twinkle**[37] 7732 5-9-1 **62** .... PatrickMathers 9 44
(I W McInnes) *a bhd* **66/1**

000- **12** *15* **Writ (IRE)**[99] 6826 7-9-1 **62** .... TomEaves 6 4
(I Semple) *chsd ldr tl over 2f out: wknd wl over 1f out* **18/1**

1m 29.97s (0.37) **Going Correction** +0.075s/f (Slow) **12** Ran SP% **119.0**
Speed ratings (Par 101): **100,98,97,97,97 96,95,95,93,92 88,71**
toteswinger: 1&2 £6.20, 1&3 £11.20, 2&3 £11.30. CSF £33.74 CT £271.44 TOTE £8.00: £2.40, £2.20, £3.90; EX 45.20 Trifecta £298.20 Part won. Pool £403.04 - 0.94 winning units..
Owner J J Staunton **Bred** Timothy Coughlan **Trained** Musley Bank, N Yorks
■ Stewards' Enquiry : Chris Catlin caution: careless riding
Paul Hanagan three-day ban: careless riding (Feb 8-10)

FOCUS
Low grade stuff but competitive nonetheless. The form is straightforward to rate through the winner to his course and distance win in November.

Namu Official explanation: jockey said mare suffered interference in running

290 LIVE CASINO GAMES @ WILLIAMHILL.COM MAIDEN FILLIES' STKS 1m 141y(P)
4:30 (4:30) (Class 5) 4-Y-O+ **£3,238** (£963; £481; £240) **Stalls** Low

Form RPR

2-20 **1** **Lady Aspen (IRE)**[15] 114 6-9-0 54 ....(t) VinceSlattery 2 59
(Ian Williams) *hld up in tch: rdn over 2f out: led ins fnl f: jst hld on* **13/2**

00/ **2** *nse* **Ludwigshafen (IRE)**[190] 4211 5-9-0 0 .... ChrisCatlin 6 59+
(John Geoghegan, Ire) *hld up in mid-div: hdwy 1f out: rdn and edgd lft ins fnl f: jst failed* **11/4**[1]

00- **3** *1¾* **Arikinui**[106] 6660 4-8-13 0 .... DarrenWilliams 4 55
(K R Burke) *hld up in tch: rdn over 1f out: r.o one pce fnl f* **50/1**

4-22 **4** *nk* **Amber Moon**[10] 175 4-8-13 50 ....(b) ShaneKelly 9 54
(J A Osborne) *chsd ldr 2f: prom: nt clr run and swtchd lft wl over 1f out: ev ch jst ins fnl f: one pce* **4/1**[3]

/00- **5** *1¼* **Bianca Capello**[46] 7620 4-8-13 60 .... AdamKirby 1 51+
(J R Fanshawe) *hld up towards rr: swtchd lft and hdwy on ins over 1f out: nvr trbld ldrs* **8/1**

324- **6** *½* **Marie Tempest**[29] 7792 4-8-13 49 .... FergusSweeney 10 50
(M R Bosley) *led: rdn over 1f out: hdd & wknd ins fnl f* **15/2**

530- **7** *½* **Snowy Indian**[156] 5232 4-8-13 65 .... JimmyQuinn 3 49
(M Botti) *hld up in mid-div: rdn over 1f out: no hdwy* **10/3**[2]

46-6 **8** *2½* **Aegean Pride**[10] 179 4-8-8 55 .... SladeO'Hara(5) 7 43
(A Berry) *sn prom: chsd ldr over 6f out: rdn to chal over 2f out: wknd ins fnl f* **25/1**

60-0 **9** *4* **Mays Louise**[23] 12 5-9-0 28 .... AndrewElliott 8 34
(B P J Baugh) *stdd s: t.k.h in rr: rdn over 2f out: no rspnse* **200/1**

/0-5 **10** *2¼* **Princess Zhukova (IRE)**[18] 80 4-8-13 36 .... GregFairley 5 29
(R J Price) *a towards rr* **40/1**

1m 51.45s (0.95) **Going Correction** +0.075s/f (Slow)
WFA 4 from 5yo+ 1lb **10** Ran SP% **114.7**
Speed ratings (Par 100): **98,97,96,96,95 94,94,91,88,86**
toteswinger: 1&2 £4.70, 1&3 £35.30, 2&3 £40.70. CSF £23.92 TOTE £8.10: £2.00, £1.60, £13.90; EX 31.30 Trifecta £240.90 Part won. Pool £325.64 - 0.10 winning units..
Owner Will Tyrrell Richard Tyrrell Andrew Dick **Bred** Michael McGlynn **Trained** Portway, Worcs

FOCUS
Another modest event, this time a weak fillies' maiden, and given the winner is an exposed 54-rated six-year-old, the form is not anything to get excited about.

291 24HR TELEPHONE BETTING @ WILLIAM HILL 0800 44 40 40 CONDITIONS STKS 7f 32y(P)
5:00 (5:01) (Class 2) 4-Y-O+
£12,462 (£3,732; £1,866; £934; £466; £234) **Stalls** High

Form RPR

005- **1** **Orchard Supreme**[36] 7740 6-9-5 97 .... DaneO'Neill 2 99
(R Hannon) *a.p: chal over 1f out: hrd rdn to ld wl ins fnl f: r.o* **4/1**[2]

31-1 **2** *hd* **Councellor (FR)**[24] 6 7-9-0 92 ....(t) MickyFenton 5 93
(Stef Liddiard) *led: rdn and hdd wl ins fnl f: r.o* **9/2**[3]

1-14 **3** *½* **Aeroplane**[15] 123 6-9-0 103 .... JamieSpencer 3 92
(S A Callaghan) *hld up in rr: hdwy on ins wl over 1f out: ev ch ins fnl f: nt qckn nr fin* **8/11**[1]

0-36 **4** *2½* **Capricorn Run (USA)**[8] 206 6-9-5 90 .... PatCosgrave 8 90
(A J McCabe) *hld up in tch: rdn over 2f out: carried wd ent st: edgd lft 1f out: one pce* **12/1**

4-41 **5** *¾* **Silver Wind**[13] 133 4-9-0 78 ....(b) JamesDoyle 7 83
(P D Evans) *hld up: hdwy on outside over 3f out: chsd ldr over 2f out tl rn wd ent st: rdn over 1f out: one pce* **25/1**

300- **6** *15* **Fire Up The Band**[79] 7218 10-9-0 57 .... SladeO'Hara 9 43
(A Berry) *sn chsng ldr: wknd over 2f out* **80/1**

/0-0 **7** *16* **Wotavadun (IRE)**[8] 204 6-9-0 36 ....(be) HollyHall 1 —
(D Flood) *nt clr run on ins and lost pl sn after s: a bhd: lost tch fnl 3f: t.o* **250/1**

1m 28.25s (-1.35) **Going Correction** +0.075s/f (Slow) **7** Ran SP% **109.3**
Speed ratings (Par 109): **110,109,109,106,105 88,70**
toteswinger: 1&2 £2.50, 1&3 £1.60, 2&3 £1.40. CSF £19.87 TOTE £5.10: £1.80, £1.90; EX 21.00 Trifecta £29.30 Pool £827.38 - 20.88 winning units. Place 6 £193.95, Place 5 £174.69..
Owner Brian C Oakley **Bred** Mrs M H Goodrich **Trained** East Everleigh, Wilts
■ Stewards' Enquiry : Dane O'Neill four-day ban: careless riding (Feb 8-11)

FOCUS
The big three players dominated the finish of this conditions race but the form looks dubious with the fifth finishing a little too close for comfort.

NOTEBOOK
Orchard Supreme got the verdict in a tight three-way finish. Although 11lb worse off with warm favourite Aeroplane than he would have been in a handicap, he is a smart performer on this surface and stayed on gamely under a strong ride to get up close home and edge out long-time leader Councellor. (op 6-1 tchd 7-2)
Councellor(FR) dictated a very steady pace but was quite keen in the early stages and that may have hindered his finishing effort, but even so, he did very well to get so close given he is rated 11lb below Aeroplane and 5lb lower than Orchard Supreme. (op 7-2)
Aeroplane was dropped out early, as is his wont, and Jamie Spencer appeared to be pretty confident turning for home, but the front two were not stopping and he was forced to get serious with his mount, who squeezed up the inside rail but could not quite get on terms. (tchd 4-5)
Capricorn Run(USA) faced a tough task on these terms and has, for the third race in succession, shaped as though he is in decent form. (op 14-1 tchd 16-1 and 11-1)
T/Plt: £217.60 to a £1 stake. Pool: £82,243.61. 275.87 winning tickets. T/Qpdt: £49.60 to a £1 stake. Pool: £6,897.92. 102.90 winning tickets. KH

286 WOLVERHAMPTON (A.W) (L-H)
Monday, January 26

OFFICIAL GOING: Standard
Wind: Nil Weather: Fine

292 ENJOY LUCKY 7 GROUP OFFER AMATEUR RIDERS' H'CAP (DIV I) 5f 216y(P)
1:55 (1:55) (Class 6) (0-60,60) 4-Y-O+ **£1,648** (£507; £253) **Stalls** Low

Form RPR

32-3 **1** **Kingsmaite**[6] 223 8-10-11 57 ....(b) MrKApark(7) 6 70
(S R Bowring) *hld up and bhd: swtchd rt over 2f out: c v wd st: hdwy and edgd lft over 1f out: led ins fnl f: rdn out* **9/2**[2]

240- **2** *3¼* **Suhayl Star (IRE)**[292] 1275 5-10-1 47 .... MrPhilipThomas(7) 2 50
(P Burgoyne) *edgd rt over 2f out: hdd and no ex ins fnl f: jst hld on for 2nd* **33/1**

-645 **3** *shd* **Mister Incredible**[10] 198 6-10-6 **50**........................(v) MissSBradley(5) 3 52
(J M Bradley) *chsd ldrs: rdn fnl f: kpt on: jst failed to take 2nd* **28/1**

2 **4** *nk* **Under Warranty (ITY)**[5] 235 5-11-7 **60**........................(tp) MrRBelluco 9 61
(F Sheridan) *t.k.h: chsd ldrs: c wd st: rdn over 1f out: kpt on towards fin* **5/4**[1]

-023 **5** *nse* **Tadlil**[10] 198 7-10-6 **52**..(v) MissHDavies(7) 10 53
(J M Bradley) *a.p: one pce fnl f* **16/1**

20-5 **6** *1* **Morse (IRE)**[12] 166 8-10-10 **56**........................(p) MissJessicaLodge(7) 1 54
(J A Osborne) *chsd ldrs: no hdwy fnl f* **14/1**

00-6 **7** *1½* **Piccolo Diamante (USA)**[11] 173 5-10-10 **54**............(t) MrBMMorris(5) 7 47
(S Parr) *s.i.s: rdn wl over 1f out: nvr trbld ldrs* **33/1**

00-2 **8** *¾* **Inca Soldier (FR)**[10] 198 6-11-0 **58**............................ MrCAHarris(5) 4 49
(R C Guest) *s.i.s: t.k.h: hdwy over 4f out: wknd wl over 1f out* **7/1**

12-3 **9** *shd* **Fantasy Fighter (IRE)**[21] 44 4-11-2 **55**........................ MrSWalker 13 45+
(J J Quinn) *bhd: carried v wd over 2f out: n.d after* **13/2**[3]

006- **10** *hd* **Briery Blaze**[42] 7686 6-10-1 **47**...................................(b) MrLJohnson(7) 5 37
(T Wall) *a bhd* **100/1**

0/0- **11** *7* **Hill Of Lujain**[364] 334 5-10-9 **55**.................................... MrJHodson(7) 11 22
(Ian Williams) *mid-div: carried wd over 2f out: bhd whn c wd st* **33/1**

1m 15.5s (0.50) **Going Correction** -0.025s/f (Stan) 11 Ran SP% **114.3**
Speed ratings (Par 101): **95,90,90,90,90 88,86,85,85,85 76**
toteswinger: 1&2 £11.60, 1&3 £19.10, 2&3 £26.00. CSF £147.74 CT £3656.23 TOTE £3.40: £1.10, £11.80, £8.10; EX 116.10 TRIFECTA Not won..
Owner S R Bowring **Bred** S R Bowring **Trained** Edwinstowe, Notts
■ The first winner for jockey Kyle Apark.
■ Stewards' Enquiry : Miss H Davies one-day ban: failed to ride to draw (Feb 14)
Mr R Belluco one-day ban: failed to ride to draw (Feb 14)

FOCUS
A moderate amateur riders' handicap but the form is sound. The winner stepped up on recent efforts.

293 GREAT OFFERS AT WOLVERHAMPTON-RACECOURSE.CO.UK CLAIMING STKS 5f 216y(P)
2:30 (2:30) (Class 6) 3-Y-O **£2,047** (£604; £302) **Stalls** Low

Form RPR

13-3 **1** **Gone Hunting**[12] 159 3-8-10 88.......................................(t) JackDean(5) 4 85
(W G M Turner) *sn chsng ldr: led jst over 1f out: sn edgd rt: rdr dropped whip ins fnl f: easily* **8/13**[1]

16-4 **2** *6* **Tillers Satisfied (IRE)**[7] 214 3-8-8 60...................... GrahamGibbons 2 59
(R Hollinshead) *sn led: hdd jst over 1f out: sn btn* **9/2**[2]

600- **3** *½* **Simple Rhythm**[87] 7113 3-8-8 66....................... EdwardCreighton 3 57
(N Tinkler) *hld up: rdn over 2f out: hdwy on outside over 1f out: kpt on ins fnl f* **16/1**

10-5 **4** *nse* **Ridgeway Silver**[25] 4 3-8-3 65 ow1.......................... HayleyTurner 5 52
(M D I Usher) *hld up in tch: rdn over 1f out: kpt on same pce fnl f* **17/2**[3]

00-2 **5** *1¼* **Weet In Nerja**[19] 75 3-8-8 59.......................................(p) ChrisCatlin 7 53
(R Hollinshead) *bhd: sme prog on ins over 1f out: nvr able to chal* **10/1**

0-02 **6** *¾* **Valdemar**[8] 207 3-8-3 49..(p) JimmyQuinn 1 46
(A D Brown) *prom: rdn over 1f out: fdd ins fnl f* **33/1**

60-3 **7** *3¼* **Dancing Welcome**[8] 207 3-8-4 0.................................... LukeMorris 6 36
(J M Bradley) *nt clr run briefly jst over 3f out: a in rr* **40/1**

450- **8** *3¼* **Premier Demon (IRE)**[145] 5614 3-7-12 48.............. CatherineGannon 8 20
(P D Evans) *led early: lost pl 4f out: bhd fnl 3f* **50/1**

1m 14.66s (-0.34) **Going Correction** -0.025s/f (Stan) 8 Ran SP% **112.9**
Speed ratings (Par 95): **101,93,92,92,90 89,85,80**
toteswinger: 1&2 £1.70, 1&3 £3.90, 2&3 £5.40. CSF £3.46 TOTE £1.40: £1.02, £1.80, £3.80; EX 4.70 Trifecta £29.80 Pool: £561.98 - 13.92 winning units..The winner was claimed by P. Grayson for £11000.
Owner E A Brook **Bred** Norman Court Stud **Trained** Sigwells, Somerset
■ Stewards' Enquiry : Edward Creighton £280 fine: failed to arrive in time to weigh out

FOCUS
A reasonable claimer but it was uncompetitive and the easy winner didn't need to improve.

294 ENJOY LUCKY 7 GROUP OFFER AMATEUR RIDERS' H'CAP (DIV II) 5f 216y(P)
3:05 (3:05) (Class 6) (0-60,58) 4-Y-0+ **£1,648** (£507; £253) **Stalls** Low

Form RPR

0-45 **1** **Muktasb (USA)**[11] 177 8-11-4 **55**..................................(v) MrsMMorris 1 65
(D Shaw) *hld up in mid-div: hdwy wl over 1f out: led ins fnl f: r.o* **15/2**[3]

141- **2** *1½* **Smirfys Systems**[31] 7782 10-11-0 **58**.......................... MissEGeorge(7) 10 64
(E S McMahon) *a.p: led wl over 2f out: hdd and nt qckn ins fnl f* **15/2**[3]

1-44 **3** *¾* **Loyal Royal (IRE)**[5] 242 6-10-13 **57**.....................(b) MissHDavies(7) 11 60+
(J M Bradley) *s.i.s: hld up in rr: swtchd rt to wd outside wl over 1f out: gd hdwy fnl f: fin wl* **15/2**[3]

04-2 **4** *nk* **Taboor (IRE)**[21] 46 11-10-11 **48**.. MrSWalker 12 50
(R M H Cowell) *hld up and bhd: rdn and hdwy 1f out: r.o ins fnl f* **12/1**

346- **5** *hd* **Spirit Of Coniston**[56] 7517 6-11-1 **57**......................... MissWGibson(5) 4 59
(P T Midgley) *broke wl: led over 2f: no ex fnl f* **7/1**[2]

04-0 **6** *½* **Briery Lane (IRE)**[11] 173 8-10-6 **48**.....................(p) MissSBradley(5) 5 48
(J M Bradley) *a.p: rdn and one pce fnl f* **25/1**

0-20 **7** *shd* **Balerno**[8] 210 10-10-5 **47**.. MissAWallace(5) 9 47
(Mrs L J Mongan) *hld up and bhd: rdn and hdwy over 1f out: no further prog fnl f* **25/1**

0-56 **8** *1* **Afton View (IRE)**[6] 222 4-10-8 **50**.............................. MrBMMorris(5) 8 46
(S Parr) *hld up in mid-div: c wd st: no hdwy fnl f* **5/1**[1]

000- **9** *½* **Hunt The Bottle (IRE)**[55] 7533 4-11-0 **56**............ MissMMullineaux(5) 3 51
(M Mullineaux) *s.i.s: nvr nr ldrs* **10/1**

4-43 **10** *hd* **Simpsons Gamble (IRE)**[12] 166 6-11-0 **58**..........(p) MrAdamWest(7) 7 52
(R A Teal) *hld up in mid-div: rdn 1f out: no rspnse* **7/1**[2]

6-20 **11** *3½* **Arfinnit (IRE)**[16] 111 8-10-3 **47**..................................(p) MrOJMurphy(7) 6 30
(Mrs A L M King) *prom: rdn wl over 1f out: sn wknd* **10/1**

0-00 **12** *nk* **Diminuto**[5] 242 5-10-10 **54**.. MissCMarelli(7) 13 36
(M D I Usher) *bhd fnl 3f* **25/1**

460- **13** *9* **Our Fugitive (IRE)**[26] 7836 7-11-1 **52**.................................(p) MrPYork 2 5
(C Gordon) *w ldr: led over 3f out tl wl over 2f out: wknd wl over 1f out* **12/1**

1m 15.54s (0.54) **Going Correction** -0.025s/f (Stan) 13 Ran SP% **122.1**
Speed ratings (Par 101): **95,93,92,91,91 90,90,89,88,88 83,83,71**
toteswinger: 1&2 £17.20, 1&3 £14.50, 2&3 £7.80. CSF £62.75 CT £451.77 TOTE £10.60: £3.30, £2.80, £2.20; EX 78.50 TRIFECTA Not won..
Owner Miss Claire Comery **Bred** Shadwell Farm LLC **Trained** Danethorpe, Notts

FOCUS
A moderate amateur riders' handicap and the winning time was almost identical to the first division. Sound form, rated around the first three.

295 PLAY BINGO @ WILLIAMHILL.COM H'CAP 1m 1f 103y(P)
3:40 (3:40) (Class 5) (0-70,68) 3-Y-O **£2,729** (£806; £403) **Stalls** Low

Form RPR

22-2 **1** **Svindal (IRE)**[9] 205 3-9-1 **65**...(b) JamieSpencer 5 67
(K A Ryan) *led: hdd over 2f out: led and hung rt wl over 1f out: sn hung rt again and bmpd: drvn out* **4/1**[3]

01-2 **2** *shd* **Mullitovermaurice**[14] 136 3-8-13 **63**............................ HayleyTurner 4 65
(J G Given) *a.p: hrd rdn and ev ch ins fnl f: r.o* **4/1**[3]

340- **3** *1¼* **Strikemaster (IRE)**[44] 7666 3-8-4 **54** oh1......................... LiamJones 6 53
(J W Hills) *hld up in rr: pushed along over 3f out: hdwy on outside over 2f out: r.o to take 3rd towards fin* **16/1**

040- **4** *¾* **Shaker Style (USA)**[39] 7718 3-8-12 **62**....................(b) GrahamGibbons 3 59
(J D Bethell) *hdwy to chse ldr over 6f out: led over 2f out: bmpd and hdd wl over 1f out: sn bdly bmpd: no ex and lost 3rd towards fin* **9/1**

052- **5** *nk* **Nicky Nutjob (GER)**[39] 7718 3-9-0 **64**............................... JimmyQuinn 8 61
(J Pearce) *hld up: rdn and hdwy 2f out: one pce fnl f* **7/2**[2]

00-4 **6** *¾* **Crazy Colours**[16] 115 3-9-1 **65**.....................................(b) PatCosgrave 2 60
(Jane Chapple-Hyam) *s.i.s: hld up in rr: nt clr run and swtchd lft ins fnl f: kpt on: nvr trbld ldrs* **9/1**

006- **7** *1¾* **Co Dependent (USA)**[89] 7073 3-9-4 **68**.............................. ShaneKelly 9 60
(J A Osborne) *t.k.h early: sn prom: rdn over 1f out: wknd ins fnl f* **3/1**[1]

40-3 **8** *4* **Helpmeronda**[14] 137 3-8-8 **58**.. ChrisCatlin 1 41
(S A Callaghan) *hld up in tch: wknd over 2f out* **28/1**

000- **9** *32* **Flashgun (USA)**[82] 7190 3-8-10 **60**............................ EdwardCreighton 7 —
(M G Quinlan) *s.i.s: hld up in rr: rdn over 3f out: sn lost tch: t.o* **66/1**

2m 2.30s (0.60) **Going Correction** -0.025s/f (Stan) 9 Ran SP% **118.0**
Speed ratings (Par 97): **96,95,94,94,93 93,91,88,59**
toteswinger: 1&2 £3.50, 1&3 £11.40, 2&3 £14.60. CSF £20.95 CT £233.18 TOTE £4.10: £1.60, £1.80, £3.50; EX 16.50 Trifecta £236.40 Pool: £485.65 - 1.52 winning units..
Owner Mrs P Good **Bred** Mrs P Good **Trained** Hambleton, N Yorks

FOCUS
A very ordinary handicap. The winner made all in a modest time.

296 HOTEL & CONFERENCING AT WOLVERHAMPTON (S) STKS 1m 141y(P)
4:10 (4:11) (Class 6) 3-Y-O **£2,047** (£604; £302) **Stalls** Low

Form RPR

340- **1** **La Diosa (IRE)**[94] 6954 3-8-7 71... ChrisCatlin 7 54
(George Baker) *hld up in mid-div: c wd st: str run on outside to ld towards fin* **11/8**[1]

000- **2** *1¼* **Cash In The Attic**[61] 7452 3-8-7 48........................... EdwardCreighton 13 52
(M R Channon) *hld up in mid-div: rdn and hdwy 2f out: led ins fnl f: hdd towards fin* **40/1**

5-26 **3** *¾* **Precocious Air (IRE)**[5] 231 3-8-8 62 ow1........................ ShaneKelly 11 51
(J A Osborne) *hld up in tch: hmpd 2f out: rdn and kpt on ins fnl f* **5/1**[2]

004- **4** *nk* **Herecomesbella**[41] 7694 3-8-9 45 ow2........................(b) MickyFenton 8 51
(Stef Liddiard) *wnt rt s: hld up and bhd: hdwy on wd outside over 2f out: c wd st: kpt on ins fnl f* **50/1**

2-60 **5** *½* **Betws Y Coed (IRE)**[14] 136 3-8-7 53..............................(p) JimmyQuinn 6 48
(A Bailey) *hld up towards rr: rdn over 1f out: r.o ins fnl f: nrst fin* **12/1**

0- **6** *1¼* **Patronne**[77] 7273 3-8-7 0.. StephenDonohoe 12 45
(Sir Mark Prescott) *chsd ldr over 6f out: led over 2f out: rdn over 1f out: hdd & wknd ins fnl f* **20/1**

2-00 **7** *shd* **King's Chorister**[6] 228 3-8-12 59..............................(v[1]) JamieSpencer 4 50
(Miss Gay Kelleway) *s.i.s: in rr: swtchd rt jst over 1f out: nvr nrr* **11/1**

40- **8** *1½* **Where You Will**[49] 7602 3-8-7 0..................................... NickyMackay 3 41
(S W Hall) *chsd ldr 2f: prom tl wknd ins fnl f* **25/1**

00-0 **9** *½* **Vodka Shot (USA)**[19] 77 3-8-7 49..................................... HayleyTurner 1 40
(M L W Bell) *hld up in tch: wknd ins fnl f* **9/1**

306- **10** *1¼* **Abhainn (IRE)**[42] 7687 3-8-12 53............................. CatherineGannon 2 42
(B Palling) *led: hdd over 2f out: sn n.m.r on ins: n.m.r again jst ins fnl f: eased whn btn towards fin* **25/1**

0-06 **11** *5* **Vien (IRE)**[14] 134 3-8-12 52.. PatDobbs 5 31
(R Hannon) *hld up in mid-div: rdn and wknd wl over 1f out* **8/1**[3]

0 **12** *7* **Whotsit (IRE)**[12] 159 3-8-12 0.. DaneO'Neill 10 15
(Miss Amy Weaver) *pushed along 7f out: a in rr* **33/1**

13 *10* **Behind Blue Eyes** 3-8-12 0... JerryO'Dwyer 9 —
(Karen George) *s.s: a in rr: eased whn no ch fnl 3f* **66/1**

1m 50.65s (0.15) **Going Correction** -0.025s/f (Stan) 13 Ran SP% **117.2**
Speed ratings (Par 95): **98,96,96,95,95 94,94,92,92,91 86,80,71**
toteswinger: 1&2 £25.80, 1&3 £3.50, 2&3 £33.70. CSF £83.43 TOTE £2.10: £1.40, £9.20, £1.70; EX 83.90 TRIFECTA Not won..The winner was bought in for 4250gns.
Owner The Betfair Radioheads **Bred** Cathal Ryan **Trained** Moreton Morrell, Warwicks

FOCUS
They went off far too fast, with Patronne and Abhainn taking each other on, and this was set up for the closers. The winner was a stone or more off her 2yo best but this could underrate her.
Precocious Air(IRE) Official explanation: jockey said filly was denied a clear run
Patronne ◆ Official explanation: jockey said filly hung left
Behind Blue Eyes Official explanation: jockey said gelding hung left throughout

297 WILLIAM HILL TELEBETTING ON 0800 44 40 40 H'CAP 7f 32y(P)
4:40 (4:40) (Class 5) (0-75,76) 4-Y-0+ **£2,729** (£806; £403) **Stalls** High

Form RPR

65-0 **1** **Cornus**[10] 191 7-9-0 **70**..(be) JamesDoyle 3 78
(A J McCabe) *hld up in rr: hdwy over 1f out: r.o u.p to ld last strides* **8/1**

3-31 **2** *nk* **Strabinios King**[7] 218 5-9-6 **76** 6ex.................................. GregFairley 7 83+
(K J Burke) *sn led: racd keenly whn taken on by loose horse: clr tl over 3f out: wnt clr again wl over 1f out: rdn fnl f: ct last strides* **15/8**[1]

1-3 **3** *2¾* **Triple Axel (IRE)**[13] 152 5-8-9 **65**.................................... ShaneKelly 1 65
(J Noseda) *hld up and bhd: hdwy 2f out: rdn over 1f out: kpt on one pce fnl f* **11/4**[2]

116- **4** *2½* **Dancing Maite**[45] 7650 4-8-12 **68** ow1.............................. DaneO'Neill 6 61
(S R Bowring) *chsd ldr over 5f out tl rdn wl over 1f out: wknd ins fnl f* **11/2**[3]

306- **5** *¾* **Lord Deevert**[26] 7834 4-8-2 **63**.. DeanHeslop(5) 4 54
(W G M Turner) *hdwy over 5f out: rdn 2f out: sn wknd* **18/1**

36-0 **6** *1* **Montiboli (IRE)**[18] 94 4-9-0 **70**....................................... JamieSpencer 5 59
(K A Ryan) *led early: prom: rdn over 2f out: wnt 2nd wl over 1f out: wknd ins fnl f* **17/2**

The Form Book, Raceform Ltd, Compton, RG20 6NL

2-53 U **Kensington (IRE)**7 218 8-8-13 74 PatrickDonaghy(5) 2 —
(P D Evans) *stmbld and uns rdr leaving stalls* 6/1
1m 28.55s (-1.05) **Going Correction** -0.025s/f (Stan) 7 Ran SP% **118.0**
Speed ratings (Par 103): **105,104,101,98,97 96,—**
toteswinger: 1&2 £3.80, 1&3 £6.00, 2&3 £1.70. CSF £24.61 TOTE £8.90: £4.00, £1.70; EX 26.60.
Owner Betfair Club ROA **Bred** G Russell **Trained** Averham Park, Notts
FOCUS
A fair handicap and they went a good pace. The winner took advantage of his lowest mark for nearly a year.
Strabinios King ◆ Official explanation: jockey said gelding ran too free

298 SPONSOR A RACE BY CALLING 01902 390009 MAIDEN STKS 7f 32y(P)
5:10 (5:11) (Class 5) 3-Y-O £2,729 (£806; £403) Stalls High

Form RPR
022- 1 **Tartan Gunna**28 7812 3-9-3 73 JoeFanning 5 78+
(M Johnston) *sn w ldr: led over 2f out: pushed clr over 1f out: easily* 2/9[1]
5 2 6 **Divine Force**12 160 3-9-3 0 ShaneKelly 3 66+
(J A Osborne) *a.p: wnt 2nd over 1f out: no ch w wnr* 7/1[2]
3 1 3/4 **Sadaska** 3-8-7 0 WilliamCarson(5) 4 52
(S C Williams) *dwlt: hld up and bhd: styd on to take 3rd wl ins fnl f* 33/1
0- 4 2 1/2 **Michael Collins (IRE)**38 7735 3-9-3 0 PatCosgrave 2 51
(Ms Maria Kelly, Ire) *led: hdd over 2f out: wknd fnl f* 14/1[3]
0-0 5 1/2 **Tiffany Lady**14 138 3-8-12 0 HayleyTurner 1 44
(M D I Usher) *prom tl wknd 2f out* 40/1
00- 6 12 **Nairana**38 7734 3-8-12 0 MickyFenton 6 12
(J G Given) *a in rr: pushed along over 3f out: sn struggling* 40/1
1m 30.25s (0.65) **Going Correction** -0.025s/f (Stan) 6 Ran SP% **108.8**
Speed ratings (Par 97): **95,88,86,83,82 69**
toteswinger: 1&2 £1.10, 1&3 £3.70, 2&3 £4.60. CSF £1.97 TOTE £1.10: £1.10, £2.10; EX 2.20.
Owner Mrs I Bird **Bred** Cheveley Park Stud Ltd **Trained** Middleham Moor, N Yorks
FOCUS
A weak and uncompetitive maiden. It is doubtful if the winner had to improve to win by this far.

299 PLAY POKER @ WILLIAMHILL.COM FILLIES' H'CAP 1m 4f 50y(P)
5:40 (5:40) (Class 5) (0-75,75) 4-Y-O+ £2,729 (£806; £403) Stalls Low

Form RPR
44-0 1 **Bluebell Ridge (IRE)**17 103 4-8-6 61 CatherineGannon 1 69
(D W P Arbuthnot) *hld up in rr: hdwy on outside to ld ent fnl f: sn edgd lft: r.o* 9/2[2]
15-4 2 1 1/4 **Eureka Moment**15 126 4-8-7 62 HayleyTurner 6 68
(E A L Dunlop) *hld up: smooth hdwy wl over 1f out: chal ent fnl f: sn shkn up and carried lft: nt qckn* 11/2
34-0 3 4 **Karmest**14 139 5-9-4 69 (b) GrahamGibbons 3 69
(A D Brown) *a.p: rdn over 1f out: wknd ins fnl f* 8/1
26-1 4 shd **Little Carmela**11 168 5-9-2 67 ChrisCatlin 2 66
(S C Williams) *hld up in tch: rdn over 1f out: wknd ins fnl f* 2/1[1]
5 hd **Mildoura (FR)**63 4-9-5 74 IanMongan 4 73
(Mrs L J Mongan) *hld up: hdwy on outside over 3f out: led 2f out: sn rdn: hdd ent fnl f: sn wknd* 22/1
524- 6 10 **Gamesters Lady**221 3176 6-8-12 63 LiamJones 5 46
(W M Brisbourne) *led over 3f: led over 6f out to 2f out: wknd over 1f out* 9/2[2]
210- 7 1 1/4 **Brave Mave**30 7797 4-9-6 75 JoeFanning 7 56
(W Jarvis) *t.k.h: prom: led over 8f out tl over 6f out: wknd wl over 1f out* 5/1[3]
2m 39.74s (-1.36) **Going Correction** -0.025s/f (Stan)
WFA 4 from 5yo+ 4lb 7 Ran SP% **117.2**
Speed ratings (Par 100): **103,102,99,99,99 92,91**
toteswinger: 1&2 £5.60, 1&3 £7.00, 2&3 £9.30. CSF £30.24 TOTE £5.90: £2.40, £2.70; EX 16.80 Place 6: £131.56 Place 5: £27.70.
Owner The Bluebell Ridge Partnership **Bred** Yeomanstown Stud **Trained** Compton, Berks
FOCUS
A modest handicap. The pace seemed just ordinary, but the first two home, who finished clear of the remainder, were held up for most of the way. The winner is rated back to her best.
T/Plt: £53.60 to a £1 stake. Pool: £62,369.34. 849.00 winning tickets. T/Qpdt: £9.10 to a £1 stake. Pool: £7,414.30. 599.24 winning tickets. KH

222 SOUTHWELL (L-H)
Tuesday, January 27

OFFICIAL GOING: Standard
Wind: Nil Weather: Misty

300 PLAY BINGO @ WILLIAMHILL.COM AMATEUR RIDERS' H'CAP (DIV I) 1m 6f (F)
12:40 (12:40) (Class 6) (0-65,65) 4-Y-O+ £1,648 (£507; £253) Stalls Low

Form RPR
6-14 1 **Sabancaya**14 148 4-10-7 59 MissGAndrews(5) 6 73
(Mrs P Sly) *hld up in tch: gd hdwy over 4f out: effrt to ld jst over 1f out: sn rdn and hmpd ins fnl f: kpt on gamely towards fin* 4/1[1]
6-15 2 nse **Sea Cliff (IRE)**11 190 5-10-12 53 MrAJBerry 9 67
(Jonjo O'Neill) *a.p: smooth hdwy to trck ldr over 4f out: led over 2f out: rdn over 1f out: drvn: hdd and edgd rt jst over 1f out: sn rallied and ev ch tl hrd drvn: hung rt and hld nr fin* 4/1[1]
10-3 3 13 **Amron Hill**14 148 6-10-4 50 MrStephenHarrison(5) 8 46
(R Hollinshead) *led: rdn along 3f out: hdd over 2f out and sn drvn: sn one pce* 9/2[2]
10-2 4 hd **Zaffeu**25 8 8-11-7 62 MrSDobson 10 58
(A G Juckes) *in tch on outer: trckd ldrs 1/2-way: effrt to chse ldrs over 3f out and sn rdn: drvn 2f out: sn one pce* 4/1[1]
04-0 5 1/2 **Reminiscent (IRE)**25 8 10-9-13 45 (p) MissAWallace(5) 12 40
(B P J Baugh) *hld up towards rr: stdy hdwy over 5f out: rdn to chse ldrs 3f out: sn drvn and one pce* 22/1
650- 6 7 **Waarid**40 5169 4-10-13 65 (p) MrJoshuaMoore(5) 7 50
(G L Moore) *trckd ldrs: pushed along over 4f out: rdn over 3f out and sn wknd* 12/1[3]
0-66 7 4 1/2 **Top Jaro (FR)**8 221 6-10-11 52 (b) MissSBrotherton 14 31
(Mrs R A Carr) *t.k.h: hld up in rr: sme hdwy over 2f out: nvr a factor* 28/1
000- 8 1/2 **Welcome Cat (USA)**217 3335 5-10-2 48 KyleJames(5) 5 26
(A D Brown) *hld up in rr: sme hdwy on outer over 4f out: nvr a factor* 28/1
4-00 9 1 1/2 **Autumn Charm**12 169 4-9-7 45 MrJPFeatherstone(5) 3 21
(Lucinda Featherstone) *a in rr* 16/1
20-4 10 5 **Mayadeen (IRE)**13 161 7-10-8 56 (v) MrBenHamilton(7) 13 25
(R A Fahey) *chsd ldrs: rdn along over 4f out: sn wknd* 14/1
00-0 11 1 1/2 **Jonquille (IRE)**4 275 4-10-0 52 MrHarryChalloner(5) 4 19
(R Ford) *in rr fr 1/2-way* 66/1
00/0 12 2 1/2 **Akash (IRE)**18 107 9-10-4 50 MrJohnEnnis(5) 2 14
(K M Prendergast) *prom: rdn along and lost pl 1/2-way: sn bhd* 50/1
00-0 13 11 **Tiegs (IRE)**17 116 7-10-4 45 (p) MrsMarieKing 1 —
(P W Hiatt) *chsd ldr: pushed along 6f out: sn wknd* 40/1
3m 10.33s (2.03) **Going Correction** +0.025s/f (Slow)
WFA 4 from 5yo+ 6lb 13 Ran SP% **115.6**
Speed ratings (Par 101): **95,94,87,87,87 83,80,80,79,76 75,74,68**
toteswinger: 1&2 £3.60, 1&3 £3.90, 2&3 £3.80. CSF £17.68 CT £74.33 TOTE £5.50: £2.20, £1.60, £1.60; EX 16.20 Trifecta £47.10 Pool: £270.24 - 4.24 winning units.
Owner David L Bayliss **Bred** Mrs M Slack **Trained** Thorney, Cambs
■ Stewards' Enquiry : Mr A J Berry four-day ban: careless riding (Feb 14,16, Mar 2, Apr 6); four-day ban: used whip with excessive frequency without giving gelding time to respond (Apr 25, May 11,18,26)
FOCUS
An uncompetitive amateur riders' staying handicap. The winning time was 0.71 seconds quicker than the second division. The first two finished clear and the form has been rated at face value.

301 PLAY BINGO @ WILLIAMHILL.COM AMATEUR RIDERS' H'CAP (DIV II) 1m 6f (F)
1:10 (1:11) (Class 6) (0-65,60) 4-Y-O+ £1,648 (£507; £253) Stalls Low

Form RPR
00-5 1 **Blue Hills**9 38 8-11-2 55 (v) MrsMarieKing 3 65
(P W Hiatt) *cl up: led after 6f: rdn clr over 2f out: styd on wl fnl f* 11/2
/120 2 1 1/2 **Safin (GER)**5 252 9-10-6 52 MissCBoxall(7) 4 60
(R Curtis) *midfield: hdwy over 4f out: chsd ldrs 3f out: wd st and rdn 2f out: styd on u.p ins fnl f* 16/1
01-5 3 3/4 **Stravita**25 8 5-10-13 59 (p) MissStefaniaGandola(7) 10 66
(R Hollinshead) *trckd ldrs: hdwy 4f out: chsd wnr 3f out: rdn wl over 1f out: drvn and kpt on same pce ins fnl f* 4/1[2]
3-03 4 hd **Spume (IRE)**6 237 5-10-9 53 (t) MrBMMorris(5) 14 60
(S Parr) *hld up in rr: hdwy over 4f out: rdn to chse ldrs over 2f out: drvn over 1f out: kpt on ins fnl f: nrst fin* 9/2[3]
600- 5 3 **Ashmolian (IRE)**131 6060 6-10-6 45 GemmaGracey-Davison 8 47
(Miss Z C Davison) *hld up towards rr: hdwy 4f out: rdn to chse ldrs over 2f out: kpt on ins fnl f: nrst fin* 40/1
6-33 6 3 1/2 **Bienheureux**14 147 8-10-10 49 (p) MissEJJones 9 46
(Miss Gay Kelleway) *trckd ldrs: hdwy 4f out: rdn over 2f out: sn no imp* 8/1
445- 7 13 **Global Traffic**314 934 5-10-8 52 MrHarryChalloner(5) 2 31
(R Ford) *chsd ldrs on inner: rdn along over 3f outr: drvn over 2f out and grad wknd* 16/1
204/ 8 4 1/2 **Just Serenade**1046 3179 10-9-13 45 MissELOwen(7) 6 18
(Mrs T J Hill) *a towards rr* 100/1
0-36 9 hd **Que Beauty (IRE)**5 252 4-9-11 49 ow4 (p) MrJohnWilley(7) 5 22
(R C Guest) *midfield on outer: rdn along over 5f out and sn wknd* 16/1
400- 10 3/4 **Bulberry Hill**121 4775 8-10-3 47 ow2 MrAWilliams(5) 1 19
(R W Price) *led 6f: cl up tl rdn along and wknd over 4f out* 40/1
10-0 11 16 **Cumbrian Knight (IRE)**25 8 11-11-4 60 MissRJefferson(3) 13 9
(J M Jefferson) *v.s.a: a bhd* 14/1
16-2 12 5 **Snowberry Hill (USA)**17 112 6-11-0 58 MrJPFeatherstone(5) 11 —
(Lucinda Featherstone) *prom: chsd wnr 1/2-way: rdn along over 4f out and sn wknd* 7/2[1]
000/ 13 45 **Blandford Flyer**32 5992 6-10-4 50 (t) MrSWandless(7) 12 —
(M J Gingell) *midsfield: rdn along and lost pl 7f out: sn bhd* 100/1
3m 11.04s (2.74) **Going Correction** +0.025s/f (Slow)
WFA 4 from 5yo+ 6lb 13 Ran SP% **118.1**
Speed ratings (Par 101): **93,92,91,91,89 87,80,77,77,77 68,65,39**
toteswinger: 1&2 £22.00, 1&3 £7.30, 2&3 £17.20. CSF £87.79 CT £392.15 TOTE £6.60: £2.50, £5.50, £2.30; EX 131.70 TRIFECTA Not won..
Owner Tom Pratt **Bred** Darley **Trained** Hook Norton, Oxon
FOCUS
A very moderate amateur riders' staying handicap. The winning time was 0.71 seconds slower than the first division. Sound form, the first four close to their marks.
Bienheureux Official explanation: jockey said gelding hung right throughout
Snowberry Hill(USA) Official explanation: jockey said gelding ran flat

302 ARENA LEISURE PLC (S) STKS 1m 4f (F)
1:40 (1:40) (Class 6) 4-Y-O+ £2,047 (£604; £302) Stalls Low

Form RPR
53-4 1 **Nawamees (IRE)**6 237 11-9-0 70 (p) PaulDoe 3 65
(P D Evans) *cl up: led over 8f out: rdn clr over 2f out: drvn and styd on strly ins fnl f* 10/1
32-0 2 1 1/4 **Rawdon (IRE)**12 172 8-9-0 74 (vt) HayleyTurner 7 63
(M L W Bell) *hld up towards rr: smooth hdwy over 4f out: trckd ldng pair over 2f out: swtchd rt and rdn to chse wnr over 1f out: sn drvn and no imp* 15/8[1]
6-33 3 3 **Ebert**11 187 6-9-0 71 PaulHanagan 11 58
(R A Fahey) *trckd ldrs: cl up 1/2-way: rdn to chse wnr over 2f out: sn drvn and kpt on same pce* 3/1[2]
00/2 4 5 **Alrafid (IRE)**13 161 10-9-0 68 (b) FergusSweeney 12 50
(G L Moore) *midfield: hdwy over 4f out: rdn over 2f out: sn drvn and kpt on same pce* 8/1
000- 5 1 1/4 **Lawyer To World**26 7613 5-9-0 35 (p) MickyFenton 5 48
(Mrs C A Dunnett) *towards rr: hdwy on inner over 4f out: rdn to chse ldrs over 2f out: sn no imp* 100/1
3-61 6 3 3/4 **Rapid City**11 187 6-9-5 67 (p) JamesDoyle 4 47
(A J McCabe) *hld up in rr: hdwy over 4f out: rdn to chse ldrs over 2f out: sn drvn and no imp* 11/1
30-0 7 2 **Daggerman**25 18 4-8-10 52 GrahamGibbons 2 39
(R Curtis) *chsd ldrs on inner: rdn along 3f out: sn drvn and wknd fnl 2f* 33/1
00-4 8 1/2 **Pembo**25 12 4-8-7 48 KevinGhunowa(3) 8 38
(R A Harris) *chsd ldrs: rdn along 3f out: no hdwy* 50/1
5-30 9 9 **Tiger's Rocket (IRE)**7 224 4-8-10 63 (v[1]) LiamJones 10 24
(S Gollings) *cl up: rdn along 3f out: grad wknd* 33/1
56-2 10 6 **St Savarin (FR)**21 66 8-9-0 82 (p) AdamKirby 6 14
(B R Johnson) *hld up in midfield: pushed along 5f out and sn wknd* 6/1[3]
6-34 11 4 1/2 **Black Falcon (IRE)**14 147 9-9-0 55 JimmyQuinn 1 7
(John A Harris) *a towards rr* 11/1
60-0 12 9 **Sir Joey**12 169 4-8-7 41 (p) DuranFentiman(3) 14 —
(B D Leavy) *a bhd* 100/1

000- **13** *1 1/4* **Art Gallery**[32] 2352 5-9-0 40 ....(p) ChrisCatlin 9 —
(R C Guest) *led over 3f: prom tl rdn along and wknd 6f out: sn bhd* **66/1**

2m 39.62s (-1.38) **Going Correction** +0.025s/f (Slow)
WFA 4 from 5yo+ 4lb **13** Ran SP% **122.3**
Speed ratings (Par 101): **105,104,102,98,98 95,94,93,87,83 80,74,74**
toteswinger: 1&2 £6.90, 1&3 £10.90, 2&3 £3.20. CSF £29.25 TOTE £14.90: £4.50, £1.10, £1.40; EX 35.00 TRIFECTA Not won..There was no bid for the winner. Rawdon was claimed by Gay Kelleway for £5,500.
Owner L G Brookes **Bred** Kilfrush Stud Ltd **Trained** Pandy, Monmouths

FOCUS
A good seller on paper and they went a strong pace, but the form is rather muddling with the fifth a lot closer than he was entitled to be. Probably not a race to take too literally.
Black Falcon(IRE) Official explanation: jockey said gelding hung left

303 WILLIAM HILL TELEBETTING ON 0800 44 40 40 H'CAP 6f (F)
2:10 (2:10) (Class 6) (0-65,65) 4-Y-0+ **£2,047** (£604; £302) **Stalls** Low

Form RPR
-045 **1** **Punching**[6] 235 5-9-2 **63** .... LPKeniry 3 73
(C R Dore) *trckd ldrs: hdwy 2f out: rdn to ld ent fnl f: styd on strly* **3/1**[1]
3565 **2** *1 1/4* **Obe Royal**[5] 245 5-9-1 **62** ....(b) PaulDoe 6 68
(P D Evans) *in tch: hdwy over 2f out: n.m.r and swtchd rt over 1f out: styd on u.p ins fnl f: could nt rch wnr* **15/2**
0-04 **3** *3/4* **Ronnie Howe**[14] 146 5-8-5 **52** ....(bt[1]) LiamJones 7 56
(S R Bowring) *led: rdn along 2f out: drvn over 1f out: hdd ent fnl f: one pce* **14/1**
3122 **4** *1 1/2* **Jordi Roper (IRE)**[7] 222 4-8-8 **55** ....(p) DaleGibson 1 54
(S Parr) *sn rdn along and bhd: hdwy 2f out: swtchd rt and drvn over 1f out: kpt on ins fnl f: nrst fin* **7/2**[2]
-644 **5** *1 1/2* **Cape Of Storms**[7] 222 6-8-4 **54** .... AndrewMullen[(3)] 10 48
(R Brotherton) *in tch: hdwy 1/2-way: rdn over 2f out: sn drvn and kpt on same pce* **5/1**[3]
0-05 **6** *shd* **Tag Team (IRE)**[14] 146 8-8-5 **52** .... ChrisCatlin 4 46
(John A Harris) *wnt lft s: sn cl up: rdn along and ev ch 2f out: sn edgd lft and wknd over 1f out* **18/1**
50-0 **7** *3/4* **Fulford**[25] 13 4-8-8 **55** .... JimmyQuinn 2 46+
(M Brittain) *dwlt and hmpd s: rr tl hdwy 2f out: sn rdn and kpt on ins fnl f: nt rch ldrs* **10/1**
00-0 **8** *3 3/4* **Trinculo (IRE)**[6] 235 12-8-7 **61** ....(b) SPRyan[(7)] 5 40
(R A Harris) *chsd ldrs: rdn along 1/2-way: sn wknd* **18/1**
502- **9** *1/2* **Angaric (IRE)**[60] 7466 6-9-4 **65** .... TomEaves 9 43
(B Smart) *chsd ldng pair: rdn along 1/2-way: sn wknd* **6/1**

1m 16.08s (-0.42) **Going Correction** +0.025s/f (Slow) **9** Ran SP% **116.2**
Speed ratings (Par 101): **103,101,100,98,96 96,95,90,89**
toteswinger: 1&2 £6.10, 1&3 £13.90, 2&3 £17.70. CSF £26.23 CT £274.36 TOTE £3.30: £1.60, £3.20, £5.50; EX 28.60 TRIFECTA Not won..
Owner Liam Breslin **Bred** Cheveley Park Stud Ltd **Trained** Cowbit, Lincs

FOCUS
This weak handicap was run at a fair pace and was the quickest of the three races over the trip. Sound form.

304 SOUTHWELL-RACECOURSE.CO.UK CLAIMING STKS 6f (F)
2:40 (2:42) (Class 6) 4-Y-0+ **£2,047** (£604; £302) **Stalls** Low

Form RPR
12-1 **1** **Back In The Red (IRE)**[14] 146 5-8-13 68 ....(b) FrankieMcDonald 2 73
(R A Harris) *cl up: led wl over 1f out and sn rdn: drvn ins fnl f and kpt on wl* **15/2**
3-42 **2** *3/4* **Grimes Faith**[14] 146 6-8-9 62 ....(p) JamieSpencer 6 67
(K A Ryan) *broke wl: sn stdd and hld up in rr: swtchd outside and pushed along 1/2-way: hdwy 2f out: rdn to chse ldrs over 1f out: drvn and ch ins fnl f: edgd lft and no ex last 75yds* **9/4**[1]
500- **3** *1 3/4* **Ballycroy Boy (IRE)**[63] 7448 4-9-3 69 .... MickyFenton 9 69
(A Bailey) *in rr and rdn along after 2f: hdwy over 2f out: sn drvn and styd on ins fnl f* **7/1**
30-0 **4** *2 1/4* **Charmel's Lad**[17] 114 4-8-13 50 ....(vt[1]) AdamKirby 5 58
(W R Swinburn) *chsd ldrs: hdwy 1/2-way: rdn 2f out: sn drvn and kpt on same pce* **40/1**
0-22 **5** *1* **Crocodile Bay (IRE)**[14] 152 6-8-12 71 ....(b) JamesO'Reilly[(5)] 4 59
(John A Harris) *sltly hmpd s: hdwy to ld after 1f: rdn along 2f out: sn hdd and grad wknd* **4/1**[2]
6-31 **6** *1/2* **Lethal**[7] 223 6-8-11 68 .... PaulHanagan 8 51
(R A Fahey) *chsd ldng pair: rdn along over 2f out: sn wknd* **9/2**[3]
3-05 **7** *3* **Savile's Delight (IRE)**[13] 165 10-8-9 70 .... RichardKingscote 7 39
(Tom Dascombe) *a towards rr* **6/1**
5-16 **8** *7* **Mafaheem**[5] 245 7-8-13 67 .... StephenDonohoe 3 21
(A B Haynes) *blind removed late: slowly away and a bhd* **16/1**
000- **9** *8* **Milloaks (IRE)**[67] 7411 4-7-9 41 ....(bt) MatthewLawson[(7)] 1 —
(Paul W Flynn, Ire) *chsd ldrs on inner: rdn along 1/2-way and sn wknd* **80/1**

1m 16.46s (-0.04) **Going Correction** +0.025s/f (Slow) **9** Ran SP% **117.1**
Speed ratings (Par 101): **101,100,97,94,93 92,88,79,68**
toteswinger: 1&2 £3.80, 1&3 £8.20, 2&3 £5.00. CSF £25.11 TOTE £8.30: £2.00, £1.60, £2.20; EX 22.60 Trifecta £409.40 Part won. Pool: £553.35 - 0.94 winning units..
Owner Mrs Ruth M Serrell **Bred** Mrs Rachanee Butler **Trained** Earlswood, Monmouths

FOCUS
An ordinary claimer. The first pair basically reproduced their previous 5f form here, although the proximity of the fourth lends doubts.
Mafaheem Official explanation: jockey said gelding never travelled

305 TWO FEBRUARY JUMPS MEETINGS AT SOUTHWELL FILLIES' H'CAP 6f (F)
3:10 (3:10) (Class 5) (0-70,67) 4-Y-0+ **£2,729** (£806; £403) **Stalls** Low

Form RPR
130- **1** **Efisio Princess**[36] 7762 6-9-1 **64** .... RichardThomas 1 70+
(J E Long) *mde all: rdn wl over 1f out: drvn ins fnl f and styd on gamely* **11/4**[3]
03-2 **2** *1 1/2* **Silk Gallery (USA)**[23] 36 4-8-4 **53** ....(t) JimmyQuinn 6 54+
(E J Alston) *trckd ldrs: hdwy on outer 2f out: swtchd lft and rdn to chse wnr over 1f out: drvn ins fnl f: no ex last 100yds* **15/8**[1]
5-00 **3** *2 1/4* **Avoca Dancer (IRE)**[13] 166 6-8-7 **56** ....(b) HayleyTurner 8 50
(Miss Gay Kelleway) *towards rr: rdn along over 2f out: drvn and styd on ins fnl f* **8/1**
6-00 **4** *nk* **Martingrange Lass (IRE)**[12] 175 4-7-11 **53** oh8(e[1]) AndrewHeffernan[(7)] 7 46
(S Parr) *cl up: rdn along over 2f out: drvn wl over 1f out and kpt on same pce* **66/1**

0-01 **5** *nse* **Dark Tara**[6] 241 4-9-3 **66** 6ex .... PaulHanagan 3 59
(R A Fahey) *chsd ldng pair: rdn over 2f out: sn drvn and kpt on same pce* **5/2**[2]
100- **6** *8* **City For Conquest (IRE)**[31] 7793 6-8-5 **54** .... ChrisCatlin 2 21
(John A Harris) *chsd ldrs on inner: rdn along over 2f out: sn wknd* **14/1**

1m 16.2s (-0.30) **Going Correction** +0.025s/f (Slow) **6** Ran SP% **109.3**
Speed ratings (Par 100): **103,101,98,97,97 86**
toteswinger: 1&2 £1.80, 1&3 £3.60, 2&3 £3.00. CSF £7.85 CT £29.84 TOTE £4.90: £3.00, £1.10; EX 10.30 Trifecta £57.70 Pool: £411.11 - 5.27 winning units..
Owner Miss M B Fernandes **Bred** Mrs A Yearley **Trained** Caterham, Surrey

FOCUS
A weakish fillies' handicap, with the proximity of the fourth from a stone wrong highlighting doubts over the strength of the form. The winner may not have had to improve on her earlier win here.

306 PLAY POKER @ WILLIAMHILL.COM MAIDEN STKS 1m (F)
3:40 (3:41) (Class 5) 3-Y-O **£2,729** (£806; £403) **Stalls** Low

Form RPR
5- **1** **Echo Dancer**[32] 7783 3-9-3 0 .... JamieSpencer 6 67+
(S A Callaghan) *sn led: rdn and hung rt over 1f out: drvn: hung lft and hdd jst ins fnl f: drvn and styd on to ld last 100yds* **9/2**[2]
0-4 **2** *3/4* **Michael Collins (IRE)**[1] 298 3-8-12 0 .... BACurtis[(5)] 3 66
(Ms Maria Kelly, Ire) *cl up: rdn 2f out: edgd rt over 1f out: drvn to ld jst ins fnl f: hdd and no ex last 100yds* **25/1**
2- **3** *nk* **Assail**[76] 7282 3-9-3 0 .... TravisBlock 8 65
(H Morrison) *trckd ldrs: hdwy over 2f out: rdn wl over 1f out: edgd lft and kpt on ins fnl f* **11/10**[1]
4 *3* **High Cross (IRE)** 3-8-12 0 .... StephenDonohoe 5 53+
(Sir Mark Prescott) *s.i.s: hdwy to chse ldrs after 2f: rdn along on outer 2f out: drvn and one pce appr fnl f* **6/1**[3]
00- **5** *5* **Dulce Domum**[51] 7593 3-8-12 0 .... JimmyQuinn 2 42
(A B Haynes) *towards rr: hdwy 3f out: sn rdn and styd on appr fnl f: nrst fin* **100/1**
3 **6** *2 1/4* **Antipodean (UAE)**[14] 151 3-9-3 0 .... JamieMoriarty 9 41
(P T Midgley) *in tch: effrt 3f out: sn rdn and no imp fnl 2f* **16/1**
7 *1 1/4* **Ettrick Mill** 3-9-3 0 .... GregFairley 12 39+
(M Johnston) *sn outpcd and bhd tl styd on fnl 2f* **7/1**
6 **8** *3 1/2* **Benozzo Gozzoli**[14] 151 3-9-3 0 .... ChrisCatlin 10 31
(H Morrison) *towards rr: sme hdwy on outer 3f out: sn rdn and nvr a factor* **33/1**
002- **9** *4* **Rockinit (IRE)**[131] 6059 3-8-9 68 .... KevinGhunowa[(3)] 11 16
(R A Harris) *plld hrd: chsd ldrs: cl up 1/2-way: rdn along 3f out and sn wknd* **12/1**
-0 **10** *6* **Unbelievable Jeff**[7] 227 3-9-3 0 .... AdamKirby 4 8
(S Parr) *in tch: rdn along over 3f out and sn wknd* **50/1**

1m 44.83s (1.13) **Going Correction** +0.025s/f (Slow) **10** Ran SP% **115.9**
Speed ratings (Par 97): **95,94,93,90,85 83,82,78,74,68**
toteswinger: 1&2 £17.10, 1&3 £2.40, 2&3 £10.80. CSF £110.42 TOTE £5.90: £1.80, £8.20, £1.10; EX 84.70 Trifecta £327.10 Part won. Pool: £442.16 - 0.50 winning units..
Owner David F O'Rourke **Bred** Plantation Stud **Trained** Newmarket, Suffolk

FOCUS
This looked a very modest maiden and is not form to be too positive about, with the runner-up the best guide. The winning time was 2.76 seconds slower than the following 61-75 handicap.
Rockinit(IRE) Official explanation: jockey said filly ran too free

307 SOUTHWELL RACECOURSE FOR CONFERENCES H'CAP 1m (F)
4:10 (4:10) (Class 5) (0-75,75) 4-Y-0+ **£2,729** (£806; £403) **Stalls** Low

Form RPR
30-0 **1** **Mcconnell (USA)**[13] 163 4-9-4 **75** .... FergusSweeney 6 84
(G L Moore) *trckd ldrs: smooth hdwy over 2f out: led wl over 1f out: sn rdn and hdd appr fnl f: drvn and rallied to ld ins fnl f: hld on gamely* **10/1**
3-11 **2** *hd* **Mrs Bun**[14] 152 4-8-9 **66** ....(b) JamieSpencer 7 75
(K A Ryan) *in tch: hdwy on outer 3f out: rdn to chal 2f out: led and edgd lft jst over 1f out: hdd ins fnl f: drvn and kpt on towards fin* **7/4**[1]
15-0 **3** *2 1/2* **What's Up Doc (IRE)**[12] 172 8-9-2 **73** .... HayleyTurner 2 76
(Mrs T J Hill) *cl up: rdn along and lost pl 3f out: hdwy on inner 2f out: drvn and kpt on fnl f* **12/1**
130- **4** *3* **My Mentor (IRE)**[166] 5018 5-9-0 **71** .... StephenDonohoe 9 67
(Sir Mark Prescott) *s.i.s: sn chsng ldrs: hdwy to ld 3f out: rdn and hdd over2f out: grad wknd* **5/2**[2]
220- **5** *nse* **Follow The Flag (IRE)**[45] 7670 5-8-6 **70** ....(p) KarenKenny[(7)] 3 66
(A J McCabe) *chsd ldrs: rdn along 3f out: drvn 2f out and sn no imp* **11/1**
00-2 **6** *nk* **Garden Party**[8] 215 5-8-9 **66** .... FrankieMcDonald 4 61
(R A Harris) *prom: hdwy and cl up 1/2-way: led over 2f out: sn rdn and hdd wl over 1f out: grad wknd* **15/2**[3]
066- **7** *8* **Flying Applause**[74] 7317 4-9-3 **74** .... ChrisCatlin 1 51
(S R Bowring) *sn led: rdn along and hdd 3f out: sn wknd* **10/1**
8 *1 3/4* **Singora Lady (IRE)**[197] 4037 4-8-0 **64** oh4 ow3 ....(p) PaulPickard[(7)] 5 37
(P T Midgley) *chsd ldrs to 1/2-way: sn wknd* **50/1**

1m 42.07s (-1.63) **Going Correction** +0.025s/f (Slow) **8** Ran SP% **112.9**
Speed ratings (Par 103): **109,108,106,103,103 102,94,93**
toteswinger: 1&2 £4.50, 1&3 £8.70, 2&3 £5.20. CSF £27.24 CT £217.44 TOTE £12.40: £2.60, £1.30, £2.70; EX 34.90 Trifecta £403.30 Pool: £675.95 - 1.24 winning units. Place 6: £30.51 Place 5: £19.91.
Owner Joe McCarthy **Bred** Hall Et Al Farm **Trained** Lower Beeding, W Sussex

FOCUS
A modest handicap, run at a sound pace. A slight personal best from the winner.
T/Jkpt: Not won. T/Plt: £104.30 to a £1 stake. Pool: £63,503.05. 444.46 winning tickets. T/Qpdt: £13.60 to a £1 stake. Pool: £4,574.14. 247.70 winning tickets. JR

[243]KEMPTON (A.W) (R-H)
Wednesday, January 28

OFFICIAL GOING: Standard
Wind: Light, half behind Weather: Drizzle

308 PANORAMIC BAR & RESTAURANT CLASSIFIED STKS 6f (P)
6:50 (6:50) (Class 7) 3-Y-0+ **£1,364** (£403; £201) **Stalls** High

Form RPR
06-3 **1** **Convince (USA)**[19] 104 8-9-1 45 .... BMcHugh[(7)] 2 52
(K M Prendergast) *awkward s: pushed along in 8th after 2f: taken to outer and urged along over 2f out: prog over 1f out: r.o to ld last 75yds* **11/2**[1]
0-00 **2** *1* **Mr Loire**[12] 198 5-9-8 45 ....(b) JerryO'Dwyer 8 49
(K G Wingrove) *s.i.s: sn chsd ldng trio: effrt on inner over 2f out: led over 1f out: drvn and hdd last 75yds* **14/1**

000- 3 ½ **Flamboyant Red (IRE)**[150] 5530 3-8-6 40 .... JimmyQuinn 11 44
(Miss Gay Kelleway) *settled in 7th on inner: gng bttr than most over 2f out: rdn and prog over 1f out: kpt on: nvr able to chal* **20/1**

00-3 4 nk **Chalentina**[25] 23 6-9-1 45 .... PNolan(7) 3 47
(J E Long) *dwlt: rdn in last trio after 2f: prog over 1f out: styd on fnl f: nrst fin* **10/1**

000- 5 1 ¾ **Viewforth**[36] 7778 11-9-8 43 .... (b) SteveDrowne 12 41
(M Wigham) *reluctant to enter stalls: led: drvn and hdd over 1f out: fdd* **6/1**[2]

560- 6 1 **Miracle Baby**[57] 7521 7-9-8 45 .... RobertHavlin 7 38
(J A Geake) *chsd ldrs: rdn and struggling over 2f out: lost pl over 1f out: plugged on again last 100yds* **15/2**[3]

04-0 7 ½ **One Way Ticket**[14] 166 9-9-8 42 .... (p) HayleyTurner 10 36
(J M Bradley) *trckd ldr: poised to chal gng wl 2f out: sn rdn and fnd nil: petered out fnl f* **11/2**[1]

0-00 8 ¾ **Szaba**[12] 192 4-9-8 42 .... NickyMackay 4 34
(J Akehurst) *sn in last pair and struggling: effrt on inner over 2f out: no real prog* **10/1**

00-6 9 ½ **Spanish Ace**[19] 104 8-9-3 45 .... (b) JackDean(5) 9 32
(J M Bradley) *chsd ldng pair: wknd 2f out* **11/2**[1]

00-0 10 ½ **Buddy Marvellous (IRE)**[14] 159 3-8-3 45 .... (b[1]) KevinGhunowa(3) 5 27
(R A Harris) *sn rdn in 6th: no prog over 2f out: steadily wknd* **14/1**

000- 11 1 ¼ **Neo's Mate (IRE)**[60] 7501 3-8-6 43 ow7 .... KrishGundowry(7) 6 30
(Paul Green) *a in rr: brief effrt 2f out: wknd over 1f out* **50/1**

-004 12 9 **Nordic Light (USA)**[14] 153 5-9-8 42 .... (bt) ChrisCatlin 1 —
(J M Bradley) *a in last pair and struggling: t.o* **8/1**

1m 13.78s (0.68) **Going Correction** +0.05s/f (Slow)
WFA 3 from 4yo+ 16lb 12 Ran SP% **121.6**
Speed ratings (Par 97): **97,95,95,94,92 90,90,89,88,87 86,74**
toteswinger: 1&2 £22.90, 1&3 £32.80, 2&3 £31.40. CSF £84.82 TOTE £7.00: £2.40, £3.90, £7.10; EX 130.00.
Owner K M Prendergast **Bred** Juddmonte Farms Inc **Trained** Sellack, H'fords

FOCUS
An open race but ordinary form for the grade at best.

309 DIGIBET.COM H'CAP 7f (P)
7:20 (7:22) (Class 6) (0-60,60) 4-Y-0+ £2,047 (£604; £302) Stalls High

Form RPR

00-1 1 **Street Power (USA)**[21] 71 4-9-3 59 .... GregFairley 13 71+
(J R Gask) *v awkward s: hld up in rr and tk fierce hold to 1/2-way: cajoled along and prog fr 2f out: r.o over 1f out to ld last 100yds: a doing enough after* **2/1**[1]

0-22 2 ½ **Duke Of Milan (IRE)**[18] 118 6-9-4 60 .... AdamKirby 14 71
(G C Bravery) *stdd s: hld up towards rr: stdy prog over 2f out gng wl: rdn to ld ins fnl f: r.o but sn hdd and outpcd* **6/1**[3]

00-0 3 2 ¾ **Ike Quebec (FR)**[14] 155 4-9-3 59 .... (b) PatCosgrave 3 62
(J R Boyle) *chsd ldrs: hrd rdn over 2f out: nt qckn over 1f out: kpt on to take 3rd nr fin* **8/1**

-116 4 ¾ **Downhill Skier (IRE)**[3] 289 5-9-4 60 .... ShaneKelly 5 61
(W M Brisbourne) *racd keenly: w ldr: led jst over 2f out: drvn over 1f out: hdd ins fnl f: wknd* **7/2**[2]

045- 5 hd **Rydal (USA)**[28] 7834 8-9-3 59 .... (v) DaneO'Neill 11 60
(Miss Jo Crowley) *trckd ldrs: effrt on inner 2f out: upsides ent fnl f: wknd* **10/1**

30-1 6 2 ½ **Takitwo**[18] 114 6-9-2 58 .... (v) SimonWhitworth 6 52
(P D Cundell) *settled in midfield: effrt over 2f out: nt qckn over 1f out: no imp after* **12/1**

660- 7 ¾ **Rio L'Oren (IRE)**[132] 6048 4-9-4 60 .... (b[1]) LukeMorris 9 52
(N J Vaughan) *reluctant to go to post: mde most to jst over 2f out: stl ch over 1f out: wknd* **25/1**

43-6 8 ½ **Light The Light (IRE)**[19] 98 4-9-2 58 .... JimCrowley 1 49
(Rae Guest) *a towards rr: shkn up and no prog over 2f out* **33/1**

34-0 9 nse **Eagle Nebula**[14] 154 5-9-4 60 .... IanMongan 4 50
(B R Johnson) *sn last: nt gng wl and unwilling 3f out: modest prog fr over 1f out* **20/1**

400- 10 ¾ **Is It Time (IRE)**[28] 7834 5-9-1 57 .... RobertHavlin 8 45
(Mrs P N Dutfield) *reluctant to go to post: trckd ldng pair: rdn over 2f out: sn lost pl and btn* **25/1**

0-62 11 6 **Ten Pole Tudor**[7] 242 4-9-0 59 .... KevinGhunowa(3) 7 31
(R A Harris) *chsd ldrs: u.p over 2f out: sn wknd* **12/1**

1m 26.34s (0.34) **Going Correction** +0.05s/f (Slow) 11 Ran SP% **120.8**
Speed ratings (Par 101): **100,99,96,95,95 92,91,90,90,90 83**
toteswinger: 1&2 £3.50, 1&3 £6.60, 2&3 £11.90. CSF £13.92 CT £84.02 TOTE £2.90: £1.60, £1.80, £3.40; EX 9.60.
Owner Horses First Racing Limited **Bred** John Hawkins **Trained** Sutton Veny, Wilts
■ Stewards' Enquiry : Pat Cosgrave four-day ban: used whip with excessive force (Feb 11-14)

FOCUS
A reasonable race for the grade. The pace seemed fair enough and the first two home raced off the gallop early. The winner stepped up on his previous course-and-distance form.

310 DIGIBET CASINO MAIDEN STKS 1m 3f (P)
7:50 (7:51) (Class 5) 3-Y-0+ £2,590 (£770; £385; £192) Stalls High

Form RPR

03- 1 **Sounds Of Jupiter (IRE)**[30] 7812 3-8-4 0 .... ChrisCatlin 1 64+
(E F Vaughan) *trckd ldng trio: effrt to chse ldr wl over 1f out: rdn to cl and led last 150yds: hld on to dwindling advantage* **9/4**[1]

2 ½ **Dream In Blue** 4-9-11 0 .... ShaneKelly 4 66+
(J A Osborne) *hld up in abt 7th: pushed along fr 5f out and green: effrt and stl green 2f out: picked up on outer jst over 1f out: r.o to take 2nd last 50yds and cl on wnr fin* **5/1**

3 ¾ **Leo The Lion (IRE)** 3-8-4 0 .... GregFairley 7 62+
(M Johnston) *settled in 5th: effrt and shkn up over 2f out: prog on wd outside whn rn green and hung lft and lost grnd over 1f out: r.o again ins fnl f: nrst fin* **4/1**[3]

050- 4 1 **Red Twist**[159] 5218 4-9-11 60 .... FergusSweeney 5 63
(M Hill) *led: tried to kick on fr over 2f out: hdd and readily outpcd last 150yds* **10/1**

4- 5 1 ¼ **Flowerbud**[41] 7713 4-9-6 0 .... JamesDoyle 10 56
(Ms J S Doyle) *trckd ldng pair: rdn over 3f out: nt qckn over 2f out: plugged on* **14/1**

604- 6 ¾ **Cozy Tiger (USA)**[107] 6703 4-9-11 68 .... StephenDonohoe 9 60
(W J Musson) *t.k.h: hld up in abt 6th: effrt over 2f out: rdn and nt qckn wl over 1f out: one pce after* **7/2**[2]

7 7 **Little Roxy (IRE)** 4-9-6 0 .... TravisBlock 6 43
(Miss A M Newton-Smith) *s.s: mostly in last pair: struggling over 3f out: n.d* **66/1**

0-3 8 5 **Oxus (IRE)**[18] 120 4-9-11 0 .... IanMongan 8 39
(B R Johnson) *mostly trckd ldr: rdn over 2f out: lost 2nd wl over 1f out and sn wknd* **18/1**

9 4 ½ **Early Girl** 4-9-1 0 .... RichardEvans(5) 2 27
(P D Evans) *s.s: a in last pair: struggling over 4f out* **33/1**

2m 25.77s (3.87) **Going Correction** +0.05s/f (Slow)
WFA 3 from 4yo 24lb 9 Ran SP% **115.1**
Speed ratings (Par 103): **87,86,86,85,84 83,78,75,71**
toteswinger: 1&2 £4.80, 1&3 £2.30, 2&3 £6.40. CSF £13.77 TOTE £3.00: £1.10, £2.90, £2.30; EX 15.00.
Owner Mohamed Obaida **Bred** Gainsborough Stud Management Ltd **Trained** Newmarket, Suffolk

FOCUS
The proximity of 60-rated Red Twist suggests the bare form is modest, but that one was allowed the run of the race at a steady pace, and some of these should rate higher particularly the first three.
Oxus(IRE) Official explanation: jockey said gelding hung left throughout

311 DIGIBET SPORTS BETTING H'CAP 1m 4f (P)
8:20 (8:22) (Class 6) (0-65,65) 4-Y-0+ £2,047 (£604; £302) Stalls Centre

Form RPR

23/0 1 **Imperial Harry**[11] 202 6-9-7 64 .... ChrisCatlin 10 77
(D E Pipe) *wl plcd in 3rd in wl strung out field: effrt to ld 2f out: drvn and styd on wl to draw clr over 1f out* **14/1**

6-56 2 5 **Epidaurian King (IRE)**[12] 194 6-9-2 59 .... DarrenWilliams 14 64
(D Shaw) *hld up in 6th and wl off the pce: prog and nt clr run briefly 3f out: effrt on inner 2f out: wnt 2nd jst over 1f out: no ch w wnr* **10/1**

43-1 3 1 **Imperium**[22] 59 8-9-4 61 .... JimCrowley 11 64
(Jean-Rene Auvray) *hld up in 5th and off the pce: clsd fr 3f out: rdn to dispute 2nd jst over 1f out: one pce after* **5/2**[1]

25-0 4 1 **Ryedale Ovation (IRE)**[25] 21 6-9-8 65 .... FergusSweeney 3 67
(M Hill) *hld up in 10th and wl off the pce: prog on outer fr 4f out: chsng ldrs and in tch over 2f out: hanging and nt keen after: plugged on* **6/1**[3]

345- 5 ½ **Penang Cinta**[54] 7563 6-9-5 62 .... (p) StephenDonohoe 13 63
(P D Evans) *wl enough plcd in 4th in wl spced out field: u.p over 3f out and looked like dropping away: plugged on* **8/1**

001- 6 nk **Eseej (USA)**[42] 7701 4-9-4 65 .... GeorgeBaker 9 66
(P W Hiatt) *led: set gd pce and spreadeagled field: drvn and hdd 2f out: steadily fdd fnl f* **6/1**[3]

60-0 7 ¾ **Resplendent Ace (IRE)**[11] 202 5-9-8 65 .... IanMongan 1 64
(P Howling) *hld up in 9th and wl off the pce: effrt 3f out: hanging and nt keen 2f out: no real prog* **5/1**[2]

200- 8 1 ¼ **Top Tiger**[16] 7715 5-9-2 59 .... (b[1]) PaulMulrennan 6 56
(M H Tompkins) *chsd clr ldr to over 2f out: wknd* **8/1**

006- 9 2 ½ **Moon Mix (FR)**[32] 7545 6-9-5 62 .... SimonWhitworth 4 55
(J R Jenkins) *s.s: hld up in last and wl off the pce: prog on wd outside over 2f out: no imp over 1f out: sn eased* **10/1**

100- 10 2 ¾ **Make Amends (IRE)**[108] 6671 4-9-3 64 .... SteveDrowne 2 53
(R J Hodges) *dwlt: hld up in last pair and wl off the pce: effrt over 2f out but sn no prog* **33/1**

530- 11 1 ¾ **Punta Galera (IRE)**[47] 7650 6-8-10 60 .... KrishGundowry(7) 12 46
(Paul Green) *hld up in 7th and wl off the pce: no prog over 2f out: sn wknd* **20/1**

/21- 12 1 **White Moss (IRE)**[60] 5262 5-9-8 65 .... RichardThomas 5 50
(Jim Best) *hld up in 8th and wl off the pce: pushed along 5f out: sn struggling: no ch over 2f out* **12/1**

2m 33.48s (-1.02) **Going Correction** +0.05s/f (Slow)
WFA 4 from 5yo+ 4lb 12 Ran SP% **136.3**
Speed ratings (Par 101): **105,101,101,100,100 99,99,98,96,94 93,93**
toteswinger: 1&2 £23.30, 1&3 £7.10, 2&3 £8.40. CSF £168.34 CT £484.66 TOTE £13.70: £3.60, £3.50, £1.80; EX 189.30.
Owner CGA Racing Partnership **Bred** Burns Farm Stud **Trained** Nicholashayne, Devon
■ David Pipe's first winner on the Flat.

FOCUS
A moderate handicap. The pace was very strong thanks to Eseej, who went quicker than when making all in a 1m3f maiden around here last time and faded in the straight. The winner is rated back to his best with the next two close to their marks.
Top Tiger Official explanation: jockey said gelding hung right throughout
White Moss(IRE) Official explanation: jockey said mare never travelled

312 KEMPTON.CO.UK H'CAP 1m (P)
8:50 (8:50) (Class 4) (0-85,83) 3-Y-O £4,727 (£1,406; £702) Stalls High

Form RPR

03-1 1 **Royal Collection (IRE)**[14] 160 3-9-0 76 .... PatCosgrave 1 82+
(J Pearce) *t.k.h: sn hld up in last: trckd ldr over 2f out: pushed along firmly and clsd to ld jst ins fnl f: readily* **7/4**[2]

41-2 2 1 **Bushveld (IRE)**[10] 209 3-9-4 80 .... GregFairley 4 83
(M Johnston) *t.k.h: led: kicked on over 2f out: nt qckn over 1f out: hdd jst ins fnl f: readily hld* **1/2**[1]

24-4 3 13 **Why Nee Amy**[14] 160 3-7-9 64 oh3 .... MatthewLawson(7) 3 37
(Miss Gay Kelleway) *dwlt: sn trckd ldr: u.p 3f out: wknd over 2f out* **10/1**[3]

1m 40.88s (1.08) **Going Correction** +0.05s/f (Slow) 3 Ran SP% **112.1**
Speed ratings (Par 99): **96,95,82**
CSF £3.26 TOTE £3.00; EX 3.40.
Owner Matthew Green **Bred** Lawn View Stud **Trained** Newmarket, Suffolk
■ Sky Gate (6/1) was withdrawn on vet's advice. R4 applies, deduct 10p in the £. New market formed.

FOCUS
Only two of these counted and, while the front pair are fair types, this rather fell into the winner's lap. There is a bit of doubt over the form, but the winner clearly improved as he beat the third much further than he did at Lingfield.

313 TURFTV H'CAP 6f (P)
9:20 (9:20) (Class 5) (0-75,73) 3-Y-O £2,590 (£770; £385; £192) Stalls High

Form RPR

5-33 1 **My Best Bet**[7] 229 3-8-10 70 .... MCGeran(5) 5 76
(M R Channon) *stdd s: hld up in 5th: prog over 2f out: swtchd to inner and wnt 2nd wl over 1f out: led ent fnl f: r.o wl* **9/4**[1]

32-3 2 1 ½ **Head Down**[19] 98 3-9-3 72 .... DaneO'Neill 1 73
(R Hannon) *led: kicked on over 2f out: hdd ent fnl f: styd on but comf hld* **11/2**[3]

03-1 3 3 **Cheap Thrills**[14] 162 3-9-1 70 .... ShaneKelly 3 62
(J A Osborne) *t.k.h: trckd ldr to wl over 1f out: sn outpcd* **4/1**[2]

150- 4 2 ¼ **Riflessione**[29] 7820 3-9-1 73 .... (p) KevinGhunowa(3) 2 57
(R A Harris) *trckd ldng trio: rdn over 2f out: nt qckn and wl outpcd over 1f out* **7/1**

404- 5 ½ **Marbled Cat (USA)**[120] 6350 3-8-11 **66** GregFairley 6 49
(M Johnston) *chsd ldng pair: rdn over 2f out: outpcd fr over 1f out* 9/4[1]
662- 6 3 ¼ **Lucky Dan (IRE)**[29] 7825 3-8-7 **62** ChrisCatlin 4 34
(Paul Green) *stdd s: t.k.h: hld up in last: pushed along over 2f out: sn wknd* 12/1
1m 13.4s (0.30) **Going Correction** +0.05s/f (Slow) **6** Ran SP% **117.1**
Speed ratings (Par 97): **100,98,94,91,90 86**
toteswinger: 1&2 £2.30, 1&3 £3.50, 2&3 £5.10. CSF £16.05 TOTE £3.70: £1.20, £3.70; EX 10.80 Place 6: £109.29; Place 5: £28.25.
Owner Phil Jen Racing **Bred** Phil Jen Racing **Trained** West Ilsley, Berks
FOCUS
A modest three-year-old sprint handicap. The winner probably only had to repeat his previous course-and-distance form.
T/Plt: £136.10 to a £1 stake. Pool: £97,712.81. 523.96 winning tickets. T/Qpdt: £23.20 to a £1 stake. Pool: £7,674.82. 244.80 winning tickets. JN

279 LINGFIELD (L-H)
Wednesday, January 28
OFFICIAL GOING: Standard
Wind: Light, behind Weather: Rain

314 "LEAFY" (S) STKS 6f (P)
12:30 (12:35) (Class 6) 4-Y-0+ **£2,047** (£604; £302) **Stalls** Low

Form RPR
-224 1 **One More Round (USA)**[6] 245 11-9-2 72 (b) RichardEvans(5) 7 70+
(P D Evans) *stdd s: patiently rdn in last: swtchd outside and shkn up 1f out: cajoled along and str run to ld fnl 50yds* 2/1[2]
100- 2 ¾ **Hart Of Gold**[51] 7611 5-9-4 64 (p) KevinGhunowa(3) 4 67
(R A Harris) *pressed ldr: led after 2f: hrd rdn fnl f: hdd and outpcd fnl 50yds* 7/1
-126 3 2 **Don Pele (IRE)**[12] 189 7-9-7 72 (p) JoeFanning 8 61
(R A Harris) *t.k.h in 4th or 5th: drvn to chse ldrs over 1f out: one pce* 6/1[3]
1-24 4 nse **C'Mon You Irons (IRE)**[5] 266 4-9-7 67 JimCrowley 2 61
(M R Hoad) *led 2f: chsd ldr after: hrd rdn over 1f out: no ex fnl 100yds* 13/8[1]
20-5 5 ¾ **Scarlet Oak**[19] 96 5-8-11 58 (p) AndrewElliott 6 48
(A M Hales) *chsd ldng pair: hrd rdn over 1f out: no ex fnl f* 8/1
6-00 6 nse **Stormburst (IRE)**[14] 153 5-8-11 43 NeilChalmers 3 48
(A J Chamberlain) *hld up towards rr: effrt ent st: nt pce to chal* 33/1
1m 12.69s (0.79) **Going Correction** +0.15s/f (Slow) **6** Ran SP% **112.3**
Speed ratings (Par 101): **100,99,96,96,95 95**
toteswinger: 1&2 £3.30, 1&3 £1.90, 2&3 £3.90. CSF £16.03 TOTE £2.70: £1.70, £4.70; EX 20.50 Trifecta £87.60 Pool: £220.25 - 1.86 winning units..There was no bid for the winner.
Owner Mrs I M Folkes **Bred** Kenneth L Ramsey And Sarah K Ramsey **Trained** Pandy, Monmouths
FOCUS
Not a bad seller, although the form is a bit muddling with the sixth close enough.

315 FOREST ROW MAIDEN STKS 6f (P)
1:00 (1:06) (Class 5) 3-Y-0+ **£2,729** (£806; £403) **Stalls** Low

Form RPR
22-2 1 **Auld Arty (FR)**[17] 127 3-8-10 77 RobertHavlin 7 69
(T G Mills) *pressed ldr: rdn over 2f out: drvn to ld fnl 100yds: a jst holding runner-up* 2/1[1]
2 hd **The Winged Assasin (USA)**[87] 7155 3-8-10 0 IanMongan 2 68
(J Akehurst) *chsd ldrs: rdn and swtchd rt jst ins fnl f: r.o to take 2nd fnl 75yds: a jst hld* 5/1[2]
5-3 3 1 **Flamsteed (IRE)**[14] 162 3-8-10 0 ShaneKelly 1 65
(M Quinn) *led: hrd rdn and hdd fnl 100yds: one pce* 2/1[1]
60- 4 nk **Hatman Jack (IRE)**[28] 7830 3-8-10 0 JamieSpencer 5 64
(B G Powell) *in tch: wnt 3rd 2f out: drvn to chal fnl f: one pce fnl 100yds* 13/2[3]
5 1 ½ **Spiritual Healing (IRE)** 3-8-5 0 ChrisCatlin 10 54+
(J A Osborne) *in midfield on outside: pushed along 1/2-way: rdn and kpt on fnl f: nvr able to chal* 14/1
6 ½ **Marina Walk** 3-8-5 0 (t) JimmyQuinn 4 53+
(H Morrison) *s.i.s: rn green and bhd: rdn and styd on fr over 1f out: nt rch ldrs* 16/1
0 7 2 **Uncle Brit**[14] 162 3-8-10 0 StephenDonohoe 9 51+
(Sir Mark Prescott) *stdd s: sn rdn along in last: nvr trbld ldrs* 40/1
00-4 8 nk **Only Hope**[8] 227 5-9-7 41 BrianReilly 3 49
(P S McEntee) *sn pushed along in 6th: n.d fr 1/2-way* 40/1
1m 13.16s (1.26) **Going Correction** +0.15s/f (Slow)
WFA 3 from 5yo 16lb **8** Ran SP% **114.1**
Speed ratings (Par 103): **97,96,95,95,93 92,89,89**
toteswinger: 1&2 £3.50, 1&3 £1.40, 2&3 £3.50. CSF £12.58 TOTE £2.20: £1.10, £2.30, £1.50; EX 10.00 Trifecta £37.40 Pool: £400.92 - 7.93 winning units..
Owner Kerr & Lillie Partnership **Bred** Ecurie Liberty **Trained** Headley, Surrey
FOCUS
Ordinary maiden form at best, and it is doubtful if the winner had to run to his best. The time was modest.

316 PLAY BINGO @ WILLIAMHILL.COM H'CAP 5f (P)
1:30 (1:36) (Class 6) (0-60,59) 3-Y-0 **£2,047** (£604; £302) **Stalls** High

Form RPR
006- 1 **Brown Lentic (IRE)**[61] 7464 3-8-0 **46** AmyBaker(5) 3 51
(Miss J Feilden) *mde all: rdn over 1f out: hld on wl fnl f* 13/2[3]
550- 2 ¾ **Speak The Truth (IRE)**[55] 7542 3-9-4 **59** PatCosgrave 7 61
(J R Boyle) *in tch: effrt ent st: r.o to take 2nd ins fnl f: a hld* 13/2[3]
0-63 3 1 **You'relikemefrank**[5] 273 3-8-4 **45** (p) AndrewElliott 1 44+
(J Balding) *prom on rail: unbalanced on bnd and bmpd over 2f out: rallied over 1f out: one pce fnl f* 10/1
3-35 4 nse **Deckchair**[7] 229 3-9-2 **57** (v) LiamJones 2 56
(H J Collingridge) *rdn along and bhd: r.o wl fnl f: nrst fin* 7/2[2]
660- 5 ½ **Piccaso's Sky**[61] 7465 3-8-11 **52** JimmyQuinn 4 49
(A B Haynes) *hld up in tch: rdn and styd on wl fr over 1f out: nvr nrr* 20/1
25-6 6 1 ½ **Dedante**[25] 34 3-8-13 **59** (b) JamesO'Reilly(5) 6 50
(D K Ivory) *chsd wnr tl wknd ins fnl f* 8/1
-522 7 2 ¾ **Sorrel Ridge (IRE)**[5] 273 3-8-12 **53** (p) NCallan 5 34
(M G Quinlan) *std s: squeezed for room and bmpd over 2f out: hrd rdn and wknd over 1f out* 6/4[1]
59.77 secs (0.97) **Going Correction** +0.15s/f (Slow) **7** Ran SP% **113.9**
Speed ratings (Par 95): **98,96,95,95,94 91,87**
toteswinger: 1&2 £7.70, 1&3 £8.50, 2&3 £10.30. CSF £46.76 TOTE £8.00: £3.10, £3.00; EX 91.00.
Owner Miss J Feilden **Bred** Niall J Donohoe **Trained** Exning, Suffolk

FOCUS
A plating-class handicap, but the time was not bad for the grade and the form seems sound.
Brown Lentic(IRE) Official explanation: trainer said, regarding apparent improvement in form, that this was the first run for her and the colt's back problem had been corrected, also a change to front running tactics.
You'relikemefrank Official explanation: jockey said colt failed to handle final bend
Sorrel Ridge(IRE) Official explanation: jockey said gelding ran flat

317 PAT EDDERY RACING VALENTINE'S GALLOPS MORNING H'CAP 7f (P)
2:05 (2:13) (Class 5) (0-75,73) 3-Y-0 **£2,900** (£856; £428) **Stalls** Low

Form RPR
000- 1 **Millway Beach (IRE)**[116] 6480 3-8-10 **65** PaulEddery 2 69
(Pat Eddery) *prom: led jst ins fnl f: drvn out* 15/2
2-22 2 ¾ **Andean Margin (IRE)**[18] 122 3-9-4 **73** (b) JamieSpencer 1 75
(S A Callaghan) *sn led: hrd drvn and edgd rt over 1f out: hdd jst ins fnl f: kpt on* 15/8[1]
420- 3 nk **Night Lily (IRE)**[41] 7718 3-8-11 **66** LukeMorris 3 67
(J Jay) *s.i.s and pushed along early: bhd: gd hdwy to press ldng pair fnl f: kpt on* 11/2[3]
012- 4 2 ¾ **Song Of Praise**[28] 7833 3-8-7 **62** JimmyQuinn 7 56
(M Blanshard) *t.k.h towards rr: hdwy and rdn 2f out: no imp* 15/2
530- 5 ½ **Caravan Of Dreams (IRE)**[33] 7784 3-9-2 **71** NCallan 5 63
(M A Jarvis) *chsd ldr: hrd rdn 2f out: no ex fnl f* 9/2[2]
00-4 6 3 ¼ **Duke Of Normandy (IRE)**[14] 154 3-8-12 **67** JoeFanning 4 51
(M Johnston) *chsd ldrs: drvn along 3f out: wknd wl over 1f out* 13/2
04-3 7 2 ¼ **Lucky Fortune (IRE)**[14] 158 3-8-9 **64** MickyFenton 6 42
(Miss Amy Weaver) *in tch: pushed along over 3f out: wknd over 2f out* 20/1
1m 25.59s (0.79) **Going Correction** +0.15s/f (Slow) **7** Ran SP% **110.0**
Speed ratings (Par 97): **101,100,99,96,96 92,89**
toteswinger: 1&2 £4.90, 1&3 £9.10, 2&3 £3.50. CSF £20.33 TOTE £8.10: £3.80, £1.50; EX 26.30.
Owner Pat Eddery Racing (Toulon) **Bred** Stone Ridge Farm **Trained** Nether Winchendon, Bucks
■ Stewards' Enquiry : Jamie Spencer caution: used whip down shoulder in forehand position
FOCUS
The clue was in the race title here. The winner was well in on the form he showed on his debut last year but did not quite have to match it here. The form seems sound.

318 WILLIAM HILL TELEBETTING ON 0800 44 40 40 H'CAP 1m (P)
2:40 (2:46) (Class 4) (0-80,78) 4-Y-0+ **£4,857** (£1,445; £722; £360) **Stalls** High

Form RPR
15-3 1 **L'Hirondelle (IRE)**[7] 232 5-9-3 **77** PaulDoe 5 89
(M J Attwater) *t.k.h: trckd ldr: led ins fnl f: rdn clr and r.o wl* 9/2[2]
4-15 2 3 ¼ **Pegasus Again (USA)**[18] 113 4-9-2 **76** (p) RobertHavlin 10 81
(T G Mills) *broke wl: led: rdn over 2f out: hdd and nt pce of wnr ins fnl f* 8/1
3 1 **Leonaldo (USA)**[119] 4-9-0 **74** ChrisCatlin 1 77
(J R Gask) *prom on rail tl hrd rdn and nt pce of ldng pair over 1f out* 25/1
2/3- 4 nk **Torch Of Freedom (IRE)**[221] 3286 4-9-4 **78** StephenDonohoe 3 80
(Sir Mark Prescott) *in tch: rdn over 2f out: styd on same pce* 7/2[1]
54-2 5 ¾ **Ocean Legend (IRE)**[7] 232 4-9-3 **77** LiamJones 11 77
(Miss J Feilden) *prom tl rdn and outpcd fnl 2f* 7/2[1]
045- 6 hd **Burnbrake**[60] 7495 4-8-6 **66** LukeMorris 6 66
(L Montague Hall) *mid-div: drvn along 3f out: styd on same pce* 12/1
0-24 7 nse **Hucking Hero (IRE)**[13] 172 4-8-12 **72** SteveDrowne 4 72
(J R Best) *dwlt: towards rr: effrt on rail and in tch ent st: no imp* 7/1[3]
15-4 8 nk **Dinner Date**[14] 157 7-8-8 **68** ShaneKelly 8 67
(T Keddy) *hld up in rr: shkn up over 1f out: nt rch chalng position* 20/1
25-6 9 shd **Napoletano (GER)**[25] 31 8-8-9 **69** (p) NickyMackay 9 68
(S Dow) *stdd s: t.k.h in midfield on outer: rdn and outpcd 3f out: styng on at fin* 16/1
00-0 10 3 ¾ **Paradise Dancer (IRE)**[18] 125 5-8-8 **68** JamieSpencer 7 58
(J A R Toller) *t.k.h in rr: mod hdwy whn nt clr run over 1f out: sn wknd* 10/1
1m 40.07s (1.87) **Going Correction** +0.15s/f (Slow) **10** Ran SP% **117.5**
Speed ratings (Par 105): **96,92,91,91,90 90,90,90,90,86**
toteswinger: 1&2 £8.00, 1&3 £17.70, 2&3 £28.60. CSF £40.77 CT £830.16 TOTE £5.40: £1.90, £2.10, £4.40; EX 43.70 Trifecta £256.60 Pool: £346.78 - 0.47 winning units..
Owner Canisbay Bloodstock **Bred** Gainsborough Stud Management Ltd **Trained** Epsom, Surrey
FOCUS
A fair handicap, run at an uneven pace and it paid to race handily with the first pair always 1-2. The race has been rated around the second but the overall form should be treated with a degree of caution.
Ocean Legend(IRE) Official explanation: trainer said gelding lost a front shoe

319 COWDEN H'CAP 1m 5f (P)
3:15 (3:20) (Class 5) (0-75,73) 4-Y-0+ **£2,900** (£856; £428) **Stalls** Low

Form RPR
41-6 1 **Mission Control (IRE)**[16] 139 4-9-1 **70** PatCosgrave 8 78+
(J R Boyle) *trckd ldrs: effrt over 2f out: wnt 2nd and clsd on ldr over 1f out: drvn to ld fnl 75yds* 9/2[2]
61-1 2 nk **Wind Flow**[14] 161 5-9-4 **68** (b) CatherineGannon 9 75
(C A Dwyer) *rdn to ld and wnt to ins rail: drvn 2 l clr ent st: hdd fnl 75yds: kpt on* 9/2[2]
050- 3 1 ½ **King's Majesty (IRE)**[37] 7758 7-9-0 **64** AndrewElliott 3 69
(A M Hales) *t.k.h in last: rdn and styd on wl fnl 2f: tk 3rd cl home* 16/1
20-2 4 nk **Star Choice**[19] 103 4-8-9 **64** JimmyQuinn 4 68
(J Pearce) *in tch: drvn to chse ldrs over 1f out: one pce* 11/4[1]
6-00 5 ¾ **Red Wine**[11] 202 10-8-10 **60** RobertWinston 7 63
(A J McCabe) *stdd s: t.k.h in rr: swtchd to rail and hdwy over 1f out: nt pce to sustain run* 14/1
020- 6 1 ¾ **Vinces**[42] 7711 5-8-13 **63** RobertHavlin 1 64
(T D McCarthy) *prom: rdn to chse ldr over 2f out: lost 2nd and wknd over 1f out* 11/1
245- 7 nk **Apache Fort**[47] 7657 6-9-9 **73** (b) ShaneKelly 5 73
(T Keddy) *travelled wl in 6th: rdn 2f out: no imp* 15/2
04-4 8 5 **Drum Major (IRE)**[19] 103 4-9-0 **69** PaulDoe 6 62
(G L Moore) *prom: hrd rdn 3f out: wknd wl over 1f out* 13/2[3]
/50- 9 39 **Nora Chrissie (IRE)**[61] 7486 7-9-5 **69** (v) JamieSpencer 2 3
(Niall Moran, Ire) *stdd s: hld up towards rr: rdn over 3f out: no rspnse: wl bhd and eased fnl 2f* 10/1
2m 46.85s (0.85) **Going Correction** +0.15s/f (Slow)
WFA 4 from 5yo+ 5lb **9** Ran SP% **118.1**
Speed ratings (Par 103): **103,102,101,101,101 100,99,96,72**
toteswinger: 1&2 £7.50, 1&3 £16.60, 2&3 £16.10. CSF £25.73 CT £300.78 TOTE £6.10: £1.90, £2.50, £5.40; EX 34.00 TRIFECTA Not won..
Owner M Khan X2 **Bred** Darley **Trained** Epsom, Surrey

FOCUS
An open handicap run at a sound pace. The winner was unexposed at the trip and the second pretty much back to his best.

320 PLAY POKER @ WILLIAMHILL.COM H'CAP 1m 2f (P)
3:50 (3:57) (Class 6) (0-60,60) 4-Y-0+ £2,047 (£604; £302) Stalls Low

Form RPR

225- 1 **Old Romney**[42] 7702 5-9-5 59 JimmyQuinn 5 71
(M Wigham) *t.k.h: in tch: effrt over 2f out: r.o to ld ins fnl f: drvn out* 7/2[2]

00-2 2 1 3/4 **Middle Of Nowhere (USA)**[18] 120 4-9-3 59 (t) ChrisCatlin 13 68
(M A Magnusson) *trckd ldrs: led over 2f out and kicked on: hdd and no ex ins fnl f* 12/1

065- 3 1/2 **Our Kes (IRE)**[49] 7620 7-9-6 60 IanMongan 14 68
(P Howling) *stdd in rr: rdn and styd on wl fnl 2f: tk 3rd fnl 75yds* 16/1

61-5 4 1 **Zalkani (IRE)**[11] 202 9-9-6 60 JerryO'Dwyer 2 66
(J Pearce) *broke wl: stdd bk into midfield: effrt 2f out: styd on to take 4th fnl 50yds* 12/1

263- 5 1 **Barton Sands (IRE)**[52] 7590 12-9-2 56 (t) JimCrowley 8 60
(Andrew Reid) *hld up in midfield: effrt and in tch ent st: one pce appr fnl f* 12/1

1-12 6 1/2 **Chalice Welcome**[5] 275 6-9-3 57 HayleyTurner 4 60+
(N B King) *patiently rdn towards rr: effrt ent st: styd on wl fnl f: nrst fin* 3/1[1]

25-6 7 1 1/2 **Siena Star (IRE)**[18] 125 11-9-6 60 MickyFenton 11 60
(Stef Liddiard) *led after 1f tl over 2f out: wknd over 1f out* 6/1[3]

55-6 8 3/4 **Media Stars**[6] 256 4-9-4 60 ShaneKelly 10 58
(J A Osborne) *hld up in rr: rdn and struggling in last 3f out: gng on again at fin* 16/1

4-23 9 2 3/4 **Broughtons Flight (IRE)**[12] 193 4-9-0 56 StephenDonohoe 12 49
(W J Musson) *in tch: rdn over 2f out: wknd over 1f out* 6/1[3]

500- 10 3 1/2 **Alfredtheordinary**[40] 7732 4-9-1 57 TonyCulhane 1 43
(M R Channon) *led 1f: prom tl hrd rdn and wknd 2f out* 16/1

06-0 11 6 **Bid Art (IRE)**[4] 285 4-9-3 59 (p) FrankieMcDonald 3 33
(Jamie Snowden) *chsd ldng trio: rdn over 4f out: sn lost pl* 50/1

600- 12 3/4 **Muraco**[76] 5145 5-9-1 55 AndrewElliott 9 27
(A M Hales) *hld up in midfield: rdn and outpcd 4f out: sn bhd* 33/1

2m 5.57s (-1.03) **Going Correction** +0.15s/f (Slow)
WFA 4 from 5yo+ 2lb 12 Ran SP% **121.4**
Speed ratings (Par 101): **110,108,108,107,106 106,105,104,102,99 94,94**
toteswinger: 1&2 £6.30, 1&3 £18.30, 2&3 £29.60. CSF £46.83 CT £610.71 TOTE £4.60: £1.80, £3.40, £4.40; EX 71.30 TRIFECTA Not won..
Owner James Crickmore **Bred** Gainsborough Stud Management Ltd **Trained** Newmarket, Suffolk

FOCUS
A competitive heat featuring a number of multiple course winners, but the early gallop was not that strong although the time was fair for the grade. Sound form overall, with the winner in line with last year's form here.

321 ASHURST WOOD APPRENTICE H'CAP 1m (P)
4:25 (4:30) (Class 6) (0-60,60) 4-Y-0+ £2,047 (£604; £302) Stalls High

Form RPR

000- 1 **Herbert Crescent**[43] 7698 4-9-5 60 JamieMoriarty 6 64
(Ollie Pears) *in tch: effrt 2f out: hung lft over 1f out: swtchd rt: r.o wl to ld nr fin* 7/1

0-42 2 hd **Nikki Bea (IRE)**[12] 192 6-8-9 53 MCGeran(3) 4 57
(Jamie Poulton) *chsd ldrs: edgd rt and led ins fnl f: kpt on u.p: jst ct* 4/1[2]

000- 3 1/2 **Shake On It**[27] 7771 5-9-2 60 (t) WilliamCarson(3) 10 63
(M J Gingell) *settled in rr and t.k.h: gd hdwy on rail over 1f out: clsd on ldrs fnl f: r.o* 16/1

30-0 4 1/2 **Riviera Red (IRE)**[17] 131 9-8-5 46 oh1 (b) LukeMorris 5 48
(L Montague Hall) *hld up in 6th: hdwy 3f out: rdn 2f out: chalng whn edgd lft ins fnl f: kpt on* 14/1

-243 5 1/2 **Red Current**[9] 221 5-8-5 51 DeanHeslop(5) 3 53+
(R A Harris) *chsd ldr: drvn to slt ld 1f out: hdd ins fnl f: cl 5th but jst hld whn squeezed out fnl 50yds* 5/1[3]

060- 6 nk **Binnion Bay (IRE)**[179] 4635 8-8-11 52 (b) TravisBlock 7 52
(J J Bridger) *s.s: t.k.h in rr: drvn along and styd on fnl 2f: nrst fin* 16/1

031- 7 1 1/4 **Wooden King (IRE)**[29] 7817 4-8-11 55 RichardEvans(3) 8 54+
(P D Evans) *led: hrd rdn and hdd 1f out: cl 6th but jst hld whn hmpd and eased fnl 75yds* 4/1[2]

4/42 8 1 3/4 **Bollywood Style**[18] 114 4-8-8 54 PNolan(5) 9 47
(J R Best) *t.k.h in rr: mod effrt and sltly wd st: sn btn* 7/2[1]

060- 9 nk **Quality Street**[70] 7392 7-8-7 55 (p) AndrewHeffernan(7) 2 47
(P Butler) *t.k.h: in tch: outpcd over 2f out: sn btn* 22/1

1m 39.92s (1.72) **Going Correction** +0.15s/f (Slow) 9 Ran SP% **114.2**
Speed ratings (Par 101): **97,96,96,95,95 95,93,92,91**
toteswinger: 1&2 £5.40, 1&3 £21.30, 2&3 £12.30. CSF £34.71 CT £434.27 TOTE £7.40: £2.00, £1.80, £4.30; EX 36.90 Trifecta £280.00 Pool: £378.45 - 0.47 winning units. Place 6: £149.03 Place 5: £66.88.
Owner Ollie Pears **Bred** Wood Hall Stud Limited **Trained** Norton, N Yorks

FOCUS
They did not go a mad gallop early and the race developed into something of a sprint, with six in with a shout half a furlong out and a bunch finish. Messy form which should not be taken too literally.
Herbert Crescent Official explanation: trainer said, regarding apparent improvement in form, that the gelding was suited by the polytrack rather than the fibresand of Southwell.
T/Plt: £238.20 to a £1 stake. Pool: £58,691.86. 179.84 winning tickets. T/Qpdt: £244.90 to a £1 stake. Pool: £5,130.04. 15.50 winning tickets. LM

300 SOUTHWELL (L-H)
Thursday, January 29

OFFICIAL GOING: Standard
Wind: Light across Weather: cloudy and dry

322 PLAY BINGO @ WILLIAMHILL.COM H'CAP 1m (F)
1:50 (1:50) (Class 5) (0-70,66) 3-Y-0 £3,070 (£906; £453) Stalls Low

Form RPR

400- 1 **Miss Fritton (IRE)**[43] 7700 3-9-3 65 JerryO'Dwyer 3 67
(M Botti) *trckd ldrs: hdwy 2f out: rdn to ld over 1f out: styd on wl* 7/1

53-2 2 1 1/4 **Solo Choice**[16] 144 3-9-4 66 TonyCulhane 4 65
(D Flood) *sn led: rdn along 2f out: drvn and hdd over 1f out: kpt on u.p ins fnl f* 5/2[1]

0-53 3 3/4 **My Best Man**[16] 149 3-8-12 63 JamesMillman(3) 1 60
(B R Millman) *cl up: effrt over 2f out: sn rdn and ev ch tl drvn and one pce ent fnl f* 7/2[3]

165- 4 3/4 **Lady Salama**[103] 6809 3-9-1 63 AndrewElliott 5 58
(K R Burke) *trckd ldng pair on outer: effrt to chal over 2f out: sn rdn and ev ch tl drvn and one pce appr fnl f* 14/1

000- 5 shd **Tae Kwon Do (USA)**[111] 6632 3-8-9 57 TomEaves 6 52
(Miss J A Camacho) *hld up: hdwy on outer 3f out: chal 2f out and ev ch tl rdn: edgd lft and wknd wl over 1f out* 9/2

641- 6 hd **Paint Splash**[44] 7694 3-8-5 58 DeanHeslop(5) 2 53
(T D Barron) *hld up: hdwy on inner 3f out: sn rdn along and ch tl drvn and wknd over 1f out* 10/3[2]

1m 42.57s (-1.13) **Going Correction** -0.25s/f (Stan) 6 Ran SP% **111.2**
Speed ratings (Par 97): **95,93,93,92,92 91**
toteswinger: 1&2 £4.60, 1&3 £5.20, 2&3 £2.00. CSF £24.33 TOTE £10.90: £4.10, £1.80; EX 29.10.
Owner Giuseppe Piccinni **Bred** Coppice Farm & Cleaboy Stud **Trained** Newmarket, Suffolk

FOCUS
A modest handicap run at a sound pace with the top-weight 4lb below the race ceiling. Most of the field had questions to answer. The winner was back to her early 2yo form.

323 WILLIAM HILL TELEBETTING ON 0800 44 40 40 MEDIAN AUCTION MAIDEN STKS 1m (F)
2:20 (2:20) (Class 6) 4-6-Y-0 £2,047 (£604; £302) Stalls Low

Form RPR

0-32 1 **More Time Tim (IRE)**[7] 255 4-9-3 66 PatCosgrave 5 77+
(J R Boyle) *trckd ldr: smooth hdwy to ld over 2f out: sn clr: heavily eased ins fnl f* 15/8[2]

2-2 2 13 **Lady Longcroft**[10] 217 4-8-12 0 JimmyQuinn 2 31
(J Pearce) *in tch: hdwy to chse ldng pair 1/2-way: rdn along over 2f out and sn no imp: tk poor 2nd nr fin* 13/8[1]

4-23 3 4 1/2 **Orpenella**[23] 58 4-8-12 54 (b) NCallan 3 45
(K A Ryan) *led: rdn along and hdd over 2f out: sn drvn and one pce: poor 2nd whn broke down wl ins fnl f: lost 2nd nr line: dead* 3/1[3]

0-55 4 15 **The Power Of Phil**[7] 247 5-9-3 42 (v[1]) RichardKingscote 1 —
(Tom Dascombe) *slwly into stride: a bhd* 11/1

5 22 **Zabellah** 4-8-12 0 PaulMulrennan 4 —
(J Balding) *chsd ldng pair: rdn along after 3f: sn outpcd and wl bhd fr wl over 2f out* 66/1

1m 41.63s (-2.07) **Going Correction** -0.25s/f (Stan) 5 Ran SP% **107.7**
Speed ratings: **100,87,82,67,45**
CSF £5.05 TOTE £2.40: £1.40, £1.30; EX 5.30.
Owner John Hopkins (t/a South Hatch Racing) **Bred** Glending Bloodstock **Trained** Epsom, Surrey

FOCUS
A weak maiden provided a simple opportunity for 66-rated More Time Tim, who appeared to put in an improved effort.
The Power Of Phil Official explanation: jockey said gelding missed the break and hung left

324 HOSPITALITY PACKAGES AVAILABLE H'CAP 1m 3f (F)
2:50 (2:50) (Class 5) (0-70,69) 4-Y-0+ £3,070 (£906; £453) Stalls Low

Form RPR

204- 1 **Edas**[40] 6551 7-8-13 61 GrahamGibbons 2 73+
(J J Quinn) *trckd ldng pair: cl up over 4f out: led 3f out: rdn clr wl over 1f out: kpt on strly* 5/1[2]

50-0 2 4 **Dancing Lyra**[14] 171 8-9-3 65 JamieMoriarty 1 70
(R A Fahey) *chsd ldrs on inner: hdwy over 3f out: chsd wnr wl over 1f out: sn drvn and no imp ins fnl f* 20/1

45-2 3 3 **Trans Sonic**[25] 40 6-9-3 65 TonyHamilton 3 65
(A J Lockwood) *led 3f: cl up: rdn along 3f out: drvn on inner wl over 1f out: kpt on same pce* 7/1[3]

0-60 4 hd **Coral Shores**[5] 285 4-8-10 61 (v) LukeMorris 4 61
(P W Hiatt) *trckd ldrs: hdwy over 3f out: rdn to chse ldng pair wl over 1f out: sn drvn and one pce* 7/1[3]

150- 5 5 **Sand Repeal (IRE)**[135] 5993 7-9-0 67 AmyBaker(5) 8 58
(Miss J Feilden) *hld up in rr: hdwy 4f out: rdn over 2f out: sn drvn and nvr nr ldrs* 15/2

40-3 6 2 **My Mirasol**[23] 66 5-8-8 56 LPKeniry 6 44
(D E Cantillon) *cl up: led after 3f: rdn and hdd 3f out: sn wknd* 9/1

254- 7 3/4 **Opera Writer (IRE)**[12] 7785 6-9-7 69 (p) JimCrowley 5 56
(R Hollinshead) *in tch and reminders after 1f: pushed along over 4f out: rdn over 3f out and sn wknd* 9/2[1]

2-30 8 2 1/4 **Thornaby Green**[10] 221 8-8-8 56 ow1 JamieSpencer 7 39
(T D Barron) *hld up towards rr: hdwy on outer 4f out: rdn to chse ldrs wl over 2f out: sn drvn and wknd: eased* 5/1[2]

65-0 9 hd **Josh You Are**[17] 139 6-9-6 68 StephenDonohoe 9 50
(Ian Williams) *hld up: a in rr* 8/1

2m 24.01s (-3.99) **Going Correction** -0.25s/f (Stan)
WFA 4 from 5yo+ 3lb 9 Ran SP% **114.2**
Speed ratings (Par 103): **104,101,98,98,95 93,93,91,91**
toteswinger: 1&2 £16.00, 1&3 £5.80, 2&3 £14.14. CSF £95.54 CT £697.28 TOTE £4.80: £1.70, £6.50, £1.90; EX 116.30 TRIFECTA Not won..
Owner S C B Limited **Bred** Stilvi Compania Financiera Sa **Trained** Settrington, N Yorks

FOCUS
Quite an open handicap and after setting off at a strong pace the gallop steadied down the back stretch. Sound form, the winner rated back to his post-3yo best.
Opera Writer(IRE) Official explanation: trainer said gelding never travelled
Thornaby Green Official explanation: jockey said gelding hung left in straight

325 PLAY POKER @ WILLIAMHILL.COM H'CAP 1m 6f (F)
3:20 (3:20) (Class 4) (0-85,84) 4-Y-0+ £5,180 (£1,541; £770; £384) Stalls Low

Form RPR

30-3 1 **Aureate**[22] 82 5-9-6 84 AnthonyBetts(7) 3 95
(B Ellison) *t.k.h: led: rdn along and hdd wl over 1f out: rallied ins fnl f: led nr line* 16/1

5-11 2 hd **El Diego (IRE)**[17] 139 5-9-5 76 NCallan 7 87
(J R Gask) *trckd ldrs: hdwy 4f out: rdn to ld wl over 1f out: drvn and edgd lft ins fnl f: hdd and no ex nr line* 4/1[2]

1-2 3 3 1/4 **Take Me There**[9] 226 6-9-1 72 JimCrowley 8 78
(John Berry) *trckd wnr: effrt 3f out: rdn and ev ch wl over 1f out: drvn and hld whn n.m.r ins fnl f* 2/1[1]

3-64 4 3 3/4 **Calculating (IRE)**[8] 233 5-8-11 68 HayleyTurner 9 69
(M D I Usher) *dwlt: hld up in rr: hdwy 5f out: rdn 3f out: chsd ldrs fnl 2f: no imp* 8/1

64-2 5 7 **Dart**[28] 3 5-8-13 70 JamieSpencer 6 61
(J R Fanshawe) *hld up in rr: hdwy on outer 6f out: rdn along 4f out: drvn over 3f out and n.d* 7/1

6-21 6 5 **Ibrox (IRE)**[14] 178 4-8-3 66 JimmyQuinn 4 50
(A D Brown) *chsd ldrs: rdn along 4f out: grad wknd* 11/2[3]

31-3 **7** 3/4 **Victory Quest (IRE)**[28] 3 9-9-1 72 (v) TomEaves 5 55
(Mrs S Lamyman) *in tch: rdn along and lost pl 1/2-way: sn bhd* **25/1**
3-14 **8** 2 **My Friend Fritz**[23] 65 9-9-0 71 LukeMorris 1 52
(P W Hiatt) *trckd ldng pair on inner: rdn along over 3f out: wknd over 2f out* **14/1**
16-4 **9** 15 **Puy D'Arnac (FR)**[9] 226 6-9-6 77 PatCosgrave 2 37
(G A Swinbank) *trckd ldrs on inner: rdn along 5f out: sn wknd* **14/1**
3m 3.70s (-4.60) **Going Correction** -0.25s/f (Stan)
WFA 4 from 5yo+ 6lb **9** Ran SP% **115.4**
Speed ratings (Par 105): **103,102,101,98,94 92,91,90,81**
toteswinger: 1&2 £14.90, 1&3 £9.60, 2&3 £3.80. CSF £78.98 CT £187.62 TOTE £28.20: £3.60, £1.60, £1.30; EX 129.00 TRIFECTA Not won..
Owner The Seasiders Again **Bred** Darley **Trained** Norton, N Yorks
FOCUS
A good-class stayers' handicap run at a a sound pace thanks to top-weight Aureate who seemed to take charge of his inexperienced rider in the back stretch. The form looks worth taking fairly positively.

326 SOUTHWELL-RACECOURSE.CO.UK H'CAP 5f (F)
3:50 (3:51) (Class 6) (0-65,69) 4-Y-0+ **£2,047** (£604; £302) **Stalls** High

Form RPR
40-2 **1** **The Geester**[14] 173 5-8-9 56 (b) JimmyQuinn 4 65
(S R Bowring) *a cl up: effrt 2f out: rdn to ld appr last: kpt on* **4/1**[2]
15-1 **2** 1/2 **Calmdownmate (IRE)**[21] 89 4-9-4 65 LukeMorris 3 72
(Mrs R A Carr) *wnt lft s and sn pushed along towards rr: hdwy 2f out and sn rdn: swtchd lft and drvn ent fnl f: kpt on* **11/4**[1]
2-00 **3** 1/2 **Colorus (IRE)**[7] 243 6-9-2 63 (p) RichardKingscote 2 68
(W J H Ratcliffe) *led: rdn along 2f out: drvn and hdd appr last: kpt on* **13/2**
0451 **4** hd **Punching**[2] 303 5-9-8 69 6ex LPKeniry 8 74
(C R Dore) *trckd ldrs: hdwy 2f out: rdn over 1f out: kpt on u.p ins fnl f* **6/1**[3]
060- **5** 1 1/2 **Cheshire Rose**[64] 7456 4-8-13 65 DeanHeslop(5) 10 64
(T D Barron) *racd wd: in tch: hdwy 2f out: sn rdn and hung lft ins fnl f: kpt on: nrst fin* **50/1**
-613 **6** 1/2 **Joss Stick**[6] 269 4-8-9 63 (p) SPRyan(7) 5 60
(R A Harris) *chsd ldrs: rdn along 2f out: drvn over 1f out and grad wknd* **20/1**
600- **7** 3/4 **Dickie Le Davoir**[117] 6486 5-9-2 63 MickyFenton 1 58
(John A Harris) *sn rdn along and outpcd on outer: hdwy 2f out: kpt on u.p ins fnl f: nrst fin* **16/1**
13-2 **8** hd **Now You See Me**[6] 269 5-9-0 61 TonyCulhane 7 55
(D Flood) *squeezed out s and rdn along in rr: hdwy over 1f out: nt rch ldrs* **6/1**[3]
5-16 **9** 1 1/2 **Spic 'n Span**[6] 269 4-9-4 65 (b) JoeFanning 6 54
(R A Harris) *cl up: rdn and ev ch 2f out: sn drvn and wknd appr fnl f* **8/1**
501- **10** 1 **Guto**[86] 7182 6-9-1 62 JamieSpencer 11 47
(W J H Ratcliffe) *prom: rdn along over 2f out and sn wknd: hmpd and eased ins fnl f* **14/1**
000- **11** 7 **Count Cougar (USA)**[58] 7534 9-8-10 60 MichaelJStainton(3) 9 20
(S P Griffiths) *sn rdn along: outpcd after 1f and bhd fr 1/2-way* **50/1**
59.73 secs (0.03) **Going Correction** +0.05s/f (Slow) **11** Ran SP% **120.9**
Speed ratings (Par 101): **101,100,99,99,96 95,94,94,91,90 79**
toteswinger: 1&2 £3.20, 1&3 £7.30, 2&3 £6.70. CSF £15.66 CT £71.07 TOTE £4.10: £1.40, £1.30, £3.00; EX 15.60 Trifecta £255.90 Part won. Pool of £345.91- 0.96 winning units..
Owner Mrs Anne & Fred Cowley **Bred** P O'Boyle **Trained** Edwinstowe, Notts
FOCUS
A modest sprint handicap with all the pace towards the centre of the track. Sound form.
Dickie Le Davoir Official explanation: jockey said, regarding running and riding, his orders were to jump out and finish as close as he could, however, he left the stalls slowly and was then flat out to the line, adding that he told the trainer that the gelding would be better suited by 6f

327 PLAY GOLF AT SOUTHWELL GOLF CLUB H'CAP 6f (F)
4:20 (4:20) (Class 6) (0-50,55) 4-Y-0+ **£2,047** (£604; £302) **Stalls** Low

Form RPR
-534 **1** **Mocha Java**[11] 210 6-8-4 48 PatrickDonaghy(5) 14 61
(M Salaman) *in tch: gd hdwy on outer wl over 2f out: rdn to ld over 1f out: drvn and edgd lft ins fnl f: kpt on strly* **7/1**
200- **2** 1 3/4 **Highland Song (IRE)**[90] 7112 6-8-7 46 oh1 FrankieMcDonald 1 53
(R F Fisher) *chsd ldr: hdwy on inner over 2f out: sn rdn and ev ch tl drvn ent fnl f and kpt on same pce* **25/1**
0-05 **3** 2 **Straight Face (IRE)**[9] 222 5-8-11 50 (e) NCallan 9 51
(Miss Gay Kelleway) *midfield: pushed along 1/2-way: wd st: rdn 2f out: styd on appr last: nrst fin* **5/1**[2]
000- **4** hd **Orange Square (IRE)**[178] 4686 4-8-8 47 ow1 TonyHamilton 8 47
(D W Barker) *chsd ldng pair: hdwy over 2f out: sn rdn and ev ch tl drvn and one pce ent fnl f* **12/1**
0-31 **5** 3/4 **Head To Head (IRE)**[9] 222 5-9-2 55 6ex (p) GrahamGibbons 4 53
(A D Brown) *chsd ldrs: rdn 2f out: drvn over 1f out: kpt on same pce* **4/1**[1]
0-56 **6** 1 1/2 **Majestic Cheer**[16] 150 5-8-9 48 ow1 (p) StephenDonohoe 6 41
(John A Harris) *midfield: hdwy 2f out: sn rdn and kpt on appr fnl f: nrst fin* **12/1**
0-24 **7** shd **Nautical**[16] 150 11-8-9 48 JerryO'Dwyer 7 40
(J R Holt) *in rr: rdn along and hdwy on outer 2f out: styd on appr fnl f: nrst fin* **9/1**
20-0 **8** 1/2 **Dubai To Barnsley**[21] 87 4-8-8 47 (p) PatrickMathers 11 38
(Garry Moss) *chsd ldrs: rdn along over 2f out: drvn wl over 1f out and sn no imp* **10/1**
0-06 **9** shd **Flying Indian**[16] 146 4-8-9 48 ow1 (v) PaulMulrennan 2 39
(J Balding) *led: rdn along 2f out: drvn and hdd over 1f out: sn wknd* **66/1**
0-03 **10** hd **Bahamian Bay**[14] 175 7-8-7 46 oh1 (v) JimmyQuinn 5 36
(M Brittain) *dwlt: sme hdwy on inner over 2f out: sn rdn and wknd wl over 1f out* **13/2**[3]
-551 **11** 1 **Vanatina (IRE)**[14] 175 5-8-7 49 DuranFentiman(3) 3 36
(W M Brisbourne) *midfield: rdn along on inner 1/2-way: sme hdwy whn n.m.r wl over 1f out: sn wknd* **8/1**
0-05 **12** 3/4 **Gone'N'Dunnett (IRE)**[15] 153 10-8-7 46 oh1 (p) AndrewElliott 10 30
(Mrs C A Dunnett) *a in rr* **22/1**
/00- **13** 6 **Royal Orissa**[372] 264 7-8-7 46 oh1 HayleyTurner 12 11
(D Haydn Jones) *a in rr* **25/1**
1m 15.76s (-0.74) **Going Correction** -0.25s/f (Stan) **13** Ran SP% **121.6**
Speed ratings (Par 101): **94,91,89,88,87 85,85,84,84,84 83,82,74**
toteswinger: 1&2 £36.60, 1&3 £7.60, 2&3 £20.50. CSF £179.03 CT £994.52 TOTE £9.90: £2.90, £8.10, £2.00; EX 183.30 Place 6: £68.15 Place 5: £30.07..
Owner Oaktree Racing **Bred** A H And C E Robinson Partnership **Trained** Upper Lambourn, Berks
FOCUS
A low-grade sprint handicap and plenty in with chances halfway up the home straight. Reliable enough form for the grade.

T/Jkpt: Not won. T/Plt: £64.70 to a £1 stake. Pool: £66,610.21. 750.94 winning tickets. T/Qpdt: £14.70 to a £1 stake. Pool: £4,423.76. 222.50 winning tickets. JR

292 WOLVERHAMPTON (A.W) (L-H)
Thursday, January 29

OFFICIAL GOING: Standard
Wind: modest across Weather: dry

328 SPONSOR A RACE BY CALLING 01902 390009 CLASSIFIED STKS 5f 20y(P)
6:50 (6:50) (Class 7) 3-Y-0+ **£1,619** (£481; £240; £120) **Stalls** Low

Form RPR
000- **1** **Honest Value (IRE)**[31] 7808 4-9-6 45 (v[1]) TravisBlock 1 52
(Mrs L C Jewell) *trckd ldrs: rdn to chse ldr wl over 1f out: led ins fnl f: rdn out* **17/2**
0004 **2** 1 **So Sublime**[7] 250 4-9-3 42 (b) AmyBaker(3) 6 48
(M C Chapman) *taken down early: racd off the pce in midfield: pushed along 3f out: hdwy ent fnl f: r.o wl to go 2nd last strides: nt rch wnr* **7/2**[1]
0040 **3** nk **Nordic Light (USA)**[1] 308 5-9-6 42 (bt) LukeMorris 13 47
(J M Bradley) *towards rr: rdn 3f out: hdwy u.p ent fnl f: r.o wl to snatch 3rd last stride: nt rch wnr* **8/1**
0-60 **4** shd **Spanish Ace**[1] 308 8-9-3 45 (b) JackDean(3) 4 47
(J M Bradley) *pressed ldr tl led over 2f out: hrd drvn over 1f out: hdd ins fnl f: no ex: lost 2 pls nr fin* **4/1**[2]
050- **5** 1 3/4 **Ace Club**[229] 3021 8-8-13 44 (b) KierenFox(7) 2 40
(Garry Moss) *led tl hdd over 2f out: rdn 2f out: wknd fnl f* **14/1**
050- **6** 2 **Gelert (IRE)**[48] 7644 4-9-3 45 (b) JamesO'Reilly(3) 11 33
(Peter Grayson) *dwlt and short of room s: chsd ldrs: hrd rdn 2f out: wknd jst over 1f out* **7/1**[3]
-006 **7** 1/2 **Desert Light (IRE)**[15] 153 8-8-13 40 (v) LeeTopliss(7) 12 31+
(D Shaw) *dropped in bhd after s: hld up wl bhd: rdn and effrt on inner wl over 1f out: short of room and swtchd rt 1f out: sn nt clr run and hmpd: swtchd rt again fnl 100yds: nvr able to chal* **9/1**
55-0 **8** 1 1/4 **Lady Hopeful (IRE)**[15] 153 7-8-13 45 (b) AndrewHeffernan(7) 3 27
(Peter Grayson) *hld up in midfield: effrt and rdn wl over 1f out: wknd ent fnl f* **12/1**
440- **9** 3 3/4 **Silver Deal**[129] 6173 4-8-13 45 DavidKenny(7) 5 13
(J A Pickering) *awkward s: a bhd: hanging rt fr 2f out* **40/1**
05-4 **10** 1 3/4 **Firewalker**[4] 286 4-9-6 45 (b) RussellKennemore 9 7
(P T Dalton) *pressed ldrs tl 1/2-way: wknd qckly u.p 2f out* **8/1**
00-0 **11** 3 1/2 **Calypso Prince**[10] 214 3-7-12 39 (p) SeanPalmer(7) 8 —
(M D I Usher) *s.i.s: alway bhd: t.o 1/2-way* **25/1**
63.62 secs (1.32) **Going Correction** +0.175s/f (Slow)
WFA 3 from 4yo+ 15lb **11** Ran SP% **118.1**
Speed ratings (Par 97): **96,94,93,93,90 87,86,84,78,76 70**
toteswinger: 1&2 £19.80, 1&3 £6.90, 2&3 £6.90. CSF £38.49 TOTE £12.50: £4.00, £1.70, £3.00; EX 43.70.
Owner Keith C Bennett **Bred** Tally-Ho Stud **Trained** Sutton Valence, Kent
FOCUS
A desperately weak race with the winner showing his best form for nearly a year.
Desert Light(IRE) Official explanation: jockey said gelding was denied a clear run
Firewalker Official explanation: jockey said filly ran flat

329 PLAY ROULETTE @ WILLIAMHILL.COM H'CAP 5f 20y(P)
7:20 (7:20) (Class 5) (0-75,75) 4-Y-0+ **£2,590** (£770; £385; £192) **Stalls** Low

Form RPR
-020 **1** **Gwilym (GER)**[7] 243 6-8-7 64 HayleyTurner 7 74
(D Haydn Jones) *hld up towards rr: hdwy 2f out: edgd lft u.p fr over 1f out: r.o wl to ld last stride* **16/1**
6-62 **2** hd **Incomparable**[7] 243 4-8-12 69 (p) StephenDonohoe 4 79
(A J McCabe) *taken down early: pressed ldr tl led 2f out: drvn over 1f out: edgd rt ins fnl f: hdd last stride* **7/2**[2]
32-0 **3** 3/4 **Figaro Flyer (IRE)**[22] 76 6-8-13 70 JimmyQuinn 8 77
(P Howling) *s.i.s: towards rr: hdwy on outer 2f out: styd on wl fnl f: wnt 3rd towards fin: nt rch ldrs* **7/1**
3114 **4** 1 1/2 **Sarah's Art (IRE)**[8] 235 6-8-11 68 MickyFenton 2 70
(Stef Liddiard) *s.i.s: sn pushed along: midfield and rdn 3f out: hdwy u.p on inner over 1f out: kpt on same pce fnl 100yds* **3/1**[1]
6-31 **5** nk **Drifting Gold**[7] 243 5-9-1 72 6ex (v) AdamKirby 1 73
(C G Cox) *chsd ldng trio: rdn and effrt 2f out: chsd ldr over 1f out tl ins fnl f: one pce fnl 100yds* **4/1**[3]
400- **6** 3 1/4 **Maryolini**[52] 7611 4-8-11 68 LukeMorris 6 57
(N J Vaughan) *racd in midfield: rdn 1/2-way: swtchd lft over 1f out: wknd ent fnl f* **14/1**
300- **7** 1/2 **Mission Impossible**[117] 6486 4-8-9 71 PatrickDonaghy(5) 5 58
(P C Haslam) *wl bhd: sme hdwy whn short of room and swtchd rt jst ins fnl f: nvr trbld ldrs* **12/1**
00-6 **8** 1 1/2 **Desert Opal**[21] 83 9-8-8 65 (b) LiamJones 9 47
(C R Dore) *a towards rr: nvr trbld ldrs* **33/1**
130- **9** nse **Fast Freddie**[55] 7562 5-8-12 72 TolleyDean(3) 10 53
(S Parr) *sn pushed up to press ldrs: rdn and unable qck over 2f out: wknd over 1f out* **25/1**
440- **10** 3 1/2 **Garlogs**[44] 7697 6-9-1 75 RussellKennemore(3) 3 44
(R Hollinshead) *led tl 2f out: sn rdn: wknd qckly jst over 1f out* **8/1**
62.58 secs (0.28) **Going Correction** +0.175s/f (Slow) **10** Ran SP% **117.9**
Speed ratings (Par 103): **104,103,102,100,99 94,93,91,91,85**
toteswinger: 1&2 £32.20, 1&3 £10.40, 2&3 £3.70. CSF £72.28 CT £442.05 TOTE £10.50: £2.20, £2.80, £1.70; EX 50.10.
Owner S Kon, D Llewelyn and J Runeckles **Bred** B Krutmann **Trained** Efail Isaf, Rhondda C Taff
FOCUS
More modest fare but the form looks pretty straightforward with the placed horses close to their marks.
Figaro Flyer(IRE) Official explanation: jockey said gelding ducked its head in stalls and missed the break
Drifting Gold Official explanation: jockey said mare was denied a clear run final furlong

330 WILLIAM HILL H'CAP 1m 4f 50y(P)
7:50 (7:50) (Class 4) (0-85,83) 4-Y-0+ **£4,727** (£1,406; £702; £351) **Stalls** Low

Form RPR
000- **1** **Transvestite (IRE)**[101] 5092 7-8-9 72 FergusSweeney 10 79+
(Miss Tor Sturgis) *stdd and dropped in bhd after s: hld up in last pair: rdn over 2f out: hdwy whn nt clr run and swtchd rt over 1f out: str run ins fnl f to ld on line* **20/1**

31-2 **2** *shd* **Heathyards Pride**^{22} [82] 9-9-3 **80** GrahamGibbons 2 87
(R Hollinshead) *chsd ldrs: wnt 2nd over 2f out: rdn to ld 1f out: drvn ins fnl f: hdd on line* **11/4**^{2}

3-11 **3** *½* **Ahlawy (IRE)**^{10} [220] 6-8-11 **74** 6ex (bt) FBranca 4 80
(F Sheridan) *in tch: chsd ldrs 5f out: rdn 2f out: edgd lft jst ins fnl f: kpt on fnl 50yds* **13/8**^{1}

06-5 **4** *1 ¼* **Friends Hope**^{14} [176] 8-8-13 **76** HayleyTurner 8 80
(R Curtis) *hld up towards rr: hdwy and rdn over 2f out: drvn and kpt on same pce fnl f* **20/1**

00- **5** *1 ¼* **Wild Desert (FR)**^{132} [6078] 4-8-13 **80** StephenDonohoe 3 82
(Ian Williams) *led: rdn 2f out: hdd 1f out: wknd ins fnl f* **12/1**

16-2 **6** *1* **Lapina (IRE)**^{18} [126] 5-8-6 **69** oh2 (b) FrankieMcDonald 6 69
(A Middleton) *t.k.h: hld up in midfield on outer: rdn and effrt 2f out: no hdwy u.p ent fnl f* **12/1**

310- **7** *5* **Flying Squad (UAE)**^{43} [7704] 5-9-6 **83** (t) SteveDrowne 9 75
(M F Harris) *t.k.h: chsd ldr: rdn 3f out: wknd u.p wl over 1f out* **28/1**

04-3 **8** *¾* **Profit's Reality (IRE)**^{15} [156] 7-9-5 **82** JimCrowley 1 73
(M J Attwater) *hld up in midfield: lost pl 5f out: rdn and struggling over 3f out: no ch fr over 1f out* **7/2**^{3}

600- **9** *6* **Quam Celerrime**^{53} [7598] 4-8-11 **83** GabrielHannon$^{(5)}$ 7 65
(R Curtis) *stdd s: a bhd: lost tch wl over 2f out* **40/1**

2m 44.0s (2.90) **Going Correction** +0.175s/f (Slow)
WFA 4 from 5yo+ 4lb **9** Ran SP% **117.8**
Speed ratings (Par 105): **97,96,96,95,94 94,90,90,86**
toteswinger: 1&2 £28.20, 1&3 not won, 2&3 £1.10. CSF £73.54 CT £145.38 TOTE £21.00: £6.20, £1.20, £1.50; EX 83.20.
Owner Delamere Racing **Bred** Rathasker Stud **Trained** Lambourn, Berks

FOCUS
Not a strong gallop to this 1m4f handicap, which wouldn't have helped Profit's Reality who was a major disappointment. The form does not look the most solid with doubts over the fourth and fifth.

331 WOLVERHAMPTON-RACECOURSE.CO.UK H'CAP 1m 141y(P)
8:20 (8:21) (Class 3) (0-95,93) 4-Y-0+
£7,352 (£2,201; £1,100; £551; £274; £138) **Stalls** Low

Form RPR

610- **1** **Wasp (AUS)**^{89} [7146] 7-8-12 **86** JoeFanning 3 94
(W Jarvis) *t.k.h: chsd ldr tl over 6f out: chsd ldng pair tl rdn and effrt over 1f out: rdn ins fnl f: r.o to ld towards fin* **11/2**^{3}

1-21 **2** *nk* **Red Somerset (USA)**^{12} [206] 6-9-0 **93** MCGeran$^{(5)}$ 5 101
(R J Hodges) *racd keenly: chsd ldr over 6f out: led wl over 1f out: rdn over 1f out: hdd towards fin* **10/11**^{1}

10-4 **3** *1 ½* **Tourist**^{6} [278] 4-8-4 **79** LukeMorris 4 83
(D Shaw) *hld up in last trio: rdn and effrt 3f out: chsd ldrs jst ins fnl f: kpt on but nt pce to chal* **6/1**

500- **4** *½* **Al Muheer (IRE)**^{43} [7703] 4-9-3 **92** (t) JimCrowley 6 95
(C E Brittain) *hld up in last pair: rdn and hdwy ent fnl 2f: drvn over 1f out: kpt on but nvr rchd ldrs* **7/2**^{2}

1-05 **5** *4* **Silver Hotspur**^{13} [195] 5-8-7 **81** LiamJones 7 75+
(C R Dore) *stdd after s: hld up in rr: outpcd 2f out: pushed along ent fnl f: nvr nr ldrs* **16/1**

43-6 **6** *5* **Gallantry**^{8} [232] 7-8-8 **85** TolleyDean$^{(3)}$ 1 67
(P Howling) *led tl rdn and hdd wl over 1f out: wknd u.p 1f out* **10/1**

030- **7** *1 ¾* **Wessex (USA)**^{327} [833] 9-8-9 **83** HayleyTurner 2 61
(R Curtis) *stdd s: t.k.h: hld up in midfield: rdn and unable qck 3f out: wl bhd fnl f* **33/1**

1m 50.29s (-0.21) **Going Correction** +0.175s/f (Slow)
WFA 4 from 5yo+ 1lb **7** Ran SP% **122.2**
Speed ratings (Par 107): **107,106,105,104,101 96,95**
toteswinger: 1&2 £4.20, 1&3 £4.30, 2&3 £1.10. CSF £11.94 TOTE £7.80: £6.50, £1.20; EX 15.60.
Owner Dr J Walker **Bred** Woodlands Stud NSW **Trained** Newmarket, Suffolk

FOCUS
A good handicap but a few of these were a bit keen suggesting the pace wasn't that strong. The form basically makes sense.

NOTEBOOK
Wasp(AUS) stayed on best to lead close home and resume his upward curve. Off since disappointing on soft ground in a hot handicap at Newmarket in November, he'd looked a horse to keep on the right side of when beating Gallantry over 7f at this venue, and he was able to race off just a 3lb higher mark here. He clearly has stamina for trips of 1m plus and, in beating a bang in-form rival, he could be one to keep on the right side of on this surface. (op 9-2 tchd 6-1)
Red Somerset(USA) ran his race and emerges with plenty of credit once again, he was ideally placed from an early stage and took over straightening up for home but he couldn't hold off the winner. He lost little in defeat. (op 11-10 tchd 11-8)
Tourist kept on from off the pace, stepping up on his all-weather debut last time, having raced a bit too freely off the steady gallop. He'll be better coming off a stronger pace and is open to further improvement being comparatively lightly raced. (op 13-2 tchd 7-1 and 11-2)
Al Muheer(IRE) was well backed beforehand but was badly positioned at the back of the field and could never get into it, although he plugged on well enough. (op 7-1)
Silver Hotspur Official explanation: jockey said gelding was denied a clear run on final bend

332 PLAY POKER @ WILLIAMHILL.COM CLAIMING STKS 1m 141y(P)
8:50 (8:50) (Class 6) 3-Y-0 **£1,942** (£578; £288; £144) **Stalls** Low

Form RPR

063- **1** **Kiyari**^{47} [7666] 3-8-4 63 HayleyTurner 3 61
(M Botti) *t.k.h: hld up in last pair: rdn on outer 2f out: drvn and ev ch jst ins fnl f: edgd lft and led fnl 100yds: r.o wl* **7/2**^{2}

1342 **2** *¾* **Hold The Bucks (USA)**^{8} [231] 3-8-13 72 LukeMorris 4 68
(J S Moore) *t.k.h: trckd ldrs tl wnt 2nd 5f out: rdn to press ldr over 2f out: drvn and ev ch ent fnl f: edgd lft and no ex fnl 50yds* **2/1**^{1}

4542 **3** *½* **Turn To Dreams**^{4} [287] 3-8-1 54 CatherineGannon 5 55
(P D Evans) *sn led: rdn and hrd pressed over 1f out: hdd and no ex fnl 100yds* **16/1**

4-31 **4** *shd* **Common Diva**^{8} [239] 3-8-4 61 JimmyQuinn 1 58
(A J McCabe) *taken down early: chsd ldr tl 5f out: rdn jst over 2f out: ev ch u.p ent fnl f: no ex fnl 100yds* **2/1**^{1}

24-3 **5** *1 ¾* **Jonnie Skull (IRE)**^{8} [231] 3-8-3 59 (b) AmyBaker$^{(5)}$ 2 58
(D R C Elsworth) *t.k.h: hld up in last pair: swtchd ins and effrt over 1f out: keeping same pce whn eased wl ins fnl f* **13/2**^{3}

1m 53.56s (3.06) **Going Correction** +0.175s/f (Slow) **5** Ran SP% **108.1**
Speed ratings (Par 95): **93,92,91,91,90**
CSF £10.49 TOTE £4.40: £1.40, £1.80; EX 10.00.Hold The Bucks was the subject of a friendly claim
Owner El Catorce **Bred** Newsells Park Stud **Trained** Newmarket, Suffolk

FOCUS
An even enough pace considering the small field, and there were four in line entering the final furlong. The form looks muddling although the runner-up and fourth ran close to course form from earlier in the month.

333 ENJOY THE LUCKY 7 GROUP OFFER H'CAP 2m 119y(P)
9:20 (9:20) (Class 5) (0-75,73) 4-Y-0+ **£2,590** (£770; £385; £192) **Stalls** Low

Form RPR

00-1 **1** **Riguez Dancer**^{10} [219] 5-9-12 **73** 6ex (t) PatrickDonaghy$^{(5)}$ 2 94+
(P C Haslam) *chsd ldr: clr of remainder: led over 8f out: 8 l clr 3f out: pushed along and drew further clr 2f out: eased ins fnl f: v easily* **15/8**^{1}

33-3 **2** *12* **Baan (USA)**^{16} [142] 6-9-7 **63** JimmyQuinn 7 64
(H J Collingridge) *racd in midfield wl off the pce: modest 3rd and rdn wl over 2f out: no imp on wnr: wnt 2nd on post* **7/2**^{2}

434- **3** *nse* **Agglestone Rock**^{34} [1364] 4-8-13 **62** HayleyTurner 5 63
(P A Kirby) *stdd after s: hld up wl bhd in last trio: hdwy over 6f out: wnt 8 l 2nd and drvn 3f out: no imp on wnr: lost 2nd on line* **13/2**

1-23 **4** *5* **Bridgewater Boys**^{10} [219] 8-9-9 **70** (b) RichardEvans$^{(5)}$ 4 65
(P D Evans) *stdd s: hld up in last trio: clsd sltly over 4f out: no prog 3f out: nvr a factor* **5/1**^{3}

642- **5** *24* **Fiddlers Ford (IRE)**^{183} [4526] 8-9-0 **56** LiamJones 6 22
(T Keddy) *chsd ldng pair: rdn over 6f out: wknd and lost pl 5f out: t.o fnl 2f: eased* **15/2**

6-44 **6** *2* **Tampa Boy (IRE)**^{7} [249] 7-9-9 **65** (b) FergusSweeney 1 29
(M F Harris) *led and clr w wnr: hdd over 8f out: rdn and struggling over 4f out: lost 2nd 3f out: wl btn and eased fnl 2f: t.o* **16/1**

10-0 **7** *14* **Capitalise (IRE)**^{18} [126] 6-9-3 **59** SteveDrowne 3 6
(Miss Gay Kelleway) *hld up wl bhd in last trio: brief effrt over 4f out: lost tch over 3f out: t.o and eased fr over 1f out* **10/1**

3m 42.19s (0.39) **Going Correction** +0.175s/f (Slow)
WFA 4 from 5yo+ 7lb **7** Ran SP% **113.7**
Speed ratings (Par 103): **106,100,100,97,86 85,79**
toteswinger: 1&2 £4.30, 1&3 £6.90, 2&3 £3.90. CSF £8.43 TOTE £3.10: £2.40, £3.30; EX 9.40 Place 6: £23.71, Place 5: £10.05..
Owner Middleham Park Racing Xii **Bred** Plantation Stud **Trained** Middleham Moor, N Yorks

FOCUS
A modest contest but the winner was impressive and is value for further.
Tampa Boy(IRE) Official explanation: jockey said gelding ran flat
T/Plt: £66.10 to a £1 stake. Pool: £110,193.43. 1,216.49 winning tickets. T/Qpdt: £6.00 to a £1 stake. Pool: £10,113.49. 1,236.64 winning tickets. SP

257 NAD AL SHEBA (L-H)
Thursday, January 29
OFFICIAL GOING: Dirt course - fast; turf course - good to firm

334a DUBAL INGOT 1600 (H'CAP) (DIRT) 1m (D)
3:15 (3:15) (90-105,105) 3-Y-0+
£45,833 (£15,277; £7,638; £3,819; £2,291; £1,527)

RPR

1 **Fares (IRE)**^{7} [261] 5-8-11 **97** (v) DO'Donohoe 8 98
(Doug Watson, UAE) *trckd ldng pair: rdn to ld 1 1/2f out: r.o wl* **25/1**

2 *1 ¼* **Grand Hombre (USA)**^{7} [263] 9-9-1 **100** KJohn 1 99+
(R Bouresly, Kuwait) *racd in rr: last 3f out: r.o wl fnl 2 1/2f: nrst fin* **16/1**

3 *1* **Fateh Field (USA)**^{14} [182] 4-9-5 **105** (v) TedDurcan 2 101
(Saeed Bin Suroor) *mid-div on rail: rdn to trck ldrs 3f out: ev ch 1 1/2f out: nt qckn fnl 110yds* **11/4**^{2}

4 *1 ¾* **Aamaaq**^{7} [261] 6-8-6 **91** RoystonFfrench 10 84
(A Al Raihe, UAE) *mid-div: rdn to chse ldrs 3 1/2f out: ev ch 2 1/2f out: nt qckn* **7/1**

5 *¾* **Art Of War (SAF)**^{14} [184] 5-9-2 **101** (b) KShea 4 92
(M F De Kock, South Africa) *trckd ldr: led 2 1/2f out: sn rdn: hdd 1 1/2f out: one pce* **11/2**^{3}

6 *1 ¼* **Firestreak**^{28} 4-8-9 **95** AhmedAjtebi 5 82
(M bin Shafya, UAE) *sn led: hdd 2 1/2f out: r.o: same pce: sn wknd* **14/1**

7 *1 ¼* **Shopton Lane (USA)**^{96} 5-9-5 **105** (t) FJara 7 89
(Doug Watson, UAE) *nvr nr to chal* **8/1**

8 *1 ¾* **Tasteyville (USA)**^{152} 6-9-3 **102** RHills 3 83
(E Charpy, UAE) *v.s.a: settled in rr: rdn 3f out: nvr able to chal* **5/2**^{1}

9 *4* **Boston Lodge**^{14} [182] 9-9-3 **102** (vt) EddieAhern 9 74
(F Nass, Bahrain) *nvr able to chal* **25/1**

10 *3 ¾* **Easy Target (FR)**^{7} [259] 4-9-1 **100** C-PLemaire 11 63
(X Nakkachdji, France) *settled in rr: rdn 4 1/2f out: nvr nr to chal* **25/1**

11 *12* **Bruges (IRE)**^{7} [260] 4-9-1 **100** (bt) RichardMullen 6 36
(A Al Raihe, UAE) *nvr able to chal* **33/1**

1m 38.86s (2.16) **Going Correction** +0.50s/f (Slow) **11** Ran SP% **121.3**
Speed ratings: **109,107,106,105,104 103,101,100,96,92 80**
.
Owner Mohammed Rashid **Bred** Darley **Trained** United Arab Emirates

FOCUS
An ordinary handicap for the level.

NOTEBOOK
Fares(IRE) went off too quickly in a race set up for the closers when a well beaten fourth over the extended 1m here the previous week, but the pace was more sensible this time and he stepped up on that effort. There might be more to come considering this was just his second start since returning from a 16-month absence, but it would be unwise to get carried away with the form.
Grand Hombre(USA) was a class act on his day - he ran fourth in the 2004 Dubai World Cup - and he showed he retains some ability when third in a decent non-Carnival handicap over this course and distance earlier in the month. Having not for the first time struggled to lay up early, he picked up well down the outside in the straight, and it briefly looked as though his momentum would take him to the front, but his effort flattened out near the line. (tchd 18-1)
Fateh Field(USA) looked worth a try on dirt judged on his quick action, running style, and US pedigree. As it turned out, he seemed to handle the surface okay, but he did not appear to go through with his effort. His only success to date was gained in a maiden. (op 5-2)
Aamaaq was well ahead of Fares when runner-up here the previous week, but that race panned out almost ideally for him and this was more competitive. (op 13-2)
Art Of War(SAF) raced keenly on the speed and looked ungainly when getting a run against the inside rail at the top of the straight. He should do better back on turf, but he doesn't look totally straightforward.
Shopton Lane(USA), ex-US trained, didn't show more on his return from three months off.

Tasteyville(USA) won a Grade 3 in the States last year, but his best form has been on a sloppy surface. He was in trouble straight away after missing the break and was a little keen when trying to recover into a more prominent position. (op 3-1)

335a DUBAL TROPHY (H'CAP) (TURF) 7f 110y(D)
3:45 (3:47) (95-110,110) 3-Y-0+

£50,000 (£16,666; £8,333; £4,166; £2,500; £1,666)

RPR

1 **Ragheed (USA)**7 [265] 5-8-9 **99**....................(vt) RHills 1 109
(E Charpy, UAE) *mid-div on rail: smooth prog to trck ldrs 2f out: led 1f out: comf* **33/1**

2 1 ¼ **Yamal (IRE)**173 [4853] 4-8-6 **96**.................... TedDurcan 6 103
(Saeed Bin Suroor) *mid-div: trckd wnr 2 1/2f out: r.o wl fnl 1 1/2f* **6/4**[1]

3 3 **Mojito Royale (IRE)**62 [7483] 5-8-10 **100**....................(p) MJKinane 5 99
(Eoin Doyle, Ire) *settled in rr: rdn 2 1/2f out: r.o wl fnl 2f: nrst fin* **20/1**

4 ¾ **Brave Tin Soldier (USA)**14 [183] 5-9-4 **108**.................... KShea 10 105
(M F De Kock, South Africa) *mid-div: rdn 2 1/2f out: r.o fnl 1 1/2f: nrst fin* **9/2**[2]

5 shd **Seihali (IRE)**14 [182] 10-9-6 **110**....................(b) WilliamBuick 16 107
(D Selvaratnam, UAE) *settled in rr: r.o wl fnl 2f: nvr able to chal* **14/1**

6 ¼ **Underworld**124 [6269] 4-8-8 **98**.................... WayneSmith 4 94
(M Al Muhairi, UAE) *sn led: hdd 1f out: kpt on same pce* **20/1**

7 1 **Lessing (FR)**14 [180] 4-8-11 **101**.................... C-PLemaire 14 95
(X Nakkachdji, France) *trckd ldr: rdn 2 1/2f out: ev ch 1f out: one pce* **20/1**

8 hd **Pointing North (SAF)**390 5-9-4 **108**.................... RichardMullen 2 101
(S Seemar, UAE) *wl away: trckd ldr: rdn to chal 2f out: wknd fnl f* **5/1**[3]

9 ¾ **Artimino**97 [6947] 5-8-8 **98**.................... DO'Donohoe 11 89
(I Mohammed, UAE) *mid-div: n.m.r 1 1/2f out on rail: eased* **14/1**

10 ½ **Keep Discovering (IRE)**141 [5795] 4-8-9 **99**....................(t) TPO'Shea 3 89
(E Charpy, UAE) *nvr bttr than mid-div* **33/1**

11 1 ¼ **Golden Riviera (SAF)**7 [259] 5-8-10 **100**....................(t) EddieAhern 13 87
(H J Brown, South Africa) *in rr of mid-div: rdn 3f out: nvr a threat* **33/1**

12 5 **Grand Vista**14 [182] 5-8-10 **100**....................(t) RyanMoore 12 75
(H J Brown, South Africa) *broke awkwardly: racd in rr: nvr able to chal* **20/1**

13 2 **Montpellier (IRE)**7 [260] 6-8-10 **100**....................(t) RoystonFfrench 9 70
(A Al Raihe, UAE) *broke awkwardly: trckd ldrs: wknd* **33/1**

14 ½ **Finicius (USA)**43 [7703] 5-9-3 **107**.................... KJManning 15 75
(Eoin Griffin, Ire) *nvr able to chal* **18/1**

15 ¼ **Ekhtiaar**7 [264] 5-8-7 **97**.................... FJara 7 65
(A Al Raihe, UAE) *rdn in mid-div 3 1/2f out: n.d* **33/1**

16 19 **Conquest (IRE)**7 [259] 5-9-4 **108**.................... AhmedAjtebi 8 28
(M bin Shafya, UAE) *nvr nr to chal* **28/1**

1m 30.78s (-0.82) **Going Correction** +0.175s/f (Good) **16** Ran SP% **130.6**
Speed ratings: **111,109,106,106,105 105,104,104,103,103 101,96,94,94,94 75**

Owner Hamdan Al Maktoum **Bred** Swordlestown Stud **Trained** United Arab Emirates

FOCUS
A competitive handicap, but the form is just ordinary for the class.

NOTEBOOK
Ragheed(USA) hardly shaped as though about to strike when ninth of 16 in a similar race over 1m here the previous week, but everything went his way in the run and he stepped up significantly on that effort. It remains to be seen if he can repeat this form next time. (op 25-1)
Yamal(IRE), the winner of five of his ten starts for Mark Johnston, was well fancied to make a winning debut for Godolphin on his return from almost six months off, with a handicap mark of 96 looking workable, but he found one too good. It's true to say he did not get the best of runs in the straight, having to wait for a gap and switch, and the winner enjoyed a much better trip, but it would be generous to call him unlucky. He obviously wasn't helped by being messed about early in the straight, and is entitled to come on for this run, but while he is surely capable of rating higher, he doesn't appeal as one to follow, particularly as he is unlikely to represent much value in the near future. (op 13-8)
Mojito Royale(IRE) stayed on from well back on his debut in Dubai. His recent runs have been on Polytrack, but he is also well suited by decent turf, and his form figures on ground 'good' or faster now read 34113. He could pick up a similar race this Carnival.
Brave Tin Soldier(USA) had a wide draw to overcome and did not get the best of trips but he was not exactly unlucky. He is vulnerable off his current sort of mark, but should find weaker races back on the dirt.
Pointing North(SAF) was a Grade 1 winner in South Africa, but he ran disappointingly on his Dubai debut. He was well enough placed if good enough, but simply failed to pick up for pressure. Admittedly this was his first run in over a year, and he might have needed it, but his new trainer has not been having the best of times in recent seasons and this one has something to prove now.
Artimino ◆, returning from three months off, was continually blocked in the straight and seemed to cross the line full of running. It's impossible to know how he might have fared with a clear run, and it will probably be unwise to get carried away, but one things for sure, he's better than he showed.

336a DUBAL POWER DASH (H'CAP) (DIRT) 5f (D)
4:15 (4:17) (90-105,105) 3-Y-0+

£45,833 (£15,277; £7,638; £3,819; £2,291; £1,527)

RPR

1 **Change Alley (USA)**6 4-8-6 **91**....................(t) RoystonFfrench 14 98
(A Al Raihe, UAE) *mid-div: rdn 2 1/2f out: r.o wl fnl 1 1/2f: led last stride* **20/1**

2 hd **Tawaassol (USA)**321 6-8-9 **95**....................(b) RHills 10 100
(E Charpy, UAE) *trckd ldrs: led 1 1/2f out: tired fnl 55yds: hdd line* **10/1**

3 2 ¼ **Bounty Quest**21 7-8-9 **95**.................... FJara 8 92
(Doug Watson, UAE) *prom in centre: ev ch 2f out: nt qckn fnl f* **8/1**

4 hd **Sarissa (BRZ)**59 6-9-0 **99**.................... C-PLemaire 3 96
(P Bary, France) *trckd ldrs* **11/2**[1]

5 1 ¼ **League Champion (USA)**6 6-9-5 **105**.................... KJohn 5 97
(R Bouresly, Kuwait) *racd in rr: r.o wl fnl 1 1/2f: nrst fin* **7/1**[3]

6 1 ¾ **New Freedom (BRZ)**157 [5347] 8-8-7 **93**.................... WayneSmith 4 78
(M Al Muhairi, UAE) *prom in centre tl 1 1/2f out: wknd* **7/1**[3]

7 1 ½ **Select Reason (BRZ)**321 5-8-9 **95**....................(bt) MJKinane 2 75
(E Martins, Bahrain) *chsd ldrs: ev ch 2 1/2f out: wknd fnl 110yds* **20/1**

8 ½ **Hammadi (IRE)**28 4-8-10 **96**....................(v) DO'Donohoe 1 74
(Doug Watson, UAE) *wl away: prom tl 1 1/2f out: wknd fnl 110yds* **25/1**

9 1 ½ **Malayeen (AUS)**21 7-8-5 **90**....................(v) TPO'Shea 16 64
(A Selvaratnam, UAE) *mid-div on rail: nvr nr to chal* **25/1**

10 2 ¼ **Charlies Island (SAF)**229 6-8-10 **96**.................... RyanMoore 7 61
(H J Brown, South Africa) *a struggling* **16/1**

11 1 **Borehan**21 6-8-7 **93**....................(v) WilliamBuick 9 54
(D Selvaratnam, UAE) *prom in centre tl 1 1/2f out: wknd* **10/1**

12 ¼ **Sound The Drum (USA)**49 7-8-7 **93**....................(bt) RichardMullen 6 53
(A Al Raihe, UAE) *nvr able to chal: racd far side* **14/1**

13 ¾ **Wingbeat (USA)**243 [2594] 4-8-8 **94**....................(t) TedDurcan 15 52
(I Mohammed, UAE) *nvr nr to chal* **13/2**[2]

14 1 **Felix (PER)**7 [258] 4-8-6 **95**....................(b) AhmedAjtebi 13 46
(M bin Shafya, UAE) *sn rdn in rr: nvr involved* **14/1**

15 4 ¾ **Strike Up The Band**7 [264] 6-9-4 **104**.................... AdrianTNicholls 12 41
(D Nicholls) *nvr able to chal* **22/1**

16 5 ¼ **Dream Impact (USA)**74 [7349] 8-8-9 **95**....................(bt) GMarcelli 11 13
(L Riccardi, Italy) *nvr able to chal* **16/1**

58.40 secs **Going Correction** +0.225s/f (Slow) **16** Ran SP% **129.7**
Speed ratings: **109,108,105,104,102 99,97,96,94,90 89,88,87,85,78 69**

Owner Hamad Mohd M Kadfoor/Abdullah Muammer Amin **Bred** Darley **Trained** UAE

FOCUS
A near-impossible race to work out beforehand. The first two were clear and there was no obvious draw bias.

NOTEBOOK
Change Alley(USA) looked shy of Carnival class on all previous evidence, and his only success prior to this had come over 7f. He had also finished over four lengths behind League Champion over 6f at Jebel Ali just six days earlier, so it's fair to say this was hard to predict. He managed to stay in touch early, but only got on top in the final few strides and ran as though he might step forward again back over another furlong.
Tawaassol(USA) travelled as well as anything, and he responded when first asked by Richard Hills, but he was entitled to get tired late on considering he had been off for 321 days.
Bounty Quest ran a creditable race and can have no excuses.
Sarissa(BRZ), runner-up behind New Freedom in this race last year, travelled kindly to a point, but her finishing effort was tame. The form of her stable remains questionable, but whatever the case she has had enough chances now and does not appeal as one to follow.

337a DUBAL BILLET 2000 (H'CAP) (DIRT) 1m 2f (D)
4:50 (4:50) (90-105,102) 3-Y-0+

£45,833 (£15,277; £7,638; £3,819; £2,291; £1,527)

RPR

1 **Dynamic Saint (USA)**28 6-9-2 **100**....................(e) RyanMoore 6 106
(Doug Watson, UAE) *trckd ldng gp: dropped to mid-div 4f out: r.o wl fnl 3f: led fnl 110yds* **7/1**[2]

2 1 ¼ **Moonquake (USA)**18 4-8-5 **90**.................... RoystonFfrench 4 94
(M bin Shafya, UAE) *led after 2 1/2f on rail: clr 4 1/2f out: rdn 1 1/2f out: one pce and hdd fnl 110yds* **14/1**

3 3 ¾ **Trust N Dustan (USA)**28 4-8-9 **95**....................(v1) DO'Donohoe 10 91
(Doug Watson, UAE) *racd in rr: nvr able to chal: r.o wl fnl 2 1/2f* **14/1**

4 6 **Bennie Blue (SAF)**7 [262] 7-8-13 **97**....................(b) KShea 14 81
(M F De Kock, South Africa) *settled in rr: rdn 3 1/2f out: chsd ldrs 3f out: r.o same pce* **7/1**[2]

5 2 ¼ **Irish Mayhem (USA)**14 [183] 4-9-3 **102**....................(v1) RichardMullen 8 82
(Saeed Bin Suroor) *racd in rr: nvr able to chal: r.o fnl 3f* **8/1**[3]

6 shd **Mister Fasliyev (IRE)**28 7-8-11 **96**....................(t) DBadel 2 74
(E Charpy, UAE) *mid-div on rail: rdn to chse ldrs 3f out: wknd* **22/1**

7 9 ¼ **Clasp**21 7-8-6 **90**....................(vt) TedDurcan 13 50
(Doug Watson, UAE) *a mid-div* **12/1**

8 11 **Singing Poet (IRE)**28 8-9-4 **102**....................(bt) TPO'Shea 5 40
(E Charpy, UAE) *mid-div on rail: rdn 3 1/2f out: sn struggling* **14/1**

9 ¼ **Igor Protti**14 [183] 7-9-2 **100**....................(b) WJSupple 11 38
(A bin Huzaim, UAE) *nvr bttr than mid-div* **14/1**

10 1 **Emirates Line (USA)**49 6-8-9 **94**.................... JRosales 9 29
(M bin Shafya, UAE) *trckd ldrs: wd: rdn over 4f out out: sn btn* **5/1**[1]

11 10 **Sgt Schultz (IRE)**19 [124] 6-8-10 **95**.................... EddieAhern 1 10
(J S Moore) *s.i.s: in rr of mid-div: nvr able to chal* **12/1**

12 8 ½ **Remaadd (USA)**41 8-8-8 **93**....................(v) WilliamBuick 7 —
(D Selvaratnam, UAE) *prom in centre tl wknd qckly over 4f out* **11/1**

13 2 **Dubai Twilight**41 5-8-8 **93**.................... AhmedAjtebi 12 —
(M bin Shafya, UAE) *nvr able to chal* **8/1**[3]

14 7 ½ **Elmustanser**34 8-8-6 **90**....................(t) RHills 15 —
(Doug Watson, UAE) *settled in rr: rdn over 4f out: nvr able to chal* **16/1**

2m 5.10s (2.80) **Going Correction** +0.50s/f (Slow)
WFA 4 from 5yo+ 2lb **15** Ran SP% **124.5**
Speed ratings: **108,107,104,99,97 97,89,81,80,80 72,65,63,57**

Owner Malih L Al Basti **Bred** Harold J Plumley **Trained** United Arab Emirates

FOCUS
An ordinary handicap for the level.

NOTEBOOK
Dynamic Saint(USA) was never too far away and he stayed on best to end a losing run stretching back to the 2007 Carnival, when he won off a 2lb higher mark over this course and distance. He looked a little hesitant when first ranging alongside Moonquake in the straight, but that one soon had little left to give. He does not appeal as one to back to follow up.
Moonquake(USA), the biggest price of the three Bin Shafya runners, faced competition for the lead early on, but he was able to dominate after a couple of furlongs or so and he opened up a clear advantage. He understandably tired late on but this was a bold effort in defeat. His course-and-distance success earlier in the month didn't amount to much, and he had since been beaten on the turf, but he was pretty useful for John Gosden last year. There could be more to come again.
Trust N Dustan(USA), a stablemate of the winner, could not lay up with the pace early on, but he made some headway mid race and kept plugging on against the inside rail in the straight.
Bennie Blue(SAF) had no excuse and it is getting on for two years since his last success.
Irish Mayhem(USA) put up a more encouraging display, especially as he seemed to meet with a little trouble at the top of the straight, but he was still some way below the pick of his Polytrack form.
Emirates Line(USA) was sent off favourite, but his two recent course wins were gained in lesser company and it seems the stable's first jockey, Ahmed Ajtebi, elected to ride Dubai Twilight. (tchd 11-2)
Sgt Schultz(IRE) simply did not take to the dirt. (op 11-1)
Dubai Twilight was well beaten having come off the bridle a long way out.

338a DUBAL POTLINE TROPHY (H'CAP) (TURF) 1m 4f (T)
5:20 (5:21) (100-110,110) 3-Y-0+

£72,916 (£24,305; £12,152; £6,076; £3,645; £2,430)

RPR

1 **Age Of Reason (UAE)**14 [185] 4-8-7 **102**.................... TedDurcan 7 109
(Saeed Bin Suroor) *trckd ldrs: rdn to ld 1f out: easily* **13/2**

2 4 ¾ **Young Mick**26 [33] 7-8-9 **101**....................(v) JohnEgan 3 99
(G G Margarson) *in rr of mid-div: rdn to chse ldrs 3f out: r.o wl: no ch w wnr* **16/1**

3 shd **Love Galore (IRE)**7 [262] 4-8-5 **100**.................... RoystonFfrench 9 99
(M Johnston) *mid-div on rail: r.o fnl 2f: nvr able to chal* **16/1**

4 2½ **Far From Old (IRE)**[14] 185 6-8-9 **101** .... FJara 4 95
(J E Hammond, France) *mid-div on rail: n.m.r after 1 1/2f: last 3f out: r.o: n.d* **4/1**[1]
5 2¾ **Bon Spiel**[40] 7741 5-8-10 **102** .... RyanMoore 12 91
(L M Cumani) *mid-div: rdn to cl 2 1/2f out: one pce fnl f* **5/1**[2]
6 shd **Arqaam**[42] 5-8-13 **105** .... RHills 6 94
(Doug Watson, UAE) *s.i.s: nvr able to chal* **12/1**
7 1½ **Al Shemali**[7] 263 5-8-5 **107** ....(t) AntiocoMurgia(10) 8 94
(M bin Shafya, UAE) *a mid-div* **11/1**
8 1¾ **Detonator (IRE)**[7] 262 4-8-7 **102** .... WJSupple 1 87
(M bin Shafya, UAE) *sn led: qcknd after 5f: hdd 2f out: wknd fnl f* **33/1**
9 4¾ **Sanbuch**[7] 262 5-9-4 **110** .... AhmedAjtebi 5 86
(M bin Shafya, UAE) *settled in last: nvr nr to chal* **11/2**[3]
10 2¼ **Before You Go (IRE)**[14] 185 6-8-9 **101** ....(v) TPO'Shea 2 74
(E Charpy, UAE) *nvr bttr than mid-div* **28/1**
11 ¾ **Crime Scene (IRE)**[14] 185 6-9-3 **109** .... JRosales 11 81
(M bin Shafya, UAE) *nvr bttr than mid-div* **6/1**
12 dist **Rohaani (USA)**[14] 185 7-8-8 **100** .... DO'Donohoe 10 —
(Doug Watson, UAE) *trckd ldr: rdn 4f out: sn btn* **14/1**

2m 31.58s (0.58) **Going Correction** +0.175s/f (Good)
WFA 4 from 5yo+ 4lb **12** Ran SP% **120.5**
Speed ratings: **105,101,101,100,98 98,97,96,92,91 90,—**

Owner Sheikh Hamdan Bin Mohammed Al Maktoum **Bred** Darley **Trained** Newmarket, Suffolk

FOCUS

This looked quite a good handicap beforehand, but the pace was steady and the form is worth treating with some caution.

NOTEBOOK

Age Of Reason(UAE), who had previously looked high enough in the weights, improved significantly on the form he showed when third behind Crime Scene (disappointing off 5lb higher mark) on his debut for Saeed Bin Suroor two weeks earlier. He won eased down and this was undoubtedly a career best. It would probably be unwise to get carried away, and things are almost sure to be tougher next time, but he's clearly capable of quite smart form.

Young Mick seemed to run in snatches a little and was left with loads to do having been caught out when the pace increased before the turn for home. He kept on, but the winner was in a different league.

Love Galore(IRE) did well to take third as, just like the previous week, he refused to settle. However, he was still beaten a long way and won't be of interest until he shows signs of relaxing early on in his races.

Far From Old(IRE) looked better than the bare form of his recent fourth behind Crime Scene (Age Of Reason third), and he again gave the impression we've yet to see the best of him out here. He should do better under a more positive ride.

Bon Spiel blew his handicap mark (he went up 12lb) when third in a 1m2f Listed race on the Polytrack at Lingfield in December, but this trip possibly stretched him in any case.

Al Shemali ◆ could not build on his promising third to Presvis over 1m2f the previous week, but he lost his place at a crucial stage under his 10lb claimer. He will be of interest if dropped back in trip with a professional aboard next time.

Sanbuch did not convince with his attitude with a full jockey back on top and is not easy to catch right.

339a AL RASHIDIYA (SPONSORED BY DUBAL) (GROUP 3) (TURF) 1m 194y(T)

5:50 (5:50) 3-Y-0+

£83,333 (£27,777; £13,888; £6,944; £4,166; £2,777)

RPR

1 **Silver Mist (SAF)**[14] 182 7-9-0 112 .... KShea 9 115
(M F De Kock, South Africa) *in rr of mid-div: smooth prog to chse ldrs 2f out: led fnl 110yds: hld on wl* **9/4**[1]
2 ¼ **Third Set (IRE)**[14] 183 6-9-0 112 ....(t) AhmedAjtebi 6 114
(M bin Shafya, UAE) *mid-div on rail: rdn to chse ldr 2f out: r.o wl* **11/2**[2]
3 ¾ **Kirklees (IRE)**[89] 7145 5-9-0 110 .... TedDurcan 3 112+
(Saeed Bin Suroor) *settled in rr: gng wl 3f out: r.o wl fnl 2f: nrst fin* **11/2**[2]
4 ½ **Mashaahed**[342] 671 6-9-0 112 ....(t) RHills 4 111
(E Charpy, UAE) *sn led: drew clr 2 1/2f out: hdd 1f out: wknd fnl 55yds* **20/1**
5 2 **With Interest**[14] 183 6-9-0 108 .... JRosales 8 107
(M bin Shafya, UAE) *in rr of main gp: nvr able to chal* **20/1**
6 ½ **Traffic Guard (USA)**[103] 6816 5-9-0 118 .... JohnEgan 2 106
(H J Brown, South Africa) *trckd ldrs: rdn 2 1/2f out: one pce fnl 1 1/2f* **6/1**[3]
7 1¼ **Familiar Territory**[124] 6287 6-9-0 108 .... DO'Donohoe 5 104
(Saeed Bin Suroor) *trckd ldrs: rdn 3f out: outpcd fnl 1 1/2f* **20/1**
8 shd **Oracle West (SAF)**[306] 1091 8-9-0 119 .... RyanMoore 1 103
(H J Brown, South Africa) *settled in rr: nvr able to chal* **8/1**
9 ¾ **Hunting Tower (SAF)**[7] 257 7-9-0 113 .... RoystonFfrench 7 102
(M F De Kock, South Africa) *mid-div: rdn 2 1/2f out: nt qckn fnl f* **7/1**
10 dist **Royal Vintage (SAF)**[14] 184 5-9-0 113 ....(b[1]) MJKinane 10 —
(M F De Kock, South Africa) *trckd ldrs: t.k.h: rdn to chal 3f out: sn btn* **11/1**

1m 50.7s (0.70) **Going Correction** +0.175s/f (Good) **10** Ran SP% **122.1**
Speed ratings: **103,102,102,101,99 99,98,98,97,—**

Owner Sheikh Rashid bin Humaid Al Nuaimi **Bred** Midlands Equine Entreprises Ltd **Trained** South Africa

FOCUS

A good, competitive Group 3, although the pace was just ordinary.

NOTEBOOK

Silver Mist(SAF) was a comfortable winner in handicap company off a mark of 106 over an extended 7f on his debut in Dubai two weeks previously and he improved on that effort to follow up in this much tougher heat, with the step back up in trip very much in his favour. This was obviously a smart effort, but it has to be noted he enjoyed one continuous run down the outside. His trainer has landed this race twice before and his 2004 winner, Right Approach, dead-heated in the Group 1 Dubai Duty Free Stakes on his next start, so it would be no surprise to see Silver Mist kept back until World Cup night. (op 5-2)

Third Set(IRE) had to switch around a furlong out after being denied a clear run and is better than the bare form. As per usual he carried his head high and, a horse with issues, he was obviously not helped by being messed around in the closing stages. He was also inclined to race a little keenly off the modest gallop, and would have preferred a stronger-run race, although the winner would also probably have been suited by a stronger tempo. The Al Fahidi Fort, Zabeel Mile and Jebel Hatta are all Group races he could be competitive in over the next few weeks.

Kirklees(IRE), returning from three months off, raced in last for much of the race and still had loads to do at the top of the straight, but he finished very nicely for third. He ran as though he will be well suited by a return to 1m2f, but unfortunately there are no Group races on the turf over that trip at the Carnival. There are a couple of open handicaps over that distance in the coming weeks that could be suitable options, although his connections stated at the start of the Carnival they hoped to try him on dirt at some stage, and it would be no surprise if the third round of Al Maktoum Challenge is on the agenda.

Mashaahed looks flattered by the bare result, but having said that he had been off for the best part of a year, so this was obviously a very creditable effort.

With Interest, a stablemate of the runner-up, had something to find in this company but ran a solid race in defeat.

Traffic Guard(USA), back for a third straight Carnival but with a new trainer, was below the pick of his form on this first run in over three months. He looks a worth a try in either blinkers or a visor.

Familiar Territory was not up to this level on his return to turf after four months off.

Oracle West(SAF), a regular at past Carnivals for Mike De Kock, was well beaten on his debut for a new trainer. He has plenty of form at around this trip (third in this in 2007), but his very best efforts have come over 1m4f.

340a DUBAL CASTHOUSE H'CAP (H'CAP) (TURF) 1m (T)

6:20 (6:22) (95-110,105) 3-Y-0+

£50,000 (£16,666; £8,333; £4,166; £2,500; £1,666)

RPR

1 **Strategic News (AUS)**[208] 6-8-13 **102** ....(bt) RyanMoore 5 106+
(H J Brown, South Africa) *in rr of mid-div: r.o wl fnl 2f: led nr line* **6/1**[1]
2 1½ **Furnace (IRE)**[104] 6783 5-8-5 **95** .... AhmedAjtebi 11 95
(M bin Shafya, UAE) *sn led: trckd ldr after 2 1/2f: led 2 1/2 out: r.o wl: hdd cl home* **6/1**[1]
3 shd **Fleeting Shadow (IRE)**[20] 5-8-5 **95** ....(t) WayneSmith 3 95
(A Al Raihe, UAE) *mid-div: smooth prog on rail 3f out: chsd ldr: ev ch 1f out: r.o wl* **20/1**
4 3¾ **Emirates Skyline (USA)**[14] 182 6-8-13 **102** .... WJSupple 6 94
(A bin Huzaim, UAE) *led main gp: ev ch 2 1/2f out: one pce* **33/1**
5 1¼ **Wise Dennis**[131] 6106 7-9-0 **104** .... TedDurcan 10 92
(A P Jarvis) *a mid-div* **6/1**[1]
6 ¼ **Yasoodd**[14] 183 6-9-0 **104** ....(e) WilliamBuick 13 92
(D Selvaratnam, UAE) *mid-div: r.o fnl 2 1/2f* **10/1**[3]
7 1¼ **River Tiber**[336] 743 6-8-13 **102** .... MJKinane 16 88
(Saeed Bin Suroor) *nvr bttr than mid-div* **10/1**[3]
8 2¾ **Halkin (USA)**[306] 1087 7-8-10 **100** .... EddieAhern 7 78
(F Nass, Bahrain) *in rr of mid-div: nvr able to chal* **20/1**
9 1¼ **Akua'Ba (IRE)**[152] 5517 5-8-13 **102** ....(tp) KJManning 1 79
(J S Bolger, Ire) *settled in rr: rdn 3f out: nvr nr to chal* **16/1**
10 7¼ **Banknote**[40] 7740 7-8-8 **98** .... FrancisNorton 15 57
(A M Balding) *racd in rr: trckd ldrs 3f out: rdn and sn btn* **8/1**[2]
11 1¼ **Mostashaar (FR)**[20] 7-8-6 **96** .... FJara 2 52
(Doug Watson, UAE) *settled in rr: nvr able to chal* **20/1**
12 ¼ **Masaalek**[14] 182 4-9-1 **105** ....(v[1]) RHills 12 60
(Doug Watson, UAE) *mid-div: rdn 2 1/2f out: nt qckn* **10/1**[3]
13 ½ **Stepping Up (IRE)**[7] 265 6-8-8 **98** ....(t) TPO'Shea 9 52
(E Charpy, UAE) *v.s.a: nvr nr to chal* **10/1**[3]
14 1¼ **Gold Sovereign (IRE)**[7] 265 5-8-10 **100** .... RichardMullen 8 51
(I Mohammed, UAE) *trckd ldr: led after 2 1/2f: hdd 2 1/2f out: one pce after* **20/1**
15 dist **Fathayer (USA)**[14] 183 4-8-13 **102** ....(bt[1]) RoystonFfrench 14 —
(A Al Raihe, UAE) *mid-div: v wd 3f out: nt rcvr* **33/1**
U **Perfect Season (SAF)**[7] 265 5-8-8 **98** .... DO'Donohoe 4 —
(H J Brown, South Africa) *mid-div on rail: uns rdr 2 1/2f out* **8/1**[2]

1m 38.58s (0.28) **Going Correction** +0.175s/f (Good) **16** Ran SP% **132.3**
Speed ratings: **105,103,103,99,98 98,96,94,92,85 84,84,83,82,— —**

Owner Snyman, Snyman, Gramenie & Cunha **Bred** Burst Pty Ltd **Trained** South Africa

FOCUS

A decent and competitive handicap run at a good, even gallop.

NOTEBOOK

Strategic News(AUS) had something to prove beforehand considering he was fitted with both a tongue-tie and blinkers, and most of the Herman Brown runners have been needing their first run, but he picked up well late on to ultimately take this in convincing fashion. He looked held halfway up the straight, but really got going inside the final 200m and was well on top at the line. He's entitled to come on for this and should be suited by a step back up in trip.

Furnace(IRE) was taken on for the lead for much of the way. Having looked beaten when coming under pressure early in the straight, he kept responding and battled on well, but he had no answer's to the winner's late surge. This was a good first effort since leaving Michael Bell.

Fleeting Shadow(IRE) back on turf, was produced with every chance but he was outbattled for second by Furnace. His only previous success came back in July 2006 and he looks best left for win-only purposes.

Emirates Skyline(USA) passed Furnace early in the straight and hit the front, but he did not go through with his effort.

Wise Dennis ◆ was nicely handicapped judged on last year's Carnival efforts, but he didn't travel as strongly as he can and got going too late. He probably would have preferred to race in a more tightly packed field, which would have allowed him to move into the race on the bridle, and he can step up on this effort.

River Tiber was not helped by a wide draw.

Banknote had a nightmare draw and did a little bit too much early, appearing to race a touch keenly with no cover over the first couple of furlongs or so.

Perfect Season(SAF) seemed to clip heels early in the straight when stuck towards the inside rail and got rid of his rider.

314 LINGFIELD (L-H)

Friday, January 30

OFFICIAL GOING: Standard

Wind: Light, behind Weather: Fine

341 HAPPY BIRTHDAY NICKY AMATEUR RIDERS' H'CAP (DIV I) 1m 4f (P)

12:40 (12:45) (Class 5) (0-70,70) 4-Y-0+ **£2,472** (£760; £380) **Stalls** Low

Form RPR

63-6 1 **Mustajed**[13] 202 8-10-13 **67** .... MrPMillman(5) 3 79
(B R Millman) *dwlt: sn settled to trck ldng pair: wnt 2nd over 4f out: led over 2f out: urged along and hld on wl* **9/2**[1]
/00- 2 ½ **Dundry**[77] 7314 8-11-2 **70** ....(p) MrJAkehurst(5) 2 81
(G L Moore) *s.s: sn wl plcd bhd ldrs: prog to chse wnr 2f out: hrd rdn and persistent chal fnl f: jst hld* **12/1**[3]
0/5- 3 4½ **Wester Lodge (IRE)**[34] 7787 7-10-1 **57** .... MrDJEustace(7) 9 61
(J M P Eustace) *plld hrd: pressed ldr: led after 4f: drew clr 5f out: hdd over 2f out: sn outpcd but clung on for 3rd* **20/1**
0-02 4 ½ **They All Laughed**[11] 219 6-11-4 **67** .... MrsMarieKing 8 70
(P W Hiatt) *hld up in rr: prog on outer fr 1/2-way to dispute 2nd 4f out: outpcd fr 2f out* **7/1**[2]
011- 5 1¼ **She's So Pretty (IRE)**[82] 7261 5-11-0 **68** ....(b) MrJoshuaMoore(5) 7 69
(G L Moore) *hld up on inner: dropped to rr 1/2-way and n.m.r sn after: prog over 2f out: one pce and no imp over 1f out* **9/2**[1]

50-1 **6** *2* **Corlough Mountain**[12] 213 5-10-2 **52** 6ex.............. MissMBryant(5) 10 54
(P Butler) *hld up in rr: effrt and cl enough 3f out: outpcd 2f out: n.d after* **16/1**

520- **7** *2 ¼* **Strike Force**[33] 7800 5-10-8 **62**......................... MissALHutchinson(5) 11 56
(Miss J Feilden) *hld up in rr: prog on wd outside 3f out to chse ldrs over 2f out: bmpd along and sn outpcd* **7/1[2]**

00-6 **8** *2 ¼* **Rock Peak (IRE)**[21] 102 4-10-4 **62**.................. MissIsabelTompsett(5) 1 53
(B J Llewellyn) *w ldrs 2f: restrained: effrt 3f out: wknd 2f out* **12/1[3]**

5-61 **9** *½* **Sunset Boulevard (IRE)**[13] 202 6-10-10 **64**......... MrAshleePrice(5) 12 54
(Miss Tor Sturgis) *hld up in rr: prog on outside fr 4f out to chse ldrs over 2f out: wknd over 1f out* **9/2[1]**

-000 **10** *1 ¼* **Autumn Charm**[3] 300 4-9-12 **56** oh11................. MrJPFeatherstone(5) 5 44
(Lucinda Featherstone) *rel to r: hld up in last: hrd rdn and btn 3f out* **40/1**

00-0 **11** *5* **Charlie Bear**[28] 8 8-10-7 **56** oh11.............. GemmaGracey-Davison 6 36
(Miss Z C Davison) *hld up wl in rr: prog to chse ldrs 3f out: wknd over 2f out* **100/1**

124- **12** *3 ¼* **Black Tor Figarro (IRE)**[270] 1871 4-10-7 **65**.................... MrMWall(5) 4 40
(B W Duke) *led 4f: chsd ldr to over 4f out: sn lost pl: last and u.p over 2f out* **14/1**

2m 34.87s (1.87) **Going Correction** +0.15s/f (Slow)
WFA 4 from 5yo+ 4lb 12 Ran SP% **115.7**
Speed ratings (Par 103): **99,98,95,95,94 93,91,90,89,89 85,83**
toteswinger: 1&2 £13.00, 1&3 £20.30, 2&3 £99.30. CSF £58.55 CT £978.32 TOTE £5.70: £2.20, £3.50, £6.50; EX 48.30 TRIFECTA Not won..
Owner Mrs L S Millman **Bred** Shadwell Estate Company Limited **Trained** Kentisbeare, Devon
■ Stewards' Enquiry : Mr J P Featherstone four-day ban: used whip with excessive force (Feb 14, 16, Mar 2, Apr 6)

FOCUS
A modest amateur riders' handicap, but it did involve three last-time winners. It was run at a stop-start pace and the first two pulled clear. The form is rated around the third and could be better than rated.

342 HAPPY BIRTHDAY NICKY AMATEUR RIDERS' H'CAP (DIV II) 1m 4f (P)
1:10 (1:15) (Class 5) (0-70,70) 4-Y-0+ **£2,472** (£760; £380) **Stalls** Low

Form RPR

0-05 **1** **William's Way**[6] 285 7-10-4 **60**.. MrCMartin(7) 8 70
(I A Wood) *trckd ldrs: rdn 4f out: prog on outer over 3f out: led over 2f out and kicked on: hld on nr fin* **11/2[3]**

2-33 **2** *½* **Augustus John (IRE)**[15] 178 6-10-13 **62**.......................(p) MrSWalker 4 71
(S Parr) *t.k.h: hld up bhd ldrs: effrt to ld jst over 3f out: hdd over 2f out and nt qckn: rallied fnl f and clsng on wnr fin* **4/1[2]**

360- **3** *4 ½* **Turner's Touch**[30] 7831 7-10-2 **56** oh11.................(b) MrJoshuaMoore(5) 2 58
(G L Moore) *hld up in rr: stdy prog over 3f out: in tch 2f out: asked for effrt and plugged on reluctantly into 3rd 1f out* **8/1**

33-1 **4** *1 ½* **Night Orbit**[21] 103 5-10-13 **67**.......................................(v) MrRBirkett(5) 1 67
(Miss J Feilden) *trckd ldrs: rdn over 3f out: stl in tch 2f out: sn outpcd* **9/4[1]**

03-1 **5** *1 ¼* **Ben Bacchus (IRE)**[8] 248 7-10-7 **56** oh7...................... MrsMarieKing 9 54
(P W Hiatt) *prom: led over 5f out to jst over 3f out: cl up tl wknd over 1f out* **7/1**

066- **6** *hd* **Caltire (GER)**[116] 6541 4-10-5 **65**..............................(b) MrJMQuinlan(7) 6 62
(M G Quinlan) *hld up in rr: bmpd along 4f out: no prog tl kpt on fnl f on inner* **20/1**

000- **7** *½* **Home**[39] 7606 4-10-2 **62**.. MissLGray(7) 5 58
(C Gordon) *prom: led briefly 1/2-way: lost pl over 3f out: struggling after* **33/1**

002- **8** *1 ½* **Papradon**[105] 6775 5-10-11 **67**............................ MrSTwiston-Davies(7) 7 61
(N A Twiston-Davies) *sn led at v stdy pce: hdd 1/2-way and pushed along: styd handy: chal again over 2f out and upsides: wknd rapidly over 1f out* **8/1**

05- **9** *1* **Munich (IRE)**[34] 7791 5-11-0 **70**.. MrTJCannon(7) 10 62
(L Wells) *heavily restrained s: hld up in last: pushed along and effrt 4f out: no prog over 2f out: sn btn* **33/1**

265/ **10** *18* **Olivino (GER)**[899] 3196 8-10-2 **56** oh11............. MissIsabelTompsett(5) 3 20
(B J Llewellyn) *in tch tl wknd over 3f out: t.o* **33/1**

2m 34.4s (1.40) **Going Correction** +0.15s/f (Slow)
WFA 4 from 5yo+ 4lb 10 Ran SP% **114.5**
Speed ratings (Par 103): **101,100,97,96,95 95,95,94,93,81**
toteswinger: 1&2 £4.40, 1&3 £5.00, 2&3 £6.70. CSF £26.06 CT £172.51 TOTE £5.00: £2.10, £1.10, £2.70; EX 22.00 Trifecta £134.80 Pool: £384.46 - 2.11 winning units..
Owner Neardown Stables **Bred** Lewis Caterers **Trained** Upper Lambourn, Berks
■ Chris Martin's first winner.

FOCUS
This was run at a muddling pace just like the first division, and the lead changed hands a number of times in the early stages. The time was slightly quicker than division one and this is straightforward form.

343 NEW CHAPEL MAIDEN STKS 1m 2f (P)
1:40 (1:45) (Class 5) 3-Y-0+ **£2,729** (£806; £403) **Stalls** Low

Form RPR

5 **1** **Bromhead (USA)**[21] 98 3-8-4 0.. GregFairley 5 70
(B J Meehan) *ponied to s (early): v keen early and trckd ldng pair: wnt 2nd 2f out: squeezed though on inner to ld jst ins fnl f: drvn out* **13/2[2]**

2 *½* **Key Regard (IRE)** 3-8-4 0.. FrankieMcDonald 6 69+
(J A Osborne) *hld up in last pair: prog 3f out to go 4th 2f out: shuffled along over 1f out: plld out last 100yds and shkn up: flashed home to take 2nd post* **10/1[3]**

0 **3** *hd* **Bomber Brown (IRE)**[13] 201 3-8-4 0.............................. PaulHanagan 3 69
(P W Chapple-Hyam) *mde most at stdy pce: pushed along 3f out: rn green whn pressed over 1f out: hdd and nt qckn jst ins fnl f: lost 2nd last stride* **2/5[1]**

6-4 **4** *2 ¾* **Kochanski (IRE)**[17] 151 3-7-6 0........................ MatthewLawson(7) 7 58
(M Johnston) *pressed ldr to 2f out: hanging and fdd fnl f* **10/1[3]**

00- **5** *5* **Myshkin**[93] 7080 3-8-1 0...(v[1]) DuranFentiman(3) 4 53
(I Semple) *mostly in same pce: u.p and wl outpcd over 2f out* **40/1**

5/0- **6** *13* **Evette**[43] 7713 4-9-6 44.. JimmyQuinn 2 27
(H J Collingridge) *trckd ldng pair tl wknd rapidly over 2f out: t.o* **50/1**

00 **7** *3 ¼* **General Sam (USA)**[16] 160 3-8-4 0.............................. RichardSmith 1 21
(R Hannon) *a in last pair: wknd 3f out: t.o* **33/1**

2m 7.22s (0.62) **Going Correction** +0.15s/f (Slow)
WFA 3 from 4yo 23lb 7 Ran SP% **110.3**
Speed ratings (Par 103): **103,102,102,100,96 85,83**
toteswinger: 1&2 £4.80, 1&3 £1.60, 2&3 £1.90. CSF £59.07 TOTE £6.80: £2.50, £3.50; EX 40.40.
Owner Atlantic Crossing **Bred** Grovendale, K Nikkel And S Robertson **Trained** Manton, Wilts
■ Stewards' Enquiry : Greg Fairley caution: careless riding

FOCUS
In all likelihood a modest maiden, but some powerful yards were represented and it produced an exciting finish.

344 PLAY BINGO @ WILLIAMHILL.COM H'CAP 1m (P)
2:10 (2:16) (Class 6) (0-65,64) 4-Y-0+ **£2,047** (£604; £302) **Stalls** High

Form RPR

6-21 **1** **General Feeling (IRE)**[14] 192 8-9-4 **64**........................ PaulHanagan 7 75
(S T Mason) *trckd ldrs: prog to ld 2f out: styd on wl to draw clr fr over 1f out: pushed out firmly* **10/3[2]**

36-6 **2** *2 ¾* **Sir Ike (IRE)**[7] 266 4-9-0 **60**..(tp) IanMongan 1 65
(W S Kittow) *hld up in tch: effrt on inner 2f out: chsd wnr jst over 1f out: kpt on but no imp* **20/1**

5-04 **3** *1 ¼* **Mountain Pass (USA)**[11] 216 7-8-9 **55**.................(p) RobertHavlin 12 57
(B J Llewellyn) *dropped in fr wd draw and hld up wl in rr: prog fr 2f out: hanging over 1f out: cajoled along and wnt 3rd ins fnl f* **14/1**

35-0 **4** *hd* **Haasem (USA)**[16] 155 6-9-2 **62**..................................(v) GeorgeBaker 11 64
(J R Jenkins) *hld up towards rr: effrt on outer 2f out: hanging bdly but styd on fnl f: jst hld for 3rd* **8/1[3]**

340- **5** *1 ½* **Johnny Friendly**[149] 5616 4-9-2 **62**................................ AndrewElliott 3 60
(K R Burke) *pressed ldr: led over 2f out to 2f out: wknd ins fnl f* **14/1**

634- **6** *¾* **The Wily Woodcock**[41] 7749 5-9-0 **60**...................(b[1]) FergusSweeney 9 56
(G L Moore) *t.k.h: hld up bhd ldrs: wnt 4th 2f out: drvn and nt qckn over 1f out: fdd* **14/1**

0-40 **7** *½* **Maybe I Wont**[15] 167 4-8-6 **59**.............................. AndrewHeffernan(7) 6 54
(Lucinda Featherstone) *hld up towards rr: rdn over 2f out: kpt on same pce u.p and n.d* **25/1**

30-0 **8** *½* **Onenightinlisbon (IRE)**[24] 60 5-9-3 **63**...................... PatCosgrave 5 57
(J R Boyle) *wl plcd: prog to chse ldng pair 2f out: nt qckn over 1f out: wknd ins fnl f* **12/1**

1323 **9** *½* **Bavarica**[6] 285 7-8-13 **64**.. AmyBaker(5) 8 57
(Miss J Feilden) *hld up and racd wdst of all: effrt 3f out: losing grnd whn wd bnd 2f out* **5/2[1]**

040- **10** *2* **Annes Rocket (IRE)**[167] 5088 4-8-13 **59**............................ PatDobbs 2 47
(J C Fox) *s.v.s: sn in tch in last pair: no prog over 2f out* **66/1**

253- **11** *nk* **Melt (IRE)**[67] 7437 4-8-11 **57**.. DaneO'Neill 4 45
(R Hannon) *dwlt: a towards rr: struggling fr 2f out* **8/1[3]**

1-64 **12** *29* **Bookiebasher Babe (IRE)**[15] 176 4-9-4 **64**.............(v) MickyFenton 10 —
(M Quinn) *set decent pce: hdd & wknd rapidly over 2f out: virtually p.u: t.o: lame* **16/1**

1m 38.28s (0.08) **Going Correction** +0.15s/f (Slow) 12 Ran SP% **117.5**
Speed ratings (Par 101): **105,102,101,100,99 98,98,97,97,95 94,65**
toteswinger: 1&2 £21.00, 1&3 £14.10, 2&3 £98.50. CSF £71.49 CT £849.10 TOTE £4.20: £1.50, £5.00, £4.70; EX 69.70 TRIFECTA Not won..
Owner Middleham Park Racing LX **Bred** John Graham And Leslie Laverty **Trained**

FOCUS
A reasonably competitive handicap run at a decent pace. The winner's best effort for three years, and fairly sound form.
Annes Rocket(IRE) Official explanation: jockey said colt missed the break
Bookiebasher Babe(IRE) Official explanation: vet said filly returned lame

345 WILLIAM HILL TELEBETTING ON 0800 44 40 40 CLAIMING STKS 7f (P)
2:45 (2:51) (Class 6) 3-Y-O **£2,047** (£604; £302) **Stalls** Low

Form RPR

13-4 **1** **Woolston Ferry (IRE)**[5] 288 3-9-3 84.......................... TonyCulhane 5 74
(M R Channon) *hld up: forced wd bnd after 3f: sn prog: rdn to dispute 2nd 2f out: narrow ld 1f out: drvn and asserted slowly* **4/6[1]**

0-15 **2** *1* **My Sweet Georgia (IRE)**[9] 239 3-8-13 71.................(b) MickyFenton 1 68
(S A Callaghan) *dwlt: rousted along to press ldr: drvn 2f out: upsides 1f out: nt qckn and hld ins fnl f* **8/1**

540- **3** *hd* **Spinight (IRE)**[85] 7205 3-8-3 63..(p) NicolPolli(5) 6 62
(M Botti) *racd keenly mde most: drvn 2f out: narrowly hdd 1f out: kpt on but a hld after* **5/1[2]**

2-51 **4** *2 ½* **Cognac Boy (USA)**[16] 159 3-9-1 64..........................(b) JimmyQuinn 2 62
(A B Haynes) *hld up towards rr: effrt on inner to chse ldng trio 2f out: fnd nil over 1f out and no imp* **7/1[3]**

1-66 **5** *2 ¼* **Art Fund (USA)**[13] 200 3-8-8 62................................... FergusSweeney 4 49
(G L Moore) *t.k.h: hld up in rr: outpcd 2f out: no imp on ldrs after* **12/1**

052- **6** *2* **Cwmni**[49] 7652 3-8-4 51... CatherineGannon 8 40
(B Palling) *hld up in last: effrt on wd outside 3f out: wknd over 2f out* **25/1**

30- **7** *8* **Wickedly Fast (USA)**[88] 7164 3-8-1 0 ow5..........(t) MatthewDavies(7) 3 22
(George Baker) *t.k.h: trckd ldng pair after 2f to over 2f out: wknd rapidly* **40/1**

0 **8** *8* **Patience Rewarded**[16] 154 3-8-3 0.................................... LukeMorris 7 —
(J S Moore) *chsd ldng pair 2f: sn lost pl u.p: last 1/2-way: sn wl bhd* **66/1**

1m 25.61s (0.81) **Going Correction** +0.15s/f (Slow) 8 Ran SP% **115.7**
Speed ratings (Par 95): **101,99,99,96,94 91,82,73**
toteswinger: 1&2 £1.90, 1&3 £2.20, 2&3 £5.90. CSF £6.93 TOTE £1.70: £1.10, £2.40, £1.60; EX 7.80 Trifecta £31.10 Pool: £841.90 - 20.01 winning units..
Owner Capital **Bred** Tim Taylor **Trained** West Ilsley, Berks

FOCUS
A fair claimer run at a strong pace and it produced a tight finish. The winner did not need to match his best, with the third and fourth the best guide to the form.

346 ASHDOWN FOREST (S) H'CAP 2m (P)
3:20 (3:25) (Class 6) (0-60,59) 4-Y-0+ **£2,047** (£604; £302) **Stalls** Low

Form RPR

2-03 **1** **Sir Liam (USA)**[8] 248 5-9-5 **53**.............................. RichardKingscote 1 60
(Tom Dascombe) *trckd ldng pair: effrt to go 2nd jst over 2f out: clsd to ld ent fnl f: drvn out and hld on* **8/1[3]**

4-22 **2** *½* **Vanquisher (IRE)**[8] 249 5-9-1 **49**.......................(t) StephenDonohoe 13 56
(Ian Williams) *hld up towards rr: prog on inner fr 3f out to go 3rd 2f out: hrd rdn to go 2nd last 150yds: clsng fin* **4/1[1]**

54-1 **3** *½* **Carlton Scroop (FR)**[20] 117 6-9-6 **54**..........................(b) LukeMorris 7 60
(J Jay) *trckd ldrs: effrt 3f out: nt qckn over 2f out: tried to cl again u.p over 1f out: gaining at fin* **8/1[3]**

060- **4** *1* **Mulaazem**[28] 2952 6-9-9 **57**...(bt[1]) AndrewElliott 2 62
(A M Hales) *trckd ldrs: on inner: rdn fr 5f out: effrt over 2f out: sn outpcd: kpt on u.p fnl f* **28/1**

-034 **5** *1* **Spume (IRE)**[3] 301 5-9-5 **53**...(t) AdamKirby 14 57+
(S Parr) *hld up in last trio: stl wl in rr over 2f out: prog on inner over 1f out: rdn and styd on fnl f: no ch of rching ldrs* **4/1[1]**

0 **6** *½* **Huck Finn (NZ)**[14] 193 9-9-2 **50**.................................... JimmyQuinn 11 53
(M Madgwick) *wl in rr: rdn over 4f out: sme prog 2f out but nt on terms: kpt on fnl f: nrst fin* **66/1**

7 ½ **Magic Kahyasi (IRE)**^{462} 6-9-3 **51** .... GeorgeBaker 9 53
(G L Moore) *hld up in rr of midfield: effrt over 3f out: outpcd u.p over 2f out: kpt on fr over 1f out: nrst fin* **7/1**^{2}

343- 8 1 **Starstruck Peter (IRE)**^{236} [2053] 5-9-5 **53** .... (b^{1}) PaulDoe 4 54
(S Curran) *led 2f: trckd ldr: led again over 3f out: drvn 2 l clr over 2f out: collared ent fnl f: wknd rapidly and eased* **7/1**^{2}

044/ 9 6 **Play Master (IRE)**^{482} [5886] 8-9-5 **53** .... (p) RobertHavlin 6 47
(B J Llewellyn) *stdd s: t.k.h early and hld up in rr: effrt 3f out but nt clr run: rchd midfield whn hmpd wl over 1f out: no prog fnl f* **22/1**

0-36 10 6 **Ten Spot (IRE)**^{7} [275] 4-8-10 **51** .... (t) MickyFenton 8 38
(Stef Liddiard) *hld up in last: struggling over 4f out: no ch fnl 2f* **16/1**

0-54 11 4 ½ **Barodine**^{14} [187] 6-9-5 **53** .... (bt) JimCrowley 10 34
(R J Hodges) *t.k.h early: prog to ld after 2f: hdd over 3f out: wknd rapidly 2f out* **14/1**

630- 12 ½ **Ocean Pride (IRE)**^{34} [7792] 6-9-2 **50** .... (b) DaneO'Neill 3 31
(L Wells) *t.k.h early: nvr beyond midfield: struggling on outer over 3f out: sn no ch* **25/1**

00-4 13 nk **Force Tradition (IRE)**^{17} [66] 4-9-0 **55** .... (b^{1}) PaulMulrennan 5 35
(M H Tompkins) *chsd ldng pair tl wknd rapidly fr 3f out* **40/1**

40-4 14 13 **Shayera**^{21} [102] 4-9-4 **59** .... (t) IanMongan 12 24
(B R Johnson) *hld up in rr: prog 1/2-way to chse ldrs: wknd 4f out: t.o* **16/1**

3m 28.2s (2.50) **Going Correction** +0.15s/f (Slow) **14** Ran SP% **121.2**
WFA 4 from 5yo+ 7lb
Speed ratings (Par 101): **99,98,98,98,97 97,97,96,93,90 88,88,87,81**
toteswinger: 1&2 £7.00, 1&3 £12.50, 2&3 £6.30. CSF £38.19 CT £273.17 TOTE £10.30: £2.20, £1.90, £3.10; EX 33.80 Trifecta £125.50 Pool: £561.59 - 3.31 winning units..Spume was the subject of a friendly claim.
Owner M Khan X2 **Bred** Keene Ridge Farm **Trained** Lambourn, Berks

FOCUS
They went a fair pace in this marathon selling handicap. The form is rated around the front pair and may not prove entirely solid.
Spume(IRE) Official explanation: jockey said gelding ran too free
Barodine Official explanation: jockey said gelding hung right

347 PLAY POKER @ WILLIAMHILL.COM H'CAP 6f (P)
3:55 (4:00) (Class 6) (0-52,52) 4-Y-O+ **£2,047** (£604; £302) **Stalls** Low

Form RPR

45-5 1 **Davids Mark**^{20} [111] 9-8-10 **50** .... SimonWhitworth 5 59
(J R Jenkins) *hld up in last trio: effrt over 1f out: swept past tightly bunched field to ld ins fnl f: sn clr* **8/1**

-560 2 1 ½ **Afton View (IRE)**^{4} [294] 4-8-11 **51** ow1 .... AdamKirby 8 55
(S Parr) *trckd ldr to 1/2-way: styd cl up: produced to chal ent fnl f and sn upsides: nt qckn* **5/1**^{2}

35-4 3 shd **Green Velvet**^{25} [46] 4-8-10 **50** .... TravisBlock 10 54
(P J Makin) *prom: chsd ldr 1/2-way: drvn to ld narrowly 1f out: sn hdd and nt qckn* **4/1**^{1}

330- 4 1 **Nawaaff**^{95} [7013] 4-8-10 **50** .... TonyCulhane 12 51
(M R Channon) *hld up: prog to dispute 2nd 1/2-way: upsides 1f out: nt qckn* **11/2**^{3}

0-00 4 dht **Faintly Hopeful**^{14} [189] 4-8-10 **50** .... DaneO'Neill 4 51
(R A Teal) *s.s: mostly in last pair: styd on u.p on outer fnl f: nrst fin* **13/2**

060- 6 nk **Inka Dancer (IRE)**^{106} [6749] 7-8-10 **50** .... CatherineGannon 6 53+
(B Palling) *towards rr: effrt over 1f out: cl up bhd ldrs whn no room and snatched up last 100yds* **12/1**

000- 7 shd **Forever Changes**^{59} [7521] 4-8-12 **52** .... JimCrowley 9 52
(L Montague Hall) *hld up in rr: prog towards outer jst over 2f out: nt qckn over 1f out: kpt on ins fnl f: nvr able to chal* **12/1**

1-0 8 ½ **Marvin Gardens**^{14} [198] 6-8-12 **52** .... (b) JerryO'Dwyer 7 50
(P S McEntee) *chsd ldrs: rdn over 2f out: styng on and cl up bhd ldrs whn no room and snatched up 150yds out* **8/1**

/00- 9 nk **Nimbelle (IRE)**^{59} [7522] 4-8-10 **50** .... (p) FrankieMcDonald 3 47
(J C Tuck) *t.k.h early: hld up in rr: shuffled along 1/2-way and again over 1f out: keeping on but no ch whn reminder nr fin* **16/1**

00-0 10 4 ½ **Metropolitan Chief**^{9} [234] 5-8-10 **50** .... MickyFenton 1 33
(P Burgoyne) *led: drvn and hdd 1f out: wknd rapidly and eased* **20/1**

1m 12.88s (0.98) **Going Correction** +0.15s/f (Slow) **10** Ran SP% **113.6**
Speed ratings (Par 101): **99,97,96,95,95 95,95,94,93,87**
toteswinger: 1&2 £7.00, 1&3 £5.10, 2&3 £5.10. CSF £46.48 CT £187.99 TOTE £7.30: £2.30, £2.20, £1.90; EX 47.80 Trifecta £237.80 Pool: £449. 91 - 1.40 winning units..
Owner Mrs Wendy Jenkins **Bred** D Lowe **Trained** Royston, Herts
■ Stewards' Enquiry : Travis Block three-day ban: careless riding (Feb 13-15)

FOCUS
A moderate handicap, but it did involve some relatively unexposed types. Only 2lb covered the whole field on official figures and the form looks straightforward.
Faintly Hopeful Official explanation: jockey said gelding missed the break
Inka Dancer(IRE) Official explanation: jockey said mare was denied a clear run
Marvin Gardens Official explanation: jockey said gelding was denied a clear run
Metropolitan Chief Official explanation: trainer said gelding bled from the nose

348 BURSTOW H'CAP 6f (P)
4:30 (4:35) (Class 6) (0-65,65) 3-Y-O **£2,047** (£604; £302) **Stalls** Low

Form RPR

06-6 1 **Rocoppelia (USA)**^{23} [74] 3-8-9 **56** .... (b^{1}) JimCrowley 5 63
(Mrs A J Perrett) *w ldr: led wl over 1f out and kicked clr: rdn out* **11/2**^{3}

6-41 2 1 ¼ **Raimond Ridge (IRE)**^{13} [200] 3-9-2 **63** .... TonyCulhane 7 66
(M R Channon) *dwlt: t.k.h and hld up in last trio: prog to go 3rd 2f out: drvn to chse wnr fnl f: styd on but unable to chal* **9/2**^{2}

2-34 3 2 ¾ **Edith's Boy (IRE)**^{12} [208] 3-9-4 **65** .... PaulDoe 8 59
(S Dow) *awkward s and wnt rt: t.k.h and hld up in last: nt clr run 2f out: kpt on fnl f to take 3rd post: no ch* **10/1**

-354 4 nse **Deckchair**^{2} [316] 3-8-5 **57** .... (v) AmyBaker$^{(5)}$ 1 51
(H J Collingridge) *dwlt: t.k.h and hld up in last trio: effrt over 1f out: plugged on but nvr on terms* **5/2**^{1}

0-33 5 nk **Mean Mr Mustard (IRE)**^{8} [246] 3-8-4 **51** .... (b) FrankieMcDonald 4 44
(J A Osborne) *led at mod pce: hdd and nt qckn wl over 1f out: fdd fnl f* **11/2**^{3}

06-5 6 nk **Lana's Charm**^{14} [188] 3-8-9 **56** .... CatherineGannon 3 48
(P J Makin) *hld up bhd ldrs: shkn up and nt qckn wl over 1f out: n.d after* **8/1**

12-5 7 3 ½ **Elusive Ronnie (IRE)**^{13} [200] 3-9-1 **62** .... (p) DaneO'Neill 6 43
(R A Teal) *racd on outer: chsd ldng pair to 2f out: wknd* **7/1**

1m 13.98s (2.08) **Going Correction** +0.15s/f (Slow) **7** Ran SP% **110.2**
Speed ratings (Par 95): **92,90,86,86,86 85,81**
toteswinger: 1&2 £5.60, 1&3 £8.20, 2&3 £5.30. CSF £27.94 CT £224.14 TOTE £7.00: £3.20, £2.40; EX 29.00 Trifecta £284.20 Pool: £768.13 - 2.00 winning units. Place 6: £301.20, Place 5: £91.83.
Owner John Connolly **Bred** James Millar & Janice Millar **Trained** Pulborough, W Sussex

FOCUS
A modest event which was quite steadily run. Nothing really got into it from behind. The winner returned to his early 2yo form.
Deckchair Official explanation: jockey said filly ran flat
T/Jkpt: £27,708.80 to a £1 stake. Pool: £58,539.90. 1.50 winning tickets. T/Plt: £591.00 to a £1 stake. Pool: £69,342.99. 85.65 winning tickets. T/Qpdt: £27.10 to a £1 stake. Pool: £7,284.18. 198.30 winning tickets. JN

^{328}WOLVERHAMPTON (A.W) (L-H)
Friday, January 30

OFFICIAL GOING: Standard
Wind: Fresh, across Weather: Overcast

349 VAUXHALL INSIGNIA CAR OF YEAR 2009 CLAIMING STKS 5f 20y(P)
6:50 (6:50) (Class 6) 4-Y-O+ **£2,729** (£806; £403) **Stalls** Low

Form RPR

3-41 1 **Harry Up**^{8} [250] 8-9-3 **87** .... (p) JamieSpencer 7 89
(K A Ryan) *mde all: rdn over 1f out: r.o* **4/6**^{1}

314- 2 2 **Blue Tomato**^{87} [7176] 8-8-8 **84** .... WilliamCarson$^{(5)}$ 3 78
(D Nicholls) *a.p: rdn to chse wnr over 1f out: no imp ins fnl f* **2/1**^{2}

-063 3 3 ¼ **Bluebok**^{16} [165] 8-9-1 **61** .... (bt) FergusSweeney 5 68
(J M Bradley) *chsd wnr over 3f: no ex fnl f* **25/1**

4 6 **Albero Di Giuda (IRE)**^{149} 4-8-12 **76** .... (t) FBranca 8 43
(F Sheridan) *hld up: rdn and wknd over 1f out* **12/1**^{3}

06-0 5 8 **Briery Blaze**^{4} [292] 6-8-3 **47** .... (p) JoshWall$^{(7)}$ 2 13
(T Wall) *rdr removed hood late: dwlt: outpcd* **100/1**

61.60 secs (-0.70) **Going Correction** +0.05s/f (Slow) **5** Ran SP% **105.8**
Speed ratings (Par 101): **107,103,98,89,76**
toteswinger: 1&2 £1.80. CSF £1.96 TOTE £1.80: £1.10, £1.30; EX 2.50.
Owner The Fishermen **Bred** J E Rose **Trained** Hambleton, N Yorks

FOCUS
A couple of fair sorts for the grade but not a competitive race. The pace was sound and the first three raced in the centre in the straight. Straightforward form, the winner not needing to match his recent best.

350 PLAY BINGO @ WILLIAMHILL.COM H'CAP 5f 20y(P)
7:20 (7:22) (Class 5) (0-75,73) 3-Y-O **£3,070** (£906; £453) **Stalls** Low

Form RPR

63-1 1 **Lady Vivien**^{17} [140] 3-8-7 **62** .... JamieSpencer 3 69
(D H Brown) *a.p: chsd ldr over 3f out: rdn to ld and edgd lft over 1f out: r.o* **15/8**^{1}

0-23 2 2 ¾ **Minotaurious (IRE)**^{22} [85] 3-9-0 **69** .... FergusSweeney 4 66
(K R Burke) *sn pushed along in rr: hdwy over 1f out: sn rdn: styd on to go 2nd nr fin: no ch w wnr* **11/4**^{3}

5-10 3 hd **Green Onions**^{9} [229] 3-8-13 **73** .... (p) GabrielHannon$^{(5)}$ 2 70
(D J S Ffrench Davis) *sn led: rdn: hung lft and hdd over 1f out: styd on same pce ins fnl f* **8/1**

00-4 4 1 ¼ **Ruby Tallulah**^{17} [140] 3-8-13 **68** .... LiamJones 1 60
(C R Dore) *chsd ldr to over 3f out: sn pushed along: rdn whn hmpd over 1f out: swtchd rt and styd on same pce ins fnl f* **9/4**^{2}

1-44 5 7 **Trick Or Two**^{17} [149] 3-8-11 **66** .... PaulMulrennan 5 33
(Mrs R A Carr) *trckd ldrs: rdn 1/2-way: wkng whn hung lft fnl f* **12/1**

62.93 secs (0.63) **Going Correction** +0.05s/f (Slow) **5** Ran SP% **111.0**
Speed ratings (Par 97): **96,91,91,89,78**
CSF £7.44 TOTE £3.10: £1.50, £1.80; EX 5.40.
Owner Ron Hull **Bred** Wheelers Land Stud **Trained** Maltby, S Yorks

FOCUS
An ordinary handicap in which the pace was reasonable throughout. The winner, a progressive sort, raced centre to far side in the straight. This probably did not take too much winning.
Trick Or Two Official explanation: jockey said gelding hung right throughout

351 WILLIAM HILL TELEBETTING ON 0800 44 40 40 H'CAP 5f 216y(P)
7:50 (7:52) (Class 4) (0-85,85) 4-Y-O+ **£5,180** (£1,541; £577; £577) **Stalls** Low

Form RPR

000- 1 **Sir Nod**^{211} [3626] 7-8-4 **71** oh1 .... PaulHanagan 9 80+
(Miss J A Camacho) *chsd ldrs: rdn to ld ins fnl f: r.o* **14/1**

030- 2 1 **Methaaly (IRE)**^{42} [7737] 6-8-6 **80** .... (e) PNolan$^{(7)}$ 8 86
(M Mullineaux) *s.i.s: hld up: r.o ins fnl f: wnt 2nd nr fin: nt rch wnr* **22/1**

063- 3 1 **Yungaburra (IRE)**^{31} [7828] 5-9-3 **84** .... (bt) AdamKirby 5 87
(S Parr) *mid-div: hdwy over 2f out: rdn and hung lft over 1f out: styd on towards fin* **7/1**

42-2 3 dht **Silvanus (IRE)**^{22} [83] 4-8-8 **75** .... PaulMulrennan 6 78
(I Semple) *led early: chsd ldr tl led over 2f out: rdn over 1f out: hdd and unable qck ins fnl f* **9/1**

050- 5 nk **Carcinetto (IRE)**^{98} [6947] 7-8-12 **84** .... RichardEvans$^{(5)}$ 3 86
(P D Evans) *sn pushed along to ld: rdn and hdd over 2f out: styd on same pce fnl f* **11/2**^{3}

4-43 6 nk **Dressed To Dance (IRE)**^{19} [128] 5-8-9 **76** .... (b) StephenDonohoe 4 77
(P D Evans) *mid-div: hdwy u.p over 1f out: one pce ins fnl f* **10/1**

-532 7 ¾ **Northern Empire (IRE)**^{7} [270] 6-8-8 **75** .... (p) JamieSpencer 7 73
(K A Ryan) *hld up: plld hrd: hdwy over 1f out: rdn ins fnl f: eased whn btn towards fin* **11/4**^{1}

05-3 8 nk **Soopacal (IRE)**^{22} [86] 4-9-4 **85** .... TomEaves 1 83
(B Smart) *chsd ldrs: rdn over 1f out: no ex fnl f* **9/2**^{2}

1-32 9 ½ **Musical Script (USA)**^{12} [212] 6-8-6 **73** .... (b) JimmyQuinn 2 69
(Mouse Hamilton-Fairley) *s.i.s: hld up: rdn over 1f out: n.d* **11/2**^{3}

1m 14.5s (-0.50) **Going Correction** +0.05s/f (Slow) **9** Ran SP% **118.2**
Speed ratings (Par 105): **105,103,102,102,101 101,100,100,99**
PL: Yungaburra £1.60, Silvanus £1.40; TRICAST: SN-M-Y £1,173.07, SN-M-S £1,455.20; toteswinger: 1&2 £40.60, 1&3 (Yungaburra) £11.10, 1&3 (Silvanus) £14.40, 2&3 (Y) £2.30, 2&3 (S) £12.70. CSF £279.42 TOTE £22.50: £6.00, £6.60; EX 253.20.
Owner Brian Nordan **Bred** B Nordan And Mrs S Camacho **Trained** Norton, N Yorks

FOCUS
Exposed performers in this fair handicap. The pace was sound and the winner raced in the centre in the straight. The form is sound with the winner taking advantage og a good mark.
Northern Empire(IRE) Official explanation: jockey said gelding was unruly in stalls and ran too freely

Musical Script(USA) Official explanation: jockey said gelding was slow into stride

352 WOLVERHAMPTON-RACECOURSE.CO.UK H'CAP 5f 216y(P)
8:20 (8:23) (Class 6) (0-60,60) 4-Y-0+ £2,047 (£604; £302) Stalls Low

Form				RPR
24	1		**Under Warranty (ITY)**[4] 292 5-9-4 **60**............(t) FBranca 6	75+
			(F Sheridan) *mde all: rdn over 1f out: r.o* **2/1**[1]	
431-	2	2 1/2	**Perlachy**[32] 7809 5-9-1 **57**............(v) LukeMorris 1	64
			(D Shaw) *trckd ldrs: racd keenly: rdn to chse wnr fnl f: edgd lft: no imp* **7/2**[2]	
603-	3	*shd*	**Elkhorn**[70] 7399 7-8-11 **60**............(v) BMcHugh(7) 7	67
			(Miss J A Camacho) *a.p: rdn and hung lft over 1f out: styd on wl towards fin* **15/2**	
060-	4	1 1/2	**Great Knight (IRE)**[98] 6956 4-8-13 **55**............ JamesDoyle 2	57
			(S Kirk) *hld up in tch: racd keenly: rdn over 1f out: styd on same pce ins fnl f* **14/1**	
140-	5	3/4	**Welcome Approach**[69] 7414 6-9-3 **59**............ JamieSpencer 8	58
			(J R Weymes) *hld up: rdn over 1f out: r.o ins fnl f: nt rch ldrs* **8/1**	
00-0	6	1	**Hunt The Bottle (IRE)**[4] 294 4-9-0 **56**............ LiamJones 10	52
			(M Mullineaux) *hld up: hdwy over 2f out: sn outpcd: r.o ins fnl f* **12/1**	
-023	7	3/4	**Wiltshire (IRE)**[8] 245 7-9-2 **58**............(v) MickyFenton 9	52
			(P T Midgley) *prom: racd keenly: rdn over 1f out: wknd fnl f* **7/1**[3]	
0-21	8	1 1/2	**Flamestone**[16] 153 5-8-6 **48**............ StephenDonohoe 3	37
			(A E Price) *hld up: rdn over 2f out: n.d* **10/1**	
00-5	9	3 1/2	**Chookie Heiton (IRE)**[22] 87 11-9-4 **60**............ TomEaves 4	38
			(I Semple) *chsd wnr tl rdn over 1f out: wknd fnl f* **20/1**	

1m 15.6s (0.60) **Going Correction** +0.05s/f (Slow) 9 Ran SP% **119.1**
Speed ratings (Par 101): **98,94,94,92,91 90,89,87,82**
toteswinger: 1&2 £4.40, 1&3 £5.80, 2&3 £3.40. CSF £9.19 CT £44.41 TOTE £3.60: £1.70, £1.10, £3.00; EX 14.70.
Owner A Zanoboni **Bred** Angelo Crucianelli **Trained** Stoke Heath, Shropshire

FOCUS
An ordinary event but just a modest pace by sprint standards, set by the winner, and those held up were at a big disadvantage. The winner raced centre to far side in the straight. The form seems pretty solid.

353 BOOK TICKETS AT WOLVERHAMPTON-RACECOURSE.CO.UK H'CAP 1m 1f 103y(P)
8:50 (8:50) (Class 6) (0-55,56) 4-Y-0+ £2,047 (£604; £302) Stalls Low

Form				RPR
05-6	1		**Snow Dancer (IRE)**[28] 18 5-8-7 **53**............(p) SladeO'Hara(5) 7	67
			(H A McWilliams) *chsd ldrs: rdn over 2f out: led over 1f out: r.o* **12/1**	
34/1	2	1 1/4	**Agilete**[8] 254 7-8-10 **51** 6ex............ JerryO'Dwyer 8	62
			(J Pearce) *a.p: chsd ldr over 2f out: sn rdn and ev ch: hung lft over 1f out: no ex towards fin* **3/1**[1]	
-451	3	3 1/4	**Ridgeway Jazz**[7] 275 4-8-13 **55** 6ex............ LukeMorris 6	60
			(M D I Usher) *hmpd s: hld up: hdwy over 2f out: sn rdn: hung lft ins fnl f: styd on* **8/1**	
0-42	4	*hd*	**Moyoko (IRE)**[11] 216 6-8-11 **52**............(b) PaulHanagan 12	56
			(M Salaman) *hmpd s: hld up: hdwy over 2f out: sn edgd lft: rdn over 1f out: styd on same pce fnl f* **9/1**	
000-	5	2	**Prince Charlemagne (IRE)**[33] 7806 6-8-9 **50**............ FergusSweeney 5	50
			(G L Moore) *wnt rt s: hld up: hung lft and r.o ins fnl f: nrst fin* **12/1**	
3-52	6	2	**Bailieborough (IRE)**[11] 221 10-9-0 **55**............ JimmyQuinn 9	51
			(B Ellison) *hld up in tch: nt clr run over 2f out: sn rdn: wkng whn hmpd fnl f* **7/2**[2]	
004-	7	1	**Altos Reales**[279] 1639 5-8-12 **53**............ RichardKingscote 3	47
			(J G Given) *chsd ldr: pushed along 6f out: led 3f out: rdn and hdd over 1f out: wknd ins fnl f* **16/1**	
0-05	8	1 1/4	**Weetfromthechaff**[9] 242 4-8-4 **53**............(p) DavidKenny(7) 13	44
			(R Hollinshead) *hld up: hdwy over 3f out: rdn: hung lft and wknd over 1f out* **33/1**	
00-5	9	2	**Bold Indian (IRE)**[11] 215 5-9-0 **55**............ TomEaves 1	42
			(I Semple) *hld up in tch: nt clr run and lost pl wl over 2f out: n.d after* **16/1**	
-012	10	2 1/2	**Ardent Prince**[7] 277 6-9-1 **56** 6ex............ JamieSpencer 10	38
			(A J McCabe) *hmpd s: hld up: nt clr run over 2f out: n.d* **9/2**[3]	
50-0	11	3 1/4	**Rampant Ronnie (USA)**[14] 186 4-8-12 **54**............ MickyFenton 4	29
			(P W D'Arcy) *chsd ldrs: rdn over 3f out: wknd wl over 2f out* **12/1**	
00-0	12	23	**Flagstone (USA)**[18] 133 5-8-8 **49**............(t) StephenDonohoe 2	—
			(Ian Williams) *led and hdd 3f out: wkng whn hmpd sn after* **33/1**	

2m 1.70s **Going Correction** +0.05s/f (Slow)
WFA 4 from 5yo+ 1lb 12 Ran SP% **127.2**
Speed ratings (Par 101): **102,100,98,97,96 94,93,92,90,88 85,64**
toteswinger: 1&2 £30.80, 1&3 £6.30, 2&3 £6.10. CSF £51.48 CT £323.14 TOTE £15.90: £2.30, £1.40, £4.10; EX 84.70.
Owner Mrs L Wohlers **Bred** Liam Queally **Trained** Cockerham, Co Durham

FOCUS
A modest handicap in which the pace was only fair and suited the prominent racers. The winner raced against the far rail in the straight and the first two pulled clear. The winner raced off a career-low mark.
Altos Reales Official explanation: jockey said mare had no more to give
Ardent Prince Official explanation: jockey said gelding was hampered at start
Rampant Ronnie(USA) Official explanation: trainer said gelding finished lame behind
Flagstone(USA) Official explanation: jockey said gelding hung right-handed throughout

354 PLAY POKER @ WILLIAMHILL.COM FILLIES' H'CAP 1m 141y(P)
9:20 (9:21) (Class 4) (0-85,89) 4-Y-0+ £5,180 (£1,541; £770; £384) Stalls Low

Form				RPR
2431	1		**Teasing**[7] 274 5-8-10 **75** 6ex............(v) RobertHavlin 2	82
			(J Pearce) *hld up: hdwy over 3f out: rdn to ld 1f out: r.o* **5/1**[3]	
51-2	2	2 3/4	**Quick Off The Mark**[15] 176 4-8-4 **70** oh2............ RichardKingscote 6	71
			(J G Given) *led: rdn and hdd 1f out: styd on same pce* **7/1**	
43-1	3	3/4	**Aphrodisia**[24] 60 5-8-5 **70** oh1............ StephenDonohoe 4	69
			(Ian Williams) *hld up: hdwy over 1f out: styd on* **10/3**[2]	
-413	4	1/2	**Mozayada (USA)**[10] 225 5-9-5 **84**............ JimmyQuinn 3	82
			(M Brittain) *chsd ldr: rdn over 2f out: styd on same pce fnl f* **5/1**[3]	
24-1	5	6	**Confidentiality (IRE)**[7] 271 5-9-10 **89** 6ex............ SteveDrowne 5	73
			(M Wigham) *chsd ldrs: rdn over 3f out: wknd fnl f* **9/4**[1]	
606-	6	27	**Perfect Act**[30] 7837 4-8-8 **74**............ LukeMorris 1	—
			(C G Cox) *hld up: plld hrd: sddle slipped and hdwy 7f out: wknd over 2f out: eased* **5/1**[3]	

1m 51.17s (0.67) **Going Correction** +0.05s/f (Slow)
WFA 4 from 5yo 1lb 6 Ran SP% **116.3**
Speed ratings (Par 102): **99,96,95,95,90 66**
toteswinger: 1&2 £6.40, 1&3 £23.20, 2&3 £13.80. CSF £39.41 TOTE £6.20: £2.70, £3.50; EX 27.80 Place 6 £212.15, Place 5 £184.61 .
Owner D Leech **Bred** Chippenham Lodge Stud Ltd **Trained** Newmarket, Suffolk

FOCUS
The best race of the night quality-wise, but one that did not take as much winning as seemed likely with the market leader disappointing. Muddling form, and not form to take too positively. The gallop was only moderate and the field came down the centre in the straight.
Confidentiality(IRE) Official explanation: jockey said mare ran flat
Perfect Act Official explanation: jockey said saddle slipped
T/Plt: £101.90 to a £1 stake. Pool: £119,300.51. 854.65 winning tickets. T/Qpdt: £61.30 to a £1 stake. Pool: £8,125.15. 98.00 winning tickets. CR

[341] LINGFIELD (L-H)
Saturday, January 31

OFFICIAL GOING: Standard
Wind: Moderate,across Weather: Fine, crisp

355 LIVE CASINO GAMES @ WILLIAMHILL.COM APPRENTICE H'CAP 7f (P)
1:10 (1:10) (Class 6) (0-65,65) 4-Y-0+ £2,047 (£604; £302) Stalls Low

Form				RPR
4-40	1		**Divertimenti (IRE)**[17] 157 5-9-5 **65**............(b) JamesO'Reilly 8	74
			(C R Dore) *t.k.h: trckd ldng pair: effrt to ld jst over 1f out: drvn and styd on wl* **4/1**[1]	
-550	2	1	**Bold Diva**[21] 118 4-8-8 **54**............(v) AmyBaker 10	60
			(A W Carroll) *hld up in 7th: clsng on ldrs whn nt clr run wl over 1f out: got through ent fnl f: kpt on to take 2nd nr fin* **10/1**	
02-5	3	*nk*	**Torquemada (IRE)**[21] 114 8-8-2 **53**............(t) KierenFox(5) 6	58
			(M J Attwater) *hld up in midfield: prog on outer 2f out: produced to chal over 1f out gng wl: fnd disappointingly little: sn btn: lost 2nd nr fin* **11/2**[3]	
026-	4	2 1/2	**Ever Cheerful**[34] 7803 8-8-12 **63**............(p) PNolan(5) 3	61
			(A B Haynes) *w ldr: narrow advantage 2f out to jst over 1f out: sn brushed aside* **11/2**[3]	
20-0	5	*nse*	**Splash The Cash**[16] 167 4-8-11 **60**............(t) DEMullins(3) 7	58
			(K A Ryan) *t.k.h: hld up in midfield: effrt on wd outside over 2f out: nt qckn over 1f out: no imp after* **11/2**[3]	
0-50	6	3 1/4	**Bridge Of Fermoy (IRE)**[11] 224 4-8-13 **62**............(bt) KylieManser(3) 4	51
			(Miss Gay Kelleway) *dwlt: mostly in last pair: detached fr rest of field over 2f out: shkn up over 1f out: r.o ins fnl f* **10/1**	
00-4	7	2 1/4	**Takaamul**[20] 130 6-8-0 **51** oh1............ AndrewHeffernan(5) 9	34
			(K A Morgan) *mde most to 2f out: nt run on* **12/1**	
2-36	8	*nk*	**Bertie Southstreet**[16] 167 6-9-4 **64**............(b) MCGeran 2	46
			(J R Boyle) *stdd s: t.k.h and sn trckd ldrs: wknd rapidly on inner over 1f out* **9/2**[2]	
306-	9	1 1/2	**Athboy Auction**[41] 7757 4-8-0 **51** oh1............ RichardRowe(5) 1	29
			(H J Collingridge) *a in last pair: detached over 2f out: no ch after* **33/1**	

1m 24.52s (-0.28) **Going Correction** +0.10s/f (Slow) 9 Ran SP% **113.2**
Speed ratings (Par 101): **105,103,103,100,100 96,94,93,92**
toteswinger: 1&2 £8.60, 1&3 £5.20, 2&3 £12.00. CSF £43.24 CT £219.86 TOTE £4.40: £1.70, £2.60, £2.00; EX 34.10 Trifecta £45.70 Pool: £283.32 - 4.58 winning units..
Owner Page, Ward, Marsh **Bred** Airlie Stud **Trained** Cowbit, Lincs
■ Stewards' Enquiry : James O'Reilly one-day ban: careless riding (Feb 14)

FOCUS
A moderate handicap restricted to apprentices who had not ridden more than 50 winners. The winner, down to a career low mark, stepped up a little on his winter form, while the placed horses were to their recent marks.
Bridge Of Fermoy(IRE) Official explanation: jockey said colt missed the break and never travelled

356 PLAY ROULETTE @ WILLIAMHILL.COM MAIDEN STKS 7f (P)
1:40 (1:41) (Class 5) 3-Y-0+ £2,729 (£806; £403) Stalls Low

Form				RPR
540-	1		**Emirates World (IRE)**[77] 7336 3-8-9 73............ JoeFanning 3	74
			(M Johnston) *trckd ldr: led jst after 2f out: pushed along and hd quite high but readily drew clr* **9/2**[3]	
000-	2	2	**Banda Sea (IRE)**[121] 6412 3-8-9 64............ FergusSweeney 10	69
			(P J Makin) *stdd s and dropped in fr wd draw: hld up at rr of main gp: prog over 1f out though hanging: styd on to snatch 2nd on line* **25/1**	
2-0	3	*shd*	**Commandingpresence (USA)**[21] 121 3-8-5 0 ow1.... MartinDwyer 4	65
			(B J Meehan) *t.k.h: cl up: nt qckn 2f out: styd on to chse wnr last 75yds: lost 2nd on post* **3/1**[2]	
3-65	4	1	**Misyaar (IRE)**[7] 280 3-8-4 65............ GregFairley 6	61
			(M A Jarvis) *t.k.h: trckd ldng pair: chsd wnr wl over 1f out: sn no imp: lost 2 pls last 75yds* **11/4**[1]	
	5	1 1/4	**West Kirk** 3-8-9 0............ NCallan 11	63+
			(W Jarvis) *dropped in fr wd draw and hld up in rr: pushed along 2f out: green but styd on steadily fr over 1f out* **8/1**	
4-42	6	1/2	**It's A Mans World**[14] 200 3-8-9 67............ TonyCulhane 5	61
			(S Dow) *t.k.h: hld up in midfield: effrt 2f out: fnd nil over 1f out* **11/2**	
	7	*nk*	**Mystic Touch** 3-8-9 0............ MickyFenton 7	60
			(Miss E C Lavelle) *hld up at bk of main gp: rn green fr 4f out: 9th over 1f out: pushed along and kpt on steadily* **20/1**	
	8	2 1/4	**Pipers Piping (IRE)** 3-8-9 0............ JimCrowley 1	54
			(J A Osborne) *dwlt: sn cl up on inner: pressing ldrs wl over 1f out: sn wknd rapidly* **16/1**	
	9	5	**El Bravo** 3-8-9 0............ SteveDrowne 8	41
			(G L Moore) *sn wl bhd in last: nvr a factor* **20/1**	
05-0	10	1	**Meg Jicaro**[8] 273 3-8-4 40............ LukeMorris 2	33
			(Mrs L Williamson) *led to jst ins 2f out: wknd rapidly* **100/1**	
0	11	10	**Would I Lie To You**[21] 115 3-8-13 0............ SimonWhitworth 9	11
			(J R Jenkins) *racd wd: in tch to 3f out: wknd rapidly: t.o* **100/1**	

1m 26.2s (1.40) **Going Correction** +0.10s/f (Slow)
WFA 3 from 5yo 18lb 11 Ran SP% **117.6**
Speed ratings (Par 103): **96,93,93,92,91 90,90,87,81,80 69**
toteswinger: 1&2 £27.50, 1&3 £3.70, 2&3 £31.30. CSF £116.66 TOTE £6.20: £2.10, £7.00, £1.70; EX 120.00 TRIFECTA Not won..
Owner Sheikh Hamdan Bin Mohammed Al Maktoum **Bred** Darley **Trained** Middleham Moor, N Yorks

FOCUS
An ordinary maiden, but the winner stepped up on his Godolphin form and there were a couple of pleasing efforts further back.
Banda Sea(IRE) Official explanation: jockey said colt hung left

El Bravo Official explanation: jockey said colt did not appreciate the kickback

357 24HR TELEPHONE BETTING @ WILLIAM HILL 0800 44 40 40 (S) STKS 1m (P)

2:15 (2:16) (Class 6) 4-Y-0+ **£2,047** (£604; £302) **Stalls** High

Form RPR

23-4 **1** **Kipchak (IRE)**[8] 274 4-8-13 60..........(p) MartinDwyer 4 68
(C E Brittain) *taken down early: mde virtually all: jnd 1f out: hung rt last 75yds: hld on u.p* **20/1**

04-1 **2** *shd* **Northern Desert (IRE)**[22] 97 10-9-5 65..........(p) DaneO'Neill 8 74
(S Curran) *hld up in last trio: prog on outer over 2f out: swtchd to inner and effrt over 1f out: jnd wnr fnl 75yds: jst hld* **11/1**

10-4 **3** *¾* **Don Pietro**[9] 244 6-9-5 69..........(p) GregFairley 5 72
(R Curtis) *trckd ldr: chal over 1f out: upsides ent fnl f: nt qckn and hld sn after* **20/1**

00-6 **4** *1½* **Bobski (IRE)**[11] 223 7-8-13 77..........(p) JamieSpencer 9 63
(Miss Gay Kelleway) *stdd s fr wd draw: hld up in last: gng strly whn nt clr run briefly 2f out: threaded through after to take 4th ins fnl f: no ch of rching ldrs* **8/1**[3]

204- **5** *1¼* **Magnitude**[240] 2761 4-9-0 83 ow1.......... GeorgeBaker 11 61
(G L Moore) *racd wd: hld up in midfield: prog over 2f out: sn drvn: hanging and reluctant over 1f out: no imp after* **8/13**[1]

00-4 **6** *2¼* **Royal Straight**[21] 119 4-8-13 59..........(v[1]) NCallan 10 55
(B N Pollock) *trckd ldrs: rdn to dispute 3rd over 2f out: steadily outpcd u.p* **22/1**

06-2 **7** *hd* **Sotik Star (IRE)**[20] 129 6-8-13 70.......... PatCosgrave 1 54
(K A Morgan) *prom: hrd rdn and cl up wl over 1f out: wknd fnl f* **7/1**[2]

646- **8** *3¼* **Convivial Spirit**[56] 7581 5-8-13 57..........(tp) JimCrowley 12 47
(E F Vaughan) *hld up towards rr on inner: effrt over 2f out: drvn over 1f out: sn wknd* **14/1**

6-00 **9** *½* **Prix Masque (IRE)**[7] 280 5-8-13 47..........(t) EdwardCreighton 3 45
(Christian Wroe) *settled towards rr: pushed along 3f out: sn struggling: outpcd over 2f out* **66/1**

060- **10** *5* **Alto Singer (IRE)**[145] 5749 4-8-8 55.......... FrankieMcDonald 7 29
(L A Dace) *prom 3f: rdn over 4f out and losing pl: struggling after* **100/1**

103- **11** *nk* **Waterside (IRE)**[324] 870 10-8-13 87.......... PaulDoe 2 33
(S Curran) *taken steadily to post: prom: rdn 3f out: sn wknd* **14/1**

1m 37.58s (-0.62) **Going Correction** +0.10s/f (Slow) **11 Ran SP% 123.6**
Speed ratings (Par 101): **107,106,106,104,103 101,100,97,97,92 91**
toteswinger: 1&2 £15.60, 1&3 £19.10, 2&3 £16.40. CSF £221.41 TOTE £22.10: £4.30, £3.40, £4.10; EX 144.40 Trifecta £384.60 Part won. Pool: £519.84 - 0.44 winning units..
Owner C E Brittain **Bred** Miss Mary Davidson & Mrs Steffi Von Schilcher **Trained** Newmarket, Suffolk

FOCUS
A good, competitive seller, even with some of the higher rated runners not performing at their best. The runner-up looks the best guide to the form.
Waterside(IRE) Official explanation: jockey said gelding made a noise

358 BETLIVE & IN-RUNNING @ WILLIAMHILL.COM MAIDEN STKS 5f (P)

2:45 (2:46) (Class 5) 3-Y-0 **£2,729** (£806; £403) **Stalls** High

Form RPR

2-2 **1** **Theatre Street (IRE)**[15] 188 3-8-12 0.......... NCallan 4 73+
(J Noseda) *led after 100yds: mde rest: reminders ins fnl f: styd on* **8/15**[1]

2 *1¾* **Under Review (IRE)** 3-9-3 0.......... JamieSpencer 5 72+
(S A Callaghan) *s.i.s: off the pce in last pair: prog to chse wnr over 2f out: tried to cl over 1f out but green: wl hld after* **3/1**[2]

0-4 **3** *3½* **Theta Wave (USA)**[20] 127 3-9-3 0.......... AdamKirby 1 59
(J R Gask) *chsd ldrs: disp 2nd over 2f out: lft bhd by ldng pair wl over 1f out* **8/1**[3]

-0 **4** *5* **Thoosa**[6] 286 3-8-12 0.......... BrianReilly 2 36
(P S McEntee) *s.i.s: off the pce in last pair: nvr a factor: passed 2 rivals fnl f* **100/1**

560- **5** *3* **Alimarr (IRE)**[44] 7719 3-8-12 60..........(p) DaleGibson 6 25
(S Parr) *fast away: led 100yds: chsd wnr to over 2f out: wknd* **20/1**

0-5 **6** *¾* **Countrywide Jaime (IRE)**[23] 85 3-8-5 0.......... HollyHall[(7)] 3 23
(S A Callaghan) *in tch to 1/2-way: sn lft wl bhd* **33/1**

59.98 secs (1.18) **Going Correction** +0.10s/f (Slow) **6 Ran SP% 110.0**
Speed ratings (Par 97): **94,91,85,77,72 71**
toteswinger: 1&2 £1.02, 1&3 £2.20, 2&3 £2.60. CSF £2.21 TOTE £1.50: £1.02, £1.70; EX 2.70.
Owner The Honorable Earle I Mack **Bred** M J Killeen **Trained** Newmarket, Suffolk

FOCUS
A modest sprint maiden, but the first two are both likely to do better.

359 LIVE CASINO GAMES @ WILLIAMHILL.COM H'CAP 5f (P)

3:20 (3:21) (Class 2) (0-100,102) 4-Y-0+ **£11,656** (£3,468; £1,733; £865) **Stalls** High

Form RPR

-013 **1** **Matsunosuke**[14] 204 7-9-6 102.......... LukeMorris 7 112
(A B Coogan) *hld up in 6th: prog on outer over 1f out: led last 150yds: powered clr* **9/2**[3]

630- **2** *2¼* **Swiss Franc**[45] 7703 4-9-4 100.......... JamieSpencer 6 102
(D R C Elsworth) *led 1f: chsd ldr: clsd to chal ent fnl f: sn outpcd by wnr* **9/4**[1]

42-2 **3** *¾* **Little Edward**[14] 204 11-8-1 88.......... MCGeran[(5)] 5 87
(R J Hodges) *chsd ldng pair: rdn and nt qckn over 1f out: kpt on same pce after* **5/1**

15-1 **4** *½* **Doubtful Sound (USA)**[14] 204 5-8-13 95..........(p) JimCrowley 2 92
(R Hollinshead) *led after 1f: kicked 2 l clr 2f out: hdd & wknd fnl 150yds* **3/1**[2]

42-0 **5** *1* **Ebraam (USA)**[14] 204 6-8-10 95.......... TolleyDean[(3)] 1 89
(P Howling) *hld up in last pair: gng strly 2f out: effrt on inner over 1f out: kpt on same pce: no ch* **8/1**

11-5 **6** *½* **Thoughtsofstardom**[8] 270 6-7-13 86 oh11.......... AmyBaker[(5)] 8 78
(P S McEntee) *hld up in last pair: rdn over 1f out: nt pce to get involved* **25/1**

00-0 **7** *4½* **Haajes**[11] 225 5-8-9 91..........(t) DaleGibson 4 67
(S Parr) *t.k.h: hld up in 5th: drvn 1/2-way: wknd 2f out* **20/1**

000- **8** *8* **Stoneacre Lad (IRE)**[112] 6653 6-9-4 100..........(b) GeorgeBaker 3 47
(Peter Grayson) *mostly in 4th tl wknd rapidly on inner over 1f out: t.o* **22/1**

58.39 secs (-0.41) **Going Correction** +0.10s/f (Slow) **8 Ran SP% 114.7**
Speed ratings (Par 109): **107,103,102,101,99 99,91,79**
toteswinger: 1&2 £3.70, 1&3 £5.10, 2&3 £3.80. CSF £14.69 CT £51.72 TOTE £6.00: £1.80, £1.20, £1.90; EX 18.20 Trifecta £173.50 Pool: £626.07 - 2.67 winning units..
Owner A B Coogan **Bred** R Coogan **Trained** Soham, Cambs

FOCUS
The pace was predictably furious, and Matsunosuke recorded another personal best.

NOTEBOOK
Matsunosuke was ideally suited by the strong gallop and picked up in fine style down the outside. Although this looked a soft enough race for the class, he was much the best and his form has reached a new level this winter, with this victory off 102 surely a career-best effort. He is now 5-15 on Polytrack, and has placed a further six times on this surface. (op 11-2 tchd 6-1)
Swiss Franc, contesting a handicap for the first time, was possibly a touch keen early on, with Jamie Spencer sensibly not wanting to get into a speed dual with Doubtful Sound. He kept on for pressure in the straight, but did not pick up anywhere near as well as the winner. (op 3-1)
Little Edward ran an honest race but simply found a couple too good. He continues to hold his form well and is a credit to his connections. (tchd 9-2)
Doubtful Sound(USA) has been a revelation since joining this yard, but he probably went off a little too fast this time and could not defy a 7lb rise for his recent success over 6f around here. A slightly more patient ride will probably suit better next time and he remains one to keep on side. (op 5-2)
Ebraam(USA) had to wait for a gap in the straight, but the response was limited when asked. (op 13-2 tchd 6-1)
Thoughtsofstardom's proximity surely confirms the form is nothing out of the ordinary, as he was forced to race off a mark of 86 (11lb out of the weights), and his best previous RPR was only 81.
Stoneacre Lad(IRE) Official explanation: jockey said horse hung left under pressure

360 PLAY ROULETTE @ WILLIAMHILL.COM H'CAP 1m 4f (P)

3:55 (3:55) (Class 2) (0-100,99) 4-Y-0+ **£11,656** (£3,468; £1,733; £865) **Stalls** Low

Form RPR

013- **1** **Robby Bobby**[33] 7814 4-8-8 89.......... GregFairley 8 96
(M Johnston) *trckd ldng pair: wnt 2nd 2f out: led over 1f out and idled briefly: pushed out firmly fnl f: jst hld on* **8/1**

150- **2** *hd* **Emerald Wilderness (IRE)**[227] 3122 5-9-4 95.......... RichardHughes 9 102+
(A King) *stdd s: keen early: hld up in last: stl there whn swtchd rt to outer over 1f out: str run fnl f: needed two more strides* **6/1**[2]

21-1 **3** *1* **Wine 'n Dine**[24] 72 4-8-5 86.......... JimmyQuinn 2 91
(G L Moore) *t.k.h early: trckd ldrs: effrt 2f out: disp 2nd 1f out: sn outpcd* **13/2**[3]

312- **4** *nk* **Lochiel**[42] 7747 5-8-9 86.......... NCallan 1 91
(G A Swinbank) *trckd ldng pair: effrt 2f out: disp 2nd 1f out: one pce* **7/1**

006- **5** *¾* **Grand Passion (IRE)**[42] 7741 9-9-8 99.......... GeorgeBaker 7 102
(C F Wall) *hld up in rr: effrt and wdst of all ent st: kpt on same pce and no threat* **17/2**

03-5 **6** *¾* **John Terry (IRE)**[21] 124 6-8-13 90.......... JimCrowley 3 92
(Mrs A J Perrett) *t.k.h: cl up: wnt 2nd 1/2-way: led over 2f out to over 1f out: wknd fnl f* **4/1**[1]

40-1 **7** *2¾* **Evident Pride (USA)**[28] 33 6-8-13 90.......... IanMongan 4 88
(B R Johnson) *hld up towards rr: effrt on inner 2f out: sn no prog: wknd fnl f* **4/1**[1]

226- **8** *¾* **War Of The Roses (IRE)**[55] 7595 6-8-5 85 oh3.......... AndrewMullen[(3)] 6 82
(R Brotherton) *hld up in last pair: effrt on outer 2f out: nt qckn wl over 1f out: wl btn after* **10/1**

060- **9** *17* **Maslak (IRE)**[104] 4742 5-8-12 89.......... DarrenWilliams 5 58
(P W Hiatt) *led: set v stdy pce to 1/2-way: hdd & wknd rapidly over 2f out: eased: t.o* **20/1**

2m 33.13s (0.13) **Going Correction** +0.10s/f (Slow)
WFA 4 from 5yo+ 4lb **9 Ran SP% 115.6**
Speed ratings (Par 109): **103,102,102,102,101 101,99,98,87**
toteswinger: 1&2 £6.70, 1&3 £4.50, 2&3 £5.20. CSF £55.29 CT £332.84 TOTE £10.60: £2.50, £1.80, £2.30; EX 72.10 Trifecta £369.60 Part won. Pool: £499.48 - 0.44 winning units..
Owner C M , B J & R F Batterham li **Bred** Highclere Stud **Trained** Middleham Moor, N Yorks

FOCUS
A good handicap, but the early pace was very steady (as usual for this trip at Lingfield), resulting in the entire field being covered by little more than three lengths at the top of the straight. The form needs treating with caution, but the winner looks as though he is capable of better still, and the runner-up looked unlucky.

NOTEBOOK
Robby Bobby was trying his furthest trip to date, but having won over 1m3f at Southwell stamina was not really an issue, especially considering the lack of pace. He was always well positioned and picked up nicely when asked, but he initially carryied his head at a slight angle and he was possibly idling late on, as he only just held on. There is apparently a race for him at Kempton on February 18. (tchd 9-1)
Emerald Wilderness(IRE) ◆ just got going too late and looked an unlucky loser. With the blinkers left off for this first run in 227 days, he was restrained well in rear after refusing to settle early on, and would undoubtedly have preferred a better gallop. He was going noticeably well turning into the straight, but was denied a clear run and found the line coming just too soon once he was switched out wide. (op 4-1)
Wine 'n Dine, attempting a hat-trick after wins in lesser company at Kempton, firstly over today's trip and then over 2m, ran well off a 5lb higher mark considering the steady pace was against him. He was keen early and would obviously have been seen in an even better light had there been more emphasis on stamina. (op 7-1 tchd 8-1 and 6-1)
Lochiel is yet another who was probably unsuited by the modest tempo and this was a creditable effort off a career-high mark. (op 8-1 tchd 9-1)
Grand Passion(IRE), dropping back to handicap company over a longer trip than usual, was produced with his chance from off the pace down the outside in the straight, but he failed to pick up. (op 10-1 tchd 11-1 and 8-1)
John Terry(IRE) won this last year but was too keen and did not see his race out. (op 9-2 tchd 7-2)
Evident Pride(USA), 2lb higher than when winning over course and distance last time, did not get the best of runs in the straight but failed to pick up when in the clear. (op 7-2)

361 24HR TELEPHONE BETTING @ WILLIAM HILL 0800 44 40 40 H'CAP 1m 2f (P)

4:25 (4:25) (Class 4) (0-80,80) 4-Y-0+ **£4,857** (£1,445; £722; £360) **Stalls** Low

Form RPR

31-1 **1** **Folio (IRE)**[16] 172 9-9-1 76.......... StephenDonohoe 8 83
(W J Musson) *trckd ldng pair: wnt 2nd 2f out: hrd rdn to cl on ldr fnl f: led nr fin* **14/1**

54-1 **2** *½* **Millie's Rock (IRE)**[21] 125 4-8-9 72.......... NCallan 7 78
(K A Ryan) *t.k.h: trckd ldr: led over 2f out and sn kicked 2 l clr: drvn fnl f: hdd nr fin* **7/2**[1]

00-5 **3** *¾* **Kestrel Cross (IRE)**[17] 163 7-8-11 72..........(t) LukeMorris 4 76
(A W Carroll) *hld up in last trio: prog on outer over 2f out: hrd rdn to cl on ldrs 1f out: kpt on: nvr quite able to chal* **20/1**

32-2 **4** *½* **Summer Winds**[17] 163 4-8-12 75.......... RobertHavlin 2 78
(T G Mills) *hld up in 6th: prog on inner over 2f out: drvn and kpt on fr over 1f out: nvr quite able to chal* **5/1**[2]

35-1 **5** *2½* **Annabelle's Charm (IRE)**[21] 120 4-8-9 72.......... JamieSpencer 1 70+
(L M Cumani) *hld up in last: prog into 7th whn hanging and rn into wall of trble 2f out: pushed along and modest prog 1f out: eased fnl 50yds* **7/2**[1]

133- **6** ½ **Action Impact (ARG)**[35] 7791 5-9-0 **75** .... GeorgeBaker 5 72
(G L Moore) *settled in midfield: rdn and effrt over 2f out: sn chsd ldng trio: no imp over 1f out: wknd* **7/2**[1]

02-0 **7** 6 **Emperor Court (IRE)**[24] 79 5-9-5 **80** .... SteveDrowne 6 65
(P J Makin) *racd freely: led to over 2f out: wknd* **9/1**[3]

040/ **8** nk **Royal Wedding**[43] 2084 7-8-12 **73** .... JimCrowley 3 57
(N J Gifford) *trckd ldng pair tl wknd on inner 3f out* **25/1**

500- **9** 1 ¾ **Cantabilly (IRE)**[98] 6898 6-8-9 **75** .... MCGeran(5) 9 56
(R J Hodges) *hld up in last trio: hrd rdn over 3f out: sn btn and bhd* **16/1**

2m 5.27s (-1.33) **Going Correction** +0.10s/f (Slow)
WFA 4 from 5yo+ 2lb **9** Ran SP% **114.5**
Speed ratings (Par 105): **109,108,108,107,105 105,100,100,98**
toteswinger: 1&2 £13.00, 1&3 £16.40, 2&3 £29.40. CSF £62.13 CT £994.10 TOTE £14.90: £3.00, £1.50, £3.90; EX 42.50 TRIFECTA Not won. .
Owner Goodey and Broughton **Bred** Lord Rothschild **Trained** Newmarket, Suffolk

FOCUS
A fair handicap run at an ordinary pace.
Annabelle's Charm(IRE) Official explanation: jockey said filly hung badly right on final bend
T/Plt: £102.60 to a £1 stake. Pool: £66,985.18. 476.33 winning tickets. T/Qpdt: £22.00 to a £1 stake. Pool: £4,295.10. 144.00 winning tickets. JN

[322]SOUTHWELL (L-H)
Sunday, February 1

OFFICIAL GOING: Standard
With snow falling, the track was harrowed between races, and there was an inspection after the fifth.
Wind: Light, half-against Weather: Snow showers

362 COME JUMP RACING TOMORROW H'CAP 1m (F)
1:20 (1:21) (Class 5) (0-70,70) 4-Y-0+ **£2,729** (£806; £403) **Stalls** Low

Form RPR

0-03 **1** **Hilbre Court (USA)**[12] 224 4-8-11 **63** .... (p) GrahamGibbons 8 73
(B P J Baugh) *hld up: hdwy 1/2-way: led over 1f out: sn rdn and edgd lft: r.o* **6/1**

-440 **2** 1 ¾ **Inside Story (IRE)**[7] 289 7-8-11 **63** .... (b) AdamKirby 9 69
(C R Dore) *prom: lost pl 5f out: hdwy u.p and hung lft fr over 1f out: r.o* **8/1**

213- **3** nk **Baratarla**[44] 7731 7-9-3 **69** .... TomEaves 2 74
(R Bastiman) *hld up in tch: rdn over 1f out: r.o* **10/1**

260- **4** nk **Lord Theo**[43] 7742 5-9-0 **66** .... LukeMorris 3 71
(N P Littmoden) *chsd ldrs: rdn 5f out: chsd wnr over 1f out: styd on* **9/1**

4-23 **5** ¾ **Betteras Bertie**[26] 63 6-8-4 **56** oh1 .... JimmyQuinn 6 59
(M Brittain) *s.s: hld up: hdwy over 1f out: nt rch ldrs* **9/2**[3]

2-22 **6** 2 ¼ **Rock Anthem (IRE)**[18] 157 5-9-1 **67** .... TonyCulhane 4 65
(Mike Murphy) *chsd ldr: led 5f out: rdn and hdd over 1f out: wknd ins fnl f* **10/3**[1]

23-1 **7** 4 **West End Lad**[12] 224 6-9-3 **69** .... (b) DaneO'Neill 7 57
(S R Bowring) *chsd ldrs: rdn 1/2-way: wknd over 2f out* **7/2**[2]

33/0 **8** 13 **Strategic Knight (USA)**[8] 280 4-8-9 **66** ow1 .... JamesO'Reilly(5) 5 25
(R C Guest) *hld up: rdn 1/2-way: sn wknd* **33/1**

010- **9** 2 ¼ **Bahamian Lad**[338] 756 4-8-11 **70** .... DavidKenny(7) 11 23
(R Hollinshead) *prom: chsd ldr over 4f out: rdn over 2f out: wknd over 1f out* **40/1**

60-4 **10** 2 ¼ **Bespoke Boy**[11] 132 4-8-1 **58** .... (t) PatrickDonaghy(5) 1 6
(P C Haslam) *sn led: hdd 5f out: rdn and wknd over 2f out* **16/1**

06-0 **11** 44 **Bury Treasure (IRE)**[17] 171 4-8-9 **61** .... JerryO'Dwyer 10 —
(Miss Gay Kelleway) *sn outpcd: bhd fnl 3f: t.o* **50/1**

1m 44.01s (0.31) **Going Correction** +0.125s/f (Slow) **11** Ran SP% **121.2**
Speed ratings (Par 103): **103,101,100,100,99 97,93,80,78,76 32**
toteswinger: 1&2 £13.30, 1&3 £16.10, 2&3 £16.60. CSF £54.47 CT £491.38 TOTE £10.10: £2.80, £3.50, £2.70; EX 50.00 TRIFECTA Not won..
Owner Saddle Up Racing **Bred** Richard Nip & Omar Trevino **Trained** Audley, Staffs

FOCUS
A modest but reasonably competitive handicap. The pace seemed fair enough and the form looks straightforward for the grade.
West End Lad Official explanation: trainer's rep had no explanation for the poor form shown

363 MEMBERSHIP AT SOUTHWELL GOLF CLUB (S) STKS 1m (F)
1:50 (1:50) (Class 6) 3-Y-O **£2,047** (£604; £302) **Stalls** Low

Form RPR

0-6 **1** **Patronne**[6] 296 3-8-6 0 .... StephenDonohoe 5 56
(Sir Mark Prescott) *led 1f: chsd ldr tl led over 1f out: sn rdn and hdd: rallied to ld ins fnl f: r.o* **13/2**

4103 **2** nk **Hawkspring (IRE)**[11] 239 3-9-2 65 .... (t) AdamKirby 8 65
(S Parr) *chsd ldrs: rdn over 3f out: led 1f out: sn hdd: unable qck towards fin* **11/8**[1]

6-30 **3** 1 ½ **Special Bond**[11] 231 3-8-6 63 .... FrankieMcDonald 3 52
(J A Osborne) *prom: outpcd over 2f out: styd on u.p fr over 1f out* **6/1**[3]

00-0 **4** 3 **Northern Shore (IRE)**[24] 92 3-8-11 20 .... (b) NCallan 9 50
(K A Ryan) *led 7f out: rdn and hdd over 1f out: hung rt and wknd ins fnl f* **33/1**

-605 **5** 6 **Betws Y Coed (IRE)**[6] 296 3-8-6 53 .... (p) NeilChalmers 6 31
(A Bailey) *hld up: styd on fr over 1f out: n.d* **15/2**

00-2 **6** 5 **Cash In The Attic**[6] 296 3-8-6 48 .... EdwardCreighton 10 19
(M R Channon) *s.s: hld up: bmpd 5f out: rdn and wknd over 3f out* **5/1**[2]

006- **7** 5 **The Canny Dove (USA)**[197] 4203 3-8-4 45 .... AdamCarter(7) 4 13
(T D Barron) *mid-div: rdn over 4f out: sn wknd* **33/1**

50-4 **8** ½ **That Boy Ronaldo**[24] 92 3-8-1 45 .... DanielleMcCreery(5) 7 7
(A Berry) *hld up: hung rt 5f out: rdn and wknd over 3f out* **40/1**

26-6 **9** shd **Kneesy Earsy Nosey**[12] 228 3-8-10 53 ow4 .... AnnStokell(5) 1 15
(Miss A Stokell) *mid-div: sn pushed along: rdn and wknd over 3f out* **25/1**

50 **10** 7 **Snoozing**[11] 231 3-8-3 0 ow4 .... AshleyMorgan(7) 2 —
(M H Tompkins) *s.i.s: a in rr: wknd over 3f out* **80/1**

1m 45.81s (2.11) **Going Correction** +0.125s/f (Slow) **10** Ran SP% **111.6**
Speed ratings (Par 95): **94,93,92,89,83 78,73,72,72,65**
toteswinger: 1&2 £3.90, 1&3 £5.70, 2&3 £2.20. CSF £14.56 TOTE £8.70: £2.40, £1.10, £2.50; EX 20.80 Trifecta £105.00 Pool: £244.15 - 1.72 winning units..The winner was sold to Ann Stokell for 3,000gns.
Owner Miss K Rausing **Bred** Miss K Rausing **Trained** Newmarket, Suffolk

FOCUS
A standard three-year-old seller, run in miserable conditions. The runner-up is the best guide to the form.

364 SOUTHWELL RACECOURSE FOR CONFERENCES MAIDEN STKS 6f (F)
2:20 (2:20) (Class 5) 3-Y-O **£2,729** (£806; £403) **Stalls** Low

Form RPR

43- **1** **Premier Lad**[117] 6548 3-9-3 0 .... TomEaves 1 75+
(T D Barron) *trckd ldrs: plld hrd: rdn to ld and hung rt over 1f out: r.o* **9/4**[2]

0- **2** 2 ¾ **Iron Out (USA)**[193] 4296 3-9-3 0 .... GrahamGibbons 8 66
(R Hollinshead) *chsd ldrs: rdn over 1f out: styd on same pce ins fnl f* **7/2**[3]

5-4 **3** 1 ¾ **Kamanja (UAE)**[23] 98 3-8-12 0 .... NCallan 5 55
(M A Jarvis) *wnt lft s: sn led: rdn and hung rt fr over 2f out: hdd over 1f out: no ex ins fnl f* **13/8**[1]

00- **4** 4 ½ **Perfect Honour (IRE)**[121] 6451 3-8-12 0 .... DarrenWilliams 2 41
(D Shaw) *prom: rdn over 2f out: wknd fnl f* **66/1**

0 **5** 1 ¾ **Brett Vale (IRE)**[11] 236 3-9-3 0 .... StephenDonohoe 4 40+
(Sir Mark Prescott) *s.i.s and hmpd s: outpcd: r.o ins fnl f: nvr nrr* **16/1**

0 **6** ½ **Sampower Shamrock (IRE)**[10] 251 3-8-13 0 ow1 .... DNolan 6 35
(D Carroll) *sn pushed along in rr: wknd over 3f out* **40/1**

00 **7** ½ **April Lady (IRE)**[7] 286 3-8-7 0 .... SladeO'Hara(5) 7 32
(A Berry) *chsd ldrs: rdn over 3f out: wknd over 2f out* **66/1**

8 9 **Geese A Laying (IRE)** 3-8-12 0 .... TPQueally 3 —
(J A Osborne) *s.i.s and hmpd s: hld up: rdn and wknd 3f out* **17/2**

1m 18.51s (2.01) **Going Correction** +0.125s/f (Slow) **8** Ran SP% **112.9**
Speed ratings (Par 97): **91,87,85,79,76 76,75,63**
toteswinger: 1&2 £3.30, 1&3 £1.70, 2&3 £2.20. CSF £10.28 TOTE £3.20: £1.10, £1.40, £1.30; EX 11.30 Trifecta £35.50 Pool: £319.84 - 6.66 winning units..
Owner J Browne **Bred** C J Murfitt **Trained** Maunby, N Yorks

FOCUS
This maiden was run in a heavy snow storm and must have been an abysmal experience for those taking part. Visibility was limited for some of the way. The winning time was 0.63 seconds slower than the following claimer (won by a filly rated 67) and form looks just modest. Not a race to view too positively.

365 PLAY GOLF AT SOUTHWELL GOLF CLUB CLAIMING STKS 6f (F)
2:50 (2:52) (Class 6) 3-Y-O **£2,047** (£604; £302) **Stalls** Low

Form RPR

0-31 **1** **Madison Belle**[26] 64 3-8-9 67 .... DarrenWilliams 3 72
(K R Burke) *s.i.s: sn trcking ldrs: led over 1f out: edgd rt ins fnl f: comf* **4/7**[1]

46-4 **2** 2 ¼ **Inthawain**[20] 137 3-8-1 61 .... DuranFentiman(3) 1 60
(N Wilson) *chsd ldr tl led over 2f out: rdn and hdd over 1f out: styd on same pce ins fnl f* **8/1**[3]

15-2 **3** 6 **Glan Lady (IRE)**[30] 10 3-8-3 53 ow3 .... (b) KevinGhunowa(3) 6 43
(G J Smith) *s.s: outpcd: rdn 1/2-way: mod late prog: nrst fin* **5/1**[2]

32-0 **4** ¾ **Bold Account (IRE)**[11] 229 3-8-1 60 .... (p) AndrewHeffernan(7) 2 42
(Garry Moss) *led: rdn and hdd over 2f out: wknd over 1f out* **9/1**

500- **5** 4 ½ **Time Loup**[75] 7372 3-8-8 49 .... AndrewElliott 5 28
(S R Bowring) *chsd ldrs: rdn over 3f out: wknd 2f out* **11/1**

1m 17.88s (1.38) **Going Correction** +0.125s/f (Slow) **5** Ran SP% **109.8**
Speed ratings (Par 95): **95,92,84,83,77**
toteswinger: 1&2 £5.50. CSF £5.77 TOTE £1.50: £1.20, £2.60; EX 6.00.
Owner Paul Sweeting & Mrs L Wright **Bred** Paul Sweeting **Trained** Middleham Moor, N Yorks

FOCUS
A modest, uncompetitive claimer with doubts over all bar the winner, who may not have had to improve.
Glan Lady(IRE) Official explanation: jockey said filly missed the break

366 SOUTHWELL-RACECOURSE.CO.UK H'CAP 7f (F)
3:20 (3:20) (Class 6) (0-60,61) 3-Y-O **£2,047** (£604; £302) **Stalls** Low

Form RPR

050- **1** **Esprit De Midas**[104] 6863 3-9-4 **60** .... NCallan 1 76+
(K A Ryan) *chsd ldr: led 5f out: rdn and hung lft over 1f out: clr whn hung rt ins fnl f* **2/1**[2]

46-1 **2** 4 ½ **Dancing Wave**[30] 10 3-8-11 **58** .... AmyBaker(5) 3 59
(M C Chapman) *s.i.s: sn rcvrd to ld: hdd 5f out: chsd wnr thereafter: rdn 1/2-way: outpcd fr over 1f out* **16/1**

50-0 **3** 6 **Pedregal**[11] 236 3-8-8 **50** .... PaulHanagan 5 35
(R A Fahey) *sn hung rt and outpcd: r.o ins fnl f: nrst fin* **9/1**

2-32 **4** 2 ¼ **Imperial Skylight**[9] 267 3-9-5 **61** .... TonyCulhane 4 40
(M R Channon) *chsd ldrs: rdn 1/2-way: wknd over 1f out* **15/8**[1]

05-3 **5** 1 ¼ **Jack's House (IRE)**[24] 92 3-8-12 **54** .... (tp) TPQueally 6 29
(Jane Chapple-Hyam) *chsd ldrs: rdn 1/2-way: wknd over 2f out* **8/1**

203- **6** 62 **Captain Cavendish (IRE)**[51] 7652 3-9-4 **60** .... (v) MickyFenton 7 —
(A Bailey) *s.s: outpcd: eased fnl 2f: t.o* **4/1**[3]

1m 32.19s (1.89) **Going Correction** +0.125s/f (Slow) **6** Ran SP% **115.1**
Speed ratings (Par 95): **94,88,82,79,78 7**
toteswinger: 1&2 £4.20, 1&3 £4.70, 2&3 £8.60. CSF £31.62 TOTE £3.10: £2.00, £4.10; EX 30.10.
Owner Joseph Ogden, J Hanson, John Ogden **Bred** Jeremy Green And Sons **Trained** Hambleton, N Yorks

FOCUS
A moderate, uncompetitive contest in which the winner made a mockery of his mark. He showed big improvement and can win again, but this form is weak.
Esprit De Midas ◆ Official explanation: trainer's rep said, regarding apparent improvement in form, that the gelding had been a backward 2yo and was having its first run on all-weather track, and benefited from being gelded
Captain Cavendish(IRE) Official explanation: jockey said gelding lost its action

367 BOOK YOUR TICKETS ON LINE AT SOUTHWELL H'CAP 5f (F)
3:50 (3:52) (Class 6) (0-55,55) 4-Y-0+ **£2,047** (£604; £302) **Stalls** High

Form RPR

0-54 **1** **Mr Rooney (IRE)**[17] 173 6-8-9 **52** .... SladeO'Hara(5) 4 59
(A Berry) *s.i.s: hdwy u.p 2f out: led ins fnl f: r.o* **8/1**

015- **2** nse **Whozart (IRE)**[89] 7176 6-9-3 **55** .... DanielTudhope 8 62
(A Dickman) *a.p: rdn over 1f out: ev ch ins fnl f: r.o* **12/1**

03-4 **3** ¾ **Argentine (IRE)**[16] 198 5-9-0 **52** .... GregFairley 2 56
(L Lungo) *s.i.s: outpcd: swtchd rt 2f out: hdwy u.p over 1f out: r.o* **4/1**[3]

60-0 **4** ½ **Blakeshall Quest**[24] 95 9-8-12 **53** .... (b) AndrewMullen(3) 9 55
(R Brotherton) *chsd ldrs: rdn to ld 1f out: sn hdd: styd on same pce* **40/1**

43-0 **5** 1 ½ **Cabopino (IRE)**[12] 222 4-9-0 **52** .... NCallan 1 49
(K R Burke) *chsd ldrs: outpcd 3f out: sn edgd lft: hdwy u.p over 1f out: styd on same pce ins fnl f* **7/1**

50-5 **6** 1 **Ace Club**[3] 328 8-8-1 **46** oh1 .... (b) AndrewHeffernan(7) 5 39
(Garry Moss) *led to 1/2-way: sn rdn: styd on same pce fnl f* **20/1**

-043 **7** *1* **Ronnie Howe**[5] 303 5-9-0 **52**...........(bt) DaneO'Neill 7 41
(S R Bowring) *hmpd s: sn chsng ldrs: led 1/2-way: rdn and hdd 1f out: wknd ins fnl f* **3/1**[1]
403- **8** *3 3/4* **Rainbow Bay**[128] 6251 6-9-1 **53**...........(p) TPQueally 6 29
(Miss Tracy Waggott) *s.i.s and hmpd s: outpcd* **8/1**
2-22 **9** *3 1/4* **Ridley Didley (IRE)**[17] 177 4-9-3 **55**........... LeeEnstone 10 19
(N Wilson) *s.i.s: sn chsng ldrs: rdn and wknd over 1f out* **7/2**[2]
000- **10** *8* **Safranine (IRE)**[159] 5374 12-8-10 **53** oh1 ow7........... AnnStokell(5) 11 —
(Miss A Stokell) *sn hung lft and outpcd* **66/1**

61.55 secs (1.85) **Going Correction** +0.40s/f (Slow) **10** Ran SP% **118.3**
Speed ratings (Par 101): **101,100,99,98,96 94,93,87,82,69**
toteswinger: 1&2 £9.00, 1&3 £7.60, 2&3 £7.80. CSF £98.45 CT £456.73 TOTE £10.60: £2.70, £2.30, £1.70; EX 101.60 Trifecta £306.60 Part won. Pool: £414.36 - 0.20 winning units..
Owner Alan Berry **Bred** Rathasker Stud **Trained** Cockerham, Lancs
■ Stewards' Enquiry : Slade O'Hara one-day ban: used whip with excessive frequency down shoulder in the forehand position (Feb 15)

FOCUS
A very moderate sprint handicap, run at a strong pace. Straightforward form.
Ridley Didley(IRE) Official explanation: jockey said gelding ran flat

368 HOSPITALITY AT SOUTHWELL RACECOURSE H'CAP 1m 4f (F)
4:20 (4:20) (Class 6) (0-60,60) 4-Y-0+ **£2,047** (£604; £302) **Stalls** Low

Form RPR
4633 **1** **General Tufto**[11] 240 4-7-11 **46** oh1...........(b) RichardRowe(7) 13 54
(C Smith) *prom: chsd ldr 9f out: led over 4f out: rdn and hung lft fr over 2f out: styd on* **20/1**
2-40 **2** *1 1/4* **Dazzling Begum**[19] 147 4-8-9 **51**........... JerryO'Dwyer 5 57
(J Pearce) *hld up: hdwy over 4f out: rdn over 2f out: chsd ldr over 1f out: edgd lft: styd on* **8/1**[2]
03-4 **3** *1/2* **Alberts Story (USA)**[16] 193 5-8-9 **48**...........(p) PaulHanagan 9 53
(R A Fahey) *hld up: hdwy over 4f out: outpcd over 2f out: rallied u.p and hung lft over 1f out: styd on* **5/1**[1]
00/0 **4** *1 1/4* **Eforetta (GER)**[30] 8 7-9-4 **57**........... LukeMorris 11 60
(A W Carroll) *prom: rdn over 2f out: styd on same pce fnl f* **8/1**[2]
0-63 **5** *7* **Norwegian**[10] 254 8-8-7 **46** oh1...........(p) StephenDonohoe 2 38
(Ian Williams) *s.i.s: hld up: hdwy u.p over 3f out: wknd over 1f out* **16/1**
00-1 **6** *2 1/4* **Raquel White**[28] 40 5-9-4 **60**........... KevinGhunowa(3) 1 48+
(J L Flint) *hld up in tch: hmpd and lost pl over 6f out: rdn over 2f out: n.d after* **8/1**[2]
24-0 **7** *hd* **Ba Dreamflight**[14] 213 4-8-12 **54**........... TravisBlock 12 42
(H Morrison) *chsd ldrs: rdn over 5f out: wknd over 1f out* **8/1**[2]
2-32 **8** *nk* **Gayanula (USA)**[19] 147 4-8-9 **58**........... BMcHugh(7) 3 45
(Miss J A Camacho) *unruly in stalls: broke wl: sn outpcd: hdwy over 4f out: rdn over 3f out: hung lft 2f out: sn wknd* **5/1**[1]
52-3 **9** *10* **Miss Understanding**[19] 145 4-8-4 **46**...........(b) JoeFanning 7 17
(J R Weymes) *hld up in tch: swtchd lft 6f out: chsd wnr 3f out: sn edgd rt: wknd 2f out* **10/1**[3]
-300 **10** *4* **Thornaby Green**[3] 324 8-8-7 **53**...........(b[1]) AdamCarter(7) 14 18
(T D Barron) *led after 1f: rdn and hdd over 4f out: hmpd and wknd over 2f out* **20/1**
-404 **11** *2 3/4* **Doctor Delta**[9] 275 4-8-4 **46**........... JimmyQuinn 10 7
(M Brittain) *hld up: pushed along 8f out: hdwy over 5f out: wknd over 2f out* **11/1**
06-5 **12** *14* **Blushing Heart**[19] 147 5-9-4 **57**........... MickyFenton 8 —
(G M Moore) *led 1f: chsd ldrs: rdn and wknd over 4f out* **12/1**
160- **13** *35* **Speagle (IRE)**[325] 863 7-9-3 **56**........... DarrenWilliams 4 —
(D Shaw) *hld up in tch: lost pl over 5f out: sn bhd: eased fnl 3f: t.o* **20/1**

2m 41.39s (0.39) **Going Correction** +0.125s/f (Slow)
WFA 4 from 5yo+ 3lb **13** Ran SP% **123.1**
Speed ratings (Par 101): **103,102,101,101,96 94,94,94,87,85 83,74,50**
toteswinger: 1&2 £45.00, 1&3 £29.10, 2&3 £11.20. CSF £172.80 CT £931.03 TOTE £26.40: £5.90, £3.10, £1.60; EX 363.80 TRIFECTA Not won. Place 6 £61.98, Place 5 £13.78.
Owner Phil Martin **Bred** Hascombe And Valiant Studs **Trained** Temple Bruer, Lincs
■ Stewards' Enquiry : Micky Fenton two-day ban: careless riding (Feb 15-16)
Richard Rowe four-day ban: careless riding (Feb 15-18)

FOCUS
Another very moderate handicap. The race is rated around the placed horses with the winner posting his best form since his early 3yo days.
T/Jkpt: Not won. T/Plt: £101.20 to a £1 stake. Pool: £65,470.96. 471.87 winning tickets. T/Qpdt: £15.10 to a £1 stake. Pool: £4,026.40. 197.30 winning tickets. CR

349 WOLVERHAMPTON (A.W) (L-H)
Monday, February 2
369 Meeting Abandoned - Snow and frost

362 SOUTHWELL (L-H)
Tuesday, February 3
OFFICIAL GOING: Standard
Wind: Light against Weather: Fine and sunny, but cold

377 ARENA LEISURE PLC AMATEUR RIDERS' H'CAP (DIV I) 1m 3f (F)
1:10 (1:11) (Class 6) (0-52,52) 4-Y-0+ **£1,648** (£507; £253) **Stalls** Low

Form RPR
426- **1** **Bright Sparky (GER)**[18] 287 6-11-3 **48**...........(b[1]) MrOGreenall 3 56
(M W Easterby) *prom: lost pl over 5f out: hdwy over 2f out: rdn to ld ins fnl f: styd on* **10/1**
4/0- **2** *1 1/4* **Ramvaswani (IRE)**[5] 330 6-10-12 **50**........... MissCTwemlow(7) 5 56
(N B King) *chsd ldr: led over 8f out: hdd over 3f out: stl ev ch fr over 1f out: unable qck towards fin* **8/1**
3-23 **3** *1 1/2* **Dontpaytheferryman (USA)**[18] 107 4-11-5 **52**...........(t) MrSDobson 12 55
(A Dickman) *hld up: racd keenly: hdwy over 7f out: led over 1f out: rdn and hdd ins fnl f: styd on same pce* **11/8**[1]
0-00 **4** *3* **Charlie Bear**[4] 341 8-11-1 **46** oh1...........(p) GemmaGracey-Davison 8 44
(Miss Z C Davison) *s.s: bhd: styd on fr over 1f out: nvr nrr* **33/1**
004- **5** *3 3/4* **Reprieved**[214] 3690 4-11-3 **50**........... MrSWalker 7 42
(Miss J A Camacho) *sn led: hdd over 8f out: chsd ldr tl led over 3f out: rdn and hdd over 1f out: wknd fnl f* **4/1**[2]
00-0 **6** *shd* **Welcome Releaf**[19] 175 6-10-8 **46** oh1........... MrSWest(7) 2 38
(P Leech) *prom: lost pl 5f out: styd on appr fnl f* **25/1**
000- **7** *1/2* **Katie Kingfisher**[65] 7265 5-10-8 **46** oh1...........(b[1]) MrJPearce(7) 10 37
(T T Clement) *s.s: hdwy 1/2-way: rdn over 2f out: wknd over 1f out* **100/1**
/60- **8** *shd* **Integration**[221] 238 9-10-8 **46** oh1........... MissCharlotteCooper(7) 4 37
(Miss M E Rowland) *plld hrd and prom: wknd over 3f out* **100/1**
050- **9** *nk* **Itsy Bitsy**[52] 7667 7-10-8 **46** oh1........... RosePearson(7) 1 36
(W J Musson) *hld up: rdn over 4f out: last and detached fr field turning for home: styd on ins fnl f* **14/1**
030- **10** *3/4* **Shenandoah Girl**[37] 7676 6-11-1 **46**...........(e) MissEJJones 6 35
(Miss Gay Kelleway) *hld up: hdwy over 3f out: wkng whn hung lft wl over 1f out* **14/1**
6-04 **11** *6* **York Cliff**[16] 213 11-11-2 **50**........... MrBenBrisbourne(3) 11 29
(W M Brisbourne) *prom: chsd ldr over 6f out: rdn over 3f out: sn wknd* **7/1**[3]
-660 **12** *hd* **Top Jaro (FR)**[7] 300 6-11-7 **52**...........(b) MissSBrotherton 9 30
(Mrs R A Carr) *mid-div: plld hrd: hdwy over 8f out: rdn and wknd 2f out* **18/1**

2m 32.45s (4.45) **Going Correction** 0.0s/f (Stan)
WFA 4 from 5yo+ 2lb **12** Ran SP% **122.2**
Speed ratings (Par 101): **83,82,81,78,76 76,75,75,75,74 70,70**
toteswinger: 1&2 £13.00, 1&3 £3.60, 2&3 £5.40. CSF £88.76 CT £181.13 TOTE £10.40: £2.00, £2.20, £1.40; EX 124.70 Trifecta £356.60 Part won. Pool: £481.95 - 0.40 winning units..
Owner D F Spence **Bred** Graf Und Grafin Von Stauffenberg **Trained** Sheriff Hutton, N Yorks

FOCUS
A very modest event, but the early pace seemed generous enough. Improved Flat form from the first two, but a weak race overall.

378 ARENA LEISURE PLC AMATEUR RIDERS' H'CAP (DIV II) 1m 3f (F)
1:40 (1:40) (Class 6) (0-52,52) 4-Y-0+ **£1,648** (£507; £253) **Stalls** Low

Form RPR
05-5 **1** **World Of Choice (USA)**[21] 152 4-11-4 **51**...........(b[1]) MrOGreenall 5 62+
(M W Easterby) *hld up: hdwy 5f out: led over 2f out: rdn over 1f out: styd on* **7/4**[1]
002- **2** *2 1/2* **Cragganmore Creek**[63] 7520 6-10-10 **46** oh1...........(v) MrBMMorris(5) 2 53
(D Morris) *prom: chsd ldr 1/2-way: led over 3f out: rdn and hdd over 2f out: styd on same pce fnl f* **2/1**[2]
00-5 **3** *nk* **Ashmolian (IRE)**[7] 301 6-11-1 **46** oh1........... GemmaGracey-Davison 6 52
(Miss Z C Davison) *prom: outpcd over 3f out: rallied over 1f out: hung rt ins fnl f: styd on* **6/1**[3]
4-05 **4** *6* **Reminiscent (IRE)**[7] 300 10-10-10 **46** oh1...........(v) MissAWallace(5) 11 42
(B P J Baugh) *s.s: hdwy to ld after 1f: hdd over 3f out: hung rt over 1f out: sn wknd* **12/1**
000- **5** *6* **Dr Light (IRE)**[200] 4173 5-10-12 **48**........... KyleJames(5) 7 34
(M A Peill) *hld up: hdwy 4f out: wknd 3f out* **16/1**
4/0- **6** *3 1/4* **Lady Asheena**[80] 7344 4-11-5 **52**........... MrSWalker 3 32
(J Jay) *prom: rdn over 4f out: wknd over 3f out* **8/1**
0/6- **7** *2 1/2* **Present**[33] 2060 5-10-12 **50**...........(t) MrJMQuinlan(7) 9 26
(M J Gingell) *sn led: hdd after 1f: chsd ldr to 1/2-way: wknd 4f out* **33/1**
/0-0 **8** *49* **Super King**[19] 174 8-11-1 **46** oh1........... MrSDobson 1 —
(A D Brown) *hld up: shkn up 8f out: rdn and wknd over 4f out* **40/1**

2m 31.55s (3.55) **Going Correction** 0.0s/f (Stan)
WFA 4 from 5yo+ 2lb **8** Ran SP% **114.0**
Speed ratings (Par 101): **87,85,84,80,76 73,72,36**
toteswinger: 1&2 £1.80, 1&3 £4.40, 2&3 £3.60. CSF £5.41 CT £15.30 TOTE £3.10: £1.40, £1.10, £2.00; EX 6.10 Trifecta £17.10 Pool: £533.05 - 23.05 winning units..
Owner D F Spence **Bred** Catesby W Clay & Runnymede Farm Inc **Trained** Sheriff Hutton, N Yorks

FOCUS
The second division of this amateurs' handicap suffered from the withdrawal of a third of the field. Half of those left were out of the handicap, although only narrowly so and the time was the faster of the two divisions by just under a second. The winner had slipped to a good mark and the second was close to the form he showed when winning this last year.

379 SOUTHWELL-RACECOURSE.CO.UK H'CAP 5f (F)
2:10 (2:10) (Class 6) (0-65,63) 3-Y-O **£2,047** (£604; £302) **Stalls** High

Form RPR
4-50 **1** **Bold Rose**[13] 229 3-9-0 **56**...........(p) DaneO'Neill 1 60
(M D I Usher) *sn outpcd: rdn 1/2-way: hdwy u.p to ld 1f out: hung rt: r.o* **9/4**[1]
50-0 **2** *1/2* **Fasliyanne (IRE)**[11] 273 3-8-3 **50**...........(bt[1]) PatrickDonaghy(5) 8 52
(K A Ryan) *chsd ldrs: led 1/2-way: sn rdn and edgd: hdd 1f out: r.o* **14/1**
5-14 **3** *1 1/2* **Forever's Girl**[11] 273 3-9-3 **62**........... DuranFentiman(3) 3 59+
(G R Oldroyd) *unruly in stalls: hood removed late and s.s: r.o u.p ins fnl f: nt rch ldrs* **10/3**[2]
0-13 **4** *hd* **Just The Lady**[11] 268 3-9-7 **63**........... StephenDonohoe 2 59
(D Nicholls) *sn outpcd: rdn over 1f out: r.o: nt rch ldrs* **5/1**[3]
56-5 **5** *shd* **Fashion Icon (USA)**[13] 236 3-8-12 **59**........... DeanHeslop(5) 4 55
(T D Barron) *chsd ldrs: rdn over 1f out: styd on same pce ins fnl f* **5/1**[3]
460- **6** *1 1/4* **Taurus Twins**[209] 3846 3-8-13 **55**........... PaulHanagan 5 47
(R J Price) *led: hdd over 3f out: rdn 1/2-way: no ex fnl f* **16/1**
-026 **7** *2* **Valdemar**[8] 293 3-8-7 **49**...........(b[1]) JimmyQuinn 7 33
(A D Brown) *chsd ldr: led over 3f out: rdn and hdd 1/2-way: edgd lft over 1f out: wknd ins fnl f* **10/1**
30-0 **8** *3* **Senora Verde**[30] 41 3-8-3 **45**...........(p) FrankieMcDonald 9 19
(P T Midgley) *in rr whn hmpd over 4f out: sn hung lft and outpcd* **40/1**
00-6 **9** *nk* **Flaming Ruby**[11] 273 3-8-3 **45**........... ChrisCatlin 6 17
(N Tinkler) *chsd ldrs: rdn 1/2-way: wknd over 1f out* **14/1**

61.77 secs (2.07) **Going Correction** +0.20s/f (Slow) **9** Ran SP% **117.9**
Speed ratings (Par 95): **91,90,87,87,87 85,82,77,76**
toteswinger: 1&2 £11.40, 1&3 £3.80, 2&3 £10.80. CSF £37.22 CT £107.14 TOTE £2.90: £1.10, £5.10, £1.30; EX 36.70 Trifecta £183.40 Pool: £359.40 - 1.45 winning units..
Owner Ushers Court **Bred** J And Mrs Bowtell **Trained** Upper Lambourn, Berks

FOCUS
A modest sprint handicap and a race of changing fortunes. All the early action was down the stands' side and the pair that raced closest to the rail seemed to hold a significant advantage at halfway, but they may have done a bit too much early. The time was slow compared to the following seller.
Forever's Girl ◆ Official explanation: jockey said after slight unruliness in stalls prior to start, he found it difficult to remove the blind and the filly missed the break.

380 BOOK YOUR TICKETS ON LINE (S) STKS 5f (F)
2:40 (2:40) (Class 6) 4-Y-0+ **£2,047** (£604; £302) **Stalls** High

Form RPR
-422 **1** **Grimes Faith**[7] 304 6-8-12 62...........(p) NCallan 2 76
(K A Ryan) *trckd ldrs: led 1f out: r.o wl: eased nr fin* **5/6**[1]
04-0 **2** *1 1/2* **Woodcote (IRE)**[26] 83 7-8-12 72...........(vt) JimmyQuinn 7 71
(P R Chamings) *s.i.s: sn trcking ldrs: led 2f out: rdn and hdd 1f out: styd on same pce* **6/1**[3]
04-3 **3** *4 1/2* **Strathmore (IRE)**[13] 235 5-8-12 64........... PaulHanagan 6 54
(R A Fahey) *w ldrs: rdn 1/2-way: wknd fnl f* **15/8**[2]

00-6 **4** 1 3/4 **She's Our Beauty (IRE)**[26] 89 6-8-12 45........(b1) FrankieMcDonald 4 48
(S T Mason) *led: rdn and hdd 2f out: wknd over 1f out* **25/1**
04-0 **5** 4 1/2 **Billy Hot Rocks (IRE)**[24] 118 4-8-10 58................(v1) KylieManser(7) 3 37
(Miss Gay Kelleway) *dwlt: outpcd* **18/1**
0-0 **6** 1 3/4 **Always Engaged**[30] 36 4-8-2 0.............................. PatrickDonaghy(5) 1 21
(J R Norton) *chsd ldrs tl rdn and wknd 1/2-way* **100/1**
60.04 secs (0.34) **Going Correction** +0.20s/f (Slow) **6** Ran SP% **113.7**
Speed ratings (Par 101): **105,102,95,92,85 82**
toteswinger: 1&2 £2.00, 1&3 £1.30, 2&3 £1.80. CSF £6.92 TOTE £2.00: £1.10, £2.20; EX 7.10.The winner was bought in for 5,500gns.
Owner Mrs Angie Bailey **Bred** John Grimes **Trained** Hambleton, N Yorks
FOCUS
This seller looked a three-horse race judged on official marks and that was reflected in the betting market. The form is rated around the winner to his winter best.

381 CALL 01636 814481 TO SPONSOR A RACE MAIDEN STKS 6f (F)
3:10 (3:13) (Class 5) 3-Y-O+ **£2,729** (£806; £403) **Stalls** Low

Form RPR
5 **1** **Spiritual Healing (IRE)**[6] 315 3-8-7 0.......................... MartinDwyer 11 65
(J A Osborne) *a.p: chsd ldr over 3f out: led 2f out: edgd rt fnl f: rdn out* **4/1**[2]
53-2 **2** *nk* **Diamond Surprise**[21] 149 3-8-7 65.......................... GrahamGibbons 5 64
(R Curtis) *dwlt: sn pushed along and prom: hung rt and racd keenly fr over 4f out: rdn to chse wnr over 1f out: r.o u.p* **4/5**[1]
3 6 **Jerusalem (IRE)** 3-8-12 0..(b1) NeilChalmers 4 50
(A Bailey) *s.s: hld up: hdwy 2f out: rdn over 1f out: styd on same pce* **33/1**
0-40 **4** 1 1/2 **Only Hope**[6] 315 5-9-8 45..(e1) JerryO'Dwyer 10 44
(P S McEntee) *sn drvn along and prom: styng on same pce whn hung lft fr over 1f out* **66/1**
60-0 **5** 1 **Imperial Djay (IRE)**[13] 242 4-9-13 55.........................(t) JimmyQuinn 7 46
(G J Smith) *hld up: hdwy 2f out: sn rdn: wknd fnl f* **16/1**
0-50 **6** *nse* **Princess Zhukova (IRE)**[9] 290 4-9-5 36......... RussellKennemore(3) 1 41
(R J Price) *s.i.s: sn prom: nt clr run over 3f out: styd on same pce fnl 2f* **100/1**
45 **7** 1/2 **Singapore Girl**[12] 251 3-8-4 0................................ DuranFentiman(3) 9 35
(G R Oldroyd) *led: rdn and hdd 2f out: wknd fnl f* **14/1**
8 2 1/2 **Chantilly Jewel (USA)** 4-9-8 0.............................. ChrisCatlin 2 31
(R M H Cowell) *w ldr tl rdn over 3f out: wknd wl over 1f out* **16/1**
00 **9** *nk* **Uncle Brit**[6] 315 3-8-12 0.. StephenDonohoe 12 31
(Sir Mark Prescott) *sn outpcd* **20/1**
10 15 **Yes Please** 4-9-13 0.. NCallan 3 —
(K A Ryan) *dwlt: outpcd* **5/1**[3]
1m 17.96s (1.46) **Going Correction** 0.0s/f (Stan)
WFA 3 from 4yo+ 15lb **10** Ran SP% **120.8**
Speed ratings (Par 103): **90,89,81,79,78 78,77,74,73,53**
toteswinger: 1&2 £2.60, 1&3 £15.90, 2&3 £11.70. CSF £7.67 TOTE £5.30: £1.30, £1.10, £7.50; EX 10.20 Trifecta £114.00 Pool: £686.00 - 4.45 winning units..
Owner Mountgrange Stud **Bred** Stephen Sullivan **Trained** Upper Lambourn, Berks
FOCUS
A weak and uncompetitive maiden in which only three mattered according to the market. The front pair pulled a long way clear, so the future doesn't look that bright for the majority of the others. The runner-up sets the modest standard.
Diamond Surprise Official explanation: jockey said filly hung right

382 PLAY GOLF AT SOUTHWELL GOLF CLUB H'CAP 6f (F)
3:40 (3:40) (Class 3) (0-90,85) 4-Y-O+ **£7,771** (£2,312; £1,155; £577) **Stalls** Low

Form RPR
010- **1** **Ingleby Arch (USA)**[44] 7756 6-8-12 79.......................... TomEaves 5 93
(T D Barron) *s.i.s: sn drvn along to chse ldr: rdn to ld over 1f out: clr fnl f: eased last strides* **9/4**[1]
0-51 **2** 3 1/4 **Xpres Maite**[28] 68 6-9-4 85..(b) DaneO'Neill 3 89+
(S R Bowring) *s.i.s: hld up: hdwy over 1f out: swtchd lft ins fnl f: wnt 2nd nr fin: no ch w wnr* **9/4**[1]
0-64 **3** *hd* **Bo McGinty (IRE)**[11] 270 8-8-9 76............................(b) PaulHanagan 2 79
(R A Fahey) *chsd ldrs: nt clr run over 4f out: edgd lft over 3f out: sn rdn: styd on same pce fnl f* **13/2**[3]
04-1 **4** 1 **Realt Na Mara (IRE)**[32] 13 6-8-6 73.......................... ChrisCatlin 6 73
(H Morrison) *hld up: rn wd over 4f out: rdn over 2f out: nvr trbld ldrs* **9/2**[2]
1-64 **5** 5 **Came Back (IRE)**[26] 86 6-8-10 82.......................... AnnStokell(5) 4 66
(Miss A Stokell) *plld hrd: led: rdn and hdd over 1f out: wkng whn hung rt ins fnl f* **8/1**
1-56 **6** 15 **Thoughtsofstardom**[3] 359 6-8-8 75..............................(e1) LukeMorris 1 11
(P S McEntee) *hld up in tch: racd keenly: hmpd and lost pl over 3f out: eased over 1f out* **14/1**
1m 15.39s (-1.11) **Going Correction** 0.0s/f (Stan) **6** Ran SP% **110.8**
Speed ratings (Par 107): **107,102,102,101,94 74**
toteswinger: 1&2 £1.80, 1&3 £3.00, 2&3 £2.90. CSF £7.11 TOTE £3.50: £2.00, £2.10; EX 7.70.
Owner Dave Scott **Bred** Alexander-Groves Thoroughbreds **Trained** Maunby, N Yorks
■ Stewards' Enquiry : Paul Hanagan two-day ban: careless riding (Feb 17-18)
FOCUS
A decent sprint handicap run at a good pace. The winner was pretty much back to the level he showed when winning this event last year.
NOTEBOOK
Ingleby Arch(USA) was well beaten at Great Leighs on his previous start, but he proved suited by the return to Southwell and took advantage of a mark 5lb lower than when winning this race last year. He recovered well from a sluggish start had this in the bag from over a furlong out. His form figures over this course and distance now read 11581 and he could return here under a penalty. (tchd 5-2)
Xpres Maite had everything go his way when winning over course and distance on his previous start and he was unable to defy a 5lb higher mark against a well-handicapped rival. (tchd 5-2)
Bo McGinty(IRE) was a little keen on the heels of the leaders early and could not sustain his effort in the straight. He looks best suited by 5f. (tchd 6-1 and 7-1)
Realt Na Mara(IRE) could not recover after getting caught on the heels of Bo McGinty at about halfway as he was forced much wider than ideal.
Came Back(IRE) was far too free in front. Official explanation: jockey said horse hung right
Thoughtsofstardom, tried in a first-time eye-shield, lost any chance he might have had when badly hampered by Bo McGinty towards the inside rail around three furlongs out. (tchd 16-1)

383 BOOK YOUR TICKETS ON LINE AT SOUTHWELL-RACECOURSE.CO.UK MAIDEN H'CAP 1m (F)
4:10 (4:11) (Class 6) (0-55,54) 3-Y-O **£2,047** (£604; £302) **Stalls** Low

Form RPR
500- **1** **Reigning In Rio (IRE)**[81] 7318 3-8-0 45.......... PatrickDonaghy(5) 11 51
(P C Haslam) *a.p: chsd ldr over 4f out: rdn to ld 2f out: sn hung lft: styd on u.p* **8/1**
004- **2** 3/4 **Litenup (IRE)**[55] 7622 3-9-0 54.. SteveDrowne 6 58
(A J Lidderdale) *mid-div: sn pushed along: hdwy 1/2-way: rdn over 2f out: styd on* **9/2**[2]
0-33 **3** 3/4 **Lady Dunhill (IRE)**[14] 228 3-8-11 51.............................. PJMcDonald 4 53
(E W Tuer) *chsd ldrs: rdn over 2f out: styd on* **15/8**[1]
0-36 **4** 2 1/2 **Rigged**[13] 239 3-8-10 50.. MartinDwyer 7 46
(J A Osborne) *sn led: rdn and hdd over 2f out: n.m.r and no ex ins fnl f* **9/1**
6055 **5** 3 1/4 **Betws Y Coed (IRE)**[2] 363 3-8-13 53..........................(p) NeilChalmers 8 42
(A Bailey) *s.i.s: hdwy over 3f out: sn rdn: styd on same pce fnl 2f* **8/1**
00-5 **6** 1 **Chantilly Dancer (IRE)**[14] 228 3-8-11 51.................(v1) LiamJones 10 38
(M Quinn) *hld up: reminders 5f out: hdwy over 3f out: nvr trbld ldrs* **14/1**
06-0 **7** *nk* **The Canny Dove (USA)**[2] 363 3-7-12 45...................... JanWilson(7) 14 31
(T D Barron) *chsd ldrs: rdn over 3f out: sn outpcd* **33/1**
0-30 **8** 3 3/4 **Royal Salsa (IRE)**[18] 196 3-8-6 46..........................(p) PaulHanagan 13 23
(R A Fahey) *prom: rdn over 3f out: sn wknd* **11/2**[3]
006- **9** 51 **Cumbrian Gold (USA)**[55] 7627 3-8-8 48..........................(v1) TomEaves 3 —
(B Smart) *s.s: sn pushed along in rr: bhd fr 1/2-way: t.o* **14/1**
600- **10** 12 **Always The Sun**[68] 7458 3-8-10 50..............................(p) MickyFenton 12 —
(P Leech) *s.i.s: a in rr: rdn 1/2-way: sn lost tch: eased over 1f out: t.o* **33/1**
1m 44.57s (0.87) **Going Correction** 0.0s/f (Stan) **10** Ran SP% **119.8**
Speed ratings (Par 95): **95,94,93,91,87 86,86,82,31,19**
toteswinger: 1&2 £7.80, 1&3 £6.90, 2&3 £3.70. CSF £45.19 CT £98.39 TOTE £10.30: £2.70, £2.00, £1.20; EX 55.00 Trifecta £221.90 Pool: £914.88 - 3.05 winning units..
Owner Mrs Alurie O'Sullivan **Bred** Kevin Foley **Trained** Middleham Moor, N Yorks
FOCUS
A very poor maiden handicap and a race in which it paid to race handily. Very few ever got into it. The form is straightforward with the winner up 8lb.
Reigning In Rio(IRE) Official explanation: trainer's rep said, regarding apparent improvement in form, filly had been a weak 2yo and had benefited from strengthening up over the winter
Always The Sun Official explanation: jockey said filly had a breathing problem

384 MEMBERSHIP AT SOUTHWELL GOLF CLUB H'CAP 1m 3f (F)
4:40 (4:40) (Class 5) (0-75,79) 4-Y-O+ **£2,729** (£806; £403) **Stalls** Low

Form RPR
0-11 **1** **Riguez Dancer**[5] 333 5-9-7 79 6ex..............(t) PatrickDonaghy(5) 2 97+
(P C Haslam) *mde all: clr over 3f out: rdn over 1f out: eased nr fin* **8/13**[1]
30-4 **2** 5 **My Mentor (IRE)**[7] 307 5-9-4 71..........................(b) StephenDonohoe 6 78
(Sir Mark Prescott) *chsd wnr thrght: rdn over 2f out: sn outpcd* **9/2**[2]
4-03 **3** *nk* **Karmest**[8] 299 5-9-2 69.. GrahamGibbons 1 75
(A D Brown) *prom: hung lft and lost pl 5f out: rallied over 1f out: one pce fnl f* **8/1**[3]
/2-4 **4** 2 1/2 **Mr Aitch (IRE)**[22] 139 7-9-6 73..............................(t) SteveDrowne 4 75
(R T Phillips) *chsd ldrs: rdn over 2f out: sn hung lft: wknd over 1f out* **10/1**
2-30 **5** 1 1/2 **Davenport (IRE)**[15] 220 7-9-1 68..............................(p) DaneO'Neill 3 67
(B R Millman) *hld up: hdwy 5f out: rdn over 3f out: wknd over 1f out* **9/1**
500- **6** *nk* **Bajan Pride**[13] 2220 5-9-1 68.. PaulHanagan 5 67
(R A Fahey) *hld up: rdn over 5f out: a in rr* **16/1**
2m 24.98s (-3.02) **Going Correction** 0.0s/f (Stan) **6** Ran SP% **116.2**
Speed ratings (Par 103): **110,106,106,104,103 103**
toteswinger: 1&2 £1.90, 1&3 £2.00, 2&3 £3.50. CSF £4.06 TOTE £1.60: £1.20, £1.70; EX 5.20 Place 6: £4.44 Place 5: £2.70.
Owner Middleham Park Racing Xii **Bred** Plantation Stud **Trained** Middleham Moor, N Yorks
FOCUS
A modest handicap but another good front-running performance from the much-improved Riguez Dancer.
T/Jkpt: £2,869.50 to a £1 stake. Pool: £16,166.74. 4.00 winning tickets. T/Plt: £4.60 to a £1 stake. Pool: £132,455.02. 20,961.75 winning tickets. T/Qpdt: £3.30 to a £1 stake. Pool: £8,745.78. 1,929.86 winning tickets. CR

308 KEMPTON (A.W) (R-H)
Wednesday, February 4

OFFICIAL GOING: Standard
Wind: Moderate, across Weather: Overcast, snowcloud

385 BOOK NOW FOR RACING POST CHASE DAY CLASSIFIED STKS 1m 4f (P)
6:50 (6:50) (Class 7) 4-Y-O+ **£1,364** (£403; £201) **Stalls** Low

Form RPR
000- **1** **Tusculum (IRE)**[153] 5651 6-9-1 45.......................... TPQueally 13 53+
(A P Stringer) *hld up in 7th: nt clr run and swtchd lft over 2f out: wnt 2nd over 1f out and reminder: sn clsd and led last 100yds: sn stamped authority* **8/11**[1]
/0-0 **2** 1 1/2 **Desert Lark**[17] 210 4-8-12 45.. NCallan 3 48
(K A Ryan) *stdd s: hld up in 9th: rdn and prog on outer over 2f out: styd on wl to take 2nd nr fin: no ch w wnr* **20/1**
50-0 **3** 1/2 **Sir Haydn**[29] 59 9-9-1 45..(v) GeorgeBaker 1 48
(J R Jenkins) *t.k.h: trckd ldr: led over 3f out: rdn abt 3 l clr 2f out: hdd last 100yds: lost 2nd nr fin* **9/1**
0-40 **4** 1 **Satindra (IRE)**[4] 147 5-9-1 45..(tp) AdamKirby 7 46
(C R Dore) *hld up in abt 5th: effrt over 2f out: disp 2nd over 1f out: nt qckn* **8/1**[3]
-230 **5** 2 1/4 **Prince Of Medina**[17] 213 6-9-1 44..............................(t) SteveDrowne 14 42
(J R Best) *trckd ldng pair: effrt over 2f out: disp 2nd over 1f out: wknd fnl f* **6/1**[2]
/66- **6** *shd* **Mucho Loco (IRE)**[22] 914 6-9-1 42.......................... DaneO'Neill 2 42
(R Curtis) *hld up in 6th: effrt over 2f out: sn one pce and no imp* **12/1**
00-0 **7** 5 **Sovietta (IRE)**[33] 8 8-8-12 45..............................(t) RussellKennemore(3) 6 34
(Ian Williams) *trckd ldng pair: chsd ldr 3f out to over 1f out: wknd rapidly fnl f* **16/1**
/4-0 **8** 34 **Lady Llanover**[13] 248 9-9-1 42.. PaulDoe 5 —
(P D Evans) *led to over 3f out: wknd rapidly: eased whn t.o fnl f* **33/1**
00-6 **9** 3 1/4 **Asmodea**[9] 130 4-8-7 45.. GabrielHannon(5) 4 —
(B G Powell) *stdd s: plld hrd and hld up in detached last: wknd over 3f out: t.o whn eased over 1f out* **40/1**
6-06 **10** *nk* **Peas 'n Beans (IRE)**[20] 168 6-9-1 45..............................(bt1) NickyMackay 8 —
(T Keddy) *hld up in 8th: rdn 4f out: wknd 3f out: eased whn t.o fnl f* **25/1**
2m 38.79s (4.29) **Going Correction** +0.175s/f (Slow)
WFA 4 from 5yo+ 3lb **10** Ran SP% **121.8**
Speed ratings (Par 97): **92,91,90,90,88 88,85,62,60,60**
toteswinger: 1&2 £6.50, 1&3 £3.10, 2&3 £24.00. CSF £24.41 TOTE £1.50: £1.10, £5.40, £2.80; EX 39.60.
Owner Curley Leisure **Bred** Gestut Schlenderhan & Abbey Bloodstock **Trained** Newmarket, Suffolk
■ Stewards' Enquiry : T P Queally six-day ban (includes four deferred days): careless riding (Feb 18-23)

FOCUS
An ordinary race. All of the contenders had been beaten more than eight lengths on their previous start but it did produce a winner who had won in Listed company and finished fifth to Sixties Icon in the 2006 St Leger when trained by Aidan O'Brien.

386 DIGIBET.COM MAIDEN STKS 1m (P)
7:20 (7:23) (Class 5) 3-Y-O+ **£2,590** (£770; £385; £192) **Stalls** High

Form RPR
64- **1** **Love Pegasus (USA)**[61] 7552 3-8-9 0 GregFairley 6 77
(M Johnston) *trckd ldr: gng much bttr whn asked to chal over 2f out: hd high and urged into narrow ld over 1f out: grad asserted* **7/4**[1]

-3 **2** *2 1/4* **Know By Now**[21] 154 3-8-9 0 MickyFenton 3 72
(T P Tate) *rousted along to ld: shkn up over 3f out: hdd over 1f out: grad outpcd fnl f* **4/1**[2]

3 *3* **National Monument (IRE)** 3-8-9 0 TPQueally 14 65+
(J A Osborne) *dwlt: sn in abt 6th: outpcd by ldng pair fr 2f out: kpt on to hold on for 3rd* **7/1**[3]

4 *nk* **Harty Boy (USA)** 3-8-10 0 ow1 NCallan 10 65
(M L W Bell) *prom: outpcd by ldng pair fr 2f out: jst lost out in battle for 3rd* **7/1**[3]

/64- **5** *4 1/2* **Apotheosis**[177] 4929 4-10-0 0 AdamKirby 4 59
(W R Swinburn) *hld up in 6th: hanging lft bnd fr 4f out: effrt over 2f out: easily lft bhd fnl 2f* **8/1**

6/4 **6** *2* **Emerald Rock (CAN)**[16] 217 4-10-0 0 LukeMorris 5 54
(N J Vaughan) *settled in 8th: shkn up and already outpcd over 2f out: plugged on but no ch* **10/1**

7 *2 1/2* **Al Jathaab (USA)** 4-10-0 0 SimonWhitworth 12 49+
(M Wigham) *s.v.s: detached in last pair early: sme prog fr 1/2-way: rchd midfield 2f out but nowhere nr ldrs: no hdwy after* **33/1**

3 **8** *nk* **Jerusalem (IRE)**[1] 381 3-8-9 0 (b) NeilChalmers 8 43
(A Bailey) *hld up in 7th: outpcd fr over 2f out: no ch after: fdd* **33/1**

9 *1 1/4* **Cherry Plum** 3-8-4 0 MartinDwyer 13 35
(A M Balding) *a wl in rr and rn green: lft bhd fnl 3f* **12/1**

10 *1 1/2* **Holoko Heights** 4-10-0 0 VinceSlattery 11 42
(N J Vaughan) *dwlt: a towards rr: wl off the pce fnl 3f* **66/1**

11 *1* **Camelot Queen** 4-9-9 0 FergusSweeney 2 34
(W S Kittow) *dwlt: a towards rr: rdn over 3f out: struggling after* **66/1**

12 *5* **Milemilia (IRE)** 3-8-4 0 ChrisCatlin 7 18
(H Morrison) *reluctant early w much tail swishing and detached in last pair: nvr a factor* **33/1**

-0 **13** *7* **Lilleput**[28] 69 4-9-9 0 JamesDoyle 1 7
(Ms J S Doyle) *prom tl wknd rapidly over 2f out* **100/1**

1m 42.2s (2.40) **Going Correction** +0.175s/f (Slow)
WFA 3 from 4yo 19lb **13** Ran SP% **122.1**
Speed ratings (Par 103): **95,92,89,89,84 82,80,80,78,77 76,71,64**
toteswinger: 1&2 £2.40, 1&3 £2.50, 2&3 £5.10. CSF £8.20 TOTE £2.90: £1.30, £1.80, £2.80; EX 8.50.
Owner M Doyle **Bred** Eaton Sales **Trained** Middleham Moor, N Yorks

FOCUS
A modest-looking maiden. The pace was steady and the two market leaders filled the first two positions all the way and finished some way clear of the rest.

387 DIGIBET SPORTS BETTING H'CAP 7f (P)
7:50 (7:50) (Class 6) (0-65,65) 4-Y-O+ **£2,047** (£604; £302) **Stalls** High

Form RPR
11-0 **1** **Tuxedo**[32] 25 4-9-0 **61** LukeMorris 8 74+
(P W Hiatt) *t.k.h: hld up towards rr: nt clr run briefly wl over 2f out: gd prog on inner fr 2f out: led 1f out: hung bdly lft but drew clr* **11/1**

001- **2** *2 1/4* **Convallaria (FR)**[77] 7383 6-8-13 **60** (b) ChrisCatlin 11 67
(C F Wall) *t.k.h and hld up in rr on inner: prog over 2f out: clsd and upsides 1f out: one pce after* **9/1**

-514 **3** *nk* **Marmooq**[10] 289 6-9-3 **64** IanMongan 3 70+
(M J Attwater) *racd wd in rr: pushed along fr 1/2-way: effrt u.p over 2f out: styd on to take 3rd ins fnl f* **7/1**

4-23 **4** *1 3/4* **Just Jimmy (IRE)**[17] 211 4-8-4 **51** oh2 CatherineGannon 7 52
(P D Evans) *w ldr to 3f out: styd prom: ch jst over 1f out: fdd fnl f* **16/1**

0-03 **5** *1 1/4* **Alucica**[29] 60 6-8-9 **56** ow1 (v) DarrenWilliams 4 54
(D Shaw) *trckd ldrs: rdn over 2f out: plugged on same pce and nvr really landed a blow* **25/1**

-401 **6** *3/4* **Divertimenti (IRE)**[4] 355 5-8-13 **65** (b) JamesO'Reilly(5) 2 61
(C R Dore) *t.k.h: hld up bhd ldrs: effrt to dispute 2nd over 2f out: nt qckn wl over 1f out: grad lost pl* **5/1**[3]

0-11 **7** *2* **Street Power (USA)**[7] 309 4-9-4 **65** 6ex GregFairley 1 56+
(J R Gask) *racd freely and wdst off all of four ldrs: led 3f out and kicked on: edgd lft fr 2f out: hdd & wknd rapidly 1f out* **2/1**[1]

1600 **8** *3/4* **Namu**[10] 289 6-9-3 **64** (p) DaneO'Neill 12 53
(Miss T Spearing) *trckd ldrs on inner: nt qckn over 2f out: steadily wknd fr over 1f out* **25/1**

-222 **9** *1/2* **Duke Of Milan (IRE)**[7] 309 6-8-13 **60** AdamKirby 9 47
(G C Bravery) *hld up in last: effrt over 2f out: sn fnd nil and no prog* **4/1**[2]

00-0 **10** *11* **Royal Orissa**[6] 327 7-8-4 **51** oh6 FrankieMcDonald 10 9
(D Haydn Jones) *led to 3f out: sn wknd: t.o* **66/1**

56-0 **11** *1 1/2* **Bishopbriggs (USA)**[14] 235 4-9-4 **65** TravisBlock 5 18
(J Ryan) *w ldrs to 3f out: wknd rapidly: t.o* **33/1**

1m 26.36s (0.36) **Going Correction** +0.175s/f (Slow) **11** Ran SP% **118.8**
Speed ratings (Par 101): **104,101,101,99,97 96,94,93,93,80 78**
toteswinger: 1&2 £21.60, 1&3 £15.70, 2&3 £21.90. CSF £103.11 CT £762.80 TOTE £12.30: £3.40, £2.80, £2.10; EX 160.70.
Owner Phil Kelly **Bred** Gainsborough Stud Management Ltd **Trained** Hook Norton, Oxon

FOCUS
A competitive event for the grade. The pace was fair and there are reasons to be positive about this form with the progressive winner back on track and the second and third pretty solid.
Royal Orissa Official explanation: jockey said gelding hung left

388 DIGIBET CASINO H'CAP 7f (P)
8:20 (8:20) (Class 2) (0-100,96) 4-Y-O+
£11,215 (£3,358; £1,679; £840; £419; £210) **Stalls** High

Form RPR
-364 **1** **Capricorn Run (USA)**[10] 291 6-8-10 **88** (v) RobertWinston 7 97
(A J McCabe) *settled in abt 6th: rdn over 3f out: u.str.p 2f out: fnlly mde prog on outer over 1f out: sustained effrt to ld fnl 75yds* **11/2**

00-5 **2** *1* **Tamagin (USA)**[18] 204 6-9-4 **96** NCallan 2 102
(K A Ryan) *led at str pce and 3 l clr after 3f: rdn over 2f out: fought on wl but grad c bk to field: hdd fnl 75yds* **11/2**

5-11 **3** *hd* **Trafalgar Square**[11] 282 7-8-5 **83** PaulDoe 4 89
(M J Attwater) *hld up in last trio: prog on inner 2f out: wnt 2nd ent fnl f and looked dangerous: nt sustain effrt fnl 100yds* **8/1**

-215 **4** *1 1/4* **Dvinsky (USA)**[17] 212 8-8-10 **88** (b) IanMongan 8 90
(P Howling) *chsd clr ldr: rdn over 2f out: clsd grad over 1f out: no ex and lost 2nd ent fnl f* **16/1**

164- **5** *1 1/2* **Opus Maximus (IRE)**[123] 6482 4-8-9 **87** GregFairley 5 85
(M Johnston) *trckd ldng pair to over 1f out: grad wknd* **4/1**[2]

0-06 **6** *nse* **Fajr (IRE)**[12] 278 7-9-1 **93** (v) SteveDrowne 1 91
(Miss Gay Kelleway) *sn last and wl off the pce: rdn over 2f out: kpt on fr over 1f out: nvr really a threat* **20/1**

1-13 **7** *3 1/2* **Southandwest (IRE)**[25] 113 5-8-11 **89** LukeMorris 3 78
(J S Moore) *stdd s: t.k.h and hld up in last trio: rdn wl over 2f out: no prog tl plugged on fnl f* **7/2**[1]

33-6 **8** *1/2* **Willkandoo (USA)**[26] 106 4-8-4 **82** ChrisCatlin 6 69
(D M Simcock) *dwlt: sn in midfield: rdn over 2f out: no prog and btn wl over 1f out: fdd* **5/1**[3]

500- **9** *2 1/2* **Geezers Colours**[243] 2794 4-8-12 **90** AndrewElliott 9 71
(K R Burke) *chsd ldng pair tl wknd rapidly over 1f out* **14/1**

1m 25.44s (-0.56) **Going Correction** +0.175s/f (Slow) **9** Ran SP% **118.1**
Speed ratings (Par 109): **110,108,108,107,105 105,101,100,98**
toteswinger: 1&2 £8.20, 1&3 £2.90, 2&3 £7.20. CSF £36.65 CT £245.95 TOTE £7.80: £2.30, £2.10, £2.20; EX 38.50.
Owner Paul J Dixon And Placida Racing **Bred** Santa Rosa Partners **Trained** Averham Park, Notts

FOCUS
A classy handicap run at a decent pace. The form reads pretty sound.

NOTEBOOK
Capricorn Run(USA) has blown the start on a few occasions recently and struggled to hit the heights that enabled him to win a conditions event at Lingfield last January. But he had tumbled down the weights, the vigorous pace here played to his strengths and he found a strong burst with a visor reapplied to pounce late and end his 12-month barren run. His slow-burning style and dependency on a strong pace make him a bit of a risky one but he is very capable of this sort of mark when things fall his way. (tchd 5-1)
Tamagin(USA) blasted into the lead and ran an excellent race on his second run back from a break. The likeable and reliable trailblazer is on a winning mark, his last four wins have been at 6f, and he could be very tough to catch back sprinting next time. (op 15-2 tchd 5-1)
Trafalgar Square was slowly away and looked in trouble at an early stage but kept battling and did really well to get as close as he did. He did well to catch one that looked like it got away last time and was not far off repeating the trick here. He remains of strong interest, despite an upwardly mobile mark. (op 6-1)
Dvinsky(USA) ran another creditable race on his 28th run in the last 12 months and gave the impression that the return to 6f would suit, the trip of ten of his last 12 successes. He should continue to run well but is often punished for his consistency, remains 4lb higher than his last winning mark and may continue to be slightly vulnerable. (op 14-1)
Opus Maximus(IRE) was in a decent position turning for home but his response to pressure was a bit limited. He may have needed the run after four months off and will be suited by the return to 1m but this still has to rate as slightly disappointing. (op 7-2)
Southandwest(IRE) did quite well to snatch third from a tough draw in his bid to complete an 11-day hat-trick last time but looked a very difficult ride here and was in serious trouble a long way out. Official explanation: jockey said gelding hung left (op 9-2)

389 "TURFTV SHOWING THE BEST RACECOURSES" H'CAP 1m 3f (P)
8:50 (8:51) (Class 4) (0-80,80) 3-Y-O **£4,727** (£1,406; £702; £351) **Stalls** High

Form RPR
51-1 **1** **Petrovsky**[23] 137 3-9-7 **80** GregFairley 6 87
(M Johnston) *led for over 1f: chsd clr ldr: clsd 3f out: drvn ahd jst over 1f out but hung lft u.p: styd on* **4/6**[1]

34-2 **2** *2 1/4* **Black N Brew (USA)**[21] 164 3-8-11 **70** RobertWinston 1 74+
(J R Best) *t.k.h early: hld up in 5th: prog over 2f out: wnt 2nd 1f out and then hmpd: no imp on wnr after* **4/1**[2]

02-3 **3** *3* **Mile High Lad (USA)**[32] 32 3-8-7 **73** MatthewDavies(7) 3 71
(George Baker) *t.k.h early: hld up in last: cl enough 3f out: drvn over 2f out: wnt 3rd ins fnl f: no imp on ldng pair* **14/1**

2-45 **4** *nk* **Supernoverre (IRE)**[17] 209 3-8-10 **69** TPQueally 2 66
(Mrs A J Perrett) *sn chsng ldng pair: nt qckn over 2f out: one pce after* **10/1**[3]

33-3 **5** *3/4* **Sign Of Approval**[25] 122 3-8-10 **74** MartinLane(5) 4 70
(K R Burke) *stdd s: plld hrd: led after 1 1/2f and sn wl clr: c bk to field 3f out: tried to kick on over 2f out: hdd jst over 1f out: wknd* **16/1**

5-51 **6** *8* **Innactualfact**[18] 205 3-8-8 **67** ChrisCatlin 5 50
(L A Dace) *t.k.h early: hld up in 4th: wknd fr jst over 2f out* **10/1**[3]

2m 23.33s (1.43) **Going Correction** +0.175s/f (Slow) **6** Ran SP% **110.7**
Speed ratings (Par 99): **101,99,97,96,96 90**
toteswinger: 1&2 £1.10, 1&3 £3.20, 2&3 £8.00. CSF £3.46 TOTE £1.40: £1.30, £1.60; EX 3.80.
Owner Sheikh Hamdan Bin Mohammed Al Maktoum **Bred** Gainsborough Stud Management Ltd **Trained** Middleham Moor, N Yorks
■ Stewards' Enquiry : Greg Fairley two-day ban: careless riding (Feb 18-19)

FOCUS
A fair handicap and the form seems sound enough despite an uneven pace. The winner should continue to progress and the second ran a clear personal best.

390 PANORAMIC BAR & RESTAURANT H'CAP 6f (P)
9:20 (9:21) (Class 6) (0-55,54) 3-Y-O **£2,047** (£604; £302) **Stalls** High

Form RPR
600- **1** **Private Passion (IRE)**[97] 7098 3-8-8 **48** PaulEddery 6 57+
(Pat Eddery) *drvn to ld: mde virtually all: kpt on wl whn chal fr 2f out: all out to hold on* **4/1**[1]

03-5 **2** *1/2* **Rocket Ruby**[12] 273 3-8-9 **49** ow1 DarrenWilliams 5 56
(D Shaw) *trckd ldrs: hrd rdn over 2f out: prog over 1f out: wnt 2nd ins fnl f and clsd on wnr at fin* **13/2**[3]

-554 **3** *1* **Sills Vincero**[13] 246 3-9-0 **54** AdamKirby 7 58
(D Shaw) *t.k.h early: trckd ldng pair: effrt on inner 2f out: wnt 2nd 1f out and cl enough: nt qckn fnl 150yds* **9/2**[2]

3-40 **4** *1 1/4* **Readily**[18] 200 3-8-11 **51** TPQueally 4 51
(J G Portman) *pressed wnr: tried to chal 2f out: hld and lost 2nd 1f out: fdd fnl 100yds* **7/1**

000- **5** *nk* **Buckle Up**[128] 6341 3-8-5 **45** ChrisCatlin 12 44+
(D K Ivory) *s.s: t.k.h and hld up in last: rdn over 2f out: prog over 1f out: styd on ins fnl f: nrst fin* **12/1**

00-0 **6** *3/4* **Pepin (IRE)**[13] 246 3-8-5 **45** (b[1]) LukeMorris 11 41
(D Haydn Jones) *dwlt: hld up in last pair: shkn up over 2f out: nt clr run and swtchd lft 1f out: r.o towards fin* **7/1**

00-3 **7** *1 1/4* **Flamboyant Red (IRE)**[7] 308 3-8-5 **45** NickyMackay 9 37
(Miss Gay Kelleway) *wnt lft s: t.k.h v early and hld up bhd ldrs: rdn over 2f out: no rspnse* **4/1**[1]

650- **8** ½ **Shirley High**[70] 7452 3-8-12 52 (t) IanMongan 3 43
(P Howling) *dwlt: hld up in last trio: rdn over 2f out: no real prog over 1f out* **25/1**

05-4 **9** 3½ **Kina Jazz**[23] 135 3-8-3 50 TobyAtkinson(7) 8 30
(M E Rimmer) *dwlt: hld up towards rr: rdn over 2f out and no prog: wknd over 1f out* **10/1**

1m 14.58s (1.48) **Going Correction** +0.175s/f (Slow) 9 Ran SP% **117.1**
Speed ratings (Par 95): **97,96,95,93,92 91,90,89,84**
toteswinger: 1&2 £8.00, 1&3 £4.90, 2&3 £6.50. CSF £30.69 CT £122.32 TOTE £5.40: £2.00, £1.40, £1.80; EX 30.80.
Owner Pat Eddery Racing (Lomond) **Bred** Ballyhane Stud **Trained** Nether Winchendon, Bucks

FOCUS
A low-grade handicap run at just a fair pace, and not many got into it from behind. The form looks decent for the lowly grade.
Private Passion(IRE) Official explanation: jockey said, regarding apparent improvement in form, gelding ran well on its first race at Bath, got upset in the stalls on its second run and got behind on its last run.
T/Plt: £88.90 to a £1 stake. Pool: £109,218.55. 896.65 winning tickets. T/Qpdt: £38.90 to a £1 stake. Pool: £7,514.65. 142.80 winning tickets. JN

355 LINGFIELD (L-H)
Wednesday, February 4

OFFICIAL GOING: Standard
Wind: virtually nil Weather: bright, very cold

391 GALLEONS LAP MAIDEN STKS — 1m 2f (P)
1:00 (1:00) (Class 5) 3-Y-O — **£2,729** (£806; £403) **Stalls** Low

Form | | | | RPR
1 **Ladies Dancing** 3-9-3 0 TPQueally 9 71
(J A Osborne) *s.i.s: hld up in last trio: hdwy over 3f out: wnt 2nd over 2f out: rdn to ld over 1f out: hung rt fnl f: styd on wl* **12/1**

25-2 **2** ½ **Mellow Mixture**[32] 32 3-9-3 77 DaneO'Neill 1 70
(R Hannon) *led at stdy gallop: rdn over 2f out: hdd over 1f out: hung lft and styd on same pce fnl f* **5/2**[2]

4 **3** 3 **Lacrosse**[12] 272 3-9-3 0 NCallan 6 64
(M A Jarvis) *trckd ldng pair: rdn jst over 2f out: outpcd by ldng pair wl over 1f out: one pce after* **8/15**[1]

00- **4** 1¾ **Majd Aljazeera**[49] 7699 3-9-3 0 (t) FergusSweeney 3 61
(D M Simcock) *hld up in tch: rdn to chse ldng trio wl over 1f out: kpt on but no real imp* **33/1**

2-0 **5** 7 **Premier Angel (USA)**[25] 121 3-8-12 0 PatCosgrave 10 42
(Jane Chapple-Hyam) *t.k.h: hld up in tch: rdn and struggling over 2f out: no ch fr over 1f out* **7/1**[3]

6 ¾ **Carrazara (IRE)** 3-8-12 0 FrankieMcDonald 8 40
(Edgar Byrne) *t.k.h: chsd ldr tl over 2f out: sn rdn and wknd* **50/1**

7 1¾ **Miami Mix** 3-9-3 0 VinceSlattery 2 42
(B N Pollock) *dwlt: hld up in rr: rdn and struggling 3f out: no ch fnl 2f* **66/1**

8 ¾ **Suhailah** 3-8-12 0 PaulDoe 5 35
(M J Attwater) *s.i.s: rn green early: a bhd: lost tch over 2f out* **20/1**

2m 9.62s (3.02) **Going Correction** +0.075s/f (Slow) 8 Ran SP% **125.2**
Speed ratings (Par 97): **90,89,87,85,80 79,78,77**
toteswinger: 1&2 £4.60, 1&3 £3.90, 2&3 £1.50. CSF £45.27 TOTE £22.90: £3.40, £1.10, £1.02; EX 95.00 Trifecta £188.70 Pool: £471.82 - 1.85 winning units..
Owner A D Spence & 12 Day Partners **Bred** P And Mrs Venner And Trickledown Stud **Trained** Upper Lambourn, Berks

FOCUS
An ordinary maiden for three-year-olds was run at a moderate early pace and the form should be treated with a little caution. The runner-up is the obvious guide to the form.

392 SANDY PIT H'CAP — 1m 2f (P)
1:30 (1:31) (Class 5) (0-75,75) 4-Y-O+ — **£2,900** (£856; £428) **Stalls** Low

Form | | | | RPR
-431 **1** **Can Can Star**[11] 285 6-9-5 75 LukeMorris 10 84
(A W Carroll) *stdd after s: hld up towards rr: hdwy on outer over 4f out: rdn over 2f out: chsd ldr jst ins fnl f: r.o wl to ld on post* **4/1**[1]

55-6 **2** nse **Kidlat**[12] 271 4-9-3 74 (t) DaneO'Neill 7 83
(B G Powell) *s.i.s: hld up in midfield: hdwy to chse ldng pair jst over 2f out: rdn to ld over 1f out: hdd on post* **13/2**[2]

526- **3** 1½ **Trifti**[64] 7526 8-9-1 71 FergusSweeney 2 77
(Miss Jo Crowley) *hld up in midfield: on inner: hdwy over 1f out: chsd ldng pair ins fnl f: kpt on* **9/1**[3]

0-00 **4** shd **Bee Stinger**[11] 283 7-8-12 68 (b) NCallan 9 74
(I A Wood) *t.k.h: hld up in tch: plld out and shuffled bk over 2f out: r.o u.p fnl f: nt rch ldrs* **16/1**

2-05 **5** 1 **Man Of Gwent (UAE)**[20] 172 5-9-2 72 PaulDoe 12 76+
(P D Evans) *stdd after s: hld up in last pl: stl last 2f out: hdwy on inner ent fnl f: kpt on: nvr nr ldrs* **16/1**

154- **6** hd **Sign Of The Cross**[39] 7791 5-9-5 75 GeorgeBaker 13 78+
(G L Moore) *t.k.h: hld up in last trio: hmpd over 2f out: hdwy over 1f out: styd on fnl f: nt rch ldrs* **4/1**[1]

32-1 **7** ¾ **Majehar**[30] 47 7-8-8 64 PaulHanagan 4 66
(A G Newcombe) *chsd ldrs: rdn over 1f out: kpt on same pce fnl f* **12/1**

640- **8** nk **Bell Island**[131] 6243 5-8-8 71 (p) BMcHugh(7) 5 72
(Lady Herries) *chsd ldrs: rdn and hld hd awkwardly wl over 1f out: edging rt and no imp fnl f* **12/1**

20-5 **9** 1 **It's My Day (IRE)**[25] 125 4-8-9 66 SamHitchcott 3 65
(C Gordon) *s.i.s: t.k.h: hld up towards rr: effrt 2f out: nt clr run and swtchd rt 1f out and again ins fnl f: nvr able to chal* **20/1**

435- **10** ½ **Parson's Punch**[44] 7758 4-8-11 68 MartinDwyer 1 66
(P D Cundell) *mde most tl rdn and hdd over 1f out: wknd qckly ins fnl f* **10/1**

6-05 **11** 10 **Direct Debit (IRE)**[16] 218 6-9-3 73 (p) AdamKirby 8 51
(M Wellings) *chsd ldr tl 2f out: sn wknd u.p: wl btn fnl f* **12/1**

160- **12** 2½ **Dr Brass**[117] 6626 4-9-4 75 VinceSlattery 11 48
(B N Pollock) *dwlt: sn in tch on outer: effrt to press ldrs and rdn 3f out: sn wknd* **33/1**

/21- **13** 1½ **Jago (SWI)**[336] 802 6-8-13 69 ChrisCatlin 6 39
(A M Hales) *t.k.h: in tch tl lost pl qckly over 2f out: wl bhd fnl f* **14/1**

2m 6.50s (-0.10) **Going Correction** +0.075s/f (Slow)
WFA 4 from 5yo+ 1lb 13 Ran SP% **121.6**
Speed ratings (Par 103): **103,102,101,101,100 100,100,99,99,98 90,88,87**
toteswinger: 1&2 £6.50, 1&3 £9.00, 2&3 £9.30. CSF £29.32 CT £227.27 TOTE £5.50: £1.40, £2.40, £3.50; EX 33.30 Trifecta £486.40 Part won..
Owner K F Coleman **Bred** A W And I Robinson **Trained** Cropthorne, Worcs

FOCUS
A competitive handicap run at a fairly steady early pace. The form is sound enough at face value.
Sign Of The Cross Official explanation: jockey said gelding ran too free
It's My Day(IRE) Official explanation: jockey said gelding had to be checked twice in straight
Parson's Punch Official explanation: jockey said gelding hung right
Direct Debit(IRE) Official explanation: jockey said gelding ran too free

393 GILLS LAP CLAIMING STKS — 1m 5f (P)
2:00 (2:01) (Class 6) 4-Y-O+ — **£2,047** (£604; £302) **Stalls** Low

Form | | | | RPR
5-60 **1** **Media Stars**[7] 320 4-8-7 59 ChrisCatlin 3 65
(J A Osborne) *t.k.h: in tch: rdn 3f out: chsd ldrs and drvn 2f out: led fnl 100yds: styd on wl* **20/1**

25-2 **2** ¾ **Quince (IRE)**[14] 237 6-9-4 78 (v) RobertHavlin 6 71
(J Pearce) *w.w in midfield: rdn and effrt over 2f out: chsd ldrs over 1f out: styd on fnl f to chse wnr fnl 75yds: no imp towards fin* **3/1**[2]

1-12 **3** 1¼ **Wind Flow**[7] 319 5-9-6 68 (b) CatherineGannon 4 71
(C A Dwyer) *led at stdy gallop: hrd pressed and rdn over 2f out: asserted again ent fnl f: hdd fnl 100yds: fdd towards fin* **11/4**[1]

5-42 **4** 1 **Eureka Moment**[9] 299 4-8-5 62 PaulHanagan 1 59
(E A L Dunlop) *chsd ldrs: effrt u.p on inner jst over 2f out: unable qck fnl f* **13/2**

0/24 **5** 1¼ **Alrafid (IRE)**[8] 302 10-8-11 68 (b) FergusSweeney 10 59
(G L Moore) *t.k.h: chsd ldrs: wnt 2nd wl over 2f out: ev ch and drvn 2f out: wknd ent fnl f* **9/1**

-234 **6** 1½ **Bridgewater Boys**[6] 333 8-9-0 72 (b) NCallan 12 59
(P D Evans) *stdd and slowly away: t.k.h: hld up in rr: swtchd to outer wl over 3f out: rdn over 2f out: kpt on over 1f out: nvr trbld ldrs* **10/3**[3]

640- **7** 2¼ **Cruise Director**[40] 5900 9-9-3 66 RussellKennemore(3) 9 62
(Ian Williams) *hld up in rr: swtchd to outer over 4f out: kpt on same pce fr over 1f out: nvr trbld ldrs* **12/1**

0-2 **8** nk **Gasat (IRE)**[25] 119 8-8-11 75 PNolan(7) 11 60
(A B Haynes) *stdd and swtchd lft sn after s: hld up in rr: rdn and unable qck over 2f out: nvr trbld ldrs* **33/1**

66-0 **9** 2¼ **Looter (FR)**[30] 42 4-8-0 45 (tp) AndrewHeffernan(7) 7 49
(P Butler) *hld up in midfield: rdn and unable qck over 2f out: no ch fr wl over 1f out* **80/1**

60/0 **10** hd **Charleston**[20] 168 8-8-4 42 RichardRowe(7) 5 49
(R Rowe) *chsd ldr tl wl over 2f out: wknd u.p 2f out* **200/1**

11 8 **Bering De Lauriere (FR)**[18] 6-8-6 0 GabrielHannon(5) 2 37
(B G Powell) *hld up in midfield: rdn and struggling 3f out: wl bhd fnl 2f* **100/1**

2m 47.84s (1.84) **Going Correction** +0.075s/f (Slow)
WFA 4 from 5yo+ 4lb 11 Ran SP% **116.2**
Speed ratings (Par 101): **97,96,95,95,94 93,92,91,90,90 85**
toteswinger: 1&2 £11.40, 1&3 £10.40, 2&3 £3.40. CSF £77.67 TOTE £23.60: £4.20, £1.60, £1.50; EX 102.90 TRIFECTA Not won..Media Stars was claimed by R. Johnson for £5,000.
Owner Getty, Green and Linden **Bred** Newsells Park Stud Limited **Trained** Upper Lambourn, Berks

FOCUS
An open contest for the class, but it was steadily run and there were the usual doubts over the form horses. The winner is rated back to his early maiden form.
Bridgewater Boys Official explanation: jockey said gelding missed the break

394 ENCHANTED PLACE MEDIAN AUCTION MAIDEN STKS — 7f (P)
2:30 (2:30) (Class 6) 3-Y-O — **£2,047** (£604; £302) **Stalls** Low

Form | | | | RPR
05- **1** **Bickersten**[35] 7830 3-9-3 0 TonyCulhane 3 65
(M R Channon) *mde virtualy all: hrd pressed wl over 1f out: hdd and rdn ins fnl f: rallied to regain ld last stride* **16/1**

0-3 **2** shd **Kiss A Prince**[21] 160 3-8-12 0 JamesO'Reilly(5) 1 65
(D K Ivory) *chsd ldrs: rdn and effrt 2f out: ev ch ent fnl f: led ins fnl f: hdd last stride* **11/1**

3 ¾ **If Only** 3-9-3 0 LukeMorris 9 63
(J Jay) *bhd: hdwy and in tch over 2f out: c wd bnd 2f out: styd on wl fnl f: wnt 3rd nr fin: nt rch ldng pair* **100/1**

050- **4** nk **Edgeworth (IRE)**[115] 6673 3-8-12 58 GabrielHannon(5) 5 62
(B G Powell) *chsd ldrs: rdn 2f out: kpt on same pce fnl f: lost 3rd nr fin* **33/1**

52 **5** 1¼ **Divine Force**[9] 298 3-9-3 0 MartinDwyer 8 59
(J A Osborne) *in tch: rdn and effrt jst over 2f out: unable qck u.p over 1f out: no imp fnl f* **6/1**[3]

6 **6** 1¼ **Dollar Express (USA)**[21] 160 3-9-3 0 TPQueally 4 55
(J Noseda) *taken down early: rrd stalls and v.s.a: sn in tch and plld hrd: shkn up on inner jst over 2f out: rdn and no hdwy over 1f out* **11/10**[1]

00- **7** 1½ **Set Em Up Mo**[49] 7708 3-8-12 0 PaulDoe 7 46
(M J Attwater) *in tch in midfield: rdn and unable qck jst over 2f out: nvr pce to threaten ldrs* **33/1**

8 nse **Georgina Macrae** 3-8-12 0 NeilChalmers 2 46
(A M Balding) *bhd: sn pushed along: rdn and detached last over 3f out: plugged on fnl f: n.d* **8/1**

23-2 **9** 3¾ **Piazza San Pietro**[10] 286 3-9-3 84 ChrisCatlin 6 41
(J R Gask) *t.k.h: chsd ldr tl over 2f out: wkng whn short of room wl over 1f out: wl btn after* **5/2**[2]

1m 26.3s (1.50) **Going Correction** +0.075s/f (Slow) 9 Ran SP% **114.5**
Speed ratings (Par 95): **94,93,93,92,91 89,88,88,83**
toteswinger: 1&2 £7.50, 1&3 £52.30, 2&3 £59.10. CSF £165.91 TOTE £20.40: £2.20, £2.40, £8.40; EX 87.40 TRIFECTA Not won..
Owner Joy And Valentine Feerick **Bred** C J M Partnership **Trained** West Ilsley, Berks

FOCUS
A modest maiden which was slowly run, and muddling form which has been rated around the front pair.
Dollar Express(USA) Official explanation: jockey said colt missed the break

395 HINDLEAP WALK H'CAP — 7f (P)
3:05 (3:07) (Class 6) (0-58,57) 4-Y-O+ — **£2,047** (£604; £302) **Stalls** Low

Form | | | | RPR
0120 **1** **Ardent Prince**[5] 353 6-9-0 55 RobertWinston 7 65
(A J McCabe) *t.k.h: in tch: chsd ldrs 2f out: rdn to ld fnl 100yds: r.o wl* **8/1**

-443 **2** ¾ **Loyal Royal (IRE)**[9] 294 6-8-10 56 (b) JackDean(5) 10 64
(J M Bradley) *stdd and dropped in bhd after s: plld hrd and hld up in rr: hdwy over 1f out: str run to go 2nd wl ins fnl f: unable to chal wnr* **8/1**

2-53 **3** ½ **Torquemada (IRE)**[4] 355 8-8-12 53 (tp) PaulDoe 6 59
(M J Attwater) *hld up wl in tch: trckd ldng pair jst over 2f out: ev ch over 1f out: rdn to ld ent fnl f: sn hdd and unable qck* **9/2**[1]

2-46 **4** ½ **Cavalry Guard (USA)**[17] 210 5-8-3 **49**........................(b) AmyBaker(5) 5 54
(T D McCarthy) *chsd ldr: ev ch and rdn 2f out tl no ex and btn ins fnl f* **9/1**
53-0 **5** 1½ **Melt (IRE)**[5] 344 4-9-2 **57**........................(p) DaneO'Neill 11 58
(R Hannon) *towards rr: rdn 3f out: hdwy over 2f out: kpt on u.p fr over 1f out: nvr pce to rch ldrs* **12/1**
05-3 **6** hd **Copperwood**[19] 192 4-8-9 **50**........................ FergusSweeney 12 50
(M Blanshard) *stdd and dropped in bhd after s: hld up in rr: stl plenty to do and n.m.r 2f out: styd on fnl f: nvr trbld ldrs* **13/2**[3]
242- **7** hd **Comrade Cotton**[38] 7801 5-9-2 **57**........................(p) AdamKirby 9 57
(J Ryan) *in tch in midfield: reminders 3f out: drvn and unable qck 2f out: kpt on same pce fnl f* **5/1**[2]
31-0 **8** 3½ **Wooden King (IRE)**[7] 321 4-9-0 **55**........................ NCallan 3 45
(P D Evans) *led: rdn 2f out: hdd over 1f out: wknd qckly fnl f* **15/2**
-150 **9** hd **Too Grand**[19] 192 4-9-0 **55**........................(v) NeilChalmers 4 45
(J J Bridger) *in tch in midfield: rdn and unable qck wl over 2f out: no ch w ldrs fnl f* **33/1**
10 ½ **Princess Teddy (IRE)**[183] 4713 6-8-7 **48**........................(b) FrankieMcDonald 8 37
(Edgar Byrne) *a towards rr: nvr nr ldrs* **25/1**
60-0 **11** 1¾ **Affirmatively**[25] 111 4-8-7 **48**........................ LukeMorris 2 32
(A W Carroll) *stdd and v.s.a: a bhd* **33/1**
36-5 **12** 5 **Kannon**[13] 256 4-9-0 **55**........................(v) DarrenWilliams 1 25
(I W McInnes) *chsd ldrs: rdn wl over 2f out: sn struggling: wl bhd fnl f* **11/1**

1m 24.34s (-0.46) **Going Correction** +0.075s/f (Slow) **12** Ran SP% **117.9**
Speed ratings (Par 101): **105,104,103,103,101 101,100,96,96,96 94,88**
toteswinger: 1&2 £18.60, 1&3 £9.60, 2&3 £9.70. CSF £68.90 CT £324.28 TOTE £9.20: £2.90, £2.30, £2.20; EX 85.40 Trifecta £379.10 Part won. Pool: £512.43 - 0.85 winning units..
Owner Barry M Fletcher **Bred** Anthem Flight Partnership **Trained** Averham Park, Notts

FOCUS
A moderate handicap but a fair race for the grade and it was very open. There was a fair pace on and the form makes enough sense.
Copperwood Official explanation: jockey said gelding ran too free and had to be checked on final bend
Princess Teddy(IRE) Official explanation: jockey said mare lost its action on the bend

396 SCOTS PINES H'CAP 6f (P)
3:35 (3:35) (Class 4) (0-85,85) 3-Y-O **£4,857** (£1,445; £722; £360) **Stalls** Low

Form RPR
-111 **1** **Five Star Junior (USA)**[10] 288 3-9-5 **85** 6ex........................ TomEaves 3 96+
(Mrs L Stubbs) *hld up in tch: hdwy to trck ldrs 2f out: qcknd to ld jst ins fnl f: r.o strly: easily* **5/4**[1]
2-43 **2** 3¼ **Satwa Street (IRE)**[18] 203 3-9-4 **84**........................ MartinDwyer 5 84
(D M Simcock) *led: rdn jst over 1f out: hdd jst ins fnl f: no ch w wnr* **7/4**[2]
3 ¾ **Vegas Baby (IRE)**[138] 6093 3-9-3 **83**........................ TPQueally 1 81
(J A Osborne) *s.i.s: racd in last pl: rdn over 2f out: outpcd over 1f out: kpt on to go 3rd ins fnl f: no ch w wnr* **9/1**
360- **4** 2½ **Mazzola**[110] 6769 3-9-1 **81**........................ TonyCulhane 6 71
(M R Channon) *chsd ldr: rdn 2f out: wknd over 1f out* **8/1**[3]
1-60 **5** 8 **Sir Geoffrey (IRE)**[18] 203 3-9-1 **81**........................(b[1]) PatCosgrave 4 45
(A J McCabe) *wnt rt s: plld hrd: chsd ldrs: rdn over 2f out: wknd 2f out: wl btn and eased ins fnl f* **25/1**

1m 11.44s (-0.46) **Going Correction** +0.075s/f (Slow) **5** Ran SP% **105.8**
Speed ratings (Par 99): **106,101,100,97,86**
toteswinger: 1&2 £2.50. CSF £3.32 TOTE £2.00: £1.10, £1.20; EX 3.00.
Owner Moyns Park Stud **Bred** Robert W Sanford **Trained** Norton, N Yorks

FOCUS
An interesting little sprint handicap in which the progressive Five Star Junior posted another personal best.
Sir Geoffrey(IRE) Official explanation: trainer said gelding had a breathing problem

397 TOP PINES H'CAP 1m (P)
4:10 (4:10) (Class 5) (0-75,70) 3-Y-O **£2,900** (£856; £428) **Stalls** High

Form RPR
000- **1** **Fong's Alibi**[138] 6086 3-9-4 **70**........................ MartinDwyer 8 74+
(J S Moore) *hld up in tch: rdn and dropped in rr over 2f out: c wd wl over 2f out: edgd lft but str run to ld wl ins fnl f: wl in command at fin* **12/1**
505- **2** ¾ **Ageebah**[114] 6697 3-8-11 **63**........................ NCallan 7 65
(C E Brittain) *chsd ldrs: wnt 2nd and rdn jst over 2f out: led narrowly 1f out: hdd and nt pce of wnr wl ins fnl f* **12/1**
20-2 **3** ½ **Captainrisk (IRE)**[14] 239 3-9-4 **70**........................(b[1]) TPQueally 3 71
(M Botti) *s.i.s: t.k.h: led after 1f out: rdn ent fnl 2f: hdd 1f out: kpt on same pce after* **4/1**[1]
36-3 **4** ½ **Diamond Twister (USA)**[28] 69 3-9-2 **68**........................(t) ChrisCatlin 4 68
(J R Best) *t.k.h: hld up in tch in rr: effrt on inner wl over 1f out: chsd ldrs ins fnl f: no imp fnl 100yds* **9/2**[2]
655- **5** ½ **Flying Lady (IRE)**[107] 6857 3-9-2 **68**........................ TonyCulhane 6 67
(M R Channon) *chsd ldr: rdn and racd awkwardly bnd 2f out: nt qckn and one pce fr over 1f out* **9/1**[3]
050- **6** ½ **Persian Buddy**[140] 6026 3-9-3 **69**........................ RobertHavlin 2 67+
(Jamie Poulton) *s.i.s: hld up in tch in rr: hdwy on outer 4f out: rdn and unable qck over 1f out: keeping on same pce whn squeezed for room ins fnl f* **12/1**
534- **7** ¾ **Bartica (IRE)**[49] 7700 3-8-13 **65**........................(p) SteveDrowne 5 61
(R Hannon) *in tch: rdn over 2f out: hanging lft after: keeping on same pce and btn whn nt clr run jst ins fnl f* **4/1**[1]
361- **8** 5 **Give Us A Song (USA)**[102] 6988 3-9-2 **68**........................ LukeMorris 1 52
(J S Moore) *t.k.h: chsd ldrs: rdn jst over 2f out: wknd u.p ent fnl f* **4/1**[1]

1m 40.01s (1.81) **Going Correction** +0.075s/f (Slow) **8** Ran SP% **111.3**
Speed ratings (Par 97): **93,92,91,91,90 90,89,84**
toteswinger: 1&2 £20.30, 1&3 £11.30, 2&3 £7.30. CSF £134.97 CT £669.46 TOTE £15.10: £3.60, £3.80, £1.50; EX 152.50 Trifecta £498.50 Part won. Pool: £673.72 - 0.45 winning units..
Owner T & Mrs J Cunningham & R Frost **Bred** Darley **Trained** Upper Lambourn, Berks
■ Stewards' Enquiry : Martin Dwyer caution: careless riding

FOCUS
A wide-open three-year-old handicap, run at a steady pace and there was a bunched finish. Modest form, but the winnre is perhaps worth a bit of extra credit.
Bartica(IRE) Official explanation: jockey said colt hung badly left
Give Us A Song(USA) Official explanation: jockey said colt ran too free

398 ASHDOWN FOREST H'CAP 1m (P)
4:40 (4:40) (Class 5) (0-75,75) 4-Y-O+ **£2,729** (£806; £403) **Stalls** High

Form RPR
02-0 **1** **Tous Les Deux**[19] 191 6-9-1 **72**........................ GeorgeBaker 10 80
(G L Moore) *stdd and dropped in bhd after s: hld up in rr: hdwy on outer 2f out: rdn over 1f out: r.o wl to ld wl ins fnl f* **9/2**[2]
00-3 **2** ½ **Shake On It**[7] 321 5-8-2 **64** oh1 ow3........................(t) WilliamCarson(5) 3 71
(M J Gingell) *stdd s: t.k.h: hld up in rr: stl plenty to do 2f out: gd hdwy over 1f out: rdn to ld ins fnl f: hdd and no ex wl ins fnl f* **18/1**
3-42 **3** shd **Wavertree Warrior (IRE)**[22] 143 7-9-1 **72**........................(b) LukeMorris 9 79
(N P Littmoden) *rn in snatches: towards rr: rdn along 3f out: drvn wl over 1f out: no hdwy tl str burst ins fnl f: fin wl: nt quite rch ldng pair* **7/1**[3]
20-2 **4** ¾ **Star Strider**[14] 238 5-9-2 **73**........................ SteveDrowne 1 78
(Miss Gay Kelleway) *s.i.s: hld up towards rr: hdwy jst over 2f out: ev ch and drvn jst ins fnl f: no ex fnl 75yds* **7/1**[3]
040- **5** ½ **King's Ransom**[54] 7650 6-8-6 **70**........................ MatthewDavies(7) 4 74
(S Gollings) *led after 1f: rdn and hdd jst over 2f out: ev ch after tl no ex fnl 100yds* **16/1**
21-3 **6** 1 **King's Colour**[21] 155 4-8-10 **67**........................ IanMongan 5 69
(B R Johnson) *chsd ldr tl led jst over 2f out: drvn over 1f out: hdd ins fnl f: wknd fnl 100yds* **4/1**[1]
051- **7** 1 **Young Bertie**[44] 7771 6-8-9 **66**........................(v) TravisBlock 11 66
(H Morrison) *led for 1f: chsd ldrs after: rdn jst over 2f out: unable qck u.p over 1f out: one pce fnl f* **8/1**
-53U **8** 1 **Kensington (IRE)**[9] 297 8-9-2 **73**........................(p) NCallan 2 70
(P D Evans) *chsd ldrs on inner: rdn and effrt 2f out: ev ch ent fnl f: wknd ins fnl f* **14/1**
420- **9** nk **Sam's Cross (IRE)**[70] 7457 4-9-4 **75**........................ DarrenWilliams 7 72
(K R Burke) *t.k.h: hld up in tch: trckd ldrs jst over 2f out: drvn and fnd little over 1f out: wknd ent fnl f* **9/2**[2]
464- **10** 5 **Straight And Level (CAN)**[44] 7771 4-8-12 **69**........................(v) DaneO'Neill 8 54
(Miss Jo Crowley) *in tch in midfield: dropped to rr and rdn 2f out: wl btn and eased ins fnl f* **11/1**

1m 37.22s (-0.98) **Going Correction** +0.075s/f (Slow) **10** Ran SP% **118.6**
Speed ratings (Par 103): **107,106,106,105,105 104,103,102,101,96**
toteswinger: 1&2 £20.60, 1&3 £9.60, 2&3 £21.80. CSF £83.01 CT £581.84 TOTE £6.90: £2.10, £5.60, £2.20; EX 77.50 Trifecta £418.70 Part won. Place 6: £67.32 Place 6: £58.62.
Owner A Grinter **Bred** G And Mrs Middlebrook **Trained** Lower Beeding, W Sussex

FOCUS
They went a fair gallop here and the first three all came from the back of the field. The form is sound.
Straight And Level(CAN) Official explanation: jockey said colt was struck into
T/Jkpt: Not won. T/Plt: £215.70 to a £1 stake. Pool: £104,073.51. 352.09 winning tickets. T/Qpdt: £77.40 to a £1 stake. Pool: £7,920.00. 75.70 winning tickets. SP

377 SOUTHWELL (L-H)
Thursday, February 5

OFFICIAL GOING: Standard
Wind: Nil Weather: Overcast and cold

399 ARENALEISUREPLC.COM H'CAP (DIV I) 1m (F)
1:00 (1:00) (Class 6) (0-50,51) 4-Y-O+ **£1,706** (£503; £252) **Stalls** Low

Form RPR
60-1 **1** **Safebreaker**[25] 130 4-8-12 **50**........................(p) RobertWinston 4 63
(K A Ryan) *trckd ldrs: pushed along over 3f out: hdwy to ld 2f out: rdn and edgd lft over 1f out: clr ins fnl f* **4/7**[1]
-240 **2** 5 **Nautical**[7] 327 11-8-10 **48**........................ GregFairley 7 49
(J R Holt) *in tch: hdwy over 3f out: rdn to chse ldng pair 2f out: drvn to chse wnr ent fnl f: sn no imp* **8/1**[3]
-050 **3** ¾ **Louisiade (IRE)**[16] 224 8-8-6 **51** ow2........................(b) BMcHugh(7) 6 50
(M C Chapman) *prom: led over 4f out: rdn along 3f out: hdd 2f out and sn drvn: one pce appr fnl f* **7/1**[2]
503- **4** 1¾ **Tour D'Amour (IRE)**[190] 4537 6-8-12 **50**........................ PaulHanagan 2 45
(R Craggs) *led 1f: cl up on inner tl rdn along over 3f out and sn one pce* **7/1**[2]
0-40 **5** 1½ **Pembo**[9] 302 4-8-7 **48**........................ KevinGhunowa(3) 9 40
(R A Harris) *chsd ldrs and sn pushed along: rdn and outpcd 1/2-way: kpt on u.p fnl 2f: n.d* **12/1**
5-00 **6** 7 **Fifth Zak**[23] 147 5-8-13 **46** oh1........................ PatrickDonaghy(5) 3 32
(S R Bowring) *dwlt: hdwy and led after 1f: hdd over 4f out: sn rdn along and wknd over 3f out* **18/1**
500- **7** 9 **Kai Mer (IRE)**[278] 1795 4-8-9 **47** oh1 ow1........................ TomEaves 8 2
(Miss J A Camacho) *dwlt: a in rr* **14/1**
0-00 **8** 7 **Fan Club**[21] 177 5-8-8 **46** oh1........................(b) AndrewElliott 11 —
(Mrs R A Carr) *cl up: rdn along 1/2-way and sn wknd* **66/1**
30-0 **9** 2¼ **Naughty Girl (IRE)**[30] 63 9-8-1 **46** oh1........................ SoniaEaton(7) 12 —
(John A Harris) *a in rr* **33/1**

1m 43.31s (-0.39) **Going Correction** -0.225s/f (Stan) **9** Ran SP% **123.8**
Speed ratings (Par 101): **92,87,86,84,83 76,67,60,57**
toteswinger: 1&2 £2.60, 1&3 £2.20, 2&3 £3.50. CSF £6.95 CT £21.79 TOTE £1.80: £1.10, £3.20, £1.30; EX 6.20 Trifecta £13.50 Pool: £286.23 - 15.61winning units..
Owner Hambleton Racing Ltd X **Bred** Gainsborough Stud Management Ltd **Trained** Hambleton, N Yorks

FOCUS
After the morning snow the track rode quite deep. A depleted field for this low-grade handicap.

400 MEMBERSHIP AT SOUTHWELL GOLF CLUB H'CAP 5f (F)
1:30 (1:30) (Class 5) (0-75,75) 4-Y-O+ **£2,729** (£806; £403) **Stalls** High

Form RPR
5111 **1** **Whiskey Creek**[13] 269 4-8-9 **73**........................(b) BMcHugh(7) 5 84+
(C A Dwyer) *cl up: led over 2f out: rdn clr ent fnl f: styd on* **3/1**[1]
-622 **2** nk **Incomparable**[7] 329 4-9-1 **72**........................ TomEaves 3 82
(A J McCabe) *cl up: rdn and ev ch over 1f out: drvn and rallied ins fnl f: kpt on wl towards fin* **10/3**[2]
-401 **3** 1 **Grand Palace (IRE)**[15] 235 6-8-10 **67**........................(v) PaulHanagan 8 73
(D Shaw) *in tch: rdn along 2f out: swtchd lft and drvn ent fnl f: styd on wl towards fin* **14/1**
-003 **4** 1 **Colorus (IRE)**[7] 326 6-8-2 **64** oh1 ow3........................(p) PatrickDonaghy(5) 4 66
(W J H Ratcliffe) *chsd ldrs: rdn along and n.m.r over 1f out: edgd lft and kpt on same pce ins fnl f* **7/1**
0-44 **5** ½ **Steel City Boy (IRE)**[14] 243 6-8-10 **67**........................ DarrenWilliams 7 68
(D Shaw) *stmbld and sltly hmpd s: towards rr tl hdwy 1/2-way: rdn over 1f out: kpt on ins fnl f: nrst fin* **7/1**
-233 **6** nk **Circle Dance (IRE)**[11] 286 4-8-12 **69**........................(v) AdamKirby 2 69
(D Shaw) *chsd ldrs on wd outside: rdn along 1/2-way: wknd over 1f out* **12/1**
5-12 **7** ½ **Calmdownmate (IRE)**[7] 326 4-8-8 **65**........................ AndrewElliott 9 63
(Mrs R A Carr) *in tch in outer: hdwy to chse ldrs 2f out: sn rdn and one pce* **7/2**[3]

40-0 **8** *6* **Garlogs**[7] 329 6-9-4 **75**.. RobertWinston 12 51
(R Hollinshead) *led: rdn along 1/2-way: sn hdd and grad wknd* **18/1**

6-33 **9** *nk* **Peter's Storm (USA)**[20] 197 4-9-2 **73**...................(p) GrahamGibbons 10 48
(K A Ryan) *in tch: rdn along 1/2-way: sn wknd* **11/1**

59.49 secs (-0.21) **Going Correction** +0.05s/f (Slow) **9** Ran SP% **123.3**
Speed ratings (Par 103): **103,102,100,99,98 98,97,87,87**
toteswinger: 1&2 £2.70, 1&3 £6.00, 2&3 £5.70. CSF £14.23 CT £127.06 TOTE £3.50: £1.30, £1.80, £3.00; EX 12.30 Trifecta £101.10 Pool: £2.83 - 386.95 winning units..
Owner Mrs L Wheeler **Bred** R J H West **Trained** Burrough Green, Cambs
■ Stewards' Enquiry : Adam Kirby caution: used whip down shoulder in forehand position.

FOCUS
The main action took place up the centre of the track.

401 SOUTHWELL-RACECOURSE.CO.UK CLAIMING STKS 6f (F)
2:00 (2:00) (Class 6) 4-Y-O+ **£2,047** (£604; £302) **Stalls** Low

Form RPR

-431 **1** **Tender Process (IRE)**[11] 289 6-8-7 65......................(v) PaulHanagan 4 72
(R A Fahey) *trckd ldrs: hdwy wl over 2f out: chal wl over 1f out: rdn to ld appr fnl f: kpt on* **7/4**[1]

5-11 **2** *1½* **Charlotte Grey**[23] 150 5-8-1 59...................................... DuranFentiman(3) 3 64
(P J McBride) *led: rdn along over 2f out: hdd wl over 1f out: drvn and rallied over 1f out and evch tl no ex ins fnl f* **9/2**[3]

5652 **3** *nk* **Obe Royal**[9] 303 5-8-4 62...................................(b) PatrickDonaghy(5) 1 68
(P D Evans) *in tch: rdn along and hdwy over 2f out: drvn over 2f out: styd on ins fnl f: nrst fin* **6/1**

1263 **4** *1¼* **Don Pele (IRE)**[8] 314 7-8-8 72...............................(b) KevinGhunowa(3) 6 66
(R A Harris) *trckd ldrs: cl up 1/2-way: rdn to ld briefly wl over 1f out: sn drvn and hdd appr fnl f: wknd* **5/2**[2]

000- **5** *2½* **Ice Planet**[41] 7780 8-8-2 66.. DeanHeslop(5) 2 54
(Mrs R A Carr) *towards rr tl styd on fnl 2f* **9/1**

330- **6** *9* **Cleveland**[155] 5601 7-8-9 60 ow2................................. GrahamGibbons 10 27
(R Hollinshead) *cl up on outer: rdn along 3f out: wknd over 2f out* **15/2**

00-0 **7** *11* **Bewdley**[23] 150 4-8-6 41... AndrewElliott 11 —
(R E Peacock) *a in rr* **50/1**

000- **8** *½* **Minimum Fuss (IRE)**[57] 7629 5-7-11 38.........................(b) AmyBaker(5) 8 —
(M C Chapman) *prom: rdn along 1/2-way and sn wknd* **80/1**

1m 15.06s (-1.44) **Going Correction** -0.225s/f (Stan) **8** Ran SP% **122.4**
Speed ratings (Par 101): **100,98,97,95,92 80,65,65**
toteswinger: 1&2 £1.70, 1&3 £2.80, 2&3 £3.00. CSF £11.15 TOTE £4.50: £1.50, £1.40, £1.40; EX 10.10 Trifecta £19.40 Pool: £371.26 - 14.13 winning units..Tender Process was claimed by J. R. Boyle for £5000.
Owner J J Staunton **Bred** Timothy Coughlan **Trained** Musley Bank, N Yorks
■ Stewards' Enquiry : Kevin Ghunowa caution: used whip with arm above shoulder height

FOCUS
A fair race by claiming standards.

402 HOSPITALITY AT SOUTHWELL RACECOURSE H'CAP 2m (F)
2:30 (2:30) (Class 6) (0-65,65) 4-Y-O+ **£2,047** (£604; £302) **Stalls** Low

Form RPR

04-1 **1** **Merrion Tiger (IRE)**[23] 147 4-9-6 **63**................................ GregFairley 12 74+
(A G Foster) *trckd ldng pair: effrt on inner 3f out: chal 2f out: rdn to ld wl over 1f out and sn edgd rt: drvn ins fnl f and kpt on wl* **6/5**[1]

0-51 **2** *½* **Blue Hills**[9] 301 8-9-10 **61** 6ex................................(b) DarrenWilliams 5 71
(P W Hiatt) *cl up: led 1/2-way: rdn along 3f out: jnd over 2f out and sn drvn: hdd wlover 1f out: rallied u.p ins fnl f: no ex towards fin* **5/1**[3]

-141 **3** *10* **Sabancaya**[9] 300 4-9-8 **65** 6ex.. MickyFenton 9 63
(Mrs P Sly) *trckd ldrs: effrt over 3f out: rdn over 2f out: drvn and outpcd fr wlover 1f out* **15/8**[2]

/0-0 **4** *6* **Up In Arms (IRE)**[27] 103 5-9-6 **64**.................................... BMcHugh(7) 8 55
(P Winkworth) *hld up in tch: tk clsr order 4f out: rdn along 3f out: sn drvn and no imp fnl 2f* **5/1**[3]

-360 **5** *18* **Que Beauty (IRE)**[9] 301 4-7-11 **47** ow2...........(p) AndrewHeffernan(7) 1 16
(R C Guest) *led to 1/2-way: cl up tl rdn along over 4f out and sn wknd* **25/1**

3m 39.75s (-5.75) **Going Correction** -0.225s/f (Stan)
WFA 4 from 5yo+ 6lb **5** Ran SP% **117.4**
Speed ratings (Par 101): **105,104,99,96,87**
toteswinger: 1&2 £4.80. CSF £8.45 TOTE £2.50: £1.20, £2.00; EX 8.30 Trifecta £12.20 Pool: £210.90 - 12.77 winning units..
Owner S C B Limited **Bred** Denis Fehan **Trained** Haddington, East Lothian

FOCUS
A depleted field with nine non-runners due to travel problems, and a very steady gallop until the final half mile.

403 PLAY GOLF AT SOUTHWELL GOLF CLUB (S) STKS 7f (F)
3:00 (3:00) (Class 6) 3-Y-O **£2,047** (£604; £302) **Stalls** Low

Form RPR

44- **1** **Kheskianto (IRE)**[55] 7652 3-8-6 57................................... NickyMackay 6 63
(M Botti) *trckd ldrs: hdwy over 2f out: rdn to ld over 1f out: edgd lft and kpt on ins fnl f* **7/2**[3]

1032 **2** *1¾* **Hawkspring (IRE)**[4] 363 3-9-3 65......................................(t) AdamKirby 7 69
(S Parr) *a.p: hdwy 3f out: led over 2f out and sn rdn: drvn and hdd over 1f out: kpt on same pce u.p ins fnl f* **5/4**[1]

155- **3** *2* **Kinigi (IRE)**[51] 7694 3-8-9 61..................................... KevinGhunowa(3) 3 59
(R A Harris) *trckd ldrs on inner: hdwy to chal 2f out and sn rdn: ev ch tl drvn and one pce ent fnl f* **7/1**

054- **4** *5* **Chocolicious (IRE)**[40] 7794 3-8-6 67.................................. GregFairley 8 40
(B Smart) *t.k.h: chsd ldrs on outer: rdn along 3f out and sn btn* **9/4**[2]

0-30 **5** *1¾* **Helpmeronda**[10] 295 3-8-3 58...................................(b[1]) DuranFentiman(3) 1 35
(S A Callaghan) *dwlt: hdwy 1/2-way: rdn and in tch 2f out: sn drvn and wknd* **17/2**

0- **6** *7* **Foxtrot Bravo (IRE)**[50] 7709 3-8-11 0................................. LukeMorris 2 21
(P Winkworth) *a in rr: bhd fr 1/2-way* **20/1**

500 **7** *2* **Royal Mischief (IRE)**[20] 196 3-8-2 45 ow1.............. PatrickDonaghy(5) 4 11
(P D Evans) *led: rdn along 3f out: hdd over 2f out and wknd qckly* **50/1**

1m 28.5s (-1.80) **Going Correction** -0.225s/f (Stan) **7** Ran SP% **127.2**
Speed ratings (Par 95): **101,99,96,91,89 81,78**
toteswinger: 1&2 £1.70, 1&3 £3.50, 2&3 £3.10. CSF £9.53 TOTE £4.70: £2.90, £1.40; EX 15.30 Trifecta £78.70 Pool: £338.20 - 3.18 winning units..The winner was bought by M.C. Chapman for 3,500gns.
Owner Giuliano Manfredini **Bred** Tinnakill Partnership II **Trained** Newmarket, Suffolk

FOCUS
Little to choose between the first three home on official ratings.

Chocolicious(IRE) Official explanation: jockey said filly hung right on bend

404 SOUTHWELL RACECOURSE FOR CONFERENCES H'CAP 7f (F)
3:30 (3:30) (Class 4) (0-80,76) 4-Y-O+ **£4,857** (£1,445; £722; £360) **Stalls** Low

Form RPR

161- **1** **Smarty Socks (IRE)**[85] 7284 5-9-1 **73**.......................... JamieMoriarty 6 79
(P T Midgley) *s.i.s and reminders s: hdwy on inner 2f out: rdn and styd on to ld ent fnl f: kpt on towards fin* **6/4**[1]

330- **2** *hd* **Flores Sea (USA)**[130] 6314 5-8-7 **70**.............................. DeanHeslop(5) 8 76
(T D Barron) *cl up tl hung rt and wd home turn: sn rdn: styd on strly on outer ins fnl f: jst hld* **6/1**[3]

53U0 **3** *1* **Kensington (IRE)**[1] 398 8-8-10 **73**......................(b) PatrickDonaghy(5) 7 76
(P D Evans) *hld up in tch: hdwy over 2f out: sn rdn: drvn over 1f out: kpt on ins fnl f* **10/1**

12-4 **4** *¾* **Captain Macarry (IRE)**[34] 9 4-9-2 **74**............................(v) TomEaves 3 75
(B Smart) *prom: effrt over 2f out and sn rdn: drvn and ev ch over 1f out: kpt on same pce ins fnl f* **7/2**[2]

0-14 **5** *1* **Tri Chara (IRE)**[23] 152 5-8-10 **68**.................................. GrahamGibbons 2 66
(R Hollinshead) *led: rdn along over 2f out: drvn over 1f out: hdd ent fnl f and wknd* **7/2**[2]

06-6 **6** *9* **Kabeer**[34] 9 11-9-4 **76**...(t) RobertWinston 4 50
(A J McCabe) *chsd ldrs: rdn along 1/2-way sn drvn and btn wl over 1f out* **12/1**

1m 27.17s (-3.13) **Going Correction** -0.225s/f (Stan) **6** Ran SP% **115.5**
Speed ratings (Par 105): **108,107,106,105,104 94**
toteswinger: 1&2 £2.80, 1&3 £3.30, 2&3 £7.40. CSF £11.66 CT £66.69 TOTE £2.00: £1.10, £4.10; EX 12.70 Trifecta £82.30 Pool: £379.70 - 3.41 winning units..
Owner R G Fell **Bred** Mick McGinn **Trained** Westow, N Yorks

FOCUS
A fair handicap run at a sound pace.

405 ARENALEISUREPLC.COM H'CAP (DIV II) 1m (F)
4:00 (4:00) (Class 6) (0-50,53) 4-Y-O+ **£1,706** (£503; £252) **Stalls** Low

Form RPR

500- **1** **Muncaster Castle (IRE)**[52] 7691 5-8-10 **48**............ FrankieMcDonald 4 54
(R F Fisher) *in tch: rdn along: hung lft and outpcd over 4f out: hdwy on inner over 2f out: rdn to ld ent fnl f: kpt on wl* **14/1**

0-00 **2** *nk* **Komreyev Star**[16] 224 7-8-7 **48**..............................(p) DuranFentiman(3) 2 53
(R E Peacock) *in tch: hdwy 3f out: rdn 2f out and sn ev ch tl drvn ins fnl f and no ex towards fin* **11/1**

-224 **3** *1* **Amber Moon**[11] 290 4-8-12 **50**...(b) TPQueally 12 53
(J A Osborne) *prom: hdwy on outer 3f out: rdn 2f out and sn ev ch: drvn over 1f out: no ex u.p wl ins fnl f* **2/1**[1]

6-30 **4** *½* **Mister Benji**[23] 150 10-8-8 **46**......................................(p) AndrewElliott 6 48
(B P J Baugh) *prom: hdwy 3f out: rdn to ld 2f out: drvn and hdd ent fnl f: one pce* **5/2**[2]

0500 **5** *4* **Government (IRE)**[16] 222 8-8-3 **46** oh1.............................. AmyBaker(5) 5 39
(M C Chapman) *led 3f: prom tl rdn along wl over 2f out and grad wknd* **28/1**

00-0 **6** *½* **Zabeel House**[29] 81 6-8-12 **50**..(p) AdamKirby 10 42
(John A Harris) *racd wd: in tch and reminders after 3f: outpcd 1/2-way: kpt on fr over 1f out: n.d* **10/1**

00-0 **7** *3¾* **Sharps Gold**[29] 71 4-8-12 **50**.......................................(bt) LukeMorris 11 33
(D Morris) *stdd s: midfield tl hdwy on bit over 3f out: swtchd rt and rdn 2f out: sn no imp* **12/1**

0-00 **8** *1¾* **Only A Grand**[23] 150 5-8-9 **47** oh1 ow1..............................(b) TomEaves 8 26
(R Bastiman) *cl up: led after 3f: rdn along 3f out: hdd 2f out and sn wknd* **12/1**

00-0 **9** *12* **Actuality**[23] 150 7-8-8 **46**.. RobertWinston 9 —
(J Balding) *midfield: rdn along over 3f out: sn drvn and wknd* **4/1**[3]

00-0 **10** *10* **Veronicas Way**[25] 131 4-8-10 **53** oh1 ow7..............(v) JamesO'Reilly(5) 3 —
(G J Smith) *cl up on inner: rdn along 1/2-way and sn wknd* **25/1**

000/ **11** *38* **King Of Dalyan (IRE)**[552] 4136 4-8-3 **46** oh1.......... PatrickDonaghy(5) 1 —
(Miss Tracy Waggott) *a in rr: bhd fr 1/2-way* **50/1**

1m 42.63s (-1.07) **Going Correction** -0.225s/f (Stan) **11** Ran SP% **130.6**
Speed ratings (Par 101): **96,95,94,94,90 89,85,84,72,62 24**
toteswinger: 1&2 £25.70, 1&3 £18.60, 2&3 £8.00. CSF £172.53 CT £460.13 TOTE £21.50: £5.70, £3.30, £1.30; EX 207.30 TRIFECTA Not won..
Owner Des Johnston **Bred** Doc Bloodstock **Trained** Ulverston, Cumbria

FOCUS
A low-grade handicap run at a sound pace. The first two stuck to the inner in the home straight and they came out best in the end.

Actuality Official explanation: jockey said gelding never travelled

406 SOUTHWELL FOR RACING AND GOLF H'CAP 1m 3f (F)
4:30 (4:30) (Class 5) (0-70,73) 4-Y-O+ **£2,729** (£806; £403) **Stalls** Low

Form RPR

3-61 **1** **Mustajed**[6] 341 8-9-9 **73** 6ex.. JamesMillman(3) 3 79
(B R Millman) *trckd ldrs on inner: effrt 3f out: rdn over 2f out: drvn and styd on ent fnl f: sn edgd rt: led fnl 100yds* **3/1**[2]

3-31 **2** *hd* **Boundless Prospect (USA)**[15] 237 10-9-1 **67**..... PatrickDonaghy(5) 1 73
(P D Evans) *hld up in rr: hdwy on outer 3f out: rdn over 1f out: styd on to chal ins fnl f: sn drvn and ev ch tl nt qckn nr fin* **8/1**

04-1 **3** *nk* **Edas**[7] 324 7-9-6 **67** 6ex.. GrahamGibbons 4 72
(J J Quinn) *trckd ldrs: hdwy to chse ldr 3f out: rdn to chal 2f out and ev ch tl drvn ent fnl f and no ex fnl 100yds* **4/7**[1]

01-6 **4** *¾* **Eseej (USA)**[8] 311 4-9-2 **65**.. DarrenWilliams 8 69
(P W Hiatt) *stmbld s: sn led: rdn along over 2f out and sn jnd: rdn over 1f out: drvn ent fnl f: hdd & wknd fnl 100yds* **12/1**

04-1 **5** *2* **Onemoreandstay**[28] 90 4-8-13 **67**...................................... MCGeran(5) 6 68
(M D Squance) *t.k.h: chsd ldr: rdn along and sltly outpcd 3f out: drvn and hdwy over 1f out: one pce ent fnl f* **7/1**[3]

2m 25.22s (-2.78) **Going Correction** -0.225s/f (Stan)
WFA 4 from 6yo+ 2lb **5** Ran SP% **120.0**
Speed ratings (Par 103): **101,100,100,100,98**
toteswinger: 1&2 £5.90. CSF £26.41 TOTE £4.10: £1.80, £1.90; EX 23.80 Trifecta £23.40 Pool: £417.78 - 13.17 winning units. Place 6: £9.16 Place 5: £7.50.
Owner Mrs L S Millman **Bred** Shadwell Estate Company Limited **Trained** Kentisbeare, Devon
■ Stewards' Enquiry : Patrick Donaghy three-day ban: used whip with excessive frequency down shoulder in forehand position (Feb 19-21)

FOCUS
A very steady pace until the final half-mile and all five were still in with a shout entering the final furlong.

Onemoreandstay Official explanation: jockey said filly ran too free

T/Jkpt: £753.70 to a £1 stake. Pool: £22,823.47. 21.50 winning tickets. T/Plt: £6.40 to a £1 stake. Pool: £85,410.01. 9,630.02 winning tickets. T/Qpdt: £4.70 to a £1 stake. Pool: £5,081.59. 785.10 winning tickets. JR

[349]WOLVERHAMPTON (A.W) (L-H)
Thursday, February 5
407 Meeting Abandoned - Snow

[334]NAD AL SHEBA (L-H)
Thursday, February 5
OFFICIAL GOING: Turf course - good; dirt course - fast

413a INTIKHAB TROPHY (H'CAP) (TURF) 7f 110y(D)
3:45 (3:47) (95-110,109) 3-Y-O+
£50,000 (£16,666; £8,333; £4,166; £2,500; £1,666)

RPR

1 **Summit Surge (IRE)**[110] 6814 5-9-5 **109**..........(t) JMurtagh 13 111
(G M Lyons, Ire) *in rr of mid-div: smooth prog to trck ldrs 1 1/2f out: led 1f out: comf* **17/2**

2 1 1/4 **Calming Influence (IRE)**[14] 260 4-9-1 **105**..........(t) LDettori 12 104
(Saeed Bin Suroor) *settled in rr: smooth prog to chal 2 1/2f out: nt qckn fnl f* **11/2**[1]

3 hd **King Jock (USA)**[14] 265 8-9-0 **104**.......... MJKinane 10 103
(A Manuel, UAE) *mid-div: trckd ldrs 2 1/2f out: r.o same pce fnl 110yds* **16/1**

4 3 1/4 **Little White Lie (IRE)**[68] 7492 5-8-13 **102**.......... WJSupple 5 93
(A bin Huzaim, UAE) *mid-div: r.o same pce fnl 2f* **20/1**

5 1 **Grantley Adams**[14] 257 6-8-11 **101**.......... TPO'Shea 3 89
(E Charpy, UAE) *s.i.s: mid-div: chsd ldrs 2 1/2f out: nt qckn* **10/1**

6 1/2 **Valedictum (AUS)**[19] 9-9-5 **109**..........(bt) TedDurcan 11 96
(Danny O'Brien, Australia) *mid-div: rdn 2 1/2f out: r.o same pce* **14/1**

7 1/2 **Glow Star (SAF)**[211] 5-8-8 **98**..........(b) RyanMoore 2 83
(H J Brown, South Africa) *nvr bttr than mid-div* **11/2**[1]

8 4 1/4 **Lion's Blood (SAF)**[14] 257 5-9-0 **104**.......... JohnEgan 8 79
(H J Brown, South Africa) *in rr of mid-div: rdn 3f out: n.d* **16/1**

9 1 **Artimino**[7] 335 5-8-8 **98**.......... FJara 7 70
(I Mohammed, UAE) *nvr able to chal* **7/1**[2]

10 3/4 **Blue Sky Basin**[189] 4553 4-8-13 **102**.......... AhmedAjtebi 9 73
(M bin Shafya, UAE) *trckd ldrs: ev ch 3f out: led briefly 3f out: sn hdd: wknd* **11/2**[1]

11 7 1/2 **Yard-Arm (SAF)**[714] 531 10-8-9 **99**.......... RMBurke 4 51
(R Bouresly, Kuwait) *trckd ldrs: led briefly 2 1/2f out: sn wknd* **40/1**

12 4 **Hallhoo (IRE)**[46] 7-8-10 **100**.......... WilliamBuick 1 42
(D Selvaratnam, UAE) *sn led: hdd 2 1/2f out: sn btn* **33/1**

13 1/2 **Prince Shaun (IRE)**[14] 265 4-9-3 **107**..........(t) DO'Donohoe 6 47
(Doug Watson, UAE) *mid-div: chsd ldrs 2 1/2f out: nt qckn* **8/1**[3]

14 17 **Tawaash (USA)**[13] 4-8-7 **97**.......... RHills 14 —
(E Charpy, UAE) *mid-div: rn wd: nvr able to chal: eased fnl f* **33/1**

1m 30.94s (-0.66) **Going Correction** +0.35s/f (Good) 14 Ran SP% **120.9**
Speed ratings: **117,115,115,112,111 110,110,106,105,104 96,92,92,75**
CSF 52.93; Tricast 750.44..
Owner W Bellew **Bred** Norelands Bloodstock **Trained** Dunsany, Co. Meath

FOCUS
There was a false running rail in place on the turf course and that, combined with some of the low-drawn runners going off too fast, resulted in those held up from high stalls dominating. This was a decent handicap.

NOTEBOOK
Summit Surge(IRE) had to concede weight to most of his rivals off a mark of 110, but that rating didn't look too harsh judged on his defeat of Prince Shaun, who has been placed off 107 at this year's Carnival (but down the field today), in a Group 3 at Leopardstown last year. He was given a fantastic ride by Murtagh, who weaved a passage towards the inside when picking up from well back, and that made all the difference as the runner-up, who was similarly held up, made his move wide. The Group 3 Zabeel Mile on February 26 could be a suitable target. (op 8-1)
Calming Influence(IRE) looked one to avoid when throwing away a winning chance by hanging in a similar race over this course and distance two weeks ago, but although again beaten into second, it was difficult to fault this effort. The strong pace suited, but he made his move very wide in the straight, whereas the winner got a run towards the inside, and that seemed to make the difference. (op 5-1 tchd 6-1)
King Jock(USA) is at his best off a decent gallop, so everything went his way and this was a solid effort.
Little White Lie(IRE) ◆ did not look at all badly handicapped judged on the pick of his British form for John Jenkins and this was a decent first effort in Dubai, faring best of those to race handy. He can win a similar race off this sort of mark.
Grantley Adams is thoroughly exposed and vulnerable in this sort of company, but he ran well and maybe should have finished even closer, as he had to force his way through a gap towards the inside rail after initially being denied a clear run. (op 9-1\n\x\x)
Valedictum(AUS), the Australian challenger, kept on but was never a threat.
Glow Star(SAF) ran reasonably and is entitled to be better for the outing having been off for 211 days.
Artimino was left with loads to do after having to switch wide at the top of the straight, but he could still have been expected to pick up better considering the early leaders got tired.
Blue Sky Basin ◆ was progressive for Andrew Balding last year, but his last three wins were gained with an uncontested lead. That was never going to be the case this time, and he got tired after doing plenty of racing early. His connections felt he would improve for the run and he has more races in him when getting an easier trip towards the front end. (op 5-1)

414a BAHRI (H'CAP) (DIRT) 7f (D)
4:15 (4:21) (90-105,104) 3-Y-O+
£45,833 (£15,277; £7,638; £3,819; £2,291; £1,527)

RPR

1 **Snaafy (USA)**[6] 5-8-7 **93**..........(v) RHills 13 96
(M Al Muhairi, UAE) *slowly away: in rr of mid-div: r.o wl fnl 2f: led nr line* **16/1**

2 1 3/4 **Noble Citizen (USA)**[14] 265 4-8-9 **95**..........(be) RichardMullen 16 93
(D M Simcock) *mid-div: rdn to chse ldrs 2 1/2f out: led briefly 110yds out: hdd cl home* **16/1**

3 3/4 **Halkin (USA)**[7] 340 7-9-1 **100**.......... EddieAhern 4 97
(F Nass, Bahrain) *trckd ldrs: led 2 1/2f out: drew clr 1 1/2f out: hdd 165yds out* **14/1**

4 3 1/2 **Bounty Quest**[7] 336 7-8-7 **93**.......... FJara 11 80
(Doug Watson, UAE) *mid-div: chsd ldrs 2 1/2f out: one pce fnl f* **10/1**

5 4 1/2 **League Champion (USA)**[7] 336 6-9-4 **104**.......... KJohn 5 78
(R Bouresly, Kuwait) *trckd ldrs: wknd fnl 2 1/2f* **16/1**

6 3/4 **Quicksand (SAF)**[14] 261 5-8-11 **97**.......... KShea 14 69
(M F De Kock, South Africa) *trckd ldrs: ev ch 3f out: r.o same pce: wknd fnl 110yds* **11/4**[1]

7 3/4 **Skywards**[35] 7-9-1 **100**..........(t) TPO'Shea 1 71
(E Charpy, UAE) *nvr bttr than mid-div* **16/1**

8 10 **Marbush (IRE)**[336] 815 8-9-1 **100**..........(e) WilliamBuick 12 44
(D Selvaratnam, UAE) *nvr nr to chal* **8/1**[3]

9 1/4 **Minted (FR)**[152] 4-8-9 **95**..........(bt) DBadel 8 38
(E Charpy, UAE) *n.d* **25/1**

10 2 3/4 **Happy Runner (BRZ)**[350] 649 6-9-1 **100**.......... MJKinane 6 36
(E Martins, Bahrain) *settled in rr: nvr able to chal* **16/1**

11 1 1/4 **Charlies Island (SAF)**[7] 336 6-8-10 **96**.......... RyanMoore 10 28
(H J Brown, South Africa) *nvr a threat* **12/1**

12 11 **Underworld**[7] 335 4-8-13 **98**.......... WayneSmith 7 1
(M Al Muhairi, UAE) *sn last: nvr nr to chal: r.o fnl 2 1/2f* **16/1**

13 3 1/4 **Flying Blue (FR)**[14] 259 4-9-1 **100**..........(tp) JMartinez 9 —
(R Martin Sanchez, Spain) *nvr able to chal* **20/1**

14 1 **Blank Cheque (SAF)**[319] 6-8-5 **90**.......... KLatham 3 —
(H J Brown, South Africa) *in rr of mid-div: n.d* **20/1**

15 1 1/2 **Iguazu Falls (USA)**[21] 182 4-9-1 **100**.......... LDettori 15 —
(Saeed Bin Suroor) *settled in rr: rn v wd 3f out: nvr nr to chal* **7/1**[2]

16 9 1/2 **Dubai Dreamer (USA)**[56] 7-8-5 **90**..........(bt) AhmedAjtebi 2 —
(A Al Raihe, UAE) *led on rail: hdd 2 1/2f out: wknd qckly: eased 1f out* **16/1**

1m 24.56s (-0.24) **Going Correction** +0.20s/f (Slow) 16 Ran SP% **128.3**
Speed ratings: **109,107,106,102,97 96,95,83,83,80 79,66,62,61,59 49**
CSF 256.91; Tricast 3,680.90..
Owner Hamdan Al Maktoum **Bred** Shadwell Farm LLC **Trained** UAE

FOCUS
They went very quick early, setting this up for those ridden with patience. This was a competitive handicap, but the form is ordinary for the level.

NOTEBOOK
Snaafy(USA) found himself well off the pace after missing the break, but that was a good thing considering the leaders went off too fast, and he picked up best when produced out wide with his challenge in the straight. This was a big step up on his recent Jebel Ali form, but things will not always pan out so kindly and a higher mark should make things tougher next time.
Noble Citizen(USA) could make no impression on the turf on his Dubai debut two weeks earlier, but this was a lot better. Like the winner, he swung wide off the final turn and had every chance in the straight.
Halkin(USA), who got warm beforehand, promised to be suited by this drop in trip, as he's a strong traveller in his race, but he doesn't do much off the bridle and seemed to find himself in front too soon after chasing the strong pace. He might be able to nick a similar race under a slightly more patient ride.
Bounty Quest was never a threat on this step back up in trip.
League Champion(USA) deserves some credit as he fared best of those who helped force the gallop. (op 14-1)
Quicksand(SAF) had too much use made of him over an extended 1m in a race set up for the closers here two weeks ago, so this drop in trip looked likely to suit, but he again did too much racing early. He was also forced three wide into the straight, although the front two were even wider, so that's no excuse. He might be able to win a similar when there is less pressure on the early lead. (op 7-2)
Marbush(IRE), expected to need this first start in almost a year, did not take the bend into the straight all that well and was in the kickback throughout, so he could leave this form behind. (op 7-1)
Iguazu Falls(USA) was unsteerable in a visor on turf three weeks earlier, so he had the headgear left off for this switch to dirt, but he produced another abysmal effort. He was never going after starting slowly and is one to have reservations about, even if a return to turf might help. (op 6-1)

415a TAMAYUZ (H'CAP) (TURF) 1m 2f (T)
4:45 (4:47) (95-110,110) 3-Y-O+
£50,000 (£16,666; £8,333; £4,166; £2,500; £1,666)

RPR

1 **Halicarnassus (IRE)**[111] 6780 5-9-4 **108**.......... TPO'Shea 4 107
(M R Channon) *mid-div: smooth prog 2 1/2f out: r.o wl fnl 1 1/2f: led cl home* **14/1**

2 3/4 **Bruges (IRE)**[7] 334 4-8-6 **96** ow1..........(bt) RHills 8 94
(A Al Raihe, UAE) *in rr of mid-div: trckd ldrs 2f out: r.o wl: nrst fin* **33/1**

3 nse **Without A Prayer (IRE)**[14] 261 4-9-0 **105**.......... LDettori 2 102
(R M Beckett) *trckd ldrs: led 1 1/2f out: r.o wl: hdd cl home* **7/1**[2]

4 1 1/4 **Bucked Off (SAF)**[14] 261 5-8-6 **96**.......... JohnEgan 12 90
(H J Brown, South Africa) *in rr of mid-div: rn wd 2 1/2f out: r.o one pce* **20/1**

5 hd **Pearly King (USA)**[14] 262 6-8-5 **95**.......... C-PLemaire 7 89
(M Al Muhairi, UAE) *mid-div: rdn to chse ldrs 2 1/2f out: nt qckn* **33/1**

6 nse **Duellant (IRE)**[103] 6992 4-8-11 **102**.......... AStarke 13 96
(P Schiergen, Germany) *sn led: hdd 1 1/2f out: kpt on same pce* **16/1**

7 1/2 **Charlie Cool**[21] 183 6-8-8 **98**.......... WilliamBuick 5 91
(D Selvaratnam, UAE) *settled in rr: sme prog 2 1/2f out: n.d* **25/1**

8 1/2 **Via Galilei (IRE)**[14] 263 4-8-10 **101**.......... KJManning 1 93
(J S Bolger, Ire) *mid-div on rail: swtchd wd 2 1/2f out: one pce* **16/1**

9 3/4 **Hawks Home (USA)**[14] 262 6-8-6 **96**..........(v) WayneSmith 9 86
(M Al Muhairi, UAE) *trckd ldrs: rdn 2 1/2f out: wknd fnl f* **20/1**

10 4 1/4 **Bound By Honour (SAF)**[14] 265 6-9-3 **107**..........(bt) RyanMoore 10 89
(H J Brown, South Africa) *settled in rr: hrd rdn 3f out: n.d* **5/4**[1]

11 1 3/4 **Feared In Flight (IRE)**[124] 6476 4-8-7 **98**.......... TedDurcan 14 76
(Saeed Bin Suroor) *mid-div: rdn to chse ldrs 2 1/2f out: one pce* **9/1**[3]

12 2 1/4 **Galactic Star**[130] 6303 6-8-10 **110**.......... AntiocoMurgia(10) 3 84
(M bin Shafya, UAE) *settled in rr: nvr nr to chal* **7/1**[2]

13 3 1/4 **Dr Faustus (IRE)**[14] 263 4-8-7 **98**..........(e) DO'Donohoe 11 65
(Doug Watson, UAE) *in rr of mid-div: n.d* **25/1**

14 3 1/2 **Varsity**[14] 263 6-8-10 **100**..........(tp) KLatham 6 60
(C F Swan, Ire) *broke v awkwardly: racd in rr: nvr involved* **20/1**

2m 6.54s (2.04) **Going Correction** +0.35s/f (Good)
WFA 4 from 5yo+ 1lb 14 Ran SP% **125.7**
Speed ratings: **105,104,104,103,103 103,102,102,101,98 96,95,92,89**
CSF 423.01; Tricast 3,494.03..
Owner M Channon **Bred** Yeomanstown Lodge Stud **Trained** West Ilsley, Berks

FOCUS
A good handicap on paper, but a steady early pace resulted in a bunch finish and the bare form is suspect. The winning time was 0.79 seconds slower than the second division won by Eastern Anthem.

NOTEBOOK

Halicarnassus(IRE) made little impression off much higher marks as last year's Carnival, but he found himself better handicapped this time around following some modest efforts when last seen in Britain and he returned to form to take full advantage. He showed a decent turn of foot to pick up off the modest gallop and was well on top at the line. This was a good prize to win, but a rise in the weights may prevent him following up.

Bruges(IRE) was unbeaten in two runs as a juvenile when trained in Ireland, including winning a Listed race, but he had lost his way badly since then. He had offered nothing in two runs since switching to Dubai this year, but finally returned to something like his two-year-old form, clearly proving suited by a steadily run 1m2f. He seems to have the ability to win a similar race, but it remains to be seen which way he'll go, especially in a stronger-run race.

Without A Prayer(IRE), no doubt glad to be back on turf, was well placed considering the lack of pace and had absolutely every chance, but this trip just stretched him, even in a slowly run race. He should be suited by a return to 1m.

Bucked Off(SAF), just as on the dirt two weeks earlier, did not help himself by carrying his head high. He had every chance, but did not convince that he went through with his effort.

Pearly King(USA) looked unlucky not to finish even closer as he had nowhere to go when about to pass rivals inside the final furlong, although it's debatable whether he had the momentum of the winner.

Duellant(IRE) got his own way at a steady pace, but it's almost impossible to make all over middle-distances on this turf track.

Via Galilei(IRE) saw even less daylight than Pearly King, as his run was blocked for most of the straight. He hardly flew home when finally in the clear near the line, and it's hard to know just how unlucky he was, but it's fair to say he probably would have finished a good deal closer with one continuous run.

Bound By Honour(SAF) had three winners from this year's Carnival (Silver Mist, Strategic News and Hunting Tower) behind when third in a Group 1 in South Africa last year, and had run a pleasing race over an inadequate 1m on his Dubai debut two week earlier. However, he never went a yard with the blinkers (also on in SA) and tongue-tie applied, and was one of the first beaten. It's fair to say his trainer's horses have been in mixed form so far this year.

Feared In Flight(IRE) offered little on his debut for Saeed Bin Suroor.

Varsity was never seen with a chance after starting very slowly.

416a CAPE VERDI SPONSORED BY DERRINSTOWN STUD (GROUP 3) (FILLIES) (TURF) — 1m (T)

5:15 (5:16) 3-Y-O+

£83,333 (£27,777; £13,888; £6,944; £4,166; £2,777)

Pos	Dist	Horse	Jockey	RPR
1		**Deem (IRE)**[41] 4-9-0 104 — (J Barton, Saudi Arabia) *trckd ldrs: hung rt: rdn to ld 1 1/2f out: r.o wl* **20/1**	FJara 6	108+
2	1 1/2	**Front House (IRE)**[194] 4-9-3 105 — (M F De Kock, South Africa) *trckd ldrs: led 2f out: r.o wl* **5/4**[1]	KShea 2	108
3	1 1/4	**Eva's Request (IRE)**[131] 6266 4-9-0 104 — (M R Channon) *mid-div on rail: chsd ldrs 2 1/2f out: r.o wl* **7/1**[3]	TedDurcan 1	102
4	1/2	**Peace Royale (GER)**[156] 5596 4-9-2 109 — (A Wohler, Germany) *mid-div: rdn to chse ldrs 2 1/2f out: r.o* **9/2**[2]	EPedroza 3	103
5	2 1/4	**Happy Spirit (SAF)**[21] 180 5-9-3 99 — (H J Brown, South Africa) *settled in rr: gng wl 4f out: r.o fnl 1 1/2f* **7/1**[3]	RyanMoore 11	99
6	1 1/4	**My Central (ITY)**[130] 5-9-0 100 — (H J Brown, South Africa) *racd in rr: nvr able to chal* **20/1**	KLatham 10	93+
7	1/2	**Jalmira (IRE)**[21] 180 8-9-0 106 — (E Charpy, UAE) *mid-div: rdn 3f out: nt qckn* **12/1**	TPO'Shea 8	92+
8	hd	**Akua'Ba (IRE)**[7] 340 5-9-0 102 — (J S Bolger, Ire) *settled in rr: nvr nr to chal* **25/1**	(tp) KJManning 9	91+
9	6 1/4	**Clifton Dancer**[21] 180 4-9-0 95 — (Tom Dascombe) *mid-div: n.d* **20/1**	WilliamBuick 4	77+
10	11	**Inca Noble (ARG)**[21] 180 5-9-0 100 — (M F De Kock, South Africa) *sn led: hdd & wknd 2f out* **16/1**	(e) JMurtagh 5	52
11	shd	**Olympic Glory (BRZ)**[11] 5-9-0 90 — (A Al Raihe, UAE) *mid-div: rdn 4f out: sn btn* **100/1**	RichardMullen 7	51+

1m 38.97s (0.67) **Going Correction** +0.35s/f (Good) 11 Ran SP% **120.3**
Speed ratings: **110,108,107,106,104 103,102,102,96,85 85**
CSF 44.23..
Owner Prince Sultan Mohammed Saud Al Kabeer **Bred** Prince Sultan Al Kabeer **Trained** Saudi Arabia

FOCUS

A decent renewal of the Cape Verdi, which has been upgraded from Listed status since last year, but the pace was just ordinary and those who raced handy seemed favoured.

NOTEBOOK

Deem(IRE) ◆ was unbeaten in three starts on the dirt in Saudi Arabia, despite having an out-and-out turf pedigree, and she showed herself to be a very smart filly on this switch to grass. It's fair to say the runner-up wants further, but the same could be said about the winner considering her sire won an Arc, and she is out of a Sadler's Wells mare, and there was no fluke whatsoever about this success. The Group 3 Balanchine (like this race upgraded from a Listed contest since last year) for fillies & mares over just short of 1m1f on February 20 looks the next logical step.

Front House(IRE) ◆ had the race put up on a plate for her by stablemate, Inca Noble, getting a good lead off that rival before swooping to take a gap against the inside rail when that one weakened at the top of the straight, but she simply lacked the speed of the winner, who was getting 3lb. There's no doubting her class - she won a Grade 2 in South Africa last year despite getting no weight allowance from a bunch of fillies around six months older than her - and she's entitled to come on for this run, but she basically needs further. She will surely get closer to today's winner if they meet again in the Balanchine later in the month, and the combination of the extra yardage and improvement for a run might be enough for her to reverse form, but we are unlikely to see the very best of her until she goes over 1m4f. (op 11-8)

Eva's Request(IRE), successful in a Listed handicap at Ascot off a mark of 99 when last seen in September, ran a good race in defeat and probably just bumped into two very smart fillies. (op 13-2)

Peace Royale(GER), a very decent German-trained filly, was just too keen for her own good but this was still a creditable effort.

Happy Spirit(SAF) ◆ was given too much to do considering both the modest pace and that she wants further than this 1m trip. She ran well considering and will be dangerous when stepped up in distance, but the Balanchine may not be far enough for her.

My Central(ITY), formerly trained in Italy, never got in a blow.

Akua'Ba(IRE) had something to find and the steady pace was no help. (op 20-1)

Clifton Dancer is not up to this class, but she looks a better filly when able to dominate.

417a AL MAKTOUM CHALLENGE R2 SPONSORED BY DERRINSTOWN STUD (GROUP 3) (DIRT) — 1m 1f (D)

5:45 (5:46) 3-Y-O+

£83,333 (£27,777; £13,888; £6,944; £4,166; £2,777)

Pos	Dist	Horse	Jockey	RPR
1		**My Indy (ARG)**[21] 184 5-9-0 113 — (Saeed Bin Suroor) *trckd ldrs: led 2f out: r.o wl: a holding on* **5/6**[1]	LDettori 6	117+
2	3/4	**Happy Boy (BRZ)**[21] 184 6-9-0 108 — (M bin Shafya, UAE) *mid-div on rail: chsd ldrs 2 1/2f out: r.o: nt qckn fnl f* **33/1**	AhmedAjtebi 2	115
3	hd	**Asiatic Boy (ARG)**[313] 1092 6-9-0 117 — (M F De Kock, South Africa) *trckd ldr: t.k.h: led 3f out: hdd 2f out r.o wl* **13/8**[2]	JMurtagh 5	115
4	5 1/4	**Gloria De Campeao (BRZ)**[21] 184 6-9-0 111 — (P Bary, France) *trckd ldrs: ev ch 2 1/2f out: nt qckn* **20/1**	JLeme 8	104
5	2 1/4	**Glen Nevis (USA)**[14] 261 5-9-0 105 — (A Al Raihe, UAE) *in rr of mid-div: nvr able to chal* **33/1**	(v) RichardMullen 9	99
6	1 1/2	**Don Renato (CHI)**[21] 184 6-9-0 109 — (J Barton, Saudi Arabia) *trckd ldrs on rail: rdn 3f out: r.o same pce* **9/1**[3]	(vt) MJKinane 3	96
7	10	**Military Power**[14] 263 4-9-0 95 — (M bin Shafya, UAE) *sn led on rail: hdd 3f out: wknd* **50/1**	JRosales 4	75
8	dist	**Fleurie**[11] 4-9-0 93 — (R Bouresly, Kuwait) *sn struggling in rr: nvr involved* **100/1**	RMBurke 7	—
9	dist	**Supaseus**[159] 5528 6-9-0 110 — (H Morrison) *s.i.s: racd in last: nvr nr to chal* **22/1**	RyanMoore 1	—

1m 50.53s (0.73) **Going Correction** +0.20s/f (Slow) 9 Ran SP% **120.6**
Speed ratings: **104,103,103,98,96 95,86,—,—**
CSF 42.79..
Owner Godolphin **Bred** Haras La Quebrada **Trained** Newmarket, Suffolk

FOCUS

The most famous winner of this race is undoubtedly subsequent World Cup winner Moon Ballad in 2003, but more often than not the overall quality falls short of the very highest level. This looked a good race, and strong form by Group 3 standards, but again probably slightly below top class.

NOTEBOOK

My Indy(ARG) looked a much-improved horse when a clear-cut winner of the first round of this series over 1m three weeks earlier and he confirmed that impression in this tougher heat, although he was understandably made to work harder. It's fair to say he enjoyed the run of the race, and was given a fine ride by Dettori, who restrained him just off the speed dual between Military Power and the free-running Asiatic Boy, and he had just enough left in the straight as a result. He didn't appear to flash his tail this time - there was no faulting his attitude - but he got tired near the line, allowing both the runner-up and third to finish closer than had looked likely a furlong out, and this looks the absolute limit of his stamina. It would be no surprise to see him take his chance in the third round of the Al Maktoum Challenge, although that his traditionally much stronger than the first two legs, and is also over an extra furlong, so it's hard to see this run continuing. (op Evs)

Happy Boy(BRZ) completely lost the plot after bolting up in the first round of this series last year for Brazilian connections, and he ran poorly in that race first-time up for this yard last month, but like so many from the Bin Shafya camp, he unexpectedly returned to form. His first-season trainer is quickly proving himself very adept at getting underachievers to produce their best, so it would be no surprise were Happy Boy to repeat this form, or even build on it next time, but things are likely to get tougher in terms of competition in the short term at least.

Asiatic Boy(ARG) had won first-time up at the last two Carnivals, but he was too free this time and got in a speed dual with Military Power. That had softened him up by the time he came off the bridle in the straight and he finished a tired horse, putting up little resistance when challenged by My Indy and wandering about under pressure. He should improve a fair bit for the run, and can be expected to reverse form with today's winner should they meet in the third round of this challenge, but we know he's vulnerable to anything top class. (tchd 7-4)

Gloria De Campeao(BRZ) is simply not quite up to winning a race like this.

Glen Nevis(USA), just as when causing a surprise in a handicap off a mark of 100 here two weeks earlier, was doing all his best work at the finish, but the leaders didn't come back to him this time. (op 25-1)

Don Renato(CHI) broke much better than is often the case, so it was disappointing he did not put up more of a show. He was stuck in behind the leaders towards the inside, which wasn't ideal, but he should still have run better.

Supaseus started slowly and was never going on this first try on dirt. (op 20-1)

418a MARJU TROPHY (H'CAP) (TURF) — 6f 110y(T)

6:15 (6:16) (100-113,113) 3-Y-O+

£72,916 (£24,305; £12,152; £6,076; £3,645; £2,430)

Pos	Dist	Horse	Jockey	RPR
1		**Hatta Fort**[14] 257 4-8-13 **108** — (Saeed Bin Suroor) *mid-div: smooth prog to trck ldrs 2f out: led 1f out: r.o wl* **3/1**[1]	(t) LDettori 10	109
2	shd	**Imbongi (SAF)**[194] 5-9-3 **112** — (M F De Kock, South Africa) *settled in rr: smooth prog to trck ldrs 1 1/2f out: r.o; nrst fin* **9/2**[2]	KShea 12	113+
3	3/4	**Balthazaar's Gift (IRE)**[14] 257 6-9-1 **110** — (R Simpson, UAE) *hmpd at s: settled last: nvr able to chal: r.o wl fnl 1 1/2f: nrst fin* **25/1**	DO'Donohoe 5	109+
4	shd	**Intrepid Jack**[117] 6645 7-9-1 **110** — (H Morrison) *in rr of mid-div: chsd wnr 2f out: nt qckn fnl f* **10/1**	RyanMoore 4	109
5	hd	**Star Crowned (USA)**[14] 264 6-9-1 **110** — (R Bouresly, Kuwait) *trckd ldrs: led 1 1/2f out: outpcd fnl f* **8/1**	(t) MJKinane 9	108
6	1 1/4	**Leandros (FR)**[14] 259 4-8-9 **105** — (G M Lyons, Ire) *broke awkwardly: mid-div: nvr able to chal* **7/1**[3]	(b) KLatham 6	99
7	1 1/2	**Beaver Patrol (IRE)**[139] 6073 7-8-8 **104** — (Eve Johnson Houghton) *trckd ldrs tl rdn 3f out: sn btn* **14/1**	(v) C-PLemaire 1	93
8	shd	**Prince Tamino**[14] 257 6-8-11 **107** — (A Al Raihe, UAE) *mid-div: nvr able to chal* **12/1**	RichardMullen 8	96
9	1/2	**Munaddam (USA)**[14] 259 7-9-1 **110** — (E Charpy, UAE) *in rr of mid-div: chsd ldrs 2 1/2f out: one pce fnl 1 1/2f* **7/1**[3]	RHills 7	98
10	1/2	**Conquest (IRE)**[7] 335 5-8-13 **108** — (M bin Shafya, UAE) *in rr of mid-div: rdn 3f out: n.d* **33/1**	AhmedAjtebi 2	95
11	1 1/2	**Drift Ice (SAF)**[14] 259 8-8-9 **105** — (M F De Kock, South Africa) *mid-div: gng wl but n.m.r 1 1/2f out: nt rcvr* **16/1**	(be) TedDurcan 3	87
12	3 1/2	**Narc (SAF)**[313] 1089 7-9-4 **113** — (H J Brown, South Africa) *sn led: t.k.h: hdd 1 1/2f out: wknd* **22/1**	FJara 11	85

1m 19.76s (2.26) **Going Correction** +0.35s/f (Good) 12 Ran SP% **119.8**
Speed ratings: **101,100,100,99,99 98,96,96,95,95 93,89**
CSF 15.50; Tricast 289.10..
Owner Godolphin **Bred** Wellsummers Farm **Trained** Newmarket, Suffolk

FOCUS

A good, competitive sprint handicap. Interestingly, just as in the opening extended 7f contest on the turf, a high draw was obviously no disadvantage.

NOTEBOOK

Hatta Fort confirmed the promise he showed when looking unlucky in a similar contest behind Prince Tamino two weeks earlier, but he only just held on. He travelled strongly throughout, but arrived on the scene sooner than ideal, with Dettori probably keen to avoid a repeat of the traffic problems from last time, and having been held together for as long as possible, before eventually being pushed out, he just found enough to hold off Imbongi.

Imbongi(SAF), a triple Grade 2 winner over slightly further in South Africa last year, produced a sustained effort on the outside and this was a fine debut in Dubai. He should be competitive in Group company back over further.

Balthazaar's Gift(IRE), an eye-catcher on his debut for this trainer two week earlier, was out the back for most of the way after a nightmare exit from the stalls, but he flashed home late on to grab third. He has plenty of talent, but is not easy to win with.
Intrepid Jack looks the type who could do well in turf handicaps in Dubai and this was a solid effort in defeat.
Star Crowned(USA) is very smart on dirt, but he's possibly even better on turf and he was not beaten far. (op 15-2)
Leandros(FR) did not build on his recent second to Munaddam, but a slightly awkward start didn't help and he was not beaten far at the finish.
Beaver Patrol(IRE) looked one or the more likely candidates beforehand but he did not feature.
Drift Ice(SAF) got absolutely no run against the inside rail all the way up the straight and this run is best ignored.

419a ALHAARTH (H'CAP) (TURF) 1m 2f (T)
6:45 (6:45) (95-110,109) 3-Y-0+

£50,000 (£16,666; £8,333; £4,166; £2,500; £1,666)

RPR
1 **Eastern Anthem (IRE)**[173] 5094 5-9-3 **107**....................(t) AhmedAjtebi 1 112+
(M bin Shafya, UAE) *racd in rr: smooth prog to trck runner-up 2f out: n.m.r 1f out: led 55yds out* **9/1**
2 1 ¼ **Fiery Lad (IRE)**[90] 7235 4-9-4 **109**.......................... JMurtagh 9 109
(G M Lyons, Ire) *mid-div on rail: trckd ldrs 1 1/2f out: led 1f out: hdd cl home* **7/1**[3]
3 4 ½ **Captain Webb**[14] 262 4-8-9 **99**....................(t) TedDurcan 10 90
(Saeed Bin Suroor) *mid-div: ev ch 2 1/2f out: r.o same pce* **9/2**[2]
4 nse **Arqaam**[7] 338 5-8-13 **102**....................(v) RHills 4 94
(Doug Watson, UAE) *sn led: drew clr 2 1/2f out: hdd 1f out: wknd* **20/1**
5 hd **Big Robert**[14] 262 5-8-7 **97** ow1.................... EddieAhern 2 88
(K R Burke) *slowly away: settled in rr: nvr nr to chal: r.o wl fnl 1 1/2f* **7/1**[3]
6 2 **Red Eye Express (IRE)**[125] 6458 4-8-9 **100**.................. MJKinane 5 87
(John M Oxx, Ire) *trckd ldrs: rdn to chse ldr 1 1/2f out: wknd 1f out* **5/2**[1]
7 1 ¾ **Love Galore (IRE)**[7] 338 4-8-8 **99**.................. RyanMoore 12 82
(M Johnston) *settled in rr: nvr nr to chal* **10/1**
8 1 ½ **Royal Prince**[14] 263 8-8-6 **96**.................. FJara 3 76
(Doug Watson, UAE) *mid-div on rail: n.d* **33/1**
9 hd **First Buddy**[147] 5851 5-8-5 **95**.................. RichardMullen 14 75
(S Seemar, UAE) *in rr of mid-div: nvr involved* **40/1**
10 1 **Bucintoro (IRE)**[90] 5-8-10 **100**..................(t) C-PLemaire 7 78
(C Theodorakis, Greece) *mid-div: gng wl 3f out: nt qckn fnl 2f* **28/1**
11 2 ½ **Mister Fasliyev (IRE)**[7] 337 7-8-11 **101**..................(t) TPO'Shea 11 74
(E Charpy, UAE) *in rr of mid-div: rn wd 3f out: nvr able to chal* **40/1**
12 1 ¾ **Yahrab (IRE)**[75] 7420 4-9-4 **109**.................. JRosales 8 78
(M bin Shafya, UAE) *broke awkwardly: trckd ldrs tl hrd rdn 2 1/2f out: wknd* **12/1**
13 ¾ **Desert Links (SAF)**[14] 265 6-9-4 **108**..................(b) KLatham 6 76
(H J Brown, South Africa) *nvr bttr than mid-div* **20/1**
14 ¾ **Tabadul (IRE)**[6] 8-8-5 **95**..................(v) WayneSmith 13 61
(M Al Muhairi, UAE) *mid-div: rn wd: nvr nr to chal* **50/1**

2m 5.75s (1.25) **Going Correction** +0.35s/f (Good)
WFA 4 from 5yo+ 1lb 14 Ran SP% **121.3**
Speed ratings: **109,108,104,104,104 102,101,100,99,99 97,95,95,94**
CSF 65.96; Tricast 328.39. PLACEPOT £472.10. Pool £21,764.92. 33.65 winning tickets. QUADPOT £35.70. Pool £1,396.55. 28.89 winning tickets..
Owner Sheikh Hamdan Bin Mohammed Al Maktoum **Bred** Darley **Trained** United Arab Emirates

FOCUS
A typical Carnival handicap; good form but most of these are exposed. The pace did not seem too steady by the usual standards for this trip on the turf course, and the winning time was 0.79 seconds quicker than the first division won by Halicarnassus.

NOTEBOOK
Eastern Anthem(IRE), who was last early, came through to ultimately score in tidy fashion. He still had loads to do early in the straight, and his path was continually blocked, but a gap eventually came towards the inside and it's fair to say the horse literally carted himself to the front when in the clear, winning with something to spare. Credit must go to Ajtebi, who is making a name for himself at this Carnival. Eastern Anthem did not really progress as one might have hoped for Godolphin, but he looked very smart on his debut for a first-season trainer who, like the jockey, is impressing.
Fiery Lad(IRE), a Listed winner on Polytrack in Ireland who was returning from a three-month break, weaved through towards the inside in the straight and picked up well, but he was simply unable to resist the winner's strong burst. He was well clear of the reminder and this was a good effort in defeat.
Captain Webb, runner-up over 1m4f around here two weeks previously, appeared unsuited by the drop back in trip.
Arqaam was given a beautiful ride from the front by Hills and briefly looked to have nicked this when kicking again early in the straight, but he could not sustain his effort, providing further evidence of just how difficult it is to make all over middle-distances on this turf track. (op 16-1)
Big Robert could not build on his recent unlucky in-running third (behind Captain Webb) over 1m4f around here last time. (tchd 15-2)
Red Eye Express(IRE), who missed his intended UAE debut with a bruised foot, was too keen for his own good after four months off and did not see his race out. A return to 1m should suit.
Love Galore(IRE) yet again refused to settle and looks one to avoid. (op 9-1)

[399]SOUTHWELL (L-H)
Friday, February 6

OFFICIAL GOING: Standard
Wind: Light behind Weather: Dry and cold

420 PLAY GOLF AT SOUTHWELL GOLF CLUB H'CAP 1m (F)
1:20 (1:21) (Class 6) (0-60,60) 4-Y-0+ **£2,047** (£604; £302) **Stalls** Low

Form RPR
060- 1 **Mudhish (IRE)**[174] 5090 4-9-4 **60**.................. NCallan 7 72
(C E Brittain) *cl up: led over 2f out: rdn and hung bdly lft over 1f out: clr fnl f* **7/1**
0-50 2 3 ½ **Moment Of Clarity**[13] 285 7-8-12 **54**..................(p) GrahamGibbons 2 58
(R C Guest) *trckd ldrs: hdwy on inner 3f out: rdn to chal 2f out and ch whn hmpd over 1f out: swtchd lft and kpt on same pce u.p fnl f* **10/3**[2]
0-06 3 1 ¾ **To Bubbles**[24] 152 4-8-10 **52**.................. FrankieMcDonald 3 52
(A G Newcombe) *in rr: hdwy 3f out: rdn along 2f out: styd on appr last: nrst fin* **28/1**
00-0 4 nk **Mont Cervin**[17] 224 4-8-8 **55**..................(b[1]) DeanHeslop[(5)] 5 54
(Mrs R A Carr) *led: rdn along 3f out: hdd over 2f out: drvn and keeping on whn hmpd and swtchd rt over 1f out: kpt on one pce: lost 3rd nr fin* **16/1**
04-0 5 1 ¼ **Pearl Dealer (IRE)**[21] 194 4-9-1 **57**.................. LukeMorris 1 53
(N J Vaughan) *s.i.s and in rr: t.k.h and in tch 1/2-way: effrt and rdn over 2f out: sn drvn and one pce* **8/1**
0-03 6 1 ¼ **Isabella's Fancy**[24] 150 4-8-3 **52**.................. DeclanCannon[(7)] 6 45
(A G Newcombe) *hld up: a towards rr* **9/2**[3]
5-00 7 10 **Desert Lover (IRE)**[18] 221 7-8-4 **46** oh1.................. NickyMackay 8 16
(R J Price) *prom: rdn along 1/2-way: sn wknd* **13/2**
546- 8 3 ¼ **Admirals Way**[117] 6685 4-8-13 **55**.................. TPQueally 10 18
(C N Kellett) *in tch on outer: rdn along over 3f out and sn wknd* **5/2**[1]

1m 42.69s (-1.01) **Going Correction** -0.15s/f (Stan) **8** Ran SP% **116.1**
Speed ratings (Par 101): **99,95,93,93,92 90,80,77**
toteswinger: 1&2 £4.80, 1&3 £15.50, 2&3 £18.10. CSF £31.10 CT £624.45 TOTE £7.00: £1.60, £1.60, £4.10; EX 39.80 TRIFECTA Not won..
Owner C E Brittain **Bred** Darley **Trained** Newmarket, Suffolk

FOCUS
A very weak handicap run at only a modest pace and doubts over the value of the form.
Isabella's Fancy Official explanation: jockey said filly hung left
Admirals Way Official explanation: trainer had no explanation for the poor form shown

421 HOSPITALITY AT SOUTHWELL RACECOURSE H'CAP 6f (F)
1:55 (1:57) (Class 6) (0-65,65) 3-Y-0 **£2,047** (£604; £302) **Stalls** Low

Form RPR
3-22 1 **Diamond Surprise**[3] 381 3-8-13 **65**.................. GabrielHannon[(5)] 3 70
(R Curtis) *t.k.h: cl up: effrt 2f out and sn pushed along: rdn to chal over 1f out: styd on u.p ins fnl f to ld nr fin* **1/1**[1]
-135 2 ½ **La Capriosa**[24] 149 3-9-3 **64**.................. RobertWinston 4 67
(A J McCabe) *led: rdn along wl over 1f out: drvn ins fnl f: hdd and no ex nr fin* **7/2**[3]
4-32 3 4 ½ **Gurteen Diamond**[16] 236 3-9-4 **65**.................. LukeMorris 2 54
(N J Vaughan) *t.k.h: trckd ldng pair: effrt on inner to chal 2f out: sn rdn and one pce appr fnl f* **5/2**[2]
500- 4 6 **Floods Of Tears**[54] 7674 3-8-12 **59**.................. ChrisCatlin 1 29
(D Flood) *chsd ldrs: rdn along over 2f out: sn wknd* **12/1**

1m 17.03s (0.53) **Going Correction** -0.15s/f (Stan) **4** Ran SP% **108.5**
Speed ratings (Par 95): **90,89,83,75**
CSF £4.79 TOTE £2.10; EX 5.40.
Owner Miss Jackie Penny **Bred** Miss Jackie Penny **Trained** Lambourn, Berks

FOCUS
A small field for this modest handicap. They went steadily until sprinting up the straight and it produced a close finish with the first two rated slight improvers.

422 MEMBERSHIP OF SOUTHWELL GOLF CLUB CLAIMING STKS 5f (F)
2:25 (2:30) (Class 6) 4-Y-0+ **£1,942** (£578; £288; £144) **Stalls** High

Form RPR
4221 1 **Grimes Faith**[3] 380 6-8-9 62..................(p) NCallan 2 76+
(K A Ryan) *t.k.h: led 1f: cl up tl led again on bit wl over 1f out: shkn up and qcknd clr ent fnl f: comf* **9/4**[2]
14-2 2 1 ¼ **Blue Tomato**[7] 349 8-8-6 84.................. WilliamCarson[(5)] 5 73
(D Nicholls) *hld up: effrt 2f out: sn rdn: edgd lft and styd on ins fnl f* **7/2**[3]
2-11 3 nk **Back In The Red (IRE)**[10] 304 5-8-13 68............(b) FrankieMcDonald 1 74
(R A Harris) *cl up: led after 1f: rdn 2f out and sn hdd: drvn and one pce ins fnl f* **2/1**[1]
-562 4 1 **Excusez Moi (USA)**[14] 266 7-9-5 99..................(b) LiamJones 4 76
(Mrs R A Carr) *chsd ldng pair: rdn along 2f out: drvn and one pce ent fnl f* **7/2**[3]

59.48 secs (-0.22) **Going Correction** -0.075s/f (Stan) **4** Ran SP% **108.5**
Speed ratings (Par 101): **98,96,95,93**
CSF £9.86 TOTE £2.80; EX 12.00.
Owner Mrs Angie Bailey **Bred** John Grimes **Trained** Hambleton, N Yorks

FOCUS
An interesting claimer despite the small field, not least because of the betting. The pair that appeared to have plenty to find on official ratings dominated the market, which suggests that punters placed proven ability to act in these conditions well ahead of handicap marks. Unfortunately the race was spoilt to a degree by the early dawdle set by Back In The Red, which is very unusual for races over this straight 5f. The winner is rated in line with his best recent effort with the runner-up and fourth below their best.

423 BOOK YOUR TICKETS ON LINE AT SOUTHWELL-RACECOURSE.CO.UK (S) STKS 1m 4f (F)
3:00 (3:00) (Class 6) 4-Y-0+ **£2,047** (£604; £302) **Stalls** Low

Form RPR
2-02 1 **Rawdon (IRE)**[10] 302 8-8-8 74..................(be[1]) KylieManser[(7)] 6 68+
(Miss Gay Kelleway) *hld up in tch: smooth hdwy 4f out: led wl over 2f out: pushed clr over 1f out: kpt on* **2/1**[1]
2 5 **Supsonic**[1] 6-9-1 65.................. RobertWinston 4 58
(R J Price) *cl up: led 1/2-way: hdd over 4f out: rdn and ev ch over 2f out: drvn over 1f out and kpt on same pce* **6/1**
20-5 3 ¾ **Calzaghe (IRE)**[16] 237 5-8-8 67..................(v) NSLawes[(7)] 3 56
(D Nicholls) *hld up in rr: hdwy over 2f out: rdn wl over 1f out: styd on ins fnl f* **7/2**[3]
-333 4 2 **Ebert**[10] 302 6-9-1 71.................. PaulHanagan 1 53
(R A Fahey) *led to 1/2-way: chsd ldrs tl rdn along and sltly outpcd wl over 2f out: rallied u.p over 1f out: sn no imp* **11/4**[2]
00-5 5 3 ¼ **Lawyer To World**[10] 302 5-9-1 35..................(v) VinceSlattery 5 48
(Mrs C A Dunnett) *trckd ldng pair: cl up 1/2-way: led over 4f out: rdn and hdd wl over 2f out and sn wknd* **40/1**
66-6 6 18 **Caltire (GER)**[7] 342 4-8-12 65..................(b) TPQueally 7 19
(M G Quinlan) *hld up towards rr: hdwy to chse ldrs 4f out: rdn along over 3f out and sn wknd* **9/1**
0/6- 7 23 **Tashkandi (IRE)**[25] 2076 9-9-1 72..................(b) JerryO'Dwyer 2 —
(Mrs S J Humphrey) *chsd ldrs: rdn along bef 1/2-way and sn wknd* **22/1**

2m 37.69s (-3.31) **Going Correction** -0.15s/f (Stan)
WFA 4 from 5yo+ 3lb **7** Ran SP% **113.3**
Speed ratings (Par 101): **105,101,101,99,97 85,70**
toteswinger: 1&2 £2.90, 1&3 £3.60, 2&3 £4.50. CSF £14.37 TOTE £2.80: £2.00, £2.60; EX 14.80.The winner was bought in for 5,500gns. Calzaghe was claimed by Frank Sheridan for £6,000.
Owner Mrs Donna Joslyn **Bred** Hascombe And Valiant Studs **Trained** Exning, Suffolk

FOCUS
A fair seller judged on official ratings but several were clearly flattered by their marks. The proximity of the fifth limits the form.

424 ARENA LEISURE PLC H'CAP 5f (F)
3:30 (3:35) (Class 4) (0-85,84) 4-Y-0+ **£4,857** (£1,445; £722; £360) **Stalls** High

Form RPR
15-4 1 **The Tatling (IRE)**[31] 67 12-9-2 **82**.................. RobertWinston 2 92
(J M Bradley) *trckd ldrs: swtchd lft and effrt over 1f out: rdn and qcknd to ld ent fnl f: sn clr* **7/1**[3]

1111 **2** *1 3/4* **Whiskey Creek**[1] [400] 4-8-6 **79** 6ex..............(b) BMcHugh(7) 6 83
(C A Dwyer) *cl up: effrt 2f out: sn rdn and ev ch tl drvn and nt qckn ins fnl f* **7/4**[1]

42-1 **3** *hd* **Wotashirtfull (IRE)**[22] [170] 4-8-13 **79**..............(p) PatCosgrave 7 82
(J R Boyle) *led: rdn 2f out: drvn over 1f out: drvn and hdd ent fnl f: kpt on u.p* **7/1**[3]

0-24 **4** *3/4* **First Order**[26] [128] 8-8-13 **84**..............(v) AnnStokell(5) 1 84
(Miss A Stokell) *cl up: effrt 2f out: sn rdn and ev ch tl wknd ent fnl f* **7/1**[3]

-643 **5** *1 1/2* **Bo McGinty (IRE)**[3] [382] 8-8-10 **76**..............(b) PaulHanagan 4 71
(R A Fahey) *cl up: rdn 2f out and ev ch tl drvn and wknd 1f out* **9/4**[2]

P-12 **6** *1* **Godfrey Street**[15] [250] 6-8-2 **75**..............(p) DeclanCannon(7) 3 66
(A G Newcombe) *cl up: rdn 2f out: ev ch tl drvn and wknd appr fnl f* **7/1**[3]

58.22 secs (-1.48) **Going Correction** -0.075s/f (Stan) **6** Ran SP% **117.1**
Speed ratings (Par 105): **108,105,104,103,101 99**
toteswinger: 1&2 £3.00, 1&3 £6.80, 2&3 £2.30. CSF £20.83 TOTE £9.50: £4.50, £1.40; EX 24.30.

Owner J M Bradley **Bred** Patrick J Power **Trained** Sedbury, Gloucs

FOCUS
By far the best race on the card and, with four of the sextet mixing it up front from the start, the winning time was 1.26 seconds faster than the claimer. The runner-up recorded a slight personal best with the third running to form.

Bo McGinty(IRE) Official explanation: jockey said gelding hung right

425 SOUTHWELL-RACECOURSE.CO.UK MAIDEN STKS 7f (F)
4:05 (4:08) (Class 5) 3-Y-O+ **£2,729** (£806; £403) **Stalls** Low

Form RPR

22-2 **1** **Boss Hog**[12] [289] 4-9-8 **65**..............GabrielHannon(5) 2 72
(R Curtis) *sn led: pushed clr over 2f out: rdn over 1f out: drvn and edgd lft ins fnl f: jst hld on* **7/4**[1]

06- **2** *nk* **Lyric Art (USA)**[128] [6391] 3-8-5 **0**..............ChrisCatlin 8 61+
(B Smart) *in tch: rdn along and outpcd 1/2-way: styd on strly appr fnl f: jst failed* **11/2**[3]

3 *1* **Royal Crest** 3-8-10 **0**..............TPQueally 6 63
(J A Osborne) *dwlt: sn trcking ldrs: hdwy on inner to chse wnr over 2f out and sn rdn: drvn and ch over 1f out: n.m.r and one pce wl ins fnl f* **4/1**[2]

4 *5* **Duke Of Urbino** 3-8-10 **0**..............NCallan 4 50+
(K A Ryan) *s.i.s: sn in tch: rdn along wl over 2f out and kpt on same pce* **10/1**

45- **5** *1/2* **Sixth Zak**[73] [7446] 4-9-13 **0**..............RobertWinston 11 53
(S R Bowring) *bhd tl styd on fnl 2f: nrst fin* **16/1**

6 *nse* **Karta (IRE)** 3-8-5 **0**..............GregFairley 3 43+
(M Johnston) *s.i.s and bhd tl styd on fnl 2f: nrst fin* **4/1**[2]

5 **7** *1* **Lively Blade**[17] [227] 3-8-10 **0**..............GrahamGibbons 5 46
(E S McMahon) *cl up: rdn along wl over 2f out and grad wknd* **18/1**

00- **8** *1* **Wahan (USA)**[114] [6731] 3-8-10 **0**..............LiamJones 13 43
(C E Brittain) *a towards rr* **18/1**

0-4 **9** *1/2* **Hint Of Honey**[29] [87] 3-8-5 **0**..............FrankieMcDonald 10 37
(A G Newcombe) *s.i.s: a in rr* **33/1**

0-5 **10** *1 1/4* **First Hand**[24] [151] 3-8-5 **0**..............DaleGibson 7 33
(M W Easterby) *prom: rdn along 3f out and sn wknd* **100/1**

000/ **11** *3 3/4* **Eastfields Lad**[605] [2535] 7-9-6 **30**..............(b) AndrewYoxall(7) 9 33
(S R Bowring) *bhd fr 1/2-way* **250/1**

30-6 **12** *1/2* **Ziggy Lee**[23] [154] 3-8-10 **0**..............(t) LukeMorris 1 27
(S C Williams) *midfield: rdn along 1/2-way: sn wknd* **33/1**

1m 29.19s (-1.11) **Going Correction** -0.15s/f (Stan)
WFA 3 from 4yo+ 17lb **12** Ran SP% **124.5**
Speed ratings (Par 103): **100,99,98,92,92 92,91,89,89,87 83,83**
toteswinger: 1&2 £6.00, 1&3 £4.20, 2&3 £7.60. CSF £12.32 TOTE £3.20: £1.30, £1.50, £2.10; EX 17.00 Trifecta £115.10 Pool: £336.11 - 2.16 winning units..

Owner Joe McCarthy **Bred** Gestut Goerlsdorf **Trained** Lambourn, Berks

FOCUS
A modest maiden on paper but a contest that featured some interesting newcomers, a couple with expensive price tags. The winner is rated to form with several of those behind likely to do better in time.

Duke Of Urbino Official explanation: jockey said colt hung left throughout

Hint Of Honey Official explanation: jockey said filly suffered interference in running

426 SPONSOR A RACE AT SOUTHWELL H'CAP 7f (F)
4:35 (4:35) (Class 5) (0-70,66) 3-Y-O **£2,729** (£806; £403) **Stalls** Low

Form RPR

50-1 **1** **Esprit De Midas**[5] [366] 3-9-5 **66** 6ex..............NCallan 5 83+
(K A Ryan) *cl up: led 1/2-way: clr over 2f out* **4/11**[1]

6-12 **2** *5* **Dancing Wave**[5] [366] 3-8-6 **58**..............AmyBaker(5) 3 58
(M C Chapman) *led: pushed along and hdd 1/2-way: sn rdn: drvn wl over 1f out and kpt on: no ch w wnr* **20/1**

-533 **3** *1 1/4* **My Best Man**[8] [322] 3-8-13 **63**..............(b1) JamesMillman(3) 4 60
(B R Millman) *in tch: pushed along 3f out: rdn over 2f out: sn one pce* **6/1**[3]

050- **4** *8* **Dahama**[112] [6785] 3-9-4 **65**..............LiamJones 1 40
(C E Brittain) *a outpcd in rr* **20/1**

40-3 **5** *2 3/4* **Spinight (IRE)**[7] [345] 3-9-2 **63**..............(b1) TPQueally 2 31
(M Botti) *trckd ldng pair: hdwy on inner 3f out: rdn over 2f out and sn wknd* **11/2**[2]

1m 28.97s (-1.33) **Going Correction** -0.15s/f (Stan) **5** Ran SP% **112.5**
Speed ratings (Par 97): **101,95,93,84,81**
CSF £10.12 TOTE £1.40: £1.10, £3.60; EX 6.80 Place 6: £109.32, Place 5: £27.42..

Owner Joseph Ogden, J Hanson, John Ogden **Bred** Jeremy Green And Sons **Trained** Hambleton, N Yorks

FOCUS
A very uncompetitive handicap and a straightforward task for the red-hot favourite. The form looks sound enough with the winner improving again.

T/Jkpt: Not won. T/Plt: £267.40 to a £1 stake. Pool: £70,639.40. 192.84 winning tickets. T/Qpdt: £25.30 to a £1 stake. Pool: £5,633.84. 164.60 winning tickets. JR

[349]WOLVERHAMPTON (A.W) (L-H)
Friday, February 6

OFFICIAL GOING: Standard
Wind: Nil Weather: Clear and cold

427 FREE ADMISSION TO RACING THIS SATURDAY APPRENTICE H'CAP 1m 1f 103y(P)
6:50 (6:50) (Class 6) (0-60,65) 4-Y-O+ **£2,047** (£604; £302) **Stalls** Low

Form RPR

453- **1** **Ghufa (IRE)**[121] [6577] 5-9-5 **60**..............PNolan 6 71
(George Baker) *s.i.s: hdwy over 6f out: led wl over 1f out: edgd lft ent fnl f: drvn out* **15/8**[1]

25-1 **2** *1/2* **Old Romney**[9] [320] 5-9-5 **65** 6ex..............TobyAtkinson(5) 10 75
(M Wigham) *stdd s: sn swtchd lft: hld up in rr: stdy prog over 3f out: rdn to chse wnr and rdr dropped whip jst over 1f out: kpt on towards fin* **7/2**[3]

55-1 **3** *5* **Giddywell**[30] [81] 5-8-10 **56**..............(p) DavidKenny(5) 2 55
(R Hollinshead) *hld up in rr: hdwy on outside 2f out: rdn and kpt on same pce fnl f* **3/1**[2]

400- **4** *nk* **Stoic Leader (IRE)**[129] [4219] 9-9-0 **60**..............AlexEdwards(5) 4 58
(R F Fisher) *hld up towards rr: swtchd rt wl over 1f out: rdn and styd on ins fnl f* **20/1**

120- **5** *hd* **Everyman**[128] [6395] 5-9-0 **58**..............KarenKenny(3) 1 56
(A W Carroll) *t.k.h in tch: lost pl over 5f out: hdwy over 1f out: kpt on one pce fnl f* **14/1**

200- **6** *1/2* **Kirstys Lad**[56] [7656] 7-9-1 **59**..............RichardRowe(3) 7 56
(M Mullineaux) *prom tl rdn and wknd over 1f out* **11/1**

50-0 **7** *5* **Carry On Cleo**[14] [275] 4-7-12 **46** oh1..............(v) DanielleMooney(7) 8 32
(A Berry) *sn chsng ldr: led over 5f out: hdd wl over 1f out: sn wknd* **50/1**

-002 **8** *8* **Spy Gun (USA)**[15] [254] 9-8-3 **51** oh1 ow5..............(p) JoshWall(7) 3 21
(T Wall) *led early: prom tl rdn and wknd over 2f out* **40/1**

4-10 **9** *6* **Ruwain**[15] [248] 5-8-9 **53**..............AndrewHeffernan(3) 9 10
(P J McBride) *sn led: hdd over 5f out: w ldr tl rdn wl over 1f out: sn wknd* **8/1**

2m 3.71s (2.01) **Going Correction** +0.20s/f (Slow) **21** Ran SP% **117.3**
Speed ratings (Par 101): **99,98,94,93,93 93,88,81,76**
toteswinger: 1&2 £2.60, 1&3 £1.10, 2&3 £2.70. CSF £8.59 CT £18.71 TOTE £3.10: £2.50, £1.10, £1.80; EX 11.20.

Owner Mrs C E S Baker **Bred** Shadwell Estate Company Limited **Trained** Moreton Morrell, Warwicks

FOCUS
A moderate handicap in which the pace was only fair and, not surprisingly given the tempo, the time was on the slow side. The first two raced against the far rail in the closing stages. The first two look up to the rating although there are doubts about how literally the form can be taken.

Old Romney Official explanation: jockey said he dropped whip 1f out.

428 GREAT OFFERS AT WOLVERHAMPTON-RACECOURSE.CO.UK H'CAP 1m 4f 50y(P)
7:20 (7:21) (Class 5) (0-75,85) 4-Y-O+ **£2,914** (£867; £433; £216) **Stalls** Low

Form RPR

0-45 **1** **Sheer Fantastic**[18] [219] 4-8-4 **65**..............(v) PatrickDonaghy(5) 7 72
(P C Haslam) *hld up in tch: wnt 2nd 3f out: rdn 2f out: led 1f out: drvn out* **7/2**[2]

3/-1 **2** *nk* **American Spin**[31] [58] 5-9-8 **75**..............AdamKirby 4 82
(L A Dace) *hld up in tch: hrd rdn and r.o ins fnl f* **2/1**[1]

33-0 **3** *1 1/4* **Morbick**[18] [220] 5-9-3 **70**..............LukeMorris 8 75
(W M Brisbourne) *hld up towards rr: hdwy on outside over 2f out: rdn over 1f out: nt qckn cl home* **7/1**

05-5 **4** *2 3/4* **Leslingtaylor (IRE)**[25] [139] 7-9-3 **70**..............GrahamGibbons 11 71
(J J Quinn) *a.p: wnt 2nd over 8f out: led over 3f out: rdn and hdd 1f out: no ex wl ins fnl f* **4/1**[3]

133/ **5** *6* **Khun John (IRE)**[610] [2397] 6-9-8 **75**..............NickyMackay 3 66
(V R A Dartnall) *t.k.h: led early: chsd ldr tl over 8f out: rdn jst over 1f out: wknd ins fnl f* **4/1**[3]

/6-0 **6** *1* **Noubian (USA)**[30] [79] 7-9-6 **73**..............LiamJones 5 62
(C R Dore) *hld up in rr: hdwy over 3f out: hmpd ent st: sn wknd* **20/1**

20-6 **7** *29* **Top Seed (IRE)**[18] [220] 8-8-12 **65**..............VinceSlattery 12 8
(Ian Williams) *a in rr: pushed along over 5f out: rdn and lost tch 3f out* **12/1**

1-0 **8** *3/4* **Anfield Road**[30] [72] 4-9-5 **75**..............TPQueally 2 17
(L Corcoran) *sn led: hdd over 3f out: n.m.r on ins wl over 2f out: sn lost pl* **16/1**

2m 41.35s (0.25) **Going Correction** +0.20s/f (Slow)
WFA 4 from 5yo+ 3lb **21** Ran SP% **126.4**
Speed ratings (Par 103): **107,106,105,104,100 99,80,79**
toteswinger: 1&2 £3.50, 1&3 £5.80, 2&3 £2.00. CSF £12.31 CT £49.88 TOTE £5.30: £1.90, £1.50, £2.10; EX 19.00.

Owner Middleham Park Racing Xviii **Bred** Newsells Park Stud Limited **Trained** Middleham Moor, N Yorks

■ Stewards' Enquiry : Adam Kirby one-day ban: careless riding (Feb 20)

FOCUS
Three of the four non-runners were recent previous winners so this race was not as strong as it looked at the final declaration stage. The pace was ordinary and the principals raced in the centre in the straight and the winner is rated as having run a slight personal-best.

Leslingtaylor(IRE) Official explanation: jockey said gelding lost its action inside final furlong
Noubian(USA) Official explanation: jockey said gelding suffered interference
Anfield Road Official explanation: jockey said gelding hung right

429 VAUXHALL INSIGNIA CAR OF THE YEAR 2009 MEDIAN AUCTION MAIDEN STKS 5f 20y(P)
7:50 (7:51) (Class 5) 3-Y-O **£2,590** (£770; £385; £192) **Stalls** Low

Form RPR

50-2 **1** **Speak The Truth (IRE)**[9] [316] 3-9-3 **59**..............PatCosgrave 2 69
(J R Boyle) *mde all: rdn over 1f out: edgd rt ins fnl f: drvn out* **7/4**[2]

2 *3/4* **Five Gold Rings (IRE)** 3-8-12 **0**..............TPQueally 8 61
(J A Osborne) *a.p: chsd wnr wl over out: rdn and edgd rt ins fnl f: r.o* **4/1**[3]

20- **3** *2 3/4* **Where's Reiley (USA)**[265] [2186] 3-9-3 **0**..............TomEaves 1 56
(T D Barron) *s.i.s: hdwy on ins over 2f out: rdn over 1f out: one pce fnl f* **11/10**[1]

4-52 **4** *1 1/4* **Wee Bizzom**[29] [91] 3-8-7 **50**..............SladeO'Hara(5) 7 47
(A Berry) *hld up: hdwy on outside over 1f out: one pce fnl f* **16/1**

0-0 **5** *5* **Cool Madam**[26] [127] 3-8-12 **0**..............JamesDoyle 3 29
(D Flood) *hld up in tch: wknd 3f out* **100/1**

0- 6 1 1/2 **Poaka Beck (IRE)**198 4289 3-9-3 0 FrankieMcDonald 4 29
(R F Fisher) *chsd wnr: ev ch over 2f out: wknd over 1f out* 33/1
64.04 secs (1.74) **Going Correction** +0.20s/f (Slow) **11** Ran SP% **113.8**
Speed ratings (Par 97): **94,92,88,86,78 76**
toteswinger: 1&2 £1.70, 1&3 £1.50, 2&3 £2.20. CSF £9.45 TOTE £2.70: £1.30, £2.30; EX 7.20.
Owner John Hopkins (t/a South Hatch Racing) **Bred** Gerard Mulligan **Trained** Epsom, Surrey
FOCUS
With the winner rated only 59, this is moderate form at best and he is the guide to the form. The pace was fair and the first four raced in the centre in the straight.

430 WOLVERHAMPTON-RACECOURSE.CO.UK H'CAP 1m 141y(P)
8:20 (8:21) (Class 4) (0-85,84) 4-Y-O+ £5,180 (£1,541; £770) Stalls Low

Form RPR
13-6 1 **Spinning**36 6 6-9-0 **80** (b) TomEaves 8 88
(T D Barron) *hld up: chal on ins over 1f out: rdn to ld ins fnl f: drvn out* 1/1[1]
5330 2 1 1/4 **Just Bond (IRE)**13 283 7-8-13 **79** PJMcDonald 7 84
(G R Oldroyd) *led: rdn and hdd ins fnl f: nt qckn* 11/8[2]
30-5 3 6 **Marning Star**21 199 4-8-10 **76** ChrisCatlin 6 67
(Ian Williams) *t.k.h: chsd ldr tl over 1f out: rdn and wknd ins fnl f* 11/2[3]
1m 52.25s (1.75) **Going Correction** +0.20s/f (Slow) **3** Ran SP% **107.5**
Speed ratings (Par 105): **100,98,93**
CSF £2.69 TOTE £1.50; EX 2.80.
Owner Mrs J Hazell **Bred** Cheveley Park Stud **Trained** Maunby, N Yorks
FOCUS
A depleted field with five non-runners. The pace was only moderate and the winner, who made his ground against the far rail entering the straight, edged into the centre in the closing stages but is rated as having run a slight personal best.

431 ENJOY THE LUCKY 7 GROUP OFFER H'CAP 5f 20y(P)
8:50 (8:51) (Class 6) (0-65,65) 4-Y-O+ £2,047 (£604; £302) Stalls Low

Form RPR
50-0 1 **Tyrannosaurus Rex (IRE)**34 22 5-8-7 **54** (v) PaulHanagan 6 68
(D Shaw) *a.p: rdn to ld ins fnl f: r.o wl* 9/2[2]
4-33 2 2 1/4 **Monte Major (IRE)**24 146 8-8-9 **56** (v) JoeFanning 11 61
(D Shaw) *a.p: led over 1f out: rdn and hdd ins fnl f: nt qckn* 5/1[3]
015- 3 1 3/4 **Multahab**99 7092 10-8-9 **63** (t) TobyAtkinson(7) 10 62+
(M Wigham) *hld up: hung rt fr over 2f out: c wd st: r.o ins fnl f: tk 3rd cl home* 20/1
0-60 4 1 **Desert Opal**8 329 9-9-4 **65** (b) LiamJones 5 60
(C R Dore) *hld up: r.o ins fnl f: hung lft towards fin* 12/1
1-25 5 2 **Admiral Bond (IRE)**14 269 4-8-12 **62** (p) DuranFentiman(3) 2 50
(G R Oldroyd) *s.i.s: bhd tl hdwy over 1f out: edgd lft jst ins fnl f: fdd* 3/1[1]
0-03 6 nk **Decider (USA)**22 173 6-8-13 **60** FrankieMcDonald 8 47
(R A Harris) *hld up in tch: wknd ins fnl f* 7/1
0-05 7 2 **Dodaa (USA)**15 250 6-8-6 **60** BMcHugh(7) 3 39
(N Wilson) *led: rdn and hdd over 1f out: wknd ins fnl f* 10/1
353- 8 3 **Triskaidekaphobia**37 7836 6-8-7 **54** (t) JamesDoyle 4 22
(Miss J R Tooth) *w ldr over 2f: rdn and wknd wl over 1f out* 10/1
20/0 9 2 1/4 **Gower**16 235 5-8-13 **60** TPQueally 1 20
(R J Price) *s.i.s: rdn wl over 1f out: a bhd* 7/1
00-6 10 1 3/4 **Fizzlephut (IRE)**15 243 7-8-10 **57** PaulFitzsimons 13 10
(Miss J R Tooth) *c v wd st: a towards rr* 16/1
61.81 secs (-0.49) **Going Correction** +0.20s/f (Slow) **10** Ran SP% **121.4**
Speed ratings (Par 101): **111,107,104,103,99 99,96,91,87,84**
toteswinger: 1&2 £5.20, 1&3 £16.00, 2&3 £8.20. CSF £28.60 CT £419.29 TOTE £6.60: £2.40, £1.60, £7.80; EX 33.30.
Owner Market Avenue Racing Club Ltd **Bred** Limestone And Tara Studs **Trained** Danethorpe, Notts
FOCUS
A modest handicap but one in which the pace was sound throughout. The first two raced in the centre in the straight and the form is rated around the first two.
Multahab Official explanation: jockey said gelding hung right on bend

432 SPONSOR A RACE BY CALLING 01902 390009 H'CAP 7f 32y(P)
9:20 (9:23) (Class 4) (0-85,82) 3-Y-O £5,180 (£1,541; £770; £384) Stalls High

Form RPR
1 1 **St Moritz (IRE)**28 98 3-9-7 **82** JoeFanning 2 95+
(M Johnston) *s.i.s and sltly hmpd: sn led: hung rt fr over 2f out: c wd st: rdn ins fnl f: r.o wl* 4/9[1]
12 2 3 1/4 **Changing The Guard**12 288 3-9-0 **75** PaulHanagan 1 79+
(R A Fahey) *led early: chsd wnr: carried v wd st: rdn and hung lft ins fnl f: one pce* 11/4[2]
25-5 3 1 1/4 **Grand Honour (IRE)**14 276 3-9-1 **76** ChrisCatlin 5 77
(P Howling) *hld up: effrt 2f out: ev ch over 1f out: rdn and one pce ins fnl f* 10/1[3]
02- 4 6 **Luckydolly (IRE)**49 7734 3-8-0 **66** BACurtis(5) 3 51
(F Costello, Ire) *wnt lft and bmpd s: hld up in tch: rdn wl over 1f out: wknd fnl f* 20/1
1m 31.25s (1.65) **Going Correction** +0.20s/f (Slow) **4** Ran SP% **109.8**
Speed ratings (Par 99): **98,94,92,86**
CSF £2.00 TOTE £1.20; EX 1.70.
Owner Mrs R J Jacobs **Bred** Newsells Park Stud Limited **Trained** Middleham Moor, N Yorks
FOCUS
Only four runners, but the most interesting runner of the evening was on show in St Moritz, who again won in good fashion, despite drifting right. The pace was ordinary and the winner ended up towards the stands' rail in the straight having come wide on the bend.
Luckydolly(IRE) Official explanation: jockey said filly lost a front shoe
T/Plt: £10.50 to a £1 stake. Pool: £104,108.03. 7,235.78 winning tickets. T/Qpdt: £6.60 to a £1 stake. Pool: £6,248.06. 698.16 winning tickets. KH

413 NAD AL SHEBA (L-H)
Friday, February 6
OFFICIAL GOING: Dirt course - fast; turf course - good to firm

433a EMPIRE HEIGHTS TROPHY (H'CAP) (TURF) 6f (T)
3:10 (3:10) (95-110,109) 3-Y-O+
£50,000 (£16,666; £8,333; £4,166; £2,500; £1,666)

RPR
1 **Diana's Choice (SAF)**15 264 5-8-13 **102** KShea 7 103
(M F De Kock, South Africa) *trckd ldrs: rdn to chal 2f out: led 55yds out: r.o wl* 3/1[1]
2 3/4 **Instant Recall (IRE)**15 257 8-9-1 **105** (v) WayneSmith 5 103
(M Al Muhairi, UAE) *led on rail: rdn clr 3f out: r.o wl: hdd cl home* 8/1
3 1 1/4 **Dohasa (IRE)**131 6315 4-9-5 **109** JMurtagh 10 105+
(G M Lyons, Ire) *settled in rr: r.o wl fnl 2 1/2f: nrst fin* 4/1[2]
4 3/4 **Nights Cross (IRE)**49 8-9-0 **104** GHind 4 96
(B Al Abed, Bahrain) *mid-div: rdn to chse ldrs 2 1/2f out: nt qckn fnl 110yds* 16/1
5 3/4 **Miss Gorica (IRE)**15 259 5-9-1 **105** TedDurcan 3 95
(Ms Joanna Morgan, Ire) *mid-div: trckd wnr 2 1/2f out: n.m.r 1 1/2f out: r.o same pce* 7/1
6 1 3/4 **Confuchias (IRE)**15 257 5-8-13 **102** MJKinane 12 88
(K R Burke) *in rr of mid-div: chsd ldrs 2 1/2f out: r.o one pce* 16/1
7 3/4 **Grand Vista**8 335 5-8-10 **100** (t) RyanMoore 1 82
(H J Brown, South Africa) *v.s.a: nvr able to chal: sme prog fnl 2 1/2f* 25/1
8 3/4 **So Will I**15 257 8-9-2 **106** (t) RHills 6 86
(Doug Watson, UAE) *trckd ldng pair tl 2 1/2f out: wknd* 13/2[3]
9 1 **Remarque (IRE)**15 259 4-8-10 **100** (bt) GMarcelli 9 77
(L Riccardi, Italy) *trckd ldr: rdn 2 1/2f out: sn btn* 16/1
10 1/2 **Benllech**93 7192 5-8-6 **96** RichardMullen 2 72
(D M Simcock) *mid-div on rail: n.m.r 1 1/2f out: eased* 10/1
11 1/2 **Ans Bach**12 6-8-9 **99** (e) WilliamBuick 8 73
(D Selvaratnam, UAE) *settled in rr: nvr able to chal* 14/1
12 3 3/4 **Desert Realm (IRE)**47 6-8-6 **96** AhmedAjtebi 11 59
(A Al Raihe, UAE) *in rr of mid-div: rdn 3f out: nvr able to chal* 28/1
1m 11.67s (-0.33) **Going Correction** +0.25s/f (Good) **12** Ran SP% **122.6**
Speed ratings: **112,111,109,108,107 105,104,103,101,101 100,95**
CSF 28.48 Tricast 101.08.
Owner Sheikh Mohammed Bin Khalifa Al Maktoum **Bred** R T Knight **Trained** South Africa
FOCUS
An ordinary sprint handicap for the level. The winning time was 0.08 seconds quicker than the second division won by the 105-rated Asset.
NOTEBOOK
Diana's Choice(SAF) was not at her best when third in a 6f Group 3 on the dirt first-time up in Dubai two weeks earlier, but the return to turf suited this South African Listed-race winner. She was always well placed and displayed a good attitude under pressure. She will probably be best off kept to the grass, but things will be tougher off a higher mark next time and she will be no good thing to follow up.
Instant Recall(IRE) was not allowed his own way up front, but he kept on surprisingly well in the straight. For so long he raced mainly on dirt, but he has now progressed into a smart type on the turf.
Dohasa(IRE) ◆ looked unlucky back in third. It's hard to be absolutely sure he would have won with a clear run, but there is no doubt whatsoever he should have finished significantly closer, as he had nowhere to go when trying to pick up from well off the pace early in the straight, and the front two had kicked for home by the time he got in the clear. This progressive Irish-trained sprinter finished well when finally in the open and should be up to winning a similar race granted a better trip. (op 9-2)
Nights Cross(IRE), a dual Listed winner a few years back for Mick Channon and now regularly successful in Bahrain, seemed to have his chance and this was a respectable effort in defeat.
Miss Gorica(IRE) might need help from the Handicapper now. (tchd 15-2)
Confuchias(IRE) was also well held, although this was an improvement on his recent course effort.
Grand Vista again ruined his chance with a slow start and is one to avoid. (op 20-1)
So Will I looked held when slightly hampered halfway up the straight. (op 6-1)
Benllech was by no means unlucky, but he's better than the beaten distance suggests as he was badly hampered against the inside rail when Dohasa switched for a run.
Ans Bach was another who possibly did not get the best of trips in the straight, although he didn't really seem to be going anywhere at the time. (tchd 16-1)

434a OXFORD (H'CAP) (TURF) 6f (T)
3:50 (3:52) (95-110,108) 3-Y-O+
£50,000 (£16,666; £8,333; £4,166; £2,500; £1,666)

RPR
1 **Asset (IRE)**15 259 6-9-1 **105** (b) LDettori 10 108+
(Saeed Bin Suroor) *in rr of mid-div: smooth prog: wd 3f out: led 1 1/2f out: r.o wl* 7/2[2]
2 1 1/2 **Lipocco**132 6289 5-8-9 **99** RyanMoore 1 98
(H J Brown, South Africa) *wl away: in rr of mid-div: smooth prog on rail 2 1/2f out: r.o fnl 1/2f: nrst fin* 11/2[3]
3 shd **Judd Street**127 6429 7-9-1 **105** (b) MJKinane 8 103
(Eve Johnson Houghton) *trckd ldrs: led 1 1/2f out: nt qckn cl home* 12/1
4 1/2 **Warsaw (IRE)**165 5347 4-9-0 **104** (b) JMurtagh 4 101
(M F De Kock, South Africa) *trckd ldrs: gng wl 3f out: n.m.r 2f out: nt qckn fnl f* 5/2[1]
5 1/4 **Black Mambazo (IRE)**82 7349 4-8-13 **102** (t) GMarcelli 11 99
(L Riccardi, Italy) *settled in rr: wd 3f out: chsd wnr 2 1/2f out: one pce ins fnl f* 12/1
6 2 1/4 **Contest (IRE)**15 259 5-9-4 **108** (b) C-PLemaire 5 97
(C Theodorakis, Greece) *sn led: hdd 1 1/2f out: one pce ins fnl f* 20/1
7 3/4 **Change Alley (USA)**8 336 4-8-6 **96** (t) RichardMullen 6 83
(A Al Raihe, UAE) *trckd ldr: rdn 3f out: sn wknd* 10/1
8 2 1/4 **Nota Bene**206 4059 7-8-10 **100** WilliamBuick 9 80
(D R C Elsworth) *trckd ldrs: ev ch 2 1/2f out: wknd fnl 1/2f* 14/1
9 1 3/4 **Santiago Atitlan**15 257 7-8-13 **102** EPedroza 7 78
(A Wohler, Germany) *in rr of mid-div: rdn 3f out: n.d* 20/1
10 hd **Valery Borzov (IRE)**15 257 5-8-10 **100** (v) AdrianTNicholls 2 74
(D Nicholls) *settled in rr: t.k.h: n.m.r after 2f: nt rcvr* 14/1
11 17 **Shmookh (USA)**7 5-8-6 **96** ow1 (t) RHills 12 19
(Doug Watson, UAE) *settled in rr: wd 3f out: nvr able to chal* 22/1
1m 11.75s (-0.25) **Going Correction** +0.25s/f (Good) **12** Ran SP% **117.9**
Speed ratings: **111,109,108,108,107 104,103,100,98,98 75**
CSF 22.44 Tricast 209.94.
Owner Godolphin **Bred** Peter Gibbons And Dermot Forde **Trained** Newmarket, Suffolk
FOCUS
The winning time was 0.08 seconds slower than the first division won by the 102-rated Diana's Choice and this was an ordinary contest for money. Most of these were forced to wait in the stalls for at least a couple of minutes after Hammadi went ballistic in box three and had to be withdrawn.
NOTEBOOK
Asset(IRE) is seriously talented, but he had become disappointing and could manage only fourth over the extended 6f here off a mark of 106 on his debut in Dubai. However, he had dropped a further pound in the weights and this was undoubtedly a weaker race. He travelled well throughout and was basically a class apart in the straight, ultimately winning quite comfortably, with none of these good enough to seriously test his resolution. He might gain some confidence from this success, but he still doesn't appeal as one to be following in a more competitive contest. (op 4-1)
Lipocco, making his debut for new connections after over four months off, made hard work of picking up and, although plugging on for second, he never threatened the winner. When trained by Ralph Beckett he was at his best when able to dominate.

Judd Street did well to hang on for third as he raced a little keenly on the pace and is probably more of a 5f horse.
Warsaw(IRE), off the track since winning a decent Polytrack handicap off a 4lb lower mark at Kempton last August, was possibly a little keener than ideal early on and only plugged on at the one pace in the straight. It might be worth noting he was drawn next to Hammadi, who played up in the stalls, and that could easily have unnerved him.
Black Mambazo(IRE), an Italian challenger, stayed on from a long way back but was never getting there.
Contest(IRE) was ridden from the front and stepped up on his recent course effort, but he was still well held.
Change Alley(USA), a winner on the dirt over 5f here off a mark of 91 the previous week, failed to prove himself as effective on this second try on turf in this tougher contest.
Nota Bene can go well fresh, but he never featured on his Dubai debut.
Valery Borzov(IRE) had to be backed out of his stall and checked over by the vet before he was allowed his chance as he was drawn next to Hammadi, who freaked out in his stall. In the race itself he pulled far too hard.

435a BLUESTONE (H'CAP) (DIRT) 1m 110y(D)
4:30 (4:30) (90-105,102) 3-Y-0+

£45,833 (£15,277; £7,638; £3,819; £2,291; £1,527)

RPR
1 **Roman's Run (USA)**[50] 5-8-13 **98**.....(t) FJara 1 100
(Doug Watson, UAE) *racd in 3rd: smooth prog 2 1/2f out: rdn: led 2f out: r.o wl* **20/1**
2 1/4 **Art Of War (SAF)**[8] 334 5-9-1 **100**..... JMurtagh 10 101
(M F De Kock, South Africa) *mid-div: hrd rdn 3f out: r.o fnl 2f: ev ch 1f out: one pce* **8/1**[3]
3 hd **Jonquil (IRE)**[351] 648 7-9-1 **100**.....(v) EddieAhern 4 101
(F Nass, Bahrain) *trckd ldr: ev ch fnl 2f: rdr dropped whip 1/2f out: one pce* **25/1**
4 1 **Jack Junior (USA)**[15] 260 5-9-1 **100**..... AdrianTNicholls 6 100+
(D Nicholls) *sn rdn in rr: hrd rdn 3 1/2f out: r.o wl: n.m.r 1f out: r.o again* **20/1**
5 hd **Trust N Dustan (USA)**[8] 337 4-8-8 **94**.....(v) RyanMoore 3 91
(Doug Watson, UAE) *in rr of mid-div: rdn 3f out: ev ch 2f out: one pce fnl f* **10/1**
6 7 3/4 **Tasteyville (USA)**[8] 334 6-9-3 **102**.....(b) RHills 12 84
(E Charpy, UAE) *wl away: sn led: hdd 1 1/2f out: wknd* **5/2**[1]
7 5 **Ketter (BRZ)**[357] 8-8-5 **90**..... WayneSmith 5 62
(R Bouresly, Kuwait) *sn stuggling in last: nvr involved* **66/1**
8 5 1/4 **Grand Hombre (USA)**[8] 334 9-9-3 **102**..... MJKinane 8 62
(R Bouresly, Kuwait) *s.i.s: r.o fnl 2f: nvr nr to chal* **8/1**[3]
9 3/4 **Naples (AUS)**[316] 6-8-11 **97**..... KShea 7 55
(M F De Kock, South Africa) *trckd ldrs: hmpd after 2f: mid-div: rdn 3f out: sn btn* **4/1**[2]
10 6 **Indiscutible (CHI)**[15] 258 4-8-4 **97** ow2..... KLatham 11 33
(M F De Kock, South Africa) *nvr nr to chal* **20/1**
11 5 1/2 **Emirates Line (USA)**[8] 337 6-8-7 **93**..... AhmedAjtebi 9 26
(M bin Shafya, UAE) *nvr nr to chal* **12/1**
12 7 **Jaffal (USA)**[28] 7-8-10 **96**.....(t) RichardMullen 2 15
(A Al Raihe, UAE) *nvr able to chal* **33/1**
13 12 **Plavius (USA)**[28] 4-8-6 **91**..... WJSupple 13 —
(A bin Huzaim, UAE) *mid-div: hrd rdn 4f out: sn btn* **8/1**[3]

1m 45.22s (1.22) **Going Correction** +0.375s/f (Slow) **13** Ran SP% **121.3**
Speed ratings: **109,108,108,107,107 100,96,91,90,85 80,74,63**
CSF 162.40 Tricast 4,019.28.
Owner Elsadig Elhag **Bred** WinStar Farm LLC **Trained** United Arab Emirates

FOCUS
They went a strong pace, but the first five still finished in a heap and this looks like ordinary form for the level.

NOTEBOOK
Roman's Run(USA) was always well positioned, close up in the chasing pack but far enough off the overly fast pace, and he kept on best in the straight. He made little impression at last year's Carnival and it will be a surprise if he follows up off a higher mark.
Art Of War(SAF) looked one to swerve when racing too keenly behind Grand Hombre over the bare 1m here the previous week, but this was a better effort with the blinkers left off.
Jonquil(IRE) deserves credit as, returning from the best part of a year off the track, he led the pack chasing the clear leader for much of the way and kept on all the way to the line in the straight.
Jack Junior(USA) came close to giving his trainer a first Carnival winner and was possibly an unlucky loser. He took an age to get going at the start, which was admittedly his own fault, but he showed good speed to move into a challenging position between the 400m pole and the 200m pole, before his path was continually blocked. He has the ability to win a similar race, but he will surely need to break quicker in future.
Trust N Dustan(USA) ran a very similar race to last time when he was third over 1m2f, as he didn't go at all early before running on in the straight. However, his effort seemed to flatten out near the line and it remains to be seen how much he wants it.
Tasteyville(USA), who was solidly backed beforehand, broke much better than last time with the blinkers re-fitted and briefly looked the winner when still clear turning into the straight, but he quickly threw in the towel when challenged. He did have to work to get the lead, and probably went off too fast, but he could still have been expected to offer more off the bridle.
Naples(AUS), a multiple winner in South Africa who had been off for 316 days, can be forgiven this as he was badly hampered by Tasteyville when that one cut across him in search of the early lead. That was basically game over, and he was making only a short-lived effort when his rider briefly dropped the reins early in the straight.

436a PARK LANE TROPHY (H'CAP) (TURF) 1m 194y(T)
5:05 (5:05) (95-115,113) 3-Y-0+

£62,500 (£20,833; £10,416; £5,208; £3,125; £2,083)

RPR
1 **Alexandros**[15] 265 4-9-5 **112**..... LDettori 5 116+
(Saeed Bin Suroor) *in rr of mid-div: smooth prog to trck ldrs 2 1/2f out: comf* **11/4**[2]
2 3 1/2 **Biarritz (SAF)**[15] 260 6-9-6 **113**.....(b) KShea 8 109
(M F De Kock, South Africa) *mid-div: trckd ldrs 3f out: led briefly 2f out: no ch w wnr* **5/1**[3]
3 1/2 **Blue Ksar (FR)**[260] 2325 6-9-5 **112**.....(t) TPO'Shea 9 107
(E Charpy, UAE) *mid-div: trckd ldrs whn n.m.r 1 1/2f out: swtchd and r.o wl* **25/1**
4 1 1/4 **With Interest**[8] 339 6-9-0 **107**..... AhmedAjtebi 1 99
(M bin Shafya, UAE) *settled in rr: nvr able to chal* **10/1**
5 1 1/4 **Kings Gambit (SAF)**[279] 5-9-5 **112**..... RyanMoore 2 102
(H J Brown, South Africa) *trckd ldrs: led briefly 2 1/2f out: hdd 2f out: wknd* **11/8**[1]
6 1/2 **Summer Doldrums (USA)**[167] 5-8-11 **105**.....(t) RHills 4 93
(Doug Watson, UAE) *mid-div on rail: rdn 3f out: n.m.r 2f out: nt rcvr* **22/1**
7 1/2 **Meydan City (USA)**[15] 263 4-8-5 **98**.....(b) JRosales 6 86
(M bin Shafya, UAE) *s.i.s: racd in rr: nvr nr to chal* **14/1**
8 8 **Apollo Star (GER)**[117] 6692 7-9-6 **113**..... SPasquier 7 84
(Ms C Erichsen, Norway) *sn led: rdn 3f out: sn wknd* **14/1**

1m 49.78s (-0.22) **Going Correction** +0.25s/f (Good) **9** Ran SP% **116.1**
Speed ratings: **110,106,106,105,104 103,103,96**
CSF 17.30 Tricast 282.07.
Owner Godolphin **Bred** Darley **Trained** Newmarket, Suffolk

FOCUS
A high-class handicap. The pace seemed ordinary until picking up just before halfway.

NOTEBOOK
Alexandros ◆ won impressively. There were mixed messages from his recent course success over the bare 1m on his debut in Dubai - some of those close up have since disappointed, but a few further back have subsequently run well - so he looked opposable in this tougher contest off a 4lb higher mark, but he produced a career best. Having promised plenty when a juvenile with Andre Fabre, Alexandros lost his way after being switched to Godolphin last year, but he is now finally fulfilling his potential for a yard who simply could not be in better form. He won a Group 3 at two and it's far to say he took this in the style of a pattern-class performer, showing a smart change of pace from off the gallop to settle this quite quickly, before being eased near the line. However, one slight note of caution, he again edged left under pressure, like he did last time, hinting that he is the type who needs to be kept sweet. (op 3-1)
Biarritz(SAF) seemed to be going well early in the straight, but if anything he might just have raced a little too enthusiastically early on, and it quickly became apparent he was no match for the winner. He might have preferred a stronger pace, but he does seem to have his limitations. (op 4-1)
Blue Ksar(FR) ran well in third considering he is probably an even better horse on easier ground.
With Interest was given too much to do, making his effort from further back than the winner, and later than that rival, and he never threatened. (op 8-1)
Kings Gambit(SAF) was a high-class performer in South Africa, where he won their Derby, and he was well backed on his debut in Dubai, but he proved most disappointing after racing keenly early on. It has to be said the Herman Brown horses, with the odd exception, have been in poor form at this year's Carnival. (op 7-4)
Summer Doldrums(USA) offered nothing. (op 20-1)
Meydan City(USA), tried in blinkers and dropped in trip, flashed his tail when hit with the whip and made no impression. He looks like one to avoid. (op 12-1)
Apollo Star(GER), a Group 3 winner on easy ground in Germany when last seen, failed to prove himself on this quicker surface, weakening tamely in the straight having led early. (op 12-1)

437a CONCOURSE 2750 (H'CAP) (TURF) 1m 5f 165y
5:40 (5:40) (95-115,113) 3-Y-0+

£62,500 (£20,833; £10,416; £5,208; £3,125; £2,083)

RPR
1 **Friston Forest (IRE)**[122] 6569 5-8-10 **104**..... TedDurcan 14 106
(Saeed Bin Suroor) *mid-div: smooth prog 2 1/2f out: r.o wl fnl 1 1/2f: led on line* **8/1**
2 nse **Veracity**[103] 7008 5-9-6 **113**..... LDettori 8 116
(Saeed Bin Suroor) *mid-div: led 1 1/2f out: r.o wl: hdd last stride* **7/2**[1]
3 1 3/4 **Mourilyan (IRE)**[54] 7682 5-9-5 **112**..... RyanMoore 6 113
(H J Brown, South Africa) *settled in rr: smooth prog to trck ldrs 2 1/2f out: ev ch: nt qckn fnl f* **6/1**[3]
4 1 1/2 **Lion Sands**[22] 185 5-9-2 **109**..... WJSupple 4 107
(A bin Huzaim, UAE) *a mid-div* **20/1**
5 shd **Fathayer (USA)**[8] 340 4-8-6 **98** ow1..... C-PLemaire 3 101
(A Al Raihe, UAE) *led main gp: led briefly 2f out: sn hdd and one pce* **50/1**
6 1 **Young Mick**[8] 338 7-8-8 **101**.....(v) JohnEgan 5 98
(G G Margarson) *mid-div: rdn to chse ldrs 3f out: r.o same pce* **6/1**[3]
7 1/4 **Basaltico (IRE)**[15] 263 5-9-1 **108**..... KLatham 1 105
(H J Brown, South Africa) *s.i.s: nvr nr to chal* **20/1**
8 shd **Leitmotiv (IRE)**[15] 262 6-8-5 **96**.....(v) WayneSmith 12 94
(M Al Muhairi, UAE) *settled last: gng wl 3f out: r.o fnl 2 1/2f: n.d* **20/1**
9 1 1/4 **New Guinea**[146] 5894 6-8-8 **101**..... TPO'Shea 13 96
(E Charpy, UAE) *in rr of mid-div: nvr able to chal* **11/1**
10 3 1/2 **Far From Old (IRE)**[8] 338 6-8-6 **99**..... FJara 2 89
(J E Hammond, France) *mid-div: rdn 2 1/2f out: eased fnl f* **9/2**[2]
11 1 **Book Of Music (IRE)**[22] 185 6-8-13 **106**.....(v) RichardMullen 7 94
(S Seemar, UAE) *settled rr: nvr nr to chal* **20/1**
12 7 1/2 **Drill Sergeant**[15] 263 4-8-6 **104**..... RHills 10 82
(M Johnston) *settled rr: nvr able to chal* **14/1**
13 8 **Classic Punch (IRE)**[102] 7017 6-8-9 **102**..... WilliamBuick 9 69+
(D R C Elsworth) *sn led: t.k.h and stdd pce after 4f: qcknd 4f out: wknd qckly 2f out* **14/1**
14 2 1/4 **Detonator (IRE)**[8] 338 4-8-5 **100**..... AhmedAjtebi 11 67+
(M bin Shafya, UAE) *trckd ldrs: wknd 2f out* **33/1**

2m 54.19s (174.19)
WFA 4 from 5yo+ 5lb **14** Ran SP% **125.7**
CSF 34.14 Tricast 189.77.
Owner Godolphin **Bred** Gainsborough Stud Management Ltd **Trained** Newmarket, Suffolk

FOCUS
A competitive staying handicap and something of a prep race for the new Dubai Racing Club Gold Cup, a Listed race which will be run over 2m on February 26. The pace was strong throughout.

NOTEBOOK
Friston Forest(IRE) edged out his stablemate Veracity by a nose after a fantastic dual. A smart stayer for Andre Fabre, he made a winning debut for his new connections in game fashion and looks a decent recruit. Most of his form in France was on easy ground, but he proved himself fully effective on this quicker surface, although it's obviously worth remembering he was getting 10lb from the runner-up.
Veracity ◆ raced close up in the chasing pack, with Dettori keen to make use of his stamina over a trip that was probably his bare minimum, and he kept on willingly in the straight, but he was just denied after changing his legs near the line. A progressive stayer towards the end of last season, this was a pleasing return under top weight after over three months off and it will take a good one to beat him in the Dubai Racing Club Gold Cup, even though he'll have a Group 3 winner's penalty. (op 4-1)
Mourilyan(IRE) had to be brave to take some tight gaps in the straight and endured a bit of a rough trip, but he didn't look unlucky. This was the furthest trip he's tried to date and it's possible his stamina gave way late on.
Lion Sands stepped up on the form he showed over 1m4f on his debut for this yard three weeks earlier and was suited by the longer trip.
Fathayer(USA) had to be switched out wide after being denied a clear run when trying to stay on in the straight, but he was not unlucky.
Young Mick had the race run to suit, but wasn't quite good enough.
Far From Old(IRE) was ridden handier this time having looked a little unlucky on his two previous starts at this year's Carnival, but that made no difference as he again enjoyed no luck in-running. He was just beginning to pick up when badly hampered 400m out, and it was race over when he again met trouble about half a furlong later.
Drill Sergeant offered little.

Classic Punch(IRE) was forced by the early attentions of Detonator to go quicker than he would have no doubt liked.

438a UAE 1000 GUINEAS SPONSORED BY GPD INVESTMENTS (LISTED RACE) (FILLIES) (DIRT) 1m (D)

6:15 (6:17) 3-Y-O

£104,166 (£34,722; £17,361; £8,680; £5,208; £3,472)

RPR

1 So Shiny (ARG)279 4-9-5 99 (t) MJKinane 1 103+
(J Barton, Saudi Arabia) *sn led: drew clr 2 1/2f out: r.o wl: comf* 16/1

2 3 Earth Living (USA)71 3-8-9 95 C-PLemaire 10 92+
(Michihiro Ogasa, Japan) *mid-div: r.o wl fnl 2f: nrst fin* 20/1

3 3/4 Purple Sage (IRE)22 181 3-8-9 89 RHills 3 90
(E Martins, Bahrain) *slowly away: trckd ldr: ev ch 2 1/2f out: r.o: wknd ins fnl f* 40/1

4 3 1/4 Ever Loved (USA)22 181 3-8-9 80 RichardMullen 5 83
(S Seemar, UAE) *mid-div: nvr able to chal* 100/1

5 1 1/4 Esta Bailando (CHI)22 181 4-9-5 96 (t) FJara 4 83
(J Barton, Saudi Arabia) *trckd ldrs: rdn 2 1/2f out: hung 1 1/2f out: r.o same pce* 33/1

6 3/4 Fire Sale (ARG)91 4-9-5 93 RyanMoore 6 81
(H J Brown, South Africa) *slowly away: racd in rr: n.m.r 3f out: nt rcvr* 33/1

7 1 Sos Brillante (CHI)22 181 4-9-5 100 (v) TedDurcan 2 79
(Saeed Bin Suroor) *trckd ldrs: gng wl 3f out: one pce fnl 2f* 5/1²

8 3 1/4 Estrela Boa (BRZ)22 180 4-9-5 95 JLeme 8 71
(P Bary, France) *settled in rr: nvr able to chal* 50/1

9 dist India Tiberina (CHI)22 181 4-9-5 98 KShea 9 —
(M F De Kock, South Africa) *in rr of mid-div: rdn 2 1/2f out: nt qckn* 9/1³

10 dist Devotee (USA)126 6463 3-8-9 96 (t) LDettori 7 —
(Saeed Bin Suroor) *mid-div: wd 3f out: hung bdly 2 1/2f out: wknd qckly* 1/3¹

1m 39.06s (2.36) **Going Correction** +0.375s/f (Slow)
WFA 3 from 4yo 19lb 10 Ran SP% **123.6**
Speed ratings: **103,100,99,96,94 94,93,89,—,—**
CSF 272.38.
Owner Prince Sultan Mohammed Saud Al Kabeer **Bred** La Quebrada **Trained** Saudi Arabia

FOCUS

This looked a good Guineas beforehand, but the winner got away with setting a pedestrian pace, and some of the more likely candidates disappointed. The end result is decidedly ordinary looking form, and it's a race to treat with caution.

NOTEBOOK

So Shiny(ARG)'s performance is not all that easy to asses. Her form in Argentina - second in a Group 1 when last seen in May - tells us she is obviously quite smart, and she deserves credit for picking up so well having racing keenly on her UAE debut. However, the reason she was inclined to pull early on was because she was setting only an ordinary pace, and she was pretty much allowed to dictate on her own terms all the way to the straight, before sealing the race when kicking clear. So on the one hand this was a noteworthy effort, but equally everything went her way and the bare form means it would be unwise to get carried away. She is unlikely to get her own way in the UAE Oaks and she also has to prove her stamina for the extra furlong.
Earth Living(USA), a wide-margin winner on her first start before finishing runner-up to the champion juvenile colt in Japan in a Grade 2, ran a fine race on her debut in Dubai. She travelled beautifully for a long way, enjoying a good trip out wide, but she still looked inexperienced when first coming under pressure and the leader was not stopping. She kept on all the way to the line and looks as though she will be well suited by the extra furlong in the Oaks. (op 16-1)
Purple Sage(IRE) could only manage third in the trial for this behind Sos Brillante and her proximity holds the form down.
Ever Loved(USA) was a 100/1 shot who was last of six in the trial for this race over 7f, so it's fair to say she is another who does little for overall form, even allowing for her improving for the return 1m.
Esta Bailando(CHI), a stablemate of the winner, had a tongue-tie fitted but didn't seem to have too many excuses. (op 25-1)
Sos Brillante(CHI) looked a classy filly when winning over 7f on her debut in Dubai three weeks earlier, a race in which she had a number of today's rivals behind, including the third, fourth and fifth, although she did display signs of waywardness on that occasion, and Dettori jumped ship to ride her stablemate. As it turned out, she ruined her chance by refusing to settle and would surely have been better off putting more pace to the race. (op 7-2)
India Tiberina(CHI) was just behind Sos Brillante over 7f here last time, but she ran no race this time. (op 8-1)
Devotee(USA) was backed as though she was as good as over the line, but she failed to run a race. She seemed to move well enough early on, but she had nothing to offer when asked for an effort and her rider could be seen looking down in the straight. A post race veterinary examination of the filly revealed she had suffered a cardiac arrhythmia. Prior to being entered to race again, a Veterinary Certificate will be required and the filly also needs to complete a satisfactory gallop in the presence of an ERA Veterinary Officer. (op 1-2)

439a MAYFAIR (H'CAP) (TURF) 1m (T)

6:45 (6:47) (95-110,110) 3-Y-O+

£50,000 (£16,666; £8,333; £4,166; £2,500; £1,666)

RPR

1 Kachgai (IRE)15 265 6-8-6 96 ow1 JMartinez 14 100
(L A Urbano-Grajales, France) *mid-div on rail: smooth prog to trck ldrs 1 1/2f out: comf* 33/1

2 1/2 Russian Sage (SAF)216 5-9-3 107 JMurtagh 7 111
(M F De Kock, South Africa) *sn led: drew clr 2 1/2f out: r.o: hdd 1/2f out: kpt on* 9/4¹

3 1/4 Vertigineux (FR)64 7550 5-9-6 110 (t) PSogorb 8 113
(Mme C Dufreche, France) *mid-div: r.o v wl fnl 2f: nrst fin* 14/1

4 2 1/2 Swop (IRE)15 265 6-8-10 100 RyanMoore 2 98
(L M Cumani) *mid-div: smooth prog to trck ldrs 2f out: one pce fnl f* 7/1

5 3/4 Wise Dennis8 340 7-9-0 104 TedDurcan 1 100
(A P Jarvis) *slowly away: mid-div in centre: n.m.r 1 1/2f out: one pce* 11/2³

6 1/4 Emirates Gold (IRE)22 182 6-8-13 102 (t) TPO'Shea 13 98
(E Charpy, UAE) *settled rr: nvr nr to chal: r.o fnl 1 1/2f* 25/1

7 1 1/4 Aqmaar12 5-8-8 98 RHills 3 91
(E Charpy, UAE) *s.i.s: in rr of mid-div: n.m.r 2 1/2f out: nt rcvr* 10/1

8 1 Naipe Marcado (URU)15 263 6-8-5 95 DBadel 4 85
(E Charpy, UAE) *trckd ldrs tl 2 1/2f out: wknd* 25/1

9 1/4 River Tiber8 340 6-8-13 102 LDettori 12 93
(Saeed Bin Suroor) *in rr of mid-div: r.o one pce fnl 3f* 14/1

10 1 1/4 Mojito Royale (IRE)8 335 5-8-10 100 (p) MJKinane 9 87
(Eoin Doyle, Ire) *settled rr: nvr able to chal* 8/1

11 3/4 T-Bird (SAF)15 265 8-8-6 96 (t) FJara 11 81
(Doug Watson, UAE) *settled in rr: nvr nr to chal* 33/1

12 1 Emirates Skyline (USA)8 340 6-8-11 101 WJSupple 10 84
(A bin Huzaim, UAE) *nvr able to chal* 20/1

13 1 Kal Barg15 265 4-8-7 97 AhmedAjtebi 5 77
(M bin Shafya, UAE) *trckd ldrs tl 2 1/2f out: sn btn* 5/1²

14 4 1/4 Royal Power (IRE)15 265 6-8-9 99 AdrianTNicholls 6 69
(D Nicholls) *trckd ldrs: rdn 3f out: wknd* 25/1

1m 38.48s (0.18) **Going Correction** +0.25s/f (Good) 14 Ran SP% **131.0**
Speed ratings: **109,108,108,105,105 104,103,102,102,101 100,99,98,93**
CSF 108.77 Tricast 1,187.05 PLACEPOT £1,503.00. Pool £19,148.73 9.30 winning tickets.
QUADPOT £730.80 Pool £987.70. 1.00 winning tickets..
Owner Mme H Devin **Bred** Henri Devin **Trained** Pau, France

FOCUS

A good, competitive handicap run at an even pace.

NOTEBOOK

Kachgai(IRE) got a run between the runner-up and the inside rail late on under an inspired ride. He lost around three lengths with a slow start, but that allowed him to switch over to the rail and he made good headway mid-race, before getting his dream run in the straight. He has some very useful form to his name in France, but had achieved an RPR of just 76 on his Dubai debut over course and distance two weeks earlier, so this was not easy to predict.
Russian Sage(SAF), a Grade 1 winner in South Africa whose home form ties in with a number of horses who have either won or run well at this year's Carnival, was ridden from the front. However, it's notoriously difficult to make all beyond sprint trips on this track, and he was reeled in by the winner. (op 5-2)
Vertigineux(FR), a regular winner in France including in Listed company, picked up well down the outside in the straight having been a long way back early and this was a smart effort under top weight.
Swop(IRE) ran much better than on his debut in Dubai and this is something to build on.
Wise Dennis again showed enough to suggest a similar race might fall his way this year, especially as he did not get the best of runs through inside the final two furlongs.
Emirates Gold(IRE) got going too late having been set plenty to do.
Aqmaar is better than he showed as he was short of room when trying to keep on in the straight. (op 16-1)
River Tiber was stuck out extremely wide in the straight.
Mojito Royale(IRE) could not build on his recent third over the extended 7f.
Kal Barg was well placed if good enough, but he disappointed.
Royal Power(IRE) offered nothing.

391 LINGFIELD (L-H)

Saturday, February 7

OFFICIAL GOING: Standard

Wind: Moderate, against Weather: Fine, cold

440 BETLIVE SPORTS TV @ WILLIAMHILL.COM MAIDEN STKS 1m (P)

12:50 (12:50) (Class 5) 3-Y-O £2,729 (£806; £403) Stalls High

Form RPR

1 Mutamaashi 3-9-3 0 LiamJones 10 82+
(W J Haggas) *dwlt: sn trckd ldng pair: effrt whn lft in ld wl over 1f out: shkn up and sn in command: pushed out* 9/4¹

2 2 Eastern Aria (UAE) 3-8-12 0 GregFairley 12 72+
(M Johnston) *led after 1f: hung bdly rt and rn wd bnd 2f out: sn hdd: kpt on to regain 2nd fnl f* 7/2³

3 3/4 Monaco Dream (IRE) 3-8-12 0 DaneO'Neill 4 71+
(W Jarvis) *s.s: hld up in last trio: pushed along and effrt over 2f out: prog to dispute 2nd over 1f out: shuffled along and kpt on* 8/1

230- 4 2 Mohanad (IRE)202 4214 3-9-3 83 TonyCulhane 5 71
(M R Channon) *s.s: trckd ldrs and rn green: effrt over 2f out: disp 2nd on inner over 1f out: fdd* 5/1

0 5 hd Ettrick Mill11 306 3-9-3 0 AndrewElliott 7 71+
(M Johnston) *led 1f: chsd ldr: trying to chal but hanging rt and carried wd bnd 2f out: lost grnd: plugged on fnl f* 12/1

6 2 1/2 So Blissful (IRE) 3-8-12 0 RobertHavlin 11 60
(T G Mills) *trckd ldrs: effrt and rn green over 2f out: disp 2nd over 1f out: sn wknd* 3/1²

7 8 Alittlemoreflair 3-8-12 0 TPQueally 9 41
(J Pearce) *dwlt: a in last trio: squeezed out 3f out: lost tch after: wl bhd fnl 2f* 33/1

5 8 nse Lyrical Intent17 230 3-9-3 0 PatCosgrave 6 46
(P Howling) *s.s: a in last trio: lost tch over 2f out: wl bhd after* 100/1

1m 39.73s (1.53) **Going Correction** +0.10s/f (Slow) 8 Ran SP% **117.4**
Speed ratings (Par 97): **96,94,93,91,91 88,80,80**
toteswinger: 1&2 £2.50, 1&3 £6.10, 2&3 £5.90. CSF £10.76 TOTE £2.50: £1.50, £2.00, £4.80; EX 12.60 Trifecta £44.20 Pool £141.85 - 2.37 winning units..
Owner Hamdan Al Maktoum **Bred** Shadwell Estate Company **Trained** Newmarket, Suffolk

FOCUS

Probably not a bad little maiden but hard to know what the form is worth.
Eastern Aria(UAE) Official explanation: jockey said filly failed to handle the final bend

441 CARL ALLINGHAM 30TH BIRTHDAY CLAIMING STKS 1m (P)

1:20 (1:21) (Class 6) 3-Y-O £2,047 (£604; £302) Stalls High

Form RPR

00 1 Whotsit (IRE)12 296 3-8-3 0 (b¹) AndrewElliott 4 57
(Miss Amy Weaver) *pushed up to chse ldng trio: dropped to 5th 2f out: sn hrd rdn on outer and no prog: styd on wl fnl f to ld last strides* 40/1

42-1 2 3/4 Desert Bump16 251 3-9-4 73 JimCrowley 7 70
(E F Vaughan) *trckd ldr: drvn to ld over 1f out: plugged on steadily u.p: hdd last strides* 6/4¹

3 3/4 Michelle (IRE) 3-7-12 0 NickyMackay 3 48
(J A Osborne) *relucatnt to enter stalls: s.i.s: hld up in 5th: effrt 2f out: tried to cl on ldrs fnl f: rn green and nt qckn* 12/1

-263 4 1/2 Precocious Air (IRE)12 296 3-7-9 59 DuranFentiman(3) 5 47
(J A Osborne) *led: shkn up 2f out: hanging and hdd over 1f out: wknd last 100yds* 11/4³

-303 5 1 Special Bond6 363 3-7-13 63 ow1 (b) FrankieMcDonald 2 49+
(J A Osborne) *trckd ldng pair: gng easily 2f out: trapped bhd hanging ldr over 1f out: swtchd rt ent fnl f: nt qckn after* 9/4²

000- 6 28 Outdroad66 7537 3-8-3 34 LiamJones 6 —
(P M Phelan) *rdn in last pair after 3f: wknd over 3f out: t.o* 66/1

00- 7 2 Farriers Gate235 3114 3-8-3 0 TobyAtkinson(7) 1 —
(M E Rimmer) *v awkward s: t.k.h and hld up in last: dropped away tamely over 3f out: t.o* 66/1

1m 38.94s (0.74) **Going Correction** +0.10s/f (Slow) 7 Ran SP% **110.6**
Speed ratings (Par 95): **100,99,98,98,97 69,67**
toteswinger: 1&2 £6.10, 1&3 £15.80, 2&3 £3.30. CSF £94.47 TOTE £44.40: £9.00, £1.60; EX 152.90.Michelle was claimed by Mr P. Butler for £5,000.
Owner Miss A Weaver **Bred** Michael J Woodlock **Trained** Newmarket, Suffolk

■ Stewards' Enquiry : Nicky Mackay caution: careless riding.

FOCUS
A messy little claimer in which Special Bond came off worst. The winner showed his first form tried in blinkers.

442 BET NOW WITH WILLIAM HILL ON 0800 444040 H'CAP 6f (P)
1:50 (1:50) (Class 4) (0-85,84) 4-Y-O+ £4,857 (£1,445; £722; £360) Stalls Low

Form RPR

-111 **1** **Mutamared (USA)**[15] 266 9-9-4 **84**.........(t) NCallan 4 89+
(K A Ryan) *trckd ldr: pushed up to chal 2f out: led over 1f out: rdn out and fnd enough fnl f* **6/5**[1]

04-5 **2** 1 **Qadar (IRE)**[22] 197 7-8-9 **75**.........(b) JamesDoyle 5 76
(N P Littmoden) *stdd s: hld up in 4th in slowly run r: effrt 2f out: coaxed along to try to cl over 1f out: wnt 2nd ins fnl f: drvn and hld by wnr last 100yds* **7/1**[3]

51-1 **3** 1 ½ **Chjimes (IRE)**[15] 270 5-8-11 **77**......... TPQueally 1 74+
(C R Dore) *stdd s: hld up in last in slowly run event: plenty to do after pce lifted over 2f out: effrt on inner over 1f out: styng on whn appeared short of room ins fnl f: tk 3rd nr fin* **9/4**[2]

04-0 **4** ½ **Storey Hill (USA)**[23] 170 4-8-6 **72**......... MartinDwyer 3 67
(D Shaw) *led: set slow pce tl past 1/2-way: rdn and hdd over 1f out: fdd fnl f* **12/1**

-566 **5** ¾ **Thoughtsofstardom**[4] 382 6-8-9 **75**......... JimCrowley 2 68
(P S McEntee) *stdd s: t.k.h: hld up in 3rd: nt qckn whn pce lifted over 2f out: hanging and nt run on fnl f* **7/1**[3]

1m 13.58s (1.68) **Going Correction** +0.10s/f (Slow) **5** Ran SP% **108.9**
Speed ratings (Par 105): **92,90,88,88,87**
CSF £9.75 TOTE £2.50: £1.50, £1.70; EX 9.10.
Owner Errigal Racing **Bred** E J Hudson Jr, Irrevocable Trust & Kilroy T'Bred **Trained** Hambleton, N Yorks

FOCUS
A farcical race from a form perspective as Storey Hill was allowed his own way in front and Martin Dwyer set very modest fractions, stacking the field up and effectively turning this into a 2f sprint. It is doubtful the winner had to improve on recent claimer wins to score.

443 CHELTENHAM ANTE-POST ODDS GUARANTEED @ HILLS H'CAP (DIV I) 1m 4f (P)
2:25 (2:25) (Class 6) (0-50,50) 4-Y-O+ £1,706 (£503; £252) Stalls Low

Form RPR

30-0 **1** **Shenandoah Girl**[4] 377 6-8-8 **46**.........(p) MartinDwyer 7 56
(Miss Gay Kelleway) *dwlt: hld up in last pair: rdn and gd prog over 2f out: swtchd to inner and chsd ldr ins fnl f: sustained effrt to ld last strides* **14/1**

403- **2** hd **Fantasy Ride**[59] 7626 7-8-12 **50**......... PatCosgrave 3 60
(J Pearce) *hld up in midfield: prog on wd outside fr 3f out: drvn to ld jst over 1f out: kpt on: hdd last strides* **9/4**[1]

63-0 **3** 1 ¾ **Itsawindup**[23] 169 5-8-8 **46** oh1.........(t) JamesDoyle 10 53
(Miss Sheena West) *trckd ldng pair: bmpd along over 4f out: wnt 2nd over 3f out: effrt to ld wl over 1f out: hdd jst over 1f out: one pce* **13/2**[3]

005- **4** 1 ¼ **Mid Valley**[57] 7647 6-8-9 **47**......... FergusSweeney 4 52+
(J R Jenkins) *t.k.h: hld up in rr: prog gng strly over 2f out: cl up bhd ldrs whn nt clr run over 1f out: keeping on but looked hld whn no room ins fnl f* **10/1**

06-6 **5** ½ **Hatch A Plan (IRE)**[28] 116 8-8-10 **48** ow1......... DaneO'Neill 12 52
(Mouse Hamilton-Fairley) *t.k.h: hld up in rr: rdn on outer over 2f out: nt qckn and no prog over 1f out: styd on ins fnl f* **13/2**[3]

26-0 **6** 1 ¼ **Maddy**[31] 78 4-8-1 **49** ow2.........(p) MatthewDavies(7) 2 51
(George Baker) *hld up in midfield: clsd on ldrs gng wl 2f out: nt qckn over 1f out and sn lost pl: one pce* **14/1**

-045 **7** 3 ¾ **Inquisitress**[20] 210 5-8-10 **48**......... NeilChalmers 11 44
(J J Bridger) *stdd s: hld up in last pair: stdy prog fr 3f out: clsd on ldrs over 1f out: sn rdn and wknd rapidly* **14/1**

04/0 **8** 2 ¼ **Just Serenade**[11] 301 10-8-8 **46** oh1......... LiamJones 8 39
(Mrs T J Hill) *led at decent pce: drvn 3f out: hdd wl over 1f out: wknd rapidly fnl f* **66/1**

06 **9** ½ **Huck Finn (NZ)**[8] 346 9-8-11 **49**.........(p) MickyFenton 9 41
(M Madgwick) *pushed up to press ldr: rdn 5f out: lost pl u.p fr over 3f out: stl in tch but btn whn eased fnl f* **20/1**

306/ **10** shd **Insignia (IRE)**[47] 666 7-8-8 **46** oh1......... FrankieMcDonald 6 38
(Mrs A M Thorpe) *settled in midfield: pushed along over 4f out: dropped to last 3f out and wl btn* **11/2**[2]

6-00 **11** 4 ½ **Looter (FR)**[3] 393 4-8-0 **46** oh1.........(tp) AmyBaker(5) 5 31
(P Butler) *chsd ldng pair: rdn 5f out: lost pl over 3f out: wknd 2f out* **10/1**

000- **12** 5 **Meohmy**[22] 5631 6-8-3 **46**......... MCGeran(5) 1 23
(M R Channon) *nvr bttr than midfield: u.p over 4f out: wknd 2f out* **33/1**

2m 33.08s (0.08) **Going Correction** +0.10s/f (Slow)
WFA 4 from 5yo+ 3lb **12** Ran SP% **120.2**
Speed ratings (Par 101): **103,102,101,100,100 99,97,95,95,95 92,88**
toteswinger: 1&2 £8.40, 1&3 £21.40, 2&3 £4.80. CSF £45.54 CT £237.59 TOTE £14.00: £3.80, £1.70, £3.10; EX 49.60 TRIFECTA Not won..
Owner Miss Gay Kelleway **Bred** Julian Czerpak And Robert Cole **Trained** Exning, Suffolk
■ Stewards' Enquiry : Pat Cosgrave three-day ban: careless riding (Feb 21-23)

FOCUS
Dreadful stuff and a bit of a surprise result.
Insignia(IRE) Official explanation: jockey said gelding hung badly left from halfway

444 CHELTENHAM ANTE-POST ODDS GUARANTEED @ HILLS H'CAP (DIV II) 1m 4f (P)
3:00 (3:00) (Class 6) (0-50,50) 4-Y-O+ £1,706 (£503; £252) Stalls Low

Form RPR

00-5 **1** **Prince Charlemagne (IRE)**[8] 353 6-8-11 **48**......... FergusSweeney 1 54
(G L Moore) *hld up towards rr: stdy prog over 2f out: rdn to ld on outer over 1f out: styd on wl* **5/2**[2]

2305 **2** 1 ¼ **Prince Of Medina**[3] 385 6-8-8 **45**.........(t) LiamJones 2 49
(J R Best) *hld up in rr: last over 2f out: prog over 1f out: wnt 2nd ins fnl f: kpt on but no real imp* **9/1**

50-2 **3** ½ **Limelight (USA)**[23] 169 4-8-7 **47**......... RichardKingscote 4 50
(Sir Mark Prescott) *cl up: rdn and effrt 2f out: tried to cl on inner 1f out: one pce after* **9/2**[3]

0/0- **4** 1 **Comeintothespace (IRE)**[115] 5917 7-8-10 **47**......... PaulDoe 10 49
(R A Farrant) *hld up in last: prog on wd outside over 2f out: wnt 2nd 1f out and looked dangerous: effrt petered out sn after* **20/1**

00-0 **5** ¾ **Historical Giant (USA)**[22] 193 4-8-9 **49**......... JimCrowley 11 49
(E F Vaughan) *trckd ldr 3f: styd prom: chal over 2f out: nrly upsides over 1f out: fdd* **2/1**[1]

00-0 **6** 2 ¾ **Usetheforce (IRE)**[29] 97 4-8-10 **50**......... MartinDwyer 6 46
(M Quinn) *tk fierce hold early: hld up tl allowed to make prog and press ldr after 3f: led narrowly 3f out: hdd & wknd over 1f out* **20/1**

00-4 **7** ½ **Goblin**[36] 8 8-8-12 **49**......... DaneO'Neill 9 44
(D E Cantillon) *in tch: drvn over 4f out: brief effrt u.p 3f out: lost pl and wl btn 2f out: hanging and looked reluctant over 1f out* **7/1**

000- **8** 5 **Steady Gaze**[206] 4085 4-8-5 **45**.........(t) NickyMackay 8 32
(M A Allen) *mde most to 3f out: stl upsides 2f out: wknd over 1f out* **66/1**

060- **9** ½ **Check Up (IRE)**[77] 7427 8-8-8 **48**.........(p) KevinGhunowa(3) 3 34
(J L Flint) *t.k.h early: cl up: rdn 3f out: wknd 2f out* **16/1**

2m 34.34s (1.34) **Going Correction** +0.10s/f (Slow)
WFA 4 from 6yo+ 3lb **9** Ran SP% **119.5**
Speed ratings (Par 101): **99,98,97,97,96 94,94,91,90**
toteswinger: 1&2 £4.30, 1&3 £2.90, 2&3 £3.00. CSF £25.65 CT £99.16 TOTE £3.80: £1.70, £2.50, £1.70; EX 17.00 Trifecta £56.00 Pool £362.92 - 4.79 winning units..
Owner A Grinter **Bred** Michael O'Mahony **Trained** Lower Beeding, W Sussex

FOCUS
Probably a bit more competitive than the first division, but very modest fare nonetheless with the runner-up rated to his recent best.
Usetheforce(IRE) Official explanation: jockey said gelding ran too free

445 WILLIAM HILL TOP TEAM FOOTBALL PRICES H'CAP 1m 2f (P)
3:35 (3:35) (Class 2) (0-100,100) 4-Y-O+ £11,656 (£3,468; £1,733; £865) Stalls Low

Form RPR

3-21 **1** **Formation (USA)**[14] 284 4-8-6 **88**......... LiamJones 2 95
(J R Boyle) *hld up in midfield on inner: effrt over 2f out: swtchd to outer over 1f out: clsd to dispute ld last 100yds: jst prevailed* **15/2**

42-5 **2** hd **Ace Of Hearts**[21] 206 10-9-0 **95**......... GeorgeBaker 3 102
(C F Wall) *led 100yds: trckd ldng pair: drvn over 2f out: styd on u.p to dispute ld last 100yds: jst hld* **5/1**[2]

5-23 **3** ½ **Baylini**[14] 284 5-8-6 **87**......... JamesDoyle 4 93+
(Ms J S Doyle) *hld up in last: stl plenty to do 2f out: prog on wd outside jst over 1f out: styd on wl: nt quite catch ldng pair* **7/1**[3]

05-4 **4** 1 **Philatelist (USA)**[28] 124 5-9-5 **100**.........(b) NCallan 7 104
(M A Jarvis) *trckd ldrs: moved up to chal 3f out: led over 2f out and drvn 2 l clr wl over 1f out: tired and hdd last 100yds* **4/1**[1]

-312 **5** 1 ½ **Lady Jane Digby**[14] 284 4-8-9 **91**......... GregFairley 10 92
(M Johnston) *trckd ldr after 1f: rdn to ld 3f out: hdd over 2f out: hld over 1f out: no ex* **4/1**[1]

00-4 **6** 1 **Al Muheer (IRE)**[9] 331 4-8-8 **90**......... MartinDwyer 11 89
(C E Brittain) *settled towards rr: rdn over 2f out: one pce and no real imp on ldrs* **9/1**

-054 **7** 2 ¼ **Internationaldebut (IRE)**[14] 284 4-8-13 **95**......... AdamKirby 5 90
(S Parr) *hld up in last pair: shkn up 2f out: no real prog over 1f out* **9/1**

3-56 **8** 3 **John Terry (IRE)**[7] 360 6-8-8 **89**......... JimCrowley 9 78
(Mrs A J Perrett) *rdn to ld after 100yds: hdd u.p 3f out: wknd over 1f out* **7/1**[3]

0- **9** 47 **Prairie Spirit (FR)**[63] 4880 5-9-0 **95**......... FergusSweeney 6 —
(C E Longsdon) *settled in midfield on outer: eased over 2f out: virtually p.u* **33/1**

2m 3.19s (-3.41) **Going Correction** +0.10s/f (Slow)
WFA 4 from 5yo+ 1lb **9** Ran SP% **116.4**
Speed ratings (Par 109): **117,116,116,115,114 113,111,109,71**
toteswinger: 1&2 £8.00, 1&3 £5.00, 2&3 £8.90. CSF £45.15 CT £276.86 TOTE £8.20: £2.20, £1.70, £2.70; EX 50.00 Trifecta £228.30 Pool £1,234.59 - 4.00 winning units..
Owner M Khan X2 **Bred** Loch Lea Farm **Trained** Epsom, Surrey

FOCUS
Easily the strongest race on the card and a mightily competitive handicap. The form looks straightforward with the winner confirming recent course form with the third and the runner-up to last year's best.

NOTEBOOK
Formation(USA) had returned to winning ways in a similar heat over course and distance last time on just his second start for his new handler. A 2lb rise for that win was never going to be a major issue and the key question was whether he was going to be able to repeat that level of form as he'd often frustrated in the past. Confirm the form he did, though, travelling strongly off the pace before making smooth headway to throw down a big challenge and lock horns with Ace Of Hearts in the final half furlong. He never looked like shirking the issue, edging out that rival close home and looking firmly on the upgrade for his new connections. (op 7-1 tchd 13-2)
Ace Of Hearts, sharper for a comeback run last month, ran a cracker in defeat, appreciating the step up in trip and going down all guns blazing. (op 13-2)
Baylini hasn't won for over a year now but she continues to run well in defeat, sticking on from well off the pace and her latest is surely going to fall her way at some point soon. (op 5-1)
Philatelist(USA) looked like he might have stolen this when kicking a couple of lengths clear turning for home but his stride shortened in the final furlong and he was swallowed up. (op 5-1)
Lady Jane Digby was in trouble early in the straight and, given she was in front of Baylini last time on similar terms, doesn't appear to have run to her best for whatever reason. (tchd 5-1)
Prairie Spirit(FR) Official explanation: jockey said gelding hung right throughout

446 WILLIAM HILL 0800 444040 - NOW OPEN 24/7 H'CAP 7f (P)
4:10 (4:10) (Class 4) (0-85,83) 4-Y-O+ £4,857 (£1,445; £722; £360) Stalls Low

Form RPR

3-66 **1** **Gallantry**[9] 331 7-9-0 **82**......... TolleyDean(3) 6 90
(P Howling) *hld up in 4th: rdn over 2f out: prog on outer to chse ldr 1f out: styd on wl to ld last 75yds* **10/3**[3]

00-5 **2** 1 **Compton's Eleven**[14] 282 8-8-10 **75**......... EdwardCreighton 3 80
(M R Channon) *hld up in last: rdn over 2f out: effrt on inner over 1f out: styd on to snatch 2nd last strides* **9/1**

-312 **3** hd **Strabinios King**[12] 297 5-8-13 **78**......... NCallan 7 83+
(K J Burke) *racd freely in ld: qcknd over 2f out and had rest in trble: 3 l clr over 1f out: tied up and hdd last 75yds* **6/4**[1]

4226 **4** 1 **Count Ceprano (IRE)**[20] 212 5-8-13 **78**......... TPQueally 2 80
(C R Dore) *trckd ldng pair: chsd clr ldr jst over 2f out: no ex and lost 2nd 1f out* **11/4**[2]

50-0 **5** 2 **Glencalvie (IRE)**[14] 283 8-8-9 **74**.........(p) MartinDwyer 5 71
(J Akehurst) *chsd ldr to jst over 2f out: sn btn* **10/1**

1m 24.56s (-0.24) **Going Correction** +0.10s/f (Slow) **5** Ran SP% **108.8**
Speed ratings (Par 105): **105,103,103,102,100**
toteswinger: 1&2 £9.10. CSF £28.34 TOTE £3.90: £1.80, £3.10; EX 19.40.
Owner The Circle Bloodstock I Limited **Bred** Cheveley Park Stud Ltd **Trained** Newmarket, Suffolk

FOCUS
The withdrawal of Trafalgar Square robbed this of much of it's competitiveness, but despite the small field Strabinios King ensured there was no hanging around. The form looks muddling and not a race to take at face value.

447 BEST ODDS GUARANTEED @ WILLIAMHILL.COM MAIDEN STKS 5f (P)
4:45 (4:45) (Class 5) 3-Y-O+ **£2,729** (£806; £403) **Stalls** High

Form RPR

5-33 **1** **Flamsteed (IRE)**[10] 315 3-8-13 71 MartinDwyer 3 65
(M Quinn) *hld up: effrt 2f out: led over 1f out: pushed clr* **2/9**[1]

500- **2** *4 ½* **Wicksy Creek**[218] 3686 4-9-13 41 FrankieMcDonald 1 55
(G C Bravery) *w ldr: led 3f out: hdd over 1f out: no ch w wnr: jst hld on for 2nd* **33/1**

-404 **3** *½* **Only Hope**[4] 381 5-9-8 45 AdamKirby 4 48
(P S McEntee) *led 100yds: outpcd and last over 2f out: lft in 3rd wl over 1f out: clsd on runner-up at fin* **16/1**

040- **4** *2* **Kalligal**[39] 7817 4-9-8 47 (p) StephenCarson 6 41+
(R Ingram) *taken down early: racd wd in tch: carried v wd bnd 2f out: no ch after* **12/1**[3]

0 **5** *5* **Geese A Laying (IRE)**[6] 364 3-8-10 0 ow2 TPQueally 2 19
(J A Osborne) *led after 100yds to 3f out: hung v wd bnd 2f out and sn wknd* **7/1**[2]

59.40 secs (0.60) **Going Correction** +0.10s/f (Slow)
WFA 3 from 4yo+ 14lb **5** Ran SP% **110.8**
Speed ratings (Par 103): **99,91,91,87,79**
toteswinger: 1&2 £9.70. CSF £11.01 TOTE £1.30: £1.02, £12.30; EX 9.20 Place 6 £55.55, Place 5 £33.83..
Owner Brian Morton **Bred** Peter Mooney **Trained** Newmarket, Suffolk

FOCUS
A desperate maiden and a penalty kick for the long odds-on winner. The winner confirmed previous course form with the third but the form is ordinary.
T/Plt: £27.00 to a £1 stake. Pool: £61,186.18. 1,649.78 winning tickets. T/Qpdt: £10.80 to a £1 stake. Pool: £4,670.28. 318.20 winning tickets. JN

427 WOLVERHAMPTON (A.W) (L-H)
Saturday, February 7

OFFICIAL GOING: Standard
Wind: Light, across Weather: Fine

448 WILLIAMHILL.COM - ODDS GUARANTEED H'CAP (DIV I) 1m 5f 194y(P)
2:10 (2:10) (Class 6) (0-60,60) 4-Y-O+ **£1,706** (£503; £252) **Stalls** Low

Form RPR

02-4 **1** **Monaadi (IRE)**[23] 178 4-9-2 60 (p) GrahamGibbons 6 68
(R Hollinshead) *hld up in tch: pushed along over 4f out: rdn over 2f out: led over 1f out: edgd rt ins fnl f: drvn out* **9/2**[2]

53-2 **2** *nk* **Terminate (GER)**[32] 59 7-9-0 53 (t) StephenDonohoe 11 61
(Ian Williams) *t.k.h towards rr: hdwy over 3f out: rdn and sustained chal fnl f: styd on* **11/4**[1]

0-31 **3** *3 ¼* **Amwell Brave**[23] 169 8-8-13 52 SimonWhitworth 12 55
(J R Jenkins) *stdd s: t.k.h in rr: hdwy on ins over 2f out: rdn and one pce ins fnl f* **9/1**

-205 **4** *¾* **Buscador (USA)**[16] 253 10-9-7 60 TomEaves 7 62
(W M Brisbourne) *led: rdn 5f out: hdd over 3f out: ev ch over 1f out: no ex ins fnl f* **11/1**

3-15 **5** *½* **Ben Bacchus (IRE)**[8] 342 7-9-0 53 ChrisCatlin 8 55
(P W Hiatt) *prom: chsd ldr after 3f out tl over 2f out: rdn and one pce fnl f* **5/1**[3]

00-5 **6** *6* **Japura (USA)**[19] 217 5-9-6 59 PaulHanagan 5 52
(T J Pitt) *chsd ldr 3f: a.p: slipped through on ins to ld over 3f out: rdn and hdd over 1f out: wknd ins fnl f* **11/1**

00- **7** *3* **Mega Steps (IRE)**[43] 7042 5-8-8 47 (p) JimmyQuinn 4 36
(Jennie Candlish) *pushed along 7f out: a bhd* **18/1**

044- **8** *¾* **Gunnadoit (USA)**[37] 3483 4-8-12 56 JerryO'Dwyer 10 44
(N B King) *a bhd: struggling fnl 3f* **12/1**

001- **9** *2 ¼* **Ruby Delta**[154] 5710 4-8-8 55 (v) RussellKennemore(3) 3 40
(A G Juckes) *hld up in mid-div: effrt over 5f out: rdn and wknd 3f out* **16/1**

036- **10** *3* **Thunderwing (IRE)**[168] 4850 7-9-5 58 PJMcDonald 2 39
(James Moffatt) *hld up in mid-div: wknd over 3f out* **12/1**

3m 6.09s (0.09) **Going Correction** +0.075s/f (Slow)
WFA 4 from 5yo+ 5lb **10** Ran SP% **114.7**
Speed ratings (Par 101): **102,101,99,99,99 95,94,93,92,90**
toteswinger: 1&2 £3.90, 1&3 £8.90, 2&3 £2.90. CSF £16.94 CT £105.67 TOTE £4.80: £1.20, £1.20, £2.20; EX 20.50.
Owner Ray Robinson **Bred** Darley **Trained** Upper Longdon, Staffs
■ Stewards' Enquiry : Stephen Donohoe one-day ban: careless riding (Feb 21)

FOCUS
Very few of these made much appeal and the form should be treated with caution.

449 WILLIAMHILL.COM - ODDS GUARANTEED H'CAP (DIV II) 1m 5f 194y(P)
2:45 (2:45) (Class 6) (0-60,59) 4-Y-O+ **£1,706** (£503; £252) **Stalls** Low

Form RPR

016- **1** **Prairie Hawk (USA)**[51] 7722 4-8-9 52 (t) TomEaves 9 64+
(Tim Vaughan) *hld up in tch: jnd ldr over 2f out: rdn to ld over 1f out: styd on wl* **15/8**[1]

/46- **2** *3 ¼* **Diktatorship (IRE)**[43] 5993 6-8-8 46 JimmyQuinn 12 54
(Jennie Candlish) *a.p: led 3f out: rdn and hdd over 1f out: no ex ins fnl f* **33/1**

-152 **3** *nk* **Sea Cliff (IRE)**[11] 300 5-9-7 59 (p) JamieMoriarty 10 67
(Jonjo O'Neill) *hld up in mid-div: hdwy 3f out: sn rdn: styd on ins fnl f* **8/1**

02-2 **4** *2 ½* **Taxman (IRE)**[16] 252 7-8-8 53 DeclanCannon(7) 8 57
(A G Newcombe) *hld up towards rr: swtchd rt and hdwy over 2f out: rdn over 1f out: one pce fnl f* **6/1**[3]

165- **5** *9* **Rebel Raider (IRE)**[58] 787 10-8-7 48 ow3 (b) RussellKennemore(3) 2 39
(B N Pollock) *rdn along and sn prom: wknd over 3f out* **33/1**

000- **6** *nse* **Bolton Hall (IRE)**[79] 6928 7-9-5 57 (t) CatherineGannon 6 48
(W K Goldsworthy) *s.v.s: hld up in rr: sme prog over 2f out: nvr nr ldrs* **66/1**

0345 **7** *¾* **Spume (IRE)**[8] 346 5-9-2 54 (t) DaleGibson 7 44
(S Parr) *t.k.h towards rr: hdwy over 3f out: rdn and wknd over 2f out* **10/1**

-222 **8** *19* **Vanquisher (IRE)**[8] 346 5-8-13 51 (t) StephenDonohoe 1 15
(Ian Williams) *hld up in mid-div: hdwy over 5f out: wknd wl over 1f out: eased ins fnl f* **9/2**[2]

3/0- **9** *5* **Born West (USA)**[75] 7042 5-9-6 58 (b) JerryO'Dwyer 3 15
(N B King) *rdn along to ld after 1f: hdd over 3f out: sn n.m.r on ins: sn wknd* **28/1**

300- **10** *24* **Bet Noir (IRE)**[117] 6703 4-9-0 57 LukeMorris 11 —
(A W Carroll) *rdn 7f out: a bhd: t.o* **22/1**

402- **11** *66* **Nounou**[73] 7455 8-9-6 58 (vt[1]) ChrisCatlin 5 —
(Miss J E Foster) *hld up and bhd: hmpd over 11f out: rdn over 7f out: t.o fnl 5f* **20/1**

00/4 **P** **Nothing Is Forever (IRE)**[28] 112 5-9-1 53 RobertWinston 4 —
(L Corcoran) *led 1f: chsd ldr: led over 3f out: sn hdd: lost action and eased over 2f out: p.u wl over 1f out* **13/2**

3m 5.28s (-0.72) **Going Correction** +0.075s/f (Slow)
WFA 4 from 5yo+ 5lb **12** Ran SP% **120.7**
Speed ratings (Par 101): **105,103,102,101,96 96,95,85,82,68 30,—**
toteswinger: 1&2 £18.40, 1&3 £5.90, 2&3 £31.80. CSF £88.61 CT £429.90 TOTE £3.90: £1.30, £10.10, £2.10; EX 91.20.
Owner J Murphy **Bred** Southern Bloodstock **Trained** Aberthin, Vale of Glamorgan

FOCUS
This was a competitive race for the class, although most of these were struggling to show their best on a consistent basis. The winning time was better than the first division.
Taxman(IRE) Official explanation: jockey said gelding never travelled
Bolton Hall(IRE) Official explanation: jockey said gelding missed the break
Vanquisher(IRE) Official explanation: jockey said gelding lost its action
Nothing Is Forever(IRE) Official explanation: jockey said gelding felt wrong throughout and pulled up

450 WILLIAM HILL 0800 444 040 - TOP FOOTBALL ODDS H'CAP 1m 1f 103y(P)
3:20 (3:20) (Class 5) (0-75,70) 3-Y-O **£2,729** (£806; £403) **Stalls** Low

Form RPR

60-6 **1** **Citizenship**[15] 276 3-9-5 68 StephenDonohoe 3 73+
(Ian Williams) *hld up and bhd: hdwy on ins wl over 1f out: sn swtchd rt: led ins fnl f: qcknd clr: comf* **6/1**

-550 **2** *2 ¼* **Autumn Morning (IRE)**[13] 287 3-8-5 59 PatrickDonaghy(5) 5 59
(P D Evans) *dwlt: hdwy over 6f out: chsd ldr over 5f out: rdn 2f out: ev ch ins fnl f: one pce* **9/2**[3]

6-60 **3** *¾* **Kneesy Earsy Nosey**[6] 363 3-8-4 53 (p) JimmyQuinn 2 51
(Miss A Stokell) *chsd ldrs: rdn over 3f out: styd on to take 3rd cl home* **28/1**

5423 **4** *nk* **Turn To Dreams**[9] 332 3-8-9 58 CatherineGannon 8 55
(P D Evans) *sn led: rdn wl over 1f out: hdd and no ex ins fnl f* **12/1**

362- **5** *2 ¼* **Miss Cracklinrosie**[95] 7172 3-8-12 61 GrahamGibbons 4 54
(J R Weymes) *led early: chsd ldr tl over 5f out: rdn over 1f out: wknd wl ins fnl f* **16/1**

6-11 **6** *2 ¼* **Fantastic Fred (IRE)**[13] 287 3-9-0 63 ChrisCatlin 6 51
(J A Osborne) *hld up: hdwy over 5f out: rdn over 2f out: wknd wl over 1f out* **13/8**[1]

435- **7** *7* **Nimmy's Special**[68] 7519 3-8-6 62 PNolan(7) 1 35
(M Mullineaux) *v awkward leaving stalls and s.s: hld up and bhd: rdn over 3f out: sn struggling* **16/1**

00-1 **8** *2* **Miss Fritton (IRE)**[9] 322 3-9-7 70 JerryO'Dwyer 7 39
(M Botti) *t.k.h: towards rr: hdwy over 5f out: rdn and wknd over 2f out* **4/1**[2]

2m 4.70s (3.00) **Going Correction** +0.075s/f (Slow) **8** Ran SP% **113.5**
Speed ratings (Par 97): **89,87,86,86,84 82,75,74**
toteswinger: 1&2 £6.80, 1&3 £25.00, 2&3 £21.50. CSF £32.53 CT £694.80 TOTE £8.40: £2.30, £1.50, £5.50; EX 53.10.
Owner Dr Marwan Koukash **Bred** Juddmonte Farms Ltd **Trained** Portway, Worcs

FOCUS
An ordinary handicap that probably took very little winning, so the impressive performance of the winner should not be taken too literally.
Citizenship ◆ Official explanation: trainer said, regarding apparent improvement in form, colt had benefited from an extended trip

451 WILLIAM HILL 0800 444 040 - 24/7 H'CAP 5f 20y(P)
3:55 (3:55) (Class 3) (0-95,95) 4-Y-O+ **£7,771** (£2,312; £1,155; £577) **Stalls** Low

Form RPR

0-00 **1** **Haajes**[7] 359 5-8-11 85 (t) DaleGibson 2 92
(S Parr) *a.p: nt clr run and swtchd rt jst over 1f out: rdn to ld last stride* **14/1**

4-30 **2** *shd* **Canadian Danehill (IRE)**[15] 270 7-8-4 78 (p) CatherineGannon 1 85
(R M H Cowell) *led 2f: led over 1f out: sn rdn and edgd rt: hdd last stride* **6/1**

5-14 **3** *shd* **Doubtful Sound (USA)**[7] 359 5-9-7 95 (p) ChrisCatlin 8 102
(R Hollinshead) *a.p: rdn and sustained chal fnl f: r.o* **2/1**[1]

6435 **4** *1 ¼* **Bo McGinty (IRE)**[1] 424 8-8-2 76 (b) PaulHanagan 10 78
(R A Fahey) *racd wd: chsd ldrs: rdn wl over 1f out: kpt on one pce ins fnl f* **4/1**[3]

0201 **5** *1 ¼* **Gwilym (GER)**[9] 329 6-7-9 76 oh8 MatthewLawson(7) 5 74
(D Haydn Jones) *plld hrd in rr: swtchd lft wl over 3f out: n.m.r on ins 2f out: rdn and effrt over 1f out: nvr able to chal* **16/1**

34-1 **6** *¾* **Pawan (IRE)**[37] 2 9-9-0 93 (b) AnnStokell(5) 6 88
(Miss A Stokell) *bhd: rdn over 1f out: nvr able to chal* **12/1**

-411 **7** *2 ¼* **Harry Up**[8] 349 8-8-8 87 (p) PatrickDonaghy(5) 4 74
(K A Ryan) *s.i.s: sn rcvrd: led 3f out: rdn and hdd over 1f out: wknd ins fnl f* **3/1**[2]

61.90 secs (-0.40) **Going Correction** +0.075s/f (Slow) **7** Ran SP% **112.9**
Speed ratings (Par 107): **106,105,105,103,101 100,96**
toteswinger: 1&2 £11.00, 1&3 £7.10, 2&3 £2.90. CSF £90.86 CT £241.20 TOTE £19.70: £6.00, £2.50; EX 165.00.
Owner Willie McKay **Bred** Irish National Stud **Trained**

FOCUS
Despite a few non-runners, this was a decent sprint.

NOTEBOOK
Haajes, winning his first race on the all weather, had been well beaten on his last three starts but responded to pressure inside the final furlong here, and just forced his head in front on the line. This win came off a stiff mark, so he will do well to follow up despite being unexposed on the surface. (op 20-1)
Canadian Danehill(IRE), who had been dropped a pound since his latest run, put up a game performance after racing prominently. He seems to be in good heart. (tchd 5-1)
Doubtful Sound(USA) looked to be going like the winner turning in and only just lost out in a tight finish. The handicapper probably just has his measure, despite the small margin of defeat. (op 9-4 tchd 15-8)
Bo McGinty(IRE), who ran the previous day, is well treated on his winning form and has been running consistently without getting his head in front. This was another fair effort but he was readily held. (op 7-1)

Gwilym(GER) won over course and distance last time but never featured in this after pulling hard early. He did keep on well once in the straight but could not be considered unlucky. (op 12-1 tchd 18-1)

Pawan(IRE) won from a good draw at Southwell last time but failed to get competitive here. (op 10-1 tchd 14-1)

Harry Up seemed to anticipate the start, which made his stall open a fraction before the others. He then lost his footing and could not take up his usual front-running role until rushed up between runners. It is probably wise to forget this run. (op 9-4)

452 WILLIAM HILL 0800 444 040 - BET NOW! CLAIMING STKS 1m 141y(P)

4:30 (4:31) (Class 6) 4-Y-0+ **£2,047** (£604; £302) **Stalls** Low

Form				RPR
5-34	**1**		**Blacktoft (USA)**[25] 143 6-8-9 72 (e) ChrisCatlin 1 (S C Williams) *hld up in rr: hdwy 2f out: led ins fnl f: rdn out* **11/8**[1]	70
1-52	**2**	1 ½	**Dancing Deano (IRE)**[15] 274 7-8-8 63 RussellKennemore(3) 3 (R Hollinshead) *t.k.h in tch: led wl over 1f out: sn edgd rt: rdn and hdd ins fnl f: nt qckn* **8/1**	69
0-64	**3**	1 ¼	**Bobski (IRE)**[7] 357 7-8-8 72 (p) PaulHanagan 9 (Miss Gay Kelleway) *hld up in rr: hdwy on outside over 2f out: rdn and one pce ins fnl f* **11/2**[3]	63
	4	5	**Johnston's Baby (IRE)**[742] 7-8-4 0 JimmyQuinn 10 (E J Alston) *hld up in mid-div: hdwy over 2f out: wknd fnl f* **66/1**	48
05-0	**5**	7	**All You Need (IRE)**[15] 277 5-8-7 47 (p) DaleGibson 2 (R Hollinshead) *hld up towards rr: prog whn hmpd ent st: n.d after* **25/1**	35
0-65	**6**	1 ¾	**Fairly Honest**[15] 275 5-8-6 46 LukeMorris 4 (P W Hiatt) *led early: prom: chsd ldr over 3f out tl rdn over 2f out: wknd wl over 1f out* **20/1**	30
05-2	**7**	hd	**Wahoo Sam (USA)**[16] 244 9-8-6 53 CatherineGannon 11 (P D Evans) *sn led: clr over 6f out: hdd wl over 1f out: sn wknd* **25/1**	29
32-0	**8**	24	**Monkey Glas (IRE)**[28] 113 5-8-11 81 (v) TravisBlock 8 (J R Gask) *sn chsng ldr: lost 2nd over 3f out: rdn and wkng whn hmpd over 2f out: eased fnl f* **5/2**[2]	—

1m 49.94s (-0.56) **Going Correction** +0.075s/f (Slow) **8** Ran SP% **111.1**
Speed ratings (Par 101): **105,103,102,98,91 90,90,68**
toteswinger: 1&2 £2.40, 1&3 £2.80, 2&3 £4.20. CSF £12.00 TOTE £2.20: £1.20, £1.40, £1.90; EX 11.70.

Owner Chris Watkins And David N Reynolds **Bred** Paradigm Thoroughbreds Inc **Trained** Newmarket, Suffolk

FOCUS
An ordinary claimer that looked to be run at a sound gallop.

All You Need(IRE) Official explanation: jockey said gelding was denied a clear run
Fairly Honest Official explanation: jockey said gelding hung left

453 WILLIAMHILL.COM - PLAY LIVE CASINO H'CAP 1m 1f 103y(P)

5:00 (5:00) (Class 4) (0-85,82) 4-Y-0+ **£4,857** (£1,445; £722; £360) **Stalls** Low

Form				RPR
1-33	**1**		**Dream Of Fortune (IRE)**[15] 271 5-9-2 77 (t) RobertWinston 7 (M G Quinlan) *stdd s: hld up in rr: hdwy on outside over 2f out: rdn to ld ins fnl f: r.o* **4/1**[2]	83
16-1	**2**	nk	**Templetuohy Max (IRE)**[22] 194 4-8-6 67 (v) JimmyQuinn 6 (J D Bethell) *hld up in tch: rdn and sustained chal fnl f: r.o* **9/2**[3]	72
0-60	**3**	1 ¼	**Count Trevisio (IRE)**[17] 232 6-9-7 82 ChrisCatlin 5 (J R Gask) *led: rdn and hdd ins fnl f: no ex* **22/1**	85
3-24	**4**	nk	**Stand Guard**[15] 271 5-9-5 80 IanMongan 4 (P Howling) *hld up: hdwy whn n.m.r over 2f out: swtchd lft wl over 1f out: sn rdn: kpt on ins fnl f* **9/4**[1]	82
3302	**5**	1 ¾	**Just Bond (IRE)**[1] 430 7-9-4 79 PJMcDonald 1 (G R Oldroyd) *chsd ldr tl rdn over 1f out: fdd wl ins fnl f* **9/2**[3]	77
65-0	**6**	10	**Princess Cocoa (IRE)**[15] 271 6-8-13 74 PaulHanagan 3 (R A Fahey) *s.i.s: hld up: bhd fnl 2f* **12/1**	51
0-53	**P**		**Kestrel Cross (IRE)**[7] 361 7-8-11 72 (t) LukeMorris 2 (A W Carroll) *hld up in tch: rdn whn wnt bdly lame over 2f out: sn p.u: dead* **15/2**	—

2m 1.90s (0.20) **Going Correction** +0.075s/f (Slow) **7** Ran SP% **110.9**
Speed ratings (Par 105): **102,101,100,100,98 89,—**
toteswinger: 1&2 £2.50, 1&3 £10.10, 2&3 £9.10. CSF £20.81 TOTE £4.10: £2.80, £2.50; EX 19.10.

Owner N J Jones **Bred** Newborough Stud **Trained** Newmarket, Suffolk

FOCUS
The pace seemed fair for this competitive handicap, so one would imagine the form will be reliable. Three looked to have a chance inside the final furlong, but that quickly went down to two.

454 WILLIAMHILL.COM - PLAY BINGO MAIDEN STKS 5f 216y(P)

5:30 (5:31) (Class 5) 3-Y-0+ **£2,729** (£806; £403) **Stalls** Low

Form				RPR
0-6	**1**		**Here Comes Danny**[20] 208 3-8-13 0 PaulHanagan 2 (M Wigham) *t.k.h in tch: wnt 2nd over 2f out: rdn and wandered fr over 1f out: led ins fnl f: r.o wl* **11/8**[1]	75+
2-36	**2**	4	**Welsh Opera**[29] 108 4-9-4 54 (v) WilliamCarson(5) 4 (S C Williams) *led 1f: led over 3f out: rdn wl over 1f out: hdd ins fnl f: sn hmpd and btn* **7/2**[3]	61
0	**3**	3 ½	**Pipers Piping (IRE)**[7] 356 3-8-13 0 ChrisCatlin 1 (J A Osborne) *in rr: struggling 3f out: tk 3rd wl ins fnl f* **8/1**	51
3-22	**4**	2 ½	**Silk Gallery (USA)**[11] 305 4-9-9 55 (t) JimmyQuinn 3 (E J Alston) *t.k.h: led after 1f: hdd over 3f out: wknd 2f out* **2/1**[2]	42

1m 15.08s (0.08) **Going Correction** +0.075s/f (Slow)
WFA 3 from 4yo 15lb **4** Ran SP% **108.8**
Speed ratings (Par 103): **102,96,92,88**
CSF £6.39 TOTE £2.50; EX 5.20 Place 6 £296.04, Place 5 £188.43..

Owner E J Evans **Bred** Mill House Stud **Trained** Newmarket, Suffolk

FOCUS
This took very little winning, so it was hardly surprising to see an unexposed sort gambled on and prove good enough to win.

Here Comes Danny Official explanation: trainer said, regarding the improved form shown, colt had run very green and was on and off the bridle last time at Kempton, adding that colt was running against higher rated horses last time and did not need to improve to win this race

Silk Gallery(USA) Official explanation: jockey said filly ran too free

T/Jkpt: Not won. T/Plt: £298.50 to a £1 stake. Pool: £74,662.02. 182.55 winning tickets. T/Qpdt: £141.90 to a £1 stake. Pool: £4,462.65. 23.27 winning tickets. KH

385 KEMPTON (A.W) (R-H)

Sunday, February 8

OFFICIAL GOING: Standard
Wind: Slight, across Weather: Sunny

455 KEMPTON.CO.UK MEDIAN AUCTION MAIDEN STKS 1m 3f (P)

2:10 (2:12) (Class 6) 3-5-Y-0 **£2,047** (£604; £302) **Stalls** High

Form				RPR
0-5	**1**		**Dubai Storming**[16] 272 3-8-5 0 JimmyQuinn 1 (E A L Dunlop) *t.k.h early: led 2f out: rdn out* **10/3**[3]	69+
3-22	**2**	2 ½	**Solo Choice**[10] 322 3-8-5 68 ChrisCatlin 7 (D Flood) *hld up: gd hdwy on outside to chal 3f out: hung lft over 1f out: no ch w wnr* **5/1**	65
00-	**3**	½	**Fielder (IRE)**[258] 2454 4-9-12 0 JimCrowley 5 (J G Portman) *sn trckd ldrs: effrt over 1f out: kpt on* **50/1**	67
3	**4**	hd	**Leo The Lion (IRE)**[11] 310 3-8-5 0 GregFairley 2 (M Johnston) *sn led: hdd after 3f: outpcd over 2f out: styd on fnl f* **2/1**[2]	64+
055-	**5**	3 ¾	**Forty Thirty (IRE)**[102] 7069 3-8-5 70 EdwardCreighton 4 (M R Channon) *t.k.h: trckd ldr: led after 3f: rdn and hdd 2f out: wknd ins fnl f* **7/4**[1]	57
	6	1	**Soul Singer** 3-8-0 0 FrankieMcDonald 6 (J G Portman) *slowly away: in rr whn checked on ins over 2f out: one pce after* **25/1**	51
00-	**7**	nk	**Moandei**[118] 6705 5-9-9 0 StephenCarson 3 (R Ingram) *hld up: a in rr* **33/1**	53
00-6	**8**	5	**Prima Fonteyn**[36] 32 3-8-2 40 ow9 JemmaMarshall(7) 8 (Miss Sheena West) *in tch tl wknd over 2f out* **50/1**	51?
0	**9**	4	**Little Roxy (IRE)**[11] 310 4-9-7 0 TravisBlock 9 (Miss A M Newton-Smith) *towards rr whn rdn over 3f out* **50/1**	38

2m 26.61s (4.71) **Going Correction** +0.25s/f (Slow)
WFA 3 from 4yo 23lb 4 from 5yo 2lb **9** Ran SP% **122.1**
Speed ratings (Par 101): **92,90,89,89,86 86,86,82,79**
toteswinger: 1&2 £2.40, 1&3 £14.80, 2&3 £17.80. CSF £20.60 TOTE £6.00: £1.30, £1.40, £7.30; EX 22.70.

Owner Salem Suhail **Bred** Gainsborough Stud Management Ltd **Trained** Newmarket, Suffolk

FOCUS
This was not a strong maiden and one would imagine that the form will be fairly weak in the long term, especially when you consider that the pace was far from strong.

456 TURFTV CLAIMING STKS 1m 3f (P)

2:40 (2:41) (Class 6) 4-Y-0+ **£2,047** (£604; £302) **Stalls** High

Form				RPR
P34-	**1**		**King's Head (IRE)**[52] 7717 6-8-9 91 (p) FergusSweeney 8 (G L Moore) *trckd ldrs: wnt 2nd 4f out: led over 1f out: rdn out* **2/1**[1]	84
1-11	**2**	1 ¼	**La Estrella (USA)**[31] 84 6-9-8 88 ChrisCatlin 4 (D E Cantillon) *hld up: hdwy on outside over 2f out: hrd rdn to go 2nd wl ins fnl f* **7/2**[2]	95
601-	**3**	1 ¼	**Bois Joli (IRE)**[106] 6991 4-8-3 77 JimmyQuinn 6 (M Botti) *trckd ldr to 4f out: rdn to go 2nd again over 1f out tl wl ins fnl f* **2/1**[1]	76
5-22	**4**	2	**Quince (IRE)**[4] 393 6-8-11 78 (v) PatCosgrave 3 (J Pearce) *a abt same pl: rdn over 3f out: kpt on one pce u.p fnl f* **6/1**[3]	79
6-54	**5**	1 ¼	**Friends Hope**[10] 330 8-8-7 77 ow1 GrahamGibbons 1 (R Curtis) *sn led: rdn and hdd over 1f out: wknd ins fnl f* **14/1**	72
4-30	**6**	1	**Profit's Reality (IRE)**[10] 330 7-9-8 81 JimCrowley 9 (M J Attwater) *hld up in rr: effrt over 2f out: sn btn* **10/1**	86

2m 25.24s (3.34) **Going Correction** +0.25s/f (Slow)
WFA 4 from 5yo+ 2lb **6** Ran SP% **118.9**
Speed ratings (Par 101): **97,96,95,93,92 92**
toteswinger: 1&2 £2.30, 1&3 £2.20, 2&3 £2.20. CSF £10.17 TOTE £3.50: £2.00, £2.00; EX 13.00.King's Head was subject of a friendly claim.

Owner The Gingerbread Men **Bred** London Thoroughbred Services Ltd **Trained** Lower Beeding, W Sussex

■ Stewards' Enquiry : Fergus Sweeney caution: used whip with excessive frequency.

FOCUS
Not many runners but this looked a decent claimer, as it featured plenty of in-form horses. However, the early gallop was not very good and it developed into a sprint up the home straight.

457 MIX BUSINESS WITH PLEASURE H'CAP 7f (P)

3:10 (3:10) (Class 5) (0-75,75) 4-Y-0+ **£2,590** (£770; £385; £192) **Stalls** High

Form				RPR
031-	**1**		**Last Sovereign**[177] 5069 5-9-4 **75** RichardHughes 11 (Jane Chapple-Hyam) *a.p on ins: led over 1f out: r.o wl* **6/1**[3]	88
01-6	**2**	2 ¾	**Millfield (IRE)**[26] 143 6-9-2 **73** GeorgeBaker 1 (P R Chamings) *c over to ins fr wd draw and in rr tl hdwy on ins over 1f out: r.o wl to go 2nd towards fin* **10/1**	79+
50-5	**3**	½	**Super Frank (IRE)**[23] 191 6-8-12 **69** JimCrowley 10 (J Akehurst) *led to rdn and hdd over 1f out: kpt on but lost 2nd towards fin* **9/4**[1]	74
06-2	**4**	1 ½	**Lend A Grand (IRE)**[36] 31 5-8-10 **67** FergusSweeney 9 (Miss Jo Crowley) *in tch: rdn and kpt on one pce fnl f* **8/1**	68
55-6	**5**	½	**Secret Dubai (IRE)**[20] 218 4-9-2 **73** (t) JerryO'Dwyer 4 (M Botti) *t.k.h in rr: effrt on outside over 2f out: kpt on fnl f but nvr nr to chal* **10/1**	72
-611	**6**	½	**Guildenstern (IRE)**[16] 277 7-8-9 **66** JimmyQuinn 2 (P Howling) *in rr: rdn over 2f out: swtchd lft wl over 1f out: kpt on but nvr nr to chal* **6/1**[3]	64
24-4	**7**	1	**Autumn Blades (IRE)**[15] 282 4-9-4 **75** (v[1]) MickyFenton 3 (A Bailey) *trckd ldrs: rdn 2f out: wknd fnl f* **9/1**	70
06-6	**8**	shd	**Geoffdaw**[28] 128 4-8-13 **70** (v) PaulDoe 8 (P D Evans) *plld hrd in tch: rdn over 2f out: sn bhd* **33/1**	65
/0-6	**9**	1	**Pharaohs Justice (USA)**[31] 94 4-8-4 **68** AlexOwen(7) 6 (N P Littmoden) *a in rr* **33/1**	60
21-3	**10**	¾	**Balata**[25] 157 4-8-13 **70** TGMcLaughlin 7 (B R Millman) *trckd ldr to 2f out: rdn and wknd over 1f out: eased ins fnl f* **4/1**[2]	65

1m 26.63s (0.63) **Going Correction** +0.25s/f (Slow) **10** Ran SP% **124.5**
Speed ratings (Par 103): **106,102,102,100,100 99,98,98,97,96**
toteswinger: 1&2 £10.40, 1&3 £4.30, 2&3 £7.30. CSF £69.11 CT £181.79 TOTE £6.60: £2.80, £3.40, £1.40; EX 74.80.

Owner Howard Spooner **Bred** Gestut Hof Ittlingen & Cheveley Park Stud Ltd **Trained** Newmarket, Suffolk

The Form Book, Raceform Ltd, Compton, RG20 6NL

FOCUS
Quite a few of these appeared to be in good form, so the race should prove a reliable guide in the future.

458 LADYBIRD STKS (LISTED RACE) 1m (P)
3:40 (3:41) (Class 1) 4-Y-0+

£22,708 (£8,608; £4,308; £2,148; £1,076; £540) Stalls High

Form RPR
16-1 1 **Premio Loco (USA)**[36] 30 5-9-0 109 GeorgeBaker 1 109
(C F Wall) *racd in tch: sustained run to ld 1f out: r.o strly* **4/5**[1]
002- 2 2 **Philario (IRE)**[50] 7740 4-9-0 97 FergusSweeney 7 104
(K R Burke) *led tl rdn and hdd 1f out: kpt on but nt pce of wnr* **8/1**
2-23 3 1 **Bonus (IRE)**[29] 123 9-9-0 107 (b) ChrisCatlin 8 102
(G A Butler) *hld up in rr: hdwy 2f out: r.o fnl f* **7/1**[2]
10-1 4 shd **Mahadee (IRE)**[16] 278 4-9-0 98 (b) JimCrowley 5 101
(C E Brittain) *in tch tl outpcd 3f out: swtchd lft 2f out: r.o ins fnl f* **7/1**[2]
1-12 5 2 **Councellor (FR)**[14] 291 7-9-0 93 (t) MickyFenton 4 97
(Stef Liddiard) *t.k.h: trckd ldr to 2f out: wknd fnl f* **14/1**
63-3 6 ½ **Samarinda (USA)**[22] 206 6-9-0 95 AdamKirby 2 96
(Mrs P Sly) *hld up: effrt 2f out: wknd fnl f* **11/1**
05-1 7 3 ¾ **Orchard Supreme**[14] 291 6-9-0 99 RichardHughes 6 87
(R Hannon) *trckd ldrs tl wknd fnl f* **15/2**[3]
0-32 8 7 **Shake On It**[4] 398 5-9-0 60 (t) WilliamCarson 3 71
(M J Gingell) *slowly away: a in rr* **66/1**
1m 39.17s (-0.63) **Going Correction** +0.25s/f (Slow) 8 Ran SP% **119.9**
Speed ratings (Par 111): **113,111,110,109,107 107,103,96**
toteswinger: 1&2 £3.80, 1&3 £2.40, 2&3 £7.50. CSF £8.83 TOTE £1.90: £1.30, £2.60, £1.90; EX 11.00.
Owner Bernard Westley **Bred** Kidder, Cole & Griggs **Trained** Newmarket, Suffolk

FOCUS
A small but select field lined up for this decent prize. The two previous winners of this contest, Medicine Path and Gentleman's Deal, turned out to be smart performers, and there is no reason to believe that this winner will not develop into a similar sort.

NOTEBOOK
Premio Loco(USA) was the classiest horse on show and played up before the start, which is usually a good sign with him, as he had done it at this course in the past before winning. Held up close to the leader, he quickened up nicely when asked to win the race and ended up a clear winner. His stamina will not be fully guaranteed for it, but he must be a player in the Winter Derby next month if asked to take up that challenge. He also has the option of the Wulfruna Stakes, which is over 7f at Wolverhampton. Later in the year, America could be on the agenda. (tchd 5-6 in places)
Philario(IRE) ran nicely in a conditions event at Lingfield last time and was allowed to lead in this. He rallied gamely for pressure once joined, but was not in the same league as the winner when he swept past. However, he is not over-raced for his age and has the scope to improve. (op 9-1)
Bonus(IRE), having his first try at 1m, was held up as usual and ran the race he virtually always does over shorter. He is probably worth another try over this distance.
Mahadee(IRE) had won three of his last five races, including a clear-cut victory at Wolverhampton last time. He had his chance but became outpaced over 2f out before staying on well inside the final furlong. One is inclined to think that he was outclassed at this level. (op 6-1)
Councellor(FR) raced a bit keenly and was slightly disappointing. He is much better than he showed here. (op 16-1)
Samarinda(USA) had finished behind Premio Loco on a couple of occasions over this course and distance and never looked like avenging those defeats. (op 12-1)
Orchard Supreme came into this on the back of a win at Wolverhampton last time (Councellor behind that day) but he reportedly missed out on work recently and weakened late on. (op 8-1)
Shake On It was predictably outclassed.

459 DAY TIME, NIGHT TIME, GREAT TIME H'CAP 2m (P)
4:10 (4:10) (Class 4) (0-85,80) 4-Y-0+ £4,727 (£1,406; £702; £351) Stalls High

Form RPR
510- 1 **Right Option (IRE)**[58] 6983 5-9-1 70 TolleyDean(3) 9 83
(J L Flint) *mid-div: hdwy over 3f out: wnt 2nd over 2f out: led over 1f out: rdn clr* **10/1**
2/42 2 9 **Kavaloti (IRE)**[18] 233 5-9-7 73 (b) GeorgeBaker 7 76
(G L Moore) *chsd ldrs: styd on to go 2nd ins fnl f* **7/4**[1]
000- 3 1 ¼ **Dreams Jewel**[262] 2245 9-8-9 61 oh1 NeilChalmers 6 62
(C Roberts) *slowly away: in rr tl hdwy on ins over 2f out: styd on to go 3rd nr fin* **50/1**
024- 4 ½ **Callisto Moon**[100] 7110 5-9-3 69 GrahamGibbons 4 69
(R Curtis) *led tl rdn and hdd over 1f out: wknd ins fnl f* **5/1**[3]
120/ 5 ½ **Cnoc Moy (IRE)**[43] 5889 5-10-0 80 JimCrowley 1 80
(O Sherwood) *wnt lft leaving stalls: in rr: styd on fr over 1f out but nvr on terms* **10/1**
240- 6 ¾ **Criterion**[185] 4784 4-9-7 79 StephenDonohoe 10 78
(Ian Williams) *chsd ldr to 7f out: rdn and sn wknd* **8/1**
-644 7 1 ¾ **Calculating (IRE)**[10] 325 5-9-0 66 (p) IanMongan 8 63
(M D I Usher) *in rr: hdwy to go 2nd 4f out: wknd over 1f out* **4/1**[2]
3 8 14 **Winged Arrow (IRE)**[17] 249 7-8-12 64 JamieMoriarty 3 44
(Jonjo O'Neill) *in tch tl wknd over 3f out* **7/1**
600/ 9 10 **Global Strategy**[80] 6666 6-9-4 70 ChrisCatlin 2 38
(O Sherwood) *in rr: lost tch over 3f out* **25/1**
3m 31.36s (1.26) **Going Correction** +0.25s/f (Slow)
WFA 4 from 5yo+ 6lb 9 Ran SP% **120.6**
Speed ratings (Par 105): **106,101,100,100,100 100,99,92,87**
toteswinger: 1&2 £5.90, 1&3 £52.50, 2&3 £24.40. CSF £29.21 CT £886.09 TOTE £14.10: £3.50, £1.10, £11.90; EX 48.80 TRIFECTA Not Won..
Owner Roy Mathias **Bred** Paul Monaghan, R Berns And P Sexton **Trained** Kenfig Hill, Bridgend

FOCUS
This looked an interesting but difficult staying event to work out before the off. It featured a mix of proven all-weather performers, fair hurdlers and unexposed types, so quite what the form will amount to is anyone's guess.

460 SPONSOR AT KEMPTON H'CAP (DIV I) 6f (P)
4:40 (4:41) (Class 6) (0-65,65) 4-Y-0+ £1,706 (£503; £252) Stalls High

Form RPR
56-0 1 **Royal Envoy (IRE)**[23] 191 6-9-1 65 TolleyDean(3) 10 75
(P Howling) *chsd ldrs: led 2f out: rdn out* **11/4**[1]
5-51 2 ¾ **Davids Mark**[9] 347 9-8-8 55 SimonWhitworth 5 63
(J R Jenkins) *hld up: hdwy to chse wnr over 1f out: kpt on* **16/1**
-451 3 shd **Muktasb (USA)**[13] 294 8-8-13 60 (v) AdamKirby 1 68+
(D Shaw) *swtchd to ins rail fr wd draw: in rr tl hdwy on ins over 1f out: r.o to go 3rd ins fnl f* **12/1**
6523 4 ¾ **Obe Royal**[3] 401 5-9-1 62 (p) PaulDoe 9 67
(P D Evans) *chsd ldr: rdn 2f out: kpt on one pce* **5/1**[3]
5-00 5 ½ **Lake Sabina**[16] 269 4-8-5 52 AndrewElliott 11 56
(M R Hoad) *mid-div: rdn 2f out: kpt on but nt qckn fnl f* **33/1**
00-6 6 ¾ **Mansii**[25] 166 4-8-13 60 RichardHughes 4 61
(P J McBride) *hld up: rdn and effrt over 1f out but no imp* **11/2**
4-13 7 2 **What Katie Did (IRE)**[17] 243 4-9-3 64 (p) JimCrowley 6 59
(J M Bradley) *t.k.h: trckd ldr to 2f out: one pce after* **4/1**[2]
004- 8 2 ¼ **My Kaiser Chief**[157] 5638 4-8-11 58 RichardKingscote 8 46
(W J H Ratcliffe) *led tl hdd 2f out: wknd fnl f* **9/1**
040- 9 2 ¼ **Prince Of Delphi**[158] 5600 6-9-3 64 GeorgeBaker 7 44
(Mrs A L M King) *prom: rdn over 2f out: sn wknd* **8/1**
1m 12.79s (-0.31) **Going Correction** +0.25s/f (Slow) 9 Ran SP% **116.3**
Speed ratings (Par 101): **112,111,110,109,109 108,105,102,99**
toteswinger: 1&2 £13.00, 1&3 £5.50, 2&3 £7.80. CSF £49.82 CT £462.06 TOTE £4.40: £1.90, £3.10, £3.70; EX 58.00.
Owner The Circle Bloodstock I Limited **Bred** Northern Lights Bloodstock **Trained** Newmarket, Suffolk

FOCUS
This looked a very competitive handicap for sprinters. Plenty of horses appeared to be fancied by connections, so the form should be sound.

461 SPONSOR AT KEMPTON H'CAP (DIV II) 6f (P)
5:10 (5:10) (Class 6) (0-65,65) 4-Y-0+ £1,706 (£503; £252) Stalls High

Form RPR
31-2 1 **Perlachy**[9] 352 5-8-10 57 (v) LukeMorris 2 66
(D Shaw) *trckd ldrs: led 2f out: rdn out* **3/1**[2]
60-4 2 ¾ **Step It Up (IRE)**[24] 167 5-9-4 65 PatCosgrave 5 72
(J R Boyle) *t.k.h: trckd ldr: ev ch 2f out: kpt on u.p fnl f* **4/1**[3]
44-0 3 nk **Mistress Cooper**[29] 118 4-8-12 59 ChrisCatlin 7 65
(W J Musson) *hld up: hd-way on ins over 1f out: r.o to go 3rd ins fnl f* **6/1**
14-0 4 nk **Littledodayno (IRE)**[18] 235 6-9-3 64 RichardHughes 9 69
(M Wigham) *trckd ldrs: rdn over 1f out: kpt on fnl f* **11/4**[1]
-400 5 ½ **Mind Alert**[19] 222 8-8-8 55 ow3 (v) JamesDoyle 10 58
(D Shaw) *hld up: r.o fnl f: nvr nrr* **10/1**
6-10 6 ½ **Hollow Jo**[18] 234 9-8-8 55 FergusSweeney 1 57+
(J R Jenkins) *blind removed late leaving stalls and lost several l: mde late hdwy fnl f* **14/1**
1-20 7 1 ¼ **Kaystar Ridge**[18] 235 4-8-8 60 (bt) JamesO'Reilly(5) 8 58
(D K Ivory) *trckd ldrs tl wknd appr fnl f* **9/1**
41-0 8 2 ½ **Brazilian Brush (IRE)**[18] 235 4-8-11 63 (t) JackDean(5) 3 53
(J M Bradley) *led tl hdd 2f out: wknd qckly* **20/1**
1m 14.62s (1.52) **Going Correction** +0.25s/f (Slow) 8 Ran SP% **116.5**
Speed ratings (Par 101): **99,98,97,97,96 95,94,90**
toteswinger: 1&2 £2.70, 1&3 £6.60, 2&3 £7.90. CSF £15.83 CT £67.46 TOTE £3.60: £1.10, £1.50, £2.00; EX 18.80 Place 6: £57.37 Place 5: 13.59.
Owner Mrs N Macauley **Bred** J James **Trained** Danethorpe, Notts

FOCUS
Much like the first division, this looked a good contest of its type, but there was a distinct lack of pace early and the form may not be completely reliable.
Hollow Jo Official explanation: jockey said he was unable to remove blindfold
T/Jkpt: Not won. T/Plt: £98.50 to a £1 stake. Pool: £153,142.02. 1,134.71 winning tickets. T/Qpdt: £13.50 to a £1 stake. Pool: £12,733.07. 695.31 winning tickets. JS

ST MORITZ (R-H)
Sunday, February 8

OFFICIAL GOING: Frozen
All races were reduced in trip owing to water on the far side of the course.

464a GP HANDELS & GEWERBEVEREIN ST MORITZ (SNOW) 4f
11:45 (11:48) 4-Y-0+ £6,275 (£2,510; £1,882; £1,255; £627)

RPR
1 **Rushing Dasher (GER)**[357] 603 7-9-0 FrauNatalieFriberg 11 75
(Natalie Friberg, Switzerland) **41/10**[2]
2 1 ¼ **Seneca Village (FR)** 5-9-4 RobertHavlin 1 73
(M Weiss, Switzerland) **145/10**
3 ½ **Princess Rose Anne (IRE)**[23] 191 4-9-1 SteveDrowne 10 67
(J R Best) **53/10**
4 1 ¾ **Spinning Crystal (IRE)**[843] 6064 5-8-10 JoeFanning 5 53
(S Szuna, Czech Republic) **15/2**
5 2 **Tobanjaro (HUN)**[357] 603 6-9-1 ow1 AFekete 9 48
(Z Nagy, Hungary) **19/1**
6 2 ½ **Tiger's Eye (FR)**[586] 6-8-11 VJanacek 2 32
(Miss A Casotti, Switzerland) **51/10**
7 2 **Assam (GER)**[312] 7-9-6 (b) GBocskai 6 31
(Carmen Bocskai, Switzerland) **7/2**[1]
8 **National Face (HUN)** 4-9-0 IRossi 3 25
(S Szabolcs, Germany) **18/1**
9 **Mina Alsalaam**[1652] 4364 7-8-11 ow1 ZVarga 4 22
(S Peto, Hungary) **12/1**
10 **Film Maker (IRE)**[135] 6239 4-9-9 GArena 7 34
(G Raveneau, Switzerland) **23/5**[3]
11 **Atlantic Dancer (GER)**[357] 603 6-9-9 MEsposito 8 34
(A Schennach, Switzerland) **26/5**
49.01 secs (49.01) 11 Ran SP% **144.3**
(including 1SF stakes): WIN 5.10; PL 2.20, 2.60, 2.70; SF 22.90. This race was programmed to be run over 5f 110y but had to be rescheduled to 4f for safety reasons..
Owner Stall Allegra Racing Club **Bred** H K Gutschow **Trained** Switzerland

465a GP AMERICAN AIRLINES (SNOW) 4f
1:15 (1:19) 4-Y-0+ £5,020 (£2,007; £1,503; £1,007; £503)

RPR
1 shd **Star Pattern (USA)**[224] 3525 4-8-11 RobertHavlin 1 —
(M Weiss, Switzerland) **67/10**
2 **Mister Minister (GER)**[146] 4-9-4 MEsposito 8 —
(C Von Der Recke, Germany) **22/5**[3]
3 6 **Song Of Victory (GER)**[371] 422 5-8-10 MiguelLopez(4) 7 —
(M Weiss, Switzerland) **23/10**[1]
4 1 **Hucking Hero (IRE)**[11] 318 4-9-11 SteveDrowne 9 —
(J R Best) **27/10**[2]
5 4 ½ **Sybelio (FR)**[103] 7063 5-9-4 GArena 11 —
(W Hefter, Germany) **47/10**
6 nk **Le Ribot (GER)**[466] 5-9-0 GBocskai 3 —
(Carmen Bocskai, Switzerland) **61/10**
7 dist **Millefeuille (FR)**[567] 7-8-11 VJanacek 4 —
(Carmen Bocskai, Switzerland) **66/10**

8 **Celesta (HUN)** 5-9-5 .... DPorcu 6 —
(S Szuna, Czech Republic) **41/5**
51.30 secs (51.30) **8** Ran SP% **144.5**
WIN 7.70; PL 2.00, 1.90, 1.40; SF 65.80. This race was programmed for one mile but was rescheduled to 4f for safety reasons..
Owner Stall Beliar **Bred** Arthur B Hancock III & Gerald F Healy **Trained** Switzerland

466a GP GUARDAVAL IMMOBILIEN (SNOW) 4f
1:45 (1:58) 4-Y-0+ **£6,275** (£2,510; £1,882; £1,255; £627)

RPR
1 **Vlavianus (CZE)**357 604 8-8-9 .... (b) MiguelLopez(4) 10 —
(M Weiss, Switzerland) **7/2**2
2 7 **Collow (GER)**357 605 9-9-3 .... RobertHavlin 3 —
(M Weiss, Switzerland) **17/10**1
3 3 **Romantic Man (GER)**893 6-9-1 .... DPorcu 9 —
(M Rulec, Germany) **42/10**
4 3 **Franziskaner (GER)**638 6-9-1 .... GArena 8 —
(W Hefter, Germany) **43/10**
5 ½ **Saraab (GER)**182 4911 7-9-3 .... IRossi 1 —
(P Vovcenko, Germany) **79/10**
6 3 **Swiss Act**22 206 5-8-13 .... JoeFanning 7 —
(M Johnston) **41/10**3
7 dist **Vegano (FR)**197 8-9-1 .... MEsposito 4 —
(C Von Der Recke, Germany) **49/10**
48.80 secs (48.80) **7** Ran SP% **145.2**
WIN 4.50; PL 1.30, 1.20, 1.30; SF 7.50. This race was programmed for 1m 1f but had to be rescheduled to 4f for safety reasons..
Owner Stall Schachen **Bred** Stall Schachen **Trained** Switzerland

455 KEMPTON (A.W) (R-H)
Monday, February 9

OFFICIAL GOING: Standard
Wind: Virtually nil Weather: Raining

467 KEMPTON.CO.UK H'CAP 5f (P)
2:10 (2:15) (Class 6) (0-55,55) 4-Y-0+ **£2,388** (£705; £352) **Stalls High**

Form RPR
-106 1 **Hollow Jo**1 461 9-9-5 55 .... (v) FergusSweeney 9 64
(J R Jenkins) *trckd ldrs on inner: hdwy 2f out: swtchd lft and effrt over 1f out: rdn and styd on to ld ins fnl f* **7/2**2
-315 2 1 **Head To Head (IRE)**11 327 5-9-1 51 .... (b) TomEaves 1 56
(A D Brown) *sn led: rdn over 1f out: drvn and hdd ins fnl f: edgd lft and kpt on* **10/1**
5-60 3 ½ **Lady Bahia (IRE)**25 177 8-8-12 49 ow1 .... (b) PatCosgrave 6 51
(Peter Grayson) *chsd ldng pair: hdwy over 1f out and sn rdn: drvn ins fnl f: edgd lft and kpt on same pce* **16/1**
-00 4 ¾ **Marvin Gardens**10 347 6-9-2 52 .... (b) AdamKirby 2 53
(P S McEntee) *outpcd and bhd: hdwy wl over 1f out: rdn and styd on strly ins fnl f: n.m.r and swtchd rt towards fin* **11/1**
200/ 5 nse **Meikle Barfil**495 5897 7-8-12 48 .... (tp) JimCrowley 3 48
(J M Bradley) *hld up towards rr: hdwy wl over 1f out: rdn to chse ldrs ent fnl f: kpt on same pce* **25/1**
600- 6 nk **Wynberg (IRE)**110 6907 4-9-5 55 .... MickyFenton 5 54
(Stef Liddiard) *in tch: rdn along wl over 1f out: kpt on same pce u.p ins fnl f* **9/4**1
00-0 7 nk **Babel**17 269 4-9-5 55 .... SimonWhitworth 7 53
(M Wigham) *hld up in tch: hdwy 2f out: rdn over 1f out: keeping on same pce whn n.m.r and swtchd rt wl ins fnl f* **5/1**3
6143 8 nk **Sherjawy (IRE)**26 153 5-8-13 49 .... (b) SamHitchcott 4 46
(Miss Z C Davison) *towards rr: pushed along 2f out: rdn over 1f out: kpt on ins fnl f: nrst fin* **11/2**
410- 9 2 **Sir Loin**351 690 8-9-3 53 .... (v) TGMcLaughlin 8 43
(P Burgoyne) *t.k.h: chsd ldr: rdn along wl over 1f out: wknd ent fnl f* **14/1**
60.57 secs (0.07) **Going Correction** +0.225s/f (Slow) **9** Ran SP% **118.9**
Speed ratings (Par 101): **108,106,105,104,104 103,103,102,99**
toteswinger: 1&2 £6.80, 1&3 £12.70, 2&3 £10.30. CSF £39.54 CT £506.52 TOTE £4.50: £1.70, £2.90, £3.70; EX 47.20.
Owner Humphrey Solomons **Bred** K J Reddington **Trained** Royston, Herts
FOCUS
A low-grade sprint handicap run at a strong pace. The form is rated around the placed horses.
Sir Loin Official explanation: trainer said gelding bled from the nose

468 TURFTV MAIDEN STKS 1m 2f (P)
2:45 (2:50) (Class 5) 3-Y-0+ **£3,238** (£963; £481; £240) **Stalls High**

Form RPR
000- 1 **Clovis**113 6403 4-9-13 65 .... (b) TomEaves 1 65
(N P Mulholland) *t.k.h: trckd ldrs: hdwy on outer over 2f out: rdn and qcknd to ld over 1f out: sn clr* **9/1**3
03-5 2 5 **Longboat Key**23 201 3-8-6 70 .... GregFairley 3 51
(M Johnston) *set stdy pce: rdn along wl over 1f out: drvn and hdd appr fnl f: one pce* **2/7**1
3 2 **Bolanderi (USA)**39 4-9-13 0 .... JimCrowley 2 51
(Andrew Turnell) *trckd ldr: hdwy and cl up 3f out: rdn wl over 1f out and ev ch tl drvn and one pce appr fnl f* **9/2**2
0 4 1¼ **Ensnare**16 280 4-9-13 0 .... MickyFenton 4 49
(A M Hales) *trckd ldrs: effrt over 2f out: sn rdn along and btn over 1f out* **14/1**
0-00 5 4 **Super King**6 378 8-10-0 36 .... (b1) JamieMoriarty 5 41
(A D Brown) *dwlt and reminders s: a in rr* **50/1**
2m 13.64s (5.64) **Going Correction** +0.225s/f (Slow)
WFA 3 from 4yo 22lb 4 from 8yo 1lb **5** Ran SP% **114.6**
Speed ratings (Par 103): **86,82,80,79,76**
CSF £12.96 TOTE £8.10: £3.10, £1.02; EX 20.10.
Owner D J Bridger **Bred** Darley **Trained** North End, Dorset
FOCUS
A very modest maiden run at a very steady pace in driving rain. Dubious form with the favourite very disappointing and the winner having looked regressive.
Bolanderi(USA) Official explanation: jockey said gelding had a breathing problem

469 MIX BUSINESS WITH PLEASURE H'CAP 1m 2f (P)
3:20 (3:27) (Class 6) (0-50,50) 4-Y-0+ **£2,047** (£604; £302) **Stalls High**

Form RPR
3-03 1 **Itsawindup**2 443 5-8-10 46 oh1 .... (t) GregFairley 11 53
(Miss Sheena West) *a.p: swtchd lft and effrt over 1f out: rdn to ld ent fnl f: sn drvn and kpt on gamely* **3/1**1
6-65 2 hd **Hatch A Plan (IRE)**2 443 8-8-11 47 .... JimCrowley 12 54
(Mouse Hamilton-Fairley) *hld up in midfield: hdwy over 3f out: effrt wl over 1f out: rdn and styd on to chal ins fnl f and ev ch tl no ex nr fin* **5/1**2
0-00 3 1½ **Golden Square**29 130 7-8-11 47 oh1 ow1 .... (v) AdamKirby 8 51
(A W Carroll) *led: rdn along wl over 1f out: drvn and hdd ent fnl f: kpt on wl u.p towards fin* **33/1**
6-65 4 ½ **Tabulate**24 193 6-9-0 50 .... PatCosgrave 14 53
(P Howling) *trckd ldrs on inner: hdwy over 2f out: swtchd lft and ch whn rdn over 1f out: drvn and one pce ins fnl f* **8/1**
-006 5 nse **Turkish Sultan (IRE)**22 211 6-8-10 46 .... (p) FergusSweeney 6 49+
(J M Bradley) *hld up in rr: hdwy on outer 2f out: rdn over 1f out: styd on ins fnl f: nrst fin* **10/1**
62-6 6 ¾ **Jiminor Mack**27 145 6-8-10 46 oh1 .... (p) RichardKingscote 10 47
(W J H Ratcliffe) *hld up and bhd: hdwy on inner 2f out: n.m.r over 1f out: sn rdn and kpt on ins fnl f: nrst fin* **25/1**
002- 7 ¾ **Poppy Dean (IRE)**57 7678 4-8-9 46 .... JamesDoyle 3 46
(J G Portman) *t.k.h: chsd ldrs: hdwy over 2f out: rdn wl over 1f out: drvn and one pce appr fnl f* **14/1**
40-6 8 ½ **Casablanca Minx (IRE)**33 78 6-8-6 49 .... (v) KylieManser(7) 4 48
(Miss Gay Kelleway) *hld up and bhd: hdwy 3f out: rdn wl over 1f out: styd on: nrst fin* **16/1**
40-3 9 nk **Magic Amigo**30 117 8-8-10 46 .... (b) SimonWhitworth 13 44
(J R Jenkins) *t.k.h: hld up in midfield: hdwy over 2f out: nt mch room and swtchd lft over 1f out: sn rdn and no imp* **8/1**
24-6 10 3 **Marie Tempest**15 290 4-8-12 49 .... VinceSlattery 9 41
(M R Bosley) *midfield: effrt over 3f out: sn rdn and wknd* **14/1**
-054 11 2 **Desert Hawk**18 248 8-8-11 47 .... (b) TGMcLaughlin 7 35
(W M Brisbourne) *hld up: a towards rr* **11/2**3
000- 12 1½ **Faraday (IRE)**81 7114 6-8-13 49 .... TomEaves 5 34
(N P Mulholland) *prom: effrt to chse ldr 3f out: rdn along over 2f out and sn wknd* **14/1**
5-50 13 ½ **Backlash**18 248 8-8-7 46 oh1 .... (b1) TolleyDean(3) 1 30
(A W Carroll) *in tch on outer: hdwy to chse ldrs 3f out: rdn along over 2f out: wknd wl over 1f out* **33/1**
0-00 14 6 **Moorside Diamond**22 211 5-8-10 46 oh1 .... JamieMoriarty 2 18
(A D Brown) *a towards rr* **50/1**
2m 9.77s (1.77) **Going Correction** +0.225s/f (Slow)
WFA 4 from 5yo+ 1lb **14** Ran SP% **125.9**
Speed ratings (Par 101): **101,100,99,99,99 98,98,97,97,94 93,92,91,86**
toteswinger: 1&2 £5.50, 1&3 £28.00, 2&3 £43.80. CSF £17.29 CT £436.85 TOTE £4.40: £2.10, £2.30, £7.90; EX 23.40.
Owner W R B Racing 46 **Bred** J A And Mrs Duffy **Trained** Falmer, E Sussex
FOCUS
A low-grade handicap in which the pace was strong early on but it soon steadied. Modest form, the first pair closely matched on their Lingfield meeting two days earlier and rated to a similar level here.
Poppy Dean(IRE) Official explanation: jockey said filly was struck into

470 DAY TIME, NIGHT TIME, GREAT TIME FILLIES' H'CAP 1m (P)
3:55 (4:02) (Class 5) (0-75,73) 4-Y-0+ **£3,238** (£963; £481; £240) **Stalls High**

Form RPR
2-43 1 **Moon Crystal**25 176 4-9-0 66 .... (t) JimCrowley 1 72
(E A L Dunlop) *set stdy pce: qcknd over 2f out: rdn over 1f out: drvn ins fnl f and hld on gamely* **7/2**3
600- 2 ¾ **Hallingdal (UAE)**69 7525 4-9-7 73 .... JamesDoyle 5 77
(Ms J S Doyle) *hld up in tch: hdwy on outer 2f out: rdn over 1f out: drvn and styd on ins fnl f: nt rch wnr* **9/4**2
6-05 3 hd **Motivated Choice**15 289 4-8-6 65 .... BMcHugh(7) 3 69
(Miss Amy Weaver) *trckd wnr: effrt on inner over 2f out: rdn over 1f out: drvn ins fnl f: nt qckn towards fin* **8/1**
06-6 4 1 **Perfect Act**10 354 4-9-7 73 .... AdamKirby 4 75
(C G Cox) *trckd ldng pair: hdwy 1/2-way: cl up 2f out and sn rdn: drvn over 1f out: wknd ent fnl f* **2/1**1
3230 5 hd **Bavarica**10 344 7-8-7 66 .... TobyAtkinson(7) 2 67
(Miss J Feilden) *hld up in rr: effrt over 2f out: sn rdn and outpcd tl styd on ins fnl f* **4/1**
1m 42.8s (3.00) **Going Correction** +0.225s/f (Slow) **5** Ran SP% **117.4**
Speed ratings (Par 100): **94,93,93,92,91**
CSF £12.62 TOTE £3.20: £1.80, £1.50; EX 9.90.
Owner Geoffrey Bishop **Bred** Eurostrait Ltd **Trained** Newmarket, Suffolk
FOCUS
A fair fillies' only handicap but the winner set just a moderate pace and the form is a bit muddling.

471 SPONSOR AT KEMPTON H'CAP 7f (P)
4:25 (4:31) (Class 6) (0-65,65) 4-Y-0+ **£2,388** (£705; £352) **Stalls High**

Form RPR
-040 1 **Red Rudy**18 245 7-8-13 60 .... AdamKirby 5 68
(A W Carroll) *t.k.h: trckd ldrs: hdwy on inner 2f out: rdn over 1f out: led jst ins fnl f and kpt on wl* **15/2**
1164 2 1 **Downhill Skier (IRE)**12 309 5-9-3 64 .... TGMcLaughlin 2 69
(W M Brisbourne) *hld up in rr: hdwy 2f out: rdn and n.m.r over 1f out: swtchd rt and squeezed through ins fnl f: kpt on towards fin* **5/2**2
03-1 3 nk **Surwaki (USA)**35 42 7-8-13 60 .... JimCrowley 3 64
(R M H Cowell) *cl up: effrt 2f out: sn rdn and ev ch tl drvn and one pce ins fnl f* **7/4**1
46-0 4 1 **Admirals Way**3 420 4-8-8 55 .... GregFairley 6 56
(C N Kellett) *led: rdn and qcknd 2f out: drvn over 1f out: edgd rt and hdd jst ins fnl f: wkng whn n.m.r towards fin* **9/2**3
0-16 5 7 **Takitwo**12 309 6-8-10 57 .... (v) SimonWhitworth 1 40
(P D Cundell) *chsd ldrs: rdn along wl over 2f out: sn wknd* **11/2**
1m 27.43s (1.43) **Going Correction** +0.225s/f (Slow) **5** Ran SP% **110.3**
Speed ratings (Par 101): **100,98,98,97,89**
toteswinger: 1&2 £9.10. CSF £26.25 TOTE £8.70: £3.70, £1.80; EX 18.50.
Owner Winding Wheel Partnership **Bred** Mrs C J Tribe **Trained** Cropthorne, Worcs
■ Stewards' Enquiry : Greg Fairley caution: used whip down shoulder in forehand position.

FOCUS
A modest handicap run at a fair pace. The winner took advantage of a good mark and the form is rated around the second.

472 BOOK NOW FOR RACING POST CHASE DAY H'CAP 6f (P)
5:00 (5:05) (Class 6) (0-50,50) 4-Y-0+ £2,047 (£604; £302) **Stalls High**

Form RPR
5-00 **1** **Jessica Wigmo**[30] 114 6-8-11 50 TolleyDean(3) 7 63
(A W Carroll) *hld up in rr: smooth hdwy 2f out: swtchd lft and effrt over 1f out: rdn and qcknd to ld ent fnl f: styd on* **10/1**
-053 **2** 1 1/4 **Straight Face (IRE)**[11] 327 5-8-13 49 (e) PatCosgrave 5 58
(Miss Gay Kelleway) *chsd ldrs: hdwy 2f out: rdn to ld over 1f: sn drvn and hdd ent fnl f: kpt on u.p* **10/3**[2]
66-0 **3** 3 1/2 **Reigning Monarch (USA)**[37] 27 6-8-12 48 SamHitchcott 2 45
(Miss Z C Davison) *chsd clr ldr: rdn 2f out and ev ch tl drvn and one pce appr fnl f* **5/1**
-210 **4** hd **Flamestone**[10] 352 5-8-12 48 RichardKingscote 4 45
(A E Price) *hld up in tch: pushed along and outpcd 1/2-way: sn rdn and styd on ins fnl f* **3/1**[1]
060- **5** 2 3/4 **Fitzwarren**[52] 7731 8-8-10 46 oh1 (b) TomEaves 1 34
(A D Brown) *led and sn clr: rdn 2f out: sn hdd & wknd* **25/1**
0-00 **6** 3 **Metropolitan Chief**[10] 347 5-8-12 48 MickyFenton 3 26
(P Burgoyne) *a towards rr* **25/1**
40-2 **7** 2 **Suhayl Star (IRE)**[14] 292 5-8-11 47 TGMcLaughlin 6 19
(P Burgoyne) *t.k.h: trckd ldrs: hdwy over 2f out: sn rdn and wknd over 1f out* **5/1**
-004 **8** 1/2 **Faintly Hopeful**[10] 347 4-9-0 50 (p) JimCrowley 8 20
(R A Teal) *towards rr: effrt over 2f out: sn rdn and nvr a factor* **7/2**[3]
1m 12.71s (-0.39) **Going Correction** +0.225s/f (Slow) **8 Ran SP% 120.4**
Speed ratings (Par 101): **111,109,104,104,100 96,94,93**
toteswinger: 1&2 £5.90, 1&3 £12.40, 2&3 £5.20. CSF £45.77 CT £192.76 TOTE £14.10: £3.10, £1.70, £1.80; EX 43.80 Place 6: £97.63, Place 5: £34.24.
Owner J Wigmore Racing Partnership **Bred** J Wigmore **Trained** Cropthorne, Worcs
FOCUS
A low-grade handicap, but it was run at a strong pace and is a solid little race for the grade.
T/Plt: £132.10 to a £1 stake. Pool: £47,605.71. 262.94 winning tickets. T/Qpdt: £25.70 to a £1 stake. Pool: £4,057.98. 116.77 winning tickets. JR

448 WOLVERHAMPTON (A.W) (L-H)
Monday, February 9

OFFICIAL GOING: Standard
Wind: Moderate against Weather: Raining

473 STAY AT THE WOLVERHAMPTON HOLIDAY INN H'CAP (DIV I) 7f 32y(P)
1:40 (1:50) (Class 6) (0-52,52) 4-Y-0+ £1,706 (£503; £252) **Stalls High**

Form RPR
-234 **1** **Just Jimmy (IRE)**[5] 387 4-8-9 49 PaulDoe 5 59
(P D Evans) *hld up towards rr: hdwy and c wd wl over 1f out: rdn to ld wl ins fnl f: r.o* **7/2**[1]
60-6 **2** 1 1/4 **Inka Dancer (IRE)**[10] 347 7-8-10 50 FrankieMcDonald 1 57
(B Palling) *led early: a.p: rdn to ld ins fnl f: sn hdd: nt qckn* **17/2**
5-54 **3** 1 **Aggbag**[17] 277 5-8-9 49 AndrewElliott 8 53
(B P J Baugh) *hld up in tch: rdn over 2f out: kpt on to take 3rd cl home* **5/1**[2]
30-4 **4** 1/2 **Outer Hebrides**[19] 234 8-8-7 52 (v) AmyBaker(5) 10 55
(J M Bradley) *sn prom: led over 2f out: rdn and hdd ins fnl f: no ex towards fin* **8/1**[3]
00-0 **5** 2 3/4 **Titus Gent**[24] 192 4-8-12 52 ChrisCatlin 4 47
(J Ryan) *a.p: hrd rdn over 2f out: fdd ins fnl f* **14/1**
-023 **6** 1/2 **Mr Rev**[18] 247 6-8-9 49 ow2 (b) RobertWinston 2 43
(J M Bradley) *hld up towards rr: n.m.r on ins jst over 3f out: rdn and sme hdwy over 1f out: no further prog fnl f* **5/1**[2]
/0-0 **7** 1/2 **Hill Of Lujain**[14] 292 5-8-12 52 StephenDonohoe 9 45
(Ian Williams) *s.i.s: hld up in rr: hung lft over 1f out: n.d* **28/1**
5510 **8** 1 1/4 **Vanatina (IRE)**[11] 327 5-8-6 49 DuranFentiman(3) 3 38
(W M Brisbourne) *mid-div: pushed along over 3f out: rdn 1f out: no imp* **16/1**
400- **9** 3/4 **Carnival Dream**[261] 2399 4-8-5 50 SladeO'Hara(5) 12 37
(H A McWilliams) *towards rr: pushed along over 3f out: rdn wl over 1f out: no rspnse* **40/1**
0163 **10** 1/2 **Stargazy**[17] 277 5-8-3 50 HollyHall(7) 11 36
(W G M Turner) *dwlt: hld up in rr: sme prog over 1f out: wknd wl ins fnl f* **9/1**
05- **11** 4 **Charlie Allnut**[59] 7654 4-8-10 50 (b) DarrenWilliams 7 25
(S Wynne) *sn led: rdn and hdd over 2f out: wknd over 1f out* **14/1**
400- **12** 4 **Capania (IRE)**[44] 7792 5-8-7 47 (p) PaulFitzsimons 6 11
(E G Bevan) *hld up in mid-div: pushed along over 3f out: sn bhd* **33/1**
1m 30.51s (0.91) **Going Correction** +0.15s/f (Slow) **12 Ran SP% 115.2**
Speed ratings (Par 101): **100,98,97,96,93 93,92,91,90,89 85,80**
toteswinger: 1&2 £5.10, 1&3 £4.70, 2&3 £7.60. CSF £31.83 CT £150.45 TOTE £4.60: £2.00, £3.20, £1.50; EX 36.90 Trifecta £212.50 Part won. Pool: £287.28 - 0.87 winning units..
Owner Richard Edwards Gwynne Williams **Bred** Richard Edwards And Gwynne Williams **Trained** Pandy, Monmouths
FOCUS
A very moderate handicap run at a good pace. The form is sound enough with the third a good guide.
Hill Of Lujain Official explanation: jockey said gelding missed the break

474 NAME A RACE TO ENHANCE YOUR BRAND H'CAP 5f 20y(P)
2:15 (2:25) (Class 6) (0-50,50) 4-Y-0+ £2,047 (£604; £302) **Stalls Low**

Form RPR
30-4 **1** **Nawaaff**[10] 347 4-8-11 49 TonyCulhane 2 55
(M R Channon) *chsd ldng quartet: chalng whn edgd rt ins fnl f: rdn to ld last strides* **3/1**[1]
0403 **2** hd **Nordic Light (USA)**[11] 328 5-8-8 46 oh1 (bt) LukeMorris 5 51
(J M Bradley) *prom: outpcd after 2f: rallied on ins wl over 1f out: rdn to ld jst ins fnl f: rdr sn dropped whip: hdd last strides* **7/1**
4-24 **3** 1/2 **Taboor (IRE)**[14] 294 11-8-10 48 ChrisCatlin 7 51
(R M H Cowell) *hld up in rr: c wd st: hdwy on outside over 1f out: rdn and r.o ins fnl f* **6/1**[3]
0-00 **4** nk **Affirmatively**[5] 395 4-8-5 48 (bt[1]) AmyBaker(5) 4 50
(A W Carroll) *s.i.s: hld up in rr: swtchd lft and hdwy on ins wl over 1f out: kpt on ins fnl f* **14/1**
0060 **5** 1 **Desert Light (IRE)**[11] 328 8-8-10 48 oh1 ow2 (v) DarrenWilliams 3 47
(D Shaw) *hld up and bhd: hdwy over 1f out: rdn and kpt on same pce fnl f* **14/1**
5-00 **6** 1 1/2 **Lady Hopeful (IRE)**[11] 328 7-8-1 46 oh1 (b) AndrewHeffernan(7) 8 39
(Peter Grayson) *s.i.s: sn swtchd lft: in rr: hdwy on ins wl over 1f out: no further prog fnl f* **50/1**
4-00 **7** 1 3/4 **Ben**[18] 245 4-8-12 50 (b[1]) SteveDrowne 1 37
(P G Murphy) *hld up: sme hdwy over 1f out: no imp fnl f* **12/1**
6453 **8** 1/2 **Mister Incredible**[14] 292 6-8-12 50 (v) RobertWinston 10 35+
(J M Bradley) *w ldrs: led over 1f out: hdd jst ins fnl f: sn wknd* **5/1**[2]
4-06 **9** 2 1/2 **Briery Lane (IRE)**[14] 294 8-8-10 48 ow1 (p) StephenDonohoe 9 24
(J M Bradley) *nt clr run and swtchd lft over 1f out: a bhd* **9/1**
600- **10** 10 **Bold Minstrel (IRE)**[96] 7197 7-8-12 50 MartinDwyer 6 —+
(M Quinn) *w ldrs: led over 3f out: rdn and hdd over 1f out: eased considerably whn btn ins fnl f: fin lame* **12/1**
666- **11** 1 3/4 **Town House**[125] 6546 7-8-10 48 AndrewElliott 13 —+
(B P J Baugh) *racd wd: led over 1f: wknd wl over 1f out* **25/1**
0-00 **12** 3/4 **Fitolini**[24] 198 4-8-12 50 (t) GrahamGibbons 11 —+
(Mrs G S Rees) *w ldrs: rdn and wknd wl over 1f out* **66/1**
63.19 secs (0.89) **Going Correction** +0.15s/f (Slow) **12 Ran SP% 114.5**
Speed ratings (Par 101): **98,97,96,96,94 92,89,88,84,68 66,64**
toteswinger: 1&2 £5.00, 1&3 £3.50, 2&3 £5.70. CSF £22.45 CT £119.30 TOTE £3.50: £1.30, £2.80, £2.60; EX 18.70 Trifecta £80.10 Pool: £257.88 - 2.38 winning units..
Owner R Bastian **Bred** Whitsbury Manor Stud & Pigeon House Stud **Trained** West Ilsley, Berks
FOCUS
The leaders went off far too fast, with Mister Incredible, Bold Minstrel, Town House and Fritolini taking each other on until about halfway, before dropping out to fill four of the bottom five places. The closers were obviously at an advantage and the form is weak.
Bold Minstrel(IRE) Official explanation: jockey said gelding finished lame

475 WOLVERHAMPTON-RACECOURSE.CO.UK (S) STKS 5f 216y(P)
2:50 (3:01) (Class 6) 3-Y-0+ £2,047 (£604; £302) **Stalls Low**

Form RPR
0/32 **1** **Stonecrabstomorrow (IRE)**[18] 245 6-9-8 63 (p) TonyHamilton 6 67
(R A Fahey) *hld up in tch: rdn wl over 1f out: led wl ins fnl f: r.o* **9/4**[2]
00-2 **2** 1/2 **Hart Of Gold**[12] 314 5-9-10 64 (p) KevinGhunowa(3) 7 70
(R A Harris) *led early: chsd ldr: led 2f out: rdn over 1f out: hdd wl ins fnl f: kpt on* **13/2**
000- **3** 5 **Orchestration (IRE)**[59] 7644 8-9-1 36 (v) AndrewHeffernan(7) 10 49
(Garry Moss) *broke wl: sn stdd into mid-div: hdwy 2f out: sn rdn: one pce fnl f* **150/1**
2241 **4** nk **One More Round (USA)**[12] 314 11-9-8 72 (b) DeanHeslop(5) 8 53
(P D Evans) *s.i.s: t.k.h towards rr: c wd st: hdwy fr over 1f out: nvr trbld ldrs* **6/4**[1]
-002 **5** nk **Mr Loire**[12] 308 5-9-8 45 (b) JerryO'Dwyer 2 47
(K G Wingrove) *hld up towards rr: rdn and hdwy over 1f out: one pce fnl f* **40/1**
06-2 **6** 4 1/2 **Angel Voices (IRE)**[34] 57 6-9-3 62 (v) MartinDwyer 11 28
(K R Burke) *prom: rdn over 2f out: wknd wl over 1f out* **11/1**
00/0 **7** 2 1/2 **Cate Washington**[24] 198 6-9-0 40 RussellKennemore(3) 1 20
(Mrs L Williamson) *prom: rdn over 2f out: wknd wl over 1f out* **250/1**
3/2- **8** 1 **Tune Up The Band**[240] 3021 5-9-8 0 SteveDrowne 5 22
(R J Hodges) *sn led: hdd 2f out: wknd qckly fnl f* **9/2**[3]
5-23 **9** 3 3/4 **Glan Lady (IRE)**[8] 365 3-8-7 53 (b) FrankieMcDonald 9 10
(G J Smith) *s.i.s: hld up and bhd: c v wd st: sn struggling: eased fnl f* **33/1**
00/0 **10** 2 1/2 **Magical Mimi**[24] 198 8-9-3 40 (t) ChrisCatlin 3 —
(K G Wingrove) *dwlt: outpcd: lost tch over 3f out* **100/1**
1m 15.54s (0.54) **Going Correction** +0.15s/f (Slow)
WFA 3 from 4yo+ 15lb **10 Ran SP% 118.0**
Speed ratings (Par 101): **102,101,94,94,93 87,84,83,78,74**
toteswinger: 1&2 £4.10, 1&3 £42.40, 2&3 £41.50. CSF £17.42 TOTE £3.90: £1.60, £2.10, £11.50; EX 17.10 Trifecta £311.70 Part won. Pool: £421.22 - 0.97 winning units..There was no bid for the winner.
Owner Miss S Bowles **Bred** P Dillon **Trained** Musley Bank, N Yorks
FOCUS
Sound selling form with the first pair clear and close to their recent best. The time was reasonable.
Glan Lady(IRE) Official explanation: jockey said filly hung right

476 HOTEL & CONFERENCING AT WOLVERHAMPTON MAIDEN STKS 1m 4f 50y(P)
3:25 (3:38) (Class 5) 4-Y-0+ £2,729 (£806; £403) **Stalls Low**

Form RPR
1 **Eighteenfifty**[90] 5-9-6 0 GeorgeBaker 4 72+
(N J Henderson) *hld up in mid-div: stdy hdwy over 6f out: rdn to ld cl home* **1/3**[1]
2 nk **Wray Castle (IRE)**[26] 4-9-3 0 StephenDonohoe 2 71
(Ian Williams) *hld up in tch: wnt 2nd over 6f out: rdn over 2f out: led jst ins fnl f: hdd cl home* **40/1**
4 **3** 3 **Johnston's Baby (IRE)**[2] 452 7-9-1 0 JimmyQuinn 8 61
(E J Alston) *t.k.h in mid-div: hdwy on ins over 2f out: led over 1f out: hdd jst ins fnl f: rdn and no ex* **16/1**
5 **4** nk **One Zero (USA)**[16] 279 4-8-12 60 TPQueally 9 61+
(M G Quinlan) *reluctant to go to post: s.i.s: in rr: nt clr run over 3f out: hdwy over 2f out: c wd st: hung lft ins fnl f: one pce* **12/1**
54-3 **5** 1 3/4 **Dusk**[16] 279 4-9-3 65 (b) ChrisCatlin 6 63
(Mrs S J Humphrey) *hld up and bhd: hmpd over 3f out: hdwy on ins over 2f out: rdn and no further prog fnl f* **7/1**[2]
0-4 **6** 3 1/4 **Waldorf (IRE)**[33] 80 4-9-3 0 MartinDwyer 1 58+
(W R Muir) *chsd ldr: led over 7f out: rdn and hdd over 1f out: wknd ins fnl f* **10/1**[3]
7 1 **Rosko**[57] 5-8-13 0 AnthonyBetts(7) 7 56
(B Ellison) *dwlt: plld hrd towards rr: nvr nr ldrs* **25/1**
656- **8** 3 1/4 **Marieschi (USA)**[80] 6550 5-9-6 48 FrankieMcDonald 11 51
(R F Fisher) *hld up towards rr: hdwy on outside over 4f out: rdn and wknd over 2f out* **50/1**
0- **9** 8 **Nomadic Warrior**[185] 4821 4-9-3 0 JerryO'Dwyer 5 38
(J R Holt) *led: hdd over 3f out: prom tl wknd over 3f out* **200/1**
0 **10** nse **Sugar State**[21] 217 4-9-3 0 IanMongan 10 38
(J L Spearing) *prom tl wknd 3f out* **150/1**
2m 45.06s (3.96) **Going Correction** +0.15s/f (Slow)
WFA 4 from 5yo+ 3lb **10 Ran SP% 119.6**
Speed ratings (Par 103): **92,91,89,89,88 86,85,83,78,78**
toteswinger: 1&2 £10.70, 1&3 £4.60, 2&3 £25.00. CSF £33.08 TOTE £1.50: £1.02, £9.10, £3.60; EX 26.60 Trifecta £150.70 Pool: £710.91 - 3.49 winning units..
Owner Richard Morecombe **Bred** Exors Of The Late K G Powter **Trained** Upper Lambourn, Berks
■ Stewards' Enquiry : Jimmy Quinn 17-day ban (takes into account previous offences; five days deferred): careless riding (Mar 6-7,13-14,16-23)

FOCUS
A modest and slowly run maiden and the form looks suspect, but the winner is a fair bumper horse and looks better than the bare result.

477 GREAT OFFERS AT WOLVERHAMPTON-RACECOURSE.CO.UK APPRENTICE H'CAP 1m 1f 103y(P)
4:00 (4:10) (Class 4) (0-80,80) 4-Y-0+ £4,857 (£1,445; £722; £360) Stalls Low

Form RPR
05-4 1 New Star (UAE)[21] 220 5-8-8 72 AndrewHeffernan(3) 5 80
(W M Brisbourne) chsd ldr tl over 5f out: led 2f out: rdn over 1f out: jst hld on 3/1[2]
0-50 2 nse Scamperdale[17] 271 7-9-5 80 SoniaEaton 3 88
(B P J Baugh) hld up: hdwy over 2f out: inclined to edge lft bhd wnr 1f out: r.o: jst failed: fin lame 7/4[1]
000- 3 ½ Monfils Monfils (USA)[63] 7606 7-8-3 67 (p) KarenKenny(3) 1 74
(A J McCabe) hld up in rr: hdwy on outside 1f out: r.o towards fin 16/1
3-63 4 3 Hucking Heat (IRE)[20] 226 5-8-9 75 (p) DavidKenny(5) 6 76
(R Hollinshead) hld up: hdwy over 2f out: sn rdn: one pce fnl f 4/1[3]
5-06 5 3¼ Princess Cocoa (IRE)[2] 453 6-8-8 74 AnthonyBetts(5) 7 68
(R A Fahey) prom: chsd ldr over 5f out: led over 3f out to 2f out: sn rdn: wknd ins fnl f 7/1
64/2 6 4 Just Observing[25] 172 6-8-5 71 (p) PaulPickard(5) 2 56
(P T Midgley) led: hdd over 3f out: wknd over 2f out 13/2
2m 2.97s (1.27) **Going Correction** +0.15s/f (Slow) 6 Ran SP% 113.1
Speed ratings (Par 105): **100,99,99,96,93 90**
toteswinger: 1&2 £2.80, 1&3 £7.70, 2&3 £6.60. CSF £8.83 TOTE £4.20: £1.60, £1.90; EX 10.30.
Owner Shropshire Wolves **Bred** Darley **Trained** Great Ness, Shropshire
FOCUS
A fair apprentice handicap run 1.20 seconds slower than the following event. The form has been rated around the winner but does not look too solid.
Scamperdale Official explanation: jockey said gelding finished lame

478 ENJOY THE LUCKY 7 GROUP OFFER H'CAP 1m 1f 103y(P)
4:30 (4:41) (Class 6) (0-65,69) 4-Y-0+ £2,047 (£604; £302) Stalls Low

Form RPR
1-21 1 Formidable Guest[18] 253 5-9-0 61 JimmyQuinn 3 71
(J Pearce) hld up in tch: wnt 2nd wl over 1f out: rdn to ld ins fnl f: drvn out 3/1[1]
5-61 2 nk Snow Dancer (IRE)[10] 353 5-8-9 61 (p) SladeO'Hara(5) 4 70
(H A McWilliams) hld up towards rr: hdwy on ins over 2f out: rdn over 1f out: r.o ins fnl f 8/1
3-12 3 shd Samurai Warrior[24] 186 4-8-6 58 DeanHeslop(5) 7 67
(P D Evans) prom: wnt 2nd 6f out: led over 3f out: rdn and hdd ins fnl f: kpt on 9/1
-055 4 2½ New Beginning (IRE)[21] 220 5-9-2 63 RobertWinston 12 67
(Mrs S Lamyman) hld up towards rr: hdwy over 3f out: rdn over 1f out: kpt on one pce fnl f 11/1
03-4 5 ½ Pelham Crescent (IRE)[18] 253 6-8-12 59 MartinDwyer 6 62
(B Palling) hld up in rr: rdn and edgd lft over 1f out: styd on fnl f: nt rch ldrs 6/1[2]
20-0 6 ½ Strike Force[10] 341 5-8-13 60 LukeMorris 5 62
(Miss J Feilden) hld up in rr: rdn and hdwy wl over 1f out: one pce fnl f 13/2[3]
3/00 7 2 Strategic Knight (USA)[8] 362 4-8-13 65 (t) JamesO'Reilly(5) 10 62
(R C Guest) hld up in mid-div: hdwy over 2f out: wknd ins fnl f 66/1
2-30 8 7 Fandango Boy[18] 253 8-9-3 64 DNolan 11 47
(D Carroll) hld up in tch: chsd ldr over 2f out tl rdn wl over 1f out: sn wknd: eased whn btn ins fnl f 33/1
00-0 9 1¼ Make Amends (IRE)[12] 311 4-9-0 61 SteveDrowne 13 41
(R J Hodges) a towards rr 50/1
-031 10 14 Hilbre Court (USA)[8] 362 4-9-8 69 6ex GrahamGibbons 1 20+
(B P J Baugh) hld up in mid-div: hmpd on ins over 3f out: n.d after 15/2
05-0 11 ¾ Spinning Ridge (IRE)[37] 25 4-8-11 61 KevinGhunowa(3) 2 10
(R A Harris) chsd ldr to 6f out: wkng whn hmpd on ins over 3f out 50/1
24-5 12 1 Keepsgettingbetter (IRE)[18] 255 4-9-1 62 (b[1]) ChrisCatlin 9 9
(J R Gask) plld hrd: prom tl lost pl on outside bnd 7f out: bhd fnl 4f 12/1
65-3 13 7 Our Kes (IRE)[12] 320 7-9-1 62 IanMongan 8 —+
(P Howling) led: hdd over 3f out: wknd 2f out: sn eased 17/2
2m 1.77s (0.07) **Going Correction** +0.15s/f (Slow) 13 Ran SP% 120.4
Speed ratings (Par 101): **105,104,104,102,101 101,99,93,92,79 79,78,72**
toteswinger: 1&2 £6.20, 1&3 £5.20, 2&3 £11.60. CSF £26.87 CT £199.55 TOTE £3.70: £1.50, £3.80, £3.30; EX 32.50 Trifecta £220.10 Pool: £449.15 - 1.51 winning units..
Owner Macniler Racing Partnership **Bred** Kingwood Bloodstock **Trained** Newmarket, Suffolk
■ Stewards' Enquiry : Jimmy Quinn caution: used whip with excessive frequency.
FOCUS
Adecent handicap for the grade, and solid form. They went a strong pace, setting this up for those held up, and the winning time was 1.20 seconds quicker than the earlier 66-80.
Our Kes(IRE) Official explanation: trainer said, regarding running and riding, mare was raced prominently following concerns by the owners regarding previous waiting tactics, adding that it seemed unsuited by change of tactics, had a restricted preparation due to inclement weather and it appeared slightly lame immediately post-race; vet said mare returned sound

479 SPONSOR A RACE BY CALLING 01902 390009 H'CAP 1m 141y(P)
5:05 (5:15) (Class 5) (0-70,70) 3-Y-O £2,729 (£806; £403) Stalls Low

Form RPR
-314 1 Common Diva[11] 332 3-9-2 68 RobertWinston 3 71
(A J McCabe) a.p: led over 1f out: sn edgd rt and rdn: r.o 11/1
025- 2 1½ Dark Oasis[149] 5914 3-8-9 61 (b) ChrisCatlin 7 61
(K A Ryan) sn chsng ldr: ev ch wl over 1f out: sn rdn: kpt on ins fnl f 7/1
1-22 3 hd Mullitovermaurice[14] 295 3-9-0 66 TPQueally 8 65
(J G Given) chsd ldrs: n.m.r briefly ent st: rdn over 1f out: sn edgd lft: kpt on ins fnl f 13/8[1]
506- 4 hd Midnight Bay[61] 7622 3-9-0 66 EdwardCreighton 5 65
(M R Channon) hld up: pushed along over 3f out: hdwy whn swtchd lft wl over 1f out: kpt on ins fnl f 9/2[3]
5502 5 3¼ Autumn Morning (IRE)[2] 450 3-8-2 59 PatrickDonaghy(5) 4 50
(P D Evans) s.i.s: hld up in rr: hdwy on outside over 2f out: rdn over 1f out: wknd fnl f 3/1[2]
4234 6 2 Turn To Dreams[2] 450 3-8-6 58 PaulDoe 2 45
(P D Evans) led: hdd over 1f out: wknd ins fnl f: eased 11/1
1m 51.48s (0.98) **Going Correction** +0.15s/f (Slow) 6 Ran SP% 110.4
Speed ratings (Par 97): **101,99,99,99,96 94**
toteswinger: 1&2 £5.20, 1&3 £2.40, 2&3 £2.60. CSF £78.02 CT £181.18 TOTE £9.50: £2.20, £3.20; EX 57.90 Trifecta £38.60 Pool: £536.32 - 10.27 winning units..
Owner Alotincommon Partnership **Bred** Llety Stud **Trained** Averham Park, Notts

FOCUS
A modest handicap run at a decent gallop. The winner defied what looked a stiffish mark but the form reads as sound.

480 STAY AT THE WOLVERHAMPTON HOLIDAY INN H'CAP (DIV II) 7f 32y(P)
5:35 (5:51) (Class 6) (0-52,52) 4-Y-0+ £1,706 (£503; £252) Stalls High

Form RPR
00-0 1 Over To You Bert[19] 234 10-8-7 52 MCGeran(5) 11 60
(R J Hodges) bolted bef s: swtchd lft sn after s: hld up in rr: hdwy over 1f out: rdn to ld wl ins fnl f: r.o 11/1
0503 2 1 Louisiade (IRE)[4] 399 8-8-2 49 (b) AndrewHeffernan(7) 3 54
(M C Chapman) led: rdn and hdd wl over 1f out: r.o ins fnl f 10/3[2]
000- 3 ½ Interchoice Star[136] 6254 4-8-5 48 DuranFentiman(3) 6 52
(R Hollinshead) w ldr: led wl over 1f out: sn rdn: hdd wl ins fnl f: nt qckn 7/2[3]
5-00 4 1½ Piermarini[25] 171 4-8-3 50 PaulPickard(7) 12 50
(P T Midgley) in rr: pushed along over 3f out: rdn and hdwy 1f out: nt rch ldrs 14/1
0235 5 ½ Tadlil[14] 292 7-8-12 52 (v) RobertWinston 1 50
(J M Bradley) a.p: rdn over 1f out: one pce 3/1[1]
00-2 6 ¾ Highland Song (IRE)[11] 327 6-8-7 47 FrankieMcDonald 5 43
(R F Fisher) t.k.h: a.p: pushed along over 2f out: swtchd lft wl over 1f out: nt clr run and swtchd rt ent fnl f: one pce 8/1
2435 7 hd Red Current[12] 321 5-8-8 51 (p) KevinGhunowa(3) 7 47
(R A Harris) chsd ldrs: pushed along over 3f out: no hdwy fnl 2f 7/1
0-6 8 8 Donard Lodge (IRE)[24] 198 4-8-10 50 AndrewElliott 9 24
(J Balding) hld up in mid-div: pushed along over 3f out: wknd over 2f out 20/1
5-00 9 4½ Harrison's Flyer (IRE)[19] 242 8-8-10 50 (b) DarrenWilliams 2 12
(J M Bradley) hld up towards rr: rdn and short-lived effrt on ins over 2f out: eased whn no ch ins fnl f 25/1
1m 30.31s (0.71) **Going Correction** +0.15s/f (Slow) 9 Ran SP% 117.5
Speed ratings (Par 101): **101,99,99,97,97 96,95,86,81**
toteswinger: 1&2 £8.90, 1&3 £9.10, 2&3 £3.10. CSF £48.53 CT £160.26 TOTE £15.10: £3.60, £1.40, £1.60; EX 63.20 Trifecta £430.60 Part won. Pool: £581.98 - 0.77 winning units. Place 6: £20.10, Place 5: £11.06.
Owner R J Hodges **Bred** J K S Cresswell **Trained** Charlton Mackrell, Somerset
■ Tobago Reef (9/1) was withdrawn after bolting before the start. R4 applies, deduct 10p in the £.
FOCUS
This moderate handicap was run at a good pace and the final time was marginally quicker than the first division. The form seems reasonable for the grade.
T/Jkpt: £2,005.40 to a £1 stake. Pool: £76,262.28. 27.00 winning tickets. T/Plt: £46.70 to a £1 stake. Pool: £79,139.78. 1,235.26 winning tickets. T/Qpdt: £14.60 to a £1 stake. Pool: £5,195.27. 262.15 winning tickets. KH

440 LINGFIELD (L-H)
Tuesday, February 10

OFFICIAL GOING: Standard
Wind: Moderate, half against Weather: fine

481 CHELSEA COTTAGE (S) STKS 5f (P)
2:10 (2:11) (Class 6) 3-Y-0+ £2,047 (£604; £302) Stalls High

Form RPR
4-02 1 Woodcote (IRE)[7] 380 7-9-7 72 (vt) GeorgeBaker 3 77+
(P R Chamings) led: shkn up appr fnl f: sn clr: eased clsng stages 8/11[1]
0-55 2 4½ Scarlet Oak[13] 314 5-9-2 57 RobertWinston 1 56
(A M Hales) dwlt: hld up in rr: hdwy over 2f out: styd on to take 2nd 1f out: no ch w wnr 8/1
2-50 3 2 Elusive Ronnie (IRE)[11] 348 3-8-12 60 (p) JimCrowley 5 53
(R A Teal) chsd ldrs: kpt on to take modest 3rd ins fnl f 12/1
-604 4 ½ Desert Opal[4] 431 9-9-7 63 (b) JamesO'Reilly(5) 2 57
(C R Dore) chsd ldrs: sn drvn along: effrt on ins over 1f out: one pce 4/1[2]
06-1 5 7 Brown Lentic (IRE)[13] 316 3-8-12 50 MickyFenton 4 26
(Miss J Feilden) w wnr: wknd appr fnl f 6/1[3]
58.27 secs (-0.53) **Going Correction** +0.175s/f (Slow)
WFA 3 from 5yo+ 14lb 5 Ran SP% 111.0
Speed ratings (Par 101): **111,103,100,99,88**
CSF £7.35 TOTE £1.80: £1.10, £5.40; EX 7.00.There was no bid for the winner.
Owner Patrick Chamings Sprint Club **Bred** Liscannor Stud Ltd **Trained** Baughurst, Hants
FOCUS
This was an uncompetitive selling stakes won in fine style by Woodcote, who sets the standard.

482 DOWN PARK CLASSIFIED STKS 1m (P)
2:40 (2:40) (Class 7) 3-Y-0+ £1,619 (£481; £240; £120) Stalls High

Form RPR
0-04 1 Riviera Red (IRE)[13] 321 9-9-7 45 (v) LukeMorris 9 51
(L Montague Hall) t.k.h in midfield: hdwy over 1f out: styd on to ld last 75yds 11/2[2]
00-4 2 1 Halsion Challenge[36] 43 4-9-7 42 (t) RobertWinston 8 49
(J R Best) led 1f: chal 2f out: led jst ins fnl f: hdd and no ex fnl 75yds 11/4[1]
4-04 3 1 Amwell House[19] 247 4-9-7 43 SimonWhitworth 6 47
(J R Jenkins) hld up towards rr: hdwy over 1f out: styd on wl ins fnl f 6/1[3]
-360 4 nk Dynamo Dave (USA)[25] 192 4-9-0 43 LeeNewnes(7) 4 46
(M D I Usher) hld up towards rr: hdwy over 1f out: kpt on wl: nvr rchd ldrs 13/2
0-00 5 2¼ Dobravany (IRE)[19] 254 5-9-7 42 (p) GeorgeBaker 10 41
(K A Morgan) chsd ldrs: outpcd and lost pl over 1f out: no threat after 6/1[3]
-500 6 hd Ma Ridge[19] 247 5-9-7 40 RobertHavlin 1 40
(T D McCarthy) led after 1f: hdd jst ins fnl f: sn wknd 16/1
0530 7 ¾ Beckenham's Secret[19] 247 5-9-7 43 ShaneKelly 2 39
(A W Carroll) sn chsng ldrs: one pce fnl 2f 9/1
46-0 8 7 Pajada[25] 193 5-9-0 44 SeanPalmer(7) 7 23
(M D I Usher) in rr: hdwy on outside over 4f out: lost pl over 1f out 25/1
-200 9 8 I Certainly May[19] 247 4-9-7 43 (p) TonyCulhane 3 4
(S Dow) s.i.s: lost pl 3f out: sn bhd 12/1
1m 39.64s (1.44) **Going Correction** +0.175s/f (Slow) 9 Ran SP% 111.4
Speed ratings (Par 97): **99,98,97,96,94 94,93,86,78**
toteswinger: 1&2 £4.10, 1&3 £4.40, 2&3 £2.60. CSF £19.88 TOTE £6.20: £1.80, £1.20, £1.90; EX 19.30.
Owner Michael S Green & Partners **Bred** Abergwaun Farms **Trained** Epsom, Surrey

FOCUS
A very weak heat but straightforward form for the grade.

483 SOUTH PARK CLAIMING STKS 1m 2f (P)
3:10 (3:10) (Class 6) 4-Y-O+ **£2,047** (£604; £302) **Stalls** Low

Form RPR

-341 **1** **Blacktoft (USA)**[3] 452 6-8-11 72.........................(e) RichardKingscote 2 76+
(S C Williams) *t.k.h early: trckd ldrs: wnt cl 2nd over 2f out: led 2f out: sn qcknd wl clr: eased towards fin* **8/13**[1]

23-4 **2** *5* **Zero Cool (USA)**[38] 29 5-8-5 73.................................. LukeMorris 5 57
(G L Moore) *led early: sn stdd and in rr: reminder 5f out: hdwy 3f out: wnt 2nd 1f out: no ch w wnr* **9/4**[2]

206- **3** *1/2* **North Parade**[10] 6400 4-9-4 77..(t) ShaneKelly 4 70
(A W Carroll) *dwlt: hld up in rr: effrt over 2f out: kpt on fnl f* **10/1**[3]

00-0 **4** *10* **Bet Noir (IRE)**[3] 449 4-7-6 57..................................... RichardRowe(7) 3 31
(A W Carroll) *dwlt: sn chsng ldr: led appr 3f out: hdd 2f out: wknd fnl f* **33/1**

605- **5** *7* **Fortune Point (IRE)**[40] 691 11-7-12 43....................(v) KarenKenny(7) 1 22
(A W Carroll) *sn led: drvn over 5f out: hdd appr 3f out: sn lost pl and bhd* **66/1**

2m 6.46s (-0.14) **Going Correction** +0.175s/f (Slow)
WFA 4 from 5yo+ 1lb **5** Ran SP% **106.2**
Speed ratings (Par 101): **107,103,102,94,89**
CSF £1.98 TOTE £1.40: £1.10, £1.50; EX 2.00.
Owner Chris Watkins And David N Reynolds **Bred** Paradigm Thoroughbreds Inc **Trained** Newmarket, Suffolk

FOCUS
This was a weak contest and the winner probably did not need to run to his best with doubts over the recent form of the placed horses.

484 MILL WOOD WINTER OPEN STKS (LISTED RACE) 1m 2f (P)
3:40 (3:41) (Class 1) 4-Y-O+ **£17,031** (£6,456; £3,231) **Stalls** Low

Form RPR

112- **1** **Suits Me**[52] 7741 6-9-1 107.. MickyFenton 5 85
(T P Tate) *led: stdd pce 5f out: kicked for home wl over 1f out: edgd rt: hld on in gritty fashion* **11/4**[2]

611- **2** *1/2* **Dansant**[52] 7741 5-9-4 114.. GeorgeBaker 2 87
(G A Butler) *hld up in last: smooth hdwy to chal on outer 2f out: pushed wd and rdn ins fnl f: no ex* **1/3**[1]

00-0 **3** *15* **Meohmy**[3] 443 6-8-10 46.. MCGeran 1 49?
(M R Channon) *chsd wnr: drvn over 2f out: sn hopelessly outpcd* **66/1**[3]

2m 9.69s (3.09) **Going Correction** +0.175s/f (Slow)
WFA 4 from 5yo+ 1lb **3** Ran SP% **103.2**
Speed ratings: **94,93,81**
CSF £4.07 TOTE £2.80; EX 2.60.
Owner D E Cook **Bred** R S A Urquhart **Trained** Tadcaster, N Yorks

FOCUS
This Listed contest was originally due to be run at Great Leighs and then at Wolverhampton's abandoned meeting last week, when a more competitive line-up had been confirmed. At it transpired the further rescheduling meant it was effectively a two-horse race, even before the two non-runners. It was unsurprisingly very tactical and the winner reversed previous course-and-distance form with the second on 1lb better terms.

NOTEBOOK
Suits Me reversed form with his old rival under a fine tactical ride. He was harried for the lead throughout last time, but was always going to get his own way in this and set the early fractions before being given a breather at halfway. He then began to quicken things up again nearing the final bend and, while it briefly appeared as though he may be swallowed up, his superior speed proved the key at the business end. This habitual front-runner was gaining a deserved first win at in such company and he has not looked back since finishing second to the classy Expresso Star last year. However, he will not always get such an easy time on the lead and would be no certainty to confirm this when faced with a bigger field again. (op 5-2)

Dansant, bidding for a hat-trick, was brought with every chance at the top of the home straight yet not that surprisingly the tactical nature of this race over a test short of his best ultimately found him out. A horse at his happiest over another 2f, he still lost little in defeat and it should be remembered he was 1lb worse off with his old rival. He remains on course for an ambitious tilt at the Santa Anita Handicap (worth $1 million) in March.

Meohmy faced an impossible task at the weights yet it has to be rated a shrewd move by her connections to have run here. Not only did she pick up over £3,000 in prizemoney for placing but was able to earn some very valuable black type in the process. (op 100-1)

485 TURNERS HILL H'CAP 1m 5f (P)
4:10 (4:10) (Class 5) (0-75,75) 4-Y-O+ **£2,729** (£806; £403) **Stalls** Low

Form RPR

34-3 **1** **Agglestone Rock**[12] 333 4-8-0 59.............................. RichardRowe(7) 8 67
(P A Kirby) *chsd ldr: led after 3f: qcknd over 2f out: styd on strly: unchal* **8/1**

50-3 **2** *2 1/4* **King's Majesty (IRE)**[13] 319 7-9-2 64.............................. ShaneKelly 2 69
(A M Hales) *hld up in midfield: effrt over 2f out: wnt 2nd over 1f out: no real imp* **11/2**[2]

-024 **3** *1 1/2* **They All Laughed**[11] 341 6-9-5 67.............................. RobertWinston 7 70
(P W Hiatt) *hld up in rr: hdwy over 2f out: kpt on to take n.d 3rd ins fnl f* **11/2**[2]

00-2 **4** *2 1/4* **Dundry**[11] 341 8-9-11 73..(p) GeorgeBaker 9 72
(G L Moore) *chsd ldrs: effrt over 2f out: one pce* **10/11**[1]

40/0 **5** *3 3/4* **Royal Wedding**[10] 361 7-9-6 68.. IanMongan 3 62
(N J Gifford) *led 3f: chal 4f out: wknd fnl f* **33/1**

3-14 **6** *2 1/4* **Night Orbit**[11] 342 5-9-4 66..(v) MickyFenton 1 56
(Miss J Feilden) *chsd ldrs: drvn 4f out: lost pl over 2f out* **7/1**[3]

211- **7** *1* **Princess Flame (GER)**[31] 6235 7-9-6 75...................... KylieManser(7) 6 64
(B G Powell) *s.i.s: hdwy 7f out: drvn 4f out: sn lost pl* **20/1**

3-13 **8** *3/4* **Imperium**[13] 311 8-8-13 61.. JimCrowley 4 49
(Jean-Rene Auvray) *t.k.h in rr: effrt 3f out: sn lost pl and bhd* **11/1**

5 **9** *2* **Aldiruos (IRE)**[34] 72 9-9-0 62.. LukeMorris 5 47
(A W Carroll) *in rr: pushed along 6f out: bhd fnl 3f* **33/1**

2m 46.81s (0.81) **Going Correction** +0.175s/f (Slow)
WFA 4 from 5yo+ 4lb **9** Ran SP% **125.7**
Speed ratings (Par 103): **104,102,101,100,98 96,96,95,94**
toteswinger: 1&2 £7.50, 1&3 £8.90, 2&3 £4.30. CSF £54.96 CT £270.92 TOTE £11.30: £2.10, £2.00, £1.60; EX 69.80.
Owner Geoff Kirby Basil Holian Michael Buckley **Bred** Mrs Fiona Denniff **Trained** Castleton, N Yorks

FOCUS
This was a moderate handicap but the form is worth taking at face value with the placed horses to recent course form.

486 DORMANS PARK H'CAP 6f (P)
4:40 (4:40) (Class 5) (0-75,75) 4-Y-O+ **£2,729** (£806; £403) **Stalls** Low

Form RPR

5-01 **1** **Cornus**[15] 297 7-9-2 73..(be) JamesDoyle 3 77
(A J McCabe) *hld up last but wl in tch: effrt on inner 2f out: slt ld fnl 100yds: all out* **3/1**[3]

0-52 **2** *nse* **Compton's Eleven**[3] 446 8-9-4 75.......................... EdwardCreighton 2 78
(M R Channon) *trckd ldrs: effrt 2f out: slt ld 1f out: hdd ins fnl f: kpt on: jst hld* **13/8**[1]

-020 **3** *3/4* **Compton Classic**[19] 243 7-7-11 61 oh1.................(p) NathanAlison(7) 4 62
(J R Boyle) *led after 1f: racd away fr running rail: hdd over 2f out: kpt on fnl 150yds: no ex* **9/4**[2]

5665 **4** *1 1/2* **Thoughtsofstardom**[3] 442 6-9-4 75.................................. LukeMorris 1 71
(P S McEntee) *t.k.h: led 1f: led over 2f out: hdd 1f out: wknd wl ins fnl f* **7/1**

1m 14.16s (2.26) **Going Correction** +0.175s/f (Slow) **4** Ran SP% **106.4**
Speed ratings (Par 103): **91,90,89,87**
CSF £8.00 TOTE £4.00; EX 6.90 Place 6: £97.18, Place 5: £66.86..
Owner Betfair Club ROA **Bred** G Russell **Trained** Averham Park, Notts

FOCUS
A tricky little handicap, run at an uneven pace but the front pair are rated close to their recent best.
T/Plt: £74.60 to a £1 stake. Pool: £70,926.37. 693.30 winning tickets. T/Qpdt: £35.60 to a £1 stake. Pool: £5,026.67. 104.37 winning tickets. WG

420 SOUTHWELL (L-H)
Tuesday, February 10

OFFICIAL GOING: Standard to slow changing to standard after race 3 (2.50)
Wind: Fresh behind Weather: Bright and dry

487 SOUTHWELL-RACECOURSE.CO.UK H'CAP 6f (F)
1:50 (1:52) (Class 6) (0-55,55) 4-Y-O+ **£2,047** (£604; £302) **Stalls** Low

Form RPR

6445 **1** **Cape Of Storms**[14] 303 6-8-11 **52**.. TomEaves 7 60
(R Brotherton) *hld up towards rr: smooth hdwy on outer over 2f out: rdn and edgd lft over 1f out: led ent fnl f: styd on* **9/2**[2]

5602 **2** *1* **Afton View (IRE)**[11] 347 4-8-11 **52** ow1........................ AdamKirby 11 57+
(S Parr) *qckly away on outer: sn led and swtchd lft: rdn along 2f out: drvn and edgd rt over 1f out: hdd ent fnl f and kpt on same pce* **7/1**[3]

0/0- **3** *nk* **Divine White**[117] 6751 6-8-5 **46** oh1.................................... JimmyQuinn 4 50
(G P Enright) *hld up towards rr: hdwy and n.m.r 1/2-way: sn swtchd rt and effrt to chse ldrs whn nt clr run over 1f out: swtchd rt and rdn ins fnl f: styd on wl towards fin* **25/1**

-003 **4** *nk* **Avoca Dancer (IRE)**[14] 305 6-9-0 **55**.............................(b) ChrisCatlin 6 58
(Miss Gay Kelleway) *hld up in rr: hdwy on wd outside over 2f out: rdn over 1f out: styd on ins fnl f: nrst fin* **12/1**

0-04 **5** *3 3/4* **Blakeshall Quest**[9] 367 9-8-9 **53**...........................(b) AndrewMullen(3) 9 44
(R Brotherton) *prom: hmpd ins first f: cl up and rdn over 2f out: drvn wl over 1f out: grad wknd* **14/1**

15-2 **6** *1* **Whozart (IRE)**[9] 367 6-9-0 **55**.. DanielTudhope 3 43+
(A Dickman) *trckd ldrs on inner: hdwy over 2f out: rdn and ev ch over 1f out: sn drvn and btn: eased ins fnl f* **11/4**[1]

0042 **7** *2 3/4* **So Sublime**[12] 328 4-8-0 **46** oh1.............................(b) AmyBaker(5) 5 25
(M C Chapman) *in tch: rdn along to chse ldrs 1/2-way: drvn and wknd 2f out* **11/1**

00-4 **8** *6* **Orange Square (IRE)**[12] 327 4-8-0 **46**.................... PatrickDonaghy(5) 1 6
(D W Barker) *cl up on inner: rdn along over 2f out and ev ch tl drvn and wknd over 1f out* **8/1**

0-60 **9** *3 1/4* **Soba Jones**[21] 222 12-8-6 **50**.. TolleyDean(3) 2 —
(J Balding) *trckd ldrs on inner: pushed along over 2f out: sn rdn and wknd* **12/1**

-056 **10** *nk* **Tag Team (IRE)**[14] 303 8-8-8 **49**.............................. StephenDonohoe 10 —
(John A Harris) *chsd ldrs: rdn along 1/2-way: sn wknd* **10/1**

635- **11** *6* **Bahamarama (IRE)**[232] 3330 4-8-8 **52**...................(p) KevinGhunowa(3) 8 —
(R A Harris) *chsd ldrs: n.m.r and rdn along 1/2-way: sn wknd* **33/1**

1m 17.47s (0.97) **Going Correction** -0.025s/f (Stan) **11** Ran SP% **114.7**
Speed ratings (Par 101): **92,90,90,89,84 83,79,71,67,67 59**
toteswinger: 1&2 £5.50, 1&3 £29.10, 2&3 £19.90. CSF £35.14 CT £716.20 TOTE £5.00: £2.20, £2.30, £8.60; EX 38.80 TRIFECTA Not won..
Owner P S J Croft **Bred** R J Turner **Trained** Elmley Castle, Worcs
■ Stewards' Enquiry : Adam Kirby four-day ban: careless riding (Feb 24-27)

FOCUS
A moderate sprint handicap run at a decent pace which suited the hold-up horses. The form is rated through the winner.

488 HAVE YOUR WEDDING AT SOUTHWELL RACECOURSE MAIDEN STKS 1m (F)
2:20 (2:22) (Class 5) 3-Y-O+ **£2,729** (£806; £403) **Stalls** Low

Form RPR

0-2 **1** **Miss Christophene (IRE)**[28] 151 3-8-3 0........................ JimmyQuinn 5 69
(Mrs S Lamyman) *trckd ldrs: pushed along and hdwy to chse ldng pair over 3f out: effrt 2f out: sn swtchd lft and drvn to ld 1f out: kpt on gamely* **7/1**[3]

4 **2** *1 1/4* **High Cross (IRE)**[14] 306 3-8-3 0.. ChrisCatlin 1 66
(Sir Mark Prescott) *led: rdn along over 2f out: drvn wl over 1f out: hdd 1f out: kpt on one pce* **4/6**[1]

3 *11* **Zarilan (IRE)**[115] 6833 4-9-13 70.................................... FergusSweeney 4 51
(Evan Williams) *cl up: shkn up 3f out: rdn over 2f out: sn drvn and btn* **5/2**[2]

0 **4** *24* **Early Girl**[13] 310 4-9-8 0.. PaulDoe 2 —
(P D Evans) *chsd ldng pair: rdn along after 3f: sn outpcd and bhd fnl 3f* **66/1**

0 **5** *53* **Croy (IRE)**[21] 227 4-9-8 0.. AdamKirby 3 —
(S Parr) *s.i.s: a outpcd and bhd* **40/1**

- **6** *dist* **Daisys Fantasy** 4-9-8 0.. DaleGibson 6 —
(S Parr) *rn v green: a bhd: t.o fr 1/2-way: virtually p.u 2f out* **33/1**

1m 44.95s (1.25) **Going Correction** -0.025s/f (Stan)
WFA 3 from 4yo 19lb **6** Ran SP% **107.9**
Speed ratings (Par 103): **92,90,79,55,2** —
toteswinger: 1&2 £1.60, 1&3 £1.70, 2&3 £1.10. CSF £11.44 TOTE £7.30: £3.20, £1.10; EX 13.10.
Owner P Lamyman **Bred** Stephen Moloney **Trained** Ruckland, Lincs

FOCUS
A weak and uncompetitive maiden. The front pair had only showed modest form previously and there are doubts over what ability the third retains.
Croy(IRE) Official explanation: vet said filly returned lame

489 SOUTHWELL GOLF CLUB (S) STKS — 7f (F)
2:50 (2:50) (Class 6) 4-Y-0+ £2,047 (£604; £302) Stalls Low

Form RPR
5234 1 **Obe Royal**[2] [460] 5-8-12 62..(b) PaulDoe 1 69
(P D Evans) *hld up in rr: hdwy 3f out: rdn to chse ldrs over 1f out: drvn ins fnl f and styd on wl to ld nr fin* **5/1**[2]
-225 2 *nk* **Hamaasy**[21] [223] 8-8-9 60..(p) KevinGhunowa(3) 11 68
(R A Harris) *trckd ldrs: smooth hdwy 2f out: rdn to ld over 1f out: drvn ins fnl f: hdd and no ex nr fin* **11/2**[3]
00-3 3 *1 1/4* **Ballycroy Boy (IRE)**[14] [304] 4-8-12 66........................(p) NeilChalmers 5 65
(A Bailey) *midfield: hdwy 3f out: rdn to chal over 1f out and ev ch tl drvn and nt qckn wl ins fnl f* **9/2**[1]
0-22 4 *1/2* **Cap St Jean (IRE)**[21] [223] 5-8-5 57........................(p) DavidKenny(7) 10 63
(R Hollinshead) *dwlt and towards rr: hdwy on wd outside over 2f out: rdn over 1f out: styd on wl fnl f: nrst fin* **6/1**
00-5 5 *1 3/4* **Ice Planet**[5] [401] 8-8-7 66.. DeanHeslop(5) 4 59
(Mrs R A Carr) *towards rr: rdn along and hdwy over 2f out: swtchd lft and styd on appr fnl f: nrst fin* **12/1**
0-43 6 *nk* **Don Pietro**[10] [357] 6-9-4 69..(p) GrahamGibbons 8 64
(R Curtis) *led: rdn over 2f out: drvn and hdd over 1f out: wknd* **11/2**[3]
2-31 7 *1 1/4* **Kingsmaite**[15] [292] 8-8-11 64..(b) AndrewYoxall(7) 9 60
(S R Bowring) *cl up: rdn along over 2f out and grad wknd* **15/2**
000- 8 *2 1/4* **Jord (IRE)**[64] [7606] 5-8-7 63.. AndrewElliott 13 43
(A J McCabe) *prom on outer: rdn along 3f out: drvn 2f out and sn wknd* **16/1**
000- 9 *hd* **Mount Usher**[44] [7723] 7-8-7 60..(b) WilliamCarson(5) 2 48
(M J Gingell) *dwlt and towards rr tl sme late hdwy* **66/1**
0-00 10 *11* **Shadow Jumper (IRE)**[22] [215] 8-8-9 40........(p) RussellKennemore(3) 3 18
(J T Stimpson) *midfield: rdn along on inner 1/2-way: sn drvn and n.d* **100/1**
000- 11 *1/2* **Last Of The Line**[111] [6895] 4-8-12 66........................ VinceSlattery 6 17
(B N Pollock) *a in rr* **25/1**
440- 12 *6* **Don Picolo**[70] [7533] 4-8-7 53..(b) GabrielHannon(5) 7 1
(R Curtis) *chsd ldrs on inner: rdn along 3f out and sn wknd* **25/1**
006- 13 *1/2* **Follow Your Spirit**[69] [7541] 4-8-12 45........................ CatherineGannon 12 —
(B Palling) *prom: rdn along 3f out: sn wknd* **66/1**

1m 29.98s (-0.32) **Going Correction** -0.025s/f (Stan) **13 Ran SP% 116.9**
Speed ratings (Par 101): **100,99,98,97,95 95,93,91,91,78 77,71,70**
toteswinger: 1&2 £5.00, 1&3 £3.80, 2&3 £7.40. CSF £30.79 TOTE £6.20: £2.50, £1.90, £2.10; EX 30.90 Trifecta £80.10 Pool: £369.54 - 3.41 winning units..There was no bid for the winner.
Owner Mrs I M Folkes **Bred** Helshaw Grange Stud Ltd **Trained** Pandy, Monmouths
■ Stewards' Enquiry : Kevin Ghunowa two-day ban: used whip above shoulder height (Feb 24-25)

FOCUS
A competitive seller contested by some solid types for the grade. The front pair were close to their recent handicap form.

490 COME JUMPING NEXT TUESDAY H'CAP — 1m (F)
3:20 (3:20) (Class 4) (0-85,85) 4-Y-0+ £4,857 (£1,445; £722; £360) Stalls Low

Form RPR
020- 1 **Exit Smiling**[129] [6482] 7-8-0 74 oh1 ow3........................ PaulPickard(7) 5 85
(P T Midgley) *prom: hdwy to chse ldr 3f out: chal 2f out: rdn to ld wl over 1f out: kpt on wl u.p ins fnl f* **8/1**
-055 2 *1 1/4* **Silver Hotspur**[12] [331] 5-8-13 80.. LiamJones 1 88
(C R Dore) *trckd ldrs: hdwy to chse ldng pair over 2f out: rdn along to chse wnr whn edgd lft 1f out: hung lft and n.g.t w effrt ins fnl f* **10/3**[1]
5/0- 3 *1* **Orpen Wide (IRE)**[18] [1816] 7-8-13 83........................(b) LeeVickers(3) 2 89
(M C Chapman) *broke early: led: rdn 2f out: drvn and hdd wl over 1f out: kpt on same pce u.p ins fnl f* **33/1**
0-01 4 *1 3/4* **Mcconnell (USA)**[14] [307] 4-8-13 80........................ FergusSweeney 10 82
(G L Moore) *towards rr: hdwy 3f out: rdn to chse ldrs wl over 1f out: sn drvn and kpt on same pce* **4/1**[2]
5-00 5 *7* **Naomh Geileis (USA)**[18] [278] 4-8-13 80........................ GregFairley 8 66
(M Johnston) *sn pushed along and outpcd in rr: hdwy over 2f out: styd on u.p appr fnl f: nvr nr ldrs* **14/1**
6-66 6 *1 1/4* **Kabeer**[5] [404] 11-8-9 76..(t) AndrewElliott 6 59
(A J McCabe) *chsd ldrs tl lost pl after 2f: swtchd ins and rdn to chse ldrs over 2f out: sn drvn and btn* **28/1**
10-0 7 *1 1/2* **Flying Squad (UAE)**[12] [330] 5-8-13 80........................ SteveDrowne 9 60
(M F Harris) *chsd ldrs: rdn along 1/2-way: sn wknd* **16/1**
/3-4 8 *4 1/2* **Torch Of Freedom (IRE)**[13] [318] 4-8-11 78........... StephenDonohoe 4 47
(Sir Mark Prescott) *in tch: hdwy to chse ldrs 3f out: rdn along over 2f out and sn wknd* **4/1**[2]
502- 9 *1 1/4* **Veiled Applause**[168] [5382] 6-9-2 83........................ GrahamGibbons 7 49
(J J Quinn) *hld up on outer: nvr a factor* **5/1**[3]
/0-0 10 *1/2* **Aviso (GER)**[31] [124] 5-9-4 85.. TPQueally 3 50
(A P Stringer) *t.k.h: chsd ldr: rdn along 3f out: sn wknd* **9/1**

1m 42.02s (-1.68) **Going Correction** -0.025s/f (Stan) **10 Ran SP% 119.8**
Speed ratings (Par 105): **107,105,104,103,96 94,93,88,87,87**
toteswinger: 1&2 £9.60, 1&3 £28.80, 2&3 £15.00. CSF £35.87 CT £856.64 TOTE £12.20: £3.10, £1.90, £5.30; EX 40.60 Trifecta £448.10 Part won..
Owner Peter Mee **Bred** Mrs D O Joly **Trained** Westow, N Yorks

FOCUS
A fair handicap run at a good pace, although the track was riding slow. The winner looked potentially well treated on sad and is rated up 6lb.

491 BOOK YOUR TICKETS ON LINE AT SOUTHWELL-RACECOURSE.CO.UK H'CAP — 6f (F)
3:50 (3:50) (Class 3) (0-95,91) 4-Y-0+ £7,771 (£2,312; £1,155; £577) Stalls Low

Form RPR
-512 1 **Xpres Maite**[7] [382] 6-9-4 85..(b) ChrisCatlin 5 92
(S R Bowring) *trckd ldng pair: hdwy to chse ldr 2f out and sn rdn: drvn ent fnl f and styd on to ld on line* **7/2**[2]
2-13 2 *shd* **Wotashirtfull (IRE)**[4] [424] 4-8-12 79........................(p) PatCosgrave 2 86
(J R Boyle) *led: rdn wl over 1f out: drvn ent fnl f: hdd on line* **13/2**
-001 3 *1/2* **Haajes**[3] [451] 5-9-10 91 6ex..(t) DaleGibson 3 96
(S Parr) *sn rdn along and outpcd in rr: drvn and hdwy 2f out: styd on wl u.p ins fnl f* **11/1**
10-1 4 *nk* **Ingleby Arch (USA)**[7] [382] 6-9-4 85 6ex........................ TomEaves 4 89
(T D Barron) *dwlt and reminders after s: chsd ldrs and pushed along whn n.m.r over 4f out: sn drvn: hdwy 2f out: hrd drvn ent fnl f and kpt on: nrst fin* **5/4**[1]
115- 5 *1* **Borasco (USA)**[159] [5635] 4-9-1 82.. NCallan 1 83
(T D Barron) *chsd ldr: effrt 2f out and sn rdn: drvn to chal ent fnl f and ev ch tl wknd fnl 100yds* **5/1**[3]
30-0 6 *8* **Wessex (USA)**[12] [331] 9-8-12 79.. GrahamGibbons 6 55
(R Curtis) *blindfold removed late and stmbld s: lost many l and a bhd* **18/1**

1m 15.46s (-1.04) **Going Correction** -0.025s/f (Stan) **6 Ran SP% 110.3**
Speed ratings (Par 107): **105,104,104,103,102 91**
toteswinger: 1&2 £3.20, 1&3 £5.90, 2&3 £6.10. CSF £24.52 TOTE £4.60: £2.10, £3.00; EX 25.30.
Owner Charterhouse Holdings Plc **Bred** S R Bowring **Trained** Edwinstowe, Notts

FOCUS
An ordinary sprint handicap for the grade with te favourite a bit disappointing. The form has been rated around the runner-up.

NOTEBOOK
Xpres Maite gradually responded to pressure and just did enough to gain his second win from his last three starts, reversing recent course-and-distance placings with Ingleby Arch in the process. He was placed off a mark of 90 less than a year ago, so he might remain competitive when reassessed. (tchd 4-1)
Wotashirtfull(IRE)'s three wins to date have all been gained over 5f, but he ran a cracker back over this extra furlong, having been able to lead, and was just denied. (op 11-2)
Haajes struggled to lay up throughout, which was a bit surprising considering he won over 5f at Wolverhampton just three days earlier, but he had shown little on his two previous tries on Fibresand and it seems he's not totally comfortable on this surface. Still, he kept on strongly in the closing stages and, all things considered, this was a decent effort considering he was 4lb wrong under his penalty. Official explanation: jockey said gelding was slowly away (tchd 10-1)
Ingleby Arch(USA) had today's winner over three lengths behind when successful over course and distance on his previous start, and he was 2lb well-in under his penalty, so this was disappointing. He received reminders not long after the start and basically made hard work of this throughout. He's surely worth another try in either blinkers or a visor. (tchd 11-10 and 11-8)
Borasco(USA) ◆'s three wins have been gained from the front over 7f on turf, so this was a respectable first effort on Fibresand after five months off. There should be more to come from her this year and she appeals as one to keep on side. (op 6-1)
Wessex(USA) lost several lengths at the start, with his rider slow to remove the blindfold, and he then stumbled, so this performance has to be excused. Official explanation: jockey said gelding was slowly away (op 16-1 tchd 20-1)

492 ARENA LEISURE PLC H'CAP — 7f (F)
4:20 (4:20) (Class 6) (0-60,72) 3-Y-0 £2,047 (£604; £302) Stalls Low

Form RPR
0-11 1 **Esprit De Midas**[4] [426] 3-10-2 72 12ex........................ NCallan 3 81+
(K A Ryan) *cl up: rdn to ld over 2f out: drvn and edgd rt over 1f out: styd on u.p ins fnl f* **1/4**[1]
-122 2 *3* **Dancing Wave**[4] [426] 3-8-11 58.. AmyBaker(5) 5 59
(M C Chapman) *led: rdn along 1/2-way: hdd over 2f out: rallied over 1f out and ev ch tl one pce ins fnl f* **9/1**[2]
41-6 3 *nk* **Paint Splash**[12] [322] 3-8-8 57.. AdamCarter(7) 4 57
(T D Barron) *dwlt: sn chsng ldng pair: effrt over 2f out and sn rdn: drvn and edgd lft ent fnl f: kpt on same pce* **10/1**[3]
52-6 4 *2* **Cwmni**[11] [345] 3-8-6 48.. CatherineGannon 6 43
(B Palling) *chsd ldrs: rdn along 1/2-way: sn outpcd* **25/1**
4-43 5 *hd* **Why Nee Amy**[13] [312] 3-9-2 58.. ChrisCatlin 1 52
(Miss Gay Kelleway) *chsd ldrs: rdn along over 2f out: sn drvn and wknd* **16/1**
00-4 6 *20* **Floods Of Tears**[4] [421] 3-9-3 59.. JimmyQuinn 2 —
(D Flood) *sn rdn along and a in rr* **33/1**

1m 29.77s (-0.53) **Going Correction** -0.025s/f (Stan) **6 Ran SP% 111.8**
Speed ratings (Par 95): **102,98,98,95,95 72**
toteswinger: 1&2 £1.30, 1&3 £2.10, 2&3 £2.20. CSF £3.31 TOTE £1.20: £1.10, £3.10; EX 2.80.
Owner Joseph Ogden, J Hanson, John Ogden **Bred** Jeremy Green And Sons **Trained** Hambleton, N Yorks

FOCUS
The winner made a bit harder work of this under his double penalty but pretty much confirmed his latest course-and-distance form with the runner-up.

493 SOUTHWELL FOR RACECOURSE CONFERENCES H'CAP — 1m 4f (F)
4:50 (4:51) (Class 6) (0-65,65) 4-Y-0+ £2,047 (£604; £302) Stalls Low

Form RPR
0-22 1 **Middle Of Nowhere (USA)**[13] [320] 4-9-1 62........................(t) ChrisCatlin 7 79+
(M A Magnusson) *t.k.h: trckd ldrs: cl up after 4f: smooth hdwy to ld wl over 2f out: rdn clr wl over 1f out: comf* **6/1**[2]
-402 2 *3 1/4* **Dazzling Begum**[9] [368] 4-8-4 51.. GregFairley 6 60
(J Pearce) *trckd ldrs on inner: hdwy over 2f out: rdn to chse wnr over 1f out: sn drvn and no imp* **6/1**[2]
53-1 3 *4 1/2* **Ghufa (IRE)**[4] [427] 5-8-9 60.. MatthewDavies(7) 10 62
(George Baker) *hld up in rr: smooth hdwy on outer over 3f out: chsd wnr 2f out: sn rdn and kpt on same pce* **13/8**[1]
40/2 4 *2 3/4* **Slew Charm (FR)**[32] [107] 7-8-13 57.. TravisBlock 5 55
(Noel T Chance) *hld up in midfield: effrt whn n.m.r over 3f out: swtchd rt and rdn over 2f out: kpt on appr fnl f: nt rch ldrs* **14/1**
5-23 5 *2* **Trans Sonic**[12] [324] 6-9-7 65..(v) TonyHamilton 2 59
(A J Lockwood) *led: rdn along over 3f out: hdd wl over 2f out and sn wknd* **20/1**
400- 6 *1 1/2* **Corrib (IRE)**[57] [7688] 6-8-7 51.. CatherineGannon 11 43
(B Palling) *hld up in rr: hdwy on outer over 3f out: rdn to chse ldrs 2f out: sn drvn and wknd* **40/1**
3-43 7 *4* **Alberts Story (USA)**[9] [368] 5-8-4 51 oh3............(p) DuranFentiman(3) 8 37
(R A Fahey) *prom on outer: rdn along over 4f out: drvn and wknd 3f out* **17/2**[3]
656- 8 *7* **Jackie Kiely**[98] [7183] 8-9-7 65..(t) NCallan 9 39
(R Brotherton) *hld up towards rr: hdwy 4f out: rdn to chse ldrs 3f out: drvn and wknd 2f out* **25/1**
-216 9 *3 3/4* **Ibrox (IRE)**[12] [325] 4-9-4 65.. JimmyQuinn 1 33
(A D Brown) *trckd ldrs on inner: rdn along over 3f out and sn wknd* **6/1**[2]
1/0- 10 *35* **Etoile D'Or (IRE)**[28] [1280] 5-8-6 55.. WilliamCarson(5) 4 —
(M J Gingell) *cl up: rdn along 1/2-way: sn wknd* **100/1**
50-0 11 *2* **Alseraaj (USA)**[19] [256] 4-8-5 52.. StephenDonohoe 3 —
(Ian Williams) *hld up: hdwy and in tch 5f out: rdn along over 4f out: sn lost pl and bhd* **25/1**

2m 37.12s (-3.88) **Going Correction** -0.025s/f (Stan)
WFA 4 from 5yo+ 3lb **11 Ran SP% 114.0**
Speed ratings (Par 101): **111,108,105,104,102 101,99,94,91,68 67**
toteswinger: 1&2 £6.80, 1&3 £4.90, 2&3 £3.60. CSF £37.93 CT £84.30 TOTE £8.50: £2.50, £2.20, £1.40; EX 45.00 Trifecta £423.70 Pool: £1,087.98 - 1.90 winning units. Place 6: £49.58, Place 5: £13.75..
Owner Eastwind Racing Ltd and Martha Trussell **Bred** Robert J Sullivan Et Al **Trained** Upper Lambourn, Berks

FOCUS
Just a modest handicap, but it was well run. The winner was value for extra and there should be more to come. The form is rated through the second.
Trans Sonic Official explanation: jockey said gelding ran too free
Jackie Kiely Official explanation: jockey said gelding never travelled
Ibrox(IRE) Official explanation: jockey said gelding had no more to give
T/Jkpt: Not won. T/Plt: £81.00 to a £1 stake. Pool: £90,957.77. 819.00 winning tickets. T/Qpdt: £19.80 to a £1 stake. Pool: £6,857.72. 255.08 winning tickets. JR

467 KEMPTON (A.W) (R-H)
Wednesday, February 11

OFFICIAL GOING: Standard
Wind: virtually nil Weather: overcast

494 DAY TIME, NIGHT TIME, GREAT TIME H'CAP 1m 2f (P)
2:05 (2:06) (Class 6) (0-55,55) 4-Y-O+ **£2,047** (£604; £302) **Stalls High**

Form RPR
05-1 **1** **Lytham (IRE)**[32] 116 8-8-11 **52**.... VinceSlattery 4 59
(A W Carroll) *hld up towards rr: hdwy on outer 3f out: rdn 2f out: styd on strly to ld wl ins fnl f* **6/1**
203- **2** *nk* **Noah Jameel**[72] 7518 7-8-13 **54**.... FergusSweeney 2 60
(A G Newcombe) *t.k.h: hld up in last pair: hdwy on outer 2f out: str run ins fnl f: wnt 2nd towards fin: nt quite rch wnr* **12/1**
6-31 **3** *nk* **Mix N Match**[26] 186 5-8-12 **53**.... FrankieMcDonald 14 59
(R M Stronge) *w.w in midfield: rdn and edgd out lft wl over 1f out: edgd lft u.p ent fnl f: pressed ldrs fnl 50yds: kpt on* **9/2**[2]
0-02 **4** *½* **Ready To Crown (USA)**[33] 100 5-8-11 **52**....(b) ChrisCatlin 11 57
(Andrew Turnell) *t.k.h: chsd ldrs: rdn and qcknd to ld wl over 1f out: 3 l clr ent fnl f: drvn fnl f: hdd wl ins fnl f: fdd and lost 3 pls nr fin* **7/2**[1]
0-42 **5** *nk* **Play Up Pompey**[26] 193 7-8-13 **54**.... RichardKingscote 9 58
(J J Bridger) *stdd and bmpd s: t.k.h: hld up in rr: hdwy on inner jst over 2f out: drvn over 1f out: chsd ldrs fnl 100yds: kpt on but nt quite pce to chal* **12/1**
006- **6** *hd* **Elliwan**[54] 7731 4-8-11 **53**....(b[1]) DaleGibson 6 57+
(M W Easterby) *in tch: rdn 3f out: unable qck and hmpd wl over 1f out: keeping on same pce whn short of room ent fnl f: nvr quite pce to chal ldrs* **5/1**[3]
-424 **7** *1 ½* **Moyoko (IRE)**[12] 353 6-8-6 **52**....(p) PatrickDonaghy[(5)] 8 53+
(M Salaman) *bmpd s: racd in midfield: rdn and hmpd wl over 1f out: kpt on fnl f: nt pce to rch ldrs* **11/1**
00/5 **8** *2 ¼* **Rough Sketch (USA)**[31] 132 4-8-13 **55**.... StephenDonohoe 1 51
(Sir Mark Prescott) *chsd ldr after 1f: led 8f out tl rdn and hdd wl over 1f out: wknd u.p fnl f* **13/2**
60-6 **9** *4* **Siryena**[26] 192 4-8-12 **54**....(tp) LukeMorris 13 42
(B I Case) *nvr bttr than midfield: plugged on same pce u.p fnl 2f* **33/1**
400- **10** *3 ¼* **Snake Skin**[40] 7355 6-8-12 **53**.... PatDobbs 5 35
(J Gallagher) *a towards rr: rdn and struggling 3f out: n.d* **33/1**
02-5 **11** *3* **Sestet**[36] 58 4-8-13 **55**.... TonyCulhane 7 31+
(S Dow) *t.k.h: chsd ldrs: wnt 2nd 7f out tl over 2f out: wkng whn bdly hmpd wl over 1f out: wl btn after* **25/1**
-035 **12** *1* **Alucica**[7] 387 6-9-0 **55**....(v) HayleyTurner 10 29
(D Shaw) *t.k.h: hld up in rr: nt clr run and shuffled bk over 2f out: nvr nr ldrs* **25/1**
0-21 **13** *9* **The Graig**[24] 211 5-8-13 **54**.... JerryO'Dwyer 3 10
(J R Holt) *restless stalls: v.s.a: a bhd* **16/1**
6-00 **14** *20* **Bid Art (IRE)**[14] 320 4-8-12 **54**....(p) AdamKirby 12 —
(Jamie Snowden) *led tl over 8f out: chsd ldrs after: rdn 1/2-way: lost pl qckly jst over 3f out: t.o* **66/1**

2m 8.25s (0.25) **Going Correction** +0.05s/f (Slow)
WFA 4 from 5yo+ 1lb **14** Ran SP% **129.4**
Speed ratings (Par 101): **101,100,100,100,99 99,98,96,93,90 88,87,80,64**
toteswinger: 1&2 £20.50, 1&3 £8.40, 2&3 £15.70. CSF £78.18 CT £368.97 TOTE £10.00: £3.20, £4.00, £1.60; EX 143.50.
Owner Patrick McGee **Bred** Mrs A S O'Brien And Lars Pearson **Trained** Cropthorne, Worcs
■ Stewards' Enquiry : Frankie McDonald two-day ban: careless riding (Feb 25-26)

FOCUS
A moderate handicap, run at a solid gallop and there was a bunched finish. The form looks pretty sound.
Play Up Pompey Official explanation: jockey said gelding missed the break
Moyoko(IRE) Official explanation: jockey said mare was denied a clear run

495 DIGIBET.COM CLAIMING STKS 7f (P)
2:35 (2:37) (Class 6) 3-Y-O+ **£2,047** (£604; £302) **Stalls High**

Form RPR
23-1 **1** **Jake The Snake (IRE)**[39] 26 8-9-7 74.... AmyBaker[(5)] 1 77
(A W Carroll) *stmbld s: dropped in bhd and hld up in last pl: t.k.h: plld out and rdn jst over 2f out: r.o to ld wl ins fnl f:* **11/8**[1]
0-51 **2** *½* **Interactive (IRE)**[20] 245 6-9-7 67.... HayleyTurner 2 71
(Andrew Turnell) *chsd ldr: drvn to ld ent fnl f: hdd and unable qck wl ins fnl f* **4/1**[3]
-053 **3** *1* **Motivated Choice**[2] 470 4-9-0 65.... JackMitchell[(3)] 4 64
(Miss Amy Weaver) *led at stdy gallop: rdn over 1f out: hdd ent fnl f: one pce after* **11/4**[2]
4-12 **4** *1 ¾* **Northern Desert (IRE)**[11] 357 10-9-7 70....(p) ChrisCatlin 5 64
(S Curran) *t.k.h: hld up in tch: rdn 2f out: kpt on same pce* **4/1**[3]
400- **5** *23* **Sunny Sprite**[29] 5964 4-9-6 64.... LukeMorris 3 —
(J M P Eustace) *hld up in tch: rdn wl obver 2f out: sn struggling: eased ins fnl f* **25/1**

1m 28.77s (2.77) **Going Correction** +0.175s/f (Slow) **5** Ran SP% **112.6**
Speed ratings (Par 101): **91,90,89,87,61**
CSF £7.50 TOTE £2.00: £1.30, £1.80; EX 5.60.
Owner D Morgan & Mrs E M Clarke **Bred** J F Tuthill **Trained** Cropthorne, Worcs

FOCUS
Not a bad little claimer but it was slowly run. The form is unconvincing.

496 DIGIBET CASINO H'CAP 7f (P)
3:05 (3:06) (Class 6) (0-55,54) 4-Y-O+ **£2,047** (£604; £302) **Stalls High**

Form RPR
60-6 **1** **Binnion Bay (IRE)**[14] 321 8-8-13 **51**....(b) JerryO'Dwyer 6 59
(J J Bridger) *hld up in midfield: rdn and effrt 2f out: drvn tover 1f out: r.o to ld fnl 100yds: drvn out* **8/1**
3/4- **2** *¾* **Mister Trickster (IRE)**[395] 149 8-9-1 **53**.... TonyCulhane 8 59
(R Dickin) *stdd s: hld up in rr: rdn and effrt over 2f out: r.o u.p fnl f to go 2nd nr fin: nt rch wnr* **9/1**
6-31 **3** *nk* **Convince (USA)**[14] 308 8-8-10 **48**.... StephenDonohoe 1 53
(K M Prendergast) *hld up in midfield: hdwy on outer wl over 2f out: drvn to ld 1f out: hdd and no ex fnl 100yds* **7/1**[3]
5502 **4** *1 ½* **Bold Diva**[11] 355 4-8-11 **54**....(v) AmyBaker[(5)] 2 55
(A W Carroll) *chsd ldrs: rdn over 2f out: ev ch over 1f out: keeping on same pce whn short of room ins fnl f: wknd fnl 100yds* **5/1**[2]
5341 **5** *1 ½* **Mocha Java**[13] 327 6-8-11 **54**.... PatrickDonaghy[(5)] 14 51
(M Salaman) *chsd ldr: rdn over 2f out: drvn and ev ch wl over 1f out: wknd ins fnl f* **4/1**[1]
3-03 **6** *¾* **Tamino (IRE)**[32] 111 6-9-2 **54**....(t) ChrisCatlin 7 49
(P Howling) *led: rdn over 2f out: drvn and hdd 1f out: wknd fnl f* **7/1**[3]
000- **7** *½* **Evenstorm (USA)**[43] 7818 4-8-9 **47**.... FrankieMcDonald 13 41
(B Gubby) *chsd ldrs: effrt and rdn over 2f out: pressed ldrs over 1f out: wknd fnl f* **16/1**
-200 **8** *nk* **Balerno**[16] 294 10-8-0 **45**.... KierenFox[(7)] 9 38
(Mrs L J Mongan) *bhd: rdn 3f out: plugged on fnl f: nvr nr ldrs* **14/1**
-465 **9** *2 ¼* **Thabaat**[21] 234 5-8-13 **54**....(b) KevinGhunowa[(3)] 11 41
(J M Bradley) *awkward leavng stalls: hld up bhd: hdwy towards inner over 2f out: rdn wl over 1f out: wknd ent fnl f* **4/1**[1]
044/ **10** *35* **Siraj**[468] 6608 10-8-7 **52**....(p) DebraEngland[(7)] 5 —
(J Ryan) *racd in midfield: bhd and rdn over 2f out: sn lost tch: t.o and eased fnl f* **16/1**

1m 26.28s (0.28) **Going Correction** +0.175s/f (Slow) **10** Ran SP% **121.2**
Speed ratings (Par 101): **105,104,103,102,100 99,98,98,96,56**
toteswinger: 1&2 £12.60, 1&3 £10.60, 2&3 £8.50. CSF £80.92 CT £549.96 TOTE £13.00: £3.40, £2.50, £2.70; EX 116.60.
Owner J J Bridger **Bred** Fieldspring Ltd **Trained** Liphook, Hants
■ Stewards' Enquiry : Kevin Ghunowa two-day ban: careless riding (Feb 26-27)

FOCUS
This weak handicap was another truly-run contest. The form is sound.
Siraj Official explanation: jockey said gelding suffered interference in running

497 DIGIBET SPORTS BETTING H'CAP 1m 4f (P)
3:35 (3:36) (Class 5) (0-70,71) 4-Y-O+ **£2,590** (£770; £385; £192) **Stalls Centre**

Form RPR
5/12 **1** **Dishdasha (IRE)**[25] 202 7-9-1 **63**....(t) ShaneKelly 3 81+
(Mrs A M Thorpe) *stdd s: hld up in last pl: smooth hdwy over 2f out: trckd ldrs gng wl 2f out: nudged ahd ins fnl f: sn clr: easily* **2/1**[2]
1-64 **2** *3* **Eseej (USA)**[6] 406 4-8-12 **63**.... TGMcLaughlin 4 75
(P W Hiatt) *chsd ldr: rdn over 2f out: drvn to ld over 1f out: hung rt and hdd ins fnl f: no ch w wnr* **7/1**[3]
2-12 **3** *3* **Colonel Sherman (USA)**[18] 285 4-9-2 **67**.... AdamKirby 6 74
(L A Dace) *led: rdn over 2f out: drvn and hdd over 1f out: wknd fnl f* **13/8**[1]
4513 **4** *3 ¼* **Ridgeway Jazz**[12] 353 4-8-4 **55**.... LukeMorris 10 57
(M D I Usher) *hld up in rr: hdwy wl over 2f out: rdn and outpcd over 2f out: no ch w ldrs after* **10/1**
3-16 **5** *3 ½* **Celtic Gold (USA)**[18] 285 5-9-6 **68**....(t) ChrisCatlin 2 64
(Andrew Turnell) *t.k.h: chsd ldrs: rdn over 2f out: wknd u.p 2f out* **10/1**
3-30 **6** *10* **Corriolanus (GER)**[18] 285 9-8-11 **66**....(p) RichardRowe[(7)] 9 46
(A M Balding) *chsd ldrs: rdn and wknd over 2f out: wl bhd fnl f* **8/1**
250- **7** *12* **Most Definitely (IRE)**[27] 1929 9-9-1 **63**....(p) FrankieMcDonald 5 24
(R M Stronge) *t.k.h: hld up in rr: rdn wl over 2f out: sn wl bhd* **16/1**
400- **8** *shd* **Royal Jasra**[140] 6210 5-9-7 **69**.... HayleyTurner 1 30
(Mrs S Leech) *chsd ldrs: rdn 1/2-way: wknd and bhd fnl 3f* **33/1**

2m 32.84s (-1.66) **Going Correction** +0.175s/f (Slow)
WFA 4 from 5yo+ 3lb **8** Ran SP% **122.0**
Speed ratings (Par 103): **112,110,108,105,103 96,88,88**
toteswinger: 1&2 £5.90, 1&3 £1.80, 2&3 £3.70. CSF £18.08 CT £28.59 TOTE £3.40: £1.20, £2.10, £1.50; EX 19.60.
Owner Tristar **Bred** Locsot S R L **Trained** Bronwydd Arms, Carmarthens
■ Stewards' Enquiry : T G McLaughlin one-day ban: careless riding (Feb 25)

FOCUS
A modest handicap, but it was run at a fair clip and the form ought to hold up. The winner impressed and can win again in a truly run race.

498 KENTUCKY DERBY CHALLENGE 18TH MARCH H'CAP 6f (P)
4:05 (4:06) (Class 5) (0-75,70) 3-Y-O **£2,590** (£770; £385; £192) **Stalls High**

Form RPR
-412 **1** **Raimond Ridge (IRE)**[12] 348 3-8-13 **65**.... TonyCulhane 4 72
(M R Channon) *s.i.s: hld up in last pl: rdn and effrt 2f out: led over 1f out: r.o strly and clr fnl f* **4/1**[3]
-222 **2** *2 ¼* **Princess Cagliari**[21] 229 3-9-2 **68**.... PatDobbs 5 68
(R Hannon) *led at stdy gallop: rdn and hdd over 1f out: no ch w wnr fnl f* **5/4**[1]
-534 **3** *hd* **Quick Single (USA)**[19] 268 3-8-5 **57**....(b) LukeMorris 1 56
(P S McEntee) *pressed ldr: rdn and unable qck over 2f out: drvn and plugged on same pce fnl f* **8/1**
60-4 **4** *1* **Hatman Jack (IRE)**[14] 315 3-9-4 **70**.... FergusSweeney 6 66
(B G Powell) *t.k.h: hld up in tch: effrt on inner 2f out: drvn and wknd ent fnl f* **7/1**
1211 **P** **Kheley (IRE)**[19] 273 3-8-12 **64**.... LiamJones 3 —
(W M Brisbourne) *lost action and p.u sn after s* **10/3**[2]

1m 15.91s (2.81) **Going Correction** +0.175s/f (Slow) **5** Ran SP% **111.1**
Speed ratings (Par 97): **88,85,84,83,—**
toteswinger: 1&2 £4.80. CSF £9.62 TOTE £5.00: £1.90, £1.20; EX 8.80.
Owner M Channon **Bred** Myles And Mrs Joan Doyle **Trained** West Ilsley, Berks

FOCUS
The race was run at just a modest early pace and turned into a sprint at the two-furlong pole so the form looks somewhat suspect, with the injury to Kheley further undermining the form.

499 GOFFS BREEZE UP SALES MARCH 6TH H'CAP 6f (P)
4:35 (4:40) (Class 5) (0-70,68) 4-Y-O+ **£2,590** (£770; £385; £192) **Stalls High**

Form RPR
4013 **1** **Grand Palace (IRE)**[6] 400 6-9-3 **67**....(v) AdamKirby 7 76
(D Shaw) *trckd ldng pair: drvn and effrt over 1f out: led ins fnl f: r.o wl* **10/3**[2]
001- **2** *1 ¼* **Atheer Dubai (IRE)**[97] 7213 4-9-4 **68**.... LPKeniry 4 73
(E F Vaughan) *pressed ldr: rdn and ev ch 2f out: led narrowly jst over 1f out: hdd ins fnl f: nt pce of wnr fnl 100yds* **13/2**[3]
4513 **3** *hd* **Muktasb (USA)**[3] 460 8-8-10 **60**....(v) DarrenWilliams 5 64
(D Shaw) *hld up in last pair: hrd rdn and effrt over 1f out: swtchd lft ins fnl f: one pce fnl 100yds* **7/4**[1]
100- **4** *½* **Music Box Express**[103] 7118 5-8-9 **66**.... MatthewDavies[(7)] 8 69
(George Baker) *t.k.h: led: rdn 2f out: hdd narrowly jst over 1f out: wknd ins fnl f* **12/1**

003- **5** 3/4 **Kingsgate Castle**[113] 6880 4-9-3 67 FergusSweeney 6 67
(Miss Gay Kelleway) *hld up in last pair: effrt on inner 2f out: no imp* **8/1**

1144 **6** 1 1/4 **Sarah's Art (IRE)**[13] 329 6-9-4 68 MickyFenton 3 64
(Stef Liddiard) *in tch in midfield: rdn and unable qck over 2f out: wknd fnl f* **10/3**[2]

1m 13.01s (-0.09) **Going Correction** +0.175s/f (Slow) **6** Ran SP% **114.7**
Speed ratings (Par 103): **107,105,105,104,103 101**
toteswinger: 1&2 £3.40, 1&3 £1.10, 2&3 £3.80. CSF £25.06 CT £48.71 TOTE £3.30: £1.20, £3.30; EX 21.10 Place 6: £132.71 Place 5: £47.91 .
Owner ownaracehorse.co.uk (Shakespeare) **Bred** D McDonnell And Tower Bloodstock **Trained** Danethorpe, Notts

FOCUS
A moderate sprint, run at a sound pace. The form looks sound, with the runner-up and the fourth close to their marks.
T/Jkpt: Not won. T/Plt: £161.80 to a £1 stake. Pool: £97,933.36. 441.70 winning tickets. T/Qpdt: £38.00 to a £1 stake. Pool: £6,848.64. 133.36 winning tickets. SP

481 LINGFIELD (L-H)
Wednesday, February 11

OFFICIAL GOING: Standard
Wind: Fresh, across Weather: Fine

500 MARSH GREEN (S) STKS — 1m 2f (P)
1:10 (1:20) (Class 6) 4-6-Y-O — **£1,978** (£584; £292) **Stalls** Low

Form RPR

560- **1** **Bombardier Wells**[56] 7707 4-8-12 58 SteveDrowne 5 63
(C J Down) *hld up in rr of main gp: hdwy over 2f out: chsd ldr over 1f out: r.o u.p to ld fnl strides* **50/1**

30-3 **2** nk **Inquest**[20] 244 4-8-12 62 JimCrowley 3 62
(Mrs A J Perrett) *chsd ldrs: n.m.r over 2f out: drvn to ld over 1f out: wnt 2 l clr: no ex fnl 50yds: hdd fnl strides* **7/2**[2]

-616 **3** 2 1/2 **Rapid City**[15] 302 6-9-5 65 (p) JamesDoyle 2 63
(A J McCabe) *s.i.s: hld up in last: swtchd wd and rapid hdwy to join ldrs 3f out: carried rt over 1f out: one pce* **5/2**[1]

6-06 **4** hd **Maddy**[4] 443 4-8-1 47 ow1 (p) MatthewDavies(7) 4 53
(George Baker) *hld up in 6th: drvn along over 2f out: hdwy to chse ldrs 1f out: one pce* **10/1**

-540 **5** 1 1/2 **Barodine**[12] 346 6-8-8 50 (bt) MCGeran(5) 9 54
(R J Hodges) *t.k.h: pressed ldr: led 3f out: hung bdly rt and hdd over 1f out: wknd* **25/1**

00-0 **6** 1/2 **Cantabilly (IRE)**[11] 361 6-8-13 70 PaulDoe 7 53
(R J Hodges) *n.m.r 1st bnd: hdwy into 5th after 2f: rdn and outpcd over 2f out: styd on same pce fnl f* **7/2**[2]

0-46 **7** 3 1/4 **Royal Straight**[11] 357 4-8-12 59 (b[1]) JimmyQuinn 8 46
(B N Pollock) *trckd ldrs: rdn over 2f out: wknd over 1f out* **8/1**[3]

406- **8** 7 **Jayyid (IRE)**[45] 7801 4-8-12 55 MartinDwyer 6 32
(C E Brittain) *towards rr: rdn over 3f out: no rspnse* **16/1**

120- **9** 1 3/4 **Sweet World**[47] 5603 5-8-13 60 RobertHavlin 1 29
(B J Llewellyn) *led tl 3f out: wknd over 2f out* **16/1**

2m 5.92s (-0.68) **Going Correction** +0.075s/f (Slow)
WFA 4 from 5yo+ 1lb **9** Ran SP% **110.8**
Speed ratings: **105,104,102,102,101 101,98,92,91**
toteswinger: 1&2 £21.60, 1&3 £20.20, 2&3 £2.30. CSF £206.70 TOTE £61.60: £6.80, £1.20, £1.50; EX 179.40 TRIFECTA Not won..There was no bid for the winner.
Owner C J Down **Bred** Brick Kiln Stud & Miss E Wright **Trained** Mutterton, Devon

FOCUS
This had the look of an open selling stakes, with doubts over the 'form' horses', so it was not a big surprise to see a 50/1 shock. The fourth and fifth look the best guides to the form.
Rapid City Official explanation: jockey said gelding hung right in straight
Barodine Official explanation: jockey said gelding hung right throughout

501 HARTFIELD MAIDEN STKS — 1m 5f (P)
1:40 (1:52) (Class 5) 4-Y-O+ — **£2,729** (£806; £403) **Stalls** Low

Form RPR

1 **Enlightenment (IRE)**[81] 9-9-7 0 GeorgeBaker 1 64+
(Evan Williams) *s.s: hdwy to ld after 2f: hdd 6f out: rdn to ld again 1f out: styd on wl* **4/1**[3]

2 **2** 2 **Dream In Blue**[14] 310 4-9-3 0 ShaneKelly 9 61+
(J A Osborne) *chsd ldrs: hrd rdn 4f out: outpcd over 2f out: styd on fnl f: tk 2nd on line* **9/4**[1]

32 **3** nse **Regal Angel**[18] 279 6-9-2 0 JimCrowley 10 56+
(Jean-Rene Auvray) *led 2f: prom after: hrd rdn over 1f out: one pce* **11/4**[2]

4 1/2 **Scandal**[27] 4-9-3 0 IanMongan 7 60
(Andrew Turnell) *s.s: bhd: gd hdwy to ld 6f out and sn increased tempo: hdd and no ex 1f out* **7/1**

005- **5** 1/2 **Rettorical Lad**[65] 7604 4-9-3 55 RobertHavlin 4 59?
(Jamie Poulton) *hld up in tch: outpcd 3f out: drvn along and hdwy over 1f out: styd on one pce* **25/1**

50-5 **6** 1 **Romantic Retreat**[33] 102 4-8-12 62 RobertWinston 6 53
(G L Moore) *hld up in 6th: pushed along 5f out: mod effrt on outside over 2f out and wd st: nt pce to chal* **10/1**

7 1/2 **Popcorn Rosie**[55] 6-9-2 0 SteveDrowne 3 52
(C J Down) *dwlt: sn chsng ldrs: hrd rdn over 3f out: outpcd and btn over 2f out* **20/1**

8 14 **Jay Ell The Trier (IRE)**[10] 5-9-7 0 TomEaves 2 36
(Tim Vaughan) *s.s: plld hrd and settled detached in last: hrd rdn 3f out: no rspnse and sn bhd* **14/1**

2m 50.34s (4.34) **Going Correction** +0.075s/f (Slow)
WFA 4 from 5yo+ 4lb **8** Ran SP% **114.3**
Speed ratings (Par 103): **89,87,87,87,87 86,86,77**
toteswinger: 1&2 £2.70, 1&3 £3.20, 2&3 £1.60. CSF £13.15 TOTE £5.70: £1.70, £1.40, £1.10; EX 14.40 Trifecta £28.90 Pool: £530.43 - 13.55 winning units..
Owner T Hywel Jones **Bred** S Wilson **Trained** Llancarfan, Vale Of Glamorgan

FOCUS
This was run at a steady pace and the bare form is very modest, which should help the winner's handicap mark.

502 ASHDOWN FOREST H'CAP — 2m (P)
2:10 (2:22) (Class 6) (0-60,59) 4-Y-O+ — **£2,047** (£604; £302) **Stalls** Low

Form RPR

16-1 **1** **Prairie Hawk (USA)**[4] 449 4-9-5 58 6ex (t) TomEaves 8 68+
(Tim Vaughan) *chsd ldrs: rdn 3f out: styd on to ld fnl 75yds* **5/6**[1]

4-64 **2** 1 1/2 **Irish Ballad**[26] 190 7-9-5 52 NickyMackay 6 60
(S Dow) *led: jnd and rdn 3f out: kpt on gamely: hdd and outpcd fnl 75yds* **6/1**[2]

/00- **3** 1 1/2 **Orchard House (FR)**[30] 436 6-9-1 48 IanMongan 3 54
(Evan Williams) *in tch: rdn to join ldrs 3f out: no ex fnl f* **25/1**

0-60 **4** 1 1/4 **Rock Peak (IRE)**[12] 341 4-9-6 59 (p) JimmyQuinn 11 64
(B J Llewellyn) *hld up towards rr: rdn 3f out: hdwy over 1f out: styd on same pce: no imp* **16/1**

60-4 **5** nse **Mulaazem**[12] 346 6-9-10 57 (bt) AndrewElliott 5 62
(A M Hales) *chsd ldrs: rdn 5f out: no ex appr fnl f* **16/1**

3052 **6** 3/4 **Prince Of Medina**[4] 444 6-8-12 45 (t) LiamJones 10 49+
(J R Best) *hld up in rr: nt clr run 3f out tl jst over 1f out: shkn up and r.o fnl f* **16/1**

R60- **7** 2 1/4 **Bella Medici**[51] 7761 4-9-6 59 SteveDrowne 7 60
(P G Murphy) *towards rr: rdn 3f out: sme hdwy over 1f out: sn wknd* **66/1**

44/0 **8** 1 1/4 **Play Master (IRE)**[12] 346 8-9-4 51 RobertHavlin 4 51
(B J Llewellyn) *stdd s: hld up in rr: mod effrt 3f out: hrd rdn ent st: nt pce to chal* **33/1**

1202 **9** 1 3/4 **Safin (GER)**[15] 301 9-9-2 54 GabrielHannon(5) 2 51
(R Curtis) *in tch: rdn 3f out: sn outpcd* **14/1**[3]

0 **10** 1 1/2 **Magic Kahyasi (IRE)**[12] 346 6-9-4 51 (p) GeorgeBaker 1 47
(G L Moore) *chsd ldrs tl wknd 2f out* **6/1**[2]

3m 25.66s (-0.04) **Going Correction** +0.075s/f (Slow)
WFA 4 from 6yo+ 6lb **10** Ran SP% **115.7**
Speed ratings (Par 101): **103,102,101,100,100 100,99,98,97,97**
toteswinger: 1&2 £2.40, 1&3 £5.80, 2&3 £18.00. CSF £5.85 CT £71.45 TOTE £1.70: £1.10, £2.00, £5.30; EX 6.90 Trifecta £128.50 Pool: £378.64 - 2.18 winning units..
Owner J Murphy **Bred** Southern Bloodstock **Trained** Aberthin, Vale of Glamorgan

FOCUS
This was a moderate staying handicap but the form looks pretty solid and the winner looks capable of improving again on the bare form.
Prince Of Medina Official explanation: jockey said gelding was denied a clear run

503 ASHURST WOOD MAIDEN STKS — 7f (P)
2:40 (2:54) (Class 5) 3-Y-O — **£2,729** (£806; £403) **Stalls** Low

Form RPR

1 **Set The Trend** 3-9-3 LPKeniry 5 77+
(A M Balding) *chsd ldrs: hmpd after 2f: wnt 2nd 2f out and drew clr w runner-up: hrd rdn fnl f: led fnl 75yds* **4/1**[2]

6-32 **2** 3/4 **Dance And Dance (IRE)**[22] 227 3-9-3 68 JimCrowley 10 75
(E F Vaughan) *led: drew clr w wnr fr 2f out: hrd rdn fnl f: hdd fnl 75yds: kpt on wl* **11/4**[1]

34-4 **3** 9 **Joannadarc (USA)**[32] 122 3-8-5 67 HollyHall(7) 6 46
(S A Callaghan) *pressed ldrs on outside: wd and lost pl on bnd 2f out: styd on to take modest 3rd ins fnl f* **8/1**

6 **4** 1/2 **Silca Meydan**[32] 121 3-9-3 EdwardCreighton 1 49
(M R Channon) *dwlt: t.k.h in rr: hdwy into midfield 4f out: outpcd fnl 2f* **5/1**[3]

5 hd **Highgate Cat** 3-9-0 JamesMillman(3) 2 49+
(B R Millman) *hld up towards rr: effrt on rail whn hmpd over 2f out: rallied to dispute modest 3rd over 1f out: one pce* **16/1**

55- **6** 2 3/4 **Cloudesley (IRE)**[43] 7823 3-9-3 MartinDwyer 7 41+
(A M Balding) *in tch: n.m.r and dropped to last over 4f out: pushed along over 3f out: modest late hdwy* **7/1**

7 hd **Viva La Vida** 3-8-12 RobertHavlin 3 36
(Jane Chapple-Hyam) *chsd ldrs: rdn over 3f out: wknd 2f out* **8/1**

0-0 **8** 1/2 **Fleuron**[28] 160 3-8-12 JimmyQuinn 9 34
(P Howling) *wd: hdwy to chse ldrs 4f out: n.m.r and wknd over 2f out* **50/1**

9 7 **Indian Story (IRE)** 3-8-12 RobertWinston 12 16
(G C Bravery) *sn pressing ldr: wknd 2f out* **25/1**

10 5 **Phoenix Rising** 3-8-12 SteveDrowne 8 2
(H Morrison) *dwlt: a in rr: pushed along over 3f out: sn struggling* **14/1**

1m 25.39s (0.59) **Going Correction** +0.075s/f (Slow) **10** Ran SP% **116.4**
Speed ratings (Par 97): **99,98,87,87,87 83,83,83,75,69**
toteswinger: 1&2 £2.70, 1&3 £8.00, 2&3 £3.80. CSF £14.30 TOTE £3.30: £1.40, £1.50, £2.80; EX 15.90 Trifecta £52.90 Pool: £342.13 - 4.78 winning units..
Owner Favourites Racing XXII **Bred** Old Suffolk Stud **Trained** Kingsclere, Hants
■ Independent James was withdrawn after refusing to enter the stalls (15/2, deduct 10p in the £ under R4.)

FOCUS
A very modest maiden overall, but the first pair finished well clear and showed fair form.
Silca Meydan Official explanation: jockey said colt hung badly right throughout
Viva La Vida Official explanation: jockey said filly ran green
Indian Story(IRE) Official explanation: jockey said filly ran green in straight

504 EDENBRIDGE CLAIMING STKS — 1m (P)
3:10 (3:20) (Class 6) 4-Y-O+ — **£2,047** (£604; £302) **Stalls** High

Form RPR

4-2 **1** **Electric Warrior (IRE)**[35] 70 6-9-1 80 DarrenWilliams 2 75
(K R Burke) *led and set slow pce: jnd by runner-up and qcknd over 2f out: sn led again: drvn clr ent fnl f* **13/8**[1]

05-6 **2** 1 3/4 **Landucci**[33] 97 8-8-11 66 (p) PaulDoe 4 67
(S Curran) *trckd wnr: disp ld and helped increase tempo over 2f out tl wl over 1f out: nt qckn fnl f* **11/2**[2]

-643 **3** shd **Bobski (IRE)**[4] 452 7-8-13 72 (p) JimCrowley 3 69
(Miss Gay Kelleway) *dwlt: hld up in 3rd: rdn 2f out: styd on fnl f: jst missed 2nd* **6/1**[3]

4311 **4** 1 1/4 **Teasing**[12] 354 5-9-0 78 (v) RobertHavlin 5 67
(J Pearce) *stdd s: hld up and a last: rdn over 2f out: one pce* **13/8**[1]

1m 43.65s (5.45) **Going Correction** +0.075s/f (Slow) **4** Ran SP% **105.9**
Speed ratings (Par 101): **75,73,73,71**
CSF £9.84 TOTE £2.20; EX 8.20.Teasing was subject to a friendly claim.
Owner Market Avenue Racing Club Ltd **Bred** Limestone Stud **Trained** Middleham Moor, N Yorks

FOCUS
They dawdled for much of this contest and the runners pretty much remained in the same positions throughout.

505 THREE BRIDGES H'CAP — 1m (P)
3:40 (3:50) (Class 5) (0-70,70) 4-Y-O+ — **£2,729** (£806; £403) **Stalls** High

Form RPR

3-41 **1** **Kipchak (IRE)**[11] 357 4-8-13 65 (p) MartinDwyer 3 73
(C E Brittain) *mde all: set modest pce: qcknd over 2f out: hrd rdn and hld on wl fnl f* **5/1**[3]

5143 **2** ½ **Marmooq**[7] 387 6-8-12 **64** IanMongan 6 71
(M J Attwater) *hld up in rr: hdwy on outside 2f out: rdn to dispute 2nd over 1f out: r.o* **6/1**
06-1 **3** ½ **Murrin (IRE)**[29] 143 5-9-4 **70** RobertHavlin 1 76
(T G Mills) *plld hrd in 3rd: rdn to dispute 2nd over 1f out: kpt on* **4/1**[2]
-320 **4** 1½ **Shake On It**[3] 458 5-8-3 **60** (t) WilliamCarson(5) 8 62
(M J Gingell) *s.i.s: plld hrd in rr: swtchd wd and rdn over 1f out: styd on: nvr rchd ldrs* **7/2**[1]
610- **5** shd **Saviour Sand (IRE)**[123] 6659 5-9-4 **70** GeorgeBaker 7 72
(M E Rimmer) *chsd wnr tl no ex appr fnl f* **9/1**
-422 **6** 1 **Nikki Bea (IRE)**[14] 321 6-8-2 **59** oh2 ow3 MCGeran(5) 2 59
(Jamie Poulton) *chsd ldrs: rdn 3f out: sn outpcd* **12/1**
-043 **7** 4 **Mountain Pass (USA)**[12] 344 7-8-4 **56** oh2 (p) JimmyQuinn 4 47
(B J Llewellyn) *s.s: hld up in rr: rdn and n.d fnl 3f* **12/1**
51-0 **8** ½ **Young Bertie**[7] 398 6-9-0 **66** (v) TravisBlock 5 56
(H Morrison) *in tch: effrt 3f out: wknd wl over 1f out* **6/1**

1m 37.6s (-0.60) **Going Correction** +0.075s/f (Slow) **8 Ran SP% 112.8**
Speed ratings (Par 103): **106,105,105,103,103 102,98,97**
toteswinger: 1&2 £5.70, 1&3 £4.10, 2&3 £4.20. CSF £33.87 CT £130.65 TOTE £6.90: £2.00, £2.20, £1.40; EX 32.70 Trifecta £41.10 Pool: £674.73 - 12.12 winning units..
Owner C E Brittain **Bred** Miss Mary Davidson & Mrs Steffi Von Schilcher **Trained** Newmarket, Suffolk

FOCUS
This was a tactical affair and very few got seriously involved. The winner set a fair pace after an early dawdle but may have been in the best place up front.

506 MARESFIELD H'CAP 1m 2f (P)
4:10 (4:20) (Class 6) (0-65,64) 3-Y-O **£2,047** (£604; £302) **Stalls** Low

Form RPR
3-16 **1** **True Britannia**[25] 205 3-9-3 **60** (v) AndrewElliott 6 64
(A M Hales) *patiently rdn in rr: swtchd wd and shkn up over 1f out: rapid hdwy to ld fnl 50yds: hld on* **15/2**
00-4 **2** hd **Good Buy Dubai (USA)**[25] 205 3-8-12 **55** RobertWinston 9 59+
(J R Best) *dwlt: towards rr: rdn and hdwy over 1f out: led briefly wl ins fnl f: rallied wl whn jnd by wnr* **3/1**[2]
003- **3** 1½ **Peintre D'Argent (IRE)**[65] 7607 3-9-1 **58** RichardKingscote 7 59
(N J Vaughan) *dwlt: hld up in last: hdwy to ld 2f out: hrd rdn and hdd wl ins fnl f: one pce* **9/2**[3]
40-0 **4** 1 **Squad**[18] 280 3-9-6 **63** NickyMackay 1 62
(S Dow) *in tch: rdn to chse ldrs 2f out: one pce appr fnl f* **20/1**
05-0 **5** ½ **Spring Quartet**[35] 77 3-8-11 **54** (v1) PaulEddery 3 52
(Pat Eddery) *led 2f: chd ldr til slt ld agn 3f out to 2f out: no ex appr fnl f* **12/1**
64-0 **6** ¾ **Maison D'Or**[32] 121 3-9-0 **57** RobertHavlin 4 54
(R Ingram) *t.k.h: led after 2f til 3f out: wknd 1f out* **6/1**
52-5 **7** 7 **Nicky Nutjob (GER)**[16] 295 3-9-7 **64** JimmyQuinn 5 47
(J Pearce) *trckd ldrs: rdn over 2f out: wknd over 1f out* **5/2**[1]
00-3 **8** 3 **Derringbay (IRE)**[29] 144 3-9-0 **64** AshleyMorgan(7) 8 41
(M H Tompkins) *hld up in tch: rdn 3f out: sn outpcd* **14/1**
0-00 **9** 1½ **Calypso Prince**[13] 328 3-7-9 **45** (p) SeanPalmer(7) 2 19
(M D I Usher) *broke wl: prom tl wknd over 2f out* **100/1**

2m 8.27s (1.67) **Going Correction** +0.075s/f (Slow) **9 Ran SP% 117.9**
Speed ratings (Par 95): **96,95,94,93,93 92,87,84,83**
toteswinger: 1&2 £3.20, 1&3 £6.30, 2&3 £2.90. CSF £30.97 CT £115.81 TOTE £8.50: £1.60, £1.50, £2.00; EX 24.70 Trifecta £145.80 Pool: £713.61 - 3.62 winning units..
Owner Brick Farm Racing **Bred** Cleaboy Farms Co **Trained** Wardington, Oxon

FOCUS
There was not much pace on in this pretty modest handicap and any number held a chance off the final bend. The winner found a bit more improvement.

507 COLEMANS HATCH H'CAP 1m 2f (P)
4:40 (4:50) (Class 5) (0-70,69) 4-Y-O+ **£2,729** (£806; £403) **Stalls** Low

Form RPR
60-0 **1** **Inch Lodge**[18] 285 7-8-11 **61** MartinDwyer 2 67
(Miss D Mountain) *hld up disputing 3rd: wnt 2nd 1f out: drvn and styd on wl fnl f: led nr fin* **4/1**[3]
1/5- **2** ½ **Cinematic (IRE)**[53] 7742 6-9-5 **69** SteveDrowne 5 74
(J R Boyle) *chsd ldr: led over 2f out: hrd rdn and kpt on fnl f: hdd nr fin* **3/1**[2]
0-50 **3** 1¼ **It's My Day (IRE)**[7] 392 4-9-1 **66** JimCrowley 1 69
(C Gordon) *hld up in rr: hrd rdn and hdwy over 1f out: styd on same pce: no imp on ldng pair* **4/1**[3]
-004 **4** ¾ **Bee Stinger**[7] 392 7-9-4 **68** (b) GeorgeBaker 4 69
(I A Wood) *hld up disputing 3rd: chsd ldr 2f out tl no ex 1f out* **6/4**[1]
06-0 **5** 12 **Moon Mix (FR)**[14] 311 6-8-10 **60** SimonWhitworth 8 37
(J R Jenkins) *dwlt: sn led and wnt 4 l clr: hdd & wknd over 2f out* **12/1**

2m 6.16s (-0.44) **Going Correction** +0.075s/f (Slow)
WFA 4 from 5yo+ 1lb **5 Ran SP% 112.7**
Speed ratings (Par 103): **104,103,102,102,92**
toteswinger: 1&2 £8.40. CSF £16.48 TOTE £7.10: £2.80, £2.20; EX 18.10 Trifecta £57.20 Pool: £188.12 - 2.43 winning units. Place 6: £13.77 Place 5: £7.93.
Owner Miss Debbie Mountain **Bred** Gainsborough Stud Management Ltd **Trained** Newmarket, Suffolk
■ Old Romney (7/4) was withdrawn on vet's advice. R4 applies, deduct 35p in the £. New market formed.

FOCUS
Despite the size of the field, this was run at a fair pace. The form looks ordinary at best with the winner taking advantage of a slipping mark.
T/Plt: £7.40 to a £1 stake. Pool: £71,999.35. 7,070.99 winning tickets. T/Qpdt: £7.10 to a £1 stake. Pool: £5,103.46. 526.40 winning tickets. LM

494 KEMPTON (A.W) (R-H)
Thursday, February 12

OFFICIAL GOING: Standard
Wind: virtually nil Weather: overcast, cold

508 KEMPTON.CO.UK CLASSIFIED STKS 5f (P)
2:20 (2:20) (Class 7) 3-Y-O+ **£1,619** (£481; £240; £120) **Stalls** High

Form RPR
000- **1** **Itshim**[146] 6085 3-7-13 45 (t) AmyBaker(5) 4 55+
(S C Williams) *chsd ldr: shkn up to ld 1f out: r.o strly and drew clr ins fnl f: comf* **9/2**[2]
0605 **2** 1¾ **Desert Light (IRE)**[3] 474 8-9-4 40 (v) DarrenWilliams 5 51
(D Shaw) *in tch: swtchd lft and effrt over 1f out: kpt on u.p to chse wnr fnl 100yds: no imp* **11/2**[3]
4-00 **3** ¾ **One Way Ticket**[15] 308 9-9-4 42 (p) HayleyTurner 6 49
(J M Bradley) *led: rdn over 1f out: hdd 1f out: nt pce of wnr ins fnl f: lost 2nd fnl 100yds* **7/1**
-604 **4** 1 **Spanish Ace**[14] 328 8-8-13 44 (b) JackDean(5) 1 45
(J M Bradley) *chsd ldrs: rdn and nt qckn wl over 1f out: plugged on same pce fnl f* **7/1**
-060 **5** 2 **Flying Indian**[14] 327 4-9-1 45 (v) RussellKennemore(3) 2 38
(J Balding) *hld up in midfield: rdn and no rspnse over 1f out: nvr trbld ldrs* **16/1**
4032 **6** 4 **Nordic Light (USA)**[3] 474 5-9-4 44 (bt) LukeMorris 8 23
(J M Bradley) *in tch in midfield: rdn and struggling 1/2-way: rdr lost whip over 2f out: no ch after* **7/4**[1]
50-0 **7** hd **Heavenly Encounter**[37] 56 4-8-13 38 (v1) MartinLane(5) 3 23
(K R Burke) *v.s.a: in rr of main gp: rdn and struggling 1/2-way: no ch after* **33/1**
-004 **8** 8 **Martingrange Lass (IRE)**[16] 305 4-9-4 45 (bt) AdamKirby 7 —
(S Parr) *v.s.a: a detached last: reminders 4f out: t.o fnl 2f* **8/1**

60.35 secs (-0.15) **Going Correction** -0.075s/f (Stan)
WFA 3 from 4yo+ 14lb **8 Ran SP% 114.9**
Speed ratings (Par 97): **98,95,94,92,89 82,82,69**
toteswinger: 1&2 £5.70, 1&3 £5.30, 2&3 £7.70. CSF £29.50 TOTE £4.20: £1.20, £1.90, £2.50; EX 19.60.
Owner Itsthem **Bred** Ambersham Stud **Trained** Newmarket, Suffolk

FOCUS
A lowly event won by the most unexposed in the field. This is probably fair form for the grade, rated through the third.
Itshim Official explanation: trainer said, regarding the apparent improvement in form, that this was the gelding's first run on all-weather surface and although it had shown ability at home, it had disappointed on the racecourse.
Martingrange Lass(IRE) Official explanation: jockey said filly never travelled

509 PANORAMIC BAR & RESTAURANT H'CAP 5f (P)
2:55 (2:55) (Class 4) (0-85,83) 3-Y-O **£5,828** (£1,734; £866; £432) **Stalls** High

Form RPR
2-60 **1** **Love You Louis**[18] 288 3-8-13 **75** (b1) SimonWhitworth 1 76
(J R Jenkins) *w ldr tl led after 1f: mde rest: hanging lft bnd over 3f out: pushed clr jst over 2f out: hung lft fnl f: jst lasted* **10/1**
03-5 **2** hd **Lesley's Choice**[34] 109 3-9-3 **79** NCallan 2 79+
(R Curtis) *led for 1f: chsd wnr after: and snatched up outpcd jst over 2f out: rallied u.p fnl f: jst hld* **7/1**
23-1 **3** nk **Comadoir (IRE)**[27] 188 3-9-3 **79** FergusSweeney 4 78
(Miss Jo Crowley) *chsd ldrs: outpcd jst over 2f out: disp 2nd and drvn over 1f out: r.o u.p fnl f* **2/1**[1]
1-35 **4** ½ **Cecily**[18] 288 3-9-6 **82** StephenDonohoe 5 79+
(Sir Mark Prescott) *hld up in tch in last pair: outpcd jst over 2f out: hdwy ent fnl f: r.o wl: nt quite rch ldrs* **3/1**[2]
0-44 **5** 3¼ **Ruby Tallulah**[13] 350 3-8-6 **68** HayleyTurner 7 53
(C R Dore) *t.k.h: hld up in tch: short of room and shuffled bk 4f out: outpcd jst over 2f out: no ch w ldrs after* **4/1**[3]
2-26 **6** ¾ **Fangfoss Girls**[22] 229 3-8-4 **66** FrankieMcDonald 6 49
(L Wells) *t.k.h: chsd ldrs: hmpd and lost grnd over 2f out: no ch w ldrs after* **7/1**

60.45 secs (-0.05) **Going Correction** -0.075s/f (Stan) **6 Ran SP% 112.4**
Speed ratings (Par 99): **97,96,96,95,90 89**
toteswinger: 1&2 £5.00, 1&3 £4.70, 2&3 £2.90. CSF £73.61 TOTE £17.20: £5.20, £3.20; EX 30.90.
Owner J Pepper **Bred** Mrs Wendy Jenkins **Trained** Royston, Herts

FOCUS
The first two home came from the two widest stalls, but the early pace was modest and that enabled them to get across in front of their rivals. There were some speedy sorts amongst the runners, so it was surprising they did not go a bit faster. An objection by the runner-up to the winner was overruled on the grounds that Callan had taken evasive action but no actual interference had occurred. Modest form.

510 BOOK NOW FOR RACING POST CHASE DAY CLAIMING STKS 6f (P)
3:30 (3:30) (Class 6) 3-Y-O+ **£1,942** (£578; £288; £144) **Stalls** High

Form RPR
4-2 **1** **Epic Odyssey**[35] 86 4-9-10 83 MartinDwyer 5 76+
(J R Boyle) *mde all: rdn ent fnl f: r.o wl and asserted ins fnl f: comf* **8/13**[1]
4-22 **2** 1 **Blue Tomato**[6] 422 8-9-4 83 WilliamCarson(5) 6 72
(D Nicholls) *trckd ldng pair: wnt 2nd over 2f out: rdn to press wnr over 1f out: drvn and unable qck ins fnl f* **9/4**[2]
44-0 **3** 2¼ **Brandywell Boy (IRE)**[25] 212 6-9-1 72 BillyCray(7) 4 64
(D J S Ffrench Davis) *s.i.s: in tch in last pl: rdn and effrt over 2f out: wnt 3rd over 1f out: outpcd by ldrs fnl f* **10/1**[3]
2104 **4** 1¾ **Flamestone**[3] 472 5-9-6 48 StephenDonohoe 1 56
(A E Price) *in tch: rdn and effrt over 2f out: outpcd u.p over 1f out: n.d fnl f* **25/1**
-503 **5** ¾ **Elusive Ronnie (IRE)**[2] 481 3-8-5 60 (p) LukeMorris 3 50
(R A Teal) *t.k.h: chsd ldr tl over 2f out: outpcd u.p wl over 1f out: n.d fnl f* **20/1**

1m 13.3s (0.20) **Going Correction** +0.10s/f (Slow)
WFA 3 from 4yo+ 15lb **5 Ran SP% 110.4**
Speed ratings (Par 101): **102,100,97,95,94**
toteswinger: 1&2 £2.40. CSF £2.22 TOTE £1.80: £1.10, £1.20; EX 2.00.Epic Odyssey was claimed by Horses First Racing Limited for £12,000.
Owner M Khan X2 **Bred** Baydon House Stud **Trained** Epsom, Surrey

FOCUS
Short on numbers, but the pair who fought out the finish set a decent standard for an all-weather claimer. The race was steadily run and the fourth limits the form.

511 GOFFS BREEZE UP MARCH 6TH H'CAP 2m (P)
4:05 (4:05) (Class 4) (0-85,81) 4-Y-O+ **£5,828** (£1,734; £866; £432) **Stalls** High

Form RPR
050- **1** **Benhego**[118] 6790 4-8-12 **71** FergusSweeney 4 83+
(G L Moore) *hld up in last trio: smooth hdwy 4f out: led 2f out: rdn and drew clr fnl f: comf* **5/4**[1]
1-61 **2** 2¼ **Mission Control (IRE)**[15] 319 4-9-1 **74** MartinDwyer 8 83+
(J R Boyle) *hld up in midfield: clsd on ldr 6f out: ev ch and drvn 2f out: nt pce of wnr fnl f* **9/4**[2]
0243 **3** 2¾ **They All Laughed**[2] 485 6-9-0 **67** LukeMorris 9 73
(P W Hiatt) *hld up in last pair: hdwy on outer over 3f out: rdn and outpcd over 2f out: plugged on same pce fnl f* **4/1**[3]

0/4- **4** *hd* **Altilhar (USA)**[400] 96 6-9-10 **77** .... GeorgeBaker 2 83
(G L Moore) *led for 2f: chsd clr ldr after: clsd on ldr 6f out: led 3f out: sn rdn: hdd 2f out: outpcd over 1f out* **20/1**

6440 **5** *3 ¾* **Calculating (IRE)**[4] 459 5-8-13 **66** .... HayleyTurner 3 67
(M D I Usher) *stdd s: hld up in last pair: hdwy over 5f out: rdn and struggling over 2f out: no ch after* **12/1**

53-5 **6** *6* **Bentley Brook (IRE)**[36] 82 7-10-0 **81** .... NCallan 7 75
(R Curtis) *t.k.h: w ldr for 1f: stdd and racd in 3rd pl after: clsd 6f out: rdn and ev ch over 2f out: wknd qckly 2f out* **16/1**

5-00 **7** *19* **Josh You Are**[14] 324 6-8-13 **66** .... StephenDonohoe 1 37
(Ian Williams) *t.k.h: hdwy to ld after 2f: sn clr: reduced advantage 6f out: hdd 3f out: sn dropped out: t.o* **16/1**

3m 33.03s (2.93) **Going Correction** +0.10s/f (Slow)
WFA 4 from 5yo+ 6lb **7 Ran SP% 119.4**
Speed ratings (Par 105): **96,94,93,93,91 88,79**
toteswinger: 1&2 £2.10, 1&3 £2.10, 2&3 £2.40. CSF £4.59 CT £8.50 TOTE £4.00: £2.20, £1.50; EX 7.00.
Owner Findlay & Bloom **Bred** Old Mill Stud **Trained** Lower Beeding, W Sussex

FOCUS
The race was not strongly run but the field was soon strung out by 20 lengths, with Josh You Are fully 12 lengths clear at halfway. The front pair are progressive and a progressive view has been taken of the form.
Josh You Are Official explanation: jockey said gelding ran too free

512 SPONSOR AT KEMPTON H'CAP 1m (P)
4:40 (4:41) (Class 6) (0-65,65) 4-Y-0+ **£2,266** (£674; £337; £168) **Stalls** High

Form RPR

0-11 **1** **Highly Regal (IRE)**[25] 210 4-9-0 **61** ....(b) LPKeniry 2 71+
(R A Teal) *chsd ldr tl led over 2f out: rdn clr wl over 1f out: drvn and styd on wl fnl f* **7/1**[3]

10-3 **2** *1* **Fine Ruler (IRE)**[40] 25 5-9-1 **62** .... GeorgeBaker 3 70
(M R Bosley) *s.i.s: t.k.h: hld up wl in tch in rr: swtchd lft and rdn ent fnl 2f out: r.o u.p to go 2nd towards fin: nt rch wnr* **9/2**[2]

00-1 **3** *½* **Lopinot (IRE)**[40] 25 6-9-1 **62** ....(v) JimCrowley 9 69
(M R Bosley) *t.k.h: hld up in tch: rdn to chse ldng pair wl over 1f out: chsd wnr fnl 100yds: no imp and lost 2nd towards fin* **8/1**

4402 **4** *1* **Inside Story (IRE)**[11] 362 7-9-2 **63** ....(b) AdamKirby 6 68
(C R Dore) *hld up in tch: rdn over 2f out: drvn and kpt on same pce fr over 1f out* **11/4**[1]

6-62 **5** *shd* **Sir Ike (IRE)**[13] 344 4-9-0 **61** ....(vt[1]) ShaneKelly 8 65
(W S Kittow) *t.k.h: hld up in tch: hdwy on inner jst over 2f out: chsd wnr over 1f out: wknd u.p fnl f* **10/1**

30-0 **6** *5* **Snowy Indian**[18] 290 4-9-1 **62** ....(p) NCallan 4 55
(M Botti) *led: rdn and hdd over 2f out: drvn and wknd over 1f out* **12/1**

05-0 **7** *1* **Alexander Guru**[21] 253 5-8-8 **55** .... FergusSweeney 5 46
(M Blanshard) *t.k.h: hld up wl in tch: rdn over 2f out: sn struggling: no ch fnl f* **8/1**

3-53 **8** *9* **Salt Of The Earth (IRE)**[22] 241 4-9-4 **65** .... RobertHavlin 7 35
(T G Mills) *dwlt: in tch towards rr: rdn and struggling 3f out: wl bhd fnl 2f* **9/2**[2]

40-0 **9** *3* **Annes Rocket (IRE)**[13] 344 4-8-10 **57** .... PatDobbs 1 20
(J C Fox) *s.i.s: t.k.h: hld up in midfield on outer: rdn and wknd over 2f out: sn bhd* **33/1**

1m 40.21s (0.41) **Going Correction** +0.10s/f (Slow) **9 Ran SP% 117.5**
Speed ratings (Par 101): **101,100,99,98,98 93,92,83,80**
toteswinger: 1&2 £5.10, 1&3 £4.50, 2&3 £7.10. CSF £39.23 CT £262.88 TOTE £6.30: £1.90, £1.70, £3.30; EX 41.30.
Owner J Morton **Bred** Mervyn Stewkesbury **Trained** Ashtead, Surrey

FOCUS
After initially looking as if there would be a good gallop, the pace slowed significantly after the first two furlongs. Regulation form for the grade.
Salt Of The Earth(IRE) Official explanation: trainer's rep said, regarding running, that the gelding became upset when loading into stalls and appeared to lose interest.

513 MIX BUSINESS WITH PLEASURE H'CAP 1m (P)
5:15 (5:16) (Class 6) (0-50,56) 4-Y-0+ **£1,942** (£578; £288; £144) **Stalls** High

Form RPR

60-1 **1** **Prince Rossi (IRE)**[21] 247 5-8-9 **47** ....(v) JimCrowley 3 55
(A E Price) *mde all: hrd pressed and drvn 2f out: hld on wl: all out* **9/1**

0-11 **2** *nse* **Safebreaker**[7] 399 4-9-4 **56** 6ex........(p) NCallan 1 64
(K A Ryan) *dwlt: sn pushed along and rcvrd: chsd ldr after 1f: rdn to chal 2f out: ev ch after: jst hld* **2/1**[1]

5-36 **3** *1* **Copperwood**[8] 395 4-8-12 **50** .... FergusSweeney 4 56
(M Blanshard) *stdd and dropped in bhd after s: hld up in last pl: stl last over 2f out: gd hdwy on inner jst over 2f out: chsd ldng pair ins fnl f: no imp fnl 50yds* **3/1**[2]

-001 **4** *1 ¾* **Jessica Wigmo**[3] 472 6-9-4 **56** 6ex........ TolleyDean 12 58
(A W Carroll) *stdd s: t.k.h: hld up towards rr: hdwy over 3f out: rdn and hdwy wl over 1f out: chsd ldrs ent fnl f: no imp after* **5/1**[3]

-616 **5** *½* **Kinsman (IRE)**[21] 247 12-8-5 **48** ....(p) AmyBaker[(5)] 13 49+
(T D McCarthy) *t.k.h: hld up towards rr: hdwy towards inner jst over 2f out: n.m.r and hmpd over 1f out: kpt on fnl f: nvr trbld ldrs* **20/1**

030- **6** *hd* **Cyfrwys (IRE)**[225] 3608 8-8-8 **46** oh1........ CatherineGannon 11 46
(B Palling) *t.k.h: chsd ldrs: rdn over 2f out: drvn and wknd ent fnl f* **33/1**

-620 **7** *1* **Dancing Duo**[22] 242 5-8-12 **50** ....(v) DarrenWilliams 14 48
(D Shaw) *hld up in tch in midfield: hdwy and rdn over 2f out: drvn and no imp wl over 1f out* **14/1**

-300 **8** *1 ½* **Baba Ghanoush**[21] 247 7-8-8 **46** oh1........(b) LukeMorris 10 41
(M J Attwater) *chsd ldrs: rdn over 2f out: wknd u.p ent fnl 2f* **16/1**

0 **9** *nk* **Princess Teddy (IRE)**[8] 395 6-8-10 **48** ....(b) FrankieMcDonald 9 42
(Edgar Byrne) *chsd ldrs: disp 2nd and drvn over 2f out: wknd wl over 1f out* **16/1**

2402 **10** *¾* **Nautical**[7] 399 11-8-9 **47** .... JerryO'Dwyer 2 39
(J R Holt) *racd wd: in tch in midfield: rdn and lost pl over 2f out: n.d after* **16/1**

000- **11** *nk* **Black Draft**[44] 7818 7-8-8 **46** oh1........ NeilChalmers 8 38
(B Forsey) *chsd ldr for 1f: in tch after tl wknd over 2f out* **33/1**

60-0 **12** *2 ½* **Alto Singer (IRE)**[12] 357 4-8-12 **50** ow2........(p) AdamKirby 5 36
(L A Dace) *hld up in rr: nvr a factor* **50/1**

00-0 **13** *3 ¼* **Almora Guru**[21] 247 5-8-8 **46** oh1........ RichardKingscote 7 24
(W M Brisbourne) *in tch in midfield on outer: rdn and struggling wl over 2f out: wl bhd fnl 2f* **50/1**

1m 40.56s (0.76) **Going Correction** +0.10s/f (Slow) **13 Ran SP% 123.9**
Speed ratings (Par 101): **100,99,98,97,96 96,95,94,93,92 92,90,86**
toteswinger: 1&2 £4.70, 1&3 £1.80, 2&3 £4.40. CSF £27.14 CT £70.99 TOTE £10.80: £3.00, £1.10, £2.00; EX 30.80 Place 6: £136.85 Place 5: £56.44 .
Owner Business Development Consultants Limited **Bred** Sir Eric Parker **Trained** Leominster, H'fords

FOCUS
The first two dominated almost throughout in this fairly weak handicap and were separated by only an inch at the winning line. The winner produced his best form since he was a 3yo.
T/Jkpt: Part won. £35,208.30 to a £1 stake. Pool: £49,589.29. 0.50 winning tickets. T/Plt: £168.80 to a £1 stake. Pool: £58,329.63. 252.20 winning tickets. T/Qpdt: £8.40 to a £1 stake. Pool: £4,960.87. 434.80 winning tickets. SP

[487] SOUTHWELL (L-H)
Thursday, February 12

OFFICIAL GOING: Standard
Wind: Virtually nil Weather: Overcast, cold and snow showers

514 SOUTHWELL-RACECOURSE.CO.UK APPRENTICE H'CAP 1m (F)
1:20 (1:20) (Class 6) (0-58,57) 4-Y-0+ **£2,047** (£604; £302) **Stalls** Low

Form RPR

6331 **1** **General Tufto**[11] 368 4-8-6 **51** 6ex........(b) HollyHall[(5)] 6 62
(C Smith) *trckd ldrs: smooth hdwy 3f out: led over 2f out: sn pushed clr: easily* **5/1**[3]

56-3 **2** *4 ½* **King Of The Beers (USA)**[27] 186 5-8-10 **55** ow1........(p) SPRyan[(5)] 3 56
(R A Harris) *hld up towards rr: hdwy 2f out: sn rdn and styd on ins fnl f: nrst fin* **17/2**

2-40 **3** *1 ¼* **Rub Of The Relic (IRE)**[23] 224 4-8-12 **57** ....(v) PaulPickard[(5)] 9 55
(P T Midgley) *prom: rdn along and outpcd over 2f out: swtchd rt and drvn over 1f out: styd on ins fnl f* **6/1**

005- **4** *1 ¾* **Lancaster Lad (IRE)**[44] 7816 4-9-0 **54** ....(p) PNolan 2 48
(A B Haynes) *midfield: hdwy 1/2-way: effrt to chse wnr wl over 1f out: sn rdn and wknd appr last* **25/1**

5005 **5** *nse* **Government (IRE)**[7] 405 8-8-2 **45** .... AndrewHeffernan[(3)] 4 39
(M C Chapman) *led 3f: sn rdn along and outpcd 1/2-way: kpt on u.p fnl 2f* **22/1**

1224 **6** *2 ¼* **Jordi Roper (IRE)**[16] 303 4-8-11 **56** .... AnthonyBetts[(5)] 8 45
(S Parr) *cl up on outer: hdwy to ld wl over 3f out: rdn and hdd over 2f out: sndrvn and wknd appr fnl f* **5/2**[1]

20-2 **7** *¾* **Fun In The Sun**[22] 234 5-8-11 **56** .... TobyAtkinson[(5)] 1 43
(A B Haynes) *hld up towards rr: hdwy on inner 3f out: rdn along 2f out and sn no imp* **11/1**

-300 **8** *11* **Tiger's Rocket (IRE)**[16] 302 4-8-11 **56** ....(v) DavidKenny[(5)] 10 18
(S Gollings) *cl up: rdn along over 4f out and sn wknd* **33/1**

5032 **9** *¾* **Louisiade (IRE)**[3] 480 8-8-4 **49** ....(b) AlexEdwards[(5)] 7 9
(M C Chapman) *t.k.h: chsd ldrs: led after 3f: pushed along and hdd wl over 2f out: sn drvn and wknd* **4/1**[2]

1m 45.45s (1.75) **Going Correction** +0.175s/f (Slow) **9 Ran SP% 109.5**
Speed ratings (Par 101): **98,93,92,90,90 88,87,76,75**
toteswinger: 1&2 £8.20, 1&3 £9.40, 2&3 £5.70. CSF £42.13 CT £239.22 TOTE £6.10: £1.70, £2.30, £2.10; EX 46.20 Trifecta £116.90 Pool: £331.86 - 2.10 winning units..
Owner Phil Martin **Bred** Hascombe And Valiant Studs **Trained** Temple Bruer, Lincs
■ Stewards' Enquiry : Andrew Heffernan two-day ban: careless riding (Feb 26-27)

FOCUS
A modest apprentice handicap, but they seemed to go a fair pace. The winner is rated back to his best form for Roger Charlton.

515 MEMBERSHIP AT SOUTHWELL GOLF CLUB (S) STKS 1m (F)
1:50 (1:50) (Class 6) 4-Y-0+ **£2,047** (£604; £302) **Stalls** Low

Form RPR

444- **1** **All In The Red (IRE)**[21] 7729 4-8-11 66........(p) JimmyQuinn 1 70
(B N Pollock) *in tch on inner: rdn along 1/2-way: hdwy over 2f out and sn drvn: styd on u.str.p ent fnl f: swtchd lft towards fin and kpt on to ld online* **14/1**[3]

1-21 **2** *hd* **Clear Sailing**[28] 171 6-9-3 75........(p) ChrisCatlin 4 76
(Ollie Pears) *led: rdn along wl over 2f out: drvn over 1f out: edgd rt wl ins fnl f: hdd on line* **11/10**[1]

-113 **3** *1 ¾* **United Nations**[20] 274 8-9-3 82........(b) LeeEnstone 8 72
(N Wilson) *cl up on outer: chsd wnr after 2f: rdn to chal over 3f out: drvn over 2f out: kpt on u.p tl no ex ins fnl f* **5/4**[2]

303- **4** *7* **Ming Vase**[156] 5776 7-8-4 48........ PaulPickard[(7)] 7 49
(P T Midgley) *chsd ldrs: rdn along 1/2-way: drvn over 2f out and no imp* **22/1**

00-0 **5** *14* **Mount Usher**[2] 489 7-8-4 60........(b) HollyHall[(7)] 3 17
(M J Gingell) *s.i.s: in tch: rdn along 3f out and sn wknd* **25/1**

-5 **6** *nse* **Redwater River**[35] 93 5-8-12 62........ DeanHeslop[(5)] 6 23
(Mrs R A Carr) *chsd ldrs: rdn along over 4f out and sn outpcd* **16/1**

4-00 **7** *8* **Countrywide Comet (IRE)**[24] 215 4-8-11 48........ TomEaves 2 —
(P Howling) *a in rr: wl bhd fnl 3f* **100/1**

1m 45.0s (1.30) **Going Correction** +0.175s/f (Slow) **7 Ran SP% 113.8**
Speed ratings (Par 101): **100,99,98,91,77 77,69**
toteswinger: 1&2 £2.40, 1&3 £1.30, 2&3 £2.50. CSF £30.04 TOTE £11.60: £3.00, £1.10; EX 29.50 Trifecta £36.90 Pool: £407.42- 8.17 winning units..There was no bid for the winner. Clear Sailing was subject to a friendly claim.
Owner Holmby Hoofbeats **Bred** John McEnery **Trained** Medbourne, Leics

FOCUS
There may have been seven runners in this claimer but punters only wanted to know about two of them in the market before the off. They were hard at it from some way out and stopped in front allowing the winner to come past.
Mount Usher Official explanation: jockey said gelding hung right

516 PLAY GOLF AT SOUTHWELL GOLF CLUB MEDIAN AUCTION MAIDEN STKS 1m 4f (F)
2:25 (2:26) (Class 6) 4-6-Y-0 **£2,047** (£604; £302) **Stalls** Low

Form RPR

2-22 **1** **Lady Longcroft**[14] 323 4-8-12 60........ JimmyQuinn 2 56+
(J Pearce) *t.k.h: hld up in rr: smooth hdwy over 4f out: chal on bit 2f out: sn led and clr: easily* **2/7**[1]

0- **2** *7* **My Mate Granite (USA)**[56] 7713 5-9-6 0........ NickyMackay 3 45
(M Wigham) *trckd ldng pair: hdwy to chse ldr 1/2-way: led 3f out and sn rdn: drvn and hdd wl over 1f out: sn one pce* **11/2**[2]

00-0 **3** *8* **Galley Slave (IRE)**[32] 132 4-9-0 43........ LeeVickers[(3)] 4 32
(M C Chapman) *led: clr after 4f: rdn along 4f out: hdd 3f out and sn wknd* **14/1**

0 4 23 **Bering De Lauriere (FR)**[8] 393 6-9-1 0 GabrielHannon(5) 1 —
(B G Powell) *chsd ldr: rdn along 1/2-way: sn lost pl and bhd* **11/1**[3]
2m 43.62s (2.62) **Going Correction** +0.175s/f (Slow)
WFA 4 from 5yo+ 3lb 4 Ran SP% **108.1**
Speed ratings: **98,93,88,72**
CSF £2.27 TOTE £1.40; EX 2.10.
Owner Jim Furlong **Bred** J R Furlong **Trained** Newmarket, Suffolk
FOCUS
As uncompetitive a maiden as you are ever likely to see and the quartet finished at very long intervals. It is very doubtful if the winner had to improve on her modest pre-race form.

517 DINE IN THE QUEEN MOTHER RESTAURANT CLAIMING STKS 1m 4f (F)
3:00 (3:00) (Class 6) 4-Y-0+ **£2,047** (£604; £302) **Stalls** Low

Form RPR
3-41 1 **Nawamees (IRE)**[16] 302 11-9-0 70 (p) PaulDoe 4 70
(P D Evans) *led: pushed along and hdd wl over 2f out: rdn wl over 1f out: drvn and rallied to ld ent fnl f: kpt on* **5/4**[2]
-021 2 *nk* **Rawdon (IRE)**[6] 423 8-8-9 70 (be) KylieManser(7) 5 72
(Miss Gay Kelleway) *cl up: effrt to ld over 2f out: rdn wl over 1f out: drvn and hdd ent fnl f: no ex* **8/11**[1]
-360 3 *11* **Ten Spot (IRE)**[13] 346 4-8-4 48 (vt) NickyMackay 1 45
(Stef Liddiard) *trckd ldng pair: rdn along 4f out: drvn wl over 2f out and sn outpcd* **20/1**[3]
2m 45.71s (4.71) **Going Correction** +0.175s/f (Slow)
WFA 4 from 8yo+ 3lb 3 Ran SP% **107.1**
Speed ratings (Par 101): **91,90,83**
CSF £2.54 TOTE £2.10; EX 2.00.
Owner Jeremiah Coffey **Bred** Kilfrush Stud Ltd **Trained** Pandy, Monmouths
FOCUS
This race cut up badly and was basically a match. The pace was modest, resulting in a winning time more than two seconds slower than the maiden. The first two did not have to improve on their recent efforts.

518 HOLD YOUR WEDDING AT SOUTHWELL RACECOURSE H'CAP 5f (F)
3:35 (3:35) (Class 5) (0-70,70) 4-Y-0+ **£2,729** (£806; £403) **Stalls** High

Form RPR
-113 1 **Back In The Red (IRE)**[6] 422 5-8-13 68 (b) KevinGhunowa(3) 3 79
(R A Harris) *chsd ldrs: rdn along after 2f: hdwy 2f out: sn chsng ldr: kpt on to ld jst ins fnl f: r.o strly* **7/2**[2]
124- 2 *2* **This Ones For Eddy**[44] 7829 4-9-3 69 DaleGibson 1 73
(S Parr) *dwlt and towards rr: sn rdn along on wd outside: hdwy over 1f out: drvnand styd on strly ins fnl f* **4/1**[3]
2-03 3 *nk* **Figaro Flyer (IRE)**[14] 329 6-9-4 70 JimmyQuinn 4 73
(P Howling) *hld up: hdwy 1/2-way: rdn to chse ldrs over 1f out: drvn and kpt on ins fnl f* **10/3**[1]
606- 4 *hd* **Efistorm**[72] 7529 8-9-4 70 (p) ChrisCatlin 6 72+
(C R Dore) *prom: rdn along and outpcd 1/2-way: styd on appr fnl f* **9/1**
-160 5 *½* **Spic 'n Span**[14] 326 4-8-12 64 (b) JoeFanning 5 64
(R A Harris) *sn led and clr at fast pce: rdn wl over 1f out: drvn and hdd jst ins fnl f: wknd* **12/1**
60-5 6 *1¼* **Cheshire Rose**[14] 326 4-8-7 64 DeanHeslop(5) 7 60
(T D Barron) *chsd ldrs: rdn along 2f out: grad wknd* **9/1**
3-40 7 *½* **Replicator**[28] 167 4-8-12 64 (v) PaulEddery 9 58
(Pat Eddery) *in tch: rdn along over 2f out: grad wknd* **8/1**
30-0 8 *hd* **Fast Freddie**[14] 329 5-9-4 70 LiamJones 2 63
(S Parr) *chsd ldrs: rdn along over 2f out: drvn over 1f out and sn wknd* **11/1**
30-3 9 *3¾* **Desperate Dan**[21] 250 8-8-11 70 (b) PNolan(7) 10 50
(A B Haynes) *s.i.s: sn swtchd lft and a in rr* **25/1**
000- 10 *¾* **Mandelieu (IRE)**[132] 6448 4-8-11 63 TonyHamilton 8 40
(Ollie Pears) *chsd ldrs to 1/2-way: sn wknd* **40/1**
59.84 secs (0.14) **Going Correction** +0.125s/f (Slow) 10 Ran SP% **118.7**
Speed ratings (Par 103): **103,99,99,99,98 96,95,95,89,87**
toteswinger: 1&2 £2.90, 1&3 £1.90, 2&3 £3.80. CSF £18.36 CT £51.06 TOTE £3.30: £1.40, £1.20, £1.90; EX 16.40 Trifecta £25.70 Pool: £448.72 - 12.92 winning units..
Owner Mrs Ruth M Serrell **Bred** Mrs Rachanee Butler **Trained** Earlswood, Monmouths
FOCUS
A competitive little sprint handicap, once again dominated by low-drawn horses, and they went a serious pace. A slight personal best from the winner and the form looks sound.

519 CALL 01636 814481 TO SPONSOR A RACE H'CAP 7f (F)
4:10 (4:10) (Class 5) (0-70,70) 4-Y-0+ **£2,729** (£806; £403) **Stalls** Low

Form RPR
2341 1 **Obe Royal**[2] 489 5-9-2 68 6ex (v1) PaulDoe 4 76
(P D Evans) *hld up: hdwy 3f out: chsd ldrs 2f out: rdn over 1f out: drvn and styd on ins fnl f to ld nr line* **11/2**[3]
/05- 2 *shd* **Tyzack (IRE)**[177] 5170 8-9-1 67 MickyFenton 8 75
(Stef Liddiard) *trckd ldrs: smooth hdwy 1/2-way: cl up over 2f out: rdn to ld 1 1/2f out: drvn ins fnl f: hdd and no ex nr line* **11/1**
1-60 3 *1¼* **Run Free**[23] 223 5-8-2 57 (p) DuranFentiman(3) 7 62
(N Wilson) *led: rdn along over 2f out: hdd 1 1/2f out: drvn and rallied ent fnl f: no ex fnl 100yds* **12/1**
-112 4 *¾* **Mrs Bun**[16] 307 4-9-4 70 (v1) RobertWinston 6 73
(K A Ryan) *cl up: effrt 2f out: sn rdn and ev ch tl drvn ins fnl f and one pce fnl 100yds* **9/2**[2]
5-55 5 *2* **Haroldini (IRE)**[23] 224 7-8-8 60 (p) JoeFanning 2 57
(J Balding) *hld up towards rr: swtchd outside 3f out: rdn and hdwy 2f out: kpt on appr fnl f: nrst fin* **9/1**
-150 6 *1* **Norcroft**[18] 289 7-8-12 64 (p) VinceSlattery 1 59
(Mrs C A Dunnett) *chsd ldrs on inner: rdn along 3f out: sn drvn and wknd* **10/1**
30-2 7 *hd* **Flores Sea (USA)**[7] 404 5-9-4 70 TomEaves 3 64
(T D Barron) *sn pushed along to go cl up: rdn along 3f out: sn drvn and wknd 2f out* **11/8**[1]
00- 8 *19* **Bright Falcon**[61] 7668 4-9-0 66 DaleGibson 5 9
(S Parr) *s.i.s: a in rr* **50/1**
1m 29.55s (-0.75) **Going Correction** +0.175s/f (Slow) 8 Ran SP% **112.7**
Speed ratings (Par 103): **111,110,109,108,106 105,104,83**
toteswinger: 1&2 £12.20, 1&3 £9.80, 2&3 £30.20. CSF £61.04 CT £693.32 TOTE £6.70: £1.90, £4.40, £3.40; EX 116.10 Trifecta £356.00 Part won. Pool: £481.16 - 0.65 winning units..
Owner Mrs I M Folkes **Bred** Helshaw Grange Stud Ltd **Trained** Pandy, Monmouths
FOCUS
Not a bad handicap for the grade even allowing for the disappointing favourite. Solid form with the winner right back to his best.
Flores Sea(USA) Official explanation: trainer said, regarding running, that the race may have come too soon.

520 ARENA LEISURE PLC H'CAP 1m (F)
4:45 (4:46) (Class 6) (0-60,60) 3-Y-0 **£2,047** (£604; £302) **Stalls** Low

Form RPR
355- 1 **Just Five (IRE)**[141] 6214 3-8-8 50 TomEaves 2 60+
(M Dods) *prom: hdwy 3f out: led over 2f out: rdn clr wl over 1f out: comf* **7/1**[3]
20-4 2 *4* **Le Petit Vigier**[23] 228 3-8-6 48 (t) AndrewElliott 3 48
(P Beaumont) *chsd ldrs: hdwy to chse wnr 2f out and sn rdn: drvn over 1f out: snedgd lft and no imp* **7/1**[3]
1-24 3 *1¾* **Kingaroo (IRE)**[18] 287 3-8-11 60 AndrewHeffernan(7) 9 56
(Garry Moss) *hld up in rr: hdwy 3f out: rdn to chse ldng pair 2f out: sn drvn and edgd lft over 1f out: no imp* **13/8**[1]
333- 4 *1¾* **Dispol Diva**[134] 6394 3-8-13 55 (v) JamieMoriarty 7 47
(P T Midgley) *in tch and sn pushed along: rdn along 3f out: hdwy u.p over 2f out: sn drvn and no imp* **4/1**[2]
40-0 5 *2½* **Where You Will**[17] 296 3-8-12 54 NickyMackay 4 40
(S W Hall) *led: rdn along 3f out: hdd over 2f out and sn wknd* **20/1**
6-00 6 *9* **The Canny Dove (USA)**[9] 383 3-7-12 47 oh1 ow1 JanWilson(7) 5 13
(T D Barron) *cl up: rdn along 3f out: grad wknd* **8/1**
0-05 7 *6* **Tiffany Lady**[17] 298 3-8-4 46 oh1 ChrisCatlin 1 —
(M D I Usher) *dwlt: effrt on inner and sme hdwy 1/2-way: rdn along wl over 2f out and sn wknd* **18/1**
04-0 8 *7* **Ringo Zaar**[26] 205 3-8-11 53 (b) JimmyQuinn 6 —
(A B Haynes) *dwlt: a in rr* **14/1**
60-5 9 *7* **Alimarr (IRE)**[12] 358 3-8-12 54 (p) DaleGibson 8 —
(S Parr) *chsd ldrs: rdn along 1/2-way: sn wknd* **20/1**
1m 44.65s (0.95) **Going Correction** +0.175s/f (Slow) 9 Ran SP% **115.7**
Speed ratings (Par 95): **102,98,96,94,92 83,77,70,63**
toteswinger: 1&2 £6.70, 1&3 £4.10, 2&3 £3.60. CSF £55.14 CT £116.37 TOTE £9.40: £2.40, £1.90, £1.50; EX 34.30 Trifecta £177.30 Pool: £261.18 - 1.09 winning units. Place 6: £88.92 Place 5: £34.63.
Owner Just Five Racing Partners **Bred** Rathbarry Stud **Trained** Denton, Co Durham
FOCUS
A moderate handicap run at only an ordinary pace and the front five pulled a mile clear of the others. The form is rated around the runner-up with more to come from the winner.
T/Plt: £166.20 to a £1 stake. Pool: £49,397.44. 216.90 winning tickets. T/Qpdt: £20.00 to a £1 stake. Pool: £3,444.31. 127.20 winning tickets. JR

433 NAD AL SHEBA (L-H)
Thursday, February 12
OFFICIAL GOING: Dirt course - fast; turf course - good

521a GNADS4U (H'CAP) (DIRT) 7f (D)
3:15 (3:15) (95-110,107) 3-Y-0+
£50,000 (£16,666; £8,333; £4,166; £2,500; £1,666)

RPR
1 **Warsaw (IRE)**[6] 434 4-9-0 104 (b) JMurtagh 8 108+
(M F De Kock, South Africa) *trckd ldr: led 2f out: r.o wl: comf* **10/3**[2]
2 *1¾* **Fervent Prince**[138] 6283 4-8-5 95 WJSupple 5 93
(A bin Huzaim, UAE) *led on rail: hdd 2f out: r.o wl fnl f* **25/1**
3 *2¼* **Green Coast (IRE)**[28] 184 6-9-3 107 FJara 1 99
(Doug Watson, UAE) *s.i.s: settled in rr: last 3f out: r.o: nvr nr to chal* **5/2**[1]
4 *½* **Royal Power (IRE)**[6] 439 6-8-9 99 AdrianTNicholls 2 90
(D Nicholls) *settled in rr: rdn 3f out: r.o fnl 1 1/2f* **20/1**
5 *¾* **Halkin (USA)**[7] 414 7-8-10 100 EddieAhern 7 89
(F Nass, Bahrain) *mid-div: rdn to chse ldrs 2 1/2f out: wknd fnl 55yds* **4/1**[3]
6 *¾* **League Champion (USA)**[7] 414 6-8-13 102 KJohn 9 90
(R Bouresly, Kuwait) *trckd ldrs: nt qckn fnl 2f* **14/1**
7 *shd* **Stepping Up (IRE)**[14] 340 6-8-5 95 (t) TPO'Shea 4 81
(E Charpy, UAE) *in rr of mid-div: rdn 3f out: n.d: r.o fnl 1 1/2f* **12/1**
8 *3¼* **Blue Sky Basin**[7] 413 4-8-13 102 JRosales 3 80
(M bin Shafya, UAE) *mid-div on rail: rdn to chse ldrs 2 1/2f out: one pce* **8/1**
9 *12* **Hamlool (AUS)**[292] 5-8-6 96 KLatham 10 41
(M F De Kock, South Africa) *mid-div: rdn 3 1/2f out: nvr able to chal* **10/1**
10 *1¼* **Select Reason (BRZ)**[14] 336 5-8-5 95 (bt) RichardMullen 6 37
(E Martins, Bahrain) *slowly away: rdn 3f out: nvr involved* **14/1**
1m 25.76s (0.96) **Going Correction** +0.325s/f (Slow) 10 Ran SP% **121.5**
Speed ratings: **107,105,102,101,101 100,100,96,82,81**
CSF £85.67 Tricast £248.43.
Owner Sheikh Mohammed Bin Khalifa Al Maktoum **Bred** Redpender Stud Ltd **Trained** South Africa
FOCUS
A very ordinary handicap for the money.
NOTEBOOK
Warsaw(IRE) hardly looked a likely candidate to take to the dirt, even considering he was a winner on his only previous try on Polytrack, as he has a turf pedigree, but he handled the surface well. Trying 7f for only the second time, he raced freely early on, more so than when fourth in a 6f turf handicap on his return from a break the previous week, but he had plenty left in the straight. He was never seriously threatened, although it's worth pointing out he enjoyed a much better trip than the third, otherwise he probably would have had to work harder.
Fervent Prince, like the winner debuting on dirt but also a winner on synthetics, ran with credit on his first start since leaving Hughie Morrison after nearly five months off. He had his chance from the front, but proved no match for Warsaw, who had the benefit of a recent run. (op 22-1)
Green Coast(IRE) ◆ is better than he was able to show as he got shuffled back to last place after a sluggish start from stall one and was eventually produced widest of all with his challenge in the straight. H remains in good order and should benefit from either a more positive ride over this trip, preferably from a wider draw, or a return a return to 1m. (op 11-4)
Royal Power(IRE), a Polytrack winner trying dirt for the first time, is maybe a length or two better than the result as he got held up when trying to make ground against the inside rail turning into the straight.
Halkin(USA)'s effort was short-lived and he looked to be feeling the effects of three quick runs. (op 9-2)
League Champion(USA) was close enough at the top of the straight if good enough, but he's another who has been kept busy lately, and in any case he's probably slightly better over shorter. (op 16-1)

Blue Sky Basin ◆ did not take to the dirt, but he remains of interest when likely to get his own way on turf. (op 15-2)

522a 4MEN TROPHY (H'CAP) (DIRT) 1m (D)

3:50 (3:50) (90-105,104) 3-Y-0+

£45,833 (£15,277; £7,638; £3,819; £2,291; £1,527)

RPR

1 **Yamal (IRE)**^{14} [335] 4-8-13 **98** .... LDettori 4 108+
(Saeed Bin Suroor) *trckd ldr: led 1 1/2f out: r.o wl* **9/4**^{1}

2 3/4 **Jonquil (IRE)**^{6} [435] 7-9-1 **100** .... (v) EddieAhern 12 109
(F Nass, Bahrain) *mid-div: rdn to chse ldrs 2 1/2f out: ev ch fnl f: r.o wl* **8/1**^{3}

3 3 1/4 **Little White Lie (IRE)**^{7} [413] 5-9-3 **102** .... WJSupple 9 103
(A bin Huzaim, UAE) *trckd ldrs: ev ch 2f out: one pce fnl f* **16/1**

4 nse **Tawaash (USA)**^{7} [413] 4-8-8 **94** .... TPO'Shea 11 94
(E Charpy, UAE) *in rr of mid-div: nvr able to chal: r.o wl fnl 2f* **33/1**

5 5 1/2 **Plavius (USA)**^{6} [435] 4-7-9 **90** .... AntiocoMurgia$^{(10)}$ 2 78
(A bin Huzaim, UAE) *trckd ldr on rail: rdn 3f out: wknd fnl 2f* **25/1**

6 shd **Naples (AUS)**^{6} [435] 6-8-11 **97** .... (t) KShea 3 84
(M F De Kock, South Africa) *sn led: hdd 1 1/2f out: one pce* **6/1**^{2}

7 2 3/4 **Escape Route (USA)**^{145} [6123] 5-8-11 **97** .... RichardMullen 1 78
(S Seemar, UAE) *last of main gp: nvr nr to chal* **16/1**

8 3/4 **Aamaaq**^{14} [334] 6-8-6 **91** .... RHills 7 71
(A Al Raihe, UAE) *nvr bttr than mid-div* **9/1**

9 1/2 **Military Power**^{7} [417] 4-8-9 **95** .... JRosales 5 73
(M bin Shafya, UAE) *trckd ldrs for 3f: sn rdn and btn* **10/1**

10 2 1/4 **Fares (IRE)**^{14} [334] 5-9-3 **102** .... (v) DO'Donohoe 10 76
(Doug Watson, UAE) *mid-div: rdn 2 1/2f out: nt qckn* **9/1**

11 dist **Sgt Schultz (IRE)**^{14} [337] 6-8-7 **93** .... WilliamBuick 6 —
(J S Moore) *slowly away: nvr able to chal* **25/1**

12 dist **Ketter (BRZ)**^{6} [435] 8-8-5 **90** .... WayneSmith 13 —
(R Bouresly, Kuwait) *s.i.s: sn rdn in distant last: nvr involved* **80/1**

13 dist **Firestreak**^{14} [334] 4-8-7 **93** .... TedDurcan 8 —
(M bin Shafya, UAE) *racd in rr: nvr nr to chal* **14/1**

U **Jet Express (SAF)**^{13} 7-9-4 **104** .... (t) RoystonFfrench 14 —
(A Al Raihe, UAE) *stmbld and uns rdr leaving stalls* **12/1**

1m 37.95s (1.25) **Going Correction** +0.325s/f (Slow) **14** Ran SP% **123.2**
Speed ratings: **106,105,102,101,96 96,93,92,92,90 —,—,—,—**
CSF £19.70 Tricast £246.10.
Owner Godolphin **Bred** Gainsborough Stud Management Ltd **Trained** Newmarket, Suffolk

FOCUS
Just ordinary form for the level. The pace seemed fair.

NOTEBOOK
Yamal(IRE) ◆ was unproven on dirt, although he did win his maiden on Polytrack and he handled this surface well. He enjoyed a lovely trip close up under an uncomplicated ride from Frankie Dettori, but appeared to idle once in front, before finding extra when the runner-up got to his hind quarters, and he looked to have something in hand. He is progressing into quite a smart type and is every bit as good (and probably even better) on turf. (op 2-1)
Jonquil(IRE) travelled nicely under a patient ride and came through to have every chance; he was simply beaten by a better one on the day.
Little White Lie(IRE) ◆ travelled well in a good, handy position for much of the way, and he looked a real threat turning for home, but was unable to pick up off the bridle on this first try on dirt. He'll be well suited by a return to turf and is one to have on side whilst in this form.
Tawaash(USA) seemed to travel okay well off the pace early (similar position to the runner-up), but he was quickly flat out in the straight and never threatened. He is another who should appreciate a return to turf.
Plavius(USA) had to be rushed up to sit handy from an unfavourable inside draw early on, but he kept on in the straight to post a respectable effort.
Naples(AUS) did not have to work too hard to get to the lead and didn't look to be over exerting himself, so it was disappointing he offered so little under pressure. The fact his connections reached for a tongue-tie is seemingly not a positive. (op 6-1, tchd 3-2)
Escape Route(USA) ◆, having his first start since leaving John Gosden, could not lay up from stall one and was soon detached, but he plugged on past beaten horses in the straight. This was his first start in five months and he is open to improvement considering he usually wears some sort of headgear and often races over further. (op 18-1)
Fares(IRE), having his third start back from an absence, was well held off a 5lb higher mark than when over C&D on his previous start. (op 8-1)
Sgt Schultz(IRE) is better suited by both middle-distances and Polytrack.

523a WHEELS 2000 (H'CAP) (DIRT) 1m 2f (D)

4:25 (4:25) (95-110,108) 3-Y-0+

£50,000 (£16,666; £6,250; £6,250; £2,500; £1,666)

RPR

1 **Art Of War (SAF)**^{6} [435] 5-8-10 **100** .... JMurtagh 8 106+
(M F De Kock, South Africa) *trckd ldr: led 2 1/2f out: drew clr 2f out: comf* **4/1**^{2}

2 8 1/2 **Familiar Territory**^{14} [339] 6-9-4 **108** .... LDettori 7 99+
(Saeed Bin Suroor) *mid-div: wd: trckd ldrs 3 1/2f out: rdn 2f out: one pce fnl f* **5/4**^{1}

3 11 **Mutasallil (USA)**^{35} 9-8-7 **97** .... (t) RHills 5 68
(Doug Watson, UAE) *sn led: hdd 2 1/2f out: r.o same pce* **16/1**

3 dht **Dynamic Saint (USA)**^{14} [337] 6-9-1 **105** .... (e) RyanMoore 3 76
(Doug Watson, UAE) *trckd ldr for 2 1/2f: mid-div: one pce fnl 3f* **9/2**^{3}

5 2 1/4 **Singing Poet (IRE)**^{14} [337] 8-8-10 **100** .... (bt) TPO'Shea 6 67
(E Charpy, UAE) *mid-div: r.o one pce fnl 2 1/2f* **20/1**

6 3 1/4 **Glen Nevis (USA)**^{7} [417] 5-9-1 **105** .... (v) RoystonFfrench 1 66
(A Al Raihe, UAE) *slowly away: racd in rr: rdn after 3f* **7/1**

7 dist **Aleutian**^{343} [817] 9-8-13 **102** .... (e) EddieAhern 4 —
(F Nass, Bahrain) *settled in last: nvr able to chal* **12/1**

2m 3.20s (0.90) **Going Correction** +0.325s/f (Slow)
WFA 4 from 5yo+ 1lb **8** Ran SP% **126.0**
Speed ratings: **109,102,93,93,91 89,—**
CSF £9.26 Tricast with Dynamic Saint £11.01; with Mutasallil £34.03..
Owner Sh Mohd Khalifa & M F De Kock **Bred** Summerhill Stud Ltd **Trained** South Africa

FOCUS
An uncompetitive handicap run at a noticeably ordinary pace.

NOTEBOOK
Art Of War(SAF) looked a difficult ride when fitted with blinkers on his first two starts in Dubai, but he ran a good race with the headgear left off over the extended 1m here the previous week and improved on that effort on this step up in trip. He was always well positioned and the steady gallop was to his benefit, with his natural speed a big asset against a field made up mainly of thorough stayers. He showed himself to be pretty smart, regardless of the way the race was run, as he had his rivals extremely well strung out and won with plenty in hand, but things will be tougher off higher marks in truer-run races. That said, he does have the option of switching to turf.
Familiar Territory won this race off a 3lb lower mark last year, but he never looked like following up. He raced further back than the winner and simply lacked that one's speed when the race got serious. He obviously retains plenty of ability, but is probably a little bit regressive now. (op 11-8)
Mutasallil(USA) had every chance from the front. (op 4-1)
Dynamic Saint(USA) was disappointing off a mark 5lb higher than when winning over course and distance last time but probably would have preferred a stronger pace. (op 4-1)
Glen Nevis(USA) can be excused this below-par showing as he lost his chance when badly hampered after appearing to get caught on heels not long after the start.

524a GNB PLATE (CONDITIONS RACE) (TURF) 6f 110y(T)

4:55 (5:01) 3-Y-0

£20,833 (£6,944; £3,472; £1,736; £1,041; £694)

RPR

1 **City Style (USA)**^{110} [6998] 3-8-9 109 .... LDettori 7 108+
(Saeed Bin Suroor) *in rr of mid-div: qcknd impressively to ld 1f out and won gng away* **1/1**^{1}

2 2 3/4 **Balcarce Nov (ARG)**^{89} 4-9-4 90 .... (t) JohnEgan 6 100+
(H J Brown, South Africa) *in rr of mid-div: n.m.r 2f out: swtchd to outside: r.o wl fnl f: nrst fin* **20/1**

3 4 1/4 **Dr Smart (IRE)**^{21} [258] 3-8-9 77 .... WilliamBuick 10 85
(M Al Muhairi, UAE) *in rr of mid-div: r.o wl fnl 2f* **66/1**

4 1/4 **Montmorency (IRE)**^{151} [5929] 3-8-9 80 .... (v) WayneSmith 11 84
(S Seemar, UAE) *mid-div: rdn to chse ldrs 2 1/2f out: one pce* **40/1**

5 3/4 **Jargelle (IRE)**^{28} [181] 3-8-5 101 .... RichardMullen 5 78
(E Martins, Bahrain) *sn led: gng wl 3f out: rdn 1 1/2f out: hdd 1f out and tired fnl 110yds* **12/1**

6 3/4 **Jose Adan (USA)**^{152} 3-8-9 105 .... (bt) TedDurcan 4 80
(Saeed Bin Suroor) *mid-div on rail: n.m.r 2f out: r.o one pce fnl 1 1/2f* **2/1**^{2}

7 1/2 **Indiscutible (CHI)**^{6} [435] 4-9-6 93 .... (b) JMurtagh 2 83
(M F De Kock, South Africa) *trckd ldrs: rdn 3f out: sn btn* **20/1**

8 3 1/4 **Versaki (IRE)**^{21} [258] 3-8-9 88 .... AdrianTNicholls 3 69
(D Nicholls) *racd in rr: nvr nr to chal* **33/1**

9 4 1/2 **Destiny Quest (USA)**^{157} [5753] 3-8-9 .... (e) TPO'Shea 8 56
(A Selvaratnam, UAE) *trckd ldrs tl 3f out: wknd* **66/1**

10 1/2 **Tishtar**^{127} [6575] 3-8-9 89 .... FJara 9 55
(Doug Watson, UAE) *mid-div: chsd ldrs 2 1/2f out: nt qckn* **33/1**

11 4 **City Queen (URU)**^{48} 4-9-0 55 .... KJohn 1 42
(O Mohammed, UAE) *sn last: nvr involved* **200/1**

12 3 1/4 **India Tiberina (CHI)**^{6} [438] 4-9-0 95 .... KShea 12 33
(M F De Kock, South Africa) *sn rdn in rr: n.d* **7/1**^{3}

1m 20.0s (2.50) **Going Correction** +0.40s/f (Good)
WFA 3 from 4yo 15lb **12** Ran SP% **124.9**
Speed ratings: **101,97,93,92,91 90,90,86,81,80 76,72**
CSF £30.93.
Owner Godolphin **Bred** Stonerside Stable **Trained** Newmarket, Suffolk

FOCUS
Loads of dross in this big-field conditions contest and the bare form is pretty limited, but the winner was a class apart.

NOTEBOOK
City Style(USA), quite a sizeable individual, had got going all too late after struggling to lay up with the early pace when fourth in the Breeders' Cup Juvenile Turf when last seen nearly four months previously, so this drop in trip looked a negative on his debut for Godolphin, but in truth his rivals simply weren't good enough to test him. Frankie Dettori was happy to sit a good six or so lengths off the early lead, even though the pace was nothing out of the ordinary, and his mount picked up in good style in the straight. However, it does have to be noted he looked quirky under pressure, both carrying his head at an awkward angle and hanging left. He will surely now take his chance in the inaugural running of the Meydan Classic, an extended 7f turf contest for three-year-olds on Super Thursday (March 5), and that should tell us more about both his temperament and just how good he could be. (op evns tchd 11/10)
Balcarce Nov(ARG), who was tried over as far as an extended 1m4f in Argentina, did not get the best of runs in the straight on his UAE debut and had to be switched a couple of times, but he was by no means unlucky. He should be suited by a step up in trip and will probably take his chance in the Meydan Classic. (op 18-1)
Dr Smart(IRE) had offered very little in three runs on dirt since switching to Dubai, but he had shown fair form on turf for Bryan Smart last year and ran with credit. However, he's still a maiden and his proximity undoubtedly limits the form.
Montmorency(IRE), off the track since winning a 6f maiden at Goodwood for Godolphin last September, made a respectable debut for new connections in a first-time visor from a wide draw.
Jargelle(IRE), reluctant to load, was not overly pressured in front, but she simply failed to stay this extended 6f and is more of a 5f filly, as she showed when winning last year's Super Sprint. (op 14-1)
Jose Adan(USA), formerly trained in the US, got messed about a bit in the straight, but that was basically as a result of him failing to take the gaps, and this was a disappointing first run for Godolphin. (op 2-1, tchd 15-8)
Versaki(IRE) was set a lot to do after taking time to find his stride and never featured.

525a INSIDEOUT TROPHY (CONDITIONS RACE) (DIRT) 5f 110y

5:30 (5:31) 4-Y-0+

£45,833 (£15,277; £7,638; £3,819; £2,291; £1,527)

RPR

1 **Force Freeze (USA)**^{21} [264] 4-8-11 105 .... (t) FJara 7 109
(Doug Watson, UAE) *trckd ldrs: led ins fnl f: r.o wl* **8/1**^{3}

2 nk **Star Crowned (USA)**^{7} [418] 6-9-1 110 .... (t) MJKinane 11 108
(R Bouresly, Kuwait) *trckd ldrs: narrow ld 2 1/2f out: ev ch and r.o wl but hdd ins fnl f: jst failed* **3/1**^{2}

3 1 1/4 **Change Alley (USA)**^{6} [434] 4-8-11 96 .... (t) RoystonFfrench 5 104
(A Al Raihe, UAE) *trckd ldrs: r.o same pce fnl 1 1/2f* **33/1**

4 3 1/4 **Sea Hunter**^{21} [264] 7-8-6 95 .... (vt) TPO'Shea 1 88
(A Al Raihe, UAE) *trckd ldrs: ev ch 1f out: one pce* **28/1**

5 6 **Taqseem (IRE)**^{335} 6-8-6 90 .... RHills 6 68
(M Al Muhairi, UAE) *sn rdn in rr: n.d* **66/1**

6 nse **J J The Jet Plane (SAF)**^{207} 5-9-4 120 .... KShea 9 80
(M F De Kock, South Africa) *wl away: led nr side: hdd 3f out: one pce* **2/5**^{1}

7 1/2 **New Freedom (BRZ)**^{14} [336] 8-8-8 93 .... WayneSmith 3 69
(M Al Muhairi, UAE) *a mid-div* **66/1**

8 1/4 **Terrific Challenge (USA)**^{21} [264] 7-8-11 105 .... (vt) TedDurcan 8 71
(S Seemar, UAE) *nvr nr to chal* **25/1**

9 2 1/2 **Malayeen (AUS)**^{14} [336] 7-8-8 90 .... DO'Donohoe 10 59
(A Selvaratnam, UAE) *nvr able to chal* **66/1**

10 1/2 **Strike Up The Band**^{14} [336] 6-8-11 100 .... (v) AdrianTNicholls 2 61
(D Nicholls) *led centre gp tl 2 1/2f out: wknd* **28/1**

11 15 **Narc (SAF)**^{7} [418] 7-8-6 109 .... KLatham 4 6
(H J Brown, South Africa) *nvr able to chal: virtually p.u* **66/1**

65.07 secs (65.07) **11** Ran SP% **127.2**
CSF £33.61.

Owner Sheikh Rashid bin Humaid Al Nuaimi **Bred** Dixiana Stables Inc **Trained** United Arab Emirates

FOCUS
The first two in the betting ran below their very best, so the form is obviously not what it might have been, but this was still a good, competitive affair, run at a predictably furious pace. The main action took place a few horse widths off the stands' rail and a middle draw was probably advantageous.

NOTEBOOK
Force Freeze(USA) produced a game effort to reverse recent 6f form with Star Crowned. Formerly trained in the US, he's well suited to this surface and is now 2-3 at Nad Al Sheba.
Star Crowned(USA) ran an honest race, but considering he would have been 5lb worse off with the winner in a handicap, and had 14lb in hand over the third, he was clearly below his official mark of 110. Stall 11 of 11 was not ideal and he had to work to keep tabs on the pacesetters more towards the centre of the track. Although clearly well suited to dirt, he's also very smart on turf and it would be nice to see more of him on the grass.
Change Alley(USA) appreciated the return to dirt and seemed to run his race. Officially rated 96, his proximity helps give the form a solid look.
Sea Hunter fared best of those drawn low and this was a respectable effort.
J J The Jet Plane(SAF), a top-class sprinter in South Africa, was all the rage beforehand, but he was in trouble by halfway and was well below his best on his UAE debut. He had won on a sand surface back home, but was unproven on this sort of track and failed to reproduce the sort of form that had seen him land three consecutive Grade 1s on the turf. Having shown some early dash, it was soon clear he wasn't able to pick up and he was left behind in the closing stages. The plan had been to go for the Golden Shaheen on World Cup night, but he'll surely be returned to the turf now and hopefully he'll be part of his trainer's British string this season, as there will be plenty of opportunities for him to show his true worth. (op 8-15)
Strike Up The Band showed tons of early speed to lead a quick field, but he couldn't keep it up. (op 25-1)

526a UAE 2000 GUINEAS - SPONSORED BY GULF NEWS (GROUP 3) (DIRT) 1m (D)
6:05 (6:05) 3-Y-O

£104,166 (£34,722; £17,361; £8,680; £5,208; £3,472)

			RPR
1		**Desert Party (USA)**[21] 258 3-8-9 108 (t) LDettori 3	112+
		(Saeed Bin Suroor) *mid-div: smooth prog to chse runner-up 1 1/2f out: led 1/2f out: comf* **6/5**[1]	
2	4 3/4	**Regal Ransom (USA)**[21] 258 3-8-9 102 (t) DO'Donohoe 6	100
		(Saeed Bin Suroor) *trckd ldrs: smooth prog to ld 1 1/2f out: hdd 1/2f out: r.o but no ch w wnr* **15/2**	
3	1 1/2	**Redding Colliery (USA)**[21] 258 3-8-9 95 (v) JohnEgan 9	97
		(H J Brown, South Africa) *sn led: hdd 1 1/2f out: r.o same pce* **14/1**	
4	5 3/4	**Vineyard Haven (USA)**[131] 6501 3-8-9 115 (v) TedDurcan 8	85
		(Saeed Bin Suroor) *trckd ldr: ev ch whn rdn 3f out: r.o fnl 1 1/2f* **9/4**[2]	
5	3 3/4	**Blues And Rock (ARG)**[21] 258 4-9-5 100 JMurtagh 7	80
		(M F De Kock, South Africa) *mid-div: wd: rdn 3 1/2f out: r.o fnl 2f: nvr able to chal* **12/1**	
6	1 3/4	**I Am The Best**[48] 3-8-9 95 (b) RoystonFfrench 10	73
		(A Al Raihe, UAE) *mid-div: rdn 3f out: r.o same pce* **66/1**	
7	hd	**Regionalista (BRZ)**[229] 4-9-5 95 JLeme 5	76
		(P Bary, France) *in rr of mid-div: rdn 4f out: n.d* **25/1**	
8	1/2	**Absent Pleasure (USA)**[21] 258 3-8-9 97 RichardMullen 4	72
		(E Martins, Bahrain) *settled in rr: nvr able to chal* **33/1**	
9	4 1/4	**Rocks Off (ARG)**[21] 258 4-9-5 107 KShea 1	66
		(M F De Kock, South Africa) *mid-div on rail: n.m.r 2 1/2f out: nvr involved after* **13/2**[3]	
10	9 1/2	**Fullback (IRE)**[21] 258 3-8-9 97 TPO'Shea 2	43
		(J S Moore) *settled in rr: n.d* **66/1**	

1m 37.62s (0.92) **Going Correction** +0.325s/f (Slow)
WFA 3 from 4yo 19lb 10 Ran SP% **125.5**
Speed ratings: **108,103,101,96,92 90,90,89,85,76**
CSF £12.45.
Owner Godolphin **Bred** David Smith & Steven Sinatra **Trained** Newmarket, Suffolk
■ A fourth UAE 2000 Guineas for trainer Saeed Bin Suroor.

FOCUS
The tenth running of the UAE 2000 Guineas and this looked a high-class contest. The winning time, although slower than the last three runnings, was 0.33 seconds quicker than the earlier older-horse handicap on the card won the 98-rated Yamal. Five of the last six renewals had gone to horses bred in the Southern Hemisphere, but it's fair to say the challenge from that part of the world was below it's usual standard this year, whereas the Northern Hemisphere was particularly well represented, and the first four home were bred in the US.

NOTEBOOK
Desert Party(USA) ◆ improved significantly on the bare form of his half-length success (gained under a 5lb penalty) in a 7f trial for this race three weeks earlier, beating the runner-up and third further than when those two filled the same positions behind him last tiome. This powerful son of Street Cry, Frankie Dettori's pick of the three Godolphin runners, produced an impressive, sustained challenge in the straight and took this in the manner of a very smart colt. It's no surprise to see he now priced at just 16/1 for the Kentucky Derby, but before then his main target is the UAE Derby. It remains to be seen whether he goes for the second leg of the Triple Crown, the Listed Al Bastakiya Stakes on Super Thursday (March 5). (op 5-4)
Regal Ransom(USA) ran his race but was left behind by the winner late on. He was not so far in front of Redding Colliery this time, but he looks to have run right up to his best and there were no excuses.
Redding Colliery(USA) settled better in front this time, with a visor replacing blinkers and he ran another honest race. It would be no surprise to see him take his chance in the next two legs of the Triple Crown, with the extra furlong in both of those races almost sure to suit, and in the longer term he looks a smart prospect for the States.
Vineyard Haven(USA) was one of the best juveniles in the US last year and had Desert Party (stumbled and squeezed start) behind when landing the first of two consecutive Grade 1 contests, although admittedly he had been beaten by today's winner earlier in his career. However, now with Godolphin, he had apparently not been showing much at home, working on a surface not too dissimilar to Polytrack, and was also said to be in need of the outing. It was hoped he would offer connections more encouragement with a run back on the dirt, but he found little once under pressure and was a long way off his two-year-old form. This might have helped wake him up a bit, and there's no doubt he was a bit rusty, but he's got something to prove now.
Blues And Rock(ARG) wasn't up to the task, but he should be capable of better over further.

527a XPRESS 2000 (H'CAP) (TURF) 1m 2f (T)
6:40 (6:40) (95-119,119) 3-Y-O+

£62,500 (£20,833; £10,416; £5,208; £3,125; £2,083)

			RPR
1		**Kirklees (IRE)**[14] 339 5-8-13 111 LDettori 8	118+
		(Saeed Bin Suroor) *mid-div: smooth prog 2 1/2f out: swtchd out 2f out: led 1 1/2f out: easily* **15/8**[1]	
2	3 1/4	**Hattan (IRE)**[138] 6286 7-8-5 113 AntiocoMurgia[(10)] 6	113
		(M bin Shafya, UAE) *mid-div: rdn 3f out: r.o wl fnl 1 1/2f: no ch w wnr* **20/1**	
3	3	**Barbaricus (AUS)**[26] 5-8-8 107 MJKinane 14	100
		(Danny O'Brien, Australia) *wl away: trckd ldrs: led 2 1/2f out: hdd 1 1/2f out: one pce* **7/2**[2]	
4	1/2	**Mr Brock (SAF)**[158] 6-8-5 102 KLatham 2	96
		(M F De Kock, South Africa) *trckd ldrs tl 3f out: n.m.r 2 1/2f out: r.o fnl 2f* **9/1**[3]	
5	1 3/4	**Once More Dubai (USA)**[95] 7263 4-8-11 111 (bt) TedDurcan 5	100
		(Saeed Bin Suroor) *mid-div: n.m.r 2f out: nt rcvr* **16/1**	
6	3 3/4	**Oracle West (SAF)**[14] 339 8-9-6 119 RyanMoore 10	100
		(H J Brown, South Africa) *mid-div: rdn 3f out: one pce* **16/1**	
7	1/2	**Hello Morning (FR)**[13] 4-8-6 106 (b[1]) TPO'Shea 3	86
		(E Charpy, UAE) *sn led: t.k.h: hdd 2 1/2f out: wknd* **25/1**	
8	1/2	**Munsef**[21] 263 7-8-5 102 AdrianTNicholls 13	83
		(D Nicholls) *settled in rr: nvr nr to chal* **40/1**	
9	3/4	**Pallodio (IRE)**[140] 6237 4-8-10 110 RHills 12	88
		(Doug Watson, UAE) *mid-div: wd 3f out: r.o same pce* **10/1**	
10	1/4	**Lion Sands**[6] 437 5-8-9 108 WJSupple 11	85
		(A bin Huzaim, UAE) *mid-div: rdn 3f out: nt qckn* **20/1**	
11	shd	**With Interest**[6] 436 6-8-7 106 RoystonFfrench 9	83
		(M bin Shafya, UAE) *settled in rr: nvr able to chal* **12/1**	
12	1/4	**Docofthebay (IRE)**[20] 278 5-8-5 100 DO'Donohoe 4	80
		(J A Osborne) *in rr of mid-div: bdly hmpd after 2f: n.d after* **14/1**	
13	1	**Anani (USA)**[55] 9-8-5 100 (vt) RichardMullen 7	78
		(S Seemar, UAE) *in rr of mid-div: nvr able to chal* **66/1**	
14	1/2	**Galactic Star**[7] 415 6-8-11 110 WayneSmith 1	83
		(M bin Shafya, UAE) *settled in rr: nvr nr to chal* **25/1**	

2m 5.04s (0.54) **Going Correction** +0.40s/f (Good)
WFA 4 from 5yo+ 1lb 14 Ran SP% **123.4**
Speed ratings: **113,110,108,107,106 103,102,102,101,101 101,101,100,100**
CSF £50.94 Tricast £132.50. Placepot: £31.80 to a £1 stake. Pool: £15,397.51. 353.18 winning units. Quadpot: £16.10 to a £1 stake. Pool: £815.38. 37.29 winning units..
Owner Godolphin **Bred** Darley **Trained** Newmarket, Suffolk

FOCUS
This looked a cracking handicap beforehand, but to say Kirklees was in a different league to his rivals would be an understatement; he absolutely bolted up. This looks like form to follow.

NOTEBOOK
Kirklees(IRE) ◆, having travelled nicely throughout in about mid-division, took over early in the straight still moving with ease and ultimately looked value for about double the winning margin. Although it's often unwise to get carried away with wide-margin handicap winners at the Carnival, mainly due to a lack of unexposed runners, this was as impressive a performance as we've seen in a race like this so far this year. A Group 1 winner in Italy as a juvenile, he's always been very talented, but he made it to the track only twice in both in 2007 and 2008, suggesting he's had some problems. However, all his issues seem well and truly behind him now and it will be a major disappointment if he cannot make his mark in Group company again this year. Unfortunately, there are no such opportunities over this trip at the Carnival. (op 2-1)
Hattan(IRE) ◆ ran a good race under his 10lb claimer on his first start since leaving Clive Brittain after nearly five months off. Many from this yard have improved for a run this year and he'll be of interest when the stable jockey, Ahmed Ajtebi, takes over in the saddle.
Barbaricus(AUS) ◆ was too keen for his own good and proved absolutely no match whatsoever for the winner. He eventually weakened into third, but he is apparently a horse who takes a lot of racing and he can be expected to improve enough on this performance to win a similar race. (op 10-3)
Mr Brock(SAF) ◆, a multiple winner in Mauritius last year, ran with credit on his UAE debut after over four months off, keeping on well after not getting the best of trips early in the straight. It would be no surprise to see the excellent Mike De Kock place him to advantage. (op 8-1)
Once More Dubai(USA) ◆, a dual Listed winner in Italy, is much better than he showed as he was continually denied a clear run in the straight, although that's not to say he would have got anywhere near Kirklees. (op 12-1)
Oracle West(SAF) did not run badly and can do better again back over 1m4f. (op 14-1)
Docofthebay(IRE) can be excused this below-par effort as he was hampered against the inside rail after a couple of furlongs or so.

500 LINGFIELD (L-H)
Friday, February 13

OFFICIAL GOING: Standard
Wind: Light, against Weather: Fine but cloudy

528 RYE APPRENTICE (S) STKS 1m 4f (P)
1:45 (1:45) (Class 6) 4-Y-O+ **£2,047** (£604; £302) **Stalls** Low

Form				RPR
346	1		**Bridgewater Boys**[9] 393 8-9-10 71 (b) LukeMorris 2	71
			(P D Evans) *s.s and needed urging to come out of stalls: hld up in rr: prog over 3f out: rdn to chse ldr jst over 2f out: narrow ld fnl f: a doing enough* **2/1**[1]	
-332	2	nk	**Augustus John (IRE)**[14] 342 6-9-5 65 TolleyDean 11	66
			(S Parr) *hld up in rr: prog 1/2-way: led 3f out and kicked on: narrowly hdd 1f out: kpt on wl but a hld* **2/1**[1]	
60-3	3	3 1/4	**Turner's Touch**[14] 342 7-9-0 54 (b) JemmaMarshall[(5)] 5	60
			(G L Moore) *stdd s: hld up in last pair: stdy prog on outer fr 3f out: tried to cl on ldrs over 1f out and wnt 3rd ent fnl f: fin weakly* **9/1**	
2-20	4	1 1/2	**Poppy Red**[22] 248 4-8-6 51 (p) AndrewHeffernan[(5)] 1	53
			(C J Gray) *disp 2nd pl to over 7f out: trapped on inner 3f out: eased out and prog to chse ldng pair 2f out: cl enough over 1f out: sn btn* **25/1**	
06-6	5	2	**Competitor**[29] 171 8-9-5 50 (v) JackMitchell 8	55
			(J Akehurst) *disp 2nd pl to over 7f out: drvn over 4f out: stl chsng ldrs over 1f out: wknd fnl f* **16/1**	
04-6	6	3	**Shouldntbethere (IRE)**[28] 187 5-8-12 50 NBazeley[(7)] 6	50
			(Mrs P N Dutfield) *s.v.s: sn in tch in last pair: effrt over 2f out: sn outpcd: plugged on one pce* **33/1**	
-155	7	1 1/4	**Ben Bacchus (IRE)**[6] 448 7-9-3 53 KierenFox[(7)] 9	53
			(P W Hiatt) *in tch: drvn 4f out: stl in tch over 2f out: sn wknd* **17/2**[3]	
43-0	8	1 1/2	**Starstruck Peter (IRE)**[14] 346 5-9-2 52 (b) WilliamCarson[(3)] 3	46
			(S Curran) *t.k.h early: prog to press ldr over 7f out: led over 5f out to 3f out: wknd u.p 2f out* **6/1**[2]	
/6-0	9	15	**Tashkandi (IRE)**[7] 423 9-9-5 72 (b) RussellKennemore 7	22
			(Mrs S J Humphrey) *led to over 5f out: wknd u.p wl over 2f out: t.o* **33/1**	

0/0- **10** *49* **Stroppi Poppi**[276] 1266 5-8-7 40.............................. CharlotteHorsley(7) 4 —
(Norma Twomey) *stdd s and lft stalls v awkwardly: prog on outer to go prom after 4f: wknd 1/2-way: sn wl t.o* **100/1**

2m 33.35s (0.35) **Going Correction** +0.225s/f (Slow)
WFA 4 from 5yo+ 3lb **10** Ran SP% **118.1**
Speed ratings (Par 101): **107,106,104,103,102 100,99,98,88,55**
toteswinger: 1&2 £1.20, 1&3 £5.20, 2&3 £5.00. CSF £5.50 TOTE £3.20: £1.60, £1.10, £2 60; EX 6.90 Trifecta £21.90 Pool: £240.43 - 8.09 winning units..The winner was bought in for 4,400 guineas. Augustus John was claimed by Roy Brotherton for £6,000.
Owner J E Abbey **Bred** Southill Stud **Trained** Pandy, Monmouths
■ Stewards' Enquiry : N Bazeley caution: used whip when out of contention

FOCUS
An ordinary seller but the form looks sound enough rated around the in-form principals.

529 EASTBOURNE MEDIAN AUCTION MAIDEN STKS 1m 2f (P)
2:15 (2:16) (Class 6) 3-Y-O **£2,729** (£806; £403) **Stalls** Low

Form RPR

6-34 **1** **Diamond Twister (USA)**[9] 397 3-9-3 68.......................(t) LukeMorris 3 71
(J R Best) *t.k.h: hld up in 6th: suddenly u.p over 3f out: prog to go 2nd wl over 1f out: sustained effrt to ld last 100yds* **11/2**[2]

0-2 **2** *1 1/4* **Badge Of Honour**[27] 201 3-9-3 0...................................... GregFairley 8 68
(M Johnston) *sn led: gng strly over 2f out: rdn and nt qckn over 1f out: hdd and put hd in air last 100yds* **4/6**[1]

3 *1 3/4* **Stormy's Prelude** 3-8-12 0...................................... JimCrowley 5 60+
(P Winkworth) *hld up in last pair: prog on inner jst over 2f out: reminder over 1f out and ins fnl f: styd on promisingly to take 3rd nr fin* **25/1**

0 **4** *hd* **El Bravo**[13] 356 3-9-3 0...................................... GeorgeBaker 7 65
(G L Moore) *hld up in last pair: pushed along and prog over 2f out: rdn to chse ldng pair ins fnl f: kpt on but lost 3rd nr fin* **14/1**

06- **5** *2* **Bishop Rock (USA)**[124] 6665 3-9-3 0...................................... NCallan 6 61
(M H Tompkins) *cl up: trckd ldr after 3f: rdn over 2f out: lost 2nd wl over 1f out: sn wknd* **10/1**

60- **6** *1 1/4* **Broughton Beck (IRE)**[83] 7422 3-9-3 0.................. FrankieMcDonald 9 58
(R F Fisher) *racd wd: in tch: effrt and cl up 3f out: steadily wknd fnl 2f* **40/1**

4 **7** *1 1/4* **Gaselee (USA)**[31] 144 3-8-12 0...................................... DaneO'Neill 2 51
(Rae Guest) *cl up: rdn to chse ldng pair 3f out to over 2f out: steadily wknd fr over 1f out* **11/1**

8 *3/4* **Garter Knight** 3-9-3 0...................................... HayleyTurner 1 54
(M L W Bell) *trckd ldr 3f: styd cl up: shkn up 3f out: btn 2f out: wkng whn hung bdly rt ins fnl f* **8/1**[3]

0 **9** *2 1/2* **Milemilia (IRE)**[9] 386 3-8-12 0...................................... SteveDrowne 4 44
(H Morrison) *in tch: pushed along and dropped to last wl over 2f out and looked like tailing off: plugged on again fnl f* **66/1**

2m 8.03s (1.43) **Going Correction** +0.225s/f (Slow) **9** Ran SP% **118.4**
Speed ratings (Par 95): **103,102,100,100,98 97,96,96,94**
toteswinger: 1&2 £1.30, 1&3 £21.10, 2&3 £7.10. CSF £9.67 TOTE £5.70: £1.80, £1.02, £7.80; EX 12.80 Trifecta £53.20 Pool: £424.23 - 5.89 winning units..
Owner John Griffin Owen Mullen **Bred** Annabel Murphy & William F Murphy **Trained** Hucking, Kent

FOCUS
An ordinary maiden in which the winner came late to catch the favourite and the third tends to limit the form.

530 BRIGHTON (S) STKS 7f (P)
2:45 (2:45) (Class 6) 3-Y-O+ **£2,047** (£604; £302) **Stalls** Low

Form RPR

-124 **1** **Northern Desert (IRE)**[2] 495 10-10-0 70.....................(p) DaneO'Neill 7 75
(S Curran) *t.k.h early: hld up in 4th: smooth prog on outer 2f out: led jst over 1f out: rdn and sn wl in command* **2/1**[1]

0322 **2** *1 1/2* **Hawkspring (IRE)**[8] 403 3-8-11 65.......................(t) NCallan 2 66
(S Parr) *trckd ldr: rdn to ld 2f out: hdd jst over 1f out: sn outpcd* **11/4**[2]

6-60 **3** *3/4* **Geoffdaw**[5] 457 4-9-8 70.......................................(v) PaulDoe 1 63
(P D Evans) *cl up on inner: effrt 2f out: kpt on same pce u.p* **11/4**[2]

650- **4** *7* **Lucky Character**[69] 7581 4-9-8 45.......................(bt[1]) GregFairley 3 44
(N J Vaughan) *led to 2f out: sn wknd* **16/1**

-426 **5** *1 3/4* **It's A Mans World**[13] 356 3-8-6 67 ow1..................... PaulFitzsimons 4 35
(S Dow) *relucatnt to r and lft 10l: jst in tch after 3f: sn lft bhd by ldrs* **11/2**[3]

000- **6** *43* **Elevate Bambina**[103] 7148 3-7-9 40................. DanielleMcCreery(5) 6 —
(A Berry) *immediately pushed along: last after 3f and wkng u.p: hopelessly t.o* **40/1**

1m 26.37s (1.57) **Going Correction** +0.225s/f (Slow)
WFA 3 from 4yo+ 17lb **6** Ran SP% **110.4**
Speed ratings (Par 101): **100,98,97,89,87 38**
toteswinger: 1&2 £1.10, 1&3 £1.70, 2&3 £2.10. CSF £7.49 TOTE £3.80: £1.60, £1.80; EX 7.40.There was no bid for the winner. It's A Mans World was claimed by K. M. Prendergast for £6,000.
Owner L Power & Miss N Henton **Bred** J P Hardiman **Trained** Hatford, Oxon

FOCUS
A fair seller but the winner scored more due to the limitations of his rivals than anything.

531 LOUIE FRENCH 21ST BIRTHDAY H'CAP 7f (P)
3:20 (3:20) (Class 6) (0-60,60) 4-Y-O+ **£2,047** (£604; £302) **Stalls** Low

Form RPR

20 **1** **Bollywood Style**[16] 321 4-8-11 53...................................... NCallan 4 62+
(J R Best) *trckd ldrs: rdn 2f out: prog towards inner over 1f out: led last 75yds: readily* **8/1**

42-0 **2** *1/2* **Shaded Edge**[37] 71 5-8-13 55...................................... HayleyTurner 7 63
(D W P Arbuthnot) *t.k.h: mostly trckd ldr to 3f out: styd prom: effrt to chal ent fnl f: nt qckn last 100yds* **7/2**[1]

04-0 **3** *nk* **Manchestermaverick (USA)**[28] 194 4-9-2 58.........(vt[1]) SteveDrowne 8 65
(H Morrison) *led: kicked on over 1f out: hdd and one pce last 75yds* **15/2**[3]

000- **4** *1 1/2* **Free Tussy (ARG)**[88] 7359 5-9-4 60.....................(bt) GeorgeBaker 6 63+
(G L Moore) *hld up in last pair: stl there 2f out: rdn and prog over 1f out: styd on wl to take 4th nr fin: no ch* **16/1**

4432 **5** *hd* **Loyal Royal (IRE)**[9] 395 6-8-9 56.....................(b) JackDean(5) 14 59+
(J M Bradley) *tk fierce hold and sddle sn slipped: plld way through on wd outside to go 2nd 3f out: stl ch 1f out: wknd* **7/1**[2]

45-5 **6** *1* **Rydal (USA)**[16] 309 8-9-1 57.......................(v) FergusSweeney 9 57
(Miss Jo Crowley) *hld up in midfield on outer: effrt 2f out: kpt on same pce: n.d* **9/1**

00-4 **7** *3/4* **Stoic Leader (IRE)**[7] 427 9-9-4 60.................. FrankieMcDonald 12 58
(R F Fisher) *t.k.h early: trckd ldrs: rdn over 2f out: nt qckn and steadily lost pl fr over 1f out* **12/1**

1-20 **8** *shd* **Mr Chocolate Drop (IRE)**[22] 256 5-9-0 56..................(b) ShaneKelly 2 54
(Miss M E Rowland) *dwlt: t.k.h: hld up towards rr: drvn and no real prog fnl 2f* **14/1**

-533 **9** *1 1/4* **Torquemada (IRE)**[9] 395 8-8-11 53.....................(tp) PaulDoe 10 47
(M J Attwater) *dwlt: t.k.h and hld up in rr: effrt on outer wl over 1f out: limited rspnse and no real prog* **9/1**

-523 **10** *nk* **Liberty Valance (IRE)**[23] 234 4-9-3 59.....................(t) JamesDoyle 1 52
(S Kirk) *no room on inner over 5f and snatched up: a in rr after: shkn up and no prog over 1f out* **9/1**

60-0 **11** *3/4* **Rio L'Oren (IRE)**[16] 309 4-9-1 57.....................(b) LukeMorris 3 48
(N J Vaughan) *t.k.h early: hld up in midfield on inner: n.m.r briefly over 5f out: rdn and no prog wl over 1f out: wknd* **25/1**

60-0 **12** *3/4* **Quality Street**[16] 321 7-8-11 53.....................(p) JimCrowley 5 42
(P Butler) *pressed ldng pair on inner to 3f out: nt qckn wl over 1f out: wknd fnl f* **22/1**

4-00 **13** *2* **Eagle Nebula**[16] 309 5-9-2 58...................................... IanMongan 11 42
(B R Johnson) *stdd s fr wd draw: hld up in last pair: drvn and struggling fr 3f out* **20/1**

1m 27.21s (2.41) **Going Correction** +0.225s/f (Slow) **13** Ran SP% **120.8**
Speed ratings (Par 101): **95,94,94,92,92 91,90,90,88,88 87,86,84**
toteswinger: 1&2 £7.40, 1&3 £14.50, 2&3 £7.90. CSF £35.43 CT £226.13 TOTE £9.70: £2.70, £1.80, £3.10; EX 47.60 TRIFECTA Not won..
Owner Miss Sara Furnival **Bred** Baroness Bloodstock & Redmyre Bloodstock **Trained** Hucking, Kent

FOCUS
A moderate but competitive handicap with the placed horses to their recent best.
Loyal Royal(IRE) Official explanation: jockey said gelding ran too free

532 PEVENSEY H'CAP 1m (P)
3:55 (3:55) (Class 4) (0-85,85) 3-Y-O **£4,857** (£1,445; £722; £360) **Stalls** High

Form RPR

22-1 **1** **Tartan Gunna**[18] 298 3-8-9 73...................................... JoeFanning 2 84+
(M Johnston) *trckd ldr: wd bnd 2f out: led over 1f out: shkn up and sn drew clr* **8/13**[1]

013- **2** *4 1/2* **Alexander Gulch (USA)**[80] 7445 3-9-7 85.....................(p) NCallan 3 83
(K A Ryan) *led and racd wl away fr inner: wd bnd 2f out: hdd over 1f out: easily outpcd* **7/1**[3]

325- **3** *nk* **Rio Royale (IRE)**[72] 7538 3-8-13 77...................................... JimCrowley 1 74
(Mrs A J Perrett) *stdd s: t.k.h in last pair: effrt on inner to chal wl over 1f out: sn brushed aside* **10/1**

1-33 **4** *1 3/4* **Doncosaque (IRE)**[26] 209 3-9-5 83...................................... IanMongan 4 76+
(P Howling) *restrained s but stl plld hrd in last pair: stl keen over 2f out: rdn and no rspnse wl over 1f out* **5/2**[2]

1m 38.9s (0.70) **Going Correction** +0.225s/f (Slow) **4** Ran SP% **112.1**
Speed ratings (Par 99): **105,100,100,98**
CSF £5.75 TOTE £1.70; EX 4.10.
Owner Mrs I Bird **Bred** Cheveley Park Stud Ltd **Trained** Middleham Moor, N Yorks

FOCUS
An interesting little handicap with the placed horses both running to previous marks.
Doncosaque(IRE) Official explanation: jockey said colt ran too free

533 LITTLEHAMPTON H'CAP 6f (P)
4:30 (4:30) (Class 4) (0-80,78) 4-Y-O+ **£4,857** (£1,445; £722; £360) **Stalls** Low

Form RPR

43-6 **1** **Resplendent Alpha**[41] 24 5-9-4 78...................................... IanMongan 2 84
(P Howling) *hld up in 4th: effrt on outer over 1f out: led narrowly ent fnl f: bustled along and fnd enough* **13/2**

2-53 **2** *nk* **Forest Dane**[20] 281 9-8-11 71...................................... HayleyTurner 1 76
(Mrs N Smith) *trckd ldng pair: gng easily 2f out: narrow ld on inner over 1f out tl ent fnl f: kpt on wl but a jst hld* **4/1**[2]

3-51 **3** *nse* **Mogok Ruby**[26] 212 5-9-4 78...................................... LukeMorris 4 83
(L Montague Hall) *awkward s: hld up in last: effrt on inner over 1f out: styd on ins fnl f: jst hld* **4/1**[2]

-541 **4** *1* **Distinctly Game**[20] 281 7-9-3 77.....................(t) NCallan 5 79+
(K A Ryan) *tk fierce hold: trckd ldr: chal and upsides over 1f out tl folded tamely ins fnl f* **11/8**[1]

00-6 **5** *3 3/4* **El Dececy (USA)**[27] 204 5-9-4 78...................................... LiamJones 3 68
(S Parr) *led: set slow pce to 1/2-way: rdn 2f out: hdd & wknd over 1f out* **11/2**[3]

1m 13.36s (1.46) **Going Correction** +0.225s/f (Slow) **5** Ran SP% **110.8**
Speed ratings (Par 105): **99,98,98,97,92**
CSF £31.27 TOTE £6.30: £2.90, £2.60; EX 19.40.
Owner The Oh So Sharp Racing Partnership **Bred** Sunley Stud **Trained** Newmarket, Suffolk

FOCUS
A fair sprint handicap and certainly competitive, despite the small field. The first two are rated to their recent best.

534 HASTINGS H'CAP 1m 5f (P)
5:00 (5:00) (Class 6) (0-65,65) 4-Y-O+ **£2,047** (£604; £302) **Stalls** Low

Form RPR

00-3 **1** **Ardmaddy (IRE)**[26] 213 5-9-0 57.....................(b) FergusSweeney 9 62
(G L Moore) *t.k.h: hld up in 4th: effrt to press ldrs 2f out: drvn over 1f out: styd on wl to ld last strides* **12/1**

0-32 **2** *nk* **King's Majesty (IRE)**[3] 485 7-9-7 64...................................... NCallan 4 69
(A M Hales) *hld up in 5th in slowly run r: prog over 2f out: drvn to chal over 1f out: narrow ld jst ins fnl f: hdd last strides* **13/8**[1]

005- **3** *nk* **Captain Mainwaring**[21] 7149 4-8-10 57.....................(b[1]) JamesDoyle 10 61
(N P Littmoden) *trckd ldr: rdn to ld 2f out: hdd narrowly jst ins fnl f: kpt on but hld after* **20/1**

-051 **4** *hd* **William's Way**[14] 342 7-9-7 64...................................... GeorgeBaker 8 68
(I A Wood) *t.k.h: hld up in 6th in slowly run r: effrt over 2f out: nt qckn over 1f out: styd on wl fnl f: gaining at fin* **5/1**[2]

1-54 **5** *nk* **Zalkani (IRE)**[16] 320 9-9-3 60...................................... JerryO'Dwyer 7 65+
(J Pearce) *hld up in 7th in slowly run r: effrt over 2f out: clsng on ldrs whn nt clr run 1f out: trying again whn no room last 100yds* **7/1**[3]

3450 **6** *1 3/4* **Spume (IRE)**[6] 449 5-8-11 54.....................(t) TolleyDean 5 55
(S Parr) *t.k.h: hld up in 8th in slowly run r: effrt over 2f out: urged along over 1f out: kpt on but no realistic ch* **10/1**

20-6 **7** *hd* **Vinces**[16] 319 5-9-4 61...................................... HayleyTurner 3 61
(T D McCarthy) *led: set pedestrian pce to 3f out: hdd 2f out: sn outpcd* **8/1**

0-00 **8** *1* **Capitalise (IRE)**[15] 333 6-9-0 57...................................... DaneO'Neill 2 56
(Miss Gay Kelleway) *stdd s: hld up in last in slowly run r: effrt on outer 2f out: nt pce to threaten* **16/1**

The Form Book, Raceform Ltd, Compton, RG20 6NL

50-5 **9** 4 1/2 **Sand Repeal (IRE)**[15] [324] 7-9-3 **65**................ AmyBaker(5) 1 57
(Miss J Feilden) *trckd ldng pair tl rdn and wknd 3f out: sn bhd* **14/1**

2m 53.26s (7.26) **Going Correction** +0.225s/f (Slow)
WFA 4 from 5yo+ 4lb **9** Ran SP% **112.5**
Speed ratings (Par 101): **86,85,85,85,85 84,84,83,80**
toteswinger: 1&2 £5.30, 1&3 £20.30, 2&3 £13.10. CSF £30.92 CT £395.33 TOTE £13.60: £4.20, £1.50, £7.00; EX 41.40 Trifecta £328.80 Part won. Pool: £444.35 - 0.20 winning units..
Owner Blue Crocodile **Bred** Frank Dunne **Trained** Lower Beeding, W Sussex

FOCUS
There was a steady pace to this handicap and it turned into a relative burn-up inside the last three furlongs. It is hard to take the form too seriously with doubts about the third.
William's Way Official explanation: jockey said gelding ran too free
Zalkani(IRE) Official explanation: jockey said gelding was denied a clear run
T/Plt: £26.80 to a £1 stake. Pool: £62,742.89. 1,704.10 winning tickets. T/Qpdt: £50.50 to a £1 stake. Pool: £3,888.89. 56.88 winning tickets. JN

473 WOLVERHAMPTON (A.W) (L-H)

Friday, February 13

OFFICIAL GOING: Standard
Wind: Nil Weather: Cloudy

535 COME TO THE 80'S PARTY NIGHT TOMORROW H'CAP 5f 20y(P)

2:25 (2:26) (Class 6) (0-60,60) 4-Y-0+ **£2,047** (£604; £302) **Stalls** Low

Form RPR
-332 **1** **Monte Major (IRE)**[7] [431] 8-9-0 **56**................(v) DarrenWilliams 1 67
(D Shaw) *chsd ldrs: wnt 2nd wl over 1f out: led ent fnl f: r.o* **15/8**[1]
0-21 **2** 3/4 **The Geester**[15] [326] 5-9-3 **59**................(b) JimmyQuinn 2 67
(S R Bowring) *t.k.h: chsd ldr: hung rt 1f out: rdn and kpt on ins fnl f* **5/1**[3]
-036 **3** nk **Decider (USA)**[7] [431] 6-9-1 **60**................(b[1]) KevinGhunowa(3) 9 67
(R A Harris) *led: hung rt 3f out: edgd lft and hdd ent fnl f: rdn and nt qckn* **16/1**
-050 **4** 1 3/4 **Weetfromthechaff**[14] [353] 4-8-6 **48**................(v) ChrisCatlin 6 49
(R Hollinshead) *hld up in rr: hdwy fr over 1f out: nt rch ldrs* **25/1**
21-6 **5** 1 **Lithaam (IRE)**[29] [177] 5-9-1 **57**................(p) RobertWinston 10 54
(J M Bradley) *s.i.s: n.m.r briefly sn after s: sn hld up in tch: pushed along over 2f out: rdn and edgd lft 1f out: one pce* **16/1**
0-01 **6** 1/2 **Tyrannosaurus Rex (IRE)**[7] [431] 5-9-4 **60** 6ex........(v) PaulHanagan 13 56
(D Shaw) *towards rr: c wd st: hung lft fnl f: kpt on: nvr able to chal* **4/1**[2]
0-04 **7** 3/4 **Teen Ager (FR)**[21] [269] 5-9-2 **58**................ LPKeniry 3 51
(P Burgoyne) *s.i.s: towards rr: hdwy on ins 2f out: rdn over 1f out: no imp fnl f* **10/1**
46-5 **8** 1/2 **Spirit Of Coniston**[18] [294] 6-8-7 **56**................ PaulPickard(7) 4 47
(P T Midgley) *mid-div: pushed along over 2f out: btn wl over 1f out* **17/2**
00-6 **9** 5 **Fire Up The Band**[19] [291] 10-8-8 **55**................ SladeO'Hara(5) 8 28
(A Berry) *pushed along over 3f out: c wd st: a towards rr* **16/1**
000- **10** 1/2 **The Thrifty Bear**[134] [6411] 6-8-4 **46** oh1................(b) AndrewElliott 7 17
(C W Fairhurst) *prom tl rdn and wknd over 2f out* **125/1**

62.25 secs (-0.05) **Going Correction** +0.075s/f (Slow) **10** Ran SP% **113.4**
Speed ratings (Par 101): **103,101,101,98,96 96,94,94,86,85**
toteswinger: 1&2 £1.40, 1&3 £10.30, 2&3 £17.50. CSF £10.72 CT £112.92 TOTE £2.90: £1.10, £2.10, £5.40; EX 9.90.
Owner Derek Shaw **Bred** B Kennedy **Trained** Danethorpe, Notts

FOCUS
A couple of previous winners but an ordinary handicap on standard ground. The pace was sound but those racing prominently were favoured, although the form looks solid enough. The principals raced centre to far side in the straight.
Spirit Of Coniston Official explanation: jockey said gelding hung left-handed in straight

536 VAUXHALL INSIGNIA CAR OF YEAR 2009 CLAIMING STKS 1m 141y(P)

2:55 (2:56) (Class 5) 4-Y-0+ **£2,978** (£886; £442; £221) **Stalls** Low

Form RPR
01-0 **1** **Carnivore**[25] [218] 7-9-3 78................ TomEaves 4 78
(T D Barron) *hld up: hdwy on ins wl over 1f out: led jst ins fnl f: drvn out: jst hld on* **11/2**[3]
45-1 **2** shd **Dichoh**[28] [195] 6-9-1 81................(tp) FBranca 6 76
(F Sheridan) *hld up in tch: carried rt over 1f out: intimidated by rival jockey's whip ins fnl f: r.o and edgd lft towards fin: jst failed* **8/15**[1]
0-26 **3** 2 1/2 **Garden Party**[17] [307] 5-8-7 62................(b) ChrisCatlin 2 62
(R A Harris) *a.p: ev ch 1f out: no ex wl ins fnl f* **4/1**[2]
-620 **4** 1 1/2 **Ten Pole Tudor**[16] [309] 4-8-5 62 ow1................ KevinGhunowa(3) 7 60
(R A Harris) *sn w ldr: led wl over 1f out: sn hung rt: hdd jst ins fnl f: one pce* **12/1**
0-00 **5** 6 **Veronicas Way**[8] [405] 4-8-0 39................(v) JimmyQuinn 5 38
(G J Smith) *led: hdd wl over 1f out: wknd fnl f* **100/1**

1m 55.18s (4.68) **Going Correction** +0.075s/f (Slow) **5** Ran SP% **109.3**
Speed ratings (Par 103): **82,81,79,78,73**
toteswinger: 1&2 £2.20. CSF £8.91 TOTE £6.00: £1.80, £1.10; EX 13.10.
Owner The Meat Eaters **Bred** Lord Halifax **Trained** Maunby, N Yorks

FOCUS
An uncompetitive event in which the pace was steady and this bare form does not look entirely reliable.

537 ENJOY THE LUCKY 7 GROUP OFFER CLASSIFIED STKS 1m 1f 103y(P)

3:30 (3:30) (Class 7) 4-Y-0+ **£1,364** (£403; £201) **Stalls** Low

Form RPR
6-60 **1** **High Five Society**[29] [174] 5-9-0 45................(bt) JimmyQuinn 4 52
(S R Bowring) *a.p: led over 3f out: rdn over 2f out: clr wl over 1f out: sn rdn and wandered: drvn out* **7/2**[1]
535- **2** 1 3/4 **Kielty's Folly**[169] [5420] 5-9-0 45................ GrahamGibbons 8 48
(B P J Baugh) *hld up towards rr: hdwy 2f out: chsd wnr over 1f out: kpt on ins fnl f* **6/1**[2]
-000 **3** hd **Desert Lover (IRE)**[7] [420] 7-9-0 45................ RobertWinston 6 48
(R J Price) *hld up in mid-div: prog on ins 4f out: rdn over 2f out: kpt on ins fnl f* **16/1**
0-02 **4** 1/2 **Desert Lark**[9] [385] 4-9-0 45................ PaulMulrennan 11 47
(K A Ryan) *t.k.h early: hld up in mid-div: hdwy 4f out: rdn 2f out: one pce fnl f* **17/2**
2-66 **5** 3/4 **Jiminor Mack**[4] [469] 6-9-0 45................(p) RichardKingscote 10 45
(W J H Ratcliffe) *hld up towards rr: hdwy on outside over 2f out: c v wd st: rdn and kpt on same pce fnl f* **8/1**[3]
0-00 **6** 1 **Bobering**[22] [254] 9-9-0 44................ AndrewElliott 9 43
(B P J Baugh) *hld up in rr: c v wd st: rdn and hdwy over 1f out: sn edgd lft: nvr trbld ldrs* **22/1**
000- **7** 5 **Little Firecracker**[61] [7678] 4-9-0 45................ AdamKirby 2 32
(Miss M E Rowland) *s.v.s: in rr: hdwy wl over 1f out: wknd ins fnl f* **33/1**
8 5 **Tunder Bool (IRE)**[38] 4-9-0 45................(bt) FBranca 12 22
(F Sheridan) *hld up towards rr: stdy prog on outside over 5f out: wknd wl over 1f out* **7/2**[1]
0-00 **9** 1 **Carry On Cleo**[7] [427] 4-8-9 45................(v) SladeO'Hara(5) 7 20
(A Berry) *hld up in tch: pushed along over 3f out: chal over 2f out: wknd wl over 1f out* **25/1**
0020 **10** 9 **Spy Gun (USA)**[7] [427] 9-8-7 43................(p) JoshWall(7) 13 —
(T Wall) *t.k.h: w ldr tl over 3f out: wknd over 2f out* **40/1**
00-0 **11** 1 3/4 **Kai Mer (IRE)**[8] [399] 4-9-0 45................(p) TomEaves 3 —
(Miss J A Camacho) *pushed along 5f out: a towards rr* **22/1**
35-3 **12** 1 **Glamoroso (IRE)**[38] [61] 4-9-0 44................ MartinDwyer 5 —
(A Kirtley) *prom tl wknd over 3f out* **17/2**
-405 **13** 1 3/4 **Pembo**[8] [399] 4-8-11 45................(p) KevinGhunowa(3) 1 —
(R A Harris) *led: hdd over 3f out: sn wknd* **20/1**

2m 3.12s (1.42) **Going Correction** +0.075s/f (Slow) **13** Ran SP% **119.5**
Speed ratings (Par 97): **96,94,94,93,93 92,87,83,82,74 72,72,70**
toteswinger: 1&2 £5.40, 1&3 £12.90, 2&3 £48.80. CSF £21.57 TOTE £4.70: £1.90, £2.70, £4.70; EX 26.40.
Owner The High Five Partnership **Bred** A C M Spalding **Trained** Edwinstowe, Notts

FOCUS
A typically weak event in which the pace was sound throughout but the form is ordinary for the grade, although relatively sound.
Jiminor Mack Official explanation: jockey said mare was slowly away
Little Firecracker Official explanation: jockey said filly was reluctant to jump out of stalls

538 WOLVERHAMPTON-RACECOURSE.CO.UK H'CAP 7f 32y(P)

4:05 (4:06) (Class 3) (0-90,94) 4-Y-0+ **£9,462** (£2,832; £1,416; £708; £352) **Stalls** High

Form RPR
/06- **1** **Flowing Cape (IRE)**[258] [2624] 4-8-13 **84**................ MickyFenton 4 96+
(R Hollinshead) *chsd ldr: led over 1f out: rdn and edgd rt whn flashed tail ins fnl f: r.o* **5/2**[1]
-130 **2** 1 1/2 **Southandwest (IRE)**[9] [388] 5-9-4 **89**................ LPKeniry 5 94
(J S Moore) *hld up: hdwy 1f out: sn rdn and edgd lft: nt trble wnr* **17/2**
3641 **3** 1/2 **Capricorn Run (USA)**[9] [388] 6-9-9 **94** 6ex................(v) RobertWinston 1 98
(A J McCabe) *hld up in tch: rdn over 2f out: swtchd lft ins fnl f: kpt on* **6/1**
-443 **4** 2 1/4 **Mister New York (USA)**[20] [283] 4-8-13 **84**................(b) MartinDwyer 6 82
(Noel T Chance) *hld up in tch: rdn wl over 1f out: one pce fnl f* **3/1**[2]
30-2 **5** 1 1/4 **Methaaly (IRE)**[14] [351] 6-8-12 **83**................(e) TomEaves 7 77
(M Mullineaux) *t.k.h in rr: hdwy on ins 1f out: sn rdn: fdd wl ins fnl f* **10/1**
2264 **6** nk **Count Ceprano (IRE)**[6] [446] 5-8-7 **78**................ ChrisCatlin 3 71
(C R Dore) *hld up: hdwy over 4f out: rdn over 1f out: wknd wl ins fnl f* **9/2**[3]
6-15 **7** 3/4 **Indian Diva (IRE)**[21] [278] 4-8-11 **82**................(t) GrahamGibbons 2 73
(R Curtis) *led: rdn and hdd over 1f out: wknd ins fnl f* **14/1**

1m 29.16s (-0.44) **Going Correction** +0.075s/f (Slow) **7** Ran SP% **112.3**
Speed ratings (Par 107): **105,103,102,100,98 98,97**
toteswinger: 1&2 £3.00, 1&3 £5.00, 2&3 £12.50. CSF £23.20 TOTE £3.70: £2.00, £4.40; EX 28.30.
Owner John L Marriott **Bred** David Maher **Trained** Upper Longdon, Staffs

FOCUS
A useful handicap but one in which the pace was only fair and the form may not be as strong as it could be. The first three home came down the centre in the straight.

NOTEBOOK
Flowing Cape(IRE) ◆, the subject of support throughout the day, was always well placed and turned in his best effort on this all-weather debut and first outing since last May, despite edging to his right and flashing his tail in the closing stages. He's a lightly raced sort who should stay 1m and will reportedly return to this track for the Lincoln Trial in March. He is capable of further improvement. (op 3-1)
Southandwest(IRE) had not been at his best after hanging left at Kempton on his previous start and, although he showed a tendency to edge left under pressure again, he fared much better against a rival that had the run of the race. A stronger overall gallop would have suited but he is likely to remain vulnerable to progressive or well-handicapped sorts from this mark. (op 10-1 tchd 8-1)
Capricorn Run(USA), who returned to winning ways with the visor refitted at Kempton the previous week, ran creditably under his penalty, despite edging to his left under pressure. He's a useful sort on this surface, will be 3lb lower in future and should continue to give a good account in this type of event. (op 9-2 tchd 7-1)
Mister New York(USA), who is largely a consistent sort who again had the blinkers fitted, left the impression that the return to 1m or a stronger overall gallop at this trip would suit and was not disgraced, but has very little margin for error from his current mark. (op 4-1)
Methaaly(IRE) was up in the weights, in grade and in distance and failed to build on his reappearance run with the headgear again fitted. He was 17lb higher than his last victory at this track and the Handicapper looks in charge. (op 8-1 tchd 13-2)
Count Ceprano(IRE) had been running consistently well but proved a disappointment this time and may be feeling the effects of a fairly busy year. (op 11-2)

539 ARENA LEISURE CATERING H'CAP 5f 20y(P)

4:40 (4:41) (Class 4) (0-80,79) 4-Y-0+ **£5,180** (£1,541; £770; £384) **Stalls** Low

Form RPR
6222 **1** **Incomparable**[8] [400] 4-8-12 **72**................ RobertWinston 2 84
(A J McCabe) *mde all: rdn over 1f out: r.o wl* **5/2**[1]
1112 **2** 1 3/4 **Whiskey Creek**[7] [424] 4-8-12 **79** 6ex................(b) BMcHugh(7) 7 85
(C A Dwyer) *a.p: ev ch over 2f out: rdn over 1f out: kpt on ins fnl f* **5/1**
-302 **3** nk **Canadian Danehill (IRE)**[6] [451] 7-9-4 **78**................(p) ChrisCatlin 6 83
(R M H Cowell) *w wnr: rdn and kpt on fnl f* **7/2**[2]
2015 **4** hd **Gwilym (GER)**[6] [451] 6-8-8 **68**................ MartinDwyer 4 72
(D Haydn Jones) *hld up and bhd: pushed along over 2f out: nt clr run and swtchd lft wl over 1f out: sn rdn: hdwy ent fnl f: kpt on* **10/1**
-315 **5** nk **Drifting Gold**[15] [329] 5-8-11 **71**................(v) AdamKirby 5 74
(C G Cox) *hld up: rdn jst over 1f out: kpt on ins fnl f* **12/1**
0-40 **6** 3 **Know No Fear**[21] [270] 4-9-1 **75**................ DarrenWilliams 3 67
(D Shaw) *hld up in tch: rdn 2f out: wknd 1f out* **20/1**
5320 **7** 2 1/2 **Northern Empire (IRE)**[14] [351] 6-9-3 **77**................(t) PaulHanagan 1 60
(K A Ryan) *plld hrd in tch: rdn over 1f out: wknd fnl f* **4/1**[3]
550- **8** 1 **Not My Choice (IRE)**[79] [7456] 4-9-3 **77**................ JimmyQuinn 8 56
(S Parr) *a in rr* **18/1**

61.92 secs (-0.38) **Going Correction** +0.075s/f (Slow) **8** Ran SP% **114.3**
Speed ratings (Par 105): **106,103,102,102,101 97,93,91**
toteswinger: 1&2 £4.10, 1&3 £2.30, 2&3 £3.20. CSF £15.29 CT £43.02 TOTE £3.60: £1.20, £1.60, £1.50; EX 13.40.
Owner Paul J Dixon & Brian Morton **Bred** Mrs Yvette Dixon **Trained** Averham Park, Notts

FOCUS
Exposed performers but a fair handicap in which the pace was sound and another race on the card in which those held up were at a disadvantage. The form looks reasonable although is limited by the proximity of the fourth. The winner came down the centre.

Northern Empire(IRE) Official explanation: jockey said gelding hung right-handed

540 STAY AT THE WOLVERHAMPTON HOLIDAY INN H'CAP 5f 216y(P)
5:10 (5:13) (Class 6) (0-60,60) 4-Y-0+ £2,047 (£604; £302) Stalls Low

Form RPR
41-2 1 **Smirfys Systems**[18] 294 10-9-3 59 StephenDonohoe 5 71+
(E S McMahon) *a.p: rdn to ld 1f out: r.o* 11/10[1]
20-5 2 ½ **Westwood Dawn**[35] 108 4-8-12 54 (v) DarrenWilliams 6 61
(D Shaw) *n.m.r sn after s: hld up in mid-div: hdwy wl over 1f out: rdn and r.o ins fnl f* 9/1
0-05 3 1¼ **Imperial Djay (IRE)**[10] 381 4-8-13 55 JimmyQuinn 9 58
(G J Smith) *sn towards rr: rdn and hdwy over 1f out: nt clr run briefly ins fnl f: r.o to take 3rd post* 33/1
20-4 4 shd **Valentino Swing (IRE)**[34] 118 6-9-2 58 AdamKirby 2 61
(Miss T Spearing) *hld up in rr: hdwy fnl f: r.o* 9/2[2]
0-05 5 3 **Splash The Cash**[13] 355 4-8-9 58 (tp) AmyRyan(7) 8 51
(K A Ryan) *led: rdn and hdd 1f out: wknd wl ins fnl f* 9/1
00-0 6 nse **Minwir (IRE)**[28] 192 4-8-11 53 (v) RobertWinston 3 46
(M Quinn) *chsd ldr tl rdn wl over 1f out: wknd wl ins fnl f* 22/1
0230 7 ½ **Wiltshire (IRE)**[14] 352 7-9-2 58 (p) JamieMoriarty 7 49
(P T Midgley) *hld up in mid-div: hdwy wl over 1f out: sn hung lft: wknd ins fnl f* 20/1
00-6 8 1½ **Wynberg (IRE)**[4] 467 4-8-13 55 MickyFenton 4 42
(Stef Liddiard) *t.k.h in mid-div: pushed along 3f out: hdwy 1f out: wknd wl ins fnl f* 10/1
40-5 9 nse **Welcome Approach**[14] 352 6-9-2 58 ChrisCatlin 10 44
(J R Weymes) *hld up in rr: pushed along 3f out: nvr nr ldrs* 10/1
03-3 10 hd **Elkhorn**[14] 352 7-9-4 60 (v) TomEaves 11 46
(Miss J A Camacho) *hld up in rr: rdn 1f out: nvr nr ldrs* 13/2[3]
2-30 11 1½ **Fantasy Fighter (IRE)**[18] 292 4-8-5 54 BMcHugh(7) 1 35
(J J Quinn) *hld up in tch: rdn over 1f out: wknd ins fnl f* 7/1
0/00 12 3¾ **Gower**[7] 431 5-8-13 60 (p) ShaneFoley(5) 12 29
(R J Price) *prom: rdn over 2f out: wknd over 1f out* 25/1

1m 14.89s (-0.11) **Going Correction** +0.075s/f (Slow) **12 Ran SP% 145.7**
Speed ratings (Par 101): **103,102,100,100,96 96,95,93,93,93 91,86**
toteswinger: 1&2 £15.00, 1&3 £30.40, 2&3 £61.50. CSF £16.16 CT £290.24 TOTE £2.40: £1.10, £3.80, £10.20; EX 37.40 Place 6: £14.38, Place 5: £8.77..
Owner Mrs Dian Plant **Bred** Gerard Bingham **Trained** Lichfield, Staffs

FOCUS
An ordinary handicap and another win on the card for a prominent racer. The pace was sound but the form is ordinary and not that solid.
T/Jkpt: £10,938.60 to a £1 stake. Pool: £38,516.29. 2.50 winning tickets. T/Plt: £33.30 to a £1 stake. Pool: £81,109.04. 1,776.60 winning tickets. T/Qpdt: £20.10 to a £1 stake. Pool: £4,412.33. 162.10 winning tickets. KH

508 KEMPTON (A.W) (R-H)
Saturday, February 14

OFFICIAL GOING: Standard
Wind: Slight, against Weather: Sunny spells

541 BEATVICTOR.COM AT KEMPTON TODAY H'CAP 1m 3f (P)
2:30 (2:32) (Class 6) (0-52,52) 4-Y-0+ £2,047 (£604; £302) Stalls High

Form RPR
/0-5 1 **Tecktal (FR)**[19] 59 6-9-2 50 IanMongan 1 54
(P M Phelan) *hld up: rdn and hdwy over 1f out: kpt on u.p to ld fnl 100yds* 8/1
043- 2 nk **Near The Front**[109] 7050 4-8-9 52 KylieManser(7) 9 56
(Miss Gay Kelleway) *mid-div: rdn to ld 1f out: hdd fnl 100yds* 12/1
0-03 3 1 **Sir Haydn**[10] 385 9-8-12 49 oh1 ow3 (v) JackMitchell(3) 3 51
(J R Jenkins) *trckd ldrs: rdn and ev ch ent fnl f: no ex towards fin* 13/2[3]
0526 4 hd **Prince Of Medina**[3] 502 6-8-12 46 (t) RobertWinston 2 48+
(J R Best) *mid-div: effrt over 1f out: r.o ins fnl f: nvr nrr* 7/2[2]
-654 5 1 **Tabulate**[5] 469 6-9-2 50 JimmyQuinn 10 50
(P Howling) *chsd ldrs: led 2f out: rdn and hdd 1f out: fdd towards fin* 7/2[2]
6 1 **Ouste (FR)**[67] 5373 7-8-5 46 oh1 DanielBlackett(7) 4 44
(Mrs S Leech) *slowly away: in rr: mde sme late hdwy* 20/1
04-0 7 6 **Altos Reales**[15] 353 5-9-4 52 RichardKingscote 8 40
(J G Given) *led tl hdd over 2f out: sn wknd* 3/1[1]
00-6 8 nk **Darley Star**[29] 193 4-8-10 49 KevinGhunowa(3) 5 37
(R A Harris) *t.k.h: trckd ldr: led briefly over 2f out: wknd over 1f out* 16/1
-004 9 shd **Charlie Bear**[11] 377 8-8-12 46 oh1 (p) SamHitchcott 6 33
(Miss Z C Davison) *v.s.a: a bhd* 25/1

2m 22.66s (0.76) **Going Correction** +0.075s/f (Slow)
WFA 4 from 5yo+ 2lb **9 Ran SP% 116.1**
Speed ratings (Par 101): **100,99,99,98,98 97,93,92,92**
toteswinger: 1&2 £20.70, 1&3 £12.00, 2&3 £14.80. CSF £98.78 CT £663.10 TOTE £10.00: £3.10, £3.30, £2.40; EX 116.20.
Owner Tony Smith **Bred** Eric Puerari & Oceanic Bloodstock **Trained** Epsom, Surrey
■ Stewards' Enquiry : Jimmy Quinn two-day ban: careless riding (Mar 1-2)

FOCUS
A moderate handicap which produced a close finish and something of a turn-up, with none of the market leaders finishing in the places.
Tecktal(FR) Official explanation: trainer said, regarding apparent improvement in form, that the mare had taken a while to find its form after producing a foal, and had been sharpened up by a recent run over hurdles.

542 LOVE TO BET WITH VICTOR CHANDLER H'CAP 7f (P)
3:00 (3:03) (Class 6) (0-65,64) 3-Y-0 £2,047 (£604; £302) Stalls High

Form RPR
-324 1 **Imperial Skylight**[13] 366 3-9-4 61 TonyCulhane 6 66
(M R Channon) *trckd ldrs: wnt 2nd 2f out: kpt on u.p to ld 1/2f out* 4/1[3]
50-4 2 nk **Edgeworth (IRE)**[10] 394 3-9-5 62 GeorgeBaker 7 66
(B G Powell) *w.w hdwy over 1f out: rdn to press wnr fnl 1/2f* 3/1[2]
43-5 3 ½ **Itsher**[33] 135 3-8-7 55 WilliamCarson(5) 4 58
(S C Williams) *led edgd lft over 1f out and hung bdly so bef hdd 1/2f out* 6/1
01-6 4 1¾ **Trusted Venture (USA)**[22] 267 3-9-3 60 RobertWinston 3 58
(J R Best) *trckd ldr to 2f out: one pce fnl f* 8/1
1 5 2 **Alexander Family (IRE)**[26] 214 3-9-7 64 LPKeniry 5 57
(E F Vaughan) *stdd s and t.k.h in rr: tk clsr order over 2f out but sn one pce* 11/4[1]
0-06 6 1¼ **Pepin (IRE)**[10] 390 3-8-2 45 (b) FrankieMcDonald 2 34
(D Haydn Jones) *prom on outside tl rdn over 2f out: wknd over 1f out* 20/1
3544 7 1¼ **Deckchair**[15] 348 3-9-0 57 (v) LiamJones 1 43
(H J Collingridge) *c over to ins fr wd draw s: a bhd* 15/2

1m 26.87s (0.87) **Going Correction** +0.075s/f (Slow) **7 Ran SP% 113.6**
Speed ratings (Par 95): **98,97,97,95,92 91,89**
toteswinger: 1&2 £2.70, 1&3 £3.90, 2&3 £4.40. CSF £16.18 TOTE £5.30: £1.90, £1.60; EX 12.90.
Owner Peter Taplin **Bred** Peter Taplin **Trained** West Ilsley, Berks

FOCUS
A modest handicap for three-year-olds which produced another good finish.
Alexander Family(IRE) Official explanation: jockey said filly ran too free
Pepin(IRE) Official explanation: jockey said gelding hung left throughout

543 LOVE TO BET AT VICTORCHANDLER.COM H'CAP 6f (P)
3:30 (3:32) (Class 4) (0-85,82) 4-Y-0+ £4,857 (£1,445) Stalls High

Form RPR
54-2 1 **Caprio (IRE)**[37] 94 4-8-8 72 RichardKingscote 1 79
(Tom Dascombe) *mde all: shkn up over 1f out: r.o wl* 4/11[1]
130- 2 3½ **Artistic License (IRE)**[124] 6699 4-9-4 82 TonyCulhane 2 78
(M R Channon) *no more than 2 l bhd wnr tl outpcd over 1f out* 13/8[2]

1m 14.11s (1.01) **Going Correction** +0.075s/f (Slow) **2 Ran SP% 111.4**
Speed ratings (Par 105): **96,91**
toteswinger: 1&2 £3.00, 1&3 £1.80, 2&3 £3.00. TOTE £1.40.
Owner M Khan X2 **Bred** P Rabbitte **Trained** Lambourn, Berks

FOCUS
A match for this fair handicap after the likely favourite was withdrawn.

544 VICTOR CHANDLER H'CAP 1m (P)
4:05 (4:06) (Class 4) (0-85,84) 4-Y-0+ £4,857 (£1,445; £722; £360) Stalls High

Form RPR
01 1 **Tous Les Deux**[10] 398 6-8-9 75 ShaneKelly 2 83+
(G L Moore) *in tch: hdwy 2f out: led on bit jst ins fnl f: pushed out* 9/1
42-4 2 hd **Saltagioo (ITY)**[29] 199 5-9-4 84 JohnEgan 7 92
(M Botti) *trckd ldrs: rdn and pressed wnr thrght fnl f but a jst hld* 9/2[3]
4-25 3 1¼ **Ocean Legend (IRE)**[17] 318 4-8-8 79 AmyBaker(5) 5 84
(Miss J Feilden) *trckd ldr: led over 2f out: rdn and hdd jst ins fnl f and sn lost 2nd* 11/4[1]
-423 4 3½ **Wavertree Warrior (IRE)**[10] 398 7-8-7 73 (b) RichardKingscote 1 70
(N P Littmoden) *sn led: hdd over 2f out: wknd appr fnl f* 7/1
0-24 5 hd **Star Strider**[10] 398 5-8-7 73 MartinDwyer 6 70
(Miss Gay Kelleway) *t.k.h: hld up: rdn over 2f out: no hdwy fr over 1f out* 6/1
1-62 6 ¾ **Millfield (IRE)**[6] 457 6-8-7 73 JimmyQuinn 4 68
(P R Chamings) *v.s.a: t.k.h: hld up: hdwy over 4f out: rdn over 2f out: one pce after* 7/2[2]
04-5 7 2¼ **Magnitude**[14] 357 4-9-1 81 ow1 GeorgeBaker 3 71
(G L Moore) *mid-div: rdn over 2f out: wknd over 1f out* 8/1

1m 39.53s (-0.27) **Going Correction** +0.075s/f (Slow) **7 Ran SP% 115.0**
Speed ratings (Par 105): **104,103,102,99,98 98,95**
toteswinger: 1&2 £6.20, 1&3 £4.00, 2&3 £3.20. CSF £49.18 TOTE £7.00: £2.80, £2.80; EX 45.00.
Owner A Grinter **Bred** G And Mrs Middlebrook **Trained** Lower Beeding, W Sussex

FOCUS
Another decent handicap but quite a tight betting heat with a couple at the head of the market backed and one notable drifter.
Millfield(IRE) Official explanation: jockey said gelding ran too free

545 VICTOR CHANDLER £50 FREE BET CLAIMING STKS 1m (P)
4:40 (4:41) (Class 5) 4-Y-0+ £2,729 (£806; £403) Stalls High

Form RPR
44-1 1 **All In The Red (IRE)**[2] 515 4-8-9 66 (p) JimmyQuinn 7 68
(B N Pollock) *trckd ldrs: led wl over 1f out: hdd briefly ins fnl f: rallied to ld again post* 9/4[1]
-165 2 nse **Takitwo**[5] 471 6-8-6 57 SimonWhitworth 6 65
(P D Cundell) *hld up in rr: hdwy to go 2nd over 1f out: led briefly ins fnl f: hdd cl home* 12/1
26-3 3 3½ **Ede's Dot Com (IRE)**[42] 28 5-8-11 62 IanMongan 4 62
(P M Phelan) *hld up: hdwy over 1f out: styd on to go 3rd ins fnl f: no ch w first 2* 9/2[2]
060- 4 6 **Wrighty Almighty (IRE)**[70] 7580 7-8-13 65 LPKeniry 2 50
(P R Chamings) *trckd ldr: led 3f out: hdd wl over 1f out: wknd appr fnl f* 10/1
-506 5 6 **Bridge Of Fermoy (IRE)**[14] 355 4-8-8 59 (bt) MartinDwyer 5 31
(Miss Gay Kelleway) *trckd ldrs tl wknd over 1f out* 11/2[3]
00-0 6 18 **Last Of The Line**[4] 489 4-8-1 66 (p) AmyBaker(5) 1 —
(B N Pollock) *led narrowly tl hdd 3f out: wknd qckly sn after* 14/1

1m 39.56s (-0.24) **Going Correction** +0.075s/f (Slow) **6 Ran SP% 87.8**
Speed ratings (Par 103): **104,103,100,94,88 70**
toteswinger: 1&2 £3.00, 1&3 £1.80, 2&3 £3.00. CSF £16.74 TOTE £2.50: £1.10, £5.50; EX 16.40.
Owner Holmby Hoofbeats **Bred** John McEnery **Trained** Medbourne, Leics
■ Red Rudy was withdrawn after rearing in the stalls. Rule 4 applies, deduct 25p in £ from all bets.

FOCUS
A tight little claimer run only marginally slower than the previous handicap and producing a desperate finish. The second favourite Red Rudy was withdrawn after getting upset and rearing up in the stalls.

546 VICTOR CHANDLER FINANCIALS H'CAP 1m 4f (P)
5:10 (5:13) (Class 6) (0-60,60) 4-Y-0+ £2,047 (£604; £302) Stalls Centre

Form RPR
0-51 1 **Prince Charlemagne (IRE)**[7] 444 6-9-2 52 GeorgeBaker 9 63
(G L Moore) *hld up in tch: hdwy 3f out: led wl over 1f out: rdn and hld on wl whn chal fnl f* 13/8[1]
4-13 2 nk **Carlton Scroop (FR)**[15] 346 6-9-5 55 (b) LiamJones 8 65
(J Jay) *mid-div: hdwy on ins to go 2nd wl over 1f out: pressed wnr fnl f but a jst hld* 9/1
640- 3 4 **Winning Show**[27] 6364 5-9-4 54 LPKeniry 10 58+
(C Gordon) *in rr: hdwy wl over 1f out: wnt 3rd ins fnl f but no ch w first 2* 20/1
400- 4 ¾ **Cape Of Luck (IRE)**[82] 7440 6-9-7 57 IanMongan 1 60
(P M Phelan) *in rr: hdwy over 1f out: nvr nrr* 11/1
400- 5 1 **Al Azy (IRE)**[246] 3004 4-9-7 60 JimmyQuinn 7 61
(D M Simcock) *prom: rdn 2f out: one pce after* 11/2[2]
-031 6 nk **Itsawindup**[5] 469 5-9-1 51 6ex (t) GregFairley 4 52
(Miss Sheena West) *led for 2f: led again over 2f out: hdd wl over 1f out: wknd appr fnl f* 6/1[3]

-313 **7** 1 1/4 **Amwell Brave**[7] 448 8-9-2 52 SimonWhitworth 6 51
(J R Jenkins) *stdd s: in rr: effrt over 1f out: nvr on terms* **7/1**

0-53 **8** 5 **Ashmolian (IRE)**[11] 378 6-8-9 45 SamHitchcott 2 36
(Miss Z C Davison) *led after 2f: hdd over 2f out: wknd over 1f out* **16/1**

0-56 **9** 1 3/4 **Japura (USA)**[7] 448 5-8-13 56 (p) LanceBetts[(7)] 5 44
(T J Pitt) *trckd ldrs: rdn over 2f out: sn wknd* **12/1**

2m 34.87s (0.37) **Going Correction** +0.075s/f (Slow)
WFA 4 from 5yo+ 3lb **9** Ran SP% **116.9**
Speed ratings (Par 101): **101,100,98,97,96 96,95,92,91**
toteswinger: 1&2 £3.90, 1&3 £11.90, 2&3 £24.20. CSF £17.61 CT £218.65 TOTE £2.30: £1.10, £2.10, £8.80; EX 12.30 Place 6: £219.05 Place 5: £44.02 .
Owner A Grinter **Bred** Michael O'Mahony **Trained** Lower Beeding, W Sussex

FOCUS
An open handicap and an interesting betting heat.
T/Plt: £140.40 to a £1 stake. Pool: £34,613.09. 179.95 winning tickets. T/Qpdt: £9.40 to a £1 stake. Pool: £1,983.80. 155.80 winning tickets. JS

528 LINGFIELD (L-H)
Saturday, February 14

OFFICIAL GOING: Standard
Wind: nil Weather: overcast

547 CHESTNUT CLAIMING STKS 1m (P)
1:25 (1:25) (Class 6) 3-Y-O **£1,978** (£584; £292) **Stalls** High

Form RPR

34-0 **1** **Bartica (IRE)**[10] 397 3-9-0 65 (b[1]) DaneO'Neill 3 67
(R Hannon) *sn pushed up to ld: mde virtually all: rdn and hung lft fr 2f out: styd on wl* **5/2[2]**

001 **2** 1 1/4 **Whotsit (IRE)**[7] 441 3-8-7 63 (b) AndrewElliott 2 57
(Miss Amy Weaver) *chsd wnr for 1f: in tch after: rdn over 2f out: chsd wnr again over 1f out: kpt on u.p but nt pce to rch wnr* **15/2[3]**

2-11 **3** 1 1/4 **Double Act**[24] 231 3-9-8 80 (t) ShaneKelly 1 69
(Evan Williams) *hld up in last pair: plld out and effrt over 1f out: rdn and styd on fnl f: no pce to rch ldrs* **5/6[1]**

0P-4 **4** 1 3/4 **Crown Affair (IRE)**[23] 251 3-9-1 0 SimonWhitworth 4 58
(J W Hills) *chsd wnr after 1f: rdn over 2f out: outpcd over 1f out: one pce fnl f* **22/1**

3 **5** 1 1/2 **Michelle (IRE)**[7] 441 3-8-3 0 NickyMackay 5 43
(P Butler) *hld up in tch in rr: effrt on inner and rdn 2f out: no imp* **11/1**

1m 41.15s (2.95) **Going Correction** +0.025s/f (Slow) **5** Ran SP% **107.6**
Speed ratings (Par 95): **86,84,83,81,80**
toteswinger: 1&2 £7.60, 1&3 £1.10, 2&3 £7.10. CSF £18.71 TOTE £2.60: £1.50, £2.70; EX 18.50.
Owner Jim McCarthy **Bred** John And Eva Peet **Trained** East Everleigh, Wilts

FOCUS
A weak claimer and with only five runners the pace was inevitably sedate, resulting in a time more than a second slower than the maiden 35 minutes later. The favourite disappointed and there are doubts about the solidity of the form.

548 MICHAEL O'DONOVAN 10TH ANNIVERSARY MEMORIAL MAIDEN STKS 1m (P)
2:00 (2:00) (Class 5) 3-Y-O **£2,729** (£806; £403) **Stalls** High

Form RPR

233- **1** **Royal Executioner (USA)**[175] 5274 3-9-3 79 FergusSweeney 2 78+
(D M Simcock) *t.k.h: trckd ldrs: wnt 2nd wl over 1f out: rdn and qcknd to ld over 1f out: clr fnl f: comf* **10/11[1]**

2 1 3/4 **Sulution** 3-9-3 0 NickyMackay 3 74+
(M Botti) *s.i.s: t.k.h: hld up wl in tch: hdwy over 1f out: r.o wl fnl f: wnt 2nd wl ins fnl f: nt rch wnr* **14/1**

2-32 **3** 1 1/4 **Head Down**[17] 313 3-9-3 75 DaneO'Neill 4 71
(R Hannon) *led at stdy gallop: rdn and qcknd jst over 2f out: hdd over 1f out: no ch w wnr fnl f: lost 2nd wl ins fnl f* **4/1[2]**

4 **4** 1 3/4 **Harty Boy (USA)**[10] 386 3-9-3 0 HayleyTurner 6 67
(M L W Bell) *pressed ldr: rdn and unable qck jst over 2f out wknd over 1f out* **5/1[3]**

4-6 **5** 1 1/2 **Green Dynasty (IRE)**[21] 280 3-9-3 0 GregFairley 7 64
(M Johnston) *chsd ldrs: rdn and struggling jst over 2f out: wknd over 1f out* **7/1**

4-0 **6** 1 1/2 **Dead Cat Bounce (IRE)**[21] 280 3-9-3 0 JerryO'Dwyer 5 60
(J Pearce) *hld up in tch on outer: effrt to chse ldrs and rdn over 2f out: wknd over 1f out* **33/1**

0-0 **7** 7 **Arabian Silk (IRE)**[28] 201 3-8-5 0 JosephineBruning[(7)] 1 39
(D M Simcock) *stdd s: hld up in tch in rr: rdn and lost tch qckly wl over 1f out* **66/1**

1m 39.97s (1.77) **Going Correction** +0.025s/f (Slow) **7** Ran SP% **112.7**
Speed ratings (Par 97): **92,90,89,87,85 84,77**
toteswinger: 1&2 £10.70, 1&3 £8.00, 2&3 £37.60. CSF £15.54 TOTE £1.60: £1.10, £5.70; EX 19.60.
Owner DXB Bloodstock Ltd **Bred** Hot Silks Racing Stable Llc **Trained** Newmarket, Suffolk

FOCUS
Just like the first race this, in effect, turned into a sprint from the 2f pole. The winner set a fair standard but it is doubtful whether he had to improve. The fourth and fifth look the best guides.

549 BETDAQ THE BETTING EXCHANGE H'CAP 1m 4f (P)
2:35 (2:35) (Class 4) (0-85,85) 4-Y-O+ **£4,727** (£1,406; £702; £351) **Stalls** Low

Form RPR

26-0 **1** **War Of The Roses (IRE)**[14] 360 6-9-3 81 TomEaves 3 90+
(R Brotherton) *hld up in tch in midfield: hdwy gng wl over 1f out: swtchd rt ins fnl f: qcknd to ld fnl 50yds: pushed out* **14/1**

33-6 **2** 1/2 **Action Impact (ARG)**[14] 361 5-8-10 74 ow1 PatDobbs 12 81
(G L Moore) *hld up in tch: hdwy over 3f out: drvn and effrt on outer wl over 1f out: pressed ldrs ins fnl f: wnt 2nd towards fin: kpt on* **12/1**

00-5 **3** 1/2 **Wild Desert (FR)**[16] 330 4-8-12 79 StephenDonohoe 8 85
(Ian Williams) *t.k.h: chsd ldr: rdn to ld wl over 1f out: drvn over 1f out: hdd and no ex fnl 50yds* **25/1**

/-12 **4** 3/4 **American Spin**[8] 428 5-8-13 77 AdamKirby 1 82
(L A Dace) *t.k.h: chsd ldng pair: rdn and effrt 2f out: ev ch ins fnl f: unable qck fnl 75yds* **4/1[2]**

32-1 **5** nse **Scarab (IRE)**[31] 156 4-9-1 82 GregFairley 4 87
(M Johnston) *t.k.h: chsd ldrs: rdn 2f out: drvn and ev ch briefly ins fnl f: nt qckn fnl 75yds* **4/1[2]**

304- **6** 1/2 **Encircled**[77] 7491 5-9-7 85 HayleyTurner 6 89
(J R Jenkins) *stdd after s: hld up in rr: rdn and effrt on inner over 1f out: r.o ins fnl f: nt rch ldrs* **12/1**

2 **7** 1 **Horseshoe Reef (AUS)**[22] 271 6-8-13 77 ChrisCatlin 5 80
(J R Gask) *led: rdn and hdd wl over 1f out: stl v ch under wknd fnl 75yds* **7/2[1]**

64-4 **8** nk **Aypeeyes (IRE)**[38] 82 5-9-1 79 (v) JimCrowley 10 81
(A King) *in tch: drvn and effrt jst over 2f out: kpt on same pce u.p fnl f* **14/1**

654- **9** nk **Sam Lord**[71] 7558 5-9-4 82 DaneO'Neill 2 84+
(A King) *hld up in midfield on inner: nt clr run fr wl over 1f out: nvr able to chal: eased towards fin* **9/1[3]**

10-0 **10** nk **Cold Turkey**[22] 271 9-8-11 82 JemmaMarshall[(7)] 11 83
(G L Moore) *hld up towards rr: rdn wl over 1f out: kpt on but nvr pce to chal* **33/1**

/00- **11** nk **Ameeq (USA)**[65] 6243 7-8-10 74 (b[1]) SteveDrowne 9 75
(G L Moore) *hld up towards rr: rdn over 2f out: nvr trbld ldrs* **25/1**

12 nk **Weststern (GER)**[32] 6-8-11 75 FergusSweeney 7 75
(G L Moore) *t.k.h: stdd after s: hld up in tch in last pl: rdn and shortlived effrt on outer wl over 2f out: nvr trbld ldrs* **25/1**

2m 32.34s (-0.66) **Going Correction** +0.025s/f (Slow)
WFA 4 from 5yo+ 3lb **12** Ran SP% **115.4**
Speed ratings (Par 105): **103,102,102,101,101 101,100,100,100,100 100,99**
toteswinger: 1&2 £12.80, 1&3 £7.10, 2&3 £4.20. CSF £158.94 CT £4099.50 TOTE £9.60: £3.10, £4.40, £7.00; EX 77.50 TRIFECTA Not won..
Owner P S J Croft **Bred** Mrs Jane Bailey **Trained** Elmley Castle, Worcs

FOCUS
A competitive handicap run at an even gallop and there were any number still in with a chance as the field entered the final furlong. There was a bunch finish and the form may not prove too reliable.
Sam Lord Official explanation: jockey said gelding was denied a clear run

550 BET FA CUP - BETDAQ H'CAP 1m 2f (P)
3:05 (3:07) (Class 4) (0-85,84) 4-Y-O+ **£4,727** (£1,406; £702; £351) **Stalls** Low

Form RPR

13P- **1** **King Olav (UAE)**[71] 6582 4-9-5 84 LukeMorris 9 93
(A W Carroll) *chsd clr ldr after 1f: rdn 4f out: clsd over 3f out: rdn to ld wl over 1f out: hrd pressed ins fnl f: styd on wl to assert towards fin* **12/1**

05-1 **2** 1 1/4 **Basra (IRE)**[31] 163 6-9-4 82 FergusSweeney 7 88
(Miss Jo Crowley) *stdd after s: t.k.h: hld up in last pl: hdwy over 2f out: swtchd lft and effrt over 1f out: pressed wnr ins fnl f: no ex towards fin* **5/1[3]**

-055 **3** nse **Man Of Gwent (UAE)**[10] 392 5-8-8 72 PaulDoe 5 78
(P D Evans) *t.k.h: hld up in midfield: rdn and effrt over 2f out: drvn over 1f out: chsd ldng pair fnl 100yds: kpt on* **7/2[1]**

1-11 **4** 1 **Folio (IRE)**[14] 361 9-9-2 80 ChrisCatlin 8 84
(W J Musson) *led for 1f: chsd ldrs after: 3rd and gng wl 2f out: drvn ent fnl f: unable qck and one pce after* **9/2[2]**

00-0 **5** hd **Alpes Maritimes**[22] 271 5-9-0 78 (p) PatDobbs 4 82
(G L Moore) *t.k.h: hld up in tch in main gp: rdn jst over 2f out: disp 2nd ent fnl f: one pce u.p fnl f* **10/1**

411- **6** 1/2 **Risque Heights**[56] 7742 5-8-11 75 DaneO'Neill 6 78
(J R Boyle) *s.i.s: t.k.h: hld up towards rr: hdwy over 2f out: c wd and rdn wl over 1f out: no imp tl styd on ins fnl f: nt pce to rch ldrs* **5/1[3]**

00-2 **7** 4 **Mataram (USA)**[29] 195 6-8-12 76 SteveDrowne 10 71
(W Jarvis) *t.k.h: hld up in midfield: rdn and unable qck jst over 2f out: n.d fr over 1f out* **5/1[3]**

00-0 **8** 2 1/4 **Allanit (GER)**[31] 156 5-9-2 80 TPQueally 11 70
(B J Curley) *s.i.s: dashed up to ld after 1f: sn clr: hung rt and hdd wl over 1f out: sn wknd* **20/1**

614- **9** 7 **Andaman Sunset**[131] 6537 4-8-10 75 TolleyDean 3 51
(J L Spearing) *hld up in rr: dropped to last wl over 2f out: sn lost tch* **16/1**

2m 6.37s (-0.23) **Going Correction** +0.025s/f (Slow)
WFA 4 from 5yo+ 1lb **9** Ran SP% **117.8**
Speed ratings (Par 105): **101,100,99,99,99 98,95,93,88**
toteswinger: 1&2 £2.10, 1&3 £2.40, 2&3 £4.60. CSF £72.34 CT £260.02 TOTE £12.90: £2.90, £1.70, £1.90; EX 97.10 TRIFECTA Not won..
Owner Cover Point Racing **Bred** Darley **Trained** Cropthorne, Worcs

FOCUS
Although Allanit went off like a scalded cat, the rest were content to let him go, and the main group didn't go a great gallop, so many were in with a chance early in the straight as the leader came back to them. The form seems sound and there should be more to come from the winner.

551 BEECH H'CAP 1m (P)
3:35 (3:35) (Class 2) (0-100,99) 4-Y-O+ **£11,527** (£3,430; £1,714; £856) **Stalls** High

Form RPR

11-2 **1** **Titan Triumph**[28] 206 5-8-10 91 (t) JimCrowley 7 101+
(W J Knight) *hld up in last pl: c wd and hdwy over 1f out: drvn to ld ins fnl f: r.o wl: drvn out* **2/1[1]**

3-22 **2** 1 1/4 **Majuro (IRE)**[25] 225 5-9-0 95 PaulHanagan 2 101
(K A Ryan) *led: rdn jst over 2f out: drvn and hdd ins fnl f: nt pce of wnr: kpt on* **4/1[2]**

0540 **3** 1/2 **Internationaldebut (IRE)**[7] 445 4-8-13 94 AdamKirby 6 99
(S Parr) *hld up in tch in last pair: c wd and sltly outpcd over 1f out: rdn and r.o fnl f: nt pce to rch ldng pair* **4/1[2]**

5-10 **4** 2 **Orchard Supreme**[6] 458 6-9-4 99 DaneO'Neill 5 99
(R Hannon) *stdd s: hld p in tch: rdn and effrt on inner 2f out: no imp fnl f* **17/2**

-212 **5** nse **Red Somerset (USA)**[16] 331 6-8-9 95 MCGeran[(5)] 3 95
(R J Hodges) *chsd ldng pair: rdn to dispute 2nd jst over 2f out: wknd jst ins fnl f* **5/1[3]**

64-5 **6** nse **Opus Maximus (IRE)**[10] 388 4-8-6 87 GregFairley 4 87
(M Johnston) *chsd ldr: rdn jst over 2f out: wknd u.p 1f out* **7/1**

1m 35.33s (-2.87) **Going Correction** +0.025s/f (Slow) course record **6** Ran SP% **113.0**
Speed ratings (Par 109): **115,113,113,111,111 111**
toteswinger: 1&2 £2.10, 1&3 £2.40, 2&3 £4.60. CSF £10.37 TOTE £3.10: £1.60, £2.00; EX 10.70.
Owner Canisbay Bloodstock **Bred** Hesmonds Stud Ltd **Trained** Patching, W Sussex

FOCUS
A decent little handicap run at a sound pace and solid form, with the runner-up the best guide.

NOTEBOOK
Titan Triumph once again displayed the kind of quickening speed that had seen him win four of his last five starts and climb 21lb in the handicap. A strong gallop in a smallish field like this would have been an ideal scenario for him. The progressive 5yo cruised round at the back of the field before moving through stylishly to throw down his challenge, then quickened away fairly comfortably in the final furlong. He is proving tough for the handicapper to get to grips with but, although it has its risks, his run style is so well suited to racing at this venue and he is proving a real star for William Knight. He will apparently now be given a break before being aimed at the Lincoln, but connections stressed that he would only take his chance if ground conditions were good or better. (tchd 9-4 and 5-2 in places)

Majuro(IRE), reverting to Polytrack off a 3lb higher mark, was responsible for the sound pace and kept on well to hold on to second. (op 7-2)

Internationaldebut(IRE), back down in trip, didn't pick up when first asked but stayed on quite well in the closing stages. (op 13-2)

Orchard Supreme had disappointingly little to give at the business end of the contest but got the best of a three-way photo for fourth. (op 10-1 tchd 8-1)

552 BET SIX NATIONS RUGBY - BETDAQ MAIDEN STKS — 6f (P)

4:10 (4:10) (Class 5) 3-Y-O+ £2,729 (£806; £403) Stalls Low

Form / RPR

5343 1 **Quick Single (USA)**[3] 498 3-8-11 57 (v1) AdamKirby 8 — 65
(P S McEntee) *chsd ldrs: rdn to chse ldr 2f out: drvn to ld 1f out: drew clr fnl 100yds: drvn out* 4/1[3]

3 2 2 1/2 **Saints Bay (IRE)**[24] 230 3-8-6 0 ChrisCatlin 9 — 52
(R Hannon) *dwlt: sn chsng ldrs: rdn 2f out: chsd wnr jst ins fnl f: nt pce of wnr fnl 100yds* 11/4[2]

-04 3 3 1/4 **Thoosa**[14] 358 3-8-6 0 LukeMorris 1 — 42
(P S McEntee) *hung rt thrght: sn rdn up to ld: rdn wl over 2f out: hdd 1f out: sn wknd: hung rt but hld on for 3rd pl* 16/1

4 3/4 **Global Village (IRE)** 4-9-7 0 WilliamCarson(5) 2 — 49
(Miss D Mountain) *bmpd s: bhd: rdn and unable qck over 2f out: styd on fnl f: snatched 4th last stride: nvr nr ldrs* 11/1

05 5 shd **Brett Vale (IRE)**[13] 364 3-8-11 0 StephenDonohoe 7 — 47+
(Sir Mark Prescott) *racd in midfield: pushed along and outpcd 2f out: keeping on same pce and wl hld whn nt clr run and eased nr fin* 11/1

6 1/2 **Crystal B Good (USA)** 3-8-6 0 HayleyTurner 3 — 38+
(J R Best) *s.i.s: racd in midfield: effrt and rn green over 1f out: kpt on fnl f: nvr trbld ldrs* 15/8[1]

00- 7 2 **Hilltop Legacy**[151] 6003 6-9-7 0 FergusSweeney 6 — 35
(J R Jenkins) *wnt lft s: a in rr: rdn over 2f out: nvr nr ldrs* 20/1

8 1 1/4 **Gingko Lady (USA)**[120] 6793 4-9-7 61 SteveDrowne 10 — 31
(J R Boyle) *s.i.s: a bhd* 8/1

00- 9 1/2 **Thumberlina**[80] 7452 3-8-6 0 (v1) AndrewElliott 5 — 26
(Mrs C A Dunnett) *bmpd s: chsd ldr tl 2f out: sn wknd* 33/1

1m 12.83s (0.93) **Going Correction** +0.025s/f (Slow)
WFA 3 from 4yo+ 15lb — **9** Ran SP% **122.8**
Speed ratings (Par 103): **94,90,86,85,85 84,81,80,79**
toteswinger: 1&2 £3.40, 1&3 £12.40, 2&3 £7.60. CSF £16.57 TOTE £8.10: £2.20, £1.10, £4.50; EX 15.10 Trifecta £22.30 Pool: £162.16 - 5.38 winning units..

Owner Miss Carmelina Favarulo **Bred** Lucky Shamrock Llc **Trained** Newmarket, Suffolk

FOCUS
A weak maiden. With the favourite disappointing and the second not progressing the winner was left with little to beat.

553 WILLOW H'CAP — 5f (P)

4:45 (4:45) (Class 2) (0-100,109) 4-Y-O+ £11,527 (£3,430; £1,714; £856) Stalls High

Form / RPR

0131 1 **Matsunosuke**[14] 359 7-9-13 109 LukeMorris 6 — 117
(A B Coogan) *hld up in last pair: hdwy to trck ldrs 2f out: rdn to ld fnl 100yds: r.o wl* 2/1[1]

2-23 2 1/2 **Little Edward**[14] 359 11-8-1 88 MCGeran(5) 3 — 94
(R J Hodges) *taken down early: t.k.h: trckd ldrs: swtchd rt 1f out: rdn and ev ch ins fnl f: no ex towards fin* 7/1[3]

2-05 3 1/2 **Ebraam (USA)**[14] 359 6-8-10 92 TolleyDean 4 — 96+
(P Howling) *hld up in last pair: swtchd rt and hdwy jst ins fnl f: r.o wl: nt quite rch ldng pair* 11/2[2]

11-2 4 hd **Turn On The Style**[35] 123 7-9-7 103 (b) PaulMulrennan 2 — 106
(J Balding) *s.i.s: pushed up to chse ldr after 1f: rdn and ev ch 2f out: drvn to ld jst ins fnl f: hdd fnl 100yds: no ex and lost 3 pls after* 2/1[1]

4110 5 1 1/4 **Harry Up**[7] 451 8-8-4 86 oh1 (p) PaulHanagan 1 — 85
(K A Ryan) *awkward s and s.i.s: pushed up to ld after 1f: rdn over 1f out: hdd jst ins fnl f: wknd fnl 100yds* 14/1

0013 6 3/4 **Haajes**[4] 491 5-8-5 87 (t) DaleGibson 5 — 83
(S Parr) *led for 1f: chsd ldrs: rdn 1/2-way: lost pl sn after: one pce u.p fnl f* 8/1

57.74 secs (-1.06) **Going Correction** +0.025s/f (Slow) — **6** Ran SP% **112.3**
Speed ratings (Par 109): **109,108,107,107,105 103**
toteswinger: 1&2 £2.60, 1&3 £2.40, 2&3 £6.10. CSF £16.89 TOTE £3.20: £2.20, £3.20; EX 23.20 Place 6: £272.95 Place 5: £101.54 .

Owner A B Coogan **Bred** R Coogan **Trained** Soham, Cambs

FOCUS
A classy contest. Unsurprisingly with Harry Up in the line-up the pace was generous; so much so that time was only half a second or so shy of the track record. Another improved effort from the smart Matsunosuke, and sound form.

NOTEBOOK
Matsunosuke is building an impressive record at this venue, this being his third win from six starts, while he's been placed on the other three. Always cantering at the back, his rider was keen not to give Turn On The Style too much of a lead approaching the distance and he was soon on the scene out wide before keeping on well enough to hold off Little Edward and Ebraam. He will now have to step into Pattern company, probably on the turf given the lack of openings for such horses on this surface, and it would be no surprise were he to transfer his improved all-weather form to grass, especially if getting the strong pace that suits him so well. (op 11-4)

Little Edwardwas 3l behind Matsunosuke here last time and on 7lb better terms closed that gap without really looking as if he might turn the form around. He has run his race once again, like the winner appreciating the decent pace.\n (op 8-1 tchd 9-1)

Ebraam(USA), also put in his place by the winner last time, attracted some good market support but he got going too late in the day and although he closed right in, he wasn't getting there (op 6-1 tchd 5-1)

Turn On The Style ran well given he tried to keep tabs on Harry Up early. He has finished in front of Matsunosuke twice this winter, once over 6f here and once on Fibresand, but a true-run 5f suits Matsunosuke better and he proved that here. Official explanation: jockey said gelding missed the break (tchd 7-4)

T/Plt: £649.90 to a £1 stake. Pool: £38,995.76. 43.80 winning tickets. T/Qpdt: £31.70 to a £1 stake. Pool: £2,930.50. 68.40 winning tickets. SP

535 WOLVERHAMPTON (A.W) (L-H)

Saturday, February 14

OFFICIAL GOING: Standard
Wind: Nil Weather: Fine

554 BACK OR LAY AT BETDAQ AMATEUR RIDERS' H'CAP — 1m 141y(P)

6:50 (6:51) (Class 6) (0-60,60) 4-Y-O+ £1,977 (£608; £304) Stalls Low

Form / RPR

200- 1 **March Mate**[68] 4679 5-10-10 54 MrDaleSwift(5) 12 — 66
(B Ellison) *hld up in mid-div: hdwy on outside over 2f out: rdn to ld over 1f out: drvn out* 8/1

-123 2 3/4 **Samurai Warrior**[5] 478 4-11-5 58 MissEFolkes 13 — 68
(P D Evans) *hld up in tch: led jst over 2f out: rdn and hdd over 1f out: r.o* 5/1[2]

05-1 3 2 1/4 **King Of Legend (IRE)**[26] 216 5-10-11 57 MrMEnnis(7) 4 — 62+
(A G Foster) *hld up in tch: nt clr run on ins and swtchd rt over 2f out: rdn over 1f out: kpt on to take 3rd wl ins fnl f* 9/2[1]

356- 4 1 1/4 **Moayed**[229] 3567 10-11-7 60 (b) MrsEmmaLittmoden 7 — 62
(N P Littmoden) *s.i.s: hld up in rr: hdwy over 2f out: rdn over 1f out: no ex and lost 3rd wl ins fnl f* 33/1

/5-3 5 1 1/4 **Wester Lodge (IRE)**[15] 341 7-10-9 55 MrHAEustace(7) 8 — 54+
(J M P Eustace) *hld up in rr: nt clr run on ins and stmbld over 2f out: hdwy fnl f: nrst fin* 12/1

4-54 6 1 **Machinate (USA)**[23] 256 7-10-13 55 MrBenBrisbourne(3) 3 — 52
(W M Brisbourne) *s.i.s: hld up in rr: hdwy on outside over 2f out: rdn wl over 1f out: wknd ins fnl f* 7/1

4506 7 3/4 **Spume (IRE)**[1] 534 5-11-0 53 (t) MissSBrotherton 1 — 48
(S Parr) *hld up in mid-div: short-lived effrt 2f out* 15/2

3-62 8 2 3/4 **Sion Hill (IRE)**[26] 216 8-11-1 54 (p) MrSWalker 5 — 43
(John A Harris) *led: hdd over 5f out: led over 3f out tl jst over 2f out: wknd wl over 1f out* 6/1[3]

610/ 9 6 **Borouj (IRE)**[29] 4070 7-10-10 56 MrJERobinson(7) 9 — 31
(Joss Saville) *s.i.s: a in rr* 50/1

00-6 10 4 **Kirstys Lad**[8] 427 7-11-0 58 MissMMullineaux(5) 11 — 24
(M Mullineaux) *a.p: w ldr over 2f out: wknd wl over 1f out* 28/1

006- 11 4 **Kirkie (USA)**[58] 7725 4-11-0 58 MrJoshuaMoore(5) 6 — 15
(S Parr) *unruly stalls: prom tl wknd over 3f out* 28/1

30-0 12 4 **Punta Galera (IRE)**[17] 311 6-11-3 56 MrSDobson 2 — 3
(Paul Green) *hld up in mid-div: reminders over 6f out: pushed along over 3f out: bhd fnl 2f* 11/1

-502 13 3 1/2 **Moment Of Clarity**[8] 420 7-10-10 54 (p) MrCAHarris(5) 10 — —
(R C Guest) *t.k.h: prom: led over 5f out tl over 3f out: rdn and wknd over 2f out* 10/1

1m 52.41s (1.91) **Going Correction** +0.125s/f (Slow) — **13** Ran SP% **121.4**
Speed ratings (Par 101): **96,95,93,92,91 90,89,87,81,78 74,71,68**
toteswinger: 1&2 £25.00, 1&3 £25.00, 2&3 £11.90. CSF £47.09 CT £213.60 TOTE £12.00: £4.20, £2.30, £2.70; EX 56.20.

Owner Ronald McCulloch **Bred** R McCulloch And B Ellison **Trained** Norton, N Yorks

FOCUS
Reasonable form for the type of race and there should be one or two winners to come out of this.

555 ENJOY THE LUCKY 7 GROUP OFFER (S) STKS — 1m 1f 103y(P)

7:20 (7:20) (Class 6) 3-Y-O £2,047 (£604; £302) Stalls Low

Form / RPR

40-1 1 **La Diosa (IRE)**[19] 296 3-8-13 66 ChrisCatlin 4 — 54
(George Baker) *bmpd s: hld up: rdn and hdwy on ins wl over 1f out: led wl ins fnl f: drvn out* 4/6[1]

2346 2 1 **Turn To Dreams**[5] 479 3-8-7 57 CatherineGannon 1 — 46
(P D Evans) *led early: a.p: rdn and ev ch fnl 2f: nt qckn towards fin* 3/1[2]

04-4 3 1 1/4 **Herecomesbella**[19] 296 3-8-10 50 ow3 (b) MickyFenton 3 — 46
(Stef Liddiard) *wnt rt s: hld up and keen early: hdwy over 3f out: led wl over 1f out: hrd rdn and hdd wl ins fnl f: no ex* 6/1[3]

65-4 4 1 1/2 **Ed's Pride (IRE)**[29] 196 3-8-12 43 (b) JamieMoriarty 5 — 45
(K A Ryan) *sltly hmpd s: sn chsng ldr: led over 5f out: hdd wl over 1f out: sn rdn: fdd ins fnl f* 10/1

400- 5 7 **Incy Wincy**[210] 4203 3-8-12 25 RobertWinston 6 — 31
(J M Bradley) *stdd s: hld up in rr: rdn and short-lived effrt 2f out* 50/1

000- 6 nk **Haafhds Delight (IRE)**[125] 6665 3-8-4 45 DuranFentiman(3) 2 — 25
(W M Brisbourne) *t.k.h: sn led: hdd over 5f out: rdn over 3f out: wknd 2f out* 40/1

2m 3.98s (2.28) **Going Correction** +0.125s/f (Slow) — **6** Ran SP% **112.8**
Speed ratings (Par 95): **94,93,92,90,84 84**
toteswinger: 1&2 £5.30, 1&3 £1.02, 2&3 £1.10. CSF £2.97 TOTE £1.70: £1.40, £1.80; EX 3.60.There was no bid for the winner.

Owner The Betfair Radioheads **Bred** Cathal Ryan **Trained** Moreton Morrell, Warwicks

FOCUS
A very ordinary seller.

556 TONIGHT IS 80'S PARTY NIGHT MAIDEN FILLIES' STKS — 1m 141y(P)

7:50 (7:50) (Class 5) 3-Y-O+ £2,729 (£806; £403) Stalls Low

Form / RPR

2- 1 **One Slick Chick (IRE)**[55] 7754 3-8-6 0 ow1 JohnEgan 5 — 70
(M Botti) *hld up: hdwy over 3f out: wnt 2nd over 2f out: rdn and edgd lft over 1f out: led ins fnl f: r.o* 4/1[2]

03-2 2 1 1/2 **Shaws Diamond (USA)**[22] 276 3-8-5 78 PaulHanagan 2 — 65
(D Shaw) *led: rdn over 1f out: wandered and hdd ins fnl f: nt qckn* 4/7[1]

626- 3 2 1/4 **Rose Cheval (USA)**[213] 4080 3-8-5 77 EdwardCreighton 1 — 60
(M R Channon) *t.k.h: in tch: nt clr run on ins over 2f out: carried hd awkwardly and one pce fnl 2f* 4/1[2]

0-00 4 nk **Mays Louise**[20] 290 5-9-9 35 DuranFentiman(3) 3 — 64?
(B P J Baugh) *hld up in rr: hdwy wl over 1f out: sn rdn: one pce fnl f* 200/1

0-0 5 7 **Flying River (IRE)**[28] 201 3-8-5 0 RichardKingscote 4 — 43
(Tom Dascombe) *prom tl wknd 3f out* 20/1[3]

00- 6 11 **Brave Optimist (IRE)**[70] 7583 4-9-5 0 KrishGundowry(7) 6 — 23
(Paul Green) *prom: w ldr 6f out tl rdn over 2f out: sn wknd* 100/1

1m 53.51s (3.01) **Going Correction** +0.125s/f (Slow)
WFA 3 from 4yo+ 21lb — **6** Ran SP% **109.9**
Speed ratings (Par 100): **91,89,87,87,81 71**
toteswinger: 1&2 £1.10, 1&3 £2.00, 2&3 £1.10. CSF £6.48 TOTE £3.20: £1.50, £1.10; EX 5.90.

Owner Miss Anita Farrell **Bred** Thomas F Hannon **Trained** Newmarket, Suffolk

FOCUS
A modest, uncompetitive maiden - the fourth was rated just 35 - and this is not form to dwell on.

557 BETDAQ.CO.UK FILLIES' H'CAP 7f 32y(P)
8:20 (8:20) (Class 5) (0-75,75) 4-Y-0+ **£2,729** (£806; £403) **Stalls** High

Form RPR
00-2 **1** **Hallingdal (UAE)**[5] 470 4-9-2 **73**.................. JamesDoyle 2 81+
(Ms J S Doyle) *hld up: hdwy over 2f out: rdn to ld ins fnl f: r.o* **5/4**[1]
06-0 **2** *nk* **Romantic Verse**[24] 241 4-8-8 **65**....................(b) GrahamGibbons 3 71
(E S McMahon) *led early: chsd ldr: led over 1f out: rdn and hdd ins fnl f: nt qckn* **7/2**[2]
1-25 **3** *2 ½* **Leading Edge (IRE)**[21] 281 4-8-13 **70**.................. TonyCulhane 1 69
(M R Channon) *a.p: rdn over 1f out: one pce* **4/1**[3]
6-06 **4** *½* **Montiboli (IRE)**[19] 297 4-8-11 **68**.................. PaulHanagan 6 66
(K A Ryan) *hld up: rdn 1f out: nvr trbld ldrs* **8/1**
204- **5** *2 ¼* **Ginger Princess (IRE)**[9] 5133 7-8-5 **69**..............(t) GJPhillips(7) 4 61
(Oliver McKiernan, Ire) *stdd s: hld up in rr: edgd lft over 1f out: n.d* **9/1**
4 **6** *3 ½* **Albero Di Giuda (IRE)**[15] 349 4-9-4 **75**..............(t) FBranca 5 57
(F Sheridan) *t.k.h: sn led: hdd over 1f out: rdn and wknd ins fnl f* **20/1**

1m 30.38s (0.78) **Going Correction** +0.125s/f (Slow) **6** Ran SP% **112.5**
Speed ratings (Par 100): **100,99,96,96,93 89**
toteswinger: 1&2 £2.00, 1&3 £2.00, 2&3 £1.02. CSF £5.88 TOTE £2.50: £1.20, £3.10; EX 13.30.
Owner W Wood **Bred** Darley **Trained** Eastbury, Berks

FOCUS
Just a modest fillies' handicap.

558 WOLVERHAMPTON-RACECOURSE.CO.UK H'CAP 1m 141y(P)
8:50 (8:50) (Class 5) (0-75,74) 4-Y-0+ **£2,729** (£806; £403) **Stalls** Low

Form RPR
40-1 **1** **Brouhaha**[26] 217 5-8-10 **66**.................. RichardKingscote 4 73
(Tom Dascombe) *sn led: set slow pce: qcknd over 2f out: clr over 1f out: sn rdn: r.o* **9/4**[1]
36-3 **2** *½* **Ours (IRE)**[26] 220 6-8-13 **69**..............(p) ChrisCatlin 5 75
(John A Harris) *hld up: str run on outside and edgd lft ins fnl f: nt rch wnr* **7/2**[3]
20-5 **3** *¾* **Follow The Flag (IRE)**[18] 307 5-8-12 **68**..............(p) RobertWinston 9 72
(A J McCabe) *hld up in tch: rdn over 2f out: chsd wnr jst over 1f out: kpt on* **11/4**[2]
00/2 **4** *½* **Ludwigshafen (IRE)**[20] 290 5-8-10 **66**.................. ShaneKelly 2 69
(John Geoghegan, Ire) *hld up: swtchd rt over 1f out: hdwy and edgd lft ins fnl f: kpt on* **8/1**
0- **5** *1 ¾* **Masterofceremonies**[24] 6487 6-8-13 **69**..............(b) PaulHanagan 6 68
(James Moffatt) *s.s: in rr whn pushed along 3f out: n.d* **40/1**
500/ **6** *5* **Sew'N'So Character (IRE)**[658] 1287 8-9-1 **71**.................. JimmyQuinn 3 58
(M Blanshard) *t.k.h in tch: rdn and wknd ins fnl f* **15/2**
544- **7** *6* **King Kenny**[124] 6744 4-9-4 **74**.................. LiamJones 1 48
(S Parr) *led early: chsd wnr: ev ch over 2f out: wknd over 1f out* **8/1**

1m 52.83s (2.33) **Going Correction** +0.125s/f (Slow) **7** Ran SP% **116.1**
Speed ratings (Par 103): **94,93,92,92,90 86,81**
toteswinger: 1&2 £2.70, 1&3 £3.70, 2&3 £3.00. CSF £10.82 CT £21.91 TOTE £5.00: £1.90, £1.70; EX 17.00.
Owner G D Newton **Bred** Mrs Rosamund Furlong **Trained** Lambourn, Berks

FOCUS
A modest handicap run at a steady pace.

559 BETDAQ ON 0870 178 1221 H'CAP 1m 4f 50y(P)
9:20 (9:20) (Class 5) (0-75,75) 4-Y-0+ **£2,729** (£806; £403) **Stalls** Low

Form RPR
21- **1** **Laurel Creek (IRE)**[94] 7293 4-9-0 **71**.................. ShaneKelly 12 88+
(M J Grassick, Ire) *hld up in tch: led over 3f out: rdn clr over 2f out: eased towards fin* **9/4**[1]
0-24 **2** *2 ½* **Star Choice**[17] 319 4-8-7 **64**.................. JimmyQuinn 7 71
(J Pearce) *hld up in mid-div: hdwy over 3f out: wnt 2nd wl over 2f out: sn rdn: no ch w wnr* **4/1**[2]
3-03 **3** *¾* **Morbick**[8] 428 5-9-2 **70**.................. LukeMorris 11 76
(W M Brisbourne) *hld up towards rr: hdwy wl over 2f out: rdn wl over 1f out: styd on ins fnl f* **8/1**
0-53 **4** *8* **Calzaghe (IRE)**[8] 423 5-8-12 **66**..............(vt) FBranca 1 59
(F Sheridan) *prom tl wknd wl over 2f out* **7/1**
-562 **5** *2 ¼* **Epidaurian King (IRE)**[17] 311 6-8-7 **61**.................. NickyMackay 10 50
(D Shaw) *stdd s: hld up in rr: c wd st: nvr nr ldrs* **20/1**
6 *1 ½* **Bariolo (FR)**[466] 5-9-0 **68**.................. SamHitchcott 4 55
(Noel T Chance) *hld up in mid-div: pushed along 3f out: sn struggling* **40/1**
6-06 **7** *1* **Noubian (USA)**[8] 428 7-9-2 **70**.................. LiamJones 6 55
(C R Dore) *hld up in rr: sme prog over 2f out: wknd wl over 1f out* **33/1**
3/01 **8** *8* **Imperial Harry**[17] 311 6-9-7 **75**.................. ChrisCatlin 2 48
(D E Pipe) *led tl over 3f out: wknd wl over 2f out* **7/1**
60-0 **9** *1 ¾* **Dr Brass**[10] 392 4-9-2 **73**..............(b) VinceSlattery 9 43
(B N Pollock) *hld up towards rr: hdwy over 6f out: wknd over 3f out* **40/1**
4-12 **10** *20* **Millie's Rock (IRE)**[14] 361 4-9-3 **74**.................. PaulHanagan 8 12
(K A Ryan) *plld hrd: chsd ldr: wknd wl over 2f out: eased ins fnl f* **11/2**[3]
5/6- **P** **Burnbank (IRE)**[29] 2361 6-8-13 **67**.................. TomEaves 5 —
(J M Jefferson) *hld up in tch: wknd over 5f out: t.o 4f out: p.u over 1f out: lame* **50/1**

2m 38.49s (-2.61) **Going Correction** +0.125s/f (Slow)
WFA 4 from 5yo+ 3lb **11** Ran SP% **116.8**
Speed ratings (Par 103): **113,111,110,105,104 103,102,97,95,82** —
toteswinger: 1&2 £15.10, 1&3 £5.10, 2&3 £21.00. CSF £10.31 CT £60.89 TOTE £3.70: £1.30, £1.90, £2.00; EX 24.30 Place 6: £4.23 Place 5: 2.28.
Owner Patrick G McKeon **Bred** Tetsu Nakata **Trained** Pollardstown, Co Kildare

FOCUS
A modest handicap but an impressive winner.
Millie's Rock(IRE) Official explanation: jockey said filly ran too free
Burnbank(IRE) Official explanation: jockey said gelding finished lame
T/Plt: £9.60 to a £1 stake. Pool: £79,721.54. 6,003.96 winning tickets. T/Qpdt: £4.30 to a £1 stake. Pool: £6,530.90. 1,106.90 winning tickets. KH

514 SOUTHWELL (L-H)
Sunday, February 15

OFFICIAL GOING: Standard
Wind: Light, across Weather: Overcast

560 MEMBERSHIP OF SOUTHWELL GOLF CLUB CLAIMING STKS 5f (F)
2:30 (2:31) (Class 6) 3-Y-0 **£2,047** (£604; £302) **Stalls** High

Form RPR
1352 **1** **La Capriosa**[9] 421 3-8-7 65 ow1.................. RobertWinston 6 67
(A J McCabe) *chsd ldr tl led 1/2-way: rdn over 1f out: edgd lft: r.o* **9/2**[2]
-134 **2** *nk* **Just The Lady**[12] 379 3-8-3 61.................. JimmyQuinn 5 62
(D Nicholls) *trckd ldrs: rdn to chse wnr fnl f: sn ev ch: r.o* **8/1**[3]
1-3 **3** *3* **Stash**[21] 288 3-9-6 79.................. GrahamGibbons 1 68
(R Hollinshead) *s.i.s: sn chsng ldrs: rdn 1/2-way: no ex ins fnl f* **8/15**[1]
05-5 **4** *2* **The Cuckoo**[33] 140 3-9-2 68.................. PatCosgrave 2 57
(M Quinn) *led to 1/2-way: rdn over 1f out: wknd ins fnl f* **10/1**
0-50 **5** *5* **Alimarr (IRE)**[3] 520 3-8-2 54..............(b[1]) CatherineGannon 3 25
(S Parr) *sn pushed along and prom: outpcd fr 1/2-way* **50/1**
660- **6** *2 ¾* **Thaumatology (USA)**[76] 7514 3-8-3 61.................. DaleGibson 4 16
(S Parr) *dwlt: outpcd* **40/1**

60.41 secs (0.71) **Going Correction** +0.025s/f (Slow) **6** Ran SP% **108.0**
Speed ratings (Par 95): **95,94,89,86,78 74**
toteswinger: 1&2 £1.40, 1&3 £1.60, 2&3 £1.20. CSF £34.97 TOTE £5.00: £1.30, £2.90; EX 17.90.
Owner Paul J Dixon **Bred** Slatch Farm Stud **Trained** Averham Park, Notts

FOCUS
An ordinary three-year-old claimer. The front pair are rated to their marks.
Thaumatology(USA) Official explanation: jockey said filly hung right

561 SOUTHWELL-RACECOURSE.CO.UK H'CAP 6f (F)
3:00 (3:00) (Class 5) (0-70,70) 4-Y-0+ **£2,590** (£770; £385; £192) **Stalls** Low

Form RPR
-120 **1** **Calmdownmate (IRE)**[10] 400 4-9-0 **66**.................. LukeMorris 7 75
(Mrs R A Carr) *trckd ldrs: racd keenly: led over 2f out: sn rdn and hung lft: styd on* **5/1**[2]
-335 **2** *1 ¼* **Whitbarrow (IRE)**[25] 241 10-8-13 **68**..............(b) JamesMillman(3) 3 73
(B R Millman) *led: rdn and hdd over 2f out: hmpd ins fnl f: styd on* **11/2**[3]
4514 **3** *nk* **Punching**[17] 326 5-9-3 **69**.................. LPKeniry 2 76+
(C R Dore) *hld up: hdwy over 2f out: carried lft fr over 1f out: hmpd ins fnl f: kpt on* **13/2**
24-2 **4** *nk* **This Ones For Eddy**[3] 518 4-9-3 **69**.................. AdamKirby 6 72
(S Parr) *s.i.s: hld up: hdwy over 2f out: rdn over 1f out: unable qckn nr fin* **11/10**[1]
00-0 **5** *2* **Dickie Le Davoir**[17] 326 5-8-10 **62**.................. RobertWinston 5 64+
(John A Harris) *s.i.s: sn pushed along in rr: hdwy over 1f out: hmpd ins fnl f: nt rcvr* **11/2**[3]
200- **6** *14* **Legendary Guest**[194] 4700 4-8-13 **65**.................. TonyHamilton 4 17
(D W Barker) *chsd ldr: ev ch 2f out: sn rdn and wknd* **33/1**
0-00 **7** *14* **Only A Game (IRE)**[27] 218 4-9-4 **70**..............(b[1]) JimmyQuinn 1 —
(Miss M E Rowland) *trckd ldrs: plld hrd: rdn and wknd over 2f out* **50/1**

1m 15.63s (-0.87) **Going Correction** -0.075s/f (Stan) **7** Ran SP% **113.3**
Speed ratings (Par 103): **102,100,99,99,96 78,59**
toteswinger: 1&2 £5.00, 1&3 £5.90, 2&3 £5.70. CSF £31.52 TOTE £6.90: £3.00, £2.30; EX 35.90.
Owner David W Chapman **Bred** J Costello **Trained** Huby, N Yorks
■ Stewards' Enquiry : Luke Morris five-day ban: careless riding (Mar 1-5)

FOCUS
The closing stages of this modest handicap were really messy, with the winner taking out pretty much half the field when hanging badly left, and the bare form needs treating with a little caution. The third has been rated to form with a clear run.
Legendary Guest Official explanation: jockey said gelding hung badly right

562 PLAY GOLF BEFORE RACING AT SOUTHWELL H'CAP 6f (F)
3:30 (3:30) (Class 4) (0-85,77) 3-Y-0 **£4,857** (£1,445; £722; £360) **Stalls** Low

Form RPR
316- **1** **Fesko**[47] 7820 3-9-4 **77**.................. GregFairley 1 87
(M Johnston) *chsd ldr tl led 2f out: sn rdn: r.o* **7/2**[3]
43-1 **2** *nk* **Premier Lad**[14] 364 3-8-12 **71**.................. TomEaves 4 80
(T D Barron) *hld up: hdwy over 2f out: rdn to chse wnr fnl f: hung lft: styd on u.p* **13/8**[1]
1 **3** *8* **Angel Song**[26] 227 3-9-3 **76**.................. StephenDonohoe 3 59
(Sir Mark Prescott) *led: rdn and hdd 2f out: wknd fnl f* **7/4**[2]
401- **4** *9* **Denton Diva**[103] 7179 3-8-10 **69**.................. DaleGibson 2 24
(M Dods) *chsd ldrs: rdn over 3f out: wknd 2f out* **17/2**

1m 15.45s (-1.05) **Going Correction** -0.075s/f (Stan) **4** Ran SP% **107.2**
Speed ratings (Par 99): **104,103,92,80**
CSF £9.42 TOTE £3.60; EX 9.70.
Owner C H Greensit & W A Greensit **Bred** C H And W A Greensit **Trained** Middleham Moor, N Yorks

FOCUS
Only four runners, but they were all recent winners (three of them last-time out) and this looked a fair three-year-old sprint handicap. The pace was good and the winning time was 0.18 seconds quicker than the earlier 56-70 older-horse handicap. The first two pulled well clear and the form has been viewed positively.

563 DINE IN THE PANTRY TODAY H'CAP 1m 3f (F)
4:00 (4:00) (Class 2) (0-100,100) 4-Y-0+ **£11,980** (£3,564; £1,781; £889) **Stalls** Low

Form RPR
06-6 **1** **Kandidate**[22] 284 7-9-6 **100**.................. RobertWinston 2 111
(C E Brittain) *sn led: rdn over 3f out: hdd over 2f out: rallied to ld 1f out: r.o* **4/1**[3]
13-1 **2** *1* **Robby Bobby**[15] 360 4-8-11 **93**.................. GregFairley 5 102
(M Johnston) *sn chsng ldr: rdn to ld over 2f out: hdd 1f out: styd on same pce ins fnl f* **1/1**[1]
-211 **3** *6* **Formation (USA)**[8] 445 4-8-9 **91**.................. PatCosgrave 1 90
(J R Boyle) *hld up in tch: rdn over 3f out: sn hung lft and outpcd* **5/2**[2]
401- **4** *shd* **Best Prospect (IRE)**[36] 7056 7-8-8 **88**.................. TomEaves 3 87
(M Dods) *broke wl: stdd to trck ldrs: rdn over 3f out: sn outpcd* **9/1**

2m 26.03s (-1.97) **Going Correction** -0.075s/f (Stan)
WFA 4 from 7yo 2lb **4** Ran SP% **108.6**
Speed ratings (Par 109): **104,103,98,98**
CSF £8.58 TOTE £4.50; EX 8.50.
Owner Mrs E W Richards **Bred** Proton Partnership **Trained** Newmarket, Suffolk

FOCUS
A good handicap, despite the small field, but the winner was allowed the run of the race. He has been rated to last season's best.

NOTEBOOK
Kandidate, easily the best horse in the race judged on back class, was allowed to dominate at a steady pace, and left behind his recent poor effort behind Formation. He had to battle when joined by the runner-up early in the straight, but he had more left in the tank than that rival, and displayed a willing attitude. A regular on the Polytrack, this was his first try on Fibresand, but having previously acted on the Nad Al Sheba dirt course, this track was never going to cause him any problems. All he did was gallop in the straight and on this evidence he will benefit from a return to 1m4f. (op 11-2)
Robby Bobby, 13lb higher than when successful over course and distance four starts back, was inclined to race just a touch keenly, and that told in the straight considering the winner had the run of the race. (op 6-5 tchd 10-11)
Formation(USA) was bidding for a hat-trick following a couple of useful wins at Lingfield, but he failed to take to the Fibresand. (op 2-1 tchd 11-4)
Best Prospect(IRE), back on the Flat after a couple of spins over hurdles, had his usual tongue-tie left off for this first try on Fibresand and never threatened. (op 7-1 tchd 10-1)

564 MEMBERSHIP AT SOUTHWELL GOLF CLUB MAIDEN FILLIES' STKS — 1m (F)
4:30 (4:30) (Class 5) 3-Y-O+ **£2,590** (£770; £385; £192) **Stalls** Low

Form RPR
2 **1** **Eastern Aria (UAE)**^{8} [440] 3-8-8 0 ... GregFairley 7 75+
(M Johnston) *chsd ldr: shkn up to ld over 2f out: clr fnl f* **7/4**^{1}
2 **2** *3* **Air Maze**^{24} [251] 3-8-8 0 ... StephenDonohoe 3 65+
(Sir Mark Prescott) *a.p: rdn over 2f out: chsd wnr over 1f out: hung rt ins fnl f: no imp* **15/2**
06-2 **3** *2 3/4* **Lyric Art (USA)**^{9} [425] 3-8-8 64 ... TomEaves 5 59+
(B Smart) *led: racd keenly: rdn and hdd over 2f out: styd on same pce appr fnl f* **5/2**^{2}
4 *nk* **Appelouse**^{71} 4-9-13 0 ... TonyHamilton 2 64
(M Dods) *s.s: hdwy u.p over 4f out: outpcd over 3f out: styd on fnl f* **66/1**
5 **5** *1 1/2* **Destinationunknown (USA)**^{32} [154] 3-8-8 0 ... LiamJones 4 55
(W J Haggas) *chsd ldrs: rdn over 2f out: styd on same pce* **4/1**^{3}
43 **6** *3 1/4* **Johnston's Baby (IRE)**^{6} [476] 7-9-13 0 ... JimmyQuinn 6 53
(E J Alston) *hld up in tch: shkn up over 2f out: wknd over 1f out* **10/1**
000- **7** *114* **Kilsyth (IRE)**^{114} [6953] 3-8-8 60 ... DaleGibson 1 —
(S Parr) *s.i.s and reluctant: sn outpcd and bhd: t.o fnl 3f: virtually p.u ins fnl f* **200/1**

1m 43.91s (0.21) **Going Correction** -0.075s/f (Stan)
WFA 3 from 4yo+ 19lb **7 Ran SP% 107.8**
Speed ratings (Par 100): **95,92,89,88,87 84,—**
toteswinger: 1&2 £2.80, 1&3 £1.70, 2&3 £2.90. CSF £13.78 TOTE £2.60: £3.20, £3.00; EX 11.00.
Owner Sheikh Hamdan Bin Mohammed Al Maktoum **Bred** Darley **Trained** Middleham Moor, N Yorks

FOCUS
A reasonable fillies' maiden, especially by the tracks usual standards, although it was steadily run and the fourth limits the form.
Lyric Art(USA) Official explanation: jockey said filly ran too free

565 COME JUMPING ON TUESDAY H'CAP — 1m (F)
5:00 (5:00) (Class 6) (0-55,55) 4-Y-O+ **£2,047** (£604; £302) **Stalls** Low

Form RPR
3311 **1** **General Tufto**^{3} [514] 4-8-4 50 ... (b) HollyHall$^{(7)}$ 1 66
(C Smith) *hld up in tch: led and hung lft over 1f out: r.o wl* **11/8**^{1}
035 **2** *3* **Very Well Red**^{28} [211] 6-8-8 47 ... JimmyQuinn 4 56
(P W Hiatt) *chsd ldr tl led over 2f out: rdn and hdd over 1f out: styd on same pce* **10/1**
-235 **3** *3 3/4* **Betteras Bertie**^{14} [362] 6-9-2 55 ... RobertWinston 8 55
(M Brittain) *s.s: bhd and drvn along: hdwy u.p over 1f out: nt trble ldrs* **9/4**^{2}
0-00 **4** *1* **Rampant Ronnie (USA)**^{16} [353] 4-9-0 53 ... LPKeniry 3 51
(P W D'Arcy) *chsd ldrs: rdn over 2f out: wknd over 1f out* **25/1**
0 **5** *hd* **Singora Lady (IRE)**^{19} [307] 4-9-2 55 ... JamieMoriarty 7 53
(P T Midgley) *hld up: rdn over 3f out: styd on ins fnl f: nvr nrr* **33/1**
400- **6** *4* **Mujma**^{181} [5152] 5-8-8 47 ... DaleGibson 9 35
(S Parr) *hld up in tch: plld hrd: rdn over 3f out: wknd over 2f out* **40/1**
6022 **7** *1* **Afton View (IRE)**^{5} [487] 4-8-12 51 ... AdamKirby 10 37
(S Parr) *led 1f: chsd ldrs: rdn over 2f out: wknd over 1f out* **8/1**^{3}
0-60 **8** *1 1/4* **Piccolo Diamante (USA)**^{20} [292] 5-8-13 52 ... (e^{1}) TolleyDean 2 35
(S Parr) *hld up: rdn over 3f out: a in rr* **40/1**
-656 **9** *nk* **Fairly Honest**^{8} [452] 5-8-7 46 oh1 ... LukeMorris 11 29
(P W Hiatt) *hld up: rdn over 3f out: a in rr* **10/1**
000- **10** *3/4* **Siena**^{123} [6735] 4-8-2 46 oh1 ... (v) AmyBaker$^{(5)}$ 6 27
(Mrs C A Dunnett) *led 7f out: rdn and hdd over 2f out: sn wknd* **50/1**

1m 41.82s (-1.88) **Going Correction** -0.075s/f (Stan) **10 Ran SP% 115.8**
Speed ratings (Par 101): **106,103,99,98,98 94,93,91,91,90**
toteswinger: 1&2 £5.30, 1&3 £1.20, 2&3 £6.00. CSF £15.55 CT £30.64 TOTE £2.60: £1.10, £2.50, £1.50; EX 16.70 Trifecta £45.10 Pool £773.65 - 12.67 winning units. Place 6 £739.32, Place 5 £189.97..
Owner Phil Martin **Bred** Hascombe And Valiant Studs **Trained** Temple Bruer, Lincs

FOCUS
A moderate handicap, but it was soundly run and the form is solid for the grade.
Piccolo Diamante(USA) Official explanation: jockey said gelding did not face the eyeshields.
T/Plt: £620.30 to a £1 stake. Pool: £73,041.11. 85.95 winning tickets. T/Qpdt: £56.10 to a £1 stake. Pool: £5,842.60. 77.00 winning tickets. CR

554 WOLVERHAMPTON (A.W) (L-H)
Monday, February 16

OFFICIAL GOING: Standard
Wind: Light half behind Weather: Fine

566 SPONSOR A RACE AT WOLVERHAMPTON AMATEUR RIDERS' H'CAP (DIV I) — 1m 4f 50y(P)
1:55 (1:55) (Class 6) (0-52,52) 4-Y-O+ **£1,648** (£507; £253) **Stalls** Low

Form RPR
0-16 **1** **Corlough Mountain**^{17} [341] 5-10-13 49 ... MissMBryant$^{(5)}$ 3 55
(P Butler) *s.i.s: sn in tch: led wl over 1f out: r.o* **10/1**
03-2 **2** *nk* **Fantasy Ride**^{9} [443] 7-11-7 52 ... MrSDobson 12 58+
(J Pearce) *stdd s: t.k.h in rr: hdwy over 3f out: rdn and hung lft fr wl over 1f out: styd on u.p to take 2nd wl ins fnl f: nt rch wnr* **6/5**^{1}
325/ **3** *1 3/4* **Conny Nobel (IRE)**^{28} [4877] 5-11-0 48 ... DonalDevereux$^{(3)}$ 4 51
(C Roberts) *led: rdn and hdd wl over 1f out: no ex and lost 2nd wl ins fnl f* **20/1**
425/ **4** *3/4* **Super Sensation (GER)**^{560} [3397] 8-10-13 49 ... (b) MrJoshuaMoore$^{(5)}$ 6 51
(G L Moore) *s.i.s: hld up towards rr: stdy prog over 6f out: rdn and hung lft wl over 1f out: one pce fnl f* **11/2**^{3}
/4-5 **5** *2 3/4* **Inn For The Dancer**^{29} [213] 7-10-13 49 ... MissSarah-JaneDurman$^{(5)}$ 8 46+
(J C Fox) *s.i.s: hld up in rr: c wd st: styd on fnl f: nrst fin* **20/1**
-040 **6** *2 1/4* **York Cliff**^{13} [377] 11-11-2 50 ... MrBenBrisbourne$^{(3)}$ 2 44
(W M Brisbourne) *hld up in mid-div: lost pl over 5f out: styd on fnl f: n.d* **14/1**
7 *3/4* **Gratuitous (IRE)**^{470} [5653] 5-10-8 46 oh1 ... MrJMQuinlan$^{(7)}$ 9 38
(L McHugh, Ire) *hld up towards rr: hdwy on outside whn swtchd lft 3f out: hrd rdn over 2f out: wknd wl over 1f out* **33/1**
8 *3* **Catai**^{26} 5-11-1 46 ... MrSWalker 11 34
(P Monteith) *prom: ev ch over 2f out: sn rdn and briefly n.m.r: wknd wl over 1f out* **5/1**^{2}
0/0- **9** *5* **Border Tale**^{114} [4630] 9-10-13 51 ... (p) MissRebeccaSparkes$^{(7)}$ 5 31
(James Moffatt) *hld up in mid-div: trapped v wd over 3f out: sn bhd* **14/1**
300- **10** *1 1/2* **Ruling Reef**^{113} [3448] 7-10-12 46 oh1 ... MrPCollington$^{(3)}$ 1 23
(M R Bosley) *prom: rdn over 4f out: wknd over 3f out* **16/1**
00-0 **11** *3 1/2* **Mega Steps (IRE)**^{9} [448] 5-11-1 46 oh1 ... (p) WilliamBiddick 10 18
(Jennie Candlish) *prom tl wknd 3f out* **40/1**

2m 47.34s (6.24) **Going Correction** +0.275s/f (Slow) **11 Ran SP% 120.7**
Speed ratings (Par 101): **90,89,88,88,86 84,84,82,78,77 75**
toteswinger: 1&2 £2.60, 1&3 £19.30, 2&3 £9.10. CSF £22.06 CT £257.39 TOTE £10.30: £3.30, £1.10, £6.70; EX 28.70 TRIFECTA Not won..
Owner Miss M Bryant **Bred** Bottisham Heath Stud **Trained** East Chiltington, E Sussex
■ Stewards' Enquiry : Mr S Dobson six-day ban: used whip with excessive frequency (Mar 2, Apr 6, Apr 25, May 11, May, 18, May 22)
Mr J M Quinlan three-day ban: used whip with excessive force (Mar 2, Apr 6, Apr 25))

FOCUS
A very moderate amateur riders' handicap and the form looks weak. The pace was ordinary and the winning time was 3.07 seconds slower than the second division.

567 SPONSOR A RACE AT WOLVERHAMPTON AMATEUR RIDERS' H'CAP (DIV II) — 1m 4f 50y(P)
2:25 (2:25) (Class 6) (0-52,52) 4-Y-O+ **£1,648** (£507; £253) **Stalls** Low

Form RPR
0-60 **1** **Casablanca Minx (IRE)**^{7} [469] 6-11-4 49 ... (v) MrSWalker 6 58
(Miss Gay Kelleway) *hld up in mid-div: hdwy over 4f out: rdn wl over 1f out: led ins fnl f: drvn out* **6/1**^{3}
0540 **2** *1/2* **Desert Hawk**^{7} [469] 8-10-13 47 ... MrBenBrisbourne$^{(3)}$ 5 55+
(W M Brisbourne) *hld up towards rr: stdy prog 5f out: rdn and edgd lft ins fnl f: styd on to take 2nd towards fin: nt rch wnr* **4/1**^{2}
46-2 **3** *2* **Diktatorship (IRE)**^{9} [449] 6-11-1 46 ... WilliamBiddick 9 51+
(Jennie Candlish) *a.p: led over 4f out: rdn over 2f out: hdd ins fnl f: no ex and lost 2nd towards fin* **5/2**^{1}
06-0 **4** *10* **Schinken Otto (IRE)**^{29} [213] 8-11-2 50 ... MissRJefferson$^{(3)}$ 4 39
(J M Jefferson) *s.s: in rr: stdy hdwy 5f out: no imp fnl 2f* **9/1**
02-2 **5** *nk* **Cragganmore Creek**^{13} [378] 6-10-10 46 oh1 ... (v) MrBMMorris$^{(5)}$ 7 34
(D Morris) *hld up in mid-div: hdwy over 5f out: wknd over 2f out* **4/1**^{2}
060- **6** *5* **Dawn Wind**^{123} [6753] 4-10-9 48 ... (bt) MrCMartin$^{(5)}$ 1 28
(I A Wood) *dwlt: sn chsng ldrs: rdn and wknd over 2f out* **25/1**
00-5 **7** *1* **Dr Light (IRE)**^{13} [378] 5-10-10 46 oh1 ... KyleJames$^{(5)}$ 11 25+
(M A Peill) *s.i.s: wl in rr 6f out: hmpd on ins wl over 1f out: nvr nr ldrs* **16/1**
6600 **8** *3/4* **Top Jaro (FR)**^{13} [377] 6-10-13 49 ... (b) MissRachelClark$^{(5)}$ 3 27
(Mrs R A Carr) *hld up in mid-div: stdy hdwy over 5f out: wknd 3f out* **20/1**
060- **9** *4* **Mr Burton**^{65} [7669] 5-10-13 49 ... MissMMullineaux$^{(5)}$ 12 20
(M Mullineaux) *t.k.h: chsd ldr: led after 3f tl over 4f out: wknd over 2f out* **40/1**
/0-2 **10** *21* **Ramvaswani (IRE)**^{13} [377] 6-11-0 52 ... (p) MissCTwemlow$^{(7)}$ 8 —
(N B King) *s.i.s: sn prom: wknd qckly wl over 5f out* **13/2**
6-05 **11** *25* **Briery Blaze**^{17} [349] 6-10-8 46 oh1 ... (p) MrLJohnson$^{(7)}$ 2 —
(T Wall) *led 3f: wknd 5f out: t.o* **66/1**
300- **12** *dist* **Grand Value (USA)**^{115} [6955] 4-10-13 52 ... MrHarryChalloner$^{(5)}$ 10 —
(R Ford) *a in rr: t.o 6f out* **16/1**

2m 44.27s (3.17) **Going Correction** +0.275s/f (Slow)
WFA 4 from 5yo+ 3lb **12 Ran SP% 130.5**
Speed ratings (Par 101): **100,99,98,91,91 88,87,86,84,70 53,—**
toteswinger: 1&2 £11.60, 1&3 £3.30, 2&3 £6.00. CSF £32.54 CT £80.41 TOTE £8.40: £1.80, £2.40, £1.10; EX 26.10 Trifecta £51.50 Pool: £139.45 - 2.00 winning units..
Owner Whispering Winds **Bred** Airlie Stud And Widden Stud **Trained** Exning, Suffolk
■ Stewards' Enquiry : Miss Rachel Clark two-day ban: careless riding (Mar 2, Apr 6); four-day ban: used whip with excessive frequency (Apr 18, Apr 25, May 3, May 9)

FOCUS
The pace was good and the winning time was 3.07 seconds quicker than the first division. The form is moderate but sound enough.
Grand Value(USA) Official explanation: jockey said filly never travelled

568 BET MULTIPLES - BETDAQ H'CAP — 5f 20y(P)
3:00 (3:00) (Class 5) (0-70,70) 3-Y-O **£2,729** (£806; £403) **Stalls** Low

Form RPR
5543 **1** **Sills Vincero**^{12} [390] 3-8-4 56 oh2 ... PaulHanagan 7 60+
(D Shaw) *racd wd: hld up in tch: carried rt over 1f out: rdn and r.o wl to ld last strides* **6/1**
0-21 **2** *1/2* **Speak The Truth (IRE)**^{10} [429] 3-8-13 65 ... (p) PatCosgrave 4 67
(J R Boyle) *w ldr: rdn to ld ins fnl f: hdd last strides* **7/2**^{2}
50-4 **3** *1 1/2* **Riflessione**^{19} [313] 3-9-1 70 ... (b^{1}) KevinGhunowa$^{(3)}$ 6 67
(R A Harris) *prom: hung rt bnd over 2f out: hung rt over 1f out: kpt on u.p to take 3rd towards fin* **11/2**^{3}
63-1 **4** *3/4* **Jolly Ranch**^{22} [286] 3-8-10 62 ... SimonWhitworth 3 56
(A G Newcombe) *led: rdn over 1f out: hdd and no ex ins fnl f* **7/2**^{2}
-445 **5** *1 1/2* **Ruby Tallulah**^{4} [509] 3-9-2 68 ... LPKeniry 2 57
(C R Dore) *hld up in tch: rdn over 1f out: one pce* **10/3**^{1}
00-1 **6** *4* **Red Cell (IRE)**^{24} [268] 3-8-10 62 ... (b) TomEaves 5 36
(I W McInnes) *t.k.h: bhd fnl 3f* **10/1**
066- **7** *4* **Black Attack (IRE)**^{66} [7649] 3-8-4 56 oh2 ... (b^{1}) ChrisCatlin 1 16
(Paul Green) *hld up: hdwy on ins 3f out: rdn and wknd over 1f out* **8/1**

63.42 secs (1.12) **Going Correction** +0.275s/f (Slow) **7 Ran SP% 117.4**
Speed ratings (Par 97): **102,101,98,97,95 88,82**
toteswinger: 1&2 £4.80, 1&3 £7.10, 2&3 £4.60. CSF £28.33 TOTE £8.90: £4.00, £2.30; EX 31.20 TRIFECTA Not won..
Owner Simon Mapletoft Racing & R G Botham **Bred** Theobalds Stud **Trained** Danethorpe, Notts
■ Stewards' Enquiry : Pat Cosgrave one-day ban: used whip with excessive frequency (Mar 2)

FOCUS
A modest sprint handicap run at a quick early pace but the form is moderate.

Riflessione Official explanation: jockey said colt hung right-handed throughout

569 HOTEL & CONFERENCING AT WOLVERHAMPTON (S) STKS 1m 141y(P)
3:35 (3:35) (Class 6) 4-Y-O+ £2,047 (£604; £302) Stalls Low

Form RPR
23-3 1 **Forbidden (IRE)**[28] 215 6-9-0 61 (t) JerryO'Dwyer 7 59
(Daniel Mark Loughnane, Ire) *hld up in mid-div: hdwy 2f out: edgd lft wl over 1f out: rdn and sn led: r.o* **8/1**
6433 2 ¾ **Bobski (IRE)**[5] 504 7-9-0 67 (p) JamieSpencer 4 57
(Miss Gay Kelleway) *hld up in mid-div: hdwy over 1f out: rdn and edgd lft ins fnl f: r.o* **3/1**[1]
5-04 3 hd **Prince Noel**[28] 215 5-8-11 67 DuranFentiman(3) 5 57
(N Wilson) *hld up in mid-div: hdwy over 1f out: rdn and r.o ins fnl f* **5/1**
-522 4 2½ **Dancing Deano (IRE)**[9] 452 7-9-3 63 RussellKennemore(3) 2 57
(R Hollinshead) *led early: chsd ldr: led over 2f out: rdn and hdd over 1f out: fdd wl ins fnl f* **4/1**[3]
0-00 5 ½ **Almora Guru**[4] 513 5-8-9 40 MartinDwyer 8 46+
(W M Brisbourne) *t.k.h: a.p: n.m.r briefly wl over 1f out: hmpd ins fnl f: one pce* **80/1**
201 6 nk **Lady Aspen (IRE)**[22] 290 6-9-1 55 (t) StephenDonohoe 6 50
(Ian Williams) *prom: rdn over 1f out: wknd ins fnl f* **8/1**
40-4 7 hd **Winged Farasi**[28] 221 5-9-0 46 (b[1]) SamHitchcott 1 49
(Miss J E Foster) *dwlt: hld up in rr: rdn and sme hdwy on ins over 1f out: n.d* **20/1**
03-4 8 nk **Artreju (GER)**[42] 42 6-9-0 63 GeorgeBaker 3 48
(G L Moore) *hld up in rr: rdn and hung lft fr over 1f out: nvr trbld ldrs* **7/2**[2]
000/ 9 14 **One Upmanship**[1262] 4960 8-8-11 36 KevinGhunowa(3) 10 16
(M Salaman) *sn led: hdd over 2f out: wknd wl over 1f out* **100/1**
0-00 10 10 **Willie Ever**[26] 238 5-9-0 68 (b[1]) DarrenWilliams 9 —
(I W McInnes) *swtchd lft sn after s: hld up in rr: hung rt bnd over 2f out: sn lost tch* **12/1**

1m 53.59s (3.09) **Going Correction** +0.275s/f (Slow) 10 Ran SP% **120.8**
Speed ratings (Par 101): **97,96,96,93,93 93,93,92,80,71**
toteswinger: 1&2 £6.10, 1&3 £6.10, 2&3 £8.00. CSF £33.23 TOTE £9.90: £2.70, £1.40, £2.20; EX 35.40 TRIFECTA Not won..The winner was bought in for £7000.
Owner Lee Suir Syndicate **Bred** Gainsborough Stud Management Ltd **Trained** Trim, Co Meath
■ Stewards' Enquiry : Kevin Ghunowa one-day ban: failed to ride to draw (Mar 2)

FOCUS
A reasonable seller, but a few of these displayed suspect attitudes and the proximity of the fifth and seventh suggests the principals ran below their marks.
Almora Guru Official explanation: jockey said mare moved badly throughout
Artreju(GER) Official explanation: jockey said gelding was unsuited by the slow gallop
Willie Ever Official explanation: jockey said gelding hung right

570 BETDAQ BETTING EXCHANGE MAIDEN STKS 1m 1f 103y(P)
4:10 (4:12) (Class 5) 3-Y-O+ £2,729 (£806; £403) Stalls Low

Form RPR
5-4 1 **Spartan Prince (USA)**[35] 138 3-8-5 0 MartinDwyer 2 67+
(T D Barron) *hld up in tch: rdn over 2f out: led ins fnl f: r.o* **6/4**[1]
5- 2 1¼ **The Staffy (IRE)**[56] 7759 4-9-12 0 LukeMorris 3 62
(N J Vaughan) *led early: a.p: rdn over 2f out: r.o ins fnl f* **5/1**[3]
0 3 nk **Rosko**[7] 476 5-9-12 0 TomEaves 4 61
(B Ellison) *hld up in tch: chsd ldr 3f out: rdn over 1f out: lost 2nd ins fnl f: kpt on* **6/1**
0 4 nk **Alittlemoreflair**[9] 440 3-8-0 0 JimmyQuinn 7 49+
(J Pearce) *t.k.h towards rr: rdn and hdwy over 2f out: kpt on ins fnl f* **33/1**
2- 5 5 **Smooth Sovereign (IRE)**[364] 610 4-9-12 0 JoeFanning 12 50
(M Johnston) *led after 1f: rdn and carried hd awkwardly over 1f out: hdd ins fnl f: wknd* **11/4**[2]
04 6 2 **Ensnare**[7] 468 4-9-12 0 AndrewElliott 1 46+
(A M Hales) *broke wl: sn hld up in mid-div: lost pl on ins over 3f out: n.d after* **20/1**
7 2 **Uncle Bertie** 4-9-12 0 VinceSlattery 5 41
(N J Vaughan) *s.i.s: nvr nr ldrs* **25/1**
- 8 1¼ **Rannoch Rose (IRE)** 3-8-0 0 CatherineGannon 6 28
(J L Spearing) *dwlt: c wd st: a in rr* **66/1**
3-0 9 1 **Fire Me Gun**[35] 138 3-7-11 0 DuranFentiman(3) 11 26
(M Mullineaux) *s.i.s: towards rr: short-lived effrt over 3f out* **50/1**
10 3¼ **Keen As Mustard** 4-9-5 0 LeeNewnes(7) 13 30
(M D I Usher) *s.i.s: a towards rr* **66/1**
60- 11 1 **Tillietudlem (FR)**[59] 7735 3-8-5 0 ChrisCatlin 10 22
(J S Goldie) *sn chsng ldr: lost 2nd over 3f out: sn wknd* **25/1**
12 7 **Simonside**[52] 6-9-5 0 LanceBetts(7) 9 13
(B Ellison) *dwlt: reminder over 4f out: c v wd st: a in rr* **8/1**
0 13 12 **Fine The World**[28] 217 5-9-7 0 FrankieMcDonald 8 —
(G A Ham) *prom: wnt 2nd briefly over 2f out: wknd over 2f out* **66/1**

2m 4.40s (2.70) **Going Correction** +0.275s/f (Slow)
WFA 3 from 4yo+ 21lb 13 Ran SP% **130.6**
Speed ratings (Par 103): **99,97,97,97,92 91,89,88,87,84 83,77,66**
toteswinger: 1&2 £3.60, 1&3 £4.50, 2&3 £9.20. CSF £9.93 TOTE £2.30: £1.10, £2.40, £2.20; EX 14.60 Trifecta £63.70 Pool: £409.00- 4.75 winning units..
Owner Harrowgate Bloodstock Ltd **Bred** Brilliant Stables Inc **Trained** Maunby, N Yorks

FOCUS
Just an ordinary maiden, but the race should produce the odd winner. The leader looked to go off to fast, which might explain why the winning time was 2.97 seconds slower than the following 51-65 handicap.
Fine The World Official explanation: jockey said mare hung right-handed throughout

571 NAME A RACE TO ENHANCE YOUR BRAND H'CAP 1m 1f 103y(P)
4:40 (4:41) (Class 6) (0-65,64) 4-Y-O+ £2,047 (£604; £302) Stalls Low

Form RPR
4/12 1 **Agilete**[17] 353 7-8-10 56 JerryO'Dwyer 13 67+
(J Pearce) *hld up in tch: wnt 2nd over 2f out: shkn up to ld ins fnl f: comf* **5/1**[3]
3-45 2 1¼ **Pelham Crescent (IRE)**[7] 478 6-8-8 59 (p) PatrickDonaghy(5) 12 66
(B Palling) *chsd ldr: led 5f out: rdn wl over 1f out: hdd ins fnl f: nt qckn* **15/2**
5/P- 3 1¾ **New England**[103] 7189 7-8-12 58 TGMcLaughlin 7 63+
(W M Brisbourne) *hld up towards rr: hdwy over 2f out: rdn over 1f out: kpt on to take 3rd cl home* **14/1**
6/46 4 ½ **Emerald Rock (CAN)**[12] 386 4-9-1 61 LukeMorris 2 63
(N J Vaughan) *a.p: rdn over 2f out: kpt on one pce fnl f* **11/2**
4024 5 shd **Inside Story (IRE)**[4] 512 7-9-3 63 (b) LPKeniry 10 65
(C R Dore) *s.i.s: t.k.h towards rr: hdwy on outside 2f out: c wd st: rdn over 1f out: one pce fnl f* **8/1**
45-5 6 ¾ **Penang Cinta**[19] 311 6-9-1 61 (p) PaulDoe 1 61
(P D Evans) *in rr: rdn wl over 1f out: kpt on fnl f: n.d* **4/1**[2]
555- 7 ½ **Rigat**[59] 7732 6-8-12 58 JoeFanning 8 57
(J S Goldie) *t.k.h in mid-div: hdwy on outside 3f out: rdn wl over 1f out: fdd wl ins fnl f* **10/1**
0-06 8 3¾ **Strike Force**[7] 478 5-8-11 60 JackMitchell(3) 4 52
(Miss J Feilden) *hld up in mid-div: swtchd rt over 2f out: swtchd lft ent st: rdn and sme prog on ins over 1f out: wknd ins fnl f* **7/2**[1]
9 6 **Fathzo (IRE)**[52] 4547 5-8-12 58 ChrisCatlin 3 37
(Gerard Keane, Ire) *s.i.s: a in rr* **16/1**
-300 10 7 **Fandango Boy**[7] 478 8-9-4 64 DNolan 6 28
(D Carroll) *prom tl rdn and wknd wl over 1f out: eased ins fnl f* **33/1**
/00- 11 4½ **Nota Liberata**[16] 7732 5-8-8 54 (bt[1]) PaulHanagan 9 9
(Ollie Pears) *plld hrd: a towards rr* **25/1**
-56 12 2¾ **Redwater River**[4] 515 5-8-11 62 DeanHeslop(5) 11 11
(Mrs R A Carr) *led: hdd 5f out: wknd wl over 2f out* **33/1**

2m 1.43s (-0.27) **Going Correction** +0.275s/f (Slow) 12 Ran SP% **128.5**
Speed ratings (Par 101): **112,110,109,108,108 108,107,104,99,92 88,86**
toteswinger: 1&2 £9.30, 1&3 £15.40, 2&3 £40.60. CSF £45.58 CT £512.07 TOTE £4.00: £2.00, £3.30, £3.40; EX 48.90 TRIFECTA Not won..
Owner Mrs M Miller **Bred** J W Parker And Lavington Stud **Trained** Newmarket, Suffolk
■ Stewards' Enquiry : T G McLaughlin six-day ban: used whip with excessive frequency without giving gelding time to respond (Mar 2-7)

FOCUS
A modest handicap but run at a good pace and the form looks sound.

572 DINE IN HORIZONS RESTAURANT MAIDEN STKS 7f 32y(P)
5:10 (5:11) (Class 5) 3-Y-O+ £2,590 (£770; £385; £192) Stalls High

Form RPR
62- 1 **Princess Zohra**[49] 7810 3-8-4 0 JimmyQuinn 3 62+
(E A L Dunlop) *t.k.h: led: hdd 5f out: chsd ldr: led over 2f out: rdn over 1f out: drvn out* **9/4**[1]
2 ¾ **Invincible Miss (IRE)**[139] 6365 3-8-4 0 NickyMackay 5 60
(M Wigham) *hld up in tch: chsd wnr over 1f out: rdn and kpt on ins fnl f* **33/1**
3 1¼ **Jawaaher (USA)** 3-8-4 0 JoeFanning 2 57+
(M Johnston) *s.i.s: sn rcvrd: hmpd on ins bnd after 1f: hld up in mid-div: hdwy on ins over 2f out: styd on ins fnl f* **5/1**
0-2 4 nk **Iron Out (USA)**[15] 364 3-8-9 0 GrahamGibbons 10 61+
(R Hollinshead) *t.k.h: sn hld up in tch: lost pl over 3f out: styd on ins fnl f* **5/2**[2]
00- 5 2¼ **Praise Of Folly**[147] 6167 3-8-4 0 SimonWhitworth 9 50
(A G Newcombe) *hld up towards rr: rdn wl over 1f out: nvr nr to chal* **50/1**
62-6 6 nse **Lucky Dan (IRE)**[19] 313 3-8-9 60 ChrisCatlin 11 55
(Paul Green) *sn prom: led 5f out tl over 2f out: wknd ins fnl f* **14/1**
42-6 7 nse **Dante Deo (USA)**[34] 144 3-8-4 0 FrankieMcDonald 12 50+
(T D Barron) *in rr: rdn and sme hdwy over 1f out: nvr trbld ldrs* **14/1**
3 8 ½ **If Only**[12] 394 3-8-9 0 LukeMorris 6 53+
(J Jay) *plld hrd: prom: rdn over 2f out: fdd ins fnl f* **4/1**[3]
0 9 ½ **Holoko Heights**[12] 386 4-9-12 0 VinceSlattery 4 58+
(N J Vaughan) *nvr nr ldrs* **50/1**
0-4 10 9 **Esteem Dancer**[26] 230 3-8-9 0 HayleyTurner 7 28
(J G Given) *prom: lost pl over 3f out: hung rt bnd over 2f out: sn bhd* **22/1**
000 11 1¼ **Uncle Brit**[13] 381 3-8-9 0 StephenDonohoe 8 24
(Sir Mark Prescott) *fly-jmpd and stmbld leaving stalls: a wl in rr* **20/1**

1m 31.75s (2.15) **Going Correction** +0.275s/f (Slow)
WFA 3 from 4yo 17lb 11 Ran SP% **125.3**
Speed ratings (Par 103): **98,97,95,95,92 92,92,92,91,81 79**
toteswinger: 1&2 £22.80, 1&3 £4.80, 2&3 £46.60. CSF £93.13 TOTE £3.40: £1.40, £8.30, £2.40; EX 172.10 Trifecta £78.00 Pool: £502.79 - 4.77 winning units..
Owner Quy, Dunlop & Gordon-Watson **Bred** Mrs J M Quy **Trained** Newmarket, Suffolk

FOCUS
A very modest maiden run at a steady pace and the form looks limited.
If Only Official explanation: jockey said colt ran too freely

573 BETDAQ.CO.UK H'CAP 7f 32y(P)
5:40 (5:40) (Class 5) (0-70,70) 4-Y-O+ £2,590 (£770; £385; £192) Stalls High

Form RPR
-11 1 **Singleb (IRE)**[28] 215 5-9-1 67 (p) JamieSpencer 2 76
(Miss Gay Kelleway) *chsd ldr 1f: wnt 2nd again over 2f out: rdn to ld ins fnl f: r.o* **15/8**[1]
1642 2 1¾ **Downhill Skier (IRE)**[7] 471 5-8-12 64 TGMcLaughlin 6 68+
(W M Brisbourne) *hld up: rdn and hdwy 2f out: kpt on to take 2nd last strides* **3/1**[2]
5-42 3 hd **Red Cape (FR)**[28] 218 6-9-1 67 (b) AndrewElliott 4 70
(Mrs R A Carr) *led: rdn over 1f out: hdd ins fnl f: no ex and lost 2nd last strides* **3/1**[2]
4016 4 11 **Divertimenti (IRE)**[12] 387 5-8-11 68 (b) JamesO'Reilly(5) 5 42
(C R Dore) *t.k.h: chsd ldr after 1f: lost 2nd and rdn over 2f out: wknd wl over 1f out* **17/2**[3]
/10- 5 dist **Mr Macattack**[270] 2333 4-9-4 70 (t) LukeMorris 1 —
(N J Vaughan) *swvd bdly lft and lost all ch s: completed crse in own time* **3/1**[2]

1m 29.98s (0.38) **Going Correction** +0.275s/f (Slow) 5 Ran SP% **120.3**
Speed ratings (Par 103): **108,106,105,93,88**
toteswinger: 1&2 £5.20. CSF £8.76 TOTE £2.40: £1.60, £1.70; EX 9.70 Place 6: £83.82 Place: £47.22.
Owner Mrs Donna Joslyn **Bred** Spratstown Stud Gm **Trained** Exning, Suffolk

FOCUS
Modest handicap form with the runner-up close to recent form.
T/Jkpt: Not won. T/Plt: £50.90 to a £1 stake. Pool: £66,584.54. 954.67 winning tickets. T/Qpdt: £25.60 to a £1 stake. Pool: £4,309.60. 124.15 winning tickets. KH

[566]WOLVERHAMPTON (A.W) (L-H)
Tuesday, February 17

OFFICIAL GOING: Standard
Wind: Light across Weather: Fine

574 GREAT OFFERS AT WOLVERHAMPTON-RACECOURSE.CO.UK CLASSIFIED STKS 5f 216y(P)
2:10 (2:10) (Class 7) 4-Y-O+ £1,364 (£403; £201) Stalls Low

Form RPR
5-05 1 **All You Need (IRE)**[10] 452 5-9-0 45 (p) HayleyTurner 8 60
(R Hollinshead) *chsd ldrs: led and edgd lft ins fnl f: r.o wl* **10/3**[1]

40-3 **2** *2 1/4* **Fraizer (IRE)**[27] 242 5-8-7 45.. IJBrennan(7) 11 53
(Adrian McGuinness, Ire) *plld hrd: prom tl stdd into mid-div after 2f: hdwy 2f out: rdn and hung lft fr over 1f out: r.o to take 2nd wl ins fnl f: nt trble wnr* **11/2**[3]

0025 **3** *1 1/2* **Mr Loire**[8] 475 5-9-0 45..(b) JerryO'Dwyer 5 48
(K G Wingrove) *hld up in mid-div: rdn and swtchd rt ins fnl f: r.o wl to take 3rd cl home* **11/2**[3]

060- **4** *hd* **Young Ivanhoe**[128] 6680 4-8-7 45.. BMcHugh(7) 1 48
(C A Dwyer) *w ldr: led wl over 1f out: rdn and hdd ins fnl f: no ex* **7/2**[2]

6044 **5** *3/4* **Spanish Ace**[5] 508 8-8-9 44..(b) JackDean(5) 13 45
(J M Bradley) *led: hdd wl over 1f out: sn rdn: fdd wl ins fnl f* **16/1**

5-00 **6** *3* **Berrymead**[28] 222 4-8-11 45 ow2.. AnnStokell(5) 12 38
(Miss A Stokell) *bhd: rdn and edgd lft fr over 1f out: nvr trbld ldrs* **33/1**

0-56 **7** *shd* **Ace Club**[16] 367 8-8-7 44..(b) AndrewHeffernan(7) 10 35
(Garry Moss) *t.k.h: prom: rdn over 1f out: wknd ins fnl f* **25/1**

-506 **8** *2* **Princess Zhukova (IRE)**[14] 381 4-8-11 45...... RussellKennemore(3) 3 29
(R J Price) *nvr nr ldrs* **25/1**

540- **9** *hd* **Geordie Dancer (IRE)**[91] 7369 7-8-9 45.. SladeO'Hara(5) 9 28
(A Berry) *towards rr: c v wd st: n.d* **28/1**

0326 **10** *1/2* **Nordic Light (USA)**[5] 508 5-9-0 44..(bt) LukeMorris 6 27
(J M Bradley) *chsd ldrs: rdn 3f out: wknd ins fnl f* **11/2**[3]

0420 **11** *1 1/2* **So Sublime**[7] 487 4-8-9 45..(b) AmyBaker(5) 2 22
(M C Chapman) *hld up in mid-div: wknd over 1f out* **9/1**

060- **12** *1/2* **Fern House (IRE)**[142] 6310 7-8-11 44.. AndrewMullen(3) 4 20
(Bruce Hellier) *s.i.s: a in rr* **16/1**

0/0- **13** *22* **Optical Seclusion (IRE)**[102] 7218 6-8-7 45............ KrishGundowry(7) 7 —
(A Berry) *a in rr: eased over 1f out* **66/1**

1m 15.06s (0.06) **Going Correction** +0.075s/f (Slow) **13** Ran SP% **128.8**
Speed ratings (Par 97): **102,99,97,96,95 91,91,88,88,88 86,85,56**
toteswinger: 1&2 £7.40, 1&3 £7.20, 2&3 £5.90. CSF £22.74 TOTE £4.20: £1.40, £2.20, £2.50; EX 26.80 Trifecta £122.50 Pool: £246.76 - 1.49 winning units..
Owner N Chapman **Bred** D J Maher **Trained** Upper Longdon, Staffs
■ Stewards' Enquiry : Jack Dean one-day ban: failed to keep straight from stalls (Mar 3)

FOCUS
An ordinary race run at a decent pace. The first five finished clear of the rest.

575 BET 1% IN RUNNING - BETDAQ H'CAP 5f 216y(P)
2:40 (2:40) (Class 6) (0-50,55) 4-Y-O+ **£2,388** (£705; £352) **Stalls** Low

Form RPR

615- **1** **Many Welcomes**[138] 6409 4-8-11 **49**.. AndrewElliott 3 57+
(B P J Baugh) *hld up towards rr: swtchd lft and hdwy on ins over 1f out: sn rdn: r.o wl to ld wl ins fnl f* **9/1**

00-3 **2** *3/4* **Interchoice Star**[8] 480 4-8-7 **48**.. RussellKennemore(3) 1 54
(R Hollinshead) *led 1f: a.p: rdn to ld briefly wl ins fnl f: kpt on* **7/4**[1]

0560 **3** *nk* **Tag Team (IRE)**[7] 487 8-8-11 **49**..(v) ChrisCatlin 13 54
(John A Harris) *led after 1f: rdn 1f out: hdd and nt qckn wl ins fnl f* **12/1**

0-62 **4** *1 1/2* **Inka Dancer (IRE)**[8] 473 7-8-12 **50**.. FrankieMcDonald 10 53+
(B Palling) *hld up towards rr: hdwy over 2f out: nt clr run and swtchd lft wl over 1f out: r.o towards fin: nt rch ldrs* **5/1**[2]

0430 **5** *hd* **Ronnie Howe**[16] 367 5-8-12 **50**..(tp) DaneO'Neill 7 50
(S R Bowring) *hld up in rr: c v wd st: rdn and hdwy whn edgd lft ins fnl f: r.o* **7/1**

-000 **6** *hd* **Diminuto**[22] 294 5-8-12 **50**.. HayleyTurner 4 49
(M D I Usher) *w ldrs: rdn and one pce fnl f* **16/1**

-060 **7** *hd* **Briery Lane (IRE)**[8] 474 8-8-9 **47**..(tp) LukeMorris 2 45
(J M Bradley) *prom: lost pl after 2f: rdn and hdwy over 1f out: no further prog fnl f* **11/1**

460- **8** *nk* **Easy Wonder (GER)**[138] 6419 4-8-5 **48**.. MartinLane(5) 6 45+
(I A Wood) *sn towards rr: nvr nrr* **12/1**

030- **9** *1 1/4* **Obe One**[77] 7529 9-8-6 **49**.. SladeO'Hara(5) 5 42
(A Berry) *hld up in mid-div: rdn over 2f out: nt clr run 1f out: n.d after* **16/1**

-006 **10** *3/4* **Metropolitan Chief**[8] 472 5-8-10 **48**..(b) JimmyQuinn 9 39
(P Burgoyne) *t.k.h: prom: hung lft fr over 1f out: wknd ins fnl f* **25/1**

05-0 **11** *shd* **Charlie Allnut**[8] 473 4-8-12 **50**..(v[1]) LeeEnstone 11 41
(S Wynne) *hld up in mid-div: hdwy on outside 3f out: c wd st: wknd over 1f out* **25/1**

0-41 **12** *1/2* **Nawaaff**[8] 474 4-9-3 **55** 6ex.. TonyCulhane 8 44
(M R Channon) *hld up in mid-div: hdwy wl over 2f out: rdn wl over 1f out: wknd ins fnl f* **11/2**[3]

1m 15.43s (0.43) **Going Correction** +0.075s/f (Slow) **12** Ran SP% **134.1**
Speed ratings (Par 101): **100,99,98,96,96 96,95,95,93,92 92,91**
toteswinger: 1&2 £5.60, 1&3 £52.10, 2&3 £8.30. CSF £28.40 CT £214.79 TOTE £10.20: £2.80, £1.40, £4.60; EX 52.00 TRIFECTA Not won..
Owner Gang Of Four **Bred** Mrs F Wilson **Trained** Audley, Staffs

FOCUS
A modest contest run at a brisk pace.
Inka Dancer(IRE) Official explanation: jockey said mare missed the break

576 ENJOY THE LUCKY 7 GROUP OFFER H'CAP 7f 32y(P)
3:10 (3:10) (Class 4) (0-80,79) 4-Y-O+ **£5,180** (£1,541; £770; £384) **Stalls** High

Form RPR

26-2 **1** **Ravi River (IRE)**[39] 106 5-9-3 **75**.. RichardKingscote 5 84+
(Tom Dascombe) *chsd ldr 1f: a.p: led jst ins fnl f: sn rdn: r.o* **9/4**[1]

6116 **2** *1* **Guildenstern (IRE)**[9] 457 7-8-8 **66**.. JimmyQuinn 4 72
(P Howling) *hld up in mid-div: hdwy on ins wl over 1f out: ev ch ins fnl f: rdn and nt qckn cl home* **5/1**[3]

3U03 **3** *hd* **Kensington (IRE)**[12] 404 8-8-10 **73**....................(v) PatrickDonaghy(5) 6 78
(P D Evans) *hld up in tch: rdn and kpt on ins fnl f* **4/1**[2]

60-1 **4** *1 1/2* **Mudhish (IRE)**[11] 420 4-8-10 **68**.. RobertWinston 8 69
(C E Brittain) *chsd ldr after 1f: led wl over 1f out: rdn and hdd jst ins fnl f: one pce* **6/1**

-011 **5** *hd* **Cornus**[7] 486 7-9-7 **79** 6ex..(be) JamesDoyle 9 80
(A J McCabe) *hld up in rr: c wd st: rdn and kpt on ins fnl f: nvr able to chal* **10/1**

-330 **6** *4 1/2* **Peter's Storm (USA)**[12] 400 4-8-13 **71**.. JamieSpencer 7 60
(K A Ryan) *hld up towards rr: pushed along 2f out: eased whn btn ins fnl f* **7/1**

000- **7** *1* **Dhhamaan (IRE)**[99] 7277 4-9-0 **72**..(b) AndrewElliott 2 58
(Mrs R A Carr) *led: hdd wl over 1f out: sn rdn and edgd rt: wknd fnl f* **33/1**

0-64 **8** *nse* **Dudley Docker (IRE)**[29] 218 7-9-4 **76**..(b) LPKeniry 3 62
(C R Dore) *s.i.s: a towards rr* **7/1**

1m 30.1s (0.50) **Going Correction** +0.075s/f (Slow) **8** Ran SP% **118.8**
Speed ratings (Par 105): **100,98,98,96,96 91,90,90**
toteswinger: 1&2 £2.70, 1&3 £3.40, 2&3 £5.10. CSF £14.46 CT £43.38 TOTE £2.40: £1.50, £1.30, £2.40; EX 18.30 Trifecta £80.00 Pool: £278.95 - 2.58 winning units..
Owner M Khan X2 **Bred** Gainsborough Stud Management Ltd **Trained** Lambourn, Berks

FOCUS
A decent handicap, most of the runners arrived here in good form. The pace was fairly steady and those who were held up may have been at a disadvantage.

577 TRY BETDAQ FOR AN EXCHANGE CLAIMING STKS 1m 1f 103y(P)
3:40 (3:40) (Class 6) 4-Y-O+ **£2,914** (£867; £433; £216) **Stalls** Low

Form RPR

3411 **1** **Blacktoft (USA)**[7] 483 6-8-11 72..(e) RichardKingscote 4 74+
(S C Williams) *hld up: hdwy to ld jst over 2f out: shkn up over 1f out: easily* **1/1**[1]

5-41 **2** *3 1/4* **New Star (UAE)**[8] 477 5-8-13 72.. GrahamGibbons 3 70+
(W M Brisbourne) *led early: chsd ldng pair tl nt clr run over 2f out tl wl over 1f out: kpt on to take 2nd ins fnl f: no ch w wnr* **10/3**[3]

5-11 **3** *nk* **Sabre Light**[26] 244 4-9-5 80..(v) JerryO'Dwyer 7 72
(J Pearce) *hld up towards rr: rdn over 5f out: hdwy on outside over 2f out: kpt on same pce fnl f* **2/1**[2]

66-0 **4** *2 1/2* **Flying Applause**[21] 307 4-8-12 70.. DaneO'Neill 5 60
(S R Bowring) *t.k.h: sn chsng ldr: chal over 2f out: sn rdn: btn 1f out* **20/1**

5-00 **5** *nse* **Alexander Guru**[5] 512 5-8-6 55.. JimmyQuinn 1 54
(M Blanshard) *hld up towards rr: hdwy 2f out: rdn over 1f out: wknd ins fnl f* **33/1**

0-60 **6** *4 1/2* **Siryena**[6] 494 4-8-6 54..(tp) ChrisCatlin 6 45
(B I Case) *stdd s: hld up in rr: no ch wl over 1f out* **80/1**

5-20 **7** *23* **Wahoo Sam (USA)**[10] 452 9-8-7 51.. PaulDoe 2 —
(P D Evans) *stmbld sltly s: t.k.h: sn led: hdd jst over 2f out: sn wknd* **40/1**

2m 1.19s (-0.51) **Going Correction** +0.075s/f (Slow) **7** Ran SP% **117.8**
Speed ratings (Par 101): **105,102,101,99,99 95,75**
.The winner was claimed by R. E. R. Williams for £8000.\n\x\x
Owner Chris Watkins And David N Reynolds **Bred** Paradigm Thoroughbreds Inc **Trained** Newmarket, Suffolk

FOCUS
A fair claimer involving three last-time-out winners who held official ratings of between 72 and 80. The three market leaders finished clear of the rest and the form looks solid.
New Star(UAE) Official explanation: jockey said gelding was denied a clear run
Sabre Light Official explanation: jockey said gelding hung left

578 STAY AT THE WOLVERHAMPTON HOLIDAY INN H'CAP (DIV I) 1m 1f 103y(P)
4:10 (4:10) (Class 6) (0-50,51) 4-Y-O+ **£2,047** (£604; £302) **Stalls** Low

Form RPR

5402 **1** **Desert Hawk**[1] 567 8-8-9 **47**.. LukeMorris 3 55
(W M Brisbourne) *hld up towards rr: c v wd st: rdn and hdwy over 1f out: edgd lft and led nr fin* **3/1**[1]

-601 **2** *nk* **High Five Society**[4] 537 5-8-10 **51** 6ex...............(bt) KevinGhunowa(3) 7 59+
(S R Bowring) *hld up: sn in tch: rdn over 2f out: led over 1f out: hung lft and hdd nr fin* **10/3**[2]

0065 **3** *2* **Turkish Sultan (IRE)**[8] 469 6-8-3 **46**..(p) MCGeran(5) 2 49+
(J M Bradley) *hld up towards rr: nt clr run on ins over 2f out: hdwy wl over 1f out: ev ch whn sn rdn and edgd rt: nt qckn whn carried lft towards fin* **9/2**[3]

2-30 **4** *1* **Miss Understanding**[16] 368 4-8-8 **46** oh1....................(b) ChrisCatlin 1 47
(J R Weymes) *hld up in mid-div: rdn and kpt on ins fnl f: nt rch ldrs* **7/1**

0-30 **5** *1 3/4* **Oxus (IRE)**[20] 310 4-8-11 **49** ow1.. AdamKirby 8 46
(B R Johnson) *hld up in rr: rdn and hdwy over 1f out: one pce ins fnl f* **14/1**

-002 **6** *1 1/2* **Komreyev Star**[12] 405 7-8-12 **50**.. JimmyQuinn 10 44
(R E Peacock) *hld up in tch: chsd ldr over 2f out tl wl over 1f out: sn rdn: wknd ins fnl f* **10/1**

00-0 **7** *nk* **Steady Gaze**[10] 444 4-8-8 **46** oh1..(t) NickyMackay 4 40
(M A Allen) *led 1f: prom tl wknd wl over 1f out* **25/1**

-004 **8** *1 1/4* **Piermarini**[8] 480 4-8-5 **50**.. PaulPickard(7) 6 41
(P T Midgley) *hld up in rr: short-lived effrt on ins wl over 1f out* **8/1**

26-0 **9** *nk* **Tapas Lad (IRE)**[41] 81 4-8-12 **50**..(v) DaneO'Neill 9 40
(G J Smith) *prom: wnt 2nd over 6f out: led over 2f out: sn rdn: hdd over 1f out: wknd fnl f* **12/1**

0200 **10** *2 3/4* **Spy Gun (USA)**[4] 537 9-8-1 **46** oh1..(p) JoshWall(7) 5 31
(T Wall) *led after 1f: hdd over 2f out: wknd wl over 1f out* **50/1**

2m 3.14s (1.44) **Going Correction** +0.075s/f (Slow) **10** Ran SP% **119.1**
Speed ratings (Par 101): **96,95,93,93,91 90,89,88,88,86**
toteswinger: 1&2 £3.10, 1&3 £4.80, 2&3 £5.70. CSF £13.38 CT £44.92 TOTE £4.80: £1.60, £1.50, £2.10; EX 14.60 Trifecta £100.80 Pool: £339.28 - 2.49 winning units..
Owner J Jones Racing Ltd **Bred** C J Mills **Trained** Great Ness, Shropshire

FOCUS
A low-grade handicap, but quite an eventful one.
High Five Society Official explanation: jockey said gelding hung left
Oxus(IRE) Official explanation: jockey said gelding hung left

579 WOLVERHAMPTON-RACECOURSE.CO.UK H'CAP 5f 216y(P)
4:40 (4:40) (Class 2) (0-100,97) 4-Y-O+
£12,462 (£3,732; £1,866; £934; £466; £234) **Stalls** Low

Form RPR

06-1 **1** **Flowing Cape (IRE)**[4] 538 4-8-11 **90** 6ex.. MickyFenton 1 101+
(R Hollinshead) *a.p: led wl over 1f out: sn shkn up: pushed out* **7/2**[2]

0-25 **2** *1/2* **Methaaly (IRE)**[4] 538 6-7-13 **83**..(be) DeanHeslop(5) 5 92
(M Mullineaux) *hld up in mid-div: rdn and hdwy whn edgd rt ins fnl f: r.o to take 2nd cl home: nt trble wnr* **14/1**

0-52 **3** *1/2* **Tamagin (USA)**[13] 388 6-9-4 **97**.. JamieSpencer 2 104
(K A Ryan) *led: hung rt fr over 2f out: hdd wl over 1f out: rdn and kpt on fnl f: lost 2nd: cl home* **5/2**[1]

612- **4** *1 1/2* **Orpenindeed (IRE)**[81] 7470 6-8-10 **89**..(p) NickyMackay 7 92
(M Botti) *a.p: ev ch wl over 1f out: sn rdn: nt qckn ins fnl f* **6/1**[3]

50-5 **5** *shd* **Carcinetto (IRE)**[18] 351 7-8-4 **83**.. PaulDoe 11 86+
(P D Evans) *prom: lost pl over 3f out: c wd st: rdn over 1f out: hmpd ins fnl f: kpt on* **22/1**

656- **6** *nk* **Orpsie Boy (IRE)**[104] 7192 6-9-4 **97**.. LukeMorris 10 98
(N P Littmoden) *sn towards rr: pushed along over 2f out: c v wd st: n.m.r on stands' rail ins fnl f: nvr nr to chal* **10/1**

4-16 **7** *1* **Pawan (IRE)**[10] 451 9-8-10 **94** ow1..(b) AnnStokell(5) 3 92
(Miss A Stokell) *chsd ldrs: rdn wl over 1f out: wknd ins fnl f* **28/1**

2154 **8** *1/2* **Dvinsky (USA)**[13] 388 8-8-9 **88**..(b) JimmyQuinn 9 85
(P Howling) *prom: hrd rdn over 1f out: wknd ins fnl f* **25/1**

-151 **9** *1 1/2* **Nightjar (USA)**[28] 225 4-9-0 **93**.. GregFairley 6 85
(M Johnston) *s.i.s: in rr: n.m.r over 2f out: rdn over 1f out: n.d* **15/2**

4-1 **10** *1 1/4* **Mrs Penny (AUS)**[32] 197 5-8-8 **87**.. ChrisCatlin 8 75
(J R Gask) *hld up in rr: swtchd violently lft over 1f out: n.d* **7/2**[2]

5624 **11** *1* **Excusez Moi (USA)**[11] 422 7-8-6 **90**.................. DanielleMcCreery(5) 4 75
(Mrs R A Carr) *s.i.s: a towards rr* **28/1**

1m 13.77s (-1.23) **Going Correction** +0.075s/f (Slow) **11** Ran SP% **129.9**
Speed ratings (Par 109): **111,110,109,107,107 107,105,105,103,101 100**
toteswinger: 1&2 £15.70, 1&3 £3.70, 2&3 £77.70. CSF £54.66 CT £150.17 TOTE £5.20: £1.70, £3.40, £1.40; EX 83.00 Trifecta £353.30 Part won. Pool: £477.55 - 0.10 winning units..
Owner John L Marriott **Bred** David Maher **Trained** Upper Longdon, Staffs
■ Stewards' Enquiry : Dean Heslop three-day ban: careless riding (Mar 3-5)

FOCUS
A classy handicap.

NOTEBOOK
Flowing Cape(IRE) showed tremendous tactical speed to race near the strong pace. He moved smoothly to the front early in the straight, found plenty for pressure and was always in control. He was well supported when making a successful all-weather debut over 7f here last week and comfortably shrugged off a penalty over this shorter trip on his eighth career start. He suffered from a stress fracture of the pelvis last year, but has looked very progressive in his two recent runs, could have quite a bit of room to successfully operate and may be aimed towards Listed company in the spring. (tchd 3-1)
Methaaly(IRE) put in a commendable effort off a mark 9lb higher than his last success. This keen type appreciated the return to 6f, got much closer to Flowing Cape than he did last week and would have to be of interest in a similar race next time. (op 16-1)
Tamagin(USA) put in a tenacious bid under trailblazing tactics over 7f last time. He blasted into the lead from stall two back over what is arguably his best trip here, looked in serous trouble when headed early in the straight but this very likeable sort showed a really feisty attitude to keep rallying and get as close to the winner as he did. (op 3-1 tchd 10-3)
Orpenindeed(IRE) ran a decent race, but could not find the gears needed in the closing stages. (op 8-1)
Carcinetto(IRE) was aiming at closed at a crucial stage. She stayed on quite well after being switched and would have finished a bit closer if she got the breaks when she needed them. She is on a fair mark and seems to be steadily finding her form after a break. Official explanation: jockey said mare suffered interference in running (op 28-1)
Orpsie Boy(IRE) came from a long way back and was a bit short of room against the stands' rail in the final furlong. This was an encouraging effort on his first run for 104 days and he should be sharper next time. Official explanation: jockey said gelding suffered interference in running (op 11-1 tchd 12-1)

580 BET API - BETDAQ H'CAP 1m 141y(P)
5:10 (5:15) (Class 6) (0-65,67) 4-Y-O+ **£2,388** (£705; £352) **Stalls** Low

Form RPR
41-2 **1** **Pab Special (IRE)**[26] 256 6-8-13 **60**.................. PatCosgrave 5 71+
(B R Johnson) *chsd ldr 2f: prom: wnt 2nd again 2f out: led over 1f out: r.o* **10/3**[2]
3-31 **2** *¾* **Forbidden (IRE)**[1] 569 6-9-6 **67** 6ex..................(t) JerryO'Dwyer 10 73
(Daniel Mark Loughnane, Ire) *hld up towards rr: hdwy on outside over 2f out: c wd st: hung lft fr over 1f out: r.o to take 2nd wl ins fnl f: nt trble wnr* **7/2**[3]
1201 **3** *1 ¾* **Ardent Prince**[13] 395 6-8-11 **58**.................. RobertWinston 6 61+
(A J McCabe) *s.i.s: hld up in rr: rdn over 1f out: hdwy fnl f: tk 3rd nr fin* **3/1**[1]
00-1 **4** *¾* **Herbert Crescent**[20] 321 4-9-3 **64**.................. JamieMoriarty 7 64
(Ollie Pears) *rrd s: hld up towards rr: rdn and hdwy over 1f out: kpt on ins fnl f* **20/1**
0-06 **5** *shd* **Stark Contrast (USA)**[27] 238 5-8-12 **59**.................. HayleyTurner 1 59
(M D I Usher) *led early: a.p: rdn and ev ch over 1f out: edgd rt ins fnl f: fdd towards fin* **8/1**
00-6 **6** *¾* **Bajan Pride**[14] 384 5-8-11 **65**.................. BMcHugh(7) 9 63
(R A Fahey) *hld up in tch: rdn over 2f out: edgd lft and wknd ins fnl f* **8/1**
64-5 **7** *½* **Apotheosis**[13] 386 4-9-2 **63**.................. AdamKirby 3 60
(W R Swinburn) *sn led: hdd over 1f out: rdn and wknd ins fnl f* **11/2**
00-0 **8** *4* **Party In The Park**[23] 289 4-8-12 **59**.................. TomEaves 2 47
(Miss J A Camacho) *t.k.h in mid-div: nt clr run jst over 1f out: n.d after* **33/1**
100- **9** *1 ¼* **Forzarzi (IRE)**[67] 7651 5-8-11 **63**.................. SladeO'Hara(5) 4 48
(H A McWilliams) *a towards rr* **33/1**
0-04 **10** *nk* **Mont Cervin**[11] 420 4-8-1 **53**..................(b) DeanHeslop(5) 11 37
(Mrs R A Carr) *t.k.h: sn prom: wnt 2nd over 6f out: ev ch over 2f out: sn rdn: wknd wl over 1f out* **20/1**

1m 50.8s (0.30) **Going Correction** +0.075s/f (Slow) **10** Ran SP% **123.3**
Speed ratings (Par 101): **101,100,98,98,98 97,96,93,92,91**
toteswinger: 1&2 £3.80, 1&3 £2.90, 2&3 £3.30. CSF £15.72 CT £39.32 TOTE £5.50: £2.10, £1.80, £1.80; EX 18.90 Trifecta £56.30 Pool: £453.13 - 5.95 winning units..
Owner T Dempsey **Bred** Ballyhane Stud **Trained** Ashtead, Surrey

FOCUS
A minor handicap, but three of the contenders had won their previous start.
Stark Contrast(USA) Official explanation: jockey said gelding hung right in home straight

581 STAY AT THE WOLVERHAMPTON HOLIDAY INN H'CAP (DIV II) 1m 1f 103y(P)
5:40 (5:45) (Class 6) (0-50,50) 4-Y-O+ **£2,047** (£604; £302) **Stalls** Low

Form RPR
4020 **1** **Nautical**[5] 513 11-8-9 **47**.................. JerryO'Dwyer 5 55
(J R Holt) *hld up towards rr: hdwy on ins over 2f out: led 1f out: rdn out* **9/2**
05-3 **2** *½* **John Potts**[25] 275 4-8-12 **50**..................(p) AndrewElliott 4 57+
(B P J Baugh) *hld up in tch: lost pl over 5f out: hdwy over 2f out: chal gng wl over 1f out: rdn and r.o ins fnl f: nt rch wnr* **11/4**[1]
400- **3** *3* **Karmei**[57] 7385 4-8-12 **50**.................. GrahamGibbons 8 51
(R Curtis) *hld up in mid-div: rdn and hdwy over 1f out: kpt on to take 3rd wl ins fnl f* **7/2**[3]
-000 **4** *¾* **Countrywide Comet (IRE)**[5] 515 4-8-10 **48**.................. TomEaves 6 47
(P Howling) *stdd sn after s: hld up towards rr: hdwy over 1f out: rdn and one pce ins fnl f* **14/1**
00-0 **5** *½* **Naledi**[33] 175 5-8-11 **49** oh1 ow3.................. PaulMulrennan 1 47
(J R Norton) *prom: pushed along over 3f out: rdn and wnt 2nd briefly wl over 1f out: wknd ins fnl f* **33/1**
-000 **6** *1 ¾* **Carry On Cleo**[4] 537 4-8-3 **46** oh1..................(v) DanielleMcCreery(5) 2 41
(A Berry) *led: hdd 1f out: wknd ins fnl f* **14/1**
0/00 **7** *5* **Magical Mimi**[8] 475 8-8-8 **46** oh1..................(b) ChrisCatlin 7 30
(K G Wingrove) *s.i.s: a in rr* **40/1**
600- **8** *7* **Ugly Betty**[121] 6836 4-8-5 **46** oh1.................. AndrewMullen(3) 3 16
(Bruce Hellier) *w ldr tl rdn over 2f out: wknd wl over 1f out* **33/1**
/0-4 **9** *8* **Comeintothespace (IRE)**[10] 444 7-8-9 **47**.................. PaulDoe 9 —
(R A Farrant) *hld up in mid-div: stdy prog 6f out: rdn and wknd over 2f out* **3/1**[2]
600- **10** *11* **Xandra (IRE)**[117] 6935 4-8-12 **50**.................. LiamJones 10 —
(W M Brisbourne) *plld hrd: prom tl wknd over 2f out* **14/1**

2m 3.20s (1.50) **Going Correction** +0.075s/f (Slow) **10** Ran SP% **120.4**
Speed ratings (Par 101): **96,95,92,92,91 90,85,79,72,62**
toteswinger: 1&2 £4.10, 1&3 £4.50, 2&3 £2.90. CSF £17.69 CT £49.44 TOTE £5.70: £1.90, £1.10, £1.70; EX 12.90 Trifecta £55.90 Pool: £530.63 - 7.02 winning units. Place 6: £8.77 Place 5: £4.74.
Owner P V Thomas **Bred** Sheikh Mohammed Bin Rashid Al Maktoum **Trained** Peckleton, Leics
■ Stewards' Enquiry : Liam Jones four-day ban: careless riding (Mar 3-6)

FOCUS
A moderate contest, but the first two pulled clear of the rest.
T/Jkpt: £32,137.20 to a £1 stake. Pool: £45,263.74. 0.50 winning tickets. T/Plt: £15.30 to a £1 stake. Pool: £79,890.15. 3,802.68 winning tickets. T/Qpdt: £5.60 to a £1 stake. Pool: £4,667.80. 611.30 winning tickets. KH

[541]KEMPTON (A.W) (R-H)
Wednesday, February 18

OFFICIAL GOING: Standard
Wind: Nil Weather: Dry

582 GOFFS BREEZE UP AT KEMPTON MARCH 6TH H'CAP 5f (P)
6:50 (6:51) (Class 5) (0-70,70) 4-Y-O+ **£2,590** (£770; £385; £192) **Stalls** High

Form RPR
-445 **1** **Steel City Boy (IRE)**[13] 400 6-8-13 **65**.................. JimCrowley 2 76
(D Shaw) *in tch in midfield: effrt and rdn over 1f out: chal 1f out: rdn to ld fnl 100yds: r.o wl* **9/2**[2]
0-42 **2** *¾* **Step It Up (IRE)**[10] 461 5-8-13 **65**.................. PatCosgrave 9 73
(J R Boyle) *chsd ldrs: swtchd lft and effrt over 1f out: drvn to ld jst ins fnl f: hdd and unable qckn fnl 100yds* **7/2**[1]
2-41 **3** *1* **Towy Valley**[31] 208 4-9-4 **70**.................. AdamKirby 7 74
(C G Cox) *chsd ldrs: short of room and jostled 4f out: hdwy over 1f out: chsd ldrs not much room briefly ins fnl f: kpt on same pce fnl 100yds* **15/2**
115- **4** *¾* **Ask Jenny (IRE)**[60] 7745 7-8-7 **59**.................. LiamJones 3 61
(Patrick Morris) *bhd: rdn and hdwy over 1f out: swtchd lft ent fnl f: r.o wl: nt rch ldrs* **10/1**
0633 **5** *½* **Bluebok**[19] 349 8-8-9 **61**..................(bt) LPKeniry 4 61
(J M Bradley) *disp ld tl 3f out: rdn to ld again over 1f out: hdd jst ins fnl f: fdd towards fin* **12/1**
2211 **6** *2 ¾* **Grimes Faith**[12] 422 6-9-4 **70**..................(p) JamieSpencer 8 60
(K A Ryan) *sn rdn along to dispute ld: rdn and hdd over 1f out: wknd ins fnl f* **7/2**[1]
4-04 **7** *nk* **Storey Hill (USA)**[11] 442 4-9-4 **70**.................. RobertWinston 6 59
(D Shaw) *restless stalls: awkward s and s.i.s: a in rr: sme hdwy u.p over 1f out: no hdwy fnl f* **5/1**[3]
00-6 **8** *1 ¼* **Maryolini**[20] 329 4-8-13 **65**.................. PaulDoe 1 49
(N J Vaughan) *wnt lft s: a bhd* **40/1**
01-0 **9** *3 ¾* **Guto**[20] 326 6-8-10 **62**.................. RichardKingscote 5 33
(W J H Ratcliffe) *chsd ldrs tl wknd u.p over 1f out* **20/1**

59.43 secs (-1.07) **Going Correction** -0.125s/f (Stan) **9** Ran SP% **115.0**
Speed ratings (Par 103): **103,101,100,99,98 93,93,91,85**
toteswinger: 1&2 £3.90, 1&3 £8.60, 2&3 £4.20. CSF £20.56 CT £115.41 TOTE £6.40: £2.20, £1.50, £1.90; EX 25.20.
Owner J Medley **Bred** Mrs A B McDonnell **Trained** Danethorpe, Notts

FOCUS
A good pace looked assured here and that is the way things panned out, with Grimes Faith, Bluebok and Guto taking each other on up front and ensuring that the race was set up for the closers. The form looks solid with the winner close to his previous best and the runner-up to form.
Towy Valley Official explanation: jockey said filly suffered interference after the start

583 DAY TIME, NIGHT TIME, GREAT TIME APPRENTICE H'CAP 6f (P)
7:20 (7:20) (Class 6) (0-55,52) 3-Y-O **£2,047** (£604; £302) **Stalls** High

Form RPR
0260 **1** **Valdemar**[15] 379 3-8-13 **49**..................(p) DeanHeslop(3) 3 50
(A D Brown) *wnt lft s: t.k.h: sn led: rdn and hdd over 1f out: kpt on u.p fnl 100yds to catch stopping ldr last stride* **7/1**
05-0 **2** *hd* **Lovely Steps (USA)**[32] 201 3-8-12 **50**..................(b[1]) ChrisHough(5) 7 53+
(D M Simcock) *t.k.h early: hld up in tch: hdwy on inner over 2f out: pushed into ld over 1f out: looked wnr tl idled bdly and ct last stride* **9/4**[1]
5-00 **3** *1 ¼* **Meg Jicaro**[18] 356 3-8-12 **45**.................. JackDean 4 41
(Mrs L Williamson) *chsd ldrs: rdn and swtchd lft over 2f out: kpt on u.p fnl f* **33/1**
0-30 **4** *3* **Flamboyant Red (IRE)**[14] 390 3-8-9 **45**.................. KylieManser(3) 6 31
(Miss Gay Kelleway) *hld up in rr: swtchd to inner and hdwy over 2f out: rdn 2f out: sn no imp* **7/2**[2]
0-0 **5** *1 ¼* **Kitty Allen**[30] 214 3-8-11 **49**.................. PaulPickard(5) 1 31
(C N Kellett) *awkward and bmpd s: racd freely and sn jnd ldr: hdd and rdn over 2f out: wknd ent fnl f* **20/1**
645- **6** *½* **Little Blacknumber**[49] 7833 3-9-0 **52**.................. CharlesEddery(5) 5 33
(R Hannon) *awkward s and s.i.s: a bhd: rdn and lost tch over 2f out: no ch after* **7/2**[2]
60-6 **7** *1 ¾* **Taurus Twins**[15] 379 3-9-4 **51**.................. MCGeran 2 26
(R J Price) *hld up in tch: rdn and hanging rt over 2f out: wknd 2f out* **9/2**[3]

1m 14.23s (1.13) **Going Correction** -0.025s/f (Stan) **7** Ran SP% **113.6**
Speed ratings (Par 95): **91,90,89,85,83 82,80**
toteswinger: 1&2 £2.60, 1&3 £11.50, 2&3 £11.60. CSF £22.86 TOTE £9.70: £3.50, £1.60; EX 31.90.
Owner John Wills **Bred** J R Wills **Trained** Yedingham, N Yorks

FOCUS
A moderate handicap for apprentice riders and the form is weak.
Meg Jicaro Official explanation: jockey said filly hung left
Little Blacknumber Official explanation: jockey said filly was hampered a furlong after the start

584 DIGIBET CLAIMING STKS 1m 4f (P)
7:50 (7:50) (Class 6) 4-Y-O+ **£2,047** (£604; £302) **Stalls** Centre

Form RPR
21-0 **1** **Cossack Prince**[32] 202 4-9-4 **68**.................. IanMongan 3 78
(Mrs L J Mongan) *racd keenly: led after 1f: sn clr: rdn and qcknd further clr over 3f out: kpt on wl u.p fr over 1f out* **9/1**
-224 **2** *1 ¼* **Quince (IRE)**[10] 456 6-9-5 **78**..................(v) JimmyQuinn 2 74
(J Pearce) *hld up wl off the pce in main gp: rdn and hdwy over 2f out: chsd clr wnr 1f out: r.o but nt rch wnr* **10/1**

-306 **3** *2* **Profit's Reality (IRE)**[10] 456 7-9-7 81 JimCrowley 7 73
(M J Attwater) *hld up wl off the pce in main gp: effrt and hdwy on inner over 2f out: wnt 3rd ins fnl f: nvr nr wnr* **8/1**[3]

2/52 **4** *½* **Bernabeu (IRE)**[27] 248 7-8-13 57 JamesDoyle 8 64
(S Curran) *led for 1f: chsd ldng pair after: 10l 3rd and rdn 3f out: kpt on but nvr able to chal* **13/2**[2]

34-1 **5** *¾* **King's Head (IRE)**[10] 456 6-9-6 91 (p) GeorgeBaker 4 70
(G L Moore) *hld up wl off the pce in last pair: rdn and hanging rt over 2f out: kpt on but nvr able to chal* **8/13**[1]

63-0 **6** *¾* **Krugerrand (USA)**[25] 285 10-8-13 65 StephenDonohoe 5 62
(W J Musson) *stdd s: hld up wl off the pce in rr: kpt on fr over 2f out: nvr trbld ldrs* **20/1**

030- **7** *1½* **Celticello (IRE)**[13] 7695 7-8-13 72 PaulDoe 6 59
(P D Evans) *t.k.h: chsd wnr clr of remainder over 8f out: rdn 3f out: wknd and lost 2nd 1f out* **25/1**

6-20 **8** *2½* **St Savarin (FR)**[22] 302 8-8-12 75 AdamKirby 1 54
(B R Johnson) *t.k.h: hld up wl off the pce in midfield: nvr trbld ldrs* **33/1**

2m 34.17s (-0.33) **Going Correction** -0.025s/f (Stan)
WFA 4 from 6yo+ 3lb **8** Ran SP% **117.0**
Speed ratings (Par 101): **100,99,97,97,97 96,95,93**
toteswinger: 1&2 £10.40, 1&3 £16.20, 2&3 £9.00. CSF £91.02 TOTE £9.80: £2.20, £1.80, £1.50; EX 109.40.King's Head was claimed by Ken McGarrity for £15,000.
Owner Mrs P J Sheen **Bred** Wyck Hall Stud Ltd **Trained** Epsom, Surrey

FOCUS
A fair claimer but the proximity of the fourth suggests the form horses were not at their best.
King's Head(IRE) Official explanation: jockey said gelding never travelled

585 DIGIBET.COM H'CAP 1m 3f (P)
8:20 (8:21) (Class 2) (0-100,98) 4-Y-0+
£11,215 (£3,358; £1,679; £840; £419; £210) **Stalls** High

Form RPR

50-2 **1** **Emerald Wilderness (IRE)**[18] 360 5-9-6 **98** JamieSpencer 5 106+
(A King) *stdd s: hld up in last pl: stl last over 2f out: swtchd lft and effrt over 1f out: pushed along and hung rt fnl f: led fnl 100yds* **11/4**[1]

-560 **2** *nk* **John Terry (IRE)**[11] 445 6-8-10 **88** JimCrowley 9 95
(Mrs A J Perrett) *t.k.h: hld up in midfield: stl travelling wl in pack 2f out: hdwy over 1f out: ev ch and drvn ins fnl f: wnt 2nd towards fin but hld by wnr* **12/1**

06-5 **3** *hd* **Grand Passion (IRE)**[18] 360 9-9-6 **98** GeorgeBaker 2 105
(C F Wall) *hld up towards rr on inner: stdy hdwy 4f out: trckd ldrs 2f out: rdn to ld jst over 1f out: drvn and hdd fnl 100yds: kpt on* **11/1**

315- **4** *1¼* **Greylami (IRE)**[124] 6784 4-8-7 **87** RobertHavlin 1 92+
(T G Mills) *hld up in midfield: stdd towards rr 7f out: hdwy over 3f out: ev ch and drvn jst ins fnl f: hld whn short of room wl ins fnl f* **4/1**[3]

0-10 **5** *2¾* **Evident Pride (USA)**[18] 360 6-8-11 **89** AdamKirby 3 89
(B R Johnson) *hld up in last pair: hdwy towards inner over 2f out: nt clr run briefly ent fnl 2f: sn rdn and one pce* **10/1**

/12- **6** *1* **Alsadaa (USA)**[60] 7558 6-8-6 **84** oh7 ChrisCatlin 4 82
(Mrs L J Mongan) *chsd ldrs tl jnd ldr over 8f out: rdn to ld 2f out: hdd jst over 1f out: wknd fnl f* **20/1**

012- **7** *2* **Cape Colony**[63] 7704 4-8-5 **85** JimmyQuinn 6 80
(R Hannon) *sn pushed along to chse ldrs: rdn 2f out: drvn and wknd ent fnl f* **13/2**

220- **8** *nse* **Halla San**[25] 4493 7-9-4 **96** MartinDwyer 7 91
(R A Fahey) *chsd ldrs: rdn over 3f out: wknd u.p 2f out* **33/1**

3-12 **9** *1¼* **Robby Bobby**[3] 563 4-8-13 **93** JoeFanning 10 86
(M Johnston) *chsd ldr tl over 8f out: chsd ldrs after: ev ch and rdn ent fnl 2f: drvn and wknd jst over 1f out* **3/1**[2]

236- **10** *½* **Maxwil**[92] 3527 4-8-6 **86** PaulDoe 8 78
(G L Moore) *stdd s: hld up in rr: hdwy on outer over 3f out: rdn and wknd over 2f out* **40/1**

0-0 **11** *10* **Prairie Spirit (FR)**[11] 445 5-9-0 **92** DaneO'Neill 11 67
(C E Longsdon) *led: jnd over 8f out: rdn and hdd 2f out: sn wknd* **66/1**

2m 18.2s (-3.70) **Going Correction** -0.025s/f (Stan)
WFA 4 from 5yo+ 2lb **11** Ran SP% **121.8**
Speed ratings (Par 109): **112,111,111,110,108 108,106,106,105,105 97**
toteswinger: 1&2 £8.40, 1&3 £8.10, 2&3 £8.20. CSF £37.10 CT £327.51 TOTE £3.10: £1.10, £4.40, £3.80; EX 42.50.
Owner Terry Warner & David Sewell **Bred** Mrs Joan Murphy **Trained** Barbury Castle, Wilts

FOCUS
A decent handicap and the form looks good. While the early lead was contested, the pace steadied markedly down the back straight before the race developed into something of a sprint in the straight, although the overall time was good for the grade.

NOTEBOOK
Emerald Wilderness(IRE) did really well to come from last to first to win. Travelling well with two furlongs to run, Spencer switched him to the outside and, despite hanging, he flew home. It was an impressive turn of foot that he showed, but he looks the type who needs to be delivered late, as he might not find a great deal once he gets his head in front. He is likely to go back hurdling now - he ran in some hot novice races last season and looks handily rated in that sphere - and connections will no doubt be looking for some decent ground for him. But he is clearly deserving of a rating in three figures on the Flat now and there could be a valuable race in the coming months. (op 15-8)
John Terry(IRE) raced keenly but really picked up late in the day. Another furlong suits him ideally, but he does not have a great strike-rate for a horse of his ability. (op 11-1 tchd 9-1)
Grand Passion(IRE) had a poor draw but Baker did a good job of getting him over to the rail and the gap on the inside opened up nicely for him in the straight. He had every chance given the way the race was run. (op 16-1)
Greylami(IRE), who has gone well fresh in the past, was having his first outing since October. Competing off a career-high mark, he ran a highly creditable race considering that he was at least two or three wide throughout. He could be in for a good season on turf this year. (op 5-1)
Evident Pride(USA) did not get the clearest of runs in the straight but he lacked the pace of the principals in the closing stages. A stronger all-round gallop would have suited him. (op 7-1)
Alsadaa(USA), who was far from disgraced from 7lb out of the handicap, went very wide around the first turn and was always to the outside of his fellow pacesetter Prairie Spirit. His next target is the County Hurdle, where he will need decent ground to be seen at his best.
Cape Colony, another running off a career-high mark, was well placed entering the straight but might just have needed this first outing for two months. (op 12-1)
Robby Bobby, making a quick reappearance after finding Kandidate too strong at Southwell three days earlier, had beaten Emerald Wilderness at Lingfield on his previous start. He got involved in an early battle for the lead here, raced too keenly and challenged wide into the straight. Not a lot went his way. (op 9-2)

586 DIGIBET H'CAP 1m (P)
8:50 (8:52) (Class 5) (0-70,74) 3-Y-O **£2,590** (£770; £385; £192) **Stalls** High

Form RPR

05-2 **1** **Ageebah**[14] 397 3-9-0 **65** MartinDwyer 5 68
(C E Brittain) *chsd ldrs: rdn ent fnl 2f: drvn to ld ins fnl f: styd on* **15/2**[3]

003- **2** *¾* **Brer Rabbit**[101] 7258 3-8-11 **62** ChrisCatlin 2 63
(B W Hills) *stdd s: t.k.h: hld up in rr: rdn 2f out: hdwy ent fnl f: r.o to go 2nd wl ins fnl f: nt rch wnr* **16/1**

06-0 **3** *¾* **Co Dependent (USA)**[23] 295 3-9-3 **68** ShaneKelly 4 67+
(J A Osborne) *stdd s: t.k.h: hld up in rr: hdwy jst over 2f out: nt clr run and edging out lft ent fnl f: in the clr and r.o fnl 75yds to snatch 3rd on line: nt rch ldrs* **9/2**[1]

00-1 **4** *nse* **Millway Beach (IRE)**[21] 317 3-9-4 **69** PaulEddery 10 68
(Pat Eddery) *in tch: effrt between horses over 1f out: ev ch u.p 1f out: unable qckn fnl 100yds* **9/2**[1]

3462 **5** *nse* **Turn To Dreams**[4] 555 3-8-6 **57** (v[1]) PaulDoe 1 56
(P D Evans) *chsd ldr: rdn to ld narrowly 2f out: hdd & wknd ins fnl f* **16/1**

063- **6** *¾* **Miss Tikitiboo (IRE)**[84] 7454 3-8-8 **59** JamieSpencer 7 56
(E F Vaughan) *in tch in midfield: hdwy and rdn ent fnl 2f out: wknd ins fnl f* **9/2**[1]

3141 **7** *hd* **Common Diva**[9] 479 3-9-9 **74** 6ex RobertWinston 11 71
(A J McCabe) *led tl over 6f out: chsd ldng pair after: rdn and effrt ent fnl 2f: ev ch 1f out: wknd ins fnl f* **7/1**[2]

2-03 **8** *¾* **Commandingpresence (USA)**[18] 356 3-9-3 **68** JamesDoyle 6 63
(Ms J S Doyle) *stdd s: hld up in last pair: rdn and effrt jst over 2f out: nvr pce to threaten ldrs* **20/1**

55-5 **9** *hd* **Flying Lady (IRE)**[14] 397 3-9-3 **68** TonyCulhane 3 63
(M R Channon) *stdd s: t.k.h: hld up in last pair: rdn and effrt jst over 2f out: kpt on but nvr pce to threaten ldrs* **11/1**

055- **10** *½* **Graycliffe (IRE)**[121] 6865 3-8-6 **57** LiamJones 9 50
(Patrick Morris) *t.k.h early: hld up in midfield: rdn and struggling over 3f out: no imp u.p fr over 2f out* **10/1**

1-64 **11** *2½* **Trusted Venture (USA)**[4] 542 3-8-9 **60** SteveDrowne 8 48
(J R Best) *chsd ldrs tl led over 6f out: j. shadow over 5f out: rdn and hdd 2f out: wknd qckly over 1f out* **12/1**

1m 39.6s (-0.20) **Going Correction** -0.025s/f (Stan) **11** Ran SP% **120.5**
Speed ratings (Par 97): **100,99,98,98,98 97,97,96,96,96 93**
toteswinger: 1&2 £18.30, 1&3 £11.00, 2&3 £24.50. CSF £123.52 CT £610.48 TOTE £8.50: £2.80, £6.50, £2.20; EX 128.60.
Owner Saeed Manana **Bred** Mrs R D Peacock **Trained** Newmarket, Suffolk

FOCUS
A modest handicap and, despite the bunch finish, the form look sound.

587 PANORAMIC BAR & RESTAURANT CLASSIFIED STKS 7f (P)
9:20 (9:20) (Class 7) 3-Y-0+ **£1,364** (£403; £201) **Stalls** High

Form RPR

0-00 **1** **Sharps Gold**[13] 405 4-9-4 45 JackMitchell(3) 4 52
(D Morris) *swtchd rt and dropped in bhd after: hdwy u.p on inner 2f out: hrd rdn to ld wl ins fnl f: all out* **40/1**

-000 **2** *nk* **Moorside Diamond**[9] 469 5-9-7 45 SteveDrowne 6 51
(A D Brown) *hld up wl in tch in midfield: effrt and hrd rdn 2f out: ev ch ins fnl f: wnt 2nd fnl 75yds: hld towards fin* **40/1**

0-42 **3** *nk* **Halsion Challenge**[8] 482 4-9-7 42 (t) RobertWinston 12 50
(J R Best) *t.k.h: trckd ldng pair: ev ch and drvn wl over 1f out: hrd rdn and hdd wl ins fnl f* **11/8**[1]

4-05 **4** *1* **Rosie Cross (IRE)**[43] 56 5-9-7 45 (p) StephenCarson 7 48
(Eve Johnson Houghton) *sn pushed up to chse ldr: ev ch and hrd rdn wl over 1f out: no ex fnl 100yds* **12/1**

5300 **5** *1¼* **Beckenham's Secret**[8] 482 5-9-7 43 ShaneKelly 9 44
(A W Carroll) *led: rdn jst over 2f out: hdd ins fnl f: fdd fnl 75yds* **15/2**

05-0 **6** *½* **Shava**[47] 14 9-9-0 45 DeclanCannon(7) 13 46+
(H J Evans) *t.k.h: in tch: chsd ldrs travelling wl whn hit on nose by rival's whip over 1f out: rdn and one pce fnl f* **13/2**[3]

2000 **7** *¾* **Balerno**[7] 496 10-9-7 45 (b) IanMongan 2 41
(Mrs L J Mongan) *swtchd rt and dropped in bhd after s: hld up in rr: effrt and rdn jst over 2f out: no imp fnl f* **11/2**[2]

3604 **8** *½* **Dynamo Dave (USA)**[8] 482 4-9-0 43 LeeNewnes(7) 10 40
(M D I Usher) *in tch: rdn 3f out: hrd rdn and wknd ent fnl f* **10/1**

50-4 **9** *3* **Lucky Character**[5] 530 4-9-7 45 (bt) PaulDoe 14 31
(N J Vaughan) *t.k.h: hld up towards rr: effrt and drvn towards inner 2f out: sn no imp* **12/1**

/0-6 **10** *nse* **Evette**[19] 343 4-9-7 44 JimmyQuinn 5 31
(H J Collingridge) *in tch in midfield: rdn 3f out: plugged on same pce* **40/1**

30-6 **11** *1* **Cyfrwys (IRE)**[6] 513 8-9-7 44 CatherineGannon 1 29+
(B Palling) *restless stalls: anticipated s and hit stalls: slowly away: t.k.h in rr: rdn on outer wl over 2f out: no hdwy* **16/1**

060- **12** *2¾* **Ramblin Bob**[125] 6751 4-9-7 45 ChrisCatlin 8 21
(W J Musson) *t.k.h: hld up in rr: bhd fnl 2f* **20/1**

1m 26.7s (0.70) **Going Correction** -0.025s/f (Stan)
WFA 3 from 4yo+ 17lb **12** Ran SP% **125.0**
Speed ratings (Par 97): **95,94,94,93,91 91,90,89,86,86 85,81**
toteswinger: 1&2 £23.80, 1&3 £27.20, 2&3 £11.90. CSF £1165.93 TOTE £81.00: £13.10, £12.20, £1.50; EX 1609.70 Place 6 £202.38, Place 5 £111.43.
Owner R Nunn **Bred** J M Beever **Trained** Newmarket, Suffolk

FOCUS
Poor form and not a race to dwell on although the form looks sound enough for the grade with the third, fourth and fifth close to their marks.
Cyfrwys(IRE) Official explanation: jockey said mare missed the break
T/Plt: £397.60 to a £1 stake. Pool: £88,575.61. 162.60 winning tickets. T/Qpdt: £71.10 to a £1 stake. Pool: £6,859.69. 71.34 winning tickets. SP

547 LINGFIELD (L-H)
Wednesday, February 18

OFFICIAL GOING: Standard
Wind: virtually nil Weather: overcast

588 COLNE (S) STKS 1m 2f (P)
1:00 (1:01) (Class 6) 4-Y-0+ **£2,047** (£604; £302) **Stalls** Low

Form RPR

263- **1** **Mystic Art (IRE)**[80] 7506 4-9-0 62 SteveDrowne 3 62+
(C R Egerton) *chsd ldrs: rdn to ld wl over 1f out: drvn clr 1f out: in command whn hung rt ins fnl f: pushed out towards fin* **3/1**[2]

0-20 **2** *1¼* **Gasat (IRE)**[14] 393 8-9-6 70 JoeFanning 1 62
(A B Haynes) *led: rdn and hdd wl over 1f out: outpcd by wnr 1f out: plugged on same pce ins fnl f* **14/1**

6163 **3** *¾* **Rapid City**[7] 500 6-9-6 65 (p) RobertWinston 5 61
(A J McCabe) *s.i.s: hld up in tch in rr on inner: swtchd rt 2f out: effrt and rdn over 1f out: styd on but nvr pce to threaten wnr* **9/4**[1]

34-5 **4** 1 1/4 **Apache Dawn**[40] [100] 5-9-1 47 GeorgeBaker 11 53
(G L Moore) *hld up in rr: hdwy on outer over 2f out: rdn and outpcd wl over 1f out: one pce after* **15/2**

6-65 **5** 3/4 **Competitor**[5] [528] 8-9-1 50 (b) DaneO'Neill 6 52
(J Akehurst) *in tch towards rr: rn in snatches: bustled along over 4f out: drvn wl over 2f out: kpt on same pce fnl 2f* **14/1**

0-32 **6** 2 3/4 **Inquest**[7] [500] 4-9-0 62 (p) JimCrowley 2 46
(Mrs A J Perrett) *trckd ldrs: travelling wl 2f out: rdn and fnd nil over 1f out: wknd tamely fnl f* **10/3**[3]

00-0 **7** 1/2 **Katie Kingfisher**[15] [377] 5-8-10 36 (b) ChrisCatlin 10 40
(T T Clement) *s.i.s: a in last pair: rdn and struggling 2f out: n.d after* **100/1**

03-0 **8** 2 3/4 **Waterside (IRE)**[18] [357] 10-9-1 80 PaulDoe 7 40
(S Curran) *chsd ldr: ev ch and rdn 2f out: sn wknd and wl btn* **14/1**

-000 **P** **Prix Masque (IRE)**[18] [357] 5-9-1 47 (t) EdwardCreighton 9 —
(Christian Wroe) *in tch in midfield tl lost action and p.u 6f out* **66/1**

2m 7.12s (0.52) **Going Correction** +0.15s/f (Slow)
WFA 4 from 5yo+ 1lb 9 Ran SP% **113.1**
Speed ratings (Par 101): **103,102,101,100,99 97,97,95,—**
toteswinger: 1&2 £9.50, 1&3 £1.90, 2&3 £11.60. CSF £43.12 TOTE £3.50: £1.90, £4.30, £1.10; EX 60.90 Trifecta £180.60 Part won. Pool: £244.17 - 0.20 winning units..The winner was bought in for 4,800gns.
Owner Longmoor Holdings Ltd **Bred** Grangecon Stud **Trained** Chaddleworth, Berks

FOCUS
A reasonable seller but the form looks messy with some moderate performers finishing close up.

589 WEY CLAIMING STKS 5f (P)
1:30 (1:33) (Class 6) 4-Y-O+ **£2,047** (£604; £302) **Stalls** High

Form RPR

4-03 **1** **Brandywell Boy (IRE)**[6] [510] 6-8-4 72 BillyCray(7) 5 77
(D J S Ffrench Davis) *racd in last trio: hdwy and pushed along on outer 2f out: rdn over 1f out: led fnl 100yds: r.o wl* **12/1**[3]

3200 **2** 3/4 **Northern Empire (IRE)**[5] [539] 6-9-4 77 JamieSpencer 4 83+
(K A Ryan) *stdd s: hld up in rr: hdwy to chse ldrs gng wl over 1f out: nt clr run briefly 1f out: squeezed between horses to chse wnr wl ins fnl f: hld hd awkwardly and hld towards fin* **11/10**[1]

-021 **3** 1/2 **Woodcote (IRE)**[8] [481] 7-8-12 70 (vt) JimCrowley 2 74
(P R Chamings) *trckd ldrs: effrt on inner wl over 1f out: drvn to ld ins fnl f: sn hdd and one pce* **9/4**[2]

2634 **4** 1/2 **Don Pele (IRE)**[13] [401] 7-8-9 68 (p) JoeFanning 3 69
(R A Harris) *chsd ldrs: drvn wl over 1f out: one pce u.p ins fnl f* **12/1**[3]

-010 **5** 2 **Ten Down**[27] [243] 4-9-2 66 MartinDwyer 7 69
(M Quinn) *led: rdn and hrd pressed over 1f out: hdd ins fnl f: fdd fnl 75yds* **22/1**

0363 **6** hd **Decider (USA)**[5] [535] 6-8-6 59 (b) KevinGhunowa(3) 6 61
(R A Harris) *racd freely: chsd ldr after 1f out: rdn over 1f out wknd jst ins fnl f* **12/1**[3]

0-34 **7** 7 **Caribbean Coral**[35] [165] 10-8-13 70 SteveDrowne 1 40
(A B Haynes) *sn outpcd in last trio: rdn 3f out: lost tch over 1f out* **14/1**

58.83 secs (0.03) **Going Correction** +0.15s/f (Slow) 7 Ran SP% **112.5**
Speed ratings (Par 101): **105,103,103,102,99 98,87**
toteswinger: 1&2 £3.30, 1&3 £4.80, 2&3 £1.10. CSF £25.02 TOTE £16.30: £4.80, £1.20; EX 43.70.
Owner P B Gallagher **Bred** Mountarmstrong Stud **Trained** Lambourn, Berks

FOCUS
A fair claimer, but the leaders went off too fast and set this up for those held up. The winner ran up to his previous all-weather form.
Northern Empire(IRE) Official explanation: jockey said gelding hung right
Decider(USA) Official explanation: jockey said gelding hung right

590 OUSE H'CAP 6f (P)
2:00 (2:01) (Class 6) (0-65,65) 4-Y-O+ **£2,047** (£604; £302) **Stalls** Low

Form RPR

-110 **1** **Street Power (USA)**[14] [387] 4-9-4 65 SteveDrowne 2 78+
(J R Gask) *stdd s: hld up in rr: rdn and hdwy on outer over 1f out: str run to ld ins fnl f: readily* **7/4**[1]

0203 **2** 1 **Compton Classic**[8] [486] 7-8-13 60 (p) PatCosgrave 8 67
(J R Boyle) *t.k.h: chsd ldrs: rdn and ev ch ent fnl f: led ins fnl f: sn hdd and no ch w wnr* **10/1**

40-0 **3** 1 1/4 **Prince Of Delphi**[10] [460] 6-9-3 64 (p) GeorgeBaker 6 67
(Mrs A L M King) *hld up in midfield: rdn and effrt over 1f out: kpt on ins fnl f: wnt 3rd last strides: no ch w wnr* **20/1**

0-22 **4** shd **Hart Of Gold**[9] [475] 5-9-0 64 (b[1]) KevinGhunowa(3) 10 67
(R A Harris) *racd freely: sn chsng ldr: drvn and ev ch wl over 1f out: led 1f out: hdd ins fnl f: no ex* **13/2**[3]

5230 **5** 1 1/4 **Liberty Valance (IRE)**[5] [531] 4-8-12 59 (t) SimonWhitworth 9 58
(S Kirk) *in tch in midfield: rdn and kpt on same pce fr wl over 1f out* **7/1**

440- **6** 2 1/4 **Radiator Rooney (IRE)**[58] [7762] 6-9-4 65 (v) JamieSpencer 4 56
(Patrick Morris) *stdd s: t.k.h: hld up in rr: effrt over 1f out: no real imp: eased whn wl btn wl ins fnl f* **9/2**[2]

6136 **7** nk **Joss Stick**[20] [326] 4-8-10 64 (p) SPRyan(7) 5 55
(R A Harris) *led: rdn and hdd 1f out: sn wknd* **12/1**

560- **8** 1/2 **Hammer Of The Gods (IRE)**[49] [7834] 9-9-0 61 (tp) AdamKirby 7 50
(G C Bravery) *chsd ldrs: rdn wl over 1f out: wknd u.p ent fnl f* **10/1**

360- **9** 2 **Maggie Kate**[172] [5510] 4-9-2 63 RobertHavlin 1 46
(R Ingram) *racd in last trio: rdn 2f out: nvr trbld ldrs* **16/1**

6-00 **10** 3 1/4 **Bishopbriggs (USA)**[14] [387] 4-9-2 63 TravisBlock 3 35
(J Ryan) *in tch in midfield: rdn and steadily lost pl 3f out: bhd fnl 2f* **25/1**

1m 12.64s (0.74) **Going Correction** +0.15s/f (Slow) 10 Ran SP% **120.7**
Speed ratings (Par 101): **101,99,98,97,96 93,92,92,89,85**
toteswinger: 1&2 £2.80, 1&3 £13.30, 2&3 £19.50. CSF £21.83 CT £281.38 TOTE £2.50: £1.40, £2.10, £4.90; EX 18.10 Trifecta £115.30 Part won. Pool: £155.94 - 0.54 winning units..
Owner Horses First Racing Limited **Bred** John Hawkins **Trained** Sutton Veny, Wilts

FOCUS
Just a modest sprint handicap run in an ordinary time, but an above-average winner. The runner-up is rated to his recent best.

591 BET UEFA CUP - BETDAQ H'CAP 2m (P)
2:35 (2:35) (Class 4) (0-85,85) 4-Y-O+ **£4,857** (£1,445; £722; £360) **Stalls** Low

Form RPR

2-44 **1** **Mr Aitch (IRE)**[15] [384] 7-9-1 73 (t) SteveDrowne 6 78
(R T Phillips) *in tch: led 2f out: sn rdn and qcknd: drvn ent fnl f: styd on wl and a holding runner up* **14/1**

3-32 **2** nk **Baan (USA)**[20] [333] 6-8-8 66 oh6 JimmyQuinn 4 71
(H J Collingridge) *chsd ldr tl 8f out: rdn and effrt over 1f out: chsd wnr ent fnl f: kpt on to press wnr wl ins fnl f: hld towards fin* **13/2**

612 **3** 2 3/4 **Mission Control (IRE)**[6] [511] 4-8-10 74 PatCosgrave 5 76
(J R Boyle) *chsd ldrs: wnt 2nd 8f out: ev ch and rdn ent fnl 2f: unable qckn over 1f out: one pce fnl f* **11/8**[1]

10-1 **4** nk **Right Option (IRE)**[10] [459] 5-9-4 76 6ex TolleyDean 8 77
(J L Flint) *stdd s: hld up in last pl: effrt on outer and rdn over 2f out: plugged on same pce fr over 1f out* **4/1**[2]

00-0 **5** nk **Ameeq (USA)**[4] [549] 7-9-2 74 (b) GeorgeBaker 3 75
(G L Moore) *hld up in tch in last pair: rdn over 2f out: kpt on fnl f: nvr pce to threaten ldrs* **10/1**

04-3 **6** 3 3/4 **Greenwich Meantime**[42] [72] 9-9-8 85 PatrickDonaghy(5) 7 81
(A King) *led tl 2f out: sn rdn: wknd over 1f out* **9/2**[3]

3m 29.18s (3.48) **Going Correction** +0.15s/f (Slow)
WFA 4 from 5yo+ 6lb 6 Ran SP% **109.4**
Speed ratings (Par 105): **97,96,95,95,95 93**
toteswinger: 1&2 £8.90, 1&3 £7.00, 2&3 £3.20. CSF £91.60 CT £190.87 TOTE £15.90: £4.80, £2.30; EX 68.30 Trifecta £125.40 Pool: 344.22 - 2.03 winning units..
Owner The Bellflower Mr Aitch Partnership **Bred** Mount Coote Stud **Trained** Adlestrop, Gloucs

FOCUS
Just the six runners, but a fair staying handicap. They went a modest pace and the form is muddling and not reliable.

592 BET MULTIPLES - BETDAQ MEDIAN AUCTION MAIDEN STKS 6f (P)
3:10 (3:12) (Class 5) 3-5-Y-O **£2,729** (£806; £403) **Stalls** Low

Form RPR

03-4 **1** **Waterloo Dock**[43] [61] 4-9-10 49 MartinDwyer 7 65
(M Quinn) *sn led: mde rest: rdn 2f out: drvn and styd on wl fnl f* **9/1**

-343 **2** 1 **Edith's Boy (IRE)**[19] [348] 3-8-9 65 IanMongan 8 58
(S Dow) *t.k.h: hld up in midfield: hdwy over 2f out: rdn to chse wnr over 1f out: kpt on but nvr quite pce to rch wnr* **6/1**[3]

32 **3** nk **Saints Bay (IRE)**[4] [552] 3-8-4 0 ChrisCatlin 4 52
(R Hannon) *chsd ldrs: rdn and unable qckn jst over 2f out: kpt on u.p fnl f: nt pce to rch wnr* **3/1**[2]

64 **4** 3 **Silca Meydan**[7] [503] 3-8-9 0 TonyCulhane 10 47
(M R Channon) *towards rr: rdn and effrt jst over 2f out: no imp and edgd lft over 1f out: wnt modest 4th ins fnl f: kpt on but nvr trbld ldrs* **5/2**[1]

6 **5** 1 **Marina Walk**[21] [315] 3-8-4 0 (t) JimmyQuinn 6 39
(H Morrison) *t.k.h: chsd ldrs on outer: rdn and hung lft over 1f out: sn wknd* **3/1**[2]

0- **6** 1 1/2 **You Avin A Laugh**[290] [1832] 3-8-9 0 PaulEddery 3 39
(C A Dwyer) *chsd ldr tl over 1f out: wknd qckly fnl f* **20/1**

7 hd **Abu Dubai (IRE)** 3-8-4 0 CatherineGannon 9 34
(C A Dwyer) *s.i.s: a bhd: effrt and rdn 2f out: edgd lft over 1f out: nvr nr ldrs* **16/1**

06- **8** 3 **Kings On The Roof**[51] [7810] 3-8-9 0 FrankieMcDonald 5 29
(G C Bravery) *in tch towards rr: rdn and struggling over 2f out: wl bhd fnl f* **100/1**

00- **9** 3/4 **Rindless**[104] [7213] 4-9-5 0 LPKeniry 2 26
(J F Panvert) *in tch: rdn 3f out: wknd u.p ent fnl 2f* **25/1**

10 3/4 **Love Allowed** 3-8-4 0 PaulDoe 1 19
(Jamie Poulton) *v.s.a: a detached in last pl: kpt on fnl f: n.d* **28/1**

1m 12.77s (0.87) **Going Correction** +0.15s/f (Slow)
WFA 3 from 4yo 15lb 10 Ran SP% **121.8**
Speed ratings (Par 103): **100,98,98,94,92 90,90,86,85,84**
toteswinger: 1&2 £10.40, 1&3 £5.60, 2&3 £1.40. CSF £62.35 TOTE £8.00: £2.50, £1.30, £2.30; EX 40.80 Trifecta £129.10 Pool: £424.25 - 2.43 winning units..
Owner M J Quinn **Bred** Norman Court Stud **Trained** Newmarket, Suffolk
■ Stewards' Enquiry : Paul Doe ten-day ban: insufficient effort (Mar 4, 5, 6, 7, 10, 11, 12, 13, 14, 16)

FOCUS
A moderate sprint maiden and the time was the slowest of the three 6f races on the card, but that said the winner seems to have improved on his official mark of 49.
Love Allowed Official explanation: jockey said orders were to jump out and settle behind the leaders and do his best thereafter, the filly jumped moderately and was outpaced in rear early on; trainer said filly has a history of leg trouble and appeared to need a longer trip, adding the filly showed signs of greenness and at this stage she is moderate and backward.

593 BET ASIAN H'CAPS - BETDAQ HANDICAP 6f (P)
3:45 (3:46) (Class 5) (0-70,71) 3-Y-O **£2,900** (£856; £428) **Stalls** Low

Form RPR

3431 **1** **Quick Single (USA)**[4] [552] 3-8-11 63 6ex (v) AdamKirby 5 69
(P S McEntee) *led briefly: dropped to last and outpcd over 3f out: hdwy u.p wl over 1f out: led ins fnl f: drew clr towards fin* **10/3**[2]

4121 **2** 2 1/2 **Raimond Ridge (IRE)**[7] [498] 3-9-5 71 6ex TonyCulhane 3 69
(M R Channon) *sn chsng ldr: rdn to ld and edgd lft over 1f out: hdd ins fnl f: wknd towards fin* **15/8**[1]

6-61 **3** 4 1/2 **Rocoppelia (USA)**[19] [348] 3-8-10 62 (b) JimCrowley 6 46
(Mrs A J Perrett) *hld up in tch: effrt to press ldrs 2f out: sn rdn and nt qckn: wknd fnl f* **15/8**[1]

2-14 **4** 2 1/4 **Romantic Queen**[44] [45] 3-9-4 70 StephenDonohoe 2 46
(E A L Dunlop) *sn led: hdd and rdn wl over 1f out: wknd fnl f* **4/1**[3]

1m 12.44s (0.54) **Going Correction** +0.15s/f (Slow) 4 Ran SP% **112.6**
Speed ratings (Par 97): **102,98,92,89**
toteswinger: 1&2: £5.90 CSF £10.23 TOTE £4.10; EX 10.80.
Owner Miss Carmelina Favarulo **Bred** Lucky Shamrock Llc **Trained** Newmarket, Suffolk
■ Stewards' Enquiry : Adam Kirby two-day ban: excessive use of the whip (Mar 4-5)

FOCUS
A modest sprint handicap with the winner rated back to his early juvenile form and the runner-up a little below his latest mark. Despite the small field, they went off fast and the winning time was 0.33 seconds quicker than earlier older-horse maiden, and 0.20 seconds faster than the 51-65.

594 THAMES H'CAP 7f (P)
4:20 (4:20) (Class 6) (0-55,55) 3-Y-O **£2,047** (£604; £302) **Stalls** Low

Form RPR

0-05 **1** **Josiah Bartlett (IRE)**[24] [287] 3-9-3 55 (bt[1]) HayleyTurner 2 62
(P S McEntee) *dwlt: hld up towards rr: swtchd rt and c wd over 1f out: chsd ldrs ent fnl f r.o strly u.p to ld towards fin* **10/1**[3]

060- **2** 3/4 **Elsie Jo (IRE)**[175] [5394] 3-8-13 51 NickyMackay 8 56
(M Wigham) *trckd ldrs: chsd ldr wl over 1f out: drvn ent fnl f: led ins fnl f: hdd and no ex towards fin* **2/1**[1]

00-1 **3** 1 1/2 **Private Passion (IRE)**[14] [390] 3-9-1 53 PaulEddery 9 54
(Pat Eddery) *s.i.s: sn rdn and hdwy: lft in ld over 5f out: drvn 2f out: hrd pressed over 1f out: hdd ins fnl f: no ex* **9/4**[2]

06-0 **4** 5 **Abhainn (IRE)**[23] [296] 3-8-13 51 MartinDwyer 1 38
(B Palling) *chsd ldrs tl hmpd and dropped to last pl over 5f out: effrt over 1f out: kpt on to go modest 4th ins fnl f: no ch w ldrs* **16/1**

40-3 **5** 1 1/4 **Tarawa Atoll**[24] 287 3-9-3 **55**........ TonyCulhane 6 39
(M R Channon) *a bhd: hdwy over 2f out: rdn ent fnl 2f out: sn wknd* **10/1**[3]
00-6 **6** 3/4 **Paymaster In Chief**[36] 149 3-8-8 **53**........ LeeNewnes(7) 4 35
(M D I Usher) *in tch on outer: effrt to chse ldrs over 2f out: rdn and wknd wl over 1f out* **10/1**[3]
5-65 **7** 1 1/2 **Fleur De'Lion (IRE)**[26] 267 3-8-10 **48**........ LPKeniry 3 29
(S Kirk) *in tch in midfield: rdn and struggling over 2f out: no ch fnl 2f: eased wl ins fnl f* **16/1**
0-04 **8** 2 **Northern Shore (IRE)**[17] 363 3-8-12 **50**........(b) JamieSpencer 11 26
(K A Ryan) *led: knapped and veered lft over 5f out: sn hdd: chsd ldr after: rdn 2f out: wknd qckly: eased wl ins fnl f* **12/1**
00-0 **9** 2 1/4 **Set Em Up Mo**[14] 394 3-9-3 **55**........ PaulDoe 7 22
(M J Attwater) *in tch: hmpd over 5f out: lost pl and rdn over 2f out: wl btn fr wl over 1f out: eased wl ins fnl f* **12/1**
30-0 **10** 8 **Wickedly Fast (USA)**[19] 345 3-9-1 **53**........(t) ChrisCatlin 5 —
(George Baker) *chsd ldrs: hmpd over 5f out: lost pl bnd jst over 2f out: wl bhd after: eased fnl f* **40/1**

1m 25.87s (1.07) **Going Correction** +0.15s/f (Slow) **10** Ran SP% **121.0**
Speed ratings (Par 95): **99,98,96,90,89 88,86,84,81,72**
toteswinger: 1&2 £6.70, 1&3 £6.80, 2&3 £2.70. CSF £31.50 CT £65.66 TOTE £14.00: £3.00, £1.40, £1.80; EX 56.70 Trifecta £287.50 Part won. Pool: £388.64 - 0.60 winning units..
Owner Playboy Kennels **Bred** Paradime Ltd **Trained** Newmarket, Suffolk

FOCUS
Just a moderate three-year-old handicap, and a bit of a turn up, but the front three were clear.

595 MEDWAY H'CAP 1m 2f (P)
4:50 (4:50) (Class 4) (0-85,84) 3-Y-O £4,857 (£1,445; £722; £360) Stalls Low

Form RPR
-334 **1** **Doncosaque (IRE)**[5] 532 3-9-6 **83**........ IanMongan 5 87
(P Howling) *stdd s: hld up in tch in rr: hdwy and rdn jst over 2f out: chal 1f out: led ins fnl f: r.o wl* **7/2**[2]
05-1 **2** 1 **Tinshu (IRE)**[37] 138 3-8-12 **75**........ PatCosgrave 3 77
(D Haydn Jones) *t.k.h: led for 1f: trckd ldr after: upsides and rdn wl over 1f out: edgd lft and led jst over 1f out: hdd and no ex ins fnl f* **9/1**
42-1 **3** 1 3/4 **Lord Chancellor (IRE)**[46] 32 3-9-7 **84**........ JoeFanning 7 82
(M Johnston) *led after 1f: set stdy gallop: jnd and rdn wl over 1f out: hdd jst over 1f out: no ex ins fnl f* **5/6**[1]
120- **4** 1 1/2 **Blue Tango (IRE)**[70] 7623 3-9-0 **77**........ JimCrowley 2 72
(Mrs A J Perrett) *chsd ldrs: rdn and effrt jst over 2f out: kpt on same pce fnl f* **5/1**[3]
013- **5** 1/2 **Orsippus (USA)**[165] 5711 3-9-3 **80**........ TonyCulhane 6 74
(M R Channon) *t.k.h: hld up in last pair: outpcd over 2f out: kpt on ins fnl f: nvr trbld ldrs* **10/1**
-516 **6** 1/2 **Innactualfact**[14] 389 3-8-4 **67**........ ChrisCatlin 4 60
(L A Dace) *in tch: rdn over 2f out: no imp fr wl over 1f out* **20/1**

2m 10.05s (3.45) **Going Correction** +0.15s/f (Slow) **6** Ran SP% **117.3**
Speed ratings (Par 99): **92,91,89,88,88 87**
toteswinger: 1&2 £4.20, 1&3 £1.50, 2&3 £2.50. CSF £34.43 TOTE £4.30: £1.30, £3.90; EX 33.10 Place 6: £673.29 Place 5: £411.54.
Owner Jo Hearn **Bred** Ammerland Verwaltung Gmbh **Trained** Newmarket, Suffolk

FOCUS
A fair handicap but hard to be confident about the form, as the pace seemed to slow noticeably at halfway and the time was moderate.
T/Plt: £1,530.30 to a £1 stake. Pool: £53,561.76. 25.55 winning tickets. T/Qpdt: £182.90 to a £1 stake. Pool: £3,707.85. 15.00 winning tickets. SP

582 KEMPTON (A.W) (R-H)
Thursday, February 19

OFFICIAL GOING: Standard
Wind: virtually nil Weather: dry

596 RACING POST CHASE THIS SATURDAY H'CAP 5f (P)
6:50 (6:52) (Class 6) (0-60,62) 4-Y-0+ £2,266 (£674; £337; £168) Stalls High

Form RPR
-362 **1** **Welsh Opera**[12] 454 4-8-9 **54**........(v) WilliamCarson(5) 9 65
(S C Williams) *chsd ldrs: rdn and effrt on inner over 1f out: drvn to ld ins fnl f: forged clr fnl 100yds* **8/1**
0-60 **2** 1 1/2 **Fizzlephut (IRE)**[13] 431 7-9-2 **56**........ PaulFitzsimons 3 62
(Miss J R Tooth) *led to s: in tch: rdn and edging rt over 1f out: r.o ins fnl f: wnt 2nd wl ins fnl f: no ch w wnr* **33/1**
1061 **3** 1/2 **Hollow Jo**[10] 467 9-9-7 **61** 6ex........(v) FergusSweeney 10 65
(J R Jenkins) *hld up in midfield: hdwy on inner over 1f out: sn rdn: plugged on ins fnl f: nt rch ldrs* **5/1**
1-65 **4** hd **Lithaam (IRE)**[6] 535 5-8-12 **57**........(p) JackDean(5) 12 60
(J M Bradley) *racd keenly: led narrowly: rdn over 1f out: hdd ins fnl f: no ex and lost 2 pls wl ins fnl f* **8/1**
33-5 **5** hd **Green Lagonda (AUS)**[47] 22 7-9-2 **56**........ MickyFenton 11 59
(Stef Liddiard) *taken down early: pressed ldr: rdn and ev ch over 1f out: wknd ins fnl f* **9/2**[3]
00/5 **6** 1 1/4 **Meikle Barfil**[10] 467 7-8-8 **48**........(tp) LukeMorris 7 46
(J M Bradley) *dwlt: short of room sn aftr s: racd in midfield: rdn and effrt over 1f out: no imp* **25/1**
03- **7** 3/4 **Rocketball (IRE)**[54] 7793 4-9-2 **56**........(v) ShaneKelly 5 51
(Patrick Morris) *hld up in rr: effrt and hanging rt over 1f out: n.d* **3/1**[1]
52-4 **8** 1 **Night Premiere (IRE)**[41] 99 4-8-13 **53**........(b) PatDobbs 2 45
(R Hannon) *wnt lft: a bhd* **10/1**
3321 **9** nk **Monte Major (IRE)**[6] 535 8-9-1 **62** 6ex........(v) LeeTopliss(7) 6 53
(D Shaw) *chsd ldrs 2f out: wknd over 1f out* **4/1**[2]

59.51 secs (-0.99) **Going Correction** -0.125s/f (Stan) **9** Ran SP% **117.9**
Speed ratings (Par 101): **102,99,98,98,98 96,94,93,92**
toteswinger: 1&2 £34.90, 1&3 £7.10, 2&3 £29.80. CSF £228.33 CT £1462.90 TOTE £10.30: £3.40, £3.80, £1.50; EX 142.30.
Owner Paul W Stevens **Bred** Usk Valley Stud **Trained** Newmarket, Suffolk
■ Stewards' Enquiry : Lee Topliss one-day ban: careless riding (Mar 5)

FOCUS
A moderate handicap producing a close finish.
Rocketball(IRE) Official explanation: jockey said gelding hung both ways
Monte Major(IRE) Official explanation: jockey said gelding lost a shoe

597 DAY TIME, NIGHT TIME, GREAT TIME H'CAP 1m 2f (P)
7:20 (7:20) (Class 5) (0-70,69) 4-Y-0+ £3,561 (£1,059; £529; £264) Stalls High

Form RPR
366- **1** **My Shadow**[82] 7495 4-9-2 **67**........ IanMongan 6 77+
(S Dow) *stdd after s: t.k.h: hld up in last pl: hdwy 3f out: c wd 2f out: str run to ld 1f out: forged ahd fnl 100yds* **14/1**
211 **2** 1 1/2 **Formidable Guest**[10] 478 5-9-3 **67** 6ex........ JimmyQuinn 9 74
(J Pearce) *hld up in midfield: hdwy to chse ldrs over 2f out: rdn to ld jst over 1f out: sn hdd: pressed wnr tl outpcd fnl 100yds* **7/2**[1]
-130 **3** 3/4 **Imperium**[9] 485 8-8-11 **61**........ JimCrowley 8 66+
(Jean-Rene Auvray) *hld up in rr: last on inner 2f out: grad swtchd to outer over 1f out: str run fnl f: wnt 3rd last stride: nt rch ldrs* **12/1**
/00- **4** shd **Gloucester**[54] 5887 6-8-11 **66**........ JackDean(5) 7 71
(M J Scudamore) *hld up in last trio: hdwy over 3f out: chsd ldrs and drvn jst over 1f out: kpt on same pce fnl f: lost 3rd last stride* **15/2**
45-6 **5** 2 **Burnbrake**[22] 318 4-9-0 **65**........ MartinDwyer 2 66
(L Montague Hall) *w ldrs for 2f: chsd ldrs after: rdn and unable qck jst over 2f out: plugged on same pce u.p after* **12/1**
60-4 **6** 1 3/4 **Lord Theo**[18] 362 5-9-2 **66**........ JamesDoyle 5 63
(N P Littmoden) *sn led: hdd over 8f out: chsd ldr after: drvn and ev ch over 1f out: wknd jst ins fnl f* **10/1**
500- **7** 5 **Director's Chair**[129] 6712 4-9-0 **65**........ HayleyTurner 1 52
(Miss J Feilden) *chsd ldrs tl led over 8f out: hrd pressed and drvn wl over 1f out: hdd jst over 1f out: wknd fnl f* **7/1**[3]
20-5 **8** 6 **Everyman**[13] 427 5-8-7 **57**........ LukeMorris 10 32
(A W Carroll) *in tch: rdn over 4f out: struggling and bhd over 2f out: eased ins fnl f* **13/2**[2]
/5-2 **9** 2 3/4 **Cinematic (IRE)**[8] 507 6-9-5 **69**........ PatCosgrave 3 39
(J R Boyle) *t.k.h: in tch: rdn and struggling over 3f out: wl bhd over 1f out: eased ins fnl f* **7/2**[1]

2m 6.09s (-1.91) **Going Correction** -0.125s/f (Stan)
WFA 4 from 5yo+ 1lb **9** Ran SP% **113.2**
Speed ratings (Par 103): **102,100,100,100,98 97,93,88,86**
toteswinger: 1&2 £7.10, 1&3 £23.20, 2&3 £9.30. CSF £61.41 CT £613.59 TOTE £17.80: £3.70, £1.30, £4.50; EX 111.50.
Owner T G Parker **Bred** Millsec Limited **Trained** Epsom, Surrey

FOCUS
A moderate, yet competitive handicap that should work out alright as positives can be taken about the first four.
Everyman Official explanation: jockey said gelding lost its action
Cinematic(IRE) Official explanation: jockey said gelding ran too free

598 SUNBURY CLASSIFIED STKS 1m (P)
7:50 (7:53) (Class 7) 3-Y-0+ £1,619 (£481; £240; £120) Stalls High

Form RPR
6560 **1** **Fairly Honest**[4] 565 5-9-2 45........ WilliamCarson(5) 3 52
(P W Hiatt) *led for 2f and again over 2f out: drvn to chal over 1f out: led ins fnl f: hld on cl home: all out* **8/1**
0-06 **2** hd **Zabeel House**[14] 405 6-9-7 45........(p) MickyFenton 13 51
(John A Harris) *hld up towards rr: nt clr run and swtchd lft 2f out: str run u.p on outer ent fnl f: ev ch fnl 50yds: hld cl home* **10/1**
-003 **3** 1/2 **Golden Square**[10] 469 7-9-7 40........(v) AdamKirby 1 50
(A W Carroll) *sn rdn along to ld and grad crossed to rail: rdn jst over 2f out: drvn and hdd ins fnl f: no ex fnl 50yds* **9/2**[2]
-423 **4** 4 **Halsion Challenge**[1] 587 4-9-7 42........(t) GeorgeBaker 7 41
(J R Best) *in tch in midfield: effrt and rdn jst over 2f out: drvn and no imp ent fnl f* **11/8**[1]
00-5 **5** 1 1/4 **Incy Wincy**[5] 555 3-8-2 25........ LukeMorris 14 32
(J M Bradley) *in tch: effrt on inner 2f out: disp 3rd and drvn over 1f out: wknd fnl f* **25/1**
-000 **6** 1/2 **Szaba**[22] 308 4-9-7 41........(p) DaneO'Neill 4 37
(J Akehurst) *chsd ldrs: rdn and effrt over 2f out: wknd fnl f* **33/1**
400- **7** 1/2 **Amatara (IRE)**[135] 6555 3-8-2 40........ JimmyQuinn 5 30
(B G Powell) *stdd after s: t.k.h: hld up in rr: swtchd ins and rdn jst over 2f out: kpt on but nvr pce to threaten ldrs* **33/1**
-043 **8** 4 1/2 **Amwell House**[9] 482 4-9-7 43........ SimonWhitworth 11 25
(J R Jenkins) *stdd s: t.k.h: hld up in rr: effrt u.p jst over 2f out: sn no hdwy and wl btn fnl f* **6/1**[3]
040- **9** 2 1/2 **Mtoto Girl**[141] 6378 5-9-7 40........ JerryO'Dwyer 2 20
(J J Bridger) *a towards rr: rdn and no hdwy wl over 2f out* **20/1**
-000 **10** 4 **Looter (FR)**[12] 443 4-9-0 45........(tp) AndrewHeffernan(7) 6 10
(P Butler) *chsd ldrs: rdn and lost pl qckly over 2f out: wl btn after* **16/1**
0-00 **11** 9 **Royal Orissa**[15] 387 7-9-7 36........(t) HayleyTurner 8 —
(D Haydn Jones) *t.k.h: in tch: hdwy to chse ldr 6f out tl over 2f out: wknd rapidly* **33/1**

1m 40.38s (0.58) **Going Correction** 0.0s/f (Stan)
WFA 3 from 4yo+ 19lb **11** Ran SP% **118.1**
Speed ratings (Par 97): **97,96,96,92,91 90,90,85,83,79 70**
toteswinger: 1&2 £14.30, 1&3 £6.90, 2&3 £14.40. CSF £78.79 TOTE £9.80: £2.60, £3.00, £2.20; EX 119.50.
Owner P W Hiatt **Bred** Whitsbury Manor Stud **Trained** Hook Norton, Oxon
■ Stewards' Enquiry : Dane O'Neill one-day ban: failed to keep straight from stalls (Mar 5); three-day ban: careless riding (Mar 6, 7, 10)

FOCUS
A seller in disguise and ordinary form despite the first three finishing clear.
Zabeel House Official explanation: jockey said gelding hung right-handed in the straight
Golden Square Official explanation: jockey said gelding hung both ways
Royal Orissa Official explanation: jockey said gelding hung left-handed

599 BOOK TICKETS ON 0844 579 3008 MEDIAN AUCTION MAIDEN STKS 1m (P)
8:20 (8:21) (Class 5) 3-5-Y-O £3,238 (£963; £481; £240) Stalls High

Form RPR
6-2 **1** **Best In Class**[40] 121 3-8-8 0........ RichardKingscote 5 66+
(Tom Dascombe) *led: hdd narrowly over 2f out: led again 2f out: rdn and edgd lft ins fnl f: hld on wl fnl 100yds* **6/4**[2]
0-0 **2** nk **Esteem Lord**[40] 121 3-8-8 0........ RobertHavlin 1 65
(Jamie Poulton) *hld up in 4th pl: outpcd over 3f out: rdn and hung rt fr 3f out: hdwy over 1f out: chal ins fnl f: nt qckn and hld fnl 100yds* **25/1**
542- **3** 2 **Fin Vin De Leu (GER)**[113] 7073 3-8-8 76........ JoeFanning 2 61
(M Johnston) *chsd wnr: rdn and led narrowly over 2f out: hdd 2f out: hld hd awkwardly u.p: v one pce fnl f* **10/11**[1]

50 **4** 1 ½ **Lyrical Intent**[12] 440 3-8-8 0........................ JimmyQuinn 3 57
(P Howling) *hld up in last pl: outpcd over 3f out: hdwy over 1f out: chsd ldrs and rdn ent fnl f: one pce after* **33/1**

5 2 ½ **Independent James (IRE)** 3-8-3 0........................ WilliamCarson(5) 4 52
(S C Williams) *chsd ldng pair: outpcd over 3f out: pushed along and rallied over 1f out: wknd ent fnl f* **8/1**[3]

1m 39.39s (-0.41) **Going Correction** 0.0s/f (Stan) **5** Ran SP% **110.3**
Speed ratings (Par 103): **102,101,99,98,95**
CSF £28.81 TOTE £2.20: £1.10, £10.60; EX 17.30.
Owner Mrs A Shone **Bred** Michael Clarke **Trained** Lambourn, Berks

FOCUS
A weak maiden and the form is muddling and hard to assess.
Esteem Lord Official explanation: jockey said gelding hung right-handed

600 TURFTV H'CAP 6f (P)
8:50 (8:50) (Class 4) (0-85,84) 4-Y-O+ **£6,476** (£1,927; £963; £481) **Stalls** High

Form RPR
-513 **1** **Mogok Ruby**[6] 533 5-9-4 **78**........................ LukeMorris 1 86
(L Montague Hall) *stdd s: hld up in rr: stl last over 1f out: plld to outer and drvn jst over 1f out: led fnl 50yds: r.o wl* **7/2**[2]

5414 **2** ½ **Distinctly Game**[6] 533 7-9-3 **77**........................(t) JoeFanning 4 83
(K A Ryan) *chsd clr ldr: clsd over 2f out: led over 1f out: sn rdn: hdd and no ex fnl 50yds* **3/1**[1]

-320 **3** 1 ½ **Musical Script (USA)**[20] 351 6-9-1 **75**........................(b) ChrisCatlin 6 77
(Mouse Hamilton-Fairley) *t.k.h: hld up towards rr: effrt on inner jst over 2f out: kpt on same pce u.p fnl f: wnt 3rd last strides* **5/1**[3]

3-61 **4** hd **Resplendent Alpha**[6] 533 5-9-10 **84** 6ex........................ IanMongan 7 85
(P Howling) *hld up towards rr: rdn and hdwy over 2f out: chsd ldr and drvn over 1f out: no ex fnl 100yds* **7/2**[2]

3-14 **5** 3 ½ **Princess Valerina**[34] 197 5-9-3 **77**........................ PatCosgrave 3 67
(D Haydn Jones) *awkward s: chsd ldrs: rdn and swtchd 2f out: wknd ent ch fnl f* **6/1**

000- **6** 1 ½ **Onceaponatime (IRE)**[127] 6734 4-9-3 **77**........................ ShaneKelly 8 62
(M D Squance) *chsd ldrs: effrt and drvn over 1f out: wknd qckly 1f out* **10/1**

06-6 **7** 4 ½ **Silver Prelude**[35] 170 8-9-0 **74**........................ JimCrowley 2 45
(S C Williams) *led and sn clr: rdn and hdd over 1f out: sn wknd* **12/1**

1m 12.25s (-0.85) **Going Correction** 0.0s/f (Stan) **7** Ran SP% **117.2**
Speed ratings (Par 105): **105,104,102,102,97 95,89**
toteswinger: 1&2 £2.90, 1&3 £4.00, 2&3 £2.20. CSF £15.07 CT £52.24 TOTE £4.20: £1.50, £2.50; EX 15.40.
Owner The Ruby Partnership **Bred** R Pain **Trained** Epsom, Surrey

FOCUS
A tight handicap and the form looks sound with the winner back to his best and the fourth to form.

601 KEMPTON.CO.UK APPRENTICE H'CAP 1m 4f (P)
9:20 (9:20) (Class 6) (0-50,55) 4-Y-O+ **£2,266** (£674; £337; £168) **Stalls** Low

Form RPR
/0-6 **1** **Lady Asheena**[16] 378 4-8-12 **50**........................ DebraEngland 2 59
(J Jay) *led after 1f: rdn and hdd jst over 2f out: kpt on fnl f to ld again nr fin* **14/1**

500- **2** nk **Phoenix Hill (IRE)**[210] 4029 7-8-10 **45**........................ CharlesEddery 10 54
(D R Gandolfo) *led for 1f: chsd wnr after: rdn to ld 2f: 1 l ld 1f out: hdd nr fin* **20/1**

60-6 **3** ¾ **Fateful Attraction**[34] 190 6-8-7 **45**........................(b) MatthewLawson(3) 8 53
(I A Wood) *hld up in rr: rdn and hdwy on outer over 2f out: chsd ldng pair jst over 1f out: r.o but nt rch ldrs* **9/2**[3]

000- **4** 4 **Ndola**[271] 1562 10-8-10 **45**........................(p) AndrewHeffernan 5 46
(P Butler) *hld up off the pce in midfield: effrt and rdn over 2f out: chsd ldng pair: sn outpcd and no ch w ldrs after* **20/1**

0-01 **5** nse **Shenandoah Girl**[10] 443 6-8-9 **49**........................(p) TobyAtkinson(5) 11 50
(Miss Gay Kelleway) *stdd s: hld up in rr: hdwy and rdn on inner over 2f out: kpt on but nvr nr ldrs* **7/1**

-665 **6** nk **Jiminor Mack**[6] 537 6-8-5 **45**........................(p) PaulPickard(5) 3 46
(W J H Ratcliffe) *racd off the pce in midfield: rdn over 3f out: plugged on fnl 2f but nvr pce to threaten ldrs* **8/1**

-652 **7** 1 **Hatch A Plan (IRE)**[10] 469 8-8-10 **45**........................ RichardRowe 13 44
(Mouse Hamilton-Fairley) *t.k.h: chsd ldrs: rdn over 2f out: wknd over 1f out* **5/2**[1]

5264 **8** ½ **Prince Of Medina**[5] 541 6-8-11 **46**........................(t) PNolan 4 44
(J R Best) *stdd s: hld up in last pl: rdn along 7f out: nvr gng wl after: nvr on terms* **3/1**[2]

0-06 **9** 2 ½ **Welcome Releaf**[16] 377 6-8-5 **45**........................ AlexEdwards(5) 6 39
(P Leech) *stdd after s: hld up towards rr: hdwy on outer over 4f out: chsd ldrs and rdn over 2f out: wknd qckly 2f out* **20/1**

-500 **10** 8 **Backlash**[10] 469 8-8-7 **45**........................ KarenKenny(3) 9 27
(A W Carroll) *chsd ldrs: rdn 3f out: wknd qckly over 2f out: wl bhd fnl f* **33/1**

2m 35.74s (1.24) **Going Correction** 0.0s/f (Stan)
WFA 4 from 5yo+ 3lb **10** Ran SP% **119.3**
Speed ratings (Par 101): **95,94,94,91,91 91,90,90,88,83**
toteswinger: 1&2 £32.50, 1&3 £10.40, 2&3 £18.10. CSF £263.25 CT £1469.17 TOTE £12.80: £5.20, £7.90, £1.70; EX 279.80 Place 6: £666.88, Place 5: £141.91.
Owner K Snell **Bred** Gainsborough Stud Management Ltd **Trained** Newmarket, Suffolk

FOCUS
A weak apprentice handicap and tricky form to pin down with the front pair the first two throughout.
T/Plt: £1,105.40 to a £1 stake. Pool: £86,316.56. 57.00 winning tickets. T/Qpdt: £91.30 to a £1 stake. Pool: £6,550.74. 53.08 winning tickets. SP

560 SOUTHWELL (L-H)
Thursday, February 19

OFFICIAL GOING: Standard
Wind: Light 1/2 behind Weather: Overcast

602 BET UEFA CUP - BETDAQ MAIDEN STKS 5f (F)
2:00 (2:01) (Class 5) 3-Y-O+ **£2,729** (£806; £403) **Stalls** High

Form RPR
2 **1** **Under Review (IRE)**[19] 358 3-8-13 0........................ JamieSpencer 10 73+
(S A Callaghan) *mde all: hung lft thrght: drvn clr appr fnl f* **8/13**[1]

2 2 ¾ **Air Lion (USA)** 3-8-13 0........................ ShaneKelly 1 59+
(R M H Cowell) *chsd wnr: kpt on same pce fnl f* **7/2**[2]

0-53 **3** 1 ½ **Beaux Yeux**[30] 227 3-8-1 0........................ PaulPickard(7) 4 49
(P T Midgley) *prom: kpt on fnl f* **25/1**

0/6- **4** 2 **Fiuntas (IRE)**[59] 7759 6-9-13 55........................(bt[1]) GrahamGibbons 5 53
(Shaun Harley, Ire) *chsd ldrs: wknd fnl f* **12/1**[3]

-402 **5** 2 ¼ **Lois Darlin (IRE)**[27] 268 3-8-5 52........................(b) KevinGhunowa(3) 7 34
(R A Harris) *sn outpcd: sme hdwy over 2f out: nvr on terms* **14/1**

-043 **6** 2 ½ **Thoosa**[5] 552 3-8-8 0........................ LukeMorris 3 25
(P S McEntee) *sn outpcd and in rr: hung rt and sme hdwy fnl f: nvr on terms* **20/1**

4043 **7** 3 ¼ **Only Hope**[12] 447 5-9-8 49........................(v) AdamKirby 6 19
(P S McEntee) *sn outpcd: bhd fnl 2f* **33/1**

0-64 **8** ¾ **Field Fantasy**[25] 286 3-8-8 0........................ PatrickMathers 8 10
(Garry Moss) *s.i.s: a towards rr* **50/1**

00-2 **9** ½ **Wicksy Creek**[12] 447 4-9-13 50........................ FrankieMcDonald 2 20
(G C Bravery) *in tch: wknd 2f out* **25/1**

60.08 secs (0.38) **Going Correction** +0.05s/f (Slow)
WFA 3 from 4yo+ 14lb **9** Ran SP% **115.9**
Speed ratings (Par 103): **98,93,91,88,84 80,75,74,73**
toteswinger: 1&2 £1.60, 1&3 £8.00, 2&3 £28.10. CSF £2.58 TOTE £1.50: £1.02, £1.90, £6.40; EX 3.60 Trifecta £63.70 Pool: £389.24 - 4.52 winning units..
Owner J Browne **Bred** James Drynan & Tom Wallace **Trained** Newmarket, Suffolk

FOCUS
A very modest and uncompetitive maiden in which the result was never really in doubt. The first four home all ended up racing towards the far side of the track. The bare form looks limited judged on the proximity of the fourth and fifth.

603 BET 1% IN RUNNING - BETDAQ (S) STKS 1m 4f (F)
2:30 (2:30) (Class 6) 4-Y-O+ **£2,047** (£604; £302) **Stalls** Low

Form RPR
032- **1** **Wabbraan (USA)**[126] 6757 4-8-6 60........................ AmyBaker(5) 6 65
(M Hill) *chsd ldrs: led over 4f out: clr 3f out: rdn out* **7/1**[3]

/33- **2** 8 **Bring It On Home**[33] 7713 5-9-0 58........................(b) FergusSweeney 9 52
(G L Moore) *prom: wnt modest 2nd over 2f out: no ch w wnr* **7/1**[3]

05/ **3** 9 **Sophist (IRE)**[21] 3299 6-9-0 50........................(be) StephenDonohoe 2 38
(Evan Williams) *mid-div: rdn 6f out: sn lost pl: styd on fnl 2f: tk modest 3rd nr fin* **16/1**

-140 **4** nk **My Friend Fritz**[21] 325 9-9-5 69........................ JamieSpencer 4 42
(P W Hiatt) *chsd ldrs: reminders after 3f: drvn over 5f out: one pce fnl 3f* **6/4**[1]

-000 **5** ¾ **Shadow Jumper (IRE)**[9] 489 8-8-11 40........(p) RussellKennemore(3) 7 36
(J T Stimpson) *hld up in tch: effrt on outer over 2f out: one pce* **66/1**

0-02 **6** 4 ½ **Dancing Lyra**[21] 324 8-9-0 65........................ PaulHanagan 1 29
(R A Fahey) *led tl over 4f out: wknd fnl 2f* **15/8**[2]

0-00 **7** 17 **Matinee Idol**[37] 148 6-8-9 32........................(b) RobertWinston 8 —
(Mrs S Lamyman) *reminders after s: hdwy on outside 7f out: lost pl over 4f out: bhd whn eased over 2f out* **50/1**

-005 **8** 26 **Super King**[10] 468 8-9-0 30........................ GrahamGibbons 3 —
(A D Brown) *hld up in rr: hdwy 7f out: lost pl over 4f out: sn bhd: virtually p.u* **80/1**

10/0 **9** 1 ¾ **Borouj (IRE)**[5] 554 7-8-7 56........................(v) DeclanCannon(7) 5 —
(Joss Saville) *s.i.s: lost pl over 4f out: sn t.o: virtually p.u* **25/1**

2m 40.58s (-0.42) **Going Correction** +0.05s/f (Slow)
WFA 4 from 5yo+ 3lb **9** Ran SP% **114.2**
Speed ratings (Par 101): **103,97,91,91,90 87,76,59,58**
toteswinger: 1&2 £7.00, 1&3 £6.80, 2&3 £13.70. CSF £52.52 TOTE £8.10: £3.00, £2.10, £4.40; EX 40.00 Trifecta £224.60 Part won. Pool: £303.63 - 0.20 winning units..The winner was bought in for 4,750gns.
Owner Martin Hill **Bred** R D Hubbard **Trained** Littlehempston, Devon
■ Stewards' Enquiry : Amy Baker caution: used whip when clearly winning.

FOCUS
A weak seller and with the two market leaders running stinkers it's debatable what the form adds up to, although the winner could be underrated..

604 BET API-BETDAQ H'CAP 1m 6f (F)
3:00 (3:00) (Class 5) (0-75,69) 4-Y-O+ **£2,729** (£806; £403) **Stalls** Low

Form RPR
1-30 **1** **Victory Quest (IRE)**[21] 325 9-9-12 **69**........................(v) RobertWinston 5 81
(Mrs S Lamyman) *chsd ldrs: rdn over 3f out: led over 1f out: hld on gamely* **8/1**

2433 **2** nk **They All Laughed**[7] 511 6-9-10 **67**........................ LukeMorris 6 79
(P W Hiatt) *hld up: hdwy on outside 4f out: chal over 1f out: no ex nr fin* **7/2**[2]

1523 **3** 3 ¼ **Sea Cliff (IRE)**[12] 449 5-9-2 **59**........................(e[1]) JamieMoriarty 2 66
(Jonjo O'Neill) *hld up in tch: effrt over 4f out: sn rdn and outpcd: kpt on fnl 2f* **3/1**[1]

-512 **4** 2 **Blue Hills**[14] 402 8-9-6 **63**........................(v) DarrenWilliams 9 68
(P W Hiatt) *led: qcknd over 8f out: hdd over 1f out: grad wknd* **9/1**

24-4 **5** 4 **Callisto Moon**[11] 459 5-9-12 **69**........................ GrahamGibbons 8 68
(R Curtis) *trckd ldrs: wknd over 1f out* **6/1**

1413 **6** 9 **Sabancaya**[14] 402 4-9-3 **65**........................ MickyFenton 4 51
(Mrs P Sly) *dwlt: mid-div: effrt over 4f out: wknd and eased over 1f out* **9/2**[3]

00-3 **7** 5 **Dreams Jewel**[11] 459 9-9-3 **60**........................ NeilChalmers 7 39
(C Roberts) *in tch on outside: effrt over 4f out: lost pl over 2f out* **18/1**

50-4 **8** 7 **Red Twist**[22] 310 4-9-0 **62**........................ FergusSweeney 1 32
(M Hill) *chsd ldrs: outpcd over 4f out: sn lost pl* **20/1**

/40- **9** 10 **Kentucky Boy (IRE)**[55] 6054 5-8-13 **56**........................ AndrewElliott 3 12
(Jedd O'Keeffe) *chsd ldrs: drvn along 8f out: lost pl over 4f out* **18/1**

3m 10.19s (1.89) **Going Correction** +0.05s/f (Slow)
WFA 4 from 5yo+ 5lb **9** Ran SP% **116.1**
Speed ratings (Par 103): **96,95,93,92,90 85,82,78,72**
toteswinger: 1&2 £8.00, 1&3 £6.90, 2&3 £3.10. CSF £36.37 CT £104.40 TOTE £7.80: £2.60, £1.60, £1.30; EX 42.90 Trifecta £187.10 Part won. Pool: £252.96 - 0.30 winning units..
Owner P Lamyman **Bred** Miss Veronica Henley **Trained** Ruckland, Lincs

FOCUS
An ordinary staying handicap, but they appeared to go a solid pace thanks to Blue Hills who made this a proper test. The solid third sets the standard.

605 TWO JUMPS MEETINGS AT SOUTHWELL IN MARCH CLAIMING STKS 6f (F)
3:35 (3:35) (Class 6) 3-Y-O **£2,047** (£604; £302) **Stalls** Low

Form RPR
-152 **1** **My Sweet Georgia (IRE)**[20] 345 3-8-12 71........................(b) JamieSpencer 3 71
(S A Callaghan) *stmbld s: led over 4f out: hrd drvn fnl 2f: hld on wl* **9/4**[1]

-311 **2** 1 **Madison Belle**[18] 365 3-9-2 70........................ DarrenWilliams 6 72
(K R Burke) *chsd ldrs: chal over 1f out: no ex ins fnl f* **5/2**[2]

3521 **3** 2 1/4 **La Capriosa**[4] 560 3-8-8 65 .... RobertWinston 4 57
(A J McCabe) *led tl over 4f out: chal over 2f out: kpt on same pce appr fnl f* **9/4**[1]

3222 **4** 2 1/2 **Hawkspring (IRE)**[6] 530 3-9-3 66 .... (t) AdamKirby 2 58+
(S Parr) *sn outpcd: kpt on fnl f* **5/1**[3]

-230 **5** 7 **Glan Lady (IRE)**[10] 475 3-8-4 52 ow3 .... (p) KevinGhunowa(3) 1 25
(G J Smith) *in rr: outpcd over 3f out: sn bhd* **25/1**

1m 17.3s (0.80) **Going Correction** +0.05s/f (Slow) **5** Ran SP% **110.6**
Speed ratings (Par 95): **96,94,91,88,79**
toteswinger: 1&2 £4.40. CSF £8.26 TOTE £3.30: £1.90, £1.40; EX 8.60.
Owner Hinge, Searchfield & Tamburro **Bred** Epona Bloodstock Ltd **Trained** Newmarket, Suffolk

FOCUS
An ordinary claimer, but the majority came into the contest in decent form. The winner ran to her January form.

606 JACK SARGENT H'CAP — 6f (F)
4:05 (4:05) (Class 5) (0-75,74) 4-Y-O+ **£2,729** (£806; £403) **Stalls** Low

Form RPR
66-4 **1** **Imprimis Tagula (IRE)**[38] 133 5-9-4 73 .... (v) RobertWinston 2 84
(A Bailey) *w ldrs: led over 1f out: styd on wl* **9/2**[3]

-233 **2** 1 **Blue Charm**[41] 106 5-9-2 71 .... TomEaves 8 79
(I W McInnes) *in rr: hdwy 2f out: styd on wl to take 2nd wl ins fnl f* **9/2**[3]

4-24 **3** 1 3/4 **This Ones For Eddy**[4] 561 4-9-0 69 .... AdamKirby 9 71
(S Parr) *mid-div: hdwy on outside over 2f out: sn chsng ldrs: kpt on same pce fnl f* **10/3**[2]

1131 **4** 1 1/4 **Back In The Red (IRE)**[7] 518 5-9-2 74 6ex .... (b) KevinGhunowa(3) 3 72
(R A Harris) *mde most: hdd over 1f out: no ex* **11/4**[1]

20-5 **5** 2 1/2 **Gainshare**[43] 76 4-8-2 62 .... DeanHeslop(5) 5 52
(Mrs R A Carr) *in rr div: hdwy 2f out: kpt on ins fnl f* **25/1**

3306 **6** 1 3/4 **Peter's Storm (USA)**[2] 576 4-8-9 71 .... AmyRyan(7) 1 56
(K A Ryan) *w ldrs: wknd over 1f out* **16/1**

260- **7** 1 **Dorn Dancer (IRE)**[197] 4736 7-9-4 73 .... TonyHamilton 6 54
(D W Barker) *in rr: sme hdwy 2f out: nvr nr ldrs* **25/1**

220- **8** hd **Royal Challenge**[89] 7428 8-9-3 72 .... PatrickMathers 10 53+
(I W McInnes) *s.i.s: stl had hood on whn stalls opened: s.s: nvr on terms* **25/1**

00-0 **9** 2 3/4 **Mission Impossible**[21] 329 4-9-0 69 .... PaulMulrennan 4 41
(P C Haslam) *chsd ldrs: wknd over 1f out* **12/1**

-050 **10** hd **Savile's Delight (IRE)**[23] 304 10-8-7 69 .... RossAtkinson(7) 7 40
(Tom Dascombe) *chsd ldrs: lost pl over 1f out* **16/1**

1m 16.74s (0.24) **Going Correction** +0.05s/f (Slow) **10** Ran SP% **117.1**
Speed ratings (Par 103): **100,98,96,94,91 89,87,87,83,83**
toteswinger: 1&2 £3.20, 1&3 £2.60, 2&3 £3.10. CSF £24.58 CT £75.40 TOTE £5.20: £1.90, £1.60, £1.70; EX 24.70 Trifecta £63.00 Pool: £305.87 - 3.59 winning units..
Owner A Bailey **Bred** Glashare House Stud **Trained** Newmarket, Suffolk

FOCUS
A competitive sprint handicap for the grade and there was no hanging about with six horses covered by about a length starting up the home straight. The winning time was over half a second quicker than the three-year-old claimer and the form looks reasonable rated through the winner to previous course form.

607 CALL 01636 814481 TO SPONSOR A RACE H'CAP — 7f (F)
4:40 (4:40) (Class 6) (0-65,65) 4-Y-O+ **£2,047** (£604; £302) **Stalls** Low

Form RPR
3415 **1** **Mocha Java**[8] 496 6-8-3 57 ow3 .... RossAtkinson(7) 4 69
(M Salaman) *mde all: hld on wl* **8/1**

-555 **2** 1/2 **Haroldini (IRE)**[7] 519 7-8-13 60 .... (b[1]) PaulMulrennan 6 71
(J Balding) *trckd ldrs: t.k.h: chal over 1f out: no ex wl ins fnl f* **17/2**

4451 **3** 1 **Cape Of Storms**[9] 487 6-8-11 58 6ex .... TomEaves 7 66
(R Brotherton) *mid-div: hdwy 2f out: kpt on wl ins fnl f* **11/1**

000- **4** 3/4 **Jebel Tara**[105] 7206 4-9-4 65 .... (t) GrahamGibbons 8 71
(A D Brown) *chsd ldrs: chal over 1f out: styd on same pce* **13/2**[3]

0533 **5** 2 1/2 **Motivated Choice**[8] 495 4-8-11 65 .... BMcHugh(7) 3 64
(Miss Amy Weaver) *mid-div: hdwy over 2f out: hung rt: kpt on same pce* **16/1**

2252 **6** nse **Hamaasy**[9] 489 8-8-10 60 .... (p) KevinGhunowa(3) 12 59
(R A Harris) *in tch on outside: outpcd over 3f out: kpt on fnl f* **5/1**[2]

-112 **7** nk **Charlotte Grey**[14] 401 5-8-9 59 .... DuranFentiman(3) 13 57
(P J McBride) *mid-div: hdwy on outer 2f out: nvr rchd ldrs* **15/2**

-603 **8** 1 3/4 **Run Free**[7] 519 5-8-10 57 .... (p) LeeEnstone 2 51
(N Wilson) *trckd ldrs on ins: wknd over 1f out* **15/2**

213- **9** nk **Ugenius**[59] 7764 5-9-0 61 .... TGMcLaughlin 9 54
(Mrs C A Dunnett) *hld up in rr: hdwy on inner over 2f out: wknd over 1f out* **9/2**[1]

2246 **10** 2 3/4 **Jordi Roper (IRE)**[7] 514 4-8-9 56 .... (p) TolleyDean 10 41
(S Parr) *s.s: nvr on terms* **12/1**

050- **11** 5 **Wiseman's Diamond (USA)**[134] 6585 4-8-10 57 .... JamieMoriarty 11 29
(P T Midgley) *a towards rr* **33/1**

0055 **12** 1 1/4 **Government (IRE)**[3] 514 8-7-13 51 oh6 .... (b) AmyBaker(5) 5 19
(M C Chapman) *w ldrs: lost pl over 2f out* **50/1**

-040 **13** 8 **Mont Cervin**[2] 580 4-8-1 53 .... (b) DeanHeslop(5) 1 —
(Mrs R A Carr) *dwlt: in rr: bhd fnl 2f* **25/1**

1m 29.0s (-1.30) **Going Correction** +0.05s/f (Slow) **13** Ran SP% **124.0**
Speed ratings (Par 101): **109,108,107,106,103 103,103,101,100,97 91,90,81**
toteswinger: 1&2 £23.10, 1&3 £18.30, 2&3 £19.70. CSF £76.25 CT £768.30 TOTE £9.80: £3.70, £3.30, £3.60; EX 77.20 TRIFECTA Not won..
Owner Oaktree Racing **Bred** A H And C E Robinson Partnership **Trained** Upper Lambourn, Berks
■ Stewards' Enquiry : Ross Atkinson three-day ban: used whip with excessive frequency (Mar 5-7)
T G McLaughlin two-day ban: used whip with excessive frequency (Mar 10-11)

FOCUS
A moderate handicap, but very open as the market would have suggested. This was a race where it paid to race handily but it looks good form for the grade.

608 SOUTHWELL RACECOURSE FOR CONFERENCES H'CAP — 1m (F)
5:10 (5:10) (Class 6) (0-52,56) 4-Y-O+ **£2,047** (£604; £302) **Stalls** Low

Form RPR
23/0 **1** **Almahaza (IRE)**[31] 221 5-9-0 52 .... NeilChalmers 2 61
(A J Chamberlain) *hld up in rr: gd hdwy on outside 2f out: r.o wl to ld towards fin* **25/1**

3111 **2** 1 **General Tufto**[4] 565 4-8-11 56 6ex .... (b) HollyHall(7) 13 63
(C Smith) *sn w ldr: led over 4f out: clr on ins 3f out: jst ct* **10/11**[1]

-304 **3** 1 3/4 **Mister Benji**[14] 405 10-8-8 46 oh1 .... (p) AndrewElliott 9 49
(B P J Baugh) *trckd ldrs: t.k.h: styd on same pce fnl f* **14/1**

4240 **4** hd **Moyoko (IRE)**[8] 494 6-9-0 52 .... (b) PaulHanagan 4 54
(M Salaman) *s.i.s: hdwy over 2f out: kpt on same pce fnl f* **10/1**[3]

4050 **5** 1/2 **Pembo**[6] 537 4-8-5 46 oh1 .... (b[1]) KevinGhunowa(3) 11 47
(R A Harris) *trckd ldrs: t.k.h: hung lft over 1f out: kpt on one pce* **33/1**

03-4 **6** 9 **Ming Vase**[7] 515 7-8-10 48 .... JamieMoriarty 6 28
(P T Midgley) *in rr: sme hdwy over 3f out: nvr nr ldrs* **14/1**

352 **7** hd **Very Well Red**[4] 565 6-8-9 47 .... RobertWinston 5 27
(P W Hiatt) *trckd ldrs: wknd appr fnl f* **3/1**[2]

-000 **8** 6 **Only A Grand**[14] 405 5-8-8 46 oh1 .... (b) TomEaves 1 12
(R Bastiman) *sn chsng ldrs: outpcd 4f out: sn lost pl* **33/1**

000- **9** 2 **Amber Ridge**[136] 6530 4-8-5 46 oh1 .... DuranFentiman(3) 10 8
(B P J Baugh) *a in rr* **66/1**

00-1 **10** 1 1/2 **Muncaster Castle (IRE)**[14] 405 5-8-13 51 .... FrankieMcDonald 8 9
(R F Fisher) *in rr: hung lft 3f out: bhd fnl 2f* **14/1**

0-05 **11** 2 1/2 **Titus Gent**[10] 473 4-8-7 52 .... RyanPowell(7) 3 4
(J Ryan) *s.i.s: nvr on terms* **66/1**

-600 **12** 2 1/4 **Piccolo Diamante (USA)**[4] 565 5-9-0 52 .... (t) TolleyDean 12 —
(S Parr) *led tl over 4f out: wkng whn hmpd 3f out* **33/1**

1m 43.2s (-0.50) **Going Correction** +0.05s/f (Slow) **12** Ran SP% **122.1**
Speed ratings (Par 101): **104,103,101,101,100 91,91,85,83,81 79,77**
toteswinger: 1&2 £10.20, 1&3 £46.60, 2&3 £4.80. CSF £48.40 CT £389.76 TOTE £43.60: £6.40, £1.20, £2.90; EX 85.20 TRIFECTA Not won. Place 6: £97.33, Place 5: £82.92..
Owner G B Heffaran **Bred** Castletown And Associates **Trained** Ashton Keynes, Wilts
■ Stewards' Enquiry : Neil Chalmers three-day ban: excessive use of the whip (Mar 12-14)

FOCUS
A very moderate handicap with the runner-up the best guide having run to recent form.
T/Plt: £203.20 to a £1 stake. Pool: £54,270.29. 194.90 winning tickets. T/Qpdt: £23.80 to a £1 stake. Pool: £4,313.54. 134.10 winning tickets. WG

521 NAD AL SHEBA (L-H)
Thursday, February 19
OFFICIAL GOING: Dirt course - fast; turf course - good

609a MUSTAQBALI H'CAP (TURF) — 7f 110y(D)
3:05 (3:05) (95-110,108) 3-Y-O+
£50,000 (£16,666; £8,333; £4,166; £2,500; £1,666)

RPR
1 **Valedictum (AUS)**[14] 413 9-9-3 107 .... (bt) TedDurcan 8 109
(Danny O'Brien, Australia) *mid-div on rail: prog to trck ldrs 2f out: swtchd 1f out: r.o wl: led fnl 55yds* **10/1**

2 1/2 **Echoes Rock (GER)**[97] 6-9-0 104 .... (t) LDettori 1 105
(Ms C Erichsen, Norway) *sn led: set stdy pce: drew clr 2 1/2f out: r.o wl: ct cl home* **5/1**[2]

3 1 3/4 **Stubbs Art (IRE)**[125] 6780 4-9-1 105 .... KShea 2 101
(M F De Kock, South Africa) *s.i.s: trckd ldrs: rdn to chse ldr 2 1/2f out: r.o same pce fnl 1 1/2f* **7/4**[1]

4 shd **Emirates Gold (IRE)**[13] 439 6-8-11 101 .... (t) TPO'Shea 7 97
(E Charpy, UAE) *in rr of mid-div: rdn to cl 2 1/2f out: ev ch 1 1/2f out: nt qckn* **10/1**

5 1 1/4 **Glow Star (SAF)**[14] 413 5-8-8 98 .... (b) RyanMoore 5 91
(H J Brown, South Africa) *racd in rr: r.o fnl 2f but nvr able to chal* **6/1**

6 hd **Stepping Up (IRE)**[7] 521 6-8-2 95 .... (t) SMGorey(3) 6 88
(E Charpy, UAE) *racd in last: nvr nr to chal but r.o same pce fnl 2f* **33/1**

7 1 1/2 **Pointing North (SAF)**[21] 335 5-9-4 108 .... RichardMullen 9 97
(S Seemar, UAE) *mid-div: rdn 3f out: one pce* **11/2**[3]

8 4 **Boston Lodge**[21] 334 9-8-11 101 ow2 .... (v) EddieAhern 3 80
(F Nass, Bahrain) *mid-div on rail: rdn 2 1/2f out: n.m.r 1 1/2f out: wknd* **40/1**

9 5 1/4 **Mojito Royale (IRE)**[13] 439 5-8-10 100 .... (p) JMurtagh 10 66
(Eoin Doyle, Ire) *trckd ldrs: rdn 3f out: sn btn* **12/1**

10 6 1/4 **Akua'Ba (IRE)**[14] 416 5-8-13 102 .... (p) KJManning 4 53
(J S Bolger, Ire) *mid-div: rdn 3f out: sn btn* **25/1**

1m 31.02s (-0.58) **Going Correction** +0.20s/f (Good) **10** Ran SP% **117.8**
Speed ratings: **110,109,107,107,106 106,104,100,95,89**
CSF £59.04 Tricast £130.82.
Owner Martin Tb/ Sinn/Mckee/Cranwell/Jaksa **Bred** Barrine Thoroughbreds, B Miller & Mrs M Miller **Trained** Australia

FOCUS
The pace was steady for much of the way and the bare form looks ordinary for the level. Although the winning time was 0.26 seconds quicker than the second division, it's probably worth noting the winner of that race, the 100-rated Swop, only got in the clear late on.

NOTEBOOK
Valedictum(AUS) found this less competitive than the course-and-distance handicap he contested first-time up at the Carnival and, 2lb lower on this occasion, he overcame the modest early tempo. He will find things tougher off higher marks, but this was a good pointer to his stablemate, Barbaricus, who looks much the better of the pair, yet is also rated 107, and that one should be able to improve on his recent third placing. (op 9/1)
Echoes Rock(GER), Listed class at best in France, very nearly nicked this from the front on his debut for Norwegian connections after a three-month break. Admittedly it's not easy making all on this turf course, but he had soft time on the lead and is no sure thing to confirm this form next time.
Stubbs Art(IRE) has loads of ability (third in last year's English and Irish 2000 Guineas), but his only win from 13 attempts coming into this was gained in a handicap off just 72, and he was disappointing on his first start since leaving David Elsworth. It's fair to say the steady pace was against him, but after recovering from a slow start to sit handy, he looked particularly laboured under pressure and just plugged on at the one speed, rather than quickening. He was briefly short of room in the straight, but that made no difference to the result. However, while it's obvious he's not totally straightforward, he should do better off a stronger gallop and his master trainer can be given another chance to get the best out of him, especially considering the horse is well treated on the pick of his form. (op 13/8)
Emirates Gold(IRE) kept on for pressure, but was never getting there and is likely to remain vulnerable in these types of races.
Glow Star(SAF) was only half a length behind today's winner over course and distance on his previous start, but he was left with a lot to do in the straight and could make no impression. He could yet be capable of better when getting a stronger pace, but his trainer is not in much form.
Stepping Up(IRE) came wide into the straight when trying to pick up from well back and he looks a little better than his finishing position indicates.

Pointing North(SAF) was far too keen early on and again failed to run anywhere near the pick of his South African form. (op 6/1)

610a AL DANA INVESTMENT PLATE (CONDITIONS RACE) (DIRT) 1m (D)
3:40 (3:40) 3-Y-0+

£45,833 (£15,277; £7,638; £3,819; £2,291; £1,527)

RPR

1 **Dijeerr (USA)**[28] [265] 5-8-3 109..........(vt) AnticoMurgia[(10)] 8 110
(M bin Shafya, UAE) *sn led: drew clr 2 1/2f out: r.o wl: comf* **11/1**[3]

2 2¼ **Tiz Now Tiz Then (USA)**[123] 4-8-9 108..........(vt) RichardMullen 2 101+
(S Seemar, UAE) *racd in rr: mid-div 3f out: r.o same pce fnl 2f: no ch w wnr* **4/1**[2]

3 8¼ **Honour Devil (ARG)**[327] [1088] 5-9-2 121.......... JMurtagh 6 89+
(M F De Kock, South Africa) *mid-div: rdn 3f out: r.o same pce* **4/9**[1]

4 ½ **Little White Lie (IRE)**[7] [522] 5-8-13 101.......... WJSupple 7 85
(A bin Huzaim, UAE) *mid-div: rdn 3f out: kpt on same pce* **11/1**[3]

5 4½ **Estihdaaf (USA)**[6] 8-8-13 91..........(bt) RHills 4 75
(A Al Raihe, UAE) *settled in rr: nvr able to chal* **50/1**

6 15 **Jaffal (USA)**[13] [435] 7-8-7 90..........(t) RoystonFfrench 1 34
(A Al Raihe, UAE) *trckd ldr on rail: rdn 4f out: sn btn* **50/1**

7 19 **Monte Alto (IRE)**[125] [6784] 5-8-7 95..........(b) TPO'Shea 3 —
(A Al Raihe, UAE) *s.i.s: nvr nr to chal* **14/1**

8 12 **Fleurie**[14] [417] 4-8-13 90..........(b) BrettDoyle 5 —
(R Bouresly, Kuwait) *trckd ldrs tl 3 1/2f out: sn btn* **66/1**

9 dist **Wingbeat (USA)**[21] [336] 4-8-9 94..........(t) FJara 9 —
(I Mohammed, UAE) *trckd ldr: wd: wknd 4f out* **20/1**

1m 37.34s (0.64) **Going Correction** +0.35s/f (Slow) 9 Ran SP% **122.8**
Speed ratings: **110,107,99,99,94 79,60,48,—**
CSF £56.75.
Owner Sheikh Ahmed Al Maktoum **Bred** Monticule **Trained** United Arab Emirates

FOCUS
The favourite ran well below form, but this was still a smart effort from the winner.

NOTEBOOK
Dijeerr(USA) ◆ had been in woeful form in two runs on turf since joining this yard, but he's bred to handle the dirt - by Danzig, out of a Deputy Minister mare - and this surface clearly suited. He was also seemingly helped the application of a first-time tongue-tie, as well as a return to front-running tactics, and was a ready winner. Having led at a decent enough-looking pace, he kicked clear off the final bend and was always doing enough, despite understandably tiring near the line. Although the bare form of his defeat of Honour Devil cannot be taken literally, this was still a smart performance and it would be unwise to underestimate him. He could go on to better things on the dirt. (op 10/1)
Tiz Now Tiz Then(USA), basically a Grade 3 standard performer when trained in the US, ran well on his UAE debut after four months off. His new stable have not been in much form lately, but there was no faulting this effort. (op 3/1)
Honour Devil(ARG), last year's UAE 2000 Guineas and Derby winner, was sent off at odds on for his first start in 11 months, but he's reportedly had a few setbacks since he was last seen and was well below his best. He won off a ten-month absence at last year's Carnival, so fitness should not have been too much of a concern, but he came under pressure before the straight and failed to pick up. While he's obviously entitled to be a lot sharper next time, there weren't many positives to take from this performance and he now looks to have little chance of making the World Cup with a realistic chance. (op 4/6)
Little White Lie(IRE) ◆ again showed good mid-race speed to briefly look a danger turning in, but once again he found little when let down. That's no surprise, as he's simply a turf horse, and might be worth a bet when returned to his favoured surface. (12/1)

611a CBD VISA INFINITE CARD TROPHY (H'CAP) (TURF) 6f (T)
4:10 (4:10) (95-110,109) 3-Y-0+

£50,000 (£16,666; £8,333; £4,166; £2,500; £1,666)

RPR

1 **Judd Street**[13] [434] 7-9-1 105..........(b) MJKinane 10 104
(Eve Johnson Houghton) *trckd ldrs: gng wl 2 1/2f out: rdn to chse ldr 2f out: led cl home* **13/2**[3]

2 ¼ **Instant Recall (IRE)**[13] [433] 8-9-1 105..........(v) WayneSmith 2 103
(M Al Muhairi, UAE) *sn led: t.k.h: rdn 3f out: r.o wl: hdd nr line* **4/1**[2]

3 shd **Nota Bene**[13] [434] 7-8-10 100.......... RichardHughes 8 98+
(D R C Elsworth) *settled in rr: swtchd wd 2 1/2f out: r.o wl fnl 1 1/2f: nrst fin* **20/1**

4 hd **So Will I**[13] [433] 8-9-1 105..........(t) RHills 6 102
(Doug Watson, UAE) *trckd ldrs: rdn 2 1/2f out: ev ch fnl 1 1/2f: nt qckn fnl 55yds* **11/1**

5 hd **Contest (IRE)**[13] [434] 5-9-2 106..........(b) JMurtagh 7 103
(C Theodorakis, Greece) *settled in rr: nvr nr to chal but r.o wl fnl 1 1/2f* **16/1**

6 ½ **Mandobi (IRE)**[28] [257] 8-8-10 100..........(vt) WilliamBuick 1 95
(D Selvaratnam, UAE) *mid-div on rail: n.m.r 2 1/2f out: r.o one pce* **25/1**

7 ½ **Miss Gorica (IRE)**[13] [433] 5-9-0 104.......... TedDurcan 3 98
(Ms Joanna Morgan, Ire) *mid-div: ev ch 2f out: one pce* **12/1**

8 1½ **Asset (IRE)**[13] [434] 6-9-5 109..........(b) LDettori 9 98
(Saeed Bin Suroor) *settled in rr: rdn to chse ldrs 2 1/2f out: nt qckn fnl f* **11/8**[1]

9 ¼ **Nights Cross (IRE)**[13] [433] 8-8-13 102.......... GHind 5 91
(B Al Abed, Bahrain) *mid-div: rdn 2 1/2f out: nt qckn fnl f* **12/1**

10 1¼ **Buachaill Dona (IRE)**[28] [259] 6-8-10 100.......... AdrianTNicholls 4 85
(D Nicholls) *s.i.s: settled in rr: nvr able to chal* **14/1**

1m 12.05s (0.05) **Going Correction** +0.20s/f (Good) 10 Ran SP% **120.3**
Speed ratings: **107,106,106,106,106 105,104,102,102,100**
CSF £33.83 Tricast £505.18.
Owner R F Johnson Houghton **Bred** R F Johnson Houghton **Trained** Blewbury, Oxon

FOCUS
A decent, competitive sprint handicap, but the pace was modest until about halfway, resulting in a bunch finish, and a few of these were denied clear runs. The bare form needs treating with some caution.

NOTEBOOK
Judd Street confirmed the promise of his recent third behind Asset (below form this time) and was a game winner. This was a good effort considering he was three wide for much of the race way, but at the same time it's worth noting a few in behind are better than they showed. (op 6/1)
Instant Recall(IRE), just as on his last two starts, was pegged back late on to fill second, having led early. He was quite free in front, but that's simply because he was setting such a pedestrian pace for the trip, and there were no excuses.
Nota Bene flashed home for third having been well back at the top of the straight and this was an improvement on his debut effort in the UAE.
So Will I seemed to have every chance. (op 10/1)
Contest(IRE) ◆ might have won with a clear run. Sporting second-time blinkers, and held up this time having failed to get home from the front in a similar race last time, he had nowhere to go for the majority of the straight, and the way he ran on when finally in the open in the last 50m or so suggests he was an unlucky loser. It's often unwise to get carried away with such types in muddling races, and he might be best left if a short price next time, but he has the ability to win a similar race if things fall right.
Mandobi(IRE) did not have that much room to manoeuvre against the inside rail in the closing stages, but he didn't look unlucky. Still, this was an improvement on his reappearance. (op 20/1)
Miss Gorica(IRE) was another who did not have much room to play with inside the final 300m or so, but she probably wasn't unlucky.
Asset(IRE) found next to nothing for pressure and was nowhere near the form he showed when successful over this course and distance off a 4lb lower mark last time. He went four wide into the straight, but the winner was similarly positioned and that's no excuse. He he has loads of ability, but is not the most reliable. (op 6/4)
Buachaill Dona(IRE) raced keenly out the back early on and then had little room in which to challenge in the straight. He would have preferred a stronger gallop and is better than he showed.

612a ATTIJARI AL ISLAMI TROPHY (H'CAP) (DIRT) 1m 2f (D)
4:55 (4:56) (90-105,102) 3-Y-0+

£45,833 (£15,277; £7,638; £3,819; £2,291; £1,527)

RPR

1 **Clasp**[21] [337] 7-8-5 90..........(vt) FJara 2 101
(Doug Watson, UAE) *trckd ldrs: led gng wl 2f out: r.o wl: comf* **16/1**

2 7¾ **Irish Mayhem (USA)**[21] [337] 4-9-0 100..........(v) LDettori 4 96
(Saeed Bin Suroor) *mid-div: rdn to chse ldrs 2 1/2f out: r.o wl: no ch w wnr* **6/1**[3]

3 6¼ **Naples (AUS)**[7] [522] 6-8-9 95..........(t) KShea 8 77
(M F De Kock, South Africa) *trckd ldrs tl rdn 4f out: kpt on same pce* **15/2**

4 1¼ **Arqaam**[14] [419] 5-9-3 102..........(v) RHills 1 83
(Doug Watson, UAE) *slowly away: in rr of mid-div: r.o wl fnl 3f but nvr able to chal* **15/2**

5 ¾ **Mutasallil (USA)**[7] [523] 9-8-9 95..........(t) WJSupple 3 73
(Doug Watson, UAE) *sn led: hdd 2f out: wknd* **16/1**

6 shd **Moonquake (USA)**[21] [337] 4-8-6 93.......... RoystonFfrench 9 71
(M bin Shafya, UAE) *trckd ldng gp: rdn 3f out: r.o same pce* **7/2**[1]

7 1¾ **Escape Route (USA)**[7] [522] 5-8-11 97..........(t) RichardMullen 13 71
(S Seemar, UAE) *trckd ldrs: one pce fnl 3f: wknd fnl f* **16/1**

8 1¾ **Jack Junior (USA)**[13] [435] 5-9-1 100.......... AdrianTNicholls 7 72
(D Nicholls) *racd in rr: nvr nr to chal* **5/1**[2]

9 18 **Grand Hombre (USA)**[13] [435] 9-9-3 102..........(t) BrettDoyle 6 38
(R Bouresly, Kuwait) *in rr of mid-div: nvr nr to chal* **14/1**

10 4¼ **Team Victory (BRZ)**[214] 5-8-13 98..........(vt) RyanMoore 12 25
(S Seemar, UAE) *slowly away: trckd ldrs for 3f: wknd* **11/1**

11 ¾ **Bucintoro (IRE)**[14] [419] 5-9-1 100..........(t) JMurtagh 10 26
(C Theodorakis, Greece) *trckd ldrs tl 4f out: wknd* **16/1**

2m 3.53s (1.23) **Going Correction** +0.35s/f (Slow)
WFA 4 from 5yo+ 1lb 11 Ran SP% **115.2**
Speed ratings: **109,102,97,96,96 96,94,93,78,75 74**
CSF £106.96 Tricast £789.27.
Owner Eerc Clasp **Bred** Taker Bloodstock **Trained** United Arab Emirates

FOCUS
Several of the more likely candidates ran below form and this was a weak handicap. The early pace seemed just ordinary by dirt racing's usual standards.

NOTEBOOK
Clasp had been well held on his two previous Carnival starts this year, so a victory was hard to predict, let alone one gained in such emphatic fashion. Unusually for a winner on this dirt course, he hugged the inside rail throughout, but he didn't seem to get all that much kickback and travelled enthusiastically in behind the leaders. Still going well early in the straight, he got a dream run against the rail and fairly bounded away to end a losing run that stretched back to the 2006 Carnival, when he won over course and distance off 94. The Handicapper will surely have him for this. (op 14/1)
Irish Mayhem(USA) is finally getting his act together for Saeed Bin Suroor and this was an improvement on his first two starts of this year. He's probably even better than the bare result, as he lost his position after getting plenty of kickback early, and had to switch out wide with his challenge, but that said, he would not have beaten the winner.
Naples(AUS) has been a bit disappointing so far in Dubai and he didn't do enough to suggest that's about to change. (op 7/1)
Arqaam followed the winner through against the inside rail for much of the way after missing the break, but he didn't pick up all that well in the straight. He can probably do better on this surface when able to dominate. (op 8/1)
Mutasallil(USA) had his chance under a positive ride.
Moonquake(USA), who had today's winner and runner-up behind when ridden from the front over course and distance last time, was not asked to try and dominate on this occasion and ran below form. (tchd 100/30)
Jack Junior(USA) was dropped in at the start, but rarely do such negative tactics pay off on the dirt.
Team Victory(BRZ), a Grade 3 winner in Brazil, was rushed up to sit handy after missing the break, but he emptied quite quickly once coming under pressure and offered noting. (op 10/1)

613a CBD FINANCIAL SERVICES (H'CAP) (TURF) 1m 4f (T)
5:25 (5:25) (95-112,111) 3-Y-0+

£62,500 (£20,833; £10,416; £5,208; £3,125; £2,083)

RPR

1 **Eastern Anthem (IRE)**[14] [419] 5-9-6 111..........(t) RoystonFfrench 2 118+
(M bin Shafya, UAE) *settled in rr: smooth prog on rail 2f out: swtchd 1 1/2f out: r.o wl: led nr line* **11/4**[1]

2 ¼ **Crime Scene (IRE)**[21] [338] 6-9-4 109.......... JRosales 6 116
(M bin Shafya, UAE) *mid-div on rail: smooth prog to ld 2f out: r.o: hdd nr line* **12/1**

3 7¼ **Sugar Ray (IRE)**[35] [185] 5-9-0 105..........(vt) LDettori 8 100
(Saeed Bin Suroor) *ssn led: set stdy pce: rdn 3f out: hdd 2f out: one pce* **9/2**[3]

4 ½ **Mr Brock (SAF)**[7] [527] 6-8-11 102.......... KShea 1 96
(M F De Kock, South Africa) *trckd ldrs: rdn to chal 2 1/2f out: r.o same pce* **7/2**[2]

5 1¼ **Colony (IRE)**[28] [262] 4-8-5 96.......... RHills 4 91
(Saeed Bin Suroor) *settled in rr: nvr nr to chal* **7/1**

6 2½ **Love Galore (IRE)**[14] [419] 4-8-5 98.......... JohnEgan 7 87
(M Johnston) *racd in 3rd: t.k.h: rdn to chse ldrs 2 1/2f out: wknd fnl 1 1/2f* **16/1**

7 1¾ **Halicarnassus (IRE)**[14] [415] 5-9-5 110.......... TedDurcan 3 95
(M R Channon) *in rr of mid-div: nvr able to chal* **9/1**

8 ½ **Bound By Honour (SAF)**[14] [415] 6-9-2 107..........(bt) RyanMoore 10 92
(H J Brown, South Africa) *settled in rr: nvr able to chal* **11/1**

9 6 1/4 **Weald**[191] [4959] 4-8-7 **100** .... FJara 5 76
(Doug Watson, UAE) *nvr bttr than mid-div* **16/1**
10 2 1/4 **Fathayer (USA)**[13] [437] 4-8-7 **100** .... MatthewHenry 9 72
(A Al Raihe, UAE) *mid-div: rdn 3 1/2f out: nvr able to chal* **25/1**

2m 31.06s (0.06) **Going Correction** +0.20s/f (Good)
WFA 4 from 5yo+ 3lb **10** Ran SP% **121.2**
Speed ratings: **107,106,102,101,100 99,98,97,93,92**
CSF £39.24 Tricast £149.77.
Owner Sheikh Hamdan Bin Mohammed Al Maktoum **Bred** Darley **Trained** United Arab Emirates

FOCUS
A decent handicap, but as usual a distinct lack of unexposed types. They seemed to go an even pace and the winning time was 3.28 seconds quicker than the slowly run second division.

NOTEBOOK
Eastern Anthem(IRE) ◆, who created such a good impression when winning off 107 over 1m2f around here two weeks earlier, proved well suited by the return to this longer trip and defied a 4lb rise. Held up out the back for most of the way, he was forced to do more work off the bridle this time (he pretty much carted himself to the front last time), but he responded willingly and just got up after having to switch off the inside rail inside the final furlong. The exact merit of this success gained off a mark of 111 is debatable considering the lack of strength in depth, but whatever, this fine, big horse is absolutely thriving right now and is on the way to fulfilling his undoubted potential. He can do better again off a proper end-to-end gallop, and also gives the impression he will improve again when stepped up to staying trips. He's earned a step up in class now, and the Group 2 Dubai City of Gold Stakes, back over this course and distance on Super Thursday (March 5) is the obvious target, but if his connections don't mind turning him out again quickly, he would be a fascinating contender in the inaugural running of the Dubai Racing Club Gold Cup, a Listed race over 2m on February 26. (op 3/1)
Crime Scene(IRE) beat just one rival in a similar race last time, but that obviously wasn't his true running and he returned to the sort of form that saw him land a course-and-distance handicap off a 5lb lower mark in January. He got a good run through against the inside rail in the straight, and had his chance, but he was pegged back by his superior stablemate near the line.
Sugar Ray(IRE) settled better in front than on his Dubai debut, but making all over this course and distance is a near impossible task.
Mr Brock(SAF) was well enough placed if good enough but he could not build on the promise of his fourth in a decent 1m2f handicap the previous week. This step up in trip should have suited, but he failed to give his true running and the race might have come too soon.
Colony(IRE), just as on his debut for this yard nearly a month earlier, never featured and offered little encouragement. (op 8/1)
Love Galore(IRE) once again simply refused to settle and that cost him his chance. (op 14/1)
Halicarnassus(IRE) was only 2lb higher than when winning over 1m2f two weeks earlier, but that success was gained in a very muddling race and he was beaten before the turn this time. (op 8/1)

614a AL FAHIDI FORT (SPONSORED BY COMMERCIAL BANK OF DUBAI) (GROUP 2) (TURF) 1m (T)
5:55 (5:55) 3-Y-O+

£104,166 (£34,722; £17,361; £8,680; £5,208; £3,472)

RPR
1 **Gladiatorus (USA)**[28] [260] 4-9-0 113 .... RoystonFfrench 6 125
(M bin Shafya, UAE) *sn led: t.k.h: drew clr 3f out: rdn 1 1/2f out: easily* **3/1**[2]
2 5 3/4 **Hunting Tower (SAF)**[21] [339] 7-9-0 112 .... LDettori 3 112
(M F De Kock, South Africa) *racd in 3rd: trckd wnr 3 1/2f out: r.o but no ch w wnr* **12/1**
3 1 1/2 **Blue Ksar (FR)**[13] [436] 6-9-0 112 .... (t) TPO'Shea 2 109
(E Charpy, UAE) *s.i.s: mid-div: rdn 3f out: r.o fnl 2f* **18/1**
4 1/2 **Imbongi (SAF)**[14] [418] 5-9-3 113 .... KShea 5 110
(M F De Kock, South Africa) *in rr of mid-div: rdn 3f out: r.o same pce* **11/8**[1]
5 1/4 **Summit Surge (IRE)**[14] [413] 5-9-0 113 .... (t) JMurtagh 1 107
(G M Lyons, Ire) *settled last: rdn 3f out: r.o same pce fnl 1 1/2f: nvr able to chal* **9/2**[3]
6 8 1/4 **Traffic Guard (USA)**[21] [339] 5-9-0 118 .... JohnEgan 4 88
(H J Brown, South Africa) *settled in rr: rdn 3f out: one pce* **6/1**
7 dist **Gold Sovereign (IRE)**[21] [340] 5-9-0 97 .... FJara 7 —
(I Mohammed, UAE) *trckd ldr: t.k.h: rdn 4f out: sn btn* **50/1**

1m 36.67s (-1.63) **Going Correction** +0.20s/f (Good) **7** Ran SP% **114.5**
Speed ratings: **116,110,108,108,108 99,—**
CSF £37.18.
Owner Sheikh Mansoor bin Mohammed al Maktoum **Bred** Az Agr Le Ferriere Di Raponi Giampaolo **Trained** United Arab Emirates

FOCUS
This looked an ordinary Group 2 beforehand, but there's certainly nothing ordinary about the winner, Gladiatorus, who thrashed his six rivals in a quick time.

NOTEBOOK
Gladiatorus(USA) ◆, formerly a smart juvenile in Italy - four Listed wins and runner-up in a Group 1 - had been off the track for over a year prior to his debut in Dubai last month, but he showed himself better than ever when breaking the track record (from the front) over the extended 7f in a handicap off 107. There had to be a danger he would bounce off the back of such a big effort, but as it turned out he bettered that performance. Again ridden from the front, he set a good pace from the off and soon had most of his rivals out of their comfort zone. He galloped on relentlessly once in the straight and was ultimately a comfortable winner; it was impossible not to be impressed. Although the opposition was ordinary for the grade, there is little doubt this was the performance of a Group 1 horse and the Dubai Duty Free on World Cup night must surely now be the main target. There's also the Group 2 Jebel Hatta on Super Thursday to consider, but it will be no surprise if connections opt to wait for the big one after two huge efforts. (op7/2)
Hunting Tower(SAF) was too keen for his own good when down the field in the Group 3 Al Rashidiya on his previous start, but he settled better this time and fared best of the rest behind the high-class winner. The Jebel Hatta is the next obvious target (the Zabeel Mile might come too soon, as he possibly needs a gap between his races) and his connections will no doubt hope to avoid today's winner. (op 9/1)
Blue Ksar(FR) ran well on his debut for these connections when third (might have been second with a better run) in a handicap off 112 and this was another decent effort. He might do better again when there's more give underfoot. (op 16/1)
Imbongi(SAF) looked to have run a nice trial for this when a short-head second off 112 over an extended 6f two weeks earlier, but he never threatened. Connections will no doubt hope for better if he takes his chance in something like the Zabeel Mile next week, or the Jebel Hatta on Super Thursday. (op 6/4)
Summit Surge(IRE) found this tougher than the handicap he won off 109 weeks earlier. (op 4/1)

615a COMMERCIAL BANK OF DUBAI (H'CAP) (TURF) 7f 110y(D)
6:25 (6:25) (95-110,108) 3-Y-O+

£50,000 (£12,500; £12,500; £4,166; £2,500; £1,666)

RPR
1 **Swop (IRE)**[13] [439] 6-8-10 **100** .... RyanMoore 10 108
(L M Cumani) *settled in last: stl in rr 3f out: r.o strly fnl 1 1/2f: led nr line* **9/2**[2]
2 1/2 **Ragheed (USA)**[21] [335] 5-9-1 **105** .... (vt) RHills 2 112
(E Charpy, UAE) *settled in rr: trckd ldrs 1 1/2f out: led briefly fnl 1/2f: hdd line* **7/1**
2 dht **Yamal (IRE)**[7] [522] 4-8-13 **102** .... LDettori 1 110
(Saeed Bin Suroor) *mid-div on rail: smooth prog to ld 2f out: r.o wl: hdd fnl stride* **2/1**[1]
4 1 **Leandros (FR)**[14] [418] 4-9-0 **104** .... (b) JMurtagh 4 109
(G M Lyons, Ire) *settled in rr: rdn 3f out: r.o same pce* **8/1**
5 1 3/4 **Perfect Season (SAF)**[21] [340] 5-8-8 **98** .... KLatham 3 98
(H J Brown, South Africa) *in rr of mid-div: nvr able to chal* **14/1**
6 1 **Banknote**[21] [340] 7-8-8 **98** .... FrancisNorton 5 96
(A M Balding) *trckd ldr: led 2 1/2f out: hdd 1f out: one pce* **20/1**
7 1/2 **Furnace (IRE)**[21] [340] 5-7-11 **97** .... AntiocoMurgia(10) 9 93
(M bin Shafya, UAE) *trckd ldrs tl 3f out: rdn and wknd* **7/1**
8 shd **Seihali (IRE)**[21] [335] 10-9-4 **108** .... WilliamBuick 6 104
(D Selvaratnam, UAE) *mid-div: n.m.r 2f out: r.o one pce* **12/1**
9 shd **Rocks Off (ARG)**[7] [526] 4-8-11 **107** .... KShea 8 97
(M F De Kock, South Africa) *in rr of mid-div: rdn 3f out: nt qckn* **13/2**[3]
10 6 **Flying Blue (FR)**[14] [414] 4-8-10 **100** .... (t) JMartinez 7 81
(R Martin Sanchez, Spain) *sn led hdd 3f out: wknd* **33/1**

1m 31.28s (-0.32) **Going Correction** +0.20s/f (Good) **10** Ran SP% **123.0**
Speed ratings: **109,108,108,107,105 104,104,104,104,98**
CSF Swop & Ragheed £19.17, Swop & Yamal £7.37 Tricast Swop, Ragheed, Yamal £42.21, Swop, Yamal, Ragheed £32.69.
Owner Mrs Angie Silver **Bred** Rathbarry Stud **Trained** Newmarket, Suffolk

FOCUS
The winning time was 0.26 seconds slower than the first division won by the 107-rated Valedictum, but this still looked a decent handicap, and the better of the two races.

NOTEBOOK
Swop(IRE) ◆ looks even better than the bare result as he had nowhere to go for much of the straight and only got in the clear with about 100m left to run. He had run unspectacularly on his first two starts in Dubai, but his latest fourth was an improvement on his initial effort and he stepped forward again. The Handicapper might just let him off lightly and he very much looks capable of following up. He is a leading fancy for the Lincoln, but is by no means a certain runner. (op 4/1)
Ragheed(USA), 1lb better off with Yamal than when beating that rival a length and a quarter over course and distance three weeks earlier, ran his race and can have no excuses. (op 6/1)
Yamal(IRE), back on turf after winning over 1m on the dirt seven days earlier, still looked to be full of running when taking over the lead two furlongs out - he touched 1.06 in-running - but he found less than expected and was reeled in late on. This was his third big effort in three weeks, so he was entitled to get tired late on. Although he has won over 1m three times, he's a horse with loads of speed (he is by Green Desert after all), and he may ultimately prove best suited by 6f-7f. (op 6/1)
Leandros(FR) had Johnny Murtagh on board this time and was up a furlong in trip, but he still didn't quite do enough. (op 15/2)
Perfect Season(SAF) again looked as though he'll be worth a try over further. (op 12/1)
Banknote ran a little better this time, but was still below his best. He will probably benefit from a more patient ride, ideally off a decent pace.
Furnace(IRE), with a 10lb claimer taking over, failed to confirm the promise he showed when second over 1m on his debut for this yard three weeks earlier.
Seihali(IRE), without the blinkers this time, was a little short of room in the straight.
Rocks Off(ARG), switched from the dirt, was too keen early on. (op 10/1)

616a AL DANA WEALTH MANAGEMENT (H'CAP) (TURF) 1m 4f (T)
6:55 (6:55) (95-110,110) 3-Y-O+

£62,500 (£20,833; £10,416; £5,208; £3,125; £2,083)

RPR
1 **Young Mick**[13] [437] 7-8-11 **101** .... (v) JohnEgan 9 106
(G G Margarson) *in rr of mid-div: chsd ldrs 2f out: n.m.r 1 1/2f out: swtchd: led 1/2f out: r.o* **6/1**[2]
2 1/2 **Classic Punch (IRE)**[13] [437] 6-8-13 **102** .... RyanMoore 4 107
(D R C Elsworth) *sn led: set stdy pce: hdd 2f out: led again 1 1/2f out: hdd ins fnl f* **16/1**
3 1 3/4 **Sanbuch**[21] [338] 5-8-10 **110** .... AntiocoMurgia(10) 6 111
(M bin Shafya, UAE) *mid-div: ev ch 2f out: nt qckn* **8/1**
4 1/4 **Captain Webb**[14] [419] 4-8-6 **98** .... (t) TedDurcan 8 100
(Saeed Bin Suroor) *trckd ldr: led 2f out: r.o same pce* **2/1**[1]
5 3/4 **Gravitas**[28] [262] 6-9-6 **110** .... WJSupple 3 110
(M bin Shafya, UAE) *mid-div: keen: gng wl 3 1/2f out: led briefly 1/2f out: one pce* **6/1**[2]
6 1/2 **Waldvogel (IRE)**[137] [6517] 5-8-13 **102** .... JMurtagh 1 102
(L M Cumani) *broke awkwardly: mid-div: gng wl 2 1/2f out: one pce fnl 1 1/2f* **7/1**[3]
7 1 1/4 **Mulaqat**[20] 6-9-3 **107** .... WilliamBuick 10 104
(D Selvaratnam, UAE) *settled in rr: nvr able to chal* **12/1**
8 1 1/4 **Munsef**[7] [527] 7-8-10 **100** .... AdrianTNicholls 5 95
(D Nicholls) *settled last: nvr nr to chal* **25/1**
9 1/4 **Desert Links (SAF)**[14] [419] 6-9-2 **106** .... (b) KLatham 2 101
(H J Brown, South Africa) *a mid-div* **14/1**
10 1 1/2 **Bruges (IRE)**[14] [415] 4-8-5 **97** .... (bt) RHills 7 90
(A Al Raihe, UAE) *settled in rr: nvr able to chal* **8/1**

2m 34.34s (3.34) **Going Correction** +0.20s/f (Good)
WFA 4 from 5yo+ 3lb **10** Ran SP% **120.7**
Speed ratings: **96,95,94,94,93 93,92,91,91,90**
CSF £100.13 Tricast £783.74. Placepot £99.30. Pool: £12187.72 - 89.55 winning units. Quadpot £59.50. Pool: £458.74 - 5.70 winning units..
Owner M F Kentish **Bred** M F Kentish **Trained** Newmarket, Suffolk

FOCUS
The field were over two seconds slower covering the opening mile than the runners in the first division, and the final time was 3.28 seconds slower the 111-rated Eastern Anthem managed earlier on the card.

NOTEBOOK
Young Mick often goes right in his races, so the narrowing of the track was to his advantage, and whether the ground was quicker on the stands' side or not is immaterial, as he was the best horse on the day.
Classic Punch(IRE) was given a terrific ride in defeat. Somehow the British champion got away with setting ridiculously slow fractions and his mount kept on in the straight, despite edging right, but he was just held.
Sanbuch would not have been suited by the slow pace, so this was a good effort in third, but he's not an easy horse to predict and is no sure thing to build on this next time.
Captain Webb was possibly at a disadvantage sticking to the far rail in the straight, but he basically made hard work of picking up and wasn't good enough on the day. He doesn't seem to be progressing as one might have expected. (op 5/2)
Gravitas was keen when winning over this course and distance a month earlier, but he was even more headstrong this time and that cost him his chance.

Waldvogel(IRE) was an out-and-out stayer when trained in Germany, so a slowly-run 1m4f was no use to him, and he did not run at all badly considering. He is entitled to come on for the run fitness wise, and he can do much better off a stronger pace.
Mulaqat was a little keen early and never featured.
Bruges(IRE) failed to build on his recent second in a muddling contest over 1m2f. (op 15/2)

602 SOUTHWELL (L-H)
Friday, February 20

OFFICIAL GOING: Standard
Wind: Light across Weather: Cloudy with sunny spells

617 BETDAQ.CO.UK CLAIMING STKS 1m (F)
1:25 (1:29) (Class 6) 4-Y-O+ **£2,047** (£604; £302) **Stalls** Low

Form RPR
06-3 **1** **North Parade**[10] 483 4-9-3 77.....(t) ShaneKelly 5 78
(A W Carroll) *hld up in tch: chsd ldr 3f out: hung lft fr over 2f out: led over 1f out: rdn out* **15/2**
-212 **2** *1 ¼* **Clear Sailing**[8] 515 6-8-12 75.....(p) ChrisCatlin 8 70
(Ollie Pears) *led after 1f: rdn: edgd lft and hdd over 1f out: styd on same pce ins fnl f* **5/6**[1]
00-0 **3** *2 ¾* **Jord (IRE)**[10] 489 5-8-4 63..... AndrewElliott 3 56
(A J McCabe) *led 1f: sn lost pl: outpcd 1/2-way: r.o wl ins fnl f* **25/1**
3-10 **4** *1 ¼* **West End Lad**[19] 362 6-8-12 69.....(b) KevinGhunowa(3) 6 64
(S R Bowring) *s.i.s: hdwy to chse ldr over 6f out: rdn over 2f out: hung lft and no ex fr over 1f out* **5/1**[3]
2-21 **5** *12* **Boss Hog**[14] 425 4-8-6 69..... GabrielHannon(5) 1 32
(R Curtis) *prom: rdn and hung lft over 2f out: wknd wl over 1f out* **7/2**[2]
-640 **6** *4 ½* **Bookiebasher Babe (IRE)**[21] 344 4-9-2 63..... MartinDwyer 2 27
(M Quinn) *sn pushed along and prom: rdn and lost pl 5f out: wknd 3f out* **28/1**

1m 42.31s (-1.39) **Going Correction** -0.175s/f (Stan) **6** Ran SP% **112.5**
Speed ratings (Par 101): **99,97,95,93,81 77**
toteswinger: 1&2 £1.80, 1&3 £25.50, 2&3 £7.60. CSF £14.43 TOTE £8.00: £4.10, £1.30; EX 18.80 Trifecta £374.00 Pool: £525.63 - 1.04 winning units..
Owner R Buckland **Bred** Le Thenney S A **Trained** Cropthorne, Worcs

FOCUS
An ordinary claimer, but several of these like to force the pace so a decent gallop was always likely. This is not form to take too positively.
Boss Hog Official explanation: jockey said gelding lost its action

618 BETDAQ THE BETTING EXCHANGE H'CAP 1m (F)
1:55 (1:55) (Class 5) (0-70,71) 4-Y-O+ **£2,729** (£806; £403) **Stalls** Low

Form RPR
-321 **1** **More Time Tim (IRE)**[22] 323 4-9-0 66..... PatCosgrave 6 82+
(J R Boyle) *chsd ldr tl led over 2f out: shkn up over 1f out: r.o* **7/4**[1]
0310 **2** *3* **Hilbre Court (USA)**[11] 478 4-9-2 68.....(p) GrahamGibbons 7 77
(B P J Baugh) *a.p: rdn to chse wnr and hung lft over 1f out: no imp fnl f* **9/2**[3]
-411 **3** *5* **Kipchak (IRE)**[9] 505 4-9-5 71 6ex..... MartinDwyer 5 69
(C E Brittain) *sn led: rdn and hdd over 2f out: wknd over 1f out* **5/1**
6-01 **4** *¾* **Royal Envoy (IRE)**[12] 460 6-9-5 71 6ex..... TolleyDean 3 67
(P Howling) *trckd ldrs: rdn over 3f out: wknd over 1f out* **14/1**
000- **5** *1* **Deadline (UAE)**[70] 4540 5-8-4 56 oh1..... JoeFanning 1 49
(P T Midgley) *sn outpcd: nvr nrr* **12/1**
05-2 **6** *½* **Tyzack (IRE)**[8] 519 8-9-1 67..... MickyFenton 8 59
(Stef Liddiard) *hld up in tch: plld hrd: rdn and wknd over 1f out* **4/1**[2]
635- **7** *12* **Time To Play**[28] 7504 4-8-8 60..... ChrisCatlin 2 25
(T T Clement) *chsd ldrs: rdn over 4f out: sn wknd* **40/1**
/66- **8** *shd* **Final Tune (IRE)**[329] 1065 6-9-1 70..... DuranFentiman(3) 4 34
(Miss M E Rowland) *hld up: bhd fr 1/2-way* **25/1**

1m 42.1s (-1.60) **Going Correction** -0.175s/f (Stan) **8** Ran SP% **111.9**
Speed ratings (Par 103): **101,98,93,92,91 90,78,78**
toteswinger: 1&2 £1.70, 1&3 £1.10, 2&3 £9.90. CSF £9.27 CT £31.26 TOTE £3.30: £1.30, £1.40, £2.30; EX 11.20 Trifecta £71.90 Pool: £376.28 - 3.87 winning units..
Owner M Khan X2 **Bred** Glending Bloodstock **Trained** Epsom, Surrey

FOCUS
Just a fair handicap run at an ordinary pace, but the winning time was still 0.21 seconds faster than the claimer. The runner-up is rated to his recent best with doubts over the strength of the race.
Tyzack(IRE) Official explanation: trainer had no explanation for the poor form shown

619 BETDAQ ON 0870 178 1221 (S) STKS 6f (F)
2:30 (2:31) (Class 6) 3-Y-O+ **£2,047** (£604; £302) **Stalls** Low

Form RPR
0-33 **1** **Ballycroy Boy (IRE)**[10] 489 4-9-8 66.....(b) MickyFenton 12 69
(A Bailey) *dwlt: sn pushed along into mid-div: hdwy u.p over 1f out: styd on to ld nr fin* **3/1**[1]
30-6 **2** *nk* **Cleveland**[15] 401 7-9-5 58..... RussellKennemore(3) 11 68
(R Hollinshead) *led over 4f out: rdn over 1f out: hdd nr fin* **10/1**[3]
2300 **3** *2* **Wiltshire (IRE)**[7] 540 7-9-8 58..... JamieMoriarty 7 61
(P T Midgley) *sn pushed along in rr: hdwy u.p over 1f out: nt rch ldrs* **16/1**
-310 **4** *1 ¼* **Kingsmaite**[10] 489 8-9-6 64.....(b) AndrewYoxall(7) 10 62
(S R Bowring) *chsd ldrs: rdn and edgd lft fr over 2f out: styd on same pce fnl f* **11/1**
0-04 **5** *nk* **Charmel's Lad**[24] 304 4-9-8 53.....(vt) RobertWinston 9 56
(W R Swinburn) *s.i.s: sn prom: rdn to chse ldr and hung lft over 1f out: no ex ins fnl f* **10/1**[3]
-600 **6** *5* **Soba Jones**[10] 487 12-9-8 50..... TomEaves 1 40
(J Balding) *prom: hmpd and lost pl after 1f: n.d after* **40/1**
0-40 **7** *½* **Kinout (IRE)**[43] 95 4-9-8 57..... PaulMulrennan 8 39
(K A Ryan) *sn led: hdd over 4f out: rdn over 2f out: wknd fnl f* **28/1**
4311 **8** *3 ¼* **Tender Process (IRE)**[15] 401 6-9-13 70.....(v) PatCosgrave 3 33
(J R Boyle) *s.i.s and hmpd s: sn drvn along in rr: n.d* **4/1**[2]
3152 **9** *shd* **Head To Head (IRE)**[11] 467 5-9-6 51.....(p) TerenceFury(7) 6 33
(A D Brown) *chsd ldrs tl rdn and wknd over 2f out* **20/1**
2526 **10** *1* **Hamaasy**[1] 607 8-9-5 60.....(p) KevinGhunowa(3) 5 25
(R A Harris) *trckd ldrs: plld hrd: n.m.r 5f out: rdn over 3f out: wknd 2f out* **3/1**[1]
/6-4 **11** *nk* **Fiuntas (IRE)**[1] 602 6-9-8 55.....(bt) GrahamGibbons 4 24
(Shaun Harley, Ire) *s.i.s and wnt lft s: outpcd* **14/1**
00/0 **12** *4 ½* **Eastfields Lad**[14] 425 7-9-8 30.....(b) ChrisCatlin 2 9
(S R Bowring) *prom: racd keenly: hmpd and lost pl after 1f: sn bhd* **150/1**

1m 16.14s (-0.36) **Going Correction** -0.175s/f (Stan) **12** Ran SP% **120.4**
Speed ratings (Par 101): **95,94,91,90,89 83,82,78,78,76 76,70**
toteswinger: 1&2 £16.70, 1&3 £17.00, 2&3 £20.90. CSF £34.09 TOTE £3.90: £1.50, £4.70, £4.80; EX 54.10 Trifecta £248.80 Part won. Pool: £336.23 - 0.44 winning units..The winner was bought by M. Rowland for 6,000gns.
Owner R T Collins **Bred** Paraic Fox **Trained** Newmarket, Suffolk

FOCUS
Quite a competitive seller and the right horse won based on adjusted official ratings, but he only had to run to his recent best to score.
Hamaasy Official explanation: jockey said gelding ran flat; trainer said regarding running, gelding ran flat

620 SHIRLEY AND WALFORD THOMAS'S GOLDEN ANNIVERSARY H'CAP 1m (F)
3:05 (3:06) (Class 6) (0-60,60) 3-Y-O **£2,047** (£604; £302) **Stalls** Low

Form RPR
42- **1** **Statute Book (IRE)**[109] 7164 3-9-2 58..... LPKeniry 6 68
(S Kirk) *trckd ldrs: lost pl 6f out: hdwy over 2f out: rdn to chse ldr over 1f out: r.o to ld wl ins fnl f: eased towards fin* **7/1**[2]
-243 **2** *1 ¼* **Kingaroo (IRE)**[8] 520 3-8-11 60..... AndrewHeffernan(7) 10 67
(Garry Moss) *led: rdn over 2f out: edgd lft over 1f out: hdd and unable qckn wl ins fnl f* **7/1**[2]
0-42 **3** *4 ½* **Le Petit Vigier**[8] 520 3-8-6 48.....(t) AndrewElliott 9 44
(P Beaumont) *s.i.s: outpcd: hdwy over 1f out: nt trble ldrs* **10/1**
55-1 **4** *1* **Just Five (IRE)**[8] 520 3-9-0 56 6ex..... TomEaves 11 50
(M Dods) *trckd ldrs: rdn 2f out: wknd fnl f* **6/4**[1]
5-44 **5** *1 ¼* **Ed's Pride (IRE)**[6] 555 3-8-4 46 oh1.....(b) ChrisCatlin 3 37
(K A Ryan) *s.s: sn drvn along and swtchd wd: hdwy 5f out: chsd ldr 3f out: sn rdn: wknd over 1f out* **12/1**
33-4 **6** *3* **Dispol Diva**[8] 520 3-8-13 55.....(v) JamieMoriarty 8 39
(P T Midgley) *chsd ldrs: sn drvn along: wknd over 2f out* **14/1**
00-1 **7** *23* **Reigning In Rio (IRE)**[17] 383 3-8-8 50..... PaulMulrennan 7 —
(P C Haslam) *chsd ldrs: rdn over 3f out: wknd over 2f out* **8/1**[3]
55-3 **8** *1* **Kinigi (IRE)**[15] 403 3-9-0 59..... KevinGhunowa(3) 5 —
(R A Harris) *hld up: a in rr: wknd over 3f out* **12/1**
00-0 **9** *2 ½* **Wahan (USA)**[14] 425 3-9-4 60..... MartinDwyer 1 —
(C E Brittain) *sn pushed along in rr: wknd over 3f out* **14/1**
0-61 **10** *4 ½* **Patronne**[19] 363 3-8-11 58 ow1..... AnnStokell(5) 4 —
(Miss A Stokell) *sn outpcd and bhd* **16/1**
550- **11** *22* **Miss Moloney (IRE)**[155] 6051 3-8-9 51 ow1..... RobertWinston 2 —
(Mrs S Lamyman) *chsd ldrs tl wknd over 2f out: virtually p.u ins fnl f* **40/1**

1m 42.63s (-1.07) **Going Correction** -0.175s/f (Stan) **11** Ran SP% **122.2**
Speed ratings (Par 95): **98,96,92,91,90 87,64,63,60,56 34**
toteswinger: 1&2 £8.20, 1&3 £14.40, 2&3 £14.40. CSF £57.71 CT £501.64 TOTE £10.50: £2.90, £2.30, £3.40; EX 134.70 TRIFECTA Not won..
Owner R J Brennan and D Boocock **Bred** R J Brennan And D Boocock **Trained** Upper Lambourn, Berks

FOCUS
A modest handicap, but several of these came into the race in reasonable form with the front pair looking better than their current marks.
Reigning In Rio(IRE) Official explanation: trainer had no explanation for the poor form shown
Patronne Official explanation: trainer said filly was never travelling
Miss Moloney(IRE) Official explanation: jockey said filly hung right and was in season

621 SOUTHWELL-RACECOURSE.CO.UK MAIDEN STKS 1m 3f (F)
3:40 (3:41) (Class 5) 3-Y-O+ **£2,729** (£806; £403) **Stalls** Low

Form RPR
200- **1** **Key Decision (IRE)**[60] 7758 5-10-0 67..... GrahamGibbons 6 75
(Shaun Harley, Ire) *hld up in tch: rdn to ld over 1f out: edgd lft ins fnl f: r.o* **9/1**
2 *2 ½* **Sambulando (FR)**[987] 6-10-0 0..... PaulMulrennan 12 71
(T R George) *chsd ldrs: led on bit over 2f out: rdn and hdd over 1f out: styd on same pce ins fnl f* **13/2**[3]
3 *6* **Miss Keck**[30] 5-9-9 0..... PJMcDonald 13 56
(G A Swinbank) *s.s: hld up: hdwy u.p over 2f out: hung rt over 1f out: nt rch ldrs* **20/1**
42 **4** *1* **High Cross (IRE)**[10] 488 3-8-1 0 ow1..... ChrisCatlin 10 51
(Sir Mark Prescott) *w ldr tl led over 8f out: rdn and hdd over 2f out: wknd fnl f* **13/8**[1]
0- **5** *6* **Diktaram**[90] 7424 3-8-5 0..... LukeMorris 3 45
(J R Weymes) *mid-div: rdn over 3f out: nvr trbld ldrs* **50/1**
36 **6** *2 ¾* **Antipodean (UAE)**[24] 306 3-8-0 0 ow2..... PaulPickard(7) 9 42
(P T Midgley) *hld up: hdwy over 4f out: rdn and wknd over 2f out* **16/1**
3-52 **7** *3 ¼* **Longboat Key**[11] 468 3-8-5 70..... JoeFanning 7 35
(M Johnston) *led: hdd over 8f out: chsd ldr tl rdn over 3f out: wknd over 2f out* **4/1**[2]
00-0 **8** *12* **Spruzzo**[39] 138 3-8-2 0..... AndrewMullen(3) 1 14
(C W Thornton) *chsd ldrs: rdn 1/2-way: wknd over 4f out* **100/1**
9 *4* **Keen Warrior**[27] 9-10-0 0..... RobertWinston 4 12
(Mrs S Lamyman) *s.i.s: hld up: rdn 7f out: sn bhd* **18/1**
00- **10** *10* **Teddy West (IRE)**[114] 7080 3-8-5 0..... MartinDwyer 11 —
(Patrick Morris) *s.i.s: hdwy 9f out: rdn over 4f out: sn wknd* **25/1**
- **11** *½* **Mochua (IRE)**[22] 6348 5-10-0 0..... JerryO'Dwyer 2 —
(Adrian Sexton, Ire) *s.s: outpcd* **16/1**
0- **12** *4 ½* **Tagalura (IRE)**[286] 1987 3-8-5 0..... FrankieMcDonald 5 —
(P T Midgley) *prom: pushed along 7f out: wknd over 4f out* **100/1**
-333 **13** *40* **Lady Dunhill (IRE)**[17] 383 3-7-9 52..... AmyBaker(5) 8 —
(E W Tuer) *sn pushed along in rr: bhd fr 1/2-way* **15/2**

2m 25.47s (-2.53) **Going Correction** -0.175s/f (Stan)
WFA 3 from 5yo+ 23lb **13** Ran SP% **122.8**
Speed ratings (Par 103): **102,100,95,95,90 88,86,77,74,67 67,63,34**
toteswinger: 1&2 £9.20, 1&3 £22.00, 2&3 £17.10. CSF £66.05 TOTE £12.70: £3.40, £2.90, £3.80; EX 72.90 Trifecta £242.90 Part won. Pool: £328.37 - 0.84 winning units..
Owner Hard Decisions Syndicate **Bred** His Highness The Aga Khan's Studs S C **Trained** Letterkenny, Co. Donegal
■ The first winner in Britain for Shaun Harley.

FOCUS
Despite the size of the field, not many counted in this modest maiden and fewer ever got involved. The pace was solid though, they finished very well spread out and a couple did offer some promise, suggesting the form could be a little better than rated.

622 PLAY GOLF AT SOUTHWELL GOLF CLUB H'CAP — 1m 3f (F)
4:15 (4:16) (Class 5) (0-70,70) 4-Y-0+ — **£2,729** (£806; £403) **Stalls** Low

Form — RPR
0245 **1** **Inside Story (IRE)**[4] 571 7-8-13 **63**.....(b) LPKeniry 5 — 70
(C R Dore) *hld up: hdwy over out: rdn over 1f out: styd on to ld wl ins fnl f* — **13/2**
4-13 **2** ½ **Edas**[15] 406 7-9-3 **67**..... GrahamGibbons 4 — 74
(J J Quinn) *chsd ldr tl led 4f out: rdn over 2f out: hdd wl ins fnl f* — **15/8**[1]
-143 **3** ½ **Mambo Sun**[29] 253 6-9-2 **66**..... RobertWinston 8 — 72
(R Curtis) *hld up: hdwy over 3f out: rdn to chse ldr over 1f out: n.m.r ins fnl f: kpt on* — **7/2**[2]
0-42 **4** 9 **My Mentor (IRE)**[17] 384 5-9-6 **70**.....(b) StephenDonohoe 2 — 60
(Sir Mark Prescott) *prom: chsd ldr over 3f out: sn rdn: wknd over 1f out* — **4/1**[3]
-235 **5** 3¾ **Trans Sonic**[10] 493 6-9-1 **65**..... TonyHamilton 7 — 49
(A J Lockwood) *chsd ldrs: rdn over 3f out: sn wknd* — **11/1**
6-04 **6** 5 **Flying Applause**[3] 577 4-9-4 **70**..... ChrisCatlin 3 — 46
(S R Bowring) *led 7f: sn rdn and wknd* — **16/1**
/12- **7** 12 **Bedouin Blue (IRE)**[170] 1184 6-9-2 **66**.....(b) WandersonD'Avila 1 — 21
(A J Lidderdale) *s.s: plld hrd and sn prom: rdn and wknd over 3f out* — **11/1**
2m 24.74s (-3.26) **Going Correction** -0.175s/f (Stan)
WFA 4 from 5yo+ 2lb — 7 Ran SP% **112.9**
Speed ratings (Par 103): **104,103,103,96,94 90,81**
toteswinger: 1&2 £4.00, 1&3 £3.60, 2&3 £2.30. CSF £18.66 CT £49.09 TOTE £10.10: £3.60, £1.80; EX 25.10 Trifecta £98.70 Pool: £404.15 - 3.03 winning units..
Owner Chris Marsh **Bred** Arthur S Phelan **Trained** Cowbit, Lincs
FOCUS
A fair little handicap, but the early pace wasn't at all strong and the field remained tightly packed until the tempo quickened half a mile from home. The winning time was still 0.73 seconds quicker than the maiden and the first three ran close to their marks, although no better.

623 SOUTHWELL RACECOURSE FOR CONFERENCES H'CAP — 1m 4f (F)
4:50 (4:50) (Class 6) (0-60,60) 4-Y-0+ — **£2,047** (£604; £302) **Stalls** Low

Form — RPR
2020 **1** **Safin (GER)**[4] 502 9-9-1 **54**..... GrahamGibbons 5 — 64
(R Curtis) *trckd ldrs: led over 2f out: rdn over 1f out: styd on wl* — **7/1**
00-0 **2** 3¼ **Top Tiger**[23] 311 5-9-4 **57**..... TonyHamilton 3 — 62
(D W Barker) *hld up: hdwy over 4f out: rdn to chse wnr over 1f out: styd on same pce* — **20/1**
430- **3** ¾ **Lisbon Lion (IRE)**[176] 5415 4-9-2 **58**..... LukeMorris 13 — 62
(N J Vaughan) *s.i.s: hld up: hdwy over 2f out: rdn over 1f out: r.o: nt rch ldrs* — **14/1**
0- **4** hd **Tyrana (GER)**[107] 7189 6-9-1 **54**..... TolleyDean 9 — 57
(J L Spearing) *hld up: hdwy and hung lft fr over 2f out: styd on* — **16/1**
0/04 **5** 3½ **Eforetta (GER)**[19] 368 7-9-3 **56**..... ShaneKelly 1 — 54
(A W Carroll) *chsd ldrs: pushed along 8f out: rdn over 3f out: wknd fnl f* — **9/2**[2]
4022 **6** 3¼ **Dazzling Begum**[10] 493 4-8-10 **52**..... JerryO'Dwyer 11 — 44
(J Pearce) *hld up: hdwy over 3f out: rdn and hung lft 2f out: wknd and eased fnl f* — **5/2**[1]
-403 **7** 6 **Rub Of The Relic (IRE)**[8] 514 4-9-1 **57**.....(v) JamieMoriarty 4 — 40
(P T Midgley) *prom: pushed along 1/2-way: wknd over 2f out* — **12/1**
300/ **8** 9 **Adversane**[243] 3969 5-9-7 **60**..... WandersonD'Avila 14 — 28
(A J Lidderdale) *chsd ldrs: led 3f out: hdd over 2f out: wknd over 1f out* — **66/1**
00-0 **9** ½ **Snake Skin**[9] 494 6-9-0 **53**..... LPKeniry 2 — 21
(J Gallagher) *s.i.s and hmpd s: sn pushed along in rr: wknd over 4f out* — **50/1**
00-5 **10** 2¾ **John Dillon (IRE)**[40] 126 5-9-7 **60**.....(v) PaulMulrennan 10 — 23
(P C Haslam) *chsd ldr 10f out: led over 4f out: hdd 3f out: wknd 2f out* — **11/2**[3]
26-1 **11** nk **Bright Sparky (GER)**[17] 377 6-8-13 **52**.....(b) DaleGibson 12 — 15
(M W Easterby) *s.s: sn drvn along: a in rr: bhd fnl 4f* — **12/1**
0-36 **12** 15 **My Mirasol**[22] 324 5-9-0 **53**.....(p) ChrisCatlin 6 — —
(D E Cantillon) *led: hdd 1/2-way: rdn over 4f out: sn wknd* — **16/1**
60-0 **13** 38 **Speagle (IRE)**[19] 368 7-8-13 **52**..... DarrenWilliams 7 — —
(D Shaw) *chsd ldrs: led 1/2-way: hdd over 4f out: sn rdn and wknd* — **33/1**
2m 38.05s (-2.95) **Going Correction** -0.175s/f (Stan)
WFA 4 from 5yo+ 3lb — 13 Ran SP% **119.6**
Speed ratings (Par 101): **102,99,99,99,96 94,90,84,84,82 82,72,47**
toteswinger: 1&2 £27.60, 1&3 £40.30, 2&3 £18.60. CSF £144.25 CT £1913.29 TOTE £6.70: £2.60, £4.70, £4.50; EX 161.40 TRIFECTA Not won. Place 6: £115.37 Place 5: £75.84.
Owner P J Hughes Developments Ltd **Bred** German American Bloodstock 1 **Trained** Lambourn, Berks
FOCUS
A modest if competitive handicap. The early pace was decent, but the leaders may have gone off too quick as the finish was dominated by those that were held up. The form looks reasonable despite the favourite disappointing.
Tyrana(GER) Official explanation: jockey said the mare hung left throughout
Dazzling Begum Official explanation: trainer had no explanation for the poor form shown
Bright Sparky(GER) Official explanation: jockey reported that the gelding was never travelling
T/Plt: £433.90 to a £1 stake. Pool: £47,052.64. 79.15 winning tickets. T/Qpdt: £104.70 to a £1 stake. Pool: £3,029.80. 21.40 winning tickets. CR

[574] WOLVERHAMPTON (A.W) (L-H)
Friday, February 20

OFFICIAL GOING: Standard
Wind: Virtually nil Weather: Started dry, light rain later

624 BET PREMIER LEAGUE FOOTBALL - BETDAQ H'CAP — 5f 20y(P)
6:50 (6:50) (Class 6) (0-60,60) 3-Y-0 — **£2,388** (£705; £352) **Stalls** Low

Form — RPR
00-1 **1** **Itshim**[8] 508 3-8-4 **51** 6ex.....(t) WilliamCarson(5) 3 — 71+
(S C Williams) *mde all: clr 2f out: eased ins fnl f: unchal* — **5/4**[1]
5431 **2** 4 **Sills Vincero**[4] 568 3-9-4 **60** 6ex..... PaulHanagan 4 — 58
(D Shaw) *chsd ldrs: wnt 2nd 1/2-way: rdn but no ch w wnr* — **7/4**[2]
6-55 **3** ½ **Fashion Icon (USA)**[17] 379 3-8-10 **57**..... DeanHeslop(5) 7 — 53
(T D Barron) *trckd ldr tl rdn and passed for 2nd 1f out* — **9/1**
56-6 **4** ¾ **Cindy Incidentally**[26] 286 3-8-11 **53**..... JimmyQuinn 5 — 47
(Miss Gay Kelleway) *hld up: sme prog 1f out but nvr in contention* — **22/1**
0-25 **5** 1¾ **Weet In Nerja**[25] 293 3-9-4 **60**.....(p) HayleyTurner 8 — 47
(R Hollinshead) *in rr and outpcd fr s* — **8/1**[3]
00- **6** 3½ **Badtanman**[139] 6489 3-7-11 **46** oh1.....(b[1]) AndrewHeffernan(7) 6 — 21
(Peter Grayson) *s.i.s: nvr on terms* — **50/1**
-524 **7** 4½ **Wee Bizzom**[14] 429 3-8-4 **51**.....(b[1]) DanielleMcCreery(5) 2 — 9
(A Berry) *chsd ldrs tl wknd over 1f out* — **18/1**
62.00 secs (-0.30) **Going Correction** +0.10s/f (Slow) — 7 Ran SP% **113.5**
Speed ratings (Par 95): **106,99,98,97,94 89,82**
toteswinger: 1&2 £1.30, 1&3 £4.10, 2&3 £2.20. CSF £3.56 CT £10.84 TOTE £2.00: £1.20, £1.40; EX 4.40.
Owner Itsthem **Bred** Ambersham Stud **Trained** Newmarket, Suffolk
FOCUS
A modest handicap run at a decent gallop, the only strongly run race on the card. The winner, who raced centre to far side in the straight, was value for at least double the winning margin. The form is rated around the second and third.
Wee Bizzom Official explanation: jockey said filly had been very unbalanced throughout race

625 GREAT OFFERS AT WOLVERHAMPTON-RACECOURSE.CO.UK H'CAP — 7f 32y(P)
7:20 (7:20) (Class 5) (0-75,81) 4-Y-0+ — **£3,070** (£906; £453) **Stalls** High

Form — RPR
2-44 **1** **Captain Macarry (IRE)**[15] 404 4-9-2 **73**.....(v) TomEaves 9 — 80
(B Smart) *in tch: wnt 2nd 4f out: swtchd lft 1f out: kpt on to ld ins fnl f: all out* — **17/2**
U033 **2** ½ **Kensington (IRE)**[3] 576 8-9-2 **73**.....(v) PaulHanagan 7 — 79
(P D Evans) *led over 5f out: hrd rdn over 1f out: hdd ins fnl f but kpt on u.p* — **9/2**
1-01 **3** ½ **Tuxedo**[16] 387 4-8-11 **68**..... LukeMorris 2 — 73
(P W Hiatt) *trckd ldrs: rdn over 2f out: kpt on ins fnl f* — **3/1**[1]
6422 **4** 3¼ **Downhill Skier (IRE)**[4] 573 5-8-4 **64**..... DuranFentiman(3) 5 — 60
(W M Brisbourne) *towards rr: hdwy on outside over 1f out but nvr on terms* — **7/2**[2]
-436 **5** 1¼ **Dressed To Dance (IRE)**[21] 351 5-9-3 **74**.....(b) PaulDoe 3 — 67
(P D Evans) *hld up: rdn over 2f out and hdwy on outside: wknd over 1f out* — **7/1**
15-2 **6** ¾ **A Big Sky Brewing (USA)**[30] 241 5-8-10 **72**.....(b) DeanHeslop(5) 6 — 62
(T D Barron) *led after 1f: hdd over 5f out: rdn over 2f out: wknd over 1f out* — **4/1**[3]
4-14 **7** 11 **Realt Na Mara (IRE)**[17] 382 6-9-2 **73**..... TravisBlock 1 — 34
(H Morrison) *led for 1f: rdn over 4f out: wknd over 2f out* — **10/1**
1m 29.56s (-0.04) **Going Correction** +0.10s/f (Slow) — 7 Ran SP% **117.5**
Speed ratings (Par 103): **104,103,102,99,97 96,84**
toteswinger: 1&2 £9.90, 1&3 £5.90, 2&3 £1.80. CSF £47.94 CT £143.73 TOTE £7.50: £2.90, £2.80; EX 45.60.
Owner Anthony D Gee **Bred** Humphrey Okeke **Trained** Hambleton, N Yorks
FOCUS
A fair handicap in which the pace was ordinary and those racing prominently were at an advantage. The first three edged towards the inside rail in the closing stages. The runner-up is the best guide to the form.

626 VAUXHALL INSIGNIA CAR OF THE YEAR 2009 MAIDEN FILLIES' STKS — 7f 32y(P)
7:50 (7:51) (Class 5) 3-Y-0+ — **£3,070** (£906; £453) **Stalls** High

Form — RPR
4 **1** **Foreign Investment (IRE)**[30] 236 3-8-7 0..... PaulDoe 4 — 65
(P D Evans) *a in tch: rdn and hdwy on outside to ld wl over 1f out: rdn out* — **15/8**[1]
2 1 **Super Academy (USA)** 3-8-8 0 ow1..... ShaneKelly 8 — 63+
(J A Osborne) *v.s.a: hdwy on ins over 2f out: kpt on to chse wnr fnl f* — **4/1**[3]
3 hd **Mosqueras Romance** 3-8-7 0..... JimmyQuinn 10 — 61+
(M Botti) *in rr: hdwy on outside over 1f out: kpt on to press runner-up ins fnl f* — **5/2**[2]
00-4 **4** 6 **Perfect Honour (IRE)**[19] 364 3-8-7 0..... PaulHanagan 2 — 45
(D Shaw) *broke wl: trckd ldrs: wknd appr fnl f* — **12/1**
00- **5** 2½ **Missed Mondays**[52] 7823 3-8-7 0..... JoeFanning 3 — 39
(Patrick Morris) *nvr bttr than mid-div* — **10/1**
0 **6** 2¾ **Camelot Queen**[16] 386 4-9-10 0..... FergusSweeney 5 — 37
(W S Kittow) *led tl hdd wl over 1f out: rdn and sn wknd* — **22/1**
6-60 **7** 3¾ **Aegean Pride**[26] 290 4-9-5 51..... SladeO'Hara(5) 6 — 27
(A Berry) *trckd ldr tl wknd wl over 1f out* — **12/1**
000- **8** 9 **Miss Medusa**[116] 7026 4-9-10 30.....(t) VinceSlattery 7 — —
(Mrs C A Dunnett) *a towards rr* — **80/1**
0 **9** 6 **Chantilly Jewel (USA)**[17] 381 4-9-10 0..... ChrisCatlin 9 — —
(R M H Cowell) *trckd ldrs early: lost pl 1/2-way* — **18/1**
1m 30.7s (1.10) **Going Correction** +0.10s/f (Slow)
WFA 3 from 4yo 17lb — 9 Ran SP% **118.7**
Speed ratings (Par 100): **97,95,95,88,85 82,78,68,61**
toteswinger: 1&2 £2.20, 1&3 £1.40, 2&3 £3.50. CSF £10.06 TOTE £2.70: £1.10, £1.50, £1.70; EX 14.40.
Owner Diamond Racing Ltd **Bred** M Duffy **Trained** Pandy, Monmouths
FOCUS
A modest maiden lacking strength in depth and just an ordinary gallop. The three market leaders, who raced centre to far side in the straight, pulled clear in the closing stages. The placed fillies can improve on the bare form.

627 BET MULTIPLES - BETDAQ H'CAP — 2m 119y(P)
8:20 (8:20) (Class 6) (0-55,55) 4-Y-0+ — **£2,388** (£705; £352) **Stalls** Low

Form — RPR
000- **1** **Bold Adventure**[20] 7169 5-9-3 **55**..... ChrisCatlin 1 — 67+
(W J Musson) *hld up in rr: stdy hdwy fr 4f out: rdn to ld ins fnl f: kpt on* — **9/2**[3]
-132 **2** 1½ **Carlton Scroop (FR)**[6] 546 6-9-3 **55**.....(b) LukeMorris 6 — 65
(J Jay) *in tch: gd hdwy to go 2nd over 3f out: led over 2f out: rdn: swished tail and hdd ins fnl f* — **3/1**[2]
/0-0 **3** 1¾ **Born West (USA)**[13] 449 5-8-13 **54**..... JackMitchell(3) 2 — 62
(N B King) *hld up: rdn over 3f out: styd on ins fnl 2f* — **14/1**
0-20 **4** 11 **Ramvaswani (IRE)**[4] 567 6-9-0 **52**..... HayleyTurner 12 — 47
(N B King) *trckd ldr: rdn over 3f out: wknd 2f out* — **10/1**
5/0- **5** 1¼ **Openide**[50] 5613 8-8-11 **49**..... DaneO'Neill 3 — 42
(B W Duke) *trckd ldrs: rdn over 4f out: sn btn* — **10/1**
00-6 **6** nk **Bolton Hall (IRE)**[13] 449 7-9-1 **53**.....(t) FergusSweeney 13 — 46
(W K Goldsworthy) *s.i.s: in rr: effrt over 2f out but nvr on terms* — **20/1**
3/2- **7** 15 **Inner Voice (USA)**[74] 5372 6-8-9 **47**.....(b) TonyCulhane 11 — 22
(J J Lambe, Ire) *in tch tl wknd over 3f out* — **11/4**[1]

8 11 **Call Me Al (IRE)**69 6260 4-8-11 55 StephenCarson 5 17
(J J Lambe, Ire) *led: rdn over 3f out: hdd over 2f out: wknd qckly* **22/1**
2-00 9 16 **Oberlin (USA)**38 148 4-8-10 54 NickyMackay 7 —
(T Keddy) *hld up in mid-div: lost tch over 3f out* **33/1**
4/4- 10 1 ½ **Conclave (IRE)**15 1792 5-8-11 49 (p) JerryO'Dwyer 9 —
(Adrian Sexton, Ire) *mid-div: rdn over 5f out: lost tch 4f out* **15/2**
45-0 P **Global Traffic**24 301 5-8-12 50 (b) MickyFenton 8 —
(R Ford) *t.k.h: trckd ldrs to 7f out: dropped out qckly and sn p.u* **28/1**
3m 41.15s (-0.65) **Going Correction** +0.10s/f (Slow)
WFA 4 from 5yo+ 6lb 11 Ran SP% **122.0**
Speed ratings (Par 101): **105,104,103,98,97 97,90,85,77,77** —
toteswinger: 1&2 £4.10, 1&3 £12.30, 2&3 £13.70. CSF £18.24 CT £181.26 TOTE £6.40: £2.20, £1.40, £4.90; EX 22.60.
Owner Mustard Cord Cads **Bred** Bricklow Ltd **Trained** Newmarket, Suffolk

FOCUS
A moderate handicap run at a just a fair gallop. The first three, who pulled clear, came down the centre in the straight. The race has been rated around the runner-up and the form is fair for the grade.
Bolton Hall(IRE) Official explanation: jockey said gelding hung left
Inner Voice(USA) Official explanation: jockey said gelding hung left throughout
Conclave(IRE) Official explanation: jockey said mare never moved well
Global Traffic Official explanation: jockey said gelding lots its action but returned sound

628 ENJOY THE LUCKY 7 GROUP OFFER H'CAP 1m 1f 103y(P)
8:50 (8:50) (Class 6) (0-65,65) 3-Y-O **£2,388** (£705; £352) **Stalls** Low

Form RPR
40-4 1 **Shaker Style (USA)**25 295 3-9-3 61 (b) JimmyQuinn 2 64
(J D Bethell) *plld hrd early: mde all: rdn over 1f out: kpt on fnl f* **11/4**2
4625 2 1 **Turn To Dreams**2 586 3-8-13 57 (v) PaulDoe 3 58
(P D Evans) *trckd ldrs: wnt 2nd 2f out: rdn and swtchd lft ins fnl f: no imp on wnr towards fin* **4/1**3
00-5 3 5 **Dulce Domum**24 306 3-8-9 53 ChrisCatlin 8 44
(A B Haynes) *in tch tl outpcd over 3f out: styd on fr over 1f out to snatch 3rd post* **16/1**
0-46 4 hd **Duke Of Normandy (IRE)**23 317 3-9-7 65 JoeFanning 7 55
(M Johnston) *trckd wnr to 2f out: rdn: fdd ins fnl f and lost 3rd post* **5/1**
10-1 5 nk **Thewaytosanjose (IRE)**44 77 3-8-13 57 JamesDoyle 5 46
(S Kirk) *hld up in rr: no hdwy u.p ins fnl 2f* **15/8**1
355- 6 12 **More Tea Vicar (IRE)**61 7754 3-9-7 65 ShaneKelly 6 29
(Patrick Morris) *s.i.s: hdwy 5f out: wknd over 2f out* **12/1**
2m 5.37s (3.67) **Going Correction** +0.10s/f (Slow) 6 Ran SP% **111.7**
Speed ratings (Par 95): **87,86,81,81,81 70**
toteswinger: 1&2 £2.70, 1&3 £8.60, 2&3 £7.80. CSF £13.89 CT £140.04 TOTE £3.30: £2.20, £1.80; EX 12.40.
Owner The Movers & Shakers **Bred** Claude Schoch **Trained** Middleham Moor, N Yorks

FOCUS
A weak handicap in which the pace was on the steady side and a race in which the market leader disappointed. The winner raced towards the centre in the straight. The runner-up is the best guide to the form.

629 BET ASIAN H'CAPS - BETDAQ HANDICAP 7f 32y(P)
9:20 (9:21) (Class 5) (0-75,79) 3-Y-O **£2,914** (£867; £433) **Stalls** High

Form RPR
0-23 1 **Captainrisk (IRE)**16 397 3-9-0 71 (v1) JerryO'Dwyer 4 73
(M Botti) *trckd ldr: led 1f out: rdn out: jst hld on* **11/2**2
5-53 2 hd **Grand Honour (IRE)**14 432 3-9-4 75 JimmyQuinn 2 76
(P Howling) *racd 3rd: hdwy appr fnl f: r.o to go 2nd wl ins fnl f: jst failed* **8/1**3
2-11 3 ½ **Tartan Gunna**7 532 3-9-8 79 6ex JoeFanning 1 79
(M Johnston) *led: rdn over 1f out: hdd 1f out: nt qckn and lost 2nd towards fin* **2/9**1
1m 31.09s (1.49) **Going Correction** +0.10s/f (Slow) 3 Ran SP% **108.3**
Speed ratings (Par 97): **95,94,94**
CSF £23.95 TOTE £5.90; EX 10.30 Place 6: £207.59 Place 5: £183.81.
Owner Giuliano Manfredini **Bred** B Walsh **Trained** Newmarket, Suffolk

FOCUS
A one-sided event on paper but a turn-up with the long odds-on favourite managing only third. The pace was only modest and the winner raced centre to far side in the straight. Messy form, rated around the runner-up.
T/Plt: £284.90 to a £1 stake. Pool: £94,121.79. 241.15 winning tickets. T/Qpdt: £57.50 to a £1 stake. Pool: £7,792.28. 100.20 winning tickets. JS

588 LINGFIELD (L-H)
Saturday, February 21

OFFICIAL GOING: Standard
Wind: Light, across Weather: Sunny

630 BET PREMIER LEAGUE FOOTBALL - BETDAQ MAIDEN STKS 1m 4f (P)
2:00 (2:00) (Class 5) 3-Y-O **£2,729** (£806; £403) **Stalls** Low

Form RPR
34 1 **Leo The Lion (IRE)**13 455 3-9-3 0 GregFairley 7 61
(M Johnston) *trckd ldrs: pushed along 3f out: led ins fnl f: rdn out* **11/2**3
02 2 1 ½ **Red Suede Shoes**29 272 3-9-0 0 JamesMillman(3) 5 58
(B R Millman) *trckd ldr: led narrowly over 2f out: rdn and edgd rt over 1f out: hdd ins fnl f: no ex* **11/4**2
0- 3 1 ½ **First Spirit**66 7708 3-8-12 0 LPKeniry 6 51
(J S Moore) *s.i.s: outpcd over 2f out: styd on fnl f to go 3rd towards fin* **25/1**
5 4 hd **Spirit Of The Glen**49 32 3-8-12 0 RobertHavlin 3 50
(Jamie Poulton) *trckd ldrs: wknd ins fnl f* **25/1**
0 5 1 **Suhailah**17 391 3-8-12 0 JimCrowley 4 49
(M J Attwater) *led tl hdd over 2f out: wknd ins fnl f* **20/1**
005- 6 ½ **Urban Space**149 6234 3-9-3 55 GeorgeBaker 1 53
(B G Powell) *in rr: rdn 4f out: nvr on terms* **14/1**
5-22 7 1 ¼ **Mellow Mixture**17 391 3-9-3 76 RichardHughes 2 51
(R Hannon) *racd 4th: rdn over 1f out: sn btn* **4/5**1
2m 38.34s (5.34) **Going Correction** +0.10s/f (Slow) 7 Ran SP% **116.7**
Speed ratings (Par 97): **86,85,84,83,83 82,82**
toteswinger: 1&2 £1.50, 1&3 £19.70, 2&3 £11.20. CSF £21.16 TOTE £5.40: £1.70, £2.00; EX 21.10.
Owner Claire Riordan And Kieran Coughlan **Bred** Kieran Coughlan And Miss Claire Riordan **Trained** Middleham Moor, N Yorks

FOCUS
A modest looking maiden featuring mainly inexperienced sorts and only three were seriously backed. The pace was slow and the favourite was disappointing, so this is dubious form. The front pair were probably not at their best.
Mellow Mixture Official explanation: trainer's rep said colt did not stay the distance

631 JOY SANDERS 50TH BIRTHDAY H'CAP 1m 5f (P)
2:30 (2:31) (Class 5) (0-70,70) 4-Y-O+ **£2,900** (£856; £428) **Stalls** Low

Form RPR
40-0 1 **Bell Island**17 392 5-9-7 69 (v1) RichardHughes 14 83
(Lady Herries) *a.p: wnt 2nd over 1f out: led wl ins fnl f: all out* **8/1**
052- 2 nk **Tyrrells Wood (IRE)**149 5406 4-9-4 70 RobertHavlin 10 84
(T G Mills) *trckd ldrs: led over 2f out: rdn and hdd wl ins fnl f* **7/1**3
41-0 3 2 ¾ **Antillia**33 219 4-9-1 67 GeorgeBaker 3 76
(C F Wall) *hld up in mid-div: hdwy over 2f out: chsd first 2 fnl f* **7/2**1
-545 4 3 **Zalkani (IRE)**8 534 9-8-12 60 ChrisCatlin 5 65
(J Pearce) *mid-div: hdwy over 2f out: kpt on one pce* **15/2**
630/ 5 4 ½ **Eastwell Smiles**57 4392 5-9-3 65 JimCrowley 12 63
(R T Phillips) *hld up: rdn 3f out: one pce fnl 2f* **33/1**
6 shd **Dantari (IRE)**74 6592 4-8-13 65 FergusSweeney 7 63
(Evan Williams) *in rr: sme hdwy over 2f out: nvr on terms* **25/1**
3-22 7 ½ **Terminate (GER)**14 448 7-8-9 57 PaulDoe 8 54
(Ian Williams) *slowly away: sn mid-div: rdn 2f out: one pce after* **8/1**
21-0 8 ½ **Jago (SWI)**17 392 6-9-5 67 LPKeniry 9 64
(A M Hales) *hld up in mid-div: effrt over 2f out: wknd appr fnl f* **16/1**
-123 9 1 **Wind Flow**17 393 5-9-1 70 (b) BMcHugh(7) 11 65
(C A Dwyer) *led after 2f: hdd over 2f out: sn wknd* **6/1**2
00/3 10 5 **Tutor (IRE)**42 112 5-9-7 69 (b) ShaneKelly 1 57
(Mrs A M Thorpe) *mid-div: rdn over 2f out: sn btn* **14/1**
-005 11 6 **Red Wine**24 319 10-8-11 59 RobertWinston 13 38
(A J McCabe) *a bhd* **16/1**
0/05 12 9 **Royal Wedding**11 485 7-9-2 64 IanMongan 2 29
(N J Gifford) *led for 2f: rdn 3f out: sn wknd* **14/1**
04-0 13 4 ½ **Flam**43 103 4-8-10 62 JamieSpencer 6 20
(A M Hales) *a bhd* **20/1**
00/0 14 47 **Maidanni (USA)**30 253 7-9-0 62 GregFairley 4 —
(J R Gask) *in tch on ins tl rdn over 4f out: sn bhd: t.o* **40/1**
2m 43.41s (-2.59) **Going Correction** +0.10s/f (Slow)
WFA 4 from 5yo+ 4lb 14 Ran SP% **122.1**
Speed ratings (Par 103): **111,110,109,107,104 104,104,103,103,100 96,90,88,59**
toteswinger: 1&2 £16.10, 1&3 £9.80, 2&3 £9.80. CSF £61.40 CT £237.34 TOTE £10.10: £3.80, £2.60, £1.70; EX 52.40 Trifecta £225.40 Part won. Pool £304.71 - 0.40 winning units..
Owner L G Lazarus **Bred** Juddmonte Farms Ltd **Trained** Patching, W Sussex

FOCUS
An ordinary handicap in which several had something to prove, but the time was fast and this looks decent form for the grade.
Antillia Official explanation: trainer said filly lost an off-fore shoe
Royal Wedding Official explanation: trainer had no explanation for the poor form shown

632 WANTABET.COM RACING TIPS TRAPPERSA H'CAP 5f (P)
3:05 (3:05) (Class 4) (0-85,81) 4-Y-O+ **£4,857** (£1,445; £722; £360) **Stalls** High

Form RPR
1-13 1 **Chjimes (IRE)**14 442 5-9-0 77 LPKeniry 3 88
(C R Dore) *hld up in tch: hdwy on ins over 1f out: rdn and r.o to ld fnl 50yds* **10/3**2
1122 2 ½ **Whiskey Creek**8 539 4-8-10 80 (b) BMcHugh(7) 1 89
(C A Dwyer) *trckd ldr: led over 1f out: strly rdn and hdd fnl 50yds* **11/4**1
-436 3 2 ½ **Fromsong (IRE)**29 270 11-8-13 81 JamesO'Reilly(5) 2 82
(D K Ivory) *led tl rdn and hdd over 1f out: one pce ins fnl f* **8/1**3
2221 4 1 **Incomparable**8 539 4-9-1 78 RobertWinston 5 76
(A J McCabe) *cl up on outside: rdn 2f out: one pce fnl f* **11/4**1
450- 5 hd **Style Award**116 7040 4-8-9 72 RichardKingscote 6 70
(W J H Ratcliffe) *in rr: sme hdwy fnl f* **8/1**3
0-00 6 3 ¼ **Fast Freddie**9 518 5-8-5 68 DaleGibson 4 55
(S Parr) *in tch to 1/2-way: outpcd fr over 1f out* **9/1**
58.01 secs (-0.79) **Going Correction** +0.10s/f (Slow) 6 Ran SP% **108.6**
Speed ratings (Par 105): **110,109,105,103,103 98**
toteswinger: 1&2 £1.60, 1&3 £8.20, 2&3 £7.90. CSF £12.01 TOTE £4.50: £2.20, £2.10; EX 15.00.
Owner Sean J Murphy **Bred** Morgan O'Flaherty **Trained** Cowbit, Lincs

FOCUS
An interesting little sprint handicap which was run to suit the winner, who is rated back to his post-2yo best.

633 BET MULTIPLES - BETDAQ CLEVES STKS (LISTED RACE) 6f (P)
3:40 (3:40) (Class 1) 4-Y-O+
£22,708 (£8,608; £4,308; £2,148; £1,076; £540) **Stalls** Low

Form RPR
1311 1 **Matsunosuke**7 553 7-9-0 112 LukeMorris 7 112
(A B Coogan) *hld up: hdwy over 1f out: str burst fnl f to ld post* **11/4**2
611- 2 shd **Duff (IRE)**66 7703 6-9-3 109 KJManning 4 115
(Edward Lynam, Ire) *trckd ldr: led 2f out: clr 1f out: kpt on: ct post* **11/10**1
56-6 3 2 ½ **Orpsie Boy (IRE)**4 579 6-9-0 97 GeorgeBaker 6 104
(N P Littmoden) *in rr: outpcd 2f out: r.o fnl f* **16/1**
30-2 4 shd **Swiss Franc**21 359 4-9-0 100 (p) JamieSpencer 1 103
(D R C Elsworth) *led tl hdd 2f out: rdn and kpt on but nt pce to chal* **12/1**
163- 5 ½ **Ceremonial Jade (UAE)**66 7703 6-9-0 105 (t) JohnEgan 2 102
(M Botti) *trckd ldrs: rdn over 2f out: wknd ins fnl f* **9/2**3
005- 6 1 ¼ **Smarten Die (IRE)**20 6-9-0 95 JimCrowley 3 98
(Frau E Mader, Germany) *in tch: rdn 2f out: wknd fnl f* **16/1**
1540 7 4 ½ **Dvinsky (USA)**4 579 8-9-0 88 (b) JimmyQuinn 5 83
(P Howling) *outpcd thrght* **50/1**
1m 10.07s (-1.83) **Going Correction** +0.10s/f (Slow) course record 7 Ran SP% **113.9**
Speed ratings (Par 111): **116,115,112,112,111 110,104**
toteswinger: 1&2 £1.60, 1&3 £9.70, 2&3 £6.40. CSF £6.08 TOTE £3.60: £1.90, £1.40; EX 7.30.
Owner A B Coogan **Bred** R Coogan **Trained** Soham, Cambs

FOCUS
A good quality Listed race that produced a terrific finish. The pace was only ordinary and neither of the first pair was quite at their best judged on the proximity of the third.

NOTEBOOK
Matsunosuke has hit a rich vein of form this winter, having now scored five times, and this completed a course hat-trick. His mark has risen from 90 to 112 in that time, which effectively rules him out of handicaps, but that is no concern at the moment. He was held up early but then came out of the pack in the straight and still had at least three lengths to make up in the last furlong. He just got there and connections will be looking at a similar race over 5f back here on Winter Derby day. (op 9-4, tchd 3-1 in a place)

Duff(IRE) came into the race unbeaten on Polytrack and looked sure to extend the sequence when kicking on off the home turn. However, he either began to idle or got tired on this first run following a break and was caught on the post. He lost nothing in defeat trying to give 3lb to a fit rival who is rated 3lb higher and it would be no surprise if he returned here for a similar race next month, although the Golden Shaheen in Dubai is a possibility. (op 11-8, tchd 6-4 in a place)
Orpsie Boy(IRE) has struggled since winning twice on Polytrack early last year and had a bit to find judged on official ratings. He ran as well as could be expected, staying on past beaten rivals, but was well behind the principals.
Swiss Franc made the early running from his inside draw but could not respond once headed by the winner turning for home. (tchd 8-1)
Ceremonial Jade(UAE) had not run since finishing third to Duff at Kempton before Christmas and faded in the closing stages, having raced on the heels of the leaders. (op 5-1 tchd 6-1)
Smarten Die(IRE), the German challenger, came into the race fit from a couple of handicap wins in his homeland but found this higher grade too much. (op 25-1)
Dvinsky(USA) Official explanation: jockey said gelding hung left

634 BETDAQ THE BETTING EXCHANGE WINTER DERBY TRIAL STKS (LISTED RACE) — 1m 2f (P)
4:10 (4:10) (Class 1) 4-Y-0+ **£22,708** (£8,608; £4,308; £2,148; £1,076) **Stalls** Low

Form				RPR
244-	**1**		**Re Barolo (IRE)**[63] [7741] 6-9-0 107 ....(t) JohnEgan 5	110
			(M Botti) *hld up in tch: hdwy appr fnl f: drvn to ld cl home* **7/4**[1]	
12-1	**2**	*nk*	**Suits Me**[11] [484] 6-9-3 107 .... MickyFenton 4	112
			(T P Tate) *led: rdn over 1f out: edgd rt ins fnl f: hdd cl home* **2/1**[2]	
305-	**3**	*3/4*	**Scintillo**[63] [7741] 4-8-13 107 .... RichardHughes 3	108
			(R Hannon) *hld up in tch: hdwy to go 2nd briefly ins fnl f: nt qckn cl home* **13/2**	
6-61	**4**	*3/4*	**Kandidate**[6] [563] 7-9-0 100 .... RobertWinston 1	107
			(C E Brittain) *trckd ldr tl rdn and no ex ins fnl f* **6/1**[3]	
/66-	**5**	*22*	**Persian Storm (GER)**[296] [1761] 5-9-0 104 .... GeorgeBaker 2	62
			(G L Moore) *plld hrd: trckd ldrs: wknd wl over 1f out: virtually p.u 1f out* **13/2**	

2m 5.76s (-0.84) **Going Correction** +0.10s/f (Slow)
WFA 4 from 5yo+ 1lb — **5** Ran SP% **110.6**
Speed ratings (Par 111): **107,106,106,105,87**
CSF £5.60 TOTE £2.80: £1.40, £1.20; EX 6.20.
Owner Effevi Snc Di Villa Felice & C **Bred** Luciano Bosio **Trained** Newmarket, Suffolk
■ Stewards' Enquiry : Micky Fenton two-day ban: careless riding (Mar 7, 10)

FOCUS
Another good-class Listed race, despite the small field, and a tight contest judged on pre-race marks. It proved as much in the race, as four of the five were in with a chance entering the last furlong. The race was rather slowly run but the form does seem to make some sense.

NOTEBOOK
Re Barolo(IRE) came from last to first to get up near the line. He had finished behind Suits Me over course and distance when last seen before Christmas but the break had freshened him up and, despite lugging in behind the leaders as he was brought to challenge, he found more than enough to get up. The Winter Derby is likely to be the target. (op 5-2 tchd 13-8)
Suits Me's only defeat in his previous six starts had been when he finished ahead of Re Barolo when runner-up two months ago, but he had reversed the form with the winner, Dansant, and got an uncontested lead again this time. He ran on gamely once challenged but could not quite hold on. (op 13-8 tchd 5-2)
Scintillo finished well behind Re Barolo and Suits Me when last seen and this was much better. He ran his race despite having the blinkers left off, but he does seem to need another furlong or two. (op 8-1)
Kandidate tends to come to himself in the early spring and scored on his Fibresand debut last time. He appeared to have every chance but looked held when squeezed out inside the final furlong. He is three from four around Kempton and is clearly one to have on-side if found a race back there. (op 5-1 tchd 7-1)
Persian Storm(GER), an ex-German performer who was a dual Group 3 winner there, was far too free on his first start for connections and, unsurprisingly, had nothing left for the closing stages. Official explanation: jockey said the gelding ran too free and hung right on the final bend (op 7-1 tchd 5-1)

635 GRANDPA PAUL'S BIRTHDAY H'CAP — 7f (P)
4:45 (4:45) (Class 2) (0-100,98) 4-Y-0+ **£11,656** (£3,468; £1,733; £865) **Stalls** Low

Form				RPR
6413	**1**		**Capricorn Run (USA)**[8] [538] 6-8-13 93 ....(v) RobertWinston 2	101
			(A J McCabe) *trckd ldr: led over 2f out: hdd ins fnl f: rallied and led again post* **11/2**[2]	
-222	**2**	*nse*	**Majuro (IRE)**[7] [551] 5-9-2 96 .... PaulHanagan 1	104
			(K A Ryan) *trckd ldr tl hdd over 2f out: led again ins fnl f: hdd post* **3/1**[1]	
1302	**3**	*2*	**Southandwest (IRE)**[8] [538] 5-8-9 89 .... LukeMorris 7	91
			(J S Moore) *slowly away: in rr: rdn and hdwy on ins over 1f out: kpt on fnl f* **6/1**[3]	
-125	**4**	*1*	**Councellor (FR)**[13] [458] 7-8-13 93 ....(t) MickyFenton 3	93
			(Stef Liddiard) *trckd ldrs: rdn 2f out: nt qckn fnl f* **9/1**	
-104	**5**	*1*	**Orchard Supreme**[7] [551] 6-9-4 98 ....(p) RichardHughes 5	95
			(R Hannon) *in tch tl rdn and wknd appr fnl f* **13/2**	
4-24	**6**	*2*	**Totally Focussed (IRE)**[31] [232] 4-8-4 84 oh4 .... ChrisCatlin 4	76
			(S Dow) *slowly away: effrt on outside 2f out: sn btn* **9/1**	
0-14	**7**	*2*	**Mahadee (IRE)**[13] [458] 4-9-4 98 ....(b) JamieSpencer 6	93
			(C E Brittain) *hld up in tch: rdn 2f out: fdd fnl f: jockey said sddle slipped* **3/1**[1]	

1m 24.27s (-0.53) **Going Correction** +0.10s/f (Slow) — **7** Ran SP% **113.0**
Speed ratings (Par 109): **107,106,104,103,102 100,97**
toteswinger: 1&2 £3.40, 1&3 £3.00, 2&3 £4.00. CSF £21.79 TOTE £5.10: £3.10, £1.90; EX 26.80.
Owner Paul J Dixon And Placida Racing **Bred** Santa Rosa Partners **Trained** Averham Park, Notts

FOCUS
A good handicap and quite a tight contest that produced another close finish. The pace was only ordinary and the front pair were always 1-2. They have both been rated up 3lb.

NOTEBOOK
Capricorn Run(USA) had a good run last winter but went up the weights and had struggled until the Handicapper relented. He rediscovered his form once that happened and gained his second success in three starts with a game victory. Always close up, he took on the runner-up off the turn but looked held halfway up the straight before battling back to get up on the line. He should not go up much for this and can remain competitive at a similar level. (op 9-2)
Majuro(IRE) has now been runner-up in his last four races but did nothing wrong and was only just beaten. He keeps creeping up the weights for getting beaten and is 7lb higher than when the sequence started. He deserves to win but may have to improve again to do so. (tchd 7-2)
Southandwest(IRE), who had finished ahead of Capricorn Run last time and was weighted to finish upsides, missed the break and was held up before staying on best of the rest, although he was never close enough to land a blow. (tchd 5-1)
Councellor(FR) had beaten Majuro in January and was a pound better off. He was always close to the pace but could not produce an extra gear. He needs a stiffer test at this trip and this track does not play to his strengths. (tchd 10-1)
Orchard Supreme usually runs his race and is capable at various trips but has been beaten 15 times at Lingfield since scoring here over two years ago. (op 7-1 tchd 8-1)
Mahadee(IRE), who was held up, was struggling when eased going into the final furlong, with his rider looking down, apparently due to a slipping saddle. Official explanation: jockey said the gelding's saddle slipped (op 7-2 tchd 11-4)

636 CORE GROUP CONDITIONS STKS — 1m (P)
5:15 (5:15) (Class 3) 4-Y-0+ **£7,771** (£2,312; £1,155; £577) **Stalls** High

Form				RPR
0-46	**1**		**Al Muheer (IRE)**[14] [445] 4-9-0 90 ....(b[1]) RobertWinston 6	99+
			(C E Brittain) *mde all: shkn up over 1f out: r.o wl* **8/1**	
03-4	**2**	*1 1/4*	**Whistledownwind**[49] [30] 4-9-0 99 .... ShaneKelly 4	96
			(J Noseda) *racd in 3rd pl: kpt on to chse wnr ins fnl f* **9/4**[2]	
5403	**3**	*nk*	**Internationaldebut (IRE)**[7] [551] 4-9-3 94 .... AdamKirby 1	98
			(S Parr) *hld up in rr: stყd on fnl f to go 3rd nr fin* **7/2**[3]	
-233	**4**	*1/2*	**Bonus (IRE)**[13] [458] 9-9-5 107 ....(b) JamieSpencer 2	99
			(G A Butler) *in rr: hdwy 2f out: kpt on but nvr looked likely to threaten* **2/1**[1]	
10-1	**5**	*nk*	**Wasp (AUS)**[23] [331] 7-9-0 89 .... JimCrowley 5	94
			(W Jarvis) *trckd wnr tl wknd ins fnl f* **6/1**	
330/	**6**	*10*	**Kaleo**[296] 5-9-0 90 .... TonyCulhane 3	71
			(S Dow) *in tch tl rdn and wknd wl over 1f out* **33/1**	

1m 39.08s (0.88) **Going Correction** +0.10s/f (Slow) — **6** Ran SP% **114.7**
Speed ratings (Par 107): **99,97,97,96,96 86**
toteswinger: 1&2 £5.40, 1&3 £6.20, 2&3 £2.40. CSF £27.14 TOTE £9.80: £2.50, £2.00; EX 38.60 Place 6 £18.55, Place 5 £4.66..
Owner Saeed Manana **Bred** Foursome Thoroughbreds **Trained** Newmarket, Suffolk

FOCUS
A good conditions race, not far short of Listed standard, but the form is dubious as the winner was allowed an easy lead. He definitley showed improvement, though.

NOTEBOOK
Al Muheer(IRE), dropping back in trip and fitted with blinkers for the first time, was kicked clear off the home turn and he never looked likely to be reeled in. He has won off 6lb higher than his current rating on turf, so could be still reasonably handicapped after reassessment, provided the headgear works as well next time. (op 12-1)
Whistledownwind has now run well here on all three starts on Polytrack and did best of the rest, but never looked like catching the winner. (op 11-4 tchd 3-1)
Internationaldebut(IRE) was held up before running on strongly in the straight, but by the time he arrived on the scene the winner was already home and hosed. He has droppped a few pounds from his peak and may be better off in handicaps again. (tchd 3-1 and 4-1)
Bonus(IRE) appeared close enough turning for home but could not pick up when asked and seems to be struggling, having gone 14 races since his last success, despite having finished in the frame on 11 occasions. (op 7-4)
Wasp(AUS) had a tough task at the weights but went in pursuit of the winner off the home turn. However, his effort flattened out in the last furlong and he was run out of the placings by the stronger finishers. Both his successes in Britain have been at Wolverhampton. (op 15-2)
Kaleo Official explanation: jockey said gelding hung right in the straight
T/Plt: £63.80 to a £1 stake. Pool: £59,528.28. 680.86 winning tickets. T/Qpdt: £4.50 to a £1 stake. Pool: £4,330.16. 699.30 winning tickets. JS

609 NAD AL SHEBA (L-H)
Friday, February 20
OFFICIAL GOING: Dirt course - fast; turf course - good to firm

637a ETISALAT WEYAK (H'CAP) (TURF) — 6f 110y(T)
3:00 (3:00) (95-110,110) 3-Y-0+
£50,000 (£16,666; £8,333; £4,166; £2,500; £1,666)

			RPR
1		**Diana's Choice (SAF)**[14] [433] 5-9-2 106 .... KShea 9	108
		(M F De Kock, South Africa) *trckd ldr: led 1 1/2f out: r.o wl: comf* **13/8**[1]	
2	*1/2*	**Munaddam (USA)**[15] [418] 7-9-6 110 .... RHills 1	111+
		(E Charpy, UAE) *in rr of mid-div on rail: swtchd 2f out: r.o wl fnl f: nrst fin* **11/2**[2]	
3	*3 1/4*	**Blue Sky Basin**[8] [521] 4-8-13 102 .... AhmedAjtebi 2	95
		(M bin Shafya, UAE) *trckd ldrs: rdn 2 1/2f out: r.o same pce* **7/1**[3]	
4	*nse*	**Benllech**[14] [433] 5-8-6 96 .... RichardMullen 7	87
		(D M Simcock) *settled in rr: mid-div whn n.m.r 1 1/2f out: r.o wl fnl f: nrst fin* **12/1**	
5	*2*	**Confuchias (IRE)**[14] [433] 5-8-10 100 .... TedDurcan 3	86
		(K R Burke) *mid-div: rdn 2 1/2f out: nt qckn* **12/1**	
6	*1 1/2*	**Keep Discovering (IRE)**[5] 4-8-9 99 ....(t) TPO'Shea 4	80
		(E Charpy, UAE) *sn led: hdd 1 1/2f out: wknd fnl f* **25/1**	
7	*nse*	**Lessing (FR)**[22] [335] 4-8-10 100 .... LDettori 5	81
		(X Nakkachdji, France) *in rr of mid-div: rdn 2 1/2f out: nvr able to chal* **10/1**	
8	*3 1/4*	**Beaver Patrol (IRE)**[15] [418] 7-9-0 104 ....(v) MJKinane 10	76
		(Eve Johnson Houghton) *a mid-div* **7/1**[3]	
9	*shd*	**Ans Bach**[14] [433] 6-8-8 98 ....(e) WilliamBuick 6	69
		(D Selvaratnam, UAE) *in rr of mid-div: n.m.r 2 1/2f out: r.o fnl f* **16/1**	
10	*2*	**Charlies Island (SAF)**[15] [414] 6-8-6 96 .... KLatham 8	62
		(H J Brown, South Africa) *settled in rr: rdn 3f out: nvr able to chal* **14/1**	

1m 17.39s (-0.11) **Going Correction** +0.225s/f (Good) — **10** Ran SP% **119.4**
Speed ratings: **109,108,104,104,102 100,100,96,96,94**
CSF £10.71 Tricast £51.28.
Owner Sheikh Mohammed Bin Khalifa Al Maktoum **Bred** R T Knight **Trained** South Africa

FOCUS
Just as for the previous day's card, the false rail was again out seven metres on the turf course but the starts were moved by a commensurate amount so all races were run over the correct distances. A decent sprint handicap and the time was good, 0.70 seconds quicker than the second division won the 110-rated Balthazaar's Gift.

NOTEBOOK
Diana's Choice(SAF) ◆ readily followed up her recent 6f success off a 4lb higher mark, despite racing keenly early on, and this was an improved performance. She was gradually being closed down near the finish, but she saw out this extra half-furlong without a bother and was always doing enough. Provided this hasn't taken too much out of her - it didn't appear to - she must be allowed her chance in the Group 3 Al Quoz Sprint, back over the bare 6f here next week, and she'll get a handy weight allowance from the colts and geldings.
Munaddam(USA) loves this course and ran a cracker in defeat behind the bang in-form winner. He had to switch off the inside rail in the straight, and finished well, but he was beaten fair and square. (op 5-1)
Blue Sky Basin ◆, dropped in trip and returned to turf, ran well considering he was unable to dominate and had little room to play with for the first half of the straight. He kept on at just the one pace when in the clear and can improve on this form when getting his own way in front back over further.

Benllech ◆, keen under restraint in last place early, had to wait for an opening at the top of the straight, before keeping on quite well. His very best form is on Polytrack and will be of interest when returned synthetics.
Confuchias(IRE) never threatened and prefers easier ground or Polytrack.
Keep Discovering(IRE), dropped in trip and ridden from the front this time, ran a little but was still well below the pick of his efforts for Mark Johnston. The tongue-tie doesn't seem to be doing him any favours.
Lessing(FR) promised to be suited by this drop in trip (her dam was a multiple sprint winner), but she found nothing for pressure after travelling well to a point.
Beaver Patrol(IRE) again failed to give his true running and offered little encouragement. (op 8-1)

638a ETISALAT BLACKBERRY (H'CAP) (TURF) 6f 110y(T)
3:35 (3:35) (95-110,110) 3-Y-0+

£50,000 (£16,666; £8,333; £4,166; £2,500; £1,666)

RPR

1 **Balthazaar's Gift (IRE)**[15] [418] 6-9-6 **110** .... RichardMullen 1 112
(R Simpson, UAE) *in rr of mid-div: n.m.r 2 1/2f out and again 1 1/2f out: r.o fnl 110yds: led nr line* **5/1**[3]

2 *shd* **Grantley Adams**[15] [413] 6-8-10 **100** .... TPO'Shea 6 102
(E Charpy, UAE) *in rr of mid-div: smooth prog 1 1/2f out: led fnl f out: hdd cl home* **10/1**

3 *hd* **Dohasa (IRE)**[14] [433] 4-9-5 **109** .... JMurtagh 4 110
(G M Lyons, Ire) *mid-div: n.m.r 2 1/2f out: r.o fnl 1 1/2f* **7/4**[1]

4 *1 ¼* **Northern Fling**[29] [264] 5-8-8 **98** .... AdrianTNicholls 9 96
(D Nicholls) *sn led: hdd 2f out: wknd* **20/1**

5 *1 ½* **League Champion (USA)**[8] [521] 6-8-13 **102** .... BrettDoyle 2 96
(R Bouresly, Kuwait) *trckd ldrs tl 3f out: wknd* **33/1**

6 *¾* **Bermuda Rye (IRE)**[110] [7162] 4-8-13 **102** .... AhmedAjtebi 5 94
(M bin Shafya, UAE) *in rr of mid-div: r.o one pce fnl 1 1/2f* **8/1**

7 *hd* **Prince Tamino**[15] [418] 6-9-1 **105** .... RoystonFfrench 7 96
(A Al Raihe, UAE) *trckd ldrs tl 1 1/2f out: wknd* **12/1**

8 *¾* **Lipocco**[14] [434] 5-8-9 **99** .... RyanMoore 8 88
(H J Brown, South Africa) *trckd ldrs tl 2 1/2f out: outpcd* **4/1**[2]

9 *5 ¼* **Artimino**[15] [413] 5-8-7 **97** .... FJara 10 70
(I Mohammed, UAE) *trckd ldrs tl 3f out* **16/1**

10 *1 ¼* **Tasdeer (USA)**[29] [260] 4-8-10 **100** ....(v) RHills 3 70
(Doug Watson, UAE) *hmpd at s: settled in last: nvr able to chal* **16/1**

1m 18.09s (0.59) **Going Correction** +0.225s/f (Good) 10 Ran SP% **120.4**
Speed ratings: **105,104,104,103,101 100,100,99,93,92**
CSF £56.05 Tricast £122.87.
Owner H E Sheikh Sultan Bin Khalifa Al Nahyan **Bred** Pat Beirne **Trained** United Arab Emirates

FOCUS
This looked a good sprint handicap, but the winning time was 0.70 seconds slower than the first division won by the 106-rated Diana's Choice.

NOTEBOOK
Balthazaar's Gift(IRE) is not the easiest to win with these days, but he got it right this time, confirming the promise he showed when flashing home after an awkward start over this course and distance on his previous start. He was very nearly unlucky again, as he had to switch off the inside rail to find a gap in the closing stages and only got in the clear in the nick of time. Like the winner of the first division, he deserves his chance in Group 3 Al Quoz Sprint next week.
Grantley Adams does not have any secrets, but he is obviously still capable of smart form and this was a fine run in defeat. He is probably slightly flattered, as both the winner and third endured troubled trips, but he did nothing wrong. (op 11-1)
Dohasa(IRE), off the same mark as when possibly an unlucky loser behind the winner of today's first division, Diana's Choice, over the bare 6f two weeks earlier, narrowly failed to gain compensation. He had to be switched right in the straight, and might have beaten the runner-up with a better trip, but the winner was the best horse on the day. (op 13-8, tchd 6-4)
Northern Fling ◆, with conditions to suit for the first time in a little while, did well to hang on for fourth considering he got very warm and had to get all the way across from stall nine to lead. He is favourably handicapped on the pick of his form and should win races back in Britain this year.
League Champion(USA) ran with credit considering he was quite free early and has been kept very busy lately. (op 25-1)
Bermuda Rye(IRE) ◆, smart over 7f-1m in France, was never competitive but this is something to build on. He came extremely wide into the straight, did not look at home on the quick ground, and gave the impression this trip was shorter than ideal. (op 15-2)
Lipocco seemed to have every chance, but he dropped out tamely and was another disappointment for the Brown yard.
Artimino is better than he showed as he raced extremely wide into the straight.

639a ETISALAT HOTSPOT TROPHY (H'CAP) (DIRT) 7f 110y(D)
4:10 (4:10) (95-110,107) 3-Y-0+

£50,000 (£16,666; £8,333; £4,166; £2,500; £1,666)

RPR

1 **Snaafy (USA)**[15] [414] 5-8-7 **97** ....(v) RHills 14 109+
(M Al Muhairi, UAE) *mid-div: smooth prog to chse ldrs 2 1/2f out: led 110yds out: comf* **5/1**[2]

2 *2 ½* **Noble Citizen (USA)**[15] [414] 4-8-6 **96** ....(be) RichardMullen 4 102
(D M Simcock) *sn led: clr 2 1/2f out: r.o: hdd 110yds out* **10/1**

3 *11* **Quicksand (SAF)**[15] [414] 5-8-6 **96** ....(t) KLatham 2 74
(M F De Kock, South Africa) *s.i.s: in rr of mid-div: r.o fnl 2 1/2f* **16/1**

4 *½* **Tasteyville (USA)**[14] [435] 6-8-10 **100** ....(b) TPO'Shea 7 77
(E Charpy, UAE) *trckd ldrs: ev ch 3f out: one pce fnl 2f* **14/1**

5 *¼* **Jonquil (IRE)**[8] [522] 7-8-11 **101** ....(v) EddieAhern 12 77
(F Nass, Bahrain) *mid-div: rdn 3f out: one pce* **7/1**[3]

6 *1 ¼* **Jet Express (SAF)**[8] [522] 7-9-0 **104** ....(t) RoystonFfrench 9 77
(A Al Raihe, UAE) *settled in rr: nvr nr to chal* **14/1**

7 *½* **Skywards**[15] [414] 7-8-5 **98** ....(t) SMGorey(3) 3 70
(E Charpy, UAE) *mid-div: rdn 3f out: r.o one pce* **16/1**

8 *4 ¼* **Brave Tin Soldier (USA)**[22] [335] 5-9-3 **107** .... KShea 11 68
(M F De Kock, South Africa) *settled in rr: rdn 3f out: nvr able to chal* **3/1**[1]

9 *3* **Fervent Prince**[8] [521] 4-8-6 **96** .... WJSupple 8 50
(A bin Huzaim, UAE) *trckd ldrs: rdn 3f out: sn wknd* **7/1**[3]

10 *½* **Fares (IRE)**[8] [522] 5-8-11 **101** ....(v) FJara 13 54
(Doug Watson, UAE) *mid-div: rdn 3 1/2f out: nvr able to chal* **16/1**

11 *9* **Minted (FR)**[15] [414] 4-8-5 **95** ....(bt) DBadel 5 25
(E Charpy, UAE) *mid-div: rdn 2 1/2f out: nt qckn* **33/1**

12 *shd* **Happy Runner (BRZ)**[15] [414] 6-8-10 **100** ....(t) JLeme 15 30
(E Martins, Bahrain) *nvr bttr than mid-div* **25/1**

13 *1 ¼* **Hamlool (AUS)**[8] [521] 5-8-6 **96** ....(bt) PDevlin 1 23
(M F De Kock, South Africa) *s.i.s: nvr able to chal* **33/1**

14 *dist* **Royal Power (IRE)**[8] [521] 6-8-8 **98** .... AdrianTNicholls 10 —
(D Nicholls) *racd in rr: nvr nr to chal* **10/1**

1m 30.07s (-1.23) **Going Correction** +0.075s/f (Slow) 14 Ran SP% **125.6**
Speed ratings: **109,106,95,95,94 93,93,88,85,85 76,76,74,—**
CSF £56.06 Tricast £763.18.
Owner Hamdan Al Maktoum **Bred** Shadwell Farm LLC **Trained** UAE

FOCUS
This looked quite a competitive handicap beforehand, but a strong pace soon sorted them out. The first two came well clear.

NOTEBOOK
Snaafy(USA) ◆ was given a lovely ride by Richard Hills, who bided his time out wide, away from the kickback, and the result was never in much doubt in the straight. This was a very useful effort off a 4lb higher mark than when winning over the bare 7f here last week and he is now 3-4 on the dirt.
Noble Citizen(USA) ◆ could not reverse recent course placings with Snaafy on 3lb better terms. Given a much more positive ride this time (his jockey probably had little choice from a low draw), he was continually harried up front but found plenty for pressure and finished a mile clear of the others who helped force the decent gallop. He has really taken to the dirt, and is also pretty useful on Polytrack, so his connections must be tempted to switch him to the US once the Carnival is over, rather than bring him back to the UK.
Quicksand(SAF) ran well considering he was slow to get going from an inside draw. (op 14-1)
Tasteyville(USA) had disappointed in two runs since switching from the US but, dropped in trip, this was a little better, even though he was still beaten a long way. (op 12-1)
Jonquil(IRE) has had a few runs in quick succession and they seem to have taken the edge off him.
Jet Express(SAF) had claims on the pick of his form, but he never really travelled and failed to run up to his best.
Brave Tin Soldier(USA) looked a player back on the dirt, but he was very disappointing. He never really travelled and was soon well behind. (op 7-2)
Fervent Prince could not dominate this time and was below the form he showed when runner-up on his previous start. (op 13-2)
Royal Power(IRE) was slowly away and never went a yard. (tchd 11-1)

640a ETISALAT MMS (H'CAP) (TURF) 1m 2f (T)
4:45 (4:45) (95-110,110) 3-Y-0+

£50,000 (£16,666; £8,333; £4,166; £2,500; £1,666)

RPR

1 **Pompeyano (IRE)**[160] [5927] 4-8-7 **98** .... RichardMullen 10 101
(S Seemar, UAE) *mid-div: wd: smooth prog to ld 1 1/2f out: r.o wl* **20/1**

2 *shd* **Strategic News (AUS)**[22] [340] 6-9-4 **108** ....(bt) RyanMoore 8 111
(H J Brown, South Africa) *in rr of main gp: smooth prog 2f out: ev ch fnl f: jst failed* **2/1**[1]

3 *3* **Fiery Lad (IRE)**[15] [419] 4-9-5 **110** .... JMurtagh 9 107
(G M Lyons, Ire) *settled in rr: rdn 2 1/2f out: r.o wl fnl 2f: nrst fin* **2/1**[1]

4 *1 ¾* **Book Of Music (IRE)**[14] [437] 6-9-0 **104** ....(e) WJSupple 1 98
(S Seemar, UAE) *slowly away: nvr bttr than mid-div* **25/1**

5 *1 ¼* **Feared In Flight (IRE)**[15] [415] 4-8-7 **98** .... TedDurcan 7 89
(Saeed Bin Suroor) *mid-div: rdn to chse ldrs 2 1/2f out: one pce fnl 1 1/2f* **20/1**

6 *½* **Duellant (IRE)**[15] [415] 4-8-11 **102** .... AStarke 3 92
(P Schiergen, Germany) *set stdy pce: rdn clr 3f out: hdd 1 1/2f out: wknd* **14/1**

7 *¾* **Bon Spiel**[22] [338] 5-8-13 **102** .... LDettori 5 92
(L M Cumani) *trckd ldrs: rdn 2 1/2f out: wknd fnl 1 1/2f* **5/1**[2]

8 *¼* **Big Robert**[15] [419] 5-8-6 **96** .... FJara 4 84
(K R Burke) *slowly away: hmpd in 4 1/2f out: nvr nr to chal* **8/1**[3]

9 *1 ¼* **Docofthebay (IRE)**[8] [527] 5-8-10 **100** .... EddieAhern 6 86
(J A Osborne) *s.i.s: mid-div: gng wl 3f out: n.m.r 2f out: nt rcvr* **20/1**

10 *1 ½* **Mister Fasliyev (IRE)**[15] [419] 7-8-8 **98** ....(t) TPO'Shea 2 81
(E Charpy, UAE) *trckd ldng duo: rdn 2 1/2f out: n.m.r 1 1/2f out: wknd* **50/1**

2m 4.89s (0.39) **Going Correction** +0.225s/f (Good)
WFA 4 from 5yo+ 1lb 10 Ran SP% **121.2**
Speed ratings: **107,106,104,103,102 101,101,100,99,98**
CSF £59.32 Tricast £124.47.
Owner Sheikh Ahmed Bin Mohammed Al Maktoum **Bred** Loughtown Stud **Trained** United Arab Emirates

FOCUS
An ordinary handicap run at a predictably modest pace early on. Despite the slow pace, the winning time was only 0.50 seconds slower than the second division won the 97-rated Charlie Cool, a race in which they looked to go off far too quick.

NOTEBOOK
Pompeyano(IRE) wanted this more than the runner-up and displayed a willing attitude on his debut for new connections, providing his trainer with a welcome Carnival winner. He should be capable of bettering this form in time, as both his breeding and his French form indicate he is best served by 1m4f-plus, and his trainer also revealed the horse has had a rushed preparation since being gelded.
Strategic News(AUS) was raised 6lb for a victory over 1m on his UAE debut, but his South African form suggested he would improve for the return to this trip. Improve he did, but he either would not, or could not go by the winner late on.
Fiery Lad(IRE) is probably plenty high enough in the weights, but he still looked to be given too much to considering there was no great pace on. Held up in second last, he was still over a length behind the runner-up at the top of the straight and it was no surprise his effort flattened out near the line. (op 9-4)
Book Of Music(IRE), with eye-shields replacing the visor, emerges with plenty of credit in fourth as he was squeezed up badly against the inside rail after a furlong or two. He also seemed to hit a bit of a flat spot halfway up the straight and his record suggests 1m4f is his optimum trip.
Feared In Flight(IRE) ran better than on his debut for this yard, but still did not shape like a winner.
Duellant(IRE) was yet another front runner to fail over a middle-distance on the Nad Al Sheba turf. He should not be judged too harshly. (op 12-1)
Bon Spiel had every chance if good enough, but he looks too high in the handicap. (op 9-2)
Big Robert was given too much to do, but in any case he was never going after being slightly squeezed against the inside rail by Fiery Lad before the turn.
Docofthebay(IRE) is better than his finishing position suggests as he did not have a great deal of room in the straight, but he was by no means unlucky. He's best suited by a strongly run race at around 1m.

641a ETISALAT WASEL TROPHY (H'CAP) (DIRT) 6f (D)
5:20 (5:20) (95-112,112) 3-Y-0+

£62,500 (£20,833; £10,416; £5,208; £3,125; £2,083)

RPR

1 **Two Step Salsa (USA)**[118] [6995] 4-9-5 **111** ....(t) LDettori 8 122+
(Saeed Bin Suroor) *prom nr side: led 2 1/2f out: r.o wl: drew clr fnl 110yds* **9/4**[1]

2 *3 ½* **Star Crowned (USA)**[8] [525] 6-9-4 **110** ....(t) BrettDoyle 2 110
(R Bouresly, Kuwait) *prom in centre: ev ch fnl 1 1/2f: outpcd fnl 110yds* **6/1**

3 *3 ¼* **Lucky Find (SAF)**[111] [7147] 6-9-6 **112** .... RyanMoore 7 102
(M F De Kock, South Africa) *outpcd in rr: r.o wl fnl 2f: n.d* **11/1**

4 ¾ **Sea Hunter**[8] 525 7-8-5 **95**.......................(vt) RoystonFfrench 6 85
(A Al Raihe, UAE) *s.i.s: prom in centre: ev ch 2f out: outpcd fnl f* **25/1**
5 1 ¼ **Frosty Secret (USA)**[36] 184 5-9-0 **106**.................... KShea 5 90
(M F De Kock, South Africa) *settled in rr: rdn 3f out: r.o same pce* **5/1**[3]
6 3 ¼ **Warsaw (IRE)**[8] 521 4-9-3 **109**....................(b) JMurtagh 3 84
(M F De Kock, South Africa) *prom for 3f: wknd fnl 1 1/2f* **5/2**[2]
7 14 **Tawaassol (USA)**[22] 336 6-8-6 **98**....................(b) RHills 10 31
(E Charpy, UAE) *prom on rail for 3f: wknd* **7/1**
8 2 ½ **Easy Target (FR)**[22] 334 4-8-5 **96**....................(b) FJara 1 22
(X Nakkachdji, France) *nvr bttr than mid-div* **50/1**
P **Ekhtiaar**[22] 335 5-8-5 **97**.................... AhmedAjtebi 9 —
(A Al Raihe, UAE) *p.u after 1 1/2f* **33/1**

1m 10.07s (-0.13) **Going Correction** +0.225s/f (Slow) 9 Ran SP% **119.9**
Speed ratings: **109,104,100,99,97 93,74,71,—**
CSF £16.89 Tricast £126.60.
Owner Godolphin **Bred** Everest Stables Inc **Trained** Newmarket, Suffolk

FOCUS
Sprint races on the dirt in Dubai usually lack strength in depth, but that certainly was not the case in this one; a cracking contest, and high-class handicap form.

NOTEBOOK
Two Step Salsa(USA) ◆ had shown all his best form in the States on synthetics, including when third in the bizarrely named Breeders' Cup Dirt Mile on his final start last year, but he handled this dirt surface beautifully and was an impressive winner on his debut for Godolphin. His very best form had been achieved at around 1m, but he displayed plenty of early speed on this drop back in trip and the result was never in much doubt when he was asked to stretch. This fine-looking individual has plenty of size, yet he is athletic with it and uses himself well, and he fairly powered clear in the manner of a high-class colt. His main target on World Cup night will likely be the Godolphin Mile, although the Golden Shaheen will probably also be considered. If his connections want to go again with him before then, there are Group 3 races over both 6f and 1m on Super Thursday (March 5). (op 5-2)
Star Crowned(USA) was a significant drifter on Betfair but ran his race and was simply beaten by a better one on the day. This effort was particularly creditable considering he has been kept very busy and probably wasn't as fresh as some of these.
Lucky Find(SAF) ◆, returning from a near four-month break over a trip short of his optimum, was unsurprisingly outpaced throughout, but he offered plenty of encouragement running on into third. The Group 3 Burj Nahaar over 1m here on Super Thursday could be a suitable target, but the Godolphin Mile is no doubt his main aim, and he should get closer today's winner if they meet again in that race.
Sea Hunter is not quite up to this sort of class, but he has bits and pieces of decent form to his name and this was another solid effort.
Frosty Secret(USA) should have been suited by the return to this trip, but he was well held off a mark 4lb higher than when winning this race last year and has to be considered disappointing.
Warsaw(IRE) won a moderately run contest over 7f first-time up on dirt the previous week, but this was a different test and a much tougher race. He had no answer from a 5lb higher mark. (tchd 11-4)
Tawaassol(USA) was heavily eased inside the final two furlongs.

642a ETISALAT APPLE SURPRISE TROPHY (H'CAP) (TURF) 1m 194y(T)
5:50 (5:51) (100-119,119) 3-Y-O+

£72,916 (£24,305; £12,152; £6,076; £3,645; £2,430)

RPR
1 **Bankable (IRE)**[111] 7147 5-9-0 **112**....................(t) JMurtagh 4 118
(M F De Kock, South Africa) *in rr of mid-div: smooth prog 2 1/2f out: r.o wl fnl 1 1/2f: led last 55yds* **11/4**[1]
2 ¾ **Emmrooz**[490] 6297 4-8-5 **104**.................... TedDurcan 1 107
(Saeed Bin Suroor) *trckd ldrs: led 1f out: r.o wl: hdd cl home* **8/1**
3 2 **Finicius (USA)**[22] 335 5-8-8 **107**....................(t) KJManning 10 106
(Eoin Griffin, Ire) *in rr of mid-div: smooth prog wd 2 1/2 f out: r.o same pce* **33/1**
4 ¾ **Kings Gambit (SAF)**[14] 436 5-9-0 **112**.................... RyanMoore 9 110
(H J Brown, South Africa) *settled last: rdn 3f out: trckd wnr 2f out: one pce* **5/1**[3]
5 ½ **Yasoodd**[22] 340 6-8-5 **102**....................(e) WilliamBuick 8 100
(D Selvaratnam, UAE) *trckd ldrs: rdn 2f out: one pce fnl 1f* **14/1**
6 hd **Mashaahed**[22] 339 6-9-0 **112**....................(t) RHills 6 109
(E Charpy, UAE) *sn led: set stdy pce: rdn 2 1/2f out: hdd 1f out: wknd* **10/1**
7 1 ½ **Macarthur**[209] 4406 5-9-6 **119**....................(b) KShea 7 112
(M F De Kock, South Africa) *mid-div: gng wl 3f out: nt qckn fnl 1 1/2f* **11/2**
8 ½ **Emirates Skyline (USA)**[14] 439 6-8-5 **100**.................... WJSupple 3 96
(A bin Huzaim, UAE) *settled in rr: n.m.r 3f out or 2f out: nt rcvr* **33/1**
9 ¾ **Yahrab (IRE)**[15] 419 4-8-10 **109**.................... AhmedAjtebi 5 99
(M bin Shafya, UAE) *s.i.s: mid-div: trckd ldrs 2 1/2f out: sn rdn and wknd* **16/1**
10 ¾ **Red Eye Express (IRE)**[15] 419 4-8-6 **101** ow1.................. MJKinane 2 94
(John M Oxx, Ire) *mid-div on rail: keen: n.m.r 2 1/2f out: nt rcvr* **7/2**[2]

1m 51.76s (1.76) **Going Correction** +0.225s/f (Good) 10 Ran SP% **119.6**
Speed ratings: **101,100,98,97,97 97,95,95,94,94**
CSF £26.39 Tricast £597.08.
Owner Ronchalon Racing (UK) Ltd **Bred** Barronstown Stud And Cobra **Trained** South Africa

FOCUS
One of the better handicaps run at this year's Carnival, but the early pace was steady, with Mashaahed allowed the run of the race in front, and that explains why the winning time was 0.67 seconds slower than the Group 3 Balanchine Stakes for fillies and mares.

NOTEBOOK
Bankable(IRE) ◆ became frustrating when trained by Luca Cumani, racking up a sequence of five straight second placings, but one of those runner-up spots was gained behind subsequent Breeders' Cup Classic winner Raven's Pass, and there was no denying his ability. He looked well treated off 113 on his debut for Mike De Kock, but the big question was whether he would go through with his effort. The answer was emphatic. The early signs were not great, as he pulled hard off the modest gallop early on, but his turn of foot in the straight was electric. It seemed Johnny Murtagh wanted to make his move between horses, which was understandable, but he soon had no choice but to switch wide into the clear, and this Medicean colt responded in the desired manner. It is interesting to note he was fitted with a tongue-tie for the first time. This performance should have done wonders for the winner's confidence and there is little doubt he is now a leading contender for the Dubai Duty Free back over this course and distance on World Cup night, particularly as a likely stronger pace will see him in an even better light. The Group 2 Jebel Hatta (also over this same course and distance) on Super Thursday is the option if his connections go again with him before the big one. (tchd 5-2)
Emmrooz was a very useful juvenile for Godolphin, but he missed his three-year-old year and was returning after 16 months off the track. He was easy to back, but ran a cracker in defeat. Okay, he is probably flattered by his proximity to the winner, but he clearly retains his ability and is entitled to come on for this run.
Finicius(USA) apparently had to be checked over by the Vet before the start, but he was passed fit to race. This was a big improvement on his first effort in Dubai, but both his career record and his breeding point to artificial surfaces suiting best.
Kings Gambit(SAF) was not quite good enough, but it's still fair to say he was set plenty to do. He was slightly impeded by the winner when that one switched out, but was not unlucky. This was better than when he disappointed as favourite on his debut in Dubai three weeks earlier.
Yasoodd did not run a bad race but he is extremely hard to win with these days. (op 12-1)
Macarthur was high class over middle-distances for Aidan O'Brien, but he seemed to be having a typical De Kock prep on his first Dubai start, racing over a trip well short of his optimum. Blinkers were also applied, and in truth he did not show a great deal, but this was a very tough ask off 119 and much better can be expected when he is returned to 1m4f. The Group 2 Dubai City of Gold Stakes on Super Thursday will surely be considered, but the Sheema Classic on World Cup night is probably his main target. (op 9-2)
Yahrab(IRE) wants further.
Red Eye Express(IRE), dropped back to a more suitable trip, was too keen tucked away towards the inside early on. A more positive ride in a truly run race should see him in a better light, but he still has something to prove and might be one to have reservations about. (op 4-1)

643a BALANCHINE (GROUP 3) (F&M) (TURF) 1m 194y(T)
6:20 (6:21) 3-Y-O+

£83,333 (£27,777; £13,888; £6,944; £4,166; £2,777)

RPR
1 **My Central (ITY)**[15] 416 5-9-0 100.................... JMurtagh 7 102
(H J Brown, South Africa) *slowly away: settled in rr: trckd 3rd 2f out: r.o wl: led fnl 55yds* **33/1**
2 1 ¼ **Front House (IRE)**[15] 416 4-9-3 110.................... KShea 8 102
(M F De Kock, South Africa) *trckd ldr: led 3f out: r.o wl: hdd cl home* **9/4**[1]
3 nse **Happy Spirit (SAF)**[15] 416 5-9-3 102.................... RyanMoore 6 102
(H J Brown, South Africa) *mid-div: rdn to chse ldrs 2 1/2f out: ev ch fnl f: nt qckn fnl 55yds* **16/1**
4 ¼ **Peace Royale (GER)**[15] 416 4-9-2 109.................... LDettori 5 100
(A Wohler, Germany) *s.i.s: settled in last: chsd ldrs 1 1/2f out: r.o* **9/1**
5 2 ½ **Deem (IRE)**[15] 416 4-9-2 110.................... FJara 1 95
(J Barton, Saudi Arabia) *sn led: t.k.h: rdn 3f out and sn hdd: r.o one pce fnl f* **11/4**[2]
6 ¾ **Varsity**[15] 415 6-9-0 100....................(t) RichardHughes 2 91
(C F Swan, Ire) *in rr of mid-div: nvr able to chal* **50/1**
7 5 **Eva's Request (IRE)**[15] 416 4-9-0 104.................... TedDurcan 4 81
(M R Channon) *in rr of mid-div: rdn 3f out: nvr able to chal* **6/1**
8 4 ¼ **Jalmira (IRE)**[15] 416 8-9-0 105.................... PJSmullen 9 72
(E Charpy, UAE) *trckd ldrs: one pce fnl 2f* **40/1**
P **Black Emblem (JPN)**[124] 4-9-0 108.................... MJKinane 3 —
(S Kojima, Japan) *mid-div on rail: rdn 3f out: p.u 1 1/2f out* **3/1**[3]

1m 51.09s (1.09) **Going Correction** +0.225s/f (Good) 9 Ran SP% **119.9**
Speed ratings: **104,102,102,102,100 99,95,91,—**
CSF £110.28.
Owner Scuderia Siba **Bred** Az Ag Antezzante Srl **Trained** South Africa

FOCUS
This looked a very good Group 3 beforehand. The first seven from the Cape Verdi re-opposed, setting up a potentially exciting re-match between the one-two from that race, Deem and Front House, and the Japanese Grade 1 winner Black Emblem provided some added spice. However, in truth, the race itself was a major disappointment, and there was a boil over, with 33/1 shot winning.

NOTEBOOK
My Central(ITY), sixth in the Cape Verdi, was unsuited by the way the race was run last time, and had also been returning from a break, so she was entitled to improve, but this was still difficult to forecast. Her record when trained in Italy was patchy - she managed just one Listed success - and a few of her main rivals are better over further, so it is hard to get excited by this victory.
Front House(IRE), runner-up in the Cape Verdi, lacked the required speed, despite being ridden handy. She was conceding 3lb to the winner and really needs 1m4f, so this wasn't a bad effort.
Happy Spirit(SAF), a stablemate of the winner, was ridden much handier this time and had her chance. Like the runner-up, she had a 3lb penalty and is better suited by further, so she emerges with some credit. (op 20-1)
Peace Royale(GER) apparently needed the run when fourth in the Cape Verdi, but she failed to find the required improvement. She looks as though she will be best served by a strong end-to-end gallop. (op 10-1)
Deem(IRE) created a favourable impression when leading home six of today's rivals in this grade last time, but she failed to reproduce that level of form. She was ridden from the front on this occasion, with her connections seemingly worried by a potential lack of pace, but she did not look at all natural in the lead. Better can be expected when more patient tactics are employed in a truer-run race. (op 5-2)
Eva's Request(IRE) was far too keen. (op 13-2)
Black Emblem(JPN) was entitled to be in the thick of things judged on the pick of her efforts in Japan, but something was amiss in the straight and she was pulled up. (10-3)

644a ETISALAT GREETUNE (H'CAP) (TURF) 1m 2f (T)
6:55 (6:55) (95-110,108) 3-Y-O+

£50,000 (£16,666; £8,333; £4,166; £2,500; £1,666)

RPR
1 **Charlie Cool**[15] 415 6-8-7 **97**.................... WilliamBuick 6 101
(D Selvaratnam, UAE) *settled in rr: gng wl 3f out: swtchd to rail 1 1/2f out: r.o to ld last 55yds* **10/1**
2 ½ **Without A Prayer (IRE)**[15] 415 4-9-0 **105**.................... PJSmullen 5 108
(R M Beckett) *mid-div: chsd ldrs 2f out: ev ch fnl 1f: nt qckn fnl 110yds* **10/3**[1]
3 1 ¼ **Summer Doldrums (USA)**[14] 436 5-9-0 **104**....................(t) RHills 10 105
(Doug Watson, UAE) *mid-div: rdn to chal 2f out: nt qckn cl home* **9/1**
4 ¾ **Wise Dennis**[14] 439 7-8-13 **102**.................... TedDurcan 1 102
(A P Jarvis) *s.i.s: settled in rr: wd 2f out: r.o wl* **9/2**[3]
5 1 ½ **Bucked Off (SAF)**[15] 415 5-8-6 **96**.................... JohnEgan 2 92
(H J Brown, South Africa) *mid-div: smooth prog to trck ldrs 2 1/2 out: hmpd nr fin* **11/2**
6 2 ¾ **Razkalla (USA)**[791] 11-8-11 **101**....................(t) BrettDoyle 4 92
(R Bouresly, Kuwait) *mid-div on rail: dropped in rr 3f out: chsd ldrs 1 1/2f out: r.o same pce* **40/1**
7 1 **Via Galilei (IRE)**[15] 415 4-8-10 **101**.................... KJManning 8 90
(J S Bolger, Ire) *settled in rr: rdn to chse ldrs 2 1/2f out: wknd fnl 1f* **5/1**
8 14 **First Buddy**[15] 419 5-8-5 **95**.................... ABouleau 3 56
(S Seemar, UAE) *sn led: clr after 2 1/2f: hdd 3f out: wknd* **25/1**
9 ½ **Eddie Jock (IRE)**[106] 7208 5-9-4 **108**.................... AhmedAjtebi 7 68
(M bin Shafya, UAE) *settled in rr: rdn 3f out: one pce* **4/1**[2]
10 dist **Before You Go (IRE)**[22] 338 6-8-6 **99**....................(v) SMGorey(3) 9 —
(E Charpy, UAE) *led main gp: rdn and wknd 3f out* **20/1**

2m 4.39s (-0.11) **Going Correction** +0.225s/f (Good)
WFA 4 from 5yo+ 1lb 10 Ran SP% **123.4**
Speed ratings: **109,108,107,107,105 103,102,91,91,—**
CSF £45.18 Tricast £326.07. Placepot: £64.30 to a £1 stake. Pool: £13.170.88. 149.41 winning tickets. Quadpot: £36.20 to a £1 stake. Pool: £569.88. 11.64 winning tickets..
Owner W J Gredley **Bred** Middle Park Stud Ltd **Trained** United Arab Emirates

FOCUS
The early leader First Buddy went off far too fast, as he covered the opening 6f in a time 2.97 seconds quicker than the runners in the first division managed, and the final time was only 0.50 seconds faster than the 98-rated Pompeyano achieved in a slowly run race earlier on the card. It's fair to say this appeared the weaker of the two races, with several of the market principals looking doubtful stayers.

NOTEBOOK
Charlie Cool was given a good ride by William Buick, who judged the pace just right, before making the horse's mind up for him in the straight, as this wise old campaigner was inclined to hang in the opposite direction to where he was being aimed. The winner continued to go right once through the gap, and did the third few favours, but the race was in safe keeping by that point and he was entitled to take this, having dropped to a mark 5lb lower than when successful at the 2007 Carnival. He does not appeal as one to back to repeat this performance any time soon.
Without A Prayer(IRE) finds this trip stretching his stamina, but there was nothing wrong with this performance and he has now posted two creditable efforts back-to-back.
Summer Doldrums(USA) proved suited by the step back up in trip and improved on his debut effort in Dubai. He was squeezed up near the line, but looked held at the time.
Wise Dennis, a winner over shorter at this meeting last year, ran okay without really proving his stamina. (op 4-1)
Bucked Off(SAF) again looked a thoroughly awkward conveyance, carrying his head high and running keen, and he's one to swerve. (op 6-1)
Via Galilei(IRE) probably owed his short price to the lack of strength in this race, but he again offered little.
Eddie Jock(IRE) looked a suspect stayer beforehand, but he failed to give his running in any case and was beaten before stamina became an issue. (op 9-2)

630 LINGFIELD (L-H)
Sunday, February 22

OFFICIAL GOING: Standard
Wind: medium against Weather: overcast

645 CHELTENHAM PREVIEW EVENING @ LINGFIELD PARK H'CAP 5f (P)
2:20 (2:21) (Class 6) (0-65,65) 4-Y-O+ **£1,878** (£558; £279; £139) **Stalls High**

Form RPR
-040 **1** **Teen Ager (FR)**^9 [535] 5-8-9 **56** JimmyQuinn 10 65
(P Burgoyne) *hld up in last pair: hdwy 2f out: chsd ldrs and swtchd rt jst ins fnl f: r.o wl to ld nr fin* **20/1**
422 **2** *hd* **Step It Up (IRE)**^4 [582] 5-9-4 **65** JamieSpencer 7 73
(J R Boyle) *racd in midfield: pushed along and hdwy 3f out: rdn to ld ent fnl f: hdd nr fin* **2/1**^1
52-2 **3** *1 1/4* **After The Show**^39 [165] 8-9-4 **65** JimCrowley 4 69+
(Rae Guest) *racd off the pce in midfield: hdwy 2f out: rdn to chse ldrs 1f out: kpt on* **5/2**^2
6335 **4** *nse* **Bluebok**^4 [582] 8-9-0 **61** (bt) LPKeniry 5 64
(J M Bradley) *chsd ldng trio: clsd jst over 2f out: ev ch 1f out: no ex ins fnl f* **10/1**
3-55 **5** *1 1/4* **Green Lagonda (AUS)**^3 [596] 7-8-9 **56** MickyFenton 1 55
(Stef Liddiard) *led at fast gallop: rdn and hdd ent fnl f: wknd fnl 75yds* **7/1**^3
0034 **6** *3/4* **Colorus (IRE)**^17 [400] 6-9-2 **63** (p) RichardKingscote 8 59
(W J H Ratcliffe) *sn rdn along in midfield: styd on fnl f: nvr pce to rch ldrs* **8/1**
3-66 **7** *1 1/2* **Magic Glade**^39 [165] 10-8-1 **55** AndrewHeffernan(7) 2 46
(Peter Grayson) *taken down early: pressed ldr tl wknd qckly over 1f out* **14/1**
-552 **8** *1 3/4* **Scarlet Oak**^12 [481] 5-8-10 **57** AndrewElliott 6 41
(A M Hales) *dwlt: bhd: effrt on inner wl over 1f out: wknd 1f out* **14/1**
3-0 **9** *2 3/4* **Triskaidekaphobia**^16 [431] 6-8-6 **53** ow1 (t) PaulFitzsimons 3 28
(Miss J R Tooth) *sn bustled up to press ldrs: rdn over 2f otu: wknd qckly over 1f out* **25/1**

59.06 secs (0.26) **Going Correction** +0.125s/f (Slow) 9 Ran SP% **116.5**
Speed ratings (Par 101): **102,101,99,99,97 96,94,91,86**
toteswinger: 1&2 £9.00, 1&3 £11.90, 2&3 £2.30. CSF £60.90 CT £143.23 TOTE £25.30: £4.70, £1.30, £1.40; EX 88.40 Trifecta £199.50 Part won. Pool: £269.69 - 0.50 winning units..
Owner L Tomlin **Bred** Haras De Beauvoir **Trained** Shepton Montague, Somerset

FOCUS
Just a modest handicap and not many of these came in here in much form. The pace was strong with a trio of runners disputing the lead and the runner-up is the best guide to the form.
Green Lagonda(AUS) Official explanation: jockey said gelding hung left
Colorus(IRE) Official explanation: jockey said gelding hung left

646 CHELTENHAM PREVIEW EVENING - THURSDAY 5TH MARCH H'CAP 6f (P)
2:50 (2:50) (Class 6) (0-55,60) 4-Y-O+ **£1,878** (£558; £279; £139) **Stalls Low**

Form RPR
0613 **1** **Hollow Jo**^3 [596] 9-9-7 **60** (v) MickyFenton 6 69
(J R Jenkins) *in tch: rdn and hdwy 2f out: rdn to ld ins fnl f: r.o wl* **8/1**^3
0-40 **2** *3/4* **Takaamul**^22 [355] 6-8-9 **48** JimmyQuinn 7 54
(K A Morgan) *t.k.h: chsd ldrs tl wnt 2nd 4f out: rdn to ld jst ins fnl f: hdd ins fnl f: one pce* **20/1**
5024 **3** *3/4* **Bold Diva**^11 [496] 4-9-1 **54** (v) ShaneKelly 3 58+
(A W Carroll) *stdd s: hld up in last pair: hdwy on outer jst over 2f out: rdn over 1f out: r.o wl fnl f: nt rch ldrs* **13/2**^2
00-3 **4** *nk* **Patavium Prince (IRE)**^43 [114] 6-9-2 **55** FergusSweeney 5 58
(Miss Jo Crowley) *in tch in midfield: rdn and hdwy over 1f out: r.o ins fnl f: nt rch ldrs* **11/2**^1
0034 **5** *1/2* **Avoca Dancer (IRE)**^12 [487] 6-9-1 **54** (v) JamieSpencer 9 55
(Miss Gay Kelleway) *led at stdy gallop tl over 4f out: chsd ldrs after: rdn wl over 1f out: drvn and one pce fnl f* **8/1**^3
004- **6** *nse* **Bateleur**^55 [7808] 5-8-13 **52** EdwardCreighton 12 53
(M R Channon) *t.k.h: chsd ldr tl led over 4f out: rdn and hdd jst ins fnl f: wknd fnl 75yds* **8/1**^3
63-0 **7** *1* **Elusive Dreams (USA)**^48 [44] 5-9-2 **55** JimCrowley 10 53+
(P Howling) *s.i.s: sn swtchd lft and dropped in bhd: rdn wl over 1f out: swtchd rt 1f out: styd on but nvr pce to rch ldrs* **9/1**
5330 **8** *1/2* **Torquemada (IRE)**^9 [531] 8-8-13 **52** (tp) PaulDoe 1 48
(M J Attwater) *t.k.h: hld up in tch towards rr: hdwy wl over 1f out: rdn ent fnl f: sn no imp* **8/1**^3
-512 **9** *nk* **Davids Mark**^14 [460] 9-9-2 **55** SimonWhitworth 8 50
(J R Jenkins) *s.i.s: hld up towards rr: hdwy 1/2-way: c wd and rdn wl over 1f out: sn wknd* **10/1**
44/0 **10** *2 1/2* **Siraj**^11 [496] 10-8-6 **52** (p) RyanPowell(7) 11 39
(J Ryan) *chsd ldrs on outer: rdn wl over 1f out: sn wknd* **50/1**
-004 **11** *1 1/4* **Marvin Gardens**^13 [467] 6-8-13 **52** (v^1) AdamKirby 4 35
(P S McEntee) *taken down early: chsd ldrs: rdn over 2f out: wknd over 1f out* **9/1**
00-0 **12** *4* **Forever Changes**^23 [347] 4-8-11 **50** (p) LukeMorris 2 21
(L Montague Hall) *a towards rr: wl bhd fr over 1f out* **12/1**

1m 13.17s (1.27) **Going Correction** +0.125s/f (Slow) 12 Ran SP% **116.7**
Speed ratings (Par 101): **96,95,94,93,92 92,91,90,90,87 85,80**
toteswinger: 1&2 £30.30, 1&3 £11.10, 2&3 £39.90. CSF £154.18 CT £1102.67 TOTE £6.50: £2.60, £8.40, £2.60; EX 255.10 TRIFECTA Not won..
Owner Humphrey Solomons **Bred** K J Reddington **Trained** Royston, Herts

FOCUS
This moderate handicap was run at a pretty sedate early pace and it proved difficult to make up much ground in the straight as a consequence. The winner is rated as a length better than recent efforts.

647 ALL-STAR PANEL @ LINGFIELD CHELTENHAM PREVIEW CLASSIFIED STKS 1m 2f (P)
3:20 (3:21) (Class 7) 3-Y-O+ **£1,619** (£481; £240; £120) **Stalls Low**

Form RPR
006/ **1** **Postage (USA)**^621 [887] 6-9-8 45 JimmyQuinn 7 51+
(K A Morgan) *t.k.h: hld up wl in tch: trckd ldrs 2f out: swtchd rt and bmpd rivals wl over 1f out: rdn to ld ins fnl f: styd on wl* **33/1**
5006 **2** *3/4* **Ma Ridge**^12 [482] 5-9-3 40 AmyBaker(5) 4 49
(T D McCarthy) *t.k.h: hld up towards rr: hdwy over 3f out: chsng ldrs and bmpd wl over 1f out: ev ch jst ins fnl f: no ex fnl 50yds* **22/1**
-033 **3** *3/4* **Sir Haydn**^8 [541] 9-9-12 49 (v) GeorgeBaker 1 52
(J R Jenkins) *stdd after s: hld up in rr: hdwy over 2f out: plld to outer and rdn over 1f out: hanging lft after: wnt 3rd ins fnl f: nt rch ldrs* **9/2**^3
000- **4** *2 1/2* **Desert Rat (IRE)**^207 [4541] 5-9-8 42 (p) FergusSweeney 6 43
(Tim Vaughan) *chsd ldrs: wnt 3rd over 4f out: effrt and ev ch whn bmpd and hmpd wl over 1f out: plugged on same pce fnl f* **4/1**^2
0316 **5** *1 1/2* **Itsawindup**^8 [546] 5-9-13 50 (t) JamesDoyle 11 45
(Miss Sheena West) *chsd ldr over 8f out: rdn and ev ch jst over 2f out: drvn to ld over 1f out: hdd ins fnl f: wknd qckly fnl 100yds* **9/2**^3
-304 **6** *hd* **Miss Understanding**^5 [578] 4-9-7 45 (v) ChrisCatlin 3 39
(J R Weymes) *in tch in midfield: rdn and unable qck over 2f out: plugged on u.p fr over 1f out: nt rch ldrs* **8/1**
0033 **7** *7* **Golden Square**^3 [598] 7-9-11 48 AdamKirby 10 28
(A W Carroll) *led: hrd pressed and drvn 2f out: hdd over 1f out: wknd rapidly fnl f* **9/1**
6040 **8** *1 3/4* **Dynamo Dave (USA)**^4 [587] 4-9-0 42 LeeNewnes(7) 14 22
(M D I Usher) *s.i.s: racd wd: a in rr: nvr trbld ldrs* **20/1**
0-60 **9** *3* **Prima Fonteyn**^14 [455] 3-8-0 45 ow7 JemmaMarshall(7) 2 23
(Miss Sheena West) *in tch in midfield: lost pl and bhd over 2f out: no ch after* **33/1**
-024 **10** *2* **Desert Lark**^9 [537] 4-9-7 45 JamieSpencer 8 12
(K A Ryan) *stdd s: hld up in rr: rdn and no rspnse over 2f out: n.d* **3/1**^1
0/0- **11** *1 1/2* **Dickie Deano**^74 [5148] 5-9-8 32 LPKeniry 5 9
(J M Bradley) *chsd ldrs: rdn over 3f out: sn struggling: bhd fnl 2f: eased ins fnl f* **100/1**
/0-0 **12** *33* **Stroppi Poppi**^9 [528] 5-9-8 39 (b^1) JimCrowley 13 —
(Norma Twomey) *s.i.s: bhd: rdn and lost tch over 3f out: t.o and eased ins fnl f* **40/1**

2m 7.45s (0.85) **Going Correction** +0.125s/f (Slow)
WFA 3 from 4yo 22lb 4 from 5yo+ 1lb 12 Ran SP% **120.9**
Speed ratings (Par 97): **101,100,99,97,96 96,90,89,87,85 84,57**
toteswinger: 1&2 £32.40, 1&3 £13.30, 2&3 £18.30. CSF £598.24 TOTE £31.10: £3.80, £5.50, £1.90; EX 434.20 TRIFECTA Not won..
Owner P Doughty **Bred** Juddmonte Farms Inc **Trained** Little Marcle, H'fords
■ Stewards' Enquiry : Jimmy Quinn two-day ban: careless riding (Mar 10-11)

FOCUS
A low-grade event which was run at a fairly steady pace. The form seems sound enough rated around the placed horses.
Desert Lark Official explanation: jockey said that the gelding was never travelling

648 FESTIVAL FEVER @ LINGFIELD PARK H'CAP 1m 2f (P)
3:55 (3:55) (Class 4) (0-85,82) 4-Y-O+ **£4,727** (£1,406; £702; £351) **Stalls Low**

Form RPR
001- **1** **Planetary Motion (USA)**^54 [7822] 4-8-10 **74** GregFairley 7 85+
(M Johnston) *mde all: stdd pce after 2f out: rdn and qcknd clr over 1f out: hung rt fnl f: styd on* **11/4**^2
400- **2** *1 1/4* **Eton Fable (IRE)**^121 [6949] 4-8-8 **72** (p) RichardKingscote 3 78
(W J H Ratcliffe) *chsd wnr: ev ch 2f out: rdn and unable qck w wnr over 1f out: kpt on ins fnl f* **16/1**
000- **3** *3/4* **Ruff Diamond (USA)**^114 [4046] 4-8-10 **74** LukeMorris 5 79+
(J S Moore) *s.i.s: hld up in rr: rdn and effrt 2f out: no real imp tl styd on ins fnl f: wnt 3rd nr fin: nvr nr wnr* **13/2**
4311 **4** *1/2* **Can Can Star**^18 [392] 6-9-3 **80** ShaneKelly 2 84
(A W Carroll) *hld up in rr: rdn and effrt 2f out: chsd ldng pair ent fnl f: kpt on one pce: lost 3rd nr fin* **2/1**^1
0-05 **5** *1 1/4* **Alpes Maritimes**^8 [550] 5-8-13 **76** (p) FergusSweeney 1 77
(G L Moore) *t.k.h: chsd ldrs: rdn and hung lft over 1f out: nvr pce to chal wnr* **3/1**^3
0-00 **6** *7* **Cold Turkey**^8 [549] 9-8-8 **78** JemmaMarshall(7) 6 65
(G L Moore) *v.s.a: hld up in tch: rdn and lost tch 2f out: wl bhd fnl f* **12/1**

2m 8.04s (1.44) **Going Correction** +0.125s/f (Slow)
WFA 4 from 5yo+ 1lb 6 Ran SP% **111.9**
Speed ratings (Par 105): **99,98,97,97,96 90**
toteswinger: 1&2 £9.10, 1&3 £3.40, 2&3 £9.40. CSF £40.19 CT £257.41 TOTE £3.40: £1.90, £5.40; EX 42.40 Trifecta £205.50 Pool: £622.14 - 2.24 winning units..
Owner Sheikh Hamdan Bin Mohammed Al Maktoum **Bred** Mellon Patch, Inc **Trained** Middleham Moor, N Yorks

FOCUS
A decent handicap, but it was a tactical race with the first pair one and two throughout. The time was slower than that for the earlier classified stakes and the form should be treated with a degree of caution, although the runner-up and fourth were close to their marks.
Alpes Maritimes Official explanation: jockey said gelding ran too free

649 BOOK CHELTENHAM PREVIEW ON 01342 834800 (S) STKS 1m (P)
4:25 (4:25) (Class 6) 3-Y-O **£1,878** (£558; £279; £139) **Stalls High**

Form RPR
2224 **1** **Hawkspring (IRE)**^3 [605] 3-9-4 66 (vt^1) AdamKirby 5 67+
(S Parr) *mde virtualy all: set stdy gallop: rdn and qcknd 5l clr jst over 2f out: kpt on: unchal after* **11/4**^2

-435 **2** 1 1/2 **Why Nee Amy**[12] 492 3-8-7 56 ChrisCatlin 3 52
(Miss Gay Kelleway) *hld up in last trio: rdn and outpcd over 2f out: styd on u.p fnl f: wnt 2nd wl ins fnl f: no ch w wnr* **14/1**

06-0 **3** 3/4 **Sweet Virginia (USA)**[28] 287 3-8-0 38 DeclanCannon(7) 8 50
(K R Burke) *t.k.h: chsd wnr: rdn and outpcd by wnr jst over 2f out: plugged on fnl f: lost 2nd wl ins fnl f: sddle slipped* **50/1**

44 **4** 3/4 **Harty Boy (USA)**[8] 548 3-8-12 0 JamieSpencer 4 54
(M L W Bell) *hld in rr: hmpd sn after s: stl last and swtchd lft 2f out: nt clr run and swtchd rt over 1f out: hung lft after: styd on fnl f: nvr nr wnr* **4/5**[1]

-514 **5** 1 3/4 **Cognac Boy (USA)**[23] 345 3-9-4 65 (b) JimmyQuinn 6 56
(A B Haynes) *hld up in last trio: nt clr run briefly on inner 2f out: sn rdn and effrt to dispute 2nd over 1f out: no imp on wnr: wknd ins fnl f* **11/2**[3]

0-56 **6** 1 3/4 **Chantilly Dancer (IRE)**[19] 383 3-8-7 49 LukeMorris 2 41
(M Quinn) *chsd ldrs: rdn and nt pce of wnr over 2f out: wknd u.p wl over 1f out* **20/1**

0-26 **7** 12 **Cash In The Attic**[21] 363 3-8-7 52 EdwardCreighton 7 13
(M R Channon) *s.i.s: hld up in tch: rdn wl over 2f out: sn struggling: wl bhd fr over 1f out* **20/1**

1m 40.73s (2.53) **Going Correction** +0.125s/f (Slow) 7 Ran SP% **115.8**
Speed ratings (Par 95): **92,90,89,89,87 85,73**
toteswinger: 1&2 £4.40, 1&3 £13.80, 2&3 £25.40. CSF £36.81 TOTE £4.00: £1.80, £4.50; EX 19.60 Trifecta £163.40 Pool: £516.72 - 2.34 winning units..There was no bid for the winner. Harty Boy was claimed by Mrs S. V. O. Leech for £10,000.
Owner Willie McKay **Bred** Mrs S M Roy **Trained**
■ Stewards' Enquiry : Edward Creighton two-day ban: careless riding (Mar 10-11)

FOCUS
A reasonable seller but tricky to pin down, with the runner-up the best guide.
Sweet Virginia(USA) Official explanation: jockey said saddle slipped

650 TOP TIPS @ CHELTENHAM PREVIEW EVENING CLAIMING STKS 1m (P)
4:55 (4:55) (Class 6) 4-Y-0+ **£1,878** (£558; £279; £139) **Stalls** High

Form RPR
4-21 **1** **Electric Warrior (IRE)**[11] 504 6-8-13 80 DarrenWilliams 3 78
(K R Burke) *chsd ldr: chal over 1f out: rdn to ld ins fnl f: drvn out* **5/4**[1]

3-60 **2** shd **Willkandoo (USA)**[18] 388 4-9-2 80 StephenDonohoe 6 81
(D M Simcock) *hld up wl in tch in last pair: rdn and effrt over 1f out: str chal wl ins fnl f: jst hld* **10/3**[3]

3-11 **3** 3/4 **Jake The Snake (IRE)**[11] 495 8-8-12 74 AmyBaker(5) 4 80
(A W Carroll) *s.i.s: t.k.h: hld up in 3rd pl on rail: shkn up jst over 2f out: rdn but nvr enough room fr wl over 1f out: kpt on to go 3rd last strides* **5/2**[2]

5-03 **4** hd **What's Up Doc (IRE)**[26] 307 8-9-2 72 FergusSweeney 2 79
(Mrs T J Hill) *led: rdn and hrd pressed fr over 1f out: hdd ins fnl f: one pce fnl 100yds: lost 3rd last strides* **9/1**

1m 37.88s (-0.32) **Going Correction** +0.125s/f (Slow) 4 Ran SP% **106.1**
Speed ratings (Par 101): **106,105,105,104**
toteswinger: 1&2 £5.30. CSF £5.40 TOTE £2.00; EX 5.20.Electric Warrior was claimed by Mr R. A. Harris for £12,000.
Owner Market Avenue Racing Club Ltd **Bred** Limestone Stud **Trained** Middleham Moor, N Yorks
■ Stewards' Enquiry : Fergus Sweeney one-day ban: failed to keep straight from stalls (Mar 10)

FOCUS
A fair claimer in which the four runners finished in the order they should have according to adjusted official figures. The pace was reasonable for such a small field but the form is a little dubious and best rated around the third and fourth.

651 CHELTENHAM PREVIEW EVENING @ LINGFIELD PARK FILLIES' H'CAP 1m (P)
5:25 (5:26) (Class 5) (0-75,74) 4-Y-0+ **£2,590** (£770; £385; £192) **Stalls** High

Form RPR
2305 **1** **Bavarica**[13] 470 7-8-2 65 TobyAtkinson(7) 1 72
(Miss J Feilden) *stdd after s: hld up in last pl: hdwy and nt clr run over 1f out: swtchd lft ent fnl f: led wl ins fnl f: hld on* **15/2**

-431 **2** shd **Moon Crystal**[13] 470 4-8-12 68 (t) JimCrowley 3 75
(E A L Dunlop) *trckd ldrs: chal gng wl 2f out: rdn to ld ent fnl f: hdd wl ins fnl f: rallied nr fin: jst hld* **4/1**[2]

154- **3** 1 1/2 **Binfield (IRE)**[267] 2622 4-9-3 73 GeorgeBaker 6 77
(B G Powell) *stdd after s: hld up in last pair: rdn and effrt on outer over 2f out: unable qck u.p over 1f out: kpt on fnl 100yds to go 3rd nr fin* **11/2**[3]

-120 **4** hd **Millie's Rock (IRE)**[8] 559 4-9-4 74 JamieSpencer 4 77
(K A Ryan) *racd keenly: led: rdn 2f out: drvn and hdd ent fnl f: btn fnl 50yds: lost 3rd nr fin* **9/4**[1]

12-3 **5** 1 3/4 **Saucy**[43] 125 8-8-9 65 RichardKingscote 2 64
(Tom Dascombe) *in tch: rdn 3f out: hdwy to chal over 1f out: wknd ins fnl f* **9/4**[1]

6-26 **6** 3 3/4 **Angel Voices (IRE)**[13] 475 6-7-11 60 (v) NoraLooby(7) 5 50
(K R Burke) *chsd ldr tl 2f out: sn wknd* **25/1**

1m 38.16s (-0.04) **Going Correction** +0.125s/f (Slow) 6 Ran SP% **112.5**
Speed ratings (Par 100): **105,104,103,103,101 97**
toteswinger: 1&2 £5.20, 1&3 £7.80, 2&3 £6.20. CSF £36.98 TOTE £9.70: £3.30, £1.60; EX 24.40 Place 6 £417.02, Place 5 £284.84.
Owner Miss J Feilden **Bred** Juddmonte Farms **Trained** Exning, Suffolk

FOCUS
A modest handicap for fillies, run at an ordinary pace. The form makes sense despite the bunch finish.
Binfield(IRE) Official explanation: jockey said filly hung right leaving the stalls
T/Plt: £384.20 to a £1 stake. Pool: £73,121.79. 138.90 winning tickets. T/Qpdt: £88.80 to a £1 stake. Pool: £3,794.08. 31.60 winning tickets. SP

464 ST MORITZ (R-H)
Sunday, February 22

OFFICIAL GOING: Frozen

652a GR CORPORATE EVENTS (SNOW) 4f
11:45 (11:49) 4-Y-0+ **£9,412** (£3,765; £2,824; £1,882; £941)

RPR
1 **Princess Rose Anne (IRE)**[14] 464 4-8-8 SteveDrowne 1 66
(J R Best) *a.p: led 1f out: r.o wl* **5/1**[1]

2 1/2 **Sahara Boy (GER)**[280] 4-9-4 FDiFede 7 74
(G Raveneau, Switzerland)

3 nk **Spinning Crystal (IRE)**[14] 464 5-8-6 IRossi 8 60
(S Szuna, Czech Republic)

4 3 **Seneca Village (FR)**[14] 464 5-8-11 RobertHavlin 3 50
(M Weiss, Switzerland)

5 1/2 **Rushing Dasher (GER)**[14] 464 7-9-9 FrauNatalieFriberg 10 60
(Natalie Friberg, Switzerland)

6 3 1/2 **Assam (GER)**[14] 464 7-9-2 GBocksai 2 35
(Carmen Bocskai, Switzerland)

7 nk **Mister Minister (GER)**[14] 465 4-9-2 MEsposito 5 34
(C Von Der Recke, Germany)

8 2 1/2 **Mina Alsalaam**[14] 464 7-8-8 ZVarga 9 13
(S Peto, Hungary)

9 8 **Mystic Ways (IRE)**[7] 5-8-9 MKolb 4 —
(Traugott Stauffer, Switzerland)

46.96 secs (46.96) **9** Ran SP% **16.7**
(including SwFr1 stake): WIN 6.00; PL 2.00, 2.90, 3.80; DF 65.40.
Owner Miss Rose-Anne Galligan **Bred** C McCarthy **Trained** Hucking, Kent
■ This Listed event was reduced in distance from 5f 110y.

653a GUEBLIN 70. GROSSER PREIS VON ST MORITZ (SNOW) 1m 2f
1:55 (2:17) 4-Y-0+ **£38,000** (£15,199; £11,399; £7,601; £3,801)

RPR
1 **Song Of Victory (GER)**[14] 465 5-9-4 MiguelLopez 3 —
(M Weiss, Switzerland)

2 1 1/4 **Collow (GER)**[14] 466 9-9-4 RobertHavlin 8 —
(M Weiss, Switzerland)

3 shd **Vlavianus (CZE)**[14] 466 8-9-2 OPlacais 11 —
(M Weiss, Switzerland)

4 6 **Thalamon (FR)**[140] 5-9-4 AStarke 13 —
(P Schiergen, Germany)

5 2 **Eiswind**[172] 5625 5-9-4 FDiFede 16 —
(G Raveneau, Switzerland)

6 3 **Hucking Hero (IRE)**[14] 465 4-8-13 SteveDrowne 12 —
(J R Best) *racd in 3rd or 4th: lost pl on fnl bnd: kpt on at one pce fr over 1f out* **123/10**[2]

7 5 **Saraab (GER)**[14] 466 7-9-0 IRossi 4 —
(P Vovcenko, Germany)

8 9 **Quiron (IRE)**[357] 8-8-12 GBocksai 14 —
(Carmen Bocskai, Switzerland)

9 1 1/4 **Salattus (GER)**[371] 605 8-9-9 VJanacek 15 —
(G Raveneau, Switzerland)

10 4 **Saldenzar (GER)**[329] 5-9-0 SGeorgiev 5 —
(Sandor Kovacs, Hungary)

11 2 **Vegano (FR)**[14] 466 8-8-12 MKolb 7 —
(C Von Der Recke, Germany)

12 17 **Romantic Man (GER)**[14] 466 6-8-12 DPorcu 10 —
(M Rulec, Germany)

13 8 **Swiss Act**[14] 466 5-8-12 JoeFanning 1 —
(M Johnston) *missed break: a bhd* **194/10**[3]

14 13 **Il Grande Ardone**[33] 226 4-8-13 MEsposito 2 —
(C Von Der Recke, Germany)

15 dist **January**[51] 17 6-8-12 WMLordan 9 —
(T M Walsh, Ire) **68/10**[1]

P **Sybelio (FR)**[14] 465 5-9-0 GArena 6 —
(W Hefter, Germany)

2m 20.36s (140.36)
WFA 4 from 5yo+ 1lb **16** Ran SP% **25.2**
WIN 5.70 (coupled with Collow); PL 3.00, 2.30, 1.70; DF 54.10.
Owner Appapays Racing Club **Bred** Gestut Elite **Trained** Switzerland

624 WOLVERHAMPTON (A.W) (L-H)
Monday, February 23

OFFICIAL GOING: Standard
Wind: Fresh, half-against Weather: Overcast

654 BET CHAMPIONS LEAGUE FOOTBALL - BETDAQ H'CAP 5f 20y(P)
2:10 (2:11) (Class 5) (0-75,75) 4-Y-0+ **£2,729** (£806; £403) **Stalls** Low

Form RPR
1-21 **1** **Perlachy**[15] 461 5-8-4 61 oh1 (v) LukeMorris 1 72
(D Shaw) *chsd ldrs: rdn to ld ins fnl f: r.o* **6/1**[2]

0-65 **2** 3/4 **El Dececy (USA)**[10] 533 5-9-4 75 AdamKirby 10 83
(S Parr) *led 4f out: rdn over 1f out: hdd ins fnl f: r.o* **12/1**

2116 **3** 1 **Grimes Faith**[5] 582 6-8-6 70 (p) AmyRyan(7) 5 75+
(K A Ryan) *chsd ldrs: ev ch over 1f out: sn rdn and rdr dropped whip: unable qck ins fnl f* **8/1**[3]

202- **4** shd **Russian Symphony (USA)**[89] 7456 8-9-1 72 (b) ShaneKelly 13 76
(C R Egerton) *mid-div: sn pushed along: rdn over 1f out: r.o wl ins fnl f* **12/1**

-406 **5** shd **Know No Fear**[10] 539 4-9-1 72 JimCrowley 6 76
(D Shaw) *mid-diviswion: hdwy u.p over 1f out: r.o* **10/1**

-016 **6** 1/2 **Tyrannosaurus Rex (IRE)**[10] 535 5-8-4 61 (v) PaulHanagan 4 63
(D Shaw) *prom: hmpd over 3f out: rdn 1/2-way: styd on same pce ins fnl f* **10/3**[1]

60-5 **7** nk **Almaty Express**[39] 170 7-8-8 72 (b) BMcHugh(7) 7 73
(J R Weymes) *sn led: hdd 4f out: chsd ldrs: rdn and edgd lft over 1f out: styd on same pce* **9/1**

400- **8** shd **Sandwith**[142] 6486 6-8-9 66 GregFairley 12 67
(A G Foster) *hld up: r.o ins fnl f: nrst fin* **8/1**[3]

3-20 **9** 1/2 **Now You See Me**[25] 326 5-8-4 61 ChrisCatlin 9 60
(D Flood) *hld up: rdn over 1f out: r.o ins fnl f: nvr nrr* **16/1**

260- **10** hd **Mayoman (IRE)**[73] 7653 4-8-1 63 DeanHeslop(5) 11 61
(M Mullineaux) *s.i.s: swtchd lft sn after s: r.o towards fin: nvr nrr* **20/1**

16-6 **11** 3/4 **Trimlestown (IRE)**[52] 20 6-9-0 71 PaulDoe 2 70+
(P D Evans) *s.i.s: a in rr* **9/1**

50-0 **12** 1/2 **Not My Choice (IRE)**[10] 539 4-9-3 74 TolleyDean 3 68
(S Parr) *hld up: shkn up over 1f out: n.d* **18/1**

44-0 **13** 5 **King Kenny**[9] 558 4-9-1 72 DarrenWilliams 8 48
(S Parr) *chsd ldrs: rdn 1/2-way: wknd over 1f out* **50/1**

62.19 secs (-0.11) **Going Correction** +0.15s/f (Slow) 13 Ran SP% **121.9**
Speed ratings (Par 103): **106,104,103,103,102 102,101,101,100,100 99,98,90**
toteswinger: 1&2 £13.70, 1&3 £9.40, 2&3 £28.10. CSF £77.92 CT £608.37 TOTE £6.40: £2.10, £6.10, £3.00; EX 87.40 TRIFECTA Not won..
Owner Mrs N Macauley **Bred** J James **Trained** Danethorpe, Notts
■ Stewards' Enquiry : Paul Doe Matter referred, in breach of Rule 157.

FOCUS
A modest sprint handicap run at a decent clip and the form looks reliable rated through the third.

Trimlestown(IRE) ◆ Official explanation: jockey said, regarding running and riding, thaty his orders were to jump out, ride a normal race and do his best, adding that the gelding started awkwardly, was outpaced mid-race, before making progress in latter stages only to be blocked inside final furlong, and gelding would be suited by a longer trip; trainer added gelding has a tendency to be slow away

655 GREAT OFFERS AT WOLVERHAMPTON-RACECOURSE.CO.UK MAIDEN STKS 5f 216y(P)
2:40 (2:40) (Class 5) 3-Y-O+ **£2,729** (£806; £403) **Stalls** Low

Form RPR

1 **Just Timmy Marcus** 3-8-12 0 GrahamGibbons 13 62+
(B P J Baugh) *dwlt: bhd: swtchd lft and hdwy 1f out: r.o to ld wl ins fnl f* **66/1**

2 ½ **Trade Centre** 4-9-13 0 MartinDwyer 6 63+
(W R Muir) *chsd ldrs: led over 1f out: rdn and hdd wl ins fnl f* **4/1[1]**

-224 3 shd **Silk Gallery (USA)**[16] 454 4-9-8 55 (t) JimmyQuinn 4 58
(E J Alston) *s.i.s: hld up: hdwy over 1f out: sn rdn: r.o* **13/2**

0504 4 hd **Weetfromthechaff**[10] 535 4-9-13 47 (v) ChrisCatlin 3 62
(R Hollinshead) *hld up in tch: racd keenly: nt clr run and lost pl over 2f out: hdwy over 1f out: rdn and ev ch ins fnl f: styd on* **10/1**

2336 5 3¼ **Circle Dance (IRE)**[18] 400 4-9-13 67 (v) JimCrowley 9 52
(D Shaw) *hld up in tch: edgd rt wl over 1f out: rdn and hung lft fnl f: no ex* **5/1[3]**

4- 6 shd **Location**[207] 4562 3-8-8 0 ow1 StephenDonohoe 10 44
(Ian Williams) *hld up: r.o ins fnl f: nrst fin* **16/1**

3 7 hd **Villaruz (IRE)**[47] 75 3-8-12 0 TonyCulhane 12 47
(D Flood) *hld up: hdwy over 2f out: rdn over 1f out: styd on same pce* **10/1**

8 ¾ **Little Lost (IRE)** 3-8-8 0 ow1 ShaneKelly 2 41
(J A Osborne) *hld up in tch: rdn over 1f out: hung lft and no ex ins fnl f* **10/1**

604- 9 2½ **Eternal Optimist (IRE)**[62] 7779 4-9-1 51 (v[1]) KrishGundowry(7) 5 37
(Paul Green) *chsd ldr: rdn over 2f out: wknd fnl f* **14/1**

-00 10 nse **Unbelievable Jeff**[27] 306 3-8-12 0 DarrenWilliams 1 37
(S Parr) *s.i.s: a in rr* **40/1**

11 3¼ **Baby Queen (IRE)** 3-8-7 0 AndrewElliott 8 23
(B P J Baugh) *chsd ldrs: ev ch over 2f out: wknd fnl f* **40/1**

-323 12 1¾ **Gurteen Diamond**[17] 421 3-8-7 65 LukeMorris 11 17
(N J Vaughan) *prom: hmpd wl over 1f out: sn rdn: wknd fnl f* **9/2[2]**

350- 13 3¾ **Chimbonda**[58] 7795 3-8-12 60 AdamKirby 7 11
(S Parr) *led: rdn and hdd over 1f out: sn wknd* **12/1**

1m 15.84s (0.84) **Going Correction** +0.15s/f (Slow)
WFA 3 from 4yo 15lb **13 Ran SP% 122.1**
Speed ratings (Par 103): **100,99,99,98,94 94,94,93,89,89 85,83,78**
toteswinger: 1&2 £75.20, 1&3 £43.60, 2&3 £5.90. CSF £323.35 TOTE £62.40: £13.60, £1.70, £2.10; EX 593.00 Trifecta £140.70 Part won. Pool: £190.22 - 0.20 winning units..
Owner C R Watts **Bred** P D Moore **Trained** Audley, Staffs

FOCUS
A moderate sprint maiden, although the front two were debutants and could rate higher.

656 ENJOY THE LUCKY 7 GROUP OFFER APPRENTICE H'CAP 1m 1f 103y(P)
3:10 (3:10) (Class 5) (0-75,75) 4-Y-O+ **£2,729** (£806; £403) **Stalls** Low

Form RPR

0-11 1 **Brouhaha**[9] 558 5-8-10 69 RossAtkinson(3) 1 79
(Tom Dascombe) *trckd ldrs: racd keenly: shkn up over 2f out: chsd wnr over 1f out: sn rdn and hung lft: r.o to ld wl ins fnl f* **6/4[1]**

13-0 2 1¼ **Supercast (IRE)**[35] 220 6-9-5 75 MCGeran 3 83
(N J Vaughan) *sn chsng ldr: led over 2f out: rdn and hung lft over 1f out: hdd wl ins fnl f* **11/2[3]**

00-3 3 5 **Monfils Monfils (USA)**[14] 477 7-8-7 68 (p) KarenKenny(5) 2 67
(A J McCabe) *prom: racd keenly: rdn over 2f out: styng on same pce whn hung lft fnl f* **8/1**

10-5 4 nk **Saviour Sand (IRE)**[12] 505 5-9-0 70 JackDean 4 68
(M E Rimmer) *led: racd keenly: hdd over 2f out: rdn and hung lft over 1f out: styd on same pce* **22/1**

0-66 5 nk **Bajan Pride**[6] 580 5-8-6 65 (p) AmyRyan(3) 7 62
(R A Fahey) *chsd ldrs: rdn and hung lft fr over 1f out: styd on same pce* **12/1**

142- 6 1 **Surprise Pension (IRE)**[31] 7039 5-8-0 61 oh1 JamieKyne(5) 6 56
(J J Quinn) *hld up: rdn over 1f out: nt clr run and swtchd rt ins fnl f: hmpd sn after: n.d* **15/2**

560- 7 ¾ **Urban Warrior**[98] 7366 5-8-8 64 WilliamCarson 8 58
(Ian Williams) *hld up: rdn over 1f out: a in rr* **12/1**

-634 8 2½ **Hucking Heat (IRE)**[14] 477 5-8-12 73 (p) DavidKenny(5) 5 62
(R Hollinshead) *dwlt: hld up: rdn over 2f out: a in rr* **5/1[2]**

2m 1.92s (0.22) **Going Correction** +0.15s/f (Slow) **8 Ran SP% 114.7**
Speed ratings (Par 103): **105,103,99,99,98 98,97,95**
toteswinger: 1&2 £2.10, 1&3 £3.00, 2&3 £4.40. CSF £10.00 CT £49.22 TOTE £2.30: £1.40, £1.90, £1.40; EX 13.60 Trifecta £70.00 Pool: £397.85 - 4.20 winning units..
Owner G D Newton **Bred** Mrs Rosamund Furlong **Trained** Lambourn, Berks

FOCUS
A modest handicap restricted to apprentices who had not ridden more than 50 winners.

657 BET ASIAN H'CAPS - BETDAQ HANDICAP 1m 141y(P)
3:40 (3:40) (Class 6) (0-60,59) 4-Y-O+ **£2,047** (£604; £302) **Stalls** Low

Form RPR

000- 1 **Ergo (FR)**[109] 6727 5-8-11 52 (v) PaulHanagan 4 59
(James Moffatt) *hld up: rdn over 2f out: r.o u.p fnl f to ld towards fin* **40/1**

02-3 2 ½ **Kargan (IRE)**[32] 256 4-9-1 56 GregFairley 10 62
(A G Foster) *hld up: hdwy on outer over 1f out: rdn and hung lft ins fnl f: sn ev ch: r.o* **4/1[2]**

-210 3 ¾ **The Graig**[12] 494 5-8-13 54 JerryO'Dwyer 12 58
(J R Holt) *chsd ldr: rdn over 3f out: led over 1f out: hdd towards fin* **20/1**

-200 4 ½ **Mr Chocolate Drop (IRE)**[10] 531 5-9-0 55 (b) AdamKirby 8 58
(Miss M E Rowland) *s.i.s: hld up: swtchd lft 1f out: r.o u.p* **14/1**

0-06 5 ½ **Hunt The Bottle (IRE)**[24] 352 4-8-7 53 DeanHeslop(5) 11 55
(M Mullineaux) *mid-div: hdwy over 6f out: rdn over 1f out: styd on* **20/1**

2341 6 1 **Just Jimmy (IRE)**[14] 473 4-8-13 54 PaulDoe 1 54
(P D Evans) *trckd ldrs: racd keenly: rdn over 2f out: no ex fnl f* **8/1[3]**

-065 7 1¼ **Stark Contrast (USA)**[6] 580 5-9-4 59 JimCrowley 9 56
(M D I Usher) *sn led: rdn and hdd over 1f out: wknd towards fin* **10/1**

/4-2 8 ½ **Mister Trickster (IRE)**[12] 496 8-8-13 54 TonyCulhane 13 50+
(R Dickin) *s.i.s: hld up: hdwy over 2f out: sn rdn: btn whn hmpd ins fnl f* **12/1**

5065 9 ¾ **Bridge Of Fermoy (IRE)**[9] 545 4-9-1 56 (vt) JamieSpencer 7 50+
(Miss Gay Kelleway) *hld up: rdn 2f out: sme hdwy and hmpd 1f out: wknd towards fin* **17/2**

-546 10 1 **Machinate (USA)**[9] 554 7-8-12 53 TGMcLaughlin 3 45
(W M Brisbourne) *prom: rdn over 2f out: wknd over 1f out* **12/1**

2013 11 3¼ **Ardent Prince**[6] 580 6-9-3 58 RobertWinston 5 42
(A J McCabe) *hld up: hdwy over 3f out: rdn: hung lft and wknd over 1f out* **9/4[1]**

-063 12 3¾ **To Bubbles**[17] 420 4-8-10 51 FrankieMcDonald 2 27
(A G Newcombe) *hld up: rdn over 3f out: a in rr* **33/1**

00-3 13 1¼ **Arikinui**[29] 290 4-8-10 51 DarrenWilliams 6 24
(K R Burke) *prom: rdn over 3f out: wknd over 2f out* **22/1**

1m 52.77s (2.27) **Going Correction** +0.15s/f (Slow) **13 Ran SP% 122.8**
Speed ratings (Par 101): **95,94,93,93,93 92,91,90,89,89 86,82,81**
toteswinger: 1&2 £31.00, 1&3 £98.60, 2&3 £21.20. CSF £189.94 CT £3491.00 TOTE £37.90: £9.10, £1.90, £4.90; EX 297.50 TRIFECTA Not won..
Owner Mrs Eileen M Milligan **Bred** Takashi Watanabe **Trained** Cartmel, Cumbria
■ Stewards' Enquiry : Dean Heslop two-day ban: careless riding (Mar 10-11)

FOCUS
A moderate but competitive handicap. The winning time was 0.61 seconds slower than the following maiden won the 70-rated Badge Of Honour.

658 STAY AT THE WOLVERHAMPTON HOLIDAY INN MEDIAN AUCTION MAIDEN STKS 1m 141y(P)
4:10 (4:11) (Class 5) 3-4-Y-O **£2,729** (£806; £403) **Stalls** Low

Form RPR

0-22 1 **Badge Of Honour**[10] 529 3-8-7 70 GregFairley 6 74
(M Johnston) *mde virtually all: hung lft fnl f: pushed out* **8/11[1]**

2 1¼ **Calling Victory (FR)** 3-8-2 0 JimmyQuinn 5 66+
(M Botti) *hld up: hdwy over 2f out: rdn to chse wnr fnl f: edgd lft: styd on* **14/1**

3 3 1 **National Monument (IRE)**[19] 386 3-8-7 0 ChrisCatlin 2 69
(J A Osborne) *w ldr tl rdn 4f out: wnt 2nd again over 2f out to 1f out: styd on same pce* **3/1[2]**

66 4 7 **Dollar Express (USA)**[19] 394 3-8-8 0 ow1 ShaneKelly 3 55+
(J Noseda) *dwlt: hld up: hdwy and hung rt fr 1/2-way: eased wl over 2f out: n.d after* **6/1[3]**

0 5 8 **Al Jathaab (USA)**[19] 386 4-10-0 0 TGMcLaughlin 4 40
(M Wigham) *prom: pushed along 5f out: wknd over 2f out* **22/1**

60-3 6 nk **Jaq's Sister**[32] 251 3-8-2 0 (b[1]) PaulHanagan 7 29
(M Blanshard) *prom: chsd wnr 4f out tl rdn over 2f out: sn wknd* **33/1**

000- 7 5 **Little Rococoa**[68] 7701 4-9-7 40 AndrewHeffernan(7) 1 28
(R J Price) *prom: rdn 1/2-way: wknd 3f out* **200/1**

1m 52.16s (1.66) **Going Correction** +0.15s/f (Slow)
WFA 3 from 4yo 21lb **7 Ran SP% 111.6**
Speed ratings (Par 103): **98,96,96,89,82 82,77**
toteswinger: 1&2 £3.30, 1&3 £1.40, 2&3 £3.80. CSF £12.18 TOTE £2.10: £1.30, £5.00; EX 10.90.
Owner Sheikh Hamdan Bin Mohammed Al Maktoum **Bred** Gainsborough Stud Management Ltd **Trained** Middleham Moor, N Yorks

FOCUS
An ordinary maiden run in a time 0.61 seconds quicker than earlier handicap won by the 52-rated Ergo.

659 BETDAQ.CO.UK MAIDEN STKS 1m 1f 103y(P)
4:40 (4:40) (Class 5) 3-Y-O **£2,729** (£806; £403) **Stalls** Low

Form RPR

3-35 1 **Sign Of Approval**[19] 389 3-8-12 74 MartinLane(5) 3 73
(K R Burke) *dwlt: rcvrd to ld 8f out: rdn and hung rt fr over 2f out: swvd rt ins fnl f: styd on* **9/4[2]**

6-4 2 2½ **Divinatore**[37] 201 3-9-3 0 AdamKirby 1 68
(D Haydn Jones) *hld up in tch: pushed along 1/2-way: rdn to chse wnr 2f out: no imp fnl f* **7/4[1]**

3 4½ **Lords A Leaping (IRE)** 3-9-3 0 ShaneKelly 5 60
(J A Osborne) *hld up: hdwy 6f out: rdn over 3f out: sn hung rt: wknd fnl f* **3/1[3]**

60-6 4 ¾ **Broughton Beck (IRE)**[10] 529 3-9-3 60 FrankieMcDonald 2 58
(R F Fisher) *led 1f: trckd wnr: racd keenly: rdn over 2f out: wknd fnl f* **7/1**

0 5 16 **Miami Mix**[19] 391 3-9-0 0 RussellKennemore(3) 6 28
(B N Pollock) *s.i.s: hld up: rdn and wknd 3f out* **33/1**

00- 6 ¾ **Stafford Charlie**[68] 7699 3-9-3 0 VinceSlattery 7 26
(J G M O'Shea) *chsd ldrs: lost pl over 5f out: wknd 3f out* **66/1**

2m 3.21s (1.51) **Going Correction** +0.15s/f (Slow) **6 Ran SP% 109.1**
Speed ratings (Par 97): **99,96,92,92,77 77**
toteswinger: 1&2 £1.90, 1&3 £3.40, 2&3 £2.40. CSF £6.17 TOTE £2.00: £1.10, £1.90; EX 5.60.
Owner Cyril Wall **Bred** Heather Raw **Trained** Middleham Moor, N Yorks
■ Martin Lane's first winner since coming over from Ireland.

FOCUS
A weak, uncompetitive maiden run at an ordinary pace.
Broughton Beck(IRE) Official explanation: jockey said gelding ran too free
Miami Mix Official explanation: jockey said colt hung right

660 SPONSOR A RACE BY CALLING 01902 390009 H'CAP 1m 4f 50y(P)
5:10 (5:10) (Class 5) (0-75,73) 4-Y-O+ **£2,729** (£806; £403) **Stalls** Low

Form RPR

-642 1 **Eseej (USA)**[12] 497 4-8-7 64 ChrisCatlin 8 73+
(P W Hiatt) *mde all: rdn clr over 1f out: styd on* **10/3[1]**

-033 2 3 **Morbick**[9] 559 5-9-2 70 LukeMorris 7 74
(W M Brisbourne) *a.p: rdn 4f out: chsd wnr over 2f out: no imp fnl f* **7/2[2]**

45-0 3 ¾ **Apache Fort**[26] 319 6-9-4 72 (b) ShaneKelly 4 75
(T Keddy) *prom: rdn over 2f out: styd on same pce fnl f* **8/1**

225- 4 2 **Thorny Mandate**[142] 6493 7-8-5 59 oh1 JimmyQuinn 10 59
(W M Brisbourne) *s.i.s: hld up: hdwy over 2f out: rdn over 1f out: styd on same pce* **20/1**

0-5 5 2¼ **Masterofceremonies**[9] 558 6-8-12 66 (b) PaulHanagan 3 62
(James Moffatt) *s.s: hld up: racd keenly: rdn and hung lft fr over 1f out: nt trble ldrs* **25/1**

5-24 6 2¼ **Hammer**[30] 279 4-8-8 65 MartinDwyer 6 58+
(R T Phillips) *chsd wnr tl rdn over 2f out: wkng whn hmpd ins fnl f* **14/1**

0553 7 ¾ **Man Of Gwent (UAE)**[9] 550 5-9-4 72 PaulDoe 2 63+
(P D Evans) *hld up: hdwy over 5f out: rdn over 2f out: wkng whn hmpd ins fnl f* **5/1[3]**

06-0 8 3½ **Sommersturm (GER)**[34] 226 5-9-5 73 MickyFenton 9 59
(B J Curley) *chsd ldrs: rdn over 3f out: wknd over 2f out* **25/1**

0212 9 nk **Rawdon (IRE)**[11] 517 8-9-3 71 (be) JamieSpencer 5 56+
(Miss Gay Kelleway) *hld up: rdn over 1f out: eased fnl f* **7/2[2]**

14-0 **10** *1 ¾* **Andaman Sunset**[9] 550 4-9-1 **72**.................... TolleyDean 1 55
(J L Spearing) *hld up: bhd fnl 4f* **28/1**
2m 41.58s (0.48) **Going Correction** +0.15s/f (Slow)
WFA 4 from 5yo+ 3lb **10** Ran SP% **117.9**
Speed ratings (Par 103): **104,102,101,100,98 97,96,94,94,92**
toteswinger: 1&2 £3.70, 1&3 £6.90, 2&3 £7.40. CSF £14.57 CT £86.87 TOTE £4.30: £1.60, £1.40, £2.70; EX 17.60 Trifecta £94.60 Pool: £796.90 - 5.84 winning units. Place 6: £85.69, Place 5: £20.27.
Owner P W Hiatt **Bred** Shadwell Farm LLC **Trained** Hook Norton, Oxon
FOCUS
A modest handicap run at a steady gallop.
Rawdon(IRE) Official explanation: trainer said gelding had a breathing problem
T/Plt: £168.50 to a £1 stake. Pool: £70,247.32. 304.20 winning tickets. T/Qpdt: £25.00 to a £1 stake. Pool: £4,683.62. 138.50 winning tickets. CR

645 LINGFIELD (L-H)
Tuesday, February 24

OFFICIAL GOING: Standard
Wind: nil Weather: overcast

661 BET ASIAN H'CAPS - BETDAQ HANDICAP (DIV I) 7f (P)
1:30 (1:32) (Class 6) (0-55,55) 4-Y-0+ **£1,706** (£503; £252) **Stalls** Low

Form RPR
0-20 **1** **Fun In The Sun**[12] 514 5-9-3 **55**.................... TPQueally 10 63
(A B Haynes) *hld up in tch: rdn and hdwy 2f out: chsd ldng pair and hanging lft fr over 1f out: led wl ins fnl f: r.o wl* **6/1**[1]
3-05 **2** *½* **Melt (IRE)**[20] 395 4-9-3 **55**....................(b[1]) DaneO'Neill 5 62
(R Hannon) *chsd ldr for 1f and again over 2f out: drvn and ev ch wl over 1f out: led ins fnl f: hdd and no ex wl ins fnl f* **8/1**
0-61 **3** *½* **Binnion Bay (IRE)**[13] 496 8-9-2 **54**....................(b) JerryO'Dwyer 6 60+
(J J Bridger) *stdd s: hld up towards rr: hdwy on inner jst over 2f out: nt clr run 1f out: squeezed through and r.o wl ins fnl f: nt rch ldrs* **7/1**[2]
00-6 **4** *¾* **Briannsta (IRE)**[2] 23 7-8-9 **47**....................(b) RichardThomas 9 51
(J E Long) *racd freely: led: hrd pressed and rdn wl over 1f out: hdd ins fnl f: no ex fnl 75yds* **14/1**
0014 **5** *1* **Jessica Wigmo**[12] 513 6-9-3 **55**.................... TolleyDean 8 56+
(A W Carroll) *t.k.h: hld up in last pair: hdwy 2f out: rdn over 1f out: r.o fnl f: nt rch ldrs* **7/1**[2]
5-06 **6** *nk* **Shava**[6] 587 9-8-5 **46** oh1.................... DuranFentiman[(3)] 1 46
(H J Evans) *chsd ldr after 1f tl over 2f out: kpt on u.p tl wknd fnl 75yds* **8/1**
3000 **7** *½* **Baba Ghanoush**[12] 513 7-8-8 **46** oh1....................(b) PaulDoe 3 45+
(M J Attwater) *chsd ldrs: rdn and unable qck jst over 2f out: kpt on same pce fnl f* **25/1**
-624 **8** *shd* **Inka Dancer (IRE)**[7] 575 7-9-0 **52**.................... FrankieMcDonald 7 51
(B Palling) *bhd: swtchd to outer over 1f out: r.o fnl f: nvr nr ldrs* **15/2**[3]
-005 **9** *3 ½* **Lake Sabina**[16] 460 4-8-12 **50**.................... JimCrowley 14 40
(M R Hoad) *in tch: rdn and unable qck over 2f out: wknd over 1f out* **12/1**
0-60 **10** *1* **Wynberg (IRE)**[11] 540 4-9-0 **52**....................(t) MickyFenton 13 40
(Stef Liddiard) *stdd and dropped in bhd after s: n.d* **12/1**
000- **11** *hd* **The Jailer**[97] 7382 6-9-1 **53**.................... VinceSlattery 11 40
(J G M O'Shea) *t.k.h: hld up in midfield: rdn and struggling 2f out: no ch after* **25/1**
60-0 **12** *hd* **Easy Wonder (GER)**[7] 575 4-8-10 **48**....................(p) ChrisCatlin 4 35
(I A Wood) *hld up in midfield: rdn and unable qck jst over 2f out: no ch fnl f* **12/1**
00-0 **13** *4* **Hilltop Legacy**[10] 552 6-8-8 **46** oh1.................... SimonWhitworth 2 23
(J R Jenkins) *racd in midfield on inner: pushed along 4f out: rdn and struggling over 2f out: wl bhd fnl f* **50/1**
00-0 **14** *1 ¼* **Siena**[9] 565 4-8-3 **46** oh1....................(v) AmyBaker[(5)] 12 20
(Mrs C A Dunnett) *towards rr: rdn 4f out: struggling over 2f out: sn wl bhd* **50/1**

1m 24.89s (0.09) **Going Correction** +0.125s/f (Slow) **14** Ran SP% **114.6**
Speed ratings (Par 101): **104,103,102,102,100 100,99,99,95,94 94,94,89,88**
toteswinger: 1&2 £9.20, 1&3 £6.40, 2&3 £8.10. CSF £48.20 CT £340.46 TOTE £5.90: £2.20, £2.40, £2.20; EX 57.40 Trifecta £214.60 Part won. Pool: £290.08 - 0.94 winning units..
Owner Ms C Berry **Bred** Miss L Johnstone **Trained** Limpley Stoke, Bath
■ Stewards' Enquiry : Dane O'Neill one-day ban: careless riding (Mar 11)
FOCUS
A moderate handicap run at a good pace. The winning time was 0.83 seconds quicker than the second division and the form is solid if limited.
Baba Ghanoush Official explanation: jockey said mare suffered interference in running

662 CHEDDAR PINK CLAIMING STKS 1m 2f (P)
2:00 (2:00) (Class 6) 3-Y-0 **£2,047** (£604; £302) **Stalls** Low

Form RPR
-454 **1** **Supernoverre (IRE)**[20] 389 3-8-9 67....................(p) JimCrowley 1 67
(Mrs A J Perrett) *led tl over 8f out: trckd ldrs after: nt clr run 2f out: rdn to chal ent fnl f: drvn to ld ins fnl f: r.o wl* **3/1**[2]
63-1 **2** *½* **Kiyari**[26] 332 3-8-4 64.................... JimmyQuinn 5 61
(M Botti) *hld up in midfield: hdwy on outer 2f out: rdn and qcknd to ld over 1f out: hdd and one pce ins fnl f* **5/2**[1]
-161 **3** *1 ¾* **True Britannia**[13] 506 3-8-10 66....................(v) AndrewElliott 4 63
(A M Hales) *hld up towards rr: hdwy on outer 2f out: rdn over 1f out: kpt on to go 3rd towards fin but nvr pce to threaten ldng pair* **11/2**[3]
51 **4** *¾* **Bromhead (USA)**[25] 343 3-9-7 67.................... GregFairley 3 73
(B J Meehan) *t.k.h: chsd ldrs: wnt 2nd over 6f out: rdn to ld jst over 2f out: hdd over 1f out: edgd rt ent fnl f: one pce after* **6/1**
603- **5** *1 ¾* **Augusta Gold (USA)**[120] 7011 3-9-5 71.................... ShaneKelly 6 67
(N P Littmoden) *trckd ldrs: effrt and hanging lft over 1f out: ev ch but one pce whn short of room and hmpd 1f out: no ch w ldrs after: eased towards fin* **7/1**
0-6 **6** *2* **Foxtrot Bravo (IRE)**[19] 403 3-8-6 0.................... LukeMorris 9 50
(P Winkworth) *t.k.h: hld up in tch towards rr: rdn 4f out: struggling u.p over 2f out: no ch w ldrs after* **50/1**
300- **7** *2 ½* **Hassadin**[99] 7353 3-8-9 62.................... TPQueally 2 48
(A B Haynes) *t.k.h: chsd ldr tl led over 8f out: rdn and hdd jst over 2f out: wknd u.p over 1f out* **12/1**
2-64 **8** *3 ¼* **Cwmni**[14] 492 3-8-1 45.................... FrankieMcDonald 7 34+
(B Palling) *awkward s and slowly away: a in rr: rdn and lost tch wl over 2f out* **33/1**
35 **9** *6* **Michelle (IRE)**[10] 547 3-8-2 0.................... ChrisCatlin 8 23
(P Butler) *t.k.h: stdd after s: hld up in last pair: rdn and lost tch over 2f out* **25/1**

2m 8.84s (2.24) **Going Correction** +0.125s/f (Slow) **9** Ran SP% **112.2**
Speed ratings (Par 95): **96,95,94,93,92 90,88,86,81**
toteswinger: 1&2 £2.90, 1&3 £4.00, 2&3 £3.70. CSF £10.36 TOTE £3.70: £1.10, £1.30, £2.00; EX 12.40 Trifecta £46.80 Pool: £311.32 - 4.05 winning units..Supernoverre was claimed by P. Howling for £8000.
Owner Cotton, James, Slade, Tracey **Bred** Derek Veitch And Saleh Ali Hammadi **Trained** Pulborough, W Sussex
■ Stewards' Enquiry : Greg Fairley two-day ban: careless riding (Mar 10-11)
FOCUS
A reasonable claimer but the early gallop was modest. The form looks reasonable with the first two rated close to their recent best.
Bromhead(USA) Official explanation: jockey said gelding ran too free
Augusta Gold(USA) Official explanation: jockey said colt hung left
Foxtrot Bravo(IRE) Official explanation: jockey said gelding hung right throughout
Cwmni Official explanation: jockey said filly missed the break

663 BLUE HEATH MAIDEN STKS 7f (P)
2:30 (2:31) (Class 5) 3-Y-0+ **£2,729** (£806; £403) **Stalls** Low

Form RPR
-322 **1** **Dance And Dance (IRE)**[13] 503 3-8-9 75.................... JamieSpencer 4 78+
(E F Vaughan) *mde all: clr after 2f out: rdn over 1f out: styd on: unchal* **8/13**[1]
-323 **2** *2 ¼* **Head Down**[10] 548 3-8-9 75.................... PatDobbs 9 72
(R Hannon) *chsd ldrs: wnt 2nd over 3f out: rdn and no imp fr over 1f out* **7/2**[2]
3 *2* **Volito** 3-8-9 0.................... JamieMoriarty 1 67+
(Jonjo O'Neill) *s.i.s: hld up towards rr: hdwy over 3f out: chsd ldng pair and rdn 2f out: hung lft and no imp fr over 1f out* **25/1**
60- **4** *5* **Sumani (FR)**[173] 5641 3-8-10 0 ow1.................... IanMongan 6 55+
(S Dow) *stdd after s: t.k.h: hld up in rr: rdn and hdwy 3f out: styd on steadily to go modest 4th ins fnl f: nvr nr ldrs* **20/1**
00- **5** *2 ½* **Alternative Choice (USA)**[120] 7011 3-8-9 0.................... JamesDoyle 7 46
(N P Littmoden) *a bhd: rdn over 2f out: nvr on terms* **14/1**
0-0 **6** *1 ¼* **Buail Isteach (IRE)**[33] 251 4-9-7 0.................... EdwardCreighton 2 44
(E J Creighton) *chsd ldrs: rdn over 2f out: wknd 2f out: sn wl btn* **66/1**
055 **7** *½* **Brett Vale (IRE)**[10] 552 3-8-9 0.................... StephenDonohoe 10 42
(Sir Mark Prescott) *a bhd: pushed along 4f out: nvr on terms* **33/1**
8 *hd* **Hector Spectre (IRE)** 3-8-9 0.................... MartinDwyer 5 41+
(B J Meehan) *s.i.s: a bhd: nudged along over 1f out: nvr on terms* **9/1**[3]
0 **9** *½* **Georgina Macrae**[20] 394 3-8-4 0.................... ChrisCatlin 3 35
(A M Balding) *chsd wnr tl over 3f out: steadily lost pl: wl bhd fnl f* **16/1**
0-0 **10** *9* **Lukatara (USA)**[31] 279 4-9-5 0.................... JemmaMarshall[(7)] 8 21
(Miss Sheena West) *racd in midfield: rdn and struggling over 3f out: t.o fnl f* **66/1**

1m 24.47s (-0.33) **Going Correction** +0.125s/f (Slow)
WFA 3 from 4yo 17lb **10** Ran SP% **121.2**
Speed ratings (Par 103): **106,103,101,95,92 91,90,90,89,79**
toteswinger: 1&2 £1.20, 1&3 £10.20, 2&3 £20.30. CSF £2.89 TOTE £1.50: £1.02, £1.40, £8.60; EX 3.40 Trifecta £34.50 Pool: £680.79 - 14.57 winning units..
Owner Mohammed Rashid **Bred** Darley **Trained** Newmarket, Suffolk
■ Stewards' Enquiry : Pat Dobbs one-day ban: used whip above shoulder height (Mar 10)
FOCUS
An ordinary maiden. Dance And Dance made all at a good pace and they finished strung out. The runner-up's recent form tends to limit things.

664 MEADOW CLARY MAIDEN STKS 6f (P)
3:00 (3:02) (Class 5) 3-Y-0 **£2,729** (£806; £403) **Stalls** Low

Form RPR
2 **1** **Five Gold Rings (IRE)**[18] 429 3-8-12 0.................... ShaneKelly 9 63+
(J A Osborne) *mde all: pushed along and in command ent fnl f: easily* **7/4**[1]
2 *1 ½* **Trip Switch** 3-9-3 0.................... MartinDwyer 1 60+
(W R Muir) *wnt rt s: chsd wnr: rdn and unable qck wl over 1f out: kpt on but nvr a threat to wnr* **6/1**[3]
3 *1 ¾* **L'Arco Baleno (IRE)** 3-8-5 0.................... HollyHall[(7)] 11 53+
(S A Callaghan) *wnt rt s and v.s.a: racd in detached last: clsd and in tch 3f out: hdwy and nt clr run wl over 1f out tl ent fnl f: r.o wl to go 3rd wl ins fnl f: nvr rchd ldrs* **16/1**
4 *¾* **Dream Catch Me (IRE)** 3-8-12 0.................... RobertHavlin 7 48
(J R Boyle) *v slwly away: bhd: rdn and hdwy 2f out: r.o fnl f: wnt 4th wl ins fnl f: nvr rchd ldrs* **16/1**
5-40 **5** *nk* **Kina Jazz**[20] 390 3-8-12 48.................... LukeMorris 8 47
(M E Rimmer) *chsd ldrs: rdn to chse ldng pair over 1f out: no imp: lost 2 pls wl ins fnl f* **12/1**
6 *1* **Keep Ringing (USA)** 3-8-9 0.................... GilmarPereira[(3)] 2 44
(W J Haggas) *s.i.s: racd in last trio: effrt on inner whn nt clr run and hmpd over 1f out: nvr nr ldrs* **11/4**[2]
00-0 **7** *1 ¼* **Thumberlina**[10] 552 3-8-12 45....................(v) TGMcLaughlin 3 40
(Mrs C A Dunnett) *in tch in midfield: rdn and effrt to chse ldrs over 1f out: wknd fnl f* **33/1**
8 *6* **Isshe A Lady** 3-8-7 0.................... JackDean[(5)] 6 22
(W G M Turner) *chsd ldrs: sn pushed along: rdn and wd bnd 2f out: sn wknd* **16/1**
9 *shd* **Peanut Girl (IRE)** 3-8-12 0.................... CatherineGannon 4 22
(B Palling) *v.s.a: a bhd: struggling u.p over 2f out* **33/1**
10 *21* **Chris's Jem** 3-8-12 0.................... SimonWhitworth 5 —
(J R Jenkins) *s.i.s: sn chsng ldrs: rdn 2f out: lost action and eased over 1f out: virtually p.u fnl f* **12/1**

1m 13.74s (1.84) **Going Correction** +0.125s/f (Slow) **10** Ran SP% **116.2**
Speed ratings (Par 97): **92,90,87,86,86 84,83,75,75,47**
toteswinger: 1&2 £2.60, 1&3 £7.00, 2&3 £17.50. CSF £12.66 TOTE £2.80: £1.10, £1.80, £5.70; EX 9.70 Trifecta £66.00 Pool: £451.07 - 5.05 winning units..
Owner P J D Pottinger & 12 Day Partners **Bred** South House Stud **Trained** Upper Lambourn, Berks
FOCUS
A field made up mainly of newcomers, and the bare form is limited ith moderate horses not that far away, but a few caught the eye.
Peanut Girl(IRE) Official explanation: jockey said filly resented the kickback

Chris's Jem Official explanation: jockey said filly lost her action

665 BET CHAMPIONS LEAGUE FOOTBALL - BETDAQ H'CAP 6f (P)
3:30 (3:30) (Class 4) (0-85,83) 4-Y-0+ **£4,857** (£1,445; £722; £360) **Stalls** Low

Form RPR

132 **1** **Wotashirtfull (IRE)**[14] 491 4-9-4 **80**.....................(p) MartinDwyer 3 86
(J R Boyle) *mde all: hrd pressed 2f out: drvn and battled on wl fnl f* **13/8**[1]

316- **2** *nk* **Louphole**[126] 6880 7-8-6 **68**..................... SimonWhitworth 5 73
(J R Jenkins) *stdd s: hld up in last pl: shkn up and hdwy 1f out: pushed along hands and heels fnl f: pressed wnr wl ins fnl f: hld last strides* **8/1**

0131 **3** *hd* **Grand Palace (IRE)**[13] 499 6-8-9 **71**.....................(v) DaneO'Neill 1 75
(D Shaw) *chsd wnr: shkn up 3f out: ev ch and drvn over 1f out: kpt pressing wnr but unable qck fnl f* **7/2**[3]

-614 **4** ½ **Resplendent Alpha**[5] 600 5-9-3 **79**..................... IanMongan 2 82
(P Howling) *stdd s: hld up in 3rd pl: effrt on inner over 1f ut: ev ch ins fnl f: no ex fnl 50yds* **7/4**[2]

1m 11.77s (-0.13) **Going Correction** +0.125s/f (Slow) 4 Ran SP% **107.8**
Speed ratings (Par 105): **105,104,104,103**
CSF £12.53 TOTE £2.20; EX 10.80.
Owner M Khan X2 **Bred** Luke O'Reilly **Trained** Epsom, Surrey

FOCUS
Ordinary form for the class, but it was still competitive and the four runners were separated by only around a length at the line.

666 BET ASIAN H'CAPS - BETDAQ HANDICAP (DIV II) 7f (P)
4:00 (4:02) (Class 6) (0-55,55) 4-Y-0+ **£1,706** (£503; £252) **Stalls** Low

Form RPR

00-0 **1** **Silidan**[46] 97 6-8-12 **50**..................... PatDobbs 12 57
(G L Moore) *stdd s: t.k.h: hld up in rr: hdwy on outer 2f out: rdn and r.o wl to ld wl ins fnl f* **7/1**[3]

0-00 **2** ½ **Rio L'Oren (IRE)**[11] 531 4-9-3 **55**.....................(b) LukeMorris 1 61
(N J Vaughan) *s.i.s: sn rcvrd and led after 1f: rdn 2f out: edgd rt u.p ins fnl f: hdd and no ex wl ins fnl f* **8/1**

-464 **3** 1¼ **Cavalry Guard (USA)**[20] 395 5-8-6 **49**.....................(b) AmyBaker(5) 14 52
(T D McCarthy) *hld up towards rr: hdwy into midfield 4f out: lost pl and rr again over 2f out: c wd over 1f out: r.o wl to go 3rd towards fin: nt rch ldrs* **11/2**[1]

06-0 **4** ½ **Running Buck (USA)**[47] 87 4-8-9 **47**.....................(v) JimmyQuinn 2 49
(A Bailey) *s.i.s: sn rcvrd to chse ldrs: rdn and effrt jst over 2f out: hrd drvn to chse ldr 1f out: lost 2nd ins fnl f: one pce* **8/1**

0-34 **5** ½ **Chalentina**[27] 308 6-8-1 **46** oh1..................... PNolan(7) 10 46+
(J E Long) *stdd s: hld up in rr on inner: nt clr run jst over 2f out tl over 1f out: rn fnl f: nt rch ldrs* **12/1**

300- **6** *nk* **Sands Of Barra (IRE)**[162] 5965 6-9-2 **54**..................... TomEaves 9 54
(I W McInnes) *t.k.h: rdn over 2f out: kpt on same pce u.p fr over 1f out* **11/2**[1]

6-04 **7** *nk* **Admirals Way**[15] 471 4-9-1 **53**..................... GregFairley 11 52
(C N Kellett) *in tch in midfield: hdwy and rdn 2f out: chsd ldrs and hrd rdn ent fnl f: one pce after* **6/1**[2]

8 *hd* **Scholars Lass (IRE)**[95] 7412 4-8-11 **49** oh1 ow3......... PaulMulrennan 4 47
(J Balding) *plld hrd: led for 1f: chsd ldrs after tl over 1f out: hrd rdn and wknd ins fnl f* **33/1**

-006 **9** ¾ **Stormburst (IRE)**[27] 314 5-8-9 **47**..................... NeilChalmers 7 44
(A J Chamberlain) *hld up in rr: swtchd rt and hdwy over 1f out: styd on but nvr nr ldrs* **16/1**

026- **10** *nk* **Never Sold Out (IRE)**[201] 4794 4-9-0 **52**..................... VinceSlattery 5 48
(J G M O'Shea) *hld up in midfield on inner: rdn and effrt over 1f out: sn no imp* **25/1**

000- **11** *nk* **Fly In Johnny (IRE)**[117] 7088 4-8-8 **46** oh1............. RichardKingscote 6 41
(J J Bridger) *in tch: rdn jst over 2f out: wknd u.p over 1f out* **16/1**

0-01 **12** ½ **Over To You Bert**[15] 480 10-8-12 **55**..................... MCGeran(5) 3 49
(R J Hodges) *t.k.h: chsd ldrs: rdn jst over 2f out: wknd over 1f out* **11/2**[1]

0/00 **13** 2¾ **Cate Washington**[15] 475 6-8-3 **46** oh1..................... DeanHeslop(5) 13 33
(Mrs L Williamson) *racd wd: a bhd: rdn and struggling over 2f out:* **66/1**

1m 25.72s (0.92) **Going Correction** +0.125s/f (Slow) 13 Ran SP% **122.9**
Speed ratings (Par 101): **99,98,97,96,95 95,95,94,94,93 93,92,89**
toteswinger: 1&2 £17.10, 1&3 £16.10, 2&3 £12.50. CSF £63.10 CT £349.54 TOTE £9.30: £3.00, £3.50, £1.80; EX 101.40 TRIFECTA Not won..
Owner Prix Mature Racing **Bred** Larkwood Stud **Trained** Lower Beeding, W Sussex

FOCUS
A moderate affair and the slower of the two divisions by 0.83 seconds. The form is limited and they finished in a bunch, with the runner-up the best guide to the form.
Scholars Lass(IRE) Official explanation: jockey said filly ran too free
Over To You Bert Official explanation: jockey said gelding ran too free

667 BET MULTIPLES - BETDAQ H'CAP 7f (P)
4:30 (4:40) (Class 6) (0-60,60) 3-Y-0 **£2,047** (£604; £302) **Stalls** Low

Form RPR

003- **1** **Sarasota Sunshine**[111] 7198 3-9-1 **57**..................... ShaneKelly 3 63
(N P Littmoden) *in tch: rdn and hdwy to chse ldng pair 2f out: plld out over 1f out: rdn and r.o wl to ld towards fin* **4/1**[2]

-644 **2** ¾ **River Rye (IRE)**[38] 200 3-9-0 **56**.....................(p) LPKeniry 7 60
(J S Moore) *chsd ldr: upsides over 2f out: rdn 2f out: drvn to ld ent fnl f: hdd and nt pce of wnr towards fin* **9/1**

60-2 **3** 1 **Elsie Jo (IRE)**[6] 594 3-8-9 **51**..................... NickyMackay 4 52+
(M Wigham) *plld hrd: sn led: jnd over 2f out: rdn wl over 1f out: hdd ent fnl f: no ex fnl 100yds* **5/4**[1]

0-40 **4** ½ **Hint Of Honey**[18] 425 3-9-1 **57**..................... TPQueally 1 57
(A G Newcombe) *in tch effrt and rdn on inner over 1f out: kpt on same pce fnl f* **14/1**

000- **5** *shd* **Daily Double**[124] 6924 3-9-1 **57**..................... DaneO'Neill 8 57+
(D K Ivory) *stdd s: hld up in last trio: rdn wl over 1f out: running on whn nt clr run and swtchd lft ins fnl f: r.o but nt rch ldrs* **8/1**[3]

60-2 **6** *nk* **Miss Mojito (IRE)**[36] 214 3-9-3 **59**..................... ChrisCatlin 5 58
(J W Hills) *t.k.h: chsd ldng pair: hdwy and ev ch whn hung rt bnd 2f out: one pce fr over 1f out* **4/1**[2]

000- **7** 5 **Lend A Light**[94] 7424 3-9-4 **60**..................... PatrickMathers 6 45
(I W McInnes) *stdd after s: plld hrd: hld up in last trio: rdn and struggling jst over 2f out* **25/1**

0-20 **8** 6 **Yellow River (USA)**[38] 200 3-9-1 **57**..................... EdwardCreighton 2 26
(E J Creighton) *awkward s: hed up in last trio: lost tch over 2f out* **33/1**

1m 28.12s (3.32) **Going Correction** +0.125s/f (Slow) 8 Ran SP% **119.0**
Speed ratings (Par 95): **86,85,84,83,83 82,77,70**
toteswinger: 1&2 £5.20, 1&3 £3.30, 2&3 £3.40. CSF £41.05 CT £70.97 TOTE £5.10: £1.10, £1.90, £1.70; EX 44.10 Trifecta £294.10 Pool: £564.38 - 1.42 winning units..
Owner Franconson Partners **Bred** London Thoroughbred S'Vces Ltd & West Bl **Trained** Newmarket, Suffolk

FOCUS
A moderate three-year-old handicap run at a very steady pace.

668 SHORE DOCK APPRENTICE H'CAP 2m (P)
5:00 (5:10) (Class 5) (0-75,75) 4-Y-0+ **£2,900** (£856; £428) **Stalls** Low

Form RPR

151- **1** **Wyeth**[84] 7520 5-8-13 **63**.....................(b) JemmaMarshall(3) 5 75+
(G L Moore) *t.k.h: hld up in tch: swtchd rt and hdwy to press ldr 2f out: led ent fnl f: pushed clr: comf* **3/1**[2]

-031 **2** 2¼ **Sir Liam (USA)**[25] 346 5-8-6 **56**..................... RossAtkinson(3) 6 63
(Tom Dascombe) *t.k.h: hld up in last pair: hdwy over 3f out: rdn to ld over 1f out: hdd ent fnl f: drvn and nt pce of wnr fnl f* **4/1**[3]

0/0- **3** 4 **Dallool**[42] 4398 8-8-12 **59**..................... JackDean 4 62
(P M Phelan) *in rr: clsd and in tch 12f out: rdn and outpcd wl over 1f out: wnt modest 3rd ins fnl f* **12/1**

5-16 **4** 1¾ **Dramatic Solo**[36] 219 4-8-13 **69**.....................(b) MartinLane(3) 8 69
(K R Burke) *in tch: chsd ldr 9f out: led over 6f out: rdn jst over 2f out: hdd over 1f out: sn wknd* **2/1**[1]

24-0 **5** 7 **Black Tor Figarro (IRE)**[25] 341 4-8-10 **63**..................... JackMitchell 3 55
(B W Duke) *chsd ldr tl 9f out: and again wl over 3f out: rdn and struggling whn short of room briefly ent fnl 2f: sn wl btn* **16/1**

0-04 **6** *shd* **Up In Arms (IRE)**[19] 402 5-8-13 **60**.....................(b) LukeMorris 2 52+
(P Winkworth) *rel to r and v.s.a: clsd and in tch 12f out: rdn and wknd over 2f out* **7/1**

0-45 **7** 28 **Mulaazem**[13] 502 6-8-10 **57**.....................(bt) TravisBlock 1 15
(A M Hales) *led: stdd pce 12f out: hdd over 6f out: drvn and wknd wl over 3f out* **10/1**

3m 25.47s (-0.23) **Going Correction** +0.125s/f (Slow)
WFA 4 from 5yo+ 6lb 7 Ran SP% **113.5**
Speed ratings (Par 103): **105,103,101,101,97 97,83**
toteswinger: 1&2 £2.40, 1&3 £8.00, 2&3 £11.90. CSF £15.17 CT £122.31 TOTE £3.10: £1.60, £2.50; EX 11.00 Trifecta £182.60 Pool: £246.86 - 0.99 winning units. Place 6: £17.92 Place 5: £8.22.
Owner D R Hunnisett **Bred** Lael Stables **Trained** Lower Beeding, W Sussex

FOCUS
The pace was muddling early and the form is weak, with the runner-up setting the standard.
T/Plt: £21.80 to a £1 stake. Pool: £58,587.26. 1,956.57 winning tickets. T/Qpdt: £8.60 to a £1 stake. Pool: £3,307.66. 282.20 winning tickets. SP

[596]KEMPTON (A.W) (R-H)
Wednesday, February 25

OFFICIAL GOING: Standard
Wind: Virtually nil

669 WEATHERBYS ALL-WEATHER "HANDS AND HEELS" APPRENTICE H'CAP 1m 3f (P)
6:50 (6:50) (Class 6) (0-55,55) 4-Y-0+ **£2,047** (£604; £302) **Stalls** High

Form RPR

5-11 **1** **Lytham (IRE)**[14] 494 8-8-12 **54**..................... TobyAtkinson(3) 9 63+
(A W Carroll) *hld up in rr: stdy hdwy over 3f out: qcknd to chal ins fnl 2f: led wl over 1f out: in command thrght fnl f: readily* **3/1**[1]

03-2 **2** 2 **Noah Jameel**[14] 494 7-8-13 **55**..................... DavidKenny(3) 7 61
(A G Newcombe) *hld up in rr: stdy hdwy fr 3f out: drvn to chse wnr jst ins fnl f: kpt on but a wl hld* **11/2**[2]

6-32 **3** 2¼ **King Of The Beers (USA)**[13] 514 5-8-12 **54**.................(p) SPRyan(3) 6 56
(R A Harris) *chsd ldrs: rdn over 2f out: styd on same pce fnl f* **11/1**

0-51 **4** ¾ **Tecktal (FR)**[11] 541 6-9-0 **53**..................... DebraEngland 14 54
(P M Phelan) *chsd ldrs: drvn to chal fr 2f out: wknd ins fnl f* **9/1**

60/5 **5** *hd* **King Gabriel (IRE)**[34] 248 7-8-10 **49**..................... CharlesEddery 3 50
(Andrew Turnell) *led: rdn over 2f out: hdd wl over 1f out: wknd ins fnl f* **12/1**

1550 **6** ½ **Ben Bacchus (IRE)**[12] 528 7-8-11 **53**..................... KierenFox(3) 13 53
(P W Hiatt) *chsd ldrs: rdn and outpcd over 2f out: kpt on again fnl f* **10/1**

4-00 **7** ¾ **Altos Reales**[11] 541 5-8-9 **51**..................... MatthewLawson(3) 12 50
(J G Given) *mid-div: rdn 3f out: hdwy 2f out: nvr rchd ldrs and sn one pce* **11/1**

-425 **8** 3 **Play Up Pompey**[14] 494 7-9-1 **54**..................... RichardRowe 10 48
(J J Bridger) *chsd ldrs: rdn over 2f out: wknd 1f out* **16/1**

14P- **9** 1½ **Bundle Up**[61] 6421 6-8-7 **49**..................... PaulPickard(3) 4 41
(P D Evans) *in rr: sme hdwy on outside 3f out: sn rdn: nvr in contention* **25/1**

0653 **10** 3½ **Turkish Sultan (IRE)**[8] 578 6-8-3 **47** ow1.................(p) JoshWall(5) 11 44+
(J M Bradley) *sddle slipped: a towards rr* **25/1**

0-63 **11** 7 **Fateful Attraction**[6] 601 6-8-8 **47** oh1 ow1.................(b) DTDaSilva 2 22
(I A Wood) *in rr: hdwy on outside 4f out: nvr rchd ldrs and wknd over 2f out* **8/1**[3]

0-56 **12** 2 **Touch Of Style (IRE)**[34] 248 5-8-11 **53**.................(p) NathanAlison(3) 1 25
(J R Boyle) *chsd ldrs: rdn over 3 out: wknd 2f out* **8/1**[3]

25-0 **13** 10 **Hennessy Island (USA)**[46] 118 4-9-0 **55**..................... PNolan 8 11
(T G Mills) *s.i.s: a bhd* **12/1**

2m 21.52s (-0.38) **Going Correction** +0.01s/f (Slow)
WFA 4 from 5yo+ 2lb 13 Ran SP% **127.3**
Speed ratings (Par 101): **101,99,97,97,97 96,96,94,93,90 85,83,76**
toteswinger: 1&2 £3.80, 1&3 £4.60, 2&3 £7.80. CSF £19.64 CT £167.34 TOTE £4.50: £1.80, £3.50, £3.20; EX 18.50.
Owner Patrick McGee **Bred** Mrs A S O'Brien And Lars Pearson **Trained** Cropthorne, Worcs
■ Stewards' Enquiry : Charles Eddery 1st incident, two-day ban: careless riding (Mar 11-12); 2nd incident, caution: careless riding.

FOCUS
A competitive race for the grade. This was restricted to apprentices who had not ridden more than the ten winners, and whips were allowed to be carried but not used. They seemed to go an even pace.
Turkish Sultan(IRE) Official explanation: jockey said saddle slipped

670 DIGIBET MEDIAN AUCTION MAIDEN STKS 1m 3f (P)
7:20 (7:22) (Class 6) 3-5-Y-0 **£2,047** (£604; £302) **Stalls** High

Form RPR

6 **1** **Soul Singer**[17] 455 3-8-0 0..................... NickyMackay 9 51
(J G Portman) *in rr: rdn and hdwy to ld ins fnl 2f: rdn out fnl f* **10/1**

-0 **2** 2 **Rannoch Rose (IRE)**[9] 570 3-8-0 0..................... CatherineGannon 6 47
(J L Spearing) *led 2f: styd chsng ldr: rdn to chal fr 2f out: outpcd by wnr fnl f* **33/1**

60-6 **3** ¾ **Dawn Wind**[9] 567 4-9-7 48 ....(bt) NCallan 5 50
(I A Wood) *in rr after 3f: hdwy 4f out: styd on fnl 2f to go 3rd ins fnl f but nvr gng pce to be competitive* **6/1**[3]

4 1¾ **Rossatron** 3-8-0 0 .... AmyBaker(5) 1 48
(T T Clement) *slowly away: plld hrd and led after 2f: rdn 3f out: hdd ins fnl 2f: hung bdly lft fnl f* **20/1**

5 ¾ **Cardinal James (IRE)**[58] 5-10-0 0 .... FergusSweeney 8 51
(Miss Tor Sturgis) *hld up in rr: stdy hdwy on outside over 3f out: rdn over 2f out: nvr gng pce to be competitive and hung lft fnl f* **4/1**[2]

55-5 **6** nse **Forty Thirty (IRE)**[17] 455 3-8-5 68 .... EdwardCreighton 2 46
(M R Channon) *t.k.h: chsd ldrs: rdn over 2f out and sn fnd no ex* **11/10**[1]

000- **7** 6 **Treasure Islands (IRE)**[270] 2613 4-9-4 55 .... DominicFox(3) 7 35
(S W Hall) *plld hrd: rdn 3f out: nvr in contention* **14/1**

00/ **8** 11 **Double Exposure**[799] 6867 5-10-0 0 .... RobertHavlin 4 20
(Jamie Poulton) *bhd most of way* **16/1**

P- **9** 17 **Wild By Nature**[151] 6280 4-9-7 0 .... JerryO'Dwyer 3 —
(P Leech) *chsd ldrs: rdn and wknd 4f out* **66/1**

2m 23.55s (1.65) **Going Correction** +0.01s/f (Slow)
WFA 3 from 4yo 23lb 4 from 5yo 2lb **9 Ran SP% 112.7**
Speed ratings (Par 101): **94,92,92,90,90 90,85,77,65**
toteswinger: 1&2 £17.00, 1&3 £9.90, 2&3 £33.80. CSF £278.99 TOTE £6.60: £1.80, £4.10, £2.00; EX 163.10.
Owner Hockham Racing **Bred** R C Dollar And Partners **Trained** Compton, Berks

FOCUS
An extremely moderate maiden contest – the winning time was 2.03 seconds slower than 46-55 handicap won by the 54-rated Lytham – and not form to dwell on.
Dawn Wind Official explanation: jockey said filly ran too free
Cardinal James(IRE) Official explanation: jockey said gelding hung left
Double Exposure Official explanation: trainer said gelding had bled from the nose

671 DIGIBET.COM CLAIMING STKS 7f (P)
7:50 (7:50) (Class 6) 3-Y-0+ **£2,047** (£604; £302) **Stalls High**

Form RPR

6-21 **1** **Ravi River (IRE)**[8] 576 5-9-12 75 .... RichardKingscote 5 85+
(Tom Dascombe) *disp 2nd: drvn and qcknd to ld 1f out: sn in command: readily* **5/4**[1]

3411 **2** 1¾ **Obe Royal**[13] 519 5-9-6 71 ....(b) PaulDoe 3 75
(P D Evans) *trckd ldrs: hdwy on ins to ld 2f out: hdd 1f out and sn one pce* **8/1**

-113 **3** ½ **Jake The Snake (IRE)**[3] 650 8-9-6 74 .... AmyBaker(5) 2 82+
(A W Carroll) *plunged stalls: slowly away and lost 10 l: rapid hdwy on outside over 2f out to dispute 2nd jst ins fnl f: sn no ex and one pce* **7/4**[2]

20-0 **4** 5 **Sam's Cross (IRE)**[21] 398 4-9-10 73 ....(v[1]) DarrenWilliams 4 65
(K R Burke) *led: rdn 3f out: hdd 2f out: wknd over 1f out* **15/2**[3]

4-06 **5** 14 **Yes One (IRE)**[40] 195 5-9-11 75 .... NCallan 1 31
(K A Ryan) *disp 2nd: rdn and wknd over 2f out* **8/1**

1m 25.73s (-0.27) **Going Correction** +0.01s/f (Slow) **5 Ran SP% 114.8**
Speed ratings (Par 101): **101,99,98,92,76**
CSF £12.19 TOTE £2.10: £1.10, £3.70; EX 6.90.
Owner M Khan X2 **Bred** Gainsborough Stud Management Ltd **Trained** Lambourn, Berks

FOCUS
A small field, but a decent claimer. Although it's hard to be sure, Jake The Snake probably would have won had he not lost around eight lengths when ducking as the stalls opened.
Jake The Snake(IRE) Official explanation: jockey said gelding missed the break

672 DIGIBET CASINO H'CAP 7f (P)
8:20 (8:20) (Class 4) (0-85,85) 3-Y-0 **£4,727** (£1,406; £702; £351) **Stalls High**

Form RPR

341- **1** **Markyg (USA)**[133] 6731 3-9-7 85 .... FergusSweeney 4 94+
(K R Burke) *trckd ldrs: rdn and str run over 1f out: led fnl 110yds: r.o strly* **2/1**[1]

-532 **2** 2 **Grand Honour (IRE)**[5] 629 3-8-11 75 .... JimmyQuinn 7 77
(P Howling) *chsd ldrs: drvn and slt ld 1f out: hdd and one pce fnl 110yds* **7/2**[2]

2-21 **3** hd **Auld Arty (FR)**[28] 315 3-8-12 76 ....(p) RobertHavlin 3 77
(T G Mills) *led: rdn over 2f out: hdd 1f out: styd on same pce ins fnl f* **7/1**

630- **4** 1 **Asian Tale (IRE)**[127] 6886 3-8-8 72 .... PaulDoe 5 70
(P D Evans) *bmpd s: bhd: pushed along over 2f out: styd on fnl f but nt rch ldrs* **33/1**

40-1 **5** 1¼ **Emirates World (IRE)**[25] 356 3-8-13 77 .... JoeFanning 2 72
(M Johnston) *chsd ldrs: rdn 2f out: fnd no ex over 1f out and sn btn* **7/2**[2]

61-0 **6** nk **Give Us A Song (USA)**[21] 397 3-8-4 68 .... LukeMorris 6 62
(J S Moore) *wnt lft s: in rr: rdn and no imp on ldrs 2f out* **12/1**

25-3 **7** 1 **Rio Royale (IRE)**[12] 532 3-8-12 76 .... JimCrowley 1 67
(Mrs A J Perrett) *t.k.h in rr: rdn over 2f out: nvr in contention* **5/1**[3]

1m 26.41s (0.41) **Going Correction** +0.01s/f (Slow) **7 Ran SP% 117.6**
Speed ratings (Par 99): **97,94,94,93,91 91,90**
toteswinger: 1&2 £2.40, 1&3 £8.20, 2&3 £4.00. CSF £9.71 TOTE £2.50: £1.60, £2.10; EX 9.60.
Owner Mrs Maura Gittins **Bred** Robert S Evans **Trained** Middleham Moor, N Yorks

FOCUS
Just a fair three-year-old handicap, but an impressive winner.

673 JUMP RACING HERE ON SATURDAY H'CAP 6f (P)
8:50 (8:51) (Class 6) (0-65,64) 3-Y-0 **£2,047** (£604; £302) **Stalls High**

Form RPR

12-4 **1** **Song Of Praise**[28] 317 3-9-2 62 .... JimmyQuinn 5 67
(M Blanshard) *hld up in tch: drvn and qcknd on rails over 2f out to ld appr fnl f: hld on all out* **9/1**

00-1 **2** hd **Perfect Class**[35] 229 3-9-3 63 .... IanMongan 8 68
(C G Cox) *chsd ldrs: rdn over 2f out: styd on wl u.p thrght fnl f nt quite get up* **9/4**[1]

525 **3** hd **Divine Force**[21] 394 3-9-1 61 .... ShaneKelly 4 65+
(J A Osborne) *hld up in rr: rapid hdwy over 1f out: str run u.p thrght fnl f: gng on cl home but nt quite get up* **11/4**[2]

630- **4** 1½ **Celtic Rebel (IRE)**[91] 7451 3-8-12 58 .... PatCosgrave 3 58
(S A Callaghan) *in rr: rdn and hdwy on ins 2f out: drvn to chse ldrs jst ins fnl f: sn one pce* **5/1**

4455 **5** 2 **Ruby Tallulah**[9] 568 3-9-4 64 .... LPKeniry 7 58
(C R Dore) *led: drvn along over 2f out: hdd & wknd appr fnl f* **16/1**

5-02 **6** 2 **Lovely Steps (USA)**[7] 583 3-8-4 50 ....(b) ChrisCatlin 2 38
(D M Simcock) *in rr: rdn and and no imp on ldrs over 2f out* **4/1**[3]

1342 **7** 2½ **Just The Lady**[10] 560 3-9-1 61 .... StephenDonohoe 6 41
(D Nicholls) *plld hrd: chsd ldrs tl wknd over 2f out* **14/1**

00-3 **8** 2¼ **Simple Rhythm**[30] 293 3-9-4 64 .... GeorgeBaker 1 37
(N Tinkler) *plld hrd: chsd ldrs: wknd qckly 2f out* **11/1**

1m 12.88s (-0.22) **Going Correction** +0.01s/f (Slow) **8 Ran SP% 125.0**
Speed ratings (Par 95): **101,100,100,98,95 93,89,86**
toteswinger: 1&2 £6.20, 1&3 £6.10, 2&3 £2.50. CSF £32.57 CT £76.05 TOTE £9.70: £3.50, £1.10, £1.50; EX 32.30.
Owner Tom Wellman **Bred** Whitsbury Manor Stud **Trained** Upper Lambourn, Berks

FOCUS
A modest but competitive sprint handicap. The early pace was just ordinary.

674 PANORAMIC BAR & RESTAURANT H'CAP 1m (P)
9:20 (9:24) (Class 6) (0-50,50) 4-Y-0+ **£2,047** (£604; £302) **Stalls High**

Form RPR

10-0 **1** **Whodunit (UAE)**[49] 81 5-8-12 50 ....(b) ChrisCatlin 10 61
(P W Hiatt) *mde all: drvn clr over 2f out: styd on strly fnl f* **11/2**[2]

35-2 **2** 2½ **Kielty's Folly**[12] 537 5-8-8 46 oh1 .... GrahamGibbons 12 52+
(B P J Baugh) *in tch: hdwy over 2f out: chsd wnr and hrd drvn over 1f out: no imp* **5/2**[1]

2243 **3** 1¼ **Amber Moon**[20] 405 4-8-12 50 ....(b) ShaneKelly 8 53
(J A Osborne) *chsd wnr: rdn over 2f out: one pce fr over 1f out* **11/2**[2]

1044 **4** nse **Flamestone**[13] 510 5-8-10 48 .... StephenDonohoe 11 51+
(A E Price) *in rr: hdwy on ins over 2f out: styd on wl fnl f: gng on cl home* **8/1**[3]

0450 **5** ½ **Inquisitress**[18] 443 5-8-9 47 ....(b[1]) NeilChalmers 5 49
(J J Bridger) *in rr tl hdwy over 2f out: styd on fnl f but nvr gng pce to rch ldrs* **8/1**[3]

0236 **6** ½ **Mr Rev**[16] 473 6-8-9 47 ....(b) LukeMorris 9 48
(J M Bradley) *chsd ldrs: rdn over 2f out: wknd fnl f* **11/1**

0-04 **7** 5 **Bet Noir (IRE)**[15] 483 4-8-12 50 .... TolleyDean 1 40
(A W Carroll) *bhd tl sme prog fnl 2f* **25/1**

000- **8** nse **Flipacoin**[231] 3847 4-8-8 46 oh1 .... NickyMackay 4 36
(S Dow) *a towards rr* **50/1**

6165 **9** 1½ **Kinsman (IRE)**[13] 513 12-8-5 48 ....(p) AmyBaker(5) 2 34
(T D McCarthy) *a towards rr* **8/1**[3]

/06- **10** 3 **Where To Now**[185] 5320 4-8-8 46 oh1 ....(v[1]) JimmyQuinn 3 26
(Mrs C A Dunnett) *nvr bttr than mid-div: bhd fnl 3f* **33/1**

0004 **11** 3½ **Countrywide Comet (IRE)**[8] 581 4-8-8 46 oh1 .... TomEaves 7 18
(P Howling) *chsd ldrs: rdn on outside 3f out: sn wknd* **20/1**

-00 **12** 5 **Daggerman**[29] 302 4-8-6 49 ow1 .... GabrielHannon(5) 13 10
(R Curtis) *chsd ldrs 5f* **12/1**

1m 39.04s (-0.76) **Going Correction** +0.01s/f (Slow) **12 Ran SP% 122.2**
Speed ratings (Par 101): **103,100,99,99,98 98,93,93,91,88 85,80**
toteswinger: 1&2 £7.40, 1&3 £6.40, 2&3 £3.40. CSF £18.75 CT £73.38 TOTE £8.20: £3.30, £1.40, £1.70; EX 20.00 Place 6: £39.66, Place 5: £19.76..
Owner Exors of the Late John Hedges **Bred** Darley **Trained** Hook Norton, Oxon

FOCUS
A moderate handicap run at a decent pace.
Whodunit(UAE) Official explanation: trainer said, regarding the apparent improvement in form, that the gelding had benefited from a break since its last run.
T/Plt: £93.60 to a £1 stake. Pool: £81,958.97. 639.02 winning tickets. T/Qpdt: £6.10 to a £1 stake. Pool: £6,543.85. 790.93 winning tickets. ST

654 WOLVERHAMPTON (A.W) (L-H)
Wednesday, February 25

OFFICIAL GOING: Standard changing to standard to fast after race 2 (3.00)
Wind: Light half-behind Weather: Fine

675 BETDAQ ON 0870 178 1221 H'CAP 5f 216y(P)
2:30 (2:31) (Class 6) (0-55,55) 4-Y-0+ **£2,047** (£604; £302) **Stalls Low**

Form RPR

60-4 **1** **Great Knight (IRE)**[26] 352 4-8-10 53 .... JamesDoyle 8 62
(S Kirk) *hld up: hdwy over 1f out: hrd rdn to ld ins fnl f: r.o wl* **6/1**

-053 **2** 2 **Imperial Djay (IRE)**[12] 540 4-8-12 55 .... RobertWinston 3 58
(G J Smith) *bhd: hdwy over 1f out: wnt 2nd ins fnl f: nt trble wnr* **9/2**[3]

15-1 **3** ¾ **Many Welcomes**[8] 575 4-8-12 55 6ex .... AndrewElliott 9 56
(B P J Baugh) *in rr: hdwy fnl f: r.o* **7/1**

0-00 **4** 1¾ **Mr Skipiton (IRE)**[40] 198 4-8-9 52 ....(v[1]) StephenCarson 12 48
(B J McMath) *a.p: rdn wl over 1f out: edgd lft and btn ins fnl f* **33/1**

3-43 **5** 1½ **Argentine (IRE)**[24] 367 5-8-9 52 .... GregFairley 5 43+
(L Lungo) *w ldrs: led over 2f out: rdn over 1f out: hdd & wknd ins fnl f* **4/1**[2]

6000 **6** nk **Piccolo Diamante (USA)**[6] 608 5-8-9 52 ....(t) DaleGibson 4 42
(S Parr) *s.i.s: in rr: sme late prog: nrst fin* **22/1**

-036 **7** 1 **Tamino (IRE)**[14] 496 6-8-10 53 ....(t) JimmyQuinn 7 40
(P Howling) *w ldrs: ev ch over 2f out: sn rdn: wknd fnl f* **13/2**

-051 **8** ½ **All You Need (IRE)**[8] 574 5-8-5 51 6ex ....(p) DuranFentiman(3) 1 37
(R Hollinshead) *hld up in tch: rdn and wknd ins fnl f* **10/3**[1]

-045 **9** 5 **Blakeshall Quest**[15] 487 9-8-9 52 ....(b) TomEaves 6 23
(R Brotherton) *led: hdd over 2f out: sn rdn: wknd wl over 1f out* **18/1**

06-0 **R** **Kirkie (USA)**[11] 554 4-8-12 55 ....(v[1]) CatherineGannon 13 —
(S Parr) *ref to r: tk no part* **33/1**

1m 14.32s (-0.68) **Going Correction** -0.025s/f (Stan) **10 Ran SP% 116.9**
Speed ratings (Par 101): **103,100,99,97,95 94,93,92,85,—**
toteswinger: 1&2 £7.20, 1&3 £8.70, 2&3 £3.20. CSF £32.58 CT £196.52 TOTE £8.90: £2.20, £2.20, £1.80; EX 49.30 Trifecta £133.10 Pool: £282.41 - 1.57 winning units..
Owner Senta Wong **Bred** Max Morris **Trained** Upper Lambourn, Berks

FOCUS
A very modest sprint handicap in which the leaders seemed to go off too fast, and the first three home came from off the pace.
Blakeshall Quest Official explanation: trainer said mare was unsuited by the Polytrack surface

676 HOTEL & CONFERENCING AT WOLVERHAMPTON (S) STKS 5f 20y(P)
3:00 (3:00) (Class 6) 4-Y-0+ **£2,047** (£604; £302) **Stalls Low**

Form RPR

0-30 **1** **Desperate Dan**[13] 518 8-9-0 67 ....(v[1]) TPQueally 1 74
(A B Haynes) *chsd ldrs: wnt 2nd wl over 1f out: rdn to ld last strides* **15/2**[3]

0213 **2** hd **Woodcote (IRE)**[7] 589 7-9-5 74 ....(vt) GeorgeBaker 7 78
(P R Chamings) *led: rdn ins fnl f: hdd last strides* **5/2**[2]

636 **3** 6 **Decider (USA)**[7] 589 6-9-0 60 ....(p) JoeFanning 8 52
(R A Harris) *chsd ldr tl wl over 1f out: sn rdn and edgd lft: wknd fnl f* **10/1**

63-3 **4** ½ **Yungaburra (IRE)**[26] 351 5-9-5 84 ....(t) RobertWinston 10 55+
(S Parr) *bhd: rdn wl over 1f out: kpt on to take 4th nr post: fin lame* **5/4**[1]

0253 **5** hd **Mr Loire**[8] 574 5-9-0 45 ....(b) JerryO'Dwyer 2 49
(K G Wingrove) *bhd: hdwy on ins wl over 1f out: one pce fnl f* **22/1**

0445 **6** 3/4 **Spanish Ace**[8] 574 8-8-9 44........(b) JackDean(5) 5 46
(J M Bradley) *chsd ldrs tl rdn and wknd over 2f out* **40/1**
030- **7** 3 3/4 **Lytton**[86] 7513 4-9-0 62........(p) PaulHanagan 9 33
(R Ford) *dwlt: a bhd* **10/1**
0-60 **8** *shd* **Fire Up The Band**[12] 535 10-8-9 52........ SladeO'Hara(5) 3 33
(A Berry) *chsd ldrs tl rdn and wknd over 2f out* **22/1**
61.35 secs (-0.95) **Going Correction** -0.025s/f (Stan) **8** Ran SP% **114.1**
Speed ratings (Par 101): **106,105,96,95,94 93,87,87**
toteswinger: 1&2 £3.50, 1&3 £9.50, 2&3 £6.00. CSF £26.03 TOTE £7.70: £1.80, £1.40, £3.90; EX 28.20 Trifecta £109.90 Pool: £398.25 - 2.68 winning units..There was no bid for the winner. Woodcote was claimed by Peter Grayson for £6,000. Yungaburra was claimed by Sean Curran for £6,000.
Owner Joe McCarthy **Bred** Sheikh Amin Dahlawi **Trained** Limpley Stoke, Bath
■ Stewards' Enquiry : George Baker one-day ban: failed to ride to draw (Mar 11)

FOCUS

A modest seller.

Yungaburra(IRE) Official explanation: jockey said gelding never moved well; vet said gelding had been lame post-race

677 BETDAQ.CO.UK H'CAP 1m 4f 50y(P)

3:30 (3:31) (Class 6) (0-65,64) 3-Y-O **£2,047** (£604; £302) **Stalls** Low

Form RPR
6-44 **1** **Kochanski (IRE)**[26] 343 3-8-13 **56**........ JoeFanning 11 56
(M Johnston) *sn led: clr over 1f out: edgd rt wl ins fnl f: r.o* **8/1**
40-3 **2** 1/2 **Strikemaster (IRE)**[30] 295 3-8-12 **55**........ SteveDrowne 8 54
(J W Hills) *hld up in tch: rdn 3f out: chsd wnr over 1f out: r.o ins fnl f* **5/1**[1]
5-05 **3** *nk* **Spring Quartet**[14] 506 3-8-10 **53**........(v) MartinDwyer 1 51
(Pat Eddery) *hld up towards rr: nt clr run wl over 1f out: rdn and hdwy over 1f out: r.o ins fnl f* **9/1**
00-5 **4** *nk* **Witch Of The Wave (IRE)**[46] 115 3-9-1 **58**........ DaneO'Neill 6 56
(Miss J S Davis) *hld up in tch: rdn over 2f out: kpt on ins fnl f* **9/1**
0-11 **5** *1* **La Diosa (IRE)**[11] 555 3-9-7 **64**........ ChrisCatlin 7 60
(George Baker) *hld up in mid-div: rdn over 1f out: styng on whn sltly hmpd wl ins fnl f* **7/1**[3]
4-5 **6** 3/4 **Key Of Fortune (IRE)**[44] 138 3-9-5 **62**........ GeorgeBaker 2 57+
(Jennie Candlish) *hld up in mid-div: swtchd lft and hdwy on ins over 1f out: one pce fnl f* **8/1**
6-04 **7** 1 1/4 **Screaming Brave**[35] 239 3-9-0 **57**........ TonyCulhane 3 50
(M R Channon) *s.i.s: hld up in rr: rdn wl over 1f out: styd on ins fnl f: n.d* **6/1**[2]
2-50 **8** 1 1/2 **Nicky Nutjob (GER)**[14] 506 3-9-6 **63**........ JimmyQuinn 12 54
(J Pearce) *rrd and s.s: a bhd* **7/1**[3]
030- **9** *1* **Saffron's Son (IRE)**[142] 6524 3-9-3 **60**........ MickyFenton 9 49
(P T Midgley) *c wd st: a towards rr* **33/1**
005- **10** 3 1/2 **Irish Saint (IRE)**[102] 7343 3-9-5 **62**........ PaulHanagan 5 45
(T J Pitt) *led early: prom: rdn wl over 1f out: wknd fnl f* **8/1**
-603 **11** 1 3/4 **Kneesy Earsy Nosey**[18] 450 3-8-3 **53**........(p) AndrewHeffernan(7) 4 34
(Miss A Stokell) *hld up in tch: rdn and wknd wl over 1f out* **40/1**
62-5 **12** *nk* **Miss Cracklinrosie**[18] 450 3-9-3 **60**........ GrahamGibbons 10 40
(J R Weymes) *chsd wnr after 2f tl over 1f out: wknd qckly ent fnl f* **18/1**
2m 44.02s (2.92) **Going Correction** -0.025s/f (Stan) **12** Ran SP% **119.9**
Speed ratings (Par 95): **89,88,88,88,87 87,86,85,84,82 81,80**
toteswinger: 1&2 £5.80, 1&3 £16.80, 2&3 £11.00. CSF £48.32 CT £375.90 TOTE £8.50: £2.70, £1.50, £4.30; EX 44.40 Trifecta £228.10 Part won. Pool: £308.26 - 0.30 winning units..
Owner J R Gough **Bred** Gainsborough Stud Management Ltd **Trained** Middleham Moor, N Yorks

FOCUS

A modest handicap and a first-class display of front-running tactics by Joe Fanning aboard the winner.

Nicky Nutjob(GER) Official explanation: jockey said colt reared at start and missed the break

678 NAME A RACE TO ENHANCE YOUR BRAND MAIDEN FILLIES' STKS 1m 1f 103y(P)

4:00 (4:01) (Class 5) 3-Y-O+ **£2,729** (£806; £403) **Stalls** Low

Form RPR
22 **1** **Air Maze**[10] 564 3-8-4 0........ ChrisCatlin 1 70+
(Sir Mark Prescott) *led 1f: sn stdd into mid-div: hdwy on ins over 2f out: led ins fnl f: rdn and r.o* **5/4**[1]
330- **2** 1 1/4 **Garra Molly (IRE)**[120] 7042 4-9-11 64........ JamieSpencer 6 70+
(G A Swinbank) *a.p: wnt 2nd over 2f out: sn rdn: led and bmpd jst over 1f out: hdd ins fnl f: nt qckn* **2/1**[2]
50-0 **3** *4* **Wusuul**[47] 105 4-9-11 59........(b[1]) RobertWinston 10 60
(R A Harris) *led after 1f: clr over 2f out: hung rt and hdd jst over 1f out: wknd fnl f* **25/1**
4-43 **4** 4 1/2 **Herecomesbella**[11] 555 3-8-4 50........(b) PaulHanagan 2 46
(Stef Liddiard) *hld up and bhd: hdwy on ins over 2f out: no further prog* **14/1**
04-0 **5** *5* **Mill Beattie**[43] 147 4-9-11 48........ AndrewElliott 3 45+
(J Mackie) *hld up in tch: wknd 3f out: bdly hmpd and rn wd ent st* **66/1**
000- **6** *3* **Thirtyfourthstreet (IRE)**[242] 3482 4-9-11 42........ MartinDwyer 4 36
(W R Muir) *a bhd* **50/1**
0-6 **7** *nk* **Happy And Glorious (IRE)**[34] 251 3-8-4 0........ SimonWhitworth 8 31
(J W Hills) *wnt rt and hmpd s: a in rr* **25/1**
6-60 **8** 1 3/4 **Give (IRE)**[33] 272 3-8-4 49........(p) JoeFanning 7 27
(R A Harris) *sn chsng ldr: lost 2nd over 2f out: sn wknd* **50/1**
9 *12* **Will Exell (IRE)**[7] 6-9-6 0........ JackDean(5) 9 10
(M J Scudamore) *hmpd s: t.k.h: sn mid-div: wknd over 2f out* **66/1**
6- **P** **Taminas Desert**[252] 3133 4-9-8 0........ JackMitchell(3) 5 —
(M Botti) *s.i.s: hld up in rr: stdy hdwy on outside over 3f out: wkng whn wnt bdly lame and p.u ent st: dead* **4/1**[3]
2m 1.30s (-0.40) **Going Correction** -0.025s/f (Stan)
WFA 3 from 4yo+ 21lb **10** Ran SP% **119.0**
Speed ratings (Par 100): **100,98,95,91,86 84,83,82,71,—**
toteswinger: 1&2 £1.50, 1&3 £10.00, 2&3 £10.50. CSF £3.82 TOTE £2.00: £1.10, £1.10, £4.40; EX 5.10 Trifecta £35.30 Pool: £470.24 - 9.83 winning units..
Owner Plantation Stud **Bred** Pontchartrain Stud And Revilo Park Stud **Trained** Newmarket, Suffolk

FOCUS

Plenty of deadwood in this modest maiden which was run at just a steady pace and was marred by the mishap to Taminas Desert.

Will Exell(IRE) Official explanation: jockey said mare hung left throughout

679 DINE IN THE HORIZONS RESTAURANT H'CAP 1m 5f 194y(P)

4:30 (4:31) (Class 6) (0-65,65) 4-Y-O+ **£2,047** (£604; £302) **Stalls** Low

Form RPR
0/50 **1** **Rough Sketch (USA)**[14] 494 4-8-9 **53**........ StephenDonohoe 3 63+
(Sir Mark Prescott) *hld up in mid-div: hdwy over 2f out: rdn to ld jst over 1f out: styd on* **7/1**[3]
2-34 **2** 1 1/4 **Generous Star**[34] 252 6-9-3 **56**........ JimmyQuinn 13 63+
(J Pearce) *hld up in rr: hdwy wl over 1f out: wnt 2nd and swtchd rt ins fnl f: styd on* **7/2**[1]
3 *3* **King De Lune (FR)**[43] 7-9-7 **60**........(b) DaneO'Neill 4 63
(C E Longsdon) *s.i.s: sn hld up in mid-div: hdwy on ins over 3f out: rdn wl over 1f out: one pce fnl f* **25/1**
0-06 **4** 1/2 **Cantabilly (IRE)**[14] 500 6-9-7 **65**........ MCGeran(5) 2 67
(R J Hodges) *hld up in tch: lost pl over 5f out: nt clr run over 2f out: hdwy over 1f out: nt clr run and swtchd lft ins fnl f: one pce* **16/1**
-000 **5** 1/2 **Capitalise (IRE)**[12] 534 6-9-2 **55**........ LukeMorris 9 56
(Miss Gay Kelleway) *hld up in rr: hdwy over 3f out: c wd st: edgd lft ins fnl f: one pce* **16/1**
30-2 **6** 2 1/4 **Ice Bellini**[41] 168 4-9-6 **64**........(v) JamieSpencer 1 62
(Miss Gay Kelleway) *a.p: led 3f out: rdn and hdd jst over 1f out: wknd ins fnl f* **7/1**[3]
0201 **7** *3* **Safin (GER)**[5] 623 9-9-7 **60** 6ex........ GrahamGibbons 6 54
(R Curtis) *hld up towards rr: stdy prog over 5f out: ev ch over 2f out: rdn and wknd wl over 1f out* **5/1**[2]
/0-0 **8** 3/4 **Border Tale**[9] 566 9-8-12 **51**........(p) PJMcDonald 11 44
(James Moffatt) *led: hdd over 7f out: prom tl wknd over 1f out* **33/1**
-060 **9** 1 1/4 **Noubian (USA)**[6] 559 7-9-12 **65**........(t) LPKeniry 12 56
(C R Dore) *prom: hmpd 3f out: wknd wl over 1f out* **16/1**
0/0- **10** 1/2 **Drumhallagh (IRE)**[59] 7807 4-8-8 **57**........ RossAtkinson(5) 10 48
(Tom Dascombe) *a in rr* **8/1**
000- **11** *7* **Dr McFab**[222] 4155 5-9-2 **55**........ ChrisCatlin 5 36
(Miss Tor Sturgis) *t.k.h early in mid-div: bhd fnl 4f* **7/1**[3]
405/ **12** *16* **Millagros (IRE)**[742] 112 9-9-9 **62**........ PaulHanagan 7 20
(I Semple) *chsd ldr: led over 7f out to 3f out: wknd 2f out* **28/1**
-000 **13** *15* **Josh You Are**[13] 511 6-9-7 **63**........ RussellKennemore(3) 8 —
(Ian Williams) *s.i.s: a in rr: t.o fnl 2f: b.b.v* **18/1**
3m 5.28s (-0.72) **Going Correction** -0.025s/f (Stan)
WFA 4 from 5yo+ 5lb **13** Ran SP% **120.6**
Speed ratings (Par 101): **101,100,98,98,98 96,95,94,93,93 89,80,71**
toteswinger: 1&2 £7.40, 1&3 £41.30, 2&3 £13.50. CSF £31.30 CT £596.09 TOTE £8.30: £3.40, £1.60, £5.70; EX 46.70 TRIFECTA Not won..
Owner Edward S A Belcher **Bred** Drama Club Syndicate **Trained** Newmarket, Suffolk
■ Stewards' Enquiry : Jimmy Quinn one-day ban: careless riding (Mar 12)

FOCUS

More modest fare and the gallop was sound. It looked a wide-open race beforehand and plenty had their chance turning for home.

Rough Sketch(USA) Official explanation: trainer's rep said, regarding the apparent improvement in form, the gelding was better suited by the longer trip.

Drumhallagh(IRE) Official explanation: jockey said gelding hung right

Josh You Are Official explanation: trainer said gelding had bled from the nose

680 WOLVERHAMPTON-RACECOURSE.CO.UK H'CAP 7f 32y(P)

5:00 (5:02) (Class 4) (0-85,85) 4-Y-O+ **£4,857** (£1,445; £722; £360) **Stalls** High

Form RPR
10-5 **1** **Mr Macattack**[9] 573 4-8-4 **71** oh1........ LukeMorris 4 88+
(N J Vaughan) *hld up: hdwy over 2f out: hrd rdn over 1f out: edgd lft and led ins fnl f: r.o wl* **9/2**[2]
4-21 **2** 4 1/2 **Caprio (IRE)**[11] 543 4-8-1 **73**........ RossAtkinson(5) 8 79
(Tom Dascombe) *w ldr: led over 3f out: rdn wl over 1f out: hdd ins fnl f: sn btn: jst hld on for 2nd* **9/1**
0115 **3** *shd* **Cornus**[8] 576 7-8-7 **74**........(be) JamesDoyle 6 80
(A J McCabe) *dwlt: hld up in rr: rdn over 1f out: hdwy fnl f: jst failed to take 2nd* **12/1**
2 **4** 3/4 **Catalan Bay (AUS)**[32] 281 5-8-8 **75**........ SteveDrowne 1 79+
(J R Gask) *led early: a.p: rdn wl over 1f out: one pce fnl f* **10/11**[1]
524- **5** 1/2 **Obezyana (USA)**[82] 7560 7-8-0 **74**........ NatashaEaton(7) 3 77
(A Bailey) *sn led: hdd 3f out: rdn and lost 2nd over 1f out: fdd* **20/1**
1162 **6** 2 1/2 **Guildenstern (IRE)**[8] 576 7-8-4 **71** oh5........ JimmyQuinn 7 68
(P Howling) *hld up: rdn wl over 1f out: no rspnse* **14/1**
/0-3 **7** 1 3/4 **Orpen Wide (IRE)**[15] 490 7-8-13 **83**........(b) LeeVickers(3) 2 75
(M C Chapman) *prom tl wknd 2f out* **18/1**
LRR- **R** **Gunfighter (IRE)**[74] 4417 6-9-4 **85**........ RobertWinston 5 —
(R A Farrant) *ref to r: tk no part* **8/1**[3]
1m 28.38s (-1.22) **Going Correction** -0.025s/f (Stan) **8** Ran SP% **116.1**
Speed ratings (Par 105): **105,99,99,98,98 95,93,—**
toteswinger: 1&2 £4.10, 1&3 £5.10, 2&3 £4.20. CSF £44.65 CT £459.22 TOTE £5.30: £2.00, £2.10, £1.70; EX 38.70 Trifecta £357.70 Part won. Pool: £483.47 - 0.74 winning units..
Owner Owen Promotions Limited **Bred** Hascombe And Valiant Studs **Trained**

FOCUS

A good-class sprint handicap reduced by one when Gunfighter refused to leave the stalls for a fourth time in a row.

681 TRY BETDAQ FOR AN EXCHANGE H'CAP 5f 20y(P)

5:30 (5:32) (Class 6) (0-60,60) 4-Y-O+ **£2,047** (£604; £302) **Stalls** Low

Form RPR
-602 **1** **Fizzlephut (IRE)**[6] 596 7-9-0 **56**........(b) PaulFitzsimons 2 67+
(Miss J R Tooth) *hld up in tch: wnt 2nd over 2f out: rdn to ld ins fnl f: r.o* **15/2**
-255 **2** 1 1/2 **Admiral Bond (IRE)**[19] 431 4-9-4 **60**........(p) PJMcDonald 3 66
(G R Oldroyd) *hld up towards rr: hdwy on ins wl over 1f out: rdn and wnt 2nd wl ins fnl f: nt trble wnr* **5/1**
-555 **3** 3/4 **Green Lagonda (AUS)**[3] 645 7-9-0 **56**........ MickyFenton 6 59
(Stef Liddiard) *hld up towards rr: hdwy over 1f out: r.o ins fnl f: tk 3rd post* **4/1**[3]
5133 **4** *hd* **Muktasb (USA)**[14] 499 8-9-4 **60**........(v) DaneO'Neill 1 62
(D Shaw) *s.i.s: in rr: hdwy on ins over 1f out: sn rdn: kpt on ins fnl f: fin 5th: plcd 4th* **7/2**[2]
3210 **5** *nk* **Monte Major (IRE)**[6] 596 8-9-4 **60**........(v) PaulHanagan 10 61
(D Shaw) *anticipated s: sn hld up in mid-div: lost pl 2f out: rdn and hdwy over 1f out: nt rch ldrs: fin 6th: plcd 5th* **3/1**[1]
0-00 **6** *1* **Trinculo (IRE)**[29] 303 12-8-11 **58**........(b) DeanHeslop(5) 5 56
(R A Harris) *chsd ldr tl over 2f out: rdn over 1f out: hld whn n.m.r cl home: fin 7th: plcd 6th* **25/1**
-541 **7** 1 1/2 **Mr Rooney (IRE)**[24] 367 6-8-8 **55**........ SladeO'Hara(5) 8 47
(A Berry) *chsd ldrs: pushed along 3f out: wknd wl over 1f out: fin 8th: plcd 7th* **16/1**
/0-0 **8** 1/2 **Stoneacre Baby (USA)**[51] 46 4-7-11 **46** oh1.... AndrewHeffernan(7) 4 36
(Peter Grayson) *t.k.h in mid-div: hdwy on ins over 2f out: rdn over 1f out: wknd fnl f: fin 9th: plcd 8th* **66/1**
66-0 **9** 1 1/4 **Town House**[16] 474 7-8-5 **47**........ AndrewElliott 11 33
(B P J Baugh) *prom tl wknd wl over 1f out: fin 10th: plcd 9th* **40/1**

4-00 **10** ½ **Stoneacre Pat (IRE)**[42] 165 4-8-10 **52**....................(b) PatrickMathers 7 36
(Peter Grayson) *s.i.s: rdn and c v wd st: a in rr: fin 11th: plcd 10th* **28/1**
3-00 **D** *nse* **Triskaidekaphobia**[3] 645 6-8-10 **52**............................(bt) JamesDoyle 9 55
(Miss J R Tooth) *led: swtchd lft after 1f: rdn over 1f out: hdd ins fnl f: no ex: fin 4th, 11/2l, ¾l & nse: disq: jockey failed to weigh in* **18/1**
61.89 secs (-0.41) **Going Correction** -0.025s/f (Stan) 11 Ran SP% **118.0**
Speed ratings (Par 101): **102,99,98,98,97 95,93,92,90,89 98**
toteswinger: 1&2 £10.40, 1&3 £6.60, 2&3 £6.40. CSF £43.71 CT £174.17 TOTE £7.70: £1.40, £1.70, £2.10; EX 42.20 Trifecta £111.70 Pool: £181.26 - 1.20 winning units..
Owner Miss J R Tooth **Bred** Tally-Ho Stud **Trained** Upper Lambourn, Berks
■ Stewards' Enquiry : James Doyle three-day ban: failed to weigh in (Mar 11-13)
FOCUS
More modest stuff, but very competitive, and the two with the worst of the draw did not line up.
Muktasb(USA) Official explanation: jockey said gelding missed the break
Monte Major(IRE) Official explanation: jockey said gelding anticipated start and hit its head on stalls

682 ARENA LEISURE CATERING APPRENTICE H'CAP 1m 141y(P)
6:00 (6:00) (Class 6) (0-58,58) 4-Y-0+ **£2,047** (£604; £151; £151) **Stalls** Low

Form RPR
0-46 **1** **Waldorf (IRE)**[16] 476 4-9-1 **56**............................ JackDean 1 64
(W R Muir) *t.k.h: a.p: wnt 2nd wl over 1f out: sn rdn: led wl ins fnl f: r.o* **9/2**[2]
0-40 **2** ½ **Stoic Leader (IRE)**[12] 531 9-9-0 **58**.................... MartinLane(3) 4 65
(R F Fisher) *a.p: led over 3f out: rdn over 1f out: edgd lft and hdd wl ins fnl f: kpt on* **6/1**
5-13 **3** 1¼ **Giddywell**[19] 427 5-8-12 **56**..........................(p) RossAtkinson(3) 2 60
(R Hollinshead) *hld up towards rr: pushed along over 4f out: rdn over 2f out: hdwy over 1f out: kpt on ins fnl f* **9/4**[1]
0-00 **3** *dht* **Make Amends (IRE)**[16] 478 4-9-2 **57**.......................... MCGeran 7 61
(R J Hodges) *hld up in mid-div: hdwy over 2f out: sn rdn: kpt on ins fnl f* **10/1**
3310 **5** 3¾ **Hurricane Coast**[37] 216 10-8-12 **58**....................(b) HollyHall(5) 6 54
(D Flood) *plld hrd towards rr: hdwy over 6f out: changed ldr over 2f out tl rdn wl over 1f out: wknd ins fnl f* **14/1**
0-00 **6** 1¼ **Hill Of Lujain**[16] 473 5-8-6 **50**..................... DeclanCannon(3) 10 44
(Ian Williams) *hld up in rr: rdn over 2f out: nvr trbld ldrs* **8/1**
-006 **7** ½ **Berrymead**[8] 574 4-8-0 **46** oh1........................ AlexEdwards(5) 5 38
(Miss A Stokell) *s.i.s: towards rr: struggling 4f out: n.d after* **25/1**
5460 **8** 1 **Machinate (USA)**[2] 657 7-8-12 **53**............................ DeanHeslop 8 43
(W M Brisbourne) *hld up in rr: rdn and c wd st: no rspnse* **11/2**[3]
0-00 **9** 2¾ **Speagle (IRE)**[5] 623 7-8-11 **52**..........................(v[1]) WilliamCarson 3 37
(D Shaw) *led: hdd over 3f out: sn rdn: wknd wl over 1f out* **12/1**
/000 **10** 1½ **Magical Mimi**[8] 581 8-8-0 **46** oh1......................(b) AndrewHeffernan(5) 9 27
(K G Wingrove) *stdd sn after s: hld up in rr: rdn over 2f out: short-lived effrt on ins wl over 1f out* **80/1**
1m 50.64s (0.14) **Going Correction** -0.025s/f (Stan) 10 Ran SP% **118.3**
Speed ratings (Par 101): **98,97,96,96,93 92,91,90,88,86**TRICAST: Waldorf, Stoic Leader, Make Amends £132.21; W, SL, Giddywell £38.40. toteswinger: W&SL £6.90, W&MA £3.60, W&G £1.80, SL&MA £4.90, SL&G £2.00. PL: MA £1.50, G £0.70. CSF £32.24 TOTE £5.90: £1.70, £2.10; EX 39.60 TRIFECTA W-SL-MA not won; W-S27 Owner.
FOCUS
Poor fare in the nightcap. They went a good gallop.
T/Jkpt: Not won. T/Plt: £137.50 to a £1 stake. Pool: £69,374.83. 368.18 winning tickets. T/Qpdt: £23.80 to a £1 stake. Pool: £4,852.55. 150.50 winning tickets. KH

617 SOUTHWELL (L-H)
Thursday, February 26

OFFICIAL GOING: Standard
Wind: Light across Weather: Overcast

683 BET SIX NATIONS RUGBY - BETDAQ APPRENTICE H'CAP 1m (F)
2:10 (2:10) (Class 5) (0-75,75) 4-Y-0+ **£2,590** (£770; £385; £192) **Stalls** Low

Form RPR
3211 **1** **More Time Tim (IRE)**[6] 618 4-9-2 **72** 6ex.................. RossAtkinson 1 84+
(J R Boyle) *trckd ldrs: wnt 2nd 3f out: led over 1f out: shkn up and sn clr: eased wl ins fnl f* **10/11**[1]
13-3 **2** ¾ **Barataria**[25] 362 7-8-13 **69**.. LanceBetts 4 76
(R Bastiman) *a.p: rdn over 2f out: styd wnr fnl f: styd on* **17/2**
4224 **3** 1¾ **Downhill Skier (IRE)**[6] 625 5-8-4 **65**................. PaulPickard(5) 2 68
(W M Brisbourne) *plld hrd and sn led: rdn and hdd over 1f out: styd on same pce ins fnl f* **16/1**
1112 **4** ¾ **General Tufto**[7] 608 4-8-6 **67** 6ex...................(b) HollyHall(5) 6 68
(C Smith) *hld up in tch: racd keenly: outpcd 3f out: hdwy and hung lft fr 2 out: no imp fnl f* **7/2**[2]
-226 **5** 3½ **Rock Anthem (IRE)**[25] 362 5-8-9 **65**......................... MartinLane 5 59
(Mike Murphy) *hld up: rdn over 3f out: wknd over 1f out* **8/1**[3]
-064 **6** 12 **Montiboli (IRE)**[12] 557 4-8-10 **66**...........................(p) AmyRyan 3 33
(K A Ryan) *led early: chsd ldr tl rdn 3f out: wknd wl over 1f out* **20/1**
600- **7** 5 **Sri Kuantan (IRE)**[285] 2200 5-9-0 **75**................... KarenKenny(5) 7 31
(R C Guest) *hld up: rdn over 3f out: sn wknd: bhd whn rdr dropped whip over 1f out* **28/1**
1m 45.48s (1.78) **Going Correction** +0.25s/f (Slow) 7 Ran SP% **110.3**
Speed ratings (Par 103): **101,100,98,97,94 82,77**
toteswinger: 1&2 £2.00, 1&3 £4.40, 2&3 £7.50. CSF £8.82 TOTE £1.80: £1.30, £3.20; EX 8.00.
Owner M Khan X2 **Bred** Glending Bloodstock **Trained** Epsom, Surrey
FOCUS
They did not go much of a pace in this handicap for apprentices, and the result was that a few failed to settle.

684 BET TEST MATCH CRICKET - BETDAQ CLAIMING STKS 7f (F)
2:40 (2:41) (Class 6) 3-Y-0 **£2,047** (£604; £302) **Stalls** Low

Form RPR
3112 **1** **Madison Belle**[7] 605 3-8-5 70........................ MartinLane(5) 7 72
(K R Burke) *chsd ldr: rdn to ld and hung lft fr over 2f out: styd on* **2/1**[2]
1521 **2** 1½ **My Sweet Georgia (IRE)**[7] 605 3-8-7 71................(b) JamieSpencer 4 66
(S A Callaghan) *led: rdn over 3 out: hdd over 2f out: styd on same pce ins fnl f* **4/5**[1]
5-35 **3** 3 **Swiss Art (IRE)**[43] 159 3-8-8 61........................... ChrisCatlin 3 59
(R A Harris) *chsd ldrs: hung lft over 4f out: sn rdn: styd on same pce fnl 2f* **8/1**[3]
60-6 **4** 10 **Thaumatology (USA)**[11] 560 3-8-2 61...................(tp) JimmyQuinn 2 28
(S Parr) *stmbld s: hld up: outpcd over 4f out: n.d after* **25/1**
-040 **5** 12 **Northern Shore (IRE)**[8] 594 3-8-10 50.......................(b) JoeFanning 1 6
(K A Ryan) *sn drvn along and prom: wknd 1/2-way: eased over 1f out* **28/1**
-505 **6** 18 **Alimarr (IRE)**[11] 560 3-8-2 50.................................. DaleGibson 5 —
(S Parr) *prom: rdn over 5f out: sn bhd: eased fnl 3f* **66/1**
1m 32.94s (2.64) **Going Correction** +0.25s/f (Slow) 6 Ran SP% **108.8**
Speed ratings (Par 95): **94,92,88,77,63 43**
toteswinger: 1&2 £1.50, 1&3 £1.70, 2&3 £1.60. CSF £3.66 TOTE £3.10: £1.50, £1.30; EX 3.70.
Owner Paul Sweeting & Mrs L Wright **Bred** Paul Sweeting **Trained** Middleham Moor, N Yorks
FOCUS
As the betting predicted this was a two-horse race from some way out.

685 BET UEFA CUP - BETDAQ H'CAP 5f (F)
3:10 (3:10) (Class 4) (0-85,82) 3-Y-0 **£4,731** (£1,416; £708; £354; £176) **Stalls** High

Form RPR
1-14 **1** **Smokey Ryder**[40] 203 3-9-6 **81**.............................. ChrisCatlin 3 90
(R A Harris) *a.p: rdn 1/2-way: r.o u.p to ld wl ins fnl f* **4/1**[2]
3-52 **2** 1¾ **Lesley's Choice**[14] 509 3-9-5 **80**.............................. NCallan 5 83
(R Curtis) *led: rdn over 1f out: hdd and unable qck wl ins fnl f* **7/2**[1]
234- **3** ½ **Dispol Grand (IRE)**[111] 7219 3-8-7 **68**......................... JoeFanning 9 69
(P T Midgley) *chsd ldrs: rdn and hung lft 2f out: styd on same pce fnl f* **12/1**
-103 **4** 1 **Green Onions**[27] 350 3-8-6 **72**.......................... GabrielHannon(5) 4 69
(D J S Ffrench Davis) *trckd ldr: rdn 2f out: no ex ins fnl f* **8/1**
-601 **5** 3½ **Love You Louis**[14] 509 3-9-2 **77**......................(b) SimonWhitworth 1 62+
(J R Jenkins) *s.i.s: sn chsng ldrs: rdn 1/2-way: wknd fnl f* **9/2**[3]
-354 **6** 2¾ **Cecily**[14] 509 3-9-7 **82**.. StephenDonohoe 2 57
(Sir Mark Prescott) *prom: rdn 1/2-way: wknd over 1f out* **7/2**[1]
216- **7** ¾ **Special Cuvee**[211] 4525 3-9-2 **77**........................... SteveDrowne 6 49
(A B Haynes) *s.i.s: outpcd* **12/1**
300- **8** 1¾ **Dispol Kylie (IRE)**[138] 6656 3-9-5 **80**..................... JamieMoriarty 7 46+
(P T Midgley) *s.i.s and hmpd s: sn outpcd* **14/1**
59.74 secs (0.04) **Going Correction** +0.05s/f (Slow) 8 Ran SP% **115.8**
Speed ratings (Par 99): **101,98,97,95,90 85,84,81**
toteswinger: 1&2 £2.60, 1&3 £8.50, 2&3 £4.60. CSF £18.70 CT £154.92 TOTE £5.10: £1.70, £1.30, £2.80; EX 18.50 Trifecta £142.00 Part won. Pool: £191.98 - 0.45 winning units..
Owner The Govin Partnership **Bred** Jeremy Hinds **Trained** Earlswood, Monmouths
FOCUS
A competitive-looking sprint.

686 HOSPITALITY AT SOUTHWELL RACECOURSE MAIDEN STKS 5f (F)
3:40 (3:41) (Class 5) 3-Y-0 **£2,590** (£770; £385; £192) **Stalls** High

Form RPR
1 **May Martin** 3-8-12 0.. ChrisCatlin 4 59
(Rae Guest) *s.i.s: outpcd: hdwy u.p over 1f out: r.o to ld wl ins fnl f* **12/1**
0-60 **2** ¾ **Taurus Twins**[8] 583 3-9-3 51.................................. PaulHanagan 7 61
(R J Price) *chsd ldr: rdn over 1f out: led ins fnl f: sn hdd: kpt on* **25/1**
2 **3** ½ **Air Lion (USA)**[7] 602 3-9-3 0................................. ShaneKelly 2 59
(R M H Cowell) *chsd ldrs: rdn 1/2-way: ev ch ins fnl f: unable qck* **2/5**[1]
0-02 **4** 2½ **Fasliyanne (IRE)**[23] 379 3-8-12 52.............................(b) NCallan 5 45
(K A Ryan) *led: rdn and hung rt over 1f out: hdd and no ex ins fnl f* **6/1**[2]
5 10 **Migliori** 3-9-3 0.. SteveDrowne 9 14
(Rae Guest) *s.i.s: sn outpcd* **10/1**[3]
6 1¼ **Ereeford** 3-9-3 0.. DaleGibson 8 —
(M W Easterby) *dwlt: outpcd* **28/1**
7 ¾ **By The Wind (IRE)** 3-9-0 0.................................. LeeVickers(3) 3 —
(T J Etherington) *s.s: outpcd* **33/1**
56- **8** *shd* **Inside Knowledge (USA)**[266] 2754 3-9-3 0................. TGMcLaughlin 6 —
(G Woodward) *sn outpcd* **18/1**
60.49 secs (0.79) **Going Correction** +0.05s/f (Slow) 8 Ran SP% **118.0**
Speed ratings (Par 97): **95,93,93,89,73 71,69,69**
toteswinger: 1&2 £11.40, 1&3 £3.00, 2&3 £6.00. CSF £253.95 TOTE £17.30: £3.50, £6.40, £1.02; EX 394.80 Trifecta £490.10 Part won. Pool: £662.37 - 0.20 winning units..
Owner Mrs A Shone **Bred** Pillar To Post Racing **Trained** Newmarket, Suffolk
FOCUS
A weak maiden run at a good pace thanks to the trailblazing Fasliyanne. The favourute did not progress and this took little winning.

687 SOUTHWELL-RACECOURSE.CO.UK H'CAP 1m 4f (F)
4:10 (4:10) (Class 4) (0-85,81) 4-Y-0+ **£4,731** (£1,416; £708; £354) **Stalls** Low

Form RPR
3063 **1** **Profit's Reality (IRE)**[8] 584 7-9-7 **81**..................... JamieSpencer 3 91+
(M J Attwater) *a.p: chsd ldr 4f out: led 2f out: sn rdn and hung lft: clr fnl f: eased nr fin* **9/2**
1-60 **2** 3¼ **Phoenix Flight (IRE)**[34] 271 4-9-1 **78**..................... StephenDonohoe 4 83
(Sir Mark Prescott) *s.s: hld up: hdwy over 3f out: sn rdn: r.o to go 2nd ins fnl f: nt rch wnr* **11/4**[3]
1-15 **3** 2¼ **Benedict Spirit (IRE)**[26] 142 4-8-10 **73**................. PaulMulrennan 2 75
(M H Tompkins) *led: rdn and hdd 2f out: wknd ins fnl f* **2/1**[1]
3-56 **4** 61 **Bentley Brook (IRE)**[14] 511 7-9-6 **80**............................ NCallan 1 —
(R Curtis) *chsd ldr tl pushed along over 4f out: wknd over 3f* **9/4**[2]
2m 41.95s (0.95) **Going Correction** +0.25s/f (Slow)
WFA 4 from 7yo 3lb 4 Ran SP% **109.0**
Speed ratings (Par 105): **106,103,102,61**
CSF £16.28 TOTE £4.00; EX 13.00.
Owner Phones Direct Partnership **Bred** Michael Munnelly **Trained** Epsom, Surrey
FOCUS
A fair handicap and quite a competitive little heat despite the disappointing turnout. The early gallop was modest, however. The winner is very useful on his day.
Bentley Brook(IRE) Official explanation: jockey said gelding never travelled

688 MEMBERSHIP OF SOUTHWELL GOLF CLUB FILLIES' H'CAP 1m 3f (F)
4:40 (4:40) (Class 5) (0-75,75) 4-Y-0+ **£2,590** (£770; £385; £192) **Stalls** Low

Form RPR
24-6 **1** **Gamesters Lady**[31] 299 6-8-3 **61** oh1..................... DuranFentiman(3) 4 66
(W M Brisbourne) *s.i.s: hdwy to chse ldr after 1f: rdn over 3f out: hung lft and outpcd over 1f out: rallied and hung rt ins fnl f: styd on to ld nr fin* **11/2**[2]
-545 **2** *nk* **Friends Hope**[18] 456 8-9-1 **75**........................... GabrielHannon(5) 3 79
(R Curtis) *hld up: hdwy to ld over 3f out: rdn and hdd nr fin* **7/1**[3]
-221 **3** 3 **Lady Longcroft**[14] 516 4-8-5 **62**................................. JimmyQuinn 1 61
(J Pearce) *s.s: hld up: racd keenly: hdwy to chse ldr 3f out: rdn and hung lft over 1f out: no ex ins fnl f* **15/8**[1]
1-22 **4** ½ **Quick Off The Mark**[27] 354 4-8-11 **68**......................... TPQueally 2 66
(J G Given) *chsd ldrs: outpcd over 2f out: rallied and edgd rt over 1f out: one pce fnl f* **15/8**[1]

510- 5 10 **Casino Night**115 7166 4-8-3 65 DeanHeslop(5) 6 45
(R Johnson) *led: rdn and hdd over 3f out: wknd 2f out* 8/1

2m 31.33s (3.33) **Going Correction** +0.25s/f (Slow)
WFA 4 from 6yo+ 2lb 5 Ran SP% **108.6**
Speed ratings (Par 100): **97,96,94,94,86**
toteswinger: 1&2 £9.70. CSF £37.83 TOTE £6.40: £2.30, £2.60; EX 36.10.
Owner Gamesters Partnership **Bred** D Timmis **Trained** Great Ness, Shropshire

FOCUS
Most of these came into the race with one question mark or another hanging over them and this was a weak race of its type. The form is rated through the third.
Gamesters Lady Official explanation: trainer said, regarding the apparent improvement in form, that on its previous run, first for six months, the mare appeared to blow up, but stripped fitter and appeared well suited by the fibresand.

689 CALL 01636 814481 TO SPONSOR A RACE H'CAP 1m (F)
5:10 (5:12) (Class 5) (0-75,73) 3-Y-O £2,590 (£770; £385; £192) Stalls Low

Form RPR
0-21 1 **Miss Christophene (IRE)**16 488 3-8-10 65 JimmyQuinn 7 73+
(Mrs S Lamyman) *hld up: hdwy over 3f out: led 1f out: styd on wl* 4/1[2]
2241 2 4 ½ **Hawkspring (IRE)**4 649 3-9-3 72 6ex (vt) NCallan 6 70
(S Parr) *chsd ldrs: led over 3f out: rdn and hdd 1f out: no ex* 6/1
-221 3 4 **Diamond Surprise**20 421 3-8-8 68 GabrielHannon(5) 4 57
(R Curtis) *hld up in tch: rdn over 3f out: chsd ldr over 2f out tl wknd over 1f out* 12/1
1-4 4 6 **Trueblue Wizard (IRE)**34 276 3-9-4 73 MartinDwyer 3 49
(W R Muir) *led: rdn and hdd over 3f out: wknd 2f out* 2/1[1]
65-4 5 3 ¼ **Lady Salama**28 322 3-8-6 61 AndrewElliott 5 30
(K R Burke) *chsd ldrs: rdn 1/2-way: wknd 2f out* 14/1
-223 6 1 **Mullitovermaurice**17 479 3-8-11 66 TPQueally 1 33
(J G Given) *sn outpcd* 11/2
16-1 7 23 **Shifting Gold (IRE)**37 228 3-8-9 64 (b) JamieSpencer 2 —
(K A Ryan) *sn drvn along to join ldr: hung rt 6f out: wknd 1/2-way* 5/1[3]

1m 45.67s (1.97) **Going Correction** +0.25s/f (Slow) 7 Ran SP% **114.0**
Speed ratings (Par 97): **100,95,91,85,82 81,58**
toteswinger: 1&2 £3.90, 1&3 £6.30, 2&3 £10.40. CSF £27.63 TOTE £4.50: £2.00, £3.00; EX 31.90 Place 6: £151.98, Place 5: £100.21..
Owner P Lamyman **Bred** Stephen Moloney **Trained** Ruckland, Lincs

FOCUS
They went a good pace here and that played into the hands of the winner, who showed marked improvement.
Shifting Gold(IRE) Official explanation: jockey said gelding hung badly right throughout
T/Plt: £77.10 to a £1 stake. Pool: £46,500.94. 440.20 winning tickets. T/Qpdt: £52.50 to a £1 stake. Pool: £2,174.50. 30.60 winning tickets. CR

675 WOLVERHAMPTON (A.W) (L-H)
Thursday, February 26

OFFICIAL GOING: Standard
Wind: Fresh, behind Weather: dry

690 HORIZONS RESTAURANT - THE PLACE TO DINE CLAIMING STKS 5f 20y(P)
6:50 (6:50) (Class 6) 3-Y-O+ £1,878 (£558; £279; £139) Stalls Low

Form RPR
1105 1 **Harry Up**12 553 8-9-0 84 (p) AmyRyan(7) 3 89
(K A Ryan) *mde all: clr and rdn over 1f out: unchal* 7/4[1]
-222 2 3 ¼ **Blue Tomato**14 510 8-9-0 78 WilliamCarson(5) 4 75
(D Nicholls) *chsd wnr thrght: rdn 2f out: drvn and wl hld fr over 1f out* 5/2[2]
4354 3 3 **Bo McGinty (IRE)**19 451 8-9-9 75 (b) PaulHanagan 1 68
(R A Fahey) *a off the pce in 3rd pl: rdn over 1f out: no imp* 5/1
600- 4 2 **White Shift (IRE)**145 6483 3-8-4 90 CatherineGannon 2 50
(P D Evans) *dwlt: sn bustled along: a last and n.d* 11/4[3]

60.95 secs (-1.35) **Going Correction** -0.025s/f (Stan)
WFA 3 from 8yo 14lb 4 Ran SP% **108.3**
Speed ratings (Par 101): **109,103,99,95**
CSF £6.32 TOTE £2.90; EX 5.00.
Owner The Fishermen **Bred** J E Rose **Trained** Hambleton, N Yorks
■ The first winner as an apprentice for former amateur rider Amy Ryan.

FOCUS
Dominated by 8yos, this was not a competitive race. A decent pace resulted in a time under the Racing Post standard. The winner edged into the centre in the closing stages.
White Shift(IRE) Official explanation: jockey said filly never travelled

691 TOMORROW IS SOUL NIGHT H'CAP 5f 216y(P)
7:20 (7:20) (Class 5) (0-75,75) 4-Y-O+ £2,590 (£770; £385; £192) Stalls Low

Form RPR
10-0 1 **Bahamian Lad**25 362 4-8-10 67 GrahamGibbons 2 81
(R Hollinshead) *t.k.h: chsd ldr tl 4f out: effrt on inner wl over 1f out: rdn to ld over 1f out: drew clr fnl 100yds: comf* 10/1
2032 2 2 ½ **Compton Classic**8 590 7-8-4 61 oh1 (p) LukeMorris 3 67
(J R Boyle) *chsd ldrs: wnt 2nd 4f out: rdn and ev ch wl over 1f out: nt pce of wnr ins fnl f* 6/1[3]
0-55 3 ½ **Gainshare**7 606 4-8-0 62 DeanHeslop(5) 6 66
(Mrs R A Carr) *taken down early: stdd after s: hld up in last pl: c wd and rdn 2f out: styd on fnl f to go 3rd nr fin: nvr nr wnr* 7/1
00-4 4 ¾ **Music Box Express**15 499 5-8-1 65 MatthewDavies(7) 4 67
(George Baker) *t.k.h: led: rdn wl over 1f out: hdd over 1f out: wknd jst ins fnl f* 5/1[2]
-033 5 1 **Figaro Flyer (IRE)**14 518 6-8-13 70 JimmyQuinn 1 69
(P Howling) *t.k.h: hld up in tch: rdn and no rspnse over 1f out: wl hld fnl f* 11/4[1]
2646 6 3 ¼ **Count Ceprano (IRE)**13 538 5-9-4 75 LPKeniry 5 63
(C R Dore) *in tch towards rr: rdn and unable qck over 2f out: no ch fnl f* 11/4[1]
4-33 7 1 ½ **Strathmore (IRE)**23 380 5-8-7 64 (p) PaulHanagan 7 48
(R A Fahey) *taken down early: t.k.h: hld up in tch in rr: rdn and effrt over 1f out: drvn and wknd ent fnl f* 10/1

1m 14.74s (-0.26) **Going Correction** -0.025s/f (Stan) 7 Ran SP% **115.0**
Speed ratings (Par 103): **100,96,96,95,93 89,87**
toteswinger: 1&2 £7.00, 1&3 £9.80, 2&3 Not won. CSF £67.93 TOTE £10.80: £4.50, £4.00; EX 93.70.
Owner R Hollinshead **Bred** J D Graham **Trained** Upper Longdon, Staffs

FOCUS
Exposed performers in this fair handicap. The pace was not a strong one and those up with the pace held the edge. The winner raced against the inside rail in the closing stages.
Count Ceprano(IRE) Official explanation: jockey said gelding failed to travel from 3f out

692 BET MULTIPLES BETDAQ H'CAP 1m 5f 194y(P)
7:50 (7:51) (Class 4) (0-85,75) 4-Y-O+ £2,590 (£770; £385; £192) Stalls Low

Form RPR
56-4 1 **Remember Ramon (USA)**43 156 6-9-10 75 NCallan 1 85
(J R Gask) *sn led: mde all: rdn clr wl over 2f out: in n.d after: rdn out* 11/4[1]
1-10 2 3 ¾ **Blockley (USA)**46 126 5-8-7 58 StephenDonohoe 7 63
(Ian Williams) *stdd s: hld up in last pl: hdwy and swtchd ins over 2f out: rdn to chse clr wnr over 1f out: no imp* 9/2[3]
2-41 3 3 ¼ **Monaadi (IRE)**19 448 4-8-9 65 (p) GrahamGibbons 4 65
(R Hollinshead) *chsd wnr for 2f: rdn 4f out: chsd wnr again and outpcd over 2f out: lost 2nd wl over 1f out: wl btn after* 3/1[2]
4405 4 4 ½ **Calculating (IRE)**14 511 5-8-12 63 DaneO'Neill 5 57
(M D I Usher) *dwlt: hld up in tch in last pair: swtchd to outer and rdn wl over 2f out: sn outpcd and wl btn* 5/1
6-14 5 6 **Little Carmela**31 299 5-9-2 67 ChrisCatlin 6 53
(S C Williams) *in tch: rdn 4f out: struggling 3f out: wl bhd fr wl over 1f out* 5/1
5124 6 nk **Blue Hills**7 604 8-8-7 63 (v) WilliamCarson(5) 8 48
(P W Hiatt) *chsd wnr after 2f tl wl over 2f out: sn drvn and wknd* 10/1

3m 2.40s (-3.60) **Going Correction** -0.025s/f (Stan)
WFA 4 from 5yo+ 5lb 6 Ran SP% **112.3**
Speed ratings (Par 105): **109,106,105,102,99 98**
toteswinger: 1&2 £11.80, 1&3 Not won, 2&3 £6.20. CSF £15.33 CT £37.77 TOTE £5.50: £2.50, £3.10; EX 21.40.
Owner Horses First Racing Limited **Bred** Bruce T Hundley **Trained** Sutton Veny, Wilts

FOCUS
Mainly exposed sorts in a race where the top-weight was 10lb below the ratings ceiling. The pace was moderate and the winner raced against the inside rail in the straight.

693 BETDAQ THE BETTING EXCHANGE H'CAP 1m 4f 50y(P)
8:20 (8:20) (Class 2) (0-100,86) 4-Y-O+
£7,352 (£2,201; £1,100; £551; £274; £138) Stalls Low

Form RPR
1230 1 **Wind Flow**5 631 5-8-6 70 (b) CatherineGannon 3 78
(C A Dwyer) *mde all: rdn wl over 1f out: hrd pressed ins fnl f: hld on gamely* 9/2[2]
1-13 2 hd **Wine 'n Dine**26 360 4-9-5 86 NCallan 1 94
(G L Moore) *trckd ldng pair: wnt 2nd 3f out: chal ent fnl f: drvn and nt qckn fnl 100yds* 4/6[1]
4111 3 6 **Blacktoft (USA)**9 577 6-9-1 79 6ex (e) ChrisCatlin 5 78
(Evan Williams) *wnt freely to s: t.k.h: hld up in tch: rdn and effrt 2f out: outpcd ent fnl f: wnt modest 3rd fnl 100yds* 8/1
01-2 4 1 ½ **Spirit Of Adjisa (IRE)**43 156 5-8-8 79 TobyAtkinson(7) 4 75
(Pat Eddery) *chsd ldr tl 3f out: rdn and outpcd over 1f out: hung lft u.p 1f out* 5/1[3]
06- 5 1 ¾ **Boo**62 7785 7-8-9 80 AlexEdwards(7) 2 74
(J W Unett) *awkward s: hld up in tch in last pair: rdn 2f out: outpcd over 1f out: wl hld whn hmpd and swtchd rt fnl 100yds* 33/1
1133 6 11 **United Nations**14 515 8-9-1 79 LeeEnstone 6 56
(N Wilson) *hld up in tch in rr: hdwy on outer 3f out: c v wd 2f out: sn wknd: eased whn no ch ins fnl f* 20/1

2m 39.91s (-1.19) **Going Correction** -0.025s/f (Stan)
WFA 4 from 5yo+ 3lb 6 Ran SP% **113.7**
Speed ratings (Par 109): **102,101,97,96,95 88**
toteswinger: 1&2 £1.10, 1&3 Not won, 2&3 £1.10. CSF £8.12 TOTE £5.90: £3.60, £1.10; EX 12.40.
Owner Super Six Partnership **Bred** Lord Halifax **Trained** Burrough Green, Cambs
■ Stewards' Enquiry : Alex Edwards one-day ban: careless riding (Mar 12)

FOCUS
A decent prize for a fair handicap but only a moderate gallop. The first two, who ended up against the inside rail, pulled clear in the straight.

NOTEBOOK
Wind Flow left a below-par effort well behind and in the process showed a tremendous attitude to notch his fourth win of the winter and his first handicap success since last May. He should continue to run well around this trip when allowed to dominate. (op 5-1)
Wine 'n Dine, a progressive sort, was well supported but, although it was a shade disappointing that he was outbattled after drawing alongside the winner in the straight, he deserves plenty of credit for an improved effort as a muddling gallop over 1m4f would not have played to his strengths. A stronger pace or a step up in distance will suit and he is well worth another chance. (op 5-6 tchd 10-11)
Blacktoft(USA), who was very free to post, settled better in the race on this first start for new connections and was not disgraced back up to this trip for only the second time. A strongly run race around 1m2f are his requirements and he will be interesting if and when sent over hurdles. (op 11-2)
Spirit Of Adjisa(IRE) had the run of the race but looked less than straightforward under pressure and failed to build on his previous run without his usual blinkers. He will be of more interest with the headgear refitted but has little margin for error from this mark. (op 9-2 tchd 11-2)
Boo's form has been patchy since his last win more than three years ago and he did not show enough on this first run after a break to suggest he would be of much immediate interest. (op 28-1)
United Nations has shown his best form around 1m on Fibresand and predictably failed to get home, even in a race run at a modest gallop. The return to that slower surface and to shorter will suit but he looks high enough in the weights. (op 16-1)

694 BETDAQ.CO.UK H'CAP 1m 141y(P)
8:50 (8:50) (Class 4) (0-85,85) 4-Y-O+ £4,727 (£1,406; £702; £351) Stalls Low

Form RPR
-661 1 **Gallantry**19 446 7-9-4 85 TolleyDean 5 94
(P Howling) *stdd and dropped in bhd after s: hld up in last pair: hdwy on inner 2f out: rdn to chse ldr over 1f out: led fnl 75yds: r.o wl* 20/1
3 2 nk **Leonaldo (USA)**29 318 4-8-7 74 ChrisCatlin 1 82
(J R Gask) *chsd ldng pair: led 2f out: sn rdn: drvn ins fnl f: hdd and no ex fnl 75yds* 6/1[3]
00-4 3 4 **Solent Ridge (IRE)**33 283 4-8-7 74 ow1 LPKeniry 3 74
(J S Moore) *racd in midfield: effrt 2f out: rdn and one pce fr over 1f out: edgd lft u.p ins fnl f* 10/1
12-1 4 2 ¼ **Plush**36 238 6-8-12 79 RichardKingscote 6 77+
(Tom Dascombe) *taken down early: stdd s: hld up in last pl: hdwy on outer 3f out: rdn and c v wd ent st: no hdwy over 1f out: wl btn whn hmpd and eased ins fnl f: fin lame* 11/8[1]
-502 5 2 ½ **Scamperdale**17 477 7-9-1 82 (p) TPQueally 7 72
(B P J Baugh) *racd in midfield: rdn and struggling over 3f out: one pce and no ch w ldrs fr over 1f out* 5/2[2]

3-40 **6** *nk* **Torch Of Freedom (IRE)**[16] 490 4-8-9 76............. StephenDonohoe 2 65
(Sir Mark Prescott) *sn pushed up to ld: clr after 1f: rdn over 3f out: drvn and hdd 2f out: wknd over 1f out* **12/1**

/60- **7** *5* **Mistress Greeley (USA)**[187] 5273 4-9-4 85.................. NCallan 4 64
(M Botti) *chsd ldr: rdn 3f out: wknd u.p wl over 1f out: sn bhd* **10/1**

1m 48.45s (-2.05) **Going Correction** -0.025s/f (Stan) **7** Ran SP% **115.6**
Speed ratings (Par 105): **108,107,104,102,99 99,95**
toteswinger: 1&2 £10.60, 1&3 £10.60, 2&3 £10.60. CSF £134.50 CT £1287.63 TOTE £17.10: £3.70, £2.40; EX 33.30.
Owner The Circle Bloodstock I Limited **Bred** Cheveley Park Stud Ltd **Trained** Newmarket, Suffolk
FOCUS
Another fair handicap in which the pace was soon sound but a race that did not take as much winning as seemed likely with both market leaders disappointing. Winner and second, who pulled clear, edged towards the centre in the closing stages.
Plush Official explanation: vet said gelding was found to be lame during routine testing post-race

695 FRIDAY NIGHTS ARE DISCO NIGHTS MAIDEN STKS 1m 141y(P)
9:20 (9:20) (Class 4) 3-Y-O+ **£2,590** (£770; £385; £192) **Stalls** Low

Form RPR
42- **1** **Gaily Noble (IRE)**[99] 7380 3-8-7 0.............................. FergusSweeney 3 74+
(A B Haynes) *mde all: clr over 2f out: in n.d fnl 2f: v easily* **4/9**[1]

2 *5* **Sullenberger (IRE)** 3-8-8 0 ow1.. ShaneKelly 1 65+
(J A Osborne) *trckd ldng pair: rdn and outpcd over 2f out: swtchd lft jst ins fnl f: kpt on to go 2nd towards fin: no ch w wnr* **10/1**[3]

50- **3** *¾* **Royal Society**[147] 6412 3-8-7 0.. JoeFanning 4 62
(M Johnston) *chsd wnr: rdn 3f out: sn outpcd by wnr: plugged on one pce: lost 2nd towards fin* **3/1**[2]

0 **4** *8* **Cherry Plum**[22] 386 3-8-2 0.. ChrisCatlin 2 46+
(A M Balding) *a last: wl in tch tl rdn and struggling over 3f out: no ch fnl 2f: eased ins fnl f* **14/1**

1m 50.21s (-0.29) **Going Correction** -0.025s/f (Stan) **4** Ran SP% **110.0**
Speed ratings (Par 105): **100,95,94,87**
CSF £5.76 TOTE £1.50; EX 6.70 Place 6 £658.36, Place 5 £244.03..
Owner Ms J Loylert **Bred** Garry Chong **Trained** Limpley Stoke, Bath
FOCUS
An uncompetitive race of its type. The pace was only fair and the winner raced just off the inside rail in the straight.
T/Plt: £428.80 to a £1 stake. Pool: £66,014.59. 112.38 winning tickets. T/Qpdt: £33.50 to a £1 stake. Pool: £6,495.68. 143.42 winning tickets. SP

637 NAD AL SHEBA (L-H)
Thursday, February 26
OFFICIAL GOING: Turf course - good to firm; dirt course - fast

696a MEYDAN BUSINESS PARK TROPHY (CONDITIONS RACE) (TURF) 6f (T)
3:15 (3:15) 3-Y-0+
£41,666 (£13,888; £6,944; £3,472; £2,083; £1,388)

RPR
1 **Beaver Patrol (IRE)**[6] 637 7-9-0 102..............................(b) MJKinane 4 104
(Eve Johnson Houghton) *mid-div: rdn to chse ldrs 2f out: led 1f out: r.o wl* **9/1**[3]

2 *1 ¾* **Lipocco**[6] 638 5-9-0 98.. RyanMoore 8 99
(H J Brown, South Africa) *sn led: rdn 2 1/2f out: hdd 1f out: r.o wl* **9/1**[3]

3 *hd* **Nota Bene**[7] 611 7-9-0 100.. RichardHughes 1 98
(D R C Elsworth) *mid-div on rail: t.k.h: ev ch whn n.m.r 1 1/2f out: r.o wl* **7/2**[1]

4 *1 ¾* **Almajd (IRE)**[160] 6073 4-9-0 100....................................... RHills 2 93
(M Al Muhairi, UAE) *slowly away: settled in rr on rail: n.m.r 2 /12f out: r.o once clr* **14/1**

5 *½* **Grantley Adams**[6] 638 6-9-0 100.. TPO'Shea 3 92
(E Charpy, UAE) *settled in rr: nvr able to chal: r.o same pce fnl f* **4/1**[2]

6 *¼* **Confuchias (IRE)**[6] 637 5-9-0 98...................................... RichardMullen 7 91
(K R Burke) *mid-div: rdn 3f out: nvr able to chal* **16/1**

7 *3 ¼* **Nights Cross (IRE)**[7] 611 8-9-0 102..................................(t) GHind 6 81
(B Al Abed, Bahrain) *in rr of mid-div: rdn to cl 2 1/2f out: wknd fnl f* **12/1**

8 *3 ½* **League Champion (USA)**[6] 638 6-9-0 100.................. WilliamBuick 5 71
(R Bouresly, Kuwait) *mid-div: rdn 3f out: sn btn* **20/1**

9 *¾* **Leandros (FR)**[7] 615 4-8-8 102.. EMcNamara(6) 10 68
(G M Lyons, Ire) *s.i.s: settled last: rdn 3f out: nt qckn* **7/2**[1]

10 *1 ¼* **Montpellier (IRE)**[11] 6-9-0 99..(t) JMurtagh 9 65
(A Al Raihe, UAE) *trckd ldr tl 3f out: sn wknd* **9/1**[3]

1m 12.56s (0.56) **Going Correction** +0.30s/f (Good) **10** Ran SP% **119.4**
Speed ratings: **108,105,105,103,102 102,97,93,92,90**
CSF £89.30..
Owner G C Stevens **Bred** Kevin B Lynch **Trained** Blewbury, Oxon
FOCUS
This race was staged at late notice to accommodate those balloted out of the Group 3 Al Quoz Sprint. The same conditions applied, but the race did not carry Group status. There wasn't much between most of these on form and this was basically just a decent conditions contest, but it paid to race handy.
NOTEBOOK
Beaver Patrol(IRE) had been below his best in two outings in handicaps so far at this year's Carnival, but his stable had a winner last week and he struck form with a clear-cut success. With second-time blinkers replacing the usual visor, he was well drawn and took full advantage of a good trip.
Lipocco was disappointing behind a couple of today's rivals over the extended 6f here the previous week, but this was better, especially considering he would have been 4lb better off with the winner in a handicap.
Nota Bene had to battle to find a gap in the straight, but he basically just took too long in picking up and was not unlucky. (op 10-3\n\x\x)
Almajd(IRE) is better than he showed as he was denied a clear run in the straight after being tucked away, well off the pace towards the inside rail. He didn't progress as one might have expected for Sir Michael Stoute, but he still showed very useful form and this was a pleasing return from over five months off, especially considering the trip was short of his optimum. (op 16-1)
Grantley Adams had today's runner-up well behind when second over the extended 6f here the previous week, but he was disappointing this time. He still had plenty to do early in the straight and ruined his chance by edging left, rather than running on. (op 9-2)
Confuchias(IRE) was a little short of room in the straight, but he was not unlucky and is basically best suited to either easy turf or Polytrack.
Nights Cross(IRE) briefly looked dangerous halfway up the straight, but he failed to see his race out, having pulled early on and gone wide into the straight.
Leandros(FR) was a disappointing joint favourite.

697a SIGNATURE MALL TROPHY (CONDITIONS RACE) (TURF) 1m (T)
3:45 (3:45) 3-Y-0+
£41,666 (£13,888; £6,944; £3,472; £2,083; £1,388)

RPR
1 **Furnace (IRE)**[7] 615 5-8-6 96................................... AntiocoMurgia(10) 3 102
(M bin Shafya, UAE) *sn led: set gd pce: styd on wl* **16/1**

2 *¾* **Kachgai (IRE)**[20] 439 6-9-2 100.. JMartinez 2 100
(L A Urbano-Grajales, France) *in rr of mid-div: r.o wl fnl 1 1/2f: nrst fin* **6/1**[3]

3 *1 ¼* **Emirates Gold (IRE)**[7] 609 6-9-2 100..............................(t) TPO'Shea 5 97
(E Charpy, UAE) *mid-div: r.o wl fnl 2f: nrst fin* **11/1**

4 *2 ¼* **Calming Influence (IRE)**[21] 413 4-9-2 106.........................(t) LDettori 6 92
(Saeed Bin Suroor) *trckd ldr: rdn to chse wnr 2 1/2f out: ev ch 1 1/2f out: one pce fnl f* **2/1**[1]

5 *1 ¼* **Mojito Royale (IRE)**[7] 609 5-9-2 98................................... RyanMoore 7 89
(Eoin Doyle, Ire) *settled in rr: nvr able to chal* **25/1**

6 *1 ¼* **King Jock (USA)**[21] 413 8-9-5 104...................................... MJKinane 11 89
(A Manuel, UAE) *settled in rr: nvr nr to chal: r.o fnl 2 1/2f* **10/1**

7 *1 ¼* **Wise Dennis**[6] 644 7-9-2 101..(v[1]) JMurtagh 9 83
(A P Jarvis) *s.i.s: mid-div: rdn 2 1/2f out: one pce* **11/2**[2]

8 *¼* **Prince Shaun (IRE)**[21] 413 4-9-2 105..........................(t) DO'Donohoe 1 83
(Doug Watson, UAE) *trckd ldr: ev ch 2 1/2f out: one pce fnl f* **12/1**

9 *2 ¼* **Fleeting Shadow (IRE)**[28] 340 5-9-2 97...............(t) RoystonFfrench 8 78
(A Al Raihe, UAE) *in rr of mid-div: n.m.r 2 1/2f out* **16/1**

10 *2 ¼* **Bermuda Rye (IRE)**[6] 638 4-9-2 102.................................. AhmedAjtebi 4 72
(M bin Shafya, UAE) *settled last: hrd rdn 3f out: nt qckn* **6/1**[3]

11 *8* **Evaluator (IRE)**[98] 8-9-2 97.. RichardMullen 12 54
(M Ramadan, UAE) *trckd ldrs for 3f: sn wknd* **50/1**

12 *17* **Bruges (IRE)**[7] 616 4-9-2 96...(bt) RHills 10 15
(A Al Raihe, UAE) *nvr nr to chal* **25/1**

1m 38.44s (0.14) **Going Correction** +0.30s/f (Good) **12** Ran SP% **123.8**
Speed ratings: **111,110,109,106,105 104,103,102,100,98 90,73**
CSF £112.20..
Owner Sheikh Mansoor bin Mohammed al Maktoum **Bred** Barouche Stud Ireland Ltd **Trained** United Arab Emirates
FOCUS
A race to accommodate those balloted out of the Group 3 Zabeel Mile. The same conditions applied, but this did not carry Group status.
NOTEBOOK
Furnace(IRE) made all after being driven to the front on leaving the stalls. His promising apprentice got the fractions absolutely spot on and was terrific value for his 10lb claim (will be 7lb when he returns to Britain). The winner, who landed a couple of decent handicaps for Michael Bell last year, was disappointing over the extended 7f here the previous, but this was a return to sort of form he showed when a good second on his debut in Dubai.
Kachgai(IRE) tried to repeat the tactics of his recent course-and-distance handicap success - hold-up ride and making much of his ground towards the inside - but he just found one too good. This was a defeat effort in defeat considering he was waited with in a race in which the winner made the running.
Emirates Gold(IRE) usually runs his race and this was a solid effort in defeat.
Calming Influence(IRE) proved unsuited by this slight step up in trip and ruined his chance by racing too keenly early on. He's rarely a value price and is one to avoid.
Mojito Royale(IRE) was left with too much to do and only got going when the race was all over.
King Jock(USA) likes to cruise into contention on the bridle, but that wasn't possible with the field strung out trying to peg back the winner.
Wise Dennis didn't take to the first-time visor, starting slowly and then racing keenly.
Prince Shaun(IRE) was another who was too keen.

698a MEYDAN HOTEL TROPHY (H'CAP) (DIRT) 1m 1f (D)
4:15 (4:15) (95-115,115) 3-Y-0
£72,916 (£24,305; £12,152; £6,076; £3,645; £2,430)

RPR
1 **Gloria De Campeao (BRZ)**[21] 417 6-9-0 **108**....................... JLeme 16 112
(P Bary, France) *trckd ldrs: gng wl 3f out: led 2f out: r.o wl: comf* **9/1**

2 *4 ¼* **Art Of War (SAF)**[14] 523 5-9-0 **108**...................................... JMurtagh 8 104
(M F De Kock, South Africa) *mid-div: chsd ldrs 3f out: trckd wnr 2f out: r.o same pce* **7/2**[1]

3 *3 ¼* **Familiar Territory**[14] 523 6-9-0 **108**...................................... LDettori 3 98
(Saeed Bin Suroor) *mid-div: rdn to chse ldrs 3f out: r.o* **7/1**

4 *¼* **Glen Nevis (USA)**[14] 523 5-8-9 **104**.........................(v) RoystonFfrench 5 92
(A Al Raihe, UAE) *in rr of mid-div: r.o fnl 2 1/2f: nrst fin* **33/1**

5 *3 ¼* **Irish Mayhem (USA)**[7] 612 4-8-6 **100**..........................(v) DO'Donohoe 9 83
(Saeed Bin Suroor) *sn rdn in rr: nvr nr to chal: r.o v wl fnl 3f* **10/1**

6 *4 ¼* **Traffic Guard (USA)**[7] 614 5-9-6 **115**................................. JohnEgan 6 89
(H J Brown, South Africa) *trckd ldrs: rdn 3 1/2f out: nt qckn* **12/1**

7 *2* **Tasteyville (USA)**[6] 639 6-8-6 **99** ow1.......................................(b) RHills 1 71
(E Charpy, UAE) *led on rail: rdn 3f out: hdd 2f out: wknd fnl 1 1/2f* **20/1**

8 *½* **Grand Hombre (USA)**[7] 612 9-8-6 **100**..............................(t) DSmith 14 70
(R Bouresly, Kuwait) *racd in rr: nvr able to chal: r.o fnl 3f* **28/1**

9 *½* **Shopton Lane (USA)**[28] 334 5-8-9 **104**.......................(t) RyanMoore 10 72
(Doug Watson, UAE) *trckd ldr: ev ch 3f out: one pce fnl 2f* **14/1**

10 *1 ¾* **Singing Poet (IRE)**[14] 523 8-8-5 **99**.................................(t) TPO'Shea 4 65
(E Charpy, UAE) *a mid-div* **33/1**

11 *dist* **Mr Brock (SAF)**[7] 613 6-8-8 **102** ow1.. KShea 15 —
(M F De Kock, South Africa) *nvr nr to chal* **14/1**

12 *dist* **Jalil (USA)**[180] 5-9-6 **115**..(t) AhmedAjtebi 12 —
(M bin Shafya, UAE) *mid-div: rn wd: rdn 3f out: nvr able to chal* **13/2**[3]

13 *dist* **Roman's Run (USA)**[20] 435 5-8-6 **100**..................................(t) FJara 11 —
(Doug Watson, UAE) *nvr bttr than mid-div* **5/1**[2]

14 *dist* **Aleutian**[14] 523 9-8-8 **102**..(e) RichardMullen 2 —
(F Nass, Bahrain) *s.i.s: trckd ldrs on rail: rdn 4f out: sn btn* **33/1**

15 *dist* **Emirates Skyline (USA)**[6] 642 6-8-6 **100**.......................... WJSupple 7 —
(A bin Huzaim, UAE) *nvr bttr than mid-div* **25/1**

16 *dist* **Jalmira (IRE)**[6] 643 8-8-6 **104**..................................... SMGorey(3) 13 —
(E Charpy, UAE) *nvr bttr than mid-div* **33/1**

1m 49.35s (-0.45) **Going Correction** +0.225s/f (Slow) **16** Ran SP% **128.7**
Speed ratings: **111,107,104,104,101 97,95,95,94,93 —,—,—,—,—, —**
CSF £39.53 Tricast £241.02..
Owner Estrela Energia Stables **Bred** Haras Santarem **Trained** Chantilly, France
FOCUS
A decent, competitive handicap, and a better race of its type than is normally the case on the Nad Al Sheba dirt. They seemed to go a decent pace.

NOTEBOOK

Gloria De Campeao(BRZ)'s last five starts in Dubai had been in Group company, and he's simply not quite up that level, but he took full advantage of this drop in class. He enjoyed the perfect trip for this track, racing close up, but three wide to ensure he avoided the kickback, and he stayed on strongly in the straight. A deserved first Carnival success for both horse and trainer. (op 8-1)

Art Of War(SAF) had to go a little wider into the straight than the winner, but that was no excuse and he had his chance. This was a solid effort off an 8lb higher mark than when winning a lesser race over 1m1f on his previous start. (op 4-1)

Familiar Territory ran better than when well behind Art Of War on previous start, especially considering he's probably ideally suited by a little further.

Glen Nevis(USA) ran his usual race, staying on strongly in the closing stages having got well behind early.

Irish Mayhem(USA) has not convinced since joining this yard and this was another unsatisfactory performance. He was detached from the main group early, but past several rivals in the straight to take fifth. It's clear he's got plenty of ability, but he has not been particularly reliable so far this year. A return to synthetics should help. (tchd 11-1)

Traffic Guard(USA), back on dirt, did not run badly considering he was stuck behind the pace towards the inside for most of the way, but he's hard to win with.

Tasteyville(USA), carrying 1lb overweight, was again well below his US form.

Mr Brock(SAF) failed to take to the dirt and only ran on past beaten horses. (op 12-1)

Jalil(USA) did not run as badly as his finishing position suggests, as he was debuting for a new stable after six months off and raced extremely wide throughout. However, he would surely have started off in the third round of the Al Maktoum Challenge if much was expected of him. (op 7-1)

Roman's Run(USA) was weighted to confirm form with Art Of War on their running from earlier in the Carnival, so this was hugely disappointing.

Emirates Skyline(USA)

699a DRC GOLD CUP SPONSORED BY MEYDAN METROPOLIS (CONDITIONS RACE) (TURF) — 2m

4:45 (4:46) 4-Y-O+

£72,916 (£24,305; £12,152; £6,076; £3,645; £2,430)

RPR

1 **Veracity**[20] [437] 5-9-2 113 .... LDettori 7 116
(Saeed Bin Suroor) *trckd ldng pair: rdn to ld 4 1/2f out: clr 2 1/2f out: r.o wl: game* **4/5**[1]

2 ½ **Mourilyan (IRE)**[20] [437] 5-9-0 112 .... RyanMoore 3 113
(H J Brown, South Africa) *settled in rr: smooth prog to chse wnr 2 1/2f out: r.o wl: ev ch 110yds out: jst failed* **7/2**[2]

3 2 ¼ **Basaltico (IRE)**[20] [437] 5-9-0 108 .... JMurtagh 9 111
(H J Brown, South Africa) *settled in rr: smooth prog to trck wnr 3f out: one pce fnl f* **14/1**

4 5 ½ **Sanbuch**[7] [616] 5-9-0 110 .... (t) AhmedAjtebi 8 104
(M bin Shafya, UAE) *settled last: rdn 3f out: rn wd 2 1/2f out: one pce* **7/1**[3]

5 4 **Galactic Star**[14] [527] 6-9-0 108 .... (t) JRosales 6 100
(M bin Shafya, UAE) *mid-div: rdn to chse ldrs 2 1/2f out: one pce fnl 1 1/2f* **20/1**

6 2 **Weald**[7] [613] 4-8-8 100 .... FJara 4 98
(Doug Watson, UAE) *mid-div: rdn to chse ldrs 2 1/2f out: one pce fnl 1 1/2f* **40/1**

7 2 ¾ **Book Of Music (IRE)**[6] [640] 6-9-0 104 .... (e) RichardMullen 1 95
(S Seemar, UAE) *mid-div: trckd wnr 3f out: nt qckn* **25/1**

8 15 **Mulaqat**[7] [616] 6-9-0 105 .... WilliamBuick 10 78
(D Selvaratnam, UAE) *mid-div: trckd wnr 3f out: nt qckn* **20/1**

9 16 **Lion Sands**[14] [527] 5-9-0 107 .... WJSupple 2 61
(A bin Huzaim, UAE) *mid-div on rail: rdn 3f out: sn btn* **14/1**

10 4 **Drill Sergeant**[20] [437] 4-8-8 102 .... RoystonFfrench 11 56
(M Johnston) *sn led: hdd 4 1/2f out: sn stuggling* **33/1**

11 dist **Fathayer (USA)**[7] [613] 4-8-8 100 .... TPO'Shea 5 —
(A Al Raihe, UAE) *trckd ldr: 3rd 5f out: rdn 3 1/2f out: wknd* **50/1**

12 dist **Detonator (IRE)**[20] [437] 4-7-12 100 .... AntiocoMurgia(10) 12 —
(M bin Shafya, UAE) *mid-div: rn wd: rdn 5f out: sn btn* **40/1**

3m 26.76s (206.76)
WFA 4 from 5yo+ 6lb **12 Ran SP% 126.8**
CSF £3.55..

Owner Godolphin **Bred** Darley **Trained** Newmarket, Suffolk

FOCUS

The inaugural running of the Dubai Racing Club Gold Cup, indeed the first-ever race over 2m at the Carnival, and this was a cracking contest. A terrific addition to the programme in Dubai and this race should go from strength to strength. The form amongst the principals looks around Listed/Group 3 standard, but a steady early pace didn't play to Veracity's strengths and he should be capable of rating even higher.

NOTEBOOK

Veracity ◆ had run a nice race under top weight in the trial for this over 1m6f around here three weeks earlier and confirmed that promise over this longer distance, despite again conceding weight all round, although he was forced to work much harder than ideal. He is an out-and-out stayer, so with the gallop steady for much of the way, he raced close up with little cover through the early stages, and was then committed for home fully half a mile out when Drill Sergeant dropped away. He looked vulnerable when strongly pressed in the straight, but he proved particularly game and was a deserving winner. Provided this has not left its mark - he had a hard race - it would be unwise to underestimate him when he contests some of the major staying races in Europe, as he can better this form when there is more emphasis on stamina. The Ascot Gold Cup must be the main aim, as he'll relish every yard of the 2m4f trip. (op 11-10)

Mourilyan(IRE) raced much further back than the winner but he was produced with absolutely every chance. He got the 2m trip okay, but not as well as Veracity, and he simply bumped into a pretty smart stayer. (op 11-4)

Basaltico(IRE), a Listed winner over 1m4f in France last year, looked well worth a try over this trip and he ran a solid race in third. (op 12-1)

Sanbuch ran in snatches for some of the way and looked an awkward ride under pressure in the straight. He has plenty of ability, but is equally quirky and looks best avoided. (op 6-1)

Galactic Star had shown little in two runs over 1m2f so far this year, but this was a better upped in trip and tried in a first-time tongue-tie. It's possible this trip stretched him, as he was one paced in the straight after travelling well, but this is still something to build on.

Weald did not run at all badly considering he was a little keen early on.

700a AL QUOZ SPRINT SPONSORED BY MEYDAN HORIZONS (GROUP 3) (TURF) — 6f (T)

5:15 (5:15) 3-Y-O+

£83,333 (£27,777; £13,888; £6,944; £4,166; £2,777)

RPR

1 **J J The Jet Plane (SAF)**[14] [525] 5-9-5 120 .... KShea 2 119
(M F De Kock, South Africa) *wl away: led for 1 1/2f: trckd ldr gng wl 1 1/2f out: led 1f out: comf* **6/4**[1]

2 1 ¼ **Hatta Fort**[21] [418] 4-9-2 110 .... (t) LDettori 7 112
(Saeed Bin Suroor) *settled in rr: n.m.r 2 1/2f out: r.o wl fnl 1 1/2f: nrst fin* **7/2**[2]

3 ¼ **Dohasa (IRE)**[6] [638] 4-9-0 109 .... JMurtagh 3 110
(G M Lyons, Ire) *mid-div on rail: rdn to chse wnr 2f out: r.o wl* **13/2**[3]

4 1 ¼ **Contest (IRE)**[7] [611] 5-9-0 106 .... (b) C-PLemaire 4 106
(C Theodorakis, Greece) *s.i.s: mid-div: n.m.r 2f out: r.o wl* **20/1**

5 1 ¼ **Instant Recall (IRE)**[7] [611] 8-9-0 105 .... (v) RoystonFfrench 10 102
(M Al Muhairi, UAE) *led after 1 1/2f: hdd 1f out: wknd* **25/1**

6 ¾ **Judd Street**[7] [611] 7-9-0 106 .... (b) MJKinane 5 99
(Eve Johnson Houghton) *a mid-div* **12/1**

7 1 ½ **Intrepid Jack**[21] [418] 7-9-2 110 .... RyanMoore 8 96
(H Morrison) *settled in rr: last 2 1/2f out: r.o same pce* **15/2**

8 1 **Prince Tamino**[6] [638] 6-9-0 104 .... (t) TPO'Shea 9 91
(A Al Raihe, UAE) *in rr of mid-div: nvr able to chal* **40/1**

9 3 **Munaddam (USA)**[6] [637] 7-9-0 111 .... RHills 6 82
(E Charpy, UAE) *in rr of mid-div: rdn 2 1/2f out: nt qckn* **10/1**

10 1 ¾ **Miss Gorica (IRE)**[7] [611] 5-8-9 102 .... WJSupple 1 71
(Ms Joanna Morgan, Ire) *trckd ldrs tl 3f out: wknd* **16/1**

1m 11.72s (-0.28) **Going Correction** +0.30s/f (Good) **10 Ran SP% 121.0**
Speed ratings: **113,111,111,109,107 106,104,103,99,97**
CSF £6.70..

Owner H Du Preez, C Strydom, L Houdalakis, C Boyens **Bred** Mrs P J Devine **Trained** South Africa

FOCUS

A reasonable Group 3 and an above-average winner for the class.

NOTEBOOK

J J The Jet Plane(SAF) relished the return to turf and was much too good for this lot, despite conceding upwards of 3lb all round. Quickly into his stride, he kept the early leader, Instant Recall, honest and found plenty when asked in the straight. He was being closed down at the finish, but was always doing enough and gave the impression he can better this form. This was a very smart effort considering he was conceding 3lb to the 110-rated runner-up, as well as 5lb to the 109-rated third, and he stopped the clock in a time 0.84 seconds quicker than the 102-rated Beaver Patrol managed carrying 5lb less in the consolation race. He is expected to form part of his trainer's string in Newmarket this year and is likely to contest some of the major European sprints.

Hatta Fort picked up smartly from a long way back and ran right up to his best; he simply bumped into a very decent type for the level.

Dohasa(IRE) was ridden a little handier this time, having not enjoyed the best of trips on his first two starts in Dubai, and he ran well upped in class. (op 11-2)

Contest(IRE), who looked an unlucky loser in a muddling race behind Judd Street over course and distance a week earlier, ran a cracking race in this much tougher heat.

Instant Recall(IRE) dead-heated in this last year, but some tough races from the front seem to have taken the edge off him.

Judd Street didn't seem to have any excuse. (tchd 11-1)

Intrepid Jack, who had no easy task under a Group win penalty, was given plenty to do and struggled to get involved. (op 17-2)

701a UAE OAKS SPONSORED BY MEYDAN CITY (LISTED RACE) (FILLIES) (DIRT) — 1m 1f (D)

5:45 (5:45) 3-Y-O

£104,166 (£34,722; £17,361; £8,680; £5,208; £3,472)

RPR

1 **Devotee (USA)**[20] [438] 3-8-9 96 .... (t) LDettori 2 103+
(Saeed Bin Suroor) *led 1 1/2f: then trckd ldr: led 2 1/2f out: r.o wl: gamely* **9/4**[2]

2 1 ¼ **Earth Living (USA)**[20] [438] 3-8-9 95 .... C-PLemaire 3 101
(Michihiro Ogasa, Japan) *in rr of mid-div: smooth prog to trck ldr 2f out: ev ch fnl 1 1/2f: nt qckn fnl 110yds* **9/2**[3]

3 11 **Sos Brillante (CHI)**[20] [438] 4-9-5 100 .... DO'Donohoe 4 82
(Saeed Bin Suroor) *mid-div: r.o fnl 3f: nvr able to chal* **7/1**

4 ¾ **So Shiny (ARG)**[20] [438] 4-9-5 102 .... (t) MJKinane 1 80
(J Barton, Saudi Arabia) *led after 1 1/2f: t.k.h: hdd 2 1/2f out: wknd* **2/1**[1]

5 6 ½ **Fire Sale (ARG)**[20] [438] 4-9-5 93 .... (t) RyanMoore 8 67
(H J Brown, South Africa) *settled in rr: nvr nr to chal* **12/1**

6 2 ¼ **Esta Bailando (CHI)**[20] [438] 4-9-5 93 .... (t) FJara 7 63
(J Barton, Saudi Arabia) *settled in rr: nvr nr to chal* **28/1**

7 ¾ **Purple Sage (IRE)**[20] [438] 3-8-9 94 .... RHills 5 58
(E Martins, Bahrain) *trckd ldrs: rdn 3f out: sn btn* **12/1**

8 dist **Ever Loved (USA)**[20] [438] 3-8-9 90 .... RichardMullen 6 —
(S Seemar, UAE) *sn rdn in rr: nvr able to chal* **33/1**

1m 51.09s (1.29) **Going Correction** +0.225s/f (Slow)
WFA 3 from 4yo 21lb **8 Ran SP% 116.6**
Speed ratings: **103,101,92,91,85 83,83,—**
CSF £13.25..

Owner Godolphin **Bred** Darley Stud **Trained** Newmarket, Suffolk

FOCUS

All eight runners in this year's UAE Oaks had contested the Guineas three weeks earlier, and the race lacked strength in depth, but the front two pulled a long way clear. They went a good pace early, but the final time was 1.74 seconds slower than the earlier handicap over this trip won the 108-rated Gloria De Campeao, a six-year-old colt.

NOTEBOOK

Devotee(USA) was sent off at odds of 1/3 in the Guineas, but she finished tailed off and was reported to have suffered a cardiac arrhythmia. However, she completed a satisfactory gallop in the presence of an ERA Veterinary Officer prior to being entered for this race and has seemingly made a full recovery. She wasn't impressive, and briefly looked a little awkward when first coming under pressure (before the runner-up) in the straight, but she ultimately knuckled down well. When trained in the States as a juvenile she was a winner on her debut, before running third in a Grade 1, and this success obviously goes some way to justifying her lofty reputation. It's probably safe to assume she won't be good enough to give the colts a race in the Derby on World Cup, so there is little left for her in Dubai this year, and she'll surely now continue her career back in the US. (op 5-2)

Earth Living(USA), who has some very smart Japanese form to her name and ran second to So Shiny in the UAE 1000 Guineas, looked all over the winner when last off the bridle in the straight - she touched 1.37 in-running - but she was simply outstayed. She was a street clear of the remainder and can do better again back over 1m. (op 5-1)

Sos Brillante(CHI) ran better than when pulling hard in a first-time visor in the Guineas, but she was still keener than ideal with the headgear left off and has not progressed as expected.

So Shiny(ARG) looked to nick the UAE 1000 Guineas, leading at modest fractions, despite pulling, but she gave herself no chance of repeating the trick. She raced with her head pointing towards the infield pretty much throughout, including under pressure in the straight, and looked a thoroughly awkward customer. (op 7-4)

Fire Sale(ARG) didn't improve for the longer trip or tongue-tie.

702a ZABEEL MILE SPONSORED BY MEYDAN RACECOURSE (GROUP 3) (TURF) 1m (T)

6:15 (6:15) 3-Y-O+

£83,333 (£27,777; £13,888; £6,944; £4,166; £2,777)

RPR

1 **Archipenko (USA)**[201] 4889 5-9-7 120.................(bt) KShea 5 118
(M F De Kock, South Africa) *trckd ldrs: led 2f out: r.o wl: comf* **9/4**[1]

2 ¾ **Vertigineux (FR)**[20] 439 5-9-4 110.................(t) PSogorb 2 113
(Mme C Dufreche, France) *trckd ldrs: ev ch 3f out: r.o: nt qckn fnl f* **9/1**

3 nse **Kalahari Gold (IRE)**[160] 6073 4-9-2 112................. RHills 3 111
(Doug Watson, UAE) *mid-div on rail: n.m.r 4 1/2f out: r.o wl fnl 2 1/2f: nrst fin* **5/1**[3]

4 2 ¼ **Brave Tin Soldier (USA)**[6] 639 5-9-2 106.................(b) C-PLemaire 1 106
(M F De Kock, South Africa) *sn led: hdd 2f out: wknd* **25/1**

5 ½ **Seihali (IRE)**[7] 615 10-9-2 106................. WilliamBuick 6 105
(D Selvaratnam, UAE) *mid-div: chsd ldrs 2 1/2f out: nt qckn fnl 110yds* **40/1**

6 ½ **My Central (ITY)**[6] 643 5-9-0 110................. RyanMoore 11 101
(H J Brown, South Africa) *slowly away: settled in rr: nvr nr to chal* **14/1**

7 hd **Tam Lin**[151] 6-9-5 113.................(t) LDettori 9 106
(Saeed Bin Suroor) *settled in rr: rn wd in mid-div 4f out: one pce fnl 2f* **9/2**[2]

8 ½ **Biarritz (SAF)**[20] 436 6-9-2 112.................(b) RoystonFfrench 10 102
(M F De Kock, South Africa) *mid-div: trckd ldrs 2 1/2f out: wknd fnl f* **16/1**

9 ½ **King Of Rome (IRE)**[151] 6324 4-9-5 111.................(t) JMurtagh 4 104
(M F De Kock, South Africa) *settled in rr: nvr able to chal* **8/1**

10 1 ¾ **Summit Surge (IRE)**[7] 614 5-9-4 113.................(t) KLatham 7 99
(G M Lyons, Ire) *in rr of mid-div: nvr able to chal* **12/1**

11 ¾ **Ragheed (USA)**[7] 615 5-9-2 106.................(vt) RichardMullen 8 95
(E Charpy, UAE) *in rr of mid-div: nvr nr to chal* **20/1**

12 2 ¾ **Golden Arrow (IRE)**[27] 6-9-2 106.................(bt) TPO'Shea 12 89
(E Charpy, UAE) *mid-div: rn wd: nvr able to chal* **25/1**

1m 39.89s (1.59) **Going Correction** +0.30s/f (Good) 12 Ran SP% **121.9**
Speed ratings: **104,103,103,100,100 99,99,99,98,97 96,93**
CSF £23.10..

Owner Sh Mohd Khalifa Al Maktoum & DR AH Parker **Bred** Eagle Holdings **Trained** South Africa

FOCUS
The winning time was 1.45 seconds slower than the earlier consolation race won by the 96-rated Furnace, but that's a result of a modest early pace and a direct comparison is misleading. For example, the field were 2.71 seconds slower over the opening 1200m than the runners in the earlier race, but went 1.26 seconds faster in the final 400m. The slow overall time should not disguise the quality of the line up for this Group 3 contest and the 'right' horses dominated. This is strong form.

NOTEBOOK
Archipenko(USA) ◆ posted a terrific performance. For a start he was conceding weight all round to some smart rivals, and he was considered only around 80% ready by his trainer, having had some time off after missing last season's Champion Stakes through soreness. On top of that, he seemed inclined to race a little keenly early on, and the steady pace, which compressed the margin of victory, did not play to his strengths, as he's a horse with a terrific cruising speed. However, he was still going well within himself when ranging upsides the early leader, Brave Tin Soldier, in the straight, and he found plenty when finally asked to stretch. His form figures since being fitted with blinkers read 131121, and those wins include a Group 1 and a couple of Group 2s. He will now aim to better last year's slightly unlucky third in the Dubai Duty Free on World Cup night. That's shaping up into quite a race, and he'll probably be joined by stablemate Bankable, who was himself quite impressive the previous week, but on this showing the top-class Archipenko is undoubtedly now the one to beat. The stronger the pace they go in that race, the better for him, and a decent gallop will almost be assured if confirmed front-runner Gladiatorus lines up. (op 5-2)
Vertigineux(FR), a multiple Listed and Group 3 winner in his native France, confirmed the promise he showed when third on his debut in Dubai with a fine run in defeat. Like a few of these, he might have preferred a stronger pace, but he was beaten fair and square.
Kalahari Gold(IRE) ◆ progressed rapidly for Andrew Balding last season, winning four of his five starts, including a Listed contest at Newbury on his final outing of 2008, and he looked the chief danger to the favourite if he continued his improvement for new connections, considering he was getting 5lb. Although not unlucky, he should improve again, as not only was the slow pace far from ideal, but he didn't have much room to play with in the straight. He's made the step up to Group company and is a terrific prospect for the year ahead. It will be fascinating to see who trains him in the longer term.
Brave Tin Soldier(USA) was allowed to set steady fractions and looks flattered.
Seihali(IRE) was not beaten far and clearly retains plenty of ability.
My Central(ITY)'s recent success against her own sex at this level didn't look to amount to all that much, but this was a fine effort in defeat against the boys.
Tam Lin didn't run badly considering he raced keenly with little cover early on but, for by no means for the first time, he carried his head high under pressure.
Biarritz(SAF) is slightly better than he showed as he was squeezed up inside the final two furlongs, although he was held at the time.
King Of Rome(IRE) ◆ made a pleasing debut for Mike De Kock over a trip short of his best. He's a horse with loads of ability and it's possible Aidan O'Brien didn't get to the bottom of him. He appeals as one to follow over 1m2f-plus. (op 7-1)

703a MEYDAN GATEWAY TOWERS TROPHY (H'CAP) (TURF) 1m 2f (T)

6:45 (6:45) (100-116,116) 3-Y-O+

£72,916 (£24,305; £12,152; £6,076; £3,645; £2,430)

RPR

1 **Presvis**[35] 263 5-9-3 **112**................. RyanMoore 10 122+
(L M Cumani) *settled last: smooth prog to chse ldr 1 1/2f out: r.o to ld last 110yds: comf* **4/6**[1]

2 3 ¼ **Yahrab (IRE)**[6] 642 4-8-9 **106**................. AhmedAjtebi 11 109
(M bin Shafya, UAE) *sn led: drew clr 3f out: ct fnl 110yds* **33/1**

3 5 ½ **Once More Dubai (USA)**[14] 527 4-9-1 **111**.................(bt) LDettori 8 104
(Saeed Bin Suroor) *settled in rr: r.o fnl 2 1/2f: nvr able to chal* **15/2**[3]

4 ¼ **Halicarnassus (IRE)**[7] 613 5-9-0 **109**................. TPO'Shea 6 101
(M R Channon) *nvr bttr than mid-div* **20/1**

5 2 ¼ **Bound By Honour (SAF)**[7] 613 6-8-9 **105**.................(bt) KShea 1 92
(H J Brown, South Africa) *settled in rr: r.o fnl 2f: nrst fin* **33/1**

6 1 ¼ **World Ruler**[157] 4-8-9 **106**................. WJSupple 2 90
(Doug Watson, UAE) *mid-div on rail: rdn 3f out: one pce* **25/1**

7 ¼ **Lion's Blood (SAF)**[21] 413 5-8-6 **101**................. JohnEgan 12 86
(H J Brown, South Africa) *in rr of main gp: rdn 3 1/2f out: nvr able to chal* **33/1**

8 1 **Eddie Jock (IRE)**[6] 644 5-8-1 **107**................. AntiocoMurgia[(10)] 9 89
(M bin Shafya, UAE) *trckd ldrs tl 2 1/2f out: wknd* **40/1**

9 ¼ **Barbaricus (AUS)**[14] 527 5-8-11 **107**.................(b) MJKinane 4 88
(Danny O'Brien, Australia) *mid-div on rail: t.k.h: chsd ldr 2 1/2f out: sn wknd* **9/2**[2]

10 1 **Hearthstead Maison (IRE)**[42] 183 5-9-4 **113**................. RoystonFfrench 7 93
(M Johnston) *nvr able to chal* **12/1**

11 4 ½ **Oracle West (SAF)**[14] 527 8-9-6 **116**................. JMurtagh 3 86
(H J Brown, South Africa) *nvr bttr than mid-div* **20/1**

12 7 **Hello Morning (FR)**[14] 527 4-8-7 **104**.................(b) RHills 5 60
(E Charpy, UAE) *led main gp: rdn 3 1/2f out: wknd* **33/1**

2m 4.20s (-0.30) **Going Correction** +0.30s/f (Good)
WFA 4 from 5yo+ 1lb 12 Ran SP% **125.2**
Speed ratings: **113,110,106,105,104 103,102,102,101,101 97,91**
CSF £42.27 Tricast £124.72. Placepot £167.50. Pool: £13,606.21 - 59.27 winning units. Quadpot £5.60. Pool: £861.78 - 112.36 winning units..

Owner L Marinopoulos **Bred** Mrs M Campbell-Andenaes **Trained** Newmarket, Suffolk

FOCUS
A decent handicap on paper, but nothing could live with the winner.

NOTEBOOK
Presvis has now won his last three starts in high-class handicaps. The sequence started with a seven-length success off 92 at Newbury, before victory off 106 on his debut in Dubai, and this time he defied the assessor off no less than 112. He's looked a Group horse in waiting for a while now and this latest success seemed every inch the performance of a gelding who can make an impression at the very top level. He was given plenty to do, not least considering the runner-up had the run of things, and he was a little keen under restraint through the first furlong, but yet again he displayed a tremendous turn of foot. The visual impression is backed up by the sectional times, as he covered the penultimate furlong in just 11.22 seconds, only 0.02 seconds slower than Archipenko (who carried 4lb more) in the earlier 1m Group 3. Take out the second, Yahrab, who got his own way, and Presvis pulled over eight lengths clear of the remainder. It would be great to see him in the Sheema Classic, but the Cumani team have that race in mind for Purple Moon, provided he runs up to expectations on Super Thursday, and they might want to keep the pair apart. Also, although he's long been regarded as a 1m4f horse in the making, and should get that trip well in time, he clearly has a ton of speed, like so many of Sakhee's progeny. If connections want to keep him at this trip, an immediate option could be the Winter Derby, for which he is entered. Wherever, he ends up, it will be brave gambler who opposes him. (op 4-5)
Yahrab(IRE) was given a really positive ride and finished a long way clear of the remainder. He obviously had the run of things, but take out the Group-class winner and he's thrashed quite a decent field. This step back up in trip suited and he's yet another one to run well for the Bin Shafya stable at the Carnival. (op 25-1)
Once More Dubai(USA) confirmed the promise he showed behind when short of room behind another highly promising type in Kirklees on his debut for Godolphin. (op 7-1)
Halicarnassus(IRE) retuned to form in fourth and helps give the form a very solid feel. (op 16-1)
Bound By Honour(SAF) ran a little better, but he was still beaten a fair way.
Eddie Jock(IRE) will be better back over shorter.
Barbaricus(AUS) once again refused to settle and was very disappointing.
Hearthstead Maison(IRE) had little chance off such a lofty mark in this company. (op 11-1)

661 LINGFIELD (L-H)

Friday, February 27

OFFICIAL GOING: Standard
Wind: Moderate, half behind Weather: Fine, mild

704 BET SIX NATIONS RUGBY - BETDAQ MAIDEN STKS 1m 4f (P)

1:45 (1:45) (Class 5) 3-Y-O+ £2,729 (£806; £403) Stalls Low

Form RPR

2 1 **Key Regard (IRE)**[28] 343 3-8-4 0................. ChrisCatlin 7 71+
(J A Osborne) *t.k.h: hld up in last: pushed along and prog over 3f out to go 3rd on outer over 2f out: led jst over 1f out: shkn up and green but sn clr* **5/6**[1]

004- 2 3 **Filun**[59] 7822 4-9-11 65................. IanMongan 2 69
(A Middleton) *stdd s: hld up in last trio: smooth prog over 3f out to go 2nd over 2f out: rdn to ld briefly over 1f out: one pce fnl f* **12/1**

4 3 2 ¼ **Scandal**[16] 501 4-9-11 0................. DaneO'Neill 4 65
(Andrew Turnell) *t.k.h: hld up in last trio: prog to ld 4f out: rdn and hdd over 1f out: sn btn* **7/1**[3]

50/ 4 7 **Tilly Shilling (IRE)**[509] 4630 5-9-9 0................. JimCrowley 1 50
(L Wells) *trckd ldrs: lft in ld briefly over 4f out: wknd 2f out* **25/1**

2 5 3 **Wray Castle (IRE)**[18] 476 4-9-11 0................. StephenDonohoe 5 50
(Ian Williams) *trckd ldng pair: pushed along over 5f out: sn lost pl: struggling over 3f out* **10/3**[2]

05 6 3 ½ **Suhailah**[6] 630 3-7-11 0 ow5................. KierenFox[(7)] 6 41+
(M J Attwater) *led: rn wd bnd over 9f out: hung violently rt bnd 5f out: sn hdd and btn* **25/1**

7 8 **Trempari**[128] 6-10-0 0................. FergusSweeney 3 33
(Mike Murphy) *sed v awkwardly: rcvrd to press ldr after 1f: wknd rapidly over 4f out: t.o* **14/1**

2m 32.53s (-0.47) **Going Correction** +0.025s/f (Slow)
WFA 3 from 4yo 24lb 4 from 5yo+ 3lb 7 Ran SP% **112.2**
Speed ratings (Par 103): **102,100,98,93,91 89,84**
toteswinger: 1&2 £3.80, 1&3 £1.90, 2&3 £9.00. CSF £12.09 TOTE £1.80: £1.20, £5.10; EX 14.50.

Owner D Margolis **Bred** D G Iceton **Trained** Upper Lambourn, Berks

FOCUS
Just a routine gallop, but good enough to show off the progress made by the winner since his promising debut.
Suhailah Official explanation: jockey said filly hung right throughout

705 BET CARLING CUP FINAL - BETDAQ H'CAP 7f (P)

2:15 (2:15) (Class 5) (0-70,68) 3-Y-O £2,900 (£856; £428) Stalls Low

Form

0-11 1 **Itshim**[7] 624 3-8-1 56 6ex.................(t) WilliamCarson[(5)] 3 69+
(S C Williams) *mde all and racd quite freely: gng much bttr than rivals 2f out: shkn up 1f out: unchal* **5/4**[1]

3241 2 3 **Imperial Skylight**[13] 542 3-9-0 64................. TonyCulhane 2 64
(M R Channon) *trckd wnr: rdn over 2f out: no imp over 1f out: readily hld after* **3/1**[3]

5-43 3 ½ **Kamanja (UAE)**[26] 364 3-8-10 60................. JimCrowley 5 59
(M J Attwater) *hld up in last: wnt 3rd on inner over 2f out: sn rdn: kpt on same pce over 1f out* **7/1**

1-06 4 4 ½ **Give Us A Song (USA)**[2] 672 3-9-4 68................. LukeMorris 6 55
(J S Moore) *trckd ldng pair: dropped to last over 2f out and sn urged along: no rspnse and wknd over 1f out* **9/4**[2]

1m 25.67s (0.87) **Going Correction** +0.025s/f (Slow) 4 Ran SP% **112.7**
Speed ratings (Par 97): **96,92,92,86**
toteswinger: 1&2 £3.00 CSF £5.56 TOTE £2.30; EX 3.00.

Owner Itsthem **Bred** Ambersham Stud **Trained** Newmarket, Suffolk

FOCUS
A taking performance from the winner to complete the hat-trick, having made all at a good solid gallop.
Give Us A Song(USA) Official explanation: jockey said colt hung left

706 CHELTENHAM PREVIEW EVENING HERE MARCH 5TH (S) STKS 1m (P)
2:50 (2:50) (Class 6) 4-Y-0+ **£2,047** (£604; £302) **Stalls** High

Form RPR
01-4 **1** **Smokey Rye**[55] 26 4-8-13 66 TolleyDean 9 69
(George Baker) *hld up: last over 1f out: rapid prog ins fnl f: wl-timed chal to ld last strides* **8/1**
-263 **2** *hd* **Garden Party**[14] 536 5-8-12 62 (p) FrankieMcDonald 1 68
(R A Harris) *dwlt: hld up in last: pushed along and prog on outer over 2f out: styd on fr over 1f out to chal nr fin: jst outpcd* **10/1**
-625 **3** *nk* **Sir Ike (IRE)**[15] 512 4-8-12 60 (tp) ShaneKelly 7 67
(W S Kittow) *hld up in midfield: prog on inner 2f out: clsd to chal fnl f: upsides 50yds out: outpcd last strides* **8/1**
3-42 **4** *nk* **Zero Cool (USA)**[17] 483 5-8-12 68 (p) FergusSweeney 5 66
(G L Moore) *mde most: hrd pressed fr over 2f out: stl narrow ld wl ins fnl f: swamped nr fin* **11/4**[1]
0-14 **5** *2* **Mudhish (IRE)**[10] 576 4-9-4 68 NCallan 2 68
(C E Brittain) *w ldr: stl upsides ent fnl f: wkng and hld whn squeezed out nr fin* **9/2**[3]
1241 **6** *1* **Northern Desert (IRE)**[14] 530 10-9-4 70 (p) DaneO'Neill 8 66
(S Curran) *mostly in midfield: rdn and effrt on outer over 2f out: tried to cl on ldrs over 1f out: nt qckn* **7/2**[2]
4350 **7** *1 ¾* **Red Current**[18] 480 5-8-7 50 JoeFanning 6 51
(R A Harris) *trckd ldng pair to over 1f out: wknd ins fnl f* **22/1**
424- **8** *1 ½* **Yakama (IRE)**[67] 7759 4-8-12 59 (b) TGMcLaughlin 10 53
(Mrs C A Dunnett) *rn in snatches: hld up in last trio: prog over 1f out: fdd ins fnl f* **16/1**
4226 **9** *8* **Nikki Bea (IRE)**[16] 505 6-8-7 54 PaulDoe 3 30
(Jamie Poulton) *chsd ldrs: rdn 1/2-way: wknd over 2f out* **14/1**
00- **10** *9* **Lucky Forteen**[102] 7363 6-8-7 0 LukeMorris 4 10
(P W Hiatt) *prom 5f: wknd rapidly over 2f out: t.o* **80/1**

1m 37.24s (-0.96) **Going Correction** +0.025s/f (Slow) **10** Ran SP% **116.5**
Speed ratings (Par 101): **105,104,104,104,102 101,99,97,89,80**
toteswinger: 1&2 £13.40, 1&3 £9.40, 2&3 £12.80. CSF £84.97 TOTE £9.70: £2.50, £3.60, £2.20; EX 109.70 Trifecta £188.10 Part Won. Pool: £254.21 - 0.85 winning units..The winner was bought in for 4,000gns
Owner The Different Partnership **Bred** Jeremy Hinds **Trained** Moreton Morrell, Warwicks
■ Stewards' Enquiry : Shane Kelly four-day ban (two-days deferred): careless riding (Mar 13-14, 16-17)

FOCUS
A good gallop set the race up for the strong finishers, with the first and second both rattling home from off the pace.
Sir Ike(IRE) Official explanation: jockey said colt hung right
Mudhish(IRE) Official explanation: jockey said gelding suffered interference in running
Nikki Bea(IRE) Official explanation: trainer said mare was in season

707 SPIKED RAMPION H'CAP 1m (P)
3:25 (3:25) (Class 6) (0-60,64) 3-Y-0 **£2,047** (£604; £302) **Stalls** High

Form RPR
2-1 **1** **Statute Book (IRE)**[7] 620 3-9-6 64 6ex DavidProbert(3) 9 76+
(S Kirk) *trckd ldrs: prog on outer 3f out: led wl over 1f out: sn rdn clr: r.o wl* **1/1**[1]
-051 **2** *4 ½* **Josiah Bartlett (IRE)**[9] 594 3-9-6 61 6ex (bt) SteveDrowne 6 59
(P S McEntee) *stdd s: hld up in last pair: prog on outer over 2f out: drvn to chse wnr 1f out: no imp and only jst hld on for 2nd* **5/1**[3]
4-30 **3** *hd* **Lucky Fortune (IRE)**[30] 317 3-8-11 59 (b) BMcHugh(7) 2 57
(Miss Amy Weaver) *led at modest pce: pressed 3f out: hdd and outpcd wl over 1f out: kpt on* **16/1**
-260 **4** *1 ¼* **Cash In The Attic**[5] 649 3-8-11 52 CatherineGannon 4 47
(M R Channon) *plld hrd early: hld up in last: effrt on inner 2f out: nt pce to threaten* **33/1**
560- **5** *shd* **Scottish Affair**[167] 5904 3-9-4 59 StephenDonohoe 5 54
(E A L Dunlop) *trckd ldrs: nt qckn over 2f out: n.d over 1f out: plugged on* **3/1**[2]
45-6 **6** *1 ½* **Little Blacknumber**[9] 583 3-8-11 52 PatDobbs 8 43
(R Hannon) *trckd ldr to 1/2-way: stl cl up 2f out: fdd* **16/1**
0-35 **7** *7* **Tarawa Atoll**[9] 594 3-9-0 55 TonyCulhane 1 30
(M R Channon) *prom: wnt 2nd 1/2-way: upsides 2f out: wknd v rapidly* **16/1**

1m 40.01s (1.81) **Going Correction** +0.025s/f (Slow) **7** Ran SP% **112.3**
Speed ratings (Par 95): **91,86,86,85,84 83,76**
toteswinger: 1&2 £1.90, 1&3 £3.90, 2&3 £13.10. CSF £6.19 CT £45.94 TOTE £2.00: £1.60, £2.20; EX 5.90 Trifecta £52.40 Pool: £327.51 - 4.62 winning units.
Owner R J Brennan and D Boocock **Bred** R J Brennan And D Boocock **Trained** Upper Lambourn, Berks

FOCUS
The pace was weak until approaching the straight, but that couldn't disguise the impressive upward curve maintained by Statute Book under a 6lb penalty.

708 TOP TIPS @ CHELTENHAM PREVIEW EVENING H'CAP 7f (P)
3:55 (3:55) (Class 5) (0-70,73) 4-Y-0+ **£2,900** (£856; £428) **Stalls** Low

Form RPR
0-53 **1** **Super Frank (IRE)**[19] 457 6-9-3 69 (p) JoeFanning 9 81
(J Akehurst) *mde all and set str pce: drvn 2f out: galloped on relentlessly fnl f* **9/2**[2]
1432 **2** *1 ¾* **Marmooq**[16] 505 6-8-13 65 IanMongan 7 72
(M J Attwater) *prom: rdn and effrt on outer over 2f out: disp 2nd jst over 1f out: claimed that pl but nvr able to chal wnr* **5/1**[3]
26-4 **3** *nk* **Ever Cheerful**[27] 355 8-8-2 61 (p) PNolan(7) 4 68
(A B Haynes) *plld hrd: wnt 2nd 5f out: jnd for pl fr 2f out: plugged on wl enough* **16/1**
-111 **4** *hd* **Singleb (IRE)**[11] 573 5-9-7 73 6ex (p) JamieSpencer 5 79
(Miss Gay Kelleway) *trckd wnr 2f: rdn to dispute 2nd again 2f out: hrd drvn and one pce over 1f out* **10/3**[1]
-013 **5** *shd* **Tuxedo**[7] 625 4-9-2 68 LukeMorris 1 74
(P W Hiatt) *hld up in midfield: rdn on inner wl over 2f out: prog to dispute 2nd jst over 1f out: one pce after* **11/2**
530- **6** *¾* **Pippbrook Gold**[89] 7507 4-9-4 70 PatCosgrave 11 74
(J R Boyle) *trckd ldrs: rdn 2f out: kpt on same pce and no real imp over 1f out* **12/1**
6-24 **7** *¾* **Lend A Grand (IRE)**[19] 457 5-9-1 67 FergusSweeney 2 69
(Miss Jo Crowley) *hld up in last trio: stl there over 2f out: rdn and kpt on fr over 1f out: nvr rchd ldrs* **10/1**
5-60 **8** *4* **Napoletano (GER)**[30] 318 8-9-2 68 (p) NCallan 6 59
(S Dow) *hld up in rr: rdn on outer 3f out: no prog: wl btn over 1f out* **12/1**
00-3 **9** *nk* **Sweet Gale (IRE)**[43] 179 5-8-11 63 FrankieMcDonald 3 53
(Mike Murphy) *s.s: rchd midfield after 2f: no prog 2f out: sn wknd* **14/1**
006- **10** *1* **Smokin Joe**[156] 6211 8-8-8 60 (b) SteveDrowne 8 47
(J R Best) *restrained into last trio sn after s: shkn up and no prog 2f out: wknd* **25/1**
05-0 **11** *5* **Munich (IRE)**[28] 342 5-8-13 65 ChrisCatlin 10 39
(L Wells) *sn detached in last: a struggling* **20/1**

1m 24.09s (-0.71) **Going Correction** +0.025s/f (Slow) **11** Ran SP% **118.9**
Speed ratings (Par 103): **105,103,102,102,102 101,100,96,95,94 88**
toteswinger: 1&2 £5.70, 1&3 £26.90, 2&3 £22.80. CSF £27.68 CT £342.45 TOTE £6.40: £2.10, £1.30, £4.90; EX 25.80 Trifecta £125.00 Part won. Pool: £168.92 - 0.10 winning units..
Owner A D Spence **Bred** A Butler **Trained** Epsom, Surrey

FOCUS
A creditable effort from the winner, who has attempted these front-running tactics in the past but got it spot-on on this occasion

709 BET IN RUNNING - BETDAQ H'CAP 6f (P)
4:30 (4:30) (Class 4) (0-85,87) 3-Y-0 **£4,857** (£1,445; £722; £360) **Stalls** Low

Form RPR
-141 **1** **Smokey Ryder**[1] 685 3-9-12 87 6ex ChrisCatlin 2 89
(R A Harris) *mde all: rdn 2f out: edgd rt but styd on steadily fnl f* **9/4**[1]
-331 **2** *¾* **Flamsteed (IRE)**[20] 447 3-8-10 71 MartinDwyer 4 71
(M Quinn) *t.k.h early: hld up in 4th: effrt 2f out: hanging and nt qckn over 1f out: r.o fnl f to take 2nd last 50yds: clsng at fin* **6/1**
2-21 **3** *¾* **Theatre Street (IRE)**[27] 358 3-8-13 74 NCallan 5 72
(J Noseda) *sn trckd wnr: rdn over 1f out: little rspnse and hld after: lost 2nd last 50yds* **10/3**[2]
3-13 **4** *¾* **Comadoir (IRE)**[15] 509 3-9-4 79 FergusSweeney 1 74
(Miss Jo Crowley) *cl up on inner: rdn 2f out: one pce fr over 1f out* **5/1**[3]
3 **5** *5* **Vegas Baby (IRE)**[23] 396 3-9-7 82 ShaneKelly 3 62
(J A Osborne) *hld up in 5th: pushed along and lost grnd 2f out: no ch whn rdn fnl f* **6/1**
4311 **6** *1 ¾* **Quick Single (USA)**[9] 593 3-8-13 74 6ex (v) SteveDrowne 6 49
(P S McEntee) *nvr gng wl: a last: wl btn fnl 2f* **15/2**

1m 12.71s (0.81) **Going Correction** +0.025s/f (Slow) **6** Ran SP% **110.9**
Speed ratings (Par 99): **95,94,93,92,85 83**
toteswinger: 1&2 £2.50, 1&3 £1.40, 2&3 £6.60. CSF £15.56 TOTE £3.10: £2.30, £3.80; EX 16.40 Place 6: £101.69 Place 5: £66.49.
Owner The Govin Partnership **Bred** Jeremy Hinds **Trained** Earlswood, Monmouths

FOCUS
Victory for the full-sister of Smokey Rye, a winner earlier on the card. However, she looks a less tricky customer than her sibling and, in stark contrast, she led all the way.
Quick Single(USA) Official explanation: trainer had no explanation for the poor form shown

710 JUMPING HERE MARCH 5TH H'CAP 5f (P)
5:05 (5:05) (Class 5) (0-70,70) 4-Y-0+ **£2,900** (£856; £428) **Stalls** High

Form RPR
6344 **1** **Don Pele (IRE)**[9] 589 7-9-2 68 (p) JoeFanning 4 78
(R A Harris) *trckd ldng pair after 2f: clsd over 1f out: drvn to ld last 100yds: styd on wl* **12/1**
0105 **2** *¾* **Ten Down**[9] 589 4-9-0 66 MartinDwyer 5 73
(M Quinn) *w ldr and sn 2 l clr of rest: led on outer wl over 1f out: hdd and no ex last 100yds* **16/1**
222 **3** *nk* **Step It Up (IRE)**[5] 645 5-8-13 65 PatCosgrave 2 71
(J R Boyle) *trckd ldng pair for 2f: rdn and effrt over 2f out: styd on to take 3rd ins fnl f* **5/2**[2]
3155 **4** *½* **Drifting Gold**[14] 539 5-9-4 70 (v) IanMongan 8 74
(C G Cox) *w.w in last pair: effrt over 2f out: styd on fr over 1f out but nvr able to rch ldrs* **9/1**
01-2 **5** *1 ¼* **Atheer Dubai (IRE)**[16] 499 4-9-2 68 (p) JamieSpencer 6 68
(E F Vaughan) *hld up towards rr: rdn over 2f out: kpt on one pce fr over 1f out* **9/4**[1]
-050 **6** *1* **Dodaa (USA)**[21] 431 6-8-2 57 DuranFentiman(3) 3 53
(N Wilson) *led but hrd pressed fr s: hdd & wknd on inner wl over 1f out* **8/1**
3621 **7** *nk* **Welsh Opera**[8] 596 4-8-3 60 6ex (v) WilliamCarson(5) 9 55
(S C Williams) *a in last pair: rdn on wd outside over 2f out and struggling: plugged on fnl f* **7/1**[3]
2-40 **8** *2 ¼* **Night Premiere (IRE)**[8] 596 4-8-4 56 oh3 (b) ChrisCatlin 1 43
(R Hannon) *towards rr: struggling sn after 1/2-way: wknd* **16/1**

58.23 secs (-0.57) **Going Correction** +0.025s/f (Slow) **8** Ran SP% **112.4**
Speed ratings (Par 103): **105,103,103,102,100 98,98,94**
toteswinger: 1&2 £13.20, 1&3 £3.70, 2&3 £9.60. CSF £173.25 CT £632.14 TOTE £12.90: £3.60, £3.30, £1.20; EX 143.40.
Owner Robert & Nina Bailey **Bred** John J Cosgrave **Trained** Earlswood, Monmouths

FOCUS
With two front-runners taking one another on, the pace was strong, and that played to the strengths of the winner.
T/Plt: £132.10 to a £1 stake. Pool: £46,251.17. 255.52 winning tickets. T/Qpdt: £43.70 to a £1 stake. Pool: £3,541.60. 59.90 winning tickets. JN

[690]WOLVERHAMPTON (A.W) (L-H)
Friday, February 27

OFFICIAL GOING: Standard
Wind: Almost nil

711 BETDAQ THE BETTING EXCHANGE APPRENTICE H'CAP 1m 1f 103y(P)
6:50 (6:50) (Class 6) (0-55,60) 4-Y-0+ **£2,388** (£705; £352) **Stalls** Low

Form RPR
5134 **1** **Ridgeway Jazz**[16] 497 4-8-7 55 SeanPalmer(7) 9 67
(M D I Usher) *stdd s: hld up towards rr: hdwy on outside 3f out: bmpd over 2f out: led wl over 1f out: rdn fnl f: r.o* **10/1**
5405 **2** *nk* **Barodine**[16] 500 6-8-6 50 KrishGundowry(3) 4 61
(R J Hodges) *hld up in rr: stdy hdwy over 5f out: nt clr run and swtchd rt over 2f out: rdn and r.o ins fnl f* **16/1**
62-0 **3** *shd* **That'll Do Nicely (IRE)**[36] 256 6-9-0 55 NSLawes 12 68+
(N G Richards) *s.i.s: hld up in mid-div: stdy prog 5f out: nt clr run 2f out: rdn over 1f out: r.o ins fnl f* **12/1**

2004 **4** 4 1/2 **Mr Chocolate Drop (IRE)**[4] 657 5-8-9 55 DavidKenny(5) 10 57
(Miss M E Rowland) *stdd s: hld up in rr: hdwy over 2f out: rdn wl over 1f out: wnt 4th wl ins fnl f: nt trble ldrs* **11/1**

5-32 **5** 1/2 **John Potts**[10] 581 4-8-9 50 (p) RichardRowe 8 52
(B P J Baugh) *a.p: ev ch 2f out: rdn over 1f out: wknd ins fnl f* **6/1**[2]

4021 **6** 3 1/2 **Desert Hawk**[10] 578 8-8-8 52 6ex MatthewLawson(3) 3 47
(W M Brisbourne) *mid-div: lost pl over 6f out: bhd 5f out: rdn and styd on fr over 1f out: n.d* **8/1**[3]

4030 **7** 3/4 **Rub Of The Relic (IRE)**[7] 623 4-8-9 55 (p) PaulPickard(5) 13 48
(P T Midgley) *prom tl wknd 3f out* **8/1**[3]

63-5 **8** 2 **Barton Sands (IRE)**[30] 320 12-8-8 54 (t) SPRyan(5) 2 44
(Andrew Reid) *hld up towards rr: nvr nr ldrs* **8/1**[3]

-111 **9** 2 1/2 **Lytham (IRE)**[2] 669 8-9-0 60 6ex TobyAtkinson(5) 5 45
(A W Carroll) *hld up in mid-div: wknd wl over 2f out* **11/10**[1]

036- **10** 2 3/4 **Duneen Dream (USA)**[243] 3524 4-8-9 55 AlexEdwards(5) 11 35
(Mrs N S Evans) *t.k.h: led after 1f tl over 7f out: led over 2f out tl wl over 1f out: sn wknd* **28/1**

00-3 **11** 2 1/4 **Karmei**[10] 581 4-8-9 50 CharlesEddery 7 25
(R Curtis) *prom: led over 4f out tl over 2f out: wknd wl over 1f out: sn eased* **20/1**

050- **12** 22 **Plaka (FR)**[371] 665 4-8-9 50 DebraEngland 6 —
(W M Brisbourne) *t.k.h: led 1f: led over 7f out tl over 4f out: wknd 3f out: eased wl over 1f out* **33/1**

2m 2.49s (0.79) **Going Correction** +0.175s/f (Slow) **12** Ran SP% **137.4**
Speed ratings (Par 101): **103,102,102,98,98 95,94,92,90,87 85,66**
toteswinger: 1&2 £22.70, 1&3 £27.30, 2&3 £38.70. CSF £179.67 CT £1999.53 TOTE £13.20: £2.50, £6.40, £4.90; EX 123.10.
Owner M D I Usher **Bred** Templeton Stud And Bricklow Ltd **Trained** Upper Lambourn, Berks
■ Sean Palmer's first winner.

FOCUS
A modest handicap and one in which the well-backed favourite disappointed. The pace was only ordinary and the first three, who came clear, raced towards the centre in the straight.
Lytham(IRE) Official explanation: jockey said gelding ran flat

712 ENJOY THE LUCKY 7 GROUP OFFER CLAIMING STKS 1m 4f 50y(P)
7:20 (7:21) (Class 5) 4-Y-0+ £2,729 (£806; £403) Stalls Low

Form RPR

2242 **1** **Quince (IRE)**[9] 584 6-9-7 78 (v) JimmyQuinn 5 62+
(J Pearce) *hld up: hdwy 3f out: wnt 2nd 2f out: rdn to ld ins fnl f: r.o* **5/4**[1]

461 **2** 1 1/2 **Bridgewater Boys**[14] 528 8-8-13 70 (b) PaulDoe 4 52+
(P D Evans) *dwlt: t.k.h: sn chsng ldr: led over 2f out: rdn wl over 1f out: hdd and nt qckn ins fnl f* **2/1**[2]

40-0 **3** 3 1/4 **Cruise Director**[23] 393 9-9-5 65 StephenDonohoe 2 53+
(Ian Williams) *chsd ldr early: a.p: rdn over 1f out: one pce* **8/1**

1633 **4** 2 1/2 **Rapid City**[9] 588 6-9-2 64 (p) RobertWinston 1 46+
(A J McCabe) *dwlt: hld up in rr: hdwy on outside wl over 2f out: sn rdn: wknd over 1f out* **4/1**[3]

000/ **5** 3 1/4 **Monroe Gold**[178] 4891 9-9-3 30 (p) GeorgeBaker 3 42
(Jennie Candlish) *set stdy pce: hdd over 2f out: wknd wl over 1f out* **33/1**

2m 47.92s (6.82) **Going Correction** +0.175s/f (Slow) **5** Ran SP% **111.8**
Speed ratings (Par 103): **84,83,80,79,77**
CSF £4.12 TOTE £2.30: £1.10, £1.60; EX 4.20.
Owner D Leech **Bred** David Ryan **Trained** Newmarket, Suffolk

FOCUS
Not a competitive race and one in which the gallop was on the steady side. Winner and second came down the centre in the straight.

713 BET 1% IN RUNNING - BETDAQ H'CAP 1m 1f 103y(P)
7:50 (7:50) (Class 4) (0-80,80) 4-Y-0+ £5,180 (£1,541; £770; £384) Stalls Low

Form RPR

-244 **1** **Stand Guard**[20] 453 5-9-4 80 TolleyDean 9 89
(P Howling) *sn chsng ldr: led 3f out: rdn wl over 1f out: r.o wl* **8/1**

0-43 **2** 1 **Tourist**[29] 331 4-9-2 78 DarrenWilliams 11 85
(D Shaw) *t.k.h early towards rr: hdwy 3f out: rdn and chsd wnr fnl f: kpt on* **15/2**[3]

0-34 **3** 1/2 **Faithful Ruler (USA)**[44] 163 5-8-9 71 PaulHanagan 3 77
(R A Fahey) *t.k.h: led 1f: a.p: chsd ldr over 2f out tl rdn over 1f out: kpt on one pce* **15/2**[3]

3-50 **4** 1/2 **Prince Golan (IRE)**[39] 220 5-7-11 66 oh1 (p) AlexEdwards(7) 2 71
(J W Unett) *t.k.h early in mid-div: styd on ins fnl f: tk 4th towards fin* **33/1**

16-0 **5** 1 **Royal Amnesty**[51] 79 6-9-1 77 (b) RobertWinston 6 80
(I Semple) *s.i.s: hld up towards rr: rdn and hdwy over 1f out: one pce ins fnl f* **9/1**

01-6 **6** hd **Theonebox (USA)**[42] 199 4-9-2 78 LukeMorris 7 81
(N J Vaughan) *hld up in mid-div: hdwy over 3f out: rdn and edgd lft over 1f out: fdd ins fnl f* **11/2**[2]

3114 **7** 1 **Teasing**[16] 504 5-9-2 78 (v) RobertHavlin 8 79
(J Pearce) *s.i.s: hld up towards rr: nvr trbld ldrs* **14/1**

-111 **8** 1/2 **Brouhaha**[4] 656 5-8-2 69 RossAtkinson(5) 1 69+
(Tom Dascombe) *prom: nt clr run on ins and lost pl over 2f out: sn swtchd rt: rdn and short-lived effrt over 1f out* **6/4**[1]

60-3 **9** 3/4 **Bull Market (IRE)**[37] 238 6-8-11 73 StephenDonohoe 10 72
(Ian Williams) *hld up: a in rr* **22/1**

4/26 **10** 7 **Just Observing**[18] 477 6-8-9 71 ow1 (p) MickyFenton 4 56
(P T Midgley) *led after 1f: pushed along and hdd 3f out: wkng whn hmpd jst over 2f out* **28/1**

6-12 **11** 40 **Templetuohy Max (IRE)**[20] 453 4-8-7 69 (v) JimmyQuinn 5 —
(J D Bethell) *hld up in mid-div: bhd fnl 2f: t.o* **11/2**[2]

2m 2.79s (1.09) **Going Correction** +0.175s/f (Slow) **11** Ran SP% **132.8**
Speed ratings (Par 105): **102,101,100,100,99 99,98,97,97,90 55**
toteswinger: 1&2 £34.80, 1&3 £19.90, 2&3 £9.90. CSF £74.30 CT £492.03 TOTE £15.30: £4.00, £2.10, £3.80; EX 66.20.
Owner The Circle Bloodstock I Limited **Bred** Juddmonte Farms Ltd **Trained** Newmarket, Suffolk
■ Stewards' Enquiry : Stephen Donohoe 10-day ban: breach of Rule 158 (Mar 13-14, Mar 16-23)
Darren Williams two-day ban: careless riding (Mar 13-14)

FOCUS
A fair handicap but another race in which the short-priced market leader disappointed. The gallop was only fair early on and the winner raced centre to far side in the straight.
Templetuohy Max(IRE) Official explanation: jockey said gelding never travelled; vet said gelding finished distressed

714 WOLVERHAMPTON-RACECOURSE.CO.UK H'CAP 5f 216y(P)
8:20 (8:20) (Class 3) (0-95,92) 4-Y-0 £9,462 (£2,832; £1,416; £708; £352) Stalls Low

Form RPR

-053 **1** **Ebraam (USA)**[13] 553 6-9-4 92 TolleyDean 9 103
(P Howling) *t.k.h in tch: rdn to ld wl ins fnl f: r.o* **7/2**[1]

1111 **2** 1 1/4 **Mutamared (USA)**[20] 442 9-8-13 87 (t) NCallan 8 94
(K A Ryan) *a.p: wnt 2nd over 3f out: led over 1f out: rdn and hdd wl ins fnl f: nt qckn* **7/1**

30-2 **3** nk **Artistic License (IRE)**[13] 543 4-8-8 82 TonyCulhane 7 88
(M R Channon) *hld up and bhd: rdn over 1f out: hdwy fnl f: tk 3rd towards fin* **20/1**

-252 **4** 1 **Methaaly (IRE)**[10] 579 6-8-4 83 (be) DeanHeslop(5) 5 86
(M Mullineaux) *s.i.s: hld up: hdwy over 2f out: rdn over 1f out: one pce* **5/1**[3]

5400 **5** 1/2 **Dvinsky (USA)**[6] 633 8-9-0 88 (b) StephenDonohoe 4 89
(P Howling) *led: rdn and hdd over 1f out: fdd towards fin* **14/1**

5-30 **6** nse **Soopacal (IRE)**[28] 351 4-8-9 83 (v[1]) PaulHanagan 6 84
(B Smart) *hld up in tch: rdn and no hdwy fr over 1f out* **8/1**

5121 **7** 1 **Xpres Maite**[17] 491 6-8-13 87 (b) JimmyQuinn 1 85
(S R Bowring) *s.i.s: hld up and bhd: rdn over 1f out: n.d* **5/1**[3]

-232 **8** 2 **Little Edward**[13] 553 11-9-1 89 GeorgeBaker 3 80
(R J Hodges) *chsd ldr tl over 3f out: wknd wl over 1f out* **4/1**[2]

5-41 **9** 4 **The Tatling (IRE)**[21] 424 12-9-0 88 RobertWinston 10 66
(J M Bradley) *hld up: c wd st: a in rr* **12/1**

1m 13.98s (-1.02) **Going Correction** +0.175s/f (Slow) **9** Ran SP% **118.3**
Speed ratings (Par 107): **113,111,110,109,108 108,107,104,99**
toteswinger: 1&2 £3.60, 1&3 £13.50, 2&3 £9.70. CSF £29.17 CT £433.01 TOTE £5.00: £1.80, £2.30, £4.70; EX 33.30.
Owner The Circle Bloodstock I Limited **Bred** Shadwell Farm LLC **Trained** Newmarket, Suffolk

FOCUS
Mainly exposed performers in this useful handicap. The pace was not overly strong in the early stages and those racing handily had the edge. The winner raced centre to far side in the straight.

NOTEBOOK
Ebraam(USA), who showed clear signs of a return to form on his previous start, appreciated the return to 6f and ran right up to his best, despite carrying his head a shade high. He should continue to give a good account away from progressive or well-handicapped sorts after reassessment. (tchd 3-1)
Mutamared(USA), who came into this race in tremendous form, was always well placed given the way this panned out, and ran right up to his best from this 3lb higher mark. He's at the top of his game and should continue to give a good account. (op 6-1)
Artistic License(IRE) fared better than on her previous run after a break and deserves extra credit attempting to come from behind where those racing handily got first run. She has little leeway from this mark, though, and her style of racing means she will always need things to drop right. (op 14-1)
Methaaly(IRE) is not the most straightforward but ran creditably after losing ground at the start and racing widest turning for home. He has little margin for error from his current mark, though. (tchd 9-2)
Dvinsky(USA) got his own way in front but, while anything but disgraced, he does not seem to be in the same form that saw him make all twice over this trip earlier in the winter. (tchd 16-1)
Soopacal(IRE) was not disgraced after racing freely early on in the first-time visor but he is going to have to show a bit more before he is a solid betting proposition from his current mark.
Xpres Maite Official explanation: jockey said gelding missed the break

715 TRY BETDAQ FOR AN EXCHANGE H'CAP 7f 32y(P)
8:50 (8:51) (Class 6) (0-60,60) 4-Y-0+ £2,388 (£705; £352) Stalls High

Form RPR

-224 **1** **Cap St Jean (IRE)**[17] 489 5-8-8 57 (p) DavidKenny(7) 2 68+
(R Hollinshead) *s.s: hld up in rr: c wd st: hdwy over 1f out: r.o to ld last strides* **7/1**[3]

4325 **2** nk **Loyal Royal (IRE)**[14] 531 6-8-10 57 (b) JackDean(5) 7 66
(J M Bradley) *s.i.s: hld up and bhd: hdwy whn swtchd rt over 1f out: rdn to ld cl home: hdd last strides* **8/1**

0-03 **3** nk **Jord (IRE)**[7] 617 5-9-3 59 RobertWinston 9 68
(A J McCabe) *hld up in mid-div: hdwy over 3f out: rdn to ld over 1f out: hdd cl home* **14/1**

4-03 **4** 2 **Manchestermaverick (USA)**[14] 531 4-9-2 58 (vt) SteveDrowne 4 62+
(H Morrison) *a.p: rdn wl over 1f out: one pce ins fnl f* **3/1**[1]

5552 **5** 1 **Haroldini (IRE)**[8] 607 7-9-1 57 (b) PaulMulrennan 12 58
(J Balding) *hld up and bhd: rdn and hdwy over 1f out: edgd lft jst ins fnl f: one pce* **11/2**[2]

000- **6** 1 1/2 **H Harrison (IRE)**[123] 7012 9-9-1 57 PatrickMathers 10 55
(I W McInnes) *hld up in mid-div: rdn and hdwy over 1f out: wknd ins fnl f* **33/1**

/000 **7** 4 **Strategic Knight (USA)**[18] 478 4-9-4 60 (t) MickyFenton 3 48
(R C Guest) *prom tl wknd wl over 1f out* **15/2**

-055 **8** 1 **Splash The Cash**[14] 540 4-9-0 56 NCallan 8 41
(K A Ryan) *sn chsng ldr: led over 2f out: rdn and hdd over 1f out: wknd ins fnl f* **7/1**[3]

40-5 **9** 2 1/4 **Johnny Friendly**[28] 344 4-9-4 60 AndrewElliott 1 40
(K R Burke) *led: rdn and hdd over 2f out: wknd over 1f out* **7/1**[3]

0-44 **10** 1 1/4 **Valentino Swing (IRE)**[14] 540 6-9-2 58 DaneO'Neill 11 35
(Miss T Spearing) *hld up and bhd: short-lived effrt on ins wl over 1f out* **11/2**[2]

1m 29.98s (0.38) **Going Correction** +0.175s/f (Slow) **10** Ran SP% **125.8**
Speed ratings (Par 101): **104,103,103,101,99 98,93,92,89,88**
toteswinger: 1&2 £14.20, 1&3 £31.10, 2&3 £16.70. CSF £66.96 CT £802.42 TOTE £9.40: £2.50, £2.60, £5.40; EX 59.70.
Owner R Hollinshead **Bred** Drumhass Stud **Trained** Upper Longdon, Staffs

FOCUS
A modest handicap but a strong pace saw the hold-up horses come to the fore in the closing stages. The first three came down the centre in the straight.
Strategic Knight(USA) Official explanation: jockey said gelding hung right-handed throughout

716 STAY AT THE WOLVERHAMPTON HOLIDAY INN MAIDEN STKS 1m 141y(P)
9:20 (9:21) (Class 5) 3-Y-0 £3,070 (£906; £453) Stalls Low

Form RPR

1 **Burza** 3-8-12 0 PaulMulrennan 7 63+
(J Mackie) *hld up: rdn and hdwy 3f out: wnt 2nd wl over 1f out: led wl ins fnl f: r.o* **33/1**

6-03 **2** hd **Co Dependent (USA)**[9] 586 3-9-3 68 ShaneKelly 2 68
(J A Osborne) *sn led: pushed clr over 2f out: rdn 1f out: hdd wl ins fnl f: r.o* **8/13**[1]

00- **3** 2 **Hypnotic Gaze (IRE)**[160] 6122 3-9-3 0 GeorgeBaker 6 63
(J Mackie) *hld up in tch: r.o one pce fnl f* **12/1**

4-65 **4** 2 **Green Dynasty (IRE)**[13] 548 3-9-3 70 JoeFanning 1 59
(M Johnston) *led early: chsd ldr: rdn over 2f out: lost 2nd wl over 1f out: one pce* **3/1**[2]

5 5 **Laminka** 3-8-12 0 LukeMorris 4 42
(G C Bravery) *prom tl wknd over 3f out* **12/1**

6 2 1/2 **Frightnight (IRE)** 3-9-3 0 RobertHavlin 3 42
(A B Haynes) *hld up in rr: pushed along 3f out: sn struggling* **10/1**[3]

060- **7** 1 1/4 **Piccolo Express**154 6246 3-9-3 34 AndrewElliott 8 39
(B P J Baugh) *t.k.h early: a bhd* **50/1**
06 **8** 8 **Petrenko**38 227 3-9-3 0 PaulHanagan 5 20
(R A Fahey) *prom tl wknd over 3f out* **20/1**
1m 53.07s (2.57) **Going Correction** +0.175s/f (Slow) **8** Ran SP% **121.1**
Speed ratings (Par 97): **95,94,93,91,86 84,83,76**
toteswinger: 1&2 £13.40, 1&3 £24.40, 2&3 £2.70. CSF £57.07 TOTE £59.90: £13.60, £1.02, £4.50; EX 91.80 Place 6: £1804.33 Place 5: £148.39.
Owner Norman A Blyth **Bred** Norman A Blyth **Trained** Church Broughton , Derbys
FOCUS
A very ordinary maiden held down by the proximity of the third. The pace was only moderate and the first two raced in the centre in the straight.
Piccolo Express Official explanation: jockey said gelding hung right-handed throughout
T/Plt: £197.40 to a £1 stake. Pool: £103,411.36. 382.39 winning tickets. T/Qpdt: £23.30 to a £1 stake. Pool: £9,346.62. 296.40 winning tickets. KH

717 - 720a (Foreign Racing) - See Raceform Interactive

704 LINGFIELD (L-H)
Sunday, March 1

OFFICIAL GOING: Standard
Wind: Moderate, across Weather: Overcast

721 APPEL (S) STKS 7f (P)
2:20 (2:20) (Class 6) 3-Y-O+ **£2,047** (£604; £302) **Stalls** Low

Form RPR
-133 **1** **Desert Dreamer (IRE)**37 266 8-10-0 75 RichardKingscote 3 75
(Tom Dascombe) *dwlt: hld up in tch: effrt 2f out: r.o to ld fnl 75yds* **7/4**1
-512 **2** 1 1/2 **Interactive (IRE)**18 495 6-10-0 67 HayleyTurner 5 71
(Andrew Turnell) *plld hrd: sn trcking ldr: led 4f out: hrd rdn and hdd 1f out: nt qckn* **9/2**2
6P-3 **3** hd **Parisian Gift (IRE)**44 189 4-9-8 77 JamieSpencer 6 64
(J R Gask) *sn led and set modest pce: hdd 4f out: led again 1f out: hdd and one pce ins fnl f* **7/4**1
-244 **4** 5 **C'Mon You Irons (IRE)**32 314 4-9-7 67 AndrewHeffernan(7) 7 57
(M R Hoad) *broke wl: stdd bk in tch: rdn over 2f out: sn btn* **14/1**
000- **5** 2 **Bigfanofthat (IRE)**164 6041 4-9-8 72 RobertWinston 4 46
(M D Squance) *in tch: effrt 3f out: rdn and wknd 2f out* **15/2**3
1m 25.92s (1.12) **Going Correction** +0.05s/f (Slow) **5** Ran SP% **109.3**
Speed ratings (Par 101): **95,93,93,87,85**
toteswinger: 1&2 £4.10. CSF £9.88 TOTE £3.00: £1.10, £1.40; EX 8.40.There was no bid for the winner.
Owner ONEWAY Partners **Bred** Gainsborough Stud Management Ltd **Trained** Lambourn, Berks
FOCUS
Not a bad seller, but a muddling affair in which the early gallop was very steady.

722 FEINT MEDIAN AUCTION MAIDEN STKS 6f (P)
2:50 (2:50) (Class 5) 3-5-Y-O **£3,070** (£906; £453) **Stalls** Low

Form RPR
2 **1** **Trip Switch**5 664 3-8-12 0 MartinDwyer 2 69+
(W R Muir) *mde all: set modest pce: qcknd over 2f out: pushed clr over 1f out: comf* **4/6**1
2 3 1/4 **Swans A Swimming (IRE)** 3-8-12 0 ShaneKelly 6 58
(J A Osborne) *hld up in rr: hdwy and wd st: r.o wl to take 2nd ins fnl f: no ch of catching wnr* **8/1**
4 **3** 3 1/4 **Dream Catch Me (IRE)**5 664 3-8-7 0 HayleyTurner 7 43
(J R Boyle) *cl up: rdn over 2f out: chsd wnr wl over 1f out tl no ex ins fnl f* **4/1**2
3432 **4** shd **Edith's Boy (IRE)**11 592 3-8-12 65 PaulDoe 1 48
(S Dow) *s.i.s: t.k.h in rr: effrt 2f out: edgd rt fnl f: styd on* **9/2**3
P0- **5** 3/4 **Wicklewood**151 6389 3-8-12 0 TGMcLaughlin 3 45
(Mrs C A Dunnett) *chsd ldrs: rdn 3f out: wknd over 1f out* **33/1**
-003 **6** 4 **Meg Jicaro**11 583 3-8-7 43 ChrisCatlin 4 27
(Mrs L Williamson) *plld hrd: chsd wnr tl wknd wl over 1f out* **16/1**
00-0 **7** 2 1/2 **Farriers Gate**22 441 3-8-7 0 (b1) EdwardCreighton 5 19
(M E Rimmer) *in tch: rdn over 2f out: wknd ent st* **66/1**
1m 12.81s (0.91) **Going Correction** +0.05s/f (Slow) **7** Ran SP% **119.6**
Speed ratings (Par 103): **95,90,86,86,85 79,76**
toteswinger: 1&2 £3.60, 1&3 £1.80, 2&3 £4.50. CSF £7.97 TOTE £1.80: £1.30, £4.60; EX 11.40.
Owner Andrew & Jo Patrick **Bred** A Saccomando **Trained** Lambourn, Berks
FOCUS
A very modest maiden but the winner can do better.

723 RIPOSTE H'CAP 2m (P)
3:20 (3:20) (Class 4) (0-85,81) 4-Y-O+ **£5,180** (£1,541; £770; £384) **Stalls** Low

Form RPR
50-1 **1** **Benhego**17 511 4-9-4 78 GeorgeBaker 5 85+
(G L Moore) *hld up towards rr: gd hdwy over 1f out: rdn to ld ins fnl f: readily* **4/5**1
-441 **2** 1 **Mr Aitch (IRE)**11 591 7-9-7 76 (t) TPQueally 7 82
(R T Phillips) *stdd s: t.k.h in rr: gd hdwy on outside to ld 2f out: hdd and nt pce of wnr ins fnl f* **11/1**
01-1 **3** 1 **Greenwich Village**39 233 6-9-12 81 JimCrowley 3 86
(W J Knight) *mainly 2nd tl no ex fnl f* **5/2**2
-322 **4** hd **Baan (USA)**11 591 6-8-9 67 JackMitchell(3) 1 72
(H J Collingridge) *led 2f: cl up tl outpcd over 2f out: styd on again fnl f* **8/1**3
112- **5** 1 **Miss Serena**132 6861 4-8-12 72 MickyFenton 6 75
(Mrs P Sly) *led after 2f and set modest pce: hdd 2f out: wknd fnl f* **8/1**3
32-1 **6** 17 **Wabbraan (USA)**10 603 4-8-2 67 AmyBaker(5) 4 50
(M Hill) *chsd ldrs: rdn 5f out: wknd 2f out* **16/1**
3m 24.93s (-0.77) **Going Correction** +0.05s/f (Slow)
WFA 4 from 5yo+ 5lb **6** Ran SP% **120.6**
Speed ratings (Par 105): **103,102,102,101,101 92**
toteswinger: 1&2 £2.50, 1&3 £1.80, 2&3 £2.70. CSF £12.72 TOTE £2.40: £1.30, £3.60; EX 16.60.
Owner Findlay & Bloom **Bred** Old Mill Stud **Trained** Lower Beeding, W Sussex
FOCUS
They went a steady pace through the early stages of this fair staying handicap.

724 FOIL H'CAP 1m (P)
3:50 (4:01) (Class 2) (0-100,95) 4-Y-O+ **£11,656** (£3,468; £1,733; £865) **Stalls** High

Form RPR
3-42 **1** **Abbondanza (IRE)**37 278 6-9-2 93 (p) PaulMulrennan 7 105
(I Semple) *mde all: set gd pce: sn 6 l clr: flagging bdly fnl f: jst lasted* **14/1**
641- **2** 3/4 **Flipando (IRE)**70 7755 8-9-2 93 JamieSpencer 8 106+
(T D Barron) *dropped out in rr s: rapid hdwy over 1f out: fin strly: catching wnr fast nr line* **7/4**1
103- **3** 3 1/4 **Bazergan (IRE)**142 6625 4-9-2 93 (tp) NCallan 10 96
(C E Brittain) *mid-div: rdn 3f out: v wd st: styd on appr fnl f: nrst fin* **11/2**3
0-15 **4** 1/2 **Wasp (AUS)**8 636 7-8-12 89 JimCrowley 9 93+
(W Jarvis) *hld up in midfield: crowded for room and lost pl over 2f out: kpt on appr fnl f* **8/1**
4-56 **5** nk **Opus Maximus (IRE)**15 551 4-8-9 86 JoeFanning 11 87
(M Johnston) *chsd wnr and clr of rest tl no ex 1f out* **12/1**
2125 **6** hd **Red Somerset (USA)**15 551 6-9-4 95 GeorgeBaker 1 96
(R J Hodges) *mid-div: effrt and sme hdwy 2f out: one pce appr fnl f* **9/1**
3023 **7** nk **Southandwest (IRE)**8 635 5-8-12 89 RobertWinston 2 89
(J S Moore) *chsd clr ldrs: one pce fnl 2f* **14/1**
4033 **8** 2 **Internationaldebut (IRE)**8 636 4-9-3 94 JohnEgan 12 90
(S Parr) *mid-div on outside: wd st: nt pce to chal* **9/2**2
3-66 **9** 3/4 **Art Man**36 283 6-8-5 82 HayleyTurner 3 76
(G L Moore) *towards rr: rdn 3f out: n.d* **10/1**
0-46 **10** 3 **Lord Theo**10 597 5-8-4 81 oh17 ChrisCatlin 5 69
(N P Littmoden) *chsd clr ldrs: rdn 3f out: sn btn* **50/1**
-233 **11** 6 **Baylini**22 445 5-8-11 88 JamesDoyle 4 62
(Ms J S Doyle) *dropped out in rr s: pushed along 3f out: sn no ch* **6/1**
1m 34.87s (-3.33) **Going Correction** +0.05s/f (Slow) course record **11** Ran SP% **137.4**
Speed ratings (Par 109): **118,117,114,113,113 113,112,110,109,106 100**
toteswinger: 1&2 £9.80, 1&3 £15.50, 2&3 £4.10. CSF £45.41 CT £175.10 TOTE £16.40: £4.40, £1.60, £2.60; EX 79.20 Trifecta £581.70 Part won. Pool £786.15 - 0.89 winning units. .
Owner Belstane Park Racing & Gordon Leckie **Bred** M Nolan **Trained** Carluke, S Lanarks
■ Kayak (16/1) was withdrawn (kicked and broke leg at start; dead).
FOCUS
A good-quality, competitive handicap on paper, but as it turned out very few got involved.
NOTEBOOK
Abbondanza(IRE) is at his best when able to dominate and, although it looked like he might have competition for that role here, he was rushed into the lead and proceeded to set a strong gallop out in front. Several lengths clear with half a mile to run, he maintained his advantage entering the straight, and, although he got noticeably tired inside the last and had very little left in the tank, the line came just in time. Credit must go to Mulrennan for his positive ride, and the winning time, just 0.12secs outside the course record, shows the merit of the winner's performance, but there will be plenty of punters wondering why the other riders allowed him so much rope. (op 12-1)
Flipando(IRE), whose SP was a disgrace compared with the price consistently available to exchange players (over 4-1) pre-race, was held up in last place and absolutely flew home down the outside in the straight. The winner's advantage was too great to claw back, but he was the best horse in the race and is clearly capable of winning off his current sort of mark. He does require a good pace to be seen at his best, though. (op 3-1, tchd 4-1 and 7-2 in places)
Bazergan(IRE) had not run since October but he was representing a stable in good form and came in for market support. He lacked Flipando's acceleration at the end of the race, but kept on well to take the minor placing, and a return to 1m2f, over which he won at Salisbury last summer, should suit. (op 10-1)
Wasp(AUS) travelled strongly but did not find a great deal under pressure. (op 9-1 tchd 10-1)
Opus Maximus(IRE) ran a bit better than his finishing position suggests, as he chased the leader for most of the way, with a gap back to the peloton. Had he been ridden more conservatively he might have finished closer.
Red Somerset(USA), who was racing off a career-high mark, found himself stuck down on the rail in the straight. (op 8-1 tchd 10-1)
Internationaldebut(IRE) was disappointing, but he saw plenty of daylight towards the outside and that probably did not suit him as he likes to be buried in the pack and delivered with a late challenge. (op 6-1 tchd 7-1)
Baylini Official explanation: jockey said mare lost its action down the hill and may have been affected by the delay.

725 BALLESTRA H'CAP 1m (P)
4:20 (4:25) (Class 6) (0-65,66) 4-Y-O+ **£2,388** (£705; £352) **Stalls** High

Form RPR
0-13 **1** **Lopinot (IRE)**17 512 6-9-2 63 (v) JimCrowley 9 72+
(M R Bosley) *hld up in midfield gng strly: smooth hdwy and edgd rt over 1f out: led ins fnl f: pushed out* **9/1**
1-21 **2** 1 1/2 **Pab Special (IRE)**12 580 6-9-2 66 JackMitchell(3) 6 72+
(B R Johnson) *t.k.h: chsd ldr: rdn 3f out: drvn to ld over 1f out: hdd and nt pce of wnr ins fnl f* **9/2**1
00-0 **3** hd **Pha Mai Blue**46 157 4-9-1 62 PatCosgrave 5 67
(J R Boyle) *t.k.h early: trckd ldrs: rdn and sltly outpcd 2f out: styd on fnl f* **5/1**2
13-0 **4** shd **Ugenius**10 607 5-9-0 61 TGMcLaughlin 11 66
(Mrs C A Dunnett) *in tch: rdn and outpcd over 2f out: rallied fnl f: r.o* **10/1**
56-4 **5** 1 1/2 **Moayed**15 554 10-8-13 60 (b) ShaneKelly 2 62
(N P Littmoden) *s.s: bhd tl rdn and r.o fnl 2f: nrst fin* **15/2**
0-32 **6** 1 **Fine Ruler (IRE)**17 512 5-9-3 64 VinceSlattery 4 64
(M R Bosley) *t.k.h in rr: hrd rdn 2f out: styd on fnl f* **12/1**
01-2 **7** hd **Convallaria (FR)**25 387 6-9-0 61 (b) GeorgeBaker 1 60
(C F Wall) *trckd ldrs: rdn over 2f out: one pce* **5/1**2
3204 **8** 1/2 **Shake On It**18 505 5-9-4 65 (t) NCallan 8 63
(M J Gingell) *swtchd lft to rail after 1f: hld up in tch gng wl: rdn over 1f out: little rspnse and sn btn* **11/2**3
5-62 **9** hd **Landucci**18 504 8-9-4 65 PaulDoe 3 63
(S Curran) *led: rdn and hdd over 1f out: sn wknd* **9/1**
/00- **10** 14 **Carole Os (IRE)**235 3845 4-8-13 60 NickyMackay 10 27
(S W Hall) *prom: rdn over 3f out: wknd over 2f out* **66/1**
0-60 **11** 9 **Pharaohs Justice (USA)**21 457 4-9-4 65 ChrisCatlin 7 12
(N P Littmoden) *sn towards rr: rdn 4f out: sn bhd* **28/1**
1m 38.75s (0.55) **Going Correction** +0.05s/f (Slow) **11** Ran SP% **120.4**
Speed ratings (Par 101): **99,97,97,97,95 94,94,94,93,79 70**
toteswinger: 1&2 £11.00, 1&3 £21.80, 2&3 £5.50. CSF £50.49 CT £231.55 TOTE £10.90: £3.40, £1.80, £2.30; EX 67.20 TRIFECTA Not won..
Owner Mrs Jean M O'Connor **Bred** G And Mrs Middlebrook **Trained** Chalfont St Giles, Bucks
■ Stewards' Enquiry : Jim Crowley two-day ban: careless riding (Mar 16-17)
FOCUS
In contrast to the previous handicap which was run at a strong gallop, this was more of a typical Lingfield race run at a steady early pace, and the winning time was a full 3.88sec slower.
Convallaria(FR) Official explanation: jockey said mare hung right throughout

726 PARRY H'CAP 1m 4f (P)
4:50 (4:53) (Class 5) (0-75,75) 4-Y-O+ **£3,885** (£1,156; £577; £288) **Stalls** Low

Form RPR
30-5 **1** **Bassinet (USA)**46 156 5-9-6 75 JimCrowley 7 83
(J A R Toller) *bhd: gd hdwy fr 2f out: str run to ld nr fin* **20/1**

400- **2** *hd* **King Supreme (IRE)**[74] 7711 4-9-3 **74**..........(b) DaneO'Neill 1 82
(R Hannon) *chsd ldrs: rdn over 2f out: r.o to narrow ld 50yds out: jst ct* **8/1**

00-2 **3** *1 ¼* **Eton Fable (IRE)**[7] 648 4-9-1 **72**..........(p) RichardKingscote 8 78
(W J H Ratcliffe) *led and clr w one rival: hdd 5f out: led 3f out: hrd rdn fnl f: hdd and no ex fnl 50yds* **12/1**

1-36 **4** *nk* **King's Colour**[25] 398 4-8-7 **67**.......... JackMitchell(3) 3 72
(B R Johnson) *bhd: gd hdwy 2f out: disp ld ins fnl f: one pce fnl 50yds* **12/1**

53-6 **5** *2 ½* **Mr Napoleon (IRE)**[57] 21 7-9-0 **69**.......... FergusSweeney 2 71
(G L Moore) *hld up in 6th: effrt 3f out: one pce fnl 2f* **14/1**

3-62 **6** *7* **Action Impact (ARG)**[15] 549 5-9-6 **75**.......... GeorgeBaker 6 66
(G L Moore) *chsd ldrs: hrd rdn 4f out: rallied u.p to press ldrs over 2f out: wknd qckly over 1f out* **13/8**[1]

1-01 **7** *4 ½* **Cossack Prince**[11] 584 4-9-1 **72**.......... PaulDoe 5 56
(Mrs L J Mongan) *pressed ldr and clr of rest: led 5f out tl 3f out: sn wknd* **15/2**[3]

5-04 **8** *4 ½* **Ryedale Ovation (IRE)**[32] 311 6-8-2 **62**.......... AmyBaker(5) 9 40
(M Hill) *hld up in rr: mod effrt 4f out: lost tch 2f out* **9/1**

1 **P** **Quite A Fella (USA)**[36] 279 4-9-4 **75**.......... ChrisCatlin 4 —
(Andrew Turnell) *mid-div: rdn and wknd rapidly over 4f out: sn wl bhd: p.u ins fnl f: lame* **9/2**[2]

2m 30.6s (-2.40) **Going Correction** +0.05s/f (Slow)
WFA 4 from 5yo+ 2lb **9** Ran SP% **116.0**
Speed ratings (Par 103): **110,109,109,108,107 102,99,96,—**
toteswinger: 1&2 £22.50, 1&3 £14.40, 2&3 £19.20. CSF £170.62 CT £2014.68 TOTE £24.00: £6.00, £3.10, £3.90; EX 160.80 TRIFECTA Not won. Place 6 £71.80, Place 5 £42.60.
Owner John Drew **Bred** Juddmonte Farms Inc **Trained** Newmarket, Suffolk

FOCUS
Eton Fable and Cossack Prince took each other on at the head of affairs and although they did not go a mad gallop out in front, they did help to set the race up for a closer.
Action Impact(ARG) Official explanation: trainer had no explanation for the poor form shown
Quite A Fella(USA) Official explanation: jockey said gelding was lame
T/Plt: £324.20 to a £1 stake. Pool: £62,866.78. 141.55 winning tickets. T/Qpdt: £96.70 to a £1 stake. Pool: £3,949.54. 30.20 winning tickets. LM

721 LINGFIELD (L-H)
Monday, March 2

OFFICIAL GOING: Standard
Wind: Fresh, across Weather: Bright, partly cloudy

727 COOT H'CAP 5f (P)
2:10 (2:11) (Class 6) (0-50,50) 4-Y-0+ **£1,878** (£558; £279; £139) **Stalls** High

Form RPR

60-0 **1** **Ramblin Bob**[12] 587 4-8-8 **46** oh1..........(bt) ChrisCatlin 4 54
(W J Musson) *mounted on crse: stdd after s: hld up in tch: hdwy ent fnl f: drvn and edgd lft fnl 100yds: r.o wl to ld towards fin* **25/1**

-306 **2** *nk* **Ishibee (IRE)**[51] 111 5-8-9 **47**..........(p) NeilChalmers 2 54
(J J Bridger) *in tch: hdwy to ld over 1f out: edgd rt u.p fnl f: hdd towards fin* **10/1**

-004 **3** *1 ¼* **Affirmatively**[21] 474 4-8-4 **47**..........(bt) AmyBaker(5) 1 49
(A W Carroll) *dwlt: hdwy into midfield 1/2-way: chsd ldrs and rdn ent fnl f: swtchd lft ins fnl f: kpt on same pce under hands and heels fnl 100yds* **10/1**

0/56 **4** *nse* **Meikle Barfil**[11] 596 7-8-8 **46** oh1..........(tp) RobertWinston 5 48
(J M Bradley) *towards rr: swtchd rt and rdn over 1f out: r.o ins fnl f: nt rch ldrs* **9/2**[2]

60-0 **5** *nse* **Our Fugitive (IRE)**[24] 294 7-8-12 **50**.......... JimCrowley 8 52
(C Gordon) *chsd ldr: ev ch 2f out: sn rdn and racd awkwardly: kpt on same pce fnl f* **15/2**

-243 **6** *1 ¾* **Taboor (IRE)**[21] 474 11-8-10 **48**..........(p) ShaneKelly 6 44
(R M H Cowell) *hld up in rr: effrt and rdn on outer over 1f out: kpt on fnl f: nvr trbld ldrs* **7/2**[1]

0-00 **7** *hd* **Forever Changes**[8] 646 4-8-12 **50**.......... MartinDwyer 3 45
(L Montague Hall) *hld up in rr: effrt on inner over 1f out: no imp ins fnl f* **8/1**

10-0 **8** *1 ¾* **Sir Loin**[21] 467 8-8-12 **50**..........(v) DaneO'Neill 7 39
(P Burgoyne) *led: rdn 2f out: hdd over 1f out: wknd fnl f* **5/1**[3]

0-64 **9** *nk* **She's Our Beauty (IRE)**[27] 380 6-8-8 **46** oh1..........(b) JoeFanning 9 33
(S T Mason) *dwlt: sn rcvrd to chse ldrs: wknd u.p over 1f out* **15/2**

58.74 secs (-0.06) **Going Correction** +0.10s/f (Slow) **9** Ran SP% **113.7**
Speed ratings (Par 101): **104,103,101,101,101 98,98,95,94**
toteswinger: 1&2 £35.20, 1&3 £19.80, 2&3 £10.50. CSF £248.39 CT £2661.01 TOTE £30.70: £7.50, £2.40, £2.80; EX 215.60 TRIFECTA Not won.
Owner The Roofing Guys **Bred** D R Tucker **Trained** Newmarket, Suffolk
■ Stewards' Enquiry : Chris Catlin caution: careless riding

FOCUS
A very weak sprint, run at a solid pace. Ramblin Bob was one of a number entitled to win on a going day.
Ramblin Bob Official explanation: trainer said, regarding apparent improvement in form, that the gelding has recently suffered from veterinary problems but seemed to benefit from being raced over the shorter trip.
Taboor(IRE) Official explanation: jockey said gelding never travelled and moved poorly throughout

728 BUZZARD H'CAP 6f (P)
2:40 (2:40) (Class 5) (0-70,68) 4-Y-0+ **£2,590** (£770; £385; £192) **Stalls** Low

Form RPR

000- **1** **Brunelleschi**[109] 7302 6-8-6 **63**..........(b) JosephineBruning(7) 4 73
(P L Gilligan) *t.k.h: chsd ldr: led wl over 1f out: hanging lft fr over 1f out: in command ins fnl f: comf* **16/1**

16-2 **2** *1 ½* **Louphole**[6] 665 7-9-4 **68**.......... FergusSweeney 1 74
(J R Jenkins) *stedaied s: t.k.h: hld up in last pl: hdwy and rdn ent fnl f: wnt 2nd fnl 100yds: no imp* **4/6**[1]

0145 **3** *¾* **Jessica Wigmo**[6] 661 6-8-5 **55**.......... HayleyTurner 2 58
(A W Carroll) *trckd ldng pair: effrt and rdn over 1f out: drvn and kpt on same pce fnl f* **3/1**[2]

0-03 **4** *½* **Prince Of Delphi**[12] 590 6-8-12 **62**..........(p) JimCrowley 6 64
(Mrs A L M King) *led at stdy gallop: rdn 2f out: sn hdd: wknd ins fnl f* **9/2**[3]

1m 12.43s (0.53) **Going Correction** +0.10s/f (Slow) **4** Ran SP% **109.1**
Speed ratings (Par 103): **100,98,97,96**
toteswinger: 1&2 £6.00. CSF £28.45 TOTE £19.50; EX 27.80.
Owner Dr Susan Barnes **Bred** Dr Susan Barnes **Trained** Newmarket, Suffolk

FOCUS
This moderate sprint was run at a modest tempo and the form is worth treating with some caution. The winner is potentially well in on the sand.

729 SPARROW HAWK MAIDEN STKS 6f (P)
3:10 (3:10) (Class 4) 3-Y-0+ **£2,590** (£770; £385; £192) **Stalls** Low

Form RPR

2 **1** **Trade Centre**[7] 655 4-9-12 0.......... MartinDwyer 3 68+
(W R Muir) *mde all: set stdy gallop: rdn and qcknd wl over 1f out: edgd rt u.p fnl f: hld on: all out* **5/6**[1]

333- **2** *hd* **Dareh (IRE)**[115] 7227 3-8-7 71.......... JoeFanning 4 62+
(M Johnston) *chsd wnr: ev ch and rdn over 1f out: unable qck and hld fnl 100yds* **2/1**[2]

3 *1 ¼* **Christmascametwice** 3-8-8 0 ow1.......... ShaneKelly 1 60
(J A Osborne) *stdd s: trckd ldrs: rdn and hung lft jst ins fnl f: kpt on but nt pce to rch ldng pair* **16/1**

4 *¾* **Wild Cat Card (USA)** 3-8-7 0.......... FergusSweeney 2 56+
(D M Simcock) *stdd and wnt rt s: a last pl: pushed along and outpcd ent fnl f: r.o fnl 100yds: styng on at fin* **7/1**[3]

1m 13.31s (1.41) **Going Correction** +0.10s/f (Slow)
WFA 3 from 4yo 14lb **4** Ran SP% **106.3**
Speed ratings (Par 105): **94,93,92,91**
CSF £2.63 TOTE £1.60; EX 2.90.
Owner K Mercer,C Edginton,S Jones,M Dawson **Bred** Usk Valley Stud **Trained** Lambourn, Berks

FOCUS
A modest maiden run in a slow time. Muddling form but the first two could be rated higher.

730 KINGFISHER CLAIMING STKS 1m (P)
3:40 (3:41) (Class 6) 4-Y-0+ **£1,878** (£558; £279; £139) **Stalls** High

Form RPR

1133 **1** **Jake The Snake (IRE)**[5] 671 8-8-9 74.......... AmyBaker(5) 3 81+
(A W Carroll) *t.k.h: hld up in 3rd pl: hdwy on inner 2f out: led wl over 1f out: clr fnl f: comf* **5/2**[2]

4-40 **2** *2 ¾* **Autumn Blades (IRE)**[22] 457 4-9-4 75.......... RobertWinston 1 79
(A Bailey) *t.k.h: hld up in last pair: hdwy on outer over 1f out: sn edging lft: wnt 2nd fnl 100yds: no ch w wnr* **7/1**

-602 **3** *1 ¼* **Willkandoo (USA)**[8] 650 4-8-13 80.......... JimCrowley 2 71
(D M Simcock) *chsd ldr: rdn and carried wd ent strt: chsd wnr over 1f out: no imp u.p: lost 2nd fnl 100yds* **1/1**[1]

1140 **4** *1* **Teasing**[3] 713 5-8-8 78..........(v) ChrisCatlin 4 64
(J Pearce) *t.k.h: hld up in last pair: rdn and effrt over 1f out: sn no imp* **9/2**[3]

5 *6* **Gold Rock (FR)**[26] 4-9-2 82.......... ShaneKelly 5 59
(A W Carroll) *led: sn clr: rdn and c towards centre 2f out: sn hdd: wknd over 1f out* **25/1**

1m 38.31s (0.11) **Going Correction** +0.10s/f (Slow) **5** Ran SP% **113.1**
Speed ratings (Par 101): **103,100,99,98,92**
CSF £19.26 TOTE £3.50: £3.00, £6.10; EX 20.70.
Owner D Morgan & M B Clarke **Bred** J F Tuthill **Trained** Cropthorne, Worcs

FOCUS
Not a bad claimer, run at an uneven pace. The winner did not need to improve on his recent form.
Autumn Blades(IRE) Official explanation: jockey said gelding hung left in final furlong

731 MARSH HARRIER MAIDEN STKS 1m (P)
4:10 (4:10) (Class 4) 3-Y-0+ **£2,590** (£770; £385; £192) **Stalls** High

Form RPR

1 **Boscage (USA)** 4-9-13 0.......... JoeFanning 2 86+
(M Johnston) *sn led: mde rest: rn green and edgd rt over 1f out: kpt on wl and a holding runner up fnl 100yds* **6/5**[1]

2- **2** *nk* **Onemix**[75] 7699 3-8-4 0.......... ChrisCatlin 3 70+
(B W Hills) *chsd wnr: carried rt over 1f out: rdn and ev ch ins fnl f: unable qck and hld fnl 100yds* **6/4**[2]

0-53 **3** *3 ¾* **Pyrus Time (IRE)**[37] 280 3-8-9 75.......... LPKeniry 5 67
(J S Moore) *stdd s: plld hrd: hld up in last pair: effrt and rdn 2f out: drvn to chse ldng pair over 1f out: sn no imp* **9/2**[3]

0 **4** *4 ½* **Aegean Rose**[54] 80 4-9-8 0.......... FergusSweeney 4 52
(M Blanshard) *hld up in 4th pl: rdn and unable qck 2f out: no ch fnl f* **40/1**

000- **5** *2* **Tightrope (IRE)**[132] 6876 3-8-4 54.......... AmyBaker(5) 1 58?
(T D McCarthy) *chsd ldng pair: rdn wl over 2f out: wknd over 1f out:* **80/1**

1m 38.25s (0.05) **Going Correction** +0.10s/f (Slow)
WFA 3 from 4yo 18lb **5** Ran SP% **107.3**
Speed ratings (Par 105): **103,102,98,94,92**
CSF £3.07 TOTE £2.00: £1.10, £1.70; EX 4.60.
Owner Sheikh Hamdan Bin Mohammed Al Maktoum **Bred** R S Evans **Trained** Middleham Moor, N Yorks
■ Stewards' Enquiry : Amy Baker one-day ban: failed to ride to draw (Mar 16)

FOCUS
The first pair came clear in this ordinary maiden and both can rate higher in due course. The fifth holds down the level to a certain extent.

732 GOLDEN PLOVER H'CAP 2m (P)
4:40 (4:41) (Class 6) (0-65,65) 4-Y-0+ **£1,878** (£558; £279; £139) **Stalls** Low

Form RPR

-642 **1** **Irish Ballad**[19] 502 7-9-4 **55**.......... NickyMackay 2 64
(S Dow) *chsd ldr: rdn over 3f out: led over 2f out: edgd rt and hld on wl ins fnl f* **4/1**[2]

00-1 **2** *½* **Bold Adventure**[10] 627 5-9-10 **61**.......... ChrisCatlin 6 69
(W J Musson) *stdd s: hld up in rr: hdwy on outer over 2f out: wnt 2nd 1f out: pressed wnr ins fnl f: unable qck and hld fnl 100yds* **9/2**[3]

25/4 **3** *3 ¾* **Super Sensation (GER)**[14] 566 8-8-12 **49**..........(b) FergusSweeney 3 53
(G L Moore) *rrd s and s.i.s: hld up in last pair: hdwy on outer 3f out: chsd wnr and drvn over 1f out: wknd jst ins fnl f* **8/1**

2640 **4** *1 ¾* **Prince Of Medina**[11] 601 6-8-8 **45**..........(t) MartinDwyer 5 47
(J R Best) *hld up in midfield: hdwy over 2f out: sltly hmpd jst over 2f out: hung lft and hdwy to chse ldrs and rdn over 1f out: wknd ent fnl f* **12/1**

-242 **5** *1 ¾* **Star Choice**[16] 559 4-9-9 **65**.......... JerryO'Dwyer 1 65
(J Pearce) *chsd ldrs: swtchd rt and n.m.r jst over 2f out: rdn wl over 1f out: no real imp* **7/2**[1]

0-23 **6** *½* **Limelight (USA)**[23] 444 4-8-5 **47**.......... HayleyTurner 4 46+
(Sir Mark Prescott) *hld up in midfield: n.m.r and shuffled bk over 2f out: effrt u.p over 1f out: nvr trbld ldrs* **8/1**

05-5 **7** *4 ½* **Rettorical Lad**[19] 501 4-8-13 **55**.......... ShaneKelly 8 49
(Jamie Poulton) *led: rdn over 3f out: hdd over 2f out: wknd wl over 1f out: wl bhd fnl f* **14/1**

0-03 **8** 3 **Born West (USA)**[10] 627 5-9-1 55 JackMitchell(3) 7 45
(N B King) *chsd ldrs: rdn 4f out: lost pl u.p over 2f out: wl bhd fnl 2f* **5/1**

3m 24.31s (-1.39) **Going Correction** +0.10s/f (Slow)
WFA 4 from 5yo+ 5lb **8** Ran SP% **113.7**
Speed ratings (Par 101): **107,106,104,104,103 102,100,99**
toteswinger: 1&2 £4.30, 1&3 £7.60, 2&3 £7.20. CSF £22.04 CT £135.37 TOTE £4.60: £1.60, £2.30, £2.50; EX 15.90 Trifecta £292.30 Part won. Pool: £395.03 - 0.94 winning units..
Owner Chua, White, Moore & Jurd **Bred** The Kingwood Partnership **Trained** Epsom, Surrey
FOCUS
This moderate staying handicap was run at a fair pace. The form looks straightforward enough with the winner rated right back to his best.

733 BITTERN H'CAP 1m 2f (P)
5:10 (5:10) (Class 5) (0-70,70) 4-Y-0+ **£2,590** (£770; £385; £192) **Stalls** Low

Form RPR
0-60 **1** **Vinces**[17] 534 5-8-7 **59** HayleyTurner 11 68
(T D McCarthy) *sn led: hdd over 7f out: chsd ldr after tl over 3f out: drvn to ld again 1f out: styd on wl fnl 100yds* **16/1**
5-12 **2** 1 **Old Romney**[24] 427 5-9-4 **70** RobertWinston 1 77
(M Wigham) *steadied after s: t.k.h: hld up in midfield: looking for room over 2f out: swtchd rt and hdwy over 1f out: pressed wnr ins fnl f: no ex fnl 75yds* **3/1**[2]
3-13 **3** ½ **Ghufa (IRE)**[20] 493 5-9-0 **66** ChrisCatlin 2 72
(George Baker) *hld up in rr: nt clr run ent fnl 2f: swtchd lft jst over 1f out: r.o wl fnl f: nt rch ldng pair* **5/2**[1]
2112 **4** ½ **Formidable Guest**[11] 597 5-9-1 **67** JerryO'Dwyer 5 72
(J Pearce) *hld up towards rr: pushed along 4f out: rdn and hdwy 2f out: chsd ldrs ent fnl f: one pce fnl 100yds* **6/1**[3]
00-1 **5** ½ **Clovis**[21] 468 4-9-2 **68** (b) ShaneKelly 6 73+
(N P Mulholland) *t.k.h: hld up towards rr: rdn jst over 2f out: stl plenty to do and swtchd rt over 1f out: r.o fnl f: nt rch ldrs* **20/1**
-424 **6** ½ **My Mentor (IRE)**[10] 622 5-9-3 **69** (b) J-PGuillambert 3 73
(Sir Mark Prescott) *sn bustled along in rr: hdwy on outer to ld over 7f out: clr over 5f out: rdn over 2f out: drvn and hdd 1f out: wknd fnl 100yds* **8/1**
64-0 **7** 1 **Straight And Level (CAN)**[26] 398 4-9-2 **68** (v) DaneO'Neill 8 70
(Miss Jo Crowley) *t.k.h: stdd after 1f and hld up in tch: rdn and unable qck wl over 1f out: one pce after* **25/1**
3/01 **8** 1 **Almahaza (IRE)**[11] 608 5-8-4 **56** (b) NeilChalmers 7 56
(A J Chamberlain) *t.k.h: chsd ldrs: wnt 2nd over 3f out tl over 1f out: wknd jst ins fnl f* **10/1**
5-30 **9** 1 ¼ **Our Kes (IRE)**[21] 478 7-8-10 **62** IanMongan 10 60
(P Howling) *t.k.h: racd on outer: hld up in midfield: rdn over 4f out: no hdwy fr over 2f out* **11/1**
00-5 **10** ¾ **Al Azy (IRE)**[16] 546 4-8-5 **57** MartinDwyer 4 53
(D M Simcock) *chsd ldrs: rdn over 2f out: wknd fnl f* **10/1**
3-40 **11** ½ **Artreju (GER)**[14] 569 6-8-10 **62** FergusSweeney 9 58
(G L Moore) *t.k.h: hld up in tch: rdn and hung lft 2f out: swtchd rt over 1f out: no hdwy fnl f* **20/1**

2m 6.71s (0.11) **Going Correction** +0.10s/f (Slow) **11** Ran SP% **124.7**
Speed ratings (Par 103): **103,102,101,101,101 100,99,99,98,97 97**
toteswinger: 1&2 £15.20, 1&3 £13.40, 2&3 £2.60. CSF £66.01 CT £170.54 TOTE £21.50: £5.00, £1.50, £2.10; EX 91.20 Trifecta £374.20 Part won. Pool: £505.69 - 0.50 winning units. Place 6: £3149.68, Place 5: £186.72.
Owner Eastwell Manor Racing Ltd **Bred** Gestut Fahrhof **Trained** Godstone, Surrey
FOCUS
A competitive handicap for the class. There was an early crawl before the sixth put pace to the race. Solid form, the winner back to the best of this winter's form.
Artreju(GER) Official explanation: jockey said gelding hung left final bend
T/Plt: £2,003.50 to a £1 stake. Pool: £52,559.75. 19.15 winning tickets. T/Qpdt: £13.50 to a £1 stake. Pool: £3,717.00. 203.40 winning tickets. SP

711 WOLVERHAMPTON (A.W) (L-H)
Monday, March 2

OFFICIAL GOING: Standard
Wind: Fresh behind Weather: Cloudy

734 ARENA LEISURE CATERING AMATEUR RIDERS' H'CAP (DIV I) 1m 5f 194y(P)
2:20 (2:20) (Class 5) (0-70,70) 4-Y-0+ **£2,307** (£709; £354) **Stalls** Low

Form RPR
0514 **1** **William's Way**[17] 534 7-10-10 **64** MrCMartin(5) 3 73
(I A Wood) *hld up: hdwy 4f out: rdn over 2f out: led ins fnl f: styd on* **6/1**[3]
5-35 **2** ¾ **Wester Lodge (IRE)**[16] 554 7-9-13 **55** MrDJEustace(7) 9 63
(J M P Eustace) *s.i.s: hld up: hdwy and hung lft fr over 1f out: styd on wl: nt rch wnr* **13/2**
4136 **3** nk **Sabancaya**[11] 604 4-10-5 **63** MissGAndrews(5) 4 71
(Mrs P Sly) *a.p: racd keenly: rdn and ev ch ins fnl f: styd on same pce* **9/2**[2]
0332 **4** 1 ¾ **Morbick**[7] 660 5-11-4 **70** MrBenBrisbourne(3) 5 75
(W M Brisbourne) *hld up: hdwy over 2f out: rdn over 1f out: styd on* **15/8**[1]
6-04 **5** nk **Schinken Otto (IRE)**[14] 567 8-9-13 **51** oh1 MissRJefferson(3) 12 56
(J M Jefferson) *s.i.s: rcvrd to chse ldr over 12f out: led over 3f out: rdn and hdd ins fnl f: no ex* **18/1**
4-55 **6** 1 ½ **Inn For The Dancer**[14] 566 7-9-11 **51** oh3 MissSarah-JaneDurman(5) 11 54
(J C Fox) *hld up: rdn over 3f out: hdwy over 1f out: nrst fin: bbv* **22/1**
6 **7** nk **Bariolo (FR)**[16] 559 5-11-2 **65** WilliamBiddick 6 67
(Noel T Chance) *hld up in tch: chsd ldr over 2f out: sn rdn: no ex fnl f* **10/1**
0-00 **8** 15 **Sovietta (IRE)**[6] 385 8-9-9 **51** oh6 (t) MrJHodson(7) 2 32
(Ian Williams) *hld up: rdn over 3f out: sn wknd* **50/1**
05-3 **9** 6 **Captain Mainwaring**[17] 534 4-10-4 **57** (b) MrsEmmaLittmoden 8 30
(N P Littmoden) *led: hdd over 3f out: sn rdn: wknd wl over 1f out* **12/1**
0-50 **10** 6 **Sand Repeal (IRE)**[17] 534 7-10-9 **63** (v) MrRBirkett(5) 1 27
(Miss J Feilden) *prom: racd keenly: rdn and wknd over 2f out* **12/1**
00-4 **11** 5 **Ndola**[11] 601 10-9-12 **52** oh6 ow1 (v) MissMBryant(5) 10 9
(P Butler) *led early: chsd ldrs: rdn over 3f out: wknd over 2f out* **50/1**

3m 8.56s (2.56) **Going Correction** +0.05s/f (Slow)
WFA 4 from 5yo+ 4lb **11** Ran SP% **118.6**
Speed ratings (Par 103): **94,93,93,92,92 91,91,82,79,75 72**
toteswinger: 1&2 £8.30, 1&3 £6.50, 2&3 £6.10. CSF £44.54 CT £193.25 TOTE £7.30: £2.00, £2.20, £1.90; EX 57.70.
Owner Neardown Stables **Bred** Lewis Caterers **Trained** Upper Lambourn, Berks
■ Stewards' Enquiry : Miss G Andrews four-day ban: careless riding (Apr 6, 18, 25, May 3)
FOCUS
There was not much of a gallop on for the first division of this moderate amateur riders' handicap.
Inn For The Dancer Official explanation: jockey said gelding bled from the nose

735 ARENA LEISURE CATERING AMATEUR RIDERS' H'CAP (DIV II) 1m 5f 194y(P)
2:50 (2:50) (Class 5) (0-70,67) 4-Y-0+ **£2,307** (£709; £354) **Stalls** Low

Form RPR
3322 **1** **Augustus John (IRE)**[17] 528 6-11-4 **64** WilliamBiddick 5 74
(R Brotherton) *hld up: hdwy over 5f out: jnd ldr wl over 1f out: led ins fnl f: rdn clr* **4/1**[1]
00-0 **2** 4 ½ **Home**[21] 342 4-10-1 **58** MissLGray(7) 4 62
(C Gordon) *hld up: hmpd over 7f out: gd hdwy on outer over 2f out: led wl over 1f out: hdd and unable qck ins fnl f* **20/1**
4/0- **3** 6 **Pertemps Power**[175] 5752 5-9-13 **48** BrianToomey(3) 9 43+
(B G Powell) *prom: n.m.r over 2f out: sn hrd rdn: styd on same pce* **4/1**[1]
-146 **4** hd **Night Orbit**[20] 485 5-11-0 **65** MrRBirkett(5) 1 60
(Miss J Feilden) *dwlt: hld up: hdwy over 5f out: hung lft over 1f out: wknd fnl f* **6/1**[3]
-054 **5** 3 ¾ **Reminiscent (IRE)**[27] 378 10-9-11 **48** oh3 (v) MissAWallace(5) 7 38
(B P J Baugh) *dwlt: hld up: hdwy over 5f out: rdn over 2f out: wknd over 1f out* **16/1**
-161 **6** ¾ **Corlough Mountain**[14] 566 5-10-1 **52** MissMBryant(5) 11 41
(P Butler) *broke wl: sn dropped into mid-div: hdwy 1/2-way: led over 2f out: hdd wl over 1f out: wknd fnl f* **8/1**
2054 **7** 15 **Buscador (USA)**[23] 448 10-10-10 **59** MrBenBrisbourne(3) 10 27
(W M Brisbourne) *chsd ldrs: rdn to ld wl over 2f out: sn hdd: wknd over 1f out* **10/1**
/00- **8** 10 **Helvetio**[30] 1482 7-11-0 **67** MrMGarnett(7) 3 21
(Micky Hammond) *s.i.s: hld up: hdwy over 5f out: wknd over 3f out: t.o* **33/1**
1246 **9** nk **Blue Hills**[4] 692 8-11-2 **62** (b) MrsMarieKing 8 15+
(P W Hiatt) *chsd ldrs: led over 7f out: rdn and hdd wl over 2f out: sn wknd: t.o* **9/2**[2]
23-0 **10** 46 **Corking (IRE)**[57] 38 4-9-10 **53** (b[1]) MrDGPrichard(7) 2 —+
(J L Flint) *plld hrd: w ldr over 3f: wknd over 7f out: t.o* **16/1**
040- **11** 75 **Jalamid (IRE)**[243] 3602 7-9-11 **48** oh3 (t) MissAngelaBarnes(5) 6 —+
(M A Barnes) *plld hrd and sn led: hdd over 7f out: wknd over 5f out: t.o* **33/1**

3m 6.25s (0.25) **Going Correction** +0.05s/f (Slow)
WFA 4 from 5yo+ 4lb **11** Ran SP% **115.1**
Speed ratings (Par 103): **101,98,95,94,92 92,83,78,77,51 8**
toteswinger: 1&2 £21.00, 1&3 £5.70, 2&3 £38.30. CSF £85.29 CT £335.73 TOTE £3.60: £1.20, £5.90, £2.40; EX 64.70.
Owner Arthur Clayton **Bred** Rizerie Syndicate **Trained** Elmley Castle, Worcs
FOCUS
The second division of a moderate amateur riders' handicap.

736 HOTEL & CONFERENCING AT WOLVERHAMPTON (S) STKS 5f 216y(P)
3:20 (3:20) (Class 6) 3-Y-0 **£2,047** (£604; £302) **Stalls** Low

Form RPR
5440 **1** **Deckchair**[16] 542 3-9-0 55 (v) DarryllHolland 10 60
(H J Collingridge) *chsd ldrs: rdn over 1f out: hung lft and r.o u.p to ld towards fin* **4/1**[1]
50-0 **2** 1 **Chimbonda**[7] 655 3-8-8 60 (v) JamesO'Reilly(5) 3 56
(S Parr) *led: rdn over 1f out: hdd towards fin* **14/1**
-255 **3** 1 ¼ **Weet In Nerja**[10] 624 3-8-13 58 (p) GrahamGibbons 8 52+
(R Hollinshead) *chsd ldrs: hmpd and lost pl over 4f out: hdwy over 2f out: hrd rdn and hung lft over 1f out: styd on* **5/1**[3]
-553 **4** shd **Fashion Icon (USA)**[10] 624 3-8-3 57 DeanHeslop(5) 11 47
(T D Barron) *chsd ldr tl rdn over 2f out: styd on u.p* **15/2**
0 **5** 1 **Peanut Girl (IRE)**[6] 664 3-8-8 0 CatherineGannon 7 43
(B Palling) *s.i.s: sn pushed along in rr: hdwy over 2f out: sn rdn: styd on* **40/1**
4555 **6** shd **Ruby Tallulah**[5] 673 3-9-0 63 NCallan 6 49
(C R Dore) *prom: chsd ldr over 2f out: rdn ins fnl f: no ex towards fin* **9/2**[2]
4025 **7** nk **Lois Darlin (IRE)**[11] 602 3-8-8 51 (b) FrankieMcDonald 4 42
(R A Harris) *sn outpcd: hdwy over 1f out: nt clr run and swtchd rt ins fnl f: r.o: nt rch ldrs* **16/1**
5220 **8** nk **Sorrel Ridge (IRE)**[33] 316 3-8-8 54 (p) NicolPolli(5) 2 46
(M G Quinlan) *hld up in tch: rdn over 1f out: edgd lft and styd on same pce ins fnl f: n.m.r sn after* **8/1**
0-30 **9** 1 ¼ **Dancing Welcome**[35] 293 3-8-3 45 MCGeran(5) 5 37
(J M Bradley) *sn outpcd: styd on ins fnl f: nvr nrr* **33/1**
0-64 **10** 10 **Thaumatology (USA)**[4] 684 3-8-8 56 TolleyDean 9 5+
(S Parr) *chsd ldrs over 3f* **20/1**
002- **11** 5 **Come On Buckers (IRE)**[96] 7451 3-9-5 62 EdwardCreighton 1 —
(E J Creighton) *sn outpcd* **7/1**

1m 16.06s (1.06) **Going Correction** +0.05s/f (Slow) **11** Ran SP% **112.9**
Speed ratings (Par 96): **94,92,91,90,89 89,89,88,86,73 66**
toteswinger: 1&2 £15.50, 1&3 £6.80, 2&3 £21.00. CSF £56.66 TOTE £5.70: £2.00, £5.50, £2.30; EX 84.60.There was no bid for the winner.
Owner Dave Clayton **Bred** Whitsbury Manor Stud **Trained** Exning, Suffolk
■ Stewards' Enquiry : Frankie McDonald three-day ban: careless riding (Mar 16-18)
FOCUS
An open seller.

737 GREAT OFFERS ONLINE AT WOLVERHAMPTON-RACECOURSE.CO.UK CLAIMING STKS 1m 1f 103y(P)
3:50 (3:50) (Class 5) 4-Y-0+ **£2,729** (£806; £403) **Stalls** Low

Form RPR
-412 **1** **New Star (UAE)**[13] 577 5-9-5 75 GrahamGibbons 3 80
(W M Brisbourne) *chsd ldrs: rdn 2f out: sn rdn: styd on u.p* **7/4**[1]
-043 **2** nk **Prince Noel**[14] 569 5-8-4 65 ow2 LanceBetts(7) 7 71
(N Wilson) *hld up: hdwy over 2f out: rdn over 1f out: r.o* **15/2**
05-0 **3** nk **Kildare Sun (IRE)**[54] 79 7-9-5 68 PaulHanagan 5 79
(J Mackie) *chsd ldr tl led over 2f out: rdn and hdd 2f out: styd on* **10/1**
6-15 **4** nk **Watson's Bay**[40] 238 4-8-11 68 JamieSpencer 8 72+
(Miss Tor Sturgis) *hld up: n.m.r over 2f out: hdwy u.p and hung lft fr over 1f out: r.o* **10/3**[2]
6-31 **5** 3 ½ **North Parade**[10] 617 4-9-7 77 (t) NCallan 2 74
(A W Carroll) *chsd ldrs: rdn over 1f out: no ex ins fnl f* **9/2**[3]
5335 **6** 7 **Motivated Choice**[11] 607 4-8-1 64 (p) MartinLane(5) 4 45
(Miss Amy Weaver) *led: hdd over 6f out: remained w ldr tl rdn 3f out: wknd wl over 1f out* **16/1**

-323 7 3 1/4 **King Of The Beers (USA)**[5] 669 5-8-8 54..............(b) DeanHeslop(5) 6 46
(R A Harris) *prom: rdn over 3f out: wknd over 2f out* **16/1**
1m 59.91s (-1.79) **Going Correction** +0.05s/f (Slow) 7 Ran SP% **110.2**
Speed ratings (Par 103): **109,108,108,108,105 98,95**
toteswinger: 1&2 £3.90, 1&3 £8.10, 2&3 £8.40. CSF £14.39 TOTE £2.10: £1.60, £3.00; EX 14.30.
Owner Shropshire Wolves **Bred** Darley **Trained** Great Ness, Shropshire
FOCUS
A modest claimer.

738 BETDAQ ON 0870 178 1221 FILLIES' H'CAP 5f 216y(P)
4:20 (4:22) (Class 5) (0-75,70) 4-Y-0+ £2,729 (£806; £403) Stalls Low

Form RPR
215- 1 **Jaconet (USA)**[203] 4922 4-9-4 70..............(b) JamieSpencer 2 83+
(T D Barron) *mde all: rdn clr 2f out: eased nr fin* **7/4[1]**
-253 2 3 3/4 **Leading Edge (IRE)**[16] 557 4-9-4 70.............. TonyCulhane 1 72
(M R Channon) *sn pushed along in rr: hdwy u.p over 2f out: wnt 2nd 1f out: no ch w wnr* **4/1[3]**
0-60 3 2 1/4 **Maryolini**[12] 582 4-8-10 62.............. PaulDoe 6 57
(N J Vaughan) *chsd ldrs: rdn 2f out: styd on same pce appr fnl f* **9/2**
4312 4 1/2 **Moon Crystal**[8] 651 4-8-11 68..............(t) RossAtkinson(5) 5 62
(E A L Dunlop) *s.i.s: hdwy 4f out: rdn over 2f out: no ex fnl f* **3/1[2]**
050- 5 13 **Andrasta**[137] 6765 4-7-13 56 oh1.............. DanielleMcCreery(5) 3 11
(A Berry) *chsd ldrs: lost pl 4f out: wknd over 2f out* **28/1**
00-0 6 9 **Just Joey**[45] 198 5-8-4 56 oh4..............(b) PaulHanagan 4 —
(J R Weymes) *chsd wnr tl rdn over 2f out: sn wknd* **12/1**
1m 14.55s (-0.45) **Going Correction** +0.05s/f (Slow) 6 Ran SP% **110.7**
Speed ratings (Par 100): **105,100,97,96,79 67**
toteswinger: 1&2 £2.00, 1&3 £2.90, 2&3 £3.90. CSF £8.81 TOTE £2.40: £1.10, £3.10; EX 9.40.
Owner R G Toes **Bred** Team Block **Trained** Maunby, N Yorks
FOCUS
This was a moderate fillies' handicap won in emphatic style by Jaconet.

739 ENJOY THE LUCKY 7 GROUP OFFER CLAIMING STKS 5f 216y(P)
4:50 (4:50) (Class 6) 4-Y-0+ £2,047 (£604; £302) Stalls Low

Form RPR
2222 1 **Blue Tomato**[4] 690 8-8-6 78.............. WilliamCarson(5) 8 85
(D Nicholls) *hld up: stl last and plenty to do turning for home: hdwy over 1f out: led ins fnl f: r.o wl* **2/1[1]**
6-41 2 3 **Imprimis Tagula (IRE)**[11] 606 5-9-3 77..............(v) MickyFenton 5 82
(A Bailey) *sn pushed along in rr: hdwy over 2f out: rdn over 1f out: styd on same pce ins fnl f* **2/1[1]**
-224 3 1 1/2 **Hart Of Gold**[12] 590 5-8-5 64..............(p) FrankieMcDonald 7 66
(R A Harris) *a.p: chsd ldr over 1f out: sn rdn: no ex ins fnl f* **9/1[3]**
-000 4 2 3/4 **Trinculo (IRE)**[5] 681 12-7-13 58 ow1..............(b) DeanHeslop(5) 2 56
(R A Harris) *led: rdn and edgd rt over 1f out: hdd & wknd ins fnl f* **40/1**
-603 5 1 1/4 **Geoffdaw**[17] 530 4-8-5 67..............(v) PaulDoe 9 54
(P D Evans) *prom: lost pl over 4f out: hdwy u.p over 2f out: hung lft and wknd over 1f out* **16/1**
-316 6 3/4 **Lethal**[34] 304 6-8-3 65.............. PaulHanagan 6 49
(R A Fahey) *chsd ldr: tl rdn over 1f out: wknd fnl f* **7/1[2]**
0500 7 hd **Savile's Delight (IRE)**[11] 606 10-8-5 65.............. RichardKingscote 1 51
(Tom Dascombe) *chsd ldr: rdn: edgd lft and ev ch over 1f out: wknd ins fnl f* **12/1**
3066 8 1/2 **Peter's Storm (USA)**[11] 606 4-9-3 68..............(p) NCallan 4 61
(K A Ryan) *prom: n.m.r and lost pl 5f out: rdn and nt clr run over 1f out: wknd ins fnl f* **25/1**
1-00 9 1 1/2 **Brazilian Brush (IRE)**[22] 461 4-8-4 60..............(t) MCGeran(5) 3 49
(J M Bradley) *chsd ldrs: rdn 1/2-way: wknd over 1f out* **33/1**
1m 14.17s (-0.83) **Going Correction** +0.05s/f (Slow) 9 Ran SP% **112.0**
Speed ratings (Par 101): **107,103,101,97,95 94,94,93,91**
toteswinger: 1&2 £1.80, 1&3 £3.20, 2&3 £2.90. CSF £5.24 TOTE £3.00: £1.10, £1.40, £2.50; EX 8.90.
Owner Dab Hand Racing **Bred** Bearstone Stud **Trained** Sessay, N Yorks
FOCUS
This looked a fair claimer.
Savile's Delight(IRE) Official explanation: jockey said gelding had no more to give

740 BETDAQ THE BETTING EXCHANGE H'CAP 1m 4f 50y(P)
5:20 (5:20) (Class 5) (0-75,72) 3-Y-0 £2,729 (£806; £403) Stalls Low

Form RPR
0-51 1 **Dubai Storming**[22] 455 3-9-4 72.............. JamieSpencer 1 77+
(E A L Dunlop) *hld up: nt clr run over 2f out: hdwy over 1f out: rdn to ld and n.m.r 1f out: edgd rt: drvn out* **11/4[1]**
03-1 2 1/2 **Sounds Of Jupiter (IRE)**[33] 310 3-8-13 67.............. StephenDonohoe 4 71+
(D M Simcock) *hld up: hdwy over 1f out: r.o to go 2nd wl ins fnl f: nt rch wnr* **11/4[1]**
463- 3 3/4 **Merton Lad**[92] 7505 3-8-12 66.............. RobertHavlin 5 67
(T G Mills) *a.p: rdn: edgd lft and ev ch 1f out: styd on* **11/2[3]**
0-41 4 2 1/2 **Shaker Style (USA)**[10] 628 3-8-11 65..............(b) DarryllHolland 2 62
(J D Bethell) *led after 1f: rdn over 2f out: hung rt and lft over 1f out: sn hdd and no etxra* **6/1**
4-56 5 7 **Key Of Fortune (IRE)**[5] 677 3-8-8 62.............. PaulHanagan 3 49
(Jennie Candlish) *led 1f: chsd ldr: chal 5f out: rdn over 2f out: wknd over 1f out* **20/1**
06-4 6 11 **Midnight Bay**[21] 479 3-8-12 66.............. TonyCulhane 6 36
(M R Channon) *trckd ldrs: racd keenly: rdn over 2f out: wkng whn hung lft over 1f out* **10/3[2]**
2m 43.1s (2.00) **Going Correction** +0.05s/f (Slow) 6 Ran SP% **110.8**
Speed ratings (Par 98): **95,94,94,92,87 80**
toteswinger: 1&2 £2.20, 1&3 £3.00, 2&3 £3.70. CSF £10.25 TOTE £2.80: £1.80, £1.70; EX 7.30.
Owner Salem Suhail **Bred** Gainsborough Stud Management Ltd **Trained** Newmarket, Suffolk
FOCUS
This had the look of a fairly decent 3yo handicap.
Midnight Bay Official explanation: jockey said gelding hung left

741 BETDAQ.CO.UK H'CAP 1m 141y(P)
5:50 (5:50) (Class 6) (0-65,65) 3-Y-0 £2,047 (£604; £302) Stalls Low

Form RPR
03-2 1 **Brer Rabbit**[12] 586 3-9-3 64.............. MichaelHills 6 69+
(B W Hills) *hld up: hdwy 3f out: chsd ldr over 2f out: sn rdn: hung lft and styd on to ld wl ins fnl f* **7/4[1]**
060- 2 3/4 **Jul's Lad (IRE)**[167] 5989 3-8-13 65.............. DeanHeslop(5) 3 68+
(M Mullineaux) *chsd ldr tl led over 2f out: rdn and hung lft over 1f out: hdd wl ins fnl f* **12/1**
2 3 3 1/2 **Invincible Miss (IRE)**[14] 572 3-9-3 64.............. PaulHanagan 7 60
(M Wigham) *chsd ldrs: rdn over 2f out: styd on same pce fnl f* **9/4[2]**
5025 4 1 **Autumn Morning (IRE)**[21] 479 3-8-13 60.............. CatherineGannon 5 54
(P D Evans) *s.s: hld up: plld hrd: hdwy u.p over 1f out: no imp fnl f* **6/1**
0-15 5 2 3/4 **Thewaytosanjose (IRE)**[10] 628 3-8-6 56.............. DavidProbert(3) 8 44
(S Kirk) *chsd ldrs: rdn over 2f out: wkng whn hung lft over 1f out* **9/2[3]**
000- 6 2 **Meydan Groove**[90] 7531 3-8-8 55.............. GrahamGibbons 1 39
(R Johnson) *hld up: a in rr: rdn over 2f out: wknd over 1f out* **14/1**
02-0 7 14 **Rockinit (IRE)**[34] 306 3-9-4 65.............. FrankieMcDonald 2 20
(R A Harris) *led: rdn and hdd over 2f out: wkng whn hmpd sn after* **16/1**
1m 52.03s (1.53) **Going Correction** +0.05s/f (Slow) 7 Ran SP% **119.8**
Speed ratings (Par 96): **95,94,91,90,87 86,73**
toteswinger: 1&2 £3.40, 1&3 £1.60, 2&3 £4.90. CSF £25.60 CT £51.17 TOTE £2.40: £1.50, £4.30; EX 21.50 Place 6: £20.85, Place 5: £7.01.
Owner S P Tindall **Bred** Redmyre Bloodstock Ltd **Trained** Lambourn, Berks
FOCUS
They went just a steady gallop for this weak handicap.
Thewaytosanjose(IRE) Official explanation: jockey said filly hung left throughout
T/Plt: £32.40 to a £1 stake. Pool: £59,375.40. 1,337.05 winning tickets. T/Qpdt: £6.00 to a £1 stake. Pool: £4,562.34. 559.96 winning tickets. CR

683 SOUTHWELL (L-H)
Tuesday, March 3

OFFICIAL GOING: Standard
Wind: Fresh across Weather: Overcast, with the odd shower

742 BACK OR LAY AT BETDAQ H'CAP 5f (F)
2:10 (2:10) (Class 5) (0-75,71) 4-Y-0+ £2,729 (£806; £403) Stalls High

Form RPR
1163 1 **Grimes Faith**[8] 654 6-8-10 70..............(p) AmyRyan(7) 3 78
(K A Ryan) *chsd ldrs: rdn over 1f out: r.o to ld towards fin* **3/1[1]**
0346 2 nk **Colorus (IRE)**[9] 645 6-8-5 63..............(p) AndreaAtzeni(5) 7 70
(W J H Ratcliffe) *sn pushed along and prom: rdn and ev ch ins fnl f: r.o* **6/1[3]**
1-00 3 nk **Guto**[13] 582 6-8-3 61.............. KellyHarrison(5) 8 67
(W J H Ratcliffe) *chsd ldrs: led 2f out: rdn and edgd lft over 1f out: hdd towards fin* **28/1**
6363 4 3 3/4 **Decider (USA)**[6] 676 6-8-7 60..............(p) ChrisCatlin 2 52
(R A Harris) *chsd ldrs: rdn 1/2-way: no ex fnl f* **4/1[2]**
1605 5 2 3/4 **Spic 'n Span**[19] 518 4-8-10 63..............(b) JoeFanning 10 46
(R A Harris) *s.i.s: sn chsng ldrs: led 3f out: hdd 2f out: sn rdn: wknd fnl f* **16/1**
000- 6 2 1/2 **The Lord**[203] 4957 9-9-0 67.............. TolleyDean 4 41+
(W G M Turner) *dwlt: outpcd: sme hdwy u.p over 1f out: wknd fnl f* **20/1**
0-00 7 1/2 **Garlogs**[26] 400 6-9-1 71.............. RussellKennemore(3) 6 43
(R Hollinshead) *led 2f: sn rdn: wknd over 1f out* **11/1**
06-4 8 3 **Efistorm**[19] 518 8-9-2 69..............(p) LPKeniry 9 30+
(C R Dore) *s.i.s: outpcd: in rr whn rdn and hung lft over 1f out* **6/1[3]**
126- 9 8 **Pride Of Northcare (IRE)**[113] 7276 5-9-3 70.............. DarrenWilliams 1 2
(D Shaw) *chsd ldrs tl wknd over 1f out: dead* **6/1[3]**
60.75 secs (1.05) **Going Correction** +0.325s/f (Slow) 9 Ran SP% **110.3**
Speed ratings (Par 103): **104,103,103,97,92 88,87,83,70**
toteswinger: 1&2 £3.20, 1&3 £14.70, 2&3 £10.80. CSF £19.55 CT £387.37 TOTE £3.30: £1.10, £2.10, £8.10; EX 21.80 Trifecta £231.50 Part won. Pool: £312.95 - 0.85 winning units..
Owner Mrs Angie Bailey **Bred** John Grimes **Trained** Hambleton, N Yorks
■ Stewards' Enquiry : Andrea Atzeni four-day ban: used whip with excessive frequency (Mar 17-20)
FOCUS
A modest but competitive sprint handicap.
Efistorm Official explanation: jockey said gelding was never travelling

743 BET IN RUNNING - BETDAQ CLAIMING STKS 1m 6f (F)
2:40 (2:40) (Class 6) 4-Y-0+ £2,047 (£604; £302) Stalls Low

Form RPR
2 1 **Supsonic**[25] 423 6-8-11 65.............. RobertWinston 9 71+
(R J Price) *hld up in tch: racd keenly: chsd ldr 6f out: led over 3f out: rdn clr fnl 2f: eased nr fin* **3/1[2]**
0-24 2 5 **Zaffeu**[35] 300 8-9-1 61.............. VinceSlattery 1 66
(A G Juckes) *s.i.s: hld up: hdwy over 4f out: sn rdn: styd on same pce fnl 2f: wnt 2nd wl ins fnl f* **8/1[3]**
4332 3 1 **They All Laughed**[12] 604 6-9-9 70.............. ChrisCatlin 6 73
(P W Hiatt) *hld up: hdwy over 5f out: rdn to chse wnr over 2f out: sn outpcd: lost 2nd wl ins fnl f* **10/11[1]**
0-03 4 11 **Cruise Director**[4] 712 9-9-9 65.............. StephenDonohoe 2 58
(Ian Williams) *prom: rdn over 3f out: wknd over 2f out* **14/1**
566- 5 20 **Mighty Kitchener (USA)**[124] 7089 6-8-11 36.............. JimmyQuinn 7 20
(P Howling) *stdd s: hld up: rdn and wknd over 3f out: t.o* **33/1**
0P/ 6 6 **Mountain Fairy**[46] 709 6-8-6 60..............(t) DaleGibson 8 8
(M W Easterby) *sn pushed along to chse ldr: led over 7f out: rdn and hdd over 3f out: wknd over 2f out: t.o* **66/1**
0/0- 7 4 1/2 **Hippodrome (IRE)**[244] 3613 7-8-13 70..............(b) MickyFenton 4 9
(John A Harris) *chsd ldrs: rdn over 4f out: sn wknd: t.o* **12/1**
0-65 8 34 **Always Certain (USA)**[48] 161 4-8-9 50.............. RobertHavlin 5 —
(P G Murphy) *led over 6f: sn rdn: wknd 5f out: t.o and eased fnl 3f* **14/1**
3m 10.57s (2.27) **Going Correction** +0.325s/f (Slow)
WFA 4 from 5yo+ 4lb 8 Ran SP% **114.0**
Speed ratings (Par 101): **106,103,102,96,84 81,78,59**
toteswinger: 1&2 £3.10, 1&3 £3.00, 2&3 £1.40. CSF £26.89 TOTE £4.90: £1.60, £2.30, £1.02; EX 22.00 Trifecta £122.20 Pool: £778.38 - 4.71 winning units..Supsonic and They All Laughed were both subject to a friendly claim.
Owner Bill Gavan **Bred** Crandon Park Stud **Trained** Ullingswick, H'fords
FOCUS
A moderate, uncompetitive claimer run at an ordinary pace.
Mountain Fairy Official explanation: jockey said mare lost its action

744 BET A.P.I. - BETDAQ (S) STKS 1m 3f (F)
3:10 (3:10) (Class 6) 4-Y-0+ £2,047 (£604; £302) Stalls Low

Form RPR
-312 1 **Boundless Prospect (USA)**[26] 406 10-8-10 67... PatrickDonaghy(5) 6 62+
(P D Evans) *dwlt: hld up: hdwy over 3f out: led over 1f out: sn rdn clr: eased nr fin* **11/10[1]**
-026 2 3 3/4 **Dancing Lyra**[12] 603 8-8-11 65.............. PaulHanagan 2 52+
(R A Fahey) *hld up: hdwy to chse ldr 3f out: led wl over 1f out: sn rdn and hdd: outpcd fnl f* **3/1[2]**

3-46 **3** 1 3/4 **Ming Vase**[12] [608] 7-8-11 48 JamieMoriarty 8 49
(P T Midgley) *chsd ldrs: led over 3f out: rdn and hdd wl over 1f out: styd on same pce* **8/1**
304- **4** 3 **Maria Antonia (IRE)**[122] [789] 6-7-13 50 AndrewHeffernan(7) 5 39
(D G Bridgwater) *plld hrd and prom: nt clr run over 3f out: sn rdn: wknd over 1f out* **12/1**
0-0 **5** hd **Stockman**[60] [11] 5-8-4 0 RyanClark(7) 7 44
(H Morrison) *sn pushed along and prom: rdn over 2f out: hung lft and wknd wl over 1f out* **28/1**
60-6 **6** 18 **Smetana**[48] [161] 4-8-10 45 EdwardCreighton 3 15
(E J Creighton) *chsd ldr over 9f out: led over 6f out: hdd over 4f out: sn rdn: wknd over 2f out: t.o* **28/1**
0005 **7** nk **Shadow Jumper (IRE)**[12] [603] 8-8-8 40 (p) RussellKennemore(3) 4 15
(J T Stimpson) *led over 4f: led again over 4f out: rdn and hdd over 3f out: sn wknd: t.o* **50/1**
436 **8** 27 **Johnston's Baby (IRE)**[16] [564] 7-8-6 59 JimmyQuinn 1 —
(E J Alston) *trckd ldrs: racd keenly: rdn and hung lft over 4f out: wknd 3f out: t.o* **11/2**[3]

2m 32.37s (4.37) **Going Correction** +0.325s/f (Slow)
WFA 4 from 5yo+ 1lb **8** Ran SP% **115.7**
Speed ratings (Par 101): **97,94,93,90,90 77,77,57**
toteswinger: 1&2 £2.20, 1&3 £4.70, 2&3 £3.90. CSF £4.46 TOTE £1.70: £1.02, £1.40, £2.90; EX 5.90 Trifecta £19.10 Pool: £1258.17 - 48.55 winning units..The winner was bought in for 3,250gns.
Owner Diamond Racing Ltd **Bred** Mrs Edgar Scott Jr & Mrs Lawrence Macelree **Trained** Pandy, Monmouths

FOCUS
A reasonable seller.
Johnston's Baby(IRE) Official explanation: trainer had no explanation for the poor form shown; jockey said mare hung left

745 SOUTHWELL-RACECOURSE.CO.UK H'CAP 1m 4f (F)
3:40 (3:40) (Class 6) (0-65,70) 4-Y-0+ £2,047 (£604; £302) Stalls Low

Form RPR
6421 **1** **Eseej (USA)**[8] [660] 4-9-10 70 6ex ChrisCatlin 5 81
(P W Hiatt) *mde all: hung rt 6f out: rdn clr fnl 2f* **2/1**[1]
044- **2** 3 3/4 **Paddy Rielly (IRE)**[129] [6991] 4-8-13 59 RobertWinston 6 64
(P D Evans) *hld up: hdwy over 3f out: rdn to chse wnr and hung lft fr over 2f out: no imp* **4/1**[3]
12-0 **3** 3 3/4 **Bedouin Blue (IRE)**[11] [622] 6-9-1 64 (p) PatrickDonaghy(5) 7 64
(A J Lidderdale) *hld up: hdwy u.p fr over 1f out: nt rch ldrs* **16/1**
56-0 **4** 2 3/4 **Jackie Kiely**[21] [493] 8-9-5 63 (t) TomEaves 2 59
(R Brotherton) *s.i.s: sn prom: rdn over 3f out: sn outpcd* **12/1**
340- **5** 9 **Sergeant Sharpe**[236] [3873] 4-9-4 64 DuranFentiman 4 46
(H J Evans) *prom: chsd ldr over 4f out: rdn and wknd over 2f out* **22/1**
0-02 **6** 1 1/2 **Top Tiger**[11] [623] 5-9-0 58 TonyHamilton 3 38
(D W Barker) *chsd ldr tl rdn over 4f out: wknd 3f out* **7/2**[2]
05-4 **7** 1 1/4 **Mid Valley**[24] [443] 6-8-6 50 oh3 JimmyQuinn 8 28
(J R Jenkins) *stdd s: hld up: hdwy over 3f out: sn rdn and wknd* **4/1**[3]

2m 44.29s (3.29) **Going Correction** +0.325s/f (Slow)
WFA 4 from 5yo+ 2lb **7** Ran SP% **113.5**
Speed ratings (Par 101): **102,99,97,95,89 88,87**
toteswinger: 1&2 £2.20, 1&3 £5.00, 2&3 £7.20. CSF £10.11 CT £95.43 TOTE £2.40: £1.30, £2.50; EX 9.00 Trifecta £40.00 Pool: £674.33 - 12.46 winning units..
Owner P W Hiatt **Bred** Shadwell Farm LLC **Trained** Hook Norton, Oxon

FOCUS
A moderate handicap.
Top Tiger Official explanation: jockey said gelding had no more to give
Mid Valley Official explanation: jockey said gelding had no more to give

746 SOUTHWELL RACECOURSE FOR CONFERENCES H'CAP 6f (F)
4:10 (4:11) (Class 6) (0-50,50) 4-Y-0+ £2,047 (£604; £302) Stalls Low

Form RPR
-313 **1** **Convince (USA)**[20] [496] 8-8-10 48 StephenDonohoe 2 57+
(K M Prendergast) *dwlt: bhd: hdwy u.p over 1f out: r.o to ld towards fin* **6/1**[2]
4530 **2** 1 **Mister Incredible**[22] [474] 6-8-7 50 (v) MCGeran(5) 9 56+
(J M Bradley) *mid-div: hdwy over 3f out: rdn to ld ins fnl f: hdd towards fin* **11/1**
0-40 **3** 1 1/2 **Orange Square (IRE)**[21] [487] 4-8-8 46 oh1 (v[1]) TonyHamilton 6 48
(D W Barker) *trckd ldrs: racd keenly: led 2f out: sn rdn and edgd lft: hdd and unable qck ins fnl f* **11/1**
0 **4** hd **Scholars Lass (IRE)**[7] [666] 4-8-8 46 oh1 GregFairley 13 47
(J Balding) *s.i.s: hdwy over 2f out: rdn over 1f out: r.o* **25/1**
0-32 **5** 5 **Interchoice Star**[14] [575] 4-8-8 49 ow1 RussellKennemore(3) 5 35+
(R Hollinshead) *hld up: hdwy 1/2-way: rdn over 1f out: wknd fnl f* **2/1**[1]
000- **6** 2 1/2 **Scruffy Skip (IRE)**[84] [7615] 4-8-12 50 VinceSlattery 7 28+
(Mrs C A Dunnett) *led: hdd over 4f out: led again over 2f out: sn hdd and hung lft: wknd over 1f out* **33/1**
/0-3 **7** 3/4 **Divine White**[21] [487] 6-8-8 46 oh1 JimmyQuinn 10 22
(G P Enright) *s.i.s: outpcd: nvr nrr* **9/1**
04-0 **8** nk **King Of Cadeaux (IRE)**[55] [78] 4-8-5 48 (b) GabrielHannon(5) 14 23
(M A Magnusson) *s.i.s: hdwy over 3f out: sn wknd* **9/1**
4305 **9** 3/4 **Ronnie Howe**[14] [575] 5-8-11 49 (bt) ChrisCatlin 4 22
(S R Bowring) *chsd ldr tl led over 4f out: rdn and hdd over 2f out: wknd over 1f out* **13/2**[3]
0060 **10** nse **Stormburst (IRE)**[7] [666] 5-8-9 47 (b[1]) NeilChalmers 1 20
(A J Chamberlain) *sn outpcd* **25/1**
5603 **11** 1/2 **Tag Team (IRE)**[14] [575] 8-8-10 48 (v) AndrewElliott 12 19
(John A Harris) *chsd ldrs: rdn over 3f out: wknd 2f out* **14/1**
6006 **12** 1 1/4 **Soba Jones**[11] [619] 12-8-8 46 oh1 PaulHanagan 8 14
(J Balding) *chsd ldrs: rdn 1/2-way: wknd 2f out* **20/1**
3260 **13** 19 **Nordic Light (USA)**[14] [574] 5-8-8 46 oh1 (bt) RobertWinston 3 —
(J M Bradley) *mid-div: rdn over 4f out: sn wknd: t.o* **33/1**

1m 18.76s (2.26) **Going Correction** +0.325s/f (Slow) **13** Ran SP% **122.6**
Speed ratings (Par 101): **97,95,93,93,86 83,82,82,81,80 80,78,53**
toteswinger: 1&2 £14.30, 1&3 £38.10, 2&3 £70.60. CSF £67.16 CT £737.36 TOTE £6.90: £1.90, £4.20, £7.20; EX 128.80 TRIFECTA Not won..
Owner K M Prendergast **Bred** Juddmonte Farms Inc **Trained** Sellack, H'fords

FOCUS
A moderate but competitive sprint handicap.
Interchoice Star Official explanation: trainer said gelding was unsuited by the going
Divine White Official explanation: trainer said mare is in season

747 BOOK TICKETS ON LINE AT SOUTHWELL-RACECOURSE.CO.UK H'CAP 1m (F)
4:40 (4:40) (Class 4) (0-85,83) 4-Y-0+ £4,857 (£1,445; £722; £360) Stalls Low

Form RPR
115- **1** **Intabih (USA)**[111] [7291] 4-9-3 82 NCallan 7 93+
(C E Brittain) *chsd ldrs: led 2f out: sn rdn and hung lft: jst hld on* **5/2**[2]
6-32 **2** hd **Ours (IRE)**[17] [558] 6-8-5 70 (p) ChrisCatlin 8 80
(John A Harris) *s.i.s: outpcd: hdwy u.p over 1f out: chsd wnr and hung rt ins fnl f: r.o* **20/1**
136- **3** 5 **Princely Hero (IRE)**[64] [7813] 5-8-13 83 AndreaAtzeni(5) 4 82
(M Botti) *trckd ldrs: lost pl over 5f out: edgd lft over 4f out: rdn over 2f out: styd on same pce appr fnl f* **14/1**
20-1 **4** 1/2 **Exit Smiling**[21] [490] 7-8-8 80 PaulPickard(7) 9 77
(P T Midgley) *chsd ldr: rdn and ev ch 2f out: no ex fnl f* **14/1**
4134 **5** 1 3/4 **Mozayada (USA)**[32] [354] 5-9-3 82 JimmyQuinn 5 76
(M Brittain) *trckd ldrs: rdn over 1f out: wknd fnl f* **12/1**
0552 **6** 1 **Silver Hotspur**[21] [490] 5-9-3 82 (p) LPKeniry 6 73
(C R Dore) *s.i.s: hld up: hdwy over 3f out: wknd fnl f* **10/1**[3]
-122 **7** 3 1/2 **Transmission (IRE)**[54] [93] 4-8-4 69 GregFairley 3 53
(B Smart) *sn led: rdn and hdd 2f out: wknd fnl f* **11/1**
-225 **8** 2 3/4 **Crocodile Bay (IRE)**[35] [304] 6-8-6 71 AndrewElliott 2 49
(John A Harris) *chsd ldrs: rdn 1/2-way: wknd 2f out* **25/1**
2111 **9** 26 **More Time Tim (IRE)**[5] [683] 4-8-3 73 RossAtkinson(5) 1 —
(J R Boyle) *hld up: hmpd over 4f out: sn rdn: bhd whn hung rt over 2f out: t.o* **13/8**[1]

1m 44.64s (0.94) **Going Correction** +0.325s/f (Slow) **9** Ran SP% **113.7**
Speed ratings (Par 105): **108,107,102,102,100 99,96,93,67**
toteswinger: 1&2 £6.70, 1&3 £8.10, 2&3 £20.20. CSF £49.90 CT £584.64 TOTE £3.20: £1.60, £4.10, £4.40; EX 58.20 TRIFECTA Not won..
Owner Saeed Manana **Bred** Dr George S Stefanis **Trained** Newmarket, Suffolk
■ Stewards' Enquiry : N Callan two-day ban: used whip down the shoulder in the forehand position (Mar 17-18)

FOCUS
A fair handicap run at a good pace.
More Time Tim(IRE) Official explanation: trainer had no explanation for the poor form shown

748 HOSPITALITY AT SOUTHWELL RACECOURSE H'CAP 7f (F)
5:10 (5:10) (Class 6) (0-50,51) 4-Y-0+ £2,047 (£604; £302) Stalls Low

Form RPR
532 **1** **Straight Face (IRE)**[22] [472] 5-8-12 50 (e) PaulHanagan 9 57
(Miss Gay Kelleway) *trckd ldrs: rdn 1/2-way: styd on u.p to ld wl ins fnl f* **3/1**[2]
-543 **2** nk **Aggbag**[22] [473] 5-8-11 49 AndrewElliott 12 55
(B P J Baugh) *a.p: led 1f out: rdn and hdd wl ins fnl f* **11/2**[3]
5-00 **3** 1 **Charlie Allnut**[14] [575] 4-8-8 46 oh1 (b) JoeFanning 8 50
(S Wynne) *chsd ldrs: led over 1f out: sn hdd: styd on same pce* **16/1**
/40- **4** 1 1/2 **Where's Killoran**[403] [306] 4-8-8 46 oh1 DuranFentiman 14 46
(E J Alston) *mid-div: hdwy u.p over 2f out: sn hung lft: kpt on* **16/1**
664- **5** 1 1/4 **Aquarian Dancer**[238] [3816] 4-8-10 48 ow1 PaulMulrennan 4 45+
(Jedd O'Keeffe) *chsd ldrs: rdn 1/2-way: hung rt over 1f out: styd on same pce* **16/1**
0-00 **6** nk **Siena**[7] [661] 4-8-3 46 oh1 (v) AndreaAtzeni(5) 7 42
(Mrs C A Dunnett) *sn outpcd: r.o ins fnl f: nvr nrr* **33/1**
0320 **7** 1 **Louisiade (IRE)**[19] [514] 8-8-5 50 (b) AndrewHeffernan(7) 5 44+
(M C Chapman) *led: rdn and hung lft over 2f out: hdd over 1f out: no ex* **10/1**
2366 **8** 1 3/4 **Mr Rev**[6] [674] 6-8-9 47 (b) RobertWinston 3 36+
(J M Bradley) *s.i.s: hdwy over 4f out: chsd ldr over 2f out: sn rdn: wknd ins fnl f* **10/1**
000- **9** 1 1/2 **Mujada**[186] [5457] 4-8-11 49 JimmyQuinn 6 35+
(M Brittain) *mid-div: rdn 1/2-way: nt trble ldrs* **33/1**
3043 **10** 1 3/4 **Mister Benji**[12] [608] 10-8-8 46 oh1 (p) GrahamGibbons 2 27+
(B P J Baugh) *chsd ldrs: n.m.r and lost pl wl over 4f out: n.d after* **5/2**[1]
0006 **11** 1 3/4 **Piccolo Diamante (USA)**[6] [675] 5-8-8 51 ow1 JamesO'Reilly(5) 11 28
(S Parr) *s.i.s: rdn 1/2-way: n.d* **20/1**
-006 **12** 1/2 **The London Gang**[40] [254] 6-8-3 46 oh1 RossAtkinson(5) 10 22
(S Wynne) *s.i.s: hdwy 1/2-way: sn rdn and wknd* **33/1**
0550 **13** 28 **Government (IRE)**[4] [607] 8-8-3 46 oh1 DanielleMcCreery(5) 1 —
(M C Chapman) *mid-div: dropped in rr over 4f out: bhd fnl 3f: eased over 1f out: t.o* **40/1**

1m 33.04s (2.74) **Going Correction** +0.325s/f (Slow) **13** Ran SP% **120.8**
Speed ratings (Par 101): **97,96,95,93,92 92,90,88,87,85 83,82,50**
toteswinger: 1&2 £5.40, 1&3 £27.30, 2&3 £23.10. CSF £18.99 CT £233.15 TOTE £4.20: £1.70, £2.90, £4.80; EX 23.00 Place 6: £57.67 Place 5: £24.24. Not won..
Owner Jon A Thompson **Bred** P J Towell **Trained** Exning, Suffolk
■ Stewards' Enquiry : Graham Gibbons trainer's representative had no explanation for the poor form shown
Paul Hanagan three-day ban: used whip with excessive frequency (Mar 17-19)

FOCUS
A moderate handicap run at a strong pace.
Mujada Official explanation: trainer said that jockey had difficulty steering filly around bends and it was found to have a sore mouth
Mister Benji Official explanation: trainer had no explanation for the poor form shown
Government(IRE) Official explanation: trainer said gelding burst a blood vessel
T/Plt: £81.90 to a £1 stake. Pool: £60,742.37. 541.36 winning tickets. T/Qpdt: £47.90 to a £1 stake. Pool: £4,062.24. 62.70 winning tickets. CR

727 LINGFIELD (L-H)
Wednesday, March 4

OFFICIAL GOING: Standard
Wind: Almost Nil Weather: Fine but cloudy

749 MARSH GREEN APPRENTICE H'CAP 1m (P)
2:10 (2:11) (Class 6) (0-55,55) 4-Y-0+ £2,047 (£604; £302) Stalls High

Form RPR
00-0 **1** **Alfredtheordinary**[35] [320] 4-9-0 54 MCGeran 9 64+
(M R Channon) *t.k.h early: hld up in midfield: pushed along and prog 2f out: styd on ins fnl f to ld last 75yds* **6/1**[3]
0-20 **2** 1 1/4 **Suhayl Star (IRE)**[23] [472] 5-8-4 47 DeclanCannon(3) 7 54
(P Burgoyne) *t.k.h: hld up bhd ldrs: prog over 2f out to ld over 1f out: 2 l clr fnl f and looked likely wnr: fin weakly and hdd last 75yds* **16/1**

4643 **3** 1 1/4 **Cavalry Guard (USA)**[8] 666 5-8-9 **49**........................(b) AndreaAtzeni 3 53
(T D McCarthy) *trckd ldr tl rdn and nt qckn 2f out: hanging and nt look keen but briefly threatened to cl again fnl f: one pce* **7/2**[1]

0243 **4** 1 1/2 **Bold Diva**[10] 646 4-8-9 **54**........................(v) TobyAtkinson(5) 6 55
(A W Carroll) *hld up in last trio: prog wl over 1f out: kpt on to take 4th nr fin: nt pce to threaten ldrs* **6/1**[3]

5601 **5** 1/2 **Fairly Honest**[13] 598 5-8-9 **49**........................ WilliamCarson 4 49
(P W Hiatt) *led to over 1f out: fdd ins fnl f* **11/2**[2]

-001 **6** 3/4 **Sharps Gold**[14] 587 4-8-7 **47**........................ KellyHarrison 8 45
(D Morris) *t.k.h: hld up in midfield: nt qckn on outer over 1f out: one pce after* **16/1**

10-0 **7** 1/2 **Copper King**[56] 71 5-8-11 **54**........................ RossAtkinson(3) 12 51
(Miss Tor Sturgis) *hld up in last trio: effrt on outer 2f out: hanging and nt qckn over 1f out: one pce after* **15/2**

0 **8** *hd* **Gingko Lady (USA)**[18] 552 4-8-10 **55**........................ NathanAlison(5) 2 52
(J R Boyle) *reluctant to enter stalls: trckd ldrs: effrt on inner over 1f out: wknd fnl f* **20/1**

650- **9** *hd* **Safe Investment (USA)**[248] 587 5-8-7 **50**........................ MartinLane(3) 1 46
(B N Pollock) *s.s: sn in tch in last trio: drvn and detached in last 3f out: no prog tl styd on fnl 100yds* **25/1**

05-4 **10** 3/4 **Lancaster Lad (IRE)**[20] 514 4-8-7 **52**........................(p) PNolan(5) 10 47
(A B Haynes) *restrained s and swtchd to inner: plld hrd in midfield: lost pl and btn over 1f out* **15/2**

006/ **11** 7 **Softly Killing Me**[511] 6106 4-9-1 **55**........................ JamesO'Reilly 11 34
(B Forsey) *racd wd: in tch: rdn over 3f out: sn wknd and wl bhd* **16/1**

1m 39.35s (1.15) **Going Correction** +0.275s/f (Slow) **11** Ran SP% **116.0**
Speed ratings (Par 101): **105,103,102,101,100 99,99,99,98,98 91**
toteswinger: 1&2 £28.80, 1&3 £5.60, 2&3 £12.70. CSF £96.08 CT £393.61 TOTE £8.10: £2.20, £6.70, £1.50; EX 154.80 TRIFECTA Not won..
Owner M Channon **Bred** Norman Court Stud **Trained** West Ilsley, Berks

FOCUS
A modest apprentice handicap, but despite what looked a reasonable pace a few of these compromised their chances by refusing to settle.

750 FOREST ROW CLAIMING STKS 1m 4f (P)
2:40 (2:40) (Class 6) 4-Y-O+ **£2,047** (£604; £302) **Stalls** Low

Form RPR

-602 **1** **Phoenix Flight (IRE)**[6] 687 4-9-5 78........................ StephenDonohoe 4 69+
(Sir Mark Prescott) *stdd s: hld up in 5th: brought to wd outside and prog 2f out: drvn to ld ins fnl f: sn wl in command* **11/10**[1]

-610 **2** 1 1/2 **Sunset Boulevard (IRE)**[33] 341 6-8-10 63........................ ChrisCatlin 5 56+
(Miss Tor Sturgis) *t.k.h: hld up in 3rd: effrt 2f out: led over 1f out to ins fnl f: sn outpcd by wnr* **3/1**[2]

5-03 **3** *nk* **Apache Fort**[9] 660 6-9-4 72........................(b) ShaneKelly 6 64
(T Keddy) *trckd ldr: led and kicked on over 2f out: hung rt bnd wl over 1f out and sn hdd: kpt on same pce* **3/1**[2]

0-33 **4** 1/2 **Turner's Touch**[19] 528 7-8-9 55........................(b) FergusSweeney 8 54
(G L Moore) *stdd s: hld up in last: effrt 2f out: clsd on ldrs 1f out: nt qckn and readily hld after* **17/2**[3]

0-40 **5** 1 **Comeintothespace (IRE)**[15] 581 7-9-0 47........................ DaneO'Neill 7 57
(R A Farrant) *hld up in 4th: effrt 2f out: n.m.r and nt qckn over 1f out: one pce after* **66/1**

0/00 **6** 7 **Charleston**[28] 393 8-8-2 45........................ RichardRowe(7) 2 42
(R Rowe) *led: set slow pce to 1/2-way: hdd over 2f out: wknd rapidly over 1f out* **100/1**

2m 39.06s (6.06) **Going Correction** +0.275s/f (Slow)
WFA 4 from 6yo+ 2lb **6** Ran SP% **110.6**
Speed ratings (Par 101): **90,89,88,88,87 83**
toteswinger: 1&2 £2.80, 1&3 £1.30, 2&3 £1.90. CSF £4.54 TOTE £1.60: £1.10, £3.30; EX 6.60 Trifecta £14.50 Pool: £490.75 - 25.01 winning units..
Owner W E Sturt - Osborne House Iv **Bred** Airlie Stud And Sir Thomas Pilkington **Trained** Newmarket, Suffolk

FOCUS
An unsatisfactory contest in some respects as they dawdled early and it developed into a sprint. However, the right horses dominated the finish as far as official ratings were concerned.

751 BET CHELTENHAM FESTIVAL - BETDAQ H'CAP 1m 5f (P)
3:10 (3:10) (Class 5) (0-70,66) 4-Y-O+ **£2,900** (£856; £428) **Stalls** Low

Form RPR

64-0 **1** **Shanafarahan (IRE)**[52] 126 4-8-6 **52**........................ JimmyQuinn 5 59
(K A Morgan) *t.k.h: trckd ldng pair: wnt 2nd 2f out: sustained chal u.p after: led last strides* **9/1**

5454 **2** *nk* **Zalkani (IRE)**[11] 631 9-9-2 **59**........................ JerryO'Dwyer 7 66
(J Pearce) *led at slow pce but unchal: wound it up fr 4f out: kpt to inner in st and styd on wl: collared last strides* **13/2**

0312 **3** *nk* **Sir Liam (USA)**[8] 668 5-8-13 **56**........................ RichardKingscote 3 63
(Tom Dascombe) *hld up in last: plenty to do whn prog fr 3f out: brought to wd outside in st: r.o wl fnl f: gaining at fin* **4/1**[2]

/501 **4** 1 **Rough Sketch (USA)**[7] 679 4-8-13 **59** 6ex............ StephenDonohoe 2 64
(Sir Mark Prescott) *hld up in 5th: effrt on outer over 2f out: nt qckn and hanging over 1f out: styd on ins fnl f* **11/4**[1]

6-26 **5** 1 1/2 **Lapina (IRE)**[34] 330 5-9-9 **66**........................(b) JamieSpencer 1 69
(A Middleton) *t.k.h early: hld up in 7th: prog 3f out: nt on terms 2f out: reminders over 1f out: fnd little and btn after* **11/2**

224- **6** 1/2 **Stoop To Conquer**[182] 5613 9-9-7 **64**........................ TonyCulhane 6 66
(A W Carroll) *t.k.h early: trckd ldrs: prog to go 2nd 4f out to 2f out: hanging and fdd* **5/1**[3]

0-00 **7** 5 **Spiritonthemount (USA)**[52] 126 4-8-10 **56**........................ ChrisCatlin 8 51
(P W Hiatt) *trckd ldr to 4f out: sn lost pl and btn* **25/1**

230- **8** *nk* **Generous Lad (IRE)**[107] 7355 6-9-0 **57**........................(p) TPQueally 4 52
(A B Haynes) *t.k.h early: hld up in 6th: pushed along over 4f out: struggling in last pair 3f out* **14/1**

2m 50.82s (4.82) **Going Correction** +0.275s/f (Slow)
WFA 4 from 5yo+ 3lb **8** Ran SP% **112.6**
Speed ratings (Par 103): **96,95,95,95,94 93,90,90**
toteswinger: 1&2 £13.40, 1&3 £8.30, 2&3 £4.00. CSF £63.59 CT £270.60 TOTE £12.80: £3.30, £2.00, £2.00; EX 82.90 Trifecta £331.50 Pool: £448.01 - 1.00 winning units..
Owner J D M Stables **Bred** Corduff Stud And J Corcoran **Trained** Little Marcle, H'fords

FOCUS
Another staying event spoilt to a degree by a lack of early pace and a few took a keen grip as a result. It was therefore an advantage to race up with the pace.

Sir Liam(USA) Official explanation: jockey said gelding hung left in straight

752 MARKSTODDART.COM INTERNATIONAL DESIGNER MAIDEN STKS 7f (P)
3:40 (3:42) (Class 5) 3-Y-O **£2,729** (£806; £403) **Stalls** Low

Form RPR

5- **1** **Fantastic Dubai (USA)**[146] 6601 3-9-3 0........................ TonyCulhane 7 66+
(M R Channon) *unsettled in stalls: t.k.h early: prom: prog to ld wl over 1f out: rn green in front and drvn: jst hld on* **8/13**[1]

2 **2** *shd* **Super Academy (USA)**[12] 626 3-8-12 0........................ ShaneKelly 9 61+
(J A Osborne) *hld up in rr: smooth prog over 2f out: brought to chal 1f out: reminder ins fnl f: nudged along nr fin and unable to overtake* **7/2**[2]

0 **3** 2 1/4 **Hector Spectre (IRE)**[8] 663 3-9-3 0........................ MartinDwyer 13 55
(B J Meehan) *trckd ldr to 2f out: sn outpcd in 4th: kpt on again to claim 3rd last strides* **14/1**

06-0 **4** *hd* **Kings On The Roof**[14] 592 3-9-3 41........................ JimCrowley 1 55
(G C Bravery) *led to wl over 1f out: steadily outpcd* **66/1**

0 **5** 1 1/2 **Abu Dubai (IRE)**[14] 592 3-8-12 0........................ CatherineGannon 6 46
(C A Dwyer) *settled in rr: 8th 2f out: pushed along and kpt on steadily wout posing a danger* **25/1**

06- **6** 1 1/2 **Valkyrie (IRE)**[159] 6253 3-8-12 0........................ JamesDoyle 2 42
(N P Littmoden) *prom: rdn over 2f out on inner: steadily fdd* **20/1**

3 **7** *nse* **Jawaaher (USA)**[16] 572 3-8-12 0........................ JoeFanning 4 41
(M Johnston) *restless stalls: dwlt: rcvrd and in tch in midfield: rn green and hanging over 1f out: fdd* **6/1**[3]

00- **8** 1 1/4 **Rubbinghousedotcom (IRE)**[110] 7312 3-9-3 0........................ IanMongan 8 43
(P M Phelan) *s.s: detached in last: modest prog on inner over 1f out: nvr a threat* **66/1**

0 **9** 1/2 **Love Allowed**[14] 592 3-8-12 0........................ RobertHavlin 12 37
(Jamie Poulton) *prom on wd outside but rn green: steadily lost grnd fr 3f out* **33/1**

10 2 **Primera Rossa** 3-8-12 0........................ LPKeniry 10 31
(J S Moore) *s.i.s: nvr gng wl and a in last pair* **66/1**

1m 27.47s (2.67) **Going Correction** +0.275s/f (Slow) **10** Ran SP% **121.1**
Speed ratings (Par 98): **95,94,92,92,90 88,88,87,86,84**
toteswinger: 1&2 £1.80, 1&3 £3.90, 2&3 £6.40 CSF £2.92 TOTE £1.60: £1.10, £1.20, £3.00; EX 3.60 Trifecta £23.70 Pool: £517.37 - 16.14 winning units..
Owner Jaber Abdullah **Bred** Gainsborough Farm Llc **Trained** West Ilsley, Berks

FOCUS
A modest maiden in which few could be given a chance and certainly not as competitive as the numbers would suggest.

Love Allowed Official explanation: jockey said filly hung left throughout

753 ASHURST WOOD H'CAP 7f (P)
4:10 (4:12) (Class 6) (0-60,59) 3-Y-O **£2,047** (£604; £302) **Stalls** Low

Form RPR

000- **1** **Green Agenda**[131] 6944 3-8-10 **51**........................ JoeFanning 6 58+
(M Johnston) *w ldr: led wl over 1f out: rdn and asserted readily fnl f* **5/1**[3]

510- **2** 2 1/2 **Bold Ring**[79] 7687 3-8-11 **59** ow1........................ SPRyan(7) 1 59
(E J Creighton) *trckd ldrs: effrt and n.m.r briefly wl over 1f out: wnt 2nd ins fnl f: no ch w wnr* **28/1**

63-6 **3** *hd* **Miss Tikitiboo (IRE)**[14] 586 3-9-4 **59**........................ JamieSpencer 5 58
(E F Vaughan) *trckd ldrs: wd bnd 2f out: drvn and styd on wl fnl f to take 3rd last stride* **9/2**[2]

0-13 **4** *nk* **Private Passion (IRE)**[14] 594 3-8-12 **53**........................ PaulEddery 4 51
(Pat Eddery) *t.k.h: narrow ld to wl over 1f out: one pce fnl f* **3/1**[1]

00-5 **5** 1/2 **Daily Double**[8] 667 3-9-2 **57**........................ DaneO'Neill 8 54
(D K Ivory) *hld up in last and racd on outer: swtchd to inner and gng wl in 7th 2f out: rdn over 1f out: effrt petered out* **8/1**

0-03 **6** 3/4 **Pedregal**[31] 366 3-8-5 **46**........................ JimmyQuinn 3 41
(R A Fahey) *trckd ldrs on inner: cl up whn nowhere to go wl over 1f out: one pce fnl f* **9/1**

00-6 **7** 1 1/2 **Sunshine Ellie**[59] 41 3-8-7 **48**........................ MartinDwyer 9 39
(D Shaw) *a in rr: struggling in last pair on outer 2f out: n.d after* **12/1**

323 **8** *nse* **Saints Bay (IRE)**[14] 592 3-9-4 **59**........................ PatDobbs 7 50
(R Hannon) *a in rr: pushed along 4f out: struggling in last pair u.p 2f out: n.d after* **5/1**[3]

00-5 **9** *nk* **Buckle Up**[28] 390 3-8-4 **45**........................ ChrisCatlin 2 35
(D K Ivory) *restless stalls: s.s: keen and sn jnd ldng pair: wknd wl over 1f out* **12/1**

1m 26.9s (2.10) **Going Correction** +0.275s/f (Slow) **9** Ran SP% **116.5**
Speed ratings (Par 96): **99,96,95,95,95 94,92,92,92**
toteswinger: 1&2 £34.80, 1&3 £5.20, 2&3 £25.00 CSF £128.74 CT £682.42 TOTE £5.70: £2.30, £7.50, £1.60; EX 191.40 TRIFECTA Not won..
Owner The Green Dot Partnership **Bred** W And R Barnett Ltd **Trained** Middleham Moor, N Yorks

FOCUS
A modest handicap in which the pace was ordinary.

Green Agenda ◆ Official explanation: trainer's rep said, regarding apparent improvement in form, it was the first time the gelding had run in a handicap and the mark given had made it competitive.

754 BETDAQ THE BETTING EXCHANGE H'CAP 5f (P)
4:40 (4:43) (Class 4) (0-85,83) 4-Y-O+ **£4,857** (£1,445; £722; £360) **Stalls** High

Form RPR

-131 **1** **Chjimes (IRE)**[11] 632 5-9-3 **82**........................ LPKeniry 3 92
(C R Dore) *trckd ldng pair: tending to hang over 1f out: sn clsd to ld last 175yds: sn rdn clr* **11/8**[1]

4-52 **2** 1 3/4 **Qadar (IRE)**[25] 442 7-8-10 **75**........................(e^1) JamesDoyle 4 79
(N P Littmoden) *racd in 4th: hrd rdn and no prog wl over 1f out: styd on ins fnl f to snatch 2nd on line* **4/1**[2]

4363 **3** *hd* **Fromsong (IRE)**[11] 632 11-8-10 **80**........................ JamesO'Reilly(5) 2 83
(D K Ivory) *chsd ldr: rdn 1/2-way: tried to cl u.p over 1f out: kpt on same pce* **9/2**[3]

000- **4** 3/4 **Merlin's Dancer**[172] 5906 9-9-4 **83**........................ TonyCulhane 1 83
(S Dow) *led at str pce: 2 l clr 2f out: hdd & wknd last 175yds* **4/1**[2]

216- **5** 1 1/4 **Wibbadune (IRE)**[126] 7066 5-8-11 **76**........................ JimCrowley 5 72
(D Shaw) *t.k.h: hld up in last: stl gng strly 2f out: effrt on inner over 1f out: keeping on but no ch whn out of room ins fnl f* **8/1**

57.95 secs (-0.85) **Going Correction** +0.275s/f (Slow) **5** Ran SP% **111.4**
Speed ratings (Par 105): **117,114,113,112,110**
toteswinger: 1&2 £3.90. CSF £7.27 TOTE £2.20: £1.10, £2.50; EX 6.60.
Owner Sean J Murphy **Bred** Morgan O'Flaherty **Trained** Cowbit, Lincs

FOCUS
A small field for this fair sprint handicap, but Merlin's Dancer made sure it was run at a true pace and the time was very quick.

755 BETDAQ ON 0870 178 1221 H'CAP 1m 2f (P)
5:10 (5:12) (Class 4) (0-85,85) 3-Y-O £4,857 (£1,445; £722; £360) Stalls Low

Form RPR
2-13 1 **Lord Chancellor (IRE)**[14] 595 3-9-6 84 GregFairley 2 93+
(M Johnston) *trckd ldr: effrt 2f out: produced to ld ent fnl f: rdn clr: decisively* **9/4**[1]
13-2 2 3 ¼ **Alexander Gulch (USA)**[19] 532 3-9-7 85 (p) NCallan 1 85
(K A Ryan) *led and sn clr: breather 1/2-way: kicked on again wl over 2f out: hdd and easily outpcd ent fnl f* **11/2**
1 3 ½ **Ladies Dancing**[28] 391 3-9-0 78 ShaneKelly 6 77
(J A Osborne) *trckd ldng pair: pushed along to dispute 2nd over 2f out: rn green and nt qckn over 1f out: one pce after* **10/3**[3]
420- 4 nk **Sgt Roberts (IRE)**[149] 6539 3-8-11 75 SimonWhitworth 5 73
(J S Moore) *hld up in last: outpcd and pushed along over 2f out: shkn up on inner over 1f out: kpt on steadily* **12/1**
00-1 5 nk **Fong's Alibi**[28] 397 3-8-13 77 MartinDwyer 3 74
(J S Moore) *hld up in 4th: pushed along 3f out: one pce fnl 2f and no imp on ldrs* **3/1**[2]
13-5 6 1 ¾ **Orsippus (USA)**[14] 595 3-9-0 78 TonyCulhane 4 72
(M R Channon) *hld up in 5th: effrt 3f out: rn green whn asked for effrt 2f out: sn btn* **6/1**

2m 8.43s (1.83) **Going Correction** +0.275s/f (Slow) **6** Ran SP% **116.2**
Speed ratings (Par 100): **103,100,100,99,99 98**
toteswinger: 1&2 £1.90, 1&3 £1.50, 2&3 £2.90 CSF £15.74 TOTE £3.00: £1.50, £1.90; EX 10.70 Place 6: £32.63 Place 5: £14.79 .
Owner Sheikh Hamdan Bin Mohammed Al Maktoum **Bred** Darley **Trained** Middleham Moor, N Yorks

FOCUS
A decent little handicap featuring some progressive and unexposed sorts and the pace was good too.
Orsippus(USA) Official explanation: jockey said colt hung right
T/Plt: £50.30 to a £1 stake. Pool: £60,881.80. 882.18 winning tickets. T/Qpdt: £15.00 to a £1 stake. Pool: £3,732.10. 183.30 winning tickets. JN

734 WOLVERHAMPTON (A.W) (L-H)
Wednesday, March 4

OFFICIAL GOING: Standard changing to standard to fast after race 1 (6.50)
Wind: Nil Weather: Fine

756 GREAT OFFERS AT WOLVERHAMPTON-RACECOURSE.CO.UK CLAIMING STKS 5f 20y(P)
6:50 (6:50) (Class 5) 3-Y-O+ £2,729 (£806; £403) Stalls Low

Form RPR
-301 1 **Desperate Dan**[7] 676 8-9-6 67 (v) TPQueally 6 81
(A B Haynes) *hld up in tch: rdn to ld wl ins fnl f: r.o* **20/1**
-413 2 1 **Towy Valley**[14] 582 4-9-4 70 JerryO'Dwyer 3 75
(C G Cox) *bhd: pushed along over 3f out: rdn over 2f out: r.o wl ins fnl f: tk 2nd post* **10/1**[3]
2221 3 nse **Blue Tomato**[2] 739 8-9-2 78 WilliamCarson(5) 4 78
(D Nicholls) *s.i.s: in rr: hdwy on ins over 1f out: rdn fnl f: r.o* **2/1**[2]
1051 4 ½ **Harry Up**[6] 690 8-9-3 84 (p) AmyRyan(7) 1 79
(K A Ryan) *led: rdn over 1f out: hdd wl ins fnl f: no ex* **10/11**[1]
-645 5 hd **Came Back (IRE)**[29] 382 6-9-5 80 AnnStokell(5) 5 78
(Miss A Stokell) *chsd ldr: rdn and ev ch ins fnl f: nt qckn* **16/1**
2132 6 2 ¾ **Woodcote (IRE)**[7] 676 7-9-7 72 (v) GeorgeBaker 2 65
(Peter Grayson) *prom: rdn over 1f out: wknd ins fnl f* **12/1**
35-0 7 7 **Bahamarama (IRE)**[22] 487 4-8-9 49 (p) KevinGhunowa(3) 7 31
(R A Harris) *in rr: pushed along over 2f out: sn struggling* **100/1**

61.01 secs (-1.29) **Going Correction** -0.125s/f (Stan) **7** Ran SP% **114.1**
Speed ratings (Par 103): **105,103,103,102,102 97,86**
toteswinger: 1&2 Not won, 1&3 £1.10, 2&3 Not won. CSF £193.74 TOTE £9.50: £3.80, £3.60; EX 120.40.
Owner Joe McCarthy **Bred** Sheikh Amin Dahlawi **Trained** Limpley Stoke, Bath

FOCUS
A fair claimer, where five of the runners held official ratings between 70 and 84. It was fast and furious.

757 BET MULTIPLES - BETDAQ H'CAP 5f 216y(P)
7:20 (7:24) (Class 5) (0-75,75) 4-Y-O+ £3,070 (£906; £453) Stalls Low

Form RPR
/321 1 **Stonecrabstomorrow (IRE)**[23] 475 6-8-6 63 (b[1]) PaulHanagan 5 73
(R A Fahey) *hld up: hdwy over 3f out: rdn to ld ins fnl f: drvn out* **8/1**
1101 2 1 ½ **Street Power (USA)**[14] 590 4-9-0 71 TPQueally 4 80+
(J R Gask) *s.i.s: hld up in rr: nt clr run briefly on ins ent st: hdwy over 1f out: rdn and r.o ins fnl f: nt trble wnr* **11/10**[1]
-423 3 1 ¼ **Red Cape (FR)**[16] 573 6-8-11 68 (b) AndrewElliott 11 70
(Mrs R A Carr) *led over 4f out: rdn over 1f out: edgd rt and hdd ins fnl f: no ex* **10/1**
0154 4 1 ½ **Gwilym (GER)**[19] 539 6-8-11 68 IanMongan 10 65
(D Haydn Jones) *hld up in mid-div: hdwy 2f out: sn rdn: one pce ins fnl f* **20/1**
1-21 5 1 ¾ **Smirfys Systems**[19] 540 10-8-7 64 GrahamGibbons 9 56
(E S McMahon) *a.p: chsd ldr over 2f out tl rdn over 1f out: wknd wl ins fnl f* **9/2**[2]
02-4 6 hd **Russian Symphony (USA)**[9] 654 8-9-1 72 (b) DaneO'Neill 3 63
(C R Egerton) *s.i.s: hld up towards rr: rdn over 2f out: hdwy over 1f out: nvr trbld ldrs* **13/2**[3]
1314 7 4 ½ **Back In The Red (IRE)**[13] 606 5-8-13 73 (b) KevinGhunowa(3) 6 51
(R A Harris) *led over 1f: chsd ldr tl rdn over 2f out: wknd wl over 1f out: eased ins fnl f* **14/1**
150- 8 1 **Flying Valentino**[195] 5207 5-9-4 75 StephenDonohoe 7 50
(Ian Williams) *a towards rr* **50/1**
4065 9 3 ½ **Know No Fear**[9] 654 4-9-1 72 TomEaves 2 36
(D Shaw) *unruly stalls: s.s: a in rr* **14/1**
-040 10 3 ¼ **Storey Hill (USA)**[14] 582 4-8-10 67 RobertWinston 1 22
(D Shaw) *rdr sltly late to remove blindfold: s.i.s: sn prom: wknd 2f out* **28/1**

1m 13.4s (-1.60) **Going Correction** -0.125s/f (Stan) **10** Ran SP% **122.8**
Speed ratings (Par 103): **105,103,101,99,97 96,90,89,84,80**
toteswinger: 1&2 £4.80, 1&3 £21.30, 2&3 £11.40. CSF £17.86 CT £100.62 TOTE £12.60: £3.70, £1.02, £3.40; EX 39.90.
Owner Miss S Bowles **Bred** P Dillon **Trained** Musley Bank, N Yorks

FOCUS
A fair handicap, involving three last-time-out winners. The pace was decent and they finished quite well strung out.
Know No Fear Official explanation: jockey said gelding missed the break
Storey Hill(USA) Official explanation: jockey said gelding had no more to give

758 SPONSOR A RACE BY CALLING 01902 390009 MAIDEN STKS 5f 20y(P)
7:50 (7:53) (Class 5) 3-Y-O+ £2,729 (£806; £403) Stalls Low

Form RPR
3365 1 **Circle Dance (IRE)**[9] 655 4-9-13 67 (v) RobertWinston 9 71
(D Shaw) *a.p: led and hung lft over 1f out: rdn fnl f: jst hld on* **5/4**[1]
644 2 hd **Silca Meydan**[14] 592 3-9-0 63 SamHitchcott 4 64
(M R Channon) *in rr: rdn and hdwy over 1f out: r.o ins fnl f: jst failed* **11/2**[3]
03-0 3 5 **Nizhoni (USA)**[59] 36 4-9-8 58 TomEaves 3 41
(B Smart) *t.k.h: led: rdn and hdd over 1f out: wknd ins fnl f* **9/2**[2]
00-6 4 nk **Badtanman**[12] 624 3-8-7 35 (b) AndrewHeffernan(7) 8 45
(Peter Grayson) *s.i.s: sn in tch: hung rt fr over 3f out: wknd 2f out* **33/1**
0 5 nse **Baby Queen (IRE)**[9] 655 3-8-9 0 AndrewElliott 1 40
(B P J Baugh) *prom tl rdn and wknd ins fnl f* **16/1**
-405 6 1 ¼ **Kina Jazz**[8] 664 3-8-9 48 (b[1]) EdwardCreighton 5 35
(M E Rimmer) *chsd ldrs: rdn and wknd wl over 1f out* **25/1**
0 7 nk **Little Lost (IRE)**[9] 655 3-8-9 0 TPQueally 6 34
(J A Osborne) *t.k.h: chsd ldr: ev ch over 2f out: wknd wl over 1f out* **11/2**[3]
8 5 **The Last Alzao (IRE)** 3-8-9 0 PaulHanagan 7 16
(R A Fahey) *s.i.s: a in rr* **9/1**

62.39 secs (0.09) **Going Correction** -0.125s/f (Stan)
WFA 3 from 4yo 13lb **8** Ran SP% **116.1**
Speed ratings (Par 103): **94,93,85,85,85 83,82,74**
toteswinger: 1&2 £2.60, 1&3 £4.80, 2&3 £2.00. CSF £8.73 TOTE £2.70: £1.10, £1.20, £2.80; EX 5.50.
Owner Simon Mapletoft Racing & R G Botham **Bred** Newberry Stud Company **Trained** Danethorpe, Notts

FOCUS
The going description was changed from standard to fast after the second race. This ordinary maiden was run at a fair pace and the two main contenders pulled clear of the rest.
Nizhoni(USA) Official explanation: jockey said filly hung right

759 BETDAQ THE BETTING EXCHANGE H'CAP 1m 1f 103y(P)
8:20 (8:20) (Class 6) (0-65,65) 3-Y-O £2,388 (£705; £352) Stalls Low

Form RPR
424 1 **High Cross (IRE)**[12] 621 3-9-4 62 StephenDonohoe 12 72+
(Sir Mark Prescott) *a.p: led over 2f out: rdn wl over 1f out: r.o wl* **5/1**[2]
-464 2 2 ½ **Duke Of Normandy (IRE)**[12] 628 3-9-6 64 JoeFanning 9 67+
(M Johnston) *t.k.h early: hld up in tch: chsd wnr wl over 1f out: rdn and hung lft ins fnl f: no imp* **12/1**
00-5 3 ¾ **Tae Kwon Do (USA)**[34] 322 3-8-11 55 TomEaves 4 57
(Miss J A Camacho) *hld up towards rr: hdwy 2f out: rdn over 1f out: edgd lft and kpt on ins fnl f* **8/1**
-650 4 2 ¼ **Fleur De'Lion (IRE)**[14] 594 3-8-2 46 JimmyQuinn 7 43
(S Kirk) *hld up in rr: plld out 2f out: sn rdn: styd on ins fnl f: tk 4th nr post* **25/1**
6252 5 shd **Turn To Dreams**[12] 628 3-9-1 59 (v) CatherineGannon 3 56
(P D Evans) *hld up in mid-div: hdwy 2f out: rdn and edgd lft over 1f out: one pce* **12/1**
55-0 6 ¾ **Graycliffe (IRE)**[14] 586 3-8-6 55 WilliamCarson(5) 5 51
(Patrick Morris) *prom: rdn over 2f out: wknd ins fnl f* **16/1**
25-2 7 1 ½ **Dark Oasis**[23] 479 3-9-4 62 (b) PaulMulrennan 1 55
(K A Ryan) *chsd ldr: led over 3f out tl over 2f out: sn rdn: wknd 1f out* **3/1**[1]
6030 8 3 ½ **Kneesy Earsy Nosey**[7] 677 3-8-9 53 (p) ChrisCatlin 2 39
(Miss A Stokell) *broke wl: stdd sn after s: lost pl over 6f out: pushed along over 4f out: n.d after* **14/1**
03-2 9 1 ¼ **Barcode**[56] 77 3-8-10 54 DaneO'Neill 6 38
(R Hannon) *hld up in mid-div: rdn over 3f out: bhd fnl 2f* **13/2**[3]
4-06 10 5 **Dead Cat Bounce (IRE)**[18] 548 3-9-7 65 JerryO'Dwyer 11 39
(J Pearce) *a in rr* **14/1**
145- 11 8 **Amazing Blue Sky**[64] 7824 3-9-7 65 PaulHanagan 10 24
(Mrs R A Carr) *led: hdd over 3f out: rdn and wknd over 2f out* **8/1**

2m 0.95s (-0.75) **Going Correction** -0.125s/f (Stan) **11** Ran SP% **115.7**
Speed ratings (Par 96): **98,95,95,93,93 92,91,87,86,82 75**
toteswinger: 1&2 £18.60, 1&3 £12.40, 2&3 Not won. CSF £62.56 CT £473.41 TOTE £7.00: £4.50, £4.10, £2.90; EX 34.00.
Owner Sir Edmund Loder **Bred** Sir E J Loder **Trained** Newmarket, Suffolk
■ Stewards' Enquiry : Paul Hanagan one-day ban: failed to ride to draw (Mar 20)

FOCUS
A modest handicap.

760 STAY AT THE WOLVERHAMPTON HOLIDAY INN H'CAP 1m 141y(P)
8:50 (8:51) (Class 6) (0-50,56) 4-Y-O+ £2,388 (£705; £352) Stalls Low

Form RPR
2433 1 **Amber Moon**[7] 674 4-8-10 50 (b) ShaneKelly 7 60
(J A Osborne) *hld up in mid-div: rdn over 5f out: hdwy over 2f out: led wl over 1f out: drvn out* **9/2**[3]
6200 2 4 ½ **Dancing Duo**[20] 513 5-8-10 50 (v) DarrenWilliams 9 51
(D Shaw) *uns rdr and got loose bef s: hld up in rr: hdwy over 2f out: rdn and chsd wnr fnl f: no imp* **16/1**
006- 3 2 ½ **Miss Clarice (USA)**[109] 7340 4-8-10 50 SimonWhitworth 11 45+
(J R Jenkins) *hld up towards rr: nt clr run over 2f out: rdn and hdwy over 1f out: tk 3rd ins fnl f: nvr nrr* **20/1**
6545 4 2 ¼ **Tabulate**[18] 541 6-8-8 48 JimmyQuinn 5 39
(P Howling) *hld up towards rr: hdwy on ins over 3f out: rdn and fnd little over 1f out* **11/2**
-005 5 2 ¼ **Almora Guru**[16] 569 5-8-9 49 MartinDwyer 4 35
(W M Brisbourne) *hld up in tch: ev ch wl over 1f out: sn rdn: wknd ins fnl f* **14/1**
0/5- 6 1 ½ **Tobago Reef**[264] 127 5-8-10 50 (p) JerryO'Dwyer 8 33+
(C W Moore) *chsd ldrs: reminder over 5f out: rdn over 2f out: wknd wl over 1f out: eased ins fnl f* **33/1**
0-30 7 3 ¾ **Karmei**[5] 711 4-8-9 49 GrahamGibbons 6 24
(R Curtis) *hld up in rr: sme hdwy on ins wl over 1f out: sn rdn: n.d* **17/2**
00-0 8 4 **Carnival Dream**[23] 473 4-8-5 50 ow2 SladeO'Hara(5) 12 16
(H A McWilliams) *ld early: chsd ldr to 6f out: wknd 3f out* **50/1**
0-01 9 1 ¾ **Whodunit (UAE)**[7] 674 5-9-2 56 6ex (b) ChrisCatlin 10 19+
(P W Hiatt) *sn led: hdd wl over 1f out: sn wknd* **3/1**[2]

000- **10** 2 3/4 **Trees Of Green (USA)**[215] 4605 5-8-10 **50**..............(b[1]) PaulHanagan 13 7
(M Wigham) *hld up in mid-div: rdn over 3f out: wknd over 2f out* **5/2**[1]
-004 **11** 29 **Mays Louise**[18] 556 5-8-10 **50**.................... DuranFentiman 3 —
(B P J Baugh) *dwlt: a in rr: eased over 1f out* **33/1**
0400 **12** 1 1/2 **Mont Cervin**[13] 607 4-8-10 **50**....................(b) PaulMulrennan 2 —
(Mrs R A Carr) *prom: rdn sn after s and sn plld hrd: chsd ldr 6f out tl rdn 3f out: wknd qckly: eased fnl 2f* **28/1**

1m 49.62s (-0.88) **Going Correction** -0.125s/f (Stan) 12 Ran SP% **126.3**
Speed ratings (Par 101): **98,94,91,89,87 86,83,79,78,75 49,48**
toteswinger: 1&2 Not won, 1&3 £17.20, 2&3 Not won. CSF £73.67 CT £1351.48 TOTE £5.00: £1.10, £7.10, £6.60; EX 49.50.
Owner Mr & Mrs G Middlebrook **Bred** G And Mrs Middlebrook **Trained** Upper Lambourn, Berks

FOCUS
An ordinary handicap in which the leaders probably went off too fast.
Whodunit(UAE) Official explanation: jockey said gelding hung right
Mays Louise Official explanation: jockey said mare was slowly away
Mont Cervin Official explanation: jockey said gelding was reluctant to race

761 BET 1% IN RUNNING - BETDAQ H'CAP 1m 4f 50y(P)
9:20 (9:21) (Class 3) (0-90,90) 4-Y-O- £9,462 (£2,832; £1,416; £708; £352) Stalls Low

Form RPR
214- **1** **Distinctive Image (USA)**[118] 7211 4-8-4 **76**.............. ChrisCatlin 3 88+
(R Hollinshead) *hld up in rr: hdwy on outside 2f out: c wd st: led over 1f out: pushed out* **9/2**[2]
5060 **2** 2 **Swiss Act**[10] 653 5-8-13 **83**.................... JoeFanning 5 90
(M Johnston) *hld up: hdwy on ins wl over 1f out: rdn and wnt 2nd ins fnl f: nt trble wnr* **7/1**[3]
251- **3** 1 3/4 **Humble Opinion**[48] 2582 7-9-6 **90**.................. MartinDwyer 7 94
(A King) *a.p: edgd lft over 3f out: led wl over 1f out: sn rdn and hdd: no ex ins fnl f* **9/2**[2]
-112 **4** 1 1/4 **La Estrella (USA)**[24] 456 6-9-4 **88**.................. DaneO'Neill 6 90
(D E Cantillon) *hld up: hdwy over 3f out: n.m.r briefly wl over 1f out: rdn whn carried rt jst ins fnl f: one pce* **9/4**[1]
60-0 **5** 6 **Maslak (IRE)**[32] 360 5-9-2 **86**...................... DarrenWilliams 1 79
(P W Hiatt) *prom: rdn over 2f out: edgd rt jst ins fnl f: wknd* **16/1**
-603 **6** 2 3/4 **Count Trevisio (IRE)**[25] 453 6-8-12 **82**............... TPQueally 4 71
(J R Gask) *led: hdd wl over 1f out: wkng whn carried rt jst ins fnl f* **8/1**
12-0 **7** nk **Cape Colony**[14] 585 4-8-13 **85**..................... PatDobbs 8 74
(R Hannon) *hld up: rdn over 3f out: bhd fnl 2f* **9/2**[2]

2m 38.41s (-2.69) **Going Correction** -0.125s/f (Stan)
WFA 4 from 5yo+ 2lb 7 Ran SP% **114.8**
Speed ratings (Par 107): **103,101,100,99,95 93,93**
toteswinger: 1&2 £3.30, 1&3 £2.60, 2&3 £4.10. CSF £35.45 CT £149.17 TOTE £6.30: £2.50, £2.80; EX 34.90 Place 6: £1,740.29 Place 5: £102.95.
Owner Stevenson Leadbeater & Hollinshead **Bred** Juddmonte Farms Inc **Trained** Upper Longdon, Staffs

FOCUS
A decent handicap in which the pace was not particularly strong.

NOTEBOOK
Distinctive Image(USA) ◆ swept from last to first down the outside in the straight and ran out an impressive winner. He will get punished for this win but could be capable of further progress and looks the type who could pick up a decent middle-distance prize on turf this spring/summer. (op 7-2 tchd 3-1)
Swiss Act had not really been firing recently since coming back from 18 months off and was well held in the snow in Switzerland the last twice. That adventure seems to have done him good and he ran a very promising race, staying on strongly to beat everything except for the progressive winner. (op 8-1)
Humble Opinion did quite well to keep battling after the winner had stormed past him early in the straight. He had not done much in three hurdle runs for his current yard but this was a fair effort trying a new trip back on the Flat off a career-high mark. (op 6-1 tchd 13-2)
La Estrella(USA) had won five consecutive claimers this winter and was second to a better-than-usual opponent who was well in at the weights last time. He was denied a run at a crucial stage and ran a bit better than the finishing position suggests, but it is unlikely that he would have posed a big threat to the emphatic winner. Official explanation: jockey said gelding was denied a clear run (op 5-2 tchd 11-4)
Maslak(IRE) compromised his chance by racing keenly. (tchd 14-1)
Count Trevisio(IRE) was allowed an easy lead but folded up quickly on his venture into unknown territory stamina-wise. (op 10-1)
T/Plt: £944.90 to a £1 stake. Pool: £95,453.08. 73.74 winning tickets. T/Qpdt: £45.10 to a £1 stake. Pool: £10,110.50. 165.80 winning tickets. KH

756 WOLVERHAMPTON (A.W) (L-H)
Thursday, March 5

OFFICIAL GOING: Standard
Wind: Nil Weather: Fine

762 DON'T MISS THE LINCOLN TRIAL ON SATURDAY (S) STKS 5f 216y(P)
6:50 (6:50) (Class 6) 4-Y-O+ £1,978 (£584; £292) Stalls Low

Form RPR
3441 **1** **Don Pele (IRE)**[6] 710 7-9-5 67..................(p) JoeFanning 5 74+
(R A Harris) *a.p: led over 1f out: rdn and edgd lft ins fnl f: r.o* **5/4**[1]
-330 **2** hd **Strathmore (IRE)**[7] 691 5-9-0 64..................(p) PaulHanagan 2 68+
(R A Fahey) *a.p: sustained chal fr over 1f out: rdn ins fnl f: r.o* **9/2**[3]
0- **3** 2 3/4 **Signora Frasi (IRE)**[119] 7206 4-8-9 67.................. SimonWhitworth 4 52
(A G Newcombe) *hld up: rdn over 1f out: kpt on to take 3rd wl ins fnl f* **14/1**
-160 **4** nk **Mafaheem**[37] 304 7-9-5 67..................(b) GeorgeBaker 1 61
(A B Haynes) *hld up and bhd: swtchd rt over 1f out: rdn and kpt on same pce fnl f* **7/2**[2]
6035 **5** 1 **Geoffdaw**[3] 739 4-9-0 67..................(p) PatCosgrave 7 53
(P D Evans) *w ldr: rdn over 1f out: wknd ins fnl f* **11/2**
1360 **6** 3 1/4 **Joss Stick**[15] 590 4-8-11 63..................(p) KevinGhunowa[(3)] 3 44
(R A Harris) *plld hrd: mde most: rdn and hdd over 1f out: wknd ins fnl f* **11/1**
2535 **7** 2 1/2 **Mr Loire**[8] 676 5-9-0 45..................(b) JerryO'Dwyer 6 36
(K G Wingrove) *hld up and bhd: rdn over 2f out: sn struggling* **40/1**

1m 15.45s (0.45) **Going Correction** +0.25s/f (Slow) 7 Ran SP% **117.7**
Speed ratings (Par 101): **107,106,103,102,101 97,93**
toteswinger: 1&2 £7.00, 1&3 not won, 2&3 not won. CSF £7.71 TOTE £2.90: £1.30, £3.60; EX 10.50.There was no bid for the winner.
Owner Robert & Nina Bailey **Bred** John J Cosgrave **Trained** Earlswood, Monmouths

FOCUS
A moderate seller, run at a sound pace and the front pair are a little better than this grade with the third setting the level.

763 FRIDAY NIGHTS ARE DISCO NIGHTS H'CAP 1m 141y(P)
7:20 (7:20) (Class 4) (0-85,83) 3-Y-O £4,727 (£1,406; £702) Stalls Low

Form RPR
51- **1** **Spring Of Fame (USA)**[170] 6000 3-9-5 **81**.................. PaulHanagan 3 90+
(M A Magnusson) *hld up: hdwy over 3f out: led 2f out: rdn and hung lft 1f out: pushed out* **5/6**[1]
01- **2** 3 **Laurie Grove (IRE)**[119] 7204 3-9-7 **83**.................. RobertHavlin 2 85
(T G Mills) *trckd ldr: lft in ld 7f out: sn hdd: led 3f out to 2f out: rdn over 1f out: one pce* **15/8**[2]
21 **3** 2 3/4 **Eastern Aria (UAE)**[18] 564 3-9-0 **76**.................. GregFairley 1 77+
(M Johnston) *led tl rn v wd bnd 7f out: sn led again: hdd 3f out: sn btn* **5/2**[3]

1m 53.9s (3.40) **Going Correction** +0.25s/f (Slow) 3 Ran SP% **117.9**
Speed ratings (Par 100): **94,91,88**
CSF £3.08 TOTE £1.80; EX 2.10.
Owner Eastwind Racing Ltd and Martha Trussell **Bred** Brushwood Stable **Trained** Upper Lambourn, Berks

FOCUS
An intriguing little handicap for three-year-olds. Not easy to rate but has been rated slightly positively.

764 MISS BLACK COUNTRY FINAL 4TH APRIL STKS (A CONDITIONS RACE) 1m 141y(P)
7:50 (7:50) (Class 4) 3-Y-O £4,984 (£1,492; £746) Stalls Low

Form RPR
454- **1** **Akhenaten**[142] 6717 3-9-0 94.................. TonyCulhane 4 93+
(M R Channon) *stdd s: hld up: hdwy over 2f out: led 1f out: rdn out* **11/10**[1]
31- **2** 2 **Splinter Cell (USA)**[210] 4780 3-8-9 87.................. AndreaAtzeni[(5)] 3 89
(M Botti) *chsd ldr: rdn wl over 1f out: nt qckn ins fnl f* **11/8**[2]
3341 **3** 2 **Doncosaque (IRE)**[15] 595 3-9-0 87.................. IanMongan 1 85
(P Howling) *led: rdn and hdd 1f out: no ex* **7/2**[3]

1m 52.38s (1.88) **Going Correction** +0.25s/f (Slow) 3 Ran SP% **111.9**
Speed ratings (Par 100): **101,99,97**
CSF £3.10 TOTE £1.40; EX 3.50.
Owner Box 41 **Bred** Netherfield House Stud **Trained** West Ilsley, Berks

FOCUS
Another interesting three-year-old handicap. The third sets the level.

765 RINGSIDE RESTAURANT - THE PLACE TO PARTY CLAIMING STKS 1m 141y(P)
8:20 (8:21) (Class 6) 4-6-Y-O £1,978 (£584; £292) Stalls Low

Form RPR
5-12 **1** **Dichoh**[20] 536 6-9-5 80..................(tp) FBranca 2 78+
(F Sheridan) *hld up: hdwy over 2f out: led on bit wl over 1f out: rdn ins fnl f: r.o* **8/11**[1]
436 **2** 1 3/4 **Don Pietro**[23] 489 6-9-3 69..................(p) GrahamGibbons 1 73
(R Curtis) *hld up: hdwy over 2f out: chsd wnr fnl f: kpt on same pce* **9/1**
4-11 **3** nk **All In The Red (IRE)**[19] 545 4-9-1 70..................(p) JimmyQuinn 6 70
(B N Pollock) *s.i.s: hld up: rdn 3f out: hdwy 2f out: kpt on towards fin* **8/1**[3]
2122 **4** 10 **Clear Sailing**[13] 617 6-9-2 74..................(p) ChrisCatlin 3 50
(Ollie Pears) *led: rdn and hdd wl over 1f out: wknd fnl f* **3/1**[2]
0-03 **5** 2 3/4 **Wusuul**[8] 678 4-8-12 59..................(b) JoeFanning 4 40
(R A Harris) *n.m.r and bmpd s: hld up in rr: rdn over 3f out: sn struggling* **20/1**
6204 **6** 16 **Ten Pole Tudor**[20] 536 4-8-12 60..................(b) KevinGhunowa[(3)] 5 10
(R A Harris) *awkward and bmpd s: sn w ldr: wknd over 2f out* **33/1**
06-0 **7** 18 **Where To Now**[8] 674 4-8-10 45..................(v) VinceSlattery 7 —
(Mrs C A Dunnett) *a in rr: rdn 4f out: t.o fnl 3f* **100/1**

1m 50.85s (0.35) **Going Correction** +0.25s/f (Slow) 7 Ran SP% **112.7**
Speed ratings (Par 101): **108,106,106,97,94 80,64**
toteswinger: 1&2 £2.50, 1&3 £12.30, 2&3 £1.40. CSF £8.11 TOTE £1.80: £1.20, £5.80; EX 7.40.The winner was subject to a friendly claim. All In The Red was claimed by A Crook for £6,000.
Owner Frank Sheridan **Bred** Red House Stud **Trained** Stoke Heath, Shropshire

FOCUS
This claimer saw the early leaders go off too quick. The winner rates value for a little further with the placed horses setting the level.

766 GREAT OFFERS AT WOLVERHAMPTON-RACECOURSE.CO.UK H'CAP 1m 1f 103y(P)
8:50 (8:50) (Class 3) (0-100,93) 4-Y-O+ £7,352 (£2,201; £1,100; £551; £274; £138) Stalls Low

Form RPR
5-11 **1** **Spectait**[48] 199 7-8-12 **87**.................. JamieMoriarty 1 100+
(Jonjo O'Neill) *hld up in mid-div: stdy prog over 4f out: led 1f out: drvn out* **5/4**[1]
-331 **2** 3 1/4 **Dream Of Fortune (IRE)**[26] 453 5-8-6 **81**..................(t) JimmyQuinn 4 86
(M G Quinlan) *s.i.s: hld up towards rr: rdn and hdwy whn hung lft over 1f out: r.o to take 2nd towards fin: nt trble wnr* **10/1**
-432 **3** hd **Tourist**[6] 713 4-8-4 **79** oh1.................. ChrisCatlin 8 84
(D Shaw) *t.k.h in tch: ev ch 1f out: rdn and one pce: lost 2nd towards fin* **4/1**[2]
300- **4** 1 **Capable Guest (IRE)**[113] 7291 7-8-13 **88**.................. TonyCulhane 5 91
(M R Channon) *hld up in mid-div: stdy prog over 4f out: rdn and hung lft fr over 1f out: one pce* **10/1**
020- **5** 1 **Hustle (IRE)**[160] 6238 4-8-11 **86**.................. AlanMunro 3 87
(Miss Gay Kelleway) *t.k.h: chsd ldr: led over 3f out: rdn and hdd 1f out: fdd wl ins fnl f* **7/1**
520- **6** 1/2 **Kingsdale Orion (IRE)**[66] 7239 5-8-7 **82**.................. PaulHanagan 2 82
(B Ellison) *prom: lost pl over 3f out: n.d after* **14/1**
00- **7** 2 **Tamimi's History**[166] 6120 5-9-4 **93**.................. PatCosgrave 6 89
(P D Evans) *set stdy pce: hdd over 3f out: wknd ins fnl f* **10/1**
42-4 **8** 9 **Pevensey (IRE)**[61] 33 7-9-1 **90**..................(p) GrahamGibbons 7 69
(J J Quinn) *a in rr: no ch fnl 3f* **6/1**[3]

2m 3.76s (2.06) **Going Correction** +0.25s/f (Slow) 8 Ran SP% **125.2**
Speed ratings (Par 107): **100,97,96,96,95 94,92,84**
toteswinger: 1&2 £3.90, 1&3 £3.70, 2&3 £12.30. CSF £17.63 CT £45.67 TOTE £2.50: £1.30, £2.10, £1.10; EX 17.00.
Owner John P McManus **Bred** Blyth Tait **Trained** Cheltenham, Gloucs

FOCUS
A good handicap, run at an uneven pace. The winner outclassed the rest and the runner-up sets the level.

NOTEBOOK
Spectait came home a decisive winner to land a hat-trick at the track. He was 3lb higher here and did not get the best of runs in midfield as he took a bump nearing the final turn. That did not stop him from picking up strongly once asked for maximum effort down the home straight and he could have been called the winner at the furlong pole. He was not short of Group class when trained by Sir Mark Prescott and, despite failing to make the grade over hurdles for current connections, has regained his enthusiasm in a big way since winning on his first outing at this venue in January. Another likely rise will make things tougher again, but he should make a bold bid for the four-timer. (op 13-8 tchd 7-4 in places)
Dream Of Fortune(IRE) ◆, 4lb higher than when winning over course and distance last time out, made a tardy start but is a confirmed hold-up performer and it made no difference to him. It was more the lack of early pace that found him out and he did well to finish as close. He looks capable of defying this mark when faced with a truly run race. (op 8-1)
Tourist proved free early on, but gamely kept to his task under pressure and ran respectably from 1lb out of the handicap. He will probably go up a few pounds, but his turn does not look far off. (op 9-2)
Capable Guest(IRE) showed more on this return from a 113-day break, but looked far from willing when put under pressure and has his own ideas. (tchd 11-1)

767 ENJOY THE LUCKY 7 GROUP OFFER MAIDEN STKS 1m 1f 103y(P)
9:20 (9:20) (Class 5) 3-Y-O+ **£2,590** (£770; £385; £192) **Stalls** Low

Form				RPR
0	**1**		**Uncle Bertie**17 570 4-10-0 0 VinceSlattery 4 (N J Vaughan) *hld up in tch: lost pl over 5f out: rdn and hdwy on outside 2f out: carried v wd ent st: edgd lft fr over 1f out: r.o wl to ld nr fin* **11/2**3	69
600-	**2**	3/4	**Campli (IRE)**221 4457 7-9-7 51 LanceBetts(7) 2 (B Ellison) *led after 1f: rdn clr 1f out: ct nr fin* **16/1**	68
03	**3**	1 1/4	**Rosko**17 570 5-10-0 0 TomEaves 8 (B Ellison) *t.k.h in tch: rdn and edgd rt over 1f out: kpt on ins fnl f* **8/1**	66
33	**4**	2 1/2	**National Monument (IRE)**10 658 3-8-8 0 ShaneKelly 9 (J A Osborne) *led 1f: chsd ldr tl over 4f out: wnt 2nd again wl over 1f out: sn rdn: fdd wl ins fnl f* **2/1**2	55
	5	1	**Hatta Diamond (IRE)** 3-8-8 0 JoeFanning 1 (M Johnston) *prom: lost pl 3f out: rallied on ins wl over 1f out: wknd wl ins fnl f* **13/8**1	53
5-2	**6**	2	**The Staffy (IRE)**17 570 4-10-0 0 GregFairley 7 (N J Vaughan) *s.v.s: a bhd* **15/2**	55
6	**7**	6	**Frightnight (IRE)**6 716 3-8-9 0 ow1 (t) RobertHavlin 6 (A B Haynes) *a bhd: rdn and hung rt 1f out* **28/1**	39
30/	**8**	2	**Lady Splodge**498 6420 5-9-2 0 MatthewDavies(7) 3 (George Baker) *s.i.s: plld hrd: hdwy over 5f out: jnd ldr over 3f out: rdn and rn wd ent st: wknd over 1f out* **10/1**	35

2m 3.51s (1.81) **Going Correction** +0.25s/f (Slow)
WFA 3 from 4yo+ 20lb **8 Ran SP% 128.1**
Speed ratings (Par 103): **101,100,99,97,96 94,89,87**
toteswinger: 1&2 £11.00, 1&3 £10.50, 2&3 £22.90. CSF £95.65 TOTE £6.70: £2.20, £5.10, £2.10; EX 177.00 Place 6: £38.47, Place 5: £24.42..
Owner Money Never Sleeps Racing **Bred** R G Percival **Trained**

FOCUS
A moderate maiden anchored by the proximity of the runner-up, although that horse has rated higher in the past.
T/Plt: £409.80 to a £1 stake. Pool: £76,547.97. 136.35 winning tickets. T/Qpdt: £83.80 to a £1 stake. Pool: £6,681.62. 59.00 winning tickets. KH

696 NAD AL SHEBA (L-H)
Thursday, March 5

OFFICIAL GOING: Turf course - good changing to good to firm after race 2 (4.10); dirt course - fast

768a AL BASTAKIYA - JAZIL (LISTED RACE) (DIRT) 1m 1f (D)
3:40 (3:40) 3-Y-O
£104,166 (£34,722; £17,361; £8,680; £5,208; £3,472)

			RPR
1		**Soy Libriano (ARG)**69 4-9-4 95 (t) WJSupple 5 (M bin Shafya, UAE) *in rr of mid-div: trckd ldrs 2 1/2f out: led 1 1/2f out: r.o wl* **12/1**	99
2	2	**Jose Adan (USA)**21 524 3-8-7 105 (vt) TedDurcan 1 (Saeed Bin Suroor) *s.i.s: trckd ldrs 3f out: ev ch fnl 2f: n.m.r 1f out: swtchd and r.o* **6/5**1	90
3	1 3/4	**I Am The Best**21 526 3-8-7 95 RoystonFfrench 7 (A Al Raihe, UAE) *mid-div: wd: trckd ldr 3f out: led 3 1/2f out: hdd 3 1/2f out: one pce* **14/1**	87
4	4 3/4	**Paso De Gloria (ARG)**194 4-9-4 95 AhmedAjtebi 2 (M bin Shafya, UAE) *trckd ldr: ev ch 3f out: one pce fnl 2f* **4/1**2	83
5	3 1/4	**Muy Ponderado (ARG)**81 4-9-4 90 JRosales 6 (M bin Shafya, UAE) *sn led: hdd 2 1/2f out: wknd* **7/1**3	76
6	dist	**Medici (CHI)**82 4-9-11 105 (t) MJKinane 4 (J Barton, Saudi Arabia) *racd in last: nvr nr to chal* **4/1**2	—

1m 52.62s (2.82) **Going Correction** +0.45s/f (Slow)
WFA 3 from 4yo 20lb **6 Ran SP% 112.3**
Speed ratings: **105,103,101,97,94** —
CSF: £27.23.
Owner Sheikh Majid Bin Mohammed al Maktoum **Bred** Haras Abolengo **Trained** United Arab Emirates

FOCUS
The second leg of the UAE Triple Crown was won by subsequent Derby winner Asiatic Boy in 2007, but this was a particularly weak renewal, and it will be a major surprise if the race has much bearing on World Cup night.

NOTEBOOK
Soy Libriano(ARG) became the fourth consecutive winner of this race bred in the Southern Hemisphere. Although a Group 3 winner when trained in Uruguay last year, he was impossible to fancy judged on his second behind today's third-placed horse, I Am The Best, in a non-Carnival conditions event over 7f in December. However, he reversed form with that rival over this longer trip and surprisingly proved good enough. He stayed well, and displayed a willing attitude, despite edging left, but this is not form to get carried away with.

Jose Adan(USA), a dual Polytrack winner in the US last year, was switched to dirt after disappointing on the turf first-time up in Dubai, but he again ran below expectations. He doesn't appeal as the type to keep making excuses for, but in his defence he endured a far from ideal trip. Firstly, he was stuck towards inside in the face of kickback from stall one (although he didn't help himself on the front with a sluggish start), and in the straight he was denied a clear run against the inside rail. He was forced to switch and that cost him vital momentum.

I Am The Best, who got a little warm, could not confirm earlier form with Soy Libriano, but this was a respectable effort over a trip that probably stretched him. He edged left in the straight (when rider used whip in right hand) and could not sustain his challenge.

Paso De Gloria(ARG), unbeaten in two runs in minor company in Peru, is by the same sire as UAE Derby winners Blues And Royals and Honour Devil, and he looked the stable first string on jockey bookings. However, he didn't travel with any fluency after stumbling on leaving the stalls and was short of room turning into the straight. He can be given another chance.

Muy Ponderado(ARG) was successful over as far as 1m2f in Argentina, so it was disappointing he dropped out tamely in the straight.

Medici(CHI) comes from a yard which won this race in 2004 with the ex-Chilean Petit Paris (subsequently close second in UAE Derby). Winner of the St Leger in Chile, he was a major disappointment, even allowing for his Group 1 penalty. He was soon detached from the main group and failed to respond to pressure.

769a MEYDAN CLASSIC - MUSTANFAR (CONDITIONS RACE) (TURF) 7f 110y(D)
4:10 (4:10) 3-Y-O
£62,500 (£20,833; £10,416; £5,208; £3,125; £2,083)

			RPR
1		**City Style (USA)**21 524 3-8-8 109 ow1 LDettori 9 (Saeed Bin Suroor) *settled in rr: smooth prog 2 1/2f out: led 1f out: comf* **1/1**1	104+
2	1 3/4	**Liberation (IRE)**152 6474 3-8-7 100 TedDurcan 4 (Saeed Bin Suroor) *in rr of mid-div: chsd ldrs 2 1/2f out: r.o wl: no ch w wnr* **7/2**2	98
3	3/4	**Naval Officer (USA)**137 6855 3-8-9 110 MJKinane 6 (J Barton, Saudi Arabia) *settled in rr: smooth prog on rail 2 1/2f out: n.m.r 2f out: r.o wl once clr: nrst fin* **11/2**3	98
4	shd	**Balcarce Nov (ARG)**21 524 4-9-4 95 (t) JohnEgan 1 (H J Brown, South Africa) *trckd ldrs on rail: led 1 1/2f out: hdd 1f out: nt qckn fnl 110yds* **12/1**	101
5	2 1/2	**Fire Sale (ARG)**7 701 4-9-0 91 (t) RyanMoore 13 (H J Brown, South Africa) *settled in rr: nvr nr to chal: r.o fnl 2f* **33/1**	91
6	1/2	**Absent Pleasure (USA)**21 526 3-8-7 97 RHills 3 (E Martins, Bahrain) *mid-div on rail: chsd ldrs 2f out: nt qckn* **33/1**	88
7	1 1/4	**Keeptheboatafloat (USA)**42 258 3-8-7 91 (b) EddieAhern 10 (K R Burke) *nvr able to chal* **50/1**	85
8	2	**Rocks Off (ARG)**14 615 4-9-11 105 (b) KShea 5 (M F De Kock, South Africa) *mid-div: trckd ldrs 2 1/2f out: led briefly 2f out: one pce fnl 1 1/2f* **16/1**	92
9	8 1/2	**Montmorency (IRE)**21 524 3-8-7 85 (v) RichardMullen 8 (S Seemar, UAE) *nvr able to chal* **16/1**	59
10	2 1/4	**Dr Smart (IRE)**21 524 3-8-7 86 RoystonFfrench 2 (M Al Muhairi, UAE) *trckd ldrs tl 3f out: wknd fnl 2f* **33/1**	53
11	3/4	**Galactos (ARG)**165 4-9-11 99 (t) AhmedAjtebi 11 (M bin Shafya, UAE) *sn led in centre: hdd 2 1/2f out: wknd qckly* **16/1**	64
12	1/4	**Classic Blade (IRE)**42 258 3-8-11 108 FJara 12 (Doug Watson, UAE) *in rr of mid-div: wd 3f out: nvr nr to chal* **16/1**	55

1m 32.35s (0.75) **Going Correction** +0.25s/f (Good)
WFA 3 from 4yo 16lb **12 Ran SP% 129.6**
Speed ratings: **106,104,103,103,100 100,99,97,88,86 85,85**
CSF: £4.83.
Owner Godolphin **Bred** Stonerside Stable **Trained** Newmarket, Suffolk

FOCUS
A new race for the Carnival and a one-two for Godolphin. They went a decent clip early and perhaps the leaders went off too quick as the last trio in the early stages ended up finishing first, third and fifth.

NOTEBOOK
City Style(USA) ◆, on whom Frankie Dettori put up 1lb overweight, had finished fourth behind Donativum in last year's Breeders' Cup Juvenile Turf and, despite hanging and showing an awkward head-carriage, was impressive on his debut for Godolphin over a shorter trip here last month when beating Balcarce Nov. Preferred by Dettori over Liberation, he was switched off near the back early before making his ground gradually, and once switched out wide to make his effort he quickened up very nicely. He did carry is head slightly awkwardly and hung to his left, but nothing like to the same degree as last time. His trainer believed that he had come on from his previous win and there may be even better things to come from him. (op 5-4)

Liberation(IRE) ◆ might be an even better long-term prospect than the winner, especially as his trainer stated beforehand that he expected him to come on for this run. Not seen since finishing fourth behind Donativum and Crowded House in the Tattersalls Timeform Million at Newmarket last October when with Mark Johnston, he was another to be ridden patiently but came through between horses to hold every chance before his race-fit stable companion engaged the afterburner. Connections believe he will appreciate further and he may now be aimed at the 1m2f sales race at the Craven meeting.

Naval Officer(USA), making his debut for the yard and racing for the first time since winning a Group 3 on easy ground at Longchamp in October, lined up for this rather than the Al Bastakiya as his prep for the UAE Derby having suffered an abscess and missed some work. Another to drop out early, he needed to be angled out after failing to find much daylight halfway up the straight and stayed on well, but he did appear to be carrying his head awkwardly and perhaps he found this surface a bit quicker than he cared for.

Balcarce Nov(ARG) was nearly three lengths behind City Style over a furlong shorter on his UAE debut last month after meeting trouble in running and was considered by his trainer to have been in need of the run. He didn't help himself by racing keenly just behind the leaders in the early stages and although he put himself right in the firing line up the home straight and battled on well, his earlier exertions probably took their toll and he didn't quite get home.

Fire Sale(ARG) disappointing in two outings on dirt here this year, was dropping back down in trip for this switch to turf. Dropped out last early, she stayed on up the inside rail in the straight but could never land a blow. A return to further looks required. (op 25-1)

Absent Pleasure(USA), a useful juvenile for Brian Meehan last year, had been disappointing in two starts on dirt for his current yard at this year's Carnival. He didn't have much room to play with when within striking distance in the home straight, but it didn't affect his chance.

Keeptheboatafloat(USA), beaten a long way on his UAE debut on dirt in January, stayed on down the wide outside and ran better in blinkers this time but he was never a threat. (op 40-1)

Rocks Off(ARG), disappointing in three outings on turf and dirt at the Carnival so far, was tried in blinkers for the first time here under his Grade 1 penalty. He was bang there with every chance passing the 400m pole, but then folded tamely. (op 14-1)

770a MAHAB AL SHIMAAL - DAYJUR (GROUP 3) (DIRT) 6f (D)

4:45 (4:45) 3-Y-0+

£83,333 (£27,777; £13,888; £6,944; £4,166; £2,777)

RPR

1 **Gayego (USA)**[95] 4-9-8 115........................(t) TedDurcan 7 121+
(Saeed Bin Suroor) *mid-div: rdn 2 1/2f out: r.o wl fnl f: led cl home* **8/1**

2 3/4 **Big City Man (USA)**[42] 264 4-9-7 112........................ JVerenzuela 5 118
(J Barton, Saudi Arabia) *wl away: led in centre: led 1 1/2f out: hdd fnl 55yds* **2/1**[2]

3 3 1/2 **Diabolical (USA)**[131] 6994 6-9-5 117........................ LDettori 4 105
(Saeed Bin Suroor) *hmpd at s: trckd ldrs* **7/4**[1]

4 1 **Diana's Choice (SAF)**[13] 637 5-9-1 110........................ KShea 1 98
(M F De Kock, South Africa) *trckd ldrs in centre: rdn 2 1/2f out: one pce fnl f* **7/1**[3]

5 2 1/4 **Change Alley (USA)**[21] 525 4-9-5 106........................(t) RoystonFfrench 6 95
(A Al Raihe, UAE) *mid-div in centre: chsd ldrs 2 1/2f out: wknd fnl f* **33/1**

6 1/4 **Artimino**[13] 638 5-9-5 100........................ DO'Donohoe 10 95
(I Mohammed, UAE) *nvr nr to chal: r.o fnl 1 1/2f* **66/1**

7 2 3/4 **Hunting Tower (SAF)**[14] 614 7-9-5 112........................ JMurtagh 12 86
(M F De Kock, South Africa) *sn rdn in rr: n.d* **8/1**

8 6 3/4 **Barbecue Eddie (USA)**[42] 264 5-9-5 108........................(bt) RHills 3 66
(Doug Watson, UAE) *broke awkwardly: trckd ldrs: rdn 3f out: nt qckn* **12/1**

9 6 **Crooner (IRE)**[69] 6-9-5 90........................(t) TPO'Shea 8 48
(A Al Raihe, UAE) *nvr able to chal* **66/1**

10 2 **Salaam Dubai (AUS)**[42] 264 8-9-5 99........................(b) FJara 14 42
(A Selvaratnam, UAE) *led nr side for 2f: sn btn* **40/1**

11 4 **Halkin (USA)**[21] 521 7-9-5 100........................ EddieAhern 11 30
(F Nass, Bahrain) *nvr able to chal* **50/1**

12 9 1/2 **New Freedom (BRZ)**[21] 525 8-9-5 90........................ WayneSmith 2 2
(M Al Muhairi, UAE) *chsd ldrs for 3f: eased fnl 1 1/2f* **66/1**

1m 11.19s (0.99) **Going Correction** +0.50s/f (Slow)
WFA 3 from 4yo+ 14lb **12** Ran SP% **123.9**
Speed ratings: **113,112,107,106,103 102,99,90,82,79 74,61**
CSF: £25.08..

Owner Godolphin **Bred** Hargus Sexton & Sandra Sexton **Trained** Newmarket, Suffolk

FOCUS

This is considered a trial for the Golden Shaheen, but the winner has a few options on World Cup night. Whatever the case, this was a high-class sprint in its own right.

NOTEBOOK

Gayego(USA) ◆, who was down the field in last season's Kentucky Derby and Preakness, before winning over an extended 6f on his final start for his previous connections, created a fine impression on his debut for Godolphin. Many considered this trip would be a bit sharp, and it was also felt he would be sharper for the run, having been off for three months, so there was plenty to like about this performance. He raced slightly away from the next three home, but Ted Durcan felt he got a good lead, and if anything that helped him, as the runner-up was softened up late on after a protracted battle with the third. This big, long-striding colt was never too far away and gradually got on top, with his stamina for further kicking in late on. He has three options on World Cup night; the Golden Shaheen back over this trip, the Godolphin Mile, or even the Dubai World Cup itself, although his stamina for the latter is questionable.

Big City Man(USA), a dual winner over this course and distance already this year, including in this grade last time, emerges with plenty of credit in second, as he had to work extremely hard to get the better of the third, and was just picked off late on by that one's stablemate, who raced away from the other principals. He should go well in the Golden Shaheen, but might find one or two too good. (op 5-2)

Diabolical(USA) ◆ ran well for a long way, despite being bumped by Barbecue Eddie leaving the stalls, before clearly getting tired late on. He was bidding to follow up last year's win in this race, but had been off for four months and needed this run. (op 6-4)

Diana's Choice(SAF) has improved to win a couple of decent turf handicaps since finishing seven lengths behind Big City Man in a Group 3 here in January, and she got a little closer this time.

Change Alley(USA) ran about as well as could have been expected.

Artimino got going all too late and is not easy to catch right.

Hunting Tower(SAF)

Barbecue Eddie(USA) started awkwardly and has lost his way.

771a BURJ NAHAAR - INTIDAB (GROUP 3) (DIRT) 1m (D)

5:15 (5:16) 3-Y-0+

£83,333 (£27,777; £13,888; £6,944; £4,166; £2,777)

RPR

1 **Snaafy (USA)**[13] 639 5-9-0 104........................(v) RHills 9 117+
(M Al Muhairi, UAE) *mid-div: smooth prog 2 1/2f out: r.o wl fnl 2f: led fnl 110yds* **8/1**

2 2 1/2 **Honour Devil (ARG)**[14] 610 5-9-0 121........................ JMurtagh 1 112
(M F De Kock, South Africa) *sn led: drew clr 2f out: hdd 110yds out: r.o* **5/2**[1]

3 3 3/4 **Green Coast (IRE)**[21] 521 6-9-0 107........................ FJara 16 105
(Doug Watson, UAE) *mid-div: wd: chsd wnr 2f out: one pce fnl f* **15/2**[3]

4 2 3/4 **Grand Hombre (USA)**[7] 698 9-9-0 98........................(t) WayneSmith 10 99
(R Bouresly, Kuwait) *racd in rr: nvr nr to chal: r.o fnl 2 1/2f: nrst fin* **100/1**

5 1/2 **Don Renato (CHI)**[28] 417 6-9-0 108........................(vt) MJKinane 11 98
(J Barton, Saudi Arabia) *in rr of mid-div: nvr able to chal: r.o fnl 3f* **16/1**

6 3/4 **Lucky Find (SAF)**[13] 641 6-9-0 112........................ KShea 13 97
(M F De Kock, South Africa) *trckd ldng gp: rdn 2 1/2f out: one pce fnl 2f* **7/2**[2]

7 2 1/4 **Jalil (USA)**[7] 698 5-9-0 113........................ AhmedAjtebi 12 92
(M bin Shafya, UAE) *mid-div: r.o one pce fnl 3f* **16/1**

8 2 1/4 **Pascal (USA)**[173] 4-9-0 100........................(t) TPO'Shea 5 88
(E Charpy, UAE) *trckd ldr tl 2 1/2f out: one pce* **33/1**

9 3/4 **Fares (IRE)**[13] 639 5-9-0 100........................(v) DO'Donohoe 8 86
(Doug Watson, UAE) *mid-div: chsd ldrs 2 1/2f out: one pce* **66/1**

10 1 1/4 **Stubbs Art (IRE)**[14] 609 4-9-0 105........................(b) BFayd'Herbe 3 84
(M F De Kock, South Africa) *racd in rr: nvr able to chal* **14/1**

11 2 3/4 **Racecar Rhapsody (USA)**[201] 4-9-0 108........................ WCMarwing 7 78
(H J Brown, South Africa) *sn rdn in rr: nvr nr to chal* **14/1**

12 5 **Jet (BRZ)**[131] 6-9-0 105........................(t) RyanMoore 2 68
(H J Brown, South Africa) *trckd ldrs: rdn and ev ch 2 1/2f out: wknd fnl f* **16/1**

13 6 **Amarna (USA)**[20] 5-9-0 100........................ RoystonFfrench 6 56
(M bin Shafya, UAE) *in rr of mid-div: rdn 4f out: n.d* **14/1**

14 dist **Gold Sovereign (IRE)**[14] 614 5-9-0 97........................ WilliamBuick 15 —
(I Mohammed, UAE) *trckd ldrs: rdn 3f out: sn btn* **66/1**

15 dist **Echoes Rock (GER)**[14] 609 6-9-0 106........................(t) LDettori 14 —
(Ms C Erichsen, Norway) *in rr of mid-div: wd 3f out: n.d* **20/1**

1m 37.0s (0.30) **Going Correction** +0.45s/f (Slow) **15** Ran SP% **123.0**
Speed ratings: **116,113,109,107,106 105,103,101,100,99 96,91,85,—,—**
CSF: £27.76..

Owner Hamdan Al Maktoum **Bred** Shadwell Farm LLC **Trained** UAE

FOCUS

A very competitive Group 3 which may have been a key trial for the Godolphin Mile and possibly for the World Cup itself. It was run at a strong pace throughout and the form looks rock-solid.

NOTEBOOK

Snaafy(USA) seems to have been transformed by the application of the visor and was up in class after winning a couple of dirt handicaps here last month. Enjoying a clear passage around the outside, he showed real grit and determination to pick up the leader and was well on top at the line. His rider believed beforehand that the very best of him may not be seen until next year, but in his current form he would have to be given plenty of respect if turning out for the Godolphin Mile.

Honour Devil(ARG) ◆, winner of last year's UAE 2000 Guineas and Derby, had been disappointing on his return to action here last month, but although he had come on from that he was expected to improve again from this race which makes this effort all the more creditable. He had little option than to go for it from the rails draw early and despite being challenged all the way up the home straight, he refused to give in until forced to give best in the very closing stages. He should be cherry-ripe now and, with the longer trip in his favour, he would have to be given a live chance in the World Cup in what appears to be an open year. (op 3-1)

Green Coast(IRE) made his effort at around the same time as the winner down the outside and it looked as though he might pick up the front pair passing the 200m pole before his effort flattened out. He was better drawn than when a beaten favourite over a furlong shorter here last month, but his trainer was still concerned about him being berthed quite so wide so this was a fine effort. (op 6-1)

Grand Hombre(USA) had been disappointing since chasing home Fares in a handicap here in January, but he put up a cracking effort here. He was last of the main group turning for home, but made up an enormous amount of late ground and this was much more encouraging.

Don Renato(CHI), third in last year's Godolphin Mile, had run only creditably in the first two rounds of the Maktoum Challenge. He was another to make up a lot of ground down the outside from well off the pace.

Lucky Find(SAF), a dual winner over a furlong further at last year's Carnival, ran an eye-catching race over an inadequate 6f on his return to action here last month and should have been more suited by this trip. He had his chance, but didn't find that much off the bridle and this was rather disappointing. (op 3-1)

Jalil(USA), a three-time winner at last year's Carnival for Godolphin, was having his first start since August when down the field on his debut for the yard seven days earlier. He showed up for a long way before fading, but it was thought that he was likely to need this outing as well so he remains capable of much better.

Pascal(USA) hadn't been seen since winning on dirt at Belmont Park in September and had a tongue tie rather than blinkers on this debut for the yard. He ran well for a long way before understandably tiring and his trainer believes that he may be more of a horse for next year.

Stubbs Art(IRE), third in both the English and Irish 2000 Guineas for David Elsworth, hadn't really shone on his debut for the yard here last month. Switched to dirt for the first time, he could never get into the race following a tardy start.

Echoes Rock(GER), a dirt debutant, was virtually pulled up at halfway as though something was amiss.

772a DUBAI CITY OF GOLD - SWAIN (GROUP 2) (TURF) 1m 4f (T)

5:45 (5:45) 4-Y-0+

£104,166 (£34,722; £17,361; £8,680; £5,208; £3,472)

RPR

1 **Front House (IRE)**[13] 643 4-8-10 110........................ KShea 16 111
(M F De Kock, South Africa) *trckd ldng pair: led 2f out: r.o wl* **8/1**

2 1/2 **Quijano (GER)**[152] 6506 7-9-5 119........................ AStarke 9 117
(P Schiergen, Germany) *in rr of mid-div: smooth prog 3f out: r.o fnl 2f: nrst fin* **12/1**

3 1/2 **King Of Rome (IRE)**[7] 702 4-9-1 111........................(t) JMurtagh 11 114
(M F De Kock, South Africa) *racd in rr: prog to chse ldrs 2 1/2f out: r.o wl fnl f* **7/1**

4 1 1/4 **Purple Moon (IRE)**[81] 7682 6-9-0 116........................ JamieSpencer 5 109
(L M Cumani) *mid-div on rail: prog to trck ldrs 3f out: ev ch 2f out: one pce fnl f* **7/2**[1]

5 1 1/2 **Kings Gambit (SAF)**[13] 642 5-9-5 111........................(t) JohnEgan 2 112
(H J Brown, South Africa) *mid-div: trckd ldrs 2 1/2f out: one pce fnl f* **16/1**

6 1/4 **Fiery Lad (IRE)**[13] 640 4-8-11 110........................ KLatham 3 105
(G M Lyons, Ire) *r.o fnl 1 1/2f: nvr able to chal* **12/1**

7 1 1/4 **Mourilyan (IRE)**[7] 699 5-9-0 112........................(p) RyanMoore 4 104
(H J Brown, South Africa) *racd in rr: r.o fnl 2f: nvr nr to chal* **6/1**[3]

8 3/4 **Macarthur**[13] 642 5-9-3 119........................(t) LDettori 6 106
(M F De Kock, South Africa) *nvr bttr than mid-div* **5/1**[2]

9 shd **Pompeyano (IRE)**[13] 640 4-8-11 102........................ RichardMullen 12 102
(S Seemar, UAE) *nvr able to chal* **25/1**

10 shd **Happy Spirit (SAF)**[13] 643 5-8-13 110........................ WCMarwing 7 102
(H J Brown, South Africa) *nvr able to chal* **20/1**

11 2 **Yahrab (IRE)**[7] 703 4-8-11 109........................ RoystonFfrench 15 99
(M bin Shafya, UAE) *sn led: set decent pce: hdd 2f out: wknd* **25/1**

12 1 3/4 **Young Mick**[14] 616 7-9-0 105........................(v) TedDurcan 13 97
(G G Margarson) *in rr of mid-div: rdn 3f out: n.d* **20/1**

13 8 **Classic Punch (IRE)**[14] 616 6-9-0 105........................ RichardHughes 10 84
(D R C Elsworth) *led main gp: rdn 3 1/2f out: btn 2 1/2f out* **20/1**

14 shd **Lion Sands**[7] 699 5-9-0 107........................ WJSupple 1 84
(A bin Huzaim, UAE) *trckd ldr: rdn 3f out: sn btn* **40/1**

15 1 **Hattan (IRE)**[21] 527 7-9-0 113........................ AhmedAjtebi 14 82
(M bin Shafya, UAE) *nvr bttr than mid-div* **14/1**

16 dist **Razkalla (USA)**[13] 644 11-9-0 101........................(t) WayneSmith 8 —
(R Bouresly, Kuwait) *racd in last: rdn 3f out: n.d* **50/1**

2m 31.7s (0.70) **Going Correction** +0.25s/f (Good)
WFA 4 from 5yo+ 2lb **16** Ran SP% **131.1**
Speed ratings: **107,106,106,105,104 104,103,103,102,102 101,100,95,94,94 —**
CSF: £98.54..

Owner Mrs John Magnier & Wilgerbosdrift Stud **Bred** Triermore Stud **Trained** South Africa

FOCUS

A trial for the Sheema Classic, but a superb contest in its own right. They seemed to go a decent enough pace, courtesy of Yahrab, and that one was kept honest by Lion Sands.

NOTEBOOK

Front House(IRE) ◆ had a fitness edge over some of her rivals, but despite that she can probably be considered even better than the bare result as, drawn in stall 16, she raced three wide around the first bend, before slotting in to sit third, just off the good gallop. She also found herself in front plenty soon enough (over 400m out) when the early leaders dropped away, but she's a through stayer at this trip, as well as a battler, and sustained her challenge to the line. She had been a beaten favourite in two races against her own sex at around 1m in Dubai this year, but this is her trip and she finally showed why she is so well regarded in her native South Africa. Mike De Kock said afterwards she has taken a while to get fit and he predicts even more improvement next time. The trainer also believes she is every bit as good as the mare, Sun Classique, whom he trained to win last year's Sheema Classic, and this one must have an outstanding chance of repeating the trick.

Quijano(GER), winner of this race in 2007 and fifth last year, finished well under joint-top weight but was never quite getting there. He's entitled to come on for this, having been off for five months, and won't have a penalty in the Sheema Classic, so he could well better last season's fourth placing in that contest, but it will still be a surprise if he doesn't find at least one too good.

King Of Rome(IRE) was said by Mike De Kock to still be short of peak fitness, despite having run over 1m here the previous week, so this was a pleasing performance. He was set plenty to do, and seemed to carry his head just a touch proud under pressure, but he kept on all the way to the line. His trainer is not afraid to reach for the headgear and blinkers or a visor might help this one.

Purple Moon(IRE), beaten just a short-head in the Hong Kong Vase when last seen in December, was well enough placed if good enough, but he failed to produce a change of pace in the straight. He is another who was said to be short of peak fitness, and his trainer is a master at improving horses with racing, but he didn't show enough to warrant confident support in the Sheema Classic, especially as he was unpenalised in this. Perhaps the stable will now let Presvis take his chance on World Cup night. (op 4-1)

Kings Gambit(SAF) tried in a tongue-tie and upped significantly in trip, seemed to have his chance under his penalty, but he didn't see his race out as well as some of these.

Fiery Lad(IRE) had something to find in this company, and he lacked the tactical speed of a few of these, even though he has done most of his racing at around 1m2f, but this was still a good effort.

Mourilyan(IRE) was set a bit to do but he basically wasn't good enough. A hard race over 2m just a week earlier no doubt took the edge off him.

Macarthur still wasn't totally wound up, but yet the trainer thought the same about third-placed King Of Rome. This one, without the blinkers he wore over an inadequate trip on his Dubai debut, but with a tongue-tie on for the first time, made only limited progress after getting messed about a bit turning for home, and going wider than ideal. (op 5-1, tchd 11-2)

773a AL MAKTOUM CHALLENGE R3 - INVASOR (GROUP 2) (DIRT) 1m 2f (D)

6:15 (6:18) 3-Y-0+

£125,000 (£41,666; £20,833; £10,416; £6,250; £4,166)

			RPR
1		**Asiatic Boy (ARG)**^{28} [417] 6-9-0 117 ... JMurtagh 15 (M F De Kock, South Africa) *trckd ldng gp: rdn 3f out: led 1f out: r.o wl* 15/8^{1}	119+
2	2 1/4	**Happy Boy (BRZ)**^{28} [417] 6-9-0 112 ... AhmedAjtebi 5 (M bin Shafya, UAE) *trckd ldr: led 2f out: hdd 1f out: r.o wl* 6/1^{3}	115
3	6 1/4	**Art Of War (SAF)**^{7} [698] 5-9-0 107 ... KShea 1 (M F De Kock, South Africa) *sn led: hdd 2f out: kpt on same pce* 10/1	104
4	3/4	**Kirklees (IRE)**^{21} [527] 5-9-0 116 ... LDettori 6 (Saeed Bin Suroor) *trckd ldr: gng wl 2 1/2f out: rdn and one pce 2f out* 9/4^{2}	102
5	3 1/4	**Muhannak (IRE)**^{81} [7682] 5-9-0 115 ... PJSmullen 16 (R M Beckett) *mid-div: chsd ldrs 3f out: one pce fnl 1 1/2f* 14/1	97
6	shd	**Dynamic Saint (USA)**^{21} [523] 6-9-0 105 ... (e) AGarcia 10 (Doug Watson, UAE) *trckd ldng gp: one pce fnl 3f* 33/1	96
7	1 1/4	**Jonquil (IRE)**^{13} [639] 7-9-0 101 ... (v) EddieAhern 4 (F Nass, Bahrain) *mid-div: trckd ldrs 2 1/2f out: one pce fnl 2f* 66/1	94
8	1 1/4	**Glen Nevis (USA)**^{7} [698] 5-9-0 102 ... (v) RoystonFfrench 14 (A Al Raihe, UAE) *a mid-div* 50/1	92
9	7	**Tiz Now Tiz Then (USA)**^{14} [610] 4-9-0 108 ... (vt) RichardMullen 3 (S Seemar, UAE) *mid-div on rail: rdn 4f out: one pce* 10/1	79
10	16	**Arqaam**^{14} [612] 5-9-0 100 ... (v) FJara 7 (Doug Watson, UAE) *slowly away: racd in rr of mid-div: nvr nr to chal* 100/1	50
11	2 1/4	**Jet Express (SAF)**^{13} [639] 7-9-0 102 ... (t) TPO'Shea 12 (A Al Raihe, UAE) *in rr of mid-div: hrd rdn over 4f out: sn btn* 100/1	46
12	12	**Merchant Marine (USA)**^{131} 5-9-0 109 ... RHills 9 (Doug Watson, UAE) *racd in rr: nvr nr to chal* 9/1	25
13	15	**Lucky Ray (ARG)**^{34} 6-9-0 102 ... (vt) DO'Donohoe 2 (Doug Watson, UAE) *trckd ldrs: n.m.r 4f out: wknd* 100/1	—
14	1 1/4	**Team Victory (BRZ)**^{14} [612] 5-9-0 98 ... (vt) WayneSmith 13 (S Seemar, UAE) *nvr able to chal* 100/1	—
15	3/4	**Pearly King (USA)**^{28} [415] 6-9-0 95 ... WilliamBuick 11 (M Al Muhairi, UAE) *racd in rr: nvr nr to chal* 100/1	—
16	dist	**Varsity**^{13} [643] 6-8-9 100 ... (tp) RichardHughes 8 (C F Swan, Ire) *sn struggling in last: n.d* 100/1	—

2m 3.03s (0.73) **Going Correction** +0.45s/f (Slow) **16** Ran SP% **127.0**

Speed ratings: **115,113,108,107,105 104,103,102,97,84 82,73,61,60,59** —

CSF: £14.40.

Owner Sheikh Mohammed Bin Khalifa Al Maktoum **Bred** Haras Arroyo De Luna **Trained** South Africa

FOCUS

Three of the last nine winners of this - Dubai Millennium, Street Cry and Electrocutionist - followed up in the Dubai World Cup, and this is a key trial, particularly with the 'big one' looking wide open this year.

NOTEBOOK

Asiatic Boy(ARG) ◆ was badly in need of the run and raced too keenly when beaten into third (Happy Boy runner-up, a head in front) in the second round of this series last time, but he settled better under a patient ride on this occasion and improved on that showing. The final time was ordinary, and it's hard to get too excited by the bare form, but Mike De Kock felt he was still "not 100% wound up". He came under pressure well before the final turn, and then had to be switched right at the top of the straight, but he picked up well once organised. It's true he took a while to master the runner-up, but he always looked like doing enough, and anyway that's understandable considering he is expected to progress again. Some will argue it will be a disappointing World Cup should Asiatic Boy prove good enough, having been beaten nearly eight lengths into second in last year's race, but there is nothing of Curlin's class to worry about this time and he goes there with as good a chance as any. Blue Square, who should be applauded for opening a market on the big race weeks ago, cut him to 5/2 and he's their second choice behind 7/4 shot Albertus Maximus. Just a side note, there was also a promising run on this card from stablemate, Honour Devil, and it will be interesting to see which one Johnny Murtagh rides. (op 15-8, tchd 7-4)

Happy Boy(BRZ) was always well placed, but he could not confirm recent form with Asiatic Boy. Still, he has now run two big races back-to-back, and having looked a lost cause when with Godolphin not so long ago, credit must go to the impressive Mubarak Bin Shafya.

Art Of War(SAF), the winner's stablemate, has really got his act together in recent starts and he ran a fine race in third. However, he enjoyed a surprisingly soft lead and is probably flattered by the bare result. (op 12-1)

Kirklees(IRE) was well worth a try on the dirt, particularly with the World Cup up for grabs, although the form of his recent impressive handicap success on the turf has not worked out as expected. He had the perfect position if good enough, but he found little when asked to stretch in the straight and was left behind by some smart dirt performers. He should be well suited by a return to turf. (op 2-1)

Muhannak(IRE), last year's Breeders' Cup Marathon winner, failed to prove himself fully effective on dirt at the first attempt, but this was not a bad effort, especially as he found himself extremely wide on the final bend.

Tiz Now Tiz Then(USA) is a disappointing sort.

Merchant Marine(USA) is extremely well-regarded but was never going on his first start since switching from the US. (op 8-1)

774a JEBEL HATTA - DAAHER (GROUP 2) (TURF) 1m 194y(T)

6:45 (6:46) 3-Y-0+

£104,166 (£26,041; £26,041; £8,680; £5,208; £3,472)

			RPR
1		**Balius (IRE)**^{81} [7685] 6-9-0 118 ... (b) WJSupple 8 (A bin Huzaim, UAE) *mid-div: gng wl 3f out: smooth prog 2f out: r.o to ld 110yds out* 7/1^{3}	120
2	1 1/4	**Jay Peg (SAF)**^{42} [260] 6-9-5 120 ... (v) WCMarwing 3 (H J Brown, South Africa) *sn led: rdn 2 1/2f out: r.o wl: hdd fnl 110yds* 8/1	122
2	dht	**Russian Sage (SAF)**^{27} [439] 5-9-5 108 ... JMurtagh 10 (M F De Kock, South Africa) *trckd ldrs: rdn to chal 2 1/2f out: r.o wl* 15/2	122
4	shd	**Imbongi (SAF)**^{14} [614] 5-9-3 113 ... KShea 4 (M F De Kock, South Africa) *in rr of mid-div: rdn 2 1/2f out: r.o wl: nrst fin* 12/1	120+
5	3/4	**Vodka (JPN)**^{95} [7511] 5-9-1 120 ... YTake 7 (Katsuhiko Sumii, Japan) *mid-div on rail: gng wl 3f out: n.m.r fnl 2f: unlucky* 7/2^{1}	116
6	2 1/4	**Valedictum (AUS)**^{14} [609] 9-9-0 111 ... (bt) TedDurcan 12 (Danny O'Brien, Australia) *in rr of mid-div: nvr able to chal* 20/1	110
7	1/2	**Strategic News (AUS)**^{13} [640] 6-9-0 111 ... (bt) RyanMoore 5 (H J Brown, South Africa) *r.o fnl 1 1/2f: nvr able to chal* 9/1	109
8	hd	**Blue Ksar (FR)**^{14} [614] 6-9-0 112 ... (t) TPO'Shea 1 (E Charpy, UAE) *r.o fnl 2f: nvr able to chal* 25/1	109
9	1/4	**Biarritz (SAF)**^{7} [702] 6-9-0 110 ... (b) BFayd'Herbe 14 (M F De Kock, South Africa) *mid-div: rdn to chse ldrs and ev ch 2 1/2f out: one pce fnl f* 25/1	108
10	1 1/4	**Vertigineux (FR)**^{7} [702] 5-9-0 113 ... (t) PSogorb 13 (Mme C Dufreche, France) *nvr able to chal* 8/1	106
11	8 1/2	**Seihali (IRE)**^{7} [702] 10-9-0 106 ... WilliamBuick 15 (D Selvaratnam, UAE) *mid-div: rdn to chse ldrs 2 1/2f out: one pce fnl 1 1/2f* 25/1	88
12	10	**Pallodio (IRE)**^{21} [527] 4-9-0 110 ... AGarcia 9 (Doug Watson, UAE) *in rr of mid-div: nvr able to chal* 33/1	67
13	1/2	**Tam Lin**^{7} [702] 6-9-3 113 ... (t) LDettori 11 (Saeed Bin Suroor) *led main gp: rdn 3f out: sn btn* 12/1	69
14	3 3/4	**Mashaahed**^{13} [642] 6-9-0 110 ... (t) RHills 16 (E Charpy, UAE) *in rr of mid-div: rdn 3f out: n.d* 25/1	58
15	5	**World Ruler**^{7} [703] 4-9-0 106 ... DO'Donohoe 6 (Doug Watson, UAE) *s.i.s: nvr nr to chal* 40/1	48
16	dist	**Third Set (IRE)**^{35} [339] 6-9-0 112 ... (t) AhmedAjtebi 2 (M bin Shafya, UAE) *settled in rr: nvr nr to chal* 6/1^{2}	—

1m 48.84s (-1.16) **Going Correction** +0.25s/f (Good) **16** Ran SP% **133.9**

Speed ratings: **115,113,113,113,113 111,110,110,110,109 101,92,92,88,84** —

CSF: Balius & Jay Peg £31.49; Balius & Russian Sage £29.80..

Owner H E Sheikh Rashid Bin Mohammed **Bred** Stilvi Compania Financiera Sa **Trained** United Arab Emirates

FOCUS

A key trial for the Dubai Duty Free, but this was a very unsatisfactory race which posed more questions than it answered as a couple of the major players got themselves into all sorts of trouble and the best horse may not have won. The pace seemed solid enough, but even so the pair that occupied the first two places early still managed to finish in the first three.

NOTEBOOK

Balius(IRE) ◆, who had made the frame in Group 1 company in his last three outings including behind Jay Peg in Singapore last May, was making his debut for the yard having been working nicely of late. He travelled really well throughout and picked up in good style when asked to go and win his race, but he enjoyed an interrupted passage whilst some of his rivals didn't and he would be no sure thing to confirm the form with them if they met again.

Jay Peg(SAF) ◆, winner of last year's Dubai Duty Free having failed to win in three previous outings at the Carnival, was expected to need his first run since winning a Group 1 in Singapore last May when returning here in January and he ran accordingly. Given his usual positive ride, he battled on very gamely when tackled and this was a step in the right direction before another crack at the Dubai Duty Free. (op 10-1)

Russian Sage(SAF), who only just failed to make all over 1m on his return to action here last month, had to be content with chasing the leader this time, but to his great credit he knuckled down to the task in hand and battled all the way to the line. This was a good effort under his penalty. (op 10-1)

Imbongi(SAF) ◆, a bit disappointing when stepped back up to a more suitable trip here last time, can be considered unfortunate not to have done even better here as he was still full of running when unable to get out passing the 200m pole and by the time he did it was too late. This was still much better.

Vodka(JPN) ◆ travelled like a dream behind the leaders on the inside rail throughout, but never saw any daylight and by the time a gap did appear on the inside it was too late. Fourth in last year's Dubai Duty Free, she hadn't been seen since finishing third in the Japan Cup in November so this at least served its purpose as prep for another crack at the big race on World Cup night, but that will be cold comfort to her backers today. (op 4-1)

Valedictum(AUS), a Group 1 winner in Australia who ended a long losing run in a handicap here last month, was over a longer trip here and perhaps his rider was mindful of that as he was switched off right out the back early. He did stay on up the home straight, but could never get to the leaders.

Strategic News(AUS), narrowly beaten over an extra furlong here last time, appeared to be preferred by Ryan Moore to Jay Peg in this contest but he could never land a blow and perhaps he found this company too hot.

Blue Ksar(FR), not disgraced in the Al Fahidi Fort last month, is highly regarded by his current trainer but although he tried to make an effort up the inside rail up the home straight he never managed to get involved.

Biarritz(SAF), who finished behind three of these rivals here the previous week, didn't run at all badly as he raced pretty keenly behind the leaders early and hung in there for longer than might have been expected. (op 33-1)

Seihali(IRE), lightly raced since winning this race in 2007, looked like playing a part in the finish when brought to challenge on the outside coming to the last 200m, but his effort then flattened out pretty quickly

[762]WOLVERHAMPTON (A.W) (L-H)

Friday, March 6

OFFICIAL GOING: Standard

Wind: Almost nil Weather: Fine

775 WEATHERBYS ALL WEATHER "HANDS AND HEELS" APPRENTICE SERIES H'CAP 1m 1f 103y(P)

6:50 (6:51) (Class 6) (0-55,61) 4-Y-0+ **£2,388** (£705; £352) **Stalls** Low

Form RPR

4052 **1** **Barodine**[7] 711 6-8-6 **50** KrishGundowry(3) 10 59
(R J Hodges) *hld up towards rr: hdwy on outside over 2f out: c v wd st: led jst ins fnl f: r.o wl* **10/3**[1]

1341 **2** 2 1/4 **Ridgeway Jazz**[7] 711 4-9-3 **61** 6ex SeanPalmer(3) 11 65
(M D I Usher) *hld up in mid-div: hdwy 3f out: ev ch 1f out: r.o one pce* **7/2**[2]

-065 **3** 1 1/4 **Hunt The Bottle (IRE)**[11] 657 4-8-12 **53** PNolan 1 54
(M Mullineaux) *s.i.s: sn chsng ldr: led over 2f out tl jst ins fnl f: no ex* **15/2**

0-04 **4** nk **Summer Bounty**[43] 254 13-8-5 **46** oh1 DTDaSilva 12 47
(F Jordan) *stdd s: sn swtchd lft: hld up in rr: hdwy wl over 1f out: kpt on one pce ins fnl f* **25/1**

0216 **5** 1 1/4 **Desert Hawk**[7] 711 8-8-11 **52** MatthewLawson 3 50
(W M Brisbourne) *prom early: sn stdd into mid-div: lost pl over 5f out: r.o ins fnl f: nt rch ldrs* **7/1**[3]

0-30 **6** shd **Magic Amigo**[7] 469 8-8-0 **46** oh1 (b) DannyBrock(5) 8 44
(J R Jenkins) *s.i.s: t.k.h early: sn chsng ldrs: btn wl over 1f out* **8/1**

-325 **7** nk **John Potts**[7] 711 4-8-13 **54** (p) RichardRowe 13 51
(B P J Baugh) *hld up in mid-div: hdwy over 3f out: ev ch over 1f out: wknd wl ins fnl f* **9/1**

-006 **8** 3/4 **Bobering**[21] 537 9-8-2 **46** oh1 PaulPickard(3) 6 42
(B P J Baugh) *hld up in rr: c wd st: nvr nr ldrs* **14/1**

00-0 **9** 1/2 **Amber Ridge**[15] 608 4-8-2 **46** oh1 KierenFox(3) 5 41
(B P J Baugh) *hld up in mid-div: hdwy 2f out: nt clr run over 1f out: n.d after* **50/1**

0-00 **10** 2 1/4 **Bewdley**[29] 401 4-8-2 **46** oh1 TobyAtkinson(3) 2 36
(R E Peacock) *led: hdd over 2f out: wknd 1f out* **50/1**

00/0 **11** nk **One Upmanship**[18] 569 8-8-2 **46** oh1 RyanClark(3) 4 35
(M Salaman) *prom tl wknd 1f out* **20/1**

6-04 **12** 6 **Running Buck (USA)**[10] 666 4-8-3 **47** (v) NatashaEaton(3) 7 24
(A Bailey) *hld up in tch: wknd over 2f out* **14/1**

2m 1.95s (0.25) **Going Correction** +0.075s/f (Slow) **12** Ran SP% **116.5**

Speed ratings (Par 101): **101,99,97,97,96 96,96,95,95,93 92,87**

toteswinger: 1&2 £4.30, 1&3 £3.80, 2&3 £9.70. CSF £14.08 CT £80.02 TOTE £4.80: £2.00, £2.00, £2.90; EX 16.00.

Owner The Gardens Entertainments Ltd **Bred** Mrs A M Jenkins And E D Kessly **Trained** Charlton Mackrell, Somerset

FOCUS

A moderate handicap for apprentices, but fair efforts for the grade from the front pair, the winner reversing recent course-and-distance form with the second.

776 BET MULTIPLES - BETDAQ CLAIMING STKS 1m 141y(P)

7:20 (7:20) (Class 5) 3-Y-O **£2,729** (£806; £403) **Stalls** Low

Form RPR

1410 **1** **Common Diva**[16] 586 3-8-7 72 RobertWinston 10 71
(A J McCabe) *hld up in tch: led on bit over 2f out: rdn over 1f out: drvn out* **3/1**[2]

5-50 **2** 1 **Flying Lady (IRE)**[16] 586 3-8-8 67 TonyCulhane 1 70
(M R Channon) *hld up: hdwy on outside 3f out: chsd wnr over 2f out: rdn wl over 1f out: kpt on same pce ins fnl f* **9/2**[3]

4541 **3** 3 **Supernoverre (IRE)**[10] 662 3-9-2 67 IanMongan 8 71
(P Howling) *hld up: hdwy over 2f out: rdn and edgd lft over 1f out: one pce* **7/1**

514 **4** hd **Bromhead (USA)**[10] 662 3-8-13 67 JamieSpencer 5 68
(B J Meehan) *hld up in rr: hdwy over 2f out: rdn whn bmpd sltly over 1f out: one pce* **5/2**[1]

0012 **5** 9 **Whotsit (IRE)**[20] 547 3-8-8 61 (b) AndrewElliott 2 42
(Miss Amy Weaver) *chsd ldr tl over 6f out: prom tl wknd over 2f out* **20/1**

6 1 **Dalrymple (IRE)** 3-9-4 0 ShaneKelly 3 50
(J A Osborne) *hld up in rr: nvr nr ldrs* **28/1**

0254 **7** hd **Autumn Morning (IRE)**[4] 741 3-8-1 60 ow2 PatrickDonaghy(5) 9 37
(P D Evans) *t.k.h early in rr: rdn over 1f out: nvr nr ldrs* **16/1**

2412 **8** 2 3/4 **Hawkspring (IRE)**[8] 689 3-9-0 66 (vt) JamesO'Reilly(5) 6 44
(S Parr) *prom: wnt 2nd over 6f out: rdn and ev ch over 2f out: wknd wl over 1f out* **11/1**

5-56 **9** 3 1/2 **Forty Thirty (IRE)**[9] 670 3-8-11 68 SamHitchcott 4 28
(M R Channon) *prom: rdn over 3f out: wknd wl over 2f out* **18/1**

2525 **10** 5 **Turn To Dreams**[2] 759 3-8-3 59 (v) CatherineGannon 7 8
(P D Evans) *led: hdd over 2f out: wknd wl over 1f out* **14/1**

1m 49.4s (-1.10) **Going Correction** +0.075s/f (Slow) **10** Ran SP% **118.6**

Speed ratings (Par 98): **107,106,103,103,95 94,94,91,88,84**

toteswinger: 1&2 £9.30, 1&3 £15.00, 2&3 £19.40. CSF £17.38 TOTE £4.10: £1.20, £2.30, £2.30; EX 17.50.

Owner Alotincommon Partnership **Bred** Llety Stud **Trained** Averham Park, Notts

FOCUS

There was a good pace on here thanks to the trailblazing Turn To Dreams. Straightforward form, rated through the winner and third.

777 BET ASIAN H'CAPS - BETDAQ HANDICAP 7f 32y(P)

7:50 (7:51) (Class 5) (0-70,76) 4-Y-0+ **£3,070** (£906; £453) **Stalls** High

Form RPR

0-51 **1** **Mr Macattack**[9] 680 4-9-10 **76** 6ex LukeMorris 3 91+
(N J Vaughan) *hld up in rr: gd hdwy on outside over 2f out: led jst over 1f out: comf* **4/6**[1]

20-0 **2** 3 3/4 **Royal Challenge**[15] 606 8-9-4 **70** PatrickMathers 6 72
(I W McInnes) *hld up in rr: hdwy over 2f out: r.o to take 2nd wl ins fnl f: no ch w wnr* **40/1**

16-4 **3** 1 **Dancing Maite**[39] 297 4-9-0 **66** ChrisCatlin 10 66
(S R Bowring) *hld up in tch: led 2f out: hdd and rdn jst over 1f out: no ex and lost 2nd wl ins fnl f* **14/1**

4113 **4** 3 1/4 **Kipchak (IRE)**[14] 618 4-9-2 **68** (p) MartinDwyer 12 60
(C E Brittain) *sn prom: led 5f out to 2f out: rdn over 1f out: wknd ins fnl f* **11/2**[2]

-666 **5** 1/2 **Kabeer**[24] 490 11-8-11 **70** KarenKenny(7) 2 61
(A J McCabe) *prom: lost pl over 4f out: n.m.r on ins over 3f out: plld out and c v wd st: rdn and r.o ins fnl f: n.d* **40/1**

-145 **6** 3/4 **Tri Chara (IRE)**[29] 404 5-9-1 **67** (p) GrahamGibbons 4 56
(R Hollinshead) *prom tl n.m.r and lost pl bnd after 1f: rdn over 1f out: n.d* **11/2**[2]

/40- **7** 1 1/4 **Rubenstar (IRE)**[304] 1900 6-9-1 **67** NCallan 5 53
(Patrick Morris) *hld up and bhd: hdwy over 3f out: nt clr run over 2f out: rdn over 1f out: wknd ins fnl f* **20/1**

46 **8** 1 1/4 **Albero Di Giuda (IRE)**[20] 557 4-9-4 **70** (t) FBranca 1 53
(F Sheridan) *led 1f: prom tl lost pl over 3f out: n.d after* **50/1**

6-02 **9** hd **Romantic Verse**[20] 557 4-8-11 **68** (b) AndreaAtzeni(5) 8 50
(E S McMahon) *t.k.h: sn in tch: rdn and wknd wl over 1f out* **12/1**[3]

00-0 **10** 3 **Sarwin (USA)**[52] 152 6-8-8 **60** RobertWinston 7 35
(G A Swinbank) *prom: nt clr run on ins 3f out: carried hd high and n.m.r: wknd 2f out* **16/1**

00-0 **11** 1 1/4 **Dhhamaan (IRE)**[17] 576 4-9-4 **70** (b) AndrewElliott 9 42
(Mrs R A Carr) *led after 1f to 5f out: rdn and wknd wl over 1f out* **100/1**

1m 29.45s (-0.15) **Going Correction** +0.075s/f (Slow) **11** Ran SP% **123.6**

Speed ratings (Par 103): **103,98,97,93,93 92,91,89,89,85 84**

toteswinger: 1&2 £12.40, 1&3 £29.00, 2&3 £0.00. CSF £53.65 CT £264.60 TOTE £1.70: £1.20, £4.90, £2.40; EX 29.80.

Owner Owen Promotions Limited **Bred** Hascombe And Valiant Studs **Trained**

■ Stewards' Enquiry : Andrea Atzeni two-day ban: careless riding (Mar 21-22)

FOCUS

Once again there was plenty of pace on, and the first two came from back of the field. The winner outclassed his field and was value for further.

778 WOLVERHAMPTON-RACECOURSE.CO.UK H'CAP 7f 32y(P)

8:20 (8:21) (Class 3) (0-95,94) 4-Y-O+ **£9,462** (£2,832; £1,416; £708; £352) **Stalls** High

Form RPR

-461 **1** **Al Muheer (IRE)**[13] 636 4-9-4 **94** (b) NCallan 3 102
(C E Brittain) *w ldr: rdn to ld and edgd lft jst over 1f out: r.o* **5/1**[3]

11 **2** 1/2 **Tous Les Deux**[20] 544 6-8-4 **80** PaulHanagan 5 87
(G L Moore) *hld up and bhd: hdwy on ins 2f out: hrd rdn and r.o wl to take 2nd nr fin* **8/1**

12-4 **3** 3/4 **Orpenindeed (IRE)**[17] 579 6-8-8 **89** (p) AndreaAtzeni(5) 1 94
(M Botti) *led: rdn and hdd jst over 1f out: nt qckn: lost 2nd nr fin* **11/4**[1]

1210 **4** 3/4 **Xpres Maite**[7] 714 6-8-11 **87** (v) ChrisCatlin 9 90
(S R Bowring) *hld up: pushed along 3f out: c wd st: rdn and r.o ins fnl f: wnt 4th towards fin* **14/1**

1112 **5** 1/2 **Mutamared (USA)**[7] 714 9-8-11 **87** (t) JamieSpencer 8 89
(K A Ryan) *hld up in rr: rdn and hung lft fr over 1f out: nvr nrr* **5/1**[3]

0330 **6** nk **Internationaldebut (IRE)**[5] 724 4-9-4 **94** MartinDwyer 2 95
(S Parr) *prom: rdn over 1f out: wknd wl ins fnl f* **3/1**[2]

000- **7** 2 **Dabbers Ridge (IRE)**[132] 6975 7-8-11 **87** RobertWinston 4 83
(I W McInnes) *prom tl wknd 2f out* **25/1**

1254 **8** nse **Councellor (FR)**[13] 635 7-9-2 **92** (t) MickyFenton 6 88
(Stef Liddiard) *prom tl wknd 2f out* **7/1**

1m 28.73s (-0.87) **Going Correction** +0.075s/f (Slow) **8** Ran SP% **119.1**

Speed ratings (Par 107): **107,106,105,104,104 103,101,101**

toteswinger: 1&2 £2.80, 1&3 £6.80, 2&3 £26.00. CSF £46.06 CT £134.19 TOTE £6.50: £2.10, £2.10, £1.50; EX 32.60.

Owner Saeed Manana **Bred** Foursome Thoroughbreds **Trained** Newmarket, Suffolk

FOCUS

Quite a competitive affair but there was a muddling early gallop. The runner-up rates a slight personal best which highlights the obvious doubt over the worth of the form.

NOTEBOOK

Al Muheer(IRE) got a prominent early pitch and was well placed to get first run on any closers. Once he had got the better of Orpenindeed he was always going to just hold off the fast-finishing Tous Les Deux. The blinkers, which he also wore to success at Lingfield last time, appear to have had a dramatically positive effect, but another rise in the weights for this could leave him vulnerable in handicaps. (op 13-2 tchd 7-1)

Tous Les Deux has been in cracking form of late, but he never got the end-to-end gallop that he needs here. It was still a good effort to close down the winner to half a length at the line, but the race simply was not run to suit him. This proves, however, that he is capable of winning off his current mark. (op 6-1)

Orpenindeed(IRE) was keen to get on with things but, once getting to the front, his rider tried to restrain him. He ended up racing keenly and, while he was well placed to kick from the front turning in, that wasted energy eventually took its toll. A drop back to sprinting will not hurt him. (op 4-1)

Xpres Maite struggled when the pace picked up but stayed on well very late. It goes without saying that a stronger all-round gallop would have suited him. (op 10-1)

Mutamared(USA) was given plenty to do given the way the race was run. He does not need to be held up so far back in the field, as Neil Callan and Jim Crowley have shown when riding him to success this winter. Official explanation: jockey said gelding fly leapt on leaving stalls (op 9-2 tchd 13-2)

Internationaldebut(IRE), below his best at Lingfield last time, was going well enough, tracking the leading pair, entering the straight, but the response under pressure was disappointing. He has been on the go for some time now and might just be in need of a break. (op 4-1)

779 HOTEL AND CONFERENCING AT WOLVERHAMPTON MAIDEN STKS 1m 4f 50y(P)

8:50 (8:51) (Class 5) 3-Y-O+ **£2,729** (£806; £403) **Stalls** Low

Form RPR

0 **1** **Simonside**[18] 570 6-9-7 0 LanceBetts(7) 6 60
(B Ellison) *a.p: rdn over 1f out: led and hung lft ins fnl f: r.o* **15/2**[3]

22 **2** 1 1/4 **Dream In Blue**[23] 501 4-9-12 0 ShaneKelly 4 58
(J A Osborne) *a.p: rdn over 4f out: kpt on to take 2nd wl ins fnl f* **10/11**[1]

00-6 **3** 1 **Thirtyfourthstreet (IRE)**[9] 678 4-9-7 42 MartinDwyer 1 51?
(W R Muir) *led: rdn over 2f out: hdd ins fnl f: no ex* **33/1**

3 **4** 1 1/2 **Miss Keck**[14] 621 5-9-9 0 PJMcDonald 8 49
(G A Swinbank) *hld up in tch: ev ch over 2f out: sn rdn: one pce fnl f* **7/2**[2]

04 **5** 1/2 **Alittlemoreflair**[18] 570 3-8-0 0 PaulHanagan 7 48
(J Pearce) *dwlt: hld up in mid-div: rdn and hung lft fr wl over 1f out: nvr able to chal* **8/1**

6 1/2 **Follow The Dream**[50] 6-9-9 0 TPQueally 3 47
(Karen George) *s.s: in rr: rdn whn swtchd rt jst over 1f out: nvr nrr* **33/1**

0-0 **7** hd **Nomadic Warrior**[25] 476 4-9-12 0 JerryO'Dwyer 10 52
(J R Holt) *hld up in rr: rdn over 3f out: sme hdwy on ins over 1f out: n.d* **66/1**

-02 **8** nk **Rannoch Rose (IRE)**[9] 670 3-8-0 0 CatherineGannon 9 47
(J L Spearing) *w ldr: ev ch over 2f out: rdn wl over 1f out: wknd ins fnl f* **20/1**

9 3 1/4 **Living The Dream**[74] 7-10-0 0 (p) MickyFenton 2 46
(Karen George) *s.s: rdn over 2f out: c wd st: a in rr* **66/1**

6- **10** *19* **Just Dennis**[354] 919 5-9-7 0 AndrewHeffernan(7) 11 16
(D G Bridgwater) *wnt rt s: hld up towards rr: lost tch and eased over 1f out* **50/1**

11 *66* **Lunar Storm (IRE)**[42] 5-10-0 0 AndrewElliott 5 —
(Mrs R A Carr) *hld up in mid-div: rdn 5f out: sn struggling: t.o fnl 3f* **20/1**

2m 42.69s (1.59) **Going Correction** +0.075s/f (Slow)
WFA 3 from 4yo 23lb 4 from 5yo+ 2lb **11** Ran SP% **117.8**
Speed ratings (Par 103): **97,96,95,94,94 93,93,93,91,78 34**
toteswinger: 1&2 £9.10, 1&3 £18.30, 2&3 £6.70. CSF £13.99 CT £222.37 TOTE £8.60: £1.80, £1.30, £7.60; EX 23.30.
Owner Racing Management & Training Ltd **Bred** Keith Richardson **Trained** Norton, N Yorks

FOCUS
A pretty desperate maiden run in a slow time. The third and fourth hold down the form.

780 BET CHELTENHAM FESTIVAL - BETDAQ H'CAP 5f 216y(P)
9:20 (9:20) (Class 4) (0-85,81) 4-Y-0+ £5,180 (£1,541; £770; £384) Stalls Low

Form RPR

0-01 **1** **Bahamian Lad**[8] 691 4-8-10 73 6ex GrahamGibbons 5 81
(R Hollinshead) *chsd ldr over 1f: a.p: rdn to ld 1f out: edgd lft wl ins fnl f: drvn out* **11/4**[1]

-145 **2** *nk* **Princess Valerina**[15] 600 5-8-13 76 TPQueally 7 83
(D Haydn Jones) *hld up in tch: rdn and edgd lft fr over 1f out: r.o* **9/1**

5131 **3** *1* **Mogok Ruby**[15] 600 5-9-4 81 LukeMorris 3 85
(L Montague Hall) *s.i.s: hld up and bhd: hdwy 2f out: sn rdn: kpt on ins fnl f* **6/1**[3]

4142 **4** *1 ½* **Distinctly Game**[15] 600 7-9-1 78 (t) NCallan 2 78
(K A Ryan) *led: rdn and hdd 1f out: no ex* **9/2**[2]

65-5 **5** *nk* **Memphis Man**[52] 141 6-8-9 72 RobertWinston 8 71
(P D Evans) *t.k.h: sn prom: chsd ldr over 4f out tl rdn wl over 1f out: one pce* **20/1**

000- **6** *shd* **Danehillsundance (IRE)**[107] 7386 5-9-2 79 TolleyDean 4 77
(S Parr) *a.p: no imp fnl f* **11/1**

1153 **7** *nse* **Cornus**[9] 680 7-9-0 77 (be) JamesDoyle 1 75
(A J McCabe) *hld up in rr: rdn over 1f out: sme late prog: n.d* **10/1**

352- **8** *2* **Credit Swap**[142] 6734 4-9-2 79 NickyMackay 6 71
(M Wigham) *a bhd* **6/1**[3]

1313 **9** *½* **Grand Palace (IRE)**[10] 665 6-8-8 71 (v) PaulHanagan 9 62
(D Shaw) *broke wl: sn stdd: a bhd* **13/2**

1m 14.59s (-0.41) **Going Correction** +0.075s/f (Slow) **9** Ran SP% **118.9**
Speed ratings (Par 105): **105,104,103,101,100 100,100,98,97**
toteswinger: 1&2 £4.60, 1&3 £10.30, 2&3 £11.10. CSF £29.60 CT £141.76 TOTE £5.30: £2.10, £2.20, £1.90; EX 42.00 Place 6: £16.79, Place 5: £10.39..
Owner R Hollinshead **Bred** J D Graham **Trained** Upper Longdon, Staffs

FOCUS
A fair sprint handicap.
T/Plt: £17.50 to a £1 stake. Pool: £112,448.78. 4,669.85 winning tickets. T/Qpdt: £7.90 to a £1 stake. Pool: £8,629.63. 802.49 winning tickets. KH

775 WOLVERHAMPTON (A.W) (L-H)
Saturday, March 7

OFFICIAL GOING: Standard
There was a tail wind in the straight.
Wind: Fresh behind Weather: Overcast

781 PLAY POKER @ WILLIAMHILL.COM LADY WULFRUNA STKS (LISTED RACE) 7f 32y(P)
2:20 (2:20) (Class 1) 4-Y-0+
£22,708 (£8,608; £4,308; £2,148; £1,076; £540) Stalls High

Form RPR

63-5 **1** **Ceremonial Jade (UAE)**[14] 633 6-9-3 105 (t) JohnEgan 8 109
(M Botti) *s.i.s: hld up: hdwy over 2f out: rdn to ld ins fnl f: edgd rt: r.o* **4/1**[1]

465- **2** *hd* **Vitznau (IRE)**[210] 4869 5-9-3 99 JimmyFortune 1 109
(R Hannon) *chsd ldrs: led over 1f out: rdn: hung rt and hdd ins fnl f: r.o* **11/2**[2]

-143 **3** *1 ½* **Aeroplane**[41] 291 6-9-3 103 (p) JamieSpencer 6 105
(S A Callaghan) *s.i.s: hld up: hdwy over 1f out: shkn up ins fnl f: eased whn hld nr fin* **4/1**[1]

003- **4** *5* **Benandonner (USA)**[168] 6103 6-9-3 94 PaulHanagan 3 93
(R A Fahey) *prom: chsd wnr 2f out: sn rdn: wknd fnl f* **11/1**

02-2 **5** *1* **Philario (IRE)**[27] 458 4-9-3 98 FergusSweeney 2 90
(K R Burke) *led: hdd over 5f out: led again 1/2-way: rdn and hdd over 1f out: wknd fnl f* **4/1**[1]

2334 **6** *3 ¾* **Bonus (IRE)**[14] 636 9-9-3 105 (p) NickyMackay 4 81
(G A Butler) *hld up: rdn and wknd over 1f out: fin lame* **6/1**[3]

320- **7** *3 ½* **Beckermet (IRE)**[231] 4188 7-9-3 108 ChrisCatlin 7 72
(R F Fisher) *chsd ldr tl led over 5f out: hdd 1/2-way: rdn over 2f out: sn wknd* **10/1**

1m 27.51s (-2.09) **Going Correction** -0.025s/f (Stan) **7** Ran SP% **107.1**
Speed ratings (Par 111): **110,109,108,102,101 96,92**
toteswinger: 1&2 £11.10, 1&3 £3.00, 2&3 £9.70. CSF £22.56 TOTE £5.20: £3.00, £2.10; EX 25.00 Trifecta £169.30 Pool: £331.89 - 1.45 winning units..
Owner Giuliano Manfredini **Bred** Darley **Trained** Newmarket, Suffolk
■ Stewards' Enquiry : Jimmy Fortune One-day ban: careless riding (Mar 21)

FOCUS
An ordinary Listed contest. The pace was fair, with Philario and Beckermet taking each other on for the lead.

NOTEBOOK
Ceremonial Jade(UAE) was slightly below his best in a 6f Listed race at Lingfield a fortnight earlier, but that was his first run for two months and it clearly put him spot on. The step back up in trip was no inconvenience and he picked up well after racing enthusiastically off the disputed lead. He didn't have much in hand at the line, but he looks slightly better than the bare result as he was taken right, towards the stands' rail, by the runner-up in the closing stages. In the long-term he will apparently be trained for a campaign in Dubai in 2010.
Vitznau(IRE) travelled well for a long way, but he was run out of it after hanging right in the closing stages. Despite that, this was close to a career best considering he would have been 6lb better off with the winner in a handicap, and also had 4lb to find with the third; a fine effort off the back of a seven-month break. (op 6-1 tchd 5-1)
Aeroplane, with cheekpieces re-fitted, missed the break but was produced with every chance from off the speed. He offered only the one pace, though, and being taken right in the straight, with the front two edging in that direction, was no excuse. After a brief good run of form, he has again become a difficult ride. (op 7-2)
Benandonner(USA) had something to find at the weights with all of these and was well held after 168 days off. (op 14-1)
Philario(IRE) failed to see his race out after being taken on for the lead by Beckermet. (op 5-1)
Bonus(IRE), with cheekpieces replacing blinkers, was the second best off at the weights, but he ran below form and was reported to have finished lame. Official explanation: vet said gelding returned lame (op 9-2)
Beckermet(IRE) was the best off at the weights (had upwards of 3lb in hand), but he had been off for 231 days, was unproven on Polytrack, and could not get his favoured uncontested lead. (op 15-2 tchd 11-1)

782 24HR TELEPHONE BETTING @ WILLIAM HILL 0800 44 40 40 H'CAP 7f 32y(P)
2:55 (2:55) (Class 4) (0-85,80) 3-Y-O £4,857 (£1,445; £722; £360) Stalls High

Form RPR

122 **1** **Changing The Guard**[29] 432 3-9-5 78 (v[1]) PaulHanagan 5 82
(R A Fahey) *hld up: hdwy over 1f out: rdn and hung lft ins fnl f: r.o to ld last strides* **15/8**[1]

3-22 **2** *nk* **Shaws Diamond (USA)**[21] 556 3-9-5 78 AdamKirby 4 81
(D Shaw) *led: rdn over 1f out: hdd last strides* **15/2**

16-1 **3** *½* **Fesko**[20] 562 3-9-7 80 GregFairley 7 82
(M Johnston) *s.i.s: sn rcvrd to chse ldr: rdn and hung lft fr over 1f out: styd on* **2/1**[2]

0-24 **4** *2 ½* **Iron Out (USA)**[19] 572 3-8-6 65 ChrisCatlin 3 61
(R Hollinshead) *prom: rdn over 2f out: styd on same pce fnl f* **8/1**

5-21 **5** *½* **Ageebah**[17] 586 3-8-10 69 MartinDwyer 2 63
(C E Brittain) *chsd ldrs: rdn over 2f out: no ex fnl f* **9/2**[3]

1m 29.83s (0.23) **Going Correction** -0.025s/f (Stan) **5** Ran SP% **109.2**
Speed ratings (Par 100): **97,96,96,93,92**
toteswinger: 1&2 £4.20 CSF £15.07 TOTE £3.10: £3.20, £9.10; EX 16.80.
Owner I L Davies **Bred** R A Bonnycastle And Marston Stud **Trained** Musley Bank, N Yorks

FOCUS
A fair three-year-old handicap, despite the small field.

783 WILLIAM HILL LINCOLN TRIAL (HERITAGE H'CAP) 1m 141y(P)
3:30 (3:31) (Class 2) (0-105,100) 4-Y-0+
£31,155 (£9,330; £4,665; £2,335; £1,165; £585) Stalls Low

Form RPR

41-2 **1** **Flipando (IRE)**[6] 724 8-9-3 93 JamieSpencer 4 103
(T D Barron) *hld up in tch: rdn and hung lft fr over 1f out: styd on u.p to ld wl ins fnl f* **9/4**[1]

2-52 **2** *¾* **Ace Of Hearts**[28] 445 10-9-4 97 JackMitchell(3) 6 105
(C F Wall) *chsd ldr tl rdn to ld over 2f out: hung lft over 1f out: hdd wl ins fnl f* **11/1**

050- **3** *1 ¼* **Whitcombe Minister (USA)**[141] 6784 4-9-2 92 JohnEgan 1 98
(M Botti) *chsd ldrs: nt clr run over 2f out: rdn over 1f out: r.o* **11/2**[2]

-140 **4** *shd* **Mahadee (IRE)**[14] 635 4-9-6 96 (b) JimmyFortune 2 102
(C E Brittain) *s.i.s: hld up: edgd lft and r.o wl u.p ins fnl f: nt rch ldrs* **13/2**

6-11 **5** *hd* **Flowing Cape (IRE)**[18] 579 4-9-5 95 GrahamGibbons 10 100
(R Hollinshead) *alway prom: rdn to chse ldr 2f out: sn ev ch: styd on same pce ins fnl f* **6/1**[3]

040- **6** *1* **Flawed Genius**[191] 5425 4-9-0 90 NCallan 7 93
(K A Ryan) *chsd ldrs: rdn over 1f out: hung lft ins fnl f: no ex towards fin* **18/1**

042- **7** *1 ¾* **Extraterrestrial**[141] 6772 5-9-2 92 TonyHamilton 11 91
(R A Fahey) *stdd and swtchd lft sn after s: hdwy u.p over 1f out: one pce ins fnl f* **25/1**

1510 **8** *½* **Nightjar (USA)**[18] 579 4-9-3 93 JoeFanning 9 91
(M Johnston) *hld up in tch: outpcd over 2f out: styd on ins fnl f:* **22/1**

3-36 **9** *1 ¼* **Samarinda (USA)**[27] 458 6-9-5 95 AdamKirby 8 91
(Mrs P Sly) *hld up: rdn over 1f out: nvr rchd ldrs* **20/1**

163- **10** *2 ¼* **Bolodenka (IRE)**[34] 6654 7-9-5 95 PaulHanagan 12 86
(R A Fahey) *hld up: rdn over 1f out: n.d* **16/1**

000- **11** *½* **Raptor (GER)**[154] 6476 6-9-10 100 FergusSweeney 5 90
(K R Burke) *hld up: rdn over 3f out: wknd 2f out* **40/1**

410- **12** *1* **Lucky Dance (BRZ)**[119] 7245 7-9-2 92 GregFairley 3 80
(A G Foster) *led: rdn and hdd over 2f out: wknd over 1f out* **9/1**

4131 **13** *5* **Capricorn Run (USA)**[14] 635 6-9-8 98 (v) RobertWinston 13 75
(A J McCabe) *chsd ldrs: rdn 3f out: wknd over 1f out* **20/1**

1m 48.4s (-2.10) **Going Correction** -0.025s/f (Stan) **13** Ran SP% **123.4**
Speed ratings (Par 109): **108,107,106,106,105 105,103,103,101,99 99,98,94**
toteswinger: 1&2 £3.20, 1&3 £4.60, 2&3 £25.70. CSF £27.49 CT £129.94 TOTE £2.70: £1.20, £3.90, £2.20; EX 24.90 Trifecta £310.30 Pool: £943.75 - 2.25 winning units..
Owner Mrs J Hazell **Bred** Denis McDonnell **Trained** Maunby, N Yorks

FOCUS
This rarely has much bearing on the Lincoln itself these days – the last horse to double up was Nimello, who won the old consolation for this race back in 2001 – but it's still a decent handicap in its own right. The pace seemed to slow down the back straight.

NOTEBOOK
Flipando(IRE) produced a very useful effort and deserves extra credit, as he raced enthusiastically in about mid-division for much of the way, suggesting he would have been even better suited by more of an end-to-end gallop. He's at the absolute top of his game and provided the ground is good he will take his chance in the Lincoln, for which he has picked up a 5lb penalty. Most bookies have him at around 16-1 for the Doncaster race. (op 3-1 tchd 10-3 and 7-2 in places)
Ace Of Hearts was unable to dominate, but he sat very handy, which was no bad thing considering how the race unfolded, and he ran on well to the line. A terrific effort considering he has never won off a mark this high and he's a credit to the Chris Wall yard. (op 9-1 tchd 17-2)
Whitcombe Minister(USA) ◆ looked slightly unlucky not to give the winner more of a race, as he got stuck behind tiring horses turning in and lost momentum when forced to switch. This was a decent first effort for the Botti yard after nearly five months off and he looks like one to keep on side. (op 8-1)
Mahadee(IRE) can be quite lazy and he found himself much further back than ideal after missing the break. He didn't enjoy the clearest of runs through when trying to pick up, and unsurprisingly could not muster the pace to pose a serious threat, but he still fared best of those held up out the back. He needs a stronger pace at this trip or 1m2f. (op 17-2)
Flowing Cape(IRE) was bidding for the hat-trick after a couple of good wins over shorter trips, but he was up a further 5lb and this was the furthest distance he has tried to date. He was also forced to race slightly wide for much of the way from stall ten, but he had his chance. This trip looked to stretch him. (op 11-2 tchd 5-1)
Flawed Genius was never the most likeable type when with Sir Michael Stoute, but he ran okay on his debut for Kevin Ryan after over six months off. (op 14-1)
Extraterrestrial, returning from nearly five months off, probably would have preferred a stronger pace. (op 20-1 tchd 18-1)

Nightjar(USA) seems better suited to Fibresand. (op 16-1)

784 LIVE CASINO GAMES: WILLIAMHILL.COM CLAIMING STKS 5f 20y(P)
4:05 (4:05) (Class 5) 3-Y-O £3,238 (£963; £481; £240) Stalls Low

Form RPR

33-1 **1** **Barnezet (GR)**[63] 34 3-8-7 73 ChrisCatlin 10 65+
(R Hannon) *sn pushed along in rr: gd hdwy fnl f: hung lft and r.o to ld nr fin* **4/1**[2]

5- **2** ½ **Pinball (IRE)**[70] 7795 3-7-11 52 AndreaAtzeni(5) 2 58
(Patrick Morris) *hld up: hdwy over 1f out: rdn to ld and edgd rt ins fnl f: hdd nr fin* **20/1**

4312 **3** *shd* **Sills Vincero**[15] 624 3-8-5 61 PaulHanagan 5 61
(D Shaw) *chsd ldrs: rdn over 1f out: ev ch ins fnl f: r.o* **11/1**

00-4 **4** ½ **White Shift (IRE)**[9] 690 3-8-12 84 JohnEgan 4 66
(P D Evans) *disp ld: rdn over 1f out: styd on* **9/2**[3]

5213 **5** *nse* **La Capriosa**[16] 605 3-8-6 66 RobertWinston 3 60
(A J McCabe) *led: rdn over 1f out: hdd and unable qck ins fnl f* **8/1**

1-33 **6** ¾ **Stash**[20] 560 3-9-3 77 GrahamGibbons 6 68
(R Hollinshead) *chsd ldrs: rdn and hung lft over 1f out: hld whn n.m.r nr fin* **6/4**[1]

0-6 **7** ½ **You Avin A Laugh**[17] 592 3-8-8 0 PaulEddery 7 57
(C A Dwyer) *hld up: hdwy over 1f out: sn rdn: no ex ins fnl f* **33/1**

-212 **8** ½ **Speak The Truth (IRE)**[19] 568 3-8-9 67 (p) MartinDwyer 9 57
(J R Boyle) *s.i.s: hdwy 1/2-way: rdn over 1f out: styng on same pce whn hung lft fnl f* **8/1**

9 *7* **Erinjay (IRE)** 3-8-10 0 TobyAtkinson(7) 1 39+
(M Wigham) *s.s: outpcd* **33/1**

61.93 secs (-0.37) **Going Correction** -0.025s/f (Stan) 9 Ran SP% **119.4**
Speed ratings (Par 98): **101,100,100,99,99 97,97,96,85**
toteswinger: 1&2 £18.60, 1&3 £5.00, 2&3 £24.50. CSF £81.85 TOTE £5.60: £2.20, £5.40, £3.00; EX 5.00 Trifecta £542.40 Part won. Pool: £733.04 - 0.10 winning units..The winner was claimed by Mr. N. M. Hanger for £10,000

Owner Robin Blunt **Bred** Stavloi Th Nanou S A **Trained** East Everleigh, Wilts

■ Stewards' Enquiry : Andrea Atzeni one-day ban: careless riding (Mar 23)
Toby Atkinson seven-day ban: in breach of Rule 158 (Mar 21-27)

FOCUS
A modest claimer in which a few of these failed to run up to their official marks and they finished in a bunch. The lead was contested and the pace was strong. Third-placed Sills Vincero (BHA mark of 61) ran her race and looks the best guide to the true merit of the form.

Erinjay(IRE) ◆ Official explanation: jockey said, regarding running and riding, that his orders were to jump out and be handy, however, the colt missed the break, a fact that he reported under instruction H24, adding that having become detached he was reluctant to put it under too much early pressure in an effort to prevent it blowing up in the latter stages; trainer confirmed, saying that the colt was fully fit to race but, through inexperience, had been slow away and that the rider appeared to freeze, also due to inexperience, he was dissatisfied with the ride.

785 BETLIVE & IN-RUNNING @ WILLIAMHILL.COM H'CAP 5f 216y(P)
4:40 (4:40) (Class 2) (0-100,112) 4-Y-O+
£11,215 (£3,358; £1,679; £840; £419; £210) Stalls Low

Form RPR

000- **1** **Thebes**[123] 7181 4-8-6 88 GregFairley 1 95
(M Johnston) *sn led: rdn and hung lft ins fnl f: jst hld on* **7/2**[1]

6-63 **2** *nk* **Orpsie Boy (IRE)**[14] 633 6-9-2 98 GeorgeBaker 3 104
(N P Littmoden) *hld up: rdn and hung lft over 1f out: r.o wl ins fnl f: nt quite get up* **6/1**[3]

2222 **3** *hd* **Majuro (IRE)**[14] 635 5-9-4 100 NCallan 7 106
(K A Ryan) *a.p: rdn to chse wnr over 2f out: r.o* **4/1**[2]

4-10 **4** 1¼ **Mrs Penny (AUS)**[18] 579 5-8-5 87 ChrisCatlin 8 89
(J R Gask) *hld up: plenty to do turning for home: r.o ins fnl f: nt trble ldrs* **10/1**

0136 **5** ½ **Haajes**[21] 553 5-8-9 91 (t) DaleGibson 4 91
(S Parr) *chsd ldrs: rdn over 2f out: hung lft fnl f: styd on* **28/1**

-143 **6** 2¾ **Doubtful Sound (USA)**[28] 451 5-8-9 96 (p) AndreaAtzeni(5) 2 88
(R Hollinshead) *chsd wnr tl rdn over 2f out: wknd ins fnl f* **4/1**[2]

3111 **7** *1* **Matsunosuke**[14] 633 7-10-2 112 LukeMorris 6 101
(A B Coogan) *hld up: plld hrd: rdn over 1f out: wkng whn hung lft fnl f* **7/2**[1]

010- **8** *8* **Hoh Hoh Hoh**[175] 5890 7-9-7 103 RobertWinston 5 68
(R J Price) *hld up in tch: rdn and wknd over 1f out* **20/1**

1m 13.33s (-1.67) **Going Correction** -0.025s/f (Stan) 8 Ran SP% **116.0**
Speed ratings (Par 109): **110,109,109,107,107 103,102,91**
toteswinger: 1&2 £8.30, 1&3 £5.20, 2&3 £7.30. CSF £25.32 CT £87.48 TOTE £5.20: £2.50, £1.20, £1.80; EX 21.40 Trifecta £68.70 Pool: £805.11 - 8.67 winning units..

Owner Sheikh Hamdan Bin Mohammed Al Maktoum **Bred** Whitsbury Manor Stud And Mrs M E Slade **Trained** Middleham Moor, N Yorks

FOCUS
A decent sprint handicap.

NOTEBOOK
Thebes was a beaten favourite at Southwell when last seen in November, but he returned from his break at the top of his game and made the most of his favourable draw. Although kept honest up front by Doubtful Sound, he was soon in a good rhythm and had enough in hand to hold off the closers in the straight, despite hanging his tongue out under pressure. He's equally effective on quick ground and his form figures over 6f on either artificial surfaces or on turf no worse than good now read 211171. (op 9-2)

Orpsie Boy(IRE), whose last success was gained in this race off a 2lb lower mark last year, finished well and very nearly followed up. He's obviously still capable of very useful form. (op 4-1 tchd 7-2)

Majuro(IRE) has never won over shorter than 7f, but he ran well on this drop in trip and there didn't seem to be any excuses. (op 6-1)

Mrs Penny(AUS) was left with a lot to do turning for home and she made her move towards the inside rail, which did not look the place to be at this meeting. (op 14-1)

Haajes didn't seem to do anything wrong, but he's high enough in the weights now. (op 20-1)

Doubtful Sound(USA) was slightly short of room on the turn into the straight, but he had already run his race by that point, having taken a bit of a grip early on, and this was a rare below-par showing. (op 7-2 tchd 3-1)

Matsunosuke raced keenly under his usual hold-up ride and could make no impression in the straight. Although he won a Listed race over this trip at Lingfield on his previous start, he's always looked best suited by a strongly run 5f, and in any case he faced a stiff task off a handicap of 112. (tchd 11-2)

Hoh Hoh Hoh Official explanation: jockey said gelding had no more to give

786 WILLIAM HILL TELEBETTING 0800 44 40 40 MAIDEN STKS 1m 141y(P)
5:15 (5:16) (Class 5) 3-Y-O+ £2,729 (£806; £403) Stalls Low

Form RPR

0- **1** **Satwa Gold (USA)**[204] 5068 3-8-8 0 StephenDonohoe 7 81+
(E A L Dunlop) *chsd ldrs: rdn over 1f out: edgd lft and r.o to ld wl ins fnl f* **20/1**

06-2 **2** *1* **Capeability (IRE)**[42] 280 3-8-8 80 EdwardCreighton 1 77+
(M R Channon) *plld hrd and prom: chsd ldr 2f out: rdn to ld over 1f out: edgd lft and hdd wl ins fnl f* **4/7**[1]

4- **3** *4* **Hypnotist (UAE)**[224] 4421 3-8-8 0 MartinDwyer 9 69+
(C E Brittain) *s.s: hld up: r.o ins fnl f: nrst fin* **7/1**[3]

0- **4** *1* **Morning Sir Alan**[235] 4062 3-8-8 0 ShaneKelly 13 66+
(S A Callaghan) *hld up: hdwy over 1f out: nt trble ldrs* **40/1**

4-2 **5** *nk* **If You Knew Suzy**[51] 178 4-9-9 0 (t) RobertWinston 4 67+
(G A Swinbank) *led: hdd 7f out: chsd ldr tl led over 2f out: rdn and hdd over 1f out: wknd ins fnl f* **12/1**

0 **6** *6* **Garter Knight**[22] 529 3-8-9 0 ow1 JamieSpencer 10 60+
(M L W Bell) *hld up: effrt and hung rt 2f out: hung lft and eased ins fnl f* **20/1**

7 1¼ **Baligha**[42] 4-9-9 0 PJMcDonald 11 52
(G A Swinbank) *prom: rdn over 2f out: sn wknd* **20/1**

2-5 **8** 4½ **Smooth Sovereign (IRE)**[19] 570 4-10-0 0 JoeFanning 5 47
(M Johnston) *w ldr: racd feely: led 7f out: rdn and hdd over 2f out: sn hung lft: wknd over 1f out* **6/1**[2]

4-6 **9** *5* **Location**[12] 655 3-8-3 0 ChrisCatlin 12 26
(Ian Williams) *dwlt: hld up: a in rr: wknd 3f out* **20/1**

10 *7* **Gozome (IRE)** 5-10-0 0 VinceSlattery 2 22
(D G Bridgwater) *mid-div: lost pl over 3f out: sn wknd* **125/1**

1m 51.08s (0.58) **Going Correction** -0.025s/f (Stan)
WFA 3 from 4yo+ 20lb 10 Ran SP% **120.4**
Speed ratings (Par 103): **96,95,91,90,90 85,83,79,75,69**
toteswinger: 1&2 £6.80, 1&3 £17.10, 2&3 £2.60. CSF £31.42 TOTE £22.20: £4.80, £1.10, £1.60; EX 44.50 TRIFECTA Not won..

Owner The Lamprell Partnership **Bred** B P Walden, L Taylor Et Al **Trained** Newmarket, Suffolk

FOCUS
A reasonable maiden for the time of year/track. They seemed to go a decent gallop.

787 PLAY ROULETTE @ WILLIAMHILL.COM H'CAP 1m 5f 194y(P)
5:45 (5:45) (Class 4) (0-85,80) 4-Y-O+ £4,857 (£1,445; £722; £360) Stalls Low

Form RPR

4-26 **1** **Salute (IRE)**[45] 233 10-9-4 74 RobertHavlin 2 83
(P G Murphy) *chsd ldrs tl led over 2f out: rdn over 1f out: styd on gamely* **7/1**[3]

453- **2** 1¼ **Pass The Port**[139] 6838 8-9-8 78 PaulHanagan 6 85
(D Haydn Jones) *hld up: hdwy over 1f out: rdn and ev ch ins fnl f: styd on same pce* **10/1**

1 **3** 2½ **Eighteenfifty**[26] 476 5-9-2 72 JamieSpencer 3 76+
(N J Henderson) *a.p: hrd rdn fr over 1f out: edgd lft and no ex ins fnl f* **10/11**[1]

2301 **4** 3¾ **Wind Flow**[9] 693 5-9-5 75 (b) CatherineGannon 7 73
(C A Dwyer) *sn drvn along to ld: hdd over 6f out: led again over 4f out: rdn and hdd over 2f out: wknd ins fnl f* **7/1**[3]

20 **5** 2½ **Horseshoe Reef (AUS)**[21] 549 6-9-6 76 MartinDwyer 1 71
(J R Gask) *chsd ldr tl led over 6f out: hdd over 4f out: rdn and ev ch over 2f out: edgd lft and wknd over 1f out* **7/2**[2]

02-0 **6** 1½ **Veiled Applause**[25] 490 6-9-10 80 GrahamGibbons 4 72
(J J Quinn) *hld up: rdn over 2f out: wknd over 1f out* **20/1**

210- **7** *57* **City Stable (IRE)**[174] 5938 4-9-6 80 JimmyFortune 5 —
(M Wigham) *s.s: a in rr: rdn over 3f out: sn wknd: t.o* **8/1**

3m 3.39s (-2.61) **Going Correction** -0.025s/f (Stan)
WFA 4 from 5yo+ 4lb 7 Ran SP% **124.6**
Speed ratings (Par 105): **106,105,103,101,100 99,66**
toteswinger: 1&2 £6.50, 1&3 £4.10, 2&3 £3.60. CSF £78.32 TOTE £6.20: £2.50, £4.70 Place 6: £56.22, Place 5: £21.00..

Owner The Golden Anorak Partnership **Bred** Ahmed M Foustok **Trained** East Garston, Berks

FOCUS
A fair staying handicap run at a reasonable pace. The first two were also 1-2 in this event in 2007.
T/Plt: £148.40 to a £1 stake. Pool: £90,191.56. 443.54 winning tickets. T/Qpdt: £14.20 to a £1 stake. Pool: £6,612.02. 343.63 winning tickets. CR

SANTA ANITA (L-H)
Saturday, March 7

OFFICIAL GOING: Pro-ride - fast; turf course - firm

789a SANTA ANITA H'CAP (GRADE 1) (PRO-RIDE) 1m 2f (D)
12:37 (1:07) 4-Y-O+ £416,666 (£138,888; £83,333; £41,666; £13,888)

RPR

1 **Einstein (BRZ)**[35] 7-8-9 JRLeparoux 7 121
(Helen Pitts-Blasi, U.S.A) **5/1**[3]

2 *1* **Champs Elysees**[27] 6-8-6 JValdiviaJr 12 116
(Robert Frankel, U.S.A) **27/1**

3 *nk* **Matto Mondo (CHI)**[28] 5-8-4 RBejarano 1 113
(Richard E Mandella, U.S.A) **47/10**[1]

4 ½ **Monba (USA)**[28] 4-8-3 (b) GKGomez 4 111
(Todd Pletcher, U.S.A) **134/10**

5 ½ **Magnum (ARG)**[27] 8-8-4 JRosario 5 111
(Darrell Vienna, U.S.A) **105/10**

6 1¼ **Dansant**[25] 484 5-8-4 TBaze 8 109
(G A Butler) *towards rear, 10th straight, never in challenging postion* **179/10**

7 ¾ **Court Vision (USA)**[34] 4-8-7 (b) RADominguez 10 110
(William Mott, U.S.A) **48/10**[2]

8 ¾ **Cowboy Cal (USA)**[28] 4-8-8 JRVelazquez 2 110
(Todd Pletcher, U.S.A) **56/10**

9 ¾ **Zambezi Sun**[13] 5-8-4 VEspinoza 11 104
(Robert Frankel, U.S.A) **41/5**

10 1¼ **Stream Cat (USA)**[47] 6-8-4 (b) ASolis 13 102
(Patrick L Biancone, U.S.A) **60/1**

11 ½ **Cause (USA)**[28] 4-8-2 (b) JKCourt 9 99
(Myung Kwon Cho, U.S.A) **70/1**

12 2 3/4 **Heroi Do Bafra (BRZ)**196 7-7-13 ....(b) MCBaze 3 90
(Peter Miller, U.S.A) **113/1**
P **Blue Exit (USA)**28 4-8-4 ....(b) RAlbarado 6 —
(Jerry Hollendorfer, U.S.A) **66/10**
2m 1.93s (2.05) **13** Ran SP% **119.1**
PARI-MUTUEL: WIN 12.00; PL (1-2) 7.00, 19.40; SHOW (1-2-3) 4.60,11.60, 5.20; SF 225.80.
Owner Midnight Cry Stable **Bred** Fazenda Mondesir **Trained** USA

742 SOUTHWELL (L-H)
Tuesday, March 10

OFFICIAL GOING: Standard
Wind: Light across Weather: Overcast

790 FREEBETS.CO.UK CHAMPION HURDLE FREE BETS APPRENTICE H'CAP 1m 4f (F)
1:25 (1:25) (Class 6) (0-55,55) 4-Y-O+ **£2,047** (£604; £302) **Stalls** Low

Form RPR
06-6 **1** **Elliwan**27 494 4-8-12 **53**....................(b) FrederikTylicki 2 65
(M W Easterby) *a.p: chsd ldr 3f out: rdn to ld 2f out: styd on wl* **15/8**1
2-25 **2** 3 1/2 **Cragganmore Creek**22 567 6-8-7 **46** oh1.................. KellyHarrison 13 53
(D Morris) *s.i.s: sn chsng ldrs: led over 4f out: sn rdn: hdd 2f out: outpcd fnl f* **9/1**3
0226 **3** 1 3/4 **Dazzling Begum**18 623 4-8-7 **51**....................(p) RossAtkinson(3) 9 55
(J Pearce) *sn pushed along in rr: hdwy over 3f out: rdn and hung lft over 2f out: styd on: nt pce to chal* **3/1**2
30-2 **4** 2 1/4 **Valentine Blue**48 240 4-8-2 **48**....................(p) PNolan(5) 4 49
(A B Haynes) *chsd ldrs: rdn over 3f out: no ex fnl f* **16/1**
454- **5** 2 3/4 **No Rules**160 6386 4-8-9 **53**.................. AshleyMorgan(3) 6 50
(M H Tompkins) *hld up: styd on u.p fr over 1f out: nvr nrr* **10/1**
460- **6** 5 **Starcross Maid**92 7608 7-8-4 **46**.................. DeclanCannon(3) 14 35
(A G Juckes) *hld up: hdwy over 4f out: rdn and wknd wl over 1f out* **20/1**
601 **7** 1 1/4 **Casablanca Minx (IRE)**22 567 6-8-11 **53**..............(v) KylieManser(3) 7 41
(Miss Gay Kelleway) *hld up: rdn over 3f out: styd on fr over 1f out: nvr nrr* **16/1**
5060 **8** 8 **Spume (IRE)**22 554 5-8-11 **50**....................(t) JamesO'Reilly 12 26
(S Parr) *hld up: rdn over 3f out: n.d* **12/1**
26-0 **9** 6 **Dark Planet**68 7 6-8-10 **49**....................(v) AmyBaker 10 16
(D W Thompson) *chsd ldr tl led 9f out: rdn and hdd over 4f out: wknd 3f out* **33/1**
36-0 **10** 7 **Bond Casino**65 38 5-8-2 **46** oh1....................(p) JamieKyne(5) 5 2
(G R Oldroyd) *led 3f: remained handy: rdn and wknd over 3f out* **40/1**
00/0 **11** 1 1/2 **Adversane**18 623 5-9-2 **55**.................. PatrickDonaghy 3 9
(A J Lidderdale) *dwlt: rdn 1/2-way: a in rr* **50/1**
5-46 **12** 2 1/2 **Pick Of The Day (IRE)**20 147 4-8-5 **46** oh1....................(v) NicolPolli 8 —
(J G Given) *chsd ldrs: rdn and wknd over 4f out* **16/1**
660- **13** 8 **Flame Creek (IRE)**91 7617 13-8-8 **52**.................. SPRyan(5) 1 —
(E J Creighton) *prom: lost pl over 7f out: sn bhd* **40/1**
2m 44.25s (3.25) **Going Correction** +0.275s/f (Slow)
WFA 4 from 5yo+ 2lb **13** Ran SP% **118.8**
Speed ratings (Par 101): **100,97,96,95,93 89,89,83,79,75 74,72,67**
toteswinger: 1&2 £5.70, 1&3 £2.20, 2&3 £5.00. CSF £18.42 CT £50.65 TOTE £2.50: £1.50, £2.80, £1.70; EX 23.30 Trifecta £72.70 Part won. Pool: £98.30 - 0.46 winning units..
Owner M W Easterby **Bred** Darley **Trained** Sheriff Hutton, N Yorks
FOCUS
A moderate handicap.

791 FREEBETS.CO.UK CHELTENHAM FESTIVAL FREE BETS CLASSIFIED CLAIMING STKS (DIV I) 1m (F)
1:55 (1:56) (Class 6) 4-Y-O+ **£1,706** (£503; £252) **Stalls** Low

Form RPR
520 **1** **Very Well Red**19 608 6-8-6 47.................. ChrisCatlin 8 59
(P W Hiatt) *chsd ldrs: led 3f out: rdn clr fnl f* **7/1**
0300 **2** 2 **Rub Of The Relic (IRE)**11 711 4-8-0 52 ow3........(v) PaulPickard(7) 10 55
(P T Midgley) *hld up: hdwy 1/2-way: sn rdn: r.o wl ins fnl f: tk 2nd on line* **10/3**2
-024 **3** nse **Magical Song**49 223 4-8-6 52.................. RobertWinston 6 54
(J Balding) *racd keenly: led: rdn and hdd 3f out: styd on u.p: lost 2nd on line* **5/2**1
3230 **4** hd **King Of The Beers (USA)**8 737 5-8-7 52..........(p) KevinGhunowa(3) 9 58
(R A Harris) *hld up: outpcd 1/2-way: hdwy u.p over 1f out: r.o wl towards fin* **4/1**3
2103 **5** nk **The Graig**15 657 5-8-9 54 ow1.................. JerryO'Dwyer 5 56
(J R Holt) *chsd ldrs: rdn 1/2-way: styd on* **8/1**
2460 **6** 6 **Jordi Roper (IRE)**19 607 4-8-10 55.................. DaleGibson 7 44
(S Parr) *hld up: rdn 1/2-way: hdwy over 2f out: nt trble ldrs* **12/1**
3046 **7** 8 **Miss Understanding**16 647 4-8-6 43....................(v) JoeFanning 2 22
(J R Weymes) *chsd ldrs: rdn over 3f out: wknd 2f out* **28/1**
0-40 **8** 6 **Winged Farasi**22 569 5-8-6 50 ow4....................(p) MarcHalford(3) 1 12
(Miss J E Foster) *s.i.s: a in rr* **28/1**
0060 **9** 11 **Berrymead**13 682 4-8-10 43 ow1....................(p) AnnStokell(5) 3 —
(Miss A Stokell) *prom: rdn 1/2-way: wknd over 3f out* **66/1**
6-00 **10** 72 **Redlynch**54 178 4-8-10 20....................(v1) TolleyDean 11 —
(S Parr) *sn outpcd: t.o fnl 3f* **66/1**
1m 46.42s (2.72) **Going Correction** +0.275s/f (Slow) **10** Ran SP% **112.8**
Speed ratings (Par 101): **97,95,94,94,94 88,80,74,63,—**
CSF £28.87 TOTE £8.30: £2.90, £1.30, £1.40; EX 36.10 Trifecta £56.30 Pool: £152.98 - 2.01 winning units.
Owner Phil Kelly **Bred** Butts Enterprises Limited **Trained** Hook Norton, Oxon
FOCUS
A poor race in which those that raced up with the pace were favoured. The front five pulled a very long way clear of the rest.
Very Well Red Official explanation: trainer said, regarding apparent improvement in form, that in hindsight the previous run may have come too soon.

792 FREEBETS.CO.UK CHELTENHAM FESTIVAL FREE BETS CLASSIFIED CLAIMING STKS (DIV II) 1m (F)
2:30 (2:30) (Class 6) 4-Y-O+ **£1,706** (£503; £252) **Stalls** Low

Form RPR
4331 **1** **Amber Moon**6 760 4-8-4 50....................(b) ChrisCatlin 4 54
(J A Osborne) *a.p: rdn over 3f out: led ins fnl f: styd on u.p* **9/4**1
0044 **2** 1/2 **Mr Chocolate Drop (IRE)**11 711 5-8-11 54 ow1.........(b) AdamKirby 8 60
(Miss M E Rowland) *hld up: hdwy over 3f out: rdn to ld over 1f out: hdd ins fnl f: styd on* **4/1**3
000- **3** 2 1/4 **Iceman George**216 4739 5-9-1 54....................(b) JackMitchell(3) 10 62
(D Morris) *sn outpcd: hdwy and hung rt fr over 3f out: sn rdn: r.o ins fnl f: wnt 3rd nr fin* **16/1**
500- **4** 1/2 **Sparky Vixen**275 2870 5-8-3 47.................. KellyHarrison(5) 7 51
(C J Teague) *led early: chsd ldr tl led over 3f out: rdn and hdd over 1f out: styd on same pce ins fnl f* **22/1**
0-00 **5** 1 1/2 **Copper King**6 749 5-8-6 54.................. JoeFanning 9 46
(Miss Tor Sturgis) *trckd ldrs: racd keenly: rdn to ld over 1f out: sn hdd: no ex ins fnl f* **11/1**
321 **6** 7 **Straight Face (IRE)**7 748 5-8-6 50....................(e) PaulHanagan 11 30
(Miss Gay Kelleway) *broke wl: sn stdd and lost pl: racd keenly: rdn over 2f out: no imp* **7/2**2
6-00 **7** 3 1/4 **Tapas Lad (IRE)**21 578 4-8-6 48 ow3..................(v) KevinGhunowa(3) 6 26
(G J Smith) *prom: rdn over 3f out: wknd 2f out* **16/1**
6012 **8** shd **High Five Society**21 578 5-8-4 54....................(bt) DuranFentiman 1 21
(S R Bowring) *s.s: a outpcd* **11/1**
0002 **9** 3 **Moorside Diamond**20 587 5-8-4 46.................. AndrewElliott 5 14
(A D Brown) *hld up: a in rr: rdn and wknd wl over 2f out* **40/1**
-036 **10** 5 **Isabella's Fancy**32 420 4-8-3 52.................. DeclanCannon(7) 3 9
(A G Newcombe) *prom: lost pl over 5f out: rdn 1/2-way: sn wknd* **16/1**
0220 **11** 2 **Afton View (IRE)**23 565 4-8-10 52 ow1.................. JamesO'Reilly(5) 2 10
(S Parr) *sn led: rdn and hdd over 3f out: wknd 2f out* **33/1**
1m 46.27s (2.57) **Going Correction** +0.275s/f (Slow) **11** Ran SP% **117.0**
Speed ratings (Par 101): **98,97,95,94,93 86,83,82,79,74 72**
toteswinger: 1&2 £3.90, 1&3 £4.40, 2&3 £3.00. CSF £10.70 TOTE £3.00: £1.50, £1.70, £4.00; EX 14.90 Trifecta £87.60 Pool: £21.84 - 178 winning units.Amber Moon claimed by Miss A. Stokell for £5,000
Owner Mr & Mrs G Middlebrook **Bred** G And Mrs Middlebrook **Trained** Upper Lambourn, Berks
■ Stewards' Enquiry : Adam Kirby caution: used whip in forehand position down shoulder
FOCUS
As in the first division, the front five pulled well clear of the others and the winning time was 0.15 seconds faster. Although the majority of the principals were handy throughout, the second and third came from off the pace.
Straight Face(IRE) Official explanation: trainer's rep said gelding lost a front plate

793 FREEBETS.CO.UK EXCLUSIVE FREE BETS (S) STKS 7f (F)
3:05 (3:05) (Class 6) 3-Y-O+ **£2,047** (£604; £302) **Stalls** Low

Form RPR
4112 **1** **Obe Royal**13 671 5-10-1 71....................(v) JamieSpencer 10 71
(P D Evans) *mid-div: hdwy and edgd lft 1/2-way: hrd rdn fr over 1f out: led ins fnl f: styd on* **9/4**1
2241 **2** 1 3/4 **Cap St Jean (IRE)**11 715 5-9-8 60....................(p) DavidKenny(7) 6 67
(R Hollinshead) *s.s: bhd: hdwy over 1f out: r.o to go 2nd on line: nt rch wnr* **8/1**3
-215 **3** hd **Boss Hog**18 617 4-9-10 69....................(p) GabrielHannon(5) 13 67
(R Curtis) *chsd ldrs: led over 2f out: rdn and hung lft over 1f out: hdd and unable qck ins fnl f: lost 2nd on line* **9/1**
-150 **4** nk **Indian Diva (IRE)**25 538 4-9-10 81....................(t) GrahamGibbons 7 61
(R Curtis) *mid-div: hdwy 1/2-way: rdn over 2f out: styd on* **3/1**2
-445 **5** 3 3/4 **Ed's Pride (IRE)**18 620 3-8-7 47....................(b) PaulHanagan 8 51+
(K A Ryan) *mid-div: hdwy whn hmpd and lost pl 1/2-way: n.d after* **25/1**
5224 **6** 1 1/4 **Dancing Deano (IRE)**22 569 7-9-12 63.......... RussellKennemore(3) 9 53
(R Hollinshead) *led: hdd 6f out: remained handy: rdn over 3f out: wknd fnl f* **17/2**
-145 **7** 6 **Mudhish (IRE)**11 706 4-9-8 67....................(b) DebraEngland(7) 5 38
(C E Brittain) *chsd ldrs: led over 4f out: hdd over 2f out: wknd over 1f out* **8/1**3
5260 **8** 2 1/4 **Hamaasy**18 619 8-9-6 59....................(p) KevinGhunowa(3) 14 27
(R A Harris) *led 6f out: hdd over 4f out: rdn and wkng whn hung lft over 1f out* **16/1**
4650 **9** nse **Thabaat**27 496 5-9-9 54....................(bt) LPKeniry 3 27
(J M Bradley) *hld up: rdn over 2f out: n.d* **16/1**
2305 **10** 3 **Glan Lady (IRE)**19 605 3-8-8 50....................(b) FrankieMcDonald 1 20
(G J Smith) *hld up: rdn 1/2-way: n.d* **80/1**
-000 **11** 19 **Only A Game (IRE)**23 561 4-9-9 65....................(p) AdamKirby 12 —
(Miss M E Rowland) *sn outpcd: drvn along 1/2-way: a in rr* **40/1**
00-0 **12** 7 **I'm Agenius**67 12 6-9-4 33.................. VinceSlattery 4 —
(D Burchell) *chsd ldrs tl rdn and wknd 1/2-way* **200/1**
000- **13** 17 **Ronnies Girl**199 5261 5-9-4 10.................. AndrewElliott 11 —
(C J Teague) *s.i.s: outpcd* **300/1**
14 3/4 **Domada** 4-8-13 0.................. KellyHarrison(5) 2 —
(W J H Ratcliffe) *hld up: racd keenly: bhd fnl 4f* **100/1**
1m 31.35s (1.05) **Going Correction** +0.275s/f (Slow)
WFA 3 from 4yo+ 16lb **14** Ran SP% **119.6**
Speed ratings (Par 101): **105,103,102,102,98 96,89,87,87,83 62,54,34,33**
toteswinger: 1&2 £2.90, 1&3 £17.10, 2&3 £30.40. CSF £20.61 TOTE £3.20: £1.50, £2.30, £2.00; EX 21.70 Trifecta £70.80 Pool: £286.17 - 2.99 winning units.There was no bid for the winner. Indian Diva was claimed by P. T. Midgley for £5,000
Owner Mrs I M Folkes **Bred** Helshaw Grange Stud Ltd **Trained** Pandy, Monmouths
FOCUS
This was a very moderate seller in which few could be given a serious chance, but they went a decent pace with Mudhish and the keen-going Hamaasy taking each other on early. As a result this rather fell into the laps of the finishers.

794 FREEBETS.CO.UK OVER £1000 IN FREE BETS H'CAP 5f (F)
3:45 (3:48) (Class 6) (0-60,60) 4-Y-O+ **£2,047** (£604; £302) **Stalls** High

Form RPR
-435 **1** **Argentine (IRE)**13 675 5-8-10 **52**.................. PaulMulrennan 4 61
(L Lungo) *a.p: rdn to chse ldr over 1f out: styd on u.p to ld ins fnl f* **7/1**3
3634 **2** nk **Decider (USA)**7 742 6-9-0 **59**....................(b) KevinGhunowa(3) 2 67
(R A Harris) *led 4f out: clr 1/2-way: rdn and hdd ins fnl f: styd on* **4/1**1
6-50 **3** 1 1/4 **Spirit Of Coniston**25 535 6-8-13 **55**.................. JamieMoriarty 12 59
(P T Midgley) *mid-div: hdwy and hung lft fr over 1f out: r.o* **22/1**
03-0 **4** hd **Rocketball (IRE)**19 596 4-9-0 **56**....................(vt) JamieSpencer 5 59
(Patrick Morris) *prom: chsd ldr 3f out: rdn over 1f out: styd on same pce* **4/1**1
2552 **5** 1 1/4 **Admiral Bond (IRE)**13 681 4-9-4 **60**....................(p) PJMcDonald 13 59
(G R Oldroyd) *sn outpcd: hdwy u.p over 1f out: nt trble ldrs* **9/1**
5-26 **6** 1 **Whozart (IRE)**28 487 6-8-10 **57**.................. KellyHarrison(5) 6 52
(A Dickman) *s.i.s: outpcd: styd on ins fnl f: nvr nrr* **9/2**2
540- **7** nk **Polish World (USA)**102 7471 5-9-0 **59**.................. LeeVickers(3) 7 53
(T J Etherington) *chsd ldrs: rdn 1/2-way: sn outpcd: no ch whn hung rt ins fnl f* **28/1**
000- **8** 1 **Supreme Speedster**272 2950 5-8-13 **55**.................. SimonWhitworth 3 45
(A G Newcombe) *sn outpcd: nvr nrr* **18/1**

-654 **9** *nk* **Litham (IRE)**[19] 596 5-9-0 56..........(p) LPKeniry 8 45
(J M Bradley) *led 1f: rdn 3f out: hung lft and wknd over 1f out* **10/1**
1520 **10** *hd* **Head To Head (IRE)**[18] 619 5-8-10 52..........(b) GrahamGibbons 11 40
(A D Brown) *sn pushed along in rr: rdn 1/2-way: no ch whn hmpd over 1f out* **25/1**
-200 **11** *2 3/4* **Now You See Me**[15] 654 5-8-11 60.......... ThomasBubb(7) 14 39+
(D Flood) *s.s: outpcd* **25/1**
0/0- **12** *5* **She's Our Dream**[243] 3868 4-8-8 50..........(t) ChrisCatlin 9 11
(R C Guest) *s.i.s: sn outpcd* **66/1**
59.85 secs (0.15) **Going Correction** +0.075s/f (Slow) **12 Ran SP% 112.0**
Speed ratings (Par 101): **101,100,98,98,96 94,94,92,92,91 87,79**
toteswinger: 1&2 £5.40, 1&3 £5.90, 2&3 £10.40. CSF £30.85 CT £586.73 TOTE £8.80: £2.70, £1.60, £5.30; EX 41.10 TRIFECTA Not won..
Owner S W Group Logistics Limited **Bred** Tony Hirschfeld & L K Piggott **Trained** Carrutherstown, D'fries & G'way
■ Stewards' Enquiry : Thomas Bubb ten-day ban: breach of Rule 158 (Mar 24-Apr 2)

FOCUS
A moderate if competitive sprint handicap and as usual the low numbers had it. With Lady Bahia (16/1) refusing to enter stall one, the front two came from the three lowest remaining gates and few got into it from off the pace.
Now You See Me Official explanation: jockey said, regarding running and riding, that the mare was slowly away and failed to pick up early stages, admitting that had he been more positive it may well have finished a great deal closer; trainer stated that he was dissatisfied with the ride and felt the mare should have been placed.

795 FREEBETS.CO.UK GOLD CUP FREE BETS H'CAP 1m 4f (F)
4:25 (4:25) (Class 5) (0-75,71) 4-Y-0+ £2,729 (£806; £403) Stalls Low

Form RPR
3323 **1** **They All Laughed**[7] 743 6-9-5 70..........(b) ChrisCatlin 2 79+
(P W Hiatt) *hld up: hdwy over 3f out: styd on u.p to ld wl ins fnl f: eased nr fin* **6/4**[1]
2120 **2** *2 1/4* **Rawdon (IRE)**[15] 660 8-8-13 71..........(bt) KylieManser(7) 5 75
(Miss Gay Kelleway) *sn trcking ldr: led over 5f out: rdn over 2f out: hdd and unable qck wl ins fnl f* **13/2**
2010 **3** *2 1/4* **Safin (GER)**[13] 679 9-8-11 62.......... GrahamGibbons 3 63
(R Curtis) *hld up in tch: chsd ldr over 4f out: rdn and ev ch over 1f out: no ex fnl f* **9/2**[3]
4-61 **4** *6* **Gamesters Lady**[12] 688 6-9-0 65.......... DuranFentiman 4 57
(W M Brisbourne) *dwlt: sn rcvrd to ld: rdn and hdd over 5f out: wknd over 2f out* **8/1**
2451 **5** *nk* **Inside Story (IRE)**[18] 622 7-9-2 67..........(b) LPKeniry 1 59
(C R Dore) *chsd ldrs: rdn over 4f out: wknd over 2f out* **3/1**[2]
2m 44.58s (3.58) **Going Correction** +0.275s/f (Slow) **5 Ran SP% 107.6**
Speed ratings (Par 103): **99,97,96,92,91**
toteswinger: 1&2 £5.70, 1&3 £25.10, 2&3 £15.60. CSF £10.87 TOTE £2.60: £1.10, £3.80; EX 10.30.
Owner Clive Roberts **Bred** T G And B B Mills **Trained** Hook Norton, Oxon

FOCUS
An ordinary handicap featuring several course regulars.

796 FREEBETS.CO.UK HORSE RACING FREE BETS MAIDEN STKS 6f (F)
5:05 (5:05) (Class 5) 3-Y-0 £2,729 (£806; £403) Stalls Low

Form RPR
326- **1** **Never Lose**[164] 6268 3-8-12 88.......... JamieSpencer 7 68
(C E Brittain) *sn led: hrd rdn and hung lft over 1f out: styd on* **4/9**[1]
2 *1 1/4* **Dontuwishitwereso** 3-9-3 0.......... RobertWinston 2 69+
(P W D'Arcy) *s.i.s: hdwy over 3f out: rdn to chse wnr and hmpd over 1f out: styd on* **28/1**
60-0 **3** *2* **Aahaygirl (IRE)**[48] 236 3-8-12 73.......... AndrewElliott 9 58
(K R Burke) *chsd ldrs: rdn and hung lft over 1f out: no ex fnl f* **10/1**[3]
-533 **4** *3/4* **Beaux Yeux**[19] 602 3-8-12 60.......... JamieMoriarty 8 55?
(P T Midgley) *trckd wnr: racd keenly: rdn over 2f out: no ex fnl f* **28/1**
4 **5** *6* **Duke Of Urbino**[32] 425 3-9-3 0.......... PaulMulrennan 1 41
(K A Ryan) *s.i.s: hdwy over 4f out: rdn over 2f out: sn wknd* **4/1**[2]
06- **6** *hd* **Solis**[132] 7082 3-9-3 0.......... GrahamGibbons 5 40
(J J Quinn) *sn outpcd* **18/1**
0-05 **7** *10* **Cool Madam**[32] 429 3-8-12 31.......... VinceSlattery 6 3
(D Flood) *s.i.s: outpcd* **100/1**
1m 17.78s (1.28) **Going Correction** +0.275s/f (Slow) **7 Ran SP% 111.5**
Speed ratings (Par 98): **102,100,97,96,88 88,75**
CSF £18.68 TOTE £1.50: £1.10, £8.80; EX 20.60 Trifecta £65.80 Pool: £407.62 - 65.80 winning units.
Owner Saeed Manana **Bred** Susan J Jensen **Trained** Newmarket, Suffolk
■ Stewards' Enquiry : Jamie Spencer two-day ban: careless riding (Mar 24-25)

FOCUS
A very uncompetitive maiden.
Aahaygirl(IRE) Official explanation: jockey said filly hung left-handed
Duke Of Urbino Official explanation: jockey said colt lost its action

797 FREEBETS.CO.UK CHELTENHAM FREE BETS H'CAP 6f (F)
5:35 (5:36) (Class 5) (0-70,70) 3-Y-O £2,729 (£806; £403) Stalls Low

Form RPR
2222 **1** **Princess Cagliari**[27] 498 3-9-3 69.......... JamieSpencer 7 74
(R Hannon) *sn pushed along in rr: hdwy over 2f out: rdn over 1f out: led and edgd lft ins fnl f: styd on* **4/1**[3]
6-42 **2** *3/4* **Inthawain**[37] 365 3-8-7 59.......... DuranFentiman 6 62
(N Wilson) *led: rdn over 2f out: hdd ins fnl f: styd on* **20/1**
0-43 **3** *1 3/4* **Riflessione**[22] 568 3-8-13 68..........(b) KevinGhunowa(3) 5 66
(R A Harris) *s.i.s: hld up: racd keenly: hdwy 1/2-way: rdn over 1f out: styd on same pce* **8/1**
610- **4** *shd* **Hit The Switch**[155] 6525 3-9-2 68.......... ChrisCatlin 3 65
(Patrick Morris) *plld hrd: trckd ldrs: rdn over 2f out: styd on same pce fnl f* **16/1**
61 **5** *2* **Here Comes Danny**[31] 454 3-9-4 70.......... PaulHanagan 4 61
(M Wigham) *plld hrd and prom: rdn over 2f out: edgd rt over 1f out: styd on same pce* **11/8**[1]
5253 **6** *8* **Divine Force**[13] 673 3-8-10 62.......... ShaneKelly 2 29
(J A Osborne) *hld up: rdn and hung lft 2f out: sn wknd* **3/1**[2]
460- **7** *5* **Blue Noodles**[143] 6811 3-8-13 65.......... TonyHamilton 1 17
(D W Barker) *trckd ldr: plld hrd: rdn and wknd 2f out* **25/1**
1m 17.1s (0.60) **Going Correction** +0.275s/f (Slow) **7 Ran SP% 112.7**
Speed ratings (Par 98): **107,106,103,103,100 90,83**
toteswinger: 1&2 £3.10, 1&3 £2.60, 2&3 £13.70. CSF £70.37 TOTE £4.40: £2.60, £6.00; EX 48.50 Place 6: £13.05 Place 5: £10.04.
Owner Richard Morecombe **Bred** Buckhurst Stud **Trained** East Everleigh, Wilts
■ Stewards' Enquiry : Jamie Spencer caution: careless riding

FOCUS
An ordinary handicap in which the winning time was 0.68 seconds faster than the maiden.
T/Plt: £16.50 to a £1 stake. Pool: £50,234.74. 2,213.24 winning tickets. T/Qpdt: £7.10 to a £1 stake. Pool: £3,069.40. 317.70 winning tickets. CR

669 KEMPTON (A.W) (R-H)
Wednesday, March 11

OFFICIAL GOING: Standard
Wind: Virtually nil Weather: Dry

798 KENTUCKY DERBY CHALLENGE NEXT WEDNESDAY H'CAP 1m 2f (P)
6:50 (6:53) (Class 5) (0-75,75) 4-Y-0+ £2,590 (£770; £385; £192) Stalls High

Form RPR
1110 **1** **Brouhaha**[12] 713 5-9-3 74.......... RichardKingscote 9 86
(Tom Dascombe) *chsd clr ldr: clsd wl over 2f out: led 2f out: hung lft after but r.o wl and a in command fnl f* **6/1**[3]
33/5 **2** *1 1/4* **Khun John (IRE)**[33] 428 6-9-1 72.......... NickyMackay 7 82
(V R A Dartnall) *chsd ldrs: rdn and effrt 2f out: chsd wnr ins fnl f: r.o but a hld* **4/1**[1]
3-02 **3** *1 1/2* **Supercast (IRE)**[16] 656 6-9-4 75.......... LukeMorris 3 82
(N J Vaughan) *hld up in midfield: effrt and rdn on outer 2f out: r.o to go 3rd fnl 100yds: nt rch ldng pair* **9/1**
00-2 **4** *3/4* **King Supreme (IRE)**[10] 726 4-9-3 74..........(b) PatDobbs 12 79
(R Hannon) *chsd ldrs: rdn 2f out: drvn and kpt on same pce fr over 1f out* **7/1**
0-15 **5** *1/2* **Clovis**[9] 733 4-8-11 68..........(b) JimCrowley 6 72
(N P Mulholland) *hmpd sn after s: bhd and niggled along early: 13th bhd a wall of horses 2f out: threaded a way through and rn wl fnl f: nvr able to rch ldrs* **20/1**
40-5 **6** *nk* **King's Ransom**[35] 398 6-8-5 69.......... MatthewDavies(7) 5 72
(S Gollings) *chsd ldng pair: rdn wl over 2f out: chsd wnr wl over 1f out: no imp and wknd ins fnl f* **25/1**
11-6 **7** *nk* **Risque Heights**[25] 550 5-9-4 75.......... SteveDrowne 11 78
(J R Boyle) *t.k.h: hld up in midfield: rdn and effrt jst over 2f out: kpt on fnl f: nvr trbld ldrs* **12/1**
3-13 **8** *1* **Aphrodisia**[40] 354 5-8-12 69.......... StephenDonohoe 10 70
(Ian Williams) *stdd s: hld up wl bhd: looking for run whn hmpd over 1f out: nvr able to chal* **14/1**
54-6 **9** *nk* **Sign Of The Cross**[35] 392 5-9-3 74.......... TonyCulhane 13 74
(G L Moore) *plld hrd: hld up in midfield on inner: edgd out off rail and rdn over 1f out: wknd ent fnl f* **5/1**[2]
-406 **10** *shd* **Torch Of Freedom (IRE)**[13] 694 4-9-3 74.......... NCallan 8 74
(Sir Mark Prescott) *racd in midfield: rdn and effrt towards inner wl over 1f out: wknd fnl f* **12/1**
66-1 **11** *8* **My Shadow**[20] 597 4-9-1 72.......... IanMongan 4 56
(S Dow) *stdd s: t.k.h: hld up in last trio: rdn jst over 2f out: no hdwy* **10/1**
0-00 **12** *7* **Allanit (GER)**[25] 550 5-8-13 70.......... TPQueally 14 40
(B J Curley) *taken down early: racd freely and sn clr ldr: hdd 2f out: sn dropped out: wl btn whn hmpd over 1f out* **14/1**
4-00 **13** *7* **Andaman Sunset**[16] 660 4-8-12 69.......... TolleyDean 1 25
(J L Spearing) *stdd s: dropped in bhd: a last: rdn and lost tch over 2f out* **33/1**
2m 5.73s (-2.27) **Going Correction** -0.15s/f (Stan) **13 Ran SP% 122.8**
Speed ratings (Par 103): **103,102,100,100,99 99,99,98,98,98 91,86,80**
toteswinger: 1&2 £6.40, 1&3 £17.30, 2&3 £9.70. CSF £30.34 CT £222.75 TOTE £8.80: £3.50, £1.50, £3.80; EX 37.80.
Owner G D Newton **Bred** Mrs Rosamund Furlong **Trained** Lambourn, Berks

FOCUS
A tight handicap, run at a decent pace.
Aphrodisia Official explanation: jockey said mare was denied a clear run
Sign Of The Cross Official explanation: jockey said gelding ran too free

799 DIGIBET H'CAP 6f (P)
7:20 (7:24) (Class 5) (0-70,70) 4-Y-0+ £2,590 (£770; £385; £192) Stalls High

Form RPR
-130 **1** **What Katie Did (IRE)**[31] 460 4-8-11 63..........(p) StephenDonohoe 10 77
(J M Bradley) *trckd ldrs: rdn and effrt 2f out: led ent fnl f: r.o wl* **13/2**
1626 **2** *1 1/4* **Guildenstern (IRE)**[14] 680 7-9-1 67.......... IanMongan 7 77
(P Howling) *hld up in midfield: hdwy towards inner jst over 2f out: chsd wnr jst ins fnl f: r.o but a hld* **6/1**[3]
60P- **3** *3* **Impromptu**[317] 1683 5-9-4 70.......... JimCrowley 9 70
(P G Murphy) *in tch: rdn and unable qck 2f out: styd on on fnl f to go 3rd fnl 75yds: nvr pce to trble ldng pair* **14/1**
5031 **4** *1/2* **Princess Rose Anne (IRE)**[17] 652 4-9-3 69.......... SteveDrowne 12 67
(J R Best) *led: rdn and hrd pressed ent fnl 2f: hdd ent fnl f: sn outpcd* **4/1**[1]
50-5 **5** *hd* **Style Award**[18] 632 4-8-13 70.......... KellyHarrison(5) 11 68
(W J H Ratcliffe) *w ldr: rdn and ev ch 2f out: outpcd jst ins fnl f: kpt on* **16/1**
-243 **6** *1* **This Ones For Eddy**[20] 606 4-9-2 68.......... TolleyDean 1 63
(S Parr) *hld up bhd: plld out and rdn 2f out: styd on ins fnl f: nvr trbld ldrs* **10/1**
6-33 **7** *hd* **Ede's Dot Com (IRE)**[25] 545 5-8-10 62.......... LukeMorris 8 56
(P M Phelan) *s.i.s: sn niggled along in rr: hdwy ent fnl 2f: no imp fnl f* **4/1**[1]
6-22 **8** *3 1/4* **Louphole**[9] 728 7-9-2 68..........(v[1]) NCallan 2 52
(J R Jenkins) *rrd s: t.k.h: hld up towards rr: rdn and effrt jst over 2f out: drvn and no prog over 1f out* **9/2**[2]
250- **9** *1 3/4* **Towy Boy (IRE)**[145] 6773 4-8-11 63..........(t) ChrisCatlin 3 41
(I A Wood) *racd in midfield on outer: rdn over 2f out: wknd wl over 1f out* **16/1**
60-0 **10** *4 1/2* **Maggie Kate**[21] 590 4-8-9 61.......... RobertHavlin 6 25
(R Ingram) *racd in midfield: rdn over 2f out: sn wknd* **33/1**
300- **11** *9* **Wee Buns**[317] 1670 4-9-2 68.......... TPQueally 5 3
(P Burgoyne) *chsd ldrs: drvn over 2f out: sn wknd: wl bhd fnl f* **28/1**
1m 12.37s (-0.73) **Going Correction** 0.0s/f (Stan) **11 Ran SP% 119.7**
Speed ratings (Par 103): **104,102,98,97,97 96,95,91,89,83 71**
toteswinger: 1&2 £6.70, 1&3 £32.70, 2&3 £31.20. CSF £46.19 CT £537.10 TOTE £9.10: £2.50, £1.70, £4.90; EX 52.20.
Owner Mr & Mrs M B Carver **Bred** Brian Williamson **Trained** Sedbury, Gloucs

FOCUS
This moderate handicap was run at a fair pace and the first pair came clear.

800 DIGIBET.COM MAIDEN STKS 1m (P)
7:50 (7:51) (Class 5) 3-Y-O+ £2,590 (£770; £385; £192) Stalls High

Form RPR
650- 1 **Sanvean (IRE)**[214] 4868 3-8-3 88 ChrisCatlin 10 67+
(M R Channon) *mde all: rdn wl over 1f out: styd on and a holding runner up fnl f* **2/7**[1]
0-02 2 1 ½ **Esteem Lord**[20] 599 3-8-8 71 RobertHavlin 7 69+
(Jamie Poulton) *chsd wnr thrght: rdn over 2f out: pressed wnr ent fnl f: one pce and a hld fnl f* **5/1**[2]
05 3 4 **Al Jathaab (USA)**[16] 658 4-9-5 0 TobyAtkinson(7) 4 66
(M Wigham) *t.k.h: hld up in tch: chsd ldng pair jst over 2f out: wknd fnl f* **25/1**
00- 4 3 ¾ **Sermons Mount (USA)**[135] 7011 3-8-8 0 NeilChalmers 1 52
(Mouse Hamilton-Fairley) *a in last pair: rdn and struggling over 2f out: sn wl bhd* **20/1**
0 5 ¾ **Keen As Mustard**[23] 570 4-9-5 0 LeeNewnes(7) 3 56
(M D I Usher) *chsd ldrs: rdn over 2f out: wknd qckly wl over 1f out* **50/1**
0- 6 ¾ **Sams Spirit**[153] 6597 3-8-5 0 JackMitchell(3) 5 48
(P J McBride) *s.i.s: a last: n.d* **8/1**[3]

1m 41.26s (1.46) **Going Correction** 0.0s/f (Stan)
WFA 3 from 4yo 18lb **6** Ran SP% **116.1**
Speed ratings (Par 103): **92,90,86,82,82 81**
toteswinger: 1&2 £1.10, 1&3 £2.90, 2&3 £3.50. CSF £2.32 TOTE £1.30: £1.02, £3.10; EX 2.00.
Owner Findlay Bloom & Channon **Bred** Ceka Ireland Limited **Trained** West Ilsley, Berks

FOCUS
Five non-runners in this very modest maiden. The winner was well below form in victory.

801 DIGIBET SPORTS BETTING H'CAP 1m 3f (P)
8:20 (8:20) (Class 2) (0-100,104) 4-Y-O+
£11,215 (£3,358; £1,679; £840; £419; £210) Stalls High

Form RPR
5-44 1 **Philatelist (USA)**[32] 445 5-9-4 99 (b) NCallan 8 112+
(M A Jarvis) *t.k.h: in tch: smooth hdwy 2f out: led over 1f out: sn pushed clr: eased fnl 100yds* **5/2**[2]
3P-1 2 2 ¾ **King Olav (UAE)**[25] 550 4-8-4 86 LukeMorris 10 94
(A W Carroll) *chsd ldrs: rdn jst over 2f out: no ch w wnr fnl f but plugged on to go 2nd ins fnl f* **14/1**
134- 3 ¾ **Dream Desert (IRE)**[265] 3157 4-8-5 87 ChrisCatlin 1 93
(M R Channon) *t.k.h: stdd s: hdwy to chse ldr 9f out: rdn over 2f out: kpt on but no ch w wnr fnl f* **11/8**[1]
-120 4 1 ½ **Robby Bobby**[21] 585 4-8-13 95 J-PGuillambert 3 99
(M Johnston) *led after 1f: rdn over 2f out: hdd over 1f out: no ch w wnr fnl f: lost 2 pls ins fnl f* **14/1**
03-3 5 ½ **Bazergan (IRE)**[10] 724 4-8-11 93 (tp) MartinDwyer 4 96
(C E Brittain) *hld up in midfield: rdn and unable qck ent fnl 2f: no ch after* **8/1**[3]
5602 6 6 **John Terry (IRE)**[11] 585 6-8-8 89 JimCrowley 2 83
(Mrs A J Perrett) *stdd s: hld up towards rr on outer: rdn and nt qckn over 2f out: wl btn after* **14/1**
231- 7 2 ¾ **Buster Hyvonen (IRE)**[259] 3375 7-9-0 95 JamieSpencer 7 84
(J R Fanshawe) *stdd sn after s: hld up in rr: n.d* **8/1**[3]
-105 8 2 **Evident Pride (USA)**[21] 585 6-8-5 89 ow1 JackMitchell(3) 6 75
(B R Johnson) *t.k.h: reluctant ldr tl hdd after 1f: chsd ldrs after tl rdn and wknd ent fnl 2f* **14/1**
11-2 9 10 **Grande Caiman (IRE)**[67] 33 5-9-6 104 (b) PatrickHills(3) 9 74
(R Hannon) *hld up towards rr: last and rdn 3f out: sn lost tch: eased: t.o* **14/1**

2m 19.0s (-2.90) **Going Correction** 0.0s/f (Stan)
WFA 4 from 5yo+ 1lb **9** Ran SP% **126.2**
Speed ratings (Par 109): **110,108,107,106,106 101,99,98,90**
toteswinger: 1&2 £36.40, 1&3 £2.50, 2&3 £15.20. CSF £41.53 CT £69.53 TOTE £3.90: £1.60, £4.40, £1.30; EX 34.50.
Owner Gary A Tanaka **Bred** Darley **Trained** Newmarket, Suffolk

FOCUS
The feature handicap and a decent prize attracted a good field. There was a sound pace on which suited the runaway winner.

NOTEBOOK
Philatelist(USA) did the business in great style. He was given time to find his stride before making up his ground off the final turn and got to the leaders firmly on the bridle. He shot clear when asked and rates value for further than the winning margin. This was his first success since landing the competitive Rosebery Handicap over course and distance last year from a 5lb lower mark and it would not be surprising to see him try to repeat that victory later this month. However, a likely rise in the handicap would mean he will probably be saddled with top weight there. (op 3-1 tchd 10-3)
King Olav(UAE), who began his career at the same stable as the winner, had bounced back to form with a ready success at Lingfield last time and had been upped 2lb. He had the run of the race, but this confirms he is in decent heart again and he can find less competitive assignments. (op 16-1)
Dream Desert(IRE) was unbeaten in two previous runs on Polytrack and was last seen running an excellent fourth in the King George V Handicap at Ascot last June. He was 2lb higher for this return to action and proved all the rage in the betting ring. He had to be ridden up after a sluggish start from his modest draw and ultimately shaped as though the run would do him good. He would be entitled to take his chance in the Rosebery back here, but it could be that he wants all of 1m4f now. (op 15-8)
Robby Bobby showed his last run over course and distance to be all wrong and returned to form with a sound effort from the front. He did get very much the run of the race, however. (op 16-1)
Bazergan(IRE) looked a possible improver over this longer trip, but he ran a funny race. He ran a little freely early on and hit a flat spot nearing the home turn. He was coming back at the placed horses from 2f out, but all too late and it is hard to know what to make of this effort.
Buster Hyvonen(IRE) was making his first appearance since winning under an ultra-confident ride by today's jockey over an extra furlong at the track back in June. He was unsurprisingly ridden out the back and failed to land a blow, looking as though the run was much needed. (op 6-1)

802 PANORAMIC BAR & RESTAURANT CLASSIFIED STKS 1m (P)
8:50 (8:51) (Class 7) 3-Y-O+ £1,364 (£403; £201) Stalls High

Form RPR
005- 1 **Wunder Strike (USA)**[146] 6755 3-8-4 45 NickyMackay 12 57+
(J R Boyle) *hld up in midfield: hdwy to join ldr gng wl 2f out: led over 1f out: rdn and a jst doing enough fnl f* **11/8**[1]
-005 2 ¾ **Dobravany (IRE)**[29] 482 5-9-8 42 (v1) NeilChalmers 9 52
(K A Morgan) *hld up towards rr: hdwy over 2f out: ev ch ent fnl f: nt qckn u.p fnl f* **16/1**
0000 3 2 ¼ **Baba Ghanoush**[15] 661 7-9-8 42 (v1) FrankieMcDonald 13 47
(M J Attwater) *t.k.h: chsd ldrs: rdn to ld 2f out: sn hdd: hrd drvn and one pce fnl f* **33/1**
6530 4 nk **Turkish Sultan (IRE)**[14] 669 6-9-8 45 (p) SaleemGolam 1 46
(J M Bradley) *stdd after s: hld up in rr: hdwy on inne rover 2f out: pressed ldrs ent fnl f: hrd drvn and one pce fnl f* **12/1**
3660 5 ¾ **Mr Rev**[8] 748 6-9-8 45 (b) PaulFitzsimons 2 45
(J M Bradley) *hld up in midfield on outer: hdwy over 2f out: rdn and nt qckn wl over 1f out: one pce fnl f* **25/1**
00-6 6 2 ¼ **Mujma**[24] 565 5-9-8 45 DaleGibson 7 40
(S Parr) *t.k.h: hld up in midfield: pushed along 4f out: hdwy to chse ldrs over 1f out: hrd drvn and no prog ent fnl f* **12/1**
-040 7 ¾ **Bet Noir (IRE)**[14] 674 4-9-8 45 JerryO'Dwyer 8 38
(A W Carroll) *hld up towards rr: rdn and effrt over 2f out: plugged on but nvr pce to rch ldrs* **8/1**[2]
0040 8 2 ½ **Countrywide Comet (IRE)**[14] 674 4-9-8 44 TonyCulhane 10 33
(P Howling) *t.k.h: hld up towards rr: nt clr run briefly ent fnl 2f: nvr trbld ldrs* **33/1**
00-2 9 2 ½ **Bad Moon Rising**[59] 131 4-9-8 45 (p) SamHitchcott 6 27
(J Akehurst) *hld up in tch: rdn over 2f out: sn lost pl: wl btn fnl 2f* **10/1**[3]
054 10 1 **Rosie Cross (IRE)**[21] 587 5-9-8 45 (p) StephenCarson 11 25
(Eve Johnson Houghton) *pressed ldr tl led 4f out: rdn and hdd 2f out: wknd qckly* **8/1**[2]
0430 11 ¾ **Amwell House**[20] 598 4-9-8 43 SimonWhitworth 3 23
(J R Jenkins) *stdd after s: plld hrd and hld up in rr: nvr a factor* **25/1**
02-0 12 1 **Poppy Dean (IRE)**[30] 469 4-9-8 45 RichardThomas 5 21
(J G Portman) *t.k.h: chsd ldrs tl rdn and wknd qckly jst over 2f out* **8/1**[2]
40-4 13 2 **Buds Dilemma**[55] 175 5-9-8 44 (b) PaulEddery 14 17
(S Gollings) *sn pushed along to ld: hdd 4f out: chsd ldr after tl jst over 2f out: sn wknd* **20/1**
0330 14 31 **Golden Square**[17] 647 7-9-8 45 (p) VinceSlattery 4 —
(A W Carroll) *dwlt: sn pushed along and hdwy to chse ldrs on outer after 1f: drvn and wknd rapidly 3f out: eased: t.o* **12/1**

1m 40.34s (0.54) **Going Correction** 0.0s/f (Stan)
WFA 3 from 4yo+ 18lb **14** Ran SP% **131.8**
Speed ratings (Par 97): **97,96,94,93,92 90,89,87,84,83 83,82,80,49**
toteswinger: 1&2 £25.00, 1&3 £65.50, 2&3 Not won. CSF £28.40 TOTE £2.80: £2.00, £6.10, £6.60; EX 42.30.
Owner Mrs B Powell B Walsh P Hughes C Murphy **Bred** Mike Abraham **Trained** Epsom, Surrey

FOCUS
A very weak affair but the winner looks a bit better than this grade.
Wunder Strike(USA) Official explanation: trainer said, regarding apparent improvement in form, that it was the gelding's first run for him, and was also a step up in trip.
Buds Dilemma Official explanation: trainer rep said mare was in season

803 KEMPTON.CO.UK APPRENTICE H'CAP 7f (P)
9:20 (9:20) (Class 6) (0-60,60) 4-Y-O+ £2,047 (£604; £302) Stalls High

Form RPR
-040 1 **Admirals Way**[15] 666 4-8-11 52 LeeNewnes 10 61+
(C N Kellett) *trckd ldrs: travelling wl: led 2f out: pushed along and asserted ins fnl f: eased nr fin* **8/1**
0444 2 ¾ **Flamestone**[14] 674 5-8-4 48 RichardRowe(3) 13 53
(A E Price) *hld up wl bhd: hdwy on inner jst over 2f out: chsd ldrs over 1f out: kpt on same pce ins fnl f: snatched 2nd last strides* **15/2**
460- 3 hd **Double Valentine**[73] 7803 6-8-13 57 DebraEngland(3) 9 62+
(R Ingram) *stdd s: hld up wl bhd: hdwy over 1f out: r.o wl fnl f: wnt 3rd last stride: nvr gng to rch wnr* **25/1**
-050 4 shd **Titus Gent**[20] 608 4-8-0 48 RyanPowell(7) 11 52
(J Ryan) *pressed ldr tl led over 2f out: rdn and narrowly hdd 2f out: stl ev ch tl unable qck ins fnl f: lost 2 pls fnl strides* **50/1**
1453 5 2 ½ **Jessica Wigmo**[9] 728 6-8-9 55 TobyAtkinson(5) 4 53
(A W Carroll) *wnt rt s: stdd and dropped in bhd: hdwy over 2f out: chsd ldrs and rdn over 1f out: wknd ins fnl f* **7/1**[3]
3252 6 nk **Loyal Royal (IRE)**[12] 715 6-8-13 59 (b) SPRyan(5) 2 56
(J M Bradley) *stdd s: t.k.h: hld up in rr: hdwy sme hdwy jst over 2f out: drvn and no prog ent fnl f* **11/2**[2]
060- 7 2 ¼ **Spent**[161] 6396 4-9-3 58 DeclanCannon 14 50
(Mouse Hamilton-Fairley) *t.k.h: hld up in midfield: rdn and effrt over 2f out: wknd ent fnl f* **16/1**
-201 8 ¾ **Fun In The Sun**[15] 661 5-9-0 58 PNolan(3) 8 48
(A B Haynes) *chsd ldrs: rdn over 3f out: wknd u.p wl over 1f out* **11/2**[2]
0-03 9 nk **Ike Quebec (FR)**[42] 309 4-9-4 59 (v) RossAtkinson 6 48
(J R Boyle) *t.k.h: chsd ldrs tl rdn and wknd 2f out* **5/1**[1]
0-44 10 ½ **Outer Hebrides**[30] 473 8-8-11 52 (v) AmyRyan 1 40
(J M Bradley) *in tch on outer: rdn wl over 2f out: wknd 2f out* **8/1**
04-0 11 hd **My Kaiser Chief**[31] 460 4-8-9 55 PaulPickard(5) 12 42
(W J H Ratcliffe) *t.k.h: hld up towards rr: rdn and effrt over 2f out: no hdwy and wl btn fnl 2f* **16/1**
00-4 12 3 ½ **Free Tussy (ARG)**[26] 531 5-9-5 60 (b) JemmaMarshall 5 39
(G L Moore) *hld up in rr: n.d* **7/1**[3]
-002 13 7 **Rio L'Oren (IRE)**[15] 666 4-9-2 57 (b) MatthewDavies 7 18
(N J Vaughan) *led narrowly tl hdd over 2f out: sn wknd* **14/1**

1m 25.84s (-0.16) **Going Correction** 0.0s/f (Stan) **13** Ran SP% **130.7**
Speed ratings (Par 101): **100,99,98,98,95 95,93,92,91,91 91,87,79**
toteswinger: 1&2 £22.60, 1&3 £28.80, 2&3 £26.10. CSF £73.44 CT £1489.62 TOTE £10.10: £3.50, £3.90, £5.50; EX 99.70 Place 6 £176.67, Place 5 £85.64.
Owner J E Titley **Bred** Juddmonte Farms Ltd **Trained** Woodlane, Staffs

FOCUS
A weak handicap, confined to apprentice riders, which had a very open look about it.
Fun In The Sun Official explanation: jockey said gelding hung left
T/Plt: £279.00 to a £1 stake. Pool: £86,458.63. 226.14 winning tickets. T/Qpdt: £65.90 to a £1 stake. Pool: £6,511.06. 73.10 winning tickets. SP

790 SOUTHWELL (L-H)
Wednesday, March 11

OFFICIAL GOING: Standard
Wind: Light across Weather: Dry and sunny

804 FREEBETS.CO.UK CHELTENHAM BETTING H'CAP 5f (F)
1:20 (1:23) (Class 6) (0-65,65) 3-Y-O £2,047 (£604; £302) Stalls High

Form RPR
-602 1 **Taurus Twins**[13] 686 3-9-1 59 RobertWinston 3 62
(R J Price) *cl up: rdn along wl over 1f out: styd on to ld ins fnl f: kpt on* **8/1**

5534 **2** *hd* **Fashion Icon (USA)**[9] 736 3-8-13 **57**.......................... JamieSpencer 2 59
(T D Barron) *chsd ldrs: rdn along over 1f out: drvn ins fnl f: styd on wl towards fin: jst hld* **7/1**

005- **3** *nse* **First Blade**[89] 7646 3-8-6 **53** ow1.......................... KevinGhunowa(3) 5 55
(S R Bowring) *chsd ldrs: rdn wl over 1f out: kpt on wl u.p ins fnl f* **50/1**

-143 **4** *1* **Forever's Girl**[36] 379 3-9-6 **64**.......................... DuranFentiman 8 63
(G R Oldroyd) *prom: effrt 2f out: rdn to ld over 1f out: hdd ins fnl f and wknd towards fin* **11/1**

300- **5** *2 1/4* **Jubilee Juggins (IRE)**[114] 7361 3-9-7 **65**.......................... LukeMorris 4 55
(N P Littmoden) *sn rdn along in rr tl styd on u.p appr fnl f: nrst fin* **13/2**[3]

3420 **6** *hd* **Just The Lady**[14] 673 3-9-2 **60**.......................... StephenDonohoe 11 50
(D Nicholls) *prom: rdn along and outpcd 1/2-way: kpt on u.p appr fnl f* **28/1**

1 **7** *1 1/4* **May Martin**[13] 686 3-9-0 **58**.......................... ChrisCatlin 7 43
(Rae Guest) *dwlt: sn rdn along and a towards rr* **5/2**[1]

-501 **8** *nk* **Bold Rose**[36] 379 3-9-2 **60**.......................... (p) IanMongan 12 44
(M D I Usher) *sn rdn along and a in rr* **20/1**

-02 **9** *3/4* **Chimbonda**[9] 736 3-9-0 **58**.......................... (v) GrahamGibbons 10 39
(S Parr) *led: rdn along 2f out: hdd over 1f out sn wknd* **28/1**

0-04 **10** *1/2* **Yes She Can Can**[52] 207 3-7-10 **47** oh1 ow1...... AndrewHeffernan(7) 1 27
(Peter Grayson) *in tch on outer tl outpcd and bhd fr 1/2-way* **100/1**

11-0 **11** *7* **Imaginary Diva**[67] 34 3-9-7 **65**.......................... AdamKirby 6 19
(G G Margarson) *chsd ldrs to 1/2-way: sn wknd* **8/1**

30-4 **U** **Celtic Rebel (IRE)**[14] 673 3-8-13 **57**.......................... (p) PatCosgrave 9 —
(S A Callaghan) *rrd bdly and uns rdr s: tk no part* **6/1**[2]

60.39 secs (0.69) **Going Correction** +0.075s/f (Slow) **12** Ran SP% **113.9**
Speed ratings (Par 96): **97,96,96,95,91 91,89,88,87,86 75,—**
toteswinger: 1&2 £14.60, 1&3 £57.30, 2&3 £57.30. CSF £57.18 CT £2596.37 TOTE £9.80: £2.50, £2.40, £10.60; EX 70.10 Trifecta £167.10 Part won. Pool: £225.84 - 0.20 winning units..
Owner G E Amey **Bred** G E Amey **Trained** Ullingswick, H'fords

■ Stewards' Enquiry : Ian Mongan one-day ban: used whip above shoulder height (Mar 25)
Kevin Ghunowa one-day ban: used whip above shoulder height (Mar 25)

FOCUS
A moderate sprint handicap marred by the ugly accident that befell the second-favourite Celtic Rebel exiting the stalls. As on the previous day the low numbers had it over this straight 5f with the first three all coming up the far side of the track.
Imaginary Diva Official explanation: trainer said filly coughed post-race

805 FREEBETS.CO.UK BEST RACING FREE BETS CLAIMING STKS 1m 3f (F)
1:55 (1:55) (Class 6) 4-Y-0+ **£2,047** (£604; £302) **Stalls** Low

Form RPR

4612 **1** **Bridgewater Boys**[12] 712 8-8-10 67.......................... (b) JamieSpencer 8 69
(P D Evans) *hld up in tch: hdwy over 3f out: rdn to chal and hung lft wl over 1f out: drvn to ld appr fnl f: styd on* **11/8**[1]

-315 **2** *2 1/4* **North Parade**[9] 737 4-9-7 77.......................... (t) ShaneKelly 9 77
(A W Carroll) *hld up in rr: hdwy over 2f out: rdn to chse ldrs and hung lft over 1f out: sn drvn and kpt on ins fnl f* **7/2**[2]

/P-3 **3** *3/4* **New England**[23] 571 7-8-11 58.......................... LukeMorris 2 65
(W M Brisbourne) *t.k.h: set stdy pce: rdn 2f out: drvn and hdd appr fnl f: kpt on same pce* **13/2**

00-0 **4** *1* **Sri Kuantan (IRE)**[13] 683 5-8-9 72.......................... KarenKenny(7) 3 69
(R C Guest) *t.k.h: cl up: effrt 2f out and ev ch whn rdn and n.m.r over 1f out: drvn and wknd ins fnl f* **50/1**

3-00 **5** *1/2* **Waterside (IRE)**[21] 588 10-9-4 75.......................... ChrisCatlin 7 70
(S Curran) *trckd ldng pair: effrt on inner over 2f out: sn rdn and ch tl drvn and wknd over 1f out* **20/1**

5452 **6** *3 1/2* **Friends Hope**[13] 688 8-8-8 77.......................... GabrielHannon(5) 6 59
(R Curtis) *hld up in tch: hdwy to chse ldrs over 3f out: rdn wl over 2f out and sn wknd* **4/1**[3]

00-0 **7** *6* **Welcome Cat (USA)**[15] 300 5-8-8 45.......................... GrahamGibbons 4 45
(A D Brown) *hld up in rr: hdwy on outer 1/2-way: rdn along over 4f out and sn wknd* **66/1**

/02- **8** *32* **Mac Don (IRE)**[180] 5877 5-8-7 68.......................... KevinGhunowa(3) 5 —
(G J Smith) *chsd ldng pair: rdn along 4f out and sn wknd* **16/1**

2m 30.23s (2.23) **Going Correction** +0.075s/f (Slow)
WFA 4 from 5yo+ 1lb **8** Ran SP% **111.8**
Speed ratings (Par 101): **94,92,91,91,90 88,83,60**
toteswinger: 1&2 £1.40, 1&3 £1.90, 2&3 £8.10. CSF £5.90 TOTE £1.80: £1.20, £1.60, £1.60; EX 6.80 Trifecta £41.60 Pool: £367.88 - 6.53 winning units..Bridgewater Boys was claimed by Tom Pitt for £6,000.
Owner J E Abbey **Bred** Southill Stud **Trained** Pandy, Monmouths

FOCUS
An ordinary claimer. The pair that set helped set the early pace managed to hang in there and finish in the first four, which shows how modest the tempo was.
Friends Hope Official explanation: jockey said mare moved poorly throughout

806 FREEBETS.CO.UK GOLD CUP BETTING H'CAP 7f (F)
2:30 (2:30) (Class 5) (0-75,77) 4-Y-0+ **£2,729** (£806; £403) **Stalls** Low

Form RPR

-402 **1** **Autumn Blades (IRE)**[9] 730 4-9-4 **75**.......................... RobertWinston 8 85
(A Bailey) *hld up: smooth hdwy on outer 3f out: rdn to chal over 1f out: led ins fnl f and kpt on wl* **9/2**

-212 **2** *1/2* **Caprio (IRE)**[14] 680 4-9-3 **74**.......................... RichardKingscote 7 83
(Tom Dascombe) *trckd ldrs: swtchd lft and hdwy 2f out: led over 1f out: rdn and hung lft ent fnl f: sn hdd: rallied and ev ch tl edgd rt and no ex last 100yds* **11/4**[1]

2332 **3** *8* **Blue Charm**[20] 606 5-9-1 **72**.......................... TomEaves 4 61
(I W McInnes) *hld up: hdwy 2f out: sn rdn and kpt on ins fnl f: nvr a factor* **7/2**[2]

30-1 **4** *1/2* **Efisio Princess**[43] 305 6-8-13 **70**.......................... RichardThomas 9 58
(J E Long) *sn led: rdn along 2f out: drvn and hdd over 1f out sn wknd* **8/1**

0332 **5** *nse* **Kensington (IRE)**[19] 625 8-8-12 **74**.......................... (v) PatrickDonaghy(5) 2 61
(P D Evans) *cl up: rdn along end ev ch 2f out: sn drvn and wknd over 1f out* **7/1**

1114 **6** *34* **Singleb (IRE)**[12] 708 5-9-2 **73**.......................... (p) JamieSpencer 5 —
(Miss Gay Kelleway) *trckd ldrs: rdn along 3f out: sn btn and eased* **4/1**[3]

1m 28.59s (-1.71) **Going Correction** +0.075s/f (Slow) **6** Ran SP% **110.7**
Speed ratings (Par 103): **112,111,102,101,101 62**
toteswinger: 1&2 £11.70, 1&3 £1.90, 2&3 £4.70. CSF £16.71 CT £44.52 TOTE £4.30: £3.40, £1.60; EX 8.30 Trifecta £48.50 Pool: £388.07 - 5.92 winning units..
Owner John Stocker **Bred** Dr D Crone & P Lafarge & P Johnston **Trained** Newmarket, Suffolk

FOCUS
They seemed to go a fair gallop in this and the leaders may have done too much early. The first two home pulled a mile clear of the others.
Singleb(IRE) Official explanation: vet said gelding had been struck into behind

807 FREEBETS.CO.UK CHELTENHAM FESTIVAL BETTING H'CAP 1m (F)
3:05 (3:05) (Class 5) (0-75,74) 4-Y-0+ **£2,729** (£806; £403) **Stalls** Low

Form RPR

-111 **1** **Highly Regal (IRE)**[27] 512 4-8-10 **66**.......................... (b) LPKeniry 7 76+
(R A Teal) *hld up in tch: smooth hdwy over 2f out: led over 1f out: kpt on* **12/1**

0-20 **2** *1/2* **Flores Sea (USA)**[27] 519 5-9-2 **72**.......................... JamieSpencer 8 80
(T D Barron) *cl up: led 3f out: rdn 2f out: hdd over 1f out: drvn and kpt on ins fnl f* **11/4**[1]

-460 **3** *1 1/4* **Lord Theo**[10] 724 5-8-8 **64**.......................... LukeMorris 6 69
(N P Littmoden) *trckd ldrs: hdwy 2f out: sn rdn and kpt on ins fnl f: nrst fin* **6/1**[3]

400- **4** *1/2* **Penchesco (IRE)**[150] 6683 4-9-2 **72**.......................... PaulEddery 4 76
(Pat Eddery) *trckd ldrs: hdwy over 2f out: snr idden and ev ch tl drvn and one pce ent fnl f* **33/1**

00-4 **5** *3/4* **Jebel Tara**[20] 607 4-8-9 **65**.......................... (t) AndrewElliott 9 68
(A D Brown) *a.p: cl up on outer 3f out: effrt 2f out and ev ch tl rdn and edgd lft ent fnl f and one pce* **11/1**

3-32 **6** *3/4* **Barataria**[13] 683 7-8-6 **69**.......................... LanceBetts(7) 10 70
(R Bastiman) *s.i.s: hdwy and in tch 1/2-way: rdn along over 2f out and sn no imp* **11/4**[1]

3102 **7** *3 1/4* **Hilbre Court (USA)**[19] 618 4-8-12 **68**.......................... (p) GrahamGibbons 3 62
(B P J Baugh) *chsd ldrs: rdn along bef 1/2-way and sn outpcd* **5/1**[2]

-104 **8** *shd* **West End Lad**[19] 617 6-8-12 **68**.......................... (b) ChrisCatlin 2 61
(S R Bowring) *led: rdn along and hdd 3f out: sn drvn and wknd* **16/1**

2243 **9** *20* **Downhill Skier (IRE)**[13] 683 5-8-1 **64**.......................... PaulPickard(7) 1 13
(W M Brisbourne) *a outpcd in rr* **20/1**

640 **10** *11* **Dudley Docker (IRE)**[22] 576 7-9-4 **74**.......................... (b) LiamJones 5 —
(C R Dore) *s.i.s: a bhd* **18/1**

1m 42.6s (-1.10) **Going Correction** +0.075s/f (Slow) **10** Ran SP% **119.2**
Speed ratings (Par 103): **108,107,106,105,105 104,101,100,80,69**
toteswinger: 1&2 £11.10, 1&3 £15.50, 2&3 £5.30. CSF £46.14 CT £226.99 TOTE £15.90: £4.20, £1.20, £2.40; EX 68.00 TRIFECTA Not won..
Owner J Morton **Bred** Mervyn Stewkesbury **Trained** Ashtead, Surrey

FOCUS
An ordinary handicap, but they went a decent pace in this and the form looks solid for the grade.
Barataria Official explanation: jockey said gelding missed the break

808 FREEBETS.CO.UK OVER £1000 IN FREE BETS (S) STKS 1m (F)
3:45 (3:46) (Class 6) 3-Y-O **£2,047** (£604; £302) **Stalls** Low

Form RPR

-353 **1** **Swiss Art (IRE)**[13] 684 3-8-12 61.......................... ChrisCatlin 5 63
(R A Harris) *midfield: hdwy over 3f out: chsd ldrs whn n.m.r and swtchd rt over 1f out: sn led and rdn whn hung bdly lft ent fnl f: kpt on* **9/2**[3]

4-35 **2** *1* **Jonnie Skull (IRE)**[41] 332 3-8-12 62.......................... (vt[1]) JerryO'Dwyer 6 62+
(P S McEntee) *chsd ldrs: rdn along 3f out: hdwy on inner wl over 1f out: ch whn hmpd enteriong fnl f: swtchd rt and kpt on towards fin* **13/2**

45-0 **3** *3 1/4* **Amazing Blue Sky**[7] 759 3-9-4 65.......................... (b[1]) PaulMulrennan 11 60
(Mrs R A Carr) *cl up on outer: effrt and ev ch over 2f out: sn rdn and kpt on same pce* **6/1**

6-10 **4** *hd* **Cause For Applause (IRE)**[50] 228 3-8-13 56.......................... (v) TomEaves 8 54
(B Smart) *cl up: led after 1f: rdn along over 2f out: hung lft wl over 1f out: drvn: n.m.r and hdd appr fnl f: sn wknd* **14/1**

4120 **5** *6* **Hawkspring (IRE)**[5] 776 3-8-13 70.......................... (t) JamesO'Reilly(5) 3 46
(S Parr) *towards rr: rdn along over 2f out: sn no imp* **2/1**[1]

5250 **6** *1/2* **Turn To Dreams**[5] 776 3-8-7 59.......................... (v) RobertWinston 10 34
(P D Evans) *cl up: rdn along over 2f out: ev ch tl drvn and wknd over 1f out* **4/1**[2]

-640 **7** *10* **Thaumatology (USA)**[9] 736 3-8-7 50.......................... LiamJones 4 12
(S Parr) *a towards rr* **50/1**

0-40 **8** *3* **Esteem Dancer**[23] 572 3-8-12 50.......................... PatCosgrave 7 10
(J G Given) *a towards rr* **33/1**

000- **9** *12* **Al Mukaala (IRE)**[134] 7052 3-8-9 62.......................... RussellKennemore(3) 1 —
(B N Pollock) *led 1f: chsd ldrs on inner: rdn along 1/2-way and sn wknd* **25/1**

1m 44.11s (0.41) **Going Correction** +0.075s/f (Slow) **9** Ran SP% **114.5**
Speed ratings (Par 96): **100,99,95,95,89 89,79,76,64**
toteswinger: 1&2 £5.20, 1&3 £5.50, 2&3 £8.10. CSF £32.77 TOTE £5.10: £2.20, £1.50, £2.50; EX 36.90 Trifecta £402.10 Part won. Pool: £543.43 - 0.46 winning units..The winner was bought in for 4,750 guineas.
Owner W Clifford **Bred** John Yarr **Trained** Earlswood, Monmouths

■ Stewards' Enquiry : Chris Catlin three-day ban: careless riding (Mar 25-27); caution: used whip down shoulder in forehand position.
James O'Reilly £290 fine: used mobile phone outside the designated area

FOCUS
A poor seller in which the winning time was 1.51 seconds slower than the preceding handicap, and also something of a dramatic race.
Hawkspring(IRE) Official explanation: jockey said colt was denied a clear run

809 FREEBETS.CO.UK FREE BETS H'CAP 1m 6f (F)
4:25 (4:25) (Class 5) (0-75,73) 4-Y-0+ **£2,729** (£806; £403) **Stalls** Low

Form RPR

-102 **1** **Blockley (USA)**[13] 692 5-8-11 **59**.......................... JamieSpencer 4 68
(Ian Williams) *hld up in rr: hdwy on outer over 4f out: rdn to chal and carried hd highover 1f out: drvn to ld ent fnl f: edgd lft and kpt on* **7/4**[1]

4054 **2** *1/2* **Calculating (IRE)**[13] 692 5-8-9 **60**.......................... DavidProbert(3) 1 69
(M D I Usher) *trckd ldr: hdwy over 3f out: rdn 2f out: led wl over 1f out: drvn and hdd ent fnl f: kpt on* **4/1**[3]

-301 **3** *2 3/4* **Victory Quest (IRE)**[20] 604 9-9-11 **73**.......................... (v) RobertWinston 5 78
(Mrs S Lamyman) *hld up in tch: hdwy over 4f out: rdn along over 3f out: drvn and kpt on same pce fnl 2f* **7/2**[2]

/045 **4** *1/2* **Eforetta (GER)**[19] 623 7-8-2 **55**.......................... AmyBaker(5) 3 59
(A W Carroll) *trckd ldrs on inner: hdwy 3f out: rdn and ch 2f out: wknd appr fnl f* **11/2**

-000 **5** *2 1/4* **Spiritonthemount (USA)**[7] 751 4-8-4 **56**.......................... LiamJones 6 57
(P W Hiatt) *led: rdn along 3f out: drvn 2f out: hdd wl over 1f out and grad wknd* **16/1**

-026 **6** *21* **Top Tiger**[8] 745 5-8-10 **58**.......................... TonyHamilton 2 29
(D W Barker) *a in rr: outpcd fnl 4f* **10/1**

66/ **7** *13* **Dream Mountain**[551] 5204 6-8-6 **54** oh9.......................... JoeFanning 7 7
(Ms J S Doyle) *cl up: rdn along over 4f out: wknd over 3f out* **20/1**

3m 10.45s (2.15) **Going Correction** +0.075s/f (Slow)
WFA 4 from 5yo+ 4lb **7** Ran SP% **113.7**
Speed ratings (Par 103): **96,95,94,93,92 80,73**
toteswinger: 1&2 £2.40, 1&3 £2.10, 2&3 £2.80. CSF £8.88 TOTE £2.60: £1.90, £2.00; EX 7.00.

Owner Ian Williams **Bred** Payson Stud Inc **Trained** Portway, Worcs

FOCUS

An ordinary staying handicap in which the early pace was fairly steady.

Dream Mountain Official explanation: trainer said gelding was unsuited by the fibresand

810 FREEBETS.CO.UK WEEKEND FOORBALL FREE BETS MAIDEN STKS 6f (F)

5:05 (5:06) (Class 5) 3-Y-O+ **£2,729** (£806; £403) **Stalls** Low

Form RPR

3 **1** **Royal Crest**[33] 425 3-8-12 0 ShaneKelly 9 62+
(J A Osborne) *chsd ldrs: hdwy on outer over 2f out: rdn over 1f out: styd on to ld ins fnl f: kpt on* **1/1**[1]

/30- **2** ½ **Bonnet O'Bonnie**[364] 862 5-9-7 43 LPKeniry 3 55
(J Mackie) *led: rdn along wl over 2f out: drvn over 1f out: hdd ins fnl f: no ex last 100yds* **16/1**

3 1 **Azharia** 3-8-7 0 SaleemGolam 2 51+
(C E Brittain) *sn pushed along in rr: n.m.r bnd over 4f out: hdwy on inner 2f out: sn rdn and styd on ins fnl furlomg: nrst fin* **13/2**[3]

00 **4** 1 ¾ **Chantilly Jewel (USA)**[19] 626 4-9-7 0 RobertWinston 4 46
(R M H Cowell) *chsd ldrs: hdwy 2f out: sn rdn and kpt on same pce appr fnl f* **33/1**

00- **5** 5 **Northern Flyer (GER)**[142] 6858 3-8-12 0 GrahamGibbons 8 32
(J J Quinn) *cl up: rdn and ev ch over 2f out: wknd wl over 1f out* **8/1**

0 **6** ½ **The Last Alzao (IRE)**[7] 758 3-8-9 0 ow2 TonyHamilton 1 28
(R A Fahey) *green and sn outpcd in rr: swtchd to outer and rdn along 1/2-way: sme late hdwy* **40/1**

7 2 ¼ **Fancy Set (IRE)** 3-8-7 0 FrankieMcDonald 7 19
(D J S Ffrench Davis) *bmpd s: a towards rr* **28/1**

5- **8** 2 ¼ **Feudal (IRE)**[139] 6923 3-8-12 0 JoeFanning 5 17
(M Johnston) *wnt rt s and sn rdn along: a towards rr* **3/1**[2]

1m 17.34s (0.84) **Going Correction** +0.075s/f (Slow)
WFA 3 from 4yo+ 14lb **8 Ran SP% 114.2**
Speed ratings (Par 103): **97,96,95,92,86 85,82,79**
toteswinger: 1&2 £2.40, 1&3 £2.10, 2&3 £2.80. CSF £19.68 TOTE £1.90: £1.10, £3.30, £1.50; EX 17.50 Trifecta £90.00 Pool: £593.52 - 4.88 winning units..

Owner J A Osborne **Bred** Cheveley Park Stud Ltd **Trained** Upper Lambourn, Berks

FOCUS

This looked a very poor and uncompetitive maiden, especially with the runner-up rated just 43, and it's unlikely that many winners will come out of it.

811 FREEBETS.CO.UK MAN UTD V LIVERPOOL FREE BETS H'CAP 6f (F)

5:40 (5:41) (Class 6) (0-60,59) 4-Y-O+ **£2,047** (£604; £302) **Stalls** Low

Form RPR

406- **1** **Gracie's Gift (IRE)**[140] 6913 7-8-8 49 GrahamGibbons 8 59
(R C Guest) *chsd ldrs: hdwy on outer 2f out: rdn wl over 1f out: edgd lft ins fnl f: hrd drvn and styd on to ld last 100yds* **9/1**

530- **2** ½ **Princess Charlmane (IRE)**[99] 7528 6-8-6 47 (t) AndrewElliott 4 56
(C J Teague) *led: rdn along 2f out: drvn over 1f out: hdd ins fnl f: no ex towards fin* **50/1**

-003 **3** 1 ½ **Charlie Allnut**[8] 748 4-8-4 45 (b) JoeFanning 6 49
(S Wynne) *prom: effrt over 2f out: sn rdn and ev ch tl drvn and one pce ent fnl f* **9/2**[2]

3003 **4** ½ **Wiltshire (IRE)**[19] 619 7-9-1 56 JamieMoriarty 11 59
(P T Midgley) *midfield: rdn along over 2f out: styd on ins fnl f: nrst fin* **14/1**

4513 **5** ¾ **Cape Of Storms**[20] 607 6-9-3 58 TomEaves 7 58
(R Brotherton) *trckd ldrs: hdwy over 2f out: rdn wl over 1f out and kpt on same pce* **11/4**[1]

0-41 **6** ½ **Great Knight (IRE)**[14] 675 4-9-1 59 DavidProbert(3) 5 58
(S Kirk) *chsd ldrs: rdn along 2f out: drvn over 1f out and kpt on same pce* **5/1**[3]

0-64 **7** 7 **Briannsta (IRE)**[15] 661 7-8-5 46 (b) RichardThomas 12 24
(J E Long) *in rr: rdn along 1/2-way: sme late hdwy* **12/1**

65F- **8** ½ **Cheery Cat (USA)**[202] 5198 5-9-3 58 TonyHamilton 10 34
(D W Barker) *chsd ldrs on outer: rdn along wl over 2f out: sn wknd* **8/1**

4-05 **9** 2 **Billy Hot Rocks (IRE)**[36] 380 4-8-10 58 KylieManser(7) 1 28
(Miss Gay Kelleway) *a in rr* **40/1**

0532 **10** nse **Imperial Djay (IRE)**[14] 675 4-9-0 55 AdamKirby 9 25
(G J Smith) *sn rdn along and a towards rr* **9/1**

30-0 **11** 1 ¼ **Lytton**[14] 676 4-9-1 56 MickyFenton 13 22
(R Ford) *midfield: effrt on outer 1/2-way: sn rdn and nvr a factor* **25/1**

0006 **12** shd **Diminuto**[22] 575 5-8-0 48 SeanPalmer(7) 3 14
(M D I Usher) *s.i.s: a bhd* **33/1**

000- **13** 21 **Owed**[85] 7698 7-9-4 59 (tp) RobertWinston 2 —
(R Bastiman) *chsd ldrs on inner: rdn along 1/2-way: sn wknd* **28/1**

1m 16.34s (-0.16) **Going Correction** +0.075s/f (Slow) **13 Ran SP% 121.6**
Speed ratings (Par 101): **104,103,101,100,99 99,89,89,86,86 84,84,56**
toteswinger: 1&2 £51.80, 1&3 £8.10, 2&3 £76.40. CSF £415.63 CT £2296.80 TOTE £11.60: £3.40, £14.10, £2.10; EX 763.50 Place 6: £118.51, Place 5: £16.31.

Owner S Hussey **Bred** Richard O'Hara **Trained** Stainforth, S Yorks

FOCUS

A modest if competitive handicap and a race dominated by those that raced handily from the start. The winning time was exactly a second faster than the maiden.

Owed Official explanation: jockey said gelding had a breathing problem, possibly as a result of tongue strap coming adrift at start

T/Plt: £229.20 to a £1 stake. Pool: £49,528.12. 157.70 winning tickets. T/Qpdt: £25.50 to a £1 stake. Pool: £4,211.06. 121.80 winning tickets. JR

798 KEMPTON (A.W) (R-H)

Thursday, March 12

OFFICIAL GOING: Standard

Wind: fresh, across Weather: dry

812 FREEBETS.CO.UK FREE BETTING FOR CHELTENHAM CLASSIFIED STKS 5f (P)

6:50 (6:50) (Class 7) 3-Y-O+ **£1,706** (£503; £252) **Stalls** High

Form RPR

/564 **1** **Meikle Barfil**[10] 727 7-9-3 45 (tp) LukeMorris 11 53
(J M Bradley) *trckd ldrs: effrt to chal over 1f out: sn led: edgd rt but rdn clr fnl f* **7/2**[1]

-006 **2** 1 ¾ **Lady Hopeful (IRE)**[31] 474 7-9-3 42 (b) LPKeniry 10 47
(Peter Grayson) *s.i.s: clsd and in midfield 1/2-way: rdn and chsd ldrs over 1f out: kpt on to go 2nd nr fin: nt trble ldr* **25/1**

4456 **3** hd **Spanish Ace**[15] 676 8-9-0 44 (b) DavidProbert(3) 12 46
(J M Bradley) *pressed ldr tl led wl over 1f out: sn rdn: hdd jst over 1f out: one pce fnl f* **4/1**[2]

-403 **4** nk **Orange Square (IRE)**[9] 746 4-9-3 44 (v) TomEaves 8 45
(D W Barker) *wnt rt s: t.k.h: hld up wl in tch: plld out and effrt over 1f out: one pce fnl f* **11/2**[3]

6-30 **5** 1 ¾ **Rightcar Lewis**[56] 177 4-9-3 45 (b) AdamKirby 1 39
(Peter Grayson) *hld up wl bhd: sme hdwy fnl f: nvr nr ldrs* **20/1**

0-00 **6** 1 **Easy Wonder (GER)**[16] 661 4-9-3 44 (b[1]) JimCrowley 6 39+
(I A Wood) *rrd s: bhd: effrt u.p wl over 1f out: keeping on but nt looking a threat whn hmpd and snatched up 1f out: no ch after* **10/1**

60-4 **7** ½ **Young Ivanhoe**[23] 574 4-9-3 45 MartinDwyer 3 33
(C A Dwyer) *chsd ldrs tl wknd u.p over 1f out* **7/2**[1]

0060 **8** 1 ½ **Metropolitan Chief**[23] 575 5-9-3 45 (p) DaneO'Neill 9 28
(P Burgoyne) *bmpd s: sn rcvrd and led narrowly tl wl over 1f out: wknd over 1f out* **8/1**

-05 **9** 4 **Kitty Allen**[22] 583 3-7-13 45 ow2 (b[1]) PaulPickard(7) 2 15
(C N Kellett) *taken down early: chsd ldrs: rdn 1/2-way: wknd 2f out* **33/1**

0-00 **10** 6 **Thumberlina**[16] 664 3-7-13 45 (v) AmyBaker(5) 7 —
(Mrs C A Dunnett) *virtually ref to r: a wl bhd* **12/1**

60.96 secs (0.46) **Going Correction** -0.05s/f (Stan)
WFA 3 from 4yo+ 13lb **10 Ran SP% 119.3**
Speed ratings (Par 97): **94,91,90,90,87 86,85,82,76,66**
toteswinger: 1&2 £8.60, 1&3 £5.30, 2&3 £18.70. CSF £97.15 TOTE £5.00: £1.10, £8.10, £2.10; EX 48.30.

Owner J M Bradley **Bred** Mrs Henry Keswick **Trained** Sedbury, Gloucs

FOCUS

A very moderate sprint. As usual, those drawn high were at an advantage, with the first three home emerging from the top three boxes. The pace was predictably fast.

Rightcar Lewis Official explanation: jockey said filly hung right

Easy Wonder(GER) Official explanation: jockey said filly suffered interference in running

Thumberlina Official explanation: jockey said filly missed the break

813 FREEBETS.CO.UK SPECIAL FREE BETS H'CAP 1m 2f (P)

7:20 (7:22) (Class 6) (0-65,65) 4-Y-O+ **£1,942** (£578; £288; £144) **Stalls** High

Form RPR

4-50 **1** **Apotheosis**[23] 580 4-8-13 60 AdamKirby 12 71+
(W R Swinburn) *chsd ldrs: wnt 2nd 2f out: chal over 1f out: led jst ins fnl f: rdn clr: comf* **5/1**[3]

0-01 **2** 1 ¾ **Inch Lodge**[29] 507 7-9-2 63 MartinDwyer 11 70
(Miss D Mountain) *chsd ldr tl led after 1f: rdn and pressed over 1f out: hdd ins fnl f: nt pce of wnr* **9/2**[2]

00-4 **3** 3 ½ **Cape Of Luck (IRE)**[26] 546 6-8-8 55 TonyCulhane 3 56+
(P M Phelan) *t.k.h: hld up in rr: pushed along and hdwy over 2f out: chsd ldrs ldrs and rdn over 1f out: sn no imp and wl hld fnl f* **4/1**[1]

200/ **4** hd **Irish Stream (USA)**[163] 831 11-7-13 51 oh6 AmyBaker(5) 14 51
(B G Powell) *stdd s: hld up bhd: swtchd lft off rail wl over 1f out: styd on wl ins fnl f: nvr trbld ldrs* **33/1**

-604 **5** nk **Coral Shores**[42] 324 4-8-10 57 (v) LukeMorris 10 57
(P W Hiatt) *chsd ldrs: rdn over 2f out: outpcd by ldng pair over 1f out: kpt on same pce fnl f* **7/1**

4505 **6** ¾ **Inquisitress**[15] 674 5-8-1 51 oh5 (b) DavidProbert(3) 2 49
(J J Bridger) *hld up in rr: plld out and gd hdwy on outer over 2f out: chsd ldng pair and rdn over 1f out: wknd fnl f* **16/1**

-062 **7** ½ **Zabeel House**[21] 598 6-8-4 51 oh3 (p) FrankieMcDonald 13 49
(John A Harris) *hld up in tch in midfield: effrt wl over 1f out: wknd fnl f* **16/1**

60-4 **8** 1 ½ **Wrighty Almighty (IRE)**[26] 545 7-9-2 63 LPKeniry 8 58
(P R Chamings) *stdd after s: t.k.h: hld up in midfield: swtchd lft and rdn over 1f out: fnd nil and no hdwy* **12/1**

4-15 **9** hd **Onemoreandstay**[35] 406 4-9-4 65 AlanMunro 7 59
(M D Squance) *led for 1f: chsd ldr after tl 2f out: wknd qckly fnl f* **6/1**

5-20 **10** ½ **Kings Topic (USA)**[49] 253 9-9-3 64 (p) TPQueally 6 58
(A B Haynes) *sonn pushed along in midfield: rdn and no hdwy 2f out* **16/1**

-503 **11** 1 ½ **It's My Day (IRE)**[29] 507 4-9-4 65 (p) JimCrowley 9 56
(C Gordon) *hld up in midfield: pushed along 3f out: rdn and fnd nil 2f out: wl btn after* **7/1**

215- **12** 6 **Mayfair's Future**[80] 7761 4-9-1 62 DaneO'Neill 4 42
(J R Jenkins) *t.k.h: hld up in rr: rdn and lost tch over 2f out* **8/1**

-006 **13** 22 **Siena**[9] 748 4-7-13 51 oh6 (v) AndreaAtzeni(5) 5 —
(Mrs C A Dunnett) *t.k.h: chsd ldrs tl rdn and wknd qckly over 2f out: t.o* **50/1**

2m 7.20s (-0.80) **Going Correction** -0.05s/f (Stan) **13 Ran SP% 135.5**
Speed ratings (Par 101): **101,99,96,96,96 95,95,94,94,93 92,87,70**
toteswinger: 1&2 £5.00, 1&3 £8.80, 2&3 £8.70. CSF £31.90 CT £107.44 TOTE £7.30: £1.80, £2.60, £3.70; EX 36.50.

Owner The Converts **Bred** Evelyn Duchess Of Sutherland **Trained** Aldbury, Herts

FOCUS

A moderate contest. A race run on the inner course, and there was a bias towards those who raced handy from high stalls.

It's My Day(IRE) Official explanation: jockey said gelding hung left

814 FREEBETS.CO.UK FREE CASINO POKER CHIPS H'CAP 5f (P)

7:50 (7:51) (Class 4) (0-85,91) 3-Y-O **£4,548** (£1,362; £681; £340) **Stalls** High

Form RPR

-522 **1** **Lesley's Choice**[14] 685 3-9-2 80 FrankieMcDonald 2 84+
(R Curtis) *chsd ldr: rdn jst over 2f out: chal ent fnl f: led ins fnl f: sn in command: comf* **7/2**[3]

412- **2** 2 **Glamorous Spirit (IRE)**[88] 7673 3-9-9 87 ChrisCatlin 5 83
(R A Harris) *led and set str pce: rdn over 1f out: hdd ins fnl f: wl hld fnl 100yds* **6/4**[1]

3546 **3** 3 **Cecily**[14] 685 3-9-2 80 StephenDonohoe 3 65
(Sir Mark Prescott) *a in 3rd pl: rdn wl over 1f out: one pce and no imp after* **4/1**

60-4 **4** 2 ½ **Mazzola**[36] 396 3-9-1 79 TonyCulhane 7 55
(M R Channon) *stdd and bmpd sn after s: t.k.h: hld up in last: rdn wl over 1f out: no prog* **5/2**[2]

59.64 secs (-0.86) **Going Correction** -0.05s/f (Stan) **4 Ran SP% 110.8**
Speed ratings (Par 100): **104,100,96,92**
toteswinger: 1&2 £2.20 CSF £9.36 TOTE £3.80; EX 9.00.

Owner B C Allen **Bred** B C Allen **Trained** Lambourn, Berks

FOCUS
An uncompetitive sprint handicap. Despite the small field, the pace was strong, courtesy of the favourite.

815 FREEBETS.CO.UK FREE GAMES BINGO MONEY CONDITIONS STKS 1m (P)
8:20 (8:20) (Class 3) 4-Y-0+ **£7,352** (£2,201; £1,100) **Stalls** High

Form RPR
120- **1** **King Of Dixie (USA)**226 4506 5-9-0 107 JimCrowley 2 98+
(W J Knight) *t.k.h: chsd ldr after 1f: cruised upsides wl over 1f out: eased ahd 1f out: nt extended* **1/3**1
205- **2** *1* **Blythe Knight (IRE)**124 6498 9-9-3 108 GrahamGibbons 3 99+
(J J Quinn) *led: rdn and qcknd jst over 2f out: jnd wl over 1f out: hdd 1f out: no ch w wnr* **3/1**2
205- **3** *4 ½* **Elna Bright**285 2624 4-9-0 88 DaneO'Neill 4 86
(P D Evans) *t.k.h: chsd ldr for 1f out: rdn and outpcd over 1f out: wl hld fnl f* **8/1**3
1m 40.19s (0.39) **Going Correction** +0.025s/f (Slow) **3** Ran SP% **111.1**
Speed ratings (Par 107): **99,98,93**
CSF £1.81 TOTE £1.20; EX 1.90.
Owner Bluehills Racing Limited **Bred** Bee Zee LLC **Trained** Patching, W Sussex
FOCUS
All three runners were returning from time off and this looked more like a racecourse gallop than a genuine contest, but King Of Dixie still created a terrific impression.
NOTEBOOK
King Of Dixie(USA), back after almost eight months off, was a little keen early on, but he travelled well into the straight and did not have to be extended at any stage. This sizeable, good-looking Kingmambo colt was having just the eighth start of his career and looks every inch a serious Group horse. He is now 3-3 on Polytrack, and it will be no surprise if his connections look at options in the US this season, but he is equally effective on turf. He should have a big year and the Doncaster Mile is apparently now the plan. (op 1-2)
Blythe Knight(IRE), who took them along at just an ordinary early pace on his return from four months off, did not receive a single backhander with the whip from his jockey, before being eased inside the final 25 yards or so, with it clear from about two furlongs out he had no chance whatsoever with the mightily impressive winner. He is in the Lincoln. (op 9-4)
Elna Bright, debuting for a new yard on his first start since last May, had loads to find with the front two at the weights and was never out of last place. (op 10-1)

816 FREEBETS.CO.UK FREE BETS FOR EVERYONE H'CAP 1m 4f (P)
8:50 (8:51) (Class 6) (0-60,60) 4-Y-0+ **£1,942** (£578; £288; £144) **Stalls** Centre

Form RPR
-511 **1** **Prince Charlemagne (IRE)**26 546 6-9-3 57 GeorgeBaker 13 66
(G L Moore) *hld up in tch: hdwy 2f out: rdn to chal ent fnl f: led ins fnl f: drvn out* **5/2**1
0333 **2** *1 ½* **Sir Haydn**18 647 9-8-2 49 (v) DannyBrock(7) 11 56
(J R Jenkins) *sn led: clr over 8f out: pushed along over 2f out: kpt on wl tl hung lft and hdd ins fnl f: one pce* **25/1**
1303 **3** *½* **Imperium**21 597 8-9-6 60 JimCrowley 2 66
(Jean-Rene Auvray) *stdd and dropped in bhd after s: hld up in rr: stl travelling wl but plenty to do 2f out: 8th and hdwy ent fnl f: r.o to go 3rd nr fin: nt rch ldrs* **12/1**
-514 **4** *nk* **Tecktal (FR)**15 669 6-8-12 52 IanMongan 12 58
(P M Phelan) *hld up in rr: hdwy over 3f out: swtchd rt ent fnl 2f: chsd ldrs and drvn over 1f out: kpt on same pce fnl f* **10/1**
44-2 **5** *1 ¾* **Paddy Rielly (IRE)**9 745 4-9-3 59 (p) RobertWinston 14 62
(P D Evans) *in tch: rdn over 2f out: chsd ldrs and drvn 2f out: kpt on one pce after* **7/2**2
150- **6** *½* **Lough Beg (IRE)**146 6775 6-9-6 60 (t) DaneO'Neill 8 62
(Miss Tor Sturgis) *t.k.h: hld up towards rr: hdwy wl over 2f out: drvn and kpt on same pce fr over 1f out* **16/1**
06/1 **7** *hd* **Postage (USA)**18 647 6-8-3 48 AndreaAtzeni(5) 1 50
(K A Morgan) *t.k.h: chsd ldrs: wnt 2nd over 7f out: clsd on ldrs over 3f out: rdn and hung rt fr 2f out: btn ins fnl f: eased towards fin* **8/1**
30-0 **8** *1 ½* **Generous Lad (IRE)**8 751 6-9-3 57 (p) TPQueally 3 57
(A B Haynes) *in tch: rdn and effrt over 2f out: drvn and no imp 2f out: wknd fnl f* **16/1**
340- **9** *4 ½* **Good Effect (USA)**85 7702 5-9-3 57 SteveDrowne 9 50
(C P Morlock) *a bhd: rdn 3f out: nvr trbld ldrs* **16/1**
3-22 **10** *5* **Fantasy Ride**24 566 7-9-0 54 TGMcLaughlin 4 39
(J Pearce) *s.i.s: sn in tch in midfield on outer: rdn over 3f out: struggling over 2f out: sn wl btn* **12/1**
5-50 **11** *3 ½* **Rettorical Lad**10 732 4-8-13 55 RobertHavlin 6 35
(Jamie Poulton) *hld up towards rr: rdn over 3f out: wl bhd fnl 2f: eased ins fnl f* **50/1**
00-2 **12** *5* **Phoenix Hill (IRE)**21 601 7-8-9 49 ChrisCatlin 7 22
(D R Gandolfo) *t.k.h: chsd ldr tl over 7f out: wknd qckly over 3f out: wl bhd fr over 2f out: eased ins fnl f* **33/1**
1322 **U** **Carlton Scroop (FR)**20 627 6-9-4 58 (b) LukeMorris 5 —
(J Jay) *rrd and uns rdr s* **6/1**3
2m 34.4s (-0.10) **Going Correction** +0.025s/f (Slow)
WFA 4 from 5yo+ 2lb **13** Ran SP% **127.1**
Speed ratings (Par 101): **101,100,99,99,98 97,97,96,93,90 88,84,—**
toteswinger: 1&2 £3.30, 1&3 £11.10, 2&3 £14.20. CSF £79.24 CT £681.01 TOTE £3.50: £1.30, £10.60, £4.70; EX 77.00.
Owner A Grinter **Bred** Michael O'Mahony **Trained** Lower Beeding, W Sussex
FOCUS
A moderate handicap, weakened when Carlton Scroop unseated his rider after rearing up as the stalls opened. The pace seemed pretty good.
Rettorical Lad Official explanation: trainer said gelding had a breathing problem

817 FREEBETS.CO.UK GRAND NATIONAL FREE BETS H'CAP 1m (P)
9:20 (9:24) (Class 6) (0-60,60) 3-Y-0 **£1,942** (£578; £288; £144) **Stalls** High

Form RPR
00-1 **1** **Green Agenda**8 753 3-9-1 57 6ex JoeFanning 8 67+
(M Johnston) *chsd ldr after 2f: rdn to ld wl over 1f out: clr ins fnl f: tiring towards fin but a holding on* **1/1**1
0-26 **2** *½* **Miss Mojito (IRE)**16 667 3-9-3 59 ChrisCatlin 13 66
(J W Hills) *s.i.s: hld up in tch in midfield: hdwy over 2f out: chsd ldng pair over 1f out: wnt 2nd ins fnl f: r.o and clsng towards fin* **14/1**
000- **3** *½* **Dark Ranger**114 7372 3-8-5 47 LukeMorris 12 52
(T J Pitt) *t.k.h: hld up in tch in midfield: rdn and sltly outpcd over 1f out: rallied and styd on u.p fnl f: nt quite rch ldng pair* **33/1**
050- **4** *½* **Fyelehk (IRE)**201 5277 3-8-12 54 TGMcLaughlin 4 58
(B R Millman) *t.k.h: led tl over 6f out: trckd ldng pair after tl wnt 2nd over 1f out: kpt on same pce and lost 2 pls ins fnl f* **33/1**
0-66 **5** *4* **Paymaster In Chief**22 594 3-8-6 48 MartinDwyer 2 43
(M D I Usher) *chsd ldrs tl led over 6f out: rdn over 2f out: hdd wl over 1f out: wknd fnl f* **20/1**
665- **6** *2 ¾* **Persian Tomcat (IRE)**206 5159 3-8-3 50 AmyBaker(5) 9 39
(Miss J Feilden) *s.i.s: sn in tch in midfield: rdn and effrt jst over 2f out: no hdwy wl over 1f out* **50/1**
4-06 **7** *3 ½* **Maison D'Or**29 506 3-8-12 54 RobertHavlin 6 35
(R Ingram) *s.i.s: hld up in rr: rdn and effrt over 2f out: nvr on terms* **8/1**3
41 **8** *1 ½* **Foreign Investment (IRE)**20 626 3-8-13 60 PatrickDonaghy(5) 5 37+
(P D Evans) *dwlt: sn in tch in midfield: c v wd and rdn bnd 3f out: sn struggling and wl btn* **2/1**2
-433 **9** *shd* **Kamanja (UAE)**13 705 3-9-3 59 JimCrowley 1 36
(M J Attwater) *s.i.s: hld up in rr: n.m.r on inner over 2f out: sn swtchd rt and drvn: no prog and wl btn after* **16/1**
04-2 **10** *4 ½* **Litenup (IRE)**37 383 3-9-1 57 SteveDrowne 11 24
(A J Lidderdale) *in tch and niggled along early: rdn and lost pl wl over 2f out: wl bhd fnl 2f* **8/1**3
-036 **11** *nk* **Pedregal**8 753 3-8-4 46 FrankieMcDonald 3 12
(R A Fahey) *in tch on outer: hanging lft bnd over 3f out: rdn and lost tch wl over 2f out* **33/1**
-155 **12** *nk* **Thewaytosanjose (IRE)**10 741 3-9-0 56 LPKeniry 10 21
(S Kirk) *in tch in midfield: rdn and struggling over 2f out: sn bhd* **20/1**
1m 40.2s (0.40) **Going Correction** +0.025s/f (Slow) **12** Ran SP% **138.4**
Speed ratings (Par 96): **99,98,98,97,93 90,87,85,85,81 80,80**
toteswinger: 1&2 £5.30, 1&3 £32.30, 2&3 £38.30. CSF £21.26 CT £391.82 TOTE £2.70: £1.30, £3.80, £13.10; EX 31.80.
Owner The Green Dot Partnership **Bred** W And R Barnett Ltd **Trained** Middleham Moor, N Yorks
FOCUS
A moderate three-year-old handicap.
Maison D'Or Official explanation: jockey said gelding missed the break
Pedregal Official explanation: jockey said gelding hung badly left
T/Plt: £99.60 to a £1 stake. Pool: £90,216.02. 660.87 winning tickets. T/Qpdt: £43.30 to a £1 stake. Pool: £5,961.56. 101.80 winning tickets. SP

804 SOUTHWELL (L-H)
Thursday, March 12

OFFICIAL GOING: Standard
Wind: Strong behind Weather: Fine and dry

818 FREEBETS.CO.UK WORLD HURDLE FREE BETS H'CAP 5f (F)
2:30 (2:30) (Class 5) (0-70,69) 4-Y-0+ **£3,412** (£1,007; £504) **Stalls** High

Form RPR
3462 **1** **Colorus (IRE)**9 742 6-8-3 61 (p) PaulPickard(7) 2 74
(W J H Ratcliffe) *sn led: rdn over 1f out: kpt on wl fnl f* **9/4**1
-003 **2** *2 ¼* **Guto**9 742 6-8-5 61 KellyHarrison(5) 5 66
(W J H Ratcliffe) *cl up: rdn along 2f out: drvn over 1f out: kpt on u.p ins fnl f* **7/1**3
5143 **3** *nk* **Punching**25 561 5-9-4 69 LPKeniry 6 73
(C R Dore) *in tch: hdwy over 2f out: rdn over 1f out: kpt on u.p ins fnl f* **5/2**2
120- **4** *nk* **Russian Rocket (IRE)**144 6840 7-9-4 69 TGMcLaughlin 11 72
(Mrs C A Dunnett) *prom: rdn along over 2f out: drvn over 1f out: kpt on same pce* **28/1**
6021 **5** *2 ¾* **Fizzlephut (IRE)**15 681 7-8-10 61 (b) PaulFitzsimons 3 54
(Miss J R Tooth) *j. awkwardly: in tch on outer: rdn along over 2f out: sn edgd lft and wknd* **9/1**
400- **6** *½* **Weet A Surprise**144 6840 4-8-6 64 DavidKenny(7) 8 55+
(R Hollinshead) *s.i.s: a in rr* **16/1**
300- **7** *½* **The Bear**159 6486 6-9-2 67 PJMcDonald 7 56
(A G Foster) *a in rr* **9/1**
-400 **8** *nk* **Replicator**28 518 4-8-11 62 (v) PaulEddery 4 50
(Pat Eddery) *cl up: rdn along 1/2-way: sn wknd* **8/1**
57.67 secs (-2.03) **Going Correction** -0.325s/f (Stan) **8** Ran SP% **112.3**
Speed ratings (Par 103): **103,99,98,98,94 93,92,91**
toteswinger: 1&2 £2.90, 1&3 £1.90, 2&3 £4.60. CSF £17.84 CT £41.03 TOTE £3.00: £1.40, £1.70, £1.30; EX 8.70 Trifecta £33.10 Pool: £284.85 - 6.35 winning units..
Owner J Sheard & W J S Ratcliffe **Bred** M Ervine **Trained** Newmarket, Suffolk
■ Bill Ratcliffe's first winner since moving to Newmarket.
FOCUS
An ordinary sprint handicap weakened by three non-runners.

819 FREEBETS.CO.UK GOLD CUP FREE BETS CLAIMING STKS 6f (F)
3:05 (3:05) (Class 6) 3-Y-0 **£2,137** (£635; £317; £158) **Stalls** Low

Form RPR
2135 **1** **La Capriosa**5 784 3-8-7 66 RobertWinston 3 67
(A J McCabe) *mde all: rdn over 1f out: kpt on* **7/1**
01-4 **2** *1 ¼* **Denton Diva**25 562 3-8-7 66 DaleGibson 2 63
(M Dods) *chsd ldrs: hdwy over 2f out: rdn wl over 1f out: kpt on u.p ins fnl f* **12/1**
1121 **3** *nk* **Madison Belle**14 684 3-8-0 77 DeclanCannon(7) 6 62
(K R Burke) *chsd wnr: rdn along 2f out: drvn over 1f out: kpt on same pce ins fnl f: lost 2nd nr line* **9/4**2
5212 **4** *3* **My Sweet Georgia (IRE)**14 684 3-8-5 71 (v1) ChrisCatlin 8 50
(S A Callaghan) *towards rr and rdn along 1/2-way: drvn 2f out: kpt on appr fnl f: nvr nr ldrs* **2/1**1
16-0 **5** *¾* **Special Cuvee**14 685 3-9-6 75 RobertHavlin 4 63
(A B Haynes) *hmpd s and bhd: rdn along 1/2-way: nvr a factor* **9/1**
3-31 **6** *3 ½* **Gone Hunting**45 293 3-8-13 88 AndrewHeffernan(7) 7 52
(Peter Grayson) *v unruly and uns rdr en route to s: chsd ldrs: rdn along 1/2-way: sn wknd* **6/1**3
7 *14* **Naywye** 3-8-12 0 PaulMulrennan 1 —
(M W Easterby) *s.i.s: a bhd* **20/1**
1m 16.11s (-0.39) **Going Correction** +0.05s/f (Slow) **7** Ran SP% **113.3**
Speed ratings (Par 96): **104,102,101,97,96 92,73**
toteswinger: 1&2 £10.60, 1&3 £5.10, 2&3 £7.90. CSF £80.80 TOTE £9.90: £2.90, £7.00; EX 89.10 Trifecta £325.80 Part won. Pool: £440.39 - 0.46 winning units..
Owner Paul J Dixon **Bred** Slatch Farm Stud **Trained** Averham Park, Notts
■ Stewards' Enquiry : Andrew Heffernan one day ban: using whip above shoulder height (Mar 26)

FOCUS
A routine claimer, but the pace was solid. The front pair both had a bit to find at the weights, but being ridden positively proved much more important on this surface.

820 FREEBETS.CO.UK BET ON DENMAN MEDIAN AUCTION MAIDEN STKS 7f (F)
3:45 (3:46) (Class 5) 3-5-Y-0 £3,412 (£1,007; £504) Stalls Low

Form RPR
52-2 1 **Elisiario (IRE)**[50] 230 4-9-12 70 PatCosgrave 8 74
(J R Boyle) *trckd ldr: hdwy to ld over 2f out and sn pushed clr: rdn over 1f out and kpt on* **3/1**[2]
-352 2 2 1/4 **Jonnie Skull (IRE)**[1] 808 3-8-10 62 (vt) JerryO'Dwyer 3 62
(P S McEntee) *led: rdn along and hdd over 2f out: sn drvn and kpt on same pce* **10/3**[3]
3 3 3 **L'Arco Baleno (IRE)**[16] 664 3-8-5 0 ChrisCatlin 7 50
(S A Callaghan) *in tch and rdn along on outer 1/2-way: drvn 2f out: styd on u.p ins fnl f: n.d* **15/8**[1]
60- 4 nse **Got Flash (FR)**[197] 5404 3-8-10 0 RobertWinston 9 54
(E J O'Neill) *chsd ldng pair: rdn along over 2f out: drvn wl over 1f out: sn one pce* **16/1**
4 5 2 1/2 **Appelouse**[25] 564 4-9-7 0 PhillipMakin 6 49
(M Dods) *dwlt and towards rr: rdn along and sme hdwy 2f out: sn no imp* **7/2**
0- 6 6 **Contemplate**[184] 5784 3-8-5 0 DaleGibson 4 28
(Dr J D Scargill) *in tch: rdn along over 2f out: sn wknd* **66/1**
7 14 **Gamegear** 4-9-7 0 AmirQuinn 1 —
(S R Bowring) *dwlt: sn chsng ldrs: rdn along over 3f out and sn wknd* **50/1**
8 1 1/4 **Napoletano (ITY)** 3-8-10 0 GrahamGibbons 2 —
(R Johnson) *s.i.s: a bhd* **22/1**

1m 30.82s (0.52) **Going Correction** +0.05s/f (Slow)
WFA 3 from 4yo 16lb 8 Ran SP% 118.8
Speed ratings (Par 103): **99,96,93,92,90 83,67,65**
toteswinger: 1&2 £1.60, 1&3 £2.40, 2&3 £2.40. CSF £13.92 TOTE £3.50: £1.30, £2.30, £1.02; EX 11.00 Trifecta £129.80 Pool: £624.82 - 3.56 winning units..
Owner John Hopkins, J-P Lim & keith Marsden **Bred** Calley House Syndicate **Trained** Epsom, Surrey

FOCUS
A moderate maiden and another race where it was vital to race up with the pace as the front pair dominated throughout.

821 FREEBETS.CO.UK BET ON KAUTO STAR H'CAP 5f (F)
4:25 (4:25) (Class 3) (0-95,94) 4-Y-0+ £9,066 (£2,697; £1,348; £673) Stalls High

Form RPR
611- 1 **Arganil (USA)**[115] 7365 4-9-4 94 NCallan 7 108+
(K A Ryan) *mde all: rdn and qcknd clr over 1f out: edgd lft and kpt on wl fnl f* **10/3**[2]
000- 2 1 1/4 **Obe Gold**[157] 6532 7-8-4 80 (v) PaulQuinn 6 89
(D Nicholls) *hld up: hdwy 2f out: sn rdn and styd on ins fnl f: nrst fin* **16/1**
3-21 3 1 1/4 **Rebel Duke (IRE)**[65] 67 5-8-10 86 (p) TonyHamilton 4 90
(D W Barker) *t.k.h: stdd s: trckd ldrs: hdwy to chse wnr 2f out: rdn over 1f out and sn one pce* **6/4**[1]
-160 4 1 1/2 **Pawan (IRE)**[23] 579 9-8-11 92 (b) AnnStokell(5) 1 91
(Miss A Stokell) *cl up on outer: rdn along 2f out: wknd over 1f out* **9/1**
-410 5 1 1/2 **The Tatling (IRE)**[13] 714 12-8-12 88 RobertWinston 8 81
(J M Bradley) *dwlt: in tch: rdn along 2f out: sn btn* **6/1**
3023 6 3/4 **Canadian Danehill (IRE)**[27] 539 7-8-4 80 oh1 (p) ChrisCatlin 3 71
(R M H Cowell) *cl up: rdn along 1/2-way: sn wknd* **9/2**[3]

57.30 secs (-2.40) **Going Correction** -0.325s/f (Stan) course record 6 Ran SP% 111.4
Speed ratings (Par 107): **106,104,102,99,97 96**
toteswinger: 1&2 £5.50, 1&3 £2.30, 2&3 £5.50. CSF £47.39 CT £106.40 TOTE £2.60: £1.10, £6.30; EX 41.00 Trifecta £100.40 Pool: £439.95 - 3.24 winning units..
Owner The Big Moment **Bred** Colt Neck Stables, Llc **Trained** Hambleton, N Yorks

FOCUS
A decent handicap run at a strong pace and the winning time was 0.37 seconds faster than the opener.

NOTEBOOK
Arganil(USA) ◆, who was in cracking form on turf and Polytrack last autumn, was 7lb higher for this return to action and Fibresand debut and was very impressive. Not that well drawn, he overcame that with a fast break and gradually edged his way towards the centre of the track. Running his rivals ragged, he had the race won from some way out and looks set for a very decent year. (op 9-4)
Obe Gold, making his Fibresand debut after five months off, ran a blinder to chase the winner home, especially as he appeared to get outpaced at halfway before staying on again. (tchd 12-1)
Rebel Duke(IRE), 6lb higher than when successful over course and distance last time, had cheekpieces on for the first time and travelled well enough for a long way. He did his best, but could never get on terms with the winner and was held inside the last furlong. (op 2-1)
Pawan(IRE), a regular at this track, was drawn in stall one when beating Rebel Duke on his last visit in January and had the plum draw again, but in the winner he was up against a more progressive rival than he normally faces in races like this and was struggling from halfway.
The Tatling(IRE), two from three over course and distance this winter, found himself drawn against the stands' rail this time and could never get involved. (op 7-1 tchd 15-2)
Canadian Danehill(IRE), 1lb wrong and therefore 5lb above his last winning mark, emerged from the horse-walk minus his jockey and proceeded to bolt to the start. He was allowed to take part, but after breaking well he gradually lost his place and for the second time at this meeting there will be a group of punters feeling aggrieved.

822 FREEBETS.CO.UK CHELTENHAM GOLD CUP FREE BETS H'CAP 1m 4f (F)
5:05 (5:05) (Class 4) (0-85,83) 4-Y-0+ £5,322 (£1,571; £786) Stalls Low

Form RPR
0602 1 **Swiss Act**[8] 761 5-9-6 83 JoeFanning 5 95+
(M Johnston) *trckd ldr: led over 2f out: rdn clr over 1f out: kpt on* **1/1**[1]
-153 2 4 1/2 **Benedict Spirit (IRE)**[14] 687 4-8-2 74 ow3 AshleyMorgan(7) 2 76
(M H Tompkins) *trckd ldng pair: hdwy on inner over 2f out and sn rdn: drvn over 1f out: kpt on u.p ins fnl f: no ch w wnr* **11/2**[3]
21 3 3 **Supsonic**[9] 743 6-8-8 71 6ex RobertWinston 1 69
(R J Price) *led: rdn along over 3f out: drvn and hdd over 2f out: sn one pce* **11/4**[2]
160/ 4 3 1/2 **Raucous (GER)**[632] 2736 6-9-3 80 PaulMulrennan 4 73
(Mrs R A Carr) *hld up in rr: sme hdwy over 3f out: sn rdn along and nvr a factor* **8/1**
500- 5 5 **Navajo Joe (IRE)**[157] 6526 4-9-3 82 PJMcDonald 3 67
(R Johnson) *t.k.h: chsd ldrs: pushed along 5f out: sn rdn and wknd over 3f out* **20/1**

2m 41.65s (0.65) **Going Correction** +0.05s/f (Slow)
WFA 4 from 5yo+ 2lb 5 Ran SP% 107.9
Speed ratings (Par 105): **99,96,94,91,88**
toteswinger: 1&2 £4.40. CSF £6.62 TOTE £1.70: £1.20, £1.80; EX 5.20.
Owner Markus Graff **Bred** Highclere Stud Ltd **Trained** Middleham Moor, N Yorks

FOCUS
A fair handicap and they went a decent pace, with the result that the five runners finished well spread out.
Supsonic Official explanation: jockey said horse hung right

823 FREEBETS.CO.UK FREE BETS H'CAP 1m (F)
5:35 (5:35) (Class 6) (0-60,60) 4-Y-0+ £3,070 (£906; £453) Stalls Low

Form RPR
043- 1 **Provost**[79] 7779 5-9-3 59 PaulMulrennan 10 74
(M W Easterby) *in tch: smooth hdwy 3f out: effrt to chal wl over 1f out: sn rdn and kpt on to ld ins fnl f* **13/8**[1]
5-13 2 1 1/4 **King Of Legend (IRE)**[26] 554 5-9-2 58 GregFairley 8 70
(A G Foster) *trckd ldrs: hdwy to ld over 2f out and sn rdn: drvn over 1f out: hdd ins fnl f and kpt on same pce* **9/2**[3]
-112 3 2 3/4 **Safebreaker**[28] 513 4-9-3 59 (p) NCallan 9 65
(K A Ryan) *a.p: effrt on outer over 2f out: sn rdn and ev ch tl drvn and one pce ent fnl f* **11/4**[2]
05 4 4 1/2 **Singora Lady (IRE)**[25] 565 4-8-10 52 JamieMoriarty 6 48
(P T Midgley) *sn rdn along and outpcd in rr: bhd 1/2-way: hdwy u.p 2f out: styd on ins fnl f: nrst fin* **33/1**
0026 5 3/4 **Komreyev Star**[23] 578 7-8-8 50 DuranFentiman 7 44
(R E Peacock) *cl up: rdn along over 3f out: drvn over 2f out and grad wknd* **33/1**
5525 6 3/4 **Haroldini (IRE)**[13] 715 7-9-4 60 (b) RobertWinston 13 53
(J Balding) *midfield: hdwy over 2f out: sn rdn along and no imp* **11/2**
6030 7 4 **Run Free**[21] 607 5-9-0 56 LeeEnstone 4 40
(N Wilson) *led: rdn along over 3f out: hdd wl over 2f out and grad wknd* **22/1**
000- 8 1 1/2 **Newgate (UAE)**[8] 3839 5-8-9 51 PJMcDonald 12 32
(Mrs R A Carr) *chsd ldrs on outer: effrt 3f out: sn rdn and wknd 2f out* **33/1**
10-5 9 3 **Casino Night**[14] 688 4-8-13 60 RossAtkinson(5) 1 34
(R Johnson) *chsd ldrs: rdn along over 3f out: sn wknd* **50/1**
656- 10 hd **Sheriff's Silk**[100] 7533 5-9-2 58 (b) PaulEddery 3 32
(Paul Mason) *chsd ldrs: rdn along over 3f out: wknd 2f out* **33/1**
046- 11 1 1/4 **Billy Bowmore**[150] 6707 4-9-1 60 LeeVickers(3) 5 31
(P A Kirby) *dwlt: a in rr* **50/1**
0201 12 1/2 **Nautical**[23] 581 11-8-9 51 JerryO'Dwyer 14 21
(J R Holt) *midfield: lost pl and in rr fr 1/2-way* **33/1**
306- 13 22 **Wilmington**[259] 3402 5-8-10 52 TonyHamilton 11 —
(Mrs J C McGregor) *chsd ldrs to 1/2-way: sn wknd* **80/1**
0/00 14 5 **Maidanni (USA)**[19] 631 7-8-8 57 (bt[1]) AshleyMorgan(7) 2 —
(J R Gask) *s.i.s: a in rr* **50/1**

1m 43.01s (-0.69) **Going Correction** +0.05s/f (Slow) 14 Ran SP% 124.5
Speed ratings (Par 101): **105,103,101,96,95 95,91,89,86,86 85,84,62,57**
toteswinger: 1&2 £5.70, 1&3 £3.40, 2&3 £3.60. CSF £8.79 CT £20.59 TOTE £2.60: £1.70, £2.50, £1.40; EX 16.30 Trifecta £26.00 Pool: £286.87 - 8.15 winning units. Place 6: £80.75, Place 5: £62.40..
Owner A G Black **Bred** Charlie Wyatt **Trained** Sheriff Hutton, N Yorks

FOCUS
A modest handicap, but despite the size of the field not many got into it. The front three pulled right away and this is probably decent form for the grade.
T/Plt: £114.90 to a £1 stake. Pool: £52,649.15. 334.28 winning tickets. T/Qpdt: £5.00 to a £1 stake. Pool: £3,769.32. 555.40 winning tickets. JR

749 LINGFIELD (L-H)
Friday, March 13

OFFICIAL GOING: Standard
Wind: Modest, behind Weather: overcast

824 FREEBETS.CO.UK GOLD CUP FREE BETS MAIDEN STKS 1m 4f (P)
1:55 (1:56) (Class 5) 3-Y-O £2,729 (£806; £403) Stalls Low

Form RPR
044- 1 **Rupestrian**[118] 7343 3-9-3 74 JoeFanning 3 70+
(M Johnston) *mde all: jnd over 2f out: rdn 2f out: forged ahd ins fnl f: styd on wl and in command towards fin* **11/4**[2]
04 2 1 **El Bravo**[28] 529 3-9-3 0 GeorgeBaker 7 68+
(G L Moore) *stdd after s: t.k.h: hld up bhd: swtchd lft over 2f out: gd hdwy ent fnl f: chsd wnr fnl 100yds: no imp towards fin* **13/2**
00 3 1/2 **Milemilia (IRE)**[28] 529 3-8-12 0 TravisBlock 9 63
(H Morrison) *chsd wnr: upsides over 2f out: rdn jst over 2f out: stl ev ch tl no ex ins fnl f* **66/1**
30-4 4 1/2 **Mohanad (IRE)**[34] 440 3-9-3 77 TonyCulhane 4 67
(M R Channon) *chsd ldng trio: wnt 3rd 3f out: nt qckn and hung lft fr over 1f out: one pce fnl f* **3/1**[3]
056 5 1/2 **Suhailah**[14] 704 3-8-12 0 JimCrowley 2 61
(M J Attwater) *t.k.h: chsd ldng pair tl 3f out: styd handy: rdn over 1f out: kpt on same pce* **66/1**
20-4 6 3/4 **Sgt Roberts (IRE)**[9] 755 3-9-3 75 SimonWhitworth 6 65+
(J S Moore) *t.k.h: hld up towards rr: hdwy on outer 3f out: wd bnd 2f out: kpt on same pce fr over 1f out* **7/4**[1]
6 7 6 **Dalrymple (IRE)**[7] 776 3-9-3 0 ChrisCatlin 10 55
(J A Osborne) *stdd s: t.k.h: hld up in midfield: rdn and wknd over 1f out* **10/1**
0-3 8 3/4 **First Spirit**[20] 630 3-8-12 0 LPKeniry 5 49
(J S Moore) *s.i.s: hld up in last pair: struggling whn hmpd over 2f out: sn lost tch* **20/1**
9 23 **Wild Lyph** 3-9-3 0 TPQueally 1 17
(N P Mulholland) *stdd s: t.k.h: hld up in midfield: wknd qckly 2f out: last and wl btn whn swvd lft jst over 1f out: eased: t.o* **33/1**

2m 38.55s (5.55) **Going Correction** +0.025s/f (Slow) 9 Ran SP% 121.1
Speed ratings (Par 98): **82,81,81,80,80 79,75,75,60**
toteswinger: 1&2 £4.40, 1&3 £32.70, 2&3 £34.40. CSF £21.46 TOTE £3.80: £1.40, £1.90, £20.50; EX 20.40 Trifecta £212.70 Pool: £336.32 - 1.17 winning units..
Owner Sheikh Hamdan Bin Mohammed Al Maktoum **Bred** Darley **Trained** Middleham Moor, N Yorks
■ Stewards' Enquiry : George Baker two-day ban: careless riding (Mar 27-28)

FOCUS
The pace was steady and the bare form is ordinary.
Mohanad(IRE) Official explanation: jockey said colt hung left

825 FREEBETS.CO.UK CHELTENHAM FESTIVAL FREE BETS CLAIMING STKS 1m 2f (P)
2:30 (2:30) (Class 6) 4-Y-0+ **£2,047** (£604; £302) **Stalls** Low

Form RPR
6334 **1** **Rapid City**[14] 712 6-8-11 59 (p) RobertWinston 6 70
(A J McCabe) *s.i.s: hld up in rr: hdwy to trck ldrs over 2f out: wnt 2nd wl over 1f out: rdn to ld ins fnl f: r.o wl* **10/1**
-113 **2** *1* **Sabre Light**[24] 577 4-9-5 78 (v) JerryO'Dwyer 1 76
(J Pearce) *chsd ldng pair: hdwy on inner to ld 2f out: rdn over 1f out: hdd and unable qck ins fnl f* **4/5**[1]
63-1 **3** *6* **Mystic Art (IRE)**[23] 588 4-8-12 60 SteveDrowne 3 58
(C R Egerton) *in tch: hdwy 3f out: ev ch and rdn over 2f out: wknd ent fnl f* **9/2**[3]
0/ **4** *6* **Beat The Odds**[36] 5-8-5 0 (tp) FBranca 4 41
(F Sheridan) *sn chsng ldr tl led 4f out: rdn and hdd 2f out: wknd qckly over 1f out* **5/2**[2]
5 **5** *43* **Gold Rock (FR)**[11] 730 4-9-11 82 LukeMorris 5 —
(A W Carroll) *t.k.h: led tl 4f out: sn rdn: lost tch 2f out: eased fr over 1f out: t.o* **50/1**
550- **R** **Love Angel (USA)**[7] 3614 7-8-4 48 (b) MarcHalford(3) 2 —
(J J Bridger) *ref to r* **66/1**
2m 4.65s (-1.95) **Going Correction** +0.025s/f (Slow) **6** Ran SP% **114.9**
Speed ratings (Par 101): **108,107,102,97,63** —
toteswinger: 1&2 £1.70, 1&3 £1.70, 2&3 £2.00. CSF £19.34 TOTE £11.50: £4.40, £1.10; EX 15.80.Sabre Light was claimed by Claes Bjorling for £12,000.
Owner Mrs M J McCabe **Bred** Juddmonte Farms Ltd **Trained** Averham Park, Notts

FOCUS
A reasonable claimer, even if this bunch can't always be relied upon to run to form, and they went a sound gallop.

826 FREEBETS.CO.UK ONLINE FREE BETS H'CAP 7f (P)
3:05 (3:05) (Class 5) (0-70,70) 3-Y-0 **£2,900** (£856; £428) **Stalls** Low

Form RPR
0-32 **1** **Kiss A Prince**[37] 394 3-8-13 **65** JimCrowley 3 69+
(D K Ivory) *dwlt: sn in tch: hdwy on inner 2f out: sn chsng ldr: sustained chal fnl f to ld last stride* **11/2**[3]
2412 **2** *nse* **Imperial Skylight**[14] 705 3-8-7 **64** MCGeran(5) 1 68
(M R Channon) *led at stdy gallop: rdn and qcknd ent fnl 2f: r.o wl tl hdd last stride* **9/2**[2]
-144 **3** *1 1/4* **Romantic Queen**[23] 593 3-9-2 **68** JimmyFortune 7 69
(E A L Dunlop) *stdd s: hld up in rr: rdn and hdwy wl over 1f out: chsd ldng pair ins fnl f: styd but nvr gng to rch ldrs* **15/2**
0512 **4** *1 1/2* **Josiah Bartlett (IRE)**[14] 707 3-8-9 **61** ow1 (bt) SteveDrowne 5 58
(P S McEntee) *s.i.s: sn in tch in midfield: rdn and effrt jst over 2f out: chsd ldng pair over 1f out: no imp and one pce after* **4/1**[1]
343- **5** *1/2* **La Verte Rue (USA)**[81] 7767 3-8-13 **65** ChrisCatlin 2 61
(J A Osborne) *t.k.h: chsd ldr for 1f: settled in 4th pl after: rdn and unable qck jst over 2f out: hld fnl f* **11/2**[3]
4-43 **6** *3/4* **Joannadarc (USA)**[30] 503 3-8-11 **63** PatCosgrave 6 57
(S A Callaghan) *chsd ldr after 1f: rdn over 2f out: wknd u.p over 1f out* **7/1**
10-2 **7** *1/2* **Bold Ring**[9] 753 3-8-6 **58** EdwardCreighton 4 51
(E J Creighton) *hld up towards rr: hdwy on outer over 2f out: wd bnd 2f out: no prog after* **16/1**
0-44 **8** *8* **Hatman Jack (IRE)**[30] 498 3-9-3 **69** MichaelHills 9 42
(B G Powell) *broke wl: sn stdd and dropped in bhd: rdn and effrt on outer over 2f out: wd and lost pl bnd 2f out: wl btn after* **20/1**
500- **9** *3/4* **Best Bidder (USA)**[148] 6760 3-9-4 **70** JamieSpencer 8 41
(Patrick Morris) *stdd and dropped in bhd after s: t.k.h: lost tch 2f out: wl btn and eased ins fnl f* **8/1**
1m 27.6s (2.80) **Going Correction** +0.025s/f (Slow) **9** Ran SP% **115.0**
Speed ratings (Par 98): **85,84,83,81,81 80,79,70,69**
toteswinger: 1&2 £3.80, 1&3 £7.40, 2&3 £4.00. CSF £30.31 CT £187.34 TOTE £5.80: £1.10, £2.00, £3.10; EX 30.20 Trifecta £65.60 Pool: £337.16 - 3.80 winning units..
Owner A Pryer **Bred** Baroness, Magnusson, Myriade, Redmyre **Trained** Radlett, Herts

FOCUS
A modest 3yo handicap and form to treat with some caution, as the pace was steady for most of the way.
La Verte Rue(USA) Official explanation: trainer's rep said filly was struck into, lost a shoe and lost action

827 FREEBETS.CO.UK NEW ONLINE BETTING FORUM CLAIMING STKS 7f (P)
3:45 (3:45) (Class 6) 3-Y-0 **£2,047** (£604; £302) **Stalls** Low

Form RPR
3-41 **1** **Woolston Ferry (IRE)**[42] 345 3-9-6 80 MCGeran(5) 2 77+
(M R Channon) *hld up wl in tch: swtchd rt and rdn over 1f out: r.o wl fnl f to ld last strides* **8/11**[1]
0-35 **2** *hd* **Spinight (IRE)**[35] 426 3-8-4 63 (p) AndreaAtzeni(5) 6 61
(M Botti) *s.i.s: t.k.h: hld up wl in tch: hdwy to press ldrs on outer over 2f out: rdn over 1f out: led ins fnl f: r.o wl tl hdd last strides* **11/4**[2]
5035 **3** *1 3/4* **Elusive Ronnie (IRE)**[29] 510 3-8-7 60 (p) AlanMunro 3 54
(R A Teal) *led at stdy gallop: rdn and qcknd jst over 2f out: edgd rt over 1f out: hdd ins fnl f: no ex* **12/1**
5145 **4** *hd* **Cognac Boy (USA)**[19] 649 3-8-9 64 (p) TGMcLaughlin 7 55
(A B Haynes) *chsd ldr: rdn over 2f out: sn ev ch tl no ex u.p fnl 100yds* **11/2**[3]
660- **5** *1 1/4* **Rapanui Belle**[171] 6191 3-8-2 47 FrankieMcDonald 1 45
(G L Moore) *t.k.h: trckd ldrs: rdn and effrt wl over 1f out: unable qck ent fnl f: wknd fnl 100yds* **50/1**
05 **6** *nk* **Abu Dubai (IRE)**[9] 752 3-8-9 0 BMcHugh(7) 4 58
(C A Dwyer) *s.i.s: hld up wl in tch in last pl: rdn jst over 2f out: kpt on same pce and no imp* **20/1**
1m 27.66s (2.86) **Going Correction** +0.025s/f (Slow) **6** Ran SP% **114.4**
Speed ratings (Par 96): **84,83,81,81,80 79**
toteswinger: 1&2 £1.40, 1&3 £1.80, 2&3 £3.30. CSF £3.08 TOTE £1.90: £1.10, £1.40; EX 3.40.Woolston Ferry was claimed by David Pinder for £14,000.
Owner Capital **Bred** Tim Taylor **Trained** West Ilsley, Berks

FOCUS
A modest 3yo claimer run at an ordinary pace early on.

828 FREEBETS.CO.UK HORSERACING FREE BETS MAIDEN STKS 1m (P)
4:25 (4:26) (Class 5) 3-Y-0 **£2,729** (£806; £403) **Stalls** High

Form RPR
640- **1** **Dalradian (IRE)**[175] 6083 3-9-3 78 JimCrowley 8 75+
(W J Knight) *stdd s: t.k.h: hld up in rr: hdwy jst over 2f out: chsd ldng pair over 1f out: qcknd and str run to ld fnl 100yds: readily* **3/1**[2]
420- **2** *3/4* **Park Lane**[162] 6426 3-9-3 80 JamieSpencer 3 70+
(B W Hills) *stdd s: t.k.h and sn chsng ldrs: wnt 2nd over 2f out: rdn to ld over 1f out: hung lft 1f out: hdd and nt pce of wnr fnl 100yds* **1/2**[1]
0 **3** *3 1/2* **Mystic Touch**[41] 356 3-9-3 0 AlanMunro 1 60
(Miss E C Lavelle) *led at stdy gallop: rdn and qcknd over 2f out: hdd over 1f out: no ch w ldng pair after* **8/1**[3]
60 **4** *3 3/4* **Benozzo Gozzoli**[45] 306 3-9-3 0 TravisBlock 7 51
(H Morrison) *chsd ldr tl over 2f out: rdn and wd bnd 2f out: wknd jst over 1f out* **50/1**
5 *hd* **Michael Laskey** 3-9-3 0 TGMcLaughlin 5 50
(B R Millman) *stdd s: hld up in rr: rdn and sme hdwy jst over 1f out: styd on fnl f: nvr nr ldrs* **33/1**
6 *1/2* **Westlin' Winds (IRE)** 3-9-3 0 SteveDrowne 2 49
(C R Egerton) *in tch: rdn and outpcd ent fnl 2f: no ch w ldrs fr over 1f out* **14/1**
0- **7** *1/2* **Pursuit Of Purpose**[175] 6076 3-8-12 0 FergusSweeney 9 43
(G L Moore) *stdd after s: hld up towards rr: rdn and struggling jst over 2f out: wl btn over 1f out* **25/1**
000- **8** *2 3/4* **Red Dagger (IRE)**[114] 7388 3-8-12 40 AmyBaker(5) 6 41
(T D McCarthy) *in tch on outer: rdn and wknd jst over 2f out* **66/1**
0- **9** *5* **Topcroft**[177] 6031 3-9-3 0 VinceSlattery 4 29
(Mrs C A Dunnett) *in tch in midfield: rdn and struggling over 2f out: sn bhd* **66/1**
1m 41.18s (2.98) **Going Correction** +0.025s/f (Slow) **9** Ran SP% **121.2**
Speed ratings (Par 98): **86,85,81,78,77 77,76,74,69**
toteswinger: 1&2 £1.20, 1&3 £2.00, 2&3 £2.40. CSF £5.00 TOTE £4.40: £1.30, £1.02, £1.90; EX 6.50 Trifecta £20.10 Pool: £280.80 - 10.35 winning units..
Owner Canisbay Bloodstock **Bred** Hesmonds Stud Ltd **Trained** Patching, W Sussex

FOCUS
This maiden lacked strength in depth.

829 FREEBETS.CO.UK RACING FREE BETS H'CAP 1m (P)
5:05 (5:05) (Class 5) (0-75,74) 3-Y-0 **£2,752** (£818; £409; £204) **Stalls** High

Form RPR
05-1 **1** **Bickersten**[37] 394 3-8-10 **66** TonyCulhane 7 73
(M R Channon) *mde all: rdn and wnt 2 l clr 2f out: drvn and styd on wl fnl f* **10/1**
402- **2** *1 3/4* **Barbarian**[130] 7170 3-8-12 **68** MichaelHills 5 71+
(B W Hills) *hld up in last trio: hdwy on outer over 2f out: wd bnd 2f out: kpt on u.p to go 2nd fnl 100yds: nvr nr wnr* **10/3**[2]
4642 **3** *3/4* **Duke Of Normandy (IRE)**[9] 759 3-8-8 **64** JoeFanning 6 66
(M Johnston) *t.k.h: chsd wnr after 1f: rdn and unable qck 2f out: drvn and no imp over 1f out: lost 2nd fnl 100yds* **4/1**[3]
0-14 **4** *1 1/4* **Millway Beach (IRE)**[23] 586 3-8-13 **69** PaulEddery 4 68
(Pat Eddery) *chsd wnr for 1f: chsd ldrs after: rdn over 2f out: uanble to qckn wl over 1f out: wknd fnl f* **5/1**
5-30 **5** *3 1/2* **Rio Royale (IRE)**[16] 672 3-9-4 **74** JimCrowley 1 65
(Mrs A J Perrett) *chsd ldr: rdn and unable qck 2f out: drvn over 1f out: wknd qckly ent fnl f* **13/2**
62-1 **6** *nse* **Princess Zohra**[25] 572 3-8-10 **66** JamieSpencer 3 57
(E A L Dunlop) *rring in stalls: awkward leaving stalls and slowly away: hld up in last pair: rdn 2f out: no hdwy* **3/1**[1]
-030 **7** *1 3/4* **Commandingpresence (USA)**[23] 586 3-8-10 **66** EdwardCreighton 2 53
(Ms J S Doyle) *stdd s: plld hrd and hld up in last pl: n.d* **20/1**
1m 38.79s (0.59) **Going Correction** +0.025s/f (Slow) **7** Ran SP% **111.9**
Speed ratings (Par 98): **98,96,95,94,90 90,88**
toteswinger: 1&2 £3.90, 1&3 £6.70, 2&3 £2.90. CSF £41.35 TOTE £12.60: £4.00, £1.90; EX 41.30.
Owner Whitwell Racing **Bred** C J M Partnership **Trained** West Ilsley, Berks

FOCUS
A fair 3yo handicap.
Princess Zohra Official explanation: trainer said filly was unsuited by the increase in trip

830 FREEBETS.CO.UK FOR FOOTBALL BETTING FILLIES' H'CAP 1m (P)
5:40 (5:41) (Class 5) (0-70,70) 4-Y-0+ **£2,752** (£818; £409; £204) **Stalls** High

Form RPR
-052 **1** **Melt (IRE)**[17] 661 4-8-4 **56** oh1 (b) SimonWhitworth 6 63
(R Hannon) *in tch in midfield: rdn and effrt 2f out: str chal jst ins fnl f: led last stride* **11/2**
3124 **2** *shd* **Moon Crystal**[11] 738 4-9-4 **70** (t) JimCrowley 8 76
(E A L Dunlop) *t.k.h: chsd ldr: rdn jst over 2f out: chal over 1f out: led 1f out: edgd lft towards fin and hdd last stride* **7/2**[2]
2434 **3** *1 1/4* **Bold Diva**[9] 749 4-8-4 **56** oh2 (v) LiamJones 7 59
(A W Carroll) *hld up in last trio: rdn and effrt on outer 2f out: r.o ins fnl f to snatch 3rd last stride: nt rch ldng pair* **9/1**
500 **4** *shd* **Too Grand**[37] 395 4-8-1 **56** oh3 DavidProbert(3) 5 59
(J J Bridger) *chsd ldrs: rdn and unable qck 2f out: kpt on again ins fnl f: wnt 4th last stride* **14/1**
- **5** *shd* **Becuille (IRE)**[142] 6918 4-8-11 **63** MartinDwyer 2 66
(B J Meehan) *led: rdn 2f out: sn hrd pressed: hdd 1f out: 3rd and btn whn short of room and eased and lost 2 pls last stride* **4/1**[3]
3051 **6** *1/2* **Bavarica**[19] 651 7-8-9 **68** TobyAtkinson(7) 4 70
(Miss J Feilden) *stdd after s: hld up in rr: effrt on inner 2f out: rdn over 1f out: no imp fnl f* **13/2**
1-41 **7** *1 1/4* **Smokey Rye**[14] 706 4-9-0 **66** TolleyDean 1 65
(George Baker) *t.k.h: hld up in tch in rr: swishing tail: rdn and nt qckn 2f out: kpt on same pce fnl f* **3/1**[1]
660- **8** *1 1/2* **Little Knickers**[75] 7803 4-8-7 **59** (b) EdwardCreighton 3 55
(E J Creighton) *t.k.h: hld up in midfield: rdn and unable qck 2f out: bhd fnl f* **20/1**
1m 41.16s (2.96) **Going Correction** +0.025s/f (Slow) **8** Ran SP% **117.4**
Speed ratings (Par 100): **86,85,84,84,84 83,82,81**
toteswinger: 1&2 £3.50, 1&3 £6.20, 2&3 £5.30. CSF £25.81 CT £154.22 TOTE £7.10: £2.60, £1.60, £2.20; EX 27.30 Trifecta £382.00 Part won. Pool: £516.27 - 0.71 winning Place 6: £36.11, Place 5: £11.72..
Owner J T Brown **Bred** London Thoroughbred Services Ltd **Trained** East Everleigh, Wilts

FOCUS
A modest fillies' handicap.

Becuille(IRE) Official explanation: jockey said filly was denied a clear run
Smokey Rye Official explanation: trainer said filly runs best when fresh
T/Plt: £61.10 to a £1 stake. Pool: £45,091.12. 537.95 winning tickets. T/Qpdt: £12.90 to a £1 stake. Pool: £3,333.13. 190.38 winning tickets. SP

781 WOLVERHAMPTON (A.W) (L-H)

Friday, March 13

OFFICIAL GOING: Standard
Wind: Light, half behind Weather: Fine

831 FREEBETS.CO.UK FRIDAY NIGHT FREE BETS H'CAP 5f 216y(P)

6:50 (6:51) (Class 6) (0-60,60) 3-Y-O **£2,217** (£654; £327) **Stalls** Low

Form RPR
030- **1** **Baby Josr**[141] 6924 3-8-13 **55** ....(t) TonyHamilton 8 60
(I A Wood) *in rr: stl last 2f out: rdn and hdwy over 2f out: r.o to ld last stride* **16/1**
30 **2** *shd* **Villaruz (IRE)**[18] 655 3-9-1 **57** .... RobertWinston 3 62
(D Flood) *s.i.s: sn rcvrd: led after 1f: led wl over 1f out: rdn fnl f: hdd last stride* **10/1**
-134 **3** *hd* **Private Passion (IRE)**[9] 753 3-8-11 **53** .... MickyFenton 13 57+
(Pat Eddery) *chsd ldrs: rdn over 1f out: r.o ins fnl f* **7/2**[2]
3-52 **4** *1 ½* **Rocket Ruby**[37] 390 3-8-10 **52** .... DaneO'Neill 6 52
(D Shaw) *hld up in tch: lost pl over 2f out: c v wd st: rdn over 1f out: kpt on fnl f* **5/1**[3]
400- **5** *½* **Dalepak Flyer (IRE)**[237] 4185 3-9-1 **60** .... RussellKennemore(3) 11 58
(Paul Mason) *hld up towards rr: rdn and hdwy over 1f out: kpt on ins fnl f* **18/1**
0-44 **6** *½* **Perfect Honour (IRE)**[21] 626 3-8-8 **50** .... PaulHanagan 7 47
(D Shaw) *w ldrs: led over 3f out tl wl over 1f out: sn rdn: fdd wl ins fnl f* **12/1**
0-23 **7** *2 ¼* **Elsie Jo (IRE)**[17] 667 3-8-12 **54** .... NickyMackay 4 44
(M Wigham) *hld up in tch: rdn over 1f out: wknd wl ins fnl f* **11/4**[1]
014- **8** *¾* **Monte Mayor Eagle**[101] 7531 3-8-13 **55** ....(b) AdamKirby 5 43
(D Haydn Jones) *s.i.s: hld up towards rr: hdwy on ins 2f out: nt clre run over 1f out: squeezed through ins fnl f: nvr trbld ldrs* **11/1**
2601 **9** *½* **Valdemar**[23] 583 3-8-4 **51** ....(p) DeanHeslop(5) 10 37
(A D Brown) *led 1f: w ldrs: rdn and wknd over 1f out* **12/1**
2553 **10** *3 ¾* **Weet In Nerja**[11] 736 3-9-2 **58** ....(v[1]) GrahamGibbons 1 33
(R Hollinshead) *s.i.s: rdn wl over 1f out: a in rr* **8/1**
00-5 **11** *1 ¾* **Missed Mondays**[21] 626 3-8-4 **51** ow1 .... WilliamCarson(5) 2 21+
(Patrick Morris) *hld up in tch: rdn over 1f out: one pce whn bdly hmpd on ins ins fnl f* **14/1**
400- **12** *10* **Twos And Eights (IRE)**[177] 6017 3-8-10 **59** .... MatthewDavies(7) 9 —
(Paul Mason) *w ldrs tl wknd over 2f out* **50/1**

1m 15.27s (0.27) **Going Correction** 0.0s/f (Stan) **12** Ran SP% **129.2**
Speed ratings (Par 96): **98,97,97,95,94 94,91,90,89,84 82,68**
toteswinger: 1&2 £18.20, 1&3 £24.20, 2&3 £7.50. CSF £181.74 CT £716.08 TOTE £25.00: £7.40, £3.30, £1.60; EX 239.70.
Owner C R Lambourne **Bred** Mrs F A Veasey **Trained** Upper Lambourn, Berks

FOCUS
A couple of unexposed sorts but a moderate race in which the market leader disappointed. The pace was sound and the winner raced centre to far side in the straight.

832 FREEBETS.CO.UK FREE BETS FOR MAN UTD V LIVERPOOL H'CAP 5f 20y(P)

7:20 (7:22) (Class 6) (0-60,60) 4-Y-O+ **£2,217** (£654; £327) **Stalls** Low

Form RPR
0166 **1** **Tyrannosaurus Rex (IRE)**[18] 654 5-9-4 **60** .... PaulHanagan 13 70
(D Shaw) *swtchd lft sn after s: hld up in rr: hdwy over 1f out: rdn to ld wl ins fnl f: r.o wl* **17/2**
5553 **2** *1 ¼* **Green Lagonda (AUS)**[16] 681 7-8-13 **55** .... MickyFenton 4 61
(Stef Liddiard) *hld up in rr: hdwy on ins wl over 1f out: ev ch ins fnl f: nt qckn: jst hld on for 2nd* **6/1**[3]
1335 **3** *hd* **Muktasb (USA)**[16] 681 8-9-4 **60** ....(v) AdamKirby 11 65
(D Shaw) *s.i.s: sn swtchd lft: in rr: gd hdwy fnl f: jst failed to take 2nd* **15/2**
6210 **4** *1 ¼* **Welsh Opera**[14] 710 4-8-12 **59** ....(v) WilliamCarson(5) 9 59
(S C Williams) *wnt lft s: chsd ldrs: rdn over 1f out: nt qckn wl ins fnl f* **7/1**
0506 **5** *½* **Dodaa (USA)**[14] 710 6-8-8 **55** .... DeanHeslop(5) 12 53+
(N Wilson) *sn led: rdn and hdd wl ins fnl f: no ex* **10/1**
3105 **6** *2 ¼* **Hurricane Coast**[16] 682 10-8-8 **57** ....(b) ThomasBubb(7) 7 47
(D Flood) *s.i.s and hmpd s: outpcd: swtchd lft ins fnl f: nvr nrr* **25/1**
450- **7** *hd* **Richardthesecond (IRE)**[263] 3332 4-9-1 **57** .... GrahamGibbons 1 47
(W M Brisbourne) *led early: chsd ldr: wknd ins fnl f* **10/1**
2106 **8** *2 ¼* **Monte Major (IRE)**[16] 681 8-9-4 **60** ....(v) LukeMorris 6 42
(D Shaw) *t.k.h in mid-div: rdn wl over 1f out: sn wknd* **5/1**[1]
22-5 **9** *hd* **Bollin Franny**[67] 46 5-8-10 **52** .... RichardThomas 5 33
(J E Long) *chsd ldrs: rdn over 1f out: wknd fnl f* **12/1**
0401 **10** *½* **Teen Ager (FR)**[19] 645 5-9-3 **59** .... RobertWinston 3 38
(P Burgoyne) *t.k.h early in mid-div: wknd fnl f* **11/2**[2]
60 **11** *¾* **Magic Glade**[19] 645 10-8-10 **52** ....(b) LPKeniry 2 28
(Peter Grayson) *mid-div: hdwy on ins wl over 1f out: sn rdn: wknd ins fnl f* **14/1**
15-4 **12** *nse* **Ask Jenny (IRE)**[23] 582 7-9-2 **58** .... AndrewElliott 10 34
(Patrick Morris) *mid-div: c wd st: wknd wl over 1f out* **10/1**
00-0 **13** *7* **Mandelieu (IRE)**[29] 518 4-9-4 **60** ....(b) TonyHamilton 8 11
(Ollie Pears) *carried lft and bmpd s: plld hrd in mid-div: dropped to rr whn rdn wl over 1f out* **33/1**

61.78 secs (-0.52) **Going Correction** 0.0s/f (Stan) **13** Ran SP% **129.5**
Speed ratings (Par 101): **104,102,101,99,98 95,94,91,91,90 89,88,77**
toteswinger: 1&2 £18.40, 1&3 £9.20, 2&3 £8.80. CSF £63.98 CT £430.60 TOTE £15.20: £3.10, £2.60, £3.70; EX 83.10.
Owner Market Avenue Racing Club Ltd **Bred** Limestone And Tara Studs **Trained** Danethorpe, Notts

FOCUS
A moderate handicap featuring exposed sorts and one in which the strong pace set things up for the hold up horses. The winner raced centre to far side in the straight.
Teen Ager(FR) Official explanation: jockey said gelding ran too freely

Mandelieu(IRE) Official explanation: jockey said gelding ran too freely

833 FREEBETS.CO.UK FREE POKER, CASINO & BINGO MEDIAN AUCTION MAIDEN STKS 1m 141y(P)

7:50 (7:51) (Class 6) 3-4-Y-O **£2,217** (£654; £327) **Stalls** Low

Form RPR
2 **1** **Sullenberger (IRE)**[15] 695 3-8-6 0 .... ChrisCatlin 6 70+
(J A Osborne) *chsd ldr over 6f out: carried hd high and led jst over 1f out: edgd lft ins fnl f: r.o* **4/1**[3]
2 **2** *shd* **Calling Victory (FR)**[18] 658 3-8-1 0 .... NickyMackay 5 64+
(M Botti) *sn led: edgd rt and hdd jst over 1f out: edgd lft ins fnl f: r.o* **1/1**[1]
5- **3** *5* **Gulf President**[245] 3926 3-8-6 0 .... SamHitchcott 7 54
(M R Channon) *pushed along over 6f out: hdwy over 5f out: one pce fnl 2f* **5/2**[2]
665- **4** *1 ¼* **Topflightrebellion**[212] 4964 4-9-7 **46** .... GrahamGibbons 1 52
(Mrs G S Rees) *t.k.h: led early: prom tl rdn and lost pl over 3f out: n.d after* **16/1**
60-0 **5** *½* **Piccolo Express**[14] 716 3-8-6 **45** .... AndrewElliott 2 50
(B P J Baugh) *plld hrd: prom tl wknd over 3f out* **50/1**
6 *3 ½* **One Scoop Or Two** 3-8-6 0 ....(t) FBranca 3 42
(F Sheridan) *stdd s: hld up in rr: short-lived effrt on outside over 2f out* **11/1**

1m 51.24s (0.74) **Going Correction** 0.0s/f (Stan)
WFA 3 from 4yo 20lb **6** Ran SP% **114.7**
Speed ratings (Par 101): **96,95,91,90,89 86**
toteswinger: 1&2 £1.20, 1&3 £1.10, 2&3 £1.02. CSF £8.73 TOTE £4.50: £3.20, £1.20; EX 6.60.
Owner J A Osborne **Bred** Highfort Stud **Trained** Upper Lambourn, Berks

FOCUS
Not a competitive maiden and one in which the gallop was on the steady side. Winner and second raced centre to far side in the straight.

834 FREEBETS.CO.UK BOOKMAKER FREE BETS H'CAP 1m 141y(P)

8:20 (8:20) (Class 3) (0-90,88) 4-Y-O **£9,462** (£2,832; £1,416; £708; £352) **Stalls** Low

Form RPR
-343 **1** **Faithful Ruler (USA)**[14] 713 5-8-4 **74** oh2 .... PaulHanagan 4 83
(R A Fahey) *hld up in tch: led over 1f out: drvn out* **8/1**
136- **2** *1 ¾* **Rainbow Mirage (IRE)**[148] 6763 5-9-3 **87** .... GrahamGibbons 1 92
(E S McMahon) *chsd ldr 2f: a.p: hrd rdn and r.o to take 2nd ins fnl f: nt trble wnr* **9/2**[3]
112 **3** *1* **Tous Les Deux**[7] 778 6-8-10 **80** .... JamieSpencer 3 83
(G L Moore) *stdd s: hld up in rr: c v wd st: rdn and r.o to take 3rd cl home* **10/11**[1]
3025 **4** *½* **Just Bond (IRE)**[34] 453 7-8-9 **79** ....(v[1]) PJMcDonald 8 81
(G R Oldroyd) *t.k.h in rr: hdwy over 3f out: rdn 2f out: one pce fnl f: lost 3rd cl home* **16/1**
4323 **5** *½* **Tourist**[8] 766 4-8-10 **80** .... LukeMorris 7 81
(D Shaw) *stdd s: hld up: rdn wl over 1f out: nvr able to chal* **7/2**[2]
1530 **6** *1 ½* **Cornus**[7] 780 7-8-6 **76** ....(be) RobertWinston 2 74
(A J McCabe) *hld up: rdn wl over 1f out: n.d* **33/1**
11 **7** *nk* **Ravi River (IRE)**[16] 671 5-8-12 **82** .... RichardKingscote 6 79
(Tom Dascombe) *led: hdd 3f out: rdn wl over 1f out: wknd ins fnl f* **7/1**
400- **8** *nk* **Scartozz**[104] 7496 7-9-4 **88** ....(b) JerryO'Dwyer 5 84
(M Botti) *prom: reminders sn after s: jnd ldr over 6f out: led 3f out: rdn and hdd over 1f out: wknd ins fnl f* **9/1**

1m 48.89s (-1.61) **Going Correction** 0.0s/f (Stan) **8** Ran SP% **135.2**
Speed ratings (Par 107): **107,105,104,104,103 102,102,101**
toteswinger: 1&2 £16.10, 1&3 £3.00, 2&3 £5.40. CSF £52.02 CT £67.93 TOTE £11.10: £3.20, £1.30, £1.10; EX 102.00.
Owner George Murray **Bred** WinStar Farm LLC **Trained** Musley Bank, N Yorks

FOCUS
A fair handicap in which the pace was only fair in the first half of the contest. The winner raced centre to far side in the straight.

NOTEBOOK
Faithful Ruler(USA) ◆ had been running creditably over further but showed improved form from just out of the handicap back over this shorter trip to register his second course-and-distance success for his current stable. A more end-to-end gallop would have suited even better and there may well be more to come.
Rainbow Mirage(IRE)'s four wins have been on turf but he showed he retains all his ability on this first start since October. He is a useful sort who is at least as effective on turf but he has little margin for error from his current rating. (op 8-1 tchd 9-1)
Tous Les Deux looked the one to beat back up in trip but he was found out in a race run at just an ordinary gallop to halfway after failing to settle and after hanging once asked for an effort. He's due to go up 2lb in future handicaps but will be worth another chance, especially when it looks as though there will be plenty of pace on. (op 5-4)
Just Bond(IRE) is a reliable sort with a fair strike-rate at this course and he was far from disgraced in the first-time visor. However, he again left the impression that he'd have to drop a bit more in the handicap before winning a race of this nature.
Tourist doesn't do anything quickly and he shaped as though a stronger overall gallop over this trip or the return to further would be in his favour. He is not one to write off just yet. (op 9-2)
Cornus had not been at his best over 6f on his previous start but, while he failed to improve for the step up to this trip for only the second time, he will have to show a bit more before he is a solid betting proposition again. (tchd 28-1)
Ravi River(IRE) Official explanation: jockey said gelding ran too freely

835 FREEBETS.CO.UK FREE FOOTBALL BETS H'CAP 2m 119y(P)

8:50 (8:50) (Class 5) (0-75,70) 4-Y-O+ **£3,070** (£906; £453) **Stalls** Low

Form RPR
0-12 **1** **Bold Adventure**[11] 732 5-9-5 **61** .... ChrisCatlin 4 72+
(W J Musson) *hld up in rr: hdwy on ins over 2f out: led ins fnl f: pushed out* **7/4**[1]
3/3- **2** *¾* **Mexican Pete**[55] 344 9-10-0 **70** .... JamieSpencer 3 79
(A King) *hld up: chsd clr ldr 3f out: led over 1f out: sn rdn and edgd lft: hdd ins fnl f: nt qckn* **2/1**[2]
-413 **3** *13* **Monaadi (IRE)**[15] 692 4-9-1 **62** ....(v[1]) GrahamGibbons 2 56
(R Hollinshead) *led: clr after 5f: rdn and hdd over 1f out: sn wknd* **4/1**[3]
0005 **4** *3 ¼* **Capitalise (IRE)**[16] 679 6-8-11 **53** .... LukeMorris 6 43
(Miss Gay Kelleway) *hld up towards rr: sme hdwy 3f out: rdn and wknd 2f out* **14/1**
-064 **5** *13* **Cantabilly (IRE)**[16] 679 6-9-4 **65** .... MCGeran(5) 5 39
(R J Hodges) *chsd ldr tl over 4f out: wknd over 3f out* **13/2**
3 **6** *5* **King De Lune (FR)**[16] 679 7-9-3 **59** ....(b) DaneO'Neill 7 27
(C E Longsdon) *hld up: disp 2nd 8f out: chsd clr ldr over 4f out to 3f out: sn wknd* **16/1**

3m 39.48s (-2.32) **Going Correction** 0.0s/f (Stan)
WFA 4 from 5yo+ 5lb **6** Ran SP% **115.6**
Speed ratings (Par 103): **105,104,98,97,90 88**
toteswinger: 1&2 £1.02, 1&3 £1.30, 2&3 £3.10. CSF £5.82 TOTE £3.10: £1.40, £2.10; EX 6.10.

Owner Mustard Cord Cads **Bred** Bricklow Ltd **Trained** Newmarket, Suffolk

FOCUS

An ordinary handicap in which the pace was only fair until the clear leader quickened things around the 4f pole. The winner raced against the inside rail in the straight.

Cantabilly(IRE) Official explanation: jockey said gelding hung badly left on the final bend

836 FREEBETS.CO.UK FREE SIX NATIONS RUGBY BETTING H'CAP 1m 4f 50y(P)
9:20 (9:20) (Class 6) (0-65,65) 4-Y-O+ **£2,217** (£654; £327) **Stalls** Low

Form RPR

2425 **1** **Star Choice**[11] 732 4-9-4 **65**..........(v[1]) RobertHavlin 6 72
(J Pearce) *hld up in tch: rdn and edgd lft over 1f out: led ins fnl f: drvn out* **3/1**[1]

56-0 **2** 3/4 **Drawn Gold**[56] 194 5-9-3 **62**.......... GrahamGibbons 5 68
(R Hollinshead) *hld up in mid-div: rdn over 2f out: hdwy 1f out: r.o to take 2nd towards fin* **8/1**

0540 **3** 3/4 **Buscador (USA)**[11] 735 10-9-0 **59**.......... RichardKingscote 12 64
(W M Brisbourne) *set stdy pce: rdn wl over 1f out: hdd ins fnl f: no ex and lost 2nd towards fin* **20/1**

-452 **4** nk **Pelham Crescent (IRE)**[25] 571 6-8-12 **60**..........(p) DavidProbert(3) 7 65
(B Palling) *a.p: swtchd lft wl over 1f out: rdn fnl f: nt qckn* **7/1**[3]

300- **5** 1/2 **Cash On (IRE)**[139] 6985 7-9-4 **63**..........(p) DaneO'Neill 1 67
(Karen George) *hld up in rr: c wd st: rdn and styng on whn edgd lft wl ins fnl f: nvr nr to chal* **33/1**

60-0 **6** 1 3/4 **Urban Warrior**[18] 656 5-9-2 **61**.......... ChrisCatlin 11 62
(Ian Williams) *hld up in tch: fdd ins fnl f* **18/1**

1-34 **7** hd **Little Richard (IRE)**[55] 202 10-9-2 **61**..........(p) AdamKirby 3 62
(M Wellings) *hld up in mid-div: rdn and no hdwy fnl f* **11/2**[2]

2-03 **8** hd **Bedouin Blue (IRE)**[10] 745 6-9-0 **64**..........(p) PatrickDonaghy(5) 10 64
(A J Lidderdale) *hld up and bhd: rdn over 1f out: n.d* **20/1**

1-00 **9** nse **Jago (SWI)**[20] 631 6-9-6 **65**.......... LPKeniry 4 65
(A M Hales) *hld up in rr: short-lived effrt on ins wl over 1f out* **7/1**[3]

530- **10** 2 1/4 **Summer Lodge**[76] 7797 6-9-0 **59**..........(p) RobertWinston 8 56
(A J McCabe) *chsd ldr: rdn 2f out: wknd over 1f out* **8/1**

-534 **11** 3 1/2 **Calzaghe (IRE)**[27] 559 5-9-5 **64**..........(vt) FBranca 2 55+
(F Sheridan) *hld up and bhd: rdn over 1f out: last whn hmpd jst ins fnl f: eased* **3/1**[1]

2m 41.71s (0.61) **Going Correction** 0.0s/f (Stan)
WFA 4 from 5yo+ 2lb **11** Ran SP% **130.3**
Speed ratings (Par 101): **97,96,96,95,95 94,94,94,94,92 90**
toteswinger: 1&2 £8.50, 1&3 £24.60, 2&3 £43.40. CSF £31.15 CT £440.84 TOTE £5.40: £2.00, £3.80, £5.10; EX 45.00 Place 6: £69.44, Place 5: £16.76..
Owner Macniler Racing Partnership **Bred** B J Warren **Trained** Newmarket, Suffolk
■ Stewards' Enquiry : Robert Winston caution: careless riding.

FOCUS

Exposed performers in this moderate handicap. The pace was only ordinary and the winner raced centre to far side in the straight.

Buscador(USA) Official explanation: vet said gelding was lame on its near-fore

Little Richard(IRE) Official explanation: jockey said gelding hung right from two out

T/Plt: £186.00 to a £1 stake. Pool: £99,900.07. 391.96 winning tickets. T/Qpdt: £6.70 to a £1 stake. Pool: £9,607.31. 1,052.30 winning tickets. KH

837 - (Foreign Racing) - See Raceform Interactive

824 LINGFIELD (L-H)
Saturday, March 14

OFFICIAL GOING: Standard
Wind: Medium, Against Weather: Overcast

838 FREEBETS.CO.UK PREMIERSHIP FOOTBALL FREE BETS (S) STKS 1m 4f (P)
2:30 (2:30) (Class 6) 4-Y-O+ **£2,047** (£604; £302) **Stalls** Low

Form RPR

6102 **1** **Sunset Boulevard (IRE)**[10] 750 6-9-7 61.......... ChrisCatlin 8 67
(Miss Tor Sturgis) *racd in last pair: hdwy over 3f out: chsd ldr over 2f out: rdn to ld narrowly over 1f out: hrd drvn and hld on wl ins fnl f* **2/1**[2]

-334 **2** nk **Turner's Touch**[10] 750 7-9-1 55..........(b) GeorgeBaker 1 60
(G L Moore) *hld up in last pl: hdwy on outer 3f out: chsd ldng pair over 2f out: rdn to chal insid efnl f: hrd rdn and nt qckn fnl 100yds* **9/2**

-202 **3** nk **Gasat (IRE)**[24] 588 8-9-7 65.......... JoeFanning 6 66
(A B Haynes) *led: clr over 8f out: reduced advatage 3f out: hdd narrowly over 1f out: ev ch tl no ex u.p fnl 100yds* **7/2**[3]

524 **4** 10 **Bernabeu (IRE)**[24] 584 7-9-1 58.......... JamesDoyle 3 45
(S Curran) *chsd ldr tl over 2f out: sn rdn and struggling: wl btn fnl f* **15/8**[1]

0-64 **5** 1 1/4 **Special Chapter (IRE)**[52] 240 4-8-2 31 ow1.......... PNolan(7) 7 39
(A B Haynes) *chsd ldrs tl rdn and wknd jst over 2f out* **66/1**

000- **6** 6 **Our Glenard**[99] 7553 10-9-1 34.......... RichardThomas 5 34
(J E Long) *early reminders: in tch tl rdn and struggling wl over 2f out: wl bhd fnl 2f* **150/1**

2m 33.88s (0.88) **Going Correction** +0.025s/f (Slow)
WFA 4 from 5yo+ 2lb **6** Ran SP% **110.7**
Speed ratings (Par 101): **98,97,97,90,90 86**
toteswinger: 1&2 £6.90, 1&3 £2.90, 2&3 £6.50. CSF £11.02 TOTE £3.20: £1.90, £1.30; EX 9.40 Trifecta £28.20 Pool: £405.98 - 10.63 winning units..There was no bid for the winner.
Owner Miss Tor Sturgis **Bred** A J Martin **Trained** Lambourn, Berks
■ Stewards' Enquiry : George Baker caution: excessive use of the whip

FOCUS

An ordinary seller.

839 FREEBETS.CO.UK FREE BETS FOR CHELSEA V MAN CITY CLAIMING STKS 1m (P)
3:00 (3:00) (Class 6) 3-Y-O **£2,047** (£604; £302) **Stalls** High

Form RPR

0-55 **1** **Daily Double**[10] 753 3-8-12 55.......... DaneO'Neill 6 63+
(D K Ivory) *hld up wl in rr: stil plenty to do 2f out: rdn and hdwy over 1f out: 7th ent fnl f: str run to ld towards fin* **16/1**

-116 **2** 3/4 **Fantastic Fred (IRE)**[35] 450 3-8-12 63.......... ChrisCatlin 11 61
(J A Osborne) *chsd ldrs: rdn and hdwy whn carried rt bnd wl over 1f out: ev ch1f out: led fnl 100yds: hdd and nt pce of wnr towards fin* **10/1**

-502 **3** 3/4 **Flying Lady (IRE)**[8] 776 3-8-8 67.......... TonyCulhane 4 56+
(M R Channon) *hld up in midfield: hdwy over 2f out: pressed ldr and carried rt bnd wl over 1f out: ev ch 1f out: one pce after* **7/4**[1]

3422 **4** 1/2 **Hold The Bucks (USA)**[44] 332 3-9-2 71.......... LukeMorris 7 63
(J S Moore) *racd in midfield: rdn over 5f out: lost pl over 3f out: rallied unde rpress 2f out: led ent fnl f: hdd and no ex fnl 100yds* **15/8**[2]

0125 **5** 2 1/4 **Whotsit (IRE)**[8] 776 3-8-4 60..........(b) KellyHarrison(5) 8 51
(Miss Amy Weaver) *s.i.s: t.k.h: hld up towards rr: hdwy over 3f out: plugged on same pce u.p fr over 1f out* **7/1**[3]

55 **6** 3/4 **Destinationunknown (USA)**[27] 564 3-8-7 0..........(b[1]) LiamJones 9 47
(W J Haggas) *led after 1f: wnt 3 l clr over 2f out: hung rt bnd wl over 1f out: sn hdd and btn* **15/2**

0 **7** 2 1/4 **Northern Champ (IRE)**[54] 214 3-8-9 47.......... WilliamCarson(5) 2 49
(Patrick G Kelly, Ire) *sn pushed up to press ldr: outpcd over 2f out: lft in ld on inner wl over 1f out: rdn and hdd ent fnl f: wknd qckly* **33/1**

0 **8** nk **Primera Rossa**[10] 752 3-8-5 0.......... MartinDwyer 3 39
(J S Moore) *s.i.s: a bhd: nvr a factor* **66/1**

P-44 **9** 3 1/4 **Crown Affair (IRE)**[28] 547 3-8-10 62.......... SimonWhitworth 10 37
(J W Hills) *in tch: rdn and effrt over 2f out: wknd over 1f out* **25/1**

000- **10** 7 **Come On Toby**[162] 6438 3-8-2 43.......... RyanPowell(7) 5 21
(Miss Amy Weaver) *led for 1f: cjhased ldrs after tl lost pl and bhd 2f out: wl btn after* **100/1**

1m 38.6s (0.40) **Going Correction** +0.025s/f (Slow) **10** Ran SP% **119.7**
Speed ratings (Par 96): **99,98,97,97,94 94,91,91,88,81**
toteswinger: 1&2 £8.90, 1&3 £6.60, 2&3 £3.30. CSF £163.77 TOTE £21.60: £4.60, £2.10, £1.50; EX 72.30 Trifecta £245.00 Part won. Pool: £331.12 - 0.56 winning units..
Owner K T Ivory **Bred** Edmond And Richard Kent **Trained** Radlett, Herts

FOCUS

They went a good gallop here with the first-time blinkered Destinationunknown and Northern Champ taking each other on at the head of affairs. The former eventually won that particular battle but both had gone too fast and simply set it up for the closers.

840 FREEBETS.CO.UK OVER £1000 IN FREE BETS H'CAP 1m 2f (P)
3:30 (3:31) (Class 4) (0-85,79) 3-Y-O **£6,476** (£1,927; £963; £481) **Stalls** Low

Form RPR

-221 **1** **Badge Of Honour**[19] 658 3-9-1 73.......... GregFairley 5 76+
(M Johnston) *sn led and set stdy gallop: qcknd jst over 2f out: hdd narrowly over 1f out: edgd rt ins fnl f: edgd lft but rallied gamely to ld again nr fin* **6/1**[3]

42-1 **2** shd **Gaily Noble (IRE)**[16] 695 3-9-6 78.......... FergusSweeney 2 81
(A B Haynes) *sn trckd wnr: ev ch 2f out: rdn and led narrowly over 1f out: edgd rt u.p ins fnl f: edgd lft and hdd nr fin* **4/1**[2]

4241 **3** 1/2 **High Cross (IRE)**[10] 759 3-8-11 69.......... ChrisCatlin 4 72+
(Sir Mark Prescott) *t.k.h: in tch: rdn and effrt 2f out: pressed ldr ins fnl f: unable qck fnl 100yds* **7/2**[1]

-511 **4** hd **Dubai Storming**[12] 740 3-9-6 78.......... JamieSpencer 6 81+
(E A L Dunlop) *s.i.s: t.k.h: hld up towards rr: rdn and unable qck wl over 1f out: hdwy u.p 1f out: clsng fnl 100yds but nvr quite getting to ldrs: short of room last strides* **7/2**[1]

5-12 **5** 3/4 **Tinshu (IRE)**[24] 595 3-9-5 77.......... MartinDwyer 1 77
(D Haydn Jones) *trckd ldng pair: rdn and effrt on inner wl over 1f out: kpt on same pce ins fnl f* **10/1**

3-56 **6** 4 **Orsippus (USA)**[10] 755 3-9-4 76.......... TonyCulhane 3 69+
(M R Channon) *stdd after s: t.k.h: hld up in last: rdn and c wd bnd 2f out: nvr trbld ldrs* **20/1**

625- **7** 1 **Wilbury Star (IRE)**[136] 7067 3-9-7 79.......... RichardHughes 7 70+
(R Hannon) *hld up in last pair: rdn over 3f out: c wd bnd 2f out: nvr nr ldrs* **6/1**[3]

20-4 **8** 1 **Blue Tango (IRE)**[24] 595 3-9-3 75.......... JimCrowley 8 64
(Mrs A J Perrett) *hld up towards rr: hdwy into midfield over 4f out: rdn 2f out: wknd over 1f out* **10/1**

2m 10.97s (4.37) **Going Correction** +0.025s/f (Slow) **8** Ran SP% **116.0**
Speed ratings (Par 100): **83,82,82,82,81 78,77,76**
toteswinger: 1&2 £4.70, 1&3 £4.70, 2&3 £3.70. CSF £30.66 CT £97.24 TOTE £6.40: £1.80, £2.10, £1.60; EX 33.90 Trifecta £160.30 Pool: £511.39 - 2.36 winning units..
Owner Sheikh Hamdan Bin Mohammed Al Maktoum **Bred** Gainsborough Stud Management Ltd **Trained** Middleham Moor, N Yorks

FOCUS

A fair handicap, although the top weight was rated 6lb below the ceiling for the race. The early pace was very steady.

841 FREEBETS.CO.UK GRAND NATIONAL FREE BETS H'CAP 1m (P)
4:05 (4:06) (Class 5) (0-70,70) 4-Y-O+ **£2,900** (£856; £428) **Stalls** High

Form RPR

0044 **1** **Bee Stinger**[31] 507 7-9-2 68..........(b) NCallan 7 81
(I A Wood) *in tch: chsd ldr over 1f out: rdn to ld 1f out: r.o strly and sn clr: comf* **8/1**

6-13 **2** 2 3/4 **Murrin (IRE)**[31] 505 5-9-4 70.......... RobertHavlin 2 77
(T G Mills) *hld up in rr: hdwy over 2f out: c wd and rdn over 1f out: r.o fnl f to go 2nd towards fin: no ch w wnr* **7/1**[3]

-014 **3** 1/2 **Royal Envoy (IRE)**[22] 618 6-9-3 69.......... TolleyDean 8 75
(P Howling) *stdd after s: hld up in last pl: hdwy on outer bnd 2f out: r.o fnl f to snatch 3rd last strides: no ch w wnr* **20/1**

-133 **4** nk **Ghufa (IRE)**[12] 733 5-9-2 68.......... DaneO'Neill 9 73
(George Baker) *trckd ldrs: pushed up to press ldr over 2f out: rdn to ld 2f out: hdd 1f out: sn outpcd by wnr: lost 2 pls towards fin* **4/1**[1]

-131 **5** nk **Lopinot (IRE)**[13] 725 6-9-2 68..........(v) JimCrowley 1 73+
(M R Bosley) *dwlt: hld up towards rr: hdwy and nt clr run briefly wl over 1f out: hdwy u.p over 1f out: kpt on but nvr a threat* **7/1**[3]

-312 **6** hd **Forbidden (IRE)**[25] 580 6-8-12 69..........(t) AndreaAtzeni(5) 10 73
(Daniel Mark Loughnane, Ire) *hld up towards rr: hdwy on outer over 2f out: rdn wl over 1f out: kpt on same pce fnl f* **8/1**

135- **7** shd **Grey Boy (GER)**[143] 6899 8-9-4 70.......... LukeMorris 5 74
(A W Carroll) *s.i.s: hld up in rr: swtchd rt jst over 2f out: rdn wl over 1f out: nvr pce to rch ldrs* **11/1**

00/6 **8** 3/4 **Sew'N'So Character (IRE)**[28] 558 8-9-2 68.......... PaulHanagan 3 70
(M Blanshard) *in tch in midfield: effrt 2f out: rdn to chse ldrs over 1f out: sn outpcd: wknd fnl 100yds* **25/1**

4322 **9** 3 1/2 **Marmooq**[15] 708 6-8-13 65.......... IanMongan 4 60
(M J Attwater) *in tch in midfield on inner: hdwy over 2f out: drvn 2f out: wknd over 1f out* **9/2**[2]

6-20 **10** 2 1/2 **Sotik Star (IRE)**[42] 357 6-8-13 65..........(p) PatCosgrave 12 54
(K A Morgan) *dwlt: sn pushe dup to chse ldrs: ev ch jst over 2f out: wknd over 1f out* **10/1**

-046 **11** 2 1/2 **Flying Applause**[22] 622 4-9-1 67.......... FergusSweeney 6 51
(S R Bowring) *sn led: rdn and hdd 2f out: sn wknd* **33/1**

6665 **12** dist **Kabeer**[8] 777 11-9-2 68.......... RobertWinston 11 —
(A J McCabe) *pressed ldr on outer tl lost pl qckly and eased jst over 2f out: virtually p.u fnl f* **25/1**

1m 37.1s (-1.10) **Going Correction** +0.025s/f (Slow) **12** Ran SP% **118.2**
Speed ratings (Par 103): **106,103,102,102,102 101,101,101,97,95 92,—**
toteswinger: 1&2 £9.30, 1&3 £37.50, 2&3 £27.80. CSF £59.75 CT £1103.56 TOTE £7.00: £2.30, £2.70, £8.10; EX 62.00 TRIFECTA Not won..

Owner Sporting Occasions No 11 **Bred** Templeton Stud **Trained** Upper Lambourn, Berks
FOCUS
A competitive handicap run at a good pace.
Kabeer Official explanation: jockey said gelding did not handle the bend

842 FREEBETS.CO.UK NEW ONLINE BETTING FORUM MEDIAN AUCTION MAIDEN STKS 6f (P)
4:40 (4:40) (Class 6) 3-5-Y-0 **£2,217** (£654; £327) **Stalls** Low

Form RPR
1 **Chasca (IRE)** 3-8-7 0 .... JimCrowley 4 66+
(Mrs A J Perrett) *sltly hmpd s: hld up in last trio: squeezed between horses and hdwy over 1f out: chsd ldr 1f out: rdn to ld ins fnl f: r.o wl* **12/1**
0- 2 ¾ **True Decision**[248] 3848 3-8-5 0 .... MatthewBirch(7) 2 69+
(S Kirk) *s.i.s: bhd: c v wd bnd 2f out: stl plenty to do ent fnl f: r.o strly after to go 2nd nr fin: nvr gng to rch wnr* **33/1**
052- 3 ½ **Robin The Till**[225] 4579 3-8-12 63 .... RichardHughes 7 67
(R Hannon) *broke wl: led and sn crossed to rail: rdn wl over 1f out: hdd ins fnl f: no ex: lost 2nd nr fin* **7/2**[2]
3 4 2¼ **Volito**[18] 663 3-8-12 0 .... JamieSpencer 1 64+
(Jonjo O'Neill) *in tch: effrt on inner 2f out: chsd ldr wl over1f out: short of room and swtchd rt over 1f out: one pce u.p fnl f* **5/6**[1]
25-0 5 nk **Twenty Score**[51] 251 3-8-7 0 .... PaulFitzsimons 8 55
(Miss J R Tooth) *in tch on outer: reminder over 2f out: chsd ldrs and rdn over 1f out: outpcd fnl f* **14/1**
3 6 1¾ **Christmascametwice**[12] 729 3-8-7 0 .... ChrisCatlin 9 49
(J A Osborne) *dwlt: racd in last trio: rdn and effrt wl over 1f out: plugged on but nvr a danger* **6/1**[3]
3/3- 7 1¾ **Tallulah Sunrise**[415] 281 4-9-2 65 .... GabrielHannon(5) 5 48
(M D I Usher) *wnt lft s: in tch in midfield: rdn and wknd over 1f out* **14/1**
P0-5 8 3¾ **Wicklewood**[13] 722 3-8-12 0 .... TGMcLaughlin 6 38
(Mrs C A Dunnett) *chsd ldrs: rdn jst over 2f out: wknd over 1f out: eased whn wl btn ins fnl f* **66/1**
9 8 **Chenin (IRE)** 3-8-0 0 .... AndrewHeffernan(7) 10 9
(Peter Grayson) *t.k.h: sn chsng ldr on outer: rdn and wknd qckly wl over 1f out: eased fnl f* **66/1**

1m 12.29s (0.39) **Going Correction** +0.025s/f (Slow)
WFA 3 from 4yo 14lb 9 Ran SP% **118.0**
Speed ratings (Par 101): **98,97,96,93,92 90,88,83,72**
toteswinger: 1&2 £23.70, 1&3 £5.80, 2&3 £26.00. CSF £315.07 TOTE £9.40: £2.50, £7.10, £1.20; EX 307.90 TRIFECTA Not won..
Owner Lady Clague **Bred** Newberry Stud Company **Trained** Pulborough, W Sussex
FOCUS
A modest maiden.

843 FREEBETS.CO.UK FREE BETS H'CAP 6f (P)
5:15 (5:15) (Class 5) (0-75,75) 4-Y-0+ **£2,900** (£856; £428) **Stalls** Low

Form RPR
-531 1 **Super Frank (IRE)**[15] 708 6-9-3 74 ....(p) JoeFanning 5 84
(J Akehurst) *dwlt: sn rcvrd and allowed easy ld: clr 2f out: r.o wl: unchal* **11/4**[1]
3211 2 2¼ **Stonecrabstomorrow (IRE)**[10] 757 6-8-13 70 ....(b) PaulHanagan 8 73
(R A Fahey) *short of room and hmpd after s: racd in midfield: rdn and effrt over 1f out: drvn 1f out: styd on to go 2nd fnl 100yds: no ch w wnr* **7/2**[2]
4411 3 ½ **Don Pele (IRE)**[9] 762 7-9-1 72 ....(p) ChrisCatlin 7 74
(R A Harris) *chsd wnr: rdn and unable qck over 1f out: no ch w wnr fnl f: lost 2nd fnl 100yds* **8/1**
040- 4 1¼ **Charles Darwin (IRE)**[120] 7315 6-8-13 70 .... LPKeniry 4 68
(M Blanshard) *t.k.h: hld up in midfield: rdn and no prog over 1f out: kpt on fnl f: nvr nr wnr* **20/1**
-522 5 2 **Qadar (IRE)**[10] 754 7-9-4 75 ....(e) JamesDoyle 9 67
(N P Littmoden) *heavily restrained after s: t.k.h: hld up towards rr: nvr a factor* **7/2**[2]
3130 6 1 **Grand Palace (IRE)**[8] 780 6-9-0 71 ....(v) AdamKirby 2 60
(D Shaw) *chsd ldng pair: rdn jst over 2f out: drvn and no prog over 1f oot: wknd ins fnl f* **13/2**[3]
000- 7 1½ **Lieutenant Pigeon**[110] 7435 4-8-10 67 .... PaulEddery 1 52
(Paul Mason) *dwlt: a bhd: n.d* **12/1**
1-00 8 1¾ **Cosmic Destiny (IRE)**[50] 270 7-8-11 68 .... JamieSpencer 6 47
(E F Vaughan) *broke wl sn heavily restrained and bhd: plld hrd: c wd wl over 2f out: no hdwy: eased ins fnl f* **16/1**

1m 11.64s (-0.26) **Going Correction** +0.025s/f (Slow) 8 Ran SP% **113.9**
Speed ratings (Par 103): **102,99,98,96,94 92,90,88**
toteswinger: 1&2 £3.10, 1&3 £6.40, 2&3 £3.40. CSF £12.35 CT £66.37 TOTE £3.80: £1.10, £2.00, £2.10; EX 13.20 Trifecta £61.80 Pool: £402.86 - 4.82 winning units..
Owner A D Spence **Bred** A Butler **Trained** Epsom, Surrey
FOCUS
A fairly ordinary handicap which the winner dominated from the front, setting his own pace.

844 FREEBETS.CO.UK FOR BETTING OFFERS H'CAP 7f (P)
5:45 (5:45) (Class 6) (0-65,65) 4-Y-0+ **£2,047** (£604; £302) **Stalls** Low

Form RPR
-202 1 **Suhayl Star (IRE)**[10] 749 5-8-4 51 oh2 .... LukeMorris 11 60
(P Burgoyne) *broke wl: sn stdd to chse ldr clr of remainder: rdn to ld ent fnl f: styd on wl* **20/1**
6-43 2 ¾ **Ever Cheerful**[15] 708 8-8-7 61 ....(p) PNolan(7) 9 68
(A B Haynes) *sn led and clr w wnr: rdn jst over 2f out: hdd ent fnl f: hld on gamely for 2nd* **7/1**[2]
2-02 3 nk **Shaded Edge**[29] 531 5-8-9 56 .... MartinDwyer 6 62+
(D W P Arbuthnot) *prom in main gp: wnt 3rd u.p over 2f out: clsd over 1f out: kpt on same pce ins fnl f* **3/1**[1]
-530 4 ½ **Salt Of The Earth (IRE)**[30] 512 4-9-4 65 .... RobertHavlin 5 70
(T G Mills) *chsd clr ldng pasir tl over 2f out: clsd u.p over 1f out: one pce ins fnl f* **12/1**
-402 5 shd **Takaamul**[20] 646 6-7-13 51 oh1 .... AndreaAtzeni(5) 2 56
(K A Morgan) *hld up off the pce in midfield: hdwy and swtchd rt over 1f out: no imp fnl 100yds* **9/1**
000- 6 shd **Trivia (IRE)**[238] 4182 5-8-8 55 .... JamesDoyle 14 59
(Ms J S Doyle) *hld up wl off the pce towards rr: hdwy jst over 2f out: styd on u.p fnl f: nt rch ldrs* **66/1**
5320 7 ½ **Imperial Djay (IRE)**[3] 811 4-8-8 55 .... JoeFanning 8 58
(G J Smith) *hld up wl off the pce in rr: hdwy on inner wl over 1f out: kpt on fnl f but nvr pce to rch ldrs* **12/1**
-240 8 ½ **Lend A Grand (IRE)**[15] 708 5-9-4 65 .... FergusSweeney 4 67
(Miss Jo Crowley) *s.i.s: t.k.h: hld up wl bhd: effrt on outer wl over 1f out: styd on but nvr a threat* **8/1**
060- 9 1 **Coeur Courageux (FR)**[276] 2930 7-8-13 60 .... SaleemGolam 12 59
(M D Squance) *s.i.s: hld up wl bhd: sme late hdwy: nvr nr ldrs* **33/1**
3-04 10 nk **Ugenius**[13] 725 5-9-0 61 .... TGMcLaughlin 3 59
(Mrs C A Dunnett) *taken down early: prom in main gp: rdn and effrt wl over 1f out: chsd ldrs 1f out: wknd qckly fnl 100yds* **15/2**[3]
0130 11 1 **Ardent Prince**[19] 657 6-8-11 58 .... RobertWinston 7 53
(A J McCabe) *t.k.h: hld up wl off the pce in midfield: awkward bnd 5f out: rdn and effrt wl over 1f out: sn edging lft and wl hld fnl f* **7/1**[2]
-345 12 2¼ **Chalentina**[18] 666 6-8-4 51 oh6 .... RichardThomas 13 40
(J E Long) *stdd after s: hld up wl bhd: nvr a factor* **50/1**
060/ 13 3¾ **Erra Go On**[44] 2874 8-8-13 60 ....(t) PatCosgrave 10 39
(G T Lynch, Ire) *racd wl off the pce in midfield: rdn over 3f out: sn struggling: wl btn fnl 2f* **14/1**
2046 14 ¾ **Ten Pole Tudor**[9] 765 4-8-13 60 .... ChrisCatlin 1 37
(R A Harris) *s.i.s: a bhd* **20/1**

1m 24.19s (-0.61) **Going Correction** +0.025s/f (Slow) 14 Ran SP% **120.8**
Speed ratings (Par 101): **104,103,102,102,102 102,101,100,99,99 98,95,91,90**
toteswinger: 1&2 £20.80, 1&3 £13.30, 2&3 £5.70. CSF £148.82 CT £552.11 TOTE £21.60: £4.80, £2.20, £1.60; EX 157.50 Trifecta £294.70 Part won. Pool: £398.34 - 0.20 winning units. .
Place 6: £184.18 Place 5: £75.70.
Owner Mrs C Leigh-Turner **Bred** John Mulhern **Trained** Shepton Montague, Somerset
FOCUS
Despite the numbers very few got into this as the winner and runner-up raced clear of the field from an early stage.
T/Plt: £92.40 to a £1 stake. Pool: £75,601.28. 596.72 winning tickets. T/Qpdt: £21.80 to a £1 stake. Pool: £4,282.89. 144.73 winning tickets. SP

788 SAINT-CLOUD (L-H)
Saturday, March 14

OFFICIAL GOING: Heavy

846a PRIX EXBURY (GROUP 3) 1m 2f
3:05 (3:05) 4-Y-0+ **£38,835** (£15,534; £11,650; £7,767; £3,883)

RPR
1 **Court Canibal**[97] 7598 4-8-11 .... OPeslier 8 107
(M Delzangles, France) *hld up in rr: 10th st: hdwy on outside to go 3rd 1 1/2f out: styd on u.str.p to ld fnl 50yds* **185/10**
2 ¾ **Diyakalanie (FR)**[93] 7643 5-8-6 .... SPasquier 5 100
(Y De Nicolay, France) *hld up in rr: 8th st: 9th on outside 1 1/2f out: fin wl to take 2nd on line* **11/1**
3 nse **Chinchon (IRE)**[170] 6237 4-8-11 .... CSoumillon 9 105
(C Laffon-Parias, France) *racd in 3rd bhd clr ldrs: clsd up 3f out: led going 2nd over 2f out: led over 1f out: hdd 50yds out: lost 2nd on line* **22/5**[2]
4 ¾ **Loup Breton (IRE)**[90] 7685 5-9-2 .... ACrastus 3 108
(E Lellouche, France) *hld up in rr: 9th st: hdwy on ins to dispute 4th 1 1/2f out: kpt on* **27/10**[1]
5 hd **Wingstar (IRE)**[21] 5-8-6 .... THuet 4 98
(Robert Collet, France) *midfield: 5th stm kpt on u.p fom over 2f out* **89/10**
6 nk **Runaway**[137] 7063 7-8-9 .... TJarnet 1 100
(R Pritchard-Gordon, France) *set str pce: 5 l clr w Lady Deauville over 3f out: hdd over 1f out: lost 3rd cl home* **15/1**
7 4 **Tardrou (FR)**[34] 463 6-8-9 .... FBlondel 11 92
(J-L Dubord, France) *racd in 5th: 4th st: rdn and one pce fr 2f out* **27/1**
8 nk **Trincot (FR)**[90] 7685 4-9-2 .... IMendizabal 7 99
(P Demercastel, France) *hld up: 6th st: rdn and nt qckn fr 2f out* **9/2**[3]
9 4 **Indian Daffodil (IRE)**[156] 6612 4-9-0 .... C-PLemaire 10 89
(J-C Rouget, France) *a in rr* **9/1**
10 8 **Lady Deauville (FR)**[97] 7598 4-8-10 .... J-PGuillambert 6 69
(R Curtis) *racd in 2nd: 5 l clr of remainder over 3f out: wknd 2 1/2f out* **30/1**
11 **Belle Et Celebre (FR)**[146] 6854 4-9-1 .... JVictoire 2 74
(A De Royer-Dupre, France) *racd in 4th: 7th and wkng ent st* **12/1**

2m 14.2s (-1.80) 11 Ran SP% **118.0**
PARI-MUTUEL: WIN 19.50; PL 4.60, 3.50, 2.10; DF 93.20.
Owner Marquise De Moratalla **Bred** Childwick Bury Stud Management Ltd **Trained** France

812 KEMPTON (A.W) (R-H)
Monday, March 16

OFFICIAL GOING: Standard
Wind: Light, behind Weather: Sunny, very mild

847 FREEBETS.CO.UK OVER £5000 IN FREE BETS H'CAP 1m 2f (P)
2:30 (2:32) (Class 4) (0-85,84) 4-Y-0+ **£4,727** (£1,406; £702; £351) **Stalls** High

Form RPR
2441 1 **Stand Guard**[17] 713 5-9-4 84 .... TolleyDean 3 93
(P Howling) *trckd ldr: rdn to ld over 2f out: kpt on u.p fr over 1f out* **11/4**[2]
5-62 2 ¾ **Kidlat**[40] 392 4-8-11 77 ....(t) DaneO'Neill 7 85
(B G Powell) *trckd ldng pair: dropped to 4th over 2f out and nt clr run sn after: rallied on inner over 1f out: wnt 2nd ins fnl f: nt quite rch wnr* **4/1**[3]
-114 3 2 **Folio (IRE)**[30] 550 9-8-13 79 .... ChrisCatlin 2 83
(W J Musson) *settled in 5th: prog over 3f out: chsd wnr wl over 1f out tl ins fnl f: fdd* **8/1**
3312 4 1 **Dream Of Fortune (IRE)**[11] 766 5-9-2 82 ....(t) AdamKirby 6 85+
(M G Quinlan) *hld up in last: pushed along 3f out: no prog tl kpt on fr over 1f out: nt pce to threaten* **8/1**
055- 5 2¾ **Lake Poet (IRE)**[389] 652 6-8-8 74 .... JamieSpencer 8 71
(C E Brittain) *led: rdn and hdd over 2f out: grad wknd fr over 1f out* **7/4**[1]
-006 6 8 **Cold Turkey**[22] 648 9-8-10 76 .... FergusSweeney 1 59
(G L Moore) *hld up in 4th: pushed along 4f out: sn dropped to last and no ch* **50/1**

2m 7.17s (-0.83) **Going Correction** +0.025s/f (Slow) 6 Ran SP% **107.2**
Speed ratings (Par 105): **104,103,101,101,98 92**
toteswinger: 1&2 £3.70, 1&3 £3.40, 2&3 £3.70. CSF £12.66 CT £62.22 TOTE £4.00: £2.60, £2.70; EX 18.00.
Owner The Circle Bloodstock I Limited **Bred** Juddmonte Farms Ltd **Trained** Newmarket, Suffolk
■ Mafeking (10/1) was withdrawn after refusing to enter the stalls. R4 applies, deduct 5p in the £.
FOCUS
A fair handicap run at a modest pace.

Dream Of Fortune(IRE) Official explanation: jockey said gelding never travelling

848 FREEBETS.CO.UK ONLINE BETTING FORUM H'CAP 1m 4f (P)
3:00 (3:02) (Class 5) (0-75,73) 4-Y-0+ **£2,590** (£770; £385; £192) **Stalls** Centre

Form RPR

04-2 **1** **Filun**[17] [704] 4-8-10 **65** .... IanMongan 4 71
(A Middleton) *s.s: t.k.h in last pair: gd prog on outer fr 3f out to ld wl over 1f out: drvn out and jst hld on* **11/2**[3]

320- **2** *hd* **Wait For The Light**[156] [6662] 5-9-3 **70** .... SteveDrowne 2 76
(Mrs S Leech) *led: set v stdy pce tl wl past 1/2-way: rdn and hdd wl over 1f out: battled on wl to press wnr fnl f: jst hld* **12/1**

/010 **3** *1 ¼* **Imperial Harry**[30] [559] 6-9-6 **73** .... ChrisCatlin 7 77
(D E Pipe) *t.k.h: trckd ldng pair: effrt on inner over 2f out: rdn over 1f out: cl enough but nt qckn fnl f: eased nr fin* **3/1**[2]

/121 **4** *2 ½* **Dishdasha (IRE)**[16] [497] 7-9-6 **73** .... (t) JamieSpencer 8 74+
(Mrs A M Thorpe) *s.s: t.k.h: hld up in 5th: trapped bhd rivals and swtchd lft over 2f out: drvn and one pce over 1f out* **6/4**[1]

6-00 **5** *4 ½* **Sommersturm (GER)**[21] [660] 5-9-3 **70** .... TPQueally 6 64
(B J Curley) *t.k.h: hld up in 6th: prog over 3f out to press ldrs over 2f out: wknd over 1f out* **20/1**

/260 **6** *2 ½* **Just Observing**[17] [713] 6-9-1 **68** .... MickyFenton 5 58
(P T Midgley) *stdd s: t.k.h in last pair: wd bnd over 3f out: sn lost tch* **20/1**

223/ **7** *hd* **Lord Oroko**[107] [6622] 5-9-1 **68** .... LukeMorris 3 58
(J G M O'Shea) *t.k.h: trckd ldr to wl over 2f out: sn wknd* **14/1**

064- **8** *6* **Mixing**[123] [7301] 7-8-6 **62** .... DavidProbert(3) 1 43
(M J Attwater) *t.k.h: hld up in 4th: wknd wl over 2f out: t.o* **9/1**

2m 39.52s (5.02) **Going Correction** +0.025s/f (Slow)
WFA 4 from 5yo+ 2lb **8** Ran SP% **114.3**
Speed ratings (Par 103): **84,83,83,81,78 76,76,72**
toteswinger: 1&2 £5.00, 1&3 £3.60, 2&3 £3.90. CSF £67.40 CT £231.32 TOTE £7.00: £1.90, £2.20, £1.60; EX 84.50.
Owner R J Matthews **Bred** Azienda Agricola Francesca **Trained** Granborough, Bucks

FOCUS
They went very steady for most of the way, resulting in a relative sprint in the straight, and this is form to treat with caution.

849 FREEBETS.CO.UK FREE BETS MAIDEN FILLIES' STKS 1m (P)
3:30 (3:33) (Class 4) 3-Y-O+ **£4,727** (£1,406; £702; £351) **Stalls** High

Form RPR

1 **Photographic** 3-8-9 0 .... MichaelHills 11 85+
(B W Hills) *dwlt: sn rcvrd into midfield: prog over 3f out to cl on ldrs: rdn to ld wl over 1f out: edgd rt after: drew clr fnl f* **2/1**[1]

3 **2** *3 ½* **Mosqueras Romance**[24] [626] 3-8-9 0 .... JohnEgan 10 75+
(M Botti) *trckd ldng pair: effrt to chal 2f out: chsd wnr after: readily lft bhd fnl f* **2/1**[1]

3 *1 ½* **Wadaat** 3-8-9 0 .... JamieSpencer 8 72+
(C E Brittain) *trckd ldr: rdn to ld jst over 2f out to wl over 1f out: rn green and sn btn: kpt on* **8/1**[3]

-035 **4** *8* **Wusuul**[11] [765] 4-9-12 58 .... (b) JoeFanning 9 59
(R A Harris) *led to jst over 2f out: wknd over 1f out* **20/1**

5 *½* **Songful (IRE)** 3-8-9 0 .... PaulEddery 13 53
(Pat Eddery) *settled in abt 9th: pushed along fr 1/2-way: styd on fr over 2f out: n.d* **50/1**

4- **6** *2* **Bishaara (IRE)**[235] [4339] 3-8-9 0 .... RobertHavlin 4 49
(J H M Gosden) *mounted outside paddock: pushed along in abt 8th after 3f: rdn and prog over 3f out: nt rch ldrs: fdd over 1f out* **7/1**[2]

0- **7** *nk* **Ocean Countess (IRE)**[206] [5241] 3-8-9 0 .... JerryO'Dwyer 3 48
(Miss J Feilden) *hld up in last pair: stl there over 2f out: pushed along and kpt on steadily: nvr nr ldrs* **66/1**

5 **8** *1 ¾* **Laminka**[17] [716] 3-8-9 0 .... LukeMorris 7 44
(G C Bravery) *pushed along towards rr bef 1/2-way: struggling after* **66/1**

9 *1 ½* **Vigorosa (IRE)** 3-8-9 0 .... TolleyDean 14 41
(P Howling) *trckd ldrs: outpcd over 3f out: grad wknd* **50/1**

10 *3 ½* **Quella** 3-8-9 0 .... NickyMackay 12 33
(J H M Gosden) *dwlt: a wl in rr: struggling fr 1/2-way* **16/1**

- **11** *10* **How Many Times (IRE)**[256] [3660] 4-9-12 65 .... ChrisCatlin 5 16
(J R Gask) *chsd ldrs tl wknd rapidly over 3f out: t.o* **14/1**

6- **12** *7* **Calling Birds (IRE)**[177] [6135] 3-8-9 0 .... SamHitchcott 6 —
(J A Osborne) *snatched up sn after s and dropped to last: nvr gng wl: t.o* **66/1**

06 **13** *7* **Camelot Queen**[24] [626] 4-9-12 0 .... FergusSweeney 1 —
(W S Kittow) *chsd ldrs 3f: sn wknd: t.o over 2f out* **100/1**

1m 39.03s (-0.77) **Going Correction** +0.025s/f (Slow)
WFA 3 from 4yo 17lb **13** Ran SP% **117.0**
Speed ratings (Par 102): **104,100,99,91,90 88,88,86,84,81 71,64,57**
toteswinger: 1&2 £2.20, 1&3 £4.80, 2&3 £4.20. CSF £4.97 TOTE £3.10: £1.60, £1.30, £2.70; EX 6.10.
Owner K Abdulla **Bred** Juddmonte Farms Ltd **Trained** Lambourn, Berks
■ Stewards' Enquiry : Michael Hills two-day ban: careless riding (Mar 30-31)

FOCUS
An interesting fillies' maiden for the time of year.

850 FREEBETS.CO.UK MIDWEEK FOOTBALL FREE BETS H'CAP 1m (P)
4:00 (4:02) (Class 4) (0-85,82) 4-Y-O+ **£4,727** (£1,406; £702; £351) **Stalls** High

Form RPR

/00- **1** **Soccerjackpot (USA)**[101] [7556] 5-9-4 **82** .... AdamKirby 5 99
(C G Cox) *mde all: comf drew clr fr over 2f out: styd on wl: unchal* **13/2**[3]

-152 **2** *4* **Pegasus Again (USA)**[47] [318] 4-8-13 **77** .... (p) RobertHavlin 4 85
(T G Mills) *chsd wnr after 100yds: rdn 3f out: clr of rest over 1f out but no imp* **11/1**

36-3 **3** *3 ½* **Princely Hero (IRE)**[13] [747] 5-8-13 **82** .... AndreaAtzeni(5) 1 81
(M Botti) *stdd s: hld up in last: stl there whn plld to wd outside wl over 1f out: rdn and r.o fnl f to take 3rd last strides* **8/1**

-660 **4** *hd* **Art Man**[15] [724] 6-9-1 **79** .... GeorgeBaker 7 78
(G L Moore) *stdd s: hld up: wnt 4th over 3f out and gng wl: one reminder wl over 1f out: nt qckn* **4/1**[2]

-246 **5** *1* **Totally Focussed (IRE)**[23] [635] 4-9-2 **80** .... IanMongan 6 77
(S Dow) *dwlt: hld up in 7th: gng wl but plenty to do whn effrt over 2f out: drvn and plugged on same pce fnl 2f* **4/1**[2]

0-00 **6** *nk* **Aviso (GER)**[34] [490] 5-9-2 **80** .... TPQueally 8 76
(B J Curley) *t.k.h: chsd wnr 100yds but sn restrained: rdn over 2f out: no imp: fdd fnl f* **25/1**

3431 **7** *2* **Faithful Ruler (USA)**[3] [834] 5-9-0 **78** 6ex .... PaulHanagan 2 69
(R A Fahey) *chsd ldng trio: first of field u.p over 3f out: sn struggling* **7/4**[1]

-253 **8** *hd* **Ocean Legend (IRE)**[30] [544] 4-9-0 **78** .... JerryO'Dwyer 3 69
(Miss J Feilden) *hld up in 5th: rdn and no prog over 2f out: fdd over 1f out* **12/1**

1m 38.16s (-1.64) **Going Correction** +0.025s/f (Slow) **8** Ran SP% **120.7**
Speed ratings (Par 105): **109,105,101,101,100 100,98,97**
toteswinger: 1&2 £12.70, 1&3 £10.80, 2&3 £8.80. CSF £77.82 CT £592.28 TOTE £7.30: £3.20, £2.60, £2.20; EX 161.40.
Owner sportaracing.com & George Houghton **Bred** Gary Chervenell **Trained** Lambourn, Berks

FOCUS
The winning time was quite good, but the winner was allowed his own way up front, only appearing to increase the pace after a furlong or so, and those who raced handy were at an advantage.
Faithful Ruler(USA) Official explanation: trainer was unable to offer any explanation for the poor form shown

851 FREEBETS.CO.UK CHAMPIONS LEAGUE FREE BETS H'CAP (LONDON MILE QUALIFIER) 1m (P)
4:30 (4:32) (Class 4) (0-85,85) 3-Y-O **£4,727** (£1,406; £702; £351) **Stalls** High

Form RPR

2-11 **1** **Statute Book (IRE)**[17] [707] 3-8-4 **74** .... DavidProbert(3) 2 76+
(S Kirk) *trckd ldng pair: effrt on outer to ld 2f out: sn looked in command: idled fnl f and drvn out* **7/1**[3]

210- **2** *½* **Pegasus Lad (USA)**[205] [5274] 3-9-2 **83** .... JoeFanning 6 84
(M Johnston) *trckd ldr: led briefly over 2f out: urged along whn hdd and nt qckn: kpt on to cl on wnr ins fnl f* **5/2**[2]

03-1 **3** *½* **Pearl Of Manacor (IRE)**[54] [236] 3-8-11 **78** .... TonyCulhane 1 79+
(M R Channon) *hld up in last: u.p and struggling 3f out: effrt on outer 2f out: kpt on fnl f but nvr able to chal* **4/5**[1]

230- **4** *¾* **Roly Boy**[142] [6970] 3-9-4 **85** .... RichardHughes 4 83
(R Hannon) *trckd ldng pair: effrt over 2f out: rdn and nt qckn wl over 1f out: pushed along fnl f but lost no further grnd* **9/1**

2 **5** *7* **The Winged Assasin (USA)**[47] [315] 3-8-7 **74** .... NickyMackay 5 57
(J Akehurst) *pushed up to ld: hdd u.p over 2f out: wknd* **25/1**

1m 39.95s (0.15) **Going Correction** +0.025s/f (Slow) **5** Ran SP% **110.5**
Speed ratings (Par 100): **100,99,99,98,91**
toteswinger: 1&2 £9.00. CSF £24.59 TOTE £5.00: £2.10, £1.10; EX 12.30.
Owner R J Brennan and D Boocock **Bred** R J Brennan And D Boocock **Trained** Upper Lambourn, Berks

FOCUS
A good three-year-old handicap despite the small field, featuring several with form on an artificial surface.
The Winged Assasin(USA) Official explanation: jockey said the colt had no more to give

852 FREEBETS.CO.UK INTERNET FREE BETS FILLIES' H'CAP 6f (P)
5:00 (5:05) (Class 4) (0-85,82) 3-Y-O+ **£4,727** (£1,406; £702; £351) **Stalls** High

Form RPR

21- **1** **Aroundthebay**[150] [6770] 3-8-7 **77** .... ChrisCatlin 2 84+
(H J L Dunlop) *pressed ldr to wl over 1f out: kpt battling away u.p: styd on fnl f to ld last strides* **4/1**[2]

300- **2** *nk* **Daddy's Gift (IRE)**[128] [7241] 3-8-11 **81** .... RichardHughes 4 87
(R Hannon) *trckd ldng pair: effrt on inner over 2f out: led over 1f out: hrd rdn fnl f: hdd last strides* **11/4**[1]

21- **3** *2* **Miss Chamanda (IRE)**[329] [1523] 3-8-8 **78** .... JamieSpencer 1 78
(P D Evans) *wnt lft s but led: drvn and hdd over 1f out: one pce* **6/1**

0-23 **4** *2* **Artistic License (IRE)**[17] [714] 4-9-11 **82** .... TonyCulhane 7 79
(M R Channon) *hld up in last: drvn and prog on outer fr 2f out to press ldrs jst over 1f out: btn ins fnl f and fin slowly* **5/1**[3]

0-21 **5** *2* **Hallingdal (UAE)**[30] [557] 4-9-6 **77** .... JamesDoyle 6 68+
(Ms J S Doyle) *hld up in 5th: effrt over 2f out: chsng ldrs over 1f out: wknd ins fnl f: eased last 75yds* **11/2**

130- **6** *8* **Polar Annie**[166] [6402] 4-9-6 **77** .... TGMcLaughlin 5 42
(M S Saunders) *t.k.h early: hld up in tch: lft wl bhd fr 2f out: t.o* **4/1**[2]

1m 12.86s (-0.24) **Going Correction** +0.025s/f (Slow)
WFA 3 from 4yo 13lb **6** Ran SP% **113.0**
Speed ratings (Par 102): **102,101,98,96,93 82**
toteswinger: 1&2 £4.00, 1&3 £3.90, 2&3 £3.60. CSF £15.59 TOTE £6.10: £2.80, £1.90; EX 26.50.
Owner The Endeavour Partnership **Bred** R G Levin **Trained** Lambourn, Berks

FOCUS
A fair fillies' sprint, but the pace was surprisingly modest.

853 FREEBETS.CO.UK FREE SPORTS BETS H'CAP (DIV I) 6f (P)
5:30 (5:35) (Class 6) (0-55,55) 4-Y-O+ **£1,706** (£503; £252) **Stalls** High

Form RPR

1430 **1** **Sherjawy (IRE)**[35] [467] 5-8-8 **47** .... (b) SamHitchcott 10 57
(Miss Z C Davison) *trckd ldrs: effrt on inner 2f out: rdn to ld jst over 1f out: jnd ins fnl f: kpt on wl* **11/1**

0-34 **2** *½* **Patavium Prince (IRE)**[22] [646] 6-9-2 **55** .... DaneO'Neill 12 64
(Miss Jo Crowley) *trckd ldrs: effrt 2f out: prog over 1f out: chal and looked likely wnr ins fnl f: n.g.t last 100yds* **11/4**[1]

4442 **3** *1* **Flamestone**[5] [803] 5-8-2 **48** .... RichardRowe(7) 4 54
(A E Price) *trckd ldrs: effrt over 2f out: bmpd along fr over 1f out: nt qckn* **11/2**[3]

3131 **4** *¾* **Convince (USA)**[13] [746] 8-8-5 **51** .... BMcHugh(7) 5 54+
(K M Prendergast) *rrd s: t.k.h and hld up in rr: prog on outer 2f out: tried to cl on ldrs 1f out: one pce* **4/1**[2]

5532 **5** *2 ½* **Green Lagonda (AUS)**[3] [832] 7-9-2 **55** .... MickyFenton 7 51
(Stef Liddiard) *plld hrd: hld up in last: prog 2f out: styd on fnl f: nvr rrr* **4/1**[2]

00-6 **6** *1* **Trivia (IRE)**[2] [844] 5-9-2 **55** .... JamesDoyle 9 48
(Ms J S Doyle) *led: drvn 2f out: hdd jst over 1f out: wknd* **25/1**

0345 **7** *shd* **Avoca Dancer (IRE)**[22] [646] 6-9-0 **53** .... (p) DarryllHolland 1 45+
(Karen George) *pressed ldr to over 1f out: losing pl whn n.m.r sn after* **10/1**

5120 **8** *1* **Davids Mark**[22] [646] 9-9-2 **55** .... SimonWhitworth 8 44+
(J R Jenkins) *hld up in rr: stdy prog fr jst over 2f out: trying to cl on ldrs whn hmpd 1f out and stmbld bdly: nt rcvr* **12/1**

00-0 **9** *¾* **The Jailer**[20] [661] 6-8-11 **50** .... VinceSlattery 3 37
(J G M O'Shea) *nvr bttr than midfield: outpcd and detached in last pair 2f out: plugged on* **50/1**

3450 **10** *¾* **Chalentina**[2] [844] 6-8-2 **48** oh1 ow2 .... PNolan(7) 2 33
(J E Long) *awkward s: hld up in last pair: detached 2f out: plugged on* **25/1**

1m 13.21s (0.11) **Going Correction** +0.025s/f (Slow) **10** Ran SP% **116.8**
Speed ratings (Par 101): **100,99,98,97,93 92,92,90,89,88**
toteswinger: 1&2 £6.70, 1&3 £4.00, 2&3 £7.70. CSF £40.85 CT £195.47 TOTE £14.30: £3.20, £1.50, £2.00; EX 55.90.

Owner Andy Irvine **Bred** Darley **Trained** Hammerwood, E Sussex
FOCUS
A moderate but competitive sprint handicap.
Davids Mark Official explanation: jockey said gelding clipped heels inside the final furlong

854 FREEBETS.CO.UK FREE SPORTS BETS H'CAP (DIV II) 6f (P)
6:00 (6:06) (Class 6) (0-55,55) 4-Y-0+ **£1,706** (£503; £252) **Stalls** High

Form RPR
-004 **1** **Mr Skipiton (IRE)**19 675 4-8-11 **50** TGMcLaughlin 7 60
(B J McMath) *swtg: trckd ldrs: wnt 2nd over 2f out: hrd rdn to cl and ld 1f out: hld on wl* **10/1**
3-00 **2** ½ **Elusive Dreams (USA)**22 646 5-9-2 **55** (v) TolleyDean 11 63
(P Howling) *s.s: hld up in last: prog on inner over 2f out: rdn to chal ent fnl f: hd high and nt qckn* **6/1**3
-640 **3** 1¼ **Briannsta (IRE)**5 811 7-8-7 **46** (b) RichardThomas 12 50
(J E Long) *in tch: prog on inner 2f out: chsd ldng pair and cl enough ins fnl f: one pce* **4/1**2
004 **4** 3¼ **Trinculo (IRE)**14 739 12-8-13 **55** (b) KevinGhunowa(3) 3 49
(R A Harris) *led: clr over 2f out: hdd & wknd 1f out* **16/1**
0-56 **5** 3¼ **Morse (IRE)**49 292 8-9-1 **54** (p) DaneO'Neill 8 37
(J A Osborne) *dwlt: mostly in last trio and nt gng that wl: effrt over 2f out: sn no prog* **9/4**1
04-6 **6** 1½ **Bateleur**22 646 5-8-12 **51** EdwardCreighton 4 29
(M R Channon) *hld up in rr: outpcd sn after 1/2-way: btn after* **8/1**
0050 **7** ¾ **Lake Sabina**20 661 4-8-11 **50** AndrewElliott 6 26
(M R Hoad) *chsd ldrs: rdn bef 1/2-way: lft bhd over 2f out* **12/1**
4/00 **8** 11 **Siraj**22 646 10-8-2 **48** (p) RyanPowell(7) 1 —
(J Ryan) *racd wd: chsd ldrs to 1/2-way: sn wknd: t.o* **50/1**
0-01 **9** 5 **Ramblin Bob**14 727 4-8-10 **49** (bt) ChrisCatlin 5 —
(W J Musson) *plld hrd: chsd ldr to over 2f out: wknd rapidly: t.o* **6/1**3
1m 12.56s (-0.54) **Going Correction** +0.025s/f (Slow) 9 Ran SP% **115.1**
Speed ratings (Par 101): **104,103,101,97,93 91,90,75,68**
toteswinger: 1&2 £13.50, 1&3 £9.20, 2&3 £4.00. CSF £68.39 CT £282.27 TOTE £13.30: £3.30, £2.30, £2.10; EX 112.60 Place 6: £118.61, Place 5: £53.51..
Owner Steve & Ros Chaplin-Brown **Bred** Darragh O'Reilly **Trained** Newmarket, Suffolk
■ Stewards' Enquiry : T G McLaughlin one-day ban: used whip with excessive frequency (Mar 30)
FOCUS
The winning time was 0.65 seconds quicker than the first division.
T/Plt: £502.00 to a £1 stake. Pool: £64,440.87. 93.70 winning tickets. T/Qpdt: £31.60 to a £1 stake. Pool: £5,010.40. 117.22 winning tickets. JN

818 SOUTHWELL (L-H)
Tuesday, March 17

OFFICIAL GOING: Standard
Wind: light 1/2 against Weather: fine but overcast

855 BRING MOTHER RACING ON MOTHERS DAY MAIDEN STKS 1m (F)
2:20 (2:21) (Class 5) 3-Y-0+ **£2,590** (£770; £385; £192) **Stalls** Low

Form RPR
1 **Clippity Clop (IRE)** 3-8-9 0 ChrisCatlin 9 70+
(J A Osborne) *chsd ldrs on outer: effrt over 2f out: wnt 2nd ins fnl f: hung bdly rt: led last strides* **7/1**2
6 **2** nk **Karta (IRE)**39 425 3-8-4 0 GregFairley 5 64+
(M Johnston) *trckd ldrs: led over 2f out: hdd nr fin* **7/4**1
5- **3** 3 **The Bully Wee**130 7221 3-8-9 0 LukeMorris 1 62
(J Jay) *w ldr: led over 3f out: hdd over 2f out: kpt on same pce appr fnl f* **8/1**3
53- **4** 1 **Magical Destiny (IRE)**95 7649 3-8-9 0 TomEaves 2 60
(B Smart) *chsd ldrs: pushed along over 4f out: hrd drvn over 2f out: hung rt: one pce* **7/4**1
5 6 **Funky Munky** 4-9-12 0 PJMcDonald 3 51
(G A Swinbank) *dwlt: sn chsng ldrs: hung rt and wknd appr fnl f* **20/1**
0 **6** 3 **Lunar Storm (IRE)**11 779 5-9-12 0 AndrewElliott 6 44
(Mrs R A Carr) *sn drvn along in rr: outpcd over 2f out: nvr a factor* **40/1**
00 **7** 12 **Gingko Lady (USA)**13 749 4-9-7 51 (v1) PatCosgrave 7 12
(J R Boyle) *led: hdd over 3f out: wknd over 2f out* **16/1**
0 **8** 3¾ **Gamegear**5 820 4-9-0 0 (b1) AndrewYoxall(7) 4 —
(S R Bowring) *in rr: drvn 5f out: nvr nr ldrs* **100/1**
9 13 **Elevate Bobbob** 3-8-5 0 ow1 SladeO'Hara(5) 8 —
(A Berry) *s.i.s: in tch: lost pl over 2f out: sn bhd* **50/1**
1m 44.06s (0.36) **Going Correction** +0.05s/f (Slow)
WFA 3 from 4yo+ 17lb 9 Ran SP% **112.4**
Speed ratings (Par 103): **100,99,96,95,89 86,74,70,57**
toteswinger: 1&2 £4.40, 1&3 £6.70, 2&3 £5.40. CSF £18.75 TOTE £5.50: £1.50, £1.20, £2.50; EX 11.00 Trifecta £94.70 Pool: £307.37 - 2.40 winning units..
Owner J A Osborne **Bred** W McCreery **Trained** Upper Lambourn, Berks
FOCUS
Just a modest maiden, but the front two pulled clear.

856 QUEEN MOTHER RESTAURANT FOR MOTHERS DAY H'CAP 6f (F)
2:55 (2:55) (Class 3) (0-95,93) 4-Y-0+ **£9,034** (£2,705; £1,352; £677) **Stalls** Low

Form RPR
5100 **1** **Nightjar (USA)**10 783 4-9-3 **92** GregFairley 3 99
(M Johnston) *trckd ldr: swtchd lft over 2f out: led over 1f out: hung rt: hld on towards fin* **1/1**1
2104 **2** hd **Xpres Maite**11 778 6-8-12 **87** (b) RobertWinston 1 93
(S R Bowring) *chsd ldrs: drvn over 2f out: hung lft 2f out: kpt on: no ex nr fin* **5/2**2
21 **3** 1¼ **Wotashirtfull (IRE)**21 665 4-8-6 **81** MartinDwyer 2 84
(J R Boyle) *led: edgd rt over 2f out: hdd over 1f out: kpt on same pce* **3/1**3
001- **4** 4½ **Invincible Force (IRE)**129 7245 5-9-4 **93** (b) ChrisCatlin 4 82
(Paul Green) *rrd s: t.k.h: sn trcking ldrs: rdn over 2f out: wknd appr fnl f* **9/1**
1m 15.78s (-0.72) **Going Correction** +0.05s/f (Slow) 4 Ran SP% **113.6**
Speed ratings (Par 107): **106,105,104,98**
CSF £4.07 TOTE £2.20; EX 4.20.
Owner Crone Stud Farms Ltd **Bred** Derry Meeting Farm & London Thoroughbred Services **Trained** Middleham Moor, N Yorks
FOCUS
A poor turnout numerically for the money, but still quite a competitive contest. They all edged right in the straight, ending up towards the stands' side.

NOTEBOOK
Nightjar(USA) extended his unbeaten record on Fibresand to four races, having been well backed to do so. His three previous wins on this surface had been gained over 7f, but he displayed sufficient speed on this drop in trip and, having mastered Wotashirtful around a furlong out, he just held off the runner-up's late challenge. (op 11-8 tchd 6-4)
Xpres Maite ran quite lazily early on, as per usual, but he responded to strong pressure in the straight and very nearly pegged back the favourite. (op 3-1)
Wotashirtfull(IRE) had no excuses and was able to lead at just an ordinary pace for the distance, albeit the winner was never too far away. (op 9-4)
Invincible Force(IRE) ran as though this first run in over four months was needed and he should do better back on turf. (op 10-1 tchd 12-1 and 8-1)

857 RACING HERE ON MOTHERS DAY H'CAP 1m 3f (F)
3:30 (3:32) (Class 6) (0-60,60) 4-Y-0+ **£1,942** (£578; £288; £144) **Stalls** Low

Form RPR
2-03 **1** **That'll Do Nicely (IRE)**18 711 6-9-4 **59** PaulMulrennan 9 70
(N G Richards) *trckd ldrs: led jst ins fnl f: hld on towards fin* **4/1**2
30-6 **2** hd **Spares And Repairs**57 217 6-8-11 **52** RobertWinston 7 63
(Mrs S Lamyman) *w ldrs: led 2f out: hdd ins fnl f: no ex nr fin* **20/1**
6-61 **3** 1¾ **Elliwan**7 790 4-8-11 **53** (b) DaleGibson 8 61
(M W Easterby) *trckd ldrs: drvn over 4f out: outpcd over 2f out: kpt on appr fnl f* **8/13**1
600- **4** 2½ **Capistrano**187 5833 6-8-4 **45** (p) PaulEddery 10 48
(Paul Mason) *led after 1f: hdd 2f out: fdd jst ins fnl f* **16/1**
6045 **5** 5 **Coral Shores**5 813 4-9-1 **57** (v) ChrisCatlin 3 51
(P W Hiatt) *t.k.h in rr: hdwy on outer 6f out: sn chsng ldrs: wknd over 1f out* **10/1**3
00-5 **6** 2 **Deadline (UAE)**25 618 5-8-13 **54** JoeFanning 2 44
(P T Midgley) *mid-div: drvn 5f out: lost pl 3f out: no ch after* **18/1**
4-05 **7** ¾ **Mill Beattie**20 678 4-8-6 **48** AndrewElliott 5 37
(J Mackie) *led 1f: chsd ldrs: rdn over 3f out: lost pl over 1f out* **25/1**
2213 **8** 2 **Lady Longcroft**19 688 4-9-4 **60** TGMcLaughlin 4 45
(J Pearce) *trckd ldrs: t.k.h: wknd over 1f out* **10/1**3
9 nk **Golden Future**911 4411 6-9-0 **55** TomEaves 1 40
(P D Niven) *in rr: nvr a factor* **66/1**
00-0 **10** 10 **Little Rococoa**22 658 4-7-12 **45** AmyBaker(5) 6 12
(R J Price) *in rr: drvn over 4f out: bhd fnl 2f* **66/1**
2m 28.48s (0.48) **Going Correction** +0.05s/f (Slow)
WFA 4 from 5yo+ 1lb 10 Ran SP% **122.8**
Speed ratings (Par 101): **100,99,98,96,93 91,91,89,89,82**
toteswinger: 1&2 £9.30, 1&3 £1.80, 2&3 £5.50. CSF £85.16 CT £112.72 TOTE £5.70: £1.50, £4.10, £1.10; EX 102.80 Trifecta £544.20 Pool: £926.77 - 1.26 winning units..
Owner J D Flood **Bred** J D Flood **Trained** Greystoke, Cumbria
■ The first Flat winner for Nicky Richards.
FOCUS
A modest handicap run at an ordinary pace, and a bit of a turn up.
Lady Longcroft Official explanation: trainer said filly finished distressed

858 VISIT NOTTINGHAMSHIRE THE HOME OF ROBIN HOOD H'CAP 1m (F)
4:05 (4:05) (Class 4) (0-85,85) 4-Y-0+ **£4,727** (£1,406; £702) **Stalls** Low

Form RPR
1 **1** **Boscage (USA)**15 731 4-9-4 **85** JoeFanning 2 97+
(M Johnston) *t.k.h: trckd ldr: lft in ld bnd over 4f out: shkn up over 1f out: r.o strly: forged clr: eased towards fin* **2/7**1
1336 **2** 8 **United Nations**19 693 8-8-9 **76** (b) LeeEnstone 5 73+
(N Wilson) *hld up in last: jnd wnr over 3f out: btn appr fnl f: eased ins fnl f* **7/2**2
600- **3** 12 **Sudden Impact (IRE)**129 7243 4-9-4 **85** ChrisCatlin 4 59+
(Paul Green) *led: t.k.h and hung bdly rt: rn wd bnd and hdd over 4f out: lost pl 3f out: bhd and eased 1f out* **22/1**3
1m 42.41s (-1.29) **Going Correction** +0.05s/f (Slow) 3 Ran SP% **104.3**
Speed ratings (Par 105): **108,100,88**
CSF £1.47 TOTE £1.30; EX 1.10.
Owner Sheikh Hamdan Bin Mohammed Al Maktoum **Bred** R S Evans **Trained** Middleham Moor, N Yorks
FOCUS
This was uncompetitive handicap and all three runners were eased in the straight once their finishing positions were established.
Sudden Impact(IRE) Official explanation: jockey said filly hung right throughout

859 RENDLESHAM H'CAP 6f (F)
4:40 (4:40) (Class 4) (0-85,86) 3-Y-0 **£4,727** (£1,406; £702; £351) **Stalls** Low

Form RPR
0-16 **1** **Takeover Bid (USA)**51 288 3-9-4 **77** JoeFanning 5 84
(M Johnston) *swvd rt s: sn led: rdn and edgd lft over 1f out: hld on wl* **9/4**2
6-13 **2** 1 **Fesko**10 782 3-9-7 **80** GregFairley 3 84
(M Johnston) *led early: effrt and edgd lft 2f out: styd on same pce fnl f* **1/1**1
5221 **3** 3 **Lesley's Choice**5 814 3-9-6 **86** 6ex ManavNem(7) 4 80
(R Curtis) *trckd ldrs: t.k.h: edgd lft over 1f out: kpt on same pce* **6/1**3
240- **4** 1¼ **Noodles Blue Boy**162 6525 3-9-2 **75** TonyHamilton 1 65
(Ollie Pears) *in tch: effrt over 2f out: kpt on ins fnl f* **20/1**
130- **5** 3¼ **Rio Cobolo (IRE)**80 7794 3-8-7 **66** (v) ChrisCatlin 2 46
(Paul Green) *hdwy over 4f out: sn chsng ldrs: edgd lft and lost pl over 1f out* **10/1**
1m 16.41s (-0.09) **Going Correction** +0.05s/f (Slow) 5 Ran SP% **108.9**
Speed ratings (Par 100): **102,100,96,95,90**
CSF £4.77 TOTE £3.30: £1.40, £1.10; EX 6.40.
Owner Sheikh Hamdan Bin Mohammed Al Maktoum **Bred** Darley **Trained** Middleham Moor, N Yorks
FOCUS
An ordinary three-year-old handicap for the grade.

860 VICTORY QUEST H'CAP 1m 6f (F)
5:10 (5:10) (Class 5) (0-75,73) 4-Y-0+ **£2,590** (£770; £385; £192) **Stalls** Low

Form RPR
0542 **1** **Calculating (IRE)**6 809 5-8-6 **60** DavidProbert(3) 4 68+
(M D I Usher) *rrd s: sn trcking ldrs: drvn 4f out: styd on to ld appr fnl f: kpt on wl* **13/8**1
5141 **2** 2½ **William's Way**15 734 7-9-4 **69** ChrisCatlin 2 74+
(I A Wood) *t.k.h: hdwy to ld and qcknd 5f out: kpt on same pce fnl f* **9/2**
3221 **3** ¾ **Augustus John (IRE)**15 735 6-9-5 **70** TomEaves 3 74+
(R Brotherton) *t.k.h: hdwy over 4f out: sn chsng wnr: styd on same pce fnl f* **3/1**2

0005 **4** 3¾ **Spiritonthemount (USA)**[6] 809 4-8-4 59 oh9..............(b) LiamJones 5 57
(P W Hiatt) *set slow pce: hdd 5f out: outpcd over 2f out* **12/1**

3013 **5** 11 **Victory Quest (IRE)**[6] 809 9-9-8 73..............(v) RobertWinston 1 56
(Mrs S Lamyman) *trckd ldrs: rdn and outpcd over 4f out: lost pl over 1f out: eased ins fnl f* **7/2**[3]

3m 16.23s (7.93) **Going Correction** +0.05s/f (Slow)
WFA 4 from 5yo+ 4lb **5** Ran SP% **111.2**
Speed ratings (Par 103): **79,77,77,75,68**
CSF £9.36 TOTE £2.60: £1.10, £3.40; EX 7.90 Place 6: £5.22, Place 5: £3.17..
Owner Brian Rogan **Bred** Darley **Trained** Upper Lambourn, Berks

FOCUS
This was run at a farcical pace early and the form is suspect.
Victory Quest(IRE) Official explanation: jockey said gelding ran flat
T/Plt: £19.40 to a £1 stake. Pool: £49,596.97. 1,858.71 winning tickets. T/Qpdt: £2.80 to a £1 stake. Pool: £3,549.60. 932.70 winning tickets. WG

847 KEMPTON (A.W) (R-H)
Wednesday, March 18

OFFICIAL GOING: Standard
Wind: virtually nil Weather: dry

861 CHURCHILL DOWNS INCORPORATED H'CAP 6f (P)
6:50 (6:50) (Class 6) (0-65,69) 4-Y-0+ **£2,047** (£604; £302) **Stalls** High

Form RPR

1301 **1** **What Katie Did (IRE)**[7] 799 4-9-8 69 6ex..............(p) JamieSpencer 2 76
(J M Bradley) *mde all: clr 4f out: rdn wl over 1f out: kpt on and jst lasted* **11/4**[1]

060- **2** *nse* **Peopleton Brook**[110] 7471 7-8-13 60..............(t) DaneO'Neill 9 67+
(B G Powell) *dwlt: hld up in midfield: plld out and rdn wl over 1f out: chsd wnr fnl 100yds: r.o wl: jst hld* **16/1**

5-40 **3** 1½ **Ask Jenny (IRE)**[5] 832 7-8-11 58.............. RichardHughes 8 60
(Patrick Morris) *t.k.h: hld up in tch: rdn and effrt 2f out: chsd wnr jst over 1f out: kpt on same pce fnl 100yds* **14/1**

2243 **4** ¾ **Hart Of Gold**[16] 739 5-8-13 63..............(p) KevinGhunowa(3) 4 63
(R A Harris) *t.k.h: chsd wnr tl jst over 1f out: kpt on one pce fnl f* **13/2**[3]

5 2 **Zars Gold (IRE)**[151] 6828 4-9-1 62.............. ChrisCatlin 5 56+
(J Gallagher) *s.i.s: hld up in last pl: edging rt looking for run fr wl over 1f out: styd on but n.d* **11/1**

-034 **6** ½ **Prince Of Delphi**[16] 728 6-8-13 60..............(p) JimCrowley 6 53+
(Mrs A L M King) *lw: chsd ldrs: rdn to dispute 2nd 2f out tl over 1f out: wknd fnl f* **8/1**

6131 **7** 1¾ **Hollow Jo**[24] 646 9-9-4 65..............(v) MickyFenton 1 52
(J R Jenkins) *slowly into strde: hld up towards rr: hdwy on outer 1/2-way: rdn over 2f out: sn no imp* **14/1**

0322 **8** ½ **Compton Classic**[20] 691 7-9-0 61..............(p) PatCosgrave 12 47
(J R Boyle) *lw: plld hrd: hld up in midfield: rdn and fnd little 2f out: wknd ent fnl f* **9/2**[2]

0215 **9** ½ **Fizzlephut (IRE)**[6] 818 7-9-0 61.............. PaulFitzsimons 11 45
(Miss J R Tooth) *stdd and hmpd sn after s: hld up towards rr: n.d* **12/1**

-266 **10** 3¼ **Angel Voices (IRE)**[24] 651 6-8-11 58..............(v) DarrenWilliams 7 33
(K R Burke) *racd in midfield: rdn over 2f out: sn struggling* **20/1**

-000 **11** *nk* **Bishopbriggs (USA)**[28] 590 4-8-13 60..............(p) ShaneKelly 10 34
(J Ryan) *t.k.h: hld up in rr: n.d* **28/1**

4-04 **12** 3½ **Littledodayno (IRE)**[38] 461 6-9-2 63.............. NickyMackay 3 26
(M Wigham) *tk t.k.h: hld up towards rr: rdn 1/2-way: bhd fnl 2f* **11/1**

1m 12.82s (-0.28) **Going Correction** +0.05s/f (Slow) **12** Ran SP% **121.1**
Speed ratings (Par 101): **103,102,100,99,97 96,94,93,92,88 88,83**
toteswinger: 1&2 £24.30, 1&3 £37.60, 2&3 £7.30. CSF £51.91 CT £550.35 TOTE £3.90: £1.50, £6.60, £4.60; EX 85.30.
Owner Mr & Mrs M B Carver **Bred** Brian Williamson **Trained** Sedbury, Gloucs
■ Stewards' Enquiry : Kevin Ghunowa one-day ban: failed to keep straight from stalls (Apr 1)
Jamie Spencer one-day ban: failed to ride to draw (Apr 1)

FOCUS
A moderate sprint handicap.
Bishopbriggs(USA) Official explanation: jockey said gelding hung right throughout

862 DIGIBET.COM MAIDEN STKS 6f (P)
7:20 (7:20) (Class 4) 3-Y-O **£4,727** (£1,406; £702; £351) **Stalls** High

Form RPR

3- **1** **Dunes Queen (USA)**[160] 6600 3-8-12 0.............. TonyCulhane 7 81+
(M R Channon) *lw: t.k.h: trckd ldng pair: rdn to ld over 1f out: clr ins fnl f: comf* **4/9**[1]

2 3½ **Lighthearted (FR)**[182] 3-8-12 0.............. AdamKirby 1 68+
(C G Cox) *w'like: chsd ldr: rdn and ev ch jst over 2f out: outpcd by wnr 1f out: 2nd and wl hld after* **25/1**

00- **3** 1½ **The Hague**[170] 6342 3-9-3 0.............. RHills 4 68+
(J H M Gosden) *s.i.s: rn green in last pair: hmpd after 1f out: rdn over 3f out: outpcd over 2f out: styd on to go 3rd ins fnl f: no ch w wnr* **17/2**[3]

323- **4** 2 **Peninsular War**[293] 2522 3-9-3 81.............. AndrewElliott 9 62
(K R Burke) *t.k.h: led at stdy gallop: jnd and rdn jst over 2f out: hdd over 1f out: wknd fnl f* **7/2**[2]

5 10 **Fravia** 3-8-7 0.............. NicolPolli(5) 5 27
(B J McMath) *leggy: unf: s.i.s and wnt rt s: a in rr: in tch tl rdn and wknd over 2f out: sn wl btn* **33/1**

04- **P** **Oceanic Dancer (IRE)**[140] 7082 3-8-12 0.............. JamieSpencer 3 —
(Patrick Morris) *lw: wnt rt s: eased and p.u sn after s* **16/1**

1m 13.41s (0.31) **Going Correction** +0.05s/f (Slow) **6** Ran SP% **114.7**
Speed ratings (Par 100): **99,94,92,89,76** —
toteswinger: 1&2 £4.30, 1&3 £2.10, 2&3 £18.90. CSF £15.94 TOTE £1.50: £1.10, £5.50; EX 19.40.
Owner Jaber Abdullah **Bred** Gainsborough Farm Llc **Trained** West Ilsley, Berks

FOCUS
The bare form of this maiden is nothing special, but the winner and the third look potentially useful and can rate much higher. The pace was just modest early on.
Oceanic Dancer(IRE) Official explanation: jockey said filly lost its action shortly after start and was pulled up

863 KENTUCKY DERBY CHALLENGE STKS (CONDITIONS STAKES) 1m 1f (P)
7:50 (7:51) (Class 2) 3-Y-O
£49,848 (£14,928; £7,464; £3,736; £1,864; £936) **Stalls** High

Form RPR

15- **1** **Mafaaz**[165] 6474 3-9-3 99..............(b[1]) RHills 7 102+
(J H M Gosden) *lw: s.i.s: sn bustled along and hdwy to r in midfield: gd hdwy 6f out: chsd ldrs over 4f out: wnt 2nd 2f out: rdn to chal over 1f out: styd on wl to ld fnl 100yds* **11/2**[2]

51-1 **2** *nk* **Spring Of Fame (USA)**[13] 763 3-9-3 89.............. ChrisCatlin 8 102+
(M A Magnusson) *lw: hld up in rr on inner: swtchd lft wl over 1f out: stl plenty to do ent fnl f: str run fnl f: wnt 2nd nr fin: nt quite get to wnr* **6/1**[3]

440- **3** *nk* **Sohcahtoa (IRE)**[165] 6474 3-9-3 97.............. RyanMoore 10 100
(R Hannon) *dashed into ld: stdd pce after 2f: rdn and qcknd 2f out: sn hrd pressed by wnr: hdd and no ex fnl 100yds* **20/1**

13- **4** *hd* **Mastery**[152] 6779 3-9-3 97.............. JoeFanning 13 100+
(M Johnston) *bit bkwd: v.s.a: towards rr: rdn and hdwy on outer over 3f out: chsd ldng pair ins fnl f: r.o wl but nvr quite getting to ldrs* **10/1**

020- **5** 1½ **Weald Park (USA)**[144] 6973 3-9-3 97.............. RichardHughes 4 97
(R Hannon) *lw: chsd ldrs: rdn jst over 2f out: kpt on same pce fnl f* **10/1**

010- **6** ½ **Shampagne**[144] 6979 3-9-3 103.............. MartinDwyer 6 96
(P F I Cole) *racd in midfield: edgd rt and effrt over 1f out: drvn ent fnl f: kpt on same pce fnl f* **12/1**

1- **7** 2¾ **Close Alliance (USA)**[160] 6597 3-9-3 90.............. JimmyFortune 5 94+
(J H M Gosden) *str: lw: s.i.s: racd in last pair: gd hdwy over 5f out: chsd ldrs and rdn 3f out: wknd ent fnl f* **7/1**

540- **8** *nk* **Agente Parmigiano (IRE)**[180] 6082 3-9-3 85.............. ShaneKelly 14 91+
(G A Butler) *hld up in tch: chsd ldrs whn nt clr run on inner and hmpd over 1f out: kpt on fnl f but nvr able to chal* **100/1**

664- **9** 1¾ **Deposer (IRE)**[153] 3-9-3 101.............. SteveDrowne 3 87+
(J R Best) *stdd towards rr sn after s: t.k.h: c v wd bnd 2f out: hmpd sn after: sme late hdwy: nvr trbld ldrs* **25/1**

41-1 **10** *shd* **Markyg (USA)**[21] 672 3-9-3 92.............. FergusSweeney 2 86
(K R Burke) *lw: dwlt: sn in midfield: t.k.h: hdwy to chse ldrs 5f out: wknd u.p over 1f out* **20/1**

536- **11** *hd* **Talking Hands**[158] 6648 3-9-3 97.............. GeorgeBaker 9 86+
(S Kirk) *chsd ldrs: tl lost pl over 3f out: bhd whn hmpd over 1f out* **25/1**

54-1 **12** 1 **Akhenaten**[13] 764 3-9-3 94.............. TonyCulhane 11 87+
(M R Channon) *lw: racd in midfield: effrt whn nt clr run and hmpd over 1f out: no ch and nt pushed after* **16/1**

4-00 **13** 2¾ **Keeptheboatafloat (USA)**[13] 769 3-9-3 92..............(b) DarrenWilliams 1 78
(K R Burke) *s.i.s: dropped in bhd: a in rr* **100/1**

1- **14** 2 **Haashed (USA)**[114] 7438 3-9-3 88.............. JamieSpencer 12 78+
(M Johnston) *leggy: attractive: chsd ldr tl 2f out: wknd u.p over 1f out: eased ins fnl f* **9/4**[1]

1m 55.13s (-0.67) **Going Correction** +0.05s/f (Slow) **14** Ran SP% **123.9**
Speed ratings (Par 104): **104,103,103,103,101 101,99,98,97,97 96,96,93,91**
toteswinger: 1&2 £8.60, 1&3 £31.40, 2&3 £44.60. CSF £36.79 TOTE £7.70: £2.30, £2.90, £6.20; EX 50.20.
Owner Hamdan Al Maktoum **Bred** The Complimentary Pass Partnership **Trained** Newmarket, Suffolk
■ Stewards' Enquiry : Richard Hughes two-day ban: careless riding (Apr 1-2)
Chris Catlin 13-day ban: (3 for careless riding and 10 under totting-up procedure - 2 days deferred for 3 months) (Apr 11-21)

FOCUS
The second running of this conditions contest - subsequent Royal Ascot winner Campanologist won last year's race - but the prize-money was bolstered significantly this season and the winner is guaranteed a run in the Kentucky Derby. The successful connections will also receive a further $100,000 if their horse makes the journey to Churchill Downs. While great initiative has been shown by all concerned to make this happen, in truth it's hard to consider this a serious trial for the 'The Run for the Roses', considering it was run around a right-handed track on Polytrack. And while a very decent field assembled, few of these looked genuine Derby types. The pace was strong early, but slowed noticeably in the middle part of the contest and it was a messy race.

NOTEBOOK
Mafaaz, who looked decent at two when winning a 7f maiden here, before running fifth in arguably the hottest juvenile race run in Britain last year at Newmarket, took well to the fitting of first-time blinkers and benefited from a terrific ride. Although caught wide into the straight, Richard Hills had made crucial headway to sit handy before the final bend, recovering well from a slow start, and his mount had just enough in hand to hold off the unlucky runner-up. The plan now is to go for the Blue Grass Stakes at Keeneland, provided he gets in, and he must have a chance there, with that race run on a synthetic surface. Provided all goes well, he'll then take in the big one, and that's when things will get really tough. (op 5-1 tchd 9-2)
Spring Of Fame(USA) ◆, held in the highest regard by his trainer, ran a massive race in defeat, confirming the impression he made when winning his last two starts on this surface. He found himself well back at the top of the straight, having been held up towards the inside early on, but he picked up in terrific style when switched widest of all, passing the majority of the field, and he probably would have got up in a few more strides. His trainer is now thinking about the European Classics, but it would be no surprise were he to still head Stateside at some stage, either to try the dirt or go for big prizes on synthetics. (op 7-1 tchd 5-1)
Sohcahtoa(IRE) ran well after 165 days off, but he looks flattered by the bare result as he was allowed the run of the race under a good front-running ride, having been favourably drawn. (op 25-1)
Mastery was unable to take advantage of his decent draw after missing the break and he got going too late in the straight to pose a threat. A respectable return from five months off and we're likely to see the best of him when he races on soft turf. He did not look great in his condition and should improve for this. (tchd 14-1)
Weald Park(USA), a stablemate of the third, ran with credit from a low draw after 144 days off and could improve. (op 14-1)
Shampagne, who was on his toes in the paddock, ran okay after around five months off, but he's pretty exposed. He looks as though he would be suited to racing in the US. (op 16-1)
Close Alliance(USA) ◆'s debut success at Great Leighs has been boosted by Redding Colliery in Dubai, but he endured a terrible trip. He didn't appear to get a particularly shrewd ride, making his move extremely wide just as the pace was increasing, and his jockey also briefly appeared to have a problem with his reins around the bend. It was no surprise the colt's effort flattened out, although his trainer said afterwards the plan had always been to make a move before the straight, with the run-in particularly short on this inner course, and it basically just didn't work out this time. This run can be safely ignored and there is much better to come from this highly regarded colt. He will apparently run at the Craven meeting. (tchd 6-1)
Agente Parmigiano(IRE) Official explanation: jockey said colt suffered interference in running
Deposer(IRE) was keen early and endured a troubled trip from stall three. Official explanation: jockey said colt suffered interference in running (op 33-1)
Markyg(USA) ◆ had little chance from stall two and can do better. Official explanation: jockey said colt suffered interference in running (op 25-1)
Akhenaten did not get much of a run in the straight and is better than he showed. (op 20-1)

Haashed(USA) had a good draw, but he was too keen early, notably so when the leader slowed things after a couple of furlongs, and in any case this trip probably stretched him. There was a suggestion he has issues with his breathing. (tchd 5-2)

864 DIGIBET DRAGONFLY STKS (LISTED RACE) 1m 4f (P)
8:20 (8:22) (Class 1) 4-Y-0+ £22,708 (£8,608; £4,308; £2,148; £1,076) Stalls Centre

Form RPR
05-3 1 **Scintillo**[25] 634 4-9-0 106 RichardHughes 6 108+
(R Hannon) *lw: stdd after s: hld up in tch: clsd on ldrs over 4f out: cruised upsides ldr over 1f out: sn shkn up to ld: rdn clr fnl f: easily* **11/8**[1]
2330 2 3 1/4 **Baylini**[17] 724 5-8-11 88 JamesDoyle 4 94
(Ms J S Doyle) *hld up in last pl: clsd and in tch over 4f out: rdn over 2f out: plugged on to go 2nd nr fin: no ch w wnr* **33/1**
350 3 nk **Big Robert**[26] 640 5-9-2 98 FergusSweeney 2 99
(K R Burke) *hld up in last pair: clsd on ldrs over 4f out: chal 2f out: sn rdn to ld: hdd over 1f out: no ch w wnr after: lost 2nd nr fin* **8/1**
052- 4 7 **Luberon**[152] 6784 6-9-2 99 JoeFanning 5 88
(M Johnston) *t.k.h: led at stdy gallop tl over 8f out: chsd ldr after tl led again over 2f out: sn rdn: hdd wl over 1f out: wknd fnl f* **3/1**[3]
0306 5 19 **Love Galore (IRE)**[27] 613 4-9-0 97 GregFairley 1 60
(M Johnston) *plld hrd: chsd ldr tl led over 8f out: sn clr: hdd over 2f out: sn wknd: t.o* **5/2**[2]

2m 32.47s (-2.03) **Going Correction** +0.05s/f (Slow)
WFA 4 from 5yo+ 2lb 5 Ran SP% **109.7**
Speed ratings (Par 111): **108,105,105,100,88**
toteswinger: 1&2 £25.40 CSF £34.74 TOTE £1.90: £1.40, £2.40; EX 14.30.
Owner White Beech Farm **Bred** Woodcote Stud Ltd **Trained** East Everleigh, Wilts

FOCUS
An ordinary Listed contest.

NOTEBOOK
Scintillo has mainly struggled since winning a Group 1 in Italy as a juvenile, but he looked on great terms with himself this time and bounded clear in the straight, ending his losing run in most willing fashion. It would be unwise to get carried away with the form considering he had 13lb in hand over the runner-up on official figures, but his confidence appeared restored and this will have helped further. (op 6-4 tchd 5-4 and 13-8 in a place)
Baylini is a pretty decent mare on her day and she ran well on this first try at 1m4f, adding to the black type she picked up when third in last year's Winter Derby Trial. She never threatened the winner, but kept on to take second inside the final furlong and got this trip without a bother.
Big Robert seemed to run slightly below his very best on his first start since returning from Dubai. (tchd 9-1)
Luberon has been running in skijoring races in St Moritz and looked very fit beforehand. He was enjoying a soft lead until passed by his stablemate, Love Galore, and that one probably cost him his chance. He is probably going to be rested until the winter, when he'll have another go on the snow. (op 15-8)
Love Galore(IRE) simply refused to settle and carted his way to the front around a mile out. He is becoming an increasing difficult ride. Official explanation: jockey said colt ran too free (op 4-1)

865 DIGIBET SPORTS BETTING H'CAP 1m 4f (P)
8:50 (8:51) (Class 5) (0-75,75) 3-Y-0 £2,590 (£770; £385; £192) Stalls Centre

Form RPR
5413 1 **Supernoverre (IRE)**[12] 776 3-9-1 69 IanMongan 3 73+
(P Howling) *hld up in last pair: swtchd lft and hdwy over 2f out: chal over 1f out: drvn to ld ins fnl f: r.o wl* **9/2**
50-3 2 3/4 **Royal Society**[20] 695 3-8-6 60 JoeFanning 4 63
(M Johnston) *lw: sn led: rdn 2f out: hdd ins fnl f: one pce* **4/1**[3]
21 3 2 **Key Regard (IRE)**[19] 704 3-9-7 75 ChrisCatlin 1 75
(J A Osborne) *lw: stdd and dropped in bhd after s: hdwy and rdn 2f out: wnt 3rd ins fnl f: kpt on same pce* **2/1**[1]
664 4 3/4 **Dollar Express (USA)**[23] 658 3-8-9 63 ShaneKelly 7 62
(J Noseda) *chsd ldr: rdn over 2f out: drvn and one pce fr over 1f out* **12/1**
63-3 5 nk **Merton Lad**[16] 740 3-9-0 68 (p) RobertHavlin 2 66
(T G Mills) *t.k.h: hld up in tch: reminder over 4f out: rdn and nt qckn over 2f out: hung rt u.p 2f out: styd on fnl f* **10/3**[2]
566- 6 8 **Lilly Blue (IRE)**[157] 6682 3-9-3 71 TonyCulhane 6 56
(M R Channon) *hld up in tch in midfield: hdwy on inner over 2f out: rdn 2f out: sn btn* **20/1**
-500 7 3 **Nicky Nutjob (GER)**[21] 677 3-8-7 61 (v[1]) LiamJones 5 42
(J Pearce) *t.k.h: trckd ldrs: rdn and hanging rt over 2f out: wknd ent fnl 2f* **12/1**

2m 35.12s (0.62) **Going Correction** +0.05s/f (Slow) 7 Ran SP% **114.7**
Speed ratings (Par 98): **99,98,97,96,96 91,89**
toteswinger: 1&2 £3.90, 1&3 £1.60, 2&3 £2.60. CSF £22.89 TOTE £6.10: £3.40, £1.90; EX 33.80.
Owner Paul Terry **Bred** Derek Veitch And Saleh Ali Hammadi **Trained** Newmarket, Suffolk

FOCUS
An ordinary three-year-old handicap run at a modest tempo.

866 PANORAMIC BAR & RESTAURANT H'CAP 7f (P)
9:20 (9:20) (Class 4) (0-85,85) 4-Y-0+ £4,727 (£1,406; £702; £351) Stalls High

Form RPR
604- 1 **Tartan Gigha (IRE)**[160] 6598 4-8-11 78 JoeFanning 2 88+
(M Johnston) *t.k.h: trckd ldng pair: wnt 2nd jst over 2f out: rdn to ld 1f out: styd on wl* **5/1**[2]
4005 2 1 **Dvinsky (USA)**[19] 714 8-9-4 85 (b) IanMongan 1 92
(P Howling) *b.hind: led: rdn and qcknd jst over 2f out: hdd 1f out: kpt on same pce fnl f* **10/1**
2122 3 1/2 **Caprio (IRE)**[7] 806 4-8-7 74 RichardKingscote 6 79
(Tom Dascombe) *lw: hld up in midfield: rdn and effrt jst over 2f out: styd on u.p to go 3rd ins fnl f: nt pce to rch ldng pair* **3/1**[1]
32 4 nk **Leonaldo (USA)**[20] 694 4-8-11 78 ChrisCatlin 5 83
(J R Gask) *lw: hld up in tch in midfield: effrt and rdn jst over 2f out: kpt on fnl f* **3/1**[1]
060- 5 1 **Carlitos Spirit (IRE)**[157] 6675 5-8-12 79 RobertWinston 4 81
(B R Millman) *t.k.h: chsd ldr tl jst over 2f out: rdn and unable qck over 1f out: eased whn btn wl ins fnl f* **14/1**
/56- 6 3/4 **Papillio (IRE)**[244] 4121 4-8-10 77 JamieSpencer 7 77
(J R Fanshawe) *hld up in tch in rr: rdn and effrt whn hung rt over 1f out: keeping on whn nt clr run ins fnl f: eased towards fin* **8/1**
-215 7 2 1/4 **Hallingdal (UAE)**[2] 852 4-8-10 77 JamesDoyle 8 72
(Ms J S Doyle) *stdd s: hld up in rr: rdn and effrt 2f out: wknd u.p over 1f out* **11/2**[3]
665- 8 8 **Non Sucre (USA)**[221] 4864 4-8-5 72 MartinDwyer 3 47
(J Gallagher) *rrd s and v.s.a: t.k.h: sn in tch in rr: rdn and hung rt jst over 2f out: sn wl btn* **33/1**

1m 26.6s (0.60) **Going Correction** +0.05s/f (Slow) 8 Ran SP% **111.9**
Speed ratings (Par 105): **98,96,96,95,94 93,91,82**
toteswinger: 1&2 £10.00, 1&3 £4.20, 2&3 £3.80. CSF £50.64 CT £173.67 TOTE £6.20: £1.90, £2.20, £1.10; EX 50.60 Place 6: £137.19 Place 5: £47.73 .
Owner Mrs I Bird **Bred** Gainsborough Stud Management Ltd **Trained** Middleham Moor, N Yorks

FOCUS
A fair handicap on paper, but the pace was steady and the bare form needs treating with some caution. It paid to race handy.
Carlitos Spirit(IRE) Official explanation: jockey said gelding hung right
Papillio(IRE) Official explanation: jockey said gelding was denied a clear run
T/Plt: £218.30 to a £1 stake. Pool: £100,524.65. 336.11 winning tickets. T/Qpdt: £39.60 to a £1 stake. Pool: £9,085.76. 169.50 winning tickets. SP

838 LINGFIELD (L-H)
Wednesday, March 18

OFFICIAL GOING: Standard
Wind: Almost nil Weather: Sunny and mild

867 FELBRIDGE APPRENTICE H'CAP 1m (P)
2:00 (2:01) (Class 6) (0-60,60) 4-Y-0+ £2,047 (£604; £302) Stalls High

Form RPR
201 1 **Very Well Red**[8] 791 6-8-7 53 6ex TobyAtkinson(5) 12 63
(P W Hiatt) *hld up in rr of midfield: hdwy over 2f out: led 1f out: pushed out* **9/1**[3]
0-01 2 1 3/4 **Alfredtheordinary**[14] 749 4-9-4 59 MatthewDavies 10 65
(M R Channon) *sn stdd towards rr: hdwy on outside 2f out: drvn to chse wnr ent fnl f f: kpt on same pce* **4/1**[1]
0003 3 2 1/2 **Baba Ghanoush**[7] 802 7-8-0 46 oh1 (v) KierenFox(5) 3 47
(M J Attwater) *chsd ldrs: n.m.r and lost pl over 2f out: styd on fnl f* **11/1**
6-45 4 2 1/4 **Moayed**[17] 725 10-8-12 58 (b) HollyHall(5) 5 56+
(N P Littmoden) *s.s: hld up in last: swtchd lft and nt clr run over 1f out: shkn up and gng on wl at fin* **7/1**[2]
0430 4 dht **Mister Benji**[15] 748 10-8-5 46 oh1 BillyCray 11 42
(B P J Baugh) *led 1f: settled in tch: n.m.r and outpcd over 2f out: styd on fnl f* **12/1**
5-22 6 1/2 **Kielty's Folly**[21] 674 5-8-2 48 PaulPickard(5) 9 43
(B P J Baugh) *mid-div: effrt on rail over 2f out: rdn to chse ldrs ent st: btn 1f out* **4/1**[1]
-600 7 1 **Pharaohs Justice (USA)**[17] 725 4-8-12 60 (b[1]) AlexOwen(7) 1 52
(N P Littmoden) *dwlt: hdwy to ld after 2f: hdd & wknd 1f out* **20/1**
0-66 8 2 1/2 **Mansii**[38] 460 4-9-2 57 AshleyMorgan 7 44
(P J McBride) *hld up in rr: rdn 3f out: sme hdwy into mod 6th over 1f out: no ex fnl f* **9/1**[3]
60-3 9 1 **Double Valentine**[7] 803 6-8-13 57 DebraEngland(3) 8 42
(R Ingram) *dwlt: hdwy to chse ldrs after 2f: wknd 2f out* **10/1**
6-50 10 2 **Kannon**[42] 395 4-8-8 52 PNolan(3) 2 32
(I W McInnes) *hdwy to press ldr after 2f: rdn over 2f out: wknd over 1f out* **20/1**
06-3 11 5 **Miss Clarice (USA)**[14] 760 4-8-1 49 DannyBrock(7) 6 18
(J R Jenkins) *plld hrd: led after 1f tl 6f out: wkng whn bmpd over 2f out* **14/1**

1m 37.39s (-0.81) **Going Correction** -0.025s/f (Stan) 11 Ran SP% **113.8**
Speed ratings (Par 101): **103,101,98,96,96 96,95,92,91,89 84**
toteswinger: 1&2 £4.90, 1&3 £8.30, 2&3 £6.50. CSF £43.37 CT £406.14 TOTE £10.20: £3.40, £1.50, £4.30; EX 35.90 Trifecta £172.40 Part won. Pool: £233.03 - 0.81 winning units..
Owner Phil Kelly **Bred** Butts Enterprises Limited **Trained** Hook Norton, Oxon
■ Stewards' Enquiry : Holly Hall ten-day ban: breach of Rule 158 (Apr 1-4, 6-9, 11-12)

FOCUS
An ordinary handicap in which they went a fair pace.
Moayed Official explanation: jockey said, regarding running and riding, that her orders were to drop the gelding out, not come wide and come through horses; trainer said he was dissatisifed with the ride, his instructions were to creep into the race and challenge between horses.

868 NEWCHAPEL (S) STKS 7f (P)
2:30 (2:33) (Class 6) 4-Y-0+ £2,047 (£604; £302) Stalls Low

Form RPR
1331 1 **Desert Dreamer (IRE)**[17] 721 8-9-3 75 AlanDaly 12 77
(Tom Dascombe) *hld up in rr: hdwy on outside over 2f out: drvn along over 1f out: r.o to ld ins fnl f* **2/1**[1]
1121 2 1 3/4 **Obe Royal**[8] 793 5-9-3 71 (b) JamieSpencer 10 72
(P D Evans) *prom: drvn to join ldr over 1f out: nt pce of wnr ins fnl f* **10/3**[2]
30-0 3 1 1/4 **Networker**[64] 143 6-8-11 67 DaneO'Neill 13 63
(P J McBride) *hld up in rr: hung bdly lft and drvn along over 1f out: styd on: nrst fin* **17/2**
-620 4 3/4 **Landucci**[17] 725 8-8-11 64 (p) JamesDoyle 9 61
(S Curran) *hld up in midfield: effrt 2f out: hrd rdn over 1f out: styd on same pce* **8/1**[3]
0203 5 1/2 **Kabis Amigos**[52] 289 7-8-11 60 (b) GregFairley 8 59+
(S T Mason) *stmbld s: plld hrd and sn in midfield: dropped to last and rdn 2f out: styd on fnl f* **14/1**
5122 6 nk **Interactive (IRE)**[17] 721 6-9-3 69 ChrisCatlin 1 64
(Andrew Turnell) *led: hrd rdn and jnd over 1f out: hdd & wknd ins fnl f* **8/1**[3]
06-0 7 1/2 **Bidable**[58] 216 5-8-3 47 DavidProbert(3) 11 52
(B Palling) *mid-div: rdn to go prom over 3f out: wknd 1f out* **22/1**
60-6 8 2 1/4 **Miracle Baby**[49] 308 7-8-6 43 RichardThomas 4 46
(J A Geake) *prom: pushed along over 3f out: wknd over 1f out* **66/1**
0016 9 3 1/2 **Sharps Gold**[14] 749 4-8-9 47 JackMitchell(3) 2 42
(D Morris) *mid-div on rail: effrt ent st: wknd over 1f out* **66/1**
2153 10 1 **Boss Hog**[8] 793 4-8-12 69 (p) GabrielHannon(5) 5 45
(R Curtis) *prom tl wknd over 2f out* **10/1**
-000 R **Willie Ever**[30] 569 5-8-11 65 (v[1]) PatrickMathers 3 —
(I W McInnes) *ref to r: tk no part* **33/1**

1m 24.61s (-0.19) **Going Correction** -0.025s/f (Stan) 11 Ran SP% **115.2**
Speed ratings (Par 101): **100,98,96,95,95 94,94,91,87,86 —**
toteswinger: 1&2 £1.20, 1&3 £8.60, 2&3 £4.70. CSF £7.86 TOTE £2.50: £1.10, £1.80, £3.20; EX 7.00 Trifecta £11.20 Pool: £782.51 - 51.59 winning units..The winner was sold to P D Evans for 7,400gns.
Owner ONEWAY Partners **Bred** Gainsborough Stud Management Ltd **Trained** Lambourn, Berks
■ A winner for Alan Daly on his final ride.

Kabis Amigos Official explanation: jockey said gelding stumbled leaving stalls

869 HAPPY BIRTHDAY ABBI FLATT MAIDEN STKS 7f (P)
3:00 (3:01) (Class 5) 3-4-Y-O £2,729 (£806; £403) Stalls Low

Form RPR
232 1 **Head Down**[22] [663] 3-8-12 73 RichardHughes 6 77+
(R Hannon) *cl up: rdn to chse ldr over 1f out: led ins fnl f: pushed out* 9/4[2]
0- 2 1¼ **Anacreon (IRE)**[138] [7106] 3-8-12 JimmyFortune 7 74+
(J H M Gosden) *trckd ldr: led 2f out tl ins fnl f: nt qckn* 13/8[1]
0- 3 5 **La Gifted**[182] [6030] 3-8-7 TonyCulhane 9 55
(M R Channon) *hld up in midfield: lost pl on outer 2f out: hung lft over 1f out: rallied and r.o fnl f* 14/1
656- 4 3½ **Gambling Jack**[78] [7817] 4-9-13 49 ShaneKelly 3 56
(A W Carroll) *prom: rdn 3f out: outpcd fnl 2f* 20/1
55- 5 nk **Ponting (IRE)**[145] [6953] 3-8-12 JimCrowley 10 54+
(R M Beckett) *t.k.h: sn stdd in 2nd last wl off the pce: shkn up and r.o fr over 1f out: nrst fin* 11/2[3]
5 6 hd **Highgate Cat**[35] [503] 3-8-12 TGMcLaughlin 11 54+
(B R Millman) *stdd in rr s: rn green and sn last wl off the pce: shkn up and r.o fr over 1f out: gng on wl at fin* 14/1
06 7 ¾ **Garter Knight**[11] [786] 3-8-12 JamieSpencer 1 48
(M L W Bell) *towards rr: rdn 3f out: nvr trbld ldrs* 14/1
00-5 8 2¼ **Tightrope (IRE)**[16] [731] 3-8-7 54 AmyBaker(5) 5 42
(T D McCarthy) *led tl 2f out: wknd over 1f out* 100/1
6 9 1 **Stylish Mover**[63] [162] 4-9-13 RobertHavlin 4 44
(R Ingram) *mid-div: outpcd over 2f out: sn btn* 66/1
00 10 2 **Holoko Heights**[30] [572] 4-9-13 VinceSlattery 8 38
(N J Vaughan) *s.i.s: a towards rr: rdn and n.d fnl 3f* 50/1
00 11 3 **Georgina Macrae**[22] [663] 3-8-7 LPKeniry 2 20
(A M Balding) *in tch: rdn over 3f out: sn wknd* 50/1

1m 25.35s (0.55) **Going Correction** -0.025s/f (Stan)
WFA 3 from 4yo 15lb 11 Ran SP% **115.4**
Speed ratings (Par 103): **95,93,87,83,83 83,82,79,78,76 73**
toteswinger: 1&2 £1.90, 1&3 £9.20, 2&3 £6.60. CSF £5.90 TOTE £3.10: £1.10, £1.30, £4.30; EX 4.70 Trifecta £71.50 Pool: £734.83 - 7.60 winning units..
Owner Jim Horgan **Bred** Hong Kong Breeders Club **Trained** East Everleigh, Wilts

FOCUS
An average little maiden and it was the two market leaders who dominated the finish.

870 ASHURST WOOD H'CAP 5f (P)
3:35 (3:36) (Class 5) (0-75,75) 4-Y-0+ £2,900 (£856; £428) Stalls High

Form RPR
1052 1 **Ten Down**[19] [710] 4-8-10 67 MartinDwyer 5 77+
(M Quinn) *flew out of stalls: mde all: rdn and responded wl fnl 2f: a in control* 5/1[3]
3543 2 1¼ **Bo McGinty (IRE)**[20] [690] 8-8-12 74 (b) FrederikTylicki(5) 1 80
(R A Fahey) *prom: rdn to chse wnr over 1f out: kpt on: a hld* 5/1[3]
-031 3 1 **Brandywell Boy (IRE)**[28] [589] 6-8-8 72 BillyCray(7) 9 74
(D J S Ffrench Davis) *s.i.s: bhd: rdn 3f out: gd hdwy to go 3rd over 1f out: nt qckn ins fnl f* 14/1
0335 4 1¼ **Figaro Flyer (IRE)**[20] [691] 6-8-11 68 ShaneKelly 4 65
(P Howling) *hld up in 6th: lost pl and dropped to 2nd last 2f out: rdn over 1f out: rallied and r.o fnl f* 5/1[3]
3011 5 ¾ **Desperate Dan**[14] [756] 8-9-4 75 (v) TPQueally 7 70
(A B Haynes) *chsd ldrs on outer: rdn over 1f out: kpt on same pce* 9/1
040- 6 ¾ **Highland Warrior**[124] [7323] 10-8-6 70 PaulPickard(7) 6 62
(P T Midgley) *s.i.s: bhd: rdn 3f out: styng on at fin* 50/1
0-55 7 nse **Style Award**[7] [799] 4-8-8 70 KellyHarrison(5) 2 63+
(W J H Ratcliffe) *chsd ldrs: 6th and btn whn squeezed for room over 1f out* 9/2[2]
16-5 8 hd **Wibbadune (IRE)**[14] [754] 5-9-4 75 AdamKirby 3 66+
(D Shaw) *hld up in 7th: hdwy on rail to chse ldrs over 1f out: no ex fnl f* 3/1[1]
6654 9 nk **Thoughtsofstardom**[36] [486] 6-9-2 73 LukeMorris 10 63
(P S McEntee) *chsd wnr tl wknd jst over 1f out* 16/1

59.02 secs (0.22) **Going Correction** -0.025s/f (Stan) 9 Ran SP% **117.7**
Speed ratings (Par 103): **97,95,93,91,90 89,88,88,88**
toteswinger: 1&2 £5.80, 1&3 £7.90, 2&3 £12.30. CSF £30.85 CT £333.51 TOTE £5.60: £1.60, £2.10, £4.70; EX 33.00 Trifecta £230.80 Pool: £595.97 - 1.59 winning units..
Owner A G MacLennan **Bred** Baydon House Stud **Trained** Newmarket, Suffolk

FOCUS
A competitive little sprint handicap on paper, but this race was won exiting the stalls.
Figaro Flyer(IRE) Official explanation: jockey said gelding suffered interference leaving stalls
Style Award Official explanation: jockey said filly was denied a clear run
Wibbadune(IRE) Official explanation: jockey said mare suffered interference leaving stalls

871 FOREST ROW H'CAP 1m 4f (P)
4:10 (4:10) (Class 6) (0-60,60) 4-Y-0+ £2,047 (£604; £302) Stalls Low

Form RPR
322U 1 **Carlton Scroop (FR)**[6] [816] 6-9-4 58 (b) LukeMorris 3 67
(J Jay) *hld up in midfield: hdwy over 1f out: led ins fnl f: rdn out* 5/1[2]
4524 2 1¼ **Pelham Crescent (IRE)**[5] [836] 6-9-3 60 DavidProbert(3) 4 67
(B Palling) *chsd ldrs: wnt 2nd 3f out: led wl over 1f out tl ins fnl f: one pce* 8/1
5-56 3 1½ **Penang Cinta**[30] [571] 6-9-5 59 (p) PaulDoe 1 64
(P D Evans) *chsd ldrs: rdn 3f out: briefly wnt 2nd over 1f out: no ex ins fnl f* 16/1
4542 4 1¾ **Zalkani (IRE)**[14] [751] 9-9-6 60 JerryO'Dwyer 6 62
(J Pearce) *hld up towards rr: hdwy in centre over 1f out: hung lft and nt qckn ins fnl f* 8/1
3123 5 1¼ **Sir Liam (USA)**[14] [751] 5-9-3 57 RichardKingscote 8 57
(Tom Dascombe) *hld up in rr: rdn and styd on fnl 2f: nvr nrr* 7/2[1]
25-4 6 ½ **Thorny Mandate**[23] [660] 7-9-3 57 JamieSpencer 10 57
(W M Brisbourne) *stdd s and swtchd to rail: hld up in rr: sme hdwy ent st: no imp fnl f* 11/1
0-43 7 1¼ **Cape Of Luck (IRE)**[6] [813] 6-9-1 55 IanMongan 9 53
(P M Phelan) *in tch: rdn 3f out: outpcd fnl 2f* 9/1
5-30 8 2¾ **Captain Mainwaring**[16] [734] 4-8-13 55 (b) JamesDoyle 13 49
(N P Littmoden) *t.k.h: chsd ldr: led over 3f out tl wl over 1f out: sn hrd rdn and wknd* 33/1
-003 9 1¼ **Make Amends (IRE)**[21] [682] 4-9-1 57 SteveDrowne 5 49
(R J Hodges) *towards rr: drvn along 4f out: mod hdwy over 1f out: n.d* 33/1
134- 10 2 **Moonshine Creek**[168] [6403] 7-9-6 60 ChrisCatlin 11 49
(P W Hiatt) *racd freely: led and set gd pce: hdd over 3f out: wknd 2f out* 15/2[3]
0/00 11 8 **Adversane**[8] [790] 5-9-1 55 (p) MartinDwyer 12 32
(A J Lidderdale) *t.k.h early: prom: rdn over 3f out: outpcd and btn over 2f out* 100/1
-300 12 2¾ **Our Kes (IRE)**[16] [733] 7-9-6 60 TonyCulhane 7 33
(P Howling) *a towards rr: rdn and struggling fnl 3f* 25/1
545- 13 4½ **Wizard Looking**[233] [4477] 8-9-6 60 JamieMoriarty 2 26
(P T Midgley) *mid-div: wknd over 3f out: sn bhd* 10/1

2m 31.1s (-1.90) **Going Correction** -0.025s/f (Stan)
WFA 4 from 5yo+ 2lb 13 Ran SP% **116.9**
Speed ratings (Par 101): **105,104,103,102,101 100,100,98,97,96 90,88,85**
toteswinger: 1&2 £12.30, 1&3 £27.10, 2&3 £32.80. CSF £42.42 CT £598.59 TOTE £5.40: £2.10, £2.70, £4.10; EX 73.40 Trifecta £276.30 Part won. Pool: £373.49 - 0.10 winning units..
Owner David Fremel **Bred** Jonathan Jay **Trained** Newmarket, Suffolk

FOCUS
They went a fair gallop in this modest handicap.
Our Kes(IRE) Official explanation: jockey said mare moved poorly throughout

872 THREE BRIDGES (S) STKS 1m 2f (P)
4:45 (4:45) (Class 6) 4-Y-0+ £2,047 (£604; £302) Stalls Low

Form RPR
2023 1 **Gasat (IRE)**[4] [838] 8-9-3 65 JoeFanning 11 73+
(A B Haynes) *mde all: set gd pce: rdn 6 l clr over 1f out: unchal* 9/2[3]
3-13 2 4½ **Mystic Art (IRE)**[5] [825] 4-9-3 60 SteveDrowne 3 65
(C R Egerton) *in tch: sltly hmpd and forced wd 4f out: hrd rdn over 2f out: kpt on to take mod 2nd ins fnl f* 9/4[1]
-424 3 nk **Zero Cool (USA)**[19] [706] 5-8-12 65 (p) FergusSweeney 8 59
(G L Moore) *hld up in midfield: drvn along 3f out: kpt on to take mod 3rd ins fnl f* 9/2[3]
4362 4 1¾ **Don Pietro**[13] [765] 6-9-3 69 (p) J-PGuillambert 1 61
(R Curtis) *prom: chsd wnr over 4f out: wknd and lost 2nd ins fnl f* 7/2[2]
05-5 5 5 **Roundthetwist (IRE)**[61] [187] 4-8-12 47 DarrenWilliams 7 47
(K R Burke) *dwlt: hld up towards rr: sme hdwy and hrd rdn ent st: wknd fnl f* 33/1
0062 6 4½ **Ma Ridge**[24] [647] 5-8-7 46 AmyBaker(5) 9 39
(T D McCarthy) *towards rr: rdn and hdwy 3f out: wknd qckly over 1f out* 33/1
020/ 7 13 **Grand Sefton**[115] [4533] 6-8-12 45 RobertHavlin 4 16+
(N R Mitchell) *in tch: wknd over 3f out: sn bhd: eased fnl 2f* 100/1
6-66 8 4½ **Caltire (GER)**[40] [423] 4-8-12 60 AdamKirby 5 7
(M G Quinlan) *bhd: hrd rdn over 4f out: no ch fnl 3f* 9/1
0 9 22 **Seven Sky (FR)**[64] [147] 6-8-12 53 (b) JamieSpencer 12 —
(P F I Cole) *chsd wnr tl rdn and wknd rapidly 4f out: bhd whn virtually p.u fnl 2f* 14/1

2m 4.40s (-2.20) **Going Correction** -0.025s/f (Stan) 9 Ran SP% **112.9**
Speed ratings (Par 101): **107,103,103,101,97 94,83,80,62**
toteswinger: 1&2 £3.80, 1&3 £5.30, 2&3 £2.90. CSF £14.52 TOTE £6.30: £1.70, £1.30, £1.30; EX 18.80 Trifecta £49.00 Pool: £431.27 - 6.51winning units..There was no bid for the winner.
Owner Ms C Berry **Bred** Scuderia Siba S P A **Trained** Limpley Stoke, Bath

FOCUS
A pretty weak seller and an all-the-way success for Gasat.
Mystic Art(IRE) Official explanation: jockey said gelding hung left

873 HARTFIELD H'CAP 1m 2f (P)
5:20 (5:20) (Class 5) (0-75,74) 4-Y-0+ £2,900 (£856; £428) Stalls Low

Form RPR
26-3 1 **Trifti**[42] [392] 8-9-1 71 DaneO'Neill 3 79+
(Miss Jo Crowley) *hld up in rr: rdn and hdwy over 1f out: drvn to ld ins fnl f: won gng away* 4/1[2]
-122 2 2¼ **Old Romney**[16] [733] 5-9-3 73 RichardHughes 8 77
(M Wigham) *hld up in rr: hdwy on bit 2f out: rdn to ld briefly ent fnl f: nt pce of wnr* 11/4[1]
-211 3 nk **General Feeling (IRE)**[47] [344] 8-9-1 71 MartinDwyer 2 74
(S T Mason) *mid-div: rdn over 3f out: crowded and lost pl over 2f out: styd on wl fnl f* 7/1[3]
4046 4 nse **Hucking Hero (IRE)**[24] [653] 4-8-12 71 MarcHalford(3) 5 74
(J R Best) *prom: nt clr run over 2f out: fnd gap in st: kpt on fnl f* 14/1
000- 5 ½ **Kindlelight Blue (IRE)**[243] [4162] 5-9-4 74 JamesDoyle 4 76
(N P Littmoden) *in tch: led over 2f out tl ent fnl f: no ex* 16/1
-601 6 3¾ **Vinces**[16] [733] 5-8-8 64 RobertHavlin 7 60
(T D McCarthy) *prom tl wknd over 1f out* 15/2
4234 7 3½ **Wavertree Warrior (IRE)**[32] [544] 7-9-2 72 (b) LukeMorris 9 61
(N P Littmoden) *t.k.h: hdwy into midfield 7f out: hrd rdn and wknd 2f out* 11/1
111- 8 7 **Lilac Moon (GER)**[214] [5105] 5-9-0 70 RichardKingscote 1 47
(N J Vaughan) *led tl over 2f out: wknd ent st* 4/1[2]

2m 5.37s (-1.23) **Going Correction** -0.025s/f (Stan) 8 Ran SP% **111.8**
Speed ratings (Par 103): **103,101,100,100,100 97,94,89**
toteswinger: 1&2 £2.70, 1&3 £5.40, 2&3 £5.90. CSF £14.70 CT £71.39 TOTE £5.70: £1.70, £1.20, £2.10; EX 14.70 Trifecta £152.90 Pool: £274.95 - 1.33 winning units..
Owner Mrs Liz Nelson **Bred** C A Cyzer **Trained** Whitcombe, Dorset

FOCUS
They went a good pace here and the race was set up for those staying on from off the gallop.
Kindlelight Blue(IRE) Official explanation: jockey said gelding hung left

874 MARSH GREEN H'CAP 7f (P)
5:50 (5:50) (Class 6) (0-55,55) 4-Y-0+ £2,047 (£604; £302) Stalls Low

Form RPR
000- 1 **Colour Of Money**[284] [2824] 4-9-0 55 SimonWhitworth 6 63+
(S A Callaghan) *trckd ldrs: hrd rdn over 1f out: led fnl 100yds: pushed out* 9/2[2]
0442 2 ¾ **Mr Chocolate Drop (IRE)**[8] [792] 5-8-13 54 (b) AdamKirby 9 60+
(Miss M E Rowland) *t.k.h in rr: rdn and hdwy over 1f out: fin wl: snatched 2nd nr fin* 5/1[3]
00-6 3 nk **H Harrison (IRE)**[19] [715] 9-9-0 55 PatrickMathers 11 60
(I W McInnes) *prom: rdn 2f out: kpt on* 16/1
2021 4 hd **Suhayl Star (IRE)**[4] [844] 5-9-0 55 6ex LukeMorris 13 60
(P Burgoyne) *trckd ldr: led over 2f out: hrd rdn fnl f: hdd and one pce fnl f* 7/2[1]
3416 5 ½ **Just Jimmy (IRE)**[23] [657] 4-8-13 54 PaulDoe 1 58
(P D Evans) *in tch: rdn over 2f out: styd on fnl f* 16/1
0-00 6 ¾ **Annes Rocket (IRE)**[34] [512] 4-8-12 53 LPKeniry 2 55
(J C Fox) *s.s: hld up towards rr: hdwy to chse ldrs over 1f out: one pce fnl f* 40/1

-613 **7** *1 1/4* **Binnion Bay (IRE)**[22] 661 8-8-13 **54**..........................(b) JerryO'Dwyer 8 53
(J J Bridger) *s.s: bhd: rdn 3f out: hdwy on rail over 1f out: nt rch ldrs* **5/1**[3]

-010 **8** *hd* **Over To You Bert**[22] 666 10-8-9 **55**.............................. MCGeran(5) 10 53
(R J Hodges) *bhd: rdn and sme hdwy over 1f out: nvr nrr* **20/1**

00-6 **9** *1* **Sands Of Barra (IRE)**[22] 666 6-8-12 **53**............................ TomEaves 4 49
(I W McInnes) *sn led: hdd over 2f out: hrd rdn and wknd over 1f out* **11/1**

06/0 **10** *2 1/4* **Softly Killing Me**[14] 749 4-8-11 **52**......................(v[1]) NeilChalmers 3 42
(B Forsey) *mid-div: pushed along over 3f out: n.d fnl 2f* **50/1**

0-06 **11** *1/2* **Buail Isteach (IRE)**[22] 663 4-8-11 **52**..................... EdwardCreighton 7 41
(E J Creighton) *towards rr: rdn 2f out: nt trble ldrs* **14/1**

0-01 **12** *1 1/2* **Silidan**[22] 666 6-8-13 **54**.................................... FergusSweeney 5 39
(G L Moore) *t.k.h towards rr: rdn 2f out: n.d* **11/1**

5-00 **13** *4* **Palais Polaire**[56] 234 7-8-11 **52**..................(tp) RichardThomas 12 27
(J A Geake) *in tch: hrd rdn 3f out: wknd wl over 1f out* **33/1**

1m 25.13s (0.33) **Going Correction** -0.025s/f (Stan) **13** Ran SP% **120.9**
Speed ratings (Par 101): **97,96,95,95,95 94,92,92,91,88 88,86,81**
toteswinger: 1&2 £2.90, 1&3 £25.60, 2&3 £12.40. CSF £26.70 CT £338.85 TOTE £5.20: £2.50, £1.90, £2.30; EX 41.20 TRIFECTA Not won. Place 6: £56.67 Place 5: £21.00 .
Owner Michael Tabor **Bred** N E Poole And Paul Trickey **Trained** Newmarket, Suffolk

FOCUS
A moderate affair won by the handicap debutant Colour Of Money.
Colour Of Money Official explanation: trainer said, regarding apparent improvement in form, that it was a drop in class, the gelding was late maturing, having had niggling health problems over the winter.
T/Plt: £57.90 to a £1 stake. Pool: £67,075.57. 844.63 winning tickets. T/Qpdt: £17.20 to a £1 stake. Pool: £4,052.58. 173.70 winning tickets. LM

861 KEMPTON (A.W) (R-H)
Thursday, March 19

OFFICIAL GOING: Standard
Wind: Virtualy nil Weather: dry, chilly

875 KEMPTON.CO.UK CLAIMING STKS 1m 2f (P)
6:50 (6:50) (Class 6) 4-Y-0+ **£1,942** (£578; £288) **Stalls** High

Form RPR

4060 **1** **Torch Of Freedom (IRE)**[8] 798 4-8-11 74................. J-PGuillambert 3 78
(Sir Mark Prescott) *t.k.h: chsd ldr for 2f: shkn up over 3f out: pushed into ld over 1f out: in command and pushed out* **11/10**[1]

300- **2** *2 3/4* **Western Roots**[167] 6450 8-8-7 68.............................. DavidProbert(3) 1 72
(A M Balding) *led at stdy gallop: rdn over 2f out: hdd over 1f out: one pce after* **5/4**[2]

0401 **3** *2 3/4* **Red Rudy**[38] 471 7-8-8 63... ShaneKelly 2 65
(A W Carroll) *plld hrd early: trckd ldr after 2f: rdn wl over 1f out: unable qck and btn over 1f out* **5/1**[3]

2m 7.67s (-0.33) **Going Correction** +0.075s/f (Slow) **3** Ran SP% **108.7**
Speed ratings (Par 101): **104,101,99**
CSF £2.85 TOTE £2.40; EX 2.30.
Owner J Fishpool - Osborne House **Bred** Kilcarn Stud **Trained** Newmarket, Suffolk

FOCUS
One can quite confidently predict that the form of this race will be meaningless. The gallop was predictably moderate.

876 DAY TIME, NIGHT TIME, GREAT TIME MAIDEN FILLIES' STKS 1m 2f (P)
7:20 (7:20) (Class 5) 3-Y-0+ **£2,590** (£770; £385; £192) **Stalls** High

Form RPR

6- **1** **Coming Back**[138] 7141 3-8-7 0.. RobertHavlin 1 77
(J H M Gosden) *stdd and swtchd rt sn after s: hld up in tch: hdwy 3f out: chal over 1f out: led 1f out: pushed out and a holding runner up after* **11/4**[2]

2-2 **2** *1/2* **Onemix**[17] 731 3-8-7 0... ChrisCatlin 4 76
(B W Hills) *w ldr: led 3f out: rdn and c clr w wnr over 1f out: hdd 1f out: one pce and a hld after* **1/1**[1]

3 *7* **Iketi (GR)** 3-8-7 0.. PaulDoe 10 62
(Jane Chapple-Hyam) *s.i.s: hld up in tch in rr: shkn up and rn green over 3f out: hdwy wl over 1f out: wnt modest 3rd 1f out: kpt on but no ch w ldng pair* **25/1**

006- **4** *1 3/4* **Triple Cee (IRE)**[175] 6231 3-8-7 71............................... TonyCulhane 3 59
(M R Channon) *trckd ldr: rdn jst over 2f out: wknd over 1f out: wl btn after* **7/1**[3]

000- **5** *3/4* **Sweet Sixteen (IRE)**[218] 4997 4-9-13 86.................. SimonWhitworth 6 61
(J R Jenkins) *v.s.a: t.k.h: hld up in last pl: rdn jst over 2f out: struggling wl over 1f out: pluged on past btn horses fnl f: n.d* **11/1**

6 *1 1/4* **Butstillitmoves (IRE)** 3-8-7 0.. NickyMackay 11 55
(J H M Gosden) *s.i.s: trckd ldrs: rdn wl over 2f out: wknd wl over 1f out* **11/1**

0- **7** *1* **Rockson (IRE)**[115] 7434 3-8-7 0.................................... RobertWinston 2 53
(B W Hills) *t.k.h: hld up in tch: wnt 2nd over 2f out: ev ch 2f out: sn rdn and outpcd by ldng pair: wknd over 1f out* **20/1**

000- **8** *4 1/2* **Pure Crystal**[130] 7258 3-8-2 55.................................... NicolPolli(5) 9 44
(M G Quinlan) *led tl hdd and rdn 3f out: wknd qckly 2f out: wl bhd fnl f* **50/1**

2m 8.85s (0.85) **Going Correction** +0.075s/f (Slow)
WFA 3 from 4yo 20lb **8** Ran SP% **116.4**
Speed ratings (Par 100): **99,98,93,91,91 90,89,85**
toteswinger: 1&2 £1.20, 1&3 £8.70, 2&3 £6.30. CSF £5.84 TOTE £4.20: £1.50, £1.10, £8.20; EX 8.60.
Owner K Abdulla **Bred** Juddmonte Farms Ltd **Trained** Newmarket, Suffolk

FOCUS
Barry Hills, John Gosden and Mick Channon are all getting their strings into gear now, which made this maiden look quite competitive. The early pace was moderate and the race only developed in the latter stages.

877 MIX BUSINESS WITH PLEASURE H'CAP 1m 4f (P)
7:50 (7:51) (Class 6) (0-65,65) 4-Y-0+ **£1,942** (£578; £288; £144) **Stalls** Centre

Form RPR

4-01 **1** **Shanafarahan (IRE)**[15] 751 4-8-7 **54**............................ TonyCulhane 4 63
(K A Morgan) *t.k.h: hld up in tch: chsd clr ldr 2f out: styd on u.p to ld ins fnl f: hld on* **11/2**[2]

3-06 **2** *nk* **Krugerrand (USA)**[29] 584 10-9-4 **63**.............................. ChrisCatlin 1 72
(W J Musson) *stdd after s: t.k.h: hld up in rr: hdwy jst over 2f out: drvn and ev ch ins fnl f: unable qck towards fin* **7/1**[3]

1110 **3** *1 1/4* **Lytham (IRE)**[20] 711 8-8-8 **60**.................................... TobyAtkinson(7) 2 67
(A W Carroll) *stdd and dropped in after s: t.k.h: hld up towards rr: hdwy over 3f out: chsd ldng pair over 1f out: plugged on same pce fnl f: wnt 3rd nr fin* **4/1**[1]

024- **4** *3/4* **Dan Tucker**[8] 7071 5-9-2 **61**.. RichardThomas 7 67
(Jim Best) *led for 2f: led again over 7f out: 7 l clr 4f out: rdn over 1f out: tired and hdd ins fnl f: wknd fnl 100yds* **4/1**[1]

-220 **5** *1/2* **Fantasy Ride**[7] 816 7-8-9 **54**...................................... TGMcLaughlin 8 59
(J Pearce) *stdd s: t.k.h: hld up in rr: hdwy over 2f out: kpt on steadily u.p fnl f: nvr quite pce to rch ldrs* **11/2**[2]

000- **6** *1* **Sweet Request**[245] 4105 5-8-4 **52** oh3 ow1............ KevinGhunowa(3) 11 55
(Dr J R J Naylor) *hld up in midfield: lost pl and towards rr over 3f out: hdwy u.p 2f out: styd on steadily fnl f: nt rch ldrs* **25/1**

3/6- **7** *5* **Mr Mischief**[329] 1589 9-9-6 **65**.................................... JimCrowley 12 60
(C Gordon) *dwlt: hld up in rr: nvr a factor* **10/1**

66-5 **8** *nse* **Mighty Kitchener (USA)**[16] 743 6-8-6 **51** oh6.................. PaulDoe 6 46
(P Howling) *hld up in midfield: rdn to go modest 4th over 3f out: no hdwy over 2f out: wl btn fnl 2f* **25/1**

600- **9** *1 3/4* **Rosy Dawn**[81] 7807 4-8-1 **51** oh6............................... DavidProbert(3) 3 44
(J J Bridger) *chsd ldrs: chsd clr ldr over 4f out tl 2f out: wknd* **20/1**

66/0 **10** *2 1/2* **Dream Mountain**[8] 809 6-8-7 **52** oh6 ow1.................... JamesDoyle 10 41
(Ms J S Doyle) *chsd ldrs: rdn and struggling over 3f out: wl btn fnl 2f* **20/1**

-000 **11** *33* **Oberlin (USA)**[27] 627 4-8-4 **51**.................................. NickyMackay 5 —
(T Keddy) *chsd ldr for over 1f: in tch tl pushed along and lost pl over 4f out: t.o and virtually p.u fnl f* **20/1**

045- **12** *dist* **Funky Town (IRE)**[83] 3602 7-8-6 **51** oh5................ SimonWhitworth 13 —
(J Akehurst) *heavily restrained s and slowly away: plld v hrd: dashed up to ld after 2f: hdd over 7f out: chsd ldr after tl lost pl qckly over 4f out: sn bhd: virtually p.u fr over 1f out: t.o* **14/1**

2m 34.76s (0.26) **Going Correction** +0.025s/f (Slow)
WFA 4 from 5yo+ 2lb **12** Ran SP% **121.0**
Speed ratings (Par 101): **100,99,98,98,98 97,94,94,92,91 69,—**
toteswinger: 1&2 £4.20, 1&3 £3.60, 2&3 £2.60. CSF £40.65 CT £172.00 TOTE £7.00: £1.80, £2.40, £1.10; EX 41.70.
Owner J D M Stables **Bred** Corduff Stud And J Corcoran **Trained** Little Marcle, H'fords

FOCUS
This looked a very competitive handicap after likely favourite Prince Charlemagne became a non-runner during the morning.
Funky Town(IRE) Official explanation: jockey said gelding ran too free

878 PANORAMIC BAR & RESTAURANT H'CAP 1m (P)
8:20 (8:20) (Class 5) (0-75,75) 4-Y-0+ **£2,590** (£770; £385; £192) **Stalls** High

Form RPR

3220 **1** **Marmooq**[5] 841 6-8-8 **65**.. LukeMorris 11 73
(M J Attwater) *in tch in midfield: rdn and effrt on outer jst over 2f out: drvn ent fnl f: r.o wl to ld nr fin* **7/2**[2]

500- **2** *hd* **Cross The Line (IRE)**[150] 6867 7-8-13 **70**................... RichardHughes 7 78
(A P Jarvis) *t.k.h: led after 1f: set stdy gallop: hrd pressed and rdn over 2f out: kpt finding ex tl hdd nr fin* **6/1**[3]

1331 **3** *1/2* **Jake The Snake (IRE)**[17] 730 8-8-13 **75**..................... AmyBaker(5) 10 81
(A W Carroll) *stdd s: t.k.h: hld up towards rr: nt clr run briefly jst over 2f out: sn rdn and hdwy between horses: ev ch ins fnl f: no ex fnl 50yds* **5/2**[1]

405- **4** *1 1/4* **Golden Prospect**[220] 4934 5-8-7 **64**............................... JamesDoyle 9 68
(J W Hills) *in tch: hdwy to join ldr jst over 2f out: hrd drvn ent fnl f: one pce fnl 100yds* **16/1**

415- **5** *1/2* **Having A Ball**[107] 7532 5-8-5 **62**............................... SimonWhitworth 4 65
(P D Cundell) *towards rr on outer: rdn and unable qck over 2f out: styd on wl fnl f: nt rch ldrs* **20/1**

05P- **6** *shd* **Marajaa (IRE)**[208] 5290 7-9-2 **73**................................. ChrisCatlin 3 75
(W J Musson) *t.k.h: hld up towards rr: rdn 2f out: kpt on ins fnl f* **8/1**

00-5 **7** *1/2* **Cactus King**[55] 266 6-9-4 **75**....................................... IanMongan 6 76
(P M Phelan) *hld up in tch in midfield: rdn and unable qck over 1f out: kpt on again u.p ins fnl f* **14/1**

54-3 **8** *hd* **Binfield (IRE)**[25] 651 4-9-2 **73**................................... JimCrowley 12 74
(B G Powell) *led for 1f: trckd ldr after tl over 2f out: wknd jst ins fnl f* **10/1**

5-40 **9** *1 1/4* **Dinner Date**[50] 318 7-8-10 **67**.................................... ShaneKelly 8 65
(T Keddy) *t.k.h: hld up in rr: swtchd rt and effrt over 2f out: no imp fnl f* **16/1**

-626 **10** *2 3/4* **Millfield (IRE)**[33] 544 6-9-3 **74**................................... GeorgeBaker 1 66
(P R Chamings) *stdd and dropped in bhd after s: t.k.h: hld up in last pl: brief effrt on inner 2f out: wl hld fnl f* **8/1**

0-05 **11** *1 1/4* **Glencalvie (IRE)**[40] 446 8-9-0 **71**........................(v) DaneO'Neill 2 60
(J Akehurst) *chsd ldrs: rdn and nt qckn 2f out: sn lost pl and bhd* **16/1**

1m 40.14s (0.34) **Going Correction** +0.025s/f (Slow) **11** Ran SP% **125.5**
Speed ratings (Par 103): **99,98,98,97,96 96,95,95,94,91 90**
toteswinger: 1&2 £6.50, 1&3 £2.80, 2&3 £4.40. CSF £26.94 CT £64.31 TOTE £5.10: £1.60, £2.50, £1.50; EX 23.90.
Owner The Attwater Partnership **Bred** Matthews Breeding And Racing Ltd **Trained** Epsom, Surrey

FOCUS
The favourite has been plying his trade successfully in claimers during the winter, so this is probably only modest form. The early pace was very moderate, which meant there was a bunch finish.
Millfield(IRE) Official explanation: jockey said gelding ran too keenly

879 KEMPTON FOR OUTDOOR EVENTS H'CAP 1m (P)
8:50 (8:50) (Class 3) (0-95,96) 4-Y-0+ **£7,771** (£2,312; £1,155; £577) **Stalls** High

Form RPR

2-42 **1** **Saltagioo (ITY)**[33] 544 5-8-9 **86**.................................. JohnEgan 2 92
(M Botti) *chsd clr ldr: clsd 1/2-way: ev ch and rdn jst over 2f out: led ins fnl f: styd on wl* **11/4**[2]

160- **2** *1/2* **Viva Vettori**[288] 2711 5-8-10 **87**................................ RichardHughes 1 92
(D R C Elsworth) *t.k.h: led: clr tl reduced advantage 1/2-way: hrd pressed 2f out: rdn over 1f out: drvn and hdd ins fnl f: no ex fnl 100yds* **13/8**[1]

3114 **3** *1* **Can Can Star**[25] 648 6-8-4 **81** oh1.............................. LukeMorris 5 84
(A W Carroll) *stdd s: hld up in last pl: rdn and hdwy 2f out: pressed ldrs ins fnl f: one pce fnl 100yds* **11/1**

221- **4** *2* **Arabian Spirit**[166] 6467 4-8-13 **90**............................... TGMcLaughlin 3 88
(E A L Dunlop) *stdd s: hld up in tch: rdn and unable qck jst over 2f out: drvn and no imp ent fnl f* **3/1**[3]

136- **5** *3/4* **Bomber Command (USA)**[216] 5051 6-9-2 **93**................ MichaelHills 7 90
(J W Hills) *in tch: rdn and effrt 2f out: wknd u.p jst ins fnl f* **7/1**

1m 38.2s (-1.60) **Going Correction** +0.025s/f (Slow) **5** Ran SP% **110.6**
Speed ratings (Par 107): **109,108,107,105,104**
toteswinger: 1&2 £3.20. CSF £7.70 TOTE £4.50: £1.60, £2.20; EX 6.90.
Owner Op - Center **Bred** Az Ag Francesca **Trained** Newmarket, Suffolk

FOCUS
None of these could be ruled out with any certainty, which made for a strong-looking race. However, one horse got an easy lead and almost held on.

NOTEBOOK
Saltagioo(ITY) was a close second over course and distance last month and a 2lb rise in the weights did not look excessive. A multiple winner in Italy, he really stuck his head out when asked for maximum effort and got his head in front just in time. He looks a real professional under pressure. (op 3-1)
Viva Vettori won twice at this track last spring and looked sure to set a decent gallop judged on previous runs. Returning from a long absence, he was a shade keen in front but still nearly landed victory. If this run has taken the freshness out of him, he can win next time. (op 5-2 tchd 11-4 in places)
Can Can Star, who has done well at Lingfield during the winter, came through to have every chance but could not quite get on terms. He is in great heart and may not have finished winning. (tchd 8-1)
Arabian Spirit, having his first run since winning over course and distance last October, had a chance turning in but soon became outpaced. (op 15-8)
Bomber Command(USA), without his now usual visor, ran well for a while on his return from an absence and should be better for the run. (op 6-1)

880 KEMPTON FOR CONFERENCES H'CAP — 6f (P)
9:20 (9:20) (Class 5) (0-75,74) 4-Y-O+ — **£2,590** (£770; £385; £192) **Stalls** High

Form — RPR
00-1 **1** **Brunelleschi**[17] 728 6-8-4 **67**..........(b) JosephineBruning[(7)] 6 — 81
(P L Gilligan) *racd in main gp: clsd on clr ldr ent fnl f: led fnl 100yds: pushed out* — **7/1**[3]
3220 **2** ½ **Compton Classic**[1] 861 7-8-5 **61**..........(p) LiamJones 1 — 73
(J R Boyle) *t.k.h: hld up in main gp: chsd clr ldr and drvn jst over 2f out: clsd u.p ent fnl f: ev ch fnl 100yds: unable qck* — **8/1**
6262 **3** ¾ **Guildenstern (IRE)**[8] 799 7-8-11 **67**.......... IanMongan 4 — 77
(P Howling) *hld up in main gp: rdn over 2f out: clsd u.p ent fnl f: wnt 3rd wl ins fnl f: one pce towards fin* — **13/8**[1]
00-6 **4** 2½ **Onceaponatime (IRE)**[28] 600 4-9-4 **74**.......... AlanMunro 3 — 76
(M D Squance) *chsd clr ldr tl jst over 2f out: kpt on same pce u.p: wknd ins fnl f* — **7/1**[3]
6-60 **5** ½ **Silver Prelude**[28] 600 8-8-13 **69**.......... J-PGuillambert 7 — 69
(S C Williams) *led and sn wl clr: 15 l clr 1/2-way: stl 8 l clr but tiring 1f out: hdd fnl 100yds: fdd rapidly* — **8/1**
-211 **6** 1½ **Perlachy**[24] 654 5-8-10 **66**..........(v) LukeMorris 2 — 61
(D Shaw) *s.i.s: in rr of main gp: rdn over 2f out: no imp u.p fr over 1f out* — **3/1**[2]
30- **7** 5 **Averoo**[238] 4329 4-8-10 **66**.......... SaleemGolam 5 — 45
(M D Squance) *rrd s and s.i.s: a bhd* — **16/1**

1m 12.72s (-0.38) **Going Correction** +0.025s/f (Slow) — **7** Ran SP% **116.2**
Speed ratings (Par 103): **103,102,101,98,97 95,88**
toteswinger: 1&2 £10.90, 1&3 £4.00, 2&3 £2.50. CSF £61.45 CT £134.35 TOTE £4.40: £5.40, £2.50; EX 52.40 Place 6: £44.44, Place 5: £20.70..
Owner Dr Susan Barnes **Bred** Dr Susan Barnes **Trained** Newmarket, Suffolk

FOCUS
A small field but everything could be given some sort of chance. The pace always looked sure to be good.
T/Jkpt: Not won. T/Plt: £84.60 to a £1 stake. Pool: £86,751.43. 747.90 winning tickets. T/Qpdt: £34.50 to a £1 stake. Pool: £7,818.33. 167.40 winning tickets. SP

855 SOUTHWELL (L-H)
Thursday, March 19

OFFICIAL GOING: Standard
Wind: Light across Weather: Overcast

881 CALL 01636 814481 TO SPONSOR A RACE MAIDEN STKS — 6f (F)
2:10 (2:10) (Class 5) 3-Y-O+ — **£2,590** (£770; £385; £192) **Stalls** Low

Form — RPR
2 **1** **Dontuwishitwereso**[9] 796 3-9-0 0.......... RobertWinston 5 — 63+
(P W D'Arcy) *hmpd s: sn trcking ldr: hdwy and cl up over 2f out: rdn to ld wl over 1f out: edgd lft and kpt on ins fnl f* — **1/4**[1]
30-2 **2** 2 **Princess Charlmane (IRE)**[8] 811 6-9-8 47..........(t) AndrewElliott 2 — 56
(C J Teague) *led: rdn along over 2f out: hdd wl over 1f out and sn drvn: kpt on same pce ins fnl f* — **11/2**[2]
3 4½ **Love In The Park** 4-9-8 0.......... TomEaves 3 — 43
(R Brotherton) *towards rr: hdwy over 2f out: rdn to chse ldng pair wl over 1f out: kpt on ins fnl f* — **14/1**[3]
00-0 **4** 3 **Minibuzz**[57] 236 3-9-0 0..........(v) GrahamGibbons 4 — 35
(Mrs G S Rees) *chsd ldng pair: rdn along 1/2-way: sn wknd* — **66/1**
5 18 **Ice Attack (IRE)**[151] 6844 3-8-9 0.......... ChrisCatlin 1 — —
(Patrick Morris) *chsd ldrs on inner: rdn along 1/2-way: sn wknd* — **14/1**[3]

1m 16.94s (0.44) **Going Correction** 0.0s/f (Stan)
WFA 3 from 4yo+ 13lb — **5** Ran SP% **110.2**
Speed ratings (Par 103): **97,94,88,84,60**
CSF £2.11 TOTE £1.10: £1.02, £2.50; EX 1.30.
Owner Paul D'Arcy **Bred** David John Brown **Trained** Newmarket, Suffolk

FOCUS
A very poor and uncompetitive maiden and the winning time was much slower than the following seller.

882 SOUTHWELL-RACECOURSE.CO.UK (S) STKS — 6f (F)
2:40 (2:40) (Class 6) 4-Y-O+ — **£2,047** (£604; £302) **Stalls** Low

Form — RPR
04-0 **1** **Swinbrook (USA)**[74] 35 8-8-12 70..........(v) JamieMoriarty 3 — 72
(R A Fahey) *hld up: hdwy on outer over 2f out: rdn to chal over 1f out: styd on to ld last 100yds* — **11/2**[2]
4113 **2** nk **Don Pele (IRE)**[5] 843 7-9-0 72..........(p) KevinGhunowa[(3)] 6 — 76
(R A Harris) *trckd ldrs: n.m.r and hmpd over 3f out: hdwy to chal over 2f out: rdn to ld over 1f out: drvn ins fnl f: hdd and nt qckn last 100yds* **8/11**[1]
3104 **3** 2¼ **Kingsmaite**[27] 619 8-8-12 62..........(b) MartinLane[(5)] 7 — 69
(S R Bowring) *cl up: led wl over 2f out: sn rdn and hdd over 1f out: drvn and one pce ins fnl f* — **6/1**[3]
0660 **4** 4 **Peter's Storm (USA)**[17] 739 4-8-12 65.......... NCallan 5 — 52
(K A Ryan) *led: rdn along 1/2-way: sn hdd and grad wknd* — **9/1**
00-6 **5** 5 **Weet A Surprise**[7] 818 4-8-7 64.......... ChrisCatlin 2 — 32
(R Hollinshead) *chsd ldrs: rdn along 1/2-way: sn wknd* — **8/1**

1m 15.49s (-1.01) **Going Correction** 0.0s/f (Stan) — **5** Ran SP% **108.7**
Speed ratings (Par 101): **106,105,102,97,90**
toteswinger: 1&2: £9.10. CSF £9.86 TOTE £6.20: £3.20, £1.02; EX 11.70.There was no bid for the winner.
Owner Mark A Leatham **Bred** Bill Bronstad **Trained** Musley Bank, N Yorks

FOCUS
A moderate seller, though the winning time was 1.45 seconds faster than the maiden.

883 SOUTHWELL RACECOURSE FOR CONFERENCES CLAIMING STKS — 1m 3f (F)
3:15 (3:15) (Class 6) 3-Y-O — **£2,047** (£604; £302) **Stalls** Low

Form — RPR
3-46 **1** **Dispol Diva**[27] 620 3-8-4 53..........(v) JoeFanning 4 — 64
(P T Midgley) *t.k.h: hld up in tch: gd hdwy on outer to ld 3f out: shkn up and clr wl over 1f out: styd on* — **7/2**[3]
03-5 **2** 4½ **Augusta Gold (USA)**[23] 662 3-9-2 71..........(b) NCallan 5 — 68
(N P Littmoden) *a.p: cl up 4f out: rdn along wl over 2f out: sn drvn and kpt on same pce* — **2/1**[1]
5-03 **3** 3½ **Amazing Blue Sky**[8] 808 3-8-7 63..........(b) AndrewElliott 2 — 52
(Mrs R A Carr) *hld up in rr: hdwy over 3f out: rdn along over 2f out: sn no imp* — **3/1**[2]
060- **4** 7 **Canucatcher (IRE)**[141] 7079 3-7-13 40 ow1.......... KellyHarrison[(5)] 6 — 37
(T D Walford) *led: rdn along 4f out: hdd 3f out and sn wknd* — **50/1**
-115 **5** hd **La Diosa (IRE)**[22] 677 3-8-1 62 ow6.......... MatthewDavies[(7)] 1 — 40
(George Baker) *trckd ldrs on inner: effrt over 4f out and sn rdn along: wknd 3f out* — **3/1**[2]
05-6 **6** 8 **Urban Space**[26] 630 3-8-10 62.......... ChrisCatlin 3 — 28
(B G Powell) *chsd ldng pair: rdn along over 4f out and sn wknd* — **20/1**

2m 28.68s (0.68) **Going Correction** 0.0s/f (Stan) — **6** Ran SP% **112.3**
Speed ratings (Par 96): **97,93,91,86,85 80**
toteswinger: 1&2 £2.20, 1&3 £3.00, 2&3 £1.90. CSF £10.96 TOTE £5.10: £2.10, £1.30; EX 11.50.La Diosa was claimed by Mrs Susan Lamyman for £5,000.
Owner W B Imison **Bred** P C Hunt **Trained** Westow, N Yorks

FOCUS
A very weak claimer and despite the pace not looking anything special they still finished well strung out.

884 PLAY GOLF AT SOUTHWELL GOLF CLUB H'CAP — 5f (F)
3:45 (3:46) (Class 6) (0-65,65) 4-Y-O+ — **£2,047** (£604; £302) **Stalls** High

Form — RPR
6055 **1** **Spic 'n Span**[16] 742 4-9-0 **61**..........(b) JoeFanning 6 — 68
(R A Harris) *dwlt: sn cl up: effrt wl over 1f out: rdn to ld appr fnl f: drvn and kpt on wl towards fin* — **8/1**
410- **2** hd **This Ones For Pat (USA)**[82] 7799 4-9-1 **62**.......... NCallan 4 — 68
(S Parr) *chsd ldrs: rdn along wl over 1f out: drvn ent fnl f: styd on wl towards fin* — **9/4**[1]
0-44 **3** hd **Music Box Express**[21] 691 5-8-10 **64**..........(t) MatthewDavies[(7)] 1 — 70
(George Baker) *chsd ldrs on outer: rdn along wl over 1f out: drvn and styd on wl fnl f* — **7/2**[2]
0032 **4** nk **Guto**[7] 818 6-8-9 **61**.......... KellyHarrison[(5)] 9 — 65
(W J H Ratcliffe) *sn rdn along towards rr: hdwy wl over 1f out: drvn and styd on strly ins fnl f: nrst fin* — **9/2**[3]
120/ **5** 1½ **Martingrange Boy (IRE)**[442] 17 4-9-4 **65**..........(t) RobertWinston 8 — 64
(J Balding) *led: rdn along wl over 1f out: drvn and hdd appr fnl f: wknd last 100yds* — **14/1**
25-3 **6** ½ **Liberty Ship**[76] 15 4-9-1 **62**..........(tp) AndrewElliott 10 — 59
(J D Bethell) *s.i.s and sn rdn along towards rr: hdwy wl over 1f out: kpt on ins fnl f: nrst fin* — **9/1**
4301 **7** 1 **Sherjawy (IRE)**[3] 853 5-8-7 **54** 6ex ow1..........(b) SamHitchcott 7 — 48
(Miss Z C Davison) *s.i.s and in rr whn swtchd rt after 2f: sn drvn and nvr a factor* — **15/2**
000- **8** 2¾ **Ducal Regancy Red**[82] 7793 5-8-0 **54** oh6 ow3.......... PaulPickard[(7)] 3 — 38
(C J Teague) *chsd ldrs: rdn along over 2f out and sn wknd* — **66/1**
5-40 **9** 1 **Firewalker**[49] 328 4-8-4 **51** oh6..........(p) DaleGibson 5 — 31
(P T Dalton) *towards rr: outpcd and bhd fr 1/2-way* — **66/1**
0-00 **10** 6 **Stoneacre Baby (USA)**[22] 681 4-8-5 **52** oh6 ow1..... PatrickMathers 2 — 11
(Peter Grayson) *towards rr: outpcd and bhd fr 1/2-way* — **40/1**

60.09 secs (0.39) **Going Correction** +0.125s/f (Slow) — **10** Ran SP% **116.1**
Speed ratings (Par 101): **101,100,100,99,97 96,95,90,89,79**
toteswinger: 1&2 £5.30, 1&3 £8.20, 2&3 £3.80. CSF £26.15 CT £76.87 TOTE £9.70: £2.50, £1.40, £1.70; EX 27.60 Trifecta £134.90 Pool: £838.92 - 4.60 winning units..
Owner Mrs Ruth M Serrell **Bred** C A Cyzer **Trained** Earlswood, Monmouths

FOCUS
A modest sprint handicap, but competitive nonetheless and there was little covering the first four at the line. The draw played its part as usual with the first three all coming down the centre of the track.

885 BOOK TICKETS ON LINE AT SOUTHWELL-RACECOURSE.CO.UK APPRENTICE H'CAP — 1m 3f (F)
4:20 (4:20) (Class 5) (0-70,68) 4-Y-O+ — **£2,590** (£770; £385; £192) **Stalls** Low

Form — RPR
1124 **1** **General Tufto**[21] 683 4-8-8 **62**..........(b) MartinLane[(5)] 5 — 70
(C Smith) *hld up in tch: stdy hdwy on outer 4f out: cl up 3f out: rdn to ld wl over 1f out: edgd lft and kpt on ins fnl f* — **9/2**[3]
1334 **2** 1¾ **Ghufa (IRE)**[5] 841 5-9-1 **68**.......... MatthewDavies[(5)] 7 — 73
(George Baker) *led: rdn along over 3f out: drvn and hdd wl over 1f out: kpt on u.p ins fnl f* — **11/4**[2]
43-1 **3** 3¼ **Provost**[7] 823 5-9-0 **65** 6ex.......... FrederikTylicki[(3)] 2 — 65
(M W Easterby) *trckd ldrs: pushed along and sltly outpcd 4f out: sn rdn: drvn and kpt on same pce fnl 2f* — **2/1**[1]
00-3 **4** ½ **Iceman George**[9] 792 5-8-6 **54**..........(b) JackMitchell 8 — 53
(D Morris) *trckd ldng pair: hdwy to chse ldr over 4f out: rdn over 2f out: drvn and wkng whn hung bdly rt over 1f out* — **9/2**[3]
0-50 **5** ½ **Everyman**[28] 597 5-8-4 **57**.......... KellyHarrison[(3)] 4 — 53
(A W Carroll) *trckd ldr on inner: rdn along 3f out: drvn 2f out and kpt on same pce* — **25/1**
0040 **6** 1 **Charlie Bear**[33] 541 8-8-3 **54** oh9..........(p) WilliamCarson[(3)] 6 — 51
(Miss Z C Davison) *dwlt and towards rr: effrt and sme hdwy on outer 1/2-way: sn rdn along and wknd over 3f out* — **66/1**
40-0 **7** 3¼ **Sularno**[58] 224 5-8-7 **62**.......... RyanClark[(7)] 3 — 54
(H Morrison) *hld up: a in rr* — **14/1**
-504 **8** ½ **Prince Golan (IRE)**[20] 713 5-8-11 **66**..........(p) AlexEdwards[(7)] 1 — 57
(J W Unett) *plld hrd: hld up in tch: pushed along whn n.m.r over 4f out: sn wknd* — **22/1**

2m 28.82s (0.82) **Going Correction** 0.0s/f (Stan)
WFA 4 from 5yo+ 1lb — **8** Ran SP% **112.7**
Speed ratings (Par 103): **97,95,93,93,92 91,89,89**
toteswinger: 1&2 £3.40, 1&3 £2.80, 2&3 £1.80. CSF £16.70 CT £31.24 TOTE £5.50: £1.80, £1.10, £1.30; EX 20.20 Trifecta £86.20 Pool: £574.67 - 4.93 winning units..
Owner Phil Martin **Bred** Hascombe And Valiant Studs **Trained** Temple Bruer, Lincs

FOCUS
An ordinary apprentice handicap in which they only went a modest gallop, which caused a few to race keenly. The winning time was 0.14 seconds slower than the earlier three-year-old claimer.

Iceman George Official explanation: trainer said gelding was struck into

886 MEMBERSHIP AT SOUTHWELL GOLF CLUB H'CAP 7f (F)
4:50 (4:50) (Class 5) (0-70,71) 4-Y-0+ **£2,590** (£770; £385; £192) **Stalls** Low

Form RPR
2436 **1** **This Ones For Eddy**[8] 799 4-9-2 **68** NCallan 5 78
(S Parr) *trckd ldrs: hdwy 2f out: rdn over 1f out: led jst ins fnl f: drvn out* **4/1**[1]

-331 **2** 1 1/4 **Ballycroy Boy (IRE)**[27] 619 4-8-13 **65** (b) MickyFenton 9 72
(Miss M E Rowland) *hld up towards rr: wd st and gd hdwy on outer 2f out: rdn to chse ldrs over 1f out: drvn and ch ins fnl f: kpt on same pce towards fin* **13/2**[3]

3352 **3** 1 **Whitbarrow (IRE)**[32] 561 10-9-2 **71** ow3 (b) JamesMillman(3) 6 75
(B R Millman) *prom whn n.m.r and hmpd over 4f out: hdwy on inner to chal 2f out: sn rdn and ev ch tl drvn ent fnl f and kpt on same pce* **10/1**

1456 **4** 1/2 **Tri Chara (IRE)**[13] 777 5-8-13 **65** (p) GrahamGibbons 12 68
(R Hollinshead) *led after 2f: rdn along over 2f out: drvn over 1f out: hdd jst ins fnl f and wknd* **4/1**[1]

5135 **5** 1 3/4 **Cape Of Storms**[8] 811 6-8-8 **60** ow2 TomEaves 2 59
(R Brotherton) *chsd ldrs: rdn along over 2f out: drvn wl over 1f out and kpt on same pce* **15/2**

0-02 **6** 2 1/4 **Royal Challenge**[13] 777 8-9-4 **70** PatrickMathers 11 63
(I W McInnes) *stdd s and hld up in rr tl styd on fnl 2f: nvr a factor* **22/1**

0-30 **7** 1 **Sweet Gale (IRE)**[20] 708 5-8-8 **60** FergusSweeney 1 51
(Mike Murphy) *dwlt: hdwy on inner wl over 2f out: rdn and in tch over 1f out: sn drvn and no imp ent fnl f* **18/1**

53-4 **8** hd **Another Genepi (USA)**[63] 179 6-8-9 **61** (b) EdwardCreighton 8 51
(E J Creighton) *prom: rdn along over 2f out and ev ch tl drvn and wknd over 1f out* **18/1**

4246 **9** shd **My Mentor (IRE)**[17] 733 5-9-2 **68** (p) PaulMulrennan 7 58
(Sir Mark Prescott) *chsd ldrs: sn rdn along and outpcd fr 1/2-way* **9/2**[2]

1-00 **10** 3 3/4 **Royal Island (IRE)**[54] 285 7-8-12 **64** VinceSlattery 10 45
(M G Quinlan) *stdd s: hld up and a in rr* **14/1**

0-00 **11** 4 **Dhhamaan (IRE)**[13] 777 4-8-10 **62** (b) AndrewElliott 4 33
(Mrs R A Carr) *led 2f: cl up tl rdn along over 2f out and sn wknd* **40/1**

1m 29.13s (-1.17) **Going Correction** 0.0s/f (Stan) **11** Ran SP% **116.4**
Speed ratings (Par 103): **106,104,103,102,100 98,97,96,96,92 87**
toteswinger: 1&2 £6.40, 1&3 £9.20, 2&3 £11.50. CSF £29.67 CT £243.51 TOTE £4.30: £1.40, £2.60, £2.80; EX 21.70 Trifecta £174.30 Pool: £605.51 - 2.57 winning units. Place 6: £5.65, Place 5: £5.30.
Owner Willie McKay **Bred** Broughton Bloodstock **Trained**

FOCUS
An ordinary event, but quite a competitive one and there were virtually four in a line across the track passing the furlong pole.
T/Plt: £13.10 to a £1 stake. Pool: £50,198.81. 2,786.98 winning tickets. T/Qpdt: £8.60 to a £1 stake. Pool: £3,480.32. 299.00 winning tickets. JR

867 LINGFIELD (L-H)
Friday, March 20

OFFICIAL GOING: Standard
The card began with a charity race, not under rules, won by John Reid on King Of Cadeaux.
Wind: medium, across Weather: bight and sunny

889 NORTH FARM STUD HOME OF HEROES H'CAP (IN HONOUR OF RAPPORTEUR & ZUCCHERO) 5f (P)
2:00 (2:01) (Class 6) (0-65,61) 3-Y-O **£2,047** (£604; £302) **Stalls** High

Form RPR
006- **1** **Iachimo**[163] 6578 3-8-9 **52** JimCrowley 9 54
(K R Burke) *chsd ldrs: wnt 2nd over 2f out: drvn over 1f out led ins fnl f: all out* **8/1**

-446 **2** hd **Perfect Honour (IRE)**[7] 831 3-8-7 **50** TonyCulhane 10 51
(D Shaw) *towards rr: hdwy on outer 3f out: hung rt and rn wd bnd 2f out: r.o strly fnl f: jst hld* **25/1**

0-60 **3** hd **You Avin A Laugh**[13] 784 3-9-3 **60** PaulEddery 7 61
(C A Dwyer) *in tch: rdn and outpcd over 1f out: hdwy u.str.p fnl f: clsng strly towards fin* **11/4**[1]

020 **4** 1 1/2 **Chimbonda**[9] 804 3-8-13 **56** NCallan 1 51
(S Parr) *t.k.h: led: rdn and edgd lft ent fnl f: hdd ins fnl f: fdd fnl 50yds* **6/1**[3]

6-15 **5** nse **Brown Lentic (IRE)**[38] 481 3-8-2 **50** AmyBaker(5) 3 45
(Miss J Feilden) *chsd ldrs: swtchd lft and effrt over 1f out: ev ch whn nt clr run jst ins fnl f: one pce whn gap opened fnl 100yds* **8/1**

5556 **6** nk **Ruby Tallulah**[18] 736 3-9-0 **57** LPKeniry 5 51
(C R Dore) *t.k.h: hld up wl in tch in rr: effrt and rdn wl over 1f out: kpt on same pce fnl f* **15/2**

60-5 **7** 1/2 **Rapanui Belle**[7] 827 3-8-4 **47** FrankieMcDonald 4 39
(G L Moore) *in tch: hdwy on inner 2f out: nt clr run and swtchd rt 1f out: keeping on but btn whn nt clr run and eased towards fin* **25/1**

3123 **8** 1 1/4 **Sills Vincero**[13] 784 3-9-4 **61** AdamKirby 8 49
(D Shaw) *hld up towards rr: hdwy on outer over 2f out: drvn and no prog over 1f out: wl hld fnl f* **9/2**[2]

545- **9** 3 **Miss Thippawan (USA)**[149] 6906 3-8-4 **47** SilvestreDeSousa 6 24
(P T Midgley) *chsd ldr tl over 2f out: sn rdn and lost pl: no ch fnl f* **9/1**

6-64 **10** 7 **Cindy Incidentally**[28] 624 3-8-8 **51** (p) ChrisCatlin 2 3
(Miss Gay Kelleway) *plld hrd: hld up wl in tch in rr: rdn wl over 1f out: sn lost tch* **16/1**

59.69 secs (0.89) **Going Correction** +0.125s/f (Slow) **10** Ran SP% **116.7**
Speed ratings (Par 96): **97,96,96,93,93 93,92,90,85,74**
toteswinger: 1&2 £15.60, 1&3 £7.60, 2&3 £15.80. CSF £185.04 CT £571.36 TOTE £8.20: £2.40, £6.50, £1.40; EX 214.30 Trifecta £262.50 Part Won Pool: £354.74 - 0.20 winning units..
Owner Philip Richards **Bred** Mrs Ann Jarvis **Trained** Middleham Moor, N Yorks
■ Stewards' Enquiry : N Callan one-day ban: careless riding (Apr 3)

FOCUS
Low-grade but competitive, producing a close finish between the first three.
Iachimo Official explanation: trainer's rep said, regarding apparent improvement in form, that it had been gelded and strengthened up over the winter.

Chimbonda Official explanation: jockey said colt hung right on bend

890 SPORTINGBET.COM MAIDEN FILLIES' STKS 7f (P)
2:30 (2:31) (Class 5) 3-Y-O+ **£2,729** (£806; £403) **Stalls** Low

Form RPR
1 **Kaabari (USA)** 3-8-9 0 NCallan 7 77
(C E Brittain) *broke wl: sn stdd to chse ldrs: rdn 2f out: styd on to ld fnl 100yds: hld on wl* **13/2**[3]

550- **2** nk **Simplification**[192] 5788 3-8-9 77 RichardHughes 3 76
(R Hannon) *chsd ldr: rdn 2f out: ev ch ins fnl f: unable qck towards fin* **4/1**[2]

6 **3** 3/4 **Keep Ringing (USA)**[24] 664 3-8-9 0 MichaelHills 4 74
(W J Haggas) *in tch in midfield: rdn 2f out: outpcd over 1f out: rallied u.p fnl f: wnt 3rd last strides* **13/2**[3]

5- **4** hd **Lady Micklegate (USA)**[88] 7767 3-8-9 0 RobertWinston 1 73
(J R Best) *chsd ldrs: rdn 2f out: hung lft over 1f out: keeping on same pce whn sltly hmpd ins fnl f: lost 3rd last strides* **9/1**

5 1 **Deraaya (IRE)**[295] 4-9-10 79 PatCosgrave 2 76
(K A Morgan) *sn led: rdn wl over 1f out: edgd lft u.p and hdd fnl 100yds: fdd after* **16/1**

6 2 1/2 **Queen Martha (USA)** 3-8-9 0 ChrisCatlin 6 64
(M A Magnusson) *hld up in last trio: rdn 2f out: sn struggling and wl btn fnl f* **11/8**[1]

7 2 **Cross Reef** 4-9-7 0 KevinGhunowa(3) 8 64?
(R A Harris) *hung rt and rn green in rr: hdwy on outer 3f out: rn wd and lost pl bnd 2f out: wl btn after* **50/1**

50- **8** 1 1/2 **Thefillyfromepsom**[100] 7622 3-8-9 0 IanMongan 5 55
(P M Phelan) *hld up in rr: rdn and lost tch 2f out: wl btn fnl f* **25/1**

1m 25.69s (0.89) **Going Correction** +0.125s/f (Slow)
WFA 3 from 4yo 15lb **8** Ran SP% **110.5**
Speed ratings (Par 100): **99,98,97,97,96 93,91,89**
toteswinger: 1&2 £4.50, 1&3 £5.20, 2&3 £4.60. CSF £30.36 TOTE £7.70: £2.00, £1.30, £2.00; EX 29.50 Trifecta £246.40 Pool: £469.54 - 1.41 winning units.
Owner Saeed Manana **Bred** Darley **Trained** Newmarket, Suffolk
■ Stewards' Enquiry : Pat Cosgrave caution: careless riding.

FOCUS
Just a pedestrian gallop, but the best horse won, and she can probably improve significantly on this.

891 DUNWOODY.CO.UK SUPPORTS HEROS CLAIMING STKS (IN HONOUR OF ADANTINO) 6f (P)
3:05 (3:06) (Class 6) 4-Y-O+ **£2,047** (£604; £302) **Stalls** Low

Form RPR
2002 **1** **Northern Empire (IRE)**[30] 589 6-8-13 77 NCallan 2 61+
(K A Ryan) *rrd s: t.k.h: chsd ldrs after 1f: led 3f out: c clr over 1f out: tiring and rdn ins fnl f: jst lasted* **4/9**[1]

2-46 **2** hd **Russian Symphony (USA)**[16] 757 8-9-0 70 (b) SteveDrowne 1 61+
(C R Egerton) *chsd ldr for 1f: rdn over 2f out: drvn and outpcd over 1f out: styd on u.p fnl f: jst hld* **9/4**[2]

00-0 **3** 2 **Fly In Johnny (IRE)**[24] 666 4-8-10 39 JimCrowley 4 51
(J J Bridger) *hld up in last pl: rdn and outpcd wl over 1f out: kpt on again u.p ins fnl f* **50/1**

55 **4** 4 **Gold Rock (FR)**[7] 825 4-9-5 75 ShaneKelly 3 48
(A W Carroll) *led tl 3f out: rdn wl over 1f out: sn outpcd: no ch fnl f* **20/1**[3]

1m 12.34s (0.44) **Going Correction** +0.125s/f (Slow) **4** Ran SP% **106.7**
Speed ratings (Par 101): **102,101,99,93**
toteswinger: 1&2 £1.60 CSF £1.63 TOTE £1.40; EX 1.60.
Owner Sunpak Potatoes **Bred** Denis McDonnell **Trained** Hambleton, N Yorks

FOCUS
An unreliable-looking claimer. The modest pace did not suit the winner, but some smart thinking and good tactical riding by Callan overcame that disadvantage.

892 VORTEX AND FAJR - LINGFIELD WINNERS H'CAP 6f (P)
3:40 (3:43) (Class 4) (0-85,85) 4-Y-O+ **£4,857** (£1,445; £722; £360) **Stalls** Low

Form RPR
00-2 **1** **Obe Gold**[8] 821 7-8-13 **80** (v) AdrianTNicholls 4 93
(D Nicholls) *chsd ldr: ev ch jst over 2f out: rdn to ld ins fnl f: drew clr fnl 50yds* **10/3**[1]

0052 **2** 2 1/4 **Dvinsky (USA)**[2] 866 8-9-4 **85** (b) IanMongan 3 91
(P Howling) *sn pushed up to ld: rdn and qcknd jst over 2f out: drvn and hdd ins fnl f: wknd towards fin* **4/1**[2]

1424 **3** 1 3/4 **Distinctly Game**[14] 780 7-8-11 **78** (t) NCallan 1 78
(K A Ryan) *t.k.h: broke wl: sn stdd to trck ldng pair: rdn and unable qck 2f out: kpt on same pce after* **5/1**[3]

21 **4** 1 1/4 **Trade Centre**[18] 729 4-8-10 **77** ShaneKelly 5 73
(W R Muir) *in tch: rdn and outpcd 2f out: styd on again u.p fnl f: no ch w ldrs* **13/2**

52-0 **5** 1 1/2 **Credit Swap**[14] 780 4-8-11 **78** NickyMackay 8 70
(M Wigham) *stdd and dropped in after s: hld up in rr: rdn 2f out: nvr trbld ldrs* **14/1**

1313 **6** 1/2 **Mogok Ruby**[14] 780 5-9-0 **81** LukeMorris 2 71
(L Montague Hall) *t.k.h: hld up in tch: rdn and unable qck jst over 2f out: n.d after* **15/2**

6144 **7** shd **Resplendent Alpha**[24] 665 5-8-13 **80** DarryllHolland 7 70
(P Howling) *stdd and swtchd lft after s: hld up in rr: rdn 2f out: wnt modest 4th over 1f out: no imp: wknd and lost 3 pls wl ins fnl f* **7/1**

3633 **8** 8 **Fromsong (IRE)**[16] 754 11-8-13 **80** JimCrowley 6 44
(D K Ivory) *dwlt: t.k.h: hld up in tch on outer: rdn and wknd over 2f out: eased ins fnl f* **11/1**

1m 12.03s (0.13) **Going Correction** +0.125s/f (Slow) **8** Ran SP% **112.3**
Speed ratings (Par 105): **104,101,98,97,95 94,94,83**
toteswinger: 1&2 £3.20, 1&3 £3.50, 2&3 £4.10. CSF £16.05 CT £63.68 TOTE £4.20: £1.60, £1.50, £1.80; EX 16.80 Trifecta £72.60 Pool: £598.28 - 6.09 winning units.
Owner D Nicholls **Bred** Mrs M Mason **Trained** Sessay, N Yorks

FOCUS
Run at a modest pace, with few significant position changes.
Fromsong(IRE) Official explanation: jockey said gelding missed the break and ran too keenly

893 SPORTINGBET.COM H'CAP (IN HONOUR OF FAJR) 1m 2f (P)
4:15 (4:15) (Class 4) (0-85,81) 4-Y-O+ **£4,857** (£1,445; £722; £360) **Stalls** Low

Form RPR
6-05 **1** **Royal Amnesty**[21] 713 6-8-13 **76** (b) RobertWinston 5 84
(I Semple) *s.i.s: hld up in last pair: hdwy 2f out: led ins fnl f: r.o wl* **15/2**

1222 **2** 1 3/4 **Old Romney**[2] 873 5-8-10 **73** RichardHughes 4 78
(M Wigham) *stdd s: last tl dashed up to ld over 8f out: sn clr: reduced advantage 5f out: pushed along and hdd ins fnl f: sn btn* **2/1**[1]

00-3 **3** *1* **Ruff Diamond (USA)**[9] 648 4-8-11 **74**............................ LukeMorris 3 77
(J S Moore) *led at crawl tl over 8f out: chsd ldrs after: clsd 5f out: rdn over 2f out: kpt on same pce fnl f* **9/2**[3]

5-12 **4** *1* **Basra (IRE)**[34] 550 6-9-4 **81**.. DaneO'Neill 2 82
(Miss Jo Crowley) *hld up in rr: swtchd rt and effrt over 1f out: one pce fnl f* **9/4**[2]

2-00 **5** *shd* **Emperor Court (IRE)**[48] 361 5-9-1 **78**........................... SteveDrowne 1 79
(P J Makin) *hld up in rr: effrt on outer bnd 2f out: one pce u.p fr over 1f out* **10/1**

5526 **6** *1 1/4* **Silver Hotspur**[17] 747 5-9-3 **80**.. LiamJones 6 79
(C R Dore) *chsd ldr: rdn 2f out: wknd ent fnl f* **16/1**

2m 11.17s (4.57) **Going Correction** +0.125s/f (Slow) **6** Ran SP% **109.0**
Speed ratings (Par 105): **86,84,83,83,82 81**
toteswinger: 1&2 £3.00, 1&3 £4.10, 2&3 £2.10. CSF £21.63 TOTE £7.30: £2.60, £1.80; EX 22.50.
Owner Mrs Francesca Mitchell **Bred** Brick Kiln Stud, Mrs L Hicks & Partners **Trained** Carluke, S Lanarks

FOCUS
A bizarre race, with the runners walking for the first furlong and Hughes on the runner-up then seizing the initiative and going eight lengths clear. After allowing the others to stack up behind him, he tried to coax his mount home on the bridle, but the winner found more in the last 150 yards.

894 SPORTINGBET.COM H'CAP (IN HONOUR OF SRI DIAMOND) 1m 5f (P)
4:50 (4:50) (Class 5) (0-75,73) 4-Y-0+ **£2,900** (£856; £428) **Stalls** Low

Form RPR

0-01 **1** **Bell Island**[27] 631 5-9-7 **73**......................................(v) RichardHughes 3 81
(Lady Herries) *chsd ldr tl c centre and sltly outpcd wl over 1f out: rdn and hdwy ent fnl f: led fnl 100yds: rdn out* **10/11**[1]

1202 **2** *1/2* **Rawdon (IRE)**[10] 795 8-8-12 **71**..............................(bt) KylieManser(7) 4 78
(Miss Gay Kelleway) *w.w in tch: hdwy to trck ldr gng wl over 1f out: chal 1f out: rdn and one pce ins fnl f* **12/1**

-164 **3** *3/4* **Dramatic Solo**[24] 668 4-8-12 **67**....................................(b) LiamJones 5 73
(K R Burke) *led: rdn over 1f out: hrd pressed ent fnl f: hdd and no ex fnl 100yds* **11/2**[3]

00-5 **4** *3* **Cash On (IRE)**[7] 836 7-8-11 **63**.................................(p) DarryllHolland 6 65
(Karen George) *racd in last pair: rdn and reminder 9f out: rdn and effrt over 2f out: chsd ldng trio over 1f out: no imp* **16/1**

300- **5** *7* **Ross Moor**[225] 4791 7-9-0 **66**... FergusSweeney 7 58
(Mike Murphy) *s.i.s: hdwy over 3f out: chsd ldrs and rdn 2f out: wknd qckly over 1f out* **14/1**

-033 **6** *4 1/2* **Apache Fort**[16] 750 6-9-4 **70**..(b) NCallan 1 56
(T Keddy) *w.w in tch: rdn and struggling over 2f out: wl btn fr over 1f out: eased ins fnl f* **7/2**[2]

2m 45.47s (-0.53) **Going Correction** +0.125s/f (Slow)
WFA 4 from 5yo+ 3lb **6** Ran SP% **110.2**
Speed ratings (Par 103): **106,105,105,103,99 96**
toteswinger: 1&2 £2.70, 1&3 £2.30, 2&3 £4.30. CSF £12.65 TOTE £2.10: £1.30, £3.80; EX 8.00.
Owner L G Lazarus **Bred** Juddmonte Farms Ltd **Trained** Patching, W Sussex

FOCUS
A typical Lingfield race, with no gallop until the pace suddenly lifted approaching the home straight.

895 BARRY DENNIS H'CAP (DIV I) 5f (P)
5:20 (5:21) (Class 6) (0-52,52) 4-Y-0+ **£1,706** (£503; £252) **Stalls** High

Form RPR

5-43 **1** **Green Velvet**[49] 347 4-8-12 **50**... TravisBlock 4 62+
(P J Makin) *in tch: rdn 2f out: hdwy u.p over 1f out: rdn ld ins fnl f: sn clr: readily* **6/1**

0043 **2** *2 1/2* **Affirmatively**[18] 727 4-8-9 **47**..(bt) ShaneKelly 10 50
(A W Carroll) *hld up bhd: c wd bnd 2f out: sn rdn: r.o wl u.p fnl f: snatched 2nd on post: no ch w wnr* **10/1**

5641 **3** *nse* **Meikle Barfil**[8] 812 7-8-13 **51** 6ex..............................(tp) LukeMorris 8 54
(J M Bradley) *hld up bhd: hdwy 2f out: drvn over 1f out: chsd wnr ins fnl f: no imp: lost 2nd on post* **7/1**

0401 **4** *1 1/4* **Admirals Way**[9] 803 4-8-7 **52**... LeeNewnes(7) 5 50
(C N Kellett) *taken down early: hld up in tch: shuffled bk 2f out: hdwy ent fnl f: styd on to go 4th on post: nt pce to threaten ldrs* **7/2**[1]

0504 **5** *shd* **Titus Gent**[9] 803 4-8-10 **48**...(p) NCallan 6 46
(J Ryan) *chsd ldrs: rdn and outpcd 2f out: edging lft u.p over 1f out: styd on again fnl 100yds* **5/1**[3]

600 **6** *1* **Magic Glade**[7] 832 10-9-0 **52**... LPKeniry 2 46
(Peter Grayson) *taken down early: chsd ldrs: rdn ent fnl f: wknd fnl 100yds* **12/1**

3062 **7** *nk* **Ishibee (IRE)**[18] 727 5-8-10 **48**.....................................(p) NeilChalmers 1 41
(J J Bridger) *sn led: rdn over 1f out: hdd ins fnl f: wknd qckly fnl 100yds* **10/1**

-305 **8** *1* **Rightcar Lewis**[8] 812 4-8-8 **46** oh1..................................(b) LiamJones 3 36
(Peter Grayson) *sn pushed up to press ldr: ev ch and rdn over 1f out: wknd qckly ent fnl f* **20/1**

5-00 **9** *1 1/4* **Bahamarama (IRE)**[16] 756 4-8-8 **49**.....................(p) KevinGhunowa(3) 7 34
(R A Harris) *in tch in midfield: lost pl and bhd 2f out: wl hld fnl f* **33/1**

5200 **10** *1/2* **Head To Head (IRE)**[10] 794 5-9-0 **52**..................(b) SilvestreDeSousa 9 35
(A D Brown) *hld up towards rr on outer: swtchd ins and rdn 2f out: no prog and wl btn fnl f* **4/1**[2]

59.34 secs (0.54) **Going Correction** +0.125s/f (Slow) **10** Ran SP% **119.3**
Speed ratings (Par 101): **100,96,95,93,93 92,91,90,88,87**
toteswinger: 1&2 £16.00, 1&3 £8.60, 2&3 £14.30. CSF £66.03 CT £446.82 TOTE £5.20: £1.80, £3.80, £1.80; EX 79.00 Trifecta £236.80 Pool: £803.27 - 2.51 winning units.
Owner Mrs P J Makin **Bred** Mrs P J Makin **Trained** Ogbourne Maisey, Wilts

FOCUS
A weak race, but the lightly-raced winner looks progressive at a realistic level and won comfortably.
Admirals Way Official explanation: jockey said gelding stumbled on leaving stalls

896 BARRY DENNIS H'CAP (DIV II) 5f (P)
5:50 (5:50) (Class 6) (0-52,52) 4-Y-0+ **£1,706** (£503; £252) **Stalls** High

Form RPR

0-66 **1** **Mujma**[9] 802 5-8-8 **46** oh1..(bt) LiamJones 5 60+
(S Parr) *stdd s: t.k.h: hld up in last trio: c wd and hdwy 2f out: str run and hung lft fr over 1f out: led ins fnl f: sn stormed clr: readily* **11/2**[3]

400- **2** *3* **Sofinella (IRE)**[160] 6658 6-9-0 **52**...................................... LukeMorris 8 55
(A W Carroll) *led briefly: sn trcking ldrs: chal on inner over 1f out: rdn to ld ent fnl f: hdd ins fnl f: no ch w wnr* **16/1**

003 **3** *1 1/4* **One Way Ticket**[36] 508 9-8-9 **47** oh1 ow1.......................(tp) ShaneKelly 6 46
(J M Bradley) *in tch: rdn and effrt 2f out: chsd ldrs and hld hd high u.p over 1f out: plugged on to go 3rd last strides* **8/1**

340- **4** *hd* **Rann Na Cille (IRE)**[162] 6595 5-8-3 **48**.......................... PaulPickard(7) 9 46
(P T Midgley) *chsd ldr: ev ch and rdn over 1f out: outpcd ins fnl f: wknd fnl 75yds and lost 3rd last strides* **7/1**

0-00 **5** *3/4* **Sir Loin**[18] 727 8-8-9 **47**...(v) FrankieMcDonald 7 42
(P Burgoyne) *in tch in midfield: effrt and rdn 2f out: one pce ent fnl f* **12/1**

0-00 **6** *nse* **Babel**[39] 467 4-9-0 **52**.. SimonWhitworth 1 47
(M Wigham) *hld up in tch on inner: swtchd rt and rdn over 1f out: no imp* **11/2**[3]

25-0 **7** *nk* **North South Divide (IRE)**[61] 208 5-9-0 **52**.................(p) DaneO'Neill 4 46
(Peter Grayson) *taken down early: s.i.s: hld up in last trio: effrt on outer bnd 2f out: nvr threatened ldrs* **5/1**[2]

-000 **8** *1/2* **Stoneacre Pat (IRE)**[23] 681 4-8-11 **49**................................ LPKeniry 10 41
(Peter Grayson) *s.i.s: bhd: hdwy over 1f out: swtchd rt 1f out: keeping on same pce and no threat whn short of room and eased wl ins fnl f* **14/1**

004 **9** *nk* **Triskaidekaphobia**[23] 681 6-8-12 **50**....................(bt) PaulFitzsimons 3 41
(Miss J R Tooth) *sn led: rdn over 1f out: hdd ent fnl f: wknd qckly* **8/1**

-410 **10** *1 1/2* **Nawaaff**[31] 575 4-8-13 **51**.. TonyCulhane 2 37
(M R Channon) *hld up in midfield: lost pl after 1f: bhd and rdn 2f out: no prog* **4/1**[1]

59.29 secs (0.49) **Going Correction** +0.125s/f (Slow) **10** Ran SP% **122.4**
Speed ratings (Par 101): **101,96,94,93,92 92,92,91,90,88**
toteswinger: 1&2 £52.40, 1&3 £39.90, 2&3 £9.90. CSF £93.58 CT £716.11 TOTE £9.00: £3.60, £3.50, £2.90; EX 201.00 Trifecta £349.20 Part won. Pool: £471.99 - 0.20 winning units. Place 6: £20.52 Place 5: £8.29.
Owner Willie McKay **Bred** Arbib Bloodstock Partnership **Trained**

FOCUS
Not a race for form students to peruse for long, but it was run at a good tempo thanks to the presence of several front-runners.
Stoneacre Pat(IRE) Official explanation: jockey said colt was denied a clear run
T/Plt: £50.60 to a £1 stake. Pool: £57,948.79. 834.84 winning tickets. T/Qpdt: £5.90 to a £1 stake. Pool: £3,559.72. 440.18 winning tickets. SP

831 WOLVERHAMPTON (A.W) (L-H)
Friday, March 20

OFFICIAL GOING: Standard changing to standard to fast after race 2 (7:20)
Wind: Nil Weather: Fine

897 STAY AT THE WOLVERHAMPTON HOLIDAY INN FILLIES' H'CAP 1m 1f 103y(P)
6:50 (6:50) (Class 5) (0-70,70) 4-Y-0+ **£2,729** (£806; £403) **Stalls** Low

Form RPR

3412 **1** **Ridgeway Jazz**[14] 775 4-8-2 **61**... SeanPalmer(7) 3 69
(M D I Usher) *a.p: led ins fnl f: pushed out* **9/1**

-612 **2** *1* **Snow Dancer (IRE)**[39] 478 5-8-13 **65**.......................(p) PaulMulrennan 9 71
(H A McWilliams) *a.p: led wl over 1f out: rdn and hdd ins fnl f: nt qckn* **9/2**[3]

1124 **3** *2 1/2* **Formidable Guest**[18] 733 5-9-1 **67**................................... RobertHavlin 1 68
(J Pearce) *hld up in rr: hdwy 3f out: rdn over 1f out: one pce fnl f* **7/2**[1]

30-2 **4** *4* **Garra Molly (IRE)**[23] 678 4-8-13 **65**................................... EddieAhern 6 59
(G A Swinbank) *hld up in tch: rdn over 2f out: wkng whn edgd lft over 1f out* **7/1**

3311 **5** *2 3/4* **Amber Moon**[10] 792 4-8-10 **67** 6ex ow4......................(b) AnnStokell(5) 5 56
(Miss A Stokell) *t.k.h: sn towards rr: rdn over 1f out: nvr trbld ldrs* **16/1**

-224 **6** *1 1/4* **Quick Off The Mark**[22] 688 4-9-1 **67**................................... TPQueally 4 53
(J G Given) *led: hdd 6f out: w ldr: led over 3f out: rdn and hdd wl over 1f out: wknd fnl f* **5/1**

060- **7** *9* **Keisha Kayleigh (IRE)**[200] 5564 6-9-4 **70**..............(v) GrahamGibbons 7 39
(B Ellison) *dwlt: rdn over 2f out: a in rr* **14/1**

05/0 **8** *3/4* **Millagros (IRE)**[23] 679 9-8-1 **58**............................... PatrickDonaghy(5) 2 26
(I Semple) *chsd ldr after 1f: led 6f out tl over 3f out: wknd over 2f out* **66/1**

-133 **9** *4 1/2* **Giddywell**[23] 682 5-8-4 **56**...(p) ChrisCatlin 8 15
(R Hollinshead) *t.k.h early in mid-div: bhd fnl 3f* **4/1**[2]

1m 59.63s (-2.07) **Going Correction** -0.10s/f (Stan) **9** Ran SP% **113.6**
Speed ratings (Par 100): **105,104,101,98,95 94,86,86,82**
toteswinger: 1&2 £7.00, 1&3 £7.00, 2&3 £5.10. CSF £48.40 CT £169.63 TOTE £11.30: £3.30, £1.60, £1.60; EX 71.90.
Owner M D I Usher **Bred** Templeton Stud And Bricklow Ltd **Trained** Upper Lambourn, Berks

FOCUS
A modest fillies' handicap.
Giddywell Official explanation: jockey said mare ran too freely

898 ENJOY THE LUCKY 7 GROUP OFFER H'CAP 1m 141y(P)
7:20 (7:20) (Class 6) (0-60,60) 4-Y-0+ **£2,047** (£604; £302) **Stalls** Low

Form RPR

00-1 **1** **Ergo (FR)**[25] 657 5-9-0 **56**..(b) DarrenMoffatt 12 71+
(James Moffatt) *t.k.h towards rr: hdwy on outside over 2f out: led over 1f out: drew clr ins fnl f: r.o wl* **14/1**

-461 **2** *4 1/2* **Waldorf (IRE)**[23] 682 4-9-4 **60**.. EddieAhern 8 66
(W R Muir) *a.p: ev ch wl over 1f out: kpt on one pce ins fnl f* **13/2**[3]

55-0 **3** *nk* **Rigat**[32] 571 6-8-13 **55**... DanielTudhope 2 60
(J S Goldie) *hld up in mid-div: nt clr run on ins over 2f out: hdwy and swtchd lft over 1f out: kpt on same pce ins fnl f* **13/2**[3]

0650 **4** *1/2* **Stark Contrast (USA)**[25] 657 5-8-12 **57**.......................... DavidProbert(3) 4 61
(M D I Usher) *hld up in tch: rdn and edgd lft ins fnl f: one pce* **7/1**

-400 **5** *1* **Maybe I Wont**[49] 344 4-9-1 **57**....................................... TGMcLaughlin 11 59
(Lucinda Featherstone) *hld up in rr: swtchd lft sn after s: rdn and hdwy fnl f: nvr nrr* **33/1**

-012 **6** *2* **Alfredtheordinary**[2] 867 4-8-12 **59**.................................... MCGeran(5) 10 57
(M R Channon) *hld up in rr: rdn wl over 1f out: styd on ins fnl f: n.d* **6/1**[2]

-030 **7** *1 1/2* **Ike Quebec (FR)**[9] 803 4-9-3 **59**......................................(b) PatCosgrave 7 54
(J R Boyle) *led: rdn over 2f out: hdd over 1f out: wknd ins fnl f* **18/1**

-132 **8** *1* **King Of Legend (IRE)**[8] 823 5-9-2 **58**............................. GregFairley 13 51
(A G Foster) *sn prom: wnt 2nd over 6f out: ev ch 2f out: rdn and wknd over 1f out* **4/1**[1]

040- **9** *1 1/2* **Whaston (IRE)**[176] 6227 4-9-2 **58**...........................(v) GrahamGibbons 5 48
(J D Bethell) *hld up in mid-div: rdn over 2f out: wknd wl over 1f out* **16/1**

45-5 **10** *3/4* **Sixth Zak**[42] 425 4-9-1 **57**... DaleGibson 1 45
(M W Easterby) *a in rr* **12/1**

310- **11** *1 1/2* **My Mate Mal**[136] 7184 5-9-4 **60**... TomEaves 6 45
(B Ellison) *t.k.h: chsd ldr 2f: prom: rdn over 2f out: wknd over 1f out* **14/1**

1300 **12** *25* **Ardent Prince**[6] 844 6-9-2 **58**... TPQueally 9 —
(A J McCabe) *hld up in mid-div: wknd qckly over 3f out: t.o* **11/1**

1m 48.62s (-1.88) **Going Correction** -0.10s/f (Stan) **12** Ran SP% **116.9**
Speed ratings (Par 101): **104,100,99,99,98 96,95,94,93,92 91,68**
toteswinger: 1&2 £20.00, 1&3 £23.30, 2&3 £14.50. CSF £100.91 CT £666.16 TOTE £22.50: £4.10, £2.80, £1.40; EX 87.90.

Owner Mrs Eileen M Milligan **Bred** Takashi Watanabe **Trained** Cartmel, Cumbria

FOCUS
A moderate yet wide-open handicap. The decent winning time prompted an official going change to "standard to fast".

King Of Legend(IRE) Official explanation: jockey said, regarding running and riding, that he was drawn 13 and had to make too much use of the gelding to obtain a prominent position, adding that it went according to plan but it failed to quicken turn into straight; trainer said he was satisfied and that the race may have come too soon.
Whaston(IRE) Official explanation: jockey said gelding hung right throughout
My Mate Mal Official explanation: jockey said gelding ran too keenly
Ardent Prince Official explanation: jockey said gelding stopped quickly

899 DINE IN THE HORIZONS RESTAURANT H'CAP 2m 119y(P)
7:50 (7:50) (Class 4) (0-85,83) 4-Y-0+ **£5,180** (£1,541; £770; £384) **Stalls** Low

Form RPR
21-1 **1** **Laurel Creek (IRE)**[34] 559 4-10-0 **83**.................. EddieAhern 3 93+
(M J Grassick, Ire) *hld up in mid-div: stdy prog over 5f out: led over 1f out: rdn and hung rt ins fnl f: drvn out* **6/4**[1]
6021 **2** ¾ **Phoenix Flight (IRE)**[16] 750 4-9-7 **76**.................. PaulMulrennan 6 85+
(Sir Mark Prescott) *stdd s: hld up in rr: hdwy on outside over 2f out: rn wd ent st: ev ch whn rdn and hung rt ins fnl f: nt qckn* **9/1**
4412 **3** 5 **Mr Aitch (IRE)**[19] 723 7-9-13 **77**..................(t) TPQueally 8 80
(R T Phillips) *hld up in mid-div: hdwy over 3f out: rdn over 2f out: ev ch over 1f out: carried rt ins fnl f: wknd* **14/1**
12-5 **4** 3 ¾ **Miss Serena**[19] 723 4-9-2 **71**.................. MickyFenton 9 70
(Mrs P Sly) *led: hdd over 1f out: wknd ins fnl f* **11/1**
123 **5** 4 **Mission Control (IRE)**[30] 591 4-9-7 **76**.................. PatCosgrave 1 70
(J R Boyle) *prom: rdn wl over 2f out: wknd wl over 1f out* **10/1**
4133 **6** 1 ½ **Monaadi (IRE)**[7] 835 4-8-7 **62**..................(v) GrahamGibbons 5 54
(R Hollinshead) *hld up in tch: wnt 2nd over 8f out: rdn and ev ch over 2f out: wknd wl over 1f out* **8/1**[3]
4-11 **7** 3 ¼ **Merrion Tiger (IRE)**[43] 402 4-8-10 **65**.................. GregFairley 7 53
(A G Foster) *chsd ldr tl over 8f out: wknd 5f out* **8/1**[3]
1-15 **8** ¾ **Zuwaar**[58] 233 4-9-2 **71**..................(t) ChrisCatlin 4 58
(Ian Williams) *hld up in rr: pushed along over 3f out: no rspnse* **7/2**[2]
106- **9** 4 ½ **Fort Churchill (IRE)**[175] 6243 8-9-2 **73**.................. MarzenaJeziorek(7) 2 55
(B Ellison) *bhd fnl 3f* **66/1**

3m 39.3s (-2.50) **Going Correction** -0.10s/f (Stan)
WFA 4 from 7yo+ 5lb 9 Ran SP% **120.0**
Speed ratings (Par 105): **101,100,98,96,94 93,92,92,89**
toteswinger: 1&2 £3.50, 1&3 £5.50, 2&3 £18.70. CSF £17.28 CT £145.81 TOTE £2.30: £1.30, £2.80, £4.60; EX 15.30.
Owner Patrick G McKeon **Bred** Tetsu Nakata **Trained** Pollardstown, Co Kildare

FOCUS
This was a fair staying handicap for the class, run at a modest pace.
Miss Serena Official explanation: jockey said filly hung right

900 ENJOY EVENING RACING WITH FRIENDS H'CAP 7f 32y(P)
8:20 (8:21) (Class 6) (0-60,60) 3-Y-O **£2,047** (£604; £302) **Stalls** High

Form RPR
4-60 **1** **Location**[13] 786 3-8-10 **52**.................. JimCrowley 6 58
(Ian Williams) *hld up towards rr: hdwy over 2f out: rdn to ld cl home* **10/1**
302 **2** nk **Villaruz (IRE)**[7] 831 3-9-1 **57**.................. EddieAhern 5 62
(D Flood) *t.k.h: chsd ldr 1f: a.p: rdn and ev ch ins fnl f: r.o* **3/1**[1]
000- **3** hd **Order Order**[155] 6761 3-9-4 **60**.................. RobertWinston 3 64
(H J L Dunlop) *a.p: rdn to ld jst ins fnl f: hdd cl home* **6/1**[3]
00-5 **4** 2 ¼ **Dalepak Flyer (IRE)**[7] 831 3-9-4 **60**.................. PaulEddery 4 58
(Paul Mason) *led: rdn and hdd jst ins fnl f: no ex towards fin* **6/1**[3]
5530 **5** 2 ¼ **Weet In Nerja**[7] 831 3-8-7 **56**..................(p) DavidKenny(7) 2 48
(R Hollinshead) *hld up towards rr: hdwy on ins wl over 1f out: rdn and one pce fnl f* **16/1**
400- **6** 1 **Key To Love (IRE)**[92] 7719 3-8-12 **57**.................. DavidProbert(3) 7 47
(A J Chamberlain) *chsd ldr after 1f to 2f out: wknd over 1f out* **16/1**
0-36 **7** ½ **Jaq's Sister**[25] 658 3-9-1 **57**.................. DaleGibson 1 45
(M Blanshard) *hld up in rr: pushed along over 2f out: nvr nr ldrs* **20/1**
1343 **8** 2 ¼ **Private Passion (IRE)**[7] 831 3-8-4 **53**.................. TobyAtkinson(7) 8 35
(Pat Eddery) *hld up in rr: c wd st: rdn over 1f out: no rspnse* **4/1**[2]
00-5 **9** 2 ¾ **Praise Of Folly**[32] 572 3-9-1 **57**.................. SteveDrowne 12 32
(A G Newcombe) *hld up in rr: rdn over 2f out: sn struggling* **16/1**
4- **10** ½ **Salgrev (IRE)**[223] 4847 3-8-10 **52**.................. PaulMulrennan 10 25
(Irene J Monaghan, Ire) *hld up: sn in tch: rdn over 2f out: wknd wl over 1f out* **33/1**
5124 **11** ¾ **Josiah Bartlett (IRE)**[7] 826 3-9-4 **60**..................(bt) ChrisCatlin 11 31
(P S McEntee) *s.i.s: sn hld up in mid-div: hdwy on outside over 3f out: wknd wl over 1f out* **7/1**

1m 30.95s (1.35) **Going Correction** -0.10s/f (Stan) 11 Ran SP% **120.5**
Speed ratings (Par 96): **88,87,87,84,82 81,80,78,74,74 73**
toteswinger: 1&2 £7.90, 1&3 £20.00, 2&3 £3.60. CSF £41.10 CT £204.06 TOTE £17.30: £4.90, £1.90, £2.10; EX 56.90.
Owner Dr Marwan Koukash **Bred** Juddmonte Farms Ltd **Trained** Portway, Worcs

FOCUS
A moderate handicap which produced a tight three-way finish.
Villaruz(IRE) Official explanation: jockey said gelding hung left throughout

901 GREAT OFFERS AT WOLVERHAMPTON-RACECOURSE.CO.UK H'CAP 5f 20y(P)
8:50 (8:50) (Class 4) (0-85,84) 4-Y-0+ **£5,180** (£1,541; £770; £384) **Stalls** Low

Form RPR
000- **1** **Northern Dare (IRE)**[182] 6069 5-9-4 **84**.................. JimCrowley 6 92
(D Nicholls) *a.p: led jst ins fnl f: sn hung lft: r.o* **4/1**[1]
045- **2** nk **Rothesay Dancer**[133] 7222 6-7-13 **70**.................. KellyHarrison(5) 11 77
(J S Goldie) *hld up towards rr: hdwy 1f out: r.o wl towards fin* **25/1**
2214 **3** 1 ¾ **Incomparable**[27] 632 4-8-12 **78**.................. RobertWinston 7 79
(A J McCabe) *chsd ldrs: rdn over 1f out: kpt on to take 3rd last strides* **4/1**[1]
501- **4** nk **Kelamon**[170] 6402 5-8-9 **75**.................. SaleemGolam 1 75
(S C Williams) *led early: chsd ldr: ev ch 1f out: rdn and no ex towards fin* **16/1**
1452 **5** 1 **Princess Valerina**[14] 780 5-8-13 **79**.................. TPQueally 12 75
(D Haydn Jones) *hld up towards rr: rdn over 1f out: late hdwy: nrst fin* **14/1**
-011 **6** ½ **Bahamian Lad**[14] 780 4-8-11 **77**.................. GrahamGibbons 2 71
(R Hollinshead) *s.i.s: sn mid-div: pushed along over 3f out: rdn and no hdwy fnl f* **4/1**[1]
2-23 **7** ¾ **Silvanus (IRE)**[49] 351 4-8-9 **75**..................(b) ChrisCatlin 9 66
(I Semple) *sn led: hdd jst ins fnl f: wknd* **11/2**[2]
6455 **8** nse **Came Back (IRE)**[16] 756 6-8-10 **81** ow2.................. AnnStokell(5) 5 72
(Miss A Stokell) *t.k.h: prom: rdn over 1f out: wknd ins fnl f* **20/1**
6540 **9** shd **Thoughtsofstardom**[2] 870 6-8-2 **73**.................. AmyBaker(5) 4 64
(P S McEntee) *nvr bttr than mid-div* **33/1**
-306 **10** ½ **Soopacal (IRE)**[21] 714 4-9-0 **80**..................(b[1]) TomEaves 8 69
(B Smart) *s.i.s: c wd st: rdn wl over 1f out: a in rr* **8/1**[3]
50-0 **11** ½ **Luscivious**[73] 68 5-8-11 **80**..................(b) DavidProbert(3) 10 67
(A J McCabe) *keen early: rdn wl over 1f out: a in rr* **14/1**

60.98 secs (-1.32) **Going Correction** -0.10s/f (Stan) 11 Ran SP% **117.3**
Speed ratings (Par 105): **106,105,102,102,100 99,98,98,98,97 96**
toteswinger: 1&2 £3.20, 1&3 £24.50, 2&3 £19.20. CSF £112.87 CT £438.16 TOTE £4.20: £1.70, £5.60, £1.90; EX 161.80.
Owner Dr Marwan Koukash **Bred** Frank Moynihan **Trained** Sessay, N Yorks

FOCUS
A fair sprint handicap, run at a strong pace.
Incomparable Official explanation: vet said gelding suffered a bad over-reach and lost a shoe

902 SPONSOR A RACE BY CALLING 01902 390009 MEDIAN AUCTION MAIDEN STKS 1m 4f 50y(P)
9:20 (9:21) (Class 6) 3-5-Y-O **£2,047** (£604; £302) **Stalls** Low

Form RPR
1 **Drussell (IRE)** 3-8-2 0.................. DavidProbert(3) 8 71+
(S Donohoe, Ire) *hld up towards rr: hdwy over 5f out: led over 2f out: rdn over 1f out: sn edgd lft: r.o wl* **5/2**[2]
3522 **2** 6 **Jonnie Skull (IRE)**[8] 820 3-8-5 62..................(t[1]) ChrisCatlin 3 61
(P S McEntee) *led early: chsd ldr tl over 3f out: regained 2nd wl over 1f out: sn rdn: no imp* **11/2**[3]
0-63 **3** 5 **Dawn Wind**[23] 670 4-9-6 50..................(bt) GeorgeBaker 4 50
(I A Wood) *hld up in tch: rdn over 2f out: wknd wl over 1f out* **12/1**
03- **4** 1 ¾ **Yonder**[301] 2363 5-9-8 0.................. SteveDrowne 5 48
(H Morrison) *prom: pushed along over 3f out: wknd over 2f out* **5/6**[1]
5 6 **Kayfour (IRE)**[181] 6144 4-9-6 59.................. EddieAhern 7 38
(M J Grassick, Ire) *hld up towards rr: rdn 4f out: sn struggling* **10/1**
4 **6** 1 ¾ **Rossatron**[23] 670 3-8-5 0.................. GregFairley 1 38
(T T Clement) *sn led: hdd over 2f out: wknd wl over 1f out* **14/1**
6-0 **7** 18 **Just Dennis**[14] 779 5-9-6 0.................. AndrewHeffernan(7) 9 11
(D G Bridgwater) *hld up in rr: rdn over 5f out: lost tch 4f out* **66/1**
0- **8** 40 **Power Of Speech**[323] 1741 4-9-11 0.................. JimCrowley 6 —
(J Gallagher) *hld up in mid-div: hdwy over 5f out: wknd 4f out: t.o* **33/1**

2m 39.43s (-1.67) **Going Correction** -0.10s/f (Stan)
WFA 3 from 4yo 22lb 4 from 5yo 2lb 8 Ran SP% **126.4**
Speed ratings (Par 101): **101,97,93,92,88 87,75,48**
toteswinger: 1&2 £4.30, 1&3 £7.90, 2&3 £9.00. CSF £18.99 TOTE £4.10: £1.30, £1.20, £3.40; EX 24.10 Place 6: £89.11 Place 5: £46.00.
Owner Mrs S Donohoe **Bred** Lynn Lodge Stud **Trained** Cootehill Road, Co. Cavan

FOCUS
A weak maiden. The placed horses set the level.
Rossatron Official explanation: jockey said colt ran too freely
Power Of Speech Official explanation: jockey said gelding hung right throughout
T/Plt: £206.70 to a £1 stake. Pool: £101,794.82. 359.38 winning tickets. T/Qpdt: £21.60 to a £1 stake. Pool: £9,449.48. 322.90 winning tickets. KH

903 - 909a (Foreign Racing) - See Raceform Interactive

889 LINGFIELD (L-H)
Saturday, March 21

OFFICIAL GOING: Standard
The track seemed to be favouring speed.
Wind: Moderate, half-against Weather: sunny and bright

910 WEATHERBYS AWT "HANDS AND HEELS" APPRENTICE SERIES (FINAL) H'CAP 1m (P)
1:35 (1:35) (Class 4) (0-85,85) 4-Y-0+ **£6,476** (£1,927; £963; £481) **Stalls** High

Form RPR
432- **1** **Fremen (USA)**[155] 6771 9-9-1 **82**.................. NSLawes 9 90+
(D Nicholls) *s.i.s: bhd: hdwy over 2f out: chsd ldng pair over 1f out: kpt on wl to ld towards fin: jst hld on* **7/1**[3]
4121 **2** nse **New Star (UAE)**[19] 737 5-8-4 **74**.................. PaulPickard(3) 1 82
(W M Brisbourne) *chsd ldr for 1f: steadily lost pl and towards rr 1/2-way: swtchd to outer 3f out: r.o wl fnl f: pressed wnr cl home: jst hld* **7/1**[3]
652 **3** ½ **El Dececy (USA)**[26] 654 5-8-10 **77**.................. KrishGundowry 5 84
(S Parr) *led for 3f: chsd ldr after: rdn to ld again 1f out: kpt on tl hdd and no ex towards fin* **8/1**
0-43 **4** 2 **Solent Ridge (IRE)**[23] 694 4-8-5 **72**.................. DTDaSilva 2 74
(J S Moore) *in tch: effrt on inner 2f out: chsd ldrs over 1f out: plugged on same pce fnl f* **8/1**
020- **5** shd **Bahiano (IRE)**[122] 7386 8-8-7 **74**..................(p) DebraEngland 6 76+
(C E Brittain) *bhd: stl last over 2f out: styd on strly fnl f: gng on wl fin but nvr gng to rch ldrs* **12/1**
000- **6** hd **Alfresco**[162] 6625 5-8-13 **85**..................(b) KathrynFerguson(5) 8 87+
(J R Best) *s.i.s w jockey struggling to remove blind: sn t.k.h and plld way into ld 5f out: hdd 1f out: fdd fnl 100yds* **11/1**
0-56 **7** hd **King's Ransom**[10] 798 6-8-4 **71** oh4.................. PNolan 3 72
(S Gollings) *dwlt: sn bustled along: chsd ldr after 1f tl 5f out: pressed ldrs after tl rdn and unable qck 2f out: plugged on same pce after* **12/1**
20-5 **8** 3 ¼ **Hustle (IRE)**[16] 766 4-9-3 **84**.................. AndrewHeffernan 10 78
(Miss Gay Kelleway) *in tch: rdn and struggling over 2f out: no ch w ldrs after* **4/1**[2]
120/ **9** 1 ½ **Padlocked (IRE)**[540] 5764 5-9-1 **85**.................. ChrisHough(3) 4 76
(D M Simcock) *stdd after s: hld up in last trio: lost tch over 2f out: no ch after* **11/4**[1]
2040 **10** 2 ¾ **Shake On It**[8] 725 5-8-4 **74** oh7 ow3..................(tp) HollyHall(3) 7 59
(M J Gingell) *s.i.s: t.k.h: hld up in tch on outer: wd and wknd bnd 2f out* **25/1**

1m 36.78s (-1.42) **Going Correction** +0.025s/f (Slow) 10 Ran SP% **121.5**
Speed ratings (Par 105): **108,107,107,105,105 105,104,101,100,97**
toteswinger: 1&2 £3.10, 1&3 £6.90, 2&3 £5.50. CSF £57.73 CT £417.57 TOTE £8.50: £2.50, £1.80, £2.70; EX 30.20 Trifecta £131.40 Pool £511.48 - 2.88 winning units..
Owner Miss C King Mrs A Seed Ms Finola Devaney **Bred** Flaxman Holdings Ltd **Trained** Sessay, N Yorks

FOCUS
A fair apprentice handicap. Whips could be carried but not used. They seemed to go a good pace and the form looks solid enough through the placed horses.

911 SPORTINGBET.COM HEVER SPRINT STKS (LISTED RACE) 5f (P)
2:05 (2:05) (Class 1) 4-Y-0+

£22,708 (£8,608; £4,308; £2,148; £1,076; £540) Stalls High

Form RPR
11-1 **1** **Arganil (USA)**[9] 821 4-9-0 94 .... NCallan 10 110
(K A Ryan) *chsd ldng pair: rdn over 1f out: chsd ldr 1f out: drvn to ld wl ins fnl f: r.o wl* **7/2**[2]
-316 **2** 3/4 **Judd Street**[23] 700 7-9-0 106 .... (b) StephenCarson 2 107
(Eve Johnson Houghton) *racd in mdfield: rdn and effrt wl over 1f out: r.o u.p ins fnl f: wnt 2nd last strides: nvr gng to rch wnr* **7/1**[3]
114- **3** nk **Judge 'n Jury**[133] 7243 5-9-0 104 .... (t) ChrisCatlin 1 106
(R A Harris) *led: rdn over 1f out: drvn and hdd wl ins fnl f: no ex: lost 2nd last strides* **17/2**
-000 **4** 1 **Strike Up The Band**[37] 525 6-9-0 100 .... AdrianTNicholls 6 103
(D Nicholls) *chsd ldr tl over 1f out: keeping on same pce whn short of room and swtchd lft ins fnl f: one pce after* **9/1**
230- **5** 1/2 **Crimson Fern (IRE)**[170] 6429 5-8-9 96 .... RichardHughes 9 96
(M S Saunders) *stdd after s: bhd: swtchd wd and rdn wl over 1f out: r.o wl ins fnl f: nt rch ldrs* **11/1**
460- **6** shd **Rowe Park**[170] 6429 6-9-0 100 .... TPQueally 4 100
(Mrs L C Jewell) *awkward s and v.s.a: wl bhd: hdwy towards inner ent fnl f: r.o wl: nvr trbld ldrs* **16/1**
100- **7** shd **Green Manalishi**[167] 6518 8-9-3 100 .... PaulHanagan 5 103
(K A Ryan) *racd in midfield: rdn and effrt bnd 2f out: kpt on same pce fnl f* **14/1**
1110 **8** nk **Matsunosuke**[14] 785 7-9-3 112 .... LukeMorris 7 102
(A B Coogan) *slowly into strde: bhd: hdwy on inner 2f out: sn rdn: chsd ldrs jst ins fnl f: no imp after* **9/4**[1]
230- **9** 1/2 **Mood Music**[13] 5-9-3 105 .... (b) RyanMoore 8 100
(Mario Hofer, Germany) *a struggling to go pce towards rr: rdn over 1f out: no imp* **7/1**[3]
00-0 **10** 1 1/4 **Stoneacre Lad (IRE)**[49] 359 6-9-3 97 .... (b) LPKeniry 3 96
(Peter Grayson) *chsd ldrs: rdn wl over 1f out: wknd fnl f* **50/1**

57.50 secs (-1.30) **Going Correction** +0.025s/f (Slow) **10** Ran SP% **121.4**
Speed ratings (Par 111): **111,109,109,107,106 106,106,106,105,103**
toteswinger: 1&2 £4.20, 1&3 £4.80, 2&3 £9.10. CSF £29.75 TOTE £4.40: £1.80, £2.20, £2.50; EX 32.20 Trifecta £115.50 Pool £714.97 - 4.58 winning units..
Owner The Big Moment **Bred** Colt Neck Stables, Llc **Trained** Hambleton, N Yorks

FOCUS
Often a decent Listed race these days - Les Arc won in 2007, and Conquest last season - and this year's race was competitive. The pace was good, but surprisingly the early lead was not contested. The progressive Arganil could have more to offer.

NOTEBOOK
Arganil(USA) ◆ extended his unbeaten record on artificial surfaces to four races with a smart effort. Stepping up in grade after a hat-trick in handicap company, he had something to find with a few of these at the weights - 10lb with the runner-up - and was not asked to try to lead this time, but he picked up in good style in the straight, having been well placed. This was only his ninth start, and there is probably a good deal more to come, making him an exciting prospect, but if he doesn't prove as effective back on turf (2-5; both wins on easy ground), he will surely be taken to the States in search of some big prizes. (op 5-1)
Judd Street, a game winner off 105 in Dubai earlier in the year, raced a little further back than ideal and took too long to get going in the straight. A return to more positive tactics should suit. (op 6-1 tchd 11-2)
Judge 'n Jury ◆ was allowed to dominate and he nearly made the most of it. Rapidly progressive late last season, much of his improvement came on easy turf, which is understandable considering he's by Pivotal, but he won his maiden over this course and distance and confirmed himself fully effective on Polytrack. He's clearly still going the right way and could be a Group-class sprinter before long. (op 7-1, tchd 11-1 and 10-1 in a place)
Strike Up The Band didn't take to dirt in Dubai, but this was better, especially considering he was unable to dominate. (op 8-1 tchd 15-2)
Crimson Fern(IRE) ◆ progressed well last season and this was a pleasing return after 170 days off. There could yet be more to come. (op 14-1 tchd 10-1)
Rowe Park, returning after nearly six months off, lost his chance with a slow start but ran on when the race was as good as over. (op 28-1)
Green Manalishi, last seen running down the field in the Abbaye (also contested the void running), had something to find with most of these on official ratings and never threatened. (op 16-1)
Matsunosuke has progressed into a very smart Polytrack sprinter this All-Weather season, but he was below form at Wolverhampton a couple of weeks ago and again failed to give his best. He's probably had enough for the time being. (op 11-4, tchd 3-1 in a place)
Mood Music, a triple Listed winner on the continent, could have been expected to fare better. (op 6-1)

912 SPORTINGBET.COM SPRING CUP (LISTED RACE) 7f (P)
2:35 (2:37) (Class 1) 3-Y-O

£34,062 (£12,912; £6,462; £3,222; £1,614; £810) Stalls Low

Form RPR
453- **1** **Nashmiah (IRE)**[169] 6439 3-8-10 99 .... JamieSpencer 12 105+
(C E Brittain) *chsd ldr after 2f: rdn to ld ent fnl f: drvn and r.o strly to go clr: readily* **7/1**[3]
111- **2** 2 3/4 **Elnawin**[196] 5693 3-9-5 110 .... PatDobbs 7 106+
(R Hannon) *t.k.h: chsd ldr for 2f: trckd ldng pair after: rdn to chse wnr 1f out: nt pce of wnr and wl hld after: hld on for 2nd* **5/2**[1]
1411 **3** nk **Smokey Ryder**[22] 709 3-8-10 91 .... KevinGhunowa 10 96
(R A Harris) *chsd ldrs: rdn over 1f out: drvn and chsd ldng pair jst ins fnl f: kpt on to press for 2nd but no ch w wnr* **20/1**
240- **4** 1 1/4 **Damien (IRE)**[159] 6713 3-9-1 112 .... MichaelHills 5 98
(B W Hills) *hld up in tch in midfield: effrt and rdn wl over 1f out: edgd rt and no imp over 1f out* **3/1**[2]
1111 **5** nk **Five Star Junior (USA)**[45] 396 3-9-1 94 .... ShaneKelly 1 97+
(Mrs L Stubbs) *stdd s: hld up towards rr: hdwy into midfield jst over 2f out: swtchd lft and rdn over 1f out: styd on steadily fnl f: nvr threatened ldrs* **10/1**
321- **6** 3/4 **Tobond (IRE)**[119] 7426 3-9-1 91 .... JohnEgan 2 96+
(M Botti) *hld up in midfield: shuffled bk and dropped to rr over 2f out: hdwy towards inner over 1f out: kpt on u.p: nvr trbld ldrs* **12/1**
000- **7** 1/2 **Icesolator (IRE)**[182] 6119 3-9-3 98 .... RichardHughes 9 96+
(R Hannon) *hld up towards rr: hdwy and c wd wl over 1f out: late hdwy but nvr nr ldrs* **12/1**
022- **8** 1 **Qalahari (IRE)**[141] 7107 3-8-10 90 .... EddieAhern 6 87+
(D J Coakley) *chsd ldrs: losing pl bnd 2f out: shkn up and no reponse over 1f out: eased fnl f* **20/1**
122- **9** 2 **Son Of The Cat (USA)**[126] 7334 3-9-1 90 .... (t) ChrisCatlin 4 87
(B Gubby) *t.k.h: hld up in midfield on inner: rdn and unable qck 2f out: no ch fnl f* **20/1**
514- **10** hd **Joe Caster**[106] 7555 3-9-1 90 .... LukeMorris 14 86
(J M P Eustace) *s.i.s: hld up in rr: n.d* **66/1**
150- **11** nk **Silver Games (IRE)**[175] 6268 3-8-10 89 .... TonyCulhane 13 81+
(M R Channon) *racd wd: in tch in midfield: rdn and v wd bnd 2f out: no ch after* **25/1**
165- **12** 1/2 **Doncaster Rover (USA)**[159] 6713 3-9-1 101 .... RyanMoore 3 84
(S Parr) *hld up in midfield: rdn and struggling jst over 2f out: wl btn fr over 1f out* **7/1**[3]
-316 **13** 1 3/4 **Gone Hunting**[9] 819 3-9-1 88 .... (t) LPKeniry 8 80
(Peter Grayson) *stdd after s: a in rr: struggling bdly 3f out* **66/1**
104- **14** 3/4 **Red Kyte**[170] 6426 3-8-10 83 .... NCallan 11 73
(K A Ryan) *led: stdd gallop after 2f: rdn and hdd ent fnl f: wknd rapidly* **25/1**

1m 23.68s (-1.12) **Going Correction** +0.025s/f (Slow) **14** Ran SP% **128.0**
Speed ratings (Par 106): **107,103,103,102,101 100,100,99,96,96 96,95,93,92**
toteswinger: 1&2 £3.80, 1&3 £44.10, 2&3 £21.10. CSF £24.34 TOTE £6.90: £2.40, £1.60, £8.00; EX 29.30 Trifecta £486.40 Part won. Pool £657.40 - 0.57 winning units..
Owner Saeed Manana **Bred** Deerpark Stud **Trained** Newmarket, Suffolk

FOCUS
Not always the strongest of Listed races, but subsequent Jersey Stakes winner Membership landed the inaugural running in 2002, and Paco Boy won a very muddling renewal last season. A maximum field of 14 lined up this year, but in truth the race lacked strength in depth, particularly with some of the better types failing to prove their stamina. The pace wasn't frantic and it paid to sit handy. There could be more improvement to come from the winner.

NOTEBOOK
Nashmiah(IRE) probably didn't have to improve a great deal on her juvenile form, with the likes of Elnawin and Damien below par, but this daughter of Elusive Quality relished the Polytrack and was a comfortable winner. She's entered in both the English and Irish fillies' Classics, and deserves her chance in a turf trial considering she has already shown smart form on the grass. However, it would be no surprise if she ultimately proves best suited by artificial surfaces, and 1m might be as far as she will want to go. (op 9-1)
Elnawin, off the track since proving a head too good for a subsequent US Grade 1 winner in a 6f Group 3 at Kempton last September, raced keenly early and did not pick up in the straight. He looked a non-stayer, which is no surprise considering he's by Elnadim, out of a dual 5f-6f winner, and he could do better back over sprint trips. Afterwards his connections said they felt he needed the run and he could now go the Greenham, but that will be over 7f. (op 11-4 tchd 3-1 and 2-1)
Smokey Ryder had plenty to find at the weights with the front two (8lb with the winner; 10lb with the runner-up), and had never previously raced beyond 6f, but she ran a cracking race in defeat, having been well placed throughout. She has progressed with almost every run since being claimed by Ron Harris in December. (op 33-1)
Damien(IRE), returning from over five months off, did not run anywhere near his official mark of 112 on this first try over 7f and debut on Polytrack. There is stamina on the dam's side of his pedigree, but he's by Namid and he might be happier back over shorter, probably on easy turf. (op 5-2 tchd 10-3 and 7-2 in a place)
Five Star Junior(USA) has progressed well over sprint trips since joining this yard, but he failed to prove himself as effective back over this longer trip, even considering he had something to find at the weights a few of his rivals. (op 8-1)
Tobond(IRE) was held up in an unpromising position for much of the way and never threatened.
Icesolator(IRE) went extremely wide into the straight. (tchd 14-1)
Qalahari(IRE) ◆ was another wider out than ideal and did not look to handle the final bend. She should do better back over sprint trips on a straight track. Official explanation: jockey said filly lost its action

913 SPORTINGBET.COM WINTER DERBY (GROUP 3) 1m 2f (P)
3:05 (3:10) (Class 1) 4-Y-O+

£56,770 (£21,520; £10,770; £5,370; £2,690; £1,350) Stalls Low

Form RPR
5-31 **1** **Scintillo**[3] 864 4-9-0 106 .... RichardHughes 10 114
(R Hannon) *hld up in tch: effrt and qcknd over 1f out: led jst ins fnl f sn hrd pressed: battled on gamely: all out* **8/1**
6-11 **2** nse **Premio Loco (USA)**[41] 458 5-9-0 109 .... GeorgeBaker 4 114
(C F Wall) *hld up in tch: hdwy 2f out: rdn to chal and hung lft over 1f out: str chal fnl f: kpt on but a jst hld* **2/1**[1]
035- **3** 1 3/4 **Bronze Cannon (USA)**[119] 7420 4-9-0 104 .... RyanMoore 5 111
(J H M Gosden) *hld up in midfield: rdn over 2f out: c wd wl over 1f out: styd on u.p to chse ldng pair ins fnl f: kpt on but nvr pce to chal* **9/2**[2]
-104 **4** 2 **Halicarnassus (IRE)**[23] 703 5-9-0 110 .... TonyCulhane 12 107
(M R Channon) *w.w in midfield: hdwy to chse ldng pair 3f out: rdn over 2f out: kpt on same pce fnl f* **20/1**
-032 **5** shd **Without A Prayer (IRE)**[29] 644 4-9-0 106 .... JimCrowley 9 107
(R M Beckett) *hld up towards rr: rdn and effrt wl over 1f out: kpt on but nvr pce to threaten ldrs* **10/1**
44-1 **6** 3 1/4 **Re Barolo (IRE)**[28] 634 6-9-0 107 .... (t) JohnEgan 7 101
(M Botti) *bustled along leaving stalls: t.k.h in midfield after 2f: rdn and unable qck jst over 2f out: no imp* **6/1**[3]
-300 **7** nse **Docofthebay (IRE)**[29] 640 5-9-0 98 .... ChrisCatlin 2 101
(J A Osborne) *s.i.s: t.k.h: hld up in rr: hdwy over 3f out: kpt on u.p fr over 1f out: nvr trbld ldrs* **25/1**
1404 **8** nk **Mahadee (IRE)**[14] 783 4-9-0 96 .... (b) JamieSpencer 11 101
(C E Brittain) *sn pushed along to chse ldr: ev ch and rdn wl over 1f out: sn hung lft: wknd over 1f out* **14/1**
3302 **9** 1/2 **Baylini**[3] 864 5-8-11 88 .... JamesDoyle 1 97
(Ms J S Doyle) *hld up in rr: rdn over 2f out: nvr nr ldrs* **66/1**
-614 **10** nse **Kandidate**[28] 634 7-9-0 105 .... NCallan 8 100
(C E Brittain) *led: stdd gallop after 2f: rdn whn j. shadow wl over 1f out: hdd jst ins fnl f: sn btn* **12/1**
2-12 **11** 3/4 **Suits Me**[28] 634 6-9-0 109 .... MickyFenton 3 103+
(T P Tate) *trckd ldrs: short of room fr wl over 1f out: nvr able to get through and sn whn snatched up ins fnl f: eased after* **13/2**
3306 **12** 9 **Internationaldebut (IRE)**[15] 778 4-9-0 94 .... AdamKirby 6 82
(S Parr) *t.k.h: hld up in rr: lost tch over 2f out* **50/1**

2m 3.79s (-2.81) **Going Correction** +0.025s/f (Slow) **12** Ran SP% **125.8**
Speed ratings (Par 113): **112,111,110,108,108 106,106,106,105,105 104,97**
toteswinger: 1&2 £6.20, 1&3 £10.30, 2&3 £3.70. CSF £25.13 TOTE £10.30: £3.20, £1.50, £1.80; EX 36.70 Trifecta £244.80 Pool £22,236.83 - 67.20 winning units..
Owner White Beech Farm **Bred** Woodcote Stud Ltd **Trained** East Everleigh, Wilts

FOCUS
The 11th running of what is the showpiece of the All-Weather season, and the fourth straight year the race has held Group 3 status. This year's race looked up to scratch. The pace seemed just modest down the back, before increasing significantly before the turn into the straight. Decent efforts from the first pair to pull clear of the third, with the revitalised Scintillo posting a personal best.

NOTEBOOK
Scintillo's confidence looked restored when he was successful in a 1m4f Listed race at Kempton three days earlier, his first win since landing a Group 1 in Italy at two, and he's right back to his best now. It's fair to say he enjoyed a much smoother path into the straight than the runner-up, but that one could easily have swamped him for speed, and he proved most willing under pressure to hold on. The plan now is the Group 3 Ormonde Stakes over an extended 1m5f at Chester in May, although the John Porter Stakes at Newbury in April may be considered. (tchd 9-1)
Premio Loco(USA) was unproven beyond 1m (not at best when sixth in last year's Cambridgeshire), but he's a brother to multiple middle-distance winner Ramsgill. Some might argue he was an unfortunate loser, as he made his move about five wide around the final bend, whereas the winner enjoyed a much better trip, but in truth he didn't help himself once in the straight. He continually edged left under pressure, forcing his rider to switch his whip to his right hand as he came close to the winner inside the final furlong. He had also raced a little keenly early and got noticeably warm, so it's hard to say he was unlucky. He got the trip okay, but it's worth remembering this was a modestly run race around a speed track, and he might ultimately prove better back over shorter. He's likely to be given a break until the summer. (op 5-2)
Bronze Cannon(USA) was being niggled along to try to keep his position before the final bend and lacked the speed of the front two. He gave the impression this run was needed to sharpen him up and better can be expected next time. (op 5-1)
Halicarnassus(IRE) had shown little on his only previous Polytrack start (at Kempton), but this was a solid effort in defeat. (op 25-1, tchd 33-1 in a place)
Without A Prayer(IRE) ran okay, but he only just gets this trip and looks best suited by 1m. (tchd 11-1 and 14-1 in a place)
Re Barolo(IRE) found this more competitive than the course-and-distance trial he win almost a month earlier. Driven along on leaving the stalls, he lacked the required speed throughout and, not for the first time, gave the impression he would be worth another try at 1m4f. If not, perhaps some headgear will sharpen him up. (tchd 13-2)
Docofthebay(IRE) was never seen with a chance after blowing the start. (tchd 33-1)
Mahadee(IRE), from the same stable as last year's winner Hattan, was given a positive ride, which was probably the right move, as he tends to hit a flat spot in his races, but he didn't look keen when asked for his effort in the straight. (op 16-1)
Suits Me, despite not being able to dominate, still looked to have something to offer in the straight, but he continually ran into the back of the weakening Kandidate. Official explanation: jockey said gelding was denied a clear run (op 8-1 tchd 6-1)
Internationaldebut(IRE) Official explanation: jockey said gelding ran too keenly

914 DAME KELLY HOLMES LEGACY TRUST MAIDEN STKS 1m 2f (P)
3:40 (3:40) (Class 4) 3-Y-O £4,857 (£1,445; £722; £360) Stalls Low

Form RPR
4- **1** **Debussy (IRE)**[129] 7289 3-9-3 0 .... RyanMoore 2 90+
(J H M Gosden) *mde all: set stdy gallop tl qcknd over 2f out: clr over 1f out: flashed tail ent fnl f: edgd rt but in n.d fnl f: v easily* **11/8**[1]
6- **2** 9 **Light Dubai (IRE)**[211] 5240 3-8-12 0 .... TonyCulhane 6 68+
(M R Channon) *hld up in tch: chsd ldrs 3f out: rdn wl over 1f out: sn no ch w wnr: wnt modest 2nd ins fnl f* **4/1**[3]
4-3 **3** 3/4 **Hypnotist (UAE)**[14] 786 3-9-3 0 .... NCallan 5 70
(C E Brittain) *dwlt: sn rcvrd to chse wnr: rdn over 2f out: outpcd by wnr wl over 1f out: no ch after: lost 2nd ins fnl f* **10/3**[2]
603- **4** hd **Makhaaleb (IRE)**[143] 7067 3-9-3 75 .... MichaelHills 1 69
(B W Hills) *t.k.h: hld up in tch: rdn jst over 2f out: outpcd wl over 1f out: plugged on same pce* **8/1**
5 5 **Mono's Only** 3-8-12 0 .... PaulEddery 7 55
(Paul Mason) *t.k.h: hld up in last pair: rdn and lost tch 3f out: no ch after* **50/1**
004- **6** 1 3/4 **Cayman Sky**[103] 7602 3-9-3 70 ....(b) RichardHughes 8 57
(R Hannon) *hld up in tch in midfield: rdn and struggling 3f out: sn wl bhd* **14/1**
64- **7** 8 **Fromthebeginning**[90] 7754 3-9-3 0 .... GeorgeBaker 4 43+
(D R C Elsworth) *stdd s: plld v hrd in rr: lost tch 3f out: eased ins fnl f* **6/1**
05 **8** nk **Miami Mix**[26] 659 3-8-12 0 .... MartinLane(5) 3 42
(B N Pollock) *in tch in midfield: rdn and struggling over 3f out: sn wl bhd* **100/1**

2m 7.93s (1.33) **Going Correction** +0.025s/f (Slow) **8** Ran SP% **120.2**
Speed ratings (Par 100): **95,87,87,87,83 81,75,75**
toteswinger: 1&2 £2.30, 1&3 £2.10, 2&3 £3.80. CSF £7.73 TOTE £2.40: £1.10, £1.80, £1.60; EX 8.60 Trifecta £18.80 Pool £457.76 - 17.95 winning units..
Owner H R H Princess Haya Of Jordan **Bred** Darley **Trained** Newmarket, Suffolk

FOCUS
The winner was allowed to lead at a steady pace, resulting in a slow time, and it's hard to know what the form is worth, but he still impressed and looks a nice type.
Fromthebeginning Official explanation: jockey said colt ran too free

915 AT THE RACES H'CAP 1m 4f (P)
4:15 (4:15) (Class 3) (0-95,94) 4-Y-O+ £9,714 (£2,890; £1,444; £721) Stalls Low

Form RPR
-300 **1** **Sgt Schultz (IRE)**[37] 522 6-9-6 94 .... LPKeniry 5 100
(J S Moore) *t.k.h: chsd ldr: ev ch and carried centre bnd 2f out: drvn fnl f: kpt on wl to ld fnl strides: jst hld on* **13/2**
14-1 **2** nse **Distinctive Image (USA)**[17] 761 4-8-8 84 .... ChrisCatlin 6 90
(R Hollinshead) *t.k.h: in tch: chsd ldrs and rdn jst over 2f out: outpcd over 1f out: rallied u.p fnl f: r.o strly: jst failed* **3/1**[1]
2113 **3** shd **Formation (USA)**[34] 563 4-9-1 91 .... GeorgeBaker 8 97
(J R Boyle) *stdd s: hld up in rr: hdwy and rdn over 1f out: str chal wl ins fnl f: r.o* **7/2**[2]
0-05 **4** nse **Maslak (IRE)**[17] 761 5-8-8 82 .... LukeMorris 2 88
(P W Hiatt) *led: rdn and c centre bnd 2f out: hrd drvn fnl f: hld on wl tl hdd and lost 3 pls fnl strides* **12/1**
540- **5** 1/2 **Beauchamp Viceroy**[182] 6120 5-9-0 88 .... EddieAhern 7 93
(G A Butler) *hld up in last trio: gd hdwy towards inner over 1f out: ev ch wl ins fnl f: no ex towards fin* **9/2**[3]
6-01 **6** 1/2 **War Of The Roses (IRE)**[35] 549 6-8-10 84 .... TomEaves 1 88
(R Brotherton) *hld up in tch: rdn and effrt over 1f out: hdwy ent fnl f: pressed ldrs ins fnl f: no imp fnl 100yds* **7/1**
4-15 **7** 2 1/4 **Confidentiality (IRE)**[50] 354 5-9-0 88 .... NickyMackay 3 89
(M Wigham) *chsd ldrs: rdn wl over 1f out: ev ch 1f out tl wknd ins fnl f* **16/1**
0-51 **8** 1 1/2 **Bassinet (USA)**[20] 726 5-8-6 80 .... KirstyMilczarek 4 79
(J A R Toller) *hld up in last pl: rdn and effrt over 1f out: no hdwy* **8/1**

2m 37.71s (4.71) **Going Correction** +0.025s/f (Slow)
WFA 4 from 5yo+ 2lb **8** Ran SP% **115.9**
Speed ratings (Par 107): **85,84,84,84,84 84,82,81**
toteswinger: 1&2 £4.30, 1&3 £6.00, 2&3 £2.40. CSF £26.75 CT £79.95 TOTE £8.10: £2.00, £1.60, £1.60; EX 38.10 Trifecta £100.40 Pool £511.97 - 3.77 winning units..
Owner Jim Barnes **Bred** Frank Dunne **Trained** Upper Lambourn, Berks
■ Stewards' Enquiry : Luke Morris one-day ban: used whip without giving gelding time to respond (Apr 4)

FOCUS
A steady pace resulted in the first six finishers being covered by little more than a length and this was a typically muddling Lingfield handicap. Not form to be relied on.

NOTEBOOK
Sgt Schultz(IRE) really didn't take to the dirt in Dubai, but Polytrack suits him much better and he won despite racing keenly and being forced wide into the straight. His trainer thinks he might still be improving and feels he would have a chance of winning an ordinary Listed race under suitable conditions. (op 6-1 tchd 11-2)
Distinctive Image(USA) ◆, like most of these unsuited by the steady pace, ran a cracker off an 8lb higher mark than when winning at Wolverhampton and is progressing nicely. (op 5-2 tchd 9-4)
Formation(USA) appreciated the return to Polytrack and was not beaten very far at all. (op 9-2, tchd 5-1 in a place)
Maslak(IRE) was allowed a very soft lead and can have no excuses.
Beauchamp Viceroy, upped in trip on his return from six months off, was given an awful lot to do considering the way the race unfolded - he was held up towards the inside with only one behind at the top of the straight - and had no chance. (op 10-1)

916 ATTHERACES.COM H'CAP 7f (P)
4:50 (4:51) (Class 2) (0-100,107) 4-Y-O+ £12,952 (£3,854; £1,926; £962) Stalls Low

Form RPR
-421 **1** **Abbondanza (IRE)**[20] 724 6-9-3 99 ....(p) TomEaves 9 109
(I Semple) *mde all: rdn over 1f out: forged clr jst ins fnl f: drvn out* **13/2**[3]
1256 **2** 1/2 **Red Somerset (USA)**[20] 724 6-8-7 94 .... MCGeran(5) 7 103
(R J Hodges) *chsd ldrs: rdn and outpcd 2f out: sltly hmpd over 1f out: rallied u.p fnl f: wnt 2nd fnl 100yds: fin wl: nt rch wnr* **16/1**
4611 **3** 1 1/4 **Al Muheer (IRE)**[15] 778 4-9-2 98 ....(b) NCallan 4 104
(C E Brittain) *chsd ldng pair: wnt 2nd over 1f out: rdn and tried to chal ent fnl f: no ex and lost 2nd fnl 100yds* **10/1**
00-1 **4** nse **Thebes**[14] 785 4-8-9 91 .... GregFairley 12 97
(M Johnston) *chsd wnr tl hung rt u.p over 1f out: one pce after* **9/1**
300- **5** 1 1/4 **Giganticus (USA)**[155] 6783 6-9-1 97 .... MichaelHills 10 99
(B W Hills) *hld up in midfield: rdn and unable qck 2f out: kpt on fnl f but nvr pce to threaten ldrs* **6/1**[2]
1433 **6** nk **Aeroplane**[14] 781 6-9-7 103 ....(p) JamieSpencer 2 105
(S A Callaghan) *stdd after s: hld up in rr: stl plenty to do 2f out: hdwy towards inner over 1f out: rdn and no imp ins fnl f* **4/1**[1]
1-04 **7** hd **Benllech**[29] 637 5-8-13 95 .... EddieAhern 3 96
(D M Simcock) *dwlt: hld up in rr: hdwy towards inner over 1f out: rdn ent fnl f: no imp after* **8/1**
1310 **8** 1/2 **Capricorn Run (USA)**[14] 783 6-9-2 98 ....(v) RobertWinston 8 98
(A J McCabe) *hld up after s: towards rr: struggling and c wd 2f out: sme hdwy fnl f: nvr trbld ldrs* **14/1**
0230 **9** 1/2 **Southandwest (IRE)**[20] 724 5-8-6 88 .... LukeMorris 1 87
(J S Moore) *dwlt: hld up in rr: rdn over 1f out: sme hdwy fnl f: n.d* **16/1**
40-6 **10** shd **Flawed Genius**[14] 783 4-8-7 89 .... PaulHanagan 5 87
(K A Ryan) *hld up in tch on inner: rdn jst over 2f out: drvn and no imp 1f out* **12/1**
14-4 **11** 2 3/4 **Atlantic Story (USA)**[63] 206 7-9-11 107 ....(bt) ChrisCatlin 11 99+
(M W Easterby) *hmpd sn after s: in tch in midfield: rdn wl over 1f out: no hdwy and wl btn fnl f* **13/2**[3]
0531 **12** 1 **Ebraam (USA)**[22] 714 6-9-1 97 .... TolleyDean 6 86+
(P Howling) *stdd s: t.k.h: hld up in rr: c v wd bnd 2f out: n.d* **16/1**
-040 **13** 6 **Jack Junior (USA)**[30] 612 5-9-3 99 .... AdrianTNicholls 13 73
(D Nicholls) *hung rt thrght: racd wd in midfield: lost pl bnd 4f out: sme hdwy 3f out: lost pl again bnd 2f out: eased fnl f* **20/1**

1m 22.43s (-2.37) **Going Correction** +0.025s/f (Slow) course record **13** Ran SP% **127.9**
Speed ratings (Par 109): **114,113,112,111,110 110,109,109,108,108 105,104,97**
toteswinger: 1&2 £24.50, 1&3 £13.20, 2&3 £32.60. CSF £114.02 CT £1061.95 TOTE £6.20: £3.10, £5.90, £2.80; EX 156.50 TRIFECTA Not won..
Owner Belstane Park Racing & Gordon Leckie **Bred** M Nolan **Trained** Carluke, S Lanarks
■ Stewards' Enquiry : Greg Fairley 21-day ban: 5 for careless riding, 16 under totting-up procedure (4 days deferred for 3 months) (Apr 11 -27)

FOCUS
A good, competitive handicap, but the winner made just about all the running, and indeed the next three finishers were always handy. A personal best from the winner, and straightforward form to rate.

NOTEBOOK
Abbondanza(IRE) was driven to the lead on leaving the stalls and was able to dominate, just as he likes to. This was a good effort off a 6lb higher mark than when defeating subsequent Lincoln Trial winner Flipando in a near course-record time over 1m here on his previous start. (op 6-1 tchd 7-1)
Red Somerset(USA) was never too far away and he kept on well in the straight. He has done most of his racing over 1m, but will have more options now he has proven himself fully effective over this shorter trip.
Al Muheer(IRE), attempting a hat-trick off an 8lb higher mark than for the first of his two wins, and 4lb higher than last time, looked to have every chance if good enough. (tchd 11-1)
Thebes, up 3lb, has won over this trip but he looks much better suited by 6f. (op 10-1 tchd 11-1)
Giganticus(USA), who had been off for five months and was trying Polytrack for the first time, made a satisfactory return. (op 7-1)
Aeroplane fared best of those held up in rear, but he's not an easy ride and this race didn't unfold to suit. (op 5-1 tchd 11-2)
Benllech looks better suited by 6f. (op 15-2)
Flawed Genius Official explanation: jockey said gelding hung left throughout
Atlantic Story(USA) has a terrific record around this track, but he wasn't at his best with the blinkers refitted this time. (tchd 15-2)
Jack Junior(USA) Official explanation: jockey said gelding hung right

917 COLEMANS HATCH MAIDEN STKS 1m (P)
5:25 (5:25) (Class 4) 3-Y-O+ £4,857 (£1,445; £722; £360) Stalls High

Form RPR
03- **1** **Legislate**[155] 6778 3-8-10 0 .... MichaelHills 9 80+
(B W Hills) *sn led: mde all: hrd pressed and rdn over 1f out: battled on gamely and hld on wl* **3/1**[2]
02- **2** hd **Jesse James (IRE)**[141] 7105 3-8-10 0 .... RyanMoore 5 80+
(J H M Gosden) *w.w in tch: effrt to chal wnr over 1f out: drvn fnl f: a jst hld* **8/15**[1]
363- **3** 3 1/4 **Princability (IRE)**[160] 6674 3-8-10 78 .... TonyCulhane 7 72
(M R Channon) *broke wl: sn stdd and chsd wnr tl wl over 1f out: sn outpcd by ldng pair: plugged on* **15/2**[3]
4 3/4 **Kloof** 3-8-10 0 .... RobertHavlin 2 70+
(J H M Gosden) *in tch in midfield: rdn and outpcd wl over 1f out: kpt on steadily ins fnl f* **14/1**
60- **5** shd **Just Like Silk (USA)**[163] 6597 3-8-10 0 .... ShaneKelly 10 70+
(G A Butler) *stdd after s: hld up in rr: c wd and rdn bnd 2f out: kpt on steadily fnl f: nvr nr ldrs* **12/1**

5- **6** *2 1/4* **Just Mustard (USA)**[169] 6443 3-8-10 0........................ EddieAhern 1 65
(G A Butler) *hld up in tch in midfield: ridded and outpcd 2f out: wknd over 1f out* **16/1**

5-0 **7** *nk* **Feudal (IRE)**[10] 810 3-8-10 0........................ JoeFanning 3 64
(M Johnston) *dwlt: a bhd: rdn wl over 1f out: no hdwy* **20/1**

000- **8** *3 3/4* **Dancing Rhythm**[161] 6660 4-9-13 40........................ MickyFenton 4 60
(M S Saunders) *chsd ldng pair: rdn and struggling jst over 2f out: sn wl bhd* **50/1**

520- **9** *dist* **Manana Manana**[83] 7802 3-8-10 67........................ TolleyDean 6 —
(S Parr) *dwlt: hld up in rr: rdn and lost tch qckly wl over 2f out: virtually p.u fnl 2f* **33/1**

1m 37.91s (-0.29) **Going Correction** +0.025s/f (Slow)
WFA 3 from 4yo+ 17lb **9** Ran SP% **131.9**
Speed ratings (Par 105): **102,101,98,97,97 95,95,91,—**
toteswinger: 1&2 £1.30, 1&3 £3.50, 2&3 £1.80. CSF £5.64 TOTE £4.50: £1.30, £1.10, £2.30; EX 6.90 Trifecta £35.20 Pool £762.00 - 16 winning units. Place 6 £37.03, Place 5 £8.88..
Owner K Abdulla **Bred** Juddmonte Farms Ltd **Trained** Lambourn, Berks

FOCUS
A reasonable maiden in which the front two pulled clear. The form could be rated higher but the relative proximity of the eighth holds it down.
T/Plt: £18.20 to a £1 stake. Pool: £100,784.03. 4,026.37 winning tickets. T/Qpdt: £3.90 to a £1 stake. Pool: £5,020.97. 941.56 winning tickets. SP

881 SOUTHWELL (L-H)
Sunday, March 22

OFFICIAL GOING: Standard
Wind: fresh 1/2 behind Weather: fine but cool and breezy

918 SOUTHWELL RACECOURSE FOR CONFERENCES APPRENTICE H'CAP — 1m 3f (F)
2:00 (2:02) (Class 6) (0-60,60) 4-Y-0+ **£2,047** (£604; £302) **Stalls** Low

Form RPR

2304 **1** **King Of The Beers (USA)**[12] 791 5-8-10 **54**........(p) SPRyan(5) 14 68
(R A Harris) *hld up in midfield: hdwy on outer 6f out: led over 4f out: clr 3f out: unchal* **7/2**[1]

-236 **2** *14* **Limelight (USA)**[20] 732 4-8-6 **46**........(p) PNolan 3 38
(Sir Mark Prescott) *chsd ldrs: drvn over 6f out: outpcd and hmpd over 4f out: styd on fnl 2f: tk modest 2nd nr fin* **7/1**

60-6 **3** *3/4* **Starcross Maid**[12] 790 7-8-6 **45**........ RichardRowe 13 35
(A G Juckes) *hld up in rr: hdwy over 4f out: wnt 2nd over 2f out: styd on same pce* **12/1**

-252 **4** *2 1/4* **Cragganmore Creek**[12] 790 6-8-8 **47**........ DebraEngland 2 34
(D Morris) *led tl over 4f out: one pce fnl 3f* **5/1**[2]

0-24 **5** *1/2* **Valentine Blue**[12] 790 4-8-7 **47**........(p) NSLawes 10 33
(A B Haynes) *hld up in rr: hdwy 4f out: outpcd 3f out: kpt on fnl f* **13/2**[3]

04-4 **6** *1 1/4* **Maria Antonia (IRE)**[19] 744 6-8-9 **48**........ AndrewHeffernan 5 32
(D G Bridgwater) *mid-div: hdwy over 3f out: one pce fnl 2f* **16/1**

0-60 **7** *1/2* **Darley Star**[36] 541 4-8-6 **49** ow2........(p) JohnCavanagh(3) 7 32
(R A Harris) *hld up in rr: hdwy 4f out: one pce* **16/1**

0-05 **8** *2 3/4* **Stockman**[19] 744 5-8-2 **46**........ RyanClark(5) 9 25
(H Morrison) *mid-div: outpcd over 3f out: no threat after* **14/1**

/0-0 **9** *2* **Hippodrome (IRE)**[19] 743 7-8-11 **55**........(p) DavidKenny(5) 4 31
(John A Harris) *prom: drvn 4f out: lost pl over 2f out* **33/1**

40-5 **10** *6* **Sergeant Sharpe**[19] 745 4-9-1 **60**........ AlexEdwards(5) 1 26
(H J Evans) *trckd ldrs: lost pl over 2f out* **20/1**

6-0R **11** *shd* **Kirkie (USA)**[25] 675 4-9-1 **55**........ KrishGundowry 6 21
(S Parr) *s.s: hdwy over 4f out: wknd 3f out* **66/1**

-405 **12** *11* **Comeintothespace (IRE)**[18] 750 7-8-11 **50**........ DTDaSilva 11 —
(R A Farrant) *chsd ldrs: lost pl over 3f out: bhd whn eased fnl f* **18/1**

-463 **13** *3* **Ming Vase**[19] 744 7-8-8 **50**........ PaulPickard(3) 8 —
(P T Midgley) *tk fierce hold: trckd ldrs: shkn up 5f out: lost pl over 3f out: sn bhd* **8/1**

2m 25.9s (-2.10) **Going Correction** 0.0s/f (Stan)
WFA 4 from 5yo+ 1lb **13** Ran SP% **116.4**
Speed ratings (Par 101): **107,96,96,94,94 93,93,91,89,85 85,77,74**
toteswinger: 1&2 £5.30, 1&3 £10.40, 2&3 £17.50. CSF £26.05 CT £265.46 TOTE £4.00: £1.70, £1.80, £4.40; EX 30.30 TRIFECTA Not Won..
Owner Dr Simon Clarke **Bred** Liberation Farm, Oratis Thoroughbreds Et Al **Trained** Earlswood, Monmouths

FOCUS
Very ordinary fare, but there was a big market move for the winner, who returned to his best.
King Of The Beers(USA) Official explanation: Stewards noted gelding lost a cheek-piece during race. No action taken.

919 HOSPITALITY AT SOUTHWELL RACECOURSE (S) STKS — 5f (F)
2:30 (2:30) (Class 6) 4-Y-0+ **£2,047** (£604; £302) **Stalls** High

Form RPR

1631 **1** **Grimes Faith**[19] 742 6-8-11 72........(p) AmyRyan(7) 3 77+
(K A Ryan) *trckd ldrs: n.m.r and swtchd lft 2f out: edgd lft and styd on to ld ins fnl f* **4/5**[1]

030- **2** *nk* **Handsinthemist (IRE)**[175] 6308 4-8-0 46........ PaulPickard(7) 2 63
(P T Midgley) *w ldr: edgd rt and led 2f out: edgd lft and hdd ins fnl f: no ex* **25/1**

460 **3** *2 3/4* **Albero Di Giuda (IRE)**[16] 777 4-8-7 65........(t) ChrisCatlin 4 53
(F Sheridan) *s.i.s: hdwy and edgd lft over 2f out: kpt on same pce* **12/1**

6342 **4** *3/4* **Decider (USA)**[12] 794 6-8-12 60........(b) JoeFanning 5 55
(R A Harris) *trckd ldrs: styd on same pce fnl 2f* **11/4**[2]

-640 **5** *3* **She's Our Beauty (IRE)**[20] 727 6-8-13 45........ FrankieMcDonald 8 46
(S T Mason) *chsd ldrs: wknd 2f out* **40/1**

00-0 **6** *3/4* **Ducal Regancy Red**[3] 884 5-8-2 41........ KellyHarrison(5) 7 37
(C J Teague) *w ldrs: wknd over 1f out* **66/1**

-000 **7** *1 1/2* **Garlogs**[19] 742 6-8-9 67........(v[1]) RussellKennemore(3) 6 36
(R Hollinshead) *led tl hdd & wknd 2f out* **7/1**[3]

58.10 secs (-1.60) **Going Correction** -0.275s/f (Stan) **7** Ran SP% **110.2**
Speed ratings (Par 101): **101,100,96,94,90 88,86**
toteswinger: 1&2 £6.90, 1&3 £3.30, 2&3 £14.50. CSF £24.07 TOTE £1.60: £1.40, £7.10; EX 21.70 Trifecta £160.90 Pool: £428.45 - 1.97 winning units.There was no bid for the winner.
Owner Mrs Angie Bailey **Bred** John Grimes **Trained** Hambleton, N Yorks

FOCUS
With Haajes a non-runner, class-dropping Grimes Faith appeared to face a fairly straightforward task and did not need to match his best. The runner-up is the key to the form.

920 CALL 01636 814481 TO SPONSOR A MAIDEN RACE FILLIES' STKS — 6f (F)
3:00 (3:00) (Class 5) 3-Y-0+ **£3,070** (£906; £453) **Stalls** Low

Form RPR

24- **1** **Hysterical Lady**[263] 3598 3-8-9 0........ AdrianTNicholls 9 59
(D Nicholls) *t.k.h: hdwy over 3f out: led appr fnl f: hld on nr fin* **3/1**[3]

0-30 **2** *hd* **Divine White**[19] 746 6-9-8 45........ AdamKirby 8 62
(G P Enright) *chsd ldrs: led over 2f out: hdd appr fnl f: no ex nr fin* **16/1**

5334 **3** *2 3/4* **Beaux Yeux**[12] 796 3-8-9 60........ JamieMoriarty 7 50
(P T Midgley) *hld up in rr: hdwy to chse ldrs over 2f out: kpt on same pce* **11/4**[2]

0040 **4** *3 3/4* **Martingrange Lass (IRE)**[38] 508 4-9-8 45........(p) MickyFenton 5 43
(S Parr) *reminders after s: led tl over 2f out: fdd fnl f* **50/1**

2243 **5** *2 3/4* **Silk Gallery (USA)**[27] 655 4-9-8 55........(t) ChrisCatlin 3 35
(E J Alston) *in rr: hung bdly rt over 4f out: swtchd wd over 2f out: nvr nr ldrs* **9/4**[1]

000- **6** *3 1/2* **Konka (USA)**[186] 6010 3-8-9 35........ JoeFanning 6 20
(E F Vaughan) *chsd ldrs: wknd over 1f out* **25/1**

65 **7** *7* **Marina Walk**[32] 592 3-8-9 0........ TravisBlock 2 —
(H Morrison) *chsd ldrs: lost pl 3f out* **6/1**

8 *1* **Placidity** 3-8-9 0........ TGMcLaughlin 4 —
(A J McCabe) *w ldr: lost pl 2f out* **16/1**

0- **9** *1/2* **Speak Freely**[140] 7148 3-8-4 0........ MartinLane(5) 1 —
(C Smith) *hld up: sme hdwy and hmpd 4f out: sn lost pl* **100/1**

1m 17.28s (0.78) **Going Correction** 0.0s/f (Stan)
WFA 3 from 4yo+ 13lb **9** Ran SP% **115.3**
Speed ratings (Par 100): **94,93,90,85,81 76,67,66,65**
toteswinger: 1&2 £9.00, 1&3 £3.60, 2&3 £8.20. CSF £48.00 TOTE £4.40: £1.30, £3.70, £1.40; EX 56.30 Trifecta £274.40 Pool: £459.90 - 1.24 winning units.
Owner Ms Finola Devaney **Bred** P And Mrs Venner And Trickledown Stud **Trained** Sessay, N Yorks

FOCUS
A plating-class fillies' maiden, the form limited by the runner-up and the fourth.
Silk Gallery(USA) Official explanation: jockey said filly ran too free

921 MEMBERSHIP AT SOUTHWELL GOLF CLUB CLASSIFIED CLAIMING STKS — 6f (F)
3:30 (3:31) (Class 6) 4-Y-0+ **£2,047** (£604; £302) **Stalls** Low

Form RPR

3166 **1** **Lethal**[20] 739 6-8-4 60........ PaulHanagan 5 63
(R A Fahey) *mde all: hrd drvn over 2f out: edgd rt: kpt on wl* **7/2**[1]

0034 **2** *2* **Wiltshire (IRE)**[11] 811 7-7-13 55 ow2........ PaulPickard(7) 6 59
(P T Midgley) *hld up in rr: hdwy and hung lft over 2f out: styd on to take 2nd nr fin* **11/2**[3]

2600 **3** *nk* **Hamaasy**[12] 793 8-8-3 57 ow1........(p) JoeFanning 12 55
(R A Harris) *mid-div: hdwy to chse ldrs over 2f out: kpt on same pce fnl f* **7/2**[1]

0-40 **4** *1/2* **Young Ivanhoe**[10] 812 4-7-11 44 ow2........(e[1]) AndrewHeffernan(7) 11 54
(C A Dwyer) *trckd ldrs: t.k.h: edgd lft and kpt on same pce fnl f* **33/1**

-266 **5** *3/4* **Whozart (IRE)**[12] 794 6-7-13 55........ KellyHarrison(5) 9 52
(A Dickman) *chsd ldrs: hung rt and one pce appr fnl f* **9/2**[2]

-400 **6** *2* **Kinout (IRE)**[30] 619 4-8-6 54........ AdrianTNicholls 3 48
(K A Ryan) *mid-div: effrt on ins over 2f out: sn chsng ldrs: fdd ins fnl f* **14/1**

1056 **7** *1 1/2* **Hurricane Coast**[9] 832 10-8-5 56........(b) WilliamCarson(5) 2 47
(D Flood) *hld up in rr: kpt on fnl 2f: nvr on terms* **14/1**

-040 **8** *1 3/4* **Ryedale Ovation (IRE)**[21] 726 6-8-11 60........(p) AmyBaker(5) 14 47
(M Hill) *awkward to load: dwlt: hdwy and c stands' side over 2f out: nvr nr ldrs* **8/1**

0-00 **9** *1 1/2* **Lytton**[11] 811 4-8-4 52........(v[1]) FrankieMcDonald 1 30
(R Ford) *mid-div: lost pl 3f out* **25/1**

060- **10** *1 1/4* **Maison Dieu**[183] 6116 6-9-0 55........ ChrisCatlin 7 36
(E J Alston) *chsd ldrs: rdn 3f out: lost pl over 1f out* **14/1**

00-0 **11** *7* **Black Draft**[38] 513 7-7-9 38........ RichardRowe(7) 4 2
(B Forsey) *hld up in rr: bhd fnl 2f* **80/1**

1m 16.42s (-0.08) **Going Correction** 0.0s/f (Stan) **11** Ran SP% **117.1**
Speed ratings (Par 101): **100,97,96,96,95 92,90,88,86,84 75**
toteswinger: 1&2 £3.60, 1&3 £4.40, 2&3 £4.20. CSF £22.34 TOTE £4.10: £1.40, £1.80, £1.80; EX 18.30 Trifecta £35.70 Pool: £284.53 - 5.89 winning units.
Owner The Matthewman One Partnership **Bred** A S Reid **Trained** Musley Bank, N Yorks

FOCUS
A modest claimer in which the winner was able to dictate. The second and fourth hold down the form.

922 BOOK TICKETS ON LINE AT SOUTHWELL-RACECOURSE.CO.UK H'CAP — 7f (F)
3:55 (3:56) (Class 4) (0-85,83) 4-Y-0+ **£4,857** (£1,445; £722; £360) **Stalls** Low

Form RPR

111- **1** **Royal Dignitary (USA)**[234] 4559 9-9-4 **83**........ AdrianTNicholls 1 90
(D Nicholls) *led: qcknd 3f out: hdd appr fnl f: kpt on wl to ld post* **10/1**

1223 **2** *nse* **Caprio (IRE)**[4] 866 4-8-12 **77**........ RichardKingscote 2 84
(Tom Dascombe) *s.i.s: sn trcking ldrs: led over 1f out: jst ct* **3/1**[2]

4021 **3** *1/2* **Autumn Blades (IRE)**[11] 806 4-9-1 **80**........ MickyFenton 7 86
(A Bailey) *hld up: stdy hdwy on outside over 3f out: chal over 1f out: no ex wl ins fnl f* **5/1**

61-1 **4** *1 3/4* **Smarty Socks (IRE)**[45] 404 5-8-11 **76**........ JamieMoriarty 6 77
(P T Midgley) *s.i.s: hdwy on ins 3f out: styd on same pce fnl f* **11/4**[1]

211 **5** *1/2* **Electric Warrior (IRE)**[28] 650 6-9-0 **79**........ LPKeniry 5 79
(C R Dore) *hld up: effrt 3f out: edgd lft and kpt on same pce appr fnl f* **11/1**

536- **6** *3 3/4* **White Deer (USA)**[154] 6841 5-8-10 **75**........ SilvestreDeSousa 3 66
(D Nicholls) *t.k.h: trckd ldr: n.m.r and lost pl over 3f out: sme hdwy and hung lft 2f out: sn wknd* **7/2**[3]

1504 **7** *1* **Indian Diva (IRE)**[12] 793 4-8-7 **79**........ PaulPickard(7) 4 67
(P T Midgley) *trckd ldrs: wknd over 1f out* **20/1**

1m 30.36s (0.06) **Going Correction** 0.0s/f (Stan) **7** Ran SP% **112.7**
Speed ratings (Par 105): **99,98,98,96,95 91,90**
toteswinger: 1&2 £5.00, 1&3 £5.70, 2&3 £3.50. CSF £38.91 TOTE £8.80: £2.80, £2.30; EX 38.60.
Owner Middleham Park Racing XXXVI **Bred** Bentley Smith, J Michael O'Farrell Jr , Joan Thor **Trained** Sessay, N Yorks
■ Stewards' Enquiry : Adrian T Nicholls one-day ban: used whip down shoulder in forehand position (Apr 6)

FOCUS
A good, competitive handicap and a tight finish. The form is solid enough.
Royal Dignitary(USA) Official explanation: one-day ban: used whip down shoulder in forehand position (Apr 6).

923 PLAY GOLF AT SOUTHWELL GOLF CLUB H'CAP — 1m 4f (F)
4:25 (4:25) (Class 5) (0-75,75) 4-Y-O+ — **£3,070** (£906; £453) **Stalls** Low

Form — RPR
2-16 **1** **Wabbraan (USA)**[21] 723 4-8-3 **65**.......... AmyBaker(5) 6 — 77
(M Hill) *chsd ldrs: led 5f out: styd on strly to draw clr fnl f* — **8/1**
1532 **2** *4 1/2* **Benedict Spirit (IRE)**[10] 822 4-8-8 **72**.......... AshleyMorgan(7) 1 — 78+
(M H Tompkins) *trckd ldrs: wnt handy 2nd over 3f out: rdn 2f out: styd on same pce* — **9/2**[3]
2606 **3** *7* **Just Observing**[6] 848 6-8-6 **68**.......... PaulPickard(7) 5 — 63
(P T Midgley) *hld up: hdwy to trck ldrs 7f out: kpt on same pce fnl 2f* **33/1**
1/0- **4** *2 1/4* **Russian Invader (IRE)**[7] 6582 5-9-6 **75**.......... ChrisCatlin 2 — 66
(R C Guest) *in rr: sn pushed along: outpcd over 4f out: kpt on fnl 2f: nvr a threat* — **33/1**
1241 **5** *12* **General Tufto**[3] 885 4-8-0 **62**..........(b) MartinLane(5) 3 — 35
(C Smith) *led 1f: chsd ldrs: drvn over 3f out: lost pl 2f out* — **11/10**[1]
060- **6** *1 1/4* **Clueless**[8] 5637 7-8-6 **61** oh2.......... PaulHanagan 7 — 33
(G A Charlton) *chsd ldrs: drvn 7f out: outpcd over 4f out: sn lost pl* — **14/1**
311- **7** *2 3/4* **Orkney (IRE)**[94] 7722 4-8-11 **68**.......... TomEaves 4 — 35
(Miss J A Camacho) *led after 1f: hdd 5f out: lost pl over 3f out* — **10/3**[2]

2m 38.06s (-2.94) **Going Correction** 0.0s/f (Stan)
WFA 4 from 5yo+ 2lb — **7** Ran SP% **112.5**
Speed ratings (Par 103): **109,106,101,99,91 91,89**
toteswinger: 1&2 £3.80, 1&3 £16.00, 2&3 £15.70. CSF £42.00 TOTE £9.60: £3.30, £2.10; EX 37.20.
Owner Martin Hill **Bred** R D Hubbard **Trained** Littlehempston, Devon

FOCUS
They went a fair pace here and it was a proper test at the trip. The consistent runner-up helps with the level.
General Tufto Official explanation: trainer said, regardingthe poor form shown, that race had come too soon for gelding
Orkney(IRE) Official explanation: trainer's rep had no explanation for the poor form shown

924 SOUTHWELL-RACECOURSE.CO.UK H'CAP — 7f (F)
4:55 (4:55) (Class 5) (0-75,75) 3-Y-O — **£3,070** (£906; £453) **Stalls** Low

Form — RPR
060- **1** **Toby Tyler**[199] 5632 3-8-10 **67**.......... JamieMoriarty 4 — 74+
(P T Midgley) *s.i.s: hdwy over 3f out: styd on to ld ins fnl f: kpt on wl* **14/1**
314- **2** *1 1/4* **Final Salute**[134] 7241 3-9-1 **72**..........(v) TomEaves 8 — 76+
(B Smart) *hld up: tk fierce hold: hdwy on outside tro trck ldrs over 3f out: led 2f out: hdd and no ex ins fnl f* — **4/1**[2]
-231 **3** *1/2* **Captainrisk (IRE)**[30] 629 3-9-2 **73**..........(v) NickyMackay 7 — 76
(M Botti) *trckd ldrs: sltly hmpd after 1f: hung rt over 1f out: styd on same pce ins fnl f* — **11/4**[1]
6-05 **4** *9* **Special Cuvee**[10] 819 3-9-1 **72**..........(v[1]) SebSanders 5 — 52
(A B Haynes) *trckd ldrs: edgd rt after 1f: led 3f out: hung bdly lft: hdd 2f out: wknd fnl f* — **9/2**[3]
0-15 **5** *nk* **Emirates World (IRE)**[25] 672 3-9-4 **75**.......... JoeFanning 1 — 54
(M Johnston) *trckd ldrs: effrt over 2f out: sn btn* — **6/1**
1205 **6** *hd* **Hawkspring (IRE)**[11] 808 3-8-11 **68**..........(t) AdamKirby 6 — 47
(S Parr) *led: hdd 3f out: wknd appr fnl f* — **6/1**
110- **7** *nk* **Nchike**[166] 6549 3-8-9 **66**.......... AdrianTNicholls 3 — 44
(D Nicholls) *trckd ldrs: n.m.r 2f out: sn wknd* — **12/1**
30-4 **8** *1* **Asian Tale (IRE)**[25] 672 3-9-0 **71**.......... PaulDoe 2 — 47
(P D Evans) *dwlt: in rr: drvn and lost pl 3f out* — **12/1**

1m 30.37s (0.07) **Going Correction** 0.0s/f (Stan) — **8** Ran SP% **115.5**
Speed ratings (Par 98): **99,97,97,86,86 86,85,84**
toteswinger: 1&2 £16.20, 1&3 £11.60, 2&3 £3.40. CSF £69.85 CT £205.01 TOTE £19.90: £5.10, £2.10, £1.30; EX 107.20 TRIFECTA Not won. Place 6 £176.98, Place 5 £73.89..
Owner Anthony D Copley **Bred** Whitsbury Manor Stud **Trained** Westow, N Yorks

FOCUS
They did not go a great pace early on and as a result one or two raced a bit keenly. This was only a modest race but the first three finished clear and this could be reasonable form for the grade.
T/Plt: £60.80 to a £1 stake. Pool: £60,356.87. 724.56 winning tickets. T/Qpdt: £22.30 to a £1 stake. Pool: £3,703.42. 122.60 winning tickets. WG

925 - 927a (Foreign Racing) - See Raceform Interactive

CURRAGH (R-H)
Sunday, March 22

OFFICIAL GOING: Soft

928a LODGE PARK STUD EUROPEAN BREEDERS FUND PARK EXPRESS STKS (GROUP 3) (F&M) — 1m
3:45 (3:46) 3-Y-O+ — **£56,883** (£16,689; £7,951; £2,708)

RPR
1 **Oh Goodness Me**[140] 7158 3-8-9 103.......... DJMoran 4 — 96
(J S Bolger, Ire) *a.p: 2nd 1/2-way: 3rd u.p 2f out: r.o strly cl home: led on line* — **12/1**[3]
2 *shd* **Firey Red (IRE)**[242] 4316 3-8-9.......... SMGorey 7 — 95
(D K Weld, Ire) *led: drvn along 1/2-way: jnd 2f out: slt advantage ins fnl f: kpt on u.p: hdd on line* — **20/1**
3 *hd* **Mad About You (IRE)**[161] 6689 4-9-10 114.......... PJSmullen 5 — 98
(D K Weld, Ire) *settled 3rd: smooth hdwy under 3f out: rdn to dispute ld 2f out: narrowly hdd ins fnl f: no ex nr fin* — **1/2**[1]
4 *1 1/4* **Russian Empress (IRE)**[140] 7157 5-9-10 93.......... JMurtagh 8 — 95
(David P Myerscough, Ire) *hld up in rr: prog 2f out: mod 4th 1f out: kpt on wl cl home* — **20/1**
5 *6* **Scarlet O'Hara (IRE)**[155] 6831 4-9-10 84.......... PShanahan 3 — 81
(D K Weld, Ire) *in tch: 5th 1/2-way: effrt over 2f out: no ex fr 1 1/2f out* — **33/1**
6 *1* **Prima Luce (IRE)**[146] 7034 4-9-13 105.......... KJManning 2 — 82
(J S Bolger, Ire) *upset in stalls: s.i.s: sn 4th on outer: rdn and no imp 3f out: wknd 2f out: eased* — **6/1**[2]
7 *12* **Indiana Gal (IRE)**[252] 4007 4-9-10 99.......... FMBerry 6 — 51
(Patrick Martin, Ire) *in tch: 6th 1/2-way: wknd fr 3f out: eased fnl f* — **20/1**

1m 47.03s (5.13) **Going Correction** +0.85s/f (Soft)
WFA 3 from 4yo+ 17lb — **7** Ran SP% **116.1**
Speed ratings: **108,107,107,106,100 99,87**
CSF £186.15 TOTE £15.50: £3.20, £5.70; DF 211.40.
Owner Mrs June Judd **Bred** Sir Eric Parker **Trained** Coolcullen, Co Carlow

FOCUS
The fourth and fifth look the best guide to the level of the form, with the unexposed runner-up rated as achieving a personal best. The favourite did not look the most genuine, but she is entitled to come on for the run and possibly needs further than this now.

NOTEBOOK
Oh Goodness Me stayed on best of all to record a narrow win. She looks sure to appreciate further and is a promising filly, especially when she gets her favoured quicker ground. The English 1,000 Guineas, Musidora Stakes, Irish 1,000 Guineas, Irish Oaks and English Oaks were all mentioned as possible targets. (op 12/1 tchd 14/1)
Firey Red(IRE) took second at the expense of her long odds-on stable companion Mad About You after making the running. Successful on her only previous start last July on quick ground, the Pivotal filly looked in trouble when pushed along after halfway, but to her credit she boxed on well against these more experienced campaigners. She can build on this creditable display. (op 20/1 tchd 25/1)
Mad About You(IRE), a Naas Listed winner last term, started a warm favourite and, approaching the three-furlong pole, looked all over the winner. However, the distress signals began to go up after the gap opened for her and she began to struggle in this ground when asked for her effort. The Group 1-placed filly had plenty going for her here having contested five Group 1 events, but the 114-rated daughter of Indian Ridge was unable to capitalise on what looked a nice opportunity in her first Group 3 event. It would come as no surprise to see the blinkers she wore when winning at Naas last October back on next time. (op 1/3)
Russian Empress(IRE) showed some improvement last year in handicaps and Listed events without winning but she could not take the next step forward in this company over a trip that could still be short of her optimum. (op 25/1)
Scarlet O'Hara(IRE) looked up against it on figures and ran accordingly.
Prima Luce(IRE), the better-fancied stable companion of the winner, was not helped when getting upset in the stalls. She then jumped away sluggishly, and last season's 33-1 Athasi Stakes heroine never looked happy at any stage. She is better than this bare form suggests. (op 11/2)
Indiana Gal(IRE) finished third in the Group 3 1,000 Guineas Trial last term. This was her first start since last July and she was not fancied in this better company. Her rider accepted the situation after the halfway stage and she was allowed to come home in her own time. (op 16/1)

929 - 931a (Foreign Racing) - See Raceform Interactive

[897]WOLVERHAMPTON (A.W) (L-H)
Monday, March 23

OFFICIAL GOING: Standard
Wind: Strong across Weather: Sunshine and showers

932 RINGSIDE CONFERENCE SUITE - 700 THEATRE STYLE APPRENTICE H'CAP — 1m 141y(P)
1:50 (1:50) (Class 5) (0-75,74) 4-Y-O+ — **£2,729** (£806; £403) **Stalls** Low

Form — RPR
0-53 **1** **Follow The Flag (IRE)**[37] 558 5-8-13 **68**..........(p) FrederikTylicki 3 — 76
(A J McCabe) *a.p: rdn to ld over 1f out: r.o* — **3/1**[2]
24-5 **2** *1/2* **Obezyana (USA)**[26] 680 7-9-0 **72**..........(p) LeeNewnes(3) 8 — 79
(A Bailey) *sn chsng ldr: led over 6f out: rdn and hdd over 1f out: kpt on ins fnl f* — **6/1**
400- **3** *2* **Black Dahlia**[150] 6950 4-9-2 **74**.......... AmyRyan(3) 6 — 77
(A J McCabe) *hld up in mid-div: rdn and styd on fnl f: tk 3rd towards fin* — **18/1**
2430 **4** *1/2* **Downhill Skier (IRE)**[12] 807 5-8-2 **62**.......... PaulPickard(5) 5 — 64
(W M Brisbourne) *hld up in rr: hdwy on outside over 2f out: rdn over 1f out: no ex ins fnl f* — **16/1**
652- **5** *3* **Indy Driver**[150] 6956 4-9-3 **72**.......... Louis-PhilippeBeuzelin 2 — 67
(J R Fanshawe) *hld up in tch: rdn over 1f out: wknd wl ins fnl f* — **9/4**[1]
0-33 **6** *3 1/4* **Monfils Monfils (USA)**[8] 656 7-8-9 **67**.......... BillyCray(3) 1 — 56
(A J McCabe) *led: hdd over 6f out: chsd ldr tl wl over 1f out: sn rdn and wknd* — **9/1**
0432 **7** *shd* **Prince Noel**[21] 737 5-8-8 **63**.......... KellyHarrison 7 — 51
(N Wilson) *hld up in tch: rdn over 1f out: wknd fnl f* — **4/1**[3]
6650 **8** *1 1/2* **Kabeer**[9] 841 11-8-7 **65**.......... RosieJessop(3) 4 — 50
(A J McCabe) *a towards rr* — **50/1**
44-0 **9** *1 1/4* **Ninth House (USA)**[61] 238 7-8-10 **65**.......... DeanHeslop 9 — 48
(Mrs R A Carr) *stdd s: rdn over 2f out: a in rr* — **16/1**

1m 52.09s (1.59) **Going Correction** +0.125s/f (Slow) — **9** Ran SP% **119.0**
Speed ratings (Par 103): **97,96,94,94,91 88,88,87,86**
toteswinger: 1&2 £3.50, 1&3 £22.90, 2&3 £71.00. CSF £22.28 CT £282.04 TOTE £5.30: £1.30, £2.10, £5.10; EX 21.40 Trifecta £183.00 Part won. Pool: £247.41 - 0.47 winning units..
Owner S Gillen **Bred** Martin Francis **Trained** Averham Park, Notts

FOCUS
A modest handicap restricted to apprentices who had not ridden more than 50 winners. The pace was fair and the form should prove reliable.

933 ENJOY THE LUCKY 7 GROUP OFFER CLAIMING STKS (DIV I) — 7f 32y(P)
2:20 (2:20) (Class 6) 4-Y-O+ — **£1,706** (£503; £252) **Stalls** High

Form — RPR
0060 **1** **The London Gang**[20] 748 6-8-8 40..........(b) JoeFanning 5 — 60
(S Wynne) *chsd ldr: led over 2f out: pushed clr over 1f out: rdn ins fnl f: r.o* — **66/1**
1212 **2** *1/2* **Obe Royal**[5] 868 5-8-10 71..........(b) DaneO'Neill 6 — 61
(P D Evans) *t.k.h early: a.p: rdn and chsd wnr wl over 1f out: edgd lft and lost 2nd ins fnl f: kpt on to regain 2nd post* — **1/1**[1]
40-0 **3** *nse* **Rubenstar (IRE)**[17] 777 6-8-7 64.......... WilliamCarson(5) 10 — 63
(Patrick Morris) *stdd s: sn swtchd lft: hld up in rr: hdwy on ins wl over 1f out: sn rdn and edgd rt: chsd wnr ins fnl f: lost 2nd post* — **12/1**
0055 **4** *2 1/4* **Almora Guru**[19] 760 5-8-1 47.......... LukeMorris 7 — 46
(W M Brisbourne) *hld up in tch: rdn over 2f out: one pce fnl f* — **16/1**
-440 **5** *1/2* **Valentino Swing (IRE)**[24] 715 6-8-9 56.......... TolleyDean 8 — 53
(Miss T Spearing) *hld up in mid-div: hdwy over 2f out: no imp fnl f* — **12/1**
2412 **6** *5* **Cap St Jean (IRE)**[13] 793 5-8-4 62..........(p) DavidKenny(7) 3 — 43
(R Hollinshead) *dwlt: in rr: struggling wl over 2f out: nvr nr ldrs* — **7/2**[2]
0-60 **7** *shd* **Cyfrwys (IRE)**[33] 587 8-7-12 44.......... DavidProbert(3) 2 — 32
(B Palling) *led: hdd over 2f out: rdn and wknd over 1f out* — **25/1**
00-0 **8** *10* **Mickys Mate**[63] 215 4-8-1 30.......... KellyHarrison(5) 4 — 13
(A Crook) *s.i.s: t.k.h: hdwy over 5f out: wknd over 3f out* — **100/1**
1/0- **9** *7* **Western Art (USA)**[303] 2409 4-8-13 100.......... PaulMulrennan 9 — 3
(M W Easterby) *bhd fnl 3f* — **11/2**[3]

1m 30.91s (1.31) **Going Correction** +0.125s/f (Slow) — **9** Ran SP% **115.2**
Speed ratings (Par 101): **97,96,96,93,93 87,87,75,67**
toteswinger: 1&2 £22.70, 1&3 £35.90, 2&3 £1.90. CSF £133.16 TOTE £28.10: £11.50, £1.10, £3.30; EX 105.00 TRIFECTA Not won..
Owner Miss Gillian Milner **Bred** Lostford Manor Stud **Trained** Whitchurch, Shropshire
■ Stewards' Enquiry : Dane O'Neill caution: careless riding.
Kelly Harrison caution: careless riding.

FOCUS
A real turn-up in this weak claimer and a difficult result to explain. A big step back up from the winner but the form has to be viewed negatively.
The London Gang Official explanation: trainer said, regarding the apparent improvement in form, that gelding jumped from the stalls better and was able to dominate.
Valentino Swing(IRE) Official explanation: jockey said gelding hung right

934 ENJOY THE LUCKY 7 GROUP OFFER CLAIMING STKS (DIV II) 7f 32y(P)
2:50 (2:50) (Class 6) 4-Y-0+ **£1,706** (£503; £252) **Stalls** High

Form RPR
2035 **1** **Kabis Amigos**^{5} 868 7-8-11 60..........(b) PaulHanagan 5 63
(S T Mason) *hld up: hdwy on outside 2f out: rdn to ld jst ins fnl f: sn edgd lft: r.o* **5/1**^{2}
412 **2** *1 1/4* **Imprimis Tagula (IRE)**^{21} 739 5-8-11 77..........(v) MickyFenton 2 60
(A Bailey) *a.p: rdn and ev ch 1f out: nt qckn* **9/4**^{1}
033 **3** *3/4* **Jord (IRE)**^{24} 715 5-8-7 60.......... RobertWinston 6 54
(A J McCabe) *rdr late removing blindfold and s.s: sn hld up in mid-div: hdwy over 1f out: swtchd lft jst ins fnl f: kpt on* **9/1**
/5- **4** *1 1/2* **Say Anything (IRE)**^{394} 684 8-8-3 38.......... RobbieEgan$^{(7)}$ 4 53
(Patrick Allen, Ire) *chsd ldr: rdn to ld wl over 1f out: hdd jst ins fnl f: no ex* **66/1**
-045 **5** *1/2* **Charmel's Lad**^{31} 619 4-8-1 53..........(tp) Louis-PhilippeBeuzelin$^{(5)}$ 7 48
(W R Swinburn) *hld up and bhd: rdn and effrt on ins over 1f out: nvr able to chal* **25/1**
6-60 **6** *1/2* **Trimlestown (IRE)**^{28} 654 6-8-13 71..........(p) DaneO'Neill 10 53
(P D Evans) *hld up in mid-div: hdwy 5f out: rdn 2f out: nt clr run briefly jst ins fnl f: one pce* **8/1**
00-0 **7** *1/2* **Xandra (IRE)**^{34} 581 4-8-2 49.......... LukeMorris 3 41
(W M Brisbourne) *hld up in tch: fdd fnl f* **50/1**
2246 **8** *1* **Dancing Deano (IRE)**^{13} 793 7-8-8 61.......... RussellKennemore$^{(3)}$ 1 47
(R Hollinshead) *led: rdn and hdd wl over 1f out: wknd ins fnl f* **11/2**^{3}
053- **9** *3 3/4* **Danish Art (IRE)**^{108} 7557 4-8-10 74.......... DaleGibson 8 36
(M W Easterby) *a bhd* **10/1**
1124 **10** *20* **Mrs Bun**^{39} 519 4-8-5 70..........(p) ChrisCatlin 9 —
(K A Ryan) *s.i.s: sn wl in rr: t.o fnl 4f* **5/1**^{2}
1m 30.49s (0.89) **Going Correction** +0.125s/f (Slow) **10** Ran SP% **117.0**
Speed ratings (Par 101): **99,97,96,95,94 93,93,92,87,65**
toteswinger: 1&2 £3.40, 1&3 £12.50, 2&3 £8.30. CSF £16.53 TOTE £7.30: £2.60, £1.30, £2.50; EX 20.70 Trifecta £501.50 Part won. Pool: £677.78 - 0.30 winning units..
Owner Ian W Glenton **Bred** Cheveley Park Stud Ltd **Trained**

FOCUS
A weak claimer run at a modest early pace, although the winning time was 0.42 seconds quicker than the first division. The form is rated through with the winner but the poor fourth holds down the race.
Jord(IRE) Official explanation: jockey said mare reared as stalls opened resulting in her being slowly away
Mrs Bun Official explanation: trainer said filly was unsuited by the Polytrack surface

935 HOTEL & CONFERENCING AT WOLVERHAMPTON CLAIMING STKS 1m 4f 50y(P)
3:25 (3:25) (Class 6) 4-Y-0+ **£2,047** (£604; £302) **Stalls** Low

Form RPR
P-33 **1** **New England**^{12} 805 7-8-13 60.......... LukeMorris 1 60+
(W M Brisbourne) *hld up in tch: rdn to ld ins fnl f: drvn out* **5/1**
/0-3 **2** *hd* **Pertemps Power**^{21} 735 5-8-11 47.......... ChrisCatlin 4 58
(B G Powell) *chsd ldr: led 2f out: rdn and hdd ins fnl f: r.o* **8/1**
6121 **3** *2 1/4* **Bridgewater Boys**^{12} 805 8-8-7 67..........(b) LanceBetts$^{(7)}$ 6 57
(T J Pitt) *hld up: c wd st: rdn and hdwy whn edgd lft over 1f out: kpt on to take 3rd wl ins fnl f* **7/2**^{3}
5340 **4** *2 1/4* **Calzaghe (IRE)**^{10} 836 5-8-9 63..........(vt) TPQueally 2 49
(F Sheridan) *a.p: rdn 2f out: one pce fnl f* **10/3**^{2}
-411 **5** *2 1/2* **Nawamees (IRE)**^{8} 517 11-8-12 70..........(p) DaneO'Neill 3 48
(P D Evans) *set stdy pce: qcknd 3f out: hdd 2f out: sn rdn: wknd ins fnl f* **15/8**^{1}
463- **6** *1/2* **Barbirolli**^{192} 5869 7-8-4 48.......... PaulPickard$^{(7)}$ 7 46
(W M Brisbourne) *t.k.h in rr: rdn over 1f out: no rspnse* **25/1**
2m 44.11s (3.01) **Going Correction** +0.125s/f (Slow)
WFA 4 from 5yo+ 2lb **6** Ran SP% **111.7**
Speed ratings (Par 101): **94,93,92,90,89 88**
toteswinger: 1&2 £4.80, 1&3 £4.50, 2&3 £6.80. CSF £41.36 TOTE £6.20: £2.40, £4.70; EX 48.40.Calzaghe was claimed by Jim Best for £3,000.
Owner Bould & Walker Racing **Bred** Darley **Trained** Great Ness, Shropshire

FOCUS
An ordinary claimer run at a modest pace. Difficult to assess, with the fifth well below form.

936 GREAT OFFERS AT WOLVERHAMPTON-RACECOURSE.CO.UK H'CAP 5f 216y(P)
4:00 (4:01) (Class 5) (0-70,70) 3-Y-O **£2,729** (£806; £403) **Stalls** Low

Form RPR
2-41 **1** **Song Of Praise**^{26} 673 3-8-12 **64**.......... DaneO'Neill 4 71
(M Blanshard) *hld up in tch: rdn to ld ins fnl f: drvn out* **12/1**
-433 **2** *nse* **Riflessione**^{13} 797 3-9-1 **67**..........(b) ChrisCatlin 2 74
(R A Harris) *hld up in tch: led jst over 1f out: rdn and hdd ins fnl f: r.o* **17/2**
301- **3** *1 3/4* **Arachnophobia (IRE)**^{137} 7205 3-9-2 **68**.......... PaulEddery 5 69
(Pat Eddery) *sn chsng ldr: rdn to ld wl over 1f out: sn hdd: no ex towards fin* **7/1**^{3}
21 **4** *1* **Trip Switch**^{22} 722 3-9-4 **70**.......... NCallan 8 68
(W R Muir) *broke wl: led early a.p: rdn 2f out: kpt on same pce fnl f* **7/4**^{1}
152- **5** *2 1/2* **Rocket Rob (IRE)**^{116} 7460 3-9-4 **70**.......... SimonWhitworth 7 60
(S A Callaghan) *hld up in tch: c wd st: wkng whn hung lft ins fnl f* **11/2**^{2}
1443 **6** *1/2* **Romantic Queen**^{10} 826 3-9-2 **68**.......... JimCrowley 3 56
(E A L Dunlop) *hld up and bhd: hdwy on ins wl over 1f out: rdn and wknd ins fnl f* **11/1**
630- **7** *1 3/4* **Captain Carey**^{110} 7538 3-8-13 **65**.......... TGMcLaughlin 6 48+
(M S Saunders) *hld up and bhd: btn whn hmpd ins fnl f* **12/1**
1351 **8** *4 1/2* **La Capriosa**^{11} 819 3-9-3 **69**.......... RobertWinston 1 37
(A J McCabe) *sn led: hdd wl over 1f out: sn rdn: wknd fnl f* **14/1**
021- **9** *1* **Freepressionist**^{117} 7452 3-9-2 **68**.......... EddieAhern 9 33
(R A Teal) *hld up in rr: rdn wl over 1f out: no rspnse* **8/1**
1m 15.29s (0.29) **Going Correction** +0.125s/f (Slow) **9** Ran SP% **116.3**
Speed ratings (Par 98): **103,102,100,99,95 95,92,86,85**
toteswinger: 1&2 £14.80, 1&3 £15.60, 2&3 £12.60. CSF £109.71 CT £775.48 TOTE £15.10: £3.00, £2.10, £3.40; EX 104.80 TRIFECTA Not won..
Owner Tom Wellman **Bred** Whitsbury Manor Stud **Trained** Upper Lambourn, Berks
■ Stewards' Enquiry : Simon Whitworth caution: careless riding.

FOCUS
A tight little 3yo sprint with just 6lb covering the entire field and it produced a very close finish. The winner is progressing and the form should work out.

937 SPONSOR A RACE BY CALLING 01902 390009 (S) STKS 5f 216y(P)
4:35 (4:35) (Class 6) 4-Y-0+ **£2,047** (£604; £302) **Stalls** Low

Form RPR
-020 **1** **Romantic Verse**^{17} 777 4-8-11 67..........(b) GrahamGibbons 5 69
(E S McMahon) *a gng wl: shkn up to ld ent fnl f: drvn clr* **9/2**^{2}
0-00 **2** *3 3/4* **Loose Caboose (IRE)**^{74} 89 4-8-11 64.......... RobertWinston 4 57
(A J McCabe) *led 1f: led over 3f out tl wl over 1f out: kpt on u.p to take 2nd last strides* **8/1**
6240 **3** *hd* **Inka Dancer (IRE)**^{27} 661 7-8-8 50.......... DavidProbert$^{(3)}$ 1 56
(B Palling) *a in tch on ins: rdn over 2f out: chsd wnr ins fnl f: no imp: lost 2nd last strides* **8/1**
1604 **4** *1* **Mafaheem**^{18} 762 7-9-2 65.......... GeorgeBaker 9 58
(A B Haynes) *hld up in rr: rdn over 2f out: hdwy 1f out: nvr nr to chal* **5/1**^{3}
3606 **5** *1/2* **Joss Stick**^{18} 762 4-9-2 62..........(p) JoeFanning 8 57
(R A Harris) *hld up and bhd: c v wd st: rdn wl over 1f out: nvr able to chal* **12/1**
00-0 **6** *3/4* **Orpen's Art (IRE)**^{61} 241 4-9-2 67.......... DaneO'Neill 6 54
(George Baker) *hld up in tch: c wd st: rdn over 1f out: no hdwy fnl f* **5/1**^{3}
6604 **7** *2* **Peter's Storm (USA)**^{4} 882 4-9-2 65.......... NCallan 7 48
(K A Ryan) *led after 1f tl over 3f out: wknd wl over 1f out* **4/1**^{1}
-325 **8** *2 1/2* **Interchoice Star**^{20} 746 4-8-8 48.......... RussellKennemore$^{(3)}$ 2 35
(R Hollinshead) *w ldrs: rdn to ld wl over 1f out: hdd ent fnl f: wknd qckly* **6/1**
1m 14.64s (-0.36) **Going Correction** +0.125s/f (Slow) **8** Ran SP% **115.7**
Speed ratings (Par 101): **107,102,101,100,99 98,96,92**
toteswinger: 1&2 £8.20, 1&3 £5.00, 2&3 £10.00. CSF £40.37 TOTE £6.20: £1.90, £3.10, £2.50; EX 41.60 Trifecta £288.40 Part won. Pool: £389.86 - 0.40 winning units..The winner was sold to Dave Grewood for 5,000 guineas. Orpen's Art was claimed by Simon Callaghan for £6,000.
Owner A McWilliam/J Yorston **Bred** Cheveley Park Stud Ltd **Trained** Lichfield, Staffs

FOCUS
A weakish seller run at a strong pace. The fairly exposed third helps set the level.

938 STAY AT THE WOLVERHAMPTON HOLIDAY INN H'CAP 1m 1f 103y(P)
5:10 (5:10) (Class 6) (0-65,64) 3-Y-O **£2,047** (£604; £302) **Stalls** Low

Form RPR
60-5 **1** **Scottish Affair**^{24} 707 3-9-1 **58**.......... JimCrowley 5 66
(E A L Dunlop) *hld up: hdwy wl over 1f out: sn swtchd rt and hung lft: rdn to ld wl ins fnl f: r.o* **13/2**
6423 **2** *2* **Duke Of Normandy (IRE)**^{10} 829 3-9-7 **64**.......... JoeFanning 3 68
(M Johnston) *hld up in tch: rdn to ld wl over 1f out: sn hung lft: hdd and nt qckn wl ins fnl f* **2/1**^{1}
0-53 **3** *3* **Tae Kwon Do (USA)**^{19} 759 3-8-12 **55**.......... TomEaves 1 53
(Miss J A Camacho) *a.p: ev ch over 1f out: one pce fnl f* **4/1**^{3}
3-12 **4** *2 1/2* **Kiyari**^{27} 662 3-9-6 **63**.......... SebSanders 2 55
(M Botti) *hld up: hdwy wl over 1f out: sn rdn: wknd wl ins fnl f* **9/4**^{2}
00-0 **5** *1 1/4* **Teddy West (IRE)**^{31} 621 3-8-7 **55**.......... WilliamCarson$^{(5)}$ 6 45
(Patrick Morris) *sn chsng ldr: led over 2f out tl wl over 1f out: carried hd high: wknd ins fnl f* **28/1**
-050 **6** *8* **Tiffany Lady**^{39} 520 3-7-13 **45**.......... DavidProbert$^{(3)}$ 7 18
(M D I Usher) *stdd s: hld up in rr: rdn and short-lived effrt on outside over 2f out: c wd st: sn struggling* **25/1**
05-0 **7** *7* **Irish Saint (IRE)**^{26} 677 3-9-3 **60**.......... PaulHanagan 4 18
(T J Pitt) *led tl over 2f out: wknd wl over 1f out* **12/1**
2m 2.59s (0.89) **Going Correction** +0.125s/f (Slow) **7** Ran SP% **112.4**
Speed ratings (Par 96): **101,99,96,94,93 86,79**
toteswinger: 1&2 £3.40, 1&3 £4.10, 2&3 £2.70. CSF £19.27 TOTE £6.30: £3.20, £1.90; EX 25.60.
Owner E A L Dunlop **Bred** Gainsborough Stud Management Ltd **Trained** Newmarket, Suffolk

FOCUS
A modest 3yo handicap. The form should work out.
Scottish Affair Official explanation: trainer's rep said, regarding the apparent improvement in form, that gelding had benefited from the step up in trip and had run creditably in its previous race.
Teddy West(IRE) Official explanation: jockey said gelding hung right
Tiffany Lady Official explanation: jockey said filly hung right

939 WOLVERHAMPTON HOSPITALITY - A PLEASURE MAIDEN STKS 1m 141y(P)
5:40 (5:40) (Class 5) 3-Y-0+ **£2,729** (£806; £403) **Stalls** Low

Form RPR
5 **1** **Hatta Diamond (IRE)**^{18} 767 3-8-5 0.......... JoeFanning 8 68+
(M Johnston) *hld up in mid-div: c wd st: hdwy jst over 1f out: sn hung lft: led wl ins fnl f: r.o* **5/2**^{1}
0-4 **2** *hd* **Morning Sir Alan**^{16} 786 3-8-5 0.......... ChrisCatlin 9 69+
(S A Callaghan) *hld up in tch: rdn and r.o wl ins fnl f* **5/2**^{1}
003- **3** *1 3/4* **Duar Mapel (USA)**^{159} 6731 3-8-5 76..........(b) PaulEddery 6 64
(Paul Mason) *chsd ldr: ev ch over 2f out: rdn wl over 1f out: nt qckn ins fnl f* **11/2**^{3}
00-3 **4** *1/2* **Hypnotic Gaze (IRE)**^{24} 716 3-8-2 66.......... DavidProbert$^{(3)}$ 2 63
(J Mackie) *a.p: rdn over 1f out: nt qckn fnl f* **13/2**
00-2 **5** *nk* **Campli (IRE)**^{18} 767 7-9-3 68.......... LanceBetts$^{(7)}$ 5 68
(B Ellison) *led: rdn over 1f out: hdd wl ins fnl f: no ex* **4/1**^{2}
444 **6** *2* **Harty Boy (USA)**^{29} 649 3-8-0 67 ow2.......... DanielBlackett$^{(7)}$ 3 60
(Mrs S Leech) *hld up in mid-div: no hdwy fnl 2f* **12/1**
50-0 **7** *1 1/4* **Plaka (FR)**^{24} 711 4-9-5 50.......... LiamJones 10 56
(W M Brisbourne) *stdd s: hld up in rr: rdn over 1f out: nvr trbld ldrs* **40/1**
05 **8** *7* **Keen As Mustard**^{12} 800 4-9-3 0.......... LeeNewnes$^{(7)}$ 1 46
(M D I Usher) *rdr slow to remove blindfold: s.v.s: a in rr* **50/1**
0 **9** *33* **Gozome (IRE)**^{16} 786 5-9-10 0.......... VinceSlattery 7 —
(D G Bridgwater) *n.m.r sn after s: t.k.h in rr: lost tch fnl 3f: t.o* **200/1**
1m 51.15s (0.65) **Going Correction** +0.125s/f (Slow)
WFA 3 from 4yo+ 19lb **9** Ran SP% **118.5**
Speed ratings (Par 103): **102,101,100,99,99 97,96,90,61**
toteswinger: 1&2 £2.70, 1&3 £3.90, 2&3 £5.80. Place 6: £679.32, Place 5: £247.62. CSF £8.94 TOTE £4.20: £1.80, £1.40, £1.70; EX 9.60 Trifecta £41.10 Pool: £317.80 - 5.71 winning units..
Owner Sheikh Hamdan Bin Mohammed Al Maktoum **Bred** Gainsborough Stud Management Ltd **Trained** Middleham Moor, N Yorks

FOCUS
The bare form of this maiden is probably just modest, but they seemed to go a decent gallop and the time was 0.94 seconds quicker than the older-horse handicap won the 68-rated Follow The Flag. The first two can probably improve on this in time.
T/Plt: £1,050.30 to a £1 stake. Pool: £59,857.39. 41.60 winning tickets. T/Qpdt: £203.40 to a £1 stake. Pool: £4,343.30. 15.80 winning tickets. KH

940 - 942a (Foreign Racing) - See Raceform Interactive

910 **LINGFIELD** (L-H)
Tuesday, March 24

OFFICIAL GOING: Standard
Wind: Moderate, against Weather: Fine

943 MARSH GREEN (S) STKS — 1m 2f (P)
2:20 (2:20) (Class 6) 3-Y-O — **£2,047** (£604; £302) **Stalls** Low

Form — RPR

5023 **1** **Flying Lady (IRE)**[10] 839 3-8-3 65 ow1 .... MCGeran[(5)] 1 59+
(M R Channon) *prom: trckd ldr 4f out: clsd to ld over 1f out: sn clr: edgd rt u.p fnl f: unchal* **13/8**[1]

-060 **2** *1 ¼* **Dead Cat Bounce (IRE)**[20] 759 3-8-12 62 .... (bt[1]) PatCosgrave 8 60
(J Pearce) *trckd ldrs: 1/2-way: struggling tl prog over 3f out: styd on to take 2nd last 100yds and cl on wnr fin* **11/2**[3]

4352 **3** *2 ¾* **Why Nee Amy**[30] 649 3-8-7 54 .... ChrisCatlin 5 50
(Miss Gay Kelleway) *t.k.h: hld up in last pair: rdn over 3f out: prog over 2f out: kpt on fr over 1f out to take 3rd last strides* **5/1**[2]

-434 **4** *hd* **Herecomesbella**[27] 678 3-8-7 50 .... (b) NickyMackay 6 50
(Stef Liddiard) *hld up: prog on outer to ld over 5f out: clr w wnr 2f out: hdd over 1f out: wknd and lost 2 pls ins fnl f* **14/1**

6-0 **5** *1* **Calling Birds (IRE)**[8] 849 3-8-8 0 ow1 .... (b[1]) ShaneKelly 2 49
(J A Osborne) *hld up in midfield: prog to chse ldng pair over 3f out: hrd rdn and no imp 2f out: wknd over 1f out* **25/1**

6-03 **6** *2 ½* **Sweet Virginia (USA)**[30] 649 3-8-2 50 .... MartinLane[(5)] 4 44
(K R Burke) *struggling in rr fr 1/2-way: nvr a factor* **16/1**

00-0 **7** *2 ¼* **Hassadin**[28] 662 3-8-12 59 .... (v[1]) TPQueally 3 45
(A B Haynes) *led to over 5f out: hrd rdn and losing pl 4f out: sn no ch* **8/1**

3-20 **8** *3 ¼* **Barcode**[20] 759 3-8-7 53 .... (b[1]) LPKeniry 9 34
(R Hannon) *dwlt: hld up in last: detached and rdn over 4f out: no ch after* **8/1**

-566 **9** *6* **Chantilly Dancer (IRE)**[30] 649 3-8-7 47 .... MartinDwyer 7 23
(M Quinn) *prom: rdn over 4f out: struggling after: wknd 3f out: t.o* **16/1**

2m 8.16s (1.56) **Going Correction** +0.075s/f (Slow) **9 Ran SP% 114.6**
Speed ratings (Par 96): **96,95,92,91 89,88,85,80**
toteswinger: 1&2 £2.10, 1&3 £2.50, 2&3 £4.30. CSF £10.47 TOTE £2.70: £1.10, £1.90, £1.60; EX 9.90 Trifecta £36.80 Pool: £481.96 - 9.68 winning units..There was no bid for the winner.
Owner M Channon **Bred** Alan Dargan **Trained** West Ilsley, Berks

FOCUS
A bad seller with four of the nine runners either trying some sort of headgear for the first time or trying a different type of equipment. The early pace was steady until picking up at around halfway. The form is limited but the idling winner can do better.

944 ASHURST WOOD MEDIAN AUCTION MAIDEN STKS — 1m (P)
2:50 (2:50) (Class 6) 3-4-Y-O — **£2,729** (£806; £403) **Stalls** High

Form — RPR

5- **1** **Muraweg (IRE)**[284] 3001 3-8-10 0 .... JimmyFortune 4 80+
(J H M Gosden) *mde virtually all: set stdy pce to 3f out: pressed and rdn 1f out: styd on wl: readily* **4/9**[1]

3 **2** *1 ¾* **Carbon Hoofprint**[66] 201 3-8-10 0 .... FergusSweeney 1 74
(P J Makin) *trckd ldng pair: effrt to chse wnr wl over 1f out on inner: cl enough sn after: rdn and one pce* **7/1**[3]

453- **3** *½* **Bagber**[197] 5754 3-8-10 77 .... EddieAhern 6 73
(H J L Dunlop) *pressed wnr: rdn and nt qckn over 2f out: lost 2nd wl over 1f out: kpt on same pce* **4/1**[2]

4 *3 ¾* **Fantastical** 3-8-5 0 .... MartinDwyer 2 60+
(C E Brittain) *s.i.s: sn chsd ldng trio: rdn 3f out: outpcd and btn over 2f out* **12/1**

60-4 **5** *7* **Sumani (FR)**[28] 663 3-8-10 64 .... ChrisCatlin 5 49
(S Dow) *t.k.h: hld up in last pair: pushed along over 2f out: nvr on terms* **25/1**

05- **6** *1 ¼* **Forced Opinion (USA)**[84] 7822 4-9-13 0 .... PatCosgrave 3 52
(K A Morgan) *t.k.h: hld up in last pair: pushed along 2f out: nvr remotely on terms* **66/1**

1m 39.17s (0.97) **Going Correction** +0.075s/f (Slow)
WFA 3 from 4yo 17lb **6 Ran SP% 114.8**
Speed ratings (Par 101): **98,96,95,92,85 83**
toteswinger: 1&2 £1.60, 1&3 £1.50, 2&3 £1.10. CSF £4.64 TOTE £1.50: £1.10, £2.30; EX 4.10.
Owner Hamdan Al Maktoum **Bred** Rozelle Bloodstock **Trained** Newmarket, Suffolk

FOCUS
An uncompetitive maiden run at a modest pace, but a few of these are probably capable of better. The winner dictated things, with the next two close to form.

945 TERRY COOK 60TH BIRTHDAY FILLIES' H'CAP — 7f (P)
3:20 (3:21) (Class 5) (0-70,70) 4-Y-O+ — **£2,729** (£806; £403) **Stalls** Low

Form — RPR

-410 **1** **Smokey Rye**[11] 830 4-8-7 66 .... MatthewDavies[(7)] 5 74
(George Baker) *cl up in 5th w usual tail swishing: prog over 2f out to go 3rd over 1f out: styd on wl fnl f to ld last 50yds* **9/2**[3]

0521 **2** *½* **Melt (IRE)**[11] 830 4-8-5 57 .... (b) ChrisCatlin 6 64
(R Hannon) *led 100yds: pressed ldr after: sustained chal over 2f out to ld narrowly over 1f out: hdd and outpcd fnl 50yds* **5/2**[2]

1242 **3** *1 ¼* **Moon Crystal**[11] 830 4-9-4 70 .... (t) JimCrowley 3 74
(E A L Dunlop) *led after 100yds: rdn and pressed over 2f out: narrowly hdd over 1f out: no ex last 100yds* **15/8**[1]

004 **4** *nk* **Too Grand**[11] 830 4-8-1 56 oh3 .... DavidProbert[(3)] 4 59
(J J Bridger) *hld up in last trio: outpcd 3f out: prog over 1f out: styd on fnl f: nrst fin* **8/1**

60-0 **5** *1 ¼* **Little Knickers**[11] 830 4-8-4 56 oh1 .... (b) MartinDwyer 7 55
(E J Creighton) *trckd ldng pair on outer: nt qckn 2f out: one pce and steadily lost pl* **8/1**

2-00 **6** *1 ½* **Poppy Dean (IRE)**[13] 802 4-8-4 56 oh11 .... FrankieMcDonald 1 51?
(J G Portman) *cl up in 4th: rdn wl over 2f out: sn lost pl and struggling* **25/1**

/0-0 **7** *4 ½* **She's Our Dream**[14] 794 4-8-4 56 oh11 .... (t) JimmyQuinn 8 39?
(R C Guest) *hld up in last trio: outpcd 3f out but stl appeared to be gng wl enough: no ch whn rdn fnl f* **50/1**

/3-0 **8** *3 ½* **Tallulah Sunrise**[10] 842 4-8-6 63 .... GabrielHannon[(5)] 2 37
(M D I Usher) *hld up in last: lft bhd fr 3f out: no ch after* **14/1**

1m 25.79s (0.99) **Going Correction** +0.075s/f (Slow) **8 Ran SP% 116.2**
Speed ratings (Par 100): **97,96,95,94,93 91,86,82**
toteswinger: 1&2 £2.70, 1&3 £3.00, 2&3 £2.10. CSF £16.50 CT £27.91 TOTE £5.20: £1.50, £1.50, £1.40; EX 19.60 Trifecta £46.00 Pool: £561.27 - 9.02 winning units..
Owner The Different Partnership **Bred** Jeremy Hinds **Trained** Moreton Morrell, Warwicks

FOCUS
An ordinary fillies' handicap with not much strength in depth. Five of these had met each other over 1m at this track 11 days earlier and they filled the first five places here.
Smokey Rye Official explanation: trainer said, regarding the apparent improvement in form, that filly was denied a clear run last time.

946 HINDLEAP WALK H'CAP — 6f (P)
3:50 (3:53) (Class 6) (0-55,56) 4-Y-O+ — **£2,047** (£604; £302) **Stalls** Low

Form — RPR

-431 **1** **Green Velvet**[4] 895 4-9-0 56 6ex .... TravisBlock 5 64+
(P J Makin) *wl plcd on inner: rdn 2f out: led 1f out: styd on wl and in command after* **2/1**[1]

4-66 **2** *1 ½* **Bateleur**[8] 854 5-8-4 51 .... (v) MCGeran[(5)] 1 55
(M R Channon) *hld up in rr: prog on inner over 2f out: clsd on ldrs over 1f out: kpt on but no imp on wnr* **11/2**[3]

2-50 **3** *½* **Bollin Franny**[11] 832 5-8-9 51 .... RichardThomas 7 53
(J E Long) *mde most: hrd pressed 2f out: hdd and nt qckn 1f out* **13/2**

-006 **4** *½* **Easy Wonder (GER)**[12] 812 4-7-13 46 oh1 .... (b) AndreaAtzeni[(5)] 4 47
(I A Wood) *settled in midfield: effrt to chse ldng quartet wl over 1f out and cl enough: nt qckn* **8/1**

000- **5** *nk* **Seductive Witch**[222] 5015 4-8-10 52 .... EddieAhern 8 52
(J Balding) *prom: pressed ldr over 2f out: upsides jst over 1f out: fdd u.p* **25/1**

0600 **6** *1* **Metropolitan Chief**[12] 812 5-8-4 46 oh1 .... (p) FrankieMcDonald 2 43
(P Burgoyne) *rrd s: t.k.h in last pair: hanging bnd 2f out: shkn up and styd on fr over 1f out: no ch* **50/1**

-002 **7** *hd* **Elusive Dreams (USA)**[8] 854 5-8-13 55 .... (v) TolleyDean 11 51+
(P Howling) *c out of stalls v late: hld up in last: shuffled along and kpt on fnl 2f: nvr nr ldrs* **4/1**[2]

04 **8** *½* **Scholars Lass (IRE)**[21] 746 4-8-1 46 oh1 .... DavidProbert[(3)] 9 41+
(J Balding) *dwlt: sn in midfield: rdn whn bmpd over 2f out: no ch after* **9/1**

0060 **9** *¾* **Diminuto**[13] 811 5-7-13 46 oh1 .... AmyBaker[(5)] 10 38
(M D I Usher) *mostly pressed ldr to over 2f out: wknd wl over 1f out* **33/1**

0-03 **10** *¾* **Fly In Johnny (IRE)**[4] 891 4-7-13 46 oh1 .... MartinLane[(5)] 12 36
(J J Bridger) *racd wd in midfield: bmpd rival over 2f out: btn after* **14/1**

00-6 **11** *1* **Scruffy Skip (IRE)**[21] 746 4-8-6 48 .... JimmyQuinn 6 35
(Mrs C A Dunnett) *a towards rr: struggling over 2f out: btn after* **20/1**

000/ **12** *8* **Pat Will (IRE)**[149] 5688 5-8-4 46 oh1 .... ChrisCatlin 3 9
(M R Hoad) *free to post: hld up in rr: wknd 1/2-way: t.o* **66/1**

1m 11.26s (-0.64) **Going Correction** +0.075s/f (Slow) **12 Ran SP% 124.8**
Speed ratings (Par 101): **107,105,104,103,103 101,101,101,100,99 97,87**
toteswinger: 1&2 £3.70, 1&3 £4.40, 2&3 £7.80. CSF £13.25 CT £66.34 TOTE £2.90: £1.40, £2.10, £2.30; EX 17.60 Trifecta £86.00 Pool: £646.81 - 5.56 winning units..
Owner Mrs P J Makin **Bred** Mrs P J Makin **Trained** Ogbourne Maisey, Wilts

FOCUS
A weak if competitive sprint handicap. The winner remains on an upward curve in a weak division.
Metropolitan Chief Official explanation: jockey said gelding reared in stalls

947 FOREST ROW MAIDEN STKS — 5f (P)
4:20 (4:20) (Class 5) 3-Y-O+ — **£2,729** (£806; £403) **Stalls** High

Form — RPR

233- **1** **Bajan Tryst (USA)**[167] 6575 3-9-0 78 .... NCallan 2 79+
(K A Ryan) *mde all: drew clr 2f out: at least 4 l up 1f out: pushed out: unchal* **8/11**[1]

2 *1* **Lenny Bee** 3-9-0 0 .... PaulMulrennan 5 78+
(D H Brown) *dwlt: rousted along on outer to rcvr: wnt 3rd 2f out but wl off the pce: styd on to take 2nd 1f out: clsd on wnr but nvr able to chal* **7/2**[2]

6- **3** *4 ½* **Vamos (IRE)**[201] 5628 3-9-0 0 .... ChrisCatlin 7 58+
(J R Gask) *chsd ldng pair but nvr on terms: lost 3rd 2f out: kpt on again to regain position ins fnl f* **12/1**

4 *3 ¾* **Fatal Attraction** 4-9-7 0 .... SebSanders 4 45
(Rae Guest) *chsd wnr and sn clr of rest: rn green and btn 2f out: wknd and lost 2 pls fnl f* **8/1**[3]

5 *4* **Trade Price (GR)** 3-9-0 0 .... ShaneKelly 1 30
(J A Osborne) *dwlt: sn outpcd: rn green and fr 1/2-way: nvr a factor* **11/1**

43 **6** *1* **Dream Catch Me (IRE)**[23] 722 3-8-4 0 .... AndreaAtzeni[(5)] 3 22
(J R Boyle) *sn outpcd in last pair: nvr a factor* **14/1**

0 **7** *1 ½* **By The Wind (IRE)**[26] 686 3-9-0 0 .... SaleemGolam 6 21
(T J Etherington) *outpcd in midfield and nvr on terms: wknd over 1f out* **66/1**

-000 **8** *4* **Thumberlina**[12] 812 3-8-9 45 .... JimmyQuinn 8 —
(Mrs C A Dunnett) *sn t.o* **50/1**

58.16 secs (-0.64) **Going Correction** +0.075s/f (Slow)
WFA 3 from 4yo 12lb **8 Ran SP% 117.4**
Speed ratings (Par 103): **108,106,99,93,86 85,82,76**
toteswinger: 1&2 £1.50, 1&3 £3.20, 2&3 £6.90. CSF £3.61 TOTE £1.70: £1.02, £1.60, £4.60; EX 4.20 Trifecta £26.30 Pool: £771.23 - 21.66 winning units..
Owner Mrs Margaret Forsyth & Mrs R G Hillen **Bred** William Patterson & James Glenn **Trained** Hambleton, N Yorks

FOCUS
A good maiden for the time of year featuring a couple with proven ability and some potentially interesting newcomers. The first two can probably do better.
Thumberlina Official explanation: jockey said filly was slowly away

948 COME JUMPING HERE THIS SATURDAY APPRENTICE H'CAP — 1m 2f (P)
4:50 (4:50) (Class 5) (0-70,68) 4-Y-O+ — **£2,729** (£806; £403) **Stalls** Low

Form — RPR

-200 **1** **Kings Topic (USA)**[12] 813 9-8-9 61 .... (p) PNolan[(3)] 3 70
(A B Haynes) *mde all: set stdy pce to 1/2-way: kicked on over 2f out: styd on wl* **11/2**[3]

0-04 **2** *2 ¾* **Sri Kuantan (IRE)**[13] 805 5-9-4 67 .... (t) AmyRyan 2 71
(R C Guest) *t.k.h: pressed wnr: nt qckn 2f out: one pce and no imp after* **3/1**[2]

0516 **3** *¾* **Bavarica**[11] 830 7-8-12 68 .... MatthewCosham[(7)] 1 71
(Miss J Feilden) *stdd s: t.k.h bhd ldrs: nt clr run briefly over 2f out: one pce u.p after* **11/2**[3]

5111 **4** *1* **Prince Charlemagne (IRE)**[12] 816 6-8-12 61 .... JemmaMarshall 5 62
(G L Moore) *hld up bhd ldrs: rdn over 2f out: nt qckn and hld after* **4/6**[1]

5056 **5** *4* **Inquisitress**[12] 813 5-8-5 54 oh7 .... MartinLane 4 48
(J J Bridger) *hld up bhd ldrs: cl up whn squeezed out over 2f out: no prog after* **12/1**

045- **6** *13* **Encore Belle**[202] 5602 4-8-7 **56** RossAtkinson 6 26
(Mouse Hamilton-Fairley) *racd wd: cl up: rdn over 3f out: sn btn: bhd fnl 2f* **12/1**

2m 7.59s (0.99) **Going Correction** +0.075s/f (Slow) **6** Ran SP% **131.1**
Speed ratings (Par 103): **99,96,96,95,92 81**
toteswinger: 1&2 £2.60, 1&3 £4.20, 2&3 £5.60. CSF £26.33 TOTE £8.70: £3.60, £1.50; EX 26.30 Place 6: £6.73 Place 5: £5.30.
Owner Ms C Berry **Bred** Marvin Delfiner And Fred Seitz **Trained** Limpley Stoke, Bath

FOCUS
A modest apprentice handicap and a very unsatisfactory race as they crawled for much of the way, which wouldn't have suited a few, and also caused a couple to pull hard. The form makes sense though.
Bavarica Official explanation: jockey said mare hung right
T/Plt: £19.60 to a £1 stake. Pool: £56,469.25. 2,096.07 winning tickets. T/Qpdt: £19.40 to a £1 stake. Pool: £3,118.20. 118.80 winning tickets. JN

875 KEMPTON (A.W) (R-H)
Wednesday, March 25

OFFICIAL GOING: Standard
Wind: Moderate, across Weather: Mostly clear

949 KEMPTON FOR CONFERENCES MAIDEN FILLIES' STKS 1m (P)
6:50 (6:50) (Class 5) 3-Y-0+ **£2,590** (£770; £385; £192) **Stalls** High

Form RPR
030- **1** **Haakima (USA)**[158] 6818 3-8-10 **86** NCallan 10 68+
(C E Brittain) *led: set v modest pce to 1/2-way: kicked on 3f out: hrd rdn and pressed wl over 1f out: kpt on* **4/5**[1]

2 *½* **Kefalonia (USA)** 3-8-10 0 WilliamBuick 8 67+
(B W Hills) *awkward s and slowly away: in tch in last trio: rdn and green over 2f out: prog over 1f out: styd on wl to take 2nd last strides* **15/2**[3]

3 *nk* **Christina Rossetti** 3-8-10 0 JimmyFortune 6 66+
(J H M Gosden) *dwlt: sn rcvrd to trck wnr: rdn to chal over 2f out: hld ent fnl f: eased last 50yds and lost 2nd last strides* **4/1**[2]

64- **4** *1 ½* **Penang Princess**[164] 6674 3-8-10 0 JimCrowley 1 63
(R M Beckett) *stdd s: hld up last in slowly run r: stl there over 1f out: nudged along and sme prog over 1f out: keeping on but no ch whn reminder ins fnl f: do bttr* **10/1**

5 *hd* **Extracurricular (USA)** 3-8-10 0 JimmyQuinn 2 62
(M Botti) *trckd ldrs: rdn wl over 2f out: kpt on one pce fnl 2f: nvr pce to threaten* **11/1**

5 **6** *2 ¼* **Songful (IRE)**[9] 849 3-8-10 0 PaulEddery 9 57?
(Pat Eddery) *hld up in last trio: hanging rt whn rdn over 2f out: no real prog after* **20/1**

00- **7** *1* **Spinning Joy**[167] 6602 3-8-10 0 PatCosgrave 7 54?
(J R Boyle) *chsd wnr 1f: 3rd after: rdn as sn as pce lifted 3f out: struggling after: wknd over 1f out* **66/1**

04 **8** *1* **Aegean Rose**[23] 731 4-9-13 0 FergusSweeney 3 52?
(M Blanshard) *racd wd: cl up: rdn wl over 2f out: sn struggling: wknd over 1f out* **50/1**

1m 44.15s (4.35) **Going Correction** +0.10s/f (Slow)
WFA 3 from 4yo 17lb **8** Ran SP% **113.0**
Speed ratings (Par 100): **82,81,81,79,79 77,76,75**
toteswinger: 1&2 £1.50, 1&3 £2.40, 2&3 £1.80. CSF £7.27 TOTE £1.80: £1.20, £2.70, £1.20; EX 8.80.
Owner Saeed Manana **Bred** R D Hubbard **Trained** Newmarket, Suffolk

FOCUS
A fairly unsatisfactory fillies' maiden which was run at a dawdling pace and turned into a sprint turning for home. The time was over six seconds above standard. The winner had the run of things but can better the bare form, and the placed horses can post better figures too.
Kefalonia(USA) ◆ Official explanation: jockey said filly missed the break
Christina Rossetti ◆ Official explanation: jockey said, regarding appearing to stop riding on run to line, that the filly's action began to shorten 50yds out and, as he felt there was something wrong, he did not persevere.

950 DIGIBET SPORTS BETTING H'CAP 1m (P)
7:20 (7:21) (Class 5) (0-75,74) 4-Y-0+ **£2,590** (£770; £385; £192) **Stalls** High

Form RPR
522- **1** **Hawaana (IRE)**[142] 7167 4-9-2 **72** PaulDoe 7 81
(Eve Johnson Houghton) *rousted along early to press ldr: drvn over 2f out: led over 1f out: edgd rt but drew clr fnl f* **5/2**[2]

110- **2** *2* **Gazboolou**[161] 6738 5-9-2 **72** FergusSweeney 1 77
(David Pinder) *t.k.h early: trckd ldng pair on outer: rdn and nt qckn 2f out: kpt on fnl f to snatch 2nd nr fin* **11/2**[3]

1111 **3** *hd* **Highly Regal (IRE)**[14] 807 4-9-1 **71** (b) LPKeniry 6 75
(R A Teal) *trckd ldng pair on inner: effrt over 2f out: disp 2nd over 1f out: one pce after* **13/8**[1]

0464 **4** *½* **Hucking Hero (IRE)**[7] 873 4-8-12 **71** MarcHalford[(3)] 4 74
(J R Best) *hld up in 5th: effrt on wd outside 2f out: disp 2nd 1f out: nt qckn after* **10/1**

6260 **5** *1 ¼* **Millfield (IRE)**[6] 878 6-9-4 **74** GeorgeBaker 2 74
(P R Chamings) *stdd s: t.k.h and hld up in last: effrt over 2f out: keeping on u.p but no ch whn run out of room ins fnl f* **12/1**

/44- **6** *1 ¼* **Magic Rush**[173] 6450 7-9-1 **71** EdwardCreighton 8 69
(Norma Twomey) *led at decent pce: urged along 2f out: hdd and fdd over 1f out* **14/1**

2-35 **7** *hd* **Sofia's Star**[60] 283 4-9-4 **74** JimCrowley 3 71
(S Dow) *hld up in 6th: drvn and effrt 2f out: sn no prog and btn* **6/1**

1m 38.95s (-0.85) **Going Correction** +0.10s/f (Slow) **7** Ran SP% **119.8**
Speed ratings (Par 103): **108,106,105,105,104 102,102**
toteswinger: 1&2 £2.60, 1&3 £1.20, 2&3 £2.60. CSF £17.85 CT £28.79 TOTE £3.90: £1.60, £3.00; EX 16.70.
Owner Elite Sports Syndicate 1 **Bred** Norelands Bloodstock, J Hanly & H Lascelles **Trained** Blewbury, Oxon
■ Stewards' Enquiry : Paul Doe caution: used whip down shoulder in forehand position.

FOCUS
A fair handicap run at an even tempo. The form looks fairly sound.

951 DIGIBET.COM MAIDEN STKS 7f (P)
7:50 (7:56) (Class 5) 3-Y-0 **£2,590** (£770; £385; £192) **Stalls** High

Form RPR
50- **1** **Seek N' Destroy (IRE)**[174] 6426 3-9-3 0 MichaelHills 5 74
(B W Hills) *trckd ldr: led over 2f out: rdn and decisive advantage over 1f out: kpt on wl* **9/4**[1]

04- **2** *1 ¼* **Woodlark Island (IRE)**[139] 7204 3-9-3 0 MartinDwyer 11 70
(M P Tregoning) *uns rdr and bolted bk towards stables bef r: sn led: rdn and hdd over 2f out: stuck on wl to hold on for 2nd* **25/1**

3 *shd* **Negotiation (IRE)** 3-9-3 0 JimmyFortune 9 70
(J H M Gosden) *prom: rdn and effrt 2f out: styd on same pce fnl f to press runner-up nr fin* **9/2**[3]

4 *½* **Danies Boy (IRE)** 3-9-3 0 DaneO'Neill 8 69
(R Hannon) *wl enough plcd on outer: effrt over 2f out: styd on fnl f to press plcd horses nr fin* **40/1**

3 **5** *1* **Azharia**[14] 810 3-8-12 0 NCallan 12 61
(C E Brittain) *prom: rdn over 2f out: no imp over 1f out: fdd ins fnl f* **9/1**

3- **6** *1 ½* **Time Medicean**[202] 5649 3-9-3 0 TonyCulhane 2 62+
(M R Channon) *sn trckd ldrs on outer: effrt over 2f out: no imp over 1f out: fdd ins fnl f* **14/1**

0- **7** *1* **Perfect Affair (USA)**[175] 6397 3-9-3 0 SebSanders 3 59+
(R M Beckett) *dwlt: wl in rr on outer: pushed along and v green over 2f out: styd on fnl f: nrst fin* **12/1**

33 **8** *1 ¾* **L'Arco Baleno (IRE)**[13] 820 3-8-5 0 HollyHall[(7)] 14 49
(S A Callaghan) *sn towards rr: sme prog and pushed along 2f out but outpcd by ldrs: no hdwy fnl f* **50/1**

30- **9** *½* **Do Be Brave (IRE)**[169] 6552 3-9-3 0 PaulEddery 13 53
(Paul Mason) *t.k.h early: hld up in midfield on inner: outpcd 2f out: fdd* **100/1**

10 *1 ¾* **Secret Hero** 3-9-3 0 PatDobbs 7 48
(R Hannon) *s.s: detached in last and pushed along: kpt on fnl 2f: nvr nrr* **40/1**

2- **11Dnse** **Pedasus (USA)**[166] 6621 3-9-3 0 RobertWinston 10 48
(T Keddy) *nvr gng wl: mostly in midfield: no prog u.p over 2f out: subs disq* **11/4**[2]

11 *1 ¼* **Rebel Woman** 3-8-12 0 ShaneKelly 6 40
(J A Osborne) *awkward to load in stalls and restless in them: dwlt: towards rr: midfield over 2f out: sn outpcd: wknd fnl f: fin 11th, plcd 12th* **10/1**

12 *nk* **Cape Melody** 3-8-12 0 SteveDrowne 1 39
(H Morrison) *sn struggling wl in rr: 13th and rdn 3f out: kpt on last 150yds: fin 13th, plcd 12th* **100/1**

3 **13** *9* **Sadaska**[58] 298 3-8-12 0 SaleemGolam 4 15
(S C Williams) *dwlt: a in rr: wknd 2f out: t.o: fin 14th, plcd 13th* **66/1**

1m 26.56s (0.56) **Going Correction** +0.10s/f (Slow) **14** Ran SP% **123.2**
Speed ratings (Par 98): **100,98,98,97,96 95,93,91,91,89 89,87,87,77**
toteswinger: 1&2 £7.50, 1&3 £2.70, 2&3 £29.50. CSF £69.31 TOTE £4.00: £1.20, £10.00, £1.70; EX 89.50.
Owner R J Arculli **Bred** James Waldron **Trained** Lambourn, Berks

FOCUS
A fair maiden featuring a very lively market, a couple with proven ability and some interesting newcomers. Pedasus was subsequently disqualified having tested positive for a prohibited substance.
Pedasus(USA) Official explanation: jockey said colt ran flat

952 DIGIBET CASINO H'CAP 1m 4f (P)
8:20 (8:24) (Class 4) (0-80,80) 4-Y-0+ **£4,727** (£1,406; £702; £351) **Stalls** Centre

Form RPR
0212 **1** **Phoenix Flight (IRE)**[5] 899 4-9-0 **76** SebSanders 4 85+
(Sir Mark Prescott) *hld up in 5th: smooth prog 4f out to ld over 2f out: kicked 3 l clr over 1f out: hrd rdn fnl f: jst lasted* **4/5**[1]

115- **2** *nk* **Right Stuff (FR)**[132] 5900 6-8-13 **73** JimCrowley 1 84+
(G L Moore) *dwlt: hld up in 7th: gng easily over 2f out: nt clr run briefly sn after: prog over 1f out: wnt 2nd ins fnl f and clsng fast on wnr fin* **14/1**

122- **3** *1 ¾* **Soundbyte**[152] 6948 4-8-11 **73** FergusSweeney 6 79
(J Gallagher) *trckd ldrs: effrt over 2f out: chsd wnr wl over 1f out but no imp: lost 2nd ins fnl f* **11/2**[2]

-625 **4** *¾* **Clear Reef**[64] 226 5-9-6 **80** PatCosgrave 5 85
(Jane Chapple-Hyam) *dwlt: hld up in 6th: drvn over 2f out: sme prog to dispute 3rd over 1f out: one pce after* **8/1**[3]

-130 **5** *3 ½* **Aphrodisia**[14] 798 5-8-9 **69** StephenDonohoe 7 69
(Ian Williams) *s.s: hld up in last: effrt and drvn over 2f out: modest prog over 1f out: no ch* **9/1**

20-2 **6** *4 ½* **Wait For The Light**[9] 848 5-8-10 **70** SteveDrowne 3 63
(Mrs S Leech) *chsd ldr to 5f out: sn pushed along: struggling over 2f out* **16/1**

4211 **7** *nk* **Eseej (USA)**[22] 745 4-9-2 **78** TGMcLaughlin 8 70
(P W Hiatt) *t.k.h early: led to over 2f out: sn wknd* **9/1**

0103 **8** *6* **Imperial Harry**[9] 848 6-8-13 **73** DaneO'Neill 2 56
(D E Pipe) *t.k.h early: prom: wnt 2nd 5f out to wl over 2f out: wknd tamely* **12/1**

2m 34.49s (-0.01) **Going Correction** +0.10s/f (Slow)
WFA 4 from 5yo+ 2lb **8** Ran SP% **122.3**
Speed ratings (Par 105): **104,103,102,102,99 96,96,92**
toteswinger: 1&2 £5.20, 1&3 £2.20, 2&3 £14.30. CSF £16.09 CT £47.04 TOTE £2.20: £1.10, £3.90, £2.10; EX 24.00.
Owner W E Sturt - Osborne House Iv **Bred** Airlie Stud And Sir Thomas Pilkington **Trained** Newmarket, Suffolk
■ The first winner for Seb Sanders since he broke his leg last August.

FOCUS
A reasonable handicap. The level looks reliable and the first two rate better than the bare form.

953 DAY TIME, NIGHT TIME, GREAT TIME H'CAP 1m 4f (P)
8:50 (8:57) (Class 6) (0-60,60) 3-Y-0 **£2,047** (£604; £302) **Stalls** Centre

Form RPR
000- **1** **Ermyn Lodge**[147] 7069 3-9-4 **60** IanMongan 11 62
(P M Phelan) *sn trckd ldr: narrow ld 2f out: hrd pressed after: battled on and jst hld on* **5/1**[3]

300- **2** *hd* **Mekong Miss**[160] 6761 3-9-3 **59** LukeMorris 12 61
(J Jay) *cl up on inner: sltly checked bnd over 8f out: pressed wnr over 1f out: persistent chal fnl f: jst hld* **16/1**

-053 **3** *¾* **Spring Quartet**[28] 677 3-8-11 **53** (v) PaulEddery 2 55+
(Pat Eddery) *dwlt: hld up in rr: checked bnd over 8f out and dropped to last pair: prog over 2f out: wnt 3rd u.p 1f out and threatened to chal: nt qckn last 100yds* **8/1**

0-42 **4** *nk* **Good Buy Dubai (USA)**[42] 506 3-9-3 **59** (t) RobertWinston 5 59+
(J R Best) *nvr gng fluently in last trio in messy affair: effrt over 2f out: keeping on whn nt clr run 1f out: styd on last 150yds* **13/8**[1]

-040 **5** *1* **Screaming Brave**[28] 677 3-8-13 **55** (v[1]) TonyCulhane 1 54
(M R Channon) *hld up in last pair in muddling r: effrt on outer 3f out: chsd ldrs 1f out: kpt on same pce after* **12/1**

0-00 **6** *¾* **Wahan (USA)**[33] 620 3-8-13 **55** NCallan 4 53
(C E Brittain) *hld up in midfield on outer: effrt over 2f out: cl enough jst over 1f out: one pce after* **10/1**

61 **7** *nse* **Soul Singer**[28] 670 3-9-0 **56** .... NickyMackay 3 53
(J G Portman) *hld up in midfield: rdn and nt qckn 2f out: one pce and no imp after* **14/1**

0-32 **8** *½* **Strikemaster (IRE)**[28] 677 3-8-13 **55** .... SteveDrowne 9 52
(J W Hills) *sn led at modest pce: rel to r bnd over 8f out: hdd 2f out: fdd* **7/2**[2]

6504 **9** *½* **Fleur De'Lion (IRE)**[21] 759 3-8-1 **46** oh1 .... DavidProbert(3) 8 42
(S Kirk) *w ldrs on outer: upsides over 2f out: fdd over 1f out* **12/1**

045 **10** *½* **Alittlemoreflair**[19] 779 3-9-4 **60** .... JimmyQuinn 10 55
(J Pearce) *dwlt: sn midfield: checked bnd over 8f out: effrt on inner over 2f out: nt qckn over 1f out: no imp after* **25/1**

000- **11** *6* **Guilin (IRE)**[187] 6081 3-8-4 **46** oh1 .... WilliamBuick 7 31
(P F I Cole) *hld up towards rr: wknd over 2f out: sn bhd* **12/1**

2m 38.89s (4.39) **Going Correction** +0.10s/f (Slow) **11** Ran SP% **136.7**
Speed ratings (Par 96): **89,88,88,88,87 87,86,86,86,85 81**
toteswinger: 1&2 £15.90, 1&3 £13.00, 2&3 £62.90. CSF £96.13 CT £670.72 TOTE £5.80: £2.10, £5.40, £2.30; EX 80.40.
Owner Ermyn Lodge Stud & Heatherwold Stud **Bred** Horizon Bloodstock Limited **Trained** Epsom, Surrey
■ Stewards' Enquiry : Paul Eddery two-day ban: used whip with excessive frequency (Apr 8-9)

FOCUS
A weak handicap. They finished in a heap and the form looks dubious.
Ermyn Lodge ◆ Official explanation: trainer said, regarding the apparent improvement in form, that last year the colt was big and weak, but had benefited from a long break and being gelded.

954 PANORAMIC BAR & RESTAURANT H'CAP 6f (P)
9:20 (9:27) (Class 4) (0-80,80) 4-Y-0+ **£4,727** (£1,406; £702; £351) **Stalls** High

Form RPR

111- **1** **Al Gillani (IRE)**[181] 6225 4-9-1 **77** .... GeorgeBaker 8 92+
(J R Boyle) *trckd ldng pair: wnt 2nd over 2f out: led over 1f out: sn rdn clr: v readily* **7/4**[1]

1440 **2** *3¼* **Resplendent Alpha**[5] 892 5-9-4 **80** .... JimmyQuinn 2 85
(P Howling) *dwlt: hld up in 6th and off the pce: prog wl over 1f out: wnt 2nd last 100yds but wnr already clr* **7/1**[3]

025- **3** *½* **Peter Island (FR)**[153] 6925 6-9-1 **77** .... (v) JimCrowley 5 81
(J Gallagher) *led at str pce: hdd over 1f out: grad fdd* **7/1**[3]

/04- **4** *1* **Stanley Goodspeed**[126] 7390 6-9-4 **80** .... JamesDoyle 4 81
(J W Hills) *stdd s: hld up in 7th and wl off the pce: asked for effrt over 2f out but limited rspnse: kpt on to take 4th wl ins fnl f* **10/1**

1-16 **5** *1* **Milne Bay (IRE)**[63] 241 4-8-4 **73** .... (t) JosephineBruning(7) 6 71
(D M Simcock) *chsd ldrs in 5th: nt qckn over 2f out: no imp after* **9/2**[2]

40-4 **6** *½* **Charles Darwin (IRE)**[11] 843 6-8-7 **69** .... LPKeniry 3 65
(M Blanshard) *chsd ldng trio: u.p over 2f out: steadily fdd* **20/1**

0313 **7** *5* **Brandywell Boy (IRE)**[7] 870 6-8-3 **72** .... BillyCray(7) 7 53
(D J S Ffrench Davis) *outpcd in last: bmpd along and no prog on wd outside over 2f out* **12/1**

5311 **8** *2½* **Super Frank (IRE)**[11] 843 6-9-4 **80** .... (p) JoeFanning 1 54
(J Akehurst) *unable to ld: chsd ldr to over 2f out: wknd rapidly* **9/2**[2]

1m 11.63s (-1.47) **Going Correction** +0.10s/f (Slow) **8** Ran SP% **119.3**
Speed ratings (Par 105): **113,108,108,106,105 104,98,94**
toteswinger: 1&2 £2.30, 1&3 £6.30, 2&3 £11.60. CSF £15.65 CT £72.59 TOTE £2.60: £1.40, £1.80, £2.10; EX 19.20 Place 6: £39.43, Place 5: £34.77..
Owner The Paddock Space Partnership **Bred** Sean Finnegan **Trained** Epsom, Surrey

FOCUS
A reasonable handicap. The time was 0.67sec quicker than standard. The progressive winner completed a five-timer in impressive fashion.
T/Plt: £110.80 to a £1 stake. Pool: £100,703.06. 662.97 winning tickets. T/Qpdt: £42.00 to a £1 stake. Pool: £8,353.99. 146.96 winning tickets. JN

943 LINGFIELD (L-H)
Wednesday, March 25

OFFICIAL GOING: Standard
Wind: Strong, half against Weather: Blustery, with showers at times

955 PREMIER SHOWFREIGHT (S) STKS 5f (P)
2:20 (2:21) (Class 6) 3-Y-O **£2,047** (£604; £302) **Stalls** High

Form RPR

2120 **1** **Speak The Truth (IRE)**[18] 784 3-9-4 67 .... (p) PatCosgrave 8 64
(J R Boyle) *in tch on outer: rdn and outpcd 2f out: hdwy over 1f out: chsd ldrs ins fnl f: r.o strly to ld towards fin* **5/2**[1]

5-54 **2** *1* **The Cuckoo**[38] 560 3-9-4 66 .... MartinDwyer 5 60
(M Quinn) *sn led: pushed clr wl over 1f out: rdn fnl f: hdd and no ex towards fin* **10/3**[2]

-024 **3** *1¼* **Fasliyanne (IRE)**[27] 686 3-8-7 52 .... (b) AlanMunro 4 45
(K A Ryan) *chsd ldrs tl hmpd and snatched up after 1f: bhd after: hdwy u.p over 1f out: swtchd rt jst ins fnl f: r.o to go 3rd fnl 100yds: no ch w ldng pair* **6/1**[3]

60-5 **4** *1¼* **Piccaso's Sky**[56] 316 3-8-12 50 .... NCallan 10 45
(A B Haynes) *hld up in midfield: rdn and effrt ent fnl 2f out: sn outpcd by ldr: plugged on same pce fnl f* **14/1**

00 **5** *hd* **Little Lost (IRE)**[21] 758 3-8-8 0 ow1 .... ShaneKelly 2 41
(J A Osborne) *in tch in midfield: hdwy to chse ldrs and rdn 2f out: sn unable qck and one pce after* **16/1**

4206 **6** *½* **Just The Lady**[14] 804 3-8-13 58 .... AdrianTNicholls 7 44
(D Nicholls) *broke wl: chsd ldr: rdn and outpcd wl over 1f out: lost 2nd ins fnl f: wknd* **7/1**

-404 **7** *1¼* **Readily**[49] 390 3-8-13 48 .... JamesDoyle 3 39
(J G Portman) *chsd ldrs tl struggling and lost pl 1/2-way: no hdwy u.p over 1f out* **9/1**

05 **8** *¾* **Geese A Laying (IRE)**[46] 447 3-8-7 0 .... FrankieMcDonald 9 31
(J A Osborne) *sn outpcd in rr: rdn 3f out: c wd bnd 2f out: nvr a factor* **66/1**

5566 **9** *1¾* **Ruby Tallulah**[5] 889 3-8-13 57 .... LPKeniry 1 30
(C R Dore) *dwlt: sn pushed up to chse ldrs on inner: rdn and wknd wl over 1f out* **13/2**

-040 **10** *1* **Yes She Can Can**[14] 804 3-8-7 34 .... KirstyMilczarek 6 21
(Peter Grayson) *a bhd: nvr a factor* **80/1**

59.43 secs (0.63) **Going Correction** -0.025s/f (Stan) **10** Ran SP% **117.0**
Speed ratings (Par 96): **93,91,89,87,87 86,84,83,80,78**
toteswinger: 1&2 £3.20, 1&3 £4.50, 2&3 £4.50. CSF £10.75 TOTE £3.40: £1.50, £1.80, £2.00; EX 10.50 Trifecta £42.50 Pool: £426.17 - 7.41 winning units..There was no bid for the winner.
Owner John Hopkins (t/a South Hatch Racing) **Bred** Gerard Mulligan **Trained** Epsom, Surrey

FOCUS
A typically modest seller, run at a sound pace. The winner was fully entitled to win this if at his best.

956 OYSTER PARTNERSHIP H'CAP 5f (P)
2:50 (2:54) (Class 6) (0-65,65) 4-Y-0+ **£2,047** (£604; £302) **Stalls** High

Form RPR

00-1 **1** **The Magic Blanket (IRE)**[79] 46 4-8-10 **57** .... TPQueally 2 76+
(Stef Liddiard) *sn clr w ldr: led 2f out: clr ent fnl f easily* **4/1**[2]

3354 **2** *2¾* **Bluebok**[31] 645 8-8-13 **60** .... (bt) LPKeniry 6 69
(J M Bradley) *chsd clr ldng pair: rdn 3f out: chsd wnr ins fnl f: no imp* **8/1**

00-6 **3** *1¼* **The Lord**[22] 742 9-8-11 **63** .... JackDean(5) 3 68
(W G M Turner) *outpcd in midfield: hdwy u.p over 1f out: wnt 3rd ins fnl f: nvr nr enough to chal wnr* **10/1**

2150 **4** *2* **Fizzlephut (IRE)**[7] 861 7-9-0 **61** .... (b) PaulFitzsimons 8 58
(Miss J R Tooth) *taken down early: bhd: wd bnd 2f out: styd on fnl f: nvr nr ldrs* **16/1**

4010 **5** *2* **Teen Ager (FR)**[12] 832 5-8-12 **59** .... JimmyQuinn 10 49
(P Burgoyne) *stdd and dropped in after s: wl bhd: hdwy and nt clr run 1f out: sn swtchd lft: styd on but n.d* **15/2**[3]

-000 **6** *½* **Brazilian Brush (IRE)**[23] 739 4-8-5 **57** .... MCGeran(5) 9 45
(J M Bradley) *a outpcd towards rr: nvr on terms* **20/1**

030- **7** *1* **Another Socket**[135] 7276 4-9-4 **65** .... GrahamGibbons 4 50
(E S McMahon) *s.i.s: sn bustled up into midfield: nvr nr ldrs* **8/1**

500- **8** *1¼* **Smokin Beau**[146] 7092 12-9-4 **65** .... JimCrowley 5 45
(N P Littmoden) *outpcd in 4th pl: wknd wl over 1f out* **25/1**

20/5 **9** *1¼* **Martingrange Boy (IRE)**[6] 884 4-9-4 **65** .... (t) RobertWinston 1 41
(J Balding) *led and clr w wnr tl hdd 2f out: wknd qckly u.p ent fnl f* **7/2**[1]

1450 **10** *2½* **Mudhish (IRE)**[15] 793 4-9-4 **65** .... (b) NCallan 7 32
(C E Brittain) *hmpd and snatched up sn after s: a outpcd in rr* **7/2**[1]

58.38 secs (-0.42) **Going Correction** -0.025s/f (Stan) **10** Ran SP% **122.0**
Speed ratings (Par 101): **102,97,95,92,89 88,86,84,82,78**
toteswinger: 1&2 £3.80, 1&3 £7.60, 2&3 £16.00. CSF £38.03 CT £307.95 TOTE £3.60: £1.40, £2.10, £3.20; EX 15.90 Trifecta £112.30 Pool: £519.35 - 3.42 winning units..
Owner David Gilbert **Bred** Mrs M Shenkin **Trained** Great Shefford, Berks

FOCUS
This was a moderate sprint handicap, run at a very strong pace. The winner looks an improved performer and the placed horses help set the standard.
Teen Ager(FR) Official explanation: jockey said gelding was denied a clear run

957 RUDRIDGE MAIDEN STKS 1m 4f (P)
3:20 (3:21) (Class 5) 3-Y-0+ **£2,729** (£806; £403) **Stalls** Low

Form RPR

0- **1** **Sehoy (USA)**[237] 4570 3-8-4 0 .... NickyMackay 3 77+
(J H M Gosden) *led at stdy gallop: hung bdly rt and hdd bnd 2f out: rallied jst over 1f out: led ins fnl f: styd on* **11/4**[1]

230- **2** *½* **Chilly Filly (IRE)**[156] 6857 3-7-13 74 .... JimmyQuinn 5 69+
(M Johnston) *t.k.h: chsd wnr for 3f: styd handy: lft cl 3rd wl over 1f out: ev ch jst ins fnl f: unable qck towards fin* **11/4**[1]

042 **3** *nk* **El Bravo**[12] 824 3-8-4 71 .... WilliamBuick 4 73
(G L Moore) *t.k.h: hld up in tch: hdwy on inner 3f out: lft in ld wl over 1f out: sn rdn: hdd and no ex ins fnl f* **3/1**[2]

05- **4** *2½* **Some Time Good (IRE)**[182] 6199 3-8-4 0 .... JoeFanning 2 69
(M R Channon) *t.k.h: chsd wnr after 3f tl carried v wd and lost pl bnd 2f out: hung lft and kpt on same pce fr over 1f out* **4/1**[3]

0565 **5** *½* **Suhailah**[12] 824 3-7-13 63 .... LukeMorris 9 63
(M J Attwater) *t.k.h: hld up in tch: lft cl 2nd wl over 1f out: ev ch u.p ent fnl f: wknd ins fnl f* **25/1**

6 **6** *16* **Follow The Dream**[19] 779 6-9-7 0 .... AlanMunro 7 38+
(Karen George) *stdd s: t.k.h: hld up in tch: hdwy to chse ldrs over 5f out: wknd qckly wl over 1f out* **33/1**

0 **7** *4½* **Living The Dream**[19] 779 7-9-12 0 .... (p) TGMcLaughlin 1 35+
(Karen George) *stdd s: hld up in tch in rr: wknd qckly jst over 2f out* **66/1**

8 *15* **Ok Katie**[162] 6-9-7 0 .... SebSanders 6 6+
(R M Beckett) *t.k.h: hld up in tch: hdwy on outer over 3f out: nt handle bnd and lost pl jst over 2f out: sn eased* **14/1**

2m 36.18s (3.18) **Going Correction** -0.025s/f (Stan)
WFA 3 from 4yo 22lb 4 from 6yo+ 2lb **8** Ran SP% **113.3**
Speed ratings (Par 103): **88,87,87,85,85 74,71,61**
toteswinger: 1&2 £3.40, 1&3 £2.30, 2&3 £2.10. CSF £10.34 TOTE £3.70: £1.40, £1.80, £1.30; EX 15.00 Trifecta £65.40 Pool: £493.01 - 5.57 winning units..
Owner George Strawbridge **Bred** George Strawbridge **Trained** Newmarket, Suffolk

FOCUS
A fair maiden, albeit a bit messy, and the winner is value for plenty further. The form seems to make sense.
Suhailah Official explanation: jockey said filly hung right on final bend

958 NICHOLAS HALL CLAIMING STKS 1m (P)
3:50 (3:50) (Class 6) 4-Y-0+ **£2,047** (£604; £302) **Stalls** High

Form RPR

-121 **1** **Dichoh**[20] 765 6-8-11 80 .... (tp) FBranca 1 79
(F Sheridan) *mde all: hrd pressed ins fnl f: hld on wl* **15/8**[2]

32-1 **2** *hd* **Fremen (USA)**[4] 910 9-9-7 82 .... AdrianTNicholls 5 88
(D Nicholls) *s.i.s: hld up in last pl: hdwy 2f out: edgd sltly lft 1f out: ev ch and rdn ins fnl f: nt qckn nr fin* **5/4**[1]

4101 **3** *1* **Smokey Rye**[1] 945 4-8-2 66 ow6 .... MatthewDavies(7) 2 74
(George Baker) *flashed tail at times: disp 2nd pl: stuck on rail and nt clr run fr over 1f out: swtchd rt ins fnl f: styd on but nvr able to chal* **4/1**[3]

4-50 **4** *10* **Magnitude**[39] 544 4-9-1 75 .... GeorgeBaker 4 68+
(G L Moore) *disp 2nd pl: niggled along fr over 4f out: rdn 2f out: keeping on same and looked btn whn bdly hmpd and snatched up 1f out: eased after* **8/1**

1m 37.91s (-0.29) **Going Correction** -0.025s/f (Stan) **4** Ran SP% **110.3**
Speed ratings (Par 101): **100,99,98,88**
CSF £4.73 TOTE £2.20; EX 3.80.Dichoh was claimed by Rae Guest for £11,000.
Owner Frank Sheridan **Bred** Red House Stud **Trained** Stoke Heath, Shropshire
■ Stewards' Enquiry : Matthew Davies three-day ban: careless riding (Apr 8-9,11)

FOCUS
A good-quality little claimer with three last-time-out winners in attendance.

Smokey Rye Official explanation: jockey said filly was denied a clear run

959 H & V SERVICEPLAN H'CAP — 1m (P)
4:20 (4:20) (Class 6) (0-65,65) 4-Y-0+ £2,047 (£604; £302) Stalls High

Form — RPR

06/2 **1** **Kilburn**[81] 25 5-9-4 **65** .... SteveDrowne 6 76+
(A J Lidderdale) *chsd ldng pair: rdn 2f out: drvn to ld ins fnl f: sn clr: comf* **7/1**[3]

-326 **2** 2 ½ **Fine Ruler (IRE)**[24] 725 5-9-3 **64** .... GeorgeBaker 7 69
(M R Bosley) *stdd s: hld up wl bhd: hdwy ent fnl f: r.o to go 2nd fnl 100yds: no ch w wnr* **7/1**[3]

4603 **3** 1 ¾ **Lord Theo**[14] 807 5-9-3 **64** .... (b[1]) LukeMorris 9 65
(N P Littmoden) *chsd ldr: rdn over 2f out: hrd rdn and ev ch briefly jst ins fnl f: sn no ch w wnr* **5/1**[2]

20-6 **4** nse **Diego Rivera**[70] 157 4-9-2 **63** .... FergusSweeney 4 64
(P J Makin) *racd in midfield: rdn and effrt wl over 1f out: kpt on fnl f: nvr nr wnr* **12/1**

414- **5** nk **Ermine Grey**[257] 3903 8-9-1 **62** .... KirstyMilczarek 3 62
(S Gollings) *racd in midfield: rdn and struggling over 3f out: kpt on u.p fnl f: nvr pce to threaten ldrs* **14/1**

540- **6** nk **Seneschal**[164] 6671 8-8-6 **60** .... PNolan(7) 8 60
(A B Haynes) *led: clr 4f out: rdn over 1f out: hdd ins fnl f: wknd fnl 100yds* **25/1**

504- **7** hd **Jo'Burg (USA)**[154] 6908 5-9-4 **65** .... SebSanders 1 64+
(Lady Herries) *stdd s: hld up in rr: swtchd ins and effrt over 1f out: n.d* **9/2**[1]

0-40 **8** ½ **Wrighty Almighty (IRE)**[13] 813 7-9-0 **61** .... JimCrowley 2 59
(P R Chamings) *chsd ldrs: rdn over 3f out: wknd u.p over 1f out* **11/1**

4332 **9** nk **Bobski (IRE)**[37] 569 7-9-4 **65** .... (p) NCallan 10 63
(Miss Gay Kelleway) *t.k.h: hld up towards rr: nvr trbld ldrs* **8/1**

-454 **10** 2 ¼ **Moayed**[7] 867 10-8-11 **58** .... (b) ShaneKelly 11 51
(N P Littmoden) *s.i.s: hld up in rr: n.d* **12/1**

-330 **11** 11 **Ede's Dot Com (IRE)**[14] 799 5-8-13 **60** .... IanMongan 12 28+
(P M Phelan) *stdd s: hld up towards rr: hdwy on outer 3f out: wknd over 1f out: eased whn btn ins fnl f* **12/1**

0-14 **12** 3 ¼ **Herbert Crescent**[36] 580 4-9-2 **63** .... JamieMoriarty 5 24+
(Ollie Pears) *racd in midfield: rdn and struggling wl over 2f out: bhd whn short of room wl over 1f out: wl bhd whn eased ins fnl f* **14/1**

1m 37.06s (-1.14) **Going Correction** -0.025s/f (Stan) **12** Ran SP% **119.5**
Speed ratings (Par 101): **104,101,99,99,99 99,98,98,98,95 84,81**
toteswinger: 1&2 £13.50, 1&3 £6.40, 2&3 £10.00. CSF £55.90 CT £271.66 TOTE £8.80: £2.00, £3.20, £2.20; EX 59.60 Trifecta £197.00 Part won. Pool: £266.27 - 0.56 winning units..
Owner Mrs A Lidderdale **Bred** B Walters **Trained** Eastbury, Berks

FOCUS
A modest handicap, but a competitive one and they went a very decent pace. The winner built on his promising return and the second sets the standard.

960 TAGWORLDWIDE.COM H'CAP — 7f (P)
4:50 (4:50) (Class 5) (0-70,70) 3-Y-0 £2,729 (£806; £403) Stalls Low

Form — RPR

651- **1** **Mr Willis**[84] 7833 3-8-12 **64** .... SteveDrowne 7 74+
(J R Best) *hld up in tch in midfield: short of room briefly 2f out: sn swtchd rt and hdwy: rdn to ld ins fnl f: r.o wl* **7/4**[1]

145- **2** 1 ¼ **Cumana Bay**[132] 7306 3-9-4 **70** .... PatDobbs 2 75
(R Hannon) *in tch: rdn and effrt on inner ent fnl f: chsd wnr fnl 100yds: kpt on but nt pce to threaten wnr* **9/1**

03-1 **3** ½ **Sarasota Sunshine**[29] 667 3-8-10 **62** .... ShaneKelly 5 66
(N P Littmoden) *hld up in last pair: c wd bnd 2f out: r.o u.p fnl f to go 3rd wl ins fnl f: nt trble wnr* **5/1**[3]

-352 **4** 1 **Spinight (IRE)**[12] 827 3-8-6 **63** .... (p) AndreaAtzeni(5) 1 64
(M Botti) *t.k.h: chsd ldr tl led 5f out: rdn over 1f out: hdd ins fnl f: no ex and lost 2 pls fnl 100yds* **8/1**

0-12 **5** ½ **Perfect Class**[28] 673 3-8-12 **64** .... AdamKirby 3 64
(C G Cox) *hld up in last pair: rdn and effrt over 1f out: no imp fnl f* **3/1**[2]

4122 **6** ½ **Imperial Skylight**[12] 826 3-8-10 **67** .... MCGeran(5) 6 65
(M R Channon) *t.k.h: led tl 5f out: chsd ldr after tl ent fnl f: wknd fnl 100yds* **11/2**

0300 **7** 7 **Commandingpresence (USA)**[12] 829 3-8-11 **63** ......(p) JamesDoyle 8 42
(Ms J S Doyle) *t.k.h: sn chsd ldng pair: rdn over 2f out: wknd over 1f out* **33/1**

1m 24.24s (-0.56) **Going Correction** -0.025s/f (Stan) **7** Ran SP% **117.5**
Speed ratings (Par 98): **102,100,100,98,98 97,89**
toteswinger: 1&2 £4.60, 1&3 £3.20, 2&3 £7.10. CSF £19.61 CT £68.94 TOTE £2.60: £1.70, £3.50; EX 24.20 Trifecta £207.00 Pool: £447.70 - 1.60 winning units..
Owner Miss Sara Furnival **Bred** John Best **Trained** Hucking, Kent

FOCUS
A modest 3yo handicap, but it was competitive and the form looks sound for the class. The winner is progressive.

961 COUNTRYSIDE CARNIVAL HERE THIS SATURDAY H'CAP — 7f (P)
5:20 (5:20) (Class 6) (0-65,65) 4-Y-0+ £2,047 (£604; £302) Stalls Low

Form — RPR

-023 **1** **Shaded Edge**[11] 844 5-8-10 **57** .... MartinDwyer 5 66
(D W P Arbuthnot) *chsd ldrs: rdn to ld ent fnl f: r.o wl and in command fnl 100yds* **3/1**[1]

06-5 **2** 2 **Lord Deevert**[58] 297 4-8-10 **62** .... JackDean(5) 1 66
(W G M Turner) *chsd ldr tl rdn to ld on inner 2f out: edgd rt u.p over 1f out: hdd ent fnl f: hld on for 2nd but wl hld by wnr after* **16/1**

-432 **3** ½ **Ever Cheerful**[11] 844 8-8-9 **63** .... (p) PNolan(7) 4 66
(A B Haynes) *sn led: rdn and hdd 2f out: stl ev ch tl nt pce of wnr fnl f: kpt on* **5/1**[2]

42-0 **4** hd **Comrade Cotton**[49] 395 5-8-8 **55** .... (p) KirstyMilczarek 6 57
(J Ryan) *hld up towards rr: hdwy on outer over 1f out: styd on ins fnl f: nt rch ldrs* **6/1**[3]

-215 **5** 1 ½ **Smirfys Systems**[21] 757 10-9-3 **64** .... GrahamGibbons 7 63
(E S McMahon) *in tch on outer: rdn and effrt over 1f out: drvn and one pce fnl f* **6/1**[3]

0-40 **6** ¾ **Free Tussy (ARG)**[14] 803 5-8-10 **57** .... (bt) FergusSweeney 11 54
(G L Moore) *stdd and dropped in bhd after s: hld up bhd: hdwy on inner wl over 1f out: kpt on: nvr nr ldrs* **14/1**

6433 **7** shd **Cavalry Guard (USA)**[21] 749 5-7-13 **51** oh2 .... (b) AmyBaker(5) 9 47
(T D McCarthy) *styd wd: a towards rr: n.d* **8/1**

6000 **8** 1 **Pharaohs Justice (USA)**[7] 867 4-8-6 **60** .... (b) AlexOwen(7) 8 54
(N P Littmoden) *hld up towards rr: n.d* **33/1**

2526 **9** nk **Loyal Royal (IRE)**[14] 803 6-8-12 **59** .... (b) LPKeniry 2 52
(J M Bradley) *t.k.h: hld up in midfield: rdn jst over 2f out: drvn and wknd ent fnl f* **9/1**

0400 **10** 2 ¾ **Shake On It**[4] 910 5-9-3 **64** .... (t) PatCosgrave 3 50
(M J Gingell) *chsd ldrs: rdn and fnd nil 2f out: wknd over 1f out* **11/1**

00-0 **11** 2 ¾ **Wee Buns**[14] 799 4-9-4 **65** .... TGMcLaughlin 10 44
(P Burgoyne) *swtchd lft sn after s: hld up towards rr: sme hdwy over 3f out: rdn and struggling over 2f out: no ch fnl f* **66/1**

1m 23.89s (-0.91) **Going Correction** -0.025s/f (Stan) **11** Ran SP% **116.7**
Speed ratings (Par 101): **104,101,101,100,99 98,98,97,96,93 90**
toteswinger: 1&2 £13.30, 1&3 £2.70, 2&3 £16.70. CSF £54.83 CT £235.52 TOTE £4.60: £1.50, £3.40, £1.70; EX 45.40 Trifecta £266.80 Pool: £382.25 - 1.06 winning units..
Owner P M Claydon **Bred** Lady Whent **Trained** Compton, Berks

FOCUS
A weak handicap which was run at a fair pace yet nothing landed a serious blow from behind. The winner is rated back to his best.
Loyal Royal(IRE) Official explanation: jockey said gelding ran too free
Shake On It Official explanation: jockey said gelding hung right in straight

962 ASHFORD ENVIRONMENTAL H'CAP — 1m 2f (P)
5:50 (5:50) (Class 5) (0-75,75) 3-Y-0 £2,729 (£806; £403) Stalls Low

Form — RPR

213 **1** **Eastern Aria (UAE)**[20] 763 3-9-4 **75** .... JoeFanning 3 83+
(M Johnston) *sn led: mde rest: rdn over 1f out: hrd pressed ins fnl f: hld on gamely* **9/4**[1]

-341 **2** nse **Diamond Twister (USA)**[40] 529 3-9-2 **73** .... (t) RobertWinston 4 78+
(J R Best) *trckd ldrs: hdwy over 2f out: rdn over 1f out: str chal ins fnl f: jst hld* **10/3**[2]

4-22 **3** 2 ¼ **Black N Brew (USA)**[49] 389 3-9-3 **74** .... SteveDrowne 6 74
(J R Best) *t.k.h early: in tch: c wd bnd 2f out: styd on u.p ins fnl f to go 3rd last strides* **5/1**[3]

0-04 **4** hd **Squad**[42] 506 3-8-6 **63** .... NickyMackay 2 63
(S Dow) *hld up in tch: hdwy over 2f out: pressed wnr and drvn jst over 1f out: wknd fnl 100yds* **10/1**

0-46 **5** 1 ¼ **Sgt Roberts (IRE)**[12] 824 3-9-3 **74** .... LPKeniry 8 71
(J S Moore) *sn chsd wnr tl over 1f out: wknd u.p ins fnl f* **11/1**

530- **6** ½ **Mutually Mine (USA)**[228] 4870 3-9-2 **73** .... MickyFenton 9 69
(Mrs P Sly) *hld up in tch in last trio: rdn and effrt over 1f out: kpt on but nvr pce to threaten ldrs* **16/1**

1613 **7** 1 ¾ **True Britannia**[29] 662 3-8-3 **65** .... (v) AndreaAtzeni(5) 1 58
(A M Hales) *broke wl and led briefly: hld up in tch: effrt on inner 2f out: drvn and pressed ldr ent fnl f: wknd fnl f* **8/1**

3-21 **8** ¾ **Brer Rabbit**[23] 741 3-8-13 **70** .... MichaelHills 5 61
(B W Hills) *hld up in last pair: effrt on inner jst over 2f out: no hdwy fr over 1f out* **15/2**

4224 **9** ¾ **Hold The Bucks (USA)**[11] 839 3-8-13 **70** .... LukeMorris 7 60
(J S Moore) *hld up in last trio: rdn along over 3f out: struggling whn jostled jst over 2f out: n.d after* **10/1**

2m 7.97s (1.37) **Going Correction** -0.025s/f (Stan) **9** Ran SP% **125.8**
Speed ratings (Par 98): **93,92,91,91,90 89,88,87,87**
toteswinger: 1&2 £2.30, 1&3 £4.00, 2&3 £3.30. CSF £10.81 CT £36.50 TOTE £4.40: £1.60, £1.40, £1.90; EX 14.90 Trifecta £36.20 Pool: £577. 54 - 11.78 winning units. Place 6: £62.04, Place 5: £45.95..
Owner Sheikh Hamdan Bin Mohammed Al Maktoum **Bred** Darley **Trained** Middleham Moor, N Yorks

FOCUS
A modest 3yo handicap, run at an average pace and it proved an advantage to race handily. The first two are clearly going the right way and this form should work out.
Brer Rabbit Official explanation: jockey said filly was unsuited by the slow pace
T/Plt: £28.00 to a £1 stake. Pool: £61,923.40. 1,613.15 winning tickets. T/Qpdt: £13.50 to a £1 stake. Pool: £3,723.86. 203.40 winning tickets. SP

[918] SOUTHWELL (L-H)
Thursday, March 26

OFFICIAL GOING: Standard
Wind: Strong, behind Weather: Bright and sunny

963 MEMBERSHIP AT SOUTHWELL GOLF CLUB MEDIAN AUCTION MAIDEN STKS — 7f (F)
2:20 (2:20) (Class 6) 3-5-Y-0 £2,047 (£604; £302) Stalls Low

Form — RPR

0-2 **1** **True Decision**[12] 842 3-8-5 0 .... MatthewBirch(7) 8 68+
(S Kirk) *hld up in tch: hdwy on outer wl over 2f out: rdn to ld over 1f out: edgd lft ins fnl f: kpt on* **9/4**[2]

03- **2** nk **Oskari**[158] 6843 4-9-13 0 .... JamieMoriarty 3 70
(P T Midgley) *s.i.s: hdwy 1/2-way: rdn along and in tch wl over 2f out: styd on to chal ent fnl f: sn drvn and no ex* **14/1**

5- **3** 5 **Crystal Feather**[97] 7734 3-8-7 0 .... LPKeniry 2 47
(E F Vaughan) *trckd ldrs: hdwy on inner over 2f out: rdn and ev ch over 1f out: sn one pce* **18/1**

200- **4** nk **Jeremiah (IRE)**[187] 6118 3-8-12 74 .... NCallan 5 51
(J G Portman) *cl up: led after 2f: rdn along 2f out: drvn and hdd appr fnl f: sn wknd* **8/11**[1]

000- **5** 3 ¾ **Just Oscar (GER)**[133] 7178 5-9-13 45 .... TGMcLaughlin 6 41
(W M Brisbourne) *t.k.h: cl up: rdn along wl over 2f out and sn wknd* **66/1**

-423 **6** 6 **Le Petit Vigier**[34] 620 3-8-7 48 .... (t) AndrewElliott 1 20
(P Beaumont) *s.i.s: a bhd* **10/1**[3]

7 2 **Apache Moon** 3-8-12 0 .... J-PGuillambert 7 19
(R Curtis) *cl up: rdn along over 3f out: sn wknd* **14/1**

00-0 **8** 44 **Ronnies Girl**[16] 793 5-9-3 9 .... (v[1]) KellyHarrison(5) 4 —
(C J Teague) *t.k.h: led 2f: rdn along and wknd bef 1/2-way: sn bhd* **250/1**

1m 31.41s (1.11) **Going Correction** +0.175s/f (Slow)
WFA 3 from 4yo+ 15lb **8** Ran SP% **118.3**
Speed ratings (Par 101): **100,99,93,93,89 82,80,29**
toteswinger: 1&2 £6.30, 1&3 £7.10, 2&3 £9.30. CSF £34.68 TOTE £2.90: £1.50, £6.10, £3.60; EX 32.10 Trifecta £160.80 Pool £434.82 - 2.00 winning units..
Owner Dr B Matalon & T R Lock **Bred** T R Lock **Trained** Upper Lambourn, Berks

FOCUS
A weak maiden in which the favourite failed to give his running. Imptoved form from the runner-up.

964 SPONSOR A RACE AT SOUTHWELL (S) STKS 1m (F)
2:55 (2:55) (Class 6) 3-Y-O **£2,047** (£604; £302) **Stalls** Low

Form RPR

3531 **1** **Swiss Art (IRE)**[15] 808 3-9-5 63 .... JoeFanning 4 70+
(R A Harris) *trckd ldrs: hdwy to chse ldr over 3f out: led wl over 1f out: sn clr* **4/6**[1]

-033 **2** *5* **Amazing Blue Sky**[7] 883 3-9-5 62 .... (b) PaulMulrennan 6 53
(Mrs R A Carr) *led: rdn along over 2f out: drvn and hdd wl over 1f out: sn one pce* **11/4**[2]

00- **3** *14* **Avrilo**[117] 7498 3-8-9 0 .... TGMcLaughlin 1 12
(M S Saunders) *prom: rdn along 3f out: drvn 2f out and sn one pce* **100/1**

-104 **4** *½* **Cause For Applause (IRE)**[15] 808 3-9-0 56 .... (v) TomEaves 8 16
(B Smart) *chsd ldrs: rdn along 3f out: sn drvn and outpcd fnl 2f* **5/1**[3]

-200 **5** *6* **Yellow River (USA)**[30] 667 3-8-9 50 .... EdwardCreighton 2 —
(E J Creighton) *dwlt and in rr: rdn along and sme hdwy 3f out: nvr a factor* **20/1**

0-55 **6** *nk* **Incy Wincy**[35] 598 3-9-0 38 .... LukeMorris 5 2
(J M Bradley) *in tch: rdn along over 3f out and sn wknd* **16/1**

00-0 **7** *7* **Amatara (IRE)**[35] 598 3-8-9 38 .... DaleGibson 3 —
(B G Powell) *a in rr* **25/1**

0-60 **8** *6* **Flaming Ruby**[51] 379 3-8-4 35 .... KellyHarrison[(5)] 7 —
(N Tinkler) *chsd ldrs: rdn along 3f out and sn wknd* **25/1**

1m 46.01s (2.31) **Going Correction** +0.175s/f (Slow) **8** Ran SP% **122.6**
Speed ratings (Par 96): **95,90,76,75,69 69,62,56**
toteswinger: 1&2 £1.70, 1&3 £15.70, 2&3 £22.30. CSF £2.93 TOTE £1.70: £1.02, £1.20, £11.60; EX 3.00 Trifecta £190.20 Pool £727.55 - 2.83 winning units..There was no bid for the winner.
Owner W Clifford **Bred** John Yarr **Trained** Earlswood, Monmouths

FOCUS
A standard seller won easily by the favourite who was value for further. The race lacked strenth in depth.

965 HOSPITALITY AT SOUTHWELL RACECOURSE CLAIMING STKS 5f (F)
3:30 (3:30) (Class 6) 4-Y-O+ **£2,047** (£604; £302) **Stalls** High

Form RPR

122 **1** **Imprimis Tagula (IRE)**[3] 934 5-8-13 77 .... (v) RobertWinston 3 73
(A Bailey) *chsd ldrs: rdn along 1/2-way: drvn over 1f out: styd on u.p ins fnl f to ld nr fin* **2/1**[1]

0551 **2** *hd* **Spic 'n Span**[7] 884 4-8-13 61 .... (b) JoeFanning 2 72
(R A Harris) *led: rdn along over 1f out: jnd ent fnl f: sn drvn and edgd lft: hdd and no ex nr fin* **8/1**

4105 **3** *nk* **The Tatling (IRE)**[14] 821 12-9-2 87 .... JackDean[(5)] 6 79
(J M Bradley) *in tch: hdwy 1/2-way: chsd ldr wl over 1f out: rdn to chal ent fnl f and ev ch tl no ex towards fin* **11/4**[2]

3060 **4** *3* **Soopacal (IRE)**[6] 901 4-9-3 80 .... TomEaves 7 64
(B Smart) *prom on wd outside: rdn along 2f out and grad wknd appr fnl f* **4/1**[3]

3140 **5** *4 ½* **Back In The Red (IRE)**[22] 757 5-8-10 72 .... (b) KevinGhunowa[(3)] 4 44
(R A Harris) *prom: rdn along 1/2-way and sn wknd* **11/2**

410- **6** *7* **Yahwudhee (FR)**[256] 3999 4-8-9 80 .... DaleGibson 1 15
(M W Easterby) *dwlt and wnt lft s: a outpcd and bhd* **16/1**

57.99 secs (-1.71) **Going Correction** -0.275s/f (Stan) **6** Ran SP% **112.4**
Speed ratings (Par 101): **102,101,101,96,89 78**
toteswinger: 1&2 £2.40, 1&3 £1.90, 2&3 £4.10. CSF £18.37 TOTE £2.50: £1.30, £3.90; EX 9.10.
Owner A Bailey **Bred** Glashare House Stud **Trained** Newmarket, Suffolk
■ Stewards' Enquiry : Kevin Ghunowa caution: used whip when out of contention

FOCUS
Just £3,000 on offer in this claimer but a well above-average contest of its type. The form is best rated through the runner-up.
Soopacal(IRE) Official explanation: vet said gelding had bled from the nose

966 ALEA CASINO H'CAP 5f (F)
4:05 (4:05) (Class 5) (0-70,67) 3-Y-O **£2,729** (£806; £403) **Stalls** High

Form RPR

30-0 **1** **Captain Carey**[3] 936 3-9-2 65 .... TGMcLaughlin 1 79+
(M S Saunders) *dwlt and sn pushed along in rr: bhd and rdn 1/2-way: styd on u.p appr fnl f: led last 100yds: sn clr* **10/1**

34-3 **2** *2 ¼* **Dispol Grand (IRE)**[28] 685 3-9-4 67 .... JoeFanning 5 72
(P T Midgley) *cl up: effrt 2f out: rdn to ld over 1f out: sn drvn and hdd ins fnl f: one pce* **13/8**[1]

20-3 **3** *1* **Where's Reiley (USA)**[48] 429 3-9-2 65 .... (b[1]) PhillipMakin 6 66+
(T D Barron) *trckd ldrs on outer: smooth hdwy 1/2-way: rdn and ev ch over 1f out tl drvn and one pce ins fnl f* **6/1**[3]

-603 **4** *3* **You Avin A Laugh**[6] 889 3-8-11 60 .... PaulEddery 3 51
(C A Dwyer) *in tch and pushed along 1/2-way: rdn to chse ldrs over 1f out: sn drvn and one pce* **7/2**[2]

0204 **5** *nk* **Chimbonda**[6] 889 3-8-6 55 .... (v) WilliamBuick 2 45
(S Parr) *led: rdn along 2f out: drvn and hdd over 1f out: sn wknd* **7/1**

600- **6** *2 ¾* **Meydan Style (USA)**[117] 7501 3-8-4 53 oh2 .... AndrewElliott 4 33
(J Balding) *in tch: rdn along over 2f out and sn wknd* **50/1**

6021 **7** *1 ½* **Taurus Twins**[15] 804 3-8-13 62 .... RobertWinston 8 36
(R J Price) *cl up: rdn along 2f out and sn wknd* **7/1**

58.76 secs (-0.94) **Going Correction** -0.275s/f (Stan) **7** Ran SP% **110.7**
Speed ratings (Par 98): **96,92,90,86,85 81,78**
toteswinger: 1&2 £4.20, 1&3 £6.90, 2&3 £2.30. CSF £25.06 CT £102.59 TOTE £20.60: £6.10, £1.10; EX 43.10 Trifecta £365.20 Part won. Pool £493.52 - 0.47 winning units..
Owner M S Saunders **Bred** B Walters **Trained** Green Ore, Somerset
■ Stewards' Enquiry : Phillip Makin caution: used whip down shoulder in forearm position

FOCUS
A low-grade sprint handicap run at a furious pace. The winner improved and the form is rated through the second.
Captain Carey Official explanation: trainer said, regarding the apparent improvement in form, that gelding may be better suited by a straight 5f.

967 BOOK TICKETS ON LINE AT SOUTHWELL-RACECOURSE.CO.UK H'CAP 2m (F)
4:40 (4:40) (Class 5) (0-70,70) 4-Y-O+ **£2,729** (£806; £403) **Stalls** Low

Form RPR

213 **1** **Supsonic**[14] 822 6-9-12 67 .... RobertWinston 1 79+
(R J Price) *trckd ldr: led over 4f out: rdn clr wl over 2f out: kpt on wl fnl f* **13/2**[3]

50-0 **2** *2* **Three Boars**[70] 168 7-9-2 57 .... (b) WilliamBuick 7 66
(S Gollings) *trckd ldrs: hdwy 4f out: chsd wnr over 3f out and sn rdn: drvn over 1f out: no imp* **9/2**[2]

0454 **3** *12* **Eforetta (GER)**[15] 809 7-8-12 53 .... (p) LukeMorris 6 48
(A W Carroll) *trckd ldrs: pushed along and outpcd whn n.m.r 4f out: drvn 3f out: kpt on u.p fnl 2f* **9/2**[2]

5014 **4** *2* **Rough Sketch (USA)**[22] 751 4-8-12 58 .... SebSanders 3 51
(Sir Mark Prescott) *hld up: effrt 4f out: rdn along over 3f out and sn btn* **5/6**[1]

/44- **5** *1 ½* **Ice And Fire**[427] 283 10-8-7 48 oh3 .... (b) FrankieMcDonald 8 39
(J T Stimpson) *hld up: gd hdwy over 4f out: chsd ldng pair 3f out: sn rdn and wknd fnl 2f* **40/1**

0054 **6** *29* **Spiritonthemount (USA)**[9] 860 4-8-1 50 .... (b) AndrewMullen[(3)] 5 6
(P W Hiatt) *led and sn clr: pushed along 5f out: sn hdd & wknd qckly* **18/1**

3m 46.12s (0.62) **Going Correction** +0.175s/f (Slow)
WFA 4 from 5yo+ 5lb **6** Ran SP% **112.0**
Speed ratings (Par 103): **105,104,98,97,96 81**
toteswinger: 1&2 £2.40, 1&3 £2.90, 2&3 £3.60. CSF £34.71 CT £143.31 TOTE £7.10: £2.20, £1.80; EX 16.80 Trifecta £72.60 Pool £489.91 - 4.99 winning units..
Owner Bill Gavan **Bred** Crandon Park Stud **Trained** Ullingswick, H'fords

FOCUS
A low-grade stayers' handicap run at a very steady pace. The winner goes well here.
Rough Sketch(USA) Official explanation: trainer's rep had no explanation for the poor form shown
Ice And Fire Official explanation: jockey said gelding hung right

968 SOUTHWELL-RACECOURSE.CO.UK H'CAP 1m (F)
5:15 (5:15) (Class 5) (0-70,62) 3-Y-O **£2,729** (£806; £403) **Stalls** Low

Form RPR

5-14 **1** **Just Five (IRE)**[34] 620 3-9-0 58 .... (t) TomEaves 1 69+
(M Dods) *cl up: rdn to ld 2f out: drvn ent fnl f: edgd rt and kpt on* **5/1**[3]

0-11 **2** *nk* **Green Agenda**[14] 817 3-9-3 61 .... JoeFanning 5 71+
(M Johnston) *stmbld s: sn trcking ldrs on outer: effrt over 2f out: rdn to chse wnr over 1f out: sn drvn and kpt on ins fnl f* **8/15**[1]

5222 **3** *6* **Jonnie Skull (IRE)**[6] 902 3-9-4 62 .... (be) AdamKirby 6 59
(P S McEntee) *led: rdn along 3f out: drvn and hdd 2f out: grad wknd* **9/2**[2]

2-50 **4** *5* **Miss Cracklinrosie**[29] 677 3-8-12 56 .... WilliamBuick 3 42
(J R Weymes) *chsd ldrs: rdn along 3f out: sn drvn and wknd over 2f out* **14/1**

600- **5** *6* **Coniston Wood**[223] 5072 3-8-8 52 .... DaleGibson 4 25
(M W Easterby) *in tch: rdn along 1/2-way: sn wknd* **50/1**

60-4 **6** *31* **Got Flash (FR)**[14] 820 3-8-12 56 .... RobertWinston 2 —
(E J O'Neill) *rrd s: a in rr: rdn along and outpcd fr over 3f out* **18/1**

1m 45.11s (1.41) **Going Correction** +0.175s/f (Slow) **6** Ran SP% **114.0**
Speed ratings (Par 98): **99,98,92,87,81 50**
toteswinger: 1&2 £2.00, 1&3 £1.70, 2&3 £1.50. CSF £8.32 TOTE £5.00: £2.20, £1.10; EX 11.60 Place 6: £71.80 Place 5: £18.90.
Owner Just Five Racing Partners **Bred** Rathbarry Stud **Trained** Denton, Co Durham

FOCUS
The top-weight was 8lb below the race ceiling in this very modest event, but the first pair finished clear and the form has been rated positively.
Got Flash(FR) Official explanation: jockey said gelding never travelled
T/Plt: £41.20 to a £1 stake. Pool: £48,905.19. 865.62 winning tickets. T/Qpdt: £15.50 to a £1 stake. Pool: £3,222.04. 153.55 winning tickets. JR

932 WOLVERHAMPTON (A.W) (L-H)
Thursday, March 26

OFFICIAL GOING: Standard
Wind: Fresh, behind Weather: Overcast

969 BETANGEL.COM H'CAP 1m 1f 103y(P)
6:50 (6:50) (Class 6) (0-55,55) 4-Y-O+ **£1,942** (£578; £288; £144) **Stalls** Low

Form RPR

1035 **1** **The Graig**[16] 791 5-8-13 54 .... GregFairley 10 60
(J R Holt) *sn chsng ldr: led 2f out: rdn over 1f out: jst hld on* **11/1**

000- **2** *hd* **Art Value**[163] 6716 4-8-9 50 .... FrancisNorton 5 56
(M Wigham) *edgd lft sn after s: led 1f: chsd ldrs: rdn over 1f out: hung lft ins fnl f: r.o* **8/1**

0052 **3** *1 ½* **Dobravany (IRE)**[15] 802 5-8-8 49 .... (v) JimmyQuinn 13 52
(K A Morgan) *a.p: rdn over 2f out: styd on* **20/1**

3-22 **4** *shd* **Noah Jameel**[29] 669 7-9-0 55 .... FergusSweeney 8 58
(A G Newcombe) *hld up: hdwy over 2f out: rdn over 1f out: nt rch ldrs* **9/4**[1]

2404 **5** *1 ¾* **Moyoko (IRE)**[35] 608 6-8-10 51 .... AlanMunro 4 50
(M Salaman) *hld up: hdwy over 1f out: nt trble ldrs* **7/1**[3]

0653 **6** *nk* **Hunt The Bottle (IRE)**[20] 775 4-8-10 51 .... EddieAhern 1 50
(M Mullineaux) *trckd ldrs: racd keenly: rdn over 1f out: styd on same pce* **6/1**[2]

0-40 **7** *nk* **Bespoke Boy**[7] 362 4-8-9 55 .... (t) PatrickDonaghy[(5)] 2 53
(P C Haslam) *trckd ldrs: plld hrd: hmpd sn after s: rdn over 1f out: no ex* **33/1**

2165 **8** *1 ¾* **Desert Hawk**[20] 775 8-8-10 51 .... LukeMorris 3 46
(W M Brisbourne) *s.i.s: hld up: rdn over 2f out: n.d* **10/1**

3250 **9** *nse* **John Potts**[20] 775 4-8-11 52 .... (p) GrahamGibbons 7 47
(B P J Baugh) *hld up: rdn over 1f out: n.d* **12/1**

0-50 **10** *1* **Al Azy (IRE)**[24] 733 4-9-0 55 .... StephenDonohoe 12 48
(D M Simcock) *led after 1f: rdn and hdd 2f out: wknd fnl f* **10/1**

054 **11** *¾* **Singora Lady (IRE)**[14] 823 4-8-9 50 .... JamieMoriarty 9 41
(P T Midgley) *hld up: hdwy 1/2-way: rdn over 2f out: wknd fnl f* **20/1**

/54- **12** *3 ½* **Dancing Wizard**[399] 643 5-8-9 50 .... LPKeniry 6 35
(Norma Twomey) *sn pushed along: a in rr* **40/1**

2m 2.19s (0.49) **Going Correction** -0.025s/f (Stan) **12** Ran SP% **117.8**
Speed ratings (Par 101): **96,95,94,94,92 92,92,90,90,89 89,86**
toteswinger: 1&2 £18.40, 1&3 Not won, 2&3 Not won. CSF £91.09 CT £1745.22 TOTE £20.80: £3.90, £2.30, £7.00; EX 116.00.
Owner J R Holt **Bred** Hedsor Stud **Trained** Peckleton, Leics

FOCUS
Not much pace for the first couple of furlongs, which saw many of these taking a keen hold and meant that it was going to be hard to come from off the pace. Pretty weak form but a slight personal best from the winner.

970 BE A BOOKIE WITH BET ANGEL MAIDEN STKS 1m 1f 103y(P)
7:20 (7:20) (Class 5) 3-Y-O+ **£2,914** (£867; £433; £216) **Stalls** Low

Form RPR

1 **Stagecoach Jade (IRE)** 3-8-2 0 .... JimmyQuinn 5 64+
(M Johnston) *trckd ldrs: plld hrd early: rdn to ld over 1f out: r.o* **15/2**[3]

033- **2** 1 1/4 **Khan Tengri (IRE)**[196] 5842 3-8-7 79 MartinDwyer 8 66
(M P Tregoning) *led: rdn and hdd over 1f out: edgd rt: styd on same pce* **4/9**[1]

3 2 **Enlist**[213] 5-9-12 0 SteveDrowne 10 66
(A J Lidderdale) *sn chsng ldr: rdn: hung lft and ev ch over 1f out: styng on same pce whn hung rt ins fnl f* **100/1**

60- **4** 3/4 **Troubletimestwo (FR)**[152] 6978 3-8-7 0 EddieAhern 3 60+
(H J L Dunlop) *hmpd s: hld up: hdwy over 2f out: rdn over 1f out: styd on* **12/1**

5 4 1/2 **Den Maschine**[34] 4-9-12 0 TomEaves 6 55
(Ollie Pears) *s.i.s: hld up: hdwy over 2f out: wknd over 1f out* **28/1**

0-00 **6** 8 **Amber Ridge**[20] 775 4-9-12 41 GrahamGibbons 11 38
(B P J Baugh) *chsd ldrs: rdn over 2f out: wknd over 1f out* **66/1**

26-3 **7** 1 3/4 **Rose Cheval (USA)**[40] 556 3-8-2 75 PaulHanagan 7 25
(M R Channon) *chsd ldrs: rdn and hung rt over 2f out: wknd over 1f out* **13/2**[2]

4-0 **8** 1/2 **Rebel Prince (IRE)**[62] 272 3-8-2 0 NicolPolli(5) 4 29
(M G Quinlan) *s.i.s: sn chsng ldrs: hmpd and lost pl over 7f out: n.d after* **40/1**

6/ **9** 2 3/4 **Magnifico (FR)**[19] 270 8-9-9 0 LeeVickers(3) 9 28
(Mrs K Waldron) *hld up: hdwy 1/2-way: rdn and wknd over 3f out* **16/1**

00 **10** 2 3/4 **Sugar State**[45] 476 4-9-12 0 SamHitchcott 1 22
(J L Spearing) *hld up: a in rr: bhd fnl 3f* **100/1**

2m 2.21s (0.51) **Going Correction** -0.025s/f (Stan)
WFA 3 from 4yo+ 19lb **10** Ran SP% **117.3**
Speed ratings (Par 103): **96,94,93,92,88 81,79,79,76,74**
toteswinger: 1&2 £2.10, 1&3 £26.40, 2&3 £14.10. CSF £11.23 TOTE £6.20: £2.00, £1.02, £19.10; EX 35.30.
Owner Mrs Jacqueline Conroy **Bred** Carradale Ltd, T Stack & W Cousis **Trained** Middleham Moor, N Yorks
■ Stewards' Enquiry : Steve Drowne four-day ban: careless riding (Apr 9, 11-13)

FOCUS
This was a modest maiden run ina slow time. Not easy to rate with the third apparently showing much-improved form.
Rose Cheval(USA) Official explanation: jockey said filly hung right throughout

971 WIN WHATEVER THE RESULT WITH BET ANGEL H'CAP 5f 20y(P)
7:50 (7:50) (Class 4) (0-80,80) 4-Y-0+ **£5,504** (£1,637; £818; £408) **Stalls** Low

Form RPR

0-50 **1** **Almaty Express**[31] 654 7-8-9 71 ow1 (b) DarryllHolland 1 82
(J R Weymes) *chsd ldrs: pushed along 1/2-way: rdn over 1f out: led ins fnl f: r.o: eased last strides* **6/1**[2]

1661 **2** 1 **Tyrannosaurus Rex (IRE)**[13] 832 5-8-4 66 oh1 PaulHanagan 5 73
(D Shaw) *hld up: hdwy over 1f out: sn rdn: r.o* **5/2**[1]

0-00 **3** nk **Luscivious**[6] 901 5-9-4 80 (b) RobertWinston 6 86
(A J McCabe) *chsd ldr: rdn and ev ch ins fnl f: kpt on* **10/1**

300- **4** 2 **Mandurah (IRE)**[208] 5493 5-8-9 71 AdrianTNicholls 4 70
(D Nicholls) *chsd ldrs: rdn 1/2-way: hung lft over 1f out: styd on* **6/1**[2]

4451 **5** 3/4 **Steel City Boy (IRE)**[36] 582 6-8-8 70 JimCrowley 2 66
(D Shaw) *hld up: rdn over 1f out: nt trble ldrs* **5/2**[1]

6-50 **6** 1 1/2 **Bookiesindex Boy**[71] 165 5-8-3 72 (v) DannyBrock(7) 3 63
(J R Jenkins) *led: rdn over 1f out: wknd and hdd ins fnl f* **16/1**

2116 **7** 3 **Perlachy**[7] 880 5-8-4 66 (v) LukeMorris 7 46
(D Shaw) *hld up: rdn 1/2-way: wknd fnl f* **8/1**[3]

60.60 secs (-1.70) **Going Correction** -0.025s/f (Stan) **7** Ran SP% **111.8**
Speed ratings (Par 105): **112,110,109,106,105 103,98**
toteswinger: 1&2 £7.50, 1&3 £23.80, 2&3 £5.90. CSF £20.42 TOTE £5.60: £3.50, £2.30; EX 23.60.
Owner Ronald Lilley **Bred** P G Airey **Trained** Middleham Moor, N Yorks
■ Stewards' Enquiry : Darryll Holland one-day ban: careless riding (Apr 9)

FOCUS
This was a modest handicap but the form looks pretty good for the grade.

972 ADVANCED DUTCHING WITH BET ANGEL H'CAP 1m 5f 194y(P)
8:20 (8:21) (Class 6) (0-60,64) 4-Y-0+ **£1,942** (£578; £288; £144) **Stalls** Low

Form RPR

5-46 **1** **Thorny Mandate**[8] 871 7-9-3 57 EddieAhern 5 64
(W M Brisbourne) *hld up: hdwy over 2f out: shkn up to ld ins fnl f: rdn out* **7/1**[3]

30-0 **2** 1 **Summer Lodge**[13] 836 6-8-13 56 DavidProbert(3) 13 62
(A J McCabe) *hld up: hdwy over 4f out: rdn to ld wl over 1f out: hdd ins fnl f: styd on* **18/1**

340 **3** 1/2 **Little Richard (IRE)**[13] 836 10-9-6 60 (p) AdamKirby 10 65
(M Wellings) *led early: chsd clr ldrs: rdn over 1f out: r.o* **10/1**

0103 **4** nk **Safin (GER)**[16] 795 9-9-6 60 GrahamGibbons 11 64
(R Curtis) *hld up: hdwy over 1f out: r.o* **14/1**

0-00 **5** 1 1/2 **Jonquille (IRE)**[58] 300 4-8-3 47 (b[1]) PaulHanagan 7 49
(T J Pitt) *hld up: hdwy over 2f out: rdn over 1f out: styd on* **66/1**

6-20 **6** nse **Snowberry Hill (USA)**[58] 301 6-9-2 56 LiamJones 1 59+
(Lucinda Featherstone) *rdr removed hood late and s.s: hld up: hdwy over 5f out: edgd lft over 3f out: hmpd and lost pl over 2f out: styd on u.p ins fnl f* **7/2**[1]

-030 **7** 3 **Bedouin Blue (IRE)**[13] 836 6-9-0 59 (p) PatrickDonaghy(5) 8 57
(A J Lidderdale) *mid-div: hdwy over 5f out: led over 2f out: rdn and hdd wl over 1f out: wknd ins fnl f* **12/1**

2263 **8** 26 **Dazzling Begum**[16] 790 4-8-6 50 (v) JimmyQuinn 4 12
(J Pearce) *chsd clr ldr after 1f: led 4f out: rdn and hdd over 2f out: sn wknd: t.o* **6/1**[2]

04-5 **9** 10 **Reprieved**[51] 377 4-8-1 48 AndrewMullen(3) 12 —
(Miss J A Camacho) *led after 1f: sn clr: hdd 4f out: wkng whn hmpd sn after* **33/1**

0-56 **10** 50 **Romantic Retreat**[43] 501 4-9-0 58 GeorgeBaker 3 —
(G L Moore) *chsd clr ldrs: rdn over 4f out: wkng whn hmpd sn after: t.o* **12/1**

0P0/ **11** 37 **Lake Wakatipu**[38] 6259 7-8-10 50 FrankieMcDonald 9 —
(R Ford) *sn pushed along in rr: bhd fnl 6f: t.o* **25/1**

3m 2.94s (-3.06) **Going Correction** -0.025s/f (Stan)
WFA 4 from 6yo+ 4lb **11** Ran SP% **93.7**
Speed ratings (Par 101): **107,106,106,105,105 105,103,88,82,54 33**
toteswinger: 1&2 Not won, 1&3 £8.20, 2&3 £13.60. CSF £68.99 CT £449.21 TOTE £6.00: £1.70, £4.70, £2.50; EX 53.40.
Owner R C Naylor **Bred** Major W R Hern And W H Carson **Trained** Great Ness, Shropshire
■ Stewards' Enquiry : Liam Jones 1st incident, two-day ban: careless riding (Apr 9,11) 2nd, two-day ban: careless riding (Apr 12-13)

FOCUS
This race lost much of its value following the withdrawal of well-backed favourite Carlton Scroop who became upset in the stalls (2/1, deduct 30p in the £ under R4). Fairly weak form.
Romantic Retreat Official explanation: jockey said filly had no more to give

973 WIN BEFORE THE OFF WITH BET ANGEL CLAIMING STKS 5f 216y(P)
8:50 (8:50) (Class 6) 3-Y-0+ **£1,942** (£578; £288; £144) **Stalls** Low

Form RPR

2213 **1** **Blue Tomato**[22] 756 8-9-0 79 WilliamCarson(5) 3 75+
(D Nicholls) *hld up: hdwy over 2f out: rdn to ld wl ins fnl f* **11/4**[2]

450- **2** 3/4 **Legal Eagle (IRE)**[210] 5433 4-9-9 77 AdrianTNicholls 5 77
(D Nicholls) *led: rdn and hung lft over 1f out: hdd wl ins fnl f* **9/1**

4-21 **3** 3 1/4 **Epic Odyssey**[42] 510 4-9-0 83 AndreaAtzeni(5) 2 63
(J R Gask) *trckd ldr to 1/2-way: rdn over 1f out: styd on same pce ins fnl f* **5/6**[1]

5225 **4** 2 **Qadar (IRE)**[12] 843 7-9-7 75 (b) GeorgeBaker 4 59
(N P Littmoden) *trckd ldrs: racd keenly: wnt 2nd 1/2-way: rdn over 1f out: no ex fnl f* **6/1**[3]

0 **5** 7 **Kenai**[7] 217 4-9-3 52 (b) FergusSweeney 1 34
(W K Goldsworthy) *hld up in tch: rdn 1/2-way: sn wknd* **100/1**

1m 14.04s (-0.96) **Going Correction** -0.025s/f (Stan) **5** Ran SP% **106.5**
Speed ratings (Par 101): **105,104,99,97,87**
CSF £22.76 TOTE £3.40: £1.30, £3.10; EX 13.30.Epic Odyssey was claimed by Mr K. R. Burke for £9,000.
Owner Dab Hand Racing **Bred** Bearstone Stud **Trained** Sessay, N Yorks

FOCUS
A fair claimer. A conservative view has been taken of the form.

974 TRY BET ANGEL AT TRY.BETANGEL.COM H'CAP 1m 141y(P)
9:20 (9:21) (Class 4) (0-85,88) 4-Y-0+ **£5,504** (£1,637; £818; £408) **Stalls** Low

Form RPR

00-1 **1** **Soccerjackpot (USA)**[10] 850 5-9-10 88 6ex AdamKirby 5 100+
(C G Cox) *mde all: shkn up over 1f out: r.o* **6/5**[1]

04-1 **2** 3/4 **Tartan Gigha (IRE)**[8] 866 4-9-6 84 6ex JoeFanning 4 92+
(M Johnston) *chsd wnr 5f: wnt 2nd again over 1f out: r.o* **11/4**[2]

50-0 **3** 2 1/4 **Flying Valentino**[22] 757 5-8-9 73 ow1 StephenDonohoe 1 77
(Ian Williams) *hld up: hdwy over 2f out: rdn over 1f out: edgd lft fnl f: styd on same pce* **40/1**

0254 **4** nk **Just Bond (IRE)**[13] 834 7-9-0 78 PJMcDonald 2 81
(G R Oldroyd) *hld up and bhd: racd keenly: rdn over 1f out: nt rch ldrs* **8/1**

324 **5** 3 1/2 **Leonaldo (USA)**[8] 866 4-9-0 78 (p) SteveDrowne 6 74
(J R Gask) *prom: chsd ldr over 3f out: rdn over 1f out: wknd fnl f* **4/1**[3]

/00- **6** 1 1/2 **Xtra Torrential (USA)**[111] 7560 7-8-11 75 FergusSweeney 3 68
(D M Simcock) *prom: rdn over 2f out: wknd over 1f out* **10/1**

1m 51.0s (0.50) **Going Correction** -0.025s/f (Stan) **6** Ran SP% **114.8**
Speed ratings (Par 105): **96,95,93,93,89 88**
toteswinger: 1&2 £1.10, 1&3 £4.40, 2&3 £6.00. CSF £4.92 TOTE £2.60: £2.50, £1.10; EX 3.80 Place 6 £189.32, Place 5 £29.21..
Owner sportaracing.com & George Houghton **Bred** Gary Chervenell **Trained** Lambourn, Berks

FOCUS
This was a decent handicap and a positive view has been taken of the principals.
T/Plt: £367.20 to a £1 stake. Pool: £101,486.77. 201.73 winning tickets. T/Qpdt: £41.00 to a £1 stake. Pool: £10,810.12. 194.74 winning tickets. CR

[963] SOUTHWELL (L-H)
Friday, March 27

OFFICIAL GOING: Standard
Wind: fresh 1/2 behind Weather: changeable and very breezy with showers

975 SOUTHWELL H'CAP 6f (F)
2:00 (2:00) (Class 6) (0-65,65) 4-Y-0+ **£2,047** (£604; £302) **Stalls** Low

Form RPR

1355 **1** **Cape Of Storms**[8] 886 6-8-11 58 (b) TomEaves 4 68
(R Brotherton) *trckd ldrs: n.m.r 3f out tl over 1f out: led 1f out: hung rt: rdn out* **7/1**

3312 **2** 1 1/4 **Ballycroy Boy (IRE)**[8] 886 4-9-4 65 (b) AdamKirby 3 71
(Miss M E Rowland) *bhd and drvn along: hdwy 2f out: styd on ins fnl f* **4/1**[1]

1043 **3** 1 1/2 **Kingsmaite**[8] 882 8-8-10 62 (v) MartinLane(5) 5 64
(S R Bowring) *trckd ldrs: led 2f out: hdd 1f out: no ex* **7/1**

4564 **4** 4 **Tri Chara (IRE)**[8] 886 5-9-4 65 (p) GrahamGibbons 6 55+
(R Hollinshead) *dwlt: in rr: effrt and n.m.r over 2f out: hung lft and kpt on: nvr trbld ldrs* **9/2**[2]

00-0 **5** 3/4 **Supreme Speedster**[17] 794 5-8-5 52 FrankieMcDonald 14 40
(A G Newcombe) *bhd: hdwy on outer 2f out: kpt on fnl f* **33/1**

00-0 **6** nk **Lieutenant Pigeon**[13] 843 4-9-4 65 PaulEddery 11 52
(Paul Mason) *trckd ldrs: outpcd 3f out: kpt on fnl f* **7/1**

6003 **7** 1/2 **Hamaasy**[5] 921 8-8-10 57 (tp) JoeFanning 13 42+
(R A Harris) *in rr-div: hdwy on wd outside 3f out: sn chsng ldrs: fdd appr fnl f* **13/2**[3]

034- **8** 3 **Avontuur (FR)**[150] 7055 7-8-8 60 DeanHeslop(5) 1 36
(Mrs R A Carr) *hld up in mid-div: effrt on inner over 2f out: wkng whn n.m.r jst ins fnl f* **18/1**

00-0 **9** 1/2 **Owed**[16] 811 7-8-11 58 (tp) RobertWinston 9 33
(R Bastiman) *trckd ldrs: led over 2f out: sn hdd: wknd 1f out* **40/1**

630- **10** 2 3/4 **Garstang**[184] 6209 6-9-1 62 PaulMulrennan 12 28
(J Balding) *chsd ldrs: wkng whn edgd lft 1f out* **33/1**

255- **11** 1/2 **Soto**[184] 6219 6-9-2 63 DaleGibson 2 28
(M W Easterby) *chsd ldr: rdn over 2f out: wkng whn n.m.r on inner jst ins fnl f* **22/1**

0-22 **12** 5 **Princess Charlmane (IRE)**[8] 881 6-8-4 51 oh1 (t) AndrewElliott 7 1
(C J Teague) *led tl over 2f out: lost pl appr fnl f* **12/1**

1m 16.54s (0.04) **Going Correction** +0.125s/f (Slow) **12** Ran SP% **114.6**
Speed ratings (Par 101): **104,102,100,95,94 93,92,88,88,84 83,77**
toteswinger: 1&2 £5.60, 1&3 £11.30, 2&3 £6.30. CSF £32.58 CT £204.14 TOTE £9.90: £3.10, £1.40, £2.80; EX 45.40 Trifecta £154.20 Pool: £312.69 - 1.50 winning units..
Owner P S J Croft **Bred** R J Turner **Trained** Elmley Castle, Worcs

FOCUS
A moderate sprint handicap, but the pace was prtty strong and the form is sound for the grade.

976 MEMBERSHIP AT SOUTHWELL GOLF CLUB H'CAP 5f (F)
2:35 (2:35) (Class 6) (0-60,60) 4-Y-0+ **£2,047** (£604; £302) **Stalls** High

Form RPR

30-2 **1** **Handsinthemist (IRE)**[5] 919 4-7-13 48 ow2 PaulPickard(7) 6 59
(P T Midgley) *w ldrs: led 3f out: edgd lft and hld on ins fnl f* **6/1**[3]

-661 **2** 3/4 **Mujma**[7] 896 5-8-9 51 6ex (bt) LiamJones 4 59
(S Parr) *chsd ldrs: hrd rdn and chsd wnr 1f out: no ex ins fnl f* **4/1**[1]

-503 **3** 1 1/4 **Spirit Of Coniston**[17] 794 6-8-13 **55** JamieMoriarty 7 59
(P T Midgley) *mid-div: outpcd over 2f out: kpt on wl fnl f* **7/1**
4351 **4** 1/2 **Argentine (IRE)**[17] 794 5-8-13 **55** PaulMulrennan 10 57
(L Lungo) *sn chsng ldrs: kpt on same pce fnl f* **12/1**
2665 **5** nse **Whozart (IRE)**[5] 921 6-8-8 **55** (b[1]) KellyHarrison(5) 1 57
(A Dickman) *chsd ldrs: edgd lft over 2f out: one pce fnl f* **4/1**[1]
3-04 **6** 3/4 **Rocketball (IRE)**[17] 794 4-8-8 **55** (vt) WilliamCarson(5) 8 54
(Patrick Morris) *sn outpcd: hdwy over 1f out: nvr nr ldrs* **11/1**
044 **7** 3 1/4 **Trinculo (IRE)**[11] 854 12-8-10 **55** (b) KevinGhunowa(3) 2 42
(R A Harris) *led 3f: edgd lft and wknd over 1f out* **16/1**
12- **8** nk **Little Eden (IRE)**[329] 1769 4-8-13 **58** NeilBrown(3) 3 44+
(T D Barron) *sn outpcd and bhd: kpt on fnl f: nvr on terms* **9/2**[2]
9 6 **Tenacious**[246] 5-8-2 **49** (t) AndreaAtzeni(5) 5 13
(F Sheridan) *mid-div: outpcd over 2f out: lost pl and eased 1f out* **14/1**

59.35 secs (-0.35) **Going Correction** -0.025s/f (Stan) **9** Ran SP% **113.5**
Speed ratings (Par 101): **101,99,97,97,96 95,90,90,80**
toteswinger: 1&2 £3.80, 1&3 £8.30, 2&3 £7.30. CSF £29.68 CT £170.76 TOTE £4.20: £1.80, £1.90, £2.40; EX 27.80 Trifecta £159.00 Pool: £309.48 - 1.44 winning units..
Owner J F Wright **Bred** Pippa Hackett **Trained** Westow, N Yorks

FOCUS
Just a moderate handicap. The form looks quite solid, with the third helping set the level.

977 HOSPITALITY AT SOUTHWELL RACECOURSE (S) STKS 1m 4f (F)
3:10 (3:10) (Class 6) 4-Y-0+ **£2,047** (£604; £302) **Stalls** Low

Form RPR
1404 **1** **My Friend Fritz**[36] 603 9-9-7 67 LukeMorris 5 69
(P W Hiatt) *trckd ldr: rdn to ld 3f out: edgd lft and hld on towards fin* **85/40**[2]
/0-4 **2** hd **Russian Invader (IRE)**[5] 923 5-9-1 75 (e[1]) GregFairley 1 63
(R C Guest) *hld up in last: effrt over 3f out: wnt handy 2nd over 2f out: kpt on wl: no ex nr fin* **2/1**[1]
10-0 **3** 4 1/2 **City Stable (IRE)**[20] 787 4-8-13 78 FrancisNorton 2 56
(M Wigham) *chsd ldrs: effrt over 3f out: sn rdn and one pce: eased towards fin* **7/1**
4115 **4** 2 1/4 **Nawamees (IRE)**[4] 935 11-9-2 70 (p) RichardEvans(5) 3 59
(P D Evans) *led: qcknd over 4f out: hdd 3f out: wkng whn eased ins fnl f* **9/4**[3]

2m 44.87s (3.87) **Going Correction** +0.125s/f (Slow)
WFA 4 from 5yo+ 2lb **4** Ran SP% **108.6**
Speed ratings (Par 101): **92,91,88,87**
CSF £6.70 TOTE £3.40; EX 8.50.There was no bid for the winner.
Owner P W Hiatt **Bred** Butts Enterprises Limited **Trained** Hook Norton, Oxon

FOCUS
An ordinary seller and the gallop was modest. The form is rated through the front pair's recent efforts.

978 PLAY GOLF AT SOUTHWELL GOLF CLUB MAIDEN STKS 1m 4f (F)
3:45 (3:46) (Class 5) 3-Y-0+ **£3,070** (£906; £453) **Stalls** Low

Form RPR
42-3 **1** **Fin Vin De Leu (GER)**[36] 599 3-8-6 73 GregFairley 9 77+
(M Johnston) *sn trcking ldrs: shkn up to ld 3f out: rdn clr fnl f* **9/4**[1]
3-52 **2** 6 **Augusta Gold (USA)**[8] 883 3-8-6 71 (b) LukeMorris 8 68
(N P Littmoden) *hld up in midfield: hdwy over 3f out: wnt 2nd 2f out: no imp* **3/1**[2]
34 **3** 1 1/2 **Miss Keck**[21] 779 5-9-9 0 PJMcDonald 10 63
(G A Swinbank) *in rr: pushed along 6f out: hdwy and rdn 4f out: one pce fnl 2f* **9/1**
6644 **4** 9 **Dollar Express (USA)**[9] 865 3-8-7 63 ow1 ShaneKelly 3 53
(J Noseda) *trckd ldr: led over 5f out: hdd 3f out: wknd over 1f out* **6/1**
0-62 **5** 6 **Spares And Repairs**[10] 857 6-10-0 52 RobertWinston 5 45
(Mrs S Lamyman) *trckd ldrs: effrt over 3f out: lost pl over 1f out* **9/2**[3]
0-2 **6** 15 **My Mate Granite (USA)**[43] 516 5-10-0 0 AdamKirby 4 23
(M E Rimmer) *led tl over 5f out: lost pl 4f out: sn bhd* **33/1**
6/ **7** 2 1/2 **Adare (GER)**[668] 2118 6-10-0 0 TomEaves 6 19
(R Brotherton) *s.i.s: t.k.h in rr: in rr and drvn 6f out: sn bhd* **25/1**
0-63 **8** 33 **Thirtyfourthstreet (IRE)**[21] 779 4-9-7 55 JimmyQuinn 1 —
(W R Muir) *restless in stalls: sn chsng ldrs: reminders 7f out: lost pl over 5f out: sn wl bhd: t.o* **16/1**
R **Furmagiatt**[57] 5-10-0 0 TPQueally 2 —
(Mrs S Leech) *ref to r: lft at s* **100/1**

2m 41.08s (0.08) **Going Correction** +0.125s/f (Slow)
WFA 3 from 4yo 22lb 4 from 5yo+ 2lb **9** Ran SP% **111.9**
Speed ratings (Par 103): **104,100,99,93,89 79,77,55,—**
toteswinger: 1&2 £2.70, 1&3 £5.20, 2&3 £6.00. CSF £8.54 TOTE £2.60: £1.20, £1.60, £2.70; EX 6.70 Trifecta £27.50 Pool: £642.15 - 17.27 winning units..
Owner R M F Curry **Bred** Newsells Park Stud Ltd **Trained** Middleham Moor, N Yorks

FOCUS
A modest maiden rated around the second and third.

979 BOOK TICKETS ON LINE AT SOUTHWELL-RACECOURSE.CO.UK H'CAP 1m (F)
4:20 (4:20) (Class 6) (0-60,60) 4-Y-0+ **£2,047** (£604; £302) **Stalls** Low

Form RPR
/010 **1** **Almahaza (IRE)**[25] 733 5-8-13 **55** NeilChalmers 2 63
(A J Chamberlain) *hld up towards rr: effrt over 2f out: edgd lft: styd on to ld nr fin* **5/1**[2]
0460 **2** nk **Ten Pole Tudor**[13] 844 4-8-9 **58** (p) SPRyan(7) 5 65
(R A Harris) *s.i.s: hdwy over 4f out: kpt on wl ins fnl f: jst hld* **33/1**
0243 **3** shd **Magical Song**[17] 791 4-8-10 **52** (b) TomEaves 8 59
(J Balding) *t.k.h: hmpd s: sn led: no ex and hdd towards fin* **9/1**
2011 **4** 1 3/4 **Very Well Red**[9] 867 6-9-0 **56** JimmyQuinn 9 59
(P W Hiatt) *led early: trckd ldr: styd on same pce fnl f* **6/1**[3]
4422 **5** shd **Mr Chocolate Drop (IRE)**[9] 874 5-8-13 **55** (b) AdamKirby 7 58
(Miss M E Rowland) *hmpd s: hld up towards rr: hdwy 2f out: styd on ins fnl f: nt rch ldrs* **7/2**[1]
3115 **6** 2 **Amber Moon**[7] 897 4-8-11 **58** ow1 (b) AnnStokell(5) 10 57
(Miss A Stokell) *chsd ldrs: edgd lft and one pce appr fnl f* **20/1**
2-50 **7** 1 1/2 **Smooth Sovereign (IRE)**[20] 786 4-9-4 **60** GregFairley 4 55
(M Johnston) *chsd ldrs: effrt 3f out: hung lft and wknd over 1f out* **10/1**
0265 **8** nk **Komreyev Star**[15] 823 7-8-6 **48** (p) LukeMorris 13 43
(R E Peacock) *chsd ldrs on outer: outpcd over 3f out: no threat after* **11/1**
-040 **9** 3 **Ugenius**[13] 844 5-9-4 **60** TGMcLaughlin 11 48
(Mrs C A Dunnett) *outpcd over 3f out: mid-div on outer: effrt over 2f out: wknd over 1f out* **11/1**
3002 **10** 2 1/2 **Rub Of The Relic (IRE)**[17] 791 4-8-3 **52** (v) PaulPickard(7) 14 35
(P T Midgley) *mid-div on outer: lost pl over 4f out: sn bhd* **10/1**
0630 **11** 5 **To Bubbles**[32] 657 4-8-8 **50** FrankieMcDonald 6 22
(A G Newcombe) *hmpd at s: hdwy over 3f out: lost pl over 1f out: sn eased* **33/1**
5256 **12** 2 **Haroldini (IRE)**[15] 823 7-9-2 **58** (p) PaulMulrennan 3 25
(J Balding) *trckd ldrs: lost pl and eased over 1f out* **15/2**
46-0 **13** 9 **Billy Bowmore**[15] 823 4-8-12 **57** ow2 LeeVickers(3) 1 4
(P A Kirby) *prom: lost pl over 4f out: sn bhd* **80/1**

1m 45.56s (1.86) **Going Correction** +0.125s/f (Slow) **13** Ran SP% **121.7**
Speed ratings (Par 101): **95,94,94,92,92 90,89,88,85,83 78,76,67**
toteswinger: 1&2 £44.20, 1&3 £14.10, 2&3 £62.50. CSF £171.53 CT £1515.77 TOTE £5.30: £1.90, £14.40, £2.80; EX 246.50 TRIFECTA Not won..
Owner G B Heffaran **Bred** Castletown And Associates **Trained** Ashton Keynes, Wilts

FOCUS
A moderate handicap run at a solid gallop. The third is as good a guide as any.

980 SOUTHWELL-RACECOURSE.CO.UK H'CAP 7f (F)
4:55 (4:55) (Class 5) (0-75,75) 4-Y-0+ **£2,729** (£806; £403) **Stalls** Low

Form RPR
-202 **1** **Flores Sea (USA)**[16] 807 5-9-3 **74** (b[1]) PhillipMakin 2 86
(T D Barron) *drvn and sn led: kpt on u.p fnl 2f: unchal* **3/1**[1]
2122 **2** 1 1/2 **Obe Royal**[4] 933 5-8-9 **71** (v) RichardEvans(5) 6 79
(P D Evans) *hld up in rr: effrt on outside over 2f out: styd on to take 2nd ins fnl f: nt rch wnr* **3/1**[1]
020- **3** 3 **Fools Gold**[150] 7048 4-9-1 **75** RussellKennemore(3) 7 76
(Paul Mason) *trckd ldrs on outside: effrt over 3f out: kpt on fnl f* **16/1**
5-65 **4** 1 **Secret Dubai (IRE)**[47] 457 4-9-0 **71** (t) TPQueally 5 69
(M Botti) *trckd ldrs: wnt 2nd 3f out: wknd ins fnl f* **7/2**[2]
3523 **5** 6 **Whitbarrow (IRE)**[8] 886 10-8-13 **73** ow5 (b) JamesMillman(3) 4 56
(B R Millman) *led early: chsd ldrs: lost pl over 1f out* **9/2**[3]
212- **6** 2 1/4 **Spin Again (IRE)**[217] 5248 4-8-10 **74** NSLawes(7) 1 52
(D Nicholls) *chsd ldrs: drvn over 4f out: lost pl 3f out* **9/1**
210- **7** 12 **Mr Toshiwonka**[185] 6186 5-8-2 **66** AdeleMulrennan(7) 3 14
(D Nicholls) *t.k.h: trckd ldrs: rdn over 3f out: lost pl over 2f out: sn bhd* **14/1**

1m 29.59s (-0.71) **Going Correction** +0.125s/f (Slow) **7** Ran SP% **113.0**
Speed ratings (Par 103): **109,107,103,102,95 93,79**
toteswinger: 1&2 £2.20, 1&3 £7.80, 2&3 £15.10. CSF £11.88 TOTE £3.30: £1.80, £1.50; EX 10.50 Place 6: £108.81 Place 5: £47.69.
Owner T D Barron **Bred** Beckie McLay-Irons **Trained** Maunby, N Yorks
■ Phillip Makin's first winner since he injured his back last June.

FOCUS
An ordinary handicap but sound form, with the second helping with the level.
T/Plt: £393.20 to a £1 stake. Pool: £70,973.11. 131.76 winning tickets. T/Qpdt: £51.40 to a £1 stake. Pool: £4,508.03. 64.90 winning tickets. WG

969 WOLVERHAMPTON (A.W) (L-H)
Friday, March 27

OFFICIAL GOING: Standard
Wind: Moderate behind Weather: Fine

981 ENJOY THE LUCKY 7 GROUP OFFER CLAIMING STKS 1m 1f 103y(P)
6:50 (6:50) (Class 6) 4-Y-0+ **£2,047** (£604; £302) **Stalls** Low

Form RPR
-113 **1** **Ahlawy (IRE)**[57] 330 6-9-1 76 (bt) AndreaAtzeni(5) 8 89
(F Sheridan) *hld up in tch: led over 1f out: edgd lft ins fnl f: drew clr: r.o wl* **9/4**[1]
3341 **2** 4 1/2 **Rapid City**[14] 825 6-8-12 70 (p) RobertWinston 5 71
(A J McCabe) *hld up towards rr: rdn and hung lft over 1f out: r.o wl to take 2nd wl ins fnl f: no ch w wnr* **7/1**[3]
5-03 **3** 1 1/4 **Kildare Sun (IRE)**[25] 737 7-9-1 70 PaulMulrennan 1 72
(J Mackie) *hld up in tch: rdn over 1f out: one pce fnl f* **9/2**[2]
-665 **4** nk **Bajan Pride**[16] 656 5-8-10 62 PaulHanagan 9 66
(R A Fahey) *sn led: hdd 7f out: led again 4f out: rdn and hdd over 1f out: one pce: lost 2nd wl ins fnl f* **20/1**
0601 **5** 1 3/4 **Torch Of Freedom (IRE)**[8] 875 4-9-2 72 SebSanders 2 68
(Sir Mark Prescott) *hld up in mid-div: rdn and hdwy 2f out: one pce fnl f* **9/2**[2]
150- **6** 1 1/2 **Lucayan Dancer**[180] 6312 9-9-6 70 AdrianTNicholls 10 69
(D Nicholls) *hld up towards rr: hdwy on outside 2f out: no imp fnl f* **16/1**
/16- **7** 4 1/2 **Thompsons Walls (IRE)**[225] 3963 4-8-10 68 TomEaves 3 50
(S T Mason) *t.k.h in mid-div: wknd 2f out* **50/1**
4121 **8** 1 1/4 **Ridgeway Jazz**[7] 897 4-8-0 61 SeanPalmer(7) 4 44
(M D I Usher) *hld up towards rr: gd hdwy over 6f out: wknd 2f out* **9/2**[2]
4200 **9** 22 **So Sublime**[38] 574 4-8-1 44 (bt) AlexEdwards(7) 6 —
(M C Chapman) *plld hrd: prom: led 7f out to 4f out: wknd 3f out: t.o* **200/1**
00-0 **10** 4 **Swallow Senora (IRE)**[82] 37 7-7-12 35 (bt) AmyBaker(5) 7 —
(M C Chapman) *dwlt: plld hrd early in rr: rdn over 2f out: sn struggling: t.o* **250/1**

1m 58.76s (-2.94) **Going Correction** -0.20s/f (Stan) **10** Ran SP% **111.3**
Speed ratings (Par 101): **105,101,99,99,98 96,92,91,72,68**
toteswinger: 1&2 £4.30, 1&3 £3.60, 2&3 £7.00. CSF £17.56 TOTE £3.20: £1.10, £3.30, £1.70; EX 20.50.Rapid City was claimed by J J Best for £8,000.
Owner Frank Sheridan **Bred** Castlemartin Stud And Skymarc Farm **Trained** Stoke Heath, Shropshire

FOCUS
A tight claimer on adjusted official ratings. The pace was steady. The winner was back to his best early-season form.
Rapid City Official explanation: jockey said gelding hung right-handed
Thompsons Walls(IRE) Official explanation: jockey said gelding ran too free

982 RINGSIDE CONFERENCE SUITE - 700 THEATRE STYLE MAIDEN STKS 5f 216y(P)
7:20 (7:20) (Class 5) 3-Y-0+ **£2,590** (£770; £385; £192) **Stalls** Low

Form RPR
222- **1** **Servoca (CAN)**[195] 5905 3-9-0 84 MichaelHills 1 90+
(B W Hills) *mde all: shkn up and wnt clr wl ins fnl f: comf* **4/7**[1]
3-22 **2** 7 **War And Peace (IRE)**[68] 208 5-9-13 73 PatCosgrave 8 77+
(Jane Chapple-Hyam) *a chsng wnr: rdn over 2f out: btn ins fnl f* **7/2**[2]
330- **3** 6 **You've Been Mowed**[158] 6863 3-8-4 65 AndreaAtzeni(5) 9 43
(R J Price) *chsd ldrs: wnt 3rd over 2f out: no ch w ldng pair whn edgd lft wl over 1f out* **20/1**
2 **4** 1/2 **Swans A Swimming (IRE)**[26] 722 3-9-0 0 ShaneKelly 2 47
(J A Osborne) *s.i.s: in rr: r.o to take modest 4th wl ins fnl f* **8/1**[3]

34 **5** 1 ¾ **Volito**[13] 842 3-9-0 0 .... JamieMoriarty 5 41
(Jonjo O'Neill) *hld up and bhd: no ch fnl 3f* **28/1**

0- **6** 3 ¼ **Guga (IRE)**[166] 6674 3-9-0 0 .... TonyCulhane 3 31
(George Baker) *s.i.s: in rr: rdn over 3f out: sn struggling* **22/1**

0 **7** nk **Placidity**[5] 920 3-8-9 0 .... RobertWinston 6 25
(A J McCabe) *in tch tl wknd over 3f out* **100/1**

04-P **8** 7 **Oceanic Dancer (IRE)**[9] 862 3-8-9 0 .... LiamJones 4 —
(Patrick Morris) *prom tl wknd over 2f out* **66/1**

3- **9** 1 ¼ **Lady Kingston**[359] 1156 3-8-9 0 .... AndrewElliott 7 —
(K R Burke) *a bhd* **100/1**

1m 12.92s (-2.08) **Going Correction** -0.20s/f (Stan)
WFA 3 from 5yo 13lb **9** Ran SP% **113.0**
Speed ratings (Par 103): **105,95,87,87,84 80,79,70,68**
toteswinger: 1&2 £3.00, 1&3 £5.30, 2&3 £8.50. CSF £2.36 TOTE £1.40: £1.02, £1.30, £4.90; EX 3.00.
Owner A L R Morton **Bred** Dermot Carty **Trained** Lambourn, Berks
■ Stewards' Enquiry : Robert Winston two-day ban: careless riding (Apr 11-12)

FOCUS
The betting suggested there would only be one winner of this maiden. Servoca is rated back to his best and this rating could underestimate him.

983 STAY AT THE WOLVERHAMPTON HOLIDAY INN H'CAP 1m 5f 194y(P)
7:50 (7:50) (Class 5) (0-75,75) 4-Y-0+ **£3,070** (£906; £453) **Stalls** Low

Form RPR

1021 **1** **Blockley (USA)**[16] 809 5-8-11 **61** ....(p) StephenDonohoe 8 62
(Ian Williams) *a.p: rdn to ld ins fnl f: styd on* **13/8**[1]

-121 **2** ½ **Bold Adventure**[14] 835 5-9-3 **67** .... TonyCulhane 7 67
(W J Musson) *hld up: hdwy 2f out: rdn over 1f out: styd on to take 2nd last strides* **7/4**[2]

200- **3** ½ **Chiff Chaff**[188] 6115 5-8-7 **57** oh6 ow1 .... LPKeniry 4 57
(C R Dore) *t.k.h: hdwy 2f out: rdn and styd on fnl f: tk 3rd last strides* **8/1**[3]

01 **4** nse **Simonside**[21] 779 6-9-4 **75** .... LanceBetts(7) 2 75
(B Ellison) *chsd ldr: led 2f out: rdn over 1f out: hdd ins fnl f: no ex and lost two pls last strides* **10/1**

00-0 **5** 3 ¼ **Helvetio**[25] 735 7-8-12 **62** .... PaulMulrennan 5 57
(Micky Hammond) *hld up in rr: pushed along over 1f out: nvr trbld ldrs* **40/1**

-614 **6** 6 **Gamesters Lady**[17] 795 6-8-13 **63** .... DuranFentiman 6 50
(W M Brisbourne) *led: rdn and hdd 2f out: wkng whn hung lft over 1f out* **14/1**

4-54 **7** 2 ¼ **Apache Dawn**[8] 588 5-8-6 **56** oh3 .... FrankieMcDonald 3 39
(A Sadik) *plld hrd: hdwy over 3f out: wknd 2f out* **14/1**

3m 5.57s (-0.43) **Going Correction** -0.20s/f (Stan) **7** Ran SP% **110.4**
Speed ratings (Par 103): **93,92,92,92,90 87,85**
toteswinger: 1&2 £1.50, 1&3 £1.90, 2&3 £2.20. CSF £4.35 CT £13.29 TOTE £3.10: £2.00, £1.30; EX 5.70.
Owner Ian Williams **Bred** Payson Stud Inc **Trained** Portway, Worcs

FOCUS
They only went an ordinary pace here but the form is solid with the front pair both in form.

984 DINE IN THE HORIZONS RESTAURANT H'CAP 7f 32y(P)
8:20 (8:20) (Class 6) (0-55,55) 4-Y-0+ **£2,047** (£604; £302) **Stalls** High

Form RPR

010- **1** **Djalalabad (FR)**[191] 6036 5-8-13 **54** ....(tp) TGMcLaughlin 3 64
(Mrs C A Dunnett) *hld up in rr: hdwy on ins whn swtchd rt over 1f out: rdn to ld wl ins fnl f: r.o* **20/1**

5432 **2** 1 ¼ **Aggbag**[24] 748 5-8-9 **50** .... AndrewElliott 5 57
(B P J Baugh) *hld up in tch: rdn wl over 1f out: ev ch ins fnl f: kpt on* **9/2**[1]

0-00 **3** ½ **Plaka (FR)**[4] 939 4-8-9 **50** .... GrahamGibbons 2 56
(W M Brisbourne) *a.p: rdn to ld 1f out: hdd wl ins fnl f: no ex* **12/1**

-440 **4** ¾ **Outer Hebrides**[16] 803 8-8-9 **50** ....(v) LukeMorris 4 54
(J M Bradley) *hld up in mid-div: swtchd rt ent st: rdn and hdwy over 1f out: kpt on one pce ins fnl f* **7/1**

3200 **5** hd **Imperial Djay (IRE)**[13] 844 4-8-13 **54** .... JimmyQuinn 1 58
(G J Smith) *hld up in mid-div: hdwy on ins wl over 1f out: ev ch ins fnl f: nt qckn* **5/1**[2]

-565 **6** 1 ¼ **Morse (IRE)**[11] 854 8-8-13 **54** ....(p) ShaneKelly 10 55
(J A Osborne) *rdn to ld after 1f: hdd 1f out: wknd ins fnl f* **16/1**

0100 **7** 1 ¾ **Over To You Bert**[9] 874 10-8-9 **55** .... MCGeran(5) 6 51
(R J Hodges) *hld up and bhd: rdn over 1f out: n.d* **7/1**

0-63 **8** ½ **H Harrison (IRE)**[9] 874 9-9-0 **55** .... PatrickMathers 8 50
(I W McInnes) *led 1f: a.p: ev ch 1f out: wknd wl ins fnl f* **8/1**

4165 **9** 3 **Just Jimmy (IRE)**[9] 874 4-8-13 **54** .... PaulDoe 7 42
(P D Evans) *hld up in mid-div: hdwy over 3f out: rdn 2f out: c wd st: wknd over 1f out* **11/2**[3]

4600 **10** ½ **Machinate (USA)**[30] 682 7-8-11 **52** .... LiamJones 12 39
(W M Brisbourne) *c wd st: a in rr* **22/1**

3200 **11** 2 ¾ **Louisiade (IRE)**[8] 748 8-8-3 **49** ....(vt[1]) AndreaAtzeni(5) 9 29
(M C Chapman) *prom: ev ch over 2f out: sn rdn: wknd over 1f out* **12/1**

1m 28.31s (-1.29) **Going Correction** -0.20s/f (Stan) **11** Ran SP% **116.7**
Speed ratings (Par 101): **99,97,97,96,95 94,92,91,88,87 84**
toteswinger: 1&2 £22.70, 1&3 £72.60, 2&3 £23.30. CSF £107.16 CT £1151.40 TOTE £23.80: £6.30, £1.40, £4.70; EX 109.70.
Owner Far Afield **Bred** Haras De Beauvoir **Trained** Hingham, Norfolk

FOCUS
They went a good gallop here and the winner came from well off the pace. Modest form.

985 BETFAIR ALL WEATHER COMPETITION H'CAP 5f 20y(P)
8:50 (8:50) (Class 3) (0-90,89) 4-Y-0 **£9,462** (£2,832; £1,416; £708; £352) **Stalls** Low

Form RPR

2320 **1** **Little Edward**[28] 714 11-8-13 **89** .... MCGeran(5) 2 98
(R J Hodges) *t.k.h in rr: hdwy on ins wl over 1f out: rdn to ld and edgd rt ins fnl f: r.o* **7/1**

5432 **2** 1 **Bo McGinty (IRE)**[9] 870 8-8-4 **75** oh1 ....(v) PaulHanagan 3 80
(R A Fahey) *hld up in mid-div: hdwy on ins 2f out: sn rdn: carried rt ins fnl f: r.o to take 2nd nr fin* **9/2**[1]

0236 **3** nk **Canadian Danehill (IRE)**[15] 821 7-8-8 **79** ....(p) ShaneKelly 6 83
(R M H Cowell) *a.p: led wl over 1f out tl ins fnl f: nt qckn* **6/1**

1311 **4** ¾ **Chjimes (IRE)**[23] 754 5-9-4 **89** .... LPKeniry 7 91
(C R Dore) *s.i.s: t.k.h in rr: hdwy 1f out: no ex towards fin* **9/1**

0514 **5** 1 ½ **Harry Up**[23] 756 8-8-7 **85** ....(p) AmyRyan(7) 10 81
(K A Ryan) *w ldr: rdn and ev ch over 1f out: one pce ins fnl f* **8/1**

024- **6** 4 ½ **Foxy Music**[158] 6859 5-8-9 **80** .... PatCosgrave 9 60
(E J Alston) *led: hdd wl over 1f out: rdn and wknd ins fnl f* **22/1**

202- **7** ½ **The Jobber (IRE)**[130] 7365 8-9-3 **88** .... JimmyQuinn 4 66
(M Blanshard) *hld up in mid-div: wknd wl over 1f out* **11/2**[3]

230- **8** shd **Northern Bolt**[175] 6449 4-8-7 **78** .... AdrianTNicholls 5 56
(D Nicholls) *chsd ldrs: rdn over 2f out: wknd wl over 1f out* **13/2**

2524 **9** 4 **Methaaly (IRE)**[28] 714 6-9-0 **85** ....(be) LiamJones 8 48
(M Mullineaux) *s.v.s: a wl in rr* **5/1**[2]

60.35 secs (-1.95) **Going Correction** -0.20s/f (Stan) **9** Ran SP% **115.8**
Speed ratings (Par 107): **107,105,104,103,101 94,93,93,86**
toteswinger: 1&2 £8.00, 1&3 £8.10, 2&3 £5.80. CSF £38.63 CT £202.96 TOTE £9.20: £2.80, £1.60, £1.80; EX 41.00.
Owner J W Mursell **Bred** J W Mursell **Trained** Charlton Mackrell, Somerset

FOCUS
A very open sprint handicap run at a good clip and in a course-record time. The form makes sense through the placed horses.

NOTEBOOK
Little Edward did not settle over 6f last time but, back down in trip and with a strong pace to chase, he travelled a lot more kindly. He came through on the inside entering the straight and picked up nicely inside the last. Despite his advancing years he remains a useful performer when getting the race run to suit. (op 15-2 tchd 8-1 and 13-2)
Bo McGinty(IRE), who had a good low draw and is on a fair mark, looked to hold solid claims, but while he kept on well he was never quite getting there. (op 4-1 tchd 5-1)
Canadian Danehill(IRE) chased the leading duo and was the first to kick for home, but he could not hang on in front for long. Nevertheless this was a return to form back at a track where he has a good record. (op 17-2)
Chjimes(IRE), winner of four of his last five starts, had been raised another 7lb since his last win and that proved too much at a track he has yet to shine on. He might yet be able to defy his new mark back at Lingfield, though. (op 11-2)
Harry Up had to work hard to get near the front from his wide draw and paid the price. (op 14-1)
Foxy Music had plenty of use made of him to lead from his wide draw. He weakened in the closing stages in the manner of a horse who needed this reappearance. (op 25-1 tchd 33-1)
The Jobber(IRE) has gone well fresh before but he was never a real threat on this seasonal return. (tchd 9-2 and 6-1)
Northern Bolt, who is entitled to come on for his seasonal reappearance, needs a right-handed rail to run against to be seen at his best. (op 9-2 tchd 7-1)
Methaaly(IRE) had his head hanging over the neighbouring stall to his right when the gates opened. Very slowly away as a result, this run can be forgotten. Official explanation: jockey said gelding hit its head on stalls (op 8-1)

986 SPONSOR A RACE BY CALLING 01902 390009 H'CAP 5f 216y(P)
9:20 (9:21) (Class 6) (0-65,65) 3-Y-0 **£2,047** (£604; £302) **Stalls** Low

Form RPR

1 **1** **Just Timmy Marcus**[32] 655 3-9-2 **63** .... GrahamGibbons 7 68+
(B P J Baugh) *s.i.s: hld up: hdwy on ins over 3f out: swtchd rt ent st: rdn over 1f out: led ins fnl f: drvn out* **10/3**[1]

540- **2** nk **Assent (IRE)**[158] 6865 3-9-1 **65** .... JamesMillman(3) 12 68
(B R Millman) *s.i.s: hld up and bhd: hdwy over 2f out: sn rdn: hung lft over 1f out: ev ch ins fnl f: r.o* **14/1**

30-1 **3** nk **Baby Josr**[14] 831 3-8-13 **60** ....(t) TonyHamilton 2 62
(I A Wood) *bhd: rdn over 1f out: hdwy fnl f: r.o wl towards fin* **9/1**

50-4 **4** shd **Fyelehk (IRE)**[15] 817 3-8-7 **54** .... AlanMunro 5 56
(B R Millman) *a.p: led wl over 1f out tl ins fnl f: no ex: fin 5th: plcd 4th* **4/1**[3]

14-0 **5** 3 **Monte Mayor Eagle**[14] 831 3-8-4 **54** ....(b) DavidProbert(3) 11 47
(D Haydn Jones) *nvr trbld ldrs: fin 6th: plcd 5th* **18/1**

1222 **6** ½ **Dancing Wave**[45] 492 3-8-6 **58** .... AmyBaker(5) 4 49
(M C Chapman) *led: hdd wl over 1f out: wknd ins fnl f: fin 7th: plcd 6th* **18/1**

0-43 **7** 3 ¾ **Theta Wave (USA)**[55] 358 3-8-13 **65** .... Louis-PhilippeBeuzelin(5) 8 45
(J R Gask) *hld up in mid-div: c wd st: bhd whn hung lft over 1f out: fin 8th: plcd 7th* **16/1**

055- **8** 8 **Port Ronan (USA)**[211] 5414 3-9-1 **62** .... TomEaves 1 18
(J S Wainwright) *w ldr: led over 3f out tl wl over 1f out: wknd fnl f: fin 9th: plcd 8th* **40/1**

21 **9** 47 **Five Gold Rings (IRE)**[31] 664 3-9-4 **65** .... ShaneKelly 10 —
(J A Osborne) *hld up: eased and virtually p.u 3f out: fin 10th: plcd 9th* **7/2**[2]

-524 **D** ¾ **Rocket Ruby**[14] 831 3-8-5 **52** .... PaulHanagan 3 52
(D Shaw) *a.p: rdn fnl f: kpt on: fin 4th, nk, nk & ¾l: disq: rdr failed to weigh in* **6/1**

1m 14.28s (-0.72) **Going Correction** -0.20s/f (Stan) **10** Ran SP% **115.1**
Speed ratings (Par 96): **96,95,95,94,90 89,84,73,11,94**
CSF £49.76 CT £396.25 TOTE £4.70: £2.30, £4.00, £3.30; EX 70.30 Place 6 £21.56, Place 5 £12.84.
Owner C R Watts **Bred** P D Moore **Trained** Audley, Staffs
■ Stewards' Enquiry : Paul Hanagan three-day ban: failed to weigh-in (Apr 11-13)

FOCUS
A modest handicap for three-year-olds. The winner built on his maiden win and is rated better than the bare form.
Five Gold Rings(IRE) Official explanation: jockey said, regarding the poor form shown, filly became upset, banged her head in the stalls, and was never travelling thereafter
T/Plt: £19.00 to a £1 stake. Pool: £109,144.81. 4185.40 winning tickets. T/Qpdt: £11.60 to a £1 stake. Pool: £9,105.96. 577.30 winning tickets. KH

987 - 993a (Foreign Racing) - See Raceform Interactive

DONCASTER (L-H)
Saturday, March 28

OFFICIAL GOING: Straight course - good to firm (good in places); round course - good (good to firm in places) (9.1)
Wind: Fresh, half bhd Weather: changeable and very breezy

994 WILLIAMHILL.COM - PLAY POKER BROCKLESBY CONDITIONS STKS 5f
2:10 (2:13) (Class 4) 2-Y-0 **£11,333** (£3,372; £1,685; £841) **Stalls** High

Form RPR

1 **Hearts Of Fire** 2-8-11 0 .... PaulEddery 14 87+
(Pat Eddery) *cl up: effrt 2f out: rdn to ld over 1f out: drvn ins fnl f and kpt on wl* **12/1**

2 2 ¼ **Archers Road (IRE)** 2-8-11 0 .... SamHitchcott 11 79+
(M R Channon) *cl up stands' side: led 1/2-way: rdn and hdd over 1f out: kpt on same pce ins fnl f* **25/1**

3 1 ¼ **Swilly Ferry (USA)** 2-8-11 0 .... MichaelHills 21 74+
(B W Hills) *stdd s and trckd ldrs on stands' rail: swtchd lft and gd hdwy over 2f out: rdn and ev ch appr fnl f: sn drvn and one pce* **9/2**[1]

4 1 ½ **Trade Secret** 2-8-11 0 .... AlanMunro 15 69+
(M Brittain) *prom nr stands' rail: rdn along 2f out: drvn over 1f out: kpt on same pce* **16/1**

5 2 3/4 **Shark Man (IRE)** 2-8-8 0 JackMitchell(3) 12 59+
(P J McBride) *dwlt and rr: hdwy and rdn whn hung lft 2f out: styd on u.p ins fnl f: nrst fin* **25/1**
6 nk **Could It Be Magic** 2-8-6 0 JackDean(5) 18 58
(W G M Turner) *racd cl to stands' rail: led: rdn along: hdd and outpcd 1/2-way: swtchd lft and drvn over 1f out: kpt on towards fin* **7/1³**
7 shd **Chicita Banana** 2-7-13 0 MatthewDavies(7) 6 53
(George Baker) *prom in centre: rdn along 2f out: grad wknd* **7/1³**
8 1 3/4 **Pullyourfingerout (IRE)** 2-8-11 0 DaneO'Neill 3 51
(B G Powell) *midfield: hdwy and in tch 1/2-way: rdn along 2f out and kpt on same pce* **50/1**
9 3/4 **Eight Hours** 2-8-11 0 PaulHanagan 4 53+
(R A Fahey) *wnt rt and hmpd s: rr tl hdwy whn hmpd 2f out: kpt on wl appr fnl f* **11/1**
10 nse **Bond Together** 2-8-11 0 TGMcLaughlin 16 48
(P D Evans) *dwlt and rr: hdwy 2f out: sn rdn and sme late hdwy* **12/1**
11 2 **Heslington** 2-8-11 0 TWilliams 2 45+
(M Brittain) *cl up on wd outside: rdn along 1/2-way: grad wknd* **33/1**
12 1/2 **Burtondale Boy (IRE)** 2-8-11 0 JamieMoriarty 8 39+
(P T Midgley) *hmpd s: sn cl up centre: rdn along over 2f out and grad wknd* **20/1**
13 nk **Take It To The Max** 2-8-11 0 PJMcDonald 22 38
(G M Moore) *in tch stands' side: rdn along 2f out: grad wknd* **12/1**
14 hd **Grace Jicaro** 2-8-1 0 DeanHeslop(5) 9 33
(Mrs L Williamson) *wnt lft s: a midfield* **100/1**
15 1 3/4 **Koo And The Gang (IRE)** 2-8-11 0 TomEaves 10 31
(B Ellison) *a towards rr* **20/1**
16 7 **Isle Of Ellis (IRE)** 2-8-11 0 RobertWinston 20 6
(A J McCabe) *s.i.s: a in rr* **16/1**
17 1 3/4 **Whippers Love (IRE)** 2-8-11 0 JoeFanning 13 —
(M Johnston) *dwlt: a towards rr* **11/2²**
18 5 **Usquaebach** 2-8-6 0 LiamJones 5 —
(H J Collingridge) *hmpd s: a bhd* **66/1**
19 13 **Reel Easy** 2-8-11 0 JerryO'Dwyer 7 —
(J R Holt) *hmpd s: a towards rr* **100/1**

59.71 secs (-0.79) **Going Correction** -0.10s/f (Good) **19** Ran SP% **127.3**
Speed ratings (Par 94): **102,98,96,94,89 89,88,86,84,84 81,80,80,80,77 66,63,55,34**
toteswinger: 1&2 £30.70, 1&3 £18.50, 2&3 £28.30 CSF £299.13 TOTE £14.70: £4.10, £6.80, £2.50; EX 282.00 TRIFECTA Not won..
Owner Pat Eddery Racing (Detroit) **Bred** Bearstone Stud **Trained** Nether Winchendon, Bucks
■ Stewards' Enquiry : Jack Mitchell one-day ban: careless riding (Apr 11)

FOCUS
This traditional early-season juvenile contest attracted a big field but very few got into contention from off the pace, and those racing nearer the stands' side appeared to hold a definite advantage over those more towards the middle of the track. The winner looks a decent recruit and the race should produce winners.

NOTEBOOK
Hearts Of Fire, a £13,000 third foal of a 5f winner from a family of sprinters, had clearly inherited plenty of speed and was backed. After tracking the leaders, he seemed to run green when striking the front but once his rider got serious he picked up well to settle the issue. There should be more to come. (op 11-1)
Archers Road(IRE), first foal of an unraced half-sister to several winners at around 1m, knew his job and showed good early pace before keeping on under pressure to hold off the favourite for second. He should be capable of winning a maiden this spring. (op 33-1)
Swilly Ferry(USA) ◆ tracked the leaders and looked the most likely winner when he was produced over a furlong out, but his effort flattened out. The son of Wiseman's Ferry will be better for the experience. (op 11-2)
Trade Secret, a cheaply bought half-brother to a 5f winner out of a multiple winning juvenile and related to several winning two-year-olds, was another to show signs of greenness. He chased the leaders and carried his head rather high, then wandered under pressure, but he did keep going and was clear of the rest. (op 12-1)
Shark Man(IRE) did best of those racing towards the centre and came from a fair way back to reach his final position. The Arakan half-brother to a couple of juvenile sprint winners is another who looks capable of winning races.
Could It Be Magic was one of the sharpest in the line-up and showed pace until fading in the last furlong. A son of Dubai Destination out of a 1m2f winner, he will appreciate longer trips in time and could make his mark in nurseries later in the season. (op 8-1)
Chicita Banana was fairly easy to back but showed plenty of pace up the centre of the track before her effort petered out. She is another who will appreciate longer trips. (tchd 6-1)
Burtondale Boy(IRE) is a half-brother to a juvenile winner and showed plenty of early pace. (op 25-1)
Whippers Love(IRE) was rather slowly into his stride and never got involved. His breeding suggests he will be a different horse when the ground is on the soft side. (op 10-1)
Usquaebach Official explanation: jockey said filly suffered interference at start

995 WILLIAM HILL SPRING MILE (H'CAP) 1m (S)
2:45 (2:48) (Class 2) 4-Y-0+

£31,155 (£9,330; £4,665; £2,335; £1,165; £585) **Stalls High**

Form RPR
0/5- 1 **Manassas (IRE)**337 [1598] 4-9-7 **92** DaneO'Neill 9 102
(B J Meehan) *racd stands' side: chsd ldrs: led over 1f out: hld on towards fin* **22/1**
42-0 2 1/2 **Extraterrestrial**21 [783] 5-9-7 **92** PaulHanagan 11 101
(R A Fahey) *hld up in rr: stdy hdwy 2f out: styd on wl ins fnl f: no ex nr fin* **16/1**
2223 3 3/4 **Majuro (IRE)**21 [785] 5-9-7 **92** NCallan 2 99+
(K A Ryan) *racd far side: chsd ldrs: led that gp over 1f out: no ex wl ins fnl f* **9/1**
241- 4 nk **The Fifth Member (IRE)**167 [6675] 5-9-3 **88** PatCosgrave 20 95
(J R Boyle) *racd stands' side: in rr: hdwy over 2f out: kpt on wl fnl f* **12/1**
10-0 5 1/2 **Lucky Dance (BRZ)**21 [783] 7-9-7 **92** RobertWinston 19 98
(A G Foster) *racd stands' side: chsd ldrs: drvn 4f out: kpt on wl fnl f* **33/1**
0-60 6 2 **Flawed Genius**7 [916] 4-9-5 **90** (t) AlanMunro 12 91
(K A Ryan) *racd stands' side: chsd ldrs on outer: edgd rt over 1f out: kpt on same pce* **20/1**
-565 7 1/2 **Opus Maximus (IRE)**27 [724] 4-9-2 **87** JoeFanning 10 87+
(M Johnston) *racd stands' side: w ldrs: one pce whn n.m.r 1f out* **25/1**
130- 8 shd **Medici Pearl**140 [7245] 5-9-5 **90** DuranFentiman 5 90
(T D Easterby) *racd far side: in rr: styd on fnl 2f: 2nd of 8 that gp* **66/1**
642- 9 3/4 **The Osteopath (IRE)**175 [6482] 6-9-2 **87** PhillipMakin 15 85
(M Dods) *racd stands' side: in rr: kpt on fnl f* **18/1**
125- 10 1 1/4 **Kings Point (IRE)**182 [6277] 8-8-9 **93** AdrianTNicholls 17 88
(D Nicholls) *led stands' side: hdd over 1f out: fdd* **28/1**
00-0 11 1 3/4 **Dabbers Ridge (IRE)**22 [778] 7-9-2 **87** DarrenWilliams 1 79
(I W McInnes) *racd far side: prom: outpcd 2f out: 3rd of 8 that gp* **66/1**
251- 12 5 **Nanton (USA)**136 [7291] 7-9-9 **94** DanielTudhope 21 75
(J S Goldie) *in rr stands' side: lost pl over 2f out* **9/1**
1001 13 1/2 **Nightjar (USA)**11 [856] 4-9-5 **90** 5ex FrancisNorton 18 70
(M Johnston) *racd stands' side: chsd ldrs: outpcd over 2f out: no threat after* **20/1**
00-0 14 nk **Raptor (GER)**21 [783] 6-9-5 **90** JimCrowley 7 69
(K R Burke) *racd far side: in tch: hdwy over 2f out: wknd 1f out: 4th of 8 that gp* **40/1**
01-4 15 4 1/2 **Invincible Force (IRE)**11 [856] 5-9-8 **93** (b) TPQueally 4 62
(Paul Green) *racd far side: trckd ldr: led that side 3f out: hdd & wknd over 1f out: 5th of 8 that gp* **40/1**
0-14 16 1 **Exit Smiling**25 [747] 7-9-8 **93** 5ex JamieMoriarty 6 60
(P T Midgley) *racd far side: prom: lost pl over 2f out: 6th of 8 that gp* **100/1**
160- 17 2 1/4 **Osteopathic Remedy (IRE)**175 [6482] 5-9-7 **92** TomEaves 8 54
(M Dods) *in rr far side: lost pl over 2f out: 7th of 8 that gp* **28/1**
103- 18 14 **Slugger O'Toole**162 [6783] 4-9-9 **94** RichardKingscote 14 25
(S C Williams) *trckd ldrs stands' side: drvn 4f out: lost pl over 2f out: bhd whn eased ins fnl f* **12/1**
1/0- 19 1/2 **Fireside**329 [1808] 4-9-7 **92** JimmyFortune 16 22
(M A Jarvis) *racd stands' side: trckd ldrs: t.k.h: lost pl over 2f out: bhd whn eased ins fnl f* **4/1¹**
012- 20 nk **Mangham (IRE)**152 [7019] 4-9-9 **94** PaulMulrennan 3 23
(D H Brown) *led 7 others far side: hdd 3f out: wknd qckly: last of 8 that gp* **8/1³**
-111 L **Spectait**23 [766] 7-9-7 **92** 5ex FMBerry 22 —
(Jonjo O'Neill) *rrd over in stalls: tk no part* **13/2²**

1m 37.97s (-1.33) **Going Correction** -0.10s/f (Good) **21** Ran SP% **127.4**
Speed ratings (Par 109): **102,101,100,100,99 97,97,97,96,95 93,88,88,87,83 82,80,66,65,65**
toteswinger: 1&2 not won, 1&3 £148.40, 2&3 £38.40 CSF £310.11 CT £3466.53 TOTE £28.20: £5.60, £4.20, £2.50, £3.80; EX 367.80 TRIFECTA Not won..
Owner Mrs R Philipps **Bred** Mrs Rebecca Philipps **Trained** Manton, Wilts

FOCUS
Another warm edition of the Lincoln's consolation race, which was introduced in 1993. There was just a 7lb spread between the top-rated runners and those at the bottom of a handicap, the latter racing off a BHA mark of 87. The field quickly split into two groups, with eight on the far side and the remainder taking the stands' side flank. The larger group held the call, with third-home Majuro doing much the best of those drawn low, although it was a case of the pace being among the high-drawn group rather than any bias.

NOTEBOOK
Manassas(IRE) was one of the few in the field who was not fully exposed and was appearing on a racecourse for just the fifth time. A Yarmouth maiden winner on his second run at two before finishing unplaced in the Group 1 Jean-Luc Lagardere at Longchamp, he ran just once last term, when last of five at Sandown in April. From stall nine, his rider made the right choice to race with the stands'-side runners, the eight drawn lower than him having taken the alternative route, and the gelding raced on the outer of the bunch, travelling well, before showing in front over a furlong out. He is clearly over his problems and could be ready for a crack at a Listed race. (op 20-1)
Extraterrestrial was held up in rear before weaving his way through and going after the winner in the final furlong. He goes well in the spring, so the Thirsk Hunt Cup, which he won last season from a 6lb lower mark, would be an obvious target. (tchd 14-1)
Majuro(IRE) ◆ had finished in the frame in a string of handicaps on sand this year, over just 6f on his latest start, and was able to race off an 8lb lower turf mark. He nearly made it tell, finishing clear on his side and looking like holding on to the overall lead at one stage, but he drifted towards the centre of the track under pressure and was worn down. This was a good effort. (op 12-1)
The Fifth Member(IRE) ◆ was put up 7lb for an impressive win at Goodwood when last seen in the autumn but there should be more improvement to come. Easier ground is perhaps ideal for him. (op 14-1)
Lucky Dance(BRZ) was another to have had a spin on sand recently. Considering he was being driven along at halfway, he did well to stick on for fifth, although he looks a little high in the weights. (tchd 40-1)
Flawed Genius ran a decent race with the tongue strap reapplied, keeping on for sixth. He is not one to trust entirely, though. (op 18-1)
Opus Maximus(IRE) ran respectably on this return to turf but was looking held when squeezed out just over a furlong from home as the runner-up burst through. He was due to be dropped 2lb before this.
Medici Pearl came through from the back of the far-side eight to finish a never-dangerous second in her group. She should be spot-on next time. (tchd 80-1 in places)
The Osteopath(IRE) was racing from a career-high mark, having been put up 5lb for finishing second at Redcar on his final run last season, and was doing his best work late on. (op 20-1 tchd 22-1 in places)
Kings Point(IRE) was responsible for the pace on the stands' flank and only relinquished the lead to the winner approaching the last furlong. (tchd 25-1)
Dabbers Ridge(IRE) was third in the far-side group but only 11th overall. He is due to go down 3lb and will be suited by a return to 7f.
Nanton(USA) ran a slightly disappointing race off a 4lb higher mark than when runner-up in last year's Cambridgeshire. (op 10-1 tchd 17-2)
Fireside, formerly with Peter Chapple-Hyam, had a similar profile to the winner, having run just once last season when striking into himself in the 2,000 Guineas. A fancy for the Lincoln before missing the cut, he was a little reluctant to enter the stalls and ran badly, coming under pressure with more than three furlongs to run and dropping out to beat one home. This was surely not his running. His rider reported that the colt was too keen. Official explanation: jockey said colt ran too keen (tchd 5-1)
Mangham(IRE) had been prominent in the Lincoln betting but missed the cut by one. He led the far-side bunch for five furlongs before backpedalling. (op 10-1)
Spectait, back on turf after a hat-trick of Wolverhampton wins, reared over backwards as the stalls opened but appeared unhurt. (tchd 6-1)

996 WILLIAMHILL.COM - PLAY LIVE CASINO CAMMIDGE TROPHY (LISTED RACE) 6f
3:20 (3:21) (Class 1) 3-Y-0+

£22,708 (£8,608; £4,308; £2,148; £1,076; £540) **Stalls High**

Form RPR
546- 1 **Prime Defender**168 [6645] 5-9-2 109 MichaelHills 6 112+
(B W Hills) *in tch: swtchd rt and hdwy wl over 1f out: rdn ins fnl f: led fnl 50yds* **3/1¹**
30U- 2 1/2 **Pusey Street Lady**239 [4586] 5-8-11 91 WilliamBuick 2 105
(J Gallagher) *chsd ldrs on outer: hdwy to ld qwl over 1f out: sn rdn and edgd lft: drvn and edgd rt ins fnl f: hdd and no ex fnl 50yds* **40/1**
411- 3 2 1/4 **Knot In Wood (IRE)**175 [6468] 7-9-2 108 PaulHanagan 4 103
(R A Fahey) *midfield: hdwy 2f out: rdn and n.m.r ent fnl f: kpt on* **10/1**
65-2 4 shd **Vitznau (IRE)**21 [781] 5-9-2 104 JimmyFortune 9 102
(R Hannon) *hld up in rr: hdwy 2f out: swtchd rt and rdn over 1f out: styd on strly ins fnl f: nrst fin* **6/1³**

312- **5** *3* **Inxile (IRE)**[209] 5556 4-9-5 108 ...... AdrianTNicholls 14 96
(D Nicholls) *cl up: led 1/2-way: rdn and hdd wl over 2f out: edgd lft and grad wknd* **9/2**[2]

1/0- **6** *shd* **Max One Two Three (IRE)**[328] 1830 4-8-11 99 ...... RichardKingscote 1 88
(Tom Dascombe) *in tch on wd outside: effrt over 2f out: sn rdn and kpt on same pce* **11/1**

/64- **7** *3/4* **Beacon Lodge (IRE)**[301] 2605 4-9-2 105 ...... AdamKirby 10 91
(C G Cox) *hld up in rr: hdwy 2f out: styd on ins fnl f* **11/1**

-523 **8** *1* **Tamagin (USA)**[39] 579 6-9-2 98 ...... NCallan 7 93+
(K A Ryan) *led: pushed along and hdd 1/2-way: rdn 2f out and sn wknd* **8/1**

-001 **9** *4* **Beaver Patrol (IRE)**[30] 696 7-9-2 104 ......(b) StephenCarson 15 76
(Eve Johnson Houghton) *towards rr and rdn along 1/2-way: nvr a factor* **15/2**

3060 **10** *nk* **Internationaldebut (IRE)**[7] 913 4-9-2 92 ...... LiamJones 13 75
(S Parr) *chsd ldrs: rdn along 2f out: sn drvn and wknd* **40/1**

530- **11** *1/2* **Quiet Elegance**[168] 6651 4-8-11 89 ...... JimmyQuinn 11 69
(E J Alston) *a towards rr* **40/1**

10-0 **12** *1/2* **Hoh Hoh Hoh**[21] 785 7-9-2 103 ...... RobertWinston 5 72
(R J Price) *prom: rdn along 2f out: sn wknd* **25/1**

-443 **13** *22* **Music Box Express**[9] 884 5-9-2 65 ......(t) MatthewDavies 16 6
(George Baker) *chsd ldrs: rdn along 2f out: sn wknd* **250/1**

1m 10.62s (-2.98) **Going Correction** -0.10s/f (Good) **13** Ran SP% **117.7**
Speed ratings (Par 111): **115,114,111,111,107 107,106,104,99,99 98,97,68**
toteswingers: 1&2 £29.20, 1&3 £9.50, 2&3 £77.00 CSF £146.17 TOTE £4.00: £1.70, £7.50, £2.40; EX 207.70 TRIFECTA Not won..
Owner S Falle, M Franklin, J Sumsion **Bred** Christopher J Mason **Trained** Lambourn, Berks

FOCUS
A big field for this Listed sprint, which featured several who had contested the race before. The time was above average for the grade, being just 0.39 secs outside the course record.

NOTEBOOK
Prime Defender, who was fourth last season and came into this race on a long losing run. That said, he was a Listed winner in 2007 and had run well in Group company last season, which made him a major player. He came out of the pack to catch the runner-up inside the last furlong and scored a little cosily. This should serve to boost his confidence and the Duke of York Stakes looks a feasible early-season target. (tchd 7-2)
Pusey Street Lady, a course-and-distance winner on soft who likes a flat track, was tuned up for this first run since August and stuck to the centre of the track from her low draw. She took a clear advantage over a furlong out but could not hold off the winner's late surge. Connections will nevertheless be consoled by the fact she earned black type, which increases her potential paddock value.
Knot In Wood(IRE) ◆ also contested this race last year and ran well on his first start since scoring on Polytrack in October. He has come back in good heart and looks one to keep on-side, especially for one of the big sprint handicaps. (op 17-2 tchd 8-1)
Vitznau(IRE) has won at 6f but his best form has been at 7f. He had been narrowly beaten in a similar contest over that trip on his return and gave a clear indication here that he needs the extra furlong, as he did all his running late. (op 11-2)
Inxile(IRE) showed plenty of pace and was a bit keen early. He stays this trip but is possibly best at 5f and did not last home. This run will have taken the fizz out of him. (op 5-1 tchd 11-2)
Max One Two Three(IRE) has been lightly raced of late but was a Listed scorer as a juvenile, when she won both her starts over this trip. She did not run too badly, finishing upsides the fifth, and should be able to make her mark at this level if building on this outing. (op 12-1)
Beacon Lodge(IRE), another who missed most of last season due to injury, stayed on nicely from the rear and could do well over 7f this term. (op 12-1 tchd 14-1)
Tamagin(USA) was fit from the all-weather and made the early running, but he never got any peace and was beaten when rather squeezed out inside the last furlong. Official explanation: jockey said, regarding appearing to ease shortly before line, that he was short of room having suffered interference and was then caught on the heels of Inxile; jockey said gelding hung right-handed. (op 12-1)
Beaver Patrol(IRE) picked up a nice prize in Dubai last time but was in trouble before halfway here. (op 7-1 tchd 8-1)

997 WILLIAM HILL LINCOLN (HERITAGE H'CAP) 1m (S)
3:55 (3:58) (Class 2) 4-Y-0+

£77,887 (£23,325; £11,662; £5,837; £2,912; £1,462) **Stalls** High

Form RPR

111- **1** **Expresso Star (USA)**[163] 6763 4-8-12 97 ...... JimmyFortune 9 113+
(J H M Gosden) *racd far side: in rr: str run to ld overall over 2f out: hrd rdn: styd on strly* **10/3**[1]

000- **2** *2 1/2* **Zaahid (IRE)**[182] 6269 5-8-11 96 ...... RobertWinston 2 106
(B W Hills) *racd far side: chsd ldrs: kpt on wl fnl f: no imp* **11/1**

1-21 **3** *1 1/4* **Flipando (IRE)**[21] 783 8-8-13 98 5ex ...... PhillipMakin 3 105
(T D Barron) *racd far side: hld up in tch: effrt over 2f out: styd on same pce fnl f* **16/1**

550- **4** *hd* **Mia's Boy**[175] 6476 5-9-3 102 ...... JimmyQuinn 20 109
(C A Dwyer) *trckd one other exclusively stands' side: led that pair over 1f out: kpt on wl: 1st of 7 gp towards stands' side* **16/1**

530- **5** *1/2* **Huzzah (IRE)**[175] 6476 4-8-13 98 ...... MichaelHills 17 104
(B W Hills) *led centre gp: kpt on wl fnl 2f: 2nd of 7 that racd towards stands' side* **12/1**

2-25 **6** *1 1/4* **Philario (IRE)**[21] 781 4-8-7 97 ...... MartinLane(5) 21 100
(K R Burke) *led one other exclusively stands' side: kpt on one pce fnl 2f: 3rd of 7 that gp* **50/1**

05-2 **7** *1 1/4* **Blythe Knight (IRE)**[16] 815 9-9-4 108 ...... FrederikTylicki(5) 6 108
(J J Quinn) *racd far side: in tch: effrt over 2f out: kpt on fnl f* **20/1**

033- **8** *shd* **Charm School**[140] 7245 4-8-11 96 ...... RichardMullen 19 96
(J H M Gosden) *racd towards centre: in rr: outpcd over 2f out: styd on wl fnl f: 4th of 7 that gp* **10/1**

3000 **9** *3* **Docofthebay (IRE)**[7] 913 5-9-4 103 ......(b) JoeFanning 18 96
(J A Osborne) *in rr centre: effrt and edgd rt over 2f out: nvr nr ldrs: 5th of 7 gp towards stands' side* **20/1**

-522 **10** *nk* **Ace Of Hearts**[21] 783 10-8-7 95 ...... JackMitchell(3) 11 88
(C F Wall) *racd far side: in rr: kpt on fnl 2f: nvr a factor* **22/1**

03-4 **11** *2* **Benandonner (USA)**[21] 781 6-8-9 94 ...... PaulHanagan 5 82
(R A Fahey) *racd far side: in tch: effrt over 2f out: one pce* **9/1**[3]

635- **12** *1 1/4* **Cobo Bay**[199] 5795 4-8-12 97 ......(p) NCallan 1 83
(K A Ryan) *led overall on far side tl over 2f out: hung rt and wknd over 1f out* **40/1**

1-30 **13** *hd* **Eva's Request (IRE)**[36] 643 4-9-0 104 ...... MCGeran(5) 7 89
(M R Channon) *racd far side: in rr: nvr a factor* **33/1**

060- **14** *hd* **Dream Lodge (IRE)**[175] 6476 5-8-13 98 ...... TPQueally 4 83
(J G Given) *racd far side: chsd ldrs: lost pl over 1f out* **40/1**

-041 **15** *3 3/4* **Swop (IRE)**[37] 615 6-9-6 105 5ex ...... DaneO'Neill 15 81
(L M Cumani) *chsd ldr centre: effrt over 2f out: lost pl over 1f out: 6th of 7 towards stands' side* **9/2**[2]

3-42 **16** *hd* **Whistledownwind**[35] 636 4-9-0 99 ......(v[1]) ShaneKelly 10 75
(J Noseda) *racd far side: in rr: effrt over 2f out: hung lft and sn btn* **28/1**

63-0 **17** *11* **Bolodenka (IRE)**[21] 783 7-8-10 95 ...... JamieMoriarty 8 47
(R A Fahey) *racd far side: mid-div: lost pl over 2f out: bhd whn eased* **50/1**

1-21 **18** *16* **Titan Triumph**[42] 551 5-8-11 96 5ex ......(t) JimCrowley 22 13
(W J Knight) *racd stands' side: in rr: wl bhd fnl 2f: last of 7 that gp* **16/1**

0040 **19** *25* **Royal Power (IRE)**[36] 639 6-9-0 99 ...... AdrianTNicholls 13 —
(D Nicholls) *racd far side: tk fierce hold: lost pl over 2f out: heavily eased* **50/1**

40R- **R** **Don't Panic (IRE)**[147] 7147 5-9-5 104 ...... AlanMunro 16 —
(P W Chapple-Hyam) *ref tro r: tk no part* **14/1**

1m 36.51s (-2.79) **Going Correction** -0.10s/f (Good) course record **20** Ran SP% **131.7**
Speed ratings (Par 109): **109,106,105,105,104 103,102,101,98,98 96,95,95,95,91 91,80,64,39,—**
toteswinger: 1&2 £35.10, 1&3 £32.90, 2&3 £58.10 CSF £37.80 CT £555.82 TOTE £4.80: £2.20, £3.80, £4.60, £3.50; EX 71.80 Trifecta £1185.30 Pool: £22959.36 - 14.33 winning units..
Owner H R H Princess Haya Of Jordan **Bred** Stonerside Stable **Trained** Newmarket, Suffolk

FOCUS
For the second year running an official rating of at least 94 was required to get into the Lincoln field. Smokey Oakey, last year's winner, was not declared because of the ground, leaving Lady Deauville to head the weights until she became a non-runner because of unsuitable underfoot conditions. The winning time was over half a second faster than for the earlier Spring Mile, and there was a very different scenario than for that race, as this time the largest group, 13-strong, raced down the far side, with five of those drawn high racing more down the centre of the track and only two runners going stands' side.

NOTEBOOK
Expresso Star(USA) ◆ came out of the same nine stall as Spring Mile winner Manassas, but unlike that horse he latched on to the larger group on the far wing. After taking the lead with a smart burst of speed, probably in front sooner than was ideal, he momentarily seemed vulnerable as he came under pressure, but he was well on top in the last half-furlong, staying on strongly as befits a horse who gets further. The ante-post favourite since the market opened in January, he only took his chance after his trainer's representatives gave the go-ahead, having walked the course following the first race. His three wins last autumn came with cut underfoot, and he will not mind a return to easier conditions. He confirmed himself a most progressive performer and is surely up to Listed level at least, with his turn of foot a useful weapon in his armoury. (op 4-1 tchd 5-1)
Zaahid(IRE) finished fourth in the Spring Mile last year, having missed the cut in this, and ran a sound race from stall two, probably having little chance against the unexposed winner on these terms. He should continue to give a good account but it should be borne in mind that he rather lost his way after taking the Victoria Cup at Ascot last May. That event is a likely target this season, with the Spring Cup at Newbury (third last year) beforehand. (op 12-1)
Flipando(IRE), penalised for his win in the Lincoln Trial at Wolverhampton earlier in the month, ran a solid race and remains in top form, but he has not won on turf since the Zetland Gold Cup at Redcar in May 2007.
Mia's Boy ◆, drawn 20, raced up the stands' rail tracking one other. He travelled well before being let down and could have done with getting a lead for longer before sticking on for a highly creditable fourth. The Newbury Spring Cup looks a realistic target. (tchd 18-1)
Huzzah(IRE) went off the boil last season after a good spring and this was an encouraging return to action. He led four others in single file down the centre of the track, a bit nearer to the stands' side than the far side, and stuck on willingly for fifth. (op 11-1 tchd 10-1)
Philario(IRE), who usually competes in Listed company and was running in only his second handicap, raced down the stands' fence, tracked by just Mia's Boy, and did well to finish sixth.
Blythe Knight(IRE) was running in the Lincoln for the fifth time - he was successful when it was held at Redcar in 2006 and finished runner-up last year. He was conceding upwards of 3lb all round and ran another creditable race.
Charm School ◆ had won a maiden at this meeting a year ago and, following a light campaign, was a fast-finishing third in a 7f handicap here on the last day of the season. Representing the same trainer and owner as Expresso Star, he looked well held with a quarter of a mile or so left, not helped by racing in the centre group of five, but found his stride when it was all over and made late gains. He is capable of picking up a nice handicap. (op 11-1)
Docofthebay(IRE) likes these big-field handicaps but could never get involved, although he was not helped by racing in the centre group. He is due to race off 6lb lower now. (op 22-1)
Ace Of Hearts, the Lincoln Trial runner-up, could never get into the action and is now set for a 4lb rise. (op 28-1)
Benandonner(USA), runner-up in the Spring Mile and the Spring Cup last year, was slightly disappointing after his promising return to action at Wolverhampton. (op 12-1)
Swop(IRE), who carried a penalty for his win over slightly shorter at Nad Al Sheba, was well supported. He was below par, coming under pressure over three furlongs out and finishing well back, but he was at a disadvantage racing in the centre-to-stands' side quintet. His return to a chilly Britain from sunnier climes may not have helped either. Official explanation: jockey said gelding did not get the run of the race (op 13-2, tchd 7-1 in a place)
Titan Triumph was another done no favours by the draw as it turned out, and never looked like transferring his red-hot streak on Polytrack over to turf. (tchd 18-1)
Royal Power(IRE) Official explanation: jockey said horse ran too keen
Don't Panic(IRE), winner of the Spring Mile 12 months ago, refused to leave the stalls, as he had done on his final appearance last year.

998 BOB BEEVERS MEMORIAL MAIDEN STKS 1m 2f 60y
4:30 (4:33) (Class 5) 3-Y-0 **£4,533** (£1,348; £674; £336) **Stalls** Low

Form RPR

4- **1** **Everynight (IRE)**[143] 7200 3-9-3 0 ...... AlanMunro 1 85
(M Botti) *trckd ldrs: hdwy 4f out: effrt over 2f out: swtchd lft and rdn to ld ins fnl f: sn drvn and jst hld on* **16/1**

05- **2** *shd* **Above Average (IRE)**[177] 6425 3-9-3 0 ...... MichaelHills 4 85
(B W Hills) *hld up in tch: hdwy over 3f out: rdn to ld over 1f out: drvn: edgd lft and hdd ins fnl f: rallied wl towards fin: jst hld* **11/4**[2]

2- **3** *shd* **Classically (IRE)**[154] 6978 3-9-3 0 ...... JimmyQuinn 10 84
(R Charlton) *hld up in midfield: stdy hdwy 3f out: rdn to chal on outer over 1f out: snd drvn and edgd lft ins fnl f: styd on wl towards fin* **13/2**[3]

2- **4** *4 1/2* **London Bridge**[154] 6977 3-9-3 0 ...... JimmyFortune 8 76
(J H M Gosden) *trckd ldrs: hdwy to chse ldr 1/2-way: cl up 4f out: rdn and ev ch over 2f out: sn drvn: n.m.r and wknd appr fnl f* **10/11**[1]

5 *3 3/4* **Amazing Tiger (GER)** 3-9-3 0 ...... JoeFanning 6 69
(M Johnston) *led: rdn along over 3f out: hdd wl over 1f out: drvn whn n.m.r appr fnl f: wknd* **14/1**

6 *2 3/4* **Outrageous Request** 3-9-3 0 ...... PaulEddery 13 64+
(Pat Eddery) *hld up towards rr: stdy hdwy 3f out: styd on appr fnl f: nrestfin* **40/1**

00- **7** *5* **Cornish Castle (USA)**[190] 6085 3-9-3 0 ...... GrahamGibbons 5 54
(T D Walford) *hld up towards rr: hdwy over 3f out: rdn over 2f out and sn wknd* **80/1**

\- **8** *nk* **Refuse Toulouse (IRE)** 3-9-3 0 ...... AdamKirby 7 53
(C G Cox) *nvr bttr than midfield* **28/1**

9 *12* **Cooperman** 3-8-10 0 ...... PaulPickard(7) 3 —
(P T Midgley) *s.i.s: t.k.h: a in rr* **200/1**

0- **10** 3 **Baheeya**[277] 3349 3-8-12 0 NCallan 2 —
(C E Brittain) *prom: rdn along 4f out: wknd over 2f out* **80/1**

50- **11** 2 ½ **Martha's Girl (USA)**[155] 6945 3-8-12 0 (t) PaulMulrennan 9 —
(D H Brown) *prom: rdn along 3f out: drvn over 2f out and sn wknd* **100/1**

63- **12** ½ **Enhancing**[230] 4896 3-8-12 0 RobertWinston 14 —
(A J McCabe) *hld up: a in rr* **50/1**

13 25 **Tarraad** 3-8-12 0 AndreaAtzeni(5) 11 —
(M Botti) *a towards rr* **80/1**

2m 13.58s (2.38) **Going Correction** +0.125s/f (Good) **13** Ran SP% **118.0**
Speed ratings (Par 98): **95,94,94,91,88 86,82,81,72,69 67,67,47**
toteswinger: 1&2 £7.20, 1&3 £8.50, 2&3 £3.00 CSF £58.62 TOTE £18.20: £2.80, £1.60, £1.80; EX 84.30 Trifecta £341.00 Pool: £889.54 - 1.93 winning units..
Owner Tenuta Dorna Di Montaltuzzo SRL **Bred** A Panetta **Trained** Newmarket, Suffolk

FOCUS
This maiden has produced the odd decent sort in recent seasons and on this occasion featured a number of unexposed performers, some from major yards. The betting suggested it was a five-horse race and that quintet dominated after the early pace was moderate.
Baheeya Official explanation: jockey said filly became unbalanced final 2f

999 WILLIAMHILL.COM - PLAY BINGO H'CAP 1m 2f 60y
5:05 (5:07) (Class 4) (0-85,85) 4-Y-O+ **£6,476** (£1,927; £963; £481) **Stalls** Low

Form RPR

320/ **1** **Spring Jim**[1280] 5496 8-8-9 **76** WilliamBuick 3 86
(J R Fanshawe) *hld up in midfield: nt clr run over 2f out: swtchd rt: str run to ld last 75yds* **10/1**

240- **2** 1 ½ **Granston (IRE)**[163] 6763 8-8-13 **80** RobertWinston 6 87
(J D Bethell) *chsd ldr: led over 2f out: hdd and no ex ins fnl f* **5/1**[2]

20-6 **3** 1 ¾ **Kingsdale Orion (IRE)**[23] 766 5-9-0 **81** TomEaves 8 85
(B Ellison) *chsd ldrs: kpt on wl fnl f* **20/1**

2-06 **4** shd **Veiled Applause**[21] 787 6-9-2 **83** GrahamGibbons 9 87
(J J Quinn) *trckd ldrs: smooth hdwy to chal over 1f out: styd on same pce ins fnl f* **12/1**

1143 **5** 2 ½ **Can Can Star**[9] 879 6-8-13 **80** ShaneKelly 2 79+
(A W Carroll) *hld up in rr: nt clr run 3f out: styd on steadily fnl f* **12/1**

120- **6** hd **Buddhist Monk**[168] 6646 4-9-4 **85** JimCrowley 11 84+
(Ian Williams) *t.k.h in rr: hdwy and nt clr run over 2f out: kpt on fnl f: sddle slipped* **7/1**[3]

336- **7** 2 ¾ **Hurlingham**[146] 7150 5-8-11 **78** PaulMulrennan 1 72
(M W Easterby) *in tch: effrt on ins and nt clr run over 2f out: nt rcvr* **20/1**

01-1 **8** 6 **Planetary Motion (USA)**[34] 648 4-8-10 **77** JoeFanning 7 60
(M Johnston) *led tl 6f out: chsd ldrs: nt clr run over 2f out: wknd over 1f out* **4/1**[1]

10-0 **9** 2 ¼ **Ellmau**[64] 271 4-9-4 **85** RichardMullen 16 64
(A J McCabe) *prom: wkng whn hmpd over 1f out* **50/1**

126- **10** 2 ¼ **Shady Gloom (IRE)**[189] 6113 4-8-12 **79** NCallan 14 54
(K A Ryan) *t.k.h: trckd ldrs: wknd over 1f out* **10/1**

/26- **11** nk **Royal Flynn**[16] 3673 7-8-6 **78** (p) KellyHarrison(5) 15 53
(Mrs K Walton) *in rr: nvr a factor* **100/1**

1143 **12** ½ **Folio (IRE)**[12] 847 9-8-11 **78** AlanMunro 20 52
(W J Musson) *in tch: effrt over 2f out: wknd over 1f out* **14/1**

400- **13** 2 ¾ **Film Festival (USA)**[146] 7150 6-8-2 **76** LanceBetts(7) 13 45
(B Ellison) *t.k.h in rr: sme hdwy over 2f out: nvr a factor* **20/1**

033- **14** 4 ½ **Jeer (IRE)**[171] 6582 5-9-1 **82** DaleGibson 19 43
(M W Easterby) *in rr: drvn over 4f out* **20/1**

611- **15** 2 ½ **La Columbina**[218] 5230 4-8-7 **77** AndrewMullen(3) 12 33
(G A Harker) *hld up in rr: nvr on terms: hmpd over 1f out* **50/1**

3235 **16** 2 **Tourist**[15] 834 4-8-12 **79** DarrenWilliams 5 32
(D Shaw) *mid-div: lost pl 3f out* **16/1**

-006 **17** 8 **Aviso (GER)**[12] 850 5-9-1 **82** TPQueally 18 20
(B J Curley) *t.k.h: sn trcking ldrs: lost pl over 1f out: eased* **50/1**

430- **18** 1 ¼ **Daaweitza**[151] 7041 6-8-13 **80** TGMcLaughlin 10 16
(B Ellison) *s.i.s: hdwy on ins over 3f out: no threat whn bdly hmpd over 1f out* **50/1**

036- **19** 7 **Bowder Stone (IRE)**[166] 6704 4-8-12 **79** JimmyQuinn 17 2
(E J Alston) *chsd ldrs: led 6f out tl over 2f out: sn wknd and eased* **25/1**

2m 10.22s (-0.98) **Going Correction** +0.125s/f (Good) **19** Ran SP% **127.0**
Speed ratings (Par 105): **108,106,105,105,103 103,100,96,94,92 92,91,89,86,84 82,76,75,69**
toteswinger: 1&2 £10.90, 1&3 £67.20, 2&3 £25.20 CSF £54.11 CT £1020.78 TOTE £12.10: £3.30, £1.50, £5.90, £3.70; EX 66.40 TRIFECTA Not won..
Owner Andrew & Julia Turner **Bred** C I T Racing Ltd **Trained** Newmarket, Suffolk
■ Stewards' Enquiry : William Buick three-day ban: careless riding (Apr 11-13)

FOCUS
A decent and competitive handicap, but the pace was only steady and there was a good deal of scrimmaging as the field bunched in the straight. Several of those who endured rough passages can be rated a good deal better than the bare form.
Buddhist Monk ◆ Official explanation: jockey said saddle had slipped
Bowder Stone(IRE) Official explanation: jockey said gelding ran too keen early on and had been struck into

1000 CROWNHOTEL-BAWTRY.COM APPRENTICE H'CAP 1m 4f
5:40 (5:40) (Class 5) (0-70,70) 4-Y-O+ **£3,412** (£1,007; £504) **Stalls** Low

Form RPR

-336 **1** **Monfils Monfils (USA)**[5] 932 7-9-1 **67** AmyRyan(3) 17 75
(A J McCabe) *mid-div: hdwy over 3f out: led over 1f out: edgd lft: hld on towards fin* **12/1**

0050 **2** ½ **Red Wine**[35] 631 10-8-12 **66** KarenKenny(5) 1 73
(A J McCabe) *s.i.s: in rr: hdwy and c wd over 2f out: styd on wl ins fnl f* **18/1**

1103 **3** ¾ **Lytham (IRE)**[9] 877 8-8-6 **60** TobyAtkinson(5) 4 66
(A W Carroll) *hld up in tch: smooth hdwy over 3f out: chal 2f out: styd on same pce ins fnl f* **16/1**

332- **4** hd **Elite Land**[37] 7695 6-8-11 **63** LanceBetts(3) 2 68
(B Ellison) *chsd ldrs: outpcd over 2f out: styd on wl ins fnl f* **5/1**[1]

006- **5** 1 ¼ **Moonwalking**[64] 2249 5-8-11 **60** MCGeran 12 63
(Jedd O'Keeffe) *mid-div: gd hdwy over 2f out: ev ch 1f out: kpt on same pce* **16/1**

450- **6** 1 ¾ **Kiho**[218] 5216 4-8-4 **62** DanielBlackett(7) 11 63
(Eve Johnson Houghton) *in rr: hdwy on outer over 2f out: kpt on wl fnl f* **25/1**

155- **7** 2 ¾ **Trip The Light**[194] 5967 4-9-1 **66** (v) FrederikTylicki 6 62+
(R A Fahey) *trckd ldrs: chal over 2f out: wknd appr fnl f: sddle slipped* **11/2**[2]

3342 **8** 1 ¼ **Ghufa (IRE)**[9] 885 5-9-4 **70** MatthewDavies(3) 10 64
(George Baker) *led 3f: chsd ldrs: led over 3f out: hdd over 1f out: sn wknd* **16/1**

352/ **9** ½ **Zefooha (FR)**[510] 6673 5-8-11 **60** KellyHarrison 3 53
(T D Walford) *trckd ldrs: hdwy on ins to chal over 3f out: wknd over 1f out* **16/1**

42-6 **10** 1 ¼ **Surprise Pension (IRE)**[33] 656 5-8-6 **60** JamieKyne(5) 13 51
(J J Quinn) *t.k.h: sn trcking ldrs: wknd 2f out* **9/1**

5/0- **11** hd **Toshi (USA)**[27] 4848 7-8-13 **62** GaryBartley 8 53
(J S Goldie) *hld up in midfield: hdwy 3f out: wknd over 1f out* **5/1**[1]

1213 **12** 1 ½ **Bridgewater Boys**[5] 935 8-9-4 **67** (b) Louis-PhilippeBeuzelin 7 56
(T J Pitt) *in rr: sme hdwy over 2f out: nvr on terms* **25/1**

006- **13** ¾ **Lady Sorcerer**[115] 7539 4-8-9 **63** MartinLane(3) 16 51
(A P Jarvis) *in rr: effrt 3f out: nvr a factor* **33/1**

4361 **14** 1 ¾ **This Ones For Eddy**[9] 886 4-8-12 **63** AndreaAtzeni 19 48
(S Parr) *a towards rr* **17/2**[3]

0-0 **15** 13 **Treetops Hotel (IRE)**[72] 169 10-8-7 **56** oh11 AmyBaker 9 20
(L R James) *in rr: bdly hanmpered on ins over 2f out* **100/1**

0-00 **16** 6 **Punta Galera (IRE)**[10] 554 6-8-2 **56** oh4 KrishGundowry(5) 18 10
(Paul Green) *chsd ldr: led after 3f tl over 3f out: wknd over 1f out* **50/1**

156- **17** 3 ½ **Dimashq**[196] 5917 7-8-2 **56** oh5 PaulPickard(5) 5 5
(P T Midgley) *prom: lost pl over 3f out* **16/1**

200- **18** 4 ½ **Plenilune (IRE)**[159] 6868 4-8-11 **62** DeanHeslop 14 4
(M Brittain) *chsd ldrs: wknd over 2f out* **66/1**

2m 35.62s (0.52) **Going Correction** +0.125s/f (Good)
WFA 4 from 5yo+ 2lb **18** Ran SP% **126.7**
Speed ratings (Par 103): **103,102,102,102,101 100,98,97,97,96 96,95,94,93,84 80,78,75**
toteswinger: 1&2 £52.30, 1&3 £52.00, 2&3 £60.00 CSF £207.47 CT £3474.38 TOTE £13.50: £3.40, £2.20, £3.60, £2.10; EX 102.00 TRIFECTA Not won. Place 6: £653.69 Place 5: £155.77.
Owner Brian Morton **Bred** Douglas McIntyre **Trained** Averham Park, Notts
■ Stewards' Enquiry : Amy Ryan two-day ban: careless riding (Apr 11-12); two-day ban: used whip in incorrect place (Apr 13-14)

FOCUS
Another large field for this apprentices' handicap which in years gone by was the opening race of the turf Flat season. It proved a good result for trainer Alan McCabe, who was responsible for the first two.
Moonwalking Official explanation: jockey said, regarding appearing to ease before win line, that he had had to take a pull because it became very tight on the rail and he was short of room after suffering interference; jockey said gelding hung left-handed.
T/Jkpt: Not won. T/Plt: £1,254.00 to a £1 stake. Pool: £194,830.77. 113.41 winning tickets. T/Qpdt: £84.70 to a £1 stake. Pool: £9,125.44. 79.66 winning tickets. WG

949 KEMPTON (A.W) (R-H)
Saturday, March 28

OFFICIAL GOING: Standard
Wind: Strong ahead Weather: Bright intervals

1001 WILLIAM HILL TELEBETTING SALE - 0800 44 40 40 H'CAP (LONDON MILE QUALIFIER) 1m (P)
1:50 (1:51) (Class 3) (0-90,90) 3-Y-O
£7,477 (£2,239; £1,119; £560; £279; £140) **Stalls** High

Form RPR

11- **1** **Saint Arch (CAN)**[142] 7214 3-9-4 **90** GregFairley 5 101+
(M Johnston) *w'like: scope: led 1f: styd pressing ldr tl led 5f out: drvn over 2f out: edgd lft fr over 1f out: styd on fnl f and won gng away* **11/4**[1]

33-1 **2** 2 ½ **Royal Executioner (USA)**[42] 548 3-8-7 **79** FergusSweeney 9 84
(D M Simcock) *swtg: hld up in tch: hdwy on ins over 2f out: chsd wnr appr fnl f: no imp and edgd lft ins fnl f* **8/1**

1221 **3** ¾ **Changing The Guard**[21] 782 3-8-9 **81** TonyHamilton 7 84
(R A Fahey) *w'like: in tch: swtchd lft and hdwy ins fnl 2f: styd on fnl f but nt rch ldng duo* **15/2**[3]

01-2 **4** 1 ¼ **Laurie Grove (IRE)**[23] 763 3-8-11 **83** SteveDrowne 2 83
(T G Mills) *chsd ldrs: rdn over 2f out: one pce fr over 1f out* **6/1**[2]

336- **5** 1 **Northern Tour**[129] 7391 3-8-9 **81** MartinDwyer 4 79
(P F I Cole) *mid-div and rdn along over 3f out: kpt on fnl f and gng on cl home* **40/1**

1- **6** ¾ **Nawaadi (USA)**[182] 6282 3-8-6 **78** RobertHavlin 6 74+
(J H M Gosden) *str: lw: slowly away: in rr: pushed along 3f out: hdwy over 1f out: styd on wl fnl f but nvr in contention* **11/4**[1]

031- **7** ¾ **Kaolak (USA)**[97] 7754 3-8-6 **78** ChrisCatlin 3 73
(J Ryan) *lw: led after 1f: kpt slt advantage tl hdd 5f out: wknd fnl f* **8/1**

510- **8** nk **Swift Chap**[190] 6082 3-8-10 **82** PaulDoe 10 76
(B R Millman) *chsd ldrs tl wknd appr fnl f* **16/1**

13- **9** ½ **Al Sabaheya**[190] 6076 3-9-2 **88** DarryllHolland 1 81
(C E Brittain) *in rr but in tch: rdn over 3f out and no rspnse* **16/1**

1- **10** 5 **Clumber Place**[341] 1515 3-8-11 **83** ow1 StephenDonohoe 8 64
(R C Guest) *leggy: attr: a towards rr* **40/1**

1m 39.21s (-0.59) **Going Correction** +0.15s/f (Slow) **10** Ran SP% **118.2**
Speed ratings (Par 102): **108,105,104,103,102 101,101,100,100,95**
toteswinger: 1&2 £3.90, 1&3 £7.70, 2&3 £14.00 CSF £26.56 CT £148.71 TOTE £4.10: £1.40, £2.30, £2.70; EX 27.60.
Owner Sheikh Hamdan Bin Mohammed Al Maktoum **Bred** Ascot Thoroughbreds **Trained** Middleham Moor, N Yorks

FOCUS
Just a routine gallop which played into the hands of the winner.

NOTEBOOK
Saint Arch(CAN), a rangy type, is now unbeaten in three races and looks set for a successful three-year-old career. From a stable in fine form, he was well suited by the step up to 1m and the way he found extra in the last 150 yards suggests he will stay a bit farther too. A strapping sort, he has plenty of potential but connections have no major plans for him yet. (op 4-1 tchd 9-2 in places)
Royal Executioner(USA) ran a sound race in defeat on this return to handicap company, with connections feeling he might have gone even closer had he found more cover. Though he goes well on Polytrack, he showed last year that he is just as at home on turf, and he should pick up a decent prize on either surface. (op 7-1)
Changing The Guard proved he stays 1m well, but he was never quite doing it fast enough in this better company. (op 10-1 tchd 11-1)
Laurie Grove(IRE) continues to perform with credit without being quite good enough off this mark. However, trainer Terry Mills feels he has taken a long time to grow up, so it is likely that he will step up on this as he matures. (op 9-2 tchd 4-1)
Northern Tour was in trouble at halfway and looks worth trying over an extra furlong or two. (op 33-1)
Nawaadi(USA), a good-bodied type making his seasonal debut, is potentially interesting over a longer trip. He got going far too late, but finished in the style of a horse who will stay 1m2f. (op 2-1)
Kaolak(USA) showed when winning easily at Great Leighs that he is capable of making his mark in handicaps, but this was a tough introduction. (op 16-1)

Swift Chap, a winner at 7f as a juvenile, may yet get 1m this year but still has it to prove. (tchd 18-1)

1002 BAMBOS CHARALAMBOUS BETVIEW MANAGER OF THE YEAR H'CAP 6f (P)

2:25 (2:26) (Class 2) (0-105,97) 3-Y-O

£11,215 (£3,358; £1,679; £840; £419; £210) **Stalls** High

Form RPR

00-2 **1** **Daddy's Gift (IRE)**[12] 852 3-8-8 **84**.................... SteveDrowne 1 89
(R Hannon) *lw: towards rr tl hdwy over 2f out: str run fr over 1f out to ld cl home* **14/1**

1115 **2** ½ **Five Star Junior (USA)**[7] 912 3-9-7 **97**.................... EddieAhern 10 100
(Mrs L Stubbs) *lw: sn chsng ldrs: rdn to chal fr 2f out: led wl ins fnl f: ct cl home* **9/4**[1]

-432 **3** ¾ **Satwa Street (IRE)**[52] 396 3-8-5 **84**.................... MarcHalford(3) 11 85
(D M Simcock) *led: drvn along whn chal fr 2f out: hdd wl ins fnl f: no ex cl home* **15/2**[3]

211- **4** ¾ **Noverre To Go (IRE)**[100] 7714 3-8-8 **89**..........(t) RossAtkinson(5) 2 88
(Tom Dascombe) *lw: rr: hdwy fr 2f out: styd on wl thrght fnl f: fin wl* **10/1**

210- **5** *hd* **Kyllachy Star**[177] 6426 3-8-4 **80**.................... ChrisCatlin 7 78
(R A Fahey) *rr: stl last 1/2-way: impr over 1f out: str run ins fnl f: fin fast* **15/2**[3]

303- **6** *1* **Effort**[152] 7024 3-8-12 **88**.................... GregFairley 6 83
(M Johnston) *sn chsng ldrs: rdn over 2f out: one pce fr over 1f out* **8/1**

3160 **7** ½ **Gone Hunting**[7] 912 3-8-9 **85**..........(t) LPKeniry 12 78
(Peter Grayson) *chsd ldrs: rdn over 2f out: wknd ins fnl f* **33/1**

103- **8** 2¼ **Top Town Girl**[170] 6603 3-8-10 **86**.................... MartinDwyer 3 72
(R M Beckett) *rr: sme hdwy whn nt clr run over 1f out: kpt on again ins fnl f* **25/1**

26-1 **9** *hd* **Never Lose**[18] 796 3-8-12 **88**..........(b[1]) DarryllHolland 4 73
(C E Brittain) *n.m.r and lost pl in rr sn after s: rdn 3f out: r.o fnl f but nvr in contention* **16/1**

4113 **10** ½ **Smokey Ryder**[7] 912 3-9-2 **95**.................... KevinGhunowa(3) 8 79
(R A Harris) *chsd ldrs: rdn over 2f out: wknd over 1f out* **11/2**[2]

14-0 **11** 4½ **Joe Caster**[7] 912 3-9-0 **90**.................... LukeMorris 5 59
(J M P Eustace) *a towards rr* **16/1**

0-00 **12** 1¼ **Versaki (IRE)**[44] 524 3-8-7 **83**.................... PaulDoe 9 48
(D Nicholls) *chsd ldr: rdn over 2f out: wkng whn hmpd 1f out* **16/1**

1m 13.45s (0.35) **Going Correction** +0.15s/f (Slow) **12** Ran SP% **121.0**
Speed ratings (Par 104): **103,102,101,100,100 98,98,95,94,94 88,86**
toteswinger: 1&2 £8.00, 1&3 £23.70, 2&3 £2.50 CSF £46.46 CT £273.90 TOTE £8.90: £2.50, £1.40, £2.80; EX 49.60 Trifecta £257.00 Part won. Pool: £104.22 - 0.70 winning units..
Owner Charlee & Hollie Allan **Bred** Vincent Dunne **Trained** East Everleigh, Wilts
■ Stewards' Enquiry : Steve Drowne one-day ban: used whip with excessive frequency (Apr 14)
Eddie Ahern caution: used whip with excessive frequency

FOCUS
Run at a good pace, with the field soon stretched out, so the form looks solid.

NOTEBOOK
Daddy's Gift(IRE), who eventually overcame the lowest stall to get up near the finish, has begun the season in fine form and, since she was 3lb higher here than when beaten last time, she appears to be still improving. A tough sort, she is well suited by a strongly-run 6f but her jockey confirmed that a return to 7f would be no problem, and trainer Richard Hannon will now target a handicap over that trip at the Craven meeting. (op 9-1 tchd 17-2)
Five Star Junior(USA) remains in cracking form and this return to handicaps after an honourable crack at Listed company nearly saw him back in the winner's enclosure. 22lb higher than when winning his first handicap in January, he goes from strength to strength. (op 7-2)
Satwa Street(IRE) put in a tremendous effort after setting such a lively tempo, only to go under near the finish. His running style always gives his opponents something to attack in the closing stages, but he is well capable of winning off this sort of mark. (op 8-1)
Noverre To Go(IRE) ◆ raced less prominently than he had last year, but he came home in good style and there seems little doubt that he has trained on. He should have a good season, with 7f looking an obvious alternative to this trip now. (op 11-2)
Kyllachy Star should stay at least another furlong. He made up a deal of ground late on, an excellent first effort on Polytrack for a horse who looked particularly well suited by soft ground last year. (op 10-1)
Never Lose Official explanation: jockey said filly hung right
Smokey Ryder, another reverting from Listed company, had a hard race over 7f the previous weekend and it may have taken the edge off her. (op 6-1 tchd 13-2)
Versaki(IRE) Official explanation: jockey said gelding hung left

1003 WILLIAMHILL.COM ROSEBERY STKS (HERITAGE H'CAP) 1m 3f (P)

3:00 (3:02) (Class 2) (0-105,98) 4-Y-O+

£24,924 (£7,464; £3,732; £1,868; £932; £468) **Stalls** High

Form RPR

15-4 **1** **Greylami (IRE)**[38] 585 4-8-12 **87**.................... ChrisCatlin 4 95
(T G Mills) *hld up in rr: str run on outside over 1f out: str burst to ld cl home* **12/1**

446- **2** *hd* **Sweet Lightning**[179] 6355 4-8-9 **84**.................... MartinDwyer 5 92
(W R Muir) *lw: rr: hdwy on outside over 2f out: hrd drvn to ld wl ins fnl f: ct cl home* **9/1**[2]

51-1 **3** *1* **Cape Express (IRE)**[80] 82 4-9-7 **96**.................... PhilipRobinson 14 102
(M A Jarvis) *lw; chsd ldrs: rdn to ld appr fnl f: hdd wl ins fnl f and sn one pce* **11/8**[1]

3020 **4** *hd* **Baylini**[7] 913 5-9-2 **90**.................... JamesDoyle 8 95
(Ms J S Doyle) *rr: stl plenty to do whn rdn and hdwy fr 2f out: fin wl: nt rch ldng trio* **33/1**

510- **5** ¾ **Albaqaa**[168] 6646 4-9-2 **91**.................... TonyHamilton 12 95
(R A Fahey) *t.k.h early: towards rr: hdwy 3f out: n.m.r 2f out: drvn and kpt on wl fnl f but nt rch ldrs* **25/1**

6021 **6** 1¼ **Swiss Act**[16] 822 5-9-2 **90**.................... EddieAhern 3 92
(M Johnston) *chsd ldrs: rdn 2f out: ev ch 1f out: wknd ins fnl f* **16/1**

131- **7** *1* **Opera Prince**[166] 6704 4-8-11 **89**.................... DavidProbert(3) 13 89
(S Kirk) *in tch: chsd ldrs 3f out: chal ins fnl 2f: wknd ins fnl f* **12/1**

4411 **8** ½ **Stand Guard**[12] 847 5-9-1 **89**.................... TolleyDean 7 88
(P Howling) *b: w ldr: led after 3f: rdn over 2f out: hdd appr fnl f: wknd ins fnl f* **16/1**

3-35 **9** *nk* **Bazergan (IRE)**[17] 801 4-9-3 **92**..........(tp) DarryllHolland 6 91
(C E Brittain) *rr: rdn over 2f out: r.o wl fnl f but nvr in contention* **16/1**

1101 **10** ½ **Brouhaha**[17] 798 5-8-2 **81**.................... RossAtkinson(5) 9 79
(Tom Dascombe) *in tch: rdn over 2f out: wknd fnl f* **16/1**

3503 **11** *nk* **Big Robert**[10] 864 5-9-7 **95**.................... FergusSweeney 11 92
(K R Burke) *rr: hdwy over 2f out: r.o fnl f but nvr in contention* **20/1**

P-12 **12** ¾ **King Olav (UAE)**[17] 801 4-8-12 **87**.................... LukeMorris 1 83
(A W Carroll) *chsd ldrs: rdn 2f out: wkng whn n.m.r and eased ins fnl f* **18/1**

00-0 **13** 3¾ **Tamimi's History**[23] 766 5-8-11 **90**.................... RichardEvans(5) 10 79
(P D Evans) *b: nvr in contention* **50/1**

6-53 **14** 2¾ **Grand Passion (IRE)**[38] 585 9-9-5 **98**.................... JPHamblett(5) 15 82
(C F Wall) *in tch whn hit rails 6f out: nvr in contention after* **16/1**

1204 **15** *8* **Robby Bobby**[17] 801 4-9-5 **94**.................... GregFairley 16 64
(M Johnston) *led 3f: styd pressing ldr: rdn 3f out: wknd ins fnl 2f* **18/1**

50-3 **16** *6* **Whitcombe Minister (USA)**[21] 783 4-9-3 **92**.................... SebSanders 2 51
(M Botti) *in tch: rdn to chse ldsrs 3f out: wknd qckly ins fnl 2f* **10/1**[3]

2m 20.75s (-1.15) **Going Correction** +0.15s/f (Slow)
WFA 4 from 5yo+ 1lb **16** Ran SP% **130.0**
Speed ratings (Par 109): **110,109,109,108,108 107,106,106,106,105 105,105,102,100,94 90**
toteswinger: 1&2 £16.30, 1&3 £12.10, 2&3 £9.20. CSF £119.30 CT £250.74 TOTE £15.20: £2.30, £2.40, £1.20, £4.90; EX 113.60 Trifecta £137.30 Pool: £426.83 - 2.30 winning units..
Owner J Daniels **Bred** Barouche Stud Ireland Ltd **Trained** Headley, Surrey

FOCUS
A good gallop set this up for the finishers, though it was only in the last furlong that things began to take shape.

NOTEBOOK
Greylami(IRE) was last, nearly 20 lengths off the lead, by halfway, but the tempo played to his strengths and he got there just in time, no bad thing since he has been known to idle in front. Trainer Terry Mills, who confirmed that he is best switched off and brought with a late run, will try to find him a handicap at Epsom from 1m2f to 1m4f. Granted a testing pace, and ridden like this, he still looks fairly handicapped. (op 14-1)
Sweet Lightning, who stays at least 1m4f, is another who was ideally suited by the strong pace. Though he just failed on this occasion, he looks well in at present and can find a similar race. (op 12-1 tchd 14-1)
Cape Express(IRE) deserves extra credit for being best of those who raced near the front. Raised 13lb for winning his first handicap in January, he put in a splendid effort in this much better company and this lightly raced sort should not be underestimated in decent races of this type. (op 6-4 tchd 15-8)
Baylini, like the first two, came home well from the rear. She has been flying high of late but this was a reminder that she can be competitive in handicaps, even off her current mark. (tchd 40-1)
Albaqaa, who had a successful time last season, made a satisfactory seasonal debut which suggests he can make his mark again this year. (op 33-1)
Swiss Act fared reasonably well but was always going to be up against it off a higher mark in this better company.
Opera Prince is beginning this season on a higher mark, but he won three times last year and this trip may have stretched his stamina a bit.
Stand Guard had a tougher task from this higher mark in a hot race, and taking on Robby Bobby for the lead at a strong gallop was the final straw.
Bazergan(IRE) runs as if likely to be suited by this trip, but attempts at it to date have been surprisingly unsuccessful. (op 20-1 tchd 22-1)
Brouhaha had won four of his previous five, but found the higher mark, better opponents and longer trip all conspiring against him.
Grand Passion(IRE) Official explanation: trainer said gelding was found to be lame and subsequently found to have a foot abscess

1004 WILLIAMHILL.COM MAGNOLIA STKS (LISTED RACE) 1m 2f (P)

3:35 (3:37) (Class 1) 4-Y-O+

£22,708 (£8,608; £4,308; £2,148; £1,076; £540) **Stalls** High

Form RPR

1-26 **1** **Dansant**[21] 789 5-9-2 113.................... EddieAhern 7 117
(G A Butler) *chsd ldrs: wnt 2nd over 2f out: drvn and styd on relentlessly to ld cl home* **9/4**[2]

6140 **2** ½ **Kandidate**[7] 913 7-8-13 105.................... DarryllHolland 2 113
(C E Brittain) *sn led: shoved along over 4f out: rdn over 2f out: styd on wl tl ct cl home* **7/1**[3]

35-3 **3** ¾ **Bronze Cannon (USA)**[7] 913 4-8-13 104.................... NickyMackay 6 112
(J H M Gosden) *chsd ldrs: rdn and outpcd over 3f out: hdwy on ins to chse ldrs 1f out: kpt on same pce ins fnl f* **13/8**[1]

4-16 **4** *5* **Re Barolo (IRE)**[7] 913 6-9-2 107..........(t) SebSanders 3 105
(M Botti) *lw: hld up towards rr: hdwy 2f out: nvr rchd ldrs and wknd ins fnl f* **9/1**

252- **5** 2½ **Alarazi (IRE)**[18] 5923 5-8-13 0..........(b) SteveDrowne 4 97
(T G Mills) *in rr: rdn over 3f out: mod prog fnl f* **50/1**

1044 **6** *1* **Halicarnassus (IRE)**[7] 913 5-8-13 110.................... TonyCulhane 1 95
(M R Channon) *in tch: hdwy to chse ldrs 1/2-way: wknd 2f out* **11/1**

346- **7** *nk* **Ajhar (USA)**[126] 7420 5-8-13 103.................... MartinDwyer 8 94
(M P Tregoning) *bit bkwd: chsd ldr tl over 2f out: sn wknd* **10/1**

3-50 **8** 3¼ **Bon Spiel**[36] 640 5-8-13 103..........(t) ChrisCatlin 5 87
(L M Cumani) *a towards rr* **25/1**

2m 6.85s (-1.15) **Going Correction** +0.075s/f (Slow) **8** Ran SP% **114.6**
Speed ratings (Par 111): **107,106,106,102,100 99,98,96**
toteswinger: 1&2 £4.70, 1&3 £1.50, 2&3 £3.20. CSF £18.56 TOTE £3.40: £1.40, £1.80, £1.10; EX 18.90 Trifecta £27.20 Pool: £678.75 - 18.46 winning units..
Owner Mrs Barbara M Keller **Bred** Mrs Cino Del Duca **Trained** Newmarket, Suffolk
■ Stewards' Enquiry : Darryll Holland caution: careless riding
Eddie Ahern caution: used whip with excessive frequency

FOCUS
The race threatened to be tactical, with Kandidate predictably having things his own way out in front. However, despite steadying it along the far side and trying to win it off the bend, he was eventually worn down by one of the proven stars of the all-weather scene.

NOTEBOOK
Dansant could have done with a better gallop but he was game under pressure and classy enough to get in front late on. His never-dangerous effort in the US last time was, on reflection, a fine effort, and back home on Polytrack he is one of the best. Trainer Gerard Butler, who praised the winner's versatility, explained that he ran here after showing a dislike for the track in Dubai last year. He will now be given a rest before returning for an autumn campaign, starting with the September Stakes here and culminating in the Breeders' Cup Marathon over 1m6f, a distance which Butler fully expects him to stay. (op 2-1 tchd 15-8)
Kandidate, last year's winner, goes well at Kempton and the lack of a rival front-runner was always likely to help his cause. He is an infrequent winner these days but these are the circumstances in which he is likely to do best. (op 17-2 tchd 9-1)
Bronze Cannon(USA) is much improved, and capable of winning in Listed company, but things conspired against him here. After being short of room at halfway, he was off the bridle disappointingly early and never found the speed to finish things off. He needs a solid gallop to bring out the best in him. (op 15-8)
Re Barolo(IRE), who would have appreciated a stronger tempo, was just short of his best. (tchd 11-1)
Alarazi(IRE) was well beaten but at least looked considerably more at home than he has done over hurdles. (tchd 66-1)
Halicarnassus(IRE) could have done with a better gallop, and can improve on this in decent company back on turf. (op 12-1 tchd 14-1)

Ajhar(USA) is undoubtedly a smart sort, but he has consistently fallen just short in Listed and Group 3 company. (op 8-1)

1005 LIVE CASINO GAMES @ WILLIAMHILL.COM EBF MAIDEN STKS 5f (P)
4:10 (4:15) (Class 4) 2-Y-O **£5,180** (£1,541; £770; £384) **Stalls** High

Form RPR

1 **Star Rover (IRE)** 2-9-3 0 .... PaulDoe 9 82+
(P D Evans) *leggy: attr: mde all: edgd lft fnl f: readily* **12/1**

2 *4* **Out The Ring (IRE)** 2-9-3 0 .... DarrylHolland 11 66
(K A Ryan) *w'like: lengthy: chsd wnr: rdn and styd towards far side: kpt on but no ch fr over 1f out* **9/4**[1]

3 *1 3/4* **Desert Auction (IRE)** 2-9-3 0 .... PatDobbs 6 59
(R Hannon) *w'like: bit bkwd: chsd ldrs: rdn 2f out: styd towards far side and one pce fr over 1f out* **5/1**[3]

4 *2* **Bould Mover** 2-9-3 0 .... FrankieMcDonald 4 51+
(R Curtis) *w'like: towards rr early: hdwy fr 2f out: styd on wl fnl f but nvr in contention* **12/1**

5 *1* **Bronze Beau** 2-9-3 0 .... EddieAhern 3 47+
(Mrs L Stubbs) *w'like: towards rr early: hdwy 2f out: styd on fnl f but nvr in contention* **16/1**

6 *1 3/4* **Black Daddy** 2-9-3 0 .... SteveDrowne 10 40
(R Hannon) *w'like: attr: lw: s.i.s: in rr: rdn and green 1/2-way: kpt on fnl f* **10/3**[2]

7 *nk* **True Red (IRE)** 2-8-12 0 .... ChrisCatlin 5 34
(B R Millman) *leggy: chsd ldrs: sn rdn: wknd over 1f out* **16/1**

8 *1/2* **Kirsty's Boy (IRE)** 2-9-3 0 .... LPKeniry 7 37
(J S Moore) *neat: chsd ldrs: rdn 1/2-way: wknd ins fnl 2f* **14/1**

9 *nk* **Red Avalanche (IRE)** 2-9-3 0 .... MartinDwyer 8 36
(P F I Cole) *str: bit bkwd: v.s.a: wl adrift 1/2-way tl mod prog fnl f* **11/2**

10 *5* **Needwood Dancer** 2-8-5 0 .... AndrewHeffernan(7) 1 11
(Peter Grayson) *leggy: unf: outpcd* **66/1**

61.21 secs (0.71) **Going Correction** +0.075s/f (Slow) **10** Ran SP% **121.2**
Speed ratings (Par 94): **97,90,87,84,83 80,79,78,78,70**
toteswinger: 1&2 £8.10, 1&3 £16.70, 2&3 £4.40. CSF £40.85 TOTE £20.60: £4.40, £1.30, £2.10; EX 67.60.
Owner Christy Leo **Bred** Yeomanstown Stud **Trained** Pandy, Monmouths

FOCUS
It was hard work getting these newcomers into the stalls, with one turning round inside them and being withdrawn, and the elongated loading process not likely to have helped any of the others. Once underway, they went a good gallop.

NOTEBOOK
Star Rover(IRE) ran as if more forward than most of his rivals, making all at a good gallop. Sprint bred, he is rated a decent sort at home and connections intend to make hay while they can. He is expected to run again soon. (op 10-1)
Out The Ring(IRE) was very agitated at the stalls and it took a number of attempts to get him in, with a blindfold finally doing the trick. Second throughout, this son of the speedy Acclamation lacked the sharpness of the winner but the market support suggests he has the pace to win a routine maiden. (op 11-4 tchd 3-1)
Desert Auction(IRE) has winners in the family from 1m to 1m4f, so probably has better long-term prospects than most of these. He showed a fair bit of speed to chase the first two throughout, and can do a bit better with the race behind him. (op 9-2 tchd 6-1)
Bould Mover is bred to be quick, but he was never going the pace in midfield and only began to find his stride too late. He needs to improve to win a maiden but should be a bit sharper for the experience. (op 11-1)
Bronze Beau is a son of the top-class sprinter Compton Place, but the family stays well beyond a mile, and the way he ran suggests that he will be suited by 6f when he gets the chance.
Black Daddy, half-brother to two speedy sorts, did not live up to expectations if the betting is any guide. However, he needed this mentally and should do better. (op 9-2 tchd 11-2)
True Red(IRE) showed more early speed than most of these and that should stand her in reasonably good stead in early season events. However, the fact that she was unsold at just 1,000gns last year is not encouraging. (tchd 14-1)

1006 PLAY POKER @ WILLIAMHILL.COM CONDITIONS STKS 6f (P)
4:45 (4:47) (Class 3) 3-Y-O+
£7,477 (£2,239; £1,119; £560; £279; £140) **Stalls** High

Form RPR

006- 1 **Eisteddfod**[196] 5897 8-9-4 97 .... EddieAhern 7 107
(P F I Cole) *chsd ldrs: led ins fnl 2f: styd on gamely whn strly chal thrght fnl f* **10/1**

034- 2 *nk* **Hogmaneigh (IRE)**[168] 6653 6-9-4 100 .... SaleemGolam 5 106
(S C Williams) *in rr tl gd hdwy appr fnl f: str run to chal ins fnl f: no ex last strides* **13/2**

100- 3 *1 1/2* **Battle Paint (USA)**[202] 5738 5-9-9 100 .... (t) RobertHavlin 9 106
(J H M Gosden) *lw: in tch: hdwy to chal appr fnl f: one pce ins fnl f* **11/2**[3]

-632 4 *1* **Orpsie Boy (IRE)**[21] 785 6-9-4 99 .... KirstyMilczarek 3 98
(N P Littmoden) *lw: chsd ldrs: rdn over 2f and styd on same pce fr over 1f out* **6/1**

000- 5 *hd* **Abraham Lincoln (IRE)**[174] 6518 5-9-4 0 .... StephenDonohoe 6 97
(D Nicholls) *in tch: rdn to chse ldrs fr 2f out: wknd ins fnl f* **11/1**

014- 6 *2* **Regal Parade**[168] 6645 5-8-13 106 .... WilliamCarson(5) 10 91+
(D Nicholls) *in rr: stl adrift over 2f out: rapid hdwy appr fnl f: fin strly* **9/4**[1]

0-55 7 *1* **Carcinetto (IRE)**[39] 579 7-8-8 83 .... RichardEvans(5) 2 83
(P D Evans) *sn led: hdd ins fnl 2f: wknd fnl f* **33/1**

-040 8 *1 1/4* **Benllech**[7] 916 5-9-4 95 .... DarrylHolland 4 84
(D M Simcock) *outpcd most of way* **5/1**[2]

005- 9 *1 3/4* **Whiskey Junction**[193] 5990 5-9-4 87 .... LPKeniry 1 78
(M Quinn) *chsd ldr early: wknd qckly over 1f out* **50/1**

1m 12.93s (-0.17) **Going Correction** +0.15s/f (Slow) **9** Ran SP% **112.8**
Speed ratings (Par 107): **107,106,104,103,103 100,99,97,95**
toteswinger: 1&2 £17.60, 1&3 £10.60, 2&3 £11.80. CSF £71.37 TOTE £9.20: £1.50, £3.80, £2.00; EX 74.70.Mac Gille Eoin was withdrawn. Price at time of withdrawal 16/1. Rule 4 does not apply.
Owner Elite Racing Club **Bred** Elite Racing Club **Trained** Whatcombe, Oxon
■ Stewards' Enquiry : Saleem Golam four-day ban: used whip with excessive force (Apr 11-14)

FOCUS
A good-quality conditions race run at a decent gallop.

NOTEBOOK
Eisteddfod's form last season was rather patchy, but he is a smart sprinter at his best, looked well, and he was very game in a close finish. It is not easy to place a horse of his current rating, but he goes well when fresh and this race was ideal. (op 11-1 tchd 9-1)
Hogmaneigh(IRE) had not run on the all-weather for over three years, but he showed then that he is no slouch on the surface. A smart handicapper in recent seasons, he looks as good as ever. (op 8-1 tchd 17-2)
Battle Paint(USA) raced only three times last season, proving somewhat disappointing in testing company. However, this was a good start to the new campaign, and if this is any guide he looks a smart sprinter after all. (op 9-2)
Orpsie Boy(IRE) came into the race in pretty good form and was just beaten by better rivals at the weights. (op 9-2)
Abraham Lincoln(IRE) steadily went downhill for Aidan O'Brien, but he looks a handy acquisition for Dandy Nicholls. Already a winner on the Dundalk Polytrack, he showed promise here and connections should have plenty of fun with him. (op 10-1)
Regal Parade was probably not ideally suited by a turning 6f on Polytrack. Carson also reported to the stewards that he had been chopped off early on, and then tried to follow instructions by coming wide out of the kickback, but without any response until it was too late. He was undoubtedly disappointing but deserves another chance given a stiffer test. Official explanation: jockey said, regarding running and riding, instructions were to jump out and take a handy position but approaching the first bend he lost his position on the inside which put him further back in the race than he wanted to be and then stayed on in home straight; trainer's rep confirmed instructions adding gelding would have benefited from being ridden more prominently early in the race (op 3-1)
Carcinetto(IRE) had it all to do in this company and was not good enough. However, she is still on a fair mark when returning to handicaps.
Benllech is high in the handicap now and that makes it harder to place him. This race should have been an ideal target, but he was rather disappointing and is capable of better. (op 7-1 tchd 15-2)

1007 PLAY ROULETTE @ WILLIAMHILL.COM QUEEN'S PRIZE (H'CAP) 2m (P)
5:20 (5:21) (Class 2) (0-105,103) 4-Y-O+
£11,215 (£3,358; £1,679; £840; £419; £210) **Stalls** High

Form RPR

626- 1 **Desert Sea (IRE)**[182] 6272 6-8-13 90 .... MartinDwyer 2 103
(D W P Arbuthnot) *in tch: hdwy to chse ldrs over 4f out: rdn 3f out: led 2f out: drvn out* **8/1**

116- 2 *1 1/2* **Gala Evening**[22] 7110 7-8-11 88 .... LPKeniry 9 99
(J A B Old) *hld up in rr: gd hdwy over 2f out: rdn and str run fnl f: tk 2nd last strides but no imp on wnr* **8/1**

051- 3 *nk* **Meshtri (IRE)**[182] 6288 4-8-13 95 .... PhilipRobinson 8 106
(M A Jarvis) *lw: led: pushed along and qcknd 4f out: rdn and hdd 2f out: kpt on ins fnl f: no ex and ct for 2nd last strides* **15/8**[1]

0-11 4 *3 1/4* **Benhego**[27] 723 4-8-3 85 .... ChrisCatlin 3 92
(G L Moore) *t.k.h early: hld up in rr: hdwy 3f out: styd on fnl 2f but nvr gng pce to rch ldrs* **11/2**[3]

010- 5 *4* **Gee Dee Nen**[17] 6817 6-9-2 93 .... PaulDoe 10 95
(Jim Best) *in tch: lost position and dropped towards rr 1/2-way: rdn and hdwy over 3f out: styd on fnl f but nvr in contention* **16/1**

000- 6 *hd* **Wicked Daze (IRE)**[140] 7244 6-8-13 90 .... StephenDonohoe 13 92
(Ian Williams) *t.k.h early: chsd ldrs: rdn over 3f out: wknd over 1f out* **25/1**

-132 7 *3 1/4* **Wine 'n Dine**[30] 693 4-8-8 90 .... SteveDrowne 11 88
(G L Moore) *chsd ldrs: rdn over 3f out: wknd fr 2f out* **8/1**

31-0 8 *1 3/4* **Buster Hyvonen (IRE)**[17] 801 7-9-3 94 .... GregFairley 4 90
(J R Fanshawe) *lw: in rr: sme prog fnl 2f* **22/1**

432- 9 *2* **Downhiller (IRE)**[182] 6272 4-8-13 95 .... EddieAhern 5 88
(J L Dunlop) *lw: chsd ldrs: grad fdd on outside fr 3f out* **9/2**[2]

600- 10 *1/2* **Land 'n Stars**[24] 6817 9-8-13 90 .... (b[1]) TolleyDean 6 83
(Jamie Poulton) *rdn 4f out: a towards rr* **66/1**

0631 11 *3/4* **Profit's Reality (IRE)**[30] 687 7-8-9 86 .... LukeMorris 1 78
(M J Attwater) *in tch: hdwy 1/2-way: wknd over 3f out* **33/1**

/30- 12 *7* **Talenti (IRE)**[63] 6817 6-9-1 92 .... SebSanders 12 75
(Miss E C Lavelle) *warm: chsd ldr: rdn 5f out: wknd over 3f out* **25/1**

3m 31.91s (1.81) **Going Correction** +0.15s/f (Slow)
WFA 4 from 5yo+ 5lb **12** Ran SP% **124.0**
Speed ratings (Par 109): **101,100,100,98,96 96,94,93,92,92 92,88**
toteswinger: 1&2 £9.40, 1&3 £6.40, 2&3 £6.00. CSF £69.60 CT £173.93 TOTE £10.10: £3.20, £2.60, £1.40; EX 66.40 Place 6: £32.84 Place 5 £15.32 .
Owner Bonusprint **Bred** Peter McGlynn **Trained** Compton, Berks

FOCUS
This traditional early-season staying handicap attracted a decent line-up, but with Robinson on Meshtri riding a canny race in front and quickening it turning out of the back, it was not easy to make ground from too far back.

NOTEBOOK
Desert Sea(IRE), whose rider was alert to the tactical tempo, put his mount into the race in plenty of time for it to pay dividends. He is lightly raced, and has proved himself on turf as well as Polytrack, so the only thing he has to overcome is his inconsistency. (tchd 15-2 and 9-1)
Gala Evening ◆, who has been in good shape over hurdles, translated that form back on the Flat but was not able to make up all the ground from the rear group. He remains an interesting runner in staying events and could develop into a Cesarewitch type. (op 6-1)
Meshtri(IRE) stayed 1m6f well last season, and gets 2m on this evidence, but he had the run of the race in front and it remains to be seen whether he will last home off a strong gallop. However, he is a likeable sort and should have a good season. (op 11-4 tchd 7-4)
Benhego was outpaced when the pace quickened, but he stayed on again and will be more effective granted a testing gallop. (op 9-2)
Gee Dee Nen came home in good style and is one to consider when facing a better test of stamina.
Wicked Daze(IRE), who has changed stables since last season, lost his way towards the end of last season. However, he had looked useful over 2m until then, and this was a satisfactory return to action. Official explanation: jockey said gelding had no more to give
Wine 'n Dine was raised 4lb for finishing second last time, and that helped to secure his fate in a competitive race. (op 10-1)
Buster Hyvonen(IRE), who has not yet reached peak form this year, needs a strong gallop to bring out the best in him. (op 20-1 tchd 25-1)
Downhiller(IRE) did not live up to last season's form, when he stayed 2m well, but he is capable of much better. (op 7-1)
T/Plt: £52.30 to a £1 stake. Pool: £94,378.66. 1,317.18 winning tickets. T/Qpdt: £13.50 to a £1 stake. Pool: £4,532.58. 247.50 winning tickets. ST

768 NAD AL SHEBA (L-H)
Saturday, March 28

OFFICIAL GOING: Dirt course - fast; turf course - good
The final day's racing at Nad Al Sheba, which is to be replaced by a new track at nearby Meydan. The dirt course seemed to favour prominent racers.

1008a GODOLPHIN MILE SPONSORED BY ETISALAT (GROUP 2) (DIRT) 1m (D)
1:40 (1:40) 3-Y-O+
£416,666 (£138,888; £69,444; £34,722; £20,833; £13,888)

RPR

1 **Two Step Salsa (USA)**[36] 641 4-9-0 118 .... (t) LDettori 4 117
(Saeed Bin Suroor) *sn led: drew clr 2f out: rdn 1f out: r.o wl* **2/1**[1]

2 *2 1/4* **Gayego (USA)**[23] 770 4-9-0 115 .... (t) TedDurcan 13 113
(Saeed Bin Suroor) *mid-div: rdn 2 1/2f out: chsd wnr 1 1/2f out: nt qckn fnl f* **3/1**[2]

3 1 3/4 **Don Renato (CHI)**^{23} [771] 6-9-0 105................................(bt) WRamos 2 109
(J Barton, Saudi Arabia) *in rr of mid-div: r.o wl fnl 2 1/2f: nrst fin* **33/1**

4 *shd* **Summer Doldrums (USA)**^{36} [644] 5-9-0 104....................(t) AGarcia 3 109
(Doug Watson, UAE) *nvr bttr than mid-div* **50/1**

5 *nse* **Brave Tin Soldier (USA)**^{15} 5-9-0 107..........................(b) C-PLemaire 9 109
(M F De Kock, South Africa) *in rr of mid-div: r.o wl fnl 2 1/2f: nrst fin* **33/1**

6 1/2 **Tiz Now Tiz Then (USA)**^{23} [773] 4-9-0 106......................(bt) EPrado 8 108
(S Seemar, UAE) *wl away: mid-div on rail: rdn 3f out: nt qckn* **20/1**

7 3 1/4 **Informed (USA)**^{48} 5-9-0 109...(bt) AGryder 11 101
(Doug O'Neill, U.S.A) *in rr of mid-div: rdn 4 1/2f out: n.d* **16/1**

8 1/2 **Green Coast (IRE)**^{23} [771] 6-9-0 106.................................... FJara 5 100
(Doug Watson, UAE) *trckd ldrs: rdn 2 1/2f out: 2nd 1f out: one pce fnl 110yds* **33/1**

9 1 **Dijeerr (USA)**^{37} [610] 5-9-0 109..................................(vt) AhmedAjtebi 15 98
(M bin Shafya, UAE) *trckd ldrs: rdn 3f out: one pce fnl 2f* **14/1**

10 2 **Art Of War (SAF)**^{23} [773] 5-9-0 105.................................... JMurtagh 10 93
(M F De Kock, South Africa) *nvr bttr than mid-div* **12/1**

11 2 1/2 **Kalahari Gold (IRE)**^{30} [702] 4-9-0 112.. RHills 6 88
(Doug Watson, UAE) *trckd ldrs on rail: ev ch 3f out: nt qckn* **9/1**^{3}

12 5 1/4 **Al Morhij (KSA)**^{43} 5-9-0 109.. RyanMoore 7 77
(B Resaque, Saudi Arabia) *mid-div: rdn 4f out: sn btn* **33/1**

13 2 **Cat Junior (USA)**^{161} [6814] 4-9-0 115.................................. JamieSpencer 1 73
(B J Meehan) *trckd ldrs tl 2 1/2f out: wknd* **12/1**

14 4 1/4 **Golden Arrow (IRE)**^{30} [702] 6-9-0 106..........................(bt) TPO'Shea 14 64
(E Charpy, UAE) *nvr nr to chal* **100/1**

15 3 1/4 **Lucky Find (SAF)**^{23} [771] 6-9-0 108.. KShea 12 57
(M F De Kock, South Africa) *mid-div: rdn 3f out: sn btn* **14/1**

1m 36.82s (0.12) **Going Correction** +0.40s/f (Slow) **15 Ran SP% 122.4**
Speed ratings: **115,112,111,110,110 110,107,106,105,103 101,95,93,89,86**
CSF: £6.99.
Owner Godolphin **Bred** Everest Stables Inc **Trained** Newmarket, Suffolk

FOCUS
The consensus beforehand was that Godolphin had this race pretty much to themselves and so it proved. The third and fourth set the level.

NOTEBOOK
Two Step Salsa(USA), for whom the presence of Dettori aboard was probably the only reason the colt went off favourite, had finished third in the Breeders' Cup Dirt Mile last autumn, and impressed when scoring over 6f here last time. On his toes and sweating beforehand, he was quickly away and soon taking the field along at a good clip. Once he had seen off fellow pacesetter Cat Junior, he kept galloping to comfortably hold off his running-on stablemate. He looks a classy performer and the Met Mile is next on the agenda, where he should be a leading candidate. (op 9-4)
Gayego(USA), who beat Golden Shaheen winner Big City Man when taking a Group 3 contest over 6f here last time, was expected to be suited by the return to a mile. Drawn out wide, he was held up off the pace in the early stages and, while staying on late, never quite looked like catching the winner. He beat the rest well enough, but his stablemate looks a class above on this evidence.
Don Renato(CHI) just edged a bunch finish for third place, repeating his performance in this race last year. He again kept on stoutly from off the pace and the stronger the pace, the better for him.
Summer Doldrums(USA), who looked up against it back on dirt, was another who got going late and ran on from way off the pace. He has won in Grade 3 company over an extended 1m1f in the past. That sort of trip probably suits him ideally.
Brave Tin Soldier(USA) was another to benefit from the strong pace, running on from the back without threatening the principals. This was a fair effort given the step up in class.
Tiz Now Tiz Then(USA), who had the blinkers back on, got a bit short of room on the inside rail in the straight and weakened having chased the pace for most of the way. He is not up to this class.
Informed(USA), who had run solid races in defeat on Pro-Ride in his last two starts, failed to replicate that form on this different dirt surface.
Green Coast(IRE) improved one position on his ninth-placed finish last year.
Dijeerr(USA) was unable to show his best as he was taken on by the winner at the head of affairs. He is a smart horse at his best but must have his own way in front.
Kalahari Gold(IRE) ran well to finish third to Archipenko on turf here last month but the experiment of trying him on dirt failed. He remains a lightly raced and progressive colt, and there are good races to be won with him this season back on turf.
Cat Junior(USA), who was up there for a long way, was another running on dirt for the first time. Although a Storm Cat, he too is likely to be happier back on grass.

1009a UAE DERBY SPONSORED BY SAEED & MOHAMMED AL NABOODAH GROUP (GROUP 2) (DIRT) 1m 1f (D)

2:15 (2:15) 3-Y-O

£833,333 (£277,777; £138,888; £69,444; £41,666; £27,777)

RPR

1 **Regal Ransom (USA)**^{44} [526] 3-8-8 102..............................(t) AGarcia 1 112
(Saeed Bin Suroor) *disp: drew clr 2 1/2f out: r.o wl* **16/1**

2 1/2 **Desert Party (USA)**^{44} [526] 3-8-8 112..................................(t) LDettori 5 111+
(Saeed Bin Suroor) *chsd ldrs: smooth prog to trck ldrs 2 1/2f out: rdn 1 1/2f out: r.o: jst hld* **2/5**^{1}

3 15 **Soy Libriano (ARG)**^{23} [768] 4-9-5 105........................(t) AhmedAjtebi 11 85
(M bin Shafya, UAE) *nvr nr to chal: r.o fnl 2f: nrst fin* **16/1**

4 1 3/4 **So Shiny (ARG)**^{30} [701] 4-9-1 102..(t) FJara 7 78
(J Barton, Saudi Arabia) *disp: hdd 2 1/2f out: kpt on same pce* **25/1**

5 5 **Lelah Dorak (KSA)**^{22} 3-8-8 102.. EPrado 3 68
(B Resaque, Saudi Arabia) *chsd ldrs: rdn 3f out: nt qckn* **20/1**

6 1 1/4 **Naval Officer (USA)**^{23} [769] 3-8-8 108..................................... MJKinane 12 65
(J Barton, Saudi Arabia) *settled in rr: r.o fnl 2 1/2f: nvr able to chal* **10/1**^{2}

7 1 1/2 **Redding Colliery (USA)**^{44} [526] 3-8-8 99.......................(t) JohnEgan 6 62
(H J Brown, South Africa) *mid-div on rail: rdn 4f out: sn btn* **18/1**

8 *hd* **Jose Adan (USA)**^{23} [768] 3-8-8 105.............................(vt) TedDurcan 10 62
(Saeed Bin Suroor) *nvr bttr than mid-div* **14/1**^{3}

9 *hd* **Ra Junior (USA)**^{162} [6779] 3-8-8 98.................................. JamieSpencer 8 61
(B J Meehan) *slowly away: settled in rr: nvr nr to chal* **25/1**

10 5 **Balcarce Nov (ARG)**^{23} [769] 4-9-5 100.........................(t) WCMarwing 9 55
(H J Brown, South Africa) *nvr bttr than mid-div* **25/1**

11 4 1/4 **I Am The Best**^{23} [768] 3-8-8 98...................................... RoystonFfrench 2 43
(A Al Raihe, UAE) *mid-div: chsd ldrs 2 1/2f out: nt qckn* **100/1**

12 *dist* **Muy Ponderado (ARG)**^{23} [768] 4-9-5 90....................... WayneSmith 4 —
(M bin Shafya, UAE) *settled in rr: nvr nr to chal* **200/1**

1m 50.0s (0.20) **Going Correction** +0.40s/f (Slow)
WFA 3 from 4yo 19lb **12 Ran SP% 122.0**
Speed ratings: **115,114,101,99,95 94,92,92,92,87 84,—**
CSF: £22.45.
Owner Godolphin **Bred** Diamond A Racing Corporation **Trained** Newmarket, Suffolk
■ Between them Saeed Bin Suroor and Mike De Kock have now won all ten runnings of the UAE Derby.

FOCUS
It's fair to say the Classic generation on the dirt this Dubai season, fillies included, have been substandard. The runner-up is rated just below form with the fourth to his previous mark.

NOTEBOOK
Regal Ransom(USA) reversed earlier form with his stable companion and the bare result sets a bit of a poser when trying to establish the worth of this form, as he had looked shy of this class when behind the runner-up in a trial in January, and in the UAE 2000 Guineas. However, even allowing for the favourite running slightly below form, the front two were a mile clear of the remainder, and this was clearly an improved performance from the Godolphin second string.
Desert Party(USA) ran into an improved performer, and finished a long way clear of the others, this was still a little disappointing, and Dettori said he felt flat. He seemed to travel well enough just in behind the leaders, and his jockey looked confident early in the straight, but for all that he found enough to pull away from the remainder, it soon became apparent he wasn't going to reel in the winner. With the benefit of hindsight his rider may have been better served by going for home sooner, especially as it turned out the track seemed to be favouring speed. Despite this slight setback, his followers can take heart from the fact his sire, Street Cry, was also beaten into second by a stablemate (when favourite) in this contest back in 2001, having won the UAE Guineas. According to connections, the front pair will both be considered for the Kentucky Derby, but their stamina for the extra furlong is questionable.
Soy Libriano(ARG), who was successful in the middle leg of the UAE Triple Crown, the Al Bastakiya, confirmed form with those who reopposed, but that was a weak renewal. His rider thinks he will benefit from a step up in distance.
So Shiny(ARG), winner of the UAE 1000 Guineas but much too keen in the Oaks, disputed the early lead with the winner but dropped away in the straight.
Lelah Dorak(KSA), the second highest earner in his native Saudi Arabia this season, recorded a quick time when winning over 1m at Janadriyah racecourse on his latest start, but he was faced with his toughest task to date and came up short.
Naval Officer(USA), a Group 3 winner in France last year, went for the Meydan Classic (on turf), rather than the Al Bastakiya on his UAE debut after suffering an abscess and missing some work. Switched to dirt this time, he raced well back early and only ran on past beaten horses.
Redding Colliery(USA), of whom better could have been expected, having been third in the Guineas, will apparently now join Kiaran McLaughlin in the US.
Jose Adan(USA), slightly unlucky when beaten into second as a short-priced favourite in the Al Bastakiya, offered little. He is not up to this class on dirt.
Ra Junior(USA), a very useful juvenile over 7f-1m on turf in Britain last year, never really got into his stride on this switch in surface and soon had no chance.

1010a DUBAI GOLDEN SHAHEEN SPONSORED BY GULF NEWS (GROUP 1) (DIRT) 6f (D)

2:55 (2:56) 3-Y-O+

£833,333 (£277,777; £138,888; £69,444; £41,666; £27,777)

RPR

1 **Big City Man (USA)**^{23} [770] 4-9-0 112.............................. JVerenzuela 2 124
(J Barton, Saudi Arabia) *trckd ldrs far side: rdn to ld ins last: r.o wl* **11/2**^{2}

2 1 1/4 **Indian Blessing (USA)**^{91} 4-8-9 117..............................(t) EPrado 12 117
(Bob Baffert, U.S.A) *trckd ldrs nr side: led 3f out: ev ch 2f out: hdd and nt qckn fnl 110yds* **11/8**^{1}

3 5 **Diabolical (USA)**^{23} [770] 6-9-0 112...................................... LDettori 3 110+
(Saeed Bin Suroor) *trckd ldrs: ev ch 2f out: one pce fnl f* **6/1**^{3}

4 1/2 **Bamboo Ere (JPN)**^{34} 6-9-0 112... YTake 11 104
(A Adachi, Japan) *mid-div: rdn 3f out: r.o fnl 1 1/2f* **16/1**

5 1/2 **Force Freeze (USA)**^{44} [525] 4-9-0 110......................................(t) FJara 1 103
(Doug Watson, UAE) *slowly away: sn led far side: hdd 2 1/2f out* **33/1**

6 3/4 **Black Seventeen (USA)**^{70} 5-9-0 115.................................(bt) CLPotts 6 100
(Brian Koriner, U.S.A) *s.i.s: swtchd far side after 1f: nvr able to chal: r.o fnl 1 1/2f* **12/1**

7 3/4 **Hammadi (IRE)**^{15} 4-9-0 105... JMurtagh 10 98
(Doug Watson, UAE) *trckd ldrs nr side: one pce fnl 1 1/2f* **100/1**

8 1/4 **Machismo (USA)**^{42} 5-9-0 105..(bt) TBaze 9 97
(John W Sadler, U.S.A) *nvr bttr than mid-div* **20/1**

9 5 1/2 **Lucky Quality (AUS)**^{48} 5-9-0 107... ODoleuze 4 81
(Y S Tsui, Hong Kong) *led nr side for 3f: outpcd fnl 2f* **14/1**

10 *shd* **Change Alley (USA)**^{23} [770] 4-9-0 105....................(t) RoystonFfrench 5 80
(A Al Raihe, UAE) *nvr able to chal* **100/1**

11 8 **Balthazaar's Gift (IRE)**^{36} [638] 6-9-0 112....................... DO'Donohoe 8 56
(R Simpson, UAE) *hmpd at s: sn rdn in rr: n.d* **28/1**

12 *shd* **Marchand D'Or (FR)**^{104} [7683] 6-9-0 121.............................. DBonilla 7 56
(F Head, France) *a in rr* **11/2**^{2}

68.93 secs (-1.27) **Going Correction** +0.225s/f (Slow) **12 Ran SP% 120.5**
Speed ratings: **117,115,108,108,107 106,105,105,97,97 86,86**
CSF: £13.14.
Owner Prince Sultan Mohammed Saud Al Kabeer **Bred** Four Horsemen's Ranch **Trained** Saudi Arabia

FOCUS
This Group 1 sprint usually goes the way of an American-trained contender, and, with the top-class American filly Indian Blessing turning up, they once again looked to hold a strong hand but she found one too good. Big City Man now heads the Global sprint division with an RPR of 124. Indian Blessing was eased close home and is rated slightly better than the bare form.

NOTEBOOK
Big City Man(USA), formerly trained in the US, but now trained by Jerry Barton in Saudi Arabia, had finished runner-up to Godolphin Mile runner-up Gayego in the Mahab Al Shimaal last time out, and Barton had suggested that the colt would improve for that outing. Drawn towards the centre of the track, he was fast away but was steadied slightly and got into a nice rhythm. When asked to pick the filly up in the closing stages he really motored and was nicely on top at the finish. While this would not be the strongest Golden Shaheen ever run, he deserves to take his chance in some of the top sprints in the states. (op 6-1)
Indian Blessing(USA), who was taking on the boys for the first time having established herself as one of the leading sprinting fillies in the US, was drawn nearest the rail. She was not best away but was soon into her stride and tracked Lucky Quality on the rail. On reflection her rider might regret moving up to take over such a long way out. In the end the filly got a bit lonely and hung left as she got tired, and the winner wore her down. She lost little in defeat, though, and retained her record of never having been out of the first two in her career.
Diabolical(USA), whom it was reasonable to expect would improve a good deal for his reappearance in the Mahab Al Shimaal, did travel well tracking the pace, but once under pressure he found no extra. This run appeared to suggest he is not quite up to it at the very top level, and he is probably better off giving weight to lesser opposition in slightly lesser company. However, he was later reported to have returned with a cut to his left fore and to have also lost a left plate.
Bamboo Ere(JPN), who won a Grade 1 over 7f in Japan last year, got outpaced before running on again late for fourth. He probably ran close to his best.
Force Freeze(USA), well beaten by the winner here in January, won a minor event over the course and distance last time, but this represented a much stiffer challenge, and he was not disgraced.
Black Seventeen(USA) won the Grade 1 Vosburgh Stakes last autumn and looked to hold a chance on that form, but he had enjoyed a far from ideal preparation for this, having failed to travel over well and missed training. In the circumstances, he probably could not have been expected to perform much better than this.
Hammadi(IRE), down the field in the Portland when last seen in Britain in September, won a 5f Listed race at Jebel Ali last time out for new connections. He showed good speed for a fair way before weakening and will be suited by a return to the minimum trip.

Lucky Quality(AUS), the Hong Kong raider, was something of an unknown quantity. He showed blistering early pace to cross over from stall four and lead on the rail, but he looked to do too much too soon and just fell in a hole.
Marchand D'Or(FR), Europe's champion sprinter, was eighth in this race in 2007 but fared even worse here after trailing from the start. It is, however, easy to forgive a poor performance by a turf horse on this surface and he should remain the one to beat in the top sprints on grass this season. (op 5-1)

1011a DUBAI DUTY FREE SPONSORED BY DUBAI DUTY FREE (GROUP 1) (TURF) 1m 194y(T)

3:55 (3:55) 3-Y-O+

£2,083,333 (£694,444; £347,222; £173,611; £104,166; £69,444)

RPR

1 **Gladiatorus (USA)**[37] 614 4-9-0 119 AhmedAjtebi 2 129
(M bin Shafya, UAE) *sn led: set decent pce: drew clr 3f out: hrd rdn 1 1/2f out: r.o wl: comf* **12/1**

2 *3 1/4* **Presvis**[30] 703 5-9-0 117 RyanMoore 16 122+
(L M Cumani) *taken to rail: settled in rr: nvr nr to chal: r.o wl fnl 1 1/2f* **10/1**

3 *2* **Alexandros**[50] 436 4-9-0 116 MJKinane 9 118
(Saeed Bin Suroor) *nvr bttr than mid-div* **40/1**

4 *3* **Niconero (AUS)**[21] 8-9-0 116 CraigAWilliams 4 112
(David Hayes, Australia) *mid-div: r.o wl fnl 2f: nrst fin* **25/1**

5 *1/2* **Bankable (IRE)**[36] 642 5-9-0 117 (t) JMurtagh 1 110
(M F De Kock, South Africa) *mid-div on rail: rdn 3f out: one pce fnl 2f* **14/1**

6 *shd* **Archipenko (USA)**[30] 702 5-9-0 120 (bt) KShea 10 110
(M F De Kock, South Africa) *mid-div: rdn 3f out: nt qckn fnl 1 1/2f* **7/2**[1]

7 *hd* **Vodka (JPN)**[23] 774 5-8-9 120 YTake 3 105
(Katsuhiko Sumii, Japan) *trckd wnr: rdn to chse 2 1/2f out: one pce fnl f* **6/1**[3]

8 *3/4* **Paco Boy (IRE)**[175] 6496 4-9-0 123 RichardHughes 13 108
(R Hannon) *in rr of mid-div: nvr nr to chal* **9/2**[2]

9 *1 3/4* **Tuesday Joy (NZ)**[21] 6-8-9 115 DarrenBeadman 11 100
(Mrs Gai Waterhouse, Australia) *nvr bttr than mid-div* **16/1**

10 *1 3/4* **Kip Deville (USA)**[55] 6-9-0 122 (bt) CVelasquez 7 101
(Richard Dutrow Jr, U.S.A) *mid-div: rdn 3 1/2f out: nt qckn* **16/1**

11 *3 3/4* **Jay Peg (SAF)**[23] 774 6-9-0 120 (v) WCMarwing 15 93
(H J Brown, South Africa) *trckd ldrs: rdn 3f out: kpt on same pce* **16/1**

12 *1/4* **Charlie Farnsbarns (IRE)**[162] 6780 5-9-0 116 JamieSpencer 14 92
(B J Meehan) *nvr nr to chal* **50/1**

13 *3/4* **Balius (IRE)**[23] 774 6-9-0 118 (b) WJSupple 8 91
(A bin Huzaim, UAE) *nvr nr to chal* **18/1**

14 *3/4* **Hyperbaric (USA)**[120] 7488 6-9-0 117 (bt) TBaze 5 89
(Julio C Canani, U.S.A) *nvr bttr than mid-div* **50/1**

15 *1 1/2* **Creachadoir (IRE)**[315] 2193 5-9-0 118 TedDurcan 6 86
(Saeed Bin Suroor) *mid-div on rail: r.o wl fnl 1 1/2f: nrst fin* **25/1**

16 *4* **Lady Marian (GER)**[174] 6521 4-8-9 119 LDettori 12 73
(Saeed Bin Suroor) *in rr of mid-div: nvr nr to chal* **16/1**

1m 46.92s (-3.08) **Going Correction** +0.10s/f (Good) **16** Ran SP% **121.0**
Speed ratings: **117,114,112,109,109 109,108,108,106,105 101,101,100,100,98 95**
CSF: £120.47.
Owner Sheikh Mansoor bin Mohammed al Maktoum **Bred** Az Agr Le Ferriere Di Raponi Giampaolo **Trained** United Arab Emirates

■ An Emirati success for Ahmed Ajtebi, still an apprentice but a Royal Ascot winner in 2008, and 2009 find Mubarak Bin Shafya.

FOCUS

It was possible to make some sort of case for most of these, and there will be few, if any, better fields assembled on the Flat this year. It was a crushing front-running display from Gladiatorus, who put up the second fastest time in ten runnings of the Duty Free and has been given the joint second highest RPR of any winner of the race, equal to Admire Moon and a pound below David Junior. He looks a force to reckon with in Europe's top mile races.

NOTEBOOK

Gladiatorus(USA) absolutely thrashed his 15 rivals with another relentless display of galloping and was a stunning winner. He never looked in any danger of being reeled in once in the straight and his rider could afford to stand up in the irons and celebrate yards from the line. While it's true he was unchallenged throughout and was allowed to build up a sizeable lead, had anything taken him on they would almost certainly have been going too quick, and this was not a fluke. For a start, the gallop he set looked a good one (backed up by a smart winning time), allowing him to build up a lead of over five lengths by the time he reached the straight, and all those who tried to keep tabs on him to an extent (the likes of Archipenko, Vodka and Jay Peg) finished out of the frame. It is not as if this was a first, as on his initial start in Dubai (after returning from a long absence and switching from Italy) he broke the extended 7f track record when defying a handicap mark of 108, and next time up he took the Group 2 Al Fahidi Fort by almost six lengths, again making all. He will now join Godolphin, and it will be fascinating to monitor his progress. He would mop up Grade 1 races if taken to North America, with the sharp, left-handed flat tracks absolutely ideal to his running style, and he already appeals as a potential winner of this year's Breeders' Cup Mile. However, one suspects he will be given the chance to prove himself elsewhere beforehand, particularly in Europe. Early season targets could include races like the Lockinge and the Queen Anne, and he should not be opposed lightly, although it remains to be seen how well he will adapt if challenged up front by a pacemaker. (op 11-1)

Presvis earned a shot at a race like this after three consecutive impressive wins in high-class handicaps, but they were all gained over 1m2f. A confirmed hold-up horse, he had little choice but to drop in from stall 16, and he had no chance with the winner considering how the race unfolded, but he displayed his customary change of pace in the straight to take a clear second. He should be suited by a return to further and his connections will consider both Hong Kong and Singapore. There's also the Prince of Wales's Stakes at Royal Ascot to think about if they opt for a domestic campaign.

Alexandros, the apparent Godolphin third string, had thrived in handicap company at the carnival and ran a fine race returned to Group company. He looks an ideal type to challenge for big-race honours at around 1m in various countries this year.

Niconero(AUS) apparently didn't travel over very well prior to his 11th placing in this race last year, but his connections had been much happier with him this time. The winner of back-to-back Group 1s in Australia coming into this, he ran a much better race than last season in a creditable fourth. Later in the year he will be targeted at Royal Ascot, and victory there will secure him a A$500,000 bonus, following his success in the Flemington Cup. Before then, he could go to either Singapore or Hong Kong.

Bankable(IRE) ran reasonably, but his main weapon, his turn of foot, was not as potent as it can be given the way the race was run. He can be given another chance. He might run next in Singapore, but will return to the UK afterwards.

Archipenko(USA) looked to have solid claims of improving on last year's unlucky third in this judged on his impressive victory in the Zabeel Mile, but he was disappointing. Although nothing managed to get in a blow at the winner, he still could have been expected to be good enough to claim second.

Vodka(JPN) looked well placed in a clear second, and she seemed the only threat to the winner in the straight, but she found little when placed under pressure.

Paco Boy(IRE) was apparently well backed with certain firms in Britain, but a wide draw was no use considering he has yet to win beyond 7f. According to Richard Hughes he was checked a couple of times and that may have cost him a place or two. He could now go for the Lockinge. (op 5-1)

Jay Peg(SAF), last year's winner, was unable to dominate and ran well below his best. (op 14-1)

Charlie Farnsbarns(IRE), having his first run since winning a Group 3 at Newmarket last backend, was out of his depth in this company.

Balius(IRE) was extremely weak on Betfair and never threatened. (op 16-1)

Creachadoir(IRE), off since winning last year's Lockinge after requiring surgery on his fractured off fore, was expected to need the run, but even allowing for that he showed very little.

Lady Marian(GER), absent since winning the Prix de l'Opera for German connections at Longchamp last year, was also said to be in need of the run, and she was reported to have over-raced in the early stages after being unable to get cover. More ground and a softer surface should suit her better.

1012a DUBAI SHEEMA CLASSIC SPONSORED BY NAKHEEL (GROUP 1) (TURF) 1m 4f (T)

4:40 (4:42) 3-Y-O+

£2,083,333 (£694,444; £347,222; £173,611; £104,166; £69,444)

RPR

1 **Eastern Anthem (IRE)**[37] 613 5-9-0 115 (t) AhmedAjtebi 2 120
(M bin Shafya, UAE) *slowly away: settled in rr: r.o wl fnl 2 1/2f: led last stride* **14/1**

2 *nse* **Spanish Moon (USA)**[143] 7193 5-9-0 113 RyanMoore 4 120
(Sir Michael Stoute) *trckd ldrs: rdn to ld 2f out: r.o wl: hdd cl home* **14/1**

3 *shd* **Purple Moon (IRE)**[23] 772 6-9-0 116 JamieSpencer 7 120
(L M Cumani) *trckd ldr: ev ch fnl 1 1/2f: jst failed* **15/2**[3]

4 *2 1/4* **Youmzain (IRE)**[174] 6522 6-9-0 125 RHills 6 116
(M R Channon) *in rr of mid-div: n.m.r 2 1/2f out and again 1 1/2f out: r.o* **7/2**[1]

5 *3 1/4* **Marsh Side (USA)**[68] 6-9-0 115 (t) EPrado 8 111
(Neil Drysdale, U.S.A) *nvr bttr than mid-div* **25/1**

6 *hd* **Quijano (GER)**[23] 772 7-9-0 119 AStarke 10 111
(P Schiergen, Germany) *mid-div: r.o wl fnl 2 1/2f: n.d* **9/1**

7 *1/2* **Deem (IRE)**[36] 643 4-8-8 110 MJKinane 9 106
(J Barton, Saudi Arabia) *settled in rr: rdn 3f out: nvr able to chal* **50/1**

8 *1 1/4* **Doctor Dino (FR)**[104] 7682 7-9-0 119 OPeslier 13 108
(R Gibson, France) *mid-div: chsd ldrs 2 1/2f out: nt qckn fnl 1 1/2f* **6/1**[2]

9 *4* **Front House (IRE)**[23] 772 4-8-8 113 KShea 1 97
(M F De Kock, South Africa) *sn led: hdd 2f out: wknd fnl f* **8/1**

10 *hd* **Kirklees (IRE)**[23] 773 5-9-0 116 LDettori 14 101
(Saeed Bin Suroor) *mid-div: nvr able to chal* **12/1**

11 *2 1/4* **Russian Sage (SAF)**[23] 774 5-9-0 118 BFayd'Herbe 3 98
(M F De Kock, South Africa) *mid-div on rail: ev ch bhd ldrs 2f out: wknd fnl f* **16/1**

12 *6 1/4* **Red Rocks (IRE)**[55] 6-9-0 117 (b) JJCastellano 12 88
(Mark Hennig, U.S.A) *mid-div: wd: t.k.h: n.d* **25/1**

13 *hd* **King Of Rome (IRE)**[23] 772 4-8-13 115 (t) JMurtagh 5 88
(M F De Kock, South Africa) *mid-div: rdn 2 1/2f out: n.m.r 2f out: sn btn* **9/1**

14 *1/2* **Macarthur**[23] 772 5-9-0 116 (t) DarrenBeadman 15 86
(M F De Kock, South Africa) *settled in rr: nvr nr to chal* **25/1**

15 *4 1/2* **Kings Gambit (SAF)**[23] 772 5-9-0 112 (t) JohnEgan 11 79
(H J Brown, South Africa) *nvr bttr than mid-div* **33/1**

2m 31.84s (0.84) **Going Correction** +0.10s/f (Good)
WFA 4 from 5yo+ 2lb **15** Ran SP% **122.7**
Speed ratings: **101,100,100,99,97 97,96,95,93,93 91,87,87,87,84**
CSF: £188.32.
Owner Sheikh Hamdan Bin Mohammed Al Maktoum **Bred** Darley **Trained** United Arab Emirates

■ Eastern Anthem completed a stunning double on the night for Emeratis Ahmed Ajtebi and Mubarak Bin Shafya.

FOCUS

Not as classy a Group 1 race as the Duty Free earlier on the card, but a competitive renewal nonetheless. A lack of pace looked a big danger on paper and that was borne out, with Front House dictating at a steady early gallop. With several of the key horses clearly compromised by the way the race was run Eastern Anthem has been given one of the lowest ratings of the last ten winners.

NOTEBOOK

Eastern Anthem(IRE), representing the stable of Mubarak Bin Shafya, who won the Duty Free with Gladiatorus, found the best turn of foot, picking up well from the back of the field and running on strongly down the outside to win in a three-way photo. Earlier in his career when with Godolphin, the winner was considered a possible Derby horse, but he never really made the grade. However, since joining his current yard he has done nothing but improve, winning his previous two starts at this track in handicap company, and this was another big step up. Bred to be special, being by Singspiel out of 1000 Guineas/Oaks winner Kazzia, he will be a fascinating contender for some of the big races back in Europe (when he will again sport the Godolphin blue) this summer.

Spanish Moon(USA), another one-time Derby hope, did not manage to win a Group race last year, but on the evidence of this seasonal return he should put that right this term. Always well placed from his low draw, he took over in front with over two furlongs to run, kept on well when strongly tackled and lost nothing in defeat. He looks a typical improver for Sir Michael Stoute and should be kept on-side this season. His effort is all the more creditable considering he was later reported to have returned with a cut to his right hind, and his mouth.

Purple Moon(IRE) suffered another heartbreakingly narrow defeat, and considering that the steady early pace would have been all against him it was another fine effort from the six-year-old. He has proved more than once that he can win at this level granted a decent gallop, and his trainer now plans to give him a break before bringing him back for another assault on the Japan Cup, Hong Kong Vase and this race. (op 7-1)

Youmzain(IRE), who finished third in this race in 2007 and fifth last year, was for the third year in succession denied a proper gallop, and once again he was doing all his best work at the finish. Denied a clear run for much of the way up the straight, the winner was already gone by the time he got into the clear, but he flew once out in the open. Not for the first time in his career he looked unlucky, but his style of running means that trouble in running is always a possibility. (op 4-1)

Marsh Side(USA), who won the Canadian International last year, was another who did not get the best of runs in the straight. He appreciated the return to 1m4f after being beaten over two furlongs shorter at Santa Anita last time, though.

Quijano(GER), who was fourth in this race last year and is a reliable type in these International Group 1s, took a while to pick up and never really got rolling. He was one of many who would have appreciated a stronger pace.

Deem(IRE), held up out the back in the early stages, never really posed a threat, although she did stay on late.

Doctor Dino(FR) had a poor draw to overcome and ended up being trapped out wide where he pulled for his head off the steady gallop. As a result it was no surprise when his challenge in the straight proved short-lived.

Front House(IRE), who won the Group 2 City Of Gold over this course and distance last time, raced a bit too freely in front, but it was still disappointing to see her drop out so early in the straight given the way the race had been run. She was by no means the only horse trained by Mike de Kock who disappointed on the night, though, and in this race in particular his runners failed to shine.

Kirklees(IRE) had his stamina to prove over this longer trip and was another drawn out in the car park. A little keen through the early stages, he gave away ground racing wider than ideal and did not get home.
Russian Sage(SAF), a late addition to this race having been initially earmarked to run in the Duty Free, returned having bled from both nostrils. (op 14-1)
Red Rocks(IRE) has been disappointing since beating Curlin last summer, but this run can be forgiven as he was poorly drawn and did not settle off the modest gallop, while all the time racing widest of all.
King Of Rome(IRE) was eased when his path on the rail was blocked by his tiring stablemate Russian Sage. He deserves rating a bit better than the bare form.
Macarthur, drawn worst of all, was held up out the back with the eventual winner, but he found little for pressure and did not look the most straightforward.

1013a DUBAI WORLD CUP SPONSORED BY EMIRATES AIRLINE (GROUP 1) (DIRT) — 1m 2f (D)
5:30 (5:30) 3-Y-O+

£2,500,000 (£833,333; £416,666; £208,333; £125,000; £83,333)

			RPR
1		**Well Armed (USA)**[48] 6-9-0 119 (t) AGryder 7 — (Eoin Harty, U.S.A) *sn led: drew clr 3f out: r.o wl: easily* **10/1**	128+
2	14	**Gloria De Campeao (BRZ)**[30] [698] 6-9-0 113 JLeme 6 — (P Bary, France) *mid-div on rail: chsd wnr 3f out: r.o: no ch w wnr* **25/1**	104
3	4 1/2	**Paris Perfect (SAF)**[36] 5-9-0 113 (t) BFayd'Herbe 13 — (N L Bruss) *in rr of mid-div: nvr able to chal: r.o wl fnl 2f* **66/1**	96
4	1/2	**Muller (ARG)**[36] 6-9-0 113 (t) WCMarwing 11 — (N L Bruss) *racd wl in rr: n.d: r.o wl fnl 2 1/2f: nrst fin* **50/1**	95
5	3 1/2	**My Indy (ARG)**[51] [417] 5-9-0 115 LDettori 14 — (Saeed Bin Suroor) *trckd ldr: ev ch 3f out: r.o: wknd fnl f* **10/1**	89
6	1 3/4	**Albertus Maximus (USA)**[56] 5-9-0 119 AGarcia 10 — (Kiaran McLaughlin, U.S.A) *mid-div: wd: t.k.h: rdn 2 1/2f out: wknd fnl 1 1/2f* **7/2**[2]	86
7	1/2	**Snaafy (USA)**[23] [771] 5-9-0 116 (v) RHills 3 — (M Al Muhairi, UAE) *s.i.s: mid-div: nt qckn fnl 2 1/2f* **12/1**	85
8	2 1/4	**Casino Drive (USA)**[34] 4-9-0 117 KAndo 8 — (Kazuo Fujisawa, Japan) *plld hard: bumped rivals after 1 1/2f: nvr bttr than mid-div* **4/1**[3]	81
9	1/2	**Happy Boy (BRZ)**[23] [773] 6-9-0 113 AhmedAjtebi 5 — (M bin Shafya, UAE) *mid-div: rdn 3 1/2f out: sn btn* **25/1**	80
10	1 1/4	**Muhannak (IRE)**[23] [773] 5-9-0 113 (b) RyanMoore 1 — (R M Beckett) *slowly away: sn rdn in last: nvr nr to chal* **50/1**	78
11	1 1/4	**Arson Squad (USA)**[56] 6-9-0 115 (t) EPrado 2 — (Richard Dutrow Jr, U.S.A) *in rr of mid-div: badly hmpd after 1 1/2f* **33/1**	76
12	3 1/4	**Asiatic Boy (ARG)**[23] [773] 6-9-0 118 JMurtagh 4 — (M F De Kock, South Africa) *s.i.s: in rr of mid-div: hmpd after 1 1/2f: rdn 4f out: sn btn* **2/1**[1]	70
13	3/4	**Joe Louis (ARG)**[36] 6-9-0 113 (t) WRamos 9 — (J Barton, Saudi Arabia) *nvr bttr than mid-div* **66/1**	69
14	7 1/2	**Anak Nakal (USA)**[56] 4-9-0 110 (t) JBravo 12 — (Nicholas Zito, U.S.A) *nvr able to chal* **100/1**	56

2m 1.01s (-1.29) **Going Correction** +0.40s/f (Slow) **14** Ran SP% **120.0**
Speed ratings: **121,109,106,105,103 101,101,99,99,98 97,94,93,87**
CSF: £238.92.
Owner WinStar Farm LLC **Bred** WinStar Farm LLC **Trained** USA

■ The last race ever run at Nad Al Sheba. The 2010 meeting is due to be held at neighbouring Meydan, still under construction.

FOCUS
A sub-standard World Cup, and certainly one of the weakest since the inaugural running in 1996. For example, coming into this not one of the 14 runners could match the race's lowest winning Racing Post Rating of 125 (Almutawakel 1999 and Captain Steve 2001), and the pick of them, Well Armed's 124, was achieved on a synthetic surface. The next best RPR was 121, boasted by both Asiatic Boy and Albertus Maximus. The lack of an outstanding performer contributed to the largest field to date, and on paper at least, that seemed to result in a much more open race than in recent seasons. As it turned out the winner was given an RPR of 128, the highest so far this year but the placed horses achieved only Listed level marks.

NOTEBOOK
Well Armed(USA) smashed the previous record margin of victory, but that only reinforces the view his rivals were simply not up to scratch. While the winner obviously deserves praise for such an achievement, it cannot be ignored that he was beaten eight lengths into third by Curlin (previous longest-margin winner) in this race last year and is exposed as short of top class. Without wishing to further knock what was clearly a fine performance on the day, it also needs pointing out that this son of Tiznow was gifted a ridiculously easy lead on a speed-favouring track. Being a gelding he can be kept on the go for as long as he is willing, but all things considered, it will be a surprise if he ever manages to top this performance.
Gloria De Campeao(BRZ) made a respectable showing, but it's hard to get too excited by his performance considering he was beaten over 16 lengths in last year's race (eight and a half lengths behind Well Armed), and his proximity provides further evidence the overall standard was well below average. His confidence probably received a boost when he landed a handicap off 108 over 1m1f here last time, but he's 0-8 in Group company outside his native Brazil.
Paris Perfect(SAF) lost a prominent early position when the winner increased the pace from the front, and was forced to switch wide in the straight, but he kept on to reverse recent placings with his stable companion.
Muller(ARG), who raced well back, finished clear of the rest but could not confirm previous form with his stable companion.
My Indy(ARG) was close enough if good enough turning in to the straight, but he was unproven over a trip this far and found little in the straight.
Albertus Maximus(USA) was representing the same connections as 2007 winner Invasor, but all his best form is at around 1m on a synthetic surface, and he was deeply unimpressive when winning the Donn Handicap (1m1f, dirt) at Gulfstream on his latest start. His rider seemed keen to hang on to him early, possibly to help him to get this longer trip, but the horse was simply much too keen. He was later reported to have returned with an inflamed off-fore tendon. (op 3-1)
Snaafy(USA) progressed rapidly at the Carnival, but his three wins this year were gained from wide draws over 7f-1m. The combination of an inside stall and this longer trip seemed to find him out. (op 14-1)
Casino Drive(USA) was far too keen under restraint and would surely have been better served by putting more pressure on the leader, especially considering the lack of pace in the race.
Happy Boy(BRZ), who had form with both My Indy and Asiatic Boy found very little under pressure.
Muhannak(IRE) is a turf/synthetic horse and did not help his chances with a slow start.
Arson Squad(USA) is much better than he was able to show as he was badly hampered on the inside rail early on by the free-running Casino Drive.
Asiatic Boy(ARG) are entitled to feel most disappointed considering he was a quarter of a length in front of today's winner when runner-up in this race last year. He raced far too far back, and was checked slightly by Casino Drive early on, but in truth there was simply no response in the straight and something seemed to be amiss. Reportedly coughing after the race, he is quite likely to race for Kieran McLaughlin in New York this summer. (op 9-4)
Joe Louis(ARG) was entitled to finish much closer on a line through the third and fourth home, but he ran a stinker. He's yet to run a good race at this course and his connections will no doubt be pleased next year's race is at Meydan.

994 DONCASTER (L-H)
Sunday, March 29

OFFICIAL GOING: Straight course - good to firm (good in places); round course - good (good to firm in places)
Wind: Moderate, half-against Weather: Fine and sunny

1014 AJA GENTLEMAN AMATEUR RIDERS' H'CAP — 1m 2f 60y
2:00 (2:00) (Class 5) (0-70,70) 4-Y-O+ **£2,498** (£774; £387; £193) **Stalls** Low

Form				RPR
00-0	1		**Director's Chair**[38] [597] 4-10-8 62 MrRBirkett(5) 11 — (Miss J Feilden) *chsd ldrs: wnt 2nd 4f out: styd on to ld 1f out: edgd rt: hld on towards fin* **25/1**	72
0-60	2	nk	**Top Seed (IRE)**[51] [428] 8-10-7 63 MrJHodson(7) 18 — (Ian Williams) *in rr: hdwy on outside over 2f out: chsd ldrs over 1f out: no ex nr fin* **16/1**	72
-560	3	3	**King's Ransom**[8] [910] 6-10-13 67 MrTFWoodside(5) 2 — (S Gollings) *led and sn wl clr: hdd 1f out: kpt on same pce* **10/1**	70
0-34	4	1/2	**Iceman George**[10] [885] 5-10-2 56 oh1 (p) MrBMMorris(5) 10 — (D Morris) *chsd ldrs: effrt on outer over 3f out: hung lft: styd on same pce appr fnl f* **14/1**	58
1412	5	1/2	**William's Way**[12] [860] 7-11-1 69 MrCMartin(5) 17 — (I A Wood) *hld up towards rr: effrt over 3f out: kpt on: nt rch ldrs* **7/1**[2]	70
-352	6	3/4	**Wester Lodge (IRE)**[27] [734] 7-10-2 58 MrDJEustace(7) 1 — (J M P Eustace) *s.i.s: hdwy on ins to chse ldrs 4f out: one pce fnl 2f* **8/1**[3]	58
-113	7	2	**All In The Red (IRE)**[24] [765] 4-11-1 67 (p) MrPCollington(3) 6 — (A Crook) *s.s: kpt on fnl 3f: nvr nr ldrs* **12/1**	63
004-	8	1 1/2	**Kalasam**[179] [6395] 5-10-10 66 MrMarkMason(7) 12 — (M W Easterby) *hld up towards rr: pushed along over 3f out: nvr nr ldrs* **25/1**	59
054/	9	3/4	**Black Beauty**[15] [4116] 6-10-9 65 (p) MrJMQuinlan(7) 7 — (M G Quinlan) *chsd ldrs: outpcd and lost pl over 2f out: styd on fnl f* **8/1**[3]	56
005/	10	3/4	**Street Warrior (IRE)**[27] [6596] 6-10-9 65 MrSeanKerr(7) 9 — (H J Evans) *t.k.h: trckd ldrs: effrt over 3f out: wknd over 1f out* **14/1**	55
6063	11	nk	**Just Observing**[7] [923] 6-11-3 66 MrSWalker 5 — (P T Midgley) *trckd clr ldr: wknd 2f out* **6/1**[1]	55
400-	12	2 1/2	**Dragon Slayer (IRE)**[120] [7502] 7-11-7 70 MrSDobson 3 — (John A Harris) *chsd ldrs: lost pl over 1f out* **11/1**	54
4/3-	13	3 1/2	**Dovedon Hero**[118] [7512] 9-10-7 63 MrSMcBride(7) 8 — (P J McBride) *s.i.s: a in rr* **16/1**	40
-526	14	2 1/4	**Bailieborough (IRE)**[58] [353] 10-10-4 58 MrDaleSwift(5) 20 — (B Ellison) *drvn to chse ldrs: effrt over 3f out: wknd 2f out* **14/1**	31
13-0	15	1 3/4	**Kingsholm**[67] [238] 7-11-3 66 MrMSeston 13 — (N Wilson) *sn chsng ldrs: lost pl 2f out* **20/1**	35

2m 11.85s (0.65) **Going Correction** -0.125s/f (Firm) **15** Ran SP% **118.3**
Speed ratings (Par 103): **92,91,89,88,88 87,86,85,84,83 83,81,78,77,75**
toteswinger: 1&2 £89.20, 1&3 £101.40, 2&3 £56.30 CSF £366.84 CT £4212.79 TOTE £20.50: £8.00, £7.30, £3.90; EX 373.10 TRIFECTA Not won..
Owner Ocean Trailers Ltd **Bred** D R Tucker **Trained** Exning, Suffolk

FOCUS
A modest amateur riders' handicap, but the vast majority of these were either fit from the All-Weather or from jumping. It proved to be an interesting race too, though not so much for each-way punters with five non-runners taking the field down to 15. The pace was decent thanks to King's Ransom, who had established a massive advantage by halfway.
King's Ransom Official explanation: jockey said, regarding appearing to ease in straight, that his orders were to jump out in front and having done so he had been run away with, adding that the gelding felt tired and was flat out at the 3f mark.

1015 SOCIETY LIFESTYLE & LEISURE MAGAZINE MAIDEN STKS — 7f
2:30 (2:34) (Class 4) 3-Y-O **£5,180** (£1,541; £770; £384) **Stalls** High

Form				RPR
2-	1		**Makaamen**[177] [6438] 3-9-3 0 MichaelHills 5 — (B W Hills) *t.k.h: cl up: led wl over 2f out: shkn up over 1f out and styd on wl* **1/2**[1]	83+
	2	3 1/2	**George Thisby** 3-9-0 0 JamesMillman(3) 6 — (B R Millman) *led: pushed along 3f out: rdn and hdd wl over 2f out: drvn and kpt on fnl f* **66/1**	74
	3	2 3/4	**African Cheetah** 3-9-3 0 JoeFanning 3 — (M Johnston) *green and sn pushed along in rr: swtchd outside and hdwy 2f out: rdn and styd on strly ins fnl fulorng: nrst fin* **8/1**[3]	66+
64-	4	2	**Feet Of Fury**[155] [6988] 3-8-12 0 JohnEgan 10 — (W M Brisbourne) *hld up: hdwy 1/2-way: n.m.r and swtchd rt wl over 1f out: effrt and n.m.r ent fnl fulorng: sn rdn and kpt on: nrst fin* **33/1**	62+
200-	5	nse	**Olympic Dream**[176] [6483] 3-9-3 79 PaulHanagan 12 — (R A Fahey) *prom: rdn along over 2f out: swtchd lft and drvn over 1f out: kpt on same pce* **6/1**[2]	61
	6	1 1/2	**Deauville Flyer** 3-9-3 0 PaulMulrennan 14 — (T D Easterby) *awkward s: sn in midfield: hdwy over 2f out: swtchd lft and rdn along wl over 1f out: kpt on same pce* **66/1**	57
360-	7	1	**Wabi Sabi (IRE)**[160] [6857] 3-8-7 63 Louis-PhilippeBeuzelin(5) 7 — (N Tinkler) *chsd ldrs: rdn along 3f out: grad wknd* **33/1**	49
0-	8	2 1/2	**Waltzing Buddy**[288] [3049] 3-8-5 0 PaulPickard(7) 9 — (P T Midgley) *chsd ldrs: rdn along 1/2-way: sn wknd* **125/1**	42
	9	3 1/4	**Flynn's Island (IRE)** 3-9-3 0 PhillipMakin 1 — (M Dods) *a towards rr* **33/1**	38
-	10	1	**Highkingofireland** 3-8-12 0 MartinLane(5) 8 — (K R Burke) *prom: rdn along 3f out: wknd over 2f out* **50/1**	36
	11	1	**Winrob** 3-9-3 0 RobertWinston 11 — (Patrick Morris) *awkward s: a in rr* **50/1**	33
234-	12	nk	**York Key Bar**[152] [7044] 3-8-10 74 AnthonyBetts(7) 2 — (B Ellison) *wnt lft s: chsd ldrs: rdn along over 3f out and sn wknd* **20/1**	32
	13	14	**Green Spirit (IRE)** 3-9-3 0 EddieAhern 4 — (Patrick Morris) *t.k.h: chsd ldrs on outer: rdn along and hung lft 1/2-way: sn wknd* **50/1**	—

1m 26.47s (0.17) **Going Correction** -0.125s/f (Firm) **13** Ran SP% **115.3**
Speed ratings (Par 100): **94,90,86,84,84 82,81,78,75,73 72,72,56**
toteswinger: 1&2 £14.00, 1&3 £2.30, 2&3 £29.90 CSF £67.92 TOTE £1.50: £1.10, £11.10, £1.80; EX 40.50 Trifecta £311.50 Part won..
Owner Hamdan Al Maktoum **Bred** Brook Stud Bloodstock Ltd **Trained** Lambourn, Berks

FOCUS
A brief look back at the history of this race suggests that not many of these runners will go on to achieve any exalted successes, but it does have to be said that plenty of the also-rans went on to win races.
Feet Of Fury ◆ Official explanation: jockey said filly was denied a clear run

1016 WILLIAMHILL.COM - PLAY BLACKJACK H'CAP 7f
3:05 (3:10) (Class 4) (0-85,85) 4-Y-O+ **£5,180** (£1,541; £770; £384) **Stalls** High

Form RPR

023- **1** **Mister Hardy**[145] 7181 4-8-11 **83**.................................. FrederikTylicki(5) 8 103
(R A Fahey) *racd far side: hld up in rr: gd hdwy to ld overall over 2f out: clr 1f out: pushed out* **9/1**[3]

31-1 **2** *6* **Last Sovereign**[49] 457 5-9-1 **82**..................................(p) JamieSpencer 1 86
(Jane Chapple-Hyam) *racd far side: chsd ldrs: kpt on same pce fnl 2f* **6/1**[1]

001- **3** *1 ¾* **Minority Report**[182] 6314 9-8-10 **80**........................... AndrewMullen(3) 9 79
(D Nicholls) *hld in rr far side: hdwy 2f out: styd on wl ins fnl f* **14/1**

003- **4** *1* **Nisaal (IRE)**[141] 7239 4-8-2 **76**..................................... JamieKyne(7) 13 73
(J J Quinn) *racd stands' side: chsd ldrs: styd on fnl f to ld that side nr fin: 1st of 9 that gp* **20/1**

/05- **5** *shd* **Trafalgar Bay (IRE)**[148] 7127 6-9-1 **82**...................... FergusSweeney 15 78
(K R Burke) *racd stands' side: chsd ldrs: led that side over 1f out: kpt on same pce: 2nd of 9 that gp* **25/1**

-441 **6** *nk* **Captain Macarry (IRE)**[37] 625 4-8-8 **75**........................(v) TomEaves 7 70
(B Smart) *racd far side: prom: one pce fnl 2f* **20/1**

400- **7** *¾* **Tiger Dream**[188] 6170 4-8-8 **75**..................................... PaulHanagan 4 68
(K A Ryan) *racd far side: trckd ldrs: styd on same pce fnl 2f* **13/2**[2]

5306 **8** *½* **Cornus**[16] 834 7-8-8 **75**..(be) JamesDoyle 5 67
(A J McCabe) *racd far side: chsd ldrs: one pce fnl 2f* **28/1**

6240 **9** *1* **Excusez Moi (USA)**[40] 579 7-8-13 **85**........................... DeanHeslop(5) 19 74
(Mrs R A Carr) *racd stands' side: in rr: hdwy over 2f out: nvr nr ldrs: 3rd of 9 that gp* **33/1**

420- **10** *¾* **Hiccups**[152] 7041 9-8-10 **77**... PhillipMakin 11 64
(M Dods) *swtchd lft s and r far side: hld up in rr: kpt on fnl 2f: nvr a factor* **20/1**

000- **11** *½* **Zomerlust**[141] 7239 7-9-1 **82**....................................... GrahamGibbons 2 68
(J J Quinn) *racd far side: prom: one pce fnl 2f* **40/1**

1045 **12** *1 ¾* **Orchard Supreme**[36] 635 6-9-4 **85**............................. JimmyFortune 10 66
(R Hannon) *racd far side: in rr: nvr a factor* **14/1**

110- **13** *2 ½* **Shotley Mac**[141] 7239 5-8-13 **80**................................. FrancisNorton 3 55
(N Bycroft) *led far side tl hdd & wknd over 2f out* **25/1**

5240 **14** *shd* **Methaaly (IRE)**[2] 985 6-9-4 **85**...................................(be) EddieAhern 12 59
(M Mullineaux) *racd stands' side: w ldrs: led that gp over 2f out: hdd & wknd over 1f out: 4th of 9 that gp* **18/1**

523 **15** *1 ¼* **El Dececy (USA)**[8] 910 5-9-0 **81**...................................... LiamJones 22 52
(S Parr) *led stands' side gp tl hdd over 2f out: wknd over 1f out: 5th of 9 that gp* **12/1**

061- **16** *¾* **Koraleva Tectona (IRE)**[208] 5589 4-8-8 **75**.................... PaulEddery 16 44
(Pat Eddery) *racd stands' side: a in rr: 6th of 9 that gp* **10/1**

1-14 **17** *nk* **Smarty Socks (IRE)**[7] 922 5-8-9 **76**.............................. JamieMoriarty 21 44
(P T Midgley) *racd stands' side: in rr: nt clr run on ins over 2f out: eased over 1f out: 7th of 9 that gp* **14/1**

60-5 **18** *4 ½* **Carlitos Spirit (IRE)**[11] 866 5-8-12 **79**....................... RobertWinston 17 35
(B R Millman) *racd stands' side: in rr: bhd fnl 2f: 8th of 9 that gp* **11/1**

400- **18** *dht* **Captain Jacksparra (IRE)**[183] 6277 5-9-0 **81**............... PaulMulrennan 6 37
(K A Ryan) *racd far side: chsd ldrs: wknd over 2f out* **25/1**

500- **20** *18* **Dream Theme**[183] 6278 6-8-11 **85**...................................... NSLawes(7) 18 —
(D Nicholls) *s.s: racd stands' side: hdwy to chse ldrs on outer after 3f: lost pl over 2f out: bhd whn eased ins fnl f: last of 9 that gp* **20/1**

1m 24.45s (-1.85) **Going Correction** -0.125s/f (Firm) **20 Ran SP% 127.4**
Speed ratings (Par 105): **105,98,96,95,94 94,93,93,91,91 90,88,85,85,84 83,82,77,77,57**
toteswinger: 1&2 £4.00, 1&3 £65.70, 2&3 £15.40 CSF £53.71 CT £794.69 TOTE £10.90: £3.50, £2.10, £4.70, £5.90; EX 49.90 Trifecta £330.70 Part won. Pool £447.02 - 0.46 winning.
Owner The Cosmic Cases **Bred** Mrs M Bryce **Trained** Musley Bank, N Yorks

FOCUS
As would have been expected, the field split into two. A larger group of 11 went far side, whilst the other nine came up the stands' rail. The far side group had the advantage, providing the first three home. This had looked a competitive handicap on paper, but the winner bolted up.
Smarty Socks(IRE) Official explanation: jockey said gelding had been denied a clear run

1017 WILLIAMHILL.COM - PLAY ROULETTE DONCASTER SHIELD (CONDITIONS STKS) 1m 4f
3:40 (3:40) (Class 2) 4-Y-O+ **£12,952** (£3,854; £1,926; £962) **Stalls** Low

Form RPR

203- **1** **Tastahil (IRE)**[141] 7244 5-9-0 98................................. MichaelHills 3 110
(B W Hills) *trckd ldng pair: smooth hdwy 4f out: led wl over 2f out: shkn up and edgd lft wl over 1f out: rdn and edgd lft ent fnl f: styd on* **6/4**[1]

-000 **2** *1 ½* **Drill Sergeant**[31] 699 4-8-12 102.................................... JoeFanning 2 107
(M Johnston) *set decent pce: pushed along 4f out and sn jnd: rdn and hdd wl over 2f out: drvn over 1f out: rallied and ev ch ent fnl f: sn no ex* **7/1**[3]

245- **3** *2 ¾* **Furmigadelagiusta**[281] 3249 5-9-0 98........................ DarrenWilliams 8 103
(K R Burke) *in tch: hdwy 1/2-way: chsd ldng pair over 2f out and sn rdn: drvn over 1f out and kpt on same pce* **10/1**

2/2- **4** *3 ¾* **Fairmile**[262] 3885 7-9-0 111.. StephenDonohoe 4 97
(Ian Williams) *hld up in rr: hdwy 4f out: rdn over 2f out: drvn and no imp fr over 1f out* **9/1**

405- **5** *2 ¼* **Hindu Kush (IRE)**[176] 6494 4-9-4 0................................... JimCrowley 6 99
(D Nicholls) *trckd ldrs: hdwy over 3f out: rdn along 2f out: sn drvn and wknd over 1f out* **8/1**

200- **6** *¾* **Carte Diamond (USA)**[141] 7244 8-9-0 97........................ TomEaves 1 92
(B Ellison) *chsd ldr: rdn along 4f out and grad wknd fnl 3f* **8/1**

7 *nk* **Valmari (IRE)**[120] 6-8-9 0... J-PGuillambert 10 87
(C E Brittain) *a towards rr* **66/1**

2610 **8** *3* **Young Mick**[24] 772 7-9-4 0...(v) JohnEgan 9 91
(G G Margarson) *hld up towards rr: hdwy over 4f out and sn rdn along: drvn on outer over 2f out and no imp* **6/1**[2]

014- **9** *4* **Lost Soldier Three (IRE)**[169] 6652 8-9-0 94.............. AdrianTNicholls 7 81
(D Nicholls) *dwlt: a in rr* **25/1**

2m 29.76s (-5.34) **Going Correction** -0.125s/f (Firm)
WFA 4 from 5yo+ 2lb **9 Ran SP% 113.4**
Speed ratings (Par 109): **112,111,109,106,105 104,104,102,99**
toteswinger: 1&2 £2.50, 1&3 £6.20, 2&3 £10.40 CSF £12.10 TOTE £2.60: £1.10, £2.40, £3.20; EX 13.00 Trifecta £112.80 Pool £440.71 - 2.89 winning units..
Owner Hamdan Al Maktoum **Bred** Darley **Trained** Lambourn, Berks

The Form Book, Raceform Ltd, Compton, RG20 6NL

FOCUS
Plenty of familiar names lined up for this decent-looking contest, although some had changed stables since the end of last season. A number had bumped into each other on various occasions before, so the form should be reasonably sound, especially as the leader appeared to set an even tempo.

NOTEBOOK
Tastahil(IRE) finished last year with a good effort in the November Handicap and, like his sire, appears to be improving with age. Always close up, he moved into the lead just over two furlongs out and kept on in really game style to be a cosy winner. The gelding operation he had after the November Handicap obviously had a positive effect, and he looks the type for staying handicaps. Considering the trainer's record at Chester, it would be no surprise to see him go for a race like the Chester Cup. (op 15-8 tchd 2-1 in places)
Drill Sergeant was well beaten in three races in Dubai ? the final two were staying events ? but bounced back to something close to his best with a gritty display. He was allowed to lead early and looked like being swamped at one point, but like so many from his stable he battled on bravely and made the winner work hard. (op 10-1)
Furmigadelagiusta finished runner-up in this last year ? a place in front of Carte Diamond ? and ran a couple of good races before his season ended in June. He moved strongly into the home straight and kept on well. This was a highly-encouraging start to 2009. (op 9-1)
Fairmile, bought at Tattersalls for 17,000 guineas, showed some very good form for Godolphin but had been off the track since chasing home Hala Bek in a conditions event at Nottingham. He has a very good record when fresh, but the trip was a slight concern, and he was easy in the betting. Held up, he came through to look dangerous but his stamina gave way and he weakened inside the final furlong. (op 15-2 tchd 10-1)
Hindu Kush(IRE) always looked an interesting prospect for Coolmore and was far from disgraced in the St Leger. He was always tried in good company and current connections had to go to 120,000 guineas to get him at the sales. The signs seemed positive, as he attracted market support, but he got outpaced two furlongs from home before running on again. One would imagine he will relish a step up in trip. (op 10-1)
Carte Diamond(USA), third in this last year, did not finish 2008 in great style but had run some respectable races earlier that season. He came through to have every chance rounding the home bend, travelling strongly, but failed to pick up when he needed to catch the leader. (op 9-1)
Valmari(IRE), an import from Greek racing, had never raced onturf before. There was not a great deal of encouragement to be taken from this effort, but she might be more interesting when moved to sand. (tchd 100-1)
Young Mick has been on the go all winter and managed a welcome success out in Dubai during February. Back in England, he was being pumped along some way from home and looked to be eased in the latter stages on the quickish ground. Official explanation: jockey said gelding hung right in straight; trainer said, regarding the poor form shown, that gelding did not come down the hill well on the fast ground and hung right in straight (op 9-2 tchd 13-2 in places)
Lost Soldier Three(IRE) made a move from well off the gallop in the home straight but still managed to finish last. (op 16-1)

1018 WILLIAMHILL.COM - PLAY BETLIVE TV H'CAP 6f
4:15 (4:18) (Class 2) (0-100,98) 4-Y-O+ **£12,952** (£3,854; £1,926; £962) **Stalls** High

Form RPR

213- **1** **Palace Moon**[149] 7109 4-8-8 **88**....................................... SteveDrowne 2 114
(H Morrison) *racd far side: trckd ldr gng wl: led overall over 1f out: sn shot clr: impressive* **5/1**[1]

004- **2** *5* **Advanced**[135] 7325 6-8-8 **95**... AmyRyan(7) 10 105
(K A Ryan) *racd far side: chsd ldrs: wnt 2nd 1f out: edgd rt: no ch w wnr* **8/1**

000- **3** *nk* **Evens And Odds (IRE)**[158] 6902 5-8-10 **90**............. AdrianTNicholls 22 99
(D Nicholls) *racd stands' side: hld up in rr: hdwy to ld that gp 2f out: kpt on wl fnl f: 1st of 11 that gp* **14/1**

622- **4** *½* **Harrison George (IRE)**[191] 6069 4-8-10 **90**................. PaulHanagan 21 97
(R A Fahey) *racd stands' side: in rr: hdwy over 1f out: styd on wl ins fnl f: 2nd of 11 that gp* **13/2**[2]

252- **5** *½* **Barney McGrew (IRE)**[141] 7245 6-9-2 **96**..................... PhillipMakin 7 101
(M Dods) *racd far side: trckd ldrs: kpt on fnl f* **12/1**

320- **6** *1 ¼* **Fathsta (IRE)**[172] 6576 4-8-12 **92**............................... StephenDonohoe 19 93
(D Nicholls) *uns rdr and rn loose to s: racd stands' side: hld up in rr: hdwy 2f out: edgd lft and styd on ins fnl f: 3rd of 11 that gp* **25/1**

3100 **7** *1 ½* **Capricorn Run (USA)**[8] 916 6-9-4 **98**.....................(b) RobertWinston 16 95
(A J McCabe) *racd stands' side: mid-div: hdwy and edgd lft over 1f out: nvr nr ldrs: 4th of 11 that gp* **33/1**

054- **8** *1 ¾* **River Falcon**[155] 6971 9-9-2 **96**................................... DanielTudhope 3 87
(J S Goldie) *rrd s: racd far side: kpt on fnl 2f: nvr a factor* **20/1**

330- **9** *1 ¼* **Joseph Henry**[183] 6289 7-8-9 **89**.. PaulQuinn 13 76
(D Nicholls) *racd stands' side: chsd ldrs on outer: edgd lft and one pce fnl 2f: 5th of 11 that gp* **20/1**

060- **10** *½* **Good Gorsoon (USA)**[211] 5509 4-8-9 **89**........................ MichaelHills 11 74
(B W Hills) *rrd and wnt lft s: racd far side: t.k.h in rr: kpt on fnl 2f: nvr on terms* **11/1**

004- **11** *hd* **Machinist (IRE)**[239] 4624 9-9-0 **97**............................. AndrewMullen(3) 4 82
(D Nicholls) *racd far side: in rr: kpt on fnl 2f: nvr a factor* **28/1**

400- **12** *¾* **Turnkey**[183] 6289 7-8-4 **91**.. AdeleMulrennan(7) 12 73
(D Nicholls) *racd stands' side: prom: outpcd fnl 2f: 6th of 11 that gp* **40/1**

000- **13** *hd* **Mastership (IRE)**[141] 7245 5-8-13 **93**........................ GrahamGibbons 1 75
(J J Quinn) *racd far side: trckd ldrs: lost pl 2f out* **14/1**

154- **14** *½* **Baldemar**[168] 6676 4-8-8 **88**... AndrewElliott 6 68
(K R Burke) *racd far side: chsd ldrs: wknd 2f out* **40/1**

400- **15** *1 ¼* **Bel Cantor**[156] 6947 6-8-4 **89**................................(p) KellyHarrison(5) 8 65
(W J H Ratcliffe) *overall ldr on far side: hdd & wknd over 1f out* **40/1**

0-04 **16** *½* **Northern Fling**[37] 638 5-9-3 **97**....................................... FrancisNorton 14 72
(D Nicholls) *racd stands' side: chsd ldrs: wknd 2f out: 7th of 11 that gp* **12/1**

365 **17** *nk* **Haajes**[22] 785 5-8-10 **90**..(bt) LiamJones 17 64
(S Parr) *racd stands' side: chsd ldrs: wandered and wknd over 2f out: 8th of 11 that gp* **33/1**

0-14 **18** *¾* **Thebes**[8] 916 4-8-11 **91**.. GregFairley 20 62
(M Johnston) *led stands' side tl hdd & wknd over 2f out: 9th of 11 that gp* **7/1**[3]

060- **19** *1 ¼* **Everymanforhimself (IRE)**[183] 6289 5-8-11 **91**........ PaulMulrennan 15 58
(K A Ryan) *racd stands' side: chsd ldrs: wkng whn hmpd over 1f out: 10th of 11 that gp* **25/1**

500- **20** *3 ¼* **Ajigolo**[225] 5109 6-8-10 **90**.. LeeEnstone 18 47
(N Wilson) *w ldr stands' side: led that gp over 2f out: sn hdd & wknd qckly: last of 11 that gp* **50/1**

1m 11.21s (-2.39) **Going Correction** -0.125s/f (Firm) **20 Ran SP% 126.5**
Speed ratings (Par 109): **110,103,102,102,101 99,97,95,93,93 93,92,91,91,89 88,88,87,85,81**
toteswinger: 1&2 £12.30, 1&3 £34.40, 2&3 £31.90 CSF £37.40 CT £557.46 TOTE £4.40: £2.10, £2.90, £5.10, £2.10; EX 59.30 TRIFECTA Not won..
Owner Miss B Swire **Bred** Miss B Swire **Trained** East Ilsley, Berks
■ Stewards' Enquiry : Robert Winston caution: careless riding.

FOCUS
A decent-quality sprint handicap and once again the field split into two, with Thebes leading a larger group of 11 up the stands' rail, whilst Bel Cantor set a decent pace for the group of nine on the far side. Again the far side had the edge, with the first two home coming from that group.

NOTEBOOK
Palace Moon ◆ took apart what had looked a tight contest. Making his handicap debut after showing good form in three starts last year, he travelled prominently in the far side group, and once Steve Drowne asked him for his effort entering the last 2f, he quickly drew clear. He was by far the least-exposed in the field and this will have delighted connections. Although he may not reach the heights of his half-brother Sakhee's Secret, he is already verging on Listed class and looks sure to progress further. (op 4-1 tchd 11-2 in places)

Advanced, now a stone lower than when winning the Ayr Gold Cup in 2007, attracted good market support beforehand and was always up there towards the far side. He tended to hang under pressure in the closing stages, but it made no difference to the result, the winner was in a different league. This was still a pleasing return and he looks capable of winning again granted easier underfoot conditions. (op 16-1)

Evens And Odds(IRE), running moderately when last seen in the autumn, was making his debut for this yard off a stone lower mark than at this time last year. He performed with plenty of credit to emerge best of the stands' side group. His new trainer should be able to find an opportunity for him in due course. (op 12-1 tchd 16-1)

Harrison George(IRE), offa career-high mark on his return to action following a successful 2008, was a big eyecatcher. He found himself last of the near-side group after a tardy start, but eventually flew home, and would have been third with a little further to go. He still looks to be a sprinter on the up. (op 8-1)

Barney McGrew(IRE), 4lb higher than when just edged out in his most recent outing here last November, had every chance in the far-side group. This was a pleasing enough return. (op 14-1)

Fathsta(IRE)deserves a lot of credit for finishing where he did. He dropped his rider going to the start before running loose. Making his debut for the yard off the back of a five-month break, he was staying on well in the latter stages. As he has done most of his recent racing over further, a step back up to 7f looks to be in order.

Capricorn Run(USA), kept very busy on sand during the winter, made some late headway in the nearside group but this trip is probably too sharp for him. He found everything happening too quickly. (tchd 28-1)

River Falcon,successful just once in four years, can go well fresh, but he could never really get involved after missing the break. (op 16-1)

Joseph Henry, usually there or thereabouts in competitive sprint handicaps, ran well for a long way in the nearside group. He remains 9lb higher than for his last win in July 2006 and could really do with some help. (op 22-1 tchd 25-1)

Haajes Official explanation: jockey said gelding had ran around in the first-time blinkers

1019 MOSSPM.CO.UK H'CAP — 1m 2f 60y
4:50 (4:51) (Class 3) (0-90,88) 3-Y-O — **£7,771** (£2,312; £1,155; £577) **Stalls** Low

Form — RPR

621- **1** **Gitano Hernando**[134] 7343 3-9-0 **84** .... JohnEgan 10 — 99
(M Botti) *hld up towards rr: hdwy on outer 4f out: rdn to chse ldr and hung lft 2f out: styd on to ld over 1f out: edgd lft ent fnl f: kpt on* **3/1**[2]

001- **2** *2 ½* **Tepmokea (IRE)**[156] 6954 3-8-4 **74** oh3 .... AndrewElliott 2 — 84
(K R Burke) *led and sn clr: pushed along over 3f out: rdn over 2f out: drvn: rallied and n.m.r ent fnl f: kpt on same pce* **8/1**[3]

021- **3** *6* **Orbitor**[151] 7069 3-8-8 **78** .... JamieSpencer 9 — 76
(M L W Bell) *hld up in rr: hdwy on outer whn edgd lft 3f out: rdn over 2f out: sn edgd lft and no imp on ldng pair appr fnl f* **11/4**[1]

-125 **4** *2 ½* **Tinshu (IRE)**[15] 840 3-8-7 **77** .... PaulHanagan 4 — 70
(D Haydn Jones) *trckd ldrs: hdwy to chse ldng pair over 3f out: rdn along over 2f out: one pce and hld whn sltly hmpd wl over 1f out* **16/1**

3-22 **5** *7* **Alexander Gulch (USA)**[25] 755 3-9-1 **85** .... DarryllHolland 3 — 64
(K A Ryan) *chsd clr ldr: cl up 4f out: rdn along 3f out: sn btn* **8/1**[3]

44-1 **6** *4* **Rupestrian**[16] 824 3-8-7 **77** .... JoeFanning 7 — 48
(M Johnston) *chsd ldng pair: rdn along over 3f out: sn drvn and grad wknd* **9/1**

250- **7** *2 ¼* **Thunderball**[156] 6946 3-8-12 **82** .... RobertWinston 5 — 49
(A J McCabe) *in midfield: rdn along 4f out and sn outpcd* **10/1**

521- **8** *3* **Madamlily (IRE)**[174] 6524 3-8-8 **78** .... GrahamGibbons 6 — 39
(J J Quinn) *in tch: rdn along 4f out: sn wknd* **10/1**

120- **9** *9* **Fol Liam**[200] 5791 3-8-11 **81** .... StephenDonohoe 1 — 24
(Ian Williams) *dwlt: a in rr* **16/1**

2m 7.25s (-3.95) **Going Correction** -0.125s/f (Firm) **9** Ran SP% **113.8**
Speed ratings (Par 102): **110,108,103,101,95 92,90,88,81**
toteswinger: 1&2 £6.30, 1&3 £3.50, 2&3 £5.50 CSF £26.86 CT £71.92 TOTE £3.80: £1.60, £2.40, £1.70; EX 31.20 Trifecta £154.90 Pool £833.22 - 3.98 winning units..

Owner Team Valor **Bred** Newsells Park Stud Limited **Trained** Newmarket, Suffolk

FOCUS
All of these had won at least one race, so this looked a very competitive handicap. The form should be followed, as the gallop set by the leader was good.

NOTEBOOK
Gitano Hernando, who landed an all-weather maiden impressively in November, was given a patient ride in this and seemed to have a lot to do turning in, but he stayed on strongly towards the middle of the course before edging left under pressure. He was nicely on top in the end and one would imagine he has more to offer, but his next target, The Belmont Stakes on the 7th of June, came as a bit of a shock. (op 5-2)

Tepmokea(IRE) was not always the most reliable at two, but he clearly had ability and managed to win on his final start of the year at Wolverhampton. Sent off in front, he kept on really well considering the pace he set and may have given the winner more to think about had he not been squeezed up by him inside the final furlong. (op 12-1)

Orbitor made good progress last year, which ended with a comfortable success at Great Leighs over 1m2f. Bred to stay, he was in the rear early but stayed on well despite seemingly wanting to hang to his left. He shaped with promise and will surely do better next time. (op 3-1)

Tinshu(IRE) had done all her racing on the all-weather, so this was her first experience of turf on a racecourse. A leggy-looking sort, she seemed a threat two out but became one-paced under pressure.

Alexander Gulch(USA) got off the mark at Pontefract asa two-year-old but then ran his next three races on the all-weather. The cheekpieces he wore on his previous two starts were missing here and, after chasing the leader, he dropped away before staying on a little inside the final furlong. (tchd 15-2)

Rupestrian was well behind Gitano Hernando when they met in a maiden, but improved on that next time when taking a 1m4f contest at Lingfield, after making all the running. However, he could not dominate here and dropped away tamely at an early stage. (op 7-1)

Thunderball was consistent in the early part of his two-year-old season but his form tailed off a little at the end. He had his chance but could not raise his game when he needed to. (op 12-1 tchd 14-1)

1020 PATEDDERYRACING.COM PROFESSIONAL RACEHORSE SYNDICATION FILLIES' H'CAP — 1m (S)
5:20 (5:20) (Class 4) (0-85,85) 4-Y-O+ — **£5,180** (£1,541; £770; £384) **Stalls** High

Form — RPR

126- **1** **Spring Goddess (IRE)**[127] 7419 8-8-5 **79** .... CharlotteKerton(7) 4 — 86
(A P Jarvis) *t.k.h in rr: gd hdwy centre over 1f out: styd on to ld nr fin* **11/1**

143- **2** *nk* **Deep Winter**[168] 6667 4-9-4 **85** .... PaulHanagan 6 — 91
(R A Fahey) *in rr: hdwy to ld 2f out: rdn and edgd lft fnl f: hdd nr fin* **11/4**[1]

1404 **3** *3 ¾* **Teasing**[27] 730 5-8-9 **76** .... (v) RobertHavlin 5 — 73
(J Pearce) *hld up towards rr: stdy hdwy over 2f out: styd on same pce appr fnl f* **14/1**

60-0 **4** *3* **Keisha Kayleigh (IRE)**[9] 897 6-7-11 **71** oh4 .... (p) JamieKyne(7) 1 — 61
(B Ellison) *s.s: detached in last: hdwy and swtchd lft over 1f out: hung lft and one pce* **12/1**

00-3 **5** *8* **Black Dahlia**[6] 932 4-8-7 **74** .... RobertWinston 8 — 46
(A J McCabe) *chsd ldrs: sn pushed along: wknd fnl f* **3/1**[2]

4-30 **6** *2 ½* **Binfield (IRE)**[10] 878 4-8-4 **71** oh1 .... ChrisCatlin 9 — 37
(B G Powell) *chsd ldrs: lost pl over 1f out* **14/1**

1204 **7** *5* **Millie's Rock (IRE)**[35] 651 4-8-6 **73** .... JoeFanning 7 — 28
(K A Ryan) *led tl hdd & wknd 2f out* **7/2**[3]

1345 **8** *4 ½* **Mozayada (USA)**[26] 747 5-8-13 **80** .... AlanMunro 2 — 24
(M Brittain) *wnt rt s: chsd ldrs on outer: wknd and eased over 1f out* **11/1**

5040 **9** *hd* **Indian Diva (IRE)**[7] 922 4-8-12 **79** .... JamieMoriarty 3 — 23
(P T Midgley) *dwlt: mid-div: effrt over 3f out: wknd over 2f out* **20/1**

1m 39.02s (-0.28) **Going Correction** -0.125s/f (Firm) **9** Ran SP% **116.3**
Speed ratings (Par 102): **96,95,91,88,80 78,73,68,68**
toteswinger: 1&2 £8.60, 1&3 £14.60, 2&3 £8.20 CSF £41.77 CT £437.42 TOTE £12.20: £2.20, £1.80, £4.20; EX 27.40 Trifecta £390.90 Pool £665.62 - 1.26 winning units. Place 6 £81.32, Place 5 £7.53..

Owner Grant & Bowman Limited **Bred** Ballyhane Stud **Trained** Middleham Moor, N Yorks

FOCUS
An ordinary fillies' handicap, but at least the pace was honest thanks to Millie's Rock, who was allowed the luxury of a soft lead. She had nothing left when collared passing the 2f pole. Only two mattered in the last furlong or so, and they were thepair that lacked a recent run.
T/Jkpt: £8,162.00 to a £1 stake. Pool: £11,495.85. 1.00 winning ticket. T/Plt: £247.50 to a £1 stake. Pool: £120,021.91. 353.89 winning tickets. T/Qpdt: £8.70 to a £1 stake. Pool: £10,659.81. 903.07 winning tickets. WG

1021 - (Foreign Racing) - See Raceform Interactive

LEOPARDSTOWN (L-H)
Sunday, March 29

OFFICIAL GOING: Good to firm

1022a LEOPARDSTOWN 2,000 GUINEAS TRIAL STKS (GROUP 3) (C&G) — 1m
3:00 (3:00) 3-Y-O — **£41,082** (£12,053; £5,742; £1,956)

RPR

1 **Recharge (IRE)**[182] 6316 3-9-0 .... CDHayes 3 — 111
(Kevin Prendergast, Ire) *trckd ldrs in 3rd: 4th 1/2-way: nt clr run early st: swtchd to outer over 1f out: r.o strly to ld 100yds out: comf* **9/4**[2]

2 *1* **Intense Focus (USA)**[162] 6815 3-9-3 119 .... (bt) KJManning 6 — 112
(J S Bolger, Ire) *trckd ldrs in 4th: 3rd on outer 1/2-way: smooth hdwy to chal early st: led 1 1/2f out: strly pressed ins fnl f: hdd 100yds out: no ex cl home* **1/1**[1]

3 *2 ½* **Born To Be King (USA)**[235] 4752 3-9-0 93 .... JAHeffernan 2 — 103
(A P O'Brien, Ire) *sn led: strly pressed appr st: hdd 2f out: kpt on same pce* **12/1**

4 *1 ¾* **Hail Caesar (IRE)**[137] 7294 3-9-0 .... JMurtagh 4 — 99
(A P O'Brien, Ire) *hld up in rr: rdn and one pce st* **5/1**[3]

5 *2 ½* **Liebermann (GER)**[153] 7029 3-9-0 103 .... PJSmullen 5 — 93
(D K Weld, Ire) *settled 2nd: chal appr st: led 2f out: hdd 1 1/2f out: no ex ins fnl f: eased cl home* **10/1**

1m 40.6s (-0.60) **Going Correction** -0.25s/f (Firm) **5** Ran SP% **114.2**
Speed ratings: **93,92,89,87,85**
CSF £5.14 TOTE £2.90: £1.60, £1.20; DF 4.50.

Owner Lady O'Reilly **Bred** Skymarc Farm & Castlemartin St **Trained** Friarstown, Co Kildare

NOTEBOOK
Recharge(IRE) got the better of his main market rival inside the final furlong and won going away. The early pace was steady in what turned into a tactical battle but full marks to the winner, who picked up well after he was switched approaching the furlong pole. A son of Cape Cross out of the stable's Group 1 winner Rebelline, he landed a Killarney maiden on his debut last August before running creditably when reaching the frame in the Beresford. He has obviously wintered well and was introduced at 33-1 for the Stan James 2,000 Guineas by Cashmans, although the Irish equivalent is likely to figure next. (op 5/2 tchd 11/4)

Intense Focus(USA) was the class act in this field having captured the Dewhurst narrowly last season. Shouldering a 3lb Group 1 penalty made this a more difficult task and he was settled in fourth place before making his move turning for home.This battle-hardened son of Giant's Causeway relishes a battle and seems to thrive on his racing, so he should be capable of better with this run behind him. His trainer was pleased with this return and either the English or French 2,000 Guineas will be next on the agenda. (op 4/5)

Born To Be King(USA), who had worked after racing at the Curragh the previous weekend, proved best of his pair after making the early running. He struggled when the two market principals went on, but improvement should be forthcoming. (op 14/1)

Hail Caesar(IRE) had finished three lengths behind Recharge in the Beresford last season and he never imposed his presence. (op 9/2 tchd 6/1)

Liebermann(GER) was attempting to provide Dermot Weld with his fourth victory in recent years after wins by Refuse To Bend(2003), Grey Swallow(2004) and Famous Name last year. The Tipperary maiden winner, who was a respectable fourth afterwards in the Killavullan Stakes last November, had ground conditions in his favour but had it all to do on figures, and, after leading briefly turning in, dropped away.

1024a LEOPARDSTOWN 1,000 GUINEAS TRIAL STKS (GROUP 3) (FILLIES) — 7f
4:05 (4:05) 3-Y-O — **£41,082** (£12,053; £5,742; £1,956)

RPR

1 **Maoineach (USA)**[175] 6519 3-9-0 102 .... KJManning 7 — 105+
(J S Bolger, Ire) *mid-div: 6th 1/2-way: pushed along bef st: hdwy 2f out: led over 1f out: styd on wl* **7/2**[2]

2 1 3/4 **Heart Shaped (USA)**[156] 6966 3-9-0 110 JMurtagh 4 98
(A P O'Brien, Ire) *hld up in tch: 8th 3f out: hdwy on inner ent st: cl 2nd and chal 1f out: no imp: eased cl home* **7/2**[2]
3 nk **Smart Coco (USA)**[182] 6318 3-9-0 WMLordan 1 97+
(T Stack, Ire) *trckd ldrs in 4th: lost pl ent st: 7th under 2f out: kpt on fnl f* **9/1**[3]
4 1 1/4 **Dance Pass (IRE)**[245] 4468 3-9-0 PJSmullen 2 94
(D K Weld, Ire) *hld up: 9th appr st: kpt on inner st* **10/1**
5 3/4 **Undaunted Affair (IRE)**[300] 2686 3-9-0 NCallan 5 92
(K A Ryan) *chsd ldrs on outer: 7th 1/2-way: rdn and lost pl early st: kpt on ins fnl f* **12/1**
6 3/4 **What's Up Pussycat (IRE)**[153] 7029 3-9-0 100 FBranca 8 90
(David Wachman, Ire) *towards rr: 10th 1f out: kpt on inner cl home* **16/1**
7 1 1/4 **Empress of France (USA)**[300] 2686 3-9-0 CO'Donoghue 3 86
(A P O'Brien, Ire) *led: hdd ent st: rdn and one pce* **16/1**
8 hd **Hallie's Comet (IRE)**[168] 6687 3-9-0 101 ShaneFoley 9 86
(A Kinsella, Ire) *prom: 3rd 1/2-way: impr to ld ent st: hdd over 1f out: wknd* **20/1**
9 1/2 **Chintz (IRE)**[182] 6318 3-9-0 109 JAHeffernan 6 85
(David Wachman, Ire) *prom: cl 2nd and chal appr st: no ex and wknd fr 2f out* **2/1**[1]
10 1 **Monivea (IRE)**[248] 4354 3-9-0 80 DJMoran 10 82
(Brian Nolan, Ire) *chsd ldrs on outer: 6th appr 1/2-way: wknd st* **50/1**
11 3 **Beauthea (IRE)**[9] 904 3-9-0 84 CDHayes 11 74
(H Rogers, Ire) *slowly away and a in rr* **50/1**

1m 27.9s (-0.80) **Going Correction** -0.25s/f (Firm) **11 Ran SP% 125.0**
Speed ratings: **103,101,100,99,98 97,96,95,95,94 90**
CSF £17.16 TOTE £4.60: £1.60, £2.00, £2.00; DF 23.30.
Owner Mrs J S Bolger **Bred** WinStar Farm LLC **Trained** Coolcullen, Co Carlow

FOCUS
A pretty decent renewal of this Group 3 event.

NOTEBOOK
Maoineach(USA), who had run poorly in the Prix Marcel Boussac after winning a 6f maiden at the Curragh on her debut, arrived with a well-timed challenge to get on top entering the final furlong. Trainer Jim Bolger puts the filly's performance at Longchamp down to her being unable to act on the very loose ground and he holds her in high regard. The Stan James 1,000 Guineas is a possible target. (op 4/1)
Heart Shaped(USA) ended last season by losing out by only a nose in the Breeders' Cup Juvenile Fillies Turf. She came through on the inside to have every chance a furlong out and, while she failed to match the winner from there to the finish, it was, nonetheless, an encouraging effort. (op 4/1 tchd 9/2)
Smart Coco(USA), fifth in a Group 3 event over the trip at the Curragh in September having won a maiden over the distance on her debut at Gowran Park, was coming back well in the final furlong after losing her place turning for home. She just failed to grab second place.
Dance Pass(IRE), fourth in a 1m maiden at the Curragh on her only start last year, was towards the back of the field into the straight and worked her way home well over the last furlong and a half. (op 12/1)
Undaunted Affair(IRE), placed at this level over 6f at Naas last season, looked a spent force early in the straight before rallying inside the final furlong.
Chintz(IRE), a consistent performer last season when she won at this level and over this trip at the Curragh, raced prominently until weakening early in the straight. Her rider reported that his mount had raced keenly early in the race and was of the opinion that the ground might have been a bit quick for the filly. Official explanation: jockey said filly ran keen early on and he felt the ground may have been a bit too fast for her (op 7/4 tchd 6/4)

1025 - 1028a (Foreign Racing) - See Raceform Interactive

[940]SAINT-CLOUD (L-H)
Sunday, March 29

OFFICIAL GOING: Soft

1029a PRIX EDMOND BLANC (GROUP 3) 1m
3:20 (3:26) 4-Y-0+ **£38,835** (£15,534; £11,650; £7,767; £3,883)

RPR
1 **Gris De Gris (IRE)**[147] 7162 5-9-2 GMosse 1 117
(A De Royer-Dupre, France) *led 1 1/2f: disputing ld gng wl st: led 2f out: r.o wl: pushed out* **41/10**[3]
2 2 **Alnadana (IRE)**[203] 5738 4-8-8 TThulliez 6 104
(A De Royer-Dupre, France) *in tch on rail: 5th st: drvn over 2f out: rdn over 1f out: styd on to go 2nd ins fnl f* **18/1**
3 1 1/2 **Racinger (FR)**[147] 7162 6-9-0 DBonilla 2 107
(F Head, France) *prom: 3rd and rdn st: wnt 2nd 1 1/2f out: styd on: jst hld 3rd* **4/1**[2]
4 shd **Verba (FR)**[22] 788 4-8-8 SPasquier 7 101
(R Gibson, France) *mid-div: disputing 6th st: drvn on ins 1 1/2f out: styd on wl ins fnl f: jst missed 3rd* **11/4**[1]
5 nk **Arcadia's Angle (USA)**[224] 5138 4-9-0 C-PLemaire 12 106
(P Bary, France) *hld up in rr: 8th st: rdn and styd on fr over 1f out: nrest at fin* **25/4**
6 1 1/2 **Full Of Gold (FR)**[162] 6816 4-9-2 DBoeuf 5 105
(Mme C Head-Maarek, France) *mid-div: disputing 6th st: rdn over 2f out: nvr in chalng position* **13/2**
7 nk **Japan (GER)**[22] 788 4-8-8 GBenoist 10 96
(D Smaga, France) *hld up: last st: sme late hdwy but n.d* **19/1**
8 3 **Chopastair (FR)**[23] 8-9-0 JVictoire 4 95
(T Lemer, France) *in tch: 4th st: drvn 1 1/2f out: one pce* **9/1**
9 3 **Mharadono (GER)**[21] 6-8-12 NRichter 8 86
(P Hirschberger, Germany) *led after 1 1/2f: jnd and rdn st: hdd 2f out: wknd fr 1 1/2f out* **23/1**
10 6 **Forthe Millionkiss (GER)**[168] 6692 5-9-2 WMongil 3 76
(Uwe Ostmann, Germany) *hld up: 9th st: n.d* **30/1**

1m 43.2s (-4.30) **10 Ran SP% 121.1**
PARI-MUTUEL: WIN 5.10; PL 2.00, 4.00, 2.20; DF 45.10.
Owner J-C Seroul **Bred** Jean-Claude Seroul **Trained** Chantilly, France

NOTEBOOK
Gris De Gris(IRE), beaten a nose in this event last year, acts well around this track. He had conditions to suit and recorded an authoritative success. The Group 2 Prix du Muguet, which he won last year, back here on May 1, will probably be his next target.
Alnadana(IRE), a stablemate of the winner, looked well in the paddock and put up a promising effort. Given a waiting race, she was brought with a late run up the far rail and second place was hers by the furlong marker. It would be not surprise if this filly is raced over a longer trip in the future.
Racinger(FR) will certainly come on for the outing. Given every chance, he raced just behind the leaders and just stayed on one-paced in the final stages. He should win a similar race later in the season.
Verba(FR), whose outside draw was a disadvantage, was at the tail of the field running down the back straight and still had plenty to do at the entrance to the straight. She did run on late, but it was still a disappointing effort as she was the only horse in the first four to have had a previous outing this season.

[955]LINGFIELD (L-H)
Monday, March 30

OFFICIAL GOING: Standard
Wind: Moderate, behind Weather: Fine

1030 HORLEY (S) STKS 1m (P)
2:30 (2:30) (Class 6) 3-Y-0+ **£2,047** (£604; £302) **Stalls High**

Form RPR
1134 1 **Kipchak (IRE)**[24] 777 4-10-0 67 (p) MartinDwyer 4 67
(C E Brittain) *sn led and set str pce: brought wd in st: rdn and styd on fr over 1f out* **1/2**[1]
3500 2 2 1/4 **Red Current**[31] 706 5-9-3 49 (p) JoeFanning 1 50
(R A Harris) *prom: chsd wnr wl over 3f out: brought wd in st: kpt on but no real imp* **8/1**[3]
6015 3 2 1/4 **Fairly Honest**[26] 749 5-9-9 49 RossAtkinson(5) 3 56
(P W Hiatt) *chsd wnr to wl over 3f out: sn u.p: styd on ins in st: one pce* **14/1**
0620 4 3 **Zabeel House**[18] 813 6-9-8 47 (p) MickyFenton 7 43
(John A Harris) *dwlt: hld up in rr: nvr on terms: plugged on one pce fr over 1f out* **16/1**
2010 5 1 **Fun In The Sun**[19] 803 5-10-0 58 StephenDonohoe 2 47
(A B Haynes) *chsd ldrs but nvr on terms: no prog fnl 2f* **11/2**[2]
60-0 6 5 **Spent**[19] 803 4-9-8 56 (b[1]) NeilChalmers 5 30
(Mouse Hamilton-Fairley) *chsd ldrs but nvr on terms: wknd over 2f out* **10/1**
45-0 7 17 **Funky Town (IRE)**[11] 877 7-9-1 45 BarryAdams(7) 6 —
(J Akehurst) *s.s: hld up in last: lost tch by 1/2-way: t.o* **40/1**

1m 37.58s (-0.62) **Going Correction** +0.05s/f (Slow) **7 Ran SP% 117.2**
Speed ratings (Par 101): **105,102,100,97,96 91,74**
toteswinger: 1&2 £2.10, 1&3 £3.20, 2&3 £6.70. CSF £5.82 TOTE £1.60: £1.10, £2.60; EX 5.00.The winner was sold to A. McCabe for 5400gns.
Owner C E Brittain **Bred** Miss Mary Davidson & Mrs Steffi Von Schilcher **Trained** Newmarket, Suffolk

FOCUS
An uncompetitive seller that concerned just the first two in the straight.
Fairly Honest Official explanation: jockey said gelding hung left
Spent Official explanation: jockey said gelding hung right in straight
Funky Town(IRE) Official explanation: jockey said gelding was slowly away

1031 FELBRIDGE MAIDEN AUCTION FILLIES' STKS 5f (P)
3:00 (3:01) (Class 5) 2-Y-0 **£2,729** (£806; £403) **Stalls High**

Form RPR
1 **Leleyf (IRE)** 2-8-10 0 TonyCulhane 7 71
(M R Channon) *chsd ldng pair: effrt on outer wl over 1f out: wnt 2nd ins fnl f: rdn and r.o to ld last strides* **4/1**[2]
2 shd **Emma Jean Lass (IRE)** 2-8-7 0 LPKeniry 8 68
(J S Moore) *sn trckd ldng pair: effrt 2f out: rdn to ld jst ins fnl f: styd on: hdd last strides* **8/1**
3 1 1/2 **Victorian Art (IRE)** 2-8-5 0 EdwardCreighton 2 60
(M A Magnusson) *led: hdd and nt qckn wl over 1f out: kpt on same pce after* **3/1**[1]
4 3/4 **My Mandy (IRE)** 2-8-10 0 StephenDonohoe 6 62
(Ian Williams) *dwlt: outpcd in last trio: pushed along firmly 3f out: prog on inner over 1f out: styd on fnl f to take 4th nr fin* **5/1**[3]
5 1/2 **Michaelmas Daisy** 2-8-5 0 AndrewElliott 3 55
(Miss Amy Weaver) *w ldr: led wl over 1f out: hdd & wknd jst ins fnl f* **20/1**
6 3/4 **French Connexion (IRE)** 2-8-4 0 LukeMorris 1 51
(J S Moore) *rrd in stalls bef s: chsd ldng quartet: hung rt and v wd bnd 2f out: styd on again fnl f* **5/1**[3]
7 2 **Patteresa Girl** 2-8-7 0 ow2 TomEaves 4 46+
(Mrs L Stubbs) *s.v.s and lost abt 10l: nvr on terms: pushed along and kpt on steadily fnl 2f: nrst fin* **15/2**
8 8 **Secret Rose** 2-7-13 0 NicolPolli(5) 5 11
(W G M Turner) *nvr on terms: bhd fr 1/2-way: t.o* **9/1**

59.92 secs (1.12) **Going Correction** +0.05s/f (Slow) **8 Ran SP% 116.0**
Speed ratings (Par 89): **93,92,90,89,88 87,84,71**
toteswinger: 1&2 £5.90, 1&3 £3.10, 2&3 £6.00. CSF £36.18 TOTE £4.00: £1.60, £2.60, £1.60; EX 33.20 Trifecta £136.60 Pool: £321.35 - 1.74 winning units..
Owner Box 41 **Bred** Mrs Noelle Walsh **Trained** West Ilsley, Berks

FOCUS
It's hard to be sure of the level, but most of these were cheapish buys and this looked a modest early season juvenile maiden and the level is fluid.

NOTEBOOK
Leleyf(IRE), one of the more expensive in the line up at 35,000euros, is a half-sister to among others prolific 5f-1m1f winner Louisiade. She was given a good ride, tracking the pace early before being produced with her chance on the outside in the straight, but she took a long time to get on top, and her stamina for further (dam 1m2f winner) was an asset. This was a pleasing introduction considering she was conceding weight to most of her rivals. (op 11-4)
Emma Jean Lass(IRE), a £12,000 half-sister to middle-distance winner Mull Of Dubai, was produced with every chance but she was just worn down in the final strides. There might be a similar race in her, with this experience likely to prove invaluable against newcomers in the next few weeks. (op 12-1)
Victorian Art(IRE), a 10,000euros purchase, was supported in the market and showed good early speed, but she did not see her race out as well as the front two. (tchd 5-2 and 7-2 in places)
My Mandy(IRE) ◆, a £26,000 buy out of a useful sprinter, was undoubtedly the eye-catcher of the race as she lost several lengths with a slow start and was outpaced for most of the way, before running on well against the usually unfavoured inside rail in the straight. She is open to a deal of improvement. (op 11-2 tchd 6-1)
Michaelmas Daisy, out of a 7f winner, showed some early speed and looked to have her chance. (op 16-1 tchd 25-1)
French Connexion(IRE), a 4,000euros Super Sprint entrant, was very green. After rearing up in the stalls, she went extremely wide around the turn into the straight and did well to finish so close all things considered. Official explanation: jockey said filly hung right (op 9-1)
Patteresa Girl, an 8,000gns purchase, was carrying 2lb overweight. She looked clueless as the stalls opened and lost around ten lengths, but she showed ability once getting the idea late on. (op 6-1)

Secret Rose, who cost just £600, was outpaced throughout and showed little. (op 12-1)

1032 THREE BRIDGES H'CAP 6f (P)
3:30 (3:30) (Class 5) (0-75,75) 3-Y-O £2,900 (£856; £428) Stalls Low

Form RPR
1212 1 **Raimond Ridge (IRE)**[40] 593 3-8-10 72 MCGeran(5) 3 74
(M R Channon) *t.k.h: trckd ldrs: shkn up and effrt over 1f out: r.o to ld last 75yds: pushed out* 15/2
52-3 2 3/4 **Robin The Till**[16] 842 3-8-8 65 RichardHughes 1 65
(R Hannon) *t.k.h: led but set mod pce: hdd over 2f out: styd on inner and led again jst ins fnl f: hdd and nt qckn last 75yds: lame* 9/2
3312 3 hd **Flamsteed (IRE)**[31] 709 3-9-2 73 MartinDwyer 2 72
(M Quinn) *pressed ldr: led over 2f out: drvn wl over 1f out and limited rspnse: hdd ins fnl f: one pce* 7/2[3]
1 4 1 1/2 **Chasca (IRE)**[16] 842 3-8-9 66 JimCrowley 5 60
(Mrs A J Perrett) *t.k.h: hld up in last in slowly run r: effrt 2f out: styd on fr over 1f out: no ch of rching ldrs* 2/1[1]
21 5 3 1/4 **Under Review (IRE)**[39] 602 3-9-4 75 JamieSpencer 4 59
(S A Callaghan) *plld hrd: hld up bhd ldrs: pushed along and no rspnse 2f out: hanging and eased after* 9/4[2]

1m 13.49s (1.59) **Going Correction** +0.05s/f (Slow) 5 Ran SP% **116.3**
Speed ratings (Par 98): **91,90,89,87,83**
CSF £40.62 TOTE £9.20: £3.20, £2.80; EX 29.90.
Owner M Channon **Bred** Myles And Mrs Joan Doyle **Trained** West Ilsley, Berks
■ Stewards' Enquiry : M C Geran three-day ban: careless riding (Apr 13-15)

FOCUS
An ordinary sprint handicap but they went a very modest pace for most of the way and this is form to treat with caution.
Robin The Till Official explanation: vet said gelding returned lame right behind

1033 HBLB H'CAP 7f (P)
4:00 (4:01) (Class 4) (0-85,81) 3-Y-O £4,857 (£1,445; £722; £360) Stalls Low

Form RPR
100- 1 **Cyflymder (IRE)**[175] 6525 3-9-0 77 RichardHughes 4 83
(R Hannon) *trckd ldr after 2f: rdn to ld narrowly jst over 1f out: drvn and asserted last 100yds* 14/1
-161 2 1 **Takeover Bid (USA)**[13] 859 3-9-4 81 JoeFanning 1 84
(M Johnston) *trckd ldr 2f: styd cl up on inner: effrt to chal over 1f out and upsides: pressed wnr fnl f: hld last 100yds* 7/1[2]
1 3 1 **Set The Trend**[47] 503 3-9-3 80 LPKeniry 3 80+
(A M Balding) *t.k.h: hld up in midfield: rdn and nt qckn wl over 1f out: styd on to take 3rd ins fnl f* 8/13[1]
216- 4 3/4 **Belated Silver (IRE)**[122] 7475 3-8-10 73 RichardKingscote 7 71+
(Tom Dascombe) *t.k.h: hld up in 7th: prog 2f out: cl up bhd ldrs over 1f out: one reminder ins fnl f: kpt on steadily: nvr nr enough to chal* 8/1[3]
F1- 5 1/2 **Geneva Geyser (GER)**[109] 7640 3-9-1 78 LukeMorris 6 75
(J M P Eustace) *racd wd: t.k.h: in tch: rdn over 2f out: nt qckn sn after: styd on fnl f: no ch* 16/1
-213 6 shd **Auld Arty (FR)**[33] 672 3-8-13 76 (p) SteveDrowne 5 73
(T G Mills) *led tl jst over 1f out: wknd ins fnl f* 14/1
613- 7 nse **Cool Art (IRE)**[122] 7472 3-9-4 81 JamieSpencer 2 78
(S A Callaghan) *t.k.h early: hld up on inner and lost pl after 3f: rdn and effrt over 1f out: no imp on ldrs* 10/1
5322 8 1 1/2 **Grand Honour (IRE)**[33] 672 3-8-13 76 JimmyQuinn 8 68
(P Howling) *t.k.h early: hld up in last: pushed along 2f out: reminder ins fnl f: no prog* 16/1

1m 25.78s (0.98) **Going Correction** +0.05s/f (Slow) 8 Ran SP% **119.7**
Speed ratings (Par 100): **96,94,93,92,92 92,92,90**
toteswinger: 1&2 £14.00, 1&3 £6.10, 2&3 £2.50. CSF £111.83 CT £153.70 TOTE £19.90: £3.20, £1.50, £1.40; EX 211.30 Trifecta £316.80 Pool: £483.86 - 1.13 winning units..
Owner Amblestock Partnership **Bred** Miss Laura G F Ferguson **Trained** East Everleigh, Wilts

FOCUS
A fair three-year-old handicap. The pace was just ordinary and it paid to race handy.

1034 NEW CHAPEL MAIDEN STKS 1m 2f (P)
4:30 (4:33) (Class 5) 3-Y-O £2,729 (£806; £403) Stalls Low

Form RPR
24- 1 **Big Bound (USA)**[165] 6759 3-9-3 0 JimmyFortune 10 80+
(J H M Gosden) *t.k.h early: pressed ldr: clr of rest over 2f out: rdn to ld over 1f out: hung rt fnl f: drvn out* 5/6[1]
3 2 3/4 **Wadaat**[14] 849 3-8-12 0 JamieSpencer 4 73+
(C E Brittain) *led: drew clr w wnr fr 3f out: hdd u.p over 1f out: edgd rt but styd on* 7/2[2]
4 3 7 **Crag Path**[65] 280 3-8-7 0 AmyBaker(5) 2 59
(D R C Elsworth) *dwlt: hld up in last pair: already wl outpcd whn effrt 3f out: rchd 5th 2f out: rdn and styd on to take 3rd nr fin* 40/1
5-3 4 1/2 **Gulf President**[17] 833 3-9-3 0 (v[1]) TonyCulhane 6 63
(M R Channon) *t.k.h early: trckd ldng pair: outpcd fr 3f out: kpt on same pce: lost 3rd nr fin* 16/1
5 2 3/4 **Gilded Age** 3-9-3 0 JoeFanning 1 58
(M Johnston) *dwlt: mostly in midfield: pushed along firmly over 3f out: sn outpcd: one pce after* 9/1[3]
336- 6 nk **Charlie Smirke (USA)**[115] 7554 3-9-3 68 GeorgeBaker 3 57
(G L Moore) *chsd ldng pair after 3f: outpcd fr 3f out: wknd fnl f* 20/1
00- 7 2 1/2 **Lennie Briscoe (IRE)**[156] 6978 3-9-3 0 RichardHughes 7 52
(S Kirk) *fractious bef ent stalls: hld up: pushed along in last over 3f out and wl outpcd: kpt on one pce fr over 2f out* 11/1
-222 8 4 **Solo Choice**[50] 455 3-9-3 68 JimCrowley 5 44
(D Flood) *hld up in rr: sme prog over 4f out: no hdwy 3f out and outpcd: wknd 2f out* 33/1
0- 9 1 3/4 **Red Margarita (IRE)**[165] 6760 3-8-12 0 AlanMunro 9 35
(D R C Elsworth) *prom on outer: rdn over 3f out: sn wknd* 66/1
10 1 1/4 **Hard Ball**[181] 6368 3-9-3 0 MartinDwyer 8 38
(M Quinn) *nvr beyond midfield: rdn 4f out: struggling after: wknd 2f out* 20/1

2m 5.45s (-1.15) **Going Correction** +0.05s/f (Slow) 10 Ran SP% **117.4**
Speed ratings (Par 98): **106,105,99,99,97 96,94,91,90,89**
toteswinger: 1&2 £1.60, 1&3 £20.20, 2&3 £31.00. CSF £3.45 TOTE £2.00: £1.20, £1.20, £8.40; EX 3.70 Trifecta £62.00 Pool: £736.70 - 8.78 winning units..
Owner Lady Rothschild **Bred** Carwell Equities Ltd **Trained** Newmarket, Suffolk

FOCUS
This maiden lacked strength in depth and the first two, who were in the front rank pretty much throughout, pulled well clear.

1035 SMALLFIELD H'CAP 1m (P)
5:00 (5:00) (Class 5) (0-75,75) 4-Y-O+ £2,900 (£856; £428) Stalls High

Form RPR
-434 1 **Solent Ridge (IRE)**[9] 910 4-8-13 70 (p) LPKeniry 1 80
(J S Moore) *mde all and allowed uncontested ld: kicked 3l clr 2f out: drvn out fnl f: unchal* 11/2
6-10 2 1 1/2 **My Shadow**[19] 798 4-8-13 70 IanMongan 3 77
(S Dow) *trckd wnr: rdn over 2f out: kpt on same pce and nvr able to chal* 12/1
-132 3 1 **Murrin (IRE)**[16] 841 5-8-13 70 StephenDonohoe 2 74
(T G Mills) *hld up bhd ldrs: rdn over 2f out: kpt on fnl f to take 3rd nr fin* 10/3[1]
0441 4 1/2 **Bee Stinger**[16] 841 7-9-4 75 (b) GeorgeBaker 4 78
(I A Wood) *hld up towards rr: urged along over 2f out: nt qckn wl over 1f out: pushed along and kpt on ins fnl f* 7/2[2]
2201 5 nse **Marmooq**[11] 878 6-8-10 67 LukeMorris 7 70
(M J Attwater) *trckd ldng pair: rdn 3f out on outer: hanging and nt qckn wl over 1f out: one pce after* 7/1
1315 6 nk **Lopinot (IRE)**[16] 841 6-8-11 68 (v) JimCrowley 6 70
(M R Bosley) *t.k.h: hld up in last: gng strly but plenty to do whn prog over 2f out: swtchd ins over 1f out: effrt petered out fnl f* 5/1[3]
2340 7 2 1/2 **Wavertree Warrior (IRE)**[12] 873 7-8-13 70 (b) KirstyMilczarek 5 67
(N P Littmoden) *hld up in rr: rdn over 3f out: no prog and struggling over 2f out* 7/1

1m 38.85s (0.65) **Going Correction** +0.05s/f (Slow) 7 Ran SP% **110.0**
Speed ratings (Par 103): **98,96,95,95,94 94,92**
toteswinger: 1&2 £10.10, 1&3 £5.40, 2&3 £8.20. CSF £60.61 TOTE £6.30: £4.50, £6.80; EX 68.40.
Owner Chris P Dineen **Bred** Glending Bloodstock **Trained** Upper Lambourn, Berks

FOCUS
A fair handicap but the winner was allowed an easy lead on a track favouring pace and this is form to treat with caution.

1036 HARTFIELD H'CAP 1m (P)
5:30 (5:31) (Class 6) (0-60,60) 3-Y-O £2,047 (£604; £302) Stalls High

Form RPR
00-3 1 **Dark Ranger**[18] 817 3-8-5 47 LukeMorris 2 57
(T J Pitt) *hld up bhd ldrs on inner: prog over 2f out: led wl over 1f out: sn clr: r.o wl* 6/1[3]
00-5 2 4 1/2 **Alternative Choice (USA)**[34] 663 3-9-4 60 JamesDoyle 3 59
(N P Littmoden) *hld up wl in rr: rdn over 2f out: prog on inner over 1f out: drvn to go 2nd ins fnl f: no ch w wnr* 8/1
65-6 3 shd **Persian Tomcat (IRE)**[18] 817 3-8-5 47 JimmyQuinn 9 46
(Miss J Feilden) *towards rr: rdn wl over 2f out: prog u.p on inner wl over 1f out: pressed runner-up fnl f* 25/1
05-1 4 1/2 **Wunder Strike (USA)**[19] 802 3-8-11 53 PatCosgrave 5 51+
(J R Boyle) *n.m.r over 5f out and snatched up: rcvrd to trck ldrs over 2f out: bdly bmpd and lost all ch wl over 1f out: styd on to press for pl cl home* 3/1[1]
000- 5 2 1/2 **Everaard (USA)**[150] 7105 3-9-3 59 AlanMunro 8 51+
(D R C Elsworth) *trckd ldrs: rdn wl over 2f out: losing pl whn nt clr run wl over 1f out: kpt on same pce after* 10/3[2]
-303 6 2 1/4 **Lucky Fortune (IRE)**[31] 707 3-8-13 58 (b) JackMitchell(3) 6 45
(Miss Amy Weaver) *led 1f: restrained: n.m.r over 4f out: cl up on outer whn nudged wl over 1f out: fdd fnl f* 8/1
035- 7 1 1/2 **Crystallize**[171] 6632 3-9-4 60 SteveDrowne 1 43
(A B Haynes) *sn cl up on inner: effrt to chal wl over 1f out: sn lft bhd by wnr: wknd rapidly fnl f* 16/1
0-46 8 nse **Floods Of Tears**[48] 492 3-8-11 53 (b[1]) MartinDwyer 10 36+
(D Flood) *trckd ldr after 1f: upsides whn nudged rival wl over 1f out and then veered wildly lft and bmpd anther: no ch after and eased: lame* 66/1
-060 9 3 1/2 **Maison D'Or**[18] 817 3-8-10 52 JimCrowley 7 27
(R Ingram) *hld up in last pair: nvr on terms no prog fnl 2f* 10/1
4330 10 1 **Kamanja (UAE)**[18] 817 3-9-1 57 JamieSpencer 4 30
(M J Attwater) *led after 1f: hung rt bnd 2f out: sn hdd & wknd rapidly* 14/1
000- 11 3 1/4 **Kaiser Willie (IRE)**[167] 6715 3-8-12 54 (t) DaneO'Neill 12 20
(B W Duke) *s.i.s: hld up in rr: prog on outer over 3f out: rdn and wknd over 2f out* 20/1
350 12 28 **Michelle (IRE)**[34] 662 3-8-7 49 RichardKingscote 11 —
(P Butler) *racd wd: prom to 1/2-way: wknd rapidly 3f out: t.o* 40/1

1m 38.84s (0.64) **Going Correction** +0.05s/f (Slow) 12 Ran SP% **118.8**
Speed ratings (Par 96): **98,93,93,92,90 88,86,86,83,82 78,50**
toteswinger: 1&2 £9.80, 1&3 £23.10, 2&3 £31.00. CSF £51.48 CT £1147.84 TOTE £7.90: £2.10, £2.80, £4.20; EX 49.80 TRIFECTA Not won. Place 6: £ 228.69 Place 5: £178.40 .
Owner Recycled Products Limited **Bred** Thomas G N Burrage **Trained** Norton, N Yorks

FOCUS
A messy race and the bare form needs treating with caution. For a start, some of these were short of room approaching the first bend, and there was even more significant bunching on the turn into the straight. The two most disadvantaged as a result of the second incident were Wunder Strike and Floods Of Tears, who collided with each other in what appeared to be general scrimmaging.
Alternative Choice(USA) Official explanation: jockey said colt suffered interference in running
Floods Of Tears Official explanation: vet said filly returned lame
Kamanja(UAE) Official explanation: jockey said filly hung right in straight
T/Plt: £89.50 to a £1 stake. Pool: £57,123.09. 465.83 winning tickets. T/Qpdt: £64.20 to a £1 stake. Pool: £3,630.50. 41.80 winning tickets. JN

981 WOLVERHAMPTON (A.W) (L-H)
Monday, March 30

OFFICIAL GOING: Standard
Wind: Light behind Weather: Cloudy

1037 DINE IN THE HORIZONS RESTAURANT APPRENTICE CLAIMING STKS 1m 141y(P)
2:20 (2:20) (Class 6) 4-Y-O+ £2,047 (£604; £302) Stalls Low

Form RPR
1013 1 **Smokey Rye**[5] 958 4-8-6 66 MatthewDavies(5) 4 64+
(George Baker) *hld up: smooth hdwy over 2f out: shkn up to ld over 1f out: comf* 5/6[1]

4013 **2** *2 ½* **Red Rudy**[11] 875 7-8-5 63 .... TobyAtkinson(7) 8 56
(A W Carroll) *hld up in rr: hdwy over 1f out: rdn to chse wnr ins fnl f: no imp* **7/1**[3]

5304 **3** *1 ¼* **Turkish Sultan (IRE)**[19] 802 6-8-9 45 ....(p) JackDean(3) 1 53
(J M Bradley) *led early: hld up in tch: kpt on one pce ins fnl f* **10/1**

0554 **4** *6* **Almora Guru**[7] 933 5-8-2 47 .... DeanHeslop(3) 9 32
(W M Brisbourne) *prom tl rdn and wknd over 2f out* **25/1**

050 **5** *nk* **Keen As Mustard**[7] 939 4-8-8 0 .... LeeNewnes(5) 7 40
(M D I Usher) *sn prom: ev ch wl over 1f out: wknd ins fnl f* **66/1**

016 **6** *hd* **Lady Aspen (IRE)**[42] 569 6-8-3 57 ow1 ....(tp) WilliamCarson(3) 3 32
(Ian Williams) *half-rrd s: hld up and bhd: hdwy on ins over 3f out: wknd over 1f out* **7/2**[2]

0601 **7** *1 ¾* **The London Gang**[7] 933 6-8-7 40 ....(b) Louis-PhilippeBeuzelin(3) 2 32
(S Wynne) *sn led: hdd over 1f out: wknd fnl f* **9/1**

000- **8** *17* **Opening Hand**[228] 4365 4-8-7 51 ....(p) AndreaAtzeni(3) 5 —
(G J Smith) *sn chsng ldr: ev ch 2f out: wknd over 1f out* **50/1**

1m 51.26s (0.76) **Going Correction** -0.05s/f (Stan) 8 Ran SP% **115.7**
Speed ratings (Par 101): **94,91,90,85,85 84,83,68**
toteswinger: 1&2 £1.20, 1&3 £3.90, 2&3 £7.90. CSF £7.54 TOTE £1.70: £1.02, £2.90, £5.10; EX 6.40.Smokey Rye was subject to a friendly claim.
Owner The Different Partnership **Bred** Jeremy Hinds **Trained** Moreton Morrell, Warwicks

FOCUS
Not the most competitive of claimers and Smokey Rye readily justified favouritism.

1038 SPONSOR A RACE BY CALLING 01902 390009 (S) STKS 5f 20y(P)
2:50 (2:50) (Class 6) 3-Y-0+ **£2,047** (£604; £302) **Stalls Low**

Form RPR

0115 **1** **Desperate Dan**[12] 870 8-9-11 73 ....(v) NCallan 3 77
(A B Haynes) *a gng wl: shkn up to ld ins fnl f: edgd rt: r.o wl* **11/8**[1]

30-0 **2** *3 ¼* **Another Socket**[5] 956 4-9-1 65 .... GrahamGibbons 4 56
(E S McMahon) *s.i.s: hld up in rr: hdwy whn swtchd rt wl over 1f out: rdn and r.o to take 2nd towards fin: nt trble wnr* **3/1**[2]

0-06 **3** *½* **Orpen's Art (IRE)**[7] 937 4-8-13 67 .... HollyHall(7) 1 59
(S A Callaghan) *led: rdn and hdd ins fnl f: no ex and lost 2nd towards fin* **9/1**

2600 **4** *2 ¾* **Nordic Light (USA)**[27] 746 5-9-6 44 ....(bt) RobertWinston 5 49
(J M Bradley) *w ldr: rdn 2f out: btn over 1f out* **50/1**

4603 **5** *hd* **Albero Di Giuda (IRE)**[8] 919 4-8-10 65 ....(t) AndreaAtzeni(5) 11 43
(F Sheridan) *racd wd: hld up in mid-div: rdn and hdwy whn edgd lft 1f out: nvr trbld ldrs* **8/1**[3]

4563 **6** *1 ¼* **Spanish Ace**[18] 812 8-9-1 44 ....(b) JackDean(5) 6 44
(J M Bradley) *hld up in mid-div: no hdwy fnl 2f* **22/1**

050- **7** *½* **Sandy Par**[227] 5074 4-9-3 46 ....(p) DavidProbert(3) 10 42
(J M Bradley) *hld up in rr: c wd st: rdn and edgd lft jst over 1f out: n.d* **66/1**

030- **8** *¾* **Distant Vision (IRE)**[189] 6159 6-8-10 43 ....(p) SladeO'Hara(5) 2 34
(H A McWilliams) *hld up in tch: rdn over 1f out: sn wknd* **40/1**

40-4 **9** *½* **Rann Na Cille (IRE)**[10] 896 5-8-8 47 .... PaulPickard(7) 9 32
(P T Midgley) *prom tl wknd over 2f out* **16/1**

1504 **10** *2 ¾* **Fizzlephut (IRE)**[5] 956 7-9-11 61 ....(b) PaulFitzsimons 8 33
(Miss J R Tooth) *w ldrs tl wknd wl over 1f out* **8/1**[3]

-000 **11** *5* **Ben**[49] 474 4-9-6 47 ....(b) RobertHavlin 7 10
(P G Murphy) *a bhd* **50/1**

61.72 secs (-0.58) **Going Correction** -0.05s/f (Stan) 11 Ran SP% **117.4**
Speed ratings (Par 101): **102,96,96,91,91 89,88,87,86,82 74**
toteswinger: 1&2 £1.10, 1&3 £11.80, 2&3 £16.10. CSF £5.07 TOTE £2.20: £1.10, £1.60, £3.10; EX 5.70.There was no bid for the winner.
Owner Joe McCarthy **Bred** Sheikh Amin Dahlawi **Trained** Limpley Stoke, Bath

FOCUS
No more than three of the runners could be given a chance in this.
Rann Na Cille(IRE) Official explanation: trainer said filly was lame the following morning

1039 ENJOY THE LUCKY 7 GROUP OFFER H'CAP 7f 32y(P)
3:20 (3:22) (Class 6) (0-60,66) 4-Y-0+ **£2,047** (£604; £302) **Stalls High**

Form RPR

0333 **1** **Jord (IRE)**[7] 934 5-9-4 60 .... RobertWinston 7 68+
(A J McCabe) *a.p: wnt 2nd over 5f out: led 2f out: rdn over 1f out: drvn out* **15/2**[2]

0430 **2** *nk* **Mountain Pass (USA)**[47] 505 7-8-12 54 ....(p) NCallan 4 61
(B J Llewellyn) *hld up towards rr: hdwy 2f out: rdn and r.o ins fnl f* **8/1**[3]

0351 **3** *2 ½* **Kabis Amigos**[7] 934 7-9-10 66 6ex ....(b) PaulHanagan 2 66
(S T Mason) *t.k.h in mid-div: hdwy 2f out: rdn 1f out: no ex wl ins fnl f* **15/2**[2]

4343 **4** *¾* **Bold Diva**[17] 830 4-8-12 54 ....(v) LiamJones 10 52
(A W Carroll) *hld up towards rr: hdwy on outside over 2f out: c wd st: edgd lft ins fnl f: kpt on* **20/1**

00-1 **5** *nk* **Colour Of Money**[12] 874 4-9-4 60 .... PatDobbs 11 57
(S A Callaghan) *hld up in tch: pushed along over 2f out: one pce fnl f* **15/8**[1]

2005 **6** *½* **Imperial Djay (IRE)**[3] 984 4-8-9 54 .... AndrewMullen(3) 1 50
(G J Smith) *hld up in mid-div: hdwy on ins wl over 1f out: rdn ins fnl f: one pce* **12/1**

2403 **7** *½* **Inka Dancer (IRE)**[7] 937 7-8-5 50 .... DavidProbert(3) 12 44
(B Palling) *sn chsng ldrs: rdn wl over 1f out: wknd ins fnl f* **14/1**

4404 **8** *nse* **Outer Hebrides**[3] 984 8-8-8 50 ....(v) WilliamBuick 8 44
(J M Bradley) *t.k.h in mid-div: bhd fnl 3f* **8/1**[3]

-005 **9** *1 ½* **Copper King**[20] 792 5-8-8 50 .... FergusSweeney 5 40
(Miss Tor Sturgis) *a bhd* **20/1**

425- **10** *½* **Imperial Sword**[179] 6411 6-8-11 60 ....(b) AdamCarter(7) 6 49
(T D Barron) *s.i.s: a bhd* **16/1**

0020 **11** *11* **Rio L'Oren (IRE)**[19] 803 4-8-10 57 ....(b) WilliamCarson(5) 9 16
(N J Vaughan) *led after 1f: rdn and hdd 2f out: wknd over 1f out* **40/1**

000- **12** *6* **August Gale (USA)**[118] 7533 4-8-8 50 ....(bt) DaleGibson 3 —
(M W Easterby) *a bhd* **8/1**[3]

1m 29.43s (-0.17) **Going Correction** -0.05s/f (Stan) 12 Ran SP% **123.8**
Speed ratings (Par 101): **98,97,94,93,93 93,92,92,90,90 77,70**
toteswinger: 1&2 £13.40, 1&3 £6.90, 2&3 £12.60. CSF £67.77 CT £484.36 TOTE £8.10: £2.00, £2.90, £2.60; EX 74.70.
Owner Paul J Dixon And The Chrystal Maze Ptn **Bred** M Channon **Trained** Averham Park, Notts

FOCUS
This was just a moderate sprint handicap.

1040 WOLVERHAMPTON-RACECOURSE.CO.UK MAIDEN STKS 1m 141y(P)
3:50 (3:50) (Class 5) 3-Y-0 **£1,767** (£1,767; £403) **Stalls Low**

Form RPR

0- **1** **Lastroarofdtiger (USA)**[159] 6910 3-9-3 0 .... DarrenWilliams 4 78
(K R Burke) *hld up: hdwy over 2f out: led wl over 1f out: sn rdn: jnd post* **9/1**

63 **1** *dht* **Keep Ringing (USA)**[10] 890 3-8-12 0 .... LiamJones 1 73
(W J Haggas) *hld up: hdwy on outside over 2f out: chal wl over 1f out: rdn ins fnl f: jnd ldr post* **9/4**[2]

03 **3** *6* **Hector Spectre (IRE)**[26] 752 3-9-3 0 .... EddieAhern 3 64
(B J Meehan) *prom tl wknd 2f out* **4/1**[3]

4- **4** *2 ½* **Dhania (IRE)**[131] 7380 3-9-3 0 .... DarryllHolland 5 58
(R A Teal) *chsd ldr: rdn to ld brief 2f out: sn wknd* **9/2**

543- **5** *15* **Heading East (IRE)**[218] 5304 3-9-3 72 .... NCallan 6 49
(K A Ryan) *hung rt thrght: led: rdn and hdd 2f out: sn wknd* **2/1**[1]

1m 50.29s (-0.21) **Going Correction** -0.05s/f (Stan) 5 Ran SP% **112.3**
Speed ratings (Par 98): **98,98,92,90,77**
WIN: Lastroarofdtiger £7.80, Keep Ringing £1.50 PL:L£5.30, KR £2.00. EX: L & KR £12.50, KR & L £28.30. CSF: LT & KR £14.94, KR &L £10.39. toteswinger: 1&2 £25.70..
Owner Cyril Wall **Bred** Gainsborough Farm Llc **Trained** Middleham Moor, N Yorks
Owner Mrs H R Slack **Bred** Pillar Investments Inc **Trained** Newmarket, Suffolk

FOCUS
This was a modest maiden and the judge proved unable to separate the two that drew clear.
Heading East(IRE) Official explanation: jockey said gelding hung right-handed throughout

1041 GREAT OFFERS AT WOLVERHAMPTON-RACECOURSE.CO.UK FILLIES' H'CAP 5f 20y(P)
4:20 (4:20) (Class 5) (0-75,74) 3-Y-0+ **£3,885** (£1,156; £577; £288) **Stalls Low**

Form RPR

2104 **1** **Welsh Opera**[17] 832 4-8-9 60 oh1 ....(v) WilliamCarson(5) 1 70
(S C Williams) *a.p: rdn to ld ins fnl f: drvn out* **4/1**[2]

0-56 **2** *1 ¼* **Cheshire Rose**[46] 518 4-8-11 62 .... DeanHeslop(5) 3 67
(T D Barron) *hld up in tch: edgd lft over 1f out: rdn and r.o to take 2nd last strides* **8/1**[3]

1230 **3** *½* **Sills Vincero**[10] 889 3-8-12 60 .... PaulHanagan 7 58
(D Shaw) *chsd ldr: led wl over 1f out: sn rdn: hdd ins fnl f: no ex and lost 2nd last strides* **8/1**[3]

1554 **4** *hd* **Drifting Gold**[31] 710 5-9-10 70 ....(v) AdamKirby 2 72
(C G Cox) *hld up: hdwy wl over 1f out: rdn and kpt on ins fnl f* **7/2**[1]

220- **5** *5* **Nomoreblondes**[220] 5250 5-9-6 66 ....(p) JamieMoriarty 4 50
(P T Midgley) *led: hdd wl over 1f out: wknd fnl f* **4/1**[2]

6-50 **6** *½* **Wibbadune (IRE)**[12] 870 5-10-0 74 .... NCallan 6 57
(D Shaw) *a bhd* **7/2**[1]

150- **7** *2 ¾* **Miacarla**[189] 6164 6-8-11 60 oh1 .... NeilBrown(3) 5 33
(H A McWilliams) *a in rr* **33/1**

61.70 secs (-0.60) **Going Correction** -0.05s/f (Stan)
WFA 3 from 4yo+ 12lb 7 Ran SP% **109.6**
Speed ratings (Par 101): **102,100,99,98,90 90,85**
toteswinger: 1&2 £13.40, 1&3 £6.90, 2&3 £12.60. CSF £32.01 CT £222.08 TOTE £5.70: £3.30, £5.10; EX 43.00.
Owner Paul W Stevens **Bred** Usk Valley Stud **Trained** Newmarket, Suffolk

FOCUS
A low-grade handicap.
Wibbadune(IRE) Official explanation: jockey said mare hung right-handed latter stages

1042 STAY AT THE WOLVERHAMPTON HOLIDAY INN H'CAP 1m 1f 103y(P)
4:50 (4:50) (Class 6) (0-65,65) 4-Y-0+ **£2,047** (£604; £302) **Stalls Low**

Form RPR

/121 **1** **Agilete**[42] 571 7-9-0 61 .... JerryO'Dwyer 6 73+
(J Pearce) *hld up in mid-div: hdwy over 2f out: rdn to ld over 1f out: r.o wl* **9/4**[1]

5242 **2** *1 ¼* **Pelham Crescent (IRE)**[12] 871 6-8-12 62 ....(p) DavidProbert(3) 10 70
(B Palling) *hld up in mid-div: hdwy over 2f out: chsd wnr fnl f: kpt on* **5/1**[2]

-154 **3** *1* **Watson's Bay**[28] 737 4-9-4 65 .... FergusSweeney 12 71
(Miss Tor Sturgis) *hld up towards rr: hdwy on outside over 1f out: sn edgd lft: tk 3rd wl ins fnl f* **7/1**[3]

-000 **4** *2 ½* **Jago (SWI)**[17] 836 6-9-0 61 .... RobertWinston 11 62
(A M Hales) *hld up in tch: rdn to ld briefly wl over 1f out: sn hung lft: fdd wl ins fnl f* **9/1**

-563 **5** *nk* **Penang Cinta**[12] 871 6-8-12 59 ....(v[1]) PaulDoe 4 59
(P D Evans) *hld up in tch: one pce fnl 2f* **7/1**[3]

0521 **6** *2 ½* **Barodine**[24] 775 6-8-3 57 ow2 .... KrishGundowry(7) 2 52
(R J Hodges) *s.i.s: hld up in rr: rdn and styd on ins fnl f: nvr nrr* **9/1**

-5 **7** *2 ¼* **Becuille (IRE)**[17] 830 4-9-2 63 .... EddieAhern 3 53
(B J Meehan) *prom: chsd ldr over 6f out tl over 3f out: wknd over 1f out* **12/1**

6504 **8** *½* **Stark Contrast (USA)**[10] 898 5-8-9 56 ....(p) WilliamBuick 9 45
(M D I Usher) *prom: wnt 2nd over 3f out: ev ch over 2f out: nt clr run wl over 1f out: sn wknd* **12/1**

554 **9** *2* **Gold Rock (FR)**[10] 891 4-8-12 59 .... ShaneKelly 5 44
(A W Carroll) *led: hdd wl over 1f out: wknd ent fnl f* **40/1**

634- **10** *¾* **Tanforan**[161] 6867 7-8-6 60 .... BillyCray(7) 1 43
(B P J Baugh) *prom tl wknd over 2f out* **28/1**

-000 **11** *2* **Royal Island (IRE)**[11] 886 7-9-2 63 .... VinceSlattery 7 42
(M G Quinlan) *hld up in mid-div: pushed along on outside over 2f out: sn wknd* **33/1**

204- **12** *3 ½* **Pitbull**[147] 7167 6-9-1 62 .... LiamJones 8 34
(Mrs G S Rees) *s.s: a in rr* **33/1**

-000 **13** *2 ¾* **Andaman Sunset**[19] 798 4-9-4 65 .... TolleyDean 13 31
(J L Spearing) *swtchd lft sn after s: rdn 3f out: a in rr* **40/1**

2m 0.26s (-1.44) **Going Correction** -0.05s/f (Stan) 13 Ran SP% **122.0**
Speed ratings (Par 101): **104,102,102,99,99 97,95,94,93,92 90,87,85**
toteswinger: 1&2 £2.90, 1&3 £7.70, 2&3 £7.70. CSF £12.39 CT £69.89 TOTE £3.40: £1.80, £1.70, £1.70; EX 12.60 Place 6: £82.67 Place 5:£58.69.
Owner S & M Supplies (Aylsham) Ltd **Bred** J W Parker And Lavington Stud **Trained** Newmarket, Suffolk

FOCUS
This was not much of a race and Agilete continued his fine run of form.
Pitbull Official explanation: jockey said gelding missed the break and hung left
T/Plt: £75.30 to a £1 stake. Pool: £60,899.25. 590.05 winning tickets. T/Qpdt: £45.60 to a £1 stake. Pool: £3,070.28. 49.76 winning tickets. KH

FONTAINEBLEAU

Monday, March 30

OFFICIAL GOING: Very soft

1043a PRIX COR DE CHASSE (LISTED RACE) 5f 110y

2:20 (2:21) 3-Y-O+ **£25,243** (£10,097; £7,573; £5,049; £2,524)

RPR

1 **Tiza (SAF)**[129] 7432 7-10-0 ....(p) GMosse 2 114
(A De Royer-Dupre, France)

2 ¾ **Contest (IRE)**[32] 700 5-9-7 ....(b) C-PLemaire 6 105
(C Theodorakis, Greece)

3 2½ **Jane Blue (FR)**[168] 6743 4-9-7 .... JVictoire 4 96
(L Larrigade, France)

4 3 **Bluster (FR)**[129] 7430 3-8-9 .... OPeslier 8 87
(Robert Collet, France)

5 ¾ **Laokoon (GER)**[129] 7432 4-9-7 .... ASuborics 7 84
(Mario Hofer, Germany)

6 nk **Judge 'n Jury**[9] 911 5-9-7 ....(t) ChrisCatlin 3 83
(R A Harris) *led to 1 1/2f out: wknd* **4/1**[1]

7 ¾ **Calbuco (FR)**[174] 6568 5-9-7 .... OPlacais 1 80
(Mme E Holmey, France)

8 6 **Ballantynes (IRE)**[119] 4-9-4 .... DBonilla 5 58
(F & S Brogi, Italy)

61.90 secs (61.90)
WFA 3 from 4yo+ 12lb **8 Ran SP% 20.0**
PARI-MUTUEL (including 1 Euro stake): WIN 2.80; PL 1.30, 1.40, 3.10;DF 6.00.
Owner J-C Seroul **Bred** Daytona Stud (pty) Ltd **Trained** Chantilly, France

NOTEBOOK
Judge 'n Jury showed good speed for a long way but was a spent force by the furlong marker.

FOLKESTONE (R-H)

Tuesday, March 31

OFFICIAL GOING: Straight course - good; round course - good to soft (good in places)
Wind: Almost Nil Weather: Fine

1044 EUROPEAN BREEDERS' FUND MAIDEN STKS 5f

2:20 (2:20) (Class 5) 2-Y-O **£3,561** (£1,059; £529; £264) **Stalls** Low

Form RPR

1 **Black Baccara** 2-8-7 0.... KellyHarrison(5) 6 65
(P S McEntee) *mde virtually all and racd one off rail: rdn and jnd ins fnl f: hld on wl* **20/1**

2 hd **Tom Folan** 2-8-12 0.... FrancisNorton 4 64
(H J Collingridge) *dwlt: rcvrd to trck ldrs and racd against rail: plld out wd over 1f out: chal and upsides ins fnl f: nt qckn nr fin* **16/1**

4 3 1¾ **Bould Mover**[3] 1005 2-9-3 0.... J-PGuillambert 1 62
(R Curtis) *racd against rail: pressed wnr: drvn over 1f out: one pce fnl f* **6/4**[1]

4 1 **Alphacino** 2-9-3 0.... SamHitchcott 3 58
(M R Channon) *trckd ldrs: shkn up 2f out: nt qckn over 1f out: one pce after* **5/1**[2]

5 2½ **Mrs Jones And Me (IRE)** 2-8-12 0.... FrankieMcDonald 5 43+
(P T Midgley) *outpcd after 2f: sn rdn and struggling: styd on fr over 1f out: nrst fin* **33/1**

6 1¼ **Maoi Chinn Tire (IRE)** 2-9-3 0.... LPKeniry 10 43+
(J S Moore) *spd on wd outside 2f: outpcd over 2f out: no ch after: plugged on* **11/1**

7 hd **Roi De Vitesse (IRE)** 2-9-0 0.... JamesMillman(3) 9 42+
(B R Millman) *dwlt: struggling in last pair: outpcd fr 1/2-way: picked up and gng on last 150yds* **10/1**[3]

8 ½ **Anjomarba (IRE)** 2-8-7 0.... JackDean(5) 8 42+
(W G M Turner) *nvr beyond midfield: outpcd 1/2-way: no ch whn n.m.r ent fnl f* **14/1**

9 1½ **Three Good Friends (IRE)** 2-8-12 0.... JamieMoriarty 7 29
(P T Midgley) *racd on outer: pressed ldrs tl wknd rapidly over 1f out* **18/1**

10 ¾ **Island Express (IRE)** 2-9-3 0.... LukeMorris 2 31
(J S Moore) *sed slowest of all: a in last pair: u.p and no prog 1/2-way* **5/1**[2]

61.69 secs (1.69) **Going Correction** +0.15s/f (Good) **10 Ran SP% 116.3**
Speed ratings (Par 92): **92,91,88,87,83 81,80,80,77,76**
toteswinger: 1&2 £55.30, 1&3 £12.60, 2&3 £8.30 CSF £301.08 TOTE £31.60: £5.00, £5.00, £1.40; EX 423.00 Trifecta £163.70 Part won. Pool: £221.27 - 0.46 winning units..
Owner Eventmaker Racehorses **Bred** Peter Balding **Trained** Newmarket, Suffolk

FOCUS
A maiden that has proved an ordinary heat over the years and this season's renewal looks modest. The third helps to set the level.

NOTEBOOK
Black Baccara cost little, but is precociously bred on her sire's side and out of a mare who scored at 1m-1m4f. She clearly knew her job as she was soon at the head of affairs and stuck her head out gamely at the business end. Her life will now be a lot tougher, but this was obviously a very pleasing start and connections are now reportedly keen to give her a break before thinking about the Queen Mary. That is surely too ambitious, however. (op 16-1)
Tom Folan ♦, a February foal, recovered from a sluggish start to race on the rail just off the early leaders and came through with a strong late challenge, but the line was always coming that bit too soon. She is bred to get further in time, but there is every reason to think she can be placed to go one better now she has the initial experience behind her. (op 12-1)
Bould Mover, fourth at Kempton three days earlier, had the advantage of the stands' rail draw, but after showing early dash he was one paced inside the final furlong and really shaped as though the run came too soon. (op 2-1 tchd 9-4 in places)
Alphacino proved too green to do himself full justice and looks just moderate, but ought to have learnt plenty from the run. (op 7-2 tchd 11-2 in places)
Mrs Jones And Me(IRE), whose dam won over 7f, caught the eye doing some nice late work and should be all the sharper for the outing. (op 22-1)

1045 LADBROKES ODDS ON LOYALTY CARD MEDIAN AUCTION MAIDEN STKS 6f

2:55 (2:55) (Class 6) 3-Y-O **£2,729** (£806; £403) **Stalls** Low

Form RPR

220- 1 **Hi Shinko**[180] 6426 3-9-3 73.... AlanMunro 7 69
(B R Millman) *wl away and grabbed nr side rail: led: hrd rdn and jnd over 1f out: forged clr last 100yds* **8/13**[1]

0 2 2¼ **Chris's Jem**[35] 664 3-8-12 0.... EddieAhern 2 57
(J R Jenkins) *hld up bhd ldrs gng wl: prog on outer to go 2nd wl over 1f out: sn jnd wnr: upsides ins fnl f: no ex last 100yds* **33/1**

0-03 3 3¼ **Aahaygirl (IRE)**[21] 796 3-8-12 75.... FergusSweeney 5 46
(K R Burke) *chsd wnr to wl over 1f out: one pce* **4/1**[2]

0- 4 ¾ **Miss Pusey Street**[257] 4126 3-8-12 0.... ChrisCatlin 4 44
(J Gallagher) *chsd ldng pair: nt qckn over 2f out: one pce after* **9/1**[3]

5 5 10 **Fravia**[13] 862 3-8-7 0.... NicolPolli(5) 1 12
(B J McMath) *racd wd in rr: prog and wl in tch 1/2-way: sn hung rt to centre of trck and wknd: t.o* **12/1**

00- 6 1½ **Wightgold**[142] 7259 3-8-5 0.... VictorSantos(7) 6 7
(H J L Dunlop) *dwlt: a in rr: wnt to centre of trck fr 1/2-way: t.o* **28/1**

0436 7 13 **Thoosa**[40] 602 3-8-7 51.... KellyHarrison(5) 8 —
(P S McEntee) *sed awkwardly: a last: t.o* **33/1**

1m 13.68s (0.98) **Going Correction** +0.15s/f (Good) **7 Ran SP% 108.9**
Speed ratings (Par 96): **99,96,91,90,77 75,58**
toteswinger: 1&2 £7.10, 1&3 £1.70, 2&3 £6.40. CSF £26.80 TOTE £1.40: £1.10, £8.40; EX 25.20 Trifecta £105.10 Pool: £657.96 - 4.63 winning units..
Owner Always Hopeful Partnership **Bred** Mrs Laura Grasby **Trained** Kentisbeare, Devon

FOCUS
An uncompetitive maiden in which the winner sets the standard.
Fravia Official explanation: jockey said filly hung right throughout
Thoosa Official explanation: jockey said filly did not handle the track

1046 LADBROKES ODDS ON CARD - GET FREE BETS (S) STKS 7f (S)

3:30 (3:30) (Class 6) 3-Y-O **£2,047** (£604; £302) **Stalls** Low

Form RPR

-054 1 **Special Cuvee**[9] 924 3-8-13 72 ow1.... SebSanders 4 58
(A B Haynes) *dwlt: hld up in last: prog 2f out: threaded through u.p and led ins fnl f: drvn clr* **2/1**[1]

6442 2 3¼ **River Rye (IRE)**[35] 667 3-8-7 58....(p) LPKeniry 9 43
(J S Moore) *t.k.h: pressed ldr: led 3f out and sn crossed to nr side rail: hdd and outpcd ins fnl f* **5/2**[2]

-665 3 2¾ **Paymaster In Chief**[19] 817 3-8-12 50.... DaneO'Neill 1 41
(M D I Usher) *trckd ldrs: effrt but nt qckn over 2f out: plugged on to take 3rd last 75yds* **11/4**[3]

0353 4 1¾ **Elusive Ronnie (IRE)**[18] 827 3-9-3 58....(p) AlanMunro 5 41
(R A Teal) *racd against rail: led to 3f out: fnd nil u.p and btn after* **15/2**

-556 5 2 **Incy Wincy**[5] 964 3-8-12 38.... LukeMorris 2 31
(J M Bradley) *in tch: outpcd over 2f out: nvr on terms after* **33/1**

000- 6 1 **Tallulah's Secret**[186] 6245 3-8-7 0.... ChrisCatlin 6 23
(J Gallagher) *racd wd: pressed ldrs: 2nd briefly over 2f out: sn wknd* **28/1**

0 7 9 **Fancy Set (IRE)**[20] 810 3-8-0 0.... BillyCray(7) 3 —
(D J S Ffrench Davis) *dwlt: wl in tch tl wknd rapidly 2f out* **18/1**

500 8 4½ **Snoozing**[58] 363 3-8-7 30....(p) FrankieMcDonald 7 —
(Mrs L C Jewell) *dwlt: rcvrd to press ldrs and racd wdst of all: wknd over 2f out: t.o* **66/1**

1m 29.47s (2.17) **Going Correction** +0.15s/f (Good) **8 Ran SP% 113.5**
Speed ratings (Par 96): **93,89,86,84,81 80,70,65**
toteswinger: 1&2 £2.20, 1&3 £2.80, 2&3 £2.70. CSF £7.06 TOTE £3.20: £1.20, £1.30, £1.80; EX 9.20 Trifecta £16.40 Pool: £569.52 - 25.63 winning units..The winner was bought in for 4,000gns.
Owner The Villains **Bred** John Brown & Megan Dennis **Trained** Limpley Stoke, Bath

FOCUS
A weak seller, run at just an ordinary pace and the proximity of the runner-up suggests the form is far from solid.

1047 LADBROKES ODDS ON CARD - GET BIGGER ODDS MAIDEN STKS 7f (S)

4:05 (4:07) (Class 5) 3-Y-O+ **£2,729** (£806; £403) **Stalls** Low

Form RPR

224- 1 **Imaam**[187] 6229 3-8-11 79.... RHills 8 75+
(J L Dunlop) *pressed ldr: led 2f out: drew rt away: easily* **4/5**[1]

500- 2 7 **My Flame**[133] 7375 4-9-12 46.... EddieAhern 1 53
(J R Jenkins) *led and racd against rail: hdd 2f out: clr of rest over 1f out but no ch w wnr* **14/1**

00 3 3 **Love Allowed**[27] 752 3-8-6 0.... FrancisNorton 6 35+
(Jamie Poulton) *trckd ldrs: lost pl 3f out but stl gng wl enough: nudged along and styd on steadily to take 3rd ins fnl f* **50/1**

6605 4 1¼ **Mr Rev**[20] 802 6-9-12 45....(b) PaulFitzsimons 2 42
(J M Bradley) *trckd ldng pair: rdn over 2f out: sn brushed aside* **28/1**

30 5 2¼ **If Only**[43] 572 3-8-11 0.... LukeMorris 14 31
(J Jay) *dwlt: t.k.h and worked way through on outer to be prom after 3f: gng strly over 2f out: sn rdn: wknd over 1f out* **10/1**

50- 6 2¾ **Aahaygran (USA)**[257] 4109 3-8-6 0.... FergusSweeney 12 19
(K R Burke) *trckd ldrs: lost pl 1/2-way: no hdwy 2f out: fdd* **5/1**[2]

0-6 7 3¾ **Sams Spirit**[20] 800 3-8-11 0.... DaneO'Neill 4 13
(P J McBride) *dwlt: mostly last and nt gng wl: kpt on fr over 1f out past btn rivals* **33/1**

6- 8 1 **Fuzzy Cat**[168] 6723 3-8-9 0 ow1.... NeilBrown(3) 9 12
(T D Barron) *racd wd: prom over 4f: sn wknd* **8/1**[3]

00- 9 ½ **Admiral Arry**[181] 6378 4-9-12 0.... LPKeniry 7 14
(J M Bradley) *a towards rr: pushed along and outpcd fr over 2f out: wknd* **100/1**

/03- 10 ¾ **Avertitop**[302] 2664 4-9-12 63.... ChrisCatlin 13 7
(J Gallagher) *racd wdst of all: prom over 4f: sn wknd and bhd* **14/1**

0- 11 1¼ **Straboe (USA)**[175] 6553 3-8-11 0.... SaleemGolam 10 4
(S C Williams) *a towards rr on outer: struggling over 2f out: wknd* **100/1**

5 12 8 **Independent James (IRE)**[40] 599 3-8-11 0.... J-PGuillambert 11 —
(S C Williams) *racd towards outer: nvr beyond midfield: wknd over 2f out: t.o* **20/1**

1m 27.8s (0.50) **Going Correction** +0.15s/f (Good)
WFA 3 from 4yo+ 15lb **12 Ran SP% 120.8**
Speed ratings (Par 103): **103,95,91,90,87 84,80,79,78,77 76,67**
toteswinger: 1&2 £4.40, 1&3 £22.60, 2&3 £73.10. CSF £13.79 TOTE £1.60: £1.10, £2.60, £10.30; EX 15.80 Trifecta £408.80 Part won. Pool: £552.53 - 0.90 winning units..
Owner Hamdan Al Maktoum **Bred** Shadwell Estate Company Limited **Trained** Arundel, W Sussex

FOCUS
No strength in depth here and the winner was different class, but did not have to run to his mark.

1048 LADBROKES ODDS ON CARD - DOUBLE POINTS DAY H'CAP 7f (S)
4:35 (4:36) (Class 5) (0-75,70) 4-Y-O+ **£3,070** (£906; £453) **Stalls** Low

Form RPR
-03 **1** **Sendreni (FR)**[77] [141] 5-9-3 **69**..............................(t) FrancisNorton 1 76
(M Wigham) *plld hrd: hld up bhd ldrs: effrt 2f out: swtchd towards ins and rdn to ld jst ins fnl f: drvn out* **7/2**[2]
260- **2** ¾ **Bere Davis (FR)**[175] [6554] 4-9-4 **70**.............................. PaulDoe 7 75
(P D Evans) *led and racd towards nr side rail: kicked on 3f out: edgd rt off rail u.p over 1f out: hdd jst ins fnl f: kpt on* **6/1**
0-03 **3** ¾ **Rubenstar (IRE)**[8] [933] 6-8-12 **64**.............................. JamieSpencer 2 67
(Patrick Morris) *stdd s: hld up in last: stl there and looking for run over 1f out: swtchd sharply rt and prog to chal ent fnl f: nt qckn last 100yds* **9/2**[3]
30-6 **4** *hd* **Pippbrook Gold**[32] [708] 4-9-3 **69**.............................. FergusSweeney 3 71
(J R Boyle) *trckd ldr: effrt 2f out on inner: nt qckn over 1f out: kpt on same pce after* **3/1**[1]
442- **5** *8* **Manere Bay**[153] [7084] 4-9-1 **67**.............................. TedDurcan 6 48
(J L Dunlop) *stdd s: racd wdst of all: trckd ldrs: fdd fr over 1f out* **3/1**[1]
400- **6** *1* **Triple Dream**[160] [6905] 4-8-12 **64**.............................. LukeMorris 5 42
(J M Bradley) *t.k.h early: pressed ldr on outer: rdn 2f out: wknd over 1f out* **12/1**

1m 28.13s (0.83) **Going Correction** +0.15s/f (Good) **6** Ran SP% **112.4**
Speed ratings (Par 103): **101,100,99,99,89 88**
toteswinger: 1&2 £3.70, 1&3 £2.50, 2&3 £4.10. CSF £24.00 TOTE £4.30: £1.80, £2.70; EX 25.60.
Owner Allan Darke **Bred** H H The Aga Khan's Studs Sc **Trained** Newmarket, Suffolk

FOCUS
A very tight handicap but the form is a bit muddling and is rated through the runner-up to the best of last summer's form.

1049 LADBROKES ODDS ON CARD - JOIN TODAY FILLIES' H'CAP 1m 4f
5:05 (5:06) (Class 5) (0-75,74) 4-Y-O+ **£3,070** (£906; £453) **Stalls** Low

Form RPR
5 **1** **Mildoura (FR)**[64] [299] 4-9-4 **74**.............................. IanMongan 1 81
(Mrs L J Mongan) *plld hrd early: hld up last: rdn and prog on outer 3f out: edgd rt over 1f out: sn led: drvn out* **13/2**
421- **2** ½ **Munlochy Bay**[170] [6672] 5-8-9 **63**.............................. FergusSweeney 6 69+
(W S Kittow) *hld up: wnt 3rd 4f out: effrt on inner 2f out: upsides jst over 1f out: styd on but a hld* **7/2**[2]
-150 **3** 1 ½ **Onemoreandstay**[19] [813] 4-8-9 **65**.............................. AlanMunro 5 69
(M D Squance) *t.k.h: hld up: rdn over 2f out: trying to cl whn squeezed for room over 1f out: styd on to take 3rd ins fnl f* **15/2**
236- **4** *4* **Sphere (IRE)**[173] [6596] 4-9-0 **70**.............................. JamieSpencer 2 68
(J R Fanshawe) *t.k.h: trckd ldr after 3f: rdn over 3f out: chal and upsides over 1f out: sn wknd* **2/1**[1]
11-0 **5** *3* **Princess Flame (GER)**[26] [485] 7-9-6 **74**.............................. SebSanders 7 67
(B G Powell) *led: kicked on over 3f out: hdd & wknd rapidly jst over 1f out* **8/1**
-265 **6** 3 ½ **Lapina (IRE)**[27] [751] 5-8-11 **65**..............................(b) DaneO'Neill 4 52
(A Middleton) *trckd ldr 3f: styd cl up: rdn 4f out: sn wknd* **4/1**[3]

2m 47.38s (6.48) **Going Correction** +0.60s/f (Yiel)
WFA 4 from 5yo+ 2lb **6** Ran SP% **111.8**
Speed ratings (Par 100): **102,101,100,98,96 93**
toteswinger: 1&2 £5.10, 1&3 £6.50, 2&3 £5.10. CSF £28.84 TOTE £8.80: £2.50, £2.40; EX 37.40.
Owner Mrs P J Sheen **Bred** H H The Aga Khan's Studs Sc **Trained** Epsom, Surrey
■ Stewards' Enquiry : Ian Mongan caution: careless riding

FOCUS
A modest fillies' handicap, run at an uneven pace, with the winner rated to her best French three-year-old form.

1050 LADBROKES ODDS ON CARD - GET REWARDED TODAY H'CAP 1m 1f 149y
5:35 (5:35) (Class 5) (0-70,69) 3-Y-O **£3,070** (£906; £453) **Stalls** Centre

Form RPR
360- **1** **Peter Grimes (IRE)**[182] [6362] 3-8-13 **64**.............................. SebSanders 8 69
(H J L Dunlop) *trckd ldrs: effrt on inner and narrow ld jst over 2f out: hdd over 1f out: styd on wl to ld again last strides* **2/1**[1]
000- **2** *hd* **Lake Kalamalka (IRE)**[194] [6058] 3-8-11 **62**.............................. EddieAhern 5 67
(J L Dunlop) *hld up in last pair: clsd 5f out: prog on outer over 3f out to chal 2f out: led over 1f out: kpt on: hdd last strides* **8/1**
004- **3** 1 ½ **Bubses Boy**[204] [5753] 3-8-4 **55**.............................. LukeMorris 7 57+
(M L W Bell) *wl in tch: trapped on inner bhd wkng rival 2f out: sn hrd rdn: styd on to take 3rd ins fnl f* **5/2**[2]
5000 **4** 2 ¾ **Nicky Nutjob (GER)**[13] [865] 3-8-7 **58**.............................. FergusSweeney 2 54
(J Pearce) *stdd s: hld up in last: prog on wd outside 3f out: drvn to chse ldrs over 1f out: no ex* **12/1**
66-6 **5** *nk* **Lilly Blue (IRE)**[13] [865] 3-9-4 **69**.............................. TonyCulhane 6 64
(M R Channon) *snatched up after 100yds and dropped to rr: last 4f out: shuffled along fnl 2f and styd on steadily: nvr nr ldrs* **12/1**
0-1 **6** 1 ¼ **Signella**[67] [272] 3-9-4 **69**.............................. AlanMunro 3 62
(P W Chapple-Hyam) *trckd ldrs: pushed along over 3f out: wnt 3rd 2f out: sn no imp and btn: wknd and eased ins fnl f* **15/2**[3]
604 **7** 4 ½ **Benozzo Gozzoli**[18] [828] 3-8-4 **55**.............................. ChrisCatlin 1 38
(H Morrison) *pressed ldr: upsides jst over 2f out: wknd u.p over 1f out* **12/1**
55-6 **8** *57* **More Tea Vicar (IRE)**[39] [628] 3-8-11 **62**.............................. JamieSpencer 4 —
(Patrick Morris) *mde most: hanging bnd over 3f out: hdd jst over 2f out: lost action and virtually p.u* **18/1**

2m 11.14s (6.24) **Going Correction** +0.60s/f (Yiel) **8** Ran SP% **113.1**
Speed ratings (Par 98): **99,98,97,95,95 94,90,45**
toteswinger: 1&2 £4.60, 1&3 £2.60, 2&3 £5.50. CSF £18.33 CT £40.46 TOTE £2.30: £1.10, £3.10, £1.80; EX 18.10 Trifecta £177.40 Place 6: £53.49 Place 5: £25.17. Pool: £803.35 - 3.35 winning units..
Owner Be Hopeful Partnership **Bred** R N Auld **Trained** Lambourn, Berks
■ Stewards' Enquiry : Seb Sanders two-day ban: excessive use of whip (Apr 14-15)

FOCUS
This could prove a fair three-year-old handicap for the class but the proximity of the previously out-of-form fifth limits how positively the form can be treated.
Lilly Blue(IRE) Official explanation: jockey said filly suffered interference just after the start
More Tea Vicar(IRE) Official explanation: jockey said gelding stopped quickly
T/Jkpt: Not won. T/Plt: £51.50 to a £1 stake. Pool: £64,242.79. 909.25 winning tickets. T/Qpdt: £8.10 to a £1 stake. Pool: £5,227.78. 472.70 winning tickets. JN

975 SOUTHWELL (L-H)
Tuesday, March 31

OFFICIAL GOING: Standard
Wind: virtually nil Weather: bright and sunny

1051 BETANGEL.COM H'CAP 1m 3f (F)
2:10 (2:10) (Class 5) (0-75,75) 4-Y-O+ **£2,590** (£770; £385; £192) **Stalls** Low

Form RPR
2-10 **1** **Majehar**[55] [392] 7-8-6 **63**.............................. RobertWinston 5 76
(A G Newcombe) *hld up off the pce: clsd on ldrs 6f out: led wl over 2f out: rdn clr over 1f out: pushed out fnl f: easily* **5/1**[3]
2415 **2** *4* **General Tufto**[9] [923] 4-8-5 **68**..............................(b) MartinLane(5) 3 73
(C Smith) *stdd s: hld up in last pl: hdwy 6f out: ev ch wl over 2f out: sn drvn: btn wl over 1f out: plugged on same pce* **5/1**[3]
205 **3** 3 ¾ **Horseshoe Reef (AUS)**[24] [787] 6-9-3 **74**..............................(p) TPQueally 2 73
(J R Gask) *pressed ldr and sn clr of remainder: led over 4f out: rdn over 3f out: hdd wl over 2f out: wknd u.p wl over 1f out* **3/1**[2]
1/- **4** 3 ½ **No Greater Love (FR)**[133] [98] 7-9-4 **75**.............................. JimCrowley 1 68
(C E Longsdon) *dwlt: sn pushed up to ld and clr w rival: hdd over 4f out: rdn and struggling over 3f out: wl btn fnl 2f* **12/1**
155- **5** 1 ¼ **Dzesmin (POL)**[136] [6288] 7-9-2 **73**.............................. PaulHanagan 4 64
(R A Fahey) *chsd clr ldng pair: clsd 6f out: rdn and struggling over 3f out: no ch fnl 2f* **11/8**[1]

2m 25.55s (-2.45) **Going Correction** -0.075s/f (Stan)
WFA 4 from 6yo+ 1lb **5** Ran SP% **108.1**
Speed ratings (Par 103): **105,102,99,96,95**
CSF £27.17 TOTE £6.90: £1.70, £2.40; EX 23.60.
Owner J R Salter **Bred** Darley **Trained** Yarnscombe, Devon

FOCUS
An uncompetitive handicap. The pace was fair and the runner-up is rated to form.
Horseshoe Reef(AUS) Official explanation: jockey said gelding hung left throughout
Dzesmin(POL) Official explanation: trainer had no explanation for the poor form shown

1052 BE THE BOOKIE WITH BET ANGEL H'CAP 5f (F)
2:40 (2:40) (Class 2) (0-100,97) 4-Y-O+
£11,215 (£3,358; £1,679; £840; £419; £210) **Stalls** High

Form RPR
520- **1** **Cheveton**[157] [6971] 5-9-3 **96**.............................. JimCrowley 4 106
(R J Price) *hld up in tch: swtchd lft 2f out: hdwy over 1f out: drvn to chal ins fnl f: styd on wl to ld last stride* **7/1**[3]
-213 **2** *shd* **Rebel Duke (IRE)**[19] [821] 5-8-6 **85**.............................. TonyHamilton 1 94
(D W Barker) *taken down early: trckd ldrs: led over 1f out: drvn ent fnl f: kpt on u.p tl hdd last stride* **5/4**[1]
5310 **3** 1 ½ **Ebraam (USA)**[10] [916] 6-9-4 **97**.............................. TolleyDean 5 101
(P Howling) *t.k.h: hld up in rr: hdwy ent fnl f: kpt on u.p to go 3rd wl ins fnl f: nvr threatened ldng pair* **9/1**
1222 **4** *nk* **Whiskey Creek**[38] [632] 4-8-1 **83** oh1..............................(b) DavidProbert(3) 7 86
(C A Dwyer) *prom: ev ch and rdn wl over 1f out: drvn ent fnl f: wknd ins fnl f* **6/1**[2]
012- **5** 1 ¾ **Tajneed (IRE)**[192] [6104] 6-9-4 **97**.............................. AdrianTNicholls 8 94
(D Nicholls) *t.k.h early: chsd ldrs: rdn 2f out: one pce and no imp fr over 1f out* **8/1**
0-00 **6** *shd* **Stoneacre Lad (IRE)**[10] [911] 6-8-9 **95**..............................(b) AndrewHeffernan(7) 2 91
(Peter Grayson) *led: rdn and hdd over 1f out: wknd ins fnl f* **14/1**
1604 **7** 1 ¼ **Pawan (IRE)**[19] [821] 9-8-9 **93** ow2..............................(b) AnnStokell(5) 9 85
(Miss A Stokell) *chsd ldrs: rdn and struggling 1/2-way: no ch fr over 1f out* **22/1**
24-6 **8** *nk* **Foxy Music**[4] [985] 5-8-4 **83** oh3.............................. JimmyQuinn 3 74
(E J Alston) *w ldr: rdn 2f out: wknd u.p over 1f out* **16/1**
010- **9** 2 ¾ **Tournedos (IRE)**[297] [2828] 7-9-1 **94**.............................. SilvestreDeSousa 6 75
(D Nicholls) *t.k.h early: hld up in tch: dropped in rr 1/2-way: wl btn fr over 1f out* **16/1**

58.96 secs (-0.74) **Going Correction** +0.075s/f (Slow) **9** Ran SP% **115.1**
Speed ratings (Par 109): **108,107,105,104,102 102,100,99,95**
toteswinger: 1&2 £3.90, 1&3 £16.20, 2&3 £6.50 CSF £16.07 CT £81.44 TOTE £8.10: £2.00, £1.30, £2.60; EX 23.50.
Owner Mrs K Oseman **Bred** Miss K Rausing **Trained** Ullingswick, H'fords
■ Stewards' Enquiry : Tolley Dean one-day ban: careless riding (Apr 14)

FOCUS
A good sprint handicap and the runner-up looks the best guide to the form, backed up by the fourth.

NOTEBOOK
Cheveton was said to be as straight as his trainer could get him for his first run in five months, and that was certainly borne out on paddock appearance, with the five-year-old looking fit and ready. This son of Most Welcome was unproven on Fibresand, but he obviously handled the surface well and was a game winner. Having tracked the pace early, he came under pressure over 2f out, before the runner-up, but he battled on well. Although not open to a great deal of improvement fitness-wise, he is generally quite a progressive sprinter and might be far off Listed class before long. (tchd 8-1)
Rebel Duke(IRE), allowed to go down to the start early, was on his toes leaving the paddock and fired up in the race itself. He showed bags of early speed and was one of the last off the bridle, but he was just worn down late on. (op 7-4 tchd 15-8, 2-1 in a place)
Ebraam(USA) has shown little on his two previous Fibresand starts, but he looked to handle the surface well this time. Having travelled nicely just in behind the speed, he appeared to have to wait longer than ideal to get a clear run and couldn't threaten the front two. (op 11-1 tchd 12-1)
Whiskey Creek, who looked well beforehand, showed good speed but found a few too strong late on, ending a seven-race sequence of top two finishes. (op 11-2 tchd 5-1)
Tajneed(IRE) had been off since finishing runner-up in last year's Ayr Gold Cup and he looked as though he would improve for the run. This was also his first start on sand. (op 5-1)
Stoneacre Lad(IRE) faded late on, but he showed plenty of early dash and will be of interest when is yard is in better form. (op 16-1)

1053 WIN WHATEVER THE RESULT WITH BET ANGEL H'CAP 6f (F)
3:15 (3:15) (Class 4) (0-85,84) 4-Y-O+ **£4,857** (£1,445; £722; £360) **Stalls** Low

Form RPR
4-01 **1** **Swinbrook (USA)**[12] [882] 8-8-4 **70** oh2..............................(v) PaulHanagan 2 82+
(R A Fahey) *hld up in tch: shkn up and jnd ldr 2f out: gng best after: rdn to ld ins fnl f: sn in command* **7/4**[2]
213 **2** 1 ¼ **Wotashirtfull (IRE)**[14] [856] 4-9-1 **81**..............................(p) PatCosgrave 4 87
(J R Boyle) *awkward s: sn led: rdn and jnd 2f out: drvn over 1f out: hdd and one pce ins fnl f* **6/4**[1]

004- **3** *3* **Regal Royale**[175] 6557 6-8-5 **71**..........(v) PatrickMathers 5 67
(Peter Grayson) *chsd ldr: rdn 3f out: ev ch over 1f out tl wknd ins fnl f* **16/1**

000- **4** *2* **Indian Trail**[157] 6971 9-9-4 **84**.......... AdrianTNicholls 1 74
(D Nicholls) *hld up in last pl: effrt on inner over 2f out: ev ch over 1f out: wknd 1f out: eased towards fin* **7/2[3]**

0-30 **5** *1/2* **Orpen Wide (IRE)**[22] 680 7-8-12 **81**..........(b) LeeVickers(3) 3 69
(M C Chapman) *a fnl pair: rdn and hld hd high wl over 2f out: nvr pce to trble ldrs* **14/1**

1m 15.81s (-0.69) **Going Correction** -0.075s/f (Stan) **5** Ran SP% **111.1**
Speed ratings (Par 105): **101,99,95,92,92**
CSF £4.83 TOTE £2.80: £1.20, £1.70; EX 4.50.
Owner Mark A Leatham **Bred** Bill Bronstad **Trained** Musley Bank, N Yorks
FOCUS
Just the five runners and this was an ordinary sprint handicap for the grade rated around the first two.

1054 BET FROM A SPREADSHEET WITH BET ANGEL MAIDEN STKS 1m (F)
3:50 (3:51) (Class 5) 3-Y-O+ **£2,590** (£770; £385; £192) **Stalls** Low

Form RPR

020- **1** **Street Devil (USA)**[176] 6537 4-9-12 70.......... DarryllHolland 4 80+
(R Curtis) *led tl over 6f out: chsd ldr after tl led again wl over 2f out: drvn clr ent fnl f: styd on* **12/1**

2 *2 3/4* **Fortunate Flame** 3-8-9 0.......... NCallan 5 67
(K A Ryan) *s.i.s: plld hrd: hdwy to ld over 6f out: clr w wnr 3f out: hdd wl over 2f out: drvn and btn ent fnl f* **4/1[3]**

3- **3** *2 1/4* **Business Class (BRZ)**[192] 6114 4-9-8 0.......... AdrianTNicholls 3 63
(D Nicholls) *chsd ldrs: rdn and outpcd by ldng pair over 3f out: styd on u.p over 1f out: nvr pce to threaten ldrs* **8/1**

00-3 **4** *nk* **The Hague**[13] 862 3-8-9 66.......... RichardMullen 2 61+
(J H M Gosden) *chsd ldrs: rdn and struggling bdly over 5f out: styd on fr over 1f out: nvr pce to threaten ldrs* **8/11[1]**

5 *5* **Elusive Glen (IRE)** 3-8-9 0.......... RoystonFfrench 6 49
(M Johnston) *dwlt: hld up in tch: hdwy to chse ldng pair over 3f out: sn hanging rt and no imp: hung to stands' rail st: lost 3rd ins fnl f: eased wl ins fnl f* **3/1[2]**

4236 **6** *15* **Le Petit Vigier**[5] 963 3-8-4 48..........(t) AndrewElliott 1 10
(P Beaumont) *a in last pair: rdn and struggling bdly 4f out: t.o fnl 2f* **50/1**

1m 42.92s (-0.78) **Going Correction** -0.075s/f (Stan)
WFA 3 from 4yo 17lb **6** Ran SP% **123.7**
Speed ratings (Par 103): **100,97,95,94,89 74**
toteswinger: 1&2 £6.70, 1&3 £14.70, 2&3 £9.40. CSF £64.20 TOTE £22.20: £5.40, £2.80; EX 75.80.
Owner John Wardle **Bred** Ramona Holt Thomson **Trained** Lambourn, Berks
FOCUS
A couple of the more interesting types ran below expectations and the bare form of this maiden is limited, with the winner the best guide.
Elusive Glen(IRE) Official explanation: jockey said colt ran green

1055 TRY BET ANGEL AT TRY.BETANGEL.COM H'CAP 5f (F)
4:25 (4:25) (Class 6) (0-52,52) 4-Y-O+ **£1,942** (£578; £288; £144) **Stalls** High

Form RPR

0-21 **1** **Handsinthemist (IRE)**[4] 976 4-8-7 **52** 6ex.......... PaulPickard(7) 11 67
(P T Midgley) *pressed ldr tl led over 2f out: mde rest: hrd pressed ins fnl f: rdn and fnd ex fnl 100yds* **4/1[1]**

3010 **2** *1 1/4* **Sherjawy (IRE)**[12] 884 5-8-11 **52**..........(b) KevinGhunowa(3) 6 62
(Miss Z C Davison) *chsd ldrs: chsd wnr and drvn wl over 1f out: hrd drvn and ev ch ins fnl f: no ex fnl 100yds* **8/1**

302 **3** *4* **Mister Incredible**[28] 746 6-8-7 **50**..........(v) MCGeran(5) 10 46
(J M Bradley) *hld up towards rr: hdwy over 2f out: rdn and kpt on same pce fr over 1f out: wnt 3rd towards fin: no ch w ldng pair* **6/1[3]**

500- **4** *shd* **She Who Dares Wins**[184] 6310 9-8-8 **46** oh1.......... TWilliams 5 41
(L R James) *led: hdd over 2f out: drvn 2f out: wknd over 1f out: lost 3rd towards fin* **50/1**

004 **5** *1 1/2* **Chantilly Jewel (USA)**[20] 810 4-8-3 **46** oh1..........(p) AndreaAtzeni(5) 2 36
(R M H Cowell) *wnt rt s and s.i.s: hdwy into midfield and rdn 1/2-way: no hdwy u.p fnl 2f* **8/1**

0-05 **6** *nk* **Our Fugitive (IRE)**[29] 727 7-8-11 **49**..........(e[1]) JimCrowley 9 38
(C Gordon) *chsd ldrs: rdn over 2f out: hld hd high u.p and wl btn over 1f out* **14/1**

4034 **7** *nk* **Orange Square (IRE)**[19] 812 4-8-8 **46** oh1..........(v) TonyHamilton 8 34
(D W Barker) *a towards rr: rdn 1/2-way: no prog u.p fnl 2f* **8/1**

5-00 **8** *2* **North South Divide (IRE)**[11] 896 5-8-12 **50**..........(p) PatrickMathers 4 30
(Peter Grayson) *taken down early: s.i.s and short of room sn after s: effrt on far side and rdn 2f out: no hdwy and wl btn after* **5/1[2]**

6413 **9** *1 3/4* **Meikle Barfil**[11] 895 7-8-12 **50**..........(tp) StephenDonohoe 7 24
(J M Bradley) *stdd s: a towards rr: rdn 2f out: no hdwy and wl btn after* **12/1**

006 **10** *1/2* **Magic Glade**[11] 895 10-8-4 **49**.......... AndrewHeffernan(7) 1 21
(Peter Grayson) *taken down early: in tch in midfield: rdn and struggling over 2f out: wl btn fnl 2f* **7/1**

59.87 secs (0.17) **Going Correction** +0.075s/f (Slow) **10** Ran SP% **113.1**
Speed ratings (Par 101): **101,99,92,92,90 89,89,85,83,82**
toteswinger: 1&2 £9.40, 1&3 £4.70, 2&3 £11.10. CSF £34.95 CT £192.02 TOTE £3.60: £1.50, £3.60, £2.30; EX 32.00.
Owner J F Wright **Bred** Pippa Hackett **Trained** Westow, N Yorks
FOCUS
A moderate sprint handicap rated through the runner-up. Unlike in the earlier 5f contest (when they raced middle to far side), the stands' rail was the place to be.
Orange Square(IRE) Official explanation: jockey said gelding would not face the kick-back

1056 WIN BET ANGEL AT WIN.BETANGEL.COM H'CAP 1m (F)
4:55 (4:58) (Class 4) (0-80,78) 3-Y-O **£4,857** (£1,445; £722; £360) **Stalls** Low

Form RPR

310- **1** **Hunterview**[158] 6946 3-9-4 **78**.......... NCallan 3 96+
(M A Jarvis) *jnd ldr after 1f: led 3f out: rdn and hung lft wl over 1f out: clr over 1f out: heavily eased fnl 100yds* **3/1[2]**

011- **2** *3 1/2* **Becausewecan (USA)**[138] 7298 3-9-2 **76**.......... RobertWinston 1 80
(M Johnston) *led: rdn and hdd 3f out: sn struggling: reagained 2nd 2f out: no ch w wnr* **6/1**

-111 **3** *3 1/4* **Statute Book (IRE)**[15] 851 3-9-1 **78**.......... DavidProbert(3) 5 74
(S Kirk) *hld up in tch: hdwy to chse wnr wl over 2f out: rdn and btn over 1f out: lost 2nd 1f out* **6/4[1]**

411- **4** *3 1/4* **Digger Derek (IRE)**[166] 6761 3-8-13 **73**.......... PaulHanagan 6 62
(R A Fahey) *in tch: rdn and struggling over 3f out: wl btn fr over 2f out* **5/1[3]**

1m 41.89s (-1.81) **Going Correction** -0.075s/f (Stan) **4** Ran SP% **96.0**
Speed ratings (Par 100): **106,102,99,96**
toteswinger: 1&2 £6.00. CSF £13.95 TOTE £3.40; EX 15.50 Place 6: £441.02 Place 5: £86.75.
Owner Sheikh Ahmed Al Maktoum **Bred** Darley **Trained** Newmarket, Suffolk
FOCUS
Only four runners, but a decent three-year-old handicap and rated positively.
T/Plt: £592.10 to a £1 stake. Pool: £54,675.77. 67.40 winning tickets. T/Qpdt: £58.30 to a £1 stake. Pool: £4,594.08. 58.30 winning tickets. SP

CATTERICK (L-H)
Wednesday, April 1

OFFICIAL GOING: Good to firm (good in places; 9.2)
Wind: virtually nil Weather: Dry with sunny periods

1057 CATTERICKBRIDGE.CO.UK (S) STKS 7f
2:20 (2:21) (Class 6) 3-4-Y-O **£2,047** (£604; £302) **Stalls** Centre

Form RPR

0550 **1** **Splash The Cash**[33] 715 4-9-4 65.......... AmyRyan(7) 14 78
(K A Ryan) *trckd ldrs: smooth hdwy over 2f out: led wl over 1f out: rdn ins fnl f and kpt on wl* **5/1[2]**

-000 **2** *1 3/4* **Lytton**[10] 921 4-9-0 52..........(v) FrederikTylicki(5) 12 67
(R Ford) *trckd ldrs: hdwy over 2f out: rdn and ev ch wl over 1f out: drvn ent fnl f and kpt on same pce* **11/1**

1-63 **3** *3 3/4* **Paint Splash**[50] 492 3-8-0 57.......... FrancisNorton 8 47
(T D Barron) *in tch on inner: hdwy over 2f out: sn rdn and kpt on ins fnl f: nrst fin* **9/2[1]**

6010 **4** *4 1/2* **Valdemar**[19] 831 3-8-5 51.......... SilvestreDeSousa 10 40
(A D Brown) *midfield: rdn along and sltly outpcd 1/2-way: hdwy 2f out: kpt on u.p appr fnl f: nrst fin* **25/1**

020- **5** *1 1/4* **Baronovici (IRE)**[182] 6382 4-9-5 58.......... TonyHamilton 6 42
(D W Barker) *cl up: effrt over 2f out: sn rdn and ev ch tl drvn and wknd over 1f out* **10/1**

205- **6** *1 1/4* **Ace Of Spies (IRE)**[69] 4919 4-9-5 52.......... PaulMulrennan 9 38
(G A Harker) *prom: rdn along over 2f out: sn drvn and grad wknd* **22/1**

00-6 **7** *shd* **Legendary Guest**[45] 561 4-9-11 65..........(p) PaulHanagan 1 44
(D W Barker) *t.k.h: towards rr: effrt and hung rt 3f out: sn rdn and styd on appr fnl f: nrst fin* **8/1**

0033 **8** *1* **Charlie Allnut**[21] 811 4-9-5 55..........(b) LeeEnstone 7 35
(S Wynne) *chsd ldrs on inner: rdn along over 2f out: drvn wl over 1f out and grad wknd* **15/2[3]**

-050 **9** *1 3/4* **Billy Hot Rocks (IRE)**[21] 811 4-9-11 55..........(b) MickyFenton 5 37
(Miss Gay Kelleway) *dwlt and in rr tl sme late hdwy* **22/1**

10 *shd* **Just Pickles**[67] 4-9-5 0.......... PJMcDonald 11 30
(G A Swinbank) *dwlt: a towards rr* **25/1**

000- **11** *9* **Rascasse**[185] 6308 4-9-5 46..........(b[1]) PhillipMakin 2 —
(Bruce Hellier) *s.i.s and a in rr* **80/1**

10-0 **12** *8* **Nchike**[10] 924 3-8-5 66.......... AdrianTNicholls 15 —
(D Nicholls) *a towards rr* **11/1**

0-50 **13** *5* **Johnny Friendly**[33] 715 4-9-11 57..........(v[1]) DarrenWilliams 13 —
(K R Burke) *chsd ldrs on outer: rdn along 1/2-way: wknd over 2f out* **10/1**

300- **14** *1 1/2* **Adab (IRE)**[288] 3117 4-9-5 63.......... GrahamGibbons 3 —
(Miss Tracy Waggott) *led: rdn along over 3f out: drvn over 2f out: sn hdd & wknd* **14/1**

1m 24.85s (-2.15) **Going Correction** -0.20s/f (Firm)
WFA 3 from 4yo 14lb **14** Ran SP% **116.9**
Speed ratings (Par 101): **104,102,97,92,91 89,89,88,86,86 76,66,61,59**
toteswinger: 1&2 £21.20, 1&3 £7.00, 2&3 £16.20. CSF £53.07 TOTE £5.40: £2.30, £3.40, £1.90; EX 81.80.There was no bid for the winner.
Owner The Armchair Jockeys **Bred** G B Turnbull Ltd **Trained** Hambleton, N Yorks
FOCUS
7mm of rain and sleet had fallen over the weekend but dry, sunny and relatively warm weather since produced ground generally good to firm. The time in this seller was good for the grade and the runner-up is rated close to his best.
Valdemar Official explanation: jockey said gelding hung left
Legendary Guest Official explanation: jockey said gelding hung right-handed throughout
Billy Hot Rocks(IRE) Official explanation: jockey said gelding had a breathing problem
Nchike Official explanation: jockey said gelding was unsuited by the good to firm (good in places) ground

1058 GORACING.CO.UK H'CAP 1m 7f 177y
2:50 (2:51) (Class 6) (0-65,65) 4-Y-O+ **£2,388** (£705; £352) **Stalls** Low

Form RPR

04-5 **1** **Daraiym (IRE)**[14] 252 4-8-2 **46**.......... FrancisNorton 2 54
(Paul Green) *trckd ldrs on inner: rdn along to chse ldng pair over 2f out: swtchd rt over 1f out: drvn ent fnl f: styd on to ld nr fin* **5/1[2]**

420/ **2** *1/2* **Sonara (IRE)**[31] 6421 5-9-6 **65**.......... FrederikTylicki(5) 1 73
(J Howard Johnson) *trckd ldr: hdwy and cl up 4f out: led over 2f out and sn rdn: drvn ent fnl f: hdd and no ex nr fin* **12/1**

115- **3** *1/2* **Bijou Dan**[238] 4735 8-9-6 **60**.......... PJMcDonald 13 67
(G M Moore) *prom: effrt to chse ldng pair 3f out: swtchd ins and gd hdwy to chal over 1f out: sn rdn and ev ch tl drvn and no ex wl ins fnl f* **12/1**

6- **4** *3 1/2* **Harcas (IRE)**[28] 3545 7-9-8 **62**..........(p) PaulMulrennan 8 65
(M Todhunter) *led at stdy pce: pushed along and qcknd over 5f out: rdn over 3f out: hdd over 2f out: sn drvn and grad wknd* **66/1**

055- **5** *3/4* **San Deng**[298] 2849 7-8-11 **51**.......... PhillipMakin 7 53
(Micky Hammond) *in tch: rdn along over 4f out: drvn over 2f out and kpt on same pce* **6/1[3]**

322- **6** *nse* **Mister Pete (IRE)**[18] 7177 6-9-8 **62**.......... AndrewElliott 9 64
(W Storey) *hld up in midfield: effrt 4f out: sn rdn along and no imp fnl 2f* **9/1**

543- **7** *3* **Aleron (IRE)**[96] 5385 11-9-0 **61**..........(p) JamieKyne(7) 10 59
(J J Quinn) *a towards rr* **7/1**

00-3 **8** *nk* **Chiff Chaff**[5] 983 5-8-13 **53**.......... LPKeniry 12 51
(C R Dore) *traked ldrs: effrt 4f out and sn rdn along: drvn over 2f out and sn btn* **9/2[1]**

000- **9** *1 1/2* **Woody Valentine (USA)**[31] 6727 8-8-7 **47**.......... PaulHanagan 3 43
(Mrs Dianne Sayer) *s.i.s: a in rr* **12/1**

600- **10** *nk* **Zabougg**[168] 4919 4-8-7 **51** ow1.......... TonyHamilton 6 47
(D W Barker) *a towards rr* **80/1**

0266 **11** *4 1/2* **Top Tiger**[21] 809 5-8-9 **52**.......... NeilBrown(3) 5 42
(D W Barker) *a in rr* **9/1**

020- 12 3½ **Coronado's Gold (USA)**[158] 6812 8-8-13 **53**.................... TomEaves 11 39
(B Ellison) *dwlt: a in rr* **10/1**

3m 32.31s (0.31) **Going Correction** -0.20s/f (Firm)
WFA 4 from 5yo+ 4lb **12** Ran SP% **116.5**
Speed ratings (Par 101): **91,90,90,88,88 88,86,86,85,85 83,81**
toteswinger: 1&2 £11.90, 1&3 £14.80, 2&3 £21.60 CSF £62.71 CT £685.33 TOTE £5.50: £2.60, £3.20, £3.90; EX 82.80.
Owner Paul Boyers **Bred** His Highness The Aga Khan's Studs S C **Trained** Lydiate, Merseyside

FOCUS
A low-grade stayers' handicap and the pace was very modest until the two leaders quickened it up coming to the final half-mile. Significantly, the first four home raced up with the pace throughout. The third sets the standard.
Chiff Chaff Official explanation: trainer said mare was unsuited by the track

1059 TED THOMPSON 80TH BIRTHDAY H'CAP 1m 5f 175y
3:20 (3:20) (Class 4) (0-85,85) 4-Y-O+ **£4,727** (£1,406; £702; £351) **Stalls** Low

Form RPR
422- 1 **Overrule (USA)**[154] 6243 5-8-10 **69**.................... GrahamGibbons 1 82+
(B Ellison) *hld up in rr: smooth hdwy over 3f out: chsd ldr over 2f out: sn chal on bit: shkn up to ld jst ins fnl f: comf* **7/4**[1]

0-31 2 1 **River Ardeche**[61] 226 4-8-10 **77**.................... PatrickDonaghy(5) 5 85
(P C Haslam) *led and sn clr: pushed along over 3f out: rdn along over 2f out: sn jnd and drvn over 1f out: hdd jst ins fnl f and one pce* **7/1**

3231 3 13 **They All Laughed**[22] 795 6-9-3 **76**....................(b) PhillipMakin 3 66
(P W Hiatt) *hld up: hdwy 4f out: rdn along 3f out: drvn over 2f out and sn one pce* **3/1**[3]

050- 4 2½ **Step This Way (USA)**[238] 4742 4-9-9 **85**.................... GregFairley 4 71
(M Johnston) *chsd clr ldr: pushed along and hdwy over 4f out: rdn along 3f out: drvn and wknd over 2f out* **11/4**[2]

/00- 5 1½ **Bergonzi (IRE)**[183] 3929 5-9-10 **83**.................... PaulMulrennan 2 67
(J Howard Johnson) *chsd clr ldr: rdn along 4f out: outpcd fnl 3f* **10/1**

2m 59.49s (-4.11) **Going Correction** -0.20s/f (Firm)
WFA 4 from 5yo+ 3lb **5** Ran SP% **109.6**
Speed ratings (Par 105): **103,102,95,93,92**
toteswinger: 1&2 £7.70. CSF £13.84 TOTE £2.70: £1.30, £2.10; EX 8.90.
Owner The Jury's Out Partnership **Bred** Avalon Farms Inc **Trained** Norton, N Yorks

FOCUS
A fair stayers' handicap run at a strong pace but something of a muddling handicap with the runner-up the best guide to the form.

1060 GODS SOLUTION H'CAP 7f
3:50 (3:50) (Class 5) (0-75,74) 4-Y-O+ **£2,590** (£770; £385; £192) **Stalls** Centre

Form RPR
000- 1 **Malcheek (IRE)**[185] 6314 7-9-2 **72**.................... DavidAllan 10 81+
(T D Easterby) *prom: effrt to chse ldr wl over 2f out: led wl over 1f out and sn rdn clr: kpt on strly* **11/1**

0-11 2 2½ **Ergo (FR)**[12] 898 5-8-8 **64**....................(b) PaulHanagan 13 66+
(James Moffatt) *hld up in midfield: hdwy over 2f out: sn rdn and styd on strly ins fnl f: nt rch wnr* **6/1**[1]

003- 3 hd **Bravely (IRE)**[148] 7175 5-9-2 **72**.................... DuranFentiman 8 74
(T D Easterby) *hld up in rr: t.k.h and n.m.r after 1 1/2f: hdwy over 2f out: sn rdn and styng on whn n.m.r over 1f out: kpt on u.p ins fnl f: nrst fin* **16/1**

606- 4 ½ **No Grouse**[156] 7021 9-8-4 **63**.................... AndrewMullen(3) 6 63
(E J Alston) *in tch: hdwy to chse ldrs 2f out and sn rdn: drvn over 1f out and kpt on same pce* **16/1**

-630 5 1 **H Harrison (IRE)**[5] 984 9-8-9 **70**.................... KellyHarrison(5) 7 68
(I W McInnes) *led 1f: cl up: rdn along over 2f out and grad wknd fr over 1f out* **10/1**

230- 6 nse **Ancient Cross**[195] 6043 5-8-10 **66**.................... DaleGibson 11 64+
(M W Easterby) *midfield: hdwy 2f out: sn rdn and n.m.r over 1f out: no imp after* **17/2**

12-6 7 ¾ **Spin Again (IRE)**[5] 980 4-9-4 **74**.................... AdrianTNicholls 3 70
(D Nicholls) *trckd ldrs on inner: hdwy over 2f out: rdn to chse ldrs whn n.m.r and swtchd rt over 1f out: sn drvn and one pce* **15/2**[2]

004- 8 nse **Stonehaugh (IRE)**[231] 4961 6-8-13 **69**.................... PaulMulrennan 15 64
(J Howard Johnson) *towards rr: hdwy over 2f out: sn rdn and no imp* **14/1**

60-0 9 ½ **Dorn Dancer (IRE)**[41] 606 7-9-3 **73**.................... TonyHamilton 14 69+
(D W Barker) *stdd and swtchd lft s: in rr and hmpd after 1f: hdwy on inner 2f out: styng on whn n.m.r and eased ins fnl f* **40/1**

1433 10 1 **Punching**[20] 818 5-8-11 **67**.................... LPKeniry 1 58
(C R Dore) *midfield: pushed along 3f out: rdn over 2f out and sn btn* **9/1**

4-25 11 nk **If You Knew Suzy**[25] 786 4-8-9 **65**....................(t) PJMcDonald 5 56
(G A Swinbank) *in tch: hdwy to chse ldrs over 2f out: sn rdn: n.m.r and hmpd over 1f out: sn wknd* **8/1**[3]

4233 12 1¾ **Red Cape (FR)**[28] 757 6-8-9 **65**....................(b) AndrewElliott 12 51
(Mrs R A Carr) *cl up: led after 1f: rdn along over 2f out: drvn and hdd wl over 1f out and sn wknd* **10/1**

000- 13 6 **Violent Velocity (IRE)**[148] 7175 6-8-7 **70**.................... JamieKyne(7) 9 40
(J J Quinn) *a towards rr* **8/1**[3]

0-00 14 2¼ **Mission Impossible**[41] 606 4-8-4 **65**.................... PatrickDonaghy(5) 2 29
(P C Haslam) *dwlt: hdwy 1/2-way: chsd ldrs over 2f out: sn rdn and wkng whn n.m.r over 1f out: sn eased* **20/1**

1m 24.98s (-2.02) **Going Correction** -0.20s/f (Firm) **14** Ran SP% **120.9**
Speed ratings (Par 103): **103,100,99,99,98 98,97,97,96,95 95,93,86,83**
toteswinger: 1&2 £10.80, 1&3 £44.60, 2&3 £26.00 CSF £75.94 CT £1075.58 TOTE £11.00: £2.80, £2.00, £8.60; EX 99.00.
Owner Mrs Susie Dicker **Bred** Carrigbeg Stud **Trained** Great Habton, N Yorks
■ Stewards' Enquiry : Adrian T Nicholls three-day ban: careless riding (Apr 15-17)

FOCUS
A competitive handicap run at a strong pace and the form looks pretty solid.

1061 TOYTOP MAIDEN STKS (DIV I) 5f 212y
4:20 (4:20) (Class 5) 3-Y-O+ **£2,266** (£674; £337; £168) **Stalls** Low

Form RPR
33- 1 **Tiger Reigns**[169] 6723 3-8-13 0.................... PhillipMakin 5 58+
(M Dods) *in tch: hdwy whn rn wd home bnd: rdn to chse ldrs wl over 1f out: styd on wl u.p ins fnl f to ld last 50yds* **15/8**[2]

2 ¾ **Street Spirit (USA)** 3-8-8 0.................... DuranFentiman 2 51
(T D Easterby) *towards rr: gd hdwy 1/2-way: chsd ldrs over 2f out: rdn to ld ent fnl f: sn drvn and edgd lft: hdd and no ex last 50yds* **12/1**

00- 3 1½ **Gore Hill (IRE)**[159] 6953 3-8-13 0.................... DarrenWilliams 10 51
(K R Burke) *prom: cl up 1/2-way: led over 2f out and sn rdn: drvn and hdd ent fnl f: kpt on same pce* **20/1**

00- 4 1¾ **Ivor Novello (IRE)**[256] 4176 3-8-13 0.................... PJMcDonald 3 45
(G A Swinbank) *chsd ldrs on inner: hdwy over 2f out: sn rdn and ev ch 1f drvn and wknd ent fnl f* **6/1**[3]

00- 5 1¾ **Nassau Beach (IRE)**[291] 3049 3-8-13 0.................... DavidAllan 1 40
(T D Easterby) *s.i.s and bhd tl styd on fnl 2f: nrst fin* **11/1**

0-00 6 1 **Mickys Mate**[9] 933 4-9-6 30.................... KellyHarrison(5) 7 39?
(A Crook) *prom: rdn along 3f out: wknd over 2f out* **100/1**

000- 7 2 **Lifetime Endeavour**[209] 5636 5-9-11 43.................... AndrewElliott 4 33?
(R E Barr) *chsd ldrs: rdn along 1/2-way: wknd over 2f out* **50/1**

00- 8 2½ **Take That**[120] 7528 4-9-8 0.................... AndrewMullen(3) 6 25?
(S P Griffiths) *led: rdn along and hdd over 2f out: sn wknd* **150/1**

035- 9 3¼ **Agent Stone (IRE)**[231] 4960 3-8-13 65....................(t) AdrianTNicholls 8 12
(D Nicholls) *dwlt: sn rdn along in rr: hung rt bnd after 2f: a in rr after* **11/8**[1]

1m 13.31s (-0.29) **Going Correction** -0.20s/f (Firm)
WFA 3 from 4yo+ 12lb **9** Ran SP% **115.6**
Speed ratings (Par 103): **93,92,90,87,85 84,81,78,73**
toteswinger: 1&2 £4.20, 1&3 £7.70, 2&3 £15.60 CSF £23.74 TOTE £2.40: £1.10, £2.50, £3.80; EX 19.80.
Owner Joe Buzzeo **Bred** Richard Green And New England Stud **Trained** Denton, Co Durham

FOCUS
A modest event for the first part of this divided sprint maiden and the form looks shaky.
Nassau Beach(IRE) Official explanation: jockey said gelding missed the break
Agent Stone(IRE) Official explanation: vet said gelding was coughing post race

1062 TOYTOP MAIDEN STKS (DIV II) 5f 212y
4:50 (4:52) (Class 5) 3-Y-O+ **£2,266** (£674; £337; £168) **Stalls** Low

Form RPR
453- 1 **Al Mugtareb (IRE)**[161] 6910 3-8-13 72.................... TPO'Shea 8 68+
(M Johnston) *trckd ldrs: hdwy over 2f out: rdn along wl over 1f out: styd on to ld ins fnl f* **5/2**[1]

43- 2 ¾ **Mister Tinktastic (IRE)**[154] 7082 3-8-13 0.................... PhillipMakin 9 66
(M Dods) *in tch: hdwy to chse ldrs 2f out: swtchd rt and rdn over 1f out: kpt on strly ins fnl f* **3/1**[2]

60-0 3 ½ **Blue Noodles**[22] 797 3-8-13 60.................... TonyHamilton 7 64
(D W Barker) *cl up: rdn to ld 2f out: drvn over 1f out: hdd and no ex ins fnl f* **28/1**

5- 4 2 **Minturno (USA)**[189] 6212 3-8-13 0.................... MickyFenton 10 58
(Mrs A Duffield) *towards rr: hdwy 2f out: sn rdn and kpt on ins fnl f: nrst fin* **15/2**

00- 5 1¾ **Smelly Cat**[256] 4202 3-8-8 0.................... DavidAllan 5 47
(T D Easterby) *t.k.hm chsd ldrs: rdn along over 2f out: sn drvn and kpt on same pce ins fnl f* **20/1**

2/0- 6 3¼ **High Profit (IRE)**[18] 7560 5-9-11 62....................(v[1]) PaulHanagan 4 45
(James Moffatt) *bhd tl rdn along and styd on fnl 2f: nvr rch ldrs* **8/1**

7 nk **Your True Love (IRE)** 3-8-8 0.................... FrancisNorton 3 36
(A Berry) *in rr: rdn along and hdwy 2f out: hung bdly rt over 1f out and wknd* **40/1**

8 hd **Pontardawe** 3-8-8 0.................... DuranFentiman 6 35
(T D Easterby) *in tch: pushed along 1/2-way and sn outpcd* **25/1**

-232 9 hd **Minotaurious (IRE)**[61] 350 3-8-8 77.................... AndrewElliott 1 34
(K R Burke) *t.k.h: led: rdn along and hdd 2f out: sn drvn and wknd* **4/1**[3]

10 ¾ **Russian Music (USA)**[11] 4-9-11 0.................... DaleGibson 2 40
(C A Mulhall) *s.i.s: a bhd* **50/1**

1m 13.21s (-0.39) **Going Correction** -0.20s/f (Firm)
WFA 3 from 4yo+ 12lb **10** Ran SP% **112.9**
Speed ratings (Par 103): **94,93,92,89,87 83,82,82,82,81**
toteswinger: 1&2 £2.80, 1&3 £13.70, 2&3 £11.10 CSF £9.01 TOTE £3.50: £1.40, £1.40, £5.50; EX 11.10.
Owner Hamdan Al Maktoum **Bred** Richard O'Hara **Trained** Middleham Moor, N Yorks

FOCUS
Marginally the quicker division and certainly more strength in depth. The form looks more solid than the first leg, with the placed horses close to their marks.
Minturno(USA) Official explanation: jockey said colt failed to handle the bend
Your True Love(IRE) Official explanation: jockey said filly hung right handed throughout

1063 TURFTV H'CAP 1m 3f 214y
5:20 (5:21) (Class 5) (0-75,74) 3-Y-O **£2,590** (£770; £385; £192) **Stalls** Low

Form RPR
4131 1 **Supernoverre (IRE)**[14] 865 3-9-1 **71**.................... IanMongan 1 78+
(P Howling) *hld up in rr: stdy hdwy 4f out: chsd ldrs over 2f out: rdn to ld wl over 1f out: drvn out* **10/3**[2]

-461 2 nk **Dispol Diva**[13] 883 3-8-4 **60**....................(v) FrankieMcDonald 5 65
(P T Midgley) *hld up towards rr: stdy hdwy over 4f out: effrt on outer 3f out: rdn to ld briefly 2f out: sn hdd and drvn: rallied ins fnl f and kpt on wl towards fin* **15/2**[3]

-566 3 3¾ **Orsippus (USA)**[18] 840 3-9-4 **74**.................... TonyCulhane 7 73
(M R Channon) *hld up in rr: gd hdwy 4f out: rdn to chse ldrs over 2f out: drvn over 1f out and kpt on same pce* **2/1**[1]

330- 4 5 **Orphaned Annie**[109] 7659 3-8-4 **60** oh2.................... PaulHanagan 6 51
(B Ellison) *trckd ldng pair: hdwy 4f out: rdn to chal over 2f out and ev ch tl drvn and one pce fr over 1f out* **14/1**

-414 5 1¼ **Shaker Style (USA)**[30] 740 3-8-9 **65**....................(b) GrahamGibbons 3 54
(J D Bethell) *chsd ldrs on inner: effrt over 2f out: sn rdn and no imp* **8/1**

0332 6 3¾ **Amazing Blue Sky**[6] 964 3-8-4 **60**....................(b) AndrewElliott 4 43
(Mrs R A Carr) *set str pce and sn clr: rdn along 4f out: drvn over 2f out: sn hdd & wknd* **16/1**

003 7 2¼ **Milemilia (IRE)**[19] 824 3-8-9 **65**.................... TravisBlock 8 44
(H Morrison) *trckd ldrs: hdwy to chse ldrs over 4f out: rdn along 3f out: drvn over 2f out and sn btn* **8/1**

6-10 8 22 **Shifting Gold (IRE)**[34] 689 3-8-8 **64**....................(b) PaulMulrennan 2 8
(K A Ryan) *chsd clr ldr: rdn along 4f out: drvn 3f out and sn wknd* **9/1**

2m 35.48s (-3.42) **Going Correction** -0.20s/f (Firm) **8** Ran SP% **112.9**
Speed ratings (Par 98): **103,102,100,96,96 93,92,77**
toteswinger: 1&2 £5.00, 1&3 £2.80, 2&3 £4.50 CSF £27.62 CT £60.79 TOTE £3.20: £1.50, £2.00, £1.20; EX 21.10.
Owner Paul Terry **Bred** Derek Veitch And Saleh Ali Hammadi **Trained** Newmarket, Suffolk

FOCUS
A modest three-year-old stayers' handicap but the leader went off very strong and the first three home came from off the pace and raced wide in the home straight. The form is rated around the placed horses.

1064 RACING UK H'CAP 5f
5:50 (5:51) (Class 6) (0-60,59) 3-Y-O **£2,183** (£644; £322) **Stalls** Low

Form RPR
0243 1 **Fasliyanne (IRE)**[7] 955 3-8-11 **52**....................(b) PaulHanagan 3 59
(K A Ryan) *wnt rt s: prom: led 1/2-way: rdn clr wl over 1f out: kpt on* **11/4**[1]

5342 **2** 2 ½ **Fashion Icon (USA)**[21] 804 3-9-1 59 NeilBrown(3) 10 57
(T D Barron) *prom: chsd wnr over 2f out: sn rdn: drvn over 1f out and no imp ins fnl f* 9/2[3]
160- **3** nse **Compton Ford**[175] 6579 3-9-4 59 PhillipMakin 2 56
(M Dods) *pushed along and outpcd in rr: hdwy 2f out: swtchd rt and rdn wl over 1f out: styd on ins fnl f* 5/1
305- **4** 2 ½ **Abbey Steps (IRE)**[187] 6247 3-9-1 56 DavidAllan 6 44
(T D Easterby) *wnt lft s: chsd ldrs: rdn along 2f out: sn drvn and kpt on same pce* 4/1[2]
536- **5** shd **Jethro Bodine (IRE)**[232] 4948 3-8-4 50 (p) KellyHarrison(5) 5 38
(W J H Ratcliffe) *hmpd s and bhd: hdwy wl over 1f out: sn rdn and kpt on ins fnl f: nrst fin* 14/1
5240 **6** 4 ½ **Wee Bizzom**[40] 624 3-8-3 49 DanielleMcCreery(5) 9 21
(A Berry) *towards rr: effrt on outer 2f out: sn rdn: edgd lft and nvr a factor* 40/1
0036 **7** 3 **Meg Jicaro**[31] 722 3-8-0 46 ow1 DeanHeslop(5) 1 7
(Mrs L Williamson) *a towards rr* 20/1
004- **8** 1 ¼ **Bold Bomber**[110] 7646 3-9-0 55 PaulMulrennan 8 12
(Paul Green) *a towards rr* 14/1
45-0 **9** nse **Miss Thippawan (USA)**[12] 889 3-8-4 45 (p) SilvestreDeSousa 7 1
(P T Midgley) *led: hdd and rdn 1/2-way: sn wknd* 13/2
0400 **10** ¾ **Yes She Can Can**[7] 955 3-7-11 45 (b) AndrewHeffernan(7) 4 —
(Peter Grayson) *hmpd s: midfield and rdn along 1/2-way: sn outpcd* 100/1

60.13 secs (0.33) **Going Correction** -0.025s/f (Good) 10 Ran SP% 116.4
Speed ratings (Par 96): **96,92,91,87,87 80,75,73,73,72**
toteswinger: 1&2 £3.20, 1&3 £4.40, 2&3 £5.90 CSF £14.88 CT £60.01 TOTE £3.30: £1.60, £1.70, £2.20; EX 10.80 Place 6: £218.73, Place 5: £106.74..
Owner Wooster Partnership **Bred** Frank Dunne **Trained** Hambleton, N Yorks

FOCUS
A low-grade three-year-old sprint handicap, a seller in all but name, and again the placed horses set the standard.
T/Jkpt: £9,340.50 to a £1 stake. Pool: £19,733.49. 1.50 winning tickets. T/Plt: £122.00 to a £1 stake. Pool: £77,747.09. 465.02 winning tickets. T/Qpdt: £9.60 to a £1 stake. Pool: £4,491.60. 346.20 winning tickets. JR

1001 KEMPTON (A.W) (R-H)
Wednesday, April 1

OFFICIAL GOING: Standard
Wind: Strong, half-against Weather: Fine

1065 KEMPTON.CO.UK CLAIMING STKS 7f (P)
6:50 (6:50) (Class 6) 4-Y-0+ £2,047 (£604; £302) Stalls High

Form RPR
0400 **1** **Ryedale Ovation (IRE)**[10] 921 6-8-10 60 FergusSweeney 7 76
(M Hill) *s.i.s: hld up: clsd 3f out: prog on inner to ld wl over 1f out: sn in command: pushed out* 10/1
10 **2** 3 ½ **Ravi River (IRE)**[19] 834 5-9-9 80 RichardKingscote 2 79
(Tom Dascombe) *t.k.h early: sn hld up bhd ldng pair: effrt to chal 2f out: sn outpcd by wnr: vain chse after* 4/6[1]
020- **3** 6 **Lady Florence**[129] 6913 4-8-5 47 LukeMorris 3 45
(A B Coogan) *led: jnd after 1f: duelled for ld tl hdd wl over 1f out: sn wknd* 50/1
6204 **4** 1 ¾ **Landucci**[14] 868 8-8-11 62 (b) JamesDoyle 6 46
(S Curran) *hld up bhd ldrs: cl enough over 2f out: sn shkn up and no rspnse: wknd over 1f out* 9/1[3]
5-56 **5** 2 **Rydal (USA)**[47] 531 8-9-0 56 (v) DaneO'Neill 1 44
(Miss Jo Crowley) *rdn in last bef 1/2-way: sn bhd* 14/1
1-01 **6** 7 **Carnivore**[47] 536 7-9-7 78 SebSanders 5 32
(T D Barron) *awkward s: rcvrd to join ldr: duelled for advantage tl wl over 1f out: wknd rapidly* 3/1[2]

1m 25.9s (-0.10) **Going Correction** +0.10s/f (Slow) 6 Ran SP% 112.7
Speed ratings (Par 101): **104,100,93,91,88 80**
toteswinger: 1&2 £1.60, 1&3 £13.90, 2&3 £10.10. CSF £17.56 TOTE £14.80: £5.00, £1.20; EX 32.40.Ryedale Ovation was claimed by G. L. Moore for £5,000.
Owner Martin Hill **Bred** Hascombe And Valiant Studs **Trained** Littlehempston, Devon

FOCUS
A surprising result to what looked a match between the two market leaders, but there did not appear to be any fluke about it. The winner is rated an improver but the form is hardly solid.
Ryedale Ovation(IRE) Official explanation: trainer said, regarding the apparent improvement in form, that the gelding appeared to be better suited by the polytrack surface than the fibresand, and appears to run best at Kempton Park.
Ravi River(IRE) Official explanation: jockey said gelding lost a front shoe

1066 DIGIBET MAIDEN FILLIES' STKS 7f (P)
7:20 (7:21) (Class 5) 3-Y-0+ £2,590 (£770; £385; £192) Stalls High

Form RPR
2- **1** **Respite**[264] 3923 3-8-12 0 MichaelHills 2 67+
(W J Haggas) *wl plcd on outer: prog to ld wl over 1f out: sn shkn up: clr ins fnl f: pushed out* 4/7[1]
54- **2** ¾ **Tikka Masala (IRE)**[149] 7168 3-8-12 0 (t) RichardKingscote 9 65+
(Tom Dascombe) *plld hrd: hld up towards rr: pushed along 3f out: reminder over 1f out: plld out and prog sn after: r.o to take 2nd last 75yds: clsng on wnr fin* 16/1
3 1 **Arrivederla (IRE)** 3-8-12 0 JamesDoyle 13 63+
(H J L Dunlop) *hld up in midfield: prog towards inner 2f out: rdn to go 2nd briefly ins fnl f: kpt on* 20/1
300- **4** hd **Sweet Possession (USA)**[185] 6305 3-8-12 74 RichardMullen 6 62
(A P Jarvis) *wnt lft s: t.k.h: hld up in midfield: prog 2f out: chsd ldrs ent fnl f: kpt on* 14/1
00- **5** ¾ **Taste Of Honey (IRE)**[160] 6933 3-8-12 0 MartinDwyer 3 60
(D W P Arbuthnot) *led to wl over 1f out: fdd and lost 3 pls fnl 100yds* 66/1
60- **6** 1 **Novastasia (IRE)**[125] 7458 3-8-12 0 RyanMoore 14 57
(W R Swinburn) *prom: effrt on inner over 2f out: cl enough over 1f out: fdd ins fnl f* 12/1
5 **7** ¾ **Zars Gold (IRE)**[14] 861 4-9-12 62 JimCrowley 11 60
(J Gallagher) *stdd s: t.k.h: hld up in midfield: effrt on inner over 2f out: reminders and hanging jst over 1f out: one pce* 10/1[3]
0- **8** ½ **Breach Of Peace (USA)**[242] 4643 3-8-12 0 SteveDrowne 7 54
(R Charlton) *fractious in preliminaries: pressed ldr: chal over 2f out: nt qckn and lost pl wl over 1f out: fdd* 6/1[2]
3 **9** 3 **Love In The Park**[13] 881 4-9-9 0 DavidProbert(3) 5 51
(R Brotherton) *carried lft s: towards rr: rapid prog on outer 4f out to press ldrs 3f out: wknd over 1f out* 50/1
0- **10** hd **Yughanni**[162] 6885 3-8-12 0 NCallan 4 45
(C E Brittain) *carried lft s: plld hrd: hld up: shkn up and no prog fr midfield over 2f out* 20/1
0- **11** 3 ¾ **Bari Bay**[162] 6877 3-8-12 0 SebSanders 10 35
(R M Beckett) *dwlt: a in last pair: struggling over 2f out* 33/1
56 **12** ½ **Songful (IRE)**[7] 949 3-8-12 0 PaulEddery 1 34
(Pat Eddery) *hld up in last pair: shuffled along and no prog over 2f out* 66/1

1m 28.41s (2.41) **Going Correction** +0.10s/f (Slow)
WFA 3 from 4yo 14lb 12 Ran SP% 124.7
Speed ratings (Par 100): **90,89,88,87,86 85,84,84,80,80 76,75**
toteswinger: 1&2 £4.60, 1&3 £10.00, 2&3 £18.70. CSF £12.12 TOTE £1.50: £1.10, £3.00, £4.90; EX 13.10.
Owner Cheveley Park Stud **Bred** Cheveley Park Stud Ltd **Trained** Newmarket, Suffolk
■ Stewards' Enquiry : Paul Eddery caution: used whip when out of contention

FOCUS
A fair fillies' maiden, run at an average pace. The first three can improve on this but the seventh sets the standard.

1067 DIGIBET.COM H'CAP (LONDON MILE QUALIFIER) 1m (P)
7:50 (7:50) (Class 4) (0-80,77) 4-Y-0+ £4,727 (£1,406; £702; £351) Stalls High

Form RPR
5P-6 **1** **Marajaa (IRE)**[13] 878 7-8-13 72 ChrisCatlin 2 82+
(W J Musson) *hld up in last: stl there 2f out: prog to go 3rd ent fnl f: urged along and r.o wl to ld last 50yds* 7/1
1522 **2** ¾ **Pegasus Again (USA)**[16] 850 4-9-4 77 (p) RobertHavlin 4 85
(T G Mills) *trckd ldr: effrt to ld over 1f out: rdn and styd on fnl f: hdd last 50yds* 7/2[2]
00-2 **3** ½ **Cross The Line (IRE)**[13] 878 7-8-12 71 RyanMoore 6 78
(A P Jarvis) *trckd ldng trio: effrt on inner 2f out: wnt 2nd jst over 1f out: hld by ldr ins fnl f and lost 2nd last 50yds* 5/2[1]
4-52 **4** 2 **Obezyana (USA)**[9] 932 7-8-6 72 (p) LeeNewnes(7) 1 74
(A Bailey) *racd on outer: trckd ldng pair: rdn and nt qckn over 2f out: kpt on again ins fnl f* 7/1
130- **5** 1 ½ **Thunder Gorge (USA)**[171] 6675 4-9-0 73 WilliamBuick 7 72
(Mouse Hamilton-Fairley) *sn led and t.k.h: kicked on over 3f out: hdd & wknd tamely over 1f out* 8/1
0-00 **6** ½ **Flying Squad (UAE)**[50] 490 5-9-2 75 SteveDrowne 8 73
(M F Harris) *hld up in 6th: cl enough on inner over 2f out: pushed along and grad lost grnd on ldrs* 20/1
20-5 **7** 1 ½ **Bahiano (IRE)**[11] 910 8-9-1 74 (p) NCallan 5 68
(C E Brittain) *settled in 5th: rdn 3f out: no real prog: wl hld whn nt clr run ins fnl f* 9/2[3]
2150 **8** 3 **Hallingdal (UAE)**[14] 866 4-9-3 76 JamesDoyle 3 63
(Ms J S Doyle) *dwlt: t.k.h: hld up in 7th: rdn on outer over 2f out: fnd nil and btn after* 14/1

1m 40.04s (0.24) **Going Correction** +0.10s/f (Slow) 8 Ran SP% 116.5
Speed ratings (Par 105): **102,101,100,98,97 96,95,92**
toteswinger: 1&2 £5.20, 1&3 £5.00, 2&3 £3.80. CSF £32.37 CT £79.69 TOTE £7.50: £2.80, £1.60, £1.10; EX 43.90.
Owner John D Jacques **Bred** Shadwell Estate Company Limited **Trained** Newmarket, Suffolk

FOCUS
This was a very tight handicap, run at an average pace, and the form looks sound and should work out.

1068 DIGIBET CASINO H'CAP 6f (P)
8:20 (8:22) (Class 4) (0-80,79) 3-Y-O £4,727 (£1,406; £702; £351) Stalls High

Form RPR
320- **1** **Ray Of Joy**[119] 7538 3-9-0 75 JimmyQuinn 11 84
(J R Jenkins) *sn wl plcd on inner: prog to go 2nd bhd clr ldr over 1f out: readily clsd and led last 100yds: won gng away* 12/1
5463 **2** 1 ¾ **Cecily**[20] 814 3-9-2 77 SebSanders 8 80
(Sir Mark Prescott) *led at decent pce: booted at least 3l clr 2f out: collared last 100yds* 16/1
110- **3** 3 **Happy Forever (FR)**[152] 7107 3-9-1 76 JohnEgan 9 69
(M Botti) *in midfield: rdn and effrt over 2f out: styd on fr over 1f out to take 3rd ins fnl f: n.d* 4/1[1]
110- **4** 2 ½ **Athania (IRE)**[179] 6477 3-9-1 76 NCallan 10 61
(A P Jarvis) *prom: rdn to go 2nd over 2f out to over 1f out: no imp on ldr and fdd fnl f* 11/1
422- **5** 3 **Ben's Dream (IRE)**[163] 6865 3-8-11 72 WilliamBuick 7 48
(A M Balding) *wl plcd bhd ldrs: rdn over 2f out: fnd nil* 5/1[3]
221 **6** 1 ½ **Princess Cagliari**[22] 797 3-8-12 73 RyanMoore 6 44
(R Hannon) *wl off the pce towards rr: modest prog fnl 2f: no ch* 5/1[3]
21 **7** hd **Dontuwishitwereso**[13] 881 3-8-4 70 Louis-PhilippeBeuzelin(5) 2 40+
(P W D'Arcy) *dwlt: wl bhd in last: styd on fnl 2f: nvr a factor: sddle slipped* 7/1
610- **8** 3 ¼ **Mary Mason**[198] 5969 3-8-13 74 ChrisCatlin 5 34
(M Hill) *racd freely: pressed ldr to 1/2-way: wknd over 2f out* 20/1
1- **9** 1 ¼ **Creshendo**[306] 2562 3-9-2 77 GeorgeBaker 3 33
(R M Beckett) *carried lft s: a in last trio and wl off the pce: nvr a factor* 12/1
340- **10** 4 **Count Paris (USA)**[144] 7241 3-9-0 75 JoeFanning 4 18
(M Johnston) *wnt lft s: nvr beyond midfield: rdn and struggling wl over 2f out: wknd* 9/2[2]
-134 **11** 3 ¾ **Comadoir (IRE)**[33] 709 3-9-4 79 FergusSweeney 1 10
(Miss Jo Crowley) *racd wd: nvr beyond midfield: struggling over 2f out: sn bhd* 25/1

1m 12.01s (-1.09) **Going Correction** +0.10s/f (Slow) 11 Ran SP% 122.2
Speed ratings (Par 100): **111,108,104,101,97 95,95,90,89,83 78**
toteswinger: 1&2 £24.30, 1&3 £9.70, 2&3 £16.90. CSF £195.53 CT £693.85 TOTE £11.40: £3.30, £5.90, £1.50; EX 80.40.
Owner Robin Stevens **Bred** D R Tucker **Trained** Royston, Herts

FOCUS
A modest three-year-old sprint handicap in which it paid to be drawn high. The runner-up is the best guide to the level.
Dontuwishitwereso Official explanation: jockey said saddle slipped

1069 MIX BUSINESS WITH PLEASURE H'CAP 2m (P)
8:50 (8:52) (Class 5) (0-75,75) 4-Y-0+ £2,590 (£770; £385; £192) Stalls High

Form RPR
/422 **1** **Kavaloti (IRE)**[41] 459 5-9-8 72 (b) RyanMoore 5 82
(G L Moore) *settled in 6th: prog 3f out to trck ldrs over 2f out: rdn to ld over 1f out: drvn clr fnl f* 13/8[1]

2213 **2** *2* **Augustus John (IRE)**[15] 860 6-9-6 **70** .... TomEaves 8 78+
(R Brotherton) *hld up in last pair: smooth prog 3f out to be cl up 2f out: urged along to go 2nd ent fnl f: limited rspnse and no imp on wnr* **8/1**

320- **3** *3* **Rose Bien**[245] 4516 7-8-7 **57** .... (p) EdwardCreighton 3 61
(P J McBride) *hld up in 5th: rdn over 3f out: prog to dispute 2nd over 2f out: nt qckn after: kpt on to take 3rd ins fnl f* **20/1**

6421 **4** *1 1/4* **Irish Ballad**[30] 732 7-8-9 **59** .... NickyMackay 6 62
(S Dow) *pressed ldr: led over 4f out: kicked on over 3f out: hdd & wknd over 1f out* **3/1**[2]

/3-2 **5** *3 3/4* **Mexican Pete**[19] 835 9-9-4 **75** .... MatthewDavies(7) 4 73
(A King) *hld up in 7th: rdn and no prog wl over 2f out: n.d after* **5/1**[3]

-145 **6** *nk* **Little Carmela**[34] 692 5-9-1 **65** .... SaleemGolam 1 63
(S C Williams) *trckd ldng pair: rdn to dispute 2nd over 3f out to 2f out: wknd* **12/1**

30/5 **7** *4* **Eastwell Smiles**[39] 631 5-8-12 **62** .... SteveDrowne 9 55
(R T Phillips) *trckd ldng pair: rdn to dispute 2nd over 3f out to 2f out: wknd: eased fnl f* **10/1**

0-54 **8** *12* **Cash On (IRE)**[12] 894 7-8-11 **61** .... (p) DarryllHolland 7 39
(Karen George) *rel to r and sharp reminders after s: in tch in last tl gave up 3f out* **16/1**

6/00 **9** *29* **Dream Mountain**[13] 877 6-8-1 **56** oh11 .... (v[1]) SophieDoyle(5) 2 —
(Ms J S Doyle) *led to over 4f out: wknd rapidly 3f out: sn t.o* **50/1**

3m 31.29s (1.19) **Going Correction** +0.10s/f (Slow) **9** Ran SP% **120.3**
Speed ratings (Par 103): **101,100,98,97,96 95,93,87,73**
toteswinger: 1&2 £2.90, 1&3 £9.60, 2&3 £11.00. CSF £16.71 CT £200.14 TOTE £2.80: £1.10, £2.80, £3.70; EX 15.20.
Owner Graham Gillespie **Bred** Mme Henri Devin **Trained** Lower Beeding, W Sussex

FOCUS
This was run at a routine pace and the second is a little better than the bare result. The form looks sound enough rated around the winner and third.
Cash On(IRE) Official explanation: jockey said gelding was reluctant to race

1070 DAY TIME, NIGHT TIME, GREAT TIME H'CAP 1m 4f (P)
9:20 (9:23) (Class 6) (0-60,60) 3-Y-O **£2,047** (£604; £302) **Stalls** Centre

Form RPR

-424 **1** **Good Buy Dubai (USA)**[7] 953 3-9-3 **59** .... RobertWinston 4 63+
(J R Best) *rn in snatches in 6th: prog to go 3rd 3f out: rdn to ld jst over 2f out: looked in command but idled in front: jst hld on* **11/4**[1]

-006 **2** *nk* **Wahan (USA)**[7] 953 3-8-13 **55** .... (t) RyanMoore 11 58+
(C E Brittain) *settled in last: rdn 3f out: taken to wd outside and rapid prog over 1f out: str run fnl f to take 2nd nr fin: jst failed to catch wnr* **9/1**

0450 **3** *3/4* **Alittlemoreflair**[7] 953 3-9-4 **60** .... JimmyQuinn 12 62
(J Pearce) *trckd ldng trio: rdn over 2f out: kpt on to take 2nd 1f out: grad clsd on wnr but lost 2nd nr fin* **25/1**

0405 **4** *2* **Screaming Brave**[7] 953 3-8-13 **55** .... (v) SamHitchcott 7 54
(M R Channon) *tended to run in snatches and drvn early: gng bttr 4f out whn effrt: nt clr run briefly 3f out and over 2f out: prog over 1f out: kpt on* **16/1**

000- **5** *3/4* **Sparkaway**[143] 7258 3-8-6 **48** .... ChrisCatlin 13 46
(W J Musson) *settled in last trio: reminders 1/2-way: struggling 3f out: prog u.p 2f out: kpt on: nt pce to threaten* **7/1**

430- **6** *1 3/4* **Extremely So**[200] 5914 3-9-2 **58** .... DaneO'Neill 5 53
(P J McBride) *trckd ldng pair to 3f out: rdn and nt qckn over 2f out: plugged on same pce* **14/1**

0533 **7** *hd* **Spring Quartet**[7] 953 3-8-11 **53** .... (v) PaulEddery 2 48
(Pat Eddery) *disp ld tl def advantage wl over 2f out: hdd jst over 2f out: wknd jst over 1f out* **8/1**

5040 **8** *nk* **Fleur De'Lion (IRE)**[7] 953 3-8-1 **46** oh1 .... DavidProbert(3) 14 40
(S Kirk) *wl enough plcd on inner: rdn over 2f out: no imp: fdd fnl f* **20/1**

040- **9** *6* **Romantic Interlude (IRE)**[171] 6682 3-9-4 **60** .... NCallan 9 45
(A P Jarvis) *hld up in abt 8th on inner: brief effrt over 2f out: eased whn btn over 1f out* **25/1**

600- **10** *2 1/4* **Strictly Royal**[260] 4063 3-8-4 **46** oh1 .... CatherineGannon 1 27
(M R Channon) *a in last trio: struggling 3f out* **50/1**

00-2 **11** *3 1/2* **Mekong Miss**[7] 953 3-9-3 **59** .... LukeMorris 3 34
(J Jay) *hld up in abt 7th: rdn 3f out: no prog: wknd 2f out* **9/2**[2]

-441 **12** *6* **Kochanski (IRE)**[35] 677 3-9-3 **59** .... JoeFanning 6 25
(M Johnston) *disp ld to wl over 2f out: wknd rapidly: t.o* **11/2**[3]

2m 36.28s (1.78) **Going Correction** +0.10s/f (Slow) **12** Ran SP% **120.8**
Speed ratings (Par 96): **98,97,97,95,95 94,94,93,89,88 86,82**
toteswinger: 1&2 £4.70, 1&3 £13.70, 2&3 £37.80. CSF £27.68 CT £528.06 TOTE £4.70: £1.80, £2.90, £11.10; EX 37.20 Place 6 £28.35, Place 5 £19.20. .
Owner John Keaty **Bred** Harold J Plumley **Trained** Hucking, Kent

FOCUS
A weak handicap, run at a fair pace but the form looks solid enough.
Mekong Miss Official explanation: jockey said filly ran flat
T/Plt: £21.90 to a £1 stake. Pool: £78,998.89. 2,631.53 winning tickets. T/Qpdt: £10.70 to a £1 stake. Pool: £6,970.28. 480.20 winning tickets. JN

1030 LINGFIELD (L-H)
Wednesday, April 1

OFFICIAL GOING: Standard
Wind: virtually nil Weather: bright, partly cloudy

1071 SPRING FAMILY FUN DAY THIS SATURDAY MAIDEN STKS 7f (P)
2:30 (2:30) (Class 5) 3-Y-O **£2,729** (£806; £403) **Stalls** Low

Form RPR

62- **1** **Secret Society**[237] 4778 3-9-3 0 .... TPQueally 5 85+
(M L W Bell) *hld up in tch: chsd ldr over 4f out: ev ch 2f out: hung lft u.p over 1f out: drvn fnl f: led last stride* **9/2**[2]

33- **2** *shd* **Shabib (USA)**[174] 6601 3-9-3 0 .... RHills 4 84+
(B W Hills) *led: rdn over 1f out: kpt on tl hdd last stride* **4/11**[1]

4 **3** *4* **Danies Boy (IRE)**[7] 951 3-9-3 0 .... RyanMoore 1 69
(R Hannon) *t.k.h: chsd ldr tl over 4f out: swtchd rt and rdn over 1f out: one pce after* **5/1**[3]

00- **4** *9* **Bright Wire (IRE)**[209] 5649 3-9-3 0 .... RobertHavlin 2 45
(M Madgwick) *dwlt: sn bustled along: in tch tl wknd u.p jst over 2f out* **100/1**

1m 25.04s (0.24) **Going Correction** +0.075s/f (Slow) **4** Ran SP% **109.2**
Speed ratings (Par 98): **101,100,96,86**
toteswinger: 1&2 £2.90. CSF £6.87 TOTE £5.50; EX 8.90.
Owner Sheikh Marwan Al Maktoum **Bred** Darley **Trained** Newmarket, Suffolk

FOCUS
Only four runners but not a bad maiden with the first three pretty much to their marks.

1072 INTERNATIONAL TRIAL THIS SATURDAY (S) STKS 6f (P)
3:00 (3:01) (Class 6) 3-Y-0+ **£2,047** (£604; £302) **Stalls** Low

Form RPR

1201 **1** **Speak The Truth (IRE)**[7] 955 3-9-1 67 .... (p) PatCosgrave 7 57
(J R Boyle) *awkward s: sn rcvrd and chsd ldrs: rdn 2f out: drvn to ld ins fnl f: hld on cl home: all out* **4/1**[2]

6065 **2** *hd* **Joss Stick**[9] 937 4-9-8 62 .... (p) ChrisCatlin 1 54
(R A Harris) *stdd s: plld v hrd: hld up in last pl: hdwy 1f out: str chal wl ins fnl f: no ex nr fin* **16/1**

266- **3** *nk* **Mannello**[225] 5166 6-9-3 52 .... (p) RichardThomas 2 48
(S W Hall) *hld up in last pair: hdwy on outer bnd 2f out: styd on u.p to press ldrs ins fnl f: one pce towards fin* **40/1**

0064 **4** *nk* **Easy Wonder (GER)**[8] 946 4-9-3 44 .... (b) NCallan 4 47
(I A Wood) *chsd ldrs: rdn 2f out: kpt on u.p to press ldrs ins fnl f: edgd lft and one pce nr fin* **33/1**

1132 **5** *1 1/4* **Don Pele (IRE)**[13] 882 7-9-13 72 .... (p) JoeFanning 3 53+
(R A Harris) *trckd ldrs on inner: short of room briefly over 1f out: rdn and effrt jst over 1f out: one pce fnl f* **4/6**[1]

-404 **6** *nse* **Young Ivanhoe**[10] 921 4-9-8 44 .... (e) DarryllHolland 5 48
(C A Dwyer) *led: rdn over 1f out: hdd ins fnl f: btn whn short of room towards fin* **10/1**

65-0 **7** *5* **Non Sucre (USA)**[14] 866 4-9-8 69 .... (b) JimCrowley 6 32
(J Gallagher) *t.k.h: chsd ldr: rdn 2f out: wknd jst ins fnl f* **8/1**[3]

1m 13.31s (1.41) **Going Correction** +0.075s/f (Slow)
WFA 3 from 4yo+ 12lb **7** Ran SP% **111.5**
Speed ratings (Par 101): **93,92,92,91,90 90,83**
toteswinger: 1&2 £7.10, 1&3 £20.90, 2&3 £19.50 CSF £57.86 TOTE £3.40: £1.60, £5.40; EX 51.00.There was no bid for the winner. Don Pele was claimed by Jeff Pearce for £6,000.
Owner John Hopkins (t/a South Hatch Racing) **Bred** Gerard Mulligan **Trained** Epsom, Surrey

FOCUS
A competitive seller but the proximity of the fourth and sixth suggests the principals were below form.

1073 LINGFIELD PARK DERBY TRIAL MAY 9TH H'CAP 1m 4f (P)
3:30 (3:30) (Class 5) (0-75,74) 4-Y-0+ **£2,900** (£856; £428) **Stalls** Low

Form RPR

1 **Manshoor (IRE)**[32] 4-9-0 **70** .... WilliamBuick 8 79
(Mrs L Wadham) *trckd ldrs: n.m.r fr jst over 2f out: drvn and squeezed between horses jst ins fnl f: led fnl 100yds: r.o strly* **16/1**

1021 **2** *2* **Sunset Boulevard (IRE)**[18] 838 6-8-7 **62** .... ChrisCatlin 3 68
(Miss Tor Sturgis) *hld up wl in tch: effrt and rdn over 1f out: ev ch ins fnl f: nt pce of wnr fnl 100yds* **10/3**[1]

4644 **3** *1/2* **Hucking Hero (IRE)**[7] 950 4-8-12 **71** .... MarcHalford(3) 9 76
(J R Best) *stdd s and dropped in bhd: hdwy on outer over 3f out: jnd ldrs over 2f out: led narrowly wl over 1f out: hdd fnl 100yds: one pce* **6/1**

0336 **4** *3* **Apache Fort**[12] 894 6-9-0 **69** .... (bt) RHills 5 69
(T Keddy) *s.i.s: hld up in rr: edgd out rt over 1f out: styd on fnl f: nvr pce to threaten ldrs* **5/1**[3]

3014 **5** *nk* **Wind Flow**[25] 787 5-9-5 **74** .... (b) CatherineGannon 7 74
(C A Dwyer) *led: jnd over 2f out: rdn ent fnl 2f: hdd wl over 1f out: wknd jst ins fnl f* **9/2**[2]

2113 **6** *1* **General Feeling (IRE)**[14] 873 8-9-2 **71** .... MartinDwyer 2 69
(S T Mason) *in tch: rdn jst over 2f out: wknd ent fnl f* **11/2**

00-3 **7** *3/4* **Fielder (IRE)**[52] 455 4-8-11 **67** .... JimCrowley 1 64
(J G Portman) *chsd ldr: ev ch and rdn jst over 2f out: wkng whn hmpd and snatched up jst ins fnl f* **14/1**

130- **8** *1 3/4* **Contrada**[170] 6703 4-8-6 **62** .... JimmyQuinn 6 56
(J A B Old) *hld up in last trio: pushed along 4f out: rdn over 1f out: no rspnse and wl hld fnl f* **8/1**

2m 35.66s (2.66) **Going Correction** +0.075s/f (Slow)
WFA 4 from 5yo+ 1lb **8** Ran SP% **111.3**
Speed ratings (Par 103): **94,92,92,90,90 89,88,87**
toteswinger: 1&2 £11.80, 1&3 £19.40, 2&3 £5.20 CSF £65.19 CT £353.69 TOTE £18.70: £4.70, £1.40, £2.60; EX 76.20 TRIFECTA Not won..
Owner Tim Wood **Bred** Liberty Road Stables **Trained** Newmarket, Suffolk
■ Stewards' Enquiry : William Buick three-day ban: careless riding (Apr 15-17)

FOCUS
A modest handicap rated around the placed horses. As usual for Lingfield, there was no real pace on for most of the way.
Fielder(IRE) Official explanation: jockey said gelding hung right

1074 ANN & BILL DUNSTAN H'CAP 7f (P)
4:00 (4:01) (Class 6) (0-60,60) 4-Y-0+ **£2,047** (£604; £302) **Stalls** Low

Form RPR

0214 **1** **Suhayl Star (IRE)**[14] 874 5-9-0 **56** .... LukeMorris 13 65
(P Burgoyne) *trckd ldng pair: wnt 2nd 2f out: chal jst ins fnl f: racd awkwardly and looked reluctant tl drvn ahd wl ins fnl f* **10/1**

40-6 **2** *3/4* **Seneschal**[7] 959 8-9-4 **60** .... TPQueally 10 67
(A B Haynes) *sn chsng ldr: led over 4f out: rdn over 1f out: jnd ins fnl f: hdd and no ex wl ins fnl f* **13/2**[3]

5212 **3** *1* **Melt (IRE)**[8] 945 4-9-1 **57** .... (b) RyanMoore 8 65+
(R Hannon) *bhd in last trio: hdwy over 1f out: nt clr run and swtchd rt jst ins fnl f: r.o but nvr gng to rch ldng pair* **6/4**[1]

140- **4** *3/4* **Zeffirelli**[142] 7270 4-9-1 **57** .... MartinDwyer 5 59
(M Quinn) *chsd ldrs: rdn over 2f out: chsd ldng pair and edgd lft jst ins fnl f: kpt on but nt pce to rch ldrs* **16/1**

-010 **5** *1/2* **Silidan**[14] 874 6-8-12 **54** .... ShaneKelly 9 55
(G L Moore) *stdd after s: hld up in rr: stl last over 1f out: rdn and hdwy fnl f: r.o: nt rch ldrs* **25/1**

-006 **6** *3/4* **Annes Rocket (IRE)**[14] 874 4-8-9 **51** .... ChrisCatlin 2 50
(J C Fox) *v.s.a: bhd: hdwy wl over 1f out: edgd lft u.p 1f out: kpt on but nvr pce to rch ldrs* **14/1**

2-04 **7** *nk* **Comrade Cotton**[7] 961 5-8-13 **55** .... (p) KirstyMilczarek 11 53
(J Ryan) *sn niggled along towards rr: nt clr run briefly wl over 1f out: styd on fnl f: nvr rchd ldrs* **9/2**[2]

504- **8** *1* **Another Try (IRE)**[119] 7536 4-9-3 **59** .... SebSanders 1 54+
(A P Jarvis) *t.k.h: hld up in midfield: rdn and no imp over 2f out: plugged on same pce after* **8/1**

500- **9** *3/4* **Seasonal Cross**[183] 6357 4-9-2 **58** .... JohnEgan 7 51
(S Dow) *a towards rr: nvr trbld ldrs* **10/1**

0354 **10** *1 3/4* **Wusuul**[16] 849 4-9-2 **58** .... (b) JoeFanning 14 47
(R A Harris) *v.s.a: hdwy into midfield over 4f out: rdn over 2f out: wknd wl over 1f out* **16/1**

0-05 **11** 3/4 **Little Knickers**[8] 945 4-8-13 **55**............................(b) EdwardCreighton 6 42
(E J Creighton) *sn led: hdd over 4f out: chsd ldr tl 2f out: sn wknd* **25/1**

600- **12** 1 1/4 **Rough Rock (IRE)**[110] 7648 4-8-10 **52**...................... CatherineGannon 3 35
(C A Dwyer) *broke wl: sn hdd: chsd ldrs: rdn over 3f out: wknd 2f out* **66/1**

1m 24.72s (-0.08) **Going Correction** +0.075s/f (Slow) **12** Ran SP% **128.4**
Speed ratings (Par 101): **103,102,101,100,99 98,98,97,96,94 93,92**
toteswinger: 1&2 £9.50, 1&3 £4.80, 2&3 £4.30 CSF £78.81 CT £158.10 TOTE £11.10: £3.10, £1.80, £1.50; EX 63.30 Trifecta £108.10 Pool: £344.89 - 2.36 winning units..
Owner Mrs C Leigh-Turner **Bred** John Mulhern **Trained** Shepton Montague, Somerset
■ Stewards' Enquiry : Kirsty Milczarek one-day ban: careless riding (Apr 15)
Ryan Moore caution: careless riding

FOCUS
A moderate but competitive handicap and the form looks sound. It paid to race handy.

1075 JOHN EBDON MEMORIAL H'CAP 7f (P)
4:30 (4:32) (Class 5) (0-70,70) 3-Y-O £2,900 (£856; £428) Stalls Low

Form RPR

51-1 **1** **Mr Willis**[7] 960 3-9-4 **70** 6ex.. SteveDrowne 6 79+
(J R Best) *hld up in tch: effrt on outer bnd 2f out: drvn to chal ins fnl f: pushed into ld on post* **15/8**[2]

5-1 **2** nse **Fantastic Dubai (USA)**[28] 752 3-9-1 **67**..................... DarryllHolland 3 76+
(M R Channon) *t.k.h: hld up in tch: plld out and chal jst over 1f out: edgd lft but rdn to ld ins fnl furlng: sn hrd pressed: hdd on post* **11/10**[1]

300- **3** 1 1/2 **Cheam Forever (USA)**[152] 7104 3-8-12 **64**.............. RichardKingscote 4 69
(R Charlton) *taken down early: led: rdn and kicked 2l clr 2f out: hrd pressed 1f out: hdd ins fnl f: no ex* **20/1**

610- **4** 4 **Global**[112] 7623 3-9-4 **70**.. RyanMoore 9 64
(R Hannon) *chsd ldrs on outer: rdn 2f out: outpcd ent fnl f: no ch w ldrs after* **8/1**[3]

400- **5** hd **Protiva**[114] 7607 3-8-8 **60**... RichardMullen 10 53
(A P Jarvis) *a towards rr: niggled along 4f out: rdn jst over 2f out: nvr pce to trble ldrs* **66/1**

505- **6** 1/2 **Spit And Polish**[168] 6732 3-9-2 **68**................................... EddieAhern 2 60
(J L Dunlop) *trckd ldrs: wnt 2nd 2f out: rdn and fnd little over 1f out: wknd jst over 1f out* **33/1**

046- **7** 1 1/4 **Deyas Dream**[139] 7306 3-8-13 **68**.................................. DavidProbert(3) 5 57
(A M Balding) *hld up towards rr: nvr trbld ldrs* **25/1**

3022 **8** 1 1/4 **Villaruz (IRE)**[12] 900 3-8-8 **60**..................................... RobertWinston 7 45
(D Flood) *taken down early: chsd ldr tl 2f out: sn wknd* **16/1**

504 **9** 1 1/2 **Lyrical Intent**[41] 599 3-8-11 **63**.. JimmyQuinn 8 44
(P Howling) *s.i.s: a bhd* **66/1**

1m 24.89s (0.09) **Going Correction** +0.075s/f (Slow) **9** Ran SP% **113.9**
Speed ratings (Par 98): **102,101,100,95,95 94,93,92,90**
toteswinger: 1&2 £1.50, 1&3 £7.70, 2&3 £6.60 CSF £3.95 CT £23.39 TOTE £3.00: £1.30, £1.10, £4.30; EX 4.50 Trifecta £50.60 Pool: £603.58 - 8.82 winning units..
Owner Miss Sara Furnival **Bred** John Best **Trained** Hucking, Kent

FOCUS
A fair three-year-old handicap for the grade and the winner looks progressive.
Lyrical Intent Official explanation: jockey said gelding was slowly into stride

1076 ASHURST WOOD H'CAP 6f (P)
5:00 (5:01) (Class 6) (0-60,63) 4-Y-O+ £2,047 (£604; £302) Stalls Low

Form RPR

0041 **1** **Mr Skipiton (IRE)**[16] 854 4-8-12 **54**............................ StephenCarson 7 65
(B J McMath) *hld up in tch: hdwy over 2f out: drvn: edgd lft and ev ch ent fnl f: kpt on to ld towards fin* **7/1**

3-41 **2** 1/2 **Waterloo Dock**[42] 592 4-9-3 **59**.. MartinDwyer 6 68
(M Quinn) *chsd ldrs: wnt 2nd over 3f out: rdn to ld over 1f out: hung lft u.p 1f out: kpt on tl hdd and no ex towards fin* **5/1**[2]

-430 **3** hd **Simpsons Gamble (IRE)**[65] 294 6-8-9 **58**.........(p) MatthewDavies(7) 9 66
(R A Teal) *hld up in midfield: hdwy 3f out: rdn and effrt wl over 1f out: pressed ldrs wl ins fnl f: kpt on same pce towards fin* **8/1**

340- **4** 1 1/4 **Truly Divine**[166] 6773 4-9-2 **58**.................................. DarryllHolland 5 62
(C A Dwyer) *awkward s and s.i.s: hld up in rr: hdwy jst over 2f out: swtchd rt over 1f out: hanging lft and hld hd high fr jst over 1f out: styd on u.p: nt rch ldrs* **7/1**

-662 **5** 1/2 **Bateleur**[8] 946 5-8-3 **50**..(v) MCGeran(5) 10 57+
(M R Channon) *stdd after s: hld up in midfield: hdwy to chse ldrs 2f out: nt clr run fr over 1f out: hmpd and snatched up jst ins fnl f: kpt on: nvr able to chal* **9/2**[1]

-503 **6** 1 1/2 **Bollin Franny**[8] 946 5-8-9 **51**.................................(p) RichardThomas 8 52+
(J E Long) *led: rdn and hdd over 1f out: keeping on same pce whn bdly hmpd and snatched up jst ins fnl f: btn after: eased towards fin* **11/2**[3]

0500 **7** 1 1/2 **Lake Sabina**[16] 854 4-8-6 **48**.. JimmyQuinn 3 41
(M R Hoad) *a in rr: reminders 3f out: styd on past btn horses ins fnl f: nvr trbld ldrs* **16/1**

50-0 **8** 1 **Towy Boy (IRE)**[21] 799 4-9-4 **60**.. NCallan 1 50+
(I A Wood) *in tch: effrt to chse ldrs 2f out: nt clr run fr over 1f out: bdly hmpd and snatched up jst ins fnl f: nt rcvr and eased after* **7/1**

5045 **9** 1 1/2 **Titus Gent**[12] 895 4-7-13 **48**...................................... RyanPowell(7) 4 33+
(J Ryan) *chsd ldr tl over 3f out: rdn 2f out: btn whn hmpd jst ins fnl f: eased after* **12/1**

-010 **10** 10 **Ramblin Bob**[16] 854 4-8-7 **49**.......................................(t) ChrisCatlin 12 2
(W J Musson) *nvr gng wl in rr: lost tch over 2f out* **16/1**

1m 12.11s (0.21) **Going Correction** +0.075s/f (Slow) **10** Ran SP% **118.3**
Speed ratings (Par 101): **101,100,100,98,97 95,93,92,90,77**
toteswinger: 1&2 £6.60, 1&3 £14.90, 2&3 £8.30. CSF £42.59 CT £290.77 TOTE £10.50: £3.00, £1.60, £2.90; EX 26.00 Trifecta £222.60 Part won. Pool: £300.82 - 0.50 winning units. Place 6: £294.56, Place 5: £47.09..
Owner Steve & Ros Chaplin-Brown **Bred** Darragh O'Reilly **Trained** Newmarket, Suffolk
■ Stewards' Enquiry : Stephen Carson three-day ban: careless riding (Apr 15-17)

FOCUS
A moderate sprint handicap, and the sort of messy race we've come to expect on the Lingfield Polytrack, with plenty of trouble in-running around a furlong out. The form is a bit messy but the winner is rated as having improved on previous effort.
Waterloo Dock Official explanation: jockey said gelding hung left
T/Plt: £76.50 to a £1 stake. Pool: £60,491.25. 577.22 winning tickets. T/Qpdt: £6.10 to a £1 stake. Pool: £6,217.38. 742.66 winning tickets. SP

1065 KEMPTON (A.W) (R-H)
Thursday, April 2

OFFICIAL GOING: Standard
Wind: modest, across Weather: sunny

1077 BLUE SQUARE MAIDEN STKS 5f (P)
5:25 (5:26) (Class 5) 3-5-Y-O £2,590 (£770; £385; £192) Stalls High

Form RPR

423- **1** **Yanza**[206] 5746 3-8-9 70.. ChrisCatlin 2 67
(J R Gask) *j. shadow sn after s: chsd ldr: ev ch fr wl over 1f out: drvn to ld fnl 100yds: styd on wl* **9/2**[3]

0- **2** 1/2 **Rathlin Light (USA)**[223] 5214 3-8-4 0.......... Louis-PhilippeBeuzelin(5) 5 65
(W R Swinburn) *led: rdn over 1f out: hdd and no ex fnl 100yds* **7/1**

23- **3** 1/2 **Keep Dancing (IRE)**[188] 6245 3-8-6 0.......................... DavidProbert(3) 8 63
(A M Balding) *t.k.h: chsd ldng pair: hung lft and lost grnd wl over 1f out: rallied u.p fnl f: wnt 3rd towards fin: nt rch ldrs* **15/8**[1]

4- **4** nk **Mac's Power (IRE)**[201] 5905 3-9-0 0.................................. RobertHavlin 7 67
(P J O'Gorman) *hld up in midfield: hdwy over 2f out: chsd ldng pair over 1f out: kpt on same pce ins fnl f: lost 3rd towards fin* **3/1**[2]

30- **5** 5 **Minnola**[210] 5636 4-9-6 0... SaleemGolam 4 49
(Rae Guest) *sn outpcd in last pl: lost tch 3f out: r.o wl fnl f: nvr nr ldrs* **20/1**

6 nse **Marzy** 3-8-9 0.. TPQueally 3 44
(M Botti) *awkward s: sn bustled up to chse ldrs: rdn over 2f out: wknd wl over 1f out* **14/1**

0- **7** hd **Alexander Loyalty (IRE)**[151] 7154 3-8-9 0........................ LPKeniry 6 43
(E F Vaughan) *stdd after s: sn struggling in last pair: sme modest hdwy fnl f: nvr nr ldrs* **6/1**

0 **8** 3/4 **Chenin (IRE)**[19] 842 3-8-2 0................................ AndrewHeffernan(7) 9 41
(Peter Grayson) *s.i.s: in tch: effrt on inner wl over 1f out: sn wknd* **33/1**

60.60 secs (0.10) **Going Correction** -0.025s/f (Stan)
WFA 3 from 4yo 11lb **8** Ran SP% **119.1**
Speed ratings (Par 103): **98,97,96,95,87 87,87,86**
toteswinger: 1&2 £4.70, 1&3 £1.40, 2&3 £4.80 CSF £37.34 TOTE £3.60: £1.30, £2.90, £1.20; EX 26.60.
Owner Horses First Racing Limited **Bred** Jeremy Green And Sons **Trained** Sutton Veny, Wilts

FOCUS
Little strength in depth for an ordinary race in which all bar one were fillies. The gallop was sound and it was an advantage to race up with the pace. The winner and runner-up raced on, or just off the inside rail throughout.
Keep Dancing(IRE) Official explanation: jockey said filly hung left

1078 BLUE SQUARE POKER H'CAP 5f (P)
5:55 (5:55) (Class 4) (0-85,85) 3-Y-O £5,459 (£1,612; £806) Stalls High

Form RPR

303- **1** **Fault**[178] 6540 3-9-4 **85**..(t) MickyFenton 8 91
(Stef Liddiard) *mde all: rdn over 1f out: styd on gamely fnl f and a holding runner up fnl 100yds* **11/1**

1- **2** 1/2 **Affluent**[155] 7082 3-8-10 **77**.. SteveDrowne 6 81
(R Charlton) *s.i.s: t.k.h: hld up towards rr: hdwy wl over 1f out: chal jst ins fnl f: rdn and unable qck fnl 100yds* **15/8**[1]

0-44 **3** 1 3/4 **Mazzola**[21] 814 3-8-9 **76**.. TonyCulhane 2 74+
(M R Channon) *broke wl: sn stdd but styd wd: bhd an dwd bnd 2f out: pushed along and hdwy over 1f out: wnt 3rd ins fnl f: nt threaten ldng pair* **16/1**

002- **4** 1/2 **Evelyn May (IRE)**[180] 6469 3-8-12 **79**.............................. WilliamBuick 4 75
(B W Hills) *stdd after s: hld up in tch: effrt and rdn over 1f out: one pce u.p fnl f* **5/1**[3]

420- **5** 3/4 **Sweet Applause (IRE)**[117] 7575 3-8-4 **76**..................... MartinLane(5) 7 70
(A P Jarvis) *chsd ldr: rdn wl over 1f out: lost 2nd jst ins fnl f: wknd fnl 100yds* **14/1**

2213 **6** 1 1/2 **Lesley's Choice**[16] 859 3-9-4 **85**.............................. FrankieMcDonald 5 73
(R Curtis) *chsd ldrs: lost pl bnd over 3f out: rdn 1/2-way: wd bnd 2f out: no hdwy after* **5/1**[3]

-605 **7** 1 1/2 **Sir Geoffrey (IRE)**[57] 396 3-8-12 **79**............................... PatCosgrave 9 62
(A J McCabe) *taken down early: awkward and s.i.s: sn pushed along and hdwy on inner to chse ldrs over 3f out: wknd u.p ent fnl f* **8/1**

500- **8** 4 1/2 **Maggie Lou (IRE)**[194] 6102 3-9-2 **83**.................................. NCallan 10 50
(K A Ryan) *s.i.s: a rdn along in rr: drvn and no prog 2f out* **9/2**[2]

59.86 secs (-0.64) **Going Correction** -0.025s/f (Stan) **8** Ran SP% **118.3**
Speed ratings (Par 100): **104,103,100,99,98 96,93,86**
toteswinger: 1&2 £5.70, 1&3 £11.30, 2&3 £4.30 CSF £33.26 CT £349.26 TOTE £22.00: £4.30, £1.20, £4.40; EX 62.60.
Owner David Gilbert **Bred** Mrs A M Vestey **Trained** Great Shefford, Berks

FOCUS
A fair handicap but, with the exception of the runner-up, this was a largely exposed field. Once again the benefit of racing up with the pace, near the inside rail over this course and distance, was well demonstrated. The pace was sound.
Maggie Lou(IRE) Official explanation: jockey said filly never travelled

1079 BLUE SQUARE CASINO CLAIMING STKS 1m (P)
6:25 (6:25) (Class 6) 4-Y-O+ £1,942 (£578; £288; £144) Stalls High

Form RPR

3313 **1** **Jake The Snake (IRE)**[14] 878 8-8-11 75......................... AmyBaker(5) 2 82
(A W Carroll) *v.s.a: clsd and in tch over 5f out: squeezed between horses and hdwy over 2f out: chsd ldr 2f out: rdn to ld ins fnl f: r.o wl* **11/4**[3]

123 **2** 3/4 **Tous Les Deux**[20] 834 6-9-4 82.. GeorgeBaker 1 83
(G L Moore) *plld hrd: hdwy to ld after 2f: rdn over 1f out: drvn and hdd ins fnl f: no ex* **9/4**[2]

2-12 **3** 2 1/4 **Fremen (USA)**[8] 958 9-9-2 84..................................... AdrianTNicholls 4 75
(D Nicholls) *hld up in tch in rr: wd and rdn bnd 3f out: nt qckn u.p jst over 2f out: kpt on same pce fnl f: wnt 3rd towards fin* **5/4**[1]

-040 **4** hd **Comrade Cotton**[1] 1074 5-7-12 55...........................(v) RyanPowell(7) 3 64
(J Ryan) *chsd ldrs: rdn and bmpd over 2f out: chsd ldng pair over 1f out: kpt on same pce fnl f: lost 3rd towards fin* **16/1**

-065 **5** 4 **Yes One (IRE)**[36] 671 5-9-1 70..(t) NCallan 6 65
(K A Ryan) *led at stdy gallop for 2f: chsd ldr after tl 2f out: wknd u.p over 1f out* **25/1**

000 **6** 8 **Gingko Lady (USA)**[16] 855 4-7-10 49 ow1..............(p) AndreaAtzeni(5) 5 32
(J R Boyle) *in tch: rdn along 5f out: lost tch over 2f out* **50/1**

1m 40.95s (1.15) **Going Correction** +0.125s/f (Slow) **6** Ran SP% **113.6**
Speed ratings (Par 101): **99,98,96,95,91 83**
toteswinger: 1&2 £1.50, 1&3 £1.20, 2&3 £1.20 CSF £9.58 TOTE £4.20: £2.90, £1.70; EX 11.30.
Owner D Morgan & M B Clarke **Bred** J F Tuthill **Trained** Cropthorne, Worcs

FOCUS
A couple of fair sorts for the grade, but a muddling gallop, the below-par run of the market leader and the proximity of the fourth means the form needs treating with caution. The winner raced up the centre in the straight.

1080 BLUE SQUARE GAMES H'CAP 1m (P)
6:55 (6:55) (Class 6) (0-65,65) 4-Y-O+ £1,942 (£578; £288; £144) Stalls High

Form RPR
15-5 **1** **Having A Ball**[14] 878 5-9-0 **61** ChrisCatlin 14 71
(P D Cundell) *towards rr: hdwy ent fnl 2f: swtchd lft ent fnl f: led fnl 100yds: r.o strly* **11/2**[2]

2400 **2** 1 3/4 **Lend A Grand (IRE)**[19] 844 5-9-2 **63** IanMongan 7 69
(Miss Jo Crowley) *hld up towards rr: swtchd to outer and rdn over 2f out: r.o wl fnl f: wnt 2nd last strides: nvr gng to rch wnr* **10/1**

5304 **3** hd **Salt Of The Earth (IRE)**[19] 844 4-9-4 **65** RobertHavlin 10 71
(T G Mills) *chsd ldng pair: rdn and outpcd by ldng pair over 3f out: rallied u.p over 1f out: kpt on wl fnl f* **8/1**

025- **4** nk **Daring Dream (GER)**[124] 7490 4-8-8 **60** (v) MartinLane(5) 11 65
(A P Jarvis) *sn led: pushed clr w rival over 3f out: edgd into centre wl over 2f out: rdn and hung lft fr 2f out: hdd ins fnl f: no ex* **14/1**

1652 **5** hd **Takitwo**[47] 545 6-8-12 **59** SebSanders 12 64
(P D Cundell) *in tch: outpcd over 3f out: hdwy on inner over 2f out: chsd ldr over 1f out: led ins fnl f: hdd fnl 100yds: no ex: lost 3 pls towards fin* **8/1**

3262 **6** 1 1/2 **Fine Ruler (IRE)**[8] 959 5-9-3 **64** GeorgeBaker 4 65
(M R Bosley) *hmpd sn after s: t.k.h: hld up bhd: rdn over 2f out: hdwy ent fnl 2f: kpt on but nvr gng to rch ldrs* **9/4**[1]

6-56 **7** shd **Debdene Bank (IRE)**[70] 253 6-8-13 **60** JimCrowley 2 61
(Mrs Mary Hambro) *chsd ldrs: rdn and outpcd by ldng pair over 3f out: rallied u.p over 1f out: kpt on same pce fnl f* **20/1**

0-64 **8** nk **Diego Rivera**[8] 959 4-9-2 **63** FergusSweeney 8 63
(P J Makin) *hld up in tch: outpcd over 3f out: kpt on same pce u.p fnl 2f* **8/1**

0126 **9** nk **Alfredtheordinary**[13] 898 4-8-8 **60** MCGeran(5) 3 59
(M R Channon) *a towards rr: rdn over 2f out: kpt on u.p fr over 1f out: nvr trbld ldrs* **10/1**

05-4 **10** 3/4 **Golden Prospect**[14] 878 5-9-2 **63** JamesDoyle 9 61
(J W Hills) *hld up in midfield: outpcd over 3f out: keeping on same pce whn sltly hmpd ent fnl f: no imp after* **6/1**[3]

-350 **11** 2 1/4 **Magic Warrior**[70] 253 9-8-9 **56** LPKeniry 1 49
(J C Fox) *stdd after s: hld up in rr: effrt towards inner jst over 2f out: n.d* **25/1**

0-30 **12** 2 1/2 **Double Valentine**[15] 867 6-8-3 **57** DebraEngland(7) 5 44
(R Ingram) *s.i.s: a bhd* **33/1**

4014 **13** 1 1/4 **Admirals Way**[13] 895 4-8-4 **56** Louis-PhilippeBeuzelin(5) 6 40
(C N Kellett) *taken down early: plld hrd: chsd ldr: clr of remainder over 3f out: rdn over 2f out: lost 2nd over 1f out: wknd qckly ent fnl f* **16/1**

1m 40.08s (0.28) **Going Correction** +0.125s/f (Slow) **13** Ran SP% **136.1**
Speed ratings (Par 101): **103,101,101,100,100 99,98,98,98,97 95,92,91**
toteswinger: 1&2 £18.00, 1&3 £16.00, 2&3 £23.10 CSF £67.24 CT £479.32 TOTE £7.60: £2.30, £3.90, £2.70; EX 106.70.
Owner Miss M C Fraser **Bred** R G Percival **Trained** Compton, Berks

FOCUS
A moderate handicap in which the pace was sound throughout. The principals raced up the centre of the track in the closing stages.
Fine Ruler(IRE) Official explanation: jockey said gelding suffered interference shortly after start
Alfredtheordinary Official explanation: jockey said gelding hung left throughout
Golden Prospect Official explanation: jockey said gelding suffered interference in running

1081 BLUE SQUARE MOBILE H'CAP 1m 4f (P)
7:25 (7:25) (Class 5) (0-70,69) 4-Y-O+ £2,590 (£770; £385; £192) Stalls Centre

Form RPR
-011 **1** **Shanafarahan (IRE)**[14] 877 4-8-6 **57** JimmyQuinn 1 68
(K A Morgan) *led after 1f: mde rest: rdn and qcknd clr 2f out: in n.d fnl f: eased towards fin* **9/2**[2]

-062 **2** 3 **Krugerrand (USA)**[14] 877 10-9-1 **65** ChrisCatlin 9 71+
(W J Musson) *t.k.h: hld up in midfield: effrt and nt clr run fr over 2f out tl 2f out: r.o u.p to go 2nd ins fnl f: no ch w wnr* **6/1**

1114 **3** 1/2 **Prince Charlemagne (IRE)**[9] 948 6-8-11 **61** FergusSweeney 3 67
(G L Moore) *hld up towards rr: hdwy and rdn over 2f out: kpt on u.p to go 3rd towards fin: no ch w wnr* **9/2**[2]

4251 **4** nk **Star Choice**[20] 836 4-9-1 **66** (v) RobertHavlin 5 71
(J Pearce) *prom: chsd wnr over 4f out: rdn and nt pce of wnr 2f out: kpt on same pce after: lost 2 pls ins fnl f* **5/1**[3]

206- **5** 2 3/4 **Tantris (IRE)**[243] 4646 4-8-11 **62** ShaneKelly 8 63
(J A Osborne) *stdd s: t.k.h: hld up in rr: effrt on inner u.p over 2f out: nvr rchd ldrs: wknd ins fnl f* **10/1**

06-0 **6** nk **Lady Sorcerer**[5] 1000 4-8-4 **60** MartinLane(5) 6 60
(A P Jarvis) *stdd s: t.k.h: hld up in rr: hdwy on outer over 3f out: rdn and no prog jst over 2f out* **9/1**

64-0 **7** 2 1/2 **Mixing**[17] 848 7-8-10 **60** KirstyMilczarek 2 56
(M J Attwater) *stdd s: hld up in tch: rdn and unable qck over 2f out: n.d fnl f* **20/1**

4-21 **8** 3 **Filun**[17] 848 4-9-4 **69** IanMongan 10 60
(A Middleton) *stdd s: t.k.h: hld up in rr: rdn over 2f out: no prog and nvr a factor* **4/1**[1]

/6-0 **9** nk **Mr Mischief**[14] 877 9-8-12 **62** JimCrowley 7 53
(C Gordon) *led for 1f: chsd wnr tl over 4f out: rdn and wknd jst over 2f out* **14/1**

0-00 **10** 3 1/2 **Steady Gaze**[44] 578 4-7-10 **54** oh9 (t) RichardRowe(7) 4 39
(M A Allen) *t.k.h: chsd ldrs: wknd over 3f out: wl bhd whn hung lft fnl 2f* **66/1**

2m 36.27s (1.77) **Going Correction** +0.125s/f (Slow)
WFA 4 from 6yo+ 1lb **10** Ran SP% **119.3**
Speed ratings (Par 103): **99,97,96,96,94 94,92,90,90,88**
toteswinger: 1&2 £4.90, 1&3 £5.80, 2&3 £5.40 CSF £32.57 CT £130.59 TOTE £5.40: £1.90, £1.90, £1.40; EX 27.60.
Owner J D M Stables **Bred** Corduff Stud And J Corcoran **Trained** Little Marcle, H'fords

FOCUS
An ordinary handicap and one in which the gallop was only moderate. The decisive winner edged towards the inside rail in the closing stages.
Filun Official explanation: trainer had no explanation for the poor form shown

1082 BLUE SQUARE H'CAP 1m (P)
7:55 (7:55) (Class 4) (0-85,84) 3-Y-O £5,180 (£1,541; £770; £384) Stalls High

Form RPR
41- **1** **Wajaha (IRE)**[162] 6901 3-9-3 **83** RHills 3 99+
(J H M Gosden) *hld up in tch: rdn and qcknd to ld over 1f out: pushed clr and in command fnl f: eased towards fin* **8/11**[1]

0-1 **2** 3 1/4 **Satwa Gold (USA)**[26] 786 3-9-3 **83** StephenDonohoe 2 88
(E A L Dunlop) *hld up in tch in rr: effrt on inner wl over 1f out: chsd wnr ins fnl f: kpt on but no imp* **14/1**

10-2 **3** 3/4 **Pegasus Lad (USA)**[17] 851 3-9-4 **84** JoeFanning 5 87
(M Johnston) *led: rdn and hdd over 1f out: no ch w wnr fnl f: lost 2nd ins fnl f* **4/1**[3]

31-0 **4** 2 1/2 **Kaolak (USA)**[5] 1001 3-8-12 **78** ChrisCatlin 4 75
(J Ryan) *chsd ldr: ev ch and rdn 2f out: wknd ent fnl f* **14/1**

3-13 **5** 1 1/4 **Pearl Of Manacor (IRE)**[17] 851 3-8-12 **78** (v[1]) TonyCulhane 1 72
(M R Channon) *hld up in tch: hdwy on outer over 3f out: rdn ent fnl 2f out: wknd over 1f out* **7/2**[2]

1m 39.38s (-0.42) **Going Correction** +0.125s/f (Slow) **5** Ran SP% **113.5**
Speed ratings (Par 100): **107,103,103,100,99**
CSF £12.63 TOTE £1.90: £1.10, £4.50; EX 7.90 Place 6: £71.99, Place 5: £44.46..
Owner Hamdan Al Maktoum **Bred** Shadwell Estate Company Limited **Trained** Newmarket, Suffolk

FOCUS
The most interesting race of the evening. The gallop was only fair and the winner raced in the centre in the last quarter mile.
T/Plt: £54.40 to a £1 stake. Pool: £57,032.46. 765.32 winning tickets. T/Qpdt: £22.60 to a £1 stake. Pool: £8,301.84. 271.22 winning tickets. SP

LEICESTER (R-H)
Thursday, April 2

OFFICIAL GOING: Good to firm
Wind: Almost nil Weather: Fine

1083 KDM FOR SUCCESSFUL MARKETING MEDIAN AUCTION MAIDEN STKS 5f 2y
2:10 (2:14) (Class 5) 2-Y-O £2,590 (£770; £385; £192) Stalls Low

Form RPR
2 **1** **Archers Road (IRE)**[5] 994 2-9-3 0 SamHitchcott 8 89+
(M R Channon) *mde all: rdn and edgd lft jst over 1f out: pushed out* **6/4**[1]

2 1 **Here Now And Why (IRE)** 2-9-3 0 NCallan 3 87+
(K A Ryan) *a.p: swtchd rt ins fnl f: r.o* **7/1**[3]

3 4 1/2 **Jack My Boy (IRE)** 2-9-3 0 PaulDoe 7 67
(P D Evans) *a.p: one pce fnl 2f* **14/1**

4 nk **Anita's Luck (IRE)** 2-9-0 0 DavidProbert(3) 6 66
(B Palling) *chsd ldrs: lost pl over 3f out: hung lft over 2f out: hdwy over 1f out: kpt on ins fnl f* **11/1**

5 10 **Ever So Bold** 2-9-3 0 MartinDwyer 2 26+
(W R Muir) *hld up and bhd: hdwy over 2f out: wknd over 1f out* **25/1**

6 3/4 **Farmer Giles (IRE)** 2-9-3 0 JamieSpencer 4 23+
(M L W Bell) *hld up: sn in tch: wknd 2f out* **7/4**[2]

7 2 1/4 **Camacho Flyer (IRE)** 2-9-3 0 JamieMoriarty 5 14
(P T Midgley) *a bhd* **66/1**

8 2 **Blue Bond** 2-8-10 0 PaulPickard(7) 1 —
(P T Midgley) *dwlt: outpcd* **125/1**

9 nk **Lucky Mellor** 2-9-3 0 StephenCarson 9 —
(D K Ivory) *sn prom: wknd wl over 1f out* **66/1**

60.98 secs (0.98) **Going Correction** -0.05s/f (Good) **9** Ran SP% **111.5**
Speed ratings (Par 92): **90,88,81,80,64 63,59,56,56**
toteswinger: 1&2 £2.50, 1&3 £2.80, 2&3 £5.50. CSF £11.93 TOTE £2.10: £1.10, £1.50, £3.10; EX 9.30 Trifecta £39.70 Pool: £383.00 - 7.13 winning units..
Owner John Webster **Bred** John Fielding **Trained** West Ilsley, Berks

FOCUS
Two of the last three winners of this early-season juvenile maiden subsequently landed the Coventry Stakes at Royal Ascot. It remains to be seen whether this year's race was quite up to that standard, especially as the winner had already had a run, but the form among the first four does look good and has been rated positively.

NOTEBOOK
Archers Road(IRE), beaten 21/4l into second in the Brocklesby at 25/1 on his debut, showed the benefit of that experience early on, breaking alertly and displaying loads of speed, but he was still green under pressure. Ridden out with mainly hands-and-heels, he edged left towards the stands' rail in the closing stages, but was always holding Here Now And Why. He would be no sure thing to confirm form with the runner-up should they meet again in the coming weeks, but he's quite useful in his own right and could pick up a novice event. (tchd 11-8)
Here Now And Why(IRE) ◆, a first runner for Hughie Morrison's 2005 July Cup winner Pastoral Pursuits, is out of a dual sprint scorer. He showed loads of natural speed to race handy throughout, and displayed a likeable attitude once switched off the rail after being crossed by the winner around a furlong out. Having received only one tap with the whip, he's open to improvement and is potentially very useful. (op 11-2 tchd 5-1)
Jack My Boy(IRE), a 17,000euros half-brother to a prolific 1m-1m4f winner in Italy, out of a multiple 6f-1m4f scorer, unseated rider on the way to the start and was loose for a short period. In the race itself, he was niggled along quite early, but he kept responding and this was a pleasing introduction from a horse who should appreciate further before long. (op 16-1 tchd 20-1)
Anita's Luck(IRE) was backed in from as big as 33/1 on course. An already gelded half-brother to among others dual 7f Polytrack winner Napoleon Dynamite, he was outpaced at halfway and switched towards the stands' side, but he kept on inside the final furlong, showing some ability in the process. (op 33-1)
Ever So Bold, an already gelded half-brother to 5f three-year-old winner Ben, could make little impression. (op 28-1 tchd 33-1)
Farmer Giles(IRE), representing the same trainer/owner as last year's winner Art Connoisseur, cost £46,000 and is by Danroad, a 6f Group 2 winner as a juvenile in New Zealand, where he has already sired a Group 1 winner. A half-brother to Pyrrha, a useful two-year-old over 6f for Chris Wall last year, he was keen for most of the way and basically looked very green. According to Michael Bell he had only done three bits of work and he's likely to improve a deal for this experience. (tchd 6-4 and 15-8 in a place)

1084 LADBROKES.COM (S) STKS 5f 218y
2:45 (2:45) (Class 6) 3-Y-O £1,942 (£578; £288; £144) Stalls Low

Form RPR
54-4 **1** **Chocolicious (IRE)**[56] 403 3-8-9 66 (v[1]) TomEaves 8 63
(B Smart) *hld up: hdwy over 3f out: led wl over 1f out: edgd rt ins fnl f: drvn out* **11/8**[1]

	2	hd	**Charlietoo** 3-9-0 0 ... RobertWinston 3 (R Hollinshead) *bhd: rdn and hdwy whn edgd lft over 1f out: r.o towards fin* **6/1**[3]	67
05	3	5	**Peanut Girl (IRE)**[31] 736 3-8-6 0 ... DavidProbert(3) 12 (B Palling) *chsd ldrs: ev ch over 2f out: rdn over 1f out: wknd ins fnl f* **9/1**	46
2200	4	3	**Sorrel Ridge (IRE)**[31] 736 3-9-0 52 ... (b[1]) AlanMunro 11 (M G Quinlan) *t.k.h: w ldrs: ev ch over 2f out: rdn and wknd over 1f out* **11/2**[2]	42
00-5	5	6	**Time Loup**[60] 365 3-9-0 46 ... MartinLane(5) 7 (S R Bowring) *w ldrs: rdn and wknd 2f out* **20/1**	28
-066	6	½	**Pepin (IRE)**[47] 542 3-9-0 40 ... (b) FrankieMcDonald 6 (D Haydn Jones) *racd alone on stands' rail: w ldrs: led over 3f out: rdn and hdd wl over 1f out: sn wknd* **14/1**	21
0-00	7	7	**Senora Verde**[58] 379 3-8-2 39 ... PaulPickard(7) 10 (P T Midgley) *t.k.h: led: hdd over 3f out: wknd qckly over 2f out* **33/1**	—
0-20	8	23	**Bold Ring**[20] 826 3-8-8 59 ow1 ... SPRyan(7) 5 (E J Creighton) *v rel to r: a t.o* **13/2**	—

1m 13.55s (0.55) **Going Correction** -0.05s/f (Good) **8** Ran SP% **109.5**
Speed ratings (Par 96): **94,93,87,83,75 74,65,34**
toteswinger: 1&2 £2.40, 1&3 £2.60, 2&3 £5.60. CSF £8.87 TOTE £1.70: £1.10, £2.40, £2.30; EX 8.80 Trifecta £18.60 Pool: £381.66 - 15.17 winning units..There was no bid for the winner. Charlietoo was claimed by E. G. Bevan for £6,000.
Owner Mrs Trisha Laughton **Bred** Ballyhane Stud **Trained** Hambleton, N Yorks

FOCUS
A fairly weak seller for three-year-olds. There is doubt as to how much ability the winner retains and he has been rated somwhere near to his 2yo form.
Sorrel Ridge(IRE) Official explanation: jockey said gelding hung right-handed
Pepin(IRE) Official explanation: jockey said gelding hung left-handed throughout

1085 LADBROKES.COM CONDITIONS STKS 5f 218y
3:20 (3:24) (Class 3) 3-Y-O £7,569 (£2,265; £1,132; £566; £282) **Stalls** Low

Form				RPR
320-	1		**Sayif (IRE)**[159] 6972 3-8-10 118 ... JamieSpencer 5 (P W Chapple-Hyam) *led 1f: w ldr: hrd rdn to ld last strides* **5/6**[1]	97
222-	2	hd	**Sneak Preview**[194] 6102 3-8-9 101 ... RichardMullen 6 (E S McMahon) *led after 1f: rdn and edgd lft ins fnl f: hdd last strides* **11/4**[2]	95
006-	3	3½	**Saucy Brown (IRE)**[194] 6118 3-9-0 94 ... RyanMoore 2 (R Hannon) *a.p: rdn over 1f out: kpt on same pce ins fnl f: tk 3rd towards fin* **10/1**	89
212-	4	¾	**Enderby Spirit (GR)**[159] 6972 3-9-0 96 ... TomEaves 1 (B Smart) *hld up in tch: rdn over 1f out: no ex ins fnl f: lost 3rd towards fin* **6/1**[3]	87
22-0	5	4	**Son Of The Cat (USA)**[12] 912 3-8-12 90 ... (t) MichaelHills 4 (B Gubby) *prom tl wknd over 2f out* **22/1**	72

1m 11.68s (-1.32) **Going Correction** -0.05s/f (Good) **5** Ran SP% **108.9**
Speed ratings (Par 102): **106,105,101,100,94**
toteswinger: 1&2 £2.60. CSF £3.24 TOTE £1.60: £1.10, £1.70; EX 3.40.
Owner Saleh Al Homaizi & Imad Al Sagar **Bred** Crandon Park Stud **Trained** Newmarket, Suffolk

FOCUS
Usually just an ordinary conditions event, but this year's race marked the return of Sayif. He was a long way below his juvenile form in scraping home.

NOTEBOOK
Sayif(IRE), although failing to win in six starts at two, was placed in four consecutive Group contests between 6f-7f, including finishing runner-up in the Middle Park. However, he had been off since failing to beat a rival (when odds on) in a Doncaster Listed race in October, and made hard work of this on his return, despite an official mark of 118 leaving him with 16lb in hand over the runner-up at these weights. He ran like a horse in need of the outing, coming under pressure around two furlongs out, and only forcing his head in front in the final few strides, and better can be expected when his yard is in full swing. Although he's entered in the Guineas, his connections think he's probably a sprinter and the plan now is the Pavilion Stakes, a Listed race for three-year-olds at Ascot on April 29. (op 8-13 tchd 10-11)
Sneak Preview, runner-up in Listed and Group 3 company over this trip as a juvenile, showed good speed throughout and looked to have the favourite in trouble for much of the closing stages, but she was finally picked off near the line. She looks flattered to finish so close to a 118-rated rival, especially considering she had 12lb in hand over third, but she showed enough to suggest she should pick up some more black type this season. Ground this quick was not sure to suit, but she handled the conditions well and is clearly versatile. (op 5-1 tchd 5-2)
Saucy Brown(IRE) had been off for 194 days and was expected to need the run. This was a creditable effort considering he had loads to find with the front two at the weights, but he could be tricky to place this year. (op 14-1 tchd 8-1)
Enderby Spirit(GR), runner-up in a Listed race over this trip at Doncaster on his final start at two, was not at his best after over five months off. This was the fastest ground he had tried to date, and it was probably quicker than he cares for. (op 5-1 tchd 9-2)
Son Of The Cat(USA) offered little in this and is another who looks hard to place. (op 25-1 tchd 20-1)

1086 LADBROKES.COM KIBWORTH H'CAP 1m 1f 218y
3:55 (3:55) (Class 3) (0-95,90) 3-Y-O £7,569 (£2,265; £1,132; £566; £282) **Stalls** High

Form				RPR
421-	1		**Kings Destiny**[118] 7552 3-9-0 83 ... PhilipRobinson 1 (M A Jarvis) *hld up: hdwy 3f out: rdn fnl f: led last strides* **15/8**[1]	91
21	2	nk	**Thief Of Time (IRE)**[68] 280 3-8-13 82 ... AlanMunro 3 (P W Chapple-Hyam) *hld up: hdwy 3f out: rdn over 1f out: ev ch fnl f: r.o* **7/1**	90
051-	3	shd	**Takaatuf (IRE)**[189] 6234 3-9-0 83 ... RHills 5 (M Johnston) *led: rdn wl over 1f out: hdd last strides* **13/2**[3]	91
321-	4	1¼	**Headline Act**[161] 6926 3-8-8 77 ... RichardMullen 4 (J H M Gosden) *sn prom: pushed along over 2f out: sn outpcd: rallied wl ins fnl f* **9/4**[2]	82
0-61	5	5	**Citizenship**[54] 450 3-8-4 73 ... AdrianTNicholls 6 (Ian Williams) *hld up: pushed along over 2f out: nvr trbld ldrs* **28/1**	68
25-0	6	1	**Wilbury Star (IRE)**[19] 840 3-8-8 77 ... RyanMoore 7 (R Hannon) *w ldr: rdn and ev ch 2f out: wknd over 1f out* **14/1**	70
31-2	7	½	**Splinter Cell (USA)**[28] 764 3-9-7 90 ... JamieSpencer 2 (M Botti) *prom tl wknd 2f out* **11/1**	82

2m 6.45s (-1.45) **Going Correction** -0.05s/f (Good) **7** Ran SP% **109.8**
Speed ratings (Par 102): **103,102,102,101,97 96,96**
toteswinger: 1&2 £2.70, 1&3 £3.10, 2&3 £4.40. CSF £14.25 TOTE £2.40: £1.40, £3.70; EX 14.30.
Owner Dennis Yardy **Bred** D A Yardy **Trained** Newmarket, Suffolk

FOCUS
A cracking early-season handicap full of progressive middle-distance three-year-olds. The pace was just ordinary, and the first four finished in a bit of a bunch - clear of the rest - but this is still form to follow with the four all capable of better.

NOTEBOOK
Kings Destiny ◆, off the track since winning an ordinary maiden over 1m on the Lingfield Polytrack last December, proved well suited by the step up in trip and was a narrow winner, getting up near the line after producing a sustained effort on the outside of runners. He's by Dubai Destination, out of a Barathea mare, so it's not unreasonable to assume he might do even better with a bit more give underfoot, although he obviously handled these quick conditions just fine. Whatever the case, he is clearly useful and should stay 1m4f. Just a side note, the winner continues to pay a big compliment to Henry Cecil's Dante/Derby entrant Father Time, who beat Kings Destiny a length when making a successful debut in a Great Leighs maiden last November. (op 9-4 tchd 11-4)
Thief Of Time(IRE)'s Lingfield maiden win over 1m has not yet worked out, but this was a big improvement on that effort. This step up in trip suited and there should be more to come. (op 11-2)
Takaatuf(IRE) ◆'s trainer had won this race for the last two years with subsequent Listed winners, and also sent out Soapy Danger to finish second in 2006. Johnston's representative this time was not allowed an easy lead, with Wilbury Star keeping him honest, but he stuck on well and is open to improvement. (op 11-2 tchd 5-1 and 7-1)
Headline Act ◆ landed his maiden at Brighton last season, despite not looking comfortable on the track, and the runner-up that day has won twice since. Returning from over five months off, he had to be driven along to take up a handy position on leaving the stalls and ran in snatches for much of the way. He also seemed to be hitting the ground quite hard, giving the impression he was uncomfortable on the quick surface around this undulating course, and it's to his credit he finished so close. He is likely to prove well suited by a step up to 1m4f, and a flat track as well as some give underfoot should also help. He remains a very useful prospect. (tchd 2-1)
Citizenship was well backed when winning last time, but that was a lesser race. (op 33-1, tchd 40-1 in a place)
Splinter Cell(USA) ◆ did not look happy on the quick ground. His maiden success was gained on a soft surface and he will be a different proposition under more suitable conditions. (tchd 12-1and 14-1 in places)

1087 LADBROKES.COM KNIGHTON MAIDEN STKS 1m 1f 218y
4:30 (4:32) (Class 5) 3-Y-O+ £3,238 (£963; £481; £240) **Stalls** High

Form				RPR
3-	1		**Bin End**[176] 6581 3-8-8 0 ... JamieSpencer 1 (M L W Bell) *racd keenly in tch: led over 2f out: rdn out* **6/1**[3]	80+
060-	2	½	**Akmal**[167] 6777 3-8-8 79 ... RHills 5 (J L Dunlop) *hld up: hdwy over 3f out: rdn to chse wnr over 1f out: kpt on ins fnl f* **16/1**	79
6-	3	2	**Cherish The Moment (IRE)**[159] 6977 3-8-8 0 ... MichaelHills 10 (B W Hills) *hld up and bhd: hdwy over 1f out: rdn and styd on ins fnl f* **9/4**[2]	75+
6-	4	1¼	**Favours Brave**[182] 6425 3-8-8 0 ... RyanMoore 3 (J H M Gosden) *led: hdd over 2f out: sn rdn: one pce* **6/4**[1]	73
66-	5	1¾	**Ateeb**[174] 6621 3-8-8 0 ... TPO'Shea 2 (M Johnston) *chsd ldr: ev ch over 2f out: sn rdn: wknd wl over 1f out* **12/1**	69
60-	6	nk	**Abulharith**[118] 7552 3-8-8 0 ... AlanMunro 11 (P W Chapple-Hyam) *hld up in mid-div: rdn over 3f out: no hdwy fnl 2f* **16/1**	68
	7	2¾	**Countenance** 3-8-8 0 ... DarryllHolland 9 (W J Haggas) *prom tl wknd over 2f out* **20/1**	65+
	8	5	**Paddy Partridge** 3-8-8 0 ... LukeMorris 8 (N J Vaughan) *s.i.s: a in rr* **20/1**	53
00	9	43	**Gozome (IRE)**[10] 939 5-9-13 0 ... VinceSlattery 4 (D G Bridgwater) *bhd fnl 6f: t.o* **150/1**	—

2m 6.48s (-1.42) **Going Correction** -0.05s/f (Good)
WFA 3 from 4yo+ 19lb **9** Ran SP% **114.7**
Speed ratings (Par 103): **103,102,101,100,98 98,96,92,57**
toteswinger: 1&2 £5.40, 1&3 £3.00, 2&3 £6.80. CSF £90.63 TOTE £4.70: £1.60, £2.40, £1.30; EX 60.30 Trifecta £250.10 Pool: £618.73 - 1.83 winning units..
Owner Chris Wright & The Hon Mrs J M Corbett **Bred** Stratford Place Stud **Trained** Newmarket, Suffolk

FOCUS
A decent maiden which has been rated through the third and fourth. Improved form from the runner-up.

1088 LADBROKES.COM MAIDEN STKS 1m 3f 183y
5:05 (5:06) (Class 5) 3-4-Y-O £3,238 (£963; £481; £240) **Stalls** High

Form				RPR
0-	1		**Lively Fling (USA)**[202] 5857 3-8-7 0 ... RyanMoore 4 (J H M Gosden) *hld up in tch: hdwy over 3f out: rdn to ld ins fnl f: r.o* **11/4**[2]	78+
0-	2	2¾	**Shemoli**[182] 6425 3-8-7 0 ... GregFairley 5 (M A Jarvis) *t.k.h: a.p: pushed along 4f out: rdn over 2f out: kpt on to take 2nd cl home* **8/1**	74+
225-	3	½	**Alhaque (USA)**[167] 6777 3-8-8 85 ow1 ... JamieSpencer 6 (P W Chapple-Hyam) *led: rdn wl over 1f out: hdd ins fnl f: no ex and lost 2nd cl home* **15/8**[1]	74
	4	nk	**Cill Rialaig**[91] 4-9-8 0 ... TravisBlock 7 (H Morrison) *a.p: hmpd wl over 1f out: sn rdn: kpt on same pce* **4/1**[3]	70+
-622	5	4	**Kidlat**[17] 847 4-9-13 80 ... (t) DaneO'Neill 1 (B G Powell) *chsd ldr: ev ch 3f out: edgd rt wl over 1f out: sn rdn and wknd* **15/2**	68
050-	6	8	**Wannarock (IRE)**[139] 7321 4-9-10 60 ... LeeVickers(3) 3 (M C Chapman) *a bhd* **200/1**	55?
25-	7	8	**Harlestone Gold**[200] 5931 4-9-13 0 ... TedDurcan 2 (J L Dunlop) *s.i.s: hld up and bhd: short-lived effrt on ins over 4f out* **20/1**	43

2m 32.96s (-0.94) **Going Correction** -0.05s/f (Good)
WFA 3 from 4yo 21lb **7** Ran SP% **109.6**
Speed ratings (Par 103): **101,99,98,98,95 90,85**
toteswinger: 1&2 £5.60, 1&3 £2.80, 2&3 £5.00. CSF £22.40 TOTE £4.20: £2.10, £3.90; EX 26.00.
Owner George Strawbridge **Bred** George Strawbridge Jr **Trained** Newmarket, Suffolk

FOCUS
An interesting maiden, but the three-year-olds starting off their campaigns over this trip seemingly aren't considered particularly speedy, and the bare form is probably just fair with the favourite below par.

1089 LADBROKES.COM H'CAP 7f 9y
5:40 (5:40) (Class 4) (0-85,85) 4-Y-O+ £4,857 (£1,445; £722; £360) **Stalls** Low

Form				RPR
-305	1		**Orpen Wide (IRE)**[2] 1053 7-8-13 83 ... (b) LeeVickers(3) 5 (M C Chapman) *a.p: led over 3f out: rdn 2f out: hld on wl ins fnl f* **33/1**	89
0213	2	1	**Autumn Blades (IRE)**[11] 922 4-8-13 80 ... RobertWinston 9 (A Bailey) *hld up and bhd: hdwy over 1f out: rdn and ev ch ins fnl f: nt qckn* **8/1**	83

3060 **3** *hd* **Cornus**[4] 1016 7-8-8 **75** ...... GregFairley 2 77
(A J McCabe) *hld up: rdn over 2f out: hdwy over 1f out: kpt on towards fin* **9/1**

/10- **4** *¾* **Pravda Street**[349] 1441 4-9-4 **85** ...... JimmyFortune 6 85
(P F I Cole) *hld up in tch: rdn and ev ch over 1f out: no ex wl ins fnl f* **2/1**[1]

005- **5** *¾* **Chartist**[177] 6557 4-8-13 **80** ...... SilvestreDeSousa 1 78
(D Nicholls) *plld hrd: led: hdd over 3f out: w ldr: ev ch over 1f out: sn rdn: no ex wl ins fnl f* **18/1**

4-12 **6** *½* **Tartan Gigha (IRE)**[7] 974 4-9-2 **83** ...... RoystonFfrench 4 80
(M Johnston) *prom: pushed along over 3f out: sltly outpcd wl over 1f out: kpt on ins fnl f* **5/2**[2]

1042 **7** *nse* **Xpres Maite**[16] 856 6-8-3 **73** ......(v) AndrewMullen(3) 7 70
(S R Bowring) *hld up and bhd: hdwy over 3f out: rdn over 1f out: fdd ins fnl f* **6/1**[3]

010- **8** *3½* **Timber Treasure (USA)**[141] 7290 5-8-13 **80** ......(b) FrancisNorton 8 67
(Paul Green) *hld up in mid-div: wknd ins fnl f* **25/1**

00-3 **9** *16* **Sudden Impact (IRE)**[16] 858 4-9-1 **82** ...... PaulMulrennan 3 26
(Paul Green) *t.k.h: chsd ldr early: wknd over 3f out* **25/1**

1m 24.86s (-1.34) **Going Correction** -0.05s/f (Good) **9** Ran SP% **113.2**
Speed ratings (Par 105): **105,103,103,102,101 101,101,97,79**
toteswinger: 1&2 £32.20, 1&3 £36.40, 2&3 £7.70. CSF £265.51 CT £2605.50 TOTE £57.30: £4.40, £1.80, £2.10; EX 241.00 TRIFECTA Not won. Place 6: £29.82 Place 5: £17.58 .
Owner Andy & Bev Wright **Bred** Mrs Marian Maguire **Trained** Market Rasen, Lincs
■ Stewards' Enquiry : Lee Vickers one-day ban: used whip with excessive frequency (Apr 16)

FOCUS
Just an ordinary handicap but the form is sound enough. The winner was pretty much back to his old turf form.
T/Plt: £69.90 to a £1 stake. Pool: £50,913.80. 531.01 winning tickets. T/Qpdt: £24.80 to a £1 stake. Pool: £2,504.92. 74.50 winning tickets. KH

BATH (L-H)
Friday, April 3

OFFICIAL GOING: Good to firm (good in places; 9.2)
Wind: Virtually nil Weather: Sunny and bright

1090 EBF/FREEBETS.CO.UK FREE BETS MAIDEN FILLIES' STKS — 5f 11y
2:10 (2:11) (Class 5) 2-Y-O — **£3,561** (£1,059; £529; £264) **Stalls** Centre

Form RPR

0 **1** **Chicita Banana**[6] 994 2-9-0 0 ...... TonyCulhane 7 68
(George Baker) *racd keenly: chsd ldr: rdn to chal ent fnl f: led ins fnl f: styd on wl and in command towards fin* **15/8**[1]

0 **2** *1* **True Red (IRE)**[6] 1005 2-9-0 0 ...... AlanMunro 5 64
(B R Millman) *led: rdn and hdd ins fnl f: kpt on same pce fnl 100yds* **14/1**

3 *¾* **Avonvalley** 2-9-0 0 ...... TGMcLaughlin 9 61+
(M S Saunders) *v.s.a: wl bhd: hdwy on outer ent fnl f: r.o wl ins fnl f: gng on fin: nt rch ldrs* **14/1**

4 *¾* **Vilnius** 2-9-0 0 ...... SamHitchcott 6 58
(M R Channon) *s.i.s: in tch: rdn 1/2-way: kpt on same pce fnl f* **25/1**

5 *shd* **Crown (IRE)** 2-9-0 0 ...... RichardHughes 3 60+
(R Hannon) *towards rr: rdn along over 3f out: edging out rt looking for clr run over 1f out: styd on wl ins fnl f: nvr threatened ldrs* **2/1**[2]

6 *shd* **Kate Skate** 2-9-0 0 ...... EddieAhern 4 57
(P F I Cole) *plld hrd: chsd ldrs: rdn wl over 1f out: kpt on same pce fnl f* **18/1**

5 **7** *½* **Michaelmas Daisy**[4] 1031 2-9-0 0 ...... DaneO'Neill 1 55
(Miss Amy Weaver) *t.k.h: chsd ldrs: lost pl 2f out: rallied over 1f out: one pce fnl f* **16/1**

8 *½* **Vaduz** 2-9-0 0 ...... EdwardCreighton 2 53+
(M R Channon) *t.k.h: hld up in tch: n.m.r fr 2f out: kpt on same pce fnl f: nvr threatened ldrs* **40/1**

9 *2½* **Country Princess (FR)** 2-9-0 0 ...... SebSanders 11 43
(R M Beckett) *s.i.s: hld up in tch: hdwy 2f out: chsd ldrs and rdn over 1f out: wknd fnl f* **11/2**[3]

10 *hd* **Dolly Will Do** 2-9-0 0 ...... JimCrowley 10 42
(N P Mulholland) *s.i.s: a in rr: n.d* **33/1**

11 *3½* **Mrs Puff (IRE)** 2-9-0 0 ...... NeilPollard 8 28
(A B Haynes) *t.k.h: chsd ldrs tl wknd 2f out* **66/1**

63.51 secs (1.01) **Going Correction** -0.025s/f (Good) **11** Ran SP% **118.7**
Speed ratings (Par 89): **90,88,87,86,85 85,84,84,80,79 74**
toteswinger: 1&2 £14.00, 1&3 £4.20, 2&3 £36.20. CSF £28.96 TOTE £2.50: £1.20, £4.50, £3.50; EX 36.20 TRIFECTA Not won..
Owner Findlay & Bloom **Bred** Highclere Stud And Floors Farming **Trained** Moreton Morrell, Warwicks

FOCUS
The ground had dried out slightly compared to that advertised and was now Good to Firm, Good in places. Three of these had the benefit of previous racecourse experience and they included the first two home. That pair were up at the front end throughout. The field finished in a heap and the form has been rated negatively.

NOTEBOOK
Chicita Banana gave the Brocklesby form, in which she finished seventh, another boost with victory here. She was always handy, if a little keen early, but responded well to pressure to get up well inside the last furlong. Connections believe she needs 6f already, but she may have another run over the minimum in the meantime and she should be able to win again before some better juveniles start to appear. (op 2-1 tchd 11-8)
True Red(IRE), well beaten on her debut on the Kempton Polytrack six days earlier, ran much better here under a positive ride and only the winner was able to get past her. An ordinary event should come her way. (op 22-1 tchd 28-1)
Avonvalley ◆ was a real eye-catcher. Having fluffed the start and raced in a detached last early, she then had to come wide around the entire field to get into the race, but finished with a rare rattle down the centre of the track to snatch third. A 4,000gns filly out of a winning juvenile sprinter, she should be winning soon with this experience under her belt. (op 33-1 tchd 12-1)
Vilnius, whose dam was a winning juvenile and a sister to six winners in Germany including the high-class Auenklang, seemed to have her chance and showed enough to suggest that a race can be found. (tchd 20-1)
Crown(IRE) was very well supported earlier in the day, but she came off the bridle at halfway before staying on again once switched off the rail. A 55,000gns foal whose dam is closely related to several winners at up to 1m4f, she performed here as though she is going to need further herself. (op 9-4 tchd 15-8 and 5-2 in a place)
Kate Skate, first foal of a multiple winning sprinter, didn't run at all badly considering she took a fierce hold early. (op 14-1 tchd 20-1)

1091 FREEBETS.CO.UK FREE SPORTS BETTING FILLIES' H'CAP — 5f 161y
2:45 (2:45) (Class 5) (0-75,70) 3-Y-O+ — **£2,590** (£770; £385; £192) **Stalls** Centre

Form RPR

0314 **1** **Princess Rose Anne (IRE)**[23] 799 4-9-10 **68** ...... SteveDrowne 6 69
(J R Best) *pressed ldrs: drvn ent fnl f: kpt on gamely u.p to ld last strides* **7/2**[2]

0-06 **2** *hd* **Just Joey**[32] 738 5-9-1 **59** ......(b) LukeMorris 3 59
(J R Weymes) *w ldr: drvn wl over 1f out: led wl ins fnl f: hdd last strides* **10/1**

0600 **3** *¾* **Berrymead**[24] 791 4-8-10 **59** oh11 ow3 ...... AnnStokell(5) 5 57?
(Miss A Stokell) *s.i.s: in tch in rr: reminder over 3f out: hdwy over 2f out: chsd ldrs ins fnl f: kpt on* **40/1**

4132 **4** *hd* **Towy Valley**[30] 756 4-9-12 **70** ...... PhilipRobinson 2 67
(C G Cox) *led narrowly: rdn over 1f out: stmbld ins fnl f: hdd and no ex wl ins fnl f* **6/4**[1]

2532 **5** *nk* **Leading Edge (IRE)**[32] 738 4-9-11 **69** ...... TonyCulhane 1 66
(M R Channon) *hld up in tch: rdn over 3f out: outpcd u.p wl over 1f out: kpt on again ins fnl f: styng on fin* **5/1**

010- **6** *3¾* **Belle Bellino (FR)**[178] 6564 4-9-1 **59** ...... SebSanders 4 43
(R M Beckett) *hld up in tch: rdn wl over 1f out: wknd jst ins fnl f* **4/1**[3]

1m 11.87s (0.67) **Going Correction** -0.025s/f (Good) **6** Ran SP% **110.4**
Speed ratings (Par 100): **94,93,92,92,92 87**
toteswinger: 1&2 £2.30, 1&3 £12.00, 2&3 £24.40. CSF £34.23 TOTE £6.10: £2.60, £6.20; EX 33.40.
Owner Miss Rose-Anne Galligan **Bred** C McCarthy **Trained** Hucking, Kent

FOCUS
A moderate sprint handicap and, as in the opener, the principals were handy throughout. The form looks very weak, however, with the third casting big doubts.
Berrymead Official explanation: jockey said filly hung right-handed
Towy Valley Official explanation: jockey said filly stumbled inside final furlong
Leading Edge(IRE) Official explanation: jockey said, regarding riding, that he eased for a stride anticipating the gap in front of him closing.

1092 FREEBETS.CO.UK GRAND NATIONAL FREE BETS MAIDEN FILLIES' STKS — 1m 2f 46y
3:20 (3:21) (Class 5) 3-Y-O+ — **£2,590** (£770; £385; £192) **Stalls** Low

Form RPR

2-22 **1** **Onemix**[15] 876 3-8-7 77 ...... MichaelHills 7 77+
(B W Hills) *chsd ldr tl led after 2f: mde rest: clr fnl 2f: easily* **5/6**[1]

55- **2** *3¼* **Teeky**[161] 6945 3-8-7 0 ...... RichardMullen 9 71
(J H M Gosden) *led for 2f: chsd wnr after: rdn over 2f out: no ch w wnr fnl 2f: plugged on* **9/2**[2]

0- **3** *¾* **Fondant Fancy**[168] 6776 3-8-7 0 ...... EddieAhern 8 69
(H J L Dunlop) *chsd ldng pair: rdn and unable qck 3f out: no ch w wnr after: plugged on ins fnl f* **17/2**

6- **4** *2½* **Am I Blue**[163] 6893 3-8-7 0 ...... FrancisNorton 5 65+
(H J L Dunlop) *s.i.s: in rr: rdn 4f out: hdwy to chse ldng trio over 1f out: kpt on but nvr nr ldrs* **14/1**

5 *5* **Atacama Sunrise** 3-8-7 0 ...... JimmyQuinn 2 55
(J Pearce) *s.i.s: bhd: rdn and struggling 5f out: swtchd rt over 1f out: kpt on past btn horses fnl f: nvr nr ldrs* **16/1**

00- **6** *2* **Eightdaysaweek**[232] 5022 3-8-7 0 ...... LPKeniry 6 51
(S Kirk) *t.k.h: in tch: rdn and struggling 3f out: wl hld fnl 2f* **33/1**

0- **7** *2½* **Carte D'Oro (IRE)**[168] 6778 3-8-7 0 ...... JimCrowley 1 47
(R M Beckett) *t.k.h: in tch: rdn and struggling 3f out: no ch fnl 2f* **15/2**[3]

0 **8** *3¾* **Quella**[18] 849 3-8-7 0 ...... NickyMackay 3 39
(J H M Gosden) *in tch in midfield: rdn 4f out: lost pl and bhd fnl 3f* **33/1**

9 *5* **Lucy's Perfect** 3-8-7 0 ...... AlanMunro 4 30
(B R Millman) *s.i.s: rn green in last pl thrght* **50/1**

2m 9.65s (-1.35) **Going Correction** -0.025s/f (Good) **9** Ran SP% **115.4**
Speed ratings (Par 100): **104,101,100,98,94 93,91,88,84**
toteswinger: 1&2 £1.20, 1&3 £3.50, 2&3 £7.80. CSF £4.62 TOTE £1.80: £1.10, £1.20, £2.60; EX 5.00 Trifecta £18.30 Pool: £335.63 - 13.53 winning units..
Owner S W Group Logistics Limited **Bred** Ken Knox **Trained** Lambourn, Berks

FOCUS
A modest early-season fillies' maiden in which the order hardly changed during the contest. The winner looks the best guide and the form should prove sound.

1093 FREEBETS.CO.UK FREE GRAND NATIONAL BETTING CONDITIONS STKS — 1m 5y
3:55 (3:56) (Class 3) 4-Y-O+ — **£8,418** (£2,505; £1,251; £625) **Stalls** Low

Form RPR

05-3 **1** **Elna Bright**[22] 815 4-9-3 84 ...... DaneO'Neill 3 91
(P D Evans) *hld up in last pl: effrt over 1f out: drvn to ld fnl 100yds: r.o wl* **18/1**

500- **2** *½* **Fanjura (IRE)**[168] 6780 4-9-3 97 ...... MichaelHills 5 90
(B W Hills) *trckd ldng pair: rdn and chal over 2f out: ev after tl unable qck towards fin* **11/4**[3]

2562 **3** *¾* **Red Somerset (USA)**[13] 916 6-8-12 94 ...... MCGeran(5) 4 88
(R J Hodges) *t.k.h: led for 1f: trckd ldr after tl shkn up to ld over 2f out: drvn ent fnl f: hdd and no ex fnl 100yds* **15/8**[2]

11 **4** *7* **Boscage (USA)**[17] 858 4-9-3 95 ...... RoystonFfrench 1 72
(M Johnston) *led after 1f: shkn up and qcknd over 3f out: rdn and hdd over 2f out: btn 1f out: eased wl ins fnl f* **5/4**[1]

1m 43.88s (3.08) **Going Correction** -0.025s/f (Good) **4** Ran SP% **111.2**
Speed ratings (Par 107): **83,82,81,74**
CSF £62.83 TOTE £21.60; EX 27.70.
Owner David Mort **Bred** D R Tucker **Trained** Pandy, Monmouths

FOCUS
A messy contest, with the early pace only modest, and a surprise result with the prize going to the horse that was by far worst in at the weights. He produced a big step up at face value but the form is dubious.

NOTEBOOK
Elna Bright, who faced an impossible task when last of three on his return from ten months off and debut for the yard in a Kempton conditions event last month, was up against it again on these terms, but he won this fair and square. His rider was content to sit last early, but when the pace eventually increased he was switched towards the inside rail and produced a turn of foot that proved too much for his rivals. He was 13lb badly in with the runner-up at the weights, so much now depends on how the handicapper views this with the future in mind, but he may turn out again at Windsor on Monday. (op 16-1)

Fanjura(IRE), well beaten in a couple of Group 3s for Jeremy Noseda last October having shown good form in a couple of outings the previous spring including winning a division of the Wood Ditton, tracked the leading pair but he was always travelling further than his rivals on the wide outside on this sharp track, so he probably did well to hang in there for so long. He obviously goes well fresh and connections will be hoping that he can hold his form for longer this time around. (op 5-2 tchd 3-1)

Red Somerset(USA), now officially rated 9lb higher than for his last win on turf at Windsor last August but running well off marks in the mid 90s in hot handicaps on Polytrack lately, looked the likely winner when moving smoothly to the front passing the 2f pole, but he couldn't get clear and was worn down. He is probably better in a more strongly run race. (op 2-1 tchd 9-4)

Boscage(USA), who had beaten a total of six rivals in the course of winning his first two starts on sand this year, got upset in the stalls but he seemed to travel well enough in front in the early stages. However, when asked to quicken up after halfway he found absolutely nothing and was already beaten when slightly hampered by the winner. Perhaps these very different conditions found him out, but this was still too bad to be true. Official explanation: jockey said, regarding running, that the colt got upset in the stalls (op 6-4)

1094 FREEBETS.CO.UK WEST INDIES V ENGLAND FREE BETS H'CAP 5f 161y

4:30 (4:30) (Class 4) (0-85,83) 4-Y-0+ £5,180 (£1,541; £770; £384) Stalls Centre

Form				RPR
-550	1		**Carcinetto (IRE)**[6] 1006 7-8-13 **83** ... RichardEvans(5) 6 (P D Evans) *pressed ldr: drvn over 1f out: kpt on gamely to ld wl ins fnl f: drvn out* **10/3**[3]	92
-234	2	3/4	**Artistic License (IRE)**[18] 852 4-8-12 **77** ... TonyCulhane 1 (M R Channon) *s.i.s: in rr: pushed along 3f out: hdwy on inner jst ins fnl f: r.o to go 2nd nr fin: unable to rch wnr* **7/1**	83+
046-	3	nk	**Blue Jack**[184] 6402 4-8-12 **77** ... MartinDwyer 3 (W R Muir) *t.k.h: trckd ldrs: led on inner 1f out: edgd rt ins fnl f: drvn and hdd wl ins fnl f: wknd towards fin* **3/1**[2]	82
000-	4	2 1/4	**Harbour Blues**[126] 7477 4-9-3 **82** ...(t) CatherineGannon 4 (A W Carroll) *led: rdn over 1f out: hdd 1f out: wknd fnl 100yds* **8/1**	80
-244	5	1 1/4	**First Order**[56] 424 8-8-13 **83** ...(v) AnnStokell(5) 7 (Miss A Stokell) *chsd ldrs: stmbld 4f out: rdn over 1f out: wknd ins fnl f* **12/1**	77
5400	6	2	**Thoughtsofstardom**[14] 901 6-8-0 **70** ... KellyHarrison(5) 2 (P S McEntee) *t.k.h: chsd ldrs: rdn over 1f out: wknd fnl f* **16/1**	57
114-	7	1	**Espy**[308] 2570 4-9-2 **81** ... GeorgeBaker 5 (S Kirk) *stdd s: hld up in rr: effrt on outer over 1f out: sn btn* **11/4**[1]	65

1m 10.26s (-0.94) **Going Correction** -0.025s/f (Good) **7 Ran SP% 111.9**
Speed ratings (Par 105): **105,104,103,100,98 96,94**
toteswinger: 1&2 £3.90, 1&3 £3.10, 2&3 £3.90. CSF £25.25 TOTE £4.90: £2.30, £1.70; EX 24.50.
Owner Mrs Sally Edwards **Bred** M A Doyle **Trained** Pandy, Monmouths

FOCUS
A fair sprint handicap, but the pace was ordinary and not for the first time at the meeting it suited those that raced handily. Despite the modest early tempo, the winning time was 1.61 seconds faster than the earlier fillies' handicap. The bare form seems pretty sound.
First Order Official explanation: jockey said gelding ran too free and clipped heels after a furlong jockey said gelding ran too free and clipped heels after a furlong

1095 FREEBETS.CO.UK HORSE RACING FREE BETS H'CAP 5f 11y

5:05 (5:05) (Class 5) (0-70,71) 3-Y-0 £2,590 (£770; £385; £192) Stalls Centre

Form				RPR
0-01	1		**Captain Carey**[8] 966 3-9-9 **71** 6ex ... TGMcLaughlin 4 (M S Saunders) *stdd and stmbld s bhd: rdn and hdwy 1/2-way: chal jst ins fnl f: led fnl 100yds: r.o strly* **4/1**[3]	74+
050-	2	2	**Billy Beetroot (USA)**[196] 6080 3-9-0 **62** ...(t) RichardKingscote 7 (S C Williams) *chsd ldr: ev ch and rdn jst over 1f out: nt pce of wnr wl ins fnl f: wnt 2nd on post* **5/1**	58
236-	3	nse	**Bees River (IRE)**[118] 7574 3-8-12 **65** ... MartinLane(5) 6 (A P Jarvis) *led: rdn over 1f out: edgd lft u.p 1f out: hdd and no ex fnl 100yds: lost 2nd on post* **10/3**[2]	61
064-	4	1 1/2	**Handcuff**[158] 7024 3-8-10 **58** ... WilliamBuick 2 (J Gallagher) *chsd ldr tl over 1f out: nt clr run thrght fnl f: swtchd rt and no joy ins fnl f: nvr able to chal* **7/1**	51+
-266	5	3 1/4	**Fangfoss Girls**[50] 509 3-9-2 **64** ... GeorgeBaker 3 (G L Moore) *hld up in tch: rdn and effrt over 1f out: drvn and btn ent fnl f* **3/1**[1]	43
310-	6	5	**August Days (IRE)**[217] 5475 3-8-11 **59** ... JimmyQuinn 5 (J Pearce) *hld up in tch: rdn 2f out: sn btn: no ch fnl f* **11/1**	20
-440	7	3 1/4	**Hatman Jack (IRE)**[21] 826 3-9-4 **66** ... SebSanders 1 (B G Powell) *bhd: rdn 1/2-way: btn over 1f out: eased wl ins fnl f* **8/1**	15

62.86 secs (0.36) **Going Correction** -0.025s/f (Good) **7 Ran SP% 116.7**
Speed ratings (Par 98): **96,92,92,90,85 77,71**
toteswinger: 1&2 £4.50, 1&3 £2.90, 2&3 £3.90. CSF £24.97 TOTE £3.90: £2.40, £3.60; EX 22.10 Place 6: £2,065.35, Place 5: £944.87..
Owner M S Saunders **Bred** B Walters **Trained** Green Ore, Somerset

FOCUS
Another ordinary sprint handicap. The winner built on his Southwell form but this would not have taken much winning. The third looks the best guide.
Handcuff Official explanation: jockey said colt was denied a clear run
Hatman Jack(IRE) Official explanation: jockey said gelding lost its action
T/Plt: £1,740.90 to a £1 stake. Pool: £42,809.17. 17.95 winning tickets. T/Qpdt: £85.30 to a £1 stake. Pool: £3,604.09. 31.26 winning tickets. SP

MUSSELBURGH (R-H)

Friday, April 3

OFFICIAL GOING: Good to firm (good in places; 8.5)
Wind: Moderate, across Weather: Early mist clearing to leave fine day

1096 TURFTV BETTING SHOP SERVICE H'CAP 5f

2:20 (2:21) (Class 5) (0-70,70) 4-Y-0+ £3,238 (£963; £481; £240) Stalls Low

Form				RPR
20-5	1		**Nomoreblondes**[4] 1041 5-9-0 **66** ...(p) JamieMoriarty 14 (P T Midgley) *mde all: rdn and edgd lft ins fnl f: hld on wl* **15/2**	76
00-0	2	hd	**Sandwith**[39] 654 6-9-4 **70** ... PJMcDonald 4 (A G Foster) *cl up: effrt and ev ch over 1f out: kpt on fnl f: jst hld* **4/1**[1]	79
204-	3	3	**Until When (USA)**[230] 5110 5-8-13 **65** ...(v) TomEaves 1 (B Smart) *midfield: drvn 1/2-way: kpt on fnl f: nt rch first two* **12/1**	63
000-	4	shd	**Twosheetstothewind**[163] 6907 5-8-4 **56** oh1 ... DaleGibson 2 (M Dods) *in tch: drvn 1/2-way: kpt on u.p fnl f* **11/1**	54
-220	5	nk	**Ridley Didley (IRE)**[61] 367 4-8-4 **56** oh2 ... DuranFentiman 13 (N Wilson) *cl up tl rdn and no ex fnl f* **12/1**	53
40-2	6	3/4	**Restless Genius (IRE)**[90] 24 4-9-1 **67** ... GrahamGibbons 7 (B Ellison) *dwlt: bhd and drvn along: hdwy over 1f out: nrst fin* **6/1**[3]	61
240-	7	3/4	**Circuit Dancer (IRE)**[256] 4239 9-9-2 **68** ... SilvestreDeSousa 8 (D Nicholls) *chsd ldrs tl rdn and no ex over 1f out* **11/2**[2]	59
006-	8	1	**Brut**[276] 3594 7-8-7 **66** ... AmyRyan(7) 10 (D W Barker) *midfield: effrt and edgd rt wl over 1f out: sn no ex* **25/1**	54
00-0	9	1	**The Bear**[22] 818 6-9-1 **67** ... PaulMulrennan 5 (A G Foster) *chsd ldrs tl rdn and wknd over 1f out* **10/1**	51
200-	10	3/4	**Thunder Bay**[147] 7225 4-8-13 **65** ... PaulHanagan 12 (R A Fahey) *bhd: shkn up and sme hdwy on outside 2f out: sn btn* **13/2**	46
000-	11	1/2	**Darcy's Pride (IRE)**[211] 5634 5-8-6 **58** ... TonyHamilton 9 (D W Barker) *chsd ldrs: drvn 1/2-way: wknd over 1f out* **25/1**	38
000-	12	6	**Howards Prince**[187] 6310 6-7-13 **58** oh11 ow2 ...(p) PaulPickard(7) 3 (D A Nolan) *towards rr: drvn and outpcd 1/2-way: sn btn* **150/1**	16

59.45 secs (-0.95) **Going Correction** -0.175s/f (Firm) **12 Ran SP% 115.9**
Speed ratings (Par 103): **100,99,94,94,94 93,91,90,88,87 86,77**
toteswinger: 1&2 £7.20, 1&3 £12.70, 2&3 £11.60. CSF £36.11 CT £365.15 TOTE £9.60: £2.90, £1.70, £3.00; EX 38.70.
Owner Anthony D Copley **Bred** P John And Redmyre Bloodstock **Trained** Westow, N Yorks

FOCUS
Morning fog threatened to impede visibility, but it had started to lift as the runners were loading into the stalls. The time of this race suggested conditions were quick, and the first two were prominent throughout. There was some bumping in the final furlong, but the interference was minimal and they finished a little way clear of the rest. Fairly sound early-season form.

1097 EUROPEAN BREEDERS' FUND MAIDEN STKS 5f

2:55 (2:56) (Class 5) 2-Y-0 £3,885 (£1,156; £577; £288) Stalls Low

Form				RPR
	1		**Monalini (IRE)** 2-9-3 0 ... TomEaves 5 (B Smart) *mde all: edgd rt ins fnl f: pushed out: comf* **2/1**[2]	72+
	2	1 3/4	**Mr Smithson (IRE)** 2-9-3 0 ... GrahamGibbons 1 (B Ellison) *in tch: effrt over 2f out: chsd wnr ins fnl f: r.o* **14/1**	65
	3	2 1/2	**Always Dixie (IRE)** 2-8-12 0 ... JoeFanning 6 (M Johnston) *cl up tl rdn and one pce fnl f* **6/1**[3]	50
	4	1 1/2	**Miss Smilla** 2-8-12 0 ... PaulMulrennan 2 (K A Ryan) *trckd ldrs tl rdn and no ex appr fnl f* **11/8**[1]	44+
	5	2 3/4	**Cariad Coch** 2-8-12 0 ... TonyHamilton 3 (Mrs L Stubbs) *prom: rdn and edgd rt over 1f out: sn outpcd* **16/1**	33
	6	13	**Miccolo** 2-9-3 0 ... JamieMoriarty 4 (P T Midgley) *t.k.h: in tch on outside: hung rt thrght: wknd fr 2f out* **14/1**	—

60.65 secs (0.25) **Going Correction** -0.175s/f (Firm) **6 Ran SP% 108.9**
Speed ratings (Par 92): **91,88,84,81,77 56**
toteswinger: 1&2 £4.40, 1&3 £1.30, 2&3 £3.80. CSF £25.84 TOTE £3.00: £1.10, £6.60; EX 29.30.
Owner Pinnacle Bertolini Partnership **Bred** Dermot Cantillon And Forenaghts Stud **Trained** Hambleton, N Yorks

FOCUS
This was probably just an ordinary maiden, though the time was not bad for debutants. The winner scored quite readily in the end.

NOTEBOOK
Monalini(IRE), who was steady in the market, broke smartly and took up the early running, and although he came under a bit of pressure a furlong out responded well and drew clear close home. This well-built colt is related to Nice Applause and Monatora, both winners at two in France and the stable has a good record with its two-year-olds, so it looks like he could win again. (tchd 7-4 and 9-4 in places)

Mr Smithson(IRE) was outpaced early but progressed mid-race and stayed on well enough without seriously threatening the winner. It was a reasonable debut from the gelding, who is bred to make his mark as a two-year-old. (op 12-1 tchd 11-1)

Always Dixie(IRE) was prominent until she could find no extra in the final furlong. A half-sister to the same stable's Parkview Love and Always Fruitful, both winners on their debut at two, she looked to need a little more time to come to herself. (tchd 11-2 and 13-2)

Miss Smilla cost 50,000 guineas as a yearling and is related to some good sprinters. With the stable's first two juvenile runners finishing second this season, she was well-backed to go one better. Looking fit, if quite lightly-made, she was never in it and was disappointing. (op 6-5 tchd 11-10)

Miccolo Official explanation: jockey said colt hung right-handed throughout

1098 MUSSELBURGHRACECOURSE.CO.UK H'CAP 7f 30y

3:30 (3:31) (Class 5) (0-70,68) 3-Y-0 £3,238 (£963; £481; £240) Stalls High

Form				RPR
-112	1		**Green Agenda**[8] 968 3-9-0 **61** ... JoeFanning 3 (M Johnston) *mde all: pushed clr fnl f* **15/8**[1]	81+
412-	2	4 1/2	**Peter's Gift (IRE)**[132] 7426 3-9-7 **68** ... PaulMulrennan 4 (K A Ryan) *chsd ldrs: drvn over 2f out: chsd wnr appr fnl f: kpt on: no imp* **9/1**	74
B52-	3	2	**Antigua Sunrise (IRE)**[167] 6809 3-9-6 **67** ... PaulHanagan 8 (R A Fahey) *dwlt: sn in tch: effrt 2f out: edgd rt: sn one pce* **11/2**[2]	67
6-23	4	3 1/2	**Lyric Art (USA)**[47] 564 3-9-2 **63** ... TomEaves 6 (B Smart) *t.k.h in midfield on outside: drvn over 2f out: no imp* **8/1**	54
-422	5	1 1/4	**Inthawain**[24] 797 3-8-13 **60** ... LeeEnstone 2 (N Wilson) *pressed wnr: rdn over 2f out: wknd appr fnl f* **16/1**	48
00-6	6	1/2	**Meydan Groove**[32] 741 3-8-5 **52** ... DuranFentiman 10 (R Johnson) *hld up on outside: drvn 3f out: nvr able to chal* **28/1**	38
1-42	7	2	**Denton Diva**[22] 819 3-9-5 **66** ... PhillipMakin 5 (M Dods) *midfield: drvn over 2f out: edgd rt and sn outpcd* **15/2**[3]	47
026-	8	hd	**Classic Contours (USA)**[211] 5632 3-9-2 **63** ... JamieMoriarty 9 (J J Quinn) *hld up: rdn 3f out: nvr on terms* **9/1**	43
400-	9	1/2	**Castle Myth (USA)**[230] 5106 3-7-12 **52** ... JamieKyne(7) 11 (B Ellison) *bhd: drvn 1/2-way: nvr on terms* **16/1**	31
004-	10	1/2	**Murrays Magic (IRE)**[150] 7172 3-8-5 **52** ... SilvestreDeSousa 1 (D Nicholls) *t.k.h: prom tl rdn and wknd fr 2f out* **18/1**	30

1m 27.64s (-2.66) **Going Correction** -0.175s/f (Firm) **10 Ran SP% 113.5**
Speed ratings (Par 98): **108,102,100,96,95 94,92,92,91,90**
toteswinger: 1&2 £4.00, 1&3 £4.10, 2&3 £4.50. CSF £18.79 CT £78.47 TOTE £2.10: £1.40, £2.00, £2.50; EX 15.40.
Owner The Green Dot Partnership **Bred** W And R Barnett Ltd **Trained** Middleham Moor, N Yorks
■ Stewards' Enquiry : Jamie Kyne one-day ban: used whip when gelding showed no response (Apr 17)

FOCUS
A modest handicap, but it was run in a good time for the grade and this looks form to be positive about with the winner improving again.

1099 BUTTY'S FINAL FURLONG (S) STKS 1m 4f 100y
4:05 (4:05) (Class 6) 4-Y-0+ £1,942 (£578; £288; £144) Stalls High

Form RPR
60/4 1 **Raucous (GER)**[22] 822 6-8-13 78 PaulMulrennan 4 69
(Mrs R A Carr) *set stdy pce: rdn clr over 1f out: unchal* 7/2[2]
2130 2 3 **Bridgewater Boys**[6] 1000 8-9-4 67 (b) PaulHanagan 7 69
(T J Pitt) *hld up: effrt whn nt clr run over 2f out: hdwy to chse wnr appr fnl f: no imp* 7/1[3]
-132 3 1 3/4 **Edas**[20] 622 7-8-11 70 JamieKyne(7) 6 66
(J J Quinn) *t.k.h: trckd ldrs: chsd wnr over 2f out to appr fnl f: one pce* 11/4[1]
000- 4 hd **Titinius (IRE)**[42] 4172 9-8-13 60 TonyHamilton 3 61
(Micky Hammond) *hld up: rdn 3f out: kpt on fnl f: no imp* 33/1
0630 5 3 1/2 **Just Observing**[5] 1014 6-8-6 66 PaulPickard(7) 2 55
(P T Midgley) *in tch: drvn and outpcd over 2f out: n.d after* 15/2
06-0 6 3 3/4 **Fort Churchill (IRE)**[14] 899 8-8-13 70 (bt) TomEaves 5 49
(B Ellison) *trckd ldrs: rdn over 2f out: wknd over 1f out* 11/4[1]
7 2 1/4 **Southern Waters (FR)**[24] 5-8-13 0 PJMcDonald 1 46
(G A Swinbank) *chsd wnr to over 2f out: sn wknd* 12/1

2m 42.83s (0.83) 7 Ran SP% 110.5
toteswinger: 1&2 £2.90, 1&3 £2.60, 2&3 £3.20. CSF £25.71 TOTE £3.90: £2.40, £2.00; EX 26.80.There was no bid for the winner.
Owner David W Chapman **Bred** Gestut Graditz **Trained** Huby, N Yorks

FOCUS
Just an ordinary seller. The winner enjoyed an easy lead and did not have to reach the level of form he showed a couple of years ago, with his two main dangers disappointing.
Just Observing Official explanation: trainer said gelding scoped dirty on return

1100 CENTRAL TAXIS H'CAP 1m
4:40 (4:40) (Class 4) (0-85,83) 4-Y-0+ £5,828 (£1,734; £866; £432) Stalls High

Form RPR
2544 1 **Just Bond (IRE)**[8] 974 7-8-13 78 PJMcDonald 1 86
(G R Oldroyd) *hld up: smooth hdwy over 2f out: shkn up to ld ins fnl f: carried hd high: all out* 7/1[3]
405- 2 shd **Celtic Change (IRE)**[144] 7278 5-8-8 73 TomEaves 3 80
(M Dods) *cl up: effrt over 2f out: kpt on wl fnl f: jst hld* 5/2[1]
442- 3 1 **Wind Shuffle (GER)**[147] 7224 6-8-8 78 GaryBartley(5) 6 83
(J S Goldie) *led 1f: cl up: lft in ld ent st: hdd ins fnl f: r.o* 10/3[2]
505- 4 1 1/4 **Moheebb (IRE)**[147] 7224 5-8-9 74 (b) JoeFanning 4 76
(Mrs R A Carr) *hld up: effrt over 2f out: kpt on fnl f* 10/1
000- 5 2 1/2 **Fortunate Isle (USA)**[31] 6582 7-8-7 72 PaulHanagan 7 68
(R A Fahey) *bhd: pushed along 3f out: kpt on fnl f: n.d* 7/1[3]
1-04 6 1/2 **Bourse (IRE)**[72] 238 4-7-11 69 oh4 JamieKyne(7) 5 64
(A G Foster) *in tch: drvn over 2f out: sn no ex* 9/1
113- 7 4 1/2 **Talk Of Saafend (IRE)**[187] 6311 4-9-2 81 PaulMulrennan 8 66
(P Monteith) *prom tl rdn and wknd over 1f out* 15/2
0- 8 2 3/4 **Arizona John (IRE)**[296] 2960 4-9-4 83 LeeEnstone 9 62
(N Wilson) *t.k.h: trckd ldrs tl rdn and wknd over 1f out* 16/1
510- 9 26 **Cigalas**[189] 6242 4-9-3 82 TonyHamilton 2 —
(Mrs J C McGregor) *led after 1f out tl rn wd bnd ent st: sn wknd* 33/1

1m 38.64s (-2.56) **Going Correction** -0.175s/f (Firm) course record 9 Ran SP% 116.3
Speed ratings (Par 105): **105,104,103,102,100 99,95,92,66**
toteswinger: 1&2 £6.00, 1&3 £5.60, 2&3 £2.80. CSF £25.06 CT £70.48 TOTE £9.50: £2.00, £1.60, £1.60; EX 35.80.
Owner R C Bond **Bred** Schwindibode Ag **Trained** Brawby, N Yorks

FOCUS
Quite a competitive handicap. The start was sluggish but the pace increased after a furlong, and they were bunched at the finish with those racing prominently filling the places. Pretty sound early-season form.
Cigalas Official explanation: jockey said gelding hung left throughout

1101 TURFTV SHOWING THE BEST RACECOURSES MAIDEN STKS 1m 1f
5:15 (5:15) (Class 5) 3-Y-0+ £2,590 (£770; £385; £192) Stalls High

Form RPR
232- 1 **Union Island (IRE)**[169] 6760 3-8-11 79 PaulMulrennan 3 69+
(K A Ryan) *chsd ldrs: drvn over 2f out: led ins fnl f: kpt on* 5/4[1]
043- 2 nk **Akbabend**[156] 7069 3-8-11 76 JoeFanning 4 68+
(M Johnston) *cl up: led over 2f out: rdn whn veered bdly lft and hdd ins fnl f: kpt on wl nr fin* 15/8[2]
234- 3 1 1/4 **Dazzling Light (UAE)**[231] 5042 4-9-9 74 DanielTudhope 1 64
(J S Goldie) *t.k.h: led to over 2f out: ev ch ins fnl f: hld nr fin* 9/2[3]
323- 4 3 1/2 **Hard Luck Story**[153] 7126 3-8-11 72 TomEaves 6 58
(I Semple) *trckd ldrs: effrt over 2f out: carried hd high: one pce appr fnl f* 10/1
0 5 2 1/4 **Baligha**[27] 786 4-9-9 0 PJMcDonald 7 52
(G A Swinbank) *hld up: effrt over 2f out: edgd rt: sn no imp* 50/1
06-0 6 1/2 **Wilmington**[22] 823 5-10-0 50 TonyHamilton 5 56?
(Mrs J C McGregor) *hld up: drvn 3f out: nvr able to chal* 100/1
06 7 18 **Lunar Storm (IRE)**[17] 855 5-10-0 0 (b[1]) AndrewElliott 2 —
(Mrs R A Carr) *s.s: nvr on terms* 100/1

1m 53.36s (-1.34) **Going Correction** -0.175s/f (Firm)
WFA 3 from 4yo+ 17lb 7 Ran SP% 110.4
Speed ratings (Par 103): **98,97,96,93,91 91,75**
toteswinger: 1&2 £1.30, 1&3 £2.00, 2&3 £1.70. CSF £3.51 TOTE £2.20: £1.10, £1.80; EX 3.40.
Owner Clipper Logistics **Bred** Barouche Stud Ireland Ltd **Trained** Hambleton, N Yorks
■ Stewards' Enquiry : P J McDonald caution: entered wrong stall

FOCUS
A reasonable maiden for the grade, though with little strength in depth. The early pace was steady and the three market leaders were able to pull a little way clear of the rest. The proximity of the sixth limits the bare form, which could have been rated around 10lb higher.
Lunar Storm(IRE) Official explanation: jockey said gelding missed the break

1102 TURFTV APPRENTICE H'CAP 2m
5:45 (5:45) (Class 5) (0-70,70) 4-Y-0+ £3,885 (£1,156; £577; £288) Stalls Low

Form RPR
021- 1 **Don't Stop Me Now (IRE)**[72] 4057 4-9-6 66 PatrickDonaghy 2 70
(J Howard Johnson) *cl up: led after 4f: edgd lft and hrd pressed ins fnl f: hld on wl* 11/8[1]
650- 2 1 **Danzatrice**[72] 6672 7-9-11 67 FrederikTylicki 6 70
(C W Thornton) *hld up: rdn and hdwy over 2f out: disp ld ins fnl f: one pce towards fin* 7/2[3]
603- 3 2 1/2 **Amir Pasha (UAE)**[20] 6708 4-8-7 58 JamieKyne(5) 7 58
(Micky Hammond) *t.k.h: in tch: rdn over 2f out: hung rt over 1f out: nt qckn fnl f* 20/1
230- 4 2 1/2 **Los Nadis (GER)**[33] 7223 5-9-11 70 AmyRyan(3) 5 67
(P Monteith) *trckd ldrs: effrt 2f out: outpcd fnl f* 5/2[2]
00- 5 13 **Francesco (FR)**[20] 7128 5-9-7 68 ALVoy(5) 3 49
(Mrs L B Normile) *trckd ldrs tl rdn and wknd wl over 1f out* 40/1
56-0 6 1/2 **Dimashq**[6] 1000 7-8-4 51 PaulPickard(5) 1 32
(P T Midgley) *chsd ldrs tl wknd fr over 2f out* 15/2
460- 7 36 **Stravonian**[5] 6309 9-8-9 51 oh6 GaryBartley 4 —
(D A Nolan) *plld hrd: led 4f: cl up tl wknd 4f out: sn lost tch* 200/1

3m 31.96s (-1.54) **Going Correction** -0.175s/f (Firm)
WFA 4 from 5yo+ 4lb 7 Ran SP% 112.4
Speed ratings (Par 103): **103,102,101,100,93 93,75**
toteswinger: 1&2 £1.80, 1&3 £4.50, 2&3 £6.00. CSF £6.28 TOTE £1.70: £1.40, £2.00; EX 6.30 Place 6: £48.80, Place 5: £19.98..
Owner Matthew Green and J H Johnson **Bred** Miss Patricia Heavey O'Connell **Trained** Billy Row, Co Durham

FOCUS
An ordinary apprentice handicap run at a steady early pace. The winner did not have to improve much and this is pretty weak form.
T/Plt: £93.90 to a £1 stake. Pool: £44,439.97. 345.30 winning tickets. T/Qpdt: £13.90 to a £1 stake. Pool: £3,666.83. 195.20 winning tickets. RY

1037 WOLVERHAMPTON (A.W) (L-H)
Friday, April 3

OFFICIAL GOING: Standard
Wind: Almost nil Weather: Fine

1103 ENJOY EVENING RACING WITH FRIENDS H'CAP 5f 216y(P)
6:50 (6:50) (Class 5) (0-70,70) 4-Y-0+ £3,238 (£963; £481; £240) Stalls Low

Form RPR
6-43 1 **Dancing Maite**[28] 777 4-9-0 66 DarryllHolland 7 78
(S R Bowring) *hld up and bhd: c wd st: hdwy over 1f out: rdn to ld towards fin* 3/1[1]
2112 2 3/4 **Stonecrabstomorrow (IRE)**[20] 843 6-8-11 70 (b) BMcHugh(7) 9 80
(R A Fahey) *hld up and bhd: hdwy on outside 2f out: rdn and edgd lft over 1f out: led ins fnl f: hdd towards fin* 3/1[1]
3354 3 1 3/4 **Figaro Flyer (IRE)**[16] 870 6-9-1 67 IanMongan 6 71
(P Howling) *hld up and bhd: hdwy jst over 1f out: kpt on same pce ins fnl f* 5/1[2]
2155 4 nse **Smirfys Systems**[9] 961 10-8-12 64 StephenDonohoe 2 68
(E S McMahon) *hld up and bhd: hdwy on ins 2f out: rdn to ld briefly ins fnl f: no ex towards fin* 9/1
1446 5 2 **Sarah's Art (IRE)**[51] 499 6-9-1 67 MickyFenton 5 65
(Stef Liddiard) *a.p: nt clr run wl over 1f out: rdn and kpt on ins fnl f tl no ex towards fin* 8/1[3]
-026 6 1/2 **Royal Challenge**[15] 886 8-9-4 70 PatrickMathers 3 66
(I W McInnes) *prom: pushed along over 2f out: lost pl wl over 1f out: sn swtchd lft: rdn and kpt on fnl f* 16/1
064- 7 1 1/4 **Comptonspirit**[174] 6658 5-8-13 65 J-PGuillambert 1 57
(B P J Baugh) *prom: led wl over 1f out tl ins fnl f: wknd* 16/1
066- 8 2 1/2 **Out Of India**[136] 7369 7-8-4 56 oh9 FrankieMcDonald 10 40
(P T Dalton) *prom: rdn 2f out: hmpd over 1f out: sn wknd* 100/1
-002 9 1/2 **Loose Caboose (IRE)**[11] 937 4-8-12 64 (p) LPKeniry 11 47
(A J McCabe) *led 1f: w ldr: rdn over 2f out: wknd wl over 1f out* 12/1
0-00 10 5 **Wee Buns**[9] 961 4-8-13 65 (b[1]) LukeMorris 8 32
(P Burgoyne) *plld hrd: led after 1f: rdn over 2f out: hdd wl over 1f out: sn wknd* 33/1

1m 14.63s (-0.37) **Going Correction** -0.075s/f (Stan) 10 Ran SP% 111.2
Speed ratings (Par 103): **99,98,95,95,92 92,90,87,86,79**
toteswinger: 1&2 £4.20, 1&3 £6.30, 2&3 £3.60. CSF £10.64 CT £40.03 TOTE £3.90: £1.30, £1.50, £2.10; EX 14.50.
Owner Stuart Burgan **Bred** S R Bowring **Trained** Edwinstowe, Notts

FOCUS
A modest sprint handicap run at a decent pace. The hold-up horses dominated and the generally progressive winner posted a personal best.

1104 RINGSIDE CONFERENCE SUITE - 700 THEATRE STYLE CLAIMING STKS 5f 20y(P)
7:20 (7:20) (Class 5) 4-Y-0+ £2,729 (£806; £403) Stalls Low

Form RPR
1151 1 **Desperate Dan**[4] 1038 8-9-0 73 (v) TPQueally 2 83
(A B Haynes) *chsd ldng pair: wnt 2nd 2f out: led ins fnl f: pushed out* 5/2[2]
5145 2 1 **Harry Up**[7] 985 8-9-1 85 (p) NeilBrown(3) 3 83
(K A Ryan) *w ldr: led over 3f out: rdn over 1f out: hdd ins fnl f: nt qckn* 2/1[1]
2131 3 1 3/4 **Blue Tomato**[8] 973 8-9-1 79 AdrianTNicholls 4 74
(D Nicholls) *s.i.s: bhd: rdn wl over 1f out: r.o to take 3rd ins fnl f* 10/3[3]
2254 4 1 **Qadar (IRE)**[8] 973 7-8-12 75 (e) LukeMorris 5 68
(N P Littmoden) *hld up and bhd: rdn over 1f out: nvr nr to chal* 7/1
-126 5 6 **Godfrey Street**[56] 424 6-8-9 74 (p) DeclanCannon(7) 1 50
(A G Newcombe) *led: hdd over 3f out: rdn and lost 2nd 2f out: wknd over 1f out* 12/1
410- 6 6 **Whinhill House**[219] 5398 9-8-7 64 JosephineBruning(7) 6 26
(T T Clement) *pushed along over 3f out: sn bhd* 40/1

61.13 secs (-1.17) **Going Correction** -0.075s/f (Stan) 6 Ran SP% 107.6
Speed ratings (Par 103): **106,104,101,100,90 80**
toteswinger: 1&2 £1.20, 1&3 £1.20, 2&3 £1.02. CSF £7.20 TOTE £3.30: £2.20, £1.60; EX 9.10.
Owner Joe McCarthy **Bred** Sheikh Amin Dahlawi **Trained** Limpley Stoke, Bath

FOCUS
A decent claimer. This was the winner's best effort for some time although the runner-up was below his best.

1105 SPONSOR A RACE BY CALLING 01902 390009 H'CAP 1m 1f 103y(P)
7:50 (7:50) (Class 4) (0-80,80) 3-Y-0 £5,180 (£1,541; £770; £384) Stalls Low

Form RPR
41- 1 **Kimberley Downs (USA)**[132] 7422 3-9-2 78 GregFairley 6 90+
(M Johnston) *chsd ldr: lost 2nd 2f out: sn outpcd and rdn: rallied 1f out: styd on to ld last strides* 13/8[1]
2413 2 shd **High Cross (IRE)**[20] 840 3-8-8 70 StephenDonohoe 5 82
(Sir Mark Prescott) *hld up in tch: led wl over 1f out: sn rdn: hdd last strides* 5/2[2]

100- **3** *2 1/4* **River Captain (IRE)**[187] 6320 3-8-13 **75**................................ LPKeniry 4 82
(S Kirk) *led: hdd wl over 1f out: one pce fnl f* **12/1**

001- **4** *2 3/4* **Thin Red Line (IRE)**[122] 7524 3-9-4 **80**................................ AlanMunro 3 81
(E A L Dunlop) *prom: rdn over 1f out: wknd fnl f* **7/2**[3]

164- **5** *2* **The Dial House**[252] 4373 3-9-2 **78**................................ ShaneKelly 1 75
(J A Osborne) *hld up in rr: rdn over 1f out: t.o* **8/1**

040- **6** *48* **Blazing Buck**[161] 6946 3-8-12 **74**................................ RobertWinston 7 —
(H J L Dunlop) *hld up: pushed along over 6f out: rdn over 3f out: sn struggling: t.o* **28/1**

1m 59.99s (-1.71) **Going Correction** -0.075s/f (Stan) **6** Ran SP% **111.1**
Speed ratings (Par 100): **104,103,101,99,97 55**
toteswinger: 1&2 £1.50, 1&3 £0.00, 2&3 £1.80. CSF £5.78 TOTE £2.40: £1.40, £1.50; EX 7.40.
Owner Favourites Racing XIX **Bred** Gaines-Gentry Thoroughbreds **Trained** Middleham Moor, N Yorks

FOCUS
A decent three-year-old handicap. They seemed to go a reasonable pace and the form should work out, with more to come from the winner.
Blazing Buck Official explanation: jockey said gelding never travelled

1106 NAME A RACE TO ENHANCE YOUR BRAND H'CAP — 1m 141y(P)
8:20 (8:20) (Class 6) (0-60,60) 3-Y-O **£2,388** (£705; £352) **Stalls** Low

Form RPR

410 **1** **Foreign Investment (IRE)**[22] 817 3-8-13 **60**........... RichardEvans(5) 4 66
(P D Evans) *chsd ldr: led 2f out: edgd rt over 1f out: sn rdn: jst hld on* **9/4**[2]

056 **2** *hd* **Abu Dubai (IRE)**[21] 827 3-9-4 **60**................................ DarryllHolland 2 65
(C A Dwyer) *a.p: rdn and edgd lft wl over 1f out: r.o u.p wl ins fnl f: jst failed* **8/1**[3]

0-31 **3** *3/4* **Dark Ranger**[4] 1036 3-8-11 **53** 6ex................................ LukeMorris 3 56
(T J Pitt) *set stdy pce: hdd 2f out: rdn over 1f out: ev ch ins fnl f: nt qckn cl home* **8/11**[1]

35-0 **4** *6* **Nimmy's Special**[55] 450 3-8-13 **60**................................ DeanHeslop(5) 1 50
(M Mullineaux) *hld up: pushed along 3f out: bhd fnl 2f* **20/1**

-036 **5** *3 3/4* **Sweet Virginia (USA)**[10] 943 3-8-1 **50**................(b[1]) DeclanCannon(7) 6 31
(K R Burke) *prom: ev ch whn hung rt bnd over 2f out: wknd wl over 1f out* **40/1**

1m 54.13s (3.63) **Going Correction** -0.075s/f (Stan) **5** Ran SP% **107.0**
Speed ratings (Par 96): **80,79,79,73,70**
toteswinger: 1&2 £9.40. CSF £17.60 TOTE £3.20: £1.40, £3.20; EX 15.30.
Owner Diamond Racing Ltd **Bred** M Duffy **Trained** Pandy, Monmouths

FOCUS
They went a very steady pace for most of the way in this modest handicap and the bare form needs treating with caution. The race only concerned three of the five runners.
Foreign Investment(IRE) Official explanation: trainer's rep said, regarding apparent improvement in form, that on its last run the filly was slowly away and lost ground by racing wide.

1107 GREAT OFFERS AT WOLVERHAMPTON-RACECOURSE.CO.UK H'CAP — 1m 1f 103y(P)
8:50 (8:50) (Class 4) (0-85,82) 4-Y-O+ **£5,180** (£1,541; £770; £384) **Stalls** Low

Form RPR

1131 **1** **Ahlawy (IRE)**[7] 981 6-8-13 **82** 6ex...........................(bt) AndreaAtzeni(5) 4 96
(F Sheridan) *a.p: chsd clr ldr 4f out: led 2f out: pushed clr fnl f* **7/2**[2]

41- **2** *4* **Empowered (IRE)**[181] 6470 4-9-4 **82**................................ TonyCulhane 6 88
(W J Haggas) *hld up: hdwy over 2f out: rdn wl over 1f out: chsd wnr fnl f: no imp* **8/13**[1]

5025 **3** *5* **Scamperdale**[36] 694 7-9-2 **80**................................ RobertWinston 5 76
(B P J Baugh) *hld up: hdwy over 2f out: rdn over 1f out: wknd ins fnl f* **16/1**

6036 **4** *3/4* **Count Trevisio (IRE)**[30] 761 6-9-2 **80**...........................(p) ChrisCatlin 1 74
(J R Gask) *led: wl clr 7f out: hdd 2f out: wknd ins fnl f* **20/1**

000- **5** *1 3/4* **Piper's Song (IRE)**[65] 7354 6-7-13 **68** oh2................................ AmyBaker(5) 2 58
(Patrick Morris) *hld up in rr: rdn over 2f out: no rspnse* **66/1**

1212 **6** *nk* **New Star (UAE)**[13] 910 5-8-11 **75**................................ LukeMorris 3 65
(W M Brisbourne) *chsd ldr to 4f out: sn rdn: wknd over 3f out* **15/2**[3]

1m 59.58s (-2.12) **Going Correction** -0.075s/f (Stan) **6** Ran SP% **108.0**
Speed ratings (Par 105): **106,102,98,97,95 95**
toteswinger: 1&2 £1.10, 1&3 £3.50, 2&3 £3.70. CSF £5.54 TOTE £4.10: £1.80, £1.40; EX 8.50.
Owner Frank Sheridan **Bred** Castlemartin Stud And Skymarc Farm **Trained** Stoke Heath, Shropshire

FOCUS
A fair handicap in which the fourth raced clear for a long way. A personal best from the winner under a claimer and the form has been rated positively.

1108 DINE IN THE HORIZONS RESTAURANT MEDIAN AUCTION MAIDEN STKS — 7f 32y(P)
9:20 (9:21) (Class 6) 3-Y-O **£2,388** (£705; £352) **Stalls** High

Form RPR

504- **1** **Seek The Fair Land**[168] 6770 3-9-3 70................................ PatCosgrave 8 72+
(J R Boyle) *w ldr: led over 2f out: hrd rdn over 1f out: clr fnl f: drvn out* **4/9**[1]

00- **2** *5* **Prince Andjo (USA)**[168] 6789 3-9-3 0...........................(t) PatrickMathers 5 58
(I W McInnes) *hld up in tch: sltly outpcd and rdn over 3f out: styd on to take 2nd ins fnl f: no ch w wnr* **33/1**

60-2 **3** *2 1/2* **Jul's Lad (IRE)**[32] 741 3-8-12 68...........................(p) DeanHeslop(5) 6 51+
(M Mullineaux) *t.k.h: led: hdd over 2f out: btn 1f out: lost 2nd ins fnl f* **9/2**[2]

0-05 **4** *1 1/2* **Piccolo Express**[21] 833 3-9-3 45................................ J-PGuillambert 3 47
(B P J Baugh) *chsd ldng pair: rdn over 2f out: one pce* **25/1**

6 **5** *7* **One Scoop Or Two**[21] 833 3-9-3 0...........................(t) NickyMackay 4 28
(F Sheridan) *a bhd* **22/1**

6 *1 1/4* **Crush (IRE)** 3-9-3 0................................ StephenDonohoe 1 25
(D M Simcock) *s.i.s: a in rr* **7/1**[3]

00- **7** *3/4* **Princess Janet**[182] 6443 3-8-12 0................................ LukeMorris 2 18
(A B Coogan) *hld up: pushed along over 3f out: sn struggling* **66/1**

8 *1 1/4* **Go Sunshine (IRE)** 3-8-12 0...........................(t) AndreaAtzeni(5) 7 20
(F Sheridan) *dwlt: a in rr* **16/1**

1m 29.99s (0.39) **Going Correction** -0.075s/f (Stan) **8** Ran SP% **118.4**
Speed ratings (Par 96): **94,88,85,83,75 74,73,72**
toteswinger: 1&2 £0.00, 1&3 £1.60, 2&3 £18.50. CSF £29.00 TOTE £1.50: £1.20, £3.50, £1.70; EX 32.50 Place 6: £4.26, Place 5: £3.35..
Owner Chris Watkins And David N Reynolds **Bred** Raimon Bloodstock **Trained** Epsom, Surrey

FOCUS
A moderate maiden run at an ordinary pace. It is doubtful if the winner had to improve too much.
T/Plt: £25.00 to a £1 stake. Pool: £79,090.18. 2,301.12 winning tickets. T/Qpdt: £12.00 to a £1 stake. Pool: £6,292.61. 386.40 winning tickets. KH

1109 - 1115a (Foreign Racing) - See Raceform Interactive

1071 LINGFIELD (L-H)
Saturday, April 4

OFFICIAL GOING: Standard
Wind: Nil Weather: Brightening up after earlier light rain

1116 FREEBETS.CO.UK GRAND NATIONAL FREE BETS H'CAP — 7f (P)
2:10 (2:10) (Class 3) (0-90,90) 4-Y-O+ **£7,771** (£2,312; £1,155; £577) **Stalls** Low

Form RPR

342- **1** **Secret Night**[133] 7419 6-8-10 **82**................................(b[1]) PhilipRobinson 1 90
(C G Cox) *hld up towards rr: hdwy 4f out: chsd ldrs 2f out: swtchd lft over 1f out: rdn to ld ins fnl f: hung bdly rt towards fin: hld on* **14/1**

2-43 **2** *1/2* **Orpenindeed (IRE)**[29] 778 6-8-12 **89**................................ AndreaAtzeni(5) 5 96
(M Botti) *led briefly: chsd ldr after: rdn to ld 2f out: hdd ins fnl f: keeping on same pce whn carried rt towards fin* **13/2**[2]

00-6 **3** *3/4* **Alfresco**[14] 910 5-8-13 **85**................................(b) RobertWinston 2 91+
(J R Best) *t.k.h: trckd ldrs: rdn and chsd ldng pair jst ins fnl f: styng on but looking hld whn nt clr run and hmpd towards fin* **10/1**[3]

1125 **4** *1 1/2* **Mutamared (USA)**[29] 778 9-9-1 **87**................................(t) NCallan 11 88
(K A Ryan) *hld up in tch: rdn and sltly outpcd 2f out: kpt on same pce u.p fnl f: nt pce to rch ldrs* **12/1**

06-5 **5** *1/2* **My Gacho (IRE)**[87] 73 7-9-1 **87**................................(b) J-PGuillambert 7 87
(M Johnston) *sn led: rdn and hdd 2f out: drvn ent fnl f: wknd fnl 100yds* **16/1**

6611 **6** *1/2* **Gallantry**[37] 694 7-9-4 **90**................................ TolleyDean 3 88
(P Howling) *stdd s: hld up wl off the pce in rr: pushed along and no hdwy over 2f out: stl plenty to do ent fnl f: r.o wl fnl f: nvr rchd ldrs* **16/1**

2300 **7** *shd* **Southandwest (IRE)**[14] 916 5-9-1 **87**................................ RichardHughes 10 85
(J S Moore) *stdd after s: hld up bhd: rdn 2f out: r.o ins fnl f: nvr threatened ldrs* **12/1**

005- **8** *1 1/4* **Lodi (IRE)**[149] 7215 4-8-9 **81**................................(t) IanMongan 8 76
(J Akehurst) *chsd ldrs: rdn jst over 2f out: wknd u.p ent fnl f* **33/1**

000- **9** *1* **Mut'Ab (USA)**[169] 6772 4-8-12 **84**................................(b) SebSanders 4 76
(C E Brittain) *hld up in tch: rdn and hung rt bnd 2f out: nt qckn and no imp fr over 1f out* **33/1**

115 **10** *13* **Electric Warrior (IRE)**[13] 922 6-8-6 **78**................................ ChrisCatlin 6 35
(C R Dore) *a bhd: lost tch over 2f out* **25/1**

0/1- **11** *16* **Cadre (IRE)**[213] 5608 4-9-0 **86**................................ JimmyFortune 9 —
(J H M Gosden) *broke wl: steadily lost pl: hung rt fr 4f out: rdn and struggling bdly over 3f out: wl btn 2f out: sn eased: t.o* **8/11**[1]

1m 22.76s (-2.04) **Going Correction** -0.125s/f (Stan) course record **11** Ran SP% **123.9**
Speed ratings (Par 107): **106,105,104,102,102 101,101,100,99,84 65**
toteswinger: 1&2 £6.80, 1&3 £34.60, 2&3 £13.60. CSF £105.85 CT £971.53 TOTE £20.40: £4.00, £2.10, £2.80; EX 72.30 TRIFECTA Not won..
Owner Hants and Herts **Bred** Worksop Manor Stud **Trained** Lambourn, Berks

FOCUS
A decent handicap run at a good pace, but not a competitive race according to the market with Cadre being sent off a very short-priced favourite. He ran no race though, which does devalue the form.

NOTEBOOK
Secret Night, who is consistent if very hard to win with, was up another 2lb on this return from five months off and had first-time blinkers replacing the usual cheekpieces. She dived through against the inside rail to make her effort in the straight, which is not normally an advantage here, but she maintained her momentum to win despite hanging violently away to her right. She has been covered by Manduro and may be in foal, and if that is the case then it is possible it contributed to this victory. (op 12-1)
Orpenindeed(IRE), whose only previous win in this country came in a claimer, was always thereabouts and kept on right to the line. He had finished no better than third in five previous visits here, so this was an improvement and he deserves to win a handicap. (op 8-1)
Alfresco ◆, who pulled far too hard on his debut for the yard off the back of a five-month absence here last time, had every chance up the straight and although he was hampered when the winner hung across him, it didn't affect the result. He is now 6lb lower than for his last win which came at this track 14 months ago, and he looks about ready to end his losing run. (tchd 14-1)
Mutamared(USA), a six-time winner on Polytrack during the winter including one over this course and distance, ran on well down the wide outside late on but, despite this effort, he does seem better over 6f. (op 10-1)
My Gacho(IRE), 2lb higher than when successful over course and distance in November, made most of the running and battled on well after being headed rounding the home turn. He was returning from a short break and may just have needed it. (tchd 20-1)
Gallantry, up another 5lb in his bid for a hat-trick, likes to come late off a strong pace but he was given an awful lot to do here. He made up a lot of late ground, but never had a prayer. Official explanation: jockey said gelding missed break
Southandwest(IRE), still 5lb above his last winning mark, also gave himself plenty to do and his late rally up the inside rail was never getting him there in time. (op 11-1)
Cadre(IRE) was sent off a very short-priced favourite. He had been gelded since beating a dual subsequent winner in a Kempton maiden on only his second outing last September, proving then that he can go well fresh. Off a mark of 86 for this handicap debut, his supporters soon knew their fate as Jimmy Fortune was getting after him before halfway but with no response, and he was eventually eased right off. His rider reported that he was never travelling and the vet reported that the gelding returned slightly lame. Official explanation: jockey said gelding was never travelling and hung right; trainer representative said gelding appeared to be lame behind; vet said gelding finished slightly lame behind (op 5-6 tchd 10-11 in places)

1117 FREEBETS.CO.UK GRAND NATIONAL BETTING SPRING H'CAP — 1m 4f (P)
2:45 (2:45) (Class 2) (0-105,103) 4-Y-O+ **£11,656** (£3,468; £1,733; £865) **Stalls** Low

Form RPR

050- **1** **Hatton Flight**[188] 6302 5-8-7 **86**................................(b) WilliamBuick 3 93
(A M Balding) *chsd ldrs: rdn 2f out: chsd ldr and drvn over 1f out: led ins fnl f: jst hld on* **16/1**

4-12 **2** *shd* **Distinctive Image (USA)**[14] 915 4-8-4 **84**................................ ChrisCatlin 5 91+
(R Hollinshead) *t.k.h early: hld up towards rr: n.m.r over 2f out: wd bnd 2f out: str run fnl f: pressed wnr wl ins fnl f: jst hld* **5/1**[3]

535- **3** *3/4* **Dansili Dancer**[175] 6646 7-9-6 **99**................................ PhilipRobinson 9 105
(C G Cox) *stdd s: hld up in rr: hdwy on wd outside bnd 2f out: r.o wl fnl f: wnt 3rd nr fin: nt quite rch ldrs* **15/2**

51-3 **4** *nk* **Humble Opinion**[31] 761 7-8-11 **90**................................ MartinDwyer 4 95
(A King) *s.i.s: towards rr: rdn 4f out: hdwy u.p on inner over 1f out: chsd ldrs jst ins fnl f: one pce fnl 100yds* **9/1**

232- **5** *1/2* **The Carlton Cannes**[173] 6698 5-8-10 **89**................................ JamieSpencer 1 94+
(M L W Bell) *trckd ldrs: lost pl over 3f out: hdwy and chsng ldrs 2f out: drvn and unable qck fnl f* **5/2**[1]

033- **6** *1 3/4* **Hunting Country**[153] 7150 4-8-8 **88**................................ JoeFanning 2 90
(M Johnston) *chsd ldr: led gng wl over 2f out: rdn over 1f out: hdd ins fnl f: wknd towards fin* **4/1**[2]

3001 **7** *5* **Sgt Schultz (IRE)**[14] [915] 6-9-1 **94**.. LPKeniry 7 88
(J S Moore) *t.k.h: hld up in tch: rdn to chse ldr over 2f out tl over 1f out: wknd 1f out: eased whn wl hld towards fin* **9/1**

1-20 **8** *6* **Grande Caiman (IRE)**[24] [801] 5-9-7 **103**....................(b) PatrickHills(3) 6 87
(R Hannon) *hld up towards rr: stdy hdwy 8f out: chsd ldrs 5f out: rdn 3f out: sn struggling: no ch fr over 1f out: eased towards fin* **9/1**

245- **9** *2 ½* **My Mate Max**[163] [6934] 4-7-13 **84** oh12.......................(p) AndreaAtzeni(5) 8 64
(R Hollinshead) *sn led: rdn over 3f out: hdd over 2f out: sn dropped out: wl bhd over 1f out: eased ins fnl f* **25/1**

2m 29.48s (-3.52) **Going Correction** -0.125s/f (Stan)
WFA 4 from 5yo+ 1lb **9** Ran SP% **116.7**
Speed ratings (Par 109): **106,105,105,105,104 103,100,96,94**
toteswinger: 1&2 £16.00, 1&3 £14.10, 2&3 £10.80. CSF £94.95 CT £662.46 TOTE £16.00: £4.00, £2.50, £3.00; EX 121.50 Trifecta £190.50 Part won. Pool £257.51 - 0.50 winning units..
Owner David Brownlow **Bred** Fittocks Stud Ltd **Trained** Kingsclere, Hants

FOCUS
A decent middle-distance handicap and although there was little covering the front five at the line, thanks to My Mate Max this was run at a more solid gallop than many races over this distance here. The winner carried over his improvement from last year.

NOTEBOOK
Hatton Flight, returning from seven months off and still 5lb higher than when completing a four-timer last summer, was always close to the pace. Having hit the front towards the inside of the track off the home bend, he looked sure to be swallowed up by the strong finishers down the centre of the track but would simply not be denied. (op 14-1)
Distinctive Image(USA) ◆, beaten a whisker by Sgt Schultz in a muddling affair over course and distance last month and meeting him on the same terms, was inclined to pull very hard in the first half of the contest despite the decent pace set by his stable companion. The fact that he still put in such a strong late challenge down the wide outside and only just failed to get up does him credit. He should be winning again before too long. (op 9-2)
Dansili Dancer, returning from six months off and still 4lb above his last winning mark, was switched off out the back early before being delivered with his effort widest of all. He finished strongly, but couldn't quite there and should be all the better with this run under his belt. (op 10-1 tchd 7-1)
Humble Opinion, nearly four lengths behind Distinctive Image at Wolverhampton last month and 8lb better off, tried to put in an effort tight against the inside rail up the home straight, which may not have been the ideal place to be, but he still finished much closer to his old rival. (op 10-1)
The Carlton Cannes, still relatively lightly raced, was 5lb higher on this return from six months off and making his debut for the yard. Tucked away on the inside for much of the way, he never had a great deal of room to play with at any stage but the gaps were there up the home straight had he the speed to take advantage of them. Unfortunately he just seemed to be lacking in that area. (op 2-1 tchd 11-4)
Hunting Country, returning from five months off and gelded in the meantime, led the field around the home bend but could never put the race to bed and was swamped. (op 7-1)
Sgt Schultz(IRE) was off the same mark as when just coming out best in a blanket finish over course and distance last month. Keen enough in a handy position early, he was close enough starting the final turn but was already under strong pressure by then and had nothing left once in line for home. (op 8-1 tchd 7-1)

1118 FREEBETS.CO.UK GRAND NATIONAL BET - INTERNATIONAL TRIAL STKS (LISTED RACE) 1m (P)
3:20 (3:21) (Class 1) 3-Y-O
£22,708 (£8,608; £4,308; £2,148; £1,076; £540) **Stalls** High

Form RPR

451- **1** **Ocean's Minstrel**[115] [7622] 3-9-0 72.................................. JerryO'Dwyer 2 98
(J Ryan) *dwlt: sn pushed up to ld: mde rest: rdn clr 2f out: styd on wl fnl f* **25/1**

64-0 **2** *2 ¼* **Deposer (IRE)**[17] [863] 3-9-0 99...................................... RobertWinston 5 93
(J R Best) *t.k.h: broke wl: sn restrained and hld up in midfield: lft 3rd bnd 2f out: sn rdn and nt qckn: chsd wnr 1f out: kpt on but no real imp* **7/2**[2]

00-0 **3** *nk* **Icesolator (IRE)**[14] [912] 3-9-0 98.................................... JimmyFortune 6 92
(R Hannon) *hld up in rr: hdwy over 2f out: lft 5th bnd 2f out: styd on u.p to go 3rd nr fin: nvr nr wnr* **7/1**

40-0 **4** *½* **Agente Parmigiano (IRE)**[17] [863] 3-9-0 91...................... EddieAhern 4 91
(G A Butler) *hld up in midfield: lft 4th bnd 2f out: wnt 3rd 1f out: kpt on same pce u.p: lost 3rd nr fin* **16/1**

000- **5** *6* **Cry Of Freedom (USA)**[161] [6979] 3-9-0 95......................... JoeFanning 1 77
(M Johnston) *disp 2nd pl: rdn and lft clr 2nd bnd 2f out: sn drvn and no imp: wknd fnl f* **9/2**[3]

230- **6** *hd* **Canwinn (IRE)**[167] [6855] 3-9-0 103.................................... TonyCulhane 7 77
(M R Channon) *hld up in last pair: rdn and hung rt bnd 2f out: no ch after* **7/1**

306- **7** *3 ¼* **Jobe (USA)**[161] [6979] 3-9-0 105..(t) NCallan 3 69
(K A Ryan) *rrd stalls: stmbld s: hung rt throughout: disp 2nd tl hung bdly rt bnd 2f out: nt rcvr and no ch after* **10/3**[1]

440- **8** *2* **Midnight Cruiser (IRE)**[161] [6973] 3-9-0 91................. RichardHughes 8 65
(R Hannon) *hung rt thrght: racd in last pair: reminders 4f out: rdn and hdwy 3f out: hung bdly rt bnd 2f out: no ch after: fin on stands rail* **9/2**[3]

1m 36.04s (-2.16) **Going Correction** -0.125s/f (Stan) course record **8** Ran SP% **116.4**
Speed ratings (Par 106): **105,102,102,101,95 95,92,90**
toteswinger: 1&2 £21.60, 1&3 £21.90, 2&3 £7.70. CSF £112.66 TOTE £34.90: £5.90, £1.80, £1.70; EX 183.00 TRIFECTA Not won..
Owner Ocean Trailers Ltd **Bred** Black Horse Farm **Trained** Newmarket, Suffolk

FOCUS
Possibly not the strongest Listed event run here and a result that is hard to make sense of. Also the way that some of these hung badly rounding the home bend was more in keeping with a field of two-year-olds. The winner showed big improvement and overall this is not a race to be too positive about.

NOTEBOOK
Ocean's Minstrel appeared to be totally out of his depth at this level as he had upwards of 19lb to find with these rivals. However, having won over 1m2f at Kempton last time his rider did the right thing in sending him straight to the front and it was obvious from some way out that none of his rivals was going to get anywhere near him. What this form adds up to is anyone's guess, but he has now landed a Listed race for connections, so they probably aren't too bothered about that. (op 33-1 tchd 40-1)
Deposer(IRE), winner of a maiden here last summer and just behind Agente Parmigiano in the Kentucky Derby Challenge at Kempton last month after an extremely troubled passage, went in pursuit of the winner up the straight, but the way he put his head in the air was a little disconcerting. (op 5-1)
Icesolator(IRE), who didn't enjoy the best of trips when only seventh in the Spring Cup here last month, was taking another step up in trip. Given a patient ride, he stayed on down the centre of the track late on but was never getting there in time. (op 13-2 tchd 11-2)
Agente Parmigiano(IRE), who like Deposer finished in mid-division after a troubled passage in the Kentucky Derby Challenge on his recent return to action, stuck to the inside rail throughout and, while that may not have been ideal, at least he didn't lose ground rounding the home bend as some of his rivals did. He may not be the easiest to place this season. (op 10-1 tchd 9-1)
Cry Of Freedom(USA), who rather lost his way as a juvenile (albeit taking on very smart company) after showing early promise, raced handily early but didn't get home and may need dropping back in trip. (tchd 5-1)
Canwinn(IRE), placed in Group and Listed company in France in the second half of last season, was given plenty to do but he was very awkward rounding the home bend and never got anywhere near. (tchd 13-2 and 8-1)
Jobe(USA), the highest rated in this field after his third in last season's Gimcrack, had a tongue tie on for this return to action over a longer trip. He didn't help himself by firstly getting upset in the stalls, then racing very keenly up with the pace before hanging badly rounding the home bend. He has questions to answer after this. Official explanation: jockey said colt hung right throughout (op 3-1 tchd 11-4 and 4-1)
Midnight Cruiser(IRE), beaten a long way in the Racing Post Trophy on his final start at two, was nonetheless popular in the market but he was the first off the bridle and was already struggling when almost running off the track turning for home. Official explanation: jockey said colt did not handle the bends and was never travelling (op 15-2 tchd 7-2)

1119 FREEBETS.CO.UK GRAND NATIONAL FREE BETTING - MAIDEN AUCTION STKS 5f (P)
3:55 (3:55) (Class 6) 2-Y-O
£2,729 (£806; £403) **Stalls** High

Form RPR

1 **Soccer (USA)** 2-9-2 0...(t) RichardKingscote 2 84+
(Tom Dascombe) *sn chsng ldr: led over 1f out: rdn and styd on wl fnl f: in command towards fin* **10/3**[3]

5 **2** *½* **Shark Man (IRE)**[7] [994] 2-8-6 0.................................. JackMitchell(3) 5 72
(P J McBride) *in tch: effrt and rdn 2f out: edging sltly lft u.p after: chsd wnr over 1f out: one pce and readily hld fnl 100yds* **11/4**[2]

3 **3** *1 ¾* **Desert Auction (IRE)**[7] [1005] 2-8-13 0......................... RichardHughes 3 69
(R Hannon) *led: sn hdd: chsd ldrs after: rdn 2f out: one pce fnl f* **7/4**[1]

4 *1 ¼* **Super Duplex** 2-8-11 0... IanMongan 4 62
(P M Phelan) *in tch: effrt on inner 2f out: wknd u.p ins fnl f* **10/1**

5 *hd* **Blue Zephyr** 2-8-11 0... MartinDwyer 6 61+
(W R Muir) *s.i.s: sn detached in rr: sme hdwy over 2f out: r.o ent fnl f: swtchd rt ins fnl f: gng on fin: nvr nr enough chal* **14/1**

6 *7* **Any Day (IRE)** 2-8-6 0.. JimCrowley 1 28
(R M Beckett) *dwlt: sn pushed up to ld: rdn and hdd over 1f out: wknd qckly ent fnl f* **8/1**

7 *3 ¼* **Captain Blake (IRE)** 2-8-11 0.. NCallan 7 20
(A B Haynes) *v.s.a: a outpcd in last pl* **16/1**

59.22 secs (0.42) **Going Correction** -0.125s/f (Stan) **7** Ran SP% **118.9**
Speed ratings (Par 90): **91,90,87,85,85 73,68**
toteswinger: 1&2 £3.10, 1&3 £1.20, 2&3 £2.00. CSF £13.75 TOTE £4.90: £2.70, £2.10; EX 12.70.
Owner Findlay & Bloom **Bred** Asiel Stables Llc **Trained** Lambourn, Berks

FOCUS
An interesting juvenile maiden featuring a couple that had already shown ability, but it went to a newcomer. He looks a nice type with the placed horses both rated as having improved on their respective debuts.

NOTEBOOK
Soccer(USA), a 40,000euros half-brother to a winning sprinter in the US, had a tongue tie on for this debut but he knew his job and, having been close to the pace from the start, quickened up nicely in the straight before showing a good attitude to hold off the runner-up. He has done well to beat two rivals with previous experience and he may now try to follow up in a novice event somewhere. (op 6-1)
Shark Man(IRE) finished fifth in the Brocklesby on his debut and that form looked very strong with the only two horses from that race to have run in the meantime both winning. He seemed to travel well enough just behind the leaders early and had his chance up the straight, but he was just inclined to hang under pressure and was always being held. He is worth another chance on a straight track back on turf. (op 9-4 tchd 3-1 7-2 and 2-1 in a place)
Desert Auction(IRE), a fair third on his debut in a maiden at Kempton the previous week from which a couple that finished behind him have subsequently been placed, raced keenly on the outside of the leaders and had every chance, but he couldn't find the required turn of foot where it mattered. (op 6-4 tchd 2-1)
Super Duplex, a £9,000 two-year-old out of a winner in Belgium, had every chance against the inside rail and showed enough to suggest that a race can be found in due course. (op 12-1 tchd 14-1 and 9-1)
Blue Zephyr, a £12,000 colt out of a triple winning sprinter, probably did well to finish as close as he did as he gave away a lot of ground at the start. He obviously has ability, but may need a bit more time.
Captain Blake(IRE) Official explanation: jockey said colt missed break

1120 GROUT INSURANCE BROKERS 25TH ANNIVERSARY MAIDEN STKS 6f (P)
4:40 (4:43) (Class 5) 3-Y-O
£2,729 (£806; £403) **Stalls** Low

Form RPR

0-2 **1** **Anacreon (IRE)**[17] [869] 3-9-3 0...................................... JimmyFortune 2 76+
(J H M Gosden) *led for 1f: chsd ldr tl led again jst over 2f out: rdn clr over 1f out: easily* **4/11**[1]

6-3 **2** *3 ¾* **Vamos (IRE)**[11] [947] 3-9-3 0... ChrisCatlin 5 64
(J R Gask) *chsd ldrs: rdn 2f out: wnt modest 2nd ins fnl f: no ch w wnr* **11/2**[2]

3 *1 ¾* **Tender Charm (USA)** 3-9-3 0... SebSanders 4 58
(R M Beckett) *s.i.s: sn rdn along in last pair: kpt on to go modest 3rd ins fnl f: nvr nr wnr* **9/1**[3]

0-50 **4** *3 ¼* **Tightrope (IRE)**[17] [869] 3-8-12 54...................................... AmyBaker(5) 6 48
(T D McCarthy) *chsd ldr tl led after 1f: hdd jst over 2f out: no ch w wnr over 1f out: wknd ins fnl f* **33/1**

5 *nse* **Moneysupermarket (IRE)** 3-8-12 0.......................... RichardHughes 3 43
(Patrick Morris) *chsd ldrs: rdn jst over 2f out: wknd ins fnl f* **12/1**

6 *½* **Honey Berry (IRE)** 3-8-9 0................................ RussellKennemore(3) 1 41
(Patrick Morris) *s.i.s: a in last pair: rdn and struggling 2f out: no ch fnl f* **28/1**

1m 11.75s (-0.15) **Going Correction** -0.125s/f (Stan) **6** Ran SP% **112.8**
Speed ratings (Par 98): **96,91,88,84,84 83**
toteswinger: 1&2 £1.60, 1&3 £1.80, 2&3 £1.60. CSF £2.92 TOTE £1.40: £1.10, £3.20; EX 2.60.
Owner H R H Princess Haya Of Jordan **Bred** S P Tindall **Trained** Newmarket, Suffolk

FOCUS
Not the most competitive of three-year-old maidens and the result was never really in much doubt. Slightly improved efforts from the front pair with the fourth too close for comfort.

1121 FREEBETS.CO.UK MAN UTD V ASTON VILLA FREE BETS H'CAP 7f (P)
5:20 (5:20) (Class 5) (0-70,70) 4-Y-O+
£2,900 (£856; £428) **Stalls** Low

Form RPR

-033 **1** **Rubenstar (IRE)**[4] [1048] 6-8-10 62.................................. JamieSpencer 3 71+
(Patrick Morris) *hld up in tch: gng wl 2f out: swtchd rt over 1f out: r.o wl to ld last strides* **9/4**[2]

0/60 **2** *hd* **Sew'N'So Character (IRE)**[21] 841 8-9-0 **66** NCallan 4 75
(M Blanshard) *in tch: hdwy to chse ldrs 2f out: sn rdn: led ins fnl f: hdd last strides* **13/2**
610- **3** *1* **Hazytoo**[235] 4946 5-9-2 **68** FergusSweeney 5 74
(P J Makin) *chsd ldr tl led jst over 2f out: rdn over 1f out: hdd ins fnl f: no ex* **8/1**
0231 **4** *2 3/4* **Shaded Edge**[10] 961 5-8-10 **62** MartinDwyer 2 61
(D W P Arbuthnot) *chsd ldrs: pushed along over 4f out: effrt u.p on inner ent fnl f: wknd fnl 100yds* **15/8**[1]
600- **5** *5* **Cativo Cavallino**[111] 7677 6-8-13 **65** RichardThomas 6 50
(J E Long) *a niggled along: in tch: sltly hmpd over 1f out: sn wl btn* **16/1**
4323 **6** *hd* **Ever Cheerful**[10] 961 8-8-11 **63** (p) SteveDrowne 1 48
(A B Haynes) *led tl jst over 2f out: sn rdn: wknd qckly ent fnl f* **9/2**[3]
0P-3 **7** *73* **Impromptu**[24] 799 5-9-4 **70** RobertHavlin 7 —
(P G Murphy) *s.i.s: a last: rdn and lost tch 3f out: virtually p.u fr wl over 1f out: b.b.v* **14/1**

1m 23.28s (-1.52) **Going Correction** -0.125s/f (Stan) **7** Ran SP% **120.7**
Speed ratings (Par 103): **103,102,101,98,92 92,9**
toteswinger: 1&2 £4.00, 1&3 £5.70, 2&3 £7.30. CSF £18.70 CT £103.71 TOTE £3.50: £1.90, £4.10; EX 24.80.
Owner Miss Sharron Pettigrew **Bred** Schwindibode Ag **Trained** Tarporley, Cheshire

FOCUS
An average handicap for the track, but the pace was sound enough. Solid form for the grade.
Impromptu Official explanation: jockey said gelding bled from both nostrils

1122 FREEBETS.CO.UK WORLD SNOOKER CHAMPIONSHIP FREE BETS H'CAP 1m 2f (P)
5:50 (5:50) (Class 6) (0-65,67) 4-Y-0+ **£2,047** (£604; £302) **Stalls** Low

Form RPR
6016 **1** **Vinces**[17] 873 5-9-2 **63** GeorgeBaker 5 71
(T D McCarthy) *in tch: effrt and rdn 2f out: chal ent fnl f: led ins fnl f: rdn out and kpt on wl* **10/3**[1]
10-4 **2** *1/2* **Solo River**[70] 285 4-9-0 **61** FergusSweeney 9 68
(P J Makin) *t.k.h: chsd ldrs: wnt 2nd 3f out: rdn to ld jst over 2f out: hdd ins fnl f: unable qckn* **5/1**[3]
0-00 **3** *2 1/2* **Alseraaj (USA)**[53] 493 4-8-4 **51** oh4 WilliamBuick 10 53
(Ian Williams) *hld up in rr: hdwy 3f out: swtchd rt over 1f out and drvn: kpt on to go 3rd last strides: nvr pce to rch ldrs* **25/1**
-100 **4** *hd* **Ruwain**[57] 427 5-8-0 **52** AndreaAtzeni(5) 4 54
(P J McBride) *dwlt: sn pushed up into midfield: hdwy over 2f out: chsd ldrs 2f out: rdn and one pce fr over 1f out: lost 3rd last strides* **12/1**
134- **5** *2 1/2* **Nassar (IRE)**[300] 2870 6-8-8 **55** KirstyMilczarek 12 52
(G Prodromou) *hld up in last pl: hdwy over 2f out: swtchd lft over 1f out: no hdwy fnl f* **13/2**
56-6 **6** *1* **Lucky Dancer**[70] 279 4-8-11 **58** (b[1]) MartinDwyer 6 53
(D R C Elsworth) *t.k.h: hld up in midfield: lost pl and bhd over 2f out: sn drvn: kpt on fnl f but nvr nr ldrs* **4/1**[2]
00-0 **7** *1 1/2* **Rosy Dawn**[16] 877 4-8-1 **51** oh6 KellyHarrison(3) 11 43
(J J Bridger) *w ldr tl led over 3f out: hdd and rdn jst over 2f out: wknd u.p over 1f out* **25/1**
3041 **8** *3* **King Of The Beers (USA)**[13] 918 5-8-13 **67** (p) SPRyan(7) 2 53
(R A Harris) *racd on outer: in tch in midfield: rdn and no prog wl over 2f out: no ch fnl 2f* **6/1**
050- **9** *15* **High 'n Dry (IRE)**[218] 5458 5-9-2 **63** SamHitchcott 3 19
(M A Allen) *led: hdd and rdn over 3f out: wl bhd fnl 2f: t.o* **16/1**
2001 **10** *18* **Kings Topic (USA)**[11] 948 9-9-5 **66** (p) SebSanders 7 —
(A B Haynes) *in tch: reminders over 5f out: rdn and btn over 2f out: virtually p.u ins fnl f: t.o: b.b.v* **7/1**

2m 5.26s (-1.34) **Going Correction** -0.125s/f (Stan) **10** Ran SP% **121.1**
Speed ratings (Par 101): **100,99,97,97,95 94,93,91,79,64**
toteswinger: 1&2 £4.30, 1&3 £23.30, 2&3 £29.30. CSF £20.99 CT £358.51 TOTE £4.10: £1.30, £2.00, £6.30; EX 22.70 Place 6 £210.68, Place 5 £54.59..
Owner Eastwell Manor Racing Ltd **Bred** Gestut Fahrhof **Trained** Godstone, Surrey

FOCUS
A modest handicap but quite a competitive one. The front pair are rated back to the pick of last season's turf form. The pace seemed decent enough with High 'N Dry and Rosie Dawn taking each other on from the start and that probably helped the first two home as they could be seen travelling best from some way out.
Kings Topic(USA) Official explanation: vet said gelding bled
T/Plt: £453.90 to a £1 stake. Pool: £50,567.05. 81.31 winning tickets. T/Qpdt: £24.00 to a £1 stake. Pool: £3,365.26. 103.50 winning tickets. SP

NEWCASTLE (L-H)
Saturday, April 4

OFFICIAL GOING: Good to firm (good in places; 8.0)
Wind: Strong, half-against Weather: Cloudy

1123 BET365 H'CAP 1m 3y(S)
2:05 (2:06) (Class 4) (0-80,80) 4-Y-0+ **£4,604** (£1,378; £689; £344; £171) **Stalls** High

Form RPR
020- **1** **Wovoka (IRE)**[182] 6482 6-8-8 **70** TonyHamilton 5 81+
(D W Barker) *hld up: nt clr run over 2f out: hdwy over 1f out: qcknd to ld wl ins fnl f: r.o* **16/1**
0-50 **2** *1 1/4* **Casino Night**[23] 823 4-8-3 **70** DeanHeslop(5) 12 75
(R Johnson) *dwlt: sn in tch: effrt over 2f out: ch wl ins fnl f: r.o* **50/1**
520- **3** *1* **We'Re Delighted**[130] 6385 4-8-10 **72** GrahamGibbons 6 75
(T D Walford) *trckd ldrs: led over 2f out: edgd lft and hdd wl ins fnl f: no ex* **8/1**
654- **4** *3 1/4* **Collateral Damage (IRE)**[222] 5360 6-9-4 **80** DavidAllan 7 75+
(T D Easterby) *cl up: disp ld over 2f out to over 1f out: no ex fnl f* **4/1**[1]
216- **5** *nk* **Handsome Falcon**[193] 6186 5-8-12 **74** PaulHanagan 11 69
(R A Fahey) *n.m.r s: sn prom: effrt over 2f out: no ex fnl f* **8/1**
503- **6** *hd* **Capucci**[174] 6675 4-8-11 **80** JamieKyne(7) 10 74
(J J Quinn) *t.k.h: prom: rdn over 2f out: no ex over 1f out* **8/1**
01-3 **7** *3/4* **Minority Report**[6] 1016 9-9-4 **80** AdrianTNicholls 1 72+
(D Nicholls) *hld up: hdwy on outside and prom over 1f out: no ex ins fnl f* **11/2**[3]
30-0 **8** *2* **Daaweitza**[7] 999 6-9-4 **80** TomEaves 8 68+
(B Ellison) *hld up: rdn over 2f out: kpt on fnl f: nvr rchd ldrs* **12/1**
300- **9** *1 3/4* **Oddsmaker (IRE)**[296] 2970 8-9-3 **79** (t) StephenDonohoe 13 63
(M A Barnes) *dwlt: sn in tch: outpcd over 2f out: no imp fnl f* **25/1**
00-0 **10** *2 1/2* **Tiger Dream**[6] 1016 4-8-13 **75** (b[1]) PaulMulrennan 9 53
(K A Ryan) *in tch tl rdn and wknd over 1f out* **7/1**
00-0 **11** *15* **Plenilune (IRE)**[7] 1000 4-8-4 **66** oh4 TWilliams 2 9
(M Brittain) *hld up on outside: drvn over 2f out: sn wknd* **100/1**
1530 **12** *6* **Boss Hog**[17] 868 4-7-13 **68** oh1 ow2 PaulPickard(7) 14 —
(P T Midgley) *t.k.h: led to over 3f out: sn wknd* **20/1**
226- **13** *2* **Mr Lu**[182] 6491 4-8-4 **66** GregFairley 15 —
(A G Foster) *t.k.h: led over 3f out to over 2f out: sn lost pl* **5/1**[2]

1m 44.09s (0.69) **Going Correction** +0.225s/f (Good) **13** Ran SP% **123.0**
Speed ratings (Par 105): **105,103,102,99,99 99,98,96,94,92 77,71,69**
toteswinger: 1&2 £56.30, 1&3 £29.30, 2&3 Not Won CSF £673.51 CT £6926.84 TOTE £25.40: £6.00, £6.30, £3.70; EX 729.80 TRIFECTA Not won..
Owner Dales Homes Ltd **Bred** Rathasker Stud **Trained** Scorton, N Yorks

FOCUS
This was a fair, competitive handicap, but it's worth pointing out there was a strong wind half against the runners and it probably explains why the hold-up horses dominated. They all raced towards the stands' side. The form is sound enough with the winner arguably a bit better than the bare form.

1124 BET365.COM H'CAP 7f
2:35 (2:36) (Class 2) (0-100,98) 4-Y-0+
£11,215 (£3,358; £1,679; £840; £419; £210) **Stalls** High

Form RPR
23-1 **1** **Mister Hardy**[6] 1016 4-8-9 **89** 6ex PaulHanagan 8 95
(R A Fahey) *t.k.h: prom: drvn to ld wl ins fnl f: hld on wl* **6/4**[1]
300- **2** *hd* **Fishforcompliments**[182] 6476 5-8-10 **90** JamieMoriarty 3 96
(R A Fahey) *led: rdn over 1f out: hdd wl ins fnl f: r.o* **18/1**
1000 **3** *nk* **Capricorn Run (USA)**[6] 1018 6-9-4 **98** (v) GrahamGibbons 9 103
(A J McCabe) *dwlt: hld up: hdwy and prom over 1f out: kpt on u.p fnl f* **16/1**
000- **4** *nk* **Sir Xaar (IRE)**[147] 7245 6-8-5 **85** (v) GregFairley 10 89
(B Smart) *hld up towards rr: hdwy 2f out: r.o u.p fnl f* **10/1**
410- **5** *3 1/4* **Quest For Success (IRE)**[133] 7418 4-8-7 **87** TonyHamilton 6 82+
(R A Fahey) *t.k.h: hld up: n.m.r 2f out: sn rdn: kpt on fnl f: no imp* **33/1**
60-0 **6** *hd* **Osteopathic Remedy (IRE)**[7] 995 5-8-11 **91** PhillipMakin 5 86
(M Dods) *stdd s: plld hrd: hdwy over 1f out: r.o fnl f: nvr rchd ldrs* **18/1**
25-0 **7** *6* **Kings Point (IRE)**[7] 995 8-8-13 **93** AdrianTNicholls 7 71
(D Nicholls) *chsd ldr: effrt 2f out: wknd ent fnl f* **14/1**
00-5 **8** *4 1/2* **Giganticus (USA)**[14] 916 6-9-2 **96** MichaelHills 4 62+
(B W Hills) *plld hrd in midfield: effrt on outside over 2f out: wknd 1f out* **5/2**[2]
0010 **9** *3 1/2* **Nightjar (USA)**[7] 995 4-8-10 **90** RoystonFfrench 1 47
(M Johnston) *cl up tl wknd over 2f out* **25/1**
3-51 **10** *10* **Ceremonial Jade (UAE)**[28] 781 6-8-12 **92** (t) JohnEgan 2 22
(M Botti) *in tch: effrt and hung lft over 2f out: sn wknd* **8/1**[3]

1m 30.3s (1.60) **Going Correction** +0.225s/f (Good) **10** Ran SP% **118.6**
Speed ratings (Par 109): **92,91,91,91,87 87,80,75,71,59**
toteswinger: 1&2 £39.10, 1&3 £6.40, 2&3 £39.10. CSF £33.47 CT £336.19 TOTE £1.90: £1.30, £5.30, £5.30; EX 34.50 TRIFECTA Not won..
Owner The Cosmic Cases **Bred** Mrs M Bryce **Trained** Musley Bank, N Yorks

FOCUS
Quite a decent handicap, but the pace was just steady early on, with the jockeys probably wary of the strong wind. As a result, the winning time was moderate. They all raced stands' side. The winner was close to his Doncaster form minus the jockey's claim.

NOTEBOOK
Mister Hardy, a six-length winner at Doncaster on his reappearance, proved good enough to defy his penalty, but he was made to work much harder this time. He enjoyed a good trip, but still only just managed to get by his stablemate and the hat-trick is probably unlikely, with a significant weight rise to come. (op 11-8)
Fishforcompliments ran a cracker on his return from six months off. Admittedly, he enjoyed an easy lead, but the wind can't have helped and he did well to hang on for so long. He has a poor strike-rate for a horse of his ability, but this effort could not be faulted. (op 25-1 tchd 33-1)
Capricorn Run(USA) is not the easiest to predict, and he had no easy task under top weight, but this was a fine effort. (op 18-1)
Sir Xaar(IRE) ran well considering he had been off for the best part of five months. (op 12-1)
Quest For Success(IRE) was a little keen early and got going too late to pose a threat after having to wait for a gap. He had been off for 133 days and should improve. (op 66-1)
Osteopathic Remedy(IRE) was far too keen. Official explanation: jockey said gelding hung left-handed final 2f (op 25-1)
Giganticus(USA) was disappointing, although he was stuck out very wide for much of the way. (op 11-4 tchd 2-1)
Ceremonial Jade(UAE) Official explanation: jockey said gelding hung right-handed throughout

1125 BEST ODDS GUARANTEED EVERY RACE AT BET365.COM H'CAP 1m 4f 93y
3:05 (3:05) (Class 5) (0-70,70) 4-Y-0+ **£2,914** (£867; £433; £216) **Stalls** Low

Form RPR
430- **1** **Herrera (IRE)**[238] 4859 4-8-11 **63** PaulHanagan 2 76
(R A Fahey) *trckd ldrs: rdn to ld 1f out: styd on strly* **8/1**
-500 **2** *2* **Smooth Sovereign (IRE)**[8] 979 4-8-6 **58** RoystonFfrench 5 67
(M Johnston) *led to 1f out: kpt on same pce u.p* **8/1**
-031 **3** *1 1/2* **That'll Do Nicely (IRE)**[18] 857 6-8-12 **63** PaulMulrennan 9 70
(N G Richards) *cl up: effrt and ev ch over 2f out: outpcd over 1f out: kpt on u.p fnl f* **7/1**[3]
455- **4** *1/2* **Destinys Dream (IRE)**[243] 4680 4-9-1 **67** GregFairley 1 73
(Miss Tracy Waggott) *in tch: effrt over 2f out: kpt on same pce ins fnl f* **33/1**
660- **5** *3* **Dechiper (IRE)**[127] 6726 7-8-4 **60** PatrickDonaghy(5) 11 61
(R Johnson) *hld up: hdwy over 2f out: kpt on fnl f: nvr rchd ldrs* **10/1**
-601 **6** *1 1/2* **Media Stars**[59] 393 4-8-4 **56** NickyMackay 4 55
(R Johnson) *in tch: drvn over 2f out: btn fnl f* **7/1**[3]
3361 **7** *1/2* **Monfils Monfils (USA)**[7] 1000 7-8-12 **70** AmyRyan(7) 7 68
(A J McCabe) *hld up: effrt over 2f out: nvr able to chal* **7/2**[1]
20-0 **8** *6* **Coronado's Gold (USA)**[3] 1058 8-8-5 **56** oh3 GrahamGibbons 10 45
(B Ellison) *missed break and swtchd lft s: hld up: effrt 3f out: btn over 1f out* **14/1**
6-00 **9** *1* **Dark Planet**[25] 790 6-7-12 **56** oh10 JamieKyne(7) 6 43
(D W Thompson) *plld hrd: prom tl wknd over 2f out* **40/1**
6-24 **10** *5* **Chookie Hamilton**[75] 219 5-8-9 **60** TomEaves 8 39
(I Semple) *t.k.h: in midfield: rdn over 2f out: sn wknd* **4/1**[2]
610- **11** *56* **Rainbow Zest**[303] 2749 6-8-12 **63** PhillipMakin 3 —
(W Storey) *plld hrd: hld up: drvn and lost tch fr 3f out* **14/1**

2m 44.91s (-0.69) **Going Correction** +0.025s/f (Good)
WFA 4 from 5yo+ 1lb **11** Ran SP% **117.2**
Speed ratings (Par 103): **103,101,100,100,98 97,97,93,92,89 51**
toteswinger: 1&2 £11.80, 1&3 £9.60, 2&3 £10.60. CSF £70.36 CT £474.48 TOTE £10.40: £3.30, £2.40, £1.70; EX 80.50 Trifecta £228.80 Part won. Pool £309.29 - 0.45 winning units..
Owner Dr Anne J F Gillespie **Bred** Dr A J F Gillespie **Trained** Musley Bank, N Yorks
■ Stewards' Enquiry : Paul Mulrennan one-day ban: careless riding (Apr 18)

FOCUS
A modest handicap. The fourth looks the best guide with the first three all open to improvement.
Monfils Monfils(USA) Official explanation: jockey said gelding ran flat

1126 EBF / GRAINGER GAMES NOVICE STKS 5f
3:45 (3:46) (Class 4) 2-Y-O **£5,018** (£1,493; £746; £372) **Stalls** High

Form RPR
21 1 **Archers Road (IRE)**[2] 1083 2-8-11 0 MCGeran(5) 7 86
(M R Channon) *mde all: hung lft and jst jnd whn lft 3l clr last 50yds* **1/1**[1]
4 2 3 **Trade Secret**[7] 994 2-8-12 0 AlanMunro 1 70
(M Brittain) *chsd ldrs: effrt 2f out: one pce whn lft 3l 2nd last 50yds* **4/1**[2]
2 3 3 ½ **Out The Ring (IRE)**[7] 1005 2-8-12 0 RichardMullen 4 56
(K A Ryan) *cl up: effrt 2f out: one pce whn lft 3rd last 50yds* **4/1**[2]
4 3 **Drumpellier (IRE)** 2-8-0 0 PaulPickard(7) 8 39+
(P T Midgley) *midfield: effrt 2f out: no imp whn lft 4th last 50yds* **66/1**
5 6 **Ignatieff (IRE)** 2-8-12 0 TomEaves 5 20
(Mrs L Stubbs) *prom: n.m.r over 2f out: sn rdn and wknd* **16/1**
6 6 **Ytartfawn (IRE)** 2-8-12 0 JamieMoriarty 6 —
(P T Midgley) *bhd and green: wknd fr 1/2-way* **80/1**
7 3 ¾ **Lily Lenor (IRE)** 2-8-7 0 GrahamGibbons 10 —
(B Ellison) *bhd and outpcd: no ch fr 1/2-way* **20/1**
8 12 **Lady Lube Rye (IRE)** 2-8-7 0 AdrianTNicholls 3 —
(N Wilson) *in tch tl rdn and wknd fr 2f out* **16/1**
9 7 **Gazamali (IRE)** 2-8-9 0 AndrewMullen(3) 2 —
(G A Harker) *s.i.s: nvr on terms* **8/1**[3]
R **Lees Anthem** 2-8-12 0 AndrewElliott 9 79+
(C J Teague) *trckd ldrs: effrt over 1f out: disputing ld and keeping on whn dived rt and crashed through rail last 50yds* **50/1**

64.68 secs (3.98) **Going Correction** +0.225s/f (Good) 10 Ran SP% **122.3**
Speed ratings (Par 94): **77,72,66,61,52 42,36,17,6,—**
toteswinger: 1&2 £2.90, 1&3 £1.50, 2&3 £4.90. CSF £5.45 TOTE £2.10: £1.10, £1.40, £1.70; EX 7.20 Trifecta £12.10 Pool £608.19 - 36.99 winning units..
Owner John Webster **Bred** John Fielding **Trained** West Ilsley, Berks

FOCUS
The first three had shown plenty of ability and this was a decent early-season juvenile contest, but the complexion of the race changed dramatically with a half a furlong to run. The runner-up is rated to his Brocklesby mark with the third a bit below his Kempton debut. Lees Anthem looks sure to win a race if none the worse.

NOTEBOOK
Archers Road(IRE) did not help his chance by edging left towards the middle of the track when hit with the whip on the right side, and that had handed the initiative to Lees Anthem, although the successful jockey felt he still would have won whatever the case. The Mick Channon runner was having his third start in eight days (second in the Brocklesby before winning his maiden at Leicester), and is tough, but this wasn't the first time he's wandered around under pressure. He's clearly still immature mentally, although the wind, which was half against him, can't have helped. He holds an entry in a similar race at Nottingham next week. (op 5-4 tchd 11-8)
Trade Secret could not reverse Brocklesby placings with the winner, but this was a respectable effort, and he finished clear of the others. (op 5-1)
Out The Ring(IRE) showed ability when second at Kempton on his debut, but found this tougher. (op 7-2 tchd 9-2)
Drumpellier(IRE) cost only £800, but she has quite a nice pedigree and showed ability.
Lees Anthem, who is out of a 6f winner, crashed through the stands' rail when appearing to hold a narrow advantage close home and had clearly been spooked. There's no way of knowing whether he would have won, but he was running a terrific race, not least because he was the only newcomer to show up prominently in the gusty conditions. He looks useful and it has to be hoped this does not leave a mental scar. (op 66-1)

1127 ST JAMES SECURITY MAIDEN STKS 1m 2f 32y
4:30 (4:38) (Class 5) 3-Y-0+ **£2,752** (£818; £409; £204) **Stalls** Low

Form RPR
23- 1 **Rafaan (USA)**[199] 6029 3-8-7 0 TPO'Shea 7 84
(M Johnston) *mde all: pushed out fnl 2f: comf* **7/4**[2]
0- 2 3 **Ruler Of All (IRE)**[184] 6425 3-8-8 0 ow1 MichaelHills 5 79
(B W Hills) *dwlt: t.k.h and sn prom: effrt and green 2f out: edgd rt and styd on fnl f: nt rch wnr* **5/4**[1]
064- 3 ¾ **Decorum (USA)**[140] 7336 3-8-7 76 (t) RichardMullen 1 76
(J H M Gosden) *trckd ldrs: effrt over 2f out: one pce fnl f: lost 2nd nr fin* **3/1**[3]
0 4 24 **Cooperman**[7] 998 3-8-0 0 PaulPickard(7) 8 28
(P T Midgley) *s.i.s: bhd: drvn over 3f out: nvr rchd ldrs* **40/1**
/00- 5 ¾ **Three Gold Leaves**[301] 2847 4-9-12 60 (t) PaulMulrennan 3 27
(D W Thompson) *plld hrd early: hld up: effrt over 2f out: sn wknd* **100/1**
6/6- 6 2 **Grail Knight**[435] 310 4-9-12 0 GregFairley 6 23
(A G Foster) *prom tl rdn and wknd fr 3f out* **50/1**
000- 7 1 ¾ **Piccolo Pete**[313] 2463 4-9-5 55 GarryWhillans(7) 4 19
(R Johnson) *bhd: struggling over 3f out: nvr on terms* **20/1**
0/0- 8 dist **Our Serendipity**[143] 7280 6-9-0 30 KarenKenny(7) 10 —
(R C Guest) *cl up tl wknd over 3f out: t.o* **150/1**

2m 13.88s (1.98) **Going Correction** +0.025s/f (Good)
WFA 3 from 4yo+ 19lb 8 Ran SP% **116.6**
Speed ratings (Par 103): **93,90,90,70,70 68,67,—**
toteswinger: 1&2 £1.10, 1&3 £1.20, 2&3 £1.20. CSF £4.33 TOTE £2.80: £1.10, £1.10, £1.10; EX 4.70 Trifecta £11.60 Pool £635.61 - 40.46 winning units..
Owner Hamdan Al Maktoum **Bred** Shadwell Farm LLC **Trained** Middleham Moor, N Yorks

FOCUS
Maidens up north are often pretty ordinary, but this was an exception and the form among the front three looks useful. They finished a mile clear.

1128 J T DOVE MAIDEN FILLIES' STKS 1m 3y(S)
5:10 (5:12) (Class 5) 3-Y-0+ **£2,719** (£809; £404; £202) **Stalls** High

Form RPR
0- 1 **Full Of Love (IRE)**[154] 7140 3-8-9 0 MichaelHills 2 66+
(B W Hills) *hld up: hdwy to ld over 1f out: edgd rt: rdn out* **11/2**[3]
0- 2 1 **Implication**[238] 4870 3-8-9 0 StephenDonohoe 1 66+
(E A L Dunlop) *swtchd to stands rail sn after s: hld up: hdwy to chse ldrs whn nt clr run over 1f out: kpt on wl fnl f: nt rch wnr* **3/1**[2]
3 ½ **Off Chance** 3-8-9 0 DuranFentiman 7 60+
(T D Easterby) *hld up: n.m.r briefly wl over 1f out: kpt on strly fnl f: nrst fin* **33/1**
0-3 4 ½ **La Gifted**[17] 869 3-8-4 0 MCGeran(5) 12 58
(M R Channon) *in tch: effrt over 2f out: kpt on u.p fnl f* **14/1**
5 shd **Jenny Potts**[140] 5-9-10 0 PaulMulrennan 8 62
(L Lungo) *s.s: hld up: hdwy on outside over 2f out: one pce fnl f* **14/1**
000- 6 3 **Knock Three Times (IRE)**[138] 7353 3-8-9 38 GrahamGibbons 14 51?
(W Storey) *trckd ldrs tl rdn and wknd ent fnl f* **66/1**

2-60 7 ½ **Dante Deo (USA)**[47] 572 3-8-9 60 TomEaves 9 50
(T D Barron) *led to over 1f out: sn no ex* **50/1**
00- 8 2 ½ **Suitably Accoutred (IRE)**[172] 6722 3-8-6 0 AndrewMullen(3) 13 44
(Mrs A Duffield) *midfield: drvn and outpcd over 2f out: n.d after* **100/1**
9 1 ½ **Carnival Fair**[31] 4-9-10 0 PaulHanagan 4 45
(R A Fahey) *bhd: pushed along 3f out: nvr rchd ldrs* **100/1**
32 10 3 ½ **Mosqueras Romance**[19] 849 3-8-9 0 JohnEgan 11 33
(M Botti) *t.k.h: cl up: ev ch over 2f out: wknd fnl f* **6/4**[1]
30 11 4 **Jawaaher (USA)**[31] 752 3-8-9 0 RoystonFfrench 6 24
(M Johnston) *in tch tl rdn and wknd over 2f out* **16/1**
0- 12 1 ¾ **Rio Carnival (USA)**[215] 5571 3-8-9 0 RichardMullen 10 20
(J H M Gosden) *prom tl wknd fr 2f out* **6/1**

1m 47.43s (4.03) **Going Correction** +0.225s/f (Good)
WFA 3 from 4yo+ 15lb 12 Ran SP% **122.3**
Speed ratings (Par 100): **88,87,86,86,85 82,82,79,78,74 70,69**
toteswinger: 1&2 £3.90, 1&3 £34.10, 2&3 £34.10. CSF £22.91 TOTE £5.20: £1.90, £1.80, £7.30; EX 29.50 Trifecta £293.90 Part won. Pool £397.24 - 0.40 winning units..
Owner Suzanne & Nigel Williams **Bred** Raymond P Doyle **Trained** Lambourn, Berks

FOCUS
The pace was just modest and the bare form of this fillies' maiden is probably only fair at best with the sixth holding it down, but the race should produce a few winners. The first two are capable of better. They all raced stands' side and conditions were still blustery.
Jenny Potts Official explanation: jockey said mare missed the break
Mosqueras Romance Official explanation: trainer's rep said filly was unsuited by the good to firm (good places) ground
T/Plt: £494.60 to a £1 stake. Pool: £58,312.34. 86.06 winning tickets. T/Qpdt: £9.00 to a £1 stake. Pool: £3,460.74. 282.20 winning tickets. RY

1103 WOLVERHAMPTON (A.W) (L-H)
Saturday, April 4

OFFICIAL GOING: Standard
Wind: Almost nil Weather: Fine

1129 FREEBETS.CO.UK CLAIMING STKS 5f 216y(P)
6:50 (6:50) (Class 6) 3-Y-0 **£2,047** (£604; £302) **Stalls** Low

Form RPR
03 1 **Pipers Piping (IRE)**[56] 454 3-9-0 0 ShaneKelly 5 65
(J A Osborne) *led 1f: chsd ldr: rdn and edgd lft jst over 1f out: r.o to ld wl ins fnl f* **9/1**
0-30 2 1 **Simple Rhythm**[38] 673 3-8-4 60 Louis-PhilippeBeuzelin(5) 3 57
(N Tinkler) *led after 1f: pushed along over 1f out: rdn and hdd wl ins fnl f: no ex* **9/2**[3]
34-0 3 4 **York Key Bar**[6] 1015 3-8-11 69 LanceBetts(7) 7 53
(B Ellison) *hld up in rr: rdn wl over 1f out: r.o to take 3rd ins fnl f: no ch w ldng pair* **4/1**[2]
5305 4 1 ¼ **Weet In Nerja**[15] 900 3-8-5 53 (p) DavidKenny(7) 8 43
(R Hollinshead) *hld up and bhd: rdn over 2f out: edgd lft over 1f out: kpt on to take 4th wl ins fnl f: n.d* **14/1**
6034 5 ¾ **You Avin A Laugh**[9] 966 3-8-7 62 (b1) BMcHugh(7) 6 43
(C A Dwyer) *prom: rdn wl over 1f out: sn wknd* **5/4**[1]
-006 6 nk **The Canny Dove (USA)**[51] 520 3-8-0 41 ow1 (b1) DeanHeslop(5) 1 33
(T D Barron) *t.k.h: prom tl rdn and wknd over 1f out* **12/1**
36 7 2 ¼ **Christmascametwice**[21] 842 3-8-13 0 TPQueally 4 34
(J A Osborne) *bhd fnl 2f* **14/1**

1m 15.33s (0.33) **Going Correction** -0.125s/f (Stan) 7 Ran SP% **113.7**
Speed ratings (Par 96): **92,90,85,83,82 82,79**
toteswinger: 1&2 £6.30, 1&3 £5.70, 2&3 £3.90. CSF £48.06 TOTE £8.40: £4.20, £1.90; EX 44.70.
Owner John Egan & 12 Day Partners **Bred** Drumhass Stud **Trained** Upper Lambourn, Berks

FOCUS
A weak claimer which concerned only two from some way out. The race has been rated around the runer-up but this is not form to take too literally or positively.

1130 GRAND NATIONAL FREE BETS MEDIAN AUCTION MAIDEN STKS 1m 141y(P)
7:20 (7:27) (Class 5) 3-Y-0 **£2,729** (£806; £403) **Stalls** Low

Form RPR
66- 1 **Puzzlemaster**[179] 6552 3-9-3 0 JimmyQuinn 4 74+
(M Botti) *s.i.s: hld up: swtchd rt ent st: hdwy over 1f out: rdn to ld towards fin* **4/1**[3]
- 2 hd **Sawab** 3-8-12 0 J-PGuillambert 5 68
(C E Brittain) *a.p: jnd ldr over 4f out: led over 1f out: rdn and hdd towards fin* **20/1**
0-42 3 4 ½ **Morning Sir Alan**[12] 939 3-9-3 72 PatCosgrave 1 63
(S A Callaghan) *hld up in tch: rdn over 1f out: one pce fnl f* **3/1**[2]
04-2 4 ½ **Woodlark Island (IRE)**[10] 951 3-9-3 74 (p) PatDobbs 3 62
(M P Tregoning) *led after 1f: rdn and hdd over 1f out: wknd wl ins fnl f* **11/10**[1]
5 3 ¾ **And A Partridge** 3-9-3 0 ShaneKelly 6 53?
(J A Osborne) *dwlt: nvr nr ldrs* **33/1**
00- 6 2 ¾ **Gibson Square (USA)**[185] 6383 3-8-12 0 WilliamCarson(5) 2 47?
(S C Williams) *led 1f: chsd ldr tl over 4f out: rdn over 3f out: wknd 2f out* **50/1**
03 7 3 ½ **Mystic Touch**[22] 828 3-9-3 0 MickyFenton 8 39
(Miss E C Lavelle) *bhd fnl 2f* **14/1**

1m 49.91s (-0.59) **Going Correction** -0.125s/f (Stan) 7 Ran SP% **108.9**
Speed ratings (Par 98): **97,96,92,92,89 86,83**
toteswinger: 1&2 £9.90, 1&3 £2.10, 2&3 £8.20. CSF £63.73 TOTE £5.00: £1.90, £6.30; EX 101.10.
Owner Norcroft Park Stud **Bred** Norcroft Park Stud **Trained** Newmarket, Suffolk

FOCUS
An ordinary maiden run in a slower time than the seller. Probably not form to be too positive about.
Mystic Touch Official explanation: jockey said gelding lost its action but returned sound

1131 OVER £1000 IN FREE BETS @ FREEBETS.CO.UK (S) STKS 1m 141y(P)
7:50 (7:54) (Class 6) 4-Y-0+ **£2,047** (£604; £302) **Stalls** Low

Form RPR
-005 1 **Waterside (IRE)**[24] 805 10-8-12 70 JamesDoyle 4 71
(S Curran) *s.i.s: hld up in rr: rdn over 1f out: r.o to ld nr fin* **7/1**
4360 2 nk **Johnston's Baby (IRE)**[32] 744 7-8-7 57 EddieAhern 6 65
(E J Alston) *hld up towards rr: hdwy over 2f out: rdn over 1f out: led wl ins fnl f: hdd nr fin* **16/1**
4320 3 2 ½ **Prince Noel**[12] 932 5-8-12 62 (v1) LeeEnstone 7 65
(N Wilson) *s.i.s: hld up in rr: hdwy over 4f out: led over 1f out: sn rdn: hdd and no ex wl ins fnl f* **3/1**[2]

40-4 **4** *6* **Where's Killoran**[32] 748 4-8-7 43 .... RobertWinston 2 46
(E J Alston) *prom: pushed along over 2f out: nt clr run wl over 1f out: sn wknd* **14/1**

6000 **5** *½* **Machinate (USA)**[8] 984 7-8-12 49 .... LiamJones 1 50
(W M Brisbourne) *hld up towards rr: hdwy on outside 2f out: c wd st: wknd over 1f out* **20/1**

1232 **6** *nk* **Samurai Warrior**[6] 554 4-8-7 62 .... RichardEvans(5) 11 49+
(P D Evans) *chsd ldr: led over 3f out: rdn and hdd over 1f out: wknd fnl f* **7/4**[1]

4304 **7** *½* **Mister Benji**[17] 867 10-8-12 45 .... TGMcLaughlin 5 48
(B P J Baugh) *hld up in mid-div: rdn and btn over 2f out* **20/1**

5260 **8** *1* **Bailieborough (IRE)**[6] 1014 10-8-5 58 .... LanceBetts(7) 9 45
(B Ellison) *hld up in rr: nvr nr ldrs* **5/1**[3]

/00- **9** *1 ¾* **Mycenean Prince (USA)**[228] 3545 6-8-12 38 .... PhillipMakin 12 41
(R C Guest) *a towards rr* **50/1**

00-6 **10** *1 ½* **Capped For Victory (USA)**[73] 7 8-8-12 47 ....(t) JimmyQuinn 13 38
(W Storey) *hld up in tch: wknd over 2f out* **33/1**

-000 **11** *7* **Bewdley**[29] 775 4-8-2 39 .... MartinLane(5) 10 17
(R E Peacock) *led: hdd over 3f out: rdn and wknd over 2f out* **50/1**

0- **12** *2 ¼* **Red Century**[308] 2620 4-8-7 0 ....(bt[1]) PaulEddery 3 12
(Paul Mason) *bhd fnl 3f* **40/1**

1m 49.03s (-1.47) **Going Correction** -0.125s/f (Stan) **12** Ran SP% **121.9**
Speed ratings (Par 101): **101,100,98,93,92 92,92,91,89,88 82,80**
toteswinger: 1&2 £7.30, 1&3 £5.60, 2&3 £10.80. CSF £103.78 TOTE £9.60: £2.50, £2.00, £1.70; EX 76.60.There was no bid for the winner.
Owner L M Power **Bred** Yeomanstown Stud **Trained** Hatford, Oxon
■ Stewards' Enquiry : Richard Evans one-day ban: failed to keep straight from stalls (Apr 18)
Martin Lane one-day ban: failed to keep straight from stalls (Apr 18)

FOCUS
A strongly run seller and the front runners dropped right out, opening the way for the hold-up horses to dominate in the final furlong. The form seems sound enough.

1132 BEST FREE BETS @ FREEBETS.CO.UK H'CAP 7f 32y(P)
8:20 (8:21) (Class 5) (0-75,73) 4-Y-0+ **£3,238** (£963; £481; £240) **Stalls** High

Form RPR

4304 **1** **Downhill Skier (IRE)**[12] 932 5-8-2 60 .... DavidProbert(3) 5 67
(W M Brisbourne) *hld up in rr: hdwy on ins 3f out: rdn to ld ins fnl f: edgd rt: r.o* **4/1**[1]

3331 **2** *hd* **Jord (IRE)**[5] 1039 5-8-10 65 6ex .... RobertWinston 3 72
(A J McCabe) *chsd ldr: rdn wl over 1f out: ev ch wl ins fnl f: r.o* **4/1**[1]

2623 **3** *hd* **Guildenstern (IRE)**[16] 880 7-9-0 69 .... JimmyQuinn 2 75
(P Howling) *a.p: swtchd lft ins fnl f: rdn and r.o* **6/1**[3]

4-00 **4** *½* **King Kenny**[40] 654 4-9-1 70 .... EddieAhern 1 75
(S Parr) *led: rdn wl over 1f out: hdd ins fnl f: nt qckn cl home* **16/1**

3513 **5** *1* **Kabis Amigos**[5] 1039 7-8-10 65 ....(b) ShaneKelly 4 67
(S T Mason) *hld up in tch: rdn over 1f out: no ex towards fin* **11/2**[2]

00-6 **6** *1 ¾* **Xtra Torrential (USA)**[9] 974 7-9-3 72 .... LPKeniry 7 69
(D M Simcock) *t.k.h towards rr: rdn over 1f out: nvr nr to chal* **11/1**

0-64 **7** *1 ¼* **Onceaponatime (IRE)**[16] 880 4-9-3 72 .... SaleemGolam 8 66
(M D Squance) *hld up: pushed along 2f out: rdn over 1f out: no hdwy* **20/1**

320- **8** *3 ¾* **Ride A White Swan**[205] 5836 4-8-9 64 ow1 .... DarrenWilliams 10 48
(D Shaw) *t.k.h: a in rr* **25/1**

300- **9** *shd* **Dream Express (IRE)**[168] 6813 4-9-4 73 .... PhillipMakin 6 56
(M Dods) *t.k.h: prom tl wknd over 2f out* **6/1**[3]

1222 **10** *½* **Obe Royal**[8] 980 5-8-12 72 ....(b) RichardEvans(5) 9 54
(P D Evans) *hld up and bhd: hdwy on outside over 4f out: pushed along over 3f out: sn wknd* **8/1**

1m 28.9s (-0.70) **Going Correction** -0.125s/f (Stan) **10** Ran SP% **117.9**
Speed ratings (Par 103): **99,98,98,97,96 94,93,89,89,88**
toteswinger: 1&2 £3.70, 1&3 £5.60, 2&3 £6.40. CSF £19.66 CT £95.98 TOTE £4.90: £2.20, £2.10, £2.40; EX 26.40.
Owner Miss P D Insull **Bred** Swettenham Stud **Trained** Great Ness, Shropshire
■ Stewards' Enquiry : Robert Winston two-day ban: used whip with excessive frequency (Apr 18-19)

FOCUS
A few in-form sorts contesting this run-of-the-mill handicap and plenty in with a chance entering the final furlong off a steady pace. Very ordinary form.

1133 GET A FREE BET AT FREEBETS.CO.UK H'CAP 1m 1f 103y(P)
8:50 (8:50) (Class 5) (0-75,75) 4-Y-0+ **£3,238** (£963; £481; £240) **Stalls** Low

Form RPR

-50 **1** **Becuille (IRE)**[5] 1042 4-8-6 63 .... EddieAhern 5 71
(B J Meehan) *chsd ldr: led 2f out: sn rdn: hdd jst ins fnl f: led last strides* **16/1**

2126 **2** *hd* **New Star (UAE)**[1] 1107 5-8-11 75 .... PaulPickard(7) 4 82
(W M Brisbourne) *hld up in tch: rdn over 1f out: led jst ins fnl f: hdd last strides* **9/2**[2]

100- **3** *1 ¼* **Bramalea**[138] 7360 4-8-9 66 .... LPKeniry 8 71
(B W Duke) *t.k.h towards rr: hdwy 2f out: c wd st: rdn over 1f out: r.o towards fin* **33/1**

1243 **4** *hd* **Formidable Guest**[15] 897 5-8-10 67 ....(v[1]) RobertHavlin 3 71
(J Pearce) *hld up in mid-div: hdwy wl over 1f out: sn rdn: kpt on towards fin* **6/1**[3]

-023 **5** *hd* **Supercast (IRE)**[24] 798 6-8-13 75 .... FrederikTylicki(5) 2 79
(N J Vaughan) *a.p: rdn wl over 1f out: nt qckn ins fnl f* **7/4**[1]

3 **6** *1 ¼* **Enlist**[9] 970 5-8-11 68 .... SteveDrowne 7 69
(A J Lidderdale) *hld up in rr: pushed along over 3f out: rdn and hdwy 1f out: swtchd lft ins fnl f: nvr able to chal* **20/1**

654- **7** *13* **Glenridding**[161] 6989 5-9-0 71 .... TPQueally 1 45
(J G Given) *led: hdd 2f out: wknd over 1f out* **8/1**

5040 **8** *4 ½* **Stark Contrast (USA)**[5] 1042 5-8-1 61 oh5 .... DavidProbert(3) 9 26
(M D I Usher) *hld up in rr: rdn over 2f out: sn struggling* **14/1**

-531 **9** *11* **Follow The Flag (IRE)**[12] 932 5-9-2 73 ....(p) RobertWinston 6 15
(A J McCabe) *t.k.h: prom: pushed along over 3f out: wknd over 2f out* **7/1**

1m 59.0s (-2.70) **Going Correction** -0.125s/f (Stan) **9** Ran SP% **112.7**
Speed ratings (Par 103): **107,106,105,105,105 104,92,88,78**
toteswinger: 1&2 £9.10, 1&3 £21.40, 2&3 £34.00. CSF £84.25 CT £2345.85 TOTE £26.90: £5.00, £1.20, £7.30; EX 128.60.
Owner Ms Susan McKeon **Bred** Tally-Ho Stud **Trained** Manton, Wilts
■ Stewards' Enquiry : Eddie Ahern one-day ban: used whip with excessive frequency (Apr 18)

FOCUS
A modest contest but another close-fought finish. Sound form with the winner back to his Irish best.

1134 VISIT FREEBETS.CO.UK H'CAP 5f 20y(P)
9:20 (9:21) (Class 6) (0-60,60) 4-Y-0+ **£2,047** (£604; £302) **Stalls** Low

Form RPR

3542 **1** **Bluebok**[10] 956 8-9-4 60 ....(bt) LPKeniry 3 73
(J M Bradley) *mde all: rdn 1f out: r.o wl* **6/1**[3]

5520 **2** *2 ¾* **Scarlet Oak**[41] 645 5-8-13 55 ....(p) RobertWinston 4 58
(A M Hales) *s.i.s: hld up in rr: hdwy on ins wl over 1f out: rdn and r.o to take 2nd wl ins fnl f: nt trble wnr* **12/1**

6612 **3** *1* **Mujma**[8] 976 5-8-12 54 ....(bt) EddieAhern 1 53
(S Parr) *a.p: chsd wnr wl over 1f out: sn rdn: no imp whn lost 2nd wl ins fnl f* **2/1**[1]

3353 **4** *1 ¼* **Muktasb (USA)**[22] 832 8-9-4 60 ....(v) TPQueally 7 55
(D Shaw) *s.i.s: hld up in rr: rdn whn swtchd rt jst over 1f out: r.o ins fnl f: nvr nrr* **7/1**

1060 **5** *shd* **Monte Major (IRE)**[22] 832 8-9-3 59 ....(v) DarrenWilliams 2 54
(D Shaw) *hld up towards rr: hdwy jst over 1f out: rdn and kpt on same pce ins fnl f* **9/1**

0000 **6** *½* **Stoneacre Pat (IRE)**[15] 896 4-8-6 48 .... PatrickMathers 13 41+
(Peter Grayson) *s.i.s: in rr: c v wd st: rdn and hdwy whn edgd lft ins fnl f: r.o* **16/1**

0432 **7** *hd* **Affirmatively**[15] 895 4-8-0 47 ....(bt) AmyBaker(5) 5 39
(A W Carroll) *prom: rdn 1f out: fdd wl ins fnl f* **12/1**

4130 **8** *2 ¼* **Meikle Barfil**[4] 1055 7-8-9 51 ow1 ....(tp) SteveDrowne 8 35
(J M Bradley) *keen early: a towards rr* **22/1**

50-0 **9** *½* **Richardthesecond (IRE)**[22] 832 4-8-13 55 .... TGMcLaughlin 9 37
(W M Brisbourne) *w wnr tl rdn and wknd wl over 1f out* **20/1**

5325 **10** *¾* **Green Lagonda (AUS)**[19] 853 7-9-0 56 ....(p) MickyFenton 6 35
(Stef Liddiard) *plld hrd in mid-div: rdn over 1f out: wkng whn n.m.r wl ins fnl f* **9/2**[2]

-400 **11** *1 ½* **Firewalker**[16] 884 4-8-4 46 oh1 ....(b) FrankieMcDonald 10 20
(P T Dalton) *prom: rdn over 1f out: wkng whn n.m.r ins fnl f* **66/1**

0040 **12** *1 ¾* **Triskaidekaphobia**[15] 896 6-8-6 48 ....(bt) PaulFitzsimons 11 16
(Miss J R Tooth) *in tch on outside: c wd st: wknd wl over 1f out* **25/1**

61.20 secs (-1.10) **Going Correction** -0.125s/f (Stan) **12** Ran SP% **124.0**
Speed ratings (Par 101): **103,98,97,95,94 94,93,90,89,88 85,82**
toteswinger: 1&2 £16.30, 1&3 £5.80, 2&3 £7.70. CSF £75.82 CT £189.86 TOTE £8.00: £1.90, £4.40, £1.70; EX 108.60 Place 6: £1,358.59 Place 5: £218.31.
Owner E A Hayward **Bred** E Duggan And D Churchman **Trained** Sedbury, Gloucs
■ Stewards' Enquiry : T G McLaughlin caution: careless riding.

FOCUS
A moderate sprint and the winner ran his rivals ragged. His performance could be rated higher but a conservative view has been taken of the form.
T/Plt: £2,576.40 to a £1 stake. Pool: £73,235.33. 20.75 winning tickets. T/Qpdt: £75.10 to a £1 stake. Pool: £7,576.11. 74.60 winning tickets. KH

1135 - 1137a (Foreign Racing) - See Raceform Interactive

925 CURRAGH (R-H)
Sunday, April 5

OFFICIAL GOING: Round course - yielding; straight course - yielding to soft

1138a BRUCE BETTING NEWBRIDGE GLADNESS STKS (GROUP 3) 7f
3:45 (3:45) 4-Y-0+ **£41,019** (£11,990; £5,679; £1,893)

RPR

1 **Mad About You (IRE)**[14] 928 4-8-11 114 ....(b) PJSmullen 1 114
(D K Weld, Ire) *trckd ldrs: 3rd 1/2-way: impr to 2nd 3f out: led over 1 1/2f out: rdn and kpt on wl ins fnl f* **9/4**[1]

2 *2 ½* **Dohasa (IRE)**[38] 700 4-9-0 109 .... KLatham 7 110
(G M Lyons, Ire) *hld up towards rr: hdwy in 5th 1 1/2f out: rdn into 2nd 1f out: kpt on fnl f: nt rch wnr* **20/1**

3 *1 ¼* **Kargali (IRE)**[218] 5524 4-9-0 105 ....(t) MJKinane 2 107
(John M Oxx, Ire) *chsd ldrs: 4th 1/2-way: 3rd 2f out: rdn and kpt on same pce fr over 1f out* **4/1**[2]

4 *3* **Lovelace**[183] 6504 5-9-6 .... JamieSpencer 9 105
(M Johnston) *prom early: sn settled mid-div: 7th 1/2-way: rdn into 4th 2f out: no ex in 5th 1f out: kpt on same pce fnl f* **7/1**

5 *hd* **Summit Surge (IRE)**[38] 702 5-9-3 111 ....(t) EJMcNamara 5 101
(G M Lyons, Ire) *mid-div: 6th 1/2-way: rdn and no imp 1 1/2f out: kpt on same pce fr over 1f out* **16/1**

6 *1 ½* **Jumbajukiba**[169] 6831 6-9-3 114 ....(b) FMBerry 3 97
(Mrs John Harrington, Ire) *sn led: rdn and hdd over 1 1/2f out: no ex over 1f out: kpt on one pce* **9/2**[3]

7 *1 ½* **Express Wish**[169] 6814 5-9-3 .... ShaneKelly 4 93
(J Noseda) *mid-div: 5th 1/2-way: rdn 2f out: no ex and wknd 1 1/2f out* **8/1**

8 *3* **Georgebernardshaw (IRE)**[231] 5130 4-9-0 109 .... JMurtagh 10 82
(A P O'Brien, Ire) *a towards rr* **6/1**

9 *14* **Tian Shan (IRE)**[154] 7157 5-9-0 106 .... PShanahan 6 44
(D K Weld, Ire) *awkward leaving stalls: sn chsd ldr: 2nd 1/2-way: rdn and wknd 3f out: trailing fnl f* **33/1**

1m 27.5s (0.40) **Going Correction** +0.40s/f (Good) **9** Ran SP% **120.4**
Speed ratings: **113,110,108,105,104 103,101,98,82**
CSF £53.71 TOTE £3.30: £1.10, £6.80, £2.40; DF 54.80.
Owner Moyglare Stud Farm **Bred** Moyglare Stud Farm Ltd **Trained** The Curragh, Co Kildare

FOCUS
The winner is rated back to her best.

NOTEBOOK
Mad About You(IRE) benefited from this better ground and the fitting of first-time blinkers to record her third career win. The headgear made her concentrate according to her trainer, following her shock defeat on her seasonal debut in the Group 3 Park Express Stakes over a furlong longer last month. Placed in four Group 1 events at two and the only filly in the line up, she travelled well before taking over after passing the two-furlong pole. For a few strides the runner-up looked like he was beginning to reel her in but to her credit she picked up again to get the job done. The Ridgewood Pearl Stakes over a mile will probably be her next target, with the Pretty Polly likely to follow afterwards. Weld considers her fully effective between 7f and 1m2f, but she failed to get 1m4f in the Irish Oaks last season. (op 2/1 tchd 5/2)
Dohasa(IRE), who enjoyed a profitable visit to Dubai, was tackling this trip for the first time. He emerged with some credit, showing no ill effect from his trip to the Emirates, and he can hopefully build on this.
Kargali(IRE), who was roughed off after scoring at Killarney last August and reportedly got a bit jarred up after that extended 1m win, was seeking his third consecutive success. Considering this was his first run since, improvement should be likely when upped slightly in trip. (op 4/1 tchd 7/2)

Lovelace, one of two British raiders in the field, could never get involved. The Group 2 penalty for winning at Baden-Baden last September made this a difficult task for the five-year-old, who was not beaten that far by Goldikova at Longchamp last year after winning a Group 2 in Germany over a mile. He should be better for this first run back. (op 8/1 tchd 9/1)
Summit Surge(IRE) had a decent season last year and was fresh from a successful trip to Dubai which yielded a win in February, but he never got in a blow.
Jumbajukiba, last year's winner, was well backed to land his eighth victory, but he probably would have preferred testing ground. He dropped away after leading for a long way on his seasonal bow. (op 6/1)
Express Wish won a Group 3 over this journey in Goodwood last September when the ground was soft. This was his first outing since October, but he was another to make little impression.
Georgebernardshaw(IRE) won his first two starts here last year, including the Loughbrown Stakes over this trip. He was held up in last place and never got involved. (op 5/1)
Tian Shan(IRE) dropped away after racing in the leading group and probably wants a longer distance according to his trainer. (op 50/1)

1139 - 1142a (Foreign Racing) - See Raceform Interactive

COLOGNE (R-H)
Sunday, April 5

OFFICIAL GOING: Soft

1143a BUCHMACHER ALBERS GRAND PRIX AUFGALOPP (GROUP 3) 1m 3f
4:20 (4:22) 4-Y-0+ **£31,068** (£9,709; £4,854; £2,913)

RPR
1 **Ostland (GER)**[189] 6324 4-9-0 ... AStarke 1 106
(P Schiergen, Germany) *6th st: hdwy appr fnl f: drvn to ld last strides* **6/5**[1]
2 *hd* **Ambassador (GER)**[115] 7643 5-8-11 ... DPorcu 7 103
(T Mundry, Germany) *a cl up: 3rd st: chal on wd outside: led ins fnl f tl ct last strides* **183/10**
3 *hd* **Zaungast (IRE)**[162] 6992 5-9-2 ... ASuborics 3 108
(W Hickst, Germany) *hld up in rr to st: gd hdwy 2f out: narrow ldr dist tl ins fnl f: ev ch tl no ex fnl strides* **22/5**[2]
4 *2* **Dwilano (GER)**[140] 6-9-0 ... NRichter 9 102
(P Remmert, Germany) *a in tch: wnt 2nd over 4f out: led over 2f out tl appr fnl f: one pce* **38/1**
5 *1 1/2* **Akiem (IRE)**[197] 6148 4-9-0 ... THellier 6 100
(Andreas Lowe, Germany) *mid-div: hdwy and 4th st: ev ch 1 1/2f out: one pce fnl f* **51/10**[3]
6 *3/4* **Simonas (IRE)**[162] 6992 10-8-11 ... JBojko 2 95
(A Wohler, Germany) *bhd: last st: prog fr over 1 1/2f out: nrest at fin* **19/1**
7 *2 1/2* **Solapur (GER)**[273] 3773 4-8-11 ... EPedroza 5 91
(A Wohler, Germany) *trckd ldr tl over 4f out: 5th and wkng st* **51/10**[3]
8 *3/4* **Stella Di Quattro**[145] 7348 5-8-11 ow1 ... WMongil 4 90
(Uwe Ostmann, Germany) *led to 1/2-way: 7th and btn st* **19/2**
9 *12* **Duellant (IRE)**[44] 640 4-9-0 ... FilipMinarik 8 73
(P Schiergen, Germany) *trckd ldr: led 1/2-way tl over 2f out: wknd qckly* **78/10**

2m 22.87s (2.07) **9** Ran SP% **130.4**
(including ten euro stakes): WIN 22; PL 13, 27, 17; SF 349.
Owner Stall Hornoldendorf **Bred** Gestut Wittekindshof **Trained** Germany

LONGCHAMP (R-H)
Sunday, April 5

OFFICIAL GOING: Good

1144a PRIX D'HARCOURT (GROUP 2) 1m 2f
2:25 (2:25) 4-Y-0+ **£71,942** (£27,767; £13,252; £8,835; £4,417)

RPR
1 **Trincot (FR)**[22] 846 4-9-1 ... SPasquier 6 119
(P Demercastel, France) *hld up in rr: 8th st: edgd out over 2f out: str run fr over 1f out: led 180yds out: drvn clr: r.o wl* **154/10**
2 *3* **The Bogberry (USA)**[112] 7682 4-8-11 ... GMosse 5 109
(A De Royer-Dupre, France) *racd in 5th to st: r.o fr over 1f out to take 2nd cl home* **71/10**
3 *hd* **Vision D'Etat (FR)**[182] 6522 4-9-4 ... IMendizabal 4 116
(E Libaud, France) *a cl up: 2nd st: led appr fnl f to 180yds out: kpt on same pce and lost 2nd cl home* **6/4**[1]
4 *shd* **Loup Breton (IRE)**[22] 846 5-9-1 ... ACrastus 1 112
(E Lellouche, France) *disp early ld then settled disputing 2nd: 3rd st: looking for a run on ins over 1f out: edgd out ins fnl f: styd on cl home* **54/10**[2]
5 *1* **Never On Sunday (FR)**[197] 6148 4-8-11 ... C-PLemaire 2 106
(J-C Rouget, France) *7th st: r.o fnl f but nvr nr to chal* **74/10**
6 *snk* **Diyakalanie (FR)**[22] 846 5-8-9 ow1 ... CSoumillon 8 104
(Y De Nicolay, France) *def ldr after 1 1/2f: hrd rdn wl over 1f out: hdd appr fnl f: one pce* **10/1**
7 *1* **Prospect Wells (FR)**[168] 6854 4-9-1 ... (b) OPeslier 7 108
(A Fabre, France) *restrained in rr early and pulling: wnt up to 4th after 3f: 4th st: briefly 3rd 1 1/2f out: one pce* **67/10**[3]
8 *1/2* **Court Canibal**[22] 846 4-8-11 ... MGuyon 3 103
(M Delzangles, France) *mid-div: 6th st: one pce fnl 2f* **16/1**
9 *1 1/2* **La Boum (GER)**[145] 7348 6-8-8 ... TJarnet 9 97
(Robert Collet, France) *last st: in last two thrght* **43/1**

2m 2.88s (-1.12) **Going Correction** -0.025s/f (Good) **9** Ran SP% **116.2**
Speed ratings: **115,112,112,112,111 111,110,110,109**
PARI-MUTUEL: WIN 16.40; PL 3.70, 2.30, 1.40; DF 73.30.
Owner S C E A Ecurie Bader **Bred** S C E A Ecurie Bader **Trained** France
■ Stewards' Enquiry : S Pasquier two-day ban: whip abuse; two-day ban: careless riding (Apr 19-22)

FOCUS
The French Rules of Racing might be changed following this spectacular victory. Up until now, cheekpieces don't have to be declared in France but they certainly made a big difference to Trincot.

NOTEBOOK
Trincot(FR) won his second Group 2 event at Longchamp in a stylish manner. Previously he had finished well behind several of the other runners at Saint-Cloud. However, fitted with cheekpieces for the first time, he was dropped right out in the early stages then was brought with a run up the centre of the track. The colt flashed past his rivals from one and a half out and won with plenty in hand. He certainly enjoys racing at Longchamp and good ground. He will now be back at the track for the Prix Ganay at the end of the month.
The Bogberry(USA) carried plenty of condition and ran a sound race. Mid-division in the early stages, he came with a progressive run from one and a half out and finished well. He had not been out since December and had a minor setback in March which led to him missing a tilt at the Dubai Duty Free. He will certainly strip fitter next time out and is likely to take on the winner again in the Ganay.
Vision D'Etat(FR) put up an excellent seasonal debut considering he was carrying a Group 1 penalty. He ran free early on but eventually settled by the straight, then went to head of affairs one and a half out before staying on one paced. This outing will have done him the power of good and his trainer was more than happy. He will be back for the Ganay where he will be at level weights with the winner and runner-up.
Loup Breton(IRE) didn't have the luckiest of runs and had nowhere to go at a crucial moment in the straight. He had been on the rail throughout from his number one draw and had problems finding a space to challenge. Once that arrived he ran on at the finish and he was probably unlucky not to have taken second position. He is now a possible for the Singapore Airways Cup in May.

1145a PRIX NOAILLES - 'LA CONVIVIALITE DU RUGBY' (GROUP 2) (C&F) 1m 2f 110y
2:55 (2:56) 3-Y-O **£71,942** (£27,767; £13,252; £8,835; £4,417)

RPR
1 **Grandcamp (FR)**[59] 3-9-2 ... C-PLemaire 2 104
(J-C Rouget, France) *mde virtually all: hrd rdn ins fnl f: drvn out* **23/5**
2 *hd* **Guest Ville (FR)**[24] 3-9-2 ... TJarnet 6 103
(Mlle S-V Tarrou, France) *racd in 5th: 6th st: hdwy 2f out: got through on rail ins fnl f: edgd out and r.o wl fnl 120yds: jst failed* **14/1**
3 *3/4* **Wajir (FR)**[22] 845 3-9-2 ... ACrastus 3 102
(E Lellouche, France) *racd in 3rd to st: rdn wl over 1f out: kpt on same pce* **9/5**[1]
4 *1/2* **Golden Sword**[168] 6846 3-9-2 ... CSoumillon 5 101
(A P O'Brien, Ire) *wnt 2nd after 2f: 2nd st: rdn 1 1/2f out: one pce* **18/5**[3]
5 *hd* **Validor (FR)**[43] 3-9-2 ... (b) GMosse 4 101
(H-A Pantall, France) *racd in 6th: last st: rdn and hdwy on outside fr over 1f out: nrest at fin* **14/1**
6 *1* **Calvados Blues (FR)**[13] 942 3-9-2 ... IMendizabal 7 99
(P Demercastel, France) *hld up in rr: hdwy and 4th st: rdn 2f out: one pce* **27/10**[2]
7 *5* **Crowfoot (IRE)**[160] 7030 3-9-2 ... CO'Donoghue 1 89
(A P O'Brien, Ire) *disp early ld: sn 2nd: 3rd after 2f: 5th st: wknd 2f out* **18/5**[3]

2m 10.77s (-2.23) **Going Correction** -0.025s/f (Good) **7** Ran SP% **137.4**
Speed ratings: **107,106,106,105,105 105,101**
PARI-MUTUEL: WIN 5.60; PL 3.20, 5.10; SF 44.00.
Owner D-Y Treves **Bred** Uwe Stallmann **Trained** Pau, France
■ Stewards' Enquiry : A Crastus two-day ban: whip abuse (Apr 19-20)

NOTEBOOK
Grandcamp(FR) was given a fine waiting in front ride by his talented jockey and was running for the first time on grass this season after a couple of victories on the all-weather at Cagnes-sur-Mer. He was asked to set a sensible pace and ran on bravely in the straight where he fended off all challenges. The colt was a great bargain as he was sold as a yearling at the Arqana October Sale for €13,000 and at the same company's Breeze-Up Sale the following year for €32,000. He has all the main engagements and it would be no surprise if he lined up for the Prix du Jockey Club in June.
Guest Ville(FR), given a waiting ride by his experienced jockey, didn't really appear on the scene until the final stages when he came with a desperate late run up the far rail. He failed by a head to catch the winner and would have had his head in front shortly after the post. This was a promising effort that bodes well for the future.
Wajir(FR), given every chance, he was rather a disappointing favourite following his Listed success over the distance at Saint-Cloud. Tucked in behind the leaders early on, he quickened from one and a half out but never really looked likely to take the lead. He ran like a horse who might prefer a longer trip and more give in the ground.
Golden Sword ran a sound race but was very one paced when the race warmed up. He was tucked in behind the winner and was given every possible chance but could not quicken before staying on one paced. The jockey felt he needed a longer trip to show his best.

1146 - (Foreign Racing) - See Raceform Interactive

WINDSOR (R-H)
Monday, April 6

OFFICIAL GOING: Good (good to firm in places)
Wind: Almost nil Weather: Fine

1147 READING EVENING POST MAIDEN STKS 5f 10y
2:20 (2:23) (Class 5) 2-Y-O **£2,729** (£806; £403) **Stalls** High

Form RPR
1 **Red Jazz (USA)** 2-9-3 0 ... MichaelHills 3 91+
(B W Hills) *sn on terms w ldrs: wnt 2nd 1/2-way: led over 1f out: scooted clr* **11/8**[1]
2 *5* **Iver Bridge Lad** 2-9-0 0 ... MarcHalford[(3)] 9 70+
(J Ryan) *pressed ldr: led wl over 2f out to over 1f out: kpt on but no ch w wnr* **12/1**
3 *2 1/2* **Thomas Baines (USA)** 2-9-3 0 ... JamieSpencer 1 61+
(M L W Bell) *dwlt: rn v green but sn swtchd to nr side rail and in tch: coaxed along to chse ldng pair over 1f out: kpt on* **4/1**[2]
4 *5* **Master Mylo (IRE)** 2-9-3 0 ... SteveDrowne 5 39
(Mrs L C Jewell) *chsd ldrs: rn green and wknd wl over 1f out* **33/1**
5 *2 1/2* **Miss Lesley** 2-8-12 0 ... StephenCarson 4 24
(D K Ivory) *s.s: outpcd and wl bhd: rn green on wd outside 2f out: n.d* **40/1**
6 *3 3/4* **Flapjack** 2-8-12 0 ... RichardHughes 8 9
(R Hannon) *dwlt: outpcd and nvr on terms* **7/1**[3]
7 *1/2* **Greenore Gordon** 2-9-3 0 ... TGMcLaughlin 7 12
(M S Saunders) *chsd ldrs: swtchd to outer and rn green 2f out: wknd rapidly* **8/1**
8 *1 3/4* **Durham Town (IRE)** 2-9-3 0 ... DaneO'Neill 6 5
(D K Ivory) *s.s: outpcd and a wl bhd* **10/1**
9 *4 1/2* **Barton Chancer** 2-8-7 0 ... JackDean[(5)] 2 —
(W G M Turner) *led to wl over 2f out: wknd rapidly* **16/1**

60.80 secs (0.50) **Going Correction** -0.025s/f (Good) **9** Ran SP% **113.8**
Speed ratings (Par 92): **95,87,83,75,71 65,64,61,54**
toteswinger: 1&2 £6.00, 1&3 £2.40, 2&3 £9.50 CSF £19.69 TOTE £2.50: £1.10, £3.20, £1.80; EX 24.90 Trifecta £106.00 Pool: £521.83 - 3.64 winning units..
Owner R J Arculli **Bred** William F Murphy & Annabel Murphy **Trained** Lambourn, Berks

FOCUS
A race for newcomers, but the potential of the winner was there for all to see.

NOTEBOOK

Red Jazz(USA) ◆, a 95,000euros Johannesburg half-brother to a multiple winner in the US, looked well beforehand, though he was on his toes and green in the paddock, and keen to post. However, once he got the hang of it he blitzed home with plenty left in the tank, and looks well above average for the time of year. He will have one more run, probably at Ascot or York, before heading to the Royal Meeting, where one of the juvenile races at either 5f or 6f is on the cards, with trainer Barry Hills confident that he will stay the extra furlong. (op 13-8)

Iver Bridge Lad, by a speedy sire but from a family with form up to 1m4f, changed hands for just 1,000gns as a yearling but this debut effort belied his bargain basement status. Though no match for the winner, he showed enough to suggest he can win a modest early maiden. (op 20-1 tchd 25-1)

Thomas Baines(USA) ◆, a 55,000gns son of Johannesburg out of a winner in the US and Canada, looked a decent sort in the paddock and will improve for the experience. Green throughout, but not knocked about when clearly held in third, he should be placed to get off the mark. (op 10-3 tchd 3-1 and 9-2)

Master Mylo(IRE), a Bertolini colt whose dam won from 7f to 1m, moved well to post. He showed early speed but was beaten too far in the end to expect big things next time, and looks more of a nursery type in due course. (tchd 28-1)

Miss Lesley, by the high-class sprinter Needwood Blade but from a family that stays up to 1m4f, missed the break and didn't have a clue for most of the race, ending up wide of the others in mid-track. She will come on with racing, but needs a bit of time yet. (tchd 33-1 and 50-1)

1148 GOLDRING SECURITY SERVICES CLAIMING STKS — 1m 2f 7y
2:50 (2:53) (Class 5) 3-Y-O — **£2,729** (£806; £403) **Stalls** Low

Form			Horse		RPR
60	**1**		**Dalrymple (IRE)**[24] 824 3-8-11 0 — TPQueally 4		55
			(N B King) *stdd s but sn prom: trckd ldr after 2f: led over 6f out: hanging lft fr 4f out: drvn and hld on fnl f*	**10/1**	
0231	**2**	*hd*	**Flying Lady (IRE)**[13] 943 3-8-6 65 — MCGeran(5) 2		55
			(M R Channon) *plld hrd: hld up in last pair: prog wl over 2f out: wnt 2nd over 1f out: chal fnl f: hanging and jst hld*	**9/4**[1]	
-551	**3**	*1 ¾*	**Daily Double**[23] 839 3-9-0 65 — DaneO'Neill 7		54
			(D K Ivory) *prom: chsd wnr 4f out to over 1f out: hanging and nt qckn*	**9/2**[3]	
2240	**4**	*shd*	**Hold The Bucks (USA)**[12] 962 3-9-0 68 — LukeMorris 8		54
			(J S Moore) *hld up in tch: effrt on wd outside 3f out: cl enough 2f out: one pce u.p*	**7/2**[2]	
0-30	**5**	*hd*	**First Spirit**[24] 824 3-8-11 63 — FergusSweeney 9		51
			(J S Moore) *hld up in tch: cl up over 3f out: nt qckn over 2f out: styd on again ins fnl f*	**16/1**	
6130	**6**	*1*	**True Britannia**[12] 962 3-8-7 64 ow1 — (v) ShaneKelly 6		45
			(A M Hales) *hld up in last pair: stdy prog on inner and cl up 2f out: nt clr run briefly over 1f out: one pce*	**6/1**	
00-0	**7**	*1 ¾*	**Guilin (IRE)**[12] 953 3-8-9 42 — (b[1]) AlanMunro 3		43
			(P F I Cole) *trckd ldr 2f: losing pl whn n.m.r over 3f out: last 2f out: plugged on*	**25/1**	
000-	**8**	*16*	**Midsummer Madness (IRE)**[161] 7023 3-8-5 51 — ChrisCatlin 1		7
			(David Pinder) *led to over 6f out: lost pl 4f out: wknd rapidly fnl 2f*	**16/1**	

2m 11.96s (3.26) **Going Correction** -0.025s/f (Good) **8** Ran SP% **110.2**
Speed ratings (Par 98): **85,84,83,83,83 82,81,68**
toteswinger: 1&2 £5.90, 1&3 £7.20, 2&3 £2.60 CSF £30.47 TOTE £11.20: £2.80, £1.10, £2.30; EX 39.30 Trifecta £153.70 Pool: £683.60 - 3.29 winning units..Dalrymple was claimed by I. Williams for £7000.

Owner Neil King **Bred** Darley **Trained** Newmarket, Suffolk

FOCUS
A weak claimer with no early pace and Queally seized control on the winner around the bend, a move which helped win the race. The proximity of the fifth and seventh suggest the form horses were not at their best.

1149 BET WITH LADBROKES GET REWARDED H'CAP — 1m 67y
3:20 (3:23) (Class 4) (0-85,90) 4-Y-O+ — **£5,180** (£1,541; £770; £384) **Stalls** High

Form			Horse		RPR
106-	**1**		**Light From Mars**[198] 6130 4-8-13 83 — JamesMillman(3) 9		92
			(B R Millman) *trckd ldr after 2f: led 1/2-way: drvn and edgd lft over 1f out: kpt on wl fnl f*	**7/1**	
1-	**2**	*1 ¼*	**The Galloping Shoe**[358] 1344 4-8-10 77 — SebSanders 12		84
			(J Noseda) *stdd s: hld up in midfield: prog over 2f out: chsd wnr over 1f out: hanging lft u.p ent fnl f: nt qckn*	**7/2**[1]	
030-	**3**	*hd*	**Mystery Star (IRE)**[198] 6128 4-8-13 80 — SaleemGolam 6		86+
			(M H Tompkins) *hld up in 9th: pushed along over 2f out: limited prog tl styd on fr over 1f out: rdn ins fnl f and fin best of all*	**18/1**	
35-0	**4**	*1 ¼*	**Grey Boy (GER)**[23] 841 8-8-4 71 oh1 — LukeMorris 7		74
			(A W Carroll) *hld up in abt 7th: effrt on outer over 2f out: drvn and kpt on same pce fr over 1f out*	**14/1**	
566-	**5**	*nse*	**Trans Siberian**[180] 6582 5-9-3 84 — JimmyFortune 10		89+
			(P F I Cole) *t.k.h: trckd ldrs: wnt 3rd 1/2-way: drvn to dispute 2nd over 1f out: hld whn tightened up jst ins fnl f: kpt on*	**4/1**[2]	
5-31	**6**	*½*	**Elna Bright**[3] 1093 4-9-9 90 6ex — DaneO'Neill 8		92
			(P D Evans) *t.k.h early: hld up in midfield: effrt on wd outside over 2f out: cl enough over 1f out: fdd fnl f*	**6/1**	
06-1	**7**	*½*	**Den's Gift (IRE)**[72] 283 5-9-1 82 — (b) PhilipRobinson 1		83
			(C G Cox) *led to 1/2-way: chsd wnr to wl over 1f out: wknd*	**5/1**[3]	
430-	**8**	*2 ¾*	**Danetime Panther (IRE)**[60] 7009 5-8-6 73 — ChrisCatlin 3		68
			(Ian Williams) *hld up in last: pushed along fr over 2f out: kpt on steadily but nvr nr ldrs*	**16/1**	
010-	**9**	*2 ¾*	**Shanzu**[176] 6675 4-8-10 77 — FergusSweeney 11		65
			(G L Moore) *chsd ldr 2f: lost pl over 3f out: struggling fnl 2f*	**20/1**	
000-	**10**	*1*	**Ivory Lace**[122] 7557 8-8-5 72 — JimmyQuinn 5		58
			(S Woodman) *hld up in 8th: rdn over 2f out: no prog*	**33/1**	
0450	**11**	*1*	**Orchard Supreme**[8] 1016 6-9-4 85 — RichardHughes 2		69
			(R Hannon) *scratchy to post: hld up in last pair: shuffled along fr 3f out: no prog and nvr nr ldrs*	**12/1**	

1m 43.03s (-1.67) **Going Correction** -0.025s/f (Good) **11** Ran SP% **118.9**
Speed ratings (Par 105): **107,105,105,104,104 103,103,100,97,96 95**
toteswinger: 1&2 £6.90, 1&3 £29.60, 2&3 £10.70 CSF £32.05 CT £439.32 TOTE £9.10: £2.90, £1.50, £5.40; EX 39.70 TRIFECTA Not won..Allanit was withdrawn. Price at time of withdrawal 66/1. Rule 4 does not apply.

Owner R K Arrowsmith **Bred** Harts Farm And Stud **Trained** Kentisbeare, Devon

FOCUS
They went a good gallop, but the winner was always near the front and deserves extra credit for that. The form looks pretty solid and should work out.

1150 THEATRE ROYAL WINDSOR "DINNERLADIES" H'CAP — 5f 10y
3:50 (3:51) (Class 4) (0-80,78) 4-Y-O+ — **£4,857** (£1,445; £722; £360) **Stalls** High

Form			Horse		RPR
6-40	**1**		**Efistorm**[34] 742 8-8-13 73 — SebSanders 11		85
			(C R Dore) *chsd ldng quintet and sn clr of rest: effrt and clr run against rail over 1f out: led jst ins fnl f: styd on wl*	**5/1**[2]	
414-	**2**	*1*	**Our Piccadilly (IRE)**[172] 6765 4-8-8 73 — Louis-PhilippeBeuzelin(5) 4		81
			(W S Kittow) *pressed ldrs: rdn to chal and upsides 1f out: outpcd by wnr last 150yds*	**8/1**	
610-	**3**	*1 ¼*	**Kyle (IRE)**[204] 5936 5-9-4 78 — FergusSweeney 1		82+
			(C R Dore) *dropped in fr wd draw: hld up last and long way off the pce: gd prog against nr side rail over 1f out: pushed along and styd on wl to take 3rd last stride*	**16/1**	
0521	**4**	*nse*	**Ten Down**[19] 870 4-8-9 69 — MartinDwyer 7		73
			(M Quinn) *led and sn racd against nr side rail: edgd lft over 1f out: drvn and hdd jst ins fnl f: fdd*	**7/2**[1]	
662-	**5**	*½*	**Digital**[196] 6164 12-8-13 73 — ChrisCatlin 6		75
			(M R Channon) *stdd s: outpcd and wl bhd: prog on outer over 1f out: kpt on fnl f*	**14/1**	
0-63	**6**	*1*	**The Lord**[12] 956 9-8-7 72 — JackDean(5) 12		70
			(W G M Turner) *pressed ldr: drvn 2f out: fdd jst over 1f out*	**14/1**	
056-	**7**	*nk*	**Zowington**[177] 6650 7-9-4 78 — SaleemGolam 3		75
			(S C Williams) *dwlt: outpcd: hrd rdn 1/2-way: plugged on fr over 1f out: nvr on terms*	**12/1**	
3130	**8**	*2 ½*	**Brandywell Boy (IRE)**[12] 954 6-7-13 66 — BillyCray(7) 10		54
			(D J S Ffrench Davis) *outpcd: effrt u.p 2f out: hanging and wknd fnl f*	**8/1**	
5544	**9**	*1*	**Drifting Gold**[7] 1041 5-8-3 70 — (b) ThomasDyer(7) 9		55
			(C G Cox) *gd spd and wl on terms: drifted bdly lft fr 1/2-way: fdd and ended up against far rail*	**11/1**	
600-	**10**	*½*	**Nusoor (IRE)**[198] 6131 6-8-5 65 — (v) KirstyMilczarek 5		48
			(Peter Grayson) *pressed ldrs to 1/2-way: sn lost pl u.p*	**18/1**	
664-	**11**	*2 ¾*	**Hereford Boy**[117] 7621 5-9-0 74 — AlanMunro 8		47
			(D K Ivory) *scratchy to post: outpcd: rdn 1/2-way: sme prog over 1f out: sn wknd*	**6/1**[3]	
5-55	**12**	*5*	**Memphis Man**[31] 780 6-8-13 78 — RichardEvans(5) 2		33
			(P D Evans) *dwlt: outpcd: marooned on wd outside 1/2-way and wl adrift after*	**14/1**	

59.54 secs (-0.76) **Going Correction** -0.025s/f (Good) **12** Ran SP% **122.6**
Speed ratings (Par 105): **105,103,101,101,100 98,98,94,92,92 87,79**
toteswinger: 1&2 £16.00, 1&3 £27.50, 2&3 £38.30 CSF £46.55 CT £620.56 TOTE £7.40: £2.70, £4.40, £6.70; EX 65.90 TRIFECTA Not won..

Owner Sean J Murphy **Bred** E Duggan And D Churchman **Trained** Cowbit, Lincs

■ Stewards' Enquiry : Thomas Dyer one-day ban: careless riding (Apr 20)

FOCUS
A good sprint gallop soon had these strung out, but horses ran well from both ends of the field, and the winner came from the chasing group. Decent form for the grade.

Brandywell Boy(IRE) Official explanation: jockey said gelding was denied a clear run

Memphis Man Official explanation: jockey said gelding was unsuited by the good, good to firm in places ground

1151 GRANT THORNTON MAIDEN STKS — 1m 2f 7y
4:20 (4:22) (Class 5) 3-Y-O — **£2,729** (£806; £403) **Stalls** Low

Form			Horse		RPR
	1		**Popmurphy** 3-9-3 0 — FergusSweeney 1		88+
			(K R Burke) *sn in 5th: prog to trck ldng pair 4f out: wnt 2nd wl over 2f out: shkn up over 1f out: styd on strly to ld last 100yds*	**11/2**	
25-	**2**	*¾*	**Souter Point (USA)**[199] 6075 3-9-3 0 — SteveDrowne 2		86
			(R Charlton) *cl up: led 3f out: rdn against nr side rail over 1f out: styd on but hdd and outpcd last 100yds*	**9/4**[1]	
0-	**3**	*5*	**Bruton Street (USA)**[174] 6720 3-9-3 0 — JimmyFortune 6		76
			(J H M Gosden) *cl up: rdn over 2f out: outpcd fnl 2f*	**3/1**[3]	
00-	**4**	*3 ½*	**Millharbour (IRE)**[157] 7105 3-9-3 0 — MichaelHills 3		69
			(B W Hills) *t.k.h leaving stalls and restrained: hld up in 6th: effrt over 3f out: wl outpcd fnl 2f*	**12/1**	
46-	**5**	*5*	**Moresco**[174] 6720 3-9-3 0 — TedDurcan 7		59
			(W R Swinburn) *led: jinked rt over 3f out: sn hdd: wknd 2f out*	**5/2**[2]	
0-	**6**	*3*	**Khayar (IRE)**[164] 6944 3-9-3 0 — SaleemGolam 5		53
			(M H Tompkins) *cl up: lost pl over 3f out: struggling 2f out: wknd*	**40/1**	
5	**7**	*2 ¼*	**Michael Laskey**[24] 828 3-9-3 0 — TGMcLaughlin 4		49
			(B R Millman) *stdd s: hld up in last: effrt on outer and in tch 3f out: wknd 2f out*	**66/1**	

2m 9.67s (0.97) **Going Correction** -0.025s/f (Good) **7** Ran SP% **111.3**
Speed ratings (Par 98): **95,94,90,87,83 81,79**
toteswinger: 1&2 £2.90, 1&3 £2.70, 2&3 £2.00 CSF £17.32 CT £19.70 TOTE £7.30: £3.10, £1.80; EX 19.70.

Owner Mogeely Stud & Mrs Maura Gittins **Bred** B Walters **Trained** Middleham Moor, N Yorks

FOCUS
A decent maiden. The pace was ordinary, but the winner scored on merit and looks potentially smart. The form makes a fair bit of sense and could rate higher.

1152 YES EVENTS H'CAP — 6f
4:50 (4:53) (Class 5) (0-75,75) 4-Y-O+ — **£2,729** (£806; £403) **Stalls** High

Form			Horse		RPR
3011	**1**		**What Katie Did (IRE)**[19] 861 4-8-8 65 — (p) JamieSpencer 9		74
			(J M Bradley) *mde all and sn crossed to nr side: clr over 2f out: drvn over 1f out: looked vulnerble ent fnl f: kpt on gamely*	**5/1**[2]	
4465	**2**	*1*	**Sarah's Art (IRE)**[3] 1103 6-8-10 67 — MickyFenton 4		73
			(Stef Liddiard) *hld up in midfield and racd on outer: prog over 2f out: chsd wnr jst over 1f out: looked dangerous ins fnl f: nt qckn*	**14/1**	
214	**3**	*½*	**Trade Centre**[17] 892 4-9-4 75 — MartinDwyer 13		79
			(W R Muir) *chsd ldrs and racd nr side: rdn over 2f out: styd on fnl f: nvr quite able to chal*	**4/1**[1]	
0143	**4**	*hd*	**Royal Envoy (IRE)**[23] 841 6-8-12 69 — TolleyDean 2		73
			(P Howling) *prom: hrd rdn 2f out: kpt on u.p: nvr able to chal*	**10/1**	
6330	**5**	*hd*	**Fromsong (IRE)**[17] 892 11-9-0 71 — StephenCarson 11		74
			(D K Ivory) *chsd wnr: no imp over 2f out: lost pl jst over 1f out: kpt on*	**25/1**	
061-	**6**	*¾*	**Gold Express**[129] 7466 6-9-2 73 — ShaneKelly 6		74+
			(P J O'Gorman) *dwlt: towards rr and racd on outer: stdy prog over 2f out: clsd on ldrs ovfer 1f out: rdn and fdd*	**8/1**	

2434 **7** ¾ **Hart Of Gold**[19] 861 5-8-11 68................(p) RichardHughes 16 66+
(R A Harris) *hld up towards rr on inner: effrt 2f out: n.m.r 1f out: kpt on: n.d* 7/1[3]
3325 **8** nk **Kensington (IRE)**[26] 806 8-9-3 74................ JimmyFortune 5 71
(P D Evans) *chsd ldrs: hrd rdn and nt qckn 2f out: one pce after* 17/2
-342 **9** 1 **Patavium Prince (IRE)**[21] 853 6-9-3 74................ DaneO'Neill 8 68
(Miss Jo Crowley) *wl plcd bhd ldrs: gng strly over 2f out: rdn over 1f out: failed to pick up: one pce after* 12/1
60-2 **10** 1 ¼ **Peopleton Brook**[19] 861 7-8-6 63................(t) ChrisCatlin 12 53
(B G Powell) *hld up wl in rr: taken towards outer 2f out: shkn up over 1f out: nvr able to get involved* 14/1
430- **11** 1 ¼ **Whiteoak Lady (IRE)**[198] 6124 4-8-8 70................ JackDean(5) 1 56
(J L Spearing) *racd wdst of all: wl in rr: sme prog over 2f out: wknd wl over 1f out* 33/1
-220 **12** ¾ **Louphole**[26] 799 7-8-10 67................ RobertHavlin 10 51
(J R Jenkins) *dwlt: wl in rr: effrt 2f out: drvn and no prog 1f out: wknd* 16/1
6-52 **13** ½ **Lord Deevert**[12] 961 4-8-6 63................ LiamJones 14 45
(W G M Turner) *nvr beyond midfield: u.p and struggling over 2f out* 14/1
404- **14** 5 **Mine Behind**[287] 3316 9-8-4 64 ow2................(t) MarcHalford(3) 7 30
(J R Best) *a in rr: struggling over 2f out* 22/1
-000 **15** 26 **Wee Buns**[3] 1103 4-8-4 61 oh1................(b) LukeMorris 15 —
(P Burgoyne) *awkward s: a wl in rr and nvr gng wl: wknd over 2f out: t.o* 40/1

1m 12.18s (-0.82) **Going Correction** -0.025s/f (Good) **15** Ran SP% **127.0**
Speed ratings (Par 103): **104,102,102,101,101 100,99,99,97,96 94,93,92,86,51**
toteswinger: 1&2 £15.20, 1&3 £5.00, 2&3 £27.20. CSF £74.25 CT £324.91 TOTE £4.70: £1.90, £5.20, £2.40; EX 94.50 Trifecta £363.20 Pool: £540.02 - 1.10 winning units. Place 6: £54.69, Place 5: £39.28..
Owner Mr & Mrs M B Carver **Bred** Brian Williamson **Trained** Sedbury, Gloucs

FOCUS
An ordinary but competitive race, won by a revitalised sprinter who has been in good form on the all-weather. Sound form.
Lord Deevert Official explanation: jockey said gelding lost his action
Wee Buns Official explanation: jockey said was unsuited by the good, good to firm in places ground
T/Plt: £153.70 to a £1 stake. Pool: £65,321.70. 310.18 winning tickets. T/Qpdt: £59.90 to a £1 stake. Pool: £4,162.60. 51.35 winning tickets. JN

1129 WOLVERHAMPTON (A.W) (L-H)
Monday, April 6

OFFICIAL GOING: Standard
Wind: Moderate half behind Weather: Fine

1153 PARADE RESTAURANT AMATEUR RIDERS' H'CAP 1m 141y(P)
2:10 (2:10) (Class 6) (0-60,61) 4-Y-O+ **£1,977** (£608; £304) **Stalls** Low

Form RPR
316- **1** **Rossini's Dancer**[180] 6585 4-10-9 55................ MrBenHamilton(7) 3 63
(R A Fahey) *t.k.h early: w ldr: rdn to ld ins fnl f: r.o* 6/1[3]
4540 **2** 1 **Moayed**[12] 959 10-11-3 56................(b) MrsEmmaLittmoden 6 62
(N P Littmoden) *s.i.s: hld up and bhd: hdwy over 2f out: rdn over 1f out: ev ch ins fnl f: nt qckn cl home* 10/1
0-60 **3** 1 ¼ **Kirstys Lad**[51] 554 7-10-11 55................ MissMMullineaux(5) 4 58
(M Mullineaux) *a.p: rdn wl over 1f out: nt clr run on ins whn swtchd rt ins fnl f: r.o* 14/1
5216 **4** ½ **Barodine**[7] 1042 6-10-13 55................ IanPopham(3) 7 57+
(R J Hodges) *hld up in mid-div: hdwy and swtchd rt over 2f out: rdn wl over 1f out: sn hung lft: styd on towards fin* 6/1[3]
00-0 **5** hd **Time To Regret**[74] 256 9-11-4 57................(p) MissFayeBramley 12 59
(I W McInnes) *led: rdn over 1f out: hdd ins fnl f: no ex towards fin* 40/1
3526 **6** ½ **Wester Lodge (IRE)**[8] 1014 7-11-1 61 ow3................ MrHAEustace(7) 2 61+
(J M P Eustace) *prom: lost pl on ins over 3f out: kpt on fnl f* 9/2[1]
-402 **7** nk **Stoic Leader (IRE)**[40] 682 9-11-7 60................ MrSWalker 8 60
(R F Fisher) *hld up in tch: wnt 2nd briefly over 2f out: rdn wl over 1f out: fdd ins fnl f* 6/1[3]
520- **8** 2 ¼ **Twist Bookie (IRE)**[219] 5512 9-10-10 56................ MrJEngland(7) 9 51
(S Lycett) *prom tl wknd over 2f out* 16/1
4302 **9** nse **Mountain Pass (USA)**[7] 1039 7-10-10 54...(p) MissIsabelTompsett(5) 13 48
(B J Llewellyn) *half-rrd and s.s: c wd bnd over 2f out: a bhd* 5/1[2]
1330 **10** 3 **Giddywell**[17] 897 5-11-0 56................(p) MissSSharratt(3) 10 43
(R Hollinshead) *half-rrd s and s.i.s: c v wd bnd over 2f out: a in rr* 16/1
046- **11** 3 **Sedge (USA)**[132] 7441 9-10-9 53................ MissWGibson(5) 11 34
(P T Midgley) *hld up and bhd: hdwy 2f out: rdn and wknd 1f out* 25/1
60-0 **12** 11 **Coeur Courageux (FR)**[23] 844 7-11-0 58................ MissMHugo(5) 5 13
(M D Squance) *hld up: hdwy on outside 6f out: wkng whn wd bnd over 2f out* 14/1

1m 51.24s (0.74) **Going Correction** -0.075s/f (Stan) **12** Ran SP% **118.2**
Speed ratings (Par 101): **93,92,91,90,90 89,89,87,87,84 82,72**
toteswinger: 1&2 £12.00, 1&3 £28.00, 2&3 £33.10 CSF £64.65 CT £811.62 TOTE £10.80: £2.20, £3.20, £7.90; EX 72.50.
Owner Lets Go Racing 1 **Bred** Heather Raw **Trained** Musley Bank, N Yorks
■ A first winner under rules for Ben Hamilton. He is the brother of jockey Tony Hamilton.
■ Stewards' Enquiry : Miss Faye Bramley four-day ban: careless riding (Apr 25, May 11, 18, 26)

FOCUS
A moderate amateur riders' handicap run at an even pace. The winner is rated to his early 3yo form with the second to his recent best.

1154 GREAT OFFERS AT WOLVERHAMPTON-RACECOURSE.CO.UK H'CAP 2m 119y(P)
2:40 (2:41) (Class 6) (0-65,65) 4-Y-O+ **£2,047** (£604; £302) **Stalls** Low

Form RPR
643- **1** **Rare Coincidence**[23] 7688 8-9-4 58................(p) NCallan 6 68+
(R F Fisher) *mde all: clr over 2f out: rdn wlover 1f out: eased cl home* 9/2[2]
505- **2** 2 ¾ **Highest Esteem**[59] 7545 5-9-9 63................(p) RyanMoore 13 69
(G L Moore) *hld up towards rr: hdwy on outside over 2f out: styd on u.p to take 2nd cl home: nt trble wnr* 8/1
-500 **3** ½ **Al Azy (IRE)**[11] 969 4-8-9 53 ow1................ StephenDonohoe 12 59
(D M Simcock) *hld up towards rr: pushed along and hdwy over 3f out: rdn to chse wnr over 1f out: styd on: lost 2nd cl home* 16/1
0-02 **4** 1 ¼ **Summer Lodge**[11] 972 6-9-0 57................ DavidProbert(3) 11 61
(A J McCabe) *hld up in rr: hdwy on outside over 2f out: rdn wl over 1f out: no ex ins fnl f* 15/2[3]
662- **5** 3 ½ **Adage**[170] 6824 6-8-7 47................(tp) FrankieMcDonald 10 47
(David Pinder) *hld up towards rr: hdwy over 4f out: rdn and wnt 2nd briefly wl over 1f out: wknd ins fnl f* 14/1
-461 **6** 1 **Thorny Mandate**[11] 972 7-9-5 59................ EddieAhern 8 58
(W M Brisbourne) *hld up in tch: rdn wl over 1f out: wknd ins fnl f* 7/2[1]
0-42 **7** 1 **Russian Invader (IRE)**[10] 977 5-9-6 65................(e) MarkCoumbe(5) 1 62
(R C Guest) *hld up in rr: sme prog fr over 1f out: n.d* 14/1
50-6 **8** 12 **Lough Beg (IRE)**[25] 816 6-9-4 58................(t) DarryllHolland 9 41
(Miss Tor Sturgis) *prom early: hld up in mid-div: hdwy over 5f out: wknd over 2f out* 9/1
5-50 **9** nk **Sixth Zak**[17] 898 4-8-10 54................ DaleGibson 3 37
(M W Easterby) *bhd fnl 3f* 33/1
0-30 **10** 4 **Chiff Chaff**[5] 1058 5-9-3 57................ LPKeniry 5 35
(C R Dore) *prom: rdn over 4f out: chsd wnr over 3f out tl rdn wl over 1f out: sn wknd* 12/1
-030 **11** 11 **Born West (USA)**[10] 732 5-8-9 52................(b) JackMitchell(3) 4 17
(N B King) *prom: rdn over 4f out: wknd over 3f out* 12/1
6/0- **12** ½ **Dee Cee Elle**[16] 7702 5-9-0 54................(p) RobertWinston 2 18
(D Burchell) *chsd wnr tl over 3f out: wknd over 2f out: eased over 1f out* 11/1

3m 39.79s (-2.01) **Going Correction** -0.075s/f (Stan)
WFA 4 from 5yo+ 4lb **12** Ran SP% **119.2**
Speed ratings (Par 101): **101,99,99,98,97 96,96,90,90,88 83,83**
toteswinger: 1&2 £5.80, 1&3 £23.60, 2&3 £33.70 CSF £40.78 CT £536.58 TOTE £4.70: £1.60, £3.20, £9.20; EX 30.80.
Owner A Kerr **Bred** D R Tucker **Trained** Ulverston, Cumbria

FOCUS
A moderate staying handicap in which the winner took advantage of a good mark from the front. The form is rated around the third and fourth.
Dee Cee Elle Official explanation: jockey said mare hung right-handed

1155 HOTEL & CONFERENCING AT WOLVERHAMPTON H'CAP 7f 32y(P)
3:10 (3:10) (Class 5) (0-75,75) 3-Y-O **£3,238** (£963; £481; £240) **Stalls** High

Form RPR
01-3 **1** **Arachnophobia (IRE)**[14] 936 3-8-11 68................ PaulEddery 7 75
(Pat Eddery) *a.p: rdn wl over 1f out: r.o to ld nr fin* 6/1
003- **2** hd **Suruor (IRE)**[205] 5883 3-9-2 73................ StephenDonohoe 3 79
(D M Simcock) *hld up in mid-div: hdwy over 2f out: rdn wl over 1f out: led ins fnl f: hdd nr fin* 9/2[2]
4101 **3** ½ **Common Diva**[31] 776 3-9-1 72................ RobertWinston 2 77
(A J McCabe) *led: rdn over 1f out: hdd ins fnl f: r.o* 9/2[2]
100- **4** 4 **One Cool Kitty**[175] 6700 3-8-11 68................ NCallan 9 62+
(M G Quinlan) *hld up in rr: hdwy over 1f out: rdn and no imp fnl f* 14/1
325- **5** 1 ¼ **Forward Feline (IRE)**[179] 6603 3-9-2 73................ DarryllHolland 5 64
(B Palling) *hld up in tch: rdn over 1f out: wknd fnl f* 12/1
40-4 **6** 1 ¾ **Noodles Blue Boy**[20] 859 3-9-2 73................ TonyHamilton 8 59
(Ollie Pears) *hld up in mid-div: hdwy on outside over 2f out: rdn and wknd wl over 1f out* 22/1
2432 **7** shd **Kingaroo (IRE)**[45] 620 3-7-13 63................ AndrewHeffernan(7) 1 49
(Garry Moss) *prom: rdn over 2f out: wknd wl over 1f out* 11/4[1]
1- **8** ½ **Peking Prince**[227] 5213 3-9-1 75................ DavidProbert(3) 6 59
(A M Balding) *hld up and bhd: effrt over 2f out: rdn and hung lft wl over 1f out: sn wknd* 11/2[3]
4446 **9** 2 **Harty Boy (USA)**[14] 939 3-8-8 65................(p) PaulHanagan 4 44
(Mrs S Leech) *hld up in rr: pushed along over 3f out: no rspnse* 20/1

1m 28.97s (-0.63) **Going Correction** -0.075s/f (Stan) **9** Ran SP% **116.2**
Speed ratings (Par 98): **100,99,99,94,93 91,91,90,88**
toteswinger: 1&2 £4.30, 1&3 £6.50, 2&3 £5.00 CSF £33.36 CT £134.38 TOTE £6.00: £2.20, £1.80, £2.20; EX 35.30.
Owner Pat Eddery Racing (Sharpo) **Bred** Michael Staunton **Trained** Nether Winchendon, Bucks

FOCUS
A fair three-year-old handicap, but the pace was just ordinary and those held up could not get involved. The first three finished clear but this race was perhaps not as strong as the bare form suggests.

1156 ENJOY THE LUCKY 7 GROUP OFFER MEDIAN AUCTION MAIDEN STKS 1m 4f 50y(P)
3:40 (3:41) (Class 5) 3-5-Y-O **£2,729** (£806; £403) **Stalls** Low

Form RPR
0423 **1** **El Bravo**[12] 957 3-8-8 71 ow3................ RyanMoore 6 80
(G L Moore) *hld up: hdwy over 4f out: led wl over 1f out: sn rdn clr: r.o wl* 11/10[1]
23- **2** 8 **Isabelonabicycle**[166] 6909 4-9-6 0................ LPKeniry 5 61
(A M Balding) *t.k.h: prom: wnt 2nd 7f out: flashed tail several times: led 3f out tl wl over 1f out: sn btn* 11/4[2]
2223 **3** 6 **Jonnie Skull (IRE)**[11] 968 3-8-5 62................(t) JoeFanning 9 55
(P S McEntee) *w ldr: led after 3f: hdd 3f out: sn rdn: wknd wl over 1f out* 7/1[3]
004- **4** hd **Telling Stories (IRE)**[114] 7666 3-8-0 51................ FrancisNorton 4 49
(B D Leavy) *hld up in rr: sme hdwy on ins over 2f out: wknd over 1f out* 33/1
05-0 **5** 5 **Aston Boy**[86] 117 4-9-11 43................ PaulHanagan 8 48
(M Blanshard) *a in rr* 50/1
0- **6** 1 ¾ **Haldibari (IRE)**[20] 1382 5-9-12 65................ JimCrowley 2 45
(S Lycett) *prom: lost pl over 6f out: rallied 5f out: rdn over 3f out: wknd over 2f out* 9/1
00-6 **7** ½ **Sweet Request**[18] 877 5-9-4 48................ KevinGhunowa(3) 7 40
(Dr J R J Naylor) *hld up and bhd: hdwy over 5f out: wknd over 3f out* 16/1
-633 **8** 3 ½ **Dawn Wind**[17] 902 4-9-6 50................(bt) NCallan 3 34
(I A Wood) *prom tl rdn and wknd over 2f out* 16/1
0-5 **9** 79 **Grange Corner**[95] 1 4-8-13 0................ AndrewHeffernan(7) 1 —
(Garry Moss) *led 3f: rdn and wknd over 5f out: t.o fnl 4f* 100/1

2m 38.13s (-2.97) **Going Correction** -0.075s/f (Stan)
WFA 3 from 4yo 21lb 4 from 5yo 1lb **9** Ran SP% **114.4**
Speed ratings (Par 103): **106,100,96,96,93 92,91,89,36**
toteswinger: 1&2 £1.50, 1&3 £2.50, 2&3 £2.10 CSF £4.01 TOTE £2.20: £1.10, £1.10, £1.70; EX 3.80.
Owner D J Deer **Bred** D J And Mrs Deer **Trained** Lower Beeding, W Sussex

FOCUS
A weak maiden. The runner-up disappointed leaving the winner with little to beat, although he probably improved.

1157 WOLVERHAMPTON HOSPITALITY - A PLEASURE H'CAP 5f 20y(P)
4:10 (4:11) (Class 6) (0-60,58) 3-Y-O £2,047 (£604; £302) Stalls Low

Form RPR
4462 1 **Perfect Honour (IRE)**[17] 889 3-8-12 52 TonyCulhane 3 58
(D Shaw) *a.p: squeezed through ent st: led over 1f out: rdn and hung lft ins fnl f: drvn out* 7/2[1]
0-50 2 1 **Rapanui Belle**[17] 889 3-8-8 48 ow1 RyanMoore 9 51
(G L Moore) *hld up and bhd: hdwy whn swtchd lft over 1f out: sn rdn: wnt 2nd wl ins fnl f: r.o* 12/1
0-64 3 ½ **Badtanman**[33] 758 3-8-5 45 PatrickMathers 6 47+
(Peter Grayson) *half-rrd and n.m.r s: hld up: hdwy on ins over 2f out: rdn and ev ch over 1f out: nt qckn whn hmpd towards fin* 40/1
5-2 4 3¾ **Pinball (IRE)**[30] 784 3-8-13 58 AndreaAtzeni(5) 5 46+
(Patrick Morris) *chsd ldrs: hmpd jst over 2f out: hung rt and rn wd ent st: kpt on to take 4th wl ins fnl f* 6/1
2066 5 ¾ **Just The Lady**[12] 955 3-8-12 55 AndrewMullen(3) 8 40+
(D Nicholls) *hld up: sn bhd: nt clr run jst over 2f out: rdn over 1f out: kpt on ins fnl f* 14/1
00-6 6 1 **Meydan Style (USA)**[11] 966 3-8-8 48 (b¹) RobertWinston 4 29
(J Balding) *prom: pushed along whn bmpd jst over 2f out: sn wknd* 11/1
0-60 7 ½ **Sunshine Ellie**[33] 753 3-8-5 45 FrancisNorton 10 24
(D Shaw) *outpcd* 20/1
-155 8 nse **Brown Lentic (IRE)**[17] 889 3-8-5 50 AmyBaker(5) 7 29
(Miss J Feilden) *wnt sltly lft s: prom: rdn and ev ch over 2f out: wknd ins fnl f* 8/1
06-1 9 2 **Iachimo**[17] 889 3-9-1 55 JimCrowley 11 27
(K R Burke) *hld up in tch: wknd wl over 1f out* 11/2[3]
2-04 10 2 **Bold Account (IRE)**[64] 365 3-9-4 58 (p) NCallan 2 23
(Garry Moss) *led: edgd rt wl over 1f out: sn hdd & wknd* 4/1[2]
540- 11 ½ **Mary West (IRE)**[168] 6863 3-8-10 55 WilliamCarson(5) 1 18
(Patrick Morris) *a bhd* 16/1

62.10 secs (-0.20) **Going Correction** -0.075s/f (Stan) 11 Ran SP% 118.8
Speed ratings (Par 96): **98,96,95,89,88 86,86,85,82,79 78**
toteswinger: 1&2 £5.40, 1&3 £15.40, 2&3 £46.50 CSF £47.13 CT £1472.80 TOTE £3.80: £1.30, £4.10, £10.00; EX 57.70.
Owner Mrs Jackie Cornwell **Bred** Country Breeders **Trained** Danethorpe, Notts
FOCUS
A moderate sprint handicap. It was strongly run and the form is probaly sound, if limited. The winner may do better.

1158 NAME A RACE AND ENHANCE YOUR BRAND MEDIAN AUCTION MAIDEN STKS 5f 20y(P)
4:40 (4:40) (Class 5) 2-Y-O £3,070 (£906; £453) Stalls Low

Form RPR
0 1 **Eight Hours**[9] 994 2-9-3 0 PaulHanagan 3 60+
(R A Fahey) *mde all: rdn ins fnl f: r.o* 11/10[1]
0 2 1½ **Bond Together**[9] 994 2-9-3 0 PaulDoe 1 50
(P D Evans) *a.p: rdn to chse wnr jst ins fnl f: nt qckn* 3/1[2]
4 3 1 **Alphacino**[6] 1044 2-9-3 0 SamHitchcott 6 46
(M R Channon) *w wnr: rdn and hung lft jst over 1f out: one pce* 3/1[2]
0 4 shd **Blue Bond**[4] 1083 2-9-3 0 JamieMoriarty 2 46
(P T Midgley) *s.i.s: bhd: rdn over 1f out: kpt on ins fnl f* 40/1
5 ½ **Zaskia (IRE)** 2-8-12 0 NCallan 5 39
(K A Ryan) *hld up in tch: rdn over 1f out: one pce* 9/1[3]

63.52 secs (1.22) **Going Correction** -0.075s/f (Stan) 5 Ran SP% 110.1
Speed ratings (Par 92): **87,84,83,82,82**
toteswinger: 1&2 £3.60 CSF £4.70 TOTE £1.60: £1.30, £2.10; EX 3.90 Place 6: £113.34 Place 5: £27.76 .
Owner Aidan J Ryan **Bred** Foxlea Farm And Stud **Trained** Musley Bank, N Yorks
FOCUS
Almost certainly just a modest juvenile maiden.
NOTEBOOK
Eight Hours did not enjoy the clearest of runs when ninth of 19 in the Brocklesby on his debut and improved on that form to take this much weaker event, having been well backed to do so. Helped by a low draw, he displayed plenty of early speed against the rail and kept on well in the straight. (op 5-4 tchd 11-8)
Bond Together was only a nose behind today's winner on his debut, but although beaten further this time, he still ran with credit. (op 5-2 tchd 9-4)
Alphacino was not helped by a wide draw, but in truth he was beaten fair and square and the race in which he ran fourth on his debut at Folkestone was an extremely moderate contest. (op 10-3 tchd 4-1)
Blue Bond was outpaced for much of the way, but he gradually got the idea and this was a big improvement on the form he showed on his debut at Leicester.
Zaskia(IRE), the only filly in the line-up, was easy to back on her debut and ran to just a moderate level. (op 7-1)
T/Plt: £123.30 to a £1 stake. Pool: £54,791.77. 324.17 winning tickets. T/Qpdt: £7.00 to a £1 stake. Pool: £4,428.60. 467.60 winning tickets. KH

PONTEFRACT (L-H)
Tuesday, April 7

OFFICIAL GOING: Good to firm (9.2)
Wind: Virtually nil Weather: Dry with sunny periods

1168 HIGH-RISE MEDIAN AUCTION MAIDEN STKS 1m 2f 6y
2:10 (2:11) (Class 4) 3-Y-O £5,180 (£1,541; £770; £384) Stalls Low

Form RPR
026- 1 **Chapter And Verse (IRE)**[165] 6944 3-9-3 81 MichaelHills 5 76
(B W Hills) *trckd ldr: hdwy 3f out: rdn wl over 1f out: drvn to ld ins fnl f: edgd lft and kpt on* 4/7[1]
560- 2 nk **Mt Kintyre (IRE)**[191] 6317 3-9-3 83 PaulMulrennan 6 76+
(M H Tompkins) *trckd ldng pair: hdwy over 2f out: effrt to chal over 1f out: rdn and ev ch wl ins fnl f whn veered bdly rt: crashed into rails and uns rdr after line* 9/2[2]
0- 3 2½ **Shaaridh (USA)**[168] 6884 3-8-12 0 RHills 4 65
(M Johnston) *set stdy pce: rdn and qcknd wl over 1f out: drvn and hdd ins fnl f: n.m.r and one pce fnl 100yds* 6/1[3]
4 9 **Gosforth Park** 3-9-3 0 AlanMunro 3 52
(M Brittain) *chsd ldrs: rdn along 3f out: sn drvn and outpcd fnl 2f* 20/1
00- 5 10 **Berriedale**[172] 6789 3-8-12 0 MickyFenton 2 27
(Mrs A Duffield) *t.k.h: a in rr* 80/1
00- 6 1½ **Marillos Proterras**[146] 7282 3-8-9 0 AndrewMullen(3) 8 24
(Mrs A Duffield) *a in rr* 33/1
7 5 **Emerald Hawk (IRE)** 3-9-3 0 NCallan 1 19+
(S Parr) *t.k.h and sltly hmpd after 1f: hld up in tch: sme hdwy 3f out: sn rdn and btn* 22/1
0- 8 23 **Herawati**[243] 4780 3-9-3 0 DavidAllan 7 —
(T D Easterby) *t.k.h: hdwy on outer 1/2-way: rdn along over 3f out and sn wknd* 33/1

2m 14.72s (1.02) **Going Correction** -0.05s/f (Good) 8 Ran SP% 112.3
Speed ratings (Par 100): **93,92,90,83,75 74,70,51**
toteswinger: 1&2 £2.00, 1&3 £2.00, 2&3 £2.00 CSF £2.94 TOTE £1.70: £1.02, £1.40, £2.00; EX 3.90.
Owner Jack Hanson & Sir Alex Ferguson **Bred** Stuart Weld **Trained** Lambourn, Berks
■ Barry Hills's 3,000th winner, almost 40 years after the first.
FOCUS
The expected three-horse race, but a dramatic finish. The form is rated through the winner with the runner-up rated a dead-heater.

1169 ANNUAL BADGE HOLDERS H'CAP 6f
2:40 (2:41) (Class 5) (0-70,74) 4-Y-O+ £3,238 (£963; £481; £240) Stalls Low

Form RPR
000- 1 **Pickering**[218] 5566 5-8-7 62 (p) AndrewMullen(3) 2 77
(E J Alston) *trckd ldrs on inner: hdwy 2f out: swtchd lft and rdn to chal over 1f out: led jst ins fnl f and kpt on wl* 12/1
0522 2 2¾ **Dvinsky (USA)**[18] 892 8-9-2 68 (b) JimmyQuinn 1 74
(P Howling) *led: rdn wl over 1f out: drvn and hdd jst ins fnl f: kpt on same pce* 9/2[1]
3311 3 1¼ **Desert Dreamer (IRE)**[20] 868 8-8-13 70 RichardEvans(5) 6 78+
(P D Evans) *s.i.s and bhd: hdwy 2f out: nt clr run and swtchd outside over 1f out: styd on strly ins fnl f* 10/1
3323 4 hd **Blue Charm**[27] 806 5-9-0 66 TomEaves 4 68
(I W McInnes) *chsd ldrs on inner: hdwy 2f out: swtchd rt and rdn over 1f out: kpt onu.p ins fnl f* 14/1
1341 5 2 **Kipchak (IRE)**[8] 1030 4-9-7 73 6ex (p) RobertWinston 11 68
(A J McCabe) *chsd ldrs: rdn along wl over 1f out: sn drvn and one pce* 14/1
610- 6 2½ **Guest Connections**[223] 5400 6-9-0 66 (v) AdrianTNicholls 12 53
(D Nicholls) *dwlt and in rr: hdwy 2f out: swtchd rt and rdn over 1f out: kpt on u.p ins fnl f: nrst fin* 20/1
-011 7 ¾ **Swinbrook (USA)**[7] 1053 8-9-8 74 6ex (v) PaulHanagan 13 59
(R A Fahey) *hld up towards rr: hdwy 2f out: rdn over 1f out: kpt on ins fnl f: nt rch ldrs* 15/2[3]
100- 8 ¾ **Moonage Daydream (IRE)**[215] 5634 4-9-2 68 (b) DavidAllan 16 50
(T D Easterby) *wnt rt after s: in tch on outer: rdn along 2f out and sn wknd* 20/1
0-05 9 1 **Dickie Le Davoir**[51] 561 5-8-13 70 MarkCoumbe(5) 14 49
(John A Harris) *dwlt and in rr tl styd on fnl 2f: nvr a factor* 12/1
-140 10 1 **Realt Na Mara (IRE)**[46] 625 6-8-11 63 TravisBlock 7 39
(H Morrison) *chsd ldrs: rdn along over 2f out: drvn wl over 1f out and grad wknd* 14/1
000- 11 shd **Flying Bantam (IRE)**[144] 7317 8-8-10 62 PaulMulrennan 8 38
(J R Norton) *midfield: effrt over 2f out: sn rdn and n.d* 40/1
466- 12 ½ **Ingleby Princess**[171] 6813 5-8-8 63 NeilBrown(3) 5 37+
(T D Barron) *a in rr* 13/2[2]
0-00 13 1 **Mandelieu (IRE)**[25] 832 4-8-10 62 TonyHamilton 17 33
(Ollie Pears) *pulld hrd early: a in rr* 66/1
350- 14 3¼ **Rio Sands**[185] 6486 4-8-11 66 MichaelJStainton(3) 15 26
(R M Whitaker) *dwlt and towards rr: swtchd ins and sme hdwy wl over 1f out: sn rdn nvr a factor* 33/1
2330 15 4 **Red Cape (FR)**[6] 1060 6-8-13 65 (b) PJMcDonald 10 13
(Mrs R A Carr) *chsd ldrs: effrt and ch 2f out: sn rdn and wknd over 1f out* 14/1
10-2 16 11 **This Ones For Pat (USA)**[19] 884 4-8-11 63 NCallan 3 —
(S Parr) *in rr fr 1/2-way* 8/1
100- 17 shd **Bid For Gold**[175] 6724 5-8-13 65 AndrewElliott 9 —
(Jedd O'Keeffe) *a in rr* 14/1

1m 15.94s (-0.96) **Going Correction** -0.05s/f (Good) 17 Ran SP% 128.6
Speed ratings (Par 103): **104,100,98,98,95 92,91,90,89,87 87,86,85,81,75 61,61**
toteswinger: 1&2 £13.50, 1&3 £20.70, 2&3 £8.40 CSF £64.68 CT £435.68 TOTE £17.50: £3.70, £1.20, £2.60, £3.60; EX 83.00.
Owner The Selebians **Bred** Mrs Rosalynd Norman **Trained** Longton, Lancs
■ Stewards' Enquiry : Richard Evans one-day ban: careless riding (Apr 21)
FOCUS
Just a modest handicap, but seriously competitive. The pace was strong and those drawn low dominated but the form looks reasonable for the grade.
Desert Dreamer(IRE) Official explanation: jockey said gelding was denied a clear run
Dickie Le Davoir Official explanation: jockey said gelding was slow away
Mandelieu(IRE) Official explanation: jockey said gelding ran too free early on
This Ones For Pat(USA) Official explanation: jockey said gelding did not handle the track

1170 DALBY STAND H'CAP 1m 4y
3:10 (3:13) (Class 3) (0-95,89) 4-Y-O+ £7,477 (£2,239; £1,119; £560; £279; £140) Stalls Low

Form RPR
003- 1 **Unbreak My Heart (IRE)**[183] 6526 4-9-4 89 PaulHanagan 4 98
(R A Fahey) *hld up towards rr: hdwy 3f out: swtchd lft wl over 1f out: swtchd rt and rdn ent fnl f: drvn and styd on wl to ld nr fin* 11/1
001- 2 hd **Bencoolen (IRE)**[186] 6446 4-9-2 87 AdrianTNicholls 6 96
(D Nicholls) *chsd ldr: tk clsr order 3f out: chal 2f out: rdn to ld 1f out: sn drvn: hdd and no ex towards fin* 16/1
5230 3 1¾ **El Dececy (USA)**[9] 1016 5-8-3 81 LanceBetts(7) 2 86
(S Parr) *led: rdn along over 2f out: sn jnd and drvn: hdd 1f out: kpt on u.p ins fnl f* 8/1
400- 4 ½ **Kavachi (IRE)**[252] 4509 6-9-2 87 GeorgeBaker 1 91
(G L Moore) *hld up towards rr: hdwy over 3f out: swtchd outside and effrt 2f out: rdn tocahse ldrs over 1f out: drvn and kpt on same pce ins fnl f* 13/2[2]
100- 5 1 **Boy Blue**[215] 5635 4-8-11 82 DaleGibson 5 84
(P Salmon) *chsd ldrs: effrt over 2f out: sn rdn and wknd over 1f out* 40/1
-064 6 nk **Veiled Applause**[10] 999 6-8-6 84 JamieKyne(7) 9 85
(J J Quinn) *hld up towards rr: hdwy 3f out: effrt and npot much room wl over 1f out: rdn and hdwy whn n.m.r 1f out: styd on ins fnl f: nrst fin* 7/1[3]
-322 7 2 **Ours (IRE)**[35] 747 6-8-4 75 (p) ChrisCatlin 12 71
(John A Harris) *bhd: hdwy over 2f out: rdn over 1f out: kpt on ins fnl f: nt rch ldrs* 14/1

056- **8** *3 ¼* **Rattan (USA)**[221] 5470 4-9-1 **86** NickyMackay 3 75
(Rae Guest) *chsd ldrs: rdn along over 2f out and grad wknd* **10/1**

462- **9** *1* **Dunn'o (IRE)**[193] 6242 4-9-1 **86** PhilipRobinson 8 72
(C G Cox) *t.k.h: chsd ldrs: effrt over 2f out: sn rdn and wknd wl over 1f out* **7/2**[1]

606- **10** *1 ¾* **Goodbye Mr Bond**[178] 6654 9-8-7 **81** AndrewMullen(3) 10 63
(E J Alston) *chsd ldrs: rdn along over 2f out and sn wknd* **25/1**

0-63 **11** *3 ¾* **Kingsdale Orion (IRE)**[10] 999 5-8-11 **82** TonyHamilton 13 56
(B Ellison) *in tch: hdwy on outer to chse ldrs 1/2-way: rdn wl over 2f out and sn wknd* **9/1**

15-1 **12** *95* **Intabih (USA)**[35] 747 4-9-4 **89** NCallan 11 —
(C E Brittain) *midfield: rdn along 3f out: wknd 2f out and sn eased* **13/2**[2]

1m 43.94s (-1.96) **Going Correction** -0.05s/f (Good) **12** Ran SP% **118.8**
Speed ratings (Par 107): **107,106,105,104,103 103,101,98,97,95 91,—**
toteswinger: 1&2 £25.60, 1&3 £22.80, 2&3 £33.70 CSF £174.93 CT £1492.34 TOTE £14.40: £4.10, £4.70, £3.40; EX 133.60.
Owner J C Parsons & J J Gilmartin **Bred** Redpender Stud Ltd **Trained** Musley Bank, N Yorks
■ Stewards' Enquiry : Lance Betts caution: excessive use of the whip

FOCUS
A competitive handicap run at a very decent pace. It featured a handful of horses who were making their debuts for new yards, and that included the first two home, both of whom were with Roger Charlton last season. The pace was good and the form looks solid.

NOTEBOOK
Unbreak My Heart(IRE), picked up for 30,000gns by current connections, was weak in the market beforehand on this return from six months off. Having been switched off at the back of the main group in the early stages, he gradually weaved through his rivals and maintained his effort to get up almost on the line. Gelded since last seen, this performance showed that he can act on a fast surface and he should continue to enjoy plenty of success for his new stable, possibly over a little further. (op 8-1 tchd 12-1)
Bencoolen(IRE), a 32,000gns recruit, was dropping back in trip on this debut for his new yard and was also returning from six months off. He was ridden much more handily than the winner and hit the front around a furlong from home before getting mugged. His new trainer should be able to find races for him. (op 14-1)
El Dececy(USA) is best when able to dominate and went off like the clappers. Considering the pace he set, he did really well to keep on battling away when challenged and eventually hang for third, though unlike those that finished around him he did have the advantage of a recent run. (op 10-1)
Kavachi(IRE), returning from nine months off and off the same mark as when fourth in last year's Royal Hunt Cup, came from a similar position to the winner and was close enough if good enough a furlong out, but couldn't quite go through with it. He has always needed his first run after a break in the past, so this was encouraging. (tchd 11-2)
Boy Blue, formerly with David Barker and returning from seven months off, was his trainer's first runner and he ran with credit having been handy from the start. (op 50-1)
Veiled Applause was racing over a shorter trip than normal, but though he stayed on late he was never getting there in time. A return to further looks to be in order. (tchd 13-2 and 8-1)
Ours(IRE), 10lb higher than when last on turf, probably did well to finish as close as he did as he struggled to go the early pace and soon found himself in a detached last. (tchd 12-1)
Dunn'o(IRE), 1lb higher than on his most recent start when runner-up to the highly progressive Mawatheeq on his first try at this trip at Ascot seven months ago, did himself no favours by taking a hold early and had little left when finally coming off the bridle. (op 9-2 tchd 5-1)
Kingsdale Orion(IRE) was always trapped out wide having started from the outside stall and looks better on softer ground in any case. (op 11-1 tchd 12-1)
Intabih(USA), up 7lb on this return to turf having won three of his last four starts on sand, ran as though something was amiss. He was reported to have been unsuited by the quick ground. Official explanation: jockey said colt was unsuited by the good to firm ground (tchd 11-2 and 7-1)

1171 JAMAICAN FLIGHT H'CAP — 2m 1f 216y
3:40 (3:40) (Class 5) (0-75,67) 4-Y-0+ **£3,238** (£963; £481; £240) **Stalls** Low

Form RPR

4-51 **1** **Daraiym (IRE)**[6] 1058 4-8-8 **52** 6ex FrancisNorton 8 59
(Paul Green) *mde most: qcknd over 2f out: rdn clr wl over 1f out: drvn ins fnl f: hld on gamely* **2/1**[1]

-206 **2** *nse* **Snowberry Hill (USA)**[12] 972 6-9-3 **56** JimmyQuinn 7 63
(Lucinda Featherstone) *hld up in rr: gd hdwy on inner over 2f out: swtchd rt to chse wnr wl over 1f out and sn rdn: drvn ent fnl f: styd on strly u.p and jst failed* **7/1**

03-4 **3** *6* **Yonder**[18] 902 5-9-10 **63** SteveDrowne 3 63
(H Morrison) *hld up in rr: hdwy on outer over 3f out: rdn and sltly outpcd 2f out: kpt on u.p ins fnl f* **13/2**[3]

1643 **4** *1 ½* **Dramatic Solo**[18] 894 4-9-9 **67** (b) AndrewElliott 2 66
(K R Burke) *t.k.h: trckd ldrs: effrt 3f out: rdn along to chse wnr 2f out: sn drvn and one pce appr fnl f* **11/2**[2]

1336 **5** *7* **Monaadi (IRE)**[18] 899 4-9-2 **60** (p) GrahamGibbons 4 51
(R Hollinshead) *chsd ldng pair: rdn along 3f out: sn drvn and wknd* **8/1**

40-0 **6** *4 ½* **Kentucky Boy (IRE)**[38] 604 5-9-0 **53** (p) NickyMackay 6 39
(Jedd O'Keeffe) *cl up: rdn along 3f out: sn drvn and wknd* **11/2**[2]

23/0 **7** *10* **Lord Oroko**[22] 848 5-9-12 **65** LukeMorris 1 40
(J G M O'Shea) *hld up in tch: smooth hdwy to trck ldrs 5f out: effrt 3f out: sn rdn and wknd 2f out* **8/1**

4m 9.97s (6.07) **Going Correction** -0.05s/f (Good)
WFA 4 from 5yo+ 5lb **7** Ran SP% **112.2**
Speed ratings (Par 103): **84,83,81,80,77 75,71**
toteswinger: 1&2 £3.90, 1&3 £4.30, 2&3 £6.90 CSF £15.84 CT £74.79 TOTE £2.80: £1.80, £3.20; EX 17.50.
Owner Paul Boyers **Bred** His Highness The Aga Khan's Studs S C **Trained** Lydiate, Merseyside

FOCUS
A moderate staying handicap and the form does not look solid, with the runner-up the best guide. The pace was noticeably steady until increasing around a mile from the finish.
Kentucky Boy(IRE) Official explanation: jockey said gelding was unsuited by the good to firm ground

1172 PADDOCK PACKAGE H'CAP — 1m 2f 6y
4:10 (4:12) (Class 2) (0-100,96) 4-Y-0+
£11,215 (£3,358; £1,679; £840; £419; £210) **Stalls** Low

Form RPR

500- **1** **Ladies Best**[150] 7244 5-8-7 **92** LanceBetts(7) 6 99
(B Ellison) *dwlt: hld up in rr: gd hdwy on inner over 1f out: sn rdn and styd on strly to ld last 100yds* **16/1**

1/1- **2** *¾* **Hawaass (USA)**[284] 3461 4-9-0 **92** GregFairley 2 98
(M Johnston) *led: rdn along and wandered over 1f out: drvn and hung rt ent fnl f: hung lft and hdd last 100yds* **6/4**[1]

10-5 **3** *¾* **Albaqaa**[10] 1003 4-8-13 **91** PaulHanagan 5 95
(R A Fahey) *t.k.h: cl up on outer: effrt to chal 2f out and sn rdn: drvn and ev ch ins fnl f tl no ex last 100yds* **15/8**[2]

55-5 **4** *1 ¼* **Lake Poet (IRE)**[22] 847 6-9-3 **95** SebSanders 1 99+
(C E Brittain) *trckd ldrs: effrt whn nt clr run over 1f out: swtchd rt and n.m.r 1f out: swtchd lft: rdn and nt clr run ins fnl f: no ch after* **8/1**

144- **5** *9* **Jabal Tariq**[234] 5111 4-8-7 **85** MichaelHills 3 69
(B W Hills) *cl up: effrt 3f out: sn rdn and wknd wl over 1f out* **11/2**[3]

2-40 **6** *15* **Pevensey (IRE)**[33] 766 7-9-4 **96** (p) GrahamGibbons 7 50
(J J Quinn) *dwlt: a in rr* **20/1**

2m 12.98s (-0.72) **Going Correction** -0.05s/f (Good) **6** Ran SP% **111.9**
Speed ratings (Par 109): **100,99,98,97,90 78**
toteswinger: 1&2 £5.00, 1&3 £5.10, 2&3 £1.60 CSF £40.55 CT £68.16 TOTE £21.80: £6.60, £1.40; EX 63.50.
Owner Koo's Racing Club **Bred** The Lavington Stud **Trained** Norton, N Yorks
■ Stewards' Enquiry : Greg Fairley two-day ban: careless riding (Apr 28-29) plus four days deferred (Apr 30-May 3)

FOCUS
A disappointing turnout numerically, and therefore not as competitive as one would expect for the grade, but still a decent race. The form looks a bit muddling.

NOTEBOOK
Ladies Best went without the tongue-tie and blinkers he had fitted when mid-division in the November Handicap on his debut for this yard, having subsequently had a wind operation and been gelded. This 32,000gns purchase from the Newmarket October sales had a 7lb claimer on for his reappearance, and Betts was instructed by his trainer not to use the whip, but he made the most of a dream trip. After getting a lovely split against the inside rail in the straight, he picked up well under hands-and-heels riding and was nicely on top at the line. This ended a losing run stretching back to October 2006 and perhaps he could finally fulfil his potential this season. (tchd 20-1)
Hawaass(USA) is well regarded, but he had been off since winning a Newmarket handicap last June, and this was just a fourth-career start, so presumably he has had some problems. Ridden from the front again, he had his chance but got tired in the straight, which was understandable. He should improve a bundle for this, but seemed to have quite a hard race and might not want to be out again too soon. (op Evens)
Albaqaa got noticeably warm and raced keenly without much cover for most of the way, so he actually ran very well in the circumstances. He is capable of better. (op 5-2)
Lake Poet(IRE), well below his turf form when unable to take advantage of a much lower All-Weather mark last time, continually had his path blocked by Hawaass in the straight, and might have finished slightly closer, but he but did not look unlucky. (op 12-1)
Jabal Tariq offered little after 234 days off. (op 7-1 tchd 15-2)
Pevensey(IRE) missed the break and no doubt found things happening much too quickly. (tchd 16-1)

1173 KEN JONES BIRTHDAY CELEBRATION MAIDEN FILLIES' STKS (DIV I) — 6f
4:40 (4:42) (Class 5) 3-Y-0 **£2,914** (£867; £433; £216) **Stalls** Low

Form RPR

620- **1** **Select (IRE)**[269] 3959 3-9-0 **91** AlanMunro 7 77+
(P W Chapple-Hyam) *cl up: hdwy to ld over 2f out: rdn clr over 1f out: kpt on wl* **13/8**[2]

0 **2** *2 ½* **Cape Melody**[13] 951 3-9-0 **0** SteveDrowne 4 69
(H Morrison) *towards rr: hdwy 1/2-way: rdn along 2f out: styd on strly appr fnl f: nrst fin* **66/1**

3 *1 ½* **La Zamora** 3-9-0 **0** PhillipMakin 3 64
(T D Barron) *chsd ldrs: hdwy over 2f out: rdn over 1f out: kpt on u.p ins fnl f* **66/1**

233- **4** *nse* **Today's The Day**[97] 7830 3-9-0 **68** (b) PhilipRobinson 8 64
(M A Jarvis) *cl up: rdn along 3f out: drvn 2f out: kpt on same pce appr fnl f* **13/2**[3]

5 *1* **Miss Porky** 3-9-0 **0** GrahamGibbons 1 61
(R Hollinshead) *chsd ldrs on inner: rdn along 3f out: drvn 2f out and sn one pce* **33/1**

66- **6** *4 ½* **Lindy Hop (IRE)**[192] 6273 3-9-0 **0** TedDurcan 6 46+
(W R Swinburn) *in tch: effrt 3f out: rdn along over 2f out: wknd over 1f out* **14/1**

05 **7** *¾* **Baby Queen (IRE)**[34] 758 3-9-0 **0** J-PGuillambert 10 44
(B P J Baugh) *in tch on outer: rdn along 1/2-way: sn wknd* **150/1**

06- **8** *¾* **Georgie Bee**[194] 6229 3-9-0 **0** DNolan 5 42
(D Carroll) *nvr bttr than midfield* **100/1**

5- **9** *1 ½* **Kasaa Ed**[182] 6565 3-9-0 **0** RHills 2 37+
(M Johnston) *led: rdn along 3f out: hdd over 2f out and sn wknd* **6/4**[1]

053- **10** *nk* **Stellarina (IRE)**[159] 7095 3-9-0 **65** RobertWinston 11 36+
(G A Swinbank) *sn rdn along and bhd tl sme late hdwy* **16/1**

300- **11** *42* **Sensacion Sensual**[208] 5835 3-9-0 **59** TPQueally 12 —
(J G Given) *s.i.s: a bhd* **66/1**

1m 16.98s (0.08) **Going Correction** -0.05s/f (Good) **11** Ran SP% **113.0**
Speed ratings (Par 95): **97,93,91,91,90 84,83,82,80,79 23**
toteswingers: 1&2 £14.10, 1&3 £19.80, 2&3 £56.90 CSF £119.40 TOTE £2.90: £1.20, £8.90, £10.30; EX 46.50.
Owner De La Warr Racing **Bred** Mohammad Al Qatami & Hugo Merry **Trained** Newmarket, Suffolk

FOCUS
An interesting fillies' maiden and a race that should produce winners. The winning time was 0.22 seconds quicker than the second division and the fourth looks the best guide to the form.
Stellarina(IRE) Official explanation: jockey said filly jumped awkwardly and was never travelling after

1174 KEN JONES BIRTHDAY CELEBRATION MAIDEN FILLIES' STKS (DIV II) — 6f
5:10 (5:11) (Class 5) 3-Y-0 **£2,914** (£867; £433; £216) **Stalls** Low

Form RPR

1 **Ingleby Lady** 3-9-0 **0** PhillipMakin 3 71+
(T D Barron) *hld up in rr: n.m.r and swtchd wd home turn: str run on outer over 1f out: led ins fnl f and styd on wl* **9/1**

2 *2 ¾* **She's In The Money** 3-9-0 **0** TPQueally 7 59
(J G Given) *towards rr: rdn and hdwy on outer over 1f out: styd on to chse wnr ins fnl f: no imp towards fin* **14/1**

0- **3** *½* **Champagne Future**[320] 2324 3-9-0 **0** TedDurcan 11 58
(W R Swinburn) *trckd ldrs: hdwy 1/2-way: rdn to ld over 1f out: drvn and hdd ins fnl f: kpt on same pce* **15/2**

35 **4** *1 ½* **Azharia**[13] 951 3-9-0 **0** NCallan 8 53
(C E Brittain) *led: rdn 2f out: drvn and hdd over 1f out: wknd ins fnl f* **3/1**[2]

- **5** *¾* **Scotch And Soda (IRE)** 3-9-0 **0** AndrewElliott 1 50
(Jedd O'Keeffe) *chsd ldrs on inner: hdwy over 2f out: rdn over 1f out: sn one pce* **25/1**

3- **6** *½* **Highly Acclaimed**[228] 5219 3-9-0 **0** MickyFenton 12 49+
(Mrs A Duffield) *chsd ldrs: hdwy on outer 1/2-way: rdn wl over 1f out and sn one pce* **9/2**[3]

0-0 **7** *¾* **Waltzing Buddy**[9] 1015 3-8-7 **0** PaulPickard(7) 9 46
(P T Midgley) *t.k.h: a midfield* **25/1**

0- **8** 1 ¼ **Off Hand**[280] 3590 3-9-0 0 .... DavidAllan 10 42
(T D Easterby) *a towards rr* **25/1**

04- **9** shd **Drum Dragon**[168] 6885 3-9-0 0 .... PaulMulrennan 6 42+
(M H Tompkins) *chsd ldrs: effrt 2f out: sn rdn and hld whn hmpd over 1f out: sn wknd* **11/4**[1]

46- **10** 3 ½ **Sleepy Valley (IRE)**[154] 7172 3-9-0 0 .... DanielTudhope 2 31
(A Dickman) *cl up: rdn along 1/2-way: wknd over 2f out* **14/1**

0- **11** 4 ½ **Sally's Swansong**[98] 7823 3-9-0 0 .... ChrisCatlin 4 16
(M Wellings) *s.i.s: a bhd* **40/1**

12 2 **Cheeky Crumpet** 3-9-0 0 .... FrancisNorton 5 10
(A Berry) *s.i.s: a bhd* **66/1**

1m 17.2s (0.30) **Going Correction** -0.05s/f (Good) **12** Ran SP% **120.4**
Speed ratings (Par 95): **96,92,91,89,88 88,87,85,85,80 74,71**
toteswinger: 1&2 £18.80, 1&3 £13.00, 2&3 £18.00 CSF £121.36 TOTE £13.00: £2.80, £3.30, £3.10; EX 202.20.
Owner Dave Scott **Bred** Hellwood Stud Farm **Trained** Maunby, N Yorks

FOCUS
The winning time was 0.22 seconds slower than the first division won by the 91-rated Select, but this was still an impressive debut from the winner. The fourth helps to set the level.
Drum Dragon Official explanation: jockey said filly was unsuited by the good to firm ground
Sleepy Valley(IRE) Official explanation: jockey said filly hing right-handed throughout

1175 BETFAIR APPRENTICE TRAINING SERIES H'CAP — 1m 4f 8y
5:40 (5:40) (Class 5) (0-75,75) 4-Y-0+ **£3,238** (£963; £481; £240) **Stalls** Low

Form RPR
0-23 **1** **Eton Fable (IRE)**[37] 726 4-9-0 **72** .... (p) PaulPickard(3) 4 81
(W J H Ratcliffe) *mde all: rdn along 2f out: styd on wl u.p ins fnl f* **11/4**[1]

3610 **2** 2 ½ **Monfils Monfils (USA)**[3] 1125 7-9-2 **70** .... AmyRyan 9 75
(A J McCabe) *hld up in tch: hdwy 3f out: chsd wnr wl over 1f out: rdn and edgd lft ins fnl f: sn no imp* **10/3**[2]

014 **3** 5 **Simonside**[11] 983 6-9-7 **75** .... LanceBetts 7 72
(B Ellison) *in tch: rdn along and sltly outpcd 3f out: kpt on u.p to take 3rd ins fnl f* **8/1**

0502 **4** ½ **Red Wine**[10] 1000 10-8-9 **68** .... KarenKenny(5) 6 64
(A J McCabe) *hld up: hdwy over 3f out: rdn to chse ldng pair over 1f out: sn edgd lft and wknd ins fnl f* **13/2**

30-0 **5** 1 ½ **Graylyn Ruby (FR)**[85] 139 4-8-13 **71** .... DebraEngland(3) 5 65
(J Jay) *chsd wnr: hdwy 3f out: rdn along over 2f out and sn btn* **10/1**

2421 **6** 4 ½ **Quince (IRE)**[39] 712 6-9-7 **75** .... (v) SimonPearce 3 62
(J Pearce) *hld up: a in rr* **5/1**[3]

2022 **7** 1 **Rawdon (IRE)**[18] 894 8-9-4 **72** .... (bt) KylieManser 2 57
(Miss Gay Kelleway) *prom: rdn along over 3f out and sn wknd* **7/1**

2m 39.26s (-1.54) **Going Correction** -0.05s/f (Good)
WFA 4 from 6yo+ 1lb **7** Ran SP% **112.4**
Speed ratings (Par 103): **103,101,98,97,96 93,93**
toteswinger: 1&2 £3.30, 1&3 £5.20, 2&3 £5.30 CSF £11.63 CT £62.20 TOTE £3.50: £2.40, £2.50; EX 13.60 Place 6: £185.15, Place 5: £160.04..
Owner The Gathering **Bred** Andrew Christy **Trained** Newmarket, Suffolk

FOCUS
A weak apprentice handicap and with few of these reliable the form is fairly weak.
T/Plt: £166.30 to a £1 stake. Pool: £86,526.45. 379.69 winning tickets. T/Qpdt: £47.10 to a £1 stake. Pool: £3,839.20. 60.20 winning tickets. JR

BRIGHTON (L-H)
Wednesday, April 8

OFFICIAL GOING: Good (good to firm in places; 8.0)
Wind: fresh, across Weather: bright, sunny

1176 FREEBETS.CO.UK NBA PLAY OFF FREE BETS MAIDEN STKS — 7f 214y
2:20 (2:22) (Class 5) 3-Y-0 **£3,238** (£963; £481; £240) **Stalls** Low

Form RPR
3- **1** **Alsahil (USA)**[145] 7312 3-9-3 0 .... RHills 1 78+
(M P Tregoning) *mde all: rdn over 1f out: rdn out and styd on wl fnl f: comf* **7/4**[2]

00- **2** 1 ½ **Brunston**[165] 6977 3-9-3 0 .... JimmyFortune 6 73
(R Charlton) *racd wd for 1f: chsd wnr after 1f: rdn over 2f out: hanging lft fr over 1f out: kpt on same pce and a hld fnl f* **6/4**[1]

32 **3** 2 **Carbon Hoofprint**[15] 944 3-9-3 0 .... SebSanders 2 68+
(P J Makin) *chsd wnr for 1f: chsd ldng pair after: hanging lft fr 2f out: kpt on same pce fnl f* **9/2**[3]

0-42 **4** 1 **Edgeworth (IRE)**[53] 542 3-9-3 64 .... GeorgeBaker 7 66
(B G Powell) *hld up in rr: swtchd rt and effrt over 2f out: hung bdly lft over 1f out: kpt on but nvr threatened ldrs* **16/1**

440- **5** 13 **Our Day Will Come**[107] 7767 3-8-12 71 .... RichardHughes 4 31
(R Hannon) *in tch in midfield: effrt over 2f out: btn wl over 1f out: no ch after* **8/1**

00-6 **6** 7 **Konka (USA)**[17] 920 3-8-7 35 .... MarkFlynn(5) 5 15
(E F Vaughan) *plld hrd: hld up in rr: c centre and effrt over 2f out: sn struggling: no ch fr wl over 1f out* **100/1**

0 **7** 75 **Wild Lyph**[26] 824 3-9-3 0 .... PaulMulrennan 3 —
(N P Mulholland) *plld hrd: chsd ldrs tl wknd qckly over 3f out: virtually p.u fnl f: t.o* **100/1**

1m 36.5s (0.50) **Going Correction** +0.025s/f (Good) **7** Ran SP% **113.5**
Speed ratings (Par 98): **98,96,94,93,80 73,—**
toteswinger: 1&2 £1.20, 1&3 £1.60, 2&3 £1.50 CSF £4.67 TOTE £2.90: £1.30, £1.60; EX 5.60.
Owner Hamdan Al Maktoum **Bred** Shadwell Farm LLC **Trained** Lambourn, Berks

FOCUS
Even though the top-rated horse with an official handicap rating was on a mark of 71, one would imagine that this was no more than a modest event. The winner did it nicely though.
Brunston Official explanation: jockey said colt ran green
Carbon Hoofprint Official explanation: jockey said gelding hung left
Edgeworth(IRE) Official explanation: jockey said gelding hung left
Wild Lyph Official explanation: jockey said gelding ran too free

1177 FREEBETS.CO.UK US MASTERS GOLF FREE BETS CLAIMING STKS — 1m 1f 209y
2:50 (2:52) (Class 6) 4-Y-0+ **£1,942** (£578; £288; £144) **Stalls** High

Form RPR
00-2 **1** **Western Roots**[20] 875 8-8-5 67 .... DavidProbert(3) 7 73
(A M Balding) *mde all: sn clr: unchal* **15/8**[1]

5322 **2** 4 ½ **Benedict Spirit (IRE)**[13] 923 4-9-5 72 .... PaulMulrennan 6 75
(M H Tompkins) *racd in 3rd pl: chsd wnr over 4f out: rdn wl over 2f out: no imp* **5/2**[2]

0-50 **3** 10 **Cactus King**[20] 878 6-8-11 73 .... IanMongan 4 47
(P M Phelan) *hld up in midfield: hdwy to chse ldng pair 4f out: hung lft and racd awkwardly fr 2f out: wl btn after* **11/4**[3]

4602 **4** 14 **Ten Pole Tudor**[12] 979 4-8-5 61 .... (p) ChrisCatlin 5 13
(R A Harris) *t.k.h: hld up in last pair: wnt modest 4th over 3f out: sn rdn and wl btn* **5/1**

00-0 **5** 12 **Flipacoin**[42] 674 4-8-1 42 .... NickyMackay 1 —
(S Dow) *t.k.h: chsd wnr tlm over 4f out: sn struggling: wl bhd fnl 2f: t.o* **25/1**

0000 **6** 7 **Looter (FR)**[24] 598 4-7-13 40 .... (tp) AmyBaker(5) 3 —
(P Butler) *a bhd: lost tch 1/2-way: t.o* **66/1**

2m 3.03s (-0.57) **Going Correction** +0.025s/f (Good) **6** Ran SP% **112.0**
Speed ratings (Par 101): **103,99,91,80,70 65**
toteswinger: 1&2 £1.30, 1&3 £1.30, 2&3 £3.00. CSF £6.85 TOTE £2.40: £1.10, £1.90; EX 6.90.
Owner I A Balding **Bred** Stratford Place Stud **Trained** Kingsclere, Hants

FOCUS
This did look quite a competitive claimer between the top three in the market, but it soon became clear that it was going to be a one-horse race. The form is best rated through the winner who may not have needed to match his best.

1178 FREEBETS.CO.UK IRISH GRAND NATIONAL FREE BETS H'CAP — 1m 3f 196y
3:20 (3:20) (Class 5) (0-85,68) 4-Y-0+ **£2,590** (£770; £385; £192) **Stalls** High

Form RPR
34-0 **1** **Moonshine Creek**[21] 871 7-8-10 **58** .... ChrisCatlin 7 65
(P W Hiatt) *chsd ldr tl led after 2f: mde rest: hrd drvn and hld on gamely fnl f* **9/2**[3]

2514 **2** ½ **Star Choice**[6] 1081 4-9-3 **66** .... (v) RobertHavlin 1 72
(J Pearce) *hld up in tch: hdwy 5f out: trckd ldr gng wl over 3f out: chal 2f out: edgd lft ent fnl f: nt qckn u.p fnl 100yds* **7/2**[2]

40-0 **3** 1 ¼ **Good Effect (USA)**[27] 816 5-8-6 **54** .... WilliamBuick 2 58
(C P Morlock) *led for 2f: chsd ldr after: pressing ldrs and rdn 3f out: hung rt and nt qckn fr over 1f out* **6/1**

-322 **4** 5 **King's Majesty (IRE)**[38] 534 7-9-3 **65** .... (p) ShaneKelly 4 61
(A M Hales) *hld up in tch in rr: hdwy over 3f out: rdn over 2f out: swtchd rt and drvn over 1f out: wknd fnl f* **11/4**[1]

21-0 **5** 6 **White Moss (IRE)**[70] 311 5-9-2 **64** .... RichardThomas 5 51
(Jim Best) *hld up in tch: rdn over 3f out: struggling over 2f out: no ch w ldrs after* **6/1**

-155 **6** 11 **Clovis**[28] 798 4-9-5 **68** .... (b) JimmyFortune 3 37
(N P Mulholland) *stdd s: hld up in tch in rr: hdwy on inner 6f out: rdn 3f out: sn struggling: no ch and eased fnl f* **7/1**

100- **7** 11 **Megalala (IRE)**[173] 6775 8-8-3 **54** .... MarcHalford(3) 6 5
(J J Bridger) *stdd s: t.k.h: disp 2nd pl after 2f: rdn and wknd qckly over 3f out: t.o and eased fnl f* **12/1**

2m 34.77s (2.07) **Going Correction** +0.025s/f (Good)
WFA 4 from 5yo+ 1lb **7** Ran SP% **115.8**
Speed ratings (Par 103): **94,93,92,89,85 78,70**
toteswinger: 1&2 £3.70, 1&3 £2.60, 2&3 £12.40. CSF £21.15 TOTE £6.50: £2.50, £2.20; EX 23.30.
Owner P W Hiatt **Bred** Lawrence Shepherd **Trained** Hook Norton, Oxon

FOCUS
A modest handicap run at an ordinary gallop. The winner is probably the best guide to the form.
King's Majesty(IRE) Official explanation: jockey said gelding did not handle the track
Clovis Official explanation: jockey said gelding stopped quickly

1179 FREEBETS.CO.UK FA CUP SEMI FINALS FREE BETS H'CAP — 1m 1f 209y
3:50 (3:53) (Class 4) (0-80,76) 4-Y-0+ **£5,504** (£1,637; £818; £408) **Stalls** High

Form RPR
0-24 **1** **King Supreme (IRE)**[28] 798 4-9-3 **75** .... (b) RichardHughes 3 86
(R Hannon) *chsd ldr: rdn to ld over 2f out: clr fnl f: styd on wl: eased towards fin* **7/4**[1]

512- **2** 3 ½ **Riqaab (IRE)**[248] 4663 4-9-1 **73** .... RHills 1 77
(E A L Dunlop) *rrd s: hld up in last pair: effrt on outer 2f out: chsd wnr over 1f out: one pce fnl f* **9/4**[2]

5163 **3** 3 ¾ **Bavarica**[15] 948 7-8-2 **67** .... MatthewCosham(7) 7 64
(Miss J Feilden) *stdd s: t.k.h: chsd ldrs after 1f: rdn to chse wnr 2f out tl over 1f out: wknd fnl f* **16/1**

4043 **4** 1 ½ **Teasing**[10] 1020 5-9-4 **76** .... (v) RobertHavlin 6 70
(J Pearce) *hld up in tch: rdn 3f out: wknd u.p over 1f out* **8/1**

400- **5** 2 **Dove Cottage (IRE)**[226] 5370 7-9-2 **74** .... ChrisCatlin 5 64
(W S Kittow) *sn led and clr: hdd and rdn over 2f out: wknd wl over 1f out* **11/2**[3]

245 **6** 4 ½ **Star Strider**[53] 544 5-9-0 **72** .... JimmyFortune 2 53
(Miss Gay Kelleway) *stdd s: hld up in last pl: rdn 2f out: sn wl btn* **15/2**

2m 4.91s (1.31) **Going Correction** +0.025s/f (Good) **6** Ran SP% **111.3**
Speed ratings (Par 105): **95,92,89,88,86 82**
toteswinger: 1&2 £1.40, 1&3 £16.80, 2&3 £5.70. CSF £5.80 TOTE £2.00: £1.90, £1.20; EX 4.30.
Owner Brian C Oakley **Bred** Miss Joan Murphy **Trained** East Everleigh, Wilts

FOCUS
A fair-looking contest. One horse got an easy lead but he was readily passed about two furlongs from home. The winner was close to the form when successful here last summer.

1180 FREEBETS.CO.UK EUROPEAN CUP RUGBY FREE BETS H'CAP — 5f 213y
4:20 (4:21) (Class 3) (0-90,88) 3-Y-0 **£8,418** (£2,505; £1,251; £625) **Stalls** Low

Form RPR
231- **1** **Green Beret (IRE)**[272] 3889 3-9-3 **87** .... JimmyFortune 7 98+
(J H M Gosden) *a travelling wl: hld up in tch: clsd 2f out: shkn up to ld 1f out: sn in comand: eased towards fin* **1/1**[1]

3123 **2** 3 **Flamsteed (IRE)**[9] 1032 3-8-4 **74** oh1 .... FrankieMcDonald 3 72
(M Quinn) *hld up in tch: n.m.r 2f out: gap sn clsd and nt clr run over 1f out tl ins fnl f: swtchd rt and pushed into 2nd towards fin: no ch w wnr* **7/1**[3]

12-2 **3** ½ **Glamorous Spirit (IRE)**[27] 814 3-9-1 **85** .... ChrisCatlin 1 81
(R A Harris) *racd freely: led: rdn 2f out: hdd 1f out: no ch w wnr after: lost 2nd towards fin* **8/1**

4632 **4** 2 **Cecily**[7] 1068 3-8-7 **77** .... WilliamBuick 6 67
(Sir Mark Prescott) *chsd ldr: rdn 2f out: unable to qckn u.p: wknd ins fnl f* **5/2**[2]

3116 **5** 4 ½ **Quick Single (USA)**[40] 709 3-7-13 **74** oh3 .... (v) AndreaAtzeni(5) 2 50
(P S McEntee) *sn outpcd in last and bustled along: c centre and drvn 2f out: no rspnse* **12/1**

69.93 secs (-0.27) **Going Correction** +0.025s/f (Good) **5** Ran SP% **109.9**
Speed ratings (Par 102): **102,98,97,94,88**
toteswinger: 1&2 £5.80. CSF £8.52 TOTE £1.80: £1.10, £3.70; EX 5.80.
Owner H R H Princess Haya Of Jordan **Bred** Denis And Mrs Teresa Bergin **Trained** Newmarket, Suffolk
■ Stewards' Enquiry : William Buick caution: careless riding

FOCUS
The gallop set by the leader was strong, and the time was good, so this form should work out. The winner can do better.
NOTEBOOK
Green Beret(IRE), absent since winning a maiden by a wide margin last July, proved a different class to his rivals and won very nicely once his jockey asked him to quicken. He will not been running in this sort of company for very long, as surely a step up in class awaits. (op 10-11 tchd 5-4)
Flamsteed(IRE), who was a pound out of the handicap, had done all of his racing on the all-weather prior to this start, almost exclusively at Lingfield, and looked unlucky not to be a bit closer in this, as he got very short of room when his jockey desperately needed it. He deserved to be second but his head came up once there. (op 12-1)
Glamorous Spirit(IRE), a place in front of Cecily when they last met, confirmed that form over this longer trip after going a good pace from the outset. She seems to progressing. (op 13-2 tchd 6-1)
Cecily failed to build on her recent second and is beginning to be disappointing. (tchd 2-1)
Quick Single(USA), who was running from 3lb out of the handicap, never got out of last place. Official explanation: trainer said gelding lost an off-fore shoe (op 16-1)

1181 FREEBETS.CO.UK RUGBY LEAGUE FREE BETS H'CAP 5f 59y
4:50 (4:50) (Class 4) (0-85,85) 4-Y-O+ **£5,504** (£1,637; £818; £408) **Stalls** Low

Form RPR
440- **1** **Magical Speedfit (IRE)**[139] 7393 4-8-4 **71** oh1................. ChrisCatlin 5 78
(G G Margarson) *bhd: hdwy on outer over 1f out: str run u.p to ld nr fin*
9/2[3]
132 **2** ½ **Wotashirtfull (IRE)**[8] 1053 4-9-0 **81**.............................(p) PatCosgrave 2 86
(J R Boyle) *dwlt: chsd ldr after 1f: rdn over 1f out: edgd lft ent fnl f: drvn and ev ch fnl 100yds: kpt on* **11/4**[2]
00-4 **3** ½ **Merlin's Dancer**[35] 754 9-9-1 **82**.................................... TonyCulhane 4 85
(S Dow) *led: rdn over 1f out: hdd nr fin: short of room on post* **13/2**
225- **4** 1 **Make My Dream**[145] 7315 6-8-6 **73**............................... WilliamBuick 6 73
(J Gallagher) *in tch: rdn and effrt 2f out: kpt on same pce ins fnl f* **5/2**[1]
05-0 **5** ¾ **Whiskey Junction**[11] 1006 5-9-4 **85**................................... LPKeniry 3 88+
(M Quinn) *chsd ldr for 1f: trckd ldrs on rail after: nt clr run fr over 1f out: nt rcvr and nvr able to chal: eased towards fin* **5/1**
4006 **6** 1¾ **Thoughtsofstardom**[5] 1094 6-8-1 **71** oh1.................. KellyHarrison(3) 1 62
(P S McEntee) *hld up in last pair: effrt 2f out: sn rdn: wknd u.p ins fnl f* **8/1**
62.53 secs (0.23) **Going Correction** +0.025s/f (Good) **6** Ran SP% **114.5**
Speed ratings (Par 105): **99,98,97,95,94 91**
toteswinger: 1&2 £2.40, 1&3 £3.20, 2&3 £1.70 CSF £17.73 TOTE £5.20: £2.80, £1.30; EX 22.60 Place 6: £13.15 Place 5: £11.09 .
Owner John Guest **Bred** John Malone **Trained** Newmarket, Suffolk
FOCUS
As could have been predicted before the off, the pace throughout was extremely strong, but the finish was very unsatisfactory. The form is best rated through the second.
Whiskey Junction Official explanation: jockey said gelding was denied a clear run
T/Plt: £29.60 to a £1 stake. Pool: £62,156.21. 1,532.72 winning tickets. T/Qpdt: £9.50 to a £1 stake. Pool: £3,711.10. 288.95 winning tickets. SP

1077 KEMPTON (A.W) (R-H)
Wednesday, April 8

OFFICIAL GOING: Standard
Wind: Moderate, half behind Weather: Fine

1182 BOOK KEMPTON TICKETS ON 0844 579 3008 H'CAP 5f (P)
6:50 (6:53) (Class 6) (0-60,66) 4-Y-O+ **£2,047** (£604; £302) **Stalls** High

Form RPR
30-0 **1** **Garstang**[12] 975 6-9-4 **60**...(b) PaulMulrennan 10 71+
(J Balding) *racd on inner: trckd ldng pair: plld out 1f out: drvn and r.o to ld nr fin* **12/1**
5421 **2** ½ **Bluebok**[4] 1134 8-9-10 **66** 6ex.......................................(bt) LPKeniry 5 75
(J M Bradley) *chsd ldr: rdn to chal over 1f out: upsides wl ins fnl f: outpcd by wnr nr fin* **5/2**[1]
065 **3** ½ **Dodaa (USA)**[26] 832 6-8-5 **54**.. BMcHugh(7) 8 61
(N Wilson) *led: hrd pressed over 1f out: kpt on tl hdd last 50yds* **5/1**[2]
00-2 **4** 3½ **Sofinella (IRE)**[19] 896 6-8-3 **52**................................ TobyAtkinson(7) 7 47
(A W Carroll) *t.k.h: hld up in midfield: rdn and nt qckn over 1f out* **20/1**
0102 **5** hd **Sherjawy (IRE)**[8] 1055 5-8-10 **52**................................(b) SamHitchcott 11 46
(Miss Z C Davison) *dwlt: drvn thrght: outpcd: kpt on fnl f* **13/2**[3]
0105 **6** 1 **Teen Ager (FR)**[14] 956 5-9-2 **58**.. JimmyQuinn 9 51+
(P Burgoyne) *dwlt: hld up in last: nvr on terms: gng wl whn nt clr run over 1f out: running on whn rn into trble ins fnl f* **8/1**
-403 **7** ¾ **Ask Jenny (IRE)**[21] 861 7-9-1 **57**................................... RichardHughes 1 45
(Patrick Morris) *racd wd: pressed ldrs: u.p over 2f out: wknd over 1f out* **8/1**
00-5 **8** 1¼ **Seductive Witch**[15] 946 4-8-10 **52**.................................... EddieAhern 2 35
(J Balding) *nvr beyond midfield and nvr on terms: struggling over 1f out* **16/1**
0652 **9** shd **Joss Stick**[7] 1072 4-9-4 **60**...(p) ChrisCatlin 4 43
(R A Harris) *hld up in last pair: nvr on terms: rdn and no prog over 1f out* **8/1**
5040 **10** ¾ **Fizzlephut (IRE)**[9] 1038 7-9-4 **60**...............................(b) PaulFitzsimons 6 40
(Miss J R Tooth) *reluctant and unruly to post: stdd s: hld up and nvr on terms: wknd fnl f* **25/1**
60.20 secs (-0.30) **Going Correction** +0.025s/f (Slow) **10** Ran SP% **114.1**
Speed ratings (Par 101): **103,102,101,95,95 93,92,90,90,89**
toteswinger: 1&2 £8.10, 1&3 £10.90, 2&3 £3.20 CSF £41.24 CT £176.77 TOTE £15.50: £5.00, £1.50, £2.20; EX 71.50.
Owner The Foulrice Twenty **Bred** Mrs S E Barclay **Trained** Scrooby, Notts
FOCUS
Nothing managed to land a blow from off the pace in this moderate sprint and the first three pretty much had it to themselves. The winner will still be well treated on his old form after this.
Teen Ager(FR) Official explanation: jockey said gelding was denied a clear run

1183 DIGIBET H'CAP 1m 2f (P)
7:20 (7:22) (Class 6) (0-60,60) 3-Y-O **£2,047** (£604; £302) **Stalls** High

Form RPR
5-06 **1** **Graycliffe (IRE)**[35] 759 3-8-11 **53**.................................. RichardHughes 6 64
(Patrick Morris) *reluctant to enter stalls: trckd ldng pair: wnt 2nd over 2f out: rdn to chal over 1f out: led last 100yds* **4/1**[1]
060- **2** ¾ **Beaubrav**[181] 6597 3-9-4 **60**... ShaneKelly 2 69
(P W D'Arcy) *led: kicked on over 3f out: hrd pressed over 1f out: worn down last 100yds* **6/1**[3]
5-63 **3** 6 **Persian Tomcat (IRE)**[9] 1036 3-8-5 **47**............................ JimmyQuinn 3 44
(Miss J Feilden) *dwlt: rcvrd and sn chsd ldr: lost 2nd over 2f out: sn no ch w ldng pair: fdd fnl f but hld on for 3rd* **13/2**
000- **4** 1¼ **Tinkerbelle (IRE)**[182] 6580 3-8-11 **53**................................ EddieAhern 1 48+
(J L Dunlop) *hld up in last trio: ldrs already gone clr whn rdn and prog to go 6th over 2f out: wnt poor 4th 1f out: styd on wl* **14/1**
124 **5** 2¾ **Kiyari**[16] 938 3-8-13 **60**... AndreaAtzeni(5) 12 49+
(M Botti) *hld up towards rr: already outpcd whn trapped on inner bhd wkng rivals over 3f out: rdn and modest prog fnl 2f: no ch* **9/2**[2]
436 **6** 1½ **Joannadarc (USA)**[26] 826 3-9-4 **60**.............................. DarryllHolland 7 46
(S A Callaghan) *hld up in rr: outpcd over 3f out: drvn and prog to go 5th 3f out: nvr on terms w ldrs: plugged on* **13/2**
0-00 **7** 1¾ **Amatara (IRE)**[13] 964 3-7-13 **46** oh1.........................(p) AmyBaker(5) 10 29
(B G Powell) *stdd s: hld up wl in rr: no ch after ldrs wnt clr 3f out: brought wd in st: plugged on* **66/1**
50-0 **8** nk **Thefillyfromepsom**[19] 890 3-9-4 **60**................................ IanMongan 8 42
(P M Phelan) *trckd ldrs: prog to go 4th 4f out: clr of rest 3f out but drvn: wknd wl over 1f out: lost 4 pls fnl f* **14/1**
06-6 **9** 10 **Valkyrie (IRE)**[35] 752 3-9-4 **60**....................................... NCallan 9 22+
(N P Littmoden) *hld up wl in rr: stl at bk of main gp whn ldrs wnt clr 3f out: no ch after: eased fnl f: t.o* **17/2**
000- **10** nk **Top Tinker**[135] 7434 3-8-13 **55**.............................. PaulMulrennan 11 16+
(M H Tompkins) *hld up in detached last: t.o and stl there and rn into trble wl over 1f out: ambled past wkng rivals nr fin* **11/1**
0-50 **11** 1 **Praise Of Folly**[19] 900 3-8-12 **54**............................ SimonWhitworth 5 13
(A G Newcombe) *a in rr: last pair and strugglingt 4f out: bhd after: t.o* **40/1**
040- **12** nse **Star Of Sophia (IRE)**[149] 7269 3-8-1 **46** oh1............ AndrewMullen(3) 4 5
(Mrs A Duffield) *t.k.h early: hld up bhd ldrs: off the bridle by 1/2-way: wknd 3f out: t.o* **33/1**
00-0 **13** 7 **Spinning Joy**[14] 949 3-8-11 **53**....................................... PatCosgrave 14 —
(J R Boyle) *trckd ldrs on inner: drvn in 5th over 3f out: sn wknd rapidly: t.o* **20/1**
2m 9.15s (1.15) **Going Correction** +0.025s/f (Slow) **13** Ran SP% **123.0**
Speed ratings (Par 96): **96,95,90,89,87 86,84,84,76,76 75,75,69**
toteswinger: 1&2 £6.00, 1&3 £65.00, 2&3 £9.60 CSF £27.83 CT £158.42 TOTE £4.80: £1.70, £2.50, £1.80; EX 33.20.
Owner Chester Racing Club Ltd **Bred** Crone Stud Farms Ltd **Trained** Tarporley, Cheshire
■ Stewards' Enquiry : Shane Kelly one-day ban: careless riding (Apr 22)
FOCUS
This poor three-year-old handicap was run at an average pace and once again it paid to race prominently. The first two came clear but this is not an easy race to rate with the second making his handicap debut and the winner and third not obviously progressive.
Top Tinker Official explanation: jockey said, regarding running and riding, his orders were to ride the race as he found it and to finish as close as possible, he was hampered shortly after start, outpaced in back straight and then was denied a clear run on final bend and in home straight; trainer's rep added that gelding would be better suited by a longer trip.

1184 DIGIBET.COM H'CAP 1m 4f (P)
7:50 (7:50) (Class 4) (0-85,85) 4-Y-O+ **£4,727** (£1,406; £702; £351) **Stalls** Centre

Form RPR
15-2 **1** **Right Stuff (FR)**[14] 952 6-8-11 **77**..................................... ShaneKelly 5 85
(G L Moore) *hld up in last: prog jst over 2f out w awkward hd carriage: wnt 2nd fnl f: sustained effrt to ld last stride* **11/10**[1]
04-6 **2** hd **Encircled**[53] 549 5-9-5 **85**.. EddieAhern 8 93
(J R Jenkins) *hld up in 5th: prog to go 3rd over 3f out: rdn to cl and led over 1f out: kpt on wout finding great deal fnl f hdd last stride* **10/1**
312 **3** ½ **River Ardeche**[7] 1059 4-8-5 **77**.......................... PatrickDonaghy(5) 2 84
(P C Haslam) *led at decent pce: drvn and hdd over 1f out: kpt on wl fnl f but a hld* **7/1**
6-41 **4** 2 **Remember Ramon (USA)**[41] 692 6-9-2 **82**........................... NCallan 6 86
(J R Gask) *t.k.h: trckd ldr: rdn over 2f out: lost 2nd wl over 1f out: nt qckn* **6/1**[3]
6254 **5** nk **Clear Reef**[14] 952 5-9-0 **80**.. PatCosgrave 7 84
(Jane Chapple-Hyam) *stdd s: t.k.h: hld up in last pair: rdn 3f out: kpt on u.p fnl 2f: nvr on terms* **9/1**
2-00 **6** 4½ **Cape Colony**[35] 761 4-9-2 **83**....................................... RichardHughes 3 79
(R Hannon) *hld up in abt 6th: rdn 3f out: sn no prog and btn: eased ins fnl f* **11/2**[2]
000- **7** 2 **Duty Free (IRE)**[223] 5423 5-8-12 **78**.................................. SteveDrowne 4 71
(C R Egerton) *t.k.h: hld up bhd ldrs: shkn up 3f out: sn lost pl and btn* **25/1**
0066 **8** 13 **Cold Turkey**[23] 847 9-8-1 **74**....................................... JemmaMarshall(7) 9 46
(G L Moore) *racd wd: trckd ldng pair to 1/2-way: sn lost pl: last and losing tch 2f out: t.o* **25/1**
2m 32.95s (-1.55) **Going Correction** +0.025s/f (Slow)
WFA 4 from 5yo+ 1lb **8** Ran SP% **116.6**
Speed ratings (Par 105): **106,105,105,104,104 101,99,91**
toteswinger: 1&2 £3.90, 1&3 £3.20, 2&3 £11.30 CSF £13.94 CT £53.03 TOTE £2.20: £1.40, £2.60, £2.40; EX 14.50.
Owner The Ashden Partnership & Partners **Bred** N P Bloodstock Ltd **Trained** Lower Beeding, W Sussex
FOCUS
A fair handicap, run at a sound pace. The form is rated around the third and fourth.

1185 DIGIBET CASINO MAIDEN STKS 7f (P)
8:20 (8:22) (Class 5) 3-Y-O+ **£3,238** (£963; £481; £240) **Stalls** High

Form RPR
30- **1** **Crown Choice**[335] 1926 4-9-12 0.. TedDurcan 11 88+
(W R Swinburn) *mde all: pushed along and 2 l clr 2f out: reminder over 1f out: styd on wl: readily* **8/1**
2 1 **Makaam (USA)** 3-8-12 0... RHills 13 80+
(M P Tregoning) *hld up in abt 8th: prog 2f out: effrt to chse wnr 1f out: styd on wl enough but no imp* **11/4**[2]
00- **3** 1½ **Eastern Empire**[180] 6621 3-8-12 0....................................... JamesDoyle 12 76
(J W Hills) *trckd ldrs on inner: rdn 2f out: wnt 3rd fnl f: styd on same pce* **50/1**
4 2¼ **Miss Glitters (IRE)** 4-9-7 0... SteveDrowne 9 70
(H Morrison) *s.i.s: sn wl in tch bhd ldrs: shkn up and nt qckn 2f out: kpt on fnl f* **25/1**
244- **5** nk **Strategic Mover (USA)**[302] 2919 4-9-12 80............... RichardHughes 10 74
(P F I Cole) *trckd ldng trio: rdn to dispute 2nd over 1f out: no imp on wnr: wknd ins fnl f* **15/2**[3]
22- **6** 2¾ **Equipe De Nuit**[236] 5066 3-8-12 0....................................... SaleemGolam 7 62
(S C Williams) *t.k.h: mostly chsd wnr to over 1f out: wknd* **2/1**[1]

452- **7** ¾ **Slant (IRE)**[163] 7015 3-8-7 75 StephenCarson 4 55
(Eve Johnson Houghton) *t.k.h: trckd ldng pair tl wknd 2f out* **8/1**

0- **8** *nse* **Conclusive**[181] 6602 3-8-12 0 JimCrowley 3 59+
(R M Beckett) *dwlt: hld up in rr: outpcd over 2f out: reminder over 1f out: kpt on: n.d* **20/1**

00- **9** *shd* **Melange (USA)**[195] 6230 3-8-5 0 DTDaSilva(7) 1 59
(P F I Cole) *hld up towards rr: outpcd over 2f out: rdn over 1f out: plugged on* **66/1**

10 *1* **The Spicer** 4-9-7 0 (t) AndreaAtzeni(5) 8 61
(F Sheridan) *dwlt: hld up wl in rr: effrt on inner over 2f out: no imp over 1f out: fdd* **33/1**

0-0 **11** ½ **Perfect Affair (USA)**[14] 951 3-8-12 0 SebSanders 2 55
(R M Beckett) *wl in rr and racd wd: nvr a factor* **9/1**

12 4½ **Rock Tech** 4-9-5 0 DannyBrock(7) 6 48
(J R Jenkins) *dwlt: hld up wl in rr: effrt 3f out: hanging and wknd over 2f out* **100/1**

13 *18* **Court Wing (IRE)** 3-8-7 0 ChrisCatlin 5 —
(George Baker) *sn last and struggling: t.o* **33/1**

1m 27.11s (1.11) **Going Correction** +0.025s/f (Slow)
WFA 3 from 4yo 14lb **13** Ran SP% **122.9**
Speed ratings (Par 103): **94,92,91,88,88 85,84,84,84,82 82,77,56**
toteswinger: 1&2 £6.00, 1&3 £36.10, 2&3 £45.90 CSF £29.63 TOTE £10.40: £3.30, £1.60, £13.80; EX 39.90.
Owner P W Harris **Bred** Howard Barton Stud **Trained** Aldbury, Herts

FOCUS
Not a bad maiden, run at a sound pace but the form is a bit muddling.
Perfect Affair(USA) Official explanation: jockey said colt hung left

1186 SPONSOR AT KEMPTON H'CAP 7f (P)
8:50 (8:50) (Class 4) (0-80,80) 4-Y-0+ **£4,727** (£1,406; £702; £351) **Stalls** High

Form RPR

2220 **1** **Obe Royal**[4] 1132 5-8-11 73 ow1 (v) RichardHughes 6 81
(P D Evans) *hld up wl in rr: eased off inner and prog 2f out: sustained effrt fnl f to ld last strides* **11/1**

650- **2** *nk* **Purus (IRE)**[129] 7507 7-8-9 71 LukeMorris 4 78
(R A Teal) *taken down early: cl up: effrt on inner 2f out: drvn ahd last 100yds: hdd fnl strides* **16/1**

412- **3** ½ **Silaah**[140] 7384 5-9-4 80 RHills 7 86
(E A L Dunlop) *trckd ldr: shkn up to ld wl over 1f out: sn pressed: hdd and jst outpcd last 100yds* **11/10**[1]

010- **4** 1¼ **Lucullus**[272] 3893 4-8-9 71 SteveDrowne 5 73+
(M Blanshard) *hld up in last: taken to wd outside 2f out and stl last of main gp: nudged along and styd on takingly fnl f* **40/1**

24-2 **5** ½ **Everybody Knows**[82] 191 4-9-1 77 IanMongan 8 78
(Miss Jo Crowley) *taken down early: led at decent pce: hdd wl over 1f out: hld whn tightened up jst ins fnl f* **5/1**[2]

22-1 **6** 2¾ **Hawaana (IRE)**[14] 950 4-9-1 77 PaulDoe 2 71
(Eve Johnson Houghton) *pressed ldng pair to 2f out: sn lost pl: fdd fnl f* **7/1**[3]

56-6 **7** ¾ **Papillio (IRE)**[21] 866 4-8-13 75 NCallan 3 66
(J R Fanshawe) *stdd s: keen early: hld up in rr: gng wl enough over 2f out: shkn up and no rspnse sn after: wknd* **12/1**

04-4 **8** ¾ **Stanley Goodspeed**[14] 954 6-9-3 79 JamesDoyle 9 68
(J W Hills) *trckd ldrs on inner: carried hd awkwardly whn n.m.r over 2f out: no prog over 1f out: wknd* **10/1**

200- **9** *23* **Greystoke Prince**[203] 6020 4-8-11 73 (p) TedDurcan 1 —
(W R Swinburn) *stdd s: t.k.h early: in trble and rdn by 1/2-way: t.o* **20/1**

1m 25.27s (-0.73) **Going Correction** +0.025s/f (Slow) **9** Ran SP% **115.0**
Speed ratings (Par 105): **105,104,104,102,102 98,98,97,70**
toteswinger: 1&2 £26.20, 1&3 £4.10, 2&3 £7.30 CSF £168.43 CT £347.91 TOTE £10.60: £2.70, £5.60, £1.10; EX 286.40.
Owner Mrs I M Folkes **Bred** Helshaw Grange Stud Ltd **Trained** Pandy, Monmouths
■ Stewards' Enquiry : R Hills caution: careless riding

FOCUS
A fair handicap that was run at a solid pace with the runner-up looking the best guide to the level.
Obe Royal Official explanation: trainer's rep said, regarding the apparent improvement in form shown, that the gelding had missed the break and then had been forced to race wide last time
Stanley Goodspeed Official explanation: jockey said gelding hung right

1187 PANORAMIC BAR & RESTAURANT H'CAP 1m (P)
9:20 (9:21) (Class 5) (0-75,75) 4-Y-0+ **£2,590** (£770; £385; £192) **Stalls** High

Form RPR

1113 **1** **Highly Regal (IRE)**[14] 950 4-9-0 71 (b) LPKeniry 5 83
(R A Teal) *sn hld up bhd ldrs: shkn up and prog on outer to ld 2f out: in command fnl f: pushed out* **7/1**[3]

4001 **2** *2* **Ryedale Ovation (IRE)**[7] 1065 6-8-9 66 6ex DarryllHolland 8 73
(G L Moore) *hld up in last pair: prog on inner 2f out: hrd rdn to chse wnr fnl f: no imp* **6/4**[1]

0132 **3** *1* **Red Rudy**[9] 1037 7-7-13 63 TobyAtkinson(7) 7 68
(A W Carroll) *plld hrd: hld up in tch: effrt over 2f out: kpt on to take 3rd ins fnl f* **12/1**

10-2 **4** ½ **Gazboolou**[14] 950 5-9-1 72 FergusSweeney 3 76
(David Pinder) *led after 2f to 2f out: fdd fnl f* **10/3**[2]

3156 **5** 1¾ **Lopinot (IRE)**[9] 1035 6-8-11 68 (v) JimCrowley 1 68
(M R Bosley) *t.k.h: hld up in rr: rdn over 2f out: plugged on one pce: n.d* **18/1**

1-54 **6** 1¼ **Upstairs**[74] 281 5-8-1 61 oh1 DavidProbert(3) 6 58
(P Henderson) *hld up: t.k.h and prog on outer to go 2nd 4f out to over 2f out: fdd* **9/1**

040- **7** *nse* **Mujood**[194] 6249 6-9-4 75 StephenCarson 2 72
(Eve Johnson Houghton) *led at stdy pce for 2f: lost pl over 2f out: sn rdn and struggling* **10/1**

50- **8** 2½ **Dubburg (USA)**[165] 6989 4-8-13 70 ChrisCatlin 9 61
(W J Musson) *cl up on inner: rdn wl over 2f out: sn btn* **16/1**

1m 40.02s (0.22) **Going Correction** +0.025s/f (Slow) **8** Ran SP% **113.5**
Speed ratings (Par 103): **99,97,96,95,93 92,92,89**
toteswinger: 1&2 £7.50, 1&3 not won, 2&3 £10.10 CSF £17.67 CT £124.31 TOTE £6.90: £1.90, £1.20, £2.70; EX 15.20 Place 6: £24.96 Place 5: £14.07 .
Owner J Morton **Bred** Mervyn Stewkesbury **Trained** Ashtead, Surrey

FOCUS
A modest handicap, run at an uneven pace but a personal best from the winner with the fourth the best guide to the level.
T/Plt: £81.30 to a £1 stake. Pool: £106,455.28. 955.21 winning tickets. T/Qpdt: £32.60 to a £1 stake. Pool: £7,810.60. 176.90 winning tickets. JN

NOTTINGHAM (L-H)
Wednesday, April 8

OFFICIAL GOING: Good to firm (good in places) changing to good to firm after race 2 (2.30)
Wind: Fresh against Weather: Cloudy with sunny spells

1188 EUROPEAN BREEDERS' FUND NOVICE STKS 5f 13y
2:00 (2:02) (Class 4) 2-Y-O **£5,018** (£1,493; £746; £372) **Stalls** High

Form RPR

1 **1** **Star Rover (IRE)**[11] 1005 2-9-5 0 PaulDoe 7 90
(P D Evans) *mde all: rdn and hung lft fr over 1f out: r.o* **11/10**[1]

0 **2** 1½ **Red Avalanche (IRE)**[11] 1005 2-8-12 0 MartinDwyer 6 77
(P F I Cole) *w wnr: rdn over 1f out: caried lft ins fnl f: unable qck towards fin* **28/1**

3 1¼ **Gillburg (USA)** 2-8-12 0 NCallan 3 72+
(K A Ryan) *s.i.s and wnt lft s: sn chsng ldrs: rdn and edgd lft over 1f out: styd on* **10/1**

4 *4* **Corporal Maddox** 2-8-12 0 FergusSweeney 8 56
(K R Burke) *s.s: rn green in rr: nt clr run over 1f out: nvr nrr* **11/4**[2]

0 **5** *shd* **Heslington**[11] 994 2-8-12 0 TWilliams 4 56
(M Brittain) *s.i.s: sn chsng ldrs: rdn 1/2-way: wknd over 1f out* **16/1**

6 *nk* **Royal Desert** 2-8-12 0 SamHitchcott 1 54
(M R Channon) *sn pushed along in mid-div: rdn 1/2-way: wknd over 1f out* **10/1**

7 2½ **Avec Moi** 2-8-7 0 JohnEgan 2 39
(Mrs C A Dunnett) *s.s: a in rr* **200/1**

6 **8** *hd* **Black Daddy**[11] 1005 2-8-12 0 PatDobbs 5 44
(R Hannon) *prom: sn drvn along: outpcd over 3f out: wknd over 1f out* **17/2**[3]

61.79 secs (0.79) **Going Correction** -0.075s/f (Good) **8** Ran SP% **112.8**
Speed ratings (Par 94): **98,95,93,87,87 86,82,82**
toteswinger: 1&2 £6.50, 1&3 £2.60, 2&3 £13.60 CSF £37.11 TOTE £1.90: £1.10, £4.80, £2.60; EX 22.30.
Owner Christy Leo **Bred** Yeomanstown Stud **Trained** Pandy, Monmouths

FOCUS
A fair novice event.

NOTEBOOK
Star Rover(IRE)'s stable won this last year with She's A Shaw Thing, who was following up a clear-cut maiden win, and this colt came here with a similar profile. Carrying a 7lb penalty, he was quickly into his stride and, despite being pushed quite hard by the runner-up for a long way, eventually finished nicely on top. He again edged left under pressure in the closing stages, and as a result a left-handed track should suit him, with the Lily Agnes looking a suitable target. (tchd Evens and 5-4)
Red Avalanche(IRE) ◆ was well behind Star Rover on his debut at Kempton, but had clearly come on a deal for that experience as he was fast away and duelled with the winner for much of the race. He could well go one better in maiden company next time. (op 20-1 tchd 33-1)
Gillburg(USA) has a fair amount of stamina in his pedigree as his dam won over about a mile and is a half-sister to that useful middle-distance performer Malt Or Mash, so this was a promising debut from him. (op 11-1 tchd 12-1)
Corporal Maddox, who cost £40,000 and is a sister to multiple 7f-1m winner Silver Hotspur, was the one they came for in the market beforehand, as he was available at prices as big as 13-2 early doors. Although a little disappointing in the circumstances, he can be expected to do better with this run under his belt. (op 5-2 tchd 9-4)
Heslington, who showed some ability in the Brocklesby, did not improve on his performance at Doncaster. (tchd 20-1)
Royal Desert, a son of July Cup winner Pastoral Pursuits and half-brother to a couple of juvenile 6f winners, was stuck on the outside and raced green. He should improve for the experience. (op 18-1)

1189 WEATHERBYS BLOODSTOCK INSURANCE CONDITIONS STKS 5f 13y
2:30 (2:30) (Class 3) 3-Y-O+ **£7,771** (£2,312; £1,155; £577) **Stalls** High

Form RPR

0-00 **1** **Hoh Hoh Hoh**[11] 996 7-9-1 101 RobertWinston 4 98
(R J Price) *s.i.s: hdwy over 3f out: swtchd lft 2f out: rdn to ld ins fnl f: r.o* **11/2**

6040 **2** *nk* **Pawan (IRE)**[8] 1052 9-8-10 91 (b) AnnStokell(5) 5 97
(Miss A Stokell) *dwlt: outpcd: hdwy over 1f out: r.o wl ins fnl f* **25/1**

3162 **3** 1½ **Judd Street**[18] 911 7-9-1 106 (b) StephenCarson 1 92
(Eve Johnson Houghton) *s.i.s: sn chsng ldrs: wnt 2nd 2f out: sn rdn: no ex ins fnl f* **2/1**[1]

0004 **4** *hd* **Strike Up The Band**[18] 911 6-9-1 108 AdrianTNicholls 6 91
(D Nicholls) *led: rdn and edgd lft over 1f out: hdd and unable qck ins fnl f* **7/2**[3]

650 **5** *7* **Haajes**[10] 1018 5-9-1 90 (vt[1]) NCallan 7 66
(S Parr) *sn pushed along and prom: wknd over 1f out* **12/1**

114- **6** *9* **Rievaulx World**[253] 4507 3-8-4 104 PaulHanagan 3 28
(K A Ryan) *w ldr to 1/2-way: sn rdn: wknd over 1f out* **5/2**[2]

61.01 secs (0.01) **Going Correction** -0.075s/f (Good)
WFA 3 from 5yo+ 11lb **6** Ran SP% **111.1**
Speed ratings (Par 107): **104,103,101,100,89 75**
toteswinger: 1&2 £8.40, 1&3 £2.30, 2&3 £6.10. CSF £100.69 TOTE £5.90: £2.70, £5.80; EX 61.70.
Owner Multi Lines 2 **Bred** D R Botterill **Trained** Ullingswick, H'fords

FOCUS
A race full of horses that like to make the running, and so it was no surprise that it was run at a strong pace and the finish was contested by a couple of horses that had been ridden more patiently. The runner-up clouds the form but has seemingly run above himself in this sort of race before.

NOTEBOOK
Hoh Hoh Hoh, beaten a head in this race last year following a down-the-field effort in the Cammidge Trophy, came here on the back of a similar preparation. The drop back to 5f and a strong pace up front suited him down to the ground and he won a shade snugly in the end from the strong-finishing runner-up. The Palace House Stakes looks the obvious next step, although whether things will work out so perfectly in that higher-class race remains to be seen. (tchd 5-1)
Pawan(IRE) had a good deal to find with the market principals on the ratings, but he stays further than this and he tends to finish his races well, so the way the race was run brought out the best in him. (tchd 28-1)
Judd Street ran a fair race at Lingfield last time but is happier when ridden more positively. Unfortunately, he found himself being dragged along at a swift pace this time and proved vulnerable to the closers in the latter part of the race. (op 7-4 tchd 13-8)
Strike Up The Band, at his best when getting his own way out in front, could have done without Rievaulx World taking him on at the head of affairs. The latter, the only three-year-old in the field, had been off the track since July. A speedy type that likes to dominate, he too found that was impossible with such stiff competition for the role. (op 3-1)

Haajes, visored for the first time, was worst in at the weights and finished up well beaten. (op 16-1)
Rievaulx World Official explanation: jockey said colt was unsuited by the good to firm, good in places, ground

1190 T DENMAN & SONS H'CAP 5f 13y
3:00 (3:13) (Class 5) (0-70,70) 3-Y-O **£2,590** (£770; £385; £192) **Stalls** High

Form RPR
505- **1** **Mattamia (IRE)**[235] 5103 3-9-1 **70**.............................. JamesMillman(3) 6 81
(B R Millman) *racd stands' side: mde all: shkn up over 1f out: r.o* **5/1**[2]
501- **2** *2 1/4* **Impressible**[173] 6788 3-8-12 **64**.............................. EddieAhern 4 67
(E J Alston) *racd stands' side: chsd wnr: rdn and edgd lft over 1f out: styd on same pce ins fnl f: 2nd of 9 in gp* **7/1**
50-2 **3** *1/2* **Billy Beetroot (USA)**[5] 1095 3-8-5 **62**...................(t) WilliamCarson(5) 3 63
(S C Williams) *racd stands' side: a.p: rdn and edgd lft over 1f out: no ex ins fnl f: 3rd of 9 in gp* **9/2**[1]
0000 **4** *3* **Thumberlina**[15] 947 3-8-4 **56** oh11.............................. AndrewElliott 15 46
(Mrs C A Dunnett) *s.s: racd stands' side: outpcd: r.o ins fnl f: nrst fin: 4th of 9 in gp* **100/1**
005- **5** *1* **Lucky Buddha**[317] 2462 3-8-8 **60**.............................. PaulHanagan 10 47
(Jedd O'Keeffe) *racd stands' side: sn outpcd: r.o ins fnl f: nt trble ldrs: 5th of 9 in gp* **17/2**
0210 **6** *1 1/4* **Taurus Twins**[13] 966 3-8-10 **62**..............................(b[1]) RobertWinston 1 44
(R J Price) *led far side pair: up w stands' side gp tl rdn 1/2-way: edgd rt over 1f out: wknd fnl f* **8/1**
2303 **7** *2* **Sills Vincero**[9] 1041 3-8-8 **60**.............................. JimCrowley 14 35
(D Shaw) *racd stands' side: prom: outpcd 1/2-way: n.d after: 6th of 9 in gp* **6/1**[3]
2045 **8** *hd* **Chimbonda**[13] 966 3-8-4 **56** oh2.............................. LiamJones 2 30
(S Parr) *chsd ldr far side: rdn 1/2-way: sn edgd rt: wknd over 1f out: last of 2 in gp* **14/1**
-542 **9** *1/2* **The Cuckoo**[14] 955 3-8-13 **65**.............................. MartinDwyer 11 38
(M Quinn) *racd stands' side: chsd ldrs tl wknd over 1f out: 7th of 9 in gp* **7/1**
00-6 **10** *3 1/2* **Key To Love (IRE)**[19] 900 3-9-1 **67**.............................. NeilChalmers 7 27
(A J Chamberlain) *racd stands' side: hld up: wknd 1/2-way: 8th of 9 in gp* **33/1**
530- **11** *8* **Capo Regime**[224] 5394 3-8-11 **63**.............................. AdrianTNicholls 12 —
(D Nicholls) *got loose and bolted bef s: s.s: racd stands' side: hld up: plld hrd: a bhd: last of 9 in gp* **12/1**

61.54 secs (0.54) **Going Correction** -0.075s/f (Good) **11** Ran SP% **114.1**
Speed ratings (Par 98): **100,96,95,90,89 87,84,83,82,77 64**
toteswinger: 1&2 £9.60, 1&3 £7.50, 2&3 £4.20. CSF £37.04 CT £147.49 TOTE £6.10: £2.60, £2.30, £1.70; EX 45.20.
Owner C Roper **Bred** H G And J R Dutfield **Trained** Kentisbeare, Devon

FOCUS
The ground was officially changed to good to firm all round. An open-looking handicap for three-year-olds and the form is sound if ordinary. The first three were always prominent and the fourth raced from 11lb wrong.
Mattamia(IRE) Official explanation: trainer said, regarding the apparent improvement in form shown, that Mattamia had been gelded over the winter and been given more time to mature
Taurus Twins Official explanation: jockey said gelding was unsuited by the good to firm ground
The Cuckoo Official explanation: jockey said colt moved poorly throughout

1191 WEATHERBYS BANK "FURTHER FLIGHT" STKS (LISTED RACE) 1m 6f 15y
3:30 (3:33) (Class 1) 4-Y-O+ **£22,708** (£8,608; £4,308; £2,148) **Stalls** Low

Form RPR
123- **1** **Fiulin**[172] 6820 4-8-11 106.............................. JohnEgan 2 107+
(M Botti) *mde all: shkn up over 2f out: c clr fnl f* **2/5**[1]
132- **2** *6* **The Betchworth Kid**[151] 7244 4-8-11 103.............................. JamieSpencer 3 99+
(M L W Bell) *a.p: chsd wnr over 3f out: rdn over 2f out: no ex fnl f* **9/2**[2]
635- **3** *1 3/4* **Presbyterian Nun (IRE)**[209] 5826 4-8-6 96.............................. RichardMullen 4 91
(J L Dunlop) *hld up: hdwy over 3f out: rdn and hung lft 2f out: eased whn btn fnl f* **8/1**[3]
624- **4** *6* **Dunaskin (IRE)**[88] 7244 9-9-0 95.............................. TonyHamilton 8 88
(B Ellison) *chsd wnr tl rdn over 3f out: wknd over 2f out* **14/1**

3m 0.08s (-4.92) **Going Correction** -0.075s/f (Good)
WFA 4 from 5yo+ 3lb **4** Ran SP% **107.4**
Speed ratings (Par 111): **111,107,106,103**
toteswinger: 1&2 £2.70. CSF £2.49 TOTE £1.50; EX 2.00.
Owner Scuderia Rencati Srl **Bred** Azienda Agricola Francesca **Trained** Newmarket, Suffolk

FOCUS
Six non-runners, four due to the ground, resulted in a rather poor turnout for this Listed race. It was straightforward for the winner who did not need to improve.

NOTEBOOK
Fiulin, who progressed through handicaps to place in Group 3 company on his final start last year, very much had the run of the race out in front, being allowed to dictate no more than a fair gallop, and kept the others comfortably at bay once asked to stretch in the straight. By Galileo out of a half-sister to Falbrav, this did not tell us a lot we did not already know about him, but he is clearly versatile ground-wise and he looks a stayer to keep on side this term. His trainer expects him to come on for the run and has already nominated the Yorkshire Cup as his next target. (op 4-6)
The Betchworth Kid needs soft ground and a decent pace to run off to be seen at his best so these conditions were far from ideal. It was a satisfactory reappearance in the circumstances and he could yet prove himself at this level on easier ground later in the year. (op 11-4)
Presbyterian Nun(IRE) did not look particularly happy on the ground and will find things less competitive back against her own sex. (op 15-2 tchd 13-2)
Dunaskin(IRE), who is not as good as he once was, had plenty on at the weights and was predictably outclassed. (tchd 12-1)

1192 DENMAN "BUILDING FOR YOU" H'CAP 1m 2f 50y
4:00 (4:01) (Class 5) (0-70,70) 4-Y-O+ **£2,590** (£770; £385; £192) **Stalls** Low

Form RPR
1130 **1** **All In The Red (IRE)**[10] 1014 4-9-1 **67**..............................(p) JoeFanning 11 75
(A Crook) *dwlt: hdwy over 7f out: lost pl 1/2-way: hdwy over 2f out: led over 1f out: edgd lft: styd on* **33/1**
52-5 **2** *3/4* **Indy Driver**[16] 932 4-9-3 **69**.............................. FrancisNorton 6 76+
(J R Fanshawe) *hld up: hdwy over 2f out: swtchd lft over 1f out: sn rdn: r.o* **15/2**[2]
0554 **3** *1* **New Beginning (IRE)**[58] 478 5-8-11 **63**.............................. RobertWinston 9 68
(Mrs S Lamyman) *chsd ldrs: rdn over 1f out: nt clr run ins fnl f: styd on same pce* **8/1**[3]
-501 **4** *2 1/4* **Apotheosis**[27] 813 4-8-13 **65**.............................. TedDurcan 8 65
(W R Swinburn) *hld up in tch: rdn over 2f out: styd on same pce fnl f* **4/1**[1]
-033 **5** *1* **Kildare Sun (IRE)**[12] 981 7-8-11 **63**.............................. PaulHanagan 14 61
(J Mackie) *trckd ldrs: led over 2f out: rdn and hdd over 1f out: wknd wl ins fnl f* **9/1**
160/ **6** *4* **King's Revenge**[25] 5810 6-9-4 **70**.............................. JamieSpencer 3 62
(A King) *hld up: hdwy over 1f out: wknd and eased ins fnl f* **4/1**[1]
266- **7** *1 1/2* **Princelywallywogan**[211] 5783 7-9-0 **66**.............................. StephenDonohoe 2 53
(John A Harris) *s.s: bhd: stl last over 2f out: r.o ins fnl f: nrst fin* **11/1**
006- **8** *1/2* **Le Corvee (IRE)**[158] 4371 7-8-10 **62**.............................. TolleyDean 4 48
(A W Carroll) *s.i.s: hld up: rdn over 4f out: n.d* **50/1**
4152 **9** *3/4* **General Tufto**[8] 1051 4-8-10 **67**..............................(b) MartinLane(5) 15 52
(C Smith) *chsd ldrs: led 8f out to 6f out: led again 3f out: sn rdn and hdd: wknd fnl f* **25/1**
056- **10** *3 1/4* **Intersky Charm (USA)**[190] 6352 5-9-0 **69**.............................. MichaelJStainton(3) 16 47
(R M Whitaker) *chsd ldrs: rdn over 2f out: wknd wl over 1f out* **20/1**
542- **11** *10* **Gala Sunday (USA)**[253] 4503 9-8-10 **62**..............................(t) DaleGibson 10 20
(M W Easterby) *mid-div: lost pl 1/2-way: sn bhd* **33/1**
00-5 **12** *16* **Ross Moor**[19] 894 7-8-11 **63**.............................. FergusSweeney 7 —
(Mike Murphy) *s.i.s: a in rr* **33/1**
1220 **13** *1 1/2* **Transmission (IRE)**[36] 747 4-9-0 **66**.............................. TomEaves 1 —
(B Smart) *hld up in tch: plld hrd: wknd over 2f out* **16/1**
5-20 **14** *nk* **Cinematic (IRE)**[48] 597 6-9-4 **70**.............................. MartinDwyer 12 —
(J R Boyle) *sn led: hdd 8f out: led again 6f out: rdn and hdd 3f out: sn wknd* **16/1**

2m 11.04s (-0.66) **Going Correction** -0.075s/f (Good) **14** Ran SP% **112.4**
Speed ratings (Par 103): **99,98,97,95,95 91,90,90,89,87 79,66,65,64**
toteswinger: 1&2 £46.00, 1&3 £41.70, 2&3 £8.60. CSF £223.37 CT £1896.21 TOTE £39.30: £8.50, £2.40, £3.60; EX 258.20 TRIFECTA Not won..
Owner Paul Fowlie & the timemaster.co.uk **Bred** John McEnery **Trained** Middleham Moor, N Yorks
■ Society Venue was withdrawn after breaking out of the stalls (12/1, deduct 5p in the £ under R4).

FOCUS
This was a low-grade handicap in which they went a steady early gallop. It was a new course record, but that was due to them racing on the inner track, which is rarely used. The winner is rated back to his best.
Princelywallywogan Official explanation: jockey said gelding hung right-handed throughout
Ross Moor Official explanation: jockey said gelding was unsuited by the good to firm ground
Cinematic(IRE) Official explanation: jockey said gelding was unsuited by the good to firm ground

1193 PADDOCKS CONFERENCE CENTRE H'CAP 1m 75y
4:30 (4:35) (Class 5) (0-70,70) 3-Y-O **£2,590** (£770; £385; £192) **Stalls** Low

Form RPR
00-0 **1** **Cornish Castle (USA)**[11] 998 3-8-12 **64**.............................. GrahamGibbons 1 76
(T D Walford) *hld up: hdwy over 2f out: edgd lft over 1f out: rdn to ld wl ins fnl f: r.o* **10/1**
002- **2** *nk* **Labisa (IRE)**[159] 7117 3-8-12 **64**.............................. SteveDrowne 12 75+
(H Morrison) *trckd ldrs: plld hrd: led and hung lft fr 2f out: hdd wl ins fnl f: r.o nr fin* **5/1**[1]
420- **3** *2 1/4* **Spinners End (IRE)**[188] 6426 3-8-12 **69**.............................. MartinLane(5) 8 75
(K R Burke) *chsd ldrs: led 3f out: rdn and hdd 2f out: styd on same pce fnl f* **13/2**[2]
0-34 **4** *2 3/4* **Hypnotic Gaze (IRE)**[16] 939 3-9-0 **66**..............................(p) PaulHanagan 6 66+
(J Mackie) *hld up in tch: rdn whn hmpd and lost pl over 1f out: styd on ins fnl f* **12/1**
440- **5** *1 1/2* **Lost In Paris (IRE)**[170] 6857 3-8-10 **62**.............................. DavidAllan 17 58
(T D Easterby) *mid-div: hdwy over 2f out: sn rdn: styd on* **16/1**
04-1 **6** *3/4* **Cool Hand Jake**[88] 115 3-9-4 **70**.............................. FergusSweeney 16 65
(P J Makin) *dwlt: sn chsng ldrs: rdn and ev ch over 2f out: wknd fnl f* **13/2**[2]
530- **7** *1 1/4* **Jobekani (IRE)**[165] 6986 3-8-7 **62** ow1.............................. RussellKennemore(3) 2 54
(Mrs L Williamson) *s.i.s: hld up: hdwy over 2f out: rdn and hung lft over 1f out: wknd fnl f* **40/1**
210- **8** *nk* **Highland River**[119] 7623 3-8-12 **64**.............................. JamieSpencer 10 55
(D R C Elsworth) *led 7f out: rdn and hdd 3f out: wknd over 1f out* **9/1**
050- **9** *shd* **Salybia Bay**[150] 7259 3-8-12 **64**.............................. PatDobbs 15 55
(R Hannon) *mid-div: rdn over 2f out: nt trble ldrs* **12/1**
000- **10** *1 1/4* **Taste The Wine (IRE)**[163] 7016 3-8-9 **61**.............................. LukeMorris 3 49
(J S Moore) *s.i.s: hld up: rdn over 2f out: n.d* **8/1**[3]
5166 **11** *7* **Innactualfact**[49] 595 3-9-1 **67**.............................. TGMcLaughlin 4 39
(L A Dace) *hld up: rdn and wknd over 2f out* **33/1**
056- **12** *1 3/4* **Very Distinguished**[158] 7142 3-8-10 **67**.............................. NicolPolli(5) 14 35
(M G Quinlan) *hld up: a in rr* **14/1**
346- **13** *39* **Naizak**[146] 7298 3-9-2 **68**.............................. TPO'Shea 11 —
(J L Dunlop) *unruly bhd stalls: sn led: hdd 7f out: chsd ldrs: rdn and wknd over 2f out* **10/1**

1m 45.89s (0.29) **Going Correction** -0.075s/f (Good) **13** Ran SP% **115.9**
Speed ratings (Par 98): **95,94,92,89,88 87,86,85,85,84 77,75,36**
toteswinger: 1&2 £11.50, 1&3 £15.70, 2&3 £8.90. CSF £57.49 CT £366.49 TOTE £10.80: £3.00, £1.90, £2.60; EX 61.40.
Owner Stephen Woodall **Bred** Juddmonte Farms Inc **Trained** Sheriff Hutton, N Yorks
■ Stewards' Enquiry : Graham Gibbons two-day ban: careless riding (Apr 22-23)

FOCUS
A race featuring a number of unexposed types, and it was a couple of handicap debutants that eventually battled it out. Probably not the strongest of races.
Cornish Castle(USA) Official explanation: trainer said, regarding the apparent improvement in form shown, that this was a less competitive race and the gelding was still maturing

1194 "NEWCOMERS NIGHT ON SATURDAY 18TH APRIL" H'CAP 1m 75y
5:00 (5:01) (Class 6) (0-65,65) 4-Y-O+ **£1,942** (£578; £288; £144) **Stalls** Low

Form RPR
0460 **1** **Flying Applause**[25] 841 4-9-1 **62**..............................(bt[1]) RobertWinston 1 71
(S R Bowring) *led 1f: plld hrd trcking ldr: led again 3f out: rdn whn jnd over 1f out: styd on gamely* **8/1**[3]
3320 **2** *hd* **Bobski (IRE)**[14] 959 7-8-9 **63**.............................. KylieManser(7) 13 72
(Miss Gay Kelleway) *s.s: hld up: hdwy over 2f out: rdn and ev ch ins fnl f: styd on* **12/1**
3610 **3** *3/4* **This Ones For Eddy**[11] 1000 4-8-13 **60**.............................. JamieSpencer 11 67+
(S Parr) *chsd ldrs: nt clr run over 1f out: swtchd lft ins fnl f: r.o* **11/2**[1]
0-45 **4** *1 1/4* **Jebel Tara**[28] 807 4-9-2 **63**..............................(t) SilvestreDeSousa 14 67
(A D Brown) *hld up: hdwy over 2f out: rdn and hung lft over 1f out: r.o* **9/1**
6033 **5** *nk* **Lord Theo**[14] 959 5-9-3 **64**..............................(b) LukeMorris 5 68
(N P Littmoden) *hld up: rdn over 3f out: hdwy over 2f out: swtchd lft over 1f out: r.o* **7/1**[2]
030- **6** *3/4* **James Pollard (IRE)**[159] 7111 4-8-12 **59**.............................. AlanMunro 6 61
(D R C Elsworth) *chsd ldrs: rdn and ev ch over 1f out: no ex wl ins fnl f* **8/1**[3]
036- **7** *1 1/2* **Aussie Blue (IRE)**[156] 7167 5-8-9 **59**.............................. MichaelJStainton(3) 12 58
(R M Whitaker) *mid-div: hdwy over 3f out: rdn over 1f out: no ex fnl f* **16/1**
1136 **8** *4 1/2* **General Feeling (IRE)**[7] 1073 8-9-0 **61**.............................. PaulHanagan 2 49
(S T Mason) *chsd ldrs: rdn over 3f out: wknd over 1f out* **8/1**[3]

0-05 **9** *1* **Time To Regret**[2] 1153 9-8-10 **57**..............................(p) DanielTudhope 3 43
(I W McInnes) *hld up: hdwy over 3f out: rdn over 1f out: wknd fnl f* **16/1**
20-3 **10** *2 ¾* **Fools Gold**[12] 980 4-8-13 **63**..............................RussellKennemore(3) 16 43
(Paul Mason) *hld up: a in rr* **20/1**
663- **11** *2 ½* **Dancing Storm**[184] 6544 6-9-0 **61**..............................FergusSweeney 17 35
(W S Kittow) *chsd ldrs: rdn over 2f out: wknd over 1f out* **10/1**
330- **12** *2 ¾* **Emperor's Well**[161] 7085 10-8-12 **59**..............................(b) DaleGibson 7 27
(M W Easterby) *hld up: rdn 1/2-way: a in rr* **50/1**
000- **13** *3* **San Silvestro (IRE)**[172] 6813 4-9-3 **64**..............................MickyFenton 8 25
(Mrs A Duffield) *prom: rdn over 3f out: wknd wl over 1f out* **20/1**
350- **14** *14* **Natural Rhythm (IRE)**[173] 6786 4-8-12 **59**..............................(b) JoeFanning 10 —
(Mrs R A Carr) *led 7f out: hdd 3f out: wknd qckly* **33/1**
10-1 **15** *6* **Djalalabad (FR)**[12] 984 5-8-10 **57**..............................(tp) TGMcLaughlin 15 —
(Mrs C A Dunnett) *s.i.s: hld up: sme hdwy over 2f out: sn wknd* **16/1**

1m 44.79s (-0.81) **Going Correction** -0.075s/f (Good) **15** Ran SP% **120.1**
Speed ratings (Par 101): **101,100,100,98,98 97,96,91,90,88 85,82,79,65,59**
toteswinger: 1&2 £22.70, 1&3 £9.20, 2&3 £13.10. CSF £95.14 CT £591.80 TOTE £7.10: £2.60, £5.50, £1.90; EX 90.10 Place 6: £319.31 Place 5: £173.56 .
Owner K Nicholls **Bred** G H Beeby And Viscount Marchwood **Trained** Edwinstowe, Notts

FOCUS
Another competitive-looking handicap and the form is solid enough, rated around the fourth and fifth.
Jebel Tara Official explanation: jockey said gelding hung left handed
General Feeling(IRE) Official explanation: vet said gelding had been struck into
T/Jkpt: Not won. T/Plt: £377.90 to a £1 stake. Pool: £67,803.47. 130.95 winning tickets. T/Qpdt: £33.90 to a £1 stake. Pool: £5,768.45. 125.85 winning tickets. CR

1044 FOLKESTONE (R-H)
Thursday, April 9

OFFICIAL GOING: Good to firm (good in places; round course 8.3, straight course - far side 7.3, stands' side 8.3)
Wind: Fresh Across Weather: Overcast

1195 RACESPONSORS.CO.UK MEDIAN AUCTION MAIDEN STKS 5f
1:40 (1:41) (Class 6) 2-Y-O £2,729 (£806; £403) Stalls Low

Form RPR
1 **Monsieur Chevalier (IRE)** 2-9-3 0..............................RichardHughes 1 96+
(R Hannon) *trckd ldrs: effrt to ld over 1f out: edgd rt and pushed clr fnl f: readily* **3/1**[1]
2 *5* **Diamond Laura** 2-8-12 0..............................PaulDoe 9 71
(P D Evans) *chsd ldrs: effrt and ev ch wl over 1f out: no ch w wnr fnl f: kpt on* **8/1**
0 **3** *2 ¼* **Anjomarba (IRE)**[9] 1044 2-8-7 0..............................WilliamCarson(5) 10 62
(W G M Turner) *chsd ldrs: rdn and effrt to press ldrs wl over 1f out: 3rd and wl outpcd fnl f* **25/1**
4 *6* **Musiara** 2-8-12 0..............................SamHitchcott 2 38
(M R Channon) *sn bustled in midfield: rdn 1/2-way: plugged on fnl f: nvr trbld ldrs* **9/1**
5 *2* **Safari Camp (IRE)** 2-9-3 0..............................JimCrowley 7 35
(P Winkworth) *led: rdn and hdd over 1f out: sn wknd* **6/1**[3]
6 *¾* **Diamond Affair (IRE)** 2-8-12 0..............................AlanMunro 6 27
(M G Quinlan) *racd keenly: chsd ldr tl rdn and wknd qckly wl over 1f out* **10/3**[2]
7 *1 ¾* **Lady Lion** 2-8-7 0..............................JackDean(5) 5 20
(W G M Turner) *dwlt: sn bustled along and in tch in midfield: rdn and struggling 1/2-way: no ch after* **66/1**
8 *1 ½* **Rufus Roughcut** 2-9-3 0..............................J-PGuillambert 3 19
(S C Williams) *s.i.s: sn rdn and wl outpcd in rr: sme late hdwy: nvr on terms* **33/1**
9 *5* **Papageno** 2-9-3 0..............................EddieAhern 14 —
(J R Jenkins) *racd in far side trio: no ch w ldrs fr 1/2-way* **16/1**
5 **10** *2 ¼* **Ever So Bold**[7] 1083 2-9-3 0..............................MartinDwyer 12 —
(W R Muir) *racd in far side trio: no ch w ldrs fr 1/2-way* **12/1**
11 *12* **Our Georgie Girl** 2-8-12 0..............................TPQueally 8 —
(G G Margarson) *s.i.s: sn wl bhd: t.o* **25/1**
12 *1 ¾* **Saachi's Vision (IRE)** 2-8-12 0..............................StephenCarson 11 —
(D K Ivory) *a last of far side trio: sn wl outpcd: t.o* **50/1**
13 *11* **Little Perc (IRE)** 2-9-3 0..............................JamieSpencer 4 —
(G L Moore) *stedaied s: sn wl outpcd in rr: t.o* **12/1**

60.88 secs (0.88) **Going Correction** +0.175s/f (Good) **13** Ran SP% **118.8**
Speed ratings (Par 90): **99,91,87,77,74 73,70,68,60,56 37,34,17**
toteswinger: 1&2 £12.60, 1&3 £10.80, 2&3 £49.20 CSF £25.89 TOTE £4.40: £1.70, £1.90, £8.60; EX 43.00 TRIFECTA Not won..
Owner Mrs Valerie Hubbard & Ian Higginson **Bred** Tally-Ho Stud **Trained** East Everleigh, Wilts
■ A first juvenile winner of the season for the powerful Hannon stable.
■ Stewards' Enquiry : Alan Munro one-day ban: failed to ride to draw (Apr 23)
Jim Crowley one-day ban: failed to ride to draw (Apr 23)

FOCUS
The riders reported that the ground was a bit softer than the official description. An interesting two-year-old maiden in which a couple showed promise for the future. The field split into two with the much larger group of ten coming stands' side, whilst the three highest-drawn horses went far side, where it soon became obvious they hadn't a prayer. The winner looks above average at this early stage.

NOTEBOOK
Monsieur Chevalier(IRE) ◆, a 17,000gns colt and closely related to a couple of winning juvenile sprinters, was well backed beforehand and showed why with a taking performance on this debut. He was always travelling nicely behind the leaders on the nearside and once the gap appeared, he was soon through it and powered right away. He looks one of the better juveniles at this stage of the season and ought to go on from here. Connections believe that he will get 7f by the end of the season. (op 4-1)
Diamond Laura, a £4,000 half-sister to a winning juvenile sprinter, was always up with the pace and kept on going to finish second, albeit well beaten by the winner. There should be a race in her. (op 13-2)
Anjomarba(IRE), well beaten on her debut here the previous week, was nonetheless backed at fancy prices. Her rider made the right decision to come stands' side despite her double-figure draw and she also kept on going to make the frame. This was certainly a much better effort. (op 66-1)
Musiara took a little while to realise what was required and came from further back than the other principals. A half-sister to a couple of winning juvenile sprinters, she should come on a bit for this. (op 10-1 tchd 17-2)
Safari Camp(IRE), a 10,000euros colt out of a multiple winning sprinter, was a springer in the market beforehand and although he dropped away after leading the stands'-side group for much of the way, there was still enough here to build on. (op 12-1)
Diamond Affair(IRE), who fetched just £2,200 as a two-year-old, is out of a dual winner at up to 1m3f. Well backed earlier in the day, she drifted on track beforehand, probably as punters saw her almost bolt to post. She showed good speed until weakening right out of it inside the last 2f, and she is probably worth another chance, as her earlier exertions cannot have done her much good. (op 2-1)

1196 SPONSOR A RACE @ RACESPONSORS.CO.UK H'CAP 6f
2:10 (2:12) (Class 5) (0-75,75) 3-Y-O £3,070 (£906; £453) Stalls Low

Form RPR
25 **1** **The Winged Assasin (USA)**[24] 851 3-9-1 **72**..............................IanMongan 1 74
(J Akehurst) *racd stands' side: in tch on stands rail: edging out rt over 1f out: drvn ent fnl f: swtchd rt ins fnl f: drvn and burst between horses to ld last stride* **9/2**[1]
00-4 **2** *shd* **Jeremiah (IRE)**[14] 963 3-8-13 **70**..............................TolleyDean 3 72
(J G Portman) *racd stands' side: chsd ldr on stands rail: rdn 2f out: battled on wl u.p to ld wl ins fnl f: hdd last stride* **25/1**
301- **3** *½* **Rare Art**[155] 7198 3-9-3 **74**..............................JamieSpencer 6 74
(S A Callaghan) *chsd ldrs: rdn over 1f out: drvn to ld 1f out: hdd wl ins fnl f: unable qck towards fin* **9/2**[1]
535- **4** *shd* **Battle**[170] 6879 3-9-0 **71**..............................RobertWinston 5 71
(H Morrison) *racd stands' side: trckd ldrs: effrt and rdn 2f out: wanting to hang rt u.p: unable qck fnl f* **13/2**[3]
325- **5** *1 ¼* **Defector (IRE)**[205] 6002 3-9-3 **74**..............................MartinDwyer 9 73+
(W R Muir) *racd stands' side: wnt lft and bmpd rival s: swtchd to stands' side after 1f: hld up bhd: hdwy ent fnl f: styng on whn no where to go towards fin: nt rch ldrs* **12/1**
050- **6** *2 ¼* **Red Rossini (IRE)**[145] 7335 3-9-1 **72**..............................RichardHughes 2 61
(R Hannon) *racd stands' side: in tch in midfield: rdn and effrt over 1f out: no imp fnl f* **11/2**[2]
0-44 **7** *½* **White Shift (IRE)**[33] 784 3-8-13 **75**..............................RichardEvans(5) 7 62
(P D Evans) *racd stands' side: overall ldr: rdn 1/2-way: hdd 1f out: btn whn hmpd and snatched up ins fnl f:* **10/1**
-125 **8** *7* **Perfect Class**[15] 960 3-8-7 **64**..............................LukeMorris 8 29+
(C G Cox) *bmpd s: swtchd to r far side: chsd far side ldr: rdn 2f out: no ch w ldrs over 1f out* **13/2**[3]
36-4 **9** *3* **Amosite**[85] 162 3-8-10 **67**..............................(v) EddieAhern 11 22+
(J R Jenkins) *racd far side: led far side gp: prom overall: rdn and hung wl over 1f out: sn btn* **33/1**
4332 **10** *¾* **Riflessione**[17] 936 3-9-1 **72**..............................(b) ChrisCatlin 4 25
(R A Harris) *racd stands' side: a bhd: no ch fnl 2f* **10/1**
021- **11** *nk* **Shadow Bay (IRE)**[126] 7547 3-9-1 **72**..............................SamHitchcott 10 24+
(Miss Z C Davison) *racd far side: chsd ldrs far side: struggling fr 1/2-way: no ch fnl 2f* **33/1**
503- **12** *38* **Mr Flannegan**[171] 6865 3-8-1 **65**..............................(v) AmyScott(7) 12 —
(H Candy) *racd far side: sn wl outpcd: t.o fr 1/2-way* **16/1**

1m 13.47s (0.77) **Going Correction** +0.175s/f (Good) **12** Ran SP% **119.9**
Speed ratings (Par 98): **101,100,100,100,98 95,94,85,81,80 80,29**
toteswinger: 1&2 £27.00, 1&3 £11.30, 2&3 £29.80 CSF £124.17 CT £546.51 TOTE £5.50: £1.90, £7.70, £2.30; EX 124.10 TRIFECTA Not won..
Owner Bill Hinge & John Searchfield **Bred** John T L Jones Jr & Bemak N V **Trained** Epsom, Surrey

FOCUS
A fair sprint handicap and, as in the opener, the larger group that raced stands' side enjoyed a huge advantage. As a result the quartet that went far side can be forgiven their efforts.

1197 JENNER REYNO H'CAP 6f
2:40 (2:42) (Class 4) (0-85,83) 4-Y-0+ £5,180 (£1,541; £770; £384) Stalls Low

Form RPR
400- **1** **Rash Judgement**[190] 6402 4-9-1 **80**..............................FergusSweeney 8 91
(W S Kittow) *chsd ldrs: rdn and hdwy wl over 1f out: ev ch over 1f out: led jst ins fnl f: hld on wl* **11/2**[3]
003- **2** *nk* **Buxton**[99] 7837 5-8-11 **76**..............................(t) RobertHavlin 1 86
(R Ingram) *chsd ldrs: hdwy 2f out: rdn to ld over 1f out: hdd jst ins fnl f: unable qck fnl 50yds* **8/1**
050- **3** *1 ¾* **Aye Aye Digby (IRE)**[152] 7239 4-9-4 **83**..............................DaneO'Neill 9 87+
(H Candy) *racd in midfield: effrt and rdn wl over 1f out: drvn over 1f out: kpt on to chse ldng pair ins fnl f: kpt on* **9/2**[1]
00-4 **4** *shd* **Vhujon (IRE)**[81] 212 4-8-12 **82**..............................RichardEvans(5) 4 86
(P D Evans) *taken down early: stdd s: hld up in midfield: looking for room and swtchd rt over 1f out: shkn up and hdwy ent fnl f: rdn and one pce fnl 100yds* **15/2**
0-50 **5** *shd* **Hustle (IRE)**[19] 910 4-9-3 **82**..............................(t) JamieSpencer 5 86+
(Miss Gay Kelleway) *bhd: nt clr run and swtchd rt and hmpd 1f out: hdwy 1f out: nt clr run and swtchd rt again ins fnl f: styd on wl and gng on fin: nvr able to rch ldrs* **12/1**
4402 **6** *2 ¼* **Resplendent Alpha**[15] 954 5-8-10 **75**..............................JimmyQuinn 11 72+
(P Howling) *swtchd lft and dropped in bhd after s: hdwy 1f out: kpt on: nvr trbld ldrs* **12/1**
2342 **7** *½* **Artistic License (IRE)**[6] 1094 4-8-12 **77**..............................TonyCulhane 7 72
(M R Channon) *sn rdn along in rr: sme hdwy and carried rt over 1f out: nvr pce to threaten ldrs* **5/1**[2]
2-05 **8** *1 ¼* **Credit Swap**[20] 892 4-8-4 **76**..............................TobyAtkinson(7) 12 67+
(M Wigham) *swtchd lft and dropped in bhd after s: hdwy wl over 1f out: edgd lft and no imp fnl f* **25/1**
04-3 **9** *½* **Regal Royale**[9] 1053 6-8-6 **71**..............................(v) PatrickMathers 10 60
(Peter Grayson) *swtchd lft and dropped in bhd after s: nvr trbld ldrs* **25/1**
000- **10** *nse* **We Have A Dream**[192] 6340 4-8-7 **72**..............................MartinDwyer 2 61
(W R Muir) *led narrowly and set fast pce: rdn over 1f out: sn hdd: wknd fnl f* **15/2**
/54- **11** *1 ¼* **For Life (IRE)**[188] 6435 7-8-10 **75**..............................RichardThomas 3 60
(J E Long) *taken down early and mounted on crse: racd freely: w ldr: rdn 2f out: wknd fnl f* **16/1**
3-16 **12** *6* **Billy Red**[75] 281 5-8-4 **69** oh2..............................(b) WilliamBuick 6 35
(J R Jenkins) *chsd ldrs: rdn 2f out: wkng whn hmpd over 1f out: eased wl ins fnl f* **16/1**

1m 12.99s (0.29) **Going Correction** +0.175s/f (Good) **12** Ran SP% **119.7**
Speed ratings (Par 105): **105,104,102,102,102 99,98,96,96,95 94,86**
toteswinger: 1&2 £9.80, 1&3 £7.30, 2&3 £9.20 CSF £49.70 CT £218.16 TOTE £6.80: £2.70, £2.80, £2.10; EX 60.60 TRIFECTA Not won..
Owner Reg Gifford **Bred** D R Tucker **Trained** Blackborough, Devon
■ Stewards' Enquiry : Richard Evans one-day ban: careless riding (Apr 23rd)

FOCUS
A fair sprint handicap and the riders had learnt from the earlier contests as the whole field came over to the stands' side. Unfortunately that contributed to trouble in running.

1198 ADVERTISE YOUR COMPANY @ RACESPONSORS.CO.UK MAIDEN FILLIES' STKS — 1m 1f 149y

3:10 (3:11) (Class 5) 3-Y-O — **£2,729** (£806; £403) **Stalls** Centre

Form / RPR

220- **1** **Three Moons (IRE)**[159] [7144] 3-9-0 82........................ RichardHughes 12 — 76
(H J L Dunlop) *chsd ldr for 1f: trckd ldng pair after: chal between horses over 1f out: led 1f out: drvn and asserted fnl 100yds: eased nr fin* **4/6**[1]

2 *1 ¼* **Invincible Isle (IRE)** 3-9-0 0........................ TPQueally 7 — 74
(H R A Cecil) *trckd ldrs: rdn and effrt over 1f out: chal ins fnl f: no ex fnl 50yds* **17/2**[2]

342- **3** *nk* **Polly's Mark (IRE)**[194] [6291] 3-9-0 75........................ PhilipRobinson 11 — 73
(C G Cox) *t.k.h: chsd ldr after 1f: ev ch and rdn 2f out: no ex wl ins fnl f* **9/1**[3]

00- **4** *¾* **Qelaan (USA)**[223] [5469] 3-9-0 0........................ WilliamBuick 4 — 71
(M P Tregoning) *led: hrd pressed and rdn 2f out: kpt on wl: hdd 1f out: one pce after* **10/1**

3 **5** *5* **Stormy's Prelude**[55] [529] 3-9-0 0........................ JimCrowley 1 — 61
(P Winkworth) *t.k.h: hld up in midfield: rdn and nt pce of ldrs wl over 1f out: one pce fnl f* **16/1**

6 *½* **Towanda (USA)** 3-9-0 0........................ JimmyFortune 14 — 60+
(J H M Gosden) *hld up in midfield: rdn and outpcd 2f out: edgd rt fr over 1f out: plugged on steadily fnl f* **12/1**

0- **7** *4* **Hold The Star**[199] [6167] 3-9-0 0........................ JamieSpencer 13 — 51
(E F Vaughan) *t.k.h: hld up wl in tch: outpcd and rdn 2f out: no ch w ldrs after* **16/1**

8 *shd* **Saa'Ida (IRE)** 3-9-0 0........................ MartinDwyer 10 — 51+
(C E Brittain) *s.i.s: detached in last pl: stl last jst over 2f out: hdwy over 1f out: r.o past btn horses fnl f: nvr nr ldrs* **33/1**

43 **9** *¾* **Crag Path**[10] [1034] 3-8-9 0........................ AmyBaker(5) 2 — 50+
(D R C Elsworth) *hld up in last trio: rdn and edgd out lft over 1f out: nvr threatened ldrs* **25/1**

0- **10** *3* **Asakusa**[171] [6858] 3-9-0 0........................ IanMongan 9 — 43
(H R A Cecil) *hld up in tch: hung lft and c wd bnd jst over 2f out: sn wknd* **50/1**

00- **11** *1* **Vita Mia**[160] [7117] 3-9-0 0........................ PaulDoe 3 — 41
(P D Evans) *s.i.s: a in rr: wd bnd 7f out: rdn and struggling 3f out* **50/1**

0-0 **12** *1 ¼* **Pursuit Of Purpose**[27] [828] 3-9-0 0........................ FergusSweeney 6 — 39
(G L Moore) *t.k.h: hld up towards rr: rdn and struggling 3f out* **66/1**

5 **13** *10* **Mono's Only**[19] [914] 3-8-11 0........................ RussellKennemore(3) 5 — 18
(Paul Mason) *hld up towards rr: rdn and struggling 3f out: wl bhd fnl 2f* **100/1**

2m 9.26s (4.36) **Going Correction** +0.325s/f (Good) **13** Ran SP% **122.3**
Speed ratings (Par 95): **95,94,93,93,89 88,85,85,84,82 81,80,72**
toteswinger: 1&2 £3.50, 1&3 £3.00, 2&3 £5.60 CSF £6.74 TOTE £1.60: £1.10, £2.50, £1.70; EX 9.20 Trifecta £37.20 Pool: £428.41 - 8.50 winning units..
Owner Mrs Ben Goldsmith **Bred** The Goldsmith Bloodstock Partnership **Trained** Lambourn, Berks

FOCUS
Probably not the strongest or competitive of maidens as the front four held those positions throughout and nothing else managed to get into it.
Asakusa Official explanation: jockey said filly hung left from the home turn
Pursuit Of Purpose Official explanation: jockey said the filly hung badly left in the straight.
Mono's Only Official explanation: trainer said filly did not handle the track

1199 BIRTHDAY SPONSORSHIP @ RACESPONSORS.CO.UK H'CAP — 1m 1f 149y

3:40 (3:41) (Class 6) (0-60,60) 4-Y-O+ — **£2,047** (£604; £302) **Stalls** High

Form / RPR

5-60 **1** **Siena Star (IRE)**[71] [320] 11-9-2 58........................ MickyFenton 12 — 68
(Stef Liddiard) *mde all and sn clr w one rival: rdn over 1f out: styd on gamely and in command fnl 100yds* **9/2**[1]

4-20 **2** *1 ½* **Mister Trickster (IRE)**[45] [657] 8-8-12 54........................ TonyCulhane 7 — 61+
(R Dickin) *s.i.s: hld up in last pl rdn and effrt 2f out: hdwy over 1f out: r.o wl to go 2nd last strides: nt rch wnr* **8/1**

4045 **3** *nk* **Moyoko (IRE)**[14] [969] 6-8-8 50........................ ShaneKelly 8 — 56
(M Salaman) *chsd clr ldng pair: clsd over 4f out: drvn over 1f out: wnt 2nd fnl 100yds: no imp on wnr: lost 2nd last strides* **11/2**[3]

004/ **4** *nk* **Murrumbidgee (IRE)**[277] [5299] 6-8-8 50........................ LPKeniry 14 — 56
(Mike Murphy) *prom in main gp: hdwy over 3f out: drvn over 1f out: kpt on to press for 2nd ins fnl f: one pce fnl 100yds* **10/1**

0-11 **5** *1* **Prince Rossi (IRE)**[56] [513] 5-8-9 51........................(v) JimCrowley 5 — 55
(A E Price) *chsd wnr clr of remainder: rdn over 1f out: btn jst ins fnl f: lost 3 pls fnl 100yds* **5/1**[2]

6-05 **6** *1* **Moon Mix (FR)**[29] [507] 6-8-8 50........................(v[1]) EddieAhern 4 — 52
(J R Jenkins) *t.k.h: hld up off the pce in midfield: hdwy on inner over 2f out: rdn jst over 1f out: fnd nil and no imp fnl f* **11/1**

2205 **7** *2* **Fantasy Ride**[21] [877] 7-8-10 52........................ TGMcLaughlin 10 — 49
(J Pearce) *s.i.s: hld up wl off the pce in rr: rdn and effrt 2f out: kpt on but nvr threatened ldrs* **11/2**[3]

542- **8** *1 ¼* **Mick Is Back**[163] [7050] 5-9-3 59........................(p) TPQueally 9 — 54
(G G Margarson) *prom in main gp: shkn up 3f out: rdn and nt qckn jst over 2f out: wl hld fnl f* **9/1**

060- **9** *½* **Libre**[173] [6821] 9-9-4 60........................ RichardHughes 1 — 54
(F Jordan) *hld up wl off the pce towards rr: hdwy 3f out: rdn and effrt 2f out: nvr pce to trble ldrs* **16/1**

005- **10** *10* **Southern Mistral**[146] [7310] 4-8-10 52........................ KirstyMilczarek 2 — 25
(Miss Gay Kelleway) *hld up off the pce in midfield: rdn and no prog 2f out: edging rt and wl btn 1f out* **12/1**

2m 7.82s (2.92) **Going Correction** +0.325s/f (Good) **10** Ran SP% **117.7**
Speed ratings (Par 101): **101,99,99,99,98 97,96,95,94,86**
toteswinger: 1&2 £10.60, 1&3 £8.00, 2&3 £9.60 CSF £40.98 CT £204.21 TOTE £4.50: £1.30, £3.10, £2.70; EX 42.80 TRIFECTA Not won..
Owner ownaracehorse.co.uk (Shefford) **Bred** Mrs T Brudenell **Trained** Great Shefford, Berks

FOCUS
A moderate handicap, but they went a decent pace and the winning time was 1.44 seconds faster than the fillies' maiden.

Southern Mistral Official explanation: jockey said the gelding hung right

1200 FREE SIGN UP WITH RACESPONSORS.CO.UK "HANDS AND HEELS" APPRENTICE SERIES H'CAP — 1m 4f

4:10 (4:11) (Class 6) (0-60,63) 4-Y-O+ — **£2,047** (£604; £302) **Stalls** Low

Form / RPR

63-6 **1** **Barbirolli**[17] [935] 7-8-8 48........................ PaulPickard 8 — 55
(W M Brisbourne) *hld up in rr: stdy hdwy 4f out: c wd st: r.o wl fnl f to ld last strides* **15/2**[3]

000- **2** *hd* **Lady Hestia (USA)**[151] [7256] 4-8-2 49........................ KatiaScallan(6) 12 — 56
(M P Tregoning) *led for 2f: chsd ldrs after: rdn to ld ins fnl f: hdd last strides* **8/1**

-500 **3** *½* **Sand Repeal (IRE)**[38] [734] 7-8-12 60........................ MatthewCosham(8) 2 — 66
(Miss J Feilden) *chsd ldr: ev ch and c centre ent st: kpt on same pce fnl f* **16/1**

4-00 **4** *nse* **Mixing**[7] [1081] 7-8-4 50........................ KierenFox(6) 3 — 56
(M J Attwater) *hld up in midfield: edgd rt 10f out: hdwy 5f out: ev ch ins fnl f: kpt on* **16/1**

-044 **5** *1 ½* **Summer Bounty**[34] [775] 13-8-6 46 oh1........................ DTDaSilva 13 — 50
(F Jordan) *stdd after s: hld up towards rr: stdy hdwy 4f out: chsd ldrs ent fnl f: no ex fnl 100yds* **28/1**

3332 **6** *shd* **Sir Haydn**[18] [816] 9-7-12 46 oh1........................(v) DannyBrock(8) 14 — 49
(J R Jenkins) *in tch: chsd ldrs 8f out: c centre st: unable qck over 1f out: one pce fnl f* **15/2**[3]

3404 **7** *hd* **Calzaghe (IRE)**[17] [935] 5-8-12 60........................ JustinHeath(8) 6 — 63+
(Jim Best) *s.i.s: in rr: c v wd bnd 2f out: 9th ent fnl f: r.o wl after: nt rch ldrs* **8/1**

0111 **8** *1 ¼* **Shanafarahan (IRE)**[7] [1081] 4-9-5 63 6ex........................ TobyAtkinson(3) 10 — 64
(K A Morgan) *chsd ldrs tl led after 2f: hrd pressed and rdn wl over 1f out: hdd ins fnl f: wknd fnl 100yds* **4/1**[1]

-630 **9** *15* **Thirtyfourthstreet (IRE)**[13] [978] 4-8-9 50........................ DebraEngland 5 — 27
(W R Muir) *hld up in midfield: lost pl 6f out: no ch fnl 2f* **25/1**

0406 **10** *nk* **Charlie Bear**[21] [885] 8-8-3 46 oh1........................(p) RyanClark(3) 7 — 23
(Miss Z C Davison) *v.s.a: a wl bhd* **40/1**

3165 **11** *2 ½* **Itsawindup**[46] [647] 5-8-5 48........................(t) JosephineBruning(3) 1 — 21
(Miss Sheena West) *racd wd in midfield: pushed along 6f out: struggling 3f out: wl btn fnl 2f* **16/1**

504- **12** *7* **Compton Charlie**[148] [6668] 5-9-0 54........................ CharlesEddery 9 — 15
(J G Portman) *t.k.h: chsd ldrs: rdn jst over 2f out: wknd over 1f out: eased ins fnl f* **11/2**[2]

5-00 **13** *12* **Funky Town (IRE)**[10] [1030] 7-8-5 53 oh1 ow7........................ BarryAdams(8) 4 — —
(J Akehurst) *v.s.a: a bhd: lost tch over 3f out: t.o* **66/1**

-046 **U** **Up In Arms (IRE)**[44] [668] 5-8-11 56........................ DanielBlackett(5) 11 — —
(P Winkworth) *hld up towards rr tl hmpd and uns rdr after 2f* **15/2**[3]

2m 46.37s (5.47) **Going Correction** +0.325s/f (Good)
WFA 4 from 5yo+ 1lb **14** Ran SP% **121.8**
Speed ratings (Par 101): **94,93,93,93,92 92,92,91,81,81 79,74,66,—**
toteswinger: 1&2 £19.20, 1&3 £38.40, 2&3 £39.80 CSF £65.25 CT £949.94 TOTE £10.60: £2.50, £2.80, £6.90; EX 107.80 TRIFECTA Not won. Place 6: £69.51 Place 5: £29.85.
Owner Mark Brisbourne **Bred** Gainsborough Stud Management Ltd **Trained** Great Ness, Shropshire

FOCUS
A moderate race, and with the pace only ordinary there were seven horses virtually in a line across the track a furlong from home.
T/Jkpt: Not won. T/Plt: £303.30 to a £1 stake. Pool: £75,872.68. 182.58 winning tickets. T/Qpdt: £32.50 to a £1 stake. Pool: £6,041.30. 137.40 winning tickets. SP

1201 - 1206a (Foreign Racing) - See Raceform Interactive

[1166] MAISONS-LAFFITTE (R-H)

Friday, April 10

OFFICIAL GOING: Good to soft

1207a PRIX DJEBEL (LISTED RACE) (C&G) (STRAIGHT) — 7f (S)

2:05 (2:15) 3-Y-O — **£26,699** (£10,680; £8,010; £5,340; £2,670)

RPR

1 **Le Havre (IRE)**[159] [7163] 3-9-2........................ C-PLemaire 4 — 111
(J-C Rouget, France) *chsd ldr towards outside: hdwy to press ldr over 1f out: led 100yds out: r.o wl* **4/1**[2]

2 *hd* **Naaqoos**[187] [6520] 3-9-2........................ DBonilla 7 — 111
(F Head, France) *sn led: hrd rdn 1 1/2f out: hdd 100yds out: kpt on* **2/5**[1]

3 *2* **Diableside (FR)**[150] [7347] 3-9-2........................ OPeslier 1 — 105
(Y Durepaire, Spain) *cl up towards ins: rdn to press ldrs over 1f out: one pce fnl 100yds* **44/5**[3]

4 *2 ½* **Stricke (FR)**[21] 3-9-2........................ DBoeuf 2 — 98
(Mme C Head-Maarek, France) *in tch in last: rdn and outpcd 1 1/2f out: edgd lft: kpt on to take 4th last 100yds* **9/1**

5 *2* **Good Bye My Friend (FR)**[22] [887] 3-9-2........................ TThulliez 6 — 93
(N Clement, France) *trckd ldr: 4th and outpcd over 1f out: lost 4th 100yds out* **4/1**[2]

6 *4* **Rock'N'Roll Dream (FR)**[181] 3-9-2........................ FSpanu 5 — 82
(A Spanu, France) *in tch on outside tl wknd over 1 1/2f out* **36/1**

7 *dist* **Rachmaninov (FR)**[157] 3-9-2........................ JAuge 3 — —
(F Doumen, France) *bolted to s then uns rdr and j. rail while loose: cl up on ins to 1/2-way: sn wknd and eased* **24/1**

1m 23.0s (-5.30) **Going Correction** -0.55s/f (Hard) **7** Ran SP% **138.3**
Speed ratings: **108,107,105,102,100 95,—**
PARI-MUTUEL: WIN 5.00 (coupled with Good Bye My Friend); PL 1.80,1.10; SF 10.90.
Owner G Augustin-Normand **Bred** Team Hogdala Ab **Trained** Pau, France

NOTEBOOK
Le Havre(IRE) was not too smartly into his stride and soon moved up to shadow the hot favourite. Brought with a progressive run from a furlong and a half out, he pulled out a little extra inside the final furlong. This was his first run since early November so further improvement can be expected. Last year's form showed he needed a good surface to show his best and he will now be aimed at the Poule d'Essai des Poulains.
Naaqoos looked pretty straight and set out to make all the running. He was asked to quicken at the two-furlong marker but couldn't draw clear, though still at the head of affairs halfway through the final furlong.This was a disappointing effort by this Group 1 winner and the colt was immediately ruled out of a tilt at the 2000 Guineas and will instead stay at home to run in the Poulains. He should be given another chance.
Diableside(FR), always well up there, lengthened his stride from two out but couldn't quicken inside the furlong. He stayed on at the one pace and is not up to this level.

Stricke(FR) still had plenty to do at the halfway stage but did run on from a furlong and a half out. He was another who was out of his depth in this class of race.

1208a PRIX IMPRUDENCE (GROUP 3) (FILLIES) (STRAIGHT) 7f (S)

2:35 (2:41) 3-Y-0 **£38,835** (£15,534; £11,650; £7,767; £3,883)

RPR

1 **Elusive Wave (IRE)**[187] 6519 3-9-0 .... C-PLemaire 3 114
(J-C Rouget, France) *mde all: rdn ins fnl f: comf* **1/1**[1]

2 2 **Entre Deux Eaux (FR)**[22] 888 3-9-0 .... IMendizabal 2 109
(Robert Collet, France) *trckd ldr in 3rd on ins: rdn to go 2nd over 1f out: styd on against ins rail but a hld* **5/1**[3]

3 2 ½ **Only Green (IRE)**[21] 3-9-0 .... OPeslier 7 102
(F Head, France) *racd in 2nd to over 1f out: one pce* **36/5**

4 1 ½ **Peach Pearl**[22] 888 3-9-0 .... SPasquier 5 98
(Y De Nicolay, France) *racd in 5th: hrd rdn to go 4th over 1f out: no imp on ldrs* **56/10**

5 1 ½ **Queen America (FR)**[179] 6713 3-9-0 .... GMosse 6 94
(Robert Collet, France) *hld up in last: effrt on outside 2f out: sn one pce* **5/1**[3]

6 ½ **Stefer (USA)**[157] 7185 3-9-0 .... DBoeuf 1 93
(D Smaga, France) *racd in 5th on ins: rdn and one pce fr over 1 1/2f out* **48/10**[2]

7 2 **Flyingwithbebe (USA)**[15] 3-9-0 .... DBonilla 4 87
(T Doumen, France) *racd in 4th tl wknd under 2f out* **16/1**

1m 23.6s (-4.70) **Going Correction** -0.55s/f (Hard) 7 Ran SP% **133.8**
Speed ratings: **104,101,98,97,95 94,92**
PARI-MUTUEL: WIN 2.00; PL 1.30, 2.20; SF 8.80.
Owner M Schwartz **Bred** Pier House Stud **Trained** Pau, France

NOTEBOOK
Elusive Wave(IRE) never gave her supporters a moment of anxiety. Smartly away, she was soon at the head of affairs and controlled the race from pillar to post. Quickening at the furlong marker, she passed the post on her own. She changed hands before her second in the Marcel Boussac and now heads for the Pouliches.
Entre Deux Eaux(FR) followed the winner virtually throughout, tried vainly to get on terms from two out and had to settle for second place. A game and consistent filly, she is not up to this class.
Only Green(IRE) was well up from the start but was left for cold by the winner and runner-up when things warmed up. She was not hard pressed to hold third place, though.
Peach Pearl put up a rather disappointing effort. She was towards the tail of the field from halfway and made little progress from then on.

1182 KEMPTON (A.W) (R-H)

Saturday, April 11

OFFICIAL GOING: Standard

The Masaka Stakes, traditionally run on this card, has been discontinued after losing its Listed status.

Wind: Moderate ahead Weather: Overcast

1209 FIND THE BEST ODDS AT ODDSCHECKER.COM H'CAP 1m (P)

2:05 (2:07) (Class 2) (0-105,99) 4-Y-0+ **£11,527** (£3,430; £1,714; £856) **Stalls** High

Form RPR

4040 1 **Mahadee (IRE)**[21] 913 4-9-4 **96** ....(b) NCallan 10 105
(C E Brittain) *trckd ldrs: rdn over 2f out: wnt 2nd over 1f out: led fnl 200yds: kpt on wl* **7/1**

140- 2 1 ¼ **Checklow (USA)**[222] 5573 4-8-10 **88** .... ShaneKelly 6 94+
(J Noseda) *in rr: rdn over 2f out: hdwy u.p over 1f out: str run fnl f to take 2nd nr fin but nt rch wnr* **14/1**

2-02 3 nk **Extraterrestrial**[14] 995 5-8-12 **95** .... FrederikTylicki(5) 1 100
(R A Fahey) *lw: in rr: rdn over 2f out: gd hdwy over 1f out: styd on wl fnl f to press for 2nd cl home but no imp on wnr* **13/2**

-360 4 nse **Samarinda (USA)**[35] 783 6-9-1 **93** .... MickyFenton 2 98
(Mrs P Sly) *pushed along to ld after 1f: 5l clr over 4f out: rdn over 2f out: hdd and no ex fnl 100yds* **12/1**

/31- 5 ½ **Cordell (IRE)**[385] 966 4-9-2 **94** .... RyanMoore 9 98
(R Hannon) *h.d.w: swtg: t.k.h: sn trcking ldr: shkn up over 2f out: lost 2nd over 1f out: fdd ins fnl f* **5/1**[2]

0400 6 1 ¼ **Jack Junior (USA)**[21] 916 5-9-7 **99** .... AdrianTNicholls 5 100
(D Nicholls) *in tch: rdn 2f out: styng on whn nt clr run ins fnl f* **25/1**

030- 7 1 ¼ **Cape Hawk (IRE)**[168] 6984 5-9-6 **98** .... RichardHughes 4 96+
(R Hannon) *b: led 1f: styd chsng ldrs: rdn over 2f out: wknd wl ins fnl f* **4/1**[1]

5650 8 ½ **Opus Maximus (IRE)**[14] 995 4-8-7 **85** .... RoystonFfrench 3 82
(M Johnston) *towards rr: rdn and sme hdwy over 2f out: no imp on ldrs over 1f out: wknd fnl f* **12/1**

-421 9 ¾ **Saltagioo (ITY)**[23] 879 5-8-10 **88** .... JohnEgan 8 84
(M Botti) *mid-div: rdn ins fnl 3f: nt pce to rch ldrs: wknd fnl f* **11/2**[3]

-210 10 1 ¼ **Titan Triumph**[14] 997 5-9-4 **96** ....(t) JimCrowley 7 89
(W J Knight) *lw: bhd most of way* **17/2**

1m 37.68s (-2.12) **Going Correction** -0.05s/f (Stan) 10 Ran SP% **114.3**
Speed ratings (Par 109): **108,106,106,106,105 104,103,102,102,100**
toteswinger: 1&2 £28.10, 1&3 £9.00, 2&3 £24.10. CSF £97.76 CT £677.98 TOTE £9.20: £2.60, £4.70, £2.50; EX 147.80 TRIFECTA Not won..
Owner Saeed Manana **Bred** Darley **Trained** Newmarket, Suffolk

FOCUS
A good handicap, but a slightly muddling race, with Samarinda allowed an uncontested lead. He wound up the pace and was upwards of five lengths clear at one stage, but he was gradually reeled in.

NOTEBOOK
Mahadee(IRE) had not totally convinced with his attitude in the Winter Derby on his previous start, but in fairness that was a big ask, and there can be no faulting this effort on his return to handicap company. He is smart on sand when things fall right, although he could be given another chance to prove himself as effective on turf. (op 8-1)
Checklow(USA) ◆, a one-time St Leger entrant, was beaten a long way in a first-time visor over 1m4f around here when last seen 222 days previously, but he had since been gelded. Not for the first time he was reluctant to enter the stalls, but his connections feel that's simply because he's such a big horse, and in the race itself he shaped encouragingly, going on nicely in the closing stages, having been outpaced when first coming under pressure. He's very talented and could do better off a stronger end-to-end gallop at this trip, but the best of him will probably be seen at around 1m2f. (op 16-1 tchd 12-1)
Extraterrestrial, dropped in from the worst stall of all, had to battle to take a narrow gap in the straight but kept on to the line. (op 5-1 tchd 7-1)
Samarinda(USA), although left alone up front, still had to use more energy than ideal to get across from stall two, and this was a respectable effort. (op 14-1)
Cordell(IRE) ◆, off the track since winning a three-year-old handicap off a mark of 85 over course and distance in March last year, was a little warm down the neck. He was not given a particularly hard time in the closing stages and looked to get tired, so better can be expected next time. (op 6-1)
Jack Junior(USA) did not get the clearest of runs in the straight, but he didn't look unlucky. (op 28-1 tchd 33-1 in a place)
Cape Hawk(IRE) looked fit enough but ran below market expectations on his return from 168 days off the track. (op 9-2 tchd 5-1)

1210 ODDSCHECKER.COM SNOWDROP FILLIES' STKS (LISTED RACE) 1m (P)

2:40 (2:41) (Class 1) 4-Y-0+

£22,708 (£8,608; £4,308; £2,148; £1,076; £540) **Stalls** High

Form RPR

015- 1 **Born Tobouggie (GER)**[163] 7099 4-8-12 102 .... TPQueally 6 106
(H R A Cecil) *lw: mde virtually all: shkn up and c clr fr 2f out: hung lft fnl f: unchal* **10/3**[2]

013- 2 2 ½ **Perfect Star**[237] 5120 5-8-12 100 .... AdamKirby 7 101
(C G Cox) *hld up towards rr but in tch: rdn 2f out: hrd rdn and styd on to chse wnr fnl f but nvr any ch: hld on wl for 2nd* **7/2**[3]

110- 3 shd **Scuffle**[189] 6484 4-8-12 100 .... RyanMoore 3 100+
(R Charlton) *h.d.w: bit bkwd: in rr but in tch: rdn along and hdwy over 2f out: styd on fnl f to disute 2nd fnl 100yds but nvr any ch w wnr* **9/4**[1]

115- 4 3 ¼ **Tactful (IRE)**[122] 7635 4-8-12 89 .... SebSanders 2 93
(R M Beckett) *chsd wnr after 2f: rdn and effrt 3f out: nvr quite upsides and wknd over 1f out* **10/1**

/01- 5 1 ¼ **Dixey**[313] 2666 4-8-12 94 .... PhilipRobinson 8 90
(M A Jarvis) *lw: chsd wnr 2f: styd chsng ldrs: rdn over 2f out: wknd qckly fnl f* **8/1**

/30- 6 2 **Festoso (IRE)**[189] 6475 4-8-12 100 .... JimmyFortune 4 86
(H J L Dunlop) *s.i.s: in rr: rdn 3f out: nvr gng pce to be competitive* **13/2**

0131 7 1 ¼ **Smokey Rye**[12] 1037 4-8-12 70 .... DaneO'Neill 5 83?
(George Baker) *nvr in contention* **33/1**

400 8 39 **Bet Noir (IRE)**[31] 802 4-8-12 44 .... TolleyDean 1 —
(A W Carroll) *towards rr for most of the way: t.o* **200/1**

1m 37.08s (-2.72) **Going Correction** -0.05s/f (Stan) 8 Ran SP% **113.0**
Speed ratings (Par 108): **111,108,108,105,103 101,100,61**
toteswinger: 1&2 £2.90, 1&3 £2.50, 2&3 £2.80. CSF £15.07 TOTE £4.60: £1.50, £1.80, £1.40; EX 17.20 Trifecta £35.10 Pool: £743.19 - 15.65 winning units..
Owner The Sticky Wicket Syndicate **Bred** Graf Und Grafin Von Stauffenberg **Trained** Newmarket, Suffolk

FOCUS
An ordinary fillies' Listed race, but a likeable effort from Born Tobouggie, who was just 0.26 seconds off the track record and was easily the quickest of the four 1m winners on the card.

NOTEBOOK
Born Tobouggie(GER) ◆, the pick of the paddock, was keen early (not for the first time), although she settled better when allowed to stride on. Pressed by Tactful approaching the straight, she then wandered around a little bit under pressure and carried her head slightly to the right, giving the impression she was idling. All things considered, she looked very smart in still managing to win decisively in such a decent time. (op 3-1 tchd 7-2)
Perfect Star ◆, warm beforehand, was no match for the winner, but she was keeping on at the finish and this was a pleasing return from 237 days off. She was only seen out three times last year, and had never raced earlier than June, so it's not unreasonable to expect better as the season progresses. (op 4-1 tchd 9-2)
Scuffle, trying Polytrack for the first time after over six months off, was being niggled before the straight and lacked the pace to threaten the winner. Not given too hard a time, she gave the impression she'll improve a good deal for this. (op 11-4 tchd 3-1)
Tactful(IRE), edgy beforehand, was a winner of her first two starts in minor company at Great Leighs before finishing in mid-division in a Deauville Listed race when last seen in December. She kept the winner honest for a fair way, but she couldn't sustain her effort. It remains to be seen whether she's up to this class, but she's open to some improvement. (tchd 8-1 and 12-1)
Dixey, off the track since winning a 7f conditions race at Leicester last June, did not pick up in the straight and weakened late on. She was entitled to need this outing and should be happier back over shorter. (tchd 17-2)
Festoso(IRE), very edgy beforehand, was trying Polytrack for the first time and offered little after six months off. (op 11-2 tchd 9-2)

1211 ODDSCHECKER.COM EASTER STKS (LISTED RACE) (C&G) 1m (P)

3:10 (3:10) (Class 1) 3-Y-0

£22,708 (£8,608; £4,308; £2,148; £1,076; £540) **Stalls** High

Form RPR

010- 1 **Pure Poetry (IRE)**[212] 5827 3-8-12 99 .... RichardHughes 8 102+
(R Hannon) *hld up towards rr: snatched up over 4f out: gd hdwy over 2f out: qcknd fnl f to ld fnl 30yds: readily* **14/1**

10-6 2 hd **Shampagne**[24] 863 3-8-12 100 .... MartinDwyer 5 101
(P F I Cole) *chsd ldrs: rdn over 2f out: led wl over 1f out: kpt on wl u.p tl hdd and outpcd fnl 30yds* **8/1**

512- 3 1 ½ **Mishrif (USA)**[173] 6860 3-8-12 93 .... AlanMunro 9 98
(P W Chapple-Hyam) *chsd ldrs: rdn over 2f out and chal fr wl over 1f out: outpcd fnl 100yds* **10/1**

1-10 4 1 **Markyg (USA)**[24] 863 3-8-12 92 .... FergusSweeney 6 95
(K R Burke) *in rr but in tch: rdn ins fnl 3f: styd on fr over 1f out and kpt on ins fnl f but nvr gng pce to trble ldng trio* **20/1**

160- 5 1 ½ **Viva Ronaldo (IRE)**[189] 6483 3-8-12 99 .... TonyHamilton 2 92
(R A Fahey) *in rr: hrd drvn over 2f out: hdwy appr fnl f: kpt on ins fnl f but nvr in contention* **16/1**

11-1 6 hd **Saint Arch (CAN)**[14] 1001 3-8-12 97 .... JoeFanning 7 91
(M Johnston) *lw: led: pushed along fr 3f out: hdd wl over 1f out: wknd fnl f* **6/4**[1]

111- 7 nse **Captain Ramius (IRE)**[183] 6637 3-9-1 104 .... JamieSpencer 1 94+
(S A Callaghan) *s.i.s: swtchd rt to ins rail: hmpd over 4f out: rapid hdwy on ins to press ldrs wl over 1f out: wknd ins fnl f* **13/2**[3]

40-3 8 1 **Sohcahtoa (IRE)**[24] 863 3-8-12 100 .... RyanMoore 3 89
(R Hannon) *lw: t.k.h: chsd ldr: rdn to chal over 2f out: wknd qckly 1f out* **4/1**[2]

2-00 9 1 **Fullback (IRE)**[58] 526 3-8-12 0 .... LPKeniry 4 87
(J S Moore) *in tch: rdn 3f out: nvr gng pce to chal and wknd over 1f out* **33/1**

1m 38.49s (-1.31) **Going Correction** -0.05s/f (Stan) 9 Ran SP% **113.8**
Speed ratings (Par 106): **104,103,102,101,99 99,99,98,97**
toteswinger: 1&2 £10.70, 1&3 £28.20, 2&3 £13.50 CSF £118.66 TOTE £18.30: £4.20, £2.00, £2.20; EX 137.30 Trifecta £444.10 Part won. Pool: £600.20 - 0.70 winning units..
Owner Mrs J Wood **Bred** R Collins And Jerry Kennedy **Trained** East Everleigh, Wilts

FOCUS
One of the lesser Classic trials and a race that rarely has much bearing on the 2000 Guineas these days, although the 2005 winner (last time the race was run on turf) Rebel Rebel went on to finish a 100-1 second at Newmarket. The lead was contested, with Saint Arch being pestered by Sohcahtoa for much of the way, but they didn't seem to go that quick and a few of those in behind were keen. The field were still well bunched halfway up the straight and the winning time was the slowest of the four 1m races on the card by some way, suggesting this is very ordinary Listed form.

NOTEBOOK
Pure Poetry(IRE) was one of those who was a little keen early, but he was still able to produce a sustained effort in the straight and gradually wore down the battling Shampagne. This was the winner's first start beyond 7f, and his two previous victories were gained over 6f, so the ordinary early pace probably helped his cause. A good start to his three-year-old season after 212 days off, but it remains to be seen what the bare form is worth. He could take his chance in the Craven Stakes and that will tell us more. (op 16-1)
Shampagne is thoroughly exposed, but he's pretty smart on sand. Another who was keen early, this was a game effort and his form figures on artificial surfaces now read 11162, compared to a record of 1-7 on turf. (op 11-1 tchd 12-1)
Mishrif(USA), on his toes beforehand, was runner-up in a Pontefract Listed race on his final start at two. He shaped encouragingly on his reappearance and is open to improvement. (op 12-1 tchd 14-1)
Markyg(USA) never featured from a poor draw in the Kentucky Derby Trial here last time, but this was better. He gives the distinct impression he can do better again off a stronger end-to-end gallop. (tchd 16-1)
Viva Ronaldo(IRE), racing beyond 6f for the first time after 189 days off, was edgy as usual and did okay considering he was last early, but he failed to prove his stamina.
Saint Arch(CAN) might not have gone off all that quick, but his chance was still compromised by the persistent pestering from Sohcahtoa. (op 11-8 tchd 6-5)
Captain Ramius(IRE), 3-3 over 7f for Mark Wallace last year, including a Dundalk Listed race on his final start of the campaign, was not at his best for new connections. Although he had made all for his last two wins, an uncontested lead was highly unlikely this time, particularly from stall one, and he was dropped in after taking a while to find his stride. He briefly looked a threat when switched for a run at the cutaway halfway up the straight, but his effort soon flattened out. (op 6-1 tchd 5-1)
Sohcahtoa(IRE) was keen early and failed to run up to the form he showed when third in the Kentucky Derby Trial after being allowed an easy lead. (op 7-2 tchd 9-2 in a place)

1212 ODDSCHECKER.COM CASINO AND POKER ROOM H'CAP 7f (P)
3:45 (3:45) (Class 2) (0-100,98) 4-Y-0+
£11,091 (£3,321; £1,660; £831; £414; £208) Stalls High

Form				RPR
004-	1		**Something (IRE)**[207] 5990 7-8-8 **88** ... PaulQuinn 5 (D Nicholls) *in rr: gd hdwy on ins over 2f out: led appr fnl f: drvn out* **20/1**	99
3-40	2	½	**Benandonner (USA)**[14] 997 6-8-12 **92** ... JamieMoriarty 7 (R A Fahey) *chsd ldrs: rdn and outpcd 2f out: str run u.p appr fnl f: styd on to chse wnr cl home but a hld* **12/1**	102
-115	3	1 ½	**Flowing Cape (IRE)**[35] 783 4-9-1 **95** ... MickyFenton 13 (R Hollinshead) *lw: chsd ldrs: chal fr ins fnl 2f: outpcd by wnr fnl f and lost 2nd cl home* **7/2**[1]	101
506-	4	1	**Spitfire**[207] 6005 4-9-0 **94** ... EddieAhern 12 (J R Jenkins) *in rr: rdn wl over 2f out: styd on appr fnl f: fin wl* **14/1**	97
20-6	5	½	**Fathsta (IRE)**[13] 1018 4-8-11 **91** ... StephenDonohoe 9 (D Nicholls) *chsd ldrs: rdn over 2f out: outpcd fnl f* **9/1**	93
5623	6	shd	**Red Somerset (USA)**[8] 1093 6-9-3 **97** ... GeorgeBaker 6 (R J Hodges) *in rr: swtchd rt and hdwy ins fnl 2f: kpt on ins fnl f but nvr gng pce to be competitive* **10/1**	99
6113	7	2	**Al Muheer (IRE)**[21] 916 4-9-4 **98** ... (b) NCallan 14 (C E Brittain) *lw: sn led: rdn 3f out: hdd ins fnl 2f: wknd over 1f out* **5/1**[2]	94
-140	8	hd	**Thebes**[13] 1018 4-8-11 **91** ... RoystonFfrench 8 (M Johnston) *chsd ldr: rdn 3f out: led ins fnl 2f: hdd & wknd appr fnl f* **12/1**	87
30-0	9	1	**Joseph Henry**[13] 1018 7-8-8 **88** ... AdrianTNicholls 4 (D Nicholls) *in rr: hdwy on ins whn sltly hmpd ins fnl 2f: rcvrd and styd on again fnl f: nvr a threat* **16/1**	81+
100-	10	1 ½	**Esteem Machine (USA)**[274] 3905 5-9-0 **94** ... RyanMoore 11 (R A Teal) *lw: nvr bttr than mid-div: bhd fr over 2f out* **10/1**	83
10-4	11	1	**Pravda Street**[9] 1089 4-8-5 **85** ... JoeFanning 3 (P F I Cole) *lw: in tch over 4f* **12/1**	71
030-	12	½	**Great Charm (IRE)**[169] 6947 4-8-7 **87** ... JamieSpencer 10 (M L W Bell) *t.k.h: chsd ldrs tl wknd qckly appr fnl 2f* **15/2**[3]	72
36-5	13	nk	**Bomber Command (USA)**[23] 879 6-8-8 **91** ... (v) PatrickHills(3) 2 (J W Hills) *in tch: rdn and wknd 3f out* **20/1**	75
420-	14	3 ½	**Brassini**[169] 6947 4-8-13 **93** ... AlanMunro 1 (B R Millman) *in tch: effrt on outside 3f out: sn wknd* **25/1**	68

1m 24.03s (-1.97) **Going Correction** -0.05s/f (Stan) **14** Ran SP% **127.8**
Speed ratings (Par 109): **109,108,106,105,105 104,102,102,101,99 98,97,97,93**
toteswinger: 1&2 £225.00, 1&3 £58.10, 2&3 £24.10. CSF £251.07 CT £1087.46 TOTE £26.70: £7.60, £3.60, £2.40; EX 366.60 Trifecta £3137.90 Pool: £153,080.88 - 36.10 winning units..
Owner Middleham Park Racing LIII **Bred** Newlands House Stud **Trained** Sessay, N Yorks
■ Stewards' Enquiry : George Baker one-day ban: careless riding (Apr 25)

FOCUS
A very competitive handicap. The pace was strong, with Al Muheer and Thebes setting the race up for those waited with.

NOTEBOOK
Something(IRE) was almost last early on, but he made good headway early in the straight and continued his progress after getting a dream run towards the inside rail. His last two victories had been gained on Polytrack in 2006 and it was a major surprise to see this was his first start on synthetics since then. His overall profile is unconvincing, but he's now unbeaten in three starts on this surface. (op 16-1)
Benandonner(USA) did best of those to race handy and this was a cracking effort. His yard is in top form.
Flowing Cape(IRE) ◆ has won over the trip, but gave the impression here that 7f in this company stretched him. He still looks reasonably treated and will be of interest back over 6f. (op 5-1)
Spitfire did not get the best of runs early in the straight, but he was in the clear in time if good enough. (op 16-1)
Fathsta(IRE) was short of room more than once in the closing stages, but he was not unlucky. (op 7-1 tchd 10-1)
Red Somerset(USA) had to be switched towards the inside in the straight and got going too late to pose a threat. (tchd 9-1)
Joseph Henry ◆ was set a hopeless task and was also squeezed against the inside rail about a furlong out. He looked to cross the line with plenty left. Official explanation: jockey said gelding suffered interference on leaving the stalls (op 20-1)
Pravda Street had no easy task from his draw and hinted that he'll be able to do better, perhaps back on easy turf. Official explanation: jockey said saddle slipped (op 10-1)
Brassini, returning from 169 days off, was stuck out extremely wide for most of the way from the worst stall of all. (tchd 28-1 and 33-1 in a place)

1213 ODDSCHECKER.COM H'CAP (LONDON MILE QUALIFIER) 1m (P)
4:15 (4:16) (Class 4) (0-85,87) 4-Y-0+ £4,727 (£1,406; £702; £351) Stalls High

Form				RPR
1/	1		**Forgotten Voice (IRE)**[535] 6436 4-9-1 **82** ... ShaneKelly 1 (J Noseda) *hld up in rr: n.m.r over 2f out: stdy hdwy over 1f out: str run under hand riding fnl f to ld last strides: cosily* **11/10**[1]	95+
2350	2	shd	**Tourist**[14] 999 4-8-12 **79** ... DarrenWilliams 10 (D Shaw) *chsd ldrs: str chal fnl f: led briefly cl home tl ct by cosy wnr last strides* **20/1**	85
032-	3	nk	**Prince Of Thebes (IRE)**[127] 7556 8-9-2 **83** ... PaulDoe 11 (M J Attwater) *lw: chsd ldrs: wnt 2nd over 4f out: chal 3f out: led 2f out: hdd cl home* **10/1**	88
1435	4	1 ½	**Can Can Star**[14] 999 6-8-13 **80** ... LukeMorris 7 (A W Carroll) *in tch: hdwy u.p over 2f out: kpt on fnl f but nvr gng pce to chal* **17/2**	82
0-63	5	2 ¼	**Alfresco**[7] 1116 5-9-3 **87** ... (b) MarcHalford(3) 8 (J R Best) *s.i.s: chsd ldrs 1/2-way: rdn over 2f out and sn btn* **11/2**[2]	84
030-	6	3 ¾	**Phluke**[197] 6250 8-7-11 **71** ... DanielBlackett(7) 5 (Eve Johnson Houghton) *chsd ldr tl over 4f out: rdn 3f out: wknd over 2f out* **25/1**	59
500-	7	1	**Gala Casino Star (IRE)**[189] 6482 4-8-12 **84** ... FrederikTylicki(5) 3 (R A Fahey) *tall: in rr: rdn over 2f out: nvr in contention* **13/2**[3]	70
11-1	8	3	**Royal Dignitary (USA)**[20] 922 9-9-4 **85** ... AdrianTNicholls 4 (D Nicholls) *led tl hdd u.p 2f out: sn wknd* **12/1**	64
005-	9	nk	**Another Bottle (IRE)**[328] 2218 8-9-0 **81** ... TPQueally 6 (Mrs S Leech) *slowly into stride: a towards rr* **40/1**	59
-006	10	hd	**Flying Squad (UAE)**[10] 1067 5-8-5 **72** ... FrankieMcDonald 2 (M F Harris) *s.i.s: a in rr* **66/1**	50
1150	11	3	**Electric Warrior (IRE)**[7] 1116 6-8-9 **76** ... LPKeniry 9 (C R Dore) *s.i.s: a in rr* **20/1**	47

1m 37.82s (-1.98) **Going Correction** -0.05s/f (Stan) **11** Ran SP% **120.9**
Speed ratings (Par 105): **107,106,106,105,102 99,98,95,94,94 91**
toteswinger: 1&2 £8.00, 1&3 £5.90, 2&3 £20.10. CSF £33.44 CT £168.95 TOTE £2.40: £1.10, £4.30, £2.60; EX 36.00.
Owner Mrs Susan Roy **Bred** Swettenham Stud And Ben Sangster **Trained** Newmarket, Suffolk

FOCUS
A good handicap run at a decent pace early on, but the gallop looked to slow approaching the straight. The heavily backed winner was value for much further.

1214 COMPARE ODDS WITH ODDSCHECKER.COM H'CAP 7f (P)
4:50 (4:50) (Class 4) (0-85,85) 3-Y-0 £4,727 (£1,406; £702; £351) Stalls High

Form				RPR
21-	1		**Laudatory**[148] 7311 3-8-10 **77** ... JamieSpencer 10 (W R Swinburn) *t.k.h: hld up in tch: n.m.r over 2f out: hdwy and hung rt 1f out: str run fnl f to ld nr fin: comf* **10/3**[1]	86+
50-1	2	¾	**Seek N' Destroy (IRE)**[17] 951 3-8-10 **77** ... MichaelHills 9 (B W Hills) *lw: plld hrd: chsd ldr: led wl over 1f out: rdn fnl f: ct nr fin* **11/2**[2]	84
1-11	3	¾	**Mr Willis**[10] 1075 3-8-6 **76** ... MarcHalford(3) 5 (J R Best) *lw: in rr but in tch: hdwy fr 2f out: edgd rt fr over 1f out: styd on cl home but nvr quite gng pce to chal* **10/3**[1]	81+
10-5	4	hd	**Kyllachy Star**[14] 1002 3-8-13 **80** ... TonyHamilton 4 (R A Fahey) *lw: in rr: hdwy fr 2f out: rdn and styd on fnl f: fin wl* **11/2**[2]	84+
565-	5	nse	**Land Hawk (IRE)**[172] 6886 3-8-4 **71** ... RoystonFfrench 6 (J Pearce) *tall: in rr: swtchd lft to outer fr 2f out: str run over 1f out: fin wl* **33/1**	75
103-	6	1	**Proclaim**[205] 6058 3-8-13 **80** ... J-PGuillambert 12 (M Johnston) *led: rdn over 2f out: hdd & wknd wl over 1f out* **9/1**[3]	82
00-1	7	2	**Cyflymder (IRE)**[12] 1033 3-9-0 **81** ... RichardHughes 7 (R Hannon) *chsd ldrs: rdn over 2f out: wkng whn hmpd jst ins fnl f* **10/1**	79+
1-	8	nk	**Charging Indian (IRE)**[312] 2696 3-9-2 **83** ... TedDurcan 2 (D R Lanigan) *in rr: pushed along over 2f out: kpt on fnl f: nvr in contention* **25/1**	78
3220	9	11	**Grand Honour (IRE)**[12] 1033 3-8-8 **75** ... JimmyQuinn 11 (P Howling) *chsd ldrs over 4f* **16/1**	41
6-10	10	3 ½	**Never Lose**[14] 1002 3-9-4 **85** ... (b) NCallan 3 (C E Brittain) *in rr: rdn towards outside 3f out: sn wknd* **25/1**	41
21-	11	2 ¾	**Efficiency**[129] 7538 3-9-1 **82** ... LPKeniry 1 (M Blanshard) *chsd ldrs 4f* **28/1**	31
16-	12	7	**Chicago Cop (IRE)**[260] 4374 3-9-4 **85** ... AdrianTNicholls 8 (D Nicholls) *s.i.s: a towards rr* **20/1**	15

1m 25.06s (-0.94) **Going Correction** -0.05s/f (Stan) **12** Ran SP% **120.7**
Speed ratings (Par 100): **103,102,101,101,101 99,97,97,84,80 77,69**
toteswinger: 1&2 £7.00, 1&3 £4.90, 2&3 £6.10. CSF £20.29 CT £68.16 TOTE £4.30: £2.00, £2.00, £1.90; EX 30.40.
Owner P W Harris **Bred** Whitsbury Manor Stud & Pigeon House Stud **Trained** Aldbury, Herts

FOCUS
A decent three-year-old handicap for the grade and the form looks strong. The first two were unexposed handicap debutants, and the third is most progressive. A race that looks worth treating positively and should work out well.
Land Hawk(IRE) Official explanation: jockey said gelding suffered interference in running

1215 TIP STAR COMPETITION AT ODDSCHECKER.COM H'CAP 2m (P)
5:25 (5:25) (Class 4) (0-85,85) 4-Y-0+ £4,727 (£1,406; £702; £351) Stalls High

Form				RPR
4221	1		**Kavaloti (IRE)**[10] 1069 5-9-2 **76** ... (b) RyanMoore 4 (G L Moore) *chsd ldrs: rdn over 2f out: styd on to ld 1f out: drvn out* **3/1**[1]	84
4123	2D	1 ¾	**Mr Aitch (IRE)**[22] 899 7-9-2 **76** ... (t) JohnEgan 8 (R T Phillips) *in rr: hdwy on ins over 2f out: styd on to chal appr fnl f: one pce ins fnl f: subs disq. (positive sample)* **13/2**[3]	82
-161	2	¾	**Wabbraan (USA)**[20] 923 4-8-4 **73** ... AmyBaker(5) 9 (M Hill) *lw: chsd ldr: led ins fnl 2f: hdd 1f out: styd on same pce* **14/1**	78
-261	3	½	**Salute (IRE)**[35] 787 10-9-5 **79** ... RobertHavlin 6 (P G Murphy) *lw: chsd ldrs: rdn and styd on same pce fr over 2f out* **14/1**	83
2-54	4	nse	**Miss Serena**[22] 899 4-8-5 **69** ... JimmyQuinn 2 (Mrs P Sly) *chsd ldrs: rdn over 2f out: styd on same pce* **9/1**	73
006-	5	1	**Crossbow Creek**[189] 6472 11-9-6 **80** ... LukeMorris 10 (M G Rimell) *in tch: rdn and styd on same pce fnl 2f* **25/1**	83
41-3	6	1	**Alnwick**[80] 233 5-8-13 **73** ... DaneO'Neill 11 (P D Cundell) *led: rdn over 3f out: hdd ins fnl 2f: wknd over 1f out* **9/2**[2]	75
-016	7	nk	**War Of The Roses (IRE)**[21] 915 6-9-8 **82** ... TomEaves 1 (R Brotherton) *rr: rdn over 3f out: mod prog fnl f* **12/1**	84

502- 9 *nk* **Mighty Moon**[39] 7128 6-8-12 77.................. FrederikTylicki(5) 5 78
(R A Fahey) *chsd ldrs: rdn over 3f out: wknd over 1f out* **9/2[2]**
324- 10 *6* **Mohawk Star (IRE)**[145] 7366 8-8-8 68..................(b) MartinDwyer 3 62
(I A Wood) *a in rr* **14/1**
3m 31.54s (1.44) **Going Correction** -0.05s/f (Stan)
WFA 4 from 5yo+ 4lb 10 Ran SP% **116.2**
Speed ratings (Par 105): **94,93,92,92,92 91,91,91,91,88**
toteswinger: 1&2 £, 1&3 £, 2&3 £ CSF £22.54 CT £236.53 TOTE £3.80: £1.20, £2.50, £5.00; EX 24.30.
Owner Graham Gillespie **Bred** Mme Henri Devin **Trained** Lower Beeding, W Sussex
FOCUS
A fair staying handicap, run at an even pace. Mr Aitch fin 2nd disq: all others promoted one place.

1216 ODDSCHECKER.COM HBLB H'CAP 1m 2f (P)
5:55 (5:55) (Class 3) (0-95,94) 4-Y-0+ **£7,771** (£2,312; £1,155; £577) **Stalls High**

Form RPR
134- 1 **Press The Button (GER)**[133] 7496 6-9-2 92.................. PatCosgrave 6 102
(J R Boyle) *hld up in tch: gd hdwy ins fnl 2f to ld 1f out: styd on wl* **8/1**
1133 2 *1* **Formation (USA)**[21] 915 4-9-1 91.................. GeorgeBaker 1 99
(J R Boyle) *hld up in rr but in tch: gd hdwy over 1f out: str run to chse wnr ins fnl f but a hld* **7/2[2]**
422- 3 *1* **Casilda (IRE)**[230] 5311 4-8-11 90.................. DavidProbert(3) 4 96
(A M Balding) *in tch: rdn and hdwy to chse ldrs ins fnl 3f: chal u.p over 1f out: wknd ins fnl f* **9/2[3]**
520- 4 *1 ½* **Ramona Chase**[105] 6984 4-9-4 94.................. IanMongan 3 97
(M J Attwater) *hld up towards rr: hdwy on outside fr 2f out: wknd over 1f out: btn whn slt hmpd wl ins fnl f* **16/1**
60-2 5 *½* **Viva Vettori**[23] 879 5-8-12 88.................. RichardHughes 2 90
(D R C Elsworth) *sn led: rdn over 2f out: hdd & wknd 1f* **9/4[1]**
013- 6 *hd* **Dance The Star (USA)**[183] 6630 4-8-11 87.................. RichardMullen 5 89+
(D M Simcock) *b: chsd ldrs: one pce whn hmpd 1f out: n.d after* **5/1**
400- 7 *4 ½* **Ballinteni**[111] 7755 7-8-12 88.................. NCallan 7 81
(D K Ivory) *lw: chsd ldrs 7f* **14/1**
2m 5.06s (-2.94) **Going Correction** -0.10s/f (Stan) 7 Ran SP% **111.5**
Speed ratings (Par 107): **107,106,105,104,103 103,100**
toteswinger: 1&2 £4.00, 1&3 £5.10, 2&3 £4.20. CSF £34.16 TOTE £10.00: £3.20, £2.10; EX 34.50 Place 6: £201.27, Place 5: £34.04 ..
Owner Brian McAtavey **Bred** Gestut Sommerberg **Trained** Epsom, Surrey
FOCUS
A fair handicap, and they seemed to go a decent pace.
NOTEBOOK
Press The Button(GER) apparently surprised his connections. Returning from a 133-day break, he quickened up after travelling well and then showed a good attitude to hold off his slightly unlucky stablemate.He could go for a handicap over this trip at Epsom on April 22. (tchd 15-2)
Formation(USA) might have beaten his stablemate with a clearer run in what was quite a rough race. Like the winner, he could go to Epsom this month. (op 11-4)
Casilda(IRE), who had been off for 230 days and was having her first start since leaving William Knight, made a pleasing return. (op 6-1)
Ramona Chase, having only his second start since leaving Sylvester Kirk, is entitled to improve, having been off for 105 days. (tchd 18-1)
Viva Vettori was slightly keen early and was continually pressured by Dance The Star. (tchd 3-1)
Dance The Star(USA) is better over further. (op 11-2 tchd 13-2)
T/Jkpt: Not won. T/Plt: £402.10 to a £1 stake. Pool: £134,288.83. 243.76 winning tickets. T/Qpdt: £125.20 to a £1 stake. Pool: £5,958.26. 35.20 winning tickets. ST

1217 - 1224a (Foreign Racing) - See Raceform Interactive

KEENELAND (L-H)
Saturday, April 11
OFFICIAL GOING: Turf course - good; polytrack - fast

1225a TOYOTA BLUE GRASS STKS (GRADE 1) (POLYTRACK) 1m 1f
10:15 (10:18) 3-Y-O **£322,917** (£104,167; £52,083; £26,042; £15,625)

RPR
1 **General Quarters (USA)**[28] 3-8-11 .... ECoa 8 117
(Thomas R McCarthy, U.S.A) **143/10**
2 *1 ½* **Hold Me Back (USA)**[21] 3-8-11 .... KDesormeaux 10 115+
(William Mott, U.S.A) **11/5[1]**
3 *1 ¼* **Massone (USA)**[56] 3-8-11 .... GKGomez 11 112
(Ronald McAnally, U.S.A) **107/10**
4 *1* **Terrain (USA)**[28] 3-8-11 .... JRLeparoux 6 110
(Albert Stall Jr, U.S.A) **73/10**
5 *1 ¼* **Join In The Dance (USA)**[28] 3-8-11 .... JRVelazquez 2 108
(Todd Pletcher, U.S.A) **143/10**
6 *1 ¼* **Loch Dubh (USA)**[21] 3-8-11 ....(b) HJTheriotII 7 105
(Jeff Talley, U.S.A) **93/1**
7 *1 ½* **Charitable Man (USA)**[210] 3-8-11 .... AGarcia 9 103
(Kiaran McLaughlin, U.S.A) **58/10[3]**
8 *1* **Mafaaz**[24] 863 3-8-11 ....(b) RHills 5 101
(J H M Gosden) *raced in 4th early, 7th straight, soon ridden and one pace* **92/10**
9 *2 ¼* **Theregoesjojo (USA)**[14] 3-8-11 .... CHBorel 3 96
(Kenneth McPeek, U.S.A) **41/10[2]**
10 *3* **Patena (USA)**[28] 3-8-11 .... RAlbarado 1 91
(Richard Dutrow Jr, U.S.A) **13/1**
11 *4 ¾* **Cliffy's Future (USA)**[21] 3-8-11 ....(b) JLCastanon 4 82
(Darrin Miller, U.S.A) **42/1**
1m 49.26s (109.26) 11 Ran SP% **119.6**
PARI-MUTUEL (including $2 stake): WIN 30.60; PL (1-2) 11.00, 4.20;SHOW (1-2-3) 7.00, 3.00, 7.20; SF 117.60.
Owner Thomas R McCarthy **Bred** Mr & Mrs R David Randal **Trained** USA

NOTEBOOK
Mafaaz, a winner of both his previous starts on Polytrack, including the race over this trip at Kempton which earned him a place in the Kentucky Derby proper, was keen early and found the step up in grade too much for him in the latter stages. It is unlikely that he will take his place at Churchill Downs now.
Theregoesjojo(USA) has been supplemented for the Epsom Derby but was well beaten here.

[1096]MUSSELBURGH (R-H)
Sunday, April 12
OFFICIAL GOING: Good to firm (firm in places) (8.7)
Wind: Virtually nil Weather: Fine and dry

1226 TOTEPLACEPOT (S) STKS 1m 1f
2:20 (2:21) (Class 6) 3-Y-O+ **£1,942** (£578; £288; £144) **Stalls High**

Form RPR
0-55 1 **Masterofceremonies**[12] 660 6-9-10 64..................(b) RoystonFfrench 9 66
(James Moffatt) *s.i.s and rel to r: bhd tl hdwy wl over 1f out: swtchd lft and rdn ent fnl f: styd on strly to ld last 100yds* **9/1**
50-6 2 *1 ¾* **Lucayan Dancer**[16] 981 9-9-10 70.................. AdrianTNicholls 3 62+
(D Nicholls) *hld up in rr: hdwy 3f out: effrt and nt clr run wl over 1f out: sn swtchd lft and styng on whn sltly hmpd ent fnl f: kpt on u.p* **5/2[2]**
0-04 3 *4* **Keisha Kayleigh (IRE)**[14] 1020 6-9-5 67..................(p) NCallan 7 49
(B Ellison) *hld up: hdwy 3f out and sn pushed along: rdn to chse ldrs 2f out: swtchd lft over 1f out: sn drvn and kpt on same pce* **2/1[1]**
610- 4 *2 ¼* **Jane Of Arc (FR)**[121] 6806 5-9-0 52.................. GaryBartley(5) 10 44
(J S Goldie) *hld up in tch: rdn along over 2f out: sn drvn and kpt on same pce* **9/2[3]**
00-4 5 *nk* **Sparky Vixen**[33] 792 5-9-2 47.................. KellyHarrison(3) 1 43
(C J Teague) *cl up: effrt 3f out: rdn to ld over 2f out: drvn over 1f out: hdd ins fnl f and wknd* **10/1**
0-05 6 *¾* **Teddy West (IRE)**[20] 938 3-8-3 52 ow1..............(b[1]) WilliamCarson(5) 2 44
(Patrick Morris) *trckd ldng pair: swtchd lft and effrt 2f out: sn rdn and hung rt over 1f out: drvn and edgd lft ent fnl f: wknd* **18/1**
40-0 7 *nk* **Jalamid (IRE)**[41] 735 7-9-10 40..................(t) TonyHamilton 5 46
(M A Barnes) *mde most tl rdn and hdd over 2f out: sn wknd* **28/1**
000- 8 *9* **Ernies Keep**[161] 7148 3-8-7 45.................. TWilliams 4 23
(W Storey) *chsd ldrs: rdn along 3f out: drvn 2f out and sn wknd* **100/1**
0 9 *¾* **Just Pickles**[11] 1057 4-9-10 0.................. PJMcDonald 8 26
(G A Swinbank) *t.k.h: hld up: a towards rr* **20/1**
1m 52.15s (-2.55) **Going Correction** -0.40s/f (Firm)
WFA 3 from 4yo+ 17lb 9 Ran SP% **113.6**
Speed ratings (Par 101): **95,93,89,87,87 86,86,78,78**
toteswinger: 1&2 £4.90, 1&3 £4.40, 2&3 £1.70. CSF £30.83 TOTE £9.00: £2.30, £1.40, £1.30; EX 33.10.There was no bid for the winner.
Owner Alan Macleod **Bred** C J Hill **Trained** Cartmel, Cumbria
FOCUS
A few of these looked ill at ease on ground that appeared to be riding very fast. An ordinary seller and the leaders went off too quick, setting this up for the closers.

1227 TOTESWINGER H'CAP 5f
2:50 (2:50) (Class 4) (0-85,84) 4-Y-O+
£6,231 (£1,866; £933; £467; £233; £117) **Stalls Low**

Form RPR
15-1 1 **Jaconet (USA)**[41] 738 4-9-1 78..................(b) PhillipMakin 6 90
(T D Barron) *trckd ldrs: n.m.r and swtchd lft wl over 1f out: rdn and hdwy ent fnl f: led last 100yds* **11/2[1]**
0-02 2 *1* **Sandwith**[9] 1096 6-8-10 73.................. GrahamGibbons 12 81
(A G Foster) *qckly away and sn cl up: rdn over 1f out and ev ch tl drvn and nt qckn last 100yds* **11/2[1]**
263- 3 *¾* **Steelcut**[226] 5467 5-8-11 74.................. TonyHamilton 4 79
(R A Fahey) *chsd ldrs: effrt whn n.m.r over 1f out: swtchd lft and rdn ent fnl f: fin wl* **8/1[3]**
45-2 4 *nse* **Rothesay Dancer**[23] 901 6-8-7 73.................. KellyHarrison(3) 3 78
(J S Goldie) *hld up towards rr: hdwy 2f out: chsd ldrs whn n.m.r over 1f out: swtchd rt and styd on ins fnl f* **10/1**
462- 5 *hd* **Le Toreador**[156] 7222 4-9-2 79.................. NCallan 2 83
(K A Ryan) *led: rdn and hung rt over 1f out: drvn ent fnl f: hdd & wknd last 100yds* **8/1[3]**
-230 6 *1 ¼* **Silvanus (IRE)**[23] 901 4-8-11 74.................. PaulMulrennan 7 74
(I Semple) *plld hrd: chsd ldrs: rdn along over 1f out: sn one pce* **7/1[2]**
1313 7 *hd* **Blue Tomato**[9] 1104 8-8-11 79.................. WilliamCarson(5) 14 78
(D Nicholls) *hld up and bhd: hdwy over 1f out: rdn and styd on ins fnl f: nrst fin* **11/1**
500- 8 *nse* **Cape Vale (IRE)**[254] 4591 4-9-7 84.................. AdrianTNicholls 9 83
(D Nicholls) *cl up: rdn along 2f out: grad wknd* **8/1[3]**
40-6 9 *2 ½* **Highland Warrior**[25] 870 10-8-12 75.................. JamieMoriarty 13 65
(P T Midgley) *a towards rr* **25/1**
1113 10 *½* **Nickel Silver**[79] 270 4-9-5 82..................(b) TomEaves 5 70
(B Smart) *hld up: plld hrd and sn in midfield: effrt wl over 1f out: sn rdn and btn* **7/1[2]**
06-0 11 *1 ½* **Brut**[9] 1096 7-7-11 65 oh1..................(p) DanielleMcCreery(5) 11 48
(D W Barker) *a in rr* **40/1**
120- 12 *4* **Harlech Castle**[143] 7394 4-9-5 82..................(b) MartinDwyer 8 50
(P F I Cole) *sn outpcd and a in rr* **12/1**
000- 13 *4 ½* **Seafield Towers**[5] 7218 9-8-8 71 oh20 ow6.......... PatrickMathers 10 23
(D A Nolan) *midfield: rdn along and wknd 1/2-way* **250/1**
57.89 secs (-2.51) **Going Correction** -0.40s/f (Firm) 13 Ran SP% **120.9**
Speed ratings (Par 105): **104,102,101,101,100 98,98,98,94,93 91,84,77**
toteswinger: 1&2 £8.60, 1&3 £12.50, 2&3 £13.40. CSF £34.47 CT £255.18 TOTE £6.90: £2.10, £2.30, £4.10; EX 45.70.
Owner R G Toes **Bred** Team Block **Trained** Maunby, N Yorks
FOCUS
A good, competitive sprint handicap, and a race that should produce some nice winners in similar company over the next few weeks.
Le Toreador ◆ Official explanation: jockey said gelding hung right in the last two furlongs
Harlech Castle Official explanation: jockey said gelding was unsuited by the good to firm, firm in places ground

1228 TOTEQUADPOT MAIDEN STKS 7f 30y
3:20 (3:22) (Class 5) 3-Y-O+ **£2,590** (£770; £385; £192) **Stalls High**

Form RPR
540- 1 **Desire To Excel (IRE)**[289] 3444 3-8-13 71.................. MartinDwyer 6 72
(P F I Cole) *mde all: rdn along 2f out: drvn over 1f out: styd on gamely* **8/1[3]**
0-25 2 *hd* **Campli (IRE)**[20] 939 7-9-6 62.................. LanceBetts(7) 7 76
(B Ellison) *hld up towards rr: hdwy over 2f out: rdn over 1f out: styd on strly ins fnl f: jst failed* **12/1**
303- 3 *nk* **Kersivay**[205] 6087 3-8-13 77.................. TonyHamilton 10 70
(D W Barker) *trckd ldrs on inner: hdwy to chal 2f out: sn rdn and ev ch tldrvn and no ex wl ins fnl f* **12/1**

00-5 **4** *3 ¼* **Olympic Dream**[14] [1015] 3-8-13 77.................. JamieMoriarty 3 61
(R A Fahey) *chsd ldrs on outer: hung lft home bnd: rdn over 2f out and kpt on same pce* **6/1**[2]

322- **5** *1* **Striker Torres (IRE)**[170] [6944] 3-8-13 81.................. TomEaves 11 59
(B Smart) *prom: effrt 3f out and sn cl up: rdn and ev ch over 2f out: drvn over 1f out: wknd ent fnl f* **8/11**[1]

0 **6** *1 ¾* **Winrob**[14] [1015] 3-8-13 0.................. NCallan 1 54
(Patrick Morris) *towards rr: hdwy 3f out: rdn along over 2f out: no imp appr fnl f* **40/1**

25- **7** *1* **Lily Jicaro (IRE)**[159] [7172] 3-8-8 0 ow3.................. RussellKennemore(3) 8 49
(Mrs L Williamson) *chsd ldrs: rdn along over 2f out: grad wknd* **50/1**

600 **8** *¾* **Aegean Pride**[51] [626] 4-9-3 46.................. SladeO'Hara(5) 9 49
(A Berry) *in tch on inner: rdn along over 2f out and sn wknd* **80/1**

5 **9** *2 ¾* **Funky Munky**[26] [855] 4-9-13 0.................. PJMcDonald 12 47
(G A Swinbank) *a towards rr* **16/1**

10 *3* **Toujours Souriante** 3-8-8 0.................. RoystonFfrench 2 29
(M Johnston) *sn outpcd and a bhd* **12/1**

11 *3 ½* **Miss Dee Lady (IRE)** 3-8-8 0.................. NeilPollard 4 19
(Patrick Morris) *green and a in rr* **125/1**

1m 28.02s (-2.28) **Going Correction** -0.40s/f (Firm)
WFA 3 from 4yo+ 14lb **11** Ran SP% **118.7**
Speed ratings (Par 103): **97,96,96,92,91 89,88,87,84,81 77**
toteswinger: 1&2 £15.70, 1&3 £9.90, 2&3 £22.60. CSF £98.76 TOTE £8.80: £2.00, £3.00, £3.10; EX 143.50.
Owner H R H Sultan Ahmad Shah **Bred** Glending Bloodstock **Trained** Whatcombe, Oxon

FOCUS
A modest maiden.
Striker Torres(IRE) Official explanation: trainer said colt was unsuited by the good to firm, firm in places ground

1229 TOTESUPER7 EASTER H'CAP 7f 30y
3:50 (3:52) (Class 4) (0-85,83) 4-Y-O+
£6,231 (£1,866; £933; £467; £233; £117) **Stalls** High

Form RPR

2400 **1** **Excusez Moi (USA)**[14] [1016] 7-9-4 83.................. (p) AndrewElliott 7 89
(Mrs R A Carr) *hld up: hdwy over 2f out: swtchd outside and rdn over 1f out: str run ins fnl f to ld nr line* **13/2**[3]

00-0 **2** *nk* **Captain Jacksparra (IRE)**[14] [1016] 5-9-0 79.................. (p) NCallan 4 84
(K A Ryan) *trckd ldrs: hdwy over 2f out: rdn over 1f out: led jst ins fnl f: sn drvn: hdd abnd no ex nr finiah* **17/2**

1122 **3** *hd* **Stonecrabstomorrow (IRE)**[9] [1103] 6-8-7 72.................. (b) TonyHamilton 6 76
(R A Fahey) *hld up in tch: hdwy over 2f out: rdn wl over 1f out: drvn and ev ch ins fnl f: edgd lft and no ex towards fin* **7/1**

05-5 **4** *2 ¼* **Chartist**[10] [1089] 4-9-1 80.................. AdrianTNicholls 9 78
(D Nicholls) *t.k.h: led: rdn and qcknd over 2f out: drvn over 1f out: hdd and one pce ins fnl f* **8/1**

5441 **5** *2* **Just Bond (IRE)**[9] [1100] 7-9-1 80.................. PJMcDonald 11 73
(G R Oldroyd) *hld up in midfield: hdwy over 2f out: sn rdn and no imp appr fnl f* **9/2**[1]

004- **6** *½* **Esoterica (IRE)**[155] [7239] 6-8-7 77.................. GaryBartley(5) 12 69
(J S Goldie) *hld up in midfield: hdwy over 2f out: sn rdn and no imp appr fnl f* **8/1**

13-0 **7** *½* **Talk Of Saafend (IRE)**[9] [1100] 4-9-1 80.................. PaulMulrennan 3 70
(P Monteith) *prom rdn along over 2f out: grad wknd* **16/1**

4416 **8** *2 ½* **Captain Macarry (IRE)**[14] [1016] 4-8-10 75.................. (v) TomEaves 8 59
(B Smart) *chsd ldr: hdwy to chal 3f out: sn rdn and wknd over 1f out* **6/1**[2]

-502 **9** *½* **Casino Night**[8] [1123] 4-8-2 72.................. DeanHeslop(5) 1 54
(R Johnson) *stdd s: hld up and a in rr* **14/1**

10-0 **10** *2* **Cigalas**[9] [1100] 4-8-11 79.................. NeilBrown(3) 5 56
(Mrs J C McGregor) *stdd s: a in rr* **66/1**

104- **11** *4 ½* **Golden Penny**[175] [6841] 4-8-10 75.................. RoystonFfrench 2 40
(A G Foster) *a in rr* **9/1**

1m 26.62s (-3.68) **Going Correction** -0.40s/f (Firm) **11** Ran SP% **115.1**
Speed ratings (Par 105): **105,104,104,101,99 99,98,95,95,92 87**
toteswinger: 1&2 £10.50, 1&3 £13.60, 2&3 £17.20. CSF £59.40 CT £398.86 TOTE £8.80: £2.40, £2.40, £2.10; EX 71.60.
Owner S B Clark **Bred** Lyons Demesne **Trained** Huby, N Yorks
■ Stewards' Enquiry : Tony Hamilton one-day ban: careless riding (Apr 26)

FOCUS
A fair handicap, and a decent pace on quick ground resulted in a time only 0.32 seconds outside the track record.

1230 TOTESPORT.COM MUSSELBURGH GOLD CUP (HANDICAP STKS) 1m 6f
4:20 (4:22) (Class 4) (0-85,83) 4-Y-O+
£12,462 (£3,732; £1,866; £934; £466; £234) **Stalls** High

Form RPR

222- **1** **Gordonsville**[156] [7223] 6-9-2 79.................. GaryBartley(5) 9 87
(J S Goldie) *hld up towards rr: hdwy 3f out: effrt on outer 2f out: rdn to ld 1f out: kpt on strly* **5/1**[2]

2121 **2** *2 ¼* **Phoenix Flight (IRE)**[18] [952] 4-9-8 83.................. SebSanders 13 88
(Sir Mark Prescott) *hld up: hdwy over 2f out: rdn and edgd rt over 1f out: swtchd lft and drvn ent fnl f: kpt on* **2/1**[1]

22-3 **3** *½* **Soundbyte**[18] [952] 4-8-12 73.................. JoeFanning 11 77
(J Gallagher) *hld up towards rr: hdwy on outer over 2f out: rdn and styd on strly ins fnl f: nrst fin* **7/1**[3]

50-4 **4** *1* **Step This Way (USA)**[11] [1059] 4-9-5 80.................. RoystonFfrench 1 83+
(M Johnston) *chsd ldrs: rdn along over 2f out: drvn and styng on whn hmpd ent fnl f: kpt on* **25/1**

00-0 **5** *½* **Film Festival (USA)**[15] [999] 6-8-8 73.................. LanceBetts(7) 7 75
(B Ellison) *chsd ldrs: rdn along 3f out: drvn 2f out: kpt on same pce* **15/2**

30-4 **6** *1 ¼* **Los Nadis (GER)**[9] [1102] 5-8-10 68.................. PhillipMakin 4 68
(P Monteith) *hld up towards rr: stdy hdwy 5f out: chsd ldrs 3f out: rdn to ld brieflyover 1f out: sn hdd & wknd ins fnl f* **11/1**

206- **7** *1 ¼* **Lets Roll**[156] [7223] 8-9-4 76.................. NCallan 2 75
(C W Thornton) *hld up in rr: sme late hdwy* **18/1**

50-2 **8** *shd* **Danzatrice**[9] [1102] 7-8-10 68.................. TomEaves 5 67
(C W Thornton) *hld up and bhd tl sme late hdwy* **14/1**

0/41 **9** *1 ¼* **Raucous (GER)**[9] [1099] 6-9-6 78.................. (b[1]) PaulMulrennan 12 75
(Mrs R A Carr) *led: rdn along 3f out: drvn 2f out: hdd & wknd over 1f out* **14/1**

110/ **10** *hd* **My Immortal**[22] [5087] 7-9-10 82.................. GrahamGibbons 14 79
(J J Quinn) *trckd ldrs on inner: effrt 3f out: rdn along 2f out: drvn and styng on whn hmpd and wknd appr fnl f* **8/1**

00-0 **11** *7* **Oddsmaker (IRE)**[8] [1123] 8-9-3 75.................. (t) TonyHamilton 8 62
(M A Barnes) *chsd ldr: effrt 3f out and sn rdn: cl up and drvn 2f out: wkng whn hmpd ent fnl f* **33/1**

2m 59.56s (-5.74) **Going Correction** -0.40s/f (Firm)
WFA 4 from 5yo+ 3lb **11** Ran SP% **119.1**
Speed ratings (Par 105): **100,98,98,97,97 96,96,96,95,95 91**
toteswinger: 1&2 £3.20, 1&3 £7.70, 2&3 £4.60. CSF £15.53 CT £71.84 TOTE £5.40: £1.90, £1.60, £2.10; EX 20.20 Trifecta £87.70 Pool: £201.70 - 1.70 winning units..
Owner Mrs Janis Macpherson **Bred** George Strawbridge **Trained** Uplawmoor, E Renfrews

FOCUS
A fair handicap and the pace seemed strong throughout.

1231 TOTESPORT 0800 221 221 MAIDEN STKS 1m 4f 100y
4:50 (4:51) (Class 5) 3-Y-O+ **£2,590** (£770; £385; £192) **Stalls** High

Form RPR

1 **Saga De Tercey (FR)**[21] 4-9-13 0.................. PJMcDonald 2 74+
(G A Swinbank) *trckd ldrs: effrt to chse ldng pair over 2f out: rdn wl over 1f out and sn rn green: drvn ins fnl f: styd on to ld last stride* **8/15**[1]

34-3 **2** *nse* **Dazzling Light (UAE)**[9] [1101] 4-9-3 73.................. GaryBartley(5) 7 69
(J S Goldie) *led: rdn along over 2f out: drvn ent fnl f: hdd on line* **10/3**[2]

-520 **3** *2 ½* **Longboat Key**[51] [621] 3-8-7 73.................. RoystonFfrench 8 68
(M Johnston) *trckd ldrs: squeezed through home bnd and sn cl up: rdn 2f out and ev ch tl drvn and wknd ins fnl f* **5/1**[3]

00-5 **4** *12* **Myshkin**[72] [343] 3-8-8 53 ow1.................. (b) TomEaves 6 51
(I Semple) *midfield: rdn along and outpcd 3f out: kpt on u.p appr fnl f: nvr a factor* **20/1**

0 **5** *1 ¼* **Carnival Fair**[8] [1128] 4-9-8 0.................. TonyHamilton 4 45
(R A Fahey) *hld up in rr: hdwy 3f out: rdn along 2f out: nvr rch ldrs* **33/1**

0-5 **6** *1 ¾* **Diktaram**[51] [621] 3-8-7 0.................. GrahamGibbons 3 46
(J R Weymes) *chsd ldrs: hmpd home turn: rdn along over 2f out and sn wknd* **33/1**

7 *24* **Bumble Rose (IRE)**[40] 6-9-9 0.................. NCallan 1 7
(A G Foster) *dwlt: hdwy to chse ldrs 1/2-way: rdn along over 3f out and sn wknd* **66/1**

8 *7* **Que Calor La Vida (FR)**[82] 5-9-9 0.................. LeeEnstone 5 —
(N Wilson) *dwlt: sn trcking ldrs: rdn along over 3f out and sn wknd* **100/1**

0- **9** *½* **Freedom Flying**[336] [1382] 6-9-9 0.................. JamieMoriarty 10 —
(Joss Saville) *a in rr* **100/1**

2m 41.97s (-0.03)
WFA 3 from 4yo 21lb 4 from 5yo+ 1lb **9** Ran SP% **119.1**
toteswinger: 1&2 £1.20, 1&3 £1.80, 2&3 £2.10. CSF £2.59 TOTE £1.70: £1.02, £1.30, £1.80; EX 3.00.
Owner Andrew Dick, Brian Dunn & Philip Holden **Bred** Haras De Tercey **Trained** Melsonby, N Yorks

FOCUS
This maiden only concerned three of the runners.
Que Calor La Vida(FR) Official explanation: jockey said gelding was unsuited by the good to firm, firm in places ground

1232 BET TOTEPOOL ON ALL UK RACING H'CAP 5f
5:20 (5:25) (Class 5) (0-75,74) 3-Y-O **£3,885** (£1,156; £577; £288) **Stalls** Low

Form RPR

451- **1** **Titus Andronicus (IRE)**[187] [6548] 3-9-7 74.................. NCallan 10 87
(K A Ryan) *cl up: led 2f out: rdn clr ent fnl f: kpt on strly* **9/1**

100- **2** *2* **Sloop Johnb**[232] [5277] 3-9-1 73.................. FrederikTylicki(5) 2 79
(R A Fahey) *chsd ldrs: rdn along wl over 1f out: kpt on ins fnl fin: nrst fin* **7/2**[2]

24-1 **3** *¾* **Hysterical Lady**[21] [920] 3-8-12 65.................. AdrianTNicholls 5 68+
(D Nicholls) *hld up towards rr: hdwy over 1f out: swtchd lft and rdn ent fnl f: styd onwl towards fin* **2/1**[1]

431- **4** *nk* **Grissom (IRE)**[156] [7219] 3-8-13 71.................. SladeO'Hara(5) 9 73
(A Berry) *chsd ldrs: hdwy on outer 2f out: sn rdn and kpt on same pce fnl f* **10/1**

0-33 **5** *½* **Where's Reiley (USA)**[17] [966] 3-8-11 64.................. (b) PhillipMakin 4 64
(T D Barron) *in tch: effrt 2f out: sn rdn and kpt on same pce* **8/1**

4-32 **6** *¾* **Dispol Grand (IRE)**[17] [966] 3-8-12 65.................. JoeFanning 8 63
(P T Midgley) *chsd ldng pair: rdn along 2f out: sn drvn and wknd appr fnl f* **5/1**[3]

310- **7** *3 ½* **Via Mia**[176] [6809] 3-9-6 73.................. MartinDwyer 1 58
(P F I Cole) *dwlt: a towards rr* **16/1**

610- **8** *¾* **Mythicism**[155] [7241] 3-9-4 71.................. (t) TomEaves 7 53
(B Smart) *a towards rr* **15/2**

-445 **9** *17* **Trick Or Two**[72] [350] 3-8-10 63.................. (b[1]) PaulMulrennan 3 —
(Mrs R A Carr) *led: rdn and hdd 2f out: sn wknd: stmbld bdly ins fnl f and eased* **25/1**

58.09 secs (-2.31) **Going Correction** -0.40s/f (Firm) **9** Ran SP% **123.9**
Speed ratings (Par 98): **102,98,97,97,96 95,89,88,61**
toteswinger: 1&2 £7.40, 1&3 £4.50, 2&3 £4.20. CSF £43.69 CT £92.46 TOTE £7.10: £2.30, £1.90, £1.60; EX 44.50 Place 6 £54.32, Place 5 £39.63.
Owner John Browne & Paddy McGinty **Bred** Tally-Ho Stud **Trained** Hambleton, N Yorks

FOCUS
A hot contest for the level, and a race that should produce a few winners.
Via Mia Official explanation: jockey said filly was unsuited by the good to firm, firm in places ground
Trick Or Two Official explanation: jockey said gelding lost it's action
T/Jkpt: £79,310.10 to a £1 stake. Pool: £111,704.47. 1.00 winning ticket. T/Plt: £75.70 to a £1 stake. Pool: £63,051.10. 607.58 winning tickets. T/Qpdt: £23.80 to a £1 stake. Pool: £4,212.90. 130.60 winning tickets. JR

1233 - 1236a (Foreign Racing) - See Raceform Interactive

1144 LONGCHAMP (R-H)
Sunday, April 12

OFFICIAL GOING: Good to soft

1237a PRIX DE LA GROTTE (GROUP 3) (FILLIES) 1m
2:50 (2:52) 3-Y-O **£38,835** (£15,534; £11,650; £7,767; £3,883)

RPR

1 **Tamazirte (IRE)**[44] 3-9-0.................. C-PLemaire 3 111
(J-C Rouget, France) *racd in 4th: wnt 2nd 1f out: led 100yds out: drvn out* **69/10**

2 *nk* **Soneva (USA)**[20] [941] 3-9-0.................. OPeslier 4 110
(Y De Nicolay, France) *racd in 5th: stl 5th 100yds out: fin wl* **37/10**[2]

3 ½ **Proportional**[189] 6519 3-9-0 .... SPasquier 1 109
(Mme C Head-Maarek, France) *racd in 2nd: disp ld jst under 2f out: rdn to ld 1 1/2f out: hdd 100yds out: one pce* **7/10**[1]

4 ¾ **Homebound (USA)**[173] 6891 3-9-0 .... IMendizabal 6 107
(J-C Rouget, France) *last to wl ins fnl f: fin wl* **12/1**

5 ½ **Rosey De Megeve**[20] 941 3-9-0 .... JMurtagh 2 106
(F Rohaut, France) *racd in 3rd: rdn and disputing 3rd ins fnl f: one pce* **19/1**

6 2 **Article Rare (USA)**[173] 6891 3-9-0 .... ACrastus 5 102
(E Lellouche, France) *set stdy pce: hdd 1 1/2f out: lost 2nd 1f out: wknd* **13/2**[3]

1m 42.78s (4.38) **Going Correction** +0.425s/f (Yiel) **6** Ran SP% **118.8**
Speed ratings: **97,96,96,95,94 92**
PARI-MUTUEL: WIN 7.90; PL 3.20, 2.70; SF 28.90.
Owner Ecurie Vallee Martigny & Mme L Rabineau **Bred** Churchtown Bloodstock Ltd **Trained** Pau, France

FOCUS
The time was three seconds slower than that for the Fontainebleau.

NOTEBOOK
Tamazirte(IRE) had previously hacked up in two minor races on the all-weather and fitness certainly played a role in her victory here. In fourth place running down the hill before the straight, she was then moved up to a challenging position a furlong and a half out. She took over from the favourite inside the final furlong and ran on well, holding on gamely in the final strides, and has now been marked down for the Pouliches.
Soneva(USA) was given rather a lot to do in a slowly run race as she was still towards the tail of the field at the entry to the straight. Engaging top gear a furlong and a half out, she made up a lot of ground and can be considered unlucky, but she will have a chance to take her revenge in the Pouliches.
Proportional, unlike the first two past the post, had not had the advantage of a previous run this season. Dropped in behind the leader, she went to the head of affairs halfway up the straight but didn't draw away from her rivals. She battled on gamely inside the final furlong and this race should certainly have brought her on. A run in the 1000 Guineas has now been ruled out and she heads for the Pouliches.
Homebound(USA), dropped out last for much of the race, had plenty to do when the field entered the straight. She suddenly switched on a furlong and a half out and finished really well.

1238a PRIX DE FONTAINEBLEAU (GROUP 3) (COLTS) 1m
3:20 (3:21) 3-Y-O **£38,835** (£15,534; £11,650; £7,767; £3,883)

RPR

1 **Silver Frost (IRE)**[20] 942 3-9-2 .... OPeslier 2 113
(Y De Nicolay, France) *racd in 3rd: hdwy to ld over 1f out: sn rdn: r.o wl* **6/4**[1]

2 ½ **Westphalia (IRE)**[169] 6998 3-9-2 .... JMurtagh 4 112
(A P O'Brien, Ire) *racd in 4th: effrt 2f out: hdwy to take 2nd ins fnl f: kpt on: nrst fin* **16/5**[2]

3 1 ½ **Oiseau De Feu (USA)**[30] 3-9-2 .... C-PLemaire 8 109
(J-C Rouget, France) *last to 1f out: fin wl* **41/10**[3]

4 snk **Set Sail (IRE)**[169] 6973 3-9-2 .... JAHeffernan 3 108
(A P O'Brien, Ire) *set str pce and sn 4 l clr: hdd over 1f out: lost 3rd cl home* **16/5**[2]

5 1 ½ **Broken In Light (FR)**[24] 887 3-9-2 ....(b) GMillet 6 105
(T Larriviere, France) *racd in 7th: kpt on steadily down ins fnl 2f* **37/1**

6 ¾ **Milanais (FR)**[20] 942 3-9-2 .... CNora 7 103
(B De Watrigant, France) *racd in 6th: one pce fnl 2f* **121/10**

7 snk **Take D'Or (FR)**[23] 3-9-2 .... DBonilla 1 103
(F Head, France) *chsd clr ldr tl wknd over 1f out* **12/1**

8 2 ½ **Sand Tiger (IRE)**[171] 3-9-2 .... MGuyon 5 97
(A Fabre, France) *racd in 5th: wknd over 1f out* **51/10**

1m 39.49s (1.09) **Going Correction** +0.425s/f (Yiel) **8** Ran SP% **141.6**
Speed ratings: **113,112,111,110,109 108,108,105**
PARI-MUTUEL: WIN 2.50; PL 1.20, 1.50, 1.40; DF 5.20.
Owner J D Cotton **Bred** Skymarc Farm **Trained** France

NOTEBOOK
Silver Frost(IRE) was suited by the decent gallop. Settled in third position in the early stages, he was brought with a well-timed run from halfway up the straight. He looked likely to be an easy winner at the furlong marker but had to be shaken up to hold the runner-up. Now the winner of three Group 3 races, he heads for the Poulains next.
Westphalia(IRE) was settled in fifth position in the early stages of this mile and was outpaced when things quickened up in the straight. He then started to run on throughout the final furlong and a half but never got a real blow in at the winner, who had already had a previous run. He could come back for the Poulains next month.
Oiseau De Feu(USA), given a waiting race, wasn't really seen until making his challenge up the centre of the track from a furlong and a half out, but he ran on really well in the dying stages. Racing in this company for the first time, it was a decent effort, but his best performances have come over shorter.
Set Sail(IRE) tried to make all the running and kept up the good work until the bitter end. He was well clear of the others before the straight and still held the advantage a furlong and a half out, but he was then one-paced until the line.

1239a PRIX LA FORCE (GROUP 3) 1m 2f
3:50 (3:49) 3-Y-O **£38,835** (£15,534; £11,650; £7,767; £3,883)

RPR

1 **On Est Bien (IRE)**[14] 1028 3-9-2 .... ACrastus 4 114
(E Lellouche, France) *racd in 3rd: 4th st: smooth hdwy to ld over 1 1/2f out: rdn ins fnl f: r.o wl* **69/10**

2 2 ½ **Topclas (FR)**[17] 3-9-2 .... SPasquier 1 109
(P Demercastel, France) *plld hrd in 5th: hdwy down outside to take 2nd under 1 1/2f out: kpt on by a hld* **11/2**

3 2 **Black Bear Island (IRE)**[251] 4884 3-9-2 .... JMurtagh 6 105+
(A P O'Brien, Ire) *racd in 4th: wnt 3rd over 4f out: no room bhd toiling ldrs under 2f out tl squeezed between them over 1f out: kpt on fnl f* **13/10**[1]

4 2 ½ **Mistaken Identity (FR)**[159] 3-9-2 .... TThulliez 5 100
(P Bary, France) *dropped out in last: stl last 1f out: styd on wl fnl f* **17/1**

5 5 **Sokar (FR)**[29] 845 3-9-2 .... OPeslier 2 90
(J Boisnard, France) *plld hrd in 2nd: wknd over 1 1/2f out* **53/10**[3]

6 ½ **War Power (USA)**[31] 3-9-2 .... C-PLemaire 3 89
(J-C Rouget, France) *set stdy pce: hdd & wknd over 1 1/2f out* **16/5**[2]

2m 9.56s (5.56) **Going Correction** +0.425s/f (Yiel) **6** Ran SP% **116.8**
Speed ratings: **106,104,102,100,96 96**
PARI-MUTUEL: WIN 7.90; PL 3.40, 3.40; SF 33.30.
Owner Mme D Lellouche **Bred** E Lellouche **Trained** Lamorlaye, France

NOTEBOOK
On Est Bien(IRE) recorded something of a surprise victory, but it was a stylish one, by a colt who is not fashionably bred. Travelling easily throughout, he quickened impressively to take control of the race halfway up the straight and then cruised to the line. This was a truly impressive performance and he could now be supplemented into the Prix du Jockey-Club.
Topclas(FR), held up towards the tail of the field in the early stages, came too late and never looked like pegging back the winner in the final furlong. He held onto second place with plenty in hand, though.
Black Bear Island(IRE), a brother to High Chaparral who won a Naas maiden on the second of his two starts last year, can be considered unlucky as he had nowhere to go when things suddenly quickened up before the final furlong. Once the space opened up he did run on, but the race for first and second place was already over. This performance is best forgotten and he should definitely be followed in the future. He looks like a type who needs to come with a progressive run.
Mistaken Identity(FR), last for much of the race, did make some progress but was never in the hunt for a first-three placing.

DUSSELDORF (R-H)
Sunday, April 12

OFFICIAL GOING: Soft

1240a RACEBETS - DUSSELDORFER STUTENPREIS (LISTED RACE) (FILLIES) 1m
4:00 (4:14) 3-Y-O **£11,650** (£4,272; £2,330; £583; £583)

RPR

1 **Norderney (GER)**[182] 3-9-2 .... AGoritz 3 102
(P Schiergen, Germany)

2 1 ¾ **Novita (FR)**[159] 7185 3-9-2 .... THellier 9 98
(P Schiergen, Germany)

3 1 ¼ **Greenisland (IRE)**[154] 7259 3-9-2 .... RobertHavlin 2 95
(H Morrison) *racd freely early: led to 1f out: one pce* **5/2**[1]

4 ¾ **Classic Summer (GER)**[168] 7006 3-8-10 .... WMongil 5 87
(M Trybuhl, Germany)

4 dht **Butterfly Lady** 3-9-2 .... EPedroza 1 93
(A Wohler, Germany)

6 nk **Ravenel (GER)** 3-8-10 .... LennartHammer-Hansen 7 87
(R Rohne, Germany)

7 ½ **Airforce (GER)** 3-8-12 .... ASuborics 6 88
(W Hickst, Germany)

8 hd **Fancy Diamond (GER)** 3-8-12 .... DPorcu 8 87
(Frau E Mader, Germany)

9 1 ¼ **First Lilly (GER)** 3-9-2 .... AHelfenbein 4 88
(Mario Hofer, Germany)

1m 40.56s (-0.60) **9** Ran SP% **28.6**
(including 10 Euro stake): WIN 57; PL 18, 13, 14; SF 109.
Owner Gestut Bona **Bred** Gestut Bona **Trained** Germany

NOTEBOOK
Greenisland(IRE), a winner over this trip on Polytrack when last seen in the autumn, is a keen sort and again made the running. She could not quite get home on the soft ground and will appreciate a return to faster but did at least earn black type.

REDCAR (L-H)
Monday, April 13

OFFICIAL GOING: Firm (10.6)
Wind: Nil Weather: Overcast

1241 MARKET CROSS JEWELLERS FILLIES' H'CAP 5f
2:00 (2:00) (Class 5) (0-70,70) 4-Y-O+ **£2,590** (£770; £385; £192) **Stalls** Centre

Form RPR

00-0 **1** **Darcy's Pride (IRE)**[10] 1096 5-8-6 **55** .... TonyHamilton 11 64
(D W Barker) *mde most: rdn over 1f out: drvn and styd on wl fnl f* **18/1**

64-0 **2** ½ **Comptonspirit**[10] 1103 5-9-2 **65** .... TomEaves 10 73
(B P J Baugh) *a.p: effrt and cl up 2f out: rdn over 1f out: drvn and ev ch ins fnl f: no ex towards fin* **7/1**[1]

234- **3** 1 ¼ **Gap Princess (IRE)**[171] 6952 5-9-0 **70** .... TimothyAyres(7) 5 73+
(R A Fahey) *towards rr: hdwy and edgd rt 2f out: effrt on outer over 1f out: styd on strly ins fnl f: nrst fin* **12/1**

4030 **4** nk **Ask Jenny (IRE)**[5] 1182 7-8-8 **57** .... RobertWinston 6 59
(Patrick Morris) *in midfield: hdwy 2f out: sn rdn and kpt on ins fnl f: nrst fin* **11/1**

400- **5** ½ **Feelin Foxy**[166] 7081 5-9-5 **68** .... PaulMulrennan 15 68
(J G Given) *chsd ldrs: rdn along wl over 1f out: kpt on same pce ins fnl f* **8/1**[2]

-211 **6** nk **Handsinthemist (IRE)**[13] 1055 4-8-2 **58** .... PaulPickard(7) 14 57
(P T Midgley) *chsd ldrs on wd outside: rdn along 2f out: kpt on same pce appr fnl f* **7/1**[1]

-550 **7** 1 ¼ **Style Award**[26] 870 4-9-2 **68** .... KellyHarrison(3) 7 63
(W J H Ratcliffe) *stmbld bdly s: sn chsng ldrs: cl up over 2f out: sn rdn and wknd over 1f out* **7/1**[1]

000- **8** 1 ½ **Toy Top (USA)**[201] 6218 6-8-9 **58** ....(b) PhillipMakin 12 47
(M Dods) *chsd ldrs: rdn 2f out: drvn and wknd over 1f out* **9/1**[3]

006- **9** 1 ¾ **Lydia's Legacy**[275] 3955 4-7-9 **51** oh6 .... MarzenaJeziorek(7) 13 34
(T J Etherington) *dwlt: nvr bttr than midfield* **100/1**

2435 **10** 2 ¼ **Silk Gallery (USA)**[22] 920 4-8-3 **55** ....(t) AndrewMullen(3) 8 30
(E J Alston) *bmpd s and towards rr: hdwy 2f out: sn rdn and no imp appr fnl f* **12/1**

000- **11** 1 ½ **Revue Princess (IRE)**[279] 3811 4-9-2 **65** .... DavidAllan 1 34
(T D Easterby) *prom on outer: rdn along 2f out and sn wknd* **18/1**

50-0 **12** nk **Miacarla**[14] 1041 6-8-8 **60** ow2 .... NeilBrown(3) 3 28
(H A McWilliams) *prom: rdn along over 2f out and sn wknd* **33/1**

100- **13** 2 ¾ **Note Perfect**[139] 7444 4-8-3 **52** ....(b) DaleGibson 4 10
(M W Easterby) *a towards rr* **33/1**

-062 **14** 3 ½ **Just Joey**[10] 1091 5-8-10 **59** ....(b) NCallan 2 5
(J R Weymes) *prom: rdn along over 2f out and sn wknd* **12/1**

58.19 secs (-0.41) **Going Correction** -0.075s/f (Good) **14** Ran SP% **107.4**
Speed ratings (Par 100): **100,99,97,96,95 95,93,91,88,84 82,81,77,71**
toteswinger: 1&2 £31.00, 1&3 £37.30, 2&3 £17.80. CSF £123.10 CT £1375.99 TOTE £19.60: £5.00, £2.30, £4.10; EX 179.80.
Owner T Shepherd & A Turton **Bred** Leo Cox **Trained** Scorton, N Yorks

FOCUS
The ground was firm but there was a good covering of grass and no jar. In a modest fillies-only sprint handicap they raced right across the track but the main action was towards the stands' side. The form looks pretty sound for the grade.
Darcy's Pride(IRE) Official explanation: trainer said, regarding the improved form shown, mare was better suited by the firm ground
Style Award Official explanation: jockey said filly stumbled on leaving the stalls

1242 FREEBETS.CO.UK HAPPY EASTER REDCAR H'CAP — 2m 4y
2:35 (2:35) (Class 6) (0-65,64) 4-Y-O+ — **£1,942** (£578; £288; £144) **Stalls** Low

Form — RPR
/01- **1** **Northern Dune (IRE)**[107] 7792 5-9-1 **53** .... MickyFenton 10 60
(B J Curley) *hld up and bhd: hdwy 4f out: effrt on outer to chse ldrs 2f out and sn rdn: drvn to chse ldr ins fnl f: edgd lft and styd on to ld nr line* **7/1**[2]
600- **2** *hd* **Sonny Sam (IRE)**[22] 5833 4-8-10 **52** .... TonyHamilton 13 59
(R A Fahey) *in tch: hdwy 4f out: led over 2f out and sn rdn: hung lft and clr over 1f out: drvn ins fnl f: hdd nr line* **9/1**[3]
43-1 **3** *3* **Rare Coincidence**[7] 1154 8-9-12 **64** 6ex........(p) NCallan 17 68
(R F Fisher) *trckd ldr: led over 7f out: rdn along over 3f out: hdd over 2f out: sn drvn and kpt on same pce* **9/1**[3]
55-5 **4** *½* **San Deng**[12] 1058 7-8-13 **51** .... PhillipMakin 9 54
(Micky Hammond) *in midfield: hdwy on inner over 3f out: rdn 2f out: drvn and styd on appr fnl f* **12/1**
343 **5** *nse* **Miss Keck**[17] 978 5-9-9 **61** .... RobertWinston 3 65+
(G A Swinbank) *trckd ldrs on inner: effrt 4f out: pushed along and slty outpcd whn n.m.r 2f out: swtchd rt and rdn over 1f out: kpt on wl u.p towards fin* **7/1**[2]
22-6 **6** *1¼* **Mister Pete (IRE)**[12] 1058 6-9-7 **62** .... DominicFox(3) 2 63
(W Storey) *in tch: hdwy over 4f out: rdn to chse ldrs over 2f out: drvn and one pce fr wl over 1f out* **14/1**
360- **7** *hd* **Categorical**[43] 7128 6-9-10 **62** .... TomEaves 1 63
(K G Reveley) *hld up towards rr: hdwy 4f out: rdn along over 2f out: styd on appr fnl f: nrst fin* **9/1**[3]
52/0 **8** *2¼* **Zefooha (FR)**[16] 1000 5-9-2 **57** .... KellyHarrison(3) 5 56
(T D Walford) *trckd ldrs: hdwy over 5f out: chal over 3f out and ev ch tl rdn over 2f out and grad wknd* **4/1**[1]
15-3 **9** *5* **Bijou Dan**[12] 1058 8-9-11 **63** .... PJMcDonald 6 56
(G M Moore) *chsd ldrs: rdn along over 3f out: wknd over 2f out* **9/1**[3]
00-0 **10** *3* **Zabougg**[12] 1058 4-8-7 **49** .... RoystonFfrench 12 38
(D W Barker) *towards rr: effrt and sme hdwy over 3f out: nvr a factor* **33/1**
03-3 **11** *5* **Amir Pasha (UAE)**[10] 1102 4-9-1 **57** .... PaulMulrennan 11 40
(Micky Hammond) *nvr bttr than midfield* **16/1**
245- **12** *1* **Blue Jet (USA)**[161] 7169 5-8-10 **51** .... MichaelJStainton(3) 15 33
(R M Whitaker) *dwlt: a in rr* **9/1**[3]
00-0 **13** *22* **Piccolo Pete**[9] 1127 4-8-3 **52** .... PaulPickard(7) 8 7
(R Johnson) *in rr fr 1/2-way* **66/1**
060/ **14** *22* **Slip Silver**[499] 6999 5-8-7 **45** .... DaleGibson 14 —
(R C Guest) *chsd ldrs: rdn along 4f out and sn wknd* **100/1**
0-0 **15** *93* **Bright Falcon**[56] 519 4-9-4 **60** ....(t) DarrenWilliams 4 —
(S Parr) *led: pushed along and hdd over 7f out: sn wknd* **80/1**
3m 29.41s (-1.99) **Going Correction** -0.075s/f (Good)
WFA 4 from 5yo+ 4lb — **15** Ran SP% **121.9**
Speed ratings (Par 101): **101,100,99,99,99 98,98,97,94,93 90,90,79,68,21**
toteswinger: 1&2 £23.10, 1&3 £19.60, 2&3 £20.80. CSF £68.55 CT £583.92 TOTE £11.20: £5.00, £3.80, £3.10; EX 156.90.
Owner Curley Leisure **Bred** Derek Iceton **Trained** Newmarket, Suffolk
FOCUS
A low-grade stayers handicap, a seller in all but name. The pace was just steady to the halfway point but increased markedly once they were in line for home. The form looks reasonable with the runner-up close to his best backed up by the fourth and sixth.
Zefooha(FR) Official explanation: jockey said mare was unsuited by the firm ground
Amir Pasha(UAE) Official explanation: jockey said gelding hung right-handed throughout

1243 FREEBETS.CO.UK BANK HOLIDAY FREE BETS (S) STKS — 7f
3:10 (3:11) (Class 6) 3-Y-O+ — **£1,942** (£578; £288; £144) **Stalls** Centre

Form — RPR
2303 **1** **El Dececy (USA)**[6] 1170 5-9-5 79 .... NCallan 10 68
(S Parr) *cl up: led after 2f: rdn wl over 1f out: drvn clr ins fnl f* **8/11**[1]
040- **2** *1¾* **Just Sam (IRE)**[188] 6562 4-8-7 46 .... BMcHugh(7) 8 58
(R E Barr) *a.p: cl up 1/2-way: rdn and ev ch 2f out tl drvn and one pce ins fnl f* **40/1**
20-5 **3** *2¾* **Baronovici (IRE)**[12] 1057 4-9-5 56 ....(p) TonyHamilton 4 56
(D W Barker) *in midfield: hdwy 2f out: rdn to chse ldng pair over 1f out: drvn and no imp ins fnl f* **28/1**
4322 **4** *2¼* **Aggbag**[17] 984 5-9-5 50 .... AndrewElliott 5 50
(B P J Baugh) *hld up towards rr: hdwy 2f out: sn rdn and styd on ins fnl f: nrst fin* **14/1**
0342 **5** *¾* **Wiltshire (IRE)**[22] 921 7-8-12 55 .... PaulPickard(7) 2 48
(P T Midgley) *towards rr: hdwy over 2f out: swtchd outside and rdn wl over 1f out: kpt on ins fnl f: nrst fin* **16/1**
00-0 **6** *1¾* **Flying Bantam (IRE)**[6] 1169 8-9-5 62 .... PaulMulrennan 6 43
(J R Norton) *towards rr: hdwy over 2f out: rdn and kpt on appr fnl f: nrst fin* **25/1**
7 *1½* **King Pin**[114] 4-9-5 0 .... PhillipMakin 16 39
(Miss Tracy Waggott) *s.i.s and bhd: hdwy 3f out: rdn wl over 1f out: kpt on ins fnl f: nrst fin* **100/1**
0-60 **8** *1* **Legendary Guest**[12] 1057 4-9-5 62 ....(v) TomEaves 18 36
(D W Barker) *in tch: hdwy over 2f out: sn rdn and no imp* **33/1**
000- **9** *nse* **Desert Hunter (IRE)**[146] 7375 6-9-2 44 .... MarkLawson(3) 9 36
(Micky Hammond) *chsd ldrs: rdn along wl over 2f out and grad wknd* **66/1**
220- **10** *¾* **Efidium**[191] 6482 11-8-12 65 .... GihanArnolda(7) 3 34+
(N Bycroft) *a towards rr* **12/1**[3]
2000 **11** *shd* **Louisiade (IRE)**[17] 984 8-9-2 45 ....(p) AndrewMullen(3) 12 34
(M C Chapman) *in midfield: rdn along 1/2-way: n.d* **66/1**
0-44 **12** *½* **Where's Killoran**[9] 1131 4-9-0 44 .... DavidAllan 14 27
(E J Alston) *chsd ldrs: rdn along 3f out: sn wknd* **33/1**
0-00 **13** *2½* **Carnival Dream**[40] 760 4-8-9 46 ....(p) SladeO'Hara(5) 19 21
(H A McWilliams) *in tch: rdn along 3f out: sn wknd* **100/1**
046- **14** *¾* **Premier Krug (IRE)**[118] 7694 3-8-0 51 ....(v) DaleGibson 13 19
(P D Evans) *a towards rr* **40/1**
0/0- **15** *1¼* **Crux**[376] 1138 7-9-2 54 .... NeilBrown(3) 7 20
(R E Barr) *s.i.s: a in rr* **40/1**
0-00 **16** *hd* **She's Our Dream**[20] 945 4-9-0 45 ....(t) SilvestreDeSousa 20 15
(R C Guest) *racd wd: in tch: rdn along 3f out and sn wknd* **100/1**
000- **17** *4* **Pennybid (IRE)**[87] 6215 7-9-5 43 ....(p) RoystonFfrench 11 9
(C R Wilson) *a in rr* **150/1**
006- **18** *½* **Andorn (GER)**[113] 7753 5-9-5 72 .... MickyFenton 17 8
(B J Curley) *chsd ldrs: rdn along wl over 2f out and sn wknd* **5/2**[2]
-006 **19** *7* **Mickys Mate**[12] 1061 4-9-2 45 .... KellyHarrison(3) 1 —
(A Crook) *a in rr* **100/1**
300- **20** *27* **Valiant Romeo**[227] 5452 9-9-5 44 .... RobertWinston 15 —
(R Bastiman) *led 2f: cl up tl rdn along 3f out and sn wknd* **100/1**
1m 23.94s (-0.56) **Going Correction** -0.075s/f (Good)
WFA 3 from 4yo+ 14lb — **20** Ran SP% **135.8**
Speed ratings (Par 101): **100,98,94,92,91 89,87,86,86,85 85,84,82,81,79 79,75,74,66,35**
toteswinger: 1&2 £16.00, 1&3 £11.70, 2&3 £42.40. CSF £60.79 TOTE £2.00: £1.40, £7.10, £5.00; EX 58.60.The winner was bought in for 13,500gns.
Owner Willie McKay **Bred** Shadwell Farm LLC **Trained**
■ Stewards' Enquiry : Paul Pickard one-day ban: careless riding (Apr 27)
FOCUS
Any price bar five and plenty of dead wood in the line-up for this non-handicap seller. The winner was in a different league but there was little solid behind.
Andorn(GER) Official explanation: jockey said horse was never travelling
Valiant Romeo Official explanation: jockey said gelding hung left-handed throughout

1244 SYD BURGESS OCTOGENARIAN H'CAP — 7f
3:45 (3:45) (Class 5) (0-70,70) 4-Y-O+ — **£2,590** (£770; £385; £192) **Stalls** Centre

Form — RPR
3415 **1** **Kipchak (IRE)**[6] 1169 4-9-1 **67** ....(p) RobertWinston 13 82
(A J McCabe) *mde all: rdn clr wl over 1f out: styd on* **7/2**[2]
60-0 **2** *1¾* **Maison Dieu**[22] 921 6-8-1 **56** oh1 .... AndrewMullen(3) 11 66
(E J Alston) *dwlt and hmpd s: in rr tl gd hdwy 2f out: sn rdn and styd on wl fnl f: nt rch wnr* **28/1**
054- **3** *3¼* **Baltimore Jack (IRE)**[185] 6628 5-8-7 **59** .... PJMcDonald 1 60
(T D Walford) *prom on outer: effrt over 2f out: sn chsng wnr: rdn over 1f out and kpt on same pce* **3/1**[1]
5F-0 **4** *nk* **Cheery Cat (USA)**[33] 811 5-8-4 **56** ....(p) RoystonFfrench 6 56
(D W Barker) *chsd ldrs: rdn along 2f out: drvn and kpt on same pce appr fnl f* **12/1**
225- **5** *¾* **Mandalay King (IRE)**[167] 7040 4-8-13 **65** .... DavidAllan 3 63
(Mrs Marjorie Fife) *hld up: hdwy over 2f out: rdn to chse ldrs over 1f out: sn one pce* **11/1**
00-0 **6** *½* **Forzarzi (IRE)**[55] 580 5-8-8 **63** ow3 .... NeilBrown(3) 9 60
(H A McWilliams) *hld up in rr: hdwy over 2f out: chsd ldrs over 1f out: sn rdn and no imp* **28/1**
026- **7** *5* **Top Tribute**[163] 7131 4-8-11 **63** .... MickyFenton 15 47
(T P Tate) *t.k.h: in tch: rdn along wl over 2f out and n.d* **8/1**[3]
566- **8** *2¾* **Buy On The Red**[120] 7675 8-9-1 **67** .... AdrianTNicholls 7 43
(D Nicholls) *hld up towards rr: sme hdwy 2f out: sn rdn and nvr a factor* **14/1**
003- **9** *1½* **Bentley**[164] 7118 5-8-10 **62** .... PaulMulrennan 8 34
(J G Given) *a in midfield* **25/1**
002- **10** *½* **Misplaced Fortune**[164] 7111 4-8-2 **59** .... Louis-PhilippeBeuzelin(5) 14 30
(N Tinkler) *a towards rr* **14/1**
160- **11** *10* **Slip Star**[193] 6419 6-8-5 **64** oh6 ow8 .... GihanArnolda(7) 12 8
(T J Etherington) *prom: rdn along 1/2-way: sn wknd* **66/1**
0- **12** *1¼* **Colombard (IRE)**[136] 7485 4-8-6 **58** .... NeilPollard 2 —
(Patrick Morris) *prom: rdn along 3f out: sn wknd* **28/1**
000- **13** *nk* **Shadowtime**[202] 6186 4-8-10 **62** .... PhillipMakin 4 2
(Miss Tracy Waggott) *prom: rdn along 3f out: sn wknd* **16/1**
-004 **14** *2½* **King Kenny**[9] 1132 4-9-4 **70** .... NCallan 10 3
(S Parr) *wnt rt s: t.k.h and sn chsng wnr: rdn along wl over 2f out and sn wknd* **8/1**[3]
1m 23.27s (-1.23) **Going Correction** -0.075s/f (Good) — **14** Ran SP% **120.4**
Speed ratings (Par 103): **104,102,98,97,97 96,90,87,85,85 73,72,72,69**
toteswinger: 1&2 £42.30, 1&3 £5.10, 2&3 £25.20. CSF £109.68 CT £342.27 TOTE £4.80: £1.90, £9.00, £1.60; EX 176.60.
Owner Timms, Lane & McCabe **Bred** Miss Mary Davidson & Mrs Steffi Von Schilcher **Trained** Averham Park, Notts
FOCUS
A modest handicap won from the front but not a strong race. The winner recorded a personal best though.
Forzarzi(IRE) Official explanation: jockey said gelding was denied a clear run
Bentley Official explanation: jockey said gelding hung right-handed throughout
Colombard(IRE) Official explanation: jockey said gelding hung left-handed throughout
Shadowtime Official explanation: jockey said gelding ran too free
King Kenny Official explanation: jockey said gelding lost its action

1245 FREEBETS.CO.UK FREE BETS MAIDEN STKS — 1m 1f
4:20 (4:20) (Class 5) 3-Y-O+ — **£2,590** (£770; £385; £192) **Stalls** Low

Form — RPR
1 **Warpedsenseofhumor (FR)** 3-8-11 0 .... IanMongan 2 76+
(H R A Cecil) *t.k.h early: mde all: shkn up and qcknd clr 2f out: rdn and edgd rt 1f out: jnd ins fnl f: kpt on wl* **85/40**[1]
5 **2** *hd* **Gilded Age**[14] 1034 3-8-11 0 .... RoystonFfrench 6 75+
(M Johnston) *trckd ldrs: hdwy on inner over 2f out: rdn to chse wnr 1f out: drvn and styd on to chal ins fnl f: no ex nr fin* **15/2**
325- **3** *3¼* **High Office**[166] 7073 3-8-11 72 .... TonyHamilton 1 68
(R A Fahey) *trckd ldrs: smooth hdwy over 3f out: chal over 2f out and sn rdn: drvn over 1f out and kpt on same pce* **9/4**[2]
00-0 **4** *2* **Vita Mia**[4] 1198 3-8-6 0 .... PaulDoe 4 59?
(P D Evans) *trckd wnr: effrt over 3f out: rdn over 2f out: sn drvn and one pce fr over 1f out* **50/1**
2 **5** *½* **Kefalonia (USA)**[19] 949 3-8-6 0 .... RobertWinston 7 58
(B W Hills) *trckd ldrs: hdwy over 3f out: rdn over 2f out: sn drvn and wknd over 1f out* **5/2**[3]
033 **6** *4½* **Rosko**[39] 767 5-9-7 66 .... LanceBetts(7) 8 57
(B Ellison) *a towards rr* **16/1**
5 **7** *3¾* **Den Maschine**[18] 970 4-10-0 0 .... TomEaves 9 48
(Ollie Pears) *a in rr* **66/1**
8 *nk* **Cosmic** 3-8-11 0 .... DavidAllan 3 44
(T D Easterby) *dwlt: a towards rr* **14/1**
1m 54.45s (1.45) **Going Correction** -0.075s/f (Good)
WFA 3 from 4yo+ 17lb — **8** Ran SP% **119.1**
Speed ratings (Par 103): **90,89,86,85,84 80,77,77**
toteswinger: 1&2 £3.50, 1&3 £2.80, 2&3 £4.00. CSF £19.91 TOTE £4.00: £1.60, £2.20, £1.30; EX 25.10.
Owner H E Sheikh Sultan Bin Khalifa Al Nahyan **Bred** Sheikh Sultan Bin Khalifa Al Nahyan **Trained** Newmarket, Suffolk

FOCUS
An interesting maiden with the third the best guide, but the time was moderate and the form may not prove reliable, although the principals can do better.
Kefalonia(USA) Official explanation: jockey said filly was unsuited by the firm ground

1246 BODDINGTONS REDCAR STRAIGHT-MILE CHAMPIONSHIP (H'CAP) (QUALIFIER) 1m
4:55 (4:55) (Class 4) (0-85,84) 4-Y-O+ **£4,857** (£1,445; £722; £360) **Stalls** Centre

Form RPR
20-1 **1** **Wovoka (IRE)**[9] 1123 6-8-9 **75**........................ TonyHamilton 4 80+
(D W Barker) *hld up in tch: hdwy on bit wl 2f out: squeezed through over 1f out: qcknd to ld ins fnl f* **11/4**[2]
651- **2** *1* **Charlie Tipple**[191] 6482 5-9-4 **84**........................(p) PaulMulrennan 5 87
(T D Easterby) *t.k.h: cl up: effrt 2f out: rdn and ev ch over 1f out: kpt on ins fnl f* **3/1**[3]
60-2 **3** *nk* **Bere Davis (FR)**[13] 1048 4-8-6 **72**........................ PaulDoe 2 74
(P D Evans) *t.k.h: set stdy pce: shkn up and qcknd 2f out: rdn and edgd lft 1f out: sn hdd and one pce* **5/2**[1]
4020 **4** *nk* **Stoic Leader (IRE)**[7] 1153 9-8-4 **70**........................ RoystonFfrench 3 71
(R F Fisher) *trckd ldrs: effrt 2f out: sn rdn and sltly hmpd appr fnl f: kpt on same pce* **10/1**
2-60 **5** *5* **Spin Again (IRE)**[12] 1060 4-8-7 **73**........................ AdrianTNicholls 7 63
(D Nicholls) *rrd s: t.k.h and sn cl up: rdn 2f out and outpcd appr fnl f* **13/2**
016- **6** *6* **Another Decree**[263] 4329 4-8-4 **70**........................ DaleGibson 6 46
(M Dods) *t.k.h: hld up in tch: pushed along over 2f out: sn rdn and btn* **12/1**

1m 37.13s (-0.87) **Going Correction** -0.075s/f (Good) **6** Ran SP% **110.4**
Speed ratings (Par 105): **101,100,99,99,94 88**
toteswinger: 1&2 £2.70, 1&3 £1.80, 2&3 £1.50. CSF £10.98 TOTE £3.50: £1.70, £2.10; EX 8.30.
Owner Dales Homes Ltd **Bred** Rathasker Stud **Trained** Scorton, N Yorks
FOCUS
The first of eight qualifiers with the £30,000 final in October. They went no gallop until after the halfway mark and the form is a bit messy.

1247 FREEBETS.CO.UK NEW LOOK WEBSITE H'CAP 5f
5:30 (5:31) (Class 6) (0-60,60) 3-Y-O **£1,942** (£578; £288; £144) **Stalls** Centre

Form RPR
36-5 **1** **Jethro Bodine (IRE)**[12] 1064 3-8-4 **49**........................(p) KellyHarrison(3) 3 56
(W J H Ratcliffe) *in tch on outer: gd hdwy 2f out: sn rdn and hung rt over 1f out: styd on to ld ins fnl f* **14/1**
2431 **2** *1 ½* **Fasliyanne (IRE)**[12] 1064 3-9-3 **59**........................(b) NCallan 4 61
(K A Ryan) *prom: led 1/2-way: rdn and edgd rt wl over 1f out: drvn ent fnl f: sn hdd and one pce* **9/4**[1]
5-24 **3** *1 ½* **Pinball (IRE)**[7] 1157 3-8-9 **58**........................ JamieKyne(7) 1 54+
(Patrick Morris) *wnt rt s: in tch: hdwy over 2f out: rdn and hung rt over 1f out: kpt on ins fnl f* **14/1**
0220 **4** *½* **Villaruz (IRE)**[12] 1075 3-9-4 **60**........................ RobertWinston 12 54+
(D Flood) *hld up in rr: hdwy over 2f out: nt clr run and swtchd lft over 1f out: sn rdn and styd on ins fnl f: nrst fin* **9/1**
0360 **5** *½* **Pedregal**[32] 817 3-8-4 **46** oh1........................ RoystonFfrench 6 39
(R A Fahey) *in rr: hdwy 2f out: sn rdn and kpt on wl fnl f: nrst fin* **8/1**[3]
004- **6** *2 ¼* **Wrens Hope**[202] 6183 3-8-9 **51**........................ TomEaves 11 36
(N Bycroft) *led to 1/2-way: sn rdn and grad wknd* **18/1**
3422 **7** *1 ¾* **Fashion Icon (USA)**[12] 1064 3-9-0 **59**........................ NeilBrown(3) 13 37
(T D Barron) *trckd ldrs: hdwy 2f out: sn rdn and btn over 1f out* **7/2**[2]
306- **8** *¾* **Chipolini (IRE)**[188] 6547 3-9-4 **60**........................ DNolan 7 36
(D Carroll) *sltly hmpd s: a towards rr* **40/1**
-302 **9** *½* **Simple Rhythm**[9] 1129 3-8-13 **60**........................ Louis-PhilippeBeuzelin(5) 9 34
(N Tinkler) *prom: rdn along 2f out: wkng whn n.m.r over 1f out* **8/1**[3]
0-54 **10** *1 ½* **Piccaso's Sky**[19] 955 3-8-8 **50**........................ NeilPollard 8 18
(A B Haynes) *wnt lft s: cl up tl rdn along 1/2-way and sn wknd* **11/1**
00-5 **11** *1 ¾* **Coniston Wood**[18] 968 3-8-6 **48**........................(b[1]) DaleGibson 10 10
(M W Easterby) *a towards rr* **25/1**

58.06 secs (-0.54) **Going Correction** -0.075s/f (Good) **11** Ran SP% **118.4**
Speed ratings (Par 96): **101,98,96,95,94 91,88,87,86,83 81**
toteswinger: 1&2 £6.80, 1&3 £18.70, 2&3 £6.90. CSF £45.93 CT £402.22 TOTE £15.10: £2.70, £1.40, £4.70; EX 37.50 Place 6 £86.23, Place 5 £24.78..
Owner J Sheard & W J S Ratcliffe **Bred** Ivan And Mrs Eileen Heanen **Trained** Newmarket, Suffolk
FOCUS
A low-grade three-year-old sprint handicap with traffic problems in running. There was no hanging about and the time was only just outside the record but the form is no more than modest.
T/Jkpt: Not won. T/Plt: £304.90 to a £1 stake. Pool: £47,855.71. 114.56 winning tickets. T/Qpdt: £17.00 to a £1 stake. Pool: £1,657.30. 71.85 winning tickets. JR

WARWICK (L-H)
Monday, April 13
OFFICIAL GOING: Good to firm (8.6)
Wind: Virtually nil Weather: Bright

1248 OFFCHURCH H'CAP 6f
2:20 (2:20) (Class 5) (0-75,74) 4-Y-O+ **£2,729** (£806; £403) **Stalls** Low

Form RPR
4652 **1** **Sarah's Art (IRE)**[7] 1152 6-8-9 **65**........................(t) TPQueally 6 71
(Stef Liddiard) *in rr: edgd lft over 3f out: gd hdwy fr 2f out: str run fnl f to ld last strides* **7/2**[2]
3113 **2** *nk* **Desert Dreamer (IRE)**[6] 1169 8-8-9 **70**........................ RichardEvans(5) 2 75
(P D Evans) *in rr and hmpd over 3f out: hdwy over 2f out: led 1f out: hdd and no ex last strides* **10/3**[1]
-222 **3** *nk* **War And Peace (IRE)**[17] 982 5-9-3 **73**........................ RichardHughes 1 77
(Jane Chapple-Hyam) *hld up towards rr: gd hdwy fr 2f out: chal fr 1f out: no ex last strides* **9/2**[3]
4340 **4** *nk* **Hart Of Gold**[7] 1152 5-8-12 **68**........................(p) AdamKirby 14 71+
(R A Harris) *in rr: hrd rdn and hdwy over 1f out: fin wl* **11/1**
000- **5** *½* **El Potro**[159] 7197 7-8-0 **61** oh10 ow1........................ MartinLane(5) 5 62
(J R Holt) *chsd ldrs: led over 2f out: hdd 1f out: wknd nr fin* **50/1**
12-0 **6** *¾* **I Confess**[87] 191 4-9-4 **74**........................ CatherineGannon 12 73
(P D Evans) *in rr: rdn and hdwy fr 2f out: styd on fnl f: nt rch ldrs* **25/1**
4430 **7** *3* **Music Box Express**[16] 996 5-8-2 **65**........................(t) MatthewDavies(7) 13 54
(George Baker) *chsd ldr: wd into st: styd chalng tl wknd fnl f* **10/1**
6003 **8** *½* **Berrymead**[10] 1091 4-8-9 **70** oh3 ow10........................(b) AnnStokell(5) 11 58
(Miss A Stokell) *chsd ldrs tl wknd fnl f* **50/1**
326- **9** *nk* **Red Amaryllis**[221] 5627 4-8-4 **60** oh1........................ RichardKingscote 9 47
(H J L Dunlop) *chsd ldrs 4f* **25/1**
0-66 **10** *1 ¼* **Trivia (IRE)**[28] 853 5-7-13 **60** oh5........................ SophieDoyle(5) 4 43
(Ms J S Doyle) *chsd ldrs 4f* **25/1**
020- **11** *2 ¾* **Baby Rock**[189] 6543 4-8-10 **66**........................ AlanMunro 7 40+
(C F Wall) *hmpd over 3f out: a in rr* **8/1**
0/1- **12** *1* **Miltons Choice**[356] 1534 6-8-4 **60**........................ LukeMorris 3 31
(J M Bradley) *hmpd over 3f out: a in rr* **20/1**
5-00 **13** *1 ¼* **Non Sucre (USA)**[12] 1072 4-8-9 **65**........................(b) TPO'Shea 10 32
(J Gallagher) *led tl hdd over 2f out: wknd rapidly* **33/1**

1m 11.25s (-0.55) **Going Correction** 0.0s/f (Good) course record **13** Ran SP% **115.2**
Speed ratings (Par 103): **103,102,102,101,101 100,96,95,95,93 89,88,86**
toteswinger: 1&2 £3.10, 1&3 £4.30, 2&3 £4.00. CSF £13.51 CT £51.70 TOTE £4.00: £1.70, £1.60, £1.90; EX 11.40.
Owner ownaracehorse.co.uk (Shefford) **Bred** Newtownbarry House Stud **Trained** Great Shefford, Berks
FOCUS
Only 5mm of rain had fallen on the track in the previous ten days and, despite putting 5mm of water on from the 7f marker, the ground was expected to ride quick. A modest handicap run at a decent pace that suited the hold-up horses but with several racing from out of the handicap not beaten far the form looks fairly ordinary.
Baby Rock Official explanation: jockey said gelding suffered interference in running

1249 BUDBROOKE (S) STKS 5f
2:55 (2:58) (Class 6) 2-Y-O **£2,047** (£604; £302) **Stalls** Low

Form RPR
1 **Transfixed (IRE)** 2-8-6 0........................ CatherineGannon 2 54
(P D Evans) *chsd ldrs: led ins fnl 2f: hung rt over 1f out: hld on all out* **5/1**[3]
0 **2** *nk* **Island Express (IRE)**[13] 1044 2-8-11 0........................ LukeMorris 4 58+
(J S Moore) *wnt rt s: in tch: rdn 2f out: hdwy: nt clr run and swtchd lft over 1f out: styd on to chse wnr ins fnl f: fin wl: jst failed* **9/4**[1]
0 **3** *1* **Vaduz**[10] 1090 2-8-6 0........................ EdwardCreighton 9 49+
(M R Channon) *chsd ldrs: rdn: chsd wnr and n.m.r appr fnl f: styd on same pce ins fnl f* **7/2**[2]
4 *1 ¾* **Needsamaite** 2-8-11 0........................ FergusSweeney 5 47
(D J S Ffrench Davis) *pushed rt s: outpcd and rdn 1/2-way: hdwy over 1f out: kpt on but nvr in contention* **12/1**
0 **5** *1 ¾* **Grace Jicaro**[16] 994 2-8-1 0........................ DeanHeslop(5) 11 35
(Mrs L Williamson) *veered rt s: sn pressing ldr: hung rt over 2f out: sn rdn: wknd fnl f* **5/1**[3]
6 *1 ¾* **Bathwick Gino** 2-8-12 0 ow1........................ SebSanders 1 34
(A B Haynes) *rdn and sn outpcd: sme hdwy fr 2f out: kpt on same pce fnl f* **15/2**
0 **7** *6* **Reel Easy**[16] 994 2-8-11 0........................ JerryO'Dwyer 3 9+
(J R Holt) *sn led: hdd ins fnl 2f: wkng whn n.m.r over 1f out* **33/1**
0 **8** *5* **Secret Rose**[14] 1031 2-8-6 0........................(t) TolleyDean 8 —
(W G M Turner) *in rr: effrt 2f out: nvr in contention and wknd over 1f out* **25/1**
U **New York Lights (IRE)** 2-8-6 0........................ JamesDoyle 12 —
(M D I Usher) *pushed rt s: continually bucked and ref to r: rdr bailed out sn after* **20/1**

61.98 secs (2.38) **Going Correction** 0.0s/f (Good) **9** Ran SP% **117.3**
Speed ratings (Par 90): **80,79,77,75,72 69,59,51,—**
toteswinger: 1&2 £5.00, 1&3 £4.20, 2&3 £3.50. CSF £16.57 TOTE £8.00: £2.00, £1.70, £1.70; EX 20.00.The winner was bought in for 6,000gns. Island Express was claimed by Miss A. Stokell for £6,000.
Owner Mrs I M Folkes **Bred** Rathasker Stud **Trained** Pandy, Monmouths
FOCUS
A very moderate seller and these two-year-olds showed their inexperience by following each other right over to the stands' rail when coming under pressure in the home straight. The form looks ordinary for the grade.
NOTEBOOK
Transfixed(IRE), who did not go off unbacked on this debut, was always close to the pace. She was one of those to hang markedly to her right when brought to challenge over a furlong from home and ended up right under the rail, but she maintained enough forward momentum to hold off the runner-up close home. A £5,000 filly out of an unraced half-sister to six winners, connections went to 6,000gns to retain her at the auction. (op 6-1 tchd 7-1)
Island Express(IRE), last of ten on his Folkestone debut despite going off second-favourite, was dropping in class here and was the subject of significant market support once again, but he handicapped himself with a slow break and then had a real problem keeping up at around halfway. He did stay on under strong pressure up the home straight and was forced to switch off the rail in order to get a run, but although he only just failed to get to the filly it would be pushing it to say he was unlucky. He is becoming expensive to follow. (op 8-1 tchd 2-1)
Vaduz, beaten less than four lengths when eighth of nine on her Bath debut, didn't have a great deal of room to play with entering the last furlong but her impetus wasn't affected and this looks as good as she is. (op 2-1)
Needsamaite, out of a dual winner at up to 7f, came from last to reach his finishing position so he deserves some credit for that even if the form of the race is weak. (op 8-1 tchd 7-1)
Grace Jicaro, 14th of the 19 runners in the Brocklesby on debut, swerved right exiting the stalls but was still able to race handily. However, she was inclined to race with her head in the air and was the first to hang right over to the stands' rail once in line for home and had little left when challenged. (op 9-1)
Reel Easy, beaten over 42 lengths when last of the 19 runners in the Brocklesby, showed much more this time but having taken the field along for a long way, he was already beaten when slightly intimidated by the winner.

1250 SNITTERFIELD MAIDEN STKS (DIV I) 7f 26y
3:30 (3:33) (Class 5) 3-Y-O **£3,070** (£906; £453) **Stalls** Low

Form RPR
1 **Mull Of Killough (IRE)** 3-9-3 0........................ AdamKirby 3 80
(J L Spearing) *hld up towards rr: stdy hdwy on ins fr 3f out: chsd ldr over 1f out: drvn to ld wl ins fnl f: r.o strly* **50/1**
66- **2** *1 ¼* **Alpha Tauri (USA)**[181] 6714 3-9-3 0........................ TPQueally 6 77
(H R A Cecil) *led after 2f: shkn up over 1f out: hdd and one pce wl ins fnl f* **9/4**[1]
43 **3** *2 ½* **Danies Boy (IRE)**[12] 1071 3-9-3 0........................ RichardHughes 2 70
(R Hannon) *led after 1f: hdd 5f out: chsd ldr tl over 1f out: sn one pce and edgd rt ins fnl f* **5/1**
2 **4** *4* **George Thisby**[15] 1015 3-9-0 0........................ JamesMillman(3) 1 59
(B R Millman) *chsd ldrs: pushed along 5f out: stl drvn along 3f out: wknd fnl f* **3/1**[2]
23- **5** *2 ½* **Arctic Freedom (USA)**[149] 7333 3-8-12 0........................ StephenDonohoe 10 47
(E A L Dunlop) *sn chsng ldrs: rdn over 3f out: wknd 2f out* **9/1**
0- **6** *2* **Desert Fever**[258] 4510 3-9-3 0........................ MichaelHills 11 47
(B W Hills) *led 1f: chsd ldrs: rdn over 3f out: wknd 2f out* **7/2**[3]
0-0 **7** *nk* **Bari Bay**[12] 1066 3-8-12 0........................ SebSanders 5 41
(R M Beckett) *chsd ldrs: sn rdn: wknd fr 1/2-way* **50/1**

The Form Book, Raceform Ltd, Compton, RG20 6NL

0- **8** *2 ¾* **Angelo Poliziano**[135] 7498 3-9-3 0 DO'Donohoe 7 39
(Mrs A Duffield) *s.i.s: hld up in rr: mod prog fr over 1f out* **66/1**

9 *1 ¼* **Royal Adelaide (IRE)** 3-8-12 0 FrankieMcDonald 4 30
(J A Osborne) *s.i.s: rdn 1/2-way: a towards rr* **50/1**

0- **10** *15* **Kirkson**[164] 7106 3-9-3 0 AlanMunro 8 —
(P W Chapple-Hyam) *a bhd* **33/1**

0-6 **11** *1 ¾* **Guga (IRE)**[17] 982 3-9-3 0 TonyCulhane 9 —
(George Baker) *a in rr* **66/1**

1m 23.94s (-0.66) **Going Correction** 0.0s/f (Good) **11** Ran SP% **116.5**
Speed ratings (Par 98): **103,101,98,94,91 89,88,85,84,66 64**
toteswinger: 1&2 £16.60, 1&3 £9.80, 2&3 £4.80. CSF £158.93 TOTE £36.90: £6.20, £1.40, £1.70; EX 422.20.
Owner Noel B Lawless **Bred** Owenstown Stud **Trained** Kinnersley, Worcs

FOCUS
An ordinary maiden on paper and a shock result, with the form best rated around the third for now.

1251 NORTON LINDSEY CONDITIONS STKS 7f 26y
4:05 (4:06) (Class 3) 4-Y-O+ **£7,771** (£2,312; £1,155; £577) **Stalls** Low

Form RPR

110- **1** **Plum Pudding (IRE)**[170] 6975 6-8-1 105 CharlesEddery(7) 6 109
(R Hannon) *mde all: clr over 3f out: rdn 2f out: hld on wl fnl f* **12/1**[3]

/53- **2** *1 ¼* **Dream Eater (IRE)**[299] 3119 4-8-8 111 (t) FrancisNorton 1 108+
(A M Balding) *hld up towards rr: hdwy on outside over 2f out: hung rt over 1f out: chsd wnr ins fnl f: clsng fast whn veered bdly lft cl home and nt rcvr* **15/8**[2]

5501 **3** *1 ½* **Carcinetto (IRE)**[10] 1094 7-8-3 87 CatherineGannon 4 97
(P D Evans) *chsd wnr: rdn over 3f out: lost 2nd over 2f out: chsd wnr again over 1f out but no ch: wknd ins fnl f and hld whn hmpd cl home* **20/1**

405- **4** *2* **Winker Watson**[198] 6270 4-8-8 115 AlanMunro 2 97
(P W Chapple-Hyam) *chsd ldrs: pushed along to chse wnr over 2f out but nvr any ch: wknd over 1f out* **8/15**[1]

000- **5** *17* **Iguacu**[303] 3033 5-8-1 37 MatthewDavies(7) 5 51?
(George Baker) *a in rr* **100/1**

1m 22.7s (-1.90) **Going Correction** 0.0s/f (Good) **5** Ran SP% **113.5**
Speed ratings (Par 107): **110,108,106,104,85**
toteswinger: 1&2 £4.70. CSF £35.85 TOTE £5.20: £2.30, £1.10; EX 24.30.
Owner Hyde Sporting Promotions Limited **Bred** Tom Deane **Trained** East Everleigh, Wilts

FOCUS
Effectively a four-horse race for this conditions event, or even a two-horse race according to the market, but ultimately a surprise result. The third is the best guide to the level with the winner not needing to run to his best.

NOTEBOOK
Plum Pudding(IRE) was given a very positive ride and reaped the benefit. Soon sent into a clear advantage, there was one stage in the home straight when it looked as though he might be caught, but he kept on finding a bit more and wanted it so much more than his rivals. All six of his previous wins have come on the Rowley Mile, but he has been only narrowly beaten a few times on turning tracks and he had no problem with the bend here. The problem for him now is that the form may be dubious with the odds-on favourite disappointing and the second-favourite proving very errant. He also had a bit to find with the two market leaders on these terms, so much now depends on whether the Handicapper takes this performance at face value. (op 8-1)
Dream Eater(IRE) was seen only twice last season when fifth in the 2000 Guineas and third in the Jersey Stakes and this was his first start since Royal Ascot. He was plenty keen enough off the pace early, but still looked the most likely of the chasing group to pick up the winner a furlong out. However, he swerved violently away to his left late on, ducking in behind the winner and hampering the third, but he was entitled to need this and connections believe he will come on plenty for it. The Group 2 Bet365 Mile at Sandown a week on Saturday may be next. (op 5-2)
Carcinetto(IRE) had a fitness advantage over her rivals, but had plenty to find with the principals at these weights. She had every chance and ran her race, but was already booked for third when getting a broadside from the runner-up. She has even more to lose than the winner if the handicapper takes the form literally, however. (tchd 25-1)
Winker Watson was disappointing as a three-year-old in view of how promising he looked at two, with his fourth of six behind Henrythenavigator in the Sussex Stakes the best of his four efforts. He didn't seem to get 1m in his two tries over it last term, but this was his first try over this trip and he was best in at the weights. The market suggested that he was expected to show much more here and he looked the part, but he didn't fire at all once the race began and never looked like getting to the winner. Connections could offer no explanation for this poor effort and he can only be watched until he shows more of his old sparkle. (tchd 1-2)

1252 SNITTERFIELD MAIDEN STKS (DIV II) 7f 26y
4:40 (4:43) (Class 5) 3-Y-O **£3,070** (£906; £453) **Stalls** Low

Form RPR

5- **1** **Maxwell Hawke (IRE)**[277] 3879 3-9-3 0 AlanMunro 1 79
(P W Chapple-Hyam) *t.k.h: trckd ldrs: wnt 2nd 2f out: chal over 1f out: drvn to ld jst ins fnl f: in command cl home* **13/8**[1]

346- **2** *½* **Izzi Mill (USA)**[165] 7097 3-8-12 72 MartinDwyer 4 73
(D R C Elsworth) *led: rdn 2f out: strly chal over 1f out: hdd jst ins fnl f: kpt on tl outpcd cl home* **10/1**

35- **3** *3 ¼* **Mister Fantastic**[273] 4014 3-9-3 0 LukeMorris 5 69
(N J Vaughan) *chsd ldr to 2f out: outpcd fnl f* **28/1**

00- **4** *¾* **Playful Asset (IRE)**[166] 7073 3-8-12 0 SebSanders 2 62
(R M Beckett) *chsd ldrs: drvn along over 3f out: one pce fnl 2f* **33/1**

06- **5** *1* **North Cape (USA)**[173] 6892 3-9-3 0 DaneO'Neill 8 65+
(H Candy) *trckd ldrs: shkn up 2f out and styd on same pce* **20/1**

3 **6** *¾* **African Cheetah**[15] 1015 3-9-3 0 J-PGuillambert 11 62+
(M Johnston) *in rr: drvn along over 3f out: styd on wl fnl f but nvr in contention* **3/1**[2]

043- **7** *nk* **Fortunate Bid (IRE)**[182] 6701 3-9-3 68 MichaelHills 10 62
(B W Hills) *chsd ldrs: rdn 3f out: wknd over 1f out* **10/1**

632- **8** *¾* **Cabernet Sauvignon**[127] 7593 3-9-3 76 EddieAhern 3 60
(J W Hills) *chsd ldrs to 2f out: sn wknd* **4/1**[3]

65- **9** *¾* **Wellesley**[117] 7709 3-9-3 0 AdamKirby 6 58+
(W R Swinburn) *broke wl: stdd towards rr but in tch tl outpcd 3f out* **20/1**

10 *29* **Dugatti** 3-9-3 0 FergusSweeney 9 —
(Mike Murphy) *plld v hrd early and stdd in rr: a bhd* **40/1**

11 *3 ¾* **Captain Peachey** 3-9-0 0 JamesMillman(3) 7 —
(B R Millman) *veered lft s and v green rdn 4f out: a towards rr: no ch fnl 2f and eased* **33/1**

1m 24.98s (0.38) **Going Correction** 0.0s/f (Good) **11** Ran SP% **122.6**
Speed ratings (Par 98): **97,96,92,91,90 89,89,88,87,54 50**
toteswinger: 1&2 £5.80, 1&3 £15.80, 2&3 £21.40. CSF £18.60 TOTE £3.40: £1.90, £2.60, £5.50; EX 28.80.
Owner The Comic Strip Heroes **Bred** Gigginstown House Stud **Trained** Newmarket, Suffolk

FOCUS
Not the strongest of maidens, but few could be ruled out entirely and betting was quite lively, with money for most of the market leaders and a couple of the newcomers attracting interest at long odds too. Nothing proved able to come from off the pace, and in a race in which a low draw looked an advantage the first four were in the first four or five from the start. The first two pulled clear of the pack, the entire field bar one having gradually crossed towards the stands' side, but the winning time was around a second slower than for the first division and the runner-up sets the level in an ordinary race.
North Cape(USA) Official explanation: jockey said filly hung right-handed
Captain Peachey Official explanation: jockey said colt ran green and hung right-handed

1253 HATTON H'CAP 7f 26y
5:15 (5:15) (Class 6) (0-60,60) 3-Y-O **£2,047** (£604; £302) **Stalls** Low

Form RPR

06-6 **1** **Solis**[34] 796 3-9-1 57 GrahamGibbons 3 64
(J J Quinn) *chsd ldrs: chal u.p over 1f out: led wl ins fnl f: hld on all out* **12/1**

360- **2** *½* **Diamond Daisy (IRE)**[178] 6785 3-9-3 59 TPQueally 6 65
(Mrs A Duffield) *towards rr: hdwy on ins fr 2f out: chal ins fnl f: kpt on but hld by wnr cl home* **14/1**

00-5 **3** *½* **Everaard (USA)**[14] 1036 3-9-3 59 AlanMunro 2 64
(D R C Elsworth) *slt ld: rdn fr 3f out: narrowly hdd wl ins fnl f: one pce cl home* **4/1**[2]

-601 **4** *1 ¼* **Location**[24] 900 3-9-0 56 StephenDonohoe 11 57+
(Ian Williams) *mid-div and in tch: rdn 3f out: hdwy over 1f out: fin wl but nt rch ldrs* **8/1**[3]

0-34 **5** *½* **La Gifted**[9] 1128 3-9-4 60 TonyCulhane 5 60+
(M R Channon) *in tch: rdn and one pce over 2f out: styd on again ins fnl f* **8/1**[3]

35-0 **6** *nk* **Crystallize**[14] 1036 3-9-2 58 SebSanders 7 57
(A B Haynes) *pressed ldr: rdn over 2f out: stl upsides over 1f out: wknd ins fnl f* **12/1**

0-54 **7** *½* **Dalepak Flyer (IRE)**[24] 900 3-9-3 59 PaulEddery 4 57
(Paul Mason) *in rr: hdwy on ins over 2f out and drvn to chal over 1f out: wknd ins fnl f* **9/1**

3000 **8** *¾* **Commandingpresence (USA)**[19] 960 3-9-3 59 (b[1]) JamesDoyle 9 55
(Ms J S Doyle) *plld hrd in rr: hdwy on ins over 2f out: rdn to press ldrs over 1f out: sn wknd* **22/1**

5-45 **9** *½* **Lady Salama**[46] 689 3-8-13 60 MartinLane(5) 10 54
(K R Burke) *in rr: rdn and sme hdwy 2f out: nvr gng pce to rch ldrs* **14/1**

-200 **10** *3 ¼* **Bold Ring**[11] 1084 3-9-1 57 EdwardCreighton 14 43
(E J Creighton) *chsd ldrs over 4f* **33/1**

3430 **11** *3 ½* **Private Passion (IRE)**[24] 900 3-9-0 56 J-PGuillambert 12 32
(Pat Eddery) *s.i.s: a towards rr* **12/1**

-262 **12** *1* **Miss Mojito (IRE)**[32] 817 3-9-4 60 MichaelHills 8 33
(J W Hills) *chsd ldrs 5f* **7/2**[1]

003- **13** *2 ½* **Rocksy**[231] 5364 3-9-4 60 TPO'Shea 13 27
(D J Coakley) *chsd ldrs tl wknd qckly over 2f out* **12/1**

1m 26.19s (1.59) **Going Correction** 0.0s/f (Good) **13** Ran SP% **125.8**
Speed ratings (Par 96): **90,89,88,87,86 86,85,85,84,80 76,75,72**
toteswinger: 1&2 £35.10, 1&3 £25.60, 2&3 £32.30. CSF £178.47 CT £609.07 TOTE £15.80: £4.80, £4.90, £2.00; EX 234.60.
Owner Ross Harmon **Bred** The Lavington Stud **Trained** Settrington, N Yorks

FOCUS
A very narrow weight range to this low-grade handicap, with only 4lb separating top from bottom, and just modest form. However, four of the 13 runners were unexposed handicap debutants, and the first two were among that quartet. Once again, a low draw looked an advantage but the form looks modest.
Solis Official explanation: trainer's rep, said regarding the improved form shown, gelding is a slow learner
Commandingpresence(USA) Official explanation: jockey said filly ran too freely
Miss Mojito(IRE) Official explanation: trainer had no explanation for the poor form shown

1254 WHITNASH H'CAP 1m 2f 188y
5:50 (5:50) (Class 6) (0-60,58) 4-Y-O+ **£2,047** (£604; £302) **Stalls** Low

Form RPR

10-0 **1** **Sagunt (GER)**[101] 18 6-8-12 52 JamesDoyle 5 58+
(S Curran) *hld up in mid-div: hdwy and nt clr run fr 2f out tl over 1f out: styng on whn bmpd jst ins fnl f: rapid hdwy to ld last stride* **16/1**

-224 **2** *nse* **Noah Jameel**[18] 969 7-9-1 55 FergusSweeney 1 61
(A G Newcombe) *chsd ldrs: rdn over 2f out: led appr fnl f: ct last stride* **3/1**[1]

45-6 **3** *¾* **Encore Belle**[20] 948 4-9-0 54 NeilChalmers 4 59
(Mouse Hamilton-Fairley) *mid-div: hdwy over 3f out: drvn to chal fr 2f out: one pce ins fnl f* **20/1**

000 **4** *hd* **Holoko Heights**[26] 869 4-9-1 55 LukeMorris 6 60+
(N J Vaughan) *hld up in rr: hdwy 3f out: trcking ldrs whn no room over 1f out: swtchd sharply rt jst ins fnl f: fin strly* **4/1**[2]

6-04 **5** *1 ¼* **Jackie Kiely**[41] 745 8-9-1 55 (t) J-PGuillambert 3 58+
(R Brotherton) *chsd ldrs: nt clr run fr over 1f out: styd on ins fnl f* **12/1**

0351 **6** *1 ¾* **The Graig**[18] 969 5-9-4 58 JerryO'Dwyer 12 58
(J R Holt) *led tl narrowly hdd 7f out: styd chalng and ev ch fr 2f out: one pce whn hmpd and wknd ins fnl f* **18/1**

5002 **7** *nse* **Red Current**[14] 1030 5-9-2 56 EddieAhern 16 55
(R A Harris) *stdd s and swtchd lft to ins: hld up in rr: hdwy on inner fr 3f out to over 2f out and ev ch over 1f out: sn wknd* **12/1**

2-60 **8** *1 ½* **Surprise Pension (IRE)**[16] 1000 5-9-3 57 GrahamGibbons 7 54
(J J Quinn) *in tch: hdwy to chse ldrs 5f out: rdn and one pce over 1f out: hmpd and wknd jst ins fnl f* **5/1**[3]

166 **9** *1 ¾* **Lady Aspen (IRE)**[14] 1037 6-9-2 56 (t) StephenDonohoe 11 50
(Ian Williams) *towards rr: rdn over 3f out: nvr bttr than mid-div* **25/1**

-560 **10** *2* **Debdene Bank (IRE)**[11] 1080 6-9-4 58 GeorgeBaker 2 52+
(Mrs Mary Hambro) *chsd ldr: slt advantage fr 7f out: rdn over 2f out: hdd over 1f out: one pce whn hmpd ins fnl f: nt rcvr and wknd qckly* **7/1**

1156 **11** *11* **Amber Moon**[17] 979 4-8-11 56 (b) AnnStokell(5) 13 28
(Miss A Stokell) *t.k.h: chsd ldrs tl wknd ins fnl 3f* **20/1**

202- **12** *1 ¼* **King Of Connacht**[133] 7518 6-9-1 55 AdamKirby 14 25
(M Wellings) *a towards rr* **12/1**

040 **13** *nse* **Aegean Rose**[19] 949 4-8-13 53 DaneO'Neill 9 23
(M Blanshard) *a towards rr* **33/1**

1-00 **14** *5* **Royal Choir**[81] 253 5-9-0 54 AlanMunro 15 15
(H E Haynes) *chsd ldrs: rdn over 3f out: wknd qckly 2f out* **16/1**

/0-0 **15** 3 1/2 **Drumhallagh (IRE)**[47] 679 4-9-1 **55**................(b[1]) RichardKingscote 10 10
(Tom Dascombe) *nvr bttr than mid-div* **14/1**

2m 22.21s (1.11) **Going Correction** 0.0s/f (Good) **15** Ran SP% **137.2**
Speed ratings (Par 101): **95,94,94,94,93 92,92,90,89,88 80,79,79,75,73**
toteswinger: 1&2 £15.20, 1&3 £47.80, 2&3 £19.10. CSF £69.00 CT £1053.58 TOTE £31.20: £7.90, £2.10, £4.90; EX 129.80 Place 6 £64.35, Place 5 £51.40..
Owner L M Power **Bred** Gestut Schlenderhan **Trained** Hatford, Oxon
■ Stewards' Enquiry : Luke Morris twenty-two day ban; careless riding (May 9, May 11-17 and 5 days deferred to Jul 1)

FOCUS
A big field in which plenty could be given a chance. The pace was steady though, which caused several to run too freely, and the form looks ordinary, although the runner-up is a pretty solid guide.
Amber Moon Official explanation: jockey said filly ran too freely
King Of Connacht Official explanation: jockey said gelding ran too freely
Drumhallagh(IRE) Official explanation: jockey said gelding ran too freely
T/Plt: £135.70 to a £1 stake. Pool: £29,852.58. 160.59 winning tickets. T/Qpdt: £108.90 to a £1 stake. Pool: £1,089.30. 7.40 winning tickets. ST

YARMOUTH (L-H)
Monday, April 13

OFFICIAL GOING: Good (7.8)
Wind: Light, half-behind Weather: Sea fret

1255 TOTEPLACEPOT MAIDEN STKS (DIV I) 1m 3y
2:15 (2:18) (Class 5) 3-Y-O+ **£3,469** (£1,038; £519; £259; £129) **Stalls High**

Form RPR
3 **1** **Negotiation (IRE)**[19] 951 3-8-12 0.............................. JimmyFortune 5 83+
(J H M Gosden) *mde all: shkn up over 1f out: edgd lft and r.o* **9/2**[3]
3- **2** 1 1/2 **Palacefield (IRE)**[167] 7054 3-8-12 0.............................. JamieSpencer 1 80
(P W Chapple-Hyam) *trckd ldrs: rdn to chse wnr over 2f out: no ex towards fin* **3/1**[2]
5- **3** 1 1/4 **Tiger Flash**[167] 7051 3-8-12 0.............................. KirstyMilczarek 8 77
(W J Haggas) *hld up in tch: rdn over 2f out: styd on* **14/1**
3- **4** 3/4 **Dukes Art**[129] 7554 3-8-12 0.............................. RobertHavlin 7 75
(J A R Toller) *chsd wnr tl rdn over 2f out: styd on same pce fnl f* **15/2**
5- **5** 5 **Dream Win**[171] 6944 3-8-12 0.............................. RyanMoore 10 64
(Sir Michael Stoute) *chsd ldrs: rdn over 2f out: wknd over 1f out* **11/10**[1]
6 hd **Red Cadeaux** 3-8-12 0.............................. TGMcLaughlin 2 63
(E A L Dunlop) *s.i.s: hld up: rdn over 2f out: nt trble ldrs* **50/1**
54- **7** 10 **Kingshill Prince**[156] 7240 3-8-12 0.............................. TedDurcan 4 40
(W J Musson) *hld up in tch: racd keenly: rdn over 2f out: sn wknd* **33/1**
8 3 1/2 **Sleepy Blue Ocean** 3-8-12 0.............................. ShaneKelly 3 32
(J Noseda) *s.s: hld up: effrt over 2f out: sn wknd and eased* **25/1**
50 **9** 3/4 **Independent James (IRE)**[13] 1047 3-8-7 0............ WilliamCarson(5) 9 31
(S C Williams) *hld up: rdn and wknd over 2f out* **100/1**

1m 40.95s (0.35) **Going Correction** -0.025s/f (Good) **9** Ran SP% **119.0**
Speed ratings (Par 103): **97,95,94,93,88 88,78,74,74**
toteswinger: 1&2 £3.50, 1&3 £10.70, 2&3 £8.30. CSF £18.66 TOTE £5.00: £1.60, £1.60, £3.70; EX 22.50 Trifecta £69.80 Part won. Pool £94.44 - 0.60 winning units..
Owner H R H Princess Haya Of Jordan **Bred** Loughbrown Stud **Trained** Newmarket, Suffolk

FOCUS
The ground was described as 'good', but the clerk of the course felt conditions might just be on the easy side, following watering from the 1m to the 1m3 1/2f start on Saturday, and 2mm of rain on Sunday. As it turned out, the winning time of this opener was 3.65 seconds outside standard, and a couple of the jockeys felt the official description was about right. A heavy mist covering much of the course restricted viewing. This looked a decent enough maiden, and the main action took place up the centre of the track.
Sleepy Blue Ocean Official explanation: jockey said colt hung right

1256 TOTESWINGER FILLIES' H'CAP 1m 3y
2:50 (2:50) (Class 5) (0-75,73) 4-Y-O+ **£3,238** (£963; £481; £240) **Stalls High**

Form RPR
246- **1** **Alsace Lorraine (IRE)**[189] 6530 4-9-4 **73**.............................. JamieSpencer 2 77
(J R Fanshawe) *hld up: hdwy 2f out: rdn to ld wl ins fnl f* **13/2**
646- **2** 1/2 **Astrodonna**[170] 6976 4-9-1 **70**.............................. RyanMoore 5 73
(M H Tompkins) *chsd ldr tl led over 1f out: rdn and hdd wl ins fnl f* **7/2**[3]
1310 **3** 3/4 **Smokey Rye**[2] 1210 4-8-12 **70**.............................. DavidProbert(3) 3 71
(George Baker) *a.p: rdn over 2f out: styd on* **5/1**
032- **4** 4 1/2 **Desert Kiss**[182] 6705 4-9-1 **70**.............................. DarryllHolland 4 61
(W R Swinburn) *led: rdn and hdd over 1f out: wknd fnl f* **9/4**[1]
440- **5** 3 **Charlevoix (IRE)**[210] 5964 4-9-1 **70**.............................. TedDurcan 1 54
(C F Wall) *chsd ldrs tl rdn and wknd over 1f out* **3/1**[2]
550- **6** 1 1/2 **Miss Bootylishes**[213] 5865 4-9-1 **70**.............................. RichardMullen 6 50
(A B Haynes) *hld up: wknd wl over 1f out* **14/1**

1m 40.98s (0.38) **Going Correction** -0.025s/f (Good) **6** Ran SP% **114.7**
Speed ratings (Par 100): **97,96,95,91,88 86**
toteswinger: 1&2 £13.80, 1&3 £7.50, 2&3 £4.90. CSF £29.95 TOTE £4.90: £3.00, £2.10; EX 16.90.
Owner Merry Fox Stud Limited **Bred** 6c Stallions Ltd **Trained** Newmarket, Suffolk

FOCUS
The mist was even thicker than in the opening race and viewing was severely restricted. Only six lined up and this looked like just a modest fillies' handicap.
Smokey Rye Official explanation: trainer's rep said filly was unsuited by the good ground

1257 TOTEPLACEPOT MAIDEN STKS (DIV II) 1m 3y
3:25 (3:27) (Class 5) 3-Y-O+ **£3,469** (£1,038; £519; £259; £129) **Stalls High**

Form RPR
52- **1** **Thousand Miles (IRE)**[187] 6580 3-8-12 0.............................. RichardMullen 7 84
(P W Chapple-Hyam) *chsd ldr tl led 5f out: rdn and edgd lft over 1f out: styd on* **5/2**[2]
00- **2** 1/2 **Putra One (IRE)**[159] 7200 3-8-12 0.............................. PhilipRobinson 1 83
(M A Jarvis) *a.p: rdn to chse wnr over 1f out: kpt on* **15/2**
4- **3** 2 3/4 **Maverin (IRE)**[171] 6944 3-8-12 0.............................. ShaneKelly 3 77
(J Noseda) *a.p: rdn to chse wnr over 2f out to over 1f out: no ex ins fnl f* **9/4**[1]
4 **4** 2 3/4 **Kloof**[23] 917 3-8-12 0.............................. JimmyFortune 10 71
(J H M Gosden) *chsd ldrs: rdn over 1f out: wknd ins fnl f* **4/1**[3]
65- **5** 1/2 **Advisor (FR)**[166] 7080 3-8-12 0.............................. JamieSpencer 2 70
(M L W Bell) *hld up: hdwy over 2f out: wknd over 1f out* **5/1**
6 3 1/4 **The Last Don (IRE)** 3-8-12 0.............................. TedDurcan 8 62+
(D R Lanigan) *dwlt: outpcd: nvr nrr* **20/1**
6- **7** shd **General Zhukov**[238] 5158 3-8-12 0.............................. JimmyQuinn 5 62
(J M P Eustace) *hld up: rdn over 3f out: n.d* **66/1**
0-0 **8** 1 3/4 **Red Margarita (IRE)**[14] 1034 3-8-2 0.............................. AmyBaker(5) 9 53
(D R C Elsworth) *hld up: rdn 1/2-way: wknd 3f out* **66/1**
9 3/4 **Fortina's Boy (USA)** 3-8-12 0.............................. DarryllHolland 6 56
(W R Swinburn) *hld up: rdn 1/2-way: sn wknd* **16/1**
10 5 **Proud Junior (USA)** 3-8-12 0.............................. JoeFanning 4 45
(S A Callaghan) *sn led: hdd 5f out: chsd wnr tl rdn over 2f out: sn wknd* **33/1**

1m 40.48s (-0.12) **Going Correction** -0.025s/f (Good) **10** Ran SP% **124.3**
Speed ratings (Par 103): **99,98,95,93,92 89,89,87,86,81**
toteswinger: 1&2 £10.60, 1&3 £2.50, 2&3 £10.70. CSF £22.81 TOTE £3.90: £2.10, £2.60, £1.80; EX 27.20 Trifecta £78.50 Part won. Pool £106.12 - 0.40 winning units..
Owner J C Fretwell **Bred** Philip Brady **Trained** Newmarket, Suffolk

FOCUS
This looked quite a decent maiden and the winning time was 0.48 seconds faster than the first division won by Negotiation.
General Zhukov Official explanation: jockey said gelding hung right-handed
Red Margarita(IRE) Official explanation: jockey said filly hung left-handed

1258 TOTESUPER7 H'CAP 7f 3y
4:00 (4:01) (Class 6) (0-65,65) 4-Y-O+ **£2,201** (£655; £327; £163) **Stalls High**

Form RPR
0-62 **1** **Seneschal**[12] 1074 8-9-1 **62**.............................. JamieSpencer 3 72
(A B Haynes) *trckd ldrs: rdn to ld over 1f out: edgd lft: r.o* **11/2**[2]
65-2 **2** nk **Elusive Hawk (IRE)**[90] 141 5-9-3 **64**.............................. JoeFanning 6 73
(B J Curley) *a.p: nt clr run and swtchd lft over 1f out: rdn and ev ch ins fnl f: r.o* **5/2**[1]
00-5 **3** 2 1/2 **Bigfanofthat (IRE)**[43] 721 4-9-1 **62**.............................. JimmyQuinn 10 64+
(M D Squance) *dwlt: sn pushed along in rr: last and plenty to do over 2f out: sn swtchd rt: r.o wl ins fnl f: nt rch ldrs* **20/1**
0400 **4** 1 3/4 **Ugenius**[17] 979 5-8-11 **58**.............................. TGMcLaughlin 14 56
(Mrs C A Dunnett) *mid-div: hdwy 1/2-way: rdn over 1f out: styd on* **14/1**
40-4 **5** 3/4 **Zeffirelli**[12] 1074 4-8-10 **57**.............................. ShaneKelly 15 53
(M Quinn) *led: rdn and hdd over 1f out: edgd lft and wknd ins fnl f* **10/1**
404- **6** 3/4 **Style Icon**[300] 3117 4-9-4 **65**.............................. RyanMoore 12 59
(Rae Guest) *trckd ldrs: rdn over 2f out: wknd ins fnl f* **15/2**
050- **7** nk **Registrar**[135] 7490 7-8-6 **58**.............................. (p) AndreaAtzeni(5) 9 51
(Mrs C A Dunnett) *chsd ldr tl rdn over 2f out: wknd fnl f* **14/1**
0-20 **8** 1 **Inca Soldier (FR)**[77] 292 6-8-8 **60** ow2.............................. MarkCoumbe(5) 5 50
(R C Guest) *hld up: rdn over 2f out: nvr nrr* **28/1**
0-03 **9** shd **Networker**[26] 868 6-8-13 **63**.............................. JackMitchell(3) 13 53
(P J McBride) *chsd ldrs: rdn over 2f out: wknd over 1f out* **7/1**[3]
006- **10** 1/2 **Chief Exec**[154] 7277 7-8-8 **58**.............................. (p) DavidProbert(3) 4 47
(J R Gask) *hld up: hdwy over 2f out: rdn and wknd over 1f out* **12/1**
525- **11** nse **Poppy's Rose**[262] 4393 5-9-4 **65**.............................. PatrickMathers 7 53
(I W McInnes) *mid-div: rdn 1/2-way: wknd over 1f out* **14/1**
000 **12** shd **Strategic Knight (USA)**[45] 715 4-8-10 **57**..............(t) KirstyMilczarek 8 45
(R C Guest) *mid-div: rdn over 2f out: n.d after* **25/1**
0-60 **13** nk **Sands Of Barra (IRE)**[26] 874 6-8-5 **59**............ AndrewHeffernan(7) 16 46
(I W McInnes) *hld up: rdn over 2f out: a in rr* **25/1**
0-00 **14** 2 1/2 **Coeur Courageux (FR)**[7] 1153 7-8-11 **58**.......................(p) JohnEgan 1 39
(M D Squance) *mid-div: rdn over 2f out: sn wknd* **25/1**
0-0 **15** 3/4 **Averoo**[25] 880 4-9-3 **64**.............................. RichardMullen 2 43
(M D Squance) *hld up: a in rr* **25/1**
40-4 **16** 2 3/4 **Truly Divine**[12] 1076 4-8-11 **58**.............................. (p) DarryllHolland 11 29
(C A Dwyer) *s.i.s: hld up: a in rr: rdn over 2f out: sn wknd* **7/1**[3]

1m 26.82s (0.22) **Going Correction** -0.025s/f (Good) **16** Ran SP% **141.1**
Speed ratings (Par 101): **97,96,93,91,90 90,89,88,88,87 87,87,87,84,83 80**
toteswinger: 1&2 £5.60, 1&3 £24.70, 2&3 £26.20. CSF £20.91 CT £301.91 TOTE £6.80: £1.70, £1.80, £4.40, £3.80; EX 25.70 Trifecta £126.40 Part won. Pool £170.93 - 0.20 winning units..
Owner P Cook **Bred** Michael E Broughton **Trained** Limpley Stoke, Bath

FOCUS
A moderate but competitive handicap in which it paid to race handy. They were spread out across the track in the closing stages.

1259 TOTEEXACTA CLAIMING STKS 6f 3y
4:35 (4:36) (Class 6) 3-Y-O+ **£1,942** (£578; £288; £144) **Stalls High**

Form RPR
1661 **1** **Lethal**[22] 921 6-9-1 60.............................. FrederikTylicki(5) 10 75
(R A Fahey) *chsd ldrs: led wl over 1f out: rdn out* **7/2**[1]
654 **2** 1 **Secret Dubai (IRE)**[17] 980 4-9-1 69.......................(t) AndreaAtzeni(5) 7 72
(M Botti) *hld up in tch: chsd wnr over 1f out: rdn and ev ch ins fnl f: nt qckn towards fin* **7/2**[1]
-640 **3** 6 **Onceaponatime (IRE)**[9] 1132 4-9-10 70.............................. JohnEgan 4 57
(M D Squance) *led: rdn and hdd wl over 1f out: no ex fnl f* **13/2**[3]
2250 **4** 1/2 **Crocodile Bay (IRE)**[41] 747 6-9-5 69.............................. MarkCoumbe(5) 11 55
(John A Harris) *hld up: hdwy u.p over 1f out: nt trble ldrs* **8/1**
000- **5** 1 3/4 **Creative (IRE)**[241] 5045 4-9-10 54.............................. TedDurcan 8 49
(M H Tompkins) *mid-div: rdn over 2f out: n.d* **14/1**
20-4 **6** 2 **Russian Rocket (IRE)**[32] 818 7-9-8 68.............................. TGMcLaughlin 6 41
(Mrs C A Dunnett) *chsd ldr: rdn over 2f out: wknd fnl f* **9/2**[2]
0450 **7** 1 3/4 **Titus Gent**[12] 1076 4-8-13 48.............................. RyanPowell(7) 1 33
(J Ryan) *racd alone towards far side tl jnd main gp 1/2-way: prom: rdn over 2f out: wknd fnl f* **40/1**
4405 **8** 4 1/2 **Valentino Swing (IRE)**[21] 933 6-9-1 54...................(b) DavidProbert(3) 5 17
(Miss T Spearing) *chsd ldrs tl rdn and wknd over 1f out* **12/1**
0404 **9** 3 1/4 **Comrade Cotton**[11] 1079 5-9-4 55.......................(v) KirstyMilczarek 13 7
(J Ryan) *sn pushed along in rr: hung rt and wknd over 2f out* **14/1**
66-3 **10** nk **Mannello**[12] 1072 6-9-0 52.............................. (p) NickyMackay 14 2
(S W Hall) *prom: rdn over 3f out: wknd over 2f out* **25/1**
000- **11** hd **Jellytot (USA)**[120] 7678 6-8-12 45.............................. PatrickMathers 12 —
(I W McInnes) *dwlt and hmpd sn after s: a in rr* **33/1**
-340 **12** 13 **Caribbean Coral**[54] 589 10-9-10 68.............................. JamieSpencer 2 —+
(A B Haynes) *hld up: a in rr: wknd and eased fnl 2f* **9/1**
00-5 **13** 8 **Viewforth**[75] 308 11-9-3 43.............................. (b) ShaneKelly 15 —
(S T Mason) *racd alone stands' side: prom to 1/2-way* **66/1**

1m 13.66s (-0.74) **Going Correction** -0.025s/f (Good) **13** Ran SP% **128.8**
Speed ratings (Par 101): **103,101,93,93,90 88,85,79,75,74 74,57,46**
toteswinger: 1&2 £6.40, 1&3 £7.50, 2&3 £8.20. CSF £16.10 TOTE £5.00: £2.00, £2.10, £2.70; EX 21.80 TRIFECTA Not won..Secret Dubai was claimed by Mrs L. Stubbs for £6,000.
Owner The Matthewman One Partnership **Bred** A S Reid **Trained** Musley Bank, N Yorks

FOCUS
A modest claimer in which the front two pulled well clear.
Comrade Cotton Official explanation: jockey said gelding lost its action

Caribbean Coral Official explanation: jockey said gelding was never travelling

1260 BET TOTEPOOL AT TOTESPORT.COM MEDIAN AUCTION MAIDEN STKS — 1m 2f 21y

5:10 (5:11) (Class 6) 3-5-Y-O — **£2,590** (£770; £385; £192) **Stalls** Low

Form — RPR

403- **1** **Holyrood**[205] 6117 3-8-9 81 ... RyanMoore 6 79+
(Sir Michael Stoute) *a.p: chsd ldr 4f out: led and edgd lft over 2f out: rdn out* **4/7**[1]

2 *2* **Time Machine (UAE)** 3-8-9 0 ... RichardMullen 11 75+
(J H M Gosden) *sn prom: chsd wnr over 1f out: hung lft ins fnl f: styd on same pce* **6/1**[3]

0- **3** *6* **Daredevil Dan**[206] 6085 3-8-9 0 ... TedDurcan 9 63
(M H Tompkins) *hld up: hdwy and hung lft fr over 1f out: nt rch ldrs and eased ins fnl f* **33/1**

5 **4** *4 ½* **Atacama Sunrise**[10] 1092 3-8-4 0 ... JimmyQuinn 4 55+
(J Pearce) *trckd ldrs: hmpd 3f out: nt clr run and lost pl wl over 1f out: r.o nr fin* **16/1**

04- **5** *hd* **Count On Guest**[259] 4488 3-8-9 0 ... JoeFanning 8 54
(G G Margarson) *led: hdd over 8f out: chsd ldr tl led again 3f out: sn rdn and hdd: wknd fnl f* **22/1**

22 **6** *nse* **Calling Victory (FR)**[31] 833 3-8-4 0 ... JohnEgan 1 49
(M Botti) *chsd ldr tl led over 8f out: rdn: hdd and edgd lft 3f out: hung rt over 1f out: sn wknd* **9/2**[2]

60- **7** *1* **Stormy Summer**[187] 6584 4-9-11 0 ... (t) JackMitchell(3) 3 56
(R W Price) *hld up: shkn up over 2f out: swtchd lft over 1f out: n.d* **66/1**

0- **8** *11* **Flannel (IRE)**[158] 7023 3-8-9 0 ... JamieSpencer 5 30
(J R Fanshawe) *mid-div: rdn 1/2-way: hung lft and wknd wl over 2f out* **12/1**

24-0 **9** *½* **Yakama (IRE)**[45] 706 4-10-0 58 ... (b) TGMcLaughlin 2 29
(Mrs C A Dunnett) *s.i.s: hdwy 8f out: rdn over 2f out: sn wknd* **25/1**

10 *26* **Roman The Emperor (IRE)** 3-8-9 0 ... NickyMackay 7 —
(S W Hall) *s.i.s: a in rr: wknd 3f out* **66/1**

11 *13* **Final Drive (IRE)**[296] 3284 3-8-9 62 ... ShaneKelly 10 —
(E J Creighton) *hld up: rdn 1/2-way: wknd 3f out* **50/1**

2m 9.62s (-0.88) **Going Correction** -0.025s/f (Good)
WFA 3 from 4yo 19lb — **11** Ran SP% **125.8**
Speed ratings (Par 101): **102,100,95,92,91 91,91,82,81,61 50**
toteswinger: 1&2 £3.30, 1&3 £12.00, 2&3 £21.90. CSF £4.75 TOTE £1.70: £1.10, £2.40, £7.50; EX 6.80 Trifecta £119.30 Pool £220.89 - 1.37 winning units..
Owner Cheveley Park Stud **Bred** Cheveley Park Stud Ltd **Trained** Newmarket, Suffolk

FOCUS
This maiden lacked strength in depth, but the front two look quite useful.
Atacama Sunrise Official explanation: jockey said filly was denied a clear run
Calling Victory(FR) Official explanation: jockey said filly hung left-handed throughout

1261 BET TOTEPOOL ON 0800 221 221 H'CAP — 1m 2f 21y

5:45 (5:45) (Class 5) (0-75,73) 4-Y-0+ — **£2,978** (£886; £442; £221) **Stalls** Low

Form — RPR

040- **1** **Agapanthus (GER)**[107] 7797 4-8-10 65 ... JoeFanning 7 77
(B J Curley) *a.p: rdn to ld ins fnl f: r.o* **4/1**[3]

042 **2** *½* **Sri Kuantan (IRE)**[20] 948 5-8-8 68 ow1 ... (t) MarkCoumbe(5) 11 79
(R C Guest) *led: clr 3f out: rdn and hdd ins fnl f: r.o* **20/1**

5-15 **3** *1 ¾* **Annabelle's Charm (IRE)**[72] 361 4-9-3 72 ... JamieSpencer 12 80+
(L M Cumani) *hld up: racd keenly: hdwy over 2f out: sn rdn: styd on same pce ins fnl f* **15/8**[1]

1211 **4** *½* **Agilete**[14] 1042 7-8-5 67 ... SimonPearce(7) 4 74
(J Pearce) *chsd ldr: rdn over 1f out: styd on same pce ins fnl f* **7/2**[2]

1503 **5** *2 ½* **Onemoreandstay**[13] 1049 4-8-12 67 ... (p) DarryllHolland 5 69+
(M D Squance) *hld up: nt clr run over 2f out: rdn: swtchd rt and hdwy over 1f out: nt trble ldrs* **10/1**

6443 **6** *1* **Hucking Hero (IRE)**[12] 1073 4-8-12 70 ... MarcHalford(3) 8 70
(J R Best) *hld up: racd keenly: rdn over 2f out: n.d* **12/1**

00-0 **7** *hd* **Dragon Slayer (IRE)**[15] 1014 7-8-7 67 ... GabrielHannon(5) 1 66
(John A Harris) *chsd ldrs: rdn over 2f out: styd on same pce appr fnl f* **14/1**

-400 **8** *hd* **Dinner Date**[25] 878 7-8-10 65 ... ShaneKelly 3 64
(T Keddy) *hld up: rdn over 2f out: styd on same pce* **20/1**

0/3- **9** *5* **Sagarich (FR)**[227] 5485 5-8-0 60 ... NicolPolli(5) 9 49
(M G Quinlan) *s.i.s: hld up: rdn over 2f out: a in rr* **16/1**

341- **10** *¾* **Carmela Maria**[200] 6227 4-8-10 65 ... KirstyMilczarek 6 52
(S C Williams) *plld hrd: trckd ldrs: rdn over 2f out: wknd over 1f out* **12/1**

2m 12.11s (1.61) **Going Correction** -0.025s/f (Good) — **10** Ran SP% **123.6**
Speed ratings (Par 103): **92,91,90,89,87 87,86,86,82,82**
toteswinger: 1&2 £22.60, 1&3 £6.40, 2&3 £11.20. CSF £85.11 CT £198.60 TOTE £6.10: £4.00, £4.30, £1.30; EX 153.00 TRIFECTA Not won. Place 6 £56.54, Place 5 £19.09..
Owner Curley Leisure **Bred** Gestut Schlenderhan **Trained** Newmarket, Suffolk

FOCUS
A modest handicap run in a moderate time and therefore some doubt over the value of the form.
Agapanthus(GER) Official explanation: trainer said, regarding the improved form shown, gelding benefited for running on turf as his previous runs had been on the all-weather surface
Annabelle's Charm(IRE) Official explanation: jockey said filly hung badly right-handed throughout
T/Plt: £51.90 to a £1 stake. Pool: £33,187.55. 465.95 winning tickets. T/Qpdt: £5.60 to a £1 stake. Pool: £1,988.80. 260.00 winning tickets. CR

1262 - 1266a (Foreign Racing) - See Raceform Interactive

[1028]SAINT-CLOUD (L-H)

Monday, April 13

OFFICIAL GOING: Soft

1267a PRIX PENELOPE (GROUP 3) (FILLIES) — 1m 2f 110y

2:20 (2:21) 3-Y-O — **£38,835** (£15,534; £11,650; £7,767; £3,883)

RPR

1 **Celimene (IRE)**[28] 3-9-0 ... YLerner 2 111
(C Lerner, France) *trckd ldr on rail: 3rd and pushed along st: drvn wl over 1f out: led 150yds out: r.o wl* **29/10**[2]

2 *1 ½* **Plumania**[190] 6519 3-9-0 ... OPeslier 3 108
(A Fabre, France) *a wl in tch: restrained early: settled disputing 4th: 4th st effrt on outside and rdn 1 1/2f out: r.o same pce fnl f* **8/5**[1]

3 *1 ½* **Villa Molitor (FR)**[51] 3-9-0 ... SPasquier 1 105
(F Rohaut, France) *led: drvn wl over 1f out: hdd 150yds out: one pce* **37/10**[3]

4 *1* **Divine Comedy (FR)**[30] 3-9-0 ... DBoeuf 4 103
(D Smaga, France) *pressed ldr on outside: 2nd st: hrd rdn 2f out: wknd appr fnl f* **7/1**

5 *nk* **Excellent Girl**[37] 3-9-0 ... TThulliez 5 103
(Y De Nicolay, France) *last to st but a wl in tch: wnt 5th over 2f out: kpt on one pce* **14/1**

6 *4* **Pearl Of Charm (FR)**[25] 3-9-0 ... GMosse 6 95
(Y De Nicolay, France) *disp 3rd to over 3f out: cl 5th on outside st: sn btn* **7/1**

2m 21.3s (1.70) — **6** Ran SP% **117.0**
PARI-MUTUEL: WIN 3.90; PL 1.80, 1.70; SF 12.80.
Owner G Laboureau **Bred** Petra Bloodstock Agency Ltd **Trained** France

NOTEBOOK
Celimene(IRE) took her unbeaten record to three, quickening up well to score. The main target is the Prix de Diane.

HANOVER (L-H)

Monday, April 13

OFFICIAL GOING: Good

1268a GROSSER PREIS VON HANNOVER 96 (LISTED RACE) (F&M) — 1m

3:45 (4:08) 4-Y-0+ — **£11,650** (£4,272; £2,330; £1,165)

RPR

1 **Waky Love (GER)**[162] 5-8-11 ... AStarke 5 89
(P Schiergen, Germany) **17/10**[1]

2 *½* **Zaya (GER)**[134] 4-8-11 ... EPedroza 1 87
(A Wohler, Germany) **4/1**

3 *1 ½* **Deep Winter**[15] 1020 4-9-4 ... JamieMoriarty 4 91
(R A Fahey) *trckd ldr: 2nd st: hrd rdn wl over 1f out: disputing 2nd ins fnl f: one pce* **27/10**[2]

4 *¾* **Magic Eye (IRE)**[162] 4-9-4 ... JiriPalik 7 89
(Andreas Lowe, Germany) **14/5**[3]

5 *1 ¼* **Porta Westfalica (IRE)**[253] 4675 4-8-11 ... PHeugl 3 79
(W Hickst, Germany) **22/1**

6 *1 ¼* **Carved Emerald**[22] 4-9-4 ... (b) RonanThomas 6 84
(R Gibson, France) **19/2**

7 *1 ¾* **Manita (IRE)**[197] 6323 4-9-4 ... AHelfenbein 2 80
(Mario Hofer, Germany) **41/5**

1m 36.84s (96.84) — **7** Ran SP% **135.1**
(including ten euro stakes): WIN 27; PL 12, 13, 13: SF 92.
Owner Gestut Brummerhof **Bred** Gestut Park Wiedingen **Trained** Germany

NOTEBOOK
Deep Winter, a well-bred filly who is versatile as regards the ground, ran her usual honest race on this step up in grade and enhanced her paddock value by earning black type in the process.

[1255]YARMOUTH (L-H)

Tuesday, April 14

OFFICIAL GOING: Good
Wind: Light across Weather: Foggy

1269 FREEBETS.CO.UK FREE BETS MEDIAN AUCTION MAIDEN FILLIES' STKS — 1m 3y

2:20 (2:24) (Class 5) 3-5-Y-O — **£4,533** (£1,348; £674; £336) **Stalls** High

Form — RPR

32 **1** **Wadaat**[15] 1034 3-8-12 0 ... NCallan 9 75+
(C E Brittain) *mde all: rdn over 1f out: styd on* **15/8**[1]

5- **2** *¾* **Astrodiva**[175] 6887 3-8-12 0 ... PaulMulrennan 6 73
(M H Tompkins) *mid-div: hdwy 1/2-way: rdn and edgd lft over 1f out: r.o* **33/1**

030- **3** *hd* **Lonely Star (IRE)**[184] 6674 3-8-12 78 ... TedDurcan 13 73
(D R Lanigan) *s.i.s: hdwy over 4f out: rdn over 1f out: styd on* **12/1**

4 *hd* **Sana Abel (IRE)** 3-8-12 0 ... RHills 3 73+
(M A Jarvis) *hld up: hdwy 2f out: chsd wnr fnl f: unable qck towards fin* **8/1**[3]

5 *2 ½* **Hisaronu (IRE)** 3-8-12 0 ... TPQueally 1 67
(H R A Cecil) *s.i.s: hdwy over 6f out: rdn over 1f out: no ex ins fnl f* **7/2**[2]

52- **6** *2 ¾* **Volochkova (USA)**[130] 7561 3-8-12 0 ... EddieAhern 14 60
(J R Fanshawe) *hld up in tch: rdn over 1f out: wknd ins fnl f* **10/1**

7 *1 ¾* **Gold Maha** 3-8-12 0 ... TonyCulhane 11 56
(M R Channon) *s.i.s: hld up: styd on appr fnl f: nvr nrr* **50/1**

8 *1* **Rowan Light** 3-8-12 0 ... PatCosgrave 5 54
(J R Boyle) *s.i.s: bhd and rdn 1/2-way: nvr nrr* **66/1**

6- **9** *3* **Markhesa**[209] 6031 3-8-12 0 ... AlanMunro 8 47
(C F Wall) *chsd ldrs: rdn over 2f out: sn wknd* **20/1**

0-0 **10** *1* **Ocean Countess (IRE)**[29] 849 3-8-12 0 ... JerryO'Dwyer 2 45
(Miss J Feilden) *mid-div: hdwy over 4f out: rdn over 2f out: edgd rt and wknd over 1f out* **33/1**

11 *1 ¾* **Whispered Wish** 3-8-12 0 ... LiamJones 12 41
(W J Haggas) *sn pushed along in rr: bhd fr 1/2-way* **33/1**

4 **12** *1 ¼* **Lady's Art (FR)**[94] 121 3-8-12 0 ... JamieSpencer 10 38
(E F Vaughan) *chsd ldrs: rdn over 2f out: wkng whn hmpd over 1f out* **8/1**[3]

32- **13** *½* **Penperth**[150] 7337 3-8-12 0 ... LukeMorris 7 37
(J M P Eustace) *s.i.s: sn pushed along: a in rr* **20/1**

0-6 **14** *1 ½* **Contemplate**[33] 820 3-8-9 0 ... DavidProbert(3) 4 33
(Dr J D Scargill) *chsd ldrs: lost pl 6f out: bhd fr 1/2-way* **100/1**

1m 40.3s (-0.30) **Going Correction** -0.125s/f (Firm) — **14** Ran SP% **118.8**
Speed ratings (Par 100): **96,95,95,94,92 89,87,86,83,82 81,79,79,77**
toteswinger: 1&2 £14.30, 1&3 £7.90, 2&3 £46.90. CSF £83.67 TOTE £2.50: £1.10, £7.30, £3.70; EX 57.50 Trifecta £153.40 Pool: £300.72 - 1.45 winning units..
Owner Saeed Manana **Bred** Jocelyn Targett **Trained** Newmarket, Suffolk

FOCUS
As was the case the previous day, a sea fret covered the track and the visibility for this opener was poor. An interesting fillies' maiden which should provide its share of winners and all the action took place down the centre of the track.
Penperth Official explanation: trainer had no explanation for the poor form shown

Contemplate Official explanation: jockey said the filly was never travelling

1270 FREEBETS.CO.UK FREE SPORTS BETTING (S) STKS 1m 3y
2:50 (2:53) (Class 6) 3-Y-O £1,942 (£578; £288; £144) Stalls High

Form RPR
0541 1 **Special Cuvee**14 [1046] 3-9-3 69 JamieSpencer 9 67+
(A B Haynes) *stdd s: hld up and bhd: hdwy over 2f out: led ins fnl f: rdn out* 9/4[1]
3523 2 3/4 **Why Nee Amy**21 [943] 3-8-4 52 (p) DavidProbert(3) 2 55
(Miss Gay Kelleway) *mid-div: hdwy over 3f out: led over 1f out: sn rdn: hdd and unable qck ins fnl f* 12/1
3 1 1/4 **Shared Moment (IRE)** 3-8-7 0 LiamJones 3 52
(S W Hall) *dwlt: hld up: hdwy over 3f out: rdn and ev ch wl over 1f out: edgd lft: styd on* 7/2[3]
5660 4 1/2 **Chantilly Dancer (IRE)**21 [943] 3-8-4 42 JackMitchell(3) 6 51
(M Quinn) *led: hdd over 5f out: outpcd over 3f out: styd on u.p fnl f* 50/1
60-0 5 3 1/4 **Wabi Sabi (IRE)**16 [1015] 3-8-2 63 Louis-PhilippeBeuzelin(5) 1 44
(N Tinkler) *hld up in tch: rdn over 1f out: wknd fnl f* 11/4[2]
056- 6 3/4 **Ba Globetrotter**134 [7519] 3-8-12 50 TonyCulhane 5 47
(M R Channon) *chsd ldr tl led over 5f out: rdn and hdd over 1f out: wknd fnl f* 33/1
00-3 7 6 **Avrilo**19 [964] 3-8-9 40 ow2 TGMcLaughlin 10 30
(M S Saunders) *prom: rdn over 3f out: wknd 2f out* 33/1
00-0 8 5 **Strictly Royal**13 [1070] 3-8-12 26 CatherineGannon 11 21
(M R Channon) *chsd ldrs: rdn 1/2-way: wknd 2f out* 66/1
00-0 9 shd **Princess Janet**11 [1108] 3-8-7 28 LukeMorris 8 16
(A B Coogan) *sn pushed along in rr: rdn 1/2-way: sn lost tch* 100/1
0602 10 27 **Dead Cat Bounce (IRE)**21 [943] 3-8-12 62 (bt) JerryO'Dwyer 4 —
(J Pearce) *chsd ldrs: rdn and wknd over 2f out: eased over 1f out* 10/1
050- 11 5 **Rose Of Coma (IRE)**104 [7833] 3-8-12 56 (p) NCallan 7 —
(Miss Gay Kelleway) *chsd ldrs tl rdn and wknd over 2f out: eased over 1f out* 12/1

1m 40.7s (0.10) **Going Correction** -0.125s/f (Firm) 11 Ran SP% 114.5
Speed ratings (Par 96): **94,93,92,91,88 87,81,76,76,49 44**
toteswinger: 1&2 £3.80, 1&3 £3.60, 2&3 £7.00 CSF £28.92 TOTE £2.60: £1.50, £2.20, £1.90; EX 23.80 Trifecta £166.20 Pool: £269.55 - 1.20 winning units..There was no bid for the winner. Shared Moment was claimed by D Cantillon for £10000.
Owner The Villains **Bred** John Brown & Megan Dennis **Trained** Limpley Stoke, Bath

FOCUS
A moderate seller in which the winning time was 0.4 seconds slower than the fillies' maiden.

1271 FREEBETS.CO.UK FREE ONLINE BINGO H'CAP 6f 3y
3:20 (3:25) (Class 5) (0-70,65) 3-Y-O £3,238 (£963; £481; £240) Stalls High

Form RPR
061- 1 **Lovely Thought**168 [7052] 3-9-4 65 (b) MichaelHills 3 87
(W J Haggas) *mde all: rdn clr fr over 1f out: eased wl ins fnl f* 7/2[2]
0-23 2 11 **Billy Beetroot (USA)**6 [1190] 3-9-1 62 (bt1) JamieSpencer 4 49
(S C Williams) *s.i.s: hld up: swtchd lft and hdwy over 2f out: rdn to chse wnr who had gone clr over 1f out: sn hung rt and no ex* 9/2[3]
10 3 nk **May Martin**34 [804] 3-8-11 58 AlanMunro 5 44
(Rae Guest) *s.i.s: sn pushed along in rr: styd on fr over 1f out: nt trble ldrs* 3/1[1]
1-00 4 1 1/2 **Imaginary Diva**34 [804] 3-9-4 65 DaneO'Neill 1 46
(G G Margarson) *prom: chsd wnr over 2f out tl rdn over 1f out: wknd fnl f* 14/1
226- 5 3/4 **Itainteasybeingme**173 [6924] 3-8-5 59 NathanAlison(7) 8 38
(J R Boyle) *sn outpcd* 9/1
346- 6 2 1/4 **Oisin's Boy**133 [7531] 3-8-12 59 PatCosgrave 6 30
(J R Boyle) *prom: rdn 1/2-way: wknd 2f out* 7/2[2]
04-5 7 3 1/2 **Silver Salsa**82 [246] 3-8-4 51 JimmyQuinn 2 11
(J R Jenkins) *free to post: trckd wnr tl rdn and wknd over 2f out* 14/1

1m 13.38s (-1.02) **Going Correction** -0.125s/f (Firm) 7 Ran SP% 111.0
Speed ratings (Par 98): **101,86,85,83,82 79,75**
toteswinger: 1&2 £2.70, 1&3 £2.60, 2&3 £3.90 CSF £18.31 CT £48.95 TOTE £4.10: £1.60, £2.40; EX 10.40 Trifecta £21.40 Pool: £380.65 - 13.16 winning units..
Owner Liam Sheridan **Bred** Whitsbury Manor Stud **Trained** Newmarket, Suffolk

FOCUS
An ordinary contest in terms of previous form, but an extremely impressive winner and not many sprint handicaps are won quite as easily as this. The form behind the winner is hard to quantify, however.
Billy Beetroot(USA) Official explanation: jockey said the gelding hung right

1272 FREEBETS.CO.UK FREE ONLINE POKER H'CAP 5f 43y
3:50 (3:51) (Class 3) (0-90,83) 3-Y-O
£10,281 (£3,078; £1,539; £770; £384; £193) Stalls High

Form RPR
010- 1 **Aakef (IRE)**228 [5466] 3-9-5 81 RHills 7 89+
(M A Jarvis) *hld up: hdwy to ld 1f out: rdn out* 11/8[1]
210- 2 nk **Bouvardia**190 [6533] 3-9-7 83 TPQueally 3 90+
(H R A Cecil) *hld up: swtchd rt and hdwy over 1f out: r.o wl towards fin* 85/40[2]
-443 3 1 **Mazzola**12 [1078] 3-8-13 75 TonyCulhane 8 78
(M R Channon) *led: hdd over 3f out: led again over 1f out: sn rdn and hdd: styd on same pce* 8/1[3]
500- 4 2 **Bahamian Ceilidh**184 [6666] 3-8-10 72 RichardKingscote 5 68
(Tom Dascombe) *chsd ldr: rdn and ev ch over 1f out: no ex ins fnl f* 12/1
23-4 5 1 3/4 **Peninsular War**27 [862] 3-9-1 77 AndrewElliott 4 67
(K R Burke) *chsd ldrs: rdn 1/2-way: no ex fnl f* 25/1
-011 6 3 1/4 **Captain Carey**11 [1095] 3-9-1 77 TGMcLaughlin 2 55
(M S Saunders) *hld up: rdn 1/2-way: wknd over 1f out* 17/2
-213 7 22 **Theatre Street (IRE)**46 [709] 3-8-12 74 NCallan 1 —
(J Noseda) *chsd ldrs: led over 3f out: hdd & wknd over 1f out* 10/1

62.69 secs (0.49) **Going Correction** -0.125s/f (Firm) 7 Ran SP% 116.4
Speed ratings (Par 102): **91,90,88,85,82 77,42**
toteswinger: 1&2 £1.90, 1&3 £3.40, 2&3 £4.00 CSF £4.63 CT £15.48 TOTE £2.70: £1.70, £1.60; EX 4.50 Trifecta £20.00 Pool: £446.17 - 16.45 winning units..
Owner Hamdan Al Maktoum **Bred** Grangecon Stud **Trained** Newmarket, Suffolk

FOCUS
A decent three-year-old sprint handicap and the front pair look likely to go on to better things. Unlike in the previous races, all the action unfolded towards the stands' rail and the pair that stayed mid-track appeared to struggle.

NOTEBOOK
Aakef(IRE) ◆, returning from eight months off and gelded since last seen, was very well backed earlier in the day. He wasn't best away, but nonetheless he was soon travelling extremely well just behind the leaders and once taking it up towards the nearside over a furlong from home, quickened up nicely. He won a shade more cosily than the margin would suggest and should go on from here. (op 6-5 tchd 13-8)
Bouvardia ◆, down to the minimum trip for the first time on this return to action, was well backed on-course. Another to travel well behind the pace-setters, she had to be switched right over to the stands' rail to make her effort but although she put in a strong finish, the winner already had the race in the bag. A return to 6f looks to be in order and it shouldn't be long before she goes one better. (op 7-2)
Mazzola, fit from the sand and 10lb lower than when last on turf, ran a game race having been handy from the start, but he is a lot more exposed than the pair that beat him. Both of his wins have been over 6f. (op 10-1)
Bahamian Ceilidh, making his debut for the yard after a six-month absence, helped force the pace until appearing to blow up. She is likely to come on for it and should be able to find easier opportunities than this. (op 14-1)
Peninsular War, the only maiden in the field, was entitled to need his first run in ten months on his recent return at Kempton and wasn't at all disgraced here. He ought to be cherry-ripe now and should find a race. (op 16-1)
Captain Carey, up 6lb on his bid for a hat-trick, was again outpaced early as he usually is, but unlike in his last two outings he could never get into the race this time. Whether he was at a disadvantage in racing down the centre of the track whilst the principals all came nearer the stands' rail is debatable, so it may not be wise to write him off just yet. (op 6-1)

1273 FREEBETS.CO.UK FREE BETTING H'CAP 2m
4:20 (4:22) (Class 5) (0-70,68) 4-Y-O+ £3,238 (£963; £481; £240) Stalls High

Form RPR
54-5 1 **No Rules**23 [790] 4-8-5 52 LiamJones 5 58
(M H Tompkins) *hld up in tch: rdn to ld 1f out: jst hld on* 6/1
0211 2 nse **Blockley (USA)**18 [983] 5-9-7 64 StephenDonohoe 10 70
(Ian Williams) *hld up: rdn over 4f out: hdwy over 2f out: styd on wl* 4/1[2]
-420 3 2 1/2 **Russian Invader (IRE)**8 [1154] 5-9-3 65 (e) MarkCoumbe(5) 6 68
(R C Guest) *prom: outpcd over 4f out: rallied over 1f out: eased whn hld nr fin* 10/1
316- 4 1 **Kokkokila**153 [7293] 5-9-7 64 RyanMoore 1 66
(Lady Herries) *hld up: hdwy u.p over 2f out: styd on same pce ins fnl f* 7/4[1]
6-66 5 3/4 **Lucky Dancer**10 [1122] 4-8-9 56 (b) AlanMunro 9 57
(D R C Elsworth) *chsd ldr: rdn to ld over 2f out: hdd 1f out: no ex* 8/1
20-3 6 2 **Rose Bien**13 [1069] 7-9-5 62 (p) EdwardCreighton 7 61
(P J McBride) *chsd ldrs: rdn over 3f out: wknd fnl f* 5/1[3]
44-5 7 2 3/4 **Ice And Fire**19 [967] 10-8-6 49 oh4 (b) FrankieMcDonald 8 44
(J T Stimpson) *hld up: rdn over 3f out: nt trble ldrs* 40/1
0-55 8 18 **Lawyer To World**67 [423] 5-8-7 50 JimmyQuinn 4 24
(Mrs C A Dunnett) *led: rdn and hdd over 2f out: wknd over 1f out* 20/1
000- 9 48 **Renege The Joker**265 [4302] 6-8-0 50 oh4 ow1 (t) RichardOld(7) 2 —
(S Regan) *hld up: bhd fnl 7f* 66/1

3m 34.84s (0.24) **Going Correction** -0.125s/f (Firm)
WFA 4 from 5yo+ 4lb 9 Ran SP% 116.2
Speed ratings (Par 103): **94,93,92,92,91 90,89,80,56**
toteswinger: 1&2 £4.20, 1&3 £11.80, 2&3 £7.70 CSF £29.96 CT £237.84 TOTE £7.40: £2.20, £1.50, £3.50; EX 35.30 Trifecta £444.10 Part won. Pool: £600.18 - 0.20 winning units..
Owner M P Bowring **Bred** R F And S D Knipe **Trained** Newmarket, Suffolk

FOCUS
The mist had descended once again and the visibility for this race was very limited. An ordinary staying handicap and the pace looked no more than ordinary.

1274 FREEBETS.CO.UK NEW ONLINE BETTING FORUM H'CAP 1m 2f 21y
4:50 (4:52) (Class 4) (0-85,85) 4-Y-O+ £5,828 (£1,734; £866; £432) Stalls Low

Form RPR
025- 1 **Serious Choice (IRE)**187 [6607] 4-8-4 71 oh1 LiamJones 2 83
(J R Boyle) *s.i.s: hld up: hdwy over 3f out: rdn to ld 1f out: r.o* 20/1
30-3 2 nk **Mystery Star (IRE)**8 [1149] 4-8-13 80 PaulMulrennan 6 91
(M H Tompkins) *hld up: hdwy over 3f out: rdn and ev ch ins fnl f: r.o* 9/2[2]
20-6 3 3 1/4 **Buddhist Monk**17 [999] 4-9-4 85 JimCrowley 7 90
(Ian Williams) *hld up: hdwy over 3f out: led over 1f out: sn rdn and hdd: styd on same pce* 4/1[1]
422 4 4 1/2 **Sri Kuantan (IRE)**1 [1261] 5-8-1 71 oh4 (t) DavidProbert(3) 1 67
(R C Guest) *chsd ldrs: led over 4f out: rdn and hdd over 1f out: wknd ins fnl f* 7/1[3]
-231 5 3/4 **Eton Fable (IRE)**7 [1175] 4-8-2 72 (p) KellyHarrison(3) 8 66
(W J H Ratcliffe) *led: hdd over 4f out: rdn and ev ch over 2f out: wknd over 1f out* 7/1[3]
/41- 6 2 1/2 **Bullet Man (USA)**118 [7712] 4-9-1 82 DaneO'Neill 4 71
(L M Cumani) *hld up in tch: outpcd 1/2-way: n.d after* 4/1[1]
460- 7 8 **Coyote Creek**192 [6479] 5-8-6 78 JPHamblett(5) 3 51
(E F Vaughan) *hld up: rdn over 3f out: n.d* 14/1
222- 8 3 3/4 **Dark Prospect**168 [7056] 4-8-12 79 PhilipRobinson 9 45
(M A Jarvis) *chsd ldr: rdn over 3f out: wknd 2f out* 9/2[2]

2m 7.86s (-2.64) **Going Correction** -0.125s/f (Firm) 8 Ran SP% 112.8
Speed ratings (Par 105): **105,104,102,98,97 95,89,86**
toteswinger: 1&2 £21.70, 1&3 £18.00, 2&3 £6.40 CSF £104.41 CT £439.93 TOTE £24.60: £5.50, £1.70, £1.40; EX 228.40 Trifecta £356.20 Pool £794.26 - 1.65 winning units. Place 6: £62.24 Place 5: £29.98.
Owner The Serious Choice Partnership **Bred** Ray Cullen **Trained** Epsom, Surrey

FOCUS
A fair handicap and the leaders may have done too much too soon as the first two home were held up out the back early. The winner looks progressive.
Eton Fable(IRE) Official explanation: jockey said gelding hung right
T/Jkpt: Not won. T/Plt: £106.80 to a £1 stake. Pool: £78,052.48. 533.50 winning tickets. T/Qpdt: £24.30 to a £1 stake. Pool: £5,373.87. 163.00 winning tickets. CR

BEVERLEY (R-H)
Wednesday, April 15

OFFICIAL GOING: Good to firm (9.5)
Wind: Moderate half behind Weather: Overcast and sunny periods

1275 RACING UK ON SKY 432 MAIDEN AUCTION STKS (DIV I) 5f
1:30 (1:38) (Class 5) 2-Y-O £2,590 (£770; £385; £192) Stalls High

Form RPR
3 1 **Jack My Boy (IRE)**13 [1083] 2-8-11 0 PaulDoe 14 77
(P D Evans) *mde most: rdn wl over 1f out: drvn and kpt on ins fnl f* 6/4[1]
05 2 2 1/4 **Heslington**7 [1188] 2-8-9 0 TWilliams 12 67
(M Brittain) *cl up: pushed along 2f out and ev ch tl drvn and one pce ent fnl f* 15/2[3]
3 1 3/4 **Tres Coronas (IRE)** 2-8-9 0 PhillipMakin 7 61
(T D Barron) *in tch: hdwy 1/2-way: rdn wl over 1f out: styd on ins fnl f: tk 3rd nr line* 16/1

5 4 nse **Bronze Beau**[18] 1005 2-8-9 0 ... TomEaves 5 60
(Mrs L Stubbs) *cl up: rdn 2f out: grad wknd appr fnl f* **11/1**

5 2 **Sharp Eclipse** 2-8-11 0 ... NCallan 11 55
(K A Ryan) *s.i.s and bhd: hdwy 1/2-way: rdn: rn green and hung bdly lft 1 1/2f out: styd on ins fnl f: nrst fin* **7/2**[2]

0 6 6 **Gazamali (IRE)**[11] 1126 2-8-13 0 ... SilvestreDeSousa 8 36
(G A Harker) *chsd ldrs: rdn along 2f out: grad wknd* **16/1**

7 nk **Bossy Kitty** 2-8-6 0 ... JoeFanning 13 28
(N Tinkler) *a in rr* **14/1**

8 1 1/4 **A Touch Of Luck** 2-8-13 0 ... DavidAllan 2 30
(T D Easterby) *in tch: rdn along 1/2-way: sn wknd* **50/1**

9 3/4 **Fairys In A Storm (IRE)** 2-8-0 0 ow3 ... PaulPickard(7) 4 21
(P T Midgley) *in tch: rdn along 2f out: sn wknd* **100/1**

0 10 3 **Captain Blake (IRE)**[11] 1119 2-8-11 0 ... FergusSweeney 3 15
(A B Haynes) *a in rr* **150/1**

11 1/2 **Ananda Kanda (USA)** 2-8-6 0 ... TonyHamilton 6 8
(B Ellison) *a in rr* **33/1**

12 19 **Strange Fiction** 2-8-9 0 ... PaulHanagan 1 —
(R A Fahey) *a in rr* **18/1**

62.92 secs (-0.58) **Going Correction** -0.225s/f (Firm) **12** Ran SP% **112.6**
Speed ratings (Par 92): **95,91,88,88,85 75,75,73,72,67 66,36**
toteswinger: 1&2 £4.20, 1&3 £9.80, 2&3 £20.50. CSF £12.16 TOTE £2.40: £1.40, £2.50, £3.60; EX 9.70.
Owner Terry Earle **Bred** Mrs Sheila Walker **Trained** Pandy, Monmouths

FOCUS
The ground had been watered but it was still on the quick side and there was quite a brisk breeze blowing half-behind. An ordinary maiden where the high draw played a part.

NOTEBOOK
Jack My Boy(IRE), third behind a subsequent winner at Leicester, had the plum high draw and soon taking them along, won going away in the end. (op 11-8 tchd 13-8)
Heslington, having his third start, matched strides with the winner from his favourable draw, but proved no match in the end. (op 17-2 tchd 9-1)
Tres Coronas(IRE) ◆, a close-coupled newcomer, shaped in pleasing fashion on his debut, picking up in good style late in the day.
Bronze Beau, who made his debut on the all-weather at Kempton, showed good speed from his low draw. He tended to edge left and faded near the line. He can be made fitter yet. (op 14-1)
Sharp Eclipse ◆, a well-made, compact newcomer, took the eye. After missing a beat at the start and showing his inexperience when asked to improve soon after halfway, he picked up in encouraging fashion. He will be a lot wiser next time and should improve and make his mark. (tchd 10-3)
A Touch Of Luck looked to be carrying plenty of condition, but he showed a glimmer of ability first time. (op 33-1)

1276 WELCOME BACK TO BEVERLEY (S) STKS 1m 100y
2:00 (2:01) (Class 5) 3-Y-O+ **£2,590** (£770; £385; £192) **Stalls** High

Form RPR

3-30 1 **Rowan Lodge (IRE)**[89] 194 7-9-13 61 ... (b) JamieMoriarty 1 59
(Ollie Pears) *hld up towards rr: swtchd lft and hdwy over 2f out: rdn over 1f out: str run ins fnl f: led nr fin* **12/1**

6654 2 nk **Bajan Pride**[19] 981 5-9-7 61 ... (v[1]) PaulHanagan 5 52
(R A Fahey) *hld up in mid-div: swtchd lft and hdwy over 2f out: rdn to chse ldr over 1f out: r.o ins fnl f* **10/3**[1]

05-6 3 nk **Ace Of Spies (IRE)**[14] 1057 4-9-7 50 ... (p) SilvestreDeSousa 13 52
(G A Harker) *led: clr over 2f out: hrd rdn over 1f out: wknd ins fnl f: ct nr fin* **11/1**

00-6 4 1 3/4 **Mister Maq**[45] 237 6-9-4 40 ... (v) KellyHarrison(3) 17 48
(A Crook) *hld up in rr: swtchd lft over 2f out: rdn and hdwy over 1f out: r.o ins fnl f: nrst fin* **150/1**

4630 5 nk **Ming Vase**[24] 918 7-9-6 47 ... PaulPickard(7) 12 53
(P T Midgley) *hld up in tch: rdn 2f out: kpt on ins fnl f* **28/1**

10-0 6 3/4 **My Mate Mal**[26] 898 5-9-6 58 ... LanceBetts(7) 16 51
(B Ellison) *hld up in tch: rdn over 2f out: kpt on same pce fnl f* **9/2**[3]

00-0 7 1/2 **Desert Hunter (IRE)**[2] 1243 6-9-7 44 ... TonyHamilton 15 44
(Micky Hammond) *t.k.h: a.p: chsd ldr 4f out tl rdn over 1f out: wknd ins fnl f* **14/1**

3203 8 1 1/2 **Prince Noel**[11] 1131 5-9-7 62 ... LeeEnstone 14 41
(N Wilson) *hld up in mid-div: pushed along whn hmpd on ins over 2f out: no imp whn nt clr run ins fnl f* **4/1**[2]

9 1 1/4 **Rosewin (IRE)**[131] 7566 3-8-1 0 ... PaulQuinn 9 29
(O Brennan) *s.s and wnt lft: in rr tl sme prog over 1f out: nvr nr ldrs* **100/1**

400 10 hd **Winged Farasi**[36] 791 5-9-7 47 ... (p) SamHitchcott 7 37
(Miss J E Foster) *hld up towards rr: rdn over 2f out: n.d* **40/1**

16-0 11 3 1/4 **Thompsons Walls (IRE)**[19] 981 4-9-13 71 ... TomEaves 10 36
(S T Mason) *prom tl hung rt and wknd over 2f out* **16/1**

000- 12 3/4 **Paint Stripper**[162] 7175 4-9-7 42 ... TWilliams 11 28
(W Storey) *hld up in mid-div: rdn over 2f out: wknd over 1f out* **200/1**

-140 13 2 1/4 **Herbert Crescent**[21] 959 4-9-7 62 ... PaulMulrennan 2 23
(Ollie Pears) *hld up in mid-div: n.m.r over 2f out: wknd wl over 1f out* **12/1**

006- 14 4 1/2 **Able Dara**[8] 7446 6-9-4 39 ... (b) MarkLawson(3) 6 13
(N Bycroft) *s.i.s: plld hrd in mid-div: bhd fnl 4f* **40/1**

060- 15 1 1/4 **Sheik'N'Knotsterd**[169] 7049 4-9-7 47 ... DavidAllan 4 10
(J F Coupland) *chsd ldr to 4f out: wkng whn n.m.r over 2f out* **125/1**

205- 16 16 **Captain Royale (IRE)**[113] 7772 4-9-7 58 ... (p) RobertWinston 3 —
(Miss Tracy Waggott) *plld hrd in mid-div on outside: c wd st: rdn over 2f out: hung rt and wknd wl over 1f out* **18/1**

6204 17 1 1/4 **Zabeel House**[16] 1030 6-9-7 46 ... (p) MickyFenton 8 —
(John A Harris) *a in rr* **16/1**

1m 46.77s (-0.83) **Going Correction** -0.075s/f (Good)
WFA 3 from 4yo+ 15lb **17** Ran SP% **119.9**
Speed ratings (Par 103): **101,100,100,98,98 97,97,95,94,94 90,90,87,83,82 66,64**
toteswinger: 1&2 £7.60, 1&3 £50.00, 2&3 £17.20. CSF £49.64 TOTE £9.10: £2.70, £1.60, £5.10; EX 44.90.There was no bid for the winner.
Owner K C West & Venture Racing **Bred** M P B Bloodstock Ltd **Trained** Norton, N Yorks
■ Stewards' Enquiry : Paul Pickard three-day ban: careless riding (Apr 29 - May 1)

FOCUS
The usual mixed bag with plenty having a lot to find on official ratings and a close finish.

1277 RACING UK ON SKY 432 MAIDEN AUCTION STKS (DIV II) 5f
2:35 (2:37) (Class 5) 2-Y-O **£2,590** (£770; £385; £192) **Stalls** High

Form RPR

1 **Fratellino** 2-8-9 0 ... RobertWinston 8 76
(A J McCabe) *cl up: edgd lft 2f out and sn rdn: edgd rt over 1f out: led and hung rt jst ins fnl f: kpt on* **20/1**

2 1 1/2 **Gower Sophia** 2-8-4 0 ... TWilliams 7 66
(M Brittain) *in tch: hdwy 2f out: swtchd lft and rdn over 1f out: styd on wl fnl f* **80/1**

2 3 1/2 **Tom Folan**[15] 1044 2-8-4 0 ... FrancisNorton 6 64
(H J Collingridge) *cl up: carried lft 2f out: sn rdn: edgd rt and led over 1f out: drvn and hdd jst ins fnl f: one pce* **3/1**[1]

4 1 **Masked Dance (IRE)** 2-8-13 0 ... NCallan 12 70
(K A Ryan) *sn led: rdn along and hung lft 2f out: hdd over 1f out: n.m.r and one pce ins fnl f* **3/1**[1]

5 nk **Maidtorun (IRE)** 2-8-6 0 ... PaulHanagan 5 64+
(R A Fahey) *dwlt: midfield and pushed along 1/2-way: hdwy over 1f out: styd on wl fnl f: nrst fin* **14/1**

6 1 1/2 **Mind Of Her Own** 2-8-5 0 ow1 ... PaulDoe 13 55
(P D Evans) *outpcd and rdn along towards rr: hdwy 2f out: styd on ins fnl f: nrst fin* **17/2**

6 dht **Oondiri (IRE)** 2-8-4 0 ... DuranFentiman 4 54
(T D Easterby) *chsd ldrs on outer: effrt 2f out: sn rdn and kpt on same pce appr fnl f* **33/1**

2 8 hd **Mr Smithson (IRE)**[12] 1097 2-8-9 0 ... GrahamGibbons 1 58
(B Ellison) *wnt rt s: a towards rr* **6/1**[2]

9 2 1/2 **Bateau Bleu** 2-8-9 0 ... PaulMulrennan 11 49
(P C Haslam) *a in rr* **25/1**

10 1 3/4 **Agent Boo** 2-8-11 0 ... PhillipMakin 9 45
(E S McMahon) *in tch: rdn along over 2f out and grad wknd* **13/2**[3]

0 11 3 1/2 **Lily Lenor (IRE)**[11] 1126 2-8-6 0 ... TonyHamilton 10 28
(B Ellison) *a in rr* **33/1**

12 nk **Dispol Kabira** 2-8-4 0 ... JoeFanning 14 24
(P T Midgley) *a in rr* **12/1**

13 1/2 **Choc'A'Moca (IRE)** 2-9-2 0 ... PatrickMathers 2 35
(I W McInnes) *a in rr* **100/1**

63.29 secs (-0.21) **Going Correction** -0.225s/f (Firm) **13** Ran SP% **119.2**
Speed ratings (Par 92): **92,89,88,87,86 84,84,84,80,77 71,71,70**
toteswinger: 1&2 £57.30, 1&3 £16.30, 2&3 £32.00. CSF £1061.38 TOTE £24.00: £3.70, £8.80, £1.60; EX 1035.80.
Owner Sale Of The Century **Bred** Llety Stud **Trained** Averham Park, Notts

FOCUS
Paddock inspection suggested this was the weaker division, confirmed by the slower time. This time the principals were drawn in the centre of the field.

NOTEBOOK
Fratellino ◆, a close-coupled newcomer, was carried wide before ducking left. He ran out a decisive winner in the end and, eliminated from the Brocklesby, will improve. (op 16-1)
Gower Sophia stayed on strongly to take second spot in the closing stages and will be wiser next time. (op 100-1)
Tom Folan, runner-up at Folkestone on her debut, lacks size and scope. She was carried wide coming to the final furlong, but this may be as good as she is. (op 9-2)
Masked Dance(IRE), drawn in double figures, took them along but he went left-handed coming to the final furlong and weakened in the closing stages. This will hopefully have taught him plenty. (op 9-4)
Maidtorun(IRE) showed ability, picking up nicely late in the day. (tchd 16-1)
Mind Of Her Own had a favourable draw, but lacked the early pace to capitalize on it. She should be sharper next time though. (op 15-2 tchd 7-1)
Mr Smithson(IRE), having his second start, had the worst of the draw. He gave problems in the stalls, dived left when they opened and never really featured. (op 7-1)

1278 SPRING INTO RACING AT BEVERLEY H'CAP 5f
3:10 (3:11) (Class 3) (0-95,95) 4-Y-O+ **£7,641** (£2,273; £1,136; £567) **Stalls** High

Form RPR

530- 1 **Fol Hollow (IRE)**[164] 7151 4-8-3 87 ... AdeleMulrennan(7) 15 97
(D Nicholls) *mde all: rdn fnl f: r.o* **6/1**[2]

000- 2 3/4 **Aegean Dancer**[164] 7151 7-8-7 84 ow1 ... TomEaves 8 92
(B Smart) *chsd ldrs: rdn and wnt 2nd ins fnl f: kpt on* **11/1**

60-0 3 1/2 **Everymanforhimself (IRE)**[17] 1018 5-8-13 90 ... (p) NCallan 13 96
(K A Ryan) *mid-div: hrd rdn over 1f out: r.o wl to take 3rd nr fin* **5/1**[1]

4322 4 1/2 **Bo McGinty (IRE)**[19] 985 8-8-4 81 oh1 ... (v) PaulHanagan 14 85
(R A Fahey) *w wnr tl rdn over 1f out: no ex ins fnl f* **7/1**[3]

0-21 5 shd **Obe Gold**[26] 892 7-8-10 87 ... (v) PaulQuinn 7 91
(D Nicholls) *mid-div: rdn over 1f out: kpt on towards fin* **14/1**

232- 6 1/2 **Supermassive Muse (IRE)**[179] 6810 4-8-12 89 .. (p) GrahamGibbons 11 91
(E S McMahon) *chsd ldrs: rdn over 1f out: one pce* **12/1**

2224 7 hd **Whiskey Creek**[15] 1052 4-8-5 82 ... (b) RobertWinston 10 83
(C A Dwyer) *w ldrs: rdn over 1f out: fdd towards fin* **8/1**

000- 8 3/4 **Lord Of The Reins (IRE)**[186] 6650 5-8-8 85 ow1 ... PaulMulrennan 6 83
(J G Given) *hld up in rr: sme late prog: nvr nrr* **66/1**

344- 9 nk **Manzila (FR)**[195] 6430 6-9-1 95 ... AndrewMullen(3) 12 92
(D Nicholls) *hld up in mid-div: no hdwy fnl f* **14/1**

-040 10 1/2 **Northern Fling**[17] 1018 5-9-4 95 ... SilvestreDeSousa 2 91
(D Nicholls) *hld up towards rr: rdn over 1f out: n.d* **16/1**

00-0 11 1 **Ajigolo**[17] 1018 6-8-11 88 ... LeeEnstone 9 80
(N Wilson) *in rr: nvr trbld ldrs* **40/1**

54-0 12 3/4 **Baldemar**[17] 1018 4-8-10 87 ... AndrewElliott 16 76
(K R Burke) *s.i.s: sn mid-div: wknd over 1f out* **12/1**

31-0 13 hd **Fyodor (IRE)**[88] 204 8-9-0 91 ... FergusSweeney 4 80
(C R Dore) *s.i.s: sn swtchd rt: a bhd* **33/1**

10-0 14 1/2 **Timber Treasure (USA)**[13] 1089 5-8-4 81 oh1 ... (b) FrancisNorton 17 68
(Paul Green) *chsd ldrs: rdn and wknd 1f out* **11/1**

030- 15 3/4 **Sunrise Safari (IRE)**[208] 6069 6-8-4 88 ... BMcHugh(7) 5 72
(R A Fahey) *a in rr* **12/1**

000- 16 1/2 **Hotham**[159] 7222 6-8-9 86 ow2 ... JamieMoriarty 3 68
(N Wilson) *a in rr* **40/1**

000- 17 4 1/2 **Nacho Libre**[162] 7176 4-8-8 85 ... DaleGibson 1 51
(M W Easterby) *a in rr* **100/1**

61.46 secs (-2.04) **Going Correction** -0.225s/f (Firm) **17** Ran SP% **123.8**
Speed ratings (Par 107): **107,105,105,104,104 103,102,101,101,100 98,97,97,96,95 94,87**
toteswinger: 1&2 £29.10, 1&3 £7.50, 2&3 £17.00. CSF £69.45 CT £375.50 TOTE £7.50: £2.10, £3.00, £1.80, £1.50; EX 118.40.
Owner Middleham Park Races **Bred** Dan O'Brien **Trained** Sessay, N Yorks
■ Stewards' Enquiry : Adele Mulrennan one-day ban: used whip in incorrect place (Apr 29)

FOCUS
A good-class sprint handicap and as is always the case over 5f here there was a mad dash to secure the favoured far side rail and those drawn high dominated.

NOTEBOOK
Fol Hollow(IRE), a winner three times at two, has drawn a blank since but he has plenty of good effort to his name. Fit and on his toes beforehand, from a favourable draw he grabbed the rail position and never really looked like being overhauled. He will not be resting on his laurels and is due to turn out again at Naas on Saturday. (tchd 11-2)
Aegean Dancer, 9lb lower than his last success, looked in good trim. Drawn in single figures, he travelled strongly on the heels of the leaders. Sent in pursuit of the winner, he was closing all the way to the line without ever threatening to get there. He has run well fresh in the past. (op 12-1)
Everymanforhimself(IRE), in first-time cheekpieces, ran a lot better than on his return. Back on his last winning mark, he stuck on strongly and is perhaps better suited by 6f. (op 11-2 tchd 9-2)

Bo McGinty(IRE) ran his usual solid race, but he is hard to win with. (op 8-1)
Obe Gold, raised 7lb after his all-weather success, had to make his effort on the wide outside and is clearly in very good heart. (op 20-1)
Supermassive Muse(IRE) improved a good deal at three and as a result resumed here 10lb higher than his last success. He looked in good trim beforehand and stuck on in solid fashion all the way to the line. (op 11-1 tchd 14-1)
Whiskey Creek has been in fine form on the all-weather, but he has yet to be placed in eight starts on turf now. (tchd 9-1)
Lord Of The Reins(IRE), who cut little ice in three starts after his victory at Newmarket in August, stayed on nicely after encountering traffic problems. (tchd 80-1)
Manzila(FR) looked short of her peak beforehand. (op 11-1)
Northern Fling, who looked very fit, had to race on the outer from stall two. (op 18-1)
Ajigolo looked very wintry. (tchd 50-1)
Sunrise Safari(IRE) looked very fit, but was always towards the rear from his low draw. (op 20-1)

1279 RAPID LAD STKS (H'CAP) — 1m 1f 207y

3:45 (3:45) (Class 5) (0-70,69) 4-Y-0+ — **£2,590** (£770; £385; £192) **Stalls** High

Form / RPR

452- **1** **Sirvino**[189] 6585 4-9-0 **65**.................... PhillipMakin 13 — 74
(T D Barron) *trckd ldrs: hdwy over 1f out: rdn ent fnl f: styd on to ld last 100yds* **4/1**[2]

5543 **2** *1* **New Beginning (IRE)**[7] 1192 5-8-12 **63**.................... RobertWinston 12 — 70
(Mrs S Lamyman) *trckd ldrs: hdwy over 2f out: rdn over 1f out: led ent fnl f: drvn: hdd and no ex last 100yds* **11/4**[1]

040- **3** *1 ¾* **King Of The Moors (USA)**[193] 6485 6-8-9 **65**........... MarkCoumbe(5) 9 — 69
(R C Guest) *hld up in midfield: hdwy on outer 3f out: rdn to chse ldrs over 1f out: kpt on ins fnl f* **28/1**

55-4 **4** *¾* **Destinys Dream (IRE)**[11] 1125 4-9-2 **67**.................... NCallan 5 — 69
(Miss Tracy Waggott) *trckd ldrs: hdwy whn n.m.r 2f out: effrt and n.m.r over 1f out: sn rdn and kpt on ins fnl f: nrst fin* **12/1**

400- **5** *nse* **Fell Pack**[50] 5361 5-8-4 **55** oh1.................... JoeFanning 11 — 57
(J J Quinn) *in rr: hdwy on wd outside wl over 1f out: rdn and styd on strly ins fnl f: nrst fin* **11/1**

035- **6** *nse* **Moonstreaker**[141] 7447 6-8-10 **64**.................... MichaelJStainton(3) 8 — 66
(R M Whitaker) *s.i.s and towards rr: hdwy on outer wl over 1f out: rdn to chse ldrs over 1f out: sn drvn and kpt on same pce* **16/1**

6122 **7** *1* **Snow Dancer (IRE)**[26] 897 5-8-12 **68**....................(p) SladeO'Hara(5) 3 — 68
(H A McWilliams) *in tch on outer: hdwy to chse ldrs 3f out: rdn over 2f out: drvn and one pce over 1f out* **14/1**

00-4 **8** *hd* **Titinius (IRE)**[12] 1099 9-8-6 **57**....................(p) TonyHamilton 16 — 56
(Micky Hammond) *chsd ldrs on inner: rdn along over 2f out: drvn over 1f out and grad wknd* **16/1**

012- **9** *nse* **Cheers For Thea (IRE)**[252] 4738 4-8-6 **57**.................... DuranFentiman 10 — 56
(T D Easterby) *led: hdd over 4f out: cl up tl led again over 2f out and sn rdn: drvn and hdd ent fnl f: wknd* **25/1**

100- **10** *1 ½* **Malinsa Blue (IRE)**[130] 7581 7-8-6 **57**....................(p) GrahamGibbons 1 — 53
(B Ellison) *in tch: hdwy to trck ldrs 3f out: rdn 2f out: n.m.r over 1f out and sn btn* **25/1**

5625 **11** *¾* **Epidaurian King (IRE)**[20] 559 6-8-9 **60** ow1.................... DarrenWilliams 7 — 55
(D Shaw) *hld up: a in rr* **16/1**

4515 **12** *1 ¾* **Inside Story (IRE)**[36] 795 7-9-0 **65**....................(b) PaulMulrennan 4 — 56
(C R Dore) *chsd ldrs: rdn along 3f out: wknd over 2f out* **20/1**

0/6- **13** *1 ¼* **Rain And Shade**[343] 1909 5-8-12 **63**.................... TomEaves 17 — 52
(E W Tuer) *cl up: led over 4f out: rdn 3f out: hdd over 2f out and sn wknd* **66/1**

00-5 **14** *1 ¾* **Fortunate Isle (USA)**[12] 1100 7-9-4 **69**.................... PaulHanagan 14 — 54
(R A Fahey) *midfield: effrt on inner 3f out: sn pushed along and wknd* **13/2**[3]

306- **15** *½* **Trouble Mountain (USA)**[168] 7085 12-8-10 **61**..............(t) DaleGibson 2 — 45
(M W Easterby) *prom tl rdn along 3f out and sn wknd* **80/1**

60-0 **16** *2 ¾* **Fern House (IRE)**[57] 574 7-8-4 **55** oh10.................... TWilliams 15 — 34
(Bruce Hellier) *hld up: a in rr* **200/1**

2m 7.52s (0.52) **Going Correction** -0.075s/f (Good) — **16** Ran SP% **119.5**
Speed ratings (Par 103): **94,93,91,91,91 91,90,90,90,88 88,86,85,84,84 81**
toteswinger: 1&2 £4.30, 1&3 £27.90, 2&3 £16.20. CSF £13.93 CT £275.61 TOTE £5.20: £1.30, £1.50, £6.60, £2.90; EX 15.80.
Owner Theo Williams and Charles Mocatta **Bred** A W J Perry **Trained** Maunby, N Yorks

FOCUS
A modest event and the pace was not strong.
Inside Story(IRE) Official explanation: jockey said gelding ran too free
Fortunate Isle(USA) Official explanation: jockey said gelding was never travelling

1280 NEW PREMIER ENCLOSURE ENTRANCE H'CAP — 1m 1f 207y

4:20 (4:20) (Class 4) (0-80,80) 3-Y-O — **£4,727** (£1,406; £702; £351) **Stalls** High

Form / RPR

232- **1** **Dubai Crest**[177] 6857 3-9-1 **77**.................... NCallan 7 — 86+
(Mrs A J Perrett) *hld up in tch: hdwy over 2f out: n.m.r over 1f out: nt clr run and swtchd outside ent fnl f: rdn and qcknd wl to ld last 100yds: sn clr* **9/4**[1]

2-12 **2** *1 ¾* **Gaily Noble (IRE)**[32] 840 3-9-4 **80**.................... FergusSweeney 6 — 82
(A B Haynes) *trckd ldrs gng wl: smooth hdwy 2f out: rdn to ld ent fnl f: drvn: hdd and one pce last 100yds* **10/1**

63-3 **3** *1 ½* **Princability (IRE)**[25] 917 3-9-0 **76**.................... SamHitchcott 5 — 75
(M R Channon) *led: rdn along and hdd 2f out: drvn over 1f out: kpt on u.p ins fnl f* **12/1**

534- **4** *1* **Tarzan (IRE)**[203] 6197 3-8-9 **71**.................... JoeFanning 3 — 68
(M Johnston) *trckd ldr: hdwy to ld 2f out and sn rdn: drvn: edgd lft and hdd ent fnl f: wknd* **7/1**[3]

11-4 **5** *1 ¾* **Digger Derek (IRE)**[15] 1056 3-8-11 **73**.................... PaulHanagan 9 — 67
(R A Fahey) *chsd ldrs: rdn along 2f out: drvn over 1f out and sn btn* **9/2**[2]

3412 **6** *1* **Diamond Twister (USA)**[21] 962 3-9-1 **77**..............(t) RobertWinston 2 — 69
(J R Best) *hld up in tch: effrt over 2f out: sn rdn: edgd rt and wknd wl over 1f out* **8/1**

150- **7** *2 ¼* **Amethyst Dawn (IRE)**[173] 6946 3-8-13 **75**.................... DavidAllan 8 — 62
(T D Easterby) *plld hrd: hld up in rr: effrt over 2f out: sn rdn and no hdwy* **7/1**[3]

5-41 **8** *2 ¾* **Spartan Prince (USA)**[58] 570 3-8-8 **70**.................... PhillipMakin 4 — 52
(T D Barron) *hld up: a in rr* **8/1**

2m 6.11s (-0.89) **Going Correction** -0.075s/f (Good) — **8** Ran SP% **113.0**
Speed ratings (Par 100): **100,98,97,96,95 94,92,90**
toteswinger: 1&2 £4.40, 1&3 £6.20, 2&3 £9.50. CSF £25.26 CT £218.67 TOTE £3.00: £1.30, £2.20, £3.10; EX 26.30.
Owner A D Spence **Bred** Bearstone Stud **Trained** Pulborough, W Sussex

FOCUS
A fair three-year-old stayers' handicap, but the pace was very steady.

1281 WHISTLEJACKETS CAFE STKS (H'CAP) — 7f 100y

4:55 (4:56) (Class 5) (0-70,75) 3-Y-O — **£2,590** (£770; £385; £192) **Stalls** High

Form / RPR

10- **1** **More Than Many (USA)**[223] 5632 3-8-9 **60**.................... PaulHanagan 13 — 76+
(R A Fahey) *midfield: swtchd lft and hdwy 2f out: rdn and strong run to ld jst ins fnl f: sn hung rt and clr* **5/2**[2]

02-2 **2** *3 ¾* **Labisa (IRE)**[7] 1193 3-8-13 **64**.................... RobertWinston 12 — 71+
(H Morrison) *trckd ldrs: hdwy over 2f out: cl up over 1f out: shkn up and ev ch whn n.m.r ent fnl f: sn rdn and hmpd: one pce after* **10/11**[1]

03-3 **3** *2 ¼* **Miss Cameo (USA)**[93] 134 3-8-4 **55** oh7.................... PaulQuinn 14 — 56
(R M Whitaker) *in rr: hdwy 2f out: rdn and styd on wl fnl f: nrst fin* **22/1**

501- **4** *shd* **Embsay Crag**[170] 7016 3-8-13 **67**.................... NeilBrown(3) 9 — 68
(Mrs K Walton) *trckd ldr: hdwy 3f out: rdn wl over 1f out: n.m.r ent fnl f and sn wknd* **10/1**[3]

-600 **5** *1* **Dante Deo (USA)**[11] 1128 3-8-4 **55**.................... FrancisNorton 4 — 53
(T D Barron) *towards rr: hdwy on outer 2f out: rdn and styd on appr fnl f: nrst fin* **28/1**

44-1 **6** *2 ½* **Kheskianto (IRE)**[69] 403 3-8-1 **59**.................... AndrewHeffernan(7) 8 — 51
(M C Chapman) *chsd ldng pair: effrt over 2f out and sn rdn: drvn and wknd over 1f out* **22/1**

2220 **7** *1 ¾* **Dancing Wave**[19] 986 3-8-3 **57**.................... KellyHarrison(3) 2 — 45
(M C Chapman) *led: rdn clr wl over 2f out: rdn over 1f out: sn hdd & wknd* **50/1**

005- **8** *1 ¼* **Nut Hand (IRE)**[203] 6213 3-8-7 **58**.................... DavidAllan 10 — 43
(T D Easterby) *a midfield* **20/1**

006- **9** *1 ¾* **Miss Gibboa (IRE)**[223] 5633 3-8-0 **56**.................... PatrickDonaghy(5) 15 — 36
(P C Haslam) *nvr nr ldrs* **22/1**

00-2 **10** *2 ½* **Prince Andjo (USA)**[12] 1108 3-8-9 **60**.................... PatrickMathers 6 — 34
(I W McInnes) *dwlt: a in rr* **33/1**

-460 **11** *2 ½* **Floods Of Tears**[16] 1036 3-8-6 **57** oh3 ow2.................... JamesDoyle 1 — 25
(D Flood) *chsd ldrs: rdn along wl over 2f out: sn wknd* **66/1**

046- **12** *1* **Hawkleaf Flier (IRE)**[196] 6381 3-8-5 **56**.................... DuranFentiman 3 — 21
(T D Easterby) *s.i.s: a in rr* **50/1**

-504 **13** *3 ¾* **Miss Cracklinrosie**[20] 968 3-8-5 **56**....................(p) GrahamGibbons 7 — 12
(J R Weymes) *chsd ldrs: rdn along over 2f out and sn wknd* **20/1**

0-60 **14** *9* **Sams Spirit**[15] 1047 3-8-7 **58**.................... TonyHamilton 11 — —
(P J McBride) *a in rr* **50/1**

1m 32.69s (-1.11) **Going Correction** -0.075s/f (Good) — **14** Ran SP% **126.4**
Speed ratings (Par 98): **103,98,96,96,94 92,90,88,86,83 80,79,75,65**
toteswinger: 1&2 £2.30, 1&3 £9.50, 2&3 £9.10. CSF £4.57 CT £42.75 TOTE £4.00: £1.50, £1.30, £4.70; EX 6.40.
Owner The Rumpole Partnership **Bred** Wall Street Thoroughbreds **Trained** Musley Bank, N Yorks
■ Stewards' Enquiry : Paul Hanagan one-day ban: careless riding (Apr 29)

FOCUS
A modest handicap run at a sound pace and a winner of some potential.
Hawkleaf Flier(IRE) Official explanation: jockey said filly was restless in the stalls and missed the break

1282 RACING HERE AGAIN NEXT THURSDAY H'CAP — 1m 4f 16y

5:30 (5:31) (Class 5) (0-70,68) 3-Y-O — **£2,590** (£770; £385; £192) **Stalls** High

Form / RPR

4612 **1** **Dispol Diva**[14] 1063 3-8-13 **63**....................(v) PhillipMakin 8 — 66
(P T Midgley) *trckd ldrs: hdwy over 2f out: rdn to ld ent fnl f: sn drvn and hld on gamely* **5/2**[1]

4410 **2** *nk* **Kochanski (IRE)**[14] 1070 3-8-7 **57**.................... JoeFanning 6 — 59
(M Johnston) *hld up: hdwy over 2f out: rdn over 1f out: styd on to chal ins fnl f: sn drvn and no ex towards fin* **14/1**

4054 **3** *4 ½* **Screaming Brave**[14] 1070 3-8-4 **54**....................(v) PaulHanagan 2 — 49
(M R Channon) *led: rdn along over 2f out: drvn and hdd ent fnl f: one pce* **15/2**

006- **4** *1 ¼* **Bollin Judith**[144] 7422 3-8-5 **55**.................... DuranFentiman 5 — 48
(T D Easterby) *hld up and bhd: hdwy over 2f out: n.m.r wl over 1f out: swtchd lft and rdn: kpt on ins fnl f: nrst fin* **9/1**

60-4 **5** *1* **Troubletimestwo (FR)**[20] 970 3-9-3 **67**.................... FrancisNorton 3 — 58
(H J L Dunlop) *chsd ldr: rdn along over 2f out: drvn and edgd rt over 1f out: sn btn* **11/2**[3]

4241 **6** *½* **Good Buy Dubai (USA)**[14] 1070 3-8-12 **62**.................... RobertWinston 7 — 53
(J R Best) *in tch: effrt 3f out: rdn along over 2f out: drvn wl over 1f out and sn btn* **10/3**[2]

30-6 **7** *1* **Extremely So**[14] 1070 3-8-7 **57**.................... TonyHamilton 1 — 46
(P J McBride) *in tch: hdwy to chse ldrs 4f out: rdn along over 2f out and sn wknd* **16/1**

30-0 **8** *3 ¼* **Saffron's Son (IRE)**[49] 677 3-7-13 **56**.................... PaulPickard(7) 4 — 40
(P T Midgley) *prom: rdn along 3f out and sn wknd* **16/1**

365- **9** *5* **Woteva**[173] 6954 3-9-4 **68**....................(p) TomEaves 9 — 44
(B Ellison) *hld up: a towards rr* **12/1**

2m 39.74s (-1.16) **Going Correction** -0.075s/f (Good) — **9** Ran SP% **114.9**
Speed ratings (Par 98): **100,99,96,95,95 94,94,92,88**
toteswinger: 1&2 £8.00, 1&3 £4.30, 2&3 £9.10. CSF £39.04 CT £232.31 TOTE £3.50: £1.10, £2.70, £2.50; EX 35.80 Place 6: £56.31, Place 5: £38.25..
Owner W B Imison **Bred** P C Hunt **Trained** Westow, N Yorks

FOCUS
Modest fare but the first two came clear.
T/Plt: £87.50 to a £1 stake. Pool: £49,099.82. 409.43 winning tickets. T/Qpdt: £17.80 to a £1 stake. Pool: £3,447.17. 142.75 winning tickets. JR

1209 KEMPTON (A.W) (R-H)

Wednesday, April 15

OFFICIAL GOING: Standard
Wind: Fresh, half behind Weather: Dull

1283 PANORAMIC BAR & RESTAURANT CLAIMING STKS — 1m (P)

6:50 (6:50) (Class 6) 4-Y-O+ — **£2,047** (£604; £302) **Stalls** High

Form / RPR

00-0 **1** **Scartozz**[33] 834 7-8-10 **85**.................... AndreaAtzeni(5) 4 — 81
(M Botti) *led main gp bhd clr ldr: clsd over 2f out: rdn to ld over 1f out: hld on wl last 100yds* **2/1**[1]

3131 **2** *½* **Jake The Snake (IRE)**[13] 1079 8-9-1 **78**.................... AmyBaker(5) 5 — 85
(A W Carroll) *hld up in 5th bhd clr ldr: prog over 2f out: urged along to go 2nd jst over 1f out: pressed wnr last 100yds: a jst hld* **5/1**[3]

-123 **3** 3 1/2 **Colonel Sherman (USA)**[63] 497 4-9-0 67 AdamKirby 3 71
(L A Dace) *led and sn at least 12 l clr: c bk over 2f out: hdd and btn over 1f out: plugged on to keep 3rd* **5/1**[3]

-123 **4** 3/4 **Fremen (USA)**[13] 1079 9-8-11 84 NSLawes[(7)] 6 73
(D Nicholls) *hld up in 4th bhd clr ldr: rdn over 2f out: no imp over 1f out: fdd* **13/2**

213- **5** 1 1/4 **Eastern Gift**[123] 7668 4-9-1 75 KylieManser[(7)] 1 74
(Miss Gay Kelleway) *hld up in 3rd bhd clr ldr: urged along and edgd lft fr over 1f out: steadily fdd* **16/1**

1232 **6** 1/2 **Tous Les Deux**[13] 1079 6-9-1 82 GeorgeBaker 2 66
(G L Moore) *stdd s: hld up in last: shkn up over 2f out: no prog: wl btn fnl f* **11/4**[2]

1m 39.33s (-0.47) **Going Correction** -0.05s/f (Stan) **6** Ran SP% **112.5**
Speed ratings (Par 101): **100,99,96,95,94 93**
toteswinger: 1&2 £2.20, 1&3 £7.80, 2&3 £3.80. CSF £12.45 TOTE £2.50: £1.50, £1.60; EX 14.60.Colonel Sherman was claimed by P Kirby for £12,000.

Owner Dioscuri Srl **Bred** Lord Halifax **Trained** Newmarket, Suffolk

FOCUS
Only a handful of runners but a couple of fair sorts for the grade. The clear leader was virtually ignored for much of the way.

1284 DIGIBET H'CAP (LONDON MILE QUALIFIER) 1m (P)
7:20 (7:21) (Class 4) (0-80,80) 3-Y-O **£4,727** (£1,406; £702; £351) **Stalls** High

Form RPR

13 **1** **Set The Trend**[16] 1033 3-9-4 **80** LPKeniry 5 94
(A M Balding) *trckd ldng pair: ready prog to ld jst over 2f out: rdn over 1f out: hrd pressed and looked vulnerable fnl f: r.o wl* **13/8**[1]

422- **2** nk **Antinori (IRE)**[175] 6892 3-9-3 **79** AdamKirby 9 92
(W R Swinburn) *hld up in 6th: smooth prog jutst over 2f out to chse wnr over 1f out: shkn up to chal fnl f: edgd lft and rt: outbattled* **4/1**[2]

50-2 **3** 4 1/2 **Simplification**[26] 890 3-8-13 **75** RyanMoore 7 78
(R Hannon) *sn in 5th: pushed along 1/2-way: under maximum press 3f out and gng nowhere: kpt on to take 3rd fnl f* **7/1**

631 **4** 1/2 **Keep Ringing (USA)**[16] 1040 3-8-13 **75** LiamJones 4 77
(W J Haggas) *s.i.s: hld up in last trio: prog 2f out to chse ldrs 1f out: effrt flattened out fnl f* **16/1**

240- **5** 1 1/4 **Hip Hip Hooray**[170] 7016 3-8-4 **66** oh1 CatherineGannon 1 65
(L A Dace) *settled in last: rdn wl over 2f out: prog wl over 1f out to go 5th ent fnl f: one pce after: n.m.r nr fin* **33/1**

631- **6** 3 3/4 **Brooksby**[161] 7190 3-8-12 **74** PatDobbs 11 64
(R Hannon) *led to over 2f out: sn lost pl and btn* **14/1**

010- **7** 1/2 **Tidal Force (USA)**[228] 5511 3-8-3 **72** DTDaSilva[(7)] 10 61
(P F I Cole) *awkward s: rcvrd to trck ldng pair on inner: rdn over 2f out: sn lost pl and btn* **25/1**

304- **8** 3/4 **Jazacosta (USA)**[208] 6086 3-9-1 **77** JimCrowley 8 64
(Mrs A J Perrett) *a in last trio: pushed along 1/2-way: no prog and struggling over 2f out* **5/1**[3]

541- **9** 1 3/4 **Herschel (IRE)**[136] 7505 3-9-0 **76** GeorgeBaker 3 59
(G L Moore) *pressed ldr: led briefly over 2f out: sn beating a retreat* **8/1**

1m 38.44s (-1.36) **Going Correction** -0.05s/f (Stan) **9** Ran SP% **117.7**
Speed ratings (Par 100): **104,103,99,98,97 93,93,92,90**
toteswinger: 1&2 £2.90, 1&3 £3.20, 2&3 £8.90. CSF £8.22 CT £35.96 TOTE £3.00: £1.40, £1.40, £2.30; EX 11.30.

Owner Favourites Racing XXII **Bred** Old Suffolk Stud **Trained** Kingsclere, Hants

FOCUS
A fair handicap run at a reasonable gallop (just outside Racing Post standard) and one in which two progressive sorts, who raced in the centre, pulled clear in the closing stages.

1285 DIGIBET.COM H'CAP 6f (P)
7:50 (7:50) (Class 6) (0-65,66) 4-Y-O+ **£2,047** (£604; £302) **Stalls** High

Form RPR

2202 **1** **Compton Classic**[27] 880 7-9-2 **63** (p) PatCosgrave 12 74
(J R Boyle) *trckd ldng trio on inner: gng strly over 2f out: led wl over 1f out: wl in command fnl f* **6/1**[3]

4500 **2** 2 1/4 **Mudhish (IRE)**[21] 956 4-9-4 **65** (b) RyanMoore 8 69
(C E Brittain) *chsd ldng trio: lost pl sltly over 3f out: effrt over 2f out on inner: wnt 2nd jst over 1f out: no imp on wnr* **8/1**

000- **3** nk **Desert Pride**[215] 5867 4-9-1 **62** IanMongan 2 65
(W S Kittow) *wl in rr on outer: u.p 1/2-way: kpt on fr 2f out to take 3rd nr fin* **20/1**

004- **4** nse **Our Blessing (IRE)**[133] 7540 5-8-11 **63** MartinLane[(5)] 11 66
(A P Jarvis) *mde most in narrow ld on inner: hdd and one pce wl over 1f out* **9/2**[1]

-520 **5** 1 1/2 **Lord Deevert**[9] 1152 4-8-11 **63** JackDean[(5)] 10 61
(W G M Turner) *w ldr to 2f out: steadily outpcd u.p* **9/1**

605- **6** hd **Gold Again (USA)**[191] 6543 4-9-0 **61** (t) AdamKirby 1 58
(W R Swinburn) *dropped in fr wd draw and hld up in last: reminder 2f out: prog fr over 1f out: pushed along and styd on steadily fnl f* **8/1**

1310 **7** 1 1/4 **Hollow Jo**[28] 861 9-9-4 **65** (v) JimCrowley 7 58
(J R Jenkins) *settled towards rr on outer: rdn over 2f out: no real prog over 1f out and whn short of room ins fnl f* **9/1**

3551 **8** 3/4 **Cape Of Storms**[19] 975 6-8-12 **64** (b) FrederikTylicki[(5)] 5 55
(R Brotherton) *chsd ldng trio: u.p over 2f out: steadily lost pl fnl 2f* **6/1**[3]

0-20 **9** 1/2 **Peopleton Brook**[9] 1152 7-9-2 **63** (t) GeorgeBaker 4 52
(B G Powell) *trckd ldng trio on outer: gng wl enough over 2f out: rdn and no rspnse 2f out: sn lost pl* **9/1**

0-0 **10** 4 1/2 **Colombard (IRE)**[2] 1244 4-9-3 **64** NeilPollard 9 39
(Patrick Morris) *stdd s: hld up towards rr: rdn 1/2-way: no prog* **25/1**

0-01 **11** 4 1/2 **Garstang**[7] 1182 6-9-5 **66** 6ex (b) EddieAhern 6 27
(J Balding) *t.k.h early: w ldng pair on outer: wknd rapidly jst over 2f out: eased* **11/2**[2]

1m 12.47s (-0.63) **Going Correction** -0.05s/f (Stan) **11** Ran SP% **123.0**
Speed ratings (Par 101): **102,99,98,98,96 96,94,93,92,86 80**
toteswinger: 1&2 £12.40, 1&3 £11.20, 2&3 £62.40. CSF £56.06 CT £939.58 TOTE £7.00: £1.60, £4.70, £3.50; EX 77.10.

Owner M Khan X2 **Bred** James Thom And Sons And Peter Orr **Trained** Epsom, Surrey

FOCUS
A modest handicap in which the pace was sound throughout. The winner raced centre to far side in the closing stages.

Garstang Official explanation: jockey said gelding ran too free

1286 DIGIBET SPORTS BETTING MAIDEN STKS 1m 4f (P)
8:20 (8:23) (Class 5) 3-Y-O+ **£2,590** (£770; £385; £192) **Stalls** Centre

Form RPR

243- **1** **It's Dubai Dolly**[165] 7142 3-8-2 80 WandersonD'Avila 10 71+
(A J Lidderdale) *t.k.h: trckd ldr: clsd gng easily to ld over 2f out: shuffled along fnl 2f: comf* **16/1**

30- **2** 2 **Dancer In Demand (IRE)**[286] 3637 4-9-13 0 RyanMoore 5 75+
(Sir Michael Stoute) *hld up off the pce in midfield: prog into 5th 4f out: rdn to cl over 2f out: kpt on at one pce to snatch 2nd last strides: no threat to wnr* **5/6**[1]

6-4 **3** hd **Favours Brave**[13] 1087 3-8-7 0 RichardMullen 6 72+
(J H M Gosden) *trckd ldng pair: pushed along over 3f out: wnt 2nd 2f out: hrd rdn and no imp on wnr after* **11/4**[2]

4 8 **King Red**[20] 5-10-0 0 RichardKingscote 2 62
(Tom Dascombe) *dwlt: t.k.h early and hld up in last: nvr anywhere nr the pce: prog fr 4f out: hung lft over 2f out: styd on: nrst fin* **16/1**

5 2 1/4 **Tabaran (FR)**[539] 6-10-0 50 AdamKirby 3 58
(L A Dace) *hld up wl in rr and nvr nr the pce but travelled wl enough: modest prog 3f out: reminder over 2f out: kpt on steadily: nrst fin* **100/1**

33-2 **6** 6 **Khan Tengri (IRE)**[20] 970 3-8-7 75 (b[1]) MartinDwyer 4 46
(M P Tregoning) *hld up in midfield: prog to go 4th 5f out: sn pushed along: reluctant u.p over 2f out and wl btn after* **9/2**[3]

7 5 **Brave Beat** 3-8-7 0 JimmyQuinn 9 38
(H J L Dunlop) *sn u.p in midfield: lost pl 1/2-way: wl in rr and off the pce 4f out: plugged on slowly* **66/1**

00 **8** 1/2 **Living The Dream**[21] 957 7-10-0 0 TGMcLaughlin 13 40
(Karen George) *led: clr after 4f: wknd rapidly and hdd over 2f out* **100/1**

66 **9** 5 **Follow The Dream**[21] 957 6-9-9 0 JerryO'Dwyer 11 27
(Karen George) *nvr beyond midfield: struggling off the pce 4f out: no ch after* **66/1**

10 2 1/2 **Qedaam (IRE)** 3-7-13 0 DavidProbert[(3)] 12 21
(Patrick Morris) *prom over 6f: u.p and wkng 4f out* **66/1**

5- **11** 11 **Lilac Wine**[214] 5913 6-9-2 0 BillyCray[(7)] 1 5
(D J S Ffrench Davis) *sn u.p in rr: nvr a factor: t.o 3f out* **50/1**

0 **12** 29 **Tarraad**[18] 998 3-8-7 0 NickyMackay 7 —
(M Botti) *dwlt: a wl in rr: eased fnl 3f: t.o* **50/1**

0 **13** 2 3/4 **Ok Katie**[21] 957 6-9-9 0 GeorgeBaker 8 —
(R M Beckett) *chsd ldrs to 1/2-way: wknd rapidly 5f out: eased and wl t.o* **50/1**

2m 34.15s (-0.35) **Going Correction** -0.05s/f (Stan)
WFA 3 from 4yo 21lb 4 from 5yo+ 1lb **13** Ran SP% **123.5**
Speed ratings (Par 103): **99,97,97,92,90 86,83,83,79,78 70,51,49**
toteswinger: 1&2 £5.10, 1&3 £7.10, 2&3 £1.30. CSF £30.94 TOTE £14.40: £2.30, £1.10, £1.30; EX 56.60.

Owner Exors Of The Late Mrs Kath Cox **Bred** R G Percival **Trained** Eastbury, Berks

FOCUS
Little strength in depth and a race in which the two market leaders were turned over by a more exposed rival. The pace was fair and the first three pulled clear.

Lilac Wine Official explanation: jockey said mare was never travelling

Tarraad Official explanation: jockey said gelding was denied a clear run

Ok Katie Official explanation: jockey said mare had no more to give

1287 BOOK KEMPTON TICKETS ON 0844 579 3008 H'CAP 1m 4f (P)
8:50 (8:54) (Class 5) (0-70,70) 4-Y-O+ **£2,590** (£770; £385; £192) **Stalls** Centre

Form RPR

646- **1** **Mista Rossa**[167] 7091 4-9-2 **67** TravisBlock 12 75
(H Morrison) *trckd ldr: rdn over 2f out: effrt to ld wl over 1f out: styd on wl* **9/1**

245- **2** 1 1/4 **Potentiale (IRE)**[118] 7715 5-9-5 **69** (p) EddieAhern 11 75
(J W Hills) *hld up towards rr: making prog and gng strly whn rn into trble 2f out: prog and got through to take 2nd fnl f: no imp wnr after* **4/1**[2]

/04- **3** 1/2 **Valvigneres (IRE)**[279] 3873 4-9-4 **69** StephenDonohoe 1 74
(E A L Dunlop) *trckd ldrs: rdn and effrt over 2f out: kpt on to dispute 2nd 1f out: one pce after* **25/1**

131- **4** 1 1/2 **Rose Row**[317] 2682 5-9-5 **69** GeorgeBaker 8 72
(Mrs Mary Hambro) *lled at stdy pce: wound it up fr over 3f out: hdd wl over 1f out: one pce and lost 2 pls fnl f* **12/1**

033- **5** 1 3/4 **Murcar**[245] 4985 4-9-3 **68** PhilipRobinson 7 68
(C G Cox) *trckd ldr: u.p over 2f out: nt qckn wl over 1f out: wknd fnl f* **9/4**[1]

-165 **6** 1 3/4 **Celtic Gold (USA)**[46] 497 5-9-2 **66** DaneO'Neill 13 63
(Andrew Turnell) *trckd ldrs: effrt over 2f out: cl enough over 1f out: wknd after* **14/1**

0/0- **7** 2 1/2 **Maximix**[29] 2245 6-8-9 **59** RyanMoore 10 52
(G L Moore) *wl in rr: shkn up 3f out: one pce and nvr on terms w ldrs* **10/1**

-004 **8** 1 **Mixing**[6] 1200 7-8-4 **57** DavidProbert[(3)] 9 49
(M J Attwater) *settled in midfield: nt qckn over 2f out: wknd over 1f out* **7/1**[3]

50-6 **9** 1/2 **Kiho**[18] 1000 4-8-11 **62** RichardMullen 3 53
(Eve Johnson Houghton) *in tch on outer: pushed along over 4f out: fnd nil over 2f out: sn wknd* **11/1**

1556 **10** 1 3/4 **Clovis**[7] 1178 4-9-3 **68** (b) JimCrowley 6 56
(N P Mulholland) *hld up in last pair: effrt on inner over 2f out: sn no prog: wknd fnl f* **16/1**

3364 **11** 3 3/4 **Apache Fort**[14] 1073 6-9-2 **66** (bt) NickyMackay 4 48
(T Keddy) *hld up in last pair: rdn and no prog wl over 2f out* **16/1**

403- **12** 7 **Starburst**[106] 7822 4-8-11 **62** MartinDwyer 2 33
(A M Balding) *hld up in rr: dropped to last 4f out and struggling: no ch after* **16/1**

2m 33.31s (-1.19) **Going Correction** -0.05s/f (Stan)
WFA 4 from 5yo+ 1lb **12** Ran SP% **126.5**
Speed ratings (Par 103): **101,100,99,98,97 96,94,94,93,92 90,85**
toteswinger: 1&2 £10.20, 1&3 £42.50, 2&3 £19.50. CSF £48.02 CT £909.58 TOTE £12.20: £3.80, £2.00, £8.10; EX 59.40.

Owner Wood Street Syndicate IV **Bred** The National Stud **Trained** East Ilsley, Berks

FOCUS
A moderate handicap in which the pace was only ordinary at best. The principals raced in the centre in the straight.

1288 KEMPTON.CO.UK H'CAP 7f (P)
9:20 (9:21) (Class 4) (0-85,85) 4-Y-O+ **£4,727** (£1,406; £702; £351) **Stalls High**

Form RPR
521- **1** **Taqdeyr**[152] 7321 4-9-4 **85**........ PhilipRobinson 1 105+
(M A Jarvis) *t.k.h early: mde all: shkn up and drtew away fr 2f out: outclassed rivals* **4/7**[1]
6-33 **2** *3½* **Princely Hero (IRE)**[30] 850 5-8-10 **82**........ AndreaAtzeni(5) 7 89
(M Botti) *n.m.r after 1f: hld up in last pair: prog on inner fr over 2f out: styd on to take 2nd wl ins fnl f: no ch w wnr* **12/1**[3]
6/21 **3** *1* **Kilburn**[21] 959 5-8-5 **72**........ WandersonD'Avila 8 76
(A J Lidderdale) *cl up: chsd wnr over 2f out: no imp: one pce and lost 2nd wl ins fnl f* **9/1**[2]
50-2 **4** *1½* **Purus (IRE)**[7] 1186 7-8-4 **71**........ LukeMorris 4 71
(R A Teal) *t.k.h early: hld up towards rr: rdn and effrt over 2f out: kpt on same pce fr over 1f out* **9/1**[2]
426- **5** *nk* **Oceana Blue**[172] 6981 4-8-6 **76**........(t) DavidProbert(3) 3 75
(A M Balding) *trckd ldng trio: rdn over 2f out: sn outpcd* **16/1**
1/0- **6** *1¼* **Kirk Michael**[175] 6911 5-8-13 **80**........ DaneO'Neill 2 76
(H Candy) *t.k.h early: hld up in midfield on outer: gng wl enough over 2f out: shkn up and sn lost pl: plugged on fnl f* **16/1**
322- **7** *2* **Woodcote Place**[193] 6471 6-9-0 **81**........ GeorgeBaker 5 72
(P R Chamings) *t.k.h early: hld up in last pair on outer: effrt over 2f out: nt qckn sn after: steadily fdd* **12/1**[3]
04-4 **8** *2* **Miss Mujanna**[89] 191 4-8-4 **71**........ NickyMackay 9 56
(J Akehurst) *hld up towards rr: effrt and sme prog over 2f out: wknd wl over 1f out* **20/1**
300- **9** *10* **King's Caprice**[138] 7470 8-8-11 **78**........(t) TravisBlock 6 36
(J A Geake) *t.k.h early: chsd wnr tl wknd rapidly over 2f out: t.o* **33/1**
1m 24.3s (-1.70) **Going Correction** -0.05s/f (Stan) **9** Ran SP% **118.5**
Speed ratings (Par 105): **107,103,101,100,99 98,96,93,82**
toteswinger: 1&2 £5.00, 1&3 £2.00, 2&3 £11.80. CSF £9.38 CT £37.83 TOTE £1.40: £1.10, £2.60, £2.70; EX 11.20 Place 6 £47.70, Place 5 £34.50.
Owner Richie Baines & Stephen Dartnell **Bred** Darley **Trained** Newmarket, Suffolk
FOCUS
A fair handicap in which the one progressive horse scored in ready fashion. The gallop was sound and the winner, who raced in the centre, posted a good time.
T/Plt: £74.40 to a £1 stake. Pool: £85,299.84. 836.64 winning tickets. T/Qpdt: £30.80 to a £1 stake. Pool: £7,454.18. 178.60 winning tickets. JN

NEWMARKET (R-H)
Wednesday, April 15
OFFICIAL GOING: Good to firm
Wind: Fresh across Weather: Misty

1289 GRAND PRIX WHITE TURF ST MORITZ MAIDEN STKS 1m 2f
1:50 (1:55) (Class 4) 3-Y-O **£5,180** (£1,541; £770; £384) **Stalls Low**

Form RPR
\- **1** **Sopranist** 3-9-3 0........ LDettori 13 88+
(J H M Gosden) *w'like: athletic: mde all at stdy pce tl qcknd over 2f out: rdn out* **7/1**[3]
2 *1¼* **Native Ruler** 3-9-3 0........ TPQueally 10 85+
(H R A Cecil) *lengthy: scope: lw: hld up in tch: chsd wnr over 2f out: sn rdn: styd on* **1/1**[1]
3 *shd* **Calypso Bay (IRE)** 3-9-3 0........ ShaneKelly 7 85+
(J Noseda) *w'like: str: lw: hld up: hdwy over 3f out: rdn over 1f out: r.o* **14/1**
0- **4** *2* **Devotion To Duty (IRE)**[208] 6083 3-9-3 0........ MichaelHills 2 81
(B W Hills) *chsd ldrs: ev ch over 2f out: sn rdn: styd on same pce ins fnl f* **5/1**[2]
5 *4* **Golden Rock (IRE)** 3-9-3 0........ SteveDrowne 4 73
(R Charlton) *w'like: b.hind: hld up: hdwy over 2f out: rdn and wknd over 1f out* **50/1**
03- **6** *½* **Monetary Fund (USA)**[180] 6777 3-9-3 0........ EddieAhern 9 72
(G A Butler) *hld up: outpcd over 2f out: styd on u.p ins fnl f* **15/2**
7 *3* **Ostaadi** 3-9-3 0........ PhilipRobinson 11 66
(M A Jarvis) *w'like: str: bit bkwd: chsd ldr 2f: remained handy tl rdn over 2f out: sn wknd* **16/1**
3- **8** *nk* **Horsley Warrior**[189] 6580 3-9-3 0........ DarryllHolland 5 65
(E S McMahon) *prom: rdn and wknd over 2f out* **20/1**
0- **9** *1½* **Jack Cool (IRE)**[236] 5246 3-9-3 0........ AlanMunro 3 62
(P W Chapple-Hyam) *edgy: prom: racd keenly: trckd wnr 8f out to 4f out: sn rdn: wknd over 2f out* **40/1**
5-3 **10** *nse* **The Bully Wee**[29] 855 3-9-3 0........ LukeMorris 12 62
(J Jay) *unruly bhd stalls: prom: rdn over 3f out: hung rt and wknd sn after* **100/1**
11 *3½* **Mac Wolf** 3-9-3 0........ TedDurcan 6 55
(M G Quinlan) *w'like: hld up: rdn and wknd over 2f out* **100/1**
12 *2¼* **Uniquely Poised (USA)** 3-9-3 0........ JimmyFortune 1 51
(J H M Gosden) *unf: hld up: hdwy over 4f out: rdn over 2f out: sn wknd* **16/1**
13 *4½* **Golden Ring** 3-9-3 0........ RobertHavlin 8 42
(P J O'Gorman) *w'like: s.s: a in rr: wknd over 2f out* **100/1**
2m 10.88s (5.08) **Going Correction** +0.40s/f (Good) **13** Ran SP% **121.5**
Speed ratings (Par 100): **95,94,93,92,89 88,86,86,84,84 82,80,76**
toteswinger: 1&2 £3.60, 1&3 £8.50, 2&3 £7.40. CSF £14.21 TOTE £8.90: £2.40, £1.20, £2.80; EX 19.30.
Owner H R H Princess Haya Of Jordan **Bred** Darley **Trained** Newmarket, Suffolk
FOCUS
Following a dry night the ground had quickened up to good to firm, but there was a strong headwind. Quite an interesting maiden, and although it was run at a steady early pace, the market principals came to the fore and dominated.

1290 BETTERBET, BOOKMAKER OF YEAR 2009 CONDITIONS STKS 5f
2:25 (2:25) (Class 3) 2-Y-O **£9,066** (£2,697; £1,348; £673) **Stalls Low**

Form RPR
1 **1** **Monsieur Chevalier (IRE)**[6] 1195 2-8-12 0........ RichardHughes 3 100+
(R Hannon) *str: good bodied: chsd ldrs: led over 1f out: shkn up and r.o wl* **5/4**[1]
1 **2** *3½* **Soccer (USA)**[11] 1119 2-8-12 0........(t) RichardKingscote 7 87+
(Tom Dascombe) *unf: chsd ldr tl led over 1f out: sn rdn and hdd: outpcd ins fnl f* **6/1**[3]
2 **3** *4* **Iver Bridge Lad**[9] 1147 2-8-9 0........ MarcHalford(3) 5 73
(J Ryan) *led: rdn and hdd over 1f out: edgd rt and wknd ins fnl f* **20/1**
1 **4** *1* **Hearts Of Fire**[18] 994 2-9-4 0........ PaulEddery 4 75
(Pat Eddery) *w'like: tall: chsd ldrs: rdn over 1f out: wknd fnl f* **2/1**[2]
5 *7* **Captain Cool (IRE)** 2-8-9 0........ RyanMoore 6 41
(R Hannon) *leggy: bit bkwd: sn outpcd* **9/1**
6 *2½* **Ant Music (IRE)** 2-8-9 0........ LPKeniry 1 32
(J S Moore) *leggy: hmpd s: outpcd* **66/1**
7 *9* **Zero Seven** 2-8-9 0........ DarryllHolland 2 —
(C E Brittain) *w'like: hmpd s: sn pushed along in rr: wknd 1/2-way* **25/1**
60.70 secs (1.60) **Going Correction** +0.40s/f (Good) **7** Ran SP% **112.2**
Speed ratings (Par 96): **103,97,91,89,78 74,59**
toteswinger: 1&2 £3.30, 1&3 £7.90, 2&3 £13.50. CSF £8.96 TOTE £2.10: £1.50, £2.90; EX 9.50.
Owner Mrs Valerie Hubbard & Ian Higginson **Bred** Tally-Ho Stud **Trained** East Everleigh, Wilts
FOCUS
The best juvenile race of the season so far, and by some way. It featured three previous winners, the most notable absentee being impressive Windsor winner Red Jazz, whose form was represented by runner-up Iver Bridge Lad. Monsieur Chevalier has been rated one of the better winners of this race and is Royal Ascot-bound.
NOTEBOOK
Monsieur Chevalier(IRE) ◆ more than confirmed the good impression he made at Folkestone by winning this far hotter contest in similar style. Chased along briefly to keep up early on, he then travelled well in behind the principals and when delivered with his challenge approaching the final furlong, he soon put the race to bed. He came away without having a hard time, looking better and better the further he went. Richard Hannon said he had seldom known a more laid back two-year-old and confirmed that he now regards him Royal Ascot material, with the proviso that he wouldn't want it too quick underfoot. The Coventry looks his race. (tchd 6-5 and 13-8)
Soccer(USA), a Lingfield winner, looked just as effective on turf and on a straight track, and he emerges with plenty of credit after finishing a clear second. He looks an above-average early-season two-year-old. (op 4-1 tchd 7-2)
Iver Bridge Lad made the running, but was put firmly in his place, eventually being beaten two and a half lengths further by the winner than he had been beaten by Red Jazz at Windsor. Connections believe he will be better at 6f. (op 33-1)
Hearts Of Fire, was the disappointment of the race, even allowing for the punitive 6lb penalty. His Brocklesby win had been franked in no uncertain terms, but having grabbed the rail, where he had every chance, he was the first of the four principals in trouble. The ground should not have been a problem, as it was on top at Doncaster, but this was not his form. (op 11-4)
Captain Cool(IRE) is a half-brother to 7f 2yo winner Welcome Return. A stablemate of the winner but expected to need the race, he did best of the newcomers, but like the others making their debuts, was in another race from before halfway. (op 8-1)
Ant Music(IRE), a £35,000 half-brother to winners from 6f to 1m, was soon outpaced. (tchd 50-1)
Zero Seven, a half-brother to the Irish 6f 2yo winner Enigma Code, struggled to go the pace, like the other two newcomers. (op 28-1)

1291 £400000 TATTERSALLS TIMEFORM 3-Y-O TROPHY 1m 2f
3:00 (3:00) (Class 2) 3-Y-O
£216,680 (£88,640; £39,440; £19,680; £9,840; £3,920) **Stalls Low**

Form RPR
1- **1** **Nehaam**[208] 6083 3-9-3 0........ RHills 18 104
(J H M Gosden) *edgy: hld up in tch: racd keenly: led over 2f out: rdn and hung lft fr over 1f out: r.o* **8/1**
361- **2** *hd* **Monitor Closely (IRE)**[172] 6977 3-9-3 **95**........ AlanMunro 15 103
(P W Chapple-Hyam) *h.d.w: a.p: racd keenly: chsd wnr over 1f out: sn rdn: edgd lft: r.o* **15/2**[3]
3 *2* **Rockhampton (IRE)**[17] 1027 3-9-3 0........ JMurtagh 5 99
(A P O'Brien, Ire) *w'like: on toes: hld up: hdwy over 1f out: sn rdn: edgd lft ins fnl f: styd on* **7/2**[2]
013- **4** *shd* **The Miniver Rose (IRE)**[193] 6473 3-8-12 **87**........ RyanMoore 1 94
(R Hannon) *lw: hld up: nt clr run 2f out: swtchd lft and hdwy over 1f out: r.o: nt rch ldrs* **20/1**
344- **5** *2¾* **Moneycantbuymelove (IRE)**[193] 6473 3-8-12 **80**........ JamieSpencer 9 89
(M L W Bell) *hld up: hmpd over 9f out: plld hrd: nt clr run over 2f out: hdwy and nt clr run over 1f out: r.o: nrst fin* **66/1**
6-22 **6** *1½* **Capeability (IRE)**[39] 786 3-9-3 **80**........ TonyCulhane 4 91?
(M R Channon) *hld up: hdwy 2f out: sn rdn: wknd fnl f* **100/1**
20-5 **7** *¾* **Weald Park (USA)**[28] 863 3-9-3 **97**........ RichardHughes 17 89
(R Hannon) *chsd ldr over 2f: remained handy: rdn over 2f out: wknd fnl f* **14/1**
44- **8** *1* **Asateer (IRE)**[243] 5066 3-9-3 0........ TPO'Shea 6 87
(B W Hills) *s.s: hld up: hdwy over 3f out: wknd fnl f* **50/1**
0 **9** *½* **Saa'Ida (IRE)**[6] 1198 3-8-12 0........ DarryllHolland 14 81
(C E Brittain) *w'like: edgy: hld up: racd keenly: hmpd over 9f out: hdwy over 2f out: sn rdn: wknd fnl f* **100/1**
32- **10** *10* **Pergamon (IRE)**[246] 4954 3-9-3 0........(b[1]) JimmyFortune 7 66
(J H M Gosden) *hld up: hmpd over 2f out: sn rdn and hung rt: n.d* **28/1**
212- **11** *1¼* **Vitoria (IRE)**[193] 6473 3-8-12 **90**........ RichardMullen 19 59
(B Smart) *mid-div: hdwy 4f out: wknd over 1f out* **16/1**
-351 **12** *hd* **Sign Of Approval**[51] 659 3-9-3 **74**........ MartinLane 13 63
(K R Burke) *mid-div: hdwy to chse ldr over 7f out: rdn to ld over 3f out: hdd over 2f out: hung lft and wknd over 1f out* **100/1**
14-2 **13** *2½* **Liberation (IRE)**[41] 769 3-9-3 **103**........ LDettori 11 58
(Saeed Bin Suroor) *lw: t.k.h: chsd ldrs: rdn over 2f out: wknd over 1f out* **9/4**[1]
1-24 **14** *4* **Laurie Grove (IRE)**[18] 1001 3-9-3 **83**........ KJManning 8 50
(T G Mills) *lw: hld up: rdn over 3f out: wkng whn hung rt over 1f out* **33/1**
6- **15** *3¼* **Sumbe (USA)**[236] 5246 3-9-3 0........ MartinDwyer 12 44
(M P Tregoning) *lw: s.i.s: hld up: hdwy over 4f out: wkng whn hmpd over 2f out* **11/1**
2-3 **16** *4* **Classically (IRE)**[18] 998 3-9-3 0........ JimmyQuinn 3 36
(R Charlton) *lw: chsd ldrs: rdn over 3f out: wknd over 2f out* **25/1**
0-21 **17** *13* **Anacreon (IRE)**[11] 1120 3-9-3 **72**........ NickyMackay 10 10
(J H M Gosden) *led: rdn and hdd over 3f out: wkng whn hmpd over 2f out* **66/1**
00-5 **18** *3* **Cry Of Freedom (USA)**[11] 1118 3-9-3 **92**........ RoystonFfrench 2 —
(M Johnston) *hld up: rdn and wknd over 3f out* **25/1**
2m 6.47s (0.67) **Going Correction** +0.40s/f (Good) **18** Ran SP% **123.5**
Speed ratings (Par 104): **113,112,111,111,108 107,107,106,105,97 96,96,94,91,89 85,75,73**
toteswinger: 1&2 £11.40, 1&3 £7.40, 2&3 £10.80. CSF £61.25 TOTE £9.20: £2.60, £2.80, £2.10; EX 45.40.
Owner Hamdan Al Maktoum **Bred** Pollards Stables **Trained** Newmarket, Suffolk
FOCUS
Restricted to graduates of the 2007 Newmarket October Yearling Sales, this was the most valuable three-year-old race outside the Classics. However, despite a good time for the grade it did not look as competitive as the numbers would suggest

NOTEBOOK

Nehaam ◆ was one of the least experienced in the line-up, but he had won over 7f on his debut here last September and with plenty of stamina in his pedigree this trip promised to bring about improvement. He looked fit and, having come through travelling really well, he quickened up to take the race before getting a little tired close home. His success was all the more noteworthy considering that he had been held up in his work recently as a result of a stone bruise, and Gosden considered that this came soon enough for him. Improvement can be expected and, having been cut to a best price of 20-1 for the Derby, his Classic credentials will be put to the test further in the Dante. With Epsom in mind, his pedigree would suggest that 1m4f should be within his range. (op 9-2)

Monitor Closely(IRE) is a half-brother to Eclipse winner Mount Nelson and was expected to be very much suited by a step up to 1m2f. Closing the winner down at the line, he came out best of the six that contested the Tattersalls Timeform Million back in October. He might be one to consider for a classic trial, too, although improvement from this run would not necessarily be guaranteed. (op 8-1)

Rockhampton(IRE), who predictably holds a stack of big-race entries, won a Leopardstown maiden on his reappearance, and that still represented the stable's only win of the season to date. He could not make that race-fitness pay and clearly has his limitations, but he will probably improve further when sent over 1m4f. (op 11-2 tchd 10-3 tchd 13-2 in a place)

The Miniver Rose(IRE), third in the Tattersalls Timeform Fillies' 800, came from well off the pace and saw her race out strongly. She will get 1m4f and is entered in the Oaks, so she looks worth a shot at a trial now, although it is worth bearing in mind that connections admit she is quirky and has attitude. (op 16-1)

Moneycantbuymelove(IRE) ◆, who looked fit for this return, was the eyecatcher, failing to settle through the early stages and then running into all sorts of trouble when asked to make up ground. By the time she got into the clear a furlong out the principals had gone, and it is probably fair to say that she deserves rating a good deal better than the bare form suggests. A maiden should be a formality. Official explanation: jockey said filly ran too free

Capeability(IRE), beaten at Wolverhampton on his last start, also did not enjoy the clearest of runs and is another capable of winning in maiden company.

Weald Park(USA) was easily beaten off and simply did not run up to the best of his two-year-old form. His stamina for this sort of trip remains in doubt.

Asateer(IRE), who carried his owner's second colours, carried his head high and did not look entirely happy on the ground. Handicaps are now an option for him.

Saa'Ida(IRE) stepped up pleasingly on her debut at Folkestone six days earlier despite racing too keenly.

Vitoria(IRE), about whom there were stamina concerns, looked fit but was disappointing as she could never land a blow. (op 20-1)

Liberation(IRE), runner-up at Nad al Sheba to stablemate City Style on his first start for Godolphin, was the biggest disappointment. He simply used up too much energy early racing keenly. Official explanation: jockey said colt ran too free (op 5-2 tchd 11-4 in places)

Classicallly(IRE) Official explanation: jockey said colt was unsuited by the good to firm ground

1292 BETTERBET EUROPEAN FREE H'CAP (LISTED RACE) 7f

3:35 (3:35) (Class 1) 3-Y-O

£25,546 (£9,684; £4,846; £2,416; £1,210; £607) Stalls Low

Form			Horse		RPR
410-	1		**Ouqba**[179] 6815 3-8-9 **104**	RHills 2	112
			(B W Hills) *lw: trckd ldrs: led 2f out: rdn and r.o wl*	**4/1**[2]	
116-	2	2 ¾	**Awinnersgame (IRE)**[199] 6317 3-8-11 **106**	JMurtagh 8	106
			(J Noseda) *swtg: hld up in tch: rdn to chse wnr and edgd lft fnl f: styd on same pce ins fnl f*	**7/2**[1]	
161-	3	½	**Penny's Gift**[166] 7107 3-8-6 **101**	RyanMoore 1	100
			(R Hannon) *lw: chsd ldrs: rdn over 2f out: styd on same pce ins fnl f*	**6/1**[3]	
240-	4	1 ¼	**Rose Diamond (IRE)**[192] 6519 3-8-5 **100**	AlanMunro 4	96
			(R Charlton) *hld up in tch: rdn over 2f out: swtchd rt over 1f out: one pce fnl f*	**14/1**	
105-	5	2 ¾	**Marine Boy (IRE)**[207] 6119 3-9-0 **109**	RichardKingscote 7	97
			(Tom Dascombe) *swtg: edgy: plld hrd: sn led: rdn and hdd 2f out: wknd ins fnl f*	**13/2**	
120-	6	nk	**Snoqualmie Girl (IRE)**[194] 6439 3-8-8 **103**	MartinDwyer 5	90
			(D R C Elsworth) *lw: hld up: hdwy over 1f out: wknd ins fnl f*	**25/1**	
120-	7	3 ¾	**Art Connoisseur (IRE)**[236] 5226 3-9-7 **116**	JamieSpencer 3	93
			(M L W Bell) *lw: hld up: plld hrd: nt clr run over 1f out: eased fnl f*	**10/1**	
525-	8	¾	**Courageous (IRE)**[172] 6973 3-8-6 **101**	RichardMullen 6	76
			(B Smart) *b.hind: plld hrd and prom: rdn over 2f out: wknd over 1f out*	**6/1**[3]	
435-	9	hd	**Wildcat Wizard (USA)**[196] 6401 3-8-5 **100**	EddieAhern 10	75
			(P F I Cole) *hld up: hdwy and hung rt over 2f out: wknd fnl f*	**25/1**	
442-	10	nk	**Saxford**[184] 6713 3-8-9 **104**	ShaneKelly 9	78
			(Mrs L Stubbs) *chsd ldrs: rdn over 2f out: wknd over 1f out*	**16/1**	

1m 27.22s (1.82) **Going Correction** +0.40s/f (Good) 10 Ran SP% **113.5**

Speed ratings (Par 106): **105,101,101,99,96 96,92,91,91,90**

toteswinger: 1&2 £5.00, 1&3 £7.20, 2&3 £3.80. CSF £17.84 CT £82.34 TOTE £5.10: £2.00, £1.80, £2.10; EX 19.80.

Owner Hamdan Al Maktoum **Bred** Highclere Stud **Trained** Lambourn, Berks

FOCUS

As has become the norm in recent years, this race did not promise to have much of an impact on either Guineas market, with none of the runners considered better than a longshot for the Classics prior to the race, and it is likely that it will prove more of a guide to sprints later in the season. There was no great pace on very early on and a number of horses failed to settle, notably Courageous, Marine Boy, Art Connoisseur and Wildcat Wizard.

NOTEBOOK

Ouqba, whose work at home had reportedly been excellent, proved more amenable to restraint than most and that helped plenty in the second half of the race. Travelling well to the front, he showed a good turn of foot to go clear and ran out an emphatic winner in the end. He will not run in the Guineas and, although entered in the French version, will probably skip that race in favour of the Jersey Stakes. He has plenty of speed and should not have any trouble dropping back to 6f as the year goes on. (tchd 9-2 in places)

Awinnersgame(IRE) kept on well enough for second and, while the Jersey could come into the equation for him as well, one gets the impression that his future lies over shorter. Indeed, he already holds an entry in the 6f Duke of York Stakes. (tchd 4-1)

Penny's Gift has a pedigree that suggests a mile should be within her compass this year and so it is probably fair to suggest that the steady early pace over this trip would not have suited her. She was staying on nicely at the end and could well take her chance in either the German or Italian Guineas. (op 11-2)

Rose Diamond(IRE)'s trainer had expressed concerns beforehand that the trip would be on the short side for her, and that is how things looked. By Daylami, the ground was in her favour but the trip, especially off a steady early pace, was inadequate.

Marine Boy(IRE) sweated up and having pulled for his head in front and did not get home. He has plenty of talent, but his energy is not being directed in the right way at the moment and he may need dropping back in trip for the time being. Official explanation: jockey said gelding hung left-handed and that gelding lost a hind shoe (op 8-1 tchd 9-1)

Snoqualmie Girl(IRE), who ran her best race in the May Hill last year, is a daughter of Montjeu and was always going to find this trip on the short side. She looked fit enough but can do better when returned to further. (op 20-1)

Art Connoisseur(IRE) did not go on after winning the Coventry and looked to have a stiff task at these weights. He did not settle at all off the steady early gallop and has plenty to prove now. (op 15-2)

Courageous(IRE), fifth in the Racing Post Trophy on his final start at two, was another who failed to shine after pulling too hard in the early stages. His rider reported that he finished lame, though, and he deserves another chance, especially over further. Official explanation: trainer said colt finished lame (op 13-2 tchd 7-1)

1293 LESLIE HARRISON MEMORIAL NELL GWYN STKS (GROUP 3) 7f

4:10 (4:10) (Class 1) 3-Y-O

£36,900 (£13,988; £7,000; £3,490; £1,748; £877) Stalls Low

Form			Horse		RPR
112-	1		**Fantasia**[200] 6268 3-8-12 113	LDettori 8	114+
			(L M Cumani) *lw: hld up: smooth hdwy to ld over 1f out: shkn up and r.o strly: impressive*	**4/5**[1]	
21-	2	7	**Damaniyat Girl (USA)**[184] 6696 3-8-12 81	JMurtagh 7	93
			(W J Haggas) *lw: a.p: jnd ldrs 3f out: sn rdn: outpcd fr over 1f out*	**10/1**[3]	
13-	3	2 ¼	**First City**[251] 4781 3-8-12 88	RyanMoore 4	87
			(D M Simcock) *s.i.s: hld up: hdwy u.p over 1f out: wnt 3rd nr fin: nt trble ldrs*	**40/1**	
041-	4	¾	**Arabian Mirage**[151] 7341 3-8-12 81	JamieSpencer 9	85
			(B J Meehan) *led: rdn over 2f out: hdd over 1f out: wknd ins fnl f*	**25/1**	
3-1	5	1 ¼	**Dunes Queen (USA)**[28] 862 3-8-12 78	TonyCulhane 2	82
			(M R Channon) *lw: hld up: rdn over 2f out: hdwy and edgd rt fr over 1f out: nt trble ldrs*	**28/1**	
013-	6	2 ¼	**Fazbee (IRE)**[213] 5937 3-8-12 86	DarryllHolland 10	76
			(P W D'Arcy) *chsd ldrs: rdn over 2f out: wknd over 1f out*	**50/1**	
41-1	7	1 ¾	**Wajaha (IRE)**[13] 1082 3-8-12 93	RHills 11	71
			(J H M Gosden) *lw: chsd ldrs tl wknd over 1f out*	**7/2**[2]	
1	8	½	**Kaabari (USA)**[26] 890 3-8-12 77	JimmyFortune 5	69
			(C E Brittain) *w'like: chsd ldr: chal 3f out: sn rdn: wknd over 1f out*	**25/1**	
120-	9	¾	**Misdaqeya**[194] 6439 3-8-12 101	TPO'Shea 6	67
			(B W Hills) *hld up: rdn over 2f out: sn wknd*	**16/1**	
141-	10	4 ½	**Summer Fete (IRE)**[172] 6982 3-8-12 100	RichardMullen 1	55
			(B Smart) *b.hind: hld up in tch: jnd ldrs 3f out: wknd over 1f out*	**10/1**[3]	
1130	11	1 ¾	**Smokey Ryder**[18] 1002 3-8-12 95	KevinGhunowa 3	51
			(R A Harris) *on toes: prom: jnd ldrs 3f out: sn rdn: wknd 2f out*	**66/1**	

1m 26.93s (1.53) **Going Correction** +0.40s/f (Good) 11 Ran SP% **118.9**

Speed ratings (Par 108): **107,99,96,95,94 91,89,89,88,83 81**

toteswinger: 1&2 £3.10, 1&3 £10.60, 2&3 £25.90. CSF £9.42 TOTE £1.70: £1.20, £2.40, £7.90; EX 9.60.

Owner George Strawbridge **Bred** Ronchalon Racing Uk Ltd **Trained** Newmarket, Suffolk

FOCUS

Not much strength in depth in what was a weak renewal overall, but the winner could hardly have been more impressive. That said, she has only been rated a marginal improver.

NOTEBOOK

Fantasia ◆, who was the only filly to give Rainbow View a race at two, was most impressive, looking different class in the preliminaries and coming back just as well, having floated to post. Ridden with plenty of confidence, despite dropping to 7f after running so well in the Fillies' Mile, she made her ground easily to lead going into the Dip and then burst clear up the hill, winning in stunning fashion by a wide margin, in a time 0.29 seconds quicker than Ouqba in the Free Handicap. It's doubtful if any of her rivals have classic pretensions, for they were mostly maiden and handicap winners, but such was the style of her win that were she would be pressing for favouritism in the 1000 Guineas were she not now in the same ownership as Rainbow View and thus seemingly more likely to go to Longchamp for the Pouliches. That race should be there for the taking, but as for the Oaks, for which she received quotes, there is lots of speed on the dam's side (granddam Blue Duster won the Cheveley Park) and she is far from certain to stay. (op 10-11 tchd Evens)

Damaniyat Girl(USA), a daughter of Guineas runner-up Dabaweyaa and a promising winner on the all-weather, beat the rest decisively, having never been too far away. She simply had no answer when the winner quickened, but this was still another step up and she could well be open to more improvement. (op 11-1)

First City, who had been off the track since her improved third in a soft-ground novice at Haydock in August, seemed to handle this quicker ground fine and came through from the rear after a slowish start to finish a creditable third. (op 33-1)

Arabian Mirage, a well-regarded Polytrack maiden winner, made the running and had every chance.

Dunes Queen(USA), a daughter of the classy two-year-old Queens Logic, was also taking a big step up in class after winning a Polytrack maiden four weeks previously. She was quite keen under restraint in the early stages, and having made some ground from the rear she then tended to edge to the right. She hardly looks a Guineas filly now. (tchd 20-1 and 33-1)

Fazbee(IRE) was well tuned up, like her stablemate Kylayne who was runner-up in this race 12 months ago. Connections were anticipating a big effort, but she never really got in a blow.

Wajaha(IRE) put up a useful effort when an easy handicap winner at Kempton off 83, and with no worries over her fitness she looked obvious place material at the least. She had her chance though, and she might be better on the artificial surfaces on which her record is two from two. (tchd 4-1 in places)

Summer Fete(IRE) was already a Listed winner so had better form than most, but that was on soft ground and she proved much less effective here. She was bandaged behind. (op 8-1 tchd 11-1)

1294 TUDDENHAM MILL FEILDEN STKS (LISTED RACE) 1m 1f

4:45 (4:46) (Class 1) 3-Y-O £25,546 (£9,684; £4,846; £2,416; £1,210) Stalls Low

Form			Horse		RPR
1-	1		**Redwood**[195] 6425 3-8-13 88	MichaelHills 3	108
			(B W Hills) *lw: s.i.s: sn trcking ldrs: pushed along and hung rt over 3f out: rdn to ld over 1f out: edgd lft: styd on wl*	**11/4**[2]	
542-	2	2	**Drumbeat (IRE)**[154] 7294 3-8-13 111	JMurtagh 1	103
			(A P O'Brien, Ire) *on toes: trckd ldrs: racd keenly: rdn and carried hd high fr over 1f out: chsd wnr fnl f: no imp*	**7/2**[3]	
121-	3	1 ½	**Heliodor (USA)**[165] 7142 3-8-13 92	RichardHughes 5	100
			(R Hannon) *hld up: rdn over 1f out: styd on to go 3rd nr fin: nt trble ldrs*	**16/1**	
231-	4	nk	**On Our Way**[180] 6779 3-8-13 103	TPQueally 4	99
			(H R A Cecil) *lw: chsd ldr: rdn to ld over 2f out: sn edgd lft: hdd over 1f out: styd on same pce*	**11/10**[1]	
133-	5	27	**Derbaas (USA)**[195] 6428 3-8-13 102	RHills 2	40
			(E A L Dunlop) *led over 6f: wknd and eased over 1f out*	**8/1**	

1m 52.73s (1.03) **Going Correction** +0.40s/f (Good) 5 Ran SP% **113.5**

Speed ratings (Par 106): **106,104,102,102,78**

CSF £12.95 TOTE £4.20: £2.70, £2.40; EX 9.90.

Owner K Abdulla **Bred** Juddmonte Farms Ltd **Trained** Lambourn, Berks

■ A 300th winner at Newmarket for veteran trainer Barry Hills.

FOCUS

Not much of a Classic trial in recent years, and the sales race earlier on the card will have no doubt poached one or two potential contenders.

NOTEBOOK

Redwood could do no more than win tidily off a sound gallop. He has a willing attitude and, being by High Chaparral out of a daughter of a French Oaks winner, is certainly bred for the job. The Dante is apparently now a possible target, but he is not in the Derby at the moment and would have to be supplemented. (tchd 9-4 tchd 3-1 in places after 9-4)

Drumbeat(IRE), who had a busy time of it last year and signed off by finishing second in the 1m2f Group 1 Criterium De Saint-Cloud, was alongside the winner for most of the race, chasing the pace. A little keen through the early stages, he showed the Montjeu in him by carrying his head a bit high in the latter part of the race. It was a sound effort, though, especially as one would imagine that he is a fair way down the pecking order at Ballydoyle. (tchd 9-2)

Heliodor(USA), who won the Zetland here on his final start at two, was ridden patiently out the back and took third late on without threatening the winner. A tough sort, if last year is anything to go by he will again be seeing plenty of the racecourse this season. (op 14-1)

On Our Way had some smart form at two, finishing third in the Royal Lodge and winning a conditions event at this track afterwards, and he ran well for a long way here. Indeed, he would have probably done better had he not got involved in a bit of duel up front with Derbaas. (op 6-4)

Derbaas(USA) had been headed when stumbling two furlongs out, and he was eased right down. He could have done with not being harassed on the front end through the early part of the race. (op 13-2)

1295 ALEX SCOTT MAIDEN STKS (C&G) 7f

5:20 (5:22) (Class 4) 3-Y-O **£5,180** (£1,541; £770; £384) **Stalls** Low

Form					RPR
3-	1		**Infiraad**[194] 6438 3-9-0 0 (B W Hills) *lw: chsd ldr tl led over 2f out: rdn out* 9/2[3]	RHills 15	92
233-	2	2	**Invincible Heart (GR)**[138] 7476 3-9-0 86 (Jane Chapple-Hyam) *swtg: a.p: chsd wnr 2f out: sn rdn and ev ch: styd on same pce ins fnl f* 16/1	JamieSpencer 13	87
4-	3	hd	**Euston Square**[262] 4446 3-9-0 0 (J H M Gosden) *bit bkwd: s.s: hld up: r.o wl ins fnl f: nrst fin* 33/1	RichardMullen 3	86
3-	4	shd	**Invisible Man**[160] 7209 3-9-0 0 (J H M Gosden) *w'like: scope: str: lw: hld up: outpcd over 2f out: swtchd rt and hdwy over 1f out: r.o: nrst fin* 6/4[1]	JimmyFortune 4	86
34-	5	¾	**Espiritu (FR)**[215] 5857 3-9-0 0 (J Noseda) *lw: chsd ldrs: rdn over 1f out: hung lft ins fnl f: styng on same pce whn hung rt towards fin* 11/4[2]	LDettori 9	84
	6	3	**Nicholas Pocock (IRE)** 3-9-0 0 (Sir Michael Stoute) *w'like: on toes: hld up: hdwy over 1f out: styd on same pce ins fnl f* 16/1	RyanMoore 7	76
	7	shd	**Brother Cha (IRE)** 3-9-0 0 (M G Quinlan) *w'like: hld up: hdwy over 1f out: egted lft and styd on ame pce ins fnl f* 100/1	AlanMunro 12	76
-022	8	2½	**Esteem Lord**[35] 800 3-9-0 71 (Jamie Poulton) *on toes: mid-div: hdwy 2f out: sn rdn: no ex fnl f* 80/1	RobertHavlin 14	69
	9	shd	**Indian Violet (IRE)** 3-9-0 0 (P F I Cole) *w'like: hld up: rdn over 2f out: n.d* 16/1	MartinDwyer 1	69
522-	10	1½	**Formula (USA)**[131] 7554 3-9-0 82 (R Hannon) *chsd ldrs: rdn over 2f out: wknd fnl f* 16/1	RichardHughes 10	65
5-6	11	nk	**Just Mustard (USA)**[25] 917 3-9-0 0 (G A Butler) *prom: rdn over 2f out: wknd fnl f* 50/1	EddieAhern 16	64
0-	12	1¼	**Hilbre Point (USA)**[166] 7106 3-9-0 0 (B J Meehan) *sn led: rdn and hdd over 2f out: wknd over 1f out* 50/1	TedDurcan 6	61
2-0	13	3½	**Pedasus (USA)**[21] 951 3-9-0 0 (T Keddy) *hld up: a in rr* 33/1	TonyCulhane 5	51
0-0	14	½	**Conclusive**[7] 1185 3-9-0 0 (R M Beckett) *mid-div: rdn over 2f out: wknd over 1f out: eased* 80/1	RichardKingscote 11	50

1m 28.11s (2.71) **Going Correction** +0.40s/f (Good) **14 Ran SP% 121.6**

Speed ratings (Par 100): **100,97,97,97,96 93,92,90,90,88 87,86,82,81**

toteswinger: 1&2 £7.50, 1&3 £24.70, 2&3 £32.60. CSF £72.48 TOTE £5.20: £1.90, £3.10, £6.10; EX 66.00.

Owner Hamdan Al Maktoum **Bred** Bearstone Stud **Trained** Lambourn, Berks

FOCUS

A decent-looking maiden that should throw up its share of winners.

1296 BETTERBET ON NEWMARKET HIGH STREET H'CAP 6f

5:55 (5:58) (Class 2) (0-100,99) 3-Y-O **£12,952** (£3,854; £1,926; £962) **Stalls** Low

Form					RPR
15-	1		**Dark Mischief**[172] 6972 3-8-10 **86** (H Candy) *hld up: hdwy over 1f out: r.o to ld wl ins fnl f* 3/1[1]	DaneO'Neill 12	95
10-	2	¾	**Enact**[172] 6982 3-8-6 **82** ow1 (Sir Michael Stoute) *h.d.w: lw: hld up: plld hrd: hdwy over 1f out: led ins fnl f: sn rdn: edgd rt and hdd: kpt on* 5/1[2]	RyanMoore 8	89
22-1	3	3¼	**Servoca (CAN)**[19] 982 3-8-8 **84** (B W Hills) *lw: racd alone on stand's side: overall ldr: rdn and hdd ins fnl f: no ex* 7/1[3]	MichaelHills 2	80
121-	4	½	**Aldermoor (USA)**[200] 6274 3-9-9 **99** (S C Williams) *lw: plld hrd and prom: rdn and ev ch over 1f out: styd on same pce* 20/1	SaleemGolam 6	94
31-1	5	¾	**Green Beret (IRE)**[7] 1180 3-9-3 **93** 6ex (J H M Gosden) *prom: rdn and ev ch over 1f out: styd on same pce* 3/1[1]	JimmyFortune 7	85
21-6	6	½	**Tobond (IRE)**[25] 912 3-9-5 **95** (M Botti) *hld up: rdn over 2f out: styd on ins fnl f: nt trble ldrs* 16/1	JohnEgan 9	86
402-	7	2½	**Dove Mews**[191] 6533 3-8-6 **82** (M L W Bell) *chsd ldrs: rdn and wknd over 1f out* 25/1	MartinDwyer 11	65
214-	8	½	**Caledonia Princess**[204] 6191 3-8-4 **80** oh5 (R Curtis) *hld up: hdwy over 2f out: rdn and ev ch over 1f out: sn wknd* 100/1	JimmyQuinn 10	61
1-	9	1¼	**Elusive Fame (USA)**[159] 7227 3-8-9 **85** (M Johnston) *w'like: chsd ldrs over 3f* 16/1	RoystonFfrench 3	62
110-	10	1¾	**Masamah (IRE)**[207] 6119 3-9-7 **97** (E A L Dunlop) *led main gp tl swtchd lft and jnd ldr stands' side over 2f out: rdn and wknd over 1f out* 12/1	(b) RHills 5	68
210-	11	4½	**Definightly**[145] 7430 3-9-2 **92** (R Charlton) *s.i.s: hld up: wknd over 2f out* 8/1	SteveDrowne 4	49

1m 14.2s (2.00) **Going Correction** +0.40s/f (Good) **11 Ran SP% 119.3**

Speed ratings (Par 104): **102,101,96,96,95 94,91,90,88,86 80**

toteswinger: 1&2 £7.70, 1&3 £6.80, 2&3 £6.80. CSF £17.78 CT £100.74 TOTE £4.10: £1.90, £1.70, £2.60; EX 26.80 Place 6: £23.98, Place 5: £16.57..

Owner First Of Many Partnership **Bred** Jeremy Green And Sons And P Bickmore **Trained** Kingston Warren, Oxon

FOCUS

This tends to be a very strong handicap - Sakhee's Secret won it two years ago and Prohibit last year - and there is no reason to think this latest running is any different, as it looked a good field on paper and plenty seemed to be fancied.

NOTEBOOK

Dark Mischief had seemed outclassed in Listed company at Doncaster at the back-end, having beaten the favourite here, Green Beret, at Windsor on his debut, but he was clearly well fancied for this, despite a suggestion he would come on for the run. Produced on the wide outside, he was too strong up the hill for Enact, who had come through with what looked a winning effort. Henry Candy has his eye on another 3yo handicap at Salisbury next month for the Namid colt, who wears special shoes after foot problems restricted him to the two runs at two. (op 4-1 tchd 11-2)

Enact was also beaten in Listed company at two after a debut win at Windsor, and she too seemed well fancied. Although free early on, she came through the pack from off the pace to look the winner, but she was inclined to drift right. She was well clear of the rest though and should have no trouble winning a similar race, although the handicapper will make her pay for this. (tchd 4-1 and 11-2)

Servoca(CAN) had made all at Wolverhampton last month following a wind operation, and he looks a solid marker for the form. He raced prominently from the start, away from the others up the stands' rail until joined by long-time leader Masamah in the last couple of furlongs. (op 11-2)

Aldermoor(USA) was always going to be vulnerable under top-weight, but he looked the part and ran a good race in the circumstances. (tchd 22-1)

Green Beret(IRE) was 3lb ahead of the handicapper despite a 6lb penalty for his easy Brighton win. He was a shade more exposed than most of those who beat him though and he had no apparent excuse. (op 11-4 tchd 7-2)

Tobond(IRE), who got loose in the pre-parade, was doing his best work at the finish.

Dove Mews hadn't come to herself and never got in a blow.

Caledonia Princess was not disgraced from out of the handicap considering her long absence.

Elusive Fame(USA) is powerfully built, but his debut win at Wolverhampton was over 7f and he did not help his chance here by being fractious at the start. (tchd 14-1)

Masamah(IRE) Official explanation: jockey said colt hung left-handed

Definightly Official explanation: jockey said colt was never travelling

T/Plt: £19.70 to a £1 stake. Pool: £93,017.81. 3,446.07 winning tickets. T/Qpdt: £8.60 to a £1 stake. Pool: £4,329.46. 370.78 winning tickets. CR

1289 NEWMARKET (R-H)

Thursday, April 16

OFFICIAL GOING: Good to firm (8.9)

Wind: Light, behind Weather: Overcast

1297 SALINITY WOOD DITTON STKS 1m

1:50 (1:52) (Class 4) 3-Y-O **£6,476** (£1,927; £963; £481) **Stalls** High

Form					RPR
	1		**Militarist (USA)** 3-9-3 0 (J H M Gosden) *w'like: tall: w ldr tl led over 2f out: rdn and edgd lft ins fnl f: r.o* 11/8[1]	JimmyFortune 4	81+
	2	¾	**Harbinger** 3-9-3 0 (Sir Michael Stoute) *str: good bodied: hld up: hdwy over 1f out: edgd rt and r.o wl ins fnl f: wnt 2nd post: nt rch wnr* 3/1[2]	RyanMoore 2	79+
	3	shd	**Big Bay (USA)** 3-9-3 0 (Jane Chapple-Hyam) *w'like: bit bkwd: s.i.s: plld hrd and sn prom: rdn over 1f out: styd on* 14/1	PatCosgrave 10	79
	4	1	**Beauchamp Xerxes** 3-9-3 0 (G A Butler) *w'like: leggy: a.p: rdn to chse wnr 2f out: styd on same pce ins fnl f* 25/1	EddieAhern 12	77
	5	nse	**Ottoman Empire (FR)** 3-9-3 0 (D R Lanigan) *s.i.s: sn chsng ldrs: rdn and edgd rt over 1f out: styd on same pce ins fnl f* 9/1	TedDurcan 5	77
	6	2¼	**Repetischa (IRE)** 3-8-12 0 (E A L Dunlop) *hld up in tch: rdn over 2f out: no ex fnl f* 20/1	StephenDonohoe 9	66
	7	1¾	**Illusive Spirit (IRE)** 3-9-3 0 (J H M Gosden) *w'like: bit bkwd: hld up: outpcd 3f out: styd on ins fnl f* 16/1	RichardMullen 8	67+
	8	5	**Dolores Ortiz (IRE)** 3-8-12 0 (S C Williams) *leggy: on toes: led: racd keenly: hdd over 2f out: wknd over 1f out* 66/1	J-PGuillambert 11	51
	9	5	**Lord Fidelio (IRE)** 3-9-3 0 (A M Balding) *leggy: s.i.s: rn green and a in rr: lost tch fr over 3f out* 16/1	MartinDwyer 3	44
	10	4½	**Errol Flynn (IRE)** 3-9-3 0 (J Noseda) *str: bit bkwd: in rr and rn green: wknd over 3f out* 15/2[3]	ShaneKelly 6	34

1m 41.39s (2.79) **Going Correction** -0.025s/f (Good) **10 Ran SP% 117.4**

Speed ratings (Par 100): **85,84,84,83,83 80,79,74,69,64**

toteswinger: 1&2 £1.80, 1&3 £5.90, 2&3 £7.90. CSF £5.22 TOTE £2.10: £1.10, £1.60, £3.80; EX 5.70.

Owner H R H Princess Haya Of Jordan **Bred** Gainsborough Farm Llc **Trained** Newmarket, Suffolk

FOCUS

The stalls were on the far side for the second day of the meeting, but they congregated towards the centre, as they had done on day one. The wind, which was not as strong, was this time pretty much behind, rather than almost into their faces. One can never tell for sure what the form of this historic newcomers' race is going to amount to, but while there is no suggestion at this stage that there were any stars in the field, it worked out pretty much according to the betting, with the market leaders first and second and another who was quietly fancied third. The early pace was steady and there were half a dozen with a chance of sorts at the furlong-marker.

1298 NGK SPARK PLUGS/COACHMAKERS MAIDEN FILLIES' STKS 5f

2:25 (2:25) (Class 4) 2-Y-O **£5,180** (£1,541; £770; £384) **Stalls** High

Form					RPR
	1		**Its Alright (IRE)** 2-9-0 0 (A Bailey) *str: good bodied: chsd ldrs: swtchd lft over 1f out: rdn to ld and edgd lft ins fnl f: r.o* 7/1	JimmyQuinn 5	84+
	2	1½	**Mijas Playa** 2-9-0 0 (C A Dwyer) *w'like: chsd ldrs: rdn and ev ch ins fnl f: styd on* 33/1	DarryllHolland 2	78
	3	1¾	**Habaayib** 2-9-0 0 (E A L Dunlop) *lengthy: scope: hld up in tch: rdn and ev ch ins fnl f: unable qck* 9/2[3]	RHills 10	72+
	4	½	**Starburst Excel** 2-9-0 0 (M G Quinlan) *unf: led: rdn over 1f out: hdd and no ex ins fnl f* 16/1	AlanMunro 4	70
	5	½	**Azif** 2-8-11 0 (Miss Gay Kelleway) *w'like: bit bkwd: prom: rdn: hung lft and outpcd over 1f out: styd on towards fin* 80/1	DavidProbert(3) 1	68+
	6	1	**Six Wives** 2-9-0 0 (W J Haggas) *str: good bodied: athletic: prom: outpcd 2f out: styd on ins fnl f* 7/2[2]	LiamJones 9	64+
5	7	½	**Crown (IRE)**[13] 1090 2-9-0 0 (R Hannon) *athletic: str: chsd ldr: rdn and ev ch over 1f out: wknd wl ins fnl f* 3/1[1]	RichardHughes 8	62
	8	3¼	**Silver Symphony (IRE)** 2-9-0 0 (P F I Cole) *unf: tall: s.i.s: rn green and a in rr* 7/1	RyanMoore 3	50+

9 1 1/4 **Zambuka (FR)** 2-9-0 0 J-PGuillambert 6 45+
(R Curtis) *leggy: s.i.s: hld up: rdn and wknd wl over 1f out* **33/1**
10 3 3/4 **Mexican Milly (IRE)** 2-9-0 0 MichaelHills 11 31
(B W Hills) *leggy: s.i.s: hld up: plld hrd: wknd wl over 1f out* **13/2**
0 11 11 **Usquaebach**[19] 994 2-9-0 0 FrancisNorton 7 —
(H J Collingridge) *str: good bodied: bit bkwd: chsd ldrs: lost pl 3f out: sn bhd* **66/1**

59.72 secs (0.62) **Going Correction** -0.025s/f (Good) **11** Ran SP% **118.2**
Speed ratings (Par 91): **94,91,88,88,87 85,84,79,77,71 54**
toteswinger: 1&2 £38.80, 1&3 £8.40, 2&3 £35.00. CSF £216.71 TOTE £8.50: £2.00, £7.80, £2.00; EX 279.30.
Owner Allan McNamee **Bred** Barouche Stud Ireland Ltd **Trained** Newmarket, Suffolk

FOCUS
A decent fillies' maiden that has been won by some classy sorts in recent years including the smart pair Flashy Wings and Silk Blossom. The winning time was nearly a second quicker than the previous day's juvenile conditions event, though the wind had turned right around since then so comparisons are misleading. Not much to go on so far as ratings are concerned, but the winner put up a taking performance and looks useful. The placed horses seemed to know their job better than some.

NOTEBOOK
Its Alright(IRE) ◆, an 8,000euros filly out of a winner over 6f, was by no means unbacked on this debut. Having been held up in the middle of the field early, once pulled out for her effort she quickened up nicely on meeting the final rise and was well on top at the line. She is now likely to head for the Lily Agnes at Chester and then, all being well, the Queen Mary. (op 10-1, tchd 12-1 in places)
Mijas Playa ◆, a 7,000gns filly out of a half-sister to a smart juvenile in France, was ridden more handily than the winner, but she never stopped trying and on this evidence a maiden looks a formality.
Habaayib was the most expensive in the field, having cost 130,000gns as a yearling. Out of a dual winner in the US, she was never that far away and put in a promising effort towards the inside rail but then lacked the finishing speed to make it count. There are races to be won with her. (tchd 4-1 and 11-2)
Starburst Excel, out of a half-sister to three winners at up to 7f, including the Great St Wilfrid and Portland-winner Cadeaux Cher, has some strengthening to do but showed decent speed from the off and she too ought to be winning races in due course. (op 20-1 tchd 22-1 and 33-1 in a place)
Azif ◆, out of a winning juvenile sprinter, ran a most promising debut. Starting from the outside stall, she saw plenty of daylight and then ran very green when put under pressure, but she was still going forward at the line and is very much one to keep on the right side. (op 66-1)
Six Wives ◆, out of a dual winning juvenile sprinter, is from the stable that took this last year. She was staying on from off the pace at the line without being by any means knocked about, and she is likely to improve. (tchd 4-1)
Crown(IRE), who seemed to find this trip inadequate on her Bath debut, was more organised this time and showed up until done for foot up the hill. She is likely to appreciate another furlong. (op 11-4 tchd 5-2)
Silver Symphony(IRE), a 12,000gns half-sister to a winning juvenile in France and also to a winning hurdler, attracted support but could never get into the race after missing the break. Still a little on the weak side, she ought to have learnt something from this and she may also appreciate a bit further in due course. (op 12-1)
Mexican Milly(IRE), who fetched only £7,600 as a two-year-old, is a half-sister to a winner over 1m2f in Italy. From the stable which took this in 2006 and 2007, she gave herself little chance by missing the break and then pulling hard in rear. (op 5-1 tchd 9-2)

1299 CONNAUGHT ACCESS FLOORING ABERNANT STKS (LISTED RACE) 6f
3:00 (3:00) (Class 1) 3-Y-0+
£25,546 (£9,684; £4,846; £2,416; £1,210; £607) **Stalls** High

Form				RPR
411-	1		**Tax Free (IRE)**[291] 3533 7-9-4 112 FrancisNorton 6	111
			(D Nicholls) *chsd ldr: led over 3f out: rdn out* **8/1**[3]	
140-	2	1/2	**Equiano (FR)**[193] 6518 4-9-4 116 MichaelHills 3	109
			(B W Hills) *lw: led: hdd over 3f out: chsd wnr thereafter: rdn and ev ch over 1f out: r.o* **3/1**[1]	
11-3	3	1	**Knot In Wood (IRE)**[19] 996 7-9-4 108 JamieMoriarty 13	106
			(R A Fahey) *swtg: hld up in tch: rdn over 1f out: r.o* **8/1**[3]	
/60-	4	shd	**Exclamation**[234] 5347 4-9-4 100 EddieAhern 9	106
			(B J Meehan) *hld up in tch: rdn over 2f out: r.o* **16/1**	
6324	5	1/2	**Orpsie Boy (IRE)**[19] 1006 6-9-4 92 KirstyMilczarek 4	104
			(N P Littmoden) *hld up: pushed along over 2f out: hdwy over 1f out: r.o* **50/1**	
010-	6	hd	**Prohibit**[145] 7421 4-9-4 103 JimmyFortune 11	103
			(J H M Gosden) *hld up: r.o u.p ins fnl f: nt trble ldrs* **8/1**[3]	
010-	7	3/4	**Edge Closer**[200] 6304 5-9-4 112 RichardHughes 14	101
			(R Hannon) *dwlt: hld up: swtchd rt and hdwy over 1f out: sn rdn: styd on same pce ins fnl f* **7/2**[2]	
/612	8	1	**Hatta Fort**[49] 700 4-9-10 112 (t) LDettori 5	104
			(Saeed Bin Suroor) *lw: hld up: rdn over 2f out: styd on ins fnl f: nt trble ldrs* **8/1**[3]	
1100	9	1	**Matsunosuke**[26] 911 7-9-8 105 LukeMorris 10	99
			(A B Coogan) *hld up: rdn over 1f out: n.d* **25/1**	
000-	10	nk	**Mac Gille Eoin**[176] 6903 5-9-4 93 JimCrowley 12	94
			(J Gallagher) *bit bkwd: chsd ldrs: rdn over 1f out: wknd ins fnl f* **40/1**	
000-	11	3	**Spirit Of Sharjah (IRE)**[173] 6971 4-9-4 92 RyanMoore 8	84
			(Miss J Feilden) *swtg: hld up: rdn and wknd over 1f out* **25/1**	
020-	12	3 1/2	**Zidane**[159] 7243 7-9-4 108 JamieSpencer 1	73
			(J R Fanshawe) *b: b.hind: lw: s.i.s: hld up and bhd: rdn over 2f out: eased fnl f* **8/1**[3]	

1m 10.3s (-1.90) **Going Correction** -0.025s/f (Good) **12** Ran SP% **120.8**
Speed ratings (Par 111): **111,110,109,108,108 107,106,105,104,103 99,95**
toteswinger: 1&2 £6.50, 1&3 £11.50, 2&3 £5.60. CSF £31.81 TOTE £7.90: £2.60, £1.70, £2.40; EX 32.70.
Owner Ian Hewitson **Bred** Denis & Mrs Teresa Bergin **Trained** Sessay, N Yorks

FOCUS
A strong renewal of this Listed race, with half the field rated 105 or above. The first two were in those positions throughout and, aided by fast ground and a tail wind, they never looked like being reeled in. The time was bang-on par for the grade.

NOTEBOOK
Tax Free(IRE) ◆, who has matured into a really imposing sprinter, had looked most effective at 5f in the past despite having won over as far as 7f. Well suited by the conditions, he took the lead off the favourite before halfway and kept going in game style. This could be his season and this consistent sort will go for the Duke Of York Stakes next. (tchd 9-1)
Equiano(FR) flew out of the gates and made the early running. However, he was taken on by the winner before halfway and Michael Hills appeared not to want to get into a battle too early. The half a length he conceded at that point he could never reduce despite running on well all the way to the line. Like the winner he has looked best at 5f, despite scoring over 7f when trained in Spain, although he could take on that rival again at York. Alternatively he could come back here for the Palace House Stakes, and then take in the Prix de Gros-Chene before attempting to repeat last season's King's Stand win at Royal Ascot. (op 7-2 tchd 4-1)
Knot In Wood(IRE), another consistent performer, is best at 6f and handles this fast ground but is usually better with some cut. He chased the principals throughout and ran on bravely up the hill, but never looked like reeling them in. He deserves to win a race at this level. (op 15-2 tchd 6-1)
Exclamation, the winner of a valuable sales race at two in 2007, was lightly raced last season and has been gelded since. He looked relaxed beforehand, chased the leaders throughout and kept going, looking more willing since his operation.
Orpsie Boy(IRE) is rather the fly in the ointment form-wise, as he looked to have a bit to find on official ratings. Fit from the all-weather and on his favoured conditions on turf, he came from the rear to finish best of all. (tchd 66-1 in places)
Prohibit, all of whose wins were at this trip and who handles fast ground, had been held in three previous tries in this grade. He moved up on the outside of his field running into the Dip but could not find another gear up the hill. (op 15-2)
Edge Closer, a dual Listed winner racing over his optimum trip, goes well enough fresh and looked fit but rather missed the break. Having made headway his effort petered out in the closing stages. (tchd 4-1 and 9-2 in places)
Hatta Fort, a Group 2 winner here in 2007, raced in the USA in 2008 but was the winner of a valuable handicap and runner-up in a Group 3 in Dubai earlier this spring. He was shouldering a 6lb penalty and in the circumstances ran respectably, having been held up. (tchd 9-1 and 10-1 in a place)
Zidane, who won this last year but had not scored since, missed the break and was struggling a fair way from home. He handles fast ground but his better recent efforts have been on good or softer. Official explanation: trainer said gelding was unsuited by the Good to Firm ground (op 15-2 tchd 9-1)

1300 BANSHAHOUSESTABLES.COM CRAVEN STKS (GROUP 3) (C&G) 1m
3:35 (3:36) (Class 1) 3-Y-0
£36,900 (£13,988; £7,000; £3,490; £1,748; £877) **Stalls** High

Form				RPR
215-	1		**Delegator**[180] 6815 3-8-12 115 JamieSpencer 7	118+
			(B J Meehan) *lw: hld up: swtchd lft: rapid hdwy to ld and edgd rt over 1f out: shkn up and r.o wl* **4/6**[1]	
1-	2	2 3/4	**Sans Frontieres (IRE)**[227] 5579 3-8-12 76 JMurtagh 5	107
			(J Noseda) *w'like: athletic: lw: trckd ldrs: plld hrd: rdn and hung rt over 2f out: styd on same pce fnl f* **12/1**	
10-1	3	3/4	**Pure Poetry (IRE)**[5] 1211 3-8-12 99 RichardHughes 8	105
			(R Hannon) *w/ prom: racd alone tl jnd main gp over 3f out: rdn and ev ch over 1f out: no ex ins fnl f* **9/1**[3]	
01-	4	shd	**Alyarf (USA)**[202] 6246 3-8-12 98 RHills 4	105
			(B W Hills) *lw: led: rdn and hdd over 1f out: no ex ins fnl f* **7/1**[2]	
01-	5	3 1/2	**Glass Harmonium (IRE)**[211] 6031 3-8-12 86 RyanMoore 3	97
			(Sir Michael Stoute) *bit bkwd: s.i.s: sn prom: rdn over 1f out: wknd fnl f* **9/1**[3]	
1-0	6	3 1/4	**Close Alliance (USA)**[29] 863 3-8-12 92 JimmyFortune 2	89
			(J H M Gosden) *swtg: chsd ldrs: rdn over 2f out: wknd over 1f out* **12/1**	
031-	7	17	**Imperial Guest**[173] 6972 3-8-12 98 TonyCulhane 1	50
			(G G Margarson) *warm: hld up: rdn over 2f out: sn wknd* **20/1**	

1m 36.56s (-2.04) **Going Correction** -0.025s/f (Good) **7** Ran SP% **112.6**
Speed ratings (Par 108): **109,106,105,105,101 98,81**
toteswinger: 1&2 £3.30, 1&3 £2.50, 2&3 £5.30. CSF £9.73 TOTE £1.60: £1.30, £2.80; EX 9.00.
Owner Mrs P Good **Bred** Mrs P Good **Trained** Manton, Wilts

FOCUS
Like the previous afternoon's Nell Gwyn, this lacked strength in depth and on paper was very one-sided following the withdrawal of City Style. Delegator looks a strong candidate for the first Classic but it is debatable if he achieved any more here than in the Dewhurst.

NOTEBOOK
Delegator won in great style, but probably did little more than his superior form entitled him to. Seemingly very much second best behind Racing Post Trophy winner Crowded House in the Manton pecking order at two after being beaten fair and square into fifth in the Dewhurst, he was a massive springer in the 2000 Guineas ante-post lists after an outstanding gallop the previous week. Held up and still last 3f out, he showed an impressive burst of speed when switched left for his effort and was already in front as they passed the furlong-marker. To his credit, he came away in style up the hill, despite pricking his ears and idling, winning in a time nearly five seconds, or 30 lengths, faster than Militarist's in the opener. Disputing Guineas favouritism as a result, he is a classy colt with a turn of foot that could be even more potent if deployed later. However, the form needs keeping in perspective and as it stands it would not match the level typically required to win the Guineas. (op 8-11)
Sans Frontieres(IRE) went into this as a once-raced Lingfield maiden winner. He could have run in a handicap off just 76 and was obviously showing much-improved form, as one would expect from such a lightly-raced son of Galileo, and one who cost 450,000gns. Though quite keen to begin with and displaying an unattractive head carriage when hanging under pressure, he is clearly useful already and he ought to go on improving. He is bred to be very well suited by further and has plenty of options. (op 17-2)
Pure Poetry(IRE) looks the most reliable guide to the form, for he got a BHA rating of 101 and an RPR of 100 after winning a weakish Easter Stakes on the Polytrack at Kempton the previous Saturday. He raced alone through the early stages, but gradually joined the pack and probably ran his race again. (op 11-1 tchd 12-1)
Alyarf(USA), last year's easy 6f Haydock winner, looked in good shape and made the running, but he has speed in his pedigree and failed to convince as a miler. (tchd 8-1)
Glass Harmonium(IRE), a Yarmouth maiden winner, is from a stoutish family and probably wants further. As he's by Verglas he possibly wants softer too, but the mere fact that Sir Michael Stoute ran him here suggests he is well regarded, so considerable improvement is on the cards. (op 8-1 tchd 10-1)
Close Alliance(USA), not seen to advantage from a poor draw in Kempton's Kentucky Derby Challenge, was racing on turf for the first time. That shouldn't have been a problem, but he was one of the first off the bridle. (op 14-1)
Imperial Guest did not run much of a race and trailed in well beaten. (tchd 25-1)

1301 WEATHERBYS EARL OF SEFTON STKS (GROUP 3) 1m 1f
4:10 (4:12) (Class 1) 4-Y-0+
£36,900 (£13,988; £7,000; £3,490; £1,748; £877) **Stalls** High

Form				RPR
401-	1		**Tazeez (USA)**[194] 6476 5-8-12 109 RHills 1	117
			(J H M Gosden) *lw: chsd ldrs tl led over 4f out: pushed clr fnl f* **9/4**[2]	
252-	2	3 1/2	**Steele Tango (USA)**[250] 4867 4-8-12 100 AlanMunro 9	109
			(R A Teal) *b b.hind: hld up: pushed along over 3f out: hdwy over 2f out: sn rdn: styd on to go 2nd wl ins fnl f* **12/1**	
102-	3	2	**Twice Over**[180] 6816 4-8-12 119 TPQueally 7	105
			(H R A Cecil) *bit bkwd: prom: chsd wnr over 2f out: sn rdn: hung rt fr over 1f out: no ex ins fnl f* **4/6**[1]	
461-	4	3 1/4	**Barshiba (IRE)**[181] 6781 5-8-9 108 RichardHughes 3	95
			(D R C Elsworth) *s.i.s: hld up: hdwy 3f out: rdn and hung lft 2f out: wknd over 1f out* **10/1**[3]	
	5	5	**Logic Way (USA)**[21] 5-8-12 108 (bt) MartinDwyer 4	87
			(Miss D Mountain) *bit bkwd: chsd clr ldr 5f: rdn over 2f out: wknd wl over 1f out* **40/1**	

0-21 **6** *12* **Emerald Wilderness (IRE)**[57] 585 5-8-12 97............ JamieSpencer 5 60
(A King) *swtg: s.i.s: hld up: rdn: hung rt and wknd 2f out* **20/1**

060/ **7** *13* **Nomoretaxes (BRZ)**[14] 7-8-12 85..........................(t) KirstyMilczarek 8 32
(Miss D Mountain) *led and sn clr: hdd & wknd over 4f out* **100/1**

1m 47.83s (-3.87) **Going Correction** -0.025s/f (Good) **7** Ran SP% **115.7**
Speed ratings (Par 113): **116,112,111,108,103 93,81**
toteswinger: 1&2 £4.20, 1&3 £1.60, 2&3 £3.00. CSF £27.63 TOTE £3.10: £1.70, £4.30; EX 29.30.
Owner Hamdan Al Maktoum **Bred** Clovelly Farms **Trained** Newmarket, Suffolk
■ Stewards' Enquiry : T P Queally one-day ban: careless riding (Apr 30)

FOCUS
A race that has been won by some top-class horses such as Shiva, Notnowcato and Manduro within the past ten years. This latest renewal was notable for a strong pace and a very decent winning time, just 0.57 seconds outside the course record. Twice Over was below form but Tazeez has clearly improved again.

NOTEBOOK
Tazeez(USA), last seen winning the Cambridgeshire over course and distance off a mark of 102 last October, was well backed for this reappearance and justified the support with a taking display. Content to sit just off the strong early pace, he took over in front at around halfway when the pacemaker wilted and from then on it was just a case of seeing his race out, which he did in game fashion. He was always finding more than enough and was well on top by the time he reached the line. A late starter, he still seems to be improving at the age of five and looks well worth a try in even higher grade. (op 3-1)
Steele Tango(USA), not seen since narrowly beaten by Tazeez off a mark of 95 in a handicap on the July Course last August, looked fit but was just being niggled along to keep in touch at halfway. He eventually found his second wind and rallied to take second spot up the final hill. Connections were thrilled by this effort and he will appreciate a return to further. (op 16-1)
Twice Over, representing last year's winning stable and last seen chasing home New Approach at a respectful distance in the Champion Stakes here last October, had been successful first time out in both of his previous campaigns including when edging out Raven's Pass in the Craven Stakes here last year. He was by far the best horse in this race judged on official ratings, but having travelled into the race very smoothly entering the final 3f he found nothing off the bridle and then hung away to his right. He appeared to be feeling the ground and may also want further now.
Official explanation: jockey said colt hung right (op 4-7 tchd 5-6 and 10-11 in places)
Barshiba(IRE), who ended a lengthy losing run when winning a fillies' Listed event on her most recent outing here last October, looked fit and raced keenly off the pace, but couldn't get involved once off the bridle and hung right over to the stands' rail, possibly because her vision in her left eye is rather better than in her right. She may be better off back in Listed company against her own sex in any case. (tchd 9-1)
Logic Way(USA), successful four times in the US last year and a good winner in Qatar last month, didn't fare too badly on this British debut even though he ended up well beaten. He should be able to find easier opportunities than this. (op 50-1 tchd 33-1 and 66-1 in a place)
Emerald Wilderness(IRE), dropping back in trip having won a Kempton Polytrack handicap off a mark of 98 last time, was dropped right out early but he never managed to get into the race at all. He faced a very stiff task on these terms, but is now officially rated 12lb higher than for his last win on turf so isn't going to be the easiest to place in the near future. (op 16-1)
Nomoretaxes(BRZ), a stable-companion of Logic Way who has a moderate strike rate despite having won in Brazil, Dubai and Qatar, went off far too fast and had run himself into the ground by halfway. He had no chance on official ratings in any case.

1302 ROSSDALES MAIDEN FILLIES' STKS — 7f
4:45 (4:47) (Class 4) 3-Y-O **£5,180** (£1,541; £770; £384) **Stalls High**

Form RPR

5- **1** **Resort**[293] 3456 3-9-0 0.. RyanMoore 9 82+
(Sir Michael Stoute) *lw: led over 2f: chsd ldr tl led again over 1f out: rdn and hrd pressed ins fnl f: hld on wl* **9/4**[2]

5- **2** *nse* **Balaagha (USA)**[181] 6776 3-9-0 0.. RHills 7 82+
(M A Jarvis) *w'like: str: s.i.s: hld up: hdwy over 2f out: rdn to chal ins fnl f: r.o* **5/4**[1]

3- **3** *2 1/2* **Spring Adventure**[191] 6565 3-9-0 0.. AlanMunro 10 75+
(E A L Dunlop) *w'like: lw: trckd ldrs: rdn over 1f out: styd on same pce ins fnl f* **7/1**[3]

45- **4** *2 1/2* **Casting Couch (IRE)**[288] 3610 3-9-0 0.. MichaelHills 3 68
(B W Hills) *lengthy: w ldr tl led over 4f out: rdn and hdd over 1f out: wknd ins fnl f* **33/1**

5 *1* **Chicora (USA)** 3-9-0 0.. RichardMullen 2 66
(J H M Gosden) *tall: scope: hld up: hdwy 1/2-way: outpcd 2f out: styd on ins fnl f* **16/1**

0 **6** *nse* **Viva La Vida**[64] 503 3-9-0 0.. KirstyMilczarek 4 65
(Jane Chapple-Hyam) *trckd ldrs: plld hrd: nt clr run over 1f out: wknd ins fnl f* **66/1**

3 **7** *1/2* **Christina Rossetti**[22] 949 3-9-0 0.. JimmyFortune 8 64
(J H M Gosden) *w'like: leggy: hld up in tch: plld hrd: wknd over 1f out* **10/1**

- **8** *3 1/2* **Angelica's Art (IRE)** 3-9-0 0.. LDettori 6 55
(B J Meehan) *str: scope: bit bkwd: hld up: shkn up over 2f out: wknd over 1f out: eased* **16/1**

2 **9** *23* **She's In The Money**[9] 1174 3-9-0 0.. TPQueally 1 —
(J G Given) *tall: scope: chsd ldrs tl wknd over 2f out* **12/1**

1m 25.77s (0.37) **Going Correction** -0.025s/f (Good) **9** Ran SP% **120.7**
Speed ratings (Par 97): **96,95,93,90,89 89,88,84,58**
toteswinger: 1&2 £2.20, 1&3 £4.60, 2&3 £3.90. CSF £5.71 TOTE £3.10: £1.60, £1.20, £2.20; EX 6.30.
Owner Cheveley Park Stud **Bred** Cheveley Park Stud Ltd **Trained** Newmarket, Suffolk

FOCUS
This fillies' maiden has produced the odd decent performer in recent years, with Yaqeen going on to finish sixth in the 1000 Guineas and Cassandra Go becoming a top-class sprinter. This year's field were a decent-looking bunch and the race produced a very close finish.
Christina Rossetti Official explanation: jockey said filly ran too free

1303 CURRAGH "HOME OF THE IRISH CLASSICS" H'CAP — 1m 2f
5:20 (5:21) (Class 3) (0-95,92) 3-Y-O **£9,714** (£2,890; £1,444; £721) **Stalls High**

Form RPR

1- **1** **Perpetually (IRE)**[265] 4394 3-8-9 **83**.. JoeFanning 1 95
(M Johnston) *chsd ldr: rdn over 1f out: edgd rt and r.o to ld post* **4/1**[2]

210- **2** *shd* **Imposing**[194] 6474 3-8-10 **84**.. RyanMoore 9 96+
(Sir Michael Stoute) *lw: hld up: hdwy over 2f out: rdn to ld ins fnl f: hdd post* **15/8**[1]

03-1 **3** *1 1/4* **Legislate**[26] 917 3-8-7 **81**.. MichaelHills 4 90
(B W Hills) *led: rdn over 1f out: hdd ins fnl f: unable qck nr fin* **15/2**

5-1 **4** *2* **Muraweg (IRE)**[23] 944 3-8-9 **83**.. RHills 11 88
(J H M Gosden) *chsd ldrs: rdn over 1f out: no ex ins fnl f* **13/2**[3]

451- **5** *5* **Tudor Key (IRE)**[209] 6085 3-9-4 **92**.. JimCrowley 10 87
(Mrs A J Perrett) *mid-div: hdwy over 3f out: rdn over 1f out: sn wknd* **16/1**

3413 **6** *2* **Doncosaque (IRE)**[42] 764 3-8-9 **83**.. TPQueally 3 74
(P Howling) *hld up: plld hrd: rdn over 2f out: n.d* **100/1**

1-6 **7** *nk* **Nawaadi (USA)**[19] 1001 3-8-4 **78**.. NickyMackay 8 68
(J H M Gosden) *lw: prom: rdn over 2f out: edgd rt and wknd over 1f out* **8/1**

4-1 **8** *1 1/4* **Everynight (IRE)**[19] 998 3-8-7 **81**.. AlanMunro 6 69
(M Botti) *hld up: rdn over 2f out: sn wknd* **10/1**

031- **9** *1 1/2* **Oasis Knight (IRE)**[209] 6086 3-8-7 **81**.. MartinDwyer 7 66
(M P Tregoning) *hld up: rdn over 3f out: wknd over 1f out* **14/1**

26-1 **10** *1 1/4* **State General (IRE)**[97] 101 3-8-5 **79**.. LiamJones 5 61
(Miss J Feilden) *swtg: hld up: rdn over 2f out: sn wknd* **33/1**

615- **11** *hd* **Zaaqya**[174] 6946 3-8-5 **79**.. RichardMullen 2 61
(J L Dunlop) *swtg: hld up: hdwy 1/2-way: rdn over 2f out: sn wknd* **14/1**

2m 2.69s (-3.11) **Going Correction** -0.025s/f (Good) **11** Ran SP% **123.2**
Speed ratings (Par 102): **111,110,109,108,104 102,102,101,100,99 99**
toteswinger: 1&2 £3.90, 1&3 £7.70, 2&3 £4.20. CSF £12.49 CT £56.84 TOTE £5.00: £2.30, £1.60, £2.20; EX 11.80 Place 6: £41.05 Place 5: £30.84.
Owner Sheikh Hamdan Bin Mohammed Al Maktoum **Bred** Gainsborough Stud Management Ltd **Trained** Middleham Moor, N Yorks

FOCUS
A race that has been won by the likes of Hazyview, Papal Bull and Bronze Cannon in recent seasons and this year's renewal looked well up to scratch, with all 11 runners successful in at least one of their last two outings. The gallop looked decent, but even so three of the first four home were up with the pace from the start and little else managed to get involved. Strong form, and the first four are all likely to be ahead of the handicapper for now.

NOTEBOOK
Perpetually(IRE) ◆, who looked fit for this return, was one of those to race handily. He came off the bridle a fair way out, but kept on responding and rallied to snatch the race near the line. He hadn't been seen since making a winning debut over 7f at York last July, but is bred to have appreciated this sort of trip and that is how things panned out. He looks a very decent middle-distance prospect and would be interesting in races like the King George V Handicap at Royal Ascot. (op 7-1 and 8-1 in places)
Imposing ◆ was last seen finishing in midfield behind Donativum in the Tattersalls Timeform Million here last October and not only has the form of that race worked out extremely well in the meantime, his previous Haydock maiden victory has also produced its share of winners. Another upped in trip here, he was the only one to make any real impact from off the pace and, despite not having much room to play with on a couple of occasions, he looked the most likely winner when hitting the front inside the last furlong before just having the prize snatched from him. He looks another progressive sort and there are some nice races to be won with him. (op 7-2)
Legislate ◆, gutsy winner of an ordinary maiden on the Lingfield Polytrack on his return to action last month, was game again here and having set a decent pace he battled on really well when challenged. Unlike the front pair, he did have the advantage of a recent run, but even so he should be winning more races this season. (op 6-1)
Muraweg(IRE) ◆, winner of an ordinary Lingfield Polytrack maiden on his return to action last month, ran a nice race over this longer trip and was another to race handily from the start. He still has scope and is one to keep on the right side. (op 6-1 tchd 15-2)
Tudor Key(IRE) ◆ ran an eye-catching race under top weight on this return to action. He travelled very powerfully behind the leaders and looked a brief threat running into the Dip, but then got tired on meeting the rising ground as lack of peak fitness rather than lack of stamina for this longer trip seemed to tell. (op 14-1)
Doncosaque(IRE), very consistent on Polytrack throughout the winter, took a keen hold out the back before running on past beaten horses late on. This was a fair effort, but he is much more exposed than the majority of his rivals and is still to prove that he is as good on grass.
Nawaadi(USA) ◆, who shaped as though he would relish this longer trip when unplaced in a handicap on the Kempton Polytrack on his return to action last month, came off the bridle nearly half a mile out but plugged on to finish a respectable seventh. A Dante entry looks very optimistic, but this was only his third start and his first on turf, so he is entitled to still have some improvement left. (op 6-1)
Everynight(IRE), successful over a similar trip in a Doncaster maiden on his return to action last month, never got involved on this handicap debut and was a bit disappointing. (op 7-1)
Oasis Knight(IRE) ◆ made an effort coming to the last couple of furlongs, but it amounted to little. He had looked a stayer when winning a 1m1f nursery off a 4lb lower mark here last September, but didn't look happy on the track then and he didn't look totally suited to it again here, so he may be worth another chance back on a flatter track with this pipe-opener under his belt. (op 12-1)
T/Plt: £133.40 to a £1 stake. Pool: £85,406.61. 467.34 winning tickets. T/Qpdt: £21.80 to a £1 stake. Pool: £5,514.77. 186.75 winning tickets. CR

RIPON (R-H)
Thursday, April 16

OFFICIAL GOING: Good to firm (9.4)
Wind: Moderate, half-against Weather: fine but cool

1304 E B F EAT SLEEP & DRINK AT NAGS HEAD PICKHILL MAIDEN STKS — 5f
2:00 (2:03) (Class 5) 2-Y-O **£4,209** (£1,252; £625; £312) **Stalls Low**

Form RPR

2 **1** **Here Now And Why (IRE)**[14] 1083 2-9-3 0.. NCallan 8 87+
(K A Ryan) *mde all: styd on strly: v readily* **2/5**[1]

2 *2* **Saucy Girl (IRE)** 2-8-12 0.. DavidAllan 5 69
(T D Easterby) *trckd ldrs: kpt on to take 2nd ins fnl f: no imp* **8/1**[2]

3 *1* **Mister Manannan (IRE)** 2-9-3 0.. SilvestreDeSousa 2 71+
(D Nicholls) *chsd ldrs: swtchd rt and chsd wnr over 2f out: rn green and hung rt: styd on same pce appr fnl f* **12/1**

4 *3 1/2* **Sheka** 2-8-12 0.. PatrickMathers 6 52+
(I W McInnes) *s.s: hdwy 2f out: nvr nr ldrs* **66/1**

5 *3/4* **Tillys Tale** 2-8-5 0.. PaulPickard(7) 7 49
(P T Midgley) *hld up in rr: hdwy on outside 2f out: nvr nr ldrs* **100/1**

6 *nk* **Senate Majority** 2-9-3 0.. DuranFentiman 9 53
(T D Easterby) *hld up in rr: kpt on fnl f* **66/1**

0 **7** *nse* **Whippers Love (IRE)**[19] 994 2-9-3 0.. RoystonFfrench 10 53
(M Johnston) *sn drvn along towards rr: hmpd over 2f out: kpt on: nvr a factor* **11/1**[3]

0 **8** *shd* **Take It To The Max**[19] 994 2-9-3 0.. PJMcDonald 1 53
(G M Moore) *t.k.h in midfield: drvn and outpcd over 2f out* **8/1**[2]

0 **9** *9* **Camacho Flyer (IRE)**[14] 1083 2-9-3 0.. MickyFenton 3 19
(P T Midgley) *chsd wnr: lost pl over 2f out: sn bhd* **100/1**

10 *3* **Chifah** 2-8-12 0.. PaulDoe 11 2
(P D Evans) *swvd rt s: sn bhd* **25/1**

61.98 secs (1.28) **Going Correction** +0.125s/f (Good) **10** Ran SP% **118.5**
Speed ratings (Par 92): **94,90,89,83,82 81,81,81,67,62**
toteswinger: 1&2 £1.10, 1&3 £2.60, 2&3 £6.50. CSF £4.41 TOTE £1.40: £1.02, £2.10, £3.10; EX 6.00 Trifecta £28.00 Pool: £248.60 - 6.56 winning units.
Owner Mrs Sandra McCarthy **Bred** Mrs Sandra McCarthy **Trained** Hambleton, N Yorks

FOCUS
An average juvenile maiden. The first three came clear and the winner sets the level and could do better.

NOTEBOOK

Here Now And Why(IRE) created a very favourable impression when just losing out to a more experienced rival on his debut at Leicester last time (has won again since) and confirmed that promise by going one better in ready fashion from the front. He still looked distinctly inexperienced though and it should be noted that he unseated his rider on the way down to post. While he was very much entitled to take this and could have been more impressive in doing so, he is in very good hands and looks sure to make his mark at a higher level. (op 8-15)

Saucy Girl(IRE) was bidding to give her stable a fourth consecutive success in the race. She was well away and ran a perfectly respectable race, but shaped very much as though the run was needed. There is plenty of speed in her pedigree and it is fair to expect her to go one better now this initial experience is behind her. (op 5-1)

Mister Manannan(IRE) ◆ cost £30,000 and is bred to make his mark at two. He proved very green throughout, but showed plenty of ability and ought to know a lot more next time. (op 16-1 tchd 11-1)

Sheka led home the chasing pack and did all of her best work towards the finish. She ought to improve a good deal for this debut experience. (tchd 50-1)

Camacho Flyer(IRE) Official explanation: jockey said the colt was unsuited by the track

1305 COPT HEWICK H'CAP 6f

2:35 (2:36) (Class 4) (0-85,83) 3-Y-O **£4,857** (£1,445; £722; £360) **Stalls** Low

Form RPR

000- **1** **Mister Laurel**[196] 6426 3-8-10 **75**.................................... PaulHanagan 6 83+
(R A Fahey) *t.k.h: trckd ldrs: effrt and swtchd outside over 1f out: r.o to ld nr fin* **5/2**[2]

144- **2** *nk* **Cheviot (USA)**[192] 6540 3-9-4 **83**.................................... PhilipRobinson 5 90
(M A Jarvis) *in rr: hdwy on outer 3f out: edgd lft and led over 1f out: hdd and no ex towards fin* **15/8**[1]

140- **3** *2 ½* **Captain Scooby**[201] 6274 3-8-7 **75**.................... MichaelJStainton(3) 4 74
(R M Whitaker) *hld up in rr: hdwy whn nt clr run and swtchd outside over 1f out: styd on same pce* **20/1**

210- **4** *2* **Dubai Hills**[173] 6970 3-9-1 **80**.................................... TomEaves 8 73
(B Smart) *w ldrs on outer: hmpd over 1f out: kpt on same pce* **14/1**

013- **5** *6* **Lucky Numbers (IRE)**[159] 7241 3-9-2 **81**.................... PaulMulrennan 3 54+
(Paul Green) *trckd ldrs on inner: nt clr run over 2f out: bdly hmpd over 1f out: nt rcvr* **16/1**

20-1 **6** *2 ¾* **Hi Shinko**[16] 1045 3-8-8 **73**.................................... RobertWinston 2 38+
(B R Millman) *led on stands' side: rail: edgd rt 2f out: edgd lft: wkng whn hdd and bdly hmpd over 1f out:* **7/2**[3]

21-3 **7** *12* **Miss Chamanda (IRE)**[31] 852 3-8-12 **77**.................................... PaulDoe 7 3+
(P D Evans) *w ldrs: keeping on same pce whn bdly hmpd over 1f out: nt rcvr: eased* **14/1**

1m 13.7s (0.70) **Going Correction** +0.125s/f (Good) 7 Ran SP% **109.6**
Speed ratings (Par 100): **100,99,96,93,85 81,65**
toteswinger: 1&2 £1.50, 1&3 £10.00, 2&3 £13.50. CSF £6.90 CT £61.64 TOTE £3.30: £2.30, £1.50; EX 7.20 Trifecta £106.30 Pool: £339.06 - 2.36 winning units.
Owner The Cosmic Cases **Bred** Mrs M Bryce **Trained** Musley Bank, N Yorks

FOCUS

An interesting three-year-old handicap in which there was a barging match at the furlong pole. The form still makes sense.

1306 RIPON SILVER BOWL CONDITIONS STKS 1m 1f 170y

3:10 (3:10) (Class 3) 4-Y-O+

£7,477 (£2,239; £1,119; £560; £279; £140) **Stalls** High

Form RPR

0446 **1** **Halicarnassus (IRE)**[19] 1004 5-9-0 107.................................... SamHitchcott 2 91+
(M R Channon) *hld up in tch: effrt over 2f out: wnt 2nd over 1f out: kpt on wl to ld last 50yds* **11/10**[1]

130- **2** *nk* **Slam**[195] 6445 4-9-0 95.................................... RobertWinston 5 90+
(B W Hills) *led 1f: t.k.h: led 3f out: sn rdn: no ex and hdd wl ins fnl f* **5/4**[2]

200- **3** *2 ½* **Just Lille (IRE)**[236] 5279 6-8-9 88.................................... MickyFenton 1 80
(Mrs A Duffield) *trckd ldrs: effrt over 4f out: sn outpcd: kpt on fnl 2f* **8/1**[3]

-140 **4** *5* **Exit Smiling**[19] 995 7-9-0 88.................................... LeeEnstone 4 75
(P T Midgley) *led after 1f: hdd 3f out: wknd ins fnl f* **20/1**

1520 **5** *1 ½* **General Tufto**[8] 1192 4-8-7 67....................................(b) RichardRowe(7) 3 72
(C Smith) *hld up in rr: effrt 4f out: nvr a factor* **66/1**

030- **6** *18* **Grethel (IRE)**[152] 7342 5-8-5 56 ow1.................................... SladeO'Hara(5) 6 32
(A Berry) *chsd ldrs: pushed along 4f out: lost pl over 2f out: sn bhd* **100/1**

2m 3.38s (-2.02) **Going Correction** -0.025s/f (Good) 6 Ran SP% **110.4**
Speed ratings (Par 107): **107,106,104,100,99 85**
toteswinger: 1&2 £1.02, 1&3 £2.10, 2&3 £1.90. CSF £2.62 TOTE £1.80: £1.10, £1.30; EX 2.60.
Owner Doric Racing **Bred** Yeomanstown Lodge Stud **Trained** West Ilsley, Berks

FOCUS

The form of this conditions event looks fair as the pace was decent. Neither of the first two are rated to their best and the form is limited by the fifth.

NOTEBOOK

Halicarnassus(IRE) had not been disgraced in Listed company on the all-weather the last twice and is happier on turf. He took time to hit top gear from 2f out, but always looked like getting on top where it mattered and only needed hands-and-heels riding to prevail. It was his second success of the year, having scored on his comeback in Dubai and, although a likely return to Group company will make life tougher again, he should continue to pay his way at least. Something like the Huxley Stakes at Chester's May meeting could be an ideal next step. (op 11-8 tchd 6-4)

Slam was well supported throughout the day for this seasonal debut. He got a little fractious down at the start and ran freely through the early parts. His rider sent him on 3f out and he looked a likely winner at the two-furlong pole, but his early exertions eventually told. This rates a decent effort against a race-fit rival who is officially rated 12lb his superior, so providing he consents to settle better he is open to further progression over this sort of trip. (tchd Evens, 11-8 in places)

Just Lille(IRE) had plenty to find at these weights with the first pair so ran a perfectly respectable comeback race and left the impression she would benefit a lot for the run. Hopefully the Handicapper will not put her up much for this as she could probably defy this mark in handicap company. (tchd 11-1)

Exit Smiling eventually got to the front and set a true pace. This was no disgrace over a trip that stretches him, but he is difficult to place at present. (op 12-1)

1307 RIPON "COCK O' NORTH" H'CAP 1m

3:45 (3:46) (Class 3) (0-95,92) 3-Y-O

£8,723 (£1,959; £1,959; £653; £326; £163) **Stalls** High

Form RPR

361- **1** **Crackdown (IRE)**[206] 6176 3-9-7 **92**.................................... RoystonFfrench 3 101
(M Johnston) *mde all: qckmd over 3f out: kpt on gamely* **10/1**

414- **2** *¾* **Firebet (IRE)**[191] 6549 3-9-0 **85**.................................... MickyFenton 9 92
(Mrs A Duffield) *t.k.h towards rr: effrt and n.m.r over 2f out: styd on fnl f* **20/1**

1 **2** *dht* **Mutamaashi**[68] 440 3-9-0 **85**.................................... TPO'Shea 6 92
(W J Haggas) *s.i.s: hdwy over 2f out: sn chsng ldrs: kpt on same pce ins fnl f* **6/5**[1]

10-1 **4** *3* **Hunterview**[16] 1056 3-9-7 **92**.................................... PhilipRobinson 1 92
(M A Jarvis) *sn chsng ldrs: effrt over 3f out: one pce fnl 2f* **7/2**[2]

01- **5** *2 ½* **Anthology**[187] 6655 3-8-13 **84**.................................... TomEaves 5 79
(B Smart) *mid-div: stdy hdwy over 3f out: chsng ldrs 2f out: fdd jst ins fnl f* **11/1**

321- **6** *nk* **On Offer (IRE)**[294] 3411 3-8-7 **78**.................................... DavidAllan 8 72
(T D Easterby) *hld up in rr: effrt over 3f out: nt clr run: kpt on: nvr nr ldrs* **28/1**

415- **7** *4 ½* **Johnmanderville**[200] 6305 3-8-5 **76**.................................... AndrewElliott 10 60
(K R Burke) *chsd ldrs: drvn over 3f out: lost pl over 1f out* **16/1**

51- **8** *3 ¼* **Trumpstoo (USA)**[184] 6723 3-8-8 **79**.................................... PaulHanagan 11 55
(R A Fahey) *mid-div: drvn over 3f out: lost pl over 2f out* **8/1**[3]

130- **9** *6* **Cook's Endeavour (USA)**[200] 6305 3-8-7 **78**.................... PaulMulrennan 7 40
(K A Ryan) *trckd ldrs: drvn 3f out: lost pl over 2f out* **12/1**

1m 40.06s (-1.34) **Going Correction** -0.025s/f (Good) **9** Ran SP% **118.0**
TOTE £12.20: £3.00 Trifecta £144.80 Part won. Po27 Owner.

FOCUS

A decent handicap with six last-time-out winners in attendance and plenty of potential improvers. There was a solid pace on and the form looks sound with the first three pulling clear and should work out.

NOTEBOOK

Crackdown(IRE) made all in typically tenacious fashion for one from his stable to get his season off to a flying start. He signed off last term by getting off the mark at Leicester in a novice event and has evidently wintered very well. This track suits one with his style of running and he looked fit for this, but further improvement cannot be ruled out as there promises to be more to come over an even stiffer test. (op 14-1 tchd 16-1)

Firebet(IRE) ◆ was successful on two of his four outings last term and turned in a career-best on this seasonal bow. He really caught the eye finishing from off the pace and, with improvement expected for the run, a more positive ride over this extra furlong ought to see him back to winning ways. (op 25-1 tchd 28-1)

Mutamaashi ◆ proved all the rage to follow up his Lingfield maiden win over this trip in February. He had to be ridden from the gates and it was clear at the furlong pole he was unlikely to get to the winner. Things simply did not pan out for him here so he should certainly not be written off when switching to a more galloping track. (op 25-1 tchd 28-1)

Hunterview had been hiked up a stone for winning at Southwell last time and that looked to find him out on this return to turf. (op 10-3 tchd 3-1)

On Offer(IRE) Official explanation: jockey said the filly was denied a clear run

1308 SKELTON MAIDEN STKS 1m

4:20 (4:23) (Class 5) 3-Y-O **£3,238** (£963; £481; £240) **Stalls** High

Form RPR

326- **1** **Mister Dee Bee (IRE)**[200] 6305 3-9-3 79.................... RobertWinston 12 79+
(B W Hills) *led tl narrowly hdd over 1f out: led jst ins fnl f: kpt on wl* **9/4**[2]

2 *1 ½* **El Loco Uno (USA)** 3-9-3 0.................................... IanMongan 9 76+
(H R A Cecil) *trckd ldrs: slt ld over 1f out: hdd jst ins fnl f: no ex* **5/4**[1]

3 *½* **Signaller (USA)** 3-9-3 0.................................... RoystonFfrench 17 75+
(M Johnston) *chsd ldrs: n.m.r over 3f out: kpt on wl ins fnl f* **6/1**[3]

4 *3 ¾* **Zouk** 3-9-3 0.................................... AdamKirby 14 66+
(W R Swinburn) *in tch: kpt on fnl 2f: improve* **14/1**

5 *4 ½* **Elusive Muse** 3-9-3 0.................................... PhillipMakin 16 56
(M Dods) *trckd ldrs: effrt over 3f out: wknd over 1f out* **20/1**

6 *2* **Steel Trade** 3-9-3 0.................................... PhilipRobinson 7 51
(M Brittain) *in rr: hdwy over 2f out: kpt on: nvr nr ldrs* **18/1**

04-0 **7** *nse* **Bold Bomber**[15] 1064 3-9-3 52.................................... SamHitchcott 5 51
(Paul Green) *trckd ldrs: effrt over 2f out: wknd over 1f out* **100/1**

8 *2* **Firsaan (IRE)**[178] 6869 3-9-3 0.................................... DarrenWilliams 8 46
(J R Norton) *mid-div: effrt over 2f out: nvr a threat* **100/1**

6 **9** *shd* **Deauville Flyer**[18] 1015 3-9-3 0.................................... PaulMulrennan 3 46
(T D Easterby) *in tch: hdwy on outer over 3f out: wknd over 2f out* **25/1**

000- **10** *1 ¾* **Addison De Witt**[170] 7038 3-8-12 49.................... PatrickDonaghy(5) 15 42
(Micky Hammond) *in tch: effrt over 2f out: sn lost pl* **100/1**

40- **11** *nk* **Scarth Hill (IRE)**[290] 3568 3-9-3 0.................................... TomEaves 13 41
(G M Moore) *a bhd* **50/1**

0- **12** *1 ½* **Saute**[130] 7593 3-9-3 0.................................... SaleemGolam 1 38
(W R Swinburn) *swtchd rt s: a in rr* **50/1**

0- **13** *10* **Tilerium's Dream (IRE)**[278] 3976 3-9-3 0.................... PaulHanagan 4 15
(K A Ryan) *chsd ldrs: lost pl over 2f out* **66/1**

14 *13* **Aldaado (IRE)** 3-9-3 0.................................... DaleGibson 11 —
(M Dods) *s.i.s: bhd and sn drvn along: t.o* **80/1**

1m 41.58s (0.18) **Going Correction** -0.025s/f (Good) **14** Ran SP% **119.7**
Speed ratings (Par 98): **98,96,96,92,87 85,85,83,83,81 81,80,70,57**
toteswinger: 1&2 £2.10, 1&3 £4.20, 2&3 £4.00. CSF £5.02 TOTE £3.60: £1.50, £1.20, £2.10; EX 7.20 Trifecta £19.40 Pool: £283.12 - 10.78 winning units.
Owner South Bank Thoroughbred Racing **Bred** Denis McDonnell **Trained** Lambourn, Berks

FOCUS

An average three-year-old maiden. The form is straightforward but somewhat limited.

1309 LEVY BOARD H'CAP 6f

4:55 (4:56) (Class 4) (0-85,83) 4-Y-O+ **£4,857** (£1,445; £722; £360) **Stalls** Low

Form RPR

200- **1** **High Curragh**[159] 7239 6-8-11 **76**....................................(p) RobertWinston 11 85
(K A Ryan) *wnt rt s: swtchd lft and overall ldr stands' side: hdd ins fnl f: r.o to ld post* **8/1**[3]

503- **2** *nse* **Pavershooz**[173] 6976 4-9-1 **80**.................................... DO'Donohoe 4 89
(N Wilson) *trckd ldrs: styd on to take narrow advantage ins fnl f: hdd post* **16/1**

00-1 **3** *½* **Pickering**[9] 1169 5-8-1 **68** 6ex....................................(p) AndrewMullen(3) 10 76
(E J Alston) *racd stands' side: chsd ldrs: upsides 1f out: no ex wl ins fnl f* **8/1**[3]

0-44 **4** *½* **Vhujon (IRE)**[7] 1197 4-9-3 **82**.................................... PaulDoe 8 88+
(P D Evans) *dwlt: racd stands' side: in rr on outer: edgd lft over 2f out: hdwy to chse ldrs and swtchd rt ins fnl f: r.o* **7/1**[2]

100- **5** *1* **Earlsmedic**[201] 6278 4-9-2 **81**.................................... SaleemGolam 2 84+
(S C Williams) *racd stands' side: hld up in rr: hdwy 2f out: styd on and carried rt and hung bdly rt ins fnl f* **9/1**

500- **6** *hd* **Ponty Rossa (IRE)**[159] 7245 5-9-4 **83**.................................... DavidAllan 16 85
(T D Easterby) *racd far side: chsd ldrs: led that gp 1f out: kpt on same pce: 1st of 4 that gp* **14/1**

300- **7** *2 ¼* **Castles In The Air**[253] 4743 4-8-8 **73**.................................... PaulHanagan 7 68
(R A Fahey) *racd stands' side: trckd ldrs: effrt over 2f out: fdd fnl f* **7/2**[1]

2400 **8** *½* **Methaaly (IRE)**[18] 1016 6-8-13 **83**....................................(be) DeanHeslop(5) 5 76
(M Mullineaux) *mid-div stands' side: kpt on fnl 2f: nvr rchd ldrs* **25/1**

500- 9 shd **Pacific Pride**[201] 6278 6-8-10 75 GrahamGibbons 13 68
(J J Quinn) *led three others stands' side tl wknd 1f out: 2nd of 4 that gp* 16/1
214- 10 1 **Leonid Glow**[258] 4595 4-8-7 77 PatrickDonaghy(5) 3 67
(M Dods) *racd stands' side: in rr: effrt over 2f out: nvr nr ldrs* 14/1
100- 11 1 1/4 **Dazzling Bay**[116] 7756 9-9-0 79 DuranFentiman 15 65
(T D Easterby) *chsd ldr far side: hdwy and upsides that gp 1f out: sn wknd: 3rd of 4 that gp* 33/1
024- 12 1/2 **Gift Horse**[186] 6680 9-9-4 83 PaulQuinn 9 67
(D Nicholls) *racd stands' side: chsd ldrs: wknds 1f out* 14/1
0-14 13 3/4 **Ingleby Arch (USA)**[65] 491 6-9-1 83 NeilBrown(3) 6 65
(T D Barron) *racd stands' side: a in rr* 12/1
355- 14 3 1/2 **Kiwi Bay**[159] 7239 4-9-3 82 PhillipMakin 12 52
(M Dods) *sltly hmpd s: mid-div on outer: wknd over 1f out* 14/1
/00- 15 3 **Spirit Of France (IRE)**[263] 4460 7-8-6 78 NeilFarley(7) 14 39
(D Carroll) *racd wd on far side: t.k.h in last that gp: edgd rt and wknd over 1f out: last of 4 that gp* 50/1
1201 16 1 1/4 **Calmdownmate (IRE)**[60] 561 4-8-8 73 (b) PaulMulrennan 1 30
(Mrs R A Carr) *racd stands' side: chsd ldrs on inner: lost pl over 1f out* 16/1

1m 12.94s (-0.06) **Going Correction** +0.125s/f (Good) 16 Ran SP% **127.7**
Speed ratings (Par 105): **105,104,104,103,102 102,99,98,98,96 95,94,93,88,84 83**
toteswinger: 1&2 £25.10, 1&3 £8.70, 2&3 £31.50. CSF £134.11 CT £1130.73 TOTE £9.60: £2.10, £4.50, £2.30, £1.80; EX 254.70 TRIFECTA Not won..
Owner J Nattrass Mrs D Davenport & R Fawcett **Bred** Wheelersland Stud **Trained** Hambleton, N Yorks
■ Stewards' Enquiry : Andrew Mullen two-day ban: used whip with excessive frequency (Apr 30, May 1)

FOCUS
A fairly tight sprint handicap and the form should work out. Four went to the far rail and the first five places were filled by those that raced towards the near side.
Earlsmedic Official explanation: jockey said gelding hung badly right handed in the final furlong
Calmdownmate(IRE) Official explanation: jockey said the gelding was unsuited by the good to firm ground

1310 BETFAIR APPRENTICE TRAINING SERIES H'CAP 5f
5:30 (5:35) (Class 5) (0-70,70) 4-Y-0+ **£3,238** (£963; £481; £240) **Stalls** Low

Form RPR
25-0 1 **Imperial Sword**[17] 1039 6-7-12 59 ow1 (b) JanWilson(10) 6 68
(T D Barron) *hld up towards rr: gd hdwy over 1f out: led ins fnl f: r.o* 12/1
3302 2 1 **Strathmore (IRE)**[42] 762 5-8-2 63 TimothyAyres(10) 11 68+
(R A Fahey) *mid-div on outer: hdwy to chal 1f out: no ex towards fin* 12/1
5033 3 1/2 **Spirit Of Coniston**[20] 976 6-7-13 56 oh1 PaulPickard(6) 3 60
(P T Midgley) *chsd ldrs on stands' side: rdn over 2f out: slt ld 1f out: hdd and no ex ins fnl f* 9/2[1]
3514 4 hd **Argentine (IRE)**[20] 976 5-8-5 56 oh1 (b[1]) SimonPearce 14 59
(L Lungo) *mid-div: hdwy over 1f out: styng on at fin* 11/1
263- 5 1 1/2 **Kyzer Chief**[270] 4216 4-9-0 65 AmyRyan 12 62+
(R E Barr) *chsd ldrs on outer: upsides 1f out: no ex* 12/1
50-0 6 nk **Rio Sands**[9] 1169 4-9-1 66 DeclanCannon 2 62
(R M Whitaker) *sn trcking ldrs: swtchd rt over 1f out: kpt on same pce* 6/1[2]
40-6 7 1 **Radiator Rooney (IRE)**[57] 590 6-8-2 56 oh4...(v) AndrewHeffernan(3) 5 49
(Patrick Morris) *chsd ldrs: one pce appr fnl f* 25/1
4621 8 shd **Colorus (IRE)**[35] 818 6-8-11 67 (p) MatthewLawson(5) 4 59
(W J H Ratcliffe) *led tl 1f out: fdd* 7/1[3]
00-4 9 1 1/2 **Mandurah (IRE)**[21] 971 5-8-13 70 NSLawes(6) 7 57
(D Nicholls) *chsd ldrs: one pce whn hmpd over 1f out* 10/1
410 10 3/4 **Mr Rooney (IRE)**[50] 681 6-8-6 57 RosieJessop 8 41
(A Berry) *chsd ldrs: fdd 1f out* 25/1
646- 11 1 1/2 **Miss Daawe**[179] 6840 5-8-8 67 AnthonyBetts(8) 16 46
(B Ellison) *unruly in stalls: rrd s: a towards rr* 14/1
-562 12 2 **Cheshire Rose**[17] 1041 4-8-4 63 AdamCarter(8) 15 35
(T D Barron) *swtchd rt after 1f and racd alone far side: wknd 1f out* 14/1
00-0 13 3/4 **George The Best (IRE)**[86] 222 8-8-5 56 oh2 LanceBetts 13 25
(Micky Hammond) *s.s: a bhd* 50/1

61.10 secs (0.40) **Going Correction** +0.125s/f (Good) 13 Ran SP% **108.5**
Speed ratings (Par 103): **101,99,98,98,95 95,93,93,91,90 87,84,83**
toteswinger: 1&2 £27.50, 1&3 £21.30, 2&3 £9.00. CSF £119.41 CT £575.93 TOTE £16.00: £5.40, £3.30, £2.50; EX 206.70 TRIFECTA Not won. Place 6: £5.56 Place 5: £4.68.
Owner Harrowgate Bloodstock Ltd **Bred** David John Brown **Trained** Maunby, N Yorks
■ Jan Wilson's first winner.
■ Stewards' Enquiry : Declan Cannon two-day ban: carelss riding (Apr 30, May 1)

FOCUS
A typically moderate sprint for apprentice riders in which four raced from out of the handicap. Just the one went over to the far side. The winner is rated in line with last year's form.
T/Plt: £4.90 to a £1 stake. Pool: £52,332.42. 7,770.41 winning tickets. T/Qpdt: £3.90 to a £1 stake. Pool: £2,695.88. 500.79 winning tickets. WG

1153 WOLVERHAMPTON (A.W) (L-H)
Thursday, April 16

OFFICIAL GOING: Standard
Wind: Almost nil Weather: Some light rain after 7.15

1311 CELEBRATE HORIZONS 2ND ANNIVERSARY H'CAP 5f 20y(P)
5:15 (5:17) (Class 5) (0-70,68) 3-Y-0 **£2,914** (£867; £433; £216) **Stalls** Low

Form RPR
0-60 1 **Ziggy Lee**[69] 425 3-8-8 63 WilliamCarson(5) 6 80
(S C Williams) *hld up in tch: rdn to ld ins fnl f: r.o wl* 3/1[1]
3510 2 2 3/4 **La Capriosa**[24] 936 3-8-13 68 FrederikTylicki(5) 2 75
(A J McCabe) *a.p: led over 1f out: hdd ins fnl f: nt qckn* 8/1
2011 3 4 1/2 **Speak The Truth (IRE)**[15] 1072 3-9-3 67 (p) PatCosgrave 1 58
(J R Boyle) *t.k.h: a.p: rdn and no ex fnl f* 7/2[2]
0-45 4 3/4 **Fyelehk (IRE)**[20] 986 3-8-4 54 JimmyQuinn 9 42
(B R Millman) *mid-div: c wd st: hung lft fr over 1f out: kpt on to take 4th cl home* 4/1[3]
36-3 5 1 1/4 **Bees River (IRE)**[13] 1095 3-8-10 65 MartinLane(5) 3 49
(A P Jarvis) *led: hdd and rdn over 1f out: wknd fnl f* 7/1
3030 6 1 1/2 **Sills Vincero**[8] 1190 3-8-10 60 SteveDrowne 4 47+
(D Shaw) *s.i.s: bhd: hdwy wl over 1f out: sn rdn: no imp whn nt clr run wl ins fnl f* 14/1
-643 7 3/4 **Badtanman**[10] 1157 3-8-5 55 oh9 ow1 PatrickMathers 11 31
(Peter Grayson) *wnt rt s: sn swtchd lft: outpcd: nvr nrr* 50/1

040- 8 2 **Tarruji (IRE)**[139] 7465 3-9-1 65 DaneO'Neill 8 33
(S A Callaghan) *bhd: rdn over 1f out: n.d* 16/1
30-3 9 1/2 **You've Been Mowed**[20] 982 3-8-13 63 CatherineGannon 10 30
(R J Price) *prom tl wknd 2f out* 10/1
1240 10 1 **Josiah Bartlett (IRE)**[27] 900 3-8-7 60 KellyHarrison(3) 12 23
(P S McEntee) *carried rt s: outpcd* 66/1
130- 11 3 1/4 **Pressed For Time (IRE)**[153] 7308 3-9-0 64 (t) EdwardCreighton 7 15
(E J Creighton) *plld hrd in mid-div: wknd 2f out* 33/1

61.72 secs (-0.58) **Going Correction** 0.0s/f (Stan) 11 Ran SP% **118.9**
Speed ratings (Par 98): **104,99,92,91,89 86,85,82,81,80 74**
toteswinger: 1&2 not won, 1&3 £8.60, 2&3 £1.80. CSF £27.87 CT £89.04 TOTE £5.10: £2.00, £5.00, £1.02; EX 37.50.
Owner Rothmere Racing Limited **Bred** Ian Allan **Trained** Newmarket, Suffolk

FOCUS
An ordinary handicap in which the pace was sound. The winner and second, who pulled clear, raced in the centre in the straight. The winner is unexposed while the runner-up posted a personal best.
Ziggy Lee ◆ Official explanation: trainer's rep said, regarding the improved form shown, gelding appears to have benefited from a nine-week break from the racecourse, and from being dropped in trip
Badtanman Official explanation: jockey said hat the colt hung right-handed throughout
Josiah Bartlett(IRE) Official explanation: jockey said the gelding had missed the break

1312 WOLVERHAMPTON-RACECOURSE.CO.UK MAIDEN AUCTION STKS 5f 20y(P)
5:45 (5:45) (Class 5) 2-Y-O **£2,914** (£867; £433; £216) **Stalls** Low

Form RPR
52 1 **Shark Man (IRE)**[12] 1119 2-8-6 0 JackMitchell(3) 3 78+
(P J McBride) *chsd ldrs: edgd lft and rdn over 1f out: led wl ins fnl f: r.o* 10/11[1]
2 1 1/4 **Dancing Freddy (IRE)** 2-8-12 0 SebSanders 1 77
(J G Given) *led: rdn over 1f out: hdd and nt qckn wl ins fnl f* 7/2[2]
3 1 1/2 **Reel Credit Crunch** 2-8-5 0 JohnEgan 6 64
(P D Evans) *chsd ldr tl wl over 1f out: sn edgd lft: kpt on towards fin: tk 3rd post* 6/1
4 nse **Bebenine (IRE)** 2-8-1 0 KellyHarrison(3) 2 63
(Patrick Morris) *a.p: ev ch 1f out: no ex towards fin: lost 3rd post* 25/1
5 8 **Absher (IRE)** 2-8-10 0 ShaneKelly 8 40
(Patrick Morris) *s.i.s: outpcd* 25/1
6 1/2 **China Bay** 2-8-4 0 RichardKingscote 5 32
(Tom Dascombe) *s.i.s: outpcd* 11/2[3]
0 7 1 3/4 **Isle Of Ellis (IRE)**[19] 994 2-8-10 0 ow1 PatCosgrave 4 32
(A J McCabe) *reminder sn after s: sn in tch: rdn over 3f out: wknd over 2f out* 16/1

63.11 secs (0.81) **Going Correction** 0.0s/f (Stan) 7 Ran SP% **117.9**
Speed ratings (Par 92): **93,91,88,88,75 74,72**
toteswinger: 1&2 £4.10, 1&3 not won, 2&3 £1.30. CSF £4.63 TOTE £1.40: £1.10, £3.10; EX 6.60.
Owner J Burns **Bred** John Grimes **Trained** Newmarket, Suffolk
■ Stewards' Enquiry : Jack Mitchell one-day ban: used whip with excessive frequency (Apr 30)

FOCUS
This looked a moderate maiden and was one that went to the most experienced runner. The gallop was sound throughout but the time was nearly a second and a half slower than the opening handicap. The principals raced in the centre in the straight and the winner sets the standard in what looks a sound enough race.

NOTEBOOK
Shark Man(IRE), who was well supported, had shown more than enough on his two previous starts to suggest he was the one to beat in this company and he did enough after getting outpaced and again edging left under pressure. He will be worth a try over 6f in due course but may struggle under a penalty. (op 11-10)
Dancing Freddy(IRE) ◆ is bred to go a bit and, after attracting support, he showed more than enough when second to the much more experienced winner to suggest a similar race can be found when the emphasis is on speed. (op 7-1)
Reel Credit Crunch is related to a couple of speedy sorts and showed ability at an ordinary level on this racecourse debut. She is entitled to improve for this experience. (op 10-3)
Bebenine(IRE), a cheaply bought first foal of a dam who was placed over middle distances, showed enough after travelling strongly for a long way to suggest she ought to be able to pick up a minor event in low-grade company. (op 33-1)
China Bay, whose yard has had a debut juvenile winner this year, started at single-figure odds but never figured after starting awkwardly. Official explanation: jockey said the filly had no more to give (tchd 5-1)

1313 HOTEL & CONFERENCING AT WOLVERHAMPTON H'CAP 5f 216y(P)
6:15 (6:15) (Class 4) (0-80,79) 4-Y-0+ **£5,180** (£1,541; £770; £384) **Stalls** Low

Form RPR
4525 1 **Princess Valerina**[27] 901 5-8-13 79 FrederikTylicki(5) 7 89
(D Haydn Jones) *hld up and bhd: hdwy on ins over 2f out: hrd rdn fr wl over 1f out: led wl ins fnl f: all out* 6/1[3]
00-4 2 nse **Harbour Blues**[13] 1094 4-8-12 73 (t) CatherineGannon 3 83
(A W Carroll) *led: rdn over 1f out: hdd wl ins fnl f: r.o* 11/2[2]
-165 3 1 3/4 **Milne Bay (IRE)**[22] 954 4-8-10 71 (t) JimmyQuinn 2 75
(D M Simcock) *t.k.h in tch: rdn and nt qckn ins fnl f* 4/1[1]
3300 4 1 **Red Cape (FR)**[9] 1169 6-8-2 68 AndreaAtzeni(5) 12 69
(Mrs R A Carr) *a.p: chsd ldr over 3f out: tl rdn wl over 1f out: one pce fnl f* 12/1
0116 5 1 1/2 **Bahamian Lad**[27] 901 4-9-2 77 DaneO'Neill 11 73
(R Hollinshead) *sn outpcd: hdwy over 2f out: rdn over 1f out: one pce fnl f* 12/1
00-1 6 6 **Sir Nod**[76] 351 7-9-2 77 TonyHamilton 6 54
(Miss J A Camacho) *s.i.s: hld up and bhd: nt clr run wl over 2f out: n.d after* 6/1[3]
011- 7 hd **Double Carpet (IRE)**[117] 7745 6-8-4 65 RichardKingscote 5 42
(G Woodward) *hld up in tch: rdn and wknd over 1f out* 10/1
-003 8 6 **Luscivious**[21] 971 5-9-4 79 (b) PatCosgrave 8 36
(A J McCabe) *hld up: hdwy over 3f out: wknd over 2f out* 14/1
2414 9 4 1/2 **One More Round (USA)**[66] 475 11-8-9 70 (b) TGMcLaughlin 4 13
(P D Evans) *s.i.s: outpcd* 20/1
4243 10 25 **Distinctly Game**[27] 892 7-9-2 77 (t) SilvestreDeSousa 1 —
(K A Ryan) *chsd ldr tl rdn over 3f out: wknd qckly wl over 2f out: t.o* 11/2[2]

1m 13.97s (-1.03) **Going Correction** 0.0s/f (Stan) 10 Ran SP% **115.2**
Speed ratings (Par 105): **106,105,103,102,100 92,92,84,78,44**
toteswinger: 1&2 £8.10, 1&3 £10.20, 2&3 £13.50. CSF £38.51 CT £151.32 TOTE £5.00: £2.50, £1.30, £2.50; EX 24.70.
Owner G J Hicks **Bred** George Joseph Hicks **Trained** Efail Isaf, Rhondda C Taff
■ Stewards' Enquiry : Frederik Tylicki five-day ban: used whip with excessive frequency (Apr 30-May 4)

FOCUS
A fair handicap featuring exposed performers. The pace was a good one and the winner raced against the inside rail in the straight. The form looks pretty sound.
Sir Nod Official explanation: jockey said the gelding was denied a clear run round the bend
Distinctly Game Official explanation: jockey said the gelding knocked itself coming out of the stalls and felt wrong behind

1314 WOLVERHAMPTON CORPORATE HOSPITALITY - A PLEASURE (S) STKS — 1m 1f 103y(P)
6:45 (6:45) (Class 6) 4-Y-0+ — £1,942 (£578; £288; £144) Stalls Low

Form — RPR
-034 **1** **What's Up Doc (IRE)**[23] 650 8-8-12 72 DaneO'Neill 9 62
(Mrs T J Hill) *chsd ldr: led over 2f out: rdn wl over 1f out: r.o wl* 5/1[3]
6/10 **2** 2 ½ **Postage (USA)**[35] 816 6-9-3 47 JimmyQuinn 4 62
(K A Morgan) *hld up in tch: chsd wnr over 1f out: rdn fnl f: no imp* 9/1
0622 **3** nk **Krugerrand (USA)**[14] 1081 10-8-12 65 EddieAhern 8 56+
(W J Musson) *hld up in mid-div: hdwy 2f out: rdn over 1f out: kpt on to take 3rd ins fnl f* 7/2[2]
-400 **4** 2 **Artreju (GER)**[45] 733 6-8-12 60 (b[1]) FergusSweeney 7 52
(G L Moore) *hld up in rr: hdwy 2f out: rdn and kpt on ins fnl f* 20/1
3624 **5** 1 **Don Pietro**[29] 872 6-9-3 69 (v[1]) J-PGuillambert 1 55
(R Curtis) *t.k.h: a.p: one pce fnl 2f* 13/2
1224 **6** 1 ¼ **Clear Sailing**[42] 765 6-8-12 70 (p) FrederikTylicki[(5)] 2 52
(Ollie Pears) *led: rdn and hdd over 2f out: wknd 1f out* 9/4[1]
0051 **7** ¾ **Waterside (IRE)**[12] 1131 10-9-3 70 JamesDoyle 3 51
(S Curran) *hld up in mid-div: pushed along 3f out: no hdwy fnl 2f* 11/1
033/ **8** 8 **Regal Tradition (IRE)**[245] 6503 4-8-7 63 AndreaAtzeni[(5)] 11 29
(G J Smith) *hld up in rr: rdn wl over 1f out: nvr nr ldrs* 66/1
06-5 **9** 2 **Tantris (IRE)**[14] 1081 4-8-12 61 ShaneKelly 10 25
(J A Osborne) *hld up in mid-div: wknd 2f out* 16/1
060 **10** 18 **Bobering**[41] 775 9-8-5 42 SoniaEaton[(7)] 12 —
(B P J Baugh) *a in rr: lost tch fnl 4f* 66/1
2m 1.74s (0.04) **Going Correction** 0.0s/f (Stan) **10 Ran SP% 115.0**
Speed ratings (Par 101): **99,96,96,94,93 92,92,84,83,67**
toteswinger: 1&2 £5.60, 1&3 £2.80, 2&3 £9.60. CSF £47.77 TOTE £6.20: £2.00, £3.30, £1.10; EX 61.60.There was no bid for the winner.
Owner M B Clarke **Bred** James J Monaghan **Trained** Aston Rowant, Oxon
FOCUS
Not the worst race of its type. The gallop was only an ordinary one and the winner raced against the inside rail in the straight. the form is not easy to pin down with the runner-up apparently a big improver.

1315 ENJOY THE LUCKY 7 GROUP OFFER FILLIES' H'CAP — 1m 1f 103y(P)
7:15 (7:16) (Class 5) (0-75,75) 3-Y-0 — £2,914 (£867; £433; £216) Stalls Low

Form — RPR
1 **1** **Stagecoach Jade (IRE)**[21] 970 3-9-1 **72** JimmyQuinn 6 73+
(M Johnston) *a.p: rdn wl over 1f out: led wl ins fnl f: r.o* 9/2[2]
0562 **2** ¾ **Abu Dubai (IRE)**[13] 1106 3-8-7 **64** ow1 FergusSweeney 4 64
(C A Dwyer) *hld up and bhd: hdwy wl over 1f out: ev ch ins fnl f: nt qckn* 66/1
221- **3** hd **Miss Beat (IRE)**[111] 7783 3-9-0 **71** EddieAhern 1 70
(B J Meehan) *t.k.h: chsd ldr: rdn wl over 1f out: ev ch ins fnl f: nt qckn* 6/1[3]
1- **4** ½ **Cascata (IRE)**[152] 7332 3-9-4 **75** DaneO'Neill 8 73+
(L M Cumani) *t.k.h: hld up in rr: hdwy on outside over 4f out: sltly outpcd and rdn wl over 1f out: styd on towards fin* 4/5[1]
2312 **5** hd **Flying Lady (IRE)**[10] 1148 3-8-3 **65** MCGeran[(5)] 11 63
(M R Channon) *swtchd lft sn after s: hld up in rr: c wd st: hdwy jst over 1f out: rdn and kpt on ins fnl f* 25/1
1013 **6** 1 ¼ **Common Diva**[10] 1155 3-8-10 **72** FrederikTylicki[(5)] 7 67
(A J McCabe) *led: rdn over 1f out: hdd and no ex wl ins fnl f* 10/1
025- **7** 1 **Peace Concluded**[198] 6358 3-8-12 **72** JamesMillman[(3)] 5 65
(B R Millman) *hld up in mid-div: hdwy 2f out: rdn over 1f out: fdd wl ins fnl f* 33/1
-210 **8** 7 **Brer Rabbit**[22] 962 3-8-12 **69** SteveDrowne 3 47
(B W Hills) *hld up in tch: rdn and wknd wl over 1f out* 33/1
062- **9** ½ **Perfect Friend**[162] 7190 3-8-11 **68** JamesDoyle 2 45
(S Kirk) *a bhd* 33/1
10- **10** 10 **Cashleen (USA)**[173] 6982 3-9-4 **75** JohnEgan 9 31
(K A Ryan) *a bhd: lost tch fnl 2f* 25/1
2m 2.52s (0.82) **Going Correction** 0.0s/f (Stan) **10 Ran SP% 115.1**
Speed ratings (Par 95): **96,95,95,94,94 93,92,86,85,76**
toteswinger: 1&2 £18.80, 1&3 £5.80, 2&3 £32.70. CSF £266.03 CT £1787.83 TOTE £5.90: £1.10, £11.20, £2.20; EX 91.80.
Owner Mrs Jacqueline Conroy **Bred** Carradale Ltd, T Stack & W Cousis **Trained** Middleham Moor, N Yorks
■ Stewards' Enquiry : Frederik Tylicki one-day ban: failed to keep straight from stalls (May 5)
FOCUS
An interesting event with two bringing unbeaten records to the table and a couple of others open to improvement. The gallop was only fair and the action unfolded in the centre. The form is a bit muddling and is rated around those just outside the frame.

1316 STAY AT THE WOLVERHAMPTON HOLIDAY INN H'CAP — 1m 141y(P)
7:45 (7:45) (Class 4) (0-80,80) 4-Y-0+ — £5,180 (£1,541; £770; £384) Stalls Low

Form — RPR
1010 **1** **Brouhaha**[19] 1003 5-9-4 **80** RichardKingscote 5 90
(Tom Dascombe) *a.p: pushed along wl over 2f out: carried rt and rdn 1f out: led ins fnl f: r.o* 7/4[1]
350- **2** ¾ **Never Ending Tale**[204] 6202 4-9-3 **79** LPKeniry 2 87
(E F Vaughan) *chsd ldr: led 2f out: carried hd high: rdn and edgd rt 1f out: hdd ins fnl f: nt qckn* 3/1[3]
P-61 **3** ½ **Marajaa (IRE)**[15] 1067 7-9-0 **76** ShaneKelly 7 83
(W J Musson) *hld up: hdwy wl over 1f out: hrd rdn fnl f: nt qckn cl home* 11/4[2]
060- **4** 8 **Justcallmehandsome**[124] 7670 7-8-8 **77** (v) BillyCray[(7)] 6 65
(D J S Ffrench Davis) *hld up in tch: led 4f out to 2f out: wknd ins fnl f* 20/1
0364 **5** ¾ **Count Trevisio (IRE)**[13] 1107 6-9-2 **78** (p) SteveDrowne 3 65
(J R Gask) *led: hdd 4f out: wknd wl over 1f out* 8/1
0-66 **6** 4 ½ **Xtra Torrential (USA)**[12] 1132 7-8-8 **70** FergusSweeney 4 46
(D M Simcock) *hld up and bhd: pushed along over 2f out: sn struggling* 14/1
4-00 **7** 5 **Ninth House (USA)**[24] 932 7-8-4 **66** oh4 (p) AndrewElliott 1 31
(Mrs R A Carr) *s.s: a in rr* 33/1
1m 50.07s (-0.43) **Going Correction** 0.0s/f (Stan) **7 Ran SP% 113.5**
Speed ratings (Par 105): **101,100,99,92,92 88,83**
toteswinger: 1&2 £5.60, 1&3 £1.10, 2&3 £2.40. CSF £7.13 TOTE £2.60: £1.10, £1.60; EX 7.20 Place 6: £30.09 Place 5: £19.06.

Owner G D Newton **Bred** Mrs Rosamund Furlong **Trained** Lambourn, Berks
FOCUS
They were exposed performers in this fair handicap. The pace was only fair and the winner raced in the centre in the straight. The first three pulled clear and the form is rated around the placed horses.
T/Plt: £153.60 to a £1 stake. Pool: £63,685.30. 302.50 winning tickets. T/Qpdt: £33.10 to a £1 stake. Pool: £8,606.21. 192.00 winning tickets. KH

[1283] KEMPTON (A.W) (R-H)
Friday, April 17

OFFICIAL GOING: Standard
Wind: Virtually nil. Weather: Heavy rain.

1317 KEMPTON.CO.UK MEDIAN AUCTION MAIDEN STKS — 5f (P)
6:35 (6:36) (Class 5) 3-5-Y-O — £2,590 (£770; £385; £192) Stalls High

Form — RPR
2 **1** **Lenny Bee**[24] 947 3-9-0 0 PaulMulrennan 3 64+
(D H Brown) *sn pushed up to trck ldng pair: rdn to chal ent fnl f: sustained chal to ld last stride* 5/4[2]
233- **2** shd **Gilt Edge Girl**[172] 7015 3-8-9 72 PhilipRobinson 7 59+
(C G Cox) *chsd ldr: rdn to ld over 1f out: hrd pressed ent fnl f: kpt on u.p tl hdd last stride* 1/1[1]
3 2 ¼ **Island Legend (IRE)** 3-9-0 0 LukeMorris 10 55
(J M Bradley) *s.i.s: in tch in midfield: hdwy on inner over 1f out: swtchd lft jst ins fnl f: styd on to go 3rd fnl 100yds: nt pce to rch ldrs* 40/1
0- **4** 1 **Maigh Eo (IRE)**[371] 1303 3-9-0 0 RichardHughes 11 51
(Patrick Morris) *t.k.h: trckd ldrs: rdn and effrt over 1f out: outpcd by ldng pair ent fnl f: kpt on same pce after* 20/1
5-5 **5** nk **Captain Flasheart (IRE)**[89] 208 3-9-0 0 SaleemGolam 9 50+
(S C Williams) *t.k.h: hld up towards rr: rdn and effrt over 1f out: styd on steadily fnl f: nvr pce to rch ldrs* 12/1
- **6** nse **Aegean King** 3-8-7 0 TobyAtkinson[(7)] 5 50+
(M Wigham) *s.i.s: hld up bhd: swtchd ins over 1f out: hdwy ent fnl f: r.o ins fnl f: nt rch ldrs* 33/1
50-0 **7** nk **Sandy Par**[18] 1038 4-9-10 44 (p) LPKeniry 8 53
(J M Bradley) *led tl rdn and hdd over 1f out: wknd ins fnl f* 50/1
53- **8** 1 **Glimpse Of Light (IRE)**[195] 6488 3-8-9 0 NeilChalmers 4 40
(A M Balding) *taken down early: hld up in midfield: rdn and unable qck over 1f out: one pce fnl f* 10/1[3]
-304 **9** 3 ¼ **Flamboyant Red (IRE)**[58] 583 3-9-0 42 (t) JimmyQuinn 6 33
(Miss Gay Kelleway) *a towards rr: rdn 2f out: no prog: wl hld fnl f* 20/1
6 **10** ½ **Honey Berry (IRE)**[13] 1120 3-8-9 0 ShaneKelly 1 26
(Patrick Morris) *stdd s: hung lft thrght: a bhd* 66/1
60.58 secs (0.08) **Going Correction** -0.025s/f (Stan)
WFA 3 from 4yo 10lb **10 Ran SP% 129.6**
Speed ratings (Par 103): **98,97,94,92,92 92,91,90,84,84**
toteswinger: 1&2 £1.50, 1&3 £13.50, 2&3 £14.80. CSF £3.04 TOTE £2.20: £1.10, £1.10, £9.10; EX 4.20.
Owner Ron Hull **Bred** Whitsbury Manor Stud & Pigeon House Stud **Trained** Maltby, S Yorks
FOCUS
The surface would have been compacted by the persistent rain, which has a tendency to produce slightly faster times than normal. There was little depth to this maiden and the pair that dominated the market fought out the finish. Possibly not the most reliable of form with the first two unlikely to have run to their best.

1318 BIG G 50TH BIRTHDAY MEMORIAL H'CAP — 1m 2f (P)
7:10 (7:10) (Class 6) (0-65,65) 4-Y-0+ — £2,047 (£604; £302) Stalls High

Form — RPR
650- **1** **Madam President**[181] 6826 4-9-4 **65** AdamKirby 8 74
(W R Swinburn) *hld up in midfield: hdwy over 3f out: chsd ldng pair over 1f out: rdn and r.o wl to ld fnl 100yds: wl in command at fin* 6/1[3]
0231 **2** 1 ½ **Gasat (IRE)**[30] 872 8-9-4 **65** SebSanders 4 71
(A B Haynes) *led over 8f out: clr 7f out: rdn and qcknd 2f out: drvn ent fnl f: hdd fnl 100yds: no ex* 7/2[1]
205- **3** ¾ **Seventh Hill**[218] 5815 4-9-1 **62** JimmyQuinn 3 67
(M Blanshard) *hld up towards rr: pushed along 4f out: hdwy 3f out: chsd clr ldr and rdn wl over 1f out: kpt on u.p but nt pce to chal* 20/1
00-5 **4** 1 ¼ **Piper's Song (IRE)**[14] 1107 6-9-4 **65** RichardHughes 2 67
(Patrick Morris) *stdd and dropped in bhd after s: hld up in last pair: stl plenty to do 2f out: c wd and hdwy over 1f out: r.o fnl f: nvr able to chal* 25/1
14-5 **5** ½ **Ermine Grey**[23] 959 8-9-1 **62** KirstyMilczarek 10 63
(S Gollings) *hld up in midfield: rdn over 2f out: hdwy to chse clr ldng trio ent fnl f: kpt on but nvr pce to rch ldrs* 11/1
620- **6** 1 **Lunar River (FR)**[153] 7342 6-9-4 **65** (t) FrankieMcDonald 1 64
(David Pinder) *stdd and dropped in bhd: hld up in last pair: stl plenty to do over 1f out: hdwy jst over 1f out: r.o: nvr threatened ldrs* 50/1
252- **7** hd **The Grey One (IRE)**[136] 7532 6-8-13 **65** (p) MCGeran[(5)] 13 64
(J M Bradley) *t.k.h: hld up in midfield: nt clr run on inner over 1f out: sn swtchd lft: styd on fnl f: nvr trbld ldrs* 16/1
1033 **8** nk **Lytham (IRE)**[20] 1000 8-8-7 **61** TobyAtkinson[(7)] 14 59
(A W Carroll) *t.k.h: hld up wl in tch: n.m.r 2f out tl wl over 1f out: sn drvn and unable qck: wknd ins fnl f* 4/1[2]
15-0 **9** 2 ¾ **Mayfair's Future**[36] 813 4-8-13 **60** JimCrowley 11 53
(J R Jenkins) *t.k.h: hld up in tch: nt clr run on inner wl over 1f out: sn swtchd lft: no prog ent fnl f* 25/1
220- **10** ½ **Gracechurch (IRE)**[220] 5783 6-8-10 **62** Louis-PhilippeBeuzelin[(5)] 6 54
(R J Hodges) *s.i.s: hld up bhd: effrt towards inner over 1f out: no prog* 16/1
1543 **11** 3 **Watson's Bay**[18] 1042 4-9-4 **65** FergusSweeney 5 51
(Miss Tor Sturgis) *in tch: hdwy over 3f out: rdn to chse clr ldr 2f out tl wl over 1f out: sn outpcd: wknd ent fnl f* 6/1[3]
1-05 **12** 14 **White Moss (IRE)**[9] 1178 5-9-3 **64** RichardThomas 12 22
(Jim Best) *led tl over 8f out: chsd ldr after tl 2f out: sn wknd: wl btn and eased ins fnl f* 25/1
41-1 **13** 7 **Sky Quest (IRE)**[104] 21 11-9-4 **65** PatCosgrave 7 9
(J R Boyle) *in tch: rdn and wkng over 2f out: towards rr whn hmpd ent fnl 2f: wl btn and eased ins fnl f* 10/1
4612 **14** 2 **Waldorf (IRE)**[28] 898 4-8-13 **60** MartinDwyer 9 —
(W R Muir) *t.k.h: chsd ldrs tl wknd u.p 3f out: wl bhd and eased ins fnl f* 7/1
2m 7.18s (-0.82) **Going Correction** -0.025s/f (Stan) **14 Ran SP% 130.7**
Speed ratings (Par 105): **102,100,100,99,98 98,97,97,95,95 92,81,75,74**
toteswinger: 1&2 £6.50, 1&3 £27.90, 2&3 £23.20. CSF £27.97 CT £423.89 TOTE £9.00: £3.20, £2.10, £7.10; EX 33.60.

Owner Mrs Doreen M Swinburn **Bred** Genesis Green Stud Ltd **Trained** Aldbury, Herts

FOCUS
Seb Sanders and Gasat appeared to set a fairly even gallop, but although they looked like nicking it from the front when kicking a couple clear early in the straight, they could not fend off the strong late surge of the winner. Pretty solid form by the look of it.

The Grey One(IRE) Official explanation: jockey said gelding ran too free early on

1319 FEDERATION OF BLOODSTOCK AGENTS (GB) H'CAP 1m 4f (P)
7:40 (7:40) (Class 4) (0-80,80) 4-Y-0+ **£4,727** (£1,406; £702; £351) **Stalls** Centre

Form RPR

320- **1** **Haarth Sovereign (IRE)**[175] 6948 5-9-0 **75**............ AdamKirby 3 86
(W R Swinburn) *hld up in midfield: rdn and effrt on inner 2f out: drvn to chal ent fnl f: led fnl 50yds: drvn out* **4/1**[2]

400- **2** *nk* **Sahrati**[201] 6302 5-8-11 **72**............(p) AlanMunro 9 83
(D R C Elsworth) *t.k.h: trckd ldrs: rdn to ld wl over 1f out: hrd pressed jst over 1f out: kpt on wl tl hdd and no ex fnl 50yds* **12/1**

121- **3** *2 ¼* **Red Merlin (IRE)**[187] 6678 4-9-0 **76**............(v) PhilipRobinson 4 83+
(C G Cox) *stdd s: t.k.h: hld up in last pl: hdwy on outer over 3f out: pressed ldrs 2f out: drvn and one pce ent fnl f* **9/2**[3]

0-33 **4** *1 ¼* **Ruff Diamond (USA)**[28] 893 4-8-11 **73**............ LukeMorris 2 78
(J S Moore) *s.i.s: hld up in last trio: shkn up over 3f out: rdn and effrt over 2f out: kpt on same pce u.p fnl f* **16/1**

5142 **5** *1 ¾* **Star Choice**[9] 1178 4-8-4 **66** oh1............(v) DO'Donohoe 8 68
(J Pearce) *hld up in midfield: hdwy 4f out: rdn to ld over 2f out: hdd wl over 1f out: wknd ent fnl f* **8/1**

-112 **6** *2 ¾* **El Diego (IRE)**[78] 325 5-9-5 **80**............ SteveDrowne 6 78
(J R Gask) *in tch: rdn 4f out: n.m.r briefly ent fnl 2f: wknd u.p over 1f out* **3/1**[1]

-510 **7** *8* **Bassinet (USA)**[27] 915 5-9-2 **77**............ KirstyMilczarek 5 62
(J A R Toller) *hld up in last trio: effrt over 2f out: wknd wl over 1f out: wl btn fnl f* **16/1**

1110 **8** *8* **Shanafarahan (IRE)**[8] 1200 4-8-4 **66** oh1............ JimmyQuinn 7 38
(K A Morgan) *chsd ldr: upsides ldrs over 5f out: wknd qckly u.p jst over 2f out: eased ins fnl f* **6/1**

26-0 **9** *9* **Shady Gloom (IRE)**[20] 999 4-9-2 **78**............ NCallan 1 36
(K A Ryan) *led: rdn and hdd over 2f out: sn wknd: t.o* **12/1**

2m 32.42s (-2.08) **Going Correction** -0.025s/f (Stan)
WFA 4 from 5yo 1lb **9** Ran SP% **115.7**
Speed ratings (Par 105): **105,104,103,102,101 99,94,88,82**
toteswinger: 1&2 £10.90, 1&3 £5.10, 2&3 £10.20. CSF £50.85 CT £224.78 TOTE £4.80: £1.90, £3.70, £2.20; EX 69.30.

Owner The Kingship **Bred** Hardys Of Kilkeel Ltd **Trained** Aldbury, Herts

■ Stewards' Enquiry : Alan Munro three-day ban: excessive use of the whip (May 1, 4-5)

FOCUS
Quite a competitive little handicap that was run at a decent pace, with the two who forced it dropping right away in the closing stages. Sound form, with the winner back to his best and the runner-up potentially well in on this surface.

1320 BOOK KEMPTON TICKETS ON 0844 579 3008 H'CAP 7f (P)
8:15 (8:15) (Class 5) (0-70,70) 4-Y-0+ **£2,590** (£770; £385; £192) **Stalls** High

Form RPR

5-04 **1** **Grey Boy (GER)**[11] 1149 8-9-4 **70**............ ShaneKelly 8 84
(A W Carroll) *hld up in tch: hdwy 2f out: rdn and qcknd to ld jst over 1f out: clr fnl f: rdn out* **5/1**[2]

44-6 **2** *2 ¼* **Magic Rush**[23] 950 7-9-3 **69**............ LPKeniry 5 77
(Norma Twomey) *stdd s: hld up in rr: stl last jst over 2f out: hdwy over 1f out: chsd wnr ins fnl f: no imp* **20/1**

/602 **3** *1* **Sew'N'So Character (IRE)**[13] 1121 8-9-2 **68**............ NCallan 6 74
(M Blanshard) *in tch in midfield: rdn and hdwy jst over 2f out: styd on u.p fnl f: nvr trbld wnr* **9/1**

1-20 **4** *nk* **Convallaria (FR)**[47] 725 6-8-9 **61**............(b) AlanMunro 11 66
(C F Wall) *hld up towards rr: hdwy jst over 2f out: nt clr run 1f out: r.o to go 4th wl ins fnl f: nvr rchd ldrs* **7/1**

25-4 **5** *¾* **Daring Dream (GER)**[15] 1080 4-8-2 **59**............(v) MartinLane[(5)] 1 62
(A P Jarvis) *stdd and swtchd rt after s: hld up bhd: hdwy on inner jst over 2f out: kpt on u.p fnl f: nvr threatened ldrs* **20/1**

2141 **6** *nk* **Suhayl Star (IRE)**[16] 1074 5-8-8 **60**............ LukeMorris 10 62
(P Burgoyne) *t.k.h: chsd ldrs: ev ch and drvn wl over 1f out: chsd wnr 1f out: no imp: wknd fnl 100yds* **10/1**

0331 **7** *¾* **Rubenstar (IRE)**[13] 1121 6-9-0 **66**............ RichardHughes 4 66
(Patrick Morris) *stdd s: hld up bhd: hdwy and rdn jst over 1f out: no imp and wknd fnl 100yds* **10/1**

-050 **8** *2* **Glencalvie (IRE)**[29] 878 8-9-2 **68**............(p) DaneO'Neill 9 63
(J Akehurst) *led: rdn over 2f out: hdd 2f out: wknd jst over 1f out* **14/1**

501- **9** *hd* **Bold Argument (IRE)**[225] 5645 6-8-7 **62**............ JackMitchell[(3)] 13 56
(Mrs P N Dutfield) *stdd s: hld up bhd: short lived effrt 2f out: nvr trbld ldrs* **18/1**

6233 **10** *½* **Guildenstern (IRE)**[13] 1132 7-9-4 **70**............ JimmyQuinn 14 63
(P Howling) *hld up in tch: rdn and effrt on inner 2f out: wknd u.p over 1f out* **6/1**[3]

10-3 **11** *nse* **Hazytoo**[13] 1121 5-9-2 **68**............ FergusSweeney 7 61
(P J Makin) *t.k.h: chsd ldr: rdn to ld 2f out: hdd jst over 1f out: wknd fnl f* **8/1**

00-6 **12** *1 ¾* **Triple Dream**[17] 1048 4-8-5 **62**............ MCGeran[(5)] 3 50
(J M Bradley) *t.k.h: chsd ldrs: rdn jst over 2f out: wknd u.p over 1f out* **50/1**

2015 **13** *2 ¾* **Marmooq**[18] 1035 6-9-1 **67**............ IanMongan 12 47
(M J Attwater) *chsd ldrs: rdn over 2f out: wknd wl over 1f out* **4/1**[1]

20-0 **14** *8* **Ride A White Swan**[13] 1132 4-8-11 **63**............ DarrenWilliams 2 22
(D Shaw) *t.k.h: hld up in midfield: rdn over 2f out: wknd over 1f out: eased ins fnl f* **40/1**

1m 24.98s (-1.02) **Going Correction** -0.025s/f (Stan) **14** Ran SP% **128.6**
Speed ratings (Par 103): **104,101,100,99,99 98,97,95,95,94 94,92,89,80**
toteswinger: 1&2 £36.20, 1&3 £17.90, 2&3 £33.60. CSF £112.16 CT £909.92 TOTE £8.10: £2.90, £8.20, £2.80; EX 60.50.

Owner Paul Downing **Bred** J Potempa **Trained** Cropthorne, Worcs

■ Stewards' Enquiry : M C Geran one-day ban: failed to ride to draw (1 May)

FOCUS
The second and third set the standard here and the form looks solid. It was another taking effort from the winner, back here for the first time since he won impressively in September.

Triple Dream Official explanation: jockey said gelding ran too free

1321 PANORAMIC BAR & RESTAURANT H'CAP 6f (P)
8:50 (8:51) (Class 3) (0-95,95) 4-Y-0+
£7,352 (£2,201; £1,100; £551; £274; £138) **Stalls** High

Form RPR

101- **1** **Mullein**[193] 6532 4-9-0 **91**............ SebSanders 8 102+
(R M Beckett) *bhd: rdn over 2f out: swtchd lft and hdwy over 1f out: drvn and str run to ld ins fnl f: edgd rt u.p: drvn out* **9/2**[2]

200- **2** *½* **Masai Moon**[160] 7245 5-8-12 **92**............ JamesMillman[(3)] 9 101
(B R Millman) *in tch in midfield: hdwy over 2f out: rdn over 1f out: chsd wnr and sltly hmpd ins fnl f: styd on wl* **7/1**

1254 **3** *2 ¼* **Mutamared (USA)**[13] 1116 9-8-9 **86**............(t) NCallan 10 88+
(K A Ryan) *trckd ldrs on inner: poised to chal whn nt clr run over 1f out tl ins fnl f: swtchd lft and r.o to go 3rd nr fin: unable to chal* **5/1**[3]

000- **4** *hd* **Baby Strange**[195] 6468 5-9-2 **93**............ DarrenWilliams 1 94
(D Shaw) *stdd and swtchd rt sn after s: hdwy and rdn on inner 2f out: ev ch ent fnl f: outpcd ins fnl f: lost 3rd last strides* **28/1**

5222 **5** *hd* **Dvinsky (USA)**[10] 1169 8-8-10 **87**............(b) JimmyQuinn 4 88
(P Howling) *led: rdn 2f out: edgd rt over 1f out: hdd ins fnl f: drvn and no ex fnl 100yds* **10/1**

140- **6** *2 ¾* **Spanish Bounty**[203] 6239 4-9-4 **95**............ TPQueally 2 87
(J G Portman) *chsd ldr: rdn over 2f out: wknd u.p jst ins fnl f* **25/1**

14-0 **7** *1* **Espy**[14] 1094 4-8-1 **81** oh2............ DavidProbert[(3)] 5 70
(S Kirk) *stdd s: hld up in rr: swtchd lft and effrt u.p ent fnl 2f: no imp* **20/1**

11-1 **8** *nk* **Al Gillani (IRE)**[23] 954 4-8-9 **86**............ PatCosgrave 3 74
(J R Boyle) *trckd ldrs: rdn and no real rspnse over 2f out: drvn and wknd over 1f out* **7/4**[1]

000- **9** *2 ½* **Victorian Bounty**[233] 5403 4-9-0 **91**............ MickyFenton 6 71
(Stef Liddiard) *puled hrd early: hld up in midfield: c wd and rdn over 2f out: no prog: wl hld fnl f* **14/1**

3201 **10** *1* **Little Edward**[21] 985 11-9-2 **93**............ GeorgeBaker 7 69
(R J Hodges) *plld hrd: chsd ldrs: rdn 2f out: sn btn: no ch fnl f* **12/1**

1m 11.67s (-1.43) **Going Correction** -0.025s/f (Stan) **10** Ran SP% **119.2**
Speed ratings (Par 107): **108,107,104,104,103 100,98,98,95,93**
toteswinger: 1&2 £6.60, 1&3 £4.00, 2&3 £6.50. CSF £35.91 CT £147.15 TOTE £5.20: £1.30, £2.60, £2.20; EX 29.80.

Owner Landmark Racing Limited **Bred** C D S Bryce And Mrs M Bryce **Trained** Whitsbury, Hants

■ Stewards' Enquiry : Jimmy Quinn seven-day ban: careless riding (May 1, May 4-9)

FOCUS
Strong fractions at the head of affairs and the race was teed up for those coming from off the pace. The winner improved again on last year's progressive form, and the runner-up ran at least as well as ever.

NOTEBOOK
Mullein ◆ made giant strides down the outside to hit the front in the final furlong and score pretty impressively. Progressive last term, she has come to hand very early this season and is a young sprinter to follow. (op 5-1)

Masai Moon ◆ is no mug at this level and he was staying on pretty strongly when slightly impeded by the winner in the closing stages. It didn't really effect the result but he's definitely one to keep on side in similar company, as he bumped into a good one here. (op 17-2 tchd 9-1)

Mutamared(USA) can be considered a little unlucky as he was chopped for room by the weakening Dvinsky up the rail at a crucial point. The winner had gone by the time he got in the clear, where he finished strongly. (tchd 7-1)

Baby Strange, who had the worst of the draw, shaped encouragingly on his first outing of the campaign and he should come on plenty for this. (op 25-1 tchd 33-1)

Espy Official explanation: jockey said gelding missed the break

Al Gillani(IRE) was the big disappointment. He came under pressure over two out but found nothing and weakened away tamely. This was clearly not his running. (tchd 6-4 and 2-1)

Little Edward refused to settle and is probably better suited by a fast run 5f. (op 10-1)

1322 FEDERATION OF BLOODSTOCK AGENTS H'CAP 6f (P)
9:20 (9:22) (Class 5) (0-70,70) 3-Y-O **£2,590** (£770; £385; £192) **Stalls** High

Form RPR

333- **1** **Jordaura**[163] 7191 3-9-4 **70**............ AdamKirby 8 76
(W R Swinburn) *mde virtually all: rdn and hung lft 2f out: drvn and edgd rt fnl f: r.o wl* **9/4**[1]

-411 **2** *1 ½* **Song Of Praise**[25] 936 3-9-4 **70**............ JimmyQuinn 9 71
(M Blanshard) *hld up bhd: rdn and hdwy wl over 1f out: drvn to chse wnr ent fnl f: no imp* **4/1**[3]

050- **3** *1 ½* **Straitjacket**[204] 6231 3-8-8 **60**............ PaulFitzsimons 7 56
(Miss J R Tooth) *squeezed out s: sn chsng ldrs: rdn to chse wnr over 1f out tl ent fnl f: edgd rt and one pce after* **22/1**

2 **4** *1 ¼* **Lighthearted (FR)**[30] 862 3-8-13 **65**............ PhilipRobinson 3 57
(C G Cox) *hld up towards rr: shkn up up and effrt 2f out: sn rdn and plugged on same pce fnl f* **11/4**[2]

404- **5** *1 ½* **Lagan Handout**[324] 2508 3-8-8 **60**............ JimCrowley 2 47
(C Gordon) *hld up in last pl: rdn and effrt wl over 1f out: nvr trbld ldrs* **25/1**

-504 **6** *nse* **Tightrope (IRE)**[13] 1120 3-7-13 **56** oh6............ AmyBaker[(5)] 5 43
(T D McCarthy) *racd keenly: sn pressing ldr: ev ch and rdn jst over 2f out: wknd over 1f out* **33/1**

0-21 **7** *6* **True Decision**[22] 963 3-8-8 **67**............ MatthewBirch[(7)] 6 35+
(S Kirk) *sddle slipped sn after s: chsd ldrs tl wknd 2f out* **9/2**

400- **8** *nk* **Mr Snowballs**[214] 5959 3-8-8 **60**............ LPKeniry 10 27
(R A Farrant) *in tch on inner: short lived effrt 2f out: sn btn* **10/1**

1m 13.76s (0.66) **Going Correction** -0.025s/f (Stan) **8** Ran SP% **115.8**
Speed ratings (Par 98): **94,92,90,88,86 86,78,77**
toteswinger: 1&2 £2.50, 1&3 £11.40, 2&3 £15.80. CSF £11.51 CT £154.11 TOTE £3.10: £1.40, £1.70, £2.40; EX 12.80 Place 6 £73.98, Place 5 £61.81..

Owner Carl Hodgson **Bred** Pendley Farm **Trained** Aldbury, Herts

■ Stewards' Enquiry : Adam Kirby caution: careless riding

FOCUS
Jordaura appeared to improve significantly on his maiden form, and it was also a slight personal best from Song Of Praise. The first three were the three highest drawn, however, and that casts a slight doubt over the depth of the form.

True Decision Official explanation: jockey said gelding's saddle slipped

T/Plt: £257.70 to a £1 stake. Pool: £63,977.26. 181.18 winning tickets. T/Qpdt: £66.60 to a £1 stake. Pool: £4,811.70. 53.40 winning tickets. SP

NEWBURY (L-H)

Friday, April 17

OFFICIAL GOING: Good to soft (soft in places in back straight; 5.4)

Wind: Virtually nil. Weather: Overcast

1323 EUROPEAN BREEDERS' FUND MAIDEN STKS — 5f 34y

1:35 (1:40) (Class 4) 2-Y-O — **£5,180** (£1,541; £770; £384) **Stalls** Centre

Form — RPR

1 — **Walkingonthemoon** 2-9-3 0 .... RichardKingscote 3 — 83+
(Tom Dascombe) *leggy: scope: mde virtually all: drvn clr over 1f out: r.o strly* **11/2**[3]

2 2 **Planet Red (IRE)** 2-9-3 0 .... RichardHughes 9 — 76+
(R Hannon) *w'like: scope: athletic: bmpd s: towards rr: rdn and one pce 1/2-way: styd on wl thrght fnl f to take 2nd cl home but no ch w wnr* **4/1**[2]

3 hd **Our Dream Queen** 2-8-12 0 .... MichaelHills 2 — 70
(B W Hills) *w'like: chsd ldrs: drvn along 1/2-way: styd on to chse wnr fnl f but no imp: ct for 2nd cl home* **9/1**

4 ½ **Di Stefano** 2-9-3 0 .... DarryllHolland 4 — 73
(M R Channon) *w'like: sn chsng ldrs: rdn 2f out: styd on same pce fnl f* **20/1**

5 1 ¾ **State Fair** 2-9-3 0 .... JamieSpencer 11 — 71+
(P F I Cole) *w'like: scope: loose bef s: hld up towards rr: hdwy and nt clr run ins fnl 2f and over 1f out: stl n.m.r but kpt on fnl f: fin wl* **12/1**

6 1 ½ **Glen Lass** 2-8-12 0 .... LPKeniry 8 — 56
(J S Moore) *w'like: leggy: chsd ldrs: rdn over 2f out: outpcd fnl f* **150/1**

0 **7** 1 **Pullyourfingerout (IRE)**[20] [994] 2-9-3 0 .... DaneO'Neill 7 — 57
(B G Powell) *leggy: pressed ldrs: rdn 3f out: wknd qckly 1f out* **16/1**

8 ¾ **Lofthouse** 2-9-3 0 .... TonyCulhane 6 — 56+
(M R Channon) *str: towards rr: hdwy whn hmpd over 1f out: nt rcvr but kpt on fnl f* **66/1**

9 ½ **Little Perisher** 2-8-12 0 .... MartinLane(5) 14 — 52
(A P Jarvis) *w'like: hdwy to chse ldrs 1/2-way: sn rdn: wknd over 1f out* **100/1**

10 2 ¼ **Angel Of Fashion (IRE)** 2-8-12 0 .... RHills 13 — 39
(B W Hills) *unf: s.i.s: outpcd* **14/1**

11 hd **Spanish Acclaim** 2-9-3 0 .... TolleyDean 10 — 43
(J G Portman) *unf: outpcd most of way* **20/1**

12 ½ **Clan Piper** 2-9-3 0 .... JimmyFortune 5 — 41
(J H M Gosden) *str: good bodied: chsd ldrs: rdn 2f out: wknd qckly ins fnl 2f* **5/2**[1]

13 5 **One Cool Buck (IRE)** 2-9-3 0 .... RyanMoore 12 — 22
(R Hannon) *leggy: unf: outpcd most of way* **16/1**

14 ¾ **Stargaze (IRE)** 2-9-3 0 .... MartinDwyer 1 — 19
(A M Balding) *w'like: bit bkwd: s.i.s: sn rdn and outpcd* **16/1**

65.58 secs (4.18) **Going Correction** +0.625s/f (Yiel) **14** Ran SP% **118.6**
Speed ratings (Par 94): **91,87,87,86,83 81,79,78,77,74 73,73,65,63**
toteswinger: 1&2 £4.90, 1&3 £10.30, 2&3 £8.90. CSF £26.20 TOTE £6.90: £2.10, £2.00, £3.50; EX 30.50.
Owner The Tipperary Partners **Bred** Dale & Ann Wilsdon **Trained** Lambourn, Berks

FOCUS

This juvenile maiden has often fallen to a decent performer, the best recent winner being Winker Watson, who went on to take the Norfolk Stakes at Royal Ascot. This year's line-up included several interesting sorts and the first four came away from the rest. The principals raced more towards the centre and afterwards the jockeys reported the going was soft. With only one runner having previous experience the level is fluid.

NOTEBOOK

Walkingonthemoon ◆, scored in convincing fashion, making all the running. Related to several sprinters out of a 7f winner, this neatly named colt was well backed and clearly knew his job, for after setting the pace he quickened clear about 2f from home and scored with something in hand. He will most likely to go for a conditions event at Ascot at the end of the month. (op 8-1 tchd 5-1)

Planet Red(IRE) ◆, who was noisy in the preliminaries, did best of those to come from off the pace. Getting the hang of things in the second half of the race, he picked up well to do best of those racing more towards the stands' side. He should be better for the experience and should be winning before long. (op 7-2 tchd 9-2)

Our Dream Queen ◆, an Oasis Dream half-sister to Spinning Queen, Shannon Springs and three other winners, raced in the slipstream of the winner throughout and kept on better than the majority of those around her. She should have no trouble winning against her own sex and will get longer trips in time. (op 8-1)

Di Stefano, a £60,000 half-brother to a dual juvenile winner, also showed a good deal of pace and looks likely to come on for the experience.

State Fair ◆, the first foal of the multiple winning sprinter Baralinka, who is a half-sister to Soviet Song among others, reared up and got rid of his rider entering the stalls before bolting down to the mile start and most of the way back to the starting gate. In the circumstances he did well to finish as close as he did, especially considering that he encountered trouble in running and had to be switched at one point. Spencer was not too hard on him once his chance had gone and, providing he settles down after this, should be up to winning races. Official explanation: jockey said colt ran very green and was denied a clear run (op 7-1)

Glen Lass, a cheaply bought half-sister to a multiple middle-distance performer out of a 1m winner, showed ability. If she goes on from this she could prove a good purchase. (op 100-1)

Pullyourfingerout(IRE), the only one with previous experience, had finished a one-paced eighth in the Brocklesby on his debut. He showed up until after halfway but then faded fairly tamely. He looks pretty limited on the evidence so far.

Lofthouse was held up off the pace and did not run badly. This half-brother to several sprint winners will know more next time.

Clan Piper, a 100,000gns half-brother to two winners at up to 1m, both of whom were successful as juveniles, was somewhat disappointing, dropping away after having every chance at halfway. He will have to improve a fair bit to justify his Group 1 entry. (op 7-2 tchd 9-4)

1324 DUBAI DUTY FREE FINEST SURPRISE H'CAP — 7f (S)

2:10 (2:11) (Class 3) (0-95,94) 3-Y-O — **£7,477** (£2,239; £1,119; £560; £279; £140) **Stalls** Centre

Form — RPR

2-1 **1** — **Makaamen**[19] [1015] 3-9-0 **90** .... TPO'Shea 15 — 100
(B W Hills) *lw: mde virtually all: edgd lft u.p over 1f out and edgd rt ins fnl f: hld on wl* **10/1**[2]

51- **2** 1 ¼ **Wannabe King**[276] [4062] 3-8-8 **84** .... TedDurcan 4 — 91
(D R Lanigan) *mid-div: hdwy over 2f out: rdn and styd on fr over 1f out: tk 2nd cl home but no imp on wnr* **10/1**[2]

312- **3** nk **Fareer**[280] [3924] 3-8-11 **87** .... RHills 3 — 93
(E A L Dunlop) *chsd ldrs: wnt 2nd u.p fnl f but a hld: lost 2nd cl home* **10/1**[2]

106- **4** ½ **Felday**[175] [6946] 3-8-8 **84** .... SteveDrowne 13 — 89
(H Morrison) *in tch: rdn and qckng fr 2f out to dispute 2nd fnl f: no ex fnl 100yds* **11/2**[1]

61- **5** 1 **Truism**[197] [6412] 3-8-7 **83** .... JimCrowley 7 — 85
(Mrs A J Perrett) *in tch: rdn to chse ldrs over 2f out: styd on same pce thrght fnl f* **11/1**[3]

321- **6** shd **Brief Encounter (IRE)**[200] [6327] 3-8-7 **83** .... LPKeniry 6 — 85
(A M Balding) *lw: in tch but rdn along fr over 3f out: edgd rt and styd on u.p fnl f: gng on cl home* **14/1**

124- **7** 1 **Key Signature**[187] [6673] 3-8-7 **83** .... PaulEddery 8 — 82
(Pat Eddery) *hld up in mid-div: hdwy to chse ldrs ins fnl 2f: no imp on ldrs ins fnl f and sn one pce* **16/1**

40-1 **8** 3 ¼ **Dalradian (IRE)**[35] [828] 3-8-5 **81** ow1 .... PaulDoe 9 — 71
(W J Knight) *in rr: rdn 3f out: sme prog fnl 2f: nvr in contention* **20/1**

321- **9** ¾ **Cloudy Start**[195] [6480] 3-8-12 **88** .... TPQueally 1 — 76
(H R A Cecil) *swtg: chsd ldrs: rdn along over 2f out: wknd fnl f* **11/2**[1]

002- **10** 2 ¼ **Indian Art (IRE)**[185] [6717] 3-8-9 **88** .... PatrickHills(3) 5 — 70
(R Hannon) *plld hrd: chsd ldrs: rdn over 2f out: wknd wl over 1f out* **25/1**

006- **11** 1 ¼ **Baycat (IRE)**[250] [4908] 3-9-0 **90** .... PatCosgrave 14 — 69
(J G Portman) *w wnr 1f: styd chsng ldrs tl wknd 2f out* **40/1**

06-3 **12** 1 ½ **Saucy Brown (IRE)**[15] [1085] 3-9-4 **94** .... RyanMoore 12 — 69
(R Hannon) *slowly away: rdn 1/2-way: a towards rr* **18/1**

11-4 **13** nse **Noverre To Go (IRE)**[20] [1002] 3-8-13 **89** .... (t) RichardKingscote 11 — 64
(Tom Dascombe) *lw: plld hrd: chsd ldrs: rdn 3f out: wknd 2f out* **11/2**[1]

50-0 **14** nk **Silver Games (IRE)**[27] [912] 3-8-13 **89** .... TonyCulhane 16 — 63
(M R Channon) *stdd in rr after 2f: nvr gng pce to be competitive after* **33/1**

114- **15** 6 **Timeteam (IRE)**[153] [7334] 3-8-12 **88** .... JamieSpencer 2 — 46
(S Kirk) *slowly away: a towards rr* **25/1**

0-21 **16** 2 ¼ **Daddy's Gift (IRE)**[20] [1002] 3-8-13 **89** .... RichardHughes 10 — 40
(R Hannon) *a outpcd* **16/1**

1m 29.45s (3.75) **Going Correction** +0.625s/f (Yiel) **16** Ran SP% **123.3**
Speed ratings (Par 102): **103,101,101,100,99 99,98,94,93,91 89,87,87,87,80 78**
toteswinger: 1&2 £25.00, 1&3 £11.30, 2&3 £25.20. CSF £100.76 CT £1084.49 TOTE £10.00: £2.50, £2.80, £2.80, £1.90; EX 128.10.
Owner Hamdan Al Maktoum **Bred** Brook Stud Bloodstock Ltd **Trained** Lambourn, Berks

FOCUS

This looked a quality handicap beforehand, but it was ruined to an extent by a very moderate early pace which didn't quicken noticeably until approaching the last quarter-mile. As a result of the slow tempo, several of these were inclined to take a pull. Nevertheless, a fairly positive view has been taken of the form.

NOTEBOOK

Makaamen found himself in front either by accident or design, but his rider made good use of the opportunity, putting pace to the race when he wanted and despite hanging about a little under pressure, he was always doing enough. He looks a nice prospect, but won't be hurried. (op 15-2)

Wannabe King, not seen since a narrow victory in a Yarmouth maiden over this trip last July, finished very nicely to snatch second and will appreciate stepping up to 1m. He is still in both the English and Irish 2000 Guineas and, whilst that is probably aiming a bit too high, he should be able to win some nice races with further improvement very likely.

Fareer, not seen since a narrow defeat in a hot Newmarket nursery last July, was preferred by Richard Hills over the winner. He had every chance and though he was almost certainly helped by racing handily in a slowly run race, he still ran with credit and is entitled to come on for it after such a long absence. (tchd 11-1)

Felday, in midfield in the red-hot sales race won by Donativum from Crowded House at Newmarket last October, was well backed on this return and was another to run well, having raced handily from the start. He didn't stay 1m in his final start at two, but the way he performed here suggests that he may do so now. (op 9-1)

Truism, who overcame traffic problems to win a Goodwood maiden over this trip on his second start at two, was staying on nicely from the middle of the field late on and is another with the scope for further improvement. (op 9-1)

Brief Encounter(IRE), progressive in three starts at two but not seen since September, was up in trip for this return to action. He appeared to get outpaced when the tempo quickened inside the last 3f, but was staying on again at the line and this was an encouraging reappearance. (tchd 16-1)

Key Signature, returning from six months off, wasn't disgraced but may need to drop a few pounds. (op 25-1)

Dalradian(IRE), making his handicap debut after winning a maiden on the Lingfield Polytrack last month that is not working out, made some modest late headway and is another that might need some help from the Handicapper. (op 16-1)

Cloudy Start, from the stable that sent out Phoenix Tower to win this race two years ago, ended last season with an easy odds-on success in a Redcar maiden. Making his handicap debut after six months off, he was up there early but gradually dropped away. However, the market vibes beforehand weren't positive so perhaps he wasn't expected to be at his very best on this return to action. (op 4-1 tchd 6-1)

Noverre To Go(IRE) Official explanation: trainer said the colt was unsuited by the good to soft ground

Daddy's Gift(IRE) Official explanation: jockey said the filly stopped quickly

1325 DUBAI DUTY FREE MULTI-MILLIONAIRE H'CAP — 5f 34y

2:40 (2:40) (Class 2) (0-110,107) 4-Y-O+ — **£11,215** (£3,358; £1,679; £840; £419; £210) **Stalls** Centre

Form — RPR

013- **1** — **Chief Editor**[160] [7243] 5-9-4 **107** .... PhilipRobinson 11 — 118+
(M A Jarvis) *hld up towards rr: t.k.h: hdwy over 1f out: str run fnl f to ld nr fin* **5/1**[2]

000- **2** ½ **Sohraab**[230] [5509] 5-8-6 **95** .... JimmyQuinn 13 — 104
(H Morrison) *in tch: hdwy fr 2f out: led wl ins fnl f: hdd cl home* **16/1**

140- **3** nk **Fullandby (IRE)**[188] [6653] 7-8-11 **100** .... RyanMoore 2 — 108
(T J Etherington) *warm bit bkwd: chsd ldrs: rdn and hdwy to chal ins fnl f: no ex cl home* **10/1**

060- **4** nk **Sonny Red (IRE)**[210] [6073] 5-8-8 **97** .... FrancisNorton 6 — 104
(D Nicholls) *lw: chsd ldrs: rdn to chal 1f out: stl ev ch u.p ins fnl f: no ex cl home* **9/1**

20-1 **5** 1 ½ **Cheveton**[17] [1052] 5-8-11 **100** .... JimCrowley 1 — 102
(R J Price) *lw: chsd ldrs: drvn to chal over 1f out: styd upsides tl wknd cl home* **13/2**[3]

436- **6** 1 ¼ **Oldjoesaid**[177] [6903] 5-8-13 **102** .... DaneO'Neill 8 — 99
(H Candy) *lw: t.k.h: in tch: pushed along and hdwy appr fnl f: kpt on cl home but nt rch ldrs* **3/1**[1]

/0-6 **7** shd **Max One Two Three (IRE)**[20] [996] 4-8-8 **97** .... RichardKingscote 4 — 94
(Tom Dascombe) *in tch: pushed along over 2f out: hdwy and nt clr run ins fnl f: kpt on cl home* **9/1**

010- **8** nk **Phantom Whisper**[160] [7245] 6-8-6 **95** .... AlanMunro 14 — 91
(B R Millman) *in tch: rdn and one pce 1/2-way: kpt on ins fnl f but nvr in contention* **33/1**

30-5 **9** ½ **Crimson Fern (IRE)**[27] 911 5-8-7 96 .... RichardHughes 5 90
(M S Saunders) *swtg: chsd ldrs: rdn to take slt ld appr fnl f: hdd & wknd qckly wl ins fnl f* **9/1**

352- **10** 1¾ **Cake (IRE)**[208] 6153 4-8-4 93 oh1 .... RichardMullen 3 81
(R Hannon) *led tl hdd appr fnl f: sn wknd* **16/1**

100- **11** 1 **Elhamri**[187] 6669 5-8-4 93 oh4 .... CatherineGannon 10 77
(S Kirk) *sn rdn and outpcd* **80/1**

121- **12** 2¼ **Holbeck Ghyll (IRE)**[314] 2828 7-8-1 93 oh3 .... DavidProbert(3) 12 69
(A M Balding) *s.i.s: outpcd* **14/1**

300- **13** 3½ **Angus Newz**[160] 7243 6-8-4 93 oh5 .... (v) MartinDwyer 7 56
(M Quinn) *pressed ldrs over 3f* **25/1**

63.03 secs (1.63) **Going Correction** +0.625s/f (Yiel) **13** Ran SP% **120.5**
Speed ratings (Par 109): **111,110,109,109,106 104,104,104,103,100 99,95,89**
toteswinger: 1&2 £27.00, 1&3 £11.70, 2&3 £24.50. CSF £82.11 CT £810.50 TOTE £6.10: £2.40, £4.90, £3.10; EX 168.50 Trifecta £444.30 Part won. Pool £600.52 - 0.10 winning units..
Owner Mrs P Good **Bred** J R And Mrs P Good **Trained** Newmarket, Suffolk

FOCUS
This high-class sprint handicap usually throws up a winner who can hold his own in Listed or even Group company, the best in recent years being Kyllachy. The race was understandably run much faster than the opening juvenile contest and produced a good finish. A smart effort from Chief Editor under top-weight, and solid form behind him.

NOTEBOOK
Chief Editor ◆, proved strongest in the closing stages. Effective at 5f-6f, and being by Tomba well suited by cut, he was 10lb higher than for his previous success (his first run for his current trainer). However, that did not stop him and, after travelling well off the pace, he picked up best inside the last furlong to get up near the line. Having won this off a mark of 107, he is already well up to Listed class and it will be no surprise to see him making his mark in Group company one day. (op 4-1)
Sohraab ◆, who is best at 5f and handles cut in the ground, was 2lb above his last winning mark and put up a fine effort on his first run since August. His form last year was a little mixed after being very consistent the year before and, if he can hold his form better, could be one to follow. (op 12-1)
Fullandby(IRE), for whom Ryan Moore was an eyecatching booking, had beaten Oldjoesaid narrowly at Beverley last season and was 2lb better off. He also ran a fine race and lost nothing in defeat, and there could be another good handicap, or even a Listed race, in him this season. (tchd 17-2)
Sonny Red(IRE), who is well suited by 5f and soft ground, was making his handicap debut having raced mainly at Group and Listed level previously. He raced prominently throughout and kept on well in the closing stages. Picked up for a bargain 5,000gns, that already looks money well spent. (op 10-1)
Cheveton, a 5f specialist, was fit from a recent win and ran well from 4lb above his previous winning mark, especially considering he had to race on the wide outside of the field. (op 11-1)
Oldjoesaid, whose trainer has targeted this race, was last year's winner and was well-backed favourite to follow up. However, he could not pick up from off the pace, only doing his best work late on. (op 7-2 tchd 4-1)
Max One Two Three(IRE), a useful juvenile in 2007, had gained both her wins at 6f but this was her first try at this trip on her handicap debut. She appeared to get slightly outpaced at around the halfway mark, but then was noted keeping on at the finish. There is a 6f fillies' Listed race at Nottingham later this spring that may suit her. (op 11-1)
Phantom Whisper, all of whose recent wins have been at 6f, was also 4lb above his last winning mark. Not surprisingly he was doing his best work late on.
Crimson Fern(IRE) is best at 5f but was 8lb above her last last winning mark. She showed up for a long way and was still in front entering the final furlong before being swamped. There is a 5f fillies' Listed race at Bath towards the end of the month that looks right up her street. (op 7-1)
Cake(IRE) also showed quite a bit of pace.
Holbeck Ghyll(IRE) Official explanation: jockey said gelding missed the break

1326 DUBAI DUTY FREE GOLF WORLD CUP CONDITIONS STKS 1m 2f 6y
3:15 (3:17) (Class 3) 3-Y-O
£7,477 (£2,239; £1,119; £560; £279; £140) **Stalls** Low

Form RPR

616- **1** **High Heeled (IRE)**[201] 6319 3-8-8 90 .... MichaelHills 6 106+
(B W Hills) *hld up towards rr: drvn and qcknd on outside fr 2f out: str run fnl f to ld fnl 40yds: readily* **12/1**

313- **2** 1¾ **Four Winds**[188] 6648 3-8-13 100 .... JamieSpencer 5 107
(M L W Bell) *lw: racd wd 3f and sn led: qcknd over 2f out: rdn and hung lft over 1f out: styd on tl hdd and outpcd fnl 40yds* **11/4**[2]

1- **3** nk **Father Time**[153] 7336 3-8-13 86 .... TPQueally 1 107
(H R A Cecil) *on toes: chsd ldrs: rdn and rn green ins fnl 2f: hung lft 1f out: kpt on ins fnl f but nvr quite gng pce to chal* **6/1**

231- **4** 1¼ **Palavicini (USA)**[190] 6602 3-8-13 96 .... EddieAhern 3 104
(J L Dunlop) *lw: sn chsng ldr: rdn over 2f out: styd on one pce fnl f* **5/1**[3]

1- **5** nk **Your Old Pal**[174] 6978 3-8-13 0 .... ShaneKelly 2 103
(J Noseda) *lw: hld up in rr: rdn and hdwy to chse ldrs ins fnl 2f: one pce ins fnl f* **6/4**[1]

426- **6** 8 **Aurorian (IRE)**[182] 6779 3-8-13 91 .... RichardHughes 4 87
(R Hannon) *hld up in rr: hdwy on ins over 3f out: nvr rchd ldrs and wknd fr 2f out* **33/1**

4-10 **7** 3½ **Akhenaten**[30] 863 3-8-13 94 .... TonyCulhane 7 80
(M R Channon) *chsd ldrs: rdn over 2f out: wknd fr 2f out* **20/1**

2m 14.39s (5.59) **Going Correction** +0.625s/f (Yiel) **7** Ran SP% **113.0**
Speed ratings (Par 102): **102,100,100,99,99 92,89**
toteswinger: 1&2 £4.90, 1&3 £9.30, 2&3 £2.90. CSF £44.01 TOTE £15.50: £4.70, £1.70; EX 37.20.
Owner Mr And Mrs Steven Jenkins **Bred** Ballylinch Stud **Trained** Lambourn, Berks

FOCUS
An interesting race, won by the subsequent Oaks-winner Light Shift two years ago, and this year's renewal featured a couple of unexposed potential improvers. However, they went no pace early and a few were inclined to race keenly as a result. In the circumstances High Heeled did well to come from off the pace, but the form, which has been rated around the runner-up, is obviously way off Oaks standard.

NOTEBOOK
High Heeled(IRE), who had not seen since finishing sixth of the 24 runners in the Goffs Million at The Curragh last September, was given a patient ride but despite having to come wide around the entire field to put in her effort she produced a decent turn of foot to hit the front well inside the last furlong. She might now go straight for the Oaks. (op 18-1 tchd 20-1)
Four Winds arguably had the best form coming into this, having been a possibly unlucky third in a Group 3 at Ascot last October, but there didn't seem to be much confidence behind him in the market. However, he soon seized the initiative and a positive ride looked like paying off until the filly's turn of foot proved too much. Connections believe that he may come on for the run. (op 9-4 tchd 3-1)
Father Time, another who was relatively weak in the market and whose stable was bidding for a hat-trick in this race, had been successful in his only previous start, a 1m Great Leighs maiden in November which has worked out extremely well. As a brother to Passage Of Time, this longer trip should have suited and he came through to hold every chance, but he then hung about all over the place and could find nothing more. Perhaps the ground had gone against him and it's far too early to write him off. (op 4-1)
Palavicini(USA), runner-up to Delegator on his debut last term and winner of a soft-ground maiden here on his final outing, is bred to have appreciated this step up in trip but he was keen early and started to struggle when the pace eventually increased. He plugged on though, and will appreciate a more strongly run race over this trip or perhaps a bit further. (tchd 9-2 and 11-2)
Your Old Pal, who bolted up in a soft-ground 1m maiden here last October that has already produced its share of winners, was well backed with the ground seemingly coming in his favour. Held up last early, he tried to creep closer once in line for home but never had much room to play with between Palavicini and hanging Father Time and lacked the pace to get himself out of trouble. This was disappointing, but he is well worth another chance to confirm the favourable impression he created last year. (op 2-1)
Aurorian(IRE), returning from six months off, is bred to be suited by this longer trip but he never got into the race.
Akhenaten, one of several not to get any sort of a run in the Kentucky Derby Challenge at Kempton last month, dropped right out after racing too keenly in the early stages. (op 33-1 tchd 18-1)

1327 BRIDGET MAIDEN FILLIES' STKS 7f (S)
3:50 (3:52) (Class 4) 3-Y-O £5,180 (£1,541; £770; £384) **Stalls** Centre

Form RPR

1 **Danehill's Pearl (IRE)** 3-9-0 0 .... RichardKingscote 13 79
(Tom Dascombe) *unf: scope: swtg: t.k.h: trckd ldrs: led appr fnl f: rdn and hld on wl fnl f* **12/1**

2 ½ **Steel Free (IRE)** 3-9-0 0 .... JamieSpencer 10 78
(M L W Bell) *unf: scope: in tch: hdwy over 2f out: drvn to chal jst ins fnl f: rdr dropped whip and no ex fnl 50yds* **8/1**[3]

3 1 **Barynya** 3-9-0 0 .... RyanMoore 8 75
(Sir Michael Stoute) *tall: rangy: lw: towards rr: but in tch: drvn and gd hdwy fr 2f out: str run fnl f: fin wl* **13/8**[1]

4 hd **Ermine And Velvet** 3-9-0 0 .... NCallan 16 74
(C E Brittain) *w'like: chsd ldrs: rdn 2f out: styd on same pce ins fnl f* **33/1**

5 ½ **Candy Ride (IRE)** 3-9-0 0 .... StephenDonohoe 4 73+
(E A L Dunlop) *w'like: towards rr: rdn and hdwy fr 2f out: moved grad rt fr 1f out: gng on cl home* **50/1**

6 ½ **Massilah** 3-9-0 0 .... RHills 11 72
(B W Hills) *athletic: lw: sn led: pushed along over 2f out: hdd appr fnl f: wknd ins fnl f* **3/1**[2]

7 1½ **La Creme (IRE)** 3-9-0 0 .... TonyCulhane 5 68
(M R Channon) *unf: chsd ldrs: rdn over 2f out: wknd fnl f* **25/1**

8 1 **Farncombe (IRE)** 3-8-7 0 .... KatiaScallan(7) 12 65
(M P Tregoning) *w'like: in tch: shkn up over 2f out: kpt on fr over 1f out but nvr in contention* **20/1**

9 3¼ **Sea Lavender** 3-9-0 0 .... JimCrowley 15 56
(R Charlton) *w'like: in tch: pushed along and styd on same pce fr 3f out* **40/1**

10 shd **Fiancee (IRE)** 3-9-0 0 .... SteveDrowne 14 56
(R Charlton) *w'like: scope: lw: s.i.s: towards rr: nvr gng pce to get into contention* **16/1**

11 ½ **La Marseillaise (IRE)** 3-9-0 0 .... MichaelHills 9 55
(B W Hills) *w'like: chsd ldrs: drvn 3f out: wknd ins fnl 2f* **16/1**

12 2½ **Bicksta** 3-9-0 0 .... RichardHughes 6 48
(E F Vaughan) *w'like: str: bit bkwd: s.i.s: a towards rr* **25/1**

13 ¾ **Wotasparkler** 3-9-0 0 .... FergusSweeney 2 46
(W S Kittow) *w'like: chsd ldrs over 4f* **50/1**

14 1½ **Fantasy Land (IRE)** 3-9-0 0 .... JimmyFortune 3 42
(B J Meehan) *w'like: scope: s.i.s: a towards rr* **8/1**[3]

15 7 **Rambling Rosie (IRE)** 3-9-0 0 .... RobertHavlin 7 23
(C Drew) *unf: in tch to 1/2-way* **100/1**

1m 31.0s (5.30) **Going Correction** +0.625s/f (Yiel) **15** Ran SP% **127.5**
Speed ratings (Par 97): **94,93,92,92,91 90,89,88,84,84 83,80,79,78,70**
toteswinger: 1&2 £13.70, 1&3 £7.20, 2&3 £7.40. CSF £102.68 TOTE £12.60: £3.00, £2.90, £1.40; EX 106.90.
Owner Paul Murphy **Bred** Azienda Agricola Mediterranea **Trained** Lambourn, Berks

FOCUS
This maiden for unraced three-year-old fillies has produced a couple of Group winners recently in Promising Lead and Silver Touch. The pace was steady and the form might not be the most solid, but there were some nice fillies on show.

1328 CHEVIOT ASSET MANAGEMENT MAIDEN STKS 1m 3f 5y
4:25 (4:25) (Class 4) 3-Y-O £5,180 (£1,541; £770; £384) **Stalls** Low

Form RPR

1 **Sight Unseen** 3-9-3 0 .... (t) EddieAhern 7 98
(H R A Cecil) *unf: scope: hld up in rr: hdwy on outside fr 3f out: led ins fnl 2f: pushed out: comf* **14/1**

43- **2** 4 **Tactic**[190] 6604 3-9-3 0 .... RHills 15 91
(J L Dunlop) *swtg: in rr: hdwy fr 3f out: styd on wl fr over 1f out to chse wnr wl ins fnl f but nvr any ch* **7/1**[3]

43- **3** 1 **Clowance House**[174] 6978 3-9-3 0 .... RichardHughes 14 89
(R Charlton) *in tch: rdn over 3f out: styd on fr 2f out to chse wnr jst ins fnl f: nvr any ch and lost 2nd nr fin* **9/2**[2]

4 2¾ **Dhushan** 3-9-3 0 .... PhilipRobinson 11 85+
(M A Jarvis) *w'like: scope: bit bkwd: chsd ldr: led ins fnl 3f: hdd ins fnl 2f: styd chsng wnr tl wknd ins fnl f* **8/1**

2- **5** nk **Hyades (USA)**[182] 6777 3-9-3 0 .... TPQueally 2 84
(H R A Cecil) *lw: chsd ldrs: drvn along over 2f out: sn one pce: wknd fnl f* **3/1**[1]

00- **6** nse **Gibb River (IRE)**[174] 6973 3-9-3 0 .... AlanMunro 9 84
(P W Chapple-Hyam) *lw: chsd ldrs: rdn over 3f out: styd on same pce fnl 2f* **25/1**

24- **7** 2½ **Lasso The Moon**[177] 6892 3-9-3 0 .... DarryllHolland 3 80
(M R Channon) *in tch: rdn over 3f out: no imp on ldrs 2f out and styd on same pce* **9/2**[2]

0-2 **8** ¾ **Ruler Of All (IRE)**[13] 1127 3-9-3 0 .... MichaelHills 4 78
(B W Hills) *chsd ldrs: rdn 3f out: wknd ins fnl 2f* **7/1**[3]

9 4½ **Time Book (IRE)** 3-9-3 0 .... JimmyFortune 1 71
(J H M Gosden) *w'like: athletic: s.i.s: in rr: shkn up and sme prog over 2f out: nvr in contention* **16/1**

63- **10** 7 **Wee Sonny (IRE)**[133] 7552 3-9-3 0 .... RichardKingscote 6 59
(Tom Dascombe) *sn led: hdd ins fnl 3f: wknd u.p 2f out* **12/1**

11 12 **The Boat Shed (IRE)** 3-9-3 0 .... LPKeniry 5 38
(B W Duke) *w'like: bit bkwd: s.i.s: sn rdn and bhd* **100/1**

12 3½ **High Severa (IRE)** 3-9-3 0 .... FergusSweeney 8 32
(K R Burke) *in rr: sme hdwy over 3f out: sn wknd* **33/1**

2m 27.63s (6.43) **Going Correction** +0.625s/f (Yiel) **12** Ran SP% **125.5**
Speed ratings (Par 100): **101,98,97,95,95 95,93,92,89,84 75,73**
toteswinger: 1&2 £18.30, 1&3 £17.50, 2&3 £5.50. CSF £113.91 TOTE £20.20: £5.40, £2.60, £2.50; EX 181.60.
Owner K Abdulla **Bred** Juddmonte Farms Ltd **Trained** Newmarket, Suffolk

FOCUS
A maiden that has thrown up some decent sorts in the past with the likes of Salford Express, Millenary, Gamut and Hala Bek successful in the past ten years. First impressions were that it may have thrown up another decent prospect this year. The only note of caution would be that, as in the earlier 1m2f conditions event, the winner made his challenge widest of all whilst the placed horses also made their efforts wide, so there may have been an advantage to those that came down the centre of the track. Worth taking a positive view of the form for now though.

1329 ROBERT SANGSTER MEMORIAL MAIDEN FILLIES' STKS 1m 2f 6y
4:55 (5:01) (Class 4) 3-Y-O £5,180 (£1,541; £770; £384) Stalls Low

Form RPR
02- 1 **Natural Flair (USA)**178 6887 3-9-0 0 AlanMunro 15 85
(P W Chapple-Hyam) *w'like: bit bkwd: trckd ldrs towards outside: drvn and styd on fr over 2f out to ld over 1f out: styd on strly* 5/1[3]
03- 2 2 3/4 **Fleurissimo**167 7141 3-9-0 0 EddieAhern 2 80
(J L Dunlop) *w'like: chsd ldrs: hrd drvn over 2f out: chsd wnr fnl f but no imp* 11/1
6-2 3 1 1/2 **Light Dubai (IRE)**27 914 3-9-0 0 TonyCulhane 3 77
(M R Channon) *in tch: hdwy 4f out: chsd ldrs u.p fr 2f out: styd on same pce ins fnl f* 18/1
4- 4 1 3/4 **Piquante**192 6559 3-9-0 0 JamieSpencer 6 73
(M L W Bell) *leggy: chsd ldrs: led appr fnl 2f: sn rdn: hdd over 1f out: wknd fnl f* 9/2[2]
0- 5 1/2 **Phillipina**210 6076 3-9-0 0 RyanMoore 11 72
(Sir Michael Stoute) *lw: hld up towards rr: hdwy fr 3f out: styd on fr over 1f out but nvr gng pce to be competitive* 13/8[1]
2- 6 shd **Hukba (IRE)**192 6559 3-9-0 0 RHills 16 72
(E A L Dunlop) *w'like: in rr: hdwy over 3f out: chsd ldrs over 2f out: wknd fnl f* 9/2[2]
7 3 1/4 **Dark Quest** 3-9-0 0 TedDurcan 12 65
(J L Dunlop) *w'like: bit bkwd: slowly away: in rr: rdn 3f out: rn green but sme prog 2f out: nvr gng pce to rch ldrs* 50/1
8 1 **Arabian Pearl (IRE)**284 3803 3-9-0 0 JimmyFortune 1 63
(P W Chapple-Hyam) *lengthy: led: rdn over 3f out: hdd over 2f out: wknd over 1f out* 50/1
0- 9 3 **Tres Chic (FR)**183 6760 3-9-0 0 SteveDrowne 9 57
(S Curran) *unf: in rr: hdwy over 3f out: nvr rchd ldrs: wknd ins fnl 2f* 125/1
3 10 13 **Iketi (GR)**29 876 3-9-0 0 PatCosgrave 4 31
(Jane Chapple-Hyam) *plld hrd in rr: hmpd on bnd 7f out: rdn 4f out: a towards rr* 50/1
11 1/2 **Rare Virtue (USA)** 3-9-0 0 TPQueally 13 30
(H R A Cecil) *w'like: scope: led to s: s.i.s: t.k.h: nvr bttr than mid-div* 14/1
0- 12 3 1/4 **Fisadara**167 7141 3-9-0 0 TPO'Shea 10 24
(B W Hills) *chsd ldrs 7f* 28/1
0- 13 4 1/2 **Haafhd Time (IRE)**297 3348 3-9-0 0 RichardKingscote 14 15
(Tom Dascombe) *a towards rr* 40/1
6 14 4 **Carrazara (IRE)**72 391 3-9-0 0 DaneO'Neill 7 7
(Edgar Byrne) *chsd ldrs 7f* 100/1

2m 15.61s (6.81) **Going Correction** +0.625s/f (Yiel) 14 Ran SP% **124.9**
Speed ratings (Par 97): **97,94,93,92,91 91,89,88,85,75 75,72,68,65**
toteswinger: 1&2 £13.40, 1&3 £11.60, 2&3 £13.40. CSF £59.62 TOTE £7.70: £2.80, £3.10, £3.90; EX 97.40 Place 6 £277.18, Place 5 £141.17..
Owner M Al-Qatami & K M Al-Mudhaf **Bred** Georgica Stable Llc & Andrew Rosen **Trained** Newmarket, Suffolk

FOCUS
An interesting fillies' maiden that has produced such good performers as Islington and Oaks winner Eswarah in the last ten years. The race was dominated by the trio with the most experience and the time was 1.22secs slower than the feature race. The proximity of the third is a slight worry, but probably decent maiden form.
T/Jkpt: Not won. T/Plt: £224.00 to a £1 stake. Pool: £92,722.82. 302.08 winning tickets. T/Qpdt: £43.40 to a £1 stake. Pool: £4,411.24. 75.10 winning tickets. ST

THIRSK (L-H)
Friday, April 17

OFFICIAL GOING: Round course - firm; straight course - good to firm (firm in places) (12.8)
Wind: Virtually nil. Weather: Sunny and dry

1330 E B F HABTON NOVICE STKS 5f
2:00 (2:00) (Class 4) 2-Y-O £5,569 (£1,657; £828; £413) Stalls High

Form RPR
11 1 **Star Rover (IRE)**9 1188 2-9-7 0 RichardEvans(5) 3 86
(P D Evans) *mde all: rdn wl over 1f out: kpt on wl u.p ins fnl f* 1/2[1]
01 2 1 1/4 **Chicita Banana**14 1090 2-8-7 0 MatthewDavies(7) 6 69
(George Baker) *trckd ldrs: hdwy 2f out: rdn over 1f out: drvn: ev ch and hung rt ins fnl f: no ex* 11/4[2]
3 1 1/2 **Gentle Beat (IRE)** 2-8-12 0 DavidAllan 7 62
(T D Easterby) *dwlt: rn green and outpcd in rr: stdy hdwy 2f out: rdn to chal over 1f out: wknd ins fnl f* 17/2[3]
4 5 **Marchin Star (IRE)** 2-8-12 0 TWilliams 4 44+
(M Brittain) *dwlt: sn cl up: rdn along over 2f out: sn edgd lft and wknd* 25/1
6 5 2 3/4 **Ytartfawn (IRE)**13 1126 2-8-12 0 JamieMoriarty 1 34
(P T Midgley) *t.k.h: cl up: rdn along 2f out: sn edgd lft and wknd* 66/1

59.94 secs (0.34) **Going Correction** -0.10s/f (Good) 5 Ran SP% **109.2**
Speed ratings (Par 94): **93,91,88,80,76**
toteswinger: 1&2 £1.30. CSF £2.08 TOTE £1.60: £1.10, £1.10; EX 1.60.
Owner Christy Leo **Bred** Yeomanstown Stud **Trained** Pandy, Monmouths
■ Stewards' Enquiry : Richard Evans one-day ban: failed to ride to draw (May 1)

FOCUS
Two previous winners lined up for this opening contest, but the race was weakened by the withdrawal of Lees Anthem. The winner did well to defy his penalty.

NOTEBOOK
Star Rover(IRE) followed up a clear-cut Kempton maiden win on his debut when dominating a 5f novice stakes event at Nottingham last time. He carried a 14lb penalty here but was heavily backed and made all after a quick move to grab the near rail from stall three. This was a professional rather than flashy performance, but the son of Camacho looks quite useful, has a very willing attitude and should be able to win more races. He is likely to head to the Lily Agnes Stakes at Chester next. (op 4-5)
Chicita Banana landed a gamble in a 5f maiden fillies race at Bath last time following her promising seventh in the Brocklesby. She has probably found some further improvement and might have posed a serious threat to the winner if she hadn't edged left during the middle part of the race. (op 2-1)
Gentle Beat(IRE) has run a very promising race on his debut and should have learned a lot from the experience. He is a 25,000gns gelding out of an unraced sister to Comfy, a very useful dual 7f winner at two and four. (op 13-2 tchd 9-1)
Marchin Star(IRE), an 8,500 euros half-brother to the prolific 5f-7f winner Kensington, was well held on his debut but he was eased in the closing stages and his jockey did take a look downwards as if he was concerned that something was amiss. (op 16-1)

1331 ROSEDALE H'CAP 1m
2:30 (2:30) (Class 5) (0-75,75) 3-Y-O £4,274 (£1,271; £635; £317) Stalls Low

Form RPR
1121 1 **Green Agenda**14 1098 3-9-1 72 JoeFanning 5 79
(M Johnston) *trckd ldng pair: hdwy to chse ldr 1/2-way: led wl over 2f out and sn rdn: drvn over 1f out and styd on strly ins fnl f* 10/11[1]
30-6 2 3 3/4 **Mutually Mine (USA)**23 962 3-8-13 70 MickyFenton 3 68
(Mrs P Sly) *cl up: pushed along and sltly outpcd whn n.m.r 3f out: swtchd rt and rdn to chse wnr over 2f out: drvn over 1f out: sn no imp* 14/1
4-21 3 2 1/4 **Avoir Choisi (IRE)**86 230 3-9-4 75 RobertWinston 6 68
(P W Chapple-Hyam) *hld up: hdwy to chse ldrs over 3f out: rdn 2f out: drvn over 1f out and kpt on same pce* 4/1[2]
16-4 4 2 3/4 **Belated Silver (IRE)**18 1033 3-8-11 73 RossAtkinson(5) 4 60
(Tom Dascombe) *s.i.s and bhd: hdwy wl over 2f out: sn rdn and nvr nr ldrs* 4/1[2]
025- 5 14 **What A Day**198 6381 3-9-0 71 GrahamGibbons 8 25
(J J Quinn) *hld up: sme hdwy on outer wl over 2f out: sn rdn and btn* 20/1
5-11 6 2 1/2 **Bickersten**35 829 3-9-1 72 SamHitchcott 7 21
(M R Channon) *sn led: rdn along and hdd wl over 2f out: sn wknd* 7/1[3]

1m 37.34s (-2.76) **Going Correction** -0.375s/f (Firm) 6 Ran SP% **116.3**
Speed ratings (Par 98): **98,94,92,89,75 72**
toteswinger: 1&2 £1.60, 1&3 £1.40, 2&3 £12.40. CSF £16.50 CT £38.74 TOTE £2.00: £1.20, £4.20; EX 18.10.
Owner The Green Dot Partnership **Bred** W And R Barnett Ltd **Trained** Middleham Moor, N Yorks

FOCUS
A fair handicap, involving three last-time-out winners. The pace was decent and they finished quite well strung out. The runner-up sets the standard.

1332 SALTERSGATE H'CAP 1m
3:05 (3:05) (Class 5) (0-70,69) 4-Y-O+ £4,274 (£1,271; £635; £317) Stalls Low

Form RPR
-454 1 **Jebel Tara**9 1194 4-8-12 63 (bt[1]) SilvestreDeSousa 14 73
(A D Brown) *trckd ldr: effrt over 2f out: rdn to ld wl over 1f out: drvn and edgd rt ins fnl f: kpt on wl towards fin* 13/2[1]
650- 2 1 1/4 **Society Music (IRE)**211 6056 7-9-2 67 PhillipMakin 10 74
(M Dods) *hld up in midfield: hdwy wl over 2f out: rdn to chal over 1f out and ev ch tl drvn: edgd rt and no ex wl ins fnl f* 16/1
0335 3 hd **Kildare Sun (IRE)**9 1192 7-8-12 63 (v[1]) PaulHanagan 16 70
(J Mackie) *hld up towards rr: hdwy over 2f out: rdn over 1f out: styd on ins fnl f: nrst fin* 15/2[3]
00-0 4 1 1/4 **Shadowtime**4 1244 4-8-11 62 RobertWinston 6 66
(Miss Tracy Waggott) *in tch: hdwy to chse ldrs 2f out: sn rdn and edgd lft ent fnl f: kpt on same pce* 25/1
-046 5 1 1/4 **Bourse (IRE)**14 1100 4-9-0 65 GrahamGibbons 4 66
(A G Foster) *in tch: hdwy over 2f out: sn rdn and styd on same pce appr fnl f* 9/1
54-0 6 3/4 **Glenridding**13 1133 5-9-4 69 TomEaves 3 68
(J G Given) *sn led: rdn along 3f out: drvn 2f out: sn hdd and grad wknd* 11/1
425- 7 1/2 **Silly Gilly (IRE)**197 6408 5-8-1 55 KellyHarrison(3) 2 53
(R E Barr) *chsd ldng pair: rdn along over 2f out: drvn and edgd lft over 1f out: grad wknd* 12/1
526- 8 nk **Resentful Angel**110 7800 4-8-13 64 PaulFitzsimons 1 61
(Pat Eddery) *chsd ldrs: pushed along 3f out: rdn and hung rt 2f out: sn drvn and btn* 7/1[2]
005- 9 3/4 **Champain Sands (IRE)**175 6951 10-8-7 61 AndrewMullen(3) 13 57
(E J Alston) *dwlt: hld up in rr tl styd on fnl 2f: nvr nr ldrs* 16/1
050- 10 1 3/4 **Summer Dancer (IRE)**179 6867 5-9-2 67 JamieMoriarty 7 58
(P T Midgley) *hld up in rr: sme hdwy on inner 2f out: sn rdn and nvr nr ldrs* 12/1
00-0 11 3/4 **Violent Velocity (IRE)**16 1060 6-9-3 68 JoeFanning 9 58
(J J Quinn) *nvr nr ldrs* 12/1
10-0 12 3/4 **Rainbow Zest**13 1125 6-8-7 61 DominicFox(3) 5 49
(W Storey) *hld up: a towards rr* 40/1
36-0 13 3/4 **Aussie Blue (IRE)**9 1194 5-8-5 59 MichaelJStainton(3) 12 45
(R M Whitaker) *towards rr: effrt and wd st: sn rdn along and nvr a factor* 12/1
0646 14 1 1/4 **Montiboli (IRE)**50 683 4-8-8 64 AmyRyan(5) 18 47
(K A Ryan) *towards rr on outer: wd st: nvr a factor* 16/1
40-0 15 1/2 **Whaston (IRE)**28 898 4-8-5 56 RoystonFfrench 17 38
(J D Bethell) *stdd s: hld up: a in rr* 28/1
233- 16 4 1/2 **Bertie Vista**171 7040 4-8-11 62 DuranFentiman 11 34
(T D Easterby) *chsd ldrs: rdn along over 2f out and sn wknd* 16/1
200- 17 5 **Complete Frontline (GER)**135 7541 4-8-4 55 oh1 AndrewElliott 8 15
(K R Burke) *a towards rr* 25/1

1m 36.45s (-3.65) **Going Correction** -0.375s/f (Firm) 17 Ran SP% **123.8**
Speed ratings (Par 103): **103,101,101,100,99 98,97,97,96,95 94,93,92,91,91 86,81**
toteswinger: 1&2 £25.20, 1&3 £12.40, 2&3 £15.10. CSF £104.98 CT £813.86 TOTE £7.70: £2.20, £4.10, £2.60, £6.80; EX 179.50.
Owner David J Sturdy **Bred** Mrs G P Booth And J Porteous **Trained** Yedingham, N Yorks

FOCUS
A modest handicap in which the winner is rated to last summer's form. It was run at a frantic pace, but not many got into it from behind.
Resentful Angel Official explanation: jockey said filly was unsuited by the good to firm ground
Whaston(IRE) Official explanation: jockey said gelding lost his action on the bend

1333 HAWNBY H'CAP 7f
3:40 (3:40) (Class 5) (0-75,75) 4-Y-O+ £4,274 (£1,271; £635; £317) Stalls Low

Form RPR
143- 1 **Turn Me On (IRE)**181 6813 6-9-1 72 GrahamGibbons 8 84
(T D Walford) *hld up in midfield: stdy hdwy over 2f out: rdn to ld and hung lft appr fnl f: sn drvn and styd on strly* 11/4[1]
36-6 2 1 3/4 **White Deer (USA)**26 922 5-9-4 75 (b) SilvestreDeSousa 6 82
(D Nicholls) *sn led: rdn over 2f out: drvn and hdd appr fnl f: kpt on wl u.p* 10/3[2]
456/ 3 hd **Diamond Lass (IRE)**590 5140 4-8-5 62 PaulHanagan 10 68
(R A Fahey) *chsd ldrs: hdwy to chse ldrs over 2f out: rdn and ch whn hmpd appr fnl f: kpt on u.p towards fin* 12/1

03-3 **4** *1* **Bravely (IRE)**[16] 1060 5-9-2 **73** DuranFentiman 1 77
(T D Easterby) *dwlt and in rr: hdwy on outer over 2f out: rdn to chse ldrs over 1f out: drvn ent fnl f and one pce* **10/1**

404- **5** *1* **Mey Blossom**[174] 6976 4-8-12 **72** MichaelJStainton(3) 4 73
(R M Whitaker) *chsd ldrs: hdwy over 2f out and sn rdn: drvn over 1f out: hld whn hmpd appr fnl f: one pce after* **15/2**

105- **6** *3/4* **Jonny Lesters Hair (IRE)**[171] 7041 4-9-4 **75** DavidAllan 9 74
(T D Easterby) *prom: effrt over 2f out and sn rdn: drvn and wkng whn n.m.r over 1f out* **6/1**[3]

06-4 **7** *1/2* **No Grouse**[16] 1060 9-8-3 **63** AndrewMullen(3) 5 61
(E J Alston) *dwlt: hld up: a towards rr* **11/1**

-522 **8** *nk* **Compton's Eleven**[66] 486 8-9-4 **75** SamHitchcott 2 72
(M R Channon) *in tch: effrt over 2f out: sn rdn and wknd* **11/1**

00-0 **9** *shd* **Dream Express (IRE)**[13] 1132 4-9-1 **72** PhillipMakin 3 69
(M Dods) *dwlt: t.k.h in rr: sme hdwy on wd outside 2f out: sn rdn and n.d* **14/1**

6305 **10** *7* **H Harrison (IRE)**[16] 1060 9-8-12 **69** RoystonFfrench 11 47
(I W McInnes) *cl up: rdn along wl over 2f out and sn wknd* **25/1**

1m 24.17s (-3.03) **Going Correction** -0.375s/f (Firm) **10** Ran SP% **119.8**
Speed ratings (Par 103): **102,100,99,98,97 96,96,95,95,87**
toteswinger: 1&2 £4.20, 1&3 £7.60, 2&3 £13.70. CSF £12.17 CT £95.97 TOTE £4.40: £1.70, £1.60, £3.30; EX 11.60.
Owner Ms M Austerfield **Bred** Brendan Lavery **Trained** Sheriff Hutton, N Yorks

FOCUS
There was a very lively market for this moderate handicap. The brisk pace seemed to set things up for finishers and the form is rated around the second and fourth.
Jonny Lesters Hair(IRE) Official explanation: jockey said gelding hung right
Dream Express(IRE) Official explanation: jockey said the gelding hung right

1334 PICKHILL H'CAP 5f
4:15 (4:15) (Class 4) (0-80,80) 4-Y-0+ **£5,569** (£1,657; £828; £413) **Stalls** High

Form RPR

63-3 **1** **Steelcut**[5] 1227 5-8-12 **74** PaulHanagan 8 85
(R A Fahey) *trckd ldrs: nt clr run and swtchd lft wl over 1f out: rdn to ld jst ins fnl f: styd on* **7/4**[1]

020- **2** *2* **Rasaman (IRE)**[149] 7384 5-8-13 **80** AmyRyan(5) 3 84
(K A Ryan) *sn cl up on outer: rdn to ld over 1f out: drvn: edgd rt and hdd jst ins fnl f: kpt on same pce* **14/1**

313- **3** *3/4* **Discanti (IRE)**[275] 4074 4-9-3 **79** (t) DavidAllan 2 80+
(T D Easterby) *trckd ldrs on outer: effrt and edgd lft wl over 1f out: sn rdn: styd on ins fnl f* **12/1**

3224 **4** *1/2* **Bo McGinty (IRE)**[2] 1278 8-8-13 **80** (b) FrederikTylicki(5) 5 79
(R A Fahey) *cl up: rdn along 2f out: grad wknd* **7/2**[2]

260- **5** *nk* **Mambo Spirit (IRE)**[140] 7477 5-9-1 **77** TomEaves 6 75
(J G Given) *dwlt and in rr: hdwy wl over 1f out: rdn and kpt on ins fnl f* **6/1**

1053 **6** *1* **The Tatling (IRE)**[22] 965 12-9-4 **80** RobertWinston 1 75
(J M Bradley) *dwlt and in rr: swtchd outside and hdwy wl over 1f out: sn rdn and kpt on ins fnl f: nt rch ldrs* **12/1**

550- **7** *6* **Angle Of Attack (IRE)**[170] 7081 4-8-8 **70** SilvestreDeSousa 7 43
(A D Brown) *qckly away and led: rdn along 2f out: hdd & wknd over 1f out* **22/1**

0-51 **8** *1 1/2* **Nomoreblondes**[14] 1096 5-8-8 **70** (p) JamieMoriarty 10 38
(P T Midgley) *chsd ldrs on rail: rdn along and outpcd fr 1/2-way* **5/1**[3]

58.45 secs (-1.15) **Going Correction** -0.10s/f (Good) **8** Ran SP% **115.9**
Speed ratings (Par 105): **105,101,100,99,99 97,88,85**
toteswinger: 1&2 £6.90, 1&3 £4.80, 2&3 £18.90. CSF £29.38 CT £233.29 TOTE £2.60: £1.40, £4.60, £2.70; EX 37.00.
Owner A Rhodes Haulage And P Timmins **Bred** Mrs B Skinner **Trained** Musley Bank, N Yorks
■ Stewards' Enquiry : Amy Ryan two-day ban: careless riding (May 1 & 4)

FOCUS
A decent 0-80 event and four of the runners had a BHA rating on the ceiling of the handicap. The winner is rated a slight improver on last year's form.

1335 HAMBLETON INN MEDIAN AUCTION MAIDEN STKS 6f
4:45 (4:46) (Class 5) 3-4-Y-0 **£4,274** (£1,271; £635; £317) **Stalls** High

Form RPR

244- **1** **Paddy Bear**[225] 5633 3-9-0 71 PaulHanagan 2 69
(R A Fahey) *prom: effrt 2f out: rdn to ld over 1f out: edgd rt ins fnl f and hdd last 50yds: drvn: edgd lft and rallied to ld again on line* **5/2**[2]

2 *shd* **Seldom (IRE)** 3-8-7 0 JohnCavanagh(7) 6 69
(M Brittain) *in midfield: hdwy on outer wl over 1f out: sn rdn and styd on strly ins fnl f to ld last 50yds: drvn: edgd rt and hdd on line* **20/1**

544- **3** *2* **Steel Stockholder**[314] 2845 3-9-0 65 TWilliams 3 62
(M Brittain) *cl up: effrt 2f out: sn rdn and ev ch tl drvn ent fnl f and kpt on same pce* **11/1**[3]

5-4 **4** *4 1/2* **Minturno (USA)**[16] 1062 3-9-0 0 PhillipMakin 11 48
(Mrs A Duffield) *led: rdn 2f out: sn hdd & wknd appr fnl f* **7/4**[1]

0- **5** *1 1/2* **Jillolini**[356] 1627 3-8-9 0 DuranFentiman 8 38
(T D Easterby) *in tch: hdwy to chse ldrs 2f out: sn rdn and no imp appr fnl f* **40/1**

-640 **6** *nk* **Field Fantasy**[57] 602 3-8-9 52 GrahamGibbons 10 37
(Garry Moss) *in midfield: pushed along 1/2-way: rdn 2f out: kpt on ins fnl f: nrst fin* **33/1**

460- **7** *1/2* **Feeling Stylish (IRE)**[205] 6214 3-8-9 53 JoeFanning 14 36
(N Tinkler) *towards rr: hdwy wl over 1f out: rdn and kpt on ins fnl f: nt rch ldrs* **16/1**

8 *2 1/4* **Hello Sunshine** 3-9-0 0 J-PGuillambert 7 33
(T J Pitt) *cl up: rdn along over 2f out and grad wknd* **20/1**

0-0 **9** *1* **Off Hand**[10] 1174 3-8-9 0 DavidAllan 4 25
(T D Easterby) *wnt lft s: a towards rr* **16/1**

343- **10** *shd* **Future Gem**[212] 6009 3-8-9 43 RobertWinston 9 25
(A Dickman) *chsd ldrs: rdn along over 2f out: sn wknd* **18/1**

6- **11** *2 1/2* **Ryedon Bye**[296] 3364 3-9-0 0 DNolan 5 22
(T D Easterby) *a in rr* **22/1**

02- **12** *2 1/2* **Fifth Amendment**[171] 7038 3-8-9 0 SladeO'Hara(5) 1 14
(A Berry) *in tch on outer: rdn along 1/2-way and sn wknd* **12/1**

000- **13** *nk* **Bluebaru**[158] 7268 3-9-0 35 (v[1]) JamieMoriarty 13 13
(L R James) *a in rr* **200/1**

14 *1/2* **The Quiet Genius** 3-9-0 0 AndrewElliott 15 11
(Jedd O'Keeffe) *dwlt: sn outpcd and a bhd* **12/1**

0 **15** *30* **Cheeky Crumpet**[10] 1174 3-8-9 0 TomEaves 12 —
(A Berry) *sn outpcd and bhd fr 1/2-way* **50/1**

1m 12.67s (-0.03) **Going Correction** -0.10s/f (Good) **15** Ran SP% **127.4**
Speed ratings (Par 103): **96,95,93,87,85 84,84,81,79,79 76,73,72,71,31**
toteswinger: 1&2 £16.20, 1&3 £5.60, 2&3 £15.70. CSF £61.19 TOTE £3.60: £1.90, £8.90, £2.50; EX 93.10 Place 6 £35.67, Place 5 £33.65..
Owner J A & Kay Campbell **Bred** The Racing Guild **Trained** Musley Bank, N Yorks

■ Stewards' Enquiry : J-P Guillambert one-day ban: failed to ride to draw (1 May)
T Williams one-day ban: failed to ride to draw (1 May)

FOCUS
A modest auction maiden. The field grouped towards the near rail and it produced an exciting finish between the main form contender and a newcomer. The first three pulled clear of the rest and the form seems sound enough.
T/Plt: £47.10 to a £1 stake. Pool: £48,319.19. 747.93 winning tickets. T/Qpdt: £23.90 to a £1 stake. Pool: £3,365.28. 103.80 winning tickets. JR

1336 - 1342a (Foreign Racing) - See Raceform Interactive

1014 DONCASTER (L-H)
Saturday, April 18

OFFICIAL GOING: Good to firm (9.3)
Wind: Light half behind Weather: Sunny and dry

1343 AJA LADY RIDERS' H'CAP 7f
4:40 (4:40) (Class 4) (0-80,87) 4-Y-0+ **£4,684** (£1,452; £726; £363) **Stalls** High

Form RPR

-140 **1** **Smarty Socks (IRE)**[20] 1016 5-9-12 **76** MissWGibson(5) 4 86
(P T Midgley) *dwlt and in rr: hdwy over 3f out: rdn to chse ldrs 2f out: styd on strly nside fnl f to ld last 50yds* **13/2**[3]

66-0 **2** *1* **Buy On The Red**[5] 1244 8-9-1 **67** (b) MissERamstrom(7) 1 74+
(D Nicholls) *cl up: led over 2f out: rdn over 1f out: hdd and no ex last 50yds* **12/1**

42-1 **3** *3/4* **Secret Night**[14] 1116 6-10-4 **77** (b) MissEJJones 5 82
(C G Cox) *t.k.h: trckd ldrs: smooth hdwy over 2f out: trckd ldr on bit over 1f out: shkn up and ev ch whn hung bdly rt ent fnl f: kpt on nr fin* **9/2**[2]

5310 **4** *1 1/4* **Follow The Flag (IRE)**[14] 1133 5-9-8 **72** (p) MissVCartmel(5) 7 74
(A J McCabe) *in tch: hdwy to chse ldrs over 2f out: sn rdn and kpt on same pce appr fnl f* **10/1**

100- **5** *1* **Middlemarch (IRE)**[175] 6989 9-10-2 **75** (v) MrsCBartley 3 74
(J S Goldie) *bhd: hdwy over 2f out: sn rdn and kpt on ins fnl f: nrst fin* **14/1**

3031 **6** *2 1/2* **El Dececy (USA)**[5] 1243 5-11-0 **87** 6ex MissNCarberry 2 80
(S Parr) *led: rdn along and hdd over 2f out: sn drvn and wknd* **7/2**[1]

-252 **7** *3 1/4* **Campli (IRE)**[6] 1228 7-9-7 **66** oh4 MissLEllison 9 50
(B Ellison) *hld up: hdwy over 2f out: sn rdn and nvr nr ldrs* **13/2**[3]

0-00 **8** *1 1/2* **Daaweitza**[14] 1123 6-9-12 **78** MissVCoates(7) 10 58
(B Ellison) *in tch on outer: rdn along over 2f out and sn wknd* **10/1**

360- **9** *hd* **Fiefdom (IRE)**[134] 7557 7-10-1 **74** MissFayeBramley 8 53
(I W McInnes) *in tch: rdn along 3f out: grad wknd* **14/1**

404- **10** *2* **Prize Fighter (IRE)**[36] 7532 7-9-7 **66** oh3 MissSBrotherton 6 40
(A Berry) *chsd ldrs: rdn along appr 1/2-way and sn wknd* **16/1**

0040 **11** *shd* **King Kenny**[5] 1244 4-9-11 **70** MrsMarieKing 11 44
(S Parr) *racd wd: prom tl rdn along wl over 2f out and sn wknd* **16/1**

1m 23.82s (-2.48) **Going Correction** -0.475s/f (Firm) **11** Ran SP% **118.0**
Speed ratings (Par 105): **95,93,93,91,90 87,83,82,81,79 79**
toteswinger: 1&2 £12.30, 1&3 £5.10, 2&3 £18.60. CSF £82.21 CT £390.35 TOTE £8.00: £2.70, £3.70, £2.30; EX 210.10.
Owner R G Fell **Bred** Mick McGinn **Trained** Westow, N Yorks

FOCUS
Firmish ground, with 17mm of water put on the track in the four days leading up to racing in order to keep conditions safe. There were typically few solid propositions in this lady riders' handicap, with plenty having to prove form, fitness or effectiveness at 7f on a firm surface and, although sound, this is not form with which to get carried away.
Secret Night Official explanation: jockey said that the mare hung right

1344 SOCIETY LIFESTYLE AND LEISURE MAGAZINE MAIDEN FILLIES' STKS 5f
5:10 (5:11) (Class 4) 2-Y-0 **£3,885** (£1,156; £577; £288) **Stalls** High

Form RPR

0 **1** **Patteresa Girl**[19] 1031 2-9-0 0 TomEaves 7 69
(Mrs L Stubbs) *trckd ldrs: pushed along and outpcd 1/2-way: hdwy wl over 1f out and sn rdn: drvn ins fnl f: edgd lft and styd on to ld nr line* **9/2**[2]

2 *1/2* **Dispol Keasha** 2-9-0 0 PhillipMakin 1 67+
(T D Barron) *in tch: hdwy on wd outside 2f out: rdn to ld ins fnl f: drvn and hdd nr line* **8/1**

4 **3** *shd* **My Mandy (IRE)**[19] 1031 2-9-0 0 JimCrowley 8 67
(Ian Williams) *cl up: led 1/2-way: rdn over 1f out: drvn and hdd ins fnl f: kpt on u.p towards fin* **7/2**[1]

0 **4** *1/2* **Lady Lube Rye (IRE)**[14] 1126 2-9-0 0 LeeEnstone 6 65
(N Wilson) *cl up: rdn 2f out: ev ch tl drvn and one pce ins fnl f* **25/1**

5 *4* **Cane Cat (IRE)** 2-9-0 0 TolleyDean 2 51+
(A W Carroll) *wnt lft s and in rr: hdwy 2f out: styd on ins fnl f: nrst fin* **20/1**

4 **6** *1/2* **Musiara**[9] 1195 2-9-0 0 SamHitchcott 3 49
(M R Channon) *cl up: rdn along over 2f out: drvn over 1f out and wknd ent fnl f* **9/2**[2]

5 **7** *4 1/2* **Mrs Jones And Me (IRE)**[18] 1044 2-9-0 0 JamieMoriarty 4 33
(P T Midgley) *a towards rr* **8/1**

5 **8** *7* **Zaskia (IRE)**[12] 1158 2-9-0 0 TedDurcan 9 7
(K A Ryan) *led: pushed along and hdd 1/2-way: sn rdn and wknd wl over 1f out* **6/1**[3]

9 *4* **Tagula Pearl (IRE)** 2-9-0 0 RoystonFfrench 5 —
(I W McInnes) *sn outpcd and a in rr* **16/1**

10 *nk* **Nidamar** 2-9-0 0 AndrewElliott 10 —
(Mrs R A Carr) *dwlt: a in rr* **12/1**

59.21 secs (-1.29) **Going Correction** -0.475s/f (Firm) **10** Ran SP% **117.3**
Speed ratings (Par 91): **91,90,90,89,82 82,74,63,57,56**
toteswinger: 1&2 £4.20, 1&3 £6.50, 2&3 £13.80. CSF £40.68 TOTE £6.50: £2.20, £2.90, £1.80; EX 42.40.
Owner Cos We Can Partnership **Bred** Cothi Bloodstock **Trained** Norton, N Yorks

FOCUS
Not an easy race to assess, with none of those to have raced having been placed but each having shaped as if there is better to come. The leading quartet fought out a tight finish and the form looks pretty modest.

NOTEBOOK
Patteresa Girl, the morning gamble, was outpaced and nudged along over 2f out, she kept on to lead near the finish. Having been very green first time out when she lost all chance at the start, she had clearly learned plenty. The way she raced here suggests she will come on again, particularly with a stiffer test and her reported target is the Hilary Needler at Beverley, where the track will suit. She is likely to be suited by 6f in time. (op 4-1)
Dispol Keasha ◆ is the one to take from the race. She was done no favours at the start and also had the disadvantage of a wide draw, seeing a fair amount of daylight, yet came through to lead around 1f out only to be caught late on. Each of the others involved in the finish had the benefit of experience so she deserves plenty of credit, and although the form of this race may be nothing ordinary, she should do better. (op 9-2)

My Mandy(IRE), the Lingfield fourth, was always to the fore on the stands' side and confirmed she has ability. (op 5-1)
Lady Lube Rye(IRE) showed up well for a long way and did better than on her debut.
Cane Cat(IRE), who went markedly left at the start and looked in need of the experience. She should improve. (op 16-1)
Musiara could not confirm the apparent promise of her debut. (tchd 5-1)

1345 OWSTON HALL HOTEL LEISURE CLUB H'CAP 6f

5:40 (5:43) (Class 3) (0-90,88) 3-Y-O **£7,771** (£2,312; £1,155; £577) **Stalls** High

Form RPR
03-6 **1** **Proclaim**[7] 1214 3-8-10 **80** RoystonFfrench 3 90
(M Johnston) *a.p: effrt and cl up 2f out: rdn to ld jst ins fnl f: drvn: edgd rt and hld on towards fin* **7/1**[2]
13-5 **2** *hd* **Lucky Numbers (IRE)**[2] 1305 3-8-6 **81** AndreaAtzeni(5) 7 90
(Paul Green) *cl up: led over 2f out and sn rdn: drvn ent fnl f and sn hdd: rallied wl u.p towards fin* **15/2**[3]
221- **3** *3 ½* **Swiss Diva**[150] 7388 3-9-1 **85** TedDurcan 12 86+
(D R C Elsworth) *hld up in rr: effrt and nt clr run whn swtchd lft and hmpd 2f out: sn rdn and kpt on ent fnl f: nrst fin* **4/1**[1]
215- **4** *nk* **Whatyouwoodwishfor (USA)**[147] 7426 3-8-9 **79** JamieMoriarty 10 76
(R A Fahey) *trckd ldrs: effrt over 2f out and sn rdn: styd on same pce ins fnl f* **7/1**[2]
400- **5** *1 ¾* **Tagula Breeze (IRE)**[220] 5794 3-8-11 **81** TomEaves 13 72+
(I W McInnes) *outpcd and in rr whn hmpd after 1f: hdwy whn bmpd 2f out: sn rdn and kpt on same pce appr fnl f* **33/1**
000- **6** *nk* **Spiritofthewest (IRE)**[161] 7241 3-8-12 **82** (t) WilliamBuick 8 72
(S Parr) *led: rdn along and hdd over 2f out: grad wknd* **33/1**
023- **7** *2 ¼* **Fivefootnumberone (IRE)**[189] 6656 3-9-0 **84** GrahamGibbons 11 67
(J J Quinn) *in tocuh: effrt over 2f out: sn rdn and wknd over 1f out* **16/1**
600- **8** *nk* **Harriet's Girl**[210] 6118 3-8-5 **75** AndrewElliott 9 57
(K R Burke) *dwlt and towards rr: effrt and sme hdwy whn n.m.r 2f out: nvr a factor* **28/1**
205- **9** *nse* **Polish Pride**[169] 7109 3-9-4 **88** AlanMunro 1 70
(M Brittain) *hld up: gd hdwy on outer over 2f out: rdn to chse ldrs wl over 1f out: sn wknd* **12/1**
04-0 **10** *5* **Red Kyte**[28] 912 3-8-13 **83** JimCrowley 2 49
(K A Ryan) *prom: rdn along over 2f out and sn wknd* **12/1**
20-1 **11** *1 ¾* **Ray Of Joy**[17] 1068 3-8-12 **82** JimmyQuinn 4 43
(J R Jenkins) *chsd ldrs: rdn along wl over 2f out and sn wknd* **9/1**
135- **12** *1 ¼* **Soul Sista (IRE)**[251] 4908 3-8-8 **78** LiamJones 6 35
(J L Spearing) *in tch to 1/2-way: sn rdn along and wknd* **33/1**

1m 10.31s (-3.29) **Going Correction** -0.475s/f (Firm) 12 Ran SP% **100.3**
Speed ratings (Par 102): **102,101,97,96,94 93,90,90,90,83 81,79**
toteswinger: 1&2 £12.60, 1&3 £6.30, 2&3 £12.60. CSF £36.42 CT £107.85 TOTE £7.90: £2.50, £2.30, £1.60; EX 53.70.
Owner Sheikh Hamdan Bin Mohammed Al Maktoum **Bred** Gainsborough Stud Management Ltd **Trained** Middleham Moor, N Yorks

FOCUS
This three-year-old handicap was undoubtedly weakened by the withdrawal of Dark Lane who reared up in the stalls. This developed into a test of early speed, suiting those who raced prominently. The form looks solid enough.

NOTEBOOK
Proclaim had run well over longer trips last season but showed he has the pace to be effective at 6f. Quickly away and always in touch, he led inside the final furlong. His in-form trainer's three-year-old handicappers often continue to improve and this relatively lightly-raced colt could well progress further. He should be as effective when stepped back up to 7f. (op 11-2)
Lucky Numbers(IRE) had lost his chance when hampered at Ripon earlier in the week and showed he has trained on with a decent effort, leading over 2f out until inside the final furlong. He progressed well as a juvenile and has clearly come on again. (op 9-1 tchd 7-1)
Swiss Diva ◆ was the real eyecatcher. The field dashed across to the stands' side and bunched, making traffic problems inevitable for a come-from-behind sprinter and she was the chief sufferer. She travelled well, but she had no room over 2f out, and had to be switched left. The first two were clear by the time she got a run and she could do little more than grab third place. It is impossible to judge where she would have finished with a clear run, but she had progressed well as a two-year-old, had looked open to considerable further improvement, and is well worth another chance next time. Official explanation: jockey said filly was denied a clear run (op 9-2 tchd 5-1)
Whatyouwoodwishfor(USA) starts his second season on a stiffish mark and probably ran as well as could be hoped for. He may need some help from the Handicapper if he is going to be competitive this year. (op 6-1)
Tagula Breeze(IRE) did not shape badly in a race not run to suit. He could well improve upon this, particularly when refitted with the tongue strap which he wore latterly last season. (op 50-1 tchd 28-1)
Spiritofthewest(IRE) showed good early speed, leading to over 2f out, but has yet to prove he stays 6f.
Polish Pride Official explanation: jockey said that the filly hung right
Red Kyte showed up well to halfway but was comfortably held on her handicap debut. (op 14-1)

1346 DONCASTER MILE STKS (LISTED RACE) 1m (R)

6:15 (6:16) (Class 1) 4-Y-O+ **£23,704** (£8,964; £4,480; £2,240) **Stalls** Low

Form RPR
600- **1** **Staying On (IRE)**[182] 6816 4-8-12 108 (t) AdamKirby 7 109
(W R Swinburn) *led: pushed along over 2f out: rdn wl over 1f out: hdd and drvn ent fnl f: rallied wl u.p to ld again last 100yds: edgd rt nr fin* **9/2**[3]
103- **2** *¾* **Unnefer (FR)**[238] 5289 4-8-12 110 IanMongan 3 108
(H R A Cecil) *trckd ldrs: swtchd rt and hdwy wl over 2f out: chal over 1f out: rdnto ld ent fnl f: hdd and no ex last 100yds* **4/1**[2]
60-0 **3** *2* **Dream Lodge (IRE)**[21] 997 5-8-12 95 (v) J-PGuillambert 4 103
(J G Given) *chsd wnr: effrt 3f out and sn cl up: rdn along over 2f out: drvn and one pce appr last* **25/1**
231- **4** *nk* **Atlantic Sport (USA)**[219] 5840 4-9-1 107 SamHitchcott 2 105
(M R Channon) *hld up: hdwy on outer 3f out: rdn 2f out: sn drvn and kpt on same pce appr last* **13/2**
20-1 **5** *1 ¼* **King Of Dixie (USA)**[37] 815 5-8-12 109 JimCrowley 6 99
(W J Knight) *s.i.s and hld up in rr: hdwy on outer wl over 2f out: rdn wl over 1f out and sn no imp* **11/8**[1]
5-20 **6** *4* **Blythe Knight (IRE)**[21] 997 9-8-12 107 GrahamGibbons 1 90
(J J Quinn) *trckd ldrs on inner: effrt over 2f out: sn rdn and wknd* **9/1**
-256 **7** *3* **Philario (IRE)**[21] 997 4-8-12 97 DarrenWilliams 5 83
(K R Burke) *trckd ldrs: pushed along over 3f out: rdn over 2f out and sn wknd* **18/1**

1m 34.46s (-6.54) **Going Correction** -0.475s/f (Firm) course record 7 Ran SP% **112.7**
Speed ratings (Par 111): **113,112,110,109,108 104,101**
toteswinger: 1&2 £14.20, 1&3 £25.90, 2&3 £29.30. CSF £22.05 TOTE £5.90: £2.90, £2.60; EX 19.20.
Owner M H Dixon **Bred** M H Dixon **Trained** Aldbury, Herts
■ Stewards' Enquiry : Adam Kirby one-day ban: used whip without allowing time for horse to respond

FOCUS
Potentially a decent listed race, with all bar two of these having already proven themselves fully effective at this level. The track record was smashed, but not many races on the round mile have occurred since the course was re-vamped, particularly when conditions are conducive to quick times. The form is limited by the proximity of the third.

NOTEBOOK
Staying On(IRE), who might have been expected to be vulnerable at this trip. He set a fair pace, winding it up in the straight and ensuring he had enough left to find extra when headed briefly around 1f out. His mount clearly had the run of the race, but this was still a most encouraging reappearance from a four-year-old who finished second over 1m2f at Royal Ascot last season. He then seemed to lose his way, but the Royal meeting is his likely destination again. (op 15-2)
Unnefer(FR) had been off the track since August, was weak in the betting, but showed he retains his ability. Always in touch, he led briefly around 1f out. He is another with form over further and is likely to be suited by a step back up in trip. (op 11-4 tchd 9-2)
Dream Lodge(IRE) had a stiff task at the weights and ran a fine race, albeit in a contest run to suit him. He was in touch from the off and kept on again to take third. (tchd 20-1)
Atlantic Sport(USA) was not disgraced as he was conceding weight all round. He tried to come from off the pace in a race which did not seem to suit such tactics. He is probably as good as ever. (tchd 6-1)
King Of Dixie(USA) was the pick of the field on Racing Post ratings, but had to come from well off the pace after a slow start and could find only one pace in the final 1f. He may have found the ground firm enough, so he could be worth another chance. (op 6-4 tchd 13-8 in a place)
Blythe Knight(IRE) is another for whom the ground may have been too firm. (op 8-1)

1347 MOSS PROPERTIES H'CAP 1m 2f 60y

6:50 (6:50) (Class 3) (0-95,94) 4-Y-O+
£7,477 (£2,239; £1,119; £560; £279; £140) **Stalls** Low

Form RPR
142- **1** **Redesignation (IRE)**[175] 6984 4-9-4 **94** JimCrowley 9 103
(R Hannon) *hld up in tch: hdwy 3f out: swtchd outside and rdn over 1f out: styd on to ld last 100yds* **5/2**[1]
40-2 **2** *¾* **Granston (IRE)**[21] 999 8-8-7 **83** GrahamGibbons 8 91
(J D Bethell) *trckd ldrs: smooth hdwy over 2f out: led over 1f out: rdn and hung lft ent fnl f: sn drvn: hdd and no ex last 100yds* **9/2**
060- **3** *2* **Demolition**[173] 7025 5-8-6 **82** PaulQuinn 6 86
(N Wilson) *hld up in rr: gd hdwy on inner 3f out: squeezed through to chal wl over 1f out and ev ch tl drvn and n.m.r ent fnl f: kpt on same pce* **20/1**
0-00 **4** *1 ¾* **Ellmau**[21] 999 4-8-7 **83** JamesDoyle 2 86+
(A J McCabe) *prom: led over 2f out: sn rdn and hdd over 1f out: cl up whn hmpd ent fnl f and no ch after* **20/1**
316- **5** *3 ½* **Princess Taylor**[183] 6781 5-8-11 **87** (t) JimmyQuinn 10 81
(M Botti) *hld up: effrt 3f out: rdn along 2f out: sn edgd lft and n.d* **10/3**[3]
20/1 **6** *2* **Spring Jim**[21] 999 8-8-7 **83** WilliamBuick 1 73
(J R Fanshawe) *trckd ldrs on inner: effrt 3f out: rdn along 2f out: sn wknd* **3/1**[2]
620- **7** *5* **Magic Echo**[203] 6293 5-8-11 **87** PhillipMakin 4 68
(M Dods) *sn led: rdn along 3f out: hdd over 2f out and sn wknd* **9/1**

2m 5.92s (-5.28) **Going Correction** -0.475s/f (Firm) 7 Ran SP% **114.4**
Speed ratings (Par 107): **102,101,99,98,95 94,90**
toteswinger: 1&2 £3.60, 1&3 £12.30, 2&3 £31.70. CSF £14.17 CT £175.33 TOTE £3.60: £2.10, £2.30; EX 14.00.
Owner Fergus Jones **Bred** D G Iceton **Trained** East Everleigh, Wilts

FOCUS
This good handicap's competitiveness was reduced by three withdrawals but the form looks solid rated around the placed horses.

NOTEBOOK
Redesignation(IRE) put up a career-best effort to defy top-weight. He deserves credit as he was only fourth entering the final 1f but stayed on well to lead close home, although his jockey felt he was saving a bit for himself. His career record is one of continual improvement and there is every indication in this performance that there could still be better to come. He appears likely to prove better at 1m2f than shorter trips, but he handles much softer ground and could be the sort to give a good account in a decent handicap this season. (op 11-4)
Granston(IRE) had been second here at the Lincoln meeting and confirmed himself in good form with another decent effort on a track where he usually runs well. Leading over 1f out, he hung left and was headed late on. (tchd 5-1)
Demolition is another who has a generally progressive profile. His come-from-behind effort was encouraging, particularly given his past record first time out. (op 16-1)
Ellmau is better than the bare form suggests as he did best of those in touch from the off and was also squeezed out inside the final furlong. This was his best effort for his new yard, and his best since being gelded, and he is worth bearing in mind. (tchd 16-1)
Princess Taylor is high enough in the weights at present. (op 5-1)
Spring Jim, for whom the ground was quicker than when he won here last month. He has had physical problems and may have found that counting against him. Official explanation: jockey said the gelding was unsuited by the good to firm ground (op 9-4 tchd 10-3 in a place)

1348 CROWNHOTEL-BAWTRY.COM FILLIES' H'CAP 1m 2f 60y

7:25 (7:25) (Class 4) (0-85,88) 4-Y-O+ **£4,857** (£1,445; £722; £360) **Stalls** Low

Form RPR
1305 **1** **Aphrodisia**[24] 952 5-8-5 **72** WilliamBuick 6 81
(Ian Williams) *hld up towards rr: hdwy on outer over 2f out: quickeend to ld appr fnl f: sn rdn and styd on wl* **8/1**
631/ **2** *1 ½* **La Rosa Nostra**[563] 5912 4-8-5 **72** RoystonFfrench 2 78+
(W R Swinburn) *trckd ldr: hdwy 3f out: effrt to chal whn n.m.r 2f out: sn rdn and led briefly over 1f out: kpt on same pce ins fnl f* **5/2**[1]
4-62 **3** *1* **Encircled**[10] 1184 5-9-7 **88** JimmyQuinn 4 92
(J R Jenkins) *trckd ldrs on inner: effrt and nt clr run over 2f out: rdn and hdwy on inner to chal over 1f out: drvn and one pce ins fnl f* **5/1**[3]
412- **4** *2 ½* **Rio Guru (IRE)**[156] 7305 4-8-11 **78** SamHitchcott 9 77
(M R Channon) *trckd ldrs: hdwy over 3f out: rdn to chal and edgd lft 2f out: sn drvn and btn appr fnl f* **4/1**[2]
0434 **5** *hd* **Teasing**[10] 1179 5-8-7 **74** (v) RobertHavlin 1 73
(J Pearce) *hld up in rr: hdwy over 2f out: sn rdn and no imp* **12/1**
-150 **6** *4* **Confidentiality (IRE)**[28] 915 5-9-2 **83** NickyMackay 5 74
(M Wigham) *hld up towards rr: hdwy 3f out: rdn to chse ldrs over 2f out: sn drvn and wknd wl over 1f out* **12/1**
0-35 **7** *1* **Black Dahlia**[20] 1020 4-8-5 **72** JamesDoyle 10 62
(A J McCabe) *set stdy pce: qcknd 4f out: rdn along 3f out: drvn and hdd wl over 1f out sn wknd* **8/1**
26-1 **8** *2 ½* **Spring Goddess (IRE)**[20] 1020 8-8-8 **82** CharlotteKerton(7) 7 67
(A P Jarvis) *in tch: hdwy on outer over 3f out: rdn over 2f out and sn wknd* **7/1**

2m 11.72s (0.52) **Going Correction** -0.475s/f (Firm) 8 Ran SP% **115.3**
Speed ratings (Par 102): **78,76,76,74,73 70,69,67**
toteswinger: 1&2 £6.40, 1&3 £8.70, 2&3 £3.20. CSF £28.65 CT £112.00 TOTE £10.30: £2.40, £1.70, £2.20; EX 46.90.
Owner bellhouseracing.com **Bred** Theobalds Stud **Trained** Portway, Worcs

FOCUS
Despite the absence of leading fancy Summer's Lease this was competitive, with plenty of horses in-form. Not a great pace early on and the form may be a bit suspect.

1349 DONCASTER SPONSORSHIP CLUB MAIDEN STKS — 1m 4f
7:55 (7:55) (Class 4) 3-Y-O — **£4,857** (£1,445; £722; £360) **Stalls** Low

Form — RPR

30-2 **1** **Chilly Filly (IRE)**[24] 957 3-8-12 73 ... JoeFanning 4 — 70
(M Johnston) *t.k.h: trckd ldrs: hdwy 3f out: led 2f out: rdn and edgd lft over 1f out: kpt on wl fnl f* **5/1**[3]

0-2 **2** *1½* **Shemoli**[16] 1088 3-9-3 0 ... TedDurcan 2 — 73
(M A Jarvis) *trckd ldrs on inner: smooth hdwy to ld 3f out: rdn and hdd 2f out: drvn and rallied ins fnl f: kpt on same pce* **11/10**[1]

60-2 **3** *½* **Akmal**[16] 1087 3-9-3 80 ... TPO'Shea 3 — 72
(J L Dunlop) *hld up in rr: hdwy over 2f out: rdn to chse wnr ent fnl f: sn drvn and no imp* **5/2**[2]

3-33 **4** *1¼* **Haljaferia (UAE)**[85] 272 3-9-3 72 ... RobertHavlin 7 — 70
(D R C Elsworth) *t.k.h: hld up in rr: hdwy 3f out: rdn to chse ldng pair wl over 1f out: sn drvn and one pce appr fnl f* **20/1**

0- **5** *1¾* **Lombok**[183] 6777 3-9-3 0 ... WilliamBuick 8 — 67
(M L W Bell) *trckd ldrs on outer: hdwy 3f out: rdn along over 2f out and sn btn* **14/1**

4 **6** *4½* **Gosforth Park**[11] 1168 3-9-3 0 ... AlanMunro 6 — 60
(M Brittain) *trckd ldr: cl up 4f out: sn rdn along: drvn and wknd wl over 2f out* **16/1**

00- **7** *27* **Acclaim To Fame (IRE)**[173] 7020 3-9-3 0 ... (t) AdamKirby 5 — 17
(S Parr) *led: rdn along 4f out: hdd 3f out and sn wknd* **14/1**

2m 34.27s (-0.83) **Going Correction** -0.475s/f (Firm) — **7** Ran SP% **116.8**
Speed ratings (Par 100): **83,82,81,80,79 76,58**
toteswinger: 1&2 £1.60, 1&3 £2.10, 2&3 £1.02. CSF £11.36 TOTE £5.20: £1.70, £1.50; EX 12.00 Place 6: £59.60, Place 5: £18.49.
Owner J Barson **Bred** Moyglare Stud Farm Ltd **Trained** Middleham Moor, N Yorks

FOCUS
A handful of these three-year-olds had form to their name and they dominated the finish. However, this maiden was run at only a modest pace and the finishing order and distances may not be a true reflection of the runners' relative merits, with the form not looking the most solid.
T/Plt: £49.20 to a £1 stake. Pool: £39,584.99. 587.17 winning tickets. T/Qpdt: £11.30 to a £1 stake. Pool: £3,834.96. 251.00 winning tickets. JR

[1323] NEWBURY (L-H)
Saturday, April 18

OFFICIAL GOING: Soft (4.4)
Wind: Moderate behind Weather: Light cloud

1350 DUBAI INTERNATIONAL AIRPORT MAIDEN STKS (DIV I) — 1m (S)
1:30 (1:38) (Class 4) 3-Y-O — **£4,857** (£1,445; £722; £360) **Stalls** Centre

Form — RPR

3- **1** **Border Patrol**[191] 6602 3-9-3 0 ... SteveDrowne 10 — 95
(R Charlton) *h.d.w: trckd ldrs: wnt 2nd 2f out: shkn up: edgd lft and led jst ins fnl f: styd on strly* **2/1**[1]

2 *¾* **South Easter (IRE)** 3-9-3 0 ... NCallan 16 — 93
(W J Haggas) *w'like: athletic: lw: galloped loose to s: trckd ldr tl led over 2f out: pushed along over 1f out and hdd jst ins fnl f: outpcd by wnr but wl clr of 3rd* **16/1**

3- **3** *6* **Ebiayn (FR)**[184] 6759 3-9-3 0 ... RHills 6 — 79
(M A Jarvis) *w'like: athletic: lw: chsd ldrs: pushed along over 2f out: readily outpcd by ldng duo appr fnl f* **3/1**[2]

0- **4** *2½* **Dreamcoat**[183] 6778 3-9-3 0 ... MartinDwyer 15 — 73
(J H M Gosden) *h.d.w: lw: led: hdd over 2f out: sn btn* **8/1**

4- **5** *6* **Bahkov (IRE)**[125] 7674 3-9-3 0 ... RichardKingscote 5 — 60
(Tom Dascombe) *in tch: rdn over 2f out: sn no ch w ldrs* **28/1**

6 *2¼* **Reportage (USA)** 3-9-3 0 ... JimmyFortune 13 — 54
(J H M Gosden) *str: bit bkwd: slowly away: pushed along over 3f out: mod prog fr over 1f out* **11/2**[3]

0- **7** *½* **Eye For The Girls**[177] 6923 3-9-3 0 ... TonyCulhane 7 — 53
(M R Channon) *leggy: chsd ldrs over 5f* **66/1**

-0 **8** *5* **Refuse Toulouse (IRE)**[21] 998 3-9-3 0 ... PhilipRobinson 3 — 42
(C G Cox) *w'like: lengthy: s.i.s: in rr tl mod prog fnl 2f* **33/1**

9 *¾* **Inside Trade (IRE)** 3-9-3 0 ... SebSanders 8 — 40
(R M Beckett) *w'like: lw: edgy: mid-div: rdn over 3f out and sn wknd* **66/1**

5- **10** *5* **Pachakutek (USA)**[183] 6778 3-9-3 0 ... DarryllHolland 4 — 29
(E F Vaughan) *a in rr* **10/1**

0- **11** *18* **Almutawaazin**[175] 6977 3-9-3 0 ... TPO'Shea 1 — —
(M P Tregoning) *lw: slowly away: sn rdn: a in rr* **33/1**

0- **12** *nk* **December**[232] 5469 3-9-3 0 ... RyanMoore 2 — —
(Sir Michael Stoute) *slowly away: a in rr* **8/1**

1m 43.05s (3.35) **Going Correction** +0.525s/f (Yiel) — **12** Ran SP% **123.2**
Speed ratings (Par 100): **104,103,97,94,88 86,86,81,80,75 57,56**
toteswinger: 1&2 £10.30, 1&3 £2.30, 2&3 £12.20 CSF £38.07 TOTE £2.90: £1.50, £4.50, £1.70; EX 51.90.
Owner Elite Racing Club **Bred** Elite Racing Club **Trained** Beckhampton, Wilts

FOCUS
After 4mm of overnight rain the official going was changed to soft. As a result there were a number of non-runners through the afternoon. This first division of a maiden that is often won by one of the major yards has thrown up Purple Moon, Diamond Tycoon and Mudawin in recent seasons. Once again, it looks strong form of its type, rated through the third.
Refuse Toulouse(IRE) Official explanation: jockey said the colt was unsuited by the soft ground
December Official explanation: jockey said the colt got upset in the stalls, was slowly away and was never travelling

1351 DUBAI TENNIS CHAMPIONSHIPS STKS (REGISTERED AS THE JOHN PORTER STAKES) (GROUP 3) — 1m 4f 5y
2:05 (2:06) (Class 1) 4-Y-O+
£36,900 (£13,988; £7,000; £3,490; £1,748; £877) **Stalls** Low

Form — RPR

454- **1** **Enroller (IRE)**[196] 6494 4-8-11 109 ... MartinDwyer 10 — 114
(W R Muir) *chsd ldrs: wnt 2nd 6f out: led over 3f out: strly chal over 2f out: forged on u.p over 1f out: styd on dourly fnl f* **12/1**

133- **2** *1½* **Centennial (IRE)**[196] 6494 4-8-11 114 ... JimmyFortune 3 — 112
(J H M Gosden) *in rr: rdn and hdwy over 3f out: styd on to chse wnr fnl f: kpt on but no imp ins fnl f* **5/1**[3]

03-1 **3** *1¼* **Tastahil (IRE)**[20] 1017 5-8-12 105 ... RHills 8 — 110
(B W Hills) *lw: sn led: rdn and hdd over 3f out: styd on fnl 2f but nvr gng pce to chal after* **9/2**[2]

303- **4** *3* **Royal And Regal (IRE)**[218] 5854 5-8-12 112 ... NCallan 6 — 105
(M A Jarvis) *lw; in tch: hdwy 5f out: drvn to chal and edgd lft over 2f out: wknd over 1f out* **6/4**[1]

/33- **5** *1¼* **Walking Talking**[208] 6171 5-8-12 94 ... TPQueally 5 — 103
(H R A Cecil) *chsd ldrs: nvr gng pce to chal and wknd u.p over 1f out* **10/1**

354- **6** *4½* **Ezdiyaad (IRE)**[197] 6444 5-8-12 102 ... TPO'Shea 1 — 96
(M P Tregoning) *lw: chsd ldrs: rdn over 3f out: wknd fr 2f out* **14/1**

-311 **7** *2½* **Scintillo**[28] 913 4-9-0 110 ... RichardHughes 2 — 95
(R Hannon) *hld up in rr: stdy hdwy fr 3f out to trck ldrs ins fnl 2f: rdn over 1f out and wknd qckly* **9/1**

104- **8** *4½* **Unleashed (IRE)**[282] 3875 4-8-11 106 ... JimmyQuinn 4 — 85
(H R A Cecil) *in tch: chsd ldrs and rdn 5f out: wknd 3f out* **20/1**

551- **9** *7* **Sereth (IRE)**[300] 3307 6-8-12 105 ... ShaneKelly 9 — 74
(B J Curley) *rdn 5f out: a in rr* **50/1**

2m 42.78s (7.28) **Going Correction** +0.525s/f (Yiel)
WFA 4 from 5yo+ 1lb — **9** Ran SP% **115.0**
Speed ratings (Par 113): **96,95,94,92,91 88,86,83,79**
toteswinger: 1&2 £12.60, 1&3 £11.70, 2&3 £4.20 CSF £70.60 TOTE £14.90: £3.60, £2.00, £1.60; EX 85.20 Trifecta £362.60 Part won. Pool: £490.12 - 0.50 winning units..
Owner D G Clarke & C L A Edginton **Bred** Mrs Denise Brophy **Trained** Lambourn, Berks

FOCUS
By no means a strong John Porter, and they went steadily, so not form to get carried away about. They raced up the middle of the track in the straight and the principals gradually came across to the stands' side. The form is a bit muddling with the second not far off his best.

NOTEBOOK
Enroller(IRE) was very much an improver at three, when he stayed well and handled soft ground, and it looks as if he has come on again. The St Leger fifth went second at halfway, and once he had nosed ahead early in the straight he always looked the likeliest winner, although favourite Royal And Regal looked a big threat when he initiated his challenge. The Yorkshire Cup is an option for the colt, whom William Muir believes could one day be his first Group 1 winner. (op 16-1 tchd 20-1)
Centennial(IRE) was a shade classier than the winner at three, when his two Group wins included the Voltigeur and he was also a close third in the Prix Niel. Held up here, he made his move in plenty of time up the stands' side of the pack and simply was not quite good enough. His stable has been in great form, so he might not improve as much as some. (op 4-1 tchd 11-2)
Tastahil(IRE), a Doncaster conditions race winner, was sweating down his neck and had much more to do. He made much of the running but looked one paced when push came to shove. The ground should not have been a problem.
Royal And Regal(IRE) won this race last year and was better in this time, as he had no penalty. Gelded since then, he looked to have everything in place for another big run, but having looked dangerous when beginning his challenge, he did not find a lot and it was soon clear that the winner was going better. He went left under pressure and was disappointing. (op 7-4 tchd 11-8)
Walking Talking, lightly raced, had a stiff task and was not disgraced. (op 11-1 tchd 12-1)
Ezdiyaad(IRE) was keen and could have done with a stronger gallop. He does not always look the most straightforward.
Scintillo came here in great form, but 1m4f in holding ground was never going to play to his strengths. He was still travelling well under cover three furlongs out but did not get home and was eased significantly when beaten. This can safely be ignored. (op 10-1 tchd 8-1)
Unleashed(IRE) had been off the track since July, so is entitled to come on for this outing. He had been improving when last seen.
Sereth(IRE), a five-times winner in Germany, including twice in Listed company at 1m6f last year, did not show much on his British debut. However, he had been off the track for 10 months and seems better with forcing tactics over further.

1352 DUBAI DUTY FREE SPRING CUP (HERITAGE H'CAP) — 1m (S)
2:35 (2:43) (Class 2) 4-Y-O+
£24,924 (£7,464; £3,732; £1,868; £932; £468) **Stalls** Centre

Form — RPR

-023 **1** **Extraterrestrial**[7] 1209 5-8-12 **95** ... FrederikTylicki(5) 20 — 104
(R A Fahey) *lw: in tch: rdn to ld appr fnl f: drvn out* **20/1**

21-4 **2** *¾* **Arabian Spirit**[30] 879 4-8-12 **90** ... TGMcLaughlin 19 — 97
(E A L Dunlop) *chsd ldrs: rdn to chal 1f out: styd on one pce: rallied to take 2nd cl home but no imp on wnr* **40/1**

30-0 **3** *hd* **Medici Pearl**[21] 995 5-8-12 **90** ... JohnEgan 24 — 97
(T D Easterby) *in tch: rdn and hdwy over 2f out: chal 1f out: styd disputing 2nd ins fnl f but nt pce of wnr: lost 2nd cl home* **20/1**

111L **4** *1* **Spectait**[21] 995 7-9-3 **95** ... GeorgeBaker 8 — 99+
(Jonjo O'Neill) *chsd ldrs: led over 2f out: sn rdn: hdd appr fnl f: kpt on same pce ins fnl f* **25/1**

00-2 **5** *nse* **Fanjura (IRE)**[15] 1093 4-9-0 **92** ... LDettori 15 — 96
(B W Hills) *chsd ldrs: rdn to chal 2f out: outpcd ins fnl f* **25/1**

50-4 **6** *2¼* **Mia's Boy**[21] 997 5-9-10 **102** ... JimmyQuinn 14 — 101
(C A Dwyer) *in rr: hdwy 3f out: n.m.r over 2f out: styd on wl fr over 1f out but pce to chal fnl f* **8/1**[3]

33-0 **7** *nk* **Charm School**[21] 997 4-9-4 **96** ... JimmyFortune 5 — 94
(J H M Gosden) *s.i.s: bhd: gd hdwy fr 2f out: styd on wl fnl f but nvr in contention* **8/1**[3]

-420 **8** *hd* **Whistledownwind**[21] 997 4-9-3 **95** ... (v) ShaneKelly 25 — 93
(J Noseda) *in rr: hdwy whn hmpd ins fnl 3f: styd on wl finak f but nvr in contention* **28/1**

30-5 **9** *1¼* **Huzzah (IRE)**[21] 997 4-9-6 **98** ... MichaelHills 23 — 93
(B W Hills) *in tch: hdwy to chse ldrs 2f out: one pce fnl f* **11/1**

52-5 **10** *2¼* **Alarazi (IRE)**[21] 1004 5-9-9 **101** ... (b) SteveDrowne 12 — 91
(T G Mills) *lw: led tl hdd over 2f out: wknd u.p fnl f* **40/1**

116- **11** *3¼* **Mawatheeq (USA)**[183] 6780 4-9-10 **102** ... TPO'Shea 6 — 84
(M P Tregoning) *chsd ldrs: chal and rdn over 2f out: wknd fnl f* **16/1**

35-0 **12** *2¼* **Cobo Bay**[21] 997 4-9-3 **95** ... (p) DarryllHolland 16 — 72
(K A Ryan) *sn chsng ldrs: stl there over 1f out: eased whn hld fnl f* **25/1**

-402 **13** *¾* **Benandonner (USA)**[7] 1212 6-9-3 **95** ... PaulHanagan 18 — 70
(R A Fahey) *sn chsng ldrs: rdn over 2f out: wknd fnl f* **12/1**

2233 **14** *3¾* **Majuro (IRE)**[21] 995 5-9-3 **95** ... NCallan 17 — 62
(K A Ryan) *chsd ldrs: rdn over 2f out: wknd over 1f out* **20/1**

003- **15** *½* **Jaser**[184] 6763 4-8-12 **90** ... RyanMoore 1 — 56
(P W Chapple-Hyam) *towards rr and hrd drvn over 3f out and nvr in contention* **15/2**[2]

/5-1 **16** *shd* **Manassas (IRE)**[21] 995 4-9-5 **97** ... DaneO'Neill 9 — 62
(B J Meehan) *in tch: hdwy to chse ldrs over 3f out: wknd insde fnl 2f* **14/1**

0-05 **17** *7* **Lucky Dance (BRZ)**[21] 995 7-9-0 **92** ... SebSanders 10 — 41
(A G Foster) *chsd ldrs: rdn 3f out: wknd 2f out* **20/1**

050- **18** *4½* **Proponent (IRE)**[210] 6120 5-9-4 **96** ... FergusSweeney 21 — 35
(R Charlton) *in rr: sme hdwy to chse ldrs 3f out: wknd over 2f out* **16/1**

00-2 **19** *1* **Zaahid (IRE)**[21] 997 5-9-7 99 RHills 13 36
(B W Hills) *lw: chsd ldrs: rdn 3f out: wknd qckly 2f out* **6/1**[1]

000- **20** *8* **European Dream (IRE)**[14] 960 6-9-1 98 (p) MarkCoumbe(5) 22 16
(R C Guest) *a towards rr* **28/1**

03-0 **21** *17* **Slugger O'Toole**[21] 995 4-9-2 94 RichardKingscote 4 —
(S C Williams) *dull in coat: chsd ldrs over 5f* **40/1**

114 **22** *2 1/4* **Boscage (USA)**[15] 1093 4-9-3 95 JoeFanning 2 —
(M Johnston) *in tch: rdn to chse ldrs over 3f out: sn wknd* **33/1**

31-5 **23** *1* **Cordell (IRE)**[7] 1209 4-9-2 94 RichardHughes 11 —
(R Hannon) *warm: s.i.s: sme hdwy and n.m.r over 3f out: sn wknd and eased fnl 2f* **25/1**

1m 42.01s (2.31) **Going Correction** +0.525s/f (Yiel) **23** Ran SP% **134.3**
Speed ratings (Par 109): **109,108,108,107,107 104,104,104,103,100 97,95,94,90,90 90,83,78,77,69 52,50,49**
toteswinger: 1&2 £75.40, 1&3 £64.20, 2&3 £37.10 CSF £653.88 CT £14998.04 TOTE £26.20: £4.70, £10.70, £4.70, £6.10; EX 1773.00 TRIFECTA Not won..
Owner G J Paver **Bred** Lostford Manor Stud **Trained** Musley Bank, N Yorks

FOCUS
A typically competitive and open contest for this natural follow-up race for horses who contested the Lincoln. The runner-up, fourth, fifth and eighth, and several others further behind, plus the first two from the Lincoln consolation race (the Spring Mile) were renewing rivalry. In recent years a double-figure draw has been an important factor and it most certainly was this time, with the first three being drawn 20, 19 and 24. The first three horses are rated as having run personal bests.

NOTEBOOK
Extraterrestrial is effective on soft ground and had finished runner-up to Manassas in Spring Mile. Aided by a useful claimer this time, he came through with the placed horses entering the last furlong and won slightly cosily. He should continue to be competitive in similar company.
Arabian Spirit, who had the trip and ground to suit, came through just ahead of the winner and stuck on well in the final furlong. He progressed last season and that has continued to do so on this evidence.
Medici Pearl, eighth in the Spring Mile on faster going, is suited by soft ground and ran her race, coming through with the first two and only just losing out on second. She will win again when conditions are in her favour. (op 22-1)
Spectait ◆, who had been in good form before rearing over backwards as the stalls opened in the Spring Mile, did best of those racing from a low draw. He looked as if he might win at one point but the trio more towards the stands' side swept past late on. He can be given extra credit considering he started from stall eight. (tchd 28-1)
Fanjura(IRE) had form at up to 1m at on a sound surface but this ground was an unknown. He ran well, though, only fading late on, and is one to bear in mind for something like the Victoria Cup, especially on a faster surface. (op 22-1)
Mia's Boy, fourth in the Lincoln and 3lb better off with the runner-up Zaahid, was settled off the pace and stayed on without looking likely to make an impression. (op 9-1 tchd 10-1)
Charm School had the ground to suit but missed the break and looked well held until making good progress in the closing stages. (tchd 9-1 in a place)
Whistledownwind, whose only win was over course and distance on soft, had slipped down the ratings but was well beaten in the Lincoln in a first-time visor. With conditions to suit and from a good draw, he ran better this time. (op 33-1)
Huzzah(IRE), fifth in the Lincoln and meeting Mia's Boy on the same terms, ran well again despite not quite matching his Doncaster effort. (op 10-1)
Alarazi(IRE), placed in Group company when trained in Ireland, had been running over jumps and on the all-weather for new connections. He was soon in front and set a decent pace up the centre, but did not drop away totally once headed probably due to the fact he gets further. (op 33-1)
Mawatheeq(USA), a lightly raced dual winner at this trip on a sound surface, ran well to a point but did not last home on this softer ground. (tchd 18-1)
Jaser acts on soft ground and, with Moore an interesting booking, was well backed. However, he never figured from the lowest draw and his rider reported that he hung right throughout. Official explanation: jockey said colt hung right handed throughout (op 8-1 tchd 7-1)
Manassas(IRE) had won the Spring Mile on fast going but was a market drifter and clearly the ground had gone against him. (op 9-1)
Zaahid(IRE) was drawn in the middle but managed to find himself right on the outside of the field over two furlongs out. He never got to the leading group but appeared to be eased in the final furlong as though something was amiss. His rider reported he was unsuited by the ground. Official explanation: jockey said horse was unsuited by the soft ground (op 8-1 tchd 11-2)
European Dream(IRE)'s rider reported the gelding was never travelling. Official explanation: jockey said gelding was never travelling (op 40-1)
Cordell(IRE) Official explanation: jockey said colt stopped quickly

1353 DUBAI DUTY FREE STKS (REGISTERED AS THE FRED DARLING STAKES) (GROUP 3) (FILLIES) 7f (S)
3:10 (3:19) (Class 1) 3-Y-O
£36,900 (£13,988; £7,000; £3,490; £1,748; £877) **Stalls** Centre

Form RPR

321- **1** **Lahaleeb (IRE)**[182] 6818 3-9-0 108 DarryllHolland 5 111
(M R Channon) *mid-div: rdn and hdwy fr 2f out: wnt 3rd over 1f out: r.o u.p fnl f: swished tail: led nr fin* **6/1**[3]

252- **2** *hd* **Super Sleuth (IRE)**[168] 7144 3-9-0 97 LDettori 4 110
(B J Meehan) *lw: hld up in midfield: smooth hdwy 3f out: led wl over 1f out and wnt 2 l clr: hrd rdn fnl f: jst ct* **8/1**

430- **3** *3* **Danehill Destiny**[197] 6441 3-9-0 102 (t) TonyCulhane 10 102
(W J Haggas) *lw: led: rdn and hdd wl over 1f out: kpt on same pce* **12/1**

1- **4** *1* **Sariska**[168] 7141 3-9-0 86 JamieSpencer 14 105+
(M L W Bell) *s.s: hld up in last: hdwy and nt clr run over 1f out: swtchd rt and r.o: nrst fin* **9/2**[2]

10- **5** *3/4* **Lassarina (IRE)**[182] 6818 3-9-0 97 MichaelHills 6 98
(B W Hills) *dwlt: hld up towards rr: rdn and hdwy over 1f out: styd on* **12/1**

150- **6** *1/2* **Please Sing**[195] 6519 3-9-0 97 EdwardCreighton 17 96
(M R Channon) *lw: hld up in rr: hrd rdn and hdwy over 1f out: no further prog fnl f* **33/1**

313- **7** *6* **Yorksters Girl (IRE)**[175] 6982 3-9-0 97 PaulHanagan 15 80
(M G Quinlan) *lw: mid-div: hrd rdn 2f out: no imp whn n.m.r over 1f out* **25/1**

10-1 **8** *3 3/4* **Maoineach (USA)**[20] 1024 3-9-0 107 KJManning 12 70
(J S Bolger, Ire) *w'like: str: b: hld up in rr: hdwy and in tch whn n.m.r over 1f out: eased whn btn fnl f* **9/4**[1]

336- **9** *1 3/4* **Touching (IRE)**[197] 6439 3-9-0 92 RyanMoore 8 65
(R Hannon) *prom: hrd rdn 2f out: sn wknd* **25/1**

30-1 **10** *4* **Haakima (USA)**[24] 949 3-9-0 86 NCallan 13 54
(C E Brittain) *chsd ldrs tl drvn and wknd 2f out* **50/1**

210- **11** *1* **Infamous Angel**[197] 6441 3-9-0 103 JimmyFortune 16 52
(R Hannon) *mid-div tl wknd over 2f out* **16/1**

624- **12** *2 1/4* **Baileys Cacao (IRE)**[182] 6818 3-9-0 103 RichardHughes 1 46
(R Hannon) *prom tl edgd lft and wknd 2f out* **14/1**

241- **13** *1/2* **Calahonda**[154] 7334 3-9-0 87 PhilipRobinson 2 44
(P W D'Arcy) *prom tl hrd rdn and wknd 2f out* **33/1**

3- **14** *1 1/2* **Sharpened Edge**[211] 6072 3-9-0 SteveDrowne 3 40
(B Palling) *s.s: sn in midfield: in tch 3f out: edgd lft over 2f out: sn wknd* **100/1**

415- **15** *nk* **Nora Mae (IRE)**[175] 6982 3-9-0 93 GeorgeBaker 9 39
(S Kirk) *dwlt: sn chsng ldrs: wknd 1/2-way: sn bhd* **50/1**

026- **16** *shd* **Favourite Girl (IRE)**[175] 6972 3-9-0 104 JohnEgan 7 39
(T D Easterby) *mid-div tl hrd rdn and wknd 2f out* **33/1**

1m 27.87s (2.17) **Going Correction** +0.525s/f (Yiel) **16** Ran SP% **123.7**
Speed ratings (Par 105): **108,107,104,103,102 101,94,90,88,84 82,80,79,78,77 77**
toteswinger: 1&2 £10.80, 1&3 £19.40, 2&3 £27.30 CSF £50.39 TOTE £6.10: £2.70, £2.60, £4.10; EX 69.10 Trifecta £377.40 Part won. Pool: £510.02 - 0.10 winning units..
Owner M Al-Qatami & K M Al-Mudhaf **Bred** Tom Twomey **Trained** West Ilsley, Berks
■ Stewards' Enquiry : L Dettori two-day ban: used whip with excessive frequency (May 4,5)

FOCUS
One of the major 1000 Guineas trials, although Wince in 1999 was the last winner to go on to take the Classic. Mick Channon had saddled three winners of this in the preceding seven years and made it four in eight with a tough and genuine filly who looks sure to give an honest account at Newmarket, although she did not run quite to her Rockfel form.

NOTEBOOK
Lahaleeb(IRE) was unplaced in three Folkestone maidens last season before winning on her handicap debut over this course and distance off a mark of 72. Since then she has come on leaps and bounds and finished last season by beating the Cheveley Park runner-up Aspen Darlin in the Rockfel. Held up off the pace, she made good headway from over a furlong out and picked up under pressure to get her head in front close home. She may not be the biggest of fillies but she is apparently quite lazy and so expected to improve. She looks sure to give a good account of herself in the 1,000 Guineas, a race in which her trainer is overdue a change of luck. (op 9-2)
Super Sleuth(IRE) ◆ looked the winner when going clear but was just touched off, as she had been in a Listed race on her final start last season. Soft ground clearly suits the daughter of Selkirk, who remains a maiden but should have no trouble winning, and possibly in Pattern company. (op 12-1)
Danehill Destiny looked pretty useful on her first two starts last season but could not quite step up to Group company. However, suited by some cut in the ground, she made the running and only tired in the final furlong. She could be the sort to pick up a Listed race back at 6f, especially on a flat track. (op 25-1)
Sariska ◆ was the unlucky horse of the race. The winner of her only previous start on easy ground, she is bred to stay much further, missed the break, and was then blocked in her run and had to be switched. She stayed on nicely and will be seen to much better effect over further with the benefit of this run. The Musidora could be on the agenda next and, depending on how she does there, the Oaks might be the target. (op 7-2 tchd 5-1)
Lassarina(IRE) beat Lahaleeb here on good ground and was subsequently seventh to her in the Rockfel. She ran pretty close to that mark, which gives substance to this form. (tchd 11-1)
Please Sing, a stablemate of the winner and successful in the Cherry Hinton last year, bounced back to something like that form on ground she handles.
Maoineach(USA) was ponied to the start. Proven on soft ground and fit from her success in Leopardstown's 1000 Guineas trial, she seemed to have no excuse but did run disappointingly on the other occasion she raced away from home, so may not be the best of travellers. (op 11-4)
Baileys Cacao(IRE) Official explanation: jokcey said the filly stopped quickly

1354 BATHWICK TYRES GREENHAM STKS (GROUP 3) (C&G) 7f (S)
3:45 (3:52) (Class 1) 3-Y-O
£36,900 (£13,988; £7,000; £3,490; £1,748; £877) **Stalls** Centre

Form RPR

1 **Vocalised (USA)**[13] 1136 3-9-0 0 (t) KJManning 12 108+
(J S Bolger, Ire) *leggy: scope: stdd towards rr: stdy hdwy over 3f out to ld 2f out: shkn up over 1f out: sn in command: readily* **2/1**[1]

212- **2** *1* **Cityscape**[203] 6267 3-9-0 110 SteveDrowne 8 105+
(R Charlton) *lw: stdd in rr: hdwy over 2f out: hrd drvn and styd on fr over 1f out to chse wnr ins fnl f: kpt on but a readily hld* **10/3**[3]

0-03 **3** *1 1/2* **Icesolator (IRE)**[14] 1118 3-9-0 98 RichardHughes 7 101
(R Hannon) *chsd ldrs: chal and rdn 2f out: outpcd ins fnl f* **25/1**

100- **4** *shd* **Sri Putra**[175] 6973 3-9-0 105 PhilipRobinson 10 101
(M A Jarvis) *bit bkwd: chsd ldrs: drvn to chal over 2f out: sn one pce but kpt on ins fnl f* **8/1**

124- **5** *1/2* **Shaweel**[182] 6815 3-9-0 118 LDettori 6 99
(Saeed Bin Suroor) *lw: chsd ldrs: drvn to chal 2 out: wknd ins fnl f* **11/4**[2]

130- **6** *4* **Nasri**[175] 6979 3-9-0 100 JamieSpencer 2 89
(B J Meehan) *led tl hdd 2f out: wknd qckly* **12/1**

10- **7** *2* **Folsomprisonblues (IRE)**[175] 6979 3-9-0 79 (t) MartinDwyer 4 83
(E J O'Neill) *hld up towards rr: hdwy to chse ldrs over 2f out: hrd rdn and wknd over 1f out* **40/1**

110- **8** *6* **War Native (IRE)**[217] 5889 3-9-0 96 RyanMoore 11 67
(J Noseda) *hld up towards rr: sme hdwy over 2f out: nvr gng pce to rch ldrs and sn wknd* **25/1**

1m 27.81s (2.11) **Going Correction** +0.525s/f (Yiel) **8** Ran SP% **112.0**
Speed ratings (Par 108): **108,106,105,105,104 99,97,90**
totewinger: 1&2 £2.30, 1&3 £7.50, 2&3 £10.10 CSF £8.41 TOTE £2.90: £1.40, £1.70, £2.60; EX 9.00 Trifecta £64.40 Pool: £531.34 - 6.10 winning units..
Owner Mrs J S Bolger **Bred** Hill 'N' Dale Farm & Edward Mc **Trained** Coolcullen, Co Carlow

FOCUS
Not a race that has a lot of significance so far as the 2000 Guineas is concerned these days - the last horse to win both races was Wollow in 1976 - and this running was weakened by the withdrawal of four runners, notable the Dewhurst second and third Lord Shanakill and Finjaan. The bare form looks pretty ordinary for the grade.

NOTEBOOK
Vocalised(USA) was held up in the smaller group that was towards the stands' rail throughout. He was in front with around two furlongs to go, and once he was shaken up to go and win his race he was firmly in command. The time was nothing special, and with the thoroughly exposed Icesolator relatively close up in third, the form can not be rated that highly. He also enjoyed a fitness advantage over many of these, having won a Listed race over this trip this year, but he is quietly progressive and Jim Bolger feels he will be better on better ground. The stable has Intense Focus for the 2000 Guineas, so he will go to Longchamp for the French equivalent. (op 5-2)
Cityscape improved with every race at two and represented the Royal Lodge form, having finished second there to the currently sidelined Jukebox Jury. He found 7f on the sharp side here and was still in rear and coming under strong pressure going into the last two furlongs, but he stuck to his task and came home a clear second, beaten only by a race-fit rival. Connections were delighted with him and hope to run him either at Newmarket or Longchamp, with Newmarket favoured. (op 3-1 tchd 5-2)
Icesolator(IRE)'s three wins at two were all at 5f, the last of them nearly a year ago. Proven on soft ground and fit after two runs on the all-weather, he returned to his best but may not be easy to place, especially if the ground dries out. (tchd 20-1)
Sri Putra was colty and on his toes in the preliminaries, and he looked as if he would be all the better for the race. A bit disappointing after winning his first two last year, he shaped much better here and can improve again when upped to 1m. However, he is unlikely to be running in the Guineas. (tchd 9-1)

Shaweel, making his debut for Godolphin, was the only representative of the Dewhurst form. Whereas Delegator gave it a boost in midweek, he hardly advertised it in finishing only fifth here, even though he was only narrowly beaten for third. Godolphin's first runner in a recognised Guineas trial, he stood out on juvenile form with a BHA rating of 118, which put him 8lb clear of Cityscape, but he weakened after having had his chance going into the last two furlongs. The ground should not have been a problem, and though he was expected to be rusty he ought to have run better. (op 3-1 tchd 7-2)

Nasri was disappointing in view of how well his stable has been going. He made the running but was beaten quickly two furlongs out. (op 9-1)

Folsomprisonblues(IRE) was well beaten in a Group 3 after a winning debut last year, but an Irish 2000 Guineas entry suggests he is regarded much better than his official mark of 79. Tongue tied for the first time here, he ran all right up to a point and would be of interest if connections opted to take advantage of his handicap mark. (op 50-1)

War Native(IRE) did not show much but both disappointments have been on softish ground and he may need it on top. (op 16-1)

1355 DUBAI INTERNATIONAL AIRPORT MAIDEN STKS (DIV II) 1m (S)
4:15 (4:22) (Class 4) 3-Y-O **£4,857** (£1,445; £722; £360) **Stalls** Centre

Form				RPR
	1		**Bridge Of Gold (USA)** 3-9-3 0 ... PaulHanagan 1 (M A Magnusson) *trckd ldrs: rdn to ld 1f out: drvn out ins fnl f* **9/1**	90+
	2	*1 3/4*	**Clockmaker (IRE)** 3-9-3 0 ... JimmyFortune 8 (J H M Gosden) *s.i.s: hld up in rr: hdwy and nt clr run 2f out: swtchd lft over 1f out and str run ins fnl f: kpt on wl but no imp on wnr* **7/2**[2]	86+
0-	**3**	*2 1/4*	**Merdaam**[229] 5579 3-9-3 0 ... RHills 3 (J L Dunlop) *in rr tl hdwy over 2f out: styd on fnl f but nt pce of ldng duo* **16/1**	81
33-	**4**	*2 1/2*	**Arabian Flame (IRE)**[260] 4600 3-9-3 0 ... DarryllHolland 9 (M R Channon) *chsd ldrs: hrd drvn over 2f out: no imp: wknd fnl f* **7/2**[2]	75
33-	**5**	*1*	**Bennelong**[188] 6677 3-9-3 0 ... SebSanders 2 (R M Beckett) *chsd ldrs: drvn to ld wl ins fnl 2f: hdd 1f out: wknd fnl f* **10/3**[1]	72
	6	*1 1/2*	**Present Alchemy** 3-9-3 0 ... TravisBlock 14 (H Morrison) *t.k.h: sn led: rdn 3f out: hdd wl ins fnl 2f: wknd fnl f* **16/1**	69
	7	*shd*	**Do The Strand (IRE)** 3-9-3 0 ... MichaelHills 13 (B W Hills) *in rr: pushed along over 3f out: styd on fr over 1f out: nvr in contention* **6/1**[3]	69+
65-	**8**	*4 1/2*	**Chic Shanique (USA)**[140] 7498 3-8-12 0 ... RichardKingscote 6 (Tom Dascombe) *chsd ldrs: rdn over 2f out: sn wknd* **22/1**	53
	9	*1/2*	**Quinsman** 3-9-3 0 ... LPKeniry 7 (J S Moore) *pressed ldrs: rdn over 2f out: sn btn* **40/1**	57
0	**10**	*8*	**Secret Hero**[24] 951 3-9-3 0 ... RichardHughes 11 (R Hannon) *chsd ldrs over 5f* **12/1**	39
0-	**11**	*1 1/2*	**Princess Soraya**[194] 6531 3-8-12 0 ... TonyCulhane 4 (R Dickin) *chsd ldrs over 5f* **100/1**	30
0-	**12**	*3 1/2*	**Ghaayer**[337] 2150 3-9-3 0 ... PatDobbs 5 (M P Tregoning) *towards rr most of way* **20/1**	27

1m 44.75s (5.05) **Going Correction** +0.525s/f (Yiel) **12** Ran SP% **123.8**
Speed ratings (Par 100): **95,93,91,88,87 86,85,81,80,72 71,67**
toteswinger: 1&2 £4.40, 1&3 £11.10, 2&3 £10.20 CSF £41.11 TOTE £9.70: £2.50, £1.80, £4.20; EX 43.20.

Owner Eastwind Racing Ltd and Martha Trussell **Bred** Hopewell Investments LLC **Trained** Upper Lambourn, Berks

■ Stewards' Enquiry : Jimmy Fortune caution: careless riding

FOCUS
The second division of this maiden was the slowest of the three races over the trip on the day, being run 1.77secs slower than the first leg. It was quite an interesting race though, with several nice newcomers, and two of them dominated the finish. The fourth and fifth are rated about 10lb below their juvenile marks but better can be expected from the first two.

1356 FINCH FAMILY H'CAP 2m
4:50 (4:51) (Class 4) (0-85,80) 4-Y-O+ **£6,476** (£1,927; £963; £481) **Stalls** Low

Form				RPR
02-0	**1**		**Mighty Moon**[7] 1215 6-9-7 **76** ... PaulHanagan 2 (R A Fahey) *trckd ldrs: slt ld 3f out: hrd rdn whn strly chal thrght fnl f: hld on gamely* **13/2**[3]	85
644-	**2**	*nse*	**Swingkeel (IRE)**[200] 6361 4-9-5 **78** ... JimmyFortune 12 (J L Dunlop) *hld up in rr: stdy hdwy over 3f out: hrd rdn to chal thrght fnl f: jst failed* **12/1**	87
020-	**3**	*1*	**Cleaver**[176] 6948 8-9-9 **78** ... RichardHughes 4 (Lady Herries) *stdd s: hld up in rr: stdy hdwy on ins over 2f out: shkn up to chse ldrs over 1f out: fnd no ex ins fnl f* **14/1**	86
100-	**4**	*9*	**Winged D'Argent (IRE)**[56] 5718 8-9-11 **80** ... (b) NCallan 1 (B J Llewellyn) *prom early: in rr and rdn 6f out: styd on to chse ldrs 3f out: wknd over 1f out* **14/1**	77
043/	**5**	*nk*	**Squadron**[61] 6131 5-9-4 **73** ... RyanMoore 3 (A King) *in rr: rdn along fr 5f out: mod prog fnl 2f* **15/8**[1]	70
113-	**6**	*2 3/4*	**Kiribati King (IRE)**[199] 6390 4-9-3 **76** ... TonyCulhane 11 (M R Channon) *in tch: chsd ldrs 6f out: drvn to chal over 3f out: wknd ins fnl 2f* **4/1**[2]	69+
0-14	**7**	*10*	**Right Option (IRE)**[59] 591 5-9-9 **78** ... LPKeniry 13 (J L Flint) *chsd ldrs: rdn 3f out: wknd over 2f out* **25/1**	59
003-	**8**	*nk*	**Ned Ludd (IRE)**[50] 7110 6-9-2 **71** ... DarryllHolland 10 (J G Portman) *in tch: rdn 5f out: nvr in contention* **12/1**	52
1613	**9**	*4*	**Wabbraan (USA)**[7] 1215 4-8-10 **74** ... AmyBaker(5) 8 (M Hill) *chsd ldr: rdn over 3f out: wknd qckly over 2f out* **14/1**	50
40-6	**10**	*8*	**Criterion**[22] 459 4-9-4 **77** ... JamieSpencer 7 (Ian Williams) *in rr tl hdwy on outside press ldrs 6f out: rdn and upsides over 3f out: sn btn* **14/1**	44
3/0-	**11**	*2 3/4*	**Cape Greko**[134] 6983 7-9-0 **69** ... MichaelHills 5 (B G Powell) *led: hdd 3f out: sn wknd* **40/1**	32
231-	**12**	*1 1/4*	**Maadraa (IRE)**[386] 1059 4-9-5 **78** ... SteveDrowne 9 (B J Llewellyn) *in tch: rdn and effrt 5f out: sn wknd* **20/1**	40

3m 42.41s (10.41) **Going Correction** +0.525s/f (Yiel)
WFA 4 from 5yo+ 4lb **12** Ran SP% **121.2**
Speed ratings (Par 105): **107,106,106,101,101 100,95,95,93,89 87,87**
toteswinger: 1&2 £6.90, 1&3 £25.20, 2&3 £11.50 CSF £82.00 CT £1070.46 TOTE £8.10: £2.70, £3.30, £3.90; EX 76.40.

Owner Enda Hunston **Bred** Angmering Park Stud **Trained** Musley Bank, N Yorks

FOCUS
An ordinary staying handicap, but three came clear in the closing stages. the winner is rated back to near his best with the runner-up still progressive and the third to his best.

1357 DUBAI DUTY FREE MILLENNIUM MILLIONAIRE H'CAP 1m 2f 6y
5:20 (5:21) (Class 4) (0-85,85) 4-Y-O+ **£5,180** (£1,541; £770; £384) **Stalls** Low

Form				RPR
030-	**1**		**Invasian (IRE)**[118] 7753 8-8-4 **76** ... Louis-PhilippeBeuzelin(5) 16 (P W D'Arcy) *led: styd alone and racd far side: drvn out fnl f* **20/1**	86
51	**2**	*hd*	**Mildoura (FR)**[18] 1049 4-8-11 **78** ... LPKeniry 13 (Mrs L J Mongan) *chsd ldrs: led main gp stands' side over 4f out: hrd rdn and edgd lft over 1f out: kpt on wl but nt rch lone wnr on far side* **20/1**	88
111-	**3**	*1 1/4*	**Moves Goodenough**[36] 6899 6-8-13 **80** ... (b) PatDobbs 1 (Andrew Turnell) *in tch: hdwy fr 3f out: styd on fnl f but nvr gng pce to chal* **12/1**	87
51/	**4**	*1/2*	**Foolin Myself**[533] 6618 4-9-4 **85** ... JamieSpencer 8 (M L W Bell) *in rr: hdwy to chse ldrs in main gp 3f out: sn rdn: kpt on same pce ins fnl f* **5/2**[1]	91+
66-5	**5**	*3 1/2*	**Trans Siberian**[12] 1149 5-9-3 **84** ... RyanMoore 7 (P F I Cole) *in rr: hdwy over 3f out: drvn to chse ldrs over 2f out: wknd ins fnl f* **9/2**[2]	83
611-	**6**	*nse*	**Liberally (IRE)**[233] 5428 4-8-11 **78** ... MartinDwyer 2 (B J Meehan) *chsd ldrs: rdn to chal over 3f out: wknd fnl f* **9/1**	77
6225	**7**	*6*	**Kidlat**[16] 1088 4-8-11 **78** ... (t) MichaelHills 3 (B G Powell) *chsd ldrs: drvn to chal 3 out: wkng whn hmpd over 1f out* **20/1**	65
312-	**8**	*1 3/4*	**Black Rain**[175] 6991 4-8-11 **78** ... JimmyFortune 10 (M Wigham) *in rr: hdwy to chse ldrs 3f out: wknd ins fnl 2f* **17/2**	61
401-	**9**	*1 1/4*	**Angel Rock (IRE)**[171] 7083 4-9-2 **83** ... DarryllHolland 6 (M Botti) *chsd ldrs: drvn to chal over 3f out: wknd 2f out* **5/1**[3]	64
1-05	**10**	*2*	**Princess Flame (GER)**[18] 1049 7-8-0 **72** ... AmyBaker(5) 11 (B G Powell) *in tch: styd chsng wnr towards far side but nvr on terms: no ch fnl 3f* **20/1**	49
30-0	**11**	*shd*	**Danetime Panther (IRE)**[12] 1149 5-8-4 **71** ... SimonWhitworth 9 (Ian Williams) *in tch 7f: wknd* **25/1**	48
203-	**12**	*3 1/4*	**Holden Eagle**[176] 6950 4-8-8 **75** ... SteveDrowne 14 (A G Newcombe) *a towards rr* **20/1**	45
146-	**13**	*shd*	**Martyr**[304] 3134 4-9-2 **83** ... RichardHughes 15 (R Hannon) *in rr: hdwy to chse ldrs over 5f out: nvr gng pce to chal and wknd ins fnl 3f* **14/1**	53

2m 13.91s (5.11) **Going Correction** +0.525s/f (Yiel) **13** Ran SP% **126.0**
Speed ratings (Par 105): **100,99,98,98,95 95,90,89,88,86 86,84,84**
toteswinger: 1&2 £41.80, 1&3 £49.10, 2&3 £30.20 CSF £356.67 CT £4961.62 TOTE £23.90: £7.00, £6.70, £2.80; EX 670.20 Place 6: £496.65, Place 5: £317.47..

Owner Paul D'Arcy **Bred** Dr Karen Monica Sanderson **Trained** Newmarket, Suffolk

FOCUS
This closing handicap featured mainly exposed types, and very few got into it as Invasion made all despite being drawn on the wide outside. The winner was well handicapped and the runner-up improved on her Folkestone form and seems quite progressive.
T/Jkpt: Not won. T/Plt: £771.30 to a £1 stake. Pool: £127,961.95. 121.10 winning tickets. T/Qpdt: £121.80 to a £1 stake. Pool: £6,419.28. 39.00 winning tickets. ST

[1188] NOTTINGHAM (L-H)
Saturday, April 18

OFFICIAL GOING: Good to firm (good in places; 8.1)
Wind: Light behind Weather: Cloudy with sunny spells

1358 RACING UK ON CHANNEL 432 MAIDEN STKS 5f 13y
5:00 (5:03) (Class 5) 2-Y-O **£2,590** (£770; £385; £192) **Stalls** High

Form				RPR
0	**1**		**Roi De Vitesse (IRE)**[18] 1044 2-9-0 0 ... JamesMillman(3) 2 (B R Millman) *chsd ldrs: outpcd 1/2-way: rallied over 1f out: r.o to ld post* **25/1**	77+
	2	*nk*	**Secret Millionaire (IRE)** 2-9-0 0 ... RussellKennemore(3) 12 (Patrick Morris) *sn led: rdn over 1f out: edgd lft fnl f: hdd post* **50/1**	76
	3	*1*	**King's Approach (IRE)** 2-9-3 0 ... DO'Donohoe 6 (R Hannon) *s.i.s: sn chsng ldrs: styd on same pce ins fnl f* **9/1**	72
	4	*2 1/2*	**Military Call** 2-9-3 0 ... RichardMullen 1 (E S McMahon) *prom: outpcd over 3f out: rallied over 1f out: no ex ins fnl f* **8/1**[3]	63+
5	**5**	*3 1/4*	**Ignatieff (IRE)**[14] 1126 2-9-3 0 ... MickyFenton 11 (Mrs L Stubbs) *sn chsng ldrs: rdn over 1f out: wknd fnl f* **14/1**	50
3	**6**	*1*	**Gillburg (USA)**[10] 1188 2-9-3 0 ... FrancisNorton 9 (K A Ryan) *chsd ldrs: rdn 1/2-way: wknd over 1f out: hung lft fnl f* **8/11**[1]	46
	7	*1 1/4*	**Kings Aphrodite** 2-9-0 0 ... DavidProbert(3) 8 (Miss Gay Kelleway) *chsd ldrs tl rdn and wknd over 1f out* **20/1**	42
5	**8**	*2 1/4*	**Absher (IRE)**[2] 1312 2-9-0 0 ... KellyHarrison(3) 3 (Patrick Morris) *sn outpcd* **100/1**	33
	9	*1*	**Amoureuse** 2-8-12 0 ... PatrickMathers 10 (I W McInnes) *s.s: outpcd* **100/1**	24
	10	*3 1/4*	**Flaneur** 2-9-3 0 ... DuranFentiman 5 (T D Easterby) *s.i.s and edgd lft s: outpcd* **66/1**	17
	11	*nk*	**Ginger Ted (IRE)** 2-9-3 0 ... PaulEddery 7 (R C Guest) *s.s: outpcd* **100/1**	16
	12	*4*	**Duke Of Rainford** 2-9-3 0 ... StephenDonohoe 4 (Ian Williams) *dwlt and hmpd s: outpcd* **11/2**[2]	—

60.38 secs (-0.62) **Going Correction** -0.425s/f (Firm) **12** Ran SP% **116.1**
Speed ratings (Par 92): **95,94,92,88,83 82,80,76,74,69 69,62**
toteswinger: 1&2 £35.90, 1&3 £23.20, 2&3 £11.40. CSF £851.76 TOTE £36.80: £4.50, £4.20, £1.90; EX 827.80.

Owner Mustajed Partnership **Bred** Tally-Ho Stud **Trained** Kentisbeare, Devon

FOCUS
The emphasis was on speed, with nothing coming from too far back, though the winner made up some ground to get there on the line. The form is rated around time compared with the later handicaps.

NOTEBOOK
Roi De Vitesse(IRE) had taken a bit too long to get going on his debut but at this second attempt the turbo kicked in just in time. He is by the classy sprinter Chineur, but his dam won over 1m as a juvenile, so races over 6f cannot come soon enough for him. (op 16-1)

Secret Millionaire(IRE) ◆ made £56,000 at the breeze-ups, and the money looks reasonably well spent. A son of the top-class sprinter Kyllachy and useful 6f winner Mithl Al Hawa, he has speed to burn, and should put it to good use in the coming months, with a similar event there for the taking. (tchd 40-1)

King's Approach(IRE), a 40,000euros yearling, made a solid debut, if never quite looking likely to win. By Fasliyev out of a dam who won twice at 7f, he will stay at least 6f before long and should win races. (op 11-2)
Military Call is a £42,000 half-brother to several sprint winners and his sire Royal Applause was a top speedster himself. With his dam also having won over 6f, he was not ideally drawn here but ran well enough to suggest that there is much better to come (tchd 15-2 and 10-1)
Ignatieff(IRE) had been beaten a fair way on his debut and, though improving a bit for that experience, looks more of a nursery type in due course. Official explanation: jockey said gelding lost its action in the latter stages (tchd 12-1)
Gillburg(USA) showed early speed but was undoubtedly disappointing in the end if the market is any guide. However, time may show that those in front of him have plenty to offer. (op Evens)

1359 BOOK YOUR HOSPITALITY @ NOTTINGHAM RACECOURSE FILLIES' H'CAP 5f 13y

5:30 (5:31) (Class 5) (0-70,70) 3-Y-O £2,590 (£770; £385; £192) Stalls High

Form RPR

6-40 **1** **Amosite**[9] [1196] 3-8-13 **65**....(v) ShaneKelly 4 71
(J R Jenkins) *mde virtually all: edgd rt 1/2-way: rdn over 1f out: styd on u.p* **16/1**

-004 **2** *1 ½* **Imaginary Diva**[4] [1271] 3-8-13 **65**.... LukeMorris 8 66
(G G Margarson) *hld up in tch: rdn: nt clr run and swtchd rt over 1f out: r.o: nt rch wnr* **10/1**[3]

045- **3** *½* **Piste**[177] [6932] 3-9-0 **66**.... TPQueally 13 65
(B J Meehan) *chsd wnr: hmpd 1/2-way: rdn and edgd lft over 1f out: unable qck wl ins fnl f* **9/2**[1]

-243 **4** *¾* **Pinball (IRE)**[5] [1247] 3-8-2 **57**.... KellyHarrison(3) 12 53
(Patrick Morris) *s.s: hld up: hdwy 2f out: sn rdn: no ex ins fnl f* **9/2**[1]

33-4 **5** *shd* **Today's The Day**[11] [1173] 3-9-2 **68**....(b) RichardMullen 2 64+
(M A Jarvis) *hmpd s: sn outpcd: r.o ins fnl f: nrst fin* **6/1**[2]

23-3 **6** *½* **Keep Dancing (IRE)**[16] [1077] 3-9-1 **70**.... DavidProbert(3) 9 64
(A M Balding) *chsd ldrs: rdn over 1f out: no ex ins fnl f* **9/2**[1]

0004 **7** *½* **Thumberlina**[10] [1190] 3-8-4 **56** oh8.... FrancisNorton 1 48
(Mrs C A Dunnett) *wnt lft s: sn in mid-div: hdwy 2f out: rdn over 1f out: no ex ins fnl f* **25/1**

4-P0 **8** *2* **Oceanic Dancer (IRE)**[22] [982] 3-8-4 **56** oh1.... FrankieMcDonald 7 41
(Patrick Morris) *chsd ldrs: rdn 1/2-way: wknd ins fnl f* **40/1**

050 **9** *½* **Baby Queen (IRE)**[11] [1173] 3-8-4 **56** oh1.... CatherineGannon 5 39
(B P J Baugh) *mid-div: sn pushed along: hdwy 1/2-way: wknd ins fnl f* **33/1**

340- **10** *4* **Eden Park**[267] [4384] 3-8-9 **61**.... DaleGibson 11 30
(M Dods) *mid-div: sn pushed along: wknd 1/2-way* **20/1**

3-11 **11** *4 ½* **Lady Vivien**[78] [350] 3-9-3 **69**.... MickyFenton 6 45+
(D H Brown) *hung lft thrght: outpcd: hdwy whn hmpd 2f out: sn wknd and eased* **6/1**[2]

10-6 **12** *9* **August Days (IRE)**[15] [1095] 3-8-5 **57**.... DO'Donohoe 3 —
(J Pearce) *mid-div: sn pushed along: lost pl 3f out: sn bhd* **33/1**

59.94 secs (-1.06) **Going Correction** -0.425s/f (Firm) **12** Ran SP% **115.0**
Speed ratings (Par 95): **99,96,95,94,94 93,92,89,88,82 75,60**
toteswinger: 1&2 £13.80, 1&3 £17.70, 2&3 £14.70. CSF £151.26 CT £856.39 TOTE £16.10: £4.30, £3.70, £2.40; EX 246.50.
Owner Rowley **Bred** Richard Kent **Trained** Royston, Herts
■ Stewards' Enquiry : Shane Kelly caution: careless riding

FOCUS
A good tactical ride by Kelly helped to win this competitive if moderate contest. The form looks sound if ordinary.
Keep Dancing(IRE) Official explanation: jockey said the filly was unsuited by the good to firm (good in places) ground
Thumberlina Official explanation: jockey said the filly hung right
Lady Vivien Official explanation: jockey said filly did not handle the track

1360 RACING UK LIVE IN YOUR LIVINGROOM H'CAP 5f 13y

6:00 (6:00) (Class 6) (0-65,65) 4-Y-O+ £2,047 (£604; £302) Stalls High

Form RPR

022- **1** **Raccoon (IRE)**[196] [6486] 9-9-3 **64**.... PJMcDonald 4 74
(Mrs R A Carr) *racd far side: led that gp: overall ldr 2f out: styd on u.p* **8/1**[3]

5-36 **2** *¾* **Liberty Ship**[30] [884] 4-8-13 **60**....(tp) PatCosgrave 5 67
(J D Bethell) *racd far side: chsd wnr: hrd rdn and ev ch fr over 1f out: styd on: 2nd of 7 in gp: r.o* **13/2**[2]

3050 **3** *nk* **Ronnie Howe**[46] [746] 5-8-11 **58**....(bt) FrancisNorton 15 64+
(S R Bowring) *racd stands' side: chsd ldr tl led that gp 2f out: rdn and hung lft fr over 1f out: styd on: 1st of 8 in gp* **11/1**

011- **4** *shd* **Todber**[202] [6308] 4-9-4 **65**....(v) RichardMullen 3 71+
(M P Tregoning) *racd far side: s.i.s: hld up: hdwy 2f out: rdn over 1f out: r.o: 3rd of 7 in gp* **10/1**

0411 **5** *¾* **Mr Skipiton (IRE)**[17] [1076] 4-8-10 **57**.... StephenCarson 6 60
(B J McMath) *racd far side: chsd ldrs: rdn over 1f out: styd on: 4th of 7 in gp* **5/1**[1]

410- **6** *1* **Top Bid**[138] [7517] 5-8-13 **60**....(b) DuranFentiman 11 60
(T D Easterby) *racd stands' side: prom: rdn to chsd ldr that side over 1f out: styd on same pce fnl f: 2nd of 8 in gp* **25/1**

0304 **7** *½* **Ask Jenny (IRE)**[5] [1241] 7-8-10 **57**.... TPQueally 9 55
(Patrick Morris) *racd stands' side: hld up: hdwy 1/2-way: rdn over 1f out: styd on same pce ins fnl f: 3rd of 8 in gp* **16/1**

500- **8** *nk* **Compton Rose**[187] [6706] 4-9-1 **62**.... FrankieMcDonald 16 59
(H Candy) *racd stands' side: chsd ldrs: rdn over 1f out: styd on same pce: 4th of 8 in gp* **12/1**

0-00 **9** *nk* **Maggie Kate**[38] [799] 4-8-11 **58**....(p) RobertHavlin 2 54
(R Ingram) *racd far side: prom: rdn over 1f out: no ex ins fnl f: 5th of 7 in gp* **22/1**

-063 **10** *¾* **Orpen's Art (IRE)**[19] [1038] 4-8-6 **60**.... HollyHall(7) 12 53
(S A Callaghan) *racd stands' side: s.i.s: hld up: hdwy over 1f out: nt trble ldrs: 5th of 8 in gp* **20/1**

12-0 **11** *1 ¾* **Little Eden (IRE)**[22] [976] 4-8-4 **56**.... DeanHeslop(5) 1 43
(T D Barron) *racd far side: sn outpcd: 6th of 7 in gp* **12/1**

0-00 **12** *3 ¼* **Richardthesecond (IRE)**[14] [1134] 4-8-10 **57**.... TGMcLaughlin 8 32
(W M Brisbourne) *racd far side: in tch: lost pl 1/2-way: wkng whn edgd rt over 1f out: last of 7 in gp* **33/1**

0324 **13** *1 ¼* **Guto**[30] [884] 6-8-11 **61**.... KellyHarrison(3) 10 31
(W J H Ratcliffe) *racd stands' side: chsd ldrs: lost pl 3f out: n.d after: 6th of 8 in gp* **9/1**

10-6 **14** *nk* **Whinhill House**[15] [1104] 9-8-9 **63**....(v) JosephineBruning(7) 14 32
(T T Clement) *racd stands' side: chsd ldrs: rdn 1/2-way: wknd over 1f out: 7th of 8 in gp* **22/1**

0/50 **15** *2 ¼* **Martingrange Boy (IRE)**[24] [956] 4-9-1 **62**....(t) MickyFenton 17 23
(J Balding) *racd stands' side: overall ldr 3f: sn rdn and wknd: last of 8 in gp* **10/1**

59.44 secs (-1.56) **Going Correction** -0.425s/f (Firm) **15** Ran SP% **119.1**
Speed ratings (Par 101): **103,101,101,101,99 98,97,97,96,95 92,87,85,84,81**
toteswinger: 1&2 £10.60, 1&3 £26.10, 2&3 £22.70. CSF £53.46 CT £594.47 TOTE £5.90: £2.50, £2.10, £5.10; EX 66.80.
Owner P D Savill **Bred** P D Savill **Trained** Huby, N Yorks

FOCUS
They split into two main groups on opposite sides of the course, with horses on the far side filling the first two places, but there was no decisive advantage. The winner looks the best guide to the form.
Martingrange Boy(IRE) Official explanation: jockey said the gelding did not handle the track

1361 NOTTINGHAMRACECOURSE.CO.UK H'CAP 1m 75y

6:35 (6:36) (Class 6) (0-65,69) 3-Y-O £2,047 (£604; £302) Stalls Low

Form RPR

0-01 **1** **Cornish Castle (USA)**[10] [1193] 3-9-8 **69**.... PJMcDonald 1 76+
(T D Walford) *hld up in tch: nt clr run and swtchd rt over 1f out: r.o u.p to ld post* **3/1**[1]

252- **2** *nk* **Victorian Tycoon (IRE)**[190] [6632] 3-9-2 **63**.... FrancisNorton 4 68
(E J O'Neill) *led: rdn and hdd over 1f out: rallied to ld 1f out: hdd post* **5/1**[2]

-424 **3** *1 ¼* **Edgeworth (IRE)**[10] [1176] 3-9-4 **65**.... GeorgeBaker 3 69+
(B G Powell) *hld up in tch: nt clr run over 1f out: sn rdn and swtchd lft: r.o* **8/1**

060 **4** *nk* **Garter Knight**[31] [869] 3-9-2 **63**.... TPQueally 16 64+
(M L W Bell) *hld up: hdwy over 2f out: led over 1f out: sn edgd rt and hdd: styng on same pce whn n.m.r nr fin* **12/1**

000- **5** *1 ¾* **Minder**[206] [6207] 3-9-2 **63**.... PatCosgrave 8 60
(J G Portman) *s.s: hld up: rdn 1/2-way: r.o ins fnl f: nt trble ldrs* **25/1**

263- **6** *hd* **West Leake (IRE)**[143] [7451] 3-8-11 **61**.... PatrickHills(3) 12 58
(B W Hills) *trckd ldrs: plld hrd: rdn over 1f out: styd on same pce ins fnl f* **7/1**[3]

051- **7** *nk* **Noble Dictator**[141] [7467] 3-9-3 **64**.... ShaneKelly 13 60
(E F Vaughan) *hld up: rdn and hung lft over 1f out: r.o ins fnl f: nrst fin* **17/2**

4320 **8** *1* **Kingaroo (IRE)**[12] [1155] 3-9-2 **63**.... FrankieMcDonald 6 57
(Garry Moss) *hld up: hdwy over 3f out: nt clr run over 1f out: no imp fnl f* **18/1**

00-3 **9** *½* **Order Order**[29] [900] 3-9-2 **63**.... DO'Donohoe 9 55
(H J L Dunlop) *s.i.s: hld up: hdwy and hung lft over 1f out: no ex ins fnl f* **16/1**

006- **10** *1 ½* **Ay Tay Tate (IRE)**[194] [6524] 3-9-3 **64**.... PatrickMathers 14 53
(I W McInnes) *trckd ldrs: racd keenly: rdn over 2f out: styd on same pce appr fnl f* **16/1**

00-0 **11** *2* **Best Bidder (USA)**[36] [826] 3-9-1 **65**.... RussellKennemore(3) 7 49
(Patrick Morris) *s.i.s: hld up: n.d* **40/1**

640- **12** *nk* **Jewelled Reef (IRE)**[204] [6240] 3-9-4 **65**.... StephenCarson 17 49
(Eve Johnson Houghton) *prom: lost pl over 4f out: hdwy over 2f out: sn rdn and edgd lft: wknd fnl f* **28/1**

4460 **13** *2 ¼* **Harty Boy (USA)**[12] [1155] 3-9-1 **62**....(v[1]) MickyFenton 2 40
(Mrs S Leech) *trckd ldr: plld hrd: rdn over 2f out: wknd over 1f out* **25/1**

0-30 **14** *6* **Derringbay (IRE)**[66] [506] 3-9-1 **62**.... SaleemGolam 11 27
(M H Tompkins) *prom: rdn over 2f out: wknd over 1f out* **40/1**

330 **15** *3 ½* **L'Arco Baleno (IRE)**[24] [951] 3-8-7 **61**.... HollyHall(7) 15 18
(S A Callaghan) *s.s: hld up: a bhd* **22/1**

1m 46.0s (-3.60) **Going Correction** -0.425s/f (Firm) **15** Ran SP% **120.9**
Speed ratings (Par 96): **101,100,99,99,97 97,96,95,95,93 91,91,89,83,79**
toteswinger: 1&2 £6.50, 1&3 £7.10, 2&3 £6.80. CSF £15.10 CT £102.45 TOTE £3.80: £1.40, £2.40, £2.80; EX 17.90.
Owner Stephen Woodall **Bred** Juddmonte Farms Inc **Trained** Sheriff Hutton, N Yorks
■ Stewards' Enquiry : P J McDonald three-day ban: careless riding (May 4-6)

FOCUS
With some relatively unexposed types on display, there were some potential improvers on show but the pace was ordinary and it was hard to come from too far behind. The winner built on his winning return over course and distance but the form looks a bit messy.
Garter Knight Official explanation: jockey said gelding hung right

1362 PADDOCKS CONFERENCE CENTRE AT NOTTINGHAM RACECOURSE MEDIAN AUCTION MAIDEN STKS 1m 2f 50y

7:10 (7:12) (Class 6) 3-Y-O £2,047 (£604; £302) Stalls Low

Form RPR

0- **1** **At A Great Rate (USA)**[168] [7141] 3-8-12 0.... TPQueally 6 59+
(H R A Cecil) *led 1f: chsd ldr tl led over 1f out: rdn out* **11/4**[2]

60-2 **2** *1* **Mt Kintyre (IRE)**[11] [1168] 3-9-3 82.... SaleemGolam 1 62+
(M H Tompkins) *trckd ldrs: rdn over 2f out: swtchd rt over 1f out: sn chsng wnr: hrd rdn and hung lft ins fnl f: no imp* **4/6**[1]

53-3 **3** *3 ½* **Bagber**[25] [944] 3-9-3 76.... SebSanders 4 55+
(H J L Dunlop) *chsd ldrs: rdn over 2f out: styd on same pce appr fnl f* **6/1**[3]

46 **4** *1 ¼* **Rossatron**[29] [902] 3-9-3 0.... JerryO'Dwyer 8 53
(T T Clement) *led after 1f: rdn over 2f out: hdd over 1f out: no ex fnl f* **66/1**

0- **5** *½* **Tropical Bachelor (IRE)**[122] [7709] 3-9-3 0.... FrancisNorton 7 52+
(T J Pitt) *hld up in tch: lost pl 5f out: styd on and hung lft fnl 2f* **33/1**

6 *2 ¾* **Emeralda** 3-8-12 0.... PaulEddery 3 42
(Pat Eddery) *hld up: hdwy over 4f out: sn rdn: wknd wl over 2f out* **18/1**

7 *11* **Kendalewood** 3-9-3 0.... PJMcDonald 9 26
(T D Walford) *hld up: a in rr: bhd fnl 4f* **25/1**

0-0 **8** *2* **Speak Freely**[27] [920] 3-8-5 0.... RichardRowe(7) 5 17
(C Smith) *s.s: a bhd* **125/1**

2m 13.16s (-1.14) **Going Correction** -0.425s/f (Firm) **8** Ran SP% **115.3**
Speed ratings (Par 96): **87,86,83,82,82 79,71,69**
toteswinger: 1&2 £1.10, 1&3 £2.10, 2&3 £1.60. CSF £4.90 TOTE £3.80: £1.10, £1.02, £1.80; EX 5.00.
Owner Niarchos Family **Bred** Flaxman Holdings Ltd **Trained** Newmarket, Suffolk
■ Stewards' Enquiry : Richard Rowe two-day ban: use of whip when out of contention (May 4-5)

FOCUS
With Rossatron setting a stop-go tempo, it became a tactical affair and the race only began in earnest in the last three furlongs. The form could be rated a good deal higher.

1363 COME RACING ON TUESDAY 28TH APRIL H'CAP — 1m 2f 50y
7:40 (7:41) (Class 6) (0-60,60) 3-Y-O — £2,047 (£604; £302) Stalls Low

Form				RPR
5-66	1		**Urban Space**[30] 883 3-9-4 60 .... GeorgeBaker 2 (B G Powell) *chsd ldrs: rdn over 2f out: led and hung lft fr over 1f out: drvn clr: eased towards fin* **25/1**	66
000-	2	2¾	**Mr Prolific**[169] 7105 3-8-9 54 .... PatrickHills(3) 14 (B W Hills) *hld up: hdwy over 2f out: rdn and hung lft fr over 1f out: styd on: nt rch wnr* **7/2**[1]	54+
060-	3	¾	**Heartsease**[233] 5432 3-9-4 60 .... PatCosgrave 6 (J G Portman) *plld hrd: led after 1f: rdn and hdd over 1f out: no ex ins fnl f* **40/1**	59
065-	4	1¼	**Susurrayshaan**[162] 7229 3-8-10 52 .... (p) DaleGibson 13 (Mrs G S Rees) *led 1f: chsd ldr: rdn to ld over 1f out: sn hdd: no ex ins fnl f* **66/1**	48
000-	5	1	**Billy Smart (IRE)**[178] 6894 3-8-10 57 .... GabrielHannon(5) 1 (D J S Ffrench Davis) *chsd ldrs: rdn over 2f out: eased whn btn ins fnl f* **8/1**	52+
-000	6	hd	**King's Chorister**[82] 296 3-9-0 56 .... (t) KirstyMilczarek 5 (Miss Gay Kelleway) *s.i.s: hld up: racd keenly: nt clr run over 2f out: swtchd rt and hdwy over 1f out: r.o ins fnl f: nvr nrr* **18/1**	55+
-061	7	½	**Graycliffe (IRE)**[10] 1183 3-9-4 60 .... ShaneKelly 4 (Patrick Morris) *s.i.s: sn mid-div: hdwy over 3f out: rdn and hung lft over 1f out: one pce fnl f* **6/1**[3]	53
40-0	8	1	**Romantic Interlude (IRE)**[17] 1070 3-9-1 57 .... SebSanders 12 (A P Jarvis) *chsd ldrs: rdn over 2f out: wknd fnl f* **16/1**	48
-565	9	shd	**Key Of Fortune (IRE)**[47] 740 3-9-2 58 .... FrancisNorton 3 (Jennie Candlish) *hld up in tch: nt clr run over 2f out: and fnl f: eased* **16/1**	51+
040-	10	¾	**Golden Games (IRE)**[193] 6565 3-9-4 60 .... TPQueally 11 (J L Dunlop) *prom: rdn over 3f out: outpcd over 2f out: styd on ins fnl f* **5/1**[2]	49+
026-	11	½	**Chalk Hill Blue**[206] 6205 3-9-3 59 .... StephenCarson 7 (Eve Johnson Houghton) *hld up: rdn over 2f out: no rspnse* **9/1**	47
0004	12	nk	**Nicky Nutjob (GER)**[18] 1050 3-8-13 55 .... JerryO'Dwyer 8 (J Pearce) *hld up: racd keenly: a in rr* **5/1**[2]	42
0-00	13	1½	**Spruzzo**[57] 621 3-8-10 52 .... PJMcDonald 10 (C W Thornton) *mid-div: hdwy over 3f out: wknd 2f out* **40/1**	36
000-	14	½	**Bertie Smalls**[208] 6165 3-9-3 59 .... SaleemGolam 16 (M H Tompkins) *s.i.s: hld up: rdn over 3f out: sn wknd* **33/1**	42
050	15	33	**Miami Mix**[28] 914 3-8-10 52 .... DO'Donohoe 9 (B N Pollock) *s.i.s: a in rr: wknd over 3f out* **80/1**	—

2m 15.09s (0.79) **Going Correction** -0.425s/f (Firm) **15** Ran SP% **122.4**
Speed ratings (Par 96): **79,76,76,75,74 74,73,73,72,72 71,71,70,70,43**
toteswinger: 1&2 £66.50, 1&3 £63.70, 2&3 £40.90. CSF £108.94 CT £3594.78 TOTE £28.60: £5.70, £1.70, £11.40; EX 149.40 Place 6: £585.11, Place 5: £33.93.
Owner Holistic Racing Ltd **Bred** Winterbeck Manor Stud **Trained** Upper Lambourn, Berks

FOCUS
As with all the races on the round course during the meeting, the pace was modest and it paid to be handy. The form looks a bit suspect with the third and fourth far from solid.
Urban Space Official explanation: trainer's representative said, regarding the apparent improvement in form, that the gelding appeared to have benefitted from racing on turf.
Billy Smart(IRE) Official explanation: jockey said the colt lost its action
Graycliffe(IRE) Official explanation: jockey said gelding hung left
Key Of Fortune(IRE) Official explanation: jockey said that the filly was denied a clear run
T/Plt: £1,620.60 to a £1 stake. Pool: £36,076.11. 16.25 winning tickets. T/Qpdt: £42.60 to a £1 stake. Pool: £4,424.10. 76.80 winning tickets. CR

1330 THIRSK (L-H)
Saturday, April 18

OFFICIAL GOING: Firm (12.7)
Wind: Light 1/2 against Weather: Fine and sunny but very cool

1364 SOWERBY CLAIMING STKS — 5f
2:00 (2:01) (Class 5) 2-Y-O — £4,274 (£1,271; £635; £317) Stalls High

Form				RPR
0	1		**Lady Lion**[9] 1195 2-8-5 0 .... JackDean(5) 6 (W G M Turner) *chsd ldr: styd on to ld last 75yds: hld on towards fin* **4/1**[3]	53
6	2	½	**Mind Of Her Own**[3] 1277 2-9-2 0 .... PaulDoe 1 (P D Evans) *chsd ldrs on outside: wl outpcd and lost pl over 3f out: edgd rt and styd on over 1f out: jst hld* **2/1**[1]	57+
	3	2¾	**Blue Rum (IRE)** 2-9-2 0 .... PatrickDonaghy(5) 3 (P C Haslam) *led: hung lft over 1f out: hdd & wknd ins fnl f* **9/2**	52
03	4	¾	**Vaduz**[5] 1249 2-8-4 0 .... CatherineGannon 5 (M R Channon) *chsd ldrs: edgd lft and wknd fnl f* **5/2**[2]	32
	5	½	**Needs A Treat** 2-8-5 0 .... KellyHarrison(3) 4 (N Tinkler) *dwlt: hdwy over 2f out: hung lft and fdd fnl f* **20/1**	34
04	6	2½	**Blue Bond**[12] 1158 2-9-5 0 .... JamieMoriarty 2 (P T Midgley) *sn chsng ldrs: hung lft over 2f out: sn wknd* **17/2**	35

61.00 secs (1.40) **Going Correction** -0.15s/f (Firm) **6** Ran SP% **115.4**
Speed ratings (Par 92): **82,81,76,75,74 70**
toteswinger: 1&2 £2.00, 1&3 £3.80, 2&3 £3.50. CSF £12.94 TOTE £5.60: £3.70, £2.10; EX 11.50.
Owner Mrs M S Teversham **Bred** Mrs Monica Teversham **Trained** Sigwells, Somerset

FOCUS
Firm ground all round and a dry, bright, sunny day. A low key start to proceedings with this juvenile claimer and the form looks weak.

NOTEBOOK
Lady Lion showed very little at Folkestone on her debut, but she had clearly come on a ton for that and was well supported. Although she tended to hang to her left from two out to one out, she had showed good speed up to that point and kept on well enough to hold off the fast-finishing Mind Of Her Own. The winner, whose dam was a 5f winner at two, is clearly getting the hang of things, and she will be in her element when the emphasis is on speed, so may well turn up at somewhere like Chester, but this form isn't very strong. (op 7-1 tchd 8-1)
Mind Of Her Own just couldn't go the pace in the early stages, but she began to roll in the closing stages and finished strongly. A step up to 6f looks on the cards now and she can win races. (op 5-2 tchd 15-8)
Blue Rum(IRE) shaped with promise, showing up well for a long way and running green in the closing stages. He should come on a bundle for this and be a big threat next time. (op 7-2 tchd 5-1)
Vaduz was a bit disappointing, weakening away in the final furlong despite carrying a very low weight. (op 2-1 tchd 3-1)

1365 CONSTANT SECURITY H'CAP — 7f
2:30 (2:30) (Class 3) (0-90,90) 4-Y-O+ — £8,159 (£2,428; £1,213; £606) Stalls Low

Form				RPR
10-5	1		**Quest For Success (IRE)**[14] 1124 4-9-1 87 .... TonyHamilton 2 (R A Fahey) *in tch: effrt over 2f out: styd on to ld ins fnl f: hld on towards fin* **12/1**	97
5013	2	nk	**Carcinetto (IRE)**[5] 1251 7-9-1 87 .... PaulDoe 4 (P D Evans) *led tl 3f out: regained ld over 1f out: hdd ins fnl f: no ex nr fin* **10/1**	96
4-40	3	hd	**Atlantic Story (USA)**[28] 916 7-9-2 88 .... (bt) AlanMunro 5 (M W Easterby) *chsd ldrs: outpcd 3f out: hdwy to chse ldrs over 1f out: kpt on towards fin* **13/2**	96
00-1	4	3¾	**Malcheek (IRE)**[17] 1060 7-8-8 80 .... DavidAllan 7 (T D Easterby) *t.k.h: sn w ldr: led 3f out: hdd over 1f out: sn wknd* **4/1**[3]	78
1-30	5	1	**Minority Report**[14] 1123 9-8-7 79 .... SilvestreDeSousa 3 (D Nicholls) *mid-div: effrt over 2f out: nvr trbld ldrs* **7/2**[2]	74
-606	6	nk	**Flawed Genius**[21] 995 4-9-2 88 .... JimCrowley 1 (K A Ryan) *hld up in mid-div: effrt on inner over 2f out: hung lft: nvr nr ldrs* **3/1**[1]	82
200-	7	1	**Bold Marc (IRE)**[137] 7534 7-8-6 78 .... AndrewElliott 6 (K R Burke) *mid-div: kpt on fnl 2f: nvr a factor* **33/1**	70
6116	8	2	**Gallantry**[14] 1116 7-9-4 90 .... TolleyDean 11 (P Howling) *hld up in rr: drvn over 3f out: nvr on terms* **22/1**	76
0-06	9	1	**Osteopathic Remedy (IRE)**[14] 1124 5-9-4 90 .... PhillipMakin 9 (M Dods) *dwlt: a in rr* **8/1**	74
6-55	10	½	**My Gacho (IRE)**[14] 1116 7-8-13 85 .... (b) J-PGuillambert 10 (M Johnston) *tk fierce hold in rr: effrt on outer over 2f out: sn wknd* **12/1**	67

1m 23.05s (-4.15) **Going Correction** -0.40s/f (Firm) **10** Ran SP% **123.4**
Speed ratings (Par 107): **107,106,106,102,101 100,99,97,96,95**
toteswinger: 1&2 £41.20, 1&3 £7.10, 2&3 £12.60. CSF £132.94 CT £865.41 TOTE £14.70: £2.80, £4.10, £2.10; EX 173.70.
Owner Morebrooke Ltd **Bred** Desmond Monaghan **Trained** Musley Bank, N Yorks

FOCUS
A warm 7f handicap run at a strong pace as Malcheek and Carcinetto duelled for the lead through the first half mile. The race was set up for something sitting just off the pace and the form looks solid with the third to last year's turf form.

NOTEBOOK
Quest For Success(IRE), fit from an initial outing at Doncaster earlier in the month, stayed on strongly to bag a fourth career win. His record suggests this ground would be plenty quick enough having posted his three previous wins on good to soft, heavy and good ground, but he handled these quick conditions fine and remains unexposed over this trip having done the majority of his racing so far over 6f. (op 10-1)
Carcinetto(IRE) looked to have been headed by Malcheek over two out, but not only did she battle back to see off that rival, she ensured Quest For Success had to pull out all the stops in the final half-furlong. Although she's never won off a mark this high, this suggests she can do just that, especially if allowed an easier time in front. (op 11-1 tchd 9-1)
Atlantic Story(USA) was below par at his beloved Lingfield last time, but he bounced back with a cracking effort in defeat here, staying on strongly down the outside, and there are surely races in him off this mark on turf. (op 6-1 tchd 15-2)
Malcheek(IRE) dropped away disappointingly in the closing stages and appeared to have no excuses. (tchd 10-3)
Minority Report kept on, but could never land a blow. (op 11-2)
Flawed Genius looks appropriately named given the way he hung, and he's not one to be getting heavily involved with. (op 9-2)

1366 SQUIRE FREDERICK BELL H'CAP — 1m 4f
3:00 (3:00) (Class 5) (0-75,71) 4-Y-O+ — £4,274 (£1,271; £635; £317) Stalls Low

Form				RPR
5-44	1		**Destinys Dream (IRE)**[3] 1279 4-9-0 67 .... PhillipMakin 2 (Miss Tracy Waggott) *led 1f: trckd ldrs: led over 1f out: hld on towards fin* **7/2**[3]	75+
1302	2	¾	**Bridgewater Boys**[15] 1099 8-8-13 65 .... (b) WilliamBuick 9 (T J Pitt) *in rr: effrt on outside 3f out: edgd lft over 1f out: styd on: no ex nr fin* **10/1**	71
50P-	3	nk	**Solas Alainn (IRE)**[277] 4057 4-9-3 70 .... RoystonFfrench 7 (M Johnston) *dwlt: sn chsng ldrs: drvn over 4f out: hung lft: kpt on same pce ins fnl f* **14/1**	76+
411-	4	¾	**Bollin Greta**[183] 6790 4-9-1 68 .... DavidAllan 6 (T D Easterby) *led after 1f: qcknd over 4f out: hdd over 1f out: kpt on same pce* **3/1**[2]	72+
6102	5	½	**Monfils Monfils (USA)**[11] 1175 7-9-0 71 .... AmyRyan(5) 4 (A J McCabe) *hld up in rr: hdwy on outside 3f out: kpt on: nvr trbld ldrs* **6/1**	75
200-	6	3½	**Sporting Gesture**[193] 6551 12-9-0 66 .... DaleGibson 8 (M W Easterby) *in rr: sn pushed along: nvr a factor* **12/1**	64
30-1	7	4½	**Herrera (IRE)**[14] 1125 4-9-3 70 .... TonyHamilton 3 (R A Fahey) *in tch: drvn over 4f out: outpcd and lost pl 3f out* **9/4**[1]	61
000-	8	1½	**Heart Of Dubai (USA)**[199] 6379 4-8-10 63 .... PJMcDonald 5 (Micky Hammond) *in tch: outpcd 3f out: sn lost pl* **25/1**	51

2m 33.73s (-2.47) **Going Correction** -0.40s/f (Firm)
WFA 4 from 7yo+ 1lb **8** Ran SP% **119.6**
Speed ratings (Par 103): **92,91,91,90,90 88,85,84**
toteswinger: 1&2 £14.80, 1&3 £31.30, 2&3 £9.80. CSF £39.74 CT £445.39 TOTE £4.90: £2.00, £2.10, £5.80; EX 48.40.
Owner H Conlon **Bred** Sean Burke **Trained** Spennymoor, Co Durham

FOCUS
Hard to know what to make of this as the gallop, set by Bollin Greta, looked pretty honest, but they finished in a bit of a heap at the line. The bare form is limited but there should be more to come from the third and fourth.
Herrera(IRE) Official explanation: jockey said filly was unsuited by the firm ground

1367 MICHAEL FOSTER MEMORIAL CONDITIONS STKS — 6f
3:35 (3:35) (Class 3) 4-Y-O+ — £7,851 (£2,351; £1,175; £588) Stalls High

Form				RPR
03-	1		**Hitchens (IRE)**[178] 6903 4-9-0 103 .... PhillipMakin 1 (T D Barron) *trckd ldrs: smooth hdwy over 1f out: qcknd to ld jst ins fnl f: sn clr: v readily* **3/1**[3]	109+
1-33	2	3	**Knot In Wood (IRE)**[2] 1299 7-9-7 108 .... TonyHamilton 3 (R A Fahey) *w ldr: led over 2f out: hdd jst ins fnl f: kpt on same pce* **11/10**[1]	106
020-	3	1½	**Wi Dud**[195] 6518 5-8-9 100 .... AmyRyan(5) 2 (K A Ryan) *led tl over 2f out: kpt on same pce* **11/4**[2]	94

135- 4 3 1/4 **Quaroma**[193] 6568 4-8-9 95 .... PatCosgrave 4 79
(Jane Chapple-Hyam) *hld up on inner: hdwy to chse ldrs 3f out: rdn over 1f out: wknd jst ins fnl f* **11/1**

1m 10.69s (-2.01) **Going Correction** -0.15s/f (Firm) 4 Ran SP% **107.6**
Speed ratings (Par 107): **107,103,101,96**
CSF £6.73 TOTE £4.10; EX 6.00.
Owner Laurence O'Kane **Bred** Curragh Bloodstock Agency Ltd **Trained** Maunby, N Yorks

FOCUS
Only four runners, and although there was little between them on adjusted ratings, Hitchens ran out an impressive winner on his first run for David Barron. The runner-up is the best guide to the form.

NOTEBOOK
Hitchens(IRE), debuting for the David Barron stable, had won a competitive handicap at Windsor on his first start of last term, and he confirmed his ability to go well fresh here, albeit for different connections. Always travelling well covered up behind his three rivals, the winner was clearly going best as the field approached the final furlong, and when the gap appeared, he burst through and skipped away in the closing stages to score in very impressive style. The big question now is whether his trainer can keep him sweet because his form dropped right away after his win last season, but he's clearly very talented when right. (tchd 10-3)
Knot In Wood(IRE) had run very well when third in a warm Listed race at Newmarket two days earlier, and he provides a solid marker to the strength of the form. He appears to have run his race once again and is capable of scoring in Pattern company this term, although probably on slightly easier ground. (op 11-8)
Wi Dud hasn't won since his juvenile days, but he was only beaten four lengths in the Group 1 Ladbrokes Sprint Cup in September and clearly retains plenty of ability. He showed good speed before weakening away, but he's better served by the minimum trip anyway and is likely to come on plenty for this and prove more competitive next time. (tchd 5-2)
Quaroma was a progressive filly last term, but she wasn't competitive here and will find easier opportunities back against her own sex. (op 6-1)

1368 THOMAS LORD STKS (H'CAP) 5f
4:10 (4:10) (Class 3) (0-90,89) 3-Y-O **£8,159** (£2,428; £1,213; £606) **Stalls** High

Form RPR
215- 1 **Brenin Taran**[183] 6769 3-8-10 **83** .... AndreaAtzeni(5) 5 90+
(D M Simcock) *trckd ldrs gng wl: shkn up to ld over 1f out: sn rdn and edgd lft: kpt on wl towards fin* **5/2**[1]
311- 2 1 1/4 **Coleorton Choice**[211] 6067 3-8-10 **83** .... AmyRyan(5) 11 86+
(K A Ryan) *dwlt: in rr: swtchd outside over 2f out: sn chsng ldrs: kpt on same pce ins fnl f* **7/2**[2]
6050 3 nse **Sir Geoffrey (IRE)**[16] 1078 3-8-9 **77** ....(t) JamesDoyle 2 79
(A J McCabe) *w ldrs: styd on same pce ins fnl f* **22/1**
114- 4 1 1/2 **Desert Falls**[192] 6575 3-9-2 **87** .... MichaelJStainton(3) 9 84+
(R M Whitaker) *sn outpcd in rr: hdwy over 1f out: styd on wl towards fin* **5/1**[3]
-440 5 3/4 **White Shift (IRE)**[9] 1196 3-8-5 **73** ow1 .... PaulDoe 1 67
(P D Evans) *swvd lft s: sn chsng ldrs: fdd jst ins fnl f* **8/1**
650- 6 2 1/2 **Caranbola**[169] 7107 3-9-6 **88** .... TWilliams 3 73
(M Brittain) *mid-div: drvn over 2f out: wknd appr fnl f* **9/1**
116- 7 3 **Metroland**[253] 4816 3-8-3 **71** .... SilvestreDeSousa 4 45
(D Nicholls) *s.i.s: nvr a factor* **10/1**
106- 8 1 **Lucky Art (USA)**[182] 6807 3-8-11 **84** .... PatrickDonaghy(5) 8 55
(J Howard Johnson) *led tl hdd & wknd over 1f out* **7/1**
00-0 9 5 **Dispol Kylie (IRE)**[51] 685 3-8-12 **80** .... DarrenWilliams 7 33
(P T Midgley) *w ldrs: lost pl over 1f out* **11/1**

58.42 secs (-1.18) **Going Correction** -0.15s/f (Firm) 9 Ran SP% **122.8**
Speed ratings (Par 102): **103,101,100,98,97 93,88,86,78**
toteswinger: 1&2 £3.10, 1&3 £11.20, 2&3 £11.50. CSF £12.09 CT £163.91 TOTE £3.20: £1.80, £2.00, £4.00; EX 14.70.
Owner Mrs Ann Simcock **Bred** D M I Simcock **Trained** Newmarket, Suffolk

FOCUS
A good little sprint run in a decent time and the form is rated fairly positively.

NOTEBOOK
Brenin Taran, despite lacking the experience of many of his rivals, confirmed the promise of his handicap debut at Kempton at the back end of last term, and he looks a sprinter to follow. Always travelling strongly just behind the speed, he came there absolutely cruising approaching the final furlong before battling on gamely, despite hanging to his left, when asked to fend off the challenges from Sir Geoffrey and Coleorton Dancer in the final half furlong. A progressive young sprinter, his high cruising speed will stand him in good stead and there looks to be loads more to come, while another furlong should be within range given his pedigree. (op 10-3 tchd 9-4)
Coleorton Choice was himself progressive in handicaps last term, although that came over 6f on much slower ground, and he shaped with real promise on seasonal return, given conditions would have been plenty quick enough. He's one to keep on side back up to 6f next time. (tchd 4-1)
Sir Geoffrey(IRE) seemed to improve for the application of a tongue-tie as he ran miles better than he has been doing on the all-weather this year. He stayed on well having been close to the pace throughout and is another who would probably prefer slightly easier ground. (op 14-1)
Desert Falls was doing his best work at the finish and he needs another furlong. (op 8-1 tchd 10-1)
White Shift(IRE), who likes to lead, could never get to the front from her wide draw. (op 17-2 tchd 7-1)
Caranbola raced 11 times as a juvenile and, although well backed, she weakened right away and might be vulnerable this year. (op 20-1)

1369 PINDER DALE H'CAP 6f
4:45 (4:45) (Class 5) (0-75,75) 4-Y-O+ **£4,274** (£1,271; £635; £317) **Stalls** High

Form RPR
0603 1 **Cornus**[16] 1089 7-9-4 **75** ....(be) JamesDoyle 9 83
(A J McCabe) *hld up in rr: hdwy and nt clr run over 1f out: str run on inner to ld nr fin* **3/1**[1]
010- 2 1 3/4 **Medici Time**[173] 7021 4-8-7 **64** ....(v) DavidAllan 6 66
(T D Easterby) *hld up: effrt and swtchd outside over 1f out: led ins fnl f: hdd and no ex towards fin* **5/1**[2]
111- 3 1 1/4 **Johnston's Glory (IRE)**[262] 4542 5-8-6 **66** ....(p) AndrewMullen(3) 5 64
(E J Alston) *t.k.h: trckd ldrs: sltly hmpd and led over 1f out: hdd ins fnl f: no ex* **6/1**[3]
056- 4 nk **Royal Composer (IRE)**[206] 6219 6-8-5 **62** oh4 ow1 .... PaulDoe 2 59
(T D Easterby) *sn chsng ldrs on outer: drvn over 2f out: kpt on same pce* **9/1**
66-0 5 nk **Ingleby Princess**[11] 1169 5-8-5 **62** .... SilvestreDeSousa 4 58
(T D Barron) *trckd ldrs: effrt over 2f out: keeping on same pce whn n.m.r over 1f out* **3/1**[1]
55-0 6 1 **Soto**[22] 975 6-8-1 **63** .... PatrickDonaghy(5) 8 56
(M W Easterby) *gave problems leaving paddock: led: drvn 3f out: hrd rdn: edgd lft and hdd over 1f out: kpt on same pce* **8/1**

160- 7 3/4 **Woodsley House (IRE)**[186] 6724 7-8-11 **71** .... NeilBrown(3) 3 62
(A G Foster) *s.s: nvr a factor: kpt on fnl f* **5/1**[2]

1m 12.56s (-0.14) **Going Correction** -0.15s/f (Firm) 7 Ran SP% **118.7**
Speed ratings (Par 103): **94,91,90,89,89 87,86**
toteswinger: 1&2 £5.30, 1&3 £3.30, 2&3 £3.80. CSF £19.39 CT £86.06 TOTE £4.20: £2.30, £3.60; EX 22.90 Place 6: £571.81, Place 5: £309.97..
Owner Betfair Club ROA **Bred** G Russell **Trained** Averham Park, Notts
■ Stewards' Enquiry : Patrick Donaghy one-day ban: careless riding (May 4)

FOCUS
Just an ordinary 6f handicap and the pace was even enough. The winner did not have to run to last year's best in a pretty weak heat.
T/Plt: £1,344.00 to a £1 stake. Pool: £52,839.95. 28.70 winning tickets. T/Qpdt: £98.70 to a £1 stake. Pool: £2,442.42. 18.30 winning tickets. WG

1370 - 1373a (Foreign Racing) - See Raceform Interactive

NAAS (L-H)
Saturday, April 18
OFFICIAL GOING: Yielding (yielding to soft in places)

1374a WOODLANDS STKS (LISTED RACE) 5f
4:20 (4:20) 3-Y-O+ **£28,441** (£8,344; £3,975; £1,354)

RPR
1 **Inxile (IRE)**[21] 996 4-9-12 .... AdrianTNicholls 2 110
(D Nicholls) *mde all on far side: strly pressed and drifted rt fr 1f out: styd on wl* **7/2**[1]
2 1/2 **Reverence**[189] 6653 8-9-9 .... WJSupple 10 105+
(E J Alston) *led stands' side gp: kpt on u.p ins fnl f wout matching wnr* **14/1**
3 3/4 **Le Cadre Noir (IRE)**[202] 6315 5-9-12 104 .... PJSmullen 8 105
(D K Weld, Ire) *chsd ldrs on stands' side: rdn and cl up whn sltly hmpd fr 1f out: no imp after and kpt on* **4/1**[2]
4 nk **Aine (IRE)**[195] 6514 4-9-6 97 .... WMLordan 12 98+
(T Stack, Ire) *towards rr on stands' side: styd on wl u.p ins fnl f wout rching 1st 3* **10/1**
5 1/2 **Judge 'n Jury**[19] 1043 5-9-9 ....(t) MJKinane 11 99
(R A Harris) *trckd ldrs on stands' side: kpt on same pce u.p ins fnl f* **7/1**[3]
6 1 **Snaefell (IRE)**[202] 6315 5-9-12 108 .... RPCleary 6 99
(M Halford, Ire) *racd on stands' side early: sn chsd ldrs in centre: kpt on same pce u.p ins fnl f* **7/1**[3]
7 1/2 **Brave Falcon (IRE)**[15] 1111 5-9-9 94 ....(p) KLatham 9 94
(Leo J Temple, Ire) *cl up stands' side: kpt on same pce u.p fr 1f out* **25/1**
8 3/4 **Benbaun (IRE)**[202] 6315 8-9-9 ....(b) FMBerry 4 91
(K A Ryan) *cl up on far side: sltly hmpd 1f out: sn no imp* **7/1**[3]
9 nk **Senor Benny (USA)**[27] 927 10-9-12 104 .... CPGeoghegan 5 93
(M McDonagh, Ire) *prom on far side: kpt on same pce u.p fr over 1f out* **25/1**
10 1 3/4 **Nanotech (IRE)**[148] 7406 5-9-9 96 .... DPMcDonogh 1 87+
(Jarlath P Fahey, Ire) *prom on far side: kpt on same pce u.p fr over 1f out* **25/1**
11 nk **Emily Blake (IRE)**[27] 927 5-9-6 104 .... JAHeffernan 3 80
(J C Hayden, Ire) *a towards rr on far side* **14/1**
12 3 1/2 **Georgebernardshaw (IRE)**[13] 1138 4-9-12 109 .... JMurtagh 7 73
(A P O'Brien, Ire) *a towards rr on stands' side: no ex fr over 1f out* **7/1**[3]

60.00 secs (-2.00) 12 Ran SP% **126.2**
CSF £56.66 TOTE £3.80: £1.70, £6.40, £2.00; DF 84.90.
Owner Ian Hewitson & D Nicholls **Bred** Denis & Mrs Teresa Bergin **Trained** Sessay, N Yorks

FOCUS
The winner has been rated to a personal best, the runner-up to roughly his 2008 level, and the fourth close to her best on her seasonal return.

NOTEBOOK
Inxile(IRE), successful over this journey on soft ground at Deauville in August, had the benefit of a recent seasonal debut run at Doncaster last month. He broke smartly from his low draw and held a narrow advantage on the far side at halfway. He then began to drift right despite his rider applying pressure with his whip in his right hand. In doing so, he slightly hampered the struggling Benbaun and Le Cadre Noir a furlong out, which prompted a stewards' enquiry. As expected, though, the placings were left to stand. Official explanation: jockey said gelding hung badly right in closing stages (op 11/4)
Reverence completed a one-two for Britain. He was seeking his tenth career win here and this was a fair effort from his high draw considering this was his first run back since last October. (op 16/1)
Le Cadre Noir(IRE), winner of the Waterford Testimonial Stakes over 6f at the Curragh last October, wasn't helped when the winner came across the track. He proved best of the domestic challenge and might prefer another furlong to be seen at his best. (op 7/2)
Aine(IRE) looked up against it on figures but the 97-rated daughter of Danehill Dancer showed plenty of speed on her seasonal bow inside the final furlong when she was doing her best work. She wasn't ignored in the market and can hopefully build on this creditable display. (op 14/1)
Judge 'n Jury, a seven-time winner last year, had winning form in similar ground. He was drawn on the nearside but he never looked likely to pose a threat when the race unfolded inside the final furlong. (op 6/1)
Benbaun(IRE) failed to win last term. The Curragh course specialist with six wins to his credit at Irish headquarters was beginning to backpedal when slightly impeded by the winner edging across the track. (op 6/1)

1375a GO RACING IN KILDARE H'CAP 5f
4:50 (4:51) (60-95,95) 3-Y-O+ **£9,392** (£2,188; £965; £557)

RPR
1 **Fol Hollow (IRE)**[3] 1278 4-9-9 92 5ex .... AdrianTNicholls 3 101+
(D Nicholls) *a.p: 2nd for much: styd on wl u.p ins fnl f to ld nr line* **9/4**[1]
2 hd **Siodul (IRE)**[7] 1217 3-8-6 85 .... MHarley(5) 4 90+
(J S Bolger, Ire) *chsd ldrs: clsd into 3rd under 2f out: rdn to ld under 1f out: styd on u.p: hdd nr line* **4/1**[2]
3 1 1/4 **Osterhase (IRE)**[320] 2685 10-9-12 90 ....(b) FMBerry 1 92
(J E Mulhern, Ire) *led: strly pressed and hdd under 1f out: sn no imp in 3rd* **20/1**
4 3 1/2 **Parc Aux Boules**[13] 1137 8-8-5 69 ow1 .... KLatham 16 58
(Adrian McGuinness, Ire) *towards rr: kpt on wout threatening u.p fr over 1f out* **12/1**
5 shd **Calm Bay (IRE)**[29] 903 3-8-5 79 .... CDHayes 13 64
(H Rogers, Ire) *mid-div: kpt on wout threatening u.p fr over 1f out* **10/1**[3]
6 nk **College Scholar (GER)**[200] 6367 5-9-1 79 .... WMLordan 12 67
(Liam McAteer, Ire) *chsd ldrs: kpt on same pce u.p fr 1 1/2f out* **16/1**
7 1 **Fly By Magic (IRE)**[29] 903 5-9-2 80 .... WJLee 5 64
(Patrick Carey, Ire) *mid-div: impr to chse ldrs fr under 2f out: kpt on same pce u.p fr over 1f out* **16/1**

8 hd **Zhukhov (IRE)**[13] 1137 6-8-11 80 .... AmyKathleenParsons(5) 14 64
(T G McCourt, Ire) *mid-div: kpt on same pce u.p fr 1 1/2f out* 10/1[3]
9 1/2 **First In Command (IRE)**[27] 927 4-9-9 87 .... (t) DPMcDonogh 15 69
(Daniel Mark Loughnane, Ire) *mid-div on outer: kpt on same pce u.p fr over 1f out* 12/1
10 1 1/4 **Fairy Flow (IRE)**[155] 7325 5-8-9 73 .... PJSmullen 11 50
(Ms Joanna Morgan, Ire) *trckd ldrs in 5th: no ex fr over 1f out* 10/1[3]
11 3/4 **Johnstown Lad (IRE)**[7] 1219 5-9-2 80 .... (t) WJSupple 2 55
(Niall Moran, Ire) *trckd ldrs in 4th: no ex u.p fr over 1f out* 14/1
12 1 **Daring Man (IRE)**[27] 927 4-9-7 85 .... (t) RPCleary 9 56
(M J P O'Brien, Ire) *mid-div: kpt on same pce u.p fr 1 1/2f out* 16/1
13 1 1/4 **Lady Meagan (IRE)**[15] 1110 4-8-3 70 .... SMGorey(3) 10 37
(Patrick Carey, Ire) *mid-div: no ex fr 1 1/2f out* 33/1
14 1 1/4 **Like Magic (IRE)**[204] 6258 3-9-7 95 .... JAHeffernan 7 53
(Patrick Martin, Ire) *a towards rr* 14/1
15 1 3/4 **Royal Intruder**[141] 7483 4-9-2 80 .... CO'Donoghue 6 36
(S Donohoe, Ire) *a towards rr* 33/1
16 2 1/2 **Point Calimere (IRE)**[29] 903 8-8-4 75 .... GFCarroll(7) 8 22
(Miss Maura McGuinness, Ire) *short of room early: sn towards rr: n.d fr under 2f out* 20/1

59.90 secs (-2.10)
WFA 3 from 4yo+ 10lb 16 Ran SP% **139.8**
CSF £11.50 CT £158.72 TOTE £3.10: £1.70, £1.90, £3.40, £2.70; DF 13.30.
Owner Middleham Park Racing Iii **Bred** Dan O'Brien **Trained** Sessay, N Yorks

FOCUS
This handicap was run in a marginally quicker time than the earlier Listed race on the card and it paid to race prominently. It has been rated through the third to the best of his 2007 form.

NOTEBOOK
Fol Hollow(IRE) defied his 5lb penalty for winning at Beverley the previous Wednesday. Always in the front rank before recording his second win since his juvenile campaign, the four-year-old coped with this ground and held off the runner-up by a head at the finish. His trainer intends returning to Ireland with the gelded son of Captain Rio, who should appreciate some better ground over the coming months. (op 5/2 tchd 11/4)

1376a SUMMER BARBEQUE EVENINGS H'CAP 7f
5:20 (5:20) (60-100,97) 3-Y-O+ £14,220 (£4,172; £1,987; £677)

RPR
1 **Joseph Henry**[7] 1212 7-9-6 88 .... AdrianTNicholls 2 100
(D Nicholls) *trckd ldr in 2nd: led fr 2f out: sn rdn clr: flashed tail and styd on wl ins fnl f: easily* 5/1[2]
2 5 **Enigma Code (UAE)**[7] 1219 4-8-6 74 .... RPCleary 11 73
(James McAuley, Ire) *racd in 6th: rdn to chse wnr fr 2f out: sn no imp and kpt on same pce* 10/1
3 1/2 **Braddock (IRE)**[13] 1137 6-7-9 73 oh1 ow1 .... (p) CPHoban(10) 1 70
(S Donohoe, Ire) *led: hdd fr 2f out: sn no imp and kpt on in 3rd* 14/1
4 shd **Kingsdale Ocean (IRE)**[27] 927 6-9-10 92 .... PJSmullen 16 89
(D K Weld, Ire) *mid-div: 9th appr st: no imp u.p in mod 4th and kpt on same pce fr over 1f out* 8/1
5 1 1/4 **Blas Ceoil (USA)**[182] 6818 3-8-11 97 .... MHarley(5) 14 86
(J S Bolger, Ire) *mid-div: 8th appr st: kpt on same pce u.p fr 2f out* 6/1[3]
6 1 1/4 **Toasted Special (USA)**[13] 1137 4-8-12 80 .... WJSupple 12 70
(W McCreery, Ire) *trckd ldrs in 3rd: wd st: kpt on same pce u.p fr under 2f out* 14/1
7 nk **Opera Music**[13] 1137 5-8-8 81 .... (b) EJMcNamara(5) 4 70
(J P Cahill, Ire) *chsd ldrs: 7th for much: kpt on same pce u.p fr 2f out* 9/1
8 hd **Ardistan (IRE)**[27] 6446 5-8-12 80 .... FMBerry 10 69
(C Roche, Ire) *towards rr: no imp u.p and kpt on wout threatening st* 9/1
9 3/4 **Worldly Wise**[12] 1163 6-8-5 80 .... GFCarroll(7) 5 67
(Patrick J Flynn, Ire) *towards rr: wd st: kpt on wout threatening u.p fr 2f out* 8/1
10 2 1/2 **Bentesina (GER)**[13] 1137 7-8-7 80 .... BACurtis(5) 13 60
(Leo J Temple, Ire) *mid-div: 10th appr st: kpt on same pce fr 2f out* 16/1
11 1 **King's Bastion (IRE)**[64] 6783 5-8-5 83 .... RPWalsh(10) 6 60
(Luke Comer, Ire) *sn settled in rr: 11th appr st: kpt on same pce fr 2f out* 25/1
12 4 1/2 **Crying Aloud (USA)**[12] 1163 4-8-12 80 .... CDHayes 15 45
(J T Gorman, Ire) *mid-div: kpt on same pce st* 14/1
13 shd **Incline (IRE)**[20] 1023 10-9-5 87 .... JMurtagh 3 52
(R McGlinchey, Ire) *racd in 5th: 4th under 3f out: sn no ex* 16/1
14 shd **Motafaany (USA)**[27] 929 4-8-12 80 .... DPMcDonogh 8 45
(Kevin Prendergast, Ire) *trckd ldrs: 3rd under 3f out: sn no ex* 3/1[1]
15 3 **Inwood (IRE)**[20] 1023 6-8-13 81 .... (tp) WMLordan 7 38
(Paul Magnier, Ire) *towards rr: wd st: sn no imp* 20/1
16 28 **Mesmerize Me**[7] 1219 4-9-5 87 .... (p) KLatham 9 —
(R McGlinchey, Ire) *towards rr: dropped bhd and eased fr under 2f out* 25/1

1m 24.1s (-3.40)
WFA 3 from 4yo+ 13lb 16 Ran SP% **151.5**
CSF £67.52 CT £746.95 TOTE £6.20: £2.30, £4.80, £3.30, £2.40; DF 232.60.
Owner Billy Hughes **Bred** John Brown & Megan Dennis **Trained** Sessay, N Yorks

FOCUS
The runner-up and third are the best guides to the level of the form, and the winner has been rated back to his very best.

NOTEBOOK
Joseph Henry turned this handicap into a procession to complete a great day for David and Adrian Nicholls with their third winner. The seven-year-old, described as 'dead unlucky' by his trainer, hadn't won a race since July 2006, but he had reached the frame several times last season and he stepped up on a couple of midfield finishes earlier this season to score here with the minimum of fuss. He took it up passing the two-furlong marker and the result was never in doubt. He's in for a hike after this but his trainer suggested he could well come back to Ireland to contest another valuable handicap before long. (op 6/1 tchd 7/2)

1377 - (Foreign Racing) - See Raceform Interactive

1116
LINGFIELD (L-H)
Sunday, April 19

OFFICIAL GOING: Standard
Wind: Virtually nil. Weather: bright

1378 HOLLOW LANE H'CAP 1m 5f (P)
2:10 (2:11) (Class 6) (0-65,60) 4-Y-O+ £1,878 (£558; £279; £139) Stalls Low

Form RPR
4040 1 **Calzaghe (IRE)**[10] 1200 5-9-8 60 .... RichardThomas 12 70
(Jim Best) *stdd after s: hld up wl in rr: stl plenty to do and plld out over 1f out: str run fnl f to ld towards fin* 8/1
143 2 3/4 **Prince Charlemagne (IRE)**[17] 1081 6-9-8 60 .... GeorgeBaker 2 69
(G L Moore) *hld up in tch: hdwy towards inner wl over 1f out: rdn to ld 1f out: r.o wl tl overwhelmed by wnr towards fin* 7/1
604- 3 1 1/2 **Jafaru**[244] 5148 5-9-8 60 .... (b) RyanMoore 13 67
(G L Moore) *led: rdn over 2f out: drvn and hdd 1f out: kpt on same pce fnl f* 7/2[1]
62-5 4 nk **Adage**[13] 1154 6-8-8 46 .... (tp) FergusSweeney 9 52
(David Pinder) *hld up in midfield: hdwy over 2f out: chsd ldrs and rdn over 1f out: edgd lft and kpt on same pce fnl f* 20/1
0455 5 1/2 **Coral Shores**[33] 857 4-9-0 53 .... (v) LukeMorris 4 58
(P W Hiatt) *hld up in tch: effrt to chse ldrs and drvn 2f out: kpt on same pce u.p fnl f* 25/1
0-02 6 1/2 **Home**[44] 735 4-9-5 58 .... JimCrowley 6 64+
(C Gordon) *hld up in midfield: effrt and nt clr run wl over 2f out: nvr enough room after and unable to chal* 16/1
300- 7 2 **Platoche (IRE)**[342] 2056 4-9-5 58 .... EddieAhern 10 60
(G A Butler) *stdd after s: hld up in midfield: pushed along and hdwy over 2f out: chsd ldrs and rdn over 1f out: no imp fnl f* 9/1
5424 8 1/2 **Zalkani (IRE)**[32] 871 9-9-0 59 .... SimonPearce(7) 8 60
(J Pearce) *hld up in midfield: hdwy on outer 3f out: chsd ldrs 2f out: rdn and unable qck over 1f out: one pce after* 13/2[3]
5-40 9 1 3/4 **Mid Valley**[47] 745 6-8-8 46 .... J-PGuillambert 11 44
(J R Jenkins) *stdd after s: hld up in last trio: effrt towards inner wl over 1f out: no hdwy 1f out: wknd ins fnl f* 33/1
222- 10 4 1/2 **Salut Saint Cloud**[358] 1459 8-8-10 55 .... JemmaMarshall(7) 14 47
(G L Moore) *hld up in last trio: pushed along and no prog over 2f out: n.d* 25/1
4050 11 shd **Comeintothespace (IRE)**[28] 918 7-8-7 45 .... WilliamBuick 7 36
(R A Farrant) *hld up towards rr: rdn 2f out: no prog and nvr trbld ldrs* 50/1
000- 12 1/2 **Medieval Maiden**[151] 7385 6-8-10 48 .... IanMongan 1 39
(Mrs L J Mongan) *dwlt: sn pushed up to chse ldr tl 6f out: rdn to press ldr again wl over 2f out: wknd qckly wl over 1f out* 50/1
4214 13 27 **Irish Ballad**[18] 1069 7-9-7 59 .... NickyMackay 3 9
(S Dow) *chsd ldrs: wnt 2nd 6f out tl wl over 2f out: btn and eased wl over 1f out: virtually p.u ins fnl f: dismntd after fin* 6/1[2]
0-03 14 4 1/2 **Good Effect (USA)**[11] 1178 5-9-0 52 .... (v[1]) SebSanders 5 —
(C P Morlock) *chsd ldrs: racd wd 8f out: rdn 5f out: wknd u.p jst over 2f out: virtually p.u fnl f* 8/1

2m 45.37s (-0.63) **Going Correction** +0.25s/f (Slow)
WFA 4 from 5yo+ 1lb 14 Ran SP% **119.8**
Speed ratings (Par 101): **111,110,109,109,109 108,107,107,106,103 103,103,86,83**
toteswinger: 1&2 £8.10, 1&3 £5.90, 2&3 £5.60. CSF £57.95 CT £234.43 TOTE £7.70: £3.50, £2.50, £1.50; EX 48.60 TRIFECTA Not won..
Owner Chipstead Racehorse Owners Club **Bred** Wentworth Racing Pty Ltd **Trained** Lewes, E Sussex

FOCUS
A modest staying handicap. The early pace looked sound, if a bit steady, but that did not stop there being a mad rush to the line inside the final two furlongs.
Home Official explanation: jockey said gelding was denied a clear run

1379 STARBOROUGH MAIDEN FILLIES' STKS 6f (P)
2:40 (2:42) (Class 5) 3-4-Y-O £2,590 (£770; £385; £192) Stalls Low

Form RPR
03- 1 **Beautiful Filly**[188] 6697 3-9-0 0 .... RichardMullen 6 60+
(D M Simcock) *chsd ldrs: rdn wl over 1f out: led 1f out: hld on wl* 7/1[2]
2- 2 1/2 **Kammaan**[263] 4534 3-9-0 0 .... PhilipRobinson 10 59+
(M A Jarvis) *chsd ldrs: rdn and ev ch 1f out: unable qck and a hld fnl f* 4/6[1]
5 3 3/4 **Deraaya (IRE)**[30] 890 4-9-11 75 .... JimmyQuinn 7 59+
(K A Morgan) *hld up towards rr: hdwy over 2f out: drvn and edgd lft over 1f out: r.o to go 3rd fnl 100yds: nt rch ldng pair* 15/2[3]
206- 4 2 1/4 **Peninsula Girl (IRE)**[201] 6362 3-9-0 67 .... TonyCulhane 9 49
(M R Channon) *led after 1f: rdn 2f out: hdd 1f out: wknd fnl 100yds* 14/1
0045 5 nk **Chantilly Jewel (USA)**[19] 1055 4-9-11 41 .... (p) JimCrowley 5 51
(R M H Cowell) *led for 1f: chsd ldr after: rdn and ev ch over 1f out: wknd ins fnl f* 80/1
- 6 1 **Langland Bay** 3-9-0 0 .... DO'Donohoe 3 45+
(W R Muir) *in rr of main gp: rdn and lost tch over 2f out: rallied ent fnl f: r.o wl: gng on at fin* 40/1
6 7 1 1/4 **Crystal B Good (USA)**[64] 552 3-8-11 0 .... MarcHalford(3) 2 41+
(J R Best) *in tch in midfield: rdn and outpcd jst over 2f out: kpt on again fnl f* 33/1
8 3/4 **King's Miracle (IRE)** 3-9-0 0 .... SteveDrowne 12 38
(J R Gask) *racd wd: in tch: rdn and no prog fr jst over 2f out* 50/1
0-0 9 16 **Yughanni**[18] 1066 3-9-0 0 .... SebSanders 1 —
(C E Brittain) *taken down early and led to s: rel to r and a t.o* 33/1
6 10 13 **Marzy**[17] 1077 3-9-0 0 .... TPQueally 11 —
(M Botti) *wnt rt s: in tch in midfield: lost pl qckly bnd jst over 2f out: t.o over 1f out* 33/1

1m 13.23s (1.33) **Going Correction** +0.25s/f (Slow)
WFA 3 from 4yo 11lb 10 Ran SP% **105.4**
Speed ratings (Par 100): **101,100,99,96,95 94,92,91,70,53**
toteswinger: 1&2 £1.10, 1&3 £3.90, 2&3 £1.80. CSF £10.06 TOTE £6.70: £1.20, £1.30, £1.60; EX 15.90 Trifecta £52.80 Pool £166.39 - 2.33 winning units..
Owner Dr Ali Ridha **Bred** Mrs C C Regalado-Gonzalez **Trained** Newmarket, Suffolk

FOCUS
Virtually all of these were unexposed but the form is probably only fair at best.
Kammaan Official explanation: trainer said filly was unsuited by the track

1380 WATERY LANE MAIDEN STKS 1m (P)
3:10 (3:12) (Class 5) 3-Y-O+ £2,590 (£770; £385; £192) Stalls High

Form RPR
22- 1 **Mohathab (IRE)**[247] 5076 4-10-0 82 .... PatCosgrave 7 77
(J R Boyle) *in tch: hdwy jst over 2f out: rdn to ld over 1f out: drvn and hld on wl fnl f* 13/8[1]
20-2 2 nk **Park Lane**[37] 828 3-9-0 79 .... PaulFitzsimons 3 72
(B W Hills) *trckd ldrs: rdn and effrt over 1f out: ev ch fnl f: unable qck and hld fnl 100yds* 4/1[3]
-2 3 1 1/2 **Sawab**[15] 1130 3-8-9 0 .... RyanMoore 2 64
(C E Brittain) *led tl over 4f out: led again wl over 2f out: rdn 2f out: hdd over 1f out: one pce fnl f* 9/4[2]
- 4 1 1/2 **King's Masque** 3-9-0 0 .... DO'Donohoe 9 71+
(W R Muir) *in tch towards outer: hmpd and lost pl bnd jst over 2f out: rallied and r.o wl fnl f: nt rch ldrs* 33/1

00- **5** 1 ½ **Murhee (USA)**[226] 5672 3-9-0 0 NeilPollard 6 62+
(D R Lanigan) *hld up towards rr: outpcd jst over 2f out: pushed along and kpt on fnl f: nvr threatened ldrs* **16/1**

6 shd **Cry Alot Boy**[79] 6-10-0 0 JimmyQuinn 10 66
(K A Morgan) *s.i.s: plld hrd: bhd: rapid hdwy on outer 3f out: edgd lft bnd 2f out: chsd ldrs and drvn wl over 1f out: wknd fnl f* **33/1**

0- **7** 2 **Matilda Poliport**[163] 7227 3-8-9 0 TedDurcan 8 52+
(W R Swinburn) *in tch in midfield: rdn and sltly hmpd bnd jst over 2f out: one pce and no ch after* **25/1**

330- **8** 1 ¼ **Caerus (USA)**[179] 6910 3-9-0 76 JimCrowley 4 54
(W J Knight) *t.k.h ealy: hld up in midfield: rdn and outpcd jst over 2f out: wl hld fnl 2f* **10/1**

9 ½ **Cardinal** 4-9-11 0 KevinGhunowa(3) 1 57
(R A Harris) *dwlt: sn pressing ldr: led over 4f out: hdd wl over 2f out: rdn and wknd qckly ent fnl 2f* **50/1**

00- **10** 11 **Royal Arthur**[220] 5812 3-9-0 0 FergusSweeney 5 28
(L A Dace) *s.i.s: a bhd* **100/1**

1m 38.66s (0.46) **Going Correction** +0.25s/f (Slow)
WFA 3 from 4yo+ 14lb **10** Ran SP% **116.5**
Speed ratings (Par 103): **107,106,105,103,102 102,100,98,98,87**
toteswinger: 1&2 £1.70, 1&3 £2.30, 2&3 £3.30. CSF £8.14 TOTE £2.50: £1.50, £1.30, £1.10; EX 8.80 Trifecta £24.50 Pool £272.58 - 8.22 winning units..
Owner M Khan X2 **Bred** Twelve Oaks Stud **Trained** Epsom, Surrey
■ Stewards' Enquiry : Pat Cosgrave three-day ban: used whip in incorrect place (May 4-6)

FOCUS
An interesting maiden.
Cry Alot Boy Official explanation: jockey said gelding missed the break and pulled hard

1381 DRY HILL FILLIES' H'CAP 1m (P)
3:40 (3:42) (Class 4) (0-85,84) 3-Y-O+ **£5,046** (£1,510; £755; £377; £188) **Stalls** High

Form RPR

213- **1** **Good Again**[203] 6305 3-9-6 80 EddieAhern 2 86+
(G A Butler) *hld up in last pl: effrt and hmpd wl over 1f out: swtchd lft jst over 1f out: qcknd to ld towards fin* **3/1**[2]

610- **2** ¾ **Fanditha (IRE)**[203] 6319 3-9-10 84 RichardHughes 3 86
(R Hannon) *led for 2f: chsd ldr after: rdn 2f out: hmpd and swtchd lft wl over 1f out: ev ch ins fnl f: unable qck towards fin* **3/1**[2]

130- **3** ½ **Something Perfect (USA)**[177] 6946 3-9-6 80 TPQueally 6 81
(H R A Cecil) *swished tail at times: chsd ldrs tl led 6f out: pushed along and hung rt wl over 2f out: sn hrd pressed: hdd and no ex towards fin* **9/2**[3]

21-2 **4** 1 **Luckier (IRE)**[97] 137 3-9-2 76 GeorgeBaker 1 75
(S Kirk) *trckd ldrs: effrt on inner 2f out: ev ch 1f out: unable qck fnl 100yds* **5/1**

014- **5** 1 **Latin Tinge (USA)**[169] 7142 3-9-10 84 RyanMoore 7 80
(P F I Cole) *taken down early: trckd ldrs: rdn 3f out: edgd lft wl over 1f out: one pce* **5/2**[1]

1m 39.81s (1.61) **Going Correction** +0.25s/f (Slow) **5** Ran SP% **113.4**
Speed ratings (Par 102): **101,100,99,98,97**
toteswinger: 1&2 £5.20. CSF £12.65 TOTE £4.40: £1.70, £2.30; EX 10.70.
Owner Future In Mind Partnership **Bred** L A Garfield **Trained** Newmarket, Suffolk

FOCUS
This looked a classy affair for three-year-old fillies. Virtually all of them came into the race unexposed, so this should be fairly strong form.

1382 FORD MANOR H'CAP 1m 2f (P)
4:10 (4:10) (Class 4) (0-80,80) 4-Y-O+ **£5,180** (£1,541; £770; £384) **Stalls** Low

Form RPR

1 **1** **Manshoor (IRE)**[18] 1073 4-9-0 76 WilliamBuick 5 84
(Mrs L Wadham) *trckd ldr: rdn to chal ent fnl f: led ins fnl f: rdn out* **7/2**[2]

-102 **2** ½ **My Shadow**[20] 1035 4-8-9 71 IanMongan 4 78
(S Dow) *led at stdy gallop: rdn and qcknd over 2f out: hrd pressed ent fnl f: hdd and no ex ins fnl f* **9/1**

6604 **3** 1 ¼ **Art Man**[34] 850 6-9-2 78 RyanMoore 3 83
(G L Moore) *hld up in tch: rdn jst over 2f out: kpt on same pce fnl f* **7/4**[1]

436 **4** 1 ¼ **Hucking Hero (IRE)**[6] 1261 4-8-5 70 MarcHalford(3) 7 72
(J R Best) *hld up in last trio: rdn and effrt over 1f out: kpt on fnl f but nt pce to threaten ldrs* **15/2**

6-31 **5** 1 ½ **Trifti**[32] 873 8-9-0 76 DaneO'Neill 1 75
(Miss Jo Crowley) *trckd ldrs: rdn and unable qck 2f out: no imp fnl f* **13/2**[3]

1430 **6** 2 **Folio (IRE)**[22] 999 9-9-0 76 AlanMunro 6 71
(W J Musson) *hld up in last trio: rdn over 1f out: no imp* **7/1**

04-0 **7** 3 ¼ **Polish Power (GER)**[86] 271 9-9-4 80 LPKeniry 2 69
(J S Moore) *s.i.s: hld up in tch in last pl: rdn over 2f out: outpcd 2f out: wl hld after* **14/1**

2m 11.2s (4.60) **Going Correction** +0.25s/f (Slow) **7** Ran SP% **112.9**
Speed ratings (Par 105): **91,90,89,88,87 85,83**
toteswinger: 1&2 £6.30, 1&3 £2.50, 2&3 £3.20. CSF £32.98 TOTE £4.60: £2.00, £3.60; EX 37.00.
Owner Tim Wood **Bred** Liberty Road Stables **Trained** Newmarket, Suffolk

FOCUS
It was difficult to rule any of these out with much certainty, which made for a tricky puzzle to solve.

1383 LADYCROSS H'CAP 2m (P)
4:40 (4:42) (Class 3) (0-95,97) 4-Y-O+
£7,477 (£2,239; £1,119; £560; £279; £140) **Stalls** Low

Form RPR

110- **1** **Keenes Day (FR)**[149] 7404 4-9-1 89 RoystonFfrench 5 99
(M Johnston) *stdd s: towards rr: reminder 10f out: hdwy on outer 3f out: rdn to ld over 1f out: edgd lft ent fnl f: clr fnl f: styd on wl* **11/4**[1]

1320 **2** 2 ½ **Wine 'n Dine**[22] 1007 4-9-1 89 RyanMoore 4 96
(G L Moore) *hld up in midfield: hdwy over 2f out: kpt on to chse wnr ins fnl f: no imp after* **10/3**[2]

00-6 **3** 1 ¼ **Carte Diamond (USA)**[21] 1017 8-9-13 97 TomEaves 9 103
(B Ellison) *t.k.h: hld up bhd: hdwy wl over 1f out: kpt on u.p to go 3rd nr fin: nvr threatened ldrs* **12/1**

016- **4** ½ **Nemo Spirit (IRE)**[148] 7429 4-9-2 90 DO'Donohoe 6 97+
(W R Muir) *led: rdn over 2f out: hdd wl over 1f out: btn whn n.m.r and swtchd rt wl ins fnl f* **11/1**

452- **5** hd **Sevenna (FR)**[217] 5938 4-9-0 88 TPQueally 2 93+
(H R A Cecil) *chsd ldrs: wnt 2nd over 2f out: rdn and ev ch 2f out: unable qck and sltly hmpd ent fnl f: edgd lft ins fnl f: wknd and lost 2 pls nr fnish* **4/1**[3]

153- **6** 10 **Jagger**[204] 6288 9-9-4 88 (p) EddieAhern 1 81
(G A Butler) *hld up in midfield: hdwy on inner over 2f out: rdn sn btn wl over 1f out: no ch after* **11/2**

0 **7** 1 ¼ **Valmari (IRE)**[21] 1017 6-9-5 89 (b[1]) J-PGuillambert 3 80
(C E Brittain) *t.k.h: sn chsng ldr tl over 2f out: sn wknd: wl bhd fr wl over 1f out* **20/1**

14-0 **8** 5 **Lost Soldier Three (IRE)**[21] 1017 8-9-10 94 AdrianTNicholls 7 79
(D Nicholls) *hld up in last pair: lost tch wl over 2f out: n.d* **14/1**

003- **9** 12 **Inchnadamph**[267] 4439 9-9-5 89 (t) JimmyQuinn 8 60
(T J Fitzgerald) *t.k.h: in tch on outer: rdn and effrt to chse ldrs 4f out: wknd over 2f out: eased fnl f: t.o* **16/1**

3m 23.35s (-2.35) **Going Correction** +0.25s/f (Slow)
WFA 4 from 6yo+ 4lb **9** Ran SP% **118.5**
Speed ratings (Par 107): **115,113,113,112,112 107,107,104,98**
toteswinger: 1&2 £2.50, 1&3 £8.40, 2&3 £10.70. CSF £12.33 CT £94.93 TOTE £3.60: £1.70, £1.40, £3.30; EX 13.80 Trifecta £141.60 Pool £359.84 - 1.88 winning units..
Owner Mrs R J Jacobs **Bred** Newsells Park Stud Ltd **Trained** Middleham Moor, N Yorks

FOCUS
An open-looking staying event, featuring plenty of familiar faces.

NOTEBOOK
Keenes Day(FR) has the look of an in-and-out performer, as he either usually wins/goes close or gets beaten a very long way. He does not seem an easy ride and was in trouble for a few strides with a circuit to go, but his jockey managed to get him back into the race and the combination won easily. It would be a brave man that always backed him at short odds. (op 3-1 tchd 5-2)
Wine 'n Dine did not really get competitive in the Queen's Prize last time at Kempton and was readily brushed aside when the winner went for home. (op 5-1)
Carte Diamond(USA), who was having his first start on Polytrack, was heavily restrained early and never posed a threat to the leaders. (op 10-1)
Nemo Spirit(IRE) ran better than his beaten distance suggests, as he was staying on again, after being headed, when finding little room at around the furlong pole. Once in the clear, he kept on nicely. (op 14-1 tchd 10-1)
Sevenna(FR) has not had much racing, so was open to a lot more improvement than most of her rivals. She looked the most likely winner two furlongs from home but her effort flattened out and she became onepaced. (op 3-1 tchd 5-1)
Jagger had a fairly consistent season in 2008 but was made to look very slow when coming off the bridle here. (op 6-1 tchd 13-2 and 5-1)
Lost Soldier Three(IRE), well beaten over 1m4f on turf last time, spent the whole race at the rear of the field. (tchd 12-1and 16-1 in a place)

1384 DERBY TRIAL HERE 9TH MAY CONDITIONS STKS 5f (P)
5:10 (5:10) (Class 3) 4-Y-O+ **£7,352** (£2,201; £1,100; £551; £274) **Stalls** High

Form RPR

60-6 **1** **Rowe Park**[29] 911 6-9-0 100 RyanMoore 3 109
(Mrs L C Jewell) *hld up in tch: rdn and hdwy over 1f out: led ins fnl f: r.o wl* **2/1**[1]

213- **2** ¾ **Masta Plasta (IRE)**[177] 6963 6-9-5 108 AdrianTNicholls 1 111
(D Nicholls) *led: rdn wl over 1f out: 2 l clr 1f out: hdd and no ex ins fnl f* **5/2**[2]

414- **3** 1 **Peace Offering (IRE)**[177] 6963 9-9-5 108 TedDurcan 4 107
(D Nicholls) *taken down early: t.k.h: chsd ldr: rdn and unable qck over 1f out: kpt on same pce fnl f* **9/2**

331- **4** hd **Icelandic**[162] 7243 7-9-0 108 (t) AndreaAtzeni(5) 5 107+
(F Sheridan) *t.k.h: hld up in tch: rdn and unable qck wl over 1f out: kpt on ins fnl f: nt pce to threaten ldrs* **3/1**[3]

-006 **5** 4 **Stoneacre Lad (IRE)**[19] 1052 6-9-5 93 (b) LPKeniry 2 92
(Peter Grayson) *chsd ldrs: rdn 2f out: wknd ent fnl f* **16/1**

59.87 secs (1.07) **Going Correction** +0.25s/f (Slow) **5** Ran SP% **111.0**
Speed ratings (Par 107): **101,99,98,97,91**
CSF £7.38 TOTE £2.60: £1.60, £1.50; EX 10.60 Place 6 £22.92, Place 5 £10.52..
Owner Mrs Sue Ashdown **Bred** J Baker **Trained** Sutton Valence, Kent

FOCUS
Not many runners but a tight-looking sprint on paper. It would be no surprise if some of these clash on a regular basis.

NOTEBOOK
Rowe Park benefited from his seasonal debut over course and distance to cut down the long-time leader inside the final furlong. He has often run well at this track and fully deserved to get his head in front. (op 3-1)
Masta Plasta(IRE), having his first start since October, did the work in front and was only just run out of it late on. He regularly goes abroad and will no doubt follow a similar path. (tchd 9-4 and 3-1)
Peace Offering(IRE) also finished last season in the same race as his stablemate. He is another sure to be campaigned in the right races, whether they be in this country or abroad. (op 7-2)
Icelandic stays much further than this trip and seems to prefer easier ground. He ran a respectable race in the circumstances. (op 5-2)
Stoneacre Lad(IRE), who had a fitness advantage on three of his rivals, never got involved. (tchd 14-1)
T/Plt: £44.00 to a £1 stake. Pool: £62,013.28. 1,026.71 winning tickets. T/Qpdt: £22.90 to a £1 stake. Pool: £3,461.30. 111.80 winning tickets. SP

1021 LEOPARDSTOWN (L-H)
Sunday, April 19

OFFICIAL GOING: Good to yielding

1388a P.W.MCGRATH MEMORIAL BALLYSAX STKS (GROUP 3) 1m 2f
3:55 (3:55) 3-Y-O **£41,082** (£12,053; £5,742; £1,956)

RPR

1 **Fame And Glory**[158] 7294 3-9-6 112 JMurtagh 4 114+
(A P O'Brien, Ire) *chsd ldrs: 5th 1/2-way: hdwy to 3rd 2f out: rdn to chal 1f out: styd on to ld fnl 100yds: kpt on wl* **4/1**[2]

2 1 **Fergus McIver (IRE)**[14] 1140 3-9-1 93 (p) KJManning 5 107
(J S Bolger, Ire) *chsd ldrs: 4th 1/2-way: 3rd 4f out: hdwy to 2nd ent st: rdn to ld over 1f out: sn chal: hdd ins fnl 100yds and no ex: jst hld on for 2nd* **5/1**[3]

3 hd **Mourayan (IRE)**[168] 7158 3-9-1 111 MJKinane 2 107+
(John M Oxx, Ire) *chsd ldrs: 3rd 1/2-way: rdn and lost pl ent st: 6th 2f out: styd into 4th 1f out: kpt on wl fnl f: jst hld for 2nd* **5/4**[1]

4 3 **Hail Caesar (IRE)**[21] 1022 3-9-1 105 JAHeffernan 7 101
(A P O'Brien, Ire) *in rr of mid-div: 8th 1/2-way: hdwy to 5th 2f out: rdn and no ex over 1f out: kpt on same pce fnl f* **14/1**

5 hd **Dixie Music (IRE)**[179] 6917 3-9-1 SMLevey 9 101
(A P O'Brien, Ire) *bhd: rdn ent st: late hdwy fnl f* **50/1**

6 1 1/4 **Grace O'Malley (IRE)**[201] 6369 3-8-12 ... PJSmullen 1 95
(D K Weld, Ire) *dwlt: sn mid-div: 7th 1/2-way: rdn and dropped to 9th 2f out: styd on to 7th 1f out: kpt on same pce fnl f* **14/1**

7 nk **Vitruvian Man**[174] 7029 3-9-1 107 ... FMBerry 10 98
(John M Oxx, Ire) *hld up towards rr: hdwy to 7th 2f out: rdn in 6th 1 1/2f out: no ex and kpt on same pce fr over 1f out* **5/1**[3]

8 3/4 **Tarankali (IRE)**[217] 5943 3-9-1 76 ... NGMcCullagh 8 96?
(John M Oxx, Ire) *chsd ldr in cl 2nd: led under 4f out: rdn and hdd over 1f out: no ex and wknd ins fnl f* **66/1**

9 1 1/4 **Nafaath (IRE)**[184] 6800 3-9-1 91 ... DPMcDonogh 3 94
(Kevin Prendergast, Ire) *mid-div: 6th 1/2-way: rdn in 8th 2f out: sn no ex: kpt on one pce* **12/1**

10 9 **Liszt (IRE)**[170] 7119 3-9-1 ... CO'Donoghue 6 76
(A P O'Brien, Ire) *led: strly pressed: hdd under 4f out: no ex in 4th 2f out: sn wknd* **16/1**

2m 7.40s (-0.80) **Going Correction** +0.225s/f (Good) **10** Ran SP% **128.1**
Speed ratings: **112,111,111,108,108 107,107,106,105,98**
CSF £27.20 TOTE £4.30: £1.60, £1.60, £1.40; DF 29.10.
Owner Derrick Smith **Bred** Ptarmigan Bloodstock & Miss K **Trained** Ballydoyle, Co Tipperary

FOCUS
This race has an impressive record for finding subsequent Group 1 winners and aside from notable previous winners like Galileo (2001), High Chaparral (2002) and Yeats (2004), several other placed runners have also gone on to better things. The third and fourth have been rated to their juvenile best, while the cosy winner, who recorded a decent time, has been rated to a personal best.

NOTEBOOK
Fame And Glory headed the Ballydoyle quartet of runners and he defied his Group 1 penalty for winning the Criterium de Saint-Cloud last November a shade comfortably in the finish. Always travelling, he crept closer to take it up on the outer inside the final furlong to underline his class and was better than the winning margin suggested. Subsequent Derby hero High Chaparral was the last winner of this race to carry a penalty and the Derrinstown Derby Trial could be next for the unbeaten son of Montjeu, who should be open to some improvement from this seasonal debut effort. (op 9/2)
Fergus McIver(IRE) shaped creditably in this better company and underlined the promise he showed when landing a decent Curragh contest after a couple of promising runs beforehand. Sinndar, runner-up in 2000, and the likes of Milan and Vinnie Roe, second and third in 2002 and Alamshar, second in 2003, stepped up on their respective displays in this race. (op 6/1)
Mourayan(IRE) looked like he should benefit from this seasonal bow. He was tapped for toe early in the straight before running on again inside the final furlong. He is an idle worker at home according to his trainer, and on this evidence he looked very much like he should relish a couple of furlongs longer. The Eyrefield Stakes winner here last season could also turn up in the Derrinstown and this seasonal debut effort should hopefully bring him on. (op 5/4 tchd 11/8)
Hail Caesar(IRE) stepped up on his seasonal debut effort behind Recharge over 1m last time.
Dixie Music(IRE) hinted enough here to suggest he should be winning his maiden before long.
Grace O'Malley(IRE), the only filly in the line-up and winner of her only start at two, missed the kick and never threatened at the business end.
Vitruvian Man, stable companion of the favourite, was also well-backed. He crept closer leaving the back but was soon going nowhere when asked a question. (op 11/2 tchd 6/1)

1389 - 1391a (Foreign Racing) - See Raceform Interactive

CAPANNELLE (R-H)
Sunday, April 19

OFFICIAL GOING: Heavy

1392a PREMIO BOTTICELLI (LISTED RACE) (C&G) 1m 2f 110y
3:00 (3:03) 3-Y-O **£19,573** (£19,573; £6,524; £3,262)

RPR

1 **Spirit Of Sport (IRE)**[14] 3-8-11 ... SDiana 1 101
(A Candi, Italy)

1 dht **Renowing (UAE)** 3-8-11 ... DVargiu 12 101
(B Grizzetti, Italy)

3 1/2 **Otello Azzy (ITY)** 3-8-11 ... SSulas 7 100
(A Cascio, Italy)

4 2 **Damiani** 3-8-11 ... MDemuro 4 96
(L Camici, Italy)

5 1/2 **Wood White (USA)**[14] 3-8-1 ... CFiocchi 9 85
(R Menichetti, Italy)

6 shd **Seul Blue (ITY)**[21] 3-8-11 ... LManiezzi 11 95
(R Menichetti, Italy)

7 1 1/2 **Masstorm (ITY)** 3-8-11 ... MMonteriso 2 92
(F Saggiomo, Italy)

8 2 **Red Kimi (IRE)**[126] 7681 3-8-11 ... MEsposito 8 88
(R Santini, Italy)

9 1 1/2 **Faidibiri (IRE)**[132] 3-8-11 ... URispoli 10 85
(G Ligas, Italy)

10 1 **Galidon (IRE)** 3-8-11 ... GBietolini 6 83
(R Brogi, Italy)

11 8 **Fanunalter**[36] 3-8-11 ... LDettori 5 68
(M Botti) *disp 5th to st: hdwy on outside to go 3rd 2 1/2f out: rdn 2f out: sn btn* **13/5**[1]

12 2 **Capo Malfatano (IRE)** 3-8-11 ... PConvertino 13 64
(R Brogi, Italy)

13 3 **Kentucky Ray (IRE)**[132] 3-8-11 ... SMulas 3 59
(Gianluca Bietolini, Italy)

2m 14.8s (134.80) **13** Ran SP% **27.8**
(including one euro stakes): Renowing WIN 3.43, PL 2.61; Spirit ofSport WIN 5.33, PL 4.09; Otello Azzy PL 9.15; DF 43.19.
Owner N Marchetti **Bred** Ugo Marchetti **Trained** Italy
Owner Scuderia Blueberry **Bred** Darley **Trained** Italy

1393a PREMIO PARIOLI MEMORIAL LORENZO BROGI (GROUP 3) (COLTS) 1m
4:10 (4:29) 3-Y-O **£82,524** (£36,311; £19,806; £9,903)

RPR

1 **Libano (IRE)**[14] 3-9-2 ... MMonteriso 9 109
(L Polito, Italy) *mde virtually all: allowed to set stdy pce: clr st: led field over to stands' side: r.o wl: unchal* **19/2**

2 4 **Sottone**[162] 7253 3-9-2 ... SMulas 8 100
(B Grizzetti, Italy) *towards rr to st: nt clr run 2f out: moved outside: r.o wl fnl f* **54/10**[3]

3 2 **Osservatorio (ITY)**[15] 3-9-2 ... LManiezzi 12 95
(R Menichetti, Italy) *towards rr to st: hdwy over 2f out: styd on same pce fnl f: reported to have fin lame* **83/10**

4 1/2 **Turati**[210] 3-9-2 ... MPasquale 4 94
(G Pucciatti, Italy) *3rd st: styd on one pce fnl 2f* **37/10**[2]

5 1/2 **Lui Rei (ITY)**[166] 7186 3-9-2 ... LDettori 13 93
(A Renzoni, Italy) *hld up disputing 8th: abt 8 l bhd wnr st: smooth prog to rch 2nd appr fnl f: no ex* **4/5**[1]

6 4 **Relco Italy (IRE)**[14] 3-9-2 ... PConvertino 7 84
(B Grizzetti, Italy) *4th st: disp 2nd 2f out: one pce* **54/10**[3]

7 2 1/2 **Desert Cry (IRE)**[21] 3-9-2 ... DVargiu 3 78
(B Grizzetti, Italy) *5th st: rdn and btn 2f out* **54/10**[3]

8 nk **Apro Lunare (IRE)**[15] 3-9-2 ... CColombi 2 77
(Laura Grizzetti, Italy) *racd in 2nd tl wknd over 1f out* **93/10**

9 1 1/4 **Ad Honores (USA)**[21] 3-9-2 ... CFiocchi 1 75
(R Menichetti, Italy) *a towards rr* **83/10**

10 3/4 **Anonimo Veneziano**[15] 3-9-2 ... MDemuro 11 73
(V Caruso, Italy) *mid-div tl btn wl over 2f out* **94/10**

11 snk **Miroslav (IRE)**[14] 3-9-2 ... URispoli 6 72
(L Camici, Italy) *in rr to st: gd hdwy to dispute 2nd 2f out: sn wknd* **37/10**[2]

12 8 **Big Tower (IRE)**[21] 3-9-2 ... PAragoni 10 71
(Giuseppe Chianese, Italy) *a towards rr* **126/1**

13 hd **Mibar (USA)**[14] 3-9-2 ... GBietolini 5 53
(Gianluca Bietolini, Italy) *a bhd* **70/1**

1m 39.8s **13** Ran SP% **197.5**
WIN 10.53; PL 3.92, 6.48, 6.15; DF 123.99.
Owner Scuderia Lucrezia **Bred** Scuderia Tamara Sas **Trained** Italy

1394a PREMIO CARLO CHIESA (GROUP 3) (F&M) 6f
4:45 (5:03) 3-Y-O+ **£38,835** (£17,087; £9,320; £4,661)

RPR

1 **L'Indiscreta**[154] 7349 4-9-2 ... DVargiu 5 103
(B Grizzetti, Italy) *mid-div: gd hdwy to ld 1f out: r.o wl* **51/10**[3]

2 2 **Lips Arrow (GER)**[196] 4-9-2 ... MDemuro 8 97
(Andreas Lowe, Germany) *a cl up: ev ch appr fnl f: kpt on one pce* **54/10**

3 1 1/2 **Ruby Dancer (IRE)**[687] 4-9-2 ... MEsposito 2 93
(Alessandro Turco, Italy) *a.p: led wl over 1f out to 1f out: one pce* **223/10**

4 3/4 **La Badia (IRE)** 3-8-5 ... GMarcelli 6 90
(L Riccardi, Italy) *a in tch: kpt on one pce fr over 1f out* **43/10**[2]

5 nk **Shoshiba (IRE)**[357] 1659 6-9-2 ... SSulas 1 72
(Alessandro Turco, Italy) *pressed ldr: led briefly 2f out: one pce* **223/10**

6 2 **Kathy Ridge (IRE)**[210] 3-8-5 ... PAragoni 9 66
(A Peraino, Italy) *in rr early: styd on fnl 2f: nvr nr to chal* **43/10**[2]

7 4 **White Rose (ITY)**[357] 1659 5-9-2 ... GBietolini 4 54
(Luigi Rosa, Italy) *in rr early: nvr nr to chal* **87/1**

8 1/2 **Crystany (IRE)**[204] 6271 4-9-2 ... LDettori 7 53
(E A L Dunlop) *in rr and u.p 1/2-way: nvr a factor* **23/10**[1]

9 nse **Docksil**[154] 7349 5-9-2 ... SMulas 3 53
(B Grizzetti, Italy) *led to 2f out: eased whn btn* **135/10**

10 nse **Eva Kant**[149] 7430 3-8-5 ... LManiezzi 15 52
(R Menichetti, Italy) *s.s: sme late prog* **96/10**

11 1/2 **Giordana (IRE)**[188] 6713 3-8-5 ... TThulliez 13 51
(P Vovcenko, Germany) *nvr a factor* **119/10**

12 3/4 **Magritte (ITY)**[154] 7349 4-9-2 ... CFiocchi 12 49
(R Menichetti, Italy) *prom: ev ch 2f out: sn wknd: eased* **96/10**

13 snk **Madda's Force (ITY)**[161] 3-8-5 ... URispoli 16 48
(R Betti, Italy) *spd to 1/2-way* **22/1**

14 1 1/4 **Lady Marmelade (ITY)**[44] 6-9-2 ... MBelli 10 45
(D Ducci, Italy) *a bhd* **131/10**

15 10 **Atalia (GER)**[185] 6767 4-9-2 ... AHelfenbein 11 43
(Mario Hofer, Germany) *bhd fnl 2f* **57/10**

1m 10.4s (0.10)
WFA 3 from 4yo+ 11lb **15** Ran SP% **169.7**
WIN 6.13; PL 2,28, 2.56, 6.95; DF 22.48.
Owner Scuderia Blueberry **Bred** Azienda Agricola Razza Del Sole **Trained** Italy

NOTEBOOK
Crystany(IRE) never got in a blow from off the pace. She is by Green Desert and this sort of ground would not be to her liking.

KREFELD (R-H)
Sunday, April 19

OFFICIAL GOING: Soft

1395a DR BUSCH MEMORIAL (GROUP 3) 1m 110y
4:00 (4:15) 3-Y-O **£31,068** (£9,709; £4,854; £2,913)

RPR

1 **Irian (GER)**[35] 3-9-2 ... ADeVries 3 116
(J Hirschberger, Germany) *a in tch: 3rd st: qcknd to ld 2f out: r.o wl* **23/5**

2 2 1/2 **Daring Tiger (GER)** 3-9-2 ... AStarke 4 110
(P Schiergen, Germany) *last to st: styd on wl fr over 1f out to take 2nd ins fnl f: nvr rchd wnr* **7/2**[2]

3 1 **King Of Sydney (USA)**[158] 7294 3-9-2 ... DBoeuf 2 108
(Mario Hofer, Germany) *hld up: 5th st: styd on fnl f* **43/10**[3]

4 2 **Globus (GER)**[182] 6853 3-9-2 ... WMongil 5 104
(Uwe Ostmann, Germany) *mid-div: cl 6th st: ev ch 2f out: no ex fnl f* **2/1**[1]

5 3 **St Moritz (IRE)**[72] 432 3-9-2 ... JoeFanning 6 97
(M Johnston) *trckd ldr to st: btn over 1f out* **66/10**

6 nk **Querari (GER)** 3-9-2 ... EPedroza 1 96
(A Wohler, Germany) *hld up: 4th st: sn one pce* **9/2**

7 4 1/2 **Sabantuy**[21] 3-9-2 ... ASuborics 7 88
(C Von Der Recke, Germany) *led to 2f out* **17/2**

1m 45.2s (-1.40) **7** Ran SP% **134.1**
(including ten euro stakes): WIN 56; PL 18, 17, 17; SF 429.
Owner Gestut Schlenderhan **Bred** *unknown **Trained** Germany

NOTEBOOK
St Moritz(IRE), winner of his previous two starts on Polytrack, was running on turf for the first time and was taking a big step up in grade, having only won a handicap off 82 last time out. He ran all right, but perhaps better ground will suit him in future.

[1168]PONTEFRACT (L-H)

Monday, April 20

OFFICIAL GOING: Firm (good to firm in places; 9.7)

Wind: Virtually nil Weather: Sunny and warm

1396 PREMIER SPORTS CAFE BAR MEDIAN AUCTION MAIDEN FILLIES' STKS — 5f

2:10 (2:11) (Class 5) 2-Y-O **£3,238** (£963; £481; £240) **Stalls** Low

Form RPR

1 **Grand Zafeen** 2-9-0 0 ... SamHitchcott 1 74+
(M R Channon) *in tch: hdwy 1/2-way: effrt to chse ldr over 1f ou: rdn to ld jst ins fnl f: kpt on wl* **3/1**[1]

03 2 ½ **Anjomarba (IRE)**[11] 1195 2-8-9 0 ... JackDean(5) 6 69
(W G M Turner) *led: rdn wl over 1f out: drvn and hdd jst ins fnl f: kpt on wl u.p* **7/2**[2]

3 5 **Duchess Dora (IRE)** 2-9-0 0 ... GrahamGibbons 4 51+
(J J Quinn) *chsd ldng pair: rdn along wl over 1f out: kpt on same pce ent fnl f* **3/1**[1]

4 1 ¼ **Elegant Dancer (IRE)** 2-9-0 0 ... PaulMulrennan 5 47
(Paul Green) *towards rr: hdwy wl over 1f out: rdn and swtchd rt ent fnl f: kpt on: nrst fin* **10/1**

5 2 **Brinscall** 2-9-0 0 ... DavidAllan 9 39
(T D Easterby) *in tch on outer: hdwy to chse ldrs 1/2-way: rdn along wl over 1f out: wknd* **11/2**[3]

4 6 1 ¾ **Drumpellier (IRE)**[16] 1126 2-9-0 0 ... JamieMoriarty 8 33
(P T Midgley) *cl up: rdn along over 2f out: sn drvn and wknd over 1f out* **17/2**

7 6 **Billy's Bid** 2-9-0 0 ... PatrickMathers 2 11
(I W McInnes) *sn outpcd and a in rr* **33/1**

8 26 **Ze Finale** 2-9-0 0 ... DuranFentiman 7 —
(T D Easterby) *chsd ldrs: rdn along 1/2-way: sn wknd* **18/1**

63.38 secs (0.08) **Going Correction** -0.225s/f (Firm) **8** Ran SP% **115.4**

Speed ratings (Par 89): **90,89,81,79,76 73,63,22**

toteswinger: 1&2 £1.20, 1&3 £3.30, 2&3 £3.10. CSF £13.86 TOTE £3.10: £1.10, £1.30, £1.50; EX 10.80.

Owner Jaber Abdullah **Bred** Rabbah Bloodstock Limited **Trained** West Ilsley, Berks

■ Stewards' Enquiry : Jack Dean one-day ban: failed to ride to draw (May 4)

FOCUS

No rain for six weeks but between half an inch and an inch of water had been put on the track and, whilst it was quick ground, there was a good cover of grass and no jar whatsoever. The form looks reasonable for the grade.

NOTEBOOK

Grand Zafeen, a daughter of first-season sire Zafeen, a Group 1 winner, out of a Fred Darling winner, is a sharp sort who looked bright and well in her coat. She took a while to get into full stride but, after pulling three horses wide turning in, she soon mastered the pacesetter and always looked in full control. The stiff five suited her and the Hilary Needler at Beverley next month must be tempting now. (op 5-2)

Anjomarba(IRE), a well-beaten third behind smart Monsieur Chevalier at Folkestone, was having her third run. She took them along and stuck to her task finishing clear second best. She can surely break her duck. (tchd 3-1)

Duchess Dora(IRE), green and noisy beforehand, came in for plenty of support. She kept tabs on the leader but tired in the final furlong and a half. She looked to be carrying plenty of condition and presumably had been showing plenty at home. (op 13-2)

Elegant Dancer(IRE), a neat daughter of Choisir, stayed on in her own time from the final turn and will be wiser next time. (op 12-1)

Brinscall, from a stable whose youngsters generally need their first run, showed ability from her outside draw. (op 5-1 tchd 6-1)

Drumpellier(IRE) tired badly in the home straight and did not improve on her debut effort. (op 8-1 tchd 15-2)

1397 CORNMARKET H'CAP — 1m 4f 8y

2:40 (2:41) (Class 5) (0-70,70) 3-Y-O **£3,238** (£963; £481; £240) **Stalls** Low

Form RPR

300- 1 **Spinning Waters**[208] 6198 3-8-11 63 ... StephenCarson 4 66
(Eve Johnson Houghton) *trckd leaer: led over 3f out: rdn clr over 1f out: styd on wl u.p* **6/1**[3]

00-0 2 1 **Addison De Witt**[4] 1308 3-7-13 56 oh7 ... PatrickDonaghy(5) 5 57
(Micky Hammond) *in tch: hdwy on outer 3f out: rdn to chse wnr 2f out: drvn and edgd lft ent fnl f: kpt on wl u.p towards fin* **40/1**

4102 3 1 ½ **Kochanski (IRE)**[5] 1282 3-8-5 57 ... RoystonFfrench 1 56
(M Johnston) *trckd ldng pair: effrt on inner 2f out and sn rdn: drvn and edgd rt over 1f out: kpt on same pce* **2/1**[2]

3-12 4 ½ **Sounds Of Jupiter (IRE)**[49] 740 3-9-4 70 ... StephenDonohoe 7 68+
(D M Simcock) *stdd s and hld up in rr: effrt whn nt clr run over 2f out: rdn and hdwy wl over 1f out: sn drvn and n.m.r appr fnl f: sn same pce* **13/8**[1]

6-65 5 1 ¾ **Lilly Blue (IRE)**[20] 1050 3-9-3 69 ... SamHitchcott 6 64
(M R Channon) *hld up towards rr: hdwy over 2f out: sn rdn and no imp* **12/1**

30-4 6 8 **Orphaned Annie**[19] 1063 3-7-12 57 ... JamieKyne(7) 2 39
(B Ellison) *trckd ldrs: effrt 3f out and sn rdn along: drvn and edgd lft wl over 1f out: sn wknd* **7/1**

50-0 7 52 **Martha's Girl (USA)**[23] 998 3-8-9 61 ... (t) PaulMulrennan 3 —
(D H Brown) *led: rdn along over 4f out: hdd over 3f out and sn wknd* **20/1**

2m 40.5s (-0.30) **Going Correction** -0.225s/f (Firm) **7** Ran SP% **113.1**

Speed ratings (Par 98): **92,91,90,90,88 83,48**

toteswinger: 1&2 £22.30, 1&3 £3.50, 2&3 £16.30. CSF £167.20 TOTE £7.70: £3.30, £23.00; EX 342.40.

Owner R Crutchley **Bred** R E Crutchley **Trained** Blewbury, Oxon

FOCUS

A modest three-year-old stayers' handicap. The pace was not strong and it turned into a tactical affair, so the form is a bit messy.

Martha's Girl(USA) Official explanation: jockey said filly hung right throughout

1398 RIU PALACE MELONERAS H'CAP — 6f

3:10 (3:11) (Class 2) (0-100,96) 4-Y-O+

£11,215 (£3,358; £1,679; £840; £419; £210) **Stalls** Low

Form RPR

04-2 1 **Advanced**[22] 1018 6-9-4 96 ... NCallan 4 105
(K A Ryan) *trckd ldr: hdwy over 2f out: rdn to ld over 1f out: hung bdly rt ins fnl f: jst hld on* **2/1**[1]

1400 2 nk **Thebes**[9] 1212 4-8-12 90 ... RoystonFfrench 8 98
(M Johnston) *in tch: hdwy over 2f out: rdn to chse wnr ent fnl f: sn drvn and evch tl nt qckn nr fin* **9/1**

-215 3 2 ¾ **Obe Gold**[5] 1278 7-8-9 87 ... (v) AdrianTNicholls 7 86
(D Nicholls) *sn pushed along in rr: hdwy over 2f out and sn rdn: drvn and kpt on ins fnl f: nrst fin* **7/2**[2]

056- 4 3 **Maze (IRE)**[276] 4145 4-8-13 91 ... TomEaves 10 81+
(B Smart) *hld up in tch: lost pl 1/2-way and sn in rr: hdwy wl over 1f out: rdn and styd on strly ins fnl f: nrst fin* **12/1**

000- 5 ¾ **Ishetoo**[178] 6947 5-9-4 96 ... SilvestreDeSousa 9 83
(A Dickman) *chsd ldrs: effrt over 2f out: rdn wl over 1f out: sn wknd* **16/1**

00-0 6 ½ **Bel Cantor**[22] 1018 6-8-7 88 ... (p) KellyHarrison(3) 5 74
(W J H Ratcliffe) *led: rdn along over 2f out: hdd and drvn over 1f out: wknd ent fnl f* **11/1**

122- 7 ½ **Fantasy Explorer**[177] 6971 6-8-10 88 ... JamieMoriarty 6 72
(J J Quinn) *chsd ldng pair: rdn along wl over 1f out: drvn appr fnl f and sn wknd* **9/1**

0100 8 4 ½ **Nightjar (USA)**[16] 1124 4-8-9 87 ... RobertWinston 2 57
(M Johnston) *s.i.s: a bhd* **8/1**[3]

1-40 9 12 **Invincible Force (IRE)**[23] 995 5-9-0 92 ... (b) FrancisNorton 3 23
(Paul Green) *chsd ldrs on inner: rdn along wl over 2f out: sn wknd* **8/1**[3]

1m 14.58s (-2.32) **Going Correction** -0.225s/f (Firm) **9** Ran SP% **119.7**

Speed ratings (Par 109): **106,105,101,97,96 96,95,89,73**

toteswinger: 1&2 £4.70, 1&3 £3.00, 2&3 £6.00. CSF £22.15 CT £62.47 TOTE £2.90: £1.10, £2.80, £1.90; EX 18.60.

Owner T Doherty and McHeen **Bred** Gestut Gorlsdorf **Trained** Hambleton, N Yorks

FOCUS

A good-class and quite valuable sprint handicap. The winner is rated to last season's form with a personal best from the runner-up.

NOTEBOOK

Advanced had shown that there was another good prize to be won with him when runner-up to handicap blot Palace Moon at Doncaster on his reappearance. Once rated as high as 114 and 109 when he took the 2007 Ayr Gold Cup, here rated 96 he ended a 16-outing blank since his big day in Scotland. Turned out in top trim, he kept tabs on the pacesetter but inside the last he edged right as if feeling the firm ground. His rider changed his whip hand twice in the blink of an eye and in the end he did just enough. He should continue to give a good account of himself and now heads for a heritage handicap at Newmarket on 2000 Guineas day. (op 3-1 tchd 10-3)

Thebes, unable to dominate, came through to chase the winner inside the last. Just held at the line, his record on turf now reads one from 11, but on the all-weather he boasts a strike-rate of four from eight. (op 8-1 tchd 15-2)

Obe Gold, drawn wide when fifth over five at Beverley last week, lacked the pace to take a good position, but he stayed on in willing fashion in the home straight without ever threatening the first two. He should continue to knock on the door. (op 10-3 tchd 9-2)

Maze(IRE), his own worst enemy at three, has slipped to a lenient mark. Skilfully restrained off the pace and towards the outer, he picked up in most encouraging fashion inside the last. If his trainer can win the battle of wills he can certainly add to his couple of juvenile wins. (op 11-1)

Ishetoo, considered a month off his best by his trainer, is much better over five. (op 14-1 tchd 12-1)

Bel Cantor showed all his old blinding speed to take them along until straightening up for home. He is still 4lb higher than for his last success and may not appreciate ground as quick as this nowadays. (op 10-1 tchd 8-1)

Fantasy Explorer, highly progressive over each of the last three seasons, is now on a career-high mark. He travelled strongly until tiring once in line for home and should find another nice handicap in due course. (op 15-2 tchd 7-1)

Nightjar(USA), who looked reluctant, is much better suited by the Fibresand surface at Southwell. (op 16-1)

1399 PONTEFRACT MARATHON H'CAP — 2m 5f 122y

3:40 (3:40) (Class 5) (0-75,74) 4-Y-O+ **£3,885** (£1,156; £577; £288) **Stalls** Low

Form RPR

251- 1 **Mr Crystal (FR)**[112] 6861 5-9-8 74 ... FrederikTylicki(5) 9 75+
(Micky Hammond) *hld up in midfield: stdy hdwy on outer over 4f out: led wl over 1f out and sn rdn: drvn and edgd lft ins fnl f: styd on wl* **3/1**[1]

0-6 2 1 ¼ **Haldibari (IRE)**[14] 1156 5-8-11 58 ... TPO'Shea 7 57
(S Lycett) *cl up: led after 2f: rdn along 4f out: drvn and hdd 2f out: kpt on gamely u.p fnl f* **20/1**

00- 3 1 ¼ **Rimsky Korsakov (IRE)**[20] 6055 5-8-8 55 oh10 ... (v) PaulMulrennan 3 53
(Micky Hammond) *trckd ldrs on inner: pushed along and sltly outpcd 3f out: rdn 2f out: styd on ent fnl f: n.m.r and kpt on wl towards fin* **16/1**

400- 4 hd **Terrasini (FR)**[61] 5399 4-8-5 58 ... RoystonFfrench 5 56
(J Howard Johnson) *t.k.h: prom: rdn along and sltly outpcd 3f out: styd on u.p fnl 2f* **5/1**[3]

0135 5 hd **Victory Quest (IRE)**[34] 860 9-9-11 72 ... (v) RobertWinston 6 70
(Mrs S Lamyman) *midfield: hdwy over 6f out: rdn to chse ldrs over 2f out: drvn and kpt on ins fnl f: nrst fin* **20/1**

-511 6 ¾ **Daraiym (IRE)**[13] 1171 4-8-3 56 ... FrancisNorton 4 53
(Paul Green) *trckd ldr: effrt to chal 3f out: sn rdn and ev ch tl drvn and one pce fr wl over 1f out* **7/2**[2]

3-43 7 2 ¾ **Yonder**[13] 1171 5-9-0 61 ... TravisBlock 8 55
(H Morrison) *trckd ldrs: effrt 4f out: rdn along 3f out: drvn 2f out and grad wknd* **6/1**

1/0- 8 4 **Hasanpour (IRE)**[9] 3250 9-9-6 67 ... (t) NCallan 10 57
(K J Burke) *hld up in rr: stdy hdwy over 4f out: rdn to chse ldrs 2f out: sn drvn and wknd* **10/1**

00-3 9 2 ¾ **Orchard House (FR)**[26] 502 6-8-8 55 oh6 ... TomEaves 1 43
(Evan Williams) *hld up: a in rr* **9/1**

0-00 10 82 **Bright Falcon**[7] 1242 4-8-7 60 ... (vt[1]) AdrianTNicholls 2 —
(S Parr) *a in rr: bhd fnl 4f* **50/1**

4m 59.12s (-9.68) **Going Correction** -0.225s/f (Firm)

WFA 4 from 5yo+ 6lb **10** Ran SP% **114.6**

Speed ratings (Par 103): **108,107,107,107,106 106,105,104,103,73**

toteswinger: 1&2 £17.30, 1&3 £17.30, 2&3 £28.50. CSF £65.81 CT £823.99 TOTE £4.30: £1.90, £5.00, £4.70; EX 79.50.

Owner Oakwood Racing Partnership **Bred** Gerard Schence **Trained** Middleham Moor, N Yorks

FOCUS

The longest handicap run on the Flat here. Modest fair but a real test with the gallop picking up from the halfway mark. The form looks messy with the third racing from 10lb out of the handicap.

Victory Quest(IRE) Official explanation: trainer said gelding was lame

Hasanpour(IRE) Official explanation: jockey said gelding hung left closing stages

1400 SUBSCRIBE ONLINE @ RACINGUK.TV MAIDEN STKS — 6f

4:10 (4:18) (Class 5) 3-Y-O+ **£3,238** (£963; £481; £240) **Stalls** Low

Form RPR

3-6 1 **Time Medicean**[26] 951 3-9-0 0 ... SamHitchcott 9 76
(M R Channon) *in tch: pushed along over 2f out: hdwy over 1f out: rdn to ld ent fnl f: styd on* **3/1**[2]

442- **2** 2 **Standpoint**[189] 6701 3-9-0 74 RobertWinston 12 70
(Sir Michael Stoute) *trckd ldrs: hdwy over 2f out: led wl over 1f out and sn rdn: hdd ent fnl f: kpt on same pce* **11/4**[1]

500- **3** 1 ¾ **Jimwil (IRE)**[182] 6857 3-9-0 63 PhillipMakin 3 64
(M Dods) *midfield: hdwy over 2f out and sn rdn: drvn over 1f out: kpt on ins fnl f: nrst fin* **7/1**

0-0 **4** hd **Angelo Poliziano**[7] 1250 3-9-0 0 MickyFenton 2 64
(Mrs A Duffield) *chsd ldrs on inner: rdn along 2f out: drvn over 1f out: kpt on same pce* **20/1**

250- **5** 2 ¾ **Virtuality (USA)**[231] 5561 4-9-6 60 TomEaves 13 53
(B Smart) *cl up on outer: rdn along 2f out: drvn over 1f out and grad wknd* **25/1**

6 1 ½ **Reject** 3-9-0 0 LiamJones 10 50+
(W J Haggas) *towards rr: hdwy wl over 1f out: kpt on ins fnl f: nrst fin* **4/1**[3]

5-0 **7** nk **Kasaa Ed**[13] 1173 3-8-9 0 TPO'Shea 16 44
(M Johnston) *prom: hdwy to ld 1/2-way: rdn and hdd wl over 1f out: sn wknd* **11/1**

06 **8** ½ **The Last Alzao (IRE)**[40] 810 3-8-9 0 JamieMoriarty 4 43+
(R A Fahey) *s.i.s and towards rr tl hdwy wl over 1f out: styd on ins fnl f* **50/1**

3-6 **9** 1 ½ **Highly Acclaimed**[13] 1174 3-8-6 0 AndrewMullen(3) 8 38
(Mrs A Duffield) *nvr bttr than midfield* **20/1**

0 **10** 6 **Russian Music (USA)**[19] 1062 4-9-11 0 DaleGibson 11 27
(C A Mulhall) *a in rr* **100/1**

2 **11** 3 ¼ **Street Spirit (USA)**[19] 1061 3-8-9 0 DavidAllan 5 8
(T D Easterby) *in tch: effrt to chse ldrs over 2f out: sn rdn and wknd* **11/1**

60 **12** 2 **Honey Berry (IRE)**[3] 1317 3-8-6 0 KellyHarrison(3) 14 —
(Patrick Morris) *dwlt: hdwy and in tch 1/2-way: rdn along over 2f out and sn wknd* **100/1**

13 15 **Ellies Inspiration** 4-9-1 0 DeanHeslop(5) 1 —
(M Mullineaux) *a in rr: outpcd and bhd fr 1/2-way* **66/1**

0 **14** 69 **Green Spirit (IRE)**[22] 1015 3-9-0 0 NCallan 7 —
(Patrick Morris) *led to 1/2-way: sn lost pl and bhd* **66/1**

1m 16.03s (-0.87) **Going Correction** -0.225s/f (Firm)
WFA 3 from 4yo 11lb **14 Ran SP% 121.1**
Speed ratings (Par 103): **96,93,91,90,87 85,84,84,82,74 69,67,47,--**
toteswinger: 1&2 £3.00, 1&3 £7.60, 2&3 £6.10. CSF £10.92 TOTE £4.40: £1.80, £1.50, £3.00; EX 15.30.
Owner Jaber Abdullah **Bred** C A Cyzer **Trained** West Ilsley, Berks
■ Stewards' Enquiry : Sam Hitchcott one-day ban: used whip in incorrect place (May 4)

FOCUS
An interesting sprint maiden likely to throw up a few future winners. The form is rated positively with the runner-up the best guide.
Green Spirit(IRE) Official explanation: jockey said gelding ran too free to post

1401 FRANK SHAW 80TH BIRTHDAY CELEBRATION H'CAP 1m 4y
4:40 (4:59) (Class 5) (0-75,75) 4-Y-O+ £3,238 (£963; £481; £240) Stalls Low

Form RPR

6103 **1** **This Ones For Eddy**[12] 1194 4-8-0 62 PatrickDonaghy(5) 6 76
(S Parr) *mde most: rdn and qcknd clr wl over 1f out: easily* **4/1**[2]

05-0 **2** 4 ½ **Champain Sands (IRE)**[3] 1332 10-8-1 61 AndrewMullen(3) 8 65+
(E J Alston) *hld up in rr: hdwy whn nt clr run 2f out and again over 1f out: rdn and squeezed through on inner ent fnl f: styd on: no ch w wnr* **7/1**

050- **3** hd **Society Venue**[276] 4172 4-8-10 67 TonyHamilton 7 70
(Jedd O'Keeffe) *chsd ldrs: hdwy on outer over 2f out: rdn wl over 1f out: drvn and one pce fnl f* **8/1**

000 **4** 1 ½ **Strategic Knight (USA)**[7] 1258 4-8-4 61 oh4 (t[1]) FrancisNorton 1 61
(R C Guest) *chsd ldrs on inner: rdn along over 2df out: drvn and wkng whn edgd lft over 1f out* **14/1**

062- **5** 3 ¾ **Ibbetson (USA)**[151] 7395 4-8-12 69 PatCosgrave 5 60
(W R Swinburn) *rrd s: sn chsng ldng pair: effrt 3f out: rdn 2f out and sn btn* **15/8**[1]

020- **6** 1 **Arctic Cape**[220] 5863 4-9-4 75 RoystonFfrench 10 64
(M Johnston) *hld up: effrt and sme hdwy over 2f out: sn rdn and n.d* **9/2**[3]

456 **7** 1 ¾ **Star Strider**[12] 1179 5-8-13 70 NCallan 4 55
(Miss Gay Kelleway) *hld up: rdn along 3f out: n.d* **12/1**

0204 **8** 2 ½ **Stoic Leader (IRE)**[7] 1246 9-8-12 69 PaulMulrennan 2 48
(R F Fisher) *t.k.h: chsd wnr: rdn along 3f out: wknd over 2f out* **9/1**

1m 43.09s (-2.81) **Going Correction** -0.225s/f (Firm) **8 Ran SP% 120.9**
Speed ratings (Par 103): **105,100,100,98,95 94,92,89**
toteswinger: 1&2 £7.30, 1&3 £8.60, 2&3 £14.60. CSF £33.96 CT £219.53 TOTE £4.40: £1.40, £2.40, £3.00; EX 32.90.
Owner Willie McKay **Bred** Broughton Bloodstock **Trained**

FOCUS
The race was much delayed after one horse lost his rider and bolted then another got loose and both were withdrawn. The form is modest with the exception of the winner, and not the most solid.
Ibbetson(USA) Official explanation: trainer's rep said gelding was unsuited by the firm (good to firm places) ground

1402 PONTEFRACT APPRENTICE H'CAP 1m 2f 6y
5:15 (5:36) (Class 5) (0-70,70) 4-Y-O+ £3,238 (£963; £481; £240) Stalls Low

Form RPR

1123 **1** **Safebreaker**[39] 823 4-8-8 59 (p) AmyRyan 4 65
(K A Ryan) *mde all: rdn wl over 1f out: drvn and styd on strly ins fnl f* **4/1**[1]

600- **2** 1 ½ **Farne Island**[14] 4540 6-8-2 56 oh8 JamieKyne(3) 7 59
(Micky Hammond) *t.k.h: chsd ldrs: hdwy wl over 1f out and sn rdn: styd on u.p ins fnl f* **6/1**[3]

4005 **3** 1 **Maybe I Wont**[31] 898 4-8-2 56 oh1 AndrewHeffernan(3) 2 57
(Lucinda Featherstone) *hld up towards rr: hdwy over 2f out: rdn over 1f out: kpt on ins fnl f: nrst fin* **16/1**

401- **4** ¾ **Neon Blue**[185] 6786 8-8-9 60 DeclanCannon 6 60
(R M Whitaker) *hld up towards rr: hdwy 2f out: rdn over 1f out: kpt on ins fnl f: nrst fin* **8/1**

0336 **5** ¾ **Rosko**[7] 1245 5-8-10 66 AnthonyBetts(5) 1 64+
(B Ellison) *plld hrd: chsd wnr: hdwy on inner and ev ch wl over 1f out: sn rdn and wknd ins fnl f* **11/2**[2]

350- **6** ¾ **Grand Art (IRE)**[20] 6312 5-9-0 70 AdamCarter(5) 10 67
(J Howard Johnson) *dwlt: hld up and bhd: hdwy on inner wl over 1f out: sn rdn and kpt on ins fnl f: nt rch ldrs* **12/1**

0-62 **7** ¾ **Lucayan Dancer**[8] 1226 9-9-2 70 NSLawes(3) 8 65
(D Nicholls) *trckd ldrs: hdwy to chal over 2f out: sn rdn and wknd wl over1f out* **4/1**[1]

500- **8** nk **Cripsey Brook**[188] 6727 11-8-8 62 RichardRowe(3) 5 56
(K G Reveley) *hld up in tch: hdwy whn carried wd st: sn rdn and no imp* **14/1**

-625 **9** 2 **Spares And Repairs**[24] 978 6-8-0 56 oh2 MatthewLawson(5) 3 46
(Mrs S Lamyman) *t.k.h: chsd ldrs: hung bdly rt home turn: sn rdn and wknd* **14/1**

42-0 **10** 12 **Gala Sunday (USA)**[12] 1192 9-8-9 60 (t) AdeleMulrennan 9 26
(M W Easterby) *a in rr* **12/1**

2m 12.82s (-0.88) **Going Correction** -0.225s/f (Firm) **10 Ran SP% 115.4**
Speed ratings (Par 103): **94,92,92,91,90 90,89,89,87,78**
toteswinger: 1&2 £5.10, 1&3 £14.40, 2&3 £23.80. CSF £27.41 CT £345.26 TOTE £4.80: £1.70, £2.70, £5.00; EX 35.70 Place 6: £161.56, Place 5: £125.17..
Owner Hambleton Racing Ltd X **Bred** Gainsborough Stud Management Ltd **Trained** Hambleton, N Yorks

FOCUS
A low-grade and much-delayed finale. The form looks less than solid with the placed horses out of the handicap.
Spares And Repairs Official explanation: jockey said gelding hung right
T/Plt: £786.30 to a £1 stake. Pool: £55,801.67. 51.80 winning tickets. T/Qpdt: £24.30 to a £1 stake. Pool: £3,747.46. 113.85 winning tickets. JR

1147 WINDSOR (R-H)
Monday, April 20

OFFICIAL GOING: Good to firm (good in places; 8.5)
Wind: Virtually nil Weather: Bright

1403 A C BECK APPRENTICE H'CAP 6f
5:10 (5:11) (Class 5) (0-75,75) 4-Y-O+ £2,729 (£806; £403) Stalls High

Form RPR

0-11 **1** **Brunelleschi**[32] 880 6-8-10 71 (b) JosephineBruning(5) 8 81
(P L Gilligan) *in tch: hdwy fr 2f out: shkn up and qcknd to ld fnl 30yds: readily* **6/1**[3]

1132 **2** 1 **Desert Dreamer (IRE)**[7] 1248 8-9-2 72 RichardEvans 9 79
(P D Evans) *s.i.s: rr tl hdwy 2f out: styd to chse ldrs ins fnl f: kpt on to take 2nd last strides but no imp on wnr* **3/1**[1]

210- **3** nse **Kyllachy Storm**[171] 7118 5-8-5 61 Louis-PhilippeBeuzelin 4 68
(R J Hodges) *chsd ldrs: rdn to ld 1f out: hdd and no ex fnl 30yds: lost 2nd fnl strides* **15/2**

62-5 **4** 2 ¼ **Digital**[14] 1150 12-9-0 73 MatthewDavies(3) 7 73
(M R Channon) *hld up in rr: hdwy on outside over 2f out: kpt on but nvr gng pce to rch ldrs* **11/1**

3305 **5** ½ **Fromsong (IRE)**[14] 1152 11-8-12 71 MarkCoumbe(3) 1 69
(D K Ivory) *chsd ldrs: rdn and ev ch over 1f out: wknd ins fnl f* **10/1**

060- **6** 2 ¾ **Stamford Blue**[236] 5400 8-8-9 70 (b) SPRyan(5) 2 59
(R A Harris) *led after 2f: rdn over 2f out: hdd 1f out: sn wknd* **14/1**

000- **7** nse **Sovereignty (JPN)**[172] 7090 7-8-5 61 oh2 AmyBaker 5 50
(D K Ivory) *free to s: rr: hdwy 2f out: nvr rchd ldrs: wknd fnl f* **20/1**

00-0 **8** nse **We Have A Dream**[11] 1197 4-8-11 70 RossAtkinson(3) 6 59
(W R Muir) *in tch: rdn over 2f out: wknd over 1f out* **8/1**

30-0 **9** hd **Whiteoak Lady (IRE)**[14] 1152 4-8-9 68 SophieDoyle(3) 3 56
(J L Spearing) *slowly away: rr: mod prog fnl f* **20/1**

000- **10** 6 **Applesnap (IRE)**[174] 7055 4-8-9 68 MartinLane(3) 11 37
(J Ryan) *rdn 1/2-way: a outpcd* **28/1**

01-4 **11** 9 **Kelamon**[31] 901 5-9-5 75 WilliamCarson 10 15
(S C Williams) *led 2f: rdn ½-wy: wknd 2f out* **4/1**[2]

1m 12.63s (-0.37) **Going Correction** +0.025s/f (Good) **11 Ran SP% 119.2**
Speed ratings (Par 103): **103,101,101,98,97 94,94,94,93,85 73**
toteswinger: 1&2 £2.50, 1&3 £25.30, 2&3 £20.70. CSF £23.97 CT £142.50 TOTE £8.90: £2.30, £1.80, £3.00; EX 22.10.
Owner Dr Susan Barnes **Bred** Dr Susan Barnes **Trained** Newmarket, Suffolk

FOCUS
A bright, warm day and ground conditions were good to firm, good in places, while the rails were in the same position as for the last meeting. Just ordinary sprint handicap form, but the pace was honest enough, thanks to the freegoing Stamford Blue and the form looks sound.
Kelamon Official explanation: jockey said gelding was unsuited by the good to firm (good in places) ground

1404 TRAINERMAGAZINE.COM MAIDEN STKS 5f 10y
5:40 (5:45) (Class 5) 2-Y-O £2,729 (£806; £403) Stalls High

Form RPR

1 **Be Invincible (IRE)** 2-9-3 0 MichaelHills 1 76
(B W Hills) *s.i.s: rr: gd hdwy over 2f out: chal appr fnl f: led ins fnl f: styd on strly* **8/1**[3]

2 1 ¼ **Monsieur Joe (IRE)** 2-9-3 0 AdamKirby 3 72+
(W R Swinburn) *hld up in rr: rdn: swtchd lft and hdwy over 1f out: styd on wl to chse wnr ins fnl f but a hld* **11/1**

3 ¾ **Pintura** 2-9-3 0 TonyCulhane 2 69
(M R Channon) *pressed ldrs: chal 2f out: slt ld appr fnl f: hdd and one pce ins fnl f* **33/1**

0 **4** 2 **Durham Town (IRE)**[14] 1147 2-9-3 0 DaneO'Neill 4 62
(D K Ivory) *disp ld to 1/2-way: sn rdn: wknd fnl f* **50/1**

4 **5** 1 **Master Mylo (IRE)**[14] 1147 2-9-3 0 SteveDrowne 11 58
(Mrs L C Jewell) *disp ld tl led over 2f out: sn rdn: hdd over 1f out: wknd ins fnl f* **33/1**

6 **6** ¾ **Maoi Chinn Tire (IRE)**[20] 1044 2-9-3 0 LPKeniry 9 55
(J S Moore) *chsd ldrs: rdn 1/2-way: wknd fnl f* **16/1**

3 **7** ¾ **Thomas Baines (USA)**[14] 1147 2-9-3 0 JamieSpencer 16 76+
(M L W Bell) *trckd ldrs on ins: nt clr run fr 2f out: fin on bridle* **11/10**[1]

8 ¾ **Travellers Kingdom (IRE)** 2-8-12 0 PaulDoe 12 45
(P D Evans) *hld up in rr: rdn and effrt 2f out: nvr gng pce to be competitive* **50/1**

9 ¾ **Hachi** 2-8-12 0 TolleyDean 13 47+
(J L Spearing) *outpcd most of way* **50/1**

5 **10** shd **Captain Cool (IRE)**[5] 1290 2-9-3 0 RichardHughes 6 47
(R Hannon) *disp ld to 1/2-way: wknd appr fnl f* **7/2**[2]

11 ½ **House Red (IRE)** 2-9-3 0 WilliamBuick 7 45+
(B W Hills) *chsd ldrs 3f* **14/1**

U **12** 3 ¾ **New York Lights (IRE)**[7] 1249 2-8-8 0 ow1 GabrielHannon(5) 15 28
(M D I Usher) *s.i.s: a in rr* **100/1**

13 1 **Bush Master** 2-9-3 0 MartinDwyer 10 28
(D K Ivory) *s.i.s: outpcd* **100/1**

14 nse **The Shuffler** 2-9-3 0 RyanMoore 8 28
(G L Moore) *outpcd* **14/1**

15 11 **Fascile** 2-9-0 0 .... AlanCreighton(3) 14 —
(E J Creighton) *drvn fr stalls: a in rr* **100/1**

61.29 secs (0.99) **Going Correction** +0.025s/f (Good) **15** Ran SP% **123.2**
Speed ratings (Par 92): **93,91,89,86,85 83,82,81,80,80 79,73,71,71,53**
toteswinger: 1&2 £30.20, 1&3 £31.40, 2&3 £31.40. CSF £91.86 TOTE £8.30: £3.30, £3.40, £9.60; EX 96.50.
Owner A L R Morton & John C Grant **Bred** Jaykayenn Syndicate **Trained** Lambourn, Berks
■ Stewards' Enquiry : Jamie Spencer caution: allowed colt to coast home approaching line

FOCUS
A strange result in so much as the first three home were drawn in stalls 1, 2 and 3 respectively, which is quite a rarity here. With little to go on the race is rated around the race averages.

NOTEBOOK
Be Invincible(IRE) powered down the outside while the favourite was suffering a nightmare passage along the inside. Despite having been niggled along early to keep his position, to hit the front inside the final furlong and stayed on strongly. The winner, who cost 80,000euros as a yearling, has quite a bit of knee action, suggesting he might be better suited by easier ground in the long term, and an entry in the valuable sales race at Doncaster in September suggests he's been showing connections plenty at home. (op 6-1 tchd 11-2)
Monsieur Joe(IRE) ◆ ran a blinder in second, switching wide to get a run having bagged a midfield position early. He stayed on takingly in the final furlong and looks a really nice prospect. (op 16-1)
Pintura ◆ ran really well and wasn't knocked about in the closing stages. He looks a certain future winner. (tchd 40-1)
Durham Town(IRE) stepped up markedly on his disappointing debut effort here, showing good speed before fading in the closing stages.
Master Mylo(IRE) also shaped with much more promise than on debut and he will do better in due course when stepped up to 6f or 7f. (op 28-1)
Thomas Baines(USA) got no run whatsoever and finished hard held as Jamie Spencer gave up the ghost inside the final furlong. He was slowly away, just as he had been on debut, which was always going to be a problem from his high draw, and Spencer simply didn't get a gap to go through until the race was all over. He clearly has plenty of ability, but at the moment he is losing his races at the start. Official explanation: jockey said colt was denied a clear run (op 10-11 tchd 5-4)

1405 P S LONDON H'CAP — 1m 67y
6:15 (6:15) (Class 4) (0-85,85) 4-Y-O+ **£5,180** (£1,541; £770; £384) **Stalls High**

Form RPR
100- 1 **Trumpet Lily**[193] 6605 4-9-1 **82** .... JimCrowley 1 91
(J G Portman) *hld up towards rr: hdwy and edgd lft ins fnl 2f: str run to ld wl ins fnl f: drvn out* **16/1**
415- 2 ¾ **Im Ova Ere Dad (IRE)**[312] 2978 6-8-11 **78** .... RyanMoore 2 86
(D E Cantillon) *hld up in rr: hdwy on outside over 2f out: rdn and str run u.p to take slt ld 1f out: hdd and no ex wl ins fnl f* **7/1**
5222 3 1 ¼ **Pegasus Again (USA)**[19] 1067 4-8-11 **78** .... (p) RobertHavlin 5 83
(T G Mills) *chsd ldrs: rdn over 2f oit: slt ld over 1f out: sn hdd: outpcd ins fnl f* **10/1**
000- 4 ½ **Salient**[165] 7215 5-8-13 **80** .... PaulDoe 12 84
(M J Attwater) *led: hrd rdn fr over 2f out: narrowly hdd over 1f out: one pce wl ins fnl f* **11/1**
065- 5 shd **Mountain Pride (IRE)**[190] 6675 4-9-2 **83** .... JimmyFortune 13 86
(J L Dunlop) *chsd ldrs: rdn to chal fr 2f out: stl ev ch whn edgd lft over 1f out: styd on same pce* **7/2**[2]
0-03 6 hd **Flying Valentino**[25] 974 5-8-8 **75** .... StephenDonohoe 7 78
(Ian Williams) *t.k.h: stdd towards rr: rdn and sme hdwy 2f out: nvr in contention* **28/1**
1-12 7 hd **Last Sovereign**[22] 1016 5-9-1 **82** .... (p) JamieSpencer 9 85
(Jane Chapple-Hyam) *s.i.s: sn sn in tch: sme hdwy whn pushed lft over 1f out: styd on same pce fnl f* **3/1**[1]
134- 8 1 ¼ **Effigy**[180] 6899 5-8-9 **76** ow1 .... DaneO'Neill 3 76
(H Candy) *hld up in rr: shkn up 2f out: styd on ins fnl f: nvr in contention* **5/1**[3]
044- 9 1 ¾ **La Coveta (IRE)**[268] 4433 4-8-12 **79** .... MartinDwyer 8 75
(B J Meehan) *chsd ldrs: rdn 3f out: wknd fr ins fnl 2f* **12/1**
1500 10 2 ¾ **Hallingdal (UAE)**[19] 1067 4-8-7 **74** .... JamesDoyle 4 63
(Ms J S Doyle) *chsd ldrs: rdn 3f out: wknd fr 2f out* **66/1**
11 7 **Rock Exhibition**[28] 6371 4-8-7 **74** .... LPKeniry 11 47
(B W Duke) *chsd ldrs: rdn 3f out: sn wknd* **66/1**
3051 12 2 ¼ **Orpen Wide (IRE)**[11] 1089 7-8-13 **85** .... (b) MarkCoumbe(5) 10 53
(M C Chapman) *a in rr: lost tch 4f out* **20/1**

1m 41.91s (-2.79) **Going Correction** -0.10s/f (Good) **12** Ran SP% **118.6**
Speed ratings (Par 105): **109,108,107,106,106 106,106,104,103,100 93,91**
toteswinger: 1&2 £40.00, 1&3 £40.00, 2&3 £37.70. CSF £120.50 CT £1191.39 TOTE £16.10: £5.10, £2.80, £3.00; EX 341.20.
Owner Mrs J Edwards-Heathcote **Bred** The Hon Mrs R Pease **Trained** Compton, Berks

FOCUS
An exposed bunch in the main but solid enough form for the grade.

1406 YES EVENTS MAIDEN FILLIES' STKS — 1m 67y
6:50 (6:52) (Class 5) 3-Y-O **£2,729** (£806; £403) **Stalls High**

Form RPR
0- 1 **Cartoon**[170] 7140 3-9-0 0 .... PhilipRobinson 1 79+
(M A Jarvis) *set mod pce after 1f: rdn over 2f out: hdd appr fnl f: rallied gamely to ld again nr fin* **9/1**
2 nk **Strawberrydaiquiri** 3-9-0 0 .... RyanMoore 5 78+
(Sir Michael Stoute) *hld up in rr tl qckнd to chse ldrs 3f out: hrd drvn to ld appr fnl f: hdd and no ex nr fin* **13/2**
4- 3 3 ¼ **Welsh Anthem**[201] 6392 3-9-0 0 .... MartinDwyer 12 71
(W R Muir) *led 1f: styd chsng ldrs: hrd rdn over 2f out: outpcd by ldng dup fnl f* **5/2**[1]
4 ½ **Saturn Girl (IRE)** 3-9-0 0 .... PatDobbs 3 69+
(S A Callaghan) *rr: shkn up and styd on fnl 2f: fin strly* **33/1**
5 hd **Sunceleb (IRE)** 3-9-0 0 .... RobertHavlin 13 71+
(H Morrison) *hld up in rr: hdwy 2f out: nt clr run ins fnl f and swtchd lft: fin wl:* **50/1**
0-0 6 1 **Breach Of Peace (USA)**[19] 1066 3-9-0 0 .... SteveDrowne 14 67
(R Charlton) *chsd ldrs: rdn over 2f out: edgd lft and wknd ins fnl f* **16/1**
0-2 7 nk **Implication**[16] 1128 3-9-0 0 .... StephenDonohoe 10 66
(E A L Dunlop) *chsd ldrs: hrd drvn and effrt over 2f out: nvr rchd ldrs: wknd fnl f* **7/2**[2]
6 8 1 **Queen Martha (USA)**[31] 890 3-9-0 0 .... PaulHanagan 2 64
(M A Magnusson) *chsd ldrs: rdn over 2f out: wknd fnl f* **4/1**[3]
9 ½ **Singbella** 3-9-0 0 .... AdamKirby 7 63+
(C G Cox) *hld up in rr: mod late prog* **25/1**
43- 10 1 **Better In Time (USA)**[120] 7754 3-9-0 0 .... KirstyMilczarek 6 60
(Jane Chapple-Hyam) *chsd ldrs: rdn over 2f out: wknd over 1f out* **14/1**
11 ½ **Kindest** 3-9-0 0 .... TedDurcan 9 59
(C F Wall) *a towards rr* **50/1**
0- 12 ¾ **Winterfell**[300] 3349 3-8-11 0 .... JackMitchell(3) 8 57
(C F Wall) *a towards rr* **100/1**
0- 13 shd **Arabian Moonlight**[241] 5240 3-9-0 0 .... LPKeniry 4 57
(E F Vaughan) *rdn over 3f out: nvr bttr than mid-div* **100/1**

1m 46.54s (1.84) **Going Correction** -0.10s/f (Good) **13** Ran SP% **119.4**
Speed ratings (Par 95): **86,85,82,81,81 80,80,79,78,77 77,76,76**
toteswinger: 1&2 £25.00, 1&3 £45.10, 2&3 £5.90. CSF £64.08 TOTE £10.90: £3.00, £2.30, £1.40; EX 38.80.
Owner Highclere Thoroughbred Racing-SunChariot **Bred** Highclere Stud **Trained** Newmarket, Suffolk

FOCUS
Yet another winner drawn in stall 1. The pace in this fillies' maiden was slow and the form does not look the most reliable.

1407 BDSB 40TH BIRTHDAY MAIDEN STKS — 1m 2f 7y
7:20 (7:22) (Class 5) 3-Y-O+ **£2,729** (£806; £403) **Stalls Low**

Form RPR
4- 1 **Libel Law**[171] 7105 3-8-11 0 .... PhilipRobinson 9 89+
(M A Jarvis) *trckd ldrs: pushed along 3f out: styd on wl fr over 1f out to ld ins fnl f: sn in command: comf* **9/2**[2]
04- 2 2 **Dubai Echo (USA)**[194] 6581 3-8-11 0 .... RyanMoore 16 85+
(Sir Michael Stoute) *chsd ldrs: rdn to ld over 1f out: hdd ins fnl f: kpt on but sn outpcd by wnr* **13/2**[3]
046- 3 4 **King's La Mont (IRE)**[187] 6731 3-8-11 77 .... JimCrowley 1 77
(Mrs A J Perrett) *in tch: hdwy fr 3f out: chsd ldng duo fnl f but nvr any ch* **20/1**
25-2 4 2 ½ **Souter Point (USA)**[14] 1151 3-8-11 85 .... SteveDrowne 11 72
(R Charlton) *chsd ldrs: drvn to ld over 2f out: hdd over 1f out: wknd qckly ins fnl f* **4/7**[1]
455- 5 2 ¼ **Gifted Leader (USA)**[194] 6584 4-10-0 73 .... StephenDonohoe 4 71
(Ian Williams) *in tch: rdn to chse ldrs 3f out: wknd over 1f out* **33/1**
6 6 ½ **Outrageous Request**[23] 998 3-8-11 0 .... PaulEddery 2 67+
(Pat Eddery) *hld up in rr: stl plenty to doover 2f out: styd on strly thrght fnl f but nvr a danger* **16/1**
U3- 7 3 ½ **Son Of My Heart (USA)**[123] 7721 4-10-0 0 .... JamieSpencer 13 63+
(P F I Cole) *sn led: rdn 3f out: hdd over 2f out: sn wknd* **20/1**
0- 8 1 ½ **Rocky Heights (IRE)**[170] 7140 3-8-6 0 .... EddieAhern 7 52+
(J L Dunlop) *chsd ldrs: pushed along 3f out: wknd fr 2f out* **66/1**
50-6 9 4 **Wannarock (IRE)**[18] 1088 4-10-0 60 .... AmirQuinn 5 52
(M C Chapman) *chsd ldrs: rdn 3f out: wknd 2f* **100/1**
10 1 ½ **Stormy Morning** 3-8-11 0 .... AdamKirby 6 46
(W R Swinburn) *a towards rr* **33/1**
0 11 ¾ **Cross Reef**[31] 890 4-9-6 0 .... KevinGhunowa(3) 3 42
(R A Harris) *hld up in rr: sme hdwy 3f out: nvr in contention* **100/1**
04- 12 1 ¼ **Deuce**[220] 5870 3-8-6 0 .... StephenCarson 14 37
(Eve Johnson Houghton) *in tch whn rdn 7f out: sn bhd* **66/1**
13 4 ½ **I'm In The Pink (FR)**[333] 5-9-9 0 .... RichardEvans(5) 10 36
(P D Evans) *s.i.s: effrt into mid-div over 3f oiy: sn wknd* **100/1**
14 1 ¾ **Bestowed**[7] 4-9-9 0 .... MarkCoumbe(5) 12 32
(M C Chapman) *a in rr* **100/1**
0-0 15 20 **Kirkson**[7] 1250 3-8-11 0 .... TedDurcan 15 —
(P W Chapple-Hyam) *hdwy to chse ldrs 6f out: wknd 4f out* **100/1**

2m 5.79s (-2.91) **Going Correction** -0.10s/f (Good)
WFA 3 from 4yo+ 17lb **15** Ran SP% **124.4**
Speed ratings (Par 103): **107,105,102,100,98 98,95,94,90,89 89,88,84,83,67**
toteswinger: 1&2 £2.60, 1&3 £9.70, 2&3 £6.80. CSF £32.50 TOTE £7.40: £2.60, £2.80, £3.90; EX 27.00.
Owner Sheikh Ahmed Al Maktoum **Bred** Darley **Trained** Newmarket, Suffolk

FOCUS
This has the potential to turn out quite a decent little maiden as, although the 85-rated Souter Point has probably not run to his best back in fourth, the field were well strung out and quite a few look nice prospects. Very few got into it in truth, with the front two close up throughout, despite the pace appearing to slacken at around halfway.
Outrageous Request ◆ Official explanation: trainer said gelding lost a near-fore shoe
Son Of My Heart(USA) Official explanation: jockey said colt was unsuited by the good to firm (good in places) ground and the track
Stormy Morning Official explanation: jockey said colt ran green

1408 ANDARA H'CAP — 1m 3f 135y
7:50 (7:51) (Class 5) (0-75,75) 3-Y-O **£3,070** (£906; £453) **Stalls Low**

Form RPR
006- 1 **Chiberta King**[228] 5641 3-8-10 **67** .... WilliamBuick 9 77
(A M Balding) *lwd tl hdd 7f out: dropped bk to 4th over 4f out: rdn and styd on to ld 2f: sn hrd drvn whn chal fr over 1f out: forged clr cl home* **20/1**
4231 2 1 ¾ **El Bravo**[14] 1156 3-9-4 **75** .... RyanMoore 7 82+
(G L Moore) *hld up in rr tl hdwy on outside fr 3f out: hrd rdn to chal ins fnl f: wknd cl home* **7/2**[1]
600- 3 hd **Admirable Duque (IRE)**[177] 6970 3-8-11 **68** .... AdamKirby 12 75
(D J S Ffrench Davis) *chsd ldrs: outpcd 4f out: hdwy 3f out: str chal fnl f: wknd cl home* **33/1**
64-4 4 2 ½ **Penang Princess**[26] 949 3-9-1 **72** .... SebSanders 8 75
(R M Beckett) *hld up in rr tl rdn and hdwy over 3f out: chsd ldrs u.p 2f out: sn one pce* **8/1**
0-1 5 ½ **Strong Storm (USA)**[93] 201 3-9-1 **72** .... ShaneKelly 15 74
(J Noseda) *chsd ldrs: squeezed through to ld on rails ins fnl 3f: hdd 2f out: hung lft u.p and wknd fnl f* **11/2**[2]
-305 6 5 **First Spirit**[14] 1148 3-8-0 **62** .... SophieDoyle(5) 5 56
(J S Moore) *rr: pushed along over 2f oit: nt clr run wl over 1f out: kpt on ins fnl f* **100/1**
60-6 7 3 ½ **Abulharith**[18] 1087 3-9-0 **71** .... JimmyFortune 6 59
(P W Chapple-Hyam) *chsd ldrs: rdn over 3f out: wknd ins fnl 2f* **6/1**[3]
601 8 1 ¾ **Dalrymple (IRE)**[14] 1148 3-8-9 **66** .... StephenDonohoe 13 52
(Ian Williams) *chsd ldrs: led 7f out tl bmpd and hdd ins fnl 3f: wknd 2f out* **20/1**
-465 9 ½ **Sgt Roberts (IRE)**[26] 962 3-9-1 **72** .... LPKeniry 4 57
(J S Moore) *chsd ldrs: rdn 4f out: wknd fr 3f out* **33/1**
0-40 10 1 ¼ **Blue Tango (IRE)**[37] 840 3-9-2 **73** .... JimCrowley 11 56
(Mrs A J Perrett) *in tch: rdn 5f out: wknd 3f out* **16/1**
344- 11 2 ½ **Persian Memories (IRE)**[180] 6901 3-9-0 **71** .... EddieAhern 1 50
(J L Dunlop) *nvr bttr than mid-div* **6/1**[3]
05-4 12 4 ½ **Some Time Good (IRE)**[26] 957 3-9-0 **71** .... TonyCulhane 10 43
(M R Channon) *chsd ldrs over a m* **9/1**

0-40 **13** *1 1/4* **Tropical Duke (IRE)**[87] 272 3-8-7 **64**........................... MartinDwyer 14 34
(D W P Arbuthnot) *a in rr* **33/1**
000- **14** *nse* **Cooper Island Kid (USA)**[171] 7106 3-8-5 **62**................ PaulHanagan 2 32
(P W D'Arcy) *bhd fr 1/2-way* **14/1**
3-35 **15** *dist* **Merton Lad**[33] 865 3-8-10 **67**.. DaneO'Neill 3 —
(T G Mills) *chsd ldrs tl wknd qckly over 4f out: t.o* **12/1**
2m 27.37s (-2.13) **Going Correction** -0.10s/f (Good) **15** Ran SP% **126.9**
Speed ratings (Par 98): **103,101,101,100,99 96,94,92,92,91 90,87,86,86,—**
toteswinger: 1&2 £39.40, 1&3 not won, 2&3 £39.40. CSF £88.21 CT £2406.27 TOTE £29.10: £7.90, £1.90, £8.50; EX 172.20 Place 6: £986.70, Place 5: £533.77..
Owner The Pink Hat Racing Partnership **Bred** Watership Down Stud **Trained** Kingsclere, Hants
■ Stewards' Enquiry : Sophie Doyle one-day ban: careless riding (May 4)
FOCUS
A lot of unexposed sorts here, many of whom were making their debut in a handicap, and a group of five finished clear. Probably form to be positive about.
Chiberta King Official explanation: trainer said, regarding apparent improvement in form, that it appeared to have benefited from being gelded during the winter.
Merton Lad Official explanation: vet said gelding bled from the nose
T/Jkpt: Not won. T/Plt: £409.70 to a £1 stake. Pool: £75,133.18. 133.86 winning tickets. T/Qpdt: £23.70 to a £1 stake. Pool: £6,685.34. 208.60 winning tickets. ST

1311 WOLVERHAMPTON (A.W) (L-H)

Monday, April 20

OFFICIAL GOING: Standard
Wind: Nil Weather: Sunny

1409 CELEBRATE YOUR BIRTHDAY AT WOLVERHAMPTON RACECOURSE CLAIMING STKS 1m 1f 103y(P)

2:20 (2:20) (Class 6) 4-Y-0+ **£2,047** (£604; £302) **Stalls** Low

Form RPR
00-2 **1** **Watchmaker**[88] 253 6-9-7 66...................................... FergusSweeney 4 73
(Miss Tor Sturgis) *hld up in tch: wnt 2nd 2f out: sn rdn: led ins fnl f: edgd lft: r.o wl* **9/4**[1]
6024 **2** *5* **Ten Pole Tudor**[12] 1177 4-8-9 60.....................................(p) NeilPollard 8 50
(R A Harris) *chsd ldr: led 3f out: rdn and edgd rt over 1f out: hdd ins fnl f: one pce and jst hld on for 2nd* **9/1**
6-06 **3** *hd* **Fort Churchill (IRE)**[17] 1099 8-8-3 65 ow3.....................(p) LanceBetts(7) 2 51
(B Ellison) *hld up: rdn 3f out: hdwy over 1f out: kpt on ins fnl f: jst failed to take 2nd* **6/1**[2]
0655 **4** *1 3/4* **Yes One (IRE)**[18] 1079 5-9-3 66.................................... DO'Donohoe 3 54
(K A Ryan) *a.p: rdn and one pce fnl 2f* **8/1**[3]
5403 **5** *2 1/4* **Buscador (USA)**[38] 836 10-8-9 58.......................... RichardKingscote 7 41
(W M Brisbourne) *led: rdn and hdd 3f out: wknd ins fnl f* **9/4**[1]
6520 **6** *1 3/4* **Hatch A Plan (IRE)**[34] 601 8-8-9 49.............................. NeilChalmers 1 38
(Mouse Hamilton-Fairley) *hld up: rdn over 2f out: no hdwy* **11/1**
7 *8* **Golden Run**[329] 6-8-5 0... DavidKenny(7) 6 24
(R Hollinshead) *dwlt: in rr: pushed along over 4f out: struggling 3f out* **25/1**
000 **8** *4* **Tapas Lad (IRE)**[41] 792 4-8-5 48 ow1.................(v) KevinGhunowa(3) 5 11
(G J Smith) *hld up: pushed along 4f out: bhd fnl 3f* **16/1**
2m 2.33s (0.63) **Going Correction** +0.05s/f (Slow) **8** Ran SP% **115.0**
Speed ratings (Par 101): **99,94,94,92,90 89,82,78**
toteswinger: 1&2 £5.50, 1&3 £8.50, 2&3 £13.30. CSF £24.62 TOTE £4.10: £1.40, £2.50, £2.00; EX 28.10 Trifecta £129.50 Pool: £325.66 - 1.86 winning units.
Owner Miss Ann Sturgis **Bred** Hesmonds Stud Ltd **Trained** Lambourn, Berks
FOCUS
An ordinary claimer and not a race to be too positive about.

1410 HOTEL & CONFERENCING AT WOLVERHAMPTON MEDIAN AUCTION MAIDEN STKS 1m 141y(P)

2:50 (2:53) (Class 5) 3-5-Y-0 **£3,070** (£906; £453) **Stalls** Low

Form RPR
303- **1** **Larkham (USA)**[202] 6359 3-8-11 77................................... SebSanders 5 79
(R M Beckett) *hld up in tch: wnt 2nd 3f out: chalng whn carried rt wl over 1f out: led jst ins fnl f: sn rdn and edgd lft: r.o* **13/8**[2]
036- **2** *hd* **Tilos Gem (IRE)**[173] 7080 3-8-11 78.............................. JoeFanning 7 78
(M Johnston) *led: j. shadow 7f out: hung rt wl over 1f out: rdn and hdd jst ins fnl f: carried lft: r.o* **10/11**[1]
65 **3** *10* **One Scoop Or Two**[17] 1108 3-8-11 0...........................(t) NickyMackay 2 55
(F Sheridan) *hld up in mid-div: rdn over 3f out: sn struggling: tk modest 3rd wl ins fnl f* **40/1**
5 **4** *1 1/4* **Extracurricular (USA)**[26] 949 3-8-6 0.............................. JimmyQuinn 6 47
(M Botti) *chsd ldr to 5f out: wknd over 1f out* **7/1**[3]
000- **5** *3 1/2* **Katie Girl**[184] 6808 3-8-6 34.. AndrewElliott 8 39
(Mrs G S Rees) *hld up in tch: chsd ldr 5f out to 3f out: wknd 2f out* **66/1**
00- **6** *2 3/4* **Zelos Diktator**[186] 6760 3-8-11 0.................................. TPQueally 1 38
(J G Given) *hld up in mid-div: wknd 3f out* **18/1**
0 **7** *1 3/4* **The Spicer**[12] 1185 4-9-7 0..................................(t) AndreaAtzeni(5) 9 37
(F Sheridan) *dwlt: a in rr* **25/1**
8 *6* **Nouailhas** 3-8-8 0... RussellKennemore(3) 4 20
(R Hollinshead) *s.i.s: a in rr* **25/1**
P00/ **9** *2 1/2* **Mega Dame (IRE)**[598] 5019 5-9-7 59............................. FrankieMcDonald 3 12
(D Haydn Jones) *prom: pushed along over 5f out: wknd over 3f out* **33/1**
1m 52.27s (1.77) **Going Correction** +0.05s/f (Slow) **9** Ran SP% **122.8**
WFA 3 from 4yo+ 15lb
Speed ratings (Par 103): **94,93,84,83,80 78,76,71,69**
toteswinger: 1&2 £1.10, 1&3 £6.80, 2&3 £13.70. CSF £3.53 TOTE £2.80: £1.10, £1.10, £12.40; EX 4.10 Trifecta £59.10 Pool: £435.39 - 5.45 winning units.
Owner R A Pegum **Bred** Elk Manor Farm **Trained** Whitsbury, Hants
■ Stewards' Enquiry : Joe Fanning caution: careless riding.
Seb Sanders caution: careless riding.
FOCUS
The two market leaders dominated this maiden and the form is straightforward with the placed horses close to their juvenile marks.
Nouailhas Official explanation: jockey said gelding hung left

1411 VERSION ONE DOCUMENT MANAGEMENT AND IMAGING FILLIES' H'CAP 5f 216y(P)

3:20 (3:20) (Class 4) (0-80,85) 4-Y-0+ **£5,180** (£1,541; £770; £384) **Stalls** Low

Form RPR
3312 **1** **Jord (IRE)**[16] 1132 5-8-8 **66**...................................... AndrewElliott 1 73
(A J McCabe) *w ldr: led after 1f: rdn wl over 1f out: jst hld on* **5/2**[2]
220- **2** *shd* **Valatrix (IRE)**[191] 6650 4-9-3 **78**.............................. JackMitchell(3) 3 85+
(C F Wall) *hld up in tch: wnt 2nd wl over 1f out: rdn wl ins fnl f: jst failed* **11/8**[1]
436- **3** *5* **Mango Music**[179] 6925 6-8-10 **68**.................................. TPQueally 4 59
(M Quinn) *led 1f: w wnr tl rdn wl over 1f out: btn whn edgd lft jst ins fnl f* **5/1**
46-0 **4** *nk* **Miss Daawe**[4] 1310 5-8-3 **68** ow1.............................. LanceBetts(7) 6 58
(B Ellison) *prom: rdn over 2f out: sn btn* **7/2**[3]
1m 14.79s (-0.21) **Going Correction** +0.05s/f (Slow) **4** Ran SP% **109.6**
Speed ratings (Par 102): **103,102,96,95**
toteswinger: 1&2 £6.40. CSF £6.44 TOTE £3.50; EX 6.40.
Owner Paul J Dixon And The Chrystal Maze Ptn **Bred** M Channon **Trained** Averham Park, Notts
FOCUS
A tight little handicap but the winner only had to run to recent form to score.

1412 WOLVERHAMPTON HOSPITALITY - A PLEASURE CLAIMING STKS 5f 20y(P)

3:50 (3:50) (Class 6) 3-Y-0+ **£2,047** (£604; £302) **Stalls** Low

Form RPR
1452 **1** **Harry Up**[17] 1104 8-9-13 82..(p) DarryllHolland 2 86
(K A Ryan) *mde all: rdn wl over 1f out: r.o wl* **15/8**[2]
1511 **2** *1 3/4* **Desperate Dan**[17] 1104 8-9-9 78.................................(v) TPQueally 5 76
(A B Haynes) *chsd wnr: edgd lft jst ins fnl f: sn rdn: no imp* **7/4**[1]
660- **3** *3/4* **Firenza Bond**[248] 5044 4-8-13 67.................................. PJMcDonald 1 63
(G R Oldroyd) *a.p: rdn wl over 1f out: one pce* **16/1**
0666 **4** *1 1/4* **Pepin (IRE)**[18] 1084 3-8-3 40....................................... FrankieMcDonald 4 55
(D Haydn Jones) *s.i.s: in rr: hung lft after 1f: hdwy over 2f out: rdn jst over 1f out: one pce* **66/1**
1324 **5** *1 1/2* **Towy Valley**[17] 1091 4-9-0 69...................................... IanMongan 3 54
(C G Cox) *chsd ldrs tl wknd 2f out* **11/4**[3]
0020 **6** *2* **Loose Caboose (IRE)**[17] 1103 4-8-5 59.......................(p) AndreaAtzeni(5) 7 43
(A J McCabe) *a bhd* **20/1**
334- **7** *2 1/2* **Our Acquaintance**[131] 7629 4-9-0 58.......................... DavidProbert(3) 6 41
(W R Muir) *hld up: rdn wl over 1f out: a bhd* **14/1**
-560 **8** *2 1/2* **Ace Club**[62] 574 8-8-10 42..(b) DominicFox(3) 8 28
(Garry Moss) *bhd fnl 3f* **66/1**
61.60 secs (-0.70) **Going Correction** +0.05s/f (Slow)
WFA 3 from 4yo+ 10lb **8** Ran SP% **118.1**
Speed ratings (Par 101): **107,104,103,101,98 95,91,87**
toteswinger: 1&2 £1.02, 1&3 £68.10, 2&3 £68.10. CSF £5.73 TOTE £2.40: £1.30, £1.50, £4.70; EX 6.50 Trifecta £49.60 Pool: £463.25 - 6.91 winning units.Firenza Bond was claimed by D. J. Flood for £5,000.
Owner The Fishermen **Bred** J E Rose **Trained** Hambleton, N Yorks
FOCUS
Not a bad claimer rated through the winner, but the proximity of the fourth does little for the form.

1413 WOLVERHAMPTON-RACECOURSE.CO.UK H'CAP 7f 32y(P)

4:20 (4:21) (Class 6) (0-65,65) 4-Y-0+ **£2,729** (£806; £403) **Stalls** High

Form RPR
-640 **1** **Diego Rivera**[18] 1080 4-8-13 **60**.................................... FergusSweeney 2 69
(P J Makin) *hld up in mid-div: hdwy over 1f out: rdn to ld last strides* **9/2**[2]
-300 **2** *nk* **Sweet Gale (IRE)**[32] 886 5-8-10 **57**.......................... FrankieMcDonald 5 65
(Mike Murphy) *hld up in tch: nt clr run over 2f out: rdn to ld nr fin: hdd last strides* **12/1**
06-1 **3** *1* **Gracie's Gift (IRE)**[40] 811 7-8-7 **54**............................ PJMcDonald 6 59
(R C Guest) *hld up in tch: rdn to ld over 1f out: sn edgd lft: hdd nr fin* **11/1**
00- **4** *2* **Lady Amberlini**[255] 4825 4-8-12 **59**................................ IanMongan 1 59
(C R Dore) *broke wl: sn hld up in tch on ins: swtchd rt jst over 1f out: kpt on ins fnl f* **11/1**
0-10 **5** *1/2* **Djalalabad (FR)**[12] 1194 5-8-10 **57**............................(tp) TGMcLaughlin 10 56+
(Mrs C A Dunnett) *hld up in rr: swtchd rt off ins rail ins fnl f: late hdwy: nrst fin* **16/1**
3434 **6** *1/2* **Bold Diva**[21] 1039 4-8-6 **53**..(v) CatherineGannon 7 50
(A W Carroll) *hld up: hdwy over 5f out: led 2f out: rdn and hdd over 1f out: wknd fnl f* **9/1**
5135 **7** *1* **Kabis Amigos**[16] 1132 7-9-4 **65**...................................(b) GeorgeBaker 12 60
(S T Mason) *hld up and bhd: c wd st: kpt on fnl f: n.d* **9/1**
3041 **8** *1 3/4* **Downhill Skier (IRE)**[16] 1132 5-8-12 **62**.................. DavidProbert(3) 3 52
(W M Brisbourne) *s.i.s: hld up and bhd: c v wd st: rdn over 1f out: nvr nr ldrs* **5/2**[1]
5-40 **9** *1/2* **Golden Prospect**[18] 1080 5-9-0 **61**............................(p) SebSanders 8 50
(J W Hills) *hld up and bhd: hdwy on outside over 3f out: rdn and wknd over 1f out* **6/1**[3]
-560 **10** *shd* **Redwater River**[63] 571 5-8-8 **55**.............................. AndrewElliott 9 43
(Mrs R A Carr) *led after 1f to 2f out: rdn and wknd over 1f out* **25/1**
640/ **11** *1 1/2* **Picture Frame**[679] 2508 5-8-12 **59**............................(p) JoeFanning 4 43
(J T Stimpson) *led 1f: prom tl wknd 1f out* **25/1**
1000 **12** *4* **Over To You Bert**[24] 984 10-8-7 **54**............................ JimmyQuinn 11 27
(R J Hodges) *sn prom: chsd ldr over 5f out tl over 2f out: wknd wl over 1f out* **25/1**
1m 29.98s (0.38) **Going Correction** +0.05s/f (Slow) **12** Ran SP% **122.8**
Speed ratings (Par 101): **99,98,97,95,94 94,92,90,90,90 88,83**
toteswinger: 1&2 £34.50, 1&3 £21.50, 2&3 £26.90. CSF £58.47 CT £558.85 TOTE £6.10: £2.20, £4.70, £2.60; EX 57.10 TRIFECTA Not won..
Owner Mrs P J Makin and Mrs R B Denny **Bred** Farmers Hill Stud **Trained** Ogbourne Maisey, Wilts
FOCUS
A moderate, but open handicap, although not the most solid form.

1414 ENJOY THE LUCKY 7 GROUP OFFER H'CAP 5f 216y(P)

4:50 (4:51) (Class 4) (0-80,79) 3-Y-0 **£5,180** (£1,541; £770; £384) **Stalls** Low

Form RPR
6324 **1** **Cecily**[12] 1180 3-9-4 **79**.. SebSanders 9 83
(Sir Mark Prescott) *mde all: rdn over 1f out: edgd lft ins fnl f: drvn out* **15/2**
25-5 **2** *1/2* **Forward Feline (IRE)**[14] 1155 3-8-11 **72**.................. CatherineGannon 6 74
(B Palling) *a.p: chsd wnr over 2f out: sn rdn: kpt on towards fin* **18/1**
2121 **3** *1/2* **Raimond Ridge (IRE)**[21] 1032 3-8-9 **75**...................... MCGeran(5) 8 76+
(M R Channon) *t.k.h in rr: hdwy wl over 1f out: rdn fnl f: kpt on towards fin but hld whn n.m.r on ins fnl strides* **8/1**
10-3 **4** *nse* **Happy Forever (FR)**[19] 1068 3-9-0 **75**........................ DarryllHolland 4 75
(M Botti) *hld up: hdwy over 2f out: sn rdn: r.o towards fin* **5/2**[1]
1232 **5** *2* **Flamsteed (IRE)**[12] 1180 3-8-12 **73**............................ TPQueally 3 67
(M Quinn) *hld up and bhd: nt clr run on ins and swtchd rt over 2f out: hdwy over 1f out: rdn and one pce ins fnl f* **4/1**[2]
10-0 **6** *3 1/2* **Via Mia**[8] 1232 3-8-12 **73**.. JimmyQuinn 7 56
(P F I Cole) *chsd ldrs: rdn 3f out: wknd over 1f out* **20/1**

324- 7 4 **Whisky Jack**[166] 7191 3-8-10 **71** DO'Donohoe 5 41
(W R Muir) *s.i.s: rdn wl over 1f out: sn edgd lft: a bhd* **10/1**
321- 8 5 **Hillside Lad**[113] 7802 3-8-11 **72** RichardKingscote 1 26
(R M Beckett) *prom: put hd in air wl over 1f out: sn wknd* **5/1**[3]
100- 9 1 1/2 **Glorious Dreams (USA)**[307] 3105 3-8-12 **73** JoeFanning 2 22
(T J Pitt) *chsd ldrs 3f* **12/1**
1m 14.53s (-0.47) **Going Correction** +0.05s/f (Slow) 9 Ran SP% **114.9**
Speed ratings (Par 100): **105,104,103,103,100 96,90,84,82**
toteswinger: 1&2 £12.30, 1&3 £4.30, 2&3 £13.60. CSF £106.05 TOTE £5.70: £2.80, £4.40, £2.80; EX 114.50 Trifecta £147.70 Part won. Pool: £199.72 - 0.10 winning units. Place 6: £191.13, Place 5: £104.45..
Owner C G Rowles Nicholson **Bred** Limestone And Tara Studs **Trained** Newmarket, Suffolk
■ Stewards' Enquiry : Seb Sanders two-day ban: careless riding (May 4-5); one-day ban: used whip with excessive frequency (May 6)
Catherine Gannon one-day ban: used whip with excessive frequency (May 4)
FOCUS
A fair three-year-old sprint for the class with the winner stepping up slightly on last year's form.
Happy Forever(FR) ◆ Official explanation: jockey said filly hung left
T/Plt: £57.10 to a £1 stake. Pool: £42,057.23. 536.91 winning tickets. T/Qpdt: £51.30 to a £1 stake. Pool: £2,976.44. 42.90 winning tickets. KH

1090 BATH (L-H)
Tuesday, April 21

OFFICIAL GOING: Good to firm (9.8)
Wind: Moderate ahead Weather: Sunny

1415 PREMIER CONSERVATORY ROOFS AND K2 H'CAP 1m 2f 46y
5:15 (5:15) (Class 5) (0-70,70) 4-Y-O+ **£2,590** (£770; £385; £192) **Stalls** Low

Form RPR
2422 1 **Pelham Crescent (IRE)**[22] 1042 6-8-8 **63** DavidProbert(3) 6 71
(B Palling) *trckd ldrs: led ins fnl 2f: drvn and hld on wl fnl f* **4/1**[1]
122- 2 1/2 **Mick's Dancer**[166] 7211 4-8-12 **64** MartinDwyer 1 71+
(W R Muir) *chsd ldr 4f: styd wl there: n.m.r 2f out and one pce: rdn and styd on fr over 1f out: fin strly but nt rch wnr* **4/1**[1]
00-3 3 1 **Bramalea**[17] 1133 4-9-0 **66** JimCrowley 9 71
(B W Duke) *chsd ldrs: rdn over 2f out: styd on to chse wnr ins fnl f: no imp and lost 2nd nr fin* **10/1**
20-1 4 2 3/4 **Street Devil (USA)**[21] 1054 4-9-4 **70** DarryllHolland 5 70
(R Curtis) *led: rdn and qcknd 3f out: hdd ins fnl 2f: wknd ins fnl f* **12/1**
0-60 5 1 1/4 **Master Mahogany**[36] 194 8-8-6 **63** MCGeran(5) 7 60
(R J Hodges) *chsd ldrs: wnt 2nd 6f out: rdn 3f out: wknd fnl f* **10/1**
040- 6 1 1/4 **Classical Rhythm (IRE)**[133] 7613 4-8-12 **64** TGMcLaughlin 2 59
(J R Boyle) *chsd ldrs: rdn over 3f out: wknd fr 2f out* **14/1**
-430 7 hd **Cape Of Luck (IRE)**[34] 871 6-8-9 **61** TonyCulhane 8 55
(P M Phelan) *in rr: sme hdwy over 2f out: nvr in contention* **11/2**[2]
040- 8 2 **Rabeera**[274] 4259 4-8-7 **59** FrancisNorton 4 49
(A M Balding) *t.k.h in rr: rdn and no prog ins fnl 3f* **6/1**[3]
06-0 9 1/2 **Le Corvee (IRE)**[13] 1192 7-8-6 **58** JimmyQuinn 3 47
(A W Carroll) *v.s.a: sme prog fr over 2f out but nvr in contention* **11/1**
-050 10 6 **Direct Debit (IRE)**[76] 392 6-9-1 **70** KevinGhunowa(3) 10 47
(M Wellings) *s.i.s: a towards rr* **18/1**
2m 9.02s (-1.98) **Going Correction** -0.05s/f (Good) 10 Ran SP% **115.8**
Speed ratings (Par 103): **105,104,103,101,100 99,99,97,97,92**
toteswinger: 1&2 £4.70, 1&3 not won, 2&3 £2.00 CSF £19.13 CT £148.85 TOTE £5.70: £1.70, £1.70, £2.70; EX 16.50.
Owner Wayne Devine **Bred** Cathal M Ryan **Trained** Tredodridge, Vale Of Glamorgan
■ Stewards' Enquiry : Kevin Ghunowa £140 fine: failed to arrive in time to weigh out
FOCUS
Following a dry night and day the ground was changed to good to firm all over. Mainly exposed performers in an ordinary handicap in which the winner and third set the standard. The pace was only moderate and those held up failed to get competitive.
Le Corvee(IRE) Official explanation: jockey said gelding missed the break and was denied a clear run home straight

1416 OAKLEY GREEN CONSERVATORIES H'CAP 1m 2f 46y
5:50 (5:53) (Class 5) (0-70,70) 3-Y-O **£2,590** (£770; £385; £192) **Stalls** Low

Form RPR
01- 1 **Lyra's Daemon**[203] 6360 3-9-4 **70** MartinDwyer 7 74
(W R Muir) *mde all: hrd rdn and styd on strly fnl f* **8/1**[3]
056- 2 3/4 **Sherman McCoy**[209] 6199 3-8-13 **65** TGMcLaughlin 1 68
(B R Millman) *chsd ldrs tl rdn and outpcd 3f out: str run on ins fr over 1f out to dispute 2nd ins fnl f but a hld: jst edgd 2nd cl home* **14/1**
000- 3 nse **Saborido (USA)**[194] 6602 3-9-1 **67** JimCrowley 12 69
(Mrs A J Perrett) *in rr but in tch: hdwy on outside 4f out: styd on strly to chse wnr 2f out: no imp fnl f and lose 2nd last stride* **10/1**
04-6 4 1 1/2 **Cayman Sky**[31] 914 3-9-0 **69** (b) PatrickHills(3) 9 68
(R Hannon) *chsd ldrs tl outpcd over 3f out: hdwy again fr 2f out: styd on fnl f but nt rch ldng duo* **25/1**
420- 5 hd **Excelsior Academy**[190] 6700 3-8-12 **69** GabrielHannon(5) 6 68
(B J Meehan) *chsd ldrs: wnt 2nd 6f out: rdn 3f out: wknd ins fnl f* **10/1**
00-0 6 1/2 **Lennie Briscoe (IRE)**[22] 1034 3-8-13 **65** JamesDoyle 10 63+
(S Kirk) *in rr whn checked 6f out: rdn 3f out: hdwy on outside fr 2f out: fin wl but nt rch ldrs* **5/1**[1]
600- 7 3/4 **Devil To Pay**[189] 6714 3-9-1 **67** TedDurcan 4 64+
(J L Dunlop) *hld up in rr: styd on fnl 2f: nvr in contention* **7/1**[2]
630- 8 nk **Mons Calpe (IRE)**[190] 6700 3-8-12 **64** DarryllHolland 3 60+
(P F I Cole) *broke wl: stdd in rr 1/2-way: gd hdwy and squeezed through ins fnl 2f: sn one pce* **5/1**[1]
1 9 4 **Clippity Clop (IRE)**[35] 855 3-9-4 **70** FrancisNorton 8 58+
(J A Osborne) *s.i.s: in rr: pushed along over 3f out: hdwy and nt clr run fr 2f out: nt rcvr* **7/1**[2]
50-0 10 nk **Salybia Bay**[13] 1193 3-8-10 **62** PatDobbs 11 49
(R Hannon) *in tch: chsd ldrs 5f out: rdn over 3f out: wknd 2f out* **14/1**
000- 11 4 1/2 **Suakin Dancer (IRE)**[199] 6473 3-8-12 **64** SteveDrowne 13 42
(H Morrison) *chsd ldr: rdn over 3f out: wkng whn hmpd ins fnl 2f* **20/1**
026- 12 6 **New Beginning (FR)**[169] 7165 3-9-1 **67** JimmyQuinn 2 33
(H J L Dunlop) *in tch: whn hmpd 6f out: sn rdn and bhd* **10/1**
00-0 13 1 1/2 **Kaiser Willie (IRE)**[22] 1036 3-8-1 **56** oh4 DavidProbert(3) 5 19
(B W Duke) *in rr: sme hdwy on outside 4f fr 3f out: sn wknd* **33/1**
2m 11.72s (0.72) **Going Correction** -0.05s/f (Good) 13 Ran SP% **121.6**
Speed ratings (Par 98): **95,94,94,93,93 92,92,91,88,88 84,79,78**
toteswinger: 1&2 not won, 1&3 not won, 2&3 not won CSF £114.19 CT £1145.79 TOTE £10.20: £4.10, £6.10, £4.90; EX 165.70.
Owner M J Caddy **Bred** Horizon Bloodstock Limited **Trained** Lambourn, Berks
■ Stewards' Enquiry : Darryll Holland caution: careless riding

FOCUS
Several unexposed sorts in another ordinary handicap. The gallop was on the steady side and those held up were again at a disadvantage. The fifth, close to last year's form, sets the level.
Mons Calpe(IRE) Official explanation: jockey said gelding hung both ways
Clippity Clop(IRE) Official explanation: jockey said gelding reared as stalls opened
Suakin Dancer(IRE) Official explanation: jockey said filly suffered interference in running
Kaiser Willie(IRE) Official explanation: jockey said colt was unsuited by the good to firm ground

1417 CR WINDOWS FILLIES' H'CAP 1m 5y
6:20 (6:21) (Class 5) (0-75,75) 4-Y-O+ **£2,590** (£770; £385; £192) **Stalls** Low

Form RPR
531- 1 **Supaverdi (USA)**[134] 7609 4-9-0 **71** SteveDrowne 1 81+
(H Morrison) *t.k.h: trckd ldrs: nt clr run over 2f out: drvn and qcknd to ld ins fnl f: drvn and r.o strly* **2/1**[2]
-306 2 1 1/2 **Binfield (IRE)**[23] 1020 4-8-11 **68** JimCrowley 5 72
(B G Powell) *chsd ldr: led wl over 2f out: sn rdn hdd and one pce ins fnl f* **12/1**
124- 3 1 3/4 **Lady Brora**[194] 6605 4-9-3 **74** WilliamBuick 2 74
(A M Balding) *in rr but in tch: rdn and hdwy on ins 3f out: chsd ldrs fr 2f out: no imp and styd on same pce ins fnl f* **15/8**[1]
2123 4 3/4 **Melt (IRE)**[20] 1074 4-8-4 **61** oh1 (b) SimonWhitworth 8 59
(R Hannon) *in rr: hdwy 4f out: rdn to chse ldrs 2f out: wknd ins fnl f* **6/1**[3]
4526 5 2 1/2 **Friends Hope**[41] 805 8-9-4 **75** DarryllHolland 6 68
(R Curtis) *in rr: pushed along over 2f out: nvr gng pce to be competitive* **8/1**
0020 6 1 1/4 **Red Current**[8] 1254 5-8-5 **62** oh5 ow1 NeilPollard 7 52
(R A Harris) *chsd ldrs: rdn over 3f out: wknd over 1f out* **10/1**
000- 7 7 **Street Diva (USA)**[191] 6683 4-8-4 **64** oh7 ow3 KevinGhunowa(3) 4 38
(R Curtis) *led: t.k.h: hdd wl over 2f out: wkng whn hmpd over 1f out* **50/1**
1m 39.42s (-1.38) **Going Correction** -0.05s/f (Good) 7 Ran SP% **112.3**
Speed ratings (Par 100): **104,102,100,100,97 96,89**
toteswinger: 1&2 £4.70, 1 & 3 £1.30, 2&3 £1.30 CSF £24.55 CT £50.02 TOTE £3.60: £1.80, £4.10; EX 28.30.
Owner Ben & Sir Martyn Arbib **Bred** Arbib Bloodstock Partnership **Trained** East Ilsley, Berks
FOCUS
Not a strong handicap but, although the gallop looked a moderate one, the time was decent. The form seems sound enough.
Street Diva(USA) Official explanation: jockey said filly ran too free

1418 KENT BUILDING PLASTICS H'CAP 5f 161y
6:50 (6:50) (Class 4) (0-85,85) 4-Y-O+ **£4,727** (£1,406; £702; £351) **Stalls** Centre

Form RPR
013- 1 **Dazed And Amazed**[190] 6699 5-8-13 **80** PatDobbs 11 88
(R Hannon) *hld up in rr: stdy hdwy on outside fr 2f out: str run fr over 1f out to ld ins fnl f: hld on wl* **13/2**
46-3 2 hd **Blue Jack**[18] 1094 4-8-10 **77** MartinDwyer 8 84
(W R Muir) *in tch: hdwy over 2f out: drvn to ld appr fnl f and sn edgd lft: hdd ins fnl f: rallied u.p but a jst hld by wnr* **10/3**[1]
0536 3 3/4 **The Tatling (IRE)**[4] 1334 12-8-8 **80** JackDean(5) 9 85
(J M Bradley) *rdn and in tch 1/2-way: styd on u.p fnl f but nvr quite gng pce to get to ldng duo* **7/1**
25-4 4 1 1/4 **Make My Dream**[13] 1181 6-8-5 **72** TPO'Shea 1 73
(J Gallagher) *disp ld tl slt advantage 3f out: sn drvn: hdd over 1f out: no ex ins fnl f* **8/1**
5-05 5 3/4 **Whiskey Junction**[13] 1181 5-9-4 **85** FrancisNorton 6 83
(M Quinn) *slt ld to 3f out: styd pressing ldr to 2f out: styd on same pce fnl f* **11/2**[2]
3420 6 3/4 **Artistic License (IRE)**[12] 1197 4-8-11 **78** TonyCulhane 2 73+
(M R Channon) *stdd towards rr: hdwy and nt clr run over 2f out: sme hdwy again and nt clr fr over 1f out and ins fnl f: nt rcvr* **6/1**[3]
060- 7 hd **Golden Dixie (USA)**[202] 6402 10-8-9 **76** NeilPollard 4 71
(R A Harris) *chsd ldrs: rdn 1/2-way: wknd fnl f* **16/1**
40-1 8 hd **Magical Speedfit (IRE)**[13] 1181 4-8-7 **74** WilliamBuick 5 68
(G G Margarson) *chsd ldrs tl lost pl and n.m.r ins fnl 2f: n.d after but kpt on ins fnl f* **15/2**
300- 9 12 **Best One**[123] 7733 5-8-9 **79** (b) KevinGhunowa(3) 3 32
(R A Harris) *slowly away: rcvr: in tch and rdn 1/2-way: sn wknd* **14/1**
1m 10.22s (-0.98) **Going Correction** -0.05s/f (Good) 9 Ran SP% **114.0**
Speed ratings (Par 105): **104,103,102,101,100 99,98,98,82**
toteswinger: 1&2 £9.70, 1&3 £6.00, 2&3 not won. CSF £28.06 CT £140.94 TOTE £8.70: £3.10, £1.90, £2.70; EX 21.10.
Owner Mrs R Ablett **Bred** Whitsbury Manor Stud & Pigeon House Stud **Trained** East Everleigh, Wilts
FOCUS
Exposed performers in this fair handicap and a race in which the gallop was sound throughout. The first two set the standard.
Artistic License(IRE) Official explanation: jockey said filly was denied a clear run

1419 RG KELLY WINDOWS MAIDEN STKS 5f 161y
7:20 (7:20) (Class 5) 3-Y-O+ **£2,590** (£770; £385; £192) **Stalls** Centre

Form RPR
0-3 1 **Champagne Future**[14] 1174 3-8-10 0 TedDurcan 6 82
(W R Swinburn) *sn led: qcknd and hung lft fnl f: readily* **4/1**[3]
342- 2 2 **Cawdor (IRE)**[221] 5860 3-9-1 74 DaneO'Neill 7 80
(H Candy) *in tch: rdn and hdwy over 2f out: chsd wnr wl over 1f out: styd on wl but a readily hld* **2/1**[1]
325- 3 2 1/2 **Frank Street**[233] 5530 3-9-1 76 JimmyQuinn 3 72
(Eve Johnson Houghton) *t.k.h: chsd ldrs: rdn over 2f out: outpcd fnl f* **7/1**
420- 4 2 **Megasecret**[145] 7458 3-9-1 71 PatDobbs 2 65
(R Hannon) *s.i.s: towards rr: hdwy over 1f out: kpt on fnl f but nvr in contention* **14/1**
22-5 5 2 1/4 **Ben's Dream (IRE)**[20] 1068 3-9-1 72 WilliamBuick 5 57
(A M Balding) *chsd ldrs: rdn 3f out: sn no imp: wknd over 1f out* **7/2**[2]
6 5 **Badge** 3-9-1 0 SteveDrowne 10 40
(R Charlton) *slowly away: a outpcd in rr* **7/1**
460- 7 3 1/4 **Tiger Trail (GER)**[272] 4313 5-9-12 57 TonyCulhane 8 32+
(Mrs N Smith) *chsd wnr tl lost action and wknd qckly ins fnl 2f* **33/1**
8 12 **Steeple Caster** 3-8-10 0 MCGeran(5) 11 —
(J M Bradley) *sn rdn and green: a in rr* **80/1**
9 56 **Supreme Glimpse** 3-8-10 0 JimCrowley 1 —
(Mrs N Smith) *v.s.a: sn t.o* **33/1**
1m 10.11s (-1.09) **Going Correction** -0.05s/f (Good)
WFA 3 from 5yo 11lb 9 Ran SP% **114.3**
Speed ratings (Par 103): **105,102,99,96,93 86,82,66,—**
toteswinger: 1&2 £4.00, 1&3 £2.90, 2&3 £6.60 CSF £12.15 TOTE £3.50: £1.10, £1.60, £2.20; EX 16.00.
Owner The Enthusiasts **Bred** P M Crane **Trained** Aldbury, Herts

FOCUS
An ordinary maiden in which the pace was reasonable. The winner is progressing and should make his mark in handicaps.
Badge Official explanation: jockey said colt missed the break
Tiger Trail(GER) Official explanation: jockey said saddle slipped leaving stalls

1420 MB FRAMES CLASSIFIED STKS — 1m 5y
7:50 (7:53) (Class 6) 3-Y-O+ — £1,978 (£584; £292) Stalls Low

Form				RPR
400-	1		**Second To Nun (IRE)**[203] 6360 3-8-7 55 JimCrowley 6 (Jean-Rene Auvray) *chsd ldrs: led over 2f out: drvn out fnl f* 7/2[2]	62+
5-14	2	½	**Wunder Strike (USA)**[22] 1036 3-8-8 53 ow1 (p) PatCosgrave 5 (J R Boyle) *in rr whn hmpd 5f out: hdwy fr 3f out: hrd rdn to chse wnr fnl f but a jst hld* 2/1[1]	61+
00-2	3	4	**Gun For Sale (USA)**[93] 211 4-9-7 49 DarryllHolland 3 (P J Makin) *t.k.h: chsd ldrs: led over 4f out: rdn and hdd over 2f out: outpcd appr fnl f* 7/2[2]	55
00-0	4	½	**Rubbinghousedotcom (IRE)**[48] 752 3-8-8 54 ow1 TonyCulhane 1 (P M Phelan) *t.k.h: chsd ldrs: pushed along 3f out: one pce fnl 2f* 14/1	51
000-	5	½	**Janshe Gold**[286] 3845 4-9-7 55 TolleyDean 8 (J G Portman) *sn slt ld: hdd over 4f out: stl ev ch 2f out: wknd over 1f out* 20/1	53
560	6	1½	**Songful (IRE)**[20] 1066 3-8-7 55 WilliamBuick 11 (Pat Eddery) *chsd ldrs: rdn 3f out: wknd ins fnl 2f* 10/1[3]	45
00-4	7	½	**Bright Wire (IRE)**[20] 1071 3-8-7 55 NeilPollard 12 (M Madgwick) *sn in tch: chsd ldrs and rdn 3f out: outpcd fnl 2f* 50/1	44
000-	8	½	**Into My Arms**[283] 3968 3-8-7 32 FrancisNorton 10 (M S Saunders) *in rr: hdwy 3f out: styd on same pce fnl 2f* 28/1	43
00-0	9	½	**Dancing Rhythm**[31] 917 4-9-7 45 TGMcLaughlin 7 (M S Saunders) *in rr tl mod prog fnl 2f* 14/1	46+
00-6	10	1½	**Wightgold**[21] 1045 3-8-7 52 JimmyQuinn 16 (H J L Dunlop) *in rr: sme hdwy over 4f out: wknd fr 3f out* 40/1	39
0505	11	½	**Keen As Mustard**[22] 1037 4-9-0 49 LeeNewnes(7) 14 (M D I Usher) *a towards rr* 40/1	41
000-	12	42	**Young Ollie**[204] 6345 4-9-2 42 SophieDoyle(5) 2 (E A Wheeler) *sddled slipped sn after s: a in rr: t.o* 100/1	—

1m 42.12s (1.32) **Going Correction** -0.05s/f (Good)
WFA 3 from 4yo 14lb — 12 Ran SP% **116.2**
Speed ratings (Par 101): **91,90,86,86,85 84,83,83,82,81 80,38**
toteswinger: 1&2 £2.50, 1&3 £5.00, 2&3 £4.30 CSF £9.98 TOTE £5.40: £2.30, £1.80, £1.90; EX 15.50 Place 6: £68.39, Place 5: £43.91..
Owner The Dragon Partnership No 2 **Bred** M J Lewin And D Grieve **Trained** Maiden Bradley, Wilts
FOCUS
A modest event in which the three market leaders filled the first three places. The gallop was a moderate one and it was another race on the card where it paid to race prominently. The placed horses are related in line with their recent all-weather form.
Gun For Sale(USA) Official explanation: jockey said gelding ran too free
Young Ollie Official explanation: jockey said saddle slipped
T/Plt: £45.10 to a £1 stake. Pool: £43,738.09. 707.62 winning tickets. T/Qpdt: £9.20 to a £1 stake. Pool: £4,806.85. 386.60 winning tickets. ST

1195 FOLKESTONE (R-H)
Tuesday, April 21

OFFICIAL GOING: Good (good to firm in places)
Wind: Light, against Weather: Sunny, warm

1421 SHEPWAY DISTRICT APPRENTICE H'CAP — 6f
2:00 (2:00) (Class 6) (0-60,60) 4-Y-O+ — £2,047 (£604; £302) Stalls Low

Form				RPR
3110	1		**Super Frank (IRE)**[27] 954 6-8-10 60 (p) BarryAdams(8) 2 (J Akehurst) *nt as wl away as others and unable to ld: racd against rail: effrt and untrbld run through to ld 1f out: edgd rt but drvn clr* 10/3[1]	73+
000-	2	2½	**Bohobe (IRE)**[186] 6792 4-8-4 54 NoelGarbutt(8) 4 (Rae Guest) *hld up in midfield: prog 2f out: styd on to take 2nd wl ins fnl f: no ch w wnr* 12/1	59
000-	3	1¼	**Bronte's Hope**[150] 7414 5-8-10 55 KatiaScallan(3) 1 (M P Tregoning) *trckd ldr but racd off nr side rail: effrt 2f out: kpt on same pce and snatched 3rd last strides* 6/1[3]	56
1200	4	hd	**Davids Mark**[36] 853 9-8-5 55 DannyBrock(8) 12 (J R Jenkins) *last and sn wl detached fr rest: taken to wd outside and styd on wl fr 2f out: nrst fin* 14/1	55+
-605	5	nse	**Silver Prelude**[33] 880 8-9-2 58 AnthonyBetts 7 (S C Williams) *taken down early: led but racd off nr side rail: hdd & wknd 1f out* 11/2[2]	58
430-	6	¾	**Who's Winning (IRE)**[155] 7359 8-8-7 54 (t) GemmaElford(5) 3 (B G Powell) *trckd ldrs: taken to outer and rdn 2f out: no imp after* 10/1	52
3450	7	¾	**Avoca Dancer (IRE)**[36] 853 6-8-11 53 (v) HollyHall 8 (Karen George) *in rr of main gp: rdn and kpt on one pce fnl 2f: n.d* 11/1	48
0-00	8	1½	**Towy Boy (IRE)**[20] 1076 4-9-4 60 TobyAtkinson 11 (I A Wood) *in rr of main gp: shkn up 2f out: one pce and no imp* 11/1	51
600-	9	3¾	**Calabaza**[113] 7808 7-8-8 53 KierenFox(3) 5 (M J Attwater) *trckd ldrs: effrt to dispute 2nd 2f out: wknd rapidly fnl f* 12/1	32
/1-0	10	shd	**Miltons Choice**[8] 1248 6-8-13 60 JoshWall(5) 13 (J M Bradley) *racd wd: in tch: effrt to dispute 2nd 2f out: sn wknd* 16/1	38
04-0	11	7	**Mine Behind**[15] 1152 9-8-10 60 (t) KathrynFerguson(8) 10 (J R Best) *no room and snatched up after 1f: racd wd in rr after: no prog 2f out: wknd rapidly* 25/1	16
023	12	1	**Mister Incredible**[21] 1055 6-8-8 50 (v) SeanPalmer 6 (J M Bradley) *mostly chsd ldr to over 1f out: wknd v rapidly* 16/1	3

1m 13.09s (0.39) **Going Correction** -0.10s/f (Good) — 12 Ran SP% **116.2**
Speed ratings (Par 101): **93,89,88,87,87 86,85,83,78,78 69,67**
toteswinger: 1&2 £14.90, 1&3 £5.40, 2&3 £34.80 CSF £43.66 CT £199.50 TOTE £3.50: £1.50, £6.60, £2.30; EX 60.60 Trifecta £172.50 Part won. Pool: £233.19 - 0.30 winning units..
Owner A D Spence **Bred** A Butler **Trained** Epsom, Surrey
■ Stewards' Enquiry : Kathryn Ferguson one-day ban: used whip when out of contention (May 5)

FOCUS
The stands' rail often proves to hold a major advantage on the straight course, and on this occasion it could not have been more evident, with the winner enjoying a dream run along the fence. The form does not look that strong.

1422 HR GO GO GO MAIDEN STKS (DIV I) — 7f (S)
2:30 (2:30) (Class 5) 3-Y-O+ — £2,388 (£705; £352) Stalls Low

Form				RPR
33-2	1		**Shabib (USA)**[20] 1071 3-8-13 83 RHills 5 (B W Hills) *mde virtually all: shkn up and stretched clr fr 2f out: eased fnl 100yds* 2/5[1]	84+
03-	2	5	**Dice (IRE)**[224] 5784 3-8-13 0 DaneO'Neill 4 (L M Cumani) *mostly chsd wnr: easily outpcd fnl 2f* 6/1[2]	68
003	3	2¾	**Love Allowed**[21] 1047 3-8-8 0 RobertWinston 1 (Jamie Poulton) *racd against rail: cl up: easily outpcd fnl 2f: kpt on* 33/1	55
00-	4	2¾	**Precious Secret (IRE)**[157] 7332 3-8-8 0 EddieAhern 2 (C F Wall) *trckd ldrs: plld out and effrt over 2f out: fdd over 1f out* 12/1	48
5/	5	1	**Muzmin (USA)**[591] 5227 4-9-12 0 TPO'Shea 7 (E A L Dunlop) *stdd s: settled wl in rr: pushed along and one pce fr over 2f out: lft bhd over 1f out* 9/1[3]	55
4	6	nk	**Global Village (IRE)**[66] 552 4-9-7 0 WilliamCarson(5) 9 (Miss D Mountain) *wl in rr: rdn over 2f out: one pce and n.d* 40/1	54
00-	7	shd	**The Scorching Wind (IRE)**[164] 7240 3-8-13 0 SaleemGolam 3 (S C Williams) *heavily stdd leaving stalls: hld up in detached last: taken to outer and sme prog 3f out: nvr on terms* 25/1	49
0-6	8	3	**Flirty (IRE)**[107] 36 3-8-8 0 NickyMackay 10 (Rae Guest) *hld up in rr: pushed along over 2f out: no prog* 150/1	36
0-	9	1	**Cake Stand**[200] 6438 3-8-13 0 RobertHavlin 8 (J A R Toller) *in tch tl lost pl 3f out: wl in rr and outpcd fnl 2f* 66/1	38
0-	10	116	**Soldier Soldier**[172] 7106 3-8-13 0 FergusSweeney 6 (J R Jenkins) *prom tl wknd rapidly wl over 2f out: virtually p.u ins fnl f* 150/1	—

1m 26.62s (-0.68) **Going Correction** -0.10s/f (Good)
WFA 3 from 4yo 13lb — 10 Ran SP% **115.4**
Speed ratings (Par 103): **99,93,90,87,85 85,85,81,80,—**
toteswingers: 1&2 £1.30, 1&3 £4.40, 2&3 £7.90 CSF £2.94 TOTE £1.40: £1.02, £1.60, £6.00; EX 3.20 Trifecta £19.00 Pool: £480.46 - 18.62 winning units..
Owner Hamdan Al Maktoum **Bred** Shadwell Farm LLC **Trained** Lambourn, Berks
FOCUS
Probably the better of the two divisions, though producing only a slightly faster time, and a maiden of varying abilities, with the winner capable of developing into a decent handicapper and some of the others likely to have to ply their trade at a much lower level. The first two are rated to their pre-race marks.
Soldier Soldier Official explanation: vet said colt broke a blood vessel

1423 HR GO GO GO MAIDEN STKS (DIV II) — 7f (S)
3:00 (3:01) (Class 5) 3-Y-O+ — £2,388 (£705; £352) Stalls Low

Form				RPR
	1		**Mastoora (IRE)** 3-8-8 0 RHills 5 (W J Haggas) *t.k.h: trckd ldrs: led wl over 1f out: cruised clr: nt extended* 11/4[1]	83+
30-	2	3½	**Safari Guide**[242] 5213 3-8-13 0 StephenCarson 9 (P Winkworth) *racd towards outer: trckd ldrs: effrt over 2f out: kpt on to take 2nd wl ins fnl f: no ch w wnr* 14/1	71
	3	¾	**Mackten** 3-8-13 0 TPQueally 6 (W J Knight) *allowed to s slowly: keen and hld up in last: stl there 2f out: gd prog over 1f out: nudged along and styd on wl to take 3rd nr fin* 11/1	69+
62	4	¾	**Karta (IRE)**[35] 855 3-8-8 0 RoystonFfrench 10 (M Johnston) *pressed ldr: pushed along over 2f out: outpcd over 1f out: plugged on* 3/1[2]	62
5-4	5	1¾	**Lady Micklegate (USA)**[32] 890 3-8-8 0 RobertWinston 7 (J R Best) *t.k.h: led and racd against rail: hrd rdn and hdd wl over 1f out: wknd fnl f* 7/2[3]	57
00-2	6	2½	**My Flame**[21] 1047 4-9-12 54 EddieAhern 1 (J R Jenkins) *trckd ldrs: cl enough 2f out: sn lft wl bhd* 7/2[3]	61
0	7	3½	**Behind Blue Eyes**[85] 296 3-8-13 0 (p) JerryO'Dwyer 3 (Karen George) *nvr gng wl: u.p after 2f in midfield: nvr on terms* 125/1	46
	8	½	**Poca A Poca (IRE)**[30] 5-9-2 0 MarkFlynn(5) 2 (G C Bravery) *hld up in rr: shkn up 2f out and rn green: sn btn* 100/1	45
00-	9	8	**Red Stiletto**[182] 6887 3-8-8 0 NickyMackay 8 (Rae Guest) *hld up in rr: pushed along and lost tch over 2f out: sn wl bhd* 66/1	18
0-0	10	21	**Straboe (USA)**[21] 1047 3-8-13 0 SaleemGolam 4 (S C Williams) *stdd s: hld up in rr: effrt on outer 1/2-way: wknd rapidly 2f out: t.o* 66/1	—

1m 26.99s (-0.31) **Going Correction** -0.10s/f (Good)
WFA 3 from 4yo+ 13lb — 10 Ran SP% **115.9**
Speed ratings (Par 103): **97,93,92,91,89 86,82,81,72,48**
toteswingers: 1&2 £7.60, 1&3 £9.90, 2&3 £15.50 CSF £41.71 TOTE £3.70: £1.30, £3.10, £2.30; EX 36.90 Trifecta £329.50 Part won. Pool: £445.35 - 0.89 winning units..
Owner Hamdan Al Maktoum **Bred** Rathbarry Stud **Trained** Newmarket, Suffolk
FOCUS
Overall, this did not look as good as division one, but it produced an equally comfortable winner and the time was only just slower. The form is a bit muddling.
Red Stiletto Official explanation: jockey said filly was unsuited by the track and became unbalanced

1424 HYTHE BAY SEAFOOD RESTAURANT (S) STKS — 5f
3:30 (3:30) (Class 6) 3-Y-O — £2,047 (£604; £302) Stalls Low

Form				RPR
21-0	1		**Shadow Bay (IRE)**[12] 1196 3-9-4 70 IanMongan 3 (Miss Z C Davison) *sn outpcd and detached in last: taken wd and prog u.p 2f out: sustained effrt fnl f to ld last 50yds* 5/1[3]	73
-232	2	1	**Billy Beetroot (USA)**[7] 1271 3-8-7 62 (b) WilliamCarson(5) 4 (S C Williams) *led and racd against rail: clr 1/2-way: edgd rt u.p fnl f: hdd last 50yds* 7/4[1]	63
100-	3	¾	**Mythical Blue (IRE)**[206] 6281 3-9-4 75 StephenDonohoe 2 (J M Bradley) *t.k.h early: chsd ldr: rdn 2f out: clsd 1f out: kpt on but lost 2nd ins fnl f* 9/4[2]	67
-300	4	½	**Dancing Welcome**[50] 736 3-8-7 45 (b[1]) LPKeniry 7 (J M Bradley) *last pair tl prog to chse ldrs 2f out: hanging and nt qckn over 1f out: kpt on last 100yds* 33/1	54
2004	5	9	**Sorrel Ridge (IRE)**[19] 1084 3-8-12 52 (b) EddieAhern 6 (M G Quinlan) *in tch 3f: hanging and wknd sn after* 8/1	27

2665 **6** 2¼ **Fangfoss Girls**[18] 1095 3-8-13 62 FergusSweeney 8 19
(G L Moore) *prom: wknd rapidly over 1f out* **7/1**

59.74 secs (-0.26) **Going Correction** -0.10s/f (Good) **6** Ran SP% **110.4**

Speed ratings (Par 96): **98,96,95,94,80 76**

CSF £13.73 TOTE £6.50: £1.50, £1.80; EX 16.30 Trifecta £23.80 Pool: £272.20 - 8.46 winning units..There was no bid for the winner.

Owner David J Bearman **Bred** Thomas Cahalan & Sophie Hayley **Trained** Hammerwood, E Sussex

■ Stewards' Enquiry : William Carson one-day ban: used whip with excessive frequency (May 5)

FOCUS

There was a strong gallop thanks to Billy Beetroot, who quickly got over to the stands' rail and set off like a scalded cat. The form is not solid and the runner-up is the best guide.

1425 SWALEHEATING.COM H'CAP 5f

4:00 (4:00) (Class 4) (0-80,79) 4-Y-0+ **£5,180** (£1,541; £770; £384) **Stalls** Low

Form RPR

3141 **1** **Princess Rose Anne (IRE)**[18] 1091 4-8-8 69 RobertWinston 3 81
(J R Best) *racd against rail: mde virtually all: def advantage over 1f out: drvn clr fnl f* **5/1**

64-0 **2** 2¼ **Hereford Boy**[15] 1150 5-8-11 72 (b) RobertHavlin 2 76
(D K Ivory) *hld up in last: rdn and prog over 1f out: wnt 2nd ins fnl f and threatened briefly: nt qckn* **15/2**

14-2 **3** 1½ **Our Piccadilly (IRE)**[15] 1150 4-9-1 76 FergusSweeney 1 75
(W S Kittow) *hld up bhd ldrs: effrt to chse wnr over 1f out tl ins fnl f: fdd* **9/4**[1]

0111 **4** 6 **What Katie Did (IRE)**[15] 1152 4-8-9 70 (p) StephenDonohoe 4 47
(J M Bradley) *w wnr to 2f out: sn rdn and wknd* **3/1**[2]

006- **5** 3¼ **What Do You Know**[182] 6881 6-8-10 71 (v) RHills 5 36
(A M Hales) *racd wd: on terms w ldrs: shkn up 2f out: wknd tamely over 1f out* **11/1**

600- **6** 2¾ **Ocean Blaze**[211] 6174 5-9-0 78 JamesMillman(3) 8 33
(B R Millman) *racd wdst of all: on terms w ldrs to 2f out: hanging and wknd rapidly sn after* **9/2**[3]

58.80 secs (-1.20) **Going Correction** -0.10s/f (Good) **6** Ran SP% **110.7**

Speed ratings (Par 105): **105,101,99,89,84 79**

toteswinger: 1&2 £5.30, 1&3 £2.30, 2&3 £3.30 CSF £38.70 CT £101.06 TOTE £5.90: £2.90, £3.00; EX 51.20 Trifecta £336.80 Pool: £555.36 - 1.22 winning units..

Owner Miss Rose-Anne Galligan **Bred** C McCarthy **Trained** Hucking, Kent

FOCUS

The previous two winners had come from slightly wider lanes, but the winner reminded everyone that the rail is usually the place to be. The winner is rated to the best of last year's form.

Ocean Blaze Official explanation: jockey said mare hung right throughout

1426 HOBBS PARKER TELECOM H'CAP 1m 7f 92y

4:30 (4:30) (Class 5) (0-75,75) 4-Y-0+ **£3,070** (£906; £453) **Stalls** Low

Form RPR

23-2 **1** **Isabelonabicycle**[15] 1156 4-8-13 65 LPKeniry 3 75
(A M Balding) *t.k.h early: trckd ldrs: prog to go 2nd 2f out and sn chalng: narrow ld and edgd rt 1f out: hld on wl* **8/1**[3]

023- **2** hd **Tobago Bay**[8] 6329 4-8-4 56 (b) NeilChalmers 6 66
(Miss Sheena West) *led: drvn and pressed 2f out: narrowly hdd and intimidated 1f out: battled on wl: jst hld* **15/8**[1]

441- **3** 3½ **Dayia (IRE)**[124] 7715 5-9-12 75 TPQueally 2 80
(J Pearce) *trckd ldrs: rdn over 3f out cl up over 2f out: nt qckn u.p: grad outpcd* **11/1**

046U **4** ¾ **Up In Arms (IRE)**[12] 1200 5-8-7 56 StephenCarson 11 60
(P Winkworth) *trckd ldrs: drvn 3f out: cl up 2f out: grad outpcd* **16/1**

0/50 **5** 2½ **Eastwell Smiles**[20] 1069 5-8-10 59 FergusSweeney 10 60
(R T Phillips) *trckd ldrs: rdn 3f out: outpcd fr 2f out: no imp after* **20/1**

/34- **6** 1½ **Whitcombe Spirit**[398] 940 4-8-8 60 RobertHavlin 4 59+
(Jamie Poulton) *hld up in last: stl there over 2f out but gng wl enough: drvn over 1f out: kpt on but nvr nr ldrs* **33/1**

-342 **7** nk **Generous Star**[55] 679 6-8-1 57 (t) SimonPearce(7) 5 55+
(J Pearce) *hld up in midfield: forced bk to rr by loose horse 6f out: rdn over 3f out: plugged on but no ch* **12/1**

222- **8** 3¼ **Epsom Salts**[120] 7770 4-9-4 70 IanMongan 9 64
(P M Phelan) *hld up in last trio: rdn and no prog fr 3f out: bhd fnl 2f* **12/1**

410- **9** shd **Go Amwell**[44] 6672 6-8-10 59 (v) StephenDonohoe 7 53
(J R Jenkins) *dwlt: hld up in last trio: rousted along 4f out: no prog after* **11/1**

100- **10** 1½ **Lupita (IRE)**[30] 2012 5-8-7 56 RobertWinston 12 48
(B G Powell) *hld up towards rr: drvn and no prog 3f out: wknd over 1f out* **33/1**

113- **11** 4½ **Rutba**[166] 7216 4-8-13 65 (v) RHills 8 51
(M P Tregoning) *trckd ldr: rdn 3f out: wknd rapidly 2f out* **11/2**[2]

5421 **U** **Calculating (IRE)**[35] 860 5-8-7 56 oh1 RoystonFfrench 1 —
(M D I Usher) *s.s: sn in tch: abt 7th whn stmbld and uns rdr bnd over 9f out* **9/1**

3m 28.03s (-1.67) **Going Correction** -0.025s/f (Good) **12** Ran SP% **119.9**

WFA 4 from 5yo+ 3lb

Speed ratings (Par 103): **103,102,101,100,99 98,98,96,96,95 93,—**

toteswinger: 1&2 £3.40, 1&3 £15.50, 2&3 £5.20 CSF £23.03 CT £170.60 TOTE £9.40: £2.90, £1.30, £3.30; EX 30.10 Trifecta £22.70 Pool: £167.34 - 5.44 winning units..

Owner J C & S R Hitchins **Bred** J C , J R And S R Hitchins **Trained** Kingsclere, Hants

■ Stewards' Enquiry : L P Keniry one-day ban, plus two deferred; careless riding (May 5-7)

FOCUS

They went a decent gallop but on this ground the leaders just kept going and it proved impossible to come from too far back. The bare form is ordinary with the third close to his all-weather mark.

Rutba Official explanation: jockey said filly stopped quickly

1427 RICHARD HOLLAND MAIDEN STKS 1m 4f

5:00 (5:00) (Class 5) 3-Y-0+ **£2,729** (£806; £403) **Stalls** Low

Form RPR

043- **1** **King Of Wands**[209] 6199 3-8-7 76 EddieAhern 1 80+
(J L Dunlop) *mde virtually all: pressed fr 4f out: rdn to assert wl over 1f out: drifted lft after: pushed out and in command fnl f* **1/1**[1]

23- **2** 1¼ **Wild Rhubarb**[256] 4821 4-9-7 0 IanMongan 5 75+
(C G Cox) *trckd ldng pair after 3f: rdn and outpcd wl over 2f out: styd on over 1f out to take 2nd last 100yds: nvr able to chal* **9/2**[3]

5- **3** 1 **Final Victory**[194] 6604 3-8-7 0 LPKeniry 2 76+
(A M Balding) *pressed wnr: persistent chal u.p fr over 3f out: hld over 1f out: swtchd rt sn after: lost 2nd last 100yds* **11/4**[2]

0 **4** 14 **Trempari**[53] 704 6-9-13 0 FergusSweeney 4 54
(Mike Murphy) *hld up in last pair: rdn wl over 3f out: sn lft bhd: tk remote 4th nr fin* **33/1**

5 ½ **Runaway Pegasus (USA)**[199] 4-9-7 0 TPQueally 6 48
(H R A Cecil) *trckd ldng pair 3f: cl up tl shkn up over 3f out: sn wknd* **7/1**

6 6 **Ullalujah**[25] 7-9-8 0 SamHitchcott 3 39
(L Wells) *s.s: a in last pair: rdn 4f out: sn lft bhd* **150/1**

2m 41.75s (0.85) **Going Correction** -0.025s/f (Good)

WFA 3 from 4yo 20lb 4 from 6yo+ 1lb **6** Ran SP% **111.0**

Speed ratings (Par 103): **96,95,94,85,84 80**

toteswinger: 1&2 £1.60, 1&3 £1.30, 2&3 £2.20 CSF £5.86 TOTE £2.10: £1.50, £2.00; EX 6.10.

Owner Normandie Stud Ltd **Bred** Normandie Stud Ltd **Trained** Arundel, W Sussex

FOCUS

A medium gallop until the increasing pace sorted them out 3f from home. They finished in two groups of three, with the leading trio all showing a solid level of form.

1428 BUY PHOTO FINISH PRINTS AT EVENTIMAGE.TV H'CAP 1m 1f 149y

5:35 (5:35) (Class 5) (0-75,75) 3-Y-0 **£3,070** (£906; £453) **Stalls** Centre

Form RPR

606- **1** **Solar Graphite (IRE)**[214] 6083 3-8-9 66 EddieAhern 8 71+
(J L Dunlop) *hld up towards rr: prog over 3f out: wnt 3rd over 1f out: drvn and styd on dourly fnl f: led last stride* **5/1**[3]

-423 **2** shd **Morning Sir Alan**[17] 1130 3-9-1 72 RobertHavlin 5 77
(S A Callaghan) *led 100yds: restrained into 3rd: chsd ldr 2f out: drvn and clsd fnl f: got up nr fin: pipped on line* **11/1**

204- **3** nk **Andhaar**[215] 6058 3-9-4 75 RHills 4 79
(E A L Dunlop) *led after 100yds: kicked on over 2f out: hrd pressed fnl f: worn down nr fin* **9/2**[2]

60-1 **4** 9 **Peter Grimes (IRE)**[21] 1050 3-8-13 70 RobertWinston 1 55
(H J L Dunlop) *trckd ldr after 100yds: drvn wl over 2f out: lost 2nd 2f out and sn wknd* **9/2**[2]

640- **5** ½ **Arrogance**[208] 6223 3-8-10 67 FergusSweeney 6 51
(G L Moore) *racd wd: hld up in midfield: pushed along fr 1/2-way: struggling over 2f out: sn lft bhd* **33/1**

51 **6** hd **Hatta Diamond (IRE)**[29] 939 3-9-2 73 IanMongan 7 57
(M Johnston) *trckd ldng trio: rdn 3f out: sn struggling: wknd 2f out* **11/4**[1]

005- **7** hd **The Saucy Snipe**[200] 6432 3-8-11 68 StephenCarson 3 51
(P Winkworth) *hld up in last pair: pushed along over 2f out: no real prog and nvr nr ldrs* **33/1**

460- **8** 1 **Mymateeric**[203] 6362 3-8-2 66 SimonPearce(7) 10 47
(J Pearce) *in tch in midfield tl lost pl over 3f out: struggling after: no ch over 1f out* **17/2**

56-0 **9** shd **Very Distinguished**[13] 1193 3-8-0 62 NicolPolli(5) 9 43
(M G Quinlan) *hld up in last pair: no prog 3f out: hrd rdn and struggling 2f out* **17/2**

2m 5.13s (0.23) **Going Correction** -0.025s/f (Good) **9** Ran SP% **115.0**

Speed ratings (Par 98): **98,97,97,90,90 89,89,88,88**

toteswinger: 1&2 £9.20, 1&3 £9.00, 2&3 £7.20 CSF £57.95 CT £261.62 TOTE £6.20: £2.70, £2.70, £1.40; EX 71.60 Trifecta £191.00 Part won. Pool: £258.19 - 28.40 winning units. Place 6: £83.43 Place 5: £46.52.

Owner Gail Brown Racing Partnership **Bred** T W Bloodstock Ltd **Trained** Arundel, W Sussex

■ Stewards' Enquiry : Eddie Ahern trainer's rep said, regarding apparent improvement in form, that it had been gelded and stepped up in trip.

FOCUS

A lively tempo, but yet again those who raced handy dominated on the round course and the winner only just got there in time. The form is rated slightly negatively for now.

Solar Graphite(IRE) Official explanation: trainer's rep said horse had been gelded and stepped up in trip

T/Plt: £97.90 to a £1 stake. Pool: £46,481.53. 346.35 winning tickets. T/Qpdt: £125.40 to a £1 stake. Pool: £3,409.71. 20.11 winning tickets. JN

1317 KEMPTON (A.W) (R-H)

Tuesday, April 21

OFFICIAL GOING: Standard

Wind: virtually nil Weather: bight and sunny

1429 MSL CLAIMING STKS 1m (P)

2:20 (2:21) (Class 6) 3-Y-0 **£2,047** (£604; £302) **Stalls** High

Form RPR

2404 **1** **Hold The Bucks (USA)**[15] 1148 3-8-6 65 (p) SophieDoyle(5) 8 68
(J S Moore) *racd in midfield: niggled along 5f out: rdn and no prog over 1f out: str run fnl 100yds to ld last strides* **11/2**[3]

4-01 **2** hd **Bartica (IRE)**[66] 547 3-8-13 70 (b) RichardHughes 5 70
(R Hannon) *dwlt: sn in tch in midfield: hdwy and hung rt fr jst over 2f out: rdn to ld over 1f out: clr ins fnl f: drvn and fdd fnl 100yds: hdd last strides* **4/1**[2]

00-5 **3** ¾ **Protiva**[20] 1075 3-8-1 58 MartinLane(5) 7 61
(A P Jarvis) *chsd ldr after 1f: rdn and unable qck wl over 1f out: chsd ldr jst ins fnl f tl fnl 75yds: kpt on* **20/1**

5144 **4** 2¼ **Bromhead (USA)**[46] 776 3-8-11 70 RyanMoore 4 61
(B J Meehan) *ponied to s: led after 1f: clr 1/2-way: rdn jst over 2f out: hdd over 1f out: wknd fnl f* **13/8**[1]

060- **5** hd **Manolito Montoya (IRE)**[191] 6674 3-8-11 67 (v[1]) GabrielHannon(5) 1 65
(J W Hills) *dwlt: hld up in rr: hdwy u.p 2f out: kpt on fnl f but nvr pce to rch ldrs* **33/1**

5513 **6** 2 **Daily Double**[15] 1148 3-8-11 65 SebSanders 2 56
(D K Ivory) *s.i.s: hld up in rr: rdn and effrt on outer over 2f out: no imp over 1f out* **11/1**

1162 **7** 1½ **Fantastic Fred (IRE)**[38] 839 3-8-9 63 ShaneKelly 3 50
(J A Osborne) *in tch in midfield: rdn wl over 2f out: drvn and wknd 2f out* **4/1**[2]

000- **8** 19 **Zaftil (IRE)**[251] 4975 3-8-4 30 CatherineGannon 6 2
(H S Howe) *led for 1f: chsd ldrs after tl over 2f out: wkng whn sltly hmpd 2f out: wl bhd after* **150/1**

1m 41.0s (1.20) **Going Correction** +0.15s/f (Slow) **8** Ran SP% **110.2**

Speed ratings (Par 96): **100,99,99,96,96 94,93,74**

toteswinger: 1&2 £3.70, 1&3 £15.90, 2&3 £12.40 CSF £25.46 TOTE £7.90: £1.90, £1.60, £3.30; EX 33.40.

Owner E Moore & J S Moore **Bred** David E Hager II **Trained** Upper Lambourn, Berks

■ Stewards' Enquiry : Sophie Doyle two-day ban: used whip with excessive frequency (May 5-6)

FOCUS

A tight claimer, five of the runners held official ratings between 65 and 70. The form looks muddling and far from solid.

Bartica(IRE) Official explanation: jockey said colt hung badly right

1430 SWINTON MAIDEN FILLIES' STKS 1m 4f (P)
2:50 (2:51) (Class 5) 3-Y-0+ **£2,590** (£770; £385; £192) **Stalls** Centre

Form RPR

6- **1** **Inhibition**214 [6081] 3-8-8 0 WilliamBuick 7 79+
(A M Balding) *chsd ldrs: edgd rt and rdn over 2f out: sn chsng ldng pair: styd on u.p fnl f to ld last stride* **15/8**1

442- **2** *shd* **Moonbeam Dancer (USA)**136 [7578] 3-8-8 68 JohnEgan 1 75
(D M Simcock) *chsd ldr after 2f: led jst over 3f out: rdn and edgd lft over 2f out: led again jst ins fnl f: hdd last stride* **6/1**3

4 **3** *nk* **Cill Rialaig**19 [1088] 4-9-13 0 SteveDrowne 3 77
(H Morrison) *stdd s: hld up in tch: hdwy to chse ldr 3f out: rdn to ld and edgd lft over 2f out: hdd ins jst ins fnl f: kpt on same pce fnl 100yds* **4/1**2

6 **4** *17* **Towanda (USA)**12 [1198] 3-8-8 0 RichardMullen 2 48
(J H M Gosden) *stdd s: hld up in last trio: hdwy on outer 4f out: chsd ldrs and rdn jst over 3f out: wknd qckly 2f out* **4/1**2

4-5 **5** *7* **Flowerbud**83 [310] 4-9-13 0 JamesDoyle 6 39
(Ms J S Doyle) *led for 1f: lost pl and towards rr 8f out: rdn over 4f out: lost tch wl over 2f out* **33/1**

6300 **6** *1 3/4* **Thirtyfourthstreet (IRE)**12 [1200] 4-9-13 47 (b) SebSanders 4 36
(W R Muir) *led tl jst over 3f: sn wknd: no ch fr over 2f out* **66/1**

323- **7** *45* **Miss Sophisticat**191 [6665] 3-8-8 75 RyanMoore 5 —
(W J Knight) *a bhd: reminders 8f out: rdn 6f out: lost tch and virtually p.u fnl 3f: t.o* **4/1**2

2m 35.28s (0.78) **Going Correction** +0.15s/f (Slow)
WFA 3 from 4yo 20lb **7** Ran SP% **113.5**
Speed ratings (Par 100): **103,102,102,91,86 85,55**
toteswinger: 1&2 £4.00, 1&3 £2.30, 2&3 £4.10 CSF £13.71 TOTE £2.30: £2.00, £2.80; EX 11.60.

Owner Kingsclere Racing CLub **Bred** Kingsclere Stud **Trained** Kingsclere, Hants

FOCUS
A modest fillies' maiden. It featured a lively market, was run at a fair pace and produced an exciting finish. The first three pulled a long way clear of the rest. The winner shaped better than the bare form.

Miss Sophisticat Official explanation: jockey said filly did not face the kickback

1431 COPART UK H'CAP 1m 4f (P)
3:20 (3:24) (Class 4) (0-85,80) 3-Y-0 **£4,727** (£1,406; £702; £351) **Stalls** Centre

Form RPR

21-4 **1** **Headline Act**19 [1086] 3-9-4 77 JimmyFortune 6 84+
(J H M Gosden) *chsd ldr for 2f: trckd ldrs after: rdn to chal 2f otu: led over 1f out: sn drvn: clr ins fnl f: styd on wl* **11/10**1

2-31 **2** *1 1/4* **Fin Vin De Leu (GER)**25 [978] 3-9-5 78 JoeFanning 5 82
(M Johnston) *led: hdd and rdn over 1f out: kpt on same pce fnl f* **7/1**

0610 **3** *3/4* **Graycliffe (IRE)**3 [1363] 3-7-11 61 oh1 AndreaAtzeni(5) 8 64
(Patrick Morris) *awkward s and s.i.s: sn in tch in midfield: reminder over 3f out: plld out and hdwy 2f out: chsd ldng pair over 1f out: kpt on fnl 100yds: nt rch ldrs* **16/1**

4126 **4** *1 1/4* **Diamond Twister (USA)**6 [1280] 3-9-4 77 (t) SteveDrowne 1 78+
(J R Best) *stdd s: hld up in last pl: plld out 2f out: stl last ent fnl f: r.o: nvr trbld ldrs* **20/1**

5114 **5** *2 1/4* **Dubai Storming**38 [840] 3-9-7 80 RyanMoore 3 77
(E A L Dunlop) *slolwly into stride: towards rr: rdn and effrt over 2f out: no imp u.p over 1f out* **6/1**2

46-5 **6** *1* **Moresco**15 [1151] 3-9-2 75 AdamKirby 7 71+
(W R Swinburn) *rn in snatches: in tch: pushed along briefly 6f out: effrt u.p on inner 2f out: no imp ent fnl f* **8/1**

304- **7** *3/4* **Sixties Swinger (USA)**174 [7080] 3-9-3 76 PhilipRobinson 4 71
(M A Jarvis) *t.k.h: chsd ldr after 2f tl over 2f out: wknd fnl f* **13/2**3

1254 **8** *shd* **Tinshu (IRE)**23 [1019] 3-9-4 77 LukeMorris 2 71
(D Haydn Jones) *in tch: hdwy to chse ldrs 4f out: rdn to chse ldr briefly over 2f out: wknd ent fnl f* **20/1**

2m 35.54s (1.04) **Going Correction** +0.15s/f (Slow) **8** Ran SP% **114.3**
Speed ratings (Par 100): **102,101,100,99,98 97,97,97**
toteswinger: 1&2 £2.60 1&3 £7.20, 2&3 £21.80 CSF £9.35 CT £76.03 TOTE £2.20: £1.40, £2.10, £3.50; EX 9.90.

Owner K Abdulla **Bred** Juddmonte Farms Ltd **Trained** Newmarket, Suffolk

FOCUS
A decent handicap, involving a number of progressive types. The form looks solid, although the winner did not have to improve on his previous mark to score.

Moresco Official explanation: jockey said colt ran in snatches throughout

1432 GROUPAMA INSURANCES H'CAP 1m 4f (P)
3:50 (3:51) (Class 4) (0-85,80) 4-Y-0+ **£4,727** (£1,406; £702; £351) **Stalls** Centre

Form RPR

312- **1** **Hendersyde (USA)**202 [6390] 4-9-4 79 AdamKirby 5 88+
(W R Swinburn) *trckd ldrs: rdn and outpcd jst over 2f out: rallied to chse ldr 1f out: drvn and r.o wl to ld on post* **3/1**2

0145 **2** *nse* **Wind Flow**20 [1073] 5-8-12 72 (v1) CatherineGannon 2 81
(C A Dwyer) *led: clr tl stdd gallop 8f out: jnd 3f out: rdn and qcknd over 2f out: fought off rival 1f out: 2l clr ins fnl f: hdd on post* **15/2**

2545 **3** *2 1/4* **Clear Reef**13 [1184] 5-9-0 79 (p) AndreaAtzeni(5) 4 84
(Jane Chapple-Hyam) *hld up in last pair: rdn and unable qck over 2f out: edgd rt after: styd on to chse ldng pair ins fnl f: nt pce to rch ldrs* **7/2**3

1-10 **4** *6* **Planetary Motion (USA)**24 [999] 4-9-1 76 LDettori 3 72
(M Johnston) *chsd ldr: ev ch 3f out: drvn over 2f out: wknd ent fnl f: eased wl ins fnl f* **2/1**1

-006 **5** *3 1/4* **Cape Colony**13 [1184] 4-9-5 80 RichardHughes 1 71
(R Hannon) *stdd s: hld up in last pl: rdn and outpcd wl over 2f out: wl btn after* **5/1**

2m 38.13s (3.63) **Going Correction** +0.15s/f (Slow)
WFA 4 from 5yo 1lb **5** Ran SP% **109.0**
Speed ratings (Par 105): **93,92,91,87,85**
CSF £22.72 TOTE £3.20: £1.50, £2.60; EX 17.90.

Owner P W Harris **Bred** Iron County Farms Inc **Trained** Aldbury, Herts

FOCUS
An interesting event. It became fairly tactical but produced a thrilling finish and the winner did well to score.

1433 OAK UNDERWRITING H'CAP (LONDON MILE QUALIFIER) 1m (P)
4:20 (4:25) (Class 3) (0-95,93) 4-Y-0+
£7,352 (£2,201; £1,100; £551; £274; £138) **Stalls** High

Form RPR

600- **1** **Dubai Dynamo**206 [6283] 4-8-11 86 JohnEgan 8 97
(P F I Cole) *hld up in tch: hdwy and rdn 2f out: drvn to ld ins fnl f: r.o strly* **8/1**

-126 **2** *1 3/4* **Tartan Gigha (IRE)**19 [1089] 4-8-12 87 JoeFanning 7 94
(M Johnston) *chsd ldr: ev ch 3f out: edgd rt u.p fr 2f out: nt pce of wnr ins fnl f: wnt 2nd towards fin* **8/1**

1/ **3** *1/2* **Wintercast**531 [6724] 4-8-12 87 AdamKirby 4 93+
(W R Swinburn) *stdd after s: hld up bhd: swtchd ins and hdwy over 2f out: chsng ldng trio whn nt clr run and swtchd lft ins fnl f: r.o to go 3rd nr fin: nvr able to chal* **8/1**

004- **4** *shd* **Vainglory (USA)**203 [6352] 5-8-6 81 RichardMullen 2 87+
(D M Simcock) *in tch in midfield on outer: effrt u.p jst over 2f out: no imp tl r.o and edgd rt ins fnl f: wnt 4th last strides* **10/1**

40-2 **5** *hd* **Checklow (USA)**10 [1209] 4-9-0 89 ShaneKelly 6 94
(J Noseda) *hld up in midfield: rdn over 2f out: hdwy over 1f out: kpt on u.p fnl f: nt rch ldrs* **11/4**1

3604 **6** *hd* **Samarinda (USA)**10 [1209] 6-9-4 93 MickyFenton 10 98
(Mrs P Sly) *sn pushed up to ld: hrd pressed and rdn over 2f out: edgd rt u.p over 1f out: hdd and nt pce of wnr ins fnl f: lost 4 pls towards fin* **13/2**2

00-0 **7** *1 1/2* **Ballinteni**10 [1216] 7-8-11 86 SebSanders 11 89+
(D K Ivory) *towards rr: hdwy over 3f out: rdn over 1f out: keeping on same pce whn hmpd ins fnl f: nt pushed after* **33/1**

5-31 **8** *3* **L'Hirondelle (IRE)**83 [318] 5-8-11 86 PaulDoe 5 83+
(M J Attwater) *in tch: rdn and effrt over 2f out: unable qck u.p: wkng whn sltly hmpd ins fnl f* **7/1**3

420- **9** *2 1/4* **The Snatcher (IRE)**176 [7019] 6-9-0 89 RichardHughes 13 78
(R Hannon) *chsd ldrs: rdn over 2f out: wknd over 1f out* **13/2**2

05-0 **10** *1 3/4* **Another Bottle (IRE)**10 [1213] 8-7-13 79 oh1 AndreaAtzeni(5) 12 64
(Mrs S Leech) *s.i.s: a bhd: rdn over 3f out: nvr trbld ldrs* **50/1**

3000 **11** *nk* **Southandwest (IRE)**17 [1116] 5-8-10 85 LukeMorris 9 69
(J S Moore) *dwlt: a towards rr: rdn wl over 2f out: wknd ent fnl 2f* **14/1**

31- **12** *3 1/2* **Aflaam (IRE)**263 [4606] 4-8-10 85 TolleyDean 1 61
(P Howling) *s.i.s: hld up bhd: effrt and rdn on outer over 3f out: sn struggling* **25/1**

1m 38.86s (-0.94) **Going Correction** +0.15s/f (Slow) **12** Ran SP% **123.7**
Speed ratings (Par 107): **110,108,107,107,107 107,105,102,100,98 98,94**
toteswinger: 1&2 £24.10, 1&3 £27.20, 2&3 £15.00 CSF £72.72 CT £542.95 TOTE £12.80: £3.70, £2.50, £2.60; EX 104.50.

Owner Mrs Fitri Hay **Bred** T K & Mrs P A Knox **Trained** Whatcombe, Oxon

■ Stewards' Enquiry : Adam Kirby one-day ban: careless riding (May 5)

FOCUS
A classy handicap which produced an authoritative display from the winner. The winner is rated back to something like his best.

NOTEBOOK
Dubai Dynamo found a sustained run against the far rail to end an 18-month losing run. He had found life tough since receiving a 19lb rise for springing a shock in a Redcar Listed sales race in October 2007, but has steadily slipped back down the ratings and stuck his neck out in determined fashion to win this with something in hand. His mark will go up again but he should run another big race next time. (op 12-1 tchd 14-1)

Tartan Gigha(IRE) worked his way into a narrow lead at the furlong marker and stayed on gamely but could not cope with the late surge by the winner. He found things happening too quickly dropped back to 7f at Leicester last time but has resumed his upward curve with a very solid effort faced with his toughest task to date. (op 9-1 tchd 10-1)

Wintercast was the eyecatcher of the race. He had not been seen since winning a 1m maiden at Nottingham in good style on his debut in November 2007 and was weak in the market, but he weaved his way past nine rivals in the straight and ran a very promising race on his handicap debut after 531 days off. (tchd 12-1)

Vainglory(USA) carried his head at an awkward angle but found a good finishing effort down the outside and ran well back from seven months off. He is very well treated on his pick of form last season but has been expensive to follow in recent times and is not certain to build on this effort next time. (op 8-1)

Checklow(USA) posted a personal best when second in a strong course-and-distance handicap on his comeback after a gelding operation this month. He tried his best to get into a threatening position here but looked a bit short of gears. He should do better over a stiffer test but it is worth noting that he threw in a few disappointments last season and his up-and-down profile makes him a risky one to follow. (tchd 5-2 and 3-1)

L'Hirondelle(IRE) could not find much cover and compromised his chance by racing keenly out wide in the early stages. (op 8-1)

The Snatcher(IRE) did not find much for pressure early in the straight and never looked like landing a gamble. (op 8-1 tchd 11-2)

1434 INSURANCEJOBS H'CAP 7f (P)
4:50 (4:52) (Class 4) (0-80,80) 3-Y-0 **£4,727** (£1,406; £702; £351) **Stalls** High

Form RPR

04-1 **1** **Seek The Fair Land**18 [1108] 3-8-10 72 PatCosgrave 6 78
(J R Boyle) *t.k.h: hld up in tch towards rr: swtchd lft and effrt jst over 2f out: led over 1f out: hld on wl fnl f* **6/1**

064- **2** *1/2* **Bobbie Soxer (IRE)**178 [6987] 3-8-10 72 RyanMoore 10 77
(J L Dunlop) *hld up in tch in midfield: rdn and gd hdwy wl over 1f out: ev ch jst over 1f out: r.o but a hld fnl f* **5/1**2

1-31 **3** *1 1/2* **Arachnophobia (IRE)**15 [1155] 3-8-9 71 PaulEddery 1 72
(Pat Eddery) *led at stdy gallop: rdn and qcknd 2f out: hdd over 1f out: kpt on same pce ins fnl f* **9/2**1

40-0 **4** *3/4* **Count Paris (USA)**20 [1068] 3-8-10 72 LDettori 8 74+
(M Johnston) *chsd ldrs: rdn and effrt on inner jst over 2f out: nt clr run and swtchd lft ins fnl f: kpt on same pce* **11/2**3

215- **5** *3/4* **Silent Hero**178 [6970] 3-9-0 76 PhilipRobinson 2 73+
(M A Jarvis) *s.i.s: bhd: hdwy on outer over 3f out: rdn 2f out: styd on fnl f: nvr pce to rch ldrs* **5/1**2

1340 **6** *1 1/2* **Comadoir (IRE)**20 [1068] 3-9-1 77 SebSanders 7 70
(Miss Jo Crowley) *hld up towards rr: edging out and looking for run whn bumping match w rival over 1f out: nt rcvr and unable to chal* **16/1**

13-0 **7** *1* **Cool Art (IRE)**22 [1033] 3-9-4 80 (b) JimmyFortune 5 70
(S A Callaghan) *in tch: rdn and unable qck 2f out: drvn and wknd over 1f out* **10/1**

423- **8** *1 1/2* **Striding Edge (IRE)**[167] 7190 3-8-8 **70**.............................. ShaneKelly 9 56+
(W R Muir) *hld up bhd: effrt and nt clr run whn bumping match w rival over 1f out: no ch and nt pushed after* **13/2**

405- **9** *nk* **Acquiesced (IRE)**[199] 6477 3-9-3 **79**.............................. RichardHughes 4 64
(R Hannon) *stdd after s: in rr: rdn and no rspnse 2f out* **14/1**

10-4 **10** *nk* **Hit The Switch**[42] 797 3-8-5 **67**.............................. JoeFanning 3 52
(Patrick Morris) *chsd ldr: ev ch jst over 2f out: sn rdn and wknd qckly* **25/1**

1m 27.12s (1.12) **Going Correction** +0.15s/f (Slow) **10** Ran SP% **120.0**
Speed ratings (Par 100): **99,98,96,95,95 93,92,90,90,89**
toteswinger: 1&2 £7.30, 1&3 £5.70, 2&3 £9.20 CSF £37.25 CT £154.16 TOTE £8.50: £2.20, £2.30, £1.80; EX 46.00.
Owner Chris Watkins And David N Reynolds **Bred** Raimon Bloodstock **Trained** Epsom, Surrey

FOCUS
A competitive event run at a solid pace and there was another very tight finish. The form looks reasonable despite the steady pace.
Striding Edge(IRE) Official explanation: jockey said gelding was denied a clear run

1435 ARC LEGAL H'CAP 2m (P)
5:20 (5:20) (Class 4) (0-85,85) 4-Y-O+ **£4,727** (£1,406; £702; £351) **Stalls** High

Form RPR

566- **1** **Judgethemoment (USA)**[143] 7493 4-9-5 **83**.............................. LDettori 1 92
(Jane Chapple-Hyam) *mde all: jnd 6f out: rdn and qcknd clr over 2f out: drvn and a holding on fnl f: eased nr finsh* **13/2**

1-30 **2** *1 1/4* **Alnwick**[10] 1215 5-8-13 **73**.............................. JoeFanning 6 81
(P D Cundell) *chsd wnr tl over 6f out and again 3f out: rdn and nt pce of wnr over 2f out: kpt on fnl f* **10/1**

0660 **3** *1 1/2* **Cold Turkey**[13] 1184 9-8-8 **68**.............................. RyanMoore 4 74+
(G L Moore) *stdd s: hld up wl in rr: hdwy on outer over 3f out: rdn over 2f out: hdwy u.p over 1f out: wnt 3rd ins fnl f: nt rch ldrs* **4/1**[2]

1212 **4** *3/4* **Phoenix Flight (IRE)**[9] 1230 4-9-5 **83**.............................. SebSanders 2 90+
(Sir Mark Prescott) *stdd s: hld up in rr: plld out and hdwy over 2f out: styd on u.p fnl f: nt rch ldrs* **11/4**[1]

-011 **5** *shd* **Bell Island**[32] 894 5-9-1 **75**..............................(v) RichardHughes 9 80
(Lady Herries) *stdd s: hld up towards rr: hdwy over 3f out: chsd ldrs and drvn over 1f out: kpt on but nvr gng to rch ldrs* **5/1**[3]

24-0 **6** *nse* **Mohawk Star (IRE)**[10] 1215 8-8-6 **66**..............................(v) RichardMullen 12 71
(I A Wood) *hld up in midfield hdwy over 3f out: chsd ldrs and drvn over 1f out: plugged on but nvr pce to rch ldrs* **16/1**

2132 **7** *6* **Augustus John (IRE)**[20] 1069 6-8-10 **70**.............................. PaulMulrennan 11 67
(R Brotherton) *hld up towards rr: hdwy 4f out: chsd ldrs 3f out: rdn and little reponse over 2f out: wknd wl over 1f out* **8/1**

2614 **8** *1 3/4* **Salute (IRE)**[10] 1215 10-9-5 **79**.............................. ShaneKelly 3 74
(P G Murphy) *chsd ldrs tl rdn and wknd over 2f out: wl btn fr over 1f out* **16/1**

21-2 **9** *3 1/2* **Munlochy Bay**[21] 1049 5-8-1 **66** oh1........... Louis-PhilippeBeuzelin(5) 10 57
(W S Kittow) *hld up in midfield: dropped to rr and rdn over 3f out: no ch after* **11/1**

00-0 **10** *4* **Land 'n Stars**[24] 1007 9-9-11 **85**..............................(b) JimmyFortune 7 71
(Jamie Poulton) *chsd ldrs tl hdwy to press wnr 6f out: rdn and wknd qckly over 2f out* **25/1**

3m 32.35s (2.25) **Going Correction** +0.15s/f (Slow)
WFA 4 from 5yo+ 4lb **10** Ran SP% **120.8**
Speed ratings (Par 105): **100,99,98,98,98 98,95,94,92,90**
toteswingers: 1&2 £7.90, 1&3 £5.30, 2&3 £8.50 CSF £72.27 CT £298.51 TOTE £8.00: £2.70, £2.30, £2.20; EX 55.80 Place 6: £219.69 Place 5: £67.34.
Owner Gordon Li **Bred** Todd Graves & Michele Graves **Trained** Newmarket, Suffolk

FOCUS
A fair marathon handicap that was weakened by the withdrawal of Kavaloti. The pace was steady and very few got into it from behind, so the form is probably worth treating with a little caution.
Bell Island Official explanation: jockey said gelding bled from the nose
Land 'n Stars Official explanation: trainer's rep said gelding bled from the nose
T/Plt: £459.90 to a £1 stake. Pool: £53,879.66. 85.52 winning tickets. T/Qpdt: £37.60 to a £1 stake. Pool: £3,804.87. 74.80 winning tickets. SP

1051 SOUTHWELL (L-H)
Tuesday, April 21

OFFICIAL GOING: Standard
Wind: Moderate behind Weather: Fine and dry

1436 SOUTHWELL-RACECOURSE.CO.UK H'CAP 7f (F)
2:10 (2:11) (Class 4) (0-80,80) 4-Y-O+ **£4,857** (£1,445; £722; £360) **Stalls** Low

Form RPR

2-21 **1** **Elisiario (IRE)**[40] 820 4-8-4 **69**.............................. JackMitchell(3) 3 80+
(J R Boyle) *t.k.h early: mde all: rdn and qcknd clr over 2f out: drvn and edgd rt ent fnl f: kpt on wl* **17/2**

2021 **2** *1* **Flores Sea (USA)**[25] 980 5-9-2 **78**..............................(b) PhillipMakin 6 86
(T D Barron) *s.i.s: gd hdwy on outer 1/2-way: rdn to chse wnr wl over 1f out: drvn ent fnl f and kpt on same pce* **7/2**[1]

2132 **3** *2* **Autumn Blades (IRE)**[19] 1089 4-8-11 **80**.............................. LeeNewnes(7) 5 83
(A Bailey) *hld up in rr: smooth hdwy on outer 1/2-way: rdn to chse ldrs 2f out: kpt onu.p fnl f: tk 3rd nr line* **6/1**[3]

2201 **4** *nk* **Obe Royal**[13] 1186 5-9-1 **77**..............................(v) JamieSpencer 9 79
(P D Evans) *trckd ldrs: hdwy 3f out: rdn to chse wnr 2f out: sn drvn: edgd lft and one pce: lost 3rd nr line* **6/1**[3]

2232 **5** *5* **Caprio (IRE)**[30] 922 4-9-2 **78**.............................. RichardKingscote 2 66
(Tom Dascombe) *trckd ldrs: hdwy over 2f out: rdn wl over 1f out and sn no imp* **6/1**[3]

0-5 **6** *7* **Navajo Joe (IRE)**[40] 822 4-9-3 **79**.............................. PJMcDonald 7 48
(R Johnson) *in tch: rdn along wl over 2f out: sn btn* **40/1**

0400 **7** *1 1/4* **Indian Diva (IRE)**[23] 1020 4-8-6 **75**.............................. PaulPickard(7) 8 41
(P T Midgley) *a towards rr* **28/1**

010- **8** *17* **Bivouac (UAE)**[309] 3090 5-8-5 **67** oh1 ow1.................. AdrianTNicholls 4 —
(G A Swinbank) *t.k.h: cl up: rdn along 3f out: sn wknd and eased over 1f out* **8/1**

0-02 **9** *4* **Captain Jacksparra (IRE)**[9] 1229 5-9-3 **79**..............................(p) NCallan 1 —
(K A Ryan) *cl up on inner: rdn along 3f out: sn wknd and eased over 1f out* **4/1**[2]

1m 28.83s (-1.47) **Going Correction** -0.025s/f (Stan) **9** Ran SP% **112.6**
Speed ratings (Par 105): **107,105,103,103,97 89,88,68,64**
toteswinger: 1&2 £3.90, 1&3 £7.10, 2&3 £3.40 CSF £37.24 CT £192.26 TOTE £10.00: £2.70, £1.90, £2.10; EX 48.00.
Owner John Hopkins, J-P Lim & keith Marsden **Bred** Calley House Syndicate **Trained** Epsom, Surrey

FOCUS
Not a bad handicap for the grade and plenty with solid form, so it's worth taking a face value.
Bivouac(UAE) Official explanation: jockey said gelding had no more to give
Captain Jacksparra(IRE) Official explanation: trainer had no explanation for the poor form shown

1437 DINE IN THE QUEEN MOTHER RESTAURANT H'CAP 6f (F)
2:40 (2:43) (Class 6) (0-60,60) 3-Y-O **£2,047** (£604; £302) **Stalls** Low

Form RPR

006- **1** **Kings Ace (IRE)**[195] 6579 3-9-1 **57**.............................. NCallan 9 59
(A P Jarvis) *chsd ldrs: effrt on outer over 2f out: sn rdn and edgd lft: drvn ent fnl f: styd on u.p to ld nr fin* **6/1**[3]

4225 **2** *1/2* **Inthawain**[18] 1098 3-9-4 **60**.............................. LeeEnstone 6 61
(N Wilson) *led: hdd 1/2-way and cl up: rdn 2f out: drvn over 1f out and ev ch tl nt qckn nr fin* **9/2**[2]

2200 **3** *hd* **Dancing Wave**[6] 1281 3-8-12 **57**.............................. KellyHarrison(3) 10 57
(M C Chapman) *cl up: led 1/2-way: rdn wl over 1f out: drvn ent fnl f: hdd and nt qckn nr fin* **7/1**

305 **4** *shd* **If Only**[21] 1047 3-9-2 **58**.............................. PaulHanagan 2 58
(J Jay) *prom: effrt 2f out and sn rdn: drvn over 1f out and ev ch tl no ex wl ins fnl f* **7/1**

4-16 **5** *hd* **Kheskianto (IRE)**[6] 1281 3-8-10 **59**.............................. AndrewHeffernan(7) 4 58+
(M C Chapman) *chsd ldrs: hdwy 2f out: rdn and n.m.r over 1f out and again ins fnl f: drvn and kpt on wl towards fin* **15/2**

05-3 **6** *1* **First Blade**[41] 804 3-8-13 **55**.............................. AmirQuinn 8 51
(S R Bowring) *chsd ldrs: hdwy over 2f out: sn rdn and ev ch tl drvn and one pce ins fnl f* **17/2**

-540 **7** *3 1/4* **Dalepak Flyer (IRE)**[8] 1253 3-9-0 **59**..............(p) RussellKennemore(3) 7 44
(Paul Mason) *sn rdn along and outpcd in rr: hdwy 2f out: swtchd lft to inner wl over 1f out and kpt on: nvr nr ldrs* **14/1**

3050 **8** *2* **Glan Lady (IRE)**[42] 793 3-8-5 **47**..............................(b) FrankieMcDonald 11 26
(G J Smith) *reminders s and sn chsng ldrs on outer: rdn along over 2f out and sn wknd* **33/1**

-633 **9** *3/4* **Paint Splash**[20] 1057 3-9-1 **57**..............................(b[1]) PhillipMakin 5 34
(T D Barron) *s.i.s: a in rr* **7/2**[1]

0-00 **10** *5* **Waltzing Buddy**[14] 1174 3-9-4 **60**.............................. JamieMoriarty 3 21
(P T Midgley) *s.i.s: a in rr* **33/1**

1m 18.07s (1.57) **Going Correction** -0.025s/f (Stan) **10** Ran SP% **114.5**
Speed ratings (Par 96): **88,87,87,86,86 85,81,78,77,70**
toteswingers: 1&2 £6.60, 1&3 £11.10, 2&3 £5.70 CSF £32.53 CT £190.70 TOTE £9.00: £2.50, £2.10, £2.50; EX 51.40.
Owner Mrs Ann Jarvis **Bred** Michael Dalton **Trained** Middleham Moor, N Yorks

FOCUS
A moderate handicap in which the first six were very closely covered at the death. The form looks sound but ordinary.
Paint Splash Official explanation: jockey said filly missed the break
Waltzing Buddy Official explanation: trainer said filly was unsuited by the track

1438 SPONSOR A RACE AT SOUTHWELL (S) STKS 7f (F)
3:10 (3:12) (Class 6) 3-Y-O+ **£2,047** (£604; £302) **Stalls** Low

Form RPR

4126 **1** **Cap St Jean (IRE)**[29] 933 5-9-5 62..............................(p) DavidKenny(7) 8 73
(R Hollinshead) *dwlt and rr: stdy hdwy on outer 3f out: rdn over 1f out: styd on strly to ld ins fnl f* **8/1**[3]

2560 **2** *2 1/4* **Haroldini (IRE)**[25] 979 7-9-7 57..............................(v[1]) PaulHanagan 10 62
(J Balding) *chsd ldrs: swtchd ins and rdn 2f out: drvn to chse ldr over 1f out: kpt on u.p ins fnl f to take 2nd nr line* **8/1**[3]

00-0 **3** *hd* **Dream Theme**[23] 1016 6-9-7 82.............................. AdrianTNicholls 12 61+
(D Nicholls) *s.i.s and bhd: rapid hdwy on outer 1/2-way: led over 2f out: rdn wlover 1f out: drvn and hdd ins fnl f: lost 2nd nr line* **5/1**[2]

4-34 **4** *3 1/4* **Elusive Warrior (USA)**[103] 94 6-9-12 65..............................(p) NCallan 4 58
(A J McCabe) *cl up: rdn over 2f out: sn drvn and grad wknd* **9/2**[1]

5300 **5** *2 3/4* **Boss Hog**[17] 1123 4-9-12 65.............................. JamieMoriarty 11 50
(P T Midgley) *midfield: rdn along 1/2-way: styd on u.p fnl 2f: n.d* **9/1**

0000 **6** *1/2* **Louisiade (IRE)**[8] 1243 8-9-0 47..............................(p) AndrewHeffernan(7) 5 44
(M C Chapman) *midfield: hdwy over 2f out and sn rdn: drvn wl over 1f out and no imp* **33/1**

3110 **7** *1/2* **Tender Process (IRE)**[60] 619 6-9-12 70..............................(v) GeorgeBaker 14 47
(J R Boyle) *midfield: hdwy 2f out: sn rdn and no imp fr over 1f out* **5/1**[2]

2433 **8** *4 1/2* **Magical Song**[25] 979 4-9-7 54..............................(b) TomEaves 7 30
(J Balding) *cl up: rdn along wl over 2f out: drvn and wknd wl over 1f out* **8/1**[3]

2000 **9** *3/4* **So Sublime**[25] 981 4-9-2 42..............................(v[1]) MarkCoumbe(5) 6 28
(M C Chapman) *chsd ldrs: rdn along 1/2-way: sn wknd* **50/1**

0433 **10** *1/2* **Kingsmaite**[25] 975 8-8-9 64.............................. KellyHarrison(3) 1 32
(S R Bowring) *a towards rr* **10/1**

3224 **11** *nk* **Aggbag**[8] 1243 5-9-0 50.............................. PaulPickard(7) 2 26
(B P J Baugh) *a towards rr* **22/1**

0030 **12** *1/2* **Hamaasy**[25] 975 8-9-7 55..............................(p) AndrewElliott 3 25
(R A Harris) *led: rdn along 3f out: sn hdd & wknd* **28/1**

060- **13** *11* **James Street (IRE)**[131] 7637 6-9-7 39..............................(v) PatrickMathers 13 —
(Peter Grayson) *a bhd* **66/1**

14 *18* **Ei Tanniola (IRE)**[110] 4-9-2 0..............................(p) FrankieMcDonald 9 —
(G J Smith) *sn rdn along and outpcd in rr: t.o fr 1/2-way* **66/1**

1m 30.05s (-0.25) **Going Correction** -0.025s/f (Stan) **14** Ran SP% **119.6**
Speed ratings (Par 101): **100,97,97,93,90 89,89,84,83,82 82,81,69,48**
toteswingers: 1&2 £39.70, 1&3 £12.30, 2&3 £21.60 CSF £66.35 TOTE £8.90: £3.30, £2.00, £2.20; EX 120.50.There was no bid for the winner.
Owner R Hollinshead **Bred** Drumhass Stud **Trained** Upper Longdon, Staffs

FOCUS
A competitive seller, run at a strong pace and the form looks reasonable for the grade.
Ei Tanniola(IRE) Official explanation: jockey said filly hung right-handed throughout

1439 SOUTHWELL RACECOURSE FOR CONFERENCES H'CAP 2m (F)
3:40 (3:41) (Class 6) (0-65,65) 4-Y-O+ **£2,047** (£604; £302) **Stalls** Low

Form RPR

4543 **1** **Eforetta (GER)**[26] 967 7-8-11 **51**.............................. LiamJones 10 63
(A W Carroll) *hld up in tch: hdwy 4f out: chal over 2f out: led wl over 1f out and sn rdn clr: styd on strly* **7/1**

0546 **2** *3* **Spiritonthemount (USA)**[26] 967 4-7-13 **46**........(b) AndrewMullen(3) 7 54
(P W Hiatt) *reminders after s and sn rdn along in rr: hdwy to chse ldrs after 6f: rdn to ld 3f out: sn drvn and hdd wl over 1f out: kpt on same pce* **22/1**

3- **3** *6* **Pinewood Legend (IRE)**[80] 7776 7-8-6 **46** oh1.........(bt) PaulHanagan 9 47
(P D Niven) *chsd ldr: rdn along and sltly outpcd 4f out: styd on on u.p fnl 2f* **6/1**[3]

301/ **4** *shd* **Pagan Starprincess**[42] 6076 5-9-2 **56**............................ PJMcDonald 14 57
(G M Moore) *hld up towards rr: stdy hdwy over 6f out: chsd ldrs over 2f out: sn rdn and kpt on appr last: tk 3rd on line* **9/2**[1]

4203 **5** *nse* **Russian Invader (IRE)**[7] 1273 5-9-5 **64**.............(e) MarkCoumbe(5) 5 65
(R C Guest) *hld up towards rr: stdy hdwy 7f out: trckd ldrs 4f out: rdn along wl over 2f out and sn one pce* **9/1**

00-0 **6** *8* **Bulberry Hill**[84] 301 8-8-6 **46** oh1.................. EdwardCreighton 2 37
(R W Price) *hld up and bhd: stdy hdwy over 6f out: in tch over 4f out: rdn along over 3f out and sn wknd* **40/1**

242 **7** *5* **Zaffeu**[49] 743 8-9-7 **61**.. VinceSlattery 12 46
(A G Juckes) *hld up towards rr: hdwy and in tch 1/2-way: rdn along 4f out and sn btn* **7/1**

036- **8** *26* **Pairumani Pat (IRE)**[185] 6824 4-8-2 **46** oh1................ DuranFentiman 4 —
(J Pearce) *hld up: a in rr* **20/1**

3-13 **9** *5* **Rare Coincidence**[8] 1242 8-9-11 **65**.................................(p) NCallan 6 13
(R F Fisher) *led: rdn along 4f out: hdd 3f out and sn wknd* **11/2**[2]

6/0 **10** *41* **Magnifico (FR)**[26] 970 8-8-6 **46** oh1....................(p) FrankieMcDonald 8 —
(Mrs K Waldron) *chsd ldrs: rdn along and lost pl 1/2-way: sn bhd* **16/1**

033- **11** *25* **River Danube**[162] 7271 6-9-7 **61**................................. JamieMoriarty 13 —
(T J Fitzgerald) *chsd ldng pair: rdn along 6f out: sn wknd and t.o fnl 2f* **12/1**

00-4 **12** *24* **Capistrano**[35] 857 6-7-13 **46** oh1..............................(p) CharlesEddery(7) 1 —
(Paul Mason) *hld up: a in rr: t.o fnl 3f* **22/1**

3m 42.74s (-2.76) **Going Correction** -0.025s/f (Stan)
WFA 4 from 5yo+ 4lb **12** Ran SP% **112.3**
Speed ratings (Par 101): **105,103,100,100,100 96,93,80,78,57 45,33**
toteswinger: 1&2 £42.20, 1&3 £7.70, 2&3 £29.70 CSF £151.21 CT £969.14 TOTE £8.70: £2.30, £7.70, £2.00; EX 187.10.
Owner John W Egan **Bred** Gestut Rietberg **Trained** Cropthorne, Worcs

FOCUS
A weak staying handicap, run at a decent gallop. The form is rated around the first two.
Rare Coincidence Official explanation: jockey said gelding hung left closing stages
River Danube Official explanation: trainer said gelding was unsuited by the standard ground

1440 BOOK YOUR HOSPITALITY PACKAGES MEDIAN AUCTION MAIDEN STKS 1m 3f (F)
4:10 (4:10) (Class 6) 3-Y-O £2,047 (£604; £302) **Stalls** Low

Form RPR

00-0 **1** **Melange (USA)**[13] 1185 3-9-3 60........................... AdrianTNicholls 8 69
(P F I Cole) *trckd ldrs: hdwy to ld over 4f out: rdn 3f out: drvn 2f out: hdd 1f out: rallied u.p ins fnl f to ld again nr fin* **10/1**

5- **2** *nk* **Repealed**[187] 6745 3-9-3 0... TravisBlock 2 68
(H Morrison) *trckd ldrs: effrt 3f out and sn rdn: styd on to ld 1f out: drvnand edgd rt ins fnl f: hdd and no ex nr fin* **3/1**[2]

036- **3** *9* **Eddie Boy**[176] 7011 3-9-3 68.. JamieSpencer 6 59
(M L W Bell) *trckd ldng pair: hdwy and cl up 4f out: rdn 3f out and ev ch tl drvn 2f out and grad wknd appr last* **15/8**[1]

2233 **4** *14* **Jonnie Skull (IRE)**[15] 1156 3-9-3 60..............................(vt) GeorgeBaker 7 29
(P S McEntee) *prom: led after 2f: rdn along and hdd over 4f out: sn drvn and outpcd fnl 3f* **7/1**

6- **5** *18* **Liberty Lodge (IRE)**[260] 4681 3-9-3 0........................... PJMcDonald 9 —
(G A Swinbank) *in tch: hdwy to trck ldrs over 4f out: rdn 3f out and ev ch tl drvn and wknd over 2f out: collapsed shortly after line* **25/1**

00- **6** *6* **Indigo Belle (IRE)**[186] 6789 3-8-12 0.............................. DO'Donohoe 4 —
(Mrs A Duffield) *in tch on inner: rdn along 4f out: wknd 3f out: b.d by faller shortly after line* **80/1**

5-30 **7** *2 ¼* **The Bully Wee**[6] 1289 3-9-3 0...................................... PaulHanagan 3 —
(J Jay) *in rr: swtchd wd and rdn along 1/2-way: nvr a factor* **4/1**[3]

00- **8** *7* **Highams Park (IRE)**[216] 6016 3-8-12 0..................... RichardKingscote 5 —
(J G Portman) *a in rr* **100/1**

000- **9** *18* **My Choice**[240] 5314 3-9-3 45.. NCallan 1 —
(A P Jarvis) *prom on inner: rdn along 1/2-way: sn wknd* **18/1**

2m 28.61s (0.61) **Going Correction** -0.025s/f (Stan) **9** Ran SP% **112.7**
Speed ratings (Par 96): **96,95,89,79,65 61,59,54,41**
toteswinger: 1&2 £6.40, 1&3 £6.60, 2&3 £2.20 CSF £38.96 TOTE £8.50: £2.30, £1.40, £1.50; EX 52.90.
Owner Frank Stella **Bred** Delehanty Stock Farm **Trained** Whatcombe, Oxon

FOCUS
A moderate maiden in which the first pair came clear in a tight finish, although the form does not look straightforward.
The Bully Wee Official explanation: jockey said colt hung left throughout
Highams Park(IRE) Official explanation: jockey said filly never travelled

1441 SOUTHWELL GOLF CLUB H'CAP 1m 3f (F)
4:40 (4:41) (Class 6) (0-60,60) 3-Y-O £2,047 (£604; £302) **Stalls** Low

Form RPR

00-6 **1** **Eightdaysaweek**[18] 1092 3-8-11 **53**............................. NCallan 10 58
(S Kirk) *in tch: hdwy to trck ldrs 4f out: rdn to chse ldr 2f out: drvn and styd on to ld jst ins fnl f: r.o* **11/1**

3326 **2** *¾* **Amazing Blue Sky**[20] 1063 3-9-2 **58**.....................(b) AndrewElliott 12 62
(Mrs R A Carr) *prom: effrt to ld 3f out: rdn clr 2f out: drvn over 1f out: hdd jst ins fnl f and kpt on same pce* **14/1**

533 **3** *1 ¼* **Tae Kwon Do (USA)**[29] 938 3-8-12 **54**.......................... TomEaves 13 56
(Miss J A Camacho) *in tch on outer: hdwy over 3f out: rdn to chse ldrs 2wf out: sn drvn and kpt on ins fnl f* **8/1**[3]

000- **4** *hd* **Dubai Diva**[157] 7337 3-9-4 **60**... GeorgeBaker 11 61
(C F Wall) *trckd ldrs: hdwy over 3f out: rdn to chse ldr over 2f out: drvn over 1f out and kpt on same pce* **10/3**[2]

660- **5** *1 ¼* **Shadows Lengthen**[209] 6214 3-9-4 **60**............................ DaleGibson 9 59
(M W Easterby) *trckd ldrs: effrt 3f out and sn rdn: drvn and one pce fnl 2f* **66/1**

04-4 **6** *nse* **Telling Stories (IRE)**[15] 1156 3-8-2 **49**.................... PatrickDonaghy(5) 6 48
(B D Leavy) *hld up in rr: hdwy and in tch over 4f out: rdn along 3f out: kpt on fnl 2f: nrst fin* **20/1**

0400 **7** *12* **Fleur De'Lion (IRE)**[20] 1070 3-8-4 **46** oh1.............. RichardKingscote 14 25
(S Kirk) *towards rr: hdwy on outer over 4f out: rdn along over 3f out and nvr nr ldrs* **33/1**

0-04 **8** *½* **Vita Mia**[8] 1245 3-8-4 **53**.. AndrewHeffernan(7) 7 31
(P D Evans) *a in midfield* **25/1**

04-3 **9** *5* **Bubses Boy**[21] 1050 3-9-2 **58**...................................... JamieSpencer 2 27
(M L W Bell) *led: rdn along 4f out: hdd 3f out and sn wknd* **7/4**[1]

00-5 **10** *2* **Berriedale**[14] 1168 3-8-6 **48**.. DO'Donohoe 5 14
(Mrs A Duffield) *v s.i.s and bhd tl sme hdwy fnl 3f* **33/1**

000- **11** *11* **Mountain Forest (GER)**[166] 7209 3-8-10 **52**................ AdrianTNicholls 1 —
(H Morrison) *trckd ldng pair on inner: effrt over 4f out: sn rdn along and wknd* **28/1**

000- **12** *3 ¾* **Shakin John**[187] 6760 3-9-0 **56**................................... PaulHanagan 4 —
(E J O'Neill) *a towards rr* **8/1**[3]

00-0 **13** *nk* **Suitably Accoutred (IRE)**[17] 1128 3-8-5 **50**............. AndrewMullen(3) 8 —
(Mrs A Duffield) *a towards rr* **66/1**

000- **14** *1 ½* **Terracotta Warrior**[126] 7693 3-8-6 **48**.............................. LiamJones 3 —
(J Jay) *a in rr* **66/1**

2m 29.22s (1.22) **Going Correction** -0.025s/f (Stan) **14** Ran SP% **119.1**
Speed ratings (Par 96): **94,93,92,92,91 91,82,82,78,77 69,66,66,65**
toteswinger: 1&2 £27.40, 1&3 £22.30, 2&3 £13.70 CSF £140.20 CT £1301.76 TOTE £12.40: £2.60, £3.90, £2.90; EX 146.90.
Owner Christopher Wright **Bred** Stratford Place Stud **Trained** Upper Lambourn, Berks

FOCUS
A competitive three-year-old handicap for the class with plenty of potential improvers. The form, which is pretty limited, is rated through the placed horses.
Eightdaysaweek Official explanation: trainer's rep said, regarding apparent improvement in form, that the filly settled better and was suited by the all-weather surface.
Bubses Boy Official explanation: trainer had no explanation for the poor form shown
Terracotta Warrior Official explanation: jockey said gelding hung left throughout

1442 SOUTHWELL-RACECOURSE.CO.UK APPRENTICE H'CAP 1m 4f (F)
5:10 (5:11) (Class 6) (0-60,60) 4-Y-O+ £2,047 (£604; £302) **Stalls** Low

Form RPR

4-25 **1** **Paddy Rielly (IRE)**[40] 816 4-9-1 **56**........................(p) AndrewHeffernan 8 65
(P D Evans) *hld up in midfield: hdwy over 4f out: effrt to chse ldr wl over 2f out: rdn to ld wl over 1f out: sn drvn clr and styd on wl* **11/4**[1]

0410 **2** *3 ¼* **King Of The Beers (USA)**[17] 1122 5-9-1 **60**...................(p) SPRyan(5) 4 64
(R A Harris) *hld up in tch: hdwy over 4f out: led 3f out and sn rdn: drvn and hdd wl over 1f out: kpt on same pce* **4/1**[2]

0/0- **3** *7* **Greenbelt**[10] 6812 8-8-7 **52**.. AdamCarter(5) 6 45
(G M Moore) *in tch: hdwy 1/2-way: led over 4f out: rdn along and hdd 3f out: sn drvn and grad wknd* **16/1**

2460 **4** *½* **Blue Hills**[26] 735 8-9-2 **59**...(b) JohnCavanagh(3) 1 51
(P W Hiatt) *bhd: hdwy 3f out: styd on fnl 2f: nrst fin* **18/1**

215- **5** *½* **Fistral**[274] 4238 5-8-10 **50**... JamieKyne 13 41
(P D Niven) *chsd ldrs: effrt 4f out: sn rdn and ev ch tl drvn and wknd over2f out* **10/1**

56-0 **6** *1 ½* **Marieschi (USA)**[71] 476 5-8-8 **48**................................... DTDaSilva 14 37
(R F Fisher) *trckd ldrs: effrt over 4f out: sn rdn and wknd 3f out* **20/1**

2524 **7** *6* **Cragganmore Creek**[30] 918 6-8-6 **46** oh1.....................(v) DebraEngland 10 25
(D Morris) *stdd s: rapid hdwy and cl up after 4f: rdn along 4f out: wknd 3f out* **7/1**[3]

000- **8** *½* **Byron Bay**[59] 6235 7-9-5 **59**....................................... GarryWhillans 2 37
(R Johnson) *in tch: hdwy on outer over 4f out: rdn along over 3f out and sn wknd* **33/1**

2630 **9** *3 ¾* **Dazzling Begum**[26] 972 4-8-0 **48**..............................(v) RyanPowell(7) 7 20
(J Pearce) *midfield: rdn along over 4f out and sn wknd* **10/1**

04/- **10** *9* **Tessie Bear**[30] 7222 4-8-5 **46** oh1.................................. CharlesEddery 11 —
(E J Creighton) *midfield: rdn along over 4f out: sn outpcd* **100/1**

60-4 **11** *9* **Rockjumper**[24] 116 4-8-9 **50**.. PaulPickard 3 —
(Mrs T J Hill) *a towards rr* **12/1**

0-00 **12** *1* **Sularno**[33] 885 5-9-0 **59**... RyanClark(5) 12 —
(H Morrison) *led: rdn along and hdd over 4f out: sn wknd* **9/1**

0/6- **13** *3* **Red River Rebel**[336] 2290 11-9-0 **54**.................................. NSLawes 5 —
(J R Norton) *a in rr: wl bhd fnl 3f* **33/1**

00-0 **14** *42* **Opening Hand**[22] 1037 4-8-1 **47**.................................(p) AlexEdwards(5) 9 —
(G J Smith) *chsd ldrs on inner: rdn along over 5f out: sn wknd* **66/1**

2m 40.7s (-0.30) **Going Correction** -0.025s/f (Stan)
WFA 4 from 5yo+ 1lb **14** Ran SP% **119.3**
Speed ratings (Par 101): **100,97,93,92,92 91,87,87,84,78 72,72,70,42**
toteswinger: 1&2 £1.70, 1&3 £13.00, 2&3 £19.40. CSF £12.18 CT £150.63 TOTE £2.90: £1.50, £2.30, £6.40; EX 15.20 Place 6: £225.75 Place 5: £105.43.
Owner M D Jones **Bred** Kilfrush Stud **Trained** Pandy, Monmouths
■ Stewards' Enquiry : Ryan Clark two-day ban: careless riding (May 5-6)

FOCUS
A weak handicap best rated through the runner-up.
T/Plt: £1,011.20 to a £1 stake. Pool: £50,215.91. 36.25 winning tickets. T/Qpdt: £153.20 to a £1 stake. Pool: £3,706.54. 17.90 winning tickets. JR

1443 - 1449a (Foreign Racing) - See Raceform Interactive

1057 CATTERICK (L-H)
Wednesday, April 22

OFFICIAL GOING: Good to firm (firm in places; 9.6)
Wind: light 1/2 behind Weather: fine and sunny

1450 MELROSE AVENUE (S) STKS 5f
2:20 (2:23) (Class 6) 2-Y-O £2,047 (£604; £302) **Stalls** Low

Form RPR

4 **1** **Vilnius**[19] 1090 2-8-6 0.. CatherineGannon 4 61
(M R Channon) *mde virtually all: kpt on strly fnl f: drvn out* **13/8**[1]

1 **2** *1 ¾* **Transfixed (IRE)**[9] 1249 2-8-7 0.............................. RichardEvans(5) 1 61
(P D Evans) *w wnr: rdn 2f out: kpt on same pce* **4/1**[3]

3 *2 ¼* **Gasparilla (IRE)** 2-8-6 0.. AndrewElliott 5 47
(A J McCabe) *chsd ldrs: kpt on fnl f* **20/1**

4 *1* **Gertmegalush (IRE)** 2-8-6 0..................................... RossAtkinson(5) 8 48+
(Tom Dascombe) *s.s: hdwy on outside 2f out: edgd lft: styd on wl ins fnl f* **5/2**[2]

5 *6* **More For Less** 2-8-11 0... PhillipMakin 10 26
(T D Barron) *chsd ldrs: outpcd and lost pl over 2f out* **10/1**

0 **6** *¾* **Needwood Dancer**[25] 1005 2-8-6 0................................ PatrickMathers 6 19
(Peter Grayson) *sn outpcd and in rr* **80/1**

7 *1 ¾* **Mostofitleft (IRE)** 2-8-6 0... PaulQuinn 2 12
(A Berry) *s.i.s: sn chsng ldrs: outpcd over 2f out: sn lost pl* **25/1**

0 **8** *6* **Nidamar**[4] 1344 2-8-3 0.. AndrewMullen(3) 9 —
(Mrs R A Carr) *prom: lost pl over 2f out: sn bhd* **50/1**

9 *1* **Aryacoddinme (IRE)** 2-8-11 0..................................... SilvestreDeSousa 7 —
(G A Harker) *s.i.s: a bhd* **14/1**

60.62 secs (0.82) **Going Correction** +0.05s/f (Good) **9** Ran SP% **114.2**
Speed ratings (Par 90): **95,92,88,87,77 76,73,63,62**
toteswinger: 1&2 £1.70, 1&3 £6.00, 2&3 £8.30 CSF £8.01 TOTE £1.90: £1.30, £1.50, £3.50; EX 5.30.The winner was bought in for 3,200gns. Gertmegalush was claimed by J. D. Bethell for £6000.
Owner P Trant **Bred** P Trant & Mike Channon Bloodstock Limited **Trained** West Ilsley, Berks

FOCUS
A baking day and ground very close to firm all round. A very ordinary seller to kick things off, and uneventful in so much as the race was dominated from the outset by the two who had shown the best form, and nothing got into it from off the pace.

NOTEBOOK

Vilnius, whose dam won at two, showed enough in a Bath maiden on her debut to suggest that she had a small race in her, and, dropped in class here, she got the job done in decent style, bouncing out to race close to leader Transfixed and stay on the stronger. She should get another furlong but the form is very modest. (op 7-4 tchd 6-4)

Transfixed(IRE), who due to Richard Evans's claim only had to concede 1lb to the winner and, although beaten this time, she has probably achieved a little more than when winning at Warwick on debut, as she kept straight and true this time. She clearly has her limitations, though. (op 3-1)

Gasparilla(IRE) only cost £800 as a yearling but she shaped with some promise here, bouncing out to track the leaders before keeping on well. If she builds on this, she can win one of these.

Gertmegalush(IRE), the most expensive horse in the line-up at £15,000, was the springer in the market beforehand but he fluffed his lines at the start and was always a long way back. To his credit he was the only one of to make up any significant ground from off the pace and, providing he learns to break better, he clearly has the ability to win a seller, at least. (op 4-1)

1451 RACESPONSORS.CO.UK MAIDEN STKS 7f

2:55 (2:57) (Class 5) 3-Y-O £2,914 (£867; £433; £216) Stalls Centre

Form RPR

03-3 **1** **Kersivay**[10] 1228 3-9-3 77 .... TonyHamilton 1 72
(D W Barker) *chsd ldrs: effrt on outer over 2f out: led jst ins fnl f: all out* **9/4**[2]

2 *hd* **Dame Anouska (IRE)** 3-8-12 0 .... PhillipMakin 2 66
(E J O'Neill) *dwlt: sn chsng ldrs: led over 2f out tl jst ins fnl f: kpt on wl: jst hld* **8/1**[3]

0-5 **3** *5* **Tropical Bachelor (IRE)**[4] 1362 3-9-3 0 .... PaulMulrennan 4 58
(T J Pitt) *in rr: hdwy on ins over 2f out: kpt on fnl f* **10/1**

2 **4** *3/4* **Fortunate Flame**[22] 1054 3-9-3 0 .... NCallan 6 56
(K A Ryan) *sn chsng ldrs: chal over 2f out: fdd fnl f* **11/8**[1]

5 **5** *nk* **Miss Porky**[15] 1173 3-8-9 0 .... RussellKennemore(3) 8 50
(R Hollinshead) *t.k.h on outer: mid-div: hdwy over 3f out: one pce fnl 2f* **10/1**

6 *5* **Cry Of Truth (IRE)** 3-8-12 0 .... PJMcDonald 10 37
(D W Barker) *sed v slow: kpt on fnl 2f: nvr on terms* **28/1**

00- **7** *4* **Kaikoura**[233] 5572 3-8-12 0 .... DuranFentiman 11 26
(T D Easterby) *swtchd lft after 1f: in rr: drvn over 3f out: nvr on terms* **40/1**

00- **8** *12* **Broomfield Buddy**[187] 6785 3-8-12 0 .... TomEaves 3 —
(D W Barker) *led tl over 2f out: lost pl over 1f out: sn bhd* **100/1**

0-04 **9** *2 1/4* **Minibuzz**[34] 881 3-9-3 38 .... (v) DaleGibson 7 —
(Mrs G S Rees) *chsd ldrs: drvn over 3f out: sn lost pl and bhd* **100/1**

1m 27.55s (0.55) **Going Correction** -0.125s/f (Firm) **9** Ran SP% **110.0**
Speed ratings (Par 98): **91,90,85,84,83 78,73,59,57**
toteswingers: 1&2 £3.30, 1&3 £5.20, 2&3 £6.70 CSF £18.52 TOTE £2.70: £1.10, £2.00, £2.80; EX 16.40.

Owner Ian Bishop **Bred** Brook Stud Bloodstock Ltd **Trained** Scorton, N Yorks

FOCUS
Not much strength in depth to this maiden

1452 TERRY BIRD AND JOE OSBORNE MEMORIAL H'CAP 7f

3:30 (3:31) (Class 6) (0-65,65) 3-Y-O £2,183 (£644; £322) Stalls Centre

Form RPR

054- **1** **Rising Kheleyf (IRE)**[198] 6525 3-8-12 59 .... PJMcDonald 7 70
(G A Swinbank) *mid-div: hdwy and swtchd to ins 2f out: hung rt and styd on to ld last 100yds: kpt on wl* **5/1**[2]

4101 **2** *1 1/4* **Foreign Investment (IRE)**[19] 1106 3-8-12 64 .... RichardEvans(5) 5 72
(P D Evans) *mid-div: effrt over 2f out: styd on to ld jst ins fnl f: sn hdd and no ex* **3/1**[1]

0-03 **3** *1 1/2* **Blue Noodles**[21] 1062 3-9-4 65 .... TonyHamilton 3 69
(D W Barker) *led after 1f: hdd jst ins fnl f: kpt on same pce* **11/2**[3]

104- **4** *3* **Top Flight Splash**[124] 7728 3-8-6 53 .... (p) DaleGibson 6 48
(Mrs G S Rees) *trckd ldrs: kpt on same pce fnl 2f* **16/1**

0104 **5** *nse* **Valdemar**[21] 1057 3-8-4 51 .... SilvestreDeSousa 8 46
(A D Brown) *led 1f: chsd ldrs: one pce fnl 2f* **11/2**[3]

150- **6** *6* **Kladester (USA)**[127] 7693 3-9-1 62 .... (t) TomEaves 4 41
(B Smart) *in rr: nvr on terms* **8/1**

0-50 **7** *2* **Wicklewood**[39] 842 3-8-4 51 oh1 .... CatherineGannon 2 25
(Mrs C A Dunnett) *in rr: nvr a factor* **25/1**

051- **8** *1/2* **Wotatomboy**[176] 7044 3-8-13 63 .... MichaelJStainton(3) 10 35
(R M Whitaker) *s.i.s: nvr on terms* **12/1**

00-5 **9** *6* **Nassau Beach (IRE)**[21] 1061 3-8-4 51 .... DuranFentiman 1 7
(T D Easterby) *s.i.s: sn chsng ldrs: lost pl 2f out* **6/1**

450- **10** *16* **Secret City (IRE)**[184] 6858 3-9-0 61 .... PaulMulrennan 9 —
(R Bastiman) *in rr: bhd and eased 2f out: t.o* **16/1**

1m 26.76s (-0.24) **Going Correction** -0.125s/f (Firm) **10** Ran SP% **121.1**
Speed ratings (Par 96): **96,94,92,89,89 82,80,79,72,54**
toteswingers: 1&2 £3.50, 1&3 £6.60, 2&3 £3.70 CSF £21.27 CT £88.24 TOTE £6.70: £2.70, £1.30, £1.80; EX 20.20.

Owner D Bamlet **Bred** J K Thoroughbreds And M Buckley **Trained** Melsonby, N Yorks

FOCUS
A strong pace to this modest 7f handicap.

1453 RICHMOND CONDITIONS STKS 1m 3f 214y

4:05 (4:05) (Class 3) 3-Y-O £7,352 (£2,201; £1,100) Stalls Low

Form RPR

1- **1** **Too Much Trouble**[251] 5029 3-9-4 87 .... TonyCulhane 1 102
(M R Channon) *hld up: wnt 2nd 7f out: shkn up and jnd ldr 4f out: drvn to ld over 2f out: plld wl clr appr fnl f* **1/3**[1]

-000 **2** *18* **Keeptheboatafloat (USA)**[35] 863 3-9-4 90 .... (b) DarrenWilliams 3 74
(K R Burke) *led after 1f and sn qcknd clr: hdd over 2f out: sn btn: heavily eased towards fin* **7/2**[2]

23-4 **3** *14* **Hard Luck Story**[19] 1101 3-8-12 70 .... TomEaves 2 43
(I Semple) *led 1f: drvn and lost 2nd 7f out: outpcd and lost pl over 4f: eased nr fin* **9/1**[3]

2m 36.84s (-2.06) **Going Correction** -0.125s/f (Firm) **3** Ran SP% **107.2**
Speed ratings (Par 102): **101,89,79**
CSF £1.81 TOTE £1.50; EX 1.40.

Owner Jaber Abdullah **Bred** Fittocks Stud **Trained** West Ilsley, Berks

FOCUS
Mick Channon had won two of the previous three runnings of this race, including with Youmzain in 2006.

NOTEBOOK

Too Much Trouble, who holds English and Irish Derby entries, ultimately had little difficulty in following in the footsteps of his stablemates. A big horse who probably wouldn't be ideally served by a track like Catterick, his rider had to change his hands a couple of times entering the turn for home, but, soon on terms with the leader, he really found his stride once in the straight and forged clear under strong driving, with his jockey clearly keen to give him a proper race. Stamina looks his strong suit (pedigree backs that up) and although it's hard to accurately evaluate the merit of this performance, the runner-up does have an official rating of 90 and he was beaten out of sight, so it might be dangerous to underestimate Too Much Trouble. Victor Chandler trimmed him into 66-1 from 100-1 for the Derby afterwards, and his rider Tony Culhane was pretty impressed, commenting that the colt was still very green but ultimately quite impressive. We will learn a lot more about him if he goes to the Dante, for which he has an entry. (tchd 4-11)

Keeptheboatafloat(USA), some of whose juvenile form was very decent, was trying a trip wasn't sure to suit on breeding, and the way he was brushed aside in the straight, albeit by a promising colt, suggests he'd be better suited by a mile to 1m2f. (op 9-2)

Hard Luck Story was struggling a long way out but he picked up £1,100 for his trouble and will probably now go handicapping. (op 17-2 tchd 8-1)

1454 SPONSOR A RACE @ RACESPONSORS.CO.UK H'CAP 1m 3f 214y

4:40 (4:40) (Class 5) (0-70,68) 4-Y-O+ £2,914 (£867; £433; £216) Stalls Low

Form RPR

55-0 **1** **Trip The Light**[25] 1000 4-9-3 66 .... (v) JamieMoriarty 7 77
(R A Fahey) *trckd ldrs: drvn 4f out: led 2f out: hld on wl* **11/4**[2]

000- **2** *1 3/4* **Saluscraggie**[43] 6812 7-8-2 53 .... KellyHarrison(3) 8 61
(R E Barr) *hld up in rr: hdwy 5f out: chal over 1f out: no ex ins fnl f* **14/1**

0-40 **3** *2 1/2* **Titinius (IRE)**[7] 1279 9-8-9 57 .... (p) TonyHamilton 3 61
(Micky Hammond) *hld up in midfield: drvn 4f out: sn outpcd: hdwy 2f out: hung lft: styd on fnl f* **13/2**

6-02 **4** *1 1/2* **Drawn Gold**[40] 836 5-9-0 62 .... NCallan 9 64
(R Hollinshead) *hld up in midfield: effrt over 3f out: one pce appr fnl f* **9/4**[1]

00/ **5** *nk* **Samizdat (FR)**[329] 3412 6-8-10 58 .... (v) TomEaves 2 59
(James Moffatt) *trckd ldrs: one pce fnl 2f* **20/1**

300- **6** *1 1/4* **Ovthenight (IRE)**[89] 5999 4-9-5 68 .... MickyFenton 5 67
(Mrs P Sly) *w ldr: reminders sn after s: sn drvn along: one pce fnl 2f: wl hld whn n.m.r on inner nr fin* **9/2**[3]

0-00 **7** *7* **Treetops Hotel (IRE)**[25] 1000 10-8-5 53 oh8 .... TWilliams 1 41
(L R James) *hld up in rr: effrt on ins over 2f out: lost pl over 1f out* **50/1**

/6-0 **8** *6* **Rain And Shade**[7] 1279 5-9-1 63 .... PaulMulrennan 4 41
(E W Tuer) *led tl hdd & wknd 2f out* **28/1**

6146 **9** *7* **Gamesters Lady**[26] 983 6-9-0 62 .... DuranFentiman 6 29
(W M Brisbourne) *s.i.s: drvn 4f out: sn lost pl* **10/1**

2m 39.77s (0.87) **Going Correction** -0.125s/f (Firm)
WFA 4 from 5yo+ 1lb **9** Ran SP% **114.9**
Speed ratings (Par 103): **92,90,89,88,87 87,82,78,73**
toteswingers: 1&2 £17.90, 1&3 £4.80, 2&3 £35.70 CSF £38.92 CT £229.77 TOTE £3.70: £1.60, £3.20, £2.20; EX 28.40.

Owner The Matthewman One Partnership **Bred** Darley **Trained** Musley Bank, N Yorks

FOCUS
The pace looked generous enough in this modest handicap.
Rain And Shade Official explanation: jockey said gelding had a breathing problem

1455 WHITE MUZZLE H'CAP 5f

5:15 (5:16) (Class 6) (0-60,59) 3-Y-O £2,183 (£644; £322) Stalls Low

Form RPR

60-3 **1** **Compton Ford**[21] 1064 3-9-4 59 .... PhillipMakin 1 65
(M Dods) *mid-div: edgd rt 3f out: sn chsng ldr: r.o to ld ins fnl f* **3/1**[2]

4312 **2** *3/4* **Fasliyanne (IRE)**[9] 1247 3-9-4 59 .... (b) NCallan 5 62
(K A Ryan) *led: edgd rt over 1f out: hdd and no ex ins fnl f* **5/2**[1]

3605 **3** *3/4* **Pedregal**[9] 1247 3-8-4 45 .... SilvestreDeSousa 10 45
(R A Fahey) *chsd ldrs: kpt on wl fnl f* **7/1**[3]

6-51 **4** *3/4* **Jethro Bodine (IRE)**[9] 1247 3-8-11 55 6ex .... (p) KellyHarrison(3) 9 53
(W J H Ratcliffe) *mid-div: hmpd 3f out: chsng ldrs over 1f out: kpt on same pce* **7/1**[3]

0040 **5** *1/2* **Thumberlina**[4] 1359 3-8-8 49 ow1 .... (v) MickyFenton 7 45
(Mrs C A Dunnett) *dwlt: sn wl outpcd and bhd: hdwy on wd outside over 1f out: styd on wl towards fin* **12/1**

0450 **6** *2 3/4* **Chimbonda**[14] 1190 3-8-8 52 .... AndrewMullen(3) 2 38
(S Parr) *chsd ldrs: fdd appr fnl f* **10/1**

000- **7** *3* **Marygate (IRE)**[331] 2462 3-8-9 50 .... TWilliams 6 25
(M Brittain) *chsd ldrs: hmpd after 2f: lost pl over 1f out* **40/1**

0-4U **8** *nk* **Celtic Rebel (IRE)**[42] 804 3-9-2 57 .... JamieMoriarty 8 31
(S A Callaghan) *restless in stalls: in rr: kpt on fnl 2f: nvr on terms* **10/1**

00-3 **9** *2 1/4* **Gore Hill (IRE)**[21] 1061 3-9-2 57 .... DarrenWilliams 4 23
(K R Burke) *chsd ldrs: hmpd and lost pl 3f out: lame* **11/1**

300- **10** *3* **Pennine Rose**[197] 6548 3-7-13 45 .... DanielleMcCreery(5) 3 —
(A Berry) *s.i.s: a outpcd and in rr* **66/1**

60.44 secs (0.64) **Going Correction** +0.05s/f (Good) **10** Ran SP% **116.7**
Speed ratings (Par 96): **96,94,93,92,91 87,82,81,78,73**
toteswingers: 1&2 £3.70, 1&3 £4.70, 2&3 £6.20. CSF £10.93 CT £48.80 TOTE £4.00: £1.20, £1.80, £2.60; EX 11.60.

Owner Septimus Racing Group **Bred** A J Coleing **Trained** Denton, Co Durham

FOCUS
A low-grade sprint run in a time only fractionally quicker than the opening seller.
Gore Hill(IRE) Official explanation: vet said gelding returned lame

1456 GO RACING AT BEVERLEY TOMORROW APPRENTICE H'CAP 5f 212y

5:50 (5:50) (Class 6) (0-65,65) 4-Y-O+ £2,183 (£644; £322) Stalls Low

Form RPR

25-5 **1** **Mandalay King (IRE)**[9] 1244 4-9-0 65 .... JohnCavanagh(5) 7 75
(Mrs Marjorie Fife) *sn outpcd and in rr: hdwy 2f out: styd on wl to ld last 50yds* **3/1**[1]

010- **2** *1 1/2* **Conjecture**[166] 7218 7-8-12 61 .... PaulPickard(3) 9 66
(R Bastiman) *trckd ldrs: led over 1f out: edgd lft: hdd and no ex wl ins fnl f* **7/1**

02-0 **3** *1/2* **Angaric (IRE)**[85] 303 6-8-12 65 .... RichardOliver(7) 3 69
(B Smart) *mid-div: hdwy over 2f out: styd on fnl f* **10/1**

00-6 **4** *3/4* **City For Conquest (IRE)**[85] 305 6-8-3 54 ow1 .... DavidKenny(5) 8 55
(John A Harris) *sn outpcd and in rr: hdwy 2f out: styd on wl ins fnl f* **28/1**

6-00 **5** *2 3/4* **Brut**[10] 1227 7-9-4 64 .... (p) LanceBetts 2 56
(D W Barker) *trckd ldrs: chal over 1f out: fdd jst ins fnl f* **9/2**[3]

-006 **6** *1/2* **Fast Freddie**[60] 632 5-8-9 55 .... AmyRyan 4 46
(S Parr) *wnt rt s: led: hdd over 1f out: sn n.m.r and edgd rt: fdd* **7/2**[2]

643- **7** *2* **Karate Queen**[140] 7541 4-8-0 51 oh1 .... AdamCarter(5) 1 35
(R E Barr) *chsd ldrs on inner: wknd jst ins fnl f* **12/1**

0-01 **8** *2 1/4* **Darcy's Pride (IRE)**[9] 1241 5-8-10 61 6ex .... AnthonyBetts(5) 10 38
(D W Barker) *sn outpcd and in rr: kpt on fnl 2f: nvr on terms* **10/1**

30-0 **9** *nse* **Obe One**[64] 575 9-8-3 **52** ... RichardRowe(3) 6 29
(A Berry) *wnt lft s: a in rr* **33/1**
00-0 **10** *3* **Royal Acclamation (IRE)**[103] 108 4-8-11 **60** ... JamieKyne(3) 5 27
(G A Harker) *hmpd s: a in rr* **7/1**

1m 13.67s (0.07) **Going Correction** -0.125s/f (Firm) **10** Ran SP% **122.7**
Speed ratings (Par 101): **94,92,91,90,86 86,83,80,80,76**
toteswinger: 1&2 £3.80, 1&3 £6.10, 2&3 £12.40 CSF £26.11 CT £197.90 TOTE £4.00: £1.50, £2.50, £3.00; EX 22.90 Place 6: £21.06 Place 5: £12.79 .
Owner R W Fife **Bred** Forenaghts Stud And Dermot Cantillon **Trained** Stillington, N Yorks

FOCUS
A strong pace to this 6f sprint but the speed collapsed over a furlong out as the hold-up horses swooped

Royal Acclamation(IRE) Official explanation: jockey said gelding was slow away
T/Plt: £19.40 to a £1 stake. Pool: £38,847.13. 1,455.15 winning tickets. T/Qpdt: £5.20 to a £1 stake. Pool: £2,400.62. 338.50 winning tickets. WG

EPSOM (L-H)

Wednesday, April 22

OFFICIAL GOING: Good (good to soft in places on round course) changing to good after race 2 (3.05) (5f 7.9, round course 7.5)
Wind: Moderate, across Weather: bright and sunny

1457 BLUE SQUARE H'CAP 5f

2:30 (2:31) (Class 3) (0-95,95) 4-Y-0+

£9,346 (£2,799; £1,399; £700; £349; £175) **Stalls** High

Form RPR

600- **1** **Fathom Five (IRE)**[180] 6947 5-9-2 **93** ... AlanMunro 6 103
(C F Wall) *trckd ldrs: shkn up and hdwy over 1f out: led ins fnl f: r.o wl: comf* **7/1**[2]
1322 **2** *3/4* **Wotashirtfull (IRE)**[14] 1181 4-8-5 **82** ... (v[1]) MartinDwyer 10 89
(J R Boyle) *led after 1f: rdn over 1f out: hdd ins fnl f: kpt on wl to hold 2nd pl* **10/1**
00-4 **3** *shd* **Indian Trail**[22] 1053 9-8-5 **82** ... (v) AdrianTNicholls 5 89
(D Nicholls) *hld up in rr: hdwy on outer wl over 1f out: r.o u.p fnl f* **15/2**[3]
2132 **4** *1/2* **Rebel Duke (IRE)**[22] 1052 5-8-11 **88** ... PaulHanagan 9 93
(D W Barker) *taken down early: hld up towards rr: hdwy 2f out: chsng ldrs and styng on whn nt clr run briefly ins fnl f: r.o fnl 100yds: unable to rch ldrs* **13/2**[1]
3103 **5** *3/4* **Ebraam (USA)**[22] 1052 6-8-13 **90** ... TolleyDean 15 92+
(P Howling) *hld up in tch: edgd out off rail and hdwy 2f out: n.m.r ent fnl f: r.o: nt rch ldrs* **9/1**
0-43 **6** *1/2* **Merlin's Dancer**[14] 1181 9-8-5 **82** ... JohnEgan 1 83
(S Dow) *sn pressing ldr: ev ch 2f out: edgd lft u.p ent fnl f: wknd fnl 100yds* **16/1**
604- **7** *3/4* **Little Pete (IRE)**[220] 5930 4-8-13 **90** ... FrancisNorton 13 88
(A M Balding) *t.k.h: hld up in tch: lost pl and towards rr over 2f out: styd on fnl f: nt trble ldrs* **9/1**
665- **8** *1* **Bertoliver**[137] 7584 5-8-11 **88** ... RichardKingscote 7 82
(Tom Dascombe) *chsd ldrs: rdn 1/2-way: wknd over 1f out* **9/1**
32-6 **9** *nk* **Supermassive Muse (IRE)**[7] 1278 4-8-12 **89** ... (p) DarryllHolland 8 82
(E S McMahon) *broke wl: led and crossed to stands rail: hdd after 1f: chsd ldrs tl rdn and wknd over 1f out* **8/1**
002- **10** *shd* **Van Bossed (CAN)**[208] 6239 4-9-4 **95** ... TPO'Shea 11 88
(D Nicholls) *hld up in rr: hdwy 2f out: nvr nr ldrs* **11/1**
300- **11** *1/2* **Misaro (GER)**[168] 7192 8-8-11 **88** ... (b) NeilPollard 14 79
(R A Harris) *a towards rr: bhd fr 1/2-way* **33/1**
02-0 **12** *2 1/2* **The Jobber (IRE)**[26] 985 8-8-10 **87** ... TedDurcan 4 69
(M Blanshard) *in tch on outer: rdn 2f out: wknd over 1f out* **33/1**
2240 **13** *9* **Whiskey Creek**[7] 1278 4-8-5 **82** ... (b) RobertWinston 12 32
(C A Dwyer) *chsd ldrs for over 1f: sn struggling and lost pl: bhd fr 1/2-way* **9/1**

55.64 secs (-0.06) **Going Correction** +0.15s/f (Good) **13** Ran SP% **117.9**
Speed ratings (Par 107): **106,104,104,103,102 101,100,99,98,98 97,93,79**
toteswinger: 1&2 £9.10, 1&3 £10.80, 2&3 £8.00 CSF £74.29 CT £540.26 TOTE £6.80: £2.30, £2.30, £2.70; EX 74.60.
Owner Hintlesham Thoroughbreds **Bred** Eamonn Connolly **Trained** Newmarket, Suffolk

FOCUS
It was a beautifully sunny day at Epsom, but there had been heavy dews overnight and the clerk of the course reported that the track dried out surprisingly little over the last couple of days. However, the ground was officially changed to good about halfway through the card. Lots of well known speedsters were chasing the prize and the pace was understandably furious.

NOTEBOOK
Fathom Five(IRE), having his first start for Chris Wall, had not won since June 2007 but was well supported on his first start of the season. He was given a great ride by Munro, who steered clear of trouble throughout. Once sent to the front, the result was never in doubt and it would be little surprise to see him enjoy a decent year. It is thought that he needs some ease in the ground so he will not be going anywhere on a really quick surface. A trip back here for the Dash will only happen if the going has some juice in it, and he may go to York before then. (op 11-1 tchd 13-2)
Wotashirtfull(IRE), wearing a visor for the first time, is extremely consistent and once again gave his supporters good value. He tried to match strides with Merlin Dancer early, which is not an easy thing to do, and kept on well down the stands-side rail. (op 11-1 tchd 9-1)
Indian Trail, with a visor back on, has dropped to a very handy mark again and attracted some market support. His draw was always going to make things difficult for him, but he ran with enough promise to suggest his turn is not far away if getting his favoured quick ground. (op 13-2 tchd 11-2)
Rebel Duke(IRE) has been racing on the Fibresand since last November and looked a shade unfortunate in this. He chased the leaders as they sped off and was in the process of making a move when the gaps close in front of him - the rider reported that he was denied a clear run. There is a decent handicap in him when things go right. Official explanation: jockey said gelding was denied a clear run (op 7-1 tchd 8-1)
Ebraam(USA) was also making his move a furlong out when finding little room. He kept on well and would have been challenging for a place with a clear passage. (op 8-1 tchd 11-1)
Merlin's Dancer showed terrific pace as usual but found the last half a furlong a bit too far. (tchd 18-1)
Little Pete(IRE) ◆, off since last September, got behind but finished well. His stable is in good heart and he could be the one to take from the race. (op 12-1)
Supermassive Muse(IRE) shaped nicely at Beverley last week on his return to action and made an early move to the stands-side rail. He quickly settled behind the pace but found little room to make a meaningful challenge. (op 7-1 tchd 17-2)
Van Bossed(CAN), having his first start since running in a 6f contest at Ascot last September, looks on a high handicap mark and could not get involved.
The Jobber(IRE) did not show much on his seasonal debut at Wolverhampton in late March but ran a bit better than his position here suggests, as his rider was far from hard on him towards the middle of the course when his chance was gone. (op 25-1)

Whiskey Creek Official explanation: jockey said gelding was unsuited by the track

1458 BLUE SQUARE GREAT METROPOLITAN H'CAP 1m 4f 10y

3:05 (3:11) (Class 3) (0-95,94) 4-Y-0+

£9,346 (£2,799; £1,399; £700; £349; £175) **Stalls** Low

Form RPR

50-1 **1** **Hatton Flight**[18] 1117 5-9-0 **88** ... (b) WilliamBuick 6 99
(A M Balding) *in tch: hdwy over 3f out: rdn to ld over 1f out: r.o wl fnl f* **9/1**
322- **2** *1 1/4* **Mezzanisi (IRE)**[197] 6563 4-8-8 **83** ... JamieSpencer 3 92
(M L W Bell) *hld up in tch: hdwy 3f out: chsd wnr jst over 1f out: hung lft u.p 1f out: kpt on same pce fnl 100yds* **6/1**[2]
330- **3** *1 1/4* **Rajeh (IRE)**[216] 6061 6-9-2 **90** ... LiamJones 10 97
(J L Spearing) *stdd after s: hld up wl bhd: swtchd rt and hdwy on outer 3f out: r.o wl fnl f: snatched 3rd last stride: nt rch ldrs* **25/1**
140- **4** *shd* **Coin Of The Realm (IRE)**[25] 5349 4-8-8 **83** ... RichardMullen 4 90
(G L Moore) *hld up in midfield: hdwy over 3f out: chsd ldrs and swtchd rt over 1f out: n.m.r briefly ins fnl f: kpt on same pce fnl 100yds* **25/1**
00-0 **5** *nk* **Group Captain**[40] 33 7-9-2 **90** ... RichardHughes 20 96
(H J Collingridge) *hld up wl bhd: hdwy jst over 2f out: r.o strly fnl f: nt rch ldrs* **25/1**
34-3 **6** *2* **Dream Desert (IRE)**[42] 801 4-8-12 **87** ... DarryllHolland 2 90
(M R Channon) *t.k.h: trckd ldrs: hdwy to ld over 2f out: sn rdn hdd over 1f out: wknd ins fnl f* **4/1**[1]
6310 **7** *2 1/2* **Profit's Reality (IRE)**[25] 1007 7-8-10 **84** ... PaulDoe 15 83
(M J Attwater) *t.k.h: chsd ldrs: wnt 2nd 8f out tl 3f out: wknd over 1f out* **33/1**
505- **8** *nk* **Record Breaker (IRE)**[193] 6652 5-9-2 **90** ... J-PGuillambert 14 89
(M Johnston) *chsd ldrs: rdn to chse ldr 3f out: ev ch 2f out: wknd u.p over 1f out* **9/1**
536- **9** *1 3/4* **Formax (FR)**[243] 5229 7-9-2 **90** ... PatDobbs 7 89+
(M P Tregoning) *stdd s: hld up wl bhd: hdwy over 2f out: styd on fnl f but nvr nr ldrs* **12/1**
0-31 **10** *1 3/4* **Aureate**[58] 325 5-9-1 **89** ... RyanMoore 19 82
(B Ellison) *hld up off the pce in midfield: effrt and rdn 3f out: wknd wl over 1f out* **12/1**
-350 **11** *2* **Bazergan (IRE)**[25] 1003 4-9-1 **90** ... (tp) SebSanders 1 80
(C E Brittain) *chsd ldr tl led 10f out: rdn over 3f out: hdd over 2f out: wknd wl over 1f out* **20/1**
01-6 **12** *1 3/4* **Paktolos (FR)**[53] 33 6-8-13 **87** ... (b) DaneO'Neill 13 74
(A King) *hld up in midfield: rdn and no prog whn sltly hmpd 3f out: nvr trbld ldrs* **28/1**
02-5 **13** *1 1/2* **Celtic Spirit (IRE)**[85] 33 6-9-5 **93** ... GeorgeBaker 9 78
(G L Moore) *stdd after s: hld up wl bhd: effrt on outer 3f out: nvr on terms* **33/1**
61-3 **14** *3 1/2* **Millville**[109] 33 9-8-13 **87** ... PhilipRobinson 18 66
(M A Jarvis) *stdd after s: hld up wl bhd: nvr on terms* **8/1**[3]
600- **15** *2 1/2* **Lancetto (FR)**[122] 7755 4-9-4 **93** ... FergusSweeney 12 68
(K R Burke) *t.k.h: led for 2f: chsd ldrs after tl rdn and wknd over 2f out: eased ins fnl f* **50/1**
062- **16** *6* **Tilt**[152] 7404 7-9-3 **91** ... FrancisNorton 8 56
(B Ellison) *stdd s: hld up in rr: nvr a factor* **20/1**
443- **17** *3/4* **Tifernati**[200] 6479 5-8-12 **86** ... SteveDrowne 5 50
(G L Moore) *hld up in midfield: rdn and effrt towards inner 3f out: wknd 2f out: eased ins fnl f* **16/1**
2040 **18** *8* **Robby Bobby**[25] 1003 4-9-3 **92** ... LDettori 11 43
(M Johnston) *in tch: rdn over 3f out: wknd over 2f out: eased ins fnl f* **14/1**

2m 38.56s (-0.34) **Going Correction** +0.15s/f (Good)
WFA 4 from 5yo+ 1lb **18** Ran SP% **125.7**
Speed ratings (Par 107): **107,106,105,105,105 103,102,101,100,99 98,97,96,93,92 88,87,82**
toteSwinger: 1&2 £10.90, 1&3 £50.60, 2&3 £29.60 CSF £54.93 CT £1342.65 TOTE £7.60: £2.20, £2.40, £4.80, £6.50; EX 73.70 Trifecta £419.70 Part won. Pool: £567.18 - 0.30 winning units..
Owner David Brownlow **Bred** Fittocks Stud Ltd **Trained** Kingsclere, Hants
■ Stewards' Enquiry : Dane O'Neill two-day ban: careless riding (May 6-7)

FOCUS
A highly-competitive handicap, as one would expect for such a historic race. The early pace did not look particularly strong, so those who sat off the gallop were at a disadvantage.

NOTEBOOK
Hatton Flight really knows how to win and the Handicapper gave him a chance after his success last time, as he only raised him 2lb. Never far away, he took his time to get to the lead but kept on powerfully once there to win comfortably. The aforementioned Handicapper will want to make his life harder now, which tempers enthusiasm for next time, but he is improving with age and loves a battle. A race like the Ebor further down the line will probably be ideal for him but it was also mentioned that he could make his way south for a race in Madrid. (op 7-1)
Mezzanisi(IRE) is a very consistent horse and managed to fill the frame again on his seasonal debut. He tracked the leaders throughout but looked awkward under pressure, as he wanted to hang left inside the final furlong. His trainer reported that he is a genuine type, so one has to conclude the track was completely against him. (op 13-2 tchd 7-1)
Rajeh(IRE) landed a couple of races over 1m6f last year and shaped well on his return to action over a trip too short for him. He is a little high in the handicap on his winning form, so this effort will not help his cause. (op 33-1)
Coin Of The Realm(IRE) looked unlucky not to go a lot closer, as he was denied a clear run on at least two occasions inside the final stages. His connections will make sure he is found the right opportunities. (op 28-1)
Group Captain, whose last run came in the County Hurdle at the Cheltenham festival, kept on really well from off the pace and should be winning again soon. (tchd 28-1)
Dream Desert(IRE) was the least exposed runner in the line-up and looked the one with most potential. He was given a good ride to have every chance but one was left with the suspicion that he will be at his best over 1m2f or possibly a mile. (tchd 9-2)
Record Breaker(IRE) has a fantastic record fresh but only shaped with a little encouragement in this. He is creeping down to a fair handicap mark again. (op 12-1)
Formax(FR) has always seemed a horse that needs finessing during a race but he was given an awful lot do from off the gallop here, and could never get involved. (op 14-1 tchd 16-1)
Millville had run a couple of fair races at Epsom in the past and was nicely treated on his best form. He was making a move forwards from the rear, without looking that dangerous, when slightly chopped for room. Official explanation: jockey said gelding did not handle the track (tchd 15-2)

Tifernati Official explanation: jockey said gelding hung right

1459 WEATHERBYS BANK BLUE RIBAND TRIAL STKS (CONDITIONS RACE) 1m 2f 18y

3:40 (3:42) (Class 2) 3-Y-O

£12,462 (£3,732; £1,866; £934; £466; £234) **Stalls** Low

Form RPR

4-1 **1** **Debussy (IRE)**[32] 914 3-9-1 90 JimmyFortune 7 108+
(J H M Gosden) *hld up in tch: hdwy over 2f out: rdn to ld over 1f out: edgd lft and styd on wl fnl f: pushed out* **11/4**[1]

314- **2** 1 1/4 **Midday**[172] 7144 3-8-10 93 TPQueally 5 97
(H R A Cecil) *trckd ldng pair: hdwy to ld on inner over 2f out: sn rdn: hdd over 1f out: kpt on tl no ex ins fnl f* **10/3**[2]

1 **3** 3/4 **Popmurphy**[16] 1151 3-9-1 89 FergusSweeney 6 101+
(K R Burke) *hld up in last pair: rdn over 3f out: wnt 3rd over 1f out: styd on steadily fnl f: unable to rch ldng pair* **6/1**

012- **4** 7 **Ouster (GER)**[172] 7142 3-9-1 92 GeorgeBaker 1 87
(D R C Elsworth) *hld up in tch: effrt and hung lft 2f out: sn no hdwy: wl hld fnl f* **7/1**

1-16 **5** 2 **Saint Arch (CAN)**[11] 1211 3-9-3 97 LDettori 3 85
(M Johnston) *led tl rdn and hdd over 2f out: wknd wl over 1f out: wl btn fnl f* **6/1**

30-6 **6** 1 3/4 **Canwinn (IRE)**[18] 1118 3-9-1 100 DarryllHolland 2 79
(M R Channon) *hld up in last pl: struggling over 3f out: lost tch 2f out* **25/1**

251- **7** 1 **Mustaqer (IRE)**[187] 6777 3-9-1 90 RHills 4 77
(B W Hills) *t.k.h: chsd ldr: ev ch and rdn wl over 2f out: wknd 2f out: sn bhd* **9/2**[3]

2m 8.92s (-0.78) **Going Correction** +0.15s/f (Good) **7** Ran SP% **112.8**
Speed ratings (Par 104): **109,108,107,101,100 98,98**
toteswingers: 1&2 £3.10, 1&3 £4.90, 2&3 £3.80 CSF £11.76 TOTE £3.10: £1.80, £2.40; EX 13.10.
Owner H R H Princess Haya Of Jordan **Bred** Darley **Trained** Newmarket, Suffolk

FOCUS
Some nice horses have won this contest in the past but it is fair to say that most of the recent winners made little impact in the Derby itself. The runners assembled for the 2009 renewal looked a potentially nice bunch, but it is difficult at this stage to envisage any of them troubling the favourites on 6th of June, although the winner is progressing into a nice type.

NOTEBOOK
Debussy(IRE), having his first taste of racing on turf, landed a 1m2f maiden last time, after being given an uncontested lead, by nine lengths. He was supplemented for the Derby after and looked good in the paddock here, so it was pleasing to see him win in such good style after travelling strongly throughout. The winning margin does not do him full justice and he should have more to come, as he looked a bit green still. Whatever his fate in the Derby, if connections take him in that direction, he is a smart sort in the making. Generally a 25/1 shot with most bookmakers, he could head to the Chester Vase next. (op 9-4 tchd 3-1 and 10-3 in places)
Midday, the only filly in the contest, tracked the leader early and went for home down the inside rail over a furlong out. However, she was no match for the winner as he came along side her and went a few lengths clear. To her credit, she stayed on well, which should mean a return visit for the Oaks. (op 5-1)
Popmurphy did not make his debut until earlier this month, but there was a lot to like about that performance, although the form has been badly let down since. He took time to get organised when his jockey asked for maximum effort, which seemed more to do with lack of experience rather than anything to do with the track, but stayed on really well inside the final furlong. He will appreciate further and one could see him surprising a few if running in the Derby. (op 7-1 tchd 15-2)
Ouster(GER), noted as being warm in the paddock, appeared to settle nicely this time but hung under pressure and was a bit disappointing. (op 11-2)
Saint Arch(CAN) set off in front but was readily reeled in when the tempo increased. (tchd 15-2)
Canwinn(IRE) was always outclassed and hung right. Official explanation: jockey said colt hung right (op 16-1)
Mustaqer(IRE) got a little warm before the race and was keen during it. His rider reported that his mount lost his action and was found to be distressed post race. Official explanation: jockey said colt lost its action; vet said colt was found to be distrressed (op 5-1)

1460 BLUE SQUARE CITY AND SUBURBAN (HERITAGE H'CAP) 1m 2f 18y

4:15 (4:20) (Class 2) (0-105,102) 4-Y-O+

£31,155 (£9,330; £4,665; £2,335; £1,165; £585) **Stalls** Low

Form RPR

160- **1** **Duncan**[172] 7145 4-9-7 99 JimmyFortune 11 113
(J H M Gosden) *hld up in midfield: hdwy over 2f out: led over 1f out: r.o strly and clr ins fnl f: readily* **8/1**[2]

5-54 **2** 2 1/2 **Lake Poet (IRE)**[15] 1172 6-9-3 95 SebSanders 3 104
(C E Brittain) *in tch: rdn to chal over 2f out: led wl over 1f out: hdd over 1f out: outpcd by wnr fnl f: kpt on for 2nd pl* **8/1**[2]

150- **3** 1/2 **Dona Alba (IRE)**[265] 4552 4-8-12 90 TedDurcan 1 98
(J L Dunlop) *dwlt: t.k.h: hld up in midfield: hdwy on inner 3f out: chsd ldrs over 1f out: styd on to press for 2nd but no ch w wnr* **14/1**

00-1 **4** 1 3/4 **Ladies Best**[15] 1172 5-9-3 95 GeorgeBaker 13 100
(B Ellison) *hld up in midfield: plld out and effrt over 2f out: hung lft fr over 1f out: chsd ldng trio jst ins fnl f: kpt on* **12/1**

03-1 **5** 3/4 **Unbreak My Heart (IRE)**[15] 1170 4-9-1 93 PaulHanagan 16 96
(R A Fahey) *hld up wl bhd: gd hdwy on inner jst over 2f out: r.o fnl f: nvr trbld ldrs* **11/1**

46-2 **6** 1/2 **Sweet Lightning**[25] 1003 4-8-9 87 MartinDwyer 20 96+
(W R Muir) *hld up bhd: hdwy and n.m.r wl over 1f out: hmpd 1f out: sn swtchd lft: r.o wl ins fnl f: nvr threatened ldrs* **11/1**

210- **7** nk **Allied Powers (IRE)**[193] 6646 4-9-6 98 JamieSpencer 14 99+
(M L W Bell) *t.k.h: hld up towards rr: hdwy on outer 4f out: rdn 3f out: no imp fnl f* **12/1**

0002 **8** nse **Drill Sergeant**[24] 1017 4-9-10 102 J-PGuillambert 17 103
(M Johnston) *chsd ldrs: wnt 2nd over 7f out: ev ch and rdn 3f out: outpcd over 1f out: one pce after* **20/1**

00-4 **9** 3/4 **Kavachi (IRE)**[15] 1170 6-8-9 87 RyanMoore 18 87
(G L Moore) *stdd and dropped in bhd after s: plld to outer and hdwy over 2f out: no imp u.p fnl f* **10/1**[3]

34-1 **10** hd **Press The Button (GER)**[11] 1216 6-9-4 96 PatCosgrave 6 95
(J R Boyle) *in tch: rdn over 2f out: unable qck u.p 2f out: plugged on same pce* **20/1**

30/6 **11** 3/4 **Kaleo**[60] 636 5-8-8 86 JohnEgan 7 86+
(S Dow) *hld up in midfield: hmpd and lost pl over 2f out: plld to outer and sme hdwy fnl f: n.d* **66/1**

/1-2 **12** 1 1/4 **Hawaass (USA)**[15] 1172 4-9-1 93 LDettori 15 88+
(M Johnston) *chsd ldr tl led 8f out: hrd pressed and drvn 3f out: hdd wl over 1f out: wknd 1f out* **6/1**[1]

01-2 **13** 2 **Bencoolen (IRE)**[15] 1170 4-8-12 90 AdrianTNicholls 12 87+
(D Nicholls) *led for 2f: trckd ldrs: nt clr run fr over 2f out tl ins fnl f: nt rcvr and nt pushed after* **20/1**

20-4 **14** hd **Ramona Chase**[11] 1216 4-9-1 93 IanMongan 5 91+
(M J Attwater) *hld up towards rr: effrt towards inner and nt clr run fr 2f: eased ins fnl f* **16/1**

5-41 **15** 3/4 **Greylami (IRE)**[25] 1003 4-8-13 91 ChrisCatlin 8 81
(T G Mills) *stdd s: t.k.h: hld up in rr: nvr a factor* **12/1**

530- **16** 1 1/4 **Goodwood Starlight (IRE)**[197] 6563 4-8-13 91 FergusSweeney 19 78
(G L Moore) *hld up in rr: nvr a factor* **66/1**

031- **17** nk **Safari Sunup (IRE)**[192] 6667 4-9-0 92 StephenCarson 2 78+
(P Winkworth) *chsd ldrs: n.m.r over 2f out: lost pl and hmpd over 1f out: no ch after* **25/1**

31-0 **18** nk **Opera Prince**[25] 1003 4-8-10 88 RichardHughes 10 87+
(S Kirk) *hld up in tch: rdn and effrt on outer 3f out: chsd ldrs over 1f out: btn and eased 1f out* **16/1**

4110 **19** 1 1/4 **Stand Guard**[25] 1003 5-8-9 87 TolleyDean 4 70
(P Howling) *trckd ldrs: rdn wl over 2f out: wknd u.p over 1f out* **33/1**

20 3 **Theocritus (USA)**[201] 6458 4-8-9 87 StephenDonohoe 9 64
(D M Simcock) *stdd s: a bhd* **33/1**

2m 8.73s (-0.97) **Going Correction** +0.15s/f (Good) **20** Ran SP% **130.8**
Speed ratings (Par 109): **109,107,106,105,104 104,103,103,103,103 102,101,99,99,99 98,97,97,96,94**
toteswinger: 1&2 £20.60, 1&3 £24.80, 2&3 £45.70 CSF £66.80 CT £915.45 TOTE £9.80: £2.50, £2.00, £4.80, £4.20; EX 77.70 Trifecta £746.70 Part won. Pool: £1009.12 - 0.50 winning units..
Owner Normandie Stud Ltd **Bred** Normandie Stud Ltd **Trained** Newmarket, Suffolk

FOCUS
The pace was not that strong for such a competitive race, and those who raced off the gallop struggled to make much impression. Plenty of those that tried suffered interference.

NOTEBOOK
Duncan looked a fascinating contender on his first start for John Gosden after leaving the John Dunlop stable. Lightly raced and a little warm in the paddock, he ranged up on the outside, going really well, and put the race to bed very quickly. Said to have improved over the winter, one would imagine that he will be tested in better company before too long. (op 12-1)
Lake Poet(IRE), beaten nearly three lengths by Ladies Best last time, has a terrific record at Epsom and had landed the Great Metropolitan on this card in 2007. A little keen early, he beat the rest of his rivals nicely but could not contain the winner. He seems sure to come back for a race at the Derby meeting. (op 7-1 tchd 13-2)
Dona Alba(IRE), a bit keen early on her first start since last July, got all the breaks up the inside rail and finished nicely. She looks capable of landing a decent contest. (tchd 16-1)
Ladies Best, who looked a picture in the paddock, tried to make ground from off the pace but started to hang, which made his task impossible. (tchd 14-1)
Unbreak My Heart(IRE) won on his first start for this stable last time, after being gelded, and was being stepped up in trip for this. He kept on well after having a clear passage, so was one of only a few with no excuses. (op 12-1)
Sweet Lightning had an awkward draw to overcome in this and met a wall of traffic when staying on. He would have undoubtedly gone closer with a clear run. Official explanation: jockey said gelding was denied a clear run (tchd 12-1)
Allied Powers(IRE) went right up through the weights last season after a superb run of form. 30lb higher than when he started handicapping, he looks in need of some respite judged on this effort. (op 16-1)
Drill Sergeant returned to form at Doncaster last time, as he showed some excellent battling qualities in the final stages, but could not sustain his challenge this time. (op 16-1)
Kavachi(IRE), not beaten far by Unbreak Your Heart and Bencoolen on his seasonal debut, made some headway down the middle of the track but never really got on terms. (op 9-1)
Kaleo ran into the back of his rivals about two out, which hampered his progress.
Hawaass(USA) got to the head of affairs nicely from his wide draw but backed out of things quickly when challenged. He reportedly failed to handle the course, which is no surprise given his size. (op 13-2 tchd 7-1 in places)
Bencoolen(IRE) was only just denied by Unbreak My Heart last time on his debut for new connections but did not have a lot of room when needed here. He can be given another chance. Official explanation: jockey said gelding was denied a clear run (op 16-1)
Ramona Chase, whose only victory came during September 2007, passed the post with plenty still to give and was another who suffered traffic problems. Official explanation: jockey said gelding was denied a clear run (op 20-1)
Greylami(IRE) landed an impressive success in Rosebery Stakes at Kempton last time but never figured in this. He failed to handle the course and became unbalanced. Official explanation: jockey said gelding was unbalanced by the track (op 11-1)
Safari Sunup(IRE) Official explanation: jockey said gelding was denied a clear run
Opera Prince Official explanation: jockey said gelding lost its action

1461 BRITANIACREST RECYCLING MAIDEN STKS 1m 114y

4:50 (4:55) (Class 5) 3-4-Y-O **£4,533** (£1,348; £674; £336) **Stalls** Low

Form RPR

2- **1** **Bothy**[195] 6604 3-8-11 0 SebSanders 10 88+
(R M Beckett) *hld up off the pce in midfield: hdwy 3f out: led over 1f out: hld on gamely fnl f: all out* **2/1**[1]

300- **2** shd **Lady Francesca**[172] 7144 3-8-6 82 MartinDwyer 2 83+
(W R Muir) *chsd clr ldr: clsd jst over 2f out: pressed wnr and ev ch fr over 1f out: jst hld* **3/1**[2]

36 **3** 4 **African Cheetah**[9] 1252 3-8-11 0 LDettori 4 77
(M Johnston) *hld up towards rr: plld out and effrt 3f out: hdwy 2f out: r.o to go 3rd ins fnl f: nvr nr ldrs* **13/2**[3]

4-4 **4** 1 1/2 **Dhania (IRE)**[23] 1040 3-8-11 0 RichardKingscote 11 73
(R A Teal) *in tch in midfield: rdn over 3f out: hdwy over 2f out: kpt on same pce u.p fnl f* **28/1**

0- **5** 1 3/4 **Ithinkbest**[173] 7105 3-8-11 0 RyanMoore 1 68
(Sir Michael Stoute) *in tch: effrt on inner over 3f out: chsd ldng pair and swtchd rt over 1f out: no imp 1f out: fdd and lost 2 pls fnl 100yds* **7/1**

46-0 **6** 3 1/2 **Deyas Dream**[21] 1075 3-8-3 66 DavidProbert(3) 5 54
(A M Balding) *mounted on crse: led and sn clr: rdn and tiring 2f out: hdd over 1f out: wknd fnl f* **20/1**

2- **7** 1 1/4 **Peaceful Rule (USA)**[227] 5716 3-8-11 0 AdrianTNicholls 9 56
(D Nicholls) *dwlt: hld up towards rr: plld out and rdn 3f out: no hdwy and nvr trbld ldrs* **14/1**

00- **8** 4 1/2 **Rowan Tiger**[179] 6978 3-8-11 0 PatCosgrave 3 43
(J R Boyle) *stdd and dropped in bhd after s: struggling over 4f out: n.d* **20/1**

42- **9** 9 **Mehendi (IRE)**[182] 6893 3-8-11 0 JamieSpencer 6 19
(B J Meehan) *s.i.s: sn pushed along and nvr gng wl: bhd: lost tch over 4f out* **7/1**

0600 **10** 2 **Maison D'Or**[23] 1036 3-8-11 49 RobertHavlin 7 14
(R Ingram) *chsd ldrs: rdn over 3f out: wknd qckly over 2f out* **200/1**

00-0 **11** 2 **Red Dagger (IRE)**[40] 828 3-8-6 40 AmyBaker(5) 8 8
(T D McCarthy) *s.i.s: bhd: lost tch over 4f out: t.o* **200/1**

0-0 **12** *1* **Hilbre Point (USA)**[7] 1295 3-8-11 0.................................. TedDurcan 12 6
(B J Meehan) *a bhd: lost tch over 4f out: t.o* **40/1**

1m 45.56s (-0.54) **Going Correction** +0.15s/f (Good) **12** Ran SP% **119.7**
Speed ratings (Par 103): **108,107,104,103,101 98,97,93,85,83 81,80**
toteswinger: 1&2 £1.80, 1&3 £3.50, 2&3 £5.60. CSF £7.40 TOTE £2.90: £1.60, £1.60, £2.20; EX 9.40.
Owner J H Richmond-Watson **Bred** Lawn Stud **Trained** Whitsbury, Hants

FOCUS
A fair-looking maiden.
Mehendi(IRE) Official explanation: jockey said gelding was unsuited by the track

1462 TROY O'CONNOR MEMORIAL H'CAP 1m 114y
5:25 (5:29) (Class 5) (0-75,75) 3-Y-O **£4,857** (£1,445; £722; £360) **Stalls** Low

Form RPR
00-3 **1** **River Captain (IRE)**[19] 1105 3-9-4 **75**.............................. RyanMoore 2 87
(S Kirk) *chsd ldrs: rdn and qcknd to ld 3f out: sn clr: unchal after* **10/1**
5-06 **2** *3 ½* **Wilbury Star (IRE)**[20] 1086 3-9-3 **74**.......................... RichardHughes 11 78
(R Hannon) *chsd ldrs: rdn and effrt 3f out: chsd clr wnr over 1f out: no imp* **10/1**
531- **3** *1 ¼* **Midnight In May (IRE)**[181] 6923 3-9-4 **75**.................... MartinDwyer 9 76+
(W R Muir) *hld up off the pce in midfield: rdn and hdwy over 2f out: kpt on u.p fr over 1f out: wnt 3rd last strides: no ch w wnr* **8/1**[3]
313- **4** *hd* **Pride Of Kings**[197] 6549 3-9-3 **74**.. LDettori 17 74
(M Johnston) *in tch: rdn and unable qck 3f out: kpt on to go 3rd 1f out: nvr pce to threaten ldrs: lost 3rd last strides* **6/1**[1]
251 **5** *1* **The Winged Assasin (USA)**[13] 1196 3-9-4 **75**............... IanMongan 15 73
(J Akehurst) *hld up in tch: hrd rdn and unable qck 3f out: kpt on u.p fr over 1f out: nvr trbld ldrs* **8/1**[3]
050- **6** *¾* **Mr Freddy (IRE)**[176] 7038 3-8-4 **61**............................... PaulHanagan 14 60+
(R A Fahey) *towards rr: rdn and hdwy over 3f out: kpt on u.p and styng on fin but nvr trbld ldrs* **15/2**[2]
040- **7** *4 ½* **Jacobite Prince (IRE)**[214] 6112 3-8-13 **70**....................... LiamJones 7 56
(M H Tompkins) *s.i.s: hld up towards rr: c wd over 4f out: hdwy 3f out: sn no imp: hung lft fnl f* **33/1**
021- **8** *1 ¾* **Young Dottie**[183] 6877 3-9-3 **74**.................................. JohnEgan 20 56
(P M Phelan) *chsd ldr: rdn over 3f out: nt pce of wnr 3f out: chsd wnr 2f out tl over 1f out: wknd* **16/1**
10-0 **9** *1* **Highland River**[14] 1193 3-8-6 **63**.................................. AlanMunro 4 43
(D R C Elsworth) *a in midfield: rdn and no prog fnl 3f* **11/1**
050- **10** *¾* **Sairaam (IRE)**[181] 6926 3-8-8 **65**.. RHills 6 43+
(J L Dunlop) *a bhd: no ch fnl 3f: sme modest late hdwy* **14/1**
000- **11** *3 ½* **Motor Home**[221] 5895 3-8-13 **70**................................. WilliamBuick 1 40
(A M Balding) *led: rdn and hdd 3f out: sn outpcd by wnr: lost 2nd 2f out: wknd over 1f out: eased ins fnl f* **8/1**[3]
406- **12** *shd* **Evening Sunset (GER)**[212] 6167 3-8-11 **68**................ EdwardCreighton 19 38
(M R Channon) *stdd and dropped in bhd after s: a bhd: nvr a factor* **16/1**
326- **13** *1* **Pokfulham (IRE)**[183] 6877 3-8-5 **67**............................ MartinLane(5) 8 34
(A P Jarvis) *chsd ldrs: pushed along 6f out: drvn over 3f out: sn struggling: no ch fnl 2f* **40/1**
65-0 **14** *1 ¾* **Ymir**[105] 74 3-8-10 **67**.. PaulDoe 16 30
(M J Attwater) *hld up in midfield: rdn 3f out: sn wknd and bhd* **66/1**
26-5 **15** *1* **Itainteasybeingme**[8] 1271 3-7-13 **61** oh2...... Louis-PhilippeBeuzelin(5) 5 22
(J R Boyle) *t.k.h: hld up in rr: lost tch over 3f out* **25/1**
46-6 **16** *½* **Oisin's Boy**[8] 1271 3-8-4 **61** oh2.................................(p) NickyMackay 3 21
(J R Boyle) *hld up towards rr: lost tch and no ch fnl 3f* **40/1**
5136 **17** *5* **Daily Double**[1] 1429 3-8-8 **65**.. ChrisCatlin 13 13
(D K Ivory) *hld up in last pl: lost tch over 3f out* **33/1**
033 **18** *1 ¾* **Hector Spectre (IRE)**[23] 1040 3-8-9 **66**........................ TedDurcan 18 10
(B J Meehan) *hld up in midfield on outer: rdn and btn over 3f out: wl bhd and eased fnl f* **16/1**

1m 46.2s (0.10) **Going Correction** +0.15s/f (Good) **18** Ran SP% **126.3**
Speed ratings (Par 98): **105,101,100,100,99 99,95,93,92,91 88,88,87,86,85 84,80,78**
toteswinger: 1&2 £16.80, 1&3 £12.40, 2&3 £21.30 CSF £103.13 CT £884.36 TOTE £10.80: £2.60, £2.90, £3.10, £1.90; EX 74.30 Place 6: £167.25 Place 5: £52.14 .
Owner S J McCay **Bred** Sean Finnegan **Trained** Upper Lambourn, Berks

FOCUS
A fiercely competitive three-year-old handicap that appeared to be run at a sound gallop. Much like earlier on the card, it proved difficult to get involved if you had plenty of ground to make up.
Ymir Official explanation: jockey said colt was unsuited by the track
T/Jkpt: Not won. T/Plt: £107.20 to a £1 stake. Pool: £124,772.04. 849.60 winning tickets. T/Qpdt: £7.60 to a £1 stake. Pool: £7,024.76. 681.20 winning tickets. SP

1429 KEMPTON (A.W) (R-H)
Wednesday, April 22

OFFICIAL GOING: Standard
Wind: Light, across Weather: Fine, warm

1463 BOOK KEMPTON TICKETS ON 0844 579 3008 H'CAP 1m 4f (P)
6:50 (6:51) (Class 6) (0-55,55) 4-Y-O+ **£2,047** (£604; £302) **Stalls** Centre

Form RPR
323- **1** **Saloon (USA)**[181] 6929 5-9-0 **55**................................(p) JamieSpencer 13 65
(Jane Chapple-Hyam) *hld up in midfield on inner: prog over 2f out: carried hd at unappealing angle but pressed ldr 1f out: cajoled along hands and heels to edge ahd last 100yds* **5/2**[1]
0-00 **2** *nk* **Generous Lad (IRE)**[41] 816 6-8-10 **51**..........................(p) SteveDrowne 11 60
(A B Haynes) *t.k.h early: trckd ldr: chal 3f out: led wl over 1f out: hdd last 100yds: kpt on wl* **7/1**[3]
0004 **3** *2* **Holoko Heights**[9] 1254 4-8-13 **55**.. LukeMorris 5 61
(N J Vaughan) *dwlt: hld up in 10th: reminder 1/2-way: prog 2f out: barged through sn after: wnt 3rd fnl f: hung lft and no imp: awkward ride* **11/4**[2]
-505 **4** *1 ½* **Everyman**[34] 885 5-8-7 **53** ow1.. MarkCoumbe(5) 14 56
(A W Carroll) *dwlt: hld up in last trio: prog and threaded through fr jst over 2f out: cl enough 1f out: one pce after* **20/1**
3130 **5** *nk* **Amwell Brave**[9] 546 8-8-9 **50**.................................. SimonWhitworth 6 53
(J R Jenkins) *hld up in last trio: stl taking t.k.h 4f out: prog 2f out: clsd on ldrs 1f out: one pce after* **14/1**
5144 **6** *1 ¼* **Tecktal (FR)**[10] 816 6-8-10 **51**.. IanMongan 4 52
(P M Phelan) *hld up towards rr: prog on outer over 3f out: pressed ldng pair 2f out: wknd fnl f* **10/1**
0-60 **7** *¾* **Lough Beg (IRE)**[16] 1154 6-9-0 **55**................................(t) DaneO'Neill 3 55
(Miss Tor Sturgis) *trckd ldrs: effrt to ld narrowly over 2f out to wl over 1f out: wknd quite qckly fnl f* **8/1**

3-61 **8** *1 ¼* **Barbirolli**[13] 1200 7-8-6 **50**.................................... DavidProbert(3) 8 48
(W M Brisbourne) *settled towards rr: effrt on outer over 2f out: stl chsng ldrs over 1f out: wknd* **10/1**
06R- **9** *1 ¼* **Chapter (IRE)**[202] 6421 7-8-9 **50**.................................... SamHitchcott 2 46
(Mrs A L M King) *stdd s: hld up in last trio: sme prog on wd outside 3f out: no hdwy over 1f out* **50/1**
-344 **10** *1 ½* **Iceman George**[24] 1014 5-8-13 **54**...........................(p) RichardMullen 7 47
(D Morris) *wl in tch: rdn over 2f out and no rspnse: wknd over 1f out* **14/1**
0400 **11** *3 ½* **Aegean Rose**[9] 1254 4-8-11 **53**................................... FergusSweeney 9 41
(M Blanshard) *trckd ldng pair: rdn over 2f out and sn lost pl* **50/1**
40-3 **12** *2* **Winning Show**[38] 546 5-8-11 **52**.. LPKeniry 10 37
(C Gordon) *t.k.h early: trckd ldrs: sing to lose pl whn bdly bmpd wl over 1f out and eased* **16/1**
433- **13** *15* **Smoothly Does It**[13] 2697 8-8-11 **52**.....................(b[1]) RichardHughes 12 13
(Jim Best) *led to over 2f out: wknd rapidly: t.o* **7/1**[3]

2m 36.5s (2.00) **Going Correction** +0.075s/f (Slow)
WFA 4 from 5yo+ 1lb **13** Ran SP% **137.4**
Speed ratings (Par 101): **96,95,94,93,93 92,91,91,90,89 86,85,75**
toteswinger: 1&2 £3.80, 1&3 £2.30, 2&3 £5.00. CSF £24.20 CT £57.72 TOTE £3.20: £2.20, £2.50, £1.40; EX 11.60.
Owner Mrs Jane Chapple-Hyam **Bred** R D Hubbard & Coolmore **Trained** Newmarket, Suffolk
■ Stewards' Enquiry : Mark Coumbe three-day ban: careless riding (May 6-7, Jun 11)

FOCUS
Little strength in depth.
Aegean Rose Official explanation: jockey said he lost his irons on leaving stalls

1464 SPONSOR AT KEMPTON MEDIAN AUCTION MAIDEN STKS 1m 3f (P)
7:20 (7:20) (Class 5) 3-5-Y-O **£2,590** (£770; £385; £192) **Stalls** High

Form RPR
1 **Tripitaka** 3-8-9 0.. PhilipRobinson 6 82+
(M A Jarvis) *hld up bhd ldng trio: prog 3f out to ld 2f out: rdn and asserted over 1f out: readily* **7/2**[2]
666- **2** *2 ¼* **Curacao**[189] 6737 3-8-9 69.. JimCrowley 5 78
(Mrs A J Perrett) *hld up in abt 6th: prog on inner 2f out: rdn to go 2nd ins fnl f: styd on but no imp on wnr* **4/1**[3]
223- **3** *1 ¾* **Rumble Of Thunder (IRE)**[154] 7391 3-8-9 76.................... MartinDwyer 1 75
(D W P Arbuthnot) *sn led: drvn and hdd 2f out: one pce after* **9/2**
5- **4** *hd* **Leulahleulahlay**[212] 6165 3-8-9 0....................................... JoeFanning 8 75
(M Johnston) *trckd ldr 2f and again 4f out to over 2f out: steadily outpcd* **8/1**
222- **5** *1 ½* **Dome Rocket**[158] 7343 3-8-9 79.. RyanMoore 4 72
(W J Knight) *trckd ldng trio: pushed along over 3f out: rdn and nt qckn over 2f out: no prog after* **6/4**[1]
040- **6** *6* **Darley Sun (IRE)**[172] 7142 3-8-9 71............................... RichardMullen 3 61
(D M Simcock) *hld up in last trio: rdn over 3f out: sn lost tch w ldrs* **20/1**
0- **7** *8* **No Sting**[230] 5650 3-8-4 0.. FrankieMcDonald 9 42
(W S Kittow) *settled in last: shkn up 4f out: sn lost tch* **66/1**
000- **8** *16* **Ma Patrice**[112] 7832 3-7-13 46.. AmyBaker(5) 2 13
(T D McCarthy) *plld hrd: wnt 2nd after 2f to 4f out: wknd rapidly over 3f out: t.o* **100/1**

2m 21.36s (-0.54) **Going Correction** +0.075s/f (Slow) **8** Ran SP% **118.8**
Speed ratings (Par 103): **104,102,101,100,99 95,89,78**
toteswinger: 1&2 £3.10, 1&3 £3.10, 2&3 £3.20. CSF £18.50 TOTE £3.40: £1.20, £1.60, £2.10; EX 18.20.
Owner The Tripitaka Partnership **Bred** Genesis Green Stud Ltd **Trained** Newmarket, Suffolk

1465 DIGIBET.COM CLASSIFIED STKS 6f (P)
7:50 (7:50) (Class 6) 3-Y-O+ **£2,047** (£604; £302) **Stalls** High

Form RPR
-454 **1** **Fyelehk (IRE)**[6] 1311 3-9-0 54... AlanMunro 8 64
(B R Millman) *trckd ldr: rdn to ld over 1f out: sn drew clr* **13/8**[1]
00-5 **2** *3 ¼* **Creative (IRE)**[9] 1259 4-9-11 54.. LiamJones 10 57
(M H Tompkins) *led: drvn and hdd over 1f out: clr of rest but sn no ch w wnr* **9/2**[2]
660- **3** *3 ½* **Sister Moonshine**[216] 6063 4-9-11 55.................................. DO'Donohoe 7 46
(W R Muir) *chsd ldng pair: u.p wl over 2f out: sn outpcd: plugged on* **10/1**
6-04 **4** *nk* **Kings On The Roof**[49] 752 3-9-0 55....................................... JimCrowley 1 42
(G C Bravery) *chsd ldrs: rdn and sme prog over 2f out: sn outpcd: plugged on* **12/1**
000- **5** *2 ½* **Lucky Bid**[272] 4321 3-9-0 26.. LPKeniry 12 34
(J M Bradley) *trckd ldrs on inner: rdn over 2f out: sn outpcd: wknd fnl f* **66/1**
000- **6** *½* **Cavitie**[154] 7388 3-9-0 50... EdwardCreighton 9 32
(E J Creighton) *plld hrd early: hld up bhd ldrs: rdn over 2f out: sn outpcd* **25/1**
00-0 **7** *1 ¼* **Lucky Forteen**[54] 706 6-9-11 30.. LukeMorris 11 31
(P W Hiatt) *hld up in midfield on inner: rdn over2f out: sn outpcd and btn: wknd fnl f* **33/1**
-404 **8** *1 ¾* **Hint Of Honey**[57] 667 3-9-0 55... DaneO'Neill 2 23
(A G Newcombe) *wl in rr: u.p on outer over 2f out: no prog* **10/1**
000- **9** *1 ¼* **Lady Lu**[194] 6621 3-9-0 53.. MartinDwyer 4 19
(P F I Cole) *v restless in stalls and missed break: a struggling in rr* **16/1**
00-4 **10** *1 ½* **Ivor Novello (IRE)**[21] 1061 3-9-0 53.................................. RobertWinston 5 14
(G A Swinbank) *wl in rr: hrd rdn on wd outside over 2f out: sn wl btn* **7/1**[3]
0-50 **11** *3 ½* **Missed Mondays**[40] 831 3-9-0 48........................(v[1]) RichardHughes 6 31+
(Patrick Morris) *hld up in midfield: abt 7th 2f out: eased over 1f out: sddle slipped* **16/1**
200- **12** *37* **Pasta Prayer**[208] 6251 4-9-11 54... ChrisCatlin 3 —
(D E Cantillon) *a last: t.o 1/2-way* **12/1**

1m 14.02s (0.92) **Going Correction** +0.075s/f (Slow)
WFA 3 from 4yo+ 11lb **12** Ran SP% **122.4**
Speed ratings (Par 101): **96,91,87,86,83 82,80,78,76,74 70,20**
toteswinger: 1&2 £2.30, 1&3 £4.80, 2&3 £11.30. CSF £8.54 TOTE £3.10: £1.40, £1.50, £2.90; EX 12.40.
Owner The Links Partnership **Bred** Camogue Stud Ltd **Trained** Kentisbeare, Devon

Cavitie Official explanation: jockey said gelding ran too free
Missed Mondays Official explanation: jockey said saddle slipped

Pasta Prayer Official explanation: jockey said gelding never travelled

1466 DIGIBET SPORTS BETTING H'CAP (LONDON MILE QUALIFIER) 1m (P)
8:20 (8:21) (Class 4) (0-80,80) 3-Y-O **£4,727** (£1,406; £702; £351) **Stalls** High

Form RPR

643- **1** **Mirrored**[189] 6737 3-8-13 **75**........ RyanMoore 11 86+
(Sir Michael Stoute) *trckd ldrs on inner: pushed along firmly to ld wl over 1f out: sn in command: styd on wl* **3/1**[2]

321- **2** *1 ¼* **Charlotte Point (USA)**[174] 7093 3-8-13 **75**........ MartinDwyer 10 83+
(P F I Cole) *plld hrd early: hld up bhd ldrs: rdn over 2f out: kpt on to take 2nd ins fnl f: n.d to wnr* **12/1**

531- **3** *¾* **Victoria Sponge (IRE)**[189] 6732 3-8-10 **72**........ DaneO'Neill 9 78
(R Hannon) *led: drvn and hdd wl over 1f out: kpt on but lost 2nd ins fnl f* **16/1**

1211 **4** *1 ¾* **Green Agenda**[5] 1331 3-9-2 **78** 6ex........ JoeFanning 8 80
(M Johnston) *pressed ldr to over 2f out: one pce u.p* **9/4**[1]

65-5 **5** *½* **Land Hawk (IRE)**[11] 1214 3-8-9 **71**........ JimmyQuinn 2 72+
(J Pearce) *forced to r wd fr wd draw: prom: drvn over 2f out: nt qckn wl over 1f out: one pce after* **3/1**[2]

-411 **6** *1 ¾* **Woolston Ferry (IRE)**[40] 827 3-9-4 **80**........ FergusSweeney 5 77
(David Pinder) *hld up wl in rr: effrt on inner 3f out: rchd midfield over 1f out but nvr on terms w ldrs* **33/1**

001- **7** *1 ¼* **Take The Micky**[183] 6876 3-8-13 **75**........ JimCrowley 1 69
(W J Knight) *s.s: mostly in last: drvn and plugged on fnl 2f: no ch* **20/1**

531- **8** *3 ½* **Pressing Matters (IRE)**[144] 7498 3-8-10 **72**........ JohnEgan 7 58
(M Botti) *hld up towards rr: shkn up over 2f out: outpcd and no ch after* **8/1**[3]

521- **9** *2 ¼* **Yellow Printer**[136] 7593 3-9-4 **80**........ RichardKingscote 3 61
(Tom Dascombe) *racd wd in rr: pushed along wl over 2f out: sn lft bhd* **12/1**

540- **10** *5* **Bandanaman (IRE)**[198] 6524 3-8-12 **74**........ RobertWinston 4 43
(G A Swinbank) *hld up wl in rr: shkn up 3f out: no prog* **66/1**

410- **11** *nk* **Sequillo**[180] 6946 3-8-12 **74**........ RichardHughes 6 43
(R Hannon) *a in rr: u.p over 3f out: sn no ch* **20/1**

1m 40.54s (0.74) **Going Correction** +0.075s/f (Slow) **11** Ran SP% **127.1**
Speed ratings (Par 100): **99,97,97,95,94 93,91,88,86,81 80**
toteswinger: 1&2 £10.90, 1&3 £17.30, 2&3 £20.90. CSF £40.65 CT £422.52 TOTE £4.90: £1.80, £2.90, £4.80; EX 53.60.
Owner K Abdulla **Bred** Millsec Limited **Trained** Newmarket, Suffolk

Woolston Ferry(IRE) Official explanation: jockey said gelding hung right
Take The Micky Official explanation: jockey said colt missed the break
Pressing Matters(IRE) Official explanation: jockey said colt ran too free
Sequillo Official explanation: jockey said colt stopped quickly

1467 DIGIBET H'CAP 7f (P)
8:50 (8:50) (Class 3) (0-95,93) 4-Y-O+
£7,352 (£2,201; £1,100; £551; £274; £138) **Stalls** High

Form RPR

21-1 **1** **Taqdeyr**[7] 1288 4-9-2 **91** 6ex........ PhilipRobinson 3 103
(M A Jarvis) *taken to post 15 minutes early: sn led: pushed along firmly whn hrd pressed ins fnl f: rdn out to assert nr fin* **1/2**[1]

655- **2** *½* **Wigram's Turn (USA)**[228] 5697 4-8-10 **85**........ WilliamBuick 6 96
(A M Balding) *hld up in 5th: prog to chse wnr over 1f out: sustained chal u.p fnl f: hld nr fin* **7/1**[3]

010- **3** *5* **Guilded Warrior**[182] 6902 6-8-13 **88**........ FergusSweeney 5 86
(W S Kittow) *t.k.h early: prom: chsd wnr over 2f out to over 1f out: readily outpcd* **20/1**

62-3 **4** *¾* **Nezami (IRE)**[105] 73 4-8-11 **86**........ JimmyQuinn 7 81
(J Akehurst) *t.k.h early: hld up in last: effrt on inner over 2f out: outpcd fr over 1f out* **12/1**

00-0 **5** *3 ¼* **Esteem Machine (USA)**[11] 1212 5-9-4 **93**........ RyanMoore 2 80
(R A Teal) *n.m.r s: hld up in last pair: drvn and no prog over 2f out* **20/1**

-432 **6** *6* **Orpenindeed (IRE)**[18] 1116 6-8-11 **91**........ AndreaAtzeni(5) 1 62
(M Botti) *t.k.h early: trckd wnr to over 2f out: wknd rapidly* **13/2**[2]

000- **7** *13* **Stevie Gee (IRE)**[215] 6069 5-8-10 **85**........ RobertWinston 4 20
(G A Swinbank) *wnt lft s: in tch tl wknd rapidly over 2f out: t.o* **20/1**

1m 24.8s (-1.20) **Going Correction** +0.075s/f (Slow) **7** Ran SP% **114.5**
Speed ratings (Par 107): **109,108,102,101,98 91,76**
toteswinger: 1&2 £1.20, 1&3 £2.40, 2&3 £11.30. CSF £4.41 TOTE £1.50: £1.30, £2.30; EX 4.60.

Owner Richie Baines & Stephen Dartnell **Bred** Darley **Trained** Newmarket, Suffolk
■ Stewards' Enquiry : Jimmy Quinn one-day ban: used whip with excessive frequency (May 6)

NOTEBOOK
Taqdeyr was weighted to win this in style being 5lb better in than in future handicaps and appearing a horse with a progressive profile. However, despite his rider dictating from the front and wishing to give the gelding as easier race as possible, he had to be very firm in the closing stages. Still tending to be keen, he clearly needs to be ridden positively, but when he steps up a grade it will make things more difficult. (op 4-9 tchd 4-7)
Wigram's Turn(USA), who was getting 6lb from the winner, showed great tenacity. He came with a rails run over a furlong out and was snapping at the winner throughout the last 110 yards. It was a career-best run, but with the third well beaten off and the immiment weight rise of the winner, a similar rise awaits. (op 11-1 tchd 12-1)
Guilded Warrior can go a decent gallop, is good fresh and only 2lb higher than his last winning mark, but was left behind from a furlong out when the leading pair settled down for their scrap. (op 25-1)
Nezami(IRE) Official explanation: jockey said gelding missed the break

1468 BOOK CONFERENCES ON 01932 753518 H'CAP 6f (P)
9:20 (9:20) (Class 5) (0-70,70) 4-Y-O+ **£2,590** (£770; £385; £192) **Stalls** High

Form RPR

502- **1** **Tudor Prince (IRE)**[161] 7288 5-8-13 **65**........ TolleyDean 9 74
(A W Carroll) *prom in chsng gp: rdn wl over 2f out: clsd to ld narrowly over 1f out: asserted ins fnl f* **7/1**

6403 **2** *½* **Onceaponatime (IRE)**[9] 1259 4-9-4 **70**........ AlanMunro 12 77
(M D Squance) *off the pce in midfield and racd wd: rdn to cl over 1f out: styd on to take 2nd nr fin* **5/1**[3]

3404 **3** *¾* **Hart Of Gold**[9] 1248 5-8-11 **63** ow1........(p) AdamKirby 3 68+
(R A Harris) *heavily restrained s: hld up in last trio and wl off the pce: prog on inner and rdn over 1f out: fin strly to take 3rd last strides: too much to do* **7/1**

2021 **4** *nk* **Compton Classic**[7] 1285 7-9-3 **69** 6ex........(p) PatCosgrave 11 73
(J R Boyle) *hld up bhd ldrs: prog on inner to dispute ld over 1f out: hld ins fnl f: wknd nr fin* **4/1**[2]

0-0 **5** *1 ¼* **Rabbit Fighter (IRE)**[110] 14 5-8-6 **58**........(v) PaulHanagan 6 58
(D Shaw) *awkward s and slowly away: towards rr: rdn and sme prog fr 2f out: nvr rchd ldrs* **11/4**[1]

000- **6** *1* **Rockfield Lodge (IRE)**[177] 7013 4-9-4 **70**........ NeilPollard 10 66
(R A Harris) *chsd clr ldr to wl over 1f out: wknd fnl f* **10/1**

250- **7** *hd* **Dualagi**[135] 7611 5-8-8 **60**........ LPKeniry 5 56+
(M R Bosley) *tk fierce hold early and hld up in last trio: nvr on terms: plugged on* **33/1**

1300 **8** *1 ¾* **Brandywell Boy (IRE)**[16] 1150 6-9-4 **70**........ RichardThomas 7 60
(D J S Ffrench Davis) *outpcd in last trio: nvr on terms: plugged on* **25/1**

1056 **9** *1 ¼* **Teen Ager (FR)**[14] 1182 5-8-6 **58**........ JimmyQuinn 1 44
(P Burgoyne) *hld up off the pce and racd wd to 1/2-way: pushed along and no real prog over 2f out: reminder over 1f out: fdd* **33/1**

-160 **10** *2* **Billy Red**[13] 1197 5-9-1 **67**........(b) FergusSweeney 2 47
(J R Jenkins) *led and sn at least 4 l clr: wknd and hdd over 1f out* **16/1**

-636 **11** *3 ¾* **The Lord**[16] 1150 9-8-8 **60**........ JohnEgan 8 28
(W G M Turner) *sn struggling to hold pl bhd ldrs: wl btn over 2f out* **12/1**

1m 12.67s (-0.43) **Going Correction** +0.075s/f (Slow) **11** Ran SP% **120.7**
Speed ratings (Par 103): **105,104,103,102,101 99,99,97,95,93 88**
toteswinger: 1&2 £7.00, 1&3 £15.50, 2&3 £11.20. CSF £42.37 CT £262.63 TOTE £6.10: £1.40, £2.00, £2.20; EX 56.40 Place 6: £44.24 Place 5: £28.59.
Owner Allan Jones **Bred** Edmond And Richard Kent **Trained** Cropthorne, Worcs

Brandywell Boy(IRE) Official explanation: jockey said gelding missed the break
T/Plt: £82.30 to a £1 stake. Pool: £70,109.63. 621.39 winning tickets. T/Qpdt: £12.80 to a £1 stake. Pool: £4,977.06. 286.90 winning tickets. JN

1275 BEVERLEY (R-H)
Thursday, April 23

OFFICIAL GOING: Good to firm (10.2)
Wind: Light, across Weather: Dry, sunny periods

1469 BEVERLEY MINSTER CLAIMING STKS 5f
2:00 (2:03) (Class 5) 3-Y-O **£2,590** (£770; £385; £192) **Stalls** High

Form RPR

5102 **1** **La Capriosa**[7] 1311 3-8-6 68........ RobertWinston 7 61
(A J McCabe) *cl up: led wl over 1f out: rdn clr ent fnl f: styd on* **2/1**[2]

-326 **2** *2* **Dispol Grand (IRE)**[11] 1232 3-8-10 65........ PhillipMakin 5 62+
(P T Midgley) *trckd ldng pair on inner: effrt and nt clr run 2f out and again over 1f out: sn swtchd lft and rdn to chse wnr ins fnl f: kpt on same pce* **6/4**[1]

30-0 **3** *½* **Pressed For Time (IRE)**[7] 1311 3-8-6 64........ EdwardCreighton 9 52
(E J Creighton) *chsd ldrs: hdwy 2f out: rdn to chse wnr appr fnl f: sn drvn and one pce* **12/1**

4-03 **4** *4 ½* **York Key Bar**[19] 1129 3-8-11 70........ DavidAllan 6 41
(B Ellison) *bolted to post: towards rr: rdn and hdwy 2f out: kpt on ins fnl f: nvr nr ldrs* **8/1**[3]

0-16 **5** *4 ½* **Red Cell (IRE)**[66] 568 3-8-6 62........(b) RoystonFfrench 8 20
(I W McInnes) *led: rdn along 1/2-way: hdd wl over 1f out and sn wknd* **8/1**[3]

2000 **6** *2* **Bold Ring**[10] 1253 3-8-8 57 ow1........ SPRyan(7) 1 21
(E J Creighton) *sltly hmpd s: a in rr* **80/1**

400- **7** *4* **Madame Jourdain (IRE)**[198] 6547 3-8-2 63........(b) DuranFentiman 2 —
(N Wilson) *hmpd s: a in rr* **16/1**

040- **8** *10* **Adozen Dreams**[157] 7361 3-8-6 62........ FrancisNorton 3 —
(N Bycroft) *wnt lft s: a bhd* **33/1**

63.31 secs (-0.19) **Going Correction** -0.075s/f (Good) **8** Ran SP% **113.3**
Speed ratings (Par 98): **98,94,94,86,79 76,70,54**
toteswinger: 1&2 £1.40, 1&3 £7.40, 2&3 £6.70 CSF £5.24 TOTE £2.70: £1.30, £1.20, £2.50; EX 5.20.
Owner Paul J Dixon **Bred** Slatch Farm Stud **Trained** Averham Park, Notts

FOCUS
The ground was described as good to firm following 7-8mm of watering over the previous two days. An ordinary claimer and some doubt over what the form is worth.

1470 VERA GREEN CELEBRATION H'CAP 1m 1f 207y
2:30 (2:32) (Class 5) (0-70,68) 3-Y-O **£2,590** (£770; £385; £192) **Stalls** High

Form RPR

004- **1** **Topolski (IRE)**[218] 6014 3-9-4 **68**........ RoystonFfrench 6 82+
(M Johnston) *hld up in rr: gd hdwy 2f out: rdn over 1f out: qcknd to ld ins fnl f: sn clr* **8/1**

624- **2** *3 ¾* **Oriental Cavalier**[185] 6857 3-9-3 **67**........ RobertWinston 10 73
(R Hollinshead) *prom: effrt over 2f out and sn rdn: led over 1f out: drvn: edgd rt and hdd ins fnl f: kpt on same pce* **5/1**[2]

52-3 **3** *1 ½* **Antigua Sunrise (IRE)**[20] 1098 3-9-3 **67**........ PaulHanagan 13 70
(R A Fahey) *hld up in tch on inner: stdy hdwy over 2f out: effrt whn n.m.r over 1f out: swtchd lft and rdn ent fnl f: kpt on same pce* **7/2**[1]

52-2 **4** *2* **Victorian Tycoon (IRE)**[5] 1361 3-8-13 **63**........ ChrisCatlin 2 62
(E J O'Neill) *sn led: rdn along over 2f out: drvn and hdd over 1f out: wkng whn n.m.r jst ins fnl f* **6/1**[3]

26-0 **5** *¾* **Classic Contours (USA)**[20] 1098 3-8-11 **61**........ JamieMoriarty 4 59
(J J Quinn) *hld up in rr: hdwy over 2f out and sn rdn: styng on whn rdr dropped rein ins fnl f: nrst fin* **20/1**

666- **6** *1* **Dreamonandon (IRE)**[204] 6383 3-9-1 **65**........ PJMcDonald 9 61
(G A Swinbank) *trckd ldrs on inner: effrt and hdwy over 2f out: rdn wl over 1f out and sn no imp* **14/1**

5-20 **7** *2 ¼* **Dark Oasis**[50] 759 3-8-12 **62**........(b) SilvestreDeSousa 5 53
(K A Ryan) *in tch: pushed along and lost pl 4f out: nvr a factor* **9/1**

300- **8** *2* **Mohawk Ridge**[185] 6858 3-8-10 **60**........ PhillipMakin 11 47
(M Dods) *hld up: a towards rr* **7/1**

000- **9** *3 ½* **Night Knight (IRE)**[191] 6714 3-8-12 **62**........ MickyFenton 3 42
(M L W Bell) *chsd ldrs: rdn along wl over 2f out and sn wknd* **40/1**

603- **10** *6* **Punch Drunk**[177] 7052 3-9-2 **66**........ TPQueally 1 34
(J G Given) *cl up on outer: pushed along and hung bdly lft home bnd: sn rdn and wknd* **14/1**

400- **11** *3 ¼* **Pilot Light**[277] 4213 3-8-4 **54**........ DuranFentiman 8 16
(T D Easterby) *a in rr* **66/1**

0-23 **12** *2 ¼* **Jul's Lad (IRE)**[20] 1108 3-8-11 **66**........ DeanHeslop(5) 7 23
(M Mullineaux) *hld up in midfield: sme hdwy on outer whn hung bdly lft and v wd home bnd: sn bhd* **28/1**

4232 **13** 2 1/4 **Duke Of Normandy (IRE)**31 938 3-9-1 **65** JoeFanning 12 18
(B P J Baugh) *prom: effrt and cl up over 3f out: rdn wl over 2f out and sn wknd* **10/1**

2m 4.40s (-2.60) **Going Correction** -0.275s/f (Firm) **13** Ran SP% **121.4**
Speed ratings (Par 98): **99,96,94,93,92 91,90,88,85,80 78,76,74**
toteswinger: 1&2 £10.20, 1&3 £6.60, 2&3 £4.70 CSF £46.98 CT £170.12 TOTE £9.80: £2.60, £2.20, £2.10; EX 69.10.
Owner Kennet Valley Thoroughbreds V **Bred** C H Wacker Iii **Trained** Middleham Moor, N Yorks
■ Stewards' Enquiry : Dean Heslop one-day ban: used whip out of contention (May 7)

FOCUS
A few unexposed sorts lined up in this solidly run handicap, and it was one of those that came out on top. The form looks good for the grade.
Punch Drunk Official explanation: jockey said filly hung left round the bend
Jul's Lad(IRE) Official explanation: jockey said the gelding hung left throughout

1471 ST GEORGE'S DAY STKS (H'CAP) 7f 100y
3:00 (3:00) (Class 3) (0-90,83) 3-Y-O **£7,641** (£2,273; £1,136; £567) **Stalls** High

Form RPR

-113 **1** **Tartan Gunna**62 629 3-9-4 **83** JoeFanning 5 93+
(M Johnston) *trckd ldrs: hdwy 2f out: rdn over 1f out: led ent fnl f: drvn out* **11/4**2

2213 **2** 1 1/4 **Changing The Guard**26 1001 3-9-2 **81** (v) PaulHanagan 2 88
(R A Fahey) *t.k.h early: chsd ldr: hdwy 2f out: rdn to chal over 1f out: ev ch whn n.m.r and hmpd ent fnl f: sn drvn and kpt on* **6/5**1

50-0 **3** 2 1/2 **Thunderball**25 1019 3-9-0 **79** RobertWinston 6 79
(A J McCabe) *led: rdn along 2f out: drvn: edgd lft and hdd ent fnl f: one pce* **11/2**3

505- **4** 1/2 **Beautiful Breeze (IRE)**215 6112 3-8-9 **74** RoystonFfrench 3 73
(M Johnston) *wnt lft s: chsd ldrs: rdn along and sltly outpcd over 3f out: styd on u.p appr fnl f* **15/2**

220- **5** 8 **Lakeman (IRE)**166 7241 3-9-3 **82** TomEaves 4 61
(B Ellison) *in tch: effrt over 2f out: sn rdn and wknd* **12/1**

1-0 **6** 3 **Clumber Place**26 1001 3-8-9 **79** MarkCoumbe(5) 1 51
(R C Guest) *a in rr* **40/1**

1m 33.08s (-0.72) **Going Correction** -0.275s/f (Firm) **6** Ran SP% **109.4**
Speed ratings (Par 102): **93,91,88,88,79 75**
toteswinger: 1&2 £1.02, 1&3 £4.90, 2&3 £1.60 CSF £6.09 TOTE £3.60: £1.80, £1.10; EX 5.60.
Owner Mrs I Bird **Bred** Cheveley Park Stud Ltd **Trained** Middleham Moor, N Yorks

FOCUS
A fair handicap, but the top-weight was rated 7lb below the ceiling for the race. The front pair have nice enough profiles.

NOTEBOOK
Tartan Gunna, turned over at heavy odds-on at Wolverhampton last time, had been given a couple of months off since and returned to form with a workmanlike success, showing he can be just as effective on turf as he is on the all-weather. He's unlikely to want much further than a mile. (op 9-4 tchd 2-1)
Changing The Guard, who had the visor back on, got squeezed up as he was challenging between the winner and third a furlong out, but for which he would have finished closer. It is unlikely that he would have won, though. (op 2-1)
Thunderball, back to a more suitable trip, got the run of the race out in front and ran a solid race in defeat. He remains high enough in the weights. (op 9-2)
Beautiful Breeze(IRE), who didn't go on last year after winning his maiden here in August, ran on after getting outpaced and might need softer ground to be seen at his best. (op 8-1 tchd 11-1)

1472 HAPPY BIRTHDAY HUGH FILLIES' H'CAP 1m 1f 207y
3:30 (3:32) (Class 5) (0-70,68) 4-Y-O+ **£2,590** (£770; £385; £192) **Stalls** High

Form RPR

040- **1** **Shekan Star**191 6727 7-8-4 **54** oh9 PaulHanagan 8 59
(K G Reveley) *trckd ldng pair on inner: effrt 2f out and sn rdn: drvn ent fnl f: styd on to ld nr fin* **8/1**

12-0 **2** 1/2 **Cheers For Thea (IRE)**8 1279 4-8-7 **57** DavidAllan 6 61
(T D Easterby) *led: pushed along 2f out: rdn over 1f out: drvn ins fnl f and sn edgd rt: hdd and no ex nr fin* **85/40**1

1220 **3** nk **Snow Dancer (IRE)**8 1279 5-9-1 **68** (p) NeilBrown(3) 1 71
(H A McWilliams) *trckd ldr: hdwy and cl up 2f out: sn rdn: drvn and ev ch ins fnl f tl no ex towards fin* **3/1**2

500- **4** 2 1/4 **Twilight Dawn**50 3552 5-9-1 **65** TomEaves 4 64
(L Lungo) *trckd ldrs: pushed along 4f out: rdn over 2f out: drvn over 1f out and kpt on same pce* **10/1**

000- **5** shd **Umverti**215 6116 4-8-5 **55** FrancisNorton 2 54
(N Bycroft) *in rr: rdn along and outpcd 3f out: styd on u.p ins fnl f: nrst fin* **18/1**

114- **6** nk **Salerosa (IRE)**139 7559 4-8-9 **62** AndrewMullen(3) 7 60
(Mrs A Duffield) *t.k.h early: hld up in rr: hdwy 3f out: rdn 2f out and kpt on same pce fnl f* **4/1**3

30-6 **7** 16 **Grethel (IRE)**7 1306 5-8-1 **56** DanielleMcCreery(5) 3 22
(A Berry) *chsd ldrs: rdn along 3f out: sn wknd* **16/1**

000- **8** 7 **Awaken**294 3644 8-8-0 **55** oh6 ow1 MartinLane(5) 5 7
(Miss Tracy Waggott) *hld up in tch: pushed along over 3f out: rdn over 2f out and sn wknd* **20/1**

2m 6.29s (-0.71) **Going Correction** -0.275s/f (Firm) **8** Ran SP% **113.1**
Speed ratings (Par 100): **91,90,90,88,88 88,75,69**
toteswinger: 1&2 £4.00, 1&3 £4.90, 2&3 £1.80 CSF £24.86 CT £62.77 TOTE £9.70: £2.20, £1.10, £1.60; EX 26.80.
Owner D Young **Bred** The Welcome Alliance **Trained** Lingdale, Redcar & Cleveland
■ Stewards' Enquiry : David Allan caution: used whip with excessive frequency

FOCUS
A modest fillies' handicap run at an ordinary pace.

1473 LEVY BOARD H'CAP 1m 4f 16y
4:00 (4:00) (Class 4) (0-85,82) 4-Y-O+ **£4,727** (£1,406; £702; £351) **Stalls** High

Form RPR

60-3 **1** **Demolition**5 1347 5-9-5 **82** (p) LeeEnstone 3 89
(N Wilson) *trckd ldng pair: smoothy hdwy to ld over 2f out: rdn over 1f out: drvn ins fnl f: edgd lft and kpt on* **3/1**3

112- **2** 1/2 **Aleatricis**248 5146 4-8-9 **73** PaulHanagan 6 79
(J J Quinn) *hld up in rr: hdwy over 3f out: rdn wl over 1f out: drvn to chse wnr ent fnl f: no ex towards fin* **9/2**

0-44 **3** 9 **Step This Way (USA)**11 1230 4-9-2 **80** RoystonFfrench 1 72
(M Johnston) *hld up: hdwy over 3f out: chsd wnr 2f out: rdn over 1f out and kpt on same pce* **5/2**2

600/ **4** 34 **Admiral (IRE)**715 1582 8-8-13 **81** PatrickDonaghy(5) 2 18
(S Parr) *cl up: rdn along over 3f out: wknd 2f out* **12/1**

/32- **5** 17 **Sir Royal (USA)**358 1728 4-8-12 **76** PJMcDonald 4 —
(G A Swinbank) *slt ld: rdn along over 3f out: drvn and hdd over 2f out and sn wknd* **2/1**1

2m 35.83s (-5.07) **Going Correction** -0.275s/f (Firm)
WFA 4 from 5yo+ 1lb **5** Ran SP% **112.8**
Speed ratings (Par 105): **105,104,98,76,64**
toteswinger: 1&2 £8.20. CSF £16.60 TOTE £4.70: £1.50, £1.80; EX 14.10.
Owner M Wormald **Bred** P D And Mrs Player **Trained** Flaxton, N Yorks
■ Stewards' Enquiry : Patrick Donaghy £140 fine: used whip that had been modified in contravention of Instriction H8

FOCUS
With Sir Royal and Admiral taking each other on at a strong pace, the race fell into the hands of the improving winner.

1474 CONSTANT SECURITY MAIDEN STKS 1m 100y
4:30 (4:31) (Class 5) 3-Y-O+ **£2,590** (£770; £385; £192) **Stalls** High

Form RPR

34- **1** **The Fonz**195 6621 3-8-11 0 RyanMoore 8 79+
(Sir Michael Stoute) *trckd ldng pair: hdwy over 2f out: rdn wl over 1f out: swtchd lft and drvn ent fnl f: styd on wl to ld nr fin* **7/4**1

032- **2** nk **Wilfred Pickles (IRE)**205 6359 3-8-11 78 SebSanders 5 78
(Mrs A J Perrett) *trckd ldr: cl up 2f out and sn rdn: drvn to ld ent fnl f: hdd and no ex nr fin* **5/2**3

324- **3** 2 1/4 **Dr Jameson (IRE)**181 6946 3-8-11 76 PaulHanagan 1 73
(R A Fahey) *set stdy pce: qcknd 3f out: rdn wl over 1f out: drvn and hdd ent fnl f: kpt on same pce* **15/8**2

5 **4** 2 1/4 **Jenny Potts**19 1128 5-9-6 0 TomEaves 7 67
(L Lungo) *chsd ldrs: rdn along 2f out: drvn over 1f out: kpt on same pce* **10/1**

5 13 **Chichen Daawe** 3-8-6 0 RoystonFfrench 2 33
(B Ellison) *a outpcd in rr* **100/1**

5 **P** **Elusive Glen (IRE)**23 1054 3-8-11 0 JoeFanning 3 —
(M Johnston) *chsd ldrs: rdn along 2f out: drvn over 1f out: hld in 4th whn p.u lame jst ins fnl f* **16/1**

1m 47.44s (-0.16) **Going Correction** -0.275s/f (Firm)
WFA 3 from 4yo+ 14lb **6** Ran SP% **115.7**
Speed ratings (Par 103): **89,88,86,84,71** —
toteswinger: 1&2 £1.90, 1&3 £1.70, 2&3 £1.50 CSF £6.86 TOTE £2.20: £1.30, £1.50; EX 6.00.
Owner Anthony & David de Rothschild **Bred** Southcourt Stud **Trained** Newmarket, Suffolk

FOCUS
A fair maiden and there is probably more to come from the winner.

1475 NEXT RACEDAY HERE MONDAY 4TH MAY H'CAP 7f 100y
5:00 (5:02) (Class 6) (0-60,60) 4-Y-O+ **£1,942** (£578; £288; £144) **Stalls** High

Form RPR

0002 **1** **Lytton**22 1057 4-8-8 **55** (v) FrederikTylicki(5) 2 67
(R Ford) *s.i.s and swtchd rt s: gd hdwy on inner 3f out: rdn over 1f out: styd on strly ins fnl f to ld nr fin* **8/1**

5-63 **2** 3/4 **Ace Of Spies (IRE)**8 1276 4-8-8 **50** (v1) SilvestreDeSousa 8 60
(G A Harker) *led and sn clr: rdn wl over 1f out: drvn ins fnl f: wknd last 100yds and hdd nr fin* **13/2**2

360- **3** 1 1/4 **Mister Jingles**149 7441 6-8-13 **58** MichaelJStainton(3) 12 65
(R M Whitaker) *chsd ldng pair: hdwy to chse ldr over 2f out: sn rdn: drvn and kpt on fnl f* **11/1**

16-1 **4** 1 **Rossini's Dancer**17 1153 4-9-4 **60** PaulHanagan 16 64
(R A Fahey) *dwlt and towards rr: stdy hdwy on inner over 2f out: rdn wl over 1f out: styd on ins fnl f: nrst fin* **7/1**3

00-0 **5** 2 1/4 **Malinsa Blue (IRE)**8 1279 7-9-1 **57** (p) J-PGuillambert 3 56
(B Ellison) *chsd ldrs: rdn along over 2f out: drvn over 1f out: kpt on same pce* **20/1**

506- **6** 1/2 **King's Icon (IRE)**135 7613 4-8-8 **50** (p) FrancisNorton 13 48+
(M Wigham) *hld up in tch: hdwy to chse ldrs over 2f out: rdn wl over 1f out and sn no imp* **5/2**1

F-04 **7** 2 1/2 **Cheery Cat (USA)**10 1244 5-9-0 **56** (p) TonyHamilton 15 47
(D W Barker) *midfield: hdwy to chse ldrs over 2f out: sn rdn and no imp* **15/2**

4-00 **8** 1/2 **Yakama (IRE)**10 1260 4-9-2 **58** TGMcLaughlin 10 48
(Mrs C A Dunnett) *towards rr: hdwy over 2f out: sn rdn and kpt on same pce appr last* **25/1**

-600 **9** 2 1/4 **Sands Of Barra (IRE)**10 1258 6-9-3 **59** (p) PatrickMathers 14 43
(I W McInnes) *in tch: hdwy over 3f out: rdn over 2f out and sn no imp* **25/1**

50-0 **9** dht **Wiseman's Diamond (USA)**63 607 4-8-13 **55** LeeEnstone 7 39
(P T Midgley) *midfield: hdwy on wd outside over 2f out: sn rdn and n.d* **40/1**

-000 **11** 1/2 **Bright Falcon**3 1399 4-8-13 **60** (bt1) PatrickDonaghy(5) 4 43
(S Parr) *s.i.s: a in rr* **66/1**

0-06 **12** 1 **Forzarzi (IRE)**10 1244 5-9-1 **60** NeilBrown(3) 11 41
(H A McWilliams) *in tch: rdn along over 2f out: sn drvn and wknd* **20/1**

6250 **13** 1 **Epidaurian King (IRE)**8 1279 6-9-3 **59** DarrenWilliams 9 37
(D Shaw) *a towards rr* **16/1**

2355 **14** 1 **Trans Sonic**30 622 6-8-11 **60** (b) JamieKyne(7) 6 36
(A J Lockwood) *a towards rr* **50/1**

00- **15** 5 **Flashy Max**181 6955 4-8-9 **51** JoeFanning 1 14
(Jedd O'Keeffe) *chsd clr ldr: rdn along 3f out: sn wknd* **33/1**

0510 **16** 1 1/2 **All You Need (IRE)**57 675 5-8-10 **52** (p) RoystonFfrench 5 11
(R Hollinshead) *in rr fr 1/2-way* **20/1**

1m 32.1s (-1.70) **Going Correction** -0.275s/f (Firm) **16** Ran SP% **122.3**
Speed ratings (Par 101): **98,97,95,94,92 91,88,88,85,85 84,83,82,81,75 74**
toteswinger: 1&2 £10.30, 1&3 £16.90, 2&3 £15.70 CSF £51.91 CT £609.69 TOTE £9.90: £2.20, £2.30, £1.90, £1.40; EX 67.60 Place 6: £13.61, Place 5: £10.40.
Owner Tarporley Turf Club **Bred** Pendley Farm **Trained** Cotebrook, Cheshire

FOCUS
A competitive-looking handicap run at a strong pace.
King's Icon(IRE) Official explanation: jockey said the gelding failed to handle the bend
T/Plt: £17.70 to a £1 stake. Pool: £59,684.27. 2,449.57 winning tickets. T/Qpdt: £5.30 to a £1 stake. Pool: £2,390.56. 331.10 winning tickets. JR

[1436]SOUTHWELL (L-H)

Thursday, April 23

OFFICIAL GOING: Standard

Wind: Light, half-behind. Weather: fine and sunny

1476 BOOK YOUR TICKETS ONLINE MEDIAN AUCTION MAIDEN STKS 7f (F)

5:20 (5:21) (Class 6) 3-4-Y-O £2,047 (£604; £302) Stalls Low

Form RPR

4 1 **Miss Glitters (IRE)**[15] [1185] 4-9-7 0 SteveDrowne 4 82+
(H Morrison) *chsd ldrs: rdn to ld appr fnl f: drew clr: readily* 2/1[2]

03-2 2 5 **Oskari**[28] [963] 4-9-12 65 JamieMoriarty 5 70
(P T Midgley) *trckd ldrs: led 3f out tl appr fnl f: no ch w wnr* 6/5[1]

5-3 3 3½ **Crystal Feather**[28] [963] 3-8-8 0 LPKeniry 6 51
(E F Vaughan) *chsd ldrs: one pce fnl 2f* 8/1[3]

4 4 **Shannon Golden** 3-8-13 0 FergusSweeney 7 45
(S R Bowring) *dwlt: hdwy to chse ldrs over 3f out: hung lft and wknd over 1f out* 28/1

-440 5 1¾ **Where's Killoran**[10] [1243] 4-9-4 44 AndrewMullen(3) 2 40
(E J Alston) *led tl 3f out: wknd over 1f out* 25/1

6 ¾ **Flaming Blaze** 3-8-13 0 AndrewElliott 8 38
(P C Haslam) *sn chsng ldrs on outer: lost pl 3f out* 9/1

7 6 **Quiet Mountain (IRE)** 4-9-12 0 PaulMulrennan 3 27
(Ollie Pears) *s.s: hdwy to chse ldrs over 4f out: lost pl over 2f out: lame* 12/1

6 8 10 **Ereeford**[56] [686] 3-8-6 0 BMcHugh(7) 1 —
(M W Easterby) *chsd ldrs: rdn and lost pl over 4f out: wl bhd fnl 3f* 66/1

1m 29.79s (-0.51) **Going Correction** -0.05s/f (Stan)
WFA 3 from 4yo 13lb 8 Ran SP% **116.4**
Speed ratings (Par 101): **100,94,90,85,83 82,76,64**
toteswinger: 1&2 £2.60, 1&3 £13.50, 2&3 £5.10 CSF £4.77 TOTE £3.50: £1.40, £1.02, £2.90; EX 4.90.
Owner Mrs M D W Morrison **Bred** Roger And Henry O'Callaghan **Trained** East Ilsley, Berks

FOCUS
A modest maiden won in impressive style. It has been rated around the runner-up being a bit below his previous course and distance form.
Quiet Mountain(IRE) Official explanation: vet said gelding was lame post-race

1477 DINE IN THE QUEEN MOTHER RESTAURANT CLAIMING STKS 6f (F)

5:50 (5:50) (Class 6) 3-Y-O+ £2,047 (£604; £302) Stalls Low

Form RPR

1221 1 **Imprimis Tagula (IRE)**[28] [965] 5-9-0 77 (v) LeeNewnes(7) 5 87
(A Bailey) *w ldrs: led over 2f out: kpt on wl* 7/4[1]

0110 2 1½ **Swinbrook (USA)**[16] [1169] 8-9-4 74 (v) JamieMoriarty 11 79
(R A Fahey) *trckd ldrs: effrt over 2f out: kpt on to take 2nd towards fin* 5/2[2]

1400 3 ¾ **Realt Na Mara (IRE)**[16] [1169] 6-9-3 72 (p) TravisBlock 9 76
(H Morrison) *hmpd s: sn chsng ldrs: chal over 1f out: kpt on same pce ins fnl f* 4/1[3]

60-0 4 10 **Sheik'N'Knotsterd**[8] [1276] 4-9-1 47 ChrisCatlin 6 42
(J F Coupland) *led tl over 2f out: lost pl over 1f out* 66/1

00-0 5 2¾ **Minimum Fuss (IRE)**[77] [401] 5-8-3 38 AndrewHeffernan(7) 10 28
(M C Chapman) *led to post: w ldrs: wknd over 1f out* 150/1

53-0 6 5 **Danish Art (IRE)**[31] [934] 4-8-11 72 BMcHugh(7) 4 20
(M W Easterby) *dwlt: lost pl over 4f out: sn bhd* 16/1

0021 7 1 **Northern Empire (IRE)**[34] [891] 6-9-6 77 NCallan 2 19
(K A Ryan) *chsd ldrs: drvn 3f out: hung bdly rt and wknd over 1f out* 6/1

10-6 8 shd **Yahwudhee (FR)**[28] [965] 4-9-4 75 DaleGibson 3 17
(N Wilson) *mid-div: drvn over 4f out: lost pl 3f out* 66/1

/0-0 9 ¾ **Western Art (USA)**[31] [933] 4-9-4 80 PaulMulrennan 7 14
(M W Easterby) *wnt rt s: towards rr: hung rt and lost pl over 4f out* 25/1

1m 16.33s (-0.17) **Going Correction** -0.05s/f (Stan) 9 Ran SP% **112.6**
Speed ratings (Par 101): **99,97,96,82,79 72,71,70,69**
toteswinger: 1&2 £1.80, 1&3 £1.80, 2&3 £2.10 CSF £5.97 TOTE £3.10: £1.10, £1.50, £1.80; EX 8.00.
Owner A Bailey **Bred** Glashare House Stud **Trained** Newmarket, Suffolk

FOCUS
The winner has an excellent record over this course and distance and this looks a personal-best effort from him, with the runner-up and third being rated close to their marks.
Northern Empire(IRE) Official explanation: jockey said the gelding hung badly right in the home straight
Western Art(USA) Official explanation: jockey said the gelding hung right

1478 SPONSOR A RACE AT SOUTHWELL H'CAP 1m 4f (F)

6:20 (6:21) (Class 5) (0-75,75) 4-Y-0+ £3,070 (£906; £453) Stalls Low

Form RPR

5035 1 **Onemoreandstay**[10] [1261] 4-8-6 63 (p) RobertWinston 9 71
(M D Squance) *sn chsng ldrs: led 3f out: hrd rdn over 1f out: hld on wl* 4/1[2]

0220 2 1 **Rawdon (IRE)**[16] [1175] 8-8-8 71 ow1 (bt) KylieManser(7) 7 77
(Miss Gay Kelleway) *trckd ldrs: smooth hdwy on ins over 2f out: chal 1f out: sn drvn and kpt on same pce wl ins fnl f* 8/1

2-44 3 1½ **Elk Trail (IRE)**[36] [93] 4-8-9 66 MickyFenton 4 70
(Mrs P Sly) *rrd s: set mod pce: qcknd over 4f out: hdd 3f out: kpt on same pce fnl 2f* 6/1[3]

100- 4 3¾ **Crimson Mitre**[228] [3393] 4-8-13 70 LukeMorris 6 68
(J Jay) *trckd ldrs: rdn over 2f out: fdd appr fnl f* 33/1

2313 5 ½ **They All Laughed**[22] [1059] 6-9-5 75 (b) ChrisCatlin 10 72
(P W Hiatt) *hld up in rr: hdwy 6f out: hrd drvn and outpcd over 3f out: kpt on fnl 2f* 11/4[1]

56-0 6 9 **Intersky Charm (USA)**[15] [1192] 5-8-10 66 PaulMulrennan 1 48
(R M Whitaker) *hld up in rr: drvn over 4f out: nvr on terms* 9/1

4P0- 7 12 **Stringsofmyheart**[209] [6248] 5-9-0 70 JamieMoriarty 3 33
(J J Quinn) *hld up in rr: drvn over 3f out: sn btn* 14/1

-005 8 1½ **Sommersturm (GER)**[38] [848] 5-8-8 64 TPQueally 5 25
(B J Curley) *trckd ldrs: tk quite t.k.h: drvn over 4f out: sn lost pl and bhd* 4/1[2]

60/0 9 1¼ **Slip Silver**[10] [1242] 5-8-2 61 oh16 (e[1]) DavidProbert(3) 2 20
(R C Guest) *trckd ldrs: drvn over 4f out: sn lost pl and bhd* 80/1

066- 10 3 **Clearing House**[360] [1669] 4-8-5 62 oh1 ow1 SaleemGolam 8 16
(R W Price) *stdd s: t.k.h in rr: hdwy 7f out: drvn and lost pl over 3f out: sn bhd* 33/1

2m 41.52s (0.52) **Going Correction** -0.05s/f (Stan)
WFA 4 from 5yo+ 1lb 10 Ran SP% **115.8**
Speed ratings (Par 103): **96,95,94,91,91 85,77,76,75,73**
toteswinger: 1&2 £12.90, 1&3 £6.80, 2&3 £5.80 CSF £35.27 CT £190.50 TOTE £5.80: £1.70, £1.80, £2.60; EX 51.20.
Owner Mrs Elizabeth Macdonald **Bred** The Duke Of Devonshire **Trained** Newmarket, Suffolk

FOCUS
This was not run at a fast pace, but it proved impossible for anything to come from behind. The runner-up and third have been rated close to their marks.
Sommersturm(GER) Official explanation: trainer's representative was unable to offer any explanation for the poor form shown

1479 SOUTHWELL GOLF CLUB H'CAP 1m (F)

6:50 (6:50) (Class 5) (0-75,75) 4-Y-O+ £2,729 (£806; £403) Stalls Low

Form RPR

1020 1 **Hilbre Court (USA)**[43] [807] 4-8-11 68 (p) RobertWinston 8 78
(B P J Baugh) *chsd ldrs on outside: drvn over 4f out: led and edgd lft over 1f out: hld on towards fin* 6/1[3]

-326 2 nk **Barataria**[43] [807] 7-8-12 69 TPQueally 6 78
(R Bastiman) *trckd ldrs: effrt between horses: upsides and hmpd appr fnl f: no ex wl ins fnl f* 8/1

0-14 3 2½ **Street Devil (USA)**[2] [1415] 4-9-4 75 DarryllHolland 9 79
(R Curtis) *w ldrs: hrd rdn to ld over 2f out: edgd rt and hdd over 1f out: kpt on same pce* 11/4[1]

6-62 4 2¼ **White Deer (USA)**[6] [1333] 5-9-2 73 (b) AdrianTNicholls 5 71
(D Nicholls) *w ldrs: led over 3f out: hdd over 2f out: one pce appr fnl f* 5/1[2]

0060 5 2 **Flying Squad (UAE)**[12] [1213] 5-8-11 68 SteveDrowne 11 62
(M F Harris) *mid-div on outer: kpt on fnl 2f: nvr rchd ldrs* 25/1

542- 6 8 **Paraguay (USA)**[205] [6352] 6-9-3 74 EdwardCreighton 7 49
(Mrs D J Sanderson) *s.s: hdwy to chse ldrs over 3f out: lost pl 2f out* 9/1

3220 7 ½ **Ours (IRE)**[16] [1170] 6-9-4 75 (p) ChrisCatlin 2 49
(John A Harris) *s.i.s: sn wl bhd: nvr on terms* 12/1

1301 8 2½ **All In The Red (IRE)**[15] [1192] 4-9-0 71 (v) TomEaves 10 39
(A Crook) *s.i.s: sn bhd: nvr on terms* 8/1

060- 9 nk **My Paris**[185] [6862] 8-8-13 70 JamieMoriarty 4 38
(Ollie Pears) *reminders after s: sn w ldrs: led over 4f out: hdd over 3f out: lost pl over 2f out* 12/1

5-51 10 3¼ **Having A Ball**[21] [1080] 5-8-8 65 SimonWhitworth 1 25
(P D Cundell) *in tch: sn drvn along: lost pl over 3f out: sn bhd* 14/1

1040 11 5 **West End Lad**[43] [807] 6-8-9 66 (b) FergusSweeney 3 15
(S R Bowring) *mde most tl over 4f out: lost pl over 3f out: sn bhd* 22/1

1m 42.68s (-1.02) **Going Correction** -0.05s/f (Stan) 11 Ran SP% **120.1**
Speed ratings (Par 103): **103,102,100,97,95 87,87,84,84,81 76**
toteswinger: 1&2 £3.50, 1&3 £3.40, 2&3 £6.80. CSF £54.65 CT £164.03 TOTE £9.90: £3.20, £2.00, £1.60; EX 70.10.
Owner Saddle Up Racing **Bred** Richard Nip & Omar Trevino **Trained** Audley, Staffs

FOCUS
There was no great pace on here and the form looks ordinary for the grade.
Ours(IRE) Official explanation: jockey said the gelding was never travelling
All In The Red(IRE) Official explanation: jockey said that the gelding missed the break
My Paris Official explanation: jockey said the gelding had no more to give
Having A Ball Official explanation: jockey said that the gelding resented the kick-back

1480 BOOK YOUR HOSPITALITY PACKAGES H'CAP 7f (F)

7:20 (7:22) (Class 5) (0-70,70) 4-Y-0+ £2,729 (£806; £403) Stalls Low

Form RPR

4330 1 **Punching**[22] [1060] 5-9-2 68 LPKeniry 10 79
(C R Dore) *trckd ldrs gng wl: nt clr run 2f out: led 1f out: hrd rdn end edgd rt: hld on towards fin* 10/1

0-00 2 ¾ **Tiger Dream**[19] [1123] 4-9-4 70 (p) NCallan 7 79
(K A Ryan) *hmpd after 100yds: hdwy to chse ldrs over 3f out: edgd lft and led over 1f out: hdd 1f out: edgd rt and no ex ins fnl f* 9/2[2]

30-6 3 hd **Ancient Cross**[22] [1060] 5-8-13 65 DaleGibson 9 73
(M W Easterby) *chsd ldrs: drvn and outpcd 4f out: chsng ldrs 2f out: crowded and no ex ins fnl f* 9/2[2]

3122 4 3¼ **Ballycroy Boy (IRE)**[27] [975] 4-9-1 67 (b) AdamKirby 4 67
(Miss M E Rowland) *prom: drvn over 4f out: chsd ldrs over 1f out: hung rt and lft: one pce* 8/1[3]

0 5 4½ **Golden Future**[37] [857] 6-8-4 56 oh5 ChrisCatlin 8 44
(P D Niven) *hmpd after s and sn wl bhd: styd on fnl 2f: nrst fin* 16/1

6611 6 1½ **Lethal**[10] [1259] 6-8-9 66 6ex FrederikTylicki(5) 12 49
(R A Fahey) *w ldrs: led over 3f out: hdd over 1f out: sn wknd* 5/2[1]

5100 7 nk **Vanatina (IRE)**[73] [473] 5-8-4 56 oh7 DuranFentiman 3 39
(W M Brisbourne) *led tl over 3f out: wknd over 1f out* 66/1

306- 8 1¼ **Big Slick (IRE)**[259] [4782] 4-8-5 57 TWilliams 2 36
(M Brittain) *reminders after s: sn w ldrs: wknd over 1f out* 20/1

2504 9 ¾ **Crocodile Bay (IRE)**[10] [1259] 6-8-12 69 (b) MarkCoumbe(5) 13 46
(John A Harris) *w ldrs: hmpd and lost pl over 1f out* 14/1

0266 10 3 **Royal Challenge**[20] [1103] 8-9-2 68 PatrickMathers 6 37
(I W McInnes) *prom: drvn and lost pl over 4f out* 40/1

000- 11 21 **Little Pandora**[188] [6791] 5-7-11 56 oh11 JamieKyne(7) 11 —
(L R James) *sn bhd and hung rt: sddle slipped and eased fnl f* 80/1

0-20 12 2½ **This Ones For Pat (USA)**[16] [1169] 4-8-11 63 (p) AdrianTNicholls 1 —
(S Parr) *prom on inner: lost pl over 4f out: bhd and eased fnl f* 14/1

26-0 13 1¼ **Top Tribute**[10] [1244] 4-8-11 63 MickyFenton 5 —
(T P Tate) *w ldrs: lost pl 3f out: heavily eased over 1f out* 8/1[3]

1m 29.27s (-1.03) **Going Correction** -0.05s/f (Stan) 13 Ran SP% **125.4**
Speed ratings (Par 103): **103,102,101,98,93 91,91,89,88,85 61,58,57**
toteswinger: 1&2 £13.00, 1&3 £13.00, 2&3 £10.80. CSF £56.27 CT £241.27 TOTE £14.10: £3.20, £2.50, £2.30; EX 77.00.
Owner Liam Breslin **Bred** Cheveley Park Stud Ltd **Trained** Cowbit, Lincs
■ Stewards' Enquiry : N Callan one-day ban: careless riding (May 7)

FOCUS
A rough race run at a sound pace, rated around the third as back to form.
Ballycroy Boy(IRE) Official explanation: jockey said the gelding hung both ways

Little Pandora Official explanation: jockey said the mare's saddle slipped

1481 SOUTHWELL-RACECOURSE.CO.UK H'CAP — 1m (F)

7:50 (7:50) (Class 6) (0-60,60) 3-Y-O — £2,047 (£604; £302) Stalls Low

Form — RPR

000- **1** **Postman**[178] 7016 3-9-0 **56** .... TomEaves 12 — 75
(B Smart) *t.k.h: w ldrs on outside: led over 3f out: shot clr ins fnl f: eased towards fin* **11/2**[2]

3-33 **2** *7* **Miss Cameo (USA)**[8] 1281 3-8-6 **48** .... PaulQuinn 11 — 50
(R M Whitaker) *chsd ldrs on outer: kpt on to take modest 2nd ins fnl f: no ch w wnr* **15/8**[1]

0-10 **3** *1 1/4* **Reigning In Rio (IRE)**[62] 620 3-8-3 **50** .... PatrickDonaghy(5) 5 — 50
(P C Haslam) *led: hdd 3f out: styd on same pce fnl 2f* **8/1**[3]

050- **4** *1/2* **On Cue (IRE)**[178] 7015 3-8-12 **54** .... LukeMorris 13 — 52
(J M P Eustace) *trckd ldrs on outside: styd on same pce fnl 2f* **10/1**

6-60 **5** *7* **Valkyrie (IRE)**[15] 1183 3-8-13 **55** .... NCallan 6 — 37
(N P Littmoden) *w ldrs: wknd over 1f out: eased* **16/1**

00-5 **6** *1* **Northern Flyer (GER)**[43] 810 3-8-13 **55** .... JamieMoriarty 9 — 35
(J J Quinn) *sn chsng ldrs towards outer: rdn over 2f out: lost pl over 1f out* **12/1**

0-66 **7** *nk* **Meydan Style (USA)**[17] 1157 3-8-4 **46** .... AndrewElliott 7 — 25
(J Balding) *hmpd s: in rr: kpt on fnl 2f: nvr on terms* **22/1**

00-0 **8** *2* **Terracotta Warrior**[2] 1441 3-8-3 **48** .... DominicFox(3) 8 — 23
(J Jay) *s.i.s: sme hdwy 2f out: hung lft: nvr a factor* **33/1**

020- **9** *hd* **Kristopher James (IRE)**[143] 7519 3-9-2 **58** .... TGMcLaughlin 10 — 32
(W M Brisbourne) *s.i.s: sn chsng ldrs: reminders over 4f out: hung lft and lost pl 2f out: eased ins fnl f* **11/2**[2]

060- **10** *nse* **Sofonisba**[168] 7207 3-9-1 **57** .... MickyFenton 3 — 31
(M L W Bell) *s.i.s: t.k.h: sn trcking ldrs: lost pl over 1f out* **10/1**

04-0 **11** *34* **Murrays Magic (IRE)**[20] 1098 3-8-8 **50** .... AdrianTNicholls 2 — —
(D Nicholls) *w ldr: lost pl over 2f out: sn eased: t.o* **20/1**

0-46 **12** *2 1/2* **Got Flash (FR)**[28] 968 3-9-0 **56** .... ChrisCatlin 1 — —
(E J O'Neill) *s.i.s: a in rr: bhd fnl 3f: t.o* **28/1**

1m 43.23s (-0.47) **Going Correction** -0.05s/f (Stan) — **12** Ran SP% **123.9**
Speed ratings (Par 96): **100,93,91,91,84 83,82,80,80,80 46,44**
toteswinger: 1&2 £5.70, 1&3 £5.70, 2&3 £3.90. CSF £16.15 CT £88.51 TOTE £5.60: £1.30, £2.00, £3.80; EX 25.20 Place 6 £17.75, Palce 5 £15.81..
Owner Crossfields Racing **Bred** Newsells Park Stud **Trained** Hambleton, N Yorks
■ Stewards' Enquiry : Paul Quinn two-day ban: used whip with excessive frequency (May 7-8)

FOCUS
Low grade stuff, but the winner showed much improved form for his first outing on this surface. The third gives the form substance.
Terracotta Warrior Official explanation: jockey said that the gelding hung left
Murrays Magic(IRE) Official explanation: jockey said the filly had no more to give
T/Plt: £67.80 to a £1 stake. Pool: £54,072.18. 581.55 winning tickets. T/Qpdt: £154.30 to a £1 stake. Pool: £4,797.86. 23.00 winning tickets. WG

CHANTILLY (R-H)

Thursday, April 23

OFFICIAL GOING: Good

1482a PRIX DE PREMIER PAS (UNRACED) — 5f

1:50 (1:57) 2-Y-O — £11,650 (£4,660; £2,495; £2,330; £1,165)

RPR

1 **Irish Cat (IRE)** 2-8-13 .... OPeslier 10 — 78
(Robert Collet, France)

2 *1/2* **Too Nice Name (FR)** 2-9-2 .... RBriard 7 — 79
(Robert Collet, France)

3 *5* **Bemboka** 2-8-13 .... MickaelForest 3 — 58
(R Pritchard-Gordon, France)

4 *3/4* **Marosh (FR)** 2-9-2 .... ShaneKelly 9 — 59
(R M H Cowell) *broke wl in centre: 6th and pushed along 1/2-way: rdn 2f out: styd on to take 4th 1f out* **63/10**[1]

5 *2* **Novlime (FR)** 2-8-13 .... GBenoist 8 — 48
(J-V Toux, France)

6 *2* **Shine A Line (FR)** 2-8-13 .... MGuyon 6 — 41
(U Suter, France)

7 *snk* **Toxeas (FR)** 2-9-2 .... GMasure 11 — 44
(C Laffon-Parias, France)

8 *3* **Lady Of Diktat (FR)** 2-8-13 .... WVion 4 — 30
(Mme C Vergne & D Sicaud, France)

9 *5* **Wo Ay Ni (BEL)** 2-8-13 .... FLefebvre 2 — 12
(Mlle M Dere, France)

10 *6* **Le Castellanais (FR)** 2-9-2 .... TPiccone 1 — —
(B Dutruel, France)

11 **Perequito (FR)** 2-9-2 .... IMendizabal 5 — —
(Peter Scotton, Germany)

59.90 secs (1.80) — **11** Ran SP% **13.7**
PARI-MUTUEL: WIN 10.10 (coupled with Too Nice Name): PL 3.60, 6.20, 12.70; DF 79.40.
Owner Mme D Ricard **Bred** Stone Ridge Farm **Trained** Chantilly, France

NOTEBOOK
Marosh(FR), rather outpaced in the early stages, learnt more and more as the race went on. He really got in to his stride in the last furlong and a half and finished really well. It was a promising first effort.

1483 - (Foreign Racing) - See Raceform Interactive

SANDOWN (R-H)

Friday, April 24

OFFICIAL GOING: Sprint course - good to firm (good in places; 8.6); round course - good (8.4)
Wind: Moderate, behind Weather: Sunny

1484 BET365.COM ESHER CUP (H'CAP) — 1m 14y

1:25 (1:27) (Class 2) (0-100,100) 3-Y-O

£15,577 (£4,665; £2,332; £1,167; £582; £292) Stalls High

Form — RPR

21- **1** **Racketeer (IRE)**[132] 7660 3-8-4 **86** oh1 .... NickyMackay 1 — 102+
(J H M Gosden) *lw: trckd ldr: clsd smoothly to ld 2f out: pushed clr fr over 1f out: r.o wl* **10/3**[2]

212 **2** *6* **Thief Of Time (IRE)**[22] 1086 3-8-5 **87** oh2 ow1 .... AlanMunro 3 — 89
(P W Chapple-Hyam) *hld up in 7th: rdn and prog on outer over 2f out: wnt 2nd over 1f out: sn brushed aside* **13/8**[1]

40-0 **3** *2* **Midnight Cruiser (IRE)**[20] 1118 3-8-9 **91** .... RichardHughes 6 — 88
(R Hannon) *lw: trckd ldng trio: gng wl enough over 2f out: rdn and effrt wl over 1f out: plugged on one pce* **14/1**

141- **4** *3 1/4* **Feeling Fab (FR)**[202] 6477 3-8-9 **91** .... JimCrowley 8 — 81
(M Johnston) *racd freely: led at gd pce: clr 1/2-way: hdd 2f out: wknd fnl f* **11/2**[3]

0-30 **5** *2 3/4* **Sohcahtoa (IRE)**[13] 1211 3-9-4 **100** .... RyanMoore 7 — 84
(R Hannon) *hld up in last and wl off the pce: rdn and prog on outer over 2f out: chsd ldrs over 1f out: wknd rapidly fnl f* **8/1**

105- **6** *3 3/4* **Cruikadyke**[189] 6779 3-8-13 **95** .... JohnEgan 5 — 70
(P F I Cole) *hld up in 6th: rdn wl over 2f out: no prog: sn btn* **14/1**

03-6 **7** *14* **Effort**[27] 1002 3-8-8 **90** .... SteveDrowne 2 — 33
(M Johnston) *dwlt: sn rcvrd to chse ldng pair: rdn over 2f out: wknd rapidly: t.o* **20/1**

420- **8** *9* **Zaffaan**[225] 5827 3-8-10 **92** .... RHills 4 — 14
(E A L Dunlop) *hld up in 5th: shkn up and no rspnse over 2f out: sn wknd and eased: t.o* **10/1**

1m 42.92s (-0.38) **Going Correction** +0.10s/f (Good) — **8** Ran SP% **114.9**
Speed ratings (Par 104): **105,99,97,93,91 87,73,64**
toteswinger: 1&2 £2.70, 1&3 £7.40, 2&3 £6.50 CSF £9.20 CT £64.08 TOTE £4.20: £1.30, £1.30, £3.70; EX 8.20 Trifecta £81.60 Pool: £331.17 - 3.00 winning units..
Owner Duke Of Roxburghe **Bred** Floors Farming **Trained** Newmarket, Suffolk

FOCUS
This is often a decent contest and the manner in which Racketeer won suggests we may have seen a future Group performer. He and the runner-up stood out on form, despite being just out of the handicap, and the race could be rated even higher.

NOTEBOOK
Racketeer(IRE), making his turf debut, having narrowly won a Southwell maiden in December, this half-brother to 1000 Guineas winner Attraction was always travelling powerfully in behind the pace-setter and was still full of running passing the two-pole. The response was impressive when asked to stretch and he powered clear inside the final furlong. Winning here off a mark of 86 (1lb out of the weights), he can expect to be hit hard for this success and it will be interesting to see where he goes next. (op 3-1 tchd 7-2)
Thief Of Time(IRE), putting up 1lb overweight and having to race from 2lb out of the handicap, was narrowly denied over 1m2f on his handicap debut at Leicester and this drop back to 1m failed to help, for all that he again ran well. He remains capable of better back up in trip and time may show he faced an impossible task trying to compete off levels against the winner. (tchd 15-8 and 7-4 in a place)
Midnight Cruiser(IRE), tried in the Group 1 Racing Post Trophy on his final start at two, hung badly right throughout on his reappearance at Lingfield, finishing last, and it was no surprise to see a better effort on this right-handed track. He travelled well for a long way and may be worth a go back at 7f. (tchd 12-1)
Feeling Fab(FR), who signed off her juvenile campaign with a hard-fought victory at Newmarket, was reappearing off a 4lb higher mark and set off in front, ensuring there was a fair gallop. She had been joined by the winner with two to run, though, and ultimately faded. (op 4-1 tchd 6-1)
Sohcahtoa(IRE), a good third at Kempton on his reappearance, failed to run to form in a Listed contest back there last time and he always looked likely to struggle here off a mark of 100, stopping quickly inside the final furlong. (op 12-1 tchd 14-1)
Zaffaan was reported to have been unsuited by the going. Official explanation: trainer's rep said gelding was unsuited by the good going (op 16-1 tchd 18-1)

1485 BET365 CLASSIC TRIAL (GROUP 3) — 1m 2f 7y

2:00 (2:00) (Class 1) 3-Y-O

£36,900 (£13,988; £7,000; £3,490; £1,748; £877) Stalls High

Form — RPR

05-2 **1** **Above Average (IRE)**[27] 998 3-9-0 80 .... MichaelHills 3 — 101
(B W Hills) *lw: s.i.s: sn rcvrd: trckd ldr 1/2-way: rdn and sustained chal fr 2f out: upsides fnl f: narrow ld nr fin* **25/1**

24-1 **2** *hd* **Big Bound (USA)**[25] 1034 3-9-0 83 .... JimmyFortune 4 — 101
(J H M Gosden) *led at mod pce: rdn and pressed 2f out: kpt on wl u.p: hdd nr fin* **6/1**[3]

3 *1 3/4* **Malibu Bay (USA)**[198] 6589 3-9-0 0 .... JMurtagh 2 — 99+
(A P O'Brien, Ire) *str: w'like: trckd ldr to 1/2-way: 3rd after: stuck in bhd ldng pair fr 3f out: plld out last 150yds: pushed along and one pce* **2/1**[2]

2- **4** *2 1/4* **Saptapadi (IRE)**[146] 7498 3-9-0 0 .... RyanMoore 6 — 93+
(Sir Michael Stoute) *unf: hld up in last trio: rdn and hanging rt fr 3f out: effrt to dispute 3rd 1f out: fdd* **13/2**

12- **5** *2* **Taameer**[195] 6648 3-9-0 104 .... RHills 5 — 89
(M P Tregoning) *hld up in last trio: effrt on outer 3f out: no imp u.p 2f out: fdd* **13/8**[1]

12-3 **6** *43* **Mishrif (USA)**[13] 1211 3-9-0 97 .... AlanMunro 1 — 3
(P W Chapple-Hyam) *hld up in last trio: rdn and wknd over 3f out: wl t.o* **12/1**

2m 10.24s (-0.26) **Going Correction** +0.10s/f (Good) — **6** Ran SP% **110.6**
Speed ratings (Par 108): **105,104,103,101,100 65**
toteswinger: 1&2 £4.10, 1&3 £3.70, 2&3 £3.30 CSF £154.66 TOTE £21.90: £4.80, £2.80; EX 68.90.
Owner J Hanson **Bred** C O P Hanbury **Trained** Lambourn, Berks

FOCUS
A race that has been an informative Derby trial in the past, but with favourite Taameer flopping, Malibu Bay looking slightly unlucky, and outsider of the field Above Average springing a surprise, it has to go down as an unsatisfactory result.

NOTEBOOK
Above Average(IRE), a maiden with an official rating of 80 coming into this, had just been touched-off at Doncaster on his reappearance and things did not start well here as he missed the break, his rider having intended to make the running. He soon came through to hold a prominent position though, and with Hills holding in the Irish raider and no other challenges coming from behind, he was able to wear down the long-time leader. This represented a massive step up on his previous achievements and it looks likely that he will improve for going up to 1m4f, but general Derby quotes of 50/1 look about right at this stage. A trip to Chester for either the Dee Stakes or Vase is next on the agenda. (op 20-1)
Big Bound(USA), workmanlike winner of a 1m2f Lingfield maiden on his seasonal reappearance, very much enjoyed the run of things out in front and kicked again over 2f out. He did not give up without a fight, battling on willingly right the way to the line, but in the end was unable to hold on. This represented a step up, for all that he did have things go his way, and perhaps he could find a small Listed race somewhere. Chester is also an option for him. (op 13-2)
Malibu Bay(USA), ridden by a 7lb claimer when making a winning debut last season, looked a solid second-favourite. He seemed nicely placed through the early stages, but got caught in behind the front pair in the straight, and he lacked a sufficient turn of foot once in the clear late on. One would imagine that victory would havebeen his had he endured a sustained run at things in the final quarter mile and he looks capable of winning a nice race, but the stable have other Derby contenders with much stronger claims. (tchd 5-2 in places)

Saptapadi(IRE) ◆, a Dante entry who finished runner-up in a 7f Wolverhampton maiden on his sole start at two, is a brother to Patkai, from the family of Islington, and was always likely to have improved from two to three. He still looked very green back in fourth, hanging under pressure, and should learn a good deal from this. There is more to come and winning an ordinary maiden should prove a formality. (op 11-2 tchd 5-1)
Taameer set a clear standard on form having finished runner-up in the Royal Lodge on his second and final outing at two. Though his trainer has yet to have a winner this season, it was surprising to see him produce such a laboured effort, coming under pressure early in the straight and finding little. His stamina was far from guaranteed at this trip, but he was beaten before that became an issue and he is left with a bit to prove now. (tchd 7-4 in places)
Mishrif(USA), a close third in the Easter Stakes on his seasonal reappearance, looked well worth a try at this extra distance, but he was a beaten horse straightening for home and the way he dropped out suggests something may have been amiss. (op 16-1 tchd 11-1)

1486 BET365 BEST ODDS GUARANTEED ON EVERY RACE H'CAP 5f 6y
2:35 (2:40) (Class 2) (0-100,97) 3-Y-O

£11,215 (£3,358; £1,679; £840; £419; £210) **Stalls** High

Form RPR
201- **1** **Master Of Disguise**[184] 6894 3-8-10 **84**........................ PhilipRobinson 9 101+
(C G Cox) *racd against rail: trckd ldng pair: plld out and rdn to ld 1f out: sn in command* **3/1**[1]
114- **2** 2 ¼ **Noble Storm (USA)**[181] 6972 3-9-1 **89**........................ GrahamGibbons 4 97
(E S McMahon) *taken down early: racd one off rail: disp ld tl def advantage wl over 1f out: hdd 1f out: styd on but no ch w wnr* **15/2**[3]
1-2 **3** 3 ¼ **Affluent**[22] 1078 3-8-6 **80**........................ SteveDrowne 10 76+
(R Charlton) *lw: rrd s: racd against rail: towards rr: prog over 1f out: kpt on to take 3rd ins fnl f: n.d* **3/1**[1]
500- **4** ½ **Able Master (IRE)**[195] 6644 3-9-9 **97**........................ RoystonFfrench 7 91+
(B Smart) *taken down early: hld up wl in rr and off the rail: nt clr run 2f out: swtchd to rail 1f out and styd on: no ch* **20/1**
2-23 **5** 1 ¼ **Glamorous Spirit (IRE)**[16] 1180 3-8-7 **84**........................ KevinGhunowa(3) 11 74
(R A Harris) *racd against rail: w ldr to wl over 1f out: wknd fnl f* **16/1**
101- **6** ½ **Cut The Cackle (IRE)**[200] 6540 3-8-11 **85**........................ JimCrowley 3 73
(P Winkworth) *dwlt: racd wd in last pair: shkn up 2f out: kpt on ins fnl f: no ch w ldrs* **10/1**
15-1 **7** 4 ½ **Brenin Taran**[6] 1368 3-8-10 **89** 6ex........................ AndreaAtzeni(5) 5 61
(D M Simcock) *taken down early: pushed along on outer bef 1/2-way: nvr bttr than midfield: wknd over 1f out* **5/1**[2]
02-4 **8** 2 ½ **Evelyn May (IRE)**[22] 1078 3-8-4 **78**........................ WilliamBuick 2 41
(B W Hills) *racd wdst of all in rr: rdn 1/2-way: sn struggling* **16/1**
050- **9** shd **Pocket's Pick (IRE)**[238] 5466 3-8-5 **79** ow1........................ AlanMunro 8 41
(G L Moore) *v free to post: pressed ldrs 3f: sn wknd* **28/1**
21-2 **10** ½ **Bobs Dreamflight**[105] 109 3-8-6 **80**........................ ChrisCatlin 1 41
(D K Ivory) *stdd s: hld up in detached last and racd wd: nvr a factor* **40/1**
610- **11** 2 **Gower Valentine**[210] 6240 3-8-7 **81**........................ TPO'Shea 6 34
(D Nicholls) *spd 2f: sn struggling: wl bhd fnl f* **10/1**

60.28 secs (-1.32) **Going Correction** -0.15s/f (Firm) 11 Ran SP% **119.0**
Speed ratings (Par 104): **104,100,95,94,92 91,84,80,80,79 76**
toteswinger: 1&2 £7.00, 1&3 £4.00, 2&3 £6.90 CSF £25.98 CT £75.47 TOTE £4.20: £1.70, £2.80, £1.70; EX 33.30.
Owner Courtenay Club **Bred** T R Lock **Trained** Lambourn, Berks

FOCUS
Time may show this to be a really decent sprint handicap.

NOTEBOOK
Master Of Disguise, who was strongly supported throughout the day, delivered in style, travelling nicely before picking up well once switched and staying on up the hill. A horse withbags of speed, he was thought a bit of at two and an opening handicap mark of 84 clearly underestimated him. Thought to be even better with a little juice in the ground, there is every reason to believe there is more to come and will be interesting to see where he goes next. (op 13-2)
Noble Storm(USA), a dual 6f soft-ground winner at Warwick last season, showed a surprising amount of speed on this seasonal return, doing well to get across from stall four, and he drew on nicely from the remainder. He was 7lb higher than when last winning, so seems to have improved from two to three, and this versatile sort should continue to pay his way in good 3yo sprints. (op 12-1 tchd 14-1)
Affluent would have been much closer had she not fluffed the start, but it has to be doubtful whether she would have beaten the winner. Up 3lb having finished second at Kempton on her seasonal reappearance, she stayed on the best she could back in third, without ever posing a serious threat, and remains of obvious interest for something similar. (op 11-4 tchd 10-3)
Able Master(IRE), who performed with credit at Pattern level on more than one occasion last season, was the eyecatcher of the race. Racing off a mark of 97, he was short of room from halfway, losing his position, and the race was all over once he found some room late on. This effort would suggest he has trained on, but he is not going to be the easiest to place with his rating.
Glamorous Spirit(IRE) has plenty of pace and she was always likely to show up for a long way, especially from the rails draw. She was unable to find any extra once passed by the winner, though, and faded out of the places in the final furlong.
Cut The Cackle(IRE), 3lb higher than when winning a 5f handicap at Windsor last October, did not have the best of draws and showed enough on this seasonal return to suggest there is a race in her off this sort of mark. (op 8-1)
Brenin Taran, shouldering a 6lb penalty for last week´s Thirsk victory, was edgy beforehand. Under pressure well over 2f out, he never looked like getting into it. (op 3-1 tchd 11-2)

1487 CASINO AT BET365.COM CONDITIONS STKS 1m 14y
3:10 (3:12) (Class 3) 3-Y-O **£7,477** (£2,239; £1,119; £560) **Stalls** High

Form RPR
143- **1** **Parthenon**[182] 6946 3-9-2 89........................ RoystonFfrench 4 102+
(M Johnston) *lw: mde all: rdn over 1f out: styd on wl: unchal and gng further clr fin* **11/10**[1]
1 **2** 4 ½ **Militarist (USA)**[8] 1297 3-9-2 0........................ JimmyFortune 5 92+
(J H M Gosden) *cl up: chsd wnr over 2f out: rdn and no imp fr over 1f out* **9/4**[2]
511- **3** 1 ¾ **Sonning Gate**[125] 7739 3-9-6 88........................ GeorgeBaker 2 92
(D R C Elsworth) *hld up in detached last: effrt to go 3rd wl over 1f out: one pce and no prog after* **8/1**
1- **4** 13 **Albaher**[271] 4446 3-9-2 0........................ RHills 3 73
(J L Dunlop) *w'like: t.k.h early: mostly chsd wnr to over 2f out: wknd rapidly and eased: t.o* **4/1**[3]

1m 44.47s (1.17) **Going Correction** +0.10s/f (Good) **4** Ran SP% **109.5**
Speed ratings (Par 102): **98,93,91,78**
CSF £3.90 TOTE £2.10; EX 3.50.
Owner Sheikh Hamdan Bin Mohammed Al Maktoum **Bred** Darley **Trained** Middleham Moor, N Yorks

FOCUS
Very little happened in this conditions stakes, Parthenon going off in front and gradually galloping his three rivals into the ground.

NOTEBOOK
Parthenon set off in front and gradually galloping his three rivals into the ground. Third off a mark of 88 at Doncaster on his third and final start at two (looked unlucky as he missed the break before staying on well late on), he seemed much happier out in front here and won in the manner of a horse that will stay at least another couple of furlongs in time. A big, long-striding horse with plenty of scope for improvement, it will be interesting to see where he goes next. (op 11-8)
Militarist(USA) created a good impression when winning at Newmarket on his debut, but he needed to have improved to beat the favourite and he was not up to doing so. This still represented a step up and he may do better in handicaps. (tchd 5-2 in places)
Sonning Gate, twice a winner at Lingfield last term, looked to have plenty to do against these, especially as he was conceding 4lb all round, and he ran about as well as could have been expected back in third. He remains an interesting horse for handicaps. (tchd 9-1)
Albaher, winner of an ordinary 6f Ascot maiden on his sole start at two, holds a 2000 Guineas engagement, and is also in the St James´s Palace Stakes, but his stamina looked far from guaranteed at this trip and he dropped right awayinside the final quarter mile, his rider reporting that he hung right. Official explanation: jockey said colt hung right (op 9-2)

1488 POKER AT BET365.COM MAIDEN FILLIES' STKS 1m 2f 7y
3:45 (3:50) (Class 4) 3-Y-O **£5,180** (£1,541; £770; £384) **Stalls** High

Form RPR
1 **Star Ruby (IRE)** 3-9-0 0........................ AlanMunro 6 96
(P W Chapple-Hyam) *str: bit bkwd: trckd ldr: led 2f out: shkn up to assert fnl f and edgd rt last 100yds: styd on wl* **9/4**[1]
4- **2** 2 ¼ **Hidden Brief**[178] 7054 3-9-0 0........................ PhilipRobinson 10 94+
(M A Jarvis) *w'like: scope: str: led: narrowly hdd 2f out: clr w wnr over 1f out: hld whn sltly hmpd last 100yds* **10/3**[2]
6- **3** 8 **Entreat**[174] 7140 3-9-0 0........................ RyanMoore 3 76
(Sir Michael Stoute) *w'like: tall: mostly in 4th tl chsd ldng pair over 2f out: lft wl bhd fr over 1f out* **4/1**[3]
0- **4** 5 **Silken Promise (USA)**[182] 6945 3-9-0 0........................ TedDurcan 8 66+
(W R Swinburn) *unf: scope: tall: hld up in 6th: wl outpcd fr 2f out: shuffled along and styd on steadily* **8/1**
0- **5** 2 ¾ **Silent Act (USA)**[174] 7141 3-9-0 0........................ JimCrowley 5 60+
(Mrs A J Perrett) *tall: lengthy: scope: hld up in 8th: nt clr run 3f out and over 2f out: already wl outpcd whn nt clr run again over 1f out: plugged on* **20/1**
6 ½ **Galilean Moon** 3-9-0 0........................ NCallan 4 59
(Sir Michael Stoute) *w'like: tall: scope: bit bkwd: settled in abt 9th: rdn on outer over 2f out: sn outpcd: no ch after* **16/1**
0- **7** ¾ **Hoboob (USA)**[258] 4870 3-9-0 0........................ RHills 11 58
(J L Dunlop) *bit bkwd: mostly chsd ldng pair to over 2f out: sn wknd* **14/1**
0- **8** 1 **My Chestnut Girl (USA)**[205] 6392 3-9-0 0........................ TPQueally 9 56
(H R A Cecil) *w'like: str: trckd ldrs in abt 5th: shkn up over 2f out: no prog whn n.m.r briefly 2f out: wl outpcd after* **16/1**
9 1 ¼ **Possibly A Ten (USA)** 3-9-0 0........................ JimmyFortune 7 53
(J H M Gosden) *b: leggy: unf: mostly in 10th: drvn 3f out: no prog and sn wl btn* **14/1**
10 3 ¾ **Cape Marien (IRE)** 3-9-0 0........................ ChrisCatlin 2 46
(D R Lanigan) *w'like: bit bkwd: s.i.s: sn pushed along and detached in last pair: nvr a factor* **40/1**
05- **11** ½ **Tomintoul Star**[185] 6884 3-9-0 0........................ IanMongan 1 45
(H R A Cecil) *leggy: settled in 7th: rdn and effrt on outer over 2f out: wknd wl over 1f out* **33/1**
12 2 ½ **Manarah (USA)** 3-9-0 0........................ TPO'Shea 12 40
(J H M Gosden) *w'like: bit bkwd: s.s: a in last pair and struggling* **33/1**

2m 9.95s (-0.55) **Going Correction** +0.10s/f (Good) **12** Ran SP% **123.1**
Speed ratings (Par 97): **106,104,97,93,91 91,90,89,88,85 85,83**
toteswinger: 1&2 £3.50, 1&3 £4.90, 2&3 £3.90 CSF £9.49 TOTE £3.80: £1.60, £1.70, £1.90; EX 13.50.
Owner Michael Tabor **Bred** Grangecon Stud **Trained** Newmarket, Suffolk
■ Stewards' Enquiry : Alan Munro one-day ban: careless riding (May 8)

FOCUS
This had the look of a good fillies´ maiden and the two that drew clear may prove to be smart.

1489 BET365.COM H'CAP 1m 2f 7y
4:20 (4:23) (Class 3) (0-90,90) 3-Y-O

£7,477 (£2,239; £1,119; £560; £279; £140) **Stalls** High

Form RPR
031- **1** **Aqwaal (IRE)**[223] 5901 3-8-4 **76**........................ TPO'Shea 6 92+
(E A L Dunlop) *lw: trckd ldng trio: clsd over 2f out: rdn and styd on to ld 1f out: readily drew clr* **9/2**[2]
42-3 **2** 2 ½ **Polly's Mark (IRE)**[15] 1198 3-8-4 **76** oh1........................ JohnEgan 1 87
(C G Cox) *trckd ldng pair: quick move to join ldr 4f out: drvn to ld narrowly 2f out: hdd and one pce 1f out* **25/1**
22-2 **3** nk **Antinori (IRE)**[9] 1284 3-8-7 **79**........................ TedDurcan 4 89
(W R Swinburn) *lw: hld up in abt 9th: prog over 2f out: gap appeared over 1f out: sn nt qckn: kpt on last 100yds* **7/2**[1]
506- **4** 1 ½ **Doctor Crane (USA)**[209] 6284 3-9-4 **90**........................ JimmyFortune 10 97
(J H M Gosden) *led after 2f: jnd 4f out: hdd 2f out: fdd ins fnl f* **16/1**
031- **5** ¾ **Jedi**[177] 7080 3-8-8 **80**........................ RyanMoore 9 86+
(Sir Michael Stoute) *hld up in abt 6th: pushed along and sme prog over 2f out: nt qckn wl over 1f out: one pce after* **7/2**[1]
011- **6** nk **Classic Vintage (USA)**[194] 6665 3-8-13 **85**........................ JimCrowley 8 90+
(Mrs A J Perrett) *hld up in abt 7th: effrt 3f out: prog to chse ldrs over 1f out: hanging and fdd fnl f* **15/2**
023- **7** 6 **Perfect Shot (IRE)**[200] 6524 3-8-6 **78**........................ EddieAhern 7 71
(J L Dunlop) *lw: hld up in 8th: shkn up and no prog wl over 2f out: n.d after* **11/1**
650- **8** 2 ¼ **Howard**[209] 6292 3-8-4 **76** oh1........................ ChrisCatlin 3 64
(J L Dunlop) *t.k.h: hld up in last pair: effrt 3f out: sn hanging and btn* **33/1**
36-5 **9** 15 **Northern Tour**[27] 1001 3-8-7 **79**........................ MartinDwyer 5 37
(P F I Cole) *chsd ldng quartet: wknd wl over 2f out: t.o* **14/1**
3-26 **10** 5 **Khan Tengri (IRE)**[9] 1286 3-8-7 **79**........................ WilliamBuick 11 27
(M P Tregoning) *reminders in last pair after 3f: a bhd: t.o* **25/1**
23-1 **11** 18 **Rafaan (USA)**[20] 1127 3-9-0 **86**........................ RHills 2 —
(M Johnston) *lw: led 2f: trckd ldr to over 4f out: wknd rapidly: eased and t.o* **6/1**[3]

2m 11.0s (0.50) **Going Correction** +0.10s/f (Good) **11** Ran SP% **120.2**
Speed ratings (Par 102): **102,100,99,98,97 97,92,91,79,75 60**
toteswinger: 1&2 £17.70, 1&3 £5.90, 2&3 £15.90 CSF £116.51 CT £445.31 TOTE £5.40: £2.30, £4.90, £1.90; EX 137.90 Place 6: £60.11, Place 5: £40.74.
Owner Hamdan Al Maktoum **Bred** Shadwell Estate Company Limited **Trained** Newmarket, Suffolk

FOCUS
This is often a competitive 3yo handicap, last year´s renewal producing subsequent St Leger/Breeders´ Cup Turf winner Conduit, and this race should produce its share of winners.

NOTEBOOK

Aqwaal(IRE), the supposed second-string of owner Hamdan Al Maktoum, came in for strong support earlier in the day before easing back out a little in the market, but his chance was there for all to see off a mark of 76 on this handicap debut and he got well on top inside the final half furlong. Winner of a 1m soft-ground maiden on his third and final start at two, he showed these different conditions were not a problem and it will be interesting to see how much further progress he is capable of, especially as it looked to some paddock judges that the run would do him good. (op 3-1 tchd 11-2)

Polly's Mark(IRE), racing from 1lb out of the handicap, posted an improved effort in second. Placed on three of her four starts in maidens, she seemed no more than reasonably treated for this handicap debut, but was taken to the front straightening for home and kept on well back in second. A small race can surely be found for her. (op 28-1 tchd 33-1)

Antinori(IRE), runner-up on each of his last three starts and due to go up 6lb from today, kept on back in third, but doesn´t look the heartiest of characters and things are only going to become more difficult for him. (tchd 4-1)

Doctor Crane(USA) did not really go on as a juvenile, struggling in better contests towards the end of the season, and a mark of 90 was always going to make things tough for him here. He ran well enough without suggesting he is ready to win off this sort of mark. (tchd 14-1)

Jedi ◆, a progressive juvenile who won his maiden in heavy ground, was always likely to find the ground conditions a bit lively and he shaped pleasingly in the circumstances. As a half-brother to High Calypso he will get further than this and certainly has more to offer. (tchd 9-2 in places)

Classic Vintage(USA), winner of a maiden here last September before following up in a novices´ stakes at Bath the following month, seemed to be making his handicap debut off a fair mark and he came with a promising-looking run over two furlongs out, but in the end got a bit tired. He should come on for this and is one to be interested in for something similar. (op 10-1)

Perfect Shot(IRE), backed beforehand, never threatened to get involved on this handicap debut. (op 25-1)

Howard, another handicap debutant, was soon well in rear and failed to make a forward move.

Rafaan(USA), who was sporting the winning owners first colours, dropped right out having been up there early and something was surely amiss. (tchd 5-1 and 13-2)

T/Plt: £161.50 to a £1 stake. Pool: £84,879.83. 383.62 winning tickets. T/Qpdt: £11.00 to a £1 stake. Pool: £5,962.81. 397.55 winning tickets. JN

1409 WOLVERHAMPTON (A.W) (L-H)

Friday, April 24

OFFICIAL GOING: Standard

Wind: Fresh half-behind Weather: Overcast

1490 DAVE "JEEVES" MORGAN - ENJOY YOUR RETIREMENT MAIDEN STKS (DIV I) 7f 32y(P)

1:50 (1:51) (Class 5) 3-Y-O **£3,238** (£963; £481; £240) **Stalls** High

Form	Pos	Dist	Horse / details	RPR
0-	1		**Smart Endeavour (USA)**[316] 2972 3-9-3 0 AdamKirby 10 (W R Swinburn) *trckd ldrs: led 2f out: rdn clr fnl f: eased nr fin* **11/10**[1]	88+
	2	7	**Ask The Oracle** 3-9-3 0 TravisBlock 11 (H Morrison) *sn pushed along in rr: hdwy over 1f out: edgd lft and r.o ins fnl f: no ch w wnr* **33/1**	64
63-0	3	1 ¾	**Enhancing**[27] 998 3-8-12 0 RobertWinston 1 (A J McCabe) *chsd ldrs: rdn to ld over 2f out: sn hdd: hung lft over 1f out: wknd fnl f* **20/1**	54
2-	4	4	**Good Humoured**[165] 7268 3-9-3 0 SebSanders 3 (Sir Mark Prescott) *chsd ldr tl rdn over 2f out: wknd fnl f* **7/2**[3]	48
4265	5	½	**It's A Mans World**[70] 530 3-9-3 67 JimmyQuinn 4 (K M Prendergast) *prom: rdn 1/2-way: wknd 2f out* **14/1**	47
60-	6	1 ¼	**The Happy Hammer (IRE)**[185] 6885 3-9-3 0 DO'Donohoe 7 (M D Squance) *sn outpcd: rdn and swtchd lft over 1f out: nvr nrr* **50/1**	43
44	7	1	**Kloof**[11] 1257 3-9-3 0 RichardMullen 2 (J H M Gosden) *led: rdn: hung rt and hdd over 2f out: sn wknd* **5/2**[2]	41
	8	nk	**Go Alone (IRE)** 3-9-3 0 PJMcDonald 5 (G A Swinbank) *mid-div: sn pushed along: wknd over 2f out* **25/1**	40
06	9	1 ¼	**Winrob**[12] 1228 3-9-3 0 LiamJones 8 (Patrick Morris) *chsd ldrs: rdn 1/2-way: wknd over 2f out* **66/1**	37
U0-	10	5	**Liberty Estelle (IRE)**[192] 6722 3-8-8 0 ow1 RichardEvans(5) 12 (P D Evans) *s.i.s: outpcd* **80/1**	19
000-	11	11	**Risky Lady (IRE)**[117] 7802 3-8-9 40 MarcHalford(3) 9 (J Ryan) *s.i.s: outpcd* **80/1**	—

1m 29.93s (0.33) **Going Correction** +0.025s/f (Slow) **11 Ran SP% 122.6**

Speed ratings (Par 98): **99,91,89,84,83 82,81,80,79,73 61**

toteswinger: 1&2 £15.50, 1&3 £10.80, 2&3 £10.60 CSF £55.55 TOTE £2.30: £1.10, £10.20, £5.10; EX 71.80 Trifecta £202.50 Pool: £298.36 - 1.09 winning units..

Owner The Lamplighters **Bred** Silverleaf Farms Inc **Trained** Aldbury, Herts

FOCUS

The market made this a three-horse race, and most of the money beforehand was for the winner, who was backed in from 11-4 in the morning. The winning time was over a second slower than the second division.

Kloof Official explanation: jockey said colt was handing badly right

Winrob Official explanation: jockey said gelding never travelled

1491 DAVE "JEEVES" MORGAN - ENJOY YOUR RETIREMENT MAIDEN STKS (DIV II) 7f 32y(P)

2:25 (2:26) (Class 5) 3-Y-O **£3,238** (£963; £481; £240) **Stalls** High

Form	Pos	Dist	Horse / details	RPR
0-	1		**Leahurst (IRE)**[260] 4792 3-9-3 0 ShaneKelly 4 (J Noseda) *chsd ldrs: led wl over 1f out: rdn out* **13/8**[2]	95+
044-	2	2 ½	**Badiat Alzaman (IRE)**[176] 7097 3-8-12 75 DarryllHolland 8 (D M Simcock) *hld up in tch: rdn over 2f out: chsd wnr fnl f: eased whn no imp towards fin* **6/4**[1]	83
000-	3	7	**Inis Boffin**[210] 6240 3-8-12 0 CatherineGannon 11 (S Kirk) *s.i.s: outpcd: rdn over 2f out: r.o ins fnl f: nrst fin* **66/1**	64+
00-	4	hd	**Sham Sheer**[176] 7098 3-9-3 0 DaneO'Neill 3 (L M Cumani) *sn pushed along in mid-div: rdn over 2f out: n.d* **6/1**[3]	69+
2-	5	hd	**Doc Jones (IRE)**[354] 1873 3-8-12 0 RichardEvans(5) 2 (P D Evans) *led: rdn and hdd wl over 1f out: wknd fnl f* **6/1**[3]	68
0-	6	nk	**All The Nines (IRE)**[189] 6788 3-8-12 0 LukeMorris 6 (Mrs D J Sanderson) *chsd ldrs: rdn 1/2-way: wkng whn hung lft fr over 1f out* **100/1**	62
536-	7	6	**Granny McPhee**[115] 7823 3-8-12 66 MickyFenton 1 (A Bailey) *prom: rdn 1/2-way: wknd over 1f out* **10/1**	46
020-	8	8	**Flute Magic**[212] 6198 3-9-3 75 FergusSweeney 9 (W S Kittow) *racd keenly: w ldr tl rdn over 2f out: wknd wl over 1f out* **16/1**	30
0-0	9	10	**Sally's Swansong**[17] 1174 3-8-12 0 AdamKirby 5 (M Wellings) *sn outpcd* **80/1**	—
0	10	½	**Go Sunshine (IRE)**[21] 1108 3-8-10 0 (t) AlexEdwards(7) 7 (F Sheridan) *s.i.s: outpcd* **100/1**	—

1m 28.87s (-0.73) **Going Correction** +0.025s/f (Slow) **10 Ran SP% 126.3**

Speed ratings (Par 98): **105,102,94,93,93 93,86,77,65,65**

toteswinger: 1&2 £1.30, 1&3 £26.80, 2&3 £30.50 CSF £4.98 TOTE £2.70: £1.10, £1.10, £14.40; EX 4.50 Trifecta £109.50 Pool: £374.51 - 2.53 winning units..

Owner Mrs Susan Roy **Bred** D And B Egan **Trained** Newmarket, Suffolk

FOCUS

There was a good pace on here and the winning time was the quicker of the two divisions by 1.06sec. The form looks solid.

1492 HOTEL & CONFERENCING AT WOLVERHAMPTON (S) STKS 7f 32y(P)

3:00 (3:00) (Class 6) 3-Y-O **£2,047** (£604; £302) **Stalls** High

Form	Pos	Dist	Horse / details	RPR
23	1		**Invincible Miss (IRE)**[53] 741 3-8-7 63 FrancisNorton 7 (M Wigham) *chsd ldrs: led over 1f out: rdn out* **3/1**[2]	59
053	2	½	**Peanut Girl (IRE)**[22] 1084 3-8-7 50 CatherineGannon 12 (B Palling) *s.i.s: hld up: hdwy over 1f out: rdn: hung lft and r.o ins fnl f* **50/1**	57
4-41	3	nk	**Chocolicious (IRE)**[22] 1084 3-8-12 66 (v) TomEaves 2 (B Smart) *hld up: hdwy over 1f out: r.o* **6/1**[3]	62
0-54	4	½	**Ridgeway Silver**[88] 293 3-8-4 60 DavidProbert(3) 1 (M D I Usher) *led: rdn: edgd rt and hdd over 1f out: styd on* **9/1**	55
4-04	5	shd	**Nun Today (USA)**[91] 267 3-8-8 46 ow1 (v[1]) DarryllHolland 10 (Karen George) *a.p: rdn over 1f out: edgd lft: styd on* **20/1**	56
5311	6	3	**Swiss Art (IRE)**[29] 964 3-9-3 70 AdamKirby 6 (R A Harris) *hld up in tch: rdn whn nt clr run over 1f out and ins fnl f: nt rcvr* **11/4**[1]	64+
2	7	1	**Charlietoo**[22] 1084 3-8-12 0 PaulFitzsimons 4 (E G Bevan) *s.i.s: hld up: hdwy over 1f out: styd on same pce fnl f* **8/1**	49
3054	8	1 ½	**Weet In Nerja**[20] 1129 3-8-5 51 (p) DavidKenny(7) 8 (R Hollinshead) *s.i.s: hld up: styd on ins fnl f: nvr nrr* **33/1**	45
6-04	9	½	**Abhainn (IRE)**[65] 594 3-8-12 49 SebSanders 5 (B Palling) *hld up: rdn over 2f out: n.d* **9/1**	44
4422	10	¾	**River Rye (IRE)**[24] 1046 3-8-7 58 (p) LPKeniry 9 (J S Moore) *chsd ldrs: rdn over 2f out: wknd fnl f* **10/1**	37
03-6	11	11	**Captain Cavendish (IRE)**[82] 366 3-8-12 59 (v) MickyFenton 11 (A Bailey) *sn pushed along to join ldr: rdn over 2f out: wknd over 1f out* **20/1**	12

1m 31.0s (1.40) **Going Correction** +0.025s/f (Slow) **11 Ran SP% 120.6**

Speed ratings (Par 96): **93,92,92,91,91 87,86,85,84,83 71**

toteswinger: 1&2 £21.10, 1&3 £3.70, 2&3 £26.10 CSF £160.63 TOTE £5.10: £1.10, £7.20, £2.50; EX 120.40 TRIFECTA Not won..There was no bid for the winner. Swiss Art was subject to a friendly claim.

Owner J M Cullinan **Bred** Mrs C S Acham **Trained** Newmarket, Suffolk

FOCUS

An ordinary seller and the form looks limited.

Chocolicious(IRE) Official explanation: jockey said filly suffered interference shortly after start

Swiss Art(IRE) Official explanation: jockey said gelding hung left throughout

1493 WOLVERHAMPTON-RACECOURSE.CO.UK H'CAP 7f 32y(P)

3:35 (3:35) (Class 5) (0-75,74) 4-Y-O+ **£3,885** (£1,156; £577; £288) **Stalls** High

Form	Pos	Dist	Horse / details	RPR
2520	1		**Campli (IRE)**[6] 1343 7-8-4 **67** LanceBetts(7) 8 (B Ellison) *hld up: hdwy over 1f out: hung lft: rdn to ld wl ins fnl f: r.o* **12/1**	76
0-24	2	¾	**Gazboolou**[16] 1187 5-9-2 **72** FergusSweeney 7 (David Pinder) *chsd ldrs: led over 2f out: rdn over 1f out: hdd wl ins fnl f* **7/1**[3]	79
6-60	3	1 ¼	**Papillio (IRE)**[16] 1186 4-9-3 **73** PatCosgrave 12 (J R Fanshawe) *hld up in tch: rdn over 1f out: edgd lft and styd on same pce ins fnl f* **12/1**	77
11-2	4	shd	**To Be Or Not To Be**[99] 179 4-8-13 **69** LukeMorris 5 (John Berry) *chsd ldrs: rdn over 1f out: edgd lft: styd on same pce ins fnl f* **7/2**[1]	72
6023	5	2	**Sew'N'So Character (IRE)**[7] 1320 8-8-12 **68** PaulHanagan 9 (M Blanshard) *hld up: hdwy and hung lft over 1f out: nt trble ldrs* **5/1**[2]	66
226-	6	2 ½	**Wing Play (IRE)**[147] 7466 4-9-0 **70** (p) TravisBlock 4 (H Morrison) *hld up: rdn over 1f out: edgd lft: nt rch ldrs* **5/1**[2]	61
3104	7	½	**Follow The Flag (IRE)**[6] 1343 5-9-2 **72** (p) RobertWinston 11 (A J McCabe) *s.i.s: hld up: shkn up over 1f out: nvr nr ldrs* **8/1**	62
106-	8	1	**Ghost Dancer**[181] 6989 5-9-2 **72** LPKeniry 3 (J M Bradley) *hld up: hdwy over 1f out: wknd ins fnl f* **20/1**	59
00-0	9	1 ¼	**Greystoke Prince**[16] 1186 4-9-3 **73** (p) AdamKirby 1 (W R Swinburn) *led 1f: chsd ldrs: rdn over 1f out: hung lft and wknd fnl f* **10/1**	57
/00-	10	5	**Call For Liberty (IRE)**[208] 6314 4-9-3 **73** TomEaves 2 (B Smart) *prom: rdn over 2f out: wknd over 1f out* **16/1**	43
2330	11	3 ½	**Guildenstern (IRE)**[7] 1320 7-9-0 **70** JimmyQuinn 10 (P Howling) *sn pushed along: a in rr* **14/1**	31
	12	2 ¾	**Soul Murmur (IRE)**[209] 6294 4-8-13 **74** (t) RichardEvans(5) 6 (F Sheridan) *led after 1f: rdn and hdd over 2f out: wknd over 1f out* **25/1**	27

1m 29.09s (-0.51) **Going Correction** +0.025s/f (Slow) **12 Ran SP% 124.8**

Speed ratings (Par 103): **103,102,100,100,98 95,94,93,92,86 82,79**

toteswinger: 1&2 £22.60, 1&3 £27.70, 2&3 £28.00 CSF £98.61 CT £1072.41 TOTE £12.90: £4.10, £2.80, £4.30; EX 185.40 TRIFECTA Not won..

Owner Racing Management & Training Ltd **Bred** Allevamento Porta Medaglia **Trained** Norton, N Yorks

FOCUS

An average handicap and the form looks straightforward.

Soul Murmur(IRE) Official explanation: jockey said gelding ran too free

1494 SPONSOR A RACE BY CALLING 01902 390009 H'CAP 5f 20y(P)

4:10 (4:11) (Class 4) (0-85,82) 4-Y-O+ **£5,180** (£1,541; £770; £384) **Stalls** Low

Form	Pos	Dist	Horse / details	RPR
-501	1		**Almaty Express**[29] 971 7-8-11 **75** (b) DarryllHolland 6 (J R Weymes) *swtg: mde all: rdn over 1f out: r.o* **11/4**[3]	86
5112	2	1 ¾	**Desperate Dan**[4] 1412 8-8-7 **78** (v) PNolan(7) 3 (A B Haynes) *sn pushed along in rr: swtchd rt 1/2-way: hdwy over 1f out: r.o to go 2nd post* **5/2**[2]	83+
233-	3	½	**Even Bolder**[147] 7477 6-9-2 **80** StephenCarson 4 (E A Wheeler) *prom: chsd wnr 2f out: sn rdn: hung lft and no ex ins fnl f: lost 2nd post* **9/4**[1]	83
1326	4	3 ¼	**Woodcote (IRE)**[51] 756 7-7-8 **72** (vt) PatrickMathers 1 (Peter Grayson) *trckd ldrs: rdn over 1f out: sn wknd* **10/1**	64

2445 **5** 2 1/4 **First Order**[21] 1094 8-8-13 **82**...(v) AnnStokell(5) 7 65
(Miss A Stokell) *prom: racd keenly: trckd wnr over 3f out to 2f out: sn rdn and wknd* **9/1**

60-3 **6** 1 **Firenza Bond**[4] 1412 4-7-13 **68** oh1..............................(b1) SophieDoyle(5) 2 48
(D Flood) *unruly to post: s.s: bhd: latched onto rr of the field 1/2-way: sn wknd* **14/1**

62.08 secs (-0.22) **Going Correction** +0.025s/f (Slow) **6** Ran SP% **111.8**
Speed ratings (Par 105): **102,99,98,93,89 88**
toteswinger: 1&2 £2.30, 1&3 £1.90, 2&3 £1.40 CSF £9.96 CT £16.32 TOTE £2.90: £1.50, £1.50; EX 8.20 Trifecta £16.40 Pool: £557.05 - 25.05 winning units..
Owner Ronald Lilley **Bred** P G Airey **Trained** Middleham Moor, N Yorks

FOCUS
A fair sprint handicap in which the winner had everything go his way.

1495 HOTEL & CONFERENCING AT WOLVERHAMPTON H'CAP 1m 141y(P)
4:45 (4:47) (Class 6) (0-65,65) 4-Y-O+ **£2,388** (£705; £352) **Stalls** Low

Form RPR

0-00 **1** **Sarwin (USA)**[49] 777 6-8-8 **55**.. RobertWinston 12 67
(G A Swinbank) *a.p: chsd ldr over 3f out: rdn to ld over 1f out: hung lft ins fnl f: styd on* **6/1**[3]

210- **2** *hd* **Steig (IRE)**[248] 5170 6-9-1 **62**.. DO'Donohoe 10 74
(George Baker) *plld hrd and prom: nt clr run and lost pl wl over 3f out: hdwy over 2f out: rdn to chse wnr fnl f: hung lft: sn ev ch: styd on* **3/1**[1]

600- **3** 3 3/4 **Hits Only Cash**[188] 6825 7-8-3 **57**.............................. SimonPearce(7) 9 60
(J Pearce) *hld up in tch: led 1/2-way: rdn and hdd over 1f out: no ex ins fnl f* **16/1**

-030 **4** 1/2 **Networker**[11] 1258 6-9-4 **65**.. DaneO'Neill 1 67+
(P J McBride) *hld up: hdwy 2f out: sn rdn: edgd lft and no ex fnl f* **8/1**

4002 **5** 1 1/2 **Lend A Grand (IRE)**[22] 1080 5-9-3 **64**.......................... FergusSweeney 11 63
(Miss Jo Crowley) *hld up in tch: rdn and ev ch over 2f out: styd on same pce appr fnl f* **9/1**

0400 **6** *nse* **Stark Contrast (USA)**[20] 1133 5-8-4 **54**...................... DavidProbert(3) 13 53
(M D I Usher) *led to 1/2-way: chsd ldrs: rdn and ev ch over 1f out: wknd ins fnl f* **16/1**

-363 **7** 1 **Copperwood**[71] 513 4-8-4 **51**.. JimmyQuinn 7 47
(M Blanshard) *hld up: hdwy over 1f out: nt trble ldrs* **7/1**

603 **8** 1 **Kirstys Lad**[18] 1153 7-8-8 **55**.. DarryllHolland 4 49
(M Mullineaux) *hld up: nt clr run over 2f out: sn rdn: nt rch ldrs* **5/1**[2]

2626 **9** 1 1/2 **Fine Ruler (IRE)**[22] 1080 5-9-3 **64**................................ VinceSlattery 2 55
(M R Bosley) *broke wl: sn stdd and lost pl: n.d after* **10/1**

300- **10** 3 **Princess Gee**[249] 5161 4-8-13 **60**.................................. StephenCarson 6 44
(B J McMath) *chsd ldrs tl rdn and wknd 3f out* **20/1**

000- **11** *nk* **Bermacha**[123] 7771 4-8-13 **60**.. RichardThomas 8 43
(J E Long) *dwlt: hld up: hdwy 3f out: sn rdn: wknd 2f out* **33/1**

56-4 **12** 1/2 **Gambling Jack**[37] 869 4-8-7 **54**.. ShaneKelly 5 36
(A W Carroll) *chsd ldrs tl rdn and wknd over 2f out* **20/1**

1m 52.78s (2.28) **Going Correction** +0.025s/f (Slow) **12** Ran SP% **122.9**
Speed ratings (Par 101): **90,89,86,86,84 84,83,82,81,78 78,78**
toteswinger: 1&2 £7.40, 1&3 £30.40, 2&3 £14.20 CSF £24.58 CT £285.86 TOTE £7.60: £3.20, £1.70, £5.00; EX 34.60 Trifecta £225.60 Pool: £335.48 - 1.10 winning units..
Owner S Rudolf **Bred** Cynthia Knight **Trained** Melsonby, N Yorks

FOCUS
They went no pace early on here, and that played into the hands of the winner who raced handily.
Hits Only Cash Official explanation: jockey said gelding ran too free
Copperwood Official explanation: jockey said gelding ran too free in a slow run race
Bermacha Official explanation: jockey said filly missed the break

1496 WOLVERHAMPTON RACECOURSE APPRENTICE H'CAP 1m 1f 103y(P)
5:15 (5:16) (Class 6) (0-55,55) 4-Y-O+ **£2,388** (£705; £352) **Stalls** Low

Form RPR

34-5 **1** **Nassar (IRE)**[20] 1122 6-8-10 **54**..................................(v) HollyHall(3) 11 66
(G Prodromou) *hld up: plld hrd: hdwy over 2f out: rdn to ld ins fnl f: r.o wl* **4/1**[1]

3500 **2** 4 1/2 **Magic Warrior**[22] 1080 9-9-0 **55**...................................... CharlesEddery 6 58
(J C Fox) *s.s: hld up: hdwy u.p over 1f out: hung lft and r.o ins fnl f: no ch w wnr* **9/1**

-050 **3** 1 1/2 **Time To Regret**[16] 1194 9-9-0 **55**............................(p) AndrewHeffernan 2 54
(I W McInnes) *trckd ldr: rdn to ld and hung lft fr over 1f out: hdd and unable qck ins fnl f* **7/1**[3]

02-0 **4** 3/4 **King Of Connacht**[11] 1254 6-9-0 **55**...........................(p) PaulPickard 8 53
(M Wellings) *hld up: hdwy over 2f out: edgd lft and r.o ins fnl f: nrst fin* **8/1**

-300 **5** *nk* **Double Valentine**[22] 1080 6-8-13 **54**................................ DebraEngland 3 51
(R Ingram) *chsd ldrs: rdn over 1f out: no etxra ins fnl f: eased last strides* **20/1**

1004 **6** 1/2 **Ruwain**[20] 1122 5-8-8 **52**.. TobyAtkinson(3) 1 48
(P J McBride) *led: rdn and hdd over 1f out: no ex ins fnl f* **11/1**

030- **7** 3/4 **Harting Hill**[169] 7217 4-8-7 **51**.. KatiaScallan(3) 5 56+
(M P Tregoning) *hld up: hdwy 2f out: nt clr run 1f out: nvr trbld ldrs* **6/1**[2]

020- **8** 2 3/4 **Just Mossie**[5] 6741 4-8-11 **55**....................................(p) RyanClark(3) 13 44
(W G M Turner) *prom: rdn over 2f out: wkng whn hung lft over 1f out* **20/1**

3300 **9** 3/4 **Giddywell**[18] 1153 5-8-10 **54**......................................(p) DavidKenny(3) 7 41
(R Hollinshead) *hld up: rdn over 2f out: nvr nrr* **8/1**

0/5- **10** 1 3/4 **Shafrons Canyon (IRE)**[321] 2855 6-8-6 **50**...................... KierenFox(3) 4 34
(P J Lally, Ire) *chsd ldrs tl rdn and wknd wl over 1f out* **20/1**

6536 **11** 1 1/4 **Hunt The Bottle (IRE)**[29] 969 4-8-6 **50**.............. MatthewLawson(3) 10 31
(M Mullineaux) *dwlt: hld up: rdn and wknd over 2f out* **8/1**

340- **12** *hd* **Josephine Malines**[165] 7267 5-8-8 **52**.....................(p) SamuelDrury(3) 12 33
(Mrs A Duffield) *hld up: hdwy over 2f out: sn rdn and wknd* **22/1**

36-0 **13** 1 1/2 **Duneen Dream (USA)**[56] 711 4-8-6 **52**.......................... BarryAdams(5) 9 29
(Mrs N S Evans) *s.i.s: rdn over 3f out: sn* **11/1**

2m 1.08s (-0.62) **Going Correction** +0.025s/f (Slow) **13** Ran SP% **125.4**
Speed ratings (Par 101): **103,99,97,97,96 96,95,93,92,90 89,89,88**
toteswinger: 1&2 £8.80, 1&3 £7.90, 2&3 £13.20 CSF £39.71 CT £255.52 TOTE £4.80: £2.10, £2.90, £3.30; EX 52.90 TRIFECTA Not won. Place 6: £126.63, Place 5: £59.82..
Owner Faisal Al-Nassar **Bred** Gigginstown House Stud **Trained** East Harling, Norfolk
■ Stewards' Enquiry : Samuel Drury one-day ban: used whip when out of contention (May 8)
Matthew Lawson caution: used whip when out of contention.

FOCUS
This looked a moderate contest with little solid recent form.
Hunt The Bottle(IRE) Official explanation: jockey said colt missed the break
Duneen Dream(USA) Official explanation: jockey said gelding missed the break
T/Plt: £359.80 to a £1 stake. Pool: £48,598.33. 98.60 winning tickets. T/Qpdt: £148.70 to a £1 stake. Pool: £4,159.85. 20.70 winning tickets. CR

1497 - 1503a (Foreign Racing) - See Raceform Interactive

HAYDOCK (L-H)
Saturday, April 25

OFFICIAL GOING: Good to firm (firm in places; 8.4)
Wind: light across Weather: Dry and sunny

1504 EUROPEAN BREEDERS' FUND MAIDEN FILLIES' STKS 5f
5:40 (5:40) (Class 5) 2-Y-O **£3,885** (£1,156; £577; £288) **Stalls** Centre

Form RPR

1 **Eternal Instinct** 2-8-9 0.. GaryBartley(5) 9 73+
(J S Goldie) *wnt lft s: in tch: swtchd rt and hdwy 2f out: rdn and styd on strly ent fnl f: led nr fin* **9/1**

43 **2** 1 **My Mandy (IRE)**[7] 1344 2-9-0 0.. JimCrowley 1 69
(Ian Williams) *racd alone far rail: led: rdn ent fnl f: sn drvn: hdd and no ex nr fin* **13/2**

3 1 3/4 **Aalsmeer** 2-9-0 0.. RichardMullen 10 62+
(E S McMahon) *prom: effrt 2f out: sn rdn and ev ch tl drvn and wknd ent fnl f* **9/4**[1]

0 **4** 5 **Tagula Pearl (IRE)**[7] 1344 2-9-0 0.............................. PatrickMathers 17 43
(I W McInnes) *in tch: rdn along and edgd lft over 2f out: styd on appr fnl f: nt rch ldrs* **50/1**

5 *nk* **Dower Glen** 2-9-0 0.. PhillipMakin 15 42
(I Semple) *towards rr and rdn along 1/2-way: sn edgd lft: styd on appr fnl f: nrst fin* **14/1**

6 1/2 **Goodbye Earl (IRE)** 2-8-9 0.. SladeO'Hara(5) 8 40
(A Berry) *hmpd s: sn chsng ldrs: rdn along over 2f out and grad wknd* **100/1**

7 *shd* **Mary Helen** 2-9-0 0.. TGMcLaughlin 12 40
(W M Brisbourne) *dwlt and towards rr tl sme late hdwy* **50/1**

8 *nk* **Mrs Boss** 2-8-13 0 ow2.. JamesMillman(3) 6 41+
(B R Millman) *wnt rt s and sn outpcd towards rr: rdn along 1/2-way: sme late hdwy* **20/1**

6 **9** *nse* **Kate Skate**[22] 1090 2-9-0 0.. EddieAhern 2 39
(P F I Cole) *prom: rdn along 2f out: sn wknd* **6/1**[3]

4 **10** 5 **Elegant Dancer (IRE)**[5] 1396 2-9-0 0................................ NeilChalmers 4 20
(Paul Green) *chsd ldrs: rdn along over 2f out: grad wknd* **12/1**

11 1 **Lewyn** 2-9-0 0.. NCallan 5 25+
(K A Ryan) *prom: rdn along 2f out: sn wknd and eased ins fnl f* **7/2**[2]

12 2 3/4 **Lady Bucket** 2-8-7 0.. KrishGundowry(7) 13 5
(Paul Green) *s.i.s and bhd: hung bdly lft 1/2-way* **18/1**

13 11 **Nuts About You (IRE)** 2-9-0 0...................................... StephenDonohoe 7 —
(A Berry) *hmprd s and s.i.s: a bhd* **100/1**

14 1 1/2 **Rivitivo** 2-9-0 0.. LiamJones 3 —
(W M Brisbourne) *towards rr: outpcd and bhd fr 1/2-way* **100/1**

60.53 secs (0.03) **Going Correction** -0.20s/f (Firm) **14** Ran SP% **121.9**
Speed ratings (Par 89): **91,89,86,78,78 77,77,76,76,68 67,62,45,42**
toteswinger: 1&2 £8.60, 1&3 £4.60, 2&3 £5.00. CSF £65.60 TOTE £9.70: £3.30, £3.00, £1.40; EX 94.90.
Owner J S Goldie **Bred** Jim Goldie **Trained** Uplawmoor, E Renfrews

FOCUS
Lightly-raced sorts and debutantes, so not easy to weigh up, but the first three finished clear and the winner looks above average.

NOTEBOOK
Eternal Instinct, by the top-class Australian sprinter Exceed and Excel and from a prolific family from 5f to 1m4f, needed a stalls blanket but made a winning debut and looks a potential improver. Though she is evidently highly strung, she did everything right in the race itself and should be even better for the experience. She is a possible runner in the Hilary Needler at Beverley or a Listed race at York's Dante meeting (op 11-1 tchd 8-1)
My Mandy(IRE) blitzed along the far rail and only gave way in the final furlong. She is getting sharper with racing and, though now qualified for nurseries, is comfortably good enough to win a typical maiden. (op 5-1 tchd 7-1)
Aalsmeer looked a picture for this debut and, though unable to justify favouritism, showed more than enough to suggest she can make amends next time. A daughter of Invincible Spirit out of a 6f winner who is a half-sister to three winners up to 1m, she has inherited plenty of their speed. (op 5-2 tchd 3-1)
Tagula Pearl(IRE), by Tagula and from a winning family up to 1m, ran much better than on her debut but will be even more effective when able to race over 6f. (tchd 80-1)
Dower Glen, a Camacho filly whose dam won three times from 5f to 1m, is related to several other good sprinters. Though taking a long time to warm up, she did some decent late work and should be significantly sharper next time. (op 20-1)
Goodbye Earl(IRE), a half-sister to Tancredi and a winning sprint juvenile in Norway, showed plenty of early speed. This was a satisfactory debut with nursieries in mind later on.
Mary Helen, a half-sister to winners from 7f to 1m4f including the hurdler Lowe Go, was going on well at the finish and already needs farther. (op 66-1)
Lewyn Official explanation: jockey said filly was unsuited by the good to firm (firm in places) ground

1505 NORTHERNRACINGCLUB.COM H'CAP 5f
6:10 (6:11) (Class 5) (0-75,75) 3-Y-O **£3,238** (£963; £481; £240) **Stalls** Centre

Form RPR

01-2 **1** **Impressible**[17] 1190 3-8-8 **65**.. EddieAhern 6 73
(E J Alston) *prom: cl up 1/2-way: rdn to ld over 1f out: drvn ins fnl f and styd on strly* **13/2**[3]

16-0 **2** 1 **Metroland**[7] 1368 3-8-13 **70**.. JimCrowley 9 75
(D Nicholls) *midfield: hdwy over 2f out: rdn to chse wnr ent fnl f: sn drvn and ev ch tl no ex last 75yds* **20/1**

31-4 **3** 1 **Grissom (IRE)**[13] 1232 3-8-8 **70**.................................... SladeO'Hara(5) 2 71
(A Berry) *in tch on wd outside: hdwy 2f out: rdn to chse ldrs over 1f out: drvn and edgd lft ins fnl f: kpt on* **16/1**

210- **4** *nse* **Red Rosanna**[210] 6274 3-9-2 **73**.................................... GrahamGibbons 7 74
(R Hollinshead) *led: rdn 2f out: drvn and hdd over 1f out: wknd wl ins fnl f* **14/1**

4405 **5** 2 **White Shift (IRE)**[7] 1368 3-8-9 **71**.............................. RichardEvans(5) 13 65
(P D Evans) *dwlt: sn chsng ldrs: cl up 1/2-way and ev ch tl rdn wl over 1f out and grad wknd* **5/1**[2]

500- **6** *nk* **Kheylide (IRE)**[259] 4857 3-8-11 **68**.............................. EdwardCreighton 1 61
(Mrs D J Sanderson) *hld up and bhd: hdwy 2f out: rdn and kpt on ins fnl f: nrst fin* **100/1**

61- **7** *hd* **Rublevka Star (USA)**[184] 6932 3-8-10 **67**........................ ShaneKelly 8 59
(J Noseda) *trckd ldrs: hdwy 2f out: sn rdn and btn over 1f out* **6/4**[1]

10- **8** 1 1/4 **Daisy Moses (IRE)**[309] 3192 3-9-4 **75**........................ AdrianTNicholls 12 63
(D Nicholls) *chsd ldrs: rdn along 2f out: sn wknd* **20/1**

215 **9** 1 1/4 **Under Review (IRE)**[26] 1032 3-9-3 **74** JamieSpencer 5 57
(S A Callaghan) *hld up towards rr: hdwy 1/2-way: swtchd rt and rdn wl over 1f out: sn btn* **11/1**
604- **10** 3/4 **Secret Venue**[172] 7173 3-8-8 **65** TonyHamilton 4 45
(Jedd O'Keeffe) *in tch: rdn along over 2f out and sn wknd* **20/1**
30-5 **11** *nk* **Rio Cobolo (IRE)**[39] 859 3-8-8 **65** ow1 (v) StephenDonohoe 11 44
(Paul Green) *a towards rr* **33/1**
23-1 **12** *39* **Yanza**[23] 1077 3-9-1 **72** SteveDrowne 10 —
(J R Gask) *dwlt: a in rr: bhd and eased appr fnl f* **8/1**

59.75 secs (-0.75) **Going Correction** -0.20s/f (Firm) **12** Ran SP% **120.2**
Speed ratings (Par 98): **98,96,94,94,91 91,90,88,86,85 85,22**
toteswinger: 1&2 £51.30, 1&3 £16.50, 2&3 £105.80. CSF £135.33 CT £2037.84 TOTE £7.50: £2.30, £5.70, £3.60; EX 75.70.
Owner Mr & Mrs G Middlebrook **Bred** Mr & Mrs G Middlebrook **Trained** Longton, Lancs

FOCUS
A moderate race for the course, but several of these should find a race in the coming months.
Yanza Official explanation: jockey said filly never travelled

1506 ST HELENS STAR H'CAP 1m 6f
6:40 (6:40) (Class 4) (0-80,77) 4-Y-O+ **£5,504** (£1,637; £818; £408) **Stalls** Low

Form RPR
-150 **1** **Zuwaar**[36] 899 4-9-0 **70** (tp) JimCrowley 11 75
(Ian Williams) *in tch: hdwy 4f out: rdn to chal 2f out: drvn to ld ent fnl f: kpt on gamely u.p towards fin* **7/1**
45-0 **2** *hd* **My Mate Max**[21] 1117 4-8-13 **72** (p) RussellKennemore(3) 1 77
(R Hollinshead) *chsd ldr: hdwy and cl up over 3f out: rdn to ld over 2f out: drvn and hdd ent fnl f: kpt on gamely u.p* **6/1**[2]
0P-3 **3** *nse* **Solas Alainn (IRE)**[7] 1366 4-9-2 **72** JoeFanning 5 77+
(M Johnston) *trckd ldrs: effrt and nt clr run wl over 1f out and again appr fnl f: sn swtchd rt and rdn to chal wl ins fnl f and ev ch tl nt qckn nr line* **6/1**[2]
4616 **4** *nk* **Thorny Mandate**[19] 1154 7-8-4 **58** LiamJones 2 63
(W M Brisbourne) *hld up in tch: hdwy over 3f out: rdn wl over 1f out and sn ev ch tl drvn ins fnl f and no ex towards fin* **12/1**
032- **5** *6* **Forrest Flyer (IRE)**[222] 5971 5-8-2 **63** oh3 ow5 LanceBetts(7) 4 59
(I Semple) *led and sn clr: pushed along 4f out: sn rdn: hdd over 2f out and sn drvn: grad wknd appr fnl f* **13/2**[3]
0/3- **6** 1/2 **Indonesia**[329] 2628 7-9-9 **77** GrahamGibbons 9 72
(T D Walford) *hld up towards rr: hdwy over 4f out: chal over 2f out: sn rdn and ev ch tl drvn and wknd ent fnl f* **3/1**[1]
100- **7** *6* **Kasban**[269] 4516 5-9-8 **76** StephenDonohoe 6 63
(Ian Williams) *hld up: a in rr* **9/1**
06-0 **8** 1 1/4 **Lets Roll**[13] 1230 8-9-6 **74** NCallan 10 59
(C W Thornton) *hld up: a in rr* **13/2**[3]
215- **9** 3 1/4 **Grandad Bill (IRE)**[175] 7128 6-8-12 **69** KellyHarrison(3) 3 50
(J S Goldie) *chsd ldng pair: hdwy over 3f out: rdn along over 2f out: wkng whn nt room wl over 1f out* **9/1**

2m 59.66s (-4.64) **Going Correction** -0.20s/f (Firm)
WFA 4 from 5yo+ 2lb **9** Ran SP% **120.4**
Speed ratings (Par 105): **105,104,104,104,101 100,97,96,94**
toteswinger: 1&2 £13.60, 1&3 £8.40, 2&3 £11.20. CSF £50.71 CT £272.88 TOTE £7.50: £2.30, £2.40, £1.90; EX 81.50.
Owner Dr Marwan Koukash **Bred** Shadwell Estate Company Limited **Trained** Portway, Worcs
■ Stewards' Enquiry : Russell Kennemore two-day ban: used whip with excessive frequency without giving gelding time to respond (May 9, 11)

FOCUS
A middling race for stayers, with a strong early pace relenting somewhat in the back straight, but still appearing to provide a stiff test. Even so, it did not appear to be easy to come from behind. The bunch finish suggests it is ordinary form.

1507 HAYDOCK PARK RAILS AND RING BOOKMAKERS H'CAP 1m 30y
7:10 (7:10) (Class 4) (0-85,85) 4-Y-O+ **£5,504** (£1,637; £818; £408) **Stalls** Low

Form RPR
360- **1** **Billy Dane (IRE)**[162] 6598 5-8-11 **78** JimCrowley 8 85
(F P Murtagh) *mde all: rdn along 2f out: drvn ins fnl f: hld on gamely* **28/1**
4415 **2** 1/2 **Just Bond (IRE)**[13] 1229 7-8-13 **80** PJMcDonald 15 86+
(G R Oldroyd) *hld up and bhd: hdwy on wd outside 2f out: rdn over 1f out: str run ins fnl f: edgd lft and kpt on towards fin* **10/1**
00-5 **3** *nk* **Boy Blue**[18] 1170 4-9-1 **82** DaleGibson 6 87
(P Salmon) *t.k.h: chsd wnr: rdn along over 2f out: drvn ins fnl f: kpt on u.p* **8/1**[3]
4/0- **4** 3/4 **Prince Evelith (GER)**[176] 6487 6-8-0 **74** JamieKyne(7) 14 77+
(J J Quinn) *hld up towards rr: hdwy 3f out: rdn along and sltly outpcd 2f out: styd on and ch ent fnl f: hld in 4th whn n.m.r and snatched up nr line* **16/1**
03-6 **5** *1* **Capucci**[21] 1123 4-8-12 **79** GrahamGibbons 4 80
(J J Quinn) *dwlt and towards rr: hdwy 3f out: rdn to chse ldrs wl over 1f out: drvn and one pce ins fnl f* **5/1**[1]
0-0 **6** *1* **Arizona John (IRE)**[22] 1100 4-8-13 **80** LeeEnstone 13 79
(N Wilson) *trckd ldrs: hdwy 4f out: rdn along over 2f out: drvn over 1f out and kpt on same pce* **33/1**
0-11 **7** *shd* **Wovoka (IRE)**[12] 1246 6-8-13 **80** TonyHamilton 1 78+
(D W Barker) *hld up in midfield: hdwy 3f out: rdn along and n.m.r over 2f out: drvn over 1f out and kpt on same pce* **7/1**[2]
-305 **8** 3/4 **Minority Report**[7] 1365 9-8-11 **78** AdrianTNicholls 11 75+
(D Nicholls) *hld up in rr: hdwy over 2f out: swtchd rt and styd on ins fnl f: nrst fin* **8/1**[3]
200- **9** 1/2 **Brasingaman Hifive**[203] 6482 4-8-11 **78** LiamJones 2 74
(Mrs G S Rees) *hld up towards rr: hdwy 3f out: rdn over 2f out: chsd ldrs and drvn over 1f out: wknd ins fnl f* **5/1**[1]
043- **10** *hd* **Wigwam Willie (IRE)**[219] 6041 7-9-0 **81** (tp) NCallan 10 76
(K A Ryan) *hld up in tch: hdwy over 3f out: rdn to chse ldrs over 2f out: drvn over 1f out and grad wknd* **8/1**[3]
5020 **11** 2 1/4 **Casino Night**[13] 1229 4-8-0 **72** DeanHeslop(5) 5 62
(R Johnson) *hld up: a towards rr* **25/1**
06-0 **12** *3* **Goodbye Mr Bond**[18] 1170 9-8-13 **80** EddieAhern 9 63
(E J Alston) *in tch: effrt on inner 3f out: sn rdn and wknd 2f out* **9/1**
410- **13** 3 3/4 **Major Magpie (IRE)**[211] 6249 7-9-4 **85** PhillipMakin 12 59
(M Dods) *prom: rdn along over 2f out: sn drvn and wknd qckly* **16/1**
3-00 **14** 2 1/4 **Talk Of Saafend (IRE)**[13] 1229 4-8-8 **78** NeilBrown(3) 3 47
(P Monteith) *chsd ldrs: rdn along 3f out: sn wknd* **14/1**

1m 42.82s (-0.98) **Going Correction** -0.20s/f (Firm) **14** Ran SP% **126.9**
Speed ratings (Par 105): **96,95,95,94,93 92,92,91,91,90 88,85,81,79**
toteswinger: 1&2 £86.60, 1&3 £62.90, 2&3 £20.80. CSF £297.27 CT £2544.96 TOTE £38.10: £8.60, £4.30, £3.50; EX 288.60.
Owner James Callow **Bred** Brian Killeen **Trained** Low Braithwaite, Cumbria
■ Stewards' Enquiry : P J McDonald three-day ban: careless riding (May 9, 11-12)
Neil Brown two-day ban: careless riding (May 9,11)

FOCUS
A modest early gallop and many of the field were too headstrong, but Crowley's judgement of pace on the winner was as good as ever.
Brasingaman Hifive Official explanation: jockey said filly was unsuited by the good to firm (firm in places) ground

1508 HAYDOCK PARK ANNUAL BADGEHOLDERS MAIDEN STKS 1m 30y
7:40 (7:44) (Class 5) 3-Y-O **£3,238** (£963; £481; £240) **Stalls** Low

Form RPR
4- **1** **African Art (USA)**[176] 7106 3-9-3 0 JamieSpencer 13 85+
(B J Meehan) *trckd ldrs: hdwy 3f out: chsd ldr 2f out: rdn to ld wl over 1f out: hung lft and styd on ins fnl f* **8/13**[1]
0- **2** 2 3/4 **Matraash (USA)**[196] 6655 3-9-3 0 TPO'Shea 7 78
(M Johnston) *trckd ldrs: smooth hdwy to ld wl over 2f out: rdn and hdd wl over 1f out: kpt on same pce* **3/1**[2]
36- **3** *2* **Justonefortheroad**[260] 4815 3-9-3 0 StephenDonohoe 10 74
(N J Vaughan) *hld up towards rr: hdwy 3f out: rdn wl over 1f out: styd on ins fnl f: nrst fin* **11/1**
6- **4** 1 1/2 **Northern Acres**[224] 5882 3-9-3 0 AdrianTNicholls 9 70
(D Nicholls) *chsd ldr: hdwy to ld 3f out: sn rdn and hdd wl over 2f out: drvn and wknd over 1f out: edgd lft ins fnl f* **10/1**[3]
5 *nk* **Una Pelota (IRE)** 3-9-3 0 JimCrowley 4 70
(N J Vaughan) *chsd ldrs: rdn along and outpcd over 2f out: styng on whn n.m.r and swtchd rt ent fnl f: kpt on towards fin* **16/1**
6 *4* **Cils Blancs (IRE)** 3-8-12 0 TomEaves 1 56
(B Smart) *chsd ldrs: rdn along wl over 2f out: sn one pce* **33/1**
7 *5* **Bobeachway (IRE)** 3-9-3 0 PhillipMakin 5 49
(M Dods) *in tch: effrt 3f out: rdn along 2f out and grad wknd* **28/1**
0 **8** 2 3/4 **Toujours Souriante**[13] 1228 3-8-12 0 JoeFanning 12 38
(M Johnston) *a towards rr* **40/1**
9 *8* **Cridda Boy** 3-9-3 0 SteveDrowne 8 24
(A G Newcombe) *a towards rr* **66/1**
06- **10** *hd* **Tahfeez (IRE)**[149] 7458 3-8-12 0 TonyHamilton 2 19
(I Semple) *led: rdn along and hdd 3f out: sn wknd* **40/1**
11 *30* **Berberi** 3-9-3 0 (t) JamieMoriarty 11 —
(A G Newcombe) *s.i.s: a bhd* **100/1**

1m 43.04s (-0.76) **Going Correction** -0.20s/f (Firm) **11** Ran SP% **124.0**
Speed ratings (Par 98): **95,92,90,88,88 84,79,76,68,68 38**
toteswinger: 1&2 £1.10, 1&3 £3.90, 2&3 £5.20. CSF £2.66 TOTE £1.70: £1.20, £1.80, £1.90; EX 2.90.
Owner Matthew Green & Sangster Family **Bred** Sean Gorman **Trained** Manton, Wilts

FOCUS
Just a medium gallop, but there should be a few winners to come from this "late developer" maiden. The winner is a nice prospect and the next three or four should be okay in handicaps.
Northern Acres Official explanation: trainer said colt lost a shoe

1509 WARRINGTON GUARDIAN H'CAP 1m 30y
8:10 (8:12) (Class 5) (0-75,75) 3-Y-O **£3,238** (£963; £481; £240) **Stalls** Low

Form RPR
565- **1** **Simon Gray**[152] 7434 3-9-3 **74** PatDobbs 4 81
(R Hannon) *trckd ldr: hdwy to ld 2f out: rdn over 1f out: jnd and drvn ins fnl f: styd on gamely towards fin* **10/3**[1]
040- **2** 1/2 **Eastern Warrior**[136] 7622 3-9-1 **72** EddieAhern 1 78
(J W Hills) *hld up: hdwy over 2f out: rdn to over 1f out: styd on to chal ins fnl f and ev ch tl edgd lft and no ex towards fin* **4/1**[3]
21- **3** 4 1/2 **Allformary**[193] 6722 3-9-2 **73** TomEaves 11 69
(B Smart) *led: rdn and hdd 2f out: sn drvn and kpt on same pce u.p fnl f* **8/1**
056- **4** 1 1/2 **Petella**[190] 6785 3-8-8 **65** PJMcDonald 8 57
(C W Thornton) *chsd ldng pair: effrt 3f out: sn rdn: drvn over 1f out and kpt on same pce* **16/1**
31- **5** *nk* **Hey Up Dad**[218] 6065 3-9-4 **75** PhillipMakin 2 66
(M Dods) *trckd ldrs: rdn along and sltly outpcd over 2f out: swtchd rt and styd on ent fnl f* **7/2**[2]
010- **6** *3* **Sharp Sovereign (USA)**[187] 6857 3-8-11 **71** NeilBrown(3) 5 55
(T D Barron) *hld up in rr: effrt 3f out: sn rdn along and nvr a factor* **8/1**
645- **7** 1 1/4 **Carter**[182] 6988 3-8-5 **62** LiamJones 10 44
(W M Brisbourne) *chsd ldrs: rdn along 3f out: sn wknd* **25/1**
60-1 **8** 1 1/4 **Toby Tyler**[34] 924 3-9-2 **73** JamieMoriarty 6 52
(P T Midgley) *t.k.h: hld up: a in rr* **7/1**
00-4 **9** 2 1/4 **Sweet Possession (USA)**[24] 1066 3-8-10 **72** MartinLane(5) 7 46
(A P Jarvis) *dwlt: a in rr* **12/1**

1m 44.16s (0.36) **Going Correction** -0.20s/f (Firm) **9** Ran SP% **117.4**
Speed ratings (Par 98): **90,89,85,83,83 80,78,77,75**
toteswinger: 1&2 £3.80, 1&3 £11.10, 2&3 £9.20. CSF £17.25 CT £99.71 TOTE £5.40: £1.70, £2.10, £2.30; EX 14.80 Place 6: £337.11, Place 5: £167.49 ..
Owner Mrs James Wigan **Bred** Mrs James Wigan **Trained** East Everleigh, Wilts

FOCUS
A weak early pace played into the hands of the prominent runners. Tricky form to pin down, but the first two were among the more interesting ones beforehand.
Simon Gray Official explanation: trainer's rep said, regarding apparent improvement in form, that the colt had strengthened up over the winter.
T/Plt: £152.60 to a £1 stake. Pool: £55,054.54. 263.36 winning tickets. T/Qpdt: £23.10 to a £1 stake. Pool: £4,198.03. 134.20 winning tickets. JR

1083 LEICESTER (R-H)
Saturday, April 25

OFFICIAL GOING: Good to firm (firm in places)
Wind: Light behind Weather: Cloudy with sunny spells

1510 TOTEPLACEPOT H'CAP 5f 218y
1:55 (1:56) (Class 4) (0-85,85) 4-Y-O+ **£4,857** (£1,445; £722; £360) **Stalls** Low

Form RPR
25-3 **1** **Peter Island (FR)**[31] 954 6-8-12 **79** (v) JimCrowley 3 94
(J Gallagher) *mde all: rdn clr fr over 1f out* **10/1**
-431 **2** *4* **Dancing Maite**[22] 1103 4-8-4 **71** JimmyQuinn 8 73
(S R Bowring) *a.p: rdn to chse wnr over 1f out: no imp* **15/2**[3]
4151 **3** 1/2 **Kipchak (IRE)**[12] 1244 4-8-9 **76** (p) RobertWinston 11 76
(A J McCabe) *chsd wnr over 2f: sn rdn: styd on same pce appr fnl f* **9/2**[1]
0-40 **4** *nk* **Pravda Street**[14] 1212 4-9-4 **85** SteveDrowne 2 84
(P F I Cole) *prom: outpcd 1/2-way: r.o ins fnl f* **13/2**[2]

300- **5** *nk* **Sparton Duke (IRE)**[197] 6627 4-8-11 **78**......................(p) JoeFanning 14 76
(K A Ryan) *s.i.s: sn prom: rdn 1/2-way: edgd lft and styd on same pce appr fnl f* **10/1**

4000 **6** *3/4* **Methaaly (IRE)**[9] 1309 6-8-8 **80**....................... DeanHeslop(5) 6 76
(M Mullineaux) *sn outpcd: r.o ins fnl f: nvr nrr* **25/1**

20-0 **7** *shd* **Harlech Castle**[13] 1227 4-9-1 **82**.........................(b) ShaneKelly 13 78
(P F I Cole) *chsd ldrs: outpcd over 3f out: rallied over 1f out: no ex ins fnl f* **33/1**

0-46 **8** *3/4* **Charles Darwin (IRE)**[31] 954 6-8-10 **77**.................... TedDurcan 7 70
(M Blanshard) *prom: rdn 1/2-way: sn outpcd* **33/1**

24-0 **9** *3/4* **Gift Horse**[9] 1309 9-8-13 **80**...................... SilvestreDeSousa 5 71
(D Nicholls) *sn outpcd: nvr nrr* **8/1**

-444 **10** *nk* **Vhujon (IRE)**[9] 1309 4-9-1 **82**.............................. JohnEgan 1 72
(P D Evans) *s.i.s: sn prom: chsd wnr over 3f out: rdn over 2f out: wknd and eased fnl f* **9/2**[1]

142- **11** *1 1/2* **Filligree (IRE)**[206] 6402 4-9-2 **83**........................ ChrisCatlin 4 68
(Rae Guest) *sn outpcd* **17/2**

0-00 **12** *2 3/4* **Timber Treasure (USA)**[10] 1278 5-8-11 **78**..............(b) TonyCulhane 10 54
(Paul Green) *hld up: rdn over 3f out: a in rr* **66/1**

-050 **13** *5* **Dickie Le Davoir**[18] 1169 5-8-4 **71** oh2.................. FrankieMcDonald 9 31
(John A Harris) *outpcd* **28/1**

69.12 secs (-3.88) **Going Correction** -0.50s/f (Hard) course record **13** Ran SP% **116.0**
Speed ratings (Par 105): **105,99,99,98,98 97,97,96,95,94 92,89,82**
toteswinger: 1&2 £26.50, 1&3 £5.30, 2&3 £9.50. CSF £76.52 CT £399.81 TOTE £9.50: £2.80, £3.20, £2.30; EX 60.10 Trifecta £131.50 Part won. Pool: £413.70 - 0.70 winning units..
Owner C R Marks (banbury) **Bred** E A R L Elevage De La Source **Trained** Chastleton, Oxon

FOCUS
This opening sprint confirmed how fast the ground was, as it was run in course record time. The stalls were positioned against the stands' rail, and with the two obvious front-runners drawn wide apart, the field split into two groups behind them. Hard to find fault with the form and it was an impressive performance from the winner, who recorded a clear personal best.
Harlech Castle Official explanation: jockey said gelding was unsuited by the good to firm (firm in places) ground
Gift Horse Official explanation: jockey said gelding ran flat

1511 TOTETENTOFOLLOW STARTS NEXT WEEKEND MEDIAN AUCTION MAIDEN STKS 5f 2y
2:30 (2:33) (Class 5) 2-Y-O £2,914 (£867; £433; £216) **Stalls** Low

Form RPR
3 **1** **King's Approach (IRE)**[7] 1358 2-9-3 0.............................. PatDobbs 4 72
(R Hannon) *w ldr tl led 3f out: rdn and edgd rt over 1f out: hdd wl ins fnl f: rallied to ld post* **6/5**[1]

6 **2** *nse* **Farmer Giles (IRE)**[23] 1083 2-9-3 0.......................... JamieSpencer 9 72
(M L W Bell) *w ldrs: rdn and hung rt fr 1/2-way: led wl ins fnl f: hdd post* **7/2**[2]

6 **3** *1/2* **Royal Desert**[17] 1188 2-9-3 0.................................. TPO'Shea 2 70
(M R Channon) *chsd ldrs: sn pushed along: outpcd wl over 1f out: r.o wl towards fin* **7/1**

4 *3/4* **Petrocelli** 2-9-3 0... PaulFitzsimons 5 67
(A J McCabe) *s.i.s: outpcd: r.o ins fnl f: nrst fin* **40/1**

5 *1* **Italian Tom (IRE)** 2-9-3 0................................... PatCosgrave 3 63
(S A Callaghan) *sn led: hdd 3f out: rdn: hung rt and ev ch over 1f out: styd on same pce ins fnl f* **9/2**[3]

6 *1/2* **Polly Macho (IRE)** 2-9-3 0..................................... JohnEgan 7 62
(P D Evans) *chsd ldrs: outpcd 1/2-way: styd on ins fnl f* **28/1**

7 *3 1/4* **George Baker (IRE)** 2-9-3 0................................ TonyCulhane 8 49
(George Baker) *s.i.s: outpcd* **20/1**

8 *2 3/4* **Pursuit Of Gold** 2-8-12 0..................................... RobertWinston 1 34
(J R Best) *s.i.s: outpcd* **25/1**

9 *17* **Bombay Mist** 2-8-7 0...................................... MarkCoumbe(5) 6 —
(R C Guest) *s.s: outpcd* **100/1**

59.81 secs (-0.19) **Going Correction** -0.50s/f (Hard) **9** Ran SP% **113.8**
Speed ratings (Par 92): **81,80,80,78,77 76,71,66,39**
toteswinger: 1&2 £1.60, 1&3 £2.30, 2&3 £4.30. CSF £4.99 TOTE £2.10: £1.20, £1.10, £2.00; EX 6.50 Trifecta £16.30 Pool: £413.70 - 18.73winning units..
Owner David & Gwyn Joseph **Bred** Sean Madigan **Trained** East Everleigh, Wilts
■ Stewards' Enquiry : Jamie Spencer one-day ban: used whip with excessive frequency (May 9)

FOCUS
Previous racecourse experience was crucial, as the only three that had raced before fought out the finish. Three early leaders set a good pace that had the trailers off the bridle from the start. The standard of this race has varied over the years, and this has provisionally been rated towards the lower end owing to the bunch finish.

NOTEBOOK
King's Approach(IRE) broke smartly and was quite keen early, but his previous experience may well have helped him hold on. He ran well for a long way before tiring at Nottingham on his debut a week earlier and just had enough in reserve here, so he might be better at this trip for now. Connections are considering giving him time off to mature. (op 13-8 tchd 7-4 and 15-8 in places)
Farmer Giles(IRE), who holds a Group 1 entry, had weakened on his debut over course and distance at the beginning of the month but, according to his trainer, he was short of work that day. He had clearly progressed in the interim and raced up with the pace, but was caught on the far side of the three leaders and it looked like he needed more cover, as he was still a bit green when asked to stride on near the finish. (op 3-1 tchd 5-2)
Royal Desert was green on his debut this month. It took a long time for the penny to drop here as well, but he eventually made good late progress. He looks a slow learner but will improve (op 11-1 tchd 6-1)
Petrocelli was green early on and still had five lengths to make up with a furlong and a half to go, but he made good late headway to finish so close to the winner. The benefit of this promising debut should soon be paying dividends. (op 33-1 tchd 25-1)
Italian Tom(IRE) showed early speed on this debut but may have just been feeling the ground when weakening in the closing stages. (op 4-1 tchd 5-1)

1512 TOTEEXACTA H'CAP 1m 3f 183y
3:05 (3:05) (Class 3) (0-95,85) 3-Y-O £9,346 (£2,799; £1,399) **Stalls** High

Form RPR
511- **1** **Holberg (UAE)**[136] 7623 3-9-7 **85**........................... JoeFanning 1 91+
(M Johnston) *chsd ldr tl led 10f out: hdd over 7f out: led again over 2f out: shkn up and edgd rt fnl f: r.o wl: eased nr fin* **5/2**[3]

0-1 **2** *1 1/4* **Lively Fling (USA)**[23] 1088 3-9-7 **85**...................... RichardMullen 2 89+
(J H M Gosden) *led: hdd 10f out: led again over 7f out: rdn and hdd over 2f out: styd on same pce fnl f* **6/4**[1]

21-3 **3** *13* **Orbitor**[27] 1019 3-9-0 **78**.......................................(t) JamieSpencer 3 72
(M L W Bell) *hld up in tch: pushed along 4f out: rdn over 2f out: wknd and eased fnl f* **7/4**[2]

2m 32.3s (-1.60) **Going Correction** -0.075s/f (Good) **3** Ran SP% **104.9**
Speed ratings (Par 102): **102,101,92**
CSF £6.13 TOTE £3.20; EX 3.20.
Owner Sheikh Hamdan Bin Mohammed Al Maktoum **Bred** Darley **Trained** Middleham Moor, N Yorks

FOCUS
A small but select field. The early pace was steady, but it picked up as they turned in when the market leaders duelled to the final furlong, drawing clear of their toiling rival. The form is a bit muddling and it is difficult to gauge how much the two principals have improved.

NOTEBOOK
Holberg(UAE) was technically on a hat-trick after two all-weather wins, although he had been off since December. Leading early, he was reportedly green after his break and was looking at the fences on the track, so his jockey took a pull behind Lively Fling and he settled much better. He showed a good turn of foot to draw clear with that rival up the home straight, before striding clear near the finish. He handled the step up in trip with ease and looks a nice progressive type. Connections feel he could be Ascot-bound this season. (op 11-4 tchd 10-3 and 9-4)
Lively Fling(USA) showed he had improved from his two-year-old days when running out a ready winner on fast ground over course and distance this month. He did nothing wrong here, and although he lacked the finishing pace of his rival, he stayed on stoutly. His Derby entry might look a tad ambitious, but he possesses plenty of stamina. (op 11-10 tchd Evens and 7-4)
Orbitor was readily outpaced before the question of whether he would appreciate the step up in trip could be answered. On official figures he was not outclassed by that much, so the fact he weakened tamely despite a first-time tongue-tie was a little worrying. (op 9-4 tchd 6-4)

1513 TOTESPORT.COM LEICESTERSHIRE STKS (LISTED RACE) 7f 9y
3:40 (3:40) (Class 1) 4-Y-O+ £22,708 (£8,608; £4,308; £2,148; £1,076) **Stalls** Low

Form RPR
-410 **1** **Asset (IRE)**[65] 611 6-9-2 108.................................(b) TedDurcan 5 111
(Saeed Bin Suroor) *racd centre: hld up in tch: wnt stands' side over 4f out: led and hung rt fr over 1f out: drvn out* **5/2**[2]

14-6 **2** *1/2* **Regal Parade**[28] 1006 5-9-2 106....................................... WilliamCarson 4 109
(D Nicholls) *racd centre: prom: wnt stands' side over 4f out: rdn to chse wnr fnl f: edgd rt: r.o* **9/4**[1]

0132 **3** *2* **Carcinetto (IRE)**[7] 1365 7-8-11 89.............................. JohnEgan 6 99
(P D Evans) *overall ldr centre: wnt stands' side over 4f out: rdn and hdd over 1f out: styng on same pce whn edgd rt ins fnl f* **13/2**[3]

0010 **4** *nse* **Beaver Patrol (IRE)**[28] 996 7-9-2 104.....................(v) StephenCarson 7 104
(Eve Johnson Houghton) *w ldr in centre: wnt stands' side over 4f out: rdn and ev ch over 1f out: styd on same pce ins fnl f* **10/1**

050- **5** *29* **Racer Forever (USA)**[189] 6814 6-9-2 105.................(b) RichardMullen 2 26
(J H M Gosden) *racd alone stands' side to over 4f out: plld hrd and prom: rdn 2f out: sn wknd and eased* **5/2**[2]

1m 22.01s (-4.19) **Going Correction** -0.50s/f (Hard) **5** Ran SP% **110.3**
Speed ratings (Par 111): **103,102,100,100,66**
toteswinger: 1&2 £3.50. CSF £8.54 TOTE £3.20: £1.90, £1.60; EX 9.30 Trifecta £28.50 Pool: £330.22 - 8.56 winning units..
Owner Godolphin **Bred** Peter Gibbons And Dermot Forde **Trained** Newmarket, Suffolk
■ A first winner of the year in Britain for Godolphin.

FOCUS
The fast ground resulted in a depleted field, but despite the small number of runners three vied for the early lead, ensuring a sound pace. The fourth looks the best guide to the form, as none of the others are that solid.

NOTEBOOK
Asset(IRE) raced keenly under a tight rein behind the early leaders in the middle of the track, but once he hit the front he veered right over to the inside rail, conceding ground to his rivals but having enough in hand at the end. This marked a return to the form he showed on his penultimate start in Dubai over 6f. His attitude has been called into question and he looks awkward in a finish, but he is very able at this level. (op 11-4 tchd 9-4)
Regal Parade, keen early tracking the leaders, went to the front with Asset and ran on well, but he was unable to capitalise when the winner gave up ground by hanging right. However, he ran well considering the ground was as fast as he would want and he will come on again for this run. (op 5-2 tchd 10-3)
Carcinetto(IRE) had little chance on official ratings but finished best of the early leaders and continues in good form. (op 8-1 tchd 6-1)
Beaver Patrol(IRE) disputed the early lead but had nothing left at the end. He goes well on fast ground and had the visor reapplied after disappointing at Doncaster last month, but he gave the impression that a bit of a break might be welcome. (op 15-2 tchd 7-1)
Racer Forever(USA) raced keenly at the head of affairs on his return from a six-month break. His lack of a recent run and stamina limitations were obvious negatives, but when his stride shortened two furlongs out it looked like he was not appreciating the fast ground, and he was soon eased. (op 11-4 tchd 9-4)

1514 TOTESWINGER H'CAP 1m 1f 218y
4:10 (4:11) (Class 5) (0-70,69) 4-Y-O+ £3,238 (£963; £481; £240) **Stalls** High

Form RPR
660- **1** **Paint The Town Red**[129] 7711 4-9-1 **69**...................... JackMitchell(3) 2 79
(H J Collingridge) *hld up: swtchd lft and hdwy 2f out: edgd rt and styd on u.p to ld towards fin* **18/1**

1656 **2** *3/4* **Celtic Gold (USA)**[10] 1287 5-9-0 **65**.............................. JimmyQuinn 7 73
(Andrew Turnell) *s.i.s: hld up: hdwy over 3f out: rdn to chse ldr over 1f out: led ins fnl f: hdd towards fin* **13/2**

036- **3** *2* **Addwaitya**[195] 6683 4-9-4 **69**.. TedDurcan 1 73
(C F Wall) *chsd ldrs: led 2f out: sn rdn and edgd rt: hdd and unable qck ins fnl f* **5/1**[3]

5635 **4** *nk* **Penang Cinta**[26] 1042 6-8-7 **58**...................................(p) JohnEgan 3 61
(P D Evans) *chsd ldrs: rdn over 3f out: styd on* **7/2**[1]

40-3 **5** *1* **King Of The Moors (USA)**[10] 1279 6-8-9 **65**............ MarkCoumbe(5) 5 66
(R C Guest) *s.i.s: hld up: hdwy u.p over 1f out: hung rt: styd on* **12/1**

50-0 **6** *2 1/2* **Dubburg (USA)**[17] 1187 4-9-1 **66**.............................. ChrisCatlin 8 62
(W J Musson) *s.i.s: hld up: hdwy over 2f out: sn lost pl: styd on ins fnl f* **20/1**

4601 **7** *nk* **Flying Applause**[17] 1194 4-9-1 **66**...........................(bt) RobertWinston 6 64
(S R Bowring) *plld hrd: led and sn clr: rdn and hdd 2f out: wknd ins fnl f* **7/2**[1]

66-0 **8** *8* **Princelywallywogan**[17] 1192 7-9-0 **65**........................... MickyFenton 4 45
(John A Harris) *hld up: hdwy and hung rt fr over 3f out: wknd over 2f out* **4/1**[2]

060- **9** *1 1/2* **Houri (IRE)**[151] 7447 4-9-0 **65**................................(p) FrankieMcDonald 9 42
(J T Stimpson) *chsd ldrs: rdn over 4f out: wknd 3f out* **40/1**

3516 **10** *9* **The Graig**[12] 1254 5-8-7 **58**.. JerryO'Dwyer 10 33
(J R Holt) *chsd ldrs: rdn over 4f out: wknd over 2f out: eased* **20/1**

2m 6.28s (-1.62) **Going Correction** -0.075s/f (Good) **10** Ran SP% **119.4**
Speed ratings (Par 103): **103,102,100,100,99 97,97,91,89,82**
toteswinger: 1&2 £17.30, 1&3 £15.00, 2&3 £8.00. CSF £130.06 CT £687.97 TOTE £22.60: £5.10, £2.20, £1.60; EX 175.30 TRIFECTA Not won..
Owner Miss C Fordham **Bred** Snailwell Stud Co Ltd **Trained** Exning, Suffolk

FOCUS
With a strong early pace set by Flying Applause, the advantage passed to the hold-up horses and the outcome was decided on a long tussle to the line. Ordinary form, but sound enough, with the winner transferring his AW form to turf and a slight personal best from the second.

Flying Applause Official explanation: jockey said gelding ran too freely
Princelywallywogan Official explanation: jockey said gelding hung right

1515 BET TOTEPOOL ON 0800 221 221 MAIDEN STKS — 1m 1f 218y
4:45 (4:45) (Class 5) 3-Y-O+ — **£3,238** (£963; £481; £240) **Stalls** High

Form — RPR

0- **1** **Serious Impact (USA)**[275] 4349 4-9-13 0 .... RobertHavlin 6 79+
(J H M Gosden) *s.i.s: hld up: outpcd over 3f out: rdn over 1f out: str run and edgd rt ins fnl f to ld towards fin* **5/2**[2]

00-4 **2** 1 1/4 **Qelaan (USA)**[16] 1198 3-8-5 74 .... TPO'Shea 4 68
(M P Tregoning) *led: rdn over 1f out: hdd towards fin* **9/2**[3]

5-3 **3** 2 1/4 **Tiger Flash**[12] 1255 3-8-10 0 .... KirstyMilczarek 3 69
(W J Haggas) *hld up: racd keenly: hdwy over 3f out: rdn over 1f out: styng on same pce whn hung rt ins fnl f* **11/10**[1]

4 1/2 **Tried And True (FR)**[350] 4-9-8 0 .... TPQueally 9 66
(H R A Cecil) *trckd ldr: plld hrd: rdn over 1f out: no ex ins fnl f* **28/1**

02- **5** 1 **Cosimo**[170] 7209 3-8-5 0 .... Louis-PhilippeBeuzelin(5) 10 67+
(Sir Michael Stoute) *chsd ldrs: rdn over 2f out: styng on same pce whn n.m.r ins fnl f* **13/2**

000- **6** 7 **Toballa**[176] 7111 4-9-8 46 .... LukeMorris 5 50
(P Leech) *prom: rdn 1/2-way: wknd over 2f out* **80/1**

0- **7** 3 3/4 **Royal Bet (IRE)**[176] 7106 3-8-10 0 .... MickyFenton 1 44
(M L W Bell) *rrd and wnt lft s: a in rr: lost tch fnl 4f* **50/1**

2m 8.21s (0.31) **Going Correction** -0.075s/f (Good)
WFA 3 from 4yo+ 17lb — **7** Ran SP% **114.3**
Speed ratings (Par 103): **95,94,92,91,91 85,82**
toteswinger: 1&2 £2.00, 1&3 £1.20, 2&3 £1.60. CSF £14.02 TOTE £3.90: £2.20, £2.10; EX 16.40 Trifecta £57.50 Pool: £547.42 - 7.04 winning units..
Owner K Abdulla **Bred** Juddmonte Farms Inc **Trained** Newmarket, Suffolk

FOCUS
Some big yards were represented in a competitive maiden, but the early pace was moderate and the form looks muddling, with the exposed sixth suggesting it is less than reliable. It has been rated around the runner-up.
Tiger Flash Official explanation: jockey said colt hung right

1516 BET TOTEPOOL AT TOTESPORT.COM H'CAP — 1m 60y
5:20 (5:26) (Class 5) (0-70,70) 3-Y-O — **£2,590** (£770; £385; £192) **Stalls** High

Form — RPR

-142 **1** **Wunder Strike (USA)**[4] 1420 3-8-4 56 oh3 ....(p) NickyMackay 1 64
(J R Boyle) *swtchd rt sn after s: hld up: nt clr run over 5f out: hdwy over 3f out: led over 1f out: rdn clr* **2/1**[1]

6-42 **2** 4 1/2 **Divinatore**[61] 659 3-9-2 68 .... RobertWinston 7 65
(D Haydn Jones) *prom: chsd ldr over 4f out: rdn over 2f out: styd on same pce fnl f* **13/2**[3]

0-62 **3** 1 1/2 **Mutually Mine (USA)**[8] 1331 3-9-4 70 .... MickyFenton 4 64
(Mrs P Sly) *led after 1f: rdn and hdd over 1f out: wknd ins fnl f* **11/4**[2]

000- **4** nk **Achromatic**[226] 5842 3-8-8 60 .... TedDurcan 5 53
(W R Swinburn) *led 1f: chsd ldrs: rdn and hung rt 2f out: styd on same pce pce* **11/4**[2]

350- **5** 3 **Surprise Party**[184] 6924 3-8-12 67 .... JackMitchell(3) 3 53
(C F Wall) *hld up: hung lft over 6f out: hmpd over 5f out: rdn and hung lft over 1f out: n.d* **9/1**

03-0 **6** 12 **Mr Flannegan**[16] 1196 3-8-5 64 .... AmyScott(7) 6 23
(H Candy) *chsd ldrs: rdn over 4f out: wknd 2f out* **28/1**

1m 43.84s (-1.26) **Going Correction** -0.075s/f (Good) — **6** Ran SP% **113.4**
Speed ratings (Par 98): **103,98,97,96,93 81**
toteswinger: 1&2 £2.90, 1&3 £1.20, 2&3 £2.40. CSF £15.81 TOTE £2.90: £1.60, £2.70; EX 11.90 Place 6: £183.33 Place 5: £69.91.
Owner Mrs B Powell B Walsh P Hughes C Murphy **Bred** Mike Abraham **Trained** Epsom, Surrey
■ Stewards' Enquiry : Nicky Mackay one-day ban: careless riding (May 9)

FOCUS
This was a moderate handicap, but the form looks sound enough, rated around the third..
Divinatore Official explanation: jockey said gelding was unsuited by the good to firm (firm in places) ground
T/Plt: £389.70 to a £1 stake. Pool: £58,530.98. 109.62 winning tickets. T/Qpdt: £105.00 to a £1 stake. Pool: £2,627.33. 18.50 winning tickets. CR

1304 RIPON (R-H)
Saturday, April 25

OFFICIAL GOING: Good to firm (9.0)
Wind: Fairly strong, half behind Weather: Overcast

1517 TOTESCOOP6 H'CAP — 6f
2:20 (2:20) (Class 3) (0-95,89) 3-Y-O
£9,346 (£2,799; £1,399; £700; £349; £175) **Stalls** Low

Form — RPR

3-61 **1** **Proclaim**[7] 1345 3-9-2 87 .... J-PGuillambert 7 99+
(M Johnston) *w ldrs: led 2f out: r.o strly fnl f: comf* **4/1**[3]

4433 **2** 2 1/2 **Mazzola**[11] 1272 3-8-4 75 .... CatherineGannon 8 79
(M R Channon) *w ldrs: rdn 2f out: kpt on fnl f: nt pce of wnr* **9/1**

123- **3** 1/2 **Parisian Pyramid (IRE)**[218] 6067 3-9-4 89 .... AdrianTNicholls 9 91
(D Nicholls) *dwlt and wnt rt s: t.k.h and hld up on outside: hdwy 1/2-way: effrt over 1f out: kpt on same pce fnl f* **9/1**

11-2 **4** 2 1/2 **Coleorton Choice**[7] 1368 3-8-13 84 .... NCallan 4 78
(K A Ryan) *slt ld to 2f out: sn rdn: no ex fnl f* **10/3**[2]

23-0 **5** 2 **Fivefootnumberone (IRE)**[7] 1345 3-8-11 82 .... GrahamGibbons 5 70
(J J Quinn) *prom: drvn along over 2f out: no ex over 1f out* **22/1**

110- **6** 5 **Mullglen**[280] 4190 3-9-0 85 .... DavidAllan 1 57
(T D Easterby) *hld up: drvn and outpcd 2f out: nvr on terms* **16/1**

210- **7** nk **Excellent Show**[311] 3123 3-9-0 85 .... TomEaves 3 56
(B Smart) *trckd ldrs tl rdn and wknd fr 2f out* **14/1**

00-1 **8** 3 1/2 **Mister Laurel**[9] 1305 3-8-8 79 .... PaulHanagan 6 39
(R A Fahey) *in tch: drvn over 2f out: sn wknd* **7/4**[1]

1m 10.61s (-2.39) **Going Correction** -0.325s/f (Firm) — **8** Ran SP% **116.3**
Speed ratings (Par 102): **102,98,98,94,92 85,84,80**
toteswinger: 1&2 £8.80, 1&3 £4.80, 2&3 £10.00. CSF £40.03 CT £254.12 TOTE £4.80: £1.40, £2.50, £2.10; EX 37.90 Trifecta £121.10 Part won. Pool: £163.70 - 0.65 winning units..
Owner Sheikh Hamdan Bin Mohammed Al Maktoum **Bred** Gainsborough Stud Management Ltd **Trained** Middleham Moor, N Yorks

FOCUS
This was a decent 3yo sprint handicap. Improved form from the winner again.

NOTEBOOK
Proclaim, who proved suited by the return to this trip at Doncaster last time, showed himself to be progressing fast by comfortably taking this off a 7lb higher mark. Soon up with the pace, he forged on two out and stayed on strongly for pressure. A further rise will follow, but there is every chance of more to come under these conditions.
Mazzola, currently 7lb lower than when last winning, has run creditably in defeat the last twice and this was another good effort. He too was up on the pace throughout and can surely be found a race before long. (op 11-1 tchd 12-1)
Parisian Pyramid(IRE) ◆ made a really pleasing reappearance. Hit hard by the handicapper after his impressive nursery win at Glorious Goodwood last year, he found himself returning 21lb higher than for that success and things did not start well as he was bumped leaving the stalls from his wide draw. He came to hold every chance, though, and in the end was found out only by the lack of arecent run. This effort suggested he is up to winning off this mark. (op 8-1)
Coleorton Choice, a progressive sort on soft ground towards the end of last season, beating Parisian Pyramid at Ayr, reappeared with a fine effort in defeat over 5f at Thirsk and perhaps this second straight run on fast ground proved too much for him. He remains capable of better with some juice in the ground. (op 7-2 tchd 3-1)
Fivefootnumberone(IRE) will become of interest once the visor he improved in last season is reapplied. (op 20-1)
Mullglen should be sharper for this first run of the season. (tchd 14-1)
Excellent Show is entitled to come on for this first outing in 2009. (tchd 16-1)
Mister Laurel, raised 4lb having won over CD on his seasonal debut, was under pressure before halfway and failed to reproduce the form. He was later found to be coughing. Official explanation: vet said colt coughed post-race (op 9-4)

1518 STOWE FAMILY LAW LLP H'CAP — 5f
2:55 (2:57) (Class 5) (0-75,75) 4-Y-O+ — **£3,238** (£963; £481; £240) **Stalls** Low

Form — RPR

63-5 **1** **Kyzer Chief**[9] 1310 4-8-4 64 .... KellyHarrison(3) 18 73
(R E Barr) *cl up: led over 1f out: rdn out* **14/1**

000- **2** 3/4 **Bahamian Ballet**[203] 6486 7-9-1 72 .... PhillipMakin 4 78+
(E S McMahon) *dwlt: sn midfield stands' side: n.m.r over 2f out: hdwy over 1f out: chsd wnr wl ins fnl f: r.o* **10/1**

-510 **3** nk **Nomoreblondes**[8] 1334 5-8-13 70 ....(p) JamieMoriarty 3 75
(P T Midgley) *prom: effrt over 2f out: kpt on u.p fnl f* **20/1**

400- **4** 3/4 **Speedy Senorita (IRE)**[187] 6859 4-8-7 71 .... JamieKyne(7) 17 73
(J J Quinn) *cl up: rdn 2f out: kpt on same pce ins fnl f* **20/1**

2306 **5** nk **Silvanus (IRE)**[13] 1227 4-9-2 73 .... TomEaves 9 74
(I Semple) *midfield: nt clr run over 2f out to over 1f out: rdn and kpt on fnl f* **10/1**

133- **6** nk **Mr Wolf**[187] 6859 8-9-4 75 .... TonyHamilton 1 75
(D W Barker) *led to over 1f out: kpt on same pce fnl f* **8/1**[3]

3022 **7** hd **Strathmore (IRE)**[9] 1310 5-8-6 63 .... PaulHanagan 15 62+
(R A Fahey) *bhd on outside: hdwy over 1f out: r.o fnl f* **7/1**[2]

500- **8** nk **Dalarossie**[164] 7288 4-8-2 62 .... AndrewMullen(3) 6 60
(E J Alston) *towards rr: hdwy over 1f out: kpt on fnl f: nvr rchd ldrs* **25/1**

500- **9** shd **Fantasy Believer**[253] 5067 11-9-1 72 .... NCallan 16 70
(J J Quinn) *hld up on outside: effrt over 2f out: kpt on fnl f: no imp* **33/1**

4-02 **10** nk **Comptonspirit**[12] 1241 5-8-11 68 .... J-PGuillambert 5 65
(B P J Baugh) *in tch: effrt over 2f out: no ex fnl f* **8/1**[3]

401- **11** 2 3/4 **Braille**[279] 4216 4-8-11 68 .... PJMcDonald 13 55
(T D Walford) *towards rr: drvn 1/2-way: nvr able to chal* **6/1**[1]

00-0 **12** 1 **Pacific Pride**[9] 1309 6-9-2 73 .... GrahamGibbons 14 56
(J J Quinn) *in tch: rdn 2f out: sn btn* **11/1**

531- **13** 2 3/4 **Embra (IRE)**[278] 4242 4-8-9 66 .... SaleemGolam 7 40
(T J Etherington) *towards rr: drvn 1/2-way: n.d* **12/1**

10-6 **14** 1 1/2 **Guest Connections**[18] 1169 6-8-8 65 ....(v) AdrianTNicholls 11 33
(D Nicholls) *dwlt: a bhd* **12/1**

00-5 **15** 6 **Feelin Foxy**[12] 1241 5-8-10 67 .... PaulMulrennan 8 14
(J G Given) *bolted bef s: chsd ldrs tl n.m.r and wknd over 2f out* **10/1**

58.66 secs (-2.04) **Going Correction** -0.325s/f (Firm) — **15** Ran SP% **123.0**
Speed ratings (Par 103): **103,101,101,100,99 99,98,98,98,97 93,91,87,84,75**
toteswinger: 1&2 £48.00, 1&3 £70.90, 2&3 £47.60. CSF £142.24 CT £2877.18 TOTE £14.40: £4.50, £4.20, £5.40; EX 275.20.
Owner Brian Morton **Bred** Mrs H F Mahr **Trained** Seamer, N Yorks

FOCUS
They all came stands´ side in what was a moderate sprint handicap. The winner did well from stall 18 and the form looks sound, with the third and fourth to their marks and the runner-up well weighted at present.
Silvanus(IRE) ◆ Official explanation: jockey said gelding was denied a clear run
Guest Connections Official explanation: jockey said gelding never travelled
Feelin Foxy Official explanation: jockey said mare bolted to post

1519 TOTETENTOFOLLOW.CO.UK H'CAP — 2m
3:30 (3:30) (Class 2) (0-100,95) 4-Y-O+
£15,577 (£4,665; £2,332; £1,167; £582; £292) **Stalls** High

Form — RPR

32-0 **1** **Downhiller (IRE)**[28] 1007 4-9-6 94 .... EddieAhern 10 105+
(J L Dunlop) *chsd clr ldrs: hdwy to ld over 2f out: sn rdn and hrd pressed: hld on wl fnl f* **5/2**[1]

111- **2** 1/2 **Wells Lyrical (IRE)**[183] 6948 4-9-1 89 .... TomEaves 6 100+
(B Smart) *chsd ldr: led over 3f out to over 2f out: rallied: kpt on fnl f: hld nr fin* **4/1**[2]

025- **3** 3 3/4 **Dolly Penrose**[201] 6527 4-8-6 80 .... CatherineGannon 2 86
(M R Channon) *hld up: effrt over 2f out: kpt on fnl f: nt rch first two* **12/1**

0-00 **4** nk **Tamimi's History**[28] 1003 5-9-2 86 .... PaulDoe 12 92
(P D Evans) *hld up in tch: hdwy and cl up over 3f out: edgd lft and one pce over 1f out* **17/2**

203- **5** 4 1/2 **Bollin Felix**[169] 7223 5-9-5 89 ....(b) DavidAllan 11 90
(T D Easterby) *hld up: pushed along and effrt over 3f out: outpcd wl over 1f out* **8/1**

100- **6** 14 **Four Miracles**[189] 6817 5-8-13 83 .... PaulMulrennan 1 67
(M H Tompkins) *bhd: pushed along whn hmpd over 2f out: sn wknd* **9/1**

430- **7** 11 **Luna Landing**[138] 6657 6-8-6 76 oh2 .... PaulHanagan 9 47
(Jedd O'Keeffe) *in tch: rdn and edgd rt over 3f out: sn wknd* **11/2**[3]

020- **8** 20 **Bogside Theatre (IRE)**[119] 6817 5-9-11 95 .... PJMcDonald 8 42
(G M Moore) *t.k.h: set decent gallop to over 3f out: wknd over 2f out* **20/1**

040- **9** 36 **Wing Collar**[246] 5229 8-9-7 91 ....(p) TonyHamilton 4 —
(T D Easterby) *bhd: struggling over 4f out: t.o* **9/1**

3m 27.98s (-3.82) **Going Correction** 0.0s/f (Good)
WFA 4 from 5yo+ 4lb — **9** Ran SP% **118.0**
Speed ratings (Par 109): **109,108,106,106,104 97,91,81,63**
toteswinger: 1&2 £2.60, 1&3 £11.60, 2&3 £9.10. CSF £12.64 CT £101.46 TOTE £3.30: £1.60, £2.10, £2.30; EX 15.10 Trifecta £210.60 Par won. Pool: £284.66 - 0.80 winning units..
Owner Windflower Overseas Holdings Inc **Bred** Windflower Overseas Holdings Inc **Trained** Arundel, W Sussex

FOCUS
This was a fair staying handicap and represents good form, with the progressive principals pulling nicely clear and expected to do better again. The third was close to last year's best and the fourth seems to have found his level now.

NOTEBOOK
Downhiller(IRE), who proved bitterly disappointing at Kempton on his seasonal reappearance, edged ahead two out and always just looked to be doing enough for the runner-up inside the final furlong. Kempton aside, he has been most progressive, and there may well be more to come over this trip or even further. (tchd 9-4 and 11-4)
Wells Lyrical(IRE) ◆ ended last term on a roll, completing a hat-trick off a 6lb lower mark at Doncaster in October, and he showed himself to have progressed further with a fine effort in defeat. He did not give in once passed, battling away doggedly, and remains capable of better still. (tchd 9-2)
Dolly Penrose was largely progressive last season and she made a satisfactory reappearance in third, keeping on well for pressure. (op 14-1)
Tamimi's History, upped markedly in trip, was backed beforehand so this improved showing was clearly not a surprise to everybody. (op 16-1 tchd 8-1)
Bollin Felix progressed well on a slow surface last term and this run will presumably bring him on.
Four Miracles Official explanation: jockey said mare hung right-handed in straight
Wing Collar Official explanation: jockey said gelding finished lame

1520 TOTESPORTCASINO.COM (S) STKS — 1m 1f 170y
4:05 (4:05) (Class 5) 3-4-Y-O — **£2,590** (£770; £385; £192) **Stalls** High

Form	Pos	Dist	Horse / Trainer / Comment	Jockey	SP	RPR
05-0	1		**Southern Mistral**16 [1199] 4-9-10 49 (Miss Gay Kelleway) *in tch: hdwy to ld 1f out: rdn and hld on wl*	(p) PaulHanagan 10	**6/1**3	61
0-00	2	1 1/2	**Whaston (IRE)**8 [1332] 4-9-10 53 (J D Bethell) *t.k.h: cl up: led and qcknd 1/2-way: hdd 1f out: rallied: hld towards fin*	(v) J-PGuillambert 5	**9/2**2	58
-064	3	1	**Maddy**73 [500] 4-8-12 49 (George Baker) *led to 1/2-way: cl up: ev ch over 2f out: edgd lft and one pce fnl f*	(p) MatthewDavies(7) 4	**3/1**1	51
50	4	2 1/4	**Den Maschine**12 [1245] 4-9-10 0 (Ollie Pears) *dwlt: bhd tl edgd rt and kpt on fr 2f out: nrst fin*	(t) TomEaves 7	**6/1**3	51
00-0	5	2	**Heart Of Dubai (USA)**7 [1366] 4-9-10 60 (Micky Hammond) *in tch tl rdn and no ex over 2f out*	PJMcDonald 9	**7/1**	47
-500	6	4	**Johnny Friendly**24 [1057] 4-9-5 55 (K R Burke) *t.k.h: cl up tl rdn and wknd over 2f out*	MartinLane(5) 3	**12/1**	39
46-0	7	3	**Premier Krug (IRE)**12 [1243] 3-8-2 47 (P D Evans) *in tch: rdn over 2f out: sn outpcd*	CatherineGannon 11	**16/1**	27
00-0	8	9	**Ernies Keep**13 [1226] 3-8-7 40 (W Storey) *bhd: drvn over 4f out: sn btn*	TWilliams 2	**50/1**	13
6020	9	18	**Dead Cat Bounce (IRE)**11 [1270] 3-8-7 62 (J Pearce) *hld up: rdn 4f out: sn wknd*	(bt) PaulMulrennan 1	**7/1**	—
0460	10	1/2	**Miss Understanding**20 [791] 4-9-2 43 (J R Weymes) *plld hrd: cl up tl wknd over 2f out: eased whn no ch*	(b) NeilBrown(3) 6	**14/1**	—

2m 6.86s (1.46) **Going Correction** 0.0s/f (Good)
WFA 3 from 4yo 17lb — **10** Ran SP% **119.0**
Speed ratings (Par 103): **94,92,92,90,88 85,83,75,61,61**
toteswinger: 1&2 £19.40, 1&3 £7.50, 2&3 £7.80. CSF £33.91 TOTE £8.20: £2.50, £1.80, £1.60; EX 36.50.There was no bid for the winner.
Owner Eugene Woods **Bred** Meon Valley Stud **Trained** Exning, Suffolk

FOCUS
This was a desperately weak contest. The runner-up looks the best guide to the race, but dubious form overall.
Premier Krug(IRE) Official explanation: jockey said filly was unsuited by the track
Miss Understanding Official explanation: jockey said filly was unsuited by thevtrack

1521 TOTESPORTGAMES.COM MAIDEN AUCTION FILLIES' STKS — 5f
4:35 (4:36) (Class 5) 2-Y-O — **£3,885** (£1,156; £577; £288) **Stalls** Low

Form	Pos	Dist	Horse / Trainer / Comment	Jockey	SP	RPR
4	1		**Sheka**9 [1304] 2-8-10 0 (I W McInnes) *in tch: rdn over 2f out: effrt and swtchd rt ent fnl f: led wl ins fnl f: jst hld on*	TomEaves 3	**9/1**	74
	2	shd	**Forbidden Paradise (IRE)** 2-8-4 0 (K R Burke) *dwlt: outpcd in rr: gd hdwy fnl f: jst failed*	AndrewElliott 8	**10/1**	68+
2	3	1/2	**Gower Sophia**10 [1277] 2-8-4 0 (M Brittain) *w ldrs tl no ex towards fin*	TWilliams 12	**5/2**1	66
4	4	3/4	**Bebenine (IRE)**9 [1312] 2-8-4 0 (Patrick Morris) *racd keenly: led wl ins fnl f: no ex*	PaulHanagan 11	**12/1**	63
3	5	3 1/2	**Reel Credit Crunch**9 [1312] 2-8-6 0 (P D Evans) *w ldrs: rdn 1/2-way: no ex whn checked ent fnl f: sn btn*	PaulDoe 6	**9/2**3	53
	6	2	**Prettiest Star (IRE)** 2-8-8 0 (K A Ryan) *dwlt: bhd and sn drvn along: nvr on terms*	PaulMulrennan 5	**11/4**2	48+
	7	10	**Santas Pal** 2-7-11 0 (C J Teague) *rn green and a outpcd*	JamieKyne(7) 2	**15/2**	8

59.71 secs (-0.99) **Going Correction** -0.325s/f (Firm) — **7** Ran SP% **112.0**
Speed ratings (Par 89): **94,93,93,91,86 83,67**
toteswinger: 1&2 £6.20, 1&3 £3.90, 2&3 £5.40. CSF £85.50 TOTE £9.50: £3.30, £4.20; EX 80.20.
Owner T Elsey, S A Elsey, R Mustill **Bred** Redmyre Bloodstock Ltd **Trained** Catwick, E Yorks
■ Stewards' Enquiry : Tom Eaves caution: careless riding.

FOCUS
A fairly modest fillies´ maiden.

NOTEBOOK
Sheka, a running-on fourth at odds of 66-1 on her recent CD debut, was having to concede weight all round, but she picked up well when switched inside the final furlong and did just enough to hang on from the fast-finishing runner-up. She is nothing special, but clearly has a good deal of speed. (op 7-1 tchd 13-2)
Forbidden Paradise(IRE), a half-sister to useful juvenile Prince Of Denmark, was green and outpaced early, but the penny finally dropped and she flashed home to just be denied. This was a really promising start and she should be capable of winning something similar. (op 11-2)
Gower Sophia nearly caused an 80-1 upset when second on her debut at Beverley and she again showed enough to suggest a small race will come her way. (op 3-1 tchd 9-4)
Bebenine(IRE) showed plenty of pace, as she had done on her debut, but once again didn´t quite see it out. (op 8-1)
Reel Credit Crunch, one place ahead of Bebenine on debut, failed to go on from that and was disappointing. (op 5-1 tchd 7-1)

Prettiest Star(IRE), who came in for good support beforehand, was soon in trouble and could only make modest late headway when the race was all over. She should learn from this, though, and will benefit from an extra furlong in time. (op 8-1)

1522 TOTESPORTBINGO.COM MAIDEN STKS — 1m 1f 170y
5:10 (5:10) (Class 5) 3-Y-O — **£3,885** (£1,156; £577; £288) **Stalls** High

Form	Pos	Dist	Horse / Trainer / Comment	Jockey	SP	RPR
3	1		**Off Chance**21 [1128] 3-8-12 0 (T D Easterby) *hld up in tch: smooth hdwy to ld 1f out: pushed out fnl f*	DuranFentiman 7	**6/1**2	65
3	2	2 1/2	**Signaller (USA)**9 [1308] 3-9-3 0 (M Johnston) *led: rdn and edgd rt fr 2f out: hdd 1f out: kpt on same pce*	J-PGuillambert 1	**1/5**1	65
000-	3	1/2	**Avitus**179 [7038] 3-8-12 50 (Micky Hammond) *trckd ldrs: rdn over 2f out: one pce fnl f*	FrederikTylicki(5) 3	**25/1**	64?
-0	4	3/4	**Highkingofireland**27 [1015] 3-9-3 0 (K R Burke) *trckd ldrs: effrt over 2f out: kpt on same pce fnl f*	DarrenWilliams 4	**33/1**	63
	5	14	**Goswick** 3-8-12 0 (Micky Hammond) *racd keenly: prom tl outpcd over 3f out: n.d after*	PaulMulrennan 6	**33/1**	30
0	6	1 3/4	**The Quiet Genius**8 [1335] 3-9-3 0 (Jedd O'Keeffe) *hld up: rdn over 3f out: sn btn*	PaulHanagan 5	**25/1**	31
0	7	17	**Cosmic**12 [1245] 3-9-3 0 (T D Easterby) *cl up tl rdn and wknd over 2f out*	DavidAllan 2	**12/1**3	—

2m 5.66s (0.26) **Going Correction** 0.0s/f (Good) — **7** Ran SP% **118.9**
Speed ratings (Par 98): **98,96,95,95,83 82,68**
toteswinger: 1&2 £1.10, 1&3 £5.80, 2&3 £3.40. CSF £7.99 TOTE £6.60: £1.80, £1.10; EX 11.80.
Owner L B Holliday **Bred** Cleaboy Farms Co **Trained** Great Habton, N Yorks

FOCUS
They went no gallop and the result was an unsatisfactory one, with the long-odds-on favourite disappointing in second and the close-up third having an official rating of just 50.
The Quiet Genius Official explanation: jockey said gelding hung left-handed throughout

1523 HARLOW OVER THE HILL F.C. 10TH ANNIVERSARY CONDITIONS STKS — 1m 4f 10y
5:45 (5:47) (Class 3) 4-Y-0+ — **£7,477** (£2,239; £1,119; £560) **Stalls** High

Form	Pos	Dist	Horse / Trainer / Comment	Jockey	SP	RPR
-020	1		**Classic Punch (IRE)**51 [772] 6-8-9 103 (D R C Elsworth) *mde all: rdn 3f out: drew clr fnl 2f: unchal*	PaulMulrennan 5	**3/1**3	107
340-	2	6	**Hobby**211 [6241] 4-8-3 100 (R M Beckett) *pressed wnr thrght: rdn over 3f out: one pce fnl 2f*	PaulHanagan 3	**7/4**2	92
320-	3	12	**Spanish Hidalgo (IRE)**154 [7429] 5-8-9 102 (J L Dunlop) *trckd ldrs: effrt whn hung bdly rt 2f out: sn wknd*	(t) J-PGuillambert 4	**5/4**1	78+
33/0	4	3 1/2	**Regal Tradition (IRE)**9 [1314] 4-8-3 60 (G J Smith) *hld up last: rdn 3f out: sn wknd*	PatrickDonaghy(5) 2	**150/1**	73?

2m 36.56s (-0.14) **Going Correction** 0.0s/f (Good)
WFA 4 from 5yo+ 1lb — **4** Ran SP% **106.5**
Speed ratings (Par 107): **100,96,88,85**
CSF £8.35 TOTE £3.10; EX 7.10 Place 6: £899.96 Place 5: £274.50.
Owner The Classic Bunch **Bred** Granham Farm **Trained** Newmarket, Suffolk

FOCUS
Only three of the five runners mattered in this and there was little between them on paper. The outclassed fourth was not beaten that far, which suggests the bare form should not be taken too literally.

NOTEBOOK
Classic Punch(IRE) galloped on relentlessly from the front to register his first success since July 2007. He showed he is still capable of useful form when finishing second off a mark of 102 in Dubai in February and this return to a right-handed track was in his favour. Races similar to this are likely to continue to represent his best chance of winning. (op 7-4)
Hobby, who got a little warm beforehand, came under strong pressure racing past the three-pole and could find no extra from over a furlong out. She is another who will not be easy to place this season. (op 9-4)
Spanish Hidalgo(IRE) was being kept in by Hobby against the rail, but when a gap opened he seemed to lose his action and continued to move poorly throughout the final furlong. His rider felt the ground was simply too fast for him. Official explanation: jockey said gelding was unsuited by the good to firm ground (op 7-4)
Regal Tradition(IRE) hung in there for a long way as a result of the steady pace.
T/Plt: £662.00 to a £1 stake. Pool: £83,576.63. 92.16 winning tickets. T/Qpdt: £18.40 to a £1 stake. Pool: £3,974.85. 159.50 winning tickets. RY

1484 SANDOWN (R-H)
Saturday, April 25

OFFICIAL GOING: Good (good to firm in places; 8.7)
Other races under Jumps rules
Wind: Light, half-against Weather: Fine

1524 CASINO AT BET365.COM FLAT V JUMP JOCKEYS H'CAP — 1m 14y
1:00 (1:04) (Class 4) (0-80,79) 4-Y-0+ — **£7,123** (£2,119; £1,059; £529) **Stalls** High

Form	Pos	Dist	Horse / Trainer / Comment	Jockey	SP	RPR
540-	1		**Twilight Star (IRE)**129 [7712] 5-11-0 75 (R A Teal) *mde all: drew at least 5 l clr 1/2-way: rdn and kpt on wl enough fnl 2f: unchal*	DarryllHolland 9	**15/2**3	84
54-4	2	1 3/4	**Collateral Damage (IRE)**21 [1123] 6-11-4 79 (T D Easterby) *hld up in 5th: rdn over 2f out: prog over 1f out: wnt 2nd ins fnl f: clsd on wnr but nvr able to chal*	(t) RWalsh 14	**11/2**2	84
000-	3	nse	**Bustan (IRE)**205 [6424] 10-11-4 79 (G C Bravery) *hld up in last trio: plenty to do whn effrt over 2f out: threaded through rivals fnl 2f and tk 3rd last 100yds: nrst fin*	SamThomas 10	**10/1**	84
2530	4	1 1/4	**Ocean Legend (IRE)**40 [850] 4-11-1 76 (Miss J Feilden) *chsd ldng pair: drvn into 2nd over 1f out: no imp onwnr: lost 2 pls ins fnl f*	RichardHughes 11	**16/1**	78
3152	5	3/4	**North Parade**45 [805] 4-11-0 75 (A W Carroll) *hld up in 9th: drvn on inner over 2f out: kpt on w limited enthusiasm: nrst fin*	(t) JamieMoore 8	**20/1**	75
-000	6	1 1/2	**Daaweitza**7 [1343] 6-11-1 76 (B Ellison) *hld up in 7th: rdn over 2f out: plugged on same pce: nvr rchd ldrs*	(p) RichardJohnson 12	**11/1**	73
0-50	7	1/2	**Carlitos Spirit (IRE)**27 [1016] 5-11-2 77 (B R Millman) *chsd clr wnr to over 1f out: wknd ins fnl f*	RobertThornton 3	**16/1**	73
30-6	8	1 1/2	**Phluke**14 [1213] 8-11-2 77 (Eve Johnson Houghton) *hld up in 6th: rdn and no prog over 2f out: nvr on terms*	JimmyFortune 2	**16/1**	69
03-4	9	3/4	**Nisaal (IRE)**27 [1016] 4-11-1 76 (J J Quinn) *hld up in 8th: hrd rdn and effrt on outer 3f out: no prog 2f out: fdd*	APMcCoy 6	**9/2**1	67

240- **10** *7* **Mount Hermon (IRE)**[224] 5908 5-11-2 **77** .... AlanMunro 13 52
(H Morrison) *hld up in last pair: no prog over 2f out: bhd after* **12/1**

421- **11** *nse* **Spotty Muldoon (IRE)**[233] 5652 4-10-12 **73** .... DaneO'Neill 4 47
(R M Beckett) *hld up in last pair: brief effrt 3f out: sn no prog and bhd* **9/2**[1]

10-0 **12** *5* **Shanzu**[19] 1149 4-11-1 **76** .... RyanMoore 7 39
(G L Moore) *chsd ldng trio: rdn 1/2-way: wknd over 2f out: t.o* **14/1**

1m 45.31s (2.01) **Going Correction** +0.15s/f (Good) **12** Ran SP% **117.7**
Speed ratings (Par 105): **95,93,93,91,91 89,89,87,86,79 79,74**
toteswinger: 1&2 £8.10, 1&3 £13.20, 2&3 £10.00 CSF £48.07 CT £425.37 TOTE £9.10: £2.90, £1.80, £3.40; EX 56.40.

Owner G M Harris **Bred** D G Hardisty Bloodstock **Trained** Ashtead, Surrey

FOCUS
This result cannot be taken completely at face value for form analysis due to the nature of the event, but it did provide viewers with an interesting comparison of raceriding styles/tactics. The well-backed and well-handicapped winner was given a good front-running ride and never looked like getting caught.

1525 BET365 MILE (GROUP 2) 1m 14y
3:45 (3:47) (Class 1) 4-Y-0+

£56,770 (£21,520; £10,770; £5,370; £2,690; £1,350) **Stalls** High

Form RPR

31-0 **1** **Paco Boy (IRE)**[28] 1011 4-9-6 124 .... RichardHughes 1 124
(R Hannon) *hld up in 4th: smooth prog over 2f out: led over 1f out: shkn up ins fnl f: a holding on* **15/8**[1]

53-2 **2** *¾* **Dream Eater (IRE)**[12] 1251 4-9-0 108 .... (t) FrancisNorton 6 116
(A M Balding) *trckd ldng pair: hemmed in on inner and lost pl over 2f out: prog over 1f out: kpt on to take 2nd nr fin* **7/1**

111- **3** *nk* **Virtual**[175] 7147 4-9-0 113 .... JimmyFortune 4 115
(J H M Gosden) *hld up in 6th: prog on outer over 2f out: upsides wnr over 1f out but nt gng as wl: hld ins fnl f: lost 2nd nr fin* **11/4**[2]

601- **4** *2 ¾* **Stotsfold**[245] 5289 6-9-0 116 .... AdamKirby 3 109
(W R Swinburn) *hld up in last: drvn on outer 2f out: plugged on but no imp on ldrs* **5/1**[3]

30-0 **5** *1 ¼* **Forthe Millionkiss (GER)**[27] 1029 5-9-0 112 .... WMongil 2 106
(Uwe Ostmann, Germany) *chsd ldr to over 2f out: sn outpcd and lost pl* **40/1**

00-4 **6** *1 ½* **Lovelace**[20] 1138 5-9-4 112 .... RoystonFfrench 7 107
(M Johnston) *s.s: rcvrd into 5th: rdn and no prog over 2f out: fdd* **7/1**

1402 **7** *6* **Kandidate**[28] 1004 7-9-0 106 .... SebSanders 8 89
(C E Brittain) *led to over 1f out: wknd rapidly: heavily eased last 150yds* **14/1**

1m 43.04s (-0.26) **Going Correction** +0.15s/f (Good) **7** Ran SP% **112.2**
Speed ratings (Par 115): **107,106,105,103,101 100,94**
toteswinger: 1&2 £2.80, 1&3 £2.00, 2&3 £4.00 CSF £15.08 TOTE £2.60: £2.10, £2.90; EX 14.20 Trifecta £29.00 Pool: £675.62 - 17.20 winning units..

Owner The Calvera Partnership No 2 **Bred** Mrs Joan Browne **Trained** East Everleigh, Wilts

FOCUS
A good field - well up to scratch in terms of both numbers and overall quality. A fine return from Paco Boy, who should be at least as good as he was last year, but the runner-up's improvement probably isn't cast iron.

NOTEBOOK
Paco Boy(IRE) had been unbeatable at 7f and stood out on form, but he had questions to answer over 1m, especially with the 6lb Group 1 penalty for his win in the Foret. He went well from the start, as he was entitled to in a race not run at a strong pace, and having had to make his move earlier than intended owing it was just a question of seeing the trip out. Richard Hughes did not need to get serious with him and he never quite looked as if he would be reeled in, but he looked as if he was tiring near the finish. According to Hughes, that was because he had not done much since his trip to Dubai, but there remain slight reservations about his stamina for a strongly-run 1m. Nevertheless, he now has the option of all the big 1m races like the Lockinge, the Queen Anne and the Sussex Stakes, plus possibly relatively easy pickings back at 7f in the Foret again. (op 13-8 tchd 2-1 in places)
Dream Eater(IRE) has always had a serious amount of ability, but he is not straightforward and had thrown away his chance by veering sharply left at Warwick last time. This time he hugged the rail, and when making his challenge up the winner's inside he had no opportunity to deviate. This was obviously a good run. (op 13-2 tchd 8-1)
Virtual improved fast on easy ground last autumn and represented a stable in great form. He looked terrific, but there was a slight question mark over him on this drying ground. Having made his effort on the outside in the straight and looked the main danger to Paco Boy approaching the final furlong, he lost second to Dream Eater in the closing stages, but this was still a very satisfactory first run of the year. He should come on for this and remains open to improvement, especially back on easier ground. (tchd 3-1)
Stotsfold looked fit and was well backed, but having been held up in rear he never quite got involved and was just one paced in the final furlong. All of his wins are over another two furlongs further. (op 13-2)
Forthe Millionkiss(GER), a German Group 2 winner, had been found out twice at Longchamp last year. Having chased front-runner Kandidate he was perhaps a shade outclassed, though not disgraced. (op 33-1)
Lovelace, another Group 2 winner in Germany, having earlier won a valuable handicap here, missed the break. (op 9-1)
Kandidate was worst in on figures and, having made the running, dropped away inside the last two furlongs. (op 16-1 tchd 11-1)

1526 BET365 GORDON RICHARDS STKS (GROUP 3) 1m 2f 7y
4:15 (4:17) (Class 1) 4-Y-0+

£36,900 (£13,988; £7,000; £3,490; £1,748; £877) **Stalls** High

Form RPR

124- **1** **Tartan Bearer (IRE)**[300] 3535 4-9-0 122 .... RyanMoore 3 120+
(Sir Michael Stoute) *hld up in 6th: prog over 2f out: rdn to chse clr ldr over 1f out: styd on wl fnl f to ld last stride* **11/10**[1]

140- **2** *shd* **Pipedreamer**[189] 6816 5-9-0 117 .... JimmyFortune 6 120
(J H M Gosden) *led 1f: restrained into 3rd: smooth prog to ld over 2f out: drew 3 l clr over 1f out: tired fnl f: hdd last stride* **9/4**[2]

116- **3** *2 ¼* **Buccellati**[132] 7682 5-9-3 114 .... (v) WilliamBuick 5 118
(A M Balding) *hld up in last pair: rdn and prog on outer over 2f out: wnt 3rd jst over 1f out: kpt on but nt pce to chal* **10/1**[3]

52-2 **4** *1* **Steele Tango (USA)**[9] 1301 4-9-0 106 .... DaneO'Neill 4 113
(R A Teal) *led after 1f to over 2f out: outpcd wl over 1f out: plugged on* **10/1**[3]

21-0 **5** *½* **Charlie Farnsbarns (IRE)**[28] 1011 5-9-3 114 .... MartinDwyer 2 115
(B J Meehan) *t.k.h: trckd ldng trio: nt qckn over 2f out: kpt on same pce fr over 1f out* **14/1**

4461 **6** *½* **Halicarnassus (IRE)**[9] 1306 5-9-0 107 .... SamHitchcott 7 111
(M R Channon) *hld up in last pair: prog on inner and cl up over 2f out: rdn whn nowhere to go and snatched up wl over 1f out: kpt on again ins fnl f* **25/1**

20- **7** *2 ¾* **Bushman**[217] 6106 5-9-0 104 .... RichardHughes 1 106
(D M Simcock) *t.k.h: trckd ldr after 1f: chal and upsides over 2f out: sn outpcd: wknd fnl f* **14/1**

530- **8** *1 ¾* **Indian Days**[203] 6476 4-9-0 100 .... AlanMunro 8 102
(J G Given) *t.k.h early: hld up in 5th: lost pl and last 2f out: struggling after* **33/1**

2m 8.65s (-1.85) **Going Correction** +0.15s/f (Good) **8** Ran SP% **116.7**
Speed ratings (Par 113): **113,112,111,110,109 109,107,105**
toteswinger: 1&2 £1.10, 1&3 £4.00, 2&3 £4.70 CSF £3.75 TOTE £2.10: £1.10, £1.60, £2.50; EX 3.30.

Owner Ballymacoll Stud **Bred** Ballymacoll Stud Farm Ltd **Trained** Newmarket, Suffolk

FOCUS
A really good field lined up for this Group 3. There was no guaranteed pacemaker prior to the off, as virtually all of those that took part had made their names being held up, and the early gallop was modest to say the least. The race developed going to two out and the classiest horses dominated the final outcome. Tartan Bearer has been rated 5lb off his Epsom mark however.

NOTEBOOK
Tartan Bearer(IRE) made a fairly rapid rise up the ladder last season, as he went from taking a Leicester maiden to winning the Dante Stakes to finishing a battling second to New Approach in the Epsom Derby. He only had one more outing afterwards and that was another good performance, despite being hampered, in the Irish Derby. Held up in midfield, Ryan Moore had looked for a minute to be caught out by an astute bit of riding by Jimmy Fortune, but he galvanised his mount inside the final furlong and they got up in the nick of time. This was a good effort over a trip that would be a bare minimum, and he looks a force to reckon with in the top races again. The Tattersalls Gold Cup at the Curragh in late May is his next target. (op 6-5 tchd 11-8 and 6-4 in a place)
Pipedreamer had been absent since a below-par effort in the Champion Stakes, but his stable have been in amazing form and it was only lack of peak fitness that cost him the race on the line after a decisive move had taken him three lengths clear inside the last two furlongs. This was a fine effort, and he looks sure to improve. (op 9-4 tchd 5-2 in places)
Buccellati improved throughout last season and claimed a Listed race and Group 3 towards the end of it. He was far from disgraced in a Group 1 out in Hong Kong on his final start but had it all to do under a penalty against these rivals. He made his bid towards the outside of the field but never quite got on terms. On official ratings, he ran as well as could have been expected, if not a bit better, and looks sure to have a good year. (op 12-1 tchd 14-1)
Steele Tango(USA) is a fantastic flag bearer for his trainer and had proved that he is still on the upgrade with a marvellous effort in the Earl of Sefton last time. This was another step in the right direction and he probably has a Group 3 in him at some stage. (op 11-1 tchd 12-1)
Charlie Farnsbarns(IRE) was pitched in at the deep end on his seasonal debut out in Dubai, where he was one of a number of horses that did not see which was Gladiatorus went in the Dubai Duty Free. Under a 3lb penalty for winning the Group 3 Darley Stakes at 50-1 last October, he did not have the speed to get on terms, but shaped well all the same. (tchd 16-1)
Halicarnassus(IRE) had fitness on his side as he had already won two races in 2009, including a small-field conditions race at Ripon the previous weekend. He did his best without making much of an impact, even allowing for the fact that he met a bit of trouble in running. (tchd 16-1)
Bushman, who looked a bit too keen, needs easier ground so this going was not ideal. One would imagine that his season will be dictated by the weather. (tchd 16-1)
Indian Days had no chance of official figures and was outclassed. (tchd 25-1)

1527 POKER AT BET365.COM H'CAP 1m 14y
4:50 (4:50) (Class 2) (0-100,93) 4-Y-0+

£11,215 (£3,358; £1,679; £840; £419; £210) **Stalls** High

Form RPR

62-0 **1** **Dunn'o (IRE)**[18] 1170 4-8-11 **86** .... AdamKirby 14 96
(C G Cox) *led at gd pce: rdn and hdd over 2f out: battled on wl u.p: led again ins fnl f* **12/1**

06-1 **2** *nk* **Light From Mars**[19] 1149 4-8-13 **88** .... AlanMunro 10 98
(B R Millman) *pressed ldr: led over 2f out whn gng bttr than wnr: clr w him sn after: rdn over 1f out: worn down ins fnl f* **10/3**[1]

445- **3** *3 ¾* **Stevie Thunder**[245] 5273 4-9-0 **89** .... DarryllHolland 4 90
(Ian Williams) *hld up in rr: rdn on outer over 2f out: prog wl over 1f out: wnt 3rd ins fnl f: nt rch ldng pair* **12/1**

654- **4** *½* **Ellemujie**[175] 7146 4-9-1 **90** .... MartinDwyer 7 90
(D K Ivory) *hld up towards rr on inner: nt clr run briefly over 2f out: prog over 1f out: kpt on fnl f: nvr able to chal* **16/1**

566- **5** *1* **Decameron (USA)**[139] 7594 4-8-10 **85** .... RyanMoore 5 83
(Sir Michael Stoute) *racd wd 1st 3f: prom: rdn to chse clr ldng pair over 1f out: no imp: fdd fnl f* **4/1**[2]

221- **6** *¾* **Isphahan**[209] 6307 6-9-0 **92** .... DavidProbert(3) 15 88
(A M Balding) *chsd ldng pair to over 2f out: steadily fdd fr over 1f out* **10/1**

1262 **7** *2* **Tartan Gigha (IRE)**[4] 1433 4-8-8 **83** .... RoystonFfrench 3 74
(M Johnston) *hld up in last pair: rdn and no prog over 2f out: kpt on u.p fr over 1f out* **7/1**

102- **8** *1 ½* **Resurge (IRE)**[185] 6900 4-8-13 **88** .... FergusSweeney 6 76
(W S Kittow) *stdd s: hld up in last pair: effrt on outer over 2f out: no real prog over 1f out* **20/1**

203- **9** *4* **Jack Dawkins (USA)**[161] 7339 4-9-4 **93** .... IanMongan 1 72
(H R A Cecil) *hld up in midfield: rdn over 2f out: sn lost tch w ldrs and no ch* **7/1**

30-0 **10** *½* **Cape Hawk (IRE)**[14] 1209 5-8-13 **88** .... RichardHughes 13 65
(R Hannon) *hld up in midfield: rdn and no prog over 2f out: wknd and eased fnl f* **13/2**[3]

00-0 **11** *11* **Mut'Ab (USA)**[21] 1116 4-8-7 **82** .... (b) DO'Donohoe 9 34
(C E Brittain) *chsd ldrs: lost pl over 2f out: sn bhd: t.o* **25/1**

311- **12** *5* **Novikov**[61] 6033 5-9-1 **90** .... JimmyFortune 8 31
(G L Moore) *hld up in last pair: shkn up over 2f out: wknd: t.o* **18/1**

1m 42.8s (-0.50) **Going Correction** +0.15s/f (Good) **12** Ran SP% **125.6**
Speed ratings (Par 109): **108,107,103,103,102 101,99,98,94,93 82,77**
toteswinger:1&2 £11.80, 1&3 £22.30, 2&3 £7.60 CSF £54.94 CT £522.66 TOTE £16.10: £3.40, £1.60, £3.00; EX 83.40 Place 6: £105.13 Place 5: £27.41.

Owner Dennis Shaw **Bred** R Hodgins **Trained** Lambourn, Berks

FOCUS
Three non-runners declared did not make this handicap any easier to solve. The first two were prominent throughout and nothing got involved from off the pace, so the form may not be completely reliable. It has provisionally been taken at face value however.

NOTEBOOK
Dunn'o(IRE) won a couple of races last season, including one over 7f here, but he did not show much sparkle on his return at Pontefract after taking a keen grip. Pulling very hard again from what seemed an ideal draw, he made the running at a decent pace but looked beaten when headed going to two out. He somehow found more for pressure, however, and got back past the runner-up inside the final furlong. He is probably the right type for some of the big 1m handicaps throughout the season, as a strong gallop set by others should help him.

Light From Mars, a previous course and distance winner, was raised 5lb for victory on his first start of this season but looked like adding to that success here when pressing on. However, the winner was in no mood to give up and came back to deny him. He is still open to plenty of improvement and should rate higher in the future. (op 4-1)
Stevie Thunder, who cost his new owners 40,000gns at Tattersalls last October, was given a bit to do from off the pace but kept on well once in the clear. (op 14-1)
Ellemujie is a really good, consistent sort but only had one win to his name. If there was an unlucky horse in the race, it was him as he was short of room up the inside rail a couple of times. (op 25-1)
Decameron(USA) represented a stable that had won this with its only two runners in the previous 10 years and would not have been kept in training unless thought capable of improving. Wide of his rivals early, he was in the firing line when the tempo increased but could not make his presence felt. (op 9-2 tchd 11-2)
Isphahan, a four-time winner in 2008 including once here over course and distance, started the season 7lb higher than he ended the last one and ran no more than a fair race on his return to action. (op 8-1)
Tartan Gigha(IRE) is a consistent sort who was making a very swift reappearance. He stayed on quite well inside the final furlong, but the leaders had gone beyond recall. (op 15-2 tchd 8-1)
Resurge(IRE), having his first start for new connections after leaving Jeremy Noseda for 22,000gns, beat Expresso Star when landing his maiden at Goodwood but seemingly did not come up to scratch afterwards. Held up, he travelled strongly but did not pick up when asked to quicken. The jockey was far from hard on him and one would imagine there is plenty more to come from the horse. (op 16-1)
Jack Dawkins(USA) ran as though the race was badly needed. (op 8-1)
Cape Hawk(IRE) reportedly did not enjoy the going. Official explanation: jockey said gelding stumbled on the undulations (op 7-1 tchd 6-1)
T/Jkpt: Not won. T/Plt: £66.60 to a £1 stake. Pool: £158,773.91. 1,739.28 winning tickets.
T/Qpdt: £22.30 to a £1 stake. Pool: £9,106.06. 301.14 winning tickets. JN

1490 WOLVERHAMPTON (A.W) (L-H)

Saturday, April 25

OFFICIAL GOING: Standard
Wind: Fresh, behind Weather: Dry with some high cloud

1528 DINE IN THE HORIZONS AMATEUR RIDERS' H'CAP 5f 216y(P)
6:50 (6:51) (Class 6) (0-60,60) 4-Y-O+ £1,977 (£608; £304) Stalls Low

Form RPR
-05 1 **Rabbit Fighter (IRE)**[3] 1468 5-11-0 **58**.................(v) MrBenHamilton(5) 4 71+
(D Shaw) *hld up in rr: hdwy on outside 2f out: led ins fnl f: sn clr* **9/4**[1]
000- 2 2 **The History Man (IRE)**[179] 7043 6-10-10 **56**.(be) MissMMullineaux(7) 10 63
(M Mullineaux) *a.p: led briefly 1f out: kpt on but nt pce of wnr* **40/1**
1-00 3 2 1/4 **Miltons Choice**[4] 1421 6-10-12 **58**.............................. MissHDavies(7) 3 57
(J M Bradley) *a.p: led 2f out to 1f out: kpt on one pce* **16/1**
3534 4 1 **Muktasb (USA)**[21] 1134 8-11-6 **59**...............................(v) MrsMMorris 11 55
(D Shaw) *in rr tl hdwy 2f out: kpt on: nvr nrr* **7/1**
/000 5 nse **Gower**[71] 540 5-10-9 **55**... MrJGoss(7) 8 51
(R J Price) *hld up: hdwy to chse ldrs over 2f out: no ex fnl f* **22/1**
-000 6 1 **Towy Boy (IRE)**[4] 1421 4-11-2 **60**...................................(t) MrCMartin(5) 1 53
(I A Wood) *in rr: mde sme late prog* **5/1**[2]
0333 7 1/2 **Spirit Of Coniston**[9] 1310 6-10-11 **55**.................... MissWGibson(5) 6 46
(P T Midgley) *in tch: rdn 2f out: fdd ins fnl f* **6/1**[3]
0560 8 1/2 **Hurricane Coast**[34] 921 10-10-8 **54**.......................(p) MissAHeath(7) 9 44
(D Flood) *mid-div: rdn and no hdwy fr over 1f out* **28/1**
101- 9 5 **Tenancy (IRE)**[158] 7369 5-10-11 **55**.......................... MrCAHarris(5) 12 29
(R C Guest) *led tl hdd 2f out: sn wknd* **20/1**
206- 10 3 1/4 **Pintano**[190] 6791 4-11-2 **60**.. MissSBradley(5) 7 23
(J M Bradley) *mid-div tl wknd 2f out* **10/1**
2660 11 3 3/4 **Angel Voices (IRE)**[38] 861 6-10-12 **56**...............(p) MissKellyBurke(5) 2 7
(K R Burke) *a bhd* **25/1**
000- 12 nk **Triumphant Welcome**[194] 6706 4-10-13 **59**.............. MrSeanKerr(7) 13 9
(H J Evans) *trckd ldr to over 2f out: sn wknd* **16/1**
036- 13 1 3/4 **Jilly Why (IRE)**[123] 7774 8-10-9 **55**........................ MissACraven(7) 5 —
(Paul Green) *a bhd* **20/1**
1m 15.15s (0.15) **Going Correction** -0.025s/f (Stan) **13** Ran SP% **118.7**
Speed ratings (Par 101): **98,95,92,91,90 89,88,88,81,77 72,71,69**
toteswinger: 1&2 £17.70, 1&3 £17.70, 2&3 £17.70. CSF £128.22 CT £1241.22 TOTE £3.50: £1.50, £11.30, £5.80; EX 201.70.
Owner Market Avenue Racing Club Ltd **Bred** Hawthorn Villa Stud **Trained** Danethorpe, Notts
■ Stewards' Enquiry : Mr J Goss one-day ban: used whip with excessive frequency (May 11)
Mr C A Harris one-day ban: failed to ride to draw (May 11)

FOCUS
A moderate amateur riders' handicap, but they went a decent pace.

1529 PLAY BINGO AT LADBROKES.COM H'CAP 5f 20y(P)
7:20 (7:21) (Class 6) (0-65,66) 3-Y-O £2,388 (£705; £352) Stalls Low

Form RPR
2204 1 **Villaruz (IRE)**[12] 1247 3-8-7 **59**..........................(b[1]) AndreaAtzeni(5) 3 65
(D Flood) *t.k.h: restrained tl hdwy on ins over 1f out: r.o to ld fnl 1/2f* **9/4**[1]
0345 2 1 1/4 **You Avin A Laugh**[21] 1129 3-8-13 **60**........................ CatherineGannon 2 61
(C A Dwyer) *led: rdn over 1f out: hdd fnl 1/2f* **11/2**[3]
6430 3 2 1/4 **Badtanman**[9] 1311 3-8-5 **52** oh6 ow1..........................(b) PatrickMathers 1 45
(Peter Grayson) *chsd ldrs: rdn over 1f out: kpt on one pce fnl f* **12/1**
060- 4 hd **Winterbourne**[211] 6244 3-8-5 **52**.................................. JimmyQuinn 12 44+
(M Blanshard) *swtchd to ins fr wd draw after 1f: styd on fr over 1f out: nvr nrr* **33/1**
4621 5 1 1/2 **Perfect Honour (IRE)**[19] 1157 3-8-9 **56**........................ TonyCulhane 7 43+
(D Shaw) *hld up: hdwy on outside 2f out: one pce appr fnl f* **4/1**[2]
2434 6 hd **Pinball (IRE)**[7] 1359 3-8-4 **56**................................ WilliamCarson(5) 4 42
(Patrick Morris) *in tch tl rdn and wknd fnl f* **4/1**[2]
045- 7 1 1/4 **Transcentral**[176] 7113 3-8-11 **65**................................ PaulPickard(7) 5 47
(W M Brisbourne) *in tch: rdn 3f out: outpcd fr over 1f out* **16/1**
-502 8 hd **Rapanui Belle**[19] 1157 3-8-4 **51** oh2.......................... WilliamBuick 10 32
(G L Moore) *prom on outside for 3f* **12/1**
1550 9 3 1/2 **Brown Lentic (IRE)**[19] 1157 3-7-11 **51** oh2........... MatthewCosham(7) 9 19
(Miss J Feilden) *in tch on outside tl wknd over 1f out* **25/1**
0306 10 nk **Sills Vincero**[9] 1311 3-8-11 **58**.. TedDurcan 8 25
(D Shaw) *trckd ldr: rdn 1/2-way wknd qckly over 1f out* **12/1**
62.21 secs (-0.09) **Going Correction** -0.025s/f (Stan) **10** Ran SP% **121.9**
Speed ratings (Par 96): **99,97,93,93,90 90,88,88,82,81**
toteswinger: 1&2 £4.70, 1&3 £9.10, 2&3 £9.10. CSF £15.71 CT £120.46 TOTE £3.10: £1.30, £2.10, £3.80; EX 28.00.
Owner S Lau **Bred** John McEnery **Trained**

FOCUS
A modest handicap in which the draw played a big part, with the first three home coming from the three inside stalls.

1530 STARPLAN ELEGANT BEDROOM FURNITURE (S) STKS 1m 141y(P)
7:50 (7:50) (Class 6) 3-Y-O+ £2,047 (£604; £302) Stalls Low

Form RPR
4-60 1 **Sign Of The Cross**[45] 798 5-10-0 73................................ DaneO'Neill 7 69
(G L Moore) *a.p on ins: led over 1f out: rdn clr ins fnl f* **6/4**[1]
0-06 2 1 1/2 **My Mate Mal**[10] 1276 5-10-0 55... DavidAllan 9 65
(B Ellison) *trckd ldrs: rdn and ev ch appr fnl f: kpt on to go 2nd towards fin* **16/1**
06-0 3 1/2 **Andorn (GER)**[12] 1243 5-9-9 66.. TPQueally 5 59
(B J Curley) *led tl hdd over 1f out: kpt on one pce but lost 2nd towards fin* **5/1**[2]
6406 4 shd **Bookiebasher Babe (IRE)**[64] 617 4-9-9 62................ FrancisNorton 3 59
(M Quinn) *mid-div: styd on fr over 1f out: nvr nrr* **16/1**
0510 5 1 3/4 **Waterside (IRE)**[9] 1314 10-10-0 68..............................(t) JamesDoyle 11 60
(S Curran) *hld up in rr: kpt on u.p fr over 1f out but nvr on terms* **12/1**
2030 6 nk **Prince Noel**[10] 1276 5-9-2 62..(v) BMcHugh(7) 12 54
(N Wilson) *nvr bttr than mid-div* **13/2**[3]
0242 7 3/4 **Ten Pole Tudor**[5] 1409 4-9-2 60...(p) SPRyan(7) 1 52
(R A Harris) *in tch: effrt on outside 2f out: sn btn* **5/1**[2]
1323 8 1/2 **Red Rudy**[17] 1187 7-9-7 63... TobyAtkinson(7) 2 56
(A W Carroll) *rrd up s and nvr got into r* **10/1**
00- 9 7 **Kathanikki Girl (IRE)**[182] 6988 3-8-3 0..................... CatherineGannon 4 30
(Mrs L Williamson) *trckd ldrs tl lost tch 2f out* **200/1**
0005 10 1 1/4 **Machinate (USA)**[21] 1131 7-9-9 49...................................... LukeMorris 8 32
(W M Brisbourne) *prom on outside tl wknd wl over 1f out* **33/1**
11 9 **Newby Abbey (IRE)**[35] 8-9-9 0..(tp) SJCraine 13 12
(D Flood) *slowly away: a bhd* **100/1**
12 11 **My Boy Nick**[13] 7-9-9 0.. LPKeniry 10 —
(D L Williams) *slowly away: a bhd* **100/1**
13 49 **Dream Street Rose (USA)**[28] 4-9-4 0.......................(t) DarrenWilliams 6 —
(K R Burke) *mid-div: rdn over 3f out: eased whn btn wl over 1f out: t.o* **100/1**
1m 50.07s (-0.43) **Going Correction** -0.025s/f (Stan)
WFA 3 from 4yo+ 15lb **13** Ran SP% **121.6**
Speed ratings (Par 101): **100,98,98,98,96 96,95,95,88,87 79,70,26**
toteswinger: 1&2 £21.30, 1&3 £4.70, 2&3 £17.10. CSF £31.65 TOTE £3.00: £1.30, £4.50, £2.60; EX 42.70.There was no bid for the winner. Andorn was claimed by P Kirby for £6,000.
Owner J L B Racing **Bred** T R G Vestey **Trained** Lower Beeding, W Sussex

FOCUS
A moderate and steadily run seller.
My Boy Nick Official explanation: jockey said gelding hung right
Dream Street Rose(USA) Official explanation: jockey said filly had a breathing problem

1531 BET IN PLAY AT LADBROKES.COM FILLIES' H'CAP 1m 141y(P)
8:20 (8:20) (Class 5) (0-70,68) 3-Y-O £3,885 (£1,156; £577; £288) Stalls Low

Form RPR
0-1 1 **Full Of Love (IRE)**[21] 1128 3-9-4 **68**................................ MichaelHills 6 75+
(B W Hills) *hld up in rr: stdy hdwy on outside fr 1/2-way: led over 1f out: pushed clr: comf* **13/8**[1]
60-2 2 2 3/4 **Diamond Daisy (IRE)**[12] 1253 3-8-11 **61**............................ TPQueally 4 62
(Mrs A Duffield) *mid-div: hmpd over 1f out: styd on to go 2nd ins fnl f* **14/1**
026- 3 nk **Chadwell Spring (IRE)**[186] 6886 3-8-11 **68**......... MatthewCosham(7) 5 68
(Miss J Feilden) *trckd ldrs: n.m.r over 1f out: kpt on fnl f* **66/1**
6014 4 hd **Location**[12] 1253 3-8-6 **56**... ChrisCatlin 8 56
(Ian Williams) *in rr: hdwy over 1f out: styd on: nvr nrr* **11/1**
5622 5 shd **Abu Dubai (IRE)**[9] 1315 3-9-2 **66**.................................. FergusSweeney 2 65+
(C A Dwyer) *mid-div tl lost pl 1/2-way: hdwy over 1f out: nvr nrr* **11/2**[3]
3125 6 1/2 **Flying Lady (IRE)**[9] 1315 3-8-10 **65**.................................. MCGeran(5) 10 63+
(M R Channon) *swtchd to ins fr wd draw s: in rr: hdwy on ins whn short of room over 1f out: swtchd rt: nt rch ldrs* **6/1**
430 7 1 1/4 **Crag Path**[16] 1198 3-8-9 **64**.. AmyBaker(5) 1 59
(D R C Elsworth) *in tch: rdn 2f out: effrt on ins bef wknd ins fnl f* **11/1**
000- 8 1/2 **Free Falling**[156] 7397 3-8-11 **61**.. DaneO'Neill 11 55
(L M Cumani) *trckd ldr: led 6f out: rdn and hdd over 1f out: wknd ins fnl f* **9/2**[2]
65-0 9 hd **Woteva**[10] 1282 3-9-1 **65**...(p) DavidAllan 9 59
(B Ellison) *in tch tl lost pl 2f out* **25/1**
240- 10 1 3/4 **Musical Maze**[191] 6761 3-9-3 **67**...................................... TGMcLaughlin 7 57
(W M Brisbourne) *led tl hdd 6f out: prom tl rdn and wknd over 1f out* **20/1**
-450 11 3 **Lady Salama**[12] 1253 3-8-9 **59**...................................... DarrenWilliams 3 42
(K R Burke) *in rr: rdn and effrt 2f out: sn btn* **50/1**
1m 51.06s (0.56) **Going Correction** -0.025s/f (Stan) **11** Ran SP% **121.3**
Speed ratings (Par 95): **96,93,93,93,93 92,91,91,90,89 86**
toteswinger: 1&2 £3.50, 1&3 £10.70, 2&3 £10.70. CSF £28.23 CT £1137.36 TOTE £2.30: £1.60, £3.00, £6.20; EX 20.80.
Owner Suzanne & Nigel Williams **Bred** Raymond P Doyle **Trained** Lambourn, Berks

FOCUS
This appeared to be a tight handicap and the pace wasn't quick, but it was won in the style of a handy filly.
Flying Lady(IRE) Official explanation: jockey said filly was denied a clear ru

1532 BET WITH LADBROKES ON 0800 777 888 MAIDEN FILLIES' STKS 1f 103y(P)
8:50 (8:52) (Class 5) 3-Y-O+ £2,729 (£806; £403) Stalls Low

Form RPR
34- 1 **Ballet Dancer (IRE)**[161] 7337 3-8-10 0........................ PhilipRobinson 10 69
(M A Jarvis) *a.p: rdn to ld over 1f out: all out* **6/5**[1]
5 2 nse **Hisaronu (IRE)**[11] 1269 3-8-10 0.. TPQueally 4 69
(H R A Cecil) *mid-div: hdwy over 2f out: pressed wnr fr over 1f out: kpt on gamely and only jst failed* **11/4**[2]
3 3 1/4 **Crimson Ribbon (USA)** 3-8-10 0..................................... NickyMackay 2 62+
(J H M Gosden) *s.i.s: in rr: c wd on bnd over 1f out: fin wl: nvr nrr* **10/1**
0- 4 1 **Frosted**[175] 7140 3-8-10 0.. RobertHavlin 3 60
(J H M Gosden) *mid-div: hung lft over 1f out: kpt on ins fnl f* **10/1**
4- 5 1 **Luthien (IRE)**[177] 7093 3-8-10 0.. TedDurcan 5 58
(W R Swinburn) *trckd ldrs: rdn over 2f out: one pce after* **11/2**[3]
00 6 1 **Cross Reef**[5] 1407 4-9-8 0... KevinGhunowa(3) 9 59
(R A Harris) *t.k.h: led 6f out: hdd & wknd over 1f out* **100/1**
0-0 7 3 3/4 **Asakusa**[16] 1198 3-8-10 0... JimmyQuinn 1 48+
(H R A Cecil) *a in rr* **40/1**
0-0 8 1 1/4 **Hold The Star**[16] 1198 3-8-5 0...................................... JPHamblett(5) 6 46
(E F Vaughan) *led: hdd 6f out: trckd ldr tl wknd over 1f out* **66/1**

0-0 **9** ½ **Rockson (IRE)**[37] 876 3-8-10 0 MichaelHills 8 44
(B W Hills) *t.k.h: hld up and a towards rr* **25/1**
6-4 **10** 3 ¼ **Am I Blue**[22] 1092 3-8-10 0 FrancisNorton 7 38
(H J L Dunlop) *in rr: lost tch over 2f out* **18/1**
2m 1.33s (-0.37) **Going Correction** -0.025s/f (Stan)
WFA 3 from 4yo 15lb **10** Ran SP% **119.7**
Speed ratings (Par 100): **100,99,97,96,95 94,91,89,89,86**
toteswinger: 1&2 £1.70, 1&3 £14.00, 2&3 £14.00. CSF £4.56 TOTE £2.60: £1.30, £1.50, £2.40; EX 4.60.
Owner Sheikh Ahmed Al Maktoum **Bred** Darley **Trained** Newmarket, Suffolk
FOCUS
Some leading yards were represented here with six of the ten runners needing one more run to be allotted a handicap mark. However, they went a muddling pace and the form is probably only ordinary.

1533 PLAY CASINO AT LADBROKES.COM H'CAP 1m 4f 50y(P)
9:20 (9:20) (Class 6) (0-65,67) 4-Y-0+ **£2,388** (£705; £352) **Stalls** Low

Form RPR
4240 **1** **Zalkani (IRE)**[6] 1378 9-8-6 **59** SimonPearce(7) 11 66
(J Pearce) *hld up in rr: hdwy over 2f out: led ins fnl f: styd on wl* **8/1**
-331 **2** ¾ **New England**[33] 935 7-8-12 **58** LukeMorris 8 64
(W M Brisbourne) *t.k.h in tch: rdn to ld 1f out: hdd ins fnl f* **5/2**[1]
6-23 **3** 1 ½ **Diktatorship (IRE)**[57] 567 6-8-5 **51** oh4 FrancisNorton 6 54
(Jennie Candlish) *t.k.h: trckd ldr: disp ld appr fnl f: nt qckn ins fnl f* **7/1**
0-00 **4** 1 **Resplendent Ace (IRE)**[87] 311 5-9-2 **62** JimmyQuinn 10 66+
(P Howling) *in rr: hdwy 3f out: short of room and hmpd wl over 1f out: styd on ins fnl f* **6/1**[3]
4035 **5** 1 ¼ **Buscador (USA)**[5] 1409 10-8-5 **58** PaulPickard(7) 2 58
(W M Brisbourne) *led: rdn clr 4f out: u.p whn hdd 1f out: fdd ins fnl f* **8/1**
0-54 **6** 2 **Piper's Song (IRE)**[8] 1318 6-9-5 **65** LPKeniry 1 62
(Patrick Morris) *in rr: rdn over 2f out: kpt on but nvr on terms* **8/1**
0/3- **7** 1 ½ **Gallantian (IRE)**[86] 2384 7-8-9 **55** (t) CatherineGannon 4 49
(David Anthony O'Brien, Ire) *mid-div: lost tch w ldrs over 2f out* **20/1**
300/ **8** 1 ¼ **Mossmann Gorge**[486] 242 7-8-5 **54** oh3 ow3 (p) KevinGhunowa(3) 9 46
(A Middleton) *towards rr: no hdwy after effrt 3f out* **50/1**
3022 **9** ½ **Bridgewater Boys**[7] 1366 8-9-7 **67** (b) WilliamBuick 7 58
(T J Pitt) *in rr: effrt 3f out: nvr got into r* **4/1**[2]
06- **10** 27 **Spanish Cross (IRE)**[238] 5525 4-8-12 **59** AdrianMcCarthy 3 7
(G Prodromou) *t.k.h: prom: rdn over 3f out: sn btn: t.o* **16/1**
0/00 **11** 18 **Slip Silver**[2] 1478 5-7-12 **51** oh6 CharlesEddery(7) 12 —
(R C Guest) *plld hrd: prom tl lost tch 4f out: t.o* **100/1**
2m 38.09s (-3.01) **Going Correction** -0.025s/f (Stan)
WFA 4 from 5yo+ 1lb **11** Ran SP% **122.3**
Speed ratings (Par 101): **109,108,107,106,106 104,103,102,102,84 72**
toteswinger: 1&2 £5.30, 1&3 £6.70, 2&3 £2.60. CSF £29.17 CT £154.67 TOTE £10.40: £2.40, £1.70, £2.20; EX 31.50 Place 6: £21.88, Place 5: £9.07..
Owner Mrs Lisa Matthews **Bred** His Highness The Aga Khan's Studs S C **Trained** Newmarket, Suffolk
FOCUS
An ordinary handicap.
Piper's Song(IRE) Official explanation: jockey said gelding was slowly away
Slip Silver Official explanation: jockey said mare hung badly left
T/Plt: £22.60 to a £1 stake. Pool: £76,911.73. 2,478.77 winning tickets. T/Qpdt: £5.90 to a £1 stake. Pool: £5,744.69. 716.90 winning tickets. JS

1176 BRIGHTON (L-H)
Sunday, April 26

OFFICIAL GOING: Good to firm (8.3)
Wind: Moderate, half-behind Weather: Sunny

1534 EUROPEAN BREEDERS' FUND MAIDEN STKS 5f 59y
2:10 (2:12) (Class 5) 2-Y-O **£4,144** (£1,233; £616; £307) **Stalls** Low

Form RPR
1 **Nadeen (IRE)** 2-9-3 0 DarryllHolland 5 76+
(M R Channon) *dwlt: hld up in 5th: rdn over 2f out: r.o to dispute ld ins fnl f: jst prevailed* **10/11**[1]
0 **2** hd **Little Perisher**[9] 1323 2-8-12 0 MartinLane(5) 4 75
(A P Jarvis) *prom: unbalanced on trck and hung lft: disp ld ins fnl f: nt qckn fnl strides* **25/1**
3 ½ **Curtains** 2-8-12 0 SebSanders 8 68+
(S Dow) *s.s: bhd: hmpd and swtchd wd over 2f out: gd hdwy over 1f out: fin wl* **25/1**
6 **4** 1 **Flapjack**[20] 1147 2-8-9 0 PatrickHills(3) 2 65
(R Hannon) *dwlt: in rr: slipped 4f out: edgd lft over 2f out: hdwy and hrd rdn over 1f out: styd on wl fnl f* **12/1**
02 **5** 3 ¼ **True Red (IRE)**[23] 1090 2-8-12 0 TGMcLaughlin 3 53
(B R Millman) *led tl over 1f out: n.m.r on rail: wknd fnl f* **7/1**[3]
5 **6** hd **Safari Camp (IRE)**[17] 1195 2-9-3 0 JimCrowley 1 57
(P Winkworth) *wnt lft s: chsd ldr: led over 1f out: edgd lft: hdd & wknd jst ins fnl f* **5/2**[2]
0 **7** 3 ¼ **Kings Aphrodite**[8] 1358 2-9-3 0 SteveDrowne 6 45
(Miss Gay Kelleway) *chsd ldrs tl wknd wl over 1f out* **33/1**
8 7 **Miss Roma (IRE)** 2-8-9 0 KevinGhunowa(3) 7 15
(R A Harris) *s.s: a bhd: hung bdly rt over 2f out: hung bdly lft over 1f out: nt act on trck* **100/1**
62.45 secs (0.15) **Going Correction** -0.125s/f (Firm) **8** Ran SP% **112.8**
Speed ratings (Par 92): **93,92,91,90,85 84,79,68**
toteswinger: 1&2 £8.80, 1&3 £3.60, 2&3 £16.50. CSF £31.46 TOTE £1.90: £1.10, £3.30, £3.10; EX 30.40 TRIFECTA Not won..
Owner Jaber Abdullah **Bred** Rabbah Bloodstock Limited **Trained** West Ilsley, Berks
■ Stewards' Enquiry : Patrick Hills one-day ban: careless riding (May 11)
FOCUS
This wouldn't have been a very strong race, with the runner-up rated as a big improver from his debut at Newbury.
NOTEBOOK
Nadeen(IRE), well backed at the head of the market, made very hard work of winning. Although by a speedy sire, he will get further than this in time and struggled to go the gallop early following a tardy start. He started to come with a good run from over a furlong out and just got the better of the runner-up close home. He will no doubt learn from the experience, but needs to improve if he is to follow up. (tchd Evens and 11-10 in a place)
Little Perisher, who shaped with a bit of promise at 100-1 before fading on his debut at Newbury, has clearly learned from that experience. He came through to hold every chance in the final furlong, briefly looking the winner, but was run out of it in the final strides. He was far from at home on this track and can find a small race. (op 20-1)
Curtains, sold for £26,000 at the breeze-up sales, had a lot of running to do passing the two-pole having been hampered, but she came home well once switched wide and may have won in another 100 yards. This was a pleasing start and she can gain compensation. (op 22-1)
Flapjack improved on her debut effort despite appearing to slip after a furlong. She stayed on well inside the final furlong, and can find a race at the right level. Official explanation: jockey said filly ran green (op 14-1 tchd 8-1)
True Red(IRE), responsible for the early pace, was readily brushed aside in the final furlong. (op 5-1)
Safari Camp(IRE), who went left coming out of the stalls, again failed to get home. (op 10-3 tchd 7-2)
Kings Aphrodite is not without ability. He may do better in low-grade nurseries later in the season. (op 25-1 tchd 20-1)
Miss Roma(IRE) Official explanation: jockey said filly hung right

1535 LITTLEWOODSGAMEON - THE TRUSTED NAME IN GAMING H'CAP 6f 209y
2:40 (2:40) (Class 6) (0-55,55) 4-Y-0+ **£2,590** (£770; £385; £192) **Stalls** Low

Form RPR
0-26 **1** **My Flame**[5] 1423 4-9-0 **54** ShaneKelly 1 62
(J R Jenkins) *led 1f: led and hrd rdn over 2f out: hdd ins fnl f: rallied to ld fnl 50yds: gamely* **8/1**[3]
0066 **2** hd **Annes Rocket (IRE)**[25] 1074 4-8-10 **50** LPKeniry 9 57
(J C Fox) *s.s: towards rr: hdwy and edgd lft 2f out: drvn to ld briefly 100yds out: kpt on* **8/1**[3]
3250 **3** 1 ¼ **Interchoice Star**[34] 937 4-8-3 **48** AndreaAtzeni(5) 12 52
(R Hollinshead) *in tch on outside: effrt over 2f out: drvn to press ldrs 1f out: kpt on same pce* **15/2**[2]
26-0 **4** nse **Never Sold Out (IRE)**[61] 666 4-8-10 **50** LukeMorris 13 54+
(J G M O'Shea) *mid-div: effrt and carried lft 2f out: in tch whn bdly hmpd 1f out: r.o ins fnl f* **28/1**
000- **5** ½ **Sun Catcher (IRE)**[172] 7194 6-9-1 **55** (p) SteveDrowne 2 57
(P G Murphy) *chsd ldrs: drvn to narrow ld ins fnl f: hdd and no ex fnl 100yds* **10/1**
-105 **6** 1 ½ **Djalalabad (FR)**[6] 1413 5-9-1 **55** (tp) TGMcLaughlin 7 53
(Mrs C A Dunnett) *sn outpcd and bhd: hdwy and hung lft over 1f out: styd on: nvr nrr* **10/1**
1650 **7** ½ **Just Jimmy (IRE)**[30] 984 4-8-13 **53** PaulDoe 6 50
(P D Evans) *in tch: drvn to chal over 1f out: hld whn n.m.r on rail ins fnl f* **7/1**[1]
4100 **8** ¾ **Nawaaff**[37] 896 4-8-5 **50** (v) MCGeran(5) 14 45
(M R Channon) *mid-div: effrt and carried lft 2f out: no imp fnl f* **16/1**
0000 **9** 4 **Over To You Bert**[6] 1413 10-8-9 **54** Louis-PhilippeBeuzelin(5) 4 38
(R J Hodges) *mid-div: outpcd and drvn along 3f out: sn btn* **25/1**
0-00 **10** 1 ¼ **The Jailer**[41] 853 6-8-5 **50** (p) WilliamCarson(5) 5 31
(J G M O'Shea) *chsd ldr: led after 1f tl over 2f out: hrd rdn and wknd wl over 1f out* **7/1**[1]
3540 **11** ¾ **Wusuul**[25] 1074 4-8-12 **55** (b) KevinGhunowa(3) 3 34
(R A Harris) *s.i.s and rdn early: wnt prom and swtchd outside over 4f out: wandered and hrd rdn over 2f out: sn wknd* **16/1**
0153 **12** 6 **Fairly Honest**[27] 1030 5-8-11 **51** ChrisCatlin 11 13
(P W Hiatt) *sn bhd: pushed along and n.d fnl 3f* **8/1**[3]
0-60 **13** 49 **Batchworth Blaise**[95] 234 6-8-13 **53** StephenCarson 16 —
(E A Wheeler) *s.s: a bhd and nvr gng wl: virtually p.u fnl 2f: lame* **17/2**
1m 21.86s (-1.24) **Going Correction** -0.125s/f (Firm) **13** Ran SP% **117.9**
Speed ratings (Par 101): **102,101,100,100,99 98,97,96,92,90 89,82,26**
toteswinger: 1&2 £13.40, 1&3 £14.40, 2&3 £16.00. CSF £69.67 CT £521.99 TOTE £8.80: £3.60, £3.60, £3.40; EX 83.70 TRIFECTA Not won..
Owner Smart K Syndicate **Bred** Mrs S Cavenagh **Trained** Royston, Herts
■ Stewards' Enquiry : Steve Drowne caution: careless riding.
FOCUS
A moderate handicap but soundly run. The winner has been rated back to his three-year-old best.
Never Sold Out(IRE) ◆ Official explanation: jockey said colt was denied a clear run
Sun Catcher(IRE) Official explanation: jockey said gelding hung left
Batchworth Blaise Official explanation: jockey said gelding finished lame

1536 MOVING YOUR GAME ON - LITTLEWOODSGAMEON.COM (S) STKS 5f 213y
3:15 (3:17) (Class 6) 3-Y-O+ **£1,942** (£578; £288; £144) **Stalls** Low

Form RPR
0316 **1** **El Dececy (USA)**[8] 1343 5-9-12 81 (p) AdamKirby 6 70
(S Parr) *led after 1f: drvn clr over 1f out: in control after: pushed out* **8/13**[1]
6520 **2** 2 ¼ **Joss Stick**[18] 1182 4-8-13 58 (p) SPRyan(7) 7 57
(R A Harris) *hld up: hdwy and nt clr run over 2f out: styd on to take 2nd jst ins fnl f: a hld* **12/1**[3]
5046 **3** 2 ¼ **Tightrope (IRE)**[9] 1322 3-8-9 52 MartinDwyer 10 47
(T D McCarthy) *plld hrd: chsd ldrs: hrd rdn 2f out: edgd lft: one pce* **66/1**
6054 **4** ½ **Mr Rev**[26] 1047 6-9-6 45 (b) LPKeniry 2 48
(J M Bradley) *led 1f: prom on rail: hrd rdn and nt pce of wnr over 1f out* **28/1**
0-60 **5** ¾ **Scruffy Skip (IRE)**[33] 946 4-9-12 45 (v[1]) TGMcLaughlin 11 56+
(Mrs C A Dunnett) *dwlt: outpcd in rr: hdwy on rail whn nt clr run over 1f out tl ins fnl f: swtchd rt: styd on* **50/1**
6-30 **6** 2 ¼ **Mannello**[13] 1259 6-9-1 50 (b) RichardThomas 1 33
(S W Hall) *t.k.h: chsd ldrs: hrd rdn 2f out: disputing 5th and btn whn hmpd ins fnl f* **20/1**
5000 **7** 1 **Lake Sabina**[25] 1076 4-9-1 46 IanMongan 16 30
(M R Hoad) *chsd ldrs 4f* **33/1**
6004 **8** 3 ¼ **Nordic Light (USA)**[27] 1038 5-9-6 46 (bt) LukeMorris 5 25
(J M Bradley) *prom: outpcd and drvn along whn rdr dropped whip wl over 1f out: 7th and btn whn n.m.r sn after* **40/1**
0644 **9** 1 **Easy Wonder (GER)**[25] 1072 4-9-1 49 (b) SebSanders 14 17
(I A Wood) *bhd: hdwy on outside 3f out: wknd 2f out* **12/1**[3]
3230 **10** 4 ½ **Saints Bay (IRE)**[53] 753 3-8-4 57 ChrisCatlin 8 —
(R Hannon) *s.s: sn wl bhd: lame* **11/2**[2]
69.86 secs (-0.34) **Going Correction** -0.125s/f (Firm)
WFA 3 from 4yo+ 11lb **10** Ran SP% **109.7**
Speed ratings (Par 101): **97,94,91,90,89 86,85,80,79,73**
toteswinger: 1&2 £1.70, 1&3 £13.70, 2&3 £19.60. CSF £6.82 TOTE £1.50: £1.10, £2.20, £12.30; EX 8.50 Trifecta £87.90 Part won. Pool £118.82 - 0.30 winning units..The winner was bought in for 23,000gns.
Owner Willie McKay **Bred** Shadwell Farm LLC **Trained**
FOCUS
This was not the most competitive of sellers.
Tightrope(IRE) Official explanation: jockey said colt hung left

Saints Bay(IRE) Official explanation: jockey said filly lost its action; vet said filly returned lame

1537 FEEL THE THRILL AT LITTLEWOODSPOKER.COM H'CAP 1m 3f 196y
3:50 (3:52) (Class 6) (0-60,66) 4-Y-0+ £2,590 (£770; £385; £192) Stalls High

Form RPR
00-2 1 **Lady Hestia (USA)**17 1200 4-8-8 **50** MartinDwyer 11 61
(M P Tregoning) *prom: effrt and edgd lft fr 2f out: styd on to ld fnl 100yds* **4/1**2
00-0 2 1 3/4 **Medieval Maiden**7 1378 6-8-5 **46** oh1 PaulDoe 2 54
(Mrs L J Mongan) *hld up in midfield: hdwy 4f out: led 2f out: hdd and outpcd fnl 100yds* **25/1**
-336 3 nk **Bienheureux**89 301 8-8-2 **46** (t) DavidProbert(3) 14 54
(Miss Gay Kelleway) *towards rr: gd hdwy over 2f out: kpt on on fnl f* **7/2**1
4555 4 nse **Coral Shores**7 1378 4-8-11 **53** (v) JimCrowley 5 60
(P W Hiatt) *t.k.h: trckd ldrs: shkn up and edgd lft 2f out: styd on same pce* **8/1**
0401 5 nk **Calzaghe (IRE)**7 1378 5-9-11 **66** 6ex RichardThomas 1 75+
(Jim Best) *towards rr: sme hdwy 5f out: rdn 4f out: effrt and hmpd ins fnl 2f: styd on fnl f* **4/1**2
6300 6 2 3/4 **Dazzling Begum**5 1442 4-8-7 **49** ow1 (v) StephenDonohoe 4 52
(J Pearce) *towards rr: hrd rdn and gd hdwy over 2f out: no ex over 1f out* **33/1**
-056 7 3 1/4 **Moon Mix (FR)**17 1199 6-8-7 **48** (v) FergusSweeney 7 45
(J R Jenkins) *s.s: bhd: sme hdwy over 2f out: nt pce to trble ldrs* **20/1**
020- 8 nse **Bob's Your Uncle**34 6668 6-9-1 **56** TolleyDean 8 53
(J G Portman) *stdd s: hld up towards rr: rdn 5f out: nvr nr to chal* **25/1**
0453 9 3 1/2 **Moyoko (IRE)**17 1199 6-8-10 **51** (p) ShaneKelly 9 43
(M Salaman) *chsd ldrs: led over 4f out tl 2f out: sn wknd* **12/1**
-030 10 3 **Good Effect (USA)**7 1378 5-8-11 **52** WilliamBuick 10 39
(C P Morlock) *led tl over 4f out: wknd over 2f out* **16/1**
-002 11 3/4 **Generous Lad (IRE)**4 1463 6-8-10 **51** (p) SteveDrowne 16 37
(A B Haynes) *prom tl wknd over 3f out* **6/1**3
1616 12 hd **Corlough Mountain**55 735 5-8-5 **51** AmyBaker(5) 6 36
(P Butler) *mid-div tl wknd 3f out* **16/1**

2m 30.9s (-1.80) **Going Correction** -0.125s/f (Firm)
WFA 4 from 5yo+ 1lb 12 Ran SP% **122.5**
Speed ratings (Par 101): **101,99,99,99,99 97,95,95,93,91 90,90**
toteswinger: 1&2 £26.00, 1&3 £4.60, 2&3 £28.50. CSF £109.28 CT £393.57 TOTE £4.50: £1.70, £6.30, £1.60; EX 186.20 TRIFECTA Not won..
Owner Mr And Mrs A E Pakenham **Bred** Shadwell Farm LLC **Trained** Lambourn, Berks

FOCUS
This was a competitive middle-distance handicap for the grade.
Bienheureux Official explanation: jockey said gelding was denied a clear run
Calzaghe(IRE) Official explanation: jockey said gelding was denied a clear run

1538 HIT, STAND, SPIN OR ROLL AT LITTLEWOODSCASINO.COM H'CAP 1m 1f 209y
4:25 (4:26) (Class 6) (0-65,65) 4-Y-0+ £2,590 (£770; £385; £192) Stalls High

Form RPR
3412 1 **Rapid City**30 981 6-9-4 **65** RichardThomas 8 71
(Jim Best) *plld hrd: chsd ldrs: narrow ld fnl 100yds: pushed out to hold runner-up* **4/1**2
4-62 2 hd **Magic Rush**9 1320 7-9-4 **65** LPKeniry 11 71
(Norma Twomey) *plld hrd in rr: rapid hdwy to ld over 4f out: hdd and jst hld fnl 100yds* **11/2**3
5-00 3 1 3/4 **Mayfair's Future**9 1318 4-8-10 **57** JimCrowley 6 59
(J R Jenkins) *set slow pce tl over 4f out: cl 3rd whn edgd lft and nt clr run on rail over 1f out: nt qckn whn gap appeared* **12/1**
1660 4 hd **Lady Aspen (IRE)**13 1254 6-8-7 **54** (t) StephenDonohoe 4 56
(Ian Williams) *chsd ldrs: drvn along over 2f out: styd on fnl f* **22/1**
2164 5 nk **Barodine**20 1153 6-8-3 **55** Louis-PhilippeBeuzelin(5) 1 56
(R J Hodges) *in tch: lost pl and rdn 4f out: rallied and r.o appr fnl f* **10/1**
5-63 6 hd **Encore Belle**13 1254 4-8-9 **56** NeilChalmers 10 57
(Mouse Hamilton-Fairley) *stdd in rr s: hrd rdn and styd on fnl 2f: nvr nrr* **14/1**
662- 7 2 1/4 **Tignello (IRE)**181 7012 4-8-13 **60** SteveDrowne 2 56
(G L Moore) *plld hrd in midfield: effrt over 2f out: no imp* **6/1**
234- 8 6 **Oronsay**192 6747 4-8-4 **51** oh2 (t) ChrisCatlin 3 35
(B R Millman) *hld up in rr: pushed along and unable to chal fnl 3f* **12/1**
-606 9 4 1/2 **Siryena**68 577 4-8-1 **51** oh2 (tp) DavidProbert(3) 7 26
(B I Case) *mid-div: hrd rdn 3f out: sn wknd* **22/1**
0-42 10 2 3/4 **Solo River**22 1122 4-9-4 **65** FergusSweeney 9 35
(P J Makin) *plld hrd: prom tl wknd qckly 2f out* **7/2**1
004 11 9 **Strategic Knight (USA)**6 1401 4-8-5 **55** ow1 (t) KevinGhunowa(3) 5 7
(R C Guest) *chsd ldrs: wknd over 4f out: sn bhd and eased: sddle slipped* **10/1**

2m 6.30s (2.70) **Going Correction** -0.125s/f (Firm) 11 Ran SP% **120.8**
Speed ratings (Par 101): **84,83,82,82,82 81,80,75,71,69 62**
toteswinger: 1&2 £4.00, 1&3 £8.10, 2&3 £12.10. CSF £27.22 CT £243.42 TOTE £4.60: £1.80, £2.00, £3.40; EX 24.60 TRIFECTA Not won..
Owner The Bad Boys **Bred** Juddmonte Farms Ltd **Trained** Lewes, E Sussex

FOCUS
This low-grade handicap was run at a very sedate gallop and many of the runners failed to settle.
Barodine Official explanation: jockey said gelding was denied a clear run
Strategic Knight(USA) Official explanation: jockey said saddle slipped

1539 MORE THAN BINGO - GAMEONBINGO.COM H'CAP 7f 214y
4:55 (4:56) (Class 5) (0-70,70) 4-Y-0+ £3,280 (£981; £490; £245; £122) Stalls Low

Form RPR
056- 1 **Driven (IRE)**301 3525 4-9-1 **67** JimCrowley 10 79
(Mrs A J Perrett) *stdd s: hld up in rr: gd hdwy over 1f out: qcknd to ld ins fnl f: won gng away* **5/1**1
-600 2 1 3/4 **Napoletano (GER)**58 708 8-8-13 **65** (p) SebSanders 7 73
(S Dow) *plld hrd: chsd ldrs: drvn to ld 1f out: hdd and nt pce of wnr ins fnl f* **8/1**
3202 3 3/4 **Bobski (IRE)**18 1194 7-8-7 **66** ow1 (t) KylieManser(7) 5 72
(Miss Gay Kelleway) *s.s: bhd: rdn into midfield over 2f out: styd on to take 3rd ins fnl f* **7/1**3
1323 4 1 **Murrin (IRE)**27 1035 5-8-11 **70** DToole(7) 6 74
(T G Mills) *towards rr: effrt on outside over 2f out: hrd rdn over 1f out: styd on wl fnl f* **7/1**3
0012 5 hd **Ryedale Ovation (IRE)**18 1187 6-9-4 **70** GeorgeBaker 8 73
(G L Moore) *t.k.h in midfield: effrt and in tch ins fnl 2f: styd on same pce* **8/1**
52-0 6 1/2 **The Grey One (IRE)**9 1318 6-8-7 **64** (p) MCGeran(5) 2 66
(J M Bradley) *bhd: rdn and styd on fnl 2f: nvr nrr* **14/1**
0-00 7 1 1/4 **Dancing Rhythm**5 1420 4-8-4 **56** oh11 WilliamBuick 12 55
(M S Saunders) *led at modest pce: qckned and drvn along 2f out: hdd 1f out: wknd fnl f* **33/1**
-212 8 1/2 **Pab Special (IRE)**56 725 6-9-0 **66** AdamKirby 3 64
(B R Johnson) *chsd ldrs: rdn over 2f out: wknd fnl f* **13/2**2
00-0 9 3/4 **Ivory Lace**20 1149 8-9-4 **70** DarryllHolland 1 67
(S Woodman) *mid-div: outpcd 3f out: n.d after* **10/1**
-621 10 3/4 **Seneschal**13 1258 8-9-1 **67** SteveDrowne 13 62
(A B Haynes) *w ldrs: hrd rdn over 1f out: wknd fnl f* **10/1**
200- 11 1 3/4 **Magroom**209 6336 5-8-10 **67** Louis-PhilippeBeuzelin(5) 9 58
(R J Hodges) *prom tl wknd over 1f out* **20/1**
5-04 12 9 **Haasem (USA)**13 344 6-8-9 **61** (v) ShaneKelly 11 31
(J R Jenkins) *chsd ldrs tl wknd 2f out: bhd and eased fnl f* **17/2**

1m 35.39s (-0.61) **Going Correction** -0.125s/f (Firm) 12 Ran SP% **120.3**
Speed ratings (Par 103): **98,96,95,94,94 93,92,92,91,90 88,79**
toteswinger: 1&2 £11.80, 1&3 £8.60, 2&3 £12.50. CSF £45.13 CT £289.69 TOTE £5.40: £2.30, £2.50, £2.50; EX 60.60 TRIFECTA Not won..
Owner A D Spence **Bred** Gestut Gorlsdorf **Trained** Pulborough, W Sussex

FOCUS
A moderate handicap.
The Grey One(IRE) Official explanation: jockey said gelding was denied a clear run
Pab Special(IRE) Official explanation: jockey said gelding ran too keen
Ivory Lace Official explanation: jockey said mare was denied a clear run
Magroom Official explanation: jockey said gelding was denied a clear run
Haasem(USA) Official explanation: jockey said gelding was unsuited by the good to firm ground

1540 INSTANT VALUE WITH GAMEONQUICKPLAY.COM H'CAP 5f 59y
5:25 (5:25) (Class 5) (0-70,70) 4-Y-0+ £3,280 (£981; £490; £245; £122) Stalls Low

Form RPR
5440 1 **Drifting Gold**20 1150 5-9-4 **70** (b) AdamKirby 4 78
(C G Cox) *chsd ldrs: effrt on ins fnl 2f: drvn to ld fnl 50yds* **9/2**2
1600 2 nk **Billy Red**4 1468 5-8-13 **65** (b) FergusSweeney 1 72
(J R Jenkins) *led: hrd rdn over 1f out: hdd fnl 50yds: kpt on* **9/1**
4212 3 2 1/4 **Bluebok**18 1182 8-9-2 **68** (bt) LPKeniry 5 67
(J M Bradley) *chsd ldr: hrd rdn over 1f out: one pce* **8/1**
030- 4 1 **Matterofact (IRE)**137 7621 6-9-3 **69** TGMcLaughlin 6 64
(M S Saunders) *mid-div: rdn over 2f out: r.o fnl f* **7/1**3
-000 5 1 **Cosmic Destiny (IRE)**43 843 7-8-9 **66** MarkFlynn(5) 2 58
(E F Vaughan) *hld up towards rr: hdwy to chse ldrs over 1f out: no ex fnl f* **12/1**
60-6 6 2 3/4 **Stamford Blue**6 1403 8-8-11 **70** (b) SPRyan(7) 10 52
(R A Harris) *mid-div: rdn over 2f out: no imp* **9/1**
15-3 7 3/4 **Multahab**79 431 10-8-3 **62** (t) TobyAtkinson(7) 9 41+
(M Wigham) *bhd: swtchd to r on stands' rail over 2f out: n.d* **8/1**
0066 8 1 **Fast Freddie**4 1456 5-8-4 **56** oh1 (e) ChrisCatlin 7 32
(S Parr) *chsd ldrs 2f* **8/1**
033 9 3 1/4 **One Way Ticket**37 896 9-8-4 **56** oh8 (tp) LukeMorris 8 20
(J M Bradley) *chsd ldrs over 2f* **25/1**
4311 10 2 **Green Velvet**33 946 4-8-10 **62** TravisBlock 11 19+
(P J Makin) *bhd: carried to stands' rail over 2f out: hmpd and swtchd lft wl over 1f out: nvr a factor* **10/3**1

61.46 secs (-0.84) **Going Correction** -0.125s/f (Firm) 10 Ran SP% **118.6**
Speed ratings (Par 103): **101,100,96,95,93 89,88,86,81,78**
toteswinger: 1&2 £11.20, 1&3 £6.10, 2&3 £17.90. CSF £45.56 CT £259.68 TOTE £6.30: £2.00, £3.90, £2.20; EX 61.00 Trifecta £150.30 Part won. Pool £203.22 - 0.10 winning units. Place 6 £59.10, Place 5 £35.87..
Owner Martin C Oliver **Bred** Witney And Warren Enterprises Ltd **Trained** Lambourn, Berks
■ Stewards' Enquiry : Toby Atkinson five-day ban: careless riding (May 11-15)

FOCUS
An open-looking sprint.
T/Jkpt: £5,007.70 to a £1 stake. Pool: £17,633.10. 2.50 winning tickets. T/Plt: £127.20 to a £1 stake. Pool: £78,391.26. 449.68 winning tickets. T/Qpdt: £22.40 to a £1 stake. Pool: £5,392.50. 177.75 winning tickets. LM

1541 - 1542a (Foreign Racing) - See Raceform Interactive

NAVAN (L-H)
Sunday, April 26

OFFICIAL GOING: Soft

1543a NAVAN SPRINT STKS (LISTED RACE) 5f 182y
3:20 (3:21) 3-Y-0+ £28,441 (£8,344; £3,975; £1,354)

RPR
1 **Jumbajukiba**21 1138 6-9-12 **114** (b) FMBerry 13 112
(Mrs John Harrington, Ire) *mde all: rdn and strly pressed 1 1/2f out: kpt on wl ins fnl f* **9/2**3
2 1 3/4 **Croisultan (IRE)**13 1264 3-8-11 **95** MCHussey 4 100
(Liam McAteer, Ire) *towards rr: hdwy to 4th 2f out: rdn to chal over 1f out: no ex ins fnl f: kpt on same pce* **25/1**
3 3/4 **Le Cadre Noir (IRE)**8 1374 5-9-10 **104** PJSmullen 3 103
(D K Weld, Ire) *hld up towards rr: hdwy in 7th 2f out: 5th 1 1/2f out: rdn into 3rd ins fnl f: kpt on same pce* **6/4**1
4 1 3/4 **Wi Dud**8 1367 5-9-7 (b) AlanMunro 12 94
(K A Ryan) *chsd ldr: 2nd 1/2-way: rdn in 4th 1 1/2f out: cl 3rd 1f out: kpt on same pce fnl f* **5/1**
5 1 1/2 **Invincible Ash (IRE)**23 1111 4-9-4 **97** RPCleary 1 88
(M Halford, Ire) *chsd ldrs: 5th 1/2-way: hdwy to 3rd 2f out: rdn to chal 1 1/2f out: no ex in 4th 1f out: kpt on same pce* **10/1**
6 3 1/2 **Abraham Lincoln (IRE)**29 1006 5-9-7 AdrianTNicholls 7 79
(D Nicholls) *chsd ldrs: 6th 1/2-way: rdn in 5th 2f out: no ex in 6th 1 1/2f out: kpt on one pce* **9/1**
7 9 **Masta Plasta (IRE)**7 1384 6-9-10 CDHayes 11 64+
(D Nicholls) *chsd ldrs: 3rd 1/2-way: rdn and no ex 2f out: eased fnl f* **7/2**2
8 2 1/2 **Tornadodancer (IRE)**23 1111 6-9-7 **88** MHarley 6 54+
(T G McCourt, Ire) *chsd ldrs: 4th 1/2-way: rdn and no ex over 2f out: wknd* **50/1**
9 8 **Fourpenny Lane**163 7325 4-9-4 **99** WJSupple 10 27+
(Ms Joanna Morgan, Ire) *towards rr: bhd fr 1/2-way* **20/1**

1m 15.6s (1.00)
WFA 3 from 4yo+ 11lb 9 Ran SP% **126.7**
CSF £116.45 TOTE £5.90: £2.00, £3.10, £1.40; DF 216.70.
Owner J P O'Flaherty **Bred** Woodcote Stud Ltd **Trained** Moone, Co Kildare

FOCUS
This was a decent sprint, but the softening ground was a big help to some and a handicap to others.
NOTEBOOK
Jumbajukiba registered his eighth career win over a trip short of his optimum on his first start at Navan. Better known as a Curragh specialist these days, with five wins over distances ranging from 7f to 1m at Irish headquarters, he was quickly into stride to lead early. The four-time Curragh Group 3 winner underlined his class, especially in this testing ground, when sticking to his task well when he met the rising ground. His trainer believes that this ground is the key to him and may consider the Greenlands Stakes at the Curragh next month should the going fall in his favour. (op 5/1 tchd 11/2)
Croisultan(IRE) put up a career-best display. This was a big step up for him bidding to add to his two sprint handicap wins at Bellewstown and here in a nursery last October in contrasting ground. He held every chance racing down the far side but couldn't wear down the leader. Official explanation: jockey said colt picked up the bit early on and hung onto the heels of another runner causing him to check
Le Cadre Noir(IRE) probably found the ground going against him. An Italian import, as he couldn't raise his game when asked to go about his business after passing the 2f marker. (op 13/8 tchd 7/4)
Wi Dud, one of two overseas challengers, held every chance and appeared still to be travelling after halfway in this rain-softened ground. When the button was pressed, the 2006 Flying Childers winner failed to answer the call and weakened. (op 5/1 tchd 11/2)
Invincible Ash(IRE) has more than paid her way on the all-weather, so was probably another inconvenienced by the rain that fell overnight. (op 12/1)
Abraham Lincoln(IRE) was beaten after halfway. (op 8/1)
Masta Plasta(IRE) proved very disappointing after racing close to the pace until halfway. He never looked happy in this ground and his rider accepted the situation entering the final furlong. Official explanation: jockey said gelding did not handle today's ground (op 4/1 tchd 9/2)

1546a VINTAGE CROP STKS (LISTED RACE) 1m 5f
5:00 (5:00) 4-Y-0+ **£28,441** (£8,344; £3,975; £1,354)

RPR
1 **Alandi (IRE)**188 6875 4-9-1 .... MJKinane 9 111+
(John M Oxx, Ire) *hld up towards rr: hdwy in 4th 3f out: 3rd over 2f out: rdn to chal 1 1/2f out: led over 1f out: kpt on strly fnl f to go clr: eased cl home* **4/1**3
2 3 ½ **Hindu Kush (IRE)**28 1017 4-9-1 .... AdrianTNicholls 1 104
(D Nicholls) *led: rdn and chal 2f out: hdd over 1f out: 3rd 1f out: kpt on same pce fnl f to go 2nd cl home* **9/1**
3 shd **The Betchworth Kid**18 1191 4-9-1 .... WJSupple 6 104
(M L W Bell) *settled bhd ldrs: 5th 1/2-way: hdwy to 2nd 4f out: rdn to chal 2f out: disp 1 1/2f out: no ex in 2nd 1f out: kpt on same pce fnl f: lost 2nd cl home* **7/2**2
4 5 ½ **Baron De'L (IRE)**21 1139 6-9-2 103........(b) FMBerry 8 98
(Edward P Harty, Ire) *hld up in rr: hdwy in 7th 3f out: rdn into mod 4th 2f out: no imp on ldrs fr 1 1/2f out: kpt on same pce* **10/1**
5 11 **Hollo Ladies (IRE)**21 1142 4-9-1 .... GFCarroll 7 79
(James Coyle, Ire) *chsd ldrs: 4th 1/2-way: rdn in 6th 3f out: no ex in mod 5th 2f out: kpt on one pce* **33/1**
6 12 **Yeats (IRE)**182 7008 8-9-9 122........ JAHeffernan 3 68
(A P O'Brien, Ire) *chsd ldr: 3rd 1/2-way: rdn in 3rd 3f out: no ex over 2f out: wknd* **4/5**1
7 4 **Tramp Stamp (IRE)**120 5-8-13 .... MHarley 5 52
(Matthieu Palussiere, Ire) *mid-div: 6th 1/2-way: rdn in 5th 3f out: no ex in 7th 2f out: wknd* **33/1**
8 2 ½ **Tale Of Two Cities (IRE)**28 1026 4-9-1 77........(t) RPWalsh 4 51
(Luke Comer, Ire) *chsd ldrs: 2nd 1/2-way: rdn and wknd ent st* **100/1**

3m 2.10s (2.10)
WFA 4 from 5yo+ 1lb **8 Ran SP% 123.7**
CSF £41.63 TOTE £5.20: £1.80, £2.80, £1.50; DF 65.90.
Owner H H Aga Khan **Bred** Hh The Aga Khan's Studs Sc **Trained** Currabeg, Co Kildare

FOCUS
A race in which all eyes were on the triple Gold Cup-winner Yeats who proved very disappointing, but the winner is unexposed.
NOTEBOOK
Alandi(IRE) made it two wins from as many starts. Winner of a 1m4f maiden at the Curragh late last season, his debut had been delayed by training problems. That maiden win was achieved on heavy ground and he again showed his liking for testing conditions here, coming from off the pace to challenge between horses and lead over 1f out. He stayed on well. (op 7/1)
Hindu Kush(IRE), a winner at this level for Aidan O'Brien over 1m2f last season also finished fourth on soft ground in the St Leger at Doncaster. He made the running and was involved in a battle for the lead until the winner challenged and got on top entering the final furlong. He was well held in the closing stages but ran a solid race. (op 7/1)
The Betchworth Kid, well-suited by soft ground and rated one pound below the runner-up on official figures, had every chance from 3f out and was vying for the lad before the winner asserted superiority. He kept on and only just lost out on second place. (op 5/2)
Baron De'L(IRE) has done all his winning at the Curragh where his six wins all came over 1m2f. Adaptable ground-wise, he achieved his first Listed succes there three weeks ago and was stepping up in distance. Held up in rear, he made headway in the straight but never reached a challenging position. (op 12/1)
Yeats(IRE) was encountering ground with an official description of "soft" for the first time since landing the Ballysax Stakes as a three-year-old. Five years on, the triple Ascot Gold Cup winner was seeking a hat-trick of wins in this event but, after racing prominently, he began to struggle early in the straight. He quickly dropped out of contention before being eased when all hope of being involved in the finish had gone. He blew a lot after the race and it is possible that he simply lacked the necessary fitness to deal with the conditions on his first start of the year. Equally so, he is now eight, and the question remains as to whether he will be able to reach the heights of past glories. Official explanation: jockey said horse became tired in closing stages and blew hard post-race; vet said horse was found to be blowing hard post-race (op 1/1)

1547 - 1548a (Foreign Racing) - See Raceform Interactive

1143 COLOGNE (R-H)
Sunday, April 26

OFFICIAL GOING: Good

1549a GERLING-PREIS (GROUP 2) 1m 4f
4:15 (4:16) 4-Y-0+ **£38,835** (£14,563; £5,825; £3,883)

RPR
1 **Kamsin (GER)**203 6522 4-9-7 .... AStarke 3 112
(P Schiergen, Germany) *mde all: drvn out* **1/2**1
2 1 ¼ **Dwilano (GER)**21 1143 6-9-0 .... NRichter 5 102
(P Remmert, Germany) *trckd wnr: 2nd st: chal over 1f out: kpt on same pce fnl 100yds* **22/1**
3 ¾ **Shawnee Saga (FR)**14 1236 4-9-0 .... WMongil 1 102
(W Baltromei, Germany) *racd in 3rd: 4th st: styd on one pce fnl 2f* **175/10**
4 1 **Ambassador (GER)**21 1143 5-9-0 .... DPorcu 2 99
(T Mundry, Germany) *racd in 4th: 5th st: hdwy on outside 2f out: kpt on one pce* **26/5**3
5 ½ **Poseidon Adventure (IRE)**133 7682 6-9-0 ....(b) KKerekes 4 98
(W Figge, Germany) *hld up in rr: last st: effrt on outside 2f out: nvr nr to chal* **7/1**
6 11 **Ostland (GER)**21 1143 4-9-0 .... THellier 6 82
(P Schiergen, Germany) *hld up in rr tl hdwy to go 3rd 4f out: btn 2f out: eased fnl f* **13/5**2

2m 31.18s (-1.72)
WFA 4 from 5yo+ 1lb **6 Ran SP% 132.8**
(Including 10 Euro stake): WIN 15; PL 14, 31; SF 293.
Owner Stall Blankenese **Bred** Gestut Karlshof **Trained** Germany

1236 LONGCHAMP (R-H)
Sunday, April 26

OFFICIAL GOING: Good

1550a PRIX VANTEAUX BEACHCOMBER HOTELS LE ROYAL PALM (GROUP 3) (FILLIES) 1m 1f 55y
2:20 (2:20) 3-Y-O **£38,835** (£15,534; £11,650; £7,767; £3,883)

RPR
1 **Denomination (USA)**21 1146 3-9-0 .... DBoeuf 2 102
(Mme C Head-Maarek, France) *mde all: r.o wl fnl f: drvn out* **9/4**1
2 nk **Celebra (FR)**13 3-9-0 .... OPeslier 1 102
(C Laffon-Parias, France) *racd in 3rd on ins: rdn to go 2nd over 1f out: styd on but hld by wnr* **6/1**
3 ¾ **Tassara (FR)**24 3-9-0 .... TThulliez 3 100
(Y De Nicolay, France) *nt settle in 4th early: 4th st: pushed along and hdwy 1 1/2f out: disputing 2nd fnl f: styd on* **10/1**
4 1 ½ **Gainful (USA)**21 1146 3-9-0 ....(b) SPasquier 6 97
(D Smaga, France) *racd in 2nd: pushed along st: rdn 2f out: wknd over 1f out* **13/2**
5 ½ **Ana Americana (FR)**21 1146 3-9-0 .... C-PLemaire 5 96
(P Demercastel, France) *racd in 5th: shkn up 2f out: no imp* **5/2**2
6 2 ½ **Becomes You**189 6855 3-9-0 .... GMosse 4 91
(M Delzangles, France) *racd in last: pushed along st: n.d* **9/2**3

1m 55.39s (-0.91) **Going Correction** +0.125s/f (Good) **6 Ran SP% 114.2**
Speed ratings: **109,108,108,106,106 104**
PARI-MUTUEL: WIN 3.50; PL 2.00, 2.90; SF 20.80.
Owner Mme Alec Head **Bred** Brookdale Thoroughbreds **Trained** Chantilly, France

NOTEBOOK
Denomination(USA) certainly appreciates good, fast ground. Once again she was asked to make all the running and her jockey injected pace into the event a furlong and a half out. She then repelled attacks from several of the other runners. It is unlikely that she will race again before the Prix de Diane on June 14th and her trainer is confident she will stay the longer distance.
Celebra(FR) didn't have the clearest of runs and ran a little free early on. Racing on the rail, things opened up well early in the straight, but then she was hampered one out before running on again inside the final furlong. (op 13-2)
Tassara(FR), a big, powerful filly, pulled a lot in the early stages and was placed in fourth position. She started her run from a furlong and a half out and stayed on one-paced in the final stages.
Gainful(USA), smartly into her stride, was well up with the winner in the early stages. She was well there a furlong and a half out but eventually dropped out of contention. (op 13-2 tchd 6-1)

1551a PRIX GANAY - GRAND PRIX AIR MAURITIUS (GROUP 1) 1m 2f 110y
2:50 (2:52) 4-Y-0+ **£166,427** (£66,583; £33,291; £16,631; £8,330)

RPR
1 **Vision D'Etat (FR)**21 1144 4-9-2 .... IMendizabal 3 121+
(E Libaud, France) *racd in 3rd on rail: wnt 2nd 2f out: pushed along over 1 1/2f out to chal: led 150yds out: comf* **13/8**1
2 ¾ **Loup Breton (IRE)**21 1144 5-9-2 .... ACrastus 6 119
(E Lellouche, France) *racd in 7th: drvn and hdwy fr 1 1/2f out: wnt 3rd ins fnl 100yds: jst got bttr of Adlerflug for 2nd fnl stages* **8/1**
3 shd **Adlerflug (GER)**231 5736 5-9-2 .... ADeVries 4 119+
(J Hirschberger, Germany) *racd in 5th: pushed along st: drvn and hdwy on rail 2f out: disputing 2nd cl home: jst missed 2nd on line* **8/1**
4 1 **Thewayyouare (USA)**329 2654 4-9-2 .... JMurtagh 1 117
(A P O'Brien, Ire) *led or disp: pushed along st: rdn over 1f out: hdd 150yds out: no ex fnl stages* **11/2**2
5 1 ½ **The Bogberry (USA)**21 1144 4-9-2 .... GMosse 7 114
(A De Royer-Dupre, France) *racd in 6th: pushed along st: n.d* **15/2**
6 nk **Cima De Triomphe (IRE)**168 7263 4-9-2 .... C-PLemaire 9 113
(L M Cumani) *hld up in last: nvr a threat* **6/1**3
7 1 **Red Rock Canyon (IRE)**183 7000 5-9-2 .... DavidMcCabe 2 111
(A P O'Brien, Ire) *racd in 2nd: plld hrd: led briefly after 3f: u.p and lost pl 2f out: wknd* **40/1**
8 1 ½ **Tajaaweed (USA)**274 4436 4-9-2 .... RHills 8 108
(Sir Michael Stoute) *racd in 4th towards outside: drvn 2f out: sn one pce* **7/1**

2m 9.43s (-3.57) **Going Correction** +0.125s/f (Good) **8 Ran SP% 116.7**
Speed ratings: **117,116,116,115,114 114,113,112**
PARI-MUTUEL: WIN 2.40; PL 1.10, 1.20, 1.60; DF 3.30.
Owner Jacques Detre **Bred** Gaetan Gilles **Trained** France
■ Stewards' Enquiry : A De Vries two-day ban: careless riding (May 10-11)

FOCUS
This was just a reasonable contest by Group 1 standards, and a little way short of top-class form. It was also a tactical affair, with Red Rock Canyon, who most assumed was in the line up to fulfil his usual pace-making duties, heavily restrained from the off, allowing stablemate Thewayyouare a very soft lead. That resulted in a steadily run race and the bare form must be treated with caution.

NOTEBOOK

Vision D'Etat(FR), the French Derby winner and Arc fifth, had only managed third in a 1m2f Group 2 on his reappearance, but this represented a return to something like his best. It's true he wasn't visually impressive, and the margin of victory means he cannot be rated particularly highly for the level, but he looks better than the bare result. For a start, a steadily run race was by no means ideal and, having tracked the pace towards the inside for most of the way, he was hemmed in by the no-hoper Red Rock Canyon early in the straight, before then being bumped by that rival with less than 400m to run. Once in the clear, he showed a smart change of pace to put his seal on the race, but idled badly once in front, continually pricking his ears, and allowing the second and third to close up near the line. All things considered, this was a thoroughly satisfactory success and he should raise his game further when faced with stiffer competition, particularly if he gets a better pace to run at. His trainer is keen to keep him at this sort of distance and mentioned the Prince Of Wales Stakes at Royal Ascot as a likely target.

Loup Breton(IRE) was 0-4 in Group 1 company coming into this. He ran well, showing a decent finishing kick to pick up from a fair way back in the straight, despite continually edging right, but this form flatters him. Not only is his proximity to the winner slightly misleading, but he would almost certainly have been third had the German raider enjoyed a better trip. Connections now have their sights on the Prix d'Ispahan and will hope there is more cut in the ground for his next race.

Adlerflug(GER) had to be switched more than once when trying to pick up from off the pace in the straight, and was then short of room after getting stuck behind the winner near the line. It's hard to know how much closer he would have finished with a clear run, and it's worth remembering Vision D'Etat did little once in front, but this was still a most encouraging reappearance. He will be well suited by a return to 1m4f and should be in for a decent season. Another not totally suited by the fast ground, he will now be heading for the Coronation Cup or the Gran Premio di Milano.

Thewayyouare(USA), last seen finishing in mid-division in the French Derby when trained by Andre Fabre, was bidding to provide Aidan O'Brien with a third straight success in this Group 1 contest, following wins from Dylan Thomas and Duke Of Marmalade. In truth, he had the race set up for him if good enough, even with the keen-running Red Rock Canyon a bit of a nuisance, but he ran like a horse both in need of the run, and even more crucially, lacking in stamina. This Lockinge entrant will benefit from a return to a 1m, the distance at which he gained his sole Group 1 success, and he is another who would prefer cut in the ground.

The Bogberry(USA) was a little keen under restraint and made only limited progress in the straight, proving unable to confirm recent form with the winner.

Cima De Triomphe(IRE), who won last year's Italian Derby, did not offer much on his debut for Luca Cumani, but he was hardly given the most positive of rides in a steadily-run affair and there should be better to come when he's fully tuned up.

Red Rock Canyon(IRE) was expected to act as a pacemaker, but instead he was heavily restrained in secind, where he pulled hard.

Tajaaweed(USA), last season's Dee Stakes winner, got warm down the neck and finished up well beaten after running a little freely close to the steady pace. This big horse was unlikely to have appreciated the lack of pace and can be given another chance, whilst his jockey also reported that the ground was too firm for him.

1552a PRIX DE BARBEVILLE (GROUP 3) — 1m 7f 110y

3:20 (3:21) 4-Y-0+ **£38,835** (£15,534; £11,650; £7,767; £3,883)

				RPR
1		**Pointilliste (USA)**[20] 1167 6-9-0 (E Lellouche, France) *led after 2f: rdn 1f out: r.o wl* **6/1**[3]	ACrastus 3	107
2	1	**La Boum (GER)**[21] 1144 6-8-13 (Robert Collet, France) *hld up: 5th 1/2-way: 5th st: drvn to take 2nd 100yds out: r.o* **14/1**	TJarnet 7	105
3	1	**Faramir (IRE)**[9] 4-8-8 (M Delcher-Sanchez, Spain) *wnt 2nd after 2f: chal 2f out: drvn and btn over 1f out: kpt on one pce fnl f* **9/1**	GMosse 6	103
4	nk	**Americain (USA)**[20] 1167 4-8-12 (A Fabre, France) *hld up: 7th st: effrt on outside fr 2f out: hrd rdn 1f out: kpt on to take 4th on line* **9/4**[2]	OPeslier 8	106
5	hd	**Quartz Jem (IRE)**[20] 1167 5-8-11 (Mme Pia Brandt, France) *disp 5th: 6th st: styd on u.p fr over 1f out: wnt 4th 100yds out: lost 4th on line* **33/1**	IMendizabal 5	101
6	1 1/2	**Caudillo (GER)**[204] 6497 6-9-2 (Dr A Bolte, Germany) *led 2f: 3rd st: disp 4th 1f out: one pce* **16/1**	SPasquier 1	104
7	snk	**Le Miracle (GER)**[20] 1167 8-8-11 (W Baltromei, Germany) *racd in 4th to st: 3rd 1f out: no ex* **8/1**	DBoeuf 2	99
8	6	**Kasbah Bliss (FR)**[45] 6497 7-9-2 (F Doumen, France) *hld up in rr: last st: bhd fr 1 1/2f out* **7/4**[1]	TThulliez 4	97

3m 21.04s (-0.46) **Going Correction** +0.125s/f (Good) **8 Ran SP% 118.0**
WFA 4 from 5yo+ 3lb
Speed ratings: **106,105,105,104,104 104,103,100**
PARI-MUTUEL: WIN 4.20; PL 1.70, 4.30, 2.60; DF 52.50.
Owner Ecurie Wildenstein **Bred** Dayton Investments Ltd **Trained** Lamorlaye, France

NOTEBOOK

Pointilliste(USA) appears to be improving with age and he impressed when making every yard of the running to win his first Group event. His jockey rode a very polished race, setting a sensible pace before quickening things up from a furlong and a half out. The horse ran on well and was not totally extended to hold off the runner-up and third. He has been entered in the Ascot Gold Cup and will first take in the Prix Vicomtesse Vigier. (op 6-1 tchd 7-1)

La Boum(GER) didn't really appear on the scene until the furlong marker having been settled in mid-division early on. She was making her seasonal debut here and trying this distance for the first time, so her effort deserves merit.

Faramir(IRE) was quickly at the head of affairs and close to the leader. Still fighting away coming into the straight, he only lost second place well inside the final furlong. The ground was certainly too firm for this colt who was attempting the distance for the first time.

Americain(USA) was given an awful lot to do and put in his best work in the dying stages of the race. Second-last from the start and into the straight, he came rattling along up the centre of the track to take fourth place late on and would have been third in a few more strides.

Kasbah Bliss(FR) Official explanation: jockey said gelding was never in a rhythm and had no other explanation for the poor form shown

SHA TIN (R-H)

Sunday, April 26

OFFICIAL GOING: Yielding

1553a CHAMPIONS MILE (GROUP 1) (TURF) — 1m

8:55 (8:55) 3-Y-0+ **£614,004** (£236,984; £107,720; £61,041; £35,907; £21,544)

				RPR
1		**Sight Winner (NZ)**[21] 6-9-0 (J Size, Hong Kong)	BrettPrebble 9	119
2	shd	**Egyptian Ra (NZ)**[42] 8-9-0 (A S Cruz, Hong Kong)	(t) FCoetzee 1	119
3	hd	**Dao Dao (AUS)**[22] 6-9-0 (Michael, Wayne & John Hawkes, Australia)	WCMarwing 2	119+
4	1/2	**Good Ba Ba (USA)**[42] 7-9-0 (A Schutz, Hong Kong)	(t) CSoumillon 10	117+
5	3/4	**Collection (IRE)**[35] 4-9-0 (J Moore, Hong Kong)	(t) DarrenBeadman 7	116
6	nk	**Imbongi (SAF)**[52] 774 5-9-0 (M F De Kock, South Africa)	KShea 3	115
7	nk	**Alexandros**[29] 1011 4-9-0 (Saeed Bin Suroor) *towards rr: 9th 1/2-way: pushed along on outside st: sn rdn: nvr able to chal SP 10-1*	LDettori 5	114
8	3/4	**More Bountiful (NZ)**[21] 5-9-0 (J Size, Hong Kong)	DWhyte 4	113
9	nk	**Armada (NZ)**[21] 8-9-0 (J Size, Hong Kong)	ESaint-Martin 11	112
10	nk	**Fellowship (NZ)**[21] 7-9-0 (P O'Sullivan, Hong Kong)	(t) ZaxPurton 6	111
11	nk	**Unique Jewellery (NZ)**[21] 5-9-0 (J Size, Hong Kong)	(b[1]) ODoleuze 8	110

1m 34.97s (0.27) **11 Ran**
(Including HK$10 stake): WIN 651.00; PL 70.00, 19.00, 80.00; DF 2,105.
Owner Mr & Mrs Wing Kun Tam **Bred** Westbury Stud Ltd **Trained** Hong Kong

NOTEBOOK

Alexandros never got into the race and proved disappointing. His rider wasn't inclined to blame the yielding ground and felt that he just wasn't good enough.

1554a AUDEMARS PIGUET QE II CUP (GROUP 1) (TURF) — 1m 2f

9:35 (9:35) 3-Y-0+ **£718,133** (£269,300; £134,650; £71,813; £40,395; £22,442)

				RPR
1		**Presvis**[29] 1011 5-9-0 (L M Cumani) *racd in last: pushed along ent st and hdwy on ins: drvn to chal 1f out: led 100yds out: r.o wl SP 29/10* **29/10**[1]	RyanMoore 8	119+
2	1	**Viva Pataca**[21] 7-9-0 (J Moore, Hong Kong)	DarrenBeadman 1	117
3	nk	**Thumbs Up (NZ)**[35] 5-9-0 (C S Shum, Hong Kong)	CSoumillon 7	116
4	1/2	**Chinchon (IRE)**[43] 846 4-9-0 (C Laffon-Parias, France) **12/1**[3]	(p) ODoleuze 5	115
5	nk	**Packing Winner (NZ)**[21] 7-9-0 (L Ho, Hong Kong)	ESaint-Martin 6	115
6	nk	**Archipenko (USA)**[29] 1011 5-9-0 (M F De Kock, South Africa) *pushed along to r promly: had to check sltly after 2f: 4th 1/2-way: rdn and 3rd 1 1/2f out: wknd fnl 100yds SP 41-10* **41/10**[2]	(bt) KShea 2	114
7	4 1/2	**Viva Macau (FR)**[35] 6-9-0 (J Moore, Hong Kong)	(tp) KTYeung 3	105
8	shd	**Niconero (AUS)**[29] 1011 8-9-0 (David Hayes, Australia)	CraigAWilliams 10	105
9	3 1/4	**Danesis (IRE)**[35] 5-9-0 (A S Cruz, Hong Kong)	(t) FCoetzee 4	99
10	1 3/4	**Bullish Cash (NZ)**[35] 7-9-0 (A S Cruz, Hong Kong)	(t) BrettPrebble 9	95

2m 2.97s (1.57) **10 Ran SP% 52.9**
WIN 39.00; PL 15.00, 11.50, 18.50; 55.00.
Owner L Marinopoulos **Bred** Mrs M Campbell-Andenaes **Trained** Newmarket, Suffolk

NOTEBOOK

Presvis has made rapid strides in the last 12 months and had improved with every race in three runs in Dubai, where he was unlucky to run up against a freakish Gladiatorus in the Duty Free on his first venture into Group company. He confirmed himself a genuine Group 1 contender here in a race run at a solid gallop, coming from last place under a confident ride and unleashing his trademark turn of foot to beat one of the local stars fair and square. He will continue to be campaigned internationally and next stop is likely to be the Singapore International Airlines Cup, then a well earned break ahead of a return here in December for the Hong Kong Cup.

Archipenko(USA) won this 12 months ago and had shown plenty of decent form since, but he was below his best when four places behind Presvis in the Dubai Duty Free and he was a bit disappointing again here.

DIELSDORF (R-H)

Sunday, April 26

OFFICIAL GOING: Good

1555a SUPER GRAND PRIX BMW — 1m 3f 110y

3:15 (3:18) 4-Y-0+ **£13,981** (£5,592; £4,194; £2,796; £1,398)

				RPR
1		**Pont Des Arts (FR)**[183] 6992 5-9-4 (K Schafflutzel, Switzerland) **23/10**[1]	OPlacais 7	—
2	5	**First Time (GER)**[337] 6-8-11 (Karin Suter, Switzerland) **56/10**[3]	TCastanheira 6	—
3	shd	**Mascarpone (GER)**[686] 2503 5-9-11 (M Weiss, Switzerland) **71/10**	MSautjeau 11	—
4	3	**Wassiljew (IRE)**[239] 5528 5-8-12 (K Schafflutzel, Switzerland) **6/1**	NGuilbert 8	—
5	nk	**Eiswind**[63] 653 5-9-4 (G Raveneau, Switzerland) **3/1**[2]	FDiFede 4	—
6	2 1/2	**Swiss Act**[29] 1003 5-9-2 (M Johnston) *disputed 2nd behind clear winner to straight, soon weakened* **89/10**	JoeFanning 10	—
7	shd	**Ailton (GER)**[434] 605 5-9-7 (G Raveneau, Switzerland) **87/10**	SFargeat 9	—
8	nk	**Golan Knight (IRE)**[315] 4-9-2 (K Schafflutzel, Switzerland) **167/10**	JCanfyn 1	—
9	1 1/2	**Simonas (IRE)**[21] 1143 10-9-4 (A Wohler, Germany) **36/5**	JBojko 3	—
10	4	**Song Of Victory (GER)**[63] 653 5-9-11 (M Weiss, Switzerland) **105/10**	MiguelLopez 2	—

2m 25.9s (145.90) **10 Ran SP% 144.0**
PARI-MUTUEL (including 1 Franc stake): WIN 3.30; PL 1.50, 1.60, 1.80;SF 18.40.
Owner A & V Krauliger **Bred** Sca De La Perrigne **Trained** Switzerland

NOTEBOOK
Swiss Act disputed second for a long way but got very tired in the straight. The ground had been watered and was a bit loose on top, but his rider did not want to use that as an excuse.

[1123]NEWCASTLE (L-H)
Monday, April 27

OFFICIAL GOING: Good to firm (firm in places; 8.4)
Wind: moderate, half against Weather: Cloudy

1556 COMPLETE FOOTBALL "HANDS AND HEELS" APPRENTICE H'CAP 1m 2f 32y
2:20 (2:21) (Class 6) (0-60,58) 4-Y-0+ **£2,320** (£685; £342) **Stalls** Low

Form RPR
000/ 1 **Mccormack (IRE)**[624] 4424 7-8-6 **45**.............................. DebraEngland 8 54+
(Miss T Jackson) *trckd ldrs: led 2f out: kpt on strly fnl f: eased nr fin* **66/1**
403- 2 ¾ **Kings Maiden (IRE)**[96] 5453 6-8-9 **48**.............................. NSLawes 4 55+
(James Moffatt) *hld up on ins: gd hdwy 2f out: kpt on fnl f: nt rch wnr* **14/1**
060/ 3 2 ¼ **Tommy Tobougg**[38] 6695 5-8-11 **50**.............................. KrishGundowry 7 52
(Miss Lucinda V Russell) *led to 2f out: kpt on same pce fnl f* **20/1**
00-2 4 ½ **Farne Island**[7] 1402 6-8-9 **48**.............................. JamieKyne 16 49
(Micky Hammond) *in tch: effrt 2f out: kpt on same pce fnl f* **3/1**[2]
60-5 5 1 ¾ **Dechiper (IRE)**[23] 1125 7-9-5 **58**.............................. GarryWhillans 3 56+
(R Johnson) *hld up: hdwy on ins over 2f out: kpt on fnl f: nvr rchd ldrs* **2/1**[1]
03-0 6 2 ¼ **Sarraaf (IRE)**[98] 216 13-8-8 **52**.............................. SFeeney(5) 13 45
(I Semple) *hld up: hdwy 2f out: kpt on fnl f: no imp* **18/1**
0-64 7 3 ¾ **Mister Maq**[12] 1276 6-8-4 **46**..............................(v) AdamCarter(3) 11 32
(A Crook) *midfield: pushed along over 2f out: sn no imp* **40/1**
-000 8 1 ¼ **Dark Planet**[23] 1125 6-8-3 **45**..............................(v) JohnCavanagh(3) 10 28
(D W Thompson) *plld hrd: cl up tl wknd fr 2f out* **12/1**
0-00 9 1 ¼ **Zabougg**[14] 1242 4-8-4 **46**..............................(p) HollyHall(3) 12 27
(D W Barker) *s.i.s: racd keenly in rr: nvr able to chal* **12/1**
/000 10 2 ½ **Cate Washington**[62] 666 6-8-3 **45**.............................. SeanPalmer(3) 2 21
(Mrs L Williamson) *t.k.h: in tch on ins tl wknd over 2f out* **100/1**
-006 11 1 ½ **Amber Ridge**[32] 970 4-8-3 **45**.............................. KierenFox(3) 5 18
(B P J Baugh) *plld hrd: cl up tl wknd over 2f out* **33/1**
060 12 1 ¼ **Lunar Storm (IRE)**[24] 1101 5-8-3 **45**..............................(p) AlexEdwards(3) 15 15
(Mrs R A Carr) *s.i.s: bhd: c wd over 2f out: nvr on terms* **50/1**
-000 13 3 ¼ **Treetops Hotel (IRE)**[5] 1454 10-8-1 **45**.............................. GemmaElford(5) 14 9
(L R James) *racd wd in rr: struggling 3f out: sn btn* **50/1**
6016 14 2 ¾ **Media Stars**[23] 1125 4-8-12 **54**..............................(p) AnthonyBetts(3) 9 12
(R Johnson) *racd keenly: hld up on ins: rdn over 2f out: sn wknd* **8/1**[3]
2500 15 1 **John Potts**[32] 969 4-8-6 **45**..............................(p) SoniaEaton 6 1
(B P J Baugh) *plld hrd: in tch tl wknd over 2f out* **12/1**

2m 14.31s (2.41) **Going Correction** +0.125s/f (Good) 15 Ran SP% **121.0**
Speed ratings (Par 101): **95,94,92,92,90 89,86,85,84,82 80,79,77,75,74**
toteswinger: 1&2 £118.60, 1&3 £237.20, 2&3 £28.90 CSF £802.67 CT £17591.17 TOTE £122.60: £19.30, £3.70, £5.10; EX 770.00 TRIFECTA Not won..
Owner R D Bickenson **Bred** Eugene O'Sullivan **Trained** Liverton, Cleveland

FOCUS
A race restricted to inexperienced apprentices, who were not allowed to use their whips, and with the field soon well-strung out, this is form to treat with caution.
Media Stars Official explanation: vet said gelding returned lame

1557 PARKLANDS GOLF CLUB H'CAP 1m 4f 93y
2:50 (2:50) (Class 4) (0-85,84) 4-Y-0+ **£5,180** (£1,541; £770; £384) **Stalls** Low

Form RPR
/410 1 **Raucous (GER)**[15] 1230 6-8-5 **70**.............................. AndrewElliott 5 75
(Mrs R A Carr) *t.k.h early: cl up: led over 2f out: hrd pressed over 1f out: hld on wl fnl f* **7/4**[1]
335- 2 1 ¼ **Rosbay (IRE)**[219] 6107 5-9-5 **84**.............................. DuranFentiman 1 87
(T D Easterby) *trckd ldrs: effrt and ev ch over 1f out: sn drvn: one pce wl ins fnl f* **15/8**[2]
000- 3 6 **Ella Woodcock (IRE)**[10] 6974 5-8-13 **78**..............................(t) TonyHamilton 4 71
(C Grant) *in tch: rdn and outpcd 3f out: rallied over 1f out: no ch w first two* **7/1**
000- 4 20 **Mister Arjay (USA)**[240] 5498 9-8-6 **71**.............................. PaulHanagan 2 32
(B Ellison) *led: rdn and hdd over 2f out: wknd over 1f out: eased whn no ch fnl f* **10/3**[3]

2m 44.95s (-0.65) **Going Correction** +0.125s/f (Good)
WFA 4 from 5yo+ 1lb 4 Ran SP% **106.7**
Speed ratings (Par 105): **107,106,102,88**
toteswinger: 1&2 £1.80. CSF £5.22 TOTE £2.80; EX 4.20.
Owner David W Chapman **Bred** Gestut Graditz **Trained** Huby, N Yorks

FOCUS
Just the four runners and this was an ordinary handicap for the class. However, despite the small field, the pace was good.

1558 COMPLETE FOOTBALL H'CAP 6f
3:20 (3:21) (Class 6) (0-52,53) 4-Y-0+ **£2,320** (£685; £342) **Stalls** High

Form RPR
-632 1 **Ace Of Spies (IRE)**[4] 1475 4-8-10 **50**..............................(p) SilvestreDeSousa 16 60+
(G A Harker) *mde all stands' side gp: clr whn hung bdly lft appr fnl f: kpt on and overall ldr towards fin: 1st of 9 stands' side gp* **2/1**[1]
0206 2 hd **Loose Caboose (IRE)**[7] 1412 4-8-8 **51**..............................(v) AndrewMullen(3) 4 60
(A J McCabe) *led far side: rdn 2f out: kpt on: hdd towards fin: 1st of 7 in gp* **16/1**
4330 3 3 ¼ **Kingsmaite**[6] 1438 8-8-12 **52**..............................(b) RobertWinston 3 51
(S R Bowring) *trckd far side ldrs: effrt over 2f out: kpt on same pce fnl f: 2nd of 7 in gp* **10/1**
-000 4 1 **Victory Spirit**[94] 277 5-8-9 **49**.............................. PaulMulrennan 1 45
(D A Nolan) *trckd far side ldrs: rdn over 2f out: r.o same pce ins fnl f: 3rd of 7 in gp* **16/1**
400- 5 hd **Not Now Lewis (IRE)**[120] 5971 5-8-12 **52**.............................. PJMcDonald 2 47
(F P Murtagh) *hld up far side: hdwy 2f out: kpt on fnl f: no imp: 4th of 7 in gp* **66/1**
216 6 8 **Straight Face (IRE)**[48] 792 5-8-6 **53** ow1..............................(b) KylieManser(7) 9 23
(Miss Gay Kelleway) *hld up stands' side: hdwy on outer of that gp fr 2f out: kpt on: no imp: 2nd of 9 in gp* **14/1**
0-00 7 2 **Piccolo Pete**[14] 1242 4-8-8 **48**..............................(p) TonyHamilton 15 11
(R Johnson) *taken early to post: dwlt: sn midfield stands' side: drvn over 2f out: sn one pce: 3rd of 9 in gp* **28/1**
006- 8 1 ½ **Avoncreek**[188] 6889 5-8-12 **52**.............................. GrahamGibbons 10 10
(B P J Baugh) *dwlet: bhd stands' side tl styd on fnl 2f: nvr rchd ldrs: 4th of 9 in gp* **16/1**
400- 9 1 ¼ **Foreign Rhythm (IRE)**[182] 7018 4-8-10 **50**..............................(v) JoeFanning 8 4
(N Tinkler) *cl up stands' side tl rdn and no ex over 1f out: 5th of 9 in gp* **40/1**
10-6 10 hd **Greek Secret**[96] 234 6-8-12 **52**.............................. AdrianTNicholls 11 6
(J O'Reilly) *bhd stands' side: drvn 1/2-way: n.d: 6th of 9 in gp* **20/1**
354- 11 3 **Angelofthenorth**[311] 3212 7-8-9 **49**.............................. AndrewElliott 5 —
(C J Teague) *chsd far side ldrs tl wknd fr 2f out: 5th of 7 in gp* **40/1**
0-00 12 1 ¼ **Fulford**[90] 303 4-8-12 **52**.............................. TWilliams 13 —
(M Brittain) *prom stands' side tl rdn and wknd over 2f out: 7th of 9 in gp* **20/1**
6625 13 4 **Bateleur**[26] 1076 5-8-7 **52**..............................(v) MCGeran(5) 12 —
(M R Channon) *prom on outside of stands' side gp tl wknd over 2f out: 8th of 9 in gp* **11/2**[2]
03-0 14 2 ¾ **Rainbow Bay**[85] 367 6-8-10 **50**..............................(v) PhillipMakin 6 —
(Miss Tracy Waggott) *in tch far side tl wknd over 2f out: 6th of 7 in gp* **16/1**
040- 15 2 ¾ **Howards Tipple**[207] 6405 5-8-12 **52**..............................(p) TomEaves 14 —
(I Semple) *trckd stands' side ldrs tl wknd over 2f out: last of 9 in gp* **12/1**
0-05 16 34 **Supreme Speedster**[31] 975 5-8-10 **50**.............................. PaulHanagan 7 —
(A G Newcombe) *hld up far side: drvn 3f out: sn wknd: t.o: last of 7 in gp* **7/1**[3]

1m 16.41s (1.21) **Going Correction** +0.125s/f (Good) 16 Ran SP% **127.5**
Speed ratings (Par 101): **96,95,91,90,89 79,76,74,72,72 68,66,61,57,54 8**
toteswinger: 1&2 £11.40, 1&3 £6.00, 2&3 £24.40 CSF £36.83 CT £297.13 TOTE £3.00: £1.40, £4.20, £2.10, £3.50; EX 48.00 TRIFECTA Not won..
Owner A S Ward **Bred** Gainsborough Stud Management Ltd **Trained** Thirkleby, N Yorks
■ Stewards' Enquiry : Kylie Manser one-day ban: careless riding (May 11)

FOCUS
Just a moderate sprint handicap and the form looks weak, but the winner may be better than the bare form.
Greek Secret Official explanation: jockey said gelding was denied a clear run
Supreme Speedster Official explanation: jockey said gelding lost its action

1559 GOSFORTH DECORATING & BUILDING SERVICES H'CAP 1m 3y(S)
3:50 (3:55) (Class 4) (0-85,85) 3-Y-O **£5,180** (£1,541; £770; £384) **Stalls** High

Form RPR
15-0 1 **Johnmanderville**[11] 1307 3-8-2 **74**.............................. MartinLane(5) 4 79
(K R Burke) *mde virtually all: rdn 2f out: hld on wl fnl f* **9/1**
0136 2 nk **Common Diva**[11] 1315 3-8-6 **73**.............................. RobertWinston 8 77
(A J McCabe) *prom: hdwy to press wnr over 2f out: sn rdn: kpt on fnl f* **16/1**
15- 3 8 **Prize Point**[284] 4108 3-8-10 **77**.............................. RichardMullen 3 63+
(K A Ryan) *unruly gng to post: t.k.h early: hld up in tch: smooth hdwy over 2f out: sn rdn: no ex over 1f out* **8/1**
413- 4 4 **Big Apple Boy (IRE)**[203] 6525 3-9-4 **85**.............................. AndrewElliott 7 61
(Jedd O'Keeffe) *hld up in tch: outpcd over 2f out: sn no imp* **8/1**
50-0 5 2 **Amethyst Dawn (IRE)**[12] 1280 3-8-5 **72**.............................. PaulHanagan 6 44
(T D Easterby) *t.k.h: hld up: rdn 3f out: nvr rchd ldrs* **4/1**[3]
231- 6 3 **Box Office**[195] 6715 3-9-4 **85**.............................. RoystonFfrench 1 50
(M Johnston) *w ldrs tl rdn and wknd fr 2f out* **10/3**[2]
521- 7 12 **Fastnet Storm (IRE)**[189] 6857 3-8-12 **79**.............................. MickyFenton 2 16
(T P Tate) *disp ld 2f: cl up tl wknd over 2f out* **3/1**[1]
F1-5 8 34 **Geneva Geyser (GER)**[28] 1033 3-8-11 **78**.............................. LukeMorris 5 —
(J M P Eustace) *dwlt and wnt lft s: bhd: lost tch fr 3f out* **10/1**

1m 43.2s (-0.20) **Going Correction** +0.125s/f (Good) 8 Ran SP% **115.3**
Speed ratings (Par 100): **106,105,97,93,91 88,76,42**
toteswinger: 1&2 £20.40, 1&3 £11.20, 2&3 £8.30 CSF £137.34 CT £1204.52 TOTE £10.80: £3.40, £2.80, £2.50; EX 121.40 TRIFECTA Not won..
Owner Jet Racing Partnership **Bred** Natton House Thoroughbreds & Mark Woodall **Trained** Middleham Moor, N Yorks
■ Stewards' Enquiry : Richard Mullen two-day ban: careless riding (May 11-12)

FOCUS
Just a fair handicap and a couple were disappointing, but they finished well spread out.
Geneva Geyser(GER) Official explanation: jockey said colt never travelled

1560 ST JAMES SECURITY H'CAP 6f
4:20 (4:22) (Class 2) (0-105,99) 4-Y-0+ **£11,656** (£3,468; £1,733; £865) **Stalls** High

Form RPR
5230 1 **Tamagin (USA)**[30] 996 6-9-6 **98**..............................(p) TedDurcan 9 106
(K A Ryan) *mde all: rdn 2f out: hld on gamely fnl f* **9/1**
30-0 2 ½ **Sunrise Safari (IRE)**[12] 1278 6-8-7 **85**..............................(v) PaulHanagan 10 91
(R A Fahey) *hld up on ins: hdwy 2f out: effrt and chsd wnr wl ins fnl f: r.o* **5/1**[2]
4002 3 ¾ **Thebes**[7] 1398 4-8-12 **90**.............................. RoystonFfrench 11 94
(M Johnston) *trckd ldrs: chsd wnr over 2f out: hrd rdn and edgd lft over 1f out: ch ins fnl f: sn no ex* **3/1**[1]
0-00 4 8 **Valery Borzov (IRE)**[80] 434 5-9-6 **98**..............................(v) AdrianTNicholls 8 76
(D Nicholls) *t.k.h: in tch: shkn up whn nt clr run over 2f out: hdwy wl over 1f out: no imp* **7/1**[3]
4001 5 3 ¼ **Excusez Moi (USA)**[15] 1229 7-8-7 **85**..............................(p) AndrewElliott 2 53
(Mrs R A Carr) *hld up: rdn and hdwy 2f out: nvr rchd ldrs* **16/1**
0003 6 7 **Capricorn Run (USA)**[23] 1124 6-9-7 **99**..............................(v) RobertWinston 5 45
(A J McCabe) *bhd and sn drvn along: nvr on terms* **14/1**
000- 7 1 **Celtic Sultan (IRE)**[170] 7245 5-8-12 **90**.............................. MickyFenton 6 32
(T P Tate) *chsd ldrs tl wknd over 2f out* **9/1**
04-0 8 nk **Machinist (IRE)**[29] 1018 9-8-10 **95**.............................. NSLawes(7) 4 36
(D Nicholls) *hld up: rdn 3f out: nvr on terms* **16/1**
330- 9 10 **Captain Dunne (IRE)**[184] 6971 4-9-6 **98**.............................. DuranFentiman 3 7
(T D Easterby) *cl up tl wknd over 2f out* **33/1**

1m 14.59s (-0.61) **Going Correction** +0.125s/f (Good) 9 Ran SP% **95.5**
Speed ratings (Par 109): **109,108,107,96,92 83,81,81,67**
toteswinger: 1&2 £6.80, 1&3 £4.00, 2&3 £2.60 CSF £36.05 CT £89.82 TOTE £9.00: £2.60, £2.10, £1.10; EX 43.40 Trifecta £164.90 Pool: £245.17 - 1.10 winning units..
Owner Tariq Al Nisf **Bred** Stonehaven Farm LLC **Trained** Hambleton, N Yorks

FOCUS
This looked a good, competitive sprint handicap, but there was once again a significant bias towards the front runner on the stands' rail, just as in the three other straight-track races.

NOTEBOOK
Tamagin(USA) took full advantage of a significant bias towards a handy ride against the stands' rail, despite being forced to go off plenty quick enough and at times looking an awkward conveyance under pressure. This is the highest mark he has ever won off, though, and considering everything went his way he must be opposed next time. (op 15-2 tchd 10-1)

Sunrise Safari(IRE) ◆ had no chance from a poor draw under a claimer at Beverley on his reappearance, but he's dropped to a very lenient mark - 15lb lower than at the start of last year - and returned to form in second. There's little doubt he probably keeps a bit back for himself, and he proved hard enough work for Paul Hanagan, but he still fared best of those to race off the pace. He looks ready to win. (op 11-2 tchd 9-2)
Thebes was unable to dominate and ran creditably considering. (op 4-1)
Valery Borzov(IRE) was a little keen early and probably wants easier ground. (tchd 15-2)
Excusez Moi(USA) could not repeat the form of his recent 7f Musselburgh win over this shorter trip on a speed-favouring track.
Capricorn Run(USA) Official explanation: jockey said gelding was unsuited by the good to firm (firm in places) ground

1561 S V RUTTER LTD H'CAP 7f
4:50 (4:50) (Class 4) (0-80,79) 3-Y-O **£5,180** (£1,541; £770; £384) **Stalls** High

Form RPR
561- **1** **Floor Show**[215] [6212] 3-8-13 **74**........................ RichardMullen 10 79+
(E S McMahon) *plld hrd: in tch: hdwy to ld over 1f out: rdn and hung lft ins fnl f: r.o* **9/2**[3]
304- **2** *1 1/4* **Richo**[193] [6756] 3-9-2 **77**........................ PaulMulrennan 9 79
(D H Brown) *led to over 1f out: kpt on same pce ins fnl f* **6/1**
305- **3** *1/2* **Dean Iarracht (IRE)**[202] [6545] 3-8-7 **68**........................ TonyHamilton 4 68+
(M Dods) *hld up: shkn up and hdwy over 1f out: r.o fnl f* **33/1**
100- **4** *3/4* **Regal Lyric (IRE)**[170] [7241] 3-8-11 **72**........................ JohnEgan 5 70
(T P Tate) *racd keenly: in tch: outpcd over 2f out: kpt on fnl f: no imp* **12/1**
12-2 **5** *hd* **Peter's Gift (IRE)**[24] [1098] 3-8-7 **68**........................ TedDurcan 1 66+
(K A Ryan) *cl up: effrt over 2f out: no ex ins fnl f* **4/1**[2]
44-3 **6** *1 1/2* **Steel Stockholder**[10] [1335] 3-8-4 **65**........................ TWilliams 6 59
(M Brittain) *stdd s: sn prom: outpcd over 2f out: rallied 1f out: no imp* **20/1**
0-1 **7** *7* **Lastroarofdtiger (USA)**[28] [1040] 3-9-4 **79**........................ DarrenWilliams 3 54
(K R Burke) *hld up: rdn over 2f out: sn btn* **14/1**
53-1 **8** *8* **Al Mugtareb (IRE)**[26] [1062] 3-8-11 **72**........................ TPO'Shea 8 25
(M Johnston) *pressed ldr tl rdn and wknd wl over 1f out* **4/1**[2]
21-6 **9** *11* **On Offer (IRE)**[11] [1307] 3-9-1 **76**........................ PaulHanagan 7 —
(T D Easterby) *cl up tl rdn and wknd fr 2f out* **7/2**[1]
1m 31.17s (2.47) **Going Correction** +0.125s/f (Good) **9 Ran SP% 116.8**
Speed ratings (Par 100): **83,81,81,80,79 78,70,61,48**
toteswinger: 1&2 £5.40, 1&3 £30.30, 2&3 £33.40 CSF £32.03 CT £799.32 TOTE £6.20: £1.80, £2.60, £8.90; EX 29.50 Trifecta £252.50 Part won. Pool: £341.32 - 0.45 winning units..
Owner J C Fretwell **Bred** Wyck Hall Stud Ltd **Trained** Lichfield, Staffs

FOCUS
A fair three-year-old handicap run at an ordinary pace.
Al Mugtareb(IRE) Official explanation: jockey said colt never travelled

1562 PARKLANDS GOLF CLUB MAIDEN STKS 1m 4f 93y
5:20 (5:21) (Class 5) 3-4-Y-O **£3,885** (£1,156; £577; £288) **Stalls** Low

Form RPR
52 **1** **Gilded Age**[14] [1245] 3-8-9 0........................ RoystonFfrench 7 72+
(M Johnston) *trckd ldrs: led over 2f out: pushed out: comf* **4/6**[1]
46 **2** *7* **Gosforth Park**[9] [1349] 3-8-2 0........................ JohnCavanagh(7) 6 61
(M Brittain) *sn chsng ldr: led 4f out to over 2f out: sn rdn: rallied to chse wnr ins fnl f: no imp* **22/1**
60 **3** *nk* **Deauville Flyer**[11] [1308] 3-8-9 0........................ JohnEgan 1 60+
(T D Easterby) *hld up: outpcd 3f out: rallied appr fnl f: nrst fin* **8/1**[3]
4 *1 1/4* **Black River Falls (USA)** 3-8-9 0........................ TomEaves 9 58
(I Semple) *hld up: hdwy to chse wnr over 1f out to ins fnl f: no ex* **12/1**
5 *3 1/2* **Caerlaverock (IRE)**[27] 4-10-0 0........................ PJMcDonald 3 53
(G A Swinbank) *hld up in tch: hdwy 1/2-way: rdn and outpcd over 2f out: n.d after* **9/4**[2]
0-00 **6** *1* **Saffron's Son (IRE)**[12] [1282] 3-8-9 52........................ MickyFenton 8 51
(P T Midgley) *bhd: rdn and edgd lft 3f out: sme late hdwy: nvr on terms* **66/1**
0 **7** *2 1/4* **Napoletano (ITY)**[46] [820] 3-8-9 0........................ TonyHamilton 4 47
(R Johnson) *trckd ldrs tl rdn and wknd fnl f* **100/1**
05 **8** *4* **Carnival Fair**[15] [1231] 4-9-9 0........................ PaulHanagan 2 36
(R A Fahey) *hld up: outpcd 4f out: sn btn* **50/1**
5044 **9** *24* **Weetfromthechaff**[29] [655] 4-9-9 55........................ SophieDoyle(5) 5 3
(M A Barnes) *led to 4f out: rdn and sn wknd: t.o* **33/1**
2m 48.93s (3.33) **Going Correction** +0.125s/f (Good)
WFA 3 from 4yo 20lb **9 Ran SP% 121.3**
Speed ratings (Par 103): **93,88,88,87,84 84,82,80,64**
toteswinger: 1&2 £3.90, 1&3 £2.80, 2&3 £12.50 CSF £24.90 TOTE £2.00: £1.60, £3.20, £1.50; EX 22.90 Trifecta £49.20 Pool: £421.15 - 6.33 winning units. Place 6: £4,019.04, Place 5: £190.36..
Owner Sheikh Hamdan Bin Mohammed Al Maktoum **Bred** Darley **Trained** Middleham Moor, N Yorks

FOCUS
A weak maiden.
Weetfromthechaff Official explanation: jockey said the gelding was unsuited by the good to firm (firm in places, loose following rain) ground
T/Plt: £925.60 to a £1 stake. Pool: £82,611.12. 65.15 winning tickets. T/Qpdt: £44.60 to a £1 stake. Pool: £6,106.10. 101.20 winning tickets. RY

1476 SOUTHWELL (L-H)
Monday, April 27

OFFICIAL GOING: Standard
Wind: Almost nil Weather: Overcast

1563 SOUTHWELL GOLF CLUB MEDIAN AUCTION MAIDEN STKS 6f (F)
5:40 (5:44) (Class 5) 3-5-Y-O **£4,094** (£1,209; £604) **Stalls** Low

Form RPR
0-6 **1** **All The Nines (IRE)**[3] [1491] 3-8-10 0........................ EdwardCreighton 9 72
(Mrs D J Sanderson) *chsd ldrs: drvn over 3f out: styd on down outer to ld over 1f out: drew clr* **33/1**
0- **2** *5* **Diamond Blade**[401] [957] 3-9-1 0........................ DNolan 6 61
(T D Easterby) *w ldrs: led 3f out tl over 1f out: kpt on same pce* **80/1**
32- **3** *hd* **Mark Of Meydan**[345] [2187] 4-9-7 0........................ FrederikTylicki(5) 12 64
(M Dods) *chsd ldrs on outer: drvn and outpcd over 3f out: hdwy over 1f out: styd on* **11/4**[2]
4 *1 1/4* **Cheyenne Red (IRE)** 3-8-10 0........................ PatrickDonaghy(5) 7 57
(M Dods) *s.i.s: sn detached in last: hdwy 2f out: styd on wl ins fnl f* **25/1**
33-0 **5** *hd* **Bertie Vista**[10] [1332] 4-9-12 62........................(b) SebSanders 1 59
(T D Easterby) *chsd ldrs: drvn over 4f out: outpcd on inner over 2f out: kpt on* **9/1**

44- **6** *1 1/2* **Choisharp (IRE)**[150] [7465] 3-8-10 0........................ AndreaAtzeni(5) 4 51
(M Botti) *rrd s: t.k.h: sn trcking ldrs: effrt over 2f out: fdd fnl f* **5/2**[1]
7 *3/4* **Bridge Note (USA)** 3-8-10 0........................ ShaneKelly 10 44
(J Noseda) *dwlt: in rr on outer: edgd lft and kpt on fnl 2f* **9/1**
0 **8** *2* **Royal Adelaide (IRE)**[14] [1250] 3-8-10 0........................ FrankieMcDonald 8 37
(J A Osborne) *in rr: sn drvn along: lost pl over 4f out* **80/1**
53-0 **9** *1/2* **Glimpse Of Light (IRE)**[10] [1317] 3-8-10 65........................ NeilChalmers 3 36
(A M Balding) *awkward s: hld up towards rr: outpcd and lost pl over 3f out* **16/1**
040 **10** *2 1/4* **Scholars Lass (IRE)**[34] [946] 4-9-4 44........................ RussellKennemore(3) 2 32
(J Balding) *gave problems befhand: led tl 3f out: lost pl over 1f out* **20/1**
0-42 **11** *9* **Jeremiah (IRE)**[18] [1196] 3-9-1 72........................ TolleyDean 11 5
(J G Portman) *mid-div: drvn over 4f out: lost pl 3f out: bhd and heavily eased ins fnl f* **9/2**[3]
1m 16.75s (0.25) **Going Correction** +0.025s/f (Slow)
WFA 3 from 4yo 11lb **11 Ran SP% 113.3**
Speed ratings (Par 103): **99,92,92,90,90 88,87,84,83,80 68**
toteswinger: 1&2 £92.20, 1&3 £18.50, 2&3 £34.10. CSF £1411.13 TOTE £33.40: £6.80, £12.10, £1.40; EX 474.80.
Owner R J Budge **Bred** Deerpark Stud **Trained** Wiseton, Notts

FOCUS
A modest maiden, though the time was similar to the later three-year-old handicap.
Royal Adelaide(IRE) Official explanation: jockey said filly ran green throughout
Jeremiah(IRE) Official explanation: jockey said gelding was unsuited by the fibresand

1564 PLAY GOLF BEFORE RACING AT SOUTHWELL CLAIMING STKS 5f (F)
6:10 (6:13) (Class 6) 3-Y-O+ **£2,388** (£705; £352) **Stalls** High

Form RPR
3240 **1** **Guto**[9] [1360] 6-8-13 61........................ KellyHarrison(3) 5 70
(W J H Ratcliffe) *rdn and wl outpcd over 2f out: hdwy over 1f out: styd on wl to ld last strides* **14/1**
5512 **2** *hd* **Spic 'n Span**[32] [965] 4-9-3 65........................(b) NeilPollard 2 70
(R A Harris) *led rdrless to post: led in centre: drifted lft ins fnl f: jst ct* **9/2**[2]
/50- **3** *1 1/4* **Peak District (IRE)**[318] [3012] 5-9-10 93........................ DaleGibson 8 73
(M W Easterby) *dwlt: hrd drvn and wl outpcd 3f out: hdwy over 1f out: styd on wl ins fnl f* **9/1**
0210 **4** *3/4* **Northern Empire (IRE)**[4] [1477] 6-9-5 77........................ NCallan 7 65
(K A Ryan) *sn chsng ldrs: hung rt and wnt 2nd over 1f out: kpt on same pce* **11/2**[3]
2116 **5** *3 3/4* **Handsinthemist (IRE)**[14] [1241] 4-8-11 58........................ JamieMoriarty 3 44
(P T Midgley) *chsd ldrs on outside: rdn and edgd lft over 2f out: one pce* **6/1**
1-00 **6** *1* **Fyodor (IRE)**[12] [1278] 8-9-10 95........................ SebSanders 9 53
(C R Dore) *dwlt: in rr: sn drvn along: nvr on terms* **15/8**[1]
3424 **7** *1 1/4* **Decider (USA)**[36] [919] 6-8-12 60........................(b) KevinGhunowa(3) 11 39
(R A Harris) *chsd ldrs: lost pl over 1f out* **25/1**
653 **8** *1 1/4* **Dodaa (USA)**[19] [1182] 6-9-0 55........................(b) LeeEnstone 6 34
(N Wilson) *trckd ldrs: wknd over 1f out* **22/1**
34-0 **9** *hd* **Our Acquaintance**[7] [1412] 4-9-1 58........................(b) ShaneKelly 4 34
(W R Muir) *sn drvn along: hung lft and lost pl over 2f out* **12/1**
60.05 secs (0.35) **Going Correction** +0.025s/f (Slow)
WFA 3 from 4yo+ 10lb **9 Ran SP% 115.2**
Speed ratings (Par 101): **98,97,95,94,88 86,84,82,82**
toteswinger: 1&2 £14.50, 1&3 £18.90, 2&3 £3.00. CSF £75.71 TOTE £18.60: £4.20, £1.90, £2.90; EX 93.60.Peak District was claimed by Kevin Ryan for £15,000.
Owner W J H Ratcliffe **Bred** H B Hughes **Trained** Newmarket, Suffolk

FOCUS
With those at the top of the weights failing to run to anywhere near their marks, this claimer did not take as much winning as had looked likely.
Fyodor(IRE) Official explanation: trainer had no explanation for the poor form shown

1565 BOOK YOUR HOSPITALITY PACKAGES H'CAP 5f (F)
6:40 (6:40) (Class 4) (0-80,79) 4-Y-O+ **£5,180** (£1,541; £770; £384) **Stalls** High

Form RPR
3543 **1** **Figaro Flyer (IRE)**[24] [1103] 6-8-5 **66**........................ JimmyQuinn 6 77
(P Howling) *dwlt: sn trcking ldrs: effrt 2f out: r.o u.p to ld last 100yds* **6/1**
6210 **2** *1 1/4* **Colorus (IRE)**[11] [1310] 6-8-3 **67**........................(p) KellyHarrison(3) 4 73
(W J H Ratcliffe) *led tl hdd and no ex ins fnl f* **3/1**[2]
4-30 **3** *2 1/4* **Regal Royale**[18] [1197] 6-8-7 **68**........................(v) PatrickMathers 8 66
(Peter Grayson) *hmpd s: sn drvn and swtchd lft: hdwy far side over 2f out: kpt on same pce appr fnl f* **25/1**
60-0 **4** *2 1/4* **Golden Dixie (USA)**[6] [1418] 10-9-1 **76**........................ NeilPollard 5 66
(R A Harris) *chsd ldrs: sn rdn along: outpcd over 2f out: hung rt and kpt on ins fnl f* **16/1**
10-3 **5** *1 3/4* **Kyle (IRE)**[21] [1150] 5-9-3 **78**........................ NCallan 1 62
(C R Dore) *chsd ldrs: effrt over 2f out: wknd over 1f out* **11/4**[1]
13-3 **6** *1 1/4* **Discanti (IRE)**[10] [1334] 4-9-4 **79**........................(t) DNolan 2 58
(T D Easterby) *w ldr: wknd over 1f out* **10/3**[3]
015- **7** *1 3/4* **Dragon Flame (IRE)**[180] [7081] 6-8-7 **68**........................ FrancisNorton 7 41
(M Quinn) *racd alone stands' side: chsd ldrs: lost pl 2f out* **12/1**
4550 **8** *9* **Came Back (IRE)**[38] [901] 6-8-12 **78**........................ AnnStokell(5) 3 18
(Miss A Stokell) *prom: rdn 3f out: sn lost pl and bhd* **10/1**
59.07 secs (-0.63) **Going Correction** +0.025s/f (Slow) **8 Ran SP% 115.5**
Speed ratings (Par 105): **106,104,100,96,94 92,89,74**
toteswinger: 1&2 £3.30, 1&3 £13.50, 2&3 £15.30. CSF £24.65 CT £423.62 TOTE £4.80: £1.80, £1.70, £5.90; EX 22.50.
Owner S J Hammond **Bred** Mohammad Al Qatami **Trained** Newmarket, Suffolk

FOCUS
An ordinary handicap.
Came Back(IRE) Official explanation: jockey said horse did not face the kick-back

1566 SOUTHWELL GOLF CLUB LADY MEMBERS FILLIES' H'CAP 1m (F)
7:10 (7:10) (Class 4) (0-80,80) 4-Y-O+ **£5,180** (£1,541; £770; £384) **Stalls** Low

Form RPR
4064 **1** **Bookiebasher Babe (IRE)**[2] [1530] 4-8-4 **66** oh4........................ FrancisNorton 5 70
(M Quinn) *drvn to sn chse ldrs: effrt on ins over 2f out: kpt on wl to ld last 50yds* **11/2**
000- **2** *1/2* **Folly Lodge**[184] [6981] 5-9-4 **80**........................ SebSanders 6 83
(R M Beckett) *trckd ldrs: t.k.h: effrt over 3f out: led 1f out: hdd and no ex wl ins fnl f* **11/8**[1]
3121 **3** *2 1/2* **Jord (IRE)**[7] [1411] 5-8-10 **72** 6ex........................ NCallan 4 69
(A J McCabe) *led: hdd 1f out: sn wknd* **11/4**[2]
-250 **4** *3 1/4* **If You Knew Suzy**[26] [1060] 4-8-4 **66** oh1........................(t) JimmyQuinn 1 56
(G A Swinbank) *trckd ldrs: drvn over 3f out: outpcd over 2f out* **5/1**[3]

1560 **5** *1* **Amber Moon**[14] [1254] 4-8-1 **66** oh12..........................(b) KellyHarrison(3) 3 53
(Miss A Stokell) *hld up in tch: outpcd and lost pl over 4f out: brought wd and kpt on fnl f* **16/1**

5265 **6** *2* **Friends Hope**[6] [1417] 8-8-8 **75**.............................. GabrielHannon(5) 2 58
(R Curtis) *dwlt: sn chsng ldrs: lost pl over 2f out* **20/1**

1m 43.19s (-0.51) **Going Correction** +0.025s/f (Slow) **6** Ran SP% **111.5**
Speed ratings (Par 102): **103,102,100,96,95 93**
toteswinger: 1&2 £2.20, 1&3 £2.60, 2&3 £1.60. CSF £13.39 TOTE £6.10: £2.70, £1.90; EX 17.90.
Owner J Henry, J Blake & A Newby **Bred** Minch Bloodstock And Castletown Stud **Trained** Newmarket, Suffolk
■ Stewards' Enquiry : N Callan £140 fine: failed to arrive in time

FOCUS
A fair little fillies' handicap.

1567 MEMBERSHIP AT SOUTHWELL GOLF CLUB H'CAP — 6f (F)

7:40 (7:40) (Class 4) (0-80,79) 3-Y-O **£5,180** (£1,541; £770; £384) **Stalls** Low

Form RPR

63-6 **1** **West Leake (IRE)**[9] [1361] 3-8-2 **60**.............................. FrancisNorton 5 68
(B W Hills) *trckd ldrs on outer: pushed along over 4f out: hdwy on wd outside 2f out: styd on wl u.p to ld last 75yds* **6/1**

031 **2** *1 3/4* **Pipers Piping (IRE)**[23] [1129] 3-8-8 **66**.............................. ShaneKelly 6 68
(J A Osborne) *w ldrs: effrt on outer over 2f out: led over 1f out: hdd and no ex ins fnl f* **22/1**

136- **3** *1* **Captain Kallis (IRE)**[136] [7645] 3-8-6 **64**.............. FrankieMcDonald 4 63
(D J S Ffrench Davis) *sn w ldrs: chal over 2f out: styd on same pce appr fnl f* **25/1**

3-12 **4** *1* **Premier Lad**[71] [562] 3-9-1 **73**.............................. PhillipMakin 1 69
(T D Barron) *t.k.h: trckd ldrs: effrt over 2f out: kpt on one pce: nvr able to chal* **6/4**[1]

01-3 **5** *1/2* **Rare Art**[18] [1196] 3-9-3 **75**.............................. SebSanders 3 69
(S A Callaghan) *trckd ldrs: effrt over 2f out: kpt on same pce: nvr a real threat* **10/3**[3]

-111 **6** *nk* **Esprit De Midas**[76] [492] 3-9-7 **79**.............................. NCallan 2 72
(K A Ryan) *led: qcknd 3f out: hdd over 1f out: wknd jst ins fnl f* **5/2**[2]

1m 16.28s (-0.22) **Going Correction** +0.025s/f (Slow) **6** Ran SP% **114.1**
Speed ratings (Par 100): **102,99,98,97,96 95**
toteswinger: 1&2 £5.40, 1&3 £7.40, 2&3 £12.90. CSF £104.32 TOTE £8.20: £3.40, £4.10; EX 35.60.
Owner Henry Barton **Bred** Rathbarry Stud **Trained** Lambourn, Berks

FOCUS
An interesting three-year-old handicap, though the market leaders were rather disappointing.
Esprit De Midas Official explanation: trainer said gelding scoped dirty post-race

1568 SOUTHWELL LADIES DAY 16TH AUGUST H'CAP — 1m 3f (F)

8:10 (8:11) (Class 6) (0-60,60) 4-Y-O+ **£2,320** (£685; £342) **Stalls** Low

Form RPR

10-6 **1** **Three Strings (USA)**[113] [40] 6-8-11 **58**..............(p) FrederikTylicki(5) 14 70
(P D Niven) *mid-div: hdwy over 4f out: led 3f out: edgd rt ins fnl f: hld on towards fin* **9/1**

1231 **2** *hd* **Safebreaker**[7] [1402] 4-8-12 **59**..............................(p) AmyRyan(5) 7 71
(K A Ryan) *dwlt: hdwy on outer 7f out: chsng ldrs over 2f out: hung lft and chal 1f out: no ex nr fin* **3/1**[1]

-045 **3** *4* **Jackie Kiely**[14] [1254] 8-9-4 **60**..............................(t) PhillipMakin 5 64
(R Brotherton) *mid-div: effrt over 4f out: sn chsng ldrs: one pce appr fnl f* **10/1**

-613 **4** *1* **Elliwan**[41] [857] 4-9-2 **58**..............................(b) DaleGibson 4 61
(M W Easterby) *chsd ldrs: kpt on same pce fnl 2f* **7/1**

050- **5** *4* **Monte Pattino (USA)**[258] [4947] 5-8-4 **46** oh1.............(vt) AndrewElliott 13 41
(C J Teague) *hld up in rr: hdwy on wd outside over 6f out: effrt over 2f out: hung lft and wknd over 1f out* **100/1**

4102 **6** *4 1/2* **King Of The Beers (USA)**[6] [1442] 5-8-11 **60**..............(p) SPRyan(7) 2 47
(R A Harris) *chsd ldrs: effrt on inner 3f out: lost pl over 1f out* **6/1**

1034 **7** *1 3/4* **Safin (GER)**[6] [972] 9-9-3 **59**.............................. GrahamGibbons 11 43
(R Curtis) *s.i.s: hdwy over 4f out: sn rdn: lost pl over 2f out* **5/1**[2]

4-5 **8** *1 1/4* **Savaronola (USA)**[113] [40] 4-9-3 **59**.............................. TPQueally 6 41
(B J Curley) *trckd ldrs: led over 2f out: sn hdd: lost pl over 1f out* **11/1**

000- **9** *nk* **Nathan Dee**[43] [2559] 4-8-4 **46**.............................. FrankieMcDonald 8 27
(M R Bosley) *chsd ldrs: drvn 6f out: lost pl over 4f out* **33/1**

-000 **10** *9* **Speagle (IRE)**[61] [682] 7-8-6 **53** ow5..............(t) MarkCoumbe(5) 1 18
(A J Chamberlain) *led tl over 3f out: hung lft and lost pl 2f out* **16/1**

3-20 **11** *3 1/4* **Fortunella**[104] [148] 4-8-12 **54**..............................(p) RobertWinston 9 13
(Miss Gay Kelleway) *sn chsng ldrs: lost pl over 1f out* **11/2**[3]

65-4 **12** *8* **Topflightrebellion**[45] [833] 4-8-4 **46**..............(p) FrancisNorton 12 —
(Mrs G S Rees) *hld up towards rr: drvn and lost pl 5f out: t.o 3f out* **20/1**

641/ **13** *1 3/4* **Norman Beckett**[158] [5862] 6-8-10 **52**.............................. JimmyQuinn 3 —
(R T Phillips) *chsd ldrs: drvn and lost pl over 5f out: t.o 3f out* **25/1**

010/ **14** *10* **Devolution (IRE)**[564] [6124] 11-9-2 **58**.............................. VinceSlattery 10 —
(Miss C Dyson) *in tch: drvn 6f out: lost pl over 4f out: sn bhd: t.o 3f out* **50/1**

2m 26.35s (-1.65) **Going Correction** +0.025s/f (Slow) **14** Ran SP% **131.6**
Speed ratings (Par 101): **107,106,103,103,100 97,95,94,94,88 85,79,78,71**
toteswinger: 1&2 £11.90, 1&3 £20.20, 2&3 £15.00. CSF £38.11 CT £298.09 TOTE £14.20: £4.70, £1.50, £5.00; EX 78.80 Place 6: £1127.31, Place 5: £376.92.
Owner Michael Paley **Bred** Gaucho Ltd **Trained** Barton-le-Street, N Yorks

FOCUS
A fair handicap run at a solid gallop.
T/Plt: £1,864.90 to a £1 stake. Pool: £56,843.43. 22.25 winning tickets. T/Qpdt: £124.60 to a £1 stake. Pool: £4,985.30. 29.60 winning tickets. WG

1403 WINDSOR (R-H)

Monday, April 27

OFFICIAL GOING: Good changing to good to soft after race 1 (5.25)
Wind: Behind, blustery races 1 & 2, light after Weather: Changeable with showers

1569 COLIN-BROWN.CO.UK BET 2 WIN LAY 2 WIN MAIDEN AUCTION FILLIES' STKS — 5f 10y

5:25 (5:26) (Class 5) 2-Y-O **£2,729** (£806; £403) **Stalls** High

Form RPR

5 **1** **Azif**[11] [1298] 2-8-1 0.............................. DavidProbert(3) 2 73
(Miss Gay Kelleway) *racd on outer: chsd ldrs: wnt 2nd over 1f out: drvn to ld narrowly ins fnl f: hld on* **8/1**

2 **2** *shd* **Diamond Laura**[18] [1195] 2-8-5 0 ow1.............................. PaulDoe 13 74
(P D Evans) *fast away: led: drvn over 1f out: hdd ins fnl f: kpt on wl: jst failed* **7/2**[2]

3 *2 3/4* **Existentialist** 2-8-10 0.............................. RichardKingscote 14 69
(J G Portman) *racd against nr side rail: pressed ldrs: disp 2nd over 1f out: one pce fnl f* **28/1**

4 *3/4* **Little Brazilien** 2-8-4 0.............................. MartinDwyer 3 60
(P F I Cole) *pressed ldrs towards outer: cl enough over 1f out: one pce after* **33/1**

5 *1 1/2* **Kings Of Leo** 2-8-8 0.............................. RichardHughes 6 58+
(R Hannon) *mostly chsd ldr to over 1f out: fdd ins fnl f* **3/1**[1]

6 *1* **Ice Cool Lady (IRE)** 2-8-8 0.............................. DarrylHolland 9 54+
(W R Swinburn) *chsd ldrs: rdn 2f out: nt on terms over 1f out: one pce after* **9/2**[3]

7 *1 1/2* **Lady Pattern (IRE)** 2-8-1 0.............................. Louis-PhilippeBeuzelin(5) 8 47+
(P W D'Arcy) *dwlt: pushed along in midfield: nvr on terms w ldrs: one pce fr over 1f out* **8/1**

6 **8** *1 1/2* **Glen Lass**[10] [1323] 2-8-4 0.............................. SimonWhitworth 4 39
(J S Moore) *sn rdn in midfield: nvr on terms w ldrs: one pce fnl 2f* **10/1**

9 *1* **Sixpenny Moon (USA)** 2-8-10 0.............................. RyanMoore 1 41
(R Hannon) *nvr beyond midfield on outer: shkn up and no prog 2f out* **12/1**

10 *nk* **Perfect Ch'I (IRE)** 2-8-4 0.............................. WilliamBuick 11 34
(I A Wood) *nvr beyond midfield: pushed along bef 1/2-way: no ch over 1f out* **66/1**

11 *1 1/2* **Rosedale** 2-8-4 0.............................. KirstyMilczarek 5 28
(J A R Toller) *dwlt: a towards rr: no prog fnl 2f* **66/1**

12 *4 1/2* **Dongola (IRE)** 2-8-6 0.............................. StephenCarson 16 13
(P Winkworth) *s.i.s: outpcd in last quartet: a bhd* **25/1**

13 *5* **Jackie Danny** 2-8-4 0.............................. CatherineGannon 15 —
(C A Dwyer) *outpcd and rn green: a bhd in last quartet* **100/1**

14 *nk* **Six Diamonds** 2-8-4 0.............................. ChrisCatlin 12 —
(H Morrison) *s.s: outpcd in last quartet: a bhd* **14/1**

15 *1* **Restyle** 2-8-10 0.............................. LPKeniry 7 —
(D K Ivory) *outpcd and rn green: a in last quartet and wl bhd* **100/1**

61.14 secs (0.84) **Going Correction** -0.10s/f (Good) **15** Ran SP% **126.3**
Speed ratings (Par 89): **89,88,84,83,80 79,76,74,72,72 69,62,54,54,52**
toteswinger: 1&2 £5.50, 1&3 £51.90, 2&3 £23.20. CSF £36.46 TOTE £11.20: £2.50, £1.80, £9.10; EX 34.40.
Owner J Ballamy,Y Mullin,R Edwards,Aggbag Ltd **Bred** Cheveley Park Stud Ltd **Trained** Exning, Suffolk

FOCUS
Despite rain turning the ground good to soft, the jockeys decided to race up the stands' side, which gave the usual bias to those drawn high and made the winner's performance all the more praiseworthy from stall two.

NOTEBOOK
Azif, showing none of the greenness of her Newmarket debut, was able to get across after a furlong, but she certainly had to do more running than some. Made to fight all the way to the line, she will be better suited by another furlong - her sire was suited by 1m-plus. In the shorter term she is likely to go for the Lily Agnes Stakes at Chester en route to the Queen Mary. (op 7-1 tchd 13-2 and 9-1)
Diamond Laura is all speed as she had shown when second on her debut in a decent race at Folkestone. Always on the pace, she only gave best near the finish and it may have been that the 1lb overweight cost her. (op 4-1 tchd 10-3)
Existentialist, who comes from a fast family, was best of the debutantes from a good draw. She looks capable of winning a similar race soon. (tchd 25-1 and 33-1)
Little Brazilien comes out of this debut with plenty of credit from a far-side draw. Like the winner, she managed to be on the pace after a furlong. She began to fade inside the last but was nursed home. (tchd 25-1 and 40-1)
Kings Of Leo, a January foal, comes from a yard that always does well with its juveniles here, although they usually come on considerably for their debuts, so she will be interesting next time. Another to show pace, she dropped away near the finish. (op 11-4 tchd 4-1)
Ice Cool Lady(IRE) was never quite going the pace of the leading bunch and, after being given a couple of taps, she stayed on well in her own time. She will be much better for this over another furlong. (tchd 11-2)
Lady Pattern(IRE), nibbled at in the market, was never going the pace but kept on and is bred to want at least another furlong. Official explanation: jockey said filly stumbled and he lost an iron (op 12-1)
Dongola(IRE) Official explanation: vet said filly finished lame

1570 TRAINERMAGAZINE.COM H'CAP — 1m 3f 135y

5:55 (5:57) (Class 5) (0-70,69) 3-Y-O **£2,729** (£806; £403) **Stalls** Centre

Form RPR

2416 **1** **Good Buy Dubai (USA)**[12] [1282] 3-8-6 **57**.............................. ChrisCatlin 9 62+
(J R Best) *pushed along and detached in last trio: sustained prog u.p fr 4f out to ld 2f out: drvn out* **9/1**

00-1 **2** *1 1/4* **Ermyn Lodge**[33] [953] 3-8-11 **62**.............................. IanMongan 11 63
(P M Phelan) *rdn and prog to go 2nd after 4f: drvn to ld over 3f out: hdd 2f out: kpt on u.p* **10/1**

4-64 **3** *1/2* **Cayman Sky**[6] [1416] 3-9-4 **69**..............................(b) RichardHughes 5 69
(R Hannon) *hld up towards rr: prog fr 4f out to chse ldrs over 2f out: sn rdn and nt qckn: kpt on* **7/1**

2220 **4** *nse* **Solo Choice**[28] [1034] 3-9-3 **68**.............................. JamesDoyle 4 68
(D Flood) *hld up in midfield: gng bttr than most 4f out: prog over 3f out: rdn and nt qckn 2f out: kpt on same pce after* **20/1**

050- **5** *4 1/2* **Rebel Swing**[158] [7397] 3-8-10 **61**.............................. MartinDwyer 3 53
(W R Muir) *sn lost prom early pl: prog 4f out: chsd ldrs over 2f out: wknd over 1f out* **7/2**[2]

0-00 **6** *3 1/4* **Red Margarita (IRE)**[14] [1257] 3-7-13 **55**.............................. AmyBaker(5) 8 42
(D R C Elsworth) *hld up in last and detached: effrt over 3f out and hanging lft: kpt on past btn rivals fr over 2f out: nvr rchd ldrs* **16/1**

060- **7** *10* **Diktalina**[182] [7023] 3-8-13 **64**.............................. DO'Donohoe 2 34
(W R Muir) *sn in last and trio and off the pce: rdn 1/2-way: nvr on terms* **40/1**

3056 **8** *7* **First Spirit**[7] [1408] 3-8-11 **62**.............................. LPKeniry 6 20
(J S Moore) *trckd ldrs: rdn 4f out: sn wknd* **20/1**

640- **9** *nk* **When Doves Cry**[158] [7397] 3-8-13 **64**.............................. MichaelHills 1 21
(B W Hills) *led at decent pce: hdd & wknd rapidly over 3f out* **5/1**[3]

050- **10** *7* **Halfway House**[181] [7051] 3-8-11 **62**.............................. JamieSpencer 10 7
(M L W Bell) *free to post: prom: rdn and wknd over 3f out: eased whn no ch* **3/1**[1]

04-5 **11** *13* **Count On Guest**[14] [1260] 3-9-2 **67**.............................. DaneO'Neill 7 —
(G G Margarson) *chsd ldr 4f: struggling 5f out: sn wknd: t.o* **16/1**

2m 33.29s (3.79) **Going Correction** +0.30s/f (Good) **11** Ran SP% **119.2**
Speed ratings (Par 98): **99,98,97,97,94 92,85,81,81,76 67**
toteswinger: 1&2 £15.30, 1&3 £10.90, 2&3 £10.20. CSF £94.32 CT £675.07 TOTE £10.40: £2.30, £3.40, £1.80; EX 77.60.

Owner John Keaty **Bred** Harold J Plumley **Trained** Hucking, Kent

FOCUS

A real puzzle, as six of these were stepping up in trip for their handicap debuts, while the changed going made this a real slog, with runners going to the far side.

Halfway House Official explanation: trainer said, regarding running, that the gelding was unsuited by the good to soft ground

1571 MAIDENHEAD ADVERTISER MISS BERKSHIRE 11TH MAY H'CAP 1m 3f 135y

6:25 (6:27) (Class 4) (0-80,80) 4-Y-0+ **£4,857** (£1,445; £722; £360) **Stalls** Centre

Form RPR

640- **1** **Run For Ede's**[146] 7526 5-8-5 **66** oh1 CatherineGannon 11 73
(P M Phelan) *t.k.h: hld up in last pair: prog on outer 3f out: rdn to ld over 1f out: jst hld on* **40/1**

21-3 **2** *nk* **Red Merlin (IRE)**[10] 1319 4-9-1 **77** (v) PhilipRobinson 9 86+
(C G Cox) *hld up in last: stl there and keen 3f out: taken to outer and prog over 2f out: wnt 2nd ins fnl f: clsng fast at fin: given too much to do* **7/4**[1]

225- **3** *1* **Plaisterer**[179] 7091 4-8-9 **71** AlanMunro 5 76
(C F Wall) *midfield early: shuffled bk on inner bnd 6f out and in last pair 4f out: prog 3f out: wnt 2nd over 1f out and tried to chal: kpt on same pce* **7/1**[3]

630- **4** *3/4* **Cyborg**[282] 4200 5-9-2 **77** MartinDwyer 8 81
(D R C Elsworth) *led at decent pce: hung lft bnd 6f out: rdn over 3f out: hdd over 2f out: kpt on wl u.p fr over 1f out* **16/1**

4125 **5** *1 3/4* **William's Way**[29] 1014 7-8-7 **68** WilliamBuick 2 69
(I A Wood) *hld up: prog to midfield 1/2-way: hdwy over 3f out to ld over 2f out: hrd rdn and hdd over 1f out: fdd* **12/1**

350- **6** *6* **Hawridge King**[187] 6898 7-9-0 **78** JamesMillman(3) 6 68
(W S Kittow) *hld up in last trio: prog into midfield over 3f out: reminder 2f out: nudged along and steadily outpcd after* **14/1**

0010 **7** *3 3/4* **Sgt Schultz (IRE)**[23] 1117 6-9-5 **80** RichardHughes 10 64
(J S Moore) *hld up: prog and wnt 4th briefly over 3f out: wknd 2f out* **9/1**

-246 **8** *2 3/4* **Hammer**[63] 660 4-7-13 **66** oh3 Louis-PhilippeBeuzelin(5) 3 45
(R T Phillips) *restless stalls: trckd clr ldrs: cl up over 3f out: nt look keen u.p and btn over 2f out* **16/1**

500- **9** *1/2* **Trachonitis (IRE)**[14] 6079 5-9-2 **77** DarryllHolland 4 55
(J R Jenkins) *chsd clr ldng trio early: lost pl on bnd 6f out: struggling in rr over 3f out: no prog* **33/1**

143- **10** *4 1/2* **Relative Strength (IRE)**[303] 3471 4-9-1 **77** LPKeniry 1 48
(A M Balding) *clr in ldng trio: chsd ldr 8f out to 3f out: wknd u.p* **3/1**[2]

0-00 **11** *25* **Dr Brass**[45] 559 4-8-8 **70** (p) EddieAhern 7 —
(B N Pollock) *chsd ldr to 8f out: wknd u.p wl over 3f out: t.o* **33/1**

2m 31.46s (1.96) **Going Correction** +0.30s/f (Good) **11** Ran SP% **118.3**

WFA 4 from 5yo+ 1lb

Speed ratings (Par 105): **105,104,104,103,102 98,95,94,93,90 74**

toteswinger: 1&2 £21.40, 1&3 £54.30, 2&3 £6.90. CSF £109.81 CT £592.49 TOTE £75.60: £11.10, £1.50, £2.90; EX 232.10.

Owner Ede's (uk) Ltd **Bred** Mrs James Wigan & London TB Services Ltd **Trained** Epsom, Surrey

FOCUS

This race was run in a time nearly two seconds faster than the previous race over course and distance by the three-year-olds.

1572 EXACTSOFTWARE.COM H'CAP 6f

6:55 (6:56) (Class 4) (0-80,80) 4-Y-0+ **£4,857** (£1,445; £722; £360) **Stalls** High

Form RPR

022- **1** **Westwood**[139] 7615 4-8-5 **67** MartinDwyer 14 77
(D Haydn Jones) *taken down early: racd centre w eventual 3rd: mde all: drifted to join main gp fnl f: hld on wl* **10/1**

240- **2** *3/4* **Superduper**[208] 6402 4-9-4 **80** RichardHughes 5 88
(R Hannon) *led main gp: pressed wnr fnl f: jst hld last 75yds* **7/1**[2]

4032 **3** *1 1/2* **Onceaponatime (IRE)**[5] 1468 4-8-5 **67** AlanMunro 15 70
(M D Squance) *chsd wnr in centre: nvr able to chal but kpt on fnl f* **5/1**[1]

131- **4** *1 1/2* **Doric Lady**[181] 7055 4-8-11 **73** KirstyMilczarek 10 75+
(J A R Toller) *trckd main gp ldrs: effrt to chal over 1f out: stl cl up whn squeezed for room 100yds out* **8/1**

030- **5** *1/2* **Carleton**[170] 7239 4-9-4 **80** ChrisCatlin 11 77
(W J Musson) *hld up in rr of main gp: prog over 2f out to chse ldrs over 1f out: no imp tl kpt on last 100yds* **12/1**

-550 **6** *3/4* **Memphis Man**[21] 1150 6-8-9 **76** RichardEvans(5) 7 70+
(P D Evans) *taken down early: stdd s: hld up in main gp: last 2f out: nt clr run briefly over 1f out: nudged along and styd on fnl f: nvr nr ldrs* **9/1**

210- **7** *nk* **Orange Pip**[273] 4483 4-9-4 **80** RyanMoore 6 73
(R Hannon) *chsd main gp ldr: rdn to chal over 1f out: hld whn short of room ins fnl f: wknd last 100yds* **8/1**

03-2 **8** *1 1/4* **Buxton**[18] 1197 5-9-4 **80** (t) RobertHavlin 2 69
(R Ingram) *chsd ldrs: rdn over 2f out: steadily fdd fr wl over 1f out* **15/2**[3]

56-0 **9** *3/4* **Zowington**[21] 1150 7-9-0 **76** SaleemGolam 3 63
(S C Williams) *chsd main gp ldrs: rdn over 2f out: wknd over 1f out* **16/1**

01-0 **10** *1* **Bold Argument (IRE)**[10] 1320 6-8-4 **69** ow2 JackMitchell(3) 1 53
(Mrs P N Dutfield) *chsd main gp ldrs: rdn over 2f out: wknd over 1f out* **14/1**

4026 **11** *2* **Resplendent Alpha**[18] 1197 5-8-13 **75** TonyCulhane 13 52
(P Howling) *stdd s: hld up in last trio: shkn up and no prog over 2f out* **11/1**

05-0 **12** *1* **Lodi (IRE)**[23] 1116 4-9-4 **80** (t) IanMongan 9 54
(J Akehurst) *a in rr: taken to centre 1/2-way: no prog 2f out* **9/1**

1m 13.52s (0.52) **Going Correction** +0.225s/f (Good) **12** Ran SP% **120.8**

Speed ratings (Par 105): **105,104,102,100,99 98,97,96,95,93 91,89**

toteswinger: 1&2 £23.80, 1&3 £6.90, 2&3 £18.70. CSF £79.93 CT £405.82 TOTE £12.30: £3.00, £3.00, £3.00; EX 123.70.

Owner Merry Llewelyn And Runeckles **Bred** D Llewelyn & J Runeckles **Trained** Efail Isaf, Rhondda C Taff

■ Stewards' Enquiry : Martin Dwyer four-day ban: careless riding (May 11-14)

FOCUS

A wide-open sprint handicap.

Memphis Man Official explanation: jockey said gelding was denied a clear run

Buxton Official explanation: jockey said gelding was denied a clear run

1573 HEART BERKSHIRE AND HAMPSHIRE MAIDEN STKS 1m 2f 7y

7:25 (7:28) (Class 5) 3-Y-0 **£2,729** (£806; £403) **Stalls** Centre

Form RPR

1 **Namibian Orator (IRE)** 3-9-3 0 RyanMoore 13 86+
(Sir Michael Stoute) *settled in rr: pushed along and prog over 3f out: chsd ldr over 1f out: drvn to ld ins fnl f: hld on wl* **9/2**[2]

66 **2** *nk* **Outrageous Request**[7] 1407 3-9-3 0 PaulEddery 2 85
(Pat Eddery) *trckd ldrs: effrt 3f out: clsd over 1f out: drvn to chal ins fnl f: jst hld* **14/1**

00-2 **3** *3/4* **Putra One (IRE)**[14] 1257 3-9-3 83 PhilipRobinson 8 83
(M A Jarvis) *led at stdy pce for 3f: led again 4f out: shkn up over 1f out: hdd and nt qckn ins fnl f* **1/1**[1]

0-3 **4** *7* **Bruton Street (USA)**[21] 1151 3-9-3 0 JimmyFortune 6 69
(J H M Gosden) *led after 3f and maintained stdy pce: hdd 4f out: stl pressing 2f out: sn outpcd* **9/1**[3]

202- **5** *1* **Threestepstoheaven**[205] 6480 3-9-3 73 MichaelHills 10 67
(B W Hills) *prom: pressing ldrs over 2f out: steadily fdd sn after* **9/2**[2]

54 **6** *1/2* **Atacama Sunrise**[14] 1260 3-8-5 0 SimonPearce(7) 15 61
(J Pearce) *hld up in midfield: prog to press ldrs in centre over 2f out: wknd over 1f out* **50/1**

0- **7** *nse* **Beauchamp Xenia**[177] 7141 3-8-12 0 DaneO'Neill 3 61
(H Candy) *nvr beyond midfield: shkn up and nt on terms w ldrs over 2f out: no prog* **20/1**

8 *1 1/2* **Lady Artemisia (IRE)** 3-8-12 0 EddieAhern 11 58
(M L W Bell) *in tch in midfield tl wknd over 2f out* **33/1**

0 **9** *4 1/2* **Stormy Morning**[7] 1407 3-9-3 0 AdamKirby 7 54
(W R Swinburn) *hld up in last trio: sme prog over 3f out: pushed along and wknd over 2f out* **66/1**

\- **10** *1* **Lady Oaksey** 3-8-12 0 FergusSweeney 14 47
(W S Kittow) *settled in last trio: pushed along and no real prog over 3f out* **100/1**

5-0 **11** *1 3/4* **Pachakutek (USA)**[9] 1350 3-9-3 0 DarryllHolland 5 48
(E F Vaughan) *prom: pushed along 4f out: steadily wknd fr over 2f out* **33/1**

12 *6* **My Bodyguard (FR)** 3-9-3 0 (t) JamesDoyle 4 36
(H J L Dunlop) *in tch: hanging and rdn bnd over 5f out: struggling in rr 3f out* **100/1**

00- **13** *28* **Jasper Cliff**[256] 5022 3-8-12 0 JackDean(5) 12 —
(Mark Gillard) *in tch tl wknd rapidly over 2f out: t.o* **100/1**

4600 **14** *14* **Floods Of Tears**[12] 1281 3-8-12 48 MartinDwyer 1 —
(D Flood) *a last: t.o over 3f out* **100/1**

2m 12.11s (3.41) **Going Correction** +0.30s/f (Good) **14** Ran SP% **121.1**

Speed ratings (Par 98): **98,97,97,91,90 90,90,89,85,84 83,78,56,44**

toteswinger: 1&2 £15.50, 1&3 £2.70, 2&3 £4.80. CSF £61.12 TOTE £5.80: £1.90, £2.60, £1.40; EX 91.60.

Owner Ballymacoll Stud **Bred** Ballymacoll Stud Farm Ltd **Trained** Newmarket, Suffolk

■ Stewards' Enquiry : Paul Eddery one-day ban: used whip with excessive frequency (May 11)

FOCUS

A muddling pace and five of the 14 starters were eligible for a mark after this outing, but it went to a newcomer who looks sure to go on to better things.

1574 D & B FINANCE TEAM H'CAP 1m 67y

7:55 (7:55) (Class 5) (0-75,74) 3-Y-0 **£3,070** (£906; £453) **Stalls** High

Form RPR

65-5 **1** **Advisor (FR)**[14] 1257 3-9-4 **74** JamieSpencer 3 80+
(M L W Bell) *hld up in 8th: prog over 2f out: hrd rdn over 1f out: led ins fnl f: drvn rt out* **4/1**[2]

02-2 **2** *1* **Barbarian**[45] 829 3-9-0 **70** MichaelHills 2 73
(B W Hills) *trckd ldrs: cl enough over 2f out: nt qckn over 1f out: kpt on fnl f to take 2nd last stride* **11/4**[1]

0-53 **3** *shd* **Everaard (USA)**[14] 1253 3-7-13 **60** AmyBaker(5) 6 63
(D R C Elsworth) *pressed ldr: led over 3f out: rdn and pressed 2f out: hdd ins fnl f: lost 2nd last stride* **15/2**

6-21 **4** *1 3/4* **Best In Class**[67] 599 3-9-2 **72** RichardKingscote 11 71
(Tom Dascombe) *prom: pressed ldr over 2f out: nt qckn over 1f out: one pce after* **7/1**

0-13 **5** *1 1/2* **Baby Josr**[31] 986 3-8-6 **62** (t) WilliamBuick 4 58
(I A Wood) *hld up in 7th: awkward bnd over 5f out: rdn and struggling 3f out: plugged on fnl f* **14/1**

045- **6** *shd* **Mitra Jaan (IRE)**[203] 6539 3-9-2 **72** (t) AdamKirby 14 67
(W R Swinburn) *dwlt: sn midfield: cl up over 2f out: outpcd over 1f out: plugged on* **6/1**

03-3 **7** *1* **Duar Mapel (USA)**[35] 939 3-9-2 **72** (b) PaulEddery 8 65
(Paul Mason) *pushed up to ld: hdd over 3f out: fdd fnl 2f* **33/1**

200- **8** *9* **Louidor**[242] 5430 3-9-0 **70** FergusSweeney 1 42
(M R Bosley) *hld up in 9th: pushed along and nt on terms over 3f out: sn bhd* **33/1**

335- **9** *4 1/2* **Admiral Sandhoe (USA)**[187] 6892 3-9-4 **74** JimCrowley 7 36
(Mrs A J Perrett) *t.k.h early: hld up bhd ldrs: wknd 2f out* **5/1**[3]

\- **10** *1 3/4* **Zepnove (IRE)**[199] 6638 3-8-11 **67** ChrisCatlin 12 25
(M Wigham) *s.i.s: hld up in detached last: rdn and btn 1/2-way* **33/1**

1m 47.1s (2.40) **Going Correction** +0.30s/f (Good) **10** Ran SP% **117.4**

Speed ratings (Par 98): **100,99,98,97,95 95,94,85,81,79**

toteswinger: 1&2 £1.80, 1&3 £12.70, 2&3 £6.10. CSF £15.29 CT £76.35 TOTE £4.40: £2.10, £1.60, £2.60; EX 11.60 Place 6: £114.48, Place 5: £27.70 ..

Owner The Royal Ascot Racing Club **Bred** Kilboy Estate **Trained** Newmarket, Suffolk

FOCUS

With five of the ten runners making their handicap debuts, this was a hard race to evaluate beforehand but the form looks pretty solid..

Advisor(FR) Official explanation: trainer said, regarding apparent improvement in form, that the colt had strengthened up over the winter, and ran well last start.

Baby Josr Official explanation: jockey said gelding hung left-handed

T/Jkpt: Not won. T/Plt: £27.80 to a £1 stake. Pool: £76,375.67. 2,001.72 winning tickets. T/Qpdt: £5.00 to a £1 stake. Pool: £6,753.10. 998.50 winning tickets. JN

SAN SIRO (R-H)

Sunday, April 26

OFFICIAL GOING: Heavy

1575a PREMIO AMBROSIANO (GROUP 3) 1m 2f

4:15 (4:47) 4-Y-0+ **£38,835** (£17,087; £9,320; £4,661)

RPR

1 **Selmis**[168] 7263 5-8-12 MDemuro 5 113
(V Caruso, Italy) *a cl up: 3rd st: led 1 1/2f out: wnt clr fnl f: pushed out: easily* **12/5**[2]

2 *6* **Papetti (ITY)**[14] 4-8-12 DVargiu 3 101
(B Grizzetti, Italy) *racd in 5th to st: styd on one pce to take 2nd in fnl f: no ch w wnr* **13/5**[3]

3 *1 3/4* **Duellant (IRE)**[21] 1143 4-8-12 GBietolini 6 98
(P Schiergen, Germany) *pressed ldr: 2nd st: c out into middle: rdn and ev ch 2f out: sn one pce* **17/1**

4 1 **Pedra Pompas**[28] 5-9-0 .... NMurru 4 98
(M Gasparini, Italy) *led: remained alone on far rail in st: hdd 1 1/2f out: one pce* **67/10**
5 7 **Zaungast (IRE)**[21] 1143 5-9-2 .... ASuborics 8 86
(W Hickst, Germany) *hld up: 6th st: no real prog: btn 2f out* **13/10**[1]
6 4 ½ **Il Divo (GER)**[205] 6461 4-8-12 .... EPedroza 1 73
(A Wohler, Germany) *disp 3rd: 4th st: wknd 2f out* **105/10**
7 1 ½ **Dovizioso (IRE)**[1071] 1870 7-8-12 .... MTellini 2 70
(P Caravati, Italy) *s.i.s and last thrght* **56/1**

2m 12.5s (5.80) **7 Ran SP% 129.7**
(Including 1 Euro stake): WIN 3.40; PL 1.82, 1.67; DF 5.55.
Owner Scuderia Incolinx **Bred** Scuderia Vittadini Srl **Trained** Italy

1576 - (Foreign Racing) - See Raceform Interactive

1415 BATH (L-H)

Tuesday, April 28

OFFICIAL GOING: Good (good to firm in places; 9.3)
Wind: Virtually nill Weather: Bright

1577 FREEBETS.CO.UK CHAMPIONS LEAGUE FREE BETS MAIDEN AUCTION STKS 5f 11y

2:10 (2:13) (Class 6) 2-Y-O **£2,266** (£674; £337; £168) **Stalls** Centre

Form RPR
1 **Raine's Cross** 2-8-9 0 .... JimCrowley 8 91+
(P Winkworth) *hld up in tch: qcknd to ld appr fnl f: sn clr: easily* **9/2**[2]
3 2 4 ½ **Avonvalley**[25] 1090 2-8-4 0 .... FrancisNorton 7 69
(M S Saunders) *pressed ldrs: led 3f out: rdn and hdd appr fnl f: sn no ch w wnr but kpt on wl for 2nd* **4/1**[1]
3 ½ **Toga Tiger (IRE)** 2-8-9 0 .... DarryllHolland 16 72
(M R Channon) *chsd ldrs: pushed along half way: kpt on fnl f to press for 2nd nr fin but no ch w wnr* **6/1**[3]
0 4 1 **Stargaze (IRE)**[11] 1323 2-8-9 0 .... MartinDwyer 14 68
(A M Balding) *chsd ldrs: rdn fr 1/2-way: styd on same pce fnl f* **7/1**
5 nk **Slice (IRE)** 2-8-9 0 .... JimmyQuinn 4 67+
(Eve Johnson Houghton) *in tch whn stmbld after 1f: rdn 1/2-way: kpt on fnl f but nvr gng pce to trble ldrs* **40/1**
6 1 ¼ **Pinnacle Lad (IRE)** 2-8-9 0 .... TolleyDean 11 62
(J L Spearing) *led to post: in tch: swtchd rt to outside and hdwy to chse ldrs ins fnl 2f: wknd ins fnl f* **16/1**
7 2 ¼ **Avon River** 2-8-11 0 .... RyanMoore 3 56+
(R Hannon) *outpcd tl swtchd to outside and hdwy over 1f out: fin wl* **8/1**
8 ¾ **Queen's Hawk** 2-8-11 0 .... TPO'Shea 6 53
(D J Coakley) *towards rr: pushed along 1/2-way: styd on fr over 1f out but nvr in contention* **66/1**
9 ¾ **Timelord (IRE)** 2-8-9 0 .... EddieAhern 10 48
(S Kirk) *in rr: pushed along 1/2-way: kpt on fnl f but nvr in contention* **11/1**
10 2 ¾ **Miss Gibbs** 2-8-5 0 ow1 .... PaulDoe 1 34
(P D Evans) *slt ld 2f: styd presing ldrs to 2f out: wknd fnl f* **20/1**
11 nse **Quaker Parrot** 2-8-6 0 .... RichardKingscote 9 35
(Tom Dascombe) *s.i.s: outpcd tl mod late prog* **12/1**
6 12 1 ¼ **French Connexion (IRE)**[29] 1031 2-8-4 0 .... ChrisCatlin 5 28
(J S Moore) *pressed ldrs 3f: sn wknd* **25/1**
13 1 ½ **Dream Of Gerontius (IRE)** 2-8-7 0 ow1 .... RichardHughes 2 25
(R Hannon) *a outpcd* **16/1**
14 nk **Tucker's Law** 2-8-9 0 .... TGMcLaughlin 15 26
(B R Millman) *a outpcd* **33/1**
15 13 **Whip Up (IRE)** 2-8-9 0 .... SteveDrowne 13 —
(J G Portman) *s.i.s: a outpcd* **40/1**

62.31 secs (-0.19) **Going Correction** +0.025s/f (Good) **15 Ran SP% 121.8**
Speed ratings (Par 90): **102,94,94,92,91 89,86,85,83,79 79,77,75,74,53**
toteswinger: 1&2 £6.10, 1&3 £6.50, 2&3 £5.80 CSF £21.29 TOTE £5.70: £2.10, £1.60, £2.80; EX 29.50 TRIFECTA Not won..
Owner David Holden **Bred** Richard C J Manning **Trained** Chiddingfold, Surrey

FOCUS
A big field for what was probably a pretty ordinary juvenile maiden, but the extremely well-backed Raine's Cross was an impressive winner and looked a class apart.

NOTEBOOK
Raine's Cross ◆, a £12,500 half-brother to smart sprinter Falcon Hill, out of a mare who was Group 3-placed in France at two, ran green early and was having to be niggled along pretty much from the off to keep tabs on the leaders. Slightly short of room at about halfway, he gradually got the idea and loomed up towards the outside going ominously well with about two furlongs to run, before bounding away when asked. The bare form looks limited, but he won this in the style of a useful colt and will apparently now go straight to Royal Ascot for the Coventry Stakes. (op 14-1)
Avonvalley had caught the eye running on strongly after a very slow start over this course and distance on her debut, and she showed the benefit of that experience with an improved performance. Much wiser this time, she showed loads of speed throughout, but simply ran into an above-average type. (tchd 9-2)
Toga Tiger(IRE), a 13,000gns purchase out of a useful 6f performer in Germany, knew his job better than some of these, but he still showed signs of inexperience and should improve enough to win an ordinary race. (op 4-1)
Stargaze(IRE) improved on the form he showed when failing to beat a rival on his debut at Newbury, but he still looked inexperienced and can do better again, especially when stepped up in trip. (op 10-1)
Slice(IRE) received an early reminder and can do better. (tchd 33-1)
Pinnacle Lad(IRE) showed ability to move into a challenging position from off the pace, before tiring. (op 25-1 tchd 33-1)
Avon River was outpaced and green for much of the way, but he made some late headway. (op 15-2 tchd 9-1)
Queen's Hawk was another to run green and never threatened, but he hinted at ability. (op 100-1)

1578 LINDLEY CATERING (S) STKS 1m 2f 46y

2:45 (2:46) (Class 6) 3-Y-O+ **£1,942** (£578; £288; £144) **Stalls** Low

Form RPR
4-40 1 **Aypeeyes (IRE)**[59] 549 5-9-9 77 .... (v) EddieAhern 13 57
(A King) *chsd ldrs: rdn and styd on fr over 1f out to chse ldr ins fnl f: kpt on u.p to ld last strides* **11/4**[1]
2312 2 hd **Gasat (IRE)**[11] 1318 8-10-0 67 .... SebSanders 7 62
(A B Haynes) *chsd ldrs: led ins fnl 4f: hrd rdn to keep advantage fr 2f out: ct last strides* **4/1**[2]
244- 3 2 **Torrens (IRE)**[121] 7806 7-9-4 56 .... (t) RichardEvans(5) 5 53
(P D Evans) *in tch: hdwy on outside to chse ldrs fr 3f out: rdn over 2f out: styd on to go 3rd ins fnl f but no imp on ldng duo* **6/1**[3]
-306 4 ¾ **Corriolanus (GER)**[76] 497 9-9-6 64 .... (p) DavidProbert(3) 10 51
(A M Balding) *in rr: hdwy towards outside 3f out: rdn and hung lft over 1f out: kpt on ins fnl f but nvr gng pce to trble ldrs* **6/1**[3]
5206 5 1 **Hatch A Plan (IRE)**[8] 1409 8-9-9 49 .... JimCrowley 4 49
(Mouse Hamilton-Fairley) *sn wl there: rdn 3f out: styd on fnl f but nvr any danger* **33/1**
0206 6 ½ **Red Current**[7] 1417 5-9-1 55 .... KevinGhunowa(3) 12 43
(R A Harris) *sn chsng ldrs: wnt 2nd over 2f out: ev ch u.p over 1f out: wknd ins fnl f* **16/1**
-132 7 ¾ **Mystic Art (IRE)**[41] 872 4-10-0 55 .... SteveDrowne 1 52
(C R Egerton) *chsd ldrs: rdn fr over 3f out: styd wl there u.p tl wknd fnl f* **17/2**
0400 8 nk **Dynamo Dave (USA)**[24] 647 4-9-2 40 .... LeeNewnes(7) 6 46
(M D I Usher) *in rr tl kpt on fr 2f out: styd on ins fnl f but nvr a threat* **100/1**
6-05 9 1 ¼ **Calling Birds (IRE)**[35] 943 3-8-1 52 .... (v[1]) JimmyQuinn 9 39
(Karen George) *s.i.s: rr: drvn along over 5f out: mod prog fr over 1f out* **50/1**
-504 10 3 **Magnitude**[34] 958 4-9-9 77 .... (b[1]) RyanMoore 11 38
(G L Moore) *t.k.h: sn in tch: rdn to chse ldrs over 2f out: sn btn* **7/1**
-050 11 10 **Cool Madam**[49] 796 3-8-1 31 .... (p) NickyMackay 3 13
(D Flood) *led after 2f: hdd ins fnl 4f: wknd fr 3f out* **100/1**
000- 12 1 ¼ **Dancelectic (IRE)**[164] 7343 3-8-6 40 .... (t) ChrisCatlin 15 15
(D R Lanigan) *a in rr* **50/1**
40- 13 5 **Almowj**[357] 1895 6-9-9 40 .... VinceSlattery 8 5
(G H Jones) *a in rr* **150/1**

2m 11.96s (0.96) **Going Correction** +0.025s/f (Good)
WFA 3 from 4yo+ 17lb **13 Ran SP% 113.7**
Speed ratings (Par 101): **97,96,95,94,93 93,92,92,91,89 81,80,76**
toteswinger: 1&2 £3.20, 1&3 £5.60, 2&3 £5.10 CSF £12.33 TOTE £3.80: £1.60, £1.40, £2.00; EX 14.30 Trifecta £189.20 Pool: £265.98 - 1.04 winning units..The winner was sold to J. Price for 8,500gns. Magnitude was claimed by M. E. Rimmer for £6,000.
Owner D A Wallace **Bred** John Malone **Trained** Barbury Castle, Wilts
■ Stewards' Enquiry : Eddie Ahern four-day ban: used whip in the incorrect place (May 12-15)

FOCUS
An ordinary but competitive seller.
Calling Birds(IRE) Official explanation: jockey said the filly was slow into her stride
Magnitude Official explanation: jockey said gelding pulled hard.
Cool Madam Official explanation: jockey said the filly moved poorly throughout

1579 WEATHERBYS FINANCE MEDIAN AUCTION MAIDEN STKS 1m 2f 46y

3:20 (3:25) (Class 5) 3-Y-O **£2,590** (£770; £385; £192) **Stalls** Low

Form RPR
3- 1 **Rosika**[167] 7289 3-8-12 0 .... RyanMoore 8 72
(Sir Michael Stoute) *trckd ldr 7f out: pushed along to ld appr fnl 2f: hrd rdn and hld on wl whn strly chal ins fnl f* **2/1**[2]
360- 2 hd **Dreamwalk (IRE)**[221] 6085 3-9-3 78 .... SebSanders 10 77
(R M Beckett) *held up in tch: hdwy towards outside fr 3f out: chsd wnr 1f out: str chal wl ins fnl f: nt quite get up* **15/2**
364- 3 1 ¾ **Coiled Spring**[193] 6777 3-9-3 87 .... JimCrowley 9 74
(Mrs A J Perrett) *in tch: chsd ldrs 3f out: rdn and ev ch over 1f out: fading whn n.m.r wl ins fnl f* **7/4**[1]
00- 4 3 ½ **Sir Freddie**[164] 7336 3-9-3 0 .... IanMongan 6 67
(Lady Herries) *t.k.h: chsd ldrs tl readily outpcd fnl 2f* **33/1**
0-3 5 2 ½ **Fondant Fancy**[25] 1092 3-8-12 0 .... EddieAhern 7 57
(H J L Dunlop) *led tl hdd appr fnl 2f: wknd qckly fnl f* **6/1**[3]
0- 6 3 ½ **Vella**[170] 7259 3-8-12 0 .... JimmyQuinn 3 50
(H J L Dunlop) *chsd ldrs tl wknd 2f out* **33/1**
0- 7 ½ **Iron Man Of Mersey (FR)**[179] 7106 3-9-3 0 .... TolleyDean 13 54
(A W Carroll) *in rr: mod prog fnl 2f* **100/1**
6 8 3 ¼ **Emeralda**[10] 1362 3-8-12 0 .... PaulEddery 2 42
(Pat Eddery) *a towards rr* **28/1**
0- 9 ½ **Gaelic Rose (IRE)**[143] 7578 3-8-12 0 .... MartinDwyer 5 41
(S Kirk) *mid-div: in tch 3f out: wknd fr 2f out* **33/1**
00 10 3 **Behind Blue Eyes**[7] 1423 3-9-3 0 .... (v[1]) TGMcLaughlin 11 40
(Karen George) *a towards rr* **200/1**
00- 11 13 **Oke Bay**[173] 7204 3-8-12 0 .... DO'Donohoe 12 9
(R M Beckett) *slowly away and rdn in rr: a wl bhd* **80/1**

2m 12.07s (1.07) **Going Correction** +0.025s/f (Good) **11 Ran SP% 110.7**
Speed ratings (Par 98): **96,95,94,91,89 86,86,83,83,81 70**
toteswinger: 1&2 £4.00, 1&3 £1.10, 2&3 £2.60 CSF £14.64 TOTE £2.90: £1.20, £1.90, £1.10; EX 19.40 Trifecta £25.20 Pool: £462.30 - 13.57 winning units..
Owner Sir Evelyn De Rothschild **Bred** Southcourt Stud **Trained** Newmarket, Suffolk

FOCUS
Just an ordinary maiden, and the winning time was 0.11sec slower than the earlier seller, as well as 1.51sec slower than the following 56-70 handicap.

1580 WEATHERBYS BANK H'CAP 1m 2f 46y

3:55 (3:56) (Class 5) (0-70,67) 3-Y-O **£2,914** (£867; £433; £216) **Stalls** Low

Form RPR
00-2 1 **Lake Kalamalka (IRE)**[28] 1050 3-9-4 67 .... EddieAhern 8 73+
(J L Dunlop) *trckd ldrs: drvn along over 2f out: rdn to chse ldr ins fnl f: kpt on u.p to assert nr fin* **5/1**[3]
0-00 2 1 **Salybia Bay**[7] 1416 3-8-13 62 .... RichardHughes 10 66
(R Hannon) *chsd ldrs: rdn over 2f out: sn pressing ldr: led wl over 1f out: kpt on tl hdd and no ex nr fin* **12/1**
-044 3 2 ¼ **Squad**[34] 962 3-9-0 63 .... NickyMackay 5 63
(S Dow) *in tch: hdwy to chse ldrs 3f out: styd on u.p to chse ldng duo ins fnl f but nvr any ch* **7/1**
206- 4 1 **Lucky Punt**[136] 7666 3-8-11 60 .... MichaelHills 3 58
(B G Powell) *chsd ldrs: chal over 3f out untl led 2f out: hdd wl over 1f out: wknd ins fnl f* **16/1**
020- 5 1 ¼ **Parc Des Princes (USA)**[194] 6745 3-8-13 62 .... (b[1]) MartinDwyer 11 57
(A M Balding) *t.k.h: stdd towards rr after 3f: hdwy over 2f out: rdn and hung lft over 1f out and again whn nt clr run ins fnl f: nt rcvr and one pce* **17/2**
400- 6 ½ **Money Money Money**[216] 6199 3-9-4 67 .... IanMongan 1 61
(P Winkworth) *sn drvn to dispute ld and led after 2f: rdn 3f out: hdd 2f out: wknd fnl f* **12/1**
00-4 7 6 **Sermons Mount (USA)**[48] 800 3-8-3 55 .... DavidProbert(3) 7 37
(Mouse Hamilton-Fairley) *towards rr: hdwy on ins to chse ldrs over 2f out: wknd over 1f out* **33/1**
0-00 8 shd **Best Bidder (USA)**[10] 1361 3-8-11 60 .... DarryllHolland 2 42
(Patrick Morris) *slowly away: in rr: sme hdwy on outside whn edgd rt over 2f out: mod late prog* **22/1**
0-51 9 3 ¾ **Scottish Affair**[36] 938 3-9-0 63 .... JimCrowley 9 37
(E A L Dunlop) *in rr: hdwy after 3f: rdn 3f out and sn wknd* **9/2**[2]

The Form Book, Raceform Ltd, Compton, RG20 6NL

056- **10** *7* **Fongoli**[149] 7505 3-8-6 **55** ow1 RobertWinston 6 15
(B G Powell) *disp ld 2f: styd chsng ldrs tl wknd over 2f out: eased whn no ch fnl f* **14/1**

00-2 **11** *5* **Mr Prolific**[10] 1363 3-8-6 **55** ChrisCatlin 12 5
(B W Hills) *chsd ldrs: rdn and towards rr whn pushed rt over 2f out* **4/1**[1]

00-6 **12** *26* **Stafford Charlie**[64] 659 3-8-0 **54** oh8 ow1 SophieDoyle(5) 13 —
(J G M O'Shea) *in tch: rn wd bnd over 5f out: sn wknd* **100/1**

4400 **13** *12* **Hatman Jack (IRE)**[25] 1095 3-9-1 **64** SebSanders 4 —
(B G Powell) *in rr: rdn: sme hdwy and wd bnd over 3f out: sn wknd and no ch whn pushed rt over 2f out* **40/1**

2m 10.56s (-0.44) **Going Correction** +0.025s/f (Good) 13 Ran SP% **116.5**
Speed ratings (Par 98): **102,101,99,98,97 97,92,92,89,83 79,58,49**
toteswinger: 1&2 £20.40, 1&3 £7.40, 2&3 £17.70 CSF £60.14 CT £422.25 TOTE £6.70: £2.20, £5.10, £2.30; EX 83.30 TRIFECTA Not won..
Owner Capt J Macdonald-Buchanan **Bred** The Lavington Stud **Trained** Arundel, W Sussex
■ Stewards' Enquiry : Richard Hughes caution: careless riding

FOCUS
A modest three-year-old handicap.
Best Bidder(USA) Official explanation: jockey said that the filly missed the break
Scottish Affair Official explanation: jockey said that the gelding was never travelling
Fongoli Official explanation: jockey said that the filly hung left
Mr Prolific Official explanation: jcokey said the gelding was never travelling
Hatman Jack(IRE) Official explanation: jockey said the gelding failed to stay the trip

1581 M.J. CHURCH H'CAP 1m 3f 144y
4:30 (4:30) (Class 5) (0-75,75) 4-Y-O+ **£3,043** (£905; £452; £226) **Stalls** Low

Form RPR

4-01 **1** **Moonshine Creek**[20] 1178 7-8-5 **61** oh2 ChrisCatlin 4 68
(P W Hiatt) *trckd ldr: drvn ahd over 2f out: styd on wl u.p fnl f* **5/2**[1]

000- **2** *1 3/4* **Invention (USA)**[198] 6671 6-8-9 **65** (t) RichardHughes 8 69
(Miss E C Lavelle) *led: rdn 3f out: hdd over 2f out: no ch w wnr fnl f but hld on wl for 2nd* **9/2**[2]

05-3 **3** *nk* **Seventh Hill**[11] 1318 4-8-6 **63** JimmyQuinn 6 67+
(M Blanshard) *in rr: hdwy whn nt clr run wl over 1f out: hdwy to chse ldrs and hung lft ins fnl f: kpt on cl home* **13/2**[3]

40-6 **4** *1 1/4* **Classical Rhythm (IRE)**[7] 1415 4-8-7 **64** EddieAhern 1 65
(J R Boyle) *hld up in tch: rdn and hdwy to chse ldrs over 2f out: nvr on terms and one pce fnl f* **7/1**

100- **5** *nk* **Colour Trooper (IRE)**[195] 6738 4-9-1 **72** JimCrowley 2 73
(P Winkworth) *chsd ldrs: rdn over 2f out: kpt on same pce fnl f* **14/1**

12-2 **6** *1* **Riqaab (IRE)**[20] 1179 4-9-2 **73** TPO'Shea 9 72+
(E A L Dunlop) *hld up in rr: hdwy and nt clr run wl over 1f out and again ins fnl f: nt pce to rcvr* **9/2**[2]

00-0 **7** *5* **Duty Free (IRE)**[20] 1184 5-9-5 **75** SteveDrowne 5 66
(C R Egerton) *stdd towards rr after 3f but in tch: rdn and effrt 3f out: nvr in contention and sn wknd* **15/2**

100- **8** *21* **Gallego**[198] 6671 7-8-11 **67** RobertWinston 3 22
(R J Price) *plld hrd: chsd ldrs after 3f: wknd qckly ins fnl 3f* **14/1**

2m 29.82s (-0.78) **Going Correction** +0.025s/f (Good)
WFA 4 from 5yo+ 1lb 8 Ran SP% **115.9**
Speed ratings (Par 103): **103,101,101,100,100 99,96,82**
toteswinger: 1&2 £4.50, 1&3 £4.00, 2&3 £5.40 CSF £13.98 CT £64.87 TOTE £3.20: £1.50, £2.00, £1.70; EX 21.40 Trifecta £199.90 Pool: £359.37 - 1.33 winning units..
Owner P W Hiatt **Bred** Lawrence Shepherd **Trained** Hook Norton, Oxon

FOCUS
A modest handicap run at a steady pace and few were ever involved.
Riqaab(IRE) Official explanation: jockey said, regarding the running and riding, that his instructions were to hold the colt up to make his run through the horses and not to see recourse to the whip unless in with a chacne in the dying strides, and that he was riding the colt for the first time and had been told that it was a quirky sort. Trainer's representative confirmed that the colt was a difficult ride and was attempting the extended trip for the first time.
Duty Free(IRE) Official explanation: jockey said that the gelding hung left

1582 EUROPEAN BREEDERS' FUND LANSDOWN FILLIES' STKS (LISTED RACE) 5f 11y
5:05 (5:06) (Class 1) 3-Y-O+
£22,708 (£8,608; £4,308; £2,148; £1,076; £540) **Stalls** Centre

Form RPR

124- **1** **Look Busy (IRE)**[220] 6121 4-9-0 103 SladeO'Hara 7 98
(A Berry) *in tch: rdn and hdwy 2f out: str run fnl f to ld last stride* **7/1**[3]

0-50 **2** *nse* **Crimson Fern (IRE)**[11] 1325 5-9-0 94 RichardHughes 12 98
(M S Saunders) *hld up in rr: hdwy over 1f out: swtchd rt and rapid hdwy fnl f: fin fast: jst failed* **6/1**[2]

320- **3** *hd* **Siren's Gift**[199] 6653 5-9-0 94 (b) DavidProbert 15 97
(A M Balding) *sn led: travelling wl 2f out: rdn over 1f out: styd on wl fnl f: ct last strides* **9/2**[1]

00-0 **4** *1 1/2* **Angus Newz**[11] 1325 6-9-4 88 DarryllHolland 2 96
(M Quinn) *chsd ldrs: rdn over 2f out: styd on same pce fnl f* **33/1**

305- **5** *3 1/2* **Bahamian Babe**[199] 6644 3-8-4 94 MartinDwyer 16 75
(M L W Bell) *chsd ldrs: rdn and edgd rt over 1f out: wknd fnl f* **8/1**

0U-2 **6** *nk* **Pusey Street Lady**[31] 996 5-9-0 99 JimCrowley 13 78
(J Gallagher) *in rr: hdwy on outside whn pushed rt over 1f out: kpt on again ins fnl f but nvr a threat* **9/2**[1]

110- **7** *1* **Gentle Guru**[227] 5884 5-9-0 85 SteveDrowne 1 75
(R T Phillips) *in rr: hdwy on ins fr 2f out: kpt on fnl f but nvr in contention* **50/1**

2/6- **8** *1/2* **La Sylvia (IRE)**[256] 5081 4-9-0 0 ChrisCatlin 8 75+
(E J O'Neill) *rr: rdn 1/2-way: hdwy on outside whn hmpd over 1f out: nt rcvr but kpt on again ins fnl f* **66/1**

44-0 **9** *nse* **Manzila (FR)**[13] 1278 6-9-0 93 AdrianTNicholls 5 73
(D Nicholls) *chsd ldrs: rdn 1/2-way: wknd fnl f* **14/1**

43P- **10** *1* **Starlit Sands**[208] 6429 4-9-0 102 SebSanders 11 69
(Sir Mark Prescott) *chsd ldrs: rdn: bmpd and wknd over 1f out* **15/2**

520- **11** *1/2* **Lucky Leigh**[256] 5055 3-8-4 95 (v[1]) JimmyQuinn 3 63
(M R Channon) *in rr: sme hdwy over 1f out: nvr in contention* **20/1**

150- **12** *hd* **Pretty Bonnie**[214] 6239 4-9-0 80 CatherineGannon 9 67
(A E Price) *chsd ldrs: rdn 1/2-way: wknd over 1f out* **66/1**

/12- **13** *1 1/2* **Speed Song**[278] 4347 4-9-0 86 MichaelHills 6 61+
(W J Haggas) *slowly away: in rr: sme hdwy on outside whn hmpd over 1f out: nt rcvr* **14/1**

1323 **14** *3/4* **Carcinetto (IRE)**[3] 1513 7-9-0 89 RichardEvans 14 59
(P D Evans) *in tch: rdn 1/2-way: wkng whn hmpd over 1f out* **12/1**

020- **15** *2* **Raggle Taggle (IRE)**[221] 6068 3-8-4 99 DO'Donohoe 17 47
(R M Beckett) *chsd ldrs: rdn and carried rt over 1f out: sn wknd* **33/1**

110- **16** *1/2* **Blades Princess**[199] 6644 3-8-4 85 GrahamGibbons 4 46
(E S McMahon) *chsd ldrs over 3f* **40/1**

61.41 secs (-1.09) **Going Correction** +0.025s/f (Good)
WFA 3 from 4yo+ 10lb 16 Ran SP% **125.1**
Speed ratings (Par 108): **109,108,108,106,100 100,98,97,97,96 95,94,92,91,88 87**
toteswinger: 1&2 £9.40, 1&3 £11.60, 2&3 £10.20 CSF £47.46 TOTE £10.60: £2.90, £2.50, £2.10; EX 44.70 Trifecta £150.50 Pool: £394.67 - 1.94 winning units..
Owner A Underwood **Bred** Tom And Hazel Russell **Trained** Cockerham, Lancs

FOCUS
More quantity than quality by Listed-race standards, but plenty of runners for this fillies' contest and it was certainly competitive.

NOTEBOOK
Look Busy(IRE) has not come in her coat yet, but she was best off at the weights, having escaped a penalty for last season's Group 3 success, and didn't have to be at her best after over seven months off. She can do better and should be set for another profitable season. (op 13-2 tchd 8-1)
Crimson Fern(IRE) only got in the clear just over a furlong out, and that allowed the winner first run. She looked a slightly unlucky loser, but that said, it's worth remembering Look Busy was probably in need of the run. Whatever, though, this was a solid effort in defeat and she could pick up a similar race this season. (tchd 5-1 and 13-2)
Siren's Gift was allowed her own way in front and travelled strongly, although she obviously still went off at a quick pace. This was a pleasing return from 199 days off and she should continue to go well in similar company. (op 7-1)
Angus Newz had no easy task under her penalty and ran about as well as could have been expected considering she had something to find with the front three at the weights. (op 25-1 tchd 22-1)
Bahamian Babe, a very useful, speedy juvenile, fared best of the three-year-olds on her return from 199 days off and this was a creditable effort. (op 12-1 tchd 7-1)
Pusey Street Lady was in trouble when bumped towards the outside over a furlong out and could not confirm the much-improved form she showed when runner-up at this level against the boys on her reappearance. Official explanation: jockey said the mare became very upset in the stalls (op 6-1)
Gentle Guru, returning from 227 days off, stayed on towards the inside but never posed a threat.
La Sylvia(IRE), who had been off for eight months and was having her first start since coming over from Ireland, was one of those hampered about a furlong out. (op 80-1)
Starlit Sands, pulled up at Newmarket when last seen about seven months previously, was bumped about a furlong out and seemed to finish quite tired. She should come on a fair bit for this. (op 8-1 tchd 13-2)
Lucky Leigh Official explanation: jockey said that the filly was slowly away
Speed Song was never in contention after starting slowly and was denied a clear run around a furlong from the finish. Official explanation: jockey said he filly reared up leaving the stalls (op 10-1)
Carcinetto(IRE) was trying to stay on from off the pace but still had work to do when badly short of room over a furlong out and that cost her any chance she might have had. (op 14-1 tchd 11-1)

1583 MOBIL 1 H'CAP 5f 11y
5:40 (5:40) (Class 5) (0-70,70) 3-Y-O **£1,890** (£1,890; £433; £216) **Stalls** Centre

Form RPR

3320 **1** **Riflessione**[19] 1196 3-9-4 **70** (b) EddieAhern 10 75
(R A Harris) *in rr tl rdn and hdwy over 1f out: str run to chal ins fnl f: styd on wl to dead heat* **5/1**[2]

0113 **1** *dht* **Speak The Truth (IRE)**[12] 1311 3-9-0 **66** (p) MartinDwyer 2 71
(J R Boyle) *chsd ldrs: led over 1f out: racd wd and styd on wl u.p to hold on for dead heat* **7/1**

6-32 **3** *1* **Vamos (IRE)**[24] 1120 3-8-8 **60** ChrisCatlin 7 61
(J R Gask) *chsd ldrs: rdn and styd on wl for 3rd fnl f but nt pce of dead heaters* **9/2**[1]

45-3 **4** *5* **Piste**[10] 1359 3-9-0 **66** SebSanders 6 48
(B J Meehan) *chsd ldrs: rdn over 1f out: one pce ins fnl f* **9/2**[1]

6-35 **5** *1 1/4* **Bees River (IRE)**[12] 1311 3-8-7 **64** (v[1]) MartinLane(5) 9 41
(A P Jarvis) *led tl hdd over 1f out: sn wknd* **12/1**

0-30 **6** *1 1/2* **You've Been Mowed**[12] 1311 3-8-8 **60** RobertWinston 8 32
(R J Price) *sn chsng ldrs: rdn 1/2-way: wknd fnl f* **8/1**

345 **7** *1/2* **Volito**[32] 982 3-8-13 **65** JamieMoriarty 5 35
(Jonjo O'Neill) *a outpcd* **11/1**

-210 **8** *1 1/4* **True Decision**[11] 1322 3-9-1 **67** RichardHughes 3 32
(S Kirk) *towards rr and rdn 1/2-way: sn wknd* **13/2**[3]

64-4 **9** *2 1/4* **Handcuff**[25] 1095 3-8-6 **58** TPO'Shea 1 15
(J Gallagher) *in tch: shkn up 1/2-way: sn wknd* **8/1**

62.77 secs (0.27) **Going Correction** +0.025s/f (Good) 9 Ran SP% **117.1**
Speed ratings (Par 98): **98,98,96,88,86 84,83,81,77**WIN: R £3.80, STT £4.30. PL R £2.30 STT £2.50 V £1.90 EX: R & STT £30.80, S&R £31.70 CSF: R&S £20.20 S&R £21.25 TRI: R,S&V £85.52 S, R&V £89.06 toteswinger: Riflessione & Speak the Truth £9.40 Riflessione & Vamos £5.30 Speak the Truth & Vamos £4.10, £27, £OwnerJohn Hopkins (t/a South Hatch Racing) Bred Trifecta £Gerard Mulligan Trained Epsom, Surrey.
Owner Paul Moulton **Bred** Tom & Evelyn Yates **Trained** Earlswood, Monmouths

FOCUS
A modest sprint handicap.
T/Plt: £29.40 to a £1 stake. Pool: £71,037.07. 1,762.48 winning tickets. T/Qpdt: £10.10 to a £1 stake. Pool: £3,667.66. 267.40 winning tickets. ST

1378 LINGFIELD (L-H)
Tuesday, April 28

OFFICIAL GOING: Standard
Wind: modest, half behind, gusty at times Weather: showery

1584 ASHDOWN FOREST CLAIMING STKS 7f (P)
2:30 (2:31) (Class 6) 3-Y-O **£2,047** (£604; £302) **Stalls** Low

Form RPR

00-5 **1** **Taste Of Honey (IRE)**[27] 1066 3-8-4 65 KirstyMilczarek 2 55
(D W P Arbuthnot) *t.k.h early: chsd ldr: rdn and nt pce of ldr over 2f out: rallied ent fnl f: edgd lft but r.o wl to ld on post* **14/1**

05-6 **2** *nse* **Spit And Polish**[27] 1075 3-8-9 66 (b) TedDurcan 3 60
(J L Dunlop) *led: rdn and qcknd clr over 2f out: drvn fnl f: hdd on post* **6/1**[3]

0-06 **3** *1/2* **Via Mia**[8] 1414 3-8-12 73 TPQueally 9 62+
(P F I Cole) *hld up towards rr: outpcd over 2f out: hdwy ent fnl f: stl only 6th ins fnl f: r.o strly and clsng rapidly at fin* **8/1**

3-00 **4** *1* **Cool Art (IRE)**[7] 1434 3-9-9 80 (b) JamieSpencer 10 70
(S A Callaghan) *stdd after s: t.k.h: hld up in last pair: hdwy on outer over 2f out: rdn 2f out: chsd ldng pair jst over 1f out: kpt on but nvr pce to rch ldrs* **15/8**[1]

35 **5** *1* **Vegas Baby (IRE)**[60] 709 3-9-4 80 ShaneKelly 1 62
(J A Osborne) *chsd ldrs: rdn and unable qck over 2f out: kpt on again fnl f: nt pce to threaten ldrs* **9/2**[2]

0000 **6** *1* **Commandingpresence (USA)**[15] [1253] 3-8-0 58.........(b) LukeMorris 6 41
(Ms J S Doyle) *t.k.h: hld up towards rr: rdn and unable qck over 2f out: plugged on fnl f: nt pce to threaten ldrs* **10/1**

7 *1* **Mister Frosty (IRE)**[347] [2181] 3-8-9 0.......................... AdrianMcCarthy 8 48
(G Prodromou) *stdd s: t.k.h: hld up in last pair: rdn and effrt jst over 2f out: kpt on pce* **16/1**

1-0 **8** *1 3/4* **Creshendo**[27] [1068] 3-9-7 75..(p) GeorgeBaker 7 55
(R M Beckett) *chsd ldrs: rdn over 2f out: sn outpcd: wknd wl over 1f out* **13/2**

50-0 **9** *5* **Premier Demon (IRE)**[92] [293] 3-7-9 43 ow2....... AndrewHeffernan(7) 4 22
(P D Evans) *chsd ldrs: rdn 3f out: wknd over 2f out: wl bhd fnl f* **50/1**

1m 25.41s (0.61) **Going Correction** +0.025s/f (Slow) **9** Ran SP% **115.3**
Speed ratings (Par 96): **97,96,96,95,94 92,91,89,84**
toteswinger: 1&2 £13.90, 1&3 £19.80, 2&3 £25.90. CSF £95.15 TOTE £16.90: £4.50, £2.20, £2.00; EX 113.10.Cool Art was claimed by P. Grayson for £15,000.
Owner Noel Cronin **Bred** N D Cronin **Trained** Compton, Berks

FOCUS
An ordinary claimer in which a few had a chance on paper.

1585 BROWNHILL INSURANCE GROUP MEDIAN AUCTION MAIDEN STKS 1m (P)

3:05 (3:06) (Class 5) 3-Y-0 **£2,729** (£806; £403) **Stalls** High

Form RPR

223- **1** **Sandor**[180] [7098] 3-9-3 80.. PatCosgrave 7 77
(P J Makin) *chsd ldr: led jst over 2f out: sn rdn: hdd narrowly 1f out: battled on gamely to ld again fnl 100yds: styd on wl* **15/8**[1]

-533 **2** *1/2* **Pyrus Time (IRE)**[57] [731] 3-9-3 75.. LukeMorris 4 76
(J S Moore) *stdd after s: hld up in midfield: hdwy to chse ldrs over 3f: rdn to chse wnr over 1f out: hung lft and led narrowly 1f out: fnd little and hdd fnl 100yds: no ex* **13/2**

022- **3** *4 1/2* **Piccolo Mondo**[189] [6877] 3-9-3 71.............................. StephenCarson 1 66
(P Winkworth) *t.k.h: led on suffernce tl over 6f out: chsd ldrs after: rdn to chse wnr 2f out tl over 1f out: outpcd fnl f* **8/1**

00- **4** *2 3/4* **Transformer (IRE)**[142] [7593] 3-9-3 0............................... ShaneKelly 12 59+
(W J Knight) *styd wd: chsd ldrs: 5th and outpcd 3f out: kpt on same pce and no imp after* **25/1**

5 *2* **Some Sunny Day** 3-8-12 0.. TravisBlock 6 50+
(H Morrison) *racd in midfield: rn green and pushed along over 4f out: sn rdn and outpcd: n.d after* **20/1**

240- **6** *1/2* **Layer Cake**[212] [6305] 3-9-3 76.. JamieSpencer 11 53
(J W Hills) *stdd s: hld up in rr: sme hdwy on outer 3f out: rdn and plugged on fnl 2f: edgd lft fnl f: n.d* **9/2**[2]

6-0 **7** *1* **General Zhukov**[15] [1257] 3-9-3 0.................................... KirstyMilczarek 8 51
(J M P Eustace) *s.i.s: t.k.h: hld up in rr struggling 4f out: no ch after* **33/1**

8 *3/4* **Bedarra Boy** 3-9-3 0.. SimonWhitworth 10 49
(D W P Arbuthnot) *s.i.s: a wl bhd: lost tch over 3f out* **33/1**

4 **9** *nse* **Fantastical**[35] [944] 3-8-12 0.. J-PGuillambert 3 44
(C E Brittain) *t.k.h: pressed ldrs tl led over 6f out: rdn and hdd jst over 2f out: wknd rapidly over 1f out* **11/1**

6 **10** *3 1/2* **The Last Don (IRE)**[15] [1257] 3-9-3 0................................ TedDurcan 9 41
(D R Lanigan) *s.i.s: sn pushed along in rr: struggling 4f out: no ch after* **6/1**[3]

- **11** *35* **Deviant Ways** 3-8-12 0... JamesDoyle 2 —
(S Kirk) *taken down early: slowly into strde: bhd and rdn over 4f out: t.o fr wl over 2f out* **25/1**

1m 37.92s (-0.28) **Going Correction** +0.025s/f (Slow) **11** Ran SP% **118.4**
Speed ratings (Par 98): **102,101,97,94,92 91,90,90,89,86 51**
toteswinger: 1&2 £2.50, 1&3 £3.10, 2&3 £5.30. CSF £13.26 TOTE £2.70: £1.50, £2.50, £3.50; EX 18.10.
Owner Keith And Brian Brackpool **Bred** Southcourt Stud **Trained** Ogbourne Maisey, Wilts

FOCUS
Quite a competitive median auction maiden on paper but a group of four broke clear leaving the back and it concerned only two entering the final furlong.

1586 ASHURST WOOD (S) STKS 1m 4f (P)

3:40 (3:40) (Class 6) 4-Y-0+ **£2,047** (£604; £302) **Stalls** Low

Form RPR

4-00 **1** **Polish Power (GER)**[9] [1382] 9-8-13 80................................ LPKeniry 10 72
(J S Moore) *trckd ldrs: rdn to chse ldr 2f out: str chal jst ins fnl f: r.o wl to ld last stride* **5/1**[2]

1154 **2** *shd* **Nawamees (IRE)**[32] [977] 11-9-5 69...........................(p) JamieSpencer 1 78
(P D Evans) *led at stdy gallop: rdn and qcknd 3f out: hrd pressed jst ins fnl f: kpt on wl tl hdd last stride* **7/1**[3]

030- **3** *4* **Royal Jet**[218] [6171] 7-8-13 89...................................... SamHitchcott 8 65
(M R Channon) *hld up in tch rdn and effrt over 2f out: chsd ldng pair jst ins fnl f: sn no imp* **8/13**[1]

-204 **4** *4 1/2* **Poppy Red**[74] [528] 4-8-0 50...............................(p) AndrewHeffernan(7) 4 53
(C J Gray) *chsd ldr tl 2f out: wknd u.p over 1f out* **25/1**

5-0 **5** *nk* **Lilac Wine**[13] [1286] 6-8-8 0... JamesDoyle 7 53
(D J S Ffrench Davis) *in tch: rdn and hung lft u.p 3f out: sn struggling and wl btn* **33/1**

0-03 **6** *1 3/4* **City Stable (IRE)**[32] [977] 4-8-5 70............................ TobyAtkinson(7) 2 55
(M Wigham) *awkward leaving stalls: hld up in tch in rr: rdn and unable qck over 2f out: nvr trbld ldrs* **16/1**

3342 **7** *1* **Turner's Touch**[45] [838] 7-8-6 55..........................(b) JemmaMarshall(7) 9 53
(G L Moore) *dwlt: hld up in tch in rr: hdwy outer 4f out: outpcd over 2f out: n.d after* **10/1**

-050 **8** *12* **Stockman**[37] [918] 5-8-6 44.. RyanClark(7) 6 34
(H Morrison) *in tch tl dropped in rr over 3f out: sn lost tch* **33/1**

2m 34.12s (1.12) **Going Correction** +0.025s/f (Slow)
WFA 4 from 5yo+ 1lb **8** Ran SP% **115.8**
Speed ratings (Par 101): **97,96,94,91,91 89,89,81**
toteswinger: 1&2 £3.70, 1&3 £2.50, 2&3 £2.10 CSF £38.80 TOTE £7.20: £1.50, £1.80, £1.10; EX 38.90.There was no bid for the winner. Royal Jet was claimed by S. V. O. Leech for £6,000.
Owner John Wells **Bred** Gestut Hofgut Mappen **Trained** Upper Lambourn, Berks
■ Stewards' Enquiry : Jamie Spencer caution: use of whip

FOCUS
A race run at a very leisurely pace and predictably it turned into a sprint turning for home.

1587 MARSH GREEN H'CAP 6f (P)

4:15 (4:16) (Class 6) (0-65,65) 4-Y-0+ **£2,306** (£681; £340) **Stalls** Low

Form RPR

1416 **1** **Suhayl Star (IRE)**[11] [1320] 5-8-13 60............................... LukeMorris 11 70
(P Burgoyne) *chsd ldr: rdn to ld ins fnl f: rdn out and r.o wl* **11/2**[3]

5002 **2** *3/4* **Mudhish (IRE)**[13] [1285] 4-9-4 65.....................................(b) JamieSpencer 5 73
(C E Brittain) *hld up in rr: hdwy over 2f out: nt clr run briefly wl over 1f out: gd hdwy on outer fnl f: edgd lft fnl f: wnt 2nd towards fin: nt threaten wnr* **9/2**[2]

0560 **3** *3/4* **Teen Ager (FR)**[6] [1468] 5-8-11 58................................ StephenCarson 1 63
(P Burgoyne) *chsd ldng pair: rdn to ld 1f out: hdd ins fnl f: no ex fnl 100yds* **14/1**

530- **4** *shd* **Bahamian Bliss**[189] [6880] 4-9-1 62...................................... KirstyMilczarek 3 67
(J A R Toller) *s.i.s: bhd: hdwy into midfield 4f out: hdwy on inner 2f out: pressed ldrs 1f out: kpt on same pce fnl 100yds* **11/2**[3]

-360 **5** *nk* **Bertie Southstreet**[87] [355] 6-9-1 62..............................(p) PatCosgrave 6 66
(J R Boyle) *stdd after s: t.k.h: hld up towards rr: hdwy to chse ldrs over 2f out: rdn over 1f out: one pce fnl f* **4/1**[1]

5-53 **6** *2 1/2* **Spoof Master (IRE)**[103] [177] 5-8-12 59................................ AdamKirby 4 55
(C R Dore) *racd in midfield: rdn and unable qck over 2f out: kpt on fnl f: nvr pce to threaten ldrs* **7/1**

4303 **7** *1 3/4* **Simpsons Gamble (IRE)**[27] [1076] 6-8-9 59..............(p) JackMitchell(3) 8 49
(R A Teal) *t.k.h early: hld up in midfield: rdn and effrt over 2f out: hung lft and no hdwy over 1f out* **6/1**

/500 **7** *dht* **Martingrange Boy (IRE)**[10] [1360] 4-8-12 59.....................(t) ShaneKelly 2 49
(J Balding) *taken down early: led at fast gallop: rdn 2f out: hdd 1f out: wknd qckly* **20/1**

0-60 **9** *3/4* **Whinhill House**[10] [1360] 9-8-7 61.......................(v) JosephineBruning(7) 7 49
(T T Clement) *chsd ldrs: rdn over 2f out: sn wknd* **50/1**

0-40 **10** *2 3/4* **Truly Divine**[15] [1258] 4-8-9 56.. TPQueally 12 35
(C A Dwyer) *hld up bhd: effrt on outer over 2f out: hung lft and wknd over 1f out* **14/1**

26-0 **11** *8* **Red Amaryllis**[15] [1248] 4-8-10 57......................................(b[1]) TedDurcan 9 11
(H J L Dunlop) *s.i.s: a detached in last pl* **16/1**

1m 11.4s (-0.50) **Going Correction** +0.025s/f (Slow) **11** Ran SP% **121.7**
Speed ratings (Par 101): **104,103,102,101,101 98,95,95,94,91 80**
toteswinger: 1&2 £4.90, 1&3 £20.00, 2&3 £13.80 CSF £31.65 CT £344.91 TOTE £7.10: £2.50, £1.70, £5.40; EX 32.00.
Owner Mrs C Leigh-Turner **Bred** John Mulhern **Trained** Shepton Montague, Somerset
■ Stewards' Enquiry : Luke Morris one-day ban: failed to ride to draw (May 18)

FOCUS
A low-grade handicap that was contested mostly by inconsistent or unreliable types. The pace was strong, though
Spoof Master(IRE) Official explanation: jockey said the gelding was denied a clear run
Red Amaryllis Official explanation: jockey said the filly did not face the blinkers

1588 EVELYN & GEORGE EVANS 50TH WEDDING ANNIVERSARY FILLIES' H'CAP 7f (P)

4:50 (4:52) (Class 5) (0-70,70) 3-Y-0 **£3,238** (£963; £481; £240) **Stalls** Low

Form RPR

52-6 **1** **Volochkova (USA)**[14] [1269] 3-9-4 70................................ FrancisNorton 9 75+
(J R Fanshawe) *s.i.s: bhd: stl plenty to do and nt clr run 2f out: hdwy on ins rail jst over 1f out: chsd ldrs and swtchd rt ins fnl f: qcknd to ld fnl 50yds: r.o wl* **9/2**[2]

62-0 **2** *nk* **Perfect Friend**[12] [1315] 3-9-0 66...................................... JamesDoyle 10 70+
(S Kirk) *hld up in rr: stl plenty to do and plld wd over 1f out: str run fnl f: pressed wnr towards fin: hld cl home* **25/1**

400- **3** *3/4* **Russian Rave**[214] [6240] 3-9-2 68.. TPQueally 12 70
(J G Portman) *t.k.h: chsd ldr after 1f: ev ch and rdn 2f out: led jst over 1f out: hdd and no ex fnl 50yds* **33/1**

60-6 **4** *1* **Novastasia (IRE)**[27] [1066] 3-8-11 63.................................. AdamKirby 2 62
(W R Swinburn) *chsd ldng pair: rdn and edgd out rt over 1f out: kpt on u.p fnl f* **6/1**[3]

030- **5** *nse* **West With The Wind (USA)**[180] [7095] 3-9-4 70................ TedDurcan 8 69
(P W Chapple-Hyam) *sn led: rdn jst over 2f out: hdd jst over 1f out: stl ev ch tl no ex fnl 100yds* **9/1**

40-2 **6** *1 1/2* **Assent (IRE)**[32] [986] 3-8-13 68................................ JamesMillman(3) 4 63
(B R Millman) *stdd s: hld up in midfield: stmbld over 4f out: rdn over 3f out: hdwy over 1f out: kpt on but nt pce to threaten ldrs* **7/1**

54-2 **7** *1 1/2* **Tikka Masala (IRE)**[27] [1066] 3-9-3 69...............(t) RichardKingscote 3 60
(Tom Dascombe) *chsd ldrs: rdn 3f out: drvn and wknd ent fnl f* **5/2**[1]

040- **8** *3/4* **Turkish Lokum**[208] [6426] 3-9-2 68...................................... LukeMorris 7 57
(J M P Eustace) *t.k.h: chsd ldrs: rdn and unable qck jst over 2f out: wknd over 1f out* **33/1**

304- **9** *1* **Corton Charlemagne (IRE)**[173] [7205] 3-8-11 63.......... SaleemGolam 6 49
(Rae Guest) *in tch in midfield on outer: rdn over 2f out: wknd u.p over 1f out* **20/1**

64-4 **10** *3/4* **Feet Of Fury**[30] [1015] 3-9-2 68.. ShaneKelly 5 52
(W M Brisbourne) *dwlt: t.k.h: in tch in midfield: rdn and wknd wl over 1f out* **7/1**

350- **11** *hd* **Countess Zara (IRE)**[174] [7190] 3-9-2 68.......................... WilliamBuick 11 52
(A M Balding) *a towards rr: rdn and no rspnse jst over 2f out: n.d* **33/1**

410- **12** *shd* **Piccolinda**[190] [6865] 3-8-8 65.. RossAtkinson(5) 1 49
(W R Muir) *dwlt: sn in tch in midfield: on inner: rdn 2f out: sn wknd* **14/1**

354 **13** *3* **Azharia**[21] [1174] 3-9-0 66.. JamieSpencer 13 41
(C E Brittain) *stdd after s: hld up in rr: n.m.r and swtchd lft wl over 1f out: n.d* **8/1**

1m 25.71s (0.91) **Going Correction** +0.025s/f (Slow) **13** Ran SP% **131.2**
Speed ratings (Par 95): **95,94,93,92,92 90,89,88,87,86 86,85,82**
toteswinger: 1&2 £22.20, 1&3 £44.70, 2&3 £161.30 CSF £127.15 CT £2235.70 TOTE £5.80: £1.90, £7.00, £11.80; EX 144.80.
Owner Mrs C C Regalado-Gonzalez **Bred** Robert N Clay & Fair Way Equine Llc **Trained** Newmarket, Suffolk

FOCUS
A race that changed dramatically in the final furlong as the hold-up horses burst onto the seen having been well served by the decent gallop.
Tikka Masala(IRE) Official explanation: jockey said the filly was never travelling
Azharia Official explanation: jockey said the filly did not face the kickback

1589 DERBY TRIAL HERE MAY 9TH H'CAP 1m 2f (P)

5:25 (5:26) (Class 6) (0-60,60) 4-Y-0+ **£2,299** (£679; £339) **Stalls** Low

Form RPR

-406 **1** **Free Tussy (ARG)**[34] [961] 5-8-13 55..............................(bt) ShaneKelly 4 63
(G L Moore) *hld up in tch towards rr: gd hdwy towards inner 2f out: led over 1f out: hung rt ins fnl f: drvn and asserted fnl 50yds* **12/1**

0030 **2** *1* **Make Amends (IRE)**[41] [871] 4-8-8 55.............................. MCGeran(5) 11 61
(R J Hodges) *hld up in midfield: hdwy on outer over 2f out: pressed wnr ins fnl f: nt pce of wnr fnl 50yds* **10/1**

4-51 **3** *3/4* **Nassar (IRE)**[4] [1496] 6-8-12 54...................................(v) AdrianMcCarthy 9 59
(G Prodromou) *s.i.s: bustled along early: t.k.h after 2f: towards rr: hdwy over 2f out: chsd ldrs ins fnl f: kpt on* **13/8**[1]

0101 **4** 1 **Almahaza (IRE)**[32] 979 5-9-4 **60** NeilChalmers 10 63
(A J Chamberlain) *bhd: rdn jst over 2f out: plld to outer over 1f out: r.o fnl f: nt rch ldrs* **7/1**[3]
4250 **5** 1 **Play Up Pompey**[62] 669 7-8-10 **52** RichardKingscote 1 53
(J J Bridger) *hld up in midfield: shuffled bk and bhd 3f out: hdwy on inner over 1f out: kpt on fnl f: nt pce to rch ldrs* **10/1**
3-00 **6** 1 1/4 **Tallulah Sunrise**[35] 945 4-8-11 **58** GabrielHannon(5) 13 58+
(M D I Usher) *t.k.h early: hld up in tch: effrt and rdn 2f out: chsd wnr 1f out: keeping on same pce whn hmpd and snatched up ins fnl f* **66/1**
005- **7** 1 **Empire Seeker (USA)**[278] 4334 4-9-1 **57** SimonWhitworth 7 53
(Mrs H S Main) *chsd ldr tl led 3f out: sn rdn: hdd over 1f out: wknd jst ins fnl f* **66/1**
3-50 **8** 1 1/2 **Barton Sands (IRE)**[60] 711 12-8-12 **54** (t) TPQueally 6 47
(Andrew Reid) *dwlt: sn in tch on outer: ev ch u.p 2f out: wknd ent fnl f* **14/1**
00-2 **9** hd **Art Value**[33] 969 4-8-11 **53** FrancisNorton 14 46
(M Wigham) *t.k.h: hld up in tch: n.m.r bnd 2f out: sn rdn and no prog* **5/1**[2]
006- **10** shd **Mr Fantozzi (IRE)**[210] 6353 4-9-2 **58** SaleemGolam 5 50
(D Donovan) *led at stdy gallop: rdn and hdd 3f out: wknd over 1f out* **25/1**
550- **11** 2 1/2 **Oops Another Act**[215] 6227 4-8-12 **54** AdamKirby 3 41
(W R Swinburn) *chsd ldrs: rdn over 2f out: wknd u.p jst over 1f out* **9/1**
-000 **12** nse **Royal Choir**[15] 1254 5-8-9 **51** LukeMorris 12 38
(H E Haynes) *hld up in tch in rr: short lived effrt on outer over 2f out: wl hld over 1f out* **20/1**
06-0 **13** 2 1/4 **Smokin Joe**[60] 708 8-8-12 **57** (b) MarcHalford(3) 2 40
(J R Best) *t.k.h: hld up in tch: rdn 3f out: sn btn: wl bhd over 1f out* **20/1**

2m 7.29s (0.69) **Going Correction** +0.025s/f (Slow) **13** Ran SP% **126.2**
Speed ratings (Par 101): **98,97,96,95,95 94,93,92,91,91 89,89,87**
toteswinger: 1&2 £28.40, 1&3 £9.80, 2&3 £13.70 CSF £126.39 CT £304.47 TOTE £12.30: £3.00, £3.90, £1.40; EX 217.50 Place 6: £151.13 Place 5: £40.05.
Owner T Bowley **Bred** Antonio Carlos Iguacel Et Al **Trained** Lower Beeding, W Sussex

FOCUS
Low-grade stuff and any number of chances as the field fanned across the track early in the straight.
T/Plt: £439.10 to a £1 stake. Pool: £51,508.39. 85.63 winning tickets. T/Qpdt: £79.00 to a £1 stake. Pool: £3,793.38. 35.50 winning tickets. SP

1358 NOTTINGHAM (L-H)
Tuesday, April 28

OFFICIAL GOING: Good to soft (good in places)
Wind: Light across Weather: Overcast

1590 RACING UK HORSERACING IN YOUR HOME MAIDEN STKS 5f 13y
5:35 (5:35) (Class 5) 2-Y-O **£3,238** (£963; £481; £240) **Stalls** High

Form RPR
02 **1** **Red Avalanche (IRE)**[20] 1188 2-9-3 0 NCallan 4 85+
(P F I Cole) *mde all: rdn clr over 1f out: eased ins fnl f* **11/4**[2]
4 **2** 4 **Military Call**[10] 1358 2-9-3 0 RichardMullen 2 64
(E S McMahon) *chsd wnr: rdn over 1f out: wknd fnl f* **9/4**[1]
3 1 3/4 **Newbury Street** 2-9-3 0 PaulHanagan 8 57+
(R A Fahey) *sn pushed along and prom: rdn: hung lft and wknd over 1f out* **9/4**[1]
0 **4** 3 1/4 **Ginger Ted (IRE)**[10] 1358 2-8-12 0 MarkCoumbe(5) 3 46
(R C Guest) *s.i.s: outpcd: styng on whn nt clr run 1f out* **200/1**
5 1 **Reignier** 2-9-3 0 AndrewElliott 5 42
(K R Burke) *trckd ldrs: racd keenly: rdn and wknd over 1f out* **22/1**
3 **6** 1 **Pintura**[8] 1404 2-9-3 0 TonyCulhane 7 38
(M R Channon) *prom: sn pushed along: rdn and hung lft 1/2-way: sn wknd* **6/1**[3]
7 6 **Regency Art (IRE)** 2-9-3 0 RobertHavlin 6 17
(D R C Elsworth) *s.s: outpcd* **20/1**

62.35 secs (1.35) **Going Correction** -0.10s/f (Good) **7** Ran SP% **112.1**
Speed ratings (Par 92): **93,86,83,78,77 75,65**
toteswinger: 1&2 £1.70, 1&3 £1.70, 2&3 £1.20 CSF £8.94 TOTE £4.50: £2.50, £2.00; EX 13.10.
Owner P de Camaret **Bred** Mrs M Purcell **Trained** Whatcombe, Oxon

FOCUS
A dry night, but after a total of 12mm of rain in the last 24 hours, the going had eased considerably. The inner course was in use and the ground seemed almost soft in the final furlong. This was probably a fair juvenile maiden but there is a doubt over the value of the form with the joint-favourites not far ahead of a cheap rag.

NOTEBOOK
Red Avalanche(IRE) paid a big compliment to his course conqueror Star Rover, now winner of all his three starts. He grabbed the stands'-side rail and looked in command some way out. He was value for more than his final winning margin. The winner carries plenty of condition and clearly relished the ease in the ground. He should improve again and follow up. (tchd 5-2)
Military Call, a respectable fourth on much quicker ground on his debut here a week ago, was heavily supported. He raced wide of the winner and proved no match. His stable know the time of day and he is well worth another chance. (op 4-1)
Newbury Street was another well supported. He looked very inexperienced but picked up in his own time late on and will be a lot wiser next time. Official explanation: trainer said colt was found to be lame post race (op 5-2 tchd 3-1)
Ginger Ted(IRE), tailed off in Military Street's race on his debut here, again lost ground at the start and was soon detached. He stayed on in his own time from halfway, and is still learning, but whether this flatters him remains to be seen.
Reignier, very weak beforehand, is a decent type and will improve a good deal. (op 20-1 tchd 25-1)
Pintura was run off his feet at halfway and did nothing for the form of the race at Windsor in which he was fourth on debut. (op 11-4)

1591 TURFTV.CO.UK H'CAP 5f 13y
6:05 (6:10) (Class 6) (0-60,60) 4-Y-O+ **£2,047** (£604; £302) **Stalls** High

Form RPR
405- **1** **Molly Two**[192] 6822 4-8-12 **54** PaulHanagan 8 71
(L A Mullaney) *racd far side: mde all: rdn clr fnl f* **14/1**
046 **2** 2 3/4 **Rocketball (IRE)**[32] 976 4-8-12 **54** PaulMulrennan 11 61+
(Patrick Morris) *led stands' side: rdn and edgd lft over 1f out: styd on to go 2nd wl ins fnl f: no ch w far side: 1st of 6 in gp* **11/1**
3250 **3** 1 **Green Lagonda (AUS)**[24] 1134 7-8-13 **55** MickyFenton 6 58
(Stef Liddiard) *racd far side: chsd ldrs: rdn and hung rt over 1f out: styd on same pce fnl f: 2nd of 8 in gp* **10/1**
0503 **4** 3/4 **Ronnie Howe**[10] 1360 5-9-3 **59** (bt) FergusSweeney 9 59
(S R Bowring) *racd far side: chsd wnr: rdn over 1f out: styd on same pce: 3rd of 8 in gp* **8/1**[2]
020- **5** nse **Paddy Jack**[247] 5307 4-8-13 **55** PhillipMakin 7 55
(J R Weymes) *racd far side: hmpd s: sn chsng ldrs: rdn over 1f out: styd on same pce: 4th of 8 in gp* **33/1**
0400 **6** 2 **Fizzlephut (IRE)**[20] 1182 7-9-2 **58** PaulFitzsimons 3 51
(Miss J R Tooth) *racd far side: prom: rdn over 1f out: no ex: 5th of 8 in gp* **22/1**
00-5 **7** 1/2 **El Potro**[15] 1248 7-9-2 **58** JerryO'Dwyer 16 49+
(J R Holt) *racd stands' side: chsd ldr: rdn over 1f out: no ex: 2nd of 6 in gp* **14/1**
63-5 **8** 1 **Ryedane (IRE)**[116] 15 7-9-1 **57** (b) DavidAllan 14 44+
(T D Easterby) *racd stands' side: dwlt: sn outpcd: nvr nrr: 3rd of 6 in gp* **7/1**[1]
0-00 **9** 1 1/4 **Miacarla**[15] 1241 6-8-11 **56** NeilBrown(3) 2 38
(H A McWilliams) *racd far side: sn pushed along in rr: n.d: 6th of 8 in gp* **50/1**
-200 **10** nk **This Ones For Pat (USA)**[5] 1480 4-9-4 **60** (bt[1]) NCallan 1 41
(S Parr) *racd far side: dwlt: outpcd: 7th of 8 in gp* **9/1**[3]
-506 **11** shd **Bookiesindex Boy**[33] 971 5-9-4 **60** TonyCulhane 17 41+
(J R Jenkins) *racd stands' side: chsd ldrs over 3f: 4th of 6 in gp* **11/1**
-000 **12** shd **Mandelieu (IRE)**[21] 1169 4-9-3 **59** TonyHamilton 4 39
(Ollie Pears) *racd far side: stdd s: plld hrd: a in rr: last of 8 in gp* **25/1**
6123 **13** 10 **Mujma**[24] 1134 5-8-12 **54** (vt) LiamJones 13 —
(S Parr) *racd stands' side: chsd ldrs: rdn 1/2-way: sn wknd: 5th of 6 in gp* **9/1**[3]
10-6 **14** 22 **Belle Bellino (FR)**[25] 1091 4-9-1 **57** GeorgeBaker 15 —
(R M Beckett) *dwlt: racd stands' side: bhd: rdn 1/2-way: sn wknd and eased: last of 6 in gp* **10/1**

61.32 secs (0.32) **Going Correction** -0.10s/f (Good) **14** Ran SP% **104.9**
Speed ratings (Par 101): **101,96,95,93,93 90,89,88,86,85 85,85,69,34**
toteswinger: 1&2 £27.30, 1&3 £26.10, 2&3 £11.10 CSF £120.77 CT £1182.97 TOTE £14.30: £3.80, £5.30, £2.50; EX 193.10.
Owner N Bulmer **Bred** N Bulmer **Trained** Great Habton, North Yorkshire

FOCUS
A low-grade sprint handicap and the majority elected to go to the far side of the track. The form looks modest rated around the runner-up to his winter all-weather level.
This Ones For Pat(USA) Official explanation: jockey said the gelding was never travelling
Belle Bellino(FR) Official explanation: jockey said the filly lost its action

1592 RACING UK £12.99 PER MONTH MAIDEN STKS 5f 13y
6:35 (6:35) (Class 5) 3-4-Y-O **£2,729** (£806; £403) **Stalls** High

Form RPR
33-2 **1** **Gilt Edge Girl**[11] 1317 3-8-12 70 PhilipRobinson 16 88
(C G Cox) *mde virtually all: edgd lft fnl f: rdn out* **7/2**[2]
2- **2** 1 1/2 **Strictly**[229] 5835 3-8-12 0 RyanMoore 13 83
(Sir Michael Stoute) *chsd ldrs: led briefly and hung lft over 1f out: styd on same pce ins fnl f* **10/11**[1]
323- **3** 4 **Mo Mhuirnin (IRE)**[227] 5904 3-8-12 71 PaulHanagan 10 68
(R A Fahey) *w ldr: rdn and ev ch over 1f out: hung lft and no ex fnl f* **14/1**
4 1 **Devil You Know (IRE)** 3-9-3 0 JimmyFortune 9 70+
(D R C Elsworth) *s.s: hung lft and styd on fr over 1f out: nvr nrr* **22/1**
46 **5** 3 3/4 **Global Village (IRE)**[7] 1422 4-9-8 0 WilliamCarson(5) 3 60
(Miss D Mountain) *s.i.s: sn pushed along in rr: n.d* **125/1**
3- **6** 2 **Apache Ridge (IRE)**[214] 6246 3-9-3 0 NCallan 6 49+
(K A Ryan) *hld up: n.d* **9/2**[3]
20 **7** 2 1/2 **Street Spirit (USA)**[8] 1400 3-8-12 0 (t) DavidAllan 4 35
(T D Easterby) *awkward leaving stalls: sn pushed along in rr: rdn and hung lft 1/2-way: n.d* **40/1**
00 **8** 3 1/4 **Russian Music (USA)**[8] 1400 4-9-13 0 (b[1]) DaleGibson 8 32
(C A Mulhall) *s.i.s: sn drvn along: a in rr* **150/1**
0 **9** 3/4 **Hello Sunshine**[11] 1335 3-9-3 0 J-PGuillambert 1 26
(T J Pitt) *prom: rdn: hung lft and wknd 1/2-way* **150/1**
4-4 **10** 3 1/4 **Mac's Power (IRE)**[26] 1077 3-9-3 0 (t) RobertHavlin 2 14
(P J O'Gorman) *hld up: wknd 1/2-way* **12/1**
0 **11** 3 3/4 **Dugatti**[15] 1252 3-9-3 0 FergusSweeney 15 —
(Mike Murphy) *dwlt: sn prom: rdn and wknd 1/2-way* **150/1**

60.43 secs (-0.57) **Going Correction** -0.10s/f (Good)
WFA 3 from 4yo 10lb **11** Ran SP% **116.7**
Speed ratings (Par 103): **108,105,99,97,91 88,84,79,78,72 66**
toteswinger: 1&2 £1.10, 1&3 £8.10, 2&3 £7.20 CSF £6.90 TOTE £5.00: £1.10, £1.90, £2.10; EX 7.90.
Owner Wood Street Syndicate V & C J Harper **Bred** Whitsbury Manor Stud **Trained** Lambourn, Berks

FOCUS
A fair sprint maiden, although plenty of dead wood, and easily the quickest of the three races run over the straight 5f course. They set off in one group, racing towards the stands' side ,but in the end the principals drifted towards the centre and far side. Those racing prominently dominated, and the fourth and sixth both shaped better than the bare form suggests.
Dugatti Official explanation: jockey said the colt lost its action

1593 GET TURFTV IN YOUR BETTING SHOP H'CAP 1m 2f 50y
7:05 (7:05) (Class 3) (0-90,90) 4-Y-O **£7,569** (£2,265; £1,132; £566; £282) **Stalls** Low

Form RPR
61- **1** **Stone Of Scone**[362] 1748 4-9-4 **90** RyanMoore 11 98+
(E A L Dunlop) *s.i.s: hld up: hdwy on outside over 1f out: rdn to ld and hung lft ins fnl f: jst hld on* **12/1**
31- **2** nk **Red Jade**[202] 6583 4-8-10 **82** DarrenWilliams 10 89+
(K R Burke) *chsd ldrs: rdn to ld and edgd lft over 1f out: hdd ins fnl f: styd on* **3/1**[1]
301- **3** 3/4 **Wiggy Smith**[196] 6721 10-8-6 **78** FergusSweeney 9 84
(H Candy) *hld up: hdwy over 1f out: r.o: nt rch ldrs* **16/1**
36-0 **4** 2 **Hurlingham**[31] 999 5-8-7 **79** ow1 PaulMulrennan 1 81
(M W Easterby) *hld up: hdwy 3f out: rdn over 1f out: styd on* **28/1**
400- **5** 1/2 **Mull Of Dubai**[171] 7244 6-9-4 **90** JohnEgan 8 91
(T P Tate) *hld up: hdwy over 3f out: rdn and hung lft fr over 1f out: styd on same pce ins fnl f* **11/1**
41-6 **6** 3 1/4 **Bullet Man (USA)**[14] 1274 4-8-9 **81** DaneO'Neill 3 75
(L M Cumani) *s.i.s: hld up: hdwy over 3f out: sn rdn: wknd over 1f out* **12/1**
120- **7** 1 1/4 **Ansells Pride (IRE)**[314] 3122 6-9-0 **86** TomEaves 2 78
(B Smart) *sn led: rdn and hdd over 1f out: wknd ins fnl f* **33/1**
321- **8** 2 **Prairie Storm**[174] 7202 4-8-9 **81** LPKeniry 7 69
(A M Balding) *chsd ldr: rdn over 2f out: wknd over 1f out* **4/1**[2]
33-6 **9** 5 **Hunting Country**[24] 1117 4-9-1 **87** RoystonFfrench 5 65
(M Johnston) *s.i.s: sn prom: rdn over 3f out: wknd over 2f out* **11/2**
33-0 **10** 1/2 **Jeer (IRE)**[31] 999 5-8-8 **80** DaleGibson 13 57
(M W Easterby) *prom: rdn over 3f out: wknd over 2f out* **50/1**

200- **11** ½ **Blue Spinnaker (IRE)**[181] 7083 10-8-4 **83** .... BMcHugh(7) 12 59
(M W Easterby) *hld up: a in rr* **80/1**

01-4 **12** 5 **Best Prospect (IRE)**[66] 563 7-9-1 **87** .... PhillipMakin 6 53
(M Dods) *s.i.s: hdwy over 8f out: rdn and wknd 2f out* **28/1**

253- **13** 6 **St Jean Cap Ferrat**[186] 6949 4-9-1 **87** ....(v) GeorgeBaker 4 41
(P J Hobbs) *s.i.s: hld up: rdn and hung out lft fr over 3f out: wknd over 2f out: eased* **9/2**[3]

2m 13.05s (-1.25) **Going Correction** +0.075s/f (Good) **13** Ran SP% **121.2**
Speed ratings (Par 107): **108,107,107,105,105 102,101,99,95,95 95,91,86**
toteswinger: 1&2 £12.70, 1&3 £50.70, 2&3 £13.00 CSF £47.04 CT £603.07 TOTE £7.00: £1.50, £3.20, £5.20; EX 63.40.
Owner Cliveden Stud **Bred** Cliveden Stud Ltd **Trained** Newmarket, Suffolk

FOCUS
A very interesting handicap but the pace was very steady until the final half-mile. The form looks decent for the grade, with the first two unexposed and the third well handicapped on his old form.

NOTEBOOK
Stone Of Scone, absent after a minor setback since taking a maiden at Great Leighs on only his second start in May, is a giant of a horse. He was friendless in the market and came from last to first from his outside draw. A half-brother to an Eclipse winner, there is much better to come and he must be kept on the right side. (op 9-2)
Red Jade, in contrast, was very well backed. Snapped up for 70,000gns after taking a maiden in good style here on only his second start, struck the front looking the likely winner only to miss out in the final strides. He looks sure to win races for his new connections. (op 9-2)
Wiggy Smith, resuming 5lb higher after signing off with success at Leicester in October, is now in the veteran stage. He too stayed on from well off the pace. He is clearly back to his best now reunited with his former trainer. (op 20-1 tchd 25-1)
Hurlingham, out of luck on his return, was another to make ground from off the pace. He raced on the inner which may have been the slowest part of the track. (op 22-1)
Mull Of Dubai showed a return to form in time for Chester, but he is 4lb higher than for his win there last May. (op 14-1 tchd 16-1)
Bullet Man(USA) stayed on from the rear. This lightly raced type will be of interest when stepped up in trip. (op 11-1)
Ansells Pride(IRE) ambled round in front before going for home on straightening up. He has yet to win beyond a mile. (tchd 40-1)
Prairie Storm, resuming from a 7lb higher mark, found this opposition much tougher than his success here in November on his final start last term. (op 17-2)
St Jean Cap Ferrat Official explanation: jockey said the gelding had no more to give

1594 NOTTINGHAMRACECOURSE.CO.UK H'CAP 1m 2f 50y
7:35 (7:37) (Class 6) (0-60,60) 3-Y-O **£2,047** (£604; £302) **Stalls** Low

Form RPR

600- **1** **Loulou (USA)**[170] 7257 3-9-0 **56** .... JimmyFortune 5 62
(S A Callaghan) *s.i.s: sn chsng ldrs: led 8f out: drvn out* **17/2**[3]

4-00 **2** 1¼ **Rebel Prince (IRE)**[33] 970 3-8-11 **53** .... EdwardCreighton 1 56
(M G Quinlan) *prom: racd keenly: rdn to chse wnr over 2f out: ev ch over 1f out: styd on same pce ins fnl f* **50/1**

-313 **3** ½ **Dark Ranger**[25] 1106 3-8-13 **55** .... RobertHavlin 15 57
(T J Pitt) *prom: lost pl over 4f out: hdwy over 2f out: rdn and hung lft over 1f out: no ex ins fnl f* **15/2**[2]

00-0 **4** 1¾ **Taste The Wine (IRE)**[20] 1193 3-9-2 **58** .... GeorgeBaker 3 57+
(J S Moore) *hld up: stl last and plenty to do over 2f out: hdwy over 1f out: hung lft ins fnl f: nt rch ldrs* **11/1**

46-0 **5** 2¼ **Hawkleaf Flier (IRE)**[13] 1281 3-8-12 **54** .... DavidAllan 2 48
(T D Easterby) *s.i.s: hld up: hdwy over 2f out: sn rdn: wknd ins fnl f* **33/1**

0006 **6** 2½ **King's Chorister**[10] 1363 3-8-13 **55** ....(t) NCallan 10 44
(Miss Gay Kelleway) *hld up: racd keenly: hdwy over 2f out: rdn over 1f out: wknd fnl f* **9/2**[1]

400- **7** 6 **Superstitious Me (IRE)**[220] 6135 3-8-13 **55** .... TonyCulhane 8 32
(B Palling) *trckd ldrs: racd keenly: rdn: hung lft and wknd over 1f out* **50/1**

0040 **8** shd **Nicky Nutjob (GER)**[10] 1363 3-8-11 **53** .... JerryO'Dwyer 4 30
(J Pearce) *hld up in tch: racd keenly: lost pl 6f out: hrd rdn over 2f out: sn wknd* **16/1**

006- **9** 1¼ **Sapphire Rose**[216] 6207 3-9-3 **59** .... TolleyDean 6 33
(J G Portman) *led 2f: chsd wnr tl rdn 3f out: wknd over 1f out* **16/1**

000- **10** 2½ **Great Western (USA)**[173] 7204 3-8-10 **52** .... TomEaves 9 21
(P F I Cole) *s.i.s: sn pushed along and prom: wknd over 2f out* **9/1**

00-0 **11** 8 **Shakin John**[7] 1441 3-9-0 **56** .... DaneO'Neill 7 9
(E J O'Neill) *s.i.s: hdwy over 6f out: rdn over 3f out: sn wknd: eased over 1f out* **33/1**

000- **P** **Mister Standfast**[182] 7051 3-8-13 **60** .... WilliamCarson(5) 16 —
(J M P Eustace) *hld up: bhd whn p.u 6f out* **40/1**

2m 17.11s (2.81) **Going Correction** +0.075s/f (Good) **12** Ran SP% **82.8**
Speed ratings (Par 96): **91,90,89,88,86 84,79,79,78,76 70,—**
toteswinger: 1&2 £20.80, 1&3 £9.50, 2&3 £6.50. CSF £183.77 CT £939.92 TOTE £7.00: £1.60, £11.80, £2.10; EX 222.00.
Owner Saleh Al Homaizi & Imad Al Sagar **Bred** Gainsborough Farm Llc **Trained** Newmarket, Suffolk

FOCUS
A low-grade three-year-old handicap and much of the interest went out of the window when the Sir Mark Prescott handicap debutant Aestival, who dominated the market, misbehaved and refused to enter the stalls. The form looks very ordinary.
Loulou(USA) Official explanation: trainer's representative said, regarding the running and riding, that the filly was having her first run on turf and had benefitted from the step up in trip./

1595 RACING AGAIN 8TH MAY H'CAP 1m 75y
8:05 (8:08) (Class 5) (0-70,70) 3-Y-O **£3,238** (£963; £481; £240) **Stalls** Low

Form RPR

00-1 **1** **Postman**[5] 1481 3-8-13 **62** 6ex .... TomEaves 10 75
(B Smart) *mde all: rdn over 1f out: styd on wl* **11/4**[1]

1421 **2** 4 **Wunder Strike (USA)**[3] 1516 3-8-10 **59** 6ex ....(p) PatCosgrave 7 62
(J R Boyle) *chsd wnr tl 7f out: wnt 2nd again over 3f out: rdn over 1f out: styd on same pce* **9/2**[2]

06-5 **3** 1½ **North Cape (USA)**[15] 1252 3-9-5 **68** .... DaneO'Neill 14 68
(H Candy) *a.p: rdn over 1f out: styd on same pce* **5/1**[3]

00-0 **4** 1¼ **Flashgun (USA)**[92] 295 3-7-13 **53** .... NicolPolli(5) 9 50
(M G Quinlan) *plld hrd and prom: rdn over 2f out: styd on same pce* **50/1**

400- **5** ½ **Dark Echoes**[222] 6051 3-8-11 **60** .... TonyHamilton 5 56
(Jedd O'Keeffe) *hld up: racd keenly: hdwy over 2f out: sn rdn: styd on same pce appr fnl f* **50/1**

030- **6** ½ **Incendo**[182] 7054 3-9-2 **65** .... NCallan 15 60+
(J R Fanshawe) *hld up: hdwy over 2f out: swtchd rt over 1f out: sn rdn: wknd fnl f* **7/1**

640- **7** 1½ **Tapis Wizard**[242] 5447 3-9-7 **70** .... PaulMulrennan 17 61+
(M W Easterby) *s.i.s: hld up: nvr nr to chal* **33/1**

55-5 **8** 1½ **Ponting (IRE)**[41] 869 3-9-1 **64** .... GeorgeBaker 4 52+
(R M Beckett) *hld up: rdn over 2f out: n.d* **9/2**[2]

003- **9** ¾ **Venture Capitalist**[176] 7170 3-8-8 **64** ow1 .... MJMurphy(7) 13 50+
(L M Cumani) *broke wl: sn stdd and lost pl: shkn up over 2f out: nvr nr to chal* **12/1**

411 **10** 2¼ **Special Cuvee**[14] 1270 3-9-6 **69** .... PhillipMakin 2 50
(A B Haynes) *hld up: rdn over 2f out: a in rr* **9/1**

5-36 **11** 12 **First Blade**[7] 1437 3-8-6 **55** .... FrankieMcDonald 6 8
(S R Bowring) *plld hrd and prom: wknd over 2f out* **40/1**

500- **12** 18 **Shanavaz**[213] 6291 3-9-5 **68** .... PaulHanagan 12 —
(Mrs G S Rees) *dwlt: hld up: a in rr: wknd over 3f out* **100/1**

-654 **13** 2¾ **Green Dynasty (IRE)**[60] 716 3-9-3 **66** .... RoystonFfrench 11 —
(M Johnston) *prom: chsd winne over 7f out tl rdn over 3f out: wknd over 2f out* **25/1**

1m 50.42s (0.82) **Going Correction** +0.075s/f (Good) **13** Ran SP% **124.0**
Speed ratings (Par 98): **98,94,92,91,90 90,88,87,86,84 72,54,51**
toteswinger: 1&2 £3.90, 1&3 £5.70, 2&3 £5.60. CSF £14.88 CT £63.98 TOTE £5.50: £1.70, £1.70, £2.10; EX 16.10 Place 6: £110.04 Place 5: £61.57.
Owner Crossfields Racing **Bred** Newsells Park Stud **Trained** Hambleton, N Yorks

FOCUS
A modest three-year-old handicap and another run at just a steady pace. The first three were in the first three throughout. It has been rated around the runner-up to his Leicester win.
Shanavaz Official explanation: jockey said the filly had a breathing proble
Green Dynasty(IRE) Official explanation: jockey said the gelding lost its action
T/Jkpt: Not won. T/Plt: £401.20 to a £1 stake. Pool: £64,169.00. 116.75 winning tickets. T/Qpdt: £12.10 to a £1 stake. Pool: £5,510.95. 334.40 winning tickets. CR

1482 CHANTILLY (R-H)
Tuesday, April 28

OFFICIAL GOING: Soft

1597a PRIX ALLEZ FRANCE (GROUP 3) (F&M) 1m 2f
2:25 (2:29) 4-Y-O+ **£38,835** (£15,534; £11,650; £7,767; £3,883)

RPR

1 **Shemima**[206] 6494 4-9-0 .... CSoumillon 2 110
(A De Royer-Dupre, France) *in midfield on outside: 5th st: rdn to ld 150yds out: r.o wl* **57/10**

2 snk **Tres Rapide (IRE)**[163] 4-8-9 .... GMosse 3 105
(H-A Pantall, France) *racd in 8th: hrd rdn in 7th 1 1/2f out: styd on u.str.p towards outside to take 2nd 80yds out: nrst fin* **17/1**

3 1½ **Albisola (IRE)**[183] 7037 4-9-0 .... JVictoire 10 107
(Robert Collet, France) *rel to r swishing tail and lost 10 l: mde contact after 3f: stl last whn swtchd outside 2f out: styd on to take 3rd cl home* **74/10**

4 hd **Salve Germania (IRE)**[198] 6691 4-8-9 .... ASuborics 8 102
(W Hickst, Germany) *hld up: 7th on ins st: effrt and n.m.r under 1 1/2f out: styd on fnl f* **46/1**

5 ½ **Danse Grecque (USA)**[19] 4-8-7 .... ACrastus 5 99
(E Lellouche, France) *racd in 3rd: 2nd st: led 1 1/2f out to 150yds out: one pce* **23/10**[1]

6 1 **Goose Bay (GER)**[183] 7037 4-9-2 .... DBonilla 4 106
(F Head, France) *racd in 2nd: 3rd st: outpcd under 2f out: kpt on again against ins rail fr over 1f out* **20/1**

7 nk **Rainbow Dancing**[22] 1166 4-8-9 .... DBoeuf 6 98
(Mlle H Van Zuylen, France) *set solid pce: hdd 1 1/2f out: one pce* **54/10**[3]

8 hd **Diyakalanie (FR)**[23] 1144 5-8-9 .... SPasquier 7 98
(Y De Nicolay, France) *racd in 9th: rdn on outside under 2f out: no imp* **19/5**[2]

9 hd **Stella Di Quattro**[23] 1143 5-8-9 .... OPeslier 9 97
(Uwe Ostmann, Germany) *in tch: 4th st: effrt and n.m.r 1 1/2f out: sn btn* **29/1**

10 ¾ **Tubular Bells (USA)**[19] 4-8-7 .... MGuyon 1 94
(H-A Pantall, France) *4th early: 6th st on ins: no room towards ins fr 1 1/2f out tl cl home: unlucky* **16/1**

2m 6.20s (1.40) **10** Ran SP% **115.3**
PARI-MUTUEL: WIN 6.70; PL 2.60, 4.30, 2.90; DF 39.40.
Owner H H Aga Khan **Bred** H H The Aga Khan's Studs Sc **Trained** Chantilly, France

NOTEBOOK
Shemima, who was winning over a distance short of her best, looks set to have a very successful four-year-old career. In mid-division early on, she came with a progressive run to take control at the furlong marker and then stayed on gamely to the end. Further improvement can certainly be expected, and she now heads for the Prix Corrida. The longer Prix Vermeille in September will certainly be a target, too.
Tres Rapide(IRE), who was given a waiting race and wasn't asked for her effort until halfway up the straight, came with a sweeping late run but could never quite peg back the winner. She certainly has a good turn of foot.
Albisola(IRE) can be considered very unlucky. She sat in the stalls and was reluctant to enter them before the race. After losing at least six lengths at the start, she raced in last position for much of the race and then came with an excellent late run up the middle of the track from a furlong and a half out. This effort augurs well for the future.
Salve Germania(IRE), seventh on the rail in the early stages, was hampered when making her challenge, before running on at the end. She was probably unlucky not to take third place.

ASCOT (R-H)
Wednesday, April 29

OFFICIAL GOING: Good to firm (good in places)
Wind: Modest, half against Weather: Bright

1598 ALAN MERRITT MEMORIAL CONDITIONS STKS 5f
2:10 (2:11) (Class 3) 2-Y-O **£6,542** (£1,959; £979; £490; £244) **Stalls** Low

Form RPR

1 **1** **Red Jazz (USA)**[23] 1147 2-9-1 0 .... MichaelHills 5 95
(B W Hills) *trckd ldrs: rdn over 1f out: r.o to ld fnl 100yds: rdn out* **1/2**[1]

211 **2** ½ **Archers Road (IRE)**[25] 1126 2-8-10 0 .... MCGeran(5) 3 93
(M R Channon) *chsd ldrs: rdn to ld and edgd lft over 1f out: hdd and no ex fnl 100yds* **10/1**[3]

02 **3** 3¼ **Little Perisher**[3] 1534 2-8-6 0 .... MartinLane(5) 1 77
(A P Jarvis) *wnt rt s and s.i.s: sn in tch: rdn to ld 2f out: hdd over 1f out: wknd fnl f* **50/1**

1 **4** 1¼ **Fratellino**[14] 1277 2-8-11 0 .... LDettori 4 72
(A J McCabe) *led: rdn and hdd 2f out: wknd ent fnl f* **16/1**

1 5 1/2 **Walkingonthemoon**[12] 1323 2-9-1 0 RichardKingscote 6 74
(Tom Dascombe) *chsd ldrs tl jst over 2f out: edgd lft and wknd jst over 1f out* **11/4**[2]

61.32 secs (0.82) **Going Correction** +0.25s/f (Good) **5** Ran SP% **110.3**
Speed ratings (Par 96): **103,102,97,95,94**
toteswinger: 1&2 £6.10. CSF £6.66 TOTE £1.50: £1.10, £3.70; EX 5.50.
Owner R J Arculli **Bred** William F Murphy & Annabel Murphy **Trained** Lambourn, Berks

FOCUS
Following a warm and sunny morning the ground was described as good to firm (good in places) and the riders reported that it was riding fast with no jar. This looked likely to be an informative juvenile contest, but it is questionable now whether it produced the Royal Ascot contender it had promised.

NOTEBOOK
Red Jazz(USA) was sent off at prohibitive odds and got the job done, but he was only workmanlike in victory and was given a real race by the more experienced runner-up. On his toes beforehand, he didn't really look to improve on his debut effort, and while he will now be aimed at the Coventry, where the extra furlong and stronger pace is expected to suit, it will be a surprise if he proves good enough to win it. (op 4-7)
Archers Road(IRE), who was arguably lucky to win at Newcastle last time, hung over to the rail under pressure so it was a good thing for him that he was drawn low. This was a solid effort under conditions that clearly suit, but he seems to have his limitations. (op 8-1 tchd 11-1)
Little Perisher, making a quick reappearance after finishing second at Brighton three days earlier, reversed Newbury form with the disappointing Walkingonthemoon on this quicker ground. Drawn nearest the stands' rail, this was probably a personal-best effort from him, although he does not really look up to this class. (op 40-1)
Fratellino, winner of a minor Beverley heat on his debut, showed pace wider out but was easily seen off. He needs to drop back in grade. (op 12-1)
Walkingonthemoon, whose trainer had warned that he might not improve a great deal for his debut when a gambled-on winner, was still disappointing. The ground was very different from that which he encountered at Newbury, though, and perhaps he needs cut to be seen at his best. (op 7-2 tchd 4-1)

1599 X FACTOR STKS (CONDITIONS RACE) (FILLIES) 1m (R)
2:45 (2:47) (Class 3) 3-Y-O

£7,477 (£2,239; £1,119; £560; £279; £140) **Stalls** High

Form				RPR
1-	1		**Apple Charlotte**[179] 7140 3-9-1 78 IanMongan 1 (H R A Cecil) *t.k.h: chsd ldr: rdn to ld wl over 1f out: r.o wl and drew clr fnl 100yds* **11/2**[3]	102+
060-	2	3 1/4	**Ahla Wasahl**[179] 7144 3-8-12 88 AhmedAjtebi(3) 4 (D M Simcock) *led: rdn over 2f out: hdd over 1f out: kpt on one pce ins fnl f* **33/1**	95
40-4	3	2 3/4	**Rose Diamond (IRE)**[14] 1292 3-9-1 100 RyanMoore 8 (R Charlton) *t.k.h: chsd ldrs: rdn and unable qckn over 2f out: plugged on same pce and no ch w ldng pair fr over 1f out* **15/8**[1]	89
251-	4	nk	**Uvinza**[208] 6432 3-8-12 98 JimCrowley 6 (W J Knight) *hld up in tch in rr: rdn and edgd rt jst over 2f out: sn drvn and no imp* **7/1**	85
	5	1 1/2	**Arwaah (IRE)** 3-8-9 0 RHills 3 (M P Tregoning) *s.i.s: t.k.h: hld up in last pair: swtchd lft and effrt jst over 2f out: no prog over 1f out: edgd rt and wknd fnl f* **4/1**[2]	79+
116-	6	2 3/4	**Honest Quality (USA)**[186] 6982 3-9-8 98 EddieAhern 5 (H R A Cecil) *t.k.h early: hld up in tch: rdn over 2f out: wknd wl over 1f out: no ch fnl f* **8/1**	85
50-1	7	4 1/2	**Sanvean (IRE)**[49] 800 3-9-1 88 DarryllHolland 7 (M R Channon) *s.i.s: hld up in last pair: rdn and no rspnse 3f out: sn lost tch* **33/1**	68
12-0	8	19	**Vitoria (IRE)**[14] 1291 3-9-1 90 RichardMullen 2 (B Smart) *in tch: rdn and struggling over 2f out: wl bhd over 1f out: eased ins fnl f: t.o* **7/1**	24

1m 43.39s (2.69) **Going Correction** +0.25s/f (Good) **8** Ran SP% **112.2**
Speed ratings (Par 99): **97,93,91,90,89 86,81,62**
toteswinger: 1&2 £23.40, 1&3 £3.60, 2&3 £12.70. CSF £145.85 TOTE £6.10: £1.80, £6.90, £1.10; EX 239.70 Trifecta £832.30 Part won. Pool: £1,124,85 - 0.55 winning units..
Owner De La Warr Racing **Bred** Hascombe And Valiant Studs **Trained** Newmarket, Suffolk

FOCUS
The rail on the final bend was out about eight metres. An interesting fillies' conditions race, but the early pace was nothing too special and it paid to race handily.

NOTEBOOK
Apple Charlotte had made a good impression when winning on her debut in a backend Newmarket maiden, and, although she had a good deal on her plate in this higher grade strictly on the ratings, her Coronation Stakes entry gave an indication of the regard in which she's held. Having stalked the leader into the straight, she picked up well when asked and eventually pulled nicely clear. Her work in the lead-up to this race had apparently not been that great and she was a bit woolly in the paddock beforehand, so improvement can be expected, and a trip to York for the Listed Michael Seely Memorial Stakes at the Dante meeting is next up for her. (tchd 7-1)
Ahla Wasahl, who didn't really go on in the second half of her two-year-old campaign, was given a good ride from the front by Ahmed Ajtebi, whose 3lb claim is a gift, on his first ride back in this country. Winding it up in the straight, the filly found the winner too classy but she finished comfortably in front of the rest. She could well struggle to confirm the form in a more strongly run race. (tchd 40-1)
Rose Diamond(IRE) appeared to set the standard and promised to be suited by the step up to a mile following her fourth over an inadequate 7f in the Free Handicap. The tactical nature of the race was not in her favour, though, and while she kept on in the straight, the first two had very much got first run on her. (op 7-4 tchd 2-1)
Uvinza, whose rating of 98 is based on finishing fifth of seven in the May Hill, hadn't run on ground this quick before. She ran no better than okay, and it remains to be seen whether she can make the grade this year. (op 10-1)
Arwaah(IRE) ◆ was the buzz horse of the race, having been well backed throughout the day. However, although evidently well regarded, this looked a big ask for a filly making her debut, especially one with a pedigree that suggests a distance closer to 1m4f would be more her thing. Her Oaks entry seemed to back that theory up, and the nail in her coffin was that she was held up towards the rear in a tactical race. She ran with plenty of promise in the circumstances, wasn't knocked about in the closing stages, and can step up on this when put over a longer trip. (op 9-2 tchd 7-2)
Honest Quality(USA) had the ground to suit but had a stiff task under her 7lb penalty, and being held up in a steadily run contest was never going to help her cause. (op 7-1 tchd 13-2)
Sanvean(IRE) Official explanation: jockey said filly lost its action

1600 BRITAIN'S GOT TALENT PARADISE STKS (LISTED RACE) 1m (S)
3:20 (3:21) (Class 1) 4-Y-O+ **£23,782** (£9,682; £5,382) **Stalls** Low

Form				RPR
160-	1		**Perfect Stride**[208] 6440 4-9-0 100 RyanMoore 7 (Sir Michael Stoute) *bmpd s: dropped in and hld up in last pl: rdn and hdwy over 2f out: ev ch over 1f out: drvn fnl f: jst hld: fin 2nd, nse: awrdd r* **11/4**[2]	113
230-	2	2 3/4	**Laa Rayb (USA)**[136] 7684 5-9-0 115 RoystonFfrench 6 (M Johnston) *wnt rt and bmpd rival s: w ldr: ev ch and rdn jst over 2f out: drvn over 1f out: wknd ins fnl f: fin 3rd, nse and 2 3/4l: plcd 2nd* **15/8**[1]	107
330-	3	nk	**Ordnance Row**[193] 6814 6-9-0 112 RichardHughes 5 (R Hannon) *led at stdy gallop: rdn and qcknd over 2f out: hdd 1f out: edgd rt and wknd ins fnl f: fin 4th, nse, 2 3/4l and nk: plcd 3rd* **4/1**	106
0R-R	R		**Don't Panic (IRE)**[32] 997 5-9-0 104 (b[1]) AlanMunro 4 (P W Chapple-Hyam) *ref to r* **16/1**	—
020-	D		**General Eliott (IRE)**[151] 7492 4-9-0 109 LDettori 3 (P F I Cole) *trckd ldng pair: rdn and effrt over 2f out: drvn and ev ch over 1f out: led 1f out: hld on gamely: fin 1st, nse: disq (banned subs in sample)* **3/1**[3]	113

1m 42.53s (1.93) **Going Correction** +0.25s/f (Good) **5** Ran SP% **112.3**
Speed ratings (Par 111): **99,97,96,—,100**
toteswinger: 1&2 £5.50. CSF £11.81 TOTE £4.00: £1.70, £1.70; EX 11.20.
Owner Saeed Suhail **Bred** Bloomsbury Stud **Trained** Newmarket, Suffolk

FOCUS
With two non-runners and Don't Panic once again failing to come out of the stalls, only four took part, and it was no surprise that the race was very tactical, with a steady early gallop and a sprint to the line.

NOTEBOOK
Perfect Stride is another who has always had a taller reputation than his racecourse performances have so far justified. Entries in the Lockinge and Queen Anne suggest connections retain the faith, and this was a good reappearance. He travels and can quicken, and rattling fast ground seems to show him at his best. (tchd 3-1)
Laa Rayb(USA), who progressed through handicaps to take a French Group 3 and a place in Group 2 company last year, had conditions to suit, but he has never looked entirely straightforward, and that was the case here. (op 9-4 tchd 5-2)
Ordnance Row had the run of the race out in front, but he needed his reappearance last year and it is probable that he will come on for this one too. (tchd 5-1)
General Eliott(IRE) and Perfect Stride both quickened up well from behind and he just got the verdict on the nod. Gelded over the winter, he has a history of going well fresh, and, while he has always been well regarded - he ran in the French Guineas last year - one would have to question whether he will build on this next time unless given a bit of a break. His trainer, however, plans to run him in a Listed race at Longchamp in ten days' time. (op 10-3 tchd 11-4)

1601 WOODCOTE STUD SAGARO STKS (GROUP 3) 2m
3:55 (3:55) (Class 1) 4-Y-O+ **£36,900** (£13,988; £7,000; £3,490; £1,748) **Stalls** High

Form				RPR
114-	1		**Patkai (IRE)**[249] 5263 4-8-11 109 RyanMoore 5 (Sir Michael Stoute) *chsd ldng pair tl wnt 2nd over 5f out: led 3f out: sn rdn clr: styd on strly and in n.d after* **2/5**[1]	116+
016-	2	9	**Mischief Making (USA)**[151] 7491 4-8-8 100 TGMcLaughlin 4 (E A L Dunlop) *hld up in 4th pl: rdn and hdwy jst over 3f out: jostled wl over 2f out: sn chsd clr wnr: no imp and edgd rt wl over 1f out* **14/1**	102
040-	3	9	**Baddam**[20] 6817 7-9-1 89 RichardHughes 2 (Ian Williams) *led for 1f: chsd ldr tl over 5f out: rdn and dropped to last pl over 3f out: sn wl btn: styd on again fnl f to go modest 3rd fnl 50yds* **33/1**	94
6100	4	2	**Young Mick**[31] 1017 7-9-1 103 (v) JohnEgan 6 (G G Margarson) *hld up in last pl: hdwy 8f out: chsd ldng pair 4f out: rdn 3f out: sn btn: tired and edgd rt over 1f out: lost 4th pl fnl 50yds* **11/1**[3]	92
150-	5	4 1/2	**Tungsten Strike (USA)**[213] 6306 8-9-1 108 (p) DarryllHolland 1 (Mrs A J Perrett) *chsd ldr tl led after 1f: rdn and hdd 3f out: edgd lft and bmpd rival wl over 2f out: sn wknd* **4/1**[2]	86

3m 30.23s (1.23) **Going Correction** +0.25s/f (Good)
WFA 4 from 6yo+ 4lb **5** Ran SP% **109.4**
Speed ratings (Par 113): **115,110,106,105,102**
toteswinger: 1&2 £5.40. CSF £7.24 TOTE £1.40: £1.10, £3.60; EX 6.70.
Owner Ballymacoll Stud **Bred** Ballymacoll Stud Farm Ltd **Trained** Newmarket, Suffolk

FOCUS
Not the strongest Group 3 race ever run, but it could be a very informative one with this season's Cup races in mind.

NOTEBOOK
Patkai(IRE), last year's Queen's Vase winner, came in for solid support on his seasonal reappearance, and he landed the odds in emphatic fashion, drawing clear from the turn in for a decisive success which saw his odds for the Gold Cup at the Royal meeting slashed to a general 4-1. He is now disputing favouritism with the reigning champ Yeats, and judged on their comeback runs their careers could well be going in opposite directions. Another half mile is likely to suit him even better as he stays particularly well, and this progressive four-year-old looks sure to prove a major contender, not only back here in June, but also in the other Cup races. He is likely to have one more outing before the Gold Cup, either in the Yorkshire Cup or the Henry II Stakes. (op 8-15 tchd 4-7 and 8-13 in a place)
Mischief Making(USA), the only filly in the field, has an official rating of 100 but she had always threatened to improve for a real stamina test, and that appears to be the case. The Park Hill would appear to be the natural long-term target for her. (tchd 16-1)
Baddam, fit from an outing over hurdles earlier in the month, is not up to this class these days. Having been left behind at the top of the straight, he was eased, only for his rider to get going again to ensure he grabbed third as Young Mick and Tungsten Strike weakened. (op 28-1 tchd 40-1)
Young Mick likes it here, but he simply did not get home over this longer distance. A drop back to 1m4f is what he needs, but his current mark leaves him difficult to place. (op 10-1 tchd 12-1)
Tungsten Strike(USA), who won this in 2007 and has gone well fresh in the past, set out to make all as usual, but he was brushed away from the turn in and might have needed this more than connections had thought. (op 10-3 tchd 3-1)

1602 CLEANEVENT PAVILION STKS (LISTED RACE) 6f
4:30 (4:30) (Class 1) 3-Y-O

£22,708 (£8,608; £4,308; £2,148; £1,076; £540) **Stalls** Low

Form				RPR
521-	1		**Total Gallery (IRE)**[207] 6483 3-9-0 103 LPKeniry 3 (J S Moore) *t.k.h: trckd ldrs on stands' rail: plld out and hdwy over 2f out: jnd ldr on bit 2f out: shkn up to ld over 1f out: drvn ent fnl f: hld on wl fnl 100yds* **11/2**	106+
12-4	2	nk	**Enderby Spirit (GR)**[27] 1085 3-8-11 96 RichardMullen 1 (B Smart) *led towards stands' rail: rdn and hdd over 1f out: kpt on gamely u.p: hld fnl 50yds* **12/1**	102
06-0	3	1 3/4	**Jobe (USA)**[25] 1118 3-8-11 105 NCallan 9 (K A Ryan) *wnt rt s: w ldr towards centre: ev ch and rdn 2f out: no ex fnl f* **14/1**	96
1152	4	1/2	**Five Star Junior (USA)**[32] 1002 3-8-11 100 ShaneKelly 4 (Mrs L Stubbs) *hld up in tch: swtchd rt and effrt over 2f out: chsd ldrs and drvn jst over 1f out: no imp fnl f* **14/1**	94
11-2	5	2 1/2	**Elnawin**[39] 912 3-9-2 110 PatDobbs 5 (R Hannon) *t.k.h: trckd ldrs: rdn and unable qck over 2f out: wknd wl over 1f out* **11/4**[2]	91
40-4	6	hd	**Damien (IRE)**[39] 912 3-8-11 107 MichaelHills 6 (B W Hills) *in tch: rdn and effrt 2f out: unable qck wl over 1f out: wknd ent fnl f* **5/2**[1]	86

260- **7** *6* **Kerrys Requiem (IRE)**[229] 5852 3-8-6 98 TPO'Shea 10 62
(M R Channon) *sltly hmpd s: t.k.h early: sn dropped in and settled: rdn over 2f out: sn wl btn* **33/1**

110- **8** *6* **Magic Cat**[200] 6644 3-9-0 107 AndrewElliott 8 50
(K R Burke) *in tch: rdn 3f out: sn struggling: no ch fnl 2f* **12/1**

05-5 **9** *20* **Marine Boy (IRE)**[14] 1292 3-8-11 109 RichardKingscote 7 —
(Tom Dascombe) *v.s.a and lost many l s: a t.o: eased fnl f* **5/1**[3]

1m 14.87s (0.47) **Going Correction** +0.25s/f (Good) **9** Ran SP% **118.9**
Speed ratings (Par 106): **106,105,103,102,99 99,91,83,56**
toteswinger: 1&2 £10.00, 1&3 £11.80, 2&3 £15.60. CSF £70.84 TOTE £6.30: £1.90, £4.20, £3.30; EX 68.70 Trifecta £711.60 Part won. Pool: £961.73 - 0.30 winning units..
Owner Coleman Bloodstock Limited **Bred** Michael Woodlock And Seamus Kennedy **Trained** Upper Lambourn, Berks
■ Stewards' Enquiry : L P Keniry one-day ban: careless riding (May 13)

FOCUS
An open Listed race for three-year-olds.

NOTEBOOK
Total Gallery(IRE) came in for support beforehand and, although it got a bit desperate close home, the way he travelled through the race suggests he's worthy of rating higher than the bare winning margin. He quickened up well approaching the furlong marker but the sixth furlong just seemed to stretch his stamina, and it's easy to see why his connections are now planning to drop him back to the minimum trip. The King's Stand, for which he's 40-1 with Coral, could now be on his agenda, providing the ground isn't too quick. (op 17-2 tchd 9-1)
Enderby Spirit(GR) was said to have needed his reappearance at Leicester and promised to strip fitter here. With the rail to help, he showed good speed throughout and battled back after being headed. Easier ground would have suited him ideally. (op 14-1 tchd 16-1)
Jobe(USA), dropping back to sprinting for the first time since the Middle Park, showed pace wider out, but gives the distinct impression that he will prove difficult to place this season. (tchd 12-1)
Five Star Junior(USA), progressive on Polytrack over the winter, ran quite well considering he had been stuffed on his previous two starts on turf. He is likely to remain a better horse on artificial surfaces, though, which is a view backed up by his pedigree. (op 20-1)
Elnawin, who was saddled with a 5lb penalty for winning a Group 3 race, raced a touch keenly and wandered around under pressure. He did not come up to expectations here, and is another who might appreciate getting back on the Polytrack, although whether an opportunity can be found for him remains to be seen. (op 9-4 tchd 2-1)
Damien(IRE) was also disappointing, but it's possible the ground was on the quick side for him. (op 10-3 tchd 7-2)
Marine Boy(IRE) lost any chance he had with a very slow start, and his list of 'issues' grows ever longer. Official explanation: jockey said gelding missed the break (op 9-2 tchd 6-1)

1603 KELTBRAY H'CAP — 1m (S)
5:05 (5:06) (Class 4) (0-85,85) 4-Y-0+ **£7,123** (£2,119; £1,059; £529) **Stalls** Low

Form RPR

05-5 **1** **Trafalgar Bay (IRE)**[31] 1016 6-9-5 82 JimCrowley 4 98
(K R Burke) *v.s.a: bhd: hdwy 3f out: gng wl looking for run over 1f out: rdn to chse ldr and edgd lft ins fnl f: r.o strly to ld fnl 75yds: gng away at fin* **8/1**[2]

006- **2** *1 1/4* **Mount Hadley (USA)**[189] 6900 5-8-9 72 (v) WilliamBuick 8 85
(G A Butler) *led: rdn jst over 2f out: clr over 1f out: hdd and no ex fnl 75yds* **6/1**[1]

023- **3** *4* **Talayeb**[287] 4085 4-8-9 72 RHills 10 76
(M P Tregoning) *chsd ldrs: rdn to chse ldr 2f out: no imp and plugged on same pce after: lost 2nd ins fnl f* **14/1**

060- **4** *1* **Last Three Minutes (IRE)**[215] 6242 4-9-5 82 TGMcLaughlin 12 84
(E A L Dunlop) *s.i.s: towards rr: hdwy into midfield over 3f out: swtchd lft and squeezed through wl over 1f out: kpt on same pce u.p: wnt 4th wl ins fnl f* **11/1**

1131 **5** *1/2* **Highly Regal (IRE)**[21] 1187 4-9-0 77 (b) LPKeniry 9 77
(R A Teal) *hld up in tch: hdwy to chse ldrs jst over 2f out: rdn and hung lft wl over 1f out: wknd ins fnl f: lost 4th pl wl ins fnl f* **14/1**

-613 **6** *1 3/4* **Marajaa (IRE)**[13] 1316 7-9-0 77 AlanMunro 14 73+
(W J Musson) *hld up towards rr and grad crossed to stands' rail: switching rt looking for run fr jst over 2f out: kpt on fnl f: nvr threatened ldrs* **16/1**

2540 **7** *1/2* **Councellor (FR)**[54] 778 7-9-1 78 (t) DO'Donohoe 11 73
(Stef Liddiard) *chsd ldrs: pushed along over 3f out: rdn jst over 2f out: wknd jst over 1f out* **33/1**

110- **8** *2* **Mister Ross**[152] 7470 4-9-3 80 RyanMoore 16 71+
(G L Moore) *sn wl bhd: clsd 1/2-way: swtchd to wd outside and hdwy over 2f out: no imp over 1f out* **12/1**

-041 **9** *1/2* **Grey Boy (GER)**[12] 1320 8-8-13 76 ShaneKelly 19 66
(A W Carroll) *wl bhd: switching out rt looking for run jst over 2f out: kpt on fnl f: nvr trbld ldrs* **14/1**

6-50 **10** *nk* **Bomber Command (USA)**[18] 1212 6-8-12 78 (v) PatrickHills(3) 3 67
(J W Hills) *in tch in midfield: rdn and unable qck whn hmpd wl over 1f out: no hdwy after: edgd lft ins fnl f* **20/1**

30-5 **11** *2 1/2* **Thunder Gorge (USA)**[28] 1067 4-8-10 73 SteveDrowne 1 56
(Mouse Hamilton-Fairley) *chsd ldrs: rdn wl over 3f out: wkng and towards rr whn bdly hmpd wl over 1f out: no ch after* **12/1**

016- **12** *1 1/4* **Blue Spartan (IRE)**[319] 3038 4-9-3 80 JamieSpencer 20 60+
(B J Meehan) *wl bhd: rdn over 4f out: styd on past btn horses fnl f: nvr a factor* **14/1**

13-5 **13** *8* **Eastern Gift**[14] 1283 4-9-8 85 NCallan 13 47
(Miss Gay Kelleway) *towards rr: hdwy towards outer over 2f out: drvn and no hdwy over 1f out: wl hld and eased fnl 100yds* **50/1**

6046 **14** *3/4* **Samarinda (USA)**[8] 1433 6-9-6 83 MartinDwyer 6 43
(Mrs P Sly) *chsd ldr tl 2f out: sn wknd u.p: eased ins fnl f* **10/1**[3]

14- **15** *3 1/4* **Priti Fabulous (IRE)**[199] 6684 4-9-6 83 DarryllHolland 15 36
(W J Haggas) *hld up towards rr: hdwy on outer jst over 2f out: drvn and no hdwy over 1f out: eased ins fnl f* **14/1**

320- **16** *1/2* **Ezdeyaad (USA)**[207] 6482 5-9-3 80 EddieAhern 5 31
(G A Swinbank) *awkward leaving stalls: sn chsng ldrs: rdn wl over 2f out: wkng whn hmpd wl over 1f out: eased ins fnl f* **16/1**

0101 **17** *28* **Brouhaha**[13] 1316 5-9-8 85 RichardKingscote 17 —
(Tom Dascombe) *chsd ldrs on outer: rdn and wknd over 2f out: eased fr over 1f out: t.o* **16/1**

143- **18** *12* **Highland Harvest**[380] 1365 5-8-13 76 RobertHavlin 2 —
(Jamie Poulton) *dwlt: sn chsng ldrs: rdn and struggling 3f out: wl bhd and eased fr over 1f out: t.o* **16/1**

221- **19** *6* **French Art**[254] 5150 4-9-7 84 LDettori 18 —
(N Tinkler) *t.k.h: hld up in midfield: rdn and wknd over 2f out: eased fr over 1f out: t.o* **20/1**

1m 42.03s (1.43) **Going Correction** +0.25s/f (Good) **19** Ran SP% **129.5**
Speed ratings (Par 105): **102,100,96,95,95 93,93,91,90,90 87,86,78,77,74 73,45,33,27**
toteswinger: 1&2 £12.50, 1&3 £25.90, 2&3 £21.30. CSF £55.07 CT £692.14 TOTE £10.50: £3.00, £2.20, £3.90, £3.50; EX 70.50 Trifecta £609.90 Part won. Pool: £824.21 - 0.20 winning units. Place 6 £92.88, Place 5 £66.08..
Owner Mogeely Stud & Mrs Maura Gittins **Bred** Patrick Hennessy **Trained** Middleham Moor, N Yorks

FOCUS
A very competitive handicap and the race developed towards the stands' side.
Highly Regal(IRE) Official explanation: jockey said gelding hung left
Bomber Command(USA) Official explanation: jockey said gelding was hampered
Brouhaha Official explanation: jockey said gelding never travelled
T/Jkpt: £10,790.60 to a £1 stake. Pool: £15,198.06. 1.00 winning ticket. T/Plt: £300.60 to a £1 stake. Pool: £101,303.20. 246.00 winning tickets. T/Qpdt: £160.00 to a £1 stake. Pool: £4,131.55. 19.10 winning tickets. SP

[1463] KEMPTON (A.W) (R-H)
Wednesday, April 29

OFFICIAL GOING: Standard
Wind: Fresh, half behind Weather: Sunny

1604 HAPPY 80TH BIRTHDAY DENNIS WRIGHT H'CAP — 1m 2f (P)
6:50 (6:50) (Class 5) (0-70,72) 4-Y-0+ **£2,590** (£770; £385; £192) **Stalls** High

Form RPR

205- **1** **Balnagore**[227] 5935 5-8-13 64 EddieAhern 10 74
(J L Dunlop) *mde all: set sedate pce: rdn and qcknd over 2f out: readily* **4/1**[1]

0330 **2** *2* **Lytham (IRE)**[12] 1318 8-8-2 60 TobyAtkinson(7) 6 66
(A W Carroll) *hld up towards rr: nt clr run over 2f out: hrd rdn and hdwy over 1f out: r.o to take 2nd fnl 75yds* **6/1**

2434 **3** *1 1/4* **Formidable Guest**[25] 1133 5-9-2 67 RobertHavlin 5 71
(J Pearce) *hld up in 5th: rdn to chse wnr wl over 1f out: one pce fnl f: lost 2nd fnl 75yds* **4/1**[1]

0-21 **4** *2 1/4* **Watchmaker**[9] 1409 6-9-7 72 6ex FergusSweeney 3 71
(Miss Tor Sturgis) *chsd ldrs: wd and lost pl bnd 2f out: kpt on again fnl f* **5/1**[2]

-200 **5** *nk* **Cinematic (IRE)**[21] 1192 6-9-4 69 PatCosgrave 4 67
(J R Boyle) *hld up in tch: rdn 3f out: disputing 6th and hld whn nt clr run over 1f out: styd on fnl f: fin lame* **25/1**

4243 **6** *shd* **Zero Cool (USA)**[42] 872 5-8-9 60 (p) SteveDrowne 9 58
(G L Moore) *prom: hrd rdn 2f out: no ex over 1f out* **11/2**[3]

0-50 **7** *3/4* **Ross Moor**[21] 1192 7-8-9 60 WilliamBuick 7 57
(Mike Murphy) *dwlt: hld up in last: rdn 2f out: sme late hdwy* **20/1**

1-10 **8** *1 1/2* **Sky Quest (IRE)**[12] 1318 11-8-6 64 NathanAlison(7) 2 58
(J R Boyle) *mid-div: hdwy on outside to chse ldrs 1/2-way: wd on bnd and wknd jst over 2f out* **20/1**

0-33 **9** *1 3/4* **Bramalea**[8] 1415 4-9-1 66 JimCrowley 8 56
(B W Duke) *t.k.h: chsd wnr tl wknd wl over 1f out* **11/2**[3]

/51- **10** *1 1/4* **Hanbrin Bhoy (IRE)**[432] 357 5-9-2 67 RoystonFfrench 1 55
(R Dickin) *stdd s: hld up towards rr: last and pushed along fnl 2f* **12/1**

2m 9.96s (1.96) **Going Correction** +0.30s/f (Slow) **10** Ran SP% **122.8**
Speed ratings (Par 103): **104,102,101,99,99 99,98,97,96,95**
toteswinger: 1&2 £5.60, 1&3 £2.90, 2&3 £5.40. CSF £29.03 CT £105.55 TOTE £6.50: £2.20, £2.50, £1.80; EX 41.10.
Owner Mrs Simon Boscawen **Bred** Mrs S A Lloyd **Trained** Arundel, W Sussex

FOCUS
A modest handicap.
Cinematic(IRE) Official explanation: vet said gelding returned lame

1605 DIGIBET MAIDEN FILLIES' STKS — 1m (P)
7:20 (7:28) (Class 5) 3-Y-0+ **£2,590** (£770; £385; £192) **Stalls** High

Form RPR

60- **1** **King's Starlet**[207] 6473 3-8-12 0 SteveDrowne 12 87
(H Morrison) *trckd ldrs on rail: rdn over 3f out: r.o to ld ins fnl f: sn clr: readily* **14/1**

2- **2** *3 1/4* **Flora Trevelyan**[165] 7341 3-8-12 0 AdamKirby 8 79
(W R Swinburn) *reluctant to enter stalls: trckd ldrs: led jst over 2f out tl ins fnl f: one pce* **7/4**[1]

62- **3** *1 3/4* **Queen Eleanor**[187] 6945 3-8-12 0 JimmyFortune 5 75
(J H M Gosden) *trckd ldrs: rdn over 3f out: wnt 3rd 1f out: styd on same pce* **9/4**[2]

4 *1 1/4* **Critical Path (IRE)** 3-8-12 0 WilliamBuick 14 72+
(A M Balding) *hld up in midfield: effrt whn hmpd on rail over 2f out: pushed along and r.o: promising* **33/1**

0- **5** *5* **Zeyadah (IRE)**[172] 7240 3-8-12 0 PhilipRobinson 13 61
(M A Jarvis) *sn rdn along in midfield: nt pce to trble ldrs fnl 2f* **8/1**

2 **6** *1 3/4* **Invincible Isle (IRE)**[20] 1198 3-8-12 0 IanMongan 4 57
(H R A Cecil) *plld hrd: w ldrs: bmpd after 2f: led 4f out tl jst over 2f out: wknd over 1f out* **3/1**[3]

\- **7** *2 3/4* **Polemica (IRE)** 3-8-12 0 StephenDonohoe 9 50
(E A L Dunlop) *s.i.s: bhd: rdn over 3f out: sme late hdwy* **50/1**

0- **8** *1 1/2* **Thegirlsgonewild (USA)**[198] 6696 3-8-12 0 JimmyQuinn 7 47
(H J L Dunlop) *bhd: pushed along 4f out: sme late hdwy* **50/1**

4 **9** *3 1/2* **Ermine And Velvet**[12] 1327 3-8-12 0 NCallan 10 39
(C E Brittain) *slt ld tl 4f out: wknd 2f out* **14/1**

0- **10** *4* **Flying Cloud (USA)**[179] 7141 3-8-12 0 MartinDwyer 6 30
(B J Meehan) *reluctant to enter stalls: w ldrs: jinked lft after 2f: wknd qckly 3f out* **50/1**

00- **11** *6* **Peace In Paradise (IRE)**[144] 7577 3-8-12 0 KirstyMilczarek 3 16
(J A R Toller) *mid-div over 3f: outpcd in rr whn wnt wd bnd 4f out: no ch after* **100/1**

12 *11* **Best Shot** 3-8-12 0 MichaelHills 1 —
(B W Hills) *outpcd in rr: wd bnd 4f out: sn wl bhd* **16/1**

0- **13** *38* **Russian Saint**[247] 5365 3-8-12 0 DarrenWilliams 2 —
(D Shaw) *mid-div 3f: wl bhd fr 1/2-way: eased fnl 2f* **100/1**

1m 41.17s (1.37) **Going Correction** +0.30s/f (Slow)
WFA 3 from 4yo 14lb **13** Ran SP% **133.3**
Speed ratings (Par 100): **105,101,100,98,93 92,89,87,84,80 74,63,25**
toteswinger: 1&2 £7.30, 1&3 £15.40, 2&3 £1.70. CSF £43.08 TOTE £23.40: £7.10, £1.10, £1.70; EX 102.60.
Owner Helena Springfield Ltd **Bred** Meon Valley Stud **Trained** East Ilsley, Berks

FOCUS
The race was delayed due to the reluctance of several of these fillies to get installed.

Ermine And Velvet Official explanation: jockey said filly had no more to give

1606 DIGIBET H'CAP 1m (P)
7:50 (7:54) (Class 6) (0-60,60) 4-Y-O+ £1,942 (£578; £288; £144) Stalls High

Form				RPR
2044	1		**Landucci**[28] 1065 8-9-4 60 ....(p) JamesDoyle 7	73
			(S Curran) *hld up towards rr: hdwy 2f out: led jst over 1f out: sn clr: edgd rt: comf* **12/1**	
5-00	2	4	**Munich (IRE)**[61] 708 5-9-4 60 .... LPKeniry 3	64
			(Norma Twomey) *prom: rdn to ld briefly over 1f out: nt pce of wnr* **25/1**	
-202	3	1 1/2	**Mister Trickster (IRE)**[20] 1199 8-8-13 55 .... RoystonFfrench 12	56+
			(R Dickin) *slowly away and lost 6 l: bhd: rdn over 2f out: hdwy and squeezed through over 1f out: nrst fin* **11/2**[2]	
054/	4	1/2	**Kickahead (USA)**[348] 2360 7-9-0 56 .... StephenDonohoe 4	55
			(Ian Williams) *mid-div: effrt over 2f out: styd on same pce* **33/1**	
6525	5	shd	**Takitwo**[27] 1080 6-9-3 59 .... SimonWhitworth 6	58
			(P D Cundell) *hld up in midfield: shkn up and hdwy over 1f out: wnt 3rd jst ins fnl f: one pce* **12/1**	
-200	6	4	**Inca Soldier (FR)**[16] 1258 6-9-1 57 .... PaulEddery 2	47
			(R C Guest) *t.k.h towards rr: rdn over 2f out: sme late hdwy: nt pce to chal* **33/1**	
30-6	7	nse	**James Pollard (IRE)**[21] 1194 4-9-2 58 .... JimmyFortune 5	48
			(D R C Elsworth) *sn led: hdd & wknd over 1f out* **11/2**[2]	
604-	8	1 3/4	**Art Market (CAN)**[262] 4910 6-9-3 59 .... DaneO'Neill 14	45
			(Miss Jo Crowley) *mid-div: lost pl over 2f out: n.d after* **12/1**	
4004	9	shd	**Ugenius**[16] 1258 5-9-2 58 .... TGMcLaughlin 11	47+
			(Mrs C A Dunnett) *t.k.h: in tch: rdn to press ldrs 2f out: n.m.r on rail over 1f out: sn lost pl* **12/1**	
0-00	10	1 3/4	**Ride A White Swan**[12] 1320 4-9-3 59 .... DarrenWilliams 9	41
			(D Shaw) *t.k.h in last: promising hdwy 2f out: hrd rdn over 1f out: sn wknd* **33/1**	
5-45	11	nk	**Daring Dream (GER)**[12] 1320 4-9-2 58 .... NCallan 10	39
			(A P Jarvis) *chsd ldrs: 4th and btn whn n.m.r over 1f out* **5/2**[1]	
04-0	12	2 1/4	**Another Try (IRE)**[28] 1074 4-8-10 57 .... MartinLane(5) 13	33
			(A P Jarvis) *prom: hrd rdn 2f out: sn wknd* **14/1**	
025-	13	8	**Cwm Rhondda (USA)**[212] 6337 4-9-3 59 ....(t) AlanMunro 1	16
			(P W Chapple-Hyam) *towards rr: rdn along fnl 5f: no ch fnl 2f* **8/1**[3]	
300-	14	7	**Robert Burns (IRE)**[195] 6762 4-9-4 60 ....(t) MartinDwyer 8	1
			(Miss D Mountain) *pressed ldrs tl wknd 2f out* **33/1**	

1m 41.91s (2.11) **Going Correction** +0.30s/f (Slow) 14 Ran SP% 123.5
Speed ratings (Par 101): **101,97,95,95,94 90,90,89,89,87 86,84,76,69**
toteswinger: 1&2 £128.40, 1&3 £25.40, 2&3 £27.60. CSF £294.76 CT £1868.43 TOTE £22.30: £5.10, £12.00, £1.90; EX 387.50.
Owner L M Power **Bred** D J And Mrs Deer **Trained** Hatford, Oxon
■ Stewards' Enquiry : Jimmy Fortune two-day ban: careless riding (May 13-14)

FOCUS
Seven of the 14 runners were maidens before the start and remain so after it.
James Pollard(IRE) Official explanation: jockey said gelding hung right

1607 DIGIBET.COM H'CAP 7f (P)
8:20 (8:21) (Class 4) (0-85,85) 4-Y-O+ £4,604 (£1,378; £689; £344; £171) Stalls High

Form				RPR
30-1	1		**Crown Choice**[21] 1185 4-8-13 80 .... AdamKirby 7	97+
			(W R Swinburn) *trckd ldr: led over 1f out: rdn clr: readily* **13/8**[1]	
22-0	2	3 3/4	**Woodcote Place**[14] 1288 6-8-12 79 .... JimCrowley 9	86
			(P R Chamings) *hld up in midfield: rdn and hdwy 2f out: wnt 2nd jst over 1f out: nt pce of wnr* **10/1**	
1312	3	3/4	**Jake The Snake (IRE)**[14] 1283 8-8-6 78 .... AmyBaker(5) 8	83
			(A W Carroll) *wnt lft s and missed break: t.k.h in rr: plld outside and rdn over 2f out: gd late hdwy* **10/1**	
32-3	4	1	**Prince Of Thebes (IRE)**[18] 1213 8-9-2 83 .... PaulDoe 5	85
			(M J Attwater) *t.k.h: prom: led 2f out tl over 1f out: no ex* **15/2**[3]	
55-2	5	1 3/4	**Wigram's Turn (USA)**[7] 1467 4-9-4 85 ....(v) WilliamBuick 6	83
			(A M Balding) *hld up in midfield: rdn 2f out: nt pce to chal* **15/8**[2]	
2225	6	1 1/4	**Dvinsky (USA)**[12] 1321 8-9-4 85 ....(b) JimmyQuinn 2	79
			(P Howling) *sn led: set modest pce early: hdd 2f out: wknd over 1f out* **20/1**	
61-6	7	1	**Gold Express**[23] 1152 6-8-6 73 .... AlanMunro 3	64
			(P J O'Gorman) *t.k.h: prom: rdn over 2f out: grad fdd* **20/1**	
0000	8	hd	**Southandwest (IRE)**[8] 1433 5-9-4 85 .... LukeMorris 4	76
			(J S Moore) *towards rr: rdn over 2f out: n.d* **20/1**	

1m 27.47s (1.47) **Going Correction** +0.30s/f (Slow) 8 Ran SP% 117.1
Speed ratings (Par 105): **103,98,97,96,94 93,92,91**
toteswinger: 1&2 £4.10, 1&3 £3.80, 2&3 £9.10. CSF £18.61 CT £117.37 TOTE £2.30: £1.60, £2.00, £2.30; EX 24.60.
Owner P W Harris **Bred** Howard Barton Stud **Trained** Aldbury, Herts

FOCUS
A useful contest.

1608 BOOK TICKETS ON 0844 579 3008 CONDITIONS STKS 6f (P)
8:50 (8:50) (Class 4) 4-Y-O £6,476 (£1,927; £963; £481) Stalls High

Form				RPR
0-00	1		**Buachaill Dona (IRE)**[69] 611 6-9-0 100 .... AdrianTNicholls 4	101
			(D Nicholls) *sluggish s and rdn leaving stalls: led after 100yds and set modest pce: rdn 5 l clr wl over 1f out: a holding late chals* **9/2**[3]	
06-1	2	1 1/2	**Eisteddfod**[32] 1006 8-9-5 103 .... EddieAhern 2	101
			(P F I Cole) *hld up in 3rd: drvn to go 2nd and cl on wnr over 1f out: no imp fnl 100yds* **9/4**[2]	
322-	3	3/4	**Diriculous**[144] 7576 5-9-0 100 .... JimmyFortune 3	94
			(T G Mills) *hld up in 4th: rdn and hdwy over 1f out: wnt 3rd ins fnl f: nt qckn* **6/5**[1]	
150/	4	3/4	**Drawnfromthepast (IRE)**[615] 4743 4-9-0 100 .... ShaneKelly 1	91?
			(J A Osborne) *hld up in rr: hung rt and outpcd over 2f out: rallied and r.o fnl f* **25/1**	
1/-	5	1 3/4	**Sammy The Snake (IRE)**[766] 779 4-9-0 0 .... DaneO'Neill 5	86?
			(B W Duke) *led 100yds: chsd wnr: rdn over 2f out: lost 2nd and no ex over 1f out* **10/1**	

1m 14.17s (1.07) **Going Correction** +0.30s/f (Slow) 5 Ran SP% 107.3
Speed ratings (Par 105): **104,102,101,100,97**
CSF £14.18 TOTE £4.90: £2.20, £1.10; EX 11.80.
Owner Mike Browne **Bred** John O Browne **Trained** Sessay, N Yorks

FOCUS
A smart contest.

1609 TURFTV H'CAP 2m (P)
9:20 (9:20) (Class 6) (0-65,65) 4-Y-O+ £1,942 (£578; £288; £144) Stalls High

Form				RPR
3-43	1		**Colourful Move**[103] 190 4-8-13 57 .... RobertHavlin 4	65
			(P G Murphy) *chsd ldrs: hrd rdn over 1f out: r.o to ld fnl 100yds* **12/1**	
-665	2	3/4	**Lucky Dancer**[15] 1273 4-8-11 55 .... AlanMunro 7	62
			(D R C Elsworth) *led: rdn 3 l clr ins fnl 2f: hdd and nt qckn fnl 100yds* **10/1**	
432	3	2 3/4	**Prince Charlemagne (IRE)**[10] 1378 6-9-6 60 .... ShaneKelly 3	64
			(G L Moore) *towards rr: hdwy 4f out: in tch and rdn over 2f out: styd on same pce* **5/1**[2]	
5233	4	hd	**Sea Cliff (IRE)**[69] 604 5-9-4 58 ....(p) JamieMoriarty 10	62+
			(Jonjo O'Neill) *towards rr: rdn and hung rt over 2f out: styd on to go 3rd 1f out: one pce* **8/1**	
/0-0	5	3 1/4	**Maximix**[14] 1287 6-9-3 57 .... GeorgeBaker 8	57
			(G L Moore) *hld up in midfield: stdy hdwy to chse ldrs over 3f out: outpcd fnl 2f* **12/1**	
1212	6	1 1/2	**Bold Adventure**[33] 983 5-9-11 65 .... ChrisCatlin 11	63
			(W J Musson) *towards rr: rdn and sme hdwy over 2f out: nt pce to chal* **5/2**[1]	
0-36	7	nk	**Rose Bien**[15] 1273 7-9-1 55 ....(p) EdwardCreighton 13	53
			(P J McBride) *stdd s: sn in tch: outpcd over 3f out: sn btn* **7/1**[3]	
6-00	8	3/4	**Mr Mischief**[27] 1081 9-9-1 55 .... JimCrowley 9	52
			(C Gordon) *bhd: hrd rdn 2f out: nvr rchd ldrs* **33/1**	
6-06	9	1/2	**Lady Sorcerer**[27] 1081 4-8-7 56 .... MartinLane(5) 12	52
			(A P Jarvis) *plld hrd in rr: rdn 3f out: nvr trbld ldrs* **33/1**	
	10	4	**Share Option**[16] 4050 7-9-0 54 .... LukeMorris 5	45
			(A W Carroll) *stdd s: hld up and bhd: drvn along 3f out: n.d* **12/1**	
5	11	3 1/2	**Tabaran (FR)**[14] 1286 6-9-6 60 .... AdamKirby 1	47
			(L A Dace) *hld up in 5th: rdn 3f out: sn wknd* **20/1**	
00/6	12	7	**Arctic Wings (IRE)**[25] 142 5-9-4 58 .... TolleyDean 2	37
			(A W Carroll) *prom tl hrd rdn and wknd over 2f out* **14/1**	
22-0	13	4 1/2	**Salut Saint Cloud**[10] 1378 8-9-1 55 ....(p) FergusSweeney 14	28
			(G L Moore) *chsd ldrs untl wknd over 3f out* **14/1**	
244-	14	6	**The Composer**[20] 6740 7-9-0 54 .... SteveDrowne 6	20
			(M Blanshard) *mid-div: rdn over 3f out: sn bhd* **33/1**	

3m 36.49s (6.39) **Going Correction** +0.30s/f (Slow)
WFA 4 from 5yo+ 4lb 14 Ran SP% 127.9
Speed ratings (Par 101): **96,95,94,94,92 91,91,91,91,89 87,83,81,78**
toteswinger: 1&2 £17.70, 1&3 £18.70, 2&3 £23.90. CSF £130.04 CT £691.26 TOTE £19.60: £3.90, £4.40, £2.70; EX 239.30 Place 6 £151.79, Place 5 £80.43.
Owner Mrs Dianne Murphy **Bred** Juddmonte Farms Ltd **Trained** East Garston, Berks
■ Stewards' Enquiry : Martin Lane one-day ban: careless riding (May 13)

FOCUS
Only a modest pace for the first half of this, which meant horses coming late faced a hopeless task.
T/Plt: £187.10 to a £1 stake. Pool: £75,988.91. 296.41 winning tickets. T/Qpdt: £42.00 to a £1 stake. Pool: £4,921.10. 86.50 winning tickets. LM

1396 PONTEFRACT (L-H)
Wednesday, April 29

OFFICIAL GOING: Good (good to firm in places; 8.4)
The ground was officially described as 'good, good to firm', but a couple of the jockeys who rode in the opener felt it was just on the slow side.
Wind: Virtually nil Weather: Fine and dry

1610 EUROPEAN BREEDERS' FUND NORTHERN RACING COLLEGE MAIDEN STKS 5f
2:20 (2:21) (Class 4) 2-Y-O £5,180 (£1,541; £770; £384) Stalls Low

Form				RPR
3	1		**Mister Manannan (IRE)**[13] 1304 2-9-3 0 .... AdrianTNicholls 8	97
			(D Nicholls) *qckly away: mde all: rdn and qcknd clr wl over 1f out: styd on wl* **4/1**[2]	
	2	7	**Kingdom Of Light** 2-9-3 0 .... PaulMulrennan 4	72+
			(J Howard Johnson) *t.k.h: prom: effrt 2f out and sn rdn: chsd wnr ins fnl f: no imp* **3/1**[1]	
	3	2 3/4	**Ghostwing** 2-9-3 0 .... MickyFenton 9	62
			(Mrs A Duffield) *prom: effrt to chse wnr 2f out: rdn over 1f out: sn no imp* **10/1**	
	4	2 1/2	**Rock Of Love (IRE)** 2-9-3 0 .... JoeFanning 7	53+
			(M Johnston) *dwlt and towards rr: hdwy on inner wl over 1f out: styd on ins fnl f: nrst fin* **11/1**	
	5	1/2	**Parbold Hill** 2-8-12 0 .... PhillipMakin 6	46
			(T D Barron) *prom: rdn along over 2f out and grad wknd* **4/1**[2]	
02	6	4 1/2	**Island Express (IRE)**[16] 1249 2-8-12 0 .... AnnStokell(5) 3	35
			(Miss A Stokell) *midfield: rdn along on inner 1/2-way: hdwy to chse ldrs 2f out: sn no imp* **50/1**	
0	7	2 1/2	**Lofthouse**[12] 1323 2-9-3 0 .... TonyCulhane 2	26
			(M R Channon) *nvr bttr than midfield* **7/1**	
	8	shd	**Hambleton** 2-9-3 0 .... TomEaves 1	26
			(B Smart) *dwlt: a towards rr* **16/1**	
	9	6	**Arch Walker (IRE)** 2-9-3 0 .... TonyHamilton 10	—
			(Jedd O'Keeffe) *a towards rr* **100/1**	
3	10	1 3/4	**Gentle Beat (IRE)**[12] 1330 2-9-3 0 .... DavidAllan 5	—
			(T D Easterby) *chsd ldrs: rdn along over 2f out: sn wknd* **13/2**[3]	
	11	8	**Dixie Bright (USA)** 2-9-3 0 .... TPQueally 11	—
			(J G Given) *chsd ldrs: rdn along 1/2-way and sn wknd* **40/1**	

63.90 secs (0.60) **Going Correction** -0.025s/f (Good) 11 Ran SP% 119.5
Speed ratings (Par 94): **94,82,78,74,73 66,62,62,52,49 37**
toteswinger: 1&2 £3.90, 1&3 £7.20, 2&3 £8.20 CSF £16.64 TOTE £5.80: £1.70, £1.80, £2.90; EX 24.40.
Owner Mrs Maureen Quayle **Bred** Mull Enterprises Ltd **Trained** Sessay, N Yorks

FOCUS
This looked a fair juvenile maiden, particularly by Pontefract's usual standards. The first three raced in the first three pretty much throughout.

NOTEBOOK

Mister Manannan(IRE) ◆ caught the eye when running green in a hot race at Ripon on his debut and confirmed that promise in no uncertain terms. He showed the benefit of that initial experience, breaking sharply from his wide draw to lead early, and he extended well in the straight for an emphatic success. He displayed a fluent, good-ground action and this very much looks his trip. He deserves his chance in something better now, and another run will tell us whether he's Royal Ascot material. (tchd 5-1)

Kingdom Of Light ◆, a £100,000 half-brother to 5f juvenile winner Brenin Taran, out of a dual 6f winner, was the talk of the racecourse and went off well backed. As it turned out, he simply ran into a useful type who had the benefit of previous experience. He should be very hard to beat in a similar race next time. (op 7-2 tchd 4-1 and 9-2 in a place)

Ghostwing, a £75,000 purchase, displayed good early speed but also showed signs of inexperience and should learn from this. (op 9-1 tchd 7-1)

Rock Of Love(IRE) ◆, a half-brother to among others smart juvenile Salsa Brava (5f winner on juvenile debut), caught the eye on his debut. He was basically in need of the whole experience and was soon in trouble after a slow start, but there was much to like about the way he kept on when switched towards the inside in the straight. A step up in trip will help in due, but he'll be a lot sharper next time. (op 12-1)

Parbold Hill ◆, the only filly in the line up, a £41,000 half-sister to among others dual 6f winner Rash Judgement, was another well backed and showed ability before getting tired. (op 15-2)

Island Express(IRE) Official explanation: jockey said colt was struck into

1611 TOTESPORT.COM MAIDEN STKS — 1m 2f 6y

2:55 (2:57) (Class 5) 3-Y-O — **£3,238** (£963; £481; £240) **Stalls** Low

Form					RPR
2	**1**		**Native Ruler**[14] 1289 3-9-3 0 (H R A Cecil) *mde most: rdn over 1f out: styd on* **8/13**[1]	TPQueally 4	94+
5	**2**	3 ¼	**Ottoman Empire (FR)**[13] 1297 3-9-3 0 (D R Lanigan) *a.p: effrt to chse wnr over 2f out: rdn wl over 1f out: drvn and one pce ins fnl f* **9/1**[3]	TedDurcan 9	87+
00-	**3**	12	**Northside Prince (IRE)**[200] 6655 3-9-3 0 (G A Swinbank) *midfield: hdwy 3f out: swtchd rt and effrt 2f out: styd on appr fnl f: n.d* **80/1**	PJMcDonald 2	63
	4	2	**Lady Luachmhar (IRE)** 3-8-12 0 (Mrs A Duffield) *hld up and bhd: hdwy 3f out: nt clr run and swtchd rt over 1f out: kpt on ins fnl f* **50/1**	MickyFenton 1	68+
	5	7	**Money Lender** 3-9-3 0 (N J Vaughan) *dwlt: sn chsng ldrs: rdn along wl over 2f out: wknd wl over 1f out* **150/1**	VinceSlattery 5	45+
0-5	**6**	¾	**Lombok**[11] 1349 3-9-3 0 (M L W Bell) *towards rr: hdwy on outer 1/2-way: rdn along 3f out: n.d* **33/1**	JoeFanning 12	44
0	**7**	1 ¾	**Rosewin (IRE)**[14] 1276 3-8-12 0 (O Brennan) *towards rr: hdwy on inner over 2f out: swtchd rt over 1f out: sn rdn and no imp* **200/1**	PaulQuinn 8	35
6-	**8**	¾	**Red China Blues (USA)**[322] 2937 3-9-3 0 (J Howard Johnson) *chsd ldrs on inner: rdn along 3f out: sn wknd* **80/1**	PaulMulrennan 3	39
6-3	**9**	5	**Cherish The Moment (IRE)**[27] 1087 3-9-3 0 (B W Hills) *cl up: rdn along over 3f out: sn wknd* **4/1**[2]	RobertWinston 13	29
04	**10**	2	**Cooperman**[25] 1127 3-9-3 0 (P T Midgley) *a in rr* **250/1**	JamieMoriarty 10	25
0	**11**	1	**Kendalewood**[11] 1362 3-9-3 0 (T D Walford) *dwlt: sn in tch: rdn along 1/2-way and sn wknd* **250/1**	GrahamGibbons 7	23
	12	hd	**Langford Decoit (IRE)** 3-9-3 0 (M R Channon) *a in rr* **100/1**	TonyCulhane 14	22
	13	15	**California Bright (IRE)** 3-8-12 0 (J G Given) *in tch: rdn along 1/2-way: sn wknd* **66/1**	SebSanders 6	—

2m 13.44s (-0.26) **Going Correction** -0.025s/f (Good) **13** Ran SP% **103.7**
Speed ratings (Par 98): **100,97,87,86,80 80,78,78,74,72 71,71,59**
toteswinger: 1&2 £2.20, 1&3 £13.70, 2&3 £31.20. CSF £5.01 TOTE £1.50: £1.02, £1.80, £14.10; EX 4.60.

Owner Lordship Stud **Bred** Lordship Stud **Trained** Newmarket, Suffolk

■ Stewards' Enquiry : Vince Slattery ten-day ban: failed to take reasonable measures to obtain best possible placing (May 13-22)

FOCUS

A reasonable three-year-old maiden in which the highly regarded Native Ruler justified his short price a time 1.45 seconds quicker than the later fillies' handicap won by the 80-rated Faldal.

Lady Luachmhar(IRE) Official explanation: jockey said filly was denied a clear run

Money Lender Official explanation: jockey said, regarding running and riding, that his orders, as it was a clumsy big colt, were to get a good start and keep it together early and see how it unfolded, adding that it had been denied a clear run and became unbalanced in the straight.

Cherish The Moment(IRE) Official explanation: jockey said colt had no more to give

1612 SKYBET.COM H'CAP — 1m 4y

3:30 (3:32) (Class 5) (0-70,70) 4-Y-O+ — **£3,238** (£963; £481; £240) **Stalls** Low

Form					RPR
3234	**1**		**Blue Charm**[22] 1169 5-9-0 66 (I W McInnes) *hld up towards rr: stdy hdwy on inner 3f out: swtchd rt and chsd ldrs over 1f out: sn rdn and styd on ins fnl f to ld nr fin* **8/1**	TomEaves 2	75
1031	**2**	hd	**This Ones For Eddy**[9] 1401 4-8-11 68 6ex (S Parr) *trckd ldr: hdwy to chal 3f out: rdn wl over 1f out: drvn to ld wl ins fnl f: hdd and no ex nr fin* **9/4**[1]	PatrickDonaghy(5) 5	77
4541	**3**	½	**Jebel Tara**[12] 1332 4-9-1 67 (A D Brown) *led: jnd 3f out: rdn 2f out: drvn over 1f out: hdd wl ins fnl f: kpt on underpress* **7/2**[2]	(bt) SilvestreDeSousa 13	75
535-	**4**	¾	**Castlebury (IRE)**[276] 4455 4-8-13 65 (G A Swinbank) *trckd ldrs: hdwy over 2f out: rdn wl over 1f out: kpt on same pce ins fnl f* **11/1**	PJMcDonald 3	71
/0-6	**5**	2 ¼	**High Profit (IRE)**[28] 1062 5-8-7 59 (James Moffatt) *hld up and bhd: hdwy on inner over 2f out: swtchd rt and rdn over 1f out: kpt on ins fnl f: nrst fin* **33/1**	(v) JoeFanning 8	60
50-0	**6**	2 ¼	**Summer Dancer (IRE)**[12] 1332 5-8-13 65 (P T Midgley) *hld up in midfield: gd hdwy on inner 2f out and sn chsng ldrs: rdn appr last and sn one pce* **14/1**	JamieMoriarty 1	61
460-	**7**	2 ½	**Royal Applord**[166] 7317 4-8-8 60 (P T Midgley) *hld up towards rr: hdwy over 2f out: rdn wl over 1f out: sn no imp* **33/1**	PaulMulrennan 11	50
0420	**8**	nse	**Xpres Maite**[27] 1089 6-9-4 70 (S R Bowring) *in rr tl sme late hdwy* **6/1**[3]	(v) RobertWinston 4	60+
0114	**9**	1 ¾	**Very Well Red**[33] 979 6-9-2 68 (P W Hiatt) *chsd ldrs: hdwy to chal 3f out: sn rdn and wknd wl over 1f out* **25/1**	ChrisCatlin 16	54
0-04	**10**	2 ½	**Shadowtime**[12] 1332 4-8-8 60 (Miss Tracy Waggott) *in tch on outer: hdwy to chse ldrs over 3f out: sn rdn along and wknd over 2f out* **10/1**	MickyFenton 15	40
010-	**11**	1 ¼	**Apache Nation (IRE)**[193] 6827 6-8-6 58 (M Dods) *in tch: rdn along over 3f out and sn wknd* **28/1**	TonyHamilton 7	35
30-0	**12**	6	**Emperor's Well**[21] 1194 10-8-5 57 (M W Easterby) *in tch: rdn along 1/2-way: sn wknd* **66/1**	DaleGibson 14	20
34-0	**13**	nse	**Tanforan**[30] 1042 7-8-0 59 (B P J Baugh) *midfield: hdwy on outer and in tch 1/2-way: rdn along 3f out and sn wknd* **33/1**	BillyCray(7) 9	22
5205	**14**	10	**General Tufto**[13] 1306 4-8-8 67 (C Smith) *chsd ldrs on outer: rdn along 3f out: sn wknd* **25/1**	(b) RichardRowe(7) 12	7

1m 46.2s (0.30) **Going Correction** -0.025s/f (Good) **14** Ran SP% **123.9**
Speed ratings (Par 103): **97,96,96,95,93 91,88,88,86,84 83,77,76,66**
toteswinger: 1&2 £6.00, 1&3 £6.20, 2&3 £3.40. CSF £25.34 CT £80.88 TOTE £9.20: £3.30, £1.90, £1.70; EX 35.10.

Owner J Morris **Bred** Mrs R Pease **Trained** Catwick, E Yorks

FOCUS

A modest but competitive handicap.

Xpres Maite Official explanation: jockey said gelding was denied a clear run

1613 LADBROKES FILLIES' H'CAP — 1m 2f 6y

4:05 (4:07) (Class 3) (0-90,90) 3-Y-O+ — **£9,346** (£2,799; £1,399; £700; £349; £175) **Stalls** Low

Form					RPR
51-	**1**		**Faldal**[144] 7577 3-8-1 80 (Tom Dascombe) *dwlt and towards rr: hdwy on outer over 3f out: effrt to chal 2f out: rdn and hung lft ins fnl f: drvn and hung lft again last 75yds: styd on to ld nr line* **5/1**[2]	AdrianMcCarthy 11	83+
16-5	**2**	nse	**Princess Taylor**[11] 1347 5-9-9 85 (M Botti) *trckd ldng pair: hdwy 3f out: rdn to ld 2f out: drvn over 1f out: edgd lft ins fnl f: hdd nr line* **11/2**[3]	SebSanders 5	91
150-	**3**	1	**Amanda Carter**[186] 6974 5-9-2 83 (R A Fahey) *hld up in tch: hdwy 2f out: rdn to chse ldng pair over 1f out: styng on whn n.m.r and swtchd rt wl ins fnl f: kpt on* **5/1**[2]	FrederikTylicki(5) 6	87
216-	**4**	nk	**Syvilla**[189] 6921 4-10-0 90 (Rae Guest) *stdd s: t.k.h: in rr: gd hdwy over 2f out: chsd ldrs over 1f out: rdn and styd on wl fnl f* **22/1**	ChrisCatlin 3	93
011-	**5**	nk	**Atabaas Allure (FR)**[195] 6756 3-8-2 81 (M Johnston) *led: rdn along and hdd 2f out: drvn and rallied ent fnl f: n.m.r and kpt on towards fin* **13/2**	FrancisNorton 9	82+
00-3	**6**	5	**Just Lille (IRE)**[13] 1306 6-9-10 86 (Mrs A Duffield) *hld up towards rr: hdwy on outer 3f out: rdn and edgd lft 2f out: sn drvn and one pce* **9/1**	(p) MickyFenton 8	79
14-5	**7**	½	**Latin Tinge (USA)**[10] 1381 3-8-5 84 (P F I Cole) *cl up: rdn along over 2f out: sn drvn and wknd* **20/1**	JoeFanning 10	73
130-	**8**	4	**Summer's Lease**[172] 7242 4-9-4 80 (M L W Bell) *trckd ldrs: effrt whn edgd rt 2f out: sn rdn and wknd over 1f out* **11/4**[1]	TPQueally 2	64
12-4	**9**	2 ½	**Rio Guru (IRE)**[11] 1348 4-9-0 76 (M R Channon) *hld up in rr: hdwy 3f out: hmpd over 2f out: bhd after* **16/1**	TonyCulhane 4	55
03-3	**10**	9	**Pension Policy (USA)**[106] 143 4-8-9 71 oh1 (J M P Eustace) *chsd ldrs: rdn along 3f out: wkng whn hmpd over 2f out: bhd after* **25/1**	LukeMorris 7	32

2m 14.89s (1.19) **Going Correction** -0.025s/f (Good)
WFA 3 from 4yo+ 17lb **10** Ran SP% **117.6**
Speed ratings (Par 104): **94,93,93,92,92 88,88,85,83,75**
toteswinger: 1&2 £10.10, 1&3 £8.70, 2&3 £6.50. CSF £31.97 CT £146.00 TOTE £5.20: £3.20, £2.40, £2.00; EX 38.00.

Owner Mrs Bernadette Quinn **Bred** Mr & Mrs J Quinn **Trained** Lambourn, Berks

■ Stewards' Enquiry : T P Queally caution: careless riding.
Micky Fenton two-day ban: careless riding (May 13-14)
Seb Sanders two-day ban: used whip with excessive frequency (May 13-14)

FOCUS

A decent fillies' handicap, although the pace seemed just ordinary and the winning time was 1.45 seconds slower than the earlier maiden by the potentially smart Native Ruler.

NOTEBOOK

Faldal looked a good prospect when winning a 1m maiden at Great Leighs on her third and final start at two and she confirmed that impression on her return from nearly five months off. She was a little keen off the modest early gallop and then, after coming about four wide into the straight, she was inclined to carry her head a little proud under pressure, just as on her previous outing despite having a sheepskin noseband fitted. As a result she made hard work of seeing off the runner-up, and gave the impression she still has some maturing to do, but that said, she does look a very useful filly in the making if going the right way. (op 3-1)

Princess Taylor went without her usual tongue-tie, but she ran a cracking race in defeat, improving on her reappearance effort. (op 6-1)

Amanda Carter ◆ was the subject of significant support on her return from six months off and looks to have returned an improved mare. She won't mind a return to further and will appeal as worth a bet in similar company next time. (op 10-1)

Syvilla ◆ stayed on from a long way back under top weight. She'll be suited by a step up in trip, as well as slightly easier ground, and must be followed when getting her conditions. (op 16-1)

Atabaas Allure(FR), upped in trip on her reappearance, had her chance from the front but found this tougher than the two Polytrack events she won last year. (op 8-1)

Just Lille(IRE) was stuck out much wider than ideal and failed to run to the form she showed at Ripon on her reappearance. (op 7-1 tchd 5-1)

Latin Tinge(USA) was a significant drifter and offered little. (op 14-1 tchd 12-1)

Summer's Lease was well backed after 172 days off, but she never posed a threat and was disappointing. (op 9-2)

1614 CORALBET BY FREEPHONE 0800 242 232 H'CAP — 1m 4f 8y

4:40 (4:42) (Class 5) (0-75,75) 3-Y-O — **£3,238** (£963; £481; £240) **Stalls** Low

Form					RPR
003-	**1**		**Cry For The Moon (USA)**[210] 6398 3-9-4 75 (Mrs A J Perrett) *hld up in rr: hdwy over 2f out: swtchd outside and rdn wl over 1f out: styd on strly to ld and hung rt wl ins fnl f: drvn out* **11/2**[2]	TPQueally 4	79
001-	**2**	nk	**Canmoss (USA)**[132] 7718 3-8-9 66 (E J O'Neill) *led: rdn wl over 2f out: drvn over 1f out: hdd wl ins fnl f: kpt on gamely u.p* **7/1**	ChrisCatlin 3	70
-661	**3**	hd	**Urban Space**[11] 1363 3-8-10 67 (B G Powell) *hld up in rr: hdwy 3f out: rdn to chse ldrs 2f out: styd on to chal over 1f out: sn drvn and ev ch tl no ex last 50yds* **12/1**	RobertWinston 8	70
30-0	**4**	4 ½	**Mons Calpe (IRE)**[8] 1416 3-8-7 64 (P F I Cole) *trckd ldr: rdn along and outpcd over 2f out: kpt on u.p fnl f* **10/1**	TomEaves 5	60
6121	**5**	10	**Dispol Diva**[14] 1282 3-8-11 68 (P T Midgley) *trckd ldrs: pushed along 3f out: rdn over 2f out and sn wknd* **10/3**[1]	(v) PhillipMakin 1	48

0-44 6 3/4 **Mohanad (IRE)**[47] 824 3-9-3 74 TonyCulhane 6 53
(M R Channon) trckd ldng pair: hdwy over 3f out: rdn wl over 2f out: grad wknd 14/1
4132 7 4 1/2 **High Cross (IRE)**[26] 1105 3-9-2 73 SebSanders 2 45
(Sir Mark Prescott) hld up towards rr: hdwy on inner over 3f out: rdn over 2f out and sn btn 10/3[1]
341 8 90 **Leo The Lion (IRE)**[67] 630 3-9-4 75 JoeFanning 7 —
(M Johnston) trckd ldrs: effrt over 3f out: sn rdn and btn: eased over 1f out 6/1[3]

2m 41.08s (0.28) **Going Correction** -0.025s/f (Good) 8 Ran SP% 111.8
Speed ratings (Par 98): **98,97,97,94,88 87,84,24**
toteswinger: 1&2 £7.30, 1&3 £12.50, 2&3 £12.40. CSF £41.27 CT £434.16 TOTE £7.20: £1.90, £2.10, £3.70; EX 55.10.
Owner A Christodoulou J H Richmond-Watson **Bred** M G Thoroughbreds **Trained** Pulborough, W Sussex

FOCUS
A pretty ordinary three-year-old handicap.
Mohanad(IRE) Official explanation: jockey said colt hung left-handed
High Cross(IRE) Official explanation: trainer had no explanation for the poor form shown
Leo The Lion(IRE) Official explanation: jockey said colt hung left-handed

1615 FRIENDS OF THE NORTHERN RACING COLLEGE H'CAP 1m 2f 6y
5:15 (5:15) (Class 5) (0-75,75) 4-Y-0+ **£3,238** (£963; £481; £120; £120) **Stalls** Low

Form RPR
235- 1 **Timocracy**[200] 6657 4-9-3 74 GrahamGibbons 1 81
(T D Walford) mde all: rdn wl over 1f out: drvn ent fnl f: styd on gamely 9/4[1]
403- 2 1 1/2 **Sudden Impulse**[127] 7777 8-8-4 61 SilvestreDeSousa 13 65
(A D Brown) hld up in midfield: hdwy over 2f out: rdn over 1f out: str run ent fnl f: kpt on same pce towards fin 33/1
4216 3 nk **Quince (IRE)**[22] 1175 6-9-3 74 (v) SebSanders 9 77
(J Pearce) hld up in rr: hdwy over 2f out: str run on outyer over 1f out: sn rdn and kpt on ins fnl f 14/1
222 4 nk **Old Romney**[40] 893 5-9-2 73 TedDurcan 7 76+
(M Wigham) s.i.s: hld up in rr: gd hdwy on inner wl over 1f out: rdn and styd on ins fnl f: nrst fin 10/1
-441 4 dht **Destinys Dream (IRE)**[11] 1366 4-9-0 71 PhillipMakin 2 74
(Miss Tracy Waggott) a.p: effrt to chse wnr 3f out: rdn wl over 1f out: drvn ent fnl f: wknd towards fin 13/2[3]
-050 6 1 1/4 **Princess Flame (GER)**[11] 1357 7-8-6 70 KylieManser(7) 8 70
(B G Powell) in tch: hdwy 3f out: rdn to chse ldrs whn n.m.r over 1f out: kpt on u.p ins fnl f 14/1
01 7 nse **Uncle Bertie**[55] 767 4-9-0 71 VinceSlattery 5 72
(N J Vaughan) chsd ldrs: rdn along 2f out: drvn over 1f out: kpt on same pce 16/1
04-0 8 nk **Kalasam**[31] 1014 5-8-8 65 DaleGibson 3 65
(M W Easterby) trckd ldrs: rdn along over 2f out: drvn over 1f out: kpt on same pce 22/1
-551 9 1 **Masterofceremonies**[17] 1226 6-8-10 67 (v[1]) TomEaves 4 66
(James Moffatt) s.i.s: towards rr: hdwy 3f out: rdn along whn nt clr run wl over 1f out: no imp after 14/1
35-6 10 1 1/2 **Moonstreaker**[14] 1279 6-8-7 64 PaulQuinn 6 59+
(R M Whitaker) s.i.s: a towards rr 12/1
622- 11 1 1/2 **Princess Rainbow (FR)**[197] 6725 4-8-13 70 JoeFanning 14 62
(Jennie Candlish) trckd ldrs: effrt on outer 3f out: sn cl up and ev ch tl rdn and wknd wl over 1f out 16/1
5432 12 32 **New Beginning (IRE)**[14] 1279 5-8-9 66 RobertWinston 11 —
(Mrs S Lamyman) prom: rdn along over 2f out: sn drvn and wknd 9/2[2]
01-4 13 11 **Neon Blue**[9] 1402 8-7-11 61 oh1 DeclanCannon(7) 10 —
(R M Whitaker) towards rr: sme hdwy on outer over 4f out: rdn and wknd over 3f out: sn bhd and eased 14/1

2m 15.24s (1.54) **Going Correction** -0.025s/f (Good) 13 Ran SP% 124.8
Speed ratings (Par 103): **92,90,90,90,90 89,89,89,88,87 85,60,51**
toteswinger: 1&2 £7.30, 1&3 £12.50, 2&3 £12.40. CSF £98.62 CT £907.96 TOTE £4.40: £2.00, £7.30, £5.40; EX 91.70 Place 6 £49.99, Place 5 £27.41.
Owner Ms J Loylert **Bred** Gainsborough Stud Management Ltd **Trained** Sheriff Hutton, N Yorks

FOCUS
A modest handicap.
Masterofceremonies Official explanation: jockey said gelding was denied a clear run
New Beginning(IRE) Official explanation: trainer had no explanation for the poor form shown
Neon Blue Official explanation: trainer had no explanation for the poor form shown
T/Plt: £123.80 to a £1 stake. Pool: £72,265.42. 426.05 winning tickets. T/Qpdt: £160.70 to a £1 stake. Pool: £3,192.59. 14.70 winning tickets. JR

1421 FOLKESTONE (R-H)
Thursday, April 30

OFFICIAL GOING: Good to firm (round 9.5; straight - stands' side 10.2, far side 9.7)
Wind: Moderate, across Weather: bright and sunny

1616 LADBROKES.COM MAIDEN AUCTION STKS 5f
2:10 (2:11) (Class 6) 2-Y-0 **£2,729** (£806; £403) **Stalls** Low

Form RPR
33 1 **Desert Auction (IRE)**[26] 1119 2-8-13 0 RichardHughes 1 80+
(R Hannon) mde all: rdn 2f out: edgd rt u.p fnl f: styd on wl fnl 100yds 10/11[1]
2 1 1/4 **Kaspirit (IRE)** 2-8-7 0 SteveDrowne 2 70
(M Wigham) restless in stalls: dwlt: hld up in last pl: swtchd rt and hdwy wl over 1f out: pressed wnr 1f out: no ex fnl 100yds 4/1[3]
3 1 1/4 **Safari Special** 2-8-10 0 JimCrowley 4 68+
(P Winkworth) trckd ldrs: ev ch wl over 1f out: rdn and rn green over 1f out: sn outpcd by ldng pair: edgd lft ins fnl f: kpt on again fnl 100yds 10/3[2]
00 4 2 3/4 **Pullyourfingerout (IRE)**[13] 1323 2-8-12 0 DaneO'Neill 3 60
(B G Powell) w ldr: rdn jst over 2f out: wknd u.p over 1f out 13/2
5 3 1/4 **Last Orders (IRE)** 2-8-13 0 AlanMunro 6 49
(M G Quinlan) chsd ldrs on outer: rdn and ev ch 2f out: wknd over 1f out 20/1

59.75 secs (-0.25) **Going Correction** -0.275s/f (Firm) 5 Ran SP% 113.6
Speed ratings (Par 90): **91,89,87,82,77**
toteswinger: 1&2 £2.20 CSF £5.19 TOTE £1.60: £1.10, £2.40; EX 5.00.
Owner A J Ilsley, K T Ivory & G Battocchi **Bred** J Kilpatrick **Trained** East Everleigh, Wilts

FOCUS
This looked an ordinary juvenile contest, which was weakened further by a couple of significant non-runners.

NOTEBOOK
Desert Auction(IRE), despite being a little weak in the market, won quite nicely after bagging the inside rail. He used his experience to good effect and got off the mark on his first start on turf. (op 4-5 tchd 8-11 and Evens)
Kaspirit(IRE), who finally made her racecourse debut after missing two previous engagements, one of which was a seller, took a while to realise what was needed but came home the best of the newcomers. There should be races to be won with her. (op 11-2 tchd 6-1)
Safari Special has a great pedigree for sprinting and showed plenty of toe before looking a little green when his jockey asked for maximum effort. He did stay on again inside the final furlong and should benefit from the outing. (op 9-2 tchd 11-2)
Pullyourfingerout(IRE) faded from a prominent position and may need an ease into selling company to get off the mark. (op 8-1)
Last Orders(IRE), representing the stable who took this contest last season, was not particularly fancied but showed some ability before losing her position. (op 16-1)

1617 LADBROKES.COM MAIDEN STKS 5f
2:45 (2:45) (Class 5) 3-Y-0+ **£2,729** (£806; £403) **Stalls** Low

Form RPR
02 1 **Chris's Jem**[30] 1045 3-8-9 0 AlanMunro 3 58
(J R Jenkins) hld up in tch: hdwy jst over 2f out: swtchd rt over 1f out: qcknd to ld ins fnl f: pushed out 3/1[2]
0-2 2 1 **Rathlin Light (USA)**[28] 1077 3-8-4 0 Louis-PhilippeBeuzelin(5) 12 56
(W R Swinburn) taken down early: flashed tail thrght: broke wl and crossed to r nr stands rail: chsd ldr tl led over 3f out: rdn wl over 1f out: hdd and no ex ins fnl f 4/1[3]
2322 3 1 3/4 **Billy Beetroot (USA)**[9] 1424 3-8-9 62 (b) WilliamCarson(5) 5 53
(S C Williams) t.k.h: led and crossed to stands rail: hdd over 3f out: chsd ldr after tl over 1f out: kpt on same pce ins fnl f 15/8[1]
0-00 4 1 1/2 **Sandy Par**[13] 1317 4-9-10 46 (b[1]) ChrisCatlin 10 52
(J M Bradley) stdd s: hld up in midfield: rdn and effrt 2f out: plugged on fnl f: nvr trbld ldrs 33/1
3050 5 nse **Rightcar Lewis**[41] 895 4-9-5 43 (b) DaneO'Neill 2 46
(Peter Grayson) bhd: rdn jst over 2f out: styd on past btn horses fnl f: nvr nr ldrs 33/1
-6 6 1 **Aegean King**[13] 1317 3-8-7 0 TobyAtkinson(7) 11 44+
(M Wigham) s.i.s: wl bhd: swtchd rt and hdwy over 1f out: rn green and edging lft after: swtchd rt again ins fnl f: r.o: nvr nr ldrs 17/2
405- 7 1/2 **Louie's Lad**[183] 7082 3-9-0 56 JerryO'Dwyer 9 42
(J J Bridger) towards rr: rdn jst over 2f out: modest late hdwy: nvr nr ldrs 40/1
00- 8 hd **Sircozy (IRE)**[173] 7240 3-9-0 0 SaleemGolam 1 41+
(S C Williams) sn totally outpcd in last pl: styd on fr over 1f out: n.d 12/1
0463 9 nk **Tightrope (IRE)**[4] 1536 3-9-0 52 MartinDwyer 14 40
(T D McCarthy) chsd ldrs on outer: rdn jst over 2f out: wknd over 1f out 20/1
5 10 1/2 **Trade Price (GR)**[37] 947 3-9-0 0 ShaneKelly 8 38+
(J A Osborne) a bhd: edging out looking for run 2f out: nvr a factor 12/1
0-20 11 1/2 **Wicksy Creek**[70] 602 4-9-5 48 MarkFlynn(5) 13 41
(G C Bravery) chsd ldrs: rdn 2f out: wknd over 1f out 50/1
450- 12 5 **Bilboa**[139] 7648 4-9-10 43 (p) AdamKirby 6 23
(J M Bradley) chsd ldrs tl wknd qckly wl over 1f out 25/1

59.25 secs (-0.75) **Going Correction** -0.275s/f (Firm)
WFA 3 from 4yo 10lb 12 Ran SP% 124.6
Speed ratings (Par 103): **95,93,90,88,88 86,85,85,84,84 83,75**
toteswinger: 1&2 £3.80, 1&3 £2.80, 2&3 £2.50 CSF £15.19 TOTE £3.80: £1.40, £2.20, £1.30; EX 11.40 Trifecta £46.00 Pool: £195.21 - 3.14 winning units..
Owner A C Murphy **Bred** Mrs V J Bjerke & Mrs E K Tope-Ottesen **Trained** Royston, Herts

FOCUS
Those with official ratings had ones that ranged from 43 to 62, so one would imagine that this was a weak maiden despite the decent winning time. The winner should at least get a decent handicap mark.
Louie's Lad Official explanation: jockey said gelding was unsuited by the good to firm ground
Trade Price(GR) Official explanation: jockey said colt was unsuited by the good to firm ground

1618 LADBROKES.COM FILLIES' H'CAP 6f
3:20 (3:30) (Class 5) (0-70,70) 3-Y-0 **£3,070** (£906; £453) **Stalls** Low

Form RPR
14 1 **Chasca (IRE)**[31] 1032 3-9-0 66 JimCrowley 8 72
(Mrs A J Perrett) trckd ldrs: swtchd rt and hdwy 2f out: led over 1f out: edgd lft fnl f: r.o wl 9/2[2]
3-45 2 1 1/4 **Today's The Day**[12] 1359 3-9-1 67 (b) PhilipRobinson 2 69
(M A Jarvis) in tch in midfield: rdn and struggling 3f out: swtchd rt over 1f out: styd on fnl f to go 2nd nr fin: no ch w wnr 5/2[1]
00-4 3 1/2 **Bahamian Ceilidh**[16] 1272 3-9-4 70 RichardKingscote 4 72+
(Tom Dascombe) uns rdr and galloped loose to s: led and crossed to stands rail: rdn wl over 1f out: hdd over 1f out: keeping on same pce and hld whn nt clr run wl ins fnl f: lost 2nd nr fin 9/2[2]
21-0 4 2 3/4 **Freepressionist**[38] 936 3-9-1 67 DaneO'Neill 10 59
(R A Teal) w ldr: ev ch and rdn wl over 1f out: wknd ins fnl f 20/1
00-4 5 7 **One Cool Kitty**[24] 1155 3-9-1 67 AlanMunro 5 36
(M G Quinlan) stdd s: in tch in midfield: rdn 2f out: sn wknd 13/2[3]
060- 6 4 1/2 **Day In Dubai**[185] 7011 3-8-5 57 ow1 NeilChalmers 3 12
(J J Bridger) stdd s: hld up in rr: struggling fr 1/2-way 50/1
436 7 9 **Dream Catch Me (IRE)**[37] 947 3-8-4 56 oh7 MartinDwyer 11 —
(J R Boyle) uns rdr and galloped loose to s: a bhd 28/1
06-4 8 1 1/2 **Peninsula Girl (IRE)**[11] 1379 3-9-1 67 TonyCulhane 9 —
(M R Channon) in tch for 2f out: sn struggling in rr 9/1

1m 11.29s (-1.41) **Going Correction** -0.275s/f (Firm) 8 Ran SP% 98.4
Speed ratings (Par 95): **98,96,95,92,82 76,64,62**
toteswinger: 1&2 £2.40, 1&3 £2.70, 2&3 £2.00 CSF £11.80 CT £31.74 TOTE £4.80: £1.40, £1.20, £1.60; EX 13.40 Trifecta £47.90 Pool: £349.86 - 5.40 winning units..
Owner Lady Clague **Bred** Newberry Stud Company **Trained** Pulborough, W Sussex
■ Abbey Belle (6/1, unruly at s) & On The Feather (12/1, unruly in stalls) were withdrawn. Deduct 15p in the 3 under R4).

FOCUS
This race went off late due to three misbehaving. The first four finished clear in this modest fillies' handicap. The runner-up looks the best guide.
Today's The Day Official explanation: jockey said filly hung right

1619 J AND J RECRUITMENT H'CAP 6f
3:55 (3:55) (Class 5) (0-75,74) 4-Y-0+ **£3,070** (£906; £453) **Stalls** Low

Form RPR
1101 1 **Super Frank (IRE)**[9] 1421 6-8-4 60 (p) ChrisCatlin 7 71
(J Akehurst) chsd ldr: ev ch and rdn wl over 1f out: led narrowly over 1f out: forged ahd ins fnl f 6/4[1]

0-00 **2** 1 ¾ **We Have A Dream**[10] 1403 4-9-0 **70** MartinDwyer 9 76
(W R Muir) *broke wl and sn crossed to stands' rail: led: rdn wl over 1f out: hdd narrowly over 1f out: kpt on wl tl no ex ins fnl f* **11/1**

4043 **3** 1 ¼ **Hart Of Gold**[6] 1468 5-8-8 **67** (p) KevinGhunowa(3) 3 69
(R A Harris) *t.k.h: trckd ldrs on stands' rail: looking for room fr over 2f out: swtchd rt and rdn over 1f out: one pce after* **9/4**[2]

-050 **4** 1 ¾ **Credit Swap**[21] 1197 4-9-4 **74** SteveDrowne 2 70
(M Wigham) *stdd s: hld up in rr: rdn 2f out: plugged on to go 4th ins fnl f: nvr trbld ldrs* **4/1**[3]

2200 **5** 3 ¾ **Louphole**[24] 1152 7-8-9 **65** RobertHavlin 1 49
(J R Jenkins) *hld up in tch: hdwy and chsd ldrs 1/2-way: rdn and fnd nil wl over 1f out: wl btn fnl f* **9/1**

-200 **6** 6 **Peopleton Brook**[15] 1285 7-8-4 **60** oh1 (t) FrankieMcDonald 4 25
(B G Powell) *stdd s: t.k.h: hld up in tch: hdwy on outer 1/2-way: chsd ldrs and rdn 2f out: wknd qckly over 1f out* **25/1**

600- **7** 5 **Black Moma (IRE)**[219] 6190 5-7-11 **60** oh2 NathanAlison(7) 8 9
(J R Boyle) *chsd ldrs: rdn 2f out: wknd qckly wl over 1f out* **33/1**

1m 10.49s (-2.21) **Going Correction** -0.275s/f (Firm) **7** Ran SP% **115.9**
Speed ratings (Par 103): **103,100,99,96,91 83,77**
toteswinger: 1&2 £4.20, 1&3 £1.20, 2&3 £3.60 CSF £20.09 CT £37.22 TOTE £2.30: £1.70, £3.80; EX 12.30 Trifecta £20.60 Pool: £339.06 - 12.17 winning units..
Owner A D Spence **Bred** A Butler **Trained** Epsom, Surrey

FOCUS
A modest-looking sprint in which the first pair were always 1-2. The winner confirmed last week's apprentice win here.

1620 LADBROKES H'CAP — 7f (S)
4:30 (4:31) (Class 6) (0-60,60) 3-Y-O **£2,047** (£604; £302) **Stalls** Low

Form RPR

503- **1** **Cavendish Road (IRE)**[143] 7600 3-9-1 **57** MartinDwyer 13 62
(W R Muir) *broke wl and sn crossed towards stands' rail: chsd ldrs tl led 2f out: drvn ent fnl f: edgd lft ins fnl f: styd on wl* **16/1**

040- **2** ½ **Fly By Nelly**[176] 7191 3-9-4 **60** SteveDrowne 2 64+
(H Morrison) *chsd ldrs on stands rail: shuffled bk and lost pl 3f out: swtchd rt and hdwy over 1f out: chal jst ins fnl f: bmpd 100yds out: one pce after* **6/1**[2]

000- **3** 1 ½ **King Of Defence**[184] 7051 3-9-3 **59** PhilipRobinson 7 59
(M A Jarvis) *dwlt: t.k.h: in midfield tl swtchd to outer 4f out: sn chsng ldrs: rdn and ev ch wl over 1f out: no ex fnl f* **8/11**[1]

060- **4** 1 **Mount Ella**[237] 5673 3-9-2 **58** ShaneKelly 3 55
(J A Osborne) *led at stdy gallop: qcknd over 2f out: hdd 2f out: sn rdn and kpt on same pce after* **33/1**

5-06 **5** 1 ½ **Crystallize**[17] 1253 3-9-1 **57** SebSanders 6 50+
(A B Haynes) *hld up in tch: chsd ldrs and nt clr run fr 2f out: nvr able to mount a chal: eased towards fin* **15/2**[3]

064- **6** ½ **Golden Pool (IRE)**[147] 7542 3-9-0 **56** DaneO'Neill 10 48
(S A Callaghan) *t.k.h: hld up in rr: plld to outer and hdwy over 2f out: chsd ldrs and rdn wl over 1f out: wknd ent fnl f* **25/1**

005- **7** 1 ½ **Kyle Of Bute**[189] 6924 3-9-0 **56** ChrisCatlin 8 44
(J L Dunlop) *hld up towards rr: effrt and hdwy jst over 2f out: rdn and no prog over 1f out: plugged on same pce* **8/1**

3300 **8** 1 ¼ **Kamanja (UAE)**[31] 1036 3-8-7 **56** KierenFox(7) 5 40
(M J Attwater) *t.k.h: hld up in rr: edging out and rdn 2f out: no real hdwy* **66/1**

50-0 **9** 3 ¼ **Rose Of Coma (IRE)**[16] 1270 3-8-9 **54** (v[1]) DavidProbert(3) 14 29
(Miss Gay Kelleway) *in tch in midfield on outer: rdn and brief effrt jst over 2f out: wknd wl over 1f out* **50/1**

606- **10** 2 ½ **Princess Rebecca**[212] 6351 3-8-12 **54** RichardKingscote 4 23
(H J Collingridge) *t.k.h: chsd ldr tl over 2f out: sn wknd* **66/1**

560- **11** 8 **Bussell Along (IRE)**[227] 5960 3-9-1 **57** RichardHughes 9 4
(M L W Bell) *hld up in rr: nvr a factor: eased wl ins fnl f* **9/1**

1m 27.3s **Going Correction** -0.275s/f (Firm) **11** Ran SP% **122.7**
Speed ratings (Par 96): **89,88,86,85,83 83,81,80,76,73 64**
toteswinger: 1&2 £2.50, 2&3 £6.80 CSF £109.98 CT £167.43 TOTE £12.70: £3.60, £1.60, £1.10; EX 76.20 Trifecta £119.50 Pool £360.29 - 2.23 winning units..
Owner C L A Edginton **Bred** Garry Chong **Trained** Lambourn, Berks

FOCUS
It was difficult to know what to make of this bunch before the off, but the favourite was heavily supported. There was little pace on early, so plenty of them pulled hard. The winning time was taken by hand. Rather muddling form, with the runner-up unlucky.
King Of Defence Official explanation: jockey said gelding was unsuited by the track
Mount Ella Official explanation: jockey said filly lost its action
Crystallize Official explanation: jockey said gelding was denied a clear run
Princess Rebecca Official explanation: jockey said filly was unsuited by the good to firm ground
Bussell Along(IRE) Official explanation: jockey said filly lost its action

1621 LADBROKES.COM H'CAP — 1m 1f 149y
5:05 (5:06) (Class 4) (0-80,79) 4-Y-O+ **£5,180** (£1,541; £770; £384) **Stalls** Centre

Form RPR

-153 **1** **Annabelle's Charm (IRE)**[17] 1261 4-8-13 **74** DaneO'Neill 3 85+
(L M Cumani) *chsd ldrs tl trckd ldr 7f out: jnd ldr 3f out: rdn to ld 2f out: in command and styd on wl fnl f* **3/1**[2]

244- **2** 1 ¼ **Special Reserve (IRE)**[153] 7474 4-9-2 **77** RichardHughes 5 83
(R Hannon) *w.w in midfield: c wd st: rdn and hdwy 2f out: drvn ent fnl f: r.o to go 2nd last strides: nvr gng to rch wnr* **2/1**[1]

240- **3** *hd* **Gaia Prince (USA)**[321] 2996 4-9-0 **75** JimCrowley 9 81
(Mrs A J Perrett) *t.k.h: chsd ldr tl 7f out: chsd ldrs after: rdn over 2f out: wnt 2nd again ins fnl f: no imp: lost 2nd last strides* **5/1**

156- **4** ½ **Constant Cheers (IRE)**[218] 6203 6-8-13 **77** DavidProbert(3) 8 82
(W R Swinburn) *led: jnd 3f out: rdn and hdd 2f out: kpt on u.p: lost 2 pls ins fnl f* **4/1**[3]

5-00 **5** 4 ½ **Another Bottle (IRE)**[9] 1433 8-9-3 **78** SteveDrowne 7 74
(Mrs S Leech) *stdd after s: hld up in last pl: rdn and no hdwy jst over 2f out* **33/1**

1050 **6** 1 **Evident Pride (USA)**[50] 801 6-9-4 **79** AdamKirby 2 73
(B R Johnson) *stdd after s: hld up in last trio: rdn and effrt jst over 2f out: no prog* **7/1**

560- **7** 1 ½ **Clipperdown (IRE)**[39] 3167 8-9-0 **75** (t) EdwardCreighton 1 66
(E J Creighton) *stdd s: hld up in last trio: rdn and no hdwy jst over 2f out* **66/1**

2m 3.69s (-1.21) **Going Correction** -0.075s/f (Good) **7** Ran SP% **111.9**
Speed ratings (Par 105): **101,100,99,99,95 95,93**
toteswinger: 1&2 £2.30, 1&3 £3.50, 2&3 £2.70 CSF £9.00 CT £26.73 TOTE £4.00: £2.00, £1.50; EX 10.10 Trifecta £49.70 Pool: £361.03 - 5.37 winning units..
Owner Merry Fox Stud Limited **Bred** Swordlestown Stud **Trained** Newmarket, Suffolk

FOCUS
The gallop was not strong early, typically for Folkestone, and a bit of a sprint ensued off the final bend. The form seems sound enough though, and the winner can probably post better figures than this.
Another Bottle(IRE) Official explanation: jockey said gelding moved poorly throughout

1622 LADBROKES.COM MEDIAN AUCTION MAIDEN STKS — 1m 1f 149y
5:40 (5:41) (Class 6) 3-4-Y-O **£2,729** (£806; £403) **Stalls** Centre

Form RPR

622- **1** **History Lesson**[197] 6731 3-8-10 **80** RichardHughes 5 81+
(R Hannon) *broke wl: mde all: stdd gallop 6f out: jnd over 4f out: rdn 2f out: drew clr ins fnl f: eased towards fin* **10/11**[1]

6-23 **2** 2 ½ **Light Dubai (IRE)**[13] 1329 3-8-5 **73** TPO'Shea 4 71
(M R Channon) *chsd ldng pair: rdn to chse wnr 2f out: no ex ent fnl f: wl hld fnl 100yds* **11/10**[2]

0- **3** 3 ½ **Cluny**[143] 7602 3-8-5 0 MartinDwyer 1 64
(J R Fanshawe) *hld up in tch: rdn to chse ldng pair wl over 1f out: sn hung lft and wknd* **16/1**[3]

0 **4** 7 **Mac Wolf**[15] 1289 3-8-5 0 NicolPolli(5) 2 55
(M G Quinlan) *s.i.s: sn bustled along: in tch in rr: rdn jst over 2f out: wknd qckly wl over 1f out* **40/1**

0 **5** 9 **Roman The Emperor (IRE)**[17] 1260 3-8-10 0 JerryO'Dwyer 7 37
(S W Hall) *t.k.h: chsd wnr: jnd wnr over 4f out tl 2f out: sn wknd* **80/1**

2m 4.00s (-0.90) **Going Correction** -0.075s/f (Good)
WFA 3 from 4yo 17lb **5** Ran SP% **109.6**
Speed ratings (Par 101): **100,98,95,89,82**
toteswinger: 1&2 £2.20 CSF £2.13 TOTE £1.90: £1.10, £1.10; EX 2.10 Place 6: £3.83 Place 5: £2.74.
Owner The Queen **Bred** The Queen **Trained** East Everleigh, Wilts

FOCUS
The winner made all, setting a stop-start pace, and is probably better than the bare form, which has been rated around the first two.
T/Jkpt: £2,366.60 to a £1 stake. Pool: £10,000.00. 3.00 winning tickets. T/Plt: £3.80 to a £1 stake. Pool: £60,555.57. 11,550.58 winning tickets. T/Qpdt: £3.60 to a £1 stake. Pool: £3,042.08. 609.90 winning tickets. SP

1241 REDCAR (L-H)
Thursday, April 30

OFFICIAL GOING: Good to firm (firm in places; 10.2)
Wind: Light, half-behind Weather: Overcast

1623 REDCAR "A COURSE FOR ALL REASONS" MAIDEN AUCTION STKS — 5f
2:00 (2:05) (Class 5) 2-Y-O **£2,590** (£770; £385; £192) **Stalls** Centre

Form RPR

04 **1** **Lady Lube Rye (IRE)**[12] 1344 2-8-4 0 PaulQuinn 7 64+
(N Wilson) *chsd ldrs: rdn along 2f out: styd on strly ins fnl f to ld nr line* **11/2**[3]

55 **2** *nk* **Ignatieff (IRE)**[12] 1358 2-8-12 0 TomEaves 5 71
(Mrs L Stubbs) *led: rdn wl over 1f out and sn edgd lft: drvn and hung lft ins fnl f: hdd and no ex nr fin* **4/1**[2]

6 **3** 1 ½ **Oondiri (IRE)**[15] 1277 2-8-4 0 DuranFentiman 1 58
(T D Easterby) *cl up on wd outside: hanging lft thrght: rdn and ev ch 2f out: drvn and one pce ent fnl f* **11/2**[3]

4 ¾ **Flow Chart (IRE)** 2-8-9 0 PhillipMakin 9 60+
(T D Barron) *dwlt: in tch: rdn along 2f out: kpt on fnl f: nrst fin* **10/3**[1]

5 6 **Rio Caribe (IRE)** 2-8-12 0 GrahamGibbons 10 41
(T D Walford) *dwlt: midfield and pushed along 1/2-way: sme late hdwy* **12/1**

6 1 ¼ **Arctic Destiny (IRE)** 2-8-12 0 AndrewElliott 8 37
(K R Burke) *wnt rt s: a midfield* **14/1**

7 1 ½ **Loss Leader (IRE)** 2-8-9 0 DavidAllan 11 28
(T D Easterby) *dwlt and wnt rt s: a towards rr* **11/1**

8 ½ **Countrywide Ice (IRE)** 2-8-9 0 RichardMullen 3 27
(K A Ryan) *s.i.s: a in rr* **8/1**

9 8 **Bring Sweets (IRE)** 2-8-9 0 JamieMoriarty 4 —
(B Ellison) *s.i.s: a in rr* **14/1**

10 20 **Miss Dreamy** 2-8-7 0 PaulMulrennan 2 —
(P C Haslam) *free to s: s.i.s and a bhd* **66/1**

57.73 secs (-0.87) **Going Correction** -0.30s/f (Firm) **10** Ran SP% **115.8**
Speed ratings (Par 92): **94,93,91,89,80 78,75,75,62,30**
toteswinger: 1&2 £3.10, 1&3 £5.50, 2&3 £4.20 CSF £27.58 TOTE £7.00: £1.90, £1.60, £2.00; EX 29.00.
Owner D & S L Tanker Transport Limited **Bred** L Fox **Trained** Flaxton, N Yorks

FOCUS
A modest juvenile in which the first three had the benefit of previous experience. The winning time was 0.54 seconds quicker than the following two-year-old seller.

NOTEBOOK
Lady Lube Rye(IRE) didn't have to improve on the form she showed when fourth at Doncaster on her previous start, but she still made hard work of this, only getting up after Ignatieff edged left. She's likely to find things much tougher from now on. (op 4-1 tchd 6-1)
Ignatieff(IRE) showed loads of speed, but ruined his winning chance by edging over towards the far rail in the closing stages. Still, this was a significant improvement on his two previous efforts. (tchd 7-2)
Oondiri(IRE) was always handy and stepped up on the form she showed on her debut from a poor draw at Beverley, despite hanging left towards the far rail. (tchd 5-1 and 6-1)
Flow Chart(IRE), an £800 first foal of a 6f winner on juvenile winner on debut, was extremely well backed, but he proved reluctant to load (needed blindfold fitted) and was fractious in the stalls. In the race itself, he lacked the sharpness of those with experience, but gradually got the idea. He showed ability and can improve, but it's worth remembering this wasn't much of a race. (op 10-1 tchd 3-1)
Rio Caribe(IRE) missed the break and never threatened, but he hinted at ability. (op 14-1)

1624 RACING UK CHANNEL 432 (S) STKS — 5f
2:30 (2:32) (Class 6) 2-Y-O **£2,047** (£604; £302) **Stalls** Centre

Form RPR

1 **House Of Frills** 2-8-9 0 ow2 PhillipMakin 2 61+
(T D Barron) *cl up: effrt to ld over 1f out: rdn and kpt on wl fnl f* **18/1**

23 **2** 1 **Out The Ring (IRE)**[26] 1126 2-8-12 0 RichardMullen 10 60
(K A Ryan) *cl up on outer: led 1/2-way: rdn and edgd rt over 1f out: sn hdd and drvn: kpt on one pce* **4/6**[1]

46 **3** 2 **Musiara**[12] 1344 2-8-7 0 SamHitchcott 6 47
(M R Channon) *chsd ldrs: rdn along 2f out: kpt on ins fnl f* **9/1**

3 **4** *hd* **Blue Rum (IRE)**^{12} [1364] 2-8-12 0 PaulMulrennan 8 52
(P C Haslam) *prom: rdn along 2f out: drvn over 1f out and kpt on same pce* **11/2**^{3}

3 **5** *11* **Gasparilla (IRE)**^{8} [1450] 2-8-7 0 RobertWinston 5 21+
(A J McCabe) *led: hdd 1/2-way: sn rdn and wknd: eased over 1f out* **5/1**^{2}

0 **6** *nk* **Mostofitleft (IRE)**^{8} [1450] 2-8-7 0 FrancisNorton 4 4
(A Berry) *a towards rr* **66/1**

5 **7** *1 1/2* **Needs A Treat**^{12} [1364] 2-8-4 0 KellyHarrison(3) 7 —
(N Tinkler) *in tch: rdn along and outpcd fr 1/2-way* **50/1**

0 **8** *2 3/4* **Ze Finale**^{10} [1396] 2-8-7 0 DavidAllan 3 —
(T D Easterby) *dwlt: a in rr* **40/1**

0 **9** *1/2* **Strange Fiction**^{15} [1275] 2-8-12 0 (b1) PaulHanagan 9 —
(R A Fahey) *wnt lft and reminders s: sn outpcd and bhd* **33/1**

58.27 secs (-0.33) **Going Correction** -0.30s/f (Firm) **9** Ran SP% **116.1**
Speed ratings (Par 90): **90,88,85,84,67 66,64,60,59**
toteswinger: 1&2 £5.20, 1&3 £12.50, 2&3 £3.20 CSF £30.81 TOTE £18.90: £3.10, £1.10, £2.20; EX 54.70.The winner was bought in for 6,200gns.
Owner M Dalby **Bred** Frilly Front Partnership **Trained** Maunby, N Yorks

FOCUS
A reasonable two-year-old seller in which the time was 0.54 seconds slower than the earlier maiden.

NOTEBOOK
House Of Frills, who is out of a multiple 5f winner, was good enough to make a successful debut, recording a time 0.54 seconds slower than the earlier maiden in the process. The David Barron yard has had two well-backed newcomers run below market expectations in maiden company over the last couple of days, but this one, seemingly unfancied, created quite a good impression in the context of this lowly grade. Carrying 2lb overweight, she showed good speed from the off and won with her ears pricked, looking slightly better than this level. (op 12-1 tchd 20-1)

Out The Ring(IRE) failed to run up to the form he showed on his debut when third at Nottingham last time, and this represented further regression. He might benefit from a return to Polytrack. (op 5-4)

Musiara never posed a threat, but is likely to find easier sellers. (op 11-1)

Blue Rum(IRE) did not build on the form he showed in a Thirsk claimer on his debut and looks extremely limited. (op 6-1 tchd 5-1)

Gasparilla(IRE) was disputing third and looking held when she appeared to lose her action just over a furlong out. Official explanation: jockey said filly lost its action and hung badly left (op 7-2 tchd 11-2)

1625 BECOME AN ANNUAL BADGE HOLDER TODAY MEDIAN AUCTION MAIDEN STKS 7f

3:05 (3:05) (Class 5) 3-Y-O **£2,590** (£770; £385; £192) **Stalls** Centre

Form RPR

2 **1** **Seldom (IRE)**^{13} [1335] 3-8-10 0 JohnCavanagh(7) 9 68
(M Brittain) *prom: hdwy 3f out: rdn to chal over 1f out: drvn to ld ins fnl f: styd on wl* **9/4**^{2}

5-44 **2** *1 1/4* **Minturno (USA)**^{13} [1335] 3-9-3 60 DO'Donohoe 1 65
(Mrs A Duffield) *hld up towards rr: stdy hdwy iover 2f out: rdn over 1f out: styd on and ch ins fnl f: drvn and one pce towards fin* **8/1**

3 *nk* **Localiser (IRE)** 3-9-3 0 AdrianTNicholls 8 64
(D Nicholls) *in tch: hdwy 1/2-way: rdn to ld over 2f out: drvn over 1f out: hdd ins fnl f: one pce towards fin* **12/1**

33- **4** *3/4* **Do The Deal (IRE)**^{194} [6808] 3-8-12 0 GrahamGibbons 2 57
(J J Quinn) *trckd ldrs: effrt and n.m.r 2f out: swtchd rt and rdn over 1f out: sn drvn and kpt on same pce* **15/8**^{1}

0-0 **5** *2 3/4* **Tilerium's Dream (IRE)**^{14} [1308] 3-9-3 0 SilvestreDeSousa 5 54
(K A Ryan) *t.k.h: prom: rdn along 3f out and sn one pce* **33/1**

-5 **6** *hd* **Scotch And Soda (IRE)**^{23} [1174] 3-8-12 0 AndrewElliott 6 49
(Jedd O'Keeffe) *cl up: rdn along 3f out: grad wknd* **10/1**

7 *2 1/4* **Kentucky Lakes** 3-9-3 0 PaulHanagan 4 48
(Jedd O'Keeffe) *in tch: rdn along over 2f out and sn btn* **15/2**^{3}

6-0 **8** *1* **Ryedon Bye**^{13} [1335] 3-9-3 0 DavidAllan 10 45
(T D Easterby) *sn led: rdn along 3f out: hdd over 2f out and sn wknd* **20/1**

9 *2* **Callis Wood** 3-8-12 0 JamieMoriarty 7 35
(Ollie Pears) *dwlt: a in rr* **50/1**

1m 23.99s (-0.51) **Going Correction** -0.30s/f (Firm) **9** Ran SP% **114.9**
Speed ratings (Par 98): **90,88,88,87,84 84,81,80,78**
toteswinger: 1&2 £4.30, 1&3 £6.30, 2&3 £9.80 CSF £20.10 TOTE £3.00: £1.50, £2.00, £4.00; EX 17.50.
Owner Mel Brittain **Bred** Stephen Moloney **Trained** Warthill, N Yorks

FOCUS
A modest maiden and not form to dwell on. With the favourite disappointing the winner probably didn't have to improve on his debut form.

1626 BODDINGTONS REDCAR STRAIGHT-MILE CHAMPIONSHIP (H'CAP) (QUALIFIER) 1m

3:40 (3:40) (Class 5) (0-75,74) 3-Y-O **£2,590** (£578; £578; £192) **Stalls** Centre

Form RPR

430- **1** **Paquerettza (FR)**^{211} [6392] 3-8-12 68 PaulMulrennan 2 80
(D H Brown) *cl up: effrt over 2f out: rdn to ld over 1f out: drvn and edgd lft ins fnl f: hld on wl* **18/1**

34-4 **2** *1/2* **Tarzan (IRE)**^{15} [1280] 3-9-1 71 RoystonFfrench 4 82
(M Johnston) *led: rdn along over 2f out: drvn and hdd over 1f out: rallied u.p towards fin* **9/2**^{3}

54-1 **2** *dht* **Rising Kheleyf (IRE)**^{8} [1452] 3-8-9 65 6ex PJMcDonald 6 76
(G A Swinbank) *trckd ldrs: hdwy over 2f out and sn cl up: effrt over 1f out: sn rdn andev ch tl drvn: edgd lft and no ex nr fin* **5/2**^{2}

-011 **4** *8* **Cornish Castle (USA)**^{12} [1361] 3-9-4 74 GrahamGibbons 3 67
(T D Walford) *hld up in tch: rdn along 3f out and sn btn* **15/8**^{1}

060- **5** *1 1/4* **Alicante**^{205} [6555] 3-8-5 61 DO'Donohoe 7 51
(Sir Mark Prescott) *t.k.h: cl up: rdn along over 2f out: grad wknd* **14/1**

01-4 **6** *nk* **Embsay Crag**^{15} [1281] 3-8-8 67 NeilBrown(3) 5 56
(Mrs K Walton) *a in rr* **8/1**

40-5 **7** *shd* **Lost In Paris (IRE)**^{22} [1193] 3-8-5 61 DuranFentiman 1 50
(T D Easterby) *trckd ldrs: rdn along over 2f out: sn wknd* **11/1**

1m 34.46s (-3.54) **Going Correction** -0.30s/f (Firm) **7** Ran SP% **112.9**
Speed ratings (Par 98): **105,104,104,96,95 94,94**
PL: Tarzan £1.30, Rising Kheleyf £1.30 EX: Paquerettza &T £62.30, P&RK £41.80 CSF: P&T £46.70 P&RK £30.69; toteswinger: P&T £13.80, T&R£3.80 P&RK £6.50 TOTE £23.20: £10.20.
Owner J B Smith & J M Smith **Bred** Newsells Park Stud **Trained** Maltby, S Yorks

FOCUS
A fair three-year-old handicap for the grade run at a strong pace. The first three came clear and the form looks sound.

1627 BOOK TICKETS ONLINE @ REDCARRACING.CO.UK FILLIES' H'CAP 5f

4:15 (4:17) (Class 4) (0-85,83) 3-Y-O+ **£4,857** (£1,445; £722; £360) **Stalls** Centre

Form RPR

5-11 **1** **Jaconet (USA)**^{18} [1227] 4-9-13 83 (b) PhillipMakin 1 94
(T D Barron) *cl up: led 2f out: rdn ent fnl f: styd on strly* **15/8**^{1}

5-24 **2** *1* **Rothesay Dancer**^{18} [1227] 6-9-0 73 KellyHarrison(3) 6 81
(J S Goldie) *hld up in tch: smooth hdwy 2f out: rdn to chal appr fnl f and ev ch tl drvn and nt qckn last 75yds* **5/1**^{3}

34-3 **3** *3/4* **Gap Princess (IRE)**^{17} [1241] 5-9-0 70 PaulHanagan 7 75
(R A Fahey) *in tch: hdwy 2f out: rdn over 1f out: kpt on ins fnl f: nrst fin* **11/4**^{2}

0-00 **4** *1* **Dispol Kylie (IRE)**^{12} [1368] 3-8-11 77 JoeFanning 8 74
(P T Midgley) *in tch on outer: hdwy 2f out: sn rdn and kpt on ins fnl f: nrst fin* **25/1**

5103 **5** *nk* **Nomoreblondes**^{5} [1518] 5-9-0 70 (p) JamieMoriarty 2 70
(P T Midgley) *led: rdn along and hdd 2f out: sn drvn and wknd appr fnl f* **15/2**

36-3 **6** *3 1/2* **Mango Music**^{10} [1411] 6-9-8 78 FrancisNorton 5 66
(M Quinn) *trckd ldrs: rdn along 2f out: sn drvn and wknd* **9/1**

-506 **7** *1* **Wibbadune (IRE)**^{31} [1041] 5-9-2 72 RobertWinston 3 56
(D Shaw) *trckd ldrs: rdn along 2f out: sn drvn and wknd over 1f out* **12/1**

8 *1/2* **Josphiel (IRE)**^{250} [5298] 4-8-8 69 oh4 SladeO'Hara(5) 4 51
(A Berry) *in tch: sn rdn along and outpcd fr 1/2-way* **40/1**

56.76 secs (-1.84) **Going Correction** -0.30s/f (Firm)
WFA 3 from 4yo+ 10lb **8** Ran SP% **113.9**
Speed ratings (Par 102): **102,100,99,97,97 91,89,89**
toteswinger: 1&2 £2.70, 1&3 £2.20, 2&3 £3.30 CSF £11.57 CT £24.72 TOTE £2.40: £1.50, £1.80, £1.20; EX 10.60.
Owner R G Toes **Bred** Team Block **Trained** Maunby, N Yorks

FOCUS
A fair sprint handicap. The winner maintained her progress with another personal best.

1628 REDCAR CONFERENCE AND EXHIBITION CENTRE APPRENTICE CLAIMING STKS 6f

4:50 (4:50) (Class 6) 3-4-Y-O **£2,047** (£604; £302) **Stalls** Centre

Form RPR

-413 **1** **Chocolicious (IRE)**^{6} [1492] 3-8-6 66 (v) GaryBartley(2) 4 68
(B Smart) *hld up: swtchd lft and hdwy over 2f out: chsd ldrs over 1f out: rdn andqcknd to ld ins fnl f: sn clr* **7/2**^{3}

1021 **2** *3 1/4* **La Capriosa**^{7} [1469] 3-8-8 68 AmyRyan(4) 8 62
(A J McCabe) *cl up: led after 1f: rdn along and edgd rt wl over 1f out: drvn and hdd ins fnl f: one pce* **13/8**^{1}

P-33 **3** *2 3/4* **Parisian Gift (IRE)**^{60} [721] 4-9-2 70 (p) AndreaAtzeni(2) 10 51
(J R Gask) *chsd ldrs: hdwy over 2f out: swtchd lft and rdn over 1f out: sn one pce* **9/4**^{2}

600- **4** *1/2* **What A Fella**^{194} [6807] 3-8-3 50 LanceBetts(4) 13 46
(Mrs A Duffield) *chsd ldrs: hdwy 2f out: sn rdn and one pce appr last* **33/1**

010- **5** *2* **Red River Boy**^{313} [3283] 4-10-0 53 KellyHarrison 3 53
(C W Fairhurst) *hld up: hdwy on outer over 2f out: rdn over 1f out: kpt on ins fnl f: nrst fin* **20/1**

6-00 **6** *1/2* **Thompsons Walls (IRE)**^{15} [1276] 4-9-2 60 (b1) PatrickDonaghy(2) 5 41
(S T Mason) *cl up: rdn along over 2f out: grad wknd* **14/1**

50-5 **7** *2 1/4* **Andrasta**^{59} [738] 4-9-1 53 SladeO'Hara(2) 12 33
(A Berry) *chsd ldrs: rdn along over 2f out: sn edgd rt and wknd* **25/1**

000 **8** *3* **She's Our Dream**^{17} [1243] 4-8-9 43 (vt1) LeeNewnes(4) 9 20
(R C Guest) *midfield: rdn along over 2f out and sn btn* **80/1**

0060 **9** *3/4* **Mickys Mate**^{17} [1243] 4-9-4 41 (p) NeilBrown 2 22
(A Crook) *a towards rr* **125/1**

000- **10** *1 3/4* **Raise All In (IRE)**^{132} [7728] 3-7-12 53 AdeleMulrennan(4) 1 9
(N Wilson) *led 1f: cl up tl rdn along over 2f out and sn wknd* **25/1**

43-0 **11** *1* **Karate Queen**^{8} [1456] 4-9-1 50 AdamCarter(4) 11 14
(R E Barr) *a in rr* **50/1**

43-0 **12** *1 1/2* **Future Gem**^{13} [1335] 3-8-0 43 JamieKyne(4) 7 3
(A Dickman) *dwlt: a in rr* **66/1**

06-0 **13** *2* **Lydia's Legacy**^{17} [1241] 4-8-13 38 MarzenaJeziorek(4) 6 1
(T J Etherington) *chsd ldrs: rdn along 1/2-way: sn wknd* **100/1**

69.77 secs (-2.03) **Going Correction** -0.30s/f (Firm)
WFA 3 from 4yo 11lb **13** Ran SP% **119.6**
Speed ratings (Par 101): **101,96,93,92,89 89,86,82,81,78 77,75,72**
toteswinger: 1&2 £2.70, 1&3 £2.30, 2&3 £1.50 CSF £8.90 TOTE £5.10: £1.70, £1.10, £1.30; EX 10.50.
Owner Mrs Trisha Laughton **Bred** Ballyhane Stud **Trained** Hambleton, N Yorks

FOCUS
A modest claimer. A personal best from the winner but the next two were probably not at their best.
Karate Queen Official explanation: trainer said filly lost a shoe

1629 GO RACING AT THIRSK THIS SATURDAY H'CAP 1m 2f

5:20 (5:22) (Class 5) (0-75,74) 3-Y-O **£2,590** (£770; £385; £192) **Stalls** Low

Form RPR

04-1 **1** **Topolski (IRE)**^{7} [1470] 3-9-7 74 6ex RoystonFfrench 3 86+
(M Johnston) *trckd ldr: effrt and pushed along 4f out: rdn to ld wl over 2f out: drvn clrwl over 1f out: styd on* **2/7**^{1}

-410 **2** *6* **Spartan Prince (USA)**^{15} [1280] 3-9-2 69 RobertWinston 9 69
(T D Barron) *led: rdn along 4f out: drvn and hdd wl over 2f out: kpt on same pce* **16/1**

366 **3** *5* **Antipodean (UAE)**^{69} [621] 3-8-4 57 oh2 JoeFanning 6 47
(P T Midgley) *trckd ldrs: effrt 4f out: rdn along 3f out: sn drvn and plugged on same pce* **28/1**

504- **4** *1 1/4* **Veronicas Boy**^{222} [6101] 3-8-12 65 PJMcDonald 5 53
(G M Moore) *hld up in rr: sme hdwy over 3f out: sn rdn and nvr a factor* **25/1**

434- **5** *1 1/4* **Hector's House**^{194} [6808] 3-9-4 71 PhillipMakin 1 56
(M Dods) *trckd ldrs on inner: hdwy 4f out: rdn 3f out and sn outpcd* **10/1**^{3}

064- **6** *1/2* **Kattar**^{157} [7438] 3-8-12 65 RichardMullen 7 49
(D M Simcock) *a in rr* **8/1**^{2}

2m 10.21s (3.11) **Going Correction** -0.30s/f (Firm) **6** Ran SP% **111.1**
Speed ratings (Par 98): **75,70,66,65,64 63**
toteswinger: 1&2 £1.80, 1&3 £5.00, 2&3 £9.50 CSF £6.42 CT £46.03 TOTE £1.40: £1.02, £3.60; EX 5.70 Place 6:£15.08 Place 5: £7.79.
Owner Kennet Valley Thoroughbreds V **Bred** C H Wacker Iii **Trained** Middleham Moor, N Yorks

FOCUS
An uncompetitive handicap run at a modest pace. The winner was 3lb well in under his penalty but is one to keep on the right side.
T/Plt: £11.00 to a £1 stake. Pool: £46,556.37. 3,077.43 winning tickets. T/Qpdt: £3.10 to a £1 stake. Pool: £3,020.17. 707.09 winning tickets. JR

1269 YARMOUTH (L-H)
Thursday, April 30

OFFICIAL GOING: Good to firm
Wind: Fresh, against Weather: Fine and sunny

1630 CREDIT ACCOUNTS WITH PREMIER RACING SERVICES EBF MAIDEN STKS 5f 43y
5:25 (5:26) (Class 5) 2-Y-O **£3,626** (£1,079; £539; £269) **Stalls** High

Form RPR
1 **Misheer** 2-8-12 0 NCallan 5 91+
(C E Brittain) *w ldr tl led 3f out: pushed clr fr over 1f out* **9/2**2
2 8 **Tiradito (USA)** 2-9-3 0 TedDurcan 4 64
(M Botti) *dwlt: outpcd: hdwy to chse wnr over 1f out: no imp fnl f* **15/2**3
30 3 3 1/2 **Thomas Baines (USA)**10 1404 2-9-3 0 JamieSpencer 1 50
(M L W Bell) *sn pushed along and prom: rdn 1/2-way: nt run on* **4/11**1
0 4 4 **Avec Moi**22 1188 2-8-12 0 CatherineGannon 7 29
(Mrs C A Dunnett) *w ldrs tl rdn wl over 2f out: wknd over 1f out* **20/1**
5 2 **Point To Prove** 2-9-3 0 PatCosgrave 6 26
(Miss Amy Weaver) *sn led: hdd 3f out: rdn and wknd over 1f out* **50/1**
0 6 1/2 **Our Georgie Girl**21 1195 2-8-12 0 JohnEgan 3 19
(G G Margarson) *prom: rdn 1/2-way: wknd wl over 1f out* **40/1**
7 1 1/4 **Southwark Newshawk** 2-8-12 0 TGMcLaughlin 2 14
(Mrs C A Dunnett) *sn outpcd* **50/1**
62.96 secs (0.76) **Going Correction** -0.10s/f (Good) 7 Ran SP% **114.4**
Speed ratings (Par 92): **89,76,70,64,61 60,58**
toteswinger: 1&2 £4.20, 1&3 £1.40, 2&3 £1.10 CSF £33.50 TOTE £7.60: £6.40, £5.30; EX 22.10.
Owner Saeed Manana **Bred** New England Stud And Partners **Trained** Newmarket, Suffolk
■ Stewards' Enquiry : Jamie Spencer caution: used whip with excessive force.

FOCUS
Following a dry night 3mm of water was placed on the track in the morning. The ground was good to firm all round. An uncompetitive opener and one that took much less winning than seemed likely with the short-priced favourite disappointing but the winner nevertheless looks a decent prospect. The pace was fair.

NOTEBOOK
Misheer ◆, the first foal of a useful 5f juvenile winner, was supported in the market and created a very favourable impression on this racecourse debut. While her task was obviously made easier by the below-par run of the market leader she could do no more than win with plenty in hand and she is the type to progress again. She will reportedly now take in a conditions or Listed race. (op 8-1)
Tiradito(USA), the third foal of a sister to a Grade 1 US winner, had reportedly been pleasing connections at home and he showed ability on this racecourse debut. He left the impression that further would suit in due course and he should be able to win a race. (op 6-1 tchd 8-1)
Thomas Baines(USA), who looked an unlucky loser at Windsor just over a week ago, was a big disappointment. He never looked happy after another tardy start and just wanted to hang and carry his head high under pressure. While he has plenty of ability and may be suited by easier ground, he looks one to tread very carefully with at present. Official explanation: jockey said colt hung left (op 2-7 tchd 2-5 in places)
Avec Moi was backed at big odds but again underlined her vulnerability in this type of event. (op 40-1)
Point To Prove was well beaten after only hinting at ability on this racecourse debut. (op 40-1 tchd 33-1)

1631 PREMIER RACING SERVICES GRAND OPENING IN LOWESTOFT CONDITIONS STKS 7f 3y
6:00 (6:02) (Class 4) 3-Y-O+ **£6,231** (£1,866; £933; £467; £233) **Stalls** High

Form RPR
1- 1 **Mutheeb (USA)**226 5995 4-9-4 82 LDettori 3 109
(Saeed Bin Suroor) *hld up in tch: led on bit 2f out: hdd ins fnl f: rallied to ld towards fin* **9/4**2
0-46 2 hd **Mia's Boy**12 1352 5-9-4 101 JimmyQuinn 5 109
(C A Dwyer) *hld up: hdwy over 2f out: led ins fnl f: sn rdn: hdd towards fin* **13/8**1
21-0 3 7 **Cloudy Start**13 1324 3-8-6 88 ow1 EddieAhern 4 86
(H R A Cecil) *prom: rdn over 2f out: wknd fnl f* **6/1**
3-00 4 1 1/4 **Charm School**12 1352 4-9-4 95 (b1) JimmyFortune 1 87
(J H M Gosden) *chsd ldr: led over 5f out: rdn and hdd 2f out: sn wknd* **10/3**3
40-0 5 9 **Mujood**22 1187 6-9-4 87 (v) StephenCarson 2 62
(Eve Johnson Houghton) *led: hdd over 5f out: chsd ldr tl rdn over 2f out: wknd over 1f out* **66/1**
1m 24.8s (-1.80) **Going Correction** -0.10s/f (Good)
WFA 3 from 4yo+ 13lb 5 Ran SP% **107.7**
Speed ratings (Par 105): **106,105,97,96,86**
toteswinger: 1&2 £3.40. CSF £6.01 TOTE £2.60: £3.00, £1.10; EX 5.10.
Owner Godolphin **Bred** Jayeff 'B' Stables **Trained** Newmarket, Suffolk

FOCUS
Not the strongest of races for the money on offer but the winner looks a most progressive sort. The pace was fair and the first two pulled clear in the final furlong. The form looks sound enough.

1632 BET WITH PREMIER RACING SERVICES MEDIAN AUCTION MAIDEN STKS 1m 3y
6:30 (6:34) (Class 6) 3-4-Y-O **£1,942** (£578; £288; £144) **Stalls** High

Form RPR
2-5 1 **Hyades (USA)**13 1328 3-8-12 0 EddieAhern 7 82+
(H R A Cecil) *trckd ldrs: led 2f out: sn rdn and hung lft: styd on wl* **8/11**1
4- 2 4 **Ithbaat (USA)**244 5469 3-8-12 0 RHills 6 72+
(J H M Gosden) *dwlt: hld up: plld hrd: swtchd lft 5f out: hdwy 3f out: rdn to chse wnr over 1f out: styd on same pce* **7/4**2
6-0 3 2 **Markhesa**16 1269 3-8-7 0 TedDurcan 4 63
(C F Wall) *hld up: racd keenly: swtchd rt and hdwy over 1f out: styd on to go 3rd wl ins fnl f: nt trble ldrs* **50/1**
3-4 4 3/4 **Dukes Art**17 1255 3-8-12 0 JamieSpencer 1 66
(J A R Toller) *led 1f: chsd ldr: rdn and ev ch 2f out: wknd ins fnl f* **11/2**3
0-0 5 7 **Topcroft**48 828 3-8-12 0 TGMcLaughlin 3 49
(Mrs C A Dunnett) *prom: pushed along 1/2-way: wknd 2f out* **150/1**
-000 6 1 **Yakama (IRE)**7 1475 4-9-12 54 JohnEgan 2 47
(Mrs C A Dunnett) *chsd ldr tl led 7f out: rdn and hdd 2f out: sn wknd* **33/1**
60- 7 3 1/2 **Dashing Daniel**201 6660 4-9-12 0 VinceSlattery 8 38
(N J Vaughan) *chsd ldrs: rdn over 2f out: sn wknd* **66/1**
1m 39.6s (-1.00) **Going Correction** -0.10s/f (Good)
WFA 3 from 4yo 14lb 7 Ran SP% **116.7**
Speed ratings (Par 101): **101,97,95,94,87 86,82**
toteswinger: 1&2 £1.10, 1&3 £5.40, 2&3 £7.30. CSF £2.36 TOTE £1.80: £1.02, £2.20; EX 2.80.
Owner Niarchos Family **Bred** Flaxman Holdings Ltd **Trained** Newmarket, Suffolk

FOCUS
An uncompetitive maiden run at just an ordinary gallop. The winner may not have had to improve with doubts over whether the runner-up was at his best.

1633 PREMIER RACING SERVICES - NEW SHOP IN LOWESTOFT H'CAP 1m 3y
7:00 (7:01) (Class 5) (0-75,75) 4-Y-O+ **£2,590** (£770; £385; £192) **Stalls** High

Form RPR
40-5 1 **Charlevoix (IRE)**17 1256 4-8-11 68 TedDurcan 2 76
(C F Wall) *hld up: nt clr run over 2f out: swtchd rt and hdwy over 1f out: r.o to ld last strides* **9/2**2
2-22 2 nk **Will He Wish**101 220 13-8-11 75 (v) MatthewDavies(7) 5 82
(S Gollings) *chsd ldrs: led wl over 1f out: sn rdn and edgd rt: hdd last strides* **10/1**
020- 3 1 1/4 **Aggravation**261 4946 7-8-11 68 RyanMoore 3 72+
(D R C Elsworth) *dwlt: hld up: hdwy and nt clr run over 1f out: swtchd rt: running on whn n.m.r ins fnl f: nvr able to chal* **6/1**
100- 4 nk **Luck Will Come (IRE)**210 6422 5-8-8 65 JimmyQuinn 7 68
(H J Collingridge) *prom: racd keenly: rdn and ev ch ins fnl f: unable qck* **10/1**
003- 5 2 1/4 **King Columbo (IRE)**181 7111 4-8-6 70 MatthewCosham(7) 4 68
(Miss J Feilden) *led: rdn over 2f out: hdd wl over 1f out: no ex ins fnl f* **11/2**3
46-2 6 4 1/2 **Astrodonna**17 1256 4-9-0 71 NCallan 1 59
(M H Tompkins) *hld up in tch: rdn over 1f out: wknd ins fnl f* **4/1**1
4341 7 2 3/4 **Solent Ridge (IRE)**31 1035 4-9-4 75 (p) LPKeniry 8 57
(J S Moore) *chsd ldrs: shkn up over 2f out: wknd over 1f out* **13/2**
000- 8 8 **Dancer's Legacy**199 6695 4-8-13 70 TGMcLaughlin 9 33
(E A L Dunlop) *s.i.s: hld up: rdn and edgd rt over 2f out: sn wknd* **16/1**
423- 9 9 **Dancing Jest (IRE)**289 4065 5-8-4 61 NickyMackay 10 3
(Rae Guest) *racd alone stands' side: tl hung lft and jnd main gp over 5f out: chsd ldrs: rdn 1/2-way: wknd over 2f out* **7/1**
1m 39.2s (-1.40) **Going Correction** -0.10s/f (Good) 9 Ran SP% **117.7**
Speed ratings (Par 103): **103,102,101,101,98 94,91,83,74**
toteswinger: 1&2 £6.50, 1&3 £4.60, 2&3 £10.10. CSF £49.61 CT £274.88 TOTE £3.50: £1.40, £3.70, £1.70; EX 67.30.
Owner M Sinclair **Bred** Farmers Hill Stud **Trained** Newmarket, Suffolk
■ Stewards' Enquiry : Matthew Cosham one-day ban: careless riding (May 14)

FOCUS
Exposed performers in this ordinary handicap. The gallop was fair and the form looks straightforward.
Aggravation Official explanation: jockey said gelding was denied a clear run

1634 PREMIER RACING SERVICES - BET WITH INDEPENDENTS H'CAP 7f 3y
7:30 (7:32) (Class 6) (0-65,65) 4-Y-O+ **£1,942** (£578; £288; £144) **Stalls** High

Form RPR
440- 1 **Hobson**174 7226 4-8-10 57 StephenCarson 4 73
(Eve Johnson Houghton) *mde all: rdn over 1f out: r.o wl* **8/1**
6-13 2 2 **Gracie's Gift (IRE)**10 1413 7-8-7 54 JohnEgan 10 65
(R C Guest) *mid-div: hdwy 1/2-way: rdn to chse wnr and hung rt fnl f: r.o* **7/1**3
0-03 3 3 **Pha Mai Blue**60 725 4-9-1 62 PatCosgrave 9 65
(J R Boyle) *chsd ldrs: rdn over 2f out: hung lft over 1f out: no ex ins fnl f* **9/1**
50 4 2 3/4 **Zars Gold (IRE)**29 1066 4-9-1 62 NCallan 3 57
(J Gallagher) *plld hrd and prom: rdn over 2f out: wknd fnl f* **8/1**
1/5- 5 1/2 **Four Tel**432 683 5-9-4 65 LukeMorris 6 59
(N J Vaughan) *s.i.s: hdwy over 5f out: outpcd over 2f out: hung lft fr over 1f out: n.d after* **7/2**2
50-0 6 3/4 **Registrar**17 1258 7-8-10 57 (p) TGMcLaughlin 1 49
(Mrs C A Dunnett) *s.i.s: hdwy over 4f out: rdn and hung lft over 1f out: wknd fnl f* **9/1**
2002 7 nk **Dancing Duo**57 760 5-8-5 52 (v) NickyMackay 5 43
(D Shaw) *n.m.r sn after s: mid-div: hdwy 1/2-way: rdn: hung lft and wknd over 1f out* **22/1**
06-0 8 1 3/4 **Athboy Auction**89 355 4-8-4 51 oh4 JimmyQuinn 7 37
(H J Collingridge) *s.i.s: rdn over 2f out: a in rr* **33/1**
0-53 9 4 **Bigfanofthat (IRE)**17 1258 4-9-1 62 DarryllHolland 12 37
(M D Squance) *hld up: hdwy 2f out: rdn over 2f out: no rspnse* **9/4**1
-605 10 4 **Scruffy Skip (IRE)**4 1536 4-8-4 51 oh6 (v) CatherineGannon 11 16
(Mrs C A Dunnett) *mid-div: hdwy 1/2-way: wknd 2f out* **12/1**
-050 11 11 **Gone'N'Dunnett (IRE)**91 327 10-7-13 53 oh6 ow2(p) MatthewCosham(7) 13 —
(Mrs C A Dunnett) *racd alone tl hung lft 1/2-way: chsd ldrs tl wknd wl over 2f out* **40/1**
1m 25.8s (-0.80) **Going Correction** -0.10s/f (Good) 11 Ran SP% **125.1**
Speed ratings (Par 101): **100,97,94,91,90 89,89,87,82,78 65**
toteswinger: 1&2 £14.20, 1&3 £24.00, 2&3 £14.80. CSF £66.06 CT £539.61 TOTE £10.00: £3.20, £1.70, £3.30; EX 80.80.
Owner Anthony Pye-Jeary And Mel Smith **Bred** Hunscote House Farm Stud **Trained** Blewbury, Oxon

FOCUS
A fair handicap for the grade although the two market leaders underperformed. The gallop was reasonable but those held up failed to land a blow. The form should prove reliable.
Bigfanofthat(IRE) Official explanation: trainer said gelding bled from the nose

1635 PREMIER RACING SERVICES CHANCE TO WIN £100 H'CAP 1m 6f 17y
8:00 (8:00) (Class 4) (0-85,83) 4-Y-O+ **£4,792** (£1,425; £712; £355) **Stalls** High

Form RPR
224 1 **Sri Kuantan (IRE)**16 1274 5-8-8 73 (t) MarkCoumbe(5) 6 79
(R C Guest) *dwlt: rcvrd to ld after 1f: set stdy pce tl qcknd over 3f out: rdn over 1f out: styd on wl* **5/1**
001- 2 3 **Aegean Prince**43 7558 5-9-9 83 JimmyQuinn 1 85
(P Howling) *hld up: hdwy 2f out: wnt 2nd ins fnl f: nt trble wnr* **14/1**
2-33 3 1 1/2 **Soundbyte**18 1230 4-8-11 73 NCallan 3 73+
(J Gallagher) *a.p: chsd wnr 2f out: sn rdn: no ex ins fnl f* **6/5**1
-334 4 2 1/4 **Ruff Diamond (USA)**13 1319 4-8-11 73 LukeMorris 5 70
(J S Moore) *trckd ldrs: wnt 2nd 10f out: rdn over 3f out: wknd fnl f* **7/2**2
3135 5 1 **They All Laughed**7 1478 6-8-13 73 (b) TGMcLaughlin 4 68
(P W Hiatt) *s.i.s: hld up: rdn over 2f out: r.o ins fnl f: nvr nrr* **20/1**

200- **6** 9 **Inchpast**[150] 7515 8-8-9 **69**.................... TedDurcan 2 52
(M H Tompkins) *led 1f: chsd wnr to 10f out: rdn over 3f out: wknd 2f out* 4/1[3]

3m 15.21s (7.61) **Going Correction** -0.10s/f (Good)
WFA 4 from 5yo+ 2lb 6 Ran SP% **115.8**
Speed ratings (Par 105): **74,72,71,70,69 64**
toteswinger: 1&2 £10.90, 1&3 £1.80, 2&3 £4.20. CSF £65.54 TOTE £5.40: £1.70, £6.20; EX 41.30 Place 6 £447.92, Place 5 £119.65..
Owner S Hussey **Bred** Pat Fullam **Trained** Stainforth, S Yorks

FOCUS
Exposed performers in this ordinary handicap, however the slow pace means this bare form is not reliable. The winner was allowed a very easy lead.
T/Plt: £580.10 to a £1 stake. Pool: £44,103.96. 55.50 winning tickets. T/Qpdt: £38.30 to a £1 stake. Pool: £7,209.26. 139.00 winning tickets. CR

1584 LINGFIELD (L-H)
Friday, May 1

OFFICIAL GOING: Standard
Wind: Moderate, behind Weather: Fine

1636 BET HEINEKEN CUP - BETDAQ MAIDEN STKS (DIV I) 7f (P)
1:40 (1:45) (Class 5) 3-4-Y-O **£3,561** (£1,059; £529; £264) **Stalls** Low

Form RPR
2- **1** **Tryst**[379] 1417 4-9-10 0.................... RyanMoore 1 87+
(Sir Michael Stoute) *s.i.s: pushed up to trck ldrs: wnt 3rd over 1f out: drvn and r.o wl fnl f to ld last strides* 11/8[1]
2 **2** *nk* **Makaam (USA)**[23] 1185 3-8-12 0.................... RHills 12 82+
(M P Tregoning) *trckd ldr after 2f: rdn to ld 1f out: r.o: hdd last strides* 7/2[3]
4-3 **3** ½ **Euston Square**[16] 1295 3-8-12 0.................... JimmyFortune 9 81+
(J H M Gosden) *stdd s: hld up towards rr: effrt 2f out: rdn and r.o wl fnl f: gaining at fin* 9/4[2]
0- **4** 2 **Francis Walsingham (IRE)**[189] 6944 3-8-12 0.................... SteveDrowne 5 76
(H Morrison) *dwlt: pushed up to ld after 1f: hdd u.p 1f out: fdd* 22/1
5 3 ¼ **Satwa Star (IRE)** 3-8-12 0.................... StephenDonohoe 3 67
(E A L Dunlop) *stdd s: hld up in last trio: sme prog on inner to go 6th over 1f out: pushed along and styd on steadily* 80/1
25- **6** ¾ **Learo Dochais (USA)**[249] 5344 3-8-12 0.................... PhilipRobinson 4 65
(M A Jarvis) *led 1f: prom tl wknd fr 2f out* 20/1
7 1 ¾ **Roar Of The King (USA)** 3-8-12 0.................... ShaneKelly 6 60
(J Noseda) *hld up in last trio: outpcd whn bmpd 2f out: nvr a factor* 20/1
246/ **8** *nse* **Mymumsaysimthebest**[617] 4743 4-9-10 85.................... GeorgeBaker 2 64
(G L Moore) *t.k.h: hld up in midfield: outpcd whn bmpd 2f out: no ch* 33/1
9 5 **Red Chieftain (FR)** 4-9-10 0.................... SimonWhitworth 7 50
(Mrs H S Main) *dwlt: rn green and a in last trio: bhd fnl 2f* 100/1
506- **10** 8 **Kappalyn (IRE)**[235] 5755 4-9-5 50.................... PatCosgrave 11 24
(J R Boyle) *reluctant to go to post: prom 4f: wknd rapidly: t.o* 100/1

1m 25.24s (0.44) **Going Correction** 0.0s/f (Stan)
WFA 3 from 4yo 12lb 10 Ran SP% **115.1**
Speed ratings (Par 103): **97,96,96,93,90 89,87,87,81,72**
toteswinger: 1&2 £1.80, 1&3 £1.20, 2&3 £2.30 CSF £5.93 TOTE £2.20: £1.30, £1.40, £1.20; EX 6.60.
Owner Cheveley Park Stud **Bred** Cheveley Park Stud Ltd **Trained** Newmarket, Suffolk

FOCUS
Not much strength in depth but a couple of fair sorts and a race that should throw up its share of winners. The pace was only moderate and the winner raced towards the centre in the straight. The fourth has been rated a big improver and the chances are that he and the fifth may set the long-term standard.
Mymumsaysimthebest Official explanation: jockey said gelding hung right

1637 DERBY TRIAL HERE MAY 9TH MAIDEN FILLIES' STKS 5f (P)
2:10 (2:10) (Class 4) 2-Y-O **£3,885** (£1,156; £577; £288) **Stalls** High

Form RPR
1 **Art Jewel (IRE)** 2-9-0 0.................... JamieSpencer 1 69
(S A Callaghan) *mde all: tail swishing furiouslt thrght: pressed 1f out: hrd rdn and kpt on wl* 11/4[1]
6 **2** 1 ¾ **Any Day (IRE)**[27] 1119 2-9-0 0.................... JimCrowley 2 63
(R M Beckett) *chsd wnr: drvn to chal and looked threatening 1f out: one pce* 11/4[1]
3 2 **Forget (IRE)** 2-9-0 0.................... SebSanders 4 56
(C E Brittain) *chsd ldng quartet: effrt 2f out: wnt 3rd and rn green over 1f out: kpt on* 7/2[2]
4 2 **Boga (IRE)** 2-9-0 0.................... TonyCulhane 5 48+
(M R Channon) *sn outpcd in 6th and bhd: styd on fr 2f out: reminder over 1f out: nrst fin* 7/2[2]
0 **5** 4 **Barton Chancer**[25] 1147 2-8-9 0.................... WilliamCarson(5) 7 34
(W G M Turner) *chsd ldrs and in tch tl wknd 2f out* 20/1
0 **6** 1 ¾ **Saachi's Vision (IRE)**[22] 1195 2-9-0 0.................... StephenCarson 3 28
(D K Ivory) *chsd ldng trio: effrt on inner 2f out: sn no prog: wknd fnl f* 40/1
7 3 ¼ **Dinky Deb** 2-9-0 0.................... TPQueally 6 16
(D K Ivory) *awkward s: sn wl bhd in last: nvr a factor* 16/1[3]

60.74 secs (1.94) **Going Correction** 0.0s/f (Stan) 7 Ran SP% **110.9**
Speed ratings (Par 92): **84,81,78,74,68 65,60**
toteswingers: 1&2 £2.60, 1&3 £2.60, 2&3 £2.70 CSF £9.82 TOTE £3.80: £1.60, £1.80; EX 8.80.
Owner Matthew Green **Bred** Mrs Jane Bailey **Trained** Newmarket, Suffolk

FOCUS
This looked an ordinary maiden. The pace was fair and the winner raced towards the centre in the straight.

NOTEBOOK
Art Jewel(IRE), a half-sister to several winners from 6f to middle distances, overcame obvious greenness and a worrying tendency to repeatedly flash her tail to beat a more experienced rival in workmanlike fashion under a strong ride on this debut. She should prove equally effective over 6f and, although capable of better, it is to be hoped temperament does not get in the way of improvement. (op 5-2 tchd 3-1)
Any Day(IRE), who showed ability before tiring on her debut over course and distance in a race that threw up winners, was well supported and turned in an improved effort. She is nothing special but should be able to pick up a minor event away from progressive sorts. (op 5-2)
Forget(IRE), from a yard that sent out an impressive first-time-out juvenile winner earlier in the week, has plenty of middle distance winners in her pedigree so it was encouraging to see her shape as she did on this racecourse debut. She will be better suited by 6f and is sure to win a race. (op 4-1 tchd 3-1)
Boga(IRE), a half-sister to a sprint winner in the US, was too green to do herself justice on this racecourse debut but was getting the hang of things as the race progressed, and she is likely to come on a fair bit for the experience. (op 4-1 tchd 9-2)
Barton Chancer, well beaten on turf on her debut, attracted a bit of support at big odds but again had her limitations firmly exposed in this grade on this all-weather debut. (op 25-1)

1638 BET HEINEKEN CUP - BETDAQ MAIDEN STKS (DIV II) 7f (P)
2:45 (2:46) (Class 5) 3-4-Y-O **£3,561** (£1,059; £529; £264) **Stalls** Low

Form RPR
1 **Secret Witness** 3-8-12 0.................... SebSanders 10 74
(J Noseda) *trckd ldng pair: rdn to ld 1f out: styd on wl to hold on nr fin* 2/1[1]
4-33 **2** *hd* **Hypnotist (UAE)**[41] 914 3-8-12 72.................... RyanMoore 6 73
(C E Brittain) *chsd ldrs: rdn in 4th over 2f out: effrt on outer over 1f out: drvn to go 2nd last 75yds and cl on wnr fin* 7/2[2]
0- **3** 1 ¼ **Silverglas (IRE)**[223] 6117 3-8-12 0.................... PatDobbs 7 70
(M P Tregoning) *trckd ldr: rdn to chal over 1f out: upsides ent fnl f: one pce* 4/1[3]
020- **4** 1 ½ **King's Sabre**[209] 6474 3-8-12 86.................... DO'Donohoe 9 66
(W R Muir) *led: rdn on inner 2f out: hdd 1f out: fdd* 9/2
5 2 ¼ **Pegasus Gold (USA)** 4-9-10 0.................... AdamKirby 2 64
(W R Swinburn) *settled midfield: gng wl enugh 3f out: chsd ldng quartet over 2f out: pushed along and kpt on steadily* 16/1
6 1 ½ **Garter Star** 4-9-5 0.................... TravisBlock 3 54
(H Morrison) *towards rr and green early: rchd 6th over 2f out but nt on terms: pushed along and kpt on steadily* 40/1
7 5 **Prince Of Johanne (IRE)** 3-8-12 0.................... ShaneKelly 5 42
(J Noseda) *s.v.s: tacked on to bk of gp after 2f: modest prog fnl 2f: n.d* 9/1
8 2 ¾ **Paul's Pet** 4-9-10 0.................... TGMcLaughlin 11 39
(Karen George) *racd wd: in tch in rr to 3f out: sn btn* 100/1
0- **9** *nse* **Peak (IRE)**[167] 7336 3-8-12 0.................... SteveDrowne 1 34
(H Morrison) *prom: pushed along over 4f out: wknd rapidly over 2f out* 40/1
6/ **10** *hd* **Dazzling Colours**[602] 5193 4-9-10 0.................... LiamJones 8 38
(T T Clement) *a towards rr: pushed along 3f out: sn struggling* 40/1
11 58 **Whispered Lands (IRE)** 3-8-8 0 ow1.................... PatCosgrave 4 —
(J R Boyle) *s.v.s: a t.o* 66/1

1m 25.14s (0.34) **Going Correction** 0.0s/f (Stan)
WFA 3 from 4yo 12lb 11 Ran SP% **119.4**
Speed ratings (Par 103): **98,97,96,94,92 90,84,81,81,81 14**
totewinger: 1&2 £2.50, 1&3 £2.50, 2&3 £3.30 CSF £8.99 TOTE £3.40: £1.60, £1.50, £1.80; EX 10.30.
Owner Cheveley Park Stud **Bred** Cheveley Park Stud Ltd **Trained** Newmarket, Suffolk

FOCUS
This did not look as strong as the first division but nevertheless a couple of interesting performances. The pace was only fair and the first three raced in the centre in the straight. It has been rated around the runner-up improving by 5lb.
Prince Of Johanne(IRE) Official explanation: jockey said colt did not face the kick back
Whispered Lands(IRE) Official explanation: jockey said filly was slowly away

1639 BETDAQ THE BETTING EXCHANGE H'CAP 6f (P)
3:20 (3:23) (Class 3) (0-90,90) 3-Y-O **£7,771** (£2,312; £1,155; £577) **Stalls** Low

Form RPR
21-3 **1** **Swiss Diva**[13] 1345 3-9-2 **85**.................... JamieSpencer 4 94+
(D R C Elsworth) *trckd ldng pair: effrt on outer 2f out: led jst ins fnl f: sn wl in command* 2/1[2]
110- **2** 1 ¼ **Crystal Moments**[217] 6240 3-9-7 **90**.................... EddieAhern 1 91
(E A L Dunlop) *trckd ldng pair: effrt on inner to press ldr over 1f out: outpcd by wnr fnl f but kpt on to take 2nd* 14/1
11- **3** *hd* **Harry Patch**[174] 7241 3-9-3 **86**.................... PhilipRobinson 2 87
(M A Jarvis) *led: pressed wl over 1f out: hdd jst ins fnl f: lost 2nd nr fin* 13/8[1]
-100 **4** ½ **Never Lose**[20] 1214 3-8-13 **82**.................... RyanMoore 3 81
(C E Brittain) *hld up in midfield: effrt 2f out: swtchd rt ent fnl f: rdn and r.o: nrst fin* 14/1
51- **5** 1 **Major Phil (IRE)**[141] 7638 3-8-10 **79**.................... DaneO'Neill 9 75+
(L M Cumani) *s.i.s: hld up in last trio: pushed along on inner 2f out: styd on steadily: nvr nr ldrs* 12/1
2-05 **6** ¾ **Son Of The Cat (USA)**[29] 1085 3-9-5 **88**.................... (t) TPQueally 8 81
(B Gubby) *hld up in midfield: effrt 2f out: rdn and kpt on one pce fr over 1f out* 14/1
4-00 **7** ½ **Joe Caster**[34] 1002 3-9-0 **88**.................... WilliamCarson(5) 6 80
(J M P Eustace) *s.i.s: hld up in last trio: prog 2f out: rdn and cl enough over 1f out: no ex* 40/1
33-1 **8** 2 ¾ **Jordaura**[14] 1322 3-8-3 **77**.................... Louis-PhilippeBeuzelin(5) 7 60
(W R Swinburn) *racd awkwardly in last trio: no prog fnl 2f* 8/1[3]
4-00 **9** 3 **Red Kyte**[13] 1345 3-8-12 **81**.................... PaulMulrennan 5 54
(K A Ryan) *pressed ldr to 2f out: wknd rapidly* 66/1

1m 11.13s (-0.77) **Going Correction** 0.0s/f (Stan) 9 Ran SP% **114.2**
Speed ratings (Par 103): **105,103,103,102,101 100,99,95,91**
toteswinger: 1&2 £6.40, 1&3 £1.10, 2&3 £5.40 CSF £29.93 CT £54.33 TOTE £3.10: £1.10, £3.20, £1.40; EX 26.70.
Owner Lordship Stud **Bred** Lordship Stud **Trained** Newmarket, Suffolk

FOCUS
A useful handicap but, although the pace was fair, those held up were at a disadvantage. The winner raced in the centre in the straight and the form looks muddling.

NOTEBOOK
Swiss Diva ◆, who shaped with plenty of promise on her reappearance, maintained her unbeaten record on Polytrack (both wins over this course and distance) with a career-best effort. This strong traveller scored with more in hand than the official margin suggests and appeals as the type to win a decent handicap this year. (op 11-4 tchd 3-1 in a place)
Crystal Moments, a progressive sort and winner of both Polytrack starts last year, shaped as though retaining at least all her ability on this first start since September. She is entitled to improve for this reappearance run but she is likely to remain vulnerable to the more progressive sorts from her current mark of 90. (op 16-1)
Harry Patch, the winner of both starts on easy and soft ground last year, looked a most interesting recruit to the all-weather ranks but, although he failed to progress in the anticipated manner after racing keenly on this reappearance and all-weather debut, he showed more than enough to suggest he can win races this term. (op 11-8 tchd 7-4)
Never Lose has been disappointing in blinkers in handicaps since her maiden win but she fared much better with the equipment left off. She shaped as though the return to 7f would suit and she is worth another chance. (op 20-1 tchd 22-1)
Major Phil(IRE) ◆ was easy to back for this handicap debut and reappearance, but was far from disgraced from his wide draw in a race that suited the prominent racers. He should have no problems with 7f and is one to keep an eye on. (op 8-1)
Son Of The Cat(USA) was not totally disgraced on this handicap debut but he looks harshly treated on a mark of 88 and is going to have to drop in the weights to offer him any realistic chance of success in this type of event. (op 25-1)

Jordaura's record coming into this race was one of steady improvement but he failed to land a blow from a higher mark in a stronger grade after racing wide at the back of the field. He too is probably worth another chance. Official explanation: jockey said colt hung right; vet said colt was lame left hind (op 13-2 tchd 6-1 and 17-2)

Red Kyte Official explanation: jockey said filly hung right throughout

1640 HARTFIELD H'CAP — 7f (P)

3:55 (3:56) (Class 2) (0-105,105) 4-Y-0+ £12,952 (£3,854; £1,926; £962) Stalls Low

Form				RPR
4211	1		**Abbondanza (IRE)**[41] 916 6-9-3 **104**....(p) PaulMulrennan 7	112
			(I Semple) *drvn to ld after 1f: mde rest: jnd ins fnl f: hld on wl* 11/4[1]	
0036	2	*hd*	**Capricorn Run (USA)**[4] 1560 6-8-12 **99**....(v) SteveDrowne 4	106
			(A J McCabe) *fast away: led 1f: trckd wnr: rdn 2f out: chal and upsides ins fnl f: jst hld nr fin* 12/1	
-510	3	*3 1/2*	**Ceremonial Jade (UAE)**[27] 1124 6-9-4 **105**....(t) JohnEgan 1	103
			(M Botti) *hld up in 6th: prog on inner to dispute 2nd wl over 1f out: nt qckn after: wknd ins fnl f* 7/2[2]	
00-0	4	*1 1/2*	**Mastership (IRE)**[33] 1018 5-8-4 **91**.... WilliamBuick 6	85
			(J J Quinn) *hld up in last: prog wl over 1f out: wnt 4th ent fnl f but nt on terms: kpt on* 8/1	
1130	5	*1 1/2*	**Al Muheer (IRE)**[20] 1212 4-8-10 **97**....(b) SebSanders 5	86
			(C E Brittain) *racd wd: trckd ldng pair to 2f out: sn btn: wknd fnl f* 9/2[3]	
2100	6	*4 1/2*	**Titan Triumph**[20] 1209 5-8-9 **96**....(t) JimCrowley 3	73
			(W J Knight) *settled in rr: rdn and no prog over 2f out: wknd over 1f out* 11/2	
01-5	7	*1/2*	**Dixey**[20] 1210 4-8-8 **95** ow1.... PhilipRobinson 2	71
			(M A Jarvis) *in tch: pushed along 1/2-way: no prog 2f out: sn wknd* 7/1	

1m 22.42s (-2.38) **Going Correction** 0.0s/f (Stan) course record 7 Ran SP% **113.8**

Speed ratings (Par 109): **113,112,108,107,105 100,99**

toteswingers: 1&2 £8.00, 1&3 £2.60, 2&3 £9.00 CSF £35.31 TOTE £2.70: £1.40, £5.80; EX 39.40.

Owner Belstane Park Racing & Gordon Leckie **Bred** M Nolan **Trained** Carluke, S Lanarks

FOCUS

Several good quality Polytrack performers and, although a couple disappointed, the front two pulled clear in the straight to post smart efforts. The time was decent (less than half a second outside the course record) and the winner raced centre to far side in the straight. The winner has been rated as recording another personal best.

NOTEBOOK

Abbondanza(IRE) doesn't look entirely straightforward given his ungainly head carriage but there's nothing wrong with his attitude and he again dug deep to post a career-best and to notch his third consecutive win at this track. Opportunities will be thin on the ground for him on Polytrack from now on, though. (op 3-1 tchd 4-1 in a place)

Capricorn Run(USA), reportedly unsuited by quick ground on turf earlier this week, showed himself in a much more favourable light back on this surface when running as well as he has ever done. He pulled clear of the rest but, as with the winner, near-to-hand opportunities for one of his rating on sand will be few and far between. (op 14-1)

Ceremonial Jade(UAE), who hung right handed throughout when well beaten on turf on his previous start, shaped much better back on his favoured Polytrack, without being at the very top of his game. This surface suits much better than turf. (op 9-2 tchd 5-1)

Mastership(IRE), a turf and dual Polytrack winner for Clive Brittain, has not scored in over two years but he is on a fair mark and shaped better than on his reappearance over 6f on turf. He is equally effective on turf and, although his losing run is a concern, he is not one to write off just yet. (op 15-2 tchd 6-1)

Al Muheer(IRE)'s run of progressive efforts on Polytrack in blinkers came to an end at Kempton on his previous start and he was again below his best. He looks best watched for now. (op 6-1)

Titan Triumph won four of his five starts over 1m at this course during the winter but he disappointed at Kempton last month and, although the longer trip probably suits best, it was a similar story back at his favourite track. He may have had enough for the time being. (op 15-2 tchd 5-1)

Dixey, a lightly raced sort from a top yard, could have been expected to improve for the return to this trip, but she was well beaten after being easy to back beforehand. She has a bit to prove at present. (op 7-2)

1641 PLAISANCE DU TOUCH CONDITIONS STKS — 1m (P)

4:30 (4:30) (Class 2) 3-Y-0+ £14,331 (£4,291; £2,145; £1,074; £535) Stalls High

Form				RPR
0-15	1		**King Of Dixie (USA)**[13] 1346 5-9-12 107.... JimCrowley 2	111
			(W J Knight) *trckd ldr: narrow ld 2f out gng wl: shkn up and readily asserted over 1f out* 1/1[1]	
-000	2	*2 1/4*	**Fullback (IRE)**[20] 1211 3-8-5 90.... LPKeniry 5	95
			(J S Moore) *led: drvn and hdd 2f out: kpt on but no match for wnr after* 8/1	
0401	3	*3/4*	**Mahadee (IRE)**[20] 1209 4-9-10 100....(b) JamieSpencer 1	102
			(C E Brittain) *chsd ldng pair: rdn over 2f out: nt qckn over 1f out: one pce after* 3/1[2]	
6236	4	*1*	**Red Somerset (USA)**[20] 1212 6-9-4 96.... GeorgeBaker 4	94
			(R J Hodges) *hld up in 4th: rdn over 2f out: nt qckn and no imp over 1f out: pushed along fnl f* 10/3[3]	
4330	5	*16*	**Cavalry Guard (USA)**[37] 961 5-9-4 49....(b) AmyBaker 3	57?
			(T D McCarthy) *hld up last: rdn sn after 1/2-way: lost tch 3f out: t.o* 200/1	

1m 36.9s (-1.30) **Going Correction** 0.0s/f (Stan)

WFA 3 from 4yo+ 13lb 5 Ran SP% **109.7**

Speed ratings (Par 109): **106,103,103,102,86**

toteswingers: 1&2 £9.20, 1&3 not won, 2&3 not won. CSF £9.74 TOTE £2.00: £1.30, £3.20; EX 9.70.

Owner Bluehills Racing Limited **Bred** Bee Zee LLC **Trained** Patching, W Sussex

FOCUS

A disappointing turnout for the money on offer. The pace was only ordinary and the winner came down the centre. The runner-up has been rated back to his two-year-old best, but the muddling pace means the form could be misleading.

NOTEBOOK

King Of Dixie(USA), a relatively lightly raced sort who was ridden closer to the pace than at Doncaster on his previous start, probably did not have to improve to maintain his unbeaten record on Polytrack with a fluent display. His best efforts have been on turf, though, and he should be able to pick up a decent handicap this year. (op 5-4)

Fullback(IRE), who had something to find at the weights, had the run of things and ran his best race of the year to divide two 100-plus rated rivals. However, he did have the rub of things to a large degree and may not be the easiest to place successfully this term. (op 10-1 tchd 11-1)

Mahadee(IRE) turned in a career-best when landing a competitive handicap at Kempton on his previous start but failed to build on that effort in a more tactical race. A more truly run race would have been more to his liking. (op 11-4 tchd 10-3)

Red Somerset(USA) has been holding his form well since the start of winter but, although not disgraced, was not seen to best effect in a muddling event. He has little margin for error from his current mark in handicaps, though. (op 11-4)

Cavalry Guard(USA) had a mountain to climb on official ratings and was predictably outclassed. (op 150-1)

1642 COLEMANS HATCH H'CAP — 1m 2f (P)

5:05 (5:05) (Class 2) (0-105,98) 4-Y-0+ £12,952 (£3,854; £1,926; £962) Stalls Low

Form				RPR
3125	1		**Lady Jane Digby**[83] 445 4-8-11 **91**.... GregFairley 9	101
			(M Johnston) *hld up towards rr: clsd on ldrs 2f out: wnt 3rd over 1f out: drvn and r.o to ld last 150yds* 6/1	
31-0	2	*1*	**Safari Sunup (IRE)**[9] 1460 4-8-12 **92**.... StephenCarson 1	100
			(P Winkworth) *trckd ldr 3f: styd prom: rdn 3f out: effrt u.p to ld over 1f out: hdd and outpcd last 150yds* 20/1	
13-	3	*1/2*	**Ancient Lights**[288] 4122 4-8-13 **93**.... IanMongan 5	100
			(H R A Cecil) *pressed ldr after 3f: led over 4f out: drvn and hdd over 1f out: kpt on but outpcd ins fnl f* 25/1	
123-	4	*4 1/2*	**Montbretia**[211] 6415 4-9-0 **94**.... TPQueally 3	92
			(H R A Cecil) *trckd ldrs: rdn on outer 3f out: outpcd 2f out: kpt on u.p to take 4th on post* 5/2[1]	
1332	5	*nse*	**Formation (USA)**[20] 1216 4-9-0 **94**.... PatCosgrave 10	92
			(J R Boyle) *hld up in last: gng wl enough 3f out: lft bhd by ldrs 2f out: wnt modest 4th 1f out: pushed along and no imp: lost pl on post* 9/2[2]	
40-5	6	*2 3/4*	**Beauchamp Viceroy**[41] 915 5-8-8 **88**.... EddieAhern 7	80
			(G A Butler) *trckd ldr: cl enough 2f out: sn shkn up and wknd tamely* 5/1[3]	
0-30	7	*1 1/2*	**Whitcombe Minister (USA)**[34] 1003 4-8-12 **92**.... JohnEgan 4	84
			(M Botti) *led to over 4f out: wknd over 1f out: eased ins fnl f* 5/1[3]	
5-10	8	*17*	**Intabih (USA)**[24] 1170 4-8-6 **89**.... AhmedAjtebi(3) 8	44
			(C E Brittain) *a in rr: rdn and wknd wl over 2f out: t.o* 11/1	
-530	9	*9*	**Grand Passion (IRE)**[34] 1003 9-9-4 **98**.... GeorgeBaker 6	35
			(C F Wall) *hld up in rr: rdn and wknd rapidly over 3f out: t.o* 7/1	

2m 2.94s (-3.66) **Going Correction** 0.0s/f (Stan) 9 Ran SP% **123.8**

Speed ratings (Par 109): **114,113,112,109,109 106,105,92,84**

toteswinger: 1&2 £27.30, 1&3 £14.50, 2&3 £29.10 CSF £122.82 CT £2820.16 TOTE £7.20: £2.40, £4.40, £5.80; EX 160.70.

Owner Miss K Rausing **Bred** Miss K Rausing **Trained** Middleham Moor, N Yorks

FOCUS

Surprisingly few progressive performers for a race of this value, but it was run at a fair gallop and the first three pulled clear. The winner raced towards the centre in the straight. The form looks sound.

NOTEBOOK

Lady Jane Digby, who showed improved form over this course and distance during the winter, was suited by the fair gallop and turned in her best effort after a near three-month break. She remains worth a try over a bit further and may be capable of better still. (op 7-1 tchd 15-2)

Safari Sunup(IRE) had shown only modest form on his two previous starts on Polytrack and was well beaten on his reappearance, but he posted a much better effort this time. He is capable of winning a race this year but he looked high enough in the weights going into this race so a further rise will leave him vulnerable to the more progressive or better handicapped sorts. (tchd 16-1)

Ancient Lights ◆, was very easy to back on this all-weather debut and first run since disappointing in a conditions event last July. He looks sure to win races on either this surface or on turf if all remains well with him. (op 22-1 tchd 20-1)

Montbretia, a progressive individual last year, was not disgraced on this all-weather debut and reappearance and left the impression that the return to 1m4f would be more to her liking. She is lightly raced enough to be open to further progress. (op 9-4 tchd 4-1)

Formation(USA), beat Lady Jane Digby in a messy race over course and distance this winter but was not at his very best this time. He is the type that needs things to drop just right. (op 4-1 tchd 7-2)

Beauchamp Viceroy failed to match his creditable reappearance run from the same mark over this shorter trip but he has not won since 2006 and does not look one to place maximum faith in. (op 7-1 tchd 15-2 and 9-2)

Whitcombe Minister(USA) Official explanation: jockey said colt lost its action in straight

1643 BET 2000 GUINEAS - BETDAQ H'CAP — 1m 4f (P)

5:35 (5:36) (Class 4) (0-80,80) 3-Y-O £5,180 (£1,541; £770; £384) Stalls Low

Form				RPR
521-	1		**Fortuni (IRE)**[140] 7649 3-9-5 **78**.... SebSanders 4	96+
			(Sir Mark Prescott) *w ldr: led over 4f out: drew clr over 3f out: unassailable 2f out: rdn out* 7/1	
0-1	2	*4*	**Sehoy (USA)**[37] 957 3-9-7 **80**.... JimmyFortune 9	91+
			(J H M Gosden) *hld up: last to 3f out: gd prog 2f out: hrd rdn to chse clr wnr over 1f out: styd on wl but no ch* 5/4[1]	
66-2	3	*3*	**Curacao**[9] 1464 3-8-10 **69**.... JimCrowley 6	75
			(Mrs A J Perrett) *hld up towards rr: prog over 3f out: chsd clr wnr over 2f out to over 1f out: one pce* 8/1	
60-5	4	*1/2*	**Just Like Silk (USA)**[28] 1113 3-8-13 **72**.... EddieAhern 5	77
			(G A Butler) *hld up towards rr: effrt over 2f out but sn wl outpcd: kpt on fr over 1f out: nrly snatched 3rd* 11/2[3]	
01-	5	*5*	**Scene Two**[133] 7735 3-9-3 **76**.... JamieSpencer 1	73
			(L M Cumani) *hld up in rr: rdn 3f and no hdwy: modest prog 2f out: nvr on terms* 5/1[2]	
1264	6	*1*	**Diamond Twister (USA)**[10] 1431 3-9-3 **76**....(t) SteveDrowne 7	72
			(J R Best) *trckd ldrs: prog to go 2nd over 3f out to over 2f out: wknd over 1f out* 33/1	
5663	7	*5*	**Orsippus (USA)**[30] 1063 3-8-13 **72**.... TonyCulhane 2	60
			(M R Channon) *trckd ldrs: wknd wl over 2f out* 50/1	
-312	8	*10*	**Fin Vin De Leu (GER)**[10] 1431 3-9-5 **78**.... GregFairley 3	50
			(M Johnston) *mde most to over 4f out: wknd over 3f out: t.o* 6/1	
43-1	9	*3 3/4*	**It's Dubai Dolly**[16] 1286 3-9-7 **80**.... WandersonD'Avila 8	46
			(A J Lidderdale) *t.k.h: prom tl wknd over 3f out: t.o* 25/1	

2m 29.09s (-3.91) **Going Correction** 0.0s/f (Stan) course record 9 Ran SP% **123.1**

Speed ratings (Par 101): **113,110,108,108,104 104,100,94,91**

toteswingers: 1&2 £4.70, 1&3 £11.90, 2&3 £5.30 CSF £17.14 CT £78.23 TOTE £8.50: £2.70, £1.40, £2.50; EX 32.20 Place 6: £5.97 Place 5: £5.58.

Owner Pacific International Management **Bred** Moyglare Stud Farm Ltd **Trained** Newmarket, Suffolk

FOCUS

A decent handicap featuring several unexposed sorts. The winner, who raced against the inside rail in the straight, put up a much-improved effort, and the time supports the view that this is decent form.

T/Plt: £8.70 to a £1 stake. Pool: £55,201.23. 4,605.86 winning tickets. T/Qpdt: £5.80 to a £1 stake. Pool: £2,999.60. 377.20 winning tickets. JN

^{1226}MUSSELBURGH (R-H)

Friday, May 1

OFFICIAL GOING: Good to firm (firm in places; 8.1) changing to good (good to firm in places) after race 1 (2.20)

Wind: Light across Weather: Overcast and showers

1644 CORNHILL BUILDING SERVICES H'CAP — 5f

2:20 (2:23) (Class 6) (0-65,65) 3-Y-O — **£2,266** (£674; £337; £168) **Stalls** Low

Form RPR

106 **1** **Taurus Twins**^{23} [1190] 3-9-4 **60**....(b) RobertWinston 7 69
(R J Price) *mde all: rdn over 1f out: kpt on strly* **7/1**

0-31 **2** 1 1/2 **Compton Ford**^{9} [1455] 3-9-9 **65** 6ex.... PhillipMakin 2 68
(M Dods) *trckd ldrs: effrt 2f out: rdn to chse wnr over 1f out: swtchd rt and drvn ins fnl f: kpt on* **4/1**^{3}

3122 **3** 1 1/4 **Fasliyanne (IRE)**^{9} [1455] 3-9-4 **60**.... NCallan 3 59
(K A Ryan) *in tch: pushed along 1/2-way: rdn and hdwy wl over 1f out: styd on ins fnl f* **3/1**^{1}

3262 **4** 3/4 **Dispol Grand (IRE)**^{8} [1469] 3-9-7 **63**.... JoeFanning 5 59
(P T Midgley) *chsd ldrs and sn pushed along: rdn 1/2-way: drvn over 1f out and sn wknd* **7/2**^{2}

00-5 **5** 1/2 **Smelly Cat**^{30} [1062] 3-8-9 **51**.... DavidAllan 4 45
(T D Easterby) *chsd ldrs: rdn wl over 1f out: kpt on same pce ins fnl f* **16/1**

6053 **6** 3/4 **Pedregal**^{9} [1455] 3-8-3 **45**.... PaulHanagan 1 37
(R A Fahey) *towards rr: hdwy 1/2-way: sn rdn: styd on ins fnl f nt rch ldrs* **9/2**

4303 **7** 1 1/2 **Badtanman**^{6} [1529] 3-8-4 **46** ow1....(b) PatrickMathers 9 32
(Peter Grayson) *sn rdn along and a bhd* **25/1**

2406 **8** 2 **Wee Bizzom**^{30} [1064] 3-8-5 **47**.... PaulQuinn 6 26
(A Berry) *a towards rr* **66/1**

-165 **9** 5 **Red Cell (IRE)**^{8} [1469] 3-9-6 **62**....(b) TomEaves 8 23
(I W McInnes) *prom: rdn along 1/2-way: sn wknd* **25/1**

59.06 secs (-1.34) **Going Correction** -0.30s/f (Firm) **9** Ran SP% **113.0**
Speed ratings (Par 97): **98,95,93,92,91 90,88,84,76**
toteswinger: 1&2 £6.80, 1&3 £5.10, 2&3 £2.50 CSF £33.71 CT £101.88 TOTE £6.90: £2.30, £1.80, £1.30; EX 41.60.
Owner G E Amey **Bred** G E Amey **Trained** Ullingswick, H'fords

FOCUS
A moderate sprint, run at a solid pace. Sound form, with a personal best from the winner.

1645 EUROPEAN BREEDERS' FUND MAIDEN STKS — 5f

2:55 (2:57) (Class 4) 2-Y-O — **£5,828** (£1,734; £866; £432) **Stalls** Low

Form RPR

2 **1** **Dispol Keasha**^{13} [1344] 2-8-12 0.... PhillipMakin 3 77+
(T D Barron) *qckly away and mde all: qcknd clr wl over 1f out: styd on* **15/8**^{2}

2 1 **Ventura Cove (IRE)** 2-9-3 0.... PaulHanagan 1 77+
(R A Fahey) *in tch: green and pushed along 1/2-way: hdwy over 1f out: styd on wl fnl f* **5/1**^{3}

2 **3** 4 1/2 **Saucy Girl (IRE)**^{15} [1304] 2-8-12 0.... DavidAllan 5 56
(T D Easterby) *chsd wnr: rdn over 2f out: sn drvn and wknd over 1f out* **11/10**^{1}

4 1/2 **Mal And Dave (IRE)** 2-9-3 0.... AdrianTNicholls 8 59
(D Nicholls) *in tch: hdwy to chse ldrs 2f out: sn rdn and no imp* **14/1**

5 hd **Cambuslang (IRE)** 2-9-3 0.... TomEaves 4 59
(I Semple) *sn rdn along and outpcd in rr: hdwy over 1f out: styd on ins fnl f: nrst fin* **25/1**

6 2 1/4 **Lord's Seat** 2-8-12 0.... SladeO'Hara$^{(5)}$ 7 51
(A Berry) *a towards rr* **100/1**

7 2 **Weetentherty** 2-8-12 0....(v^{1}) GaryBartley$^{(5)}$ 6 43
(J S Goldie) *a in rr: pushed along and outpcd fr 1/2-way* **40/1**

59.44 secs (-0.96) **Going Correction** -0.30s/f (Firm) **7** Ran SP% **113.0**
Speed ratings (Par 95): **95,93,86,85,85 81,78**
toteswinger: 1&2 £2.30, 2&3 £1.10 CSF £11.29 TOTE £2.90: £1.60, £2.70; EX 12.40.
Owner W B Imison **Bred** D Powell, Petches Farm & Trickledown Stud **Trained** Maunby, N Yorks

FOCUS
The ground was officially eased to good, good to firm in places after the opener.

NOTEBOOK
Dispol Keasha showed the real benefit of her debut second at Doncaster 13 days earlier and made all, showing a bundle of early dash. She had done her best work at the finish first time up, but she was very smartly away here and had her rivals in trouble from an early stage. She could have been called the winner in between the final two furlongs and did the job without need for the whip, rating value for better than the bare result. Her connections are fully entitled to look for something more valuable now and the Hilary Needler at Beverley later this month would look a logical next step. That represents a stiffer 5f, but it will take a very speedy filly to lead her there. (op 2-1)
Ventura Cove(IRE) ◆ at £80,000 was by far the most expensive of these at the sales and is precociously bred. He ran a very encouraging debut race considering he found things happening so quickly early on, and ought to prove hard to beat next time now he has the run behind him. (op 15-2)
Saucy Girl(IRE)'s debut second at Ripon has worked out well and she looked sure to take some beating. The winner's early dash proved too strong for her, however, and she paid the price for tracking that rival late on. Her rider was not hard on her inside the final furlong and there ought to be a race for her, but this somewhat confirms her limitations. (tchd Evens)
Mal And Dave(IRE), whose dam won over this trip at two, got markedly outpaced off the strong early fractions and was never seriously involved. He ran on nicely towards the finish though and should be all the wiser for the run. (tchd 11-1 and 16-1)
Cambuslang(IRE), whose dam was a 5f juvenile winner, got the hang of things from 2f out and can be expected to get closer now he has the initial experience under his belt. Official explanation: jockey said colt hung right final half furlong (tchd 22-1 and 28-1)

1646 CORE (OIL AND GAS) LIMITED-PHILIZMA H'CAP — 1m 1f

3:30 (3:30) (Class 4) (0-80,80) 4-Y-O+ — **£5,180** (£1,541; £770; £384) **Stalls** High

Form RPR

52-1 **1** **Sirvino**^{16} [1279] 4-8-10 **72**.... PhillipMakin 2 82+
(T D Barron) *prom on outer: hdwy 3f out: effrt 2f out: rdn to ld ent fnl f: kpt on wl* **5/2**^{1}

-051 **2** 1 1/2 **Royal Amnesty**^{42} [893] 6-9-4 **80**....(b) RobertWinston 6 88+
(I Semple) *hld up: smooth hdwy on inner 3f out: effrt and nt clr run over 1f out: rdn to chse wnr ins fnl f: kpt on* **12/1**

42-3 **3** 3/4 **Wind Shuffle (GER)**^{28} [1100] 6-8-11 **78**.... GaryBartley$^{(5)}$ 9 83
(J S Goldie) *led: rdn along and edgd lft wl over 1f out: drive: hdd and edgd rt ent fnl f: one pce* **6/1**

551- **4** 1 3/4 **Wind Star**^{228} [5968] 6-9-1 **80**.... NeilBrown$^{(3)}$ 3 82
(G A Swinbank) *hld up in tch: hdwy on outer 3f out: rdn to chse ldrs 2f out: sn drvn and kpt on same pce appr last* **5/1**^{3}

0465 **5** 3 1/4 **Bourse (IRE)**^{14} [1332] 4-7-11 **66** oh3.... JamieKyne$^{(7)}$ 1 61
(A G Foster) *towards rr: hdwy wl over 2f out: sn rdn and kpt on ins fnl f: nt rch ldrs* **9/1**

04-0 **6** 3 1/4 **Golden Penny**^{19} [1229] 4-8-12 **74**.... NCallan 8 62
(A G Foster) *trckd ldrs: hdwy 1/2-way: cl up 3f out and sn rdn: drvn wl over 1f out and grad wknd* **12/1**

0200 **7** 1 1/4 **Casino Night**^{6} [1507] 4-8-5 **72**.... DeanHeslop$^{(5)}$ 4 57
(R Johnson) *a towards rr* **28/1**

05-2 **8** 1/2 **Celtic Change (IRE)**^{28} [1100] 5-8-12 **74**....(v) TomEaves 5 58
(M Dods) *hld up in tch: hdwy 3f out: chsd ldrs whn n.m.r 2f out: sn rdn and wknd* **3/1**^{2}

0-00 **9** 1 1/2 **Cigalas**^{19} [1229] 4-8-13 **75**.... TonyHamilton 7 56
(Mrs J C McGregor) *t.k.h: prom: rdn along over 3f out and sn wknd* **80/1**

1m 51.11s (-3.59) **Going Correction** -0.30s/f (Firm) **9** Ran SP% **114.6**
Speed ratings (Par 105): **103,101,101,99,96 93,92,92,90**
toteswinger: 1&2 £6.40, 1&3 £2.80, 2&3 £7.40 CSF £33.57 CT £164.26 TOTE £3.60: £1.30, £3.20, £2.40; EX 34.70.
Owner Theo Williams and Charles Mocatta **Bred** A W J Perry **Trained** Maunby, N Yorks

FOCUS
A good handicap for the grade and the form looks pretty solid. The winner is progressing and the second was better than ever.
Celtic Change(IRE) Official explanation: vet said gelding returned in a distressed state

1647 POMMERY CHAMPAGNE BAR AT MUSSELBURGH RACECOURSE CONDITIONS STKS — 5f

4:05 (4:05) (Class 2) 3-Y-O+ — **£12,462** (£3,732; £1,866; £934; £466; £234) **Stalls** Low

Form RPR

500- **1** **Spin Cycle (IRE)**^{202} [6644] 3-8-12 102.... TomEaves 7 109
(B Smart) *trckd ldrs: hdwy 2f out: sswtchd rt and rdn ent fnl f: qcknd wl to ld nr fin* **6/1**

0-15 **2** 1/2 **Cheveton**^{14} [1325] 5-8-12 100.... RobertWinston 6 102
(R J Price) *t.k.h: chsd ldrs: hdwy to chal over 1f out: rdn to ld ins fnl f: drvn: hdd and no ex nr line* **15/8**^{1}

21- **3** 1 3/4 **City Dancer (IRE)**^{208} [6507] 3-8-2 95.... PaulHanagan 8 91
(A Berry) *cl up: led 2f out: rdn ent fnl f: sn hdd and one pce towards fin* **20/1**

010- **4** nk **Hamish McGonagall**^{188} [6971] 4-8-12 100.... DavidAllan 1 95
(T D Easterby) *chsd ldrs: rdn whn n.m.r over 1f out: kpt on u.p ins fnl f* **7/2**^{3}

54-0 **5** 1 1/4 **River Falcon**^{33} [1018] 9-8-12 95.... DanielTudhope 9 90
(J S Goldie) *in rr and outpcd: hdwy 2f out: styd on ins fnl f: nrst fin* **9/1**

0-11 **6** 2 1/4 **Fol Hollow (IRE)**^{13} [1375] 4-8-12 100.... AdrianTNicholls 4 82
(D Nicholls) *hld: rdn and hdd 2f out: sn wknd* **10/3**^{2}

0402 **7** 3 1/2 **Pawan (IRE)**^{23} [1189] 9-8-12 92....(b) AnnStokell 2 69
(Miss A Stokell) *a in rr* **33/1**

00-0 **8** 6 **Seafield Towers**^{19} [1227] 9-8-12 41....(b) PatrickMathers 5 48
(D A Nolan) *a in rr* **200/1**

57.66 secs (-2.74) **Going Correction** -0.30s/f (Firm)
WFA 3 from 4yo+ 9lb **8** Ran SP% **112.6**
Speed ratings (Par 109): **109,108,105,104,102 99,93,84**
toteswinger: 1&2 £7.70, 1&3 £39.80, 2&3 £15.80 CSF £17.12 TOTE £6.80: £2.00, £1.20, £3.30; EX 24.40.
Owner H E Sheikh Rashid Bin Mohammed **Bred** Mrs Lisa Kelly **Trained** Hambleton, N Yorks

FOCUS
A competitive conditions event that had decent prize money on offer and was won last year by subsequent Group 1 winner Borderlescott. The time and the proximity of the third cast slight doubts over the form, but it does seem an improved effort from the winner.

NOTEBOOK
Spin Cycle(IRE) had the highest BHB rating, boasting a mark of 102 due to his narrow defeat in the Norfolk Stakes last year. His form rather tailed off thereafter, but he showed he has done well during the off-season and this was a decent effort as a 3yo against his elders. He shaped like a horse in need of the run 2f out, but picked up strongly once given a few smacks and completed the task a touch cosily in the end. He has now won both of his races over C&D and this ground was likely perfect for him. Where he goes from here is uncertain and things will be tougher, but this was the best possible start to his campaign. (op 8-1 tchd 11-2)
Cheveton came here in great heart and ran right up to his best. The easing of underfoot conditions was ideal for his needs and there should be a decent pot in him at some stage this term. (op 5-2 tchd 7-4)
City Dancer(IRE), last seen getting off the mark at Dundalk in October, was making her British debut for new connections and ran a blinder in defeat. Nothing was travelling better 2f out, but she just began to feel the pinch after the furlong pole. Along with the winner she was the only other 3yo in attendance and, remembering her trainer did so well with the filly Look Busy last term, looks set for a profitable year. (op 18-1 tchd 16-1)
Hamish McGonagall, closely matched with the runner-up on C&D form last year, did very little wrong on this seasonal return and looks set to come on a lot for the outing. (op 5-1)
River Falcon produced a very eyecatching display. He was taken off his feet early on, but his rider hardly moved a muscle through the first half of the race. The manner in which he eventually stayed on suggests he could have finished a deal closer under a more vigorous ride and he clearly still retains ability. Official explanation: jockey said, regarding running and riding, that his orders were to drop the gelding in, take his time and stalk the field, adding that he dropped in from a wide draw and felt outpaced early stages; trainer confirmed, adding that it was outpaced early and would benefit from a step up to 5 1/2f. (tchd 17-2)
Fol Hollow(IRE) was not disgraced in this quest for the hat-trick, but found things too hot and is not going to prove that simple to place now. (op 9-4 tchd 2-1)

1648 BOOGIE IN THE MORNING H'CAP — 1m 6f

4:40 (4:40) (Class 5) (0-70,69) 4-Y-O+ — **£3,885** (£1,156; £577; £288) **Stalls** Low

Form RPR

0313 **1** **That'll Do Nicely (IRE)**^{27} [1125] 6-9-5 **63**.... TomEaves 4 70+
(N G Richards) *hld up in rr: hdwy over 3f out: n.m.r and swtchd outside 2f out: rdn and str run ent fnl f: led last 100yds* **13/2**

-110 **2** 1 1/4 **Merrion Tiger (IRE)**^{42} [899] 4-9-5 **64**.... NCallan 9 69
(A G Foster) *a.p: hdwy 3f out: led over 2f out and sn rdn: drvn ent fnl f: hdd and no ex last 100yds* **11/1**

00-2 **3** 3/4 **Sonny Sam (IRE)**^{18} [1242] 4-8-10 **55**.... PaulHanagan 7 59+
(R A Fahey) *hld up towards rr: stdy hdwy over 3f out: hmpd 2f out and sn swtchd lft: rdn to chse ldrs over 1f out: kpt on ins fnl f* **4/1**^{2}

11-4 **4** 1 1/2 **Bollin Greta**^{13} [1366] 4-9-10 **69**.... DavidAllan 3 71
(T D Easterby) *t.k.h: hld up in tch: hdwy over 3f out: rdn to chal over 1f out and ev ch tl drvn and one pce ins fnl f* **3/1**^{1}

2/00 **5** ½ **Zefooha (FR)**[18] 1242 5-8-12 **56** GrahamGibbons 8 57
(T D Walford) *hld up in tch: hdwy over 3f out: rdn 2f out: sn drvn and kpt on same pce* **13/2**

3435 **6** shd **Miss Keck**[18] 1242 5-9-3 **61** PJMcDonald 2 62
(G A Swinbank) *in tch: hdwy over 3f out: rdn to chse ldrs wl over 2f out: sn drvn and kpt on same pce* **11/2**[3]

0-46 **7** 2¼ **Los Nadis (GER)**[8] 1230 5-9-6 **64** PhillipMakin 5 62
(P Monteith) *hld up and bhd: hdwyu on inner 3f out: effrt whn nt clr run 2f out: sn rdn and no imp* **11/2**[3]

10-4 **8** ¾ **Jane Of Arc (FR)**[19] 1226 5-8-5 **52** KellyHarrison(3) 6 49
(J S Goldie) *prom: effrt 3f out: sn rdn and wknd over 2f out* **25/1**

/6-6 **9** 10 **Grail Knight**[27] 1127 4-7-12 **50** JamieKyne(7) 10 33
(A G Foster) *led: rdn along over 3f out: drvn: wandered and hdd over 2f out: sn wknd* **100/1**

446- **10** 42 **Hugs Destiny (IRE)**[158] 5869 8-8-0 **49** oh4 (t) SophieDoyle(5) 1 —
(M A Barnes) *cl up: rdn along 5f out: sn wknd* **40/1**

3m 4.41s (-0.89) **Going Correction** -0.30s/f (Firm)
WFA 4 from 5yo+ 1lb **10** Ran SP% **118.0**
Speed ratings (Par 103): **90,89,88,88,87 87,86,85,80,56**
toteswinger: 1&2 £6.20, 1&3 £4.80, 2&3 £5.60 CSF £75.10 CT £325.50 TOTE £7.20: £2.20, £2.60, £1.40; EX 56.60.
Owner J D Flood **Bred** J D Flood **Trained** Greystoke, Cumbria
■ Stewards' Enquiry : Graham Gibbons two-day ban: careless riding (May 15-16)

FOCUS
A moderate staying handicap, run at an average pace and a bit muddling in consequence. The winner could have a bit more to offer as a stayer.

1649 ISS FACILITIES SERVICES H'CAP 7f 30y
5:15 (5:15) (Class 3) (0-90,90) 4-Y-0+
£7,477 (£2,239; £1,119; £560; £279; £140) **Stalls** High

Form RPR

6500 **1** **Opus Maximus (IRE)**[20] 1209 4-8-13 **82** JoeFanning 11 94
(M Johnston) *chsd ldr: hdwy to ld 2f out: sn rdn and edgd rt appr last: sn clr and styd on strly* **3/1**[1]

00-5 **2** 3¼ **Jewelled Dagger (IRE)**[114] 70 5-9-2 **85** (b) LeeEnstone 3 88
(I Semple) *led: pushed along 3f out: rdn and hdd 2f out: swtchd lft and drvn ent fnl f: kpt on: no ch w wnr* **9/1**

0212 **3** ½ **Flores Sea (USA)**[10] 1436 5-8-9 **78** (b) PhillipMakin 4 80
(T D Barron) *hld up: hdwy wl over 2f out: rdn wl over 1f out: kpt on ins fnl f: nrst fin* **5/1**[2]

0-00 **4** ½ **Dabbers Ridge (IRE)**[34] 995 7-8-13 **82** RobertWinston 2 83
(I W McInnes) *hld up towards rr: hdwy and in tch 3f out: effrt to chse ldrs 2f out: sn rdn and kpt on same pce appr fnl f* **18/1**

620- **5** ¾ **Mujaadel (USA)**[211] 6424 4-9-1 **84** AdrianTNicholls 7 83+
(D Nicholls) *hld up in rr: hdwy on wd outside 3f out: rdn 2f out: drvn and no imp appr fnl f* **20/1**

05-6 **6** ½ **Jonny Lesters Hair (IRE)**[14] 1333 4-8-5 **74** PaulHanagan 5 71
(T D Easterby) *chsd ldng pair: effrt 3f out: rdn over 2f out: sn drvn and no imp* **15/2**

-020 **7** 1¾ **Captain Jacksparra (IRE)**[10] 1436 5-8-11 **80** (p) NCallan 12 73
(K A Ryan) *chsd ldrs: hdwy 3f out: rdn over 2f out: sn drvn and grad wknd* **12/1**

04-6 **8** ½ **Esoterica (IRE)**[19] 1229 6-8-4 **76** KellyHarrison(3) 9 67
(J S Goldie) *in rr tl sme late hdwy* **14/1**

655- **9** 2¼ **Hinton Admiral**[131] 7755 5-8-13 **82** TonyHamilton 10 67
(R A Fahey) *a towards rr* **7/1**[3]

020/ **10** 4 **Commando Scott (IRE)**[538] 6758 8-9-7 **90** PatrickMathers 8 64
(I W McInnes) *chsd ldrs: rdn along over 3f out and sn wknd* **40/1**

3123 **11** ½ **Strabinios King**[83] 446 5-8-5 **79** ow1 SladeO'Hara(5) 6 52
(A Berry) *in tch on inner: hdwy to chse ldrs over 3f out: rdn wl over 2f out and sn wknd* **16/1**

00-4 **12** 9 **Sir Xaar (IRE)**[27] 1124 6-9-2 **85** (v) TomEaves 1 34
(B Smart) *a towards rr: bhd and eased over 1f out* **10/1**

1m 26.9s (-3.40) **Going Correction** -0.30s/f (Firm) **12** Ran SP% **117.7**
Speed ratings (Par 107): **107,103,102,102,101 100,98,98,95,91 90,80**
toteswingers: 1&2 £7.80, 1&3 £7.80, 2&3 £2.80 CSF £30.05 CT £134.27 TOTE £3.30: £2.00, £3.90, £1.70; EX 33.50.
Owner Jim McGrath **Bred** Mrs Anne Marie Burns **Trained** Middleham Moor, N Yorks

FOCUS
A decent handicap which was run at a sound early pace. The front pair were always 1-2 and the form should work out.

NOTEBOOK
Opus Maximus(IRE) got back to winning ways with a straightforward display. He was never far from the early lead from his decent draw and showed a likeable attitude when asked to win the race. He had slipped in the weights, but had run respectably in defeat since resuming this year and everything went right here. He would have to be entitled to respect if turned out under a penalty. (op 4-1 tchd 11-4)
Jewelled Dagger(IRE) set out to make all at a strong pace and deserves plenty of credit for keeping on for second place. His form figures at the track read 11122 and he should improve nicely for this first run in 114 days. (op 8-1 tchd 10-1)
Flores Sea(USA), back on turf, stayed on gamely for pressure down the home straight without threatening and helps to set the level. (op 11-2)
Dabbers Ridge(IRE) performed creditably from his low draw on ground he would have found lively enough. He is now very well handicapped on his previous best efforts and it was his best run for current connections. (op 16-1)
Mujaadel(USA) ◆, having his first outing for seven months, really caught the eye staying on from way off the pace. He was pretty much detached after being restrained early on and did show a slightly awkward head carriage down the home straight. He motored home inside the final furlong and, while it is not the first time he has done this, there is surely another race in him back over an extra furlong. (op 14-1)
Sir Xaar(IRE) (op 8-1 tchd 15-2)

1650 ARTHRITIS CARE SUPPORTING YOU IN SCOTLAND H'CAP 7f 30y
5:50 (5:52) (Class 6) (0-65,65) 4-Y-0+ **£2,266** (£674; £337; £168) **Stalls** High

Form RPR

2-03 **1** **Angaric (IRE)**[9] 1456 6-9-4 **65** TomEaves 5 72
(B Smart) *trckd ldr: hdwy 3f out: rdn to chal 2f out: sn led and edgd rt over 1f out: drvn ins fnl f and hld on gamely* **8/1**[3]

2-32 **2** nse **Kargan (IRE)**[67] 657 4-8-13 **60** GrahamGibbons 12 66
(A G Foster) *trckd ldrs on inner: hdwy over 2f out: rdn and ev ch whn nt clr run over 1f out: drvn and styd on strly ins fnl f: jst failed* **8/1**[3]

0-02 **3** nse **Maison Dieu**[18] 1244 6-8-13 **60** DavidAllan 2 66
(E J Alston) *hld up: hdwy over 2f out: rdn to chse ldrs wl over 1f out: drvn to chal ins fnl f and ev ch tl no ex nr line* **15/2**[2]

200- **4** shd **Optical Illusion (USA)**[150] 7533 5-8-6 **53** PaulHanagan 4 59
(R A Fahey) *hld up towards rr: hdwy over 2f out: swtchd lft and rdn over 1f out: styd on strly ins fnl f* **14/1**

334- **5** 2½ **Grand Diamond (IRE)**[123] 7224 5-9-3 **64** (p) DanielTudhope 11 63
(J S Goldie) *led: rdn along 3f out: drvn 2f out and sn hdd: kpt on same pce appr fnl f* **7/2**[1]

0-53 **6** 2¾ **Baronovici (IRE)**[18] 1243 4-8-9 **56** (p) TonyHamilton 6 48
(D W Barker) *in tch: hdwy to chse ldrs 3f out: rdn along over 2f out: sn drvn and grad wknd* **14/1**

26-0 **7** 1 **Mr Lu**[27] 1123 4-9-3 **64** NCallan 3 53
(A G Foster) *chsd ldrs: rdn along and sltly outpcd wl over 2f out: hdwy u.p wl over 1f out: no imp ent fnl f* **12/1**

5-51 **8** nk **Mandalay King (IRE)**[9] 1456 4-8-10 **64** JohnCavanagh(7) 8 52
(Mrs Marjorie Fife) *hld up towards rr: hdwy 3f out: rdn over 2f out and sn no imp* **7/2**[1]

0-00 **9** ½ **Wiseman's Diamond (USA)**[8] 1475 4-8-9 **56** ow1 (p) PhillipMakin 10 43
(P T Midgley) *a towards rr* **9/1**

25-0 **10** 1½ **Poppy's Rose**[18] 1258 5-9-3 **64** (p) PatrickMathers 1 47
(I W McInnes) *a in rr* **25/1**

246- **11** 12 **Red Skipper (IRE)**[182] 7111 4-9-1 **62** LeeEnstone 7 13
(N Wilson) *chsd ldrs on outer: rdn along 3f out and sn wknd* **18/1**

1m 28.27s (-2.03) **Going Correction** -0.30s/f (Firm) **11** Ran SP% **118.6**
Speed ratings (Par 101): **99,98,98,98,95 92,91,91,90,89 75**
toteswingers: 1&2 £7.10, 1&3 £13.40, 2&3 £9.30 CSF £71.18 CT £513.51 TOTE £9.80: £3.00, £2.60, £2.90; EX 40.00 Place 6: £71.29 Place 5: £47.92.
Owner B Smart **Bred** Humphrey Okeke **Trained** Hambleton, N Yorks

FOCUS
The first four came home in a blanket finish in this moderate handicap, which was run at a solid pace. They were clear of the remainder. Straightforward form.
T/Jkpt: Not won. T/Plt: £58.60 to a £1 stake. Pool: £74,306.44. 924.62 winning tickets. T/Qpdt: £17.00 to a £1 stake. Pool: £4,446.59. 193.30 winning tickets. JR

1563 SOUTHWELL (L-H)
Friday, May 1

OFFICIAL GOING: Standard
Wind: fresh 1/2 against Weather: fine but quite breezy

1651 BET AFTER THE OFF AT LADBROKES.COM APPRENTICE H'CAP 1m 3f (F)
2:30 (2:30) (Class 6) (0-55,49) 4-Y-0+ **£2,388** (£705; £352) **Stalls** Low

Form RPR

3326 **1** **Sir Haydn**[22] 1200 9-8-9 **49** (v) DannyBrock(5) 6 56
(J R Jenkins) *t.k.h: hdwy to trck ldrs after 3f: led over 3f out: rdn clr fnl 2f* **7/2**[1]

0-63 **2** 5 **Starcross Maid**[40] 918 7-8-10 **45** DavidKenny 2 44
(A G Juckes) *hld up in rr: hdwy over 3f out: wnt 2nd 2f out: no ch w wnr* **13/2**

6656 **3** 4½ **Jiminor Mack**[71] 601 6-8-10 **45** (p) JosephineBruning 4 36
(W J H Ratcliffe) *hld up: hdwy to chse ldrs 5f out: brought wd over 2f out: tk modest 3rd 1f out* **14/1**

00-6 **4** 2¼ **Corrib (IRE)**[80] 493 6-9-0 **49** HollyHall 3 36
(B Palling) *t.k.h: w ldrs: one pce fnl 3f* **6/1**[3]

5 nk **Crazy Bold (GER)**[18] 6-8-12 **47** TobyAtkinson 8 34
(A W Carroll) *in rr: drvn 6f out: one pce fnl 3f* **9/2**[2]

636- **6** 9 **Pretty Officer (USA)**[248] 5379 4-8-9 **49** NoelGarbutt(5) 1 20
(Rae Guest) *hld up in rr: drvn 5f out: sn lost pl* **7/1**

2/0- **7** 1¼ **Doonigan (IRE)**[36] 6550 5-8-13 **48** SeanPalmer 9 17
(G Brown) *in rr: hdwy u.p on outside 6f out: lost pl 5f out* **20/1**

200- **8** 22 **Cecina Marina**[219] 6215 6-8-10 **45** (p) MatthewLawson 7 —
(Mrs K Walton) *mde most tl over 5f out: sn lost pl: bhd and eased 2f out: t.o* **40/1**

0643 **9** 1 **Maddy**[6] 1520 4-9-0 **49** (p) MJMurphy 5 —
(George Baker) *w ldrs: led over 5f out: hdd over 3f out: sn lost pl: t.o* **9/2**[2]

2m 27.79s (-0.21) **Going Correction** -0.10s/f (Stan) **9** Ran SP% **112.6**
Speed ratings (Par 101): **96,92,89,87,87 80,79,63,63**
toteswinger: 1&2 £5.80, 1&3 £36.70, 2&3 £56.50 CSF £25.65 CT £277.71 TOTE £3.90: £1.20, £2.60, £5.30; EX 22.50 Trifecta £230.70 Part won. Pool: £311.89 - 0.45 winning units..
Owner A C Murphy **Bred** D Leggate, Miss N Kent & Helshaw Grange Stud **Trained** Royston, Herts

FOCUS
A very moderate apprentice handicap indeed with the four top-weights officially rated just 49. The early pace was decent though, with three horses taking each other on for the lead and the tempo certainly appeared to find out a few. It is doubtful if the winner had to improve on his recent efforts.
Maddy Official explanation: jockey said filly had no more to give

1652 BET WITH LADBROKES ON 0800 777888 CLAIMING STKS 6f (F)
3:05 (3:05) (Class 6) 3-Y-O **£2,047** (£604; £302) **Stalls** Low

Form RPR

30-0 **1** **Capo Regime**[23] 1190 3-9-7 63 (v[1]) SilvestreDeSousa 4 76
(D Nicholls) *t.k.h: trckd ldrs: effrt on inner over 2f out: styd on wl to ld last 75yds* **7/1**[3]

1213 **2** 2½ **Madison Belle**[50] 819 3-8-12 75 DarrenWilliams 7 59
(K R Burke) *w ldr: led over 2f out: edgd lft: hdd and no ex ins fnl f* **10/11**[1]

6664 **3** 4 **Pepin (IRE)**[11] 1412 3-8-7 40 FrankieMcDonald 5 41
(D Haydn Jones) *dwlt: mid-div: hung bdly lft 2f out: kpt on* **12/1**

-420 **4** 7 **Denton Diva**[28] 1098 3-8-12 65 (p) DaleGibson 8 24
(M Dods) *drvn to chse ldrs: rdn over 2f out: sn btn* **11/4**[2]

-040 **5** 1¾ **Bold Account (IRE)**[25] 1157 3-8-0 53 (p) AndrewHeffernan(7) 6 13
(Garry Moss) *led tl over 2f out: wknd over 1f out* **14/1**

250- **6** 1½ **Royal Premium**[172] 7266 3-8-8 50 AndreaAtzeni(5) 3 14
(Mrs G S Rees) *chsd ldrs: wknd over 2f out* **33/1**

0 **7** 1¼ **Naywye**[50] 819 3-8-2 0 DuranFentiman 1 —
(M W Easterby) *s.s: a in rr* **50/1**

0360 **8** hd **Meg Jicaro**[30] 1064 3-8-2 43 CatherineGannon 10 —
(Mrs L Williamson) *chsd ldrs on outside: sn drvn along: lost pl 3f out* **40/1**

00 **9** 12 **Fancy Set (IRE)**[31] 1046 3-8-2 0 (b[1]) ChrisCatlin 9 —
(D J S Ffrench Davis) *in rr: lost pl over 4f out: sn bhd* **50/1**

1m 15.87s (-0.63) **Going Correction** -0.10s/f (Stan) **9** Ran SP% **115.2**
Speed ratings (Par 97): **100,96,91,82,79 77,76,75,59**
oteswinger: 1&2 £1.20, 1&3 £5.30, 2&3 £6.00 CSF £13.60 TOTE £11.10: £2.40, £1.02, £3.10; EX 18.10 Trifecta £80.80 Pool: £381.33 - 3.49 winning units..
Owner Martin Love **Bred** Mason Gill Racing **Trained** Sessay, N Yorks
■ Stewards' Enquiry : Frankie McDonald caution: used whip down shoulder in forehand position

FOCUS
A weak claimer in which only a couple appeared to hold realistic claims at the weights, but a race run at a decent tempo produced a bit of a turn up. A much-improved effort from the winner in the visor.

Pepin(IRE) Official explanation: jockey said gelding hung badly left
Denton Diva Official explanation: jockey said filly ran flat

1653 PLAY POKER AT LADBROKES.COM MEDIAN AUCTION MAIDEN STKS 5f (F)
3:40 (3:40) (Class 6) 2-Y-O £2,729 (£806; £403) Stalls High

Form RPR
0 1 **Lucky Mellor**[29] 1083 2-9-3 0 ChrisCatlin 2 67
(D K Ivory) *racd towards far side: w ldrs: led jst ins fnl f: jst hld on* 14/1
0 2 hd **Koo And The Gang (IRE)**[34] 994 2-8-12 0 LanceBetts[(5)] 4 66
(B Ellison) *led: hdd jst ins fnl f: kpt on wl: jst hld* 7/2[2]
00 3 4 **Usquaebach**[15] 1298 2-8-12 0 (v[1]) FrancisNorton 1 47
(H J Collingridge) *racd far side: w wnr: one pce appr fnl f* 40/1
4 nk **Midnight Uno** 2-8-12 0 JackDean[(5)] 5 51
(W G M Turner) *chsd ldrs: kpt on same pce appr fnl f* 10/1[3]
4 5 1 **Masked Dance (IRE)**[16] 1277 2-9-3 0 RichardMullen 11 47+
(K A Ryan) *racd stands' side: chsd ldrs: one pce fnl 2f* 4/6[1]
0 6 2 **Chifah**[15] 1304 2-8-12 0 PaulDoe 3 35
(P D Evans) *dwlt: sn chsng ldrs: wknd fnl f* 14/1
7 3 **Magneto (IRE)** 2-9-3 0 EdwardCreighton 10 29+
(E J Creighton) *sn outpcd and in rr: nvr on terms* 66/1
8 3 1/2 **Miss Marani (IRE)** 2-8-12 0 TolleyDean 8 12
(W G M Turner) *s.i.s: a outpcd and in rr* 25/1
5 9 1 3/4 **Cariad Coch**[28] 1097 2-8-12 0 RichardKingscote 6 5
(Mrs L Stubbs) *racd towards stands' side: chsd ldrs: lost pl over 1f out* 10/1[3]
10 1 1/2 **Pong Ping** 2-8-12 0 DuranFentiman 9 —
(T D Easterby) *s.i.s: a outpcd and in rr: edgd rt fnl 2f* 20/1
11 3 **Val's Princess** 2-8-5 0 DannyBrock[(7)] 7 —
(J R Jenkins) *dwlt: a outpcd and bhd* 28/1

59.85 secs (0.15) **Going Correction** -0.175s/f (Stan) 11 Ran SP% 129.7
Speed ratings (Par 91): **91,90,84,83,82 79,74,68,65,63 58**
toteswinger: 1&2 £5.70, 2&3 £44.70 1&3 not won. CSF £66.28 TOTE £34.50: £4.50, £2.10, £15.50; EX 147.30 TRIFECTA Not won..
Owner L M Baker **Bred** Mr And Mrs L Baker **Trained** Radlett, Herts

FOCUS
A moderate juvenile maiden and once again over this straight 5f the draw played a huge part with the first three home starting from the four lowest stalls. Very few ever got into it.

NOTEBOOK
Lucky Mellor had finished last of nine on his Leicester debut, but he did show some early speed there and that wasn't a bad race as the first three home all won their next starts. He made good use of his decent draw here and having been disputing the lead from the start, kept on going to hang on with nothing to spare. (op 16-1)
Koo And The Gang(IRE) had been beaten a long way in the Brocklesby on debut, but he was the subject of quite a gamble here which suggested that much better was expected. Another to race up at the sharp end from a low draw from the start, albeit more towards the nearside of the track, he almost justified the market confidence and may have got back up in another stride. (op 15-2)
Usquaebach, beaten a very long way in her first two starts in much classier contests than this, including when behind Koo And The Gang in the Brocklesby, ran much better here in the first-time visor though she benefited greatly from racing prominently and starting from the plum draw. (op 33-1)
Midnight Uno, a half-brother to the multiple 5f-7f winner Sea Salt, showed up for a long way and fared best of the newcomers, so deserves credit for that. (op 14-1 tchd 20-1)
Masked Dance(IRE), representing last year's winning stable, had shown plenty of early pace when fourth on his Beverley debut and he was all the rage here, but he found himself starting from the dreaded stands'-rails draw. Unfortunately for him, he didn't break too well and as a result he was forced to race tight against the rail throughout. He did his best, but could never land a blow and it's probably best to put a line through this effort. (op 8-13 tchd Evens, tchd 11-10 in a place)
Cariad Coch Official explanation: jockey said filly was unsuited by the fibresand

1654 BETTER PRICES, BIGGER WINS AT LADBROKES.COM H'CAP 1m 4f (F)
4:15 (4:16) (Class 6) (0-65,64) 4-Y-O+ £2,388 (£705; £352) Stalls Low

Form RPR
5-51 1 **World Of Choice (USA)**[48] 378 4-8-8 54 (b) DaleGibson 4 66
(M W Easterby) *hld up in midfield: hdwy to trck ldrs 6f out: shkn up to ld over 1f out: hrd drvn: kpt on towards fin* 16/1
/0-3 2 1 **Greenbelt**[10] 1442 8-8-6 52 ChrisCatlin 8 62
(G M Moore) *chsd ldrs: sn pushed along: led over 3f out: hdd over 1f out: no ex ins fnl f* 9/2[3]
-251 3 1 1/4 **Paddy Rielly (IRE)**[10] 1442 4-8-10 56 (p) PaulDoe 3 64
(P D Evans) *trckd ldrs: rdn over 2f out: hung rt and kpt on same pce fnl f* 5/6[1]
-320 4 6 **Gayanula (USA)**[89] 368 4-8-5 58 ow1 (p) BMcHugh[(7)] 1 57
(Miss J A Camacho) *hld up towards rr: stdy hdwy 6f out: effrt and chsng ldrs 3f out: wknd appr fnl f* 20/1
221- 5 5 **Art Exhibition (IRE)**[51] 1710 4-9-1 64 JamesMillman[(3)] 7 55
(B R Millman) *chsd ldrs: drvn and lost pl 5f out: no threat after* 4/1[2]
45-0 6 2 1/2 **Wizard Looking**[44] 871 8-8-9 55 JamieMoriarty 2 42
(P T Midgley) *hld up in rr: effrt 3f out: nvr nr ldrs* 25/1
632/ 7 4 **Impeccable Guest (IRE)**[47] 6551 6-8-4 50 oh5 DuranFentiman 5 30
(J Mackie) *in rr: hdwy to chse ldrs 6f out: outpcd over 3f out: sn lost pl* 20/1
00-6 8 7 **Sporting Gesture**[13] 1366 12-8-12 63 LanceBetts[(5)] 6 32
(M W Easterby) *led: qcknd over 4f out: hdd over 3f out: sn lost pl* 25/1

2m 40.22s (-0.78) **Going Correction** -0.10s/f (Stan) 8 Ran SP% 115.8
Speed ratings (Par 101): **98,97,96,92,89 87,84,80**
toteswinger: 1&2 not won, 1&3 £5.20, 2&3 £2.60 CSF £81.28 CT £127.49 TOTE £27.80: £3.50, £1.90, £1.10; EX 101.70 Trifecta £390.10 Pool: £606.29 - 1.15 winning units..
Owner Mrs Jean Turpin **Bred** Catesby W Clay & Runnymede Farm Inc **Trained** Sheriff Hutton, N Yorks

FOCUS
A modest middle-distance handicap and although the pace looked ordinary, they finished very well spread out behind the leading trio. The winner is rated back to his best with the well-in favourite not that far off his best.
Paddy Rielly(IRE) Official explanation: trainer's rep said he had no explanation for the gelding's run

1655 LADIES DAY AT SOUTHWELL 16TH AUGUST H'CAP 7f (F)
4:50 (4:50) (Class 6) (0-60,59) 4-Y-O+ £2,047 (£604; £302) Stalls Low

Form RPR
132 1 **Gracie's Gift (IRE)**[1] 1634 7-8-8 54 MarkCoumbe[(5)] 9 63
(R C Guest) *hld up in rr: hdwy on wd outside over 2f out: wnt 2nd 1f out: r.o to ld nr fin* 11/4[1]
4346 2 3/4 **Bold Diva**[11] 1413 4-8-12 53 (v) TolleyDean 10 60
(A W Carroll) *trckd ldrs on outer: led over 2f out: hdd towards fin* 8/1
5602 3 1 1/4 **Haroldini (IRE)**[10] 1438 7-8-13 57 (v) JackMitchell[(3)] 2 61
(J Balding) *in rr: nt clr run and swtchd outside over 2f out: styd on same pce fnl f* 9/2[2]
0050 4 2 1/2 **Copper King**[32] 1039 5-8-7 48 ChrisCatlin 14 45
(Miss Tor Sturgis) *mid-div: hdwy over 2f out: sn chsng ldrs: kpt on one pce* 11/1
0006 5 4 1/2 **Louisiade (IRE)**[10] 1438 8-7-13 47 ow1 (p) AndrewHeffernan[(7)] 4 32
(M C Chapman) *chsd ldrs: drvn 3f out: wknd over 1f out* 16/1
4330 6 nk **Magical Song**[10] 1438 4-8-13 54 (b) EdwardCreighton 5 38
(J Balding) *in tch: drvn over 4f out: wknd over 1f out* 7/1
05-0 7 2 **Captain Royale (IRE)**[16] 1276 4-9-0 55 (p) MickyFenton 11 34
(Miss Tracy Waggott) *led tl over 2f out: wknd over 1f out* 20/1
34-0 8 1/2 **Avontuur (FR)**[35] 975 7-9-1 59 MichaelJStainton[(3)] 13 37
(Mrs R A Carr) *chsd ldrs: lost pl over 1f out* 16/1
66-0 9 1 1/4 **Out Of India**[28] 1103 7-8-6 47 FrankieMcDonald 3 21
(P T Dalton) *mid-div: hdwy over 3f out: sn chsng ldrs: lost pl 2f out* 50/1
020/ 10 1/2 **Legal Lover (IRE)**[597] 5330 7-8-12 56 RussellKennemore[(3)] 12 29
(R Hollinshead) *chsd ldrs: drvn 3f out: wknd over 1f out* 5/1[3]
050- 11 12 **Young Gladiator (IRE)**[213] 6353 4-9-1 56 (p) JamieMoriarty 1 —
(Miss J A Camacho) *mid-div: drvn over 2f out: sn lost pl and bhd* 20/1
000- 12 11 **Osteopathic Care (IRE)**[287] 4168 5-8-1 47 ow1 MartinLane[(5)] 6 —
(Miss Tracy Waggott) *s.i.s: in rr and sn drvn along: bhd fnl 3f* 66/1

1m 29.12s (-1.18) **Going Correction** -0.10s/f (Stan) 12 Ran SP% 118.2
Speed ratings (Par 101): **102,101,99,96,91 91,89,88,87,86 72,60**
toteswinger: 1&2 £4.00, 1&3 £2.00, 2&3 £6.40 CSF £24.14 CT £99.31 TOTE £3.70: £1.40, £2.80, £1.90; EX 28.40 Trifecta £37.50 Pool: £431.33 - 8.49 winning units..
Owner S Hussey **Bred** Richard O'Hara **Trained** Stainforth, S Yorks

FOCUS
A moderate handicap, but a competitive one and most of these know their way around here. Straightforward form.

1656 GOLF SOCIETY DAYS - SOUTHWELL GOLF CLUB H'CAP 7f (F)
5:25 (5:25) (Class 5) (0-75,75) 3-Y-O £3,070 (£906; £453) Stalls Low

Form RPR
2-25 1 **Peter's Gift (IRE)**[4] 1561 3-8-11 68 RichardMullen 9 75
(K A Ryan) *chsd ldrs on outer: led over 1f out: styd on wl ins fnl f* 5/1[3]
-141 2 1 1/2 **Just Five (IRE)**[36] 968 3-8-2 64 PatrickDonaghy[(5)] 4 67+
(M Dods) *s.i.s: hdwy on ins over 2f out: kpt on to take 2nd ins fnl f: no imp* 7/2[2]
6-44 3 hd **Belated Silver (IRE)**[14] 1331 3-9-0 71 RichardKingscote 2 73
(Tom Dascombe) *led: edgd lft and hdd over 1f out: kpt on same pce* 12/1
0000 4 hd **Uncle Brit**[74] 572 3-8-4 61 oh1 ChrisCatlin 5 63+
(Sir Mark Prescott) *drvn along to sn chse ldrs: rdn over 3f out: kpt on same pce appr fnl f* 25/1
0-10 5 1 1/4 **Toby Tyler**[6] 1509 3-9-2 73 JamieMoriarty 6 71
(P T Midgley) *in rr: hdwy over 2f out: kpt on: nvr rchd ldrs* 16/1
002- 6 9 **Thurston (IRE)**[140] 7649 3-8-8 70 GabrielHannon[(5)] 8 44
(D J S Ffrench Davis) *chsd ldrs: wknd over 1f out: eased ins fnl f* 50/1
210 7 4 1/2 **Dontuwishitwereso**[30] 1068 3-8-9 66 FrancisNorton 7 28
(P W D'Arcy) *chsd ldrs: drvn over 3f out: lost pl over 2f out: eased ins fnl f* 7/1
01- 8 12 **Captain Dancer (IRE)**[182] 7106 3-9-4 75 MichaelHills 3 5
(B W Hills) *sn chsng ldrs on ins: drvn over 3f out: lost pl over 2f out: eased over 1f out* 4/5[1]
30-0 9 2 1/4 **Do Be Brave (IRE)**[37] 951 3-8-8 65 PaulEddery 1 —
(Paul Mason) *s.i.s: in rr: bhd fnl 3f* 66/1

1m 29.34s (-0.96) **Going Correction** -0.10s/f (Stan) 9 Ran SP% 127.8
Speed ratings (Par 99): **101,99,99,98,97 87,81,68,65**
toteswinger: 1&2 £2.50, 1&3 £3.80, 2&3 £7.60 CSF £25.38 CT £213.01 TOTE £7.70: £2.10, £1.40, £1.90; EX 26.30 Trifecta £228.50 Pool: £444.70 - 1.44 winning units. Place 6: £67.12 Place 5: £29.40.
Owner Mr & Mrs Julian And Rosie Richer **Bred** T C Chiang **Trained** Hambleton, N Yorks

FOCUS
An ordinary handicap, run in a time 0.22 seconds slower than the preceding handicap for older horses, and the front five pulled miles clear of the others. The form is rated around the third.
Captain Dancer(IRE) Official explanation: trainer's rep said, regarding running, that the gelding moved poorly throughout
T/Plt: £176.70 to a £1 stake. Pool: £48,895.35. 201.93 winning tickets. T/Qpdt: £38.10 to a £1 stake. Pool: £3,351.33. 65.00 winning tickets. WG

1267 SAINT-CLOUD (L-H)
Friday, May 1

OFFICIAL GOING: Soft

1657a PRIX CLEOPATRE (GROUP 3) (FILLIES) 1m 2f 110y
2:20 (2:20) 3-Y-O £38,835 (£15,534; £11,650; £7,767; £3,883)

RPR
1 **Flying Cloud (IRE)**[29] 3-8-9 MGuyon 1 102+
(A Fabre, France) *racd in 3rd bhd ldr: looking for gap between 2nd and 3rd fr 1 1/2f out: swtchd to rails ins fnl f: drvn to ld 80yds out: r.o wl* 31/10[2]
2 nk **Board Meeting (IRE)**[26] 3-8-9 ACrastus 4 100
(E Lellouche, France) *cl 2nd on outside: drvn 1 1/2f out: sltly hmpd jst ins fnl f: r.o at one pce: fin 3rd: plcd 2nd* 7/10[1]
3 1 **Excellent Girl**[18] 1267 3-8-9 CSoumillon 2 100
(Y De Nicolay, France) *led: drvn 1 1/2f out: hung rt off rail 1f out: hdd 80yds out: one pce: fin 2nd: disqualified: plcd 3rd* 9/2[3]
4 2 1/2 **Golden Clou (FR)**[29] 3-8-9 SPasquier 3 93
(P Demercastel, France) *racd in 4th: kpt on at same pce fr wl over 1f out* 41/5
5 nk **Black Crystal (USA)**[7] 3-8-9 OPeslier 5 93
(Robert Collet, France) *last thrght* 18/1

2m 13.6s (-6.00) 5 Ran SP% 117.5
PARI-MUTUEL: WIN 4.10; PL 1.30, 1.10; SF 5.30.
Owner Sheikh Mohammed **Bred** Gainsborough Stud Management Ltd **Trained** Chantilly, France

NOTEBOOK
Flying Cloud(IRE), an inexperienced filly, enjoyed some good luck but also displayed an excellent turn of foot to land this Group 3 event. Quickening up well when a gap appeared on the rail, she was going away from the others at the post. She is pretty certain to stay further and, while entered in the Prix de Diane, could be supplemented into the Oaks at Epsom.

Board Meeting(IRE) never seemed to be going well and proved disappointing. She challenged for the lead from a furlong and a half out but then just stayed on one-paced. Hampered at the furlong marker by the runner-up, the places were later reversed, but her trainer felt that she didn't show her best.
Excellent Girl, wearing cheekpieces for the first time, tried to make every yard of the running and was still going well at the entrance to the straight. She came under strong pressure a furlong and a half out and hung right, even though her jockey had his whip in the correct hand. She battled on gamely for second place but was then demoted as the stewards decided that she had prevented the third past the post from obtaining her best possible prize money.
Golden Clou(FR), who is not up to this class, was held up early on but couldn't quicken when things warmed up in the straight.

1658a PRIX DU MUGUET (GROUP 2) 1m
2:50 (2:50) 4-Y-O+ £71,942 (£27,767; £13,252; £8,835; £4,417)

RPR
1 **Vertigineux (FR)**57 [774] 5-8-12 .... PSogorb 4 116
(Mme C Dufreche, France) *racd in 3rd: hdwy against ins rail to press ldrs 1 1/2f out: led narrowly 1f out: drvn out* **109/10**
2 3/4 **Gris De Gris (IRE)**33 [1029] 5-9-1 .... GMosse 2 117
(A De Royer-Dupre, France) *led 1f then racd in 2nd: led narrowly 1 1/2f out to 1f out: kpt on* **6/4**1
3 2 1/2 **Precious Boy (GER)**215 [6322] 4-9-1 .... ASuborics 6 111
(W Hickst, Germany) *unruly bhd stalls: racd in 6th: kpt on steadily u.p fr 2f out to take 3rd 100yds out* **41/10**2
4 2 **Racinger (FR)**33 [1029] 6-8-12 .... (b) DBonilla 3 104
(F Head, France) *missed break: rcvrd to ld after 1f: set str pce: hdd 1 1/2f out: one pce* **49/10**3
5 2 1/2 **Alnadana (IRE)**33 [1029] 4-8-8 .... CSoumillon 7 94
(A De Royer-Dupre, France) *hld up in last: nvr a factor* **49/10**3
6 1 1/2 **Arcadia's Angle (USA)**33 [1029] 4-8-12 .... C-PLemaire 5 94
(P Bary, France) *racd in 5th: outpcd fnl 2f* **12/1**
7 2 **Putney Bridge (USA)**25 [1166] 4-8-12 .... SPasquier 1 90
(Mme C Head-Maarek, France) *racd in 4th: outpcd fnl 2f* **10/1**

1m 37.9s (-9.60) **7** Ran SP% **118.7**
PARI-MUTUEL: WIN 11.90; PL 4.20, 1.70; SF 34.40.
Owner Mme C & P Dufreche **Bred** Patrick Dufreche **Trained** France
■ Stewards' Enquiry : P Sogorb 100euro fine: whip abuse

NOTEBOOK
Vertigineux(FR), who looked well and was given an excellent ride, had beaten the runner-up in a Group 3 here in November, and he franked the form. He quickened well when a gap opened up on the rail at the furlong marker and stayed on with great gusto to the line. He will now be given a rest and then possibly aimed at a Group 1 race like the Jacques le Marois. He is a very consistent and good-looking individual.
Gris De Gris(IRE) ran his heart out and lost nothing in defeat. He took over from the leader halfway up the straight but could do nothing when the winner came shooting through on his inside. He would probably have preferred softer ground, and a tilt at the Lockinge Stakes at Newbury has not been totally ruled out, but the going would need to be on the soft side.
Precious Boy(GER) wasn't seen until the latter stages of this mile. Sixth for the early part of the race and with plenty still to do in the straight, he was putting in his best work at the finish. This race will certainly have done him good, and another race in this category will surely come his way during the season.
Racinger(FR), who had the blinkers back on, made a good effort to go from pillar to post, but he hung right under pressure a furlong and a half out and could then only stay on one-paced. He is better than this performance suggests.

1392 CAPANNELLE (R-H)
Friday, May 1

OFFICIAL GOING: Good

1659a PREMIO REGINA ELENA (GROUP 3) (FILLIES) 1m
4:00 (4:04) 3-Y-O £82,524 (£36,311; £19,806; £9,903)

RPR
1 **My Sweet Baby (USA)**19 3-8-11 .... CFiocchi 2 103
(R Menichetti, Italy) *a.p: 4th st: smooth hdwy wl over 2f out: led 1 1/2f out: rdn clr fnl f: r.o wl* **22/5**2
2 3/4 **Aria Di Festa (IRE)**19 3-8-11 .... DVargiu 1 101
(B Grizzetti, Italy) *broke wl: trckd ldr early: 3rd st: rdn and outpcd 2f out: styd on fnl f* **7/1**
3 1/2 **Louise Aron (IRE)**19 3-8-11 .... TThulliez 9 100
(G Dolfi, Italy) *a cl up: 5th st: hdwy 3f out: rdn over 2f out: styd on to take 3rd cl home* **53/10**3
4 shd **Alta Fedelta**18 3-8-11 .... MDemuro 12 100
(V Caruso, Italy) *plld hrd: rushed up to go 2nd after 2f: led 2f out: sn rdn: hdd 1 1/2f out: lost 3rd cl home* **19/20**1
5 2 **Going For Gold (ITY)**18 3-8-11 .... PConvertino 7 95
(M Marcialis, Italy) *mid-div: hdwy 2f out: styd on u.p: one pce fnl f* **20/1**
6 3/4 **Nannarella (IRE)** 3-8-11 .... MSanna 13 93
(P Giannotti, Italy) *mid-div: hdwy to dispute 6th over 2f out: rdn and swished tail wl over 1f out: one pce* **57/1**
7 1 1/2 **Piperita**320 3-8-11 .... MMonteriso 6 90
(F & L Camici, Italy) *towards rr to st: hdwy on ins wl over 2f out: disp 4th over 1f out: sn wknd* **21/1**
8 2 **The Blue God (IRE)**19 3-8-11 .... GBietolini 15 85
(R Brogi, Italy) *nvr nr to chal* **15/1**
9 3/4 **Desert Nice (IRE)**19 3-8-11 .... GMarcelli 10 84
(G Angellotti, Italy) *a towards rr* **88/1**
10 1 **Tillerdan (IRE)** 3-8-11 .... PAragoni 3 81
(A Peraino, Italy) *6th st: rdn wl over 3f out: sn btn* **184/1**
11 1 **Destination Place (IRE)**18 3-8-11 .... LManiezzi 8 79
(R Menichetti, Italy) *a towards rr: last and drvn over 2f out* **22/5**2
12 1 1/2 **Diva Cattiva**173 3-8-11 .... MJKinane 5 75
(B Grizzetti, Italy) *towards rr tl sme hdwy over 3f out: btn 2f out* **103/10**
13 3 **Fine Island (IRE)** 3-8-11 .... MVargiu 11 69
(A Cascio, Italy) *led to 2f out* **98/1**
14 nk **Passavanti (IRE)**19 3-8-11 .... SDiana 14 68
(F & L Camici, Italy) *a in rr* **66/1**
15 4 **Taurakina** 3-8-11 .... ASanna 16 59
(E Borromeo, Italy) *7th st: wknd wl over 2f out* **103/10**

1m 38.3s (-1.50) **15** Ran SP% **155.8**
(Including 1 Euro stake): WIN 5.41 (coupled with Destination Place);PL 2.40, 2.40, 2.23; DF 23.67.
Owner Razza Dell'Olmo **Bred** Azienda Agricola Le Ferriere Di Raponi **Trained** Italy

1343 DONCASTER (L-H)
Saturday, May 2

OFFICIAL GOING: Good (good to firm in places; 8.6)
Wind: Nil Weather: Fine and dry

1660 DONCASTER FREE PRESS GARY GRIFFITHS APPRENTICE H'CAP 1m 2f 60y
5:40 (5:41) (Class 4) (0-85,87) 4-Y-O+ £4,857 (£1,445; £722; £360) Stalls Low

Form RPR
41-2 1 **Empowered (IRE)**29 [1107] 4-9-4 82 .... MatthewDavies 5 94+
(W J Haggas) *t.k.h: trckd ldrs: hdwy 4f out: pushed along 3f out and sn hung rt: rdn over 2f out: styd on to ld over 1f out: styd on* **11/8**1
150- 2 2 3/4 **Tufton**231 [5910] 6-8-3 74 .... LeeTopliss(7) 10 80
(R A Fahey) *dwlt: sn in tch: hdwy to trck ldrs 5f out: effrt 3f out: rdn and squeezed through to ld over 2f out: drvn: edgd rt and hdd over 1f out: one pce* **22/1**
0646 3 2 **Veiled Applause**25 [1170] 6-9-2 83 .... JamieKyne(3) 1 85
(J J Quinn) *trckd ldrs on inner: hdwy 4f out: sn cl up: rdn and ev ch over 2f out: drvn and one pce fr wl over 1f out* **4/1**2
0235 4 1/2 **Supercast (IRE)**28 [1133] 6-8-8 75 .... PaulPickard(3) 6 76
(N J Vaughan) *cl up: led over 4f out: rdn along: edgd lft and hdd over 2f out: sn drvnand grad wknd* **16/1**
-001 5 1 **Polish Power (GER)**4 [1586] 9-9-2 85 6ex .... MatthewBirch(5) 3 84
(J S Moore) *hld up in rr: hdwy 3f out: styd on appr last: nrst fin* **11/1**
000- 6 4 1/2 **Sinbad The Sailor**212 [6416] 4-8-5 69 .... LanceBetts 4 59
(J W Hills) *led 3f: cl up tl rdn along over 3f out and sn wknd* **7/1**3
26-0 7 2 3/4 **Royal Flynn**35 [999] 7-8-8 75 .... (p) NSLawes(3) 8 60
(Mrs K Walton) *a towards rr* **100/1**
3161 8 1/2 **El Dececy (USA)**6 [1536] 5-9-6 87 6ex .... (p) GarryWhillans(3) 9 71
(S Parr) *midfield: rdn along over 3f out and sn btn* **16/1**
-624 9 5 **White Deer (USA)**9 [1479] 5-8-11 75 .... (v1) AdeleMulrennan 7 50
(D Nicholls) *prom: led after 3f: rdn along and hdd over 4f out: wknd 3f out* **14/1**

2m 7.79s (-3.41) **Going Correction** -0.20s/f (Firm) **9** Ran SP% **106.7**
Speed ratings (Par 105): **105,102,101,100,100 96,94,93,89**
toteswingers: 1&2 not won, 1&3 £2.00, 2&3 not won CSF £31.15 CT £75.03 TOTE £1.70: £1.30, £4.90, £1.40; EX 27.30.
Owner Cheveley Park Stud **Bred** Marengo Investments & Knighton House Ltd & M Kina **Trained** Newmarket, Suffolk

FOCUS
This was a fair handicap, confined to apprentice riders. The form looks sound enough behind the unexposed winner, who has been rated as taking quite a big step forward.

1661 DONCASTER FREE PRESS SHARON SMITH MAIDEN STKS 5f
6:10 (6:11) (Class 5) 2-Y-O £3,238 (£963; £481; £240) Stalls High

Form RPR
1 **King Of Axum (IRE)** 2-9-3 0 .... RoystonFfrench 3 78+
(M Johnston) *green and outpcd in rr: hdwy 2f out: swtchd lft and rdn whn n.m.r ent fnl f: sn idden and edgd lft: jst hld on* **10/3**2
2 shd **Little Scotland** 2-8-12 0 .... AlanMunro 9 73+
(T D Easterby) *hld up in tch: hdwy 2f out: rdn to chal and ev ch whn edgd lft ent fnl f: sn drvn and styd on strly: jst failed* **4/1**
0 3 3 **Lees Anthem**28 [1126] 2-9-3 0 .... AndrewElliott 4 67+
(C J Teague) *led: pushed along 2f out and sn hung lft: rdn and hung bdly rt over 1f out: hd high and wandered ent fnl f: sn hdd & wknd* **11/4**1
4 nk **Final Ovation (IRE)** 2-9-3 0 .... GrahamGibbons 8 66
(J J Quinn) *trckd ldrs: hdwy over 2f out: rdn over 1f out: n.m.r ent fnl f and kpt on same pce* **7/2**3
5 1/2 **Whozthecat (IRE)** 2-9-3 0 .... DNolan 1 64+
(D Carroll) *cl up: effrt whn sltly hmpd over 1f out: sn rdn and wknd ent fnl f* **16/1**
6 1/2 **Emeralds Spirit (IRE)** 2-8-12 0 .... StephenDonohoe 2 57
(J R Weymes) *trckd ldrs: hdwy 2f out: styng on wl whn nt clr run and hmpd 1f out: nt rcvr* **8/1**
P **Captain Sachin (IRE)** 2-9-0 0 .... LeeVickers(3) 5 —
(T J Etherington) *unruly stalls: dwlt and dived violently lft s and rdr lost irons: bhd tl p.u 2f out* **16/1**

60.72 secs (0.22) **Going Correction** -0.20s/f (Firm) **7** Ran SP% **114.8**
Speed ratings (Par 93): **90,89,85,84,83 82,—**
toteswingers: 1&2 £2.00, 1&3 £2.40, 2&3 £2.50 CSF £17.21 TOTE £3.60: £2.70, £2.60; EX 15.80.
Owner Mark Johnston Racing Ltd **Bred** Keatly Overseas Ltd **Trained** Middleham Moor, N Yorks

FOCUS
An ordinary juvenile maiden which saw the first pair come clear.

NOTEBOOK
King Of Axum(IRE) showed a likeable attitude when the gun was put to his head and got his career off to a winning start. He knew his job as he was well away and looked suited by the underfoot conditions. Bred to get a good bit further in time, he should learn a bundle for the experience and it will be interesting to see where he is pitched in next. (op 3-1 tchd 11-4 and 7-2)
Little Scotland ◆ took time to get the hang of things, but was motoring home on the stands' rail inside the final furlong and only just missed out. Her dam was a 6f winner at two and that is likely to prove her optimum trip this year, but there is evidently a race to be won with her in the coming weeks. (op 3-1 tchd 5-2 and 9-2)
Lees Anthem was still in with every chance before crashing through the rails on his debut and, after showing decent early pace, was the one to catch here nearing the final furlong. He advertised his quirks by downing tools when put under pressure, however, and, while he has talent, he is clearly one to tread very carefully with. Official explanation: jockey said colt hung right (op 5-2 tchd 3-1)
Final Ovation(IRE), well backed, was far from disgraced but shaped as though this initial experience was needed. (op 8-1)
Emeralds Spirit(IRE) Official explanation: jockey said filly was denied a clear run

1662 DONCASTER FREE PRESS GILLIAN LILLEY MEDIAN AUCTION MAIDEN STKS 6f
6:45 (6:45) (Class 5) 3-4-Y-O £3,238 (£963; £481; £240) Stalls High

Form RPR
35-0 1 **Agent Stone (IRE)**31 [1061] 3-9-2 65 .... (v1) SilvestreDeSousa 2 74
(D Nicholls) *trckd ldrs: hdwy over 2f out: rdn to ld wl over 1f out: drvn and kpt on wl fnl f* **14/1**
3 2 3/4 **La Zamora**25 [1173] 3-8-11 0 .... PhillipMakin 11 67
(T D Barron) *trckd ldrs on inner: swtchd lft and hdwy 2f out: rdn over 1f out: drvn and kpt on ins fnl f* **11/10**1

20-0 **3** *2 3/4* **Manana Manana**[42] 917 3-9-2 65................(b[1]) JohnEgan 6 63
(S Parr) *dwlt and towards rr: hdwy 1/2-way: effrt on outer 2f out: sn rdn and ev ch tl drvn ent fnl f and one pce* **12/1**

30- **4** *4 1/2* **Breakevie (IRE)**[185] 7082 3-8-4 0................ TimothyAyres(7) 9 44+
(R A Fahey) *towards rr: stdy hdwy 1/2-way: rdn 2f out: no imp appr fnl f* **9/1**

0- **5** *3/4* **Iron Max (IRE)**[154] 7501 3-9-2 0................ StephenDonohoe 10 46+
(N J Vaughan) *hld up and towards rr tl styd on fnl 2f: nrst fin* **50/1**

30-0 **6** *nk* **Caerus (USA)**[13] 1380 3-9-2 72................ NCallan 8 45
(W J Knight) *led: rdn along over 2f out: hdd wl over 1f out and grad wknd* **9/2[2]**

46-0 **7** *4 1/2* **Sleepy Valley (IRE)**[25] 1174 3-8-12 55 ow1................ DanielTudhope 4 27
(A Dickman) *a towards rr* **22/1**

0- **8** *1 3/4* **Brynfa Boy**[147] 7574 3-9-2 0................(t) MickyFenton 5 25
(P W D'Arcy) *cl up: rdn along wl over 2f out: sn drvn and wknd* **13/2[3]**

0-4 **9** *1 1/2* **Maigh Eo (IRE)**[15] 1317 3-8-13 0................ RussellKennemore(3) 7 20
(Patrick Morris) *prom: rdn along 1/2-way: sn wknd* **28/1**

00 **10** *9* **The Spicer**[12] 1410 4-9-7 0................(t) AndreaAtzeni(5) 1 —
(F Sheridan) *s.i.s: a in rr* **50/1**

000- **11** *1/2* **Alyseve**[187] 7026 4-9-2 30................ AmyBaker(5) 3 —
(Mrs C A Dunnett) *chsd ldrs to 1/2-way: sn wknd* **100/1**

1m 12.35s (-1.25) **Going Correction** -0.20s/f (Firm)
WFA 3 from 4yo 10lb **11** Ran SP% **116.2**
Speed ratings (Par 103): **100,99,95,89,88 87,81,79,77,65 64**
toteswingers: 1&2 £4.60, 1&3 £8.80, 2&3 £4.00 CSF £28.72 TOTE £10.20: £1.90, £1.50, £2.70; EX 19.70.
Owner The Untouchable Partnership **Bred** P Kelly **Trained** Sessay, N Yorks

FOCUS
A moderate maiden and an improved effort from the winner in a visor. It has been rated around the third to his All-Weather form.
Brynfa Boy Official explanation: jockey said gelding hung left

1663 DONCASTER FREE PRESS TOM CARDWELL H'CAP 6f
7:15 (7:15) (Class 3) (0-90,90) 4-Y-O+ **£7,771** (£2,312; £1,155; £577) **Stalls** High

Form RPR

122- **1** **High Standing (USA)**[291] 4060 4-8-13 **85**................ RyanMoore 3 97+
(W J Haggas) *hld up towards rr: gd hdwy over 2f out: rdn to ld over 1f out: edgd rt ins fnl f: styd on* **9/4[1]**

303- **2** *1/2* **Solar Spirit (IRE)**[265] 4900 4-8-8 **80**................ GrahamGibbons 10 90+
(J J Quinn) *hld up in midfield: smooth hdwy to trckd ldrs 2f out: effrt over 1f out: rdn ent fnl f and kpt on wl towards fin* **16/1**

000- **3** *2* **Wyatt Earp (IRE)**[175] 7245 8-9-0 **86**................ DaleGibson 2 90
(P Salmon) *hld up: hdwy 2f out: sn rdn and styd on ins fnl f: nrst fin* **33/1**

00-1 **4** *nk* **High Curragh**[16] 1309 6-8-8 **80**................(p) NCallan 13 83
(K A Ryan) *cl up: led over 2f out: sn rdn and hdd over 1f out: wknd ins fnl f* **9/2[2]**

12-3 **5** *shd* **Silaah**[24] 1186 5-8-10 **82**................ TPO'Shea 11 85
(E A L Dunlop) *hmpd and slowly away: in rr tl hdwy 2f out: rdn over 1f out: styd on wl fnl f* **6/1**

2211 **6** *2 3/4* **Imprimis Tagula (IRE)**[9] 1477 5-8-2 **77**................(v) DavidProbert(3) 6 71
(A Bailey) *prom: rdn along over 2f out: drvn wl over 1f out and grad wknd* **12/1**

55-0 **7** *1 1/4* **Kiwi Bay**[16] 1309 4-8-9 **81** ow1................ PhillipMakin 12 71
(M Dods) *wnt lft s and bhd: effrt whn nt clr run 2f out: kpt on ins fnl f: nvr afactor* **33/1**

20-0 **8** *3 1/4* **Brassini**[21] 1212 4-9-4 **90**................ AlanMunro 8 69
(B R Millman) *hld up in tch: effrt over 2f out: sn rdn and btn* **16/1**

00-0 **9** *3/4* **Victorian Bounty**[15] 1321 4-9-3 **89**................ MickyFenton 1 66
(Stef Liddiard) *prom on wd outside: rdn along over 2f out and sn wknd* **33/1**

0-06 **10** *1 1/4* **Bel Cantor**[12] 1398 6-8-12 **87**................(p) KellyHarrison(3) 14 60
(W J H Ratcliffe) *led: rdn along and hdd over 2f out: sn wknd* **18/1**

-140 **11** *shd* **Ingleby Arch (USA)**[16] 1309 6-8-2 **79**................ DeanHeslop(5) 7 52
(T D Barron) *a towards rr* **16/1**

5-54 **12** *22* **Chartist**[20] 1229 4-8-7 **79**................ AdrianTNicholls 9 —
(D Nicholls) *cl up: rdn along over 2f out and sn wknd* **5/1[3]**

1m 11.16s (-2.44) **Going Correction** -0.20s/f (Firm) **12** Ran SP% **119.3**
Speed ratings (Par 107): **108,107,104,104,104 100,98,94,93,91 91,62**
toteswingers: 1&2 not won, 1&3 £19.70, 2&3 not won CSF £42.74 CT £935.19 TOTE £3.00: £1.90, £4.80, £4.50; EX 55.50.
Owner Findlay & Bloom **Bred** Dr Melinda Blue **Trained** Newmarket, Suffolk

FOCUS
This was a fair sprint handicap, run at a solid pace, and it has been rated around the fourth to his Ripon win.

NOTEBOOK
High Standing(USA) ◆ was well backed and rewarded his supporters in ready fashion. He was not the best away, but the decent pace played into his hands. He made his challenge on the outside and won without his rider having to get really serious. He is unbeaten in three outings at this trip and, entitled to come on for the run, there could well be a decent prize within his grasp during the summer. (op 7-2)
Solar Spirit(IRE) ◆ was making his seasonal debut for a new stable and showed himself to be nicely handicapped with a solid effort in defeat. He should go close next time out. (tchd 20-1)
Wyatt Earp(IRE) was another making his debut for a new trainer and racing without his usual blinkers. He was never a serious threat, but posted a very respectable return to the track and ought to be placed to advantage in due course. (op 25-1)
High Curragh did nothing wrong under his usual positive ride, but was found out by his latest 4lb rise for scoring at Ripon. (op 7-1)
Silaah did little to help his cause with a sluggish start on this drop back in distance and was keeping on all too late. He is worth another chance to show his worth over this trip. (op 4-1)
Chartist Official explanation: jockey said gelding hung left

1664 DONCASTER FREE PRESS TONY FREEMAN CONDITIONS STKS 7f
7:50 (7:54) (Class 3) 3-Y-0 **£7,477** (£2,239; £1,119; £560; £279) **Stalls** High

Form RPR

6-30 **1** **Saucy Brown (IRE)**[15] 1324 3-8-11 90................ PatrickHills(3) 1 93
(R Hannon) *sn led: qckned 2f out: rdn over 1f out: drvn and edgd lft wl ins fnl f: hld on gamely towards fin* **9/1**

10- **2** *nk* **Exceptional Art**[251] 5330 3-9-0 0................ AlanMunro 5 92
(P W Chapple-Hyam) *t.k.h early: trckd ldr: shkn up over 1f out: rdn to chal ent fnl f and ev ch tl drvn and nt qckn nr fin* **5/6[1]**

10-0 **3** *shd* **War Native (IRE)**[14] 1354 3-9-2 94................ RyanMoore 7 94
(J Noseda) *cl up: effrt 2f out: sn shkn up and ev ch: rdn ent fnl f: drvn and nt qckn towards fin* **9/4[2]**

13-6 **4** *12* **Fazbee (IRE)**[17] 1293 3-8-4 86................ DavidProbert(3) 6 53
(P W D'Arcy) *trckd ldrs: effrt over 2f out: sn rdn and outpcd over 1f out* **7/1[3]**

\- **5** *30* **It Must Be Love** 3-7-13 0................ AndreaAtzeni(5) 4 —
(D Flood) *sn outpcd and a wl bhd* **100/1**

1m 24.6s (-1.70) **Going Correction** -0.20s/f (Firm) **5** Ran SP% **108.8**
Speed ratings (Par 103): **101,100,100,86,52**
toteswingers: 1&2 £6.60 CSF £16.96 TOTE £8.40: £2.20, £1.10; EX 20.80.
Owner The Heffer Syndicate **Bred** Churchtown House Stud **Trained** East Everleigh, Wilts

FOCUS
This was a very interesting conditions event, featuring some enigmatic performers. The first three came home in a blanket finish.

NOTEBOOK
Saucy Brown(IRE) proved the most resolute where it mattered and relished the return to quicker ground. He was given a no-nonsense ride and, much better away from the gates here, the drop back to 6f proved ideal. Everything went right this time but a likely rise for this should make him very hard to place successfully again. (tchd 7-1)
Exceptional Art had flopped on his final outing at two, but that was when pitched into Group 1 company in France after winning on his debut. He was gelded during the off-season, but still proved too keen through the early stages and, although he finished well, did not appear the most straightforward of rides. (op Evens tchd 11-10)
War Native(IRE) showed his quirks when finishing last on his final two outings last term in Group company. He settled better than the second and had his chance against the stands' rail, but for all his talent he appears another who will be tricky to place this season. (tchd 15-8)
Fazbee(IRE) found the principals in a different league and this was too sharp for him. (op 11-2 tchd 5-1)

1665 DONCASTER FREE PRESS ALEC AND GARY STARR H'CAP 1m 6f 132y
8:20 (8:20) (Class 4) (0-85,79) 4-Y-O+ **£4,857** (£1,445; £722; £360) **Stalls** Low

Form RPR

122- **1** **Hawk Mountain (UAE)**[208] 6529 4-9-1 **71**................ GrahamGibbons 6 82+
(J J Quinn) *trckd ldr: hdwy 3f out: cl up 2f out: riidden to ld over 1f out: drvn ins fnl f and styd on wl* **7/2[2]**

5024 **2** *1 1/4* **Red Wine**[25] 1175 10-8-8 **67**................ AndreaAtzeni(5) 7 73
(A J McCabe) *hld up in rr: gd hdwy over 4f out: effrt 3f out: riudden to chal 2f out and ev ch tl edgd lft and no ex ins fnl f* **16/1**

2315 **3** *1 1/2* **Eton Fable (IRE)**[18] 1274 4-9-0 **77**................(p) PaulPickard(7) 3 81
(W J H Ratcliffe) *led and sn clr: pushed along 3f out: rdn and hdd 2f out: drvn and rallied over 1f out: one pce ins fnl f* **14/1**

22-1 **4** *shd* **Overrule (USA)**[31] 1059 5-9-11 **79**................ RyanMoore 8 83
(B Ellison) *hld up in rr: hdwy 5f out: tk cl order over 3f out: swtchd lft and led briefly 2f out: sn rdn and hdd: drvn over 1f out and one pce* **2/1[1]**

423/ **5** *3* **Dansimar**[53] 6341 5-8-7 **61**................ SteveDrowne 5 61
(Miss Venetia Williams) *chsd ldrs: hdwy over 3f out: rdn over 2f out: sn drvn and plugged on same pce* **9/2[3]**

5-01 **6** *11* **Trip The Light**[10] 1454 4-9-2 **72**................(v) PaulHanagan 2 56
(R A Fahey) *hld up: hdwy 5f out: rdn along over 3f out: sn drvn and wknd* **9/2[3]**

1025 **7** *1 3/4* **Monfils Monfils (USA)**[14] 1366 7-8-12 **71**................ AmyRyan(5) 4 53
(A J McCabe) *hld up in tch: effrt and hdwy on outer 4f out: rdn 3f out and sn wknd* **12/1**

00/4 **8** *20* **Admiral (IRE)**[9] 1473 8-9-9 **77**................ JohnEgan 1 31
(S Parr) *t.k.h: chsd ldrs: rdn along over 4f out: wknd over 3f out* **33/1**

3m 7.83s (1.13) **Going Correction** -0.20s/f (Firm)
WFA 4 from 5yo+ 2lb **8** Ran SP% **115.1**
Speed ratings (Par 105): **88,87,86,86,84 79,78,67**
toteswingers: 1&2 £6.00, 1&3 £9.90, 2&3 £8.40 CSF £56.42 CT £697.90 TOTE £6.50: £2.20, £1.10, £5.10; EX 96.90 Place 6: £77.01, Place 5: £54.45..
Owner P Morrison & N Luck **Bred** Darley **Trained** Settrington, N Yorks

FOCUS
A modest staying handicap rated around the exposed runner-up, who runs well here.
Admiral(IRE) Official explanation: jockey said gelding had no more to give
T/Plt: £75.60 to a £1 stake. Pool: £66,463.83. 641.06 winning tickets. T/Qpdt: £38.70 to a £1 stake. Pool: £4,386.97. 83.88 winning tickets. JR

GOODWOOD (R-H)
Saturday, May 2

OFFICIAL GOING: Good (good to firm in places; 8.6)
Wind: Light, across Weather: Fine

1666 TOTESWINGER STKS (H'CAP) 1m 1f 192y
2:20 (2:20) (Class 3) (0-90,86) 4-Y-O+ **£9,714** (£2,890; £1,444; £721) **Stalls** High

Form RPR

0-32 **1** **Mystery Star (IRE)**[18] 1274 4-9-3 **85**................ GeorgeBaker 2 91+
(M H Tompkins) *hld up in 4th: prog on outer 3f out: hanging rt but led over 1f out: in command fnl f and pushed out* **7/4[1]**

-120 **2** *2 1/4* **King Olav (UAE)**[35] 1003 4-9-4 **86**................ SebSanders 6 88
(A W Carroll) *led: set stdy pce to 4f out: rdn and hrd pressed over 2f out: hdd over 1f out: kpt on* **9/2[3]**

44-5 **3** *nse* **Jabal Tariq**[25] 1172 4-9-2 **84**................ RobertWinston 4 87+
(B W Hills) *t.k.h: trckd ldr: chal 3f out: nt qckn 2f out: hld in 3rd whn short of room briefly 1f out: kpt on* **13/2**

600- **4** *1 1/4* **Dear Maurice**[231] 5903 5-8-13 **81**................ TGMcLaughlin 5 80
(E A L Dunlop) *t.k.h: hld up in 5th: effrt and rdn over 2f out: one pce and no real imp* **6/1**

206- **5** *1/2* **Cupid's Glory**[124] 7814 7-9-0 **82**................ FergusSweeney 1 80
(G L Moore) *hld up in last: effrt on outer over 2f out: one pce and sn no imp* **16/1**

-241 **6** *1 1/4* **King Supreme (IRE)**[24] 1179 4-8-13 **81**................(b) PatDobbs 3 77
(R Hannon) *trckd ldng pair: rdn on inner wl over 2f out: fdd fr over 1f out* **10/3[2]**

2m 11.57s (3.57) **Going Correction** +0.15s/f (Good) **6** Ran SP% **111.1**
Speed ratings (Par 107): **91,89,89,88,87 86**
toteswingers: 1&2 £1.80, 1&3 £2.90, 2&3 £4.40 CSF £9.72 TOTE £2.70: £1.60, £2.50; EX 8.80.
Owner John Brenchley **Bred** R Coffey **Trained** Newmarket, Suffolk

FOCUS
This was not a strong race for the grade and the pace was steady, resulting in a slower time than the later three-year-old handicap, and it only lifted once they had left the half-mile pole behind. The winner is improving.

NOTEBOOK
Mystery Star(IRE), who was gelded over the winter, had run two solid races in defeat already this term and, although 5lb higher than when runner-up at Yarmouth, came in for some good support. Well away, but soon settled in fourth place, he was not best suited by the lack of a true gallop but nevertheless won well, hanging a little when coming to challenge before clearing away to win with a bit in hand. He should continue on the up and his trainer thinks he is the type for the John Smith's Cup at York in July. (op 11-4 tchd 3-1 in a place)

King Olav(UAE), reverting to turf, made the running and tried to wind things up in the home straight. He could not resist the winner's challenge but stuck on well enough, just holding on for second. He does not have many miles on the clock and there may be a little improvement still in him. (op 11-2 tchd 6-1)
Jabal Tariq often leads but tracked the pace here. He had every chance, but was under pressure when slightly impeded by the winner a furlong or so out, which probably cost him second place. He is still 3lb higher than for last year's two Ripon wins. (tchd 6-1)
Dear Maurice, who wore first-time blinkers on his final start last season, has been gelded since then. He drifted in the market beforehand and could only keep on from the rear without getting in a blow, not really proving his stamina for this trip. (op 7-2)
Cupid's Glory plugged on from the back of the field and should be sharper for this first run in four months. (op 14-1)
King Supreme(IRE) was raised 6lb to a career-high mark of 81 following his Brighton win last month. After tracking the leading pair, he could not pick up when the pace quickened. (op 3-1 tchd 7-2)

1667 E B F CONQUEROR STKS (LISTED RACE) 1m
2:55 (2:55) (Class 1) 3-Y-O+

£22,708 (£8,608; £4,308; £2,148; £1,076; £540) **Stalls High**

Form RPR
-300 **1** **Eva's Request (IRE)**[35] [997] 4-9-9 103 .... EdwardCreighton 6 110
(M R Channon) *hld up in last pair: waiting for clr run fr over 2f out tl got through over 1f out: pushed firmly into ld ins fnl f: powered clr* **10/1**
00-2 **2** 2 1/4 **Lady Francesca**[10] [1461] 3-8-7 81 .... DO'Donohoe 1 99
(W R Muir) *hld up in midfield: prog on outer over 2f out: cl up over 1f out: styd on to take 2nd last 100yds but readily outpcd by wnr* **20/1**
15-1 **3** 1 **Born Tobouggie (GER)**[21] [1210] 4-9-9 105 .... TPQueally 7 103
(H R A Cecil) *led: rdn 2f out: hdd and outpcd ins fnl f* **2/1**[1]
10-0 **4** 1 1/2 **Infamous Angel**[14] [1353] 3-8-7 103 .... PatDobbs 4 93
(R Hannon) *hld up in midfield: prog and swtchd to inner over 2f out: chsd ldr wl over 1f out: fdd fnl f* **12/1**
13-2 **5** 3/4 **Perfect Star**[21] [1210] 5-9-6 100 .... IanMongan 5 94
(C G Cox) *sn restrained into 4th: effrt on outer over 2f out: disp 2nd over 1f out: fdd* **11/4**[2]
10-3 **6** 1 3/4 **Scuffle**[21] [1210] 4-9-6 100 .... GeorgeBaker 2 90
(R Charlton) *trckd ldr: shkn up 3f out: hanging and nt qckn 2f out: sn lost pl and btn* **7/2**[3]
0- **7** 3 1/2 **Cassique Lady (IRE)**[218] [6261] 4-9-6 93 .... WilliamBuick 3 82
(Mrs L Wadham) *hld up in last pair: rdn 1/2-way: no prog: no ch fnl 2f* **9/1**
-23 **8** 23 **Sawab**[13] [1380] 3-8-7 0 .... RobertWinston 8 26+
(C E Brittain) *t.k.h: trckd ldng pair: rdn and losing pl whn squeezed out over 2f out: sn bhd: t.o* **40/1**

1m 38.76s (-1.14) **Going Correction** +0.15s/f (Good)
WFA 3 from 4yo+ 13lb **8 Ran SP% 116.2**
Speed ratings (Par 111): **111,108,107,106,105 103,100,77**
toteswingers: 1&2 £35.40, 1&3 £5.00, 2&3 £20.50 CSF £182.08 TOTE £12.70: £2.10, £3.10, £1.60; EX 161.20.
Owner Liam Mulryan **Bred** Ballylinch Stud **Trained** West Ilsley, Berks

FOCUS
A decent Listed fillies' race which was run at a strong pace, and both the winner, who looks better than ever, and second came through from the rear.

NOTEBOOK
Eva's Request(IRE) had to wait for a run in the straight, but the gap appeared for her around a furlong out and she showed a nice turn of foot to cut down the leader. She is a little inconsistent and was never a factor in the Lincoln on her return from a spell in Dubai, but is a smart filly when on song, capable of winning again in this grade. She will be aimed at the Group 2 Windsor Forest Stakes at Royal Ascot. Official explanation: trainer had no explanation for the apparent improvement in form (op 9-1 tchd 17-2)
Lady Francesca made her move at the same time as the winner, in her case down the outside, and kept on well for second. She will not remain a maiden for long and may stay further than this. (op 33-1)
Born Tobouggie(GER) had made all when landing a similar event on the Kempton Polytrack (from Perfect Star and Scuffle) and she adopted the same tactics, but she did not have things all her own way up front this time and her exertions told late on as she edged off the rail and was collared. This was still a solid effort and she confirmed her superiority over her Kempton opponents. Like the winner she has been given a Windsor Forest entry. (op 15-8 tchd 13-8 and 9-4 in a place)
Infamous Angel, winner of a rearranged Lowther Stakes at Newmarket last summer, was well held in the Fred Darling at Newbury on her return and was taking a step up in trip. She ran respectably, albeit causing one or two problems when switching to the rail for a run, but did not really see out the extra furlong. (tchd 14-1)
Perfect Star was 3lb better off with Born Tobouggie on their Kempton meeting but was unable to turn around the form. She appeared to have no obvious excuses. (op 7-2 tchd 4-1 in a place)
Scuffle tracked the generous pace, which probably did for her as she faded after coming under pressure with over two to run. This was a little disappointing. (op 3-1 tchd 5-2)
Cassique Lady(IRE), representing last season's winning stable, was always in rear on this seasonal debut. Her two wins for Tommy Stack in Ireland last season came over further. (op 14-1)
Sawab, placed in a couple of sand maidens, was outclassed on this turf debut and was already in trouble when hampered against the rail.

1668 TOTESCOOP6 STKS (H'CAP) 6f
3:30 (3:31) (Class 4) (0-85,86) 4-Y-O+ £4,857 (£1,445; £722; £360) **Stalls Low**

Form RPR
50-3 **1** **Aye Aye Digby (IRE)**[23] [1197] 4-9-2 **83** .... FergusSweeney 4 95
(H Candy) *prom: wnt 2nd over 3f out: clsd to ld over 1f out: sn pressed: styd on wl fnl f* **3/1**[2]
00-1 **2** 1 **Rash Judgement**[23] [1197] 4-9-4 **85** .... IanMongan 1 94
(W S Kittow) *hld up off the pce: pushed along and prog fr wl over 2f out: wnt 2nd and chal 1f out: styd on but hld last 100yds* **11/2**
3136 **3** 4 1/2 **Mogok Ruby**[43] [892] 5-9-0 **81** .... RobertWinston 6 75
(L Montague Hall) *dwlt: outpcd and bhd: drvn fr 1/2-way: stl only 6th 1f out: styd on wl to snatch 3rd last strides* **14/1**
13-1 **4** 1/2 **Dazed And Amazed**[11] [1418] 5-9-1 **82** .... PatDobbs 11 75
(R Hannon) *hld up: smooth prog fr 1/2-way to trck ldrs over 1f out: rdn and cl up ent fnl f: wknd bdly* **4/1**[3]
2-54 **5** 3/4 **Digital**[12] [1403] 12-8-5 **72** ....(v) EdwardCreighton 5 62
(M R Channon) *chsd ldrs: stl cl enough 2f out: wl outpcd after: plugged on nr fin* **16/1**
5-31 **6** 1/2 **Peter Island (FR)**[7] [1510] 6-9-5 **86** ....(v) ChrisCatlin 9 75
(J Gallagher) *led at fast pce to over 1f out: wknd qckly* **9/4**[1]
010- **7** 2 1/4 **Choreography**[254] [5207] 6-8-13 **80** .... RichardThomas 8 62
(Jim Best) *v awkward s: wl bhd in last: nvr a factor* **20/1**
0-42 **8** 4 1/2 **Harbour Blues**[16] [1313] 4-8-13 **80** ....(t) CatherineGannon 7 47
(A W Carroll) *chsd ldr over 2f: sn wknd* **13/2**

1m 12.18s (-0.02) **Going Correction** +0.15s/f (Good) **8 Ran SP% 121.8**
Speed ratings (Par 105): **106,104,98,98,97 96,93,87**
toteswingers: 1&2 £4.00, 1&3 £5.60, 2&3 £18.40 CSF £21.49 CT £207.02 TOTE £4.30: £1.70, £1.90, £3.80; EX 23.30 Trifecta £358.30 Part won. Pool: 484.32 - 0.50 winning units..
Owner Trolley Action **Bred** G J King **Trained** Kingston Warren, Oxon

FOCUS
A fair sprint which was run at a good clip. The first two, who met at Folkestone last month, came clear in the end.
Choreography Official explanation: jockey said gelding missed the break

1669 GOODWOOD HOTEL MAIDEN STKS 5f
4:05 (4:05) (Class 5) 2-Y-O £3,238 (£963; £481; £240) **Stalls Low**

Form RPR
0 **1** **Kirsty's Boy (IRE)**[35] [1005] 2-9-3 0 .... LPKeniry 7 74
(J S Moore) *prom on outer: reminder after 2f: led 1/2-way: rdn over 1f out: kpt on wl fnl f* **25/1**
2 hd **Oil Strike** 2-9-3 0 .... StephenCarson 3 73+
(P Winkworth) *jst in tch at bk of main gp: rdn 2f out: swtchd to nr side rail over 1f out: r.o fnl f: gaining at fin* **6/1**
3 1 1/4 **Admin (IRE)** 2-9-3 0 .... SebSanders 1 69
(R M Beckett) *sltly outpcd early: taken to wd outside and prog bef 1/2-way: chal over 1f out: hrd rdn and no ex last 100yds* **5/1**[3]
4 **4** 1/2 **Di Stefano**[15] [1323] 2-9-3 0 .... TonyCulhane 6 67
(M R Channon) *chsd ldrs: nrly upsides 2f out: nt qckn u.p over 1f out: one pce* **11/4**[2]
5 2 **Russian Rock (IRE)** 2-9-3 0 .... RichardKingscote 5 60
(R A Teal) *prom: upsides and rdn 2f out: fdd fnl f* **12/1**
6 3/4 **Riffelalp (IRE)** 2-8-12 0 .... JimmyQuinn 8 52
(Eve Johnson Houghton) *s.i.s: outpcd and wl bhd: r.o last 150yds: fin wl* **25/1**
7 4 1/2 **Reddy To Star (IRE)** 2-9-3 0 .... IanMongan 2 41
(C G Cox) *s.s: outpcd and virtually t.o after 1f: nvr a factor: modest late prog* **5/2**[1]
8 1/2 **Bob Goes Electric (IRE)** 2-9-3 0 .... RobertWinston 4 39+
(J R Best) *led to 1/2-way: hanging after: wkng whn hmpd on inner over 1f out* **6/1**
9 7 **Silvee** 2-8-12 0 .... NeilChalmers 9 9
(J J Bridger) *swvd rt and slowly away: a wl bhd* **40/1**

59.69 secs (1.29) **Going Correction** +0.15s/f (Good) **9 Ran SP% 118.3**
Speed ratings (Par 93): **95,94,92,91,88 87,80,79,68**
toteswingers: 1&2 £67.10, 1&3 £16.70, 2&3 £11.30 CSF £168.89 TOTE £28.00: £5.10, £2.10, £2.10; EX 241.00.
Owner F J Stephens **Bred** Edmond Kent **Trained** Upper Lambourn, Berks

FOCUS
Just an ordinary maiden. Only two of the field had previous experience and several of the runners were notably green.

NOTEBOOK
Kirsty's Boy(IRE), one of the two with a previous race under their belt, had shown pace before fading to finish eighth of ten on the sand at Kempton in late March. Loaded with the help of a rug, he knew his job here and, smartly away and always prominent, he held off a couple of challengers after edging ahead. Out of a winner over 6f who was a half-sister to smart two-year-old Magic Ring, he looks a nursery type for later in the season. (op 28-1)
Oil Strike, whose yard landed a big gamble with juvenile debutant Raine's Cross at Bath in the week, is a half-brother to a couple of winners over sprint distances at two. He hung before running on well against the rail, needing a few more strides. A maiden should come his way. (op 9-1)
Admin(IRE) ◆ was one of the greener runners and it took him some time to realise what was required of him. He was drawn alongside the stands' rail, but ended up being switched around the field for his challenge, briefly looking a threat to the winner and not being given too hard a time when held. Sprint-bred, he will have learnt from the run and should improve. (op 7-1)
Di Stefano, who was fourth at Newbury on his debut on easy ground, still appeared green in the preliminaries. He had his chance but did not find a great deal for pressure. (op 2-1)
Russian Rock(IRE) is a half-brother to listed-winning sprinter Contest out of a half-sister to Irish 1,000 Guineas winner Tarascon. He showed ability and should make his mark at an ordinary level in time. (op 14-1)
Riffelalp(IRE) finished a lot closer in the end than appeared likely for the first two-thirds of the race and definitely has improvement in her. (op 28-1)
Reddy To Star(IRE) is a half-brother to several sprinters including the smart March Star. He was well supported, but missed the break and trailed throughout. There were signs late on that he was getting the hang of things and he should leave this form behind, perhaps on easier ground. Official explanation: jockey said colt was slowly away (tchd 2-1)
Bob Goes Electric(IRE) is a half-brother to four winners, notably the useful Granston. He showed good early pace to lead, but did not put up much of a fight when headed at halfway and was beaten when hampered against the rail by the runner-up. (op 7-1)
Silvee Official explanation: jockey said filly was slowly away

1670 ROYAL SUSSEX REGIMENT H'CAP 1m 1f 192y
4:40 (4:40) (Class 5) (0-70,68) 3-Y-O £3,238 (£963; £481; £240) **Stalls High**

Form RPR
00-0 **1** **Devil To Pay**[11] [1416] 3-9-2 **66** .... SebSanders 12 71+
(J L Dunlop) *hld up in rr: n.m.r 3f out and looked in trble: gd prog on outer 2f out: drvn to ld last 100yds: styd on wl* **13/8**[1]
035- **2** 1 **Breadstick**[184] [7093] 3-9-4 **68** .... RobertWinston 4 71
(H Morrison) *hld up in last quartet: prog on wd outside wl over 2f out: led wl over 1f out: hdd and outpcd last 100yds* **8/1**[3]
305- **3** 1/2 **Lucky Score (IRE)**[201] [6700] 3-9-2 **66** .... WilliamBuick 7 68
(Mouse Hamilton-Fairley) *prom: effrt 3f out: rdn and w wnr wl over 1f out: nt qckn and hld sn after: styd on* **14/1**
40-5 **4** 1 3/4 **Arrogance**[11] [1428] 3-9-1 **65** .... FergusSweeney 6 63
(G L Moore) *t.k.h bhd ldrs: nt qckn 2f out: styd on same pce fr over 1f out: nvr able to chal* **16/1**
4041 **5** 1 **Hold The Bucks (USA)**[11] [1429] 3-8-12 **67** .... SophieDoyle(5) 8 63
(J S Moore) *hld up in last trio: brought to wd outside over 3f out: hanging further to outer fr 2f out: styd on but nvr on terms w ldrs* **14/1**
001- **6** nk **Nice Time (IRE)**[168] [7337] 3-9-4 **68** .... GeorgeBaker 5 63+
(M H Tompkins) *hld up in last trio: pushed along and effrt 3f out: kpt on fnl 2f but nvr able to rch ldrs* **14/1**
0-45 **7** nk **Sumani (FR)**[39] [944] 3-8-11 **61** .... IanMongan 14 56
(S Dow) *t.k.h: hld up in midfield: rdn over 3f out: plugged on same pce* **14/1**
60-3 **8** 1/2 **Heartsease**[14] [1363] 3-8-10 **60** .... RichardKingscote 15 54
(J G Portman) *trckd ldr 4f: prom tl grad wknd fnl 2f* **12/1**
40-0 **9** 1 3/4 **Jewelled Reef (IRE)**[14] [1361] 3-8-12 **62** .... StephenCarson 13 52
(Eve Johnson Houghton) *nvr beyond midfield: u.p 3f out: no prog* **18/1**
500- **10** 3 **Harlestone Snake**[200] [6720] 3-9-3 **67** .... JimmyQuinn 3 51
(J L Dunlop) *dwlt: rcvrd on outer to chse ldr after 4f: chal 3f out: upsides 2f out: sn wknd* **14/1**
030 **11** nk **Mystic Touch**[28] [1130] 3-8-13 **63** .... LPKeniry 16 47
(Miss E C Lavelle) *mde most to wl over 1f out: wknd rapidly* **20/1**

-655 **12** *2* **Lilly Blue (IRE)**[12] 1397 3-9-3 **67** .... TonyCulhane 1 47
(M R Channon) *dropped in fr outside draw and hld up wl in rr: pushed along and effrt on inner 3f out: no prog 2f out: wknd over 1f out* **14/1**
0-06 **13** *9* **Lennie Briscoe (IRE)**[11] 1416 3-9-0 **64** ....(b[1]) PatDobbs 10 26
(S Kirk) *s.s: rcvrd on inner to trck ldrs after 4f: wknd over 2f out* **6/1**[2]
00-0 **14** *14* **Royal Arthur**[13] 1380 3-8-4 **54** oh9.... CatherineGannon 11 —
(L A Dace) *s.s: a last: t.o* **50/1**
2m 10.33s (2.33) **Going Correction** +0.15s/f (Good) **14** Ran SP% **129.1**
Speed ratings (Par 99): **96,95,94,93,92 92,92,91,90,87 87,86,78,67**
toteswingers: 1&2 £3.90, 1&3 £10.30, 2&3 £21.20 CSF £15.78 CT £154.45 TOTE £2.60: £1.30, £2.80, £4.80; EX 19.90.
Owner Mark Armitage **Bred** G Russell **Trained** Arundel, W Sussex
■ Stewards' Enquiry : Sophie Doyle two-day ban: used whip with excessive frequency (May 17-18)

FOCUS
Just a modest handicap and perhaps not a likely source of too many winners in the near future.
Devil To Pay Official explanation: trainer's rep said, regarding apparent improvement in form, that the colt had improved physically and stepped up in trip since last year, and did not have the best of runs last time out.

1671 FESTIVAL OF SPEED MEDIAN AUCTION MAIDEN STKS 7f
5:15 (5:15) (Class 5) 3-Y-O **£3,238** (£963; £481; £240) **Stalls** High

Form RPR
0- **1** **Sir Isaac**[252] 5271 3-9-3 0.... KirstyMilczarek 8 75
(W J Haggas) *wl in tch: chsd ldng pair 3f out: rdn 2f out: styd on wl fnl f to ld last 50yds* **16/1**
55- **2** *½* **Mabuya (UAE)**[212] 6412 3-9-3 0.... SebSanders 2 74
(P J Makin) *led: pushed along firmly and jnd 2f out: kpt on wl fnl f: hdd last 50yds* **5/2**[2]
0 **3** *hd* **Farncombe (IRE)**[15] 1327 3-8-12 0.... PatDobbs 1 68
(M P Tregoning) *trckd ldr: upsides 2f out gng wl: pushed along and stl upsides 1f out: rdn and nt qckn last 100yds* **4/1**[3]
4 *2½* **Perfect Secret** 3-8-12 0.... WilliamBuick 4 61
(A M Balding) *chsd ldrs: shkn up over 2f out: nt on terms fr over 1f out: kpt on* **8/1**
00- **5** *¾* **Golden Flight (IRE)**[204] 6620 3-9-3 0.... GeorgeBaker 9 64
(J W Hills) *stdd s: hld up towards rr: pushed along and hanging over 2f out: one pce* **14/1**
00- **6** *3* **Ethics Girl (IRE)**[186] 7051 3-8-12 0.... CatherineGannon 7 51
(John Berry) *a in midfield: shkn up and no imp on ldrs over 2f out* **40/1**
00- **7** *2¾* **Arlene Phillips**[214] 6358 3-8-12 0.... JimmyQuinn 5 44
(R Hannon) *dwlt: rn green in rr: shkn up and no real prog over 2f out* **16/1**
25-5 **8** *1¾* **Defector (IRE)**[23] 1196 3-9-3 74.... DO'Donohoe 6 53
(W R Muir) *plld hrd: hld up in last: brief effrt on outer 3f out: no prog 2f out: eased fnl f* **2/1**[1]
5-00 **9** *33* **Ymir**[10] 1462 3-9-3 63.... PaulDoe 10 —
(M J Attwater) *t.k.h: chsd ldng pair to 3f out: wknd rapidly: t.o and gng v slowly 1f out* **25/1**
1m 29.14s (1.74) **Going Correction** +0.15s/f (Good) **9** Ran SP% **117.7**
Speed ratings (Par 99): **96,95,95,92,91 88,84,82,45**
toteswingers: 1&2 £9.20, 1&3 £12.40, 2&3 £2.20 CSF £57.25 TOTE £22.70: £4.10, £1.40, £1.90; EX 82.10.
Owner Mr & Mrs R Scott **Bred** Mr & Mrs R & P Scott **Trained** Newmarket, Suffolk

FOCUS
A modest maiden lacking strength in depth and the second horse looks the best guide to the form.
Defector(IRE) Official explanation: jockey said colt hung badly left throughout
Ymir Official explanation: jockey said colt stopped quickly

1672 GOLF AT GOODWOOD STKS (H'CAP) 5f
5:45 (5:45) (Class 3) (0-90,90) 4-Y-0+ **£7,771** (£2,312; £1,155; £577) **Stalls** Low

Form RPR
52-0 **1** **Cake (IRE)**[15] 1325 4-9-4 **90**.... PatDobbs 9 98
(R Hannon) *pressed ldrs and grad taken fr wd outside to inner: rdn to ld over 1f out: hld on wl* **8/1**
04-0 **2** *½* **Little Pete (IRE)**[10] 1457 4-9-3 **89**.... FrancisNorton 7 95
(A M Balding) *chsd ldrs: struggling 1/2-way and dropped to last trio sn after: rallied over 1f out: wnt 2nd ins fnl f: pressed wnr nr fin* **11/4**[1]
112- **3** *1¼* **Rocker**[191] 6925 5-8-6 **78**.... FergusSweeney 10 80
(G L Moore) *nsettled in last trio: prog fr 2f out: drvn and styd on fnl f to take 3rd nr fin* **7/1**[3]
00-0 **4** *nk* **Elhamri**[15] 1325 5-9-2 **88**.... RichardKingscote 6 88
(S Kirk) *prom: led 1/2-way to over 1f out: no ex ins fnl f* **17/2**
3-31 **5** *nk* **Steelcut**[15] 1334 5-8-9 **81**.... TonyHamilton 1 80
(R A Fahey) *chsd ldrs: effrt nr side 2f out: drvn and kpt on same pce* **7/1**[3]
00-0 **6** *¾* **Spirit Of Sharjah (IRE)**[16] 1299 4-9-4 **90**.... GeorgeBaker 4 87
(Miss J Feilden) *hld up last: taken to outer 2f out: reminder over 1f out: kpt on: nvr nr ldrs* **11/1**
1411 **7** *¾* **Princess Rose Anne (IRE)**[11] 1425 4-8-5 **77** ow1.... RobertWinston 8 71
(J R Best) *w ldrs to over 1f out: lost pl and btn fnl f* **4/1**[2]
00-0 **8** *2¼* **Misaro (GER)**[10] 1457 8-8-13 **85**....(b) LPKeniry 3 71
(R A Harris) *sn led on nr side: hdd 1/2-way: lost pl and struggling wl over 1f out* **16/1**
00-0 **9** *12* **Lord Of The Reins (IRE)**[17] 1278 5-8-11 **83**.... TPQueally 2 26
(J G Given) *s.s: a in last pair: hanging and wknd over 1f out: t.o* **8/1**
58.66 secs (0.26) **Going Correction** +0.15s/f (Good) **9** Ran SP% **118.6**
Speed ratings (Par 107): **103,102,100,99,99 98,96,93,74**
toteswingers: 1&2 £5.30, 1&3 £12.00, 2&3 £9.30 CSF £31.19 CT £166.69 TOTE £10.90: £2.30, £1.80, £1.90; EX 41.50 Place 6: £118.22, Place 5: £70.10..
Owner Des Anderson **Bred** Carpet Lady Partnership **Trained** East Everleigh, Wilts

FOCUS
A decent sprint handicap, despite an ordinary time, which should provide winners in the coming weeks.

NOTEBOOK
Cake(IRE), a Listed winner at two, proved hard to place last year and dropped away after showing good pace on her reappearance. Drawn wide here, she managed to work her way to the fence to lead and held off the runner-up's late challenge. A rise for the win will rule her out of this grade and she may not be easy to place again in the near future. (op 9-1 tchd 11-1)
Little Pete(IRE), who made a promising comeback at Epsom last month, has gained both his career wins during May on his second run of the season. He came close to repeating the trick, but after having to wait for a run he was never quite able to get to the filly, although he should not be regarded as unlucky. He is clearly in good heart and is handicapped to win something similar before long. (op 10-3)
Rocker ended last season in fine form and made a very encouraging reappearance, finishing well down the outside for third. He is 6lb above his highest winning mark but that should not stop him from adding to his tally. (tchd 6-1)
Elhamri had finished a length behind Cake when they were making their respective seasonal debuts at Newbury and was 2lb better off here. A winner over course and distance in this month last year, when 3lb lower, he showed plenty of pace and was only run out of second spot inside the last. (op 12-1)
Steelcut won well at Thirsk but could not defy a 7lb rise, fading after chasing the pace near the rail. (op 11-2 tchd 15-2)
Princess Rose Anne(IRE) came here on a hat-trick, but the rise in grade coupled with a career-high mark did for her chances. (op 5-1 tchd 7-2)
T/Plt: £416.80 to a £1 stake. Pool: £76,400.36. 133.80 winning tickets. T/Qpdt: £144.20 to a £1 stake. Pool: £3,879.89. 19.90 winning tickets. JN

[1297] NEWMARKET (R-H)
Saturday, May 2

OFFICIAL GOING: Good to firm (8.8)
Wind: fresh, behind Weather: bright, partly cloudy, breezy

1673 STANJAMES.COM SUFFOLK STKS (HERITAGE H'CAP) 1m 1f
2:00 (2:02) (Class 2) 3-Y-O+
£31,155 (£9,330; £4,665; £2,335; £1,165; £585) **Stalls** Low

Form RPR
/54- **1** **Confront**[230] 5941 4-9-10 **105**.... RyanMoore 6 114
(Sir Michael Stoute) *hld up towards rr stands' side: hdwy over 3f out: drvn to chse ldrs over 1f out: styd on u.p to ld ins fnl f: forged clr fnl 50yds* **8/1**[3]
0-25 **2** *1¼* **Viva Vettori**[21] 1216 5-8-6 **87**.... MartinDwyer 4 93
(D R C Elsworth) *chsd ldrs on stands' side: chsd overall ldr over 2f out: led over 1f out: drvn and hdd ins fnl f: no ex fnl 50yds* **28/1**
060- **3** *¾* **Kay Gee Be (IRE)**[169] 7313 5-8-9 **90**.... AlanMunro 13 94
(W Jarvis) *chsd ldrs in centre gp: led that gp over 3f out: chsd ldrs whn gps merged 3f out: kpt on same pce u.p fnl f* **20/1**
-213 **4** *¾* **Flipando (IRE)**[35] 997 8-9-3 **98**.... JamieSpencer 7 101
(T D Barron) *lw: stdd s: hld up in rr on stands' side: hdwy 3f out: swtchd sharply lft wl over 1f out: chsd ldrs and drvn ent fnl f: wknd fnl 100yds* **8/1**[3]
3500 **5** *¾* **Bazergan (IRE)**[10] 1458 4-8-3 **87**....(tp) AhmedAjtebi[(3)] 15 88
(C E Brittain) *b.hind: trckd ldrs in centre gp: chsd ldrs whn gps merged 3f out: drvn and one pce over 1f out: wknd ins fnl f* **12/1**
600- **6** *1* **King Charles**[203] 6649 5-9-0 **95**.... JimmyFortune 3 97+
(E A L Dunlop) *hld up in midfield on stands' side: shuffled bk and towards rr jst over 2f out: rdn whn bdly hmpd wl over 1f out: styd on fnl f: unable to rch ldrs* **7/1**[2]
0-40 **7** *¾* **Ramona Chase**[10] 1460 4-8-11 **92**.... PhilipRobinson 2 89
(M J Attwater) *hld up in tch on stands' side: rdn and unable qck over 2f out: plugged on same pce fnl f* **9/1**
0-03 **8** *nk* **Dream Lodge (IRE)**[14] 1346 5-9-5 **100**....(v) J-PGuillambert 8 97
(J G Given) *chsd overall ldr on stands' side: rdn over 4f out: lost 2nd over 2f out: struggling whn bmpd wl over 1f out: no ch w ldrs after* **20/1**
50-0 **9** *½* **Proponent (IRE)**[14] 1352 5-8-13 **94**.... SteveDrowne 10 89
(R Charlton) *lw: t.k.h early: in tch in centre gp: rdn and unable qck over 2f out: plugged on same pce fr over 1f out* **8/1**[3]
54-6 **10** *1* **Ezdiyaad (IRE)**[14] 1351 5-9-6 **101**.... RHills 12 94
(M P Tregoning) *lw: led centre gp tl over 3f out: rdn and struggling over 2f out: n.d fnl 2f* **8/1**[3]
0/3- **11** *nk* **Road To Love (IRE)**[367] 1724 6-9-0 **95**.... JoeFanning 1 88
(M Johnston) *led overall on stands' side: rdn and hung rt fr over 2f out: hdd over 1f out: wknd fnl f* **16/1**
51/4 **12** *nk* **Foolin Myself**[14] 1357 4-8-5 **86**.... RichardMullen 5 78
(M L W Bell) *lw: hld up towards rr on stands' side: rdn and effrt over 2f out: btn wl over 1f out: bhd fnl f* **11/2**[1]
405- **13** *nk* **Heron Bay**[252] 5264 5-9-5 **100**.... EddieAhern 11 91
(C F Wall) *hld up towards rr of stands' side gp: rdn and little rspnse over 3f out: nvr threatened ldrs* **16/1**
3-23 **14** *2½* **Deep Winter**[19] 1268 4-8-9 **90**.... TonyHamilton 14 76
(R A Fahey) *hld up in rr of centre gp: rdn and effrt 3f out: no prog: wl btn fnl f* **16/1**
22-1 **15** *35* **Mohathab (IRE)**[13] 1380 4-8-1 **82**.... NickyMackay 9 —
(J R Boyle) *chsd ldrs on stands' side: rdn over 4f out: wknd wl over 2f out: virtually p.u fnl f: t.o* **12/1**
1m 50.17s (-1.53) **Going Correction** +0.075s/f (Good) **15** Ran SP% **128.3**
Speed ratings (Par 109): **109,107,107,106,105 105,104,104,103,102 102,102,101,99,68**
toteswingers: 1&2 £73.30, 1&3 £40.80, 2&3 £151.00 CSF £229.88 CT £4422.15 TOTE £8.00: £3.10, £13.80, £6.40; EX 302.50 TRIFECTA Not won..
Owner K Abdulla **Bred** Juddmonte Farms Ltd **Trained** Newmarket, Suffolk
■ Stewards' Enquiry : Ahmed Ajtebi three-day ban: used whip with excessive frequency (May 17-19)

FOCUS
A competitive handicap. The field split into two, with the larger group of ten racing against the stands' rail, while the other five raced more towards the centre. The two groups had merged by the time they reached the two-furlong pole. It was a slightly rough race, though, with the winner having to be switched left to avoid the errant Road To Love passing the two-furlong pole, in the process carrying Flipando to his left who in turned badly hampered King Charles. The winner looked well treated on his juvenile defeat of Stimulation and the runner-up matched his AW form. Both can do better again.

NOTEBOOK
Confront ◆, a one-time classic hope, was restricted to just two outings last term and had been gelded since disappointing in his most recent outing at Great Leighs last September. Fit enough for his reappearance, he raced in the nearside group and came off the bridle a fair way out, but after being switched he found his stride on meeting the rising ground and powered away. Handicaps may be out for him now, with a fair rise in the weights likely, but he is still unexposed and can surely go on to better things. (op 6-1)
Viva Vettori, whose best form has come on Polytrack, has raced keenly and did so again in a prominent position just behind the leader in the nearside group. Despite being carried away to his right as Road To Love began to hang, he kept on for pressure and just found the unexposed winner too strong. There are more races to be won with him, especially when he learns to settle. (op 25-1)
Kay Gee Be(IRE) was having his first outing since November, although he has won after a much longer layoff. He raced keenly near the front of the far-side group early but kept on going to the line and this was an encouraging return. (op 18-1 tchd 16-1)
Flipando(IRE), in fine form on Polytrack and turf in recent months including when finishing third in the Lincoln off this mark last time, was given his usual patient ride before staying on and though he wasn't done many favours passing the two-furlong pole, it would be pushing it to say his finishing position was affected that much. His latest win on turf came over an extra furlong in the 2007 Zetland Gold Cup and he may be worth another try over that trip. Official explanation: jockey said gelding hung right throughout (op 7-1 tchd 6-1)

Bazergan(IRE), down to a career-low mark and dropping back in trip, saw plenty of daylight out in the centre of the track and though he plugged on, he lacked speed where it mattered. His best trip is yet to be established. (op 20-1)

King Charles ◆, on his toes beforehand, was 1lb lower than when third to Proponent in this race last year, but he had been racing in Dubai before that and on this occasion he was returning from seven months off. He finished well and would surely have been even closer had he not been so badly interfered with. He is very much one to keep an eye on. (op 10-1)

Ramona Chase, who often pulls far too hard for his own good, made some late progress up the stands' rail, but he has won only once and that was in September 2007. (op 14-1 tchd 16-1 in a place)

Proponent(IRE), beaten a long way in the Newbury Spring Cup on much softer ground on his return last month, was 4lb higher than when taking this race last year, but having raced in the far side group he never looked like following up. (op 9-1)

Ezdiyaad(IRE) was well beaten in the John Porter at Newbury on his return to action last month, his first start since being gelded, and he attracted good market support here but faded after showing up prominently in the far-side group. (op 14-1)

Road To Love(IRE) looked fit beforehand on his first outing for a year. (op 14-1)

Foolin Myself, who beat Tartan Bearer here in his second and final start at two, was having his first start since when fourth in a Newbury handicap on much softer ground last month. He failed to make any real impact here and there may be a chance that he suffered from the bounce. Official explanation: jockey said colt was unsuited by the good to firm ground (op 5-1 tchd 6-1 in a place)

Mohathab(IRE), a springer in the market, was successful in a Lingfield maiden on his debut for the yard last month, his first start since being gelded, and was making his handicap debut here. He dropped right out entering the last couple of furlongs and something must surely have been amiss. Official explanation: jockey said gelding lost its action (op 25-1)

1674 STANJAMES.COM JOCKEY CLUB STKS (GROUP 2) 1m 4f

2:30 (2:38) (Class 1) 4-Y-O+ **£56,770** (£21,520; £10,770) **Stalls** High

Form RPR

5-33 **1** **Bronze Cannon (USA)**[35] 1004 4-8-12 105 JimmyFortune 3 119
(J H M Gosden) *trckd ldr: c wd and racd off the rail fr over 3f out: led over 2f out: rdn over 1f out: drvn ent fnl f: edgd lft but styd on wl to assert ins fnl f* **7/1**[2]

132- **2** *3* **Casual Conquest (IRE)**[307] 3535 4-8-12 0 PJSmullen 1 114
(D K Weld, Ire) *lw: trckd rivals: followed wnr and racd off the rail over 3f out: rdn and effrt wl over 1f out: ev ch and drvn over 1f out: no ex and btn ins fnl f* **10/11**[1]

0020 **3** *3* **Drill Sergeant**[10] 1460 4-8-12 101 JoeFanning 4 109
(M Johnston) *led: rdn and hdd over 2f out: outpcd wl over 1f out: kpt on same pce u.p after* **20/1**[3]

2m 30.7s (-2.80) **Going Correction** +0.075s/f (Good) **3** Ran SP% **69.6**
Speed ratings (Par 115): **112,110,108**
CSF £5.61 TOTE £4.30; EX 4.30.
Owner A E Oppenheimer **Bred** Hascombe And Valiant Studs **Trained** Newmarket, Suffolk

FOCUS

A race that has been won by some high-class performers, with Silver Patriarch, Millenary, Marienbard, Shirocco and Sixties Icon all successful within the past ten years. However, this year's renewal proved very unsatisfactory, with All The Aces withdrawn because of the ground and Spanish Moon refusing to enter the stalls for a third time and earning what will effectively be a ban of at least six months before he can race again in Britain. The pace was ordinary at best, and the form probably should not be taken too literally.

NOTEBOOK

Bronze Cannon(USA), who looked a bit dull in his coat, was always travelling well just behind the leader. Sent to the front passing the two-furlong pole, he quickly took control and despite edging away to his left up the hill, he was always doing more than enough. He was fit, having made the frame in a couple of decent contests on Polytrack during March, but had failed to make an impact in his only previous try at this trip in last season's King Edward VII Stakes at Royal Ascot. This muddling contest didn't prove his stamina either, but he shapes as though he would still get it in a more strongly run race. (tchd 6-1 and 15-2)

Casual Conquest(IRE) appeared to face a straightforward task after Spanish Moon refused to enter the stalls, but he too proved troublesome when being loaded. At least he took part, but after seemingly travelling well in last place for much of the way, the response was very limited when his rider got after him entering the last couple of furlongs. He hadn't been seen since finishing second in last year's Irish Derby, having been third to New Approach at Epsom before that, but he had been successful first time out in both of his previous seasons, so it's hard to blame lack of fitness and he may just have found the ground too quick. There is also a chance that 1m2f might eventually turn out to be his best trip. (op Evens tchd 11-10)

Drill Sergeant, placed in Listed company but comfortably held in an Epsom handicap last time, had plenty on against these rivals and was firmly put in his place, having had the run of the race out in front. He might not be the easiest horse to place. (tchd 16-1 and 25-1)

1675 STANJAMES.COM 2000 GUINEAS STKS (201ST RUNNING) (GROUP 1) (ENTIRE COLTS & FILLIES) 1m

3:10 (3:15) (Class 1) 3-Y-O

£241,840 (£91,675; £45,880; £22,876; £11,459; £5,751) **Stalls** Centre

Form RPR

1- **1** **Sea The Stars (IRE)**[216] 6316 3-9-0 112 MJKinane 1 124+
(John M Oxx, Ire) *str: w'like: scope: lengthy: lw: hld up in tch: hdwy to trck ldrs gng wl over 2f out: rdn and ev ch over 1f out: led jst ins fnl f: r.o wl to assert fnl 50yds* **8/1**

15-1 **2** *1 ½* **Delegator**[16] 1300 3-9-0 115 JamieSpencer 15 120
(B J Meehan) *lw: hld up towards rr on outer: hdwy over 2f out: rdn and qcknd to ld over 1f out: sn hung lft u.p: hdd jst ins fnl f: no ex and btn fnl 50yds* **3/1**[1]

2- **3** *¾* **Gan Amhras (IRE)**[216] 6317 3-9-0 111 KJManning 14 119+
(J S Bolger, Ire) *w'like: leggy: chsd ldrs: wnt 2nd and rdn over 2f out: outpcd u.p jst over 1f out: kpt on again fnl 100yds* **15/2**

10- **4** *nk* **Rip Van Winkle (IRE)**[196] 6815 3-9-0 115 JMurtagh 5 118+
(A P O'Brien, Ire) *lw: hld up towards rr: rdn and switching rt looking for run fr 2f out: drvn and kpt on fin: styng on fin: nt pce to rch ldrs* **9/2**[2]

114- **5** *1 ¾* **Mastercraftsman (IRE)**[209] 6520 3-9-0 112 PJSmullen 12 114
(A P O'Brien, Ire) *swtg: in tch: rdn and unable qck whn sltly short of room wl over 1f out: sn outpcd: plugged on again ins fnl f* **7/1**

311- **6** *hd* **Evasive**[189] 6979 3-9-0 108 RyanMoore 13 113+
(Sir Michael Stoute) *lw: chsd ldr tl led 3f out: rdn ent fnl 2f: hdd over 1f out: 3rd and one pce whn short of room jst over 1f out: wknd fnl 100yds* **13/2**[3]

0-13 **7** *1 ¾* **Pure Poetry (IRE)**[16] 1300 3-9-0 101 RichardHughes 16 109
(R Hannon) *hld up in rr: rdn and effrt over 2f out: styd on steadily u.p fr over 1f out: nvr pce to threaten ldrs* **66/1**

61-2 **8** *½* **Monitor Closely (IRE)**[17] 1291 3-9-0 101 AlanMunro 11 108
(P W Chapple-Hyam) *lw: t.k.h early: in tch tl stdd to rr after 1f: rdn jst over 2f out: kpt on steadily fnl f: nvr trbld ldrs* **28/1**

103- **9** *2* **Finjaan**[196] 6815 3-9-0 118 TPO'Shea 8 104
(M P Tregoning) *swtg: t.k.h: chsd ldrs: ev ch over 2f out: rdn 2f out: wknd qckly over 1f out* **25/1**

51-1 **10** *1 ¼* **Ocean's Minstrel**[28] 1118 3-9-0 102 JerryO'Dwyer 6 101
(J Ryan) *led tl 3f out: sn rdn: wknd wl over 1f out* **100/1**

10-1 **11** *1* **Ouqba**[17] 1292 3-9-0 112 RHills 17 99
(B W Hills) *lw: chsd ldrs: rdn and struggling over 2f out: wl hld fnl f* **25/1**

512- **12** *6* **Lord Shanakill (USA)**[196] 6815 3-9-0 118 JimCrowley 10 85
(K R Burke) *swtg: t.k.h: stdd after s: hld up in rr: effrt and rdn jst over 2f out: drvn and btn wl over 1f out* **14/1**

216- **13** *1 ¼* **Ashram (IRE)**[196] 6815 3-9-0 115 LDettori 2 82
(Saeed Bin Suroor) *hld up in rr: effrt over 2f out: drvn and wl btn wl over 1f out* **16/1**

12-2 **14** *5* **Cityscape**[14] 1354 3-9-0 110 SteveDrowne 9 70
(R Charlton) *in tch in midfield: rdn 3f out: sn struggling* **16/1**

31-0 **15** *49* **Imperial Guest**[16] 1300 3-9-0 98 JohnEgan 3 —
(G G Margarson) *swtg: a bhd: rdn and toiling over 4f out: t.o fnl 2f* **150/1**

1m 35.88s (-2.72) **Going Correction** +0.075s/f (Good) **15** Ran SP% **124.6**
Speed ratings (Par 113): **116,114,113,113,111 111,109,109,107,106 105,99,97,92,43**
toteswingers: 1&2 £9.70, 1&3 £12.10, 2&3 £9.00 CSF £31.74 TOTE £10.60: £3.10, £1.90, £3.60; EX 49.80 Trifecta £360.30 Pool: £42,004.06 - 86.25 winning units.
Owner Christopher Tsui **Bred** Sunderland Holdings **Trained** Currabeg, Co Kildare

FOCUS

This was a solid enough renewal, but on paper it lacked a true star, with just one Group 1 winner in the line-up, all 15 runners having been beaten at least once, and two-thirds of the field covered by only 9lb on Racing Post Ratings. However, while it would be difficult to rate it an exceptional 2,000 Guineas, at least the finish was dominated by the classiest and least exposed runners, and several of them, the winner included, look set to do even better when they are stepped up in trip. Unless something exceptional happens in the Dante, Sea The Stars is likely to line-up the form choice at Epsom. Derlagator improved again in second and there were steps up too from Gan Amhras and Rip Van Winkle.

NOTEBOOK

Sea The Stars(IRE) ◆ has the pedigree - he is a half-brother to Derby winner Galileo, out of Arc winner Urban Sea - and he looked the part too. He was a classy two-year-old, when a Group 2 winner on unsuitably soft ground, but it was only recently that connections had started to make more encouraging noises about him, his preparation having been held up by a temperature in March and then soft ground at home. Drawn on the nearside wing of the field, he could soon be seen travelling well, tracking Ocean's Minstrel, and once he made his move and tackled Delegator going to the furlong pole he always looked the stronger stayer. Having come here without a prep race, he was maintaining a very strong trend, as 11 of the previous 15 winners were also making their reappearance. A colt of real quality, with improvement to come, Sea The Stars goes straight to the Derby, for which Guineas sponsors Stan James make him a 4-1 chance. The Cape Cross side of the pedigree sounds a note of caution, but there is plenty of stamina on the dam's side and connections sound reasonably confident he will stay. (op 9-1 tchd 11-1 in a place and 10-1 in places)

Delegator's impressive Craven win may have been more about style than substance, but he confirmed here he is a top-class miler. Drawn on the opposite flank to the winner, he travelled strongly at the back of the field and quickened impressively to lead before the furlong marker. Once in front, however, he hung left, possibly feeling the ground, which had been a concern to connections, and he was then always looking likely to come off second best. The Irish 2000 Guineas is the obvious race for him, but he has had two quick races on fast ground and there is no hurry to commit him. He has no pretensions to staying further, so the St James's Palace would be the alternative. (op 7-2 tchd 4-1)

Gan Amhras(IRE) ◆ was heavily backed once it emerged he was running here rather than stablemate Intense Focus, and he ran a fine race, all the better considering his pedigree has middle-distance colt written all over it. Having raced handily, he got a touch outpaced but then kept on well, running a very good trial for the Derby, which will evidently be his next race. (op 10-1)

Rip Van Winkle(IRE), whose only previous defeat came under unsatisfactory circumstances when a hot favourite for the Dewhurst, had his preparation held up by a bruised foot. He came from off the pace and stayed on so well that he only just failed to snatch third. It's impossible to say how much the hold-up cost him, but it can not have helped and he still probably has improvement in him. It's debatable how far he will stay, but while he will surely get further than this, he is by no means sure to get the Derby trip. (op 4-1 tchd 5-1)

Mastercraftsman(IRE), a dual Group 1 winner and beaten only in the Jean-Luc Lagardere, stayed in closer touch but was already in trouble when a bit short of room approaching the furlong pole. He stayed on again after getting a bit outpaced, and is another who looks sure to appreciate further without being certain to get 1m4f. (op 6-1 tchd 8-1 in a place)

Evasive was up there helping force it from the start, as expected. He ran well but appeared to be beaten on merit under conditions that were expected to suit him. The Irish 2000 Guineas is likely to be next for him. (op 8-1)

Pure Poetry(IRE) ran right up to form in seventh, if never dangerous. (op 100-1)

Monitor Closely(IRE) was far from disgraced in eighth, looking as if he needs returning to further. Connections intend returning him to 1m2f and dropping his sights to Listed company, possibly at Royal Ascot. (op 25-1 tchd 33-1 in a place)

Finjaan looked one of the more suspect stayers, and he ran as though he had stamina limitations too. The Jersey Stakes would be an obvious race for him.

Ocean's Minstrel, a rank outsider despite his shock win in a Listed race on Polytrack at Lingfield, ran every bit as well as he was entitled to, making much of the running and finishing closer than many must have anticipated.

Ouqba, supplemented after his Free Handicap win, has more speed than stamina but ought to have lasted longer than he did. (tchd 28-1)

Lord Shanakill(USA) was a big disappointment, although he was relatively exposed and always likely to prove vulnerable. He had never run a bad race at two but was a bit keen here and, having been steadied, never looked like getting back into it. (op 16-1)

Ashram(IRE) made an inauspicious start for new connections. (tchd 20-1 in a place)

Cityscape had never run on ground this quick and was in trouble a long way out.

Imperial Guest, on his toes beforehand, ran no sort of race, even allowing for his stiff task.

1676 STANJAMES.COM PALACE HOUSE STKS (GROUP 3) 5f

3:45 (3:49) (Class 1) 3-Y-O+

£36,900 (£13,988; £7,000; £3,490; £1,748; £877) **Stalls** Low

Form RPR

111- **1** **Amour Propre**[203] 6644 3-8-7 109 DaneO'Neill 13 119+
(H Candy) *trckd ldr tl rdn to ld over 1f out: styd on strly to draw clr ins fnl f: impressive* **7/1**

-001 **2** *2 ½* **Hoh Hoh Hoh**[24] 1189 7-8-13 101 JimCrowley 16 111
(R J Price) *in tch: rdn and hdwy jst over 2f out: hrd drvn and kpt on fnl f to snatch 2nd on post: no ch w wnr* **25/1**

131- **3** *nse* **Borderlescott**[190] 6963 7-8-13 116 PatCosgrave 3 111
(R Bastiman) *chsd ldrs: rdn jst over 2f out: chsd wnr jst ins fnl f: no imp: lost 2nd on post* **4/1**[1]

305- **4** *½* **Strike The Deal (USA)**[216] 6304 4-8-13 109 (v) RyanMoore 8 109
(J Noseda) *racd off the pce in midfield: rdn and hdwy 1/2-way: hrd drvn and kpt on fnl furlng: styng on fin: no ch w wnr* **13/2**

14-6 **5** *¾* **Rievaulx World**[24] 1189 3-8-4 102 RichardMullen 10 102
(K A Ryan) *swtg: led at fast gallop: rdn and hdd over 1f out: lost 2nd jst ins fnl f: wknd fnl 100yds* **66/1**

0-61 **6** *1 ½* **Rowe Park**[13] 1384 6-8-13 104 SteveDrowne 12 101
(Mrs L C Jewell) *swtg: s.i.s: bhd: hdwy 1/2-way: kpt on u.p fr over 1f out: nvr threatened ldrs* **33/1**

201- **7** *½* **King's Apostle (IRE)**[216] 6304 5-9-5 112 LiamJones 15 105
(W J Haggas) *lw: s.i.s: sn wl outpcd in rr: r.o fr over 1f out: nvr nr ldrs* **16/1**

0-00 **8** *¾* **Ajigolo**[17] 1278 6-8-13 86 DarryllHolland 14 96
(N Wilson) *s.i.s: bhd: sme late hdwy: nvr threatened ldrs* **100/1**

300- **9** *shd* **Dandy Man (IRE)**[209] 6518 6-8-13 110 (t) LDettori 5 96
(Saeed Bin Suroor) *chsd ldrs: rdn over 2f out: drvn and wknd ent fnl f* **6/1**[3]

2/0- **10** *nk* **Group Therapy**[332] 2712 4-8-13 97 ShaneKelly 6 95
(N P Littmoden) *s.i.s: bhd: sme late hdwy: nvr a factor* **100/1**

-365 **11** *½* **Judge 'n Jury**[14] 1374 5-8-13 107 (t) KevinGhunowa 4 93
(R A Harris) *chsd ldrs: rdn and struggling jst over 2f out: wknd over 1f out* **28/1**

1000 **12** *1 ½* **Matsunosuke**[16] 1299 7-8-13 102 JimmyFortune 2 88
(A B Coogan) *s.i.s: sn wl bhd: nvr a factor* **40/1**

34-2 **13** *½* **Hogmaneigh (IRE)**[35] 1006 6-8-13 106 SaleemGolam 9 86
(S C Williams) *s.i.s: a wl bhd* **25/1**

120- **14** *1* **Moorhouse Lad**[139] 7683 6-9-2 112 TomEaves 1 85
(B Smart) *swtg: racd alone stands' rail: chsd ldrs tl rdn and wknd over 2f out: wl bhd fnl f* **12/1**

005- **15** *7* **Fat Boy (IRE)**[275] 4550 4-8-13 110 RichardHughes 7 57
(P W Chapple-Hyam) *a towards rr: wl bhd fnl 2f* **13/2**

13-1 **F** **Chief Editor**[15] 1325 5-8-13 109 PhilipRobinson 11 —
(M A Jarvis) *racd in midfield: rdn and struggling whn fell 2f out* **9/2**[2]

57.73 secs (-1.37) **Going Correction** +0.075s/f (Good)
WFA 3 from 4yo+ 9lb **16** Ran SP% **125.2**
Speed ratings (Par 113): **113,109,108,108,106 104,103,102,102,101 101,98,97,96,85** —
toteswingers: 1&2 £37.40, 1&3 £8.40, 2&3 £22.20 CSF £182.04 TOTE £7.60: £2.90, £6.40, £1.90; EX 302.70 Trifecta £890.50 Pool: £2,166.18 -1.80 winning units.
Owner Simon Broke And Partners **Bred** Mrs Sheila Oakes **Trained** Kingston Warren, Oxon

FOCUS
A very competitive renewal of this Group 3 contest which has been won by some top-class sprinters, with Kyllachy and Avonbridge among the best of those victorious within the last ten years. The vast majority of the field raced centre to stands' side, while one ploughed a lone furrow up the stands' rail. Three-year-olds had been successful in two of the past three years, but only two from that age group lined up this time and one of them ran out a most impressive winner in a very fast time. Some of the older horses were clearly below their best, but sound form overall.

NOTEBOOK
Amour Propre ◆, who looked pretty fit, ran out a most impressive winner despite weakness in the market. He was most progressive at two, culminating in a game all-the-way victory in the Group 3 Cornwallis Stakes at Ascot in October, and having been handy in the centre of the track from the start here, he quickened up smartly when asked to go and win his race. From a yard with a great record with high-class sprinters over the years, this was a fine start to his second season and there is no telling how far he can go. The Temple Stakes and then the King's Stand are his likely targets. (op 6-1)

Hoh Hoh Hoh came into the race off the back of a win in a Nottingham conditions event, but he had been comfortably held when tried in Pattern company before. Never far off the pace out in the centre of the track, he never stopped trying and this was by far his best effort at this sort of level. If he can repeat it, he should be able to pick up a Listed race at least. (op 33-1)

Borderlescott, on his toes beforehand, has a great record fresh, so his absence since October wasn't a concern. Successful in last season's rearranged Nunthorpe at Newmarket, had that race been more than nine days later he would have had to carry an 8lb penalty for that Group 1 victory. Never far away, he seemed to have every chance and his consistency means he should be able to hit the target more than once during the current campaign. (tchd 7-2, 9-2 in a place)

Strike The Deal(USA), winless since the Group 2 Richmond Stakes in August 2007 though far from disgraced on several occasions last season, was staying on well from off the pace in the closing stages and will be suited by stepping back up to 6f. He may now go for the Duke Of York. (op 15-2 tchd 8-1)

Rievaulx World, the other three-year-old in the line up, was useful last season but was very disappointing behind Hoh Hoh Hoh at Nottingham on his return. However, he ran much better here, having led for a long way, and he should be found an opportunity in due course. (op 50-1)

Rowe Park, winner of a conditions event on the Lingfield Polytrack last time but held at this level since winning a Group 3 at Newbury in September 2007, kept on in the closing stages and was by no means disgraced. (tchd 40-1 in a place)

King's Apostle(IRE) ◆, carrying a 6lb penalty for his win in last season's Diadem, was trying the minimum trip for the first time in his 18th outing. Not surprisingly, he found everything happening too quickly, but he was doing some good late work and is one to watch out for when back up to 6f. (op 20-1)

Dandy Man(IRE), successful in this race three years ago, hasn't managed a victory in over two years and he faded rather tamely after racing handily. His best days seem to be behind him. (tchd 13-2)

Moorhouse Lad had failed to sparkle over an extra furlong in Hong Kong when last seen in December, but he had finished runner-up in the Prix de l'Abbaye and been successful at Group 3 level at Newbury before that, which earned him a 3lb penalty here. Representing last year's winning stable, he raced alone up the stands' rail and how much that contributed to this moderate effort is hard to say. (tchd 14-1)

Fat Boy(IRE) Official explanation: jockey said colt moved poorly throughout

1677 BEST ODDS GUARANTEED AT STAN JAMES H'CAP 7f

4:20 (4:25) (Class 2) (0-100,98) 3-Y-O **£12,952** (£3,854; £1,926; £962) **Stalls** Low

Form RPR

3-1 **1** **Infiraad**[17] 1295 3-8-10 **90** RHills 2 104+
(B W Hills) *lw: mde all: hung rt fr over 2f out: clr ent fnl f: styd on strly: comf* **10/11**[1]

14-2 **2** *4* **Firebet (IRE)**[16] 1307 3-8-8 **88** MickyFenton 7 91
(Mrs A Duffield) *in tch: rdn and effrt jst over 2f out: no ch w wnr fnl f: kpt on to go 2nd towards fin* **4/1**[2]

35-0 **3** *¾* **Wildcat Wizard (USA)**[17] 1292 3-9-4 **98** JimmyFortune 6 99
(P F I Cole) *in tch: rdn and effrt jst over 2f out: chsd wnr over 1f out: no imp ent fnl f: lost 2nd towards fin* **16/1**

213- **4** *3* **Aunt Nicola**[308] 3496 3-8-8 **88** JamieSpencer 4 81
(M L W Bell) *b: wnt rt s: t.k.h: chsd wnr tl over 1f out: sn struggling: wknd fnl f* **10/1**[3]

02-0 **5** *2 ¼* **Indian Art (IRE)**[15] 1324 3-7-13 **86** CharlesEddery(7) 1 73
(R Hannon) *hld up in last pair: rdn and no rspnse 2f out: wl btn after* **20/1**

10-0 **6** *½* **Folsomprisonblues (IRE)**[14] 1354 3-8-5 **85** (t) MartinDwyer 3 70
(E J O'Neill) *hld up in last pair: hdwy 3f out: rdn and disp 2nd 2f out: wknd over 1f out* **11/1**

1m 25.2s (-0.20) **Going Correction** +0.075s/f (Good) **6** Ran SP% **100.5**
Speed ratings (Par 105): **104,99,98,95,92 92**
toteswingers: 1&2 £1.10, 1&3 £3.40, 2&3 £6.40 CSF £3.51 CT £16.08 TOTE £1.50: £1.20, £2.00; EX 3.10.
Owner Hamdan Al Maktoum **Bred** Bearstone Stud **Trained** Lambourn, Berks

FOCUS
This race has been won by horses that have gone on to better things within the past ten years, notably Reel Buddy and New Seeker, but this year's field looked ordinary for the money and was weakened further by the withdrawal of Calligrapher, who refused to enter the stalls. It may have been won by a very nice prospect, however.

NOTEBOOK
Infiraad ◆ was making his handicap debut after winning a course-and-distance maiden in convincing style last month. Soon bowling along in front under Richard Hills, he quickened up most impressively when asked to stretch and was able to take things easy near the line. Connections believe he will get 1m without any problem and depending on what the handicapper does, he may now be aimed at the Britannia. In the longer term, he should be Listed class at least. (op 5-4 tchd 5-6)

Firebet(IRE) ◆, who ran a blinder at decent odds when runner-up over 1m at Ripon on his recent return to action, wasn't sure to be suited by this drop back in trip and that is how it looked. He was never far off the winner, but became slightly outpaced running into the Dip before running on again up the hill. He should be winning again when put back over further and he almost certainly ran into a decent rival here. (op 9-2 tchd 7-2)

Wildcat Wizard(USA), held in Listed company since winning his first two starts at two including in the Free Handicap on his return, had his chance. He wasn't disgraced, but he was more exposed than most in this race and probably needs to drop a few more pounds. (op 14-1 tchd 20-1)

Aunt Nicola, not seen since finishing third in a Listed race on the July course last June, was trying this trip for the first time. She showed up for a long way before fading and lack of peak fitness rather than lack of stamina may have found her out. (op 11-1 tchd 9-1)

Indian Art(IRE), who pulled far too hard early when well beaten on his return at Newbury last month, never looked happy at the back of the field here and started to hang after coming off the bridle at halfway. He is starting to look exposed. (op 16-1 tchd 25-1)

Folsomprisonblues(IRE), twice held in Group 3 company since winning on his debut at Newcastle just under a year ago, drifted ominously in the market. Off the bridle passing the three-furlong pole, he then started to hang and his chance was soon gone. His win came on fast ground, but he didn't appear to handle it here. (op 13-2 tchd 12-1)

1678 STANJAMES.COM NEWMARKET STKS (LISTED RACE) (C&G) 1m 2f

4:55 (4:59) (Class 1) 3-Y-O
£28,385 (£10,760; £5,385; £2,685; £1,345; £675) **Stalls** Low

Form RPR

1-5 **1** **Your Old Pal**[15] 1326 3-8-12 97 ShaneKelly 4 107
(J Noseda) *hld up in tch: hdwy to trck ldrs 3f out: rdn to ld 2f out: edgd rt over 1f out: hrd pressed ins fnl f: hld on gamely* **13/2**

31-4 **2** *hd* **Palavicini (USA)**[15] 1326 3-8-12 97 EddieAhern 3 107
(J L Dunlop) *lw: stdd s: hld up in tch in rr: hdwy 3f out: chsd wnr over 1f out: str chal ins fnl f: kpt on but a jst hld* **9/2**[3]

1-12 **3** *3 ¾* **Spring Of Fame (USA)**[45] 863 3-8-12 101 LDettori 7 100
(Saeed Bin Suroor) *chsd ldr: rdn jst over 2f out: edgd lft u.p and outpcd by ldng pair ent fnl f* **9/4**[1]

1-06 **4** *1 ¼* **Close Alliance (USA)**[16] 1300 3-8-12 92 RichardMullen 6 97
(J H M Gosden) *lw: led: rdn and hdd 2f out: wknd u.p over 1f out* **20/1**

613- **5** *½* **Alazeyab (USA)**[203] 6647 3-8-12 97 RHills 5 96
(M A Jarvis) *lw: t.k.h: chsd ldrs: rdn and unable qck over 1f out: wl hld fnl f* **10/1**

21-3 **6** *nk* **Heliodor (USA)**[17] 1294 3-8-12 100 RichardHughes 2 95
(R Hannon) *stdd s: hld up in tch in rr: effrt 2f out: no imp fnl f* **6/1**

-1 **7** *3 ½* **Sopranist**[17] 1289 3-8-12 0 JimmyFortune 1 88
(J H M Gosden) *lw: t.k.h: hld up in tch: rdn 2f out: sn drvn and hung rt: no prog* **11/4**[2]

2m 4.91s (-0.89) **Going Correction** +0.075s/f (Good) **7** Ran SP% **117.1**
Speed ratings (Par 107): **106,105,102,101,101 101,98**
toteswingers: 1&2 £7.80, 1&3 £4.80, 2&3 £2.40 CSF £36.83 TOTE £9.70: £3.70, £3.10; EX 52.00.

Owner Raffles Racing **Bred** Meon Valley Stud **Trained** Newmarket, Suffolk

■ Stewards' Enquiry : Eddie Ahern one-day ban: used whip without giving colt time to respond (May 17)

FOCUS
This race hasn't produced any superstars in recent years, but there were a couple of interesting sorts in the line-up who could go on to better things. The field switched to race down the centre of the track, although they soon split into two groups with four racing centre-to-far side, while the other three raced centre-to-nearside. They had merged by around halfway, however. Decent Listed form, and improvement from both the first two.

NOTEBOOK
Your Old Pal had been very impressive in his one start at two, but was rather disappointing on his Newbury return last month when just behind Palavicini despite being well supported in the market. He threatened to compromise his chances by taking a keen hold early on here, but his rider managed to settle him behind the leaders in the far side group and he was soon back on an even keel. He travelled into the race very smoothly and despite edging away to his right under pressure up the hill, he kept on finding just enough to keep his old rival at bay. Now he has proved himself on this quicker ground, he may head to Royal Ascot for either the Group 2 King Edward VII Stakes or the Listed Hampton Court Stakes. (op 6-1 tchd 8-1)

Palavicini(USA) came from further back than the winner, but put in a determined effort towards the far side of the track and despite giving it his all, he was always just held. He appeared to improve for the better ground and looks capable of winning a nice prize given a strongly run race and/or a longer trip. (op 5-1 tchd 6-1)

Spring Of Fame(USA), having his first start for Godolphin, appeared to have every chance but hung when put under pressure and was make to look very one-paced by the front pair from the furlong pole. He had appeared to be a very unlucky second in the Kentucky Derby Trial at Kempton last month on his last start for his previous trainer, but although several have run from that race since, nothing has won, so perhaps the form isn't as strong as it looked at the time. There must also be the possibility that he is just better suited to an artificial surface. (op 11-4 tchd 7-2)

Close Alliance(USA), rather disappointing on his turf debut in the Craven here last month and behind Spring Of Fame at Kempton before that, took the field along in the far side group, but had little in reserve when challenged and was left behind up the hill. He has plenty to prove. (tchd 16-1 and 25-1 in a place)

Alazeyab(USA), minus the tongue tie for this return to action, is bred to be suited by this longer trip and raced prominently towards the nearside of the field before finding nothing off the bridle. Perhaps the run was needed. (tchd 9-1 and 12-1)

Heliodor(USA), a fair third of five over a furlong shorter on his return here last month, was successful in the Zetland Stakes over course and distance at the end of last season, so his stamina wasn't in doubt, but he never managed to get involved from off the pace. This was disappointing. (op 15-2 tchd 9-2)

Sopranist, successful from a subsequent winner when able to dominate in a slowly run maiden over course and distance last month, was ridden differently this time but he hung all over the place when coming under pressure and failed to pick up. This was a much stiffer task, but it was only his second outing, so it's probably too early to write him off. Official explanation: jockey said colt pulled hard early (tchd 15-8 and 3-1 in a place)

1679 CALL STAN JAMES 08000 351135 H'CAP — 1m

5:30 (5:31) (Class 2) (0-105,100) 3-Y-O **£12,952** (£3,854; £1,926; £962) **Stalls** Low

Form — RPR

1 **1** **Photographic**[47] 849 3-8-7 **84** .... MichaelHills 3 91+
(B W Hills) *lw: stdd s: t.k.h: hld up in tch: hdwy to join ldrs gng wl 2f out: led over 1f out: rdn and r.o wl fnl f* **3/1**[2]

0-62 **2** ½ **Shampagne**[21] 1211 3-9-9 **100** .... MartinDwyer 1 106
(P F I Cole) *t.k.h hld up in tch in rr: rdn and effrt 2f out: hdwy u.p ent fnl f: r.o to go 2nd wl ins fnl f: nt rch wnr* **10/1**

410- **3** *1* **Ave**[211] 6439 3-8-11 **88** .... RyanMoore 5 92
(Sir Michael Stoute) *trckd ldrs: rdn and effrt over 2f out: pressed wnr fr over 1f out: kpt on same pce u.p fnl f* **11/4**[1]

13-1 **4** *1* **Good Again**[13] 1381 3-8-8 **85** .... EddieAhern 2 86
(G A Butler) *t.k.h: hld up in tch in rr: rdn and effrt over 2f out: pressed wnr jst over 1f out: wknd ins fnl f* **3/1**[2]

-122 **5** *2¼* **Gaily Noble (IRE)**[17] 1280 3-8-6 **83** .... DaneO'Neill 6 79
(A B Haynes) *w ldr tl led over 2f out: sn rdn: hdd over 1f out: wknd ent fnl f* **8/1**[3]

-100 **6** ½ **Akhenaten**[15] 1326 3-9-2 **93** .... DarryllHolland 7 88
(M R Channon) *stdd and dropped in bhd after s: t.k.h: hld up in last pl: short lived effrt 2f out: nvr trbld ldrs* **16/1**

021- **7** *10* **Baariq**[214] 6359 3-8-5 **82** .... GregFairley 4 54
(P W Chapple-Hyam) *swtg: plld hrd: led narrowly tl over 2f out: rdn and wknd qckly wl over 1f out: wl bhd fnl f* **8/1**[3]

1m 38.0s (-0.60) **Going Correction** +0.075s/f (Good) 7 Ran SP% **113.9**
Speed ratings (Par 105): **106,105,104,103,101 100,90**
toteswingers: 1&2 £4.20, 1&3 £3.70, 2&3 £4.10 CSF £31.69 TOTE £3.40: £2.00, £3.00; EX 19.60 Place 6: £1,093.41, Place 5: £153.31..
Owner K Abdulla **Bred** Juddmonte Farms Ltd **Trained** Lambourn, Berks

FOCUS
This race tends to go to a useful three-year-old - none more so than 2005 winner Notnowcato - but the latest running attracted just a smallish field and they went only steadily, which contributed to a time more than two seconds slower than the 2,000 Guineas. The unexposed winner did it nicely.

NOTEBOOK
Photographic ◆ looks a decent prospect because she was making only her second appearance and won more convincingly than the bare margin suggests. Hardest of all to evaluate and open to any amount of improvement following her debut win on the all-weather at Kempton, she travelled well, held up, and having made her effort towards the far side of the septet she was last off the bridle. She was given a couple of smacks to make sure, but was always in charge and earned a trip to Royal Ascot for the Listed Sandringham Handicap, for which she looks sure to be a leading contender. (op 5-2 tchd 10-3)
Shampagne's best form had been on the all-weather, but he was clearly well fancied and he ran an excellent race under his big weight, making his challenge up the nearside and going down fighting. (op 8-1 tchd 11-2)
Ave, off the track seven months, was another who had won on the all-weather. Dropped in class after running in a Group 3 on her final start at two, she improved to have her chance but seemed to be beaten fair and square, although she is entitled to come on for the run. (op 3-1)
Good Again, who had won on turf and the all-weather, threatened for a moment but weakened in the final furlong. (op 4-1)
Gaily Noble(IRE), up 5lb and dropping back two furlongs, raced prominently but was always likely to be vulnerable in this company. (op 12-1)
Akhenaten, given a patient ride, also found this company too demanding. (op 12-1)
Baariq was potentially interesting off bottom weight, but he played up in the preliminaries and was too keen. He should do better off a stronger pace, but needs to settle down. (op 10-1 tchd 12-1)
T/Jkpt: Not won. T/Plt: £1,838.00 to a £1 stake. Pool: £194,509.91. 77.25 winning tickets. T/Qpdt: £28.00 to a £1 stake. Pool: £10,390.63. 274.50 winning tickets. SP

1364 THIRSK (L-H)

Saturday, May 2

OFFICIAL GOING: Good to firm (10.7)
Wind: light, half behind Weather: fine

1680 BET ON TOTESCOOP6 AT TOTESPORT.COM EUROPEAN BREEDERS' FUND NOVICE STKS — 5f

1:55 (2:00) (Class 4) 2-Y-O **£5,569** (£1,657; £828) **Stalls** High

Form — RPR

21 **1** **Here Now And Why (IRE)**[16] 1304 2-9-5 0 .... NCallan 1 87+
(K A Ryan) *mde all: clr over 1f out: v easily* **2/11**[1]

463 **2** *5* **Musiara**[2] 1624 2-8-7 0 .... SamHitchcott 3 47
(M R Channon) *chsd wnr: drvn over 2f out: sn hopelessly outclassed* **16/1**[2]

3 *1¾* **Cassidy K** 2-8-7 0 .... PaulMulrennan 4 40
(J Howard Johnson) *outpcd and hung lft after 1f* **25/1**[3]

59.66 secs (0.06) **Going Correction** -0.30s/f (Firm) 3 Ran SP% **94.3**
Speed ratings (Par 95): **87,79,76**
CSF £1.63 TOTE £1.10; EX 1.30.
Owner Mrs Sandra McCarthy **Bred** Mrs Sandra McCarthy **Trained** Hambleton, N Yorks

FOCUS
This race has been won by some talented juveniles in the past, so the winner is probably one to keep on the right side of, even allowing for the fact that he would have done more at home than he did here.

NOTEBOOK
Here Now And Why(IRE) was only just beaten on his debut but got off the mark next time very easily at Ripon. After the withdrawal of what looked his only serious challenger, who herself had only won a seller, he got the job done readily under his 7lb penalty and should be competitive in some decent early season contests. He should find his way to Royal Ascot but may have another outing before. (op 4-11)
Musiara has been beaten in some moderate events, including a seller, and gave a bit of trouble at the stalls before consenting to go in. She sat just behind the winner early but had no response as he quickened clear. (tchd 14-1 and 18-1)
Cassidy K, who did not cost a lot at the sales, is by Zafeen and attracted no obvious support on her first outing. She was none too quick away from the stalls and showed very little. (op 16-1 tchd 14-1)

1681 BIGGER ODDS AT TOTESPORT.COM MAIDEN STKS — 1m 4f

2:25 (2:26) (Class 5) 3-Y-O+ **£4,274** (£1,271; £635; £317) **Stalls** Low

Form — RPR

-334 **1** **Haljaferia (UAE)**[14] 1349 3-8-8 74 .... RobertHavlin 4 76
(D R C Elsworth) *hld up: hdwy 8f out: styd on to ld ins fnl f* **5/1**

24-0 **2** *1¼* **Lasso The Moon**[15] 1328 3-8-8 85 .... SamHitchcott 8 74
(M R Channon) *in tch: hdwy over 4f out: led over 2f out: wandered: hdd and npo ex ins fnl f* **11/4**[2]

60- **3** *nse* **Ruud Revenge (USA)**[296] 3888 3-8-8 0 .... SilvestreDeSousa 9 74
(Mrs D J Sanderson) *hld up in rr: hdwy and swvd rt 2f out: edgd lft and styd on fnl f: crowded and eased nr finsh* **66/1**

0 **4** *7* **I'm In The Pink (FR)**[12] 1407 5-9-8 0 .... AndreaAtzeni(5) 6 63
(P D Evans) *hld up in rr: hdwy 4f out: sn chsng ldrs: wknd over 1f out* **20/1**

6- **5** ½ **Grey Granite (IRE)**[186] 7054 3-8-8 0 .... TedDurcan 2 62
(W Jarvis) *chsd ldrs: effrt and hmpd 3f out: wkng whn bmpd 2f out* **7/4**[1]

6 *¾* **Autumn Harvest**[48] 5-9-13 0 .... (t) JamesDoyle 5 61
(A J McCabe) *t.k.h: trckd ldr: led over 3f out: hdd over 2f out: wknd over 1f out* **28/1**

7 *27* **Terrymene Prince** 3-8-3 0 ow2 .... GihanArnolda(7) 3 20
(L A Mullaney) *prom: hmpd and lost pl over 8f out: sn drvn: lost pl 5f out: t.o 3f out* **80/1**

8 *2¾* **Saveiro (FR)**[28] 5-9-13 0 .... PaulMulrennan 10 13
(G A Swinbank) *sn chsng ldrs: drvn 7f out: hung rt and lost pl over 3f out: sn eased: t.o* **7/2**[3]

0 **9** *17* **Que Calor La Vida (FR)**[20] 1231 5-9-8 0 .... LeeEnstone 1 —
(N Wilson) *led tl over 3f out: sn lost pl and eased: t.o* **100/1**

2m 32.16s (-4.04) **Going Correction** -0.30s/f (Firm)
WFA 3 from 4yo+ 19lb 9 Ran SP% **113.8**
Speed ratings (Par 103): **101,100,100,95,95 94,76,74,63**
toteswingers: 1&2 £3.80, 1&3 £4.70, 2&3 £54.70 CSF £18.26 TOTE £4.60: £1.40, £1.10, £12.00; EX 12.40.
Owner The Howarting's Partnership **Bred** Darley **Trained** Newmarket, Suffolk

FOCUS
An ordinary-looking maiden, in which more than half of those who took part had raced under jumps rules. The early pace was fairly slow. It is not hard to have doubts over the strength of the form, and the winner has been used as the guide.
Saveiro(FR) Official explanation: jockey said gelding hung right throughout

1682 BET IN-PLAY AT TOTESPORT.COM H'CAP — 7f

3:05 (3:05) (Class 4) (0-85,83) 4-Y-O+ **£5,569** (£1,657; £828; £413) **Stalls** Low

Form — RPR

120- **1** **Horatio Carter**[237] 5717 4-9-1 **80** .... (p) NCallan 9 93
(K A Ryan) *chsd ldr: led appr fnl f: drvn out* **9/1**

00-0 **2** *2½* **Bold Marc (IRE)**[14] 1365 7-8-12 **77** .... AndrewElliott 2 83
(K R Burke) *led tl hdd appr fnl f: no ex* **12/1**

460- **3** *¾* **Novellen Lad (IRE)**[224] 6124 4-8-11 **76** .... WJSupple 5 80
(E J Alston) *in tch: effrt over 2f out: styd on fnl f* **10/1**

-505 **4** *1¼* **Hustle (IRE)**[23] 1197 4-9-3 **82** .... (t) PaulHanagan 10 83+
(Miss Gay Kelleway) *t.k.h in midfield: effrt on ins over 2f out: kpt on: nvr trbld ldrs* **10/3**[1]

2-06 **5** *1* **I Confess**[19] 1248 4-8-3 **73** .... (b) AndreaAtzeni(5) 4 71
(P D Evans) *chsd ldrs: drvn 3f out: one pce* **11/2**[2]

00-6 **6** *2¼* **Ponty Rossa (IRE)**[16] 1309 5-9-3 **82** .... TedDurcan 15 74
(T D Easterby) *hld up in midfield on outer: kpt on fnl 2f: nvr nr ldrs* **15/2**

5220 **7** ½ **Compton's Eleven**[15] 1333 8-8-10 **75** .... SamHitchcott 12 65
(M R Channon) *hld up in rr: kpt on fnl 2f: nvr nrr* **20/1**

0006 **8** ½ **Methaaly (IRE)**[7] 1510 6-8-7 **77** .... DeanHeslop(5) 14 66+
(M Mullineaux) *hld up in rr: hdwy on outer over 2f out: kpt on: nvr nr ldrs* **16/1**

00-0 **9** *1¼* **Zomerlust**[34] 1016 7-9-1 **80** .... GrahamGibbons 13 66
(J J Quinn) *chsd ldrs: one pce fnl 3f* **22/1**

00-0 **10** *¾* **Spirit Of France (IRE)**[16] 1309 7-8-9 **74** ow1 .... DNolan 6 58
(D Carroll) *swtchd lft s: bhd: sme hdwy over 2f out: nvr on terms* **66/1**

100- **11** ½ **Game Lad**[186] 7041 7-9-4 **83** .... (t) DuranFentiman 1 65
(T D Easterby) *chsd ldrs: effrt over 2f out: sn fdd* **40/1**

6031 **12** *nk* **Cornus**[14] 1369 7-9-1 **80** .... (be) JamesDoyle 7 62
(A J McCabe) *hld up: a towards rr: swtchd wd ins fnl f* **6/1**[3]

222- **13** *¾* **Sam's Secret**[310] 3403 7-9-2 **81** .... PJMcDonald 16 61
(G A Swinbank) *hld up: a in rr* **8/1**

14-0 **14** *6* **Leonid Glow**[16] 1309 4-8-11 **76** .... PaulMulrennan 11 39
(M Dods) *stmbld s: t.k.h in rr: bhd and eased fnl f* **22/1**

1m 23.86s (-3.34) **Going Correction** -0.30s/f (Firm) 14 Ran SP% **125.7**
Speed ratings (Par 105): **107,104,103,101,100 98,97,97,95,94 94,93,92,86**
toteswingers: 1&2 £20.10, 1&3 £19.90, 2&3 £10.90 CSF £110.37 CT £1124.64 TOTE £12.60: £3.90, £3.80, £3.50; EX 151.50.
Owner T Alderson **Bred** Mrs T Brudenell **Trained** Hambleton, N Yorks

FOCUS
A really competitive handicap on paper but very few got into the race, mainly due to the lack of any early pace. Nothing seemed to find any trouble in running. The runner-up is a pretty solid performer when allowed to lead and the race has been rated around him.
Leonid Glow Official explanation: jockey said filly ran too free

1683 TOTESPORTCASINO.COM MAIDEN STKS — 7f

3:40 (3:44) (Class 4) 3-Y-O **£5,569** (£1,657; £828; £413) **Stalls** Low

Form — RPR

320- **1** **Ishe Mac**[208] 6525 3-8-5 78 .... MatthewLawson(7) 8 75
(N Bycroft) *led tl narowly hdd appr fnl f: kpt on wl to ld last stride* **12/1**[3]

3-2 **2** *nse* **Palacefield (IRE)**[19] 1255 3-9-3 0 .... TedDurcan 12 80
(P W Chapple-Hyam) *trckd ldrs: slt ld appr fnl f: sn rdn: hdd post* **8/13**[1]

0 **3** *3¾* **Fantasy Land (IRE)**[15] 1327 3-8-12 0 .... (t) NCallan 5 65
(B J Meehan) *in tch: effrt and edgd rt over 2f out: hung bdly rt over 1f out: kpt on same pce* **14/1**

2- **4** *5* **Royal Defence (IRE)**[231] 5882 3-9-3 0 .... AdrianTNicholls 7 56
(D Nicholls) *trckd ldrs: effrt over 2f out: wknd over 1f out* **9/4**[2]

6 **5** *1¼* **Steel Trade**[16] 1308 3-8-10 0 .... JohnCavanagh(7) 10 53+
(M Brittain) *s.i.s: sn bhd: hdwy on outside over 2f out: styd on wl fnl f* **22/1**

6 ½ **Catch Key (IRE)** 3-8-12 0 .... DuranFentiman 9 47
(T D Easterby) *hld up in rr: kpt on fnl 2f* **66/1**

0 **7** ½ **Flynn's Island (IRE)**[34] 1015 3-9-3 0 .... PhillipMakin 3 50
(M Dods) *chsd ldrs: drvn over 2f out: one pce* **50/1**

6 **8** ½ **Cry Of Truth (IRE)**[10] 1451 3-8-12 0 .... PaulHanagan 2 44
(D W Barker) *in tch: one pce fnl 3f* **40/1**
9 8 **Two Turtle Doves (IRE)** 3-8-7 0 .... DeanHeslop(5) 1 22
(M Mullineaux) *s.s: reminders after 1f: sn bhd* **100/1**
00- **10** 4½ **Luckette**[337] 2584 3-8-5 0 .... BMcHugh(7) 11 10
(M Brittain) *mid-div: lost pl 3f out: sn bhd* **80/1**
11 4 **Elusive Style (IRE)** 3-8-9 0 .... MichaelJStainton(3) 13 —
(S P Griffiths) *s.i.s: swvd rt after 1f: sn bhd* **100/1**
60- **12** 3¾ **Smitain**[248] 5394 3-8-10 0 .... AndrewHeffernan(7) 6 —
(Mrs S Lamyman) *unruly s: t.k.h in rr* **100/1**
5- **13** 3 **Golden Kiss**[176] 7220 3-8-9 0 .... KellyHarrison(3) 14 —
(Paul Murphy) *hld up in rr: bhd fnl 3f* **100/1**

1m 25.1s (-2.10) **Going Correction** -0.30s/f (Firm) **13** Ran SP% **122.5**
Speed ratings (Par 101): **100,99,95,89,88 87,87,86,77,72 67,63,60**
toteswingers: 1&2 £2.10, 1&3 £12.40, 2&3 £4.80 CSF £20.26 TOTE £12.20: £2.20, £1.02, £3.60; EX 28.00.
Owner N Bycroft **Bred** P And Mrs J Clark **Trained** Brandsby, N Yorks

FOCUS
Hardly any of these could have been given an obvious chance on what they had done before taking part, so the form looks a bit weak. The race has been rated around the winner to her nursery form.

1684 TOTESPORT.COM THIRSK HUNT CUP (H'CAP) 1m
4:15 (4:16) (Class 2) (0-100,94) 4-Y-O+ **£12,045** (£3,584; £1,791; £894) **Stalls** Low

Form RPR
6066 **1** **Flawed Genius**[14] 1365 4-8-10 **86** .... (t) NCallan 3 95
(K A Ryan) *s.i.s: sn trcking ldrs: nt clr run on inner 2f out: swtchd and led jst ins fnl f: hld on wl* **8/1**
320- **2** ½ **Webbow (IRE)**[224] 6130 7-8-8 **89** .... Louis-PhilippeBeuzelin(5) 4 97
(N Tinkler) *trckd ldrs: t.k.h: chal appr fnl f: no ex towards fin* **16/1**
1-20 **3** ½ **Bencoolen (IRE)**[10] 1460 4-9-0 **90** .... AdrianTNicholls 14 97
(D Nicholls) *chsd ldr: drvn over 3f out: styd on same pce ins fnl f* **9/2**[1]
2330 **4** nk **Majuro (IRE)**[14] 1352 5-9-4 **94** .... TedDurcan 10 100+
(K A Ryan) *slipped s: hld up in rr: gd hdwy on wd outside over 1f out: fin strly* **15/2**[3]
51-2 **5** 2 **Charlie Tipple**[19] 1246 5-8-8 **84** .... (p) WJSupple 9 86
(T D Easterby) *mid-div: effrt over 2f out: kpt on wl fnl f* **10/1**
5-00 **6** hd **Kings Point (IRE)**[28] 1124 8-9-1 **91** .... SilvestreDeSousa 11 92
(D Nicholls) *chsd ldrs: styd on same pce appr fnl f* **20/1**
12-0 **7** ½ **Mangham (IRE)**[35] 995 4-9-4 **94** .... PaulMulrennan 5 94
(D H Brown) *led tl hdd & wknd jst ins fnl f* **14/1**
20-0 **8** 1 **Ansells Pride (IRE)**[4] 1593 6-8-10 **86** .... PaulHanagan 6 84
(B Smart) *t.k.h in midfield: kpt on fnl 2f: nvr nr ldrs* **11/2**[2]
6/2- **9** nse **Ilie Nastase (FR)**[259] 5115 5-8-7 **86** .... AndrewMullen(3) 12 84
(D Nicholls) *hld up in rr: kpt on fnl 2f: nvr a factor* **14/1**
-154 **10** ½ **Wasp (AUS)**[62] 724 7-8-12 **88** .... RobertHavlin 15 84
(W Jarvis) *mid-div: kpt on fnl 2f: nvr a threat* **16/1**
4152 **11** 1 **Just Bond (IRE)**[7] 1507 7-8-5 **81** .... PJMcDonald 1 75
(G R Oldroyd) *hld up in rr: effrt on outside over 2f out: nvr on terms* **11/1**
0-03 **12** ½ **Medici Pearl**[14] 1352 5-9-2 **92** .... DuranFentiman 8 85
(T D Easterby) *hld up in rr: nvr a factor* **12/1**
42-0 **13** nk **The Osteopath (IRE)**[35] 995 6-8-11 **87** .... RoystonFfrench 13 79
(M Dods) *s.i.s: racd wd: nvr on terms* **20/1**
000- **14** nk **Summon Up Theblood (IRE)**[231] 5907 4-8-13 **89** .... SamHitchcott 7 81
(M R Channon) *chsd ldrs: effrt on ins over 2f out: wknd fnl f* **20/1**
-060 **15** 1 **Osteopathic Remedy (IRE)**[14] 1365 5-8-12 **88** .... PhillipMakin 16 77
(M Dods) *s.i.s: a in rr* **9/1**
360- **16** 23 **Green Park (IRE)**[189] 6971 6-8-10 **86** .... DNolan 2 22
(D Carroll) *trckd ldrs: lost pl over 2f out: eaased whn bhd over 1f out: t.o* **66/1**

1m 36.41s (-3.69) **Going Correction** -0.30s/f (Firm) **16** Ran SP% **132.4**
Speed ratings (Par 109): **106,105,105,104,102 102,102,101,100,100 99,98,98,97 74**
toteswingers: 1&2 £40.20, 1&3 £9.10, 2&3 £25.10 CSF £134.83 CT £694.47 TOTE £11.00: £2.30, £5.20, £1.90, £2.10; EX 142.70.
Owner Dubai's Finest **Bred** Darley **Trained** Hambleton, N Yorks
■ Stewards' Enquiry : N Callan caution: used whip down shoulder in forehand position.

FOCUS
A competitive renewal of this historic handicap, which was run at a good pace and produced a tight finish.

NOTEBOOK
Flawed Genius, who has not looked straightforward in the past, had the tongue-tie fitted again, an aid his trainer believes has made plenty of difference. His jockey needed to be patient here, as he was stuck behind a wall of horses before getting the breaks. The gaps came in plenty of time and there was no signs of waywardness this time.
Webbow(IRE), having his first outing for Nigel Tinkler, can go well fresh and did so once again. After sitting close to the pace, he made a relentless charge towards the middle of the track but never quickened and was caught inside the final furlong.
Bencoolen(IRE) had run a couple of fair races since joining these connections from Roger Charlton and was really well backed. He rewarded those who had played each-way on him and he showed his toughness once again. (op 15-2)
Majuro(IRE), who reportedly slipped in the stalls, finished third in the Spring Mile but disappointed in the Spring Cup last time at Newbury. He was flying home all too late, after taking an age to get going, and would have made a bigger impact in another 100 yards. Official explanation: jockey said horse slipped on leaving stalls (op 9-1 tchd 10-1)
Charlie Tipple ran really well at Redcar fairly recently but lacked any change of gears in this off quite a high handicap mark. (op 17-2 tchd 8-1)
Kings Point(IRE), who was fourth in this race back in 2007 when with another stable, still looked a little high in the handicap but put up a satisfactory effort without ever looking likely to win. (op 18-1)
Mangham(IRE) was well beaten on his seasonal debut but returned to something better here after making most early. (op 16-1)
Ansells Pride(IRE) had a nice pipe-opener the previous Tuesday over a trip too far but could never get on terms here, hard though his jockey tried. (op 15-2 tchd 8-1)
Ilie Nastase(FR), having his first start in Britain, won a few races for Richard Gibson in France on good ground and on the all-weather at around this distance and shaped with a bit of promise. (op 20-1 tchd 25-1)
Osteopathic Remedy(IRE), who enjoyed a purple patch last summer, met trouble when trying to make up ground from the rear. (op 11-1)

1685 TOTESPORTGAMES.COM H'CAP 5f
4:50 (4:50) (Class 4) (0-80,80) 4-Y-O+ **£5,569** (£1,657; £828; £413) **Stalls** High

Form RPR
0-40 **1** **Mandurah (IRE)**[16] 1310 5-8-6 **68** .... SilvestreDeSousa 4 87
(D Nicholls) *racd far side: w ldr: racd keenly: led that gp over 1f out: r.o wl to go clr overall ins fnl f* **11/1**
50-2 **2** 3¾ **Legal Eagle (IRE)**[37] 973 4-9-4 **80** .... AdrianTNicholls 10 85
(D Nicholls) *chsd ldrs stands' side: kpt on to ld that gp nr fin: no ch w wnr on other side* **12/1**
62-5 **3** ½ **Le Toreador**[20] 1227 4-9-3 **79** .... NCallan 1 82
(K A Ryan) *swtchd rt after s and led stands' side gp: hung lft and hdd nr fin* **8/1**
450- **4** ¾ **Blazing Heights**[176] 7222 6-8-4 **69** .... KellyHarrison(3) 15 70
(J S Goldie) *racd stands' side: hld up in rr: hdwy over 1f out: fin strly* **12/1**
60-5 **5** hd **Mambo Spirit (IRE)**[15] 1334 5-9-0 **76** .... PaulMulrennan 11 76
(J G Given) *racd stands' side: in tch: kpt on wl fnl f* **8/1**
2244 **6** 1 **Bo McGinty (IRE)**[15] 1334 8-8-11 **80** .... BMcHugh(7) 8 76
(R A Fahey) *racd stands' side: mid-div: rdn over 2f out: kpt on fnl f* **12/1**
00-2 **7** hd **Bahamian Ballet**[7] 1518 7-8-11 **73** .... TedDurcan 9 68
(E S McMahon) *racd stands' side: in rr: styd on fnl f* **15/2**[3]
233- **8** nk **Artsu**[176] 7222 4-8-13 **75** .... PhillipMakin 3 69
(M Dods) *racd far side: chsd ldrs: kpt on ins fnl f* **20/1**
330- **9** hd **Equuleus Pictor**[222] 6174 5-8-13 **80** .... JackDean(5) 5 74
(J L Spearing) *racd stands' side: chsd ldrs: styd on same pce appr fnl f* **16/1**
011- **10** shd **Invincible Lad (IRE)**[189] 6990 5-9-1 **77** .... WJSupple 2 70
(E J Alston) *led three others on far side: hung lft and hdd over 1f out: fdd: 3rd of 4 that gp* **7/1**[2]
-022 **11** ½ **Sandwith**[20] 1227 6-8-12 **74** .... PaulHanagan 13 66
(A G Foster) *racd stands' side: chsd ldrs: drvn 2f out: no imp* **9/2**[1]
000- **12** hd **Divine Spirit**[194] 6859 8-9-0 **76** .... DaleGibson 14 67
(M Dods) *racd stands' side: a in rr* **33/1**
554- **13** ¾ **King Of Swords (IRE)**[185] 7081 5-8-2 **69** ... Louis-PhilippeBeuzelin(5) 12 57
(N Tinkler) *racd stands' side: chsd ldrs on outer: edgd lft over 1f out: sn fdd* **22/1**
0-60 **14** ¾ **Highland Warrior**[20] 1227 10-8-11 **73** .... JamieMoriarty 6 58
(P T Midgley) *swtchd lft s and racd far side: a struggling last of 4 that gp* **50/1**
002- **15** hd **Dig Deep (IRE)**[194] 6859 7-9-0 **76** .... DanielTudhope 7 61
(J J Quinn) *racd stands' side: chsd ldrs on outer: lost pl over 1f out* **14/1**
444- **16** 1½ **Glasshoughton**[182] 7129 6-8-12 **74** .... PJMcDonald 16 53
(M Dods) *racd stands' side: a towards rr* **10/1**

57.64 secs (-1.96) **Going Correction** -0.30s/f (Firm) **16** Ran SP% **131.7**
Speed ratings (Par 105): **103,97,96,95,94 93,92,92,91,91 91,90,89,88,87 85**
toteswingers: 1&2 £42.90, 1&3 £27.90, 2&3 £11.90 CSF £142.28 CT £1190.92 TOTE £18.40: £3.90, £2.70, £2.60, £4.40; EX 107.50.
Owner Martin Hignett **Bred** Michael Lyons **Trained** Sessay, N Yorks
■ Stewards' Enquiry : Jack Dean one-day ban: failed to ride to draw (May 17)

FOCUS
A wide-open sprint. The field predictably split and, although most of them came to the near-side rail, the winner did it all himself towards the far side of the track (he raced near three others but not with them) and won with plenty in hand. The form has been rated around the first two.
Mandurah(IRE) Official explanation: trainer said, regarding apparent improvement in form, that the gelding was better suited by the track.
Le Toreador Official explanation: jockey said gelding hung badly left

1686 TOTESPORTBINGO.COM H'CAP 6f
5:20 (5:21) (Class 5) (0-75,75) 3-Y-O **£4,274** (£1,271; £635; £317) **Stalls** High

Form RPR
4-13 **1** **Hysterical Lady**[20] 1232 3-8-8 **65** .... AdrianTNicholls 3 74+
(D Nicholls) *mde all: kpt on wl fnl f: won gng away* **10/3**[2]
1213 **2** 2 **Raimond Ridge (IRE)**[12] 1414 3-8-13 **75** .... MCGeran(5) 8 78
(M R Channon) *dwlt: hld up in rr: nt clr run over 2f out: chsd wnr over 1f out: styd on same pce* **9/1**
40-3 **3** 2½ **Captain Scooby**[16] 1305 3-9-1 **75** .... MichaelJStainton(3) 7 70
(R M Whitaker) *hld up in rr: nt clr run 2f out: kpt on wl fnl f* **9/2**[3]
055- **4** 1½ **Legal Legacy**[186] 7038 3-8-4 **61** oh1 .... DaleGibson 6 51
(M Dods) *dwlt: hld up in rr and sn pushed along: kpt on fnl 2f: nvr a threat* **8/1**
-033 **5** 1 **Blue Noodles**[10] 1452 3-8-8 **65** .... PJMcDonald 2 52
(D W Barker) *w ldrs: wkng whn hmpd appr fnl f* **8/1**
210- **6** nk **Moonlight Affair (IRE)**[222] 6172 3-9-3 **74** .... TedDurcan 4 60
(E S McMahon) *mid-div: lost pl over 1f out* **12/1**
44-1 **7** 10 **Paddy Bear**[15] 1335 3-9-0 **71** .... PaulHanagan 9 39
(R A Fahey) *chsd ldrs: hung bdly lft and lost pl over 1f out: eased ins fnl f* **5/2**[1]
060- **8** 4 **Bermondsey Bob (IRE)**[189] 6987 3-8-11 **68** .... TolleyDean 5 9
(J L Spearing) *chsd ldrs: lost pl 2f out* **16/1**
522- **9** 16 **Liberty Diamond**[212] 6407 3-9-1 **72** .... DarrenWilliams 1 —
(K R Burke) *chsd ldrs: wknd 2f out: sn eased and bhd: t.o* **25/1**

1m 10.96s (-1.74) **Going Correction** -0.30s/f (Firm) **9** Ran SP% **119.5**
Speed ratings (Par 99): **99,96,93,91,89 89,75,70,49**
toteswingers: 1&2 £7.00, 1&3 £3.70, 2&3 £3.70 CSF £34.73 CT £139.47 TOTE £3.50: £1.40, £2.10, £2.20; EX 23.80 Place 6: £220.89, Place 5: £198.71..
Owner Ms Finola Devaney **Bred** P And Mrs Venner And Trickledown Stud **Trained** Sessay, N Yorks
■ Stewards' Enquiry : P J McDonald one-day ban: careless riding (May 17)

FOCUS
The field was not big enough to split, so they all hurtled down the stands'-side rail. The form has been rated around the runner-up to a marginal personal best.
Paddy Bear Official explanation: jockey said colt hung badly left
T/Plt: £169.20 to a £1 stake. Pool: £55,593.70. 239.85 winning tickets. T/Qpdt: £150.80 to a £1 stake. Pool: £2,934.94. 14.40 winning tickets. WG

1763 CHURCHILL DOWNS (L-H)
Saturday, May 2
OFFICIAL GOING: Turf course - good; dirt course - sloppy (sealed)

1688a KENTUCKY DERBY PRESENTED BY YUM! BRANDS (GRADE 1) (DIRT) 1m 2f (D)
11:24 (11:28) 3-Y-O **£984,167** (£277,778; £138,889; £69,444; £41,667)

RPR
1 **Mine That Bird (USA)**[34] 3-9-0 .... CHBorel 8 121
(Bennie L Woolley Jr, U.S.A) *last, 6 lengths behind field 4f out, rapid headway on rail & 8th straight, switched back to rail and squeezed through to lead over 1f out, ran on well* **51/1**
2 7 **Pioneerof The Nile (USA)**[28] 3-9-0 .... GKGomez 15 109
(Bob Baffert, U.S.A) *disputed 3rd on outside, 3rd straight, disputed lead briefly over 1f out, just holding on for 2nd when hung right 100yds out, kept on* **63/10**[3]

3 *nse* **Musket Man (USA)**[28] 3-9-0 .... ECoa 2 109
(Derek S Ryan, U.S.A) *raced in 8th, 7th straight on outside, 4th but pressing for 2nd when carried right 100yds out, kept on to take 3rd on line* **19/1**

4 *hd* **Papa Clem (USA)**[21] 3-9-0 .... RBejarano 7 109
(Gary Stute, U.S.A) *always close up racing keenly, taken to outside and 5th straight, pressing for 2nd when bumped 100yds out, lost 3rd on line* **122/10**

5 *6* **Chocolate Candy (USA)**[28] 3-9-0 .... MESmith 11 98
(Jerry Hollendorfer, U.S.A) *towards rear, headway under 3f out, 6th and taken to outside entering straight, kept on at same pace* **10/1**

6 *hd* **Summer Bird (USA)**[21] 3-9-0 .... CRosier 16 97
(Tim Ice, U.S.A) *raced in 16th, headway under 3f out, 10th straight towards outside, kept on final 1 1/2f* **44/1**

7 *1 1/4* **Join In The Dance (USA)**[21] 1225 3-9-0 .... CDeCarlo 9 95
(Todd Pletcher, U.S.A) *set strong pace to over 1f out, weakened* **51/1**

8 *1/2* **Regal Ransom (USA)**[35] 1009 3-9-0 .... AGarcia 10 94
(Saeed Bin Suroor) *raced in 2nd til weakened over 1 1/2f out* **226/10**

9 *3/4* **West Side Bernie (USA)**[28] 3-9-0 .... StewartElliott 1 93
(Kelly Breen, U.S.A) *towards rear, never a factor* **33/1**

10 *2* **General Quarters (USA)**[21] 1225 3-9-0 .... JRLeparoux 12 89
(Thomas R McCarthy, U.S.A) *raced keenly early, never better than midfield* **103/10**

11 *1 1/2* **Dunkirk (USA)**[35] 3-9-0 .... EPrado 14 87
(Todd Pletcher, U.S.A) *stumbled after start, always midfield* **26/5**[2]

12 *1 1/2* **Hold Me Back (USA)**[21] 1225 3-9-0 .... KDesormeaux 5 84
(William Mott, U.S.A) *towards rear early, headway on inside to go 5th after 4f, 4th straight on inside, soon weakened* **127/10**

13 *1/2* **Advice (USA)**[14] 3-9-0 .... RRDouglas 4 83
(Todd Pletcher, U.S.A) *always in rear* **49/1**

14 *3/4* **Desert Party (USA)**[35] 1009 3-9-0 .... RADominguez 18 82
(Saeed Bin Suroor) *bumped start, raced in 5th or 6th til weakened 2f out* **148/10**

15 *1 1/4* **Mr. Hot Stuff (USA)**[28] 3-9-0 .... JRVelazquez 3 79
(Eoin Harty, U.S.A) *always in rear* **28/1**

16 *8* **Atomic Rain (USA)**[28] 3-9-0 ....(b) JBravo 13 64
(Kelly Breen, U.S.A) *raced in 9th or 10th on inside, 11th straight, soon weakened* **55/1**

17 *3 1/2* **Nowhere To Hide (USA)**[28] 3-9-0 ....(b) SXBridgmohan 17 58
(Nicholas Zito, U.S.A) *broke awkwardly, in touch to 4f out* **46/1**

18 *7* **Friesan Fire (USA)**[49] 3-9-0 ....(b) GSaez 6 44
(J Larry Jones, U.S.A) *raced in 6th or 7th, weakened over 2f out* **19/5**[1]

19 *1 1/4* **Flying Private (USA)**[21] 3-9-0 ....(b) RAlbarado 19 42
(D Wayne Lukas, U.S.A) *in touch til weakened over 4f out* **47/1**

2m 2.66s (1.47) **19 Ran SP% 119.5**
PARI-MUTUEL: WIN 103.20; PL (1-2) 54.00, 8.40; SHOW (1-2-3) 25.80,6.40, 12.00; SF 2074.80.

Owner Double Eagle Ranch & Bueno Suerte Equine **Bred** Lamantia, Blackburn And Needham/Betz Thoroughbreds **Trained** USA

■ Calvin Borel became only the seventh rider to win both the Kentucky Derby and Oaks in the same season.

FOCUS

For a number of reasons this was a deeply disappointing renewal of the Kentucky Derby. The likes of Midshipman, Old Fashioned and Quality Road missed the race through injury, and morning line favourite I Want Revenge joined that trio on the sidelines when scratched just hours from the off. The race itself was farcical, with the leaders going off far too fast and, on a sloppy track, the inside rail was akin to a golden highway.

NOTEBOOK

Mine That Bird(USA) had gained all of his previous wins on Polytrack in Canada and looked one of the least likely winners on all known form coming into the race. However, having sat in a detached last early on, a good six lengths off the main pack, the suicidal gallop played into his hands, and just as significant was the route charted by his jockey, who deserves plenty of credit. Calvin Borel kept his mount tight against the rail whenever possible - very much the brave-man's route in a 19-runner field - and the tactics paid dividends in no uncertain terms, with the inside of the track almost certainly riding significantly quicker than elsewhere. All things considered, the winner, for all that he is obviously talented, looks badly flattered by the bare form, and he seems extremely unlikely to follow up in the Preakness. Later on, the 1m4f trip in the third leg of the Triple Crown, the Belmont Stakes, should suit this strong stayer, but one cannot help but think he'll struggle to ever match this level of form again.

Pioneerof The Nile(USA) ◆, who had won four straight Graded races on synthetics since joining the Baffert yard, emerges with loads of credit on this first try on dirt. He basically had far too much use made of him by the usually reliable Garrett Gomez, and it's to the horse's credit he held on for second. This fine-looking colt should be a danger to all in the Preakness.

Musket Man(USA) outstayed his pedigree with a fine run in third, and in the process looked a better horse than his victories in the Tampa Bay and Illinois Derbies implied.

Papa Clem(USA) ◆ didn't help his chance by racing keenly close to the frantic pace, and he was also bumped near the line. A fine effort all things considered, and this improver won't mind dropping in trip for the Preakness.

Regal Ransom(USA) likes to race handy, so it's hard to blame his rider, but he basically had no chance considering how the race developed.

Dunkirk(USA)'s chance cannot have been helped by a stumble a couple of strides after the start, and he could make no impression whatsoever. It turned out he injured his left hind hoof and he's out of consideration for the Preakness. However, this extremely talented son of Unbridled's Song can be given another chance and could be one for the Belmont Stakes.

Desert Party(USA) didn't see his race out after sitting close to the mad gallop. It later transpired he returned with filling and soreness in his left front ankle and x-rays revealed a displaced chip which requires surgery and a period of time out of training. His connections hope to get him back later in the year.

Friesan Fire(USA) was heavily eased in the straight having endured an extremely rough trip, and he returned with a total of nine cuts to all four of his legs.

HAMILTON (R-H)

Sunday, May 3

OFFICIAL GOING: Good (good to firm in places; 8.8)

Wind: Fresh, across Weather: Cloudy, bright

1689 HAMILTON PARK SUPER SIX CLAIMING STKS 6f 5y

2:25 (2:25) (Class 5) 4-6-Y-0 **£2,729** (£806; £403) **Stalls** Low

Form RPR

1223 1 **Stonecrabstomorrow (IRE)**[21] 1229 6-8-11 73.......(b) PaulHanagan 10 78
(R A Fahey) *hld up in tch: effrt 2f out: led ins fnl f: rdn out* **5/2**[1]

0-03 2 *1 1/4* **Dream Theme**[12] 1438 6-8-10 78.. FrancisNorton 8 73
(D Nicholls) *dwlt: t.k.h and sn prom: effrt and ev ch ins fnl f: r.o* **5/2**[1]

050- 3 *1 1/2* **Makshoof (IRE)**[128] 7782 5-8-9 78.. AmyRyan(5) 9 73
(K A Ryan) *w ldrs: led over 1f out to ins fnl f: kpt on* **3/1**[2]

3065 4 *3/4* **Silvanus (IRE)**[8] 1518 4-9-2 72.. TomEaves 7 72
(I Semple) *racd keenly: hld up: hdwy over 1f out: kpt on fnl f: nrst fin* **7/1**[3]

542 5 *nse* **Secret Dubai (IRE)**[20] 1259 4-8-7 67.. KristinStubbs(7) 6 70
(Mrs L Stubbs) *racd keenly: led tl edgd rt and hdd over 1f out: nt qckn* **7/1**[3]

00-0 6 *3 1/4* **Nacho Libre**[18] 1278 4-9-4 77.. DaleGibson 3 64
(M W Easterby) *bhd: drvn 1/2-way: kpt on fnl f: n.d* **33/1**

0-50 7 *nk* **Andrasta**[3] 1628 4-8-5 56 ow3.. SladeO'Hara(5) 2 55
(A Berry) *in tch: drvn and outpcd over 2f out: no imp over 1f out* **66/1**

30-0 8 *8* **Distant Vision (IRE)**[34] 1038 6-8-3 43..............................(p) IanCraven(7) 1 29
(H A McWilliams) *hld up: rdn over 2f out: n.d* **125/1**

00-0 9 *2 3/4* **Lifetime Endeavour**[32] 1061 5-8-7 43.. RoystonFfrench 5 17
(R E Barr) *cl up tl rdn and wknd fr 2f out* **100/1**

000 10 *3* **She's Our Dream**[3] 1628 4-7-9 43..............................(vt) JamieKyne(7) 4 3
(R C Guest) *dwlt: sn cl up: rdn and wknd fr 2f out* **100/1**

1m 12.47s (0.27) **Going Correction** +0.125s/f (Good) **10 Ran SP% 114.4**
Speed ratings: **103,101,99,98,98 93,93,82,79,75**
toteswingers: 1&2 £2.00, 1&3 £1.70, 2&3 £2.50 CSF £8.69 TOTE £3.60: £1.20, £1.60, £1.50; EX 10.90.

Owner Miss S Bowles **Bred** P Dillon **Trained** Musley Bank, N Yorks

FOCUS

Only half of these looked to have any prospects of winning, and so it proved as the first five in the betting pulled clear of the remainder. Indeed, there was almost four in a line with a furlong to go. Quite straightforward form to rate, with the winner the guide.

1690 WELCOME TO HAMILTON PARK ANNUAL JUMP JOCKEYS H'CAP (QUALIFIER FOR SCOTTISH TROPHY H'CAP SERIES) 1m 65y

3:00 (3:00) (Class 5) (0-70,70) 4-Y-0+ **£3,238** (£963; £481; £240) **Stalls** High

Form RPR

-112 1 **Ergo (FR)**[32] 1060 5-10-13 65..............................(b) DenisO'Regan 5 76+
(James Moffatt) *in tch: smooth hdwy over 2f out: swtchd lft and shkn up to ld ins fnl f: edgd rt: comf* **5/1**[2]

3365 2 *1 1/4* **Rosko**[13] 1402 5-10-12 64.. GLee 9 71
(B Ellison) *racd keenly in midfield: effrt over 2f out: styd on wl fnl f: wnt 2nd nr fin* **9/1**

0312 3 *1/2* **This Ones For Eddy**[4] 1612 4-11-3 69.. BarryKeniry 15 74
(S Parr) *led to over 3f out: rallied and ev ch ins fnl f: kpt on: lost 2nd cl home* **5/2**[1]

620- 4 *hd* **Papa's Princess**[245] 5538 5-10-5 57.. BrianHarding 16 62
(J S Goldie) *hld up on ins: hdwy over 2f out: edgd lft and styd on fnl f: nrst fin* **16/1**

060- 5 *1 3/4* **Shy Glance (USA)**[225] 6108 7-11-1 67.. WilsonRenwick 10 68
(P Monteith) *hld up: hdwy and shkn up 2f out: kpt on fnl f: nrst fin* **25/1**

10-2 6 *nse* **Steig (IRE)**[9] 1495 6-11-4 70.. AndrewTinkler 2 71
(George Baker) *w ldr: led over 3f out to ins fnl f: kpt on same pce* **10/1**

0000 7 *1* **Bright Falcon**[10] 1475 4-10-4 56 oh4..............................(bt) SJCraine 1 55
(S Parr) *hld up: rdn over 3f out: kpt on fnl f: n.d* **125/1**

350- 8 *2* **Desert Destiny**[208] 6551 9-11-3 69.. RichardMcGrath 13 63
(C Grant) *towards rr: hdwy over 2f out: no ex fnl f* **22/1**

040- 9 *1* **Jordan's Light (USA)**[176] 6161 6-10-4 56 oh2.......... DougieCostello 14 48
(P Monteith) *midfield: drvn over 3f out: no imp fnl 2f* **20/1**

020- 10 *3/4* **Marvo**[195] 6867 5-11-2 68.. DaveCrosse 7 58
(M H Tompkins) *trckd ldrs: effrt over 2f out: one pce fnl f* **9/1**

060- 11 *1/2* **Hawkit (USA)**[227] 6040 8-10-7 59.. PeterBuchanan 4 48
(P Monteith) *hld up: rdn 4f out: kpt on fnl f: n.d* **40/1**

500- 12 *3* **Baizically (IRE)**[266] 4895 6-11-2 68.. BrianHughes 12 50
(G A Swinbank) *dwlt: sn midfield: outpcd over 2f out: n.d after* **15/2**[3]

350- 13 *1/2* **Five Wishes**[28] 7202 5-10-10 62..............................(v[1]) PAspell 8 43
(G A Harker) *hld up on outside: rdn 3f out: sn btn* **25/1**

1233 14 *1/2* **Colonel Sherman (USA)**[18] 1283 4-11-1 67.. PhilKinsella 3 47
(P A Kirby) *hld up on outside: rdn 3f out: sn outpcd* **12/1**

0-60 15 *3 1/4* **Grethel (IRE)**[10] 1472 5-10-4 56 oh2.. KennyJohnson 11 28
(A Berry) *racd wd in rr: rdn 4f out: nvr on terms* **80/1**

203- 16 *4* **Primo Way**[223] 6161 8-10-11 63..............................(t) GaryBerridge 6 26
(D A Nolan) *chsd ldrs tl rdn and wknd fr 2f out* **33/1**

1m 49.96s (1.56) **Going Correction** +0.025s/f (Good) **16 Ran SP% 123.9**
Speed ratings (Par 103): **93,91,91,91,89 89,88,86,85,84 84,81,80,80,76 72**
toteswingers: 1&2 £7.50, 1&3 £3.70, 2&3 £6.80 CSF £45.91 CT £147.91 TOTE £5.40: £1.60, £1.90, £1.60, £2.60; EX 46.00.

Owner Mrs Eileen M Milligan **Bred** Takashi Watanabe **Trained** Cartmel, Cumbria

FOCUS

A fair-looking handicap that provided the Jump jockeys with a chance to put there skills to use on the Flat. Straightforward form, with the third running close to his Pontefract rating, and the fourth to his mark.

1691 CANCER RESEARCH (S) STKS 1m 65y

3:35 (3:35) (Class 5) 3-Y-O **£2,590** (£770; £385; £192) **Stalls** High

Form RPR

000- 1 **Blessing Belle (IRE)**[194] 6884 3-8-7 45.. SaleemGolam 1 57
(M H Tompkins) *hld up: hdwy over 2f out: led appr fnl f: r.o wl* **11/1**

-200 2 *2* **Dark Oasis**[10] 1470 3-8-12 60..............................(p) PaulMulrennan 10 57
(K A Ryan) *pressed ldr: ev ch over 3f out: sn rdn: kpt on u.p fnl f* **13/8**[1]

6330 3 *1/2* **Paint Splash**[12] 1437 3-8-2 50.. DeanHeslop(5) 2 51
(T D Barron) *hld up: hdwy to ld over 2f out: hdd appr fnl f: one pce* **6/1**[3]

3-43 4 *5* **Hard Luck Story**[11] 1453 3-8-12 68..............................(p) TomEaves 11 44
(I Semple) *led to over 3f out: sn rdn: wknd over 1f out* **5/2**[2]

00-6 5 *2 1/2* **Knock Three Times (IRE)**[29] 1128 3-8-4 50.............. KellyHarrison(3) 3 34
(W Storey) *in tch: hdwy and cl up over 2f out: rdn and wknd over 1f out* **10/1**

-056 6 *hd* **Teddy West (IRE)**[21] 1226 3-8-12 52..............................(v[1]) PaulHanagan 6 38
(Patrick Morris) *t.k.h: chsd ldrs: n.m.r over 2f out: sn rdn and hung rt: no imp over 1f out* **20/1**

05- 7 *4* **Desdamona (IRE)**[183] 7126 3-8-5 0 ow3.. SladeO'Hara(5) 8 27
(A Berry) *hld up: effrt whn stmbld over 2f out: n.d* **66/1**

4506 8 *3* **Chimbonda**[11] 1455 3-8-9 50.. JackMitchell(3) 7 22
(S Parr) *t.k.h: in tch: hdwy 1/2-way: wknd over 1f out* **9/1**

1m 50.78s (2.38) **Going Correction** +0.025s/f (Good) **8 Ran SP% 114.6**
Speed ratings (Par 99): **89,87,86,81,79 78,74,71**
toteswingers: 1&2 £3.80, 1&3 £17.30, 2&3 £1.50 CSF £29.48 TOTE £14.50: £2.30, £1.40, £1.40; EX 37.70.There was no bid for the winner.

Owner M P Bowring **Bred** M J Foley **Trained** Newmarket, Suffolk

FOCUS
This, by any standards, was a very moderate seller, and it should not pay to be positive about the form. The runner-up is the guide.

1692 DAILY RECORD H'CAP 1m 5f 9y
4:10 (4:10) (Class 4) (0-80,77) 4-Y-O+ **£6,476** (£1,927; £963; £481) **Stalls** High

Form RPR
-240 **1** **Chookie Hamilton**[29] 1125 5-7-9 **58** oh2 JamieKyne(7) 5 65
(I Semple) *in tch: led over 2f out: drvn out fnl f* **11/2**
0220 **2** *3* **Bridgewater Boys**[8] 1533 8-8-11 **67** (b) J-PGuillambert 7 70
(T J Pitt) *dwlt: hld up: hdwy over 2f out: chsd wnr ins fnl f: kpt on* **16/1**
/41- **3** *½* **Legion D'Honneur (UAE)**[44] 1950 4-9-5 **75** PaulMulrennan 6 77
(L Lungo) *chsd ldrs: outpcd over 2f out: kpt on u.p fnl f* **5/1**[3]
6-40 **4** *nse* **Puy D'Arnac (FR)**[94] 325 6-9-7 **77** PJMcDonald 3 79
(G A Swinbank) *hld up: hdwy and prom over 2f out: one pce fnl f* **16/1**
32-4 **5** *2* **Elite Land**[14] 1000 6-8-8 **64** TomEaves 4 63
(B Ellison) *hld up in midfield: niggled over 4f out: effrt over 2f out: one pce fnl f* **4/1**[1]
15-0 **6** *2* **Grandad Bill (IRE)**[8] 1506 6-8-7 **66** KellyHarrison(3) 10 62
(J S Goldie) *hld up: rdn 3f out: kpt on fnl f: no imp* **8/1**
0-00 **7** *2* **Oddsmaker (IRE)**[21] 1230 8-8-12 **68** (t) DavidAllan 8 61
(M A Barnes) *mde most to over 2f out: btn fnl f* **10/1**
232- **8** *½* **Signalman**[106] 6727 5-8-3 **59** ow1 RoystonFfrench 2 51
(P Monteith) *in tch tl wknd over 2f out* **9/2**[2]
156- **9** *14* **Keelung (USA)**[232] 5887 8-9-4 **74** PhillipMakin 11 45
(R Ford) *cl up tl rdn and wknd over 2f out* **11/1**
10 *34* **Oh Landino (GER)**[266] 4-8-2 **58** oh8 FrancisNorton 9 —
(P Monteith) *bhd: struggling 4f out: sn btn* **28/1**
00-2 **P** **Saluscraggie**[11] 1454 7-8-2 **58** oh3 PaulHanagan 1 —
(R E Barr) *bhd: broke leg after 2f: dead* **20/1**

2m 50.98s (-2.92) **Going Correction** +0.025s/f (Good) **11** Ran SP% **118.7**
Speed ratings (Par 105): **109,107,106,106,105 104,103,102,94,73** —
toteswingers: 1&2 £13.70, 1&3 £5.20, 2&3 £12.40 CSF £90.69 CT £472.84 TOTE £6.80: £2.10, £3.80, £2.00; EX 58.40.
Owner Hamilton Park Members Syndicate **Bred** D And J Raeburn **Trained** Carluke, S Lanarks
■ Stewards' Enquiry : Paul Mulrennan two-day ban: used whip with excessive frequency (May 17-18)
P J McDonald one-day ban: careless riding (May 18)

FOCUS
All of these are pretty much exposed handicappers. The early pace was much too quick and the chasing pack got on top in the final stages. It has been rated around the winner to the best of last year's turf form, and the third to his win her last May.
Chookie Hamilton Official explanation: trainer's rep said, regarding apparent improvement in form, that the gelding was better suited by the easier ground.
Signalman Official explanation: jockey said gelding slipped on bend turn into home straight

1693 GARY OWEN MEDIAN AUCTION MAIDEN STKS 1m 3f 16y
4:45 (4:45) (Class 5) 3-5-Y-O **£2,729** (£806; £403) **Stalls** High

Form RPR
5 **1** **Caerlaverock (IRE)**[6] 1562 4-9-12 0 TomEaves 7 80
(G A Swinbank) *prom: outpcd over 2f out: kpt on strly fnl f to ld post* **8/1**
04- **2** *nse* **Stanstill (IRE)**[201] 6723 3-8-9 0 PJMcDonald 1 78
(G A Swinbank) *trckd ldrs: rdn to ld ins fnl f: hdd post* **16/1**
4-32 **3** *3* **Dazzling Light (UAE)**[21] 1231 4-9-2 72 GaryBartley(5) 6 69
(J S Goldie) *led to ins fnl f: sn no ex* **7/2**[3]
0-22 **4** *1 ¼* **Mt Kintyre (IRE)**[15] 1362 3-8-9 81 PaulMulrennan 4 71
(M H Tompkins) *cl up: disp ld 3f out: carried hd awkwardly and hung rt u.p 2f out: nt run on fnl f* **11/10**[1]
5 *2 ½* **Act Of Kalanisi (IRE)** 3-8-9 0 RoystonFfrench 5 67+
(M Johnston) *in tch: rn green and outpcd over 3f out: r.o fnl f: n.d* **10/3**[2]
6 *4 ½* **Flora's Pride**[49] 5-9-7 0 PaulHanagan 2 55
(K G Reveley) *hld up: rdn and outpcd 3f out: n.d after* **40/1**
00-0 **7** *31* **Rascasse**[32] 1057 4-9-7 44 (b) SladeO'Hara(5) 3 8
(Bruce Hellier) *hld up in tch: outpcd over 3f out: sn wknd* **200/1**

2m 24.89s (-0.71) **Going Correction** +0.025s/f (Good) **7** Ran SP% **112.8**
WFA 3 from 4yo+ 17lb
Speed ratings (Par 103): **103,102,100,99,98 94,72**
toteswingers: 1&2 £8.10, 1&3 £5.70, 2&3 £7.40 CSF £113.61 TOTE £13.20: £3.60, £4.90; EX 53.30.
Owner Mr & Mrs Duncan Davidson **Bred** Ger Hayes **Trained** Melsonby, N Yorks

FOCUS
Even though the top-rated horse had a mark of 81, one would imagine that this was no more than just an average maiden. The form is difficult to evaluate, with the third and fourth far from solid markers.

1694 RACING UK H'CAP 6f 5y
5:20 (5:22) (Class 5) (0-70,70) 4-Y-O+ **£2,590** (£770; £385; £192) **Stalls** Low

Form RPR
0-60 **1** **Guest Connections**[8] 1518 6-8-8 **60** (v) SilvestreDeSousa 15 77
(D Nicholls) *hld up: gd hdwy to ld over 1f out: edgd lft: sn clr* **8/1**
5-01 **2** *4* **Imperial Sword**[17] 1310 6-8-11 **63** (b) PhillipMakin 3 67
(T D Barron) *hld up: hdwy 2f out: chsd wnr ins fnl f: no imp* **13/2**[3]
6-02 **3** *1 ¾* **Buy On The Red**[15] 1343 8-9-3 **69** (b) FrancisNorton 11 68
(D Nicholls) *mde most tl edgd rt and hdd over 1f out: sn no ex* **5/1**[2]
11-3 **4** *1 ½* **Johnston's Glory (IRE)**[15] 1369 5-9-0 **66** DavidAllan 1 60
(E J Alston) *midfield: rdn over 2f out: r.o fnl f: nrst fin* **10/1**
10-2 **5** *1 ½* **Conjecture**[11] 1456 7-8-7 **62** JackMitchell(3) 14 51
(R Bastiman) *cl up: ev ch and rdn over 2f out: no ex over 1f out* **14/1**
60-0 **6** *nk* **Woodsley House (IRE)**[15] 1369 7-9-1 **70** NeilBrown(3) 4 58
(A G Foster) *hld up: hdwy over 1f out: nvr rchd ldrs* **33/1**
5501 **7** *½* **Splash The Cash**[32] 1057 4-8-10 **67** AmyRyan(5) 13 53
(K A Ryan) *prom: effrt over 2f out: btn fnl f* **3/1**[1]
50-5 **8** *1 ¼* **Virtuality (USA)**[13] 1400 4-8-8 **60** TomEaves 12 42
(B Smart) *in tch: rdn and edgd lft over 2f out: sn no ex* **18/1**
0-00 **9** *4 ½* **Royal Acclamation (IRE)**[11] 1456 4-7-13 **58** JamieKyne(7) 5 26
(G A Harker) *midfield: rdn after 2f: edgd rt and wknd over 2f out* **40/1**
560- **10** *1 ½* **Musca (IRE)**[294] 4001 5-9-4 **70** RoystonFfrench 7 33
(J Wade) *missed break: bhd tl sme late hdwy: nvr on terms* **40/1**
00-0 **11** *2 ½* **Thunder Bay**[30] 1096 4-8-10 **62** PaulHanagan 8 17
(R A Fahey) *sn outpcd: nvr on terms* **14/1**
300 **12** *½* **Music Box Express**[20] 1248 5-8-5 **64** (t) MatthewDavies(7) 6 18
(George Baker) *spd tl wknd fr 2f out* **25/1**
0-00 **13** *3 ¾* **The Bear**[30] 1096 6-8-13 **65** PJMcDonald 9 7
(D A Nolan) *sn prom: drvn 1/2-way: sn wknd* **12/1**
0400 **14** *2 ½* **King Kenny**[15] 1343 4-9-1 **67** (vt[1]) J-PGuillambert 16 1
(S Parr) *cl up tl wknd fr 2f out: eased whn no ch* **33/1**

1m 12.12s (-0.08) **Going Correction** +0.125s/f (Good) **14** Ran SP% **116.1**
Speed ratings (Par 103): **105,99,97,95,93 92,92,90,84,82 79,78,73,70**
toteswingers: 1&2 £8.90, 1&3 £11.30, 2&3 £6.30 CSF £51.71 CT £257.32 TOTE £9.50: £2.90, £2.80, £2.20; EX 69.40.
Owner Hall Farm Racing & D Nicholls **Bred** The Lavington Stud **Trained** Sessay, N Yorks

FOCUS
A big field of handicappers rattled up the straight 6f, and the form has been rated around the winner as back to last year's best.
Musca(IRE) Official explanation: jockey said gelding missed the break
King Kenny Official explanation: jockey said gelding had no more to give

1695 SPRING OFFICE PARTY NIGHT ON FRIDAY H'CAP 5f 4y
5:50 (5:52) (Class 6) (0-60,57) 4-Y-O+ **£2,729** (£806; £403) **Stalls** Low

Form RPR
462 **1** **Rocketball (IRE)**[5] 1591 4-9-1 **54** PaulHanagan 8 64
(Patrick Morris) *mde all: rdn and hung lft appr fnl f: kpt on strly* **9/4**[1]
0-52 **2** *1 ¼* **Creative (IRE)**[11] 1465 4-8-13 **52** SaleemGolam 7 57
(M H Tompkins) *in tch: rdn over 2f out: styd on to go 2nd nr fin: nt rch wnr* **5/1**[2]
5144 **3** *nk* **Argentine (IRE)**[17] 1310 5-9-2 **55** (b) PaulMulrennan 15 59
(L Lungo) *prom: rdn over 2f out: edgd lft appr fnl f: kpt on u.p* **6/1**[3]
6655 **4** *hd* **Whozart (IRE)**[37] 976 6-8-12 **54** KellyHarrison(3) 10 57
(A Dickman) *cl up: rdn whn n.m.r briefly appr fnl f: kpt on fin* **8/1**
000- **5** *¾* **Sunley Sovereign**[142] 7218 5-8-8 **47** (be) AndrewElliott 2 48
(Mrs R A Carr) *towards rr: drvn and hdwy 2f out: r.o fnl f: nrst fin* **40/1**
0-50 **6** *1* **Chookie Heiton (IRE)**[93] 352 11-9-4 **57** TomEaves 6 54
(I Semple) *bhd and pushed along: hdwy over 1f out: r.o fnl f* **16/1**
0030 **7** *½* **Berrymead**[20] 1248 4-8-13 **57** (b) AnnStokell(5) 14 52
(Miss A Stokell) *prom: effrt over 2f out: no ex fnl f* **25/1**
0-60 **8** *1 ½* **Radiator Rooney (IRE)**[17] 1310 6-8-13 **52** (v) PhillipMakin 9 42
(Patrick Morris) *in tch: drvn 1/2-way: one pce over 1f out* **14/1**
00-0 **9** *nk* **Foreign Rhythm (IRE)**[6] 1558 4-8-11 **50** (v) DaleGibson 1 39
(N Tinkler) *bhd and sn drvn along: kpt on fnl f: nvr on terms* **40/1**
100 **10** *¾* **Mr Rooney (IRE)**[17] 1310 6-8-11 **55** SladeO'Hara(5) 13 41
(A Berry) *towards rr: effrt over 2f out: sn no imp* **18/1**
000- **11** *½* **Cross Of Lorraine (IRE)**[249] 5392 6-9-3 **56** (b) RoystonFfrench 12 40
(J Wade) *towards rr: pckd and outpcd after 1f: n.d* **20/1**
1230 **12** *nse* **Mujma**[5] 1591 5-9-1 **54** (t) J-PGuillambert 4 38
(S Parr) *in tch tl rdn and wknd wl over 1f out* **14/1**
-000 **13** *½* **Miacarla**[5] 1591 6-9-0 **56** NeilBrown(3) 11 38
(H A McWilliams) *t.k.h: hld up: rdn over 2f out: sn btn* **20/1**
01-0 **14** *1* **Tenancy (IRE)**[8] 1528 5-9-2 **55** PAspell 5 34
(R C Guest) *bhd: shortlived effrt 1/2-way: btn over 1f out* **22/1**

60.45 secs (0.45) **Going Correction** +0.125s/f (Good) **14** Ran SP% **119.9**
Speed ratings (Par 101): **101,99,98,98,97 95,94,92,91,90 89,89,88,87**
toteswingers: 1&2 £2.70, 1&3 £3.90, 2&3 £7.60 CSF £10.91 CT £62.00 TOTE £3.10: £1.80, £2.00, £2.40; EX 13.70 Place 6 £314.51, Place 5 £263.92..
Owner Miss Sharron Pettigrew **Bred** John Morris **Trained** Tarporley, Cheshire
■ Stewards' Enquiry : Paul Mulrennan two-day ban: careless riding (May 19-20)

FOCUS
A poor but wide-open sprint handicap. The runner-up and third are the best guides to the form.
Radiator Rooney(IRE) Official explanation: jockey said gelding hung right
T/Plt: £645.00 to a £1 stake. Pool: £65,429.74. 74.05 winning tickets. T/Qpdt: £195.10 to a £1 stake. Pool: £3,216.58. 12.20 winning tickets. RY

[1673] NEWMARKET (R-H)
Sunday, May 3

OFFICIAL GOING: Good to firm (firm in places; 9.7)
Wind: Fresh to strong, behind Weather: Bright spells, breezy

1696 CALL STAN JAMES 08000 351135 STKS (HERITAGE H'CAP) 1m 4f
2:00 (2:02) (Class 2) (0-105,104) 4-Y-O+
£31,155 (£9,330; £4,665; £2,335; £1,165; £585) **Stalls** High

Form RPR
0-11 **1** **Hatton Flight**[11] 1458 5-9-0 **94** (b) WilliamBuick 12 102
(A M Balding) *in tch: hdwy over 2f out: chsd ldr over 1f out: rdn to ld wl over 1f out: styd on wl fnl f* **6/1**[3]
42-1 **2** *1 ¼* **Redesignation (IRE)**[15] 1347 4-9-3 **97** RichardHughes 5 103
(R Hannon) *lw: t.k.h: hld up in tch: hdwy on rail 2f out: kpt on u.p to go 2nd wl ins fnl f: unable to chal wnr* **9/2**[1]
501- **3** *¾* **Boz**[202] 6698 5-8-11 **91** JamieSpencer 4 96
(L M Cumani) *bit bkwd: trckd ldrs: hdwy and rdn over 2f out: ev ch fr wl over 1f out tl no ex fnl 100yds: lost 2nd wl ins fnl f* **16/1**
35-3 **4** *nk* **Dansili Dancer**[29] 1117 7-9-5 **99** AdamKirby 13 103
(C G Cox) *lw: hld up in rr: hdwy 3f out: chsd ldrs and drvn over 1f out: kpt on same pce fnl f* **7/1**
100- **5** *1 ¼* **Night Crescendo (USA)**[155] 7491 6-9-0 **94** JimCrowley 16 96
(Mrs A J Perrett) *t.k.h: hld up in rr: hdwy jst over 2f out: kpt on fnl f but nvr pce to rch ldrs* **20/1**
444- **6** *3 ¼* **Resplendent Light**[213] 6427 4-9-2 **96** MartinDwyer 11 93
(W R Muir) *led: hrd pressed 3f out: rdn and hdd wl over 1f out: wknd jst over 1f out* **20/1**
311- **7** *½* **Precision Break (USA)**[177] 7230 4-8-13 **93** JohnEgan 6 89
(P F I Cole) *in tch: effrt to press ldrs 3f out: sn rdn: wknd jst over 1f out* **16/1**
05-0 **8** *hd* **Record Breaker (IRE)**[11] 1458 5-8-9 **89** GregFairley 14 85
(M Johnston) *hld up in midfield: rdn and unable qck over 2f out: no imp u.p fnl 2f* **15/2**
0204 **9** *¾* **Baylini**[36] 1003 5-8-0 **85** SophieDoyle(5) 2 80
(Ms J S Doyle) *t.k.h: hld up towards rr: gd hdwy on outer 4f out: jnd ldrs 3f out: sn rdn: wknd wl over 1f out* **33/1**
-122 **10** *3 ¼* **Distinctive Image (USA)**[29] 1117 4-8-5 **85** ChrisCatlin 15 75
(R Hollinshead) *hld up bhd: rdn and effrt 3f out: no prog and wl hld fnl 2f* **8/1**
116- **11** *nse* **Storyland (USA)**[185] 7100 4-8-11 **91** KirstyMilczarek 3 81+
(W J Haggas) *lw: hld up towards rr: stl bhd and n.m.r over 2f out: swtchd rt to far rail 2f out: n.d* **5/1**[2]
51-0 **12** *1 ¼* **Sereth (IRE)**[15] 1351 6-9-10 **104** TPQueally 9 92
(B J Curley) *hld up towards rr: rdn and struggling over 3f out: wl bhd fnl 2f* **50/1**
-406 **13** *8* **Pevensey (IRE)**[26] 1172 7-8-13 **93** (p) GrahamGibbons 8 68
(J J Quinn) *chsd ldr tl jst over 3f out: sn wknd: wl bhd fnl 2f* **25/1**

13-6 **14** 3¾ **Dance The Star (USA)**[22] 1216 4-8-3 **86**...................... AhmedAjtebi(3) 1 55
(D M Simcock) *t.k.h: in tch in midfield: rdn over 4f out: wknd over 3f out: wl bhd fnl 2f* **16/1**

2m 32.47s (-1.03) **Going Correction** -0.15s/f (Firm) **14** Ran SP% **120.4**
Speed ratings (Par 109): **97,96,95,95,94 92,92,92,91,89 89,88,83,80**
toteswingers: 1&2 £4.20, 1&3 £16.80, 2&3 £10.40 CSF £30.81 CT £420.61 TOTE £6.30: £2.40, £2.00, £3.20; EX 21.80 Trifecta £167.50 Pool £966.52 - 4.40 winning units..

Owner David Brownlow **Bred** Fittocks Stud Ltd **Trained** Kingsclere, Hants

FOCUS

Continued sunshine along with a strong wind made for drying conditions. This was a valuable and competitive handicap, but they went a pretty steady gallop which only picked up with around three furlongs to run. It paid to to race handily. Hatton Flight continues to improve, and it was a good return from Boz, who can do better again this year.

NOTEBOOK

Hatton Flight raced more prominently than he sometimes does and, although briefly looking in trouble when the sprint for home began, he picked up well to hold off the challenge of the third and make it three out of three for the season and seven wins in his last ten starts. Raised 6lb for his victory in the Great Metropolitan at Epsom last month, he doesn't win his races by far and remains hard for the handicapper to get to grips with. \n\x\x He should continue to progress and a handicap at Epsom on Derby day and the Duke of Edinburgh at Royal Ascot will come under consideration. The Ebor may be a suitable target come August. (op 5-1 tchd 8-1 in places)

Redesignation(IRE), put up only 3lb for his Doncaster win first time out and well backed here, was one of a number who raced freely off the slow gallop. Tackling 1m4f for only the second time, he kept on against the rail to go second near the finish. It will be interesting to see how he fares in a truly run race over this trip. (op 7-1 tchd 4-1)

Boz looked a big threat to the winner at one stage, but edged to his right under pressure and was just held. This was a fine seasonal return and he can win a good handicap this season, but he must have fast ground on turf. (op 12-1)

Dansili Dancer comes in for credit as the first home to come from the rear, but having improved to have his chance his effort flattened out late on. The drying ground was in his favour and he remains difficult to actually win with. (op 6-1)

Night Crescendo(USA) ◆ travelled strongly in midfield but lacked a change of pace late on. This was a pleasing return and he will be sharper for the return of cheekpieces, which he wore on his last four starts of last term. Official explanation: jockey said gelding was denied a clear run (tchd 18-1, 25-1 in places)

Resplendent Light set the modest pace and stuck on for sixth. This outing should take some of the freshness from him, but he is currently 18lb higher than when last successful and may prove tricky to place this year. (tchd 25/1 in a place)

Precision Break(USA) had an excellent time of it in 2008, successful seven times, but those wins came either on Polytrack or easy ground, and the last four of them were over further than he tackled today. He was reported to have lost a shoe, and in the circumstances he ran quite well. Official explanation: jockey said colt lost a shoe (op 12-1 tchd 10-1)

Record Breaker(IRE), who was unplaced in Hatton Flight's Epsom race on his reappearance, is now only 1lb higher than when last winning. He has not fared badly on either start this term but a bit more is required. (op 9-1 tchd 10-1)

Distinctive Image(USA) settled reasonably well but could never get into the picture. He has been very progressive on sand, but this was just his second run on turf (the first came on heavy) and he has yet to fully prove himself on this surface. (op 9-1)

Storyland(USA) was well supported with trip and ground to suit, but the lack of a true gallop was against her. She was switched to the rail after being impeded when in last place around three furlongs out, but could make no real inroads. (op 7-1)

1697 STANJAMES.COM DAHLIA STKS (GROUP 3) (F&M) 1m 1f
2:35 (2:36) (Class 1) 4-Y-0+ **£36,900** (£13,988; £7,000; £3,490) **Stalls** Low

Form RPR

345- **1** **Heaven Sent**[211] 6475 6-8-12 111...................................... RyanMoore 4 104+
(Sir Michael Stoute) *hld up in last pl: rdn and qcknd to ld wl over 1f out: in command fnl f: rdn out* **4/11**[1]

22-3 **2** 1¼ **Casilda (IRE)**[22] 1216 4-8-12 90...................................... WilliamBuick 5 101
(A M Balding) *led: rdn and qcknd jst over 2f out: hdd wl over 1f out: nt pce of wnr jst over 1f out: kpt on* **14/1**[3]

61-4 **3** 2 **Barshiba (IRE)**[17] 1301 5-8-12 106............................... RichardHughes 2 97
(D R C Elsworth) *stdd s: t.k.h: trckd ldrs: rdn jst over 2f out: kpt on same pce fr over 1f out* **4/1**[2]

120- **4** 7 **Moon Sister (IRE)**[198] 6781 4-8-12 100............................... AlanMunro 3 89
(W Jarvis) *trckd ldr: rdn jst over 2f out: outpcd jst over 1f out: btn and eased ins fnl f* **14/1**[3]

1m 47.98s (-3.72) **Going Correction** -0.15s/f (Firm) **4** Ran SP% **106.6**
Speed ratings (Par 113): **110,108,107,100**
CSF £6.02 TOTE £1.30; EX 3.40.

Owner Cheveley Park Stud **Bred** Cheveley Park Stud Ltd **Trained** Newmarket, Suffolk

FOCUS

A weak turnout for this distaff Group 3, with forecast second favourite Changing Skies a late absentee. The four runners raced down the centre of the track and the pace was not bad considering the small field.

NOTEBOOK

Heaven Sent was faced with what looked a straightforward task on paper and she duly followed up last season's victory in this event. Held up last of the four, she needed to be firmly pushed along to take the lead but was comfortably on top in the end, although a length and a quarter beating of a filly officially 21lb her inferior suggests she was well below her best. She failed to win again last year, finishing second in the Group 2 Windsor Forest at Ascot, which is her likely target next month. It could be that she she will come up just short at the top level again. (op 1-2)

Casilda(IRE) made a satisfactory debut for new connections on the Kempton Polytrack and she ran well here, not being allowed an uncontested lead but setting a reasonable gallop and sticking on for second. She is flattered to have finished as close as she did to the winner but picked up some valuable black type. (op 11-1 tchd 10-1)

Barshiba(IRE) raced keenly once again on the far side of the quartet. She could not quicken when the race to the line began but was keeping on for third, the position she filled behind Heaven Sent in a six-runner renewal of this event a year ago. She has won only one of her last 17 starts and is without a victory in 14 runs at Group level, despite some creditable efforts. (op 7-2 tchd 9-2)

Moon Sister(IRE) had her chance but was the first of the four beaten. She may have needed this but her Listed second at Yarmouth last September remains the best form she has posted. (op 10-1)

1698 STANJAMES.COM 1000 GUINEAS STKS (GROUP 1) (FILLIES) 1m
3:15 (3:16) (Class 1) 3-Y-0
£227,080 (£86,080; £43,080; £21,480; £10,760; £5,400) **Stalls** Centre

Form RPR

31- **1** **Ghanaati (USA)**[188] 7011 3-9-0 85.. RHills 8 115
(B W Hills) *lw: a.p: led 2f out: rdn and clr over 1f out: r.o wl and in command fnl f* **20/1**

120- **2** 1½ **Cuis Ghaire (IRE)**[259] 5132 3-9-0 108............................... KJManning 14 112
(J S Bolger, Ire) *racd keenly: w ldr tl led 4f out: rdn and hdd 2f out: drvn and nt pce of wnr over 1f out: kpt on wl but readily hld by wnr* **12/1**[3]

52-2 **3** 1¼ **Super Sleuth (IRE)**[15] 1353 3-9-0 107.............................. MartinDwyer 3 109+
(B J Meehan) *lw: stdd s: hld up bhd: hdwy over 2f out: stl plenty to do over 1f out: r.o wl fnl f: wnt 3rd towards fin: nvr threatened ldrs* **33/1**

52-2 **4** nse **Heart Shaped (USA)**[35] 1024 3-9-0 110.............................. JMurtagh 10 109
(A P O'Brien, Ire) *hld up in tch in midfield: hdwy 3f out: rdn and hanging rt fr over 1f out: styd on fnl f: nvr pce to threaten wnr* **14/1**

111- **5** hd **Rainbow View (USA)**[218] 6268 3-9-0 118..................... JimmyFortune 6 108
(J H M Gosden) *lw: in tch: rdn and unable qck over 2f out: drvn and no prog over 1f out: hdwy ins fnl f: styng on fin but nvr pce to threaten ldrs* **8/11**[1]

61-3 **6** hd **Penny's Gift**[18] 1292 3-9-0 101.................................. RichardHughes 15 108
(R Hannon) *lw: led narrowly tl over 6f out: styd w ldrs: 3rd and rdn 2f out: outpcd u.p over 1f out: wknd ins fnl f* **66/1**

111- **7** 2½ **Serious Attitude (IRE)**[212] 6441 3-9-0 111........................ PJSmullen 12 102
(Rae Guest) *t.k.h: hld up in tch: rdn and unable qck 2f out: plugged on same pce u.p fnl f* **8/1**[2]

30- **8** 4½ **Pursuit Of Glory (IRE)**[191] 6967 3-9-0 107........................ WMLordan 9 92
(David Wachman, Ire) *hld up in tch in midfield: rdn and unable qck 3f out: no ch w ldrs fnl 2f* **33/1**

53-1 **9** 4 **Nashmiah (IRE)**[43] 912 3-9-0 103.................................. JamieSpencer 13 83
(C E Brittain) *hld up towards rr: hdwy into midfield 4f out: rdn 3f out: sn struggling: no ch and eased fr over 1f out* **20/1**

21-1 **10** 1 **Lahaleeb (IRE)**[15] 1353 3-9-0 108.............................. DarryllHolland 4 80
(M R Channon) *towards rr: rdn 4f out: sn struggling: no ch fnl 2f* **14/1**

12- **11** 2½ **Shimah (USA)**[245] 5549 3-9-0 110.............................. DPMcDonogh 5 75
(Kevin Prendergast, Ire) *w'like: small: rdn and struggling over 3f out: wl bhd fr over 2f out* **16/1**

341- **12** 4½ **Seradim**[150] 7549 3-9-0 99.. SPasquier 1 64
(P F I Cole) *in tch in midfield: rdn and losing pl 3f out: wl bhd fr over 2f out* **100/1**

01 **13** 2¼ **Devotee (USA)**[66] 701 3-9-0 107.......................................(t) LDettori 7 59
(Saeed Bin Suroor) *w ldrs tl led narrowly over 6f out: hdd 4f out: sn dropped out: wl bhd fr over 2f out* **50/1**

122- **P** **Aspen Darlin (IRE)**[197] 6818 3-9-0 109........................(p) JimmyQuinn 11 —
(A Bailey) *plld hrd: hld up in midfield tl p.u 4f out* **40/1**

1m 34.22s (-4.38) **Going Correction** -0.15s/f (Firm) course record **14** Ran SP% **118.2**
Speed ratings (Par 110): **115,113,112,112,112 111,109,104,100,99 97,92,90,—**
toteswingers: 1&2 £32.60, 1&3 £71.80, 2&3 £49.50 CSF £224.43 CT £7833.64 TOTE £26.00: £6.70, £4.20, £8.80; EX 227.20 Trifecta £7479.00 Part won. Pool £10,106.82 - 0.10 winning units..

Owner Hamdan Al Maktoum **Bred** Shadwell Farm LLC **Trained** Lambourn, Berks

FOCUS

A fascinating 1,000 Guineas, with a strong line-up headed by a filly who was among the very best juveniles of her sex in the last 20 years and a supporting cast that included the Cheveley Park winner, also unbeaten, and three of her closest pursuers that day, plus a really tough filly who had won both the Rockfel and the Fred Darling, a Royal Ascot winner, and a Godolphin filly who had landed the UAE Oaks but had yet to race on turf. Although Polytrack maiden winner Ghanaati deserves enormous credit for an emphatic win on just her third start and her first on turf, there was inevitably a sense of anti-climax when Rainbow View ran such a flat race and Serious Attitude faded right out of contention. While she has the potential for further improvement, Ghanaati can be rated no more than an average Guineas winner, and one has to wonder how the runaway Nell Gwyn winner Fantasia, now in the same ownership as Rainbow View, might have fared.

NOTEBOOK

Ghanaati(USA) ◆, a good-looking filly from the outstanding family of Nashwan and co, had not been out since her stylish all-weather maiden win at Kempton six months previously, but she had been the subject of good recent reports and she was clearly well primed for this massive step up in class. In the firing line from the word go, she took it up two furlongs out and was already clear at the furlong marker. She will stay further than this, but with Giant's Causeway for her sire she would not be guaranteed to stay 1m4f and the Coronation Stakes is likely to be her next race, as Barry Hills does not see much to be gained by going to Ireland for their 1,000 Guineas. From a family that go on improving, there could still be plenty more to come, and she ought to take some beating at Royal Ascot. In the long-term Hills sees her as a Champion Stakes type, as he expects significant improvement for the extra two furlongs. (tchd 22-1 in places)

Cuis Ghaire(IRE), successful at Royal Ascot and second to Rip Van Winkle at Leopardstown last summer, brought solid but unexceptional form to the race, and she looks to have improved again. She, too, raced with the leaders from the start, and there is no faulting the way she stuck on. She will get further than this too. (op 11-1 tchd 14-1 in a place)

Super Sleuth(IRE) ◆ did tremendously well in third, as she came from much further back than any of the other principals, having been just about last still with only three furlongs to run. Still a maiden but arguably beaten only by lack of hard fitness when second to Lahaleeb in the Fred Darling, she is now likely to go for the Prix de Diane, where she ought to get the easier ground that connections feel she will appreciate. She is clearly a very smart filly. (op 28-1 tchd 40-1 in a place)

Heart Shaped(USA) also enjoyed the benefit of a prep race, and she was among those who looked sure to appreciate the fast ground. She appeared to have a sound each-way chance, but she was inclined to hang and just lost out in a three-way battle for third. She should win a nice prize somewhere along the way, and one could see her returning for the Breeders' Cup, in whch she was second last year.

Rainbow View(USA) came here unbeaten and stood out so far on her juvenile form that this looked hers to lose. The temperament worries proved unfounded, as she was unusually calm throughout the preliminaries, but having raced in touch from the start she was being niggled along at halfway and just plugged on at one pace. Jimmy Fortune reported she would not let herself down on the drying ground, and John Gosden had no hesitation in attributing her indifferent perfomance to the conditions. However, while the ground is a perfectly plausible explanation, there will be a nagging suspicion until she proves otherwise that her contemporaries may now have been caught up, or else she has lost some of the fire that characterised her succession of spectacular wins at two. Her next race will be either the Irish Guineas or the Oaks, and she would almost certainly get an easier surface than this in either. Official explanation: jockey said filly was unsuited by the good to firm (firm in places) ground (op 10-11 tchd 11-10 in a place and Evens in places)

Penny's Gift was among the race's more doubtful stayers, and she ran accordingly without being in the slightest disgraced. (tchd 100-1 in a place and 80-1 in a place)

Serious Attitude(IRE), who did not look great in her coat beforehand, also ran like a non-stayer, for having raced in touch, possibly a shade keen early on, she was left behind when the principals quickened. Although she has an Oaks entry, one can see her reverting to sprinting before long. She would need supplementing for the Golden Jubilee though. (op 15-2)

Pursuit Of Glory(IRE), a close third to Serious Attitude in the Cheveley Park last year, did not advertise that form either.

Nashmiah(IRE), who had impressed in a Listed race on the Polytrack at Lingfield, could manage only the briefest of efforts and was never better than mid-field. Official explanation: jockey said filly was unsuited by the good to firm (firm in places) ground (op 25-1)

Lahaleeb(IRE), who had beaten Super Sleuth at Newbury, was a big disappointment, for she was among the first beaten. (tchd 16-1, 11-1 in a place)

Shimah(USA) is only small and she was one of the least taking in the paddock. She showed little in the race. (op 14-1)

Seradim lost her place from three furlongs out and trailed in well beaten.

Devotee(USA) raced with the leaders to halfway but dropped right out. She reportedly had a cardiac problem in the UAE Guineas before landing the Oaks there, and something may have been amiss again. The ground could have been a factor on her turf debut and she was reported to have lost her action. Official explanation: jockey said filly lost its action

Aspen Darlin(IRE), the Cheveley Park second and a Group 3 winner on heavy ground at Ayr, was sadly pulled up at around halfway, having strained a tendon. She will not race again but has been saved for stud. (tchd 50-1)

1699 BEST ODDS GUARANTEED AT STAN JAMES STKS (HERITAGE H'CAP) 6f

3:50 (3:53) (Class 2) 3-Y-0+

£31,155 (£9,330; £4,665; £2,335; £1,165; £585) **Stalls** Low

Form RPR

00-3 **1** **Evens And Odds (IRE)**[35] 1018 5-8-11 **90** AdrianTNicholls 1 106
(D Nicholls) *lw: towards rr: rdn and hdwy fr 1/2-way: led jst ins fnl f: r.o strly and sn clr* **7/1**[3]

0023 **2** 3 1/4 **Thebes**[6] 1560 4-8-12 **91** GregFairley 7 97
(M Johnston) *chsd ldrs tl led over 2f out: rdn wl over 1f out: hdd jst ins fnl f: nt pce of wnr but kpt on to hold 2nd pl* **8/1**

60-4 **3** 1 **Exclamation**[17] 1299 4-9-7 **100** EddieAhern 10 103
(B J Meehan) *hld up off the pce in midfield: rdn and effrt 2f out: swtchd rt over 1f out: styd on u.p fnl f to go 3rd nr fin: nvr trbld ldrs* **11/2**[1]

3245 **4** nse **Orpsie Boy (IRE)**[17] 1299 6-9-5 **98** LDettori 6 101
(N P Littmoden) *bhd: rdn 2f out: hdwy u.p 1f out: styd on wl: nt rch ldrs* **6/1**[2]

032- **5** hd **Wise Melody**[249] 5403 4-8-8 **87** WilliamBuick 3 89
(W J Haggas) *broke wl: led for 1f: trckd ldrs after: rdn to chse ldr 2f out tl ent fnl f: one pce after: lost 2 pls nr fin* **20/1**

00-0 **6** 1/2 **Mac Gille Eoin**[17] 1299 5-9-0 **93** JimCrowley 18 93
(J Gallagher) *lw: pressed ldrs: rdn over 2f out: outpcd jst over 1f out: plugged on same pce fnl f* **16/1**

2543 **7** 2 **Mutamared (USA)**[16] 1321 9-8-8 **87** ow1 (t) NCallan 17 81
(K A Ryan) *chsd ldrs: rdn over 2f out: wknd u.p over 1f out* **16/1**

36-6 **8** 1 **Oldjoesaid**[16] 1325 5-9-8 **101** FergusSweeney 8 92
(H Candy) *dwlt and short of room sn after s: a towards rr: rdn and effrt over 2f out: kpt on but nvr nr ldrs* **14/1**

403- **9** 1/2 **Shifting Star (IRE)**[191] 6947 4-9-5 **98** AdamKirby 11 87
(W R Swinburn) *s.i.s: a towards rr: rdn and hdwy jst over 2f out: no prog fnl f* **11/1**

40-6 **10** 3/4 **Spanish Bounty**[16] 1321 4-9-1 **94** TPQueally 16 81
(J G Portman) *chsd ldr tl led after 1f: rdn 1/2-way: sn hdd: wknd over 1f out* **20/1**

10-6 **11** 2 1/4 **Prohibit**[17] 1299 4-9-10 **103** JimmyFortune 14 83
(J H M Gosden) *broke wl: stdd into midfield after 1f: grad lost pl and bhd 1/2-way: no ch whn nt clr run ins fnl f* **12/1**

22-0 **12** nk **Fantasy Explorer**[13] 1398 6-8-8 **87** PatCosgrave 2 66
(J J Quinn) *stdd s: hld up in tch: rdn and nt qckn 2f out: wknd fnl f* **20/1**

00-4 **13** 2 1/2 **Baby Strange**[16] 1321 5-8-13 **92** DarrenWilliams 15 63
(D Shaw) *racd off the pce in midfield: shortlived effrt over 2f out: sn wl btn* **12/1**

-550 **14** 1 **My Gacho (IRE)**[15] 1365 7-8-4 **83** (b) JimmyQuinn 13 50
(M Johnston) *chsd ldrs: rdn 1/2-way: sn losing pl: wl bhd over 1f out* **40/1**

6-32 **15** 1 **Blue Jack**[12] 1418 4-7-8 **78** AndreaAtzeni(5) 4 42
(W R Muir) *t.k.h: hld up bhd: nvr a factor* **20/1**

510- **16** 6 **Countdown**[170] 7313 7-8-5 **84** ow1 AlanMunro 19 29
(M D Squance) *s.i.s: a outpcd in last pair* **66/1**

40-3 **17** 1/2 **Fullandby (IRE)**[16] 1325 7-9-7 **100** RyanMoore 21 43
(T J Etherington) *lw: s.i.s: sn outpcd and detached in last pl* **8/1**

69.90 secs (-2.30) **Going Correction** -0.15s/f (Firm) course record **17** Ran SP% **129.5**
Speed ratings (Par 109): **109,104,103,103,103 102,99,98,97,96 93,93,89,88,87 79,78**
toteswingers: 1&2 £6.70, 1&3 £5.90, 2&3 £7.70 CSF £59.61 CT £356.16 TOTE £7.50: £2.20, £2.40, £2.10, £2.00; EX 79.40 Trifecta £400.80 Pool £1,625.10 - 3 winning units..

Owner Dab Hand Racing **Bred** Old Carhue Stud **Trained** Sessay, N Yorks

FOCUS

A competitive heritage handicap, and solid form, with the winner right back to his best. The field raced up the centre.

NOTEBOOK

Evens And Odds(IRE), who had been first home on his side on his debut for Nicholls at Doncaster, raced on the near side of the bunch out of stall 1. He came under pressure earlier than most, but picked up really well and powered away after leading inside the last. After falling in the weights by a stone over the past year he will be hit by the handicapper for this, but he could be well handicapped if turning out quickly in the Victoria Cup and in the longer term should still be competitive in races like the Wokingham and Stewards' Cup this summer. He is clearly fully effective without headgear. (op 8-1 tchd 13-2 and 9-1 in a place)

Thebes led travelling smoothly, and although he could not hold on after edging slightly to his left, it was no disgrace to find only the well handicapped winner too strong. He is well capable if he feels like it but is not always on a going day, although there has not been much wrong with his last few efforts. (op 10-1 tchd 11-1)

Exclamation ran well in the Listed Abernant Stakes won by Evens And Odds's stablemate Tax Free at the Craven meeting and this was another good run, as he kept on down the far side of the pack to snatch third. Winner of a big pot in a sales race here at two, he has run only seven times in his life and has improvement in him. (op 6-1 tchd 5-1)

Orpsie Boy(IRE), put up 5lb following his good run in the Abernant, ran on steadily from the rear for fourth. This was a good run, but he is without a turf win since July 2007 and his current mark will not make it easy for him to put that right. (op 10-1)

Wise Melody got a flyer as her stall, and that of Blue Jack, opened fractionally ahead of the others. Always prominent and only run out of third place close home, this was a satisfactory first run since August. (op 16-1)

Mac Gille Eoin showed his customary bright pace and should prove competitive from a favourable mark in the coming weeks, perhaps at downhill tracks like Epsom and Goodwood.

Mutamared(USA) won this race three years ago and was second the following season. He is not quite as good as he was then, but he has come down the weights and this was still a creditable return to turf following a profitable winter on the sand.

Oldjoesaid, whose yard's sprinters are in good form, could never get into the race following a slow start but was keeping on at the end. (tchd 16-1 in places)

Shifting Star(IRE) was progressive last season, winning three times, but never really figured on this seasonal bow. He has a fine record at Ascot and is being targeted at the Wokingham there next month. (op 12-1)

Spanish Bounty disputed the lead with Mac Gille Eoin but faded going to the final furlong. He continues to look vulnerable off this sort of mark. (op 18-1 tchd 16-1)

Prohibit showed a rather awkward head carriage. He lost his pitch at halfway but was in the process of running on when he ran out of room around a furlong out. With a current three-figure mark he may prove difficult to place. Official explanation: jockey said gelding was unsuited by the good to firm (firm in places) ground

Fantasy Explorer

Baby Strange, 5lb higher than when fourth in this last year - he went on to win next time out - was one of the first beaten and was disappointing. He was reported to have been unsuited by the ground. Official explanation: jockey said gelding was unsuited by the good to firm (firm in places) ground (tchd 14-1)

Fullandby(IRE) who has been given speculative entries in the King's Stand and Golden Jubilee at Ascot, was third in this in 2008 but trailed throughout this time and failed to give his running. Official explanation: jockey said gelding was unsuited by the good to firm (firm in places) ground (op 17-2 tchd 9-1)

1700 STANJAMES.COM MAIDEN STKS 5f

4:25 (4:26) (Class 2) 2-Y-O **£9,714** (£2,890; £1,444; £721) **Stalls** Low

Form RPR

1 **High Spice (USA)** 2-8-12 0 EddieAhern 2 85+
(R M H Cowell) *str: lw: mde all: rdn 2f out: r.o wl fnl f* **10/1**

2 1 1/4 **Radiohead** 2-9-3 0 JamieSpencer 6 86+
(B J Meehan) *w'like: leggy: rn green and sn detached in last pl: gd hdwy jst over 2f out: chsd wnr wl over 1f out: rdn and tried to chal 1f out: sn hung rt and one pce* **6/4**[1]

3 3 3/4 **Izaaj (USA)** 2-9-3 0 (t) LDettori 4 72
(Saeed Bin Suroor) *w'like: athletic: outpcd in last pair: pushed along over 3f out: hdwy and rdn over 2f out: chsd ldng pair ent fnl f: sn hung lft and no prog* **4/1**[3]

4 1 1/2 **Ejaab** 2-9-3 0 RHills 1 67
(W J Haggas) *w'like: scope: sn bustled along: in tch: rdn jst over 2f out: outpcd over 1f out: wl btn fnl f* **9/2**

5 3 **Mahiki** 2-8-12 0 MartinDwyer 5 51
(S A Callaghan) *w'like: leggy: t.k.h: chsd ldrs: rdn and rn green 2f out: wknd over 1f out* **25/1**

6 2 1/4 **Footstepsofspring (FR)** 2-9-3 0 RichardHughes 7 48
(R Hannon) *w'like: str: bit bkwd: chsd wnr tl lost pl qckly wl over 1f out: wl bhd fnl f* **7/2**[2]

59.03 secs (-0.07) **Going Correction** -0.15s/f (Firm) **6** Ran SP% **113.3**
Speed ratings (Par 99): **94,92,86,83,78 75**
toteswingers: 1&2 £4.80, 1&3 £4.20, 2&3 £2.20 CSF £26.09 TOTE £13.10: £3.60, £1.60; EX 24.40.

Owner Khalifa Dasmal **Bred** Dell Ridge Farm Llc **Trained** Six Mile Bottom, Cambs

FOCUS

A reasonable maiden contested by six newcomers, although it is unlikely there was anything in the field as good as last year's winner Finjaan. The field finished strung out.

NOTEBOOK

High Spice(USA) ◆, a $110,000 yearling, has an American dirt pedigree. She knew her job and showed good pace, burning off Footstepsofspring before pulling out more to repel the runner-up. She looks a decent early juvenile and is probably good enough to take her chance in the Queen Mary at Royal Ascot, where she is likely to head next. (op 9-1 tchd 14-1)

Radiohead ◆, a 78,000gns yearling, was markedly green. Slow to break and detached in last at halfway, he cut through the pack to deliver a challenge to the winner but hung and was not really helping his rider. His yard's juveniles often improve for their debut experience and he should be no exception, with an ordinary maiden surely there for the taking. (op 15-8 tchd 2-1)

Izaaj(USA), a rare early two-year-old runner for Godolphin, took time to pick up what was understood of him but was staying on late. Out of a high-class dirt mare who was a half-sister to the smart filly Karen's Caper, he holds a Derby entry and will need further than this in time. (tchd 7-2)

Ejaab is a half-brother to several winners, but none of them as juveniles. He seems a real sprinter on looks and pedigree but he will need to improve on what he showed here. (tchd 4-1 and 5-1)

Mahiki, who cost £12,000 as a yearling, raced rather freely and was in trouble with a quarter of a mile left. (op 20-1)

Footstepsofspring(FR), a 72,000gns yearling, is out of a mare who is closely related to German 2,000 Guineas winners Dupont and Pacino. He showed early pace to bustle up the leader but faded to finish well beaten. (tchd 100-30)

1701 STANJAMES.COM PRETTY POLLY STKS (LISTED RACE) (FILLIES) 1m 2f

5:00 (5:00) (Class 1) 3-Y-O

£28,385 (£10,760; £5,385; £2,685; £1,345; £675) **Stalls** Low

Form RPR

01- **1** **Take The Hint**[194] 6887 3-8-12 86 JimmyFortune 4 106
(J H M Gosden) *lw: in tch: rdn wl over 2f out: hdwy u.p 2f out: led over 1f out: edgd lft u.p fnl f: styd on wl* **15/2**[3]

20-1 **2** 1 1/4 **Three Moons (IRE)**[24] 1198 3-8-12 82 LDettori 8 103
(H J L Dunlop) *chsd ldrs tl led over 2f out: rdn and hdd over 1f out: kpt on u.p tl no ex wl ins fnl f* **16/1**

44-5 **3** 5 **Moneycantbuymelove (IRE)**[18] 1291 3-8-12 90 JamieSpencer 2 93
(M L W Bell) *lw: stdd and dropped in bhd after s: rdn and effrt wl over 2f out: no ch w ldng pair over 1f out: styd on u.p to go modest 3rd nr fin* **8/1**

13-4 **4** shd **The Miniver Rose (IRE)**[18] 1291 3-8-12 93 RichardHughes 5 93
(R Hannon) *chsd ldr: rdn over 3f out: drvn wl over 2f out: outpcd by ldng pair wl over 1f out: modest 3rd over 1f out tl nr fin* **11/4**[1]

104- **5** 4 1/2 **Pachattack (USA)**[212] 6439 3-8-12 98 EddieAhern 1 84
(G A Butler) *racd alone on stands' side: in tch: rdn 3f out: no ch w ldrs fnl 2f* **11/2**[2]

15- **6** 2 **Golden Stream (IRE)**[218] 6268 3-8-12 98 RyanMoore 7 80
(Sir Michael Stoute) *lw: led: rdn over 3f out: drvn and hdd over 2f out: wknd over 1f out: eased whn no ch ins fnl f* **11/4**[1]

02-1 **7** 24 **Natural Flair (USA)**[16] 1329 3-8-12 81 AlanMunro 6 32
(P W Chapple-Hyam) *in tch tl wknd qckly 3f out: eased fr 2f out: t.o* **10/1**

20-6 **8** 22 **Snoqualmie Girl (IRE)**[18] 1292 3-9-3 102 MartinDwyer 3 —
(D R C Elsworth) *hld up in rr: rdn 4f out: sn bhd: t.o and eased fnl 2f* **12/1**

2m 1.93s (-3.87) **Going Correction** -0.15s/f (Firm) **8** Ran SP% **114.3**
Speed ratings (Par 104): **109,108,104,103,100 98,79,61**
toteswingers: 1&2 £10.20, 1&3 £8.50, 2&3 £6.90 CSF £114.49 TOTE £8.00: £2.30, £2.40, £2.10; EX 102.50.

Owner K Abdulla **Bred** Juddmonte Farms Ltd **Trained** Newmarket, Suffolk

FOCUS

This looked an up-to-scratch renewal of the Pretty Polly beforehand, but the finish was fought out by two of the three fillies with the lowest official ratings, with the three highest rated out the back, so the form does not look too strong and the race is unlikely to have much of a bearing on the Oaks. The first pair showed improvement and the form has been rated around the third and fourth. All bar Pachattack raced up the centre of the course.

NOTEBOOK

Take The Hint, who accounted for Natural Flair when winning a Yarmouth maiden on her second run at two, came under pressure over a quarter of a mile out before coming with a sweeping run to challenge the leader. She had to work a bit to get on top but stayed on well and showed improved form. She could go for the Oaks, in which her grandam All At Sea finished second, but has a lot to find still and her yard has Rainbow View for Epsom, so the Ribblesdale looks a more suitable target. She should stay 1m4f. (op 13-2 tchd 6-1)

Three Moons(IRE), successful in a maiden on her reappearance and by the same sire as the winner, showed improved form and went down fighting. This looks her trip and she can pick up a race in this grade. (op 14-1)
Moneycantbuymelove(IRE) stayed on quite well for third after becoming outpaced, without troubling the front pair. Turning around previous form with The Miniver Rose, she should not remain a maiden for too long and may benefit for a step up to 1m4f. (tchd 11-1)
The Miniver Rose(IRE) had twice finished ahead of Moneycantbuymelove but was just caught for third by that filly, after the front pair had pulled clear of her. Now might be the time to step her up in trip. (op 7-2)
Pachattack(USA), the subject of good recent reports, raced solo down the stands' side and was beaten with two furlongs to run. She may be worth another chance but still has to prove that she stays this far. (op 9-1)
Golden Stream(IRE), reportedly in season when fifth in the Fillies' Mile on her second run at two, set the pace but dropped out disappointingly, after briefly looking to have her rivals in trouble. She has plenty to prove now. (op 5-2 tchd 3-1 in a place)
Natural Flair(USA) faced a difficult task on these terms but clearly failed to reproduce her Yarmouth form from last season with Take The Hint on this different ground. (op 9-1 tchd 11-1)
Snoqualmie Girl(IRE) was giving away 5lb all round but was expected to improve for the step up to this trip. She dropped right away to finish tailed off and failed to handle the ground. Official explanation: jockey said filly was unsuited by the good to firm (firm in places) ground (op 10-1)

1702 TEXT STANS TO 89700 H'CAP — 1m 2f
5:35 (5:35) (Class 2) (0-100,90) 3-Y-£12,462 (£3,732; £1,866; £934; £466) Stalls Low

Form — RPR
51-3 **1** **Takaatuf (IRE)**[31] 1086 3-8-13 85 ... RHills 8 — 91
(M Johnston) *mde all: rdn 2f out: hrd pressed and edgd lft 1f out: styd on wl u.p to assert fnl 100yds* **9/4**[2]
32-1 **2** 1 1/4 **Dubai Crest**[18] 1280 3-9-1 87 ... JimCrowley 4 — 91
(Mrs A J Perrett) *lw: w.w in tch: rdn and effrt 3f out: ev ch and drvn ent fnl f: no ex and btn fnl 100yds* **2/1**[1]
01- **3** 3 1/2 **Opinion Poll (IRE)**[201] 6720 3-9-3 89 ... LDettori 3 — 88+
(M A Jarvis) *hld up in tch: hdwy to trck ldrs 4f out: rdn 3f out: hdwy to press ldrs jst over 1f out: wknd ins fnl f* **11/4**[3]
120- **4** 1 3/4 **Guestofthenation (USA)**[186] 7067 3-8-13 85 ... GregFairley 2 — 78
(M Johnston) *chsd ldr: rdn over 3f out: drvn and wknd over 1f out* **7/1**
13-0 **5** 8 **Al Sabaheya**[36] 1001 3-9-0 86 ... NCallan 1 — 63
(C E Brittain) *hld up in tch: effrt and rdn 3f out: wknd u.p wl over 1f out: eased ins fnl f* **12/1**

2m 3.42s (-2.38) **Going Correction** -0.15s/f (Firm) — **5** Ran SP% **111.0**
Speed ratings (Par 105): **103,102,99,97,91**
toteswingers: 1&2 £3.70 CSF £7.24 TOTE £3.50: £1.80, £1.70; EX 6.40 Place 6 £648.76, Place 5 £276.87..
Owner Hamdan Al Maktoum **Bred** Ballyreddin Stud **Trained** Middleham Moor, N Yorks

FOCUS
With four non-runners owing to the fast ground, including the Hannon pair who would have shared top weight, there was not much of a turnout for this fairly valuable prize. The action again took place down the centre. The winner made all and has more to offer.

NOTEBOOK
Takaatuf(IRE), his owner's second string before the withdrawal of Mutamaashi, made all the running at just a steady gallop and kept pulling out extra to hold off a couple of challengers. He was put up 2lb for a good reappearance effort at Leicester, but the handicapper has clearly not got a hold of him just yet and he remains admirably progressive. A step up to 1m4f should not trouble him and he might be the type for the King George V Handicap at Royal Ascot. (op 2-1 tchd 11-4)
Dubai Crest was raised 10lb for his Beverley win and that told in the end, although he had every chance. A truer gallop would have benefited him but he has something to prove from his elevated mark. (op 5-2)
Opinion Poll(IRE) ran respectably over this longer trip but wandered in the latter stages, as if unhappy on the fast ground, and was eased. His Leicester maiden win at the back-end had come on an easier surface. (op 2-1)
Guestofthenation(USA) chased his winning stablemate on this seasonal bow before weakening out of contention inside the final two furlongs. His two previous runs on turf had been in soft ground and these firm conditions may not have been ideal for him. (op 10-1 tchd 13-2)
Al Sabaheya, another who had yet to tackle fast conditions, was the first beaten. She may not have stayed here but her two runs this year have not proved that she has trained on. (op 14-1 tchd 9-1)
T/Jkpt: Not won. T/Plt: £508.20 to a £1 stake. Pool: £165,953.62. 238.35 winning tickets. T/Qpdt: £255.90 to a £1 stake. Pool: £6,605.96. 19.10 winning tickets. SP

SALISBURY (R-H)
Sunday, May 3
OFFICIAL GOING: Good to firm (firm in places; 9.6)
Wind: Fresh against Weather: Sunny

1703 TOTEPLACEPOT MAIDEN STKS (DIV I) — 6f
1:10 (1:14) (Class 5) 3-Y-O+ £3,885 (£1,156; £577; £288) Stalls High

Form — RPR
1 **Romanticize** 3-8-9 0 ... TedDurcan 2 — 69
(Dr J D Scargill) *hld up bhd: struggling and running green 3f out: str run ent fnl f: edgd rt: led nr fin* **33/1**
02 **2** 3/4 **Cape Melody**[26] 1173 3-8-9 0 ... SteveDrowne 11 — 67
(H Morrison) *trckd ldrs: rdn 2f out: kpt on to ld ins fnl f: hdd nr fin* **4/1**[2]
24 **3** 3/4 **George Thisby**[20] 1250 3-8-11 0 ... JamesMillman(3) 13 — 69
(B R Millman) *led: rdn and drifted lft over 1f out: hdd ins fnl f: no ex* **9/2**[3]
20- **4** nse **The Desert Saint**[353] 2124 3-8-11 0 ... DavidProbert(3) 4 — 69
(A M Balding) *mid-div: swtchd lft 2f out: sn rdn: r.o fnl f: clsng at fin* **6/1**
06- **5** 2 1/4 **Ariadnes Filly (IRE)**[205] 6620 3-8-9 0 ... TonyCulhane 12 — 57
(Mrs A J Perrett) *mid-div: hdwy 2f out: sn rdn: kpt on same pce fnl f* **10/1**
3 **6** nk **Tender Charm (USA)**[29] 1120 3-9-0 0 ... SebSanders 1 — 61
(R M Beckett) *s.i.s: bhd: rdn 3f out: styd on fnl f: nvr a danger* **12/1**
0- **7** 3/4 **Spring Green**[286] 4251 3-8-9 0 ... TravisBlock 7 — 54+
(H Morrison) *w ldr: rdn and ev ch whn drifted lft over 1f out: fdd ins fnl f* **12/1**
0 **8** 3/4 **Cardinal**[14] 1380 4-9-7 0 ... KevinGhunowa(3) 10 — 59
(R A Harris) *hld up towards rr: rdn 3f out: sme late prog: nvr a factor* **33/1**
/00- **9** 1 3/4 **Shybutwilling (IRE)**[242] 5608 4-9-5 39 ... TGMcLaughlin 8 — 49
(Mrs P N Dutfield) *a towards rr* **100/1**
10 6 **Zip Lock (IRE)** 3-9-0 0 ... ShaneKelly 14 — 31
(J Noseda) *trckd ldrs: rdn over 2f out: hung lft and wknd over 1f out* **15/8**[1]
060 **11** 3/4 **Camelot Queen**[48] 849 4-9-5 40 ... IanMongan 5 — 27
(W S Kittow) *trckd ldrs: rdn over 2f out: sn wknd* **50/1**
12 70 **Santefisio** 3-9-0 0 ... DO'Donohoe 6 — —
(P J Makin) *dwlt: a wl bhd* **33/1**

1m 14.21s (-0.59) **Going Correction** -0.075s/f (Good)
WFA 3 from 4yo 10lb — **12** Ran SP% **123.5**
Speed ratings (Par 103): **100,99,98,97,94 94,93,92,90,82 81,—**
toteswingers: 1&2 £50.90, 1&3 £41.50, 2&3 £4.40 CSF £164.66 TOTE £54.90: £10.10, £1.90, £2.10; EX 268.30.
Owner Mrs Susan Scargill **Bred** Cheveley Park Stud Ltd **Trained** Newmarket, Suffolk

FOCUS
An ordinary sprint maiden in which the main action took place more towards the centre of the course. The race has been rated through the placed horses, but the proximity of the eighth and ninth limits the form.
Santefisio Official explanation: jockey said gelding missed the break

1704 TOTEPLACEPOT MAIDEN STKS (DIV II) — 6f
1:45 (1:45) (Class 5) 3-Y-O+ £3,885 (£1,156; £577; £288) Stalls High

Form — RPR
0- **1** **Rapid Water**[198] 6776 3-9-0 0 ... LPKeniry 11 — 75+
(A M Balding) *trckd ldrs: swtchd lft 2f out: led over 1f out: kpt on wl: pushed out* **4/1**[2]
42- **2** 3 **Hajoum (IRE)**[269] 4792 3-9-0 0 ... (t) TedDurcan 4 — 65+
(Saeed Bin Suroor) *raced keenly trcking ldrs: led over 2f out: rdn and hdd over 1f out: sn hld: fading nr fin* **4/5**[1]
3 1/2 **Hightime Heroine (IRE)** 3-8-9 0 ... ShaneKelly 3 — 59+
(J Noseda) *t.k.h in tch: bmpd 3f out: swtchd rt over 2f out: sn rdn: styd on ins fnl f* **9/1**
4-5 **4** nk **Bahkov (IRE)**[15] 1350 3-9-0 0 ... RichardKingscote 13 — 63
(Tom Dascombe) *led for 3f: sn rdn to chse ldrs: kpt on gamely ins fnl f* **11/1**
-000 **5** 3/4 **Dancing Rhythm**[7] 1539 4-9-10 44 ... TolleyDean 10 — 63
(M S Saunders) *w ldr: led 3f: sn rdn and hdd: kpt on but no ex fr over 1f out* **66/1**
0 **6** 1/2 **Wotasparkler**[16] 1327 3-8-9 0 ... MickyFenton 5 — 54
(W S Kittow) *hld up towards rr: hdwy 3f out: sn rdn and hung rt: styd on same pce fnl f* **33/1**
60-0 **7** 4 **Tiger Trail (GER)**[12] 1419 5-9-10 57 ... GeorgeBaker 6 — 49
(Mrs N Smith) *hld up towards rr: hdwy whn nt clr run over 2f out: sme late prog: nvr trbld ldrs* **25/1**
8 4 1/2 **Viva Averti** 4-9-10 0 ... RichardThomas 2 — 35
(Christian Wroe) *hung rt fr over 2f out: mainly towards rr* **50/1**
04- **9** nk **Print (IRE)**[227] 6062 3-9-0 0 ... TonyCulhane 1 — 31
(M R Channon) *trckd ldrs: rdn over 2f out: wknd over 1f out* **8/1**[3]
0 **10** 3 **Captain Peachey**[20] 1252 3-9-0 0 ... TGMcLaughlin 7 — 21
(B R Millman) *trckd ldrs: rdn over 3f out: sn wknd and hung rt* **50/1**
0 **11** 1 3/4 **Phoenix Rising**[81] 503 3-8-9 0 ... TravisBlock 9 — 10
(H Morrison) *s.i.s: sn mid-div: outpcd 3f out* **33/1**

1m 13.7s (-1.10) **Going Correction** -0.075s/f (Good)
WFA 3 from 4yo+ 10lb — **11** Ran SP% **120.1**
Speed ratings (Par 103): **104,100,99,98,97 97,91,85,85,81 79**
toteswingers: 1&2 £1.60, 1&3 £5.60, 2&3 £3.00 CSF £7.39 TOTE £5.30: £1.60, £1.10, £2.70; EX 11.20.
Owner J C Smith **Bred** Littleton Stud **Trained** Kingsclere, Hants

FOCUS
This second division of the maiden looked another average affair. It was run in a time nearly a second quicker than the opener. The proximity of the fifth raises doubts over the level of the form, though.
Bahkov(IRE) Official explanation: jockey said colt was unsuited by the track
Viva Averti Official explanation: jockey said gelding hung left-handed

1705 TOTESUPER7 H'CAP — 6f
2:15 (2:17) (Class 2) (0-100,99) 3-Y-O
£12,462 (£3,732; £1,866; £934; £466; £234) Stalls High

Form — RPR
602- **1** **Instalment**[214] 6399 3-9-7 99 ... PatDobbs 6 — 103
(R Hannon) *racd keenly: trckd ldr: led wl over 1f out: hrd pressed thrght fnl f: hld on: rdn out* **12/1**
14-0 **2** nk **Timeteam (IRE)**[16] 1324 3-8-7 85 ... LPKeniry 3 — 88
(S Kirk) *in tch: tk clsr order over 2f out: rdn and ev ch thrght fnl f: kpt on but no ex nr fin* **20/1**
44-2 **3** nk **Cheviot (USA)**[17] 1305 3-8-8 86 ... (p) ShaneKelly 5 — 88+
(M A Jarvis) *hld up: tk clsr order over 1f out: swtchd lft ent fnl f: rdn and r.o wl: nt quite get up* **9/2**[3]
061- **4** 1 **Global City (IRE)**[200] 6739 3-9-2 94 ... (t) TedDurcan 4 — 94+
(Saeed Bin Suroor) *trckd ldrs: rdn but n.m.r fr over 1f out: nt pce to mount chal: hld whn squeezed out nr fin* **13/2**
15-1 **5** 1 **Dark Mischief**[18] 1296 3-9-3 95 ... DaneO'Neill 10 — 91
(H Candy) *led: rdn and hdd wl over 1f out: kpt on but no ex* **6/4**[1]
1300 **6** nse **Smokey Ryder**[18] 1293 3-9-0 95 ... KevinGhunowa(3) 8 — 91
(R A Harris) *chsd ldrs: rdn over 2f out: kpt on same pce* **28/1**
-210 **7** hd **Daddy's Gift (IRE)**[16] 1324 3-8-7 85 ... RichardMullen 9 — 80
(R Hannon) *hld up: hdwy and nt clr run bhd wall of horses 2f out: rdn and kpt on wout ever threatening* **14/1**
06-4 **8** 6 **Felday**[16] 1324 3-8-6 84 ... SteveDrowne 2 — 60
(H Morrison) *trckd ldrs: rdn over 2f out: wkng whn squeezed out ent fnl f* **7/2**[2]
305- **9** 18 **Countrywide City (IRE)**[200] 6739 3-7-13 80 oh1 ... DavidProbert(3) 1 — —
(Jane Southcombe) *in tch: rdn 3f out: sn btn* **66/1**

1m 14.08s (-0.72) **Going Correction** -0.075s/f (Good) — **9** Ran SP% **117.8**
Speed ratings (Par 105): **101,100,100,98,97 97,97,89,65**
toteswingers: 1&2 £34.20, 1&3 £8.30, 2&3 £23.40 CSF £217.03 CT £1248.25 TOTE £11.80: £2.70, £5.80, £1.90; EX 205.80 TRIFECTA Not won..
Owner The Queen **Bred** The Queen **Trained** East Everleigh, Wilts

FOCUS
This was a decent three-year-old sprint handicap, run at a solid pace. The first seven were closely covered at the finish and the form looks muddling.

NOTEBOOK
Instalment got his new campaign off to a winning start and has now scored first time up in successive seasons. He proved game to fend off rivals at the business end, despite having failed to settle early on, and his success is made more meritorious as he carried top weight. His pedigree suggests he will enjoy racing over further, but the drop back in distance actually helped and he has a future as a sprinter. However, his connections are reportedly hopeful he may take in the Jersey Stakes at Royal Ascot next month, back over another furlong. Whichever way he goes, there should be more to come from him. (op 10-1 tchd 8-1)
Timeteam(IRE) showed the benefit of his seasonal return 16 days earlier and shaped much better for the furlong-shorter trip. He travelled sweetly and is capable of winning this term. (op 25-1)

Cheviot(USA), 3lb higher, was equipped with first-time cheekpieces and got heavily restrained early on. He took an age to pick up and does look to have his quirks, but this was still another personal-best effort. He helps to set the level of the form and can no doubt defy this sort of mark at some stage during the summer. (op 6-1 tchd 7-1)

Global City(IRE) performed close to his mark on this seasonal debut and is a little better than the bare margin, as he endured a rough passage nearing the final furlong. He should come on for the run and likely has a bit more to offer as a three-year-old. (op 17-2 tchd 10-1)

Dark Mischief was 9lb higher than when winning on his return at Newmarket 18 days earlier, but still had a very unexposed look about him and is from a yard that has excelled with such types. He simply proved too free on the early pace and was cooked at the furlong pole, but it would be unwise to write him off on the back of this run. (op 11-10 tchd 7-4)

Smokey Ryder enjoyed the drop back in class and shaped a little better than the bare form, as she did not get the best of passages against the far rail. She may not be weighted out of winning again just yet and does relish racing off a decent pace. (op 33-1 tchd 25-1)

Daddy's Gift(IRE) was unable to confirm Kempton form with the fifth, but she made a sluggish start and did not get the best of runs late on. She was far from disgraced in the circumstances. (op 10-1 tchd 9-1)

Felday proved unsuited by this sharper test, but got restless in the stalls and had no cover through the race. He is better than this on his day. Official explanation: jockey said colt suffered interference in running (op 5-1 tchd 11-2)

1706 TOTESWINGER FILLIES' CONDITIONS STKS 5f

2:50 (2:50) (Class 3) 2-Y-O **£6,799** (£2,023; £1,011; £505) **Stalls** High

Form RPR

1 **1** **Leleyf (IRE)**[34] 1031 2-8-9 0 TonyCulhane 5 77
(M R Channon) *mde all: edgd rt u.p ins fnl f: kpt on: drvn out* **5/2**[2]

2 ½ **Kurtanella** 2-8-7 0 ow1 DaneO'Neill 4 73
(R Hannon) *s.i.s: bhd: rdn 2f out: r.o wl but drifted rt ins fnl f: wnt 2nd nr fin* **6/1**

0 **3** *nk* **Mrs Boss**[8] 1504 2-8-10 0 ow4 JamesMillman[(3)] 2 78
(B R Millman) *wnt lft and bmpd s: cl up: rdn to chse wnr 2f out: kpt on but no ex whn lost 2nd nr fin* **16/1**

4 3½ **White Daffodil (IRE)** 2-8-6 0 PatDobbs 1 59
(R Hannon) *wnt rt and bmpd s: hld up: rdn and drifted lft fr over 2f out: wnt 4th ins fnl f: nvr on terms* **13/2**

01 **5** 3¾ **Lady Lion**[15] 1364 2-8-5 0 ow1 JackDean[(5)] 3 49
(W G M Turner) *chsd wnr: rdn over 2f out: wknd ent fnl f* **12/1**

2 **6** *1* **Emma Jean Lass (IRE)**[34] 1031 2-8-9 0 LPKeniry 7 44
(J S Moore) *chsd ldrs: rdn over 2f out: wknd over 1f out* **5/1**[3]

7 *nk* **Lutine Lady** 2-8-6 0 StephenCarson 6 40
(P Winkworth) *plld v hrd trcking ldrs: rough passage early on: rdn 2f out: wknd ent fnl f* **9/4**[1]

62.37 secs (1.37) **Going Correction** -0.075s/f (Good) 7 Ran SP% **117.2**
Speed ratings (Par 94): **84,83,82,77,71 69,69**
toteswingers: 1&2 £3.10, 1&3 £10.20, 2&3 £12.50 CSF £18.63 TOTE £3.50: £2.10, £3.00; EX 20.30.
Owner Box 41 **Bred** Mrs Noelle Walsh **Trained** West Ilsley, Berks

FOCUS
A fair little conditions event featuring two previous winners.

NOTEBOOK
Leleyf(IRE) looked to possess a bit of stamina when just getting up to pip Emma Jean Lass on her Lingfield Polytrack debut in March, so this stiffer track was always likely to play to her strengths. Soon in front, she made every yard and showed a good attitude through the last furlong to hold on. She looks worth another step up in class and should appreciate another furlong. (tchd 11-4)

Kurtanella ◆, a £20,000 filly, has a very speedy pedigree. Representing a stable with an excellent record in this race, she didn't break too well and took a while to realise what was required, but she eventually gathered herself together and finished in good style to run the winner close. She ought to have learned plenty from this outing and shouldn't take long in going one better. (tchd 7-1)

Mrs Boss, whose rider put up 4lb overweight, was much more organised than on her Haydock debut and stayed on nicely. Another step forward should enable her to hit the target before too long. (op 14-1 tchd 12-1)

White Daffodil(IRE), a stablemate of the runner-up, is a 35,000euros half-sister to four winners, including the smart Lady Links. Like her stablemate, she looked green, probably more so, as she hung markedly away to her left as the race developed, but she did show some ability and should leave this behind. (op 6-1 tchd 5-1)

Lutine Lady met strong support ahead of this racecourse bow and is clearly well regarded, but she gave herself little chance by refusing to settle. Official explanation: jockey said filly had a breathing problem (op 3-1 tchd 100-30)

1707 TOTEEXACTA H'CAP 1m 1f 198y

3:25 (3:26) (Class 4) (0-85,83) 3-Y-O **£4,857** (£1,445; £722; £360) **Stalls** High

Form RPR

00-2 **1** **Brunston**[25] 1176 3-8-12 **74** SebSanders 2 81+
(R Charlton) *hld up towards rr: hdwy over 4f out: led 2f out: sn rdn: wandered ent fnl f: kpt on wl: rdn out* **7/2**[1]

-221 **2** ¾ **Barwell Bridge**[105] 209 3-9-7 **83** JamesDoyle 3 88
(S Kirk) *hld up bhd: rdn over 2f out: little imp tl styd on strly ins fnl f: snatched 2nd nr fin* **10/1**

4136 **3** *nk* **Doncosaque (IRE)**[17] 1303 3-9-3 **79** IanMongan 5 83
(P Howling) *hld up bhd: swtchd lft and stdy prog whn rdn over 2f out: styd on strly to chse wnr wl ins fnl f: lost 2nd nr fin* **12/1**

1-60 **4** *2* **Nawaadi (USA)**[17] 1303 3-9-0 **76** RichardMullen 10 76
(J H M Gosden) *led: rdn and hdd 2f out: kpt on same pce* **4/1**[2]

63-1 **5** *hd* **Ultimate**[110] 151 3-9-0 **76** SteveDrowne 6 76
(H Morrison) *trckd ldr: rdn and ev ch 2f out: kpt on same pce* **13/2**

3-33 **6** *nse* **Princability (IRE)**[18] 1280 3-9-0 **76** TonyCulhane 4 76
(M R Channon) *hld up towards rr: pushed along and hdwy 3f out: sn rdn: chsd ldrs ent fnl f: kpt on same pce* **6/1**[3]

04-0 **7** 3¼ **Jazacosta (USA)**[18] 1284 3-8-13 **75** (p) TedDurcan 7 68
(Mrs A J Perrett) *trckd ldrs: rdn over 2f out: wknd ins fnl f* **7/1**

0-15 **8** 1½ **Fong's Alibi**[60] 755 3-9-0 **76** LPKeniry 9 66
(J S Moore) *trckd ldrs: rdn over 2f out: sn btn* **25/1**

4232 **9** *hd* **Morning Sir Alan**[12] 1428 3-9-0 **76** (p) ShaneKelly 1 66
(S A Callaghan) *in tch: rdn to chal over 2f out: wknd over 1f out* **8/1**

2m 9.84s (-0.06) **Going Correction** -0.075s/f (Good) 9 Ran SP% **114.1**
Speed ratings (Par 101): **97,96,96,94,94 94,91,90,90**
toteswingers: 1&2 £5.10, 1&3 £9.60, 2&3 £12.40 CSF £38.41 CT £375.40 TOTE £3.20: £1.60, £3.00, £4.30; EX 21.30.
Owner Seasons Holidays **Bred** Seasons Holidays **Trained** Beckhampton, Wilts

FOCUS
A fairly tight three-year-old handicap. Despite there being just a moderate early pace, the first three all came from behind and the form makes sense rated through the runner-up and third to their All-Weather marks.

1708 BET TOTEPOOL AT TOTESPORT.COM MAIDEN STKS 1m 4f

4:00 (4:01) (Class 5) 3-Y-O **£3,885** (£1,156; £577; £288) **Stalls** High

Form RPR

43-3 **1** **Clowance House**[16] 1328 3-9-3 79 TedDurcan 7 78+
(R Charlton) *mde all: rdn 2f out: styd on wl to assert fnl f: eased nr fin* **2/7**[1]

2 2¼ **Talimos (IRE)** 3-9-3 0 SebSanders 8 75+
(R M Beckett) *s.i.s: hld up: gd prog to chse wnr over 3f out: wandered u.p 2f out: kpt on for clr 2nd but a hld by wnr* **7/1**[2]

0-0 **3** *11* **Haafhd Time (IRE)**[16] 1329 3-8-12 0 RichardKingscote 5 52
(Tom Dascombe) *trckd wnr tl over 3f out: sn rdn: wknd ent fnl f* **20/1**

0 **4** 1¾ **Lucy's Perfect**[30] 1092 3-8-12 0 TGMcLaughlin 4 49
(B R Millman) *in tch: rdn over 3f out: sn btn: regained 4th ins fnl f* **20/1**

500- **5** *1* **Googoobarabajagal (IRE)**[193] 6893 3-9-3 52 IanMongan 6 53
(W S Kittow) *rrd leaving stalls: t.k.h in rr: hdwy 3f out: sn rdn: wknd over 1f out* **20/1**

6 *27* **Comprimario (IRE)** 3-9-3 0 PatDobbs 3 9
(J L Dunlop) *slowly away: a in rr: reminders over 5f out: sn lost tch* **9/1**[3]

00-0 **7** *8* **Jasper Cliff**[6] 1573 3-8-12 0 JackDean[(5)] 1 —
(Mark Gillard) *chsd ldrs: rdn over 5f out: wknd 3f out: t.o* **66/1**

2m 38.38s (0.38) **Going Correction** -0.075s/f (Good) 7 Ran SP% **116.0**
Speed ratings (Par 99): **95,93,86,85,84 66,61**
toteswingers: 1&2 £1.10, 1&3 £2.60, 2&3 £8.50 CSF £2.70 TOTE £1.40: £1.10, £2.00; EX 3.20.
Owner Seasons Holidays **Bred** Seasons Holidays **Trained** Beckhampton, Wilts

FOCUS
A modest maiden, run at a fair pace. The first two came well clear and the form has been rated around the fifth.

1709 BET TOTEPOOL ON 0800 221 221 H'CAP 1m 6f 21y

4:35 (4:36) (Class 2) (0-105,97) 4-Y-O+ **£11,215** (£3,358; £1,679; £840; £419) **Stalls** Far side

Form RPR

002- **1** **Woolfall Treasure**[37] 5054 4-9-0 **87** GeorgeBaker 3 94
(G L Moore) *racd in cl 4th: hdwy over 3f out: led 2f out: styd on wl ins fnl f: rdn out* **7/2**[3]

306- **2** 2¼ **Cool Judgement (IRE)**[204] 6646 4-9-10 **97** TedDurcan 1 101
(M A Jarvis) *hld up last of 5: hdwy over 2f out: rdn to chse wnr over 1f out: hld thrght fnl f* **9/4**[2]

30-3 **3** *nk* **Rajeh (IRE)**[11] 1458 6-9-5 **91** LiamJones 4 94
(J L Spearing) *trckd ldr: led over 3f out: sn rdn: hdd 2f out: sn lost 2nd: styd on towards fin* **13/8**[1]

-200 **4** *12* **Grande Caiman (IRE)**[29] 1117 5-9-7 **93** (b) PatDobbs 5 80
(R Hannon) *trckd ldrs: chal 3f out: wknd 2f out* **10/1**

53-6 **5** *20* **Jagger**[14] 1383 9-9-2 **88** ShaneKelly 6 47
(G A Butler) *led tl over 3f out: sn wknd and eased* **7/1**

3m 3.13s (-4.27) **Going Correction** -0.075s/f (Good)
WFA 4 from 5yo+ 1lb 5 Ran SP% **112.7**
Speed ratings (Par 109): **109,107,107,100,89**
toteswingers: 1&2 £5.50 CSF £12.05 TOTE £4.50: £2.10, £1.60; EX 12.40.
Owner Findlay & Bloom **Bred** Serpentine Bloodstock Et Al **Trained** Lower Beeding, W Sussex

FOCUS
A good-quality staying handicap, run at an average pace and rated around the winner.

NOTEBOOK
Woolfall Treasure did not progress as might have been expected over hurdles and had become a tricky ride in that sphere. This was his first run on the Flat since finishing second off a 1lb lower mark at Newbury last August and he went one better with a ready success. The ground looked ideal for him and, despite wandering a touch when in front, there was little faulting his attitude. He could well be an Ebor contender this season. (op 4-1)

Cool Judgement(IRE) was patiently ridden and came through to have his chance around two furlongs out. He found the weight concession to the winner beyond him and still has to prove he truly gets this far, but it was still a very respectable start to his campaign. (op 11-4 tchd 3-1)

Rajeh(IRE)'s last-time-out third to Hatton Flight looked better after that rival went in again at Newmarket earlier in the afternoon and he was well backed on this return to a stiffer test. He was ridden up to dispute the lead around five furlongs out and did not look to have any excuses, so perhaps he needs respite from the handicapper. (op 7-4 tchd 2-1)

Grande Caiman(IRE) was unable to go with the principals when it mattered on this return to turf and is struggling for form. (op 8-1 tchd 11-1)

Jagger, with the cheekpieces abandoned, was closely matched with the winner on Newbury form last year and was entitled to have improved for his comeback run a fortnight earlier. He stopped quickly around three furlongs out, however, and failed to run his race. (op 11-2 tchd 5-1)

1710 TOTESPORT HOME OF POOL BETTING LADY RIDERS' H'CAP 6f 212y

5:10 (5:10) (Class 6) (0-65,64) 4-Y-O+ **£2,935** (£910; £454; £227) **Stalls** High

Form RPR

2314 **1** **Shaded Edge**[29] 1121 5-10-7 **62** GemmaGracey-Davison 15 76
(D W P Arbuthnot) *chsd ldrs: led over 2f out: r.o wl: readily* **13/2**[2]

-034 **2** 4½ **Manchestermaverick (USA)**[65] 715 4-9-12 **58**(vt) MissVCartmel[(5)] 10 60
(H Morrison) *prom: rdn to chse wnr fr over 1f out: kpt on but a being hld: jst hld on for 2nd* **3/1**[1]

6130 **3** *hd* **Binnion Bay (IRE)**[46] 874 8-9-5 **53** oh1 ow3 (b) MrsNParry[(7)] 9 54
(J J Bridger) *s.i.s: bhd: stdy prog fr 2f out: styd on wl fnl f: jst failed to snatch 2nd* **20/1**

-600 **4** ¾ **Batchworth Blaise**[7] 1535 6-9-5 **53** MissCNosworthy[(7)] 2 52
(E A Wheeler) *hld up bhd: hdwy over 1f out: styd on wl fnl f* **33/1**

0-60 **5** ½ **Triple Dream**[16] 1320 4-9-13 **59** (p) MissSBradley[(5)] 6 57
(J M Bradley) *in tch: rdn over 2f out: kpt on fnl f* **28/1**

1234 **6** 1¼ **Melt (IRE)**[12] 1417 4-10-5 **60** (b) MrsSMoore 1 55
(R Hannon) *s.i.s: sn mid-div: rdn over 2f out: styd on fnl f* **7/1**[3]

2420 **7** ½ **Ten Pole Tudor**[8] 1530 4-10-4 **59** (p) MissADeniel 17 52
(R A Harris) *s.i.s: nvr bttr than mid-div* **16/1**

1226 **8** *3* **Interactive (IRE)**[46] 868 6-10-5 **60** MissEJJones 13 45
(Andrew Turnell) *chsd ldrs tl wknd over 1f out* **8/1**

4151 **9** ½ **Mocha Java**[73] 607 6-9-12 **60** MissLGray[(7)] 16 44
(M Salaman) *prom: led 4f out: hdd over 2f out: wknd ent fnl f* **10/1**

6160 **10** *1* **Corlough Mountain**[7] 1537 5-9-11 **57** ow6 MissMBryant[(5)] 7 38
(P Butler) *a towards rr* **16/1**

010- **11** 1½ **Zazous**[167] 7360 8-9-11 **52** MissLEllison 18 29
(J J Bridger) *chsd ldrs tl wknd 2f out* **14/1**

0360 **12** 1¾ **Tamino (IRE)**[67] 675 6-10-0 **60** (t) MissAWallace[(5)] 5 32
(P Howling) *chsd ldrs tl wknd 2f out* **16/1**

2-06 **13** ½ **The Grey One (IRE)**[7] 1539 6-10-2 **64** (p) MissHDavies[(7)] 11 35
(J M Bradley) *s.i.s: a towards rr* **11/1**

06-0 **14** *5* **Pintano**[8] 1528 4-10-3 **58**.. MissSBrotherton 8 15
(J M Bradley) *in tch tl wknd 2f out* **25/1**
0360 **15** *shd* **Isabella's Fancy**[54] 792 4-9-9 **50**........................ MissCHannaford 12 —
(A G Newcombe) *led tl 4f out: wknd 2f out* **28/1**
00-0 **16** *9* **Sovereignty (JPN)**[13] 1403 7-9-10 **58**.................. MissECrossman(7) 3 —
(D K Ivory) *hung bdly rt over 2f out: a in rr* **16/1**

1m 28.89s (-0.11) **Going Correction** -0.075s/f (Good) **16** Ran SP% **128.0**
Speed ratings (Par 101): **97,91,91,90,90 88,88,84,84,83 81,79,78,73,72 62**
toteswingers: 1&2 £6.60, 1&3 £38.90, 2&3 £24.10 CSF £25.68 CT £394.71 TOTE £9.20: £2.30, £1.40, £4.70, £5.70; EX 33.50 Place 6 £80.31, Place 5 £34.29..
Owner P M Claydon **Bred** Lady Whent **Trained** Compton, Berks

FOCUS
A typically wide-open race of its type, run at a routine pace. The level of the form is a bit guessy, but the runner-up looks a fairly solid guide.
T/Plt: £37.90 to a £1 stake. Pool: £42,915.66. 826.20 winning tickets. T/Qpdt: £15.10 to a £1 stake. Pool: £2,834.80. 138.30 winning tickets. TM

1711 - 1717a (Foreign Racing) - See Raceform Interactive

FRANKFURT (L-H)
Sunday, May 3

OFFICIAL GOING: Soft

1718a FRUHJAHRSPREIS DES BANKHAUSES METZLER (GROUP 3) 1m 2f
4:05 (4:16) 3-Y-O **£31,068** (£9,709; £4,854; £2,913)

RPR
1 **Glad Panther**[243] 3-9-2 .... WMongil 2 99
(Uwe Ostmann, Germany) *disp 4th: 4th st: chal appr fnl f: drvn to ld 100yds out: r.o* **11/2**[3]
2 *3/4* **Saphir (GER)** 3-9-2 .... AStarke 3 97
(P Schiergen, Germany) *led to 100yds out: no ex* **11/10**[1]
3 *1/2* **Night Magic (GER)**[224] 3-8-13 .... KKerekes 6 93
(W Figge, Germany) *hld up: 6th and c wd st: styd on fr over 1f out: nrest at fin* **44/5**
4 *2 1/2* **Torres (GER)** 3-9-2 .... JiriPalik 5 91
(Frau E Mader, Germany) *disputing 2nd and pulling early: 3rd st: one pce fr over 1f out* **16/5**[2]
5 *1* **Enzio (GER)**[196] 6853 3-9-2 .... EPedroza 7 89
(A Wohler, Germany) *disp 2nd: 2nd st: one pce fr wl over 1f out* **58/10**
6 *1/2* **Quo Dubai (GER)**[191] 3-9-2 ....(b) AHelfenbein 4 88
(Mario Hofer, Germany) *hld up in rr: hdwy and rn wd st: sn btn* **117/10**
7 *3 1/2* **Asian Tiger (GER)** 3-9-2 .... FilipMinarik 1 81
(P Schiergen, Germany) *disp 4th: 5th st: wknd qckly* **7/1**

2m 8.38s (-0.19) **7** Ran SP% **132.1**
(including ten euro stakes): WIN 65; PL 23, 14, 20; SF 294.
Owner Gestuet Auenquelle **Bred** Gestut Auenquelle **Trained** Germany

1469 BEVERLEY (R-H)
Monday, May 4

OFFICIAL GOING: Good to firm (firm in places; 10.6)
Wind: Light across Weather: Overcast

1719 TURFTV MEDIAN AUCTION MAIDEN STKS 5f
1:50 (1:50) (Class 6) 2-Y-O **£1,942** (£578; £288; £144) **Stalls** High

Form RPR
5 **1** **Maidtorun (IRE)**[19] 1277 2-8-12 0.. PaulHanagan 1 67+
(R A Fahey) *cl up on outer: rdn along and sltly outpcd 1/2-way: hdwy to chal wl over 1f out: drvn to ld ins fnl f: kpt on wl* **9/2**[3]
2 *hd* **The Hermitage (IRE)** 2-8-12 0.. JoeFanning 5 67+
(M Johnston) *sn led: rdn along 2f out: drvn and hdd ins fnl f: rallied wl u.p towards fin* **13/8**[1]
4 **3** *3 3/4* **Petrocelli**[9] 1511 2-9-3 0.. PaulFitzsimons 4 58
(A J McCabe) *cl up: effrt 2f out and ev ch tl rdn: hung lft and wknd appr fnl f* **7/4**[2]
00 **4** *nk* **Lily Lenor (IRE)**[19] 1277 2-8-12 0.. J-PGuillambert 6 52
(B Ellison) *chsd ldrs: rdn over 2f out: kpt on ins fnl f: nrst fin* **50/1**
5 **5** *2* **More For Less**[12] 1450 2-9-3 0.. MickyFenton 7 50
(T D Barron) *in tch: rdn along 1/2-way: no imp* **18/1**
0 **6** *1* **Dispol Kabira**[19] 1277 2-8-12 0.. JamieMoriarty 8 41
(P T Midgley) *sn rdn along and a in rr* **40/1**
7 *nse* **Rose Bed (IRE)** 2-8-12 0.. EdwardCreighton 3 41
(M G Quinlan) *dwlt and a in rr* **12/1**
8 *1/2* **Daft Lad** 2-9-3 0.. DuranFentiman 2 44
(L A Mullaney) *dwlt and wnt rt s: a in rr* **33/1**

65.67 secs (2.17) **Going Correction** +0.225s/f (Good) **8** Ran SP% **112.9**
Speed ratings (Par 91): **91,90,84,84,81 79,79,78**
toteswingers: 1&2 £2.30, 1&3 £1.70, 2&3 £1.30 CSF £11.91 TOTE £5.70: £1.60, £1.10, £1.10; EX 13.20.
Owner Mrs H Steel **Bred** M J Wiley **Trained** Musley Bank, N Yorks

FOCUS
The ground was described as 'very quick but with a good cover of grass' by the riders after this opener. There were three newcomers in the line-up for what was probably just a modest event.

NOTEBOOK
Maidtorun(IRE), who showed ability when a staying-on fifth on her debut here two weeks earlier, had the worst of the draw. She kept tabs on the two leaders and showed real battling qualities to gain the upper hand near the line. She will be even better suited by 6f and should improve again. (op 4-1)
The Hermitage(IRE), a well-touted newcomer, knew her job. She helped take them along but after seeing off the attentions of Petrocelli she missed out in the final strides. She has plenty of speed and will have no difficulty going one better. (tchd 15-8)
Petrocelli, fourth at Leicester first time, matched strides with the leader but tended to hang left and in the end was readily shaken off. He may be better suited by 6f. (op 2-1)
Lily Lenor(IRE), about ten lengths behind the winner here on her second start, showed a lot more. Soon driven along, she was putting in her best work at the finish and is crying out for an extra furlong. (tchd 40-1)
Rose Bed(IRE) missed the break and raced widest of all. She showed a glimmer of ability, staying on from the rear when it was all over. (tchd 14-1)

1720 MAYDAY RACEDAY STKS (H'CAP) 5f
2:20 (2:20) (Class 5) (0-75,73) 3-Y-O **£2,752** (£818; £409; £204) **Stalls** High

Form RPR
00-2 **1** **Sloop Johnb**[22] 1232 3-9-4 **73**.. PaulHanagan 6 81+
(R A Fahey) *stmbld s: trckd ldrs: effrt and nt clr run 2f out: swtchd lft and rdn over 1f out: qcknd to ld ins fnl f: kpt on* **10/11**[1]
00-6 **2** *nk* **Kheylide (IRE)**[9] 1505 3-8-10 **65**.. EdwardCreighton 7 72
(Mrs D J Sanderson) *hld up in rr: hdwy whn nt clr run 2f out: effrt and n.m.r over 1f out: rdn and styd on strly ins fnl f: jst hld* **10/1**
2624 **3** *3 1/2* **Dispol Grand (IRE)**[3] 1644 3-8-10 **65**.. JoeFanning 1 59
(P T Midgley) *cl up: led 2f out: rdn and hung rt over 1f out: drvn and hdd ins fnl f: one pce* **8/1**[3]
51-0 **4** *1/2* **Wotatomboy**[12] 1452 3-8-5 **60**.. PaulQuinn 3 53
(R M Whitaker) *chsd ldrs: rdn along over 2f out: drvn and n.m.r over 1f out: sn btn* **25/1**
52-5 **5** *nk* **Rocket Rob (IRE)**[42] 936 3-8-7 **69**.. HollyHall(7) 5 61
(S A Callaghan) *chsd ldrs: hdwy on outer 1/2-way: rdn wl over 1f out and grad wknd* **6/1**[2]
0212 **6** *1 1/2* **La Capriosa**[4] 1628 3-8-10 **68**.. AndrewMullen(3) 4 54
(A J McCabe) *trckd ldrs: hdwy 2f out: rdn and n.m.r over 1f out: sn btn* **6/1**[2]
10-4 **7** *2* **Red Rosanna**[9] 1505 3-9-0 **72**.. RussellKennemore(3) 2 51
(R Hollinshead) *led: pushed along and hdd 2f out: drvn and wknd over 1f out* **10/1**

64.65 secs (1.15) **Going Correction** +0.225s/f (Good) **7** Ran SP% **114.1**
Speed ratings (Par 99): **99,98,92,92,91 89,86**
toteswingers: 1&2 £3.80, 1&3 £2.10, 2&3 £10.20 CSF £11.23 TOTE £1.90: £1.60, £6.60; EX 17.00.
Owner Jonathan Gill **Bred** Manor Farm Stud (rutland) **Trained** Musley Bank, N Yorks

FOCUS
Modest fair, but the first two came clear in the end after both had encountered traffic problems. Further improvement from the winner with the second getting back to something like his 2yo best.

1721 BEVERLEY ROTARY CLUB H'CAP 1m 1f 207y
2:50 (2:50) (Class 4) (0-80,79) 4-Y-O+ **£4,759** (£1,416; £707; £353) **Stalls** High

Form RPR
100- **1** **Snowed Under**[36] 6203 8-9-4 **79**.. FrancisNorton 6 83
(J D Bethell) *led: pushed along over 2f out: rdn over 1f out: edgd lft ent fnl f: sn drvn and kpt on gamely* **7/1**
3222 **2** *nk* **Benedict Spirit (IRE)**[26] 1177 4-8-11 **72**.. JoeFanning 8 75
(M H Tompkins) *trckd ldrs on outer: effrt 2f out: rdn to chse wnr ent fnl f: sn drvn to chal and ev ch tl no ex nr fin* **9/4**[1]
50-3 **3** *3/4* **Society Venue**[14] 1401 4-8-4 **65**.. AndrewElliott 9 67
(Jedd O'Keeffe) *trckd ldrs on inner: effrt 2f out: rdn and edgd lft ent fnl f: sn drvn and kpt on same pce* **3/1**[2]
024- **4** *1 1/4* **Fujin Dancer (FR)**[12] 3911 4-8-12 **73**.. PaulHanagan 7 72
(R A Fahey) *trckd wnr: effrt 3f out and sn pushed along: rdn 2f out: drvn over 1f out and kpt on same pce* **10/3**[3]
460- **5** *1 1/2* **Smugglers Bay (IRE)**[23] 6551 5-8-9 **70**....................(b) DuranFentiman 5 66
(T D Easterby) *t.k.h: hld up in rr: effrt and hdwy over 2f out: sn rdn and one pce* **17/2**
00-5 **6** *hd* **Bergonzi (IRE)**[33] 1059 5-9-3 **78**..(t) JamieMoriarty 1 74
(J Howard Johnson) *hld up in rr: hdwy on outer over 2f out: rdn wl over 1f out: no imp appr fnl f* **9/1**

2m 8.58s (1.58) **Going Correction** -0.25s/f (Firm) **6** Ran SP% **111.9**
Speed ratings (Par 105): **83,82,82,81,79 79**
toteswingers: 1&2 £2.70, 1&3 £3.40, 2&3 £1.90 CSF £22.98 CT £56.45 TOTE £8.90: £2.20, £1.70; EX 24.40.
Owner Mrs G Fane **Bred** Mrs G Fane **Trained** Middleham Moor, N Yorks

FOCUS
A depleted field and a very steady gallop, with the winner given an easy lead. He is rated to last year's best.

1722 GARDEN FETE IN THE COURSE ENCLOSURE H'CAP 1m 100y
3:20 (3:20) (Class 4) (0-85,85) 4-Y-O+ **£4,759** (£1,416; £707; £353) **Stalls** High

Form RPR
2620 **1** **Tartan Gigha (IRE)**[9] 1527 4-9-0 **81**.. JoeFanning 1 94
(M Johnston) *trckd ldrs: hdwy on outer 3f out: rdn to ld appr fnl f: sn edgd rt and clr* **7/2**[1]
16-5 **2** *3 1/4* **Handsome Falcon**[30] 1123 5-8-6 **73**.. PaulHanagan 9 82+
(R A Fahey) *trckd ldr: effrt whn nt clr run on inner 2f out and again over 1f out: swtchd lft and rdn ent fnl f: kpt on: nt rch wnr* **4/1**[2]
0-23 **3** *nk* **Bere Davis (FR)**[21] 1246 4-7-12 **72**.. AndrewHeffernan(7) 2 77
(P D Evans) *sn led: rdn along 2f out: drvn and edgd lft over 1f out: sn hdd and edgd rt: kpt on same pce* **10/1**
1404 **4** *2 1/4* **Exit Smiling**[18] 1306 7-9-2 **83**.. JamieMoriarty 4 83
(P T Midgley) *prom: effrt over 2f out: sn chal and ev ch tl rdn and hld whn n.m.r appr fnl f* **14/1**
05-4 **5** *3/4* **Moheebb (IRE)**[31] 1100 5-8-7 **74**..(b) AndrewElliott 5 72+
(Mrs R A Carr) *hld up in rr: gd hdwy on inner over 2f out: rdn to chse ldrs over 1f out: sn one pce* **7/1**
43-0 **6** *1* **Wigwam Willie (IRE)**[9] 1507 7-8-13 **80**..(tp) FrancisNorton 10 76
(K A Ryan) *chsd ldrs: rdn along over 2f out: sn drvn and one pce* **7/1**
0510 **7** *1/2* **Orpen Wide (IRE)**[14] 1405 7-9-1 **85**..(b) LeeVickers(3) 11 80
(M C Chapman) *hld up towards rr: sme hdwy over 2f out: sn rdn and no imp* **20/1**
256- **8** *1 1/2* **Admiral Dundas (IRE)**[210] 6526 4-9-1 **82**.. J-PGuillambert 7 73
(W Jarvis) *a towards rr* **5/1**[3]
650- **9** *4 1/2* **Toto Skyllachy**[310] 3493 4-9-1 **82**.. MickyFenton 3 63
(T P Tate) *sltly hmpd s: a in rr* **12/1**
10-0 **10** *11* **Major Magpie (IRE)**[9] 1507 7-9-3 **84**.. LeeEnstone 8 40
(M Dods) *in tch: effrt over 2f out: sn rdn and wknd* **28/1**

1m 44.3s (-3.30) **Going Correction** -0.25s/f (Firm) **10** Ran SP% **115.5**
Speed ratings (Par 105): **106,102,102,100,99 98,97,96,91,80**
toteswingers: 1&2 £2.90, 1&3 £8.70, 2&3 £8.50 CSF £17.17 CT £129.95 TOTE £4.70: £1.70, £1.80, £2.90; EX 18.50.
Owner Mrs I Bird **Bred** Gainsborough Stud Management Ltd **Trained** Middleham Moor, N Yorks

FOCUS
A 72-85 handicap run at just a steady pace with nothing getting into it from the rear. Straightforward form.

1723 GO RACING IN YORKSHIRE SUMMER FESTIVAL H'CAP 7f 100y
3:50 (3:50) (Class 5) (0-75,73) 4-Y-O+ **£2,752** (£818; £409; £204) **Stalls** High

Form RPR

4160 **1** **Captain Macarry (IRE)**[22] 1229 4-9-4 **73**.....................(v) JoeFanning 11 89+
(B Smart) *trckd ldrs on inner: effrt and nt clr run 2f out: swtchd lft and rdn over 1f out: qckndto ld ent fnl f and sn clr: comf* **4/1**[1]

14-6 **2** *5* **Salerosa (IRE)**[11] 1472 4-8-6 **61**........................ FrancisNorton 7 64
(Mrs A Duffield) *chsd ldrs: hdwy 3f out: rdn to chal 2f out: drvn and led briefly appr fnl f: hdd ent fnl f: kpt on: no ch w wnr* **15/2**[3]

60-3 **3** *3 1/4* **Mister Jingles**[11] 1475 6-8-4 **59** oh1........................ PaulQuinn 10 54
(R M Whitaker) *trckd ldrs: hdwy 3f out: rdn 2f out and sn edgd rt: drvn over 1f out and kpt on same pce* **4/1**[1]

60-0 **4** *1/2* **Fiefdom (IRE)**[16] 1343 7-9-4 **73**........................ PatrickMathers 4 67
(I W McInnes) *hld up in midfield: hdwy 2f out: swtchd rt and rdn over 1f out: kpt on u.p ins fnl f: nrst fin* **14/1**

04-0 **5** *3/4* **Stonehaugh (IRE)**[33] 1060 6-8-13 **68**........................(t) PaulHanagan 6 60
(J Howard Johnson) *led: rdn along 3f out: drvn 2f out: hdd appr fnl f and wknd* **4/1**[1]

5040 **6** *2 1/4* **Crocodile Bay (IRE)**[11] 1480 6-8-8 **68**........................ MarkCoumbe(5) 9 54
(John A Harris) *hld up in rr: effrt over 2f out and sn rdn: kpt on ins fnl f: nvr nr ldrs* **8/1**

3-05 **7** *1/2* **Bertie Vista**[7] 1563 4-8-7 **62**........................(b) DuranFentiman 2 47
(T D Easterby) *prom: rdn along over 2f out: wknd wl over 1f out* **20/1**

20-0 **8** *3/4* **Efidium**[21] 1243 11-8-3 **65** ow1........................ GihanArnolda(7) 1 48
(N Bycroft) *towards rr: hdwy on outer 3f out: sn rdn and wknd* **33/1**

0-00 **9** *shd* **Fern House (IRE)**[19] 1279 7-8-1 **59** oh14........................ AndrewMullen(3) 5 42
(Bruce Hellier) *hld up: a in rr* **100/1**

1322 **10** *26* **Desert Dreamer (IRE)**[14] 1403 8-8-12 **72**........................ RichardEvans(5) 3 —
(P D Evans) *s.i.s and bhd: rapid hdwy on outer to join ldrs 1/2-way: rdn along and wknd qckly over 2f out: eased* **9/2**[2]

1m 31.37s (-2.43) **Going Correction** -0.25s/f (Firm) **10** Ran SP% **116.4**
Speed ratings (Par 103): **103,97,93,93,92 89,89,88,88,58**
toteswingers: 1&2 £4.60, 1&3 £5.40, 2&3 £6.90 CSF £33.81 CT £118.44 TOTE £5.20: £1.60, £2.50, £1.80; EX 52.90.

Owner Anthony D Gee **Bred** Humphrey Okeke **Trained** Hambleton, N Yorks

FOCUS
A 59-73 handicap run at a sound pace. The form is ratedaround the second and the clear-cut winner's performance could be worth more.

Captain Macarry(IRE) Official explanation: trainer's rep said, regarding apparent improvement in form, that the gelding was better suited by the uphill finish.

Desert Dreamer(IRE) Official explanation: jockey said buckle on right rein became undone on leaving stalls

1724 GO RACING AT CATTERICK TOMORROW CLASSIFIED STKS 1m 4f 16y
4:20 (4:21) (Class 6) 3-Y-O+ **£2,013** (£594; £297) **Stalls** High

Form RPR

0-50 **1** **Berriedale**[13] 1441 3-8-4 45........................ FrancisNorton 1 54
(Mrs A Duffield) *hld up in rr and pushed wd bnd after s: stdy hdwy into midfield over 6f out: effrt on outer 3f out: rdn to ld over 1f out: kpt on wl undcer press fnl f* **40/1**

00-0 **2** *1 1/4* **Pure Crystal**[46] 876 3-7-13 52........................(b[1]) NicolPolli(5) 5 52
(M G Quinlan) *t.k.h: in tch: hdwy 3f out: rdn 2f out and sn ev ch: drvn and kpt on ins fnl f* **33/1**

06-4 **3** *hd* **Bollin Judith**[19] 1282 3-8-4 55........................ PaulQuinn 10 54+
(T D Easterby) *hld up towards rr: hdwy 1/2-way: rdn along and outpcd over 2f out: swtchd outside and drvn over 1f out: styd on strly ins fnl f* **9/4**[1]

00-5 **4** *shd* **Fell Pack**[19] 1279 5-9-9 55........................ JamieMoriarty 3 54
(J J Quinn) *in tch: hdwy 3f out: rdn to chse ldrs 2f out: drvn over 1f out: kpt on wl u.p ins fnl f* **4/1**[2]

5650 **5** *nse* **Key Of Fortune (IRE)**[16] 1363 3-8-4 55........................ PaulHanagan 9 52
(Jennie Candlish) *hld up and bhd: hdwy over 3f out: rdn 2f out: styd on wl u.p ins fnl f: nrst fin* **7/1**

0-60 **6** *2* **Wannarock (IRE)**[14] 1407 4-9-6 55........................ LeeVickers(3) 6 51
(M C Chapman) *hld up in rr: hdwy over 3f out: rdn 2f out: drvn and kpt on appr fnl f: nrst fin* **10/1**

06-0 **7** *1/2* **Miss Gibboa (IRE)**[19] 1281 3-8-1 53........................ KellyHarrison(3) 4 48
(P C Haslam) *chsd ldrs: effrt 3f out: rdn and ch 2f out: sn drvn and grad wknd* **14/1**

0-00 **8** *2 3/4* **Suitably Accoutred (IRE)**[13] 1441 3-8-1 46........................ AndrewMullen(3) 8 44
(Mrs A Duffield) *trckd ldrs: effrt 3f out: rdn over 2f out: sn drvn and grad wknd* **18/1**

060- **9** *1/2* **Swing It Ruby (IRE)**[199] 6789 3-8-6 54 ow2........................ EdwardCreighton 7 45
(Mrs D J Sanderson) *hld up and bhd: effrt 3f out: rdn along 2f out and n.d* **22/1**

00-0 **10** *hd* **Pilot Light**[11] 1470 3-8-4 50........................(p) DuranFentiman 11 42
(T D Easterby) *led: rdn along over 2f out: drvn and hdd over 1f out: wknd ins fnl f* **22/1**

000- **11** *nse* **Step Fast (USA)**[185] 7117 3-8-4 50........................ JoeFanning 2 42
(M Johnston) *cl up: pushed along 3f out: rdn over 2f out: drvn and wknd over 1f out* **9/2**[3]

00-6 **12** *nk* **Marillos Proterras**[27] 1168 3-8-4 50........................ AdrianMcCarthy 12 42
(Mrs A Duffield) *chsd ldrs: rdn along over 2f out: drvn and wknd over 1f out* **25/1**

2m 41.62s (0.72) **Going Correction** -0.25s/f (Firm)
WFA 3 from 4yo+ 19lb **12** Ran SP% **120.4**
Speed ratings (Par 101): **95,94,94,93,93 92,92,90,90,89 89,89**
toteswingers: 1&2 £80.90, 1&3 £22.50, 2&3 £24.70 CSF £977.54 TOTE £47.70: £8.80, £4.70, £1.40; EX 496.80.

Owner Evelyn Duchess Of Sutherland **Bred** Evelyn Duchess Of Sutherland **Trained** Constable Burton, N Yorks

■ Stewards' Enquiry : Nicol Polli one-day ban: used whip with excessive frequency (May 18)

FOCUS
The rain had arrived and this 0-55 classified stakes produced a shock result, but it was no fluke. Overall this is not a race to be with.

Berriedale Official explanation: trainer said, regarding apparent improvement in form, that the filly had put her best foot forward in a poor race.

1725 WHITE RABBIT H'CAP 7f 100y
4:50 (4:52) (Class 6) (0-60,60) 3-Y-O **£1,910** (£568; £284; £141) **Stalls** High

Form RPR

6005 **1** **Dante Deo (USA)**[19] 1281 3-8-12 **54**........................ JoeFanning 10 59
(T D Barron) *chsd ldrs: hdwy 3f out: cl up 2f out: rdn over 1f out: drvn and styd on ins fnl f to ld nr fin* **4/1**[2]

-165 **2** *nk* **Kheskianto (IRE)**[13] 1437 3-8-10 **59**........................ AndrewHeffernan(7) 1 63+
(M C Chapman) *chsd ldrs: hdwy on outer 3f out: rdn 2f out: led over 1f out: drvn and edgd lft ent fnl f: sn hung rt and hdd nr fin* **16/1**

2003 **3** *1 3/4* **Dancing Wave**[13] 1437 3-8-12 **57**........................ LeeVickers(3) 16 57
(M C Chapman) *trckd ldrs: effrt 2f out: rdn and styd on ent fnl f: one pce towards fin* **12/1**

400- **4** *2 1/4* **Ask Dan (IRE)**[142] 7659 3-9-4 **60**........................ PaulHanagan 14 54
(B Smart) *midfield: hdwy over 2f out: rdn over 1f out: sn drvn and styd on ins fnl f: nrst fin* **5/1**[3]

400- **5** *3/4* **Sardan Dansar (IRE)**[226] 6112 3-8-12 **54**........................ AdrianMcCarthy 15 47
(Mrs A Duffield) *chsd ldrs: rdn along over 2f out: drvn over 1f out and kpt on same pce* **28/1**

06-0 **6** *hd* **Georgie Bee**[27] 1173 3-8-13 **55**........................ DNolan 5 47
(D Carroll) *midfield: hdwy over 2f out: rdn wl over 1f out: kpt on ins fnl f: nrst fin* **22/1**

606- **7** *1 3/4* **Kiama Bay (IRE)**[188] 7038 3-9-1 **57**........................ JamieMoriarty 8 45
(J J Quinn) *hld up towards rr: hdwy over 2f out: sn rdn and kpt on ins fnl f: nt rch ldrs* **9/1**

5-00 **8** *1 3/4* **Irish Saint (IRE)**[42] 938 3-9-0 **56**........................ J-PGuillambert 7 39
(T J Pitt) *midfield: effrt 3f out and sn rdn along: drvn over 1f out and sn no imp* **18/1**

60-0 **9** *1/2* **Feeling Stylish (IRE)**[17] 1335 3-8-8 **53**........................ MichaelJStainton(3) 6 35
(N Tinkler) *cl up: rdn along 3f out: led briefly 2f out: sn drvn and hdd: wknd over 1f out* **25/1**

045- **10** *1 1/2* **Monaco Mistress (IRE)**[199] 6785 3-9-1 **60**........................(t) KellyHarrison(3) 3 38
(P C Haslam) *hld up in rr: effrt and sme hdwy over 2f out: sn rdn and no imp* **20/1**

040- **11** *3/4* **Venetian Lady**[191] 6987 3-9-2 **58**........................ FrancisNorton 4 41+
(Mrs A Duffield) *a in midfield* **33/1**

062- **12** *2* **Dillenda**[198] 6811 3-9-2 **58**........................ LeeEnstone 12 29
(T D Easterby) *t.k.h: in tch: hdwy to chse ldrs 1/2-way: rdn along wl over 2f out: sn drvn and wknd* **14/1**

3-60 **13** *3 3/4* **Highly Acclaimed**[14] 1400 3-9-3 **59**........................ MickyFenton 11 21
(Mrs A Duffield) *led: rdn along 3f out: drvn and hdd 2f out: sn wknd* **11/1**

0-00 **14** *nk* **Off Hand**[17] 1335 3-8-13 **55**........................ DuranFentiman 2 16
(T D Easterby) *hld up: a bhd* **33/1**

000- **15** *36* **Oneofthesedayz (IRE)**[221] 6229 3-8-13 **55**........................ EdwardCreighton 9 —
(Mrs D J Sanderson) *a in rr: wl bhd fnl 3f* **33/1**

-332 **P** **Miss Cameo (USA)**[11] 1481 3-8-13 **55**........................ PaulQuinn 13 —
(R M Whitaker) *chsd ldrs tl lost pl qckly 3f out: p.u and dismntd 2f out: dead* **7/2**[1]

1m 34.29s (0.49) **Going Correction** -0.25s/f (Firm) **16** Ran SP% **128.0**
Speed ratings (Par 97): **87,86,84,82,81 81,79,77,76,74 73,71,67,66,25** —
toteswingers: 1&2 £24.00, 1&3 £9.80, 2&3 £22.00 CSF £64.01 CT £754.24 TOTE £5.00: £2.30, £3.90, £2.70, £2.10; EX 100.20 Place 6 £13.46, Place 5 £12.43..

Owner Patrick Toes & R G Toes **Bred** Katalpa Farm & William L S Landes, III **Trained** Maunby, N Yorks

■ Stewards' Enquiry : Joe Fanning caution: careless riding.
Andrew Heffernan two-day ban: careless riding (May 18-19)

FOCUS
A low-grade finale, a 46-60 three-year-old handicap run at a sound pace. The first three met over C/D last month and finished in the same order.

Highly Acclaimed Official explanation: jockey said filly was unsuited by the good to firm (firm in places) ground

Oneofthesedayz(IRE) Official explanation: jockey said filly hung badly left throughout

T/Plt: £22.50 to a £1 stake. Pool: £57,925.40. 1,871.41 winning tickets. T/Qpdt: £11.10 to a £1 stake. Pool: £2,945.84. 195.00 winning tickets. JR

1604 KEMPTON (A.W) (R-H)
Monday, May 4

OFFICIAL GOING: Standard
Wind: Moderate, across Weather: Overcast

1726 WILLIAMHILL.COM - BEST FOOTBALL ODDS FACT! E B F MAIDEN STKS 5f (P)
2:00 (2:00) (Class 4) 2-Y-O **£5,018** (£1,493; £746; £186; £186) **Stalls** High

Form RPR

0 **1** **Avon River**[6] 1577 2-9-3 0........................ JimmyFortune 2 72+
(R Hannon) *wnt lft s: sn led: kpt up to work and r.o wl fnl f* **11/4**[2]

2 *2 1/4* **Paradise Dream** 2-9-3 0........................ ShaneKelly 3 64+
(J Noseda) *trckd wnr after 2f: hld appr fnl f but kpt on wl* **9/4**[1]

0 **3** *3 1/2* **Dream Of Gerontius (IRE)**[6] 1577 2-8-12 0........................ DaneO'Neill 5 46
(R Hannon) *broke wl: sn hdd: rdn over 1f out: kpt on but wl hld fnl f* **20/1**

4 *nk* **Radio City** 2-9-3 0........................ NCallan 6 50
(R M Beckett) *slowly away: effrt on outside over 1f out: no ex ins fnl f* **4/1**

4 *dht* **Mind The Monarch** 2-8-12 0........................ LPKeniry 4 45
(R A Teal) *in tch: pushed along 1/2-way no ex fnl f* **16/1**

6 *3/4* **Knightfire (IRE)** 2-9-3 0........................ AdamKirby 1 48+
(W R Swinburn) *sltly hmpd s: w.w but in tch: outpcd over 1f out* **3/1**[3]

64.00 secs (3.50) **Going Correction** +0.175s/f (Slow) **6** Ran SP% **113.1**
Speed ratings (Par 95): **79,75,69,69,69 68**
toteswingers: 1&2 £1.30, 1&3 £8.80, 2&3 £11.10 CSF £9.53 TOTE £3.20: £2.20, £1.90; EX 7.00.

Owner Jim Horgan **Bred** Poulton Stud **Trained** East Everleigh, Wilts

FOCUS
This maiden was contested by a majority of newcomers. The early pace was steady and it turned into a short sprint in the straight.

NOTEBOOK
Avon River got outpaced before finishing quite strongly when just over nine lengths seventh at 8-1 in a Bath maiden on debut. That experience seemed to give him an edge here and he showed a willing attitude and good turn of speed to score decisively under a shrewd front-running ride. (tchd 5-2 and 3-1)

Paradise Dream showed promise on this debut. He was a bit flat-footed when the pace quickened and never really looked like challenging the winner, but pulled clear of the rest. He cost 110,000gns last October, is out of Wunders Dream a high-class sprinter who won the Flying Childers, and could improve significantly for this initial experience. (tchd 11-4)

Dream Of Gerontius(IRE) struggled for speed in a Bath maiden on debut last month. She travelled with a bit more fluency here, plugged on quite well in the straight and gave the impression that a step up in trip will suit. (op 16-1)
Mind The Monarch, out of a half-sister to Richmond Stakes winner Always Hopeful, ran just a fair race on this debut. (op 6-1)
Radio City ran very green, but should have learned a lot from the experience. He was forced wide in the straight but stayed on steadily and showed some signs of ability on his first run. (op 6-1)
Knightfire(IRE) attracted support in the market, but compromised his chance by starting slowly and taking a fierce hold off the pedestrian pace on this debut. (op 5-2)

1727 WILLIAMHILL.COM - CAN SHEARER SAVE NEWCASTLE? H'CAP 5f (P)
2:30 (2:30) (Class 4) (0-85,85) 3-Y-O **£4,727** (£1,406; £702; £351) **Stalls** High

Form RPR
-235 **1** **Glamorous Spirit (IRE)**[10] 1486 3-8-12 **82**............ KevinGhunowa(3) 9 91
(R A Harris) *mde all: rdn and r.o wl fnl f* **7/1**[3]
21 **2** *1 ¼* **Lenny Bee**[17] 1317 3-8-9 **76**.............. JamieSpencer 8 81+
(D H Brown) *s.i.s: t.k.h: rdn and hdwy over 1f out to go 2nd ins fnl f* **15/8**[1]
20-5 **3** *2* **Sweet Applause (IRE)**[32] 1078 3-8-0 **74**.............. CharlotteKerton(7) 4 71
(A P Jarvis) *in tch: rdn to go 2nd over 1f out tl ins fnl f* **16/1**
3241 **4** *5* **Cecily**[14] 1414 3-9-0 **81**.............. DO'Donohoe 6 60
(Sir Mark Prescott) *chsd ldrs: rdn 1/2-way: one pce fr over 1f out* **7/1**[3]
14-1 **5** *1* **Desert Strike**[111] 140 3-8-9 **76**.............. LPKeniry 3 52
(P F I Cole) *hld up: styd on fnl f but nvr on terms* **7/1**[3]
001- **6** *2 ½* **Rebecca De Winter**[179] 7212 3-9-4 **85**.............. FergusSweeney 7 52
(David Pinder) *chsd wnr tl over 1f out: wknd* **16/1**
33-1 **7** *27* **Bajan Tryst (USA)**[41] 947 3-8-11 **78**.............. NCallan 5 —
(K A Ryan) *rdn and outpcd after 1f: lost tch over 1f out: t.o* **2/1**[2]

60.35 secs (-0.15) **Going Correction** +0.175s/f (Slow) **7** Ran SP% **117.4**
Speed ratings (Par 101): **108,106,102,94,93 89,46**
toteswingers: 1&2 £3.80, 1&3 £31.20, 2&3 £7.10 CSF £21.48 CT £208.49 TOTE £8.80: £3.70, £1.70; EX 22.40.
Owner Robert Bailey **Bred** Carlo Soria **Trained** Earlswood, Monmouths

FOCUS
A fair handicap, involving four last-time-out winners. It was run at a furious pace with the winner making most of her optimum draw to post a personal best.
Bajan Tryst(USA) Official explanation: jockey said colt got upset in stalls

1728 WILLIAMHILL.COM - WANNA BET MAN UTD? H'CAP 1m 2f (P)
3:00 (3:02) (Class 6) (0-65,65) 4-Y-O+ **£2,047** (£604; £302) **Stalls** High

Form RPR
00-0 **1** **Megalala (IRE)**[26] 1178 8-8-5 **52** oh1 ow1.............. NeilChalmers 7 64
(J J Bridger) *mde all: edgd lft u.p over 1f out: all out* **12/1**
-126 **2** *½* **Chalice Welcome**[21] 320 6-8-10 **60**.............. JackMitchell(3) 12 71+
(N B King) *mid-div: hdwy over 2f out: rdn to press wnr ins fnl f* **7/1**
5430 **3** *2 ¼* **Watson's Bay**[17] 1318 4-9-4 **65**.............. FergusSweeney 10 72
(Miss Tor Sturgis) *mid-div: hdwy 2f out: kpt on fnl f but little ch w first 2* **7/2**[1]
30-0 **4** *3 ½* **Harting Hill**[10] 1496 4-8-4 **51**.............. DO'Donohoe 2 51
(M P Tregoning) *in rr: rdn over 1f out and mde late hdwy* **6/1**[3]
5-01 **5** *½* **Southern Mistral**[9] 1520 4-8-12 **59**..............(p) NCallan 3 58
(Miss Gay Kelleway) *a.p: ev ch over 1f out: wknd ins fnl f* **7/1**
3005 **6** *1 ¼* **Double Valentine**[10] 1496 6-8-6 **53**.............. KirstyMilczarek 9 49
(R Ingram) *slowly away: t.k.h in rr: hdwy over 1f out: styd on* **12/1**
064- **7** *3 ½* **Felicia**[168] 7367 4-8-4 **51** oh1.............. RichardThomas 11 40
(J E Long) *mid-div: rdn over 2f out: one pce after* **16/1**
00-0 **8** *shd* **Princess Gee**[10] 1495 4-8-9 **56** ow1..............(v[1]) TedDurcan 8 45
(B J McMath) *t.k.h: trckd wnr: rdn over 2f out: wknd over 1f out* **20/1**
-400 **9** *shd* **Mid Valley**[15] 1378 6-8-4 **51** oh6.............. NickyMackay 13 40
(J R Jenkins) *t.k.h: nvr bttr than mid-div* **12/1**
0-00 **10** *nk* **Rosy Dawn**[30] 1122 4-8-1 **51** oh6.............. DavidProbert(3) 14 39
(J J Bridger) *mid-div: hdwy to trck ldrs 1/2-way: wknd over 1f out* **25/1**
230- **11** *14* **Cyril The Squirrel**[435] 695 5-8-4 **51** oh2.............. NeilPollard 6 11
(Karen George) *t.k.h: prom tl rdn and wknd 2f out* **14/1**
5002 **12** *nse* **Magic Warrior**[10] 1496 9-8-10 **57**.............. LPKeniry 5 17
(J C Fox) *in tch tl rdn and wknd over 2f out* **11/2**[2]
0000 **13** *55* **Andaman Sunset**[35] 1042 4-8-13 **60**.............. TolleyDean 1 —
(J L Spearing) *c over to ins fr wd draw and in rr: t.o over 3f out* **25/1**

2m 9.37s (1.37) **Going Correction** +0.175s/f (Slow) **13** Ran SP% **125.0**
Speed ratings (Par 101): **101,100,98,96,95 94,91,91,91,91 80,80,36**
toteswingers: 1&2 £44.60, 1&3 £24.10, 2&3 £5.80 CSF £95.65 CT £364.69 TOTE £14.50: £4.10, £2.60, £1.70; EX 130.90.
Owner Tommy Ware **Bred** Joseph Gallagher **Trained** Liphook, Hants

FOCUS
A modest handicap, run at a steady pace and not many got into it from behind. Sound enough form.
Double Valentine Official explanation: vet said mare lost a front shoe

1729 WILLIAMHILL.COM - ARE YOU ON ARSENAL? MAIDEN STKS (DIV I) 1m (P)
3:30 (3:37) (Class 4) 3-Y-O **£4,403** (£1,310; £654; £327) **Stalls** High

Form RPR
1 **Rainbow Peak (IRE)** 3-9-3 0.............. NCallan 3 92
(M A Jarvis) *a.p: rdn to ld 1f out: drvn out* **25/1**
- **2** *1* **Sovereign Remedy (USA)** 3-9-3 0.............. TedDurcan 7 90
(Saeed Bin Suroor) *a.p: rdn and ev ch 1f out: kpt on* **7/2**[2]
3 *1* **Mohtashem (IRE)** 3-9-3 0.............. RHills 13 87+
(Sir Michael Stoute) *w.w: hdwy over 2f out: r.o wl fnl f: nvr nrr* **6/1**[3]
3-4 **4** *2* **Invisible Man**[19] 1295 3-9-3 0.............. JimmyFortune 1 83
(J H M Gosden) *a.p: rdn 2f out: nt qckn fr over 1f out* **6/4**[1]
2 **5** *nk* **El Loco Uno (USA)**[18] 1308 3-9-3 0.............. TPQueally 5 82
(H R A Cecil) *led after 2f: hdd 1f out: wknd ins fnl f* **7/2**[2]
6 *nk* **Mared (USA)** 3-9-3 0.............. ShaneKelly 4 81+
(J Noseda) *mid-div: rdn 2f out: styd on fr over 1f out: nvr nr to chal* **20/1**
0 **7** *7* **Lord Fidelio (IRE)**[18] 1297 3-9-3 0.............. LPKeniry 9 65
(A M Balding) *mid-div: rdn and wknd over 1f out* **80/1**
8 *2 ½* **M'Lady Rousseur (IRE)** 3-8-12 0.............. RobertHavlin 8 55
(D R C Elsworth) *s.i.s: a towards rr* **100/1**
0-0 **9** *2 ¼* **Saute**[18] 1308 3-9-3 0.............. AdamKirby 6 54
(W R Swinburn) *a bhd* **66/1**
10 *2* **Spensley (IRE)** 3-9-3 0.............. DaneO'Neill 11 50
(J R Fanshawe) *slowly away: a bhd* **20/1**
0 **11** *13* **Indian Violet (IRE)**[19] 1295 3-9-3 0.............. JamieSpencer 2 20
(P F I Cole) *led for 2f: wknd over 2f out* **33/1**
00- **12** *19* **Pethers Dancer (IRE)**[157] 7465 3-9-3 0.............. DO'Donohoe 10 —
(W R Muir) *mid-div tl rdn and wknd over 2f out* **200/1**
0 **13** *6* **Rambling Rosie (IRE)**[17] 1327 3-8-12 0.............. RichardThomas 12 —
(C Drew) *a bhd* **200/1**

1m 40.35s (0.55) **Going Correction** +0.175s/f (Slow) **13** Ran SP% **119.8**
Speed ratings (Par 101): **104,103,102,100,99 99,92,89,87,85 72,53,47**
toteswingers: 1&2 £63.80, 1&3 £47.90, 2&3 £4.50 CSF £107.34 TOTE £36.30: £6.30, £1.70, £2.20; EX 191.10.
Owner P D Savill **Bred** P D Savill **Trained** Newmarket, Suffolk

FOCUS
A strong maiden run in a good time. The favourite set a useful standard and several powerful yards were represented by newcomers. The race could throw a number of future winners.
Indian Violet(IRE) Official explanation: jockey said gelding hung left-handed in straight

1730 WILLIAMHILL.COM - ARE YOU ON ARSENAL? MAIDEN STKS (DIV II) 1m (P)
4:00 (4:07) (Class 4) 3-Y-O **£4,403** (£1,310; £654; £327) **Stalls** High

Form RPR
0 **1** **Uniquely Poised (USA)**[19] 1289 3-9-3 0.............. JimmyFortune 10 92+
(J H M Gosden) *trckd ldrs: led over 1f out: pushed clr fnl f* **14/1**
0- **2** *5* **Sam Sharp (USA)**[325] 3001 3-9-3 0.............. TPQueally 13 80+
(H R A Cecil) *mid-div: hdwy over2f out: r.o to go 2nd nr fin* **5/1**[3]
3 **3** *½* **Big Bay (USA)**[18] 1297 3-9-3 0.............. JamieSpencer 3 79
(Jane Chapple-Hyam) *trckd ldr: rdn and lost 2nd nr fin* **7/4**[1]
4-3 **4** *¾* **Maverin (IRE)**[21] 1257 3-9-3 0.............. ShaneKelly 1 77
(J Noseda) *led tl rdn and hdd over 1f out: kpt on one pce fnl f* **11/2**
5 *1 ½* **Thabit (USA)** 3-9-3 0.............. RHills 5 74+
(M A Jarvis) *slowly away: in rr: styd on fnl 2f: n.d* **4/1**[2]
6 *½* **Senses (USA)** 3-9-3 0.............. NCallan 8 73
(J Noseda) *chsd ldrs: hung lft fr 3f out: no hdwy fnl 2f* **16/1**
-4 **7** *¾* **King's Masque**[15] 1380 3-9-0 0.............. DavidProbert(3) 2 71
(W R Muir) *towards rr: sme hdwy over 3f out: nvr on terms* **12/1**
6 **8** *3 ¼* **Red Cadeaux**[21] 1255 3-9-3 0.............. TGMcLaughlin 11 63+
(E A L Dunlop) *a towards rr* **40/1**
0 **9** *nk* **Fortina's Boy (USA)**[21] 1257 3-9-3 0.............. AdamKirby 14 63
(W R Swinburn) *a bhd* **40/1**
06- **10** *½* **Hi Fling**[199] 6778 3-9-3 0.............. TedDurcan 6 62
(B J Meehan) *in tch tl lost pl over 4f out* **33/1**
11 *1 ¼* **Peace Corps** 3-9-3 0.............. DaneO'Neill 12 59
(J R Fanshawe) *slowly away: a bhd* **20/1**
2-4 **12** *4* **Good Humoured**[10] 1490 3-9-3 0.............. DO'Donohoe 9 50
(Sir Mark Prescott) *prom tl rdn and wknd over 2f out* **20/1**

1m 40.84s (1.04) **Going Correction** +0.175s/f (Slow) **12** Ran SP% **126.0**
Speed ratings (Par 101): **101,96,95,94,93 92,92,88,88,87 86,82**
toteswingers: 1&2 £24.10, 1&3 £14.80, 2&3 £4.90 CSF £83.13 TOTE £20.50: £4.40, £2.70, £1.30; EX 75.90.
Owner Malih L Al Basti **Bred** B Wayne Hughes **Trained** Newmarket, Suffolk

FOCUS
This second division of the maiden looked another potentially decent contest, although the time was a little slower than for division one. There was arguably morestrength in depth to the first division, but the form of this race looks more solid.
Big Bay(USA) ◆ Official explanation: vet said colt suffered an overreach on left-fore
King's Masque Official explanation: jockey said gelding hung left-handed

1731 WILLIAMHILL.COM - CHOOSING CHELSEA? JUBILEE H'CAP (LONDON MILE QUALIFIER) 1m (P)
4:30 (4:36) (Class 3) (0-90,90) 4-Y-O+ **£7,477** (£2,239; £1,119; £560; £279; £140) **Stalls** High

Form RPR
1/1 **1** **Forgotten Voice (IRE)**[23] 1213 4-9-4 **90**.............. ShaneKelly 3 108
(J Noseda) *w.w: hdwy and shkn up to ld over 1f out: sn clr: easily* **4/5**[1]
115- **2** *3* **Multakka (IRE)**[171] 7313 6-8-13 **85**.............. RHills 1 96
(M P Tregoning) *in rr: hdwy over 2f out: r.o to chse wnr ins fnl f* **16/1**
20-0 **3** *3 ½* **The Snatcher (IRE)**[13] 1433 6-9-1 **87**.............. JimmyFortune 2 90
(R Hannon) *trckd ldr: rdn over 2f out: kpt on fr over 1f out* **33/1**
41-4 **4** *2* **The Fifth Member (IRE)**[37] 995 5-8-10 **89**.............. NathanAlison(7) 4 87
(J R Boyle) *prom: wnt 2nd over 2f out tl wknd over 1f out* **6/1**[3]
456- **5** *hd* **Mr Hichens**[189] 7019 4-9-0 **86**.............. DarryllHolland 5 84
(Karen George) *led tl hdd over 1f out: wknd ins fnl f* **66/1**
3502 **6** *6* **Tourist**[23] 1213 4-8-8 **80**.............. TedDurcan 6 64
(D Shaw) *t.k.h: trckd ldr tl rdn and wknd 2f out* **16/1**
660- **7** *4 ½* **Pride Of Nation (IRE)**[184] 7146 7-8-13 **85**.............. JamieSpencer 7 59
(J W Hills) *towards rr: swtchd rt and hdwy 2f out: wknd appr fnl f* **14/1**
00-1 **8** *½* **Dubai Dynamo**[13] 1433 4-9-4 **90**.............. JohnEgan 10 63
(P F I Cole) *prom: rdn 2f out: sn btn* **4/1**[2]
1211 **9** *5* **Dichoh**[40] 958 6-8-3 **80**..............(p) WilliamCarson(5) 9 41
(Rae Guest) *hld up: rdn 1/2-way: a bhd* **22/1**
16/ **10** *10* **Bold Alaska (IRE)**[1074] 1990 6-8-11 **83**.............. DaneO'Neill 8 21
(Peter Grayson) *a in rr* **100/1**

1m 39.33s (-0.47) **Going Correction** +0.175s/f (Slow) **10** Ran SP% **118.0**
Speed ratings (Par 107): **109,106,102,100,100 94,89,89,84,74**
toteswingers: 1&2 £4.20, 1&3 £8.20, 2&3 £10.00 CSF £16.70 CT £263.92 TOTE £2.00: £1.30, £2.10, £4.70; EX 13.40.
Owner Mrs Susan Roy **Bred** Swettenham Stud And Ben Sangster **Trained** Newmarket, Suffolk

FOCUS
A decent handicap and an impressive performance by the unexposed winner, who will be hit for this but will still be a contender for some of the top handicaps if he is as effective on turf. The runner-up beat the rest convincingly.

NOTEBOOK
Forgotten Voice(IRE) ◆ made a successful debut in a 7f Lingfield maiden in October 2007 and navigated his way past plenty of traffic problems in a course-and-distance handicap on his return from 535 days off last month. He was heavily backed to make it three from three and did the job in really good style. He had to work to gain the initiative in the straight, but quickened well and eventually ran out a wide-margin winner. He looks highly progressive and looks an interesting contender for some of the prestigious 1m handicaps this summer. (op 8-13)
Multakka(IRE) swooped late when winning back-to-back handicaps last autumn and had an excuse when slowly away and keen in a steadily run race last time. He was given quite a bit to do in the straight, but stayed on in pleasing fashion and pulled clear of the third. This was a solid display behind the useful winner on his comeback from six months off. (op 14-1)
The Snatcher(IRE) could not get into his usual front-running position from stall two, but ran respectably and seemed to step up on his slightly disappointing reappearance run. (op 16-1)
The Fifth Member(IRE) was a close fourth in the Spring Mile on his return last month. He relentlessly climbed the handicap ranks last year and ran a fair race switched to Polytrack, but is going to need to summon some further improvement this season to strike off his current mark. (op 9-1)
Mr Hichens got an uncontested lead, but was a sitting duck in the closing stages. The handicapper has looked in control since his hat-trick of wins last summer and he could continue to find things difficult in these competitive handicaps.

Dubai Dynamo cashed in on a sliding mark in a course-and-distance handicap on his reappearance last month, but could only find a short-lived effort off 4lb higher here and dropped away tamely. Official explanation: jockey said gelding had no more to give (op 13-2)

1732 WILLIAMHILL.COM - BACKING BARCA? H'CAP 2m (P)

5:00 (5:04) (Class 5) (0-75,75) 4-Y-O+ **£2,590** (£770; £385; £192) **Stalls** High

Form RPR

5431 **1** **Eforetta (GER)**[13] 1439 7-8-7 **58**........ ShaneKelly 7 67+
(A W Carroll) *hld up in rr: hdwy on nside over 1f out: rdn to ld ins fnl f: drvn out* **15/2**

41-3 **2** *1* **Dayia (IRE)**[13] 1426 5-9-10 **75**........ JerryO'Dwyer 2 83
(J Pearce) *hld up: hdwy on outside 3f out: rdn to ld 1f out: hdd ins fnl f* **3/1**[2]

2112 **3** *1 1/4* **Blockley (USA)**[20] 1273 5-9-1 **66**........(p) JamieSpencer 3 73
(Ian Williams) *hld up: hdwy on ins 2f out: led briefly appr fnl f: nt qckn ins fnl f* **2/1**[1]

-302 **4** *1 1/4* **Alnwick**[13] 1435 5-9-10 **75**........ DaneO'Neill 6 80
(P D Cundell) *led tl rdn and hdd appr fnl f: no ex ins fnl f* **9/2**[3]

0-26 **5** *1* **Wait For The Light**[40] 952 5-9-6 **71**........ TPQueally 5 75
(Mrs S Leech) *in tch: wnt 2nd over 2f out: wknd fnl f* **12/1**

13-0 **6** *12* **Rutba**[13] 1426 4-8-11 **65**........(v) TedDurcan 8 54
(M P Tregoning) *trckd ldrs: rdn over 3f out: wknd 2f out* **7/1**

4041 **7** *8* **My Friend Fritz**[38] 977 9-9-6 **71**........ LPKeniry 1 51
(P W Hiatt) *trckd ldr tl rdn and wknd over 2f out* **16/1**

3m 33.93s (3.83) **Going Correction** +0.175s/f (Slow)
WFA 4 from 5yo+ 3lb **7** Ran SP% **114.4**
Speed ratings (Par 103): **97,96,95,95,94 88,84**
toteswingers: 1&2 £5.20, 1&3 £3.20, 2&3 £2.00 CSF £30.22 CT £62.08 TOTE £9.90: £3.80, £2.50; EX 35.70.
Owner John W Egan **Bred** Gestut Rietberg **Trained** Cropthorne, Worcs

FOCUS
There was a thrilling finish to this 2m handicap which was run at just an even gallop. Straightforard form, rated through the runner-up.

1733 WILLIAMHILL.COM - BETLIVE AND IN-PLAY! FILLIES' H'CAP 6f (P)

5:30 (5:33) (Class 4) (0-85,84) 4-Y-O+ **£4,727** (£1,406; £702; £351) **Stalls** High

Form RPR

50-0 **1** **Pretty Bonnie**[6] 1582 4-9-0 **80**........ KirstyMilczarek 2 90
(A E Price) *in rr but a cl up: hdwy 2f out: drvn to ld ins fnl f: kpt on wl* **9/1**

10-0 **2** *1 3/4* **Orange Pip**[7] 1572 4-9-0 **80**........ JimmyFortune 6 84
(R Hannon) *led tl rdn and hdd ins fnl f: jst hld on for 2nd* **7/2**[3]

031- **3** *shd* **Romany Princess (IRE)**[163] 7419 4-9-4 **84**........ DaneO'Neill 3 88
(R Hannon) *trckd ldrs: rdn and kpt on one pce fnl f* **4/1**

26-5 **4** *1/2* **Oceana Blue**[19] 1288 4-8-6 **75**........(vt) DavidProbert(3) 4 77
(A M Balding) *chsd ldrs: nt qckn ins fnl f* **3/1**[2]

20-2 **5** *6* **Valatrix (IRE)**[14] 1411 4-8-9 **78**........ JackMitchell(3) 1 61
(C F Wall) *in tch on outside: rdn over 2f out: wknd over 1f out* **11/4**[1]

1m 13.82s (0.72) **Going Correction** +0.175s/f (Slow) **5** Ran SP% **103.9**
Speed ratings (Par 102): **102,99,99,98,90**
toteswingers: 1&2 £18.40 CSF £31.83 TOTE £10.80: £4.20, £1.80; EX 33.70 Place 6 £41.84, Place 5 £27.31..
Owner Mrs P Field **Bred** P And Mrs A G Venner & Alpha Bloodstock Ltd **Trained** Leominster, H'fords

■ Hurricane Harriet was withdrawn (5/1 ref to ent stalls). R4 applies, deduct 15p in the £.

FOCUS
A fair handicap for fillies, featuring a very open market. The winner maintained last season's improvement and the form seems sound.
T/Plt: £67.50 to a £1 stake. Pool: £59,132.24. 638.69 winning tickets. T/Qpdt: £38.10 to a £1 stake. Pool: £2,933.86. 56.90 winning tickets. JS

1556 NEWCASTLE (L-H)

Monday, May 4

OFFICIAL GOING: Good to soft (soft in places; 6.6)
Wind: Fairly strong, across Weather: Overcast, dull

1734 PARKLANDS GOLFCOURSE APPRENTICE CLAIMING STKS 7f

2:15 (2:17) (Class 6) 4-Y-O+ **£1,942** (£578; £288; £144) **Stalls** Low

Form RPR

2166 **1** **Straight Face (IRE)**[7] 1558 5-8-7 52........(v) JamieKyne(5) 13 61
(Miss Gay Kelleway) *bhd: pushed along 1/2-way: gd hdwy 2f out: led ins fnl f: sn clr* **12/1**

-016 **2** *7* **Carnivore**[33] 1065 7-9-5 78........ AdamCarter(5) 15 54+
(T D Barron) *hld up: smooth hdwy to ld over 2f out: clr over 1f out: hung lft and hdd ins fnl f: no ex* **13/2**

40-2 **3** *2 1/2* **Just Sam (IRE)**[21] 1243 4-8-4 57........ AnthonyBetts(5) 10 32
(R E Barr) *trckd ldrs: led over 3f out to over 2f out: sn one pce* **15/2**

00-0 **4** *2 1/2* **Paint Stripper**[19] 1276 4-8-5 42........ JohnCavanagh(5) 12 27
(W Storey) *in tch: hdwy and cl up over 2f out: sn rdn and no ex over 1f out* **66/1**

0/0- **5** *3 1/2* **Just Crystal**[487] 33 5-8-4 39........ BillyCray(3) 11 14
(B P J Baugh) *dwlt: hdwy and prom 1/2-way: rdn and wknd fr 2f out* **100/1**

256- **6** *nse* **Stellite**[276] 4605 9-8-10 68........ GaryBartley 3 17
(J S Goldie) *hld up: pushed along 1/2-way: kpt on fr 2f out: nvr rchd ldrs* **11/2**[3]

6116 **7** *1 1/2* **Lethal**[11] 1480 6-8-5 69........ LeeTopliss(7) 2 15
(R A Fahey) *led to over 3f out: wknd 2f out* **4/1**[1]

0 **8** *nk* **King Pin**[21] 1243 4-8-11 0........ NSLawes(5) 14 18
(Miss Tracy Waggott) *dwlt: bhd: shortlived effrt 3f out: sn btn* **33/1**

6000 **9** *10* **Aegean Pride**[22] 1228 4-8-7 47 ow2........ KrishGundowry(5) 8 —
(A Berry) *dwlt: towards rr: drvn and edgd lft 3f out: sn wknd* **80/1**

31 **10** *8* **Sendreni (FR)**[34] 1048 5-9-5 73........(t) TobyAtkinson(5) 9 —
(M Wigham) *prom tl rdn and wknd over 2f out* **9/2**[2]

306- **11** *2* **Morristown Music (IRE)**[214] 6405 5-8-0 44........ NoraLooby(7) 6 —
(J S Wainwright) *cl up tl rdn and wknd over 2f out* **33/1**

5-00 **12** *8* **Captain Royale (IRE)**[3] 1655 4-8-9 55........ DeclanCannon(5) 5 —
(Miss Tracy Waggott) *prom tl edgd lft and wknd fr 3f out* **16/1**

-000 **13** *13* **Piccolo Pete**[7] 1558 4-9-0 48........(p) SladeO'Hara 7 —
(R Johnson) *slowly away: a bhd* **40/1**

1400 **14** *1/2* **Herbert Crescent**[19] 1276 4-8-9 60........(p) LanceBetts(3) 1 —
(Ollie Pears) *midfield: drvn after 2f: struggling fr 1/2-way* **14/1**

030- **15** *45* **Morocchius (USA)**[178] 7226 4-8-10 58 ow1........(p) MJMurphy(5) 4 —
(Miss J A Camacho) *dwlt: bhd: lost tch fr 1/2-way* **11/1**

1m 31.72s (3.02) **Going Correction** +0.575s/f (Yiel) **15** Ran SP% **119.3**
Speed ratings (Par 101): **98,90,87,84,80 80,78,78,66,57 55,46,31,30,—**
toteswingers: 1&2 £17.20, 1&3 £33.40, 2&3 £24.10 CSF £84.17 TOTE £13.20: £5.00, £2.30, £1.80; EX 135.00.
Owner KingsClubSyndicate **Bred** P J Towell **Trained** Exning, Suffolk

FOCUS
A low-grade apprentice riders' handicap to kick things off and all of the runners edged over to the far side initially, but the action took place down the middle of the track in the closing stages. The leader fell in a hole in the last 100 yards and the form does not look too solid.
Sendreni(FR) Official explanation: jockey said gelding was unsuited by the good to soft (soft in places) ground
Morocchius(USA) Official explanation: vet said gelding was lame on left-fore

1735 EUROPEAN BREEDERS' FUND MEDIAN AUCTION MAIDEN STKS 5f

2:45 (2:45) (Class 5) 2-Y-O **£3,238** (£963; £481; £240) **Stalls** Low

Form RPR

3 **1** **Tres Coronas (IRE)**[19] 1275 2-9-3 0........ PhillipMakin 5 69
(T D Barron) *cl up: rdn 2f out: styd on to ld nr fin* **9/4**[2]

54 **2** *nk* **Bronze Beau**[19] 1275 2-9-3 0........ TomEaves 1 68
(Mrs L Stubbs) *led: rdn over 1f out: kpt on: hdd cl home* **9/2**[3]

5 **3** *1* **Sharp Eclipse**[19] 1275 2-9-3 0........ PaulMulrennan 4 65+
(K A Ryan) *trckd ldrs: rdn and outpcd over 1f out: rallied ins fnl f: no further imp last 50yds* **85/40**[1]

0 **4** *7* **A Touch Of Luck**[19] 1275 2-9-3 0........ RoystonFfrench 7 39
(T D Easterby) *prom tl rdn and outpcd fr 2f out* **20/1**

5 *1 1/2* **Fibs And Flannel** 2-9-3 0........ DavidAllan 8 34
(T D Easterby) *dwlt: hld up in tch: shkn up over 2f out: sn no imp* **10/1**

6 *nk* **Wallgate** 2-8-12 0........ TonyHamilton 3 28
(Miss J A Camacho) *dwlt: bhd: rdn after 2f: btn over 1f out* **12/1**

7 *6* **Lady Navara (IRE)** 2-8-12 0........ TWilliams 6 6
(M Brittain) *dwlt: sn in tch and rdn along: wknd fr 1/2-way* **10/1**

8 *1* **Ron The Don** 2-8-12 0........ SladeO'Hara(5) 2 7
(A Berry) *sn outpcd in rr: nvr on terms* **33/1**

64.33 secs (3.63) **Going Correction** +0.575s/f (Yiel) **8** Ran SP% **114.5**
Speed ratings (Par 93): **93,92,90,79,77 76,67,65**
toteswingers: 1&2 £1.50, 1&3 £1.10, 2&3 £2.70 CSF £12.95 TOTE £2.70: £1.20, £1.60, £1.60; EX 13.00.
Owner J Cringan & D Pryde **Bred** Denis McDonnell **Trained** Maunby, N Yorks

FOCUS
Very ordinary maiden form and the first three, who filled those positions throughout, finished clear.

NOTEBOOK
Tres Coronas(IRE), who had shaped encouragingly at Beverley on debut, is bred to want a much stiffer test of stamina than this (dam was a 1m4f winner at three), but the soft ground would have helped to bring his staying power into play and he ground out victory, staying on to get the better of long-time leader Bronze Beau in the final 50 yards. He already wants at least another furlong, but the likelihood is we'll not see the best of him until upped to trips of a mile plus next season. (op 2-1)
Bronze Beau, having his third start, showed good speed to lead and take them along at a decent clip and he kept on very well, only succumbing in the closing stages. He looks the type to make an impact in nurseries off what is likely to be a pretty lowly mark, especially when the emphasis is more on speed.
Sharp Eclipse kept on for pressure having been close up throughout and he, like the winner, shapes as though another furlong would be ideal. (op 5-2 tchd 11-4)
A Touch Of Luck looks more of a long-term prospect. (op 33-1 tchd 18-1)
Fibs And Flannel, who is quite speedily bred, shaped with some promise before not really picking up in the final 2f, possibly on ground softer than ideal. He could fare much better on a sounder surface, especially with this pipe-opener under his belt. (op 6-1)

1736 GOSFORTH DECORATING & BUILDING SERVICES H'CAP 6f

3:15 (3:17) (Class 5) (0-70,70) 3-Y-O **£2,849** (£847; £423; £211) **Stalls** Low

Form RPR

-335 **1** **Where's Reiley (USA)**[22] 1232 3-8-7 **62**........ NeilBrown(3) 13 67
(T D Barron) *prom centre: rdn to ld that gp over 1f out: kpt on wl fnl f* **7/1**[2]

6-61 **2** *3/4* **Solis**[21] 1253 3-8-9 **61**........ GrahamGibbons 8 63+
(J J Quinn) *prom far side: rdn to ld that gp ins fnl f: kpt on: nt pce of wnr* **8/1**[3]

05-5 **3** *nk* **Lucky Buddha**[26] 1190 3-8-6 **58**........ TonyHamilton 12 59
(Jedd O'Keeffe) *plld hrd: cl up centre: effrt 2f out: kpt on u.p fnl f* **25/1**

05-4 **4** *shd* **Abbey Steps (IRE)**[33] 1064 3-8-4 **56** oh1........(b) DaleGibson 11 57
(T D Easterby) *t.k.h: cl up centre: hung lft over 2f out: r.o fnl f* **18/1**

540- **5** *shd* **Fathey (IRE)**[214] 6426 3-8-11 **70**........ BMcHugh(7) 10 71
(R A Fahey) *led centre gp to over 1f out: kpt on u.p fnl f* **16/1**

4-36 **6** *2 1/2* **Steel Stockholder**[7] 1561 3-8-13 **65**........ TWilliams 1 58
(M Brittain) *led far side to ins fnl f: sn btn* **12/1**

306- **7** *shd* **Le Reve Royal**[212] 6481 3-8-7 **59**........ DavidAllan 4 51
(G R Oldroyd) *prom far side: outpcd over 2f out: r.o fnl f: no imp* **16/1**

43-2 **8** *nse* **Mister Tinktastic (IRE)**[33] 1062 3-9-1 **67**........ PhillipMakin 7 59+
(M Dods) *hld up far side: drvn and effrt over 2f out: nvr rchd ldrs* **7/2**[1]

560- **9** *2 1/4* **Red Max (IRE)**[209] 6549 3-8-4 **56** oh1........ DarrenMoffatt 2 41
(T D Easterby) *chsd far side ldrs tl rdn and wknd over 1f out* **20/1**

11 **10** *1 3/4* **Just Timmy Marcus**[38] 986 3-9-1 **67**........ DanielTudhope 5 46
(B P J Baugh) *dwlt: hld up far side: drvn over 2f out: n.d* **10/1**

33-2 **11** *6* **Dareh (IRE)**[63] 729 3-9-3 **69**........ RoystonFfrench 6 29
(M Johnston) *sn bhd far side: rdn 1/2-way: nvr on terms* **7/2**[1]

0-46 **12** *2 3/4* **Noodles Blue Boy**[28] 1155 3-9-4 **70**........ PaulMulrennan 9 21
(Ollie Pears) *prom far side tl wknd fr 2f out* **22/1**

55-0 **13** *1 1/4* **Port Ronan (USA)**[38] 986 3-8-8 **60**........ SaleemGolam 3 7
(J S Wainwright) *dwlt: a bhd far side* **66/1**

10-0 **14** *14* **Mythicism**[22] 1232 3-9-2 **68**........(t) TomEaves 14 —
(B Smart) *racd alone stands' side: wknd fr 3f out* **10/1**

1m 17.93s (2.73) **Going Correction** +0.575s/f (Yiel) **14** Ran SP% **132.0**
Speed ratings (Par 99): **104,103,102,102,102 99,98,98,95,93 85,81,80,61**
toteswingers: 1&2 £5.60, 1&3 £39.10, 2&3 £0.00 CSF £65.81 CT £1381.62 TOTE £10.00: £3.40, £3.70, £4.50; EX 90.50.
Owner Harrowgate Bloodstock Ltd **Bred** Overbrook Farm **Trained** Maunby, N Yorks

■ Stewards' Enquiry : Neil Brown caution: careless riding.

FOCUS
The finish was fought out by horses from both sides, but all four of the group that stayed down the middle figured in the finish, as opposed to just the sole representative of the main group on the far side. Just modest form.

1737 MILL VOLVO H'CAP 7f
3:45 (3:47) (Class 5) (0-75,75) 4-Y-0+ £2,866 (£846; £423) Stalls Low

Form RPR
020- 1 **Celtic Lynn (IRE)**[228] 6043 4-9-1 72 TonyHamilton 14 83
(M Dods) *t.k.h: hld up: smooth hdwy 2f out: led ins fnl f: r.o wl* 16/1
-002 2 1 3/4 **Tiger Dream**[11] 1480 4-8-12 72 (p) NeilBrown(3) 6 79
(K A Ryan) *led: rdn and hdd ins fnl f: kpt on same pce* 7/1[2]
0-00 3 hd **Dream Express (IRE)**[17] 1333 4-8-13 70 PhillipMakin 2 76
(M Dods) *in tch: effrt over 2f out: kpt on u.p* 16/1
0-63 4 1 3/4 **Ancient Cross**[11] 1480 5-8-10 67 (b) DaleGibson 11 73+
(M W Easterby) *midfield: outpcd 3f out: rallied whn nt clr run over 1f out: r.o fnl f* 7/1[2]
20-3 5 shd **We'Re Delighted**[30] 1123 4-9-1 72 GrahamGibbons 3 73
(T D Walford) *hld up: hdwy and in tch 2f out: kpt on same pce ins fnl f* 4/1[1]
000- 6 3/4 **Sunnyside Tom (IRE)**[198] 6813 5-8-5 69 BMcHugh(7) 4 68
(R A Fahey) *cl up: ev ch over 2f out: wknd ins fnl f* 14/1
043- 7 1 1/4 **Island Music (IRE)**[178] 7224 4-8-3 67 JamieKyne(7) 13 63
(J J Quinn) *hld up: hdwy over 2f out: sn rdn and no imp over 1f out* 12/1
010- 8 1/2 **Apollo Shark (IRE)**[199] 6792 4-8-12 69 PaulMulrennan 15 63
(J Howard Johnson) *midfield: rdn over 2f out: no ex over 1f out* 12/1
046- 9 1 3/4 **Al Wasef (USA)**[308] 3548 4-8-13 70 DanielTudhope 7 60
(J S Goldie) *hld up: shkn up and stdy hdwy over 1f out: nvr nr to chal* 16/1
614- 10 6 **Infinity Bond**[277] 4560 4-8-6 63 SilvestreDeSousa 5 36
(G R Oldroyd) *prom tl rdn and wknd fr 2f out* 33/1
343- 11 3/4 **Hippolytus**[271] 4737 4-8-12 69 RoystonFfrench 8 40
(J J Quinn) *bhd: drvn after 2f: nvr on terms* 10/1
051 12 1 3/4 **Rabbit Fighter (IRE)**[9] 1528 5-8-12 69 (v) DarrenWilliams 16 36
(D Shaw) *dwlt: bhd: drvn over 2f out: nvr on terms* 15/2[3]
640- 13 1/2 **Ubenkor (IRE)**[184] 7131 4-8-13 70 TomEaves 10 35
(B Smart) *t.k.h: prom tl wknd fr 2f out* 20/1
00-0 14 3 1/2 **Moonage Daydream (IRE)**[27] 1169 4-8-10 67 (bt) DavidAllan 9 23
(T D Easterby) *in tch tl rdn and wknd fr 3f out* 20/1
0-56 15 7 **Navajo Joe (IRE)**[13] 1436 4-9-4 75 AdrianTNicholls 12 12
(R Johnson) *racd keenly in rr: rdn 3f out: sn wknd* 33/1
200- 16 7 **Grey Command (USA)**[223] 6188 4-8-5 69 JohnCavanagh(7) 1 —
(M Brittain) *in tch: drvn 1/2-way: sn wknd: eased whn no ch fnl f* 33/1
1m 32.17s (3.47) **Going Correction** +0.575s/f (Yiel) 16 Ran SP% 123.9
Speed ratings (Par 103): **95,93,92,90,90 89,88,87,85,78 78,76,75,71,63 55**
toteswingers: 1&2 £52.40, 1&3 £32.70, 2&3 £35.90 CSF £118.13 CT £1906.22 TOTE £21.40: £4.80, £2.20, £3.50, £2.00; EX 199.90.
Owner P Taylor **Bred** Mrs Miriam O'Donnell **Trained** Denton, Co Durham
■ Stewards' Enquiry : Phillip Makin one-day ban: careless riding (May 18)

FOCUS
A competitive 7f handicap in which the field all went far side, but they drifted towards the centre just after halfway. The time was slower than for the claimer, but the form looks sound enough.
Grey Command(USA) Official explanation: jockey said colt lost its action

1738 COMPLETE FOOTBALL H'CAP 1m 4f 93y
4:15 (4:16) (Class 5) (0-70,69) 4-Y-0+ £2,978 (£886; £442; £221) Stalls Low

Form RPR
0-55 1 **Dechiper (IRE)**[7] 1556 7-8-7 58 GrahamGibbons 2 70+
(R Johnson) *hld up: smooth hdwy to ld over 1f out: sn clr: easily* 3/1[1]
-546 2 4 1/2 **Piper's Song (IRE)**[9] 1533 6-8-13 64 SaleemGolam 6 66
(Patrick Morris) *hld up: hdwy over 2f out: chsd wnr ins fnl f: r.o: no imp* 10/1
/00- 3 nse **Cote D'Argent**[39] 6862 6-9-0 65 TomEaves 1 68+
(L Lungo) *hld up in tch: nt clr run over 2f out: swtchd rt and hdwy over 1f out: kpt on fnl f* 17/2
0-26 4 4 **Ice Bellini**[68] 679 4-8-11 62 (v) PhillipMakin 9 58
(Miss Gay Kelleway) *hld up: hdwy outside over 2f out: wknd fnl f* 9/2[3]
00/5 5 1 3/4 **Samizdat (FR)**[12] 1454 6-8-4 55 (v) DarrenMoffatt 8 48
(James Moffatt) *cl up: led 3f to over 1f out: wknd ent fnl f* 8/1
0-05 6 2 3/4 **Graylyn Ruby (FR)**[27] 1175 4-9-1 69 NeilBrown(3) 3 58
(J Jay) *chsd ldrs: effrt over 2f out: wknd appr fnl f* 15/2
652/ 7 1 1/2 **Majestic Chief**[9] 3907 5-8-8 59 ow1 (tp) PaulMulrennan 7 44
(Miss Lucinda V Russell) *led to 3f out: wknd over 1f out* 33/1
15-5 8 nk **Fistral**[13] 1442 5-8-4 55 oh6 RoystonFfrench 10 41
(P D Niven) *prom tl rdn and wknd over 2f out* 7/2[2]
5/00 9 12 **Millagros (IRE)**[45] 897 9-8-4 55 oh1 AdrianTNicholls 5 22
(I Semple) *hld up in tch: drvn and outpcd 3f out: sn btn* 25/1
2m 51.41s (5.81) **Going Correction** +0.575s/f (Yiel) 9 Ran SP% 114.7
Speed ratings (Par 103): **103,100,99,97,96 94,93,93,85**
toteswingers: 1&2 £14.60, 1&3 £8.60, 2&3 £18.40 CSF £33.55 CT £229.53 TOTE £3.50: £1.90, £3.80, £1.80; EX 48.10.
Owner L Armstrong **Bred** Tommy Burns **Trained** Newburn, Tyne & Wear

FOCUS
Not a strong handicap by any means, but the pace seemed even enough. The winner is rated back to his best.

1739 MILLVOLVO.CO.UK MAIDEN STKS 1m 2f 32y
4:45 (4:46) (Class 5) 3-Y-0+ £2,719 (£809; £404; £202) Stalls Low

Form RPR
363 1 **African Cheetah**[12] 1461 3-8-11 76 RoystonFfrench 3 71
(M Johnston) *hld up in tch: hdwy to ld over 1f out: drvn clr* 11/8[2]
2- 2 6 **Taarab**[188] 7054 3-8-11 0 SaleemGolam 9 59
(Saeed Bin Suroor) *trckd ldr: led 3f to over 1f out: kpt on same pce* 1/1[1]
3 3/4 **Johnny Rocket (IRE)**[51] 4-9-9 0 NeilBrown(3) 1 58
(K A Ryan) *hld up: effrt over 2f out: kpt on fnl f: no imp* 14/1[3]
0 4 shd **Aldaado (IRE)**[18] 1308 3-8-11 0 PhillipMakin 2 57
(M Dods) *trckd ldrs: effrt and edgd lft over 1f out: kpt on same pce fnl f* 33/1
0- 5 5 **Eborbrav**[317] 3277 3-8-11 0 DavidAllan 8 47
(T D Easterby) *led to 3f out: wknd over 1f out* 40/1
0 6 1 **Bumble Rose (IRE)**[22] 1231 6-9-7 0 (p) GrahamGibbons 4 41
(A G Foster) *prom tl rdn and wknd over 2f out* 50/1
00 7 17 **Napoletano (ITY)**[7] 1562 3-8-11 0 TonyHamilton 5 11
(R Johnson) *racd keenly in rr: lost tch fr 1/2-way: t.o* 33/1
0- 8 nk **Rogalt (IRE)**[200] 6759 3-8-11 0 TomEaves 6 10
(B Smart) *bhd: struggling over 3f out: t.o* 16/1
2m 20.03s (8.13) **Going Correction** +0.575s/f (Yiel)
WFA 3 from 4yo+ 15lb 8 Ran SP% 114.9
Speed ratings (Par 103): **90,85,84,84,80 79,66,65**
toteswingers: 1&2 £1.02, 1&3 £5.70, 2&3 £7.30 CSF £2.98 TOTE £2.70: £1.20, £1.02, £3.10; EX 3.60.
Owner Sheikh Hamdan Bin Mohammed Al Maktoum **Bred** Sheikh Abdulla Bin Isa Al-Khalifa **Trained** Middleham Moor, N Yorks

FOCUS
A weakish maiden which looked a match on paper, but the favourite was very disappointing and the winner was left with little to beat. It was slowly run.
Eborbrav Official explanation: jockey said bit slipped through gelding's mouth

1740 DIGIBET.COM H'CAP 1m (R)
5:15 (5:17) (Class 5) (0-70,70) 3-Y-0 £2,978 (£886; £442; £221) Stalls Low

Form RPR
33-1 1 **Tiger Reigns**[33] 1061 3-9-2 68 PhillipMakin 3 80
(M Dods) *hld up: hdwy over 2f out: led appr fnl f to ins fnl f: rallied to regain ld nr fin* 7/2[2]
50-6 2 hd **Mr Freddy (IRE)**[12] 1462 3-8-8 60 TonyHamilton 7 72
(R A Fahey) *hld up in tch: stdy hdwy 3f out: disp ld appr fnl f: led ins fnl f: hdd nr fin* 13/8[1]
000- 3 5 **Speed Dating**[206] 6620 3-8-7 59 PaulMulrennan 9 59
(Sir Mark Prescott) *sn pushed along and prom: effrt and led briefly over 1f out: outpcd ins fnl f* 11/2[3]
056- 4 1 **Hawkeyethenoo (IRE)**[206] 6632 3-8-4 56 DaleGibson 4 54
(M W Easterby) *t.k.h: hld up in tch: hdwy and cl up over 1f out: no ex ins fnl f* 22/1
40-0 5 1/2 **Tapis Wizard**[6] 1595 3-9-4 70 TomEaves 8 67
(M W Easterby) *hld up: pushed along 3f out: hdwy over 1f out: no imp fnl f* 8/1
04- 6 1/2 **Haulage Lady (IRE)**[202] 6722 3-8-11 63 RoystonFfrench 2 59
(Karen McLintock) *hld up: outpcd over 2f out: nvr rchd ldrs* 22/1
2-21 7 2 1/2 **Svindal (IRE)**[98] 295 3-9-1 70 (b) NeilBrown(3) 5 60
(K A Ryan) *led to over 1f out: sn wknd* 9/1
633- 8 9 **Island Chief**[139] 7694 3-8-10 62 DavidAllan 6 31
(K A Ryan) *chsd ldrs: rdn 3f out and wknd 2f out* 16/1
0-40 9 35 **Hit The Switch**[13] 1434 3-8-13 65 SaleemGolam 1 —
(Patrick Morris) *chsd ldrs tl wknd fr 2f out* 18/1
1m 47.62s (4.22) **Going Correction** +0.575s/f (Yiel) 9 Ran SP% 116.7
Speed ratings (Par 99): **103,102,97,96,96 95,93,84,49**
toteswingers: 1&2 £1.20, 1&3 £4.80, 2&3 £4.90 CSF £9.67 CT £28.62 TOTE £5.10: £1.60, £1.10, £2.10; EX 12.10 Place 6: £165.38, Place 5: £42.41..
Owner Joe Buzzeo **Bred** Richard Green And New England Stud **Trained** Denton, Co Durham

FOCUS
A modest handicap and the clear pick of the times on the round course. Good efforts from the first two to pull clear.
Svindal(IRE) Official explanation: jockey said gelding hung badly right throughout
Hit The Switch Official explanation: jockey said gelding hung right throughout
T/Plt: £76.40 to a £1 stake. Pool: £66,594.02. 636.12 winning tickets. T/Qpdt: £12.30 to a £1 stake. Pool: £3,922.88. 235.38 winning tickets. RY

1248 WARWICK (L-H)
Monday, May 4

OFFICIAL GOING: Good to firm (8.9)
Wind: Light across

1741 KNOWLE APPRENTICE H'CAP 1m 22y
2:10 (2:14) (Class 6) (0-60,63) 4-Y-0+ £2,047 (£604; £302) Stalls Low

Form RPR
0662 1 **Annes Rocket (IRE)**[8] 1535 4-8-2 50 GemmaElford(7) 7 59
(J C Fox) *hld up: plld hrd: hdwy over 1f out: hung rt and r.o to ld wl ins fnl f* 8/1[3]
200- 2 nk **Al Rayanah**[176] 7261 6-8-8 52 (p) JemmaMarshall(3) 11 60
(G Prodromou) *hld up: hdwy 1/2-way: rdn to ld and hung rt fr over 1f out: hdd wl ins fnl f* 12/1
00-0 3 1 **Seasonal Cross**[33] 1074 4-8-7 53 NathanAlison(5) 14 59
(S Dow) *dwlt: outpcd and bhd: rapid hdwy fnl f: running on wl whn n.m.r nr fin* 25/1
3400 4 2 1/2 **Wavertree Warrior (IRE)**[35] 1035 7-8-9 57 (b) AlexOwen(7) 10 57
(N P Littmoden) *s.i.s and rdr lost iron s: hld up: hdwy over 1f out: nt trble ldrs* 14/1
3033 5 3/4 **Imperium**[53] 816 8-9-5 60 Louis-PhilippeBeuzelin 1 59
(Jean-Rene Auvray) *hld up in tch: rdn over 2f out: styd on same pce fnl f* 5/1[2]
0-06 6 1/2 **Flying Bantam (IRE)**[21] 1243 8-8-11 57 DavidKenny(5) 3 54
(J R Norton) *prom: hmpd and outpcd 3f out: styng on whn nt clr run and swtchd rt ins fnl f* 20/1
2503 7 3/4 **Interchoice Star**[8] 1535 4-8-4 48 RosieJessop(3) 5 44
(R Hollinshead) *led: clr 3f out: rdn and hdd over 1f out: edgd rt and wknd ins fnl f* 8/1[3]
026- 8 1/2 **Reve Vert (FR)**[187] 7072 4-8-6 50 MartinLane(3) 12 45
(Tim Vaughan) *prom: lost pl over 6f out: rdn and hung lft over 1f out: nt trble ldrs* 9/2[1]
300- 9 hd **Jay Gee Wigmo**[217] 6332 4-8-9 50 AmyBaker 8 44
(A W Carroll) *hld up: rdn over 1f out: n.d* 28/1
5-40 10 1 1/2 **Lancaster Lad (IRE)**[61] 749 4-8-5 49 (p) PNolan(3) 4 40
(A B Haynes) *prom: chsd ldr 1/2-way: rdn over 2f out: wknd over 1f out* 14/1
6500 11 7 **Just Jimmy (IRE)**[8] 1535 4-8-12 53 AndreaAtzeni 13 28
(P D Evans) *hld up: wknd over 3f out* 12/1
6-04 12 14 **Never Sold Out (IRE)**[8] 1535 4-8-9 50 MCGeran 6 —
(J G M O'Shea) *hld up in tch: rdn and wknd over 3f out* 10/1
-003 13 11 **Plaka (FR)**[38] 984 4-8-8 49 DeanHeslop 9 —
(W M Brisbourne) *chsd ldrs: wkng whn carried rt 3f out* 25/1
004- 14 47 **Ryan's Rock**[261] 5086 4-8-6 50 RossAtkinson(3) 2 —
(R J Price) *bolted a circ bef s: chsd ldr to 1/2-way: hung rt and wknd 3f out* 25/1

4030 15 2 3/4 **Inka Dancer (IRE)**[35] 1039 7-8-9 **50** .... WilliamCarson 15 —
(B Palling) *unruly in stalls: s.i.s: sn prom: rdn over 5f out: wkng whn carried rt 3f out* **33/1**

1m 40.76s (-0.24) **Going Correction** -0.075s/f (Good) **15** Ran SP% **117.6**
Speed ratings (Par 101): **98,97,96,94,93 92,92,91,91,90 83,69,58,11,8**
toteswingers: 1&2 £26.50, 1&3 £35.60, 2&3 £47.00 CSF £87.35 CT £2335.24 TOTE £8.00: £3.00, £3.70, £7.60; EX 136.50.
Owner The Cross Keys Racing Club **Bred** S Coughlan **Trained** Collingbourne Ducis, Wilts
■ Gemma Elford's first winner.

FOCUS
They went a decent gallop in this moderate apprentices' handicap, and the form is sound.
Ryan's Rock Official explanation: trainer said gelding returned lame near-fore
Inka Dancer(IRE) Official explanation: jockey said mare never travelled

1742 EUROPEAN BREEDERS' FUND PRIMROSE MAIDEN FILLIES' STKS 5f
2:40 (2:41) (Class 5) 2-Y-O **£3,885** (£1,156; £577; £288) **Stalls** Low

Form RPR
5 1 **Kings Of Leo**[7] 1569 2-9-0 0 .... PatDobbs 8 74+
(R Hannon) *chsd ldrs: led over 1f out: r.o wl* **7/4**[2]
0 2 1 1/4 **Angel Of Fashion (IRE)**[17] 1323 2-9-0 0 .... MichaelHills 7 70
(B W Hills) *hldup in tch: rdn and ev ch over 1f out: styd on same pce ins fnl f* **15/2**[3]
6 3 nk **Six Wives**[18] 1298 2-9-0 0 .... LiamJones 5 68
(W J Haggas) *wnt rt s: led: rdn and hdd over 1f out: edgd rt fnl f: styd on same pce* **11/8**[1]
4 1 1/2 **Pepi Royal (IRE)** 2-9-0 0 .... PaulEddery 4 63
(Pat Eddery) *chsd ldrs: pushed along and wandered 2f out: sn outpcd: styd on ins fnl f* **20/1**
5 shd **Two Kisses (IRE)** 2-9-0 0 .... StephenCarson 6 63
(B G Powell) *s.i.s: outpcd: r.o ins fnl f: nrst fin* **50/1**
6 7 **Chinese Democracy (USA)** 2-9-0 0 .... MartinDwyer 2 37
(P F I Cole) *chsd ldr: pushed along whn bmpd 2f out: wkng whn hung rt fnl f* **17/2**
7 1 **Desert Aisling (IRE)** 2-8-9 0 .... MartinLane(5) 3 34
(Edgar Byrne) *s.i.s: outpcd* **80/1**
8 nk **Moonlight Serenade** 2-9-0 0 .... TonyCulhane 9 33
(W G M Turner) *s.s: outpcd* **40/1**

59.91 secs (0.31) **Going Correction** -0.175s/f (Firm) **8** Ran SP% **111.2**
Speed ratings (Par 90): **90,88,87,85,84 73,72,71**
toteswingers: 1&2 £3.10, 1&3 £1.10, 2&3 £3.00 CSF £13.86 TOTE £2.60: £1.10, £2.00, £1.20; EX 16.40.
Owner J F Perryman **Bred** Mrs C R Philipson & Mrs H G Lascelles **Trained** East Everleigh, Wilts

FOCUS
An ordinary fillies' maiden.

NOTEBOOK
Kings Of Leo, who showed plenty of speed before fading on her debut at Windsor, again travelled strongly up with the pace and was driven to the front over a furlong out. She stuck on well for pressure, seeing the trip out this time, and remains open to further improvement. (op 15-8 tchd 2-1)
Angel Of Fashion(IRE), slowly away and always outpaced on her debut at Newbury, was a lot sharper this time and came with a strong-looking challenge, but the winner proved too good in the end. This was a big step forward and she will appreciate an extra furlong in time. (op 8-1)
Six Wives showed a good bit of ability when sixth on her debut at Newmarket and this was expected to prove easier. She went right out of the stalls, but was still able to lead and in the end was just done for speed. (op 5-4 tchd 6-5)
Pepi Royal(IRE), a cheaply bought purchase representing the yard responsible for the Brocklesby winner, travelled kindly in behind the speed and showed more than enough on this debut to suggest she will be winning something similar. (op 25-1)
Two Kisses(IRE) was outpaced from the word go and still last turning in, only to run on well down the straight. Her trainer is hardly renowned for success with juveniles and she will do better over further. (op 40-1 tchd 33-1)
Chinese Democracy(USA), related to several useful performers in the US, showed bright early speed before tiring in the straight and should benefit from the experience. (op 9-1 tchd 10-1)

1743 QUANTUM MANUFACTURING FILLIES' H'CAP 7f 26y
3:10 (3:11) (Class 5) (0-70,68) 3-Y-O+ **£3,238** (£963; £481; £240) **Stalls** Low

Form RPR
2-02 1 **Perfect Friend**[6] 1588 3-9-2 **66** .... EddieAhern 6 70+
(S Kirk) *hld up: hdwy 3f out: rdn to ld over 1f out: edgd rt ins fnl f: r.o* **11/4**[1]
26-0 2 3/4 **Resentful Angel**[17] 1332 4-9-10 **62** .... PaulEddery 2 68
(Pat Eddery) *led 6f out: edgd rt over 2f out: rdn and hdd over 1f out: r.o* **9/2**[3]
53-0 3 1/2 **Stellarina (IRE)**[27] 1173 3-9-1 **65** .... RobertWinston 14 65
(G A Swinbank) *led 1f: chsd ldrs: rdn over 1f out: r.o* **7/2**[2]
240- 4 1/2 **Turfwolke (GER)**[204] 6671 4-9-10 **62** .... SimonWhitworth 3 65
(Mrs H S Main) *hld up: racd keenly: hdwy over 2f out: rdn over 1f out: r.o* **16/1**
66-6 5 1/2 **Lindy Hop (IRE)**[27] 1173 3-8-12 **67** .... Louis-PhilippeBeuzelin(5) 5 65
(W R Swinburn) *s.i.s: hld up: hdwy over 1f out: r.o: nt rch ldrs* **8/1**
560- 6 6 **Ailsa Craig (IRE)**[222] 6198 3-9-0 **64** .... PatDobbs 7 45
(R Hannon) *hld up: rdn over 1f out: n.d* **12/1**
000- 7 2 1/4 **Barbee (IRE)**[212] 6477 3-9-4 **68** .... StephenDonohoe 10 43
(E A L Dunlop) *edgd rt s: hld up: rdn over 1f out: n.d* **14/1**
410- 8 shd **Ken's Girl**[189] 7021 5-9-11 **66** .... JamesMillman(3) 13 45
(W S Kittow) *prom: rdn over 2f out: wknd over 1f out* **14/1**
5605 9 1 1/4 **Amber Moon**[7] 1566 4-8-11 **54** ....(b) AnnStokell(5) 12 30
(Miss A Stokell) *edgd lft s: mid-div: sn pushed along: wknd over 2f out* **33/1**
46-0 10 1 1/2 **Naizak**[26] 1193 3-9-3 **67** ....(b[1]) TPO'Shea 4 35
(J L Dunlop) *trckd ldrs: rdn over 2f out: hung lft and wknd over 1f out* **16/1**
11 3/4 **Summer Capers (USA)**[157] 7479 4-9-0 **52** oh1 .... JimCrowley 8 22
(J Gallagher) *trckd ldrs: rdn over 2f out: sn wknd* **20/1**
0-00 12 21 **Lucky Forteen**[12] 1465 6-9-0 **52** oh7 .... ChrisCatlin 11 —
(P W Hiatt) *hmpd sn after s: outpcd* **80/1**

1m 24.51s (-0.09) **Going Correction** -0.075s/f (Good)
WFA 3 from 4yo+ 12lb **12** Ran SP% **119.9**
Speed ratings (Par 100): **97,96,95,95,94 87,85,84,83,81 80,56**
toteswingers: 1&2 £3.50, 1&3 £2.20, 2&3 £4.80 CSF £14.86 CT £45.82 TOTE £3.30: £1.30, £2.40, £2.00; EX 17.50.
Owner Lady Davis **Bred** Speedlith Group **Trained** Upper Lambourn, Berks

FOCUS
They went just a fair gallop in this and the gambled-on Perfect Friend got the job done. The form is rated around the second and fourth but is a bit muddling.

1744 BETFAIR H'CAP (FOR THE COVENTRY CUP) 7f 26y
3:40 (3:40) (Class 4) (0-80,80) 3-Y-O **£5,828** (£1,734; £866; £432) **Stalls** Low

Form RPR
03-2 1 **Suruor (IRE)**[28] 1155 3-8-13 **75** .... StephenDonohoe 3 84
(D M Simcock) *s.i.s: hld up: hdwy over 1f out: rdn to ld ins fnl f: hung rt: r.o wl* **9/1**[3]
0-03 2 2 3/4 **Thunderball**[11] 1471 3-9-1 **77** ....(p) RobertWinston 6 79
(A J McCabe) *led 6f out: sn hdd: rdn to ld 2f out: hung lft and hdd ins fnl f: styd on same pce* **9/1**[3]
21- 3 3/4 **Glen Molly (IRE)**[261] 5097 3-9-2 **78** .... MichaelHills 5 78
(B W Hills) *hld up in tch: rdn to chse ldr over 1f out: styd on same pce ins fnl f* **11/8**[1]
102- 4 2 1/4 **My Kingdom (IRE)**[193] 6924 3-9-3 **79** ....(t) TravisBlock 7 73
(H Morrison) *hld up: hdwy over 2f out: rdn over 1f out: styd on same pce* **12/1**
0-40 5 1 3/4 **Asian Tale (IRE)**[43] 924 3-8-7 **69** .... PaulDoe 9 58
(P D Evans) *s.i.s: bhd and rdn 3f out: r.o ins fnl f: nrst fin* **40/1**
214 6 1/2 **Trip Switch**[42] 936 3-8-8 **70** .... MartinDwyer 2 58
(W R Muir) *led 1f: chsd ldrs: rdn and wknd over 1f out* **8/1**[2]
31-3 7 1/2 **Victoria Sponge (IRE)**[12] 1466 3-8-11 **73** .... PatDobbs 10 59
(R Hannon) *hld up: rdn over 2f out: n.d* **12/1**
-132 8 3/4 **Fesko**[48] 859 3-9-4 **80** .... GregFairley 4 64
(M Johnston) *s.i.s: sn pushed along in rr: sme hdwy over 1f out: wknd ins fnl f* **8/1**[2]
25-3 9 15 **Frank Street**[13] 1419 3-8-13 **75** .... StephenCarson 11 19
(Eve Johnson Houghton) *hld up: wknd 3f out* **20/1**
-000 10 1/2 **Versaki (IRE)**[37] 1002 3-9-3 **79** .... JimCrowley 1 22
(D Nicholls) *led over 5f out: rdn and hdd 2f out: sn wknd* **11/1**
540- 11 8 **Viking Awake (IRE)**[191] 6988 3-8-10 **72** .... ChrisCatlin 8 —
(J W Unett) *prom to 1/2-way: eased* **80/1**

1m 23.5s (-1.10) **Going Correction** -0.075s/f (Good) **11** Ran SP% **116.5**
Speed ratings (Par 101): **103,99,99,96,94 93,93,92,75,74 65**
toteswingers: 1&2 £13.20, 1&3 £3.80, 2&3 £6.30 CSF £85.10 CT £179.74 TOTE £11.20: £2.60, £3.20, £1.30; EX 94.60.
Owner Dr Marwan Koukash **Bred** Shadwell Estate Company Limited **Trained** Newmarket, Suffolk

FOCUS
This was a competitive-looking handicap and a fair race for the grade. The winner is improved this year for a new yard.
Versaki(IRE) Official explanation: jockey said gelding hung right and lost its action

1745 PATEDDERYRACING.COM PROFESSIONAL RACEHORSE SYNDICATION MEDIAN AUCTION MAIDEN FILLIES' STKS 1m 22y
4:10 (4:10) (Class 5) 3-5-Y-O **£2,914** (£867; £433; £216) **Stalls** Low

Form RPR
44-2 1 **Badiat Alzaman (IRE)**[10] 1491 3-8-12 75 .... JimCrowley 9 79
(D M Simcock) *hld up: racd keenly: hdwy 3f out: led wl over 1f out: hung rt fnl f: r.o wl: eased nr fin* **6/4**[1]
24- 2 5 **Storming Sioux**[178] 7227 3-8-12 0 .... LiamJones 5 68
(W J Haggas) *dwlt: hld up: hdwy and hung rt over 3f out: led 2f out: sn hdd: outpcd fnl f* **7/4**[2]
00 3 2 **Toujours Souriante**[9] 1508 3-8-12 0 .... GregFairley 1 63
(M Johnston) *chsd ldrs: rdn and hung rt fnl f over 1f out: no ex fnl f* **28/1**
4 1 3/4 **Tisifone** 3-8-12 0 .... EddieAhern 2 59
(C G Cox) *prom: lost pl over 5f out: hdwy over 1f out: hung rt ins fnl f: nt trble ldrs* **8/1**
0 5 10 **La Creme (IRE)**[17] 1327 3-8-12 0 .... TonyCulhane 3 36
(M R Channon) *chsd ldrs: hung rt over 3f out: rdn and hung lft 2f out: sn wknd* **6/1**[3]
0 6 3 1/2 **Poca A Poca (IRE)**[13] 1423 5-9-6 0 .... MarkFlynn(5) 10 28
(G C Bravery) *dwlt: hld up: effrt over 2f out: sn wknd* **100/1**
60 7 1 3/4 **Carrazara (IRE)**[17] 1329 3-8-7 0 .... MartinLane(5) 7 24
(Edgar Byrne) *sn pushed along to chse ldr: rdn and ev ch over 2f out: sn wknd* **80/1**
0- 8 7 **Cativo**[216] 6360 3-8-10 0 ow1 .... JamesMillman(3) 8 9
(B R Millman) *hld up: wknd over 3f out* **100/1**
0- 9 27 **Houdella**[266] 4923 3-8-12 0 .... MichaelHills 6 —
(B W Hills) *hld up: rdn and hdd 2f out: sn wknd* **20/1**
0-00 10 7 **Xandra (IRE)**[42] 934 4-9-11 45 .... MartinDwyer 4 —
(W M Brisbourne) *chsd ldrs over 4f* **100/1**

1m 40.28s (-0.72) **Going Correction** -0.075s/f (Good)
WFA 3 from 4yo+ 13lb **10** Ran SP% **114.2**
Speed ratings (Par 100): **100,95,93,91,81 77,76,69,42,35**
toteswingers: 1&2 £1.10, 1&3 £9.80, 2&3 £13.60 CSF £4.04 TOTE £2.30: £1.40, £1.20, £3.90; EX 4.80.
Owner Sultan Ali **Bred** Michael Woodlock & Seamus Kennedy **Trained** Newmarket, Suffolk

FOCUS
An uncompetitive maiden won in good style by the favourite. Straightforward form, the winner close to her Wolverhampton effort.
Cativo Official explanation: jockey said filly hung right

1746 TURFTV H'CAP 1m 22y
4:40 (4:41) (Class 6) (0-60,63) 3-Y-O **£2,047** (£604; £302) **Stalls** Low

Form RPR
-533 1 shd **Everaard (USA)**[7] 1574 3-9-4 **60** .... MartinDwyer 1 67+
(D R C Elsworth) *sn led: rdn: hung rt and hdd over 1f out: ev ch whn hmpd ins fnl f: styd on gamely: fin 2nd: awrdd the r* **3/1**[2]
000- 2 **Bob Stock (IRE)**[196] 6865 3-9-4 **60** .... ChrisCatlin 4 67+
(W J Musson) *hld up in tch: plld hrd: rdn to ld and hung rt fr over 1f out: hdd ins fnl f: rallied to ld wl ins fnl f: all out: fin 1st: plcd 2nd* **11/4**[1]
30-0 3 3/4 **Jobekani (IRE)**[26] 1193 3-9-3 **59** .... StephenDonohoe 3 64
(Mrs L Williamson) *s.i.s: hdwy over 2f out: hung rt over 1f out: rdn to ld ins fnl f: hmpd sn after: hdd wl ins fnl f: unable qck nr fin* **25/1**
-345 4 4 1/2 **La Gifted**[21] 1253 3-9-4 **60** .... TonyCulhane 5 55
(M R Channon) *prom: rdn over 2f out: wknd fnl f* **10/1**
000- 5 1 1/4 **Almazar**[209] 6553 3-9-4 **60** .... TPO'Shea 10 52
(J L Dunlop) *chsd ldrs: rdn over 2f out: wknd over 1f out* **9/1**
4600 6 3/4 **Harty Boy (USA)**[16] 1361 3-9-2 **58** ....(p) StephenCarson 9 48
(Mrs S Leech) *hld up and bhd: hdwy u.p over 1f out: nt trble ldrs* **33/1**
606- 7 3 1/4 **Spring Secret**[200] 6745 3-9-4 **60** .... FrankieMcDonald 2 43
(B Palling) *s.i.s: hld up: rdn over 2f out: n.d* **33/1**
04-5 8 5 **Lagan Handout**[17] 1322 3-9-2 **58** .... JimCrowley 8 29
(C Gordon) *hld up: rdn over 2f out: n.d* **25/1**

-040 **9** *2 ½* **Vita Mia**[13] 1441 3-9-1 **57** .... PaulDoe 11 22
(P D Evans) *s.i.s: hmpd over 6f out: rdn over 3f out: n.d* **20/1**
00-4 **10** *6* **Achromatic**[9] 1516 3-8-11 **58** .... (v[1]) Louis-PhilippeBeuzelin(5) 7 10
(W R Swinburn) *chsd ldr: rdn and ev ch over 2f out: wknd wl over 1f out* **8/1**
1255 **11** *5* **Whotsit (IRE)**[51] 839 3-8-13 **58** .... (b) MarcHalford(3) 6 —
(Miss Amy Weaver) *s.i.s: hmpd over 6f out: a in rr* **22/1**
3036 **12** *3 ¾* **Lucky Fortune (IRE)**[35] 1036 3-8-10 **57** .... (b) MartinLane(5) 16 —
(Miss Amy Weaver) *s.i.s: sn prom: rdn and wknd over 2f out* **50/1**
600- **13** *4* **Eager To Bow (IRE)**[209] 6553 3-9-1 **57** .... GregFairley 14 —
(P R Chamings) *mid-div: hmpd over 6f out: rdn over 3f out: wknd over 2f out* **18/1**
450- **14** *1* **Call Me Courageous (IRE)**[222] 6207 3-8-8 **57** .... PNolan(7) 15 —
(A B Haynes) *chsd ldrs: edgd lft over 6f out: wknd over 2f out* **100/1**
56-0 **15** *2 ¾* **Jhinga Palak (IRE)**[122] 19 3-9-4 **60** .... PaulEddery 17 —
(Mrs K Waldron) *hld up: a in rr: wknd 3f out* **50/1**
03-1 **16** *1 ¼* **Cavendish Road (IRE)**[4] 1620 3-9-2 **63** 6ex .... RossAtkinson(5) 13 —
(W R Muir) *prom: lost pl over 6f out: bhd fnl 3f* **15/2**[3]
600- **17** *108* **May Need A Spell**[212] 6488 3-9-2 **58** .... RobertWinston 12 —
(J G M O'Shea) *hld up in tch: hmpd over 6f out: wknd over 3f out: eased fnl 2f* **66/1**

1m 41.39s (0.39) **Going Correction** -0.075s/f (Good) **17** Ran SP% **128.0**
Speed ratings (Par 97): **94,95,94,89,88 87,84,79,76,70 65,62,58,57,54 53,—**
toteswingers: 1&2 £3.90, 1&3 £25.50, 2&3 £19.30 CSF £10.92 CT £178.28 TOTE £4.00: £1.40, £1.10, £6.10, £2.50; EX 14.20.
Owner D R C Elsworth **Bred** F & F Investments **Trained** Newmarket, Suffolk
■ Stewards' Enquiry : Chris Catlin five-day ban, inc two deferred: careless riding (May 18-22)

FOCUS
This low-grade handicap that produced a controversial finish, with the heavily-gambled first-past-the-post Bob Stock hanging right once hitting the front and hampering Everaard on several occasions. He was disqualified but can rate higher. The first three finished clear but the form is only \n\x\x ordinary.
May Need A Spell Official explanation: jockey said gelding was unsuited by the good to firm ground

1747 EDGECOTE H'CAP — 1m 4f 134y
5:10 (5:12) (Class 5) (0-70,70) 3-Y-O — **£2,914** (£867; £433; £216) **Stalls** Low

Form — RPR
00-3 **1** **Admirable Duque (IRE)**[14] 1408 3-9-4 **70** .... StephenDonohoe 1 76
(D J S Ffrench Davis) *sn pushed along to chse ldrs: led and hung rt 2f out: rdn clr fnl f: eased nr fin* **11/2**[3]
00-3 **2** *3 ¼* **Saborido (USA)**[13] 1416 3-9-2 **68** .... JimCrowley 3 69
(Mrs A J Perrett) *chsd ldrs: rdn 4f out: styd on same pce fnl f* **5/2**[1]
20-5 **3** *¾* **Excelsior Academy**[13] 1416 3-9-2 **68** .... RobertWinston 8 68
(B J Meehan) *prom: rdn and lost pl over 7f out: rallied over 2f out: styd on* **14/1**
650- **4** *1* **Strathcal**[180] 7190 3-9-0 **66** .... TravisBlock 9 64
(H Morrison) *dwlt: hld up: styd on fr over 2f out: nt rch ldrs* **20/1**
01-2 **5** *½* **Canmoss (USA)**[5] 1614 3-9-0 **66** .... ChrisCatlin 5 64
(E J O'Neill) *chsd ldr: rdn 3f out: no ex fnl f* **3/1**[2]
00-1 **6** *nse* **Spinning Waters**[14] 1397 3-9-2 **68** .... StephenCarson 11 66
(Eve Johnson Houghton) *hld up: rdn over 2f out: nt rch ldrs* **12/1**
40-0 **7** *10* **Golden Games (IRE)**[16] 1363 3-8-6 **58** .... EddieAhern 10 40
(J L Dunlop) *broke wl: sn stdd and lost pl: n.d after* **9/1**
0-01 **8** *8* **Melange (USA)**[13] 1440 3-9-0 **66** .... MartinDwyer 2 35
(P F I Cole) *led: rdn and hdd whn hmpd 2f out: sn wknd* **12/1**
053- **9** *4 ½* **Play To Win (IRE)**[137] 7718 3-8-10 **62** .... MichaelHills 7 24
(D R C Elsworth) *hld up: hdwy over 7f out: rdn over 3f out: wknd 2f out: eased fnl f* **8/1**
060- **10** *2 ½* **Aziz (IRE)**[173] 7282 3-8-4 **56** oh11 .... (b) PaulEddery 4 14
(Miss D Mountain) *hld up: rdn whn stmbld wl over 2f out: a in rr* **100/1**
0-54 **11** *22* **Witch Of The Wave (IRE)**[68] 677 3-8-6 **58** .... (v[1]) FrankieMcDonald 6 —
(Miss J S Davis) *trckd ldrs: racd keenly: rdn and wknd over 3f out: n.m.r sn after* **33/1**

2m 44.28s (-0.32) **Going Correction** -0.075s/f (Good) **11** Ran SP% **120.8**
Speed ratings (Par 99): **97,95,94,93,93 93,87,82,79,78 64**
toteswingers: 1&2 £2.40, 1&3 £11.70, 2&3 £12.50 CSF £19.89 CT £189.32 TOTE £6.70: £2.50, £2.00, £2.20; EX 31.10 Place 6 £13.45, Place 5 £2.12..
Owner Brian W Taylor **Bred** Airlie Stud And R N Clay **Trained** Lambourn, Berks

FOCUS
This was a modest middle-distance handicap. The form looks sound and makes sense.
Strathcal Official explanation: jockey said gelding stopped quickly
T/Jkpt: £2,309.50 to a £1 stake. Pool: £34,155.74. 10.50 winning tickets. T/Plt: £20.90 to a £1 stake. Pool: £69,468.63. 2,423.28 winning tickets. T/Qpdt: £3.50 to a £1 stake. Pool: £3,213.40. 669.50 winning tickets. CR

1569 WINDSOR (R-H)
Monday, May 4
OFFICIAL GOING: Good to firm (good in places; 8.5)
Wind: Brisk across Weather: Dull

1748 BETFAIR APPRENTICE TRAINING SERIES H'CAP — 6f
2:25 (2:25) (Class 5) (0-75,72) 4-Y-O+ — **£2,729** (£806; £403) **Stalls** High

Form — RPR
5500 **1** **Style Award**[21] 1241 4-8-9 **65** .... (p) PaulPickard(3) 8 71
(W J H Ratcliffe) *trckd ldr 1/2-way: chal fr 2f out: hung lft over 1f out: led ins fnl f: hld on all out* **7/1**[3]
04-4 **2** *hd* **Our Blessing (IRE)**[19] 1285 5-8-10 **63** .... MatthewDavies 5 68
(A P Jarvis) *sn led: rdn 2f out: hdd ins fnl f: styd pressing wnr: no ex last strides* **7/1**[3]
1544 **3** *1 ½* **Gwilym (GER)**[61] 757 6-8-12 **68** .... DebraEngland(3) 1 68
(D Haydn Jones) *t.k.h: chsd ldrs: ev ch 2f out: sn rdn: outpcd fnl f* **5/1**[1]
1025 **4** *hd* **Sherjawy (IRE)**[26] 1182 5-8-0 **58** oh4 .... (b) AlexEdwards(5) 9 58
(Miss Z C Davison) *t.k.h: shkn up and outpcd over 2f out: kpt on again fnl f: kpt on cl home* **16/1**
-400 **5** *½* **Golden Prospect**[14] 1413 5-8-3 **59** .... CharlesEddery(3) 4 57
(J W Hills) *in tch: rdn and effrt 2f out: nvr gng pce to rch ldrs* **5/1**[1]
060- **6** *½* **Lunces Lad (IRE)**[25] 6650 5-9-3 **70** .... LeeNewnes 7 66
(G Brown) *s.i.s: sn rcvrd to chse ldrs: rdn half way: wknd fnl f* **14/1**
3230 **7** *1* **Red Rudy**[9] 1530 7-8-6 **59** .... SimonPearce 3 52
(A W Carroll) *chsd ldrs: rdn over 2f out: wknd fnl f* **5/1**[1]
600- **8** *3 ½* **Luminous Gold**[188] 7055 4-9-2 **69** .... JPHamblett 2 51+
(C F Wall) *t.k.h: chsd ldrs: ev ch 2f out: sn wknd* **11/2**[2]
420- **9** *3 ¾* **Polmaily**[184] 7143 4-9-0 **72** .... BarryAdams(5) 6 42
(J Akehurst) *s.i.s: sn rdn and managed to get in tch w main gp 1/2-way: sn wknd* **9/1**

1m 13.51s (0.51) **Going Correction** +0.10s/f (Good) **9** Ran SP% **112.9**
Speed ratings (Par 103): **100,99,97,97,96 96,94,90,85**
toteswingers: 1&2 £14.40, 1&3 £14.80, 2&3 £9.30 CSF £53.76 CT £267.31 TOTE £7.40: £2.20, £2.50, £1.90; EX 55.80 Trifecta £185.40.
Owner Bolton Hall Partnership 1 **Bred** Mrs S F Dibben **Trained** Newmarket, Suffolk

FOCUS
A tricky opening handicap, confined to apprentice riders. The race developed more towards the middle of the track and the form is ordinary and somewhat muddling.

1749 GOLDRING SECURITY SERVICES MAIDEN STKS — 5f 10y
2:55 (2:58) (Class 5) 2-Y-O — **£2,729** (£806; £403) **Stalls** High

Form — RPR
50 **1** **Crown (IRE)**[18] 1298 2-8-12 0 .... RichardHughes 3 82+
(R Hannon) *w ldr: led ins fnl 3f: rdn over 1f out: hld on wl cl home* **11/4**[2]
2 *1* **Tawaabb** 2-9-3 0 .... RyanMoore 7 84+
(M R Channon) *sn led: hdd ins fnl 3f: rdn and qcknd to chal 1f out: hung lft and nt qckn ins fnl f* **5/6**[1]
3 *4* **Deal (IRE)** 2-8-12 0 .... RichardSmith 5 64
(R Hannon) *chsd ldrs: rdn 1/2-way: outpcd by ldng duo fr over 1f out* **10/1**
4 *7* **Ballyvonane (USA)** 2-9-3 0 .... IanMongan 1 44
(L A Dace) *chsd ldrs: rdn 1/2-way: wknd fr 2f out* **33/1**
5 *7* **Underworld Dandy** 2-9-3 0 .... RichardKingscote 4 19
(Tom Dascombe) *sn rdn and outpcd in rr* **13/2**[3]
6 *¾* **Polebrook** 2-9-3 0 .... RichardMullen 6 16
(J R Jenkins) *slowly away: a outpcd* **14/1**

61.07 secs (0.77) **Going Correction** +0.10s/f (Good) **6** Ran SP% **113.3**
Speed ratings (Par 93): **97,95,89,77,66 65**
toteswingers: 1&2 £1.10, 1&3 £2.40, 2&3 £3.80 CSF £5.51 TOTE £4.00: £2.40, £1.10; EX 6.00.
Owner Mrs J Wood **Bred** Shortgrove Manor Stud **Trained** East Everleigh, Wilts

FOCUS
An interesting little juvenile maiden, but few seriously got involved off the decent pace and the first pair dominated down the home straight.

NOTEBOOK
Crown(IRE) was the only runner in attendance with any previous form and that counted for plenty as she shed her maiden tag at the third time of asking. She had contested a hotter event at Newmarket last time when well held, but this flatter track was more to her liking and she knuckled down well at the business end. Another furlong should suit ideally in due course, but her life will be tougher now. (op 15-8)
Tawaabb ◆ cost 82,000gns, is bred to make his mark at two and came in for strong support. He knew his job as he was well away, but hit a flat spot before keeping on again and really lost out through inexperience. He lost ground by drifting under pressure, but should be a lot wiser next time. (op 13-8 tchd 7-4)
Deal(IRE), a stablemate to the winner, looked the second string using betting as a guide. She showed early dash, but could not raise her game from 2f out. This debut experience will not be lost on her. (op 8-1)
Ballyvonane(USA) is bred to appreciate further and shaped accordingly. (op 28-1 tchd 25-1)
Underworld Dandy, whose stable have hit the ground running with its juveniles, has speed in his pedigree yet was taken off his feet through the early stages. He was too green to do himself justice. (op 5-1 tchd 9-2)
Polebrook, out of a dam who has thrown up some useful winners, did not go unbacked for this racecourse debut, but fell out the gates and appeared clueless through the race. He should learn a deal for the outing, but already looks to want a stiffer test. (tchd 9-1)

1750 OMM PRINT H'CAP — 1m 2f 7y
3:25 (3:26) (Class 4) (0-85,84) 4-Y-O+ — **£5,180** (£1,541; £770; £384) **Stalls** Low

Form — RPR
46-0 **1** **Martyr**[16] 1357 4-9-1 **81** .... RichardHughes 1 91
(R Hannon) *led 2f: styd trcking ldr: rdn to chal over 1f out: slt ld ins fnl f: styd on wl* **4/1**[3]
6-55 **2** *¾* **Trans Siberian**[16] 1357 5-9-3 **83** .... RyanMoore 6 92
(P F I Cole) *t.k.h: led after 2f: rdn over 2f out: hdd ins fnl f: styd on same pce u.p* **9/4**[1]
0-00 **3** *¾* **Ballinteni**[13] 1433 7-9-4 **84** .... WilliamBuick 3 91
(D K Ivory) *in tch: pushed along and hdwy fr 3f out: rdn to chse ldrs ins fnl 2f: kpt on but nvr quite gng pce to chal* **10/3**[2]
4354 **4** *1 ¾* **Can Can Star**[23] 1213 6-8-13 **79** .... JamesDoyle 2 83
(A W Carroll) *t.k.h: sn chsng ldrs: rdn and bmpd over 1f out: sn one pce u.p* **15/2**
-124 **5** *3* **Basra (IRE)**[45] 893 6-9-1 **81** .... IanMongan 5 79
(Miss Jo Crowley) *in tch: rdn and hdwy 2f out: edgd lft over 1f out: wknd ins fnl f* **15/2**
-055 **6** *3 ¼* **Alpes Maritimes**[71] 648 5-8-6 **72** .... (p) RichardMullen 8 63
(G L Moore) *a towards rr* **16/1**
0-53 **7** *7* **Marning Star**[87] 430 4-8-9 **75** .... RichardKingscote 4 59
(Ian Williams) *t.k.h: chsd ldrs to 3f out: sn wknd* **14/1**
560- **8** *26* **Zaif (IRE)**[275] 4645 6-8-8 **74** ow2 .... SteveDrowne 7 —
(D J S Ffrench Davis) *a bhd* **16/1**

2m 6.93s (-1.77) **Going Correction** -0.05s/f (Good) **8** Ran SP% **115.8**
Speed ratings (Par 105): **105,104,103,102,100 97,91,71**
toteswingers: 1&2 £3.60, 1&3 £2.50, 2&3 £1.60 CSF £13.64 CT £32.71 TOTE £6.30: £1.90, £1.60, £1.60; EX 16.50 Trifecta £117.00.
Owner Highclere Thoroughbred Racing (Delilah) **Bred** D Maroun **Trained** East Everleigh, Wilts

FOCUS
This was a fair handicap run at a good pace, and the form is sound.
Zaif(IRE) Official explanation: trainer said gelding bled from the nose

1751 WYCOMBE WANDERERS FC H'CAP — 1m 67y
3:55 (3:56) (Class 3) (0-90,88) 3-Y-O — **£8,095** (£2,408; £1,203; £601) **Stalls** High

Form — RPR
21- **1** **Desert Creek (IRE)**[188] 7051 3-8-9 **79** .... RyanMoore 10 93+
(Sir Michael Stoute) *t.k.h: trckd ldrs: led appr fnl 4f: drvn and hld on wl fr over 1f out* **7/4**[1]
221- **2** *1 ¾* **Emirates Roadshow (USA)**[185] 7105 3-8-9 **82** .... AhmedAjtebi(3) 11 92+
(Saeed Bin Suroor) *led tl hdd appr fnl 4f: styd chsng wnr: rdn and kpt on same pce fnl 2f* **7/2**[2]
31- **3** *2 ¼* **December Draw (IRE)**[147] 7602 3-8-12 **82** .... RichardKingscote 9 87
(W J Knight) *chsd ldrs: rdn 3f out: styd on to chse ldng duo ins fnl f but nvr any ch* **14/1**
11-3 **4** *1 ½* **Sonning Gate**[10] 1487 3-9-4 **88** .... GeorgeBaker 6 89+
(D R C Elsworth) *towards rr: rdn: hdwy and hung lft over 2f out: kpt on cl home but nvr any threat* **12/1**

331- **5** *hd* **Hail Promenader (IRE)**[212] 6481 3-8-11 **81**.................... WilliamBuick 4 82
(B W Hills) *chsd ldrs: pushed along over 3f out: one pce 2f out: wknd fnl f* **20/1**

51-2 **6** *2* **Wannabe King**[17] 1324 3-9-2 **86**.................... RichardMullen 5 82
(D R Lanigan) *broke wl: stdd towards rr after 2f: rdn 3f out: sme hdwy over 2f out: nvr in contention* **4/1**[3]

431- **7** *2½* **Calaloo (IRE)**[194] 6892 3-8-10 **80**.................... SteveDrowne 3 71
(C R Egerton) *in rr tl sme hdwy fnl 2f* **40/1**

231- **8** *½* **Officer In Command (USA)**[187] 7073 3-8-10 **80**..........(t) JamesDoyle 2 69
(J S Moore) *in tch: hdwy on outside 3f out: chsd ldrs 2f out: wknd qckly over 1f out* **28/1**

30-4 **9** *1¾* **Roly Boy**[49] 851 3-8-13 **83**.................... RichardHughes 12 68
(R Hannon) *rdn and hung bdly lft fr ins fnl 3f: no rspnse* **17/2**

206- **10** *¾* **Perfect Citizen (USA)**[204] 6673 3-8-13 **83**.................... IanMongan 1 67
(W R Swinburn) *chsd ldrs: wd into st: wknd qckly 2f out* **20/1**

40-5 **11** *shd* **Hip Hip Hooray**[19] 1284 3-8-1 **74** oh10.................... GilmarPereira(3) 8 57
(L A Dace) *slowly away: in rr: wd into st and sme hdwy 3f out: nvr rchd ldrs and wknd 2f out* **66/1**

1m 43.66s (-1.04) **Going Correction** -0.05s/f (Good) **11** Ran SP% **120.4**
Speed ratings (Par 103): **103,101,99,97,97 95,92,92,90,89 89**
toteswingers: 1&2 £1.60, 1&3 £12.20, 2&3 £4.70 CSF £7.39 CT £66.49 TOTE £2.40: £1.40, £1.50, £4.30; EX 7.30 Trifecta £81.40.
Owner Saeed Suhail **Bred** Mount Coote Stud And M H Dixon **Trained** Newmarket, Suffolk

FOCUS
A fascinating 3yo handicap featuring six last-time-out maiden winners. The first pair both had decent draws and the race should produce plenty of future winners. The form is sound and there is more to come from the first two.

NOTEBOOK
Desert Creek(IRE) ◆ looked to have got in lightly off a mark of 79 for his handicap debut and so it proved, as he did the job readily against the stands' rail. He proved a little fresh on this return, but was soon in a good rhythm and took a split on the inside 4f out to dispute the lead. He sealed the race when asserting 2f out without needing to be fully asked and was always doing enough inside the final furlong. The step up to this trip suited, as did the sound surface, and there should be plenty more to come from this choicely-bred colt. The Britannia Stakes at Royal Ascot next month looks an ideal next target and a likely rise for this should just get him in there. (op 13-8 tchd 2-1)

Emirates Roadshow(USA) took four runs to get off the mark last term, but did have some useful form and met support for his seasonal return. He set out to make all, but lacked the tactical speed of the winner and although coming back at that rival late on, was always being held. This rates a pleasing start to his 3yo campaign and he should not be long in resuming winning ways, but may prefer an even stiffer test now. (op 7-1)

December Draw(IRE) ◆ had got off the mark in a moderate Lingfield maiden on his final outing at two, but his debut third at Great Leighs has worked out very well. Making his turf bow, he posted a highly encouraging return to the track and looks sure to benefit a deal for the outing. His pedigree suggests speed, but all of his three runs have been at this distance and he shaped as though he may get a little further. Official explanation: jockey said gelding hung left (op 12-1 tchd 11-1)

Sonning Gate was making his handicap debut after running with credit on his return in a decent little conditions event at Sandown ten days earlier. He ran respectably in defeat, considering this may have come soon enough, and is the type his trainer does very well with. (op 10-1 tchd 14-1)

Hail Promenader(IRE), off the mark at the fourth attempt last term, proved easy to back despite his yard being in excellent form. He ran as though the race was needed and got the extra furlong well enough. (op 16-1)

Wannabe King ran a cracker on his comeback on easier ground at Newbury 17 days earlier and proved himself on fast ground as a juvenile. He did not get the best of runs through the race, but was disappointingly one-paced when under pressure and it is hard to tell if he stayed the extra furlong. His entry in the Irish 2000 Guineas is aiming too high, but this was probably not his true running and it would be unwise to judge him fully on this effort. (op 9-2 tchd 5-1)

Calaloo(IRE), a Bath maiden winner at this trip on his third and final outing last season, endured a troubled passage early on. He was keeping on when the race was all but over and can be expected to step up on this when upped in distance. This ground was also probably lively enough for him. (op 33-1)

1752 AMELIA MAY LAYE HURST 91ST BIRTHDAY MEDIAN AUCTION MAIDEN STKS 1m 67y
4:25 (4:26) (Class 5) 3-4-Y-O **£2,729** (£806; £403) **Stalls** High

Form RPR

2- **1** **Farleigh**[215] 6375 3-8-10 0.................... WilliamBuick 7 69
(A M Balding) *w ldr: t.k.h: slt ld over 4f out: rdn 2f out: edgd lft u.p ins fnl f: sn narrowly hdd: rallied to ld again last stride: all out* **5/1**[3]

22-0 **2** *shd* **Formula (USA)**[19] 1295 3-9-1 79.................... RichardHughes 5 74
(R Hannon) *sn slt ld: narrowly hdd over 4f out: styd pressing wnr: edgd lft ins fnl f and sn slt ld: ct last stride* **9/4**[2]

3 *½* **Voortrekker** 3-9-1 0.................... NickyMackay 9 73+
(D J Coakley) *s.i.s: in rr: hdwy over 2f out: str run fnl f: fin wl* **40/1**

003- **4** *nse* **Nesayem (IRE)**[213] 6432 3-8-7 75.................... AhmedAjtebi(3) 11 68
(D M Simcock) *chsd ldrs: rdn and str chal ins fnl f: no ex nr fin* **10/1**

4 **5** *2* **Zouk**[18] 1308 3-9-1 0.................... RyanMoore 8 68
(W R Swinburn) *trckd ldrs: rdn over 2f out: styd on same pce fnl f* **2/1**[1]

550- **6** *hd* **Fajita**[208] 6574 3-9-1 68.................... GeorgeBaker 4 67
(G L Moore) *in rr: hdwy towards outside 3f out: styd on same pce fnl 2f* **20/1**

033- **7** *2* **Darwin's Dragon**[147] 7602 3-9-1 71.................... JosedeSouza 3 63
(P F I Cole) *plld hrd: chsd ldrs: rdn over 2f out: wknd fnl f* **20/1**

8 *nse* **Young Star Gazer** 3-9-1 0.................... IanMongan 6 63
(H R A Cecil) *chsd ldrs: rdn over 2f out: wknd over 1f out* **7/1**

0-0 **9** *4* **Tres Chic (FR)**[17] 1329 3-8-10 0.................... SteveDrowne 10 49
(S Curran) *in tch: sme prog 3f out: wknd fr 2f out* **33/1**

10 *3½* **Final Son** 4-9-7 0.................... MatthewDavies(7) 13 45
(A P Jarvis) *a towards rr* **16/1**

11 *3* **Scarlett Angel (IRE)** 3-8-10 0.................... RichardKingscote 2 34
(W J Knight) *s.i.s: a in rr* **25/1**

12 *12* **Dancing Again** 3-8-9 0 ow6.................... LeeNewnes(7) 1 12
(E A Wheeler) *slowly away: chsd ldrs on outside 4f out: sn wknd* **66/1**

1m 45.44s (0.74) **Going Correction** -0.05s/f (Good)
WFA 3 from 4yo 13lb **12** Ran SP% **128.5**
Speed ratings (Par 103): **94,93,93,93,91 91,89,89,85,81 78,66**
toteswingers: 1&2 £2.10, 1&3 £19.80, 2&3 £42.30 CSF £16.92 TOTE £5.90: £2.20, £1.50, £9.30; EX 16.00 Trifecta £188.30.
Owner Farleigh Partnership **Bred** Pollards Stables **Trained** Kingsclere, Hants
■ Stewards' Enquiry : William Buick caution: careless riding.

FOCUS
An average maiden, run at an ordinary pace and the first four were closely covered at the finish. Very ordinary form. There was a stewards' enquiry as the first pair came close late on, but the placings rightly remained unaltered.

1753 AW CREATIVE H'CAP 1m 3f 135y
4:55 (4:56) (Class 4) (0-85,81) 4-Y-0+ **£5,180** (£1,541; £770; £384) **Stalls** Low

Form RPR

610- **1** **Shimoni**[214] 6415 5-9-4 **81**.................... RyanMoore 1 88
(G L Moore) *trckd ldrs: drvn to cl up 3f out: led and edgd lft wl over 1f out: rdn out* **4/1**

2416 **2** *1¼* **King Supreme (IRE)**[2] 1666 4-9-4 **81**....................(b) RichardHughes 3 86
(R Hannon) *chsd ldr: led over 2f out: rdn and hdd wl over 1f out: styd on one pce ins fnl f* **3/1**[2]

100- **3** *1½* **Look To This Day**[206] 6630 4-8-12 **75**.................... SteveDrowne 2 77
(R Charlton) *led: rdn and hdd over 2f out: styd pressing ldrs tl appr fnl f: wknd ins fnl f* **12/1**

421- **4** *3¾* **Dakiyah (IRE)**[332] 2799 5-9-4 **81**.................... IanMongan 6 77
(Mrs L J Mongan) *in tch: rdn to chse ldrs and hung lft over 2f out: wknd over 1f out* **7/2**[3]

010- **5** *1½* **Russian Epic**[22] 6035 5-9-1 **78**.................... RichardKingscote 5 71
(Andrew Turnell) *in rr but in tch: rdn over 3f out: nvr in contention and sn wknd* **7/1**

0 **6** *19* **Theocritus (USA)**[12] 1460 4-9-0 **80**.................... AhmedAjtebi(3) 4 39
(D M Simcock) *chsd ldrs: rdn 3f out: wknd qckly over 2f out: b.b.v* **5/2**[1]

2m 30.53s (1.03) **Going Correction** -0.05s/f (Good) **6** Ran SP% **116.0**
Speed ratings (Par 105): **94,93,92,89,88 76**
toteswingers: 1&2 £2.70, 1&3 £8.20, 2&3 £4.60 CSF £17.05 TOTE £4.10: £2.70, £1.50; EX 12.60 Place 6: £23.82, Place 5: £9.43.
Owner The Welldiggers Partnership **Bred** Lakin Bloodstock And H And W Thornton **Trained** Lower Beeding, W Sussex

FOCUS
This was a very tight little handicap with 6lb covering the field. It was run at a fair pace and the form is ordinary for the grade.
Theocritus(USA) Official explanation: trainer said gelding bled from the nose
T/Plt: £17.90 to a £1 stake. Pool: £65,852.64. 2,681.77 winning tickets. T/Qpdt: £8.70 to a £1 stake. Pool: £3,538.30. 298.50 winning tickets. ST

1754 - (Foreign Racing) - See Raceform Interactive

1135 CURRAGH (R-H)
Monday, May 4

OFFICIAL GOING: Heavy

1755a DYLAN THOMAS EUROPEAN BREEDER FUND TETRARCH STKS (GROUP 3) (ENTIRE COLTS & FILLIES) 7f
2:30 (2:31) 3-Y-O **£53,723** (£15,762; £7,509; £2,558)

RPR

1 **Vocalised (USA)**[16] 1354 3-9-1 111....................(t) KJManning 7 109
(J S Bolger, Ire) *trckd ldrs in 3rd: pushed along to go 2nd 2f out: led over 1f out: rdn clr ins fnl f: styd on wl* **8/15**[1]

2 *1¾* **Chief Lone Eagle (USA)**[183] 7155 3-9-1 .... JMurtagh 3 104+
(A P O'Brien, Ire) *sn led: rdn and hdd 3f out: sn dropped to 3rd: kpt on into 2nd nr fin wout troubling wnr* **9/2**[2]

3 *½* **Count John (IRE)**[13] 1447 3-9-1 91.................... CDHayes 9 103
(J T Gorman, Ire) *sn trckd ldr in 2nd: led 3f out: strly pressed and hdd over 1f out: no imp and kpt on same pce ins fnl f: dropped to 3rd nr fin* **16/1**

4 *2½* **Ohiyesa (IRE)**[29] 1136 3-8-12 94.................... KLatham 5 93
(G M Lyons, Ire) *towards rr: short of room 3f out: hdwy into 4th 2f out: no imp and kpt on same pce u.p fr 1f out* **16/1**

5 *½* **What's Up Pussycat (IRE)**[29] 1136 3-8-12 97.................... WMLordan 8 92
(David Wachman, Ire) *sn racd in 4th: 5th 2f out: no imp u.p and kpt on same pce fr over 1f out* **6/1**[3]

6 *10* **Lastkingofscotland (IRE)**[13] 1447 3-9-1 .... FMBerry 1 69
(Charles O'Brien, Ire) *towards rr: rdn fr 2f out: sn no imp: eased under 1f out* **16/1**

7 *1¾* **Little Arrows (IRE)**[164] 7408 3-9-1 83....................(b[1]) WJSupple 2 64
(W McCreery, Ire) *sn chsd ldrs: lost pl fr 2f out: sn no imp u.p: eased ins fnl f* **100/1**

8 *1½* **Three Way Stretch (IRE)**[29] 1136 3-9-1 90....................(t) DPMcDonogh 4 60
(J T Gorman, Ire) *towards rr: clsd to trck ldrs 3f out: 6th 2f out: sn no imp u.p: eased over 1f out* **33/1**

1m 34.8s (7.70) **Going Correction** +1.025s/f (Soft) **8** Ran SP% **119.3**
Speed ratings: **97,95,94,91,91 79,77,75**
CSF £3.61 TOTE £1.50: £1.10, £1.60, £4.20; DF 4.30.
Owner Mrs J S Bolger **Bred** Hill 'N' Dale Farm & Edward Mc **Trained** Coolcullen, Co Carlow

FOCUS
The fourth and fifth help set the standard for the form, which should work out.

NOTEBOOK
Vocalised(USA) maintained his unbeaten record for the season. Last month's Greenham winner at Newbury had previously won a Listed race over this course and distance and, while he didn't look in love with this heavy ground, his class got him through when he got to the front from Count John after halfway. He ran into 2,000 Guineas winner Sea The Stars on his debut but is clearly going the right way and should be even more effective when he encounters a decent surface. The Boylesports Irish 2,000 Guineas could figure in plans now. (op 4/9 tchd 4/7)

Chief Lone Eagle(USA) had got off the mark first time out at Leopardstown last autumn in a maiden that worked out well after he beat his better-fancied stable companion Rockhampton into fourth. The Ballydoyle colt, half-brother to 1,000 Guineas winner Virginia Waters and to the Group 1-placed pair Chevalier and Alexander Of Hales, broke smartly to take them along up front before Count John took over three furlongs out, clearly relishing these testing conditions. He looked destined for third before staying on again to snatch second close home, and he'll appreciate a longer journey on this evidence. Good ground should also bring out the best in him in due course. (op 4/1)

Count John(IRE) is clearly improving and this was another creditable effort from the dual Limerick winner on his favoured ground. He only ran out of puff inside the final furlong and he might prefer a drop back in trip.

Ohiyesa(IRE) Official explanation: jockey said filly checked off heels approx 3f out

1756a ORATORIO EUROPEAN BREEDERS FUND ATHASI STKS (GROUP 3) (F&M) 7f
3:00 (3:01) 3-Y-O+ **£53,640** (£15,679; £7,427; £2,475)

RPR

1 **Emily Blake (IRE)**[16] 1374 5-9-9 104.................... JMurtagh 8 106
(J C Hayden, Ire) *sn led: rdn 1 1/2f out: styd on best ins fnl f* **9/1**

The Form Book, Raceform Ltd, Compton, RG20 6NL

2 1 3/4 **Mad About You (IRE)**[29] 1138 4-9-12 114........................(b) PJSmullen 4 104
(D K Weld, Ire) *sn trckd ldrs: 2nd over 2f out: rdn 1 1/2f out: no imp ins fnl f and kpt on same pce* **5/4**[1]

3 3 1/2 **Girouette (IRE)**[183] 7157 4-9-9 97........................ PShanahan 7 92+
(Tracey Collins, Ire) *towards rr: rdn over 2f out: sn no imp: wnt mod 5th over 1f out: kpt on wout threatening* **20/1**

4 nk **Kalidaha (IRE)**[171] 7328 4-9-9 99........................ MJKinane 9 91
(John M Oxx, Ire) *prom: rdn in 3rd over 2f out: sn no imp and kpt on same pce* **5/1**[3]

5 2 1/2 **Pollen (IRE)**[29] 1139 4-9-9 96........................ WMLordan 6 84
(T Stack, Ire) *sn chsd ldrs: 6th and rdn over 2f out: sn no imp: kpt on same pce* **7/1**

6 nk **Choose Me (IRE)**[13] 1447 3-8-11 93........................ DPMcDonogh 1 79
(Kevin Prendergast, Ire) *hld up in rr and sn pushed along: dropped bhd u.p over 2f out: kpt on wout threatening ins fnl f* **33/1**

7 4 **Patio**[25] 1202 4-9-9 99........................ CO'Donoghue 5 72
(David Marnane, Ire) *prom: dropped to 5th and rdn over 2f out: sn no ex* **20/1**

8 10 **Russian Empress (IRE)**[43] 928 5-9-9 97........................ FMBerry 3 45
(David P Myerscough, Ire) *towards rr: clsr in 4th and rdn over 2f out: wknd fr over 1f out* **14/1**

9 5 **Maoineach (USA)**[16] 1353 3-9-0 107........................(t) KJManning 2 31
(J S Bolger, Ire) *ponied to s and slow to load: sn chsd ldrs: 7th and rdn over 2f out: sn wknd* **9/2**[2]

1m 32.7s (5.60) **Going Correction** +1.025s/f (Soft)
WFA 3 from 4yo+ 12lb **9** Ran SP% **120.9**
Speed ratings: **109,107,103,102,99 99,94,83,77**
CSF £21.26 TOTE £10.40: £1.80, £1.10, £5.40; DF 36.00.
Owner Stephen Hayden **Bred** Francis J O'Toole **Trained** Kilcullen, Co Kildare

FOCUS
The race has been rated through the winner to her best form. The third and fourth are both entitled to improve for the run.

NOTEBOOK
Emily Blake(IRE), who ran second in this event last year, went one better here, making all and showing her liking for the testing ground. She had the measure of her rivals from over a furlong out and kept on well in the closing stages. A three-time handicap winner, she is likely to drop back to 6f in the Group 3 Ballyogan Stakes, another fillies' and mares' event, at Leopardstown. (op 8/1)
Mad About You(IRE) had won the Group 3 Gladness Stakes over this course and trip on yielding ground early last month. The more testing conditions were probably not ideal for her this time and, after closing to go second a furlong and a half out, it was soon obvious that she was not going to trouble the winner. (op 11/10)
Girouette(IRE), a maiden winner over the trip and also Listed placed last season, made steady progress from the back of the field inside the last two furlongs and stayed on for third. It was an encouraging start to her year as the first two had both had a couple of runs each.
Kalidaha(IRE), runner-up to Mad About You in a 1m Listed event on soft ground at Naas last year, was making her reappearance and was close up for most of the way until tiring from a furlong out. (op 6/1 tchd 13/2)
Maoineach(USA), disappointing at Newbury on her previous start following her Group 3 win at Leopardstown, was again ponied to the start where she played up a bit before being loaded. She was fighting a losing battle from over two furlongs out and, although she won a Group 3 on soft here last year, her Leopardstown victory was on fast ground and the very testing conditions here were probably against her. Official explanation: vet said filly was found to be blowing hard post-race (op 100/30)

1758a HIGH CHAPARRAL EUROPEAN BREEDERS FUND MOORESBRIDGE STKS (GROUP 3) 1m 2f
4:00 (4:00) 4-Y-0+ **£53,640** (£15,679; £7,427; £2,475)

RPR

1 **Curtain Call (FR)**[294] 4042 4-9-1........................ FMBerry 7 115
(L M Cumani) *mde all: rdn clr st: drifted lft and styd on wl ins fnl f* **3/1**[3]

2 3 **Famous Name**[189] 7034 4-9-1 120........................ PJSmullen 1 109+
(D K Weld, Ire) *in tch towards rr in 6th: 5th over 3f out: sent to chse wnr 1 1/2f out: mod 2nd over 1f out: kpt on wout troubling wnr* **5/2**[2]

3 nk **Moiqen (IRE)**[232] 5944 4-9-1 108........................ DPMcDonogh 4 108
(Kevin Prendergast, Ire) *racd in 5th: wnt mod 2nd 2f out: kpt on same pce u.p in 3rd fr over 1f out* **25/1**

4 3 **Shreyas (IRE)**[198] 6819 4-9-1 108........................(t) KJManning 3 102+
(J S Bolger, Ire) *in rr: mod last and no imp u.p fr 2f out: kpt on wout threatening* **16/1**

5 hd **Perks (IRE)**[226] 6106 4-9-1........................ JMurtagh 6 102
(J L Dunlop) *trckd ldrs in 3rd: rdn st: no imp fr 2f out: 4th and kpt on same pce fr over 1f out* **11/2**

6 4 1/2 **Lady Deauville (FR)**[51] 846 4-9-1........................ WMLordan 2 93
(R Curtis) *trckd ldrs: rdn st: dropped to mod 5th and no imp fr 2f out: kpt on same pce* **14/1**

7 1 1/4 **Kargali (IRE)**[15] 1387 4-9-1 110........................(t) MJKinane 5 91
(John M Oxx, Ire) *trckd ldr in 2nd: rdn st: lost pl and no imp fr 2f out* **9/4**[1]

2m 24.7s (15.20) **Going Correction** +1.775s/f (Heav) **7** Ran SP% **116.1**
Speed ratings: **110,107,107,104,104 101,100**
CSF £11.32 TOTE £3.20: £1.90, £2.50; DF 12.70.
Owner Mrs P K Cooper and Partners **Bred** Famille Niarchos **Trained** Newmarket, Suffolk

FOCUS
The race was run in a slow time compared to the handicap over the same trip, and the race has been rated through the winner to his best.

NOTEBOOK
Curtain Call(FR), returning to the Curragh for the first time since his controversial fifth behind Frozen Fire in the Irish Derby last June, benefited from a positive ride to land this race. Supplemented at a cost of €8,500 last week, he broke smartly to lead and, when Fran Berry quickened the tempo into the straight, it proved a telling move on this ground. His chasing rivals were soon in trouble and, despite drifting left close home, this was more like the real Curtain Call, with the prevailing conditions certainly bringing out the best in him. His trainer Luca Cumani will go next to "wherever it rains", with the Tattersalls Gold Cup back here in under three weeks time on the shortlist. (op 5/2)
Famous Name, successful first time out in the last two seasons, looked a threat when sent after the winner in the straight. Just pipped in the French Derby last year, he didn't have his ground conditions for his first run back since landing a Leopardstown 1m2f Listed contest last October and it told in the end. He'll be better judged this term when he gets his ground. (op 5/2 tchd 100/30)
Moiqen(IRE) looked up against it on official figures but he wasn't disgraced given that this was his first run since last September, and he also didn't have underfoot conditions in his favour. His couple of below-par runs last term also came in similar ground.
Shreyas(IRE) proved disappointing on heavy ground last term and never got in a blow here, although she did stay on for a share of the minor honours. This comeback run should stand her in good stead when she encounters better ground conditions.
Perks(IRE) raced up with the pace until the distress signals went up on him. (op 11/2 tchd 5/1)
Lady Deauville(FR) dropped out in similar fashion once the winner picked up the pace.
Kargali(IRE) proved a big disappointment. He got the better of the progressive Three Rocks at Leopardstown over 1m, resulting in a 3lb hike to a mark of 110, but he ran to nothing like that figure on this heavy ground, stepping up to this trip for the first time. After tracking the leader, he dropped right out. Official explanation: trainer later said colt was found to have quarter crack post-race (op 11/4)

1759 - 1760a (Foreign Racing) - See Raceform Interactive

1550 LONGCHAMP (R-H)
Monday, May 4

OFFICIAL GOING: Good

1761a PRIX HOCQUART (GROUP 2) (C&F) 1m 3f
2:20 (2:21) 3-Y-O **£71,942** (£27,767; £13,252; £8,835; £4,417)

RPR

1 **Wajir (FR)**[29] 1145 3-9-2........................ ACrastus 2 105
(E Lellouche, France) *racd in 3rd to st: swtchd to rails appr fnl f: led 130yds out: r.o wl* **5/1**

2 1/2 **Telluride**[160] 3-9-2........................ GMosse 3 105
(J E Hammond, France) *hld up in rr: last st: hdwy on outside fr over 1f out to take 2nd cl home* **89/10**

3 snk **Claremont (IRE)**[29] 3-9-2........................ MGuyon 5 104
(A Fabre, France) *trckd ldr: 2nd st: narrow ldr ins fnl 2f to 1 1/2f out: rdn and ev ch ins fnl f: one pce* **7/5**[1]

4 3/4 **Guest Ville (FR)**[29] 1145 3-9-2........................ TJarnet 4 103
(Mlle S-V Tarrou, France) *racd in 4th to st: sn wnt 3rd: led 1 1/2f out to 130yds out: one pce* **7/2**[3]

5 8 **Grandcamp (FR)**[29] 1145 3-9-2........................ C-PLemaire 1 89
(J-C Rouget, France) *led to wl over 1f out* **14/5**[2]

2m 17.6s (-2.30) **Going Correction** +0.15s/f (Good) **5** Ran SP% **117.0**
Speed ratings: **114,113,113,112,107**
PARI-MUTUEL: WIN 6.00; PL 2.70, 3.60; SF 44.00.
Owner Ecurie Wildenstein **Bred** Dayton Investments Ltd **Trained** Lamorlaye, France

NOTEBOOK
Wajir(FR) looked much better in the preliminaries on this occasion and produced an excellent turn of foot in the straight. He had to wait for a gap to open between the long-time leader and the favourite before making his final effort just over one out, but quickened well on the rail and stayed on well in the final stages. He has now won four of his six races and is now likely to go for the Prix du Jockey Club.
Telluride put up an excellent performance considering this was his first race for over five months. Slightly hampered by the winner after the gates opened, he settled in last place and remained there until the straight. He needed a little time to be balanced before making his challenge up the centre of the track but finally finished best of all. He looks a horse to follow in the future and it would be no surprise if he went for the Jockey Club, and then the Grand Prix de Paris.
Claremont(IRE) was a disappointing favourite. He was given every chance by his young jockey and settled in second place in the early part of the race but proved one-paced in the final stages. He may well be better suited by a longer distance, which is suggested by his exceptional pedigree.
Guest Ville(FR) burst into the lead halfway up the straight, but not for long as things had changed by the furlong marker. He ran on gamely and was only beaten a length and a half, but maybe he will be better suited by a shorter distance.

1762a PRIX D'HEDOUVILLE (GROUP 3) 1m 4f
2:50 (2:56) 4-Y-O+ **£38,835** (£15,534; £11,650; £7,767; £3,883)

RPR

1 **Magadan (IRE)**[22] 1236 4-8-11........................ ACrastus 7 115
(E Lellouche, France) *hld up: 8th st: hdwy on outside over 1f out: led ins fnl f: r.o wl* **7/5**[1]

2 2 **Coastal Path**[253] 5333 5-9-4........................ SPasquier 8 119
(A Fabre, France) *hld up: 7th st: styd on fr over 1f out to take 2nd wl ins fnl f* **43/10**[2]

3 3/4 **Winkle (IRE)**[194] 6921 4-8-7 ow1........................ CSoumillon 6 107
(M Delzangles, France) *4th st: disp 3rd over 1f out: kpt on same pce* **68/10**[3]

4 snk **Candy Gift (ARG)**[22] 1236 6-8-9........................ TJarnet 1 108
(T Clout, France) *6th st: styd on fr wl over 1f out: disp 3rd appr fnl f: one pce* **9/1**

5 hd **Tempelstern (GER)**[22] 1236 5-8-11........................(b) GMosse 9 110
(M Delzangles, France) *trckd ldr: led 5f out to ins fnl f: one pce* **38/1**

6 1 1/2 **Timos (GER)**[42] 940 4-8-9........................ DBonilla 2 106
(T Doumen, France) *hld up: last st: styd on fnl 2f: nvr a factor* **9/1**

7 1/2 **Prospect Wells (FR)**[29] 1144 4-9-4........................(b) OPeslier 4 114
(A Fabre, France) *racd in 3rd: wnt 2nd over 3f out: wknd over 1f out* **9/1**

8 2 **Mondovino (FR)**[22] 1236 6-8-9........................ CStefan 3 102
(Rod Collet, France) *hld up: 8th st: sn one pce* **32/1**

9 2 1/2 **Tangaspeed (FR)**[22] 1236 4-8-6........................ MGuyon 10 95
(R Laplanche, France) *5th st: sn btn* **10/1**

10 20 **Petrograd (IRE)**[22] 1236 8-8-9........................ YBourgois 5 66
(E Lellouche, France) *led to 5f out: 3rd st: sn wknd* **7/5**[1]

2m 29.8s (-0.60) **Going Correction** +0.15s/f (Good) **10** Ran SP% **159.7**
Speed ratings: **110,108,108,108,107 106,106,105,103,90**
PARI-MUTUEL: WIN 2.40 (coupled with Petrograd); PL 1.20, 1.80, 1.90;DF 6.90.
Owner Ecurie Wildenstein **Bred** Kilcarn Stud **Trained** Lamorlaye, France

NOTEBOOK
Magadan(IRE) is turning into a top class middle-distance performer and one with an outstanding turn of foot. Held up early on, he still had plenty to do entering the straight and wasn't asked for an effort until halfway up the straight. His challenge came up the centre of the track from a furlong and a half out and he mowed down his rivals to win with something in hand. He needs a true pace to show his best and had a pacemaker to help him here. The Grand Prix de Chantilly and Grand Prix de Saint Cloud are next up for him, and he is beginning to look like a candidate for the Prix de l'Arc de Triomphe.
Coastal Path, who was conceding 7lb to the winner and probably racing over a trip short of his best, put up a fine effort considering he had not been out since the Prix Kergolay at the end of August. He was held up in the early stages and, always close to the winner, came with a progressive run from a furlong and a half out. He stayed on but never looked like catching the winner. His connections now have options - they could go for another tilt at the Ascot Gold Cup or keep him to middle distances.
Winkle(IRE) put up her best performance to date. She went in pursuit of the leaders from halfway up the straight and stayed on well in the final stages. She fought well to retain third place as the race came to a close and looks capable of winning a similar race in the future.
Candy Gift(ARG), who was supplemented into the race, made a forward move from a furlong and a half out, together with the third, and only lost that position at the end of the race.

CHURCHILL DOWNS (L-H)

Friday, May 1

OFFICIAL GOING: Turf course - good; dirt course - fast

1763a KENTUCKY OAKS (GRADE 1) (FILLIES) (DIRT) 1m 1f (D)

10:45 (10:45) 3-Y-O

£233,968 (£75,474; £37,737; £18,869; £11,321; £3,851)

RPR

1 **Rachel Alexandra (USA)**[26] 3-8-9 .... CHBorel 6 124+
(Hal R Wiggins, U.S.A) **30/100**[1]

2 20 **Stone Legacy (USA)**[41] 3-8-9 ....(b) KDesormeaux 3 86
(D Wayne Lukas, U.S.A) **25/1**

3 4 1/4 **Flying Spur (USA)**[48] 3-8-9 .... GKGomez 8 78
(William Mott, U.S.A) **53/10**[2]

4 1 **Be Fair (USA)**[27] 3-8-9 .... RBejarano 2 76
(D Wayne Lukas, U.S.A) **197/10**

5 nk **Nan (USA)**[27] 3-8-9 ....(b) CNakatani 7 75
(Craig Dollase, U.S.A) **155/10**

6 3 1/2 **Gabby's Golden Gal (USA)**[33] 3-8-9 .... VEspinoza 4 69
(Bob Baffert, U.S.A) **79/10**[3]

7 22 **Tweeter (USA)** 3-8-9 ....(b) MMena 1 27
(D Wayne Lukas, U.S.A) **227/10**

1m 48.87s (108.87) **7 Ran SP% 123.0**

PARI-MUTUEL (including $2 stake): WIN 2.60; PL (1-2) 2.20, 11.00;SHOW (1-2-3) 2.10, 5.00, 2.80; SF 45.20.

Owner L & M Partners LLC **Bred** Dolphus C Morrison **Trained** North America

FOCUS

The winner looks a brilliant filly.

NOTEBOOK

Rachel Alexandra(USA) looked a pretty special filly in the making pre race, but in truth this performance exceeded all expectations - she was a quite breathtaking winner. The margin of victory and the final time, both most impressive anyway, would have been even greater had she been so much as nudged out, but her jockey sat pretty much motionless throughout. Her connections are not tempted by the two remaining legs of the Triple Crown, but it's hoped she'll be tested against the colts one day.

1450 CATTERICK (L-H)

Tuesday, May 5

OFFICIAL GOING: Good to firm (good in places)

Wind: Fresh 1/2 against Weather: Overcast , cool and very breezy

1764 ALPHA RADIO MAIDEN AUCTION STKS 5f

6:05 (6:05) (Class 6) 2-Y-O **£2,183** (£644; £322) **Stalls** Low

Form RPR

3 1 **Duchess Dora (IRE)**[15] 1396 2-8-8 0........................ GrahamGibbons 10 76
(J J Quinn) *chsd ldrs: led 1f out: hld on towards fin* **5/1**[3]

2 2 nk **Dancing Freddy (IRE)**[19] 1312 2-8-13 0........................ PaulMulrennan 3 80
(J G Given) *led: hdd 1f out: kpt on wl: no ex towards fin* **85/40**[1]

20 3 3 1/4 **Mr Smithson (IRE)**[20] 1277 2-8-9 0........................ TomEaves 1 64
(B Ellison) *chsd ldrs: styd on same pce fnl 2f* **7/2**[2]

5 4 4 **Tillys Tale**[19] 1304 2-8-0 0 ow3........................ PaulPickard(7) 6 48
(P T Midgley) *chsd ldrs: hung rt and wknd over 1f out* **10/1**

0 5 1 **Agent Boo**[20] 1277 2-8-11 0........................ StephenDonohoe 4 48
(E S McMahon) *chsd ldrs: wkng whn carried rt over 1f out* **14/1**

6 1/2 **Belle Eponine** 2-8-4 0 ow5........................ LanceBetts(5) 9 44
(E J O'Neill) *mid-div: kpt on fnl 2f: nvr on terms* **16/1**

7 1 1/2 **Regardless** 2-8-6 0........................ DarrenMoffatt 12 36
(Mrs G S Rees) *swvd bdly rt s: hung rt and sme hdwy over 2f out: nvr a factor* **33/1**

8 3/4 **Bluie** 2-8-9 0........................ AdrianTNicholls 11 36
(D Nicholls) *sn outpcd and in rr: sme hdwy 2f out: nvr on terms* **8/1**

0 9 3/4 **Amoureuse**[17] 1358 2-8-8 0........................ PatrickMathers 8 32
(I W McInnes) *in tch: sn drvn along: lost pl 2f out* **50/1**

10 3 **London Girl (IRE)** 2-8-5 0 ow1........................ AndrewElliott 2 19
(A J McCabe) *sn towards rr* **25/1**

11 8 **Another Sold** 2-8-4 0........................ FrancisNorton 5 —
(A Berry) *s.s: a bhd* **33/1**

12 3/4 **Countrymans Dream** 2-8-11 0........................ PhillipMakin 7 —
(J R Weymes) *sn outpcd and wl bhd* **33/1**

60.70 secs (0.90) **Going Correction** -0.025s/f (Good) **12 Ran SP% 118.3**

Speed ratings (Par 91): **91,90,85,78,77 76,74,72,71,66 54,52**

toteswinger: 1&2 £5.30, 1&3 £3.50, 2&3 £1.60. CSF £15.16 TOTE £7.50: £2.00, £1.40, £1.60; EX 15.70.

Owner The Clay Family **Bred** Glending Bloodstock **Trained** Settrington, N Yorks

FOCUS

Following a dry 24 hours and a fairly strong headwind the ground was altered to good to firm, good in places before the first. An ordinary race in which the horses with experience dominated. The pace was sound but nothing got into the race from behind.

NOTEBOOK

Duchess Dora(IRE), well backed when showing promise on her debut, was relatively easy in the market this time but showed improved form and a decent attitude to get off the mark. She should stay 6f and she appeals physically as the type to win more races. (op 9-2 tchd 11-2)

Dancing Freddy(IRE), from a yard that has struggled for winners so far this season, again showed bags of foot from a good draw on this turf debut and again showed more than enough to suggest a similar event can be found when the emphasis is on speed. (op 3-1 tchd 100-30 in a place)

Mr Smithson(IRE), who failed to confirm debut promise from a poor draw at Beverley last time, returned to form and is capable of picking up a small event but is vulnerable to the better types in this grade. (op 9-2)

Tillys Tale's debut run has worked out well but, while far from disgraced, she again had her limitations exposed in this grade. She left the impression that this ground was plenty quick enough. (op 6-1)

Agent Boo did not seem particularly well suited by this test of speed and his pedigree suggests easier ground will suit. He may improve but will need to before he is a solid betting proposition. (op 11-1)

Belle Eponine, a half-sister to a fair juvenile sprinter, fared the best of the newcomers. She should improve for the experience and is likely to be suited by a stiffer test of stamina. (op 12-1 tchd 11-1)

Regardless, who was noticeably green, hinted at ability from the widest draw and she should have learned plenty from this experience. (tchd 25-1)

Amoureuse Official explanation: jockey said filly was unsuited by the track

1765 BOOK RACEDAY HOSPITALITY ON 01748 810165 CLAIMING STKS 1m 3f 214y

6:35 (6:35) (Class 6) 4-Y-O+ **£2,047** (£604; £302) **Stalls** Low

Form RPR

50-6 1 **Grand Art (IRE)**[15] 1402 5-8-9 69........................ PaulMulrennan 7 67
(J Howard Johnson) *hld up towards rr: hdwy over 3f out: led over 1f out: hld on towards fin* **9/2**[3]

-620 2 hd **Lucayan Dancer**[15] 1402 9-8-10 67........................ AdeleMulrennan(7) 4 75
(D Nicholls) *trckd ldrs: t.k.h: chal over 1f out: no ex nr fin* **7/2**[2]

-063 3 3 1/2 **Fort Churchill (IRE)**[15] 1409 8-8-7 61........................(p) TomEaves 8 59
(B Ellison) *trckd ldrs: t.k.h: chal over 1f out: kpt on one pce* **7/1**

4101 4 nk **Raucous (GER)**[8] 1557 6-9-3 70........................ AndrewElliott 3 69
(Mrs R A Carr) *w ldr: rdn to ld over 3f out: hdd over 1f out: one pce: lame* **11/10**[1]

5 7 **Obara D'Avril (FR)**[373] 7-9-3 0........................ MHNaughton 5 57
(S G West) *in rr: hdwy over 4f out: sn rdn and outpcd* **150/1**

45-0 6 7 **Blue Jet (USA)**[22] 1242 5-9-0 48........................(v[1]) MichaelJStainton(3) 1 46
(R M Whitaker) *gave problems gng down: led: t.k.h: hdd over 3f out: wandered and wknd fnl 2f* **12/1**

0000 7 20 **Dark Planet**[8] 1556 6-8-7 44........................(v) ChrisCatlin 6 4
(D W Thompson) *in rr: drvn over 5f out: sn lost pl: t.o 3f out: lame* **40/1**

2m 38.3s (-0.60) **Going Correction** -0.025s/f (Good) **7 Ran SP% 111.3**

Speed ratings (Par 101): **101,100,98,98,93 89,75**

toteswinger: 1&2 £3.10, 1&3 £3.10, 2&3 £5.70 CSF £19.43 TOTE £4.00: £1.70, £2.60; EX 22.90.Grand Art was claimed by P T Midgley for £6,000. Fort Churchill was claimed by J J Best for £5,000.

Owner Matthew Green and J H Johnson **Bred** Mrs Teresa Bergin & Mrs Anne Fitzgerald **Trained** Billy Row, Co Durham

■ A rare finish fought out by husband and wife.

■ Stewards' Enquiry : Adele Mulrennan two-day ban: excessive use of the whip (May 21-22)
Paul Mulrennan one-day ban: excessive use of the whip (May 21)

FOCUS

A moderate claimer in which the market leader proved a shade disappointing. The gallop was only fair.

Raucous(GER) Official explanation: vet said gelding finished lame left-fore

Dark Planet Official explanation: vet said gelding finished lame right-fore

1766 WHY NOT TRY A SUMMER PACKAGE H'CAP 7f

7:05 (7:05) (Class 4) (0-80,80) 4-Y-O+ **£4,727** (£1,406; £702; £351) **Stalls** Centre

Form RPR

43-1 1 **Turn Me On (IRE)**[18] 1333 6-9-1 77........................ GrahamGibbons 6 85+
(T D Walford) *hld up in mid-div: hdwy over 2f out: led over 1f out: jst hld on* **2/1**[1]

335- 2 nk **Barricado (FR)**[248] 5491 4-8-10 72........................ ChrisCatlin 13 79
(E J O'Neill) *s.s: sn wl bhd: gd hdwy over 1f out: hung lft and fin wl: jst hld* **17/2**

5201 3 1 **Campli (IRE)**[11] 1493 7-8-4 71........................ LanceBetts(5) 11 75
(B Ellison) *bhd: hdwy 3f out: chsng ldrs appr fnl f: styd on same pce ins fnl f* **10/1**

20-0 4 1 **Hiccups**[37] 1016 9-8-13 75........................ PhillipMakin 10 77
(M Dods) *hld up in rr: smooth hdwy and swtchd rt over 1f out: kpt on same pce ins fnl f* **13/2**[3]

04-5 5 2 **Mey Blossom**[18] 1333 4-8-7 72........................ MichaelJStainton(3) 12 68
(R M Whitaker) *mid-div: effrt on wd outside over 2f out: one pce appr fnl f* **8/1**

3050 6 2 **H Harrison (IRE)**[18] 1333 9-8-2 67........................ KellyHarrison(3) 7 58
(I W McInnes) *led tl hdd & wknd over 1f out* **11/1**

1513 7 2 3/4 **Kipchak (IRE)**[10] 1510 4-9-0 76........................(p) RobertWinston 14 59
(A J McCabe) *s.i.s: sn chsng ldrs: chal over 2f out: hung lft and wknd over 1f out* **7/2**[2]

60-5 8 hd **Fitzwarren**[85] 472 8-8-4 66 oh21........................(v) SilvestreDeSousa 4 49
(A D Brown) *chsd ldrs: lost pl over 1f out* **100/1**

0-06 9 1 3/4 **Arizona John (IRE)**[10] 1507 4-9-2 78........................(b) LeeEnstone 8 56
(N Wilson) *chsd ldrs: rdn over 2f out: lost pl over 1f out* **10/1**

460- 10 1 1/4 **Kalhan Sands (IRE)**[325] 3050 4-8-13 75........................ JamieMoriarty 5 50
(J J Quinn) *sn in rr: hdwy on ins 3f out: lost pl over 1f out* **28/1**

1m 25.57s (-1.43) **Going Correction** -0.025s/f (Good) **10 Ran SP% 121.5**

Speed ratings (Par 105): **107,106,105,104,102 99,96,96,94,93**

toteswinger: 1&2 £5.90, 1&3 £10.00, 2&3 £15.10. CSF £21.29 CT £148.26 TOTE £2.70: £1.10, £3.50, £4.10; EX 26.90.

Owner Ms M Austerfield **Bred** Brendan Lavery **Trained** Sheriff Hutton, N Yorks

■ Stewards' Enquiry : Chris Catlin caution: used whip down shoulder in forehand position

FOCUS

Mainly exposed performers in just a fair handicap. The pace was sound and the front runners did not get home.

1767 LIVE MUSIC EVENING H'CAP 1m 7f 177y

7:35 (7:37) (Class 6) (0-65,62) 4-Y-O+ **£2,388** (£705; £352) **Stalls** Centre

Form RPR

5-30 1 **Bijou Dan**[22] 1242 8-9-12 62........................ TomEaves 1 71+
(G M Moore) *trckd ldrs: hmpd over 2f out: led ins fnl f: styd on wl* **12/1**

43-0 2 1 3/4 **Aleron (IRE)**[34] 1058 11-9-10 60........................(p) GrahamGibbons 14 66
(J J Quinn) *trckd ldrs: led 2f out: hdd and no ex ins fnl f* **20/1**

36-0 3 1 3/4 **Thunderwing (IRE)**[11] 448 7-9-5 55........................ DarrenMoffatt 11 59
(James Moffatt) *mid-div: t.k.h: effrt over 3f out: sn chsng ldrs: hung lft and styd on same pce fnl f* **40/1**

/31- 4 1 1/2 **Lady Pilot**[19] 7455 7-9-10 60........................ RichardThomas 12 62
(Jim Best) *in tch: effrt over 4f out: sn chsng ldrs: one pce whn edgd lft wl ins fnl f* **11/4**[1]

6-4 5 nse **Harcas (IRE)**[28] 1058 7-9-11 61........................(p) PaulMulrennan 5 63
(M Todhunter) *led: qcknd over 4f out: hdd 2f out: one pce whn hmpd nr fin* **50/1**

200- 6 10 **Its Moon (IRE)**[52] 7039 5-9-7 57........................(b) JamieMoriarty 4 47
(T D Walford) *drvn early to sn chse ldrs: effrt 4f out: wknd over 1f out* **10/1**

5003 7 2 1/4 **Al Azy (IRE)**[29] 1154 4-8-13 52........................ StephenDonohoe 8 39
(D M Simcock) *hld up in mid-div: effrt over 2f out: sn wknd* **9/1**[3]

00-1 8 1 1/4 **Tusculum (IRE)**[90] 385 6-9-2 52........................ TPQueally 6 38
(B J Curley) *in tch: rdn and lost pl over 2f out* **11/4**[1]

200- 9 hd **Wulimaster (USA)**[199] 6812 6-8-8 49........................ AmyRyan(5) 13 35
(D W Barker) *s.i.s: hdwy 4f out: effrt on wd outside over 2f out: edgd lft and sn wknd* **14/1**

0-00 10 3/4 **Coronado's Gold (USA)**[31] 1125 8-8-9 50........................(p) LanceBetts(5) 9 35
(B Ellison) *reluctant to go to s: rr-div: sme hdwy 3f out: sn btn* **12/1**

044- **11** *3 ¾* **Hunting Haze**[146] 7630 6-8-10 **46**................................ AndrewElliott 3 26
(A Crook) *hld up in rr: hdwy on outer 4f out: lost pl over 2f out* **40/1**

0000 **12** *12* **Josh You Are**[69] 679 6-8-12 **51**......................... RussellKennemore(3) 7 17
(Ian Williams) *w ldr: t.k.h: drvn 4f out: lost pl over 2f out* **50/1**

5462 **13** *14* **Spiritonthemount (USA)**[14] 1439 4-8-9 **48**...................(b) ChrisCatlin 2 —
(P W Hiatt) *unruly and reluctant to go to s: in rr: pushed along after 6f: sn bhd: t.o 3f out* **6/1[2]**

3m 31.81s (-0.19) **Going Correction** -0.025s/f (Good)
WFA 4 from 5yo+ 3lb **13** Ran SP% **122.3**
Speed ratings (Par 101): **99,98,97,96,96 91,90,89,89,89 87,81,74**
toteswinger: 1&2 £22.10, 1&3 £120.40, 2&3 £88.50. CSF £238.40 CT £8950.14 TOTE £13.20: £2.50, £4.70, £9.90; EX 180.20.

Owner Bert Markey **Bred** James Thom And Sons **Trained** Middleham Moor, N Yorks

FOCUS
A moderate handicap in which an ordinary gallop increased in the last half-mile.

Spiritonthemount(USA) Official explanation: jockey said gelding was unsuited by the good to firm (good in places) ground

1768 DON'T MISS TOTESPORT SATURDAY 23RD MAY H'CAP 5f
8:05 (8:05) (Class 5) (0-70,70) 4-Y-O+ **£3,070** (£906; £453) **Stalls** Low

Form RPR

-362 **1** **Liberty Ship**[17] 1360 4-8-10 **62**..........................(bt[1]) GrahamGibbons 4 74
(J D Bethell) *mid-div: hdwy 2f out: styd on to ld jst ins fnl f: kpt on wl* **7/2[1]**

0-50 **2** *1 ¼* **Feelin Foxy**[10] 1518 5-8-13 **65**................................ PaulMulrennan 3 72
(J G Given) *chsd ldrs: kpt on fnl f: no real imp* **14/1**

22-1 **3** *2 ¾* **Raccoon (IRE)**[17] 1360 9-9-2 **68**................................ AndrewElliott 6 65
(Mrs R A Carr) *tubed: led: hdd jst ins fnl f: wknd towards fin* **15/2**

-010 **4** *shd* **Darcy's Pride (IRE)**[13] 1456 5-8-8 **60**.......................... TonyHamilton 5 56
(D W Barker) *chsd ldrs: rdn and outpcd over 2f out: styd on fnl f* **12/1**

40-0 **5** *1 ½* **Circuit Dancer (IRE)**[32] 1096 9-9-1 **67**........................ AdrianTNicholls 10 58
(D Nicholls) *in rr: swtchd lft after 1f: hdwy 2f out: kpt on: nvr trbld ldrs* **6/1[2]**

0-26 **6** *1 ¾* **Restless Genius (IRE)**[32] 1096 4-9-1 **67**.......................... TomEaves 8 51
(B Ellison) *mid-div: kpt on fnl 2f: nvr a threat* **17/2**

50-0 **7** *nse* **Angle Of Attack (IRE)**[18] 1334 4-9-2 **68**................. SilvestreDeSousa 2 52
(A D Brown) *w ldr: wknd fnl f* **7/1[3]**

0-06 **8** *1* **Rio Sands**[19] 1310 4-8-9 **64**................................ MichaelJStainton(3) 1 44
(R M Whitaker) *chsd ldrs on ins: one pce fnl 2f* **8/1**

020- **9** *1* **Baybshambles (IRE)**[223] 6218 5-9-2 **68**.......................... PhillipMakin 15 44
(R E Barr) *mid-div: effrt on outside 2f out: nvr nr ldrs* **11/1**

100- **10** *1* **Joyeaux**[179] 7218 7-9-1 **67**... DuranFentiman 13 39
(Ollie Pears) *in rr: nvr a factor* **25/1**

00-0 **11** *nse* **Nusoor (IRE)**[29] 1150 6-8-11 **63**.............................(v) PatrickMathers 12 35
(Peter Grayson) *s.i.s: nvr on terms* **20/1**

000- **12** *11* **Coconut Moon**[199] 6823 7-8-5 **62** ow2........................ SladeO'Hara(5) 9 —
(A Berry) *chsd ldrs on outer: lost pl over 1f out: bhd whn eased ins fnl f* **33/1**

240- **13** *1 ¼* **Cayman Fox**[137] 7733 4-9-4 **70**.................................. DarrenMoffatt 14 —
(James Moffatt) *w ldrs on outer: lost pl over 1f out* **33/1**

59.63 secs (-0.17) **Going Correction** -0.025s/f (Good) **13** Ran SP% **119.6**
Speed ratings (Par 103): **100,98,93,93,91 88,88,86,84,83 83,65,63**
toteswinger: 1&2 £15.90, 1&3 £4.10, 2&3 £24.80. CSF £53.01 CT £348.97 TOTE £4.30: £2.30, £3.30, £3.70; EX 58.50.

Owner M W Territt **Bred** Mrs R D Peacock **Trained** Middleham Moor, N Yorks

FOCUS
An ordinary handicap but, although strongly run, those coming from off the pace and those in the top half of the draw were at a disadvantage.

1769 CATTERICKBRIDGE.CO.UK MAIDEN STKS 7f
8:35 (8:36) (Class 5) 3-Y-O+ **£2,914** (£867; £433; £216) **Stalls** Centre

Form RPR

0- **1** **Cotswolds**[210] 6566 4-9-12 0.. GregFairley 8 80+
(M Johnston) *trckd ldrs: led and edgd rt over 1f out: drew clr* **4/1[3]**

2- **2** *5* **Proud Times (USA)**[277] 4593 3-9-0 0.............................. RobertWinston 7 62
(G A Swinbank) *chsd ldrs: pushed along over 4f out: kpt on to take modest 2nd wl ins fnl f* **4/5[1]**

3-3 **3** *1* **Business Class (BRZ)**[35] 1054 4-9-11 0........................ AdrianTNicholls 12 63
(D Nicholls) *chsd ldr: led over 2f out: hdd over 1f out: kpt on same pce* **3/1[2]**

040- **4** *4 ½* **Oscar Wild**[129] 6055 7-9-12 52..................................... DarrenMoffatt 13 52+
(James Moffatt) *s.i.s: drvn 4f out: kpt on fnl 2f: nvr nr ldrs* **100/1**

/00- **5** *nk* **Call Me Rosy (IRE)**[331] 2870 5-9-7 47............................. TomEaves 10 46
(B Smart) *trckd ldrs: one pce fnl 2f* **28/1**

/0-0 **6** *2 ½* **Crux**[22] 1243 7-9-7 50... LanceBetts(5) 9 44
(R E Barr) *s.i.s: hdwy 4f out: kpt on fnl 2f: nvr nr ldrs* **25/1**

600- **7** *5* **Hettie Hubble**[222] 6229 3-8-9 59.................................. AndrewElliott 11 22
(D W Thompson) *led tl over 2f out: wknd over 1f out* **80/1**

8 *25* **Majaji** 5-9-7 0... DaleGibson 2 —
(P Salmon) *s.s: reluctant detached in last: sn t.o* **33/1**

005- **R** **Cherries On Top (IRE)**[242] 5679 4-9-12 45............ SilvestreDeSousa 4 —
(D Nicholls) *ref to r: tk no part* **12/1**

1m 26.28s (-0.72) **Going Correction** -0.025s/f (Good)
WFA 3 from 4yo+ 12lb **9** Ran SP% **120.7**
Speed ratings (Par 103): **103,97,96,91,90 87,82,53,—**
toteswinger: 1&2 £1.30, 1&3 £1.10, 2&3 £1.40. CSF £7.81 TOTE £4.70: £1.60, £1.10, £1.40; EX 9.00 Place 6 £201.79, Place 5 £165.65..

Owner Sheikh Hamdan Bin Mohammed Al Maktoum **Bred** Gainsborough Stud Management Ltd **Trained** Middleham Moor, N Yorks

FOCUS
Not the strongest of maidens and one that did not take as much winning as seemed likely with the market leader proving a disappointment. The pace was only fair and the proximity of the fourth and fifth holds the form down.

T/Plt: £142.70 to a £1 stake. Pool: £69,742.97. 356.73 winning tickets. T/Qpdt: £41.60 to a £1 stake. Pool: £4,064.73. 72.20 winning tickets. WG

CHEPSTOW (L-H)
Tuesday, May 5

OFFICIAL GOING: Good to firm (8.7)
Wind: Moderate across Weather: Dull

1770 WYVERN ICES CLAIMING STKS 1m 2f 36y
2:10 (2:11) (Class 6) 4-Y-O+ **£1,942** (£578; £288; £144) **Stalls** Low

Form RPR

021- **1** **Gross Prophet**[155] 6908 4-9-11 75.............................. RichardKingscote 4 82
(Tom Dascombe) *trckd ldr: rdn and lost 2nd over 2f out: rdn and styd on to ld fnl 100yds edgd rt: readily* **8/1**

5/ **2** *2* **Castellina**[7] 5-8-0 94.. NickyMackay 12 53
(P J Hobbs) *chsd ldrs in 3rd: rdn to go 2nd over 2f out: chal over 1f out: sn no imp and one pce: styd on again to chse wnr wl ins fnl f* **4/1[2]**

0-21 **3** *3* **Western Roots**[27] 1177 8-8-10 67................................ DavidProbert(3) 5 60+
(A M Balding) *led: sn clr: rdn over 2f out: kpt narrow advantage tl hdd & wknd fnl 100yds* **13/8[1]**

100- **4** *3* **Personify**[186] 7112 7-8-5 50 ow3.............................(p) KevinGhunowa(3) 2 49
(J L Flint) *chsd ldng trio: rdn over 3f out: styd on fr over 1f out: nvr in contention* **16/1**

2066 **5** *½* **Red Current**[7] 1578 5-8-5 55 ow1................................ EddieAhern 10 45+
(R A Harris) *in rr: rdn fr 3f out: styd on fr over 1f out but nvr in contention* **15/2[3]**

0500 **6** *1 ¼* **Comeintothespace (IRE)**[16] 1378 7-7-12 42........(p) SimonPearce(7) 11 43
(R A Farrant) *in rr: rdn and mod prog fnl 2f* **50/1**

44-3 **7** *¾* **Torrens (IRE)**[7] 1578 7-8-5 56..............................(t) KirstyMilczarek 8 41
(P D Evans) *towards rr: rdn 3f out: sme hdwy 2f out: nver anywhere nr ldrs* **4/1[2]**

3043 **8** *4 ½* **Turkish Sultan (IRE)**[9] 1037 6-8-6 49 ow1..............(p) FergusSweeney 9 33
(J M Bradley) *a towards rr* **25/1**

00/4 **9** *2* **Irish Stream (USA)**[12] 813 11-8-5 50..................(v[1]) CatherineGannon 6 28
(B G Powell) *a towards rr* **50/1**

6R-0 **10** *4* **Chapter (IRE)**[13] 1463 7-8-6 47 ow1.............................. SamHitchcott 1 21
(Mrs A L M King) *s.i.s: a in rr* **50/1**

2044 **11** *6* **Poppy Red**[7] 1586 4-7-7 50...............................(p) CharlotteKerton(7) 7 —
(C J Gray) *sn bhd* **33/1**

2m 10.23s (-0.37) **Going Correction** -0.075s/f (Good) **11** Ran SP% **119.5**
Speed ratings (Par 101): **98,96,94,91,91 90,89,86,84,81 76**
toteswinger: 1&2 £4.60, 1&3 £3.90, 2&3 £2.50. CSF £39.35 TOTE £9.30: £2.80, £1.60, £1.30; EX 40.10 Trifecta £55.90 Pool: £407.19 - 5.39 winning units..Castellina was claimed by E J Creighton for £5,000.

Owner Alan Solomon **Bred** A David Solomon **Trained** Lambourn, Berks

FOCUS
A fair claimer on paper, but a bizarre race to watch, with Western Roots going off at a strong pace and soon stretching the field out by 20 lengths-plus. Those held up were never involved.

1771 WINEAUX.CO.UK MAIDEN STKS 1m 2f 36y
2:40 (2:46) (Class 5) 3-Y-O+ **£2,719** (£809; £404; £202) **Stalls** Low

Form RPR

3/ **1** **Made To Ransom**[579] 5951 4-9-13 0............................ JimmyFortune 9 94+
(J H M Gosden) *mde all: shkn up 2f out: and styd clr: unchal* **8/13[1]**

353- **2** *5* **Decision**[188] 7080 3-8-12 79.. IanMongan 5 80
(C G Cox) *trckd ldrs in 3rd: chsd wnr over 3f out: rdn and styd on fnl 2f but nvr any ch* **7/2[2]**

04 **3** *6* **I'm In The Pink (FR)**[3] 1681 5-9-8 0.......................... RichardEvans(5) 8 67
(P D Evans) *in rr: hdwy and pushed along over 3f out: styd on fnl f but nvr any ch w ldng duo* **22/1**

4 *1 ¾* **Game Stalker (USA)** 3-8-12 0................................... TedDurcan 10 63+
(Saeed Bin Suroor) *s.i.s: sn pushed along and in tch: rdn to chse ldrs 3f out: nvr anywhere nr wnr: wknd over 1f out* **7/1[3]**

04- **5** *nk* **Heart Of Tuscany**[223] 6205 3-8-8 0 ow1........................ JimCrowley 4 58+
(W J Knight) *towards rr: hdwy and drvn 4f out: no imp: mod prog u.p fnl f* **16/1**

6 *1 ¼* **Pallaton** 3-8-12 0.. RichardKingscote 6 59+
(R M Beckett) *towards rr: rdn and hdwy over 3f out: styd on fnl 2f but nvr anywhere nr ldrs* **33/1**

7 *6* **Giant Sequoia (USA)**[923] 6182 5-9-13 0........................ EddieAhern 3 48
(K J Burke) *in rr: sme prog over 3f out: no further prog* **33/1**

0- **8** *hd* **Little Sark (IRE)**[409] 961 4-9-13 0.......................... CatherineGannon 1 48
(P D Evans) *in rr: mod late prog* **80/1**

50 **9** *1 ¼* **Michael Laskey**[29] 1151 3-8-12 0................................ TGMcLaughlin 12 45
(B R Millman) *a towards rr* **100/1**

00- **10** *11* **Smart Tazz**[243] 5652 4-9-13 0.................................... FergusSweeney 2 24
(H J Evans) *chsd ldrs over 7f* **125/1**

0- **11** *19* **Aspirational (IRE)**[181] 7200 3-8-12 0............................ TonyCulhane 7 —
(B Palling) *a in rr* **100/1**

000- **12** *18* **Hill Of Clare (IRE)**[45] 4365 7-9-8 44............................. NickyMackay 11 —
(G H Jones) *chsd wnr tl over 3f out: wknd quicky* **200/1**

2m 9.29s (-1.31) **Going Correction** -0.075s/f (Good)
WFA 3 from 4yo+ 15lb **12** Ran SP% **117.3**
Speed ratings (Par 103): **102,98,93,91,91 90,85,85,84,75 60,46**
toteswinger: 1&2 £2.10, 1&3 £6.70, 2&3 £8.00. CSF £2.16 TOTE £1.70: £1.10, £1.20, £3.00; EX 3.40 Trifecta £14.20 Pool: £815.41 - 42.30 winning units..

Owner Normandie Stud Ltd **Bred** Normandie Stud Ltd **Trained** Newmarket, Suffolk

FOCUS
A maiden that lacked strength in depth.

1772 BET365.COM H'CAP 6f 16y
3:10 (3:15) (Class 6) (0-65,65) 3-Y-O **£2,266** (£674; £337; £168) **Stalls** High

Form RPR

5010 **1** **Bold Rose**[55] 804 3-8-13 **60**.......................................(p) DaneO'Neill 13 67
(M D I Usher) *mde virtually all: rdn and styd on gamely fnl 2f* **18/1**

36-3 **2** *¾* **Captain Kallis (IRE)**[8] 1567 3-8-12 **59**................... FrankieMcDonald 14 64
(D J S Ffrench Davis) *in tch: hdwy to chse ldrs 1/2-way: chsd wnr ins fnl 2f: kpt on wl fnl f but a hld* **15/2**

0532 **3** *3 ¼* **Peanut Girl (IRE)**[11] 1492 3-9-1 **62**.......................... CatherineGannon 3 56+
(B Palling) *in rr: hdwy 1/2-way: hrd drvn and styd on to chse ldng duo ins fnl f but nvr gng pce to be competitive* **10/1**

004- **4** *2 ¾* **Noverre To Hide (USA)**[233] 5939 3-9-4 **65**.................. SteveDrowne 9 50
(J R Best) *in tch: hrd drvn over 2f out: styd on fnl f but nvr gng pce to rch ldrs* **11/2[2]**

00-0 **5** *nk* **Zaftil (IRE)**[14] 1429 3-8-4 **51** oh6 KirstyMilczarek 4 35
(H S Howe) *in tch: rdn to chse ldrs 2f out: nvr gng pce to chal and one pce fnl f* **50/1**

3004 **6** *nk* **Dancing Welcome**[14] 1424 3-8-6 **53** (b) FergusSweeney 6 36
(J M Bradley) *chsd ldrs: rdn over 2f out: wknd fnl f* **16/1**

-544 **7** *hd* **Ridgeway Silver**[11] 1492 3-8-10 **64** LeeNewnes(7) 1 47
(M D I Usher) *sn chsng ldrs: pushed along over 2f out: wknd appr fnl f* **12/1**

600- **8** *1* **Now**[211] 6539 3-9-1 **62** JimCrowley 5 46+
(P Winkworth) *in tch: n.m.r and lost plcd 2f out: styd on again ins fnl f* **6/1**[3]

66P- **9** *1* **Miss Kadee**[164] 7425 3-8-11 **58** SimonWhitworth 2 34
(J S Moore) *s.i.s: styd on fr over 1f out* **28/1**

6-42 **10** *½* **Tillers Satisfied (IRE)**[99] 293 3-9-1 **62** DO'Donohoe 8 37
(R Hollinshead) *chsd ldrs: rdn over 2f out: wknd over 1f out* **12/1**

0006 **11** *nk* **Bold Ring**[12] 1469 3-8-6 **53** EdwardCreighton 11 27
(E J Creighton) *in rr: sme hdwy and in tch fr 1/2-way: wknd ins fnl 2f* **50/1**

505- **12** *2¾* **Compton Blue**[186] 7105 3-9-4 **65** RichardHughes 10 30
(R Hannon) *pressed wnr: rdn 2f out: wknd qckly wl over 1f out* **9/4**[1]

000- **13** *2* **Sharp Discovery**[285] 4321 3-8-1 **51** oh6 (p) DavidProbert(3) 12 10
(J M Bradley) *sn outpcd* **80/1**

000- **14** *1* **Fly Butterfly**[233] 5937 3-8-10 **57** TonyCulhane 15 12
(M R Channon) *outpcd* **16/1**

0-60 **15** *6* **Key To Love (IRE)**[27] 1190 3-9-3 **64** NeilChalmers 7 —
(A J Chamberlain) *spd to 1/2-way* **33/1**

1m 12.13s (0.13) **Going Correction** -0.075s/f (Good) **15** Ran SP% **125.3**
Speed ratings (Par 97): **102,101,96,93,92 92,91,90,89,88 88,84,81,80,72**
toteswinger: 1&2 £24.20, 1&3 £28.90, 2&3 £7.00. CSF £148.40 CT £1494.74 TOTE £25.50: £6.50, £2.10, £2.40; EX 185.30 TRIFECTA Not won..
Owner Ushers Court **Bred** J And Mrs Bowtell **Trained** Upper Lambourn, Berks

FOCUS
A moderate sprint handicap for three-year-olds. They raced middle to stands' side, and a high draw looked an advantage.
Peanut Girl(IRE) Official explanation: jockey said filly hung left
Now Official explanation: jockey said, regarding running and riding, that his orders were to jump out and take a handy position, which he was able to do, adding that in the closing stages the filly was short of room and he was unable to ride out vigorously, further adding that it might benefit from a step back up in trip.
Bold Ring Official explanation: jockey said filly was unsuited by the track

1773 WYVERN ICES H'CAP — 1m 14y
3:40 (3:43) (Class 6) (0-65,64) 4-Y-O+ **£2,266** (£674; £337; £168) **Stalls** High

Form RPR

-115 **1** **Prince Rossi (IRE)**[26] 1199 5-8-6 **52** ow1 (v) EddieAhern 2 60
(A E Price) *racd towards centre trck: mde virtually all: hld on wl thrght fnl f* **5/1**[2]

4025 **2** *2¼* **Takaamul**[52] 844 6-8-5 **51** DO'Donohoe 13 54
(K A Morgan) *t.k.h towards rr: hdwy 3f out: styd on u.p to chse wnr fnl f but no imp* **18/1**

0060 **3** *nk* **Amber Ridge**[8] 1556 4-8-4 **50** oh5 CatherineGannon 15 52
(B P J Baugh) *chsd ldrs: rdn over 2f out: styd on fnl f but nt pce of wnr* **50/1**

40-1 **4** *1½* **Hobson**[5] 1634 4-9-3 **63** 6ex StephenCarson 1 62
(Eve Johnson Houghton) *racd along towards far side and w wnr: rdn over 2f out: wknd ins fnl f* **4/1**[1]

-226 **5** *¾* **Kielty's Folly**[48] 867 5-8-1 **50** oh2 DavidProbert(3) 11 47
(B P J Baugh) *in tch: chsd ldrs and rdn 3f out: wknd ins fnl f* **11/2**[3]

63-0 **6** *1½* **Dancing Storm**[27] 1194 6-9-0 **60** FergusSweeney 6 54
(W S Kittow) *chsd ldrs: rdn 3f out: wknd fnl f* **11/2**[3]

20-0 **7** *1¼* **Gracechurch (IRE)**[18] 1318 6-8-9 **60** WilliamCarson(5) 8 51
(R J Hodges) *chsd ldrs: rdn over 3f out: wknd appr fnl f* **11/1**

006 **8** *2¾* **Cross Reef**[10] 1532 4-8-13 **62** KevinGhunowa(3) 4 46
(R A Harris) *chsd ldrs towards centre crse: rdn 3f out: wknd ins fnl 2f* **40/1**

60-0 **9** *shd* **Libre**[26] 1199 9-8-12 **58** PaulFitzsimons 9 42
(F Jordan) *s.i.s: in rr: drvn 1/2-way: mod prog fnl f* **11/1**

2326 **10** *shd* **Samurai Warrior**[31] 1131 4-8-11 **62** RichardEvans(5) 16 46
(P D Evans) *sn in tch: rdn over 3f out: wknd fr 2f out* **9/1**

312- **11** *¾* **Croeso Cusan**[201] 6746 4-9-4 **64** SteveDrowne 7 46
(J L Spearing) *outpcd most of way* **8/1**

060- **12** *2* **Tara's Garden**[193] 6956 4-8-10 **56** ow1 DaneO'Neill 5 34
(M Blanshard) *outpcd most of way* **25/1**

000/ **13** *30* **Days Of Thunder (IRE)**[647] 3947 4-8-4 **50** oh5 NickyMackay 14 —
(B R Summers) *chsd ldrs to 1/2-way* **50/1**

1m 35.99s (-0.21) **Going Correction** -0.075s/f (Good) **13** Ran SP% **120.7**
Speed ratings (Par 101): **98,95,95,93,93 91,90,87,87,87 86,84,54**
toteswinger: 1&2 £19.30, 1&3 £50.00, 2&3 £80.70. CSF £89.64 CT £4123.22 TOTE £8.20: £2.90, £5.20, £11.80; EX 120.50 TRIFECTA Not won..
Owner Business Development Consultants Limited **Bred** Sir Eric Parker **Trained** Leominster, H'fords

FOCUS
A moderate handicap. They raced in two groups early, with three runners positioned more towards the far side, but they were all pretty well spread out in the closing stages, and the main action took place up the middle of the track.
Kielty's Folly Official explanation: jockey said gelding was unsuited by the track
Tara's Garden Official explanation: jockey said filly hung left
Days Of Thunder(IRE) Official explanation: jockey said gelding lost its action

1774 LINDLEY CATERING H'CAP — 1m 14y
4:10 (4:11) (Class 4) (0-80,78) 3-Y-O **£4,857** (£1,445; £722; £360) **Stalls** High

Form RPR

061- **1** **Roar Of Applause**[177] 7258 3-8-7 **67** EddieAhern 6 74+
(B J Meehan) *hld up towards rr but in tch: hdwy on bit to trck ldrs 2f out: drvn to ld appr fnl f: readily* **8/1**

0-10 **2** *1¾* **Dalradian (IRE)**[18] 1324 3-9-4 **78** JimCrowley 8 78
(W J Knight) *hld up in rr: in tch but stl last over 2f out: gd hdwy over 1f out: drvn to chse wnr ins fnl f: kpt on but a readily hld* **7/2**[2]

21-0 **3** *½* **Yellow Printer**[13] 1466 3-9-4 **78** RichardKingscote 3 77
(Tom Dascombe) *led: rdn over 2f out: hdd and outpcd by wnr appr fnl f: lost 2nd ins fnl f but clr for 3rd* **8/1**

5333 **4** *5* **My Best Man**[88] 426 3-8-4 **64** oh1 CatherineGannon 4 51
(B R Millman) *s.i.s: sn recovered to chse ldrs: rdn over 2f out: wknd qckly fnl f* **18/1**

-062 **5** *nk* **Wilbury Star (IRE)**[13] 1462 3-9-1 **75** RichardHughes 7 62
(R Hannon) *chsd ldrs: hrd drvn and outpcd 1/2-way: styd on to chse ldrs but nvr on terms over 2f out: hung lft and wknd fnl f* **11/8**[1]

06-0 **6** *2¾* **Evening Sunset (GER)**[13] 1462 3-8-5 **65** EdwardCreighton 1 45
(M R Channon) *in tch: rdn over 3f out: no imp on ldrs: sn no ch* **20/1**

6-30 **7** *4½* **Rose Cheval (USA)**[40] 970 3-8-12 **72** TonyCulhane 5 42
(M R Channon) *chsd ldrs tl wknd over 2f out* **25/1**

00-0 **8** *nse* **Motor Home**[13] 1462 3-8-4 **67** (p) DavidProbert(3) 2 37
(A M Balding) *pressed ldr over 4f: sn wknd qckly over 2f out* **6/1**[3]

1m 34.92s (-1.28) **Going Correction** -0.075s/f (Good) **8** Ran SP% **114.7**
Speed ratings (Par 101): **103,101,100,95,95 92,88,88**
toteswinger: 1&2 £4.30, 1&3 £6.80, 2&3 £3.90. CSF £36.27 CT £234.84 TOTE £5.90: £1.70, £1.60, £2.80; EX 28.00 Trifecta £225.10 Pool: £748.33 - 2.46 winning units..
Owner Raymond Tooth **Bred** Southcourt Stud **Trained** Manton, Wilts

FOCUS
A fair three-year-old handicap.
Wilbury Star(IRE) Official explanation: jockey said colt never travelled

1775 CHEPSTOW RACECOURSE WINE CLUB AT WINEAUX.CO.UK H'CAP — 7f 16y
4:40 (4:41) (Class 5) (0-70,70) 4-Y-O+ **£2,914** (£867; £433; £216) **Stalls** High

Form RPR

560- **1** **Bold Cross (IRE)**[217] 6363 6-8-13 **65** PaulFitzsimons 8 76
(E G Bevan) *slowly away: rcvrd after 3f and sn trcking ldrs: led ins fnl 3f: hrd drvn and styd on wl but difted lft ins fnl f* **10/1**

000- **2** *1½* **Millfields Dreams**[162] 7436 10-8-13 **65** JimCrowley 12 73+
(G C Bravery) *chsd ldrs: wnt 2nd 1f out: pressed wnr and carried lft ins fnl f* **14/1**

3301 **3** *3¼* **Punching**[12] 1480 5-9-0 **66** FergusSweeney 2 64
(C R Dore) *in tch: rdn and hdwy over 2f out: chsd ldrs fnl f but no imp* **7/2**[1]

00-3 **4** *3¼* **Desert Pride**[20] 1285 4-8-10 **62** RichardKingscote 11 51
(W S Kittow) *in tch 1/2-way: rdn and styd on same pce fnl 2f* **6/1**[2]

606- **5** *1* **Full Victory (IRE)**[159] 6544 7-9-0 **66** DaneO'Neill 7 53+
(R A Farrant) *in rr: stl plenty to do over 2f out: r.o wl fr over 1f out: nt rch ldrs* **15/2**[3]

3020 **6** *2* **Mountain Pass (USA)**[29] 1153 7-8-2 **57** (p) DavidProbert(3) 1 38
(B J Llewellyn) *s.i.s: in rr: sme prog fnl 2f but nvr in contention* **12/1**

06-0 **7** *2¼* **Ghost Dancer**[11] 1493 5-9-4 **70** GeorgeBaker 10 45
(J M Bradley) *in rr: hdwy over 2f out: kpt on but nvr gng pce to be competitive* **10/1**

-600 **8** *4½* **Cyfrwys (IRE)**[43] 933 8-8-4 **56** oh10 FrankieMcDonald 5 19
(B Palling) *slowly away and bhd: sme late hdwy* **33/1**

400- **9** *nse* **Bahamian Kid**[164] 7428 4-9-4 **70** (p) DO'Donohoe 16 33
(R Hollinshead) *chsd ldrs: drvn to chal 3f out: wknd wl over 1f out* **9/1**

015- **10** *shd* **Out Of Nothing**[176] 7267 6-8-4 **61** AmyKathleenParsons(5) 6 24
(K M Prendergast) *chsd ldrs: rdn 1/2-way: sn wknd* **8/1**

030- **11** *¾* **Charlie Delta**[202] 6734 6-9-1 **70** (b) KevinGhunowa(3) 9 31
(R A Harris) *chsd ldrs: upsides 3f out: wknd fr 2f out* **9/1**

06- **12** *¾* **Sawpit Sunshine (IRE)**[344] 2451 4-8-12 **64** SteveDrowne 4 23
(J L Spearing) *in tch: rdn 3f out: wknd fr 2f out* **20/1**

06-0 **13** *3* **Follow Your Spirit**[84] 489 4-8-4 **56** oh11 CatherineGannon 13 7
(B Palling) *chsd ldrs over 4f* **40/1**

000- **14** *32* **Mr Funshine**[181] 7197 4-8-4 **56** oh8 NickyMackay 15 —
(R J Hodges) *led tl hdd ins fnl 3f: sn wknd: eased whn no ch fnl f: t.o* **28/1**

1m 22.16s (-1.04) **Going Correction** -0.075s/f (Good) **14** Ran SP% **125.5**
Speed ratings (Par 103): **102,100,96,92,91 89,86,81,81,81 80,79,76,39**
toteswinger: 1&2 £40.90, 1&3 £11.50, 2&3 £21.30. CSF £142.91 CT £615.98 TOTE £13.80: £4.60, £5.30, £1.40; EX 236.80 TRIFECTA Not won. Place 6: £275.60, Place 5: £188.78..
Owner E G Bevan **Bred** M Hosokawa **Trained** Ullingswick, H'fords
■ Stewards' Enquiry : Paul Fitzsimons three-day ban: careless riding (May 19-21)

FOCUS
A modest handicap in which they all raced towards the stands' side.
T/Jkpt: Not won. T/Plt: £184.00 to a £1 stake. Pool: £68,275.13. 270.74 winning tickets. T/Qpdt: £86.20 to a £1 stake. Pool: £3,111.79. 26.70 winning tickets. ST

1651 SOUTHWELL (L-H)
Tuesday, May 5

OFFICIAL GOING: Standard
Wind: Moderate, half behind Weather: Cloudy and dry

1776 NSPCC CHILD VOICE APPEAL H'CAP — 5f (F)
2:30 (2:30) (Class 5) (0-75,72) 4-Y-O+ **£3,756** (£1,117; £558; £278) **Stalls** High

Form RPR

2010 **1** **Calmdownmate (IRE)**[19] 1309 4-9-2 **70** PaulMulrennan 8 80
(Mrs R A Carr) *chsd ldrs: hdwy 1/2-way: chsd ldr wl over 1f out and sn rdn: drvn ins fnl f and styd on to ld last 100yds* **5/1**[2]

5122 **2** *1¼* **Spic 'n Span**[8] 1564 4-8-11 **65** (b) JoeFanning 10 71
(R A Harris) *led: rdn over 1f out: drvn ins fnl f: hdd and no ex last 100yds* **11/2**[3]

-303 **3** *2¾* **Regal Royale**[8] 1565 6-9-0 **68** (v) PatrickMathers 2 64
(Peter Grayson) *in tch on outer: rdn along and outpcd after 1f: bhd 1/2-way: hdwy u.p wl over 1f out: drvn and kpt on ins fnl f* **5/1**[2]

0-46 **4** *1¼* **Russian Rocket (IRE)**[22] 1259 7-8-13 **67** TPQueally 1 59
(Mrs C A Dunnett) *chsd ldrs on outer: rdn along 1/2-way: sn drvn and kpt on same pce* **7/1**

2102 **5** *1¼* **Colorus (IRE)**[8] 1565 6-8-6 **67** (p) PaulPickard(7) 6 54
(W J H Ratcliffe) *chsd ldr: effrt 2f out: sn rdn and wknd appr fnl f* **11/4**[1]

2401 **6** *1¼* **Guto**[8] 1564 6-8-10 **67** 6ex KellyHarrison(3) 7 50
(W J H Ratcliffe) *chsd ldr: rdn along 1/2-way and sn outpcd* **12/1**

2-23 **7** *6* **After The Show**[72] 645 8-8-11 **65** NCallan 4 26
(Rae Guest) *dwlt: a in rr* **6/1**

000- **8** *nk* **Inspainagain (USA)**[225] 6164 5-9-2 **70** PaulEddery 3 30
(Paul Mason) *in tch: rdn along after 1f: sn lost pl and bhd* **33/1**

506- **9** *7* **Namir (IRE)**[192] 6990 7-9-0 **68** (vt) PaulHanagan 9 3
(D Shaw) *a in rr* **25/1**

57.73 secs (-1.97) **Going Correction** -0.30s/f (Stan) **9** Ran SP% **116.6**
Speed ratings (Par 103): **103,101,96,94,92 90,81,80,69**
toteswinger: 1&2 £7.50, 1&3 £8.80, 2&3 £5.50. CSF £32.99 CT £146.41 TOTE £8.20: £2.60, £1.90, £1.60; EX 51.90.
Owner Ruth Carr Racing **Bred** J Costello **Trained** Huby, N Yorks

FOCUS
A routine Southwell sprint handicap, but unusually for races over this straight 5f the high draws held sway, though the front pair were able to gradually edge over towards the centre of the track. Straightforward form.

Colorus(IRE) Official explanation: vet said gelding finished distressed

1777 ROSELANDGROUP.COM CLAIMING STKS 1m (F)
3:00 (3:01) (Class 6) 4-Y-O+ **£2,729** (£806; £403) **Stalls** Low

Form RPR

1-10 **1** **Royal Dignitary (USA)**[24] 1213 9-9-7 85 AdrianTNicholls 7 87
(D Nicholls) *mde all: rdn along 2f out: drvn ent fnl f: styd on wl* **5/4**[1]

520- **2** *¾* **Moonlight Man**[148] 7610 8-8-12 75 (t) NCallan 8 76
(C R Dore) *trckd ldrs: pushed along 3f out: chsd wnr wl over 1f out: rdn and edgd lft ent fnl f: sn drvn and no ex last 100yds* **11/2**[2]

2504 **3** *2½* **If You Knew Suzy**[8] 1566 4-8-1 65 KellyHarrison(3) 9 62
(G A Swinbank) *in tch: smooth hdwy 3f out and sn trcking ldng pair: effrt over 1f out: shkn up ent fnl f and sn no imp* **6/1**[3]

000- **4** *3½* **Brother Barry (USA)**[200] 6792 4-9-0 55 RobertWinston 4 64
(G A Swinbank) *chsd ldrs: rdn along wl over 2f out: sn drvn and one pce* **20/1**

0-30 **5** *5* **Fools Gold**[27] 1194 4-8-9 72 MCGeran(5) 5 53
(Paul Mason) *chsd ldrs: rdn along 1/2-way: sn drvn and wknd over 2f out* **6/1**[3]

6542 **6** *3¼* **Bajan Pride**[20] 1276 5-8-11 60 (v) PaulHanagan 1 42
(R A Fahey) *s.i.s and bhd: hdwy and in tch on outer 1/2-way: sn rdn and nvr a factor* **8/1**

0-45 **7** *2¾* **Sparky Vixen**[23] 1226 5-8-6 47 FrancisNorton 3 31
(C J Teague) *chsd ldrs: rdn along bef 1/2-way: sn wknd* **25/1**

-400 **8** *38* **Truly Divine**[7] 1587 4-8-11 56 DarryllHolland 6 —
(C A Dwyer) *s.i.s and bhd: rapid hdwy to chse ldrs on outer after 2f: rdn along 3f out and sn wknd* **22/1**

000- **9** *¾* **Bertie Boo**[222] 6226 4-8-7 47 ChrisCatlin 2 —
(G J Smith) *sn outpcd and alway wl bhd* **100/1**

1m 42.73s (-0.97) **Going Correction** -0.025s/f (Stan) **9** Ran SP% **113.5**
Speed ratings (Par 101): **103,102,99,96,91 88,85,47,46**
toteswinger: 1&2 £1.90, 1&3 £2.90, 2&3 £4.30. CSF £7.66 TOTE £2.30: £1.30, £1.10, £2.60; EX 8.30.

Owner Middleham Park Racing XXXVI **Bred** Bentley Smith, J Michael O'Farrell Jr , Joan Thor **Trained** Sessay, N Yorks

FOCUS
A moderate claimer outside the first two in which only a few had any real chance at the weights, and they basically finished in the order that adjusted official ratings suggested they should.

1778 BET CHAMPIONS LEAGUE FOOTBALL - BETDAQ FILLIES' H'CAP 1m (F)
3:30 (3:30) (Class 4) (0-80,80) 4-Y-O+ **£6,476** (£1,927; £963; £481) **Stalls** Low

Form RPR

0641 **1** **Bookiebasher Babe (IRE)**[8] 1566 4-8-5 **67** 6ex FrancisNorton 6 74
(M Quinn) *trckd ldrs: hdwy to chal 2f out: sn led and rdn clr over 1f out: eased towards fin* **11/2**

24-3 **2** *2* **Lady Brora**[14] 1417 4-8-12 **74** WilliamBuick 7 74
(A M Balding) *chsd ldrs on outer: hdwy and cl up 3f out: rdn and sltly outpcd 2f out: kpt on u.p ins fnl f: no ch w wnr* **7/4**[1]

000- **3** *2¼* **Mafasina (USA)**[228] 6090 4-8-4 **66** oh4 RoystonFfrench 4 61
(B Smart) *prom: rdn along over 2f out: drvn wl over 1f out and kpt on same pce* **10/1**

3450 **4** *7* **Mozayada (USA)**[37] 1020 5-9-4 **80** NCallan 2 59
(M Brittain) *mde most tl rdn 2f out and sn hdd: drvn and wknd over 1f out* **11/4**[2]

0-50 **5** *8* **Grange Corner**[29] 1156 4-8-1 **66** oh21 DominicFox(3) 1 26
(Garry Moss) *sn rdn along and a bhd* **200/1**

0 **6** *2* **Rock Exhibition**[15] 1405 4-8-6 **68** RichardMullen 5 24
(B W Duke) *in tch: rdn along 3f out: sn wknd* **20/1**

56/3 **7** *4* **Diamond Lass (IRE)**[18] 1333 4-8-4 **66** oh4 PaulHanagan 3 13
(R A Fahey) *cl up and sn pushed along: rdn 1/2-way: sn lost pl and bhd* **7/2**[3]

1m 42.63s (-1.07) **Going Correction** -0.025s/f (Stan) **7** Ran SP% **115.0**
Speed ratings (Par 102): **104,102,99,92,84 82,78**
toteswinger: 1&2 £2.90, 1&3 £10.00, 2&3 £3.70. CSF £15.78 TOTE £4.90: £2.40, £2.00; EX 11.20.

Owner J Henry, J Blake & A Newby **Bred** Minch Bloodstock And Castletown Stud **Trained** Newmarket, Suffolk

FOCUS
Not the most competitive of fillies' handicaps with three of the seven runners out of the weights. The pace seemed fair enough with four horses disputing the lead until well past halfway. The winner produced a personal best at face value, but it is not hard to pick holes in the form.

1779 BET TEST MATCH CRICKET - BETDAQ H'CAP 1m 3f (F)
4:00 (4:00) (Class 4) (0-85,83) 4-Y-O+ **£5,828** (£1,734; £866; £432) **Stalls** Low

Form RPR

22-0 **1** **Persian Peril**[105] 226 5-8-11 **76** RobertWinston 4 87
(G A Swinbank) *trckd ldrs: smooth hdwy over 4f out: led 3f out: rdn over 2f out: drvn and edgd lft appr fnl f: kpt on* **6/1**[2]

41-4 **2** *1¾* **Taikoo**[112] 142 4-9-3 **82** TravisBlock 6 90
(H Morrison) *cl up: pushed along and sltly outpcd 4f out: hdwy to chse wnr over 2f out: sn drvn and kpt on same pce ins fnl f* **5/2**[1]

445- **3** *4½* **Buddy Holly**[189] 7056 4-9-1 **80** PatDobbs 3 80
(Pat Eddery) *chsd ldrs: rdn along over 3f out: drvn over 2f out: plugged on same pce u.p: tk 3rd nr line* **9/1**

3100 **4** *nk* **Profit's Reality (IRE)**[13] 1458 7-9-4 **83** DarryllHolland 5 82
(M J Attwater) *hld up in tch: hdwy after 4f: led 1/2-way: rdn along and hdd 3f out: drvn over 2f out: sn one pce: lost 3rd nr fin* **5/2**[1]

3010 **5** *3½* **All In The Red (IRE)**[12] 1479 4-8-6 **71** (p) JoeFanning 9 64
(A Crook) *hld up: hdwy to chse ldrs 1/2-way: rdn along 4f out: drvn and outpcd fr 3f out* **9/1**

-054 **6** *13* **Maslak (IRE)**[45] 915 5-9-3 **82** ChrisCatlin 1 52
(P W Hiatt) *chsd ldrs and rdn along whn n.m.r bnd after 1f: sn bhd and swtchd wd 1/2-way: nvr a factor* **7/1**[3]

30-1 **7** *17* **Invasian (IRE)**[17] 1357 8-8-11 **81** Louis-PhilippeBeuzelin(5) 2 20
(P W D'Arcy) *sn led: rdn along and hdd 1/2-way: sn wknd* **8/1**

2m 25.01s (-2.99) **Going Correction** -0.025s/f (Stan) **7** Ran SP% **115.0**
Speed ratings (Par 105): **109,107,104,104,101 92,79**
toteswinger: 1&2 £3.50, 1&3 £7.10, 2&3 £6.60. CSF £21.68 CT £134.58 TOTE £8.00: £4.60, £1.10; EX 26.60.

Owner Mrs J Porter **Bred** Mrs P Lewis **Trained** Melsonby, N Yorks

FOCUS
A fair handicap and they went a decent pace from the start with the result that they finished very well spread out. Good efforts from the first two, who finished clear.

Maslak(IRE) Official explanation: jockey said gelding never travelled

1780 BETDAQ.CO.UK MAIDEN STKS 1m 3f (F)
4:30 (4:30) (Class 4) 3-Y-O+ **£4,857** (£1,445; £722; £360) **Stalls** Low

Form RPR

0 **1** **Ostaadi**[20] 1289 3-8-10 0 WilliamBuick 8 75+
(M A Jarvis) *hld up in tch: hdwy 5f out: effrt to ld over 2f out: rdn wl over 1f out: edgd lft ins fnl f: eased nr fin* **3/1**[3]

3-0 **2** *¾* **Horsley Warrior**[20] 1289 3-8-10 0 DarryllHolland 5 71
(E S McMahon) *chsd ldrs: hdwy on outer 1/2-way: cl up over 4f out: led over 3f out: rdn and hdd over 2f out and sn drvn: swtchd rt ins fnl f and kpt on u.p towards fin* **9/4**[1]

3 *hd* **Birdinthehand (FR)** 3-8-7 0 ow2 TPQueally 6 67
(H R A Cecil) *hld up in tch: hdwy 5f out: chsd ldrs 3f out: rdn and ev ch tlsltly outpcd over 1f out: kpt on u.p ins fnl f* **7/1**

50-5 **4** *11* **Monte Pattino (USA)**[8] 1568 5-9-13 20 (vt) PaulHanagan 2 51
(C J Teague) *sn led: hdd 1/2-way and sn pushed along: rdn over 3f out and sn outpcd* **80/1**

0 **5** *nk* **The Boat Shed (IRE)**[18] 1328 3-8-10 0 PatDobbs 4 50
(B W Duke) *chsd ldrs tl rdn along and outpcd 1/2-way: hdwy u.p 3f out: drvn over 2f out: plugged on same pce* **66/1**

32-0 **6** *6* **Pergamon (IRE)**[20] 1291 3-8-10 83 (b) RichardMullen 7 39
(J H M Gosden) *trckd ldrs: hdwy to ld 1/2-way: rdn along and hdd over 4f out: drvn over 3f out and sn wknd* **5/2**[2]

7 *34* **Peters Pride**[35] 7-9-13 0 DaleGibson 3 —
(M W Easterby) *sn outpcd and a wl bhd* **25/1**

U3-0 **8** *56* **Son Of My Heart (USA)**[15] 1407 4-9-13 0 NCallan 1 —
(P F I Cole) *chsd ldrs: rdn along over 5f out: sn wknd and bhd fnl 3f* **8/1**

2m 26.94s (-1.06) **Going Correction** -0.025s/f (Stan)
WFA 3 from 4yo+ 17lb **8** Ran SP% **114.5**
Speed ratings (Par 105): **102,101,101,93,93 88,64,23**
toteswinger: 1&2 £3.00, 1&3 £4.50, 2&3 £4.60. CSF £10.13 TOTE £5.00: £2.00, £1.40, £1.80; EX 11.90.

Owner Sheikh Ahmed Al Maktoum **Bred** Snailwell Stud Co Ltd **Trained** Newmarket, Suffolk

FOCUS
Probably not a bad older-horse maiden for the track with a few of these open to improvement. The fourth had shown nothing previously and the sixth was well below form, though. The winning time was 1.93 seconds slower than the preceding handicap.

Pergamon(IRE) Official explanation: trainer's rep said gelding was unsuited by the track

Son Of My Heart(USA) Official explanation: trainer had no explanation for the poor form shown

1781 PARTY IN THE PADDOCK 27TH MAY H'CAP 6f (F)
5:00 (5:02) (Class 7) (0-50,50) 4-Y-O+ **£2,183** (£644; £322) **Stalls** Low

Form RPR

4040 **1** **Outer Hebrides**[36] 1039 8-8-5 **48** (v) AmyBaker(5) 13 56
(J M Bradley) *in tch: hdwy to chse ldrs over 2f out: rdn over 1f out: kpt on u.p ins fnl f to ld last 75yds* **11/1**

2000 **2** *¾* **Head To Head (IRE)**[46] 895 5-8-12 **50** (bt) DarryllHolland 6 56
(A D Brown) *chsd ldrs: hdwy 3f out: rdn to ld 2f out: drvn and edgd lft ent fnl f: hdd and no ex last 75yds* **12/1**

6440 **3** *1¼* **Easy Wonder (GER)**[9] 1536 4-8-11 **49** (b) JoeFanning 10 51
(I A Wood) *hld up in rr: hdwy over 2f out: swtchd lft and rdn over 1f out: styd on strly ins fnl f* **16/1**

6030 **4** *shd* **Tag Team (IRE)**[63] 746 8-8-5 **48** (p) MarkCoumbe(5) 11 49
(John A Harris) *cl up: led 3f out: rdn and hdd 2f out: sn drvn and kpt on u.p fnl f* **20/1**

00-5 **5** *shd* **Iguacu**[22] 1251 5-8-5 **50** MatthewDavies(7) 12 51
(George Baker) *hld up in rr: gd hdwy on wd outside 2f out: rdn to chse ldrs and edgd lft ins fnl f: kpt on: nrst fin* **11/2**[3]

5100 **6** *2¾* **All You Need (IRE)**[12] 1475 5-8-7 **50** (p) AndreaAtzeni(5) 9 42
(R Hollinshead) *midfield: rdn along 1/2-way: hdwy 2f out: drvn and no imp appr fnl f* **15/2**

230 **7** *1¾* **Mister Incredible**[14] 1421 6-8-6 **49** (v) MCGeran(5) 14 36
(J M Bradley) *midfield: effrt 3f out: rdn over 2f out: sn drvn and no imp* **9/2**[2]

1000 **8** *1½* **Vanatina (IRE)**[12] 1480 5-8-11 **49** DuranFentiman 3 31
(W M Brisbourne) *nvr bttr than midfield* **16/1**

4046 **9** *½* **Young Ivanhoe**[34] 1072 4-8-5 **50** (e) AndrewHeffernan(7) 5 30
(C A Dwyer) *chsd ldrs on inner: rdn along 3f out: drvn over 2f out and grad wknd* **16/1**

30-2 **10** *1¼* **Bonnet O'Bonnie**[55] 810 5-8-10 **48** NCallan 7 24
(J Mackie) *prom: rdn along over 2f out: drvn and edgd lft over 1f out: sn wknd and eased ins fnl f* **4/1**[1]

00-0 **11** *1¾* **Mujada**[63] 748 4-8-4 **49** JohnCavanagh(7) 4 20
(M Brittain) *dwlt and a in rr* **40/1**

-220 **12** *1¼* **Princess Charlmane (IRE)**[39] 975 6-8-12 **50** (t) PaulHanagan 8 17
(C J Teague) *led: rdn along and hdd 3f out: sn wknd* **12/1**

5360 **13** *3½* **Hunt The Bottle (IRE)**[11] 1496 4-8-11 **49** (p) TPQueally 2 4
(M Mullineaux) *a in rr* **14/1**

00-0 **14** *10* **Note Perfect**[22] 1241 4-8-12 **50** (b) DaleGibson 1 —
(M W Easterby) *midfield: rdn along 1/2-way: sn wknd* **20/1**

1m 16.98s (0.48) **Going Correction** -0.025s/f (Stan) **14** Ran SP% **125.3**
Speed ratings (Par 97): **95,94,92,92,92 88,86,84,83,81 79,77,73,59**
toteswinger: 1&2 £31.40, 1&3 £42.80, 2&3 £43.80. CSF £138.97 CT £2193.19 TOTE £12.00: £4.20, £4.40, £5.60; EX 207.40 Place 6: £98.75, Place 5: £36.68..

Owner Asterix Partnership **Bred** St Clare Hall Stud **Trained** Sedbury, Gloucs

FOCUS
A dreadful contest which would have once been called a banded race. There was only a 2lb weight range covering the whole field and ten of the 14 runners were wearing some kind of headgear. They went a decent pace given the context of the race and not that many ever got into it. The form is straightforward.

Bonnet O'Bonnie Official explanation: jockey said mare resented kick-back

Note Perfect Official explanation: jockey said he lost iron at the start

T/Plt: £183.90 to a £1 stake. Pool: £66,952.54. 265.69 winning tickets. T/Qpdt: £114.10 to a £1 stake. Pool: £3,007.35. 19.50 winning tickets. JR

[1577]BATH (L-H)
Wednesday, May 6

OFFICIAL GOING: Good to firm (9.4)
Wind: Strong ahead Weather: Dull

1782 LINDLEY CATERING MAIDEN AUCTION STKS 5f 11y
2:00 (2:02) (Class 5) 2-Y-O **£2,719** (£809; £404; £202) **Stalls** Centre

Form RPR
63 **1** **Royal Desert**[11] [1511] 2-9-0 0 .... TonyCulhane 2 86+
(M R Channon) *mde all: shkn up over 1f out: styd on strly ins fnl f* **11/10**[1]
2 2 **Yer Woman (IRE)** 2-8-6 0 .... RichardSmith 4 71+
(R Hannon) *chsd ldrs: wnt 2nd u.p over 1f out: kpt on but nvr gng pce of wnr* **8/1**
3 **3** 1 ¼ **Curtains**[10] [1534] 2-8-12 0 .... NickyMackay 8 72
(S Dow) *chsd ldrs: rdn and effrt 2f out: nvr on terms: kpt on same pce fnl f* **9/4**[2]
4 3 ¼ **Daniella De Bruijn (IRE)** 2-8-4 0 ow2 .... PNolan(7) 5 60+
(A B Haynes) *slowly away: outpcd and sn pushed along: stl plenty to do 2f out: styd on wl appr fnl f: fin wl: promising* **33/1**
0 **5** 1 ½ **Dolly Will Do**[33] [1090] 2-8-4 0 .... FrankieMcDonald 6 47
(N P Mulholland) *chsd wnr: rdn over 2f oit: wknd appr fnl f* **33/1**
5 **6** 2 ½ **Cane Cat (IRE)**[18] [1344] 2-8-6 0 .... TolleyDean 1 40
(A W Carroll) *chsd ldrs: rdn 3f out: wknd wl over 1f out* **6/1**[3]
0 **7** 20 **Whip Up (IRE)**[8] [1577] 2-8-10 0 .... RichardKingscote 7 —
(J G Portman) *s.i.s: sn rdn to get in tch: wknd qckly bef 1/2-way* **100/1**

63.81 secs (1.31) **Going Correction** +0.10s/f (Good) **7 Ran SP% 110.7**
Speed ratings (Par 93): **93,89,87,82,80 76,44**
toteswingers: 1&2 £2.40, 1&3 £1.10, 2&3 £3.40 CSF £10.07 TOTE £1.80: £1.50, £3.60; EX 10.60 Trifecta £17.90 Pool: £543.33 - 22.36 winning units..
Owner Jaber Abdullah **Bred** D R Tucker **Trained** West Ilsley, Berks

FOCUS
A modest juvenile maiden and the winning time was only 0.20 seconds quicker than the following two-year-old seller.

NOTEBOOK
Royal Desert was the clear form pick and he ran out a decisive winner, confirming the ability he showed when a close third at Leicester on his second start. He's progressing, but looks just fair at best at the moment. (op 6-4)
Yer Woman(IRE), a 7,500gns half-sister to dual 6f-7f juvenile winner Palazzone, made a pleasing enough introduction. She's entitled to improve plenty for this experience and ought to be hard to beat in similar company next time, particularly with her stable's juveniles in such good form. (op 6-1)
Curtains looked uncomfortable on the track and didn't appear to improve on the form she showed when third in an ordinary Brighton maiden on her debut. She gives the impression easier ground and a flatter course will suit better. (tchd 5-2)
Daniella De Bruijn(IRE), a £16,000 half-sister to 5f two-year-old winner First Choice, out of a 1m winner, was outpaced for most of the way after starting slowest of all but she ran on quite nicely late on. She should be all the better for this experience. (op 50-1)
Dolly Will Do looks pretty limited, but this still looked an improvement on her debut effort. (op 40-1)
Cane Cat(IRE) did not progress from the form she showed first-time up at Doncaster. (op 9-2 tchd 13-2)

1783 LINDLEY CATERING (S) STKS 5f 11y
2:35 (2:35) (Class 6) 2-Y-O **£1,942** (£578; £288; £144) **Stalls** Centre

Form RPR
4 **1** **Boga (IRE)**[5] [1637] 2-8-6 0 .... TPO'Shea 4 61+
(M R Channon) *in tch: drvn along 1/2-way: styd on wl fr over 1f out to ld fnl 50yds: readily* **10/3**[2]
60 **2** 1 ¼ **Kate Skate**[11] [1504] 2-8-4 0 ow5 .... DTDaSilva(7) 8 61
(P F I Cole) *s.i.s: hdwy to trck ldrs 1/2-way: led jst ins fnl f: sn shkn up: hdd and outpcd fnl 50yds* **8/1**
12 **3** 1 ½ **Transfixed (IRE)**[14] [1450] 2-8-7 0 ow1 .... RichardEvans(5) 9 57
(P D Evans) *trckd ldrs: led 1/2-way: sn hrd drvn: hdd over 1f out: wknd cl home* **11/4**[1]
6 **4** nk **Bathwick Gino**[23] [1249] 2-8-11 0 .... SteveDrowne 2 55
(A B Haynes) *sn in tch: hung lft over 2f out: swtchd rt and styd on over 1f out: kpt on but nvr gng pce to rch ldng trio* **25/1**
025 **5** ¾ **True Red (IRE)**[10] [1534] 2-8-6 0 .... AlanMunro 7 47
(B R Millman) *chsd ldrs: rdn over 2f out: one pce fnl f* **11/4**[1]
56 **6** 1 ¼ **Safari Camp (IRE)**[10] [1534] 2-8-11 0 .... StephenCarson 10 49+
(P Winkworth) *trckd ldrs: led over 1f out: hdd over 1f out: sn wknd* **5/1**[3]
7 1 ¼ **Southern Goddess (IRE)** 2-8-6 0 .... CatherineGannon 5 38
(P D Evans) *outpcd: mod prog ins fnl f* **33/1**
0 **8** 5 **Miss Marani (IRE)**[5] [1653] 2-8-6 0 .... TolleyDean 1 20
(W G M Turner) *sn outpcd* **33/1**
U0 **9** 1 ½ **New York Lights (IRE)**[16] [1404] 2-8-3 0 .... DavidProbert(3) 6 14
(M D I Usher) *s.i.s: sn in tch: wknd 1/2-way* **100/1**
0 **10** 10 **Little Perc (IRE)**[27] [1195] 2-8-11 0 ....(b[1]) FergusSweeney 3 —
(G L Moore) *led to 1/2-way: sn wknd* **33/1**

64.01 secs (1.51) **Going Correction** +0.10s/f (Good) **10 Ran SP% 117.8**
Speed ratings (Par 91): **91,89,86,86,84 82,80,72,70,54**
toteswinger: 1&2 £5.60, 1&3 £2.40, 2&3 £5.70 CSF £28.59 TOTE £3.80: £1.80, £2.60, £1.50; EX 24.70 Trifecta £98.90 Pool: £354.29 - 2.65 winning units..The winner was bought in for 15,000gns.
Owner Findlay & Bloom **Bred** Cathal Ennis **Trained** West Ilsley, Berks

FOCUS
A reasonable two-year-old seller run in a time only 0.20 seconds slower than the earlier juvenile maiden.

NOTEBOOK
Boga(IRE) improved significantly on the form she showed on her debut on the Lingfield Polytrack five days earlier. She lacked the mid-race speed of a few of her rivals, but gradually responded to pressure and was nicely on top at the line. Bought in for 15,000gns at the subsequent auction, her connections are obviously anticipating better again and she is open to further improvement, particularly over 6f. (op 3-1 tchd 9-4)
Kate Skate recovered well from a sluggish start and looked the winner about a furlong out, but she was reeled in close home, with her rider's 5lb overweight arguably the decisive factor. (op 6-1)
Transfixed(IRE) was always prominent and had every chance if good enough. (op 7-2)
Bathwick Gino lacked the required pace and was inclined to edge left in the closing stages. Still, this looked a slight improvement on his debut effort. Official explanation: jockey said colt hung left (op 33-1 tchd 40-1)
True Red(IRE) proved a major disappointment on this drop into selling company and is looking increasingly flattered by her second placing here back in April. (op 3-1 tchd 4-1 and 5-2)
Safari Camp(IRE) had every chance if good enough but he again failed to see his race out. (op 7-1 tchd 9-2)
New York Lights(IRE) Official explanation: jockey said filly was unsuited by the good to firm ground

1784 EVENT MOBILE CATERING (S) STKS 5f 161y
3:05 (3:06) (Class 6) 3-Y-O+ **£2,183** (£644; £322) **Stalls** Centre

Form RPR
4365 **1** **Dressed To Dance (IRE)**[75] [625] 5-8-10 83 ....(b) RichardEvans(5) 6 54
(P D Evans) *stdd s: rr: hdwy on outside over 2f out: styd on wl thrght fnl f to ld last strides* **6/4**[1]
3400 **2** nk **Caribbean Coral**[23] [1259] 10-9-6 66 .... GeorgeBaker 16 58
(A B Haynes) *in tch: chsd ldrs 1/2-way: led over 1f out: continually hung lft u.p: hdd last strides* **9/1**
0544 **3** 1 ½ **Mr Rev**[10] [1536] 6-9-6 45 ....(b) AdamKirby 10 53
(J M Bradley) *rrm hdwy on outside over 2f out: chsd ldr ins fnl f: no imp: outpcd for 2nd nr fin* **14/1**
000- **4** ¾ **Talamahana**[202] [6751] 4-9-1 42 .... TGMcLaughlin 7 45
(A B Haynes) *in rr: rdn and hdwy fr 2f out: kpt on wl cl home* **40/1**
-200 **5** 3 ¼ **Arfinnit (IRE)**[100] [294] 8-9-6 47 ....(p) KirstyMilczarek 5 39
(Mrs A L M King) *in rr: pushed along 1/2-way: rdn and styd on fnl f but nvr in contention* **25/1**
00-6 **6** hd **Rockfield Lodge (IRE)**[14] [1468] 4-9-3 67 ....(b) KevinGhunowa(3) 13 39
(R A Harris) *w ldrs: led over 2f out: hdd over 1f out: sn btn* **7/2**[2]
005 **7** ¾ **Beckenham's Secret**[77] [587] 5-9-6 42 ....(v) TolleyDean 3 36
(A W Carroll) *in rr tl hdwy appr fnl f: kpt on cl home* **18/1**
5636 **8** 1 ¼ **Spanish Ace**[37] [1038] 8-9-1 44 ....(p) JackDean(5) 1 32
(J M Bradley) *s.i.s: sn qcknd to ld: hdd over 2f out: wknd fnl f* **33/1**
2503 **9** 1 ¼ **Green Lagonda (AUS)**[8] [1591] 7-9-6 55 .... MickyFenton 2 28
(Stef Liddiard) *chsd ldrs: rdn over 2f out: wknd over 1f out* **5/1**[3]
0040 **10** 1 ¼ **Nordic Light (USA)**[10] [1536] 5-9-6 46 ....(bt) ChrisCatlin 15 23
(J M Bradley) *chsd ldrs: wknd over 1f out* **40/1**
1000 **11** 1 ¼ **Nawaaff**[10] [1535] 4-9-7 50 .... MCGeran(5) 4 25
(M R Channon) *chsd ldrs over 3f* **14/1**
00-0 **12** 15 **Admiral Arry**[36] [1047] 4-9-6 45 ....(v[1]) SteveDrowne 14 —
(J M Bradley) *chsd ldrs over 3f* **40/1**

1m 12.34s (1.14) **Going Correction** +0.10s/f (Good)
WFA 3 from 4yo+ 10lb **12 Ran SP% 121.6**
Speed ratings (Par 101): **96,95,93,92,88 88,87,85,83,82 80,60**
toteswinger: 1&2 £7.70, 1&3 £12.90, 2&3 £29.00 CSF £16.08 TOTE £2.30: £1.10, £2.50, £3.10; EX 14.30 Trifecta £86.90 Pool: £129.27 - 1.10 winning units..Dressed to Dance was bought by R. Harris by 7,200gns.
Owner R Piff **Bred** John Doyle **Trained** Pandy, Monmouths

FOCUS
A reasonable, competitive seller and it is more than likely that the winner and second ran below their marks.
Green Lagonda(AUS) Official explanation: jockey said gelding was denied a clear run

1785 PATRICIA BIFFEN BIRTHDAY H'CAP 1m 2f 46y
3:45 (3:45) (Class 6) (0-65,71) 4-Y-O+ **£2,388** (£705; £352) **Stalls** Low

Form RPR
2-04 **1** **King Of Connacht**[12] [1496] 6-8-7 **54** ....(p) LiamJones 9 62
(M Wellings) *mid-div: rdn over 3f out: hdwy over 2f out: styd on u.p fnl f to ld cl home* **25/1**
-601 **2** nk **Siena Star (IRE)**[27] [1199] 11-9-1 **62** .... MickyFenton 4 69
(Stef Liddiard) *chsd ldrs: str chal fr 2f out and stl upsides thrght fnl f: no ex last strides* **8/1**
240- **3** hd **Auntie Mame**[172] [7342] 5-9-0 **61** .... TPO'Shea 7 68
(D J Coakley) *chsd ldrs: led 2f out: rdn and kpt on wl fr over 1f out: hdd and nt qckn cl home* **5/1**[1]
04-0 **4** 2 ¾ **Jo'Burg (USA)**[42] [959] 5-8-12 **64** .... Louis-PhilippeBeuzelin(5) 2 65
(Lady Herries) *led to s: hld up in rr: hdwy fr 3f out: drvn to chse ldrs ins fnl 2f: outpcd fnl f* **7/1**[3]
5054 **5** 1 **Everyman**[14] [1463] 5-8-2 **52** .... DavidProbert(3) 16 51
(A W Carroll) *chsd ldrs: rdn 3f out: styd on same pce fnl 2f* **12/1**
0302 **6** 1 ¼ **Make Amends (IRE)**[8] [1589] 4-8-3 **55** .... MCGeran(5) 10 52
(R J Hodges) *in tch: wd into stride and one pce: styd on again fnl f: gng on cl home* **8/1**
4004 **7** hd **Artreju (GER)**[20] [1314] 6-8-13 **60** .... FergusSweeney 6 56
(G L Moore) *chsd ldrs: rdn 3f out: wknd over 1f out* **14/1**
5560 **8** hd **Clovis**[21] [1287] 4-9-3 **64** ....(bt) ChrisCatlin 1 60
(N P Mulholland) *in rr: hrd drvn fr 3f out: hdwy fr 2f out: gng on u.p cl home* **25/1**
300- **9** 1 **Feasible**[182] [7194] 4-9-0 **61** ....(b) TolleyDean 8 55
(J G Portman) *t.k.h: led: hdd 2f out: sn wknd* **50/1**
0-4 **10** 1 ¾ **Tyrana (GER)**[75] [623] 6-8-5 **57** ow3 .... JackDean(5) 5 47
(G F Bridgwater) *s.i.s: mod prog fnl 2f* **25/1**
-605 **11** 1 ¾ **Master Mahogany**[15] [1415] 8-9-1 **62** .... KirstyMilczarek 3 49
(R J Hodges) *in tch: rdn to chse ldrs over 3f out: wknd over 1f out* **14/1**
4121 **12** 1 ½ **Rapid City**[10] [1538] 6-9-10 **71** 6ex .... RichardThomas 11 55
(Jim Best) *in rr: rapid hdwy on outside over 4f out: chsd ldrs 3f out: sn rdn: wknd 2f out* **11/2**[2]
/102 **13** ½ **Postage (USA)**[20] [1314] 6-9-4 **65** .... GeorgeBaker 15 48
(K A Morgan) *chsd ldrs: rdn over 2f out: wknd wl over 1f out* **16/1**
60-0 **14** 7 **Houri (IRE)**[11] [1514] 4-9-0 **61** ....(b[1]) FrankieMcDonald 12 30
(J T Stimpson) *in rr: mod hdwy on outside 3f out: nvr rchd ldrs and sn wknd* **33/1**
-636 **15** 1 ½ **Encore Belle**[10] [1538] 4-8-9 **56** .... NeilChalmers 14 22
(Mouse Hamilton-Fairley) *in rr: sme hdwy on outside 3f out: one pce whn bmpd and wknd 2f out* **9/1**

2m 8.93s (-2.07) **Going Correction** -0.125s/f (Firm) **15 Ran SP% 120.1**
Speed ratings (Par 101): **103,102,102,100,99 98,98,98,97,96 94,93,93,87,86**
toteswinger: 1&2 £55.30, 1&3 £32.60, 2&3 £6.60 CSF £203.73 CT £1183.59 TOTE £37.50: £7.30, £3.50, £2.30; EX 310.90 TRIFECTA Not won..
Owner Ann Lindsay,Francis Lindsay,Jim O'Connor **Bred** B Burrough **Trained** Six Ashes, Shropshire

FOCUS
A moderate handicap run at a good pace and the form is sound and straightforward.
Make Amends(IRE) Official explanation: jockey said filly hung right
Tyrana(GER) Official explanation: jockey said mare hung left

1786 EVENT MOBILE CATERING H'CAP 1m 3f 144y
4:20 (4:21) (Class 5) (0-70,69) 4-Y-O+ **£2,914** (£867; £433; £216) **Stalls** Low

Form RPR
4221 **1** **Pelham Crescent (IRE)**[15] [1415] 6-8-13 **67** .... DavidProbert(3) 5 75
(B Palling) *in tch: rdn over 3f out: hdwy over 2f out: led jst ins fnl f: drvn out* **7/2**[2]

-220 **2** ¾ **Terminate (GER)**[46] 631 7-8-4 **55** oh1..............................(t) TPO'Shea 9 61
(Ian Williams) *in rr: hdwy fr 4f out: chsd ldrs fr 2f out: kpt on fnl f but nt pce of wnr* **8/1**[3]

/05- **3** ¾ **Party Palace**[12] 2641 5-8-4 **55** oh10.............................. CatherineGannon 3 60
(H S Howe) *in rr: hdwy over 2f out: nt clera run on ins 1f out: swtchd rt ins fnl f: kpt on cl home* **50/1**

3/00 **4** nk **Lord Oroko**[29] 1171 5-8-9 **60**.............................. TGMcLaughlin 2 64
(J G M O'Shea) *s.i.s: hdwy over 2f out: styd on fnl f: gng on cl home* **16/1**

500- **5** ½ **Great View (IRE)**[193] 6983 10-8-10 **61**..................(p) KirstyMilczarek 13 65
(Mrs A L M King) *in rr: hdwy over 2f out: kpt on ins fnl f: nt pce to rch ldrs* **16/1**

00-3 **6** hd **Double Spectre (IRE)**[67] 168 7-9-0 **65**.............................. RobertHavlin 1 69+
(Jean-Rene Auvray) *mid-div: hdwy over 2f out: styng on whn n.m.r jst ins fnl f: sn one pce* **10/1**

565- **7** ¾ **Kashmina**[148] 6437 4-8-10 **61**.............................. JamesDoyle 7 63
(Miss Sheena West) *chsd ldrs: led over 1f out: hdd jst ins fnl f and sn btn* **10/1**

011 **8** nk **Moonshine Creek**[8] 1581 7-9-0 **65** 6ex.............................. ChrisCatlin 4 66
(P W Hiatt) *chsd ldrs: rdn over 2f out: wknd fnl f* **3/1**[1]

1542 **9** 5 **Nawamees (IRE)**[8] 1586 11-8-13 **69**..................(p) RichardEvans(5) 10 62
(P D Evans) *led tl hdd 7f out: led again over 3f out: hdd & wknd 2f out* **11/1**

350- **10** 3¼ **Fourth Dimension (IRE)**[139] 7715 10-8-12 **63**.............. AdamKirby 12 50
(Miss T Spearing) *in rr: mod prog whn rdn 2f over out: nvr in contention and sn wknd* **10/1**

0000 **11** 5 **Speagle (IRE)**[9] 1568 7-8-5 **56** oh7 ow1..................(t) NeilChalmers 8 35
(A J Chamberlain) *t.k.h: led 7f out: hdd over 3f out: sn wknd* **50/1**

010- **12** 6 **Lady Jinks**[236] 5868 4-8-4 **60** ow4.............................. MCGeran(5) 6 29
(R J Hodges) *bhd fr 1/2-way* **20/1**

-005 **13** 14 **Jonquille (IRE)**[41] 972 4-8-0 **56** oh8 ow1..................(b) MartinLane(5) 11 —
(T J Pitt) *bhd fr 1/2-way* **22/1**

2m 28.42s (-2.18) **Going Correction** -0.125s/f (Firm) **13** Ran SP% **118.7**
Speed ratings (Par 103): **102,101,101,100,100 100,99,99,96,94 90,86,77**
toteswinger: 1&2 £7.10, 1&3 £50.90, 2&3 £33.20 CSF £30.24 CT £1189.25 TOTE £4.30: £1.40, £2.90, £11.10; EX 36.50 TRIFECTA Not won..

Owner Wayne Devine **Bred** Cathal M Ryan **Trained** Tredodridge, Vale Of Glamorgan

■ Stewards' Enquiry : David Probert two-day ban: careless riding (May 20-21)

FOCUS
A modest handicap, but they seemed to go a decent enough gallop. Despite the good pace the form is limited.

Party Palace Official explanation: jockey said mare was denied a clear run

1787 DIGIBET.CO.UK H'CAP 5f 11y
4:50 (4:55) (Class 6) (0-65,63) 4-Y-0+ **£2,266** (£674; £337; £168) **Stalls** Low

Form RPR

10-3 **1** **Kyllachy Storm**[16] 1403 5-8-11 **61**.............. Louis-PhilippeBeuzelin(5) 14 74+
(R J Hodges) *hld up towards rr: hdwy 2f out: qcknd to ld fnl 100yds* **3/1**[1]

-605 **2** 1¾ **Triple Dream**[3] 1710 4-9-0 **59**..................(p) SteveDrowne 5 66
(J M Bradley) *chsd ldrs: rdn and styd on to chse wnr fnl f: no imp* **11/1**

000- **3** 1¼ **Mr Forthright**[190] 7049 5-8-4 **49** oh2.............................. LiamJones 9 51
(J M Bradley) *bhd: hdwy on outside over 1f out: styd on wl but nt rch ldng duo* **33/1**

5202 **4** 1¼ **Joss Stick**[10] 1536 4-8-10 **58**..................(p) KevinGhunowa(3) 16 56
(R A Harris) *chsd ldrs on outside: rdn over 2f out: styd on same pce ins fnl f* **11/1**

30-6 **5** shd **Who's Winning (IRE)**[15] 1421 8-8-8 **53**..................(t) StephenCarson 3 53+
(B G Powell) *in rr: nt clr run over 1f out: swtchd rt and hdwy fnl f: fin wl* **16/1**

0-24 **6** ½ **Sofinella (IRE)**[28] 1182 6-8-0 **50**.............................. AmyBaker(5) 15 45
(A W Carroll) *chsd ldrs: slt ld fr ins fnl 2f: sn rdn: hdd & wknd fnl 100yds* **11/1**

1300 **7** shd **Meikle Barfil**[32] 1134 7-8-4 **49**..................(tp) CatherineGannon 1 44
(J M Bradley) *in rr: hdwy on ins and n.m.r 1f out: styd on cl home but nvr in contention* **40/1**

-000 **8** 1 **Maggie Kate**[18] 1360 4-8-12 **57**..................(p) RobertHavlin 6 48
(R Ingram) *chsd ldrs: rdn 3f out: one pce fnl f* **14/1**

04-6 **9** nk **Style Icon**[23] 1258 4-9-4 **63**.............................. ChrisCatlin 2 53+
(Rae Guest) *rr: hdwy and n.m.r over 1f out: kpt on ins fnl f: nvr in contention* **14/1**

0005 **10** nk **Gower**[11] 1528 5-8-6 **54**.............................. DavidProbert(3) 10 43
(R J Price) *in rr: rdn 3f out: styd on fnl f but nvr in contention* **17/2**[3]

0346 **11** ½ **Prince Of Delphi**[49] 861 6-9-0 **59**..................(p) KirstyMilczarek 11 46
(Mrs A L M King) *in rr: rdn and sme hdwy fr 2f out: nvr gng pce to be competitive* **11/1**

000- **12** ½ **Miss Firefly**[205] 6711 4-8-8 **58**.............................. MCGeran(5) 13 44
(R J Hodges) *chsd ldrs: rdn over 2f out: wknd fnl f* **16/1**

0-60 **13** 1 **Pegasus Dancer (FR)**[103] 269 5-8-10 **55**..................(p) MickyFenton 8 37+
(R H York) *chsd ldrs over 3f* **20/1**

00-0 **14** ¾ **Compton Rose**[18] 1360 4-9-1 **60**.............................. FrankieMcDonald 12 39+
(H Candy) *chsd ldrs over 3f* **8/1**[2]

400- **15** ¾ **Rathmolyon**[155] 7528 4-8-10 **55**.............................. FergusSweeney 7 32
(D Haydn Jones) *chsd ldrs: str chal fr over 2f out tl wknd qckly jst ins fnl f* **14/1**

330 **16** 1 **One Way Ticket**[10] 1540 9-8-4 **49** oh1..................(tp) TPO'Shea 4 22
(J M Bradley) *led tl hdd ins fnl 2f: wknd qckly* **33/1**

62.67 secs (0.17) **Going Correction** +0.10s/f (Good) **16** Ran SP% **124.8**
Speed ratings (Par 101): **102,99,97,95,95 94,94,92,92,91 90,89,88,87,85 84**
toteswinger: 1&2 £10.60, 1&3 £32.40, 2&3 £64.60 CSF £35.18 CT £987.45 TOTE £3.50: £1.70, £2.70, £8.70, £2.60; EX 40.70 Trifecta £201.50 Part won. Pool: £272.36 - 0.20 winning unit. Place 6: £58.60 Place 5: £38.44 .

Owner Mrs Angela Hart **Bred** Sir Eric Parker **Trained** Charlton Mackrell, Somerset

FOCUS
A moderate but competitive sprint handicap with the third rated to last year's form.

Pegasus Dancer(FR) Official explanation: jockey said gelding was denied a clear run

T/Plt: £53.60 to a £1 stake. Pool: £52,554.13. 714.97 winning tickets. T/Qpdt: £17.20 to a £1 stake. Pool: £2,736.28. 117.10 winning tickets. ST

CHESTER (L-H)
Wednesday, May 6

OFFICIAL GOING: Good to firm (good in places)
Wind: Fresh across Weather: Fine

1788 MANOR HOUSE STABLES LILY AGNES CONDITIONS STKS 5f 16y
1:45 (1:47) (Class 2) 2-Y-O
£13,085 (£3,918; £1,959; £980; £489; £245) **Stalls** Low

Form RPR

111 **1** **Star Rover (IRE)**[19] 1330 2-9-7 0.............................. JohnEgan 5 95
(P D Evans) *mde all: hung rt thrght: rdn over 1f out: r.o u.p* **13/2**

2112 **2** hd **Archers Road (IRE)**[7] 1598 2-9-1 0.............................. SamHitchcott 7 88
(M R Channon) *lw: pressed wnr thrght: rdn over 1f out: sn carried rt: r.o u.p* **3/1**[2]

23 **3** 3¾ **Tom Folan**[21] 1277 2-8-7 0.............................. MartinDwyer 2 67
(H J Collingridge) *racd keenly: trckd ldrs: rdn over 1f out: sn edgd rt: nt pce of front pair ins fnl f* **12/1**

6 **4** nk **Goodbye Earl (IRE)**[11] 1504 2-8-7 0.............................. FrancisNorton 1 66
(A Berry) *leggy: wnt rt s: towards rr: styd on fnl f: nt pce to chal* **20/1**

2 **5** hd **Mijas Playa**[20] 1298 2-8-8 0 ow1.............................. DarryllHolland 3 66
(C A Dwyer) *lw: midfield: pushed along on outside 3f out: effrt over 1f out: keeping on whn bmpd ins fnl f: no imp after* **9/4**[1]

432 **6** 1½ **My Mandy (IRE)**[11] 1504 2-8-7 0.............................. JimCrowley 9 60
(Ian Williams) *in rr: sn pushed along: kpt on ins fnl f: nvr able to chal* **16/1**

14 **7** nk **Fratellino**[7] 1598 2-8-12 0.............................. RobertWinston 4 64+
(A J McCabe) *bmpd s: sn chsd ldrs: rdn and nt qckn whn n.m.r and hmpd ins fnl f: sn eased* **11/1**

51 **8** 2¼ **Kings Of Leo**[2] 1742 2-8-10 0.............................. RichardHughes 6 53
(R Hannon) *w'like: fly-jmpd s: racd keenly in rr: nvr on terms* **4/1**[3]

60.48 secs (-0.52) **Going Correction** -0.05s/f (Good) **8** Ran SP% **115.8**
Speed ratings (Par 99): **102,101,95,95,94 92,92,88**
toteswinger: 1&2 £2.80, 1&3 £6.10, 2&3 £6.50 CSF £26.71 TOTE £6.80: £2.00, £1.50, £2.90; EX 16.00 TRIFECTA Not won..

Owner Christy Leo **Bred** Yeomanstown Stud **Trained** Pandy, Monmouths

■ Stewards' Enquiry : Martin Dwyer two-day ban: careless riding (May 20-21)

FOCUS
Seven of the previous nine winners had been drawn in one of the bottom three stalls, but those who had the best of the draw lacked experience, and with quick breaks the top two in the weights were able to cross over from stalls five and seven respectively to make the running.

NOTEBOOK
Star Rover(IRE) has great pace from the gate and around here it helped him gain the best position on the rail. This track always promised to suit, and despite racing keenly, he responded well to pressure in the straight and held off his only serious rival, to whom he was conceding 6lb, in gritty fashion. He has plenty of heart and is clearly a smart early two-year-old, but he probably wouldn't be up to winning at Royal Ascot and the valuable sales races at Newbury and Redcar are apparently the long-term aim. He is in at Goodwood today and the plan is to run if all is well with him. (op 5-1)

Archers Road(IRE) ran well in a decent contest at Ascot last time but, from trap seven here, he was never going to get the rail. Always on the winner's outside, he pushed him all the way to the line, but was just being held. A consistent sort, he is the guide to the level of the form. (tchd 10-3)

Tom Folan had not achieved a great deal in her first two starts and quick ground did not look ideal for this daughter of Namid, but she got to the rail from stall two and tracked the winner through. She ran a sound race and can do better with some cut. (op 16-1 tchd 11-1)

Goodbye Earl(IRE), who showed some ability on her debut, had the plum draw. Held up towards the rear, but crucially on the rail, she kept on for a creditable fourth, but this competition was a bit hot for her. (tchd 22-1)

Mijas Playa finished runner-up in a fillies' maiden at Newmarket on her debut and that form has been working out well. However, she challenged wide round the bend into the straight and struggled to land a blow. (op 3-1)

My Mandy(IRE) never threatened. (tchd 20-1 in places)

Fratellino, who raced wide through the early stages, got squeezed up between Mijas Playa and Tom Folan inside the last and deserves rating a bit better than the bare form. (op 20-1)

Kings Of Leo, a winner two days earlier, fly-jumped the start, raced keenly and never got involved. A return to a more conventional track ought to suit her. (tchd 7-2 and 9-2 in places)

1789 WEATHERBYS BANK CHESHIRE OAKS (FOR THE ROBERT SANGSTER MEMORIAL CUP) (LISTED RACE) (FILLIES) 1m 3f 79y
2:15 (2:15) (Class 1) 3-Y-O
£22,708 (£8,608; £4,308; £2,148; £1,076; £540) **Stalls** Low

Form RPR

40- **1** **Perfect Truth (IRE)**[25] 1222 3-8-12 **95**.............................. JMurtagh 2 103
(A P O'Brien, Ire) *mde all: drew clr 6f out: rdn over 1f out: jst hld on* **9/1**

0-5 **2** shd **Phillipina**[19] 1329 3-8-12 0.............................. RyanMoore 6 103+
(Sir Michael Stoute) *lw: chsd ldrs: pushed along 4f out: r.o to take 2nd ins fnl f: fin wl: jst failed* **9/2**[3]

3 1¾ **Roses For The Lady (IRE)**[38] 1021 3-8-12 **91**.............................. MJKinane 5 100
(John M Oxx, Ire) *racd keenly: chsd ldrs: rdn over 2f out: chsd wnr over 1f out tl ins fnl f: styd on same pce* **11/4**[2]

4-2 **4** 3 **Hidden Brief**[12] 1488 3-8-12 0.............................. LDettori 3 94+
(M A Jarvis) *lw: racd keenly: chsd wnr: pushed along over 4f out: lost 2nd over 1f out: no ex* **2/1**[1]

51- **5** 6 **Simple Solution (USA)**[247] 5570 3-8-12 **86**.............................. MichaelHills 7 83
(B W Hills) *racd keenly towards rr: pushed along 4f out: nvr on terms* **5/1**

1- **6** 57 **Hazy Dancer**[208] 6622 3-8-12 **77**.............................. MartinDwyer 1 —
(M P Tregoning) *in rr: sn niggled along: lost tch 3f out: t.o* **16/1**

34- **P** **Mystical Spirit (IRE)**[162] 7445 3-8-12 0.............................. RobertWinston 4 —
(J R Weymes) *bhd: lost tch over 7f out: t.o whn p.u over 5f out* **150/1**

2m 22.17s (-4.43) **Going Correction** -0.05s/f (Good) course record **7** Ran SP% **111.4**
Speed ratings (Par 104): **114,113,112,110,106 64,—**
toteswinger: 1&2 £7.60, 1&3 £5.40, 2&3 £2.60 CSF £46.15 TOTE £9.60: £3.70, £2.70; EX 54.60.

Owner Mrs A M O'Brien **Bred** Whisperview Trading Ltd **Trained** Ballydoyle, Co Tipperary

FOCUS
This did not look much of an Oaks trial, but it was run at a good gallop and was a proper test at the distance. The winning time broke the course record by 0.38sec. The runner-up is open to more improvement though.

NOTEBOOK

Perfect Truth(IRE) has plenty of stamina in her pedigree and she made full use of it by being given a positive ride from the front. Unsurprisingly, she got tired in the closing stages, but she had just enough in hand to hold on narrowly at the line. It has taken her eight starts to get off the mark, but she has clearly improved for this further step up in trip and return to quick ground, and she deserves a crack at a Group race now. She was cut to 25-1 for the Oaks, and it wouldn't be a surprise to see her line up at Epsom, but it's difficult to see her being good enough to win. (tchd 8-1 and 10-1)

Phillipina had been backed into 16-1 for the Oaks in the previous few days and clearly a bold bid was expected on this step up in distance and switch to faster ground. She got the trip well, closing all the way to the line, but is unlikely to be going to the Oaks now, and the Ribblesdale might be a more realistic target. (tchd 4-1 and 5-1)

Roses For The Lady(IRE) prefers some cut so the ground was a bit of a concern. She had beaten the Perfect Truth by two lengths when winning her maiden at Leopardstown last time, but couldn't confirm the form here. Her connections should not be too disappointed, though, as she picked up some black type and they appear to have a stronger candidate for the Oaks in Beauty O'Gwaun. (tchd 5-2 after early 10-3)

Hidden Brief, second in what looked a hot maiden on her debut, didn't see out the trip as well as might have been expected. A daughter of Barathea, this was the quickest ground she has encountered to date and a return to an easier surface should suit her. (op 5-2 tchd 11-4 in places)

Simple Solution(USA), who is bred to appreciate this sort of trip, was disappointing for a stable that tends to target this race. (tchd 11-2)

Hazy Dancer's dam and granddam won this race, but she had only won a moderate Lingfield maiden and never threatened. (op 14-1)

Mystical Spirit(IRE) Official explanation: jockey said filly hung right

1790 TOTESPORT.COM CHESTER CUP (HERITAGE H'CAP) 2m 2f 147y

2:45 (2:46) (Class 2) 4-Y-0+

£74,772 (£22,392; £11,196; £5,604; £2,796; £1,404) **Stalls** High

Form RPR

310- **1** **Daraahem (IRE)**^{200} [6817] 4-9-0 99 .... RHills 4 106
(B W Hills) *lw: trckd ldrs: wnt 2nd over 2f out: rdn to ld ins fnl f: kpt on wl* **7/1**^{2}

000- **2** *nk* **Ajaan**^{179} [7244] 5-9-0 95 .... (b) TPQueally 8 102
(H R A Cecil) *midfield: pushed along over 3f out: hdwy over 2f out: pressed wnr ins fnl f: hld cl home* **11/1**

20-0 **3** *nk* **Halla San**^{18} [585] 7-9-0 95 .... PaulHanagan 7 102
(R A Fahey) *lw: midfield: rdn and hdwy 3f out: r.o towards fin* **20/1**

26-1 **4** *1 1/2* **Desert Sea (IRE)**^{39} [1007] 6-9-0 95 .... MartinDwyer 6 100
(D W P Arbuthnot) *led after 1f: hdd after 2f: remained prom: regained ld over 5f out: rdn over 1f out: hdd ins fnl f: no ex cl home* **14/1**

112- **5** *1/2* **Amerigo (IRE)**^{201} [3196] 4-8-13 98 .... JMurtagh 16 102+
(M A Jarvis) *lw: hld up: rdn 4f out: hdwy over 3f out: hung lft ins fnl f: styd on wl nrst fin* **8/1**^{3}

03-0 **6** *3/4* **Inchnadamph**^{17} [1383] 9-8-8 89 .... (t) RobertWinston 12 93
(T J Fitzgerald) *in tch: effrt to chse ldrs 2f out: one pce fnl 100yds* **50/1**

2-01 **7** *2* **Downhiller (IRE)**^{11} [1519] 4-8-12 97 3ex .... EddieAhern 11 99+
(J L Dunlop) *lw: midfield: hdwy over 3f out: chsd ldrs on outside over 2f out: eased whn no ex wl ins fnl f* **9/2**^{1}

16-2 **8** *nk* **Gala Evening**^{20} [1007] 7-8-10 91 .... RichardHughes 10 92+
(J A B Old) *hld up: rdn over 1f out: styd on ins fnl f: nt rch ldrs* **14/1**

063- **9** *1/2* **Double Banded (IRE)**^{207} [6652] 5-8-7 88 .... StephenDonohoe 2 89
(Ian Williams) *in tch: effrt over 2f out: fdd ins fnl f* **11/1**

250- **10** *shd* **Som Tala**^{280} [4516] 6-8-13 94 .... DarryllHolland 3 95+
(M R Channon) *hld up: hdwy 2f out: no imp whn n.m.r ins fnl f: n.d after* **10/1**

5-52 **11** *hd* **Hindu Kush (IRE)**^{10} [1546] 4-9-5 104 .... JimCrowley 14 104
(D Nicholls) *led 1f: trckd ldrs: wnt 2nd 4f out tl over 2f out: sn rdn: wknd fnl f* **14/1**

36-0 **12** *1* **Formax (FR)**^{14} [1458] 7-8-9 90 .... PatDobbs 19 89+
(M P Tregoning) *hld up in rr: pushed along over 2f out: nvr on terms* **20/1**

24-4 **13** *2 3/4* **Dunaskin (IRE)**^{28} [1191] 9-8-12 93 .... TonyHamilton 17 89
(B Ellison) *led after 2f: clr after 5f: hdd over 5f out: wknd 2f out* **50/1**

62-0 **14** *6* **Tilt**^{14} [1458] 7-8-10 91 .... (p) RyanMoore 5 81
(B Ellison) *a bhd* **11/1**

0-63 **15** *18* **Carte Diamond (USA)**^{17} [1383] 8-9-2 97 .... TomEaves 9 67
(B Ellison) *a bhd* **25/1**

224/ **16** *11* **Warsaw Pact (IRE)**^{18} [4997] 6-8-8 89 .... JamieSpencer 15 47
(P J Hobbs) *midfield: rdn 4f out: sn wknd: eased ins fnl f* **10/1**

4m 4.01s (-0.79) **Going Correction** -0.05s/f (Good)
WFA 4 from 5yo+ 4lb **16** Ran SP% **122.3**
Speed ratings (Par 109): **99,98,98,98,97 97,96,96,96,96 96,95,94,92,84 79**
toteswinger: 1&2 £18.10, 1&3 £40.10, 2&3 £39.40 CSF £76.87 CT £1483.20 TOTE £5.70: £2.00, £2.70, £5.40, £3.30; EX 67.60 Trifecta £476.60 Pool: £2499.32 - 3.88 winning units..
Owner Hamdan Al Maktoum **Bred** Shadwell Estate Company Limited **Trained** Lambourn, Berks

FOCUS

Nothing drawn low wanted to make the running so they pottered about until Dunaskin had crossed over to take up pace-setting duties. Once in front, he set an ordinary gallop and it proved a big advantage to race prominently. The form appears sound enough but is limited by the proximity of the sixth.

NOTEBOOK

Daraahem(IRE) succeeded in getting a lead and was settled on the rail behind the pace. He was always in prime position to strike and, once a gap appeared on the inside entering the straight, he took full advantage. The Cesarewitch proved all to much for him last year as a three-year-old, but he has been gelded since and promises to play a big part in the valuable staying handicaps to come this term, with the Northumberland Plate next up. A bit of cut is thought to suit him ideally. (tchd 8-1)

Ajaan, who has not always looked straightforward, deserves plenty of credit for doing best of those held up off the pace. He didn't really go on after a promising start to last year's campaign, but as a result he had dropped back to his last winning mark. He can cope with a little rise in the weights and clearly stays particularly well. (op 14-1)

Halla San, runner-up in the Northumberland Plate last year, got a nice run through towards the inside in the straight and looks to have performed close to his best. A return to hurdling is apparently on the cards now, though. (op 16-1)

Desert Sea(IRE), raised 5lb to a career-high mark for winning at Kempton last time, was always well placed in a race not run at a strong gallop, as he was at the head of the main pack behind the leader for much of the race. The bare form may flatter him.

Amerigo(IRE), whose last run on the Flat saw him finish second in the Queen's Vase, had a poor draw and didn't have the race run to suit, so in the circumstances he was far from disgraced. He will have possibilities off his current mark on a fairer track. (tchd 15-2)

Inchnadamph was another to benefit from racing prominently off a relatively modest gallop.

Downhiller(IRE) was 2lb well in at the weights under his 3lb penalty for winning at Ripon last time, but he was under pressure some way out and this course didn't see him at his best. A return to a more galloping track will suit. Official explanation: jockey said colt was unsuited by the track (op 11-2 tchd 6-1 in places)

Gala Evening, another with a career-high mark to defy, could never get competitive.

Double Banded(IRE), fourth in this race last year for John Dunlop off a 1lb higher mark, held a good pitch throughout but his stamina seemed to run out from the turn in. (op 12-1)

Som Tala, who looked fit, continues to be held up in his races despite recording two of his three career wins from the front. (op 12-1)

1791 BOODLES DIAMOND ROULETTE H'CAP 5f 16y

3:15 (3:16) (Class 2) (0-105,100) 4£13,877 (£4,153; £2,076; £1,038; £517) **Stalls** Low

Form RPR

00-2 **1** **Sohraab**^{19} [1325] 5-9-3 **96** .... EddieAhern 4 106
(H Morrison) *chsd ldrs: wnt 2nd over 1f out: led ins fnl f: r.o* **11/4**^{1}

0044 **2** *1 1/4* **Strike Up The Band**^{28} [1189] 6-9-7 **100** .... AdrianTNicholls 1 106
(D Nicholls) *lw: led: rdn over 1f out: hdd ins fnl f: nt qckn* **7/2**^{2}

0-04 **3** *1/2* **Angus Newz**^{8} [1582] 6-8-9 **88** .... DarryllHolland 6 92
(M Quinn) *w ldr tl rdn over 1f out: r.o same pce ins fnl f* **8/1**

10-0 **4** *1/2* **Tournedos (IRE)**^{36} [1052] 7-9-5 **98** .... SilvestreDeSousa 9 100
(D Nicholls) *in tch: rdn over 1f out: styd on same pce ins fnl f* **20/1**

00-0 **5** *1* **Green Manalishi**^{46} [911] 8-9-7 **100** .... NCallan 13 99+
(K A Ryan) *midfield: rdn over 1f out: one pce ins fnl f* **18/1**

60-0 **6** *1* **Good Gorsoon (USA)**^{38} [1018] 4-8-9 **88** .... MichaelHills 3 88+
(B W Hills) *lw: s.i.s: plld hrd in midfield: n.m.r and hmpd over 2f out: nvr able to chal* **6/1**^{3}

400- **7** *nse* **An Tadh (IRE)**^{33} [1111] 6-8-13 **92** .... JMurtagh 11 87+
(G M Lyons, Ire) *hld up: nt clr run 2f out: shkn up over 1f out: kpt on ins fnl f: eased whn no imp towards fin* **16/1**

3230 **8** *1* **Carcinetto (IRE)**^{8} [1582] 7-9-2 **95** .... RyanMoore 5 86+
(P D Evans) *towards rr: rdn over 1f out: nvr on terms w ldrs* **20/1**

0600 **9** *nk* **Internationaldebut (IRE)**^{39} [996] 4-8-10 **89** .... JohnEgan 14 79
(S Parr) *chsd ldrs: rdn and wknd 1f out: eased whn btn towards fin* **50/1**

00-1 **10** *1/2* **Northern Dare (IRE)**^{47} [901] 5-8-9 **88** .... JimCrowley 8 76+
(D Nicholls) *towards rr: rdn over 1f out: nvr on terms* **15/2**

0-04 **11** *6* **Elhamri**^{4} [1672] 5-8-9 **88** .... RichardHughes 7 55
(S Kirk) *midfield tl rdn and wknd over 1f out* **12/1**

-400 **12** *4 1/2* **Invincible Force (IRE)**^{16} [1398] 5-8-10 **89** .... (b) FrancisNorton 12 40
(Paul Green) *rrd s: a bhd* **33/1**

59.59 secs (-1.41) **Going Correction** -0.05s/f (Good) **12** Ran SP% **119.3**
Speed ratings (Par 109): **109,107,106,105,103 102,102,100,100,99 89,82**
toteswinger: 1&2 £2.60, 1&3 £6.30, 2&3 £6.10 CSF £11.49 CT £69.59 TOTE £4.10: £1.70, £1.80, £2.30; EX 11.60 Trifecta £39.90 Pool: £1154.72 - 21.40 winning units..
Owner Pangfield Racing **Bred** T J Billington **Trained** East Ilsley, Berks

FOCUS

No horse drawn higher than stall eight had placed in this race in the last ten years, and that stat was upheld for another year. Nevertheless, a solid handicap with the placed horses close to previous form.

NOTEBOOK

Sohraab had shaped very well when runner-up at Newbury on his reappearance and, off just a 1lb higher mark and from a good, low draw, he got the perfect pitch tracking the leader on the rail. In a race in which few got competitive, he wore down the Nicholls horse inside the last and won a shade cosily. He was fully entitled to win off this mark. (op 7-2)

Strike Up The Band had the best of the draw and that was always going to suit him given his preferred style of running. Fast away, he led into the first turn, but he had Angus Newz hassling him on his outside and that probably resulted in him going a stride too quick, which in turn set things up for the winner. (op 3-1)

Angus Newz, who was drawn in stall six, is a natural front-runner, but with Strike Up The Band drawn in stall one she was always going to struggle to bag the rail. She ended up racing one off the rail until straightening up, and ran a sound race in the circumstances. (op 6-1)

Tournedos(IRE), all the better for his reappearance, was quickly away and got to race alongside the winner to his outside. Twice a previous course-and-distance winner, he once again showed his liking for the track.

Green Manalishi, whose last three wins have come at this track, had a tough draw to overcome and could never land a blow. (op 20-1 tchd 16-1)

Good Gorsoon(USA) forfeited his decent draw one off the rail (Fyodor, who had been scheduled to race from stall two, was a non-runner) by being slowly away. He then failed to settle, pulling much too hard in midfield, and gave himself little chance. He is not completely straightforward. (op 11-2 tchd 13-2)

An Tadh(IRE) often makes the running but his rider had no option but to drop him in from his tough draw and hope that the leaders went off too quick. That didn't happen and he ran about as well as one could expect. (op 18-1 tchd 14-1)

Carcinetto(IRE) is handicapped up to the hilt. (op 28-1)

Internationaldebut(IRE) raced wide and can be forgiven his effort. (tchd 40-1)

Elhamri also gave up plenty of ground racing wide.

1792 STELLAR GROUP H'CAP 1m 4f 66y

4:00 (4:01) (Class 3) (0-95,86) 3-Y-0 **£10,037** (£2,986; £1,492; £745) **Stalls** Low

Form RPR

01- **1** **Braveheart Move (IRE)**^{222} [6253] 3-9-1 **78** .... StephenDonohoe 2 90+
(Sir Mark Prescott) *w'like: str: lw: a.p: rdn over 1f out: r.o to ld towards fin* **9/2**^{2}

10- **2** *1/2* **Quai D'Orsay**^{207} [6648] 3-9-6 **83** .... LDettori 5 95
(M Johnston) *led: rdn over 1f out: hdd and nt qckn towards fin* **7/1**

31-5 **3** *1 1/2* **Jedi**^{12} [1489] 3-9-3 **80** .... RyanMoore 4 89+
(Sir Michael Stoute) *lw: trckd ldrs: rdn and nt qckn over 2f out: kpt on wout troubling front pair ins fnl f* **11/2**^{3}

21-1 **4** *1 3/4* **Kings Destiny**^{34} [1086] 3-9-9 **86** .... NCallan 7 92+
(M A Jarvis) *lw: hld up: hdwy over 7f out: chsd ldrs on outside 3f out: rdn over 1f out: one pce ins fnl f* **11/4**^{1}

-615 **5** *nk* **Citizenship**^{34} [1086] 3-8-7 **70** .... JimCrowley 11 76
(Ian Williams) *hld up in rr: hdwy on outside 3f out: rdn over 1f out: kpt on ins fnl f: nt pce to trble ldrs* **40/1**

41-1 **6** *1/2* **Kimberley Downs (USA)**^{33} [1105] 3-9-7 **84** .... GregFairley 3 89
(M Johnston) *chsd ldrs: pushed along over 3f out: outpcd 2f out* **7/1**

1-41 **7** *shd* **Headline Act**^{15} [1431] 3-9-5 **82** .... JimmyFortune 10 87
(J H M Gosden) *hld up: rdn ins fnl f: nvr able to chal* **9/2**^{2}

23-3 **8** *hd* **Rumble Of Thunder (IRE)**^{14} [1464] 3-8-12 **75** .... MartinDwyer 8 81+
(D W P Arbuthnot) *racd keenly in midfield: outpcd 2f out: eased whn no real imp fnl 100yds* **40/1**

1-45 **9** *17* **Digger Derek (IRE)**^{21} [1280] 3-8-9 **72** .... PaulHanagan 6 50
(R A Fahey) *midfield: wknd over 3f out* **20/1**

2m 38.18s (-1.72) **Going Correction** -0.05s/f (Good) **9** Ran SP% **113.1**
Speed ratings (Par 103): **103,102,101,100,100 99,99,99,88**
toteswinger: 1&2 £9.20, 1&3 £6.90, 2&3 £6.60 CSF £34.19 CT £173.84 TOTE £5.60: £2.20, £2.30, £2.00; EX 44.10.
Owner Moyglare Stud Farm Ltd **Bred** Moyglare Stud Farm Ltd **Trained** Newmarket, Suffolk

FOCUS

A race made up mainly of unexposed three-year-old handicappers, and it should throw up a few winners. It was something of a tactical affair, though, with Dettori setting a stop-start gallop on Quai d'Orsay up front, so the form is a bit muddling.

NOTEBOOK

Braveheart Move(IRE) ◆ let the leader get first run, but he was still able to pick him up, and he clearly has plenty of talent. There is plenty more to come from the son of Cape Cross, and the King George V Handicap at the Royal meeting looks an ideal target for him. While he handled this track perfectly well, he's a fine, big horse and Ascot ought to suit him better, as will a stronger all-round pace. He looks one to follow (tchd 5-1)

Quai D'Orsay was given a fine ride by Dettori, who set fractions to suit himself and, having kicked off the final bend, would have no doubt expected to collect in most races. He bumped into one here, but it was a sound effort, and, as a close relative of Foreign Affairs, who won 12 races for this race's winning trainer Sir Mark Prescott, he can be expected to improve and get further with time. (op 8-1)

Jedi ◆ ran well given the tactical nature of the race. Easier ground would probably be in his favour, and one would expect that the Bibury Cup at Salisbury will be on his agenda next month. (op 5-1)

Kings Destiny, a winner at Leicester on his reappearance, had only been put up 3lb for that and looked to hold sound claims. He was held up off the steady early gallop, though, and gave away ground by racing wide, so it wasn't a great surprise that after coming to challenge three wide on the home turn, he was soon beaten off. He could well regain the winning thread back on a more conventional track. (tchd 5-2)

Citizenship, well beaten by Kings Destiny at Leicester, got some experience of this track as a two-year-old, and he did much better back here, despite not exactly enjoying the run of the race. (op 33-1)

Kimberley Downs(USA), not for the first time, struggled to keep up when the pace increased. He could have done with the gallop being stronger on his turf debut, and he is not one to write off back on a more galloping track. (op 17-2 tchd 9-1)

Headline Act stayed on late but this race just wasn't run to suit. He will be seen to much better effect off a stronger pace. (op 5-1)

1793 HULL CITY A.F.C. PREMIER DREAM MAIDEN STKS — 1m 2f 75y

4:35 (4:36) (Class 4) 3-Y-O — **£7,123** (£2,119; £1,059; £529) **Stalls** High

Form	Pos	Dist	Horse / Details	RPR
2	1		**Harbinger**[20] 1297 3-9-3 0 ... RyanMoore 10 (Sir Michael Stoute) *lw: a.p: led over 1f out: qcknd away ins fnl f: impressive* 6/4[1]	94+
	2	3	**Changingoftheguard (IRE)**[191] 7030 3-9-3 0 ... JMurtagh 1 (A P O'Brien, Ire) *w'like: str: lw: midfield: nt clr run 2f out: rdn and hdwy over 1f out: wnt 2nd jst ins fnl f: nt pce of wnr* 3/1[3]	88+
5	3	3 ¾	**Una Pelota (IRE)**[11] 1508 3-9-3 0 ... JimCrowley 7 (N J Vaughan) *w'like: flat ldrs: rdn jst ins fnl f: sn one pce* 40/1	80
4	4	shd	**Beauchamp Xerxes**[20] 1297 3-9-3 0 ... EddieAhern 9 (G A Butler) *hld up: rdn and hdwy 1f out: styd on wl towards fin* 25/1	82+
53-	5	1 ¼	**Norwegian Dancer (UAE)**[215] 6451 3-9-3 0 ... RichardMullen 11 (E S McMahon) *prom: led over 3f out: rdn and hdd over 1f out: wknd ins fnl f* 50/1	78
44-0	6	¾	**Asateer (IRE)**[21] 1291 3-9-3 89 ... RHills 2 (B W Hills) *racd keenly in midfield: hung bdly lft fr over 1f out: eased whn difficult to ride ins fnl f* 11/4[2]	76+
3	7	1 ¼	**Calypso Bay (IRE)**[21] 1289 3-9-3 0 ... ShaneKelly 14 (J Noseda) *lw: in rr: pushed along 3f out: effrt and swtchd rt over 1f out: sn hung lft and no imp on ldrs* 6/1	74+
0	8	8	**Paddy Partridge**[34] 1087 3-9-3 0 ... StephenDonohoe 8 (N J Vaughan) *w'like: str: lw: dwlt: a towards rr* 200/1	58
	9	1 ¼	**Annes Sound (IRE)**[194] 6959 3-8-12 0 ... PaulHanagan 13 (Patrick Morris) *in rr: pushed along over 1f out: nvr on terms* 200/1	50
6-4	10	½	**Northern Acres**[11] 1508 3-9-3 0 ... AdrianTNicholls 12 (D Nicholls) *in tch: chsd ldrs over 3f out: rdn and chal 2f out: wknd over 1f out: eased ins fnl f* 50/1	54
U0-0	11	16	**Liberty Estelle (IRE)**[12] 1490 3-8-12 0 ... JohnEgan 4 (P D Evans) *led: hdd over 3f out: wknd over 2f out* 200/1	17

2m 10.19s (-2.01) **Going Correction** -0.05s/f (Good) **11** Ran SP% **117.7**

Speed ratings (Par 101): **106,103,100,100,99 98,97,91,90,90 77**

toteswinger: 1&2 £3.00, 1&3 £16.70, 2&3 £20.30 CSF £6.14 TOTE £2.80: £1.20, £1.50, £5.30; EX 7.20 Place 6: £227.64 Place 5: £97.99 .

Owner Highclere Thoroughbred Racing (Adm. Rous) **Bred** Mrs A K H Ooi **Trained** Newmarket, Suffolk

■ Stewards' Enquiry : Paul Hanagan Fine: £140. Vaccinations in passport did not meet requirements of Rules of Racing.

FOCUS

This looked a pretty decent maiden on paper, and Sir Michael Stoute's success with Harbinger means that nine of the last ten winners of this race have now been trained by either Stoute, Barry Hills or John Gosden. The winner was impressive but the third and fifth may limit the form in time.

Asateer(IRE) Official explanation: jockey said colt hung left

Northern Acres Official explanation: jockey said colt hung right

T/Jkpt: Not won. T/Plt: £267.80 to a £1 stake. Pool: £168,621.75. 459.50 winning tickets. T/Qpdt: £27.70 to a £1 stake. Pool: £8,806.80. 235.20 winning tickets. DO

1794 - 1797a (Foreign Racing) - See Raceform Interactive

1788 CHESTER (L-H)

Thursday, May 7

OFFICIAL GOING: Good to firm (8.0)

Rail out 3yds from the 4f marker to the 1.5f marker, adding 6 yds to each circuit.

Wind: Moderate half against Weather: Fine

1798 BOODLES DIAMOND VELOCITY H'CAP — 1m 2f 75y

1:45 (1:45) (Class 2) (0-100,99) 4-Y-O+ **£14,193** (£4,248; £2,124; £1,062; £528) **Stalls** High

Form	Pos	Dist	Horse / Details	RPR
600-	1		**Cheshire Prince**[213] 6536 5-8-4 85 oh2 ... LiamJones 5 (W M Brisbourne) *chsd ldr: led over 2f out: kicked on over 1f out: jst hld on towards fin* 25/1	94
133-	2	shd	**Kingdom Of Fife**[212] 6563 4-8-6 87 oh2 ow2 ... (v[1]) RyanMoore 3 (Sir Michael Stoute) *lw: midfield: chsd ldrs 7f out: wnt 2nd ent fnl f: r.o and gaining on wnr towards fin: jst failed* 11/4[1]	96+
0400	3	2 ½	**Robby Bobby**[15] 1458 4-8-5 86 ... GregFairley 7 (M Johnston) *lw: midfield: rdn and hdwy over 1f out: styd on ins fnl f: nt pce to rch front pair* 18/1	90+
00-0	4	½	**Gala Casino Star (IRE)**[26] 1213 4-8-4 85 oh2 ... PaulHanagan 4 (R A Fahey) *chsd ldrs: rdn over 2f out: chsd wnr fr over 1f out tl ent fnl f: no ex fnl 75yds* 14/1	88
4-10	5	½	**Press The Button (GER)**[15] 1460 6-8-11 92 ... JimmyFortune 2 (J R Boyle) *b: chsd ldrs: nt clr run wl over 1f out: styd on same pce ins fnl f* 7/1	94
04-4	6	½	**Vainglory (USA)**[16] 1433 5-8-1 85 oh4 ... AhmedAjtebi(3) 10 (D M Simcock) *lw: midfield: niggled along and hdwy 3f out: kpt on same pce ins fnl f* 10/1	86
0-25	7	½	**Fanjura (IRE)**[19] 1352 4-8-11 92 ... MichaelHills 1 (B W Hills) *midfield: pushed along 2f out: nt clr run wl over 1f out: hung lft and kpt on ins fnl f: nvr able to chal* 9/2[2]	92+
4-36	8	1	**Dream Desert (IRE)**[15] 1458 4-8-6 87 ... EdwardCreighton 12 (M R Channon) *towards rr: effrt on outside 2f out: no imp ins fnl f* 6/1[3]	85
00-5	9	4 ½	**Mull Of Dubai**[9] 1593 6-8-9 90 ... JohnEgan 11 (T P Tate) *swtchd lft s: hld up: rdn over 1f out: eased whn n.d ins fnl f* 7/1	79
1610	10	10	**El Dececy (USA)**[5] 1660 5-8-6 87 6ex ... MartinDwyer 8 (S Parr) *lw: occasionally hung-rt: led: rdn and hdd over 2f out: wknd over 1f out: eased ins fnl f* 50/1	56
000-	11	28	**Humungous (IRE)**[243] 5694 6-9-4 99 ... JamieSpencer 9 (C R Egerton) *s.i.s: swtchd lft s: a bhd: eased whn n.d fnl f* 20/1	12
653-	12	1 ½	**Bee Sting**[14] 6698 5-8-6 87 ... (b) GrahamGibbons 6 (Mrs L Williamson) *sn pushed along: a bhd: eased fnl f* 20/1	—

2m 8.40s (-3.80) **Going Correction** -0.15s/f (Firm) **12** Ran SP% **120.5**

Speed ratings (Par 109): **109,108,106,106,106 105,105,104,100,92 70,69**

toteswinger: 1&2 £20.80, 1&3 £62.70, 2&3 £17.00 CSF £91.26 CT £1331.64 TOTE £21.60: £4.20, £1.80, £4.70; EX 178.90 TRIFECTA Not won..

Owner D C Rutter & H Clewlow **Bred** The National Stud **Trained** Great Ness, Shropshire

■ Stewards' Enquiry : Ryan Moore one-day ban: used whip with excessive frequency (May 21)

FOCUS

Despite half a millimetre of rain overnight, the ground had quickened up a shade to Good to Firm all round. A competitive handicap on paper and they went a very decent pace. Very few ever really got into this and the form looks a bit suspect

NOTEBOOK

Cheshire Prince, whose last three wins had come here, was returning from seven months off and has tended to need his first run back following a break, but not this time and plenty of credit must go to his jockey who rode a fine tactical race. He was in the ideal position to strike when the leader started to fade and having gone to the front inside the last 3f, was set alight and took the contest by the scruff of the neck from that point. Things got a little tight towards the end, but he always looked like holding on and he is now likely to be aimed at the Old Newton Cup at Haydock in early July. (op 20-1)

Kingdom Of Fife was the subject of quite a plunge beforehand. Back down to probably his best trip and visored for the first time on this return from seven months off, he raced kindly in the middle of the field before asked a question and, although he finished strongly, the line was always just going to beat him. Many will point to the 2lb overweight making the difference, but that would be a little unkind to the winner. (op 9-2)

Robby Bobby ◆, in good form on sand during the winter but very disappointing in his last two starts, was down 6lb here and ran much better. He stayed on well to snatch third in a race where it was an advantage to be handy and he looks capable of winning again off this sort of mark. (op 16-1)

Gala Casino Star(IRE), well beaten on Polytrack on his return from six months off last month, performed better here though he was probably helped by racing handily in the main group.

Press The Button(GER), who was off the same mark as when successful on the Kempton Polytrack two starts back, was also probably helped by racing handily in the main group. (op 8-1 tchd 13-2)

Vainglory(USA), an eye-catcher on his return to action on the Kempton Polytrack last month, was 4lb out of the handicap here but was still 4lb lower than when third behind Mull Of Dubai in this race last year. He made some late progress down the outside without being able to land a blow, but wasn't disgraced given the way the race was run. (op 9-1)

Fanjura(IRE), trying this trip for the first time, seemed to be ridden with that in mind and was another to make a little late headway. (op 4-1)

Dream Desert(IRE) was trapped out a little wide on this drop back down in trip. He is still relatively unexposed and is worth another chance. (op 15-2)

Mull Of Dubai Official explanation: jockey said gelding had no more to give

Humungous(IRE) was edgy beforehand. Official explanation: trainer's rep said gelding missed the break and ran too freely early stages (op 16-1)

Bee Sting Official explanation: jockey said gelding never travelled

1799 EXTRABET.COM HUXLEY STKS (FOR THE TRADESMAN'S CUP) (GROUP 3) — 1m 2f 75y

2:15 (2:15) (Class 1) 4-Y-O+

£36,900 (£13,988; £7,000; £3,490; £1,748; £877) **Stalls** High

Form	Pos	Dist	Horse / Details	RPR
440-	1		**Doctor Fremantle**[236] 5892 4-9-0 113 ... RyanMoore 8 (Sir Michael Stoute) *racd keenly: chsd ldrs: 4th wd on bnd wl over 7f out: rdn and lugged lft fr over 1f out: led ent fnl f: all out* 1/1[1]	110+
00-1	2	shd	**Staying On (IRE)**[19] 1346 4-9-0 110 ... (t) AdamKirby 3 (W R Swinburn) *led: rdn over 1f out: hdd ent fnl f: continued to chal: r.o u.p* 6/1[3]	110
11-1	3	½	**Expresso Star (USA)**[40] 997 4-9-0 107 ... JimmyFortune 1 (J H M Gosden) *lw: chsd ldrs: awkward on bnd wl over 7f out: rdn over 1f out: sn chalng strly between horses: nt qckn cl home* 11/4[2]	109
/2-4	4	1 ¼	**Fairmile**[39] 1017 7-9-0 105 ... StephenDonohoe 4 (Ian Williams) *midfield: rdn and hdwy over 1f out: cl 4th ins fnl f: looking hld whn n.m.r and hmpd cl home* 40/1	107+
30-0	5	1	**Indian Days**[12] 1526 4-9-0 100 ... AlanMunro 6 (J G Given) *lw: hld up: rdn over 1f out: flashed tail ent fnl f: r.o towards fin: nt pce of ldrs* 50/1	104+
20-0	6	2	**Bushman**[12] 1526 5-9-0 104 ... JamieSpencer 5 (D M Simcock) *bhd: pushed along and hdwy 4f out: wknd over 1f out* 20/1	100
0020	7	½	**Yahrab (IRE)**[46] 4-9-0 109 ... AhmedAjtebi 9 (Saeed Bin Suroor) *prom: rdn and losing pl whn n.m.r over 1f out: wknd ins fnl f* 14/1	99
4616	8	shd	**Halicarnassus (IRE)**[12] 1526 5-9-0 108 ... SamHitchcott 7 (M R Channon) *racd keenly in midfield: forced wd bnd wl over 7f out: pushed along 3f out: wknd over 1f out* 20/1	99
5	9	1 ¼	**Logic Way (USA)**[21] 1301 5-9-0 100 ... (bt) MartinDwyer 2 (Miss D Mountain) *b.hind: lw: midfield: forced wd on bnd over 7f out: pushed along over 3f out: wknd over 2f out* 50/1	96

2m 10.04s (-2.16) **Going Correction** -0.15s/f (Firm) **9** Ran SP% **113.5**

Speed ratings (Par 113): **102,101,101,100,99 98,97,97,96**

toteswinger: 1&2 £2.50, 1&3 £1.20, 2&3 £2.90 CSF £6.83 TOTE £2.10: £1.10, £1.50, £1.30; EX 7.80 Trifecta £14.80 Pool: £881.66 - 44.00 winning units..

Owner K Abdulla **Bred** Juddmonte Farms Ltd **Trained** Newmarket, Suffolk

FOCUS

An interesting Group 3 featuring a couple of established Pattern-class performers and a few progressive types, but three dominated the market and they eventually dominated the finish also. The early pace was nothing special though, and the winning time was 1.64 seconds slower than the opening handicap. The runner-up is the best guide to the form with the winner not needing to be at his best.

NOTEBOOK

Doctor Fremantle, representing the stable that had won this race four times since 2001 and the winner of the Chester Vase on this card last year, hadn't been seen since failing to stay in the St Leger. Relaxed in the paddock, he was always in a prominent position if a little wide in the race itself. He hit the front a furlong out and seemed likely to win comfortably, but the rallying runner-up made sure he had to fight hard and in the end he only just scraped home. His trainer believes that he is better suited by 1m4f and the Coronation Cup seems the most likely option now.\ (op 6-4)

Staying On(IRE), who smashed the course record when winning a 1m Doncaster Listed event on his return to action last month, is yet to win over this trip but he very much had his own way out in front here until taken on by Yahrab a good half a mile from home. He managed to shake him off, but looked likely to be comfortably beaten when the favourite was unleashed a furlong out. However, he never gave up and was coming right back at the line. A Group race looks within his grasp now. (op 5-1)

Expresso Star(USA), trying Pattern company for the first time after his impressive win in the Lincoln, had proved himself over this trip last season so there were no worries over his stamina. Never far away, he kept on trying between the front pair all the way to the line and he too should have little trouble finding a Pattern race in due course. (op 5-2 tchd 3-1 in places)

Fairmile, who has managed just two well-spaced-out appearances since November 2007 and who failed to see out the extra 2f on his debut for the yard at Doncaster in March, performed much better here and he stayed on well after being switched over to the inside rail turning in. If he can be kept sound, there should be another decent prize in him. (op 33-1)

Indian Days, well held in his previous tries on Group company and behind both Halicarnassus and Bushman when last of eight at Sandown last month, deserves credit for this effort as he was stone last on the run to the final bend but finished in good style after having to be switched around the entire field. (tchd 40-1)

Bushman, who pulled too hard at Sandown, didn't seem to be handling the track early on here and, though he made some progress at around halfway, he failed to get involved. He probably needs softer ground in any case. Official explanation: jockey said gelding was unsuited by the track (op 16-1)

Yahrab(IRE), running with credit in Dubai and Abu Dhabi so far this year, dropped out after sitting just behind the runner-up for a long way. (op 12-1)

Halicarnassus(IRE), who had the advantage in fitness when just in front of Bushman at Sandown last month, never got into it.

Logic Way(USA) is yet to show that he is up to this level in this country. (tchd 40-1)

1800 VIRGIN MONEY CHESTER VASE (GROUP 3) (C&G) — 1m 4f 66y

2:45 (2:47) (Class 1) 3-Y-O

£39,739 (£15,064; £7,539; £3,759; £1,883; £945) **Stalls** Low

Form — RPR

5-4 **1** **Golden Sword**[32] 1145 3-8-12 105 .... CO'Donoghue 5 114
(A P O'Brien, Ire) *lw: mde all: pushed along over 3f out: abt 4l clr 2f out: drvn out and styd on* **25/1**

30- **2** *2* **Masterofthehorse (IRE)**[194] 6973 3-8-12 111 .... JMurtagh 4 113+
(A P O'Brien, Ire) *patiently rdn and wl bhd: hdwy 2f out: rdn over 1f out: wnt 2nd ins fnl f: r.o: nvr able to rch wnr: too much to do* **13/8**[1]

4-11 **3** *1 1/2* **Debussy (IRE)**[15] 1459 3-8-12 101 .... JimmyFortune 7 108
(J H M Gosden) *lw: racd keenly in midfield: hdwy 2f out: rdn to chse ldrs over 1f out: styd on whn hung lft ins fnl f: no imp towards fin* **11/4**[2]

1 **4** *1 3/4* **Sight Unseen**[20] 1328 3-8-12 0 .... (t) TPQueally 6 105
(H R A Cecil) *midfield: hdwy 5f out: rdn to chse wnr over 2f out tl ins fnl f: sn hmpd whn btn* **5/1**[3]

2-4 **5** *shd* **Saptapadi (IRE)**[13] 1485 3-8-12 0 .... RyanMoore 8 108+
(Sir Michael Stoute) *stdd s: hld up: nt clr run over 2f out: hdwy over 1f out: styd on ins fnl f: nvr able to land a blow* **11/1**

1-1 **6** *8* **Too Much Trouble**[15] 1453 3-8-12 102 .... DarryllHolland 2 92
(M R Channon) *lw: racd keenly: chsd ldrs: wnt 2nd over 4f out: pushed along over 3f out: lost 2nd over 2f out: wknd over 1f out* **8/1**

5-21 **7** *14* **Above Average (IRE)**[13] 1485 3-8-12 103 .... MichaelHills 3 70
(B W Hills) *chsd wnr: lost 2nd wl over 4f out: sn n.m.r: wknd over 2f out: eased whn btn over 1f out* **12/1**

204 **8** *56* **Solo Choice**[10] 1570 3-8-12 68 .... (b[1]) JamesDoyle 1 —
(D Flood) *chsd ldrs: rdn and wknd over 4f out: sn bhd: t.o* **100/1**

2m 33.86s (-6.04) **Going Correction** -0.15s/f (Firm) **8 Ran SP% 113.4**

Speed ratings (Par 109): **114,112,111,110,110 105,95,58**

toteswingers: 1&2 £6.90, 1&3 £8.70, 2&3 £2.10 CSF £65.25 TOTE £24.60: £3.60, £1.40, £1.50; EX 46.90 Trifecta £441.30 Pool: £894.54 - 1.50 winning units..

Owner M Tabor, D Smith & Mrs John Magnier **Bred** T E Pocock And Morton Bloodstock **Trained** Ballydoyle, Co Tipperary

FOCUS

A race that has produced some top-class performers over the years with Millenary, Papal Bull and Soldier Of Fortune amongst the best of those successful since 2000, but no subsequent Derby winner had taken this since Shergar in 1981. They went a decent pace but there is little solid to go on form-wise, with the third probably the best guide.

NOTEBOOK

Golden Sword was sent straight into the lead and set a decent pace, but not many would have expected him to still be in front at the line. As soon as his rider asked him to stretch away from his nearest rivals passing the 3f pole, it became obvious that it would have taken something special to catch him and that never looked like happening. He had run well to finish fourth in a French Group 2 on his seasonal reappearance last month, and this step up to 1m4f proved to be no problem at all. It also showed that he doesn't need soft ground and it's probably worth taking a positive view of this form, but he is still a top-priced 40-1 for the Derby with Ladbrokes. (tchd 20-1)

Masterofthehorse(IRE), disappointing in the Racing Post Trophy on his final start at two but beaten less than a length into third behind the 2000 Guineas-winner Sea The Stars in the Beresford Stakes before that, was ridden in total contrast to his stablemate, being held up in last place from the off. He still had a good ten lengths to find on the winner passing the 2f pole and, although he finished strongly down the wide outside once into the straight, he never had a prayer of getting there. Admittedly the winner did have the advantage of a recent run, but the feeling is that this result isn't necessarily an accurate measure of their respective abilities and his next outing should be much more enlightening. Official explanation: jockey said, regarding running and riding, that his orders were to settle the colt early stages, as it had failed to come home in its last race, adding that he had attempted to take closer order from 4f out, but had been unable to reach the winner. (tchd 15-8 in places)

Debussy(IRE), who has improved with each run and was the cosy winner of the Blue Riband Trial at Epsom last time, was also given a patient ride though not to the same extent as the favourite. He did stay on over the last couple of furlongs without quite being able to land a blow and might be better suited by a more galloping track. His trainer was delighted by this effort and believed that he didn't really handle the fast ground. He will now head to Epsom. (op 3-1 tchd 10-3)

Sight Unseen, an easy winner of a maiden on his racecourse debut at Newbury last month which has already produced a couple of winners, came off the bridle a long way from home. He kept staying on under pressure, though he was beaten when intimidated by the third horse in the very closing stages. This was a tough task given his inexperience and he still looks capable of making the grade as he becomes more streetwise. He also may prefer a more galloping track. (op 7-1)

Saptapadi(IRE), over four lengths behind Above Average in the Sandown Classic Trial last month, managed to reverse that form but although he made some late progress, he could never get near the leaders. This was only his third start - he still showed signs of greenness in the paddock beforehand - and he is another that may well continue to progress with racing. (op 10-1 tchd 12-1)

Too Much Trouble attracted market support but after racing handily he came off the bridle half a mile from home and gradually dropped away. He had won both of his previous starts, but had only beaten a total of six horses and he may need his sights lowering. (op 11-1)

Above Average(IRE), up in trip after narrowly winning the Sandown Classic Trial last time, was relaxed in the paddock but weak in the market. Having tracked the winner early, he was ridden passing the 4f pole and eventually dropped right out. Michael Hills reported that he was unsuited by the track. Official explanation: jockey said colt was unsuited by the track (op 9-1 tchd 8-1)

Solo Choice, blinkered for the first time but rated just 68, was predictably outclassed.

1801 BOODLES DIAMOND ETERNITY H'CAP — 7f 122y

3:15 (3:15) (Class 2) (0-100,97) 3-Y-O **£14,193** (£4,248; £2,124; £1,062; £528) **Stalls** Low

Form — RPR

12-3 **1** **Fareer**[20] 1324 3-8-9 88 .... RHills 3 96+
(E A L Dunlop) *lw: hld up: hdwy over 1f out: rdn and hung lft whn led ins fnl f: r.o and on top towards fin* **7/2**[1]

1131 **2** *1 1/4* **Tartan Gunna**[14] 1471 3-8-9 88 .... JoeFanning 4 93
(M Johnston) *in tch: effrt to chal over 1f out: carried lft ins fnl f: hld cl home* **4/1**[2]

306- **3** *1/2* **Foundation Room (IRE)**[223] 6240 3-8-9 88 .... MartinDwyer 2 95+
(A M Balding) *in tch: nt clr run over 1f out: swtchd rt ins fnl f: gng on towards fin* **11/1**

60-5 **4** *1 1/4* **Viva Ronaldo (IRE)**[26] 1211 3-9-4 97 .... TonyHamilton 6 98
(R A Fahey) *awkward leaving stalls: hld up: nt clr run briefly over 1f out: sn carried hd high: styd on and prog ins fnl f: nt pce to rch ldrs* **8/1**

5 *hd* **Imco Spirit (IRE)**[20] 1341 3-8-6 85 .... (b[1]) KLatham 7 85
(G M Lyons, Ire) *racd keenly w ldr: nosed ahd over 1f out: hdd ins fnl f: no ex fnl 75yds* **14/1**

0-14 **6** *3/4* **Hunterview**[21] 1307 3-8-11 90 .... TedDurcan 8 88
(M A Jarvis) *in rr and nvr travelling wl: kpt on ins fnl f: unable to chal ldrs: eased towards fin* **8/1**

5-1 **7** *2 1/4* **Resort**[21] 1302 3-8-6 85 ow2 .... RyanMoore 9 86+
(Sir Michael Stoute) *lw: racd keenly: trckd ldrs: lost clr run over 1f out: sn cl up: n.m.r and squeezed out ins fnl f: sn eased and dropped away* **4/1**[2]

314- **8** *1* **Goliaths Boy (IRE)**[163] 7449 3-8-10 89 .... PaulHanagan 5 84+
(R A Fahey) *led: rdn and hdd over 1f out: losing pl whn squeezed out ins fnl f: sn eased* **9/2**[3]

1m 32.47s (-1.33) **Going Correction** -0.15s/f (Firm) **8 Ran SP% 117.6**

Speed ratings (Par 105): **100,98,98,97,96 96,93,92**

toteswinger: 1&2 £3.30, 1&3 £7.40, 2&3 £13.20 CSF £18.25 CT £128.92 TOTE £4.90: £1.80, £1.80, £3.00; EX 21.90 Trifecta £260.20 Pool: £1055.14 - 3.00 winning units..

Owner Hamdan Al Maktoum **Bred** Bishopswood Bloodstock & Trickledown Stud **Trained** Newmarket, Suffolk

■ Stewards' Enquiry : R Hills four-day ban: careless riding (May 21-24)

FOCUS

A competitive three-year-old handicap and a couple were seriously backed, but there were several still in with a chance passing the furlong pole and a couple met trouble in running. However, the form looks decent rated around the second and fourth.

NOTEBOOK

Fareer, an eye-catcher when third at Newbury last month on his return from a lengthy absence, was the paddock pick, enjoyed a clear run and was produced with a strong late effort down the wide outside. He did edge left under pressure late on, but he kept on finding just enough and is now likely to be aimed at the Britannia. (op 4-1 tchd 10-3)

Tartan Gunna, a winner three times already this year, was never far off the pace and after having every chance went down with all guns blazing. He was 5lb higher than when making a successful return to turf at Beverley last month, but on this evidence his current mark isn't beyond him. (op 7-2)

Foundation Room(IRE) ◆, returning from seven months off but successful on her racecourse debut last term, was the unlucky horse of the race. Having travelled sweetly on the inside of the track throughout, she found herself with a wall of horses in front of her a furlong out with apparently plenty more to give, but by the time she was switched out wide it was too late. She can be rated a good deal better than the bare form. (op 12-1)

Viva Ronaldo(IRE), a winner over 6f here last August and making his handicap debut after a couple of tries in Listed company, looked the stable's second string but he was nonetheless a springer in the market. On his toes beforehand, he was held up at the back early and stayed on over the last couple of furlongs but could never quite get there. (op 14-1 tchd 7-1)

Imco Spirit(IRE), who was having his first outing away from Dundalk, had blinkers on for the first time. Prominent on the outside from the off, he had every chance and there seemed no real excuses.

Hunterview, relaxed beforehand, was another to be held up out the back. He made a little late progress but was never getting there in time. He was 12lb higher then when bolting up in a four-runner handicap on the Southwell Fibresand two starts back, but he probably needs a more testing surface than this. (tchd 9-1 and 11-1 in a place)

Resort, the least exposed in the field and making her handicap debut after scraping home in a Newmarket fillies' maiden on her return to action last month, had to be ridden along early to take a handy position from the outside stall. She appeared to be in the ideal place to attack when the false rail ended over a furlong from home, but she didn't find as much as had looked likely and with not much room to play with against the rail, she was eased right off once her chance had gone. (op 3-1)

Goliaths Boy(IRE), not disgraced in a French Listed event on his final start at two, was making his handicap debut after six months off. Preferred by Hanagan over Viva Ronaldo, he was well supported in the market and set a decent pace but he was already on the retreat when squeezed right out well inside the last furlong. (op 8-1)

1802 MOSCOW EIGHT E B F MAIDEN STKS — 5f 16y

4:00 (4:01) (Class 3) 2-Y-O **£8,418** (£2,505; £1,251; £625) **Stalls** Low

Form — RPR

1 **Metal Soldier (IRE)** 2-9-3 0 .... GrahamGibbons 3 74+
(J J Quinn) *w'like: athletic: trckd ldrs: qcknd to chal over 1f out: led ins fnl f: r.o* **9/1**[3]

35 **2** *1* **Reel Credit Crunch**[12] 1521 2-8-12 0 .... JohnEgan 2 65
(P D Evans) *led: rdn and hdd 1f out: kpt on ins fnl f: a hld* **16/1**

3 **3** *1 1/4* **Swilly Ferry (USA)**[40] 994 2-9-3 0 .... MichaelHills 6 66
(B W Hills) *lw: bmpd s: chsd ldrs: rdn to ld 1f out: hdd ins fnl f: no ex cl home* **4/7**[1]

4 *2* **Angelena Ballerina (IRE)** 2-8-12 0 .... MickyFenton 10 54+
(A Bailey) *w'like: leggy: dwlt: towards rr: hdwy 1/2-way: kpt on ins fnl f: nt pce to chal* **14/1**

0 **5** *shd* **Bossy Kitty**[22] 1275 2-8-12 0 .... JoeFanning 4 53
(N Tinkler) *leggy: pressed ldr tl checked over 1f out: fdd ins fnl f* **20/1**

6 *1* **Ramamara (IRE)** 2-8-12 0 .... TPQueally 7 50+
(P D Evans) *leggy: carried rt s: midfield: outpcd over 1f out: nvr trbld ldrs* **33/1**

44 **7** *1* **Bebenine (IRE)**[12] 1521 2-8-12 0 .... JamieSpencer 5 46+
(Patrick Morris) *wnt rt s: in tch: rdn and outpcd over 1f out: eased whn btn towards fin* **8/1**[2]

8 3 ½ **Psychopathicsandra (IRE)** 2-8-7 0 .... SladeO'Hara(5) 8 34
(A Berry) *w/like: carried rt s: a towards rr* **50/1**

9 11 **Johnnyleary (IRE)** 2-9-3 0 .... StephenDonohoe 1 —
(D Nicholls) *cmpt: missed break: sn in midfield: pushed along and outpcd 2f out* **8/1[2]**

06 10 1 ¾ **Needwood Dancer**[15] 1450 2-8-12 0 .... PatrickMathers 9 —
(Peter Grayson) *bmpd sn after s: a bhd* **100/1**

11 1 **Whistling Wind** 2-8-10 0 .... KrishGundowry(7) 11 —
(Paul Green) *w/like: missed break: a outpcd* **50/1**

61.38 secs (0.38) **Going Correction** -0.15s/f (Firm) **11 Ran SP% 121.0**
Speed ratings (Par 97): **90,88,86,83,83 81,79,74,56,53 52**
toteswinger: 1&2 £12.50, 1&3 £3.30, 2&3 £4.00 CSF £136.29 TOTE £13.20: £2.50, £3.40, £1.10; EX 113.50.
Owner The Clay Family **Bred** James And Joe Brannigan **Trained** Settrington, N Yorks

FOCUS
A fair maiden, won by some decent sorts in the past ten years including the subsequent Middle-Park winner Dark Angel two years ago. Every winner of this race since 2001 had previously made the frame, but this time it went to a newcomer.

NOTEBOOK
Metal Soldier(IRE), a 10,000euros half-brother to Crocodile Bay, was by no means unbacked on this debut and having tracked the pace throughout, he produced a good turn of foot up the inside after the false rail ran out and was well on top at the line. The form may not be that strong, but he could hardly have made a better start to his career. (op 14-1)
Reel Credit Crunch, well behind Bebenine at Ripon last time having finished ahead of her at Wolverhampton the time before, made good use of her low draw after the horse drawn in stall one had missed the break. Battling on really well from the front, she wasn't worn down until late and should be up to winning an ordinary race. Her rider reported that she had hung right. Official explanation: jockey said filly hung right (op 12-1)
Swilly Ferry(USA), third in the Brocklesby on debut which has produced its far share of winners in the meantime, was representing the stable that had won this race three years in a row up until 2007. Always in a prominent position on the outside, he looked to have been produced at just the right time but could never put his stamp on the race and was worried out of it. This was a bit disappointing. (op 4-6 tchd 4-5 in places)
Angelena Ballerina(IRE) ◆, a half-sister to three winners including as two-year-olds, was noted staying on late from off the pace and is worth keeping an eye on. (op 10-1)
Bossy Kitty, well beaten on her Beverley debut, was given a positive ride from her good draw and hung in there until well inside the last furlong, but it remains to be seen how much of an improvement this was. (op 16-1)
Ramamara(IRE) ◆, a half-sister to a useful winning sprinter, was another noted doing her best work late and better can be expected in due course.
Whistling Wind looked fit enough beforehand but was coltish in the paddock. (op 33-1)

1803 HALLIWELL JONES BMW Z4 H'CAP 6f 18y
4:35 (4:36) (Class 3) (0-90,89) 3-Y-O **£10,361** (£3,083; £1,540; £384; £384) **Stalls Low**

Form RPR

33-2 1 **Invincible Heart (GR)**[22] 1295 3-9-1 **86** .... JamieSpencer 1 95
(Jane Chapple-Hyam) *mde all: qcknd over 1f out: r.o wl* **7/2[1]**

3-52 2 2 ½ **Lucky Numbers (IRE)**[19] 1345 3-9-2 **87** .... JohnEgan 2 88
(Paul Green) *lw: trckd ldrs: wnt 2nd over 1f out: nt pce of wnr ins fnl f* **4/1[2]**

213- 3 2 **The Kyllachy Kid**[184] 7173 3-9-0 **85** .... MickyFenton 5 80
(T P Tate) *racd in midfield: rdn and hdwy on inner over 1f out: kpt on ins fnl f: lost pl w ldrs* **25/1**

3-05 4 1 **Fivefootnumberone (IRE)**[12] 1517 3-8-7 **78** .... GrahamGibbons 3 70
(J J Quinn) *pressed wnr tl over 1f out: rdr sn dropped whip: no ex ins fnl f* **13/2[3]**

0-10 4 dht **Cyflymder (IRE)**[26] 1214 3-8-10 **81** .... RyanMoore 4 73+
(R Hannon) *towards rr: rdn over 1f out: hdwy whn nt clr run ins fnl f: no imp towards fin* **4/1[2]**

3-31 6 nk **Kersivay**[15] 1451 3-8-7 **78** .... TonyHamilton 15 69
(D W Barker) *lw: swtchd lft s: hld up: hdwy ent fnl f: nt pce to get competitive* **66/1**

10-1 7 1 **Aakef (IRE)**[23] 1272 3-9-1 **86** .... RHills 8 74+
(M A Jarvis) *lw: hld up: effrt on wd outside over 1f out: sn no imp* **7/2[1]**

024- 8 1 **Moscow Eight (IRE)**[140] 7714 3-8-11 **82** .... MartinDwyer 10 66
(E J O'Neill) *unruly in stalls: in tch: rdn and outpcd over 1f out: wknd ins fnl f* **33/1**

000- 9 ¾ **Mister Green (FR)**[211] 6575 3-8-6 **82** ....(b[1]) AndreaAtzeni(5) 6 64
(D Flood) *in tch: rdn over 1f out: wknd ins fnl f* **28/1**

14-4 10 1 ¼ **Desert Falls**[19] 1368 3-8-13 **87** .... MichaelJStainton(3) 7 65
(R M Whitaker) *w ldrs: rdn whn checked over 1f out: wknd ent fnl f* **18/1**

23-3 11 10 **Parisian Pyramid (IRE)**[12] 1517 3-9-4 **89** .... AdrianTNicholls 11 35
(D Nicholls) *bhd: nt clr run over 1f out and ins fnl f: sn eased* **12/1**

1m 12.9s (-0.90) **Going Correction** -0.15s/f (Firm) **11 Ran SP% 122.5**
Speed ratings (Par 103): **100,96,94,92,92 92,90,89,88,86 73**
toteswinger: 1&2 £4.30, 1&3 £8.80, 2&3 £13.30 CSF £17.87 CT £313.37 TOTE £5.20: £1.50, £1.60, £5.90; EX 15.20 Place 6: £12.73 Place 5: £4.37.
Owner Gordon Li **Bred** Stavloi Th Nanou S A **Trained** Newmarket, Suffolk

FOCUS
A race affected by the five non-runners who would incidentally have been starting from stalls 9, 12, 13, 14 and 16, but still a competitive sprint handicap for three-year-olds despite the absentees. The winner could rate higher and the placed horses were close to previous form.

NOTEBOOK
Invincible Heart(GR) made all for a convincing success having made full use of the rails draw. He was making his handicap debut after a string of near misses, including when chasing home the subsequently impressive Infiraad in a Newmarket maiden last month, and this was a welcome victory after his run of placings. He is now likely to go to Hong Kong. (op 4-1 tchd 9-2 in places)
Lucky Numbers(IRE), raised 6lb after splitting a pair of subsequent winners at Doncaster last time, raced handily and ran on to finish a clear second best. He is already due to go up another 3lb so will still need to improve from this in order to go one better off his new mark. (op 7-2 tchd 10-3, 9-2 and 3-1 in places)
The Kyllachy Kid, who looked fit for his reappearance, stayed on well up the inside rail late on and this was a decent effort considering he has shown his very best form on softer ground. (op 22-1 tchd 20-1)
Fivefootnumberone(IRE), behind Parisian Pyramid at Ripon last time, ran his race having always been handy from his low draw. (op 8-1 tchd 17-2, 10-1 in places)
Cyflymder(IRE), a winner over course and distance on much softer ground for James Given last August, was back down in trip after a couple of recent outings over 7f on Polytrack for his new stable. Given plenty to do, he made late progress up the inside rail but could never get there. On this evidence a step back up in trip may be in order. (op 8-1 tchd 17-2, 10-1 in places)
Kersivay didn't have much go right after having inherited the outside stall. Dropped in behind horses from the start, he stayed on from off the pace late on but could never land a blow. His previous six outings had all been over 7f and a return to that trip looks required (op 50-1)
Aakef(IRE), raised 5lb for his cosy win on his return to action over 5f at Yarmouth last month but successful over this trip last season, was always trapped out wide and couldn't get involved. It may be worth forgiving him this. (tchd 4-1, 9-2 in places)

Parisian Pyramid(IRE), an eye-catcher on his Ripon return last month, was weak in the market here. Another to be tucked in after starting from a wide draw, he wouldn't have been involved in the finish but would have been closer had he not run into traffic problems when trying to stay on inside the last furlong. His rider reported that he had lost his action. Official explanation: jockey said gelding lost its action (op 8-1)
T/Jkpt: Not won. T/Plt: £17.30 to a £1 stake. Pool: £152,069.55. 6,406.63 winning tickets. T/Qpdt: £5.50 to a £1 stake. Pool: £7,479.18. 994.70 winning tickets. DO

1666 GOODWOOD (R-H)
Thursday, May 7

OFFICIAL GOING: Good to firm (8.0)
Wind: Brisk ahead Weather: Dull

1804 PIONEERPOINT MAIDEN STKS 1m
2:00 (2:00) (Class 5) 3-Y-O+ **£3,238** (£963; £481; £240) **Stalls High**

Form RPR

00-3 1 **Eastern Empire**[29] 1185 3-9-0 72 .... RichardHughes 4 87
(J W Hills) *mde all: drvn and styd on strly fr 2f out: in command thrght fnl f* **11/1[3]**

02-2 2 ¾ **Jesse James (IRE)**[47] 917 3-9-0 80 .... RichardMullen 9 85
(J H M Gosden) *s.i.s: sn mid-div: rdn and hdwy over 2f out: chsd wnr fnl f: kpt on but a hld* **8/13[1]**

3 3 ¼ **Maria Nunziata** 3-8-9 0 .... EddieAhern 6 73+
(J Noseda) *sn chsng wnr: rdn over 2f out: sn no imp: wknd and lost 2nd fnl f* **7/1[2]**

00- 4 3 ½ **Flapper (IRE)**[173] 7332 3-8-9 0 .... ChrisCatlin 10 64+
(J W Hills) *plld hrd towards rr: hdwy fr 3f out: nvr quite gng pce to chal: wknd fnl f* **66/1**

5 1 ¼ **Stravella (IRE)** 4-9-8 0 .... GeorgeBaker 3 65
(R M Beckett) *slowly away and swtchd rt: pushed along and hdwy over 3f out: nvr rchd ldrs: wknd over 1f out* **20/1**

6 ¾ **Dubai Gem** 3-8-9 0 .... RobertHavlin 2 60
(Jamie Poulton) *in rr: sme hdwy fr 3f out: nvr rchd ldrs: wknd fr 2f out* **100/1**

50- 7 hd **Mejala (IRE)**[230] 6076 3-8-9 0 .... ShaneKelly 11 59
(J L Dunlop) *in rr: pushed along on outside over 3f out: styd on fnl f: nvr in contention* **16/1**

3 8 ½ **Monaco Dream (IRE)**[89] 440 3-8-9 0 .... WilliamBuick 5 58+
(W Jarvis) *chsd ldrs: rdn 3f out: hung lft 2f out: sn wknd* **12/1**

9 1 ½ **Dream On Connie** 3-9-0 0 .... JimCrowley 1 60
(W J Knight) *nvr bttr than mid-div* **66/1**

0- 10 2 **In Secret**[245] 5643 3-8-9 0 .... SebSanders 12 50
(J L Dunlop) *in tch: chsd ldrs 4f out: wknd over 2f out* **20/1**

0-0 11 4 ½ **Eye For The Girls**[19] 1350 3-9-0 0 .... TonyCulhane 7 45
(M R Channon) *in rr: sme prog 3f out: nvr in contention: sn wknd* **50/1**

12 2 ¾ **Mutawarath (IRE)** 3-9-0 0 .... TPO'Shea 8 39
(W J Haggas) *a in rr* **20/1**

1m 41.83s (1.93) **Going Correction** +0.20s/f (Good)
WFA 3 from 4yo 13lb **12 Ran SP% 116.5**
Speed ratings (Par 103): **98,97,94,90,89 88,88,87,86,84 79,77**
toteswinger: 1&2 £3.10, 1&3 £7.90, 2&3 £2.70 CSF £16.88 TOTE £11.70: £2.70, £1.10, £2.10; EX 23.00.
Owner Wai Kuen Chan **Bred** Rockwell Bloodstock **Trained** Upper Lambourn, Berks

FOCUS
This looked a fair maiden, although the bare result needs treating with a little caution considering the winner was able to dictate at a steady pace.
In Secret Official explanation: jockey said filly was unbalanced
Eye For The Girls Official explanation: jockey said gelding hung right

1805 EMPIRE PROPERTY GROUP INTERNATIONAL CONDITIONS STKS 5f
2:30 (2:30) (Class 2) 2-Y-O **£8,723** (£2,612; £1,306; £653) **Stalls Low**

Form RPR

331 1 **Desert Auction (IRE)**[7] 1616 2-8-12 0 .... RichardHughes 1 84
(R Hannon) *t.k.h early: trckd ldrs: rdn and swtchd lft to rail 1f out: styd on u.p ins fnl f: led last strides* **11/2[3]**

1 2 nk **Grand Zafeen**[17] 1396 2-8-7 0 .... TonyCulhane 3 78
(M R Channon) *s.i.s: t.k.h: sn w ldr: drvn and hung lft and led over 1f out: kpt slt advantage tl hdd last strides* **5/4[1]**

1111 3 ½ **Star Rover (IRE)**[1] 1788 2-9-7 0 .... RichardMullen 2 90
(P D Evans) *t.k.h: led: drvn and hung rt fr 3f out: hdd appr fnl f: styd chalng tl no ex nr fin* **11/8[2]**

4 17 **Hairs Vital (IRE)** 2-8-8 0 .... ChrisCatlin 4 16
(E J O'Neill) *s.i.s: sn rcvrd and t.k.h: wknd fr 1/2-way* **14/1**

59.57 secs (1.17) **Going Correction** +0.20s/f (Good) **4 Ran SP% 108.6**
Speed ratings (Par 99): **98,97,96,69**
CSF £12.92 TOTE £6.40; EX 14.90.
Owner A J Ilsley, K T Ivory & G Battocchi **Bred** J Kilpatrick **Trained** East Everleigh, Wilts

FOCUS
An interesting conditions contest, but the bare form doesn't look anything special for the grade.

NOTEBOOK
Desert Auction(IRE)'s recent Folkestone success didn't amount to a great deal, but he bettered that form under an astute ride. Richard Hughes let his two mains rivals, Grand Zafeen and Star Rover, take each other on from an early stage, racing in their slipstream, before producing his mount with an expertly timed run up the inside rail. Although the winner clearly had plenty go his way, he's progressive and promises to improve again when stepped up to 6f. (op 9-2 tchd 4-1)
Grand Zafeen's debut success looked just a fair effort at best, even with the third home subsequently successful, but this was a solid effort in defeat. She battled well to get the better of the David Evans horse, but was caught with a sucker punch when the winner, waited with early, nipped up the inside. (tchd 6-4)
Star Rover(IRE) showed improved form to win the Lily Agnes just a day earlier, and came into this chasing a remarkable five-timer, but he had no easy task conceding upwards of 9lb all round. In the race itself, he was inclined to edge off the inside rail, not looking totally comfortable on the track, and was pressured by Grand Zafeen on his outside much earlier than he would have liked. Official explanation: jockey said colt hung right (op 7-4)
Hairs Vital(IRE), a £16,000 first foal of a 5f winner (juvenile debut), finished up well beaten but hinted at ability, displaying good mid-race speed to recover from a slow start, before dropping out. (op 12-1)

1806 NOVOCAPITAL STKS (H'CAP) 6f
3:00 (3:01) (Class 4) (0-80,80) 4-Y-O+ **£5,180** (£1,541; £770; £384) **Stalls Low**

Form RPR

2325 1 **Caprio (IRE)**[16] 1436 4-9-1 77 .... PatCosgrave 8 86
(J R Boyle) *towards rr: pushed along 1/2-way: rdn and hdwy over 1f out: styd on strly u.p to ld nr fin* **15/2[3]**

5363 **2** ¾ **The Tatling (IRE)**[16] 1418 12-8-12 79 JackDean(5) 2 86
(J M Bradley) *hld up in tch: hdwy over 1f out: led fnl 110yds: hdd nr fin* **8/1**

0-00 **3** ¾ **Harlech Castle**[12] 1510 4-9-3 79 EddieAhern 1 84
(P F I Cole) *s.i.s: sn in tch: rdn 1/2-way: outpcd over 2f out: hdwy and n.m.r over 1f out: swtchd lft ins fnl f: fin wl to take 3rd last strides but no imp on ldng duo* **9/1**

4206 **4** *hd* **Artistic License (IRE)**[16] 1418 4-9-2 78 TonyCulhane 7 82
(M R Channon) *trckd ldrs: upsides over 3f out: led 2f out: styd on u.p tl hdd and no ex fnl 110yds* **6/1**[2]

0260 **5** 1 ¾ **Resplendent Alpha**[10] 1572 5-8-13 75 IanMongan 6 73
(P Howling) *s.i.s: rr but in tch: rdn and hdwy fr 2f out: nvr gng pce to chal and one pce ins fnl f* **12/1**

40-2 **6** 5 **Superduper**[10] 1572 4-9-4 80 RichardHughes 4 62
(R Hannon) *t.k.h: in tch: rdn and effrt over 2f out: nvr gng pce to rch ldrs: wknd fnl f* **11/8**[1]

4-00 **7** 1 ¼ **Espy**[20] 1321 4-9-1 77 WilliamBuick 5 55
(S Kirk) *pressed ldr after 2f: stl ev ch 2f out: hung rt u.p sn after and wknd fnl f* **8/1**

126- **8** ½ **Stand In Flames**[164] 7436 4-8-13 75 ShaneKelly 3 52
(Pat Eddery) *led tl hdd 2f out: sn wknd* **14/1**

1m 12.54s (0.34) **Going Correction** +0.20s/f (Good) **8** Ran SP% **114.7**
Speed ratings (Par 105): **105,104,103,102,100 93,92,91**
toteswinger: 1&2 £8.70, 1&3 £12.70, 2&3 £6.40 CSF £65.35 CT £555.34 TOTE £10.10: £2.50, £2.20, £2.20; EX 82.20.

Owner M Khan X2 **Bred** P Rabbitte **Trained** Epsom, Surrey

FOCUS
An ordinary sprint handicap for the grade. They raced stands' side, but the main action took place a few horse widths off the rail. The winner has been rated as recording a personal best, with the fourth to her turf form.

Espy Official explanation: jockey said gelding stopped quickly

1807 GATEWAY PROJECT SERVICES STKS (H'CAP) 1m 4f
3:35 (3:39) (Class 5) (0-75,73) 4-Y-0+ **£3,238** (£963; £481; £240) **Stalls** Low

Form RPR

-010 **1** **Cossack Prince**[17] 726 4-8-7 62 PaulDoe 7 73
(Mrs L J Mongan) *mde all: sn clr advantage and 10 ahd fr 1/2-way: pushed along over 3f out: kpt on wl: unchal* **5/2**[2]

46-1 **2** 9 **Mista Rossa**[22] 1287 4-9-4 73 TravisBlock 3 70
(H Morrison) *racd in 2nd thrght and nvr anywhere nr unchal wnr: rdn fr 5f out: kpt on for 2nd whn chal for that position ins fnl 3f* **11/2**

45-2 **3** 1 **Potentiale (IRE)**[22] 1287 5-9-4 73 (p) ChrisCatlin 2 68
(J W Hills) *hld up in rr bhd unchal wnr: rdn and sme prog over 3f out: tk wl hld 3rd fnl f* **9/2**[3]

4300 **4** 3 ¾ **Cape Of Luck (IRE)**[16] 1415 6-8-4 59 (b[1]) CatherineGannon 5 48
(P M Phelan) *racd in 3rd and nvr anywhere nr unchal wnr: styd on to press for 2nd 3f out: hld for that position 2f out: wknd into 4th fnl f* **14/1**

16-4 **5** 33 **Kokkokila**[23] 1273 5-8-9 64 (p) RichardHughes 6 —
(Lady Herries) *s.i.s: a in rr and nvr anywhere nr unchal wnr: rdn and lost action over 3f out: eased: t.o* **9/4**[1]

000- **6** 26 **Royal Premier (IRE)**[24] 6775 6-8-9 64 (vt) SebSanders 1 —
(H J Collingridge) *rdn in rr fr stalls: a wl bhd: lost tch fr 5f out: t.o* **12/1**

2m 39.7s (1.30) **Going Correction** +0.20s/f (Good) **6** Ran SP% **107.3**
Speed ratings (Par 103): **103,97,96,93,71 54**
toteswingers: 1&2 £2.80, 1&3 £2.40, 2&3 £2.20 CSF £14.76 CT £47.59 TOTE £2.80: £1.90, £2.40; EX 17.30.

Owner Mrs P J Sheen **Bred** Wyck Hall Stud Ltd **Trained** Epsom, Surrey

FOCUS
A race to treat with real caution as the winner was allowed far too much rope in front. The winner has been rated to his best turf mark.

Potentiale(IRE) Official explanation: trainer said gelding lost a front shoe

Kokkokila Official explanation: jockey said mare was unsuited by the good to firm ground

Royal Premier(IRE) Official explanation: jockey said gelding never travelled

1808 DALLAS CHURCHILL INTERNATIONAL FILLIES' STKS (H'CAP) 1m
4:10 (4:11) (Class 4) (0-85,84) 3-Y-0 **£5,180** (£1,541; £770; £384) **Stalls** High

Form RPR

21-2 **1** **Charlotte Point (USA)**[15] 1466 3-8-11 77 EddieAhern 5 84
(P F I Cole) *fly j. s: t.k.h: trckd ldrs: led jst ins fnl 2f: rdn and hld on wl fr over 1f out* **7/2**[1]

45-2 **2** ¾ **Cumana Bay**[43] 960 3-8-7 73 ow2 RichardHughes 8 78
(R Hannon) *trckd ldrs and t.k.h: rdn and styd on fr 2f out: wnt 2nd ins fnl f but a hld by wnr* **4/1**[2]

234- **3** ¾ **Sterling Sound (USA)**[258] 5214 3-8-7 73 PatDobbs 4 76
(M P Tregoning) *stdd s: hld up towards rr: hdwy on outside over 2f out: styd on wl fnl f and gng on cl home but a hld by ldng duo* **10/1**

0-00 **4** *nk* **Silver Games (IRE)**[20] 1324 3-9-4 84 TonyCulhane 6 87
(M R Channon) *in tch hdwy on ins over 2f out: styd on to chse wnr 1f out: no imp and outpcd ins fnl f* **6/1**

1- **5** *nk* **Iasia (GR)**[160] 7465 3-8-10 76 PatCosgrave 9 78
(Jane Chapple-Hyam) *in tch: hdwy and n.m.r appr fnl 2f: styd on fr over 1f out: kpt on cl home but nvr gng pce to be competitive* **11/2**

10-4 **6** 6 **Athania (IRE)**[36] 1068 3-8-3 74 MartinLane(5) 7 62
(A P Jarvis) *plld hrd: chsd ldr: rdn over 2f out: sn btn* **11/1**

441- **7** 2 **King's Siren (IRE)**[189] 7095 3-8-4 70 oh2 WilliamBuick 1 53
(A M Balding) *led: rdn 3f out: hdd jst ins fnl 2f: sn hung rt and wknd* **5/1**[3]

310- **8** 3 ¾ **Accede**[223] 6240 3-9-2 82 TolleyDean 3 57
(J G Portman) *in rr: sme hdwy on outside fr 3f oit: nvr in contention and sn wknd* **33/1**

103- **9** ½ **Foxtrot Alpha (IRE)**[269] 4925 3-8-7 73 JimCrowley 2 47
(P Winkworth) *t.k.h in rr: hdwy on outside whn nt clr run appr fnl 2f: sn btn* **12/1**

1m 42.04s (2.14) **Going Correction** +0.20s/f (Good) **9** Ran SP% **116.6**
Speed ratings (Par 98): **97,96,95,95,94 88,86,83,82**
toteswinger: 1&2 £3.00, 1&3 £7.40, 2&3 £8.90 CSF £17.73 CT £128.60 TOTE £2.90: £1.50, £2.00, £2.90; EX 11.20.

Owner C Wright & The Hon Mrs J M Corbett **Bred** Douglas S Arnold **Trained** Whatcombe, Oxon

■ Stewards' Enquiry : Pat Cosgrave two-day ban: careless riding (May 21-22)

FOCUS
A fair fillies' handicap on paper, but the pace was steady, resulting in some of these racing keenly, before a relative dash to the line. The form is muddling and the winner didn't have to improve to score. The runner-up has been rated to form, with the fourth to her two-year-old best.

1809 LONDON AND REGENT MAIDEN STKS 1m 4f
4:45 (4:45) (Class 5) 3-Y-0+ **£3,238** (£963; £481; £240) **Stalls** Low

Form RPR

43-2 **1** **Tactic**[20] 1328 3-8-9 81 TPO'Shea 6 89+
(J L Dunlop) *sn trcking ldrs: rdn to ld and edgd rt 2f out: kpt on u.p fnl f* **1/1**[1]

00-6 **2** 1 **Gibb River (IRE)**[20] 1328 3-8-9 76 AdrianMcCarthy 1 87+
(P W Chapple-Hyam) *sn led: hdd over 3f out: n.m.r and swtchd lft 2f out: rallied to chse wnr jst ins last: kpt on but a hld* **7/1**[3]

43 **3** 7 **Cill Rialaig**[16] 1430 4-9-9 0 SteveDrowne 7 73
(H Morrison) *chsd ldr: led over 3f out: hdd 2f out: sn one pce: lost 2nd and wknd fnl f* **17/2**

2 **4** 5 **Time Machine (UAE)**[24] 1260 3-8-9 0 RichardMullen 2 68
(J H M Gosden) *sn pushed along to chse ldrs: rdn over 3f out: sn outpcd: wknd fr 2f out* **3/1**[2]

46-3 **5** 7 **King's La Mont (IRE)**[17] 1407 3-8-9 76 JimCrowley 8 57
(Mrs A J Perrett) *chsd ldrs: rdn 3f out: sn wknd* **7/1**[3]

0 **6** 4 **Langford Decoit (IRE)**[8] 1611 3-8-9 0 TonyCulhane 4 50
(M R Channon) *rr: sme hdwy over 4f out: nvr in contention: wknd over 2f out* **80/1**

6- **7** 15 **Warrior Conquest**[218] 6378 4-10-0 0 GeorgeBaker 3 26
(W J Knight) *slowly away: sme hdwy to cl on ldng gp 5f out: wknd 3f out* **40/1**

0-0 **8** 48 **Almutawaazin**[19] 1350 3-8-9 0 DO'Donohoe 5 —
(M P Tregoning) *rdn fr stalls and a wl bhd: t.o* **33/1**

2m 38.2s (-0.20) **Going Correction** +0.20s/f (Good)
WFA 3 from 4yo 19lb **8** Ran SP% **117.1**
Speed ratings (Par 103): **108,107,102,99,94 92,82,50**
toteswinger: 1&2 £2.90, 1&3 £2.30, 2&3 £7.30 CSF £9.25 TOTE £1.90: £1.10, £2.20, £1.80; EX 10.40 Place 6: £191.90 Place 5: £151.82.

Owner Hamdan Al Maktoum **Bred** Shadwell Estate Company Limited **Trained** Arundel, W Sussex

FOCUS
A fair maiden in which the front two, both useful types, finished clear. The form looks solid with the third being rated close to her previous Flat form.

T/Plt: £127.20 to a £1 stake. Pool: £46,788.02. 268.49 winning tickets. T/Qpdt: £22.10 to a £1 stake. Pool: £3,366.25. 112.55 winning tickets. S

1748 WINDSOR (R-H)
Thursday, May 7

OFFICIAL GOING: Good to firm (good in places; 8.4)
Wind: Virtually nil Weather: overcast

1810 JETCARD EUROPEAN BREEDERS' FUND MAIDEN FILLIES' STKS 5f 10y
5:30 (5:36) (Class 5) 2-Y-0 **£3,561** (£1,059; £529; £264) **Stalls** High

Form RPR

3 **1** **Existentialist**[10] 1569 2-9-0 0 RichardKingscote 11 79+
(J G Portman) *mde all: clr over 1f out: pushed out fnl f: comf* **11/8**[1]

2 2 **Bell's Ocean (USA)** 2-9-0 0 JerryO'Dwyer 4 72+
(J Ryan) *chsd ldrs: hdwy to chse wnr over 1f out: drvn and one pce ent fnl f: kpt on* **20/1**

3 2 ¼ **La Pantera** 2-8-11 0 PatrickHills(3) 3 64+
(R Hannon) *chsd ldrs: rdn to chse ldng pair jst over 1f out: no imp fnl f* **9/1**

0 **4** 2 **Country Princess (FR)**[34] 1090 2-9-0 0 SebSanders 1 57+
(R M Beckett) *chsd ldrs: rdn and edgd lft wl over 1f out: wknd ent fnl f* **10/3**[2]

5 3 **Itwasonlyakiss (IRE)** 2-8-11 0 DavidProbert(3) 2 46
(J W Hills) *chsd wnr tl over 1f out: wknd u.p jst over 1f out* **33/1**

6 2 ¼ **Aegean Destiny** 2-9-0 0 RichardSmith 6 38+
(R Hannon) *s.i.s: hld up in rr: shkn up and rn green 1/2-way: hung rt fr 2f out: styd on fnl f: n.d* **12/1**

7 ¾ **Angie's Nap (USA)** 2-9-0 0 TGMcLaughlin 10 35
(E A L Dunlop) *racd in midfield: rdn and hung lft 2f out: sn wknd* **20/1**

8 ¾ **Xaara Star (IRE)** 2-9-0 0 StephenCarson 8 32
(Eve Johnson Houghton) *uns rdr and galloped loose to s: dwlt: sn rdn along: hdwy into midfield over 3f out: wknd 1/2-way* **33/1**

9 3 **Zinjbar (USA)** 2-9-0 0 J-PGuillambert 7 21
(C E Brittain) *sn rdn along towards rr: n.d* **8/1**[3]

0 **10** 1 **Silvee**[5] 1669 2-9-0 0 NeilChalmers 13 18
(J J Bridger) *wnt rt s and s.i.s: a bhd* **66/1**

11 7 **Jasmine Scent (IRE)** 2-9-0 0 ShaneKelly 5 —
(J A Osborne) *racd in midfield: wknd 1/2-way: wl btn and eased fnl f* **28/1**

12 6 **Billie Jean** 2-9-0 0 RobertWinston 9 —
(B W Hills) *s.i.s: a detached last* **10/1**

60.03 secs (-0.27) **Going Correction** -0.20s/f (Firm) **12** Ran SP% **123.4**
Speed ratings (Par 90): **94,90,87,84,79 75,74,73,68,66 55,46**
toteswinger: 1&2 £8.50, 1&3 £5.40, 2&3 £62.20. CSF £40.39 TOTE £2.60: £1.50, £5.60, £3.90; EX 58.40.

Owner Paul Moulton **Bred** R F And S D Knipe **Trained** Compton, Berks

FOCUS
An ordinary fillies' maiden. Few got into it from off the pace.

NOTEBOOK
Existentialist made all to open her account in good style. Third on debut over course and distance ten days earlier, she had no trouble with this quicker surface. She still looked green under pressure so can be expected to go forward from this again, but her life will be plenty tougher now wherever she goes. (op 7-4 tchd 15-8 in a place)

Bell's Ocean(USA), looked in need of the run, but was backed at long odds and rewarded each-way support with a solid debut effort. She never looked a serious threat to the winner, but was a clear second best and looks well up to winning one of these, despite being bred to appreciate further. (op 50-1 tchd 66-1)

La Pantera, whose pedigree is a mix of speed and stamina, was the second string from her stable according to jockey bookings yet met support. She proved too green to do herself full justice, but was getting the hang of things late on and ought to prove plenty sharper next time. (op 8-1 tchd 10-1)

Country Princess(FR) met solid support despite being housed in stall 1. She was much better away than on her Bath debut last month and showed up more encouragingly, but her early exertions told when it mattered. (op 9-2)

Zinjbar(USA) Official explanation: jockey said filly ran green

Silvee Official explanation: jockey said filly was slowly into its stride

1811 JET MAX LUBES CLAIMING STKS 1m 2f 7y
6:00 (6:03) (Class 6) 3-Y-O £2,388 (£705; £352) Stalls Low

Form RPR

000- **1** **Hollow Green (IRE)**[145] 7659 3-8-6 52 CatherineGannon 12 60
(P D Evans) *stdd after s: hld up towards rr: rdn and hdwy 3f out: led 1f out: styd on strly* **16/1**

0330 **2** 1 ½ **Hector Spectre (IRE)**[15] 1462 3-8-7 63 RobertWinston 6 58
(B J Meehan) *chsd ldrs: rdn to ld 2f out: hdd 1f out: kpt on same pce fnl f* **7/1**[3]

400- **3** 2 ¾ **Primo Dilettante**[197] 6892 3-8-11 55 RichardKingscote 10 58
(W J Knight) *chsd ldrs: rdn and effrt over 2f out: edgd lft 2f out: outpcd ent fnl f: kpt on* **14/1**

4344 **4** ½ **Herecomesbella**[44] 943 3-8-4 52 (b) NickyMackay 4 50
(Stef Liddiard) *t.k.h: in tch: swtchd rt over 2f out: chsd ldrs and drvn over 1f out: outpcd fnl f* **20/1**

6010 **5** 2 ¼ **Dalrymple (IRE)**[17] 1408 3-8-12 65 PaulDoe 1 53
(Ian Williams) *led for 2f: in tch: effrt to chse ldrs over 2f out: drvn 2f out: wknd over 1f out* **9/2**[2]

6653 **6** ½ **Paymaster In Chief**[37] 1046 3-8-6 50 DavidProbert(3) 15 49
(M D I Usher) *chsd ldrs: rdn over 2f out: keeping on same pce whn swtchd rt over 1f out: sn wknd* **16/1**

0006 **7** 1 ¼ **Commandingpresence (USA)**[9] 1584 3-8-4 58 (t) SaleemGolam 13 42
(Ms J S Doyle) *stdd s: hld up in rr: effrt and rdn over 2f out: drvn over 1f out: nvr threatened ldrs* **25/1**

1360 **8** ½ **Daily Double**[15] 1462 3-8-11 63 SebSanders 3 48
(D K Ivory) *racd in midfield: edging out lft and effrt jst over 2f out: drvn and wknd over 1f out* **14/1**

3116 **9** 3 ½ **Swiss Art (IRE)**[13] 1492 3-8-8 70 KevinGhunowa(3) 2 41
(R A Harris) *hld up in midfield: hung lft and hdwy on outer 6f out: drvn and ev ch 2f out: wknd over 1f out* **8/1**

0-53 **10** ½ **Dulce Domum**[76] 628 3-8-10 49 RobertHavlin 8 39
(A B Haynes) *stdd s: hld up in rr: rdn and effrt over 2f out: nvr trbld ldrs* **33/1**

0-04 **11** 6 **Rubbinghousedotcom (IRE)**[16] 1420 3-8-11 51 IanMongan 16 28
(P M Phelan) *chsd ldr tl led after 2f: rdn and hdd 2f out: sn wknd: wl btn and eased fnl f* **20/1**

0-45 **12** 2 ¼ **Troubletimestwo (FR)**[22] 1282 3-8-13 66 TGMcLaughlin 9 25
(H J L Dunlop) *a towards rr: sn pushed along: rdn 4f out: n.d* **10/3**[1]

5 **13** 1 ½ **And A Partridge**[33] 1130 3-8-11 0 ShaneKelly 11 20
(J A Osborne) *t.k.h: hld up in tch: rdn and wknd qckly over 2f out* **33/1**

-300 **14** ¾ **Derringbay (IRE)**[19] 1361 3-8-13 59 LiamJones 7 21
(M H Tompkins) *chsd ldr after 2f: ev ch and rdn over 2f out: hung lft and sn wknd* **33/1**

1620 **15** 20 **Fantastic Fred (IRE)**[16] 1429 3-8-9 63 ChrisCatlin 5 —
(J A Osborne) *racd in midfield: lost pl and in rr 4f out: sn rdn and lost tch: t.o and eased over 1f out* **14/1**

2m 10.12s (1.42) **Going Correction** -0.05s/f (Good) **15 Ran SP% 118.8**
Speed ratings (Par 97): **92,90,89,88,86 86,85,85,82,81 77,75,74,73,57**
toteswinger: 1&2 £29.70, 1&3 £10.60, 2&3 £22.50. CSF £110.84 TOTE £18.40: £5.20, £1.90, £7.80; EX 214.10.Hector Spectre was claimed by K. M. Prendergast for £4,000. Hollow Green was the subject of a friendly claim of £8,000.
Owner P D Evans **Bred** R N Auld **Trained** Pandy, Monmouths

FOCUS
This three-year-old claimer was a poor heat and wide open.
Swiss Art(IRE) Official explanation: jockey said gelding hung left
Rubbinghousedotcom(IRE) Official explanation: jockey said gelding hung left
And A Partridge Official explanation: jockey said gelding had no more to give
Derringbay(IRE) Official explanation: jockey said gelding hung left

1812 JET HELP FOR HEROES H'CAP 1m 2f 7y
6:30 (6:30) (Class 4) (0-80,80) 4-Y-O+ £5,180 (£1,541; £770; £384) Stalls Low

Form RPR

44-2 **1** **Special Reserve (IRE)**[7] 1621 4-9-1 77 RichardHughes 9 87
(R Hannon) *stdd s: hld up off the pce in midfield: hdwy to trck ldrs gng wl over 2f out: chal ent fnl f: shkn up to ld ins fnl f: pushed out* **3/1**[1]

663- **2** 1 **Indian Skipper (IRE)**[161] 7462 4-8-11 73 SaleemGolam 3 81
(M H Tompkins) *chsd ldrs: rdn and effrt over 2f out: led over 1f out: edgd lft u.p: hdd and no ex ins fnl f* **9/1**[3]

4364 **3** 1 ¼ **Hucking Hero (IRE)**[18] 1382 4-8-6 68 RobertWinston 7 73
(J R Best) *stdd s: hld up in last pair: gd hdwy on outer over 2f out: ev ch over 1f out: kpt on same pce fnl f* **10/1**

1525 **4** 1 ¾ **North Parade**[12] 1524 4-8-12 74 (t) ShaneKelly 1 76
(A W Carroll) *stdd s: t.k.h: hld up in rr: hdwy over 2f out: hld hd high and hanging lft fr over 1f out: chsd ldng trio ins fnl f: nvr gng pce to rch ldrs* **8/1**[2]

130- **5** 4 ½ **Wogan's Sister**[245] 5630 4-8-6 68 RobertHavlin 4 61
(D R C Elsworth) *chsd ldng pair: rdn to chse ldr wl over 2f out: ev ch 2f out: wknd over 1f out* **10/1**

22-2 **6** 2 ½ **Mick's Dancer**[16] 1415 4-8-2 67 DavidProbert(3) 8 55
(W R Muir) *plunged leaving stalls: sn led: rdn 2f out: hdd over 1f out: wknd qckly jst over 1f out* **3/1**[1]

000- **7** nse **By Command**[213] 6526 4-9-4 80 SebSanders 10 67
(J W Hills) *stdd s: t.k.h: hld up in rr: shkn up and no rspnse 2f out: n.d* **12/1**

4306 **8** ½ **Folio (IRE)**[18] 1382 9-8-12 74 ChrisCatlin 2 60
(W J Musson) *stdd s: hld up in rr: rdn and effrt over 1f out: no hdwy and wl btn fnl f* **14/1**

2250 **9** 3 **Kidlat**[19] 1357 4-9-0 76 (t) StephenCarson 6 56
(B G Powell) *chsd ldr tl wl over 2f out: wknd qckly wl over 1f out* **10/1**

010- **10** 14 **Maybe I Will (IRE)**[232] 6028 4-8-9 71 NickyMackay 5 37
(S Dow) *stdd s: racd in midfield: rdn 3f out: wknd qckly 2f out: wl btn and eased ins fnl f* **25/1**

2m 6.98s (-1.72) **Going Correction** -0.05s/f (Good) **10 Ran SP% 116.6**
Speed ratings (Par 105): **104,103,102,100,97 95,95,94,92,81**
toteswinger: 1&2 £12.50, 1&3 £14.20, 2&3 £24.70. CSF £31.40 CT £241.67 TOTE £3.10: £1.30, £2.00, £3.60; EX 30.70.
Owner Mrs J Wood **Bred** David Magnier And Cobra Bloodstock **Trained** East Everleigh, Wilts

FOCUS
A modest handicap, run at a solid pace.
Mick's Dancer Official explanation: trainer said, regarding running, that the gelding was not suited by tactics of making the running

1813 CONOCOPHILLIPS WHOLESALE H'CAP 1m 67y
7:05 (7:05) (Class 4) (0-85,83) 4-Y-O+ £5,180 (£1,541; £770; £384) Stalls High

Form RPR

4-25 **1** **Everybody Knows**[29] 1186 4-8-12 77 IanMongan 6 84
(Miss Jo Crowley) *taken down early: mde all: hrd pressed and rdn 2f out: styd on wl fnl f* **15/2**

34-0 **2** 1 ½ **Effigy**[17] 1405 5-8-10 75 FergusSweeney 8 79
(H Candy) *chsd ldrs: rdn and effrt jst over 2f out: chsd wnr over 1f out: kpt on same pce ins fnl f* **11/4**[1]

1-46 **3** ½ **The Cayterers**[111] 191 7-8-4 74 MCGeran(5) 5 77
(A W Carroll) *stdd after s: t.k.h: hld up in tch in rr: hdwy on inner ent fnl f: r.o: nt rch ldrs* **16/1**

650- **4** hd **Kinsya**[176] 7291 6-9-4 83 SaleemGolam 1 85
(M H Tompkins) *t.k.h: hld up in tch: rdn and unable qck over 2f out: drvn over 1f out: styd on ins fnl f: nt rch ldrs* **15/2**

-350 **5** hd **Sofia's Star**[43] 950 4-8-5 73 ow1 JackMitchell(3) 7 75
(S Dow) *s.i.s: hld up in rr: hdwy and nt clr run 2f out: sn swtchd lft: drvn to chse ldrs ent fnl f: one pce fnl 100yds* **10/1**

2-16 **6** 1 ¼ **Hawaana (IRE)**[29] 1186 4-8-12 77 ChrisCatlin 3 76
(Eve Johnson Houghton) *t.k.h: chsd wnr: ev ch and drvn wl over 1f out: wknd fnl f* **11/2**[3]

2-34 **7** 1 ¾ **Prince Of Thebes (IRE)**[8] 1607 8-9-4 83 PaulDoe 4 78
(M J Attwater) *stdd after s: hld up in tch in rr: rdn and effrt 3f out: chsd ldrs and drvn over 1f out: wknd fnl f* **9/2**[2]

/213 **8** 1 **Kilburn**[22] 1288 5-8-7 72 WandersonD'Avila 2 65
(A J Lidderdale) *chsd ldrs on outer: ev ch and rdn 2f out: wknd over 1f out* **8/1**

1m 43.3s (-1.40) **Going Correction** -0.05s/f (Good) **8 Ran SP% 109.8**
Speed ratings (Par 105): **105,103,103,102,102 101,99,98**
toteswinger: 1&2 £5.40, 1&3 £11.20, 2&3 £15.10. CSF £26.19 CT £296.48 TOTE £8.20: £2.80, £1.80, £6.00; EX 29.30.
Owner Mrs Liz Nelson **Bred** Middle Park Stud Ltd **Trained** Whitcombe, Dorset

FOCUS
A fair handicap, run at a sound pace.

1814 CONOCOPHILLIPS JET DISTRIBUTORS H'CAP 6f
7:35 (7:36) (Class 5) (0-75,76) 3-Y-O £2,914 (£867; £433; £216) Stalls High

Form RPR

3-21 **1** **Gilt Edge Girl**[9] 1592 3-9-5 76 6ex AdamKirby 14 90+
(C G Cox) *trckd ldng pair: led 2f out: rdn and clr 1f out: styd on strly: readily* **7/2**[2]

64-2 **2** 3 ½ **Bobbie Soxer (IRE)**[16] 1434 3-9-4 75 TedDurcan 9 78
(J L Dunlop) *s.i.s: bhd: rdn 3f out: hdwy over 2f out: edgd lft over 1f out: chsd wnr jst ins fnl f: no imp: kpt on* **11/2**[3]

42-2 **3** 1 **Cawdor (IRE)**[16] 1419 3-9-4 75 FergusSweeney 11 75
(H Candy) *in tch: rdn 2f out: plugged on u.p to go 3rd nr fin: no ch w wnr* **10/3**[1]

46-2 **4** nse **Izzi Mill (USA)**[24] 1252 3-9-2 73 RobertHavlin 6 72
(D R C Elsworth) *led tl rdn and hdd 2f out: no ch w wnr after: lost 2 pls ins fnl f* **9/1**

130- **5** ¾ **Leadenhall Lass (IRE)**[223] 6240 3-9-2 73 IanMongan 5 70
(P M Phelan) *chsd ldr tl over 2f out: plugged on same pce u.p fnl 2f* **25/1**

2132 **6** ¾ **Raimond Ridge (IRE)**[5] 1686 3-8-13 75 MCGeran(5) 1 70
(M R Channon) *hld up in midfield: effrt on outer jst over 2f out: kpt on same pce fnl 2f* **10/1**

1-20 **7** hd **Bobs Dreamflight**[13] 1486 3-9-4 75 ChrisCatlin 10 69
(D K Ivory) *bhd: swtchd lft over 2f out: rdn ent fnl f: sme late hdwy: nvr trbld ldrs* **20/1**

020- **8** nk **Miss Hollybell**[154] 7546 3-9-4 75 TPO'Shea 12 68
(J Gallagher) *stdd s: hld up in midfield: rdn over 1f out: plugged on but nvr pce to rch ldrs* **50/1**

61- **9** ½ **Merry Diva**[198] 6885 3-9-1 75 JackMitchell(3) 16 66
(C F Wall) *stdd s: hld up towards rr on inner: rdn and shortlived effrt 2f out: nvr a factor* **12/1**

35-4 **10** ½ **Battle**[28] 1196 3-9-1 72 SteveDrowne 15 62
(H Morrison) *in tch: rdn jst over 2f out: drvn and no prog over 1f out: wknd fnl f* **6/1**

-420 **11** 2 ¾ **Jeremiah (IRE)**[10] 1563 3-9-1 72 TolleyDean 2 53
(J G Portman) *racd in midfield on outer: rdn and effrt over 2f out: wknd over 1f out* **25/1**

50-0 **12** 7 **Pocket's Pick (IRE)**[13] 1486 3-9-4 75 GeorgeBaker 3 34
(G L Moore) *stdd and swtchd rt after s: a bhd: eased whn wl btn ins fnl f* **33/1**

1m 11.93s (-1.07) **Going Correction** -0.20s/f (Firm) **12 Ran SP% 119.1**
Speed ratings (Par 99): **99,94,93,92,91 90,90,90,89,88 85,75**
toteswinger: 1&2 £4.50, 1&3 £3.60, 2&3 £4.10. CSF £21.65 CT £70.53 TOTE £3.90: £1.80, £2.80, £1.90; EX 30.40.
Owner Wood Street Syndicate V & C J Harper **Bred** Whitsbury Manor Stud **Trained** Lambourn, Berks
■ Stewards' Enquiry : Robert Havlin one-day ban: failed to ride to draw (May 21)

FOCUS
A very tight handicap. The form should work out.
Pocket's Pick(IRE) Official explanation: jockey said gelding had no more to give

1815 CONOCOPHILLIPS HELP FOR HEROES H'CAP 1m 3f 135y
8:10 (8:10) (Class 5) (0-75,75) 4-Y-O+ £2,914 (£867; £433; £216) Stalls Low

Form RPR

31-0 **1** **Maadraa (IRE)**[19] 1356 4-9-4 75 SteveDrowne 3 79
(B J Llewellyn) *chsd ldr after 2f tl over 3f out: rdn to ld 2f out: drvn over 1f out: edgd lft u.p ins fnl f: hld on wl* **14/1**

6223 **2** ½ **Krugerrand (USA)**[21] 1314 10-8-8 65 ChrisCatlin 4 68
(W J Musson) *stdd s: t.k.h: hld up in rr: hdwy on outer 2f out: sn rdn: drvn and str chal ins fnl f: carried lft fnl 100yds: hld towards fin* **8/1**

4345 **3** 1 ½ **Teasing**[19] 1348 5-9-1 72 (v) RobertHavlin 1 72
(J Pearce) *stdd s: hld up in last pl: hdwy on outer 2f out: rdn over 1f out: pressed ldrs ins fnl f: no ex and btn whn eased towards fin* **16/1**

220- **4** ¾ **Into The Light**[171] 7366 4-8-11 68 ow1 AdamKirby 2 67
(E S McMahon) *t.k.h: led for 2f: stdd to chse ldrs after: rdn and nt qckn over 2f out: styd on again ins fnl f* **5/1**[3]

000- **5** ½ **Northern Spy (USA)**[228] 5349 5-9-3 74 SebSanders 6 72
(S Dow) *t.k.h: led after 2f: rdn and hdd 2f out: drvn over 1f out: wknd and edgd lft ins fnl f* **9/2**[2]

The Form Book, Raceform Ltd, Compton, RG20 6NL

60/6 **6** *shd* **King's Revenge**[29] 1192 6-8-10 **67**................................ RichardHughes 7 65
(A King) *hld up in midfield: hdwy to trck ldrs 4f out: rdn 2f out: drvn and unable qck over 1f out: wknd ins fnl f* **3/1**[1]

062/ **7** *1* **Annambo**[524] 6971 9-8-6 **66** ow2................................ JackMitchell(3) 5 62
(Andrew Reid) *t.k.h: hld up in midfield: lost pl over 2f out: nt clr run 2f out: swtchd lft over 1f out: drvn and kpt on same pce fnl f* **9/1**

202 **8** *¾* **Rawdon (IRE)**[14] 1478 8-8-9 **73**................................(bt) KylieManser(7) 8 68
(Miss Gay Kelleway) *hld up towards rr: pushed along and effrt on inner wl over 1f out: no prog* **12/1**

2053 **9** *21* **Horseshoe Reef (AUS)**[37] 1051 6-9-1 **72**........................(p) TedDurcan 9 29
(J R Gask) *t.k.h: chsd ldrs tl jnd ldr over 3f out: hung lft and wknd qckly over 2f out: eased over 1f out* **13/2**

2m 31.48s (1.98) **Going Correction** -0.05s/f (Good) **9** Ran SP% **114.5**
Speed ratings (Par 103): **91,90,89,88 88,88,87,73**
toteswinger: 1&2 £25.20, 1&3 Not won, 2&3 £25.20. CSF £119.42 CT £1810.90 TOTE £21.20: £3.00, £1.30, £5.50; EX 140.20 Place 6 £323.49, Place 5 £174.52..
Owner Terry Warner **Bred** Darley **Trained** Fochriw, Caerphilly

FOCUS
A modest handicap, run at a routine pace.
Horseshoe Reef(AUS) Official explanation: trainer said gelding was unsuited by the track
T/Plt: £212.80 to a £1 stake. Pool: £54,620.74. 187.30 winning tickets. T/Qpdt: £25.50 to a £1 stake. Pool: £4,361.92. 126.32 winning tickets. SP

1816 - 1820a (Foreign Racing) - See Raceform Interactive

[1798] CHESTER (L-H)
Friday, May 8

OFFICIAL GOING: Good to firm
Rail out 6yds from the 6f marker to the 1.5f marker adding 12dys to each circuit.
Wind: Strong half against Weather: Bright intervals

1821 SURRENDA-LINK EARL GROSVENOR STKS (HERITAGE H'CAP) 7f 122y
1:45 (1:46) (Class 2) (0-105,103) 4**£25,232** (£7,552; £3,776; £1,888; £940) **Stalls** Low

Form RPR

3-11 **1** **Mister Hardy**[34] 1124 4-8-8 **92**................................ FrederikTylicki(5) 6 103+
(R A Fahey) *lw: chsd ldrs: lost pl 2f out: rallied and prog over 1f out: led ins fnl f: r.o wl* **7/2**[1]

5001 **2** *1 ¼* **Opus Maximus (IRE)**[7] 1649 4-8-9 **88** 6ex........................ JoeFanning 16 96+
(M Johnston) *lw: hld up: nt clr run fr 2f out tl rdn and hdwy over 1f out: r.o towards fin: nt rch wnr* **14/1**

0-65 **3** *nk* **Fathsta (IRE)**[27] 1212 4-8-11 **90**................................ StephenDonohoe 10 97
(D Nicholls) *midfield: hdwy on outside 3f out: led 2f out: rdn and hdd ins fnl f: nt qckn towards fin* **7/1**

-006 **4** *½* **Kings Point (IRE)**[6] 1684 8-8-12 **91**........................ SilvestreDeSousa 13 97
(D Nicholls) *midfield: pushed along over 3f out: hdwy over 1f out: chsd ldrs ins fnl f: styd on* **25/1**

6000 **5** *hd* **Internationaldebut (IRE)**[2] 1791 4-8-10 **89**.................... EddieAhern 15 94+
(S Parr) *hld up: nt clr run 2f out: swtchd lft whn rdn and hdwy over 1f out: styd on wl towards fin* **50/1**

2-01 **6** *1* **Dunn'o (IRE)**[13] 1527 4-8-13 **92**................................ LDettori 17 95
(C G Cox) *racd keenly: chsd ldrs: rdn over 1f out: no ex fnl 75yds* **11/1**

0661 **7** *nk* **Flawed Genius**[6] 1684 4-8-13 **92** 6ex.................................(t) NCallan 4 94
(K A Ryan) *lw: s.i.s: sn in midfield: rdn over 1f out: one pce ins fnl f* **5/1**[2]

00-0 **8** *shd* **Celtic Sultan (IRE)**[11] 1560 5-8-11 **90**............................ MickyFenton 1 92
(T P Tate) *led: hdd 2f out: rdn over 1f out: fdd fnl 75yds* **6/1**[3]

2640 **9** *nk* **Leandros (FR)**[71] 696 4-9-10 **103**................................(b) JMurtagh 7 104+
(G M Lyons, Ire) *dwlt: bhd: effrt over 1f out: sn lugged lft: eased whn no imp fnl 100yds* **14/1**

/2-0 **10** *¾* **Ilie Nastase (FR)**[6] 1684 5-8-7 **86**................................ AdrianTNicholls 8 85+
(D Nicholls) *bhd: swtchd lft and hdwy over 1f out: checked whn nt clr run ins fnl f: denied a run again fnl 75yds* **16/1**

3-50 **11** *8* **Eastern Gift**[9] 1603 4-8-3 **85**................................(p) DavidProbert(3) 9 64
(Miss Gay Kelleway) *midfield: effrt on outside 2f out: wknd fnl f* **40/1**

-022 **12** *¾* **Noble Citizen (USA)**[77] 639 4-9-2 **98**........................(b) AhmedAjtebi(3) 3 75
(D M Simcock) *s.i.s: hld up: rdn over 1f out: no imp* **7/1**

-316 **13** *¾* **Elna Bright**[32] 1149 4-9-1 **94**................................ JohnEgan 2 82+
(P D Evans) *chsd ldrs: rdn over 1f out: sn wknd: eased ins fnl f* **14/1**

4000 **14** *12* **Invincible Force (IRE)**[2] 1791 5-8-10 **89**.................(b) RobertWinston 5 34
(Paul Green) *chsd ldr: pushed along 3f out: lost 2nd over 2f out: wknd over 1f out: sn eased* **25/1**

1m 32.55s (-1.25) **Going Correction** +0.05s/f (Good) **14** Ran SP% **124.5**
Speed ratings (Par 109): **108,106,106,105,105 104,104,104,104,103 95,94,93,81**
toteswinger: 1&2 £8.70, 1&3 £9.30, 2&3 £20.80 CSF £55.47 CT £348.71 TOTE £4.10: £1.80, £4.30, £3.50; EX 51.70 Trifecta £775.50 Part won. Pool: £1,047.98 - 0.50 winning units..
Owner The Cosmic Cases **Bred** Mrs M Bryce **Trained** Musley Bank, N Yorks

FOCUS
This is traditionally a competitive handicap and once again there was any number in with a chance on paper, but it was the hat-trick chasing Mister Hardy that came out on top. The form looks solid with the third and fourth close to previous course form.

NOTEBOOK
Mister Hardy, who bolted up at Doncaster on his reappearance, narrowly got the job done under a 6lb penalty at Newcastle just a few days later. He was 3lb higher for this hat-trick bid, but his very capable rider claimed a handy 5lb and soon obtained a good position, on the rail just behind the leaders. He briefly met trouble and got shuffled back a couple of spots as they started to turn for home, but really picked up once asked for his effort and swept through inside the final furlong to win going away. This highly-progressive colt is not far off Listed level on this evidence and his rating may force connections that way with him before long. (op 9-2 tchd 5-1 in places)
Opus Maximus(IRE), who had stall 16 to deal with, ran a huge race in second. Shouldering a 6lb penalty for last week´s win at Musselburgh, he was towards rear early and had to be switched having met trouble turning in, but stayed on really strongly inside the final furlong to grab second. He can be rated a good bit better than the bare form and is clearly progressing. (op 12-1)
Fathsta(IRE), a course winner who was progressive in a busy campaign last term, came with his challenge a little wide and probably went for home sooner than ideal, getting run out of it inside the final furlong. He is a horse with plenty of speed and a more waiting ride will help in future. Official explanation: jockey said gelding hung right (op 10-1 tchd 13-2)
Kings Point(IRE) couldn´t take up his usual prominent position from stall 13 and was under pressure sooner than most, but he kept finding and stayed on to just sneak fourth.
Internationaldebut(IRE) , far from disgraced over 5f at the course a couple of days earlier, had to be dropped in from his wide draw and still looked to be going well turning for home. He stayed on without threatening to win the race and is not on a bad mark at present.
Dunn'o(IRE), 6lb higher than when winning at Sandown last month, did mightily well to get across and grab such a good position, but he came under strong pressure turning in and could only keep on at the one pace. (op 12-1)
Flawed Genius, another recent winner shouldering a penalty, never got into it following a slow start. (op 11-2 tchd 6-1)
Celtic Sultan(IRE), 10lb lower than when winning the race a year ago, had to be rousted to lead from stall one, and he ran well to a point, but could find no extra inside the final furlong. (tchd 11-2)
Leandros(FR) was closing at the finish, despite looking unhappy on the track, and could pick up a race once dropped a few pounds. (tchd 12-1)
Ilie Nastase(FR) caught the eye of the stewards. Settled in rear, he looked far from happy on the track, but kept on well down the straight despite managing to find trouble. He was eased inside the final half furlong and the general feeling was that he should have finished a good bit closer, but there was veterinary evidence to suggest the horse wasn´t 100%. Official explanation: jockey said, regarding running and riding, that his orders were to get a good break and sit 2nd if possible, adding that the gelding missed the break and never travelled, merely staying on in latter stages, having been denied a clear run; vet said gelding was found to be coughing post-race and scoped dirty.

1822 ADDLESHAW GODDARD DEE STKS (GROUP 3) 1m 2f 75y
2:15 (2:17) (Class 1) 3-Y-O

£39,739 (£15,064; £7,539; £3,759; £1,883; £945) **Stalls** High

Form RPR

2 **1** **South Easter (IRE)**[20] 1350 3-8-12 0................................ NCallan 4 105
(W J Haggas) *chsd ldrs: rdn to chal 1f out: r.o to ld fnl 75yds: all out* **6/1**[3]

21-1 **2** *hd* **Gitano Hernando**[40] 1019 3-8-12 92................................ JohnEgan 3 105
(M Botti) *lw: hld up: nt clr run over 3f out and 2f out: swtchd lft and hdwy over 1f out: str chal ins fnl f: r.o* **7/2**[2]

42-2 **3** *hd* **Drumbeat (IRE)**[23] 1294 3-8-12 111................................ JMurtagh 7 105
(A P O'Brien, Ire) *hld up towards rr: effrt and hdwy whn carried hd high 1f out: r.o u.p towards fin* **11/10**[1]

4-02 **4** *nk* **Deposer (IRE)**[34] 1118 3-8-12 99................................ RobertWinston 5 104
(J R Best) *racd keenly: led: pushed along over 2f out: hdd 75yds out: hld fnl stride* **33/1**

4-12 **5** *3 ¼* **Big Bound (USA)**[14] 1485 3-8-12 102........................ JimmyFortune 6 98
(J H M Gosden) *racd keenly: chsd ldr tl rdn over 1f out: no ex ins fnl f* **9/1**

4-1 **6** *shd* **Libel Law**[18] 1407 3-8-12 88................................ LDettori 8 97
(M A Jarvis) *in tch: effrt to chse ldrs 2f out: no ex ins fnl f* **7/1**

0-4 **7** *27* **Devotion To Duty (IRE)**[23] 1289 3-8-12 0........................ MichaelHills 2 43
(B W Hills) *s.i.s: a bhd: pushed along 4f out: lost tch 2f out: t.o* **16/1**

2m 10.21s (-1.99) **Going Correction** +0.05s/f (Good) **7** Ran SP% **115.5**
Speed ratings (Par 109): **109,108,108,108,105 105,84**
toteswinger: 1&2 £3.60, 1&3 £2.40, 2&3 £2.20 CSF £27.73 TOTE £6.50: £3.40, £2.30; EX 26.20 Trifecta £101.90 Pool: £537.56 - 3.90 winning units..
Owner Markus Jooste & Bernard Kantor **Bred** Tarworth Bloodstock Investments Ltd **Trained** Newmarket, Suffolk
■ Stewards' Enquiry : N Callan two-day ban: careless riding (May 22-23); two-day ban: used whip with excessive frequency without giving colt time to respond (May 24-25)

FOCUS
This certainly looked one of the weaker renewals in recent times, especially in the absence of unbeaten Royal Ascot winner Free Agent, and the bunched finish only seemed to confirm that impression. They went a steady gallop early and the form does not look worth much as a Classic trial.

NOTEBOOK
South Easter(IRE), runner-up in a Newbury maiden on debut, was taking a jump in class today, but he is certainly bred for the job and showed a determined attitude to score. He was always likely to improve for the rise in distance, his debut effort having been over 1m, and Callan secured an excellent position on the rail just behind the leaders. He was briefly tapped for toe when the pace quickened, but came strong in the straight, and, having fought his way to the front, stuck out a willing head to hold the late challenge of the unlucky runner-up. There is every reason to expect further progress from the son of Galileo as he goes up to 1m4f, but he won´t be winning a Derby on this evidence. He is generally around a 40/1 for Epsom. (op 7-1)
Gitano Hernando's connections objected following the race, the winner having cut across him after about 100 yards, and that combined with the trouble he met straightening for home has to mark him down as being unlucky. Winner of a Doncaster handicap off 84 on his reappearance, he was the pick of the paddock, backed beforehand and still very nearly got up, marking himself down as a smart performer. There should be more to come from the son of Hernando and he is still on course for an ambitious crack at the Belmont Stakes. (op 11-2)
Drumbeat(IRE), who returned with a satisfactory effort in the Feilden Stakes, set a strong standard on the evidence of last year´s second to stablemate Fame And Glory in a Group 1 at Saint-Cloud. He briefly met with trouble turning in, but was still produced to have every chance and stayed on well enough to the line despite again holding his head high. He is most unlikely to be making an impact at Epsom. (op Evens tchd 5-4)
Deposer(IRE), who had finished second in a 1m Listed contest at Lingfield last time, set just a steady gallop and briefly looked to have stolen a march turning in, but he found it half a furlong too far and could not hold on. He was no doubt flattered to finish so close. (op 25-1)
Big Bound(USA), narrowly denied by Thursday´s Vase seventh Above Average in the Sandown Classic Trial, couldn´t get an uncontested lead and did not get home, having raced keenly. (op 17-2 tchd 8-1)
Libel Law was up markedly in grade and didn´t look up to it. (op 15-2 tchd 6-1)
Devotion To Duty(IRE) was never travelling following a sluggish start. (op 12-1)

1823 BETCHRONICLE.COM ORMONDE STKS (GROUP 3) 1m 5f 89y
2:45 (2:45) (Class 1) 4-Y-0+ **£42,577** (£16,140; £8,077) **Stalls** Low

Form RPR

16-3 **1** **Buccellati**[13] 1526 5-9-3 115................................(v) WilliamBuick 4 116
(A M Balding) *crawled along in 2nd tl whole field virtually p.u after 1f: sn tk ld at sedate pce: qcknd over 3f out: rdn over 1f out: r.o wl* **15/8**[2]

3110 **2** *3* **Scintillo**[20] 1351 4-9-3 114................................ RichardHughes 1 111
(R Hannon) *lw: led at crawl tl virtually p.u after 1f: racd in 2nd pl at sedate pce: lost 2nd 5f out: chsd wnr again 3f out: edgd lft ins fnl f: no imp fnl 150yds* **6/1**[3]

010- **3** *8* **Frozen Fire (GER)**[237] 5892 4-9-0 119................................ JMurtagh 2 96
(A P O'Brien, Ire) *crawled along in last pl tl whole field virtually p.u after 1f: continued in last pl at sedate pce: chsd wnr fr 5f out tl 3f out: sn pushed along: lost tch w front pair ins fnl f: sn eased* **8/11**[1]

3m 45.91s (52.71) **Going Correction** +0.05s/f (Good) **3** Ran SP% **107.0**
CSF £8.94 TOTE £2.50; EX 6.90.
Owner Mr & Mrs P McMahon & Mr & Mrs R Gorell **Bred** Burton Agnes Stud Co Ltd **Trained** Kingsclere, Hants

FOCUS
A race that has fallen the way of some really classy individuals in recent times, but this year´s renewal was quite simply a joke, the three remaining participants from the eight declared barely breaking into a trot for the first three-quarters of a mile. They dawdled until about three furlongs out and the form is worth nothing.

NOTEBOOK
Buccellati started to quicken off the front from three out. He was in control from over a furlong out and ran on well to win with a bit in hand, but the form is worth absolutely nothing. There is no doubting he is a progressive horse, though, his reappearance third behind Tartan Bearer suggesting as much, and it will be interesting to see where he goes next. Official explanation: jockey said, regarding running and riding, that his orders were not to be in front as the horse's best form had been when held up, but was unable to prevent this from occurring. (op 2-1 tchd 7-4)

Scintillo, who struggled in soft ground at Newbury last time, quickened past Frozen Fire to emerge as the threat to the winner, but he was always coming off second-best. He may struggle to match his all-weather Group 3 winning-effort on turf. Official explanation: jockey said, regarding running and riding, that the colt had previously disappointed when attempting to make the running and had show its best form when held up. (op 7-1 tchd 5-1)

Frozen Fire(GER) would have been least-suited by the complete lack of pace. A beaten-favourite in last season's St Leger, he closed over half a mile out, but began to carry his head high (a trait he has shown in the past) and was quickly beaten. He looks to have done well physically over the winter and can safely be afforded another chance to show what he is capable of. Official explanation: jockey said, regarding running and riding, that his orders were to sit last and get the colt to finish and it was its first race of the season. (op 4-6 tchd 5-6 tchd 10-11 in places)

1824 HAWKER BEECHCRAFT H'CAP 5f 16y

3:15 (3:16) (Class 2) (0-100,95) 3-Y-0+ **£14,193** (£4,248; £2,124; £1,062; £528) **Stalls** Low

Form RPR

241- **1** **Doctor Parkes**[254] 5394 3-8-7 **79**........ EddieAhern 1 86
(E J Alston) *lw: chsd ldrs: wnt 2nd over 1f out: led wl ins fnl f: r.o* **7/2**[1]

14-2 **2** *½* **Noble Storm (USA)**[14] 1486 3-9-6 **92**........ GrahamGibbons 7 97
(E S McMahon) *lw: led: rdn 1f out: hdd wl ins fnl f: hld cl home* **4/1**[2]

21-3 **3** *nk* **City Dancer (IRE)**[7] 1647 3-9-4 **95**........ SladeO'Hara(5) 2 99+
(A Berry) *missed break: bhd: hdwy over 1f out: r.o ins fnl f: a looking hld* **9/2**[3]

241- **4** *3* **Saif Al Fahad (IRE)**[144] 7689 3-8-5 **77**........ MartinDwyer 3 70
(E J O'Neill) *chsd ldrs: rdn over 1f out: styd on same pce ins fnl f* **16/1**

1-15 **5** *½* **Green Beret (IRE)**[23] 1296 3-9-8 **94**........ JimmyFortune 5 86+
(J H M Gosden) *lw: hld up: c wd ent st wl over 1f out: kpt on ins fnl f: nt pce to chal* **5/1**

03-1 **6** *nk* **Fault**[36] 1078 3-9-4 **90**........(t) MickyFenton 8 80
(Stef Liddiard) *lw: chsd ldr tl rdn over 1f out: edgd rt ins fnl f: fdd* **25/1**

3-30 **7** *1 ½* **Parisian Pyramid (IRE)**[1] 1803 3-9-3 **89**........ AdrianTNicholls 4 74
(D Nicholls) *towards rr: hdwy 1/2-way: rdn over 1f out whn no imp: wknd ins fnl f* **7/1**

-522 **8** *4* **Lucky Numbers (IRE)**[1] 1803 3-9-1 **87**........ JohnEgan 6 62
(Paul Green) *in tch: rdn on outside 1/2-way: wknd ins fnl f: eased* **8/1**

323 **9** *1* **Satwa Street (IRE)**[41] 1002 3-8-10 **85**........ AhmedAjtebi(3) 10 52
(D M Simcock) *hld up: effrt whn carried wd ent st wl over 1f out: sn btn* **40/1**

10-0 **10** *2 ¼* **Masamah (IRE)**[23] 1296 3-9-9 **95**........ RHills 11 54
(E A L Dunlop) *swtchd lft sn after s: a wl bhd* **16/1**

60.06 secs (-0.94) **Going Correction** +0.05s/f (Good) **10** Ran SP% **118.7**
Speed ratings (Par 105): **109,108,107,102,102 101,99,92,91,87**
toteswinger: 1&2 £4.60, 1&3 £4.70, 2&3 £4.80 CSF £17.84 CT £66.32 TOTE £5.40: £1.70, £2.00, £1.70; EX 22.30 Trifecta £44.10 Pool: £1,061.08 - 17.80 winning units..
Owner Joseph Heler **Bred** Joseph Heler **Trained** Longton, Lancs

FOCUS
A decent-looking sprint handicap that was run at a fast pace. The form looks worth being positive about.

NOTEBOOK
Doctor Parkes, making his debut for the yard, looked fit beforehand, was nicely berthed in stall one and soon held a perfect position just in behind the speed. He responded well once pulled out to challenge and got on top in plenty of time. The 5f trip seems to suit him well and he is open to further progress. (op 9-2 tchd 5-1 in places)
Noble Storm(USA), a progressive juvenile who finished second to a useful sort on his reappearance at Sandown, had been nudged up 3lb but still looked a major player. He set a good gallop and found plenty when challenged, but the winner eventually wore him down. He too has more to come, especially back on a slower surface. (op 7-2 tchd 9-2)
City Dancer(IRE) would have gone very close to winning had she not blown the start. Third at Musselburgh on her debut for the yard, this ex-Irish filly got a lot further back than her rider would have liked and kept on without ever looking likely to get there. She can be rated better than the bare form. (op 4-1 tchd 7-2)
Saif Al Fahad(IRE), also declared at Nottingham today, made a satisfactory reappearance back in fourth and is entitled to be sharper for the run. (op 20-1)
Green Beret(IRE) got knocked wide coming into the straight and did not run too badly considering. Official explanation: jockey said gelding hung right (op 11-2 tchd 6-1 tchd 7-1 in places)
Fault failed to last home having been produced to hold every chance in the straight. (op 33-1 tchd 20-1)
Parisian Pyramid(IRE), never involved from a bad draw at the course 24 hours earlier, had a kinder stall berth on this occasion, but never posed a threat. (op 13-2)
Lucky Numbers(IRE) had finished second in the same race the day before, but he couldn´t reproduce the form. Official explanation: jockey said colt hung right (op 12-1)
Masamah(IRE) Official explanation: jockey said colt hung left

1825 CHARLES RODGERS CHESHIRE REGIMENT MAIDEN FILLIES' STKS 7f 2y

4:00 (4:01) (Class 4) 3-Y-O **£7,123** (£2,119; £1,059; £529) **Stalls** Low

Form RPR

5-2 **1** **Balaagha (USA)**[22] 1302 3-9-0 0........ RHills 12 79+
(M A Jarvis) *lw: dismntd and walked to post: dwlt: sn in midfield: hdwy over 2f out: led ins fnl f: r.o and edgd lft towards fin* **1/1**[1]

02- **2** *1 ¼* **Miss Tango Hotel**[265] 5099 3-9-0 0........ JimmyFortune 4 75
(J H M Gosden) *chsd ldrs: rdn over 1f out: sn chal: nt qckn towards fin* **5/2**[2]

0 **3** *1 ¼* **La Marseillaise (IRE)**[21] 1327 3-9-0 0........ RobertWinston 6 72
(B W Hills) *chsd ldr tl rdn over 1f out: styd on same pce ins fnl f* **33/1**

6 **4** *shd* **Massilah**[21] 1327 3-9-0 0........ MichaelHills 9 72
(B W Hills) *lw: sn led: rdn over 1f out: hdd ins fnl f: kpt on same pce towards fin* **5/1**[3]

06 **5** *1* **Viva La Vida**[22] 1302 3-9-0 0........ KirstyMilczarek 7 69
(Jane Chapple-Hyam) *n.m.r and lost pl 5f out: rdn over 1f out: kpt on ins fnl f: nt pce to chal* **20/1**

0- **6** *¾* **Aphrodite's Rock**[189] 7104 3-9-0 0........ RichardHughes 10 67
(Miss Gay Kelleway) *hld up: rdn and hdwy over 1f out: kpt on ins fnl f: nvr able to chal* **33/1**

7 *2 ½* **Riley Queen Bee (USA)** 3-9-0 0........ AndrewElliott 5 60
(K R Burke) *w'like: s.i.s: n.m.r after 1f: towards rr: rdn and hung lft over 1f out: unable to rch ldrs* **33/1**

646- **8** *3 ¾* **Bella Rowena**[248] 5584 3-9-0 72........ WilliamBuick 11 50
(A M Balding) *in tch: rdn 2f out: wknd over 1f out* **16/1**

9 *7* **Jeannie (IRE)** 3-9-0 0........ NeilChalmers 14 31
(A Bailey) *w'like: leggy: racd on outside: midfield: effrt 3f out: wknd over 2f out* **33/1**

00- **10** *12* **Diamond Jo (IRE)**[189] 7117 3-9-0 0........ EddieAhern 13 —
(Patrick Morris) *w'like: dwlt: a wl bhd* **33/1**

0 **11** *2 ¾* **Bicksta**[21] 1327 3-9-0 0........ NCallan 1 —
(E F Vaughan) *a towards rr* **25/1**

5 **12** *4* **Moneysupermarket (IRE)**[34] 1120 3-9-0 0........ JMurtagh 3 —
(Patrick Morris) *racd in midfield early: eased whn bhd over 2f out: fin lame* **16/1**

1m 27.16s (0.66) **Going Correction** +0.05s/f (Good) **12** Ran SP% **130.3**
Speed ratings (Par 98): **98,96,95,95,93 93,90,85,77,64 61,56**
toteswinger: 1&2 £1.80, 1&3 £13.60, 2&3 £16.70 CSF £3.63 TOTE £2.30: £1.10, £1.50, £8.70; EX 4.70.
Owner Hamdan Al Maktoum **Bred** Brereton C Jones **Trained** Newmarket, Suffolk

FOCUS
This was not the strongest of maidens but the form seems to make sense rated around the runner-up, fourth and fifth.
Moneysupermarket(IRE) Official explanation: vet said filly returned lame

1826 CRUISE NIGHTCLUB H'CAP 1m 4f 66y

4:35 (4:35) (Class 4) (0-85,85) 4-Y-0+ **£4,957** (£4,957; £1,136; £567) **Stalls** Low

Form RPR

1-21 **1** **Empowered (IRE)**[6] 1660 4-9-1 **82**........ JMurtagh 4 93+
(W J Haggas) *lw: chsd ldr: outpcd by ldr over 2f out: clsd ins fnl f: r.o to dispute ld post* **1/1**[1]

1-32 **1** *dht* **Red Merlin (IRE)**[11] 1571 4-8-10 **77**........(v) RichardHughes 5 88
(C G Cox) *hld up: rapid hdwy to ld wl over 2f out: rdn 1f out: hrd pressed towards fin: jnd post* **11/4**[2]

0-63 **3** *4* **Buddhist Monk**[24] 1274 4-9-3 **84**........ StephenDonohoe 3 89
(Ian Williams) *lw: midfield: hdwy and swtchd lft 2f out: wnt 3rd over 1f out: no imp on front pair fnl f* **7/1**[3]

3051 **4** *1 ¼* **Aphrodisia**[20] 1348 5-8-10 **77**........ WilliamBuick 6 80
(Ian Williams) *hld up: hdwy on outside over 2f out: rdn over 1f out: kpt on ins fnl f: nt pce to chal* **16/1**

004- **5** *1 ¾* **Birkside**[160] 7499 6-9-1 **82**........ DNolan 2 82
(Ollie Pears) *chsd ldrs: pushed along 2f out: wknd ins fnl f* **25/1**

-310 **6** *6* **Aureate**[16] 1458 5-9-4 **85**........(b[1]) JimmyFortune 1 76
(B Ellison) *racd keenly: chsd ldrs: lost pl wl over 2f out: sn btn* **9/1**

36-0 **7** *1 ¾* **Bowder Stone (IRE)**[41] 999 4-8-12 **79**........ EddieAhern 8 67
(E J Alston) *a bhd* **12/1**

0/40 **8** *27* **Admiral (IRE)**[6] 1665 8-8-7 **77**........ AndrewMullen(3) 7 22
(S Parr) *led: hdd wl over 2f out: sn wknd* **33/1**

2m 37.58s (-2.32) **Going Correction** +0.05s/f (Good) **8** Ran SP% **119.5**
Speed ratings (Par 105): **109,109,106,105,104 100,99,81**WIN: Empowered £1.00, Red Merlin £1.90. PL: E 1.10, RM 1.40, Buddhist Monk £1.90. EX: E-RM £2.20, RM-E £3.20. CSF: E-RM £2.04, RM-E 3.08 TRI: E-RM-BM £6.26, RM-E-BM £8.36. toteswinger: E-RM £1.40, E-BM £2.60, RM-BM £4.50 Place 6: £40.82 Place 5:27 Owner.
Owner Reid's Allstars **Bred** Keatly Overseas Ltd **Trained** Lambourn, Berks

FOCUS
They went a steady gallop in what was an ordinary handicap and the judge was unable to separate Red Merlin and Empowered. The form looks reasonably sound though with the third and fourth setting the level.
T/Jkpt: £2,526.30 to a £1 stake. Pool: £69,384.98. 19.50 winning tickets. T/Plt: £47.00 to a £1 stake. Pool: £159,356.38. 2,470.96 winning tickets. T/Qpdt: £5.40 to a £1 stake. Pool: £7,470.94. 1,020.56 winning tickets. DO

1689 HAMILTON (R-H)

Friday, May 8

OFFICIAL GOING: Good to soft (7.9)
Wind: Fairly strong, across Weather: Cloudy, bright

1827 BRAVEHEART NIGHT NEXT WEEK MAIDEN STKS 5f 4y

6:10 (6:11) (Class 5) 2-Y-O **£2,590** (£770; £385; £192) **Stalls** Low

Form RPR

06 **1** **Dispol Kabira**[4] 1719 2-8-12 0........ TonyCulhane 2 56
(P T Midgley) *sn pushed along in tch: hdwy and swtchd rt over 1f out: edgd lft and styd on wl ins fnl f to ld post* **66/1**

5 **2** *nse* **Dower Glen**[13] 1504 2-8-12 0........ TomEaves 3 56
(I Semple) *led: rdn ent fnl f: kpt on: hdd post* **9/2**[3]

4 **3** *1 ½* **Midnight Uno**[7] 1653 2-8-12 0........ JackDean(5) 5 55
(W G M Turner) *cl up: drvn fr 2f out: kpt on same pce ins fnl f* **7/1**

4 **4** *½* **Rock Of Love (IRE)**[9] 1610 2-9-3 0........ JoeFanning 1 54
(M Johnston) *cl up: pushed along 1/2-way: effrt over 1f out: one pce fnl f* **4/5**[1]

5 *3 ½* **Valantino Oyster (IRE)** 2-9-3 0........ PaulMulrennan 6 41
(J Howard Johnson) *prom: rn green and outpcd after 2f: n.d after* **20/1**

6 *½* **Charity Fair** 2-8-12 0........ DarrenMoffatt 4 34
(A Berry) *sn outpcd and bhd: plugged on fnl f: nvr on terms* **80/1**

7 *2 ¼* **Olympic Ceremony** 2-9-3 0........ PaulHanagan 7 31
(R A Fahey) *wnt rt s: cl up tl rdn and wknd fr 2f out* **4/1**[2]

64.15 secs (4.15) **Going Correction** +0.525s/f (Yiel) **7** Ran SP% **113.7**
Speed ratings (Par 93): **87,86,84,83,78 77,73**
toteswinger: 1&2 £14.50, 1&3 £14.80, 2&3 £2.60 CSF £333.45 TOTE £47.70: £7.60, £2.20; EX 188.30.
Owner W B Imison **Bred** Silfield Bloodstock **Trained** Westow, N Yorks

FOCUS
Very ordinary maiden form, run in a time nearly 6sec slower than Racing Post standard, suggesting the rain had changed the ground fairly significantly.

NOTEBOOK
Dispol Kabira got up right on the line to collar Dower Glen. Outpaced early, just as she had been on both previous starts, she began to find her stride once switched out to the middle of the track and she stayed on well in the final furlong, shaping as though she already wants another furlong. Her previous two starts had both been on quick ground, so it may be that this slower terrain suited her, but the stiff finish definitely helped and, although probably only modest, she will do better over another furlong or two. (op 80-1)
Dower Glen stayed on well at Haydock on her debut but she ran a different sort of race here, showing much more early toe and looking like she was going to keep them all at bay until close home. (op 7-2 tchd 10-3)
Midnight Uno kept on well enough. (tchd 9-1 in a place)
Rock Of Love(IRE) was a bit disappointing, coming under pressure over a furlong out and never really getting to grips with the pacesetting Dower Glen. (op 10-11 tchd 5-2)

Olympic Ceremony, who was the most expensive of these at £50,000, showed good speed out wide for the first three furlongs before getting tired, and he looks the type to do much better. (tchd 5-1)

1828 HAMILTON-PARK.CO.UK CONDITIONS STKS 6f 5y
6:45 (6:46) (Class 3) 3-Y-O

£8,723 (£2,612; £1,306; £653; £326; £163) **Stalls** Low

Form RPR

6-03 **1** **Jobe (USA)**[9] 1602 3-8-12 105 .... JoeFanning 4 96
(K A Ryan) *mde all: rdn and edgd rt over 2f out: hld on wl fnl f* **4/5**[1]

00-4 **2** 1 ¼ **Able Master (IRE)**[14] 1486 3-9-2 95 .... TomEaves 1 96
(B Smart) *trckd ldrs: effrt and edgd rt over 1f out: wnt 2nd ins fnl f: kpt on fin* **4/1**[2]

0-04 **3** 2 **Agente Parmigiano (IRE)**[34] 1118 3-8-9 95 .... PaulHanagan 6 83
(G A Butler) *pressed wnr tl no ex ins fnl f* **6/1**[3]

103- **4** 6 **Blown It (USA)**[205] 6739 3-8-9 80 .... PaulMulrennan 2 64
(I Semple) *dwlt: hld up in tch: effrt over 2f out: sn no imp* **22/1**

3-15 **5** ½ **Dunes Queen (USA)**[23] 1293 3-8-7 90 .... TonyCulhane 5 60
(M R Channon) *in tch tl rdn and outpcd over 2f out* **6/1**[3]

6 44 **Our Girl Ally (IRE)** 3-8-1 0 .... DarrenMoffatt 3 —
(A Berry) *prom tl wknd qckly over 3f out* **125/1**

1m 15.49s (3.29) **Going Correction** +0.525s/f (Yiel) **6** Ran SP% **109.3**
Speed ratings (Par 103): **99,97,94,86,86 27**
toteswinger: 1&2 £1.50, 1&3 £2.00, 2&3 £3.00 CSF £4.02 TOTE £1.90: £1.50, £1.40; EX 4.20.
Owner J & L Duddy A Bailey B McDonald A Heeney **Bred** David Garvin **Trained** Hambleton, N Yorks

FOCUS
Not a bad little conditions race in which the field soon tacked over middle to far side despite the stalls being up the stands' rail. The form looks muddling, but has been rated through the third to his two-year-old turf form.

NOTEBOOK
Jobe(USA), last year's Gimcrack third, was easily the best treated on these terms and he had shaped with real encouragement in an Ascot Listed event last time. Having also proved himself on ground with juice in it as a two-year-old everything was in place for a good run here and, soon to the fore, he ground this out from the front. A mark of 100 means he could be something of a twilight horse this term so connections will probably need to be cute with their placing of him, but this looks his optimum trip and he has now confirmed his ability to handle ground with cut. (op 6-5 tchd 5-4)
Able Master(IRE) ran an excellent race in defeat given that his penalty meant he was 9lb worse off with the winner than he would have been in a handicap. A further negative was the softening of the ground, as he has proved himself much more effective on a sound surface. In the circumstances he shaped with real promise for his in-form yard. (tchd 5-1 in a place)
Agente Parmigiano(IRE) was taking a big drop in trip having run well in a 1m Listed race last time, and, although he showed up well for a long way, he couldn't match the speed of the front two in the final furlong. He might appreciate going back up in trip. (op 5-1 tchd 9-2)
Blown It(USA) was slow from the gates and could never land a blow, but he had little chance on these terms anyway and will be found more suitable opportunities. (op 18-1 tchd 9-1)
Dunes Queen(USA), whose Irish 1,000 Guineas entry looks more than a touch ambitious on this evidence, could also never get into it and couldn't build on the promise she showed in the Nell Gwyn, although conditions were much slower here. She might be worth another chance back on better ground and up in trip. Official explanation: jockey said filly was unsuited by the good to soft ground (op 7-2 tchd 7-1)

1829 MITIE H'CAP 1m 4f 17y
7:15 (7:15) (Class 5) (0-70,69) 3-Y-O

£3,238 (£963; £481; £240) **Stalls** High

Form RPR

6-05 **1** **Classic Contours (USA)**[15] 1470 3-8-5 60 .... JamieKyne(7) 10 64
(J J Quinn) *in tch: effrt and rdn over 3f out: led over 1f out: drvn out* **4/1**[2]

505- **2** 2 ¼ **New Tricks**[229] 6151 3-8-11 59 .... TomEaves 5 59
(I Semple) *hld up: drvn 4f out: rallied over 2f out: styd on to go 2nd nr fin: nt rch wnr* **14/1**

1215 **3** ½ **Dispol Diva**[9] 1614 3-8-13 68 ....(v) PaulPickard(7) 2 67
(P T Midgley) *led to over 1f out: kpt on same pce: lost 2nd nr fin* **12/1**

10-6 **4** *nk* **Sharp Sovereign (USA)**[13] 1509 3-9-3 68 .... NeilBrown(3) 9 67
(T D Barron) *hld up: hdwy over 2f out: r.o fnl f: nrst fin* **11/1**

1023 **5** 5 **Kochanski (IRE)**[18] 1397 3-8-13 61 .... JoeFanning 7 52
(M Johnston) *cl up: ev ch 3f out: wknd over 1f out* **9/1**[3]

5-40 **6** 5 **Some Time Good (IRE)**[18] 1408 3-9-7 69 .... TonyCulhane 8 52
(M R Channon) *plld hrd early: in tch: rdn 3f out: edgd rt and outpcd fnl 2f* **22/1**

400- **7** 3 **Blackstone Vegas**[268] 4960 3-9-5 67 .... PaulMulrennan 1 45
(J Howard Johnson) *trckd ldrs tl edgd rt and wknd fr 3f out* **22/1**

0-56 **8** 8 **Diktaram**[26] 1231 3-8-4 52 .... SilvestreDeSousa 3 17
(J R Weymes) *hld up: drvn over 3f out: nvr on terms* **25/1**

460- **9** 3 ¾ **Royal Diamond (IRE)**[210] 6621 3-9-7 69 .... SebSanders 6 28
(Sir Mark Prescott) *hld up in tch: rdn over 3f out: sn wknd: eased whn no ch ins fnl f* **1/1**[1]

2m 47.31s (8.71) **Going Correction** +0.725s/f (Yiel) **9** Ran SP% **115.2**
Speed ratings (Par 99): **99,97,97,96,93 90,88,82,80**
toteswinger: 1&2 £28.00, 1&3 £8.40, 2&3 £14.30 CSF £55.11 CT £617.76 TOTE £6.00: £1.40, £3.00, £2.20; EX 70.40.
Owner Elsa Crankshaw Gordon Allan **Bred** Hopewell Investments LLC **Trained** Settrington, N Yorks

FOCUS
Just ordinary handicap form in which warm favourite Royal Diamond bombed out badly and the jury has to be out on him now. Despite the pace slowing markedly mid-race, allowing the field to close up on the leader, not a great deal got into it. The form looks sound rated around the runner-up and third improving slightly.
Blackstone Vegas Official explanation: jockey said gelding hung right throughout
Royal Diamond(IRE) Official explanation: jockey said gelding was unsuited by the good to soft ground

1830 HAMILTON PARK SUPER SIX H'CAP 1m 1f 36y
7:50 (7:51) (Class 4) (0-80,80) 4-Y-O+

£5,180 (£1,541; £770; £384) **Stalls** High

Form RPR

20-6 **1** **Arctic Cape**[18] 1401 4-8-11 73 .... JoeFanning 7 81
(M Johnston) *trckd ldrs: rdn 3f out: led 1f out: hld on wl* **9/2**[3]

2-33 **2** *nk* **Wind Shuffle (GER)**[7] 1646 6-8-11 78 .... GaryBartley(5) 2 85
(J S Goldie) *led to over 2f out: rallied and swtchd lft over 1f out: kpt on wl towards fin* **9/4**[1]

0-35 **3** 2 **King Of The Moors (USA)**[13] 1514 6-8-4 66 oh1 ....(p) PaulHanagan 6 69
(R C Guest) *hld up in tch: rdn and outpcd over 2f out: styd on wl fnl f* **4/1**[2]

/0-4 **4** ½ **Prince Evelith (GER)**[13] 1507 6-8-5 74 .... JamieKyne(7) 4 76+
(J J Quinn) *hld up: rdn 4f out: hdwy to ld over 2f out: hung rt: hdd 1f out: no ex ins fnl f* **7/1**

35-4 **5** 16 **Castlebury (IRE)**[9] 1612 4-8-4 66 oh1 .... SilvestreDeSousa 3 33
(G A Swinbank) *prom tl rdn and wknd over 2f out* **4/1**[2]

-000 **6** 24 **Talk Of Saafend (IRE)**[13] 1507 4-8-13 75 .... PaulMulrennan 5 —
(P Monteith) *trckd ldrs tl wknd qckly over 3f out* **10/1**

2m 4.97s (5.27) **Going Correction** +0.725s/f (Yiel) **6** Ran SP% **110.5**
Speed ratings (Par 105): **105,104,102,102,88 66**
toteswinger: 1&2 £2.70, 1&3 £3.10, 2&3 £2.20 CSF £14.57 CT £40.00 TOTE £5.00: £2.50, £2.10; EX 14.90.
Owner Mrs Christine Brown **Bred** Mrs R D Peacock **Trained** Middleham Moor, N Yorks

FOCUS
A reduced field and another modest contest. The winner probably only had to match the best of his three-year-old form to score, while the consistent runner-up has been rated to his mark.

1831 BACK2BLACK MAIDEN STKS 6f 5y
8:20 (8:21) (Class 5) 3-5-Y-O

£2,590 (£770; £385; £192) **Stalls** Low

Form RPR

3-6 **1** **Apache Ridge (IRE)**[10] 1592 3-9-0 0 .... JoeFanning 2 76+
(K A Ryan) *chsd ldrs: led over 2f out: edgd rt: styd on strly* **3/1**[2]

240- **2** 3 **Asserting**[219] 6381 3-8-9 56 .... PaulMulrennan 6 61
(J A McShane) *w ldr: led briefly 1/2-way: kpt on same pce fnl f* **18/1**

23-3 **3** 1 ¼ **Mo Mhuirnin (IRE)**[10] 1592 3-8-9 71 .... PaulHanagan 8 57
(R A Fahey) *led to 1/2-way: sn rdn: one pce fr over 1f out* **11/8**[1]

5-60 **4** 8 **Just Mustard (USA)**[23] 1295 3-9-0 70 .... TomEaves 1 36
(G A Butler) *hld up: effrt over 2f out: sn no imp* **10/3**[3]

-000 **5** 4 ½ **North South Divide (IRE)**[38] 1055 5-9-10 47 ....(p) PatrickMathers 4 22
(Peter Grayson) *prom tl rdn and wknd over 2f out* **22/1**

0 **6** 2 **Your True Love (IRE)**[37] 1062 3-8-9 0 .... TonyCulhane 7 11
(A Berry) *unruly in stalls: t.k.h: hld up in tch: hung rt and outpcd over 3f out: sn btn* **40/1**

6- **7** ½ **Bootleg**[231] 6065 3-9-0 0 .... SilvestreDeSousa 5 14
(D Nicholls) *dwlt: sn chsng ldrs: rdn and wknd qckly over 2f out* **10/1**

1m 15.93s (3.73) **Going Correction** +0.525s/f (Yiel)
WFA 3 from 5yo 10lb **7** Ran SP% **111.3**
Speed ratings (Par 103): **96,92,90,79,73 71,70**
toteswinger: 1&2 £7.00, 1&3 £1.80, 2&3 £4.40 CSF £48.56 TOTE £4.60: £2.20, £4.60; EX 55.90.

Owner Aidan Heeney **Bred** Allevamento Ficomontanino Srl **Trained** Hambleton, N Yorks
■ Stewards' Enquiry : Paul Mulrennan caution: used whip with excessive frequency

FOCUS
A pretty weak maiden and the race was over as a contest well over a furlong out. The form is tricky to pin down with the favourite disappointing.

1832 CONFERENCE AND EVENTS AT HAMILTON PARK H'CAP 6f 5y
8:50 (8:50) (Class 5) (0-75,74) 3-Y-O+

£3,412 (£1,007; £504) **Stalls** Low

Form RPR

00-0 **1** **Castles In The Air**[22] 1309 4-9-10 72 .... PaulHanagan 4 88
(R A Fahey) *pressed ldr: led appr fnl f: pushed out* **5/1**

000- **2** 2 **Bonnie Prince Blue**[197] 6925 6-9-12 74 .... SilvestreDeSousa 3 83
(D Nicholls) *led to appr fnl f: kpt on same pce* **10/3**[1]

4131 **3** 2 **Chocolicious (IRE)**[8] 1628 3-8-8 66 ....(v) TomEaves 2 66
(B Smart) *prom: effrt and edgd rt over 1f out: sn no ex* **4/1**[3]

-012 **4** 1 ¼ **Imperial Sword**[5] 1694 6-8-12 63 ....(b) NeilBrown(3) 8 62
(T D Barron) *dwlt: hld up: hdwy 2f out: sn rdn: no imp fnl f* **7/2**[2]

342- **5** 1 **Heureux (USA)**[280] 4605 6-9-3 65 ....(b) PaulMulrennan 1 61
(J Howard Johnson) *prom tl edgd lft and outpcd over 1f out* **10/1**

0-00 **6** 2 ¼ **Obe One**[16] 1456 9-8-12 60 oh10 .... JoeFanning 5 49
(A Berry) *hld up in tch: rdn and outpcd over 2f out: n.d after* **33/1**

0-06 **7** ½ **Woodsley House (IRE)**[5] 1694 7-9-1 70 .... JamieKyne(7) 6 57
(A G Foster) *in tch: rdn over 2f out: wknd over 1f out* **9/2**

4000 **8** 8 **Indian Diva (IRE)**[17] 1436 4-9-4 73 ....(t) PaulPickard(7) 7 34
(P T Midgley) *s.s: sme hdwy over 3f out: sn rdn and wknd* **33/1**

1m 14.81s (2.61) **Going Correction** +0.525s/f (Yiel)
WFA 3 from 4yo+ 10lb **8** Ran SP% **115.1**
Speed ratings (Par 103): **103,100,97,96,94 91,91,80**
toteswinger: 1&2 £3.80, 1&3 £3.50, 2&3 £3.90 CSF £22.22 CT £71.46 TOTE £5.10: £1.90, £2.30, £1.50; EX 33.60 Place 6: £281.13, Place 5: £45.05.
Owner Jim McGrath **Bred** Newgate Stud Company **Trained** Musley Bank, N Yorks

FOCUS
A decent pace to this 6f handicap and it looks a decent race for the grade, with the third rated close to her form, and the fourth with solid course and distance efforts to his name.
Indian Diva(IRE) Official explanation: jockey said filly missed the break
T/Plt: £292.00 to a £1 stake. Pool: £45,312.01. 113.25 winning tickets. T/Qpdt: £35.20 to a £1 stake. Pool: £4,094.74. 86.00 winning tickets. RY

1636 LINGFIELD (L-H)
Friday, May 8

OFFICIAL GOING: Turf course - good to firm (straight course 8.7; round course 8.9) all-weather - standard
Wind: strong, across Weather: bright, breezy

1833 BET MULTIPLES - BETDAQ H'CAP 1m (P)
1:35 (1:35) (Class 5) (0-70,73) 4-Y-O+

£3,070 (£906; £453) **Stalls** High

Form RPR

-033 **1** **Pha Mai Blue**[8] 1634 4-8-10 62 ....(v) PatCosgrave 6 71
(J R Boyle) *t.k.h: hld up in tch: rdn and effrt jst over 2f out: led over 1f out: edgd rt u.p fnl 100yds: r.o wl* **8/1**[3]

56-1 **2** ¾ **Driven (IRE)**[12] 1539 4-9-7 73 6ex .... JimCrowley 1 80
(Mrs A J Perrett) *trckd ldrs gng wl on inner: rdn and effrt over 1f out: drvn and chsd wnr 1f out: kpt on but nt pce to get to wnr* **5/2**[1]

20-3 **3** 1 ¼ **Aggravation**[8] 1633 7-9-2 68 .... RobertHavlin 5 72
(D R C Elsworth) *hld up in midfield: hdwy jst over 2f out: chsd ldng pair and drvn jst ins fnl f: kpt on same pce fnl 100yds* **7/2**[2]

1565 **4** 1 ¼ **Lopinot (IRE)**[30] 1187 6-9-1 67 ....(v) RichardKingscote 4 68
(M R Bosley) *hld up in midfield: rdn and hdwy towards inner jst over 1f out: r.o fnl f: nt rch ldrs* **14/1**

0235 **5** 1 **Sew'N'So Character (IRE)**[14] 1493 8-9-1 67 .... LPKeniry 10 66
(M Blanshard) *racd in midfield on outer: rdn and effrt jst over 2f out: styd on same pce fnl f* **10/1**

130- **6** ¾ **April Fool**[170] 7390 5-9-3 69 ....(v) RichardThomas 12 66
(J A Geake) *taken down early: w ldr: rdn to ld jst over 2f out: hdd over 1f out: wknd 1f out* **20/1**

6401 **7** *hd* **Diego Rivera**[18] 1413 4-8-11 63 .... FergusSweeney 9 60
(P J Makin) *in tch: rdn and effrt jst over 2f out: edgd lft u.p over 1f out: plugged on same pce after* **9/1**

3-30 **8** 1/2 **Pension Policy (USA)**9 1613 4-9-4 **70**........................(b1) ShaneKelly 7 66
(J M P Eustace) *stdd s: hld up in last pl: c wd and hdwy wl over 1f out: nvr threatened ldrs* **14/1**

9 3/4 **Hidden Door (IRE)**278 4672 4-8-13 **70**....... Louis-PhilippeBeuzelin(5) 11 64
(Jane Chapple-Hyam) *s.i.s: hld up in last trio: rdn 2f out: nvr threatened ldrs* **12/1**

06-5 **10** nk **What Do You Know**17 1425 6-8-10 **67**.............................. NicolPolli(5) 8 60
(A M Hales) *hld up in last trio: effrt on inner over 1f out: no prog fnl f* **33/1**

0500 **11** 2 1/4 **Glencalvie (IRE)**21 1320 8-9-0 **66**....................................(p) AdamKirby 2 54
(J Akehurst) *led tl rdn and hdd over 1f out: wknd fnl f* **12/1**

0-54 **12** 1 1/2 **Saviour Sand (IRE)**30 656 5-8-13 **68**.......................... MarcHalford(3) 3 53
(T Keddy) *sn pushed up to press ldrs: rdn over 2f out: wknd over 1f out* **20/1**

1m 36.83s (-1.37) **Going Correction** -0.025s/f (Stan) **12** Ran SP% **122.2**
Speed ratings (Par 103): **105,104,103,101,100 100,99,99,98,98 96,94**
toteswinger: 1&2 £8.60, 1&3 £14.60, 2&3 £4.20 CSF £28.38 CT £88.16 TOTE £6.90: £2.90, £2.10, £1.20; EX 29.50 TRIFECTA Not won..
Owner Bluefriar Construction Ltd **Bred** Chippenham Lodge Stud Ltd **Trained** Epsom, Surrey

FOCUS
A modest handicap made up of largely exposed performers. There was a sound pace on and the form makes sense rated through the runner-up and third.
Pension Policy(USA) Official explanation: jockey said filly was slowly away and never travelled

1834 BETDAQ THE BETTING EXCHANGE FILLIES' H'CAP — 1m 2f (P)
2:10 (2:12) (Class 5) (0-70,70) 3-Y-0+ **£3,070** (£906; £453) **Stalls** Low

Form RPR

20-6 **1** **Lunar River (FR)**21 1318 6-9-9 **63**...........................(t) FergusSweeney 13 71
(David Pinder) *stdd s: hld up in rr: stdy hdwy 3f out: rdn over 1f out: qcknd to ld fnl 100yds: sn in command* **14/1**

430- **2** 1 1/4 **Demeanour (USA)**231 6081 3-9-1 **70**................................. AdamKirby 3 75
(E A L Dunlop) *chsd ldrs: chsd ldr wl over 1f out: rdn to ld ins fnl f: hdd and nt pce of wnr fnl 100yds* **4/11**

-501 **3** 1 1/4 **Becuille (IRE)**34 1133 4-9-7 **66**...................... Louis-PhilippeBeuzelin(5) 9 69
(B J Meehan) *t.k.h: hld up in midfield: effrt on inner 2f out: pressed ldrs and drvn jst ins fnl f: one pce after* **13/2**

-420 **4** 3/4 **Solo River**12 1538 4-9-11 **65**.. ChrisCatlin 2 67
(P J Makin) *chsd ldrs: wnt 2nd over 3f out: rdn to ld ent fnl 2f out: drvn and hdd ins fnl f: outpcd fnl 100yds* **12/1**

4343 **5** 1/2 **Formidable Guest**9 1604 5-9-6 **67**........................... SimonPearce(7) 11 68
(J Pearce) *hld up towards rr: hdwy over 3f out: chsd ldrs jst over 2f out: rdn over 1f out: nt qckn and no imp fnl f* **11/23**

100- **6** 2 1/4 **Oriental Girl**189 7111 4-9-12 **66**................................(p) RichardThomas 6 62
(J A Geake) *in tch in midfield: shuffled bk and pushed along over 4f out: rdn over 2f out: styd on fnl f: nvr trbld ldrs* **40/1**

1633 **7** 1/2 **Bavarica**30 1179 7-9-6 **67**................................... MatthewCosham(7) 8 62
(Miss J Feilden) *stdd after s: t.k.h: hld up bhd on inner: grad switching to outer over 2f out: c v wd bnd 2f out: r.o fnl f: nvr trbld ldrs* **16/1**

41-0 **8** 1 **Carmela Maria**25 1261 4-9-8 **62**............................... RichardKingscote 1 55
(S C Williams) *chsd ldr tl over 3f out: wknd u.p over 1f out* **12/1**

44-0 **9** 1 1/4 **Persian Memories (IRE)**18 1408 3-9-0 **69**.................... JimCrowley 7 59
(J L Dunlop) *hld up in midfield early: hdwy 7f out: chsd ldrs over 5f out: rdn and one pce whn hmpd over 1f out: wknd fnl f* **9/22**

0-53 **10** 3/4 **Protiva**17 1429 3-8-5 **60**.. EdwardCreighton 12 48
(A P Jarvis) *sn led: rdn and hdd ent fnl 2f out: wknd wl over 1f out* **25/1**

65-0 **11** 3 3/4 **Chic Shanique (USA)**20 1355 3-8-2 **57**.................... CatherineGannon 4 38
(Tom Dascombe) *t.k.h early: chsd ldrs tl stdd into midfield 7f out: rdn whn short of room and lost pl bnd jst over 2f out: no ch after* **7/1**

-006 **12** 3 1/2 **Tallulah Sunrise**10 1589 4-8-13 **58**......................... GabrielHannon(5) 10 33
(M D I Usher) *s.i.s: bhd: hdwy into midfield over 3f out: rdn and struggling jst over 2f out: wl btn fnl f* **40/1**

660 **13** 3/4 **Innactualfact**30 1193 3-8-3 **65**.............................. JemmaMarshall(7) 14 37
(L A Dace) *a bhd* **33/1**

040/ **14** 45 **Lady Calido (USA)**653 3834 4-9-4 **58**.............................. DO'Donohoe 5 —
(Sir Mark Prescott) *racd in midfield: pushed along and losing pl over 7f out: rdn and dropped to last 5f out: t.o fnl 3f* **8/1**

2m 6.34s (-0.26) **Going Correction** -0.025s/f (Stan)
WFA 3 from 4yo+ 15lb **14** Ran SP% **130.1**
Speed ratings (Par 100): **100,99,98,97,97 95,94,94,93,92 89,86,86,50**
toteswinger: 1&2 £14.70, 1&3 £23.60, 2&3 £4.40 CSF £73.04 CT £420.99 TOTE £16.90: £4.50, £2.30, £2.20; EX 168.90 TRIFECTA Not won..
Owner The Little Farm Partnership **Bred** M Daguzan-Garros & Rolling Hills Farm **Trained** Kingston Lisle, Oxon

FOCUS
This moderate fillies' handicap was a wide-open affair. It was run at a good pace and the form looks sound enough with the winner rated back to her best and the third and fourth close to their marks.
Bavarica Official explanation: jockey said mare ran too free
Tallulah Sunrise Official explanation: jockey said filly lost its action

1835 EUROPEAN BREEDERS' FUND MAIDEN STKS — 5f
2:40 (2:40) (Class 5) 2-Y-0 **£3,561** (£1,059; £529; £264) **Stalls** High

Form RPR

04 **1** **Stargaze (IRE)**10 1577 2-9-3 0.. LPKeniry 7 80+
(A M Balding) *mde all: rdn over 1f out: clr and in total command fnl f: eased towards fin: easily* **6/41**

2 4 1/2 **I'Malwaysright (IRE)** 2-9-3 0.. RobertHavlin 6 61
(D R C Elsworth) *stdd s: in tch: shkn up ent fnl 2f out: rdn over 1f out: chsd wnr jst ins fnl f: no imp* **5/13**

6 **3** 1 **Diamond Affair (IRE)**29 1195 2-8-12 0.................... EdwardCreighton 3 52
(M G Quinlan) *stdd s: plld hrd: hld up in tch: rdn and effrt wl over 1f out: plugged on same pce fnl f* **13/2**

4 3/4 **Khanivorous** 2-9-3 0.. PatCosgrave 1 55+
(J R Boyle) *s.i.s: rn green in rr: reminders 3f out: rdn over 2f out: styd on ins fnl f: nvr trbld ldrs* **7/22**

0 **5** nk **Jackie Danny**11 1569 2-8-12 0...................................... CatherineGannon 5 48
(C A Dwyer) *chsd wnr: rdn over 2f out: nt pce of wnr over 1f out: lost 2nd pl and wknd ins fnl f* **50/1**

6 nk **Strike Shot** 2-9-3 0.. DO'Donohoe 4 52
(W R Muir) *a in last pair: pushed along early: rdn 2f out: kpt on same pce and no imp after* **5/13**

58.12 secs (-0.08) **Going Correction** -0.125s/f (Firm) **6** Ran SP% **110.8**
Speed ratings (Par 93): **95,87,86,85,84 84**
toteswinger: 1&2 £4.70, 1&3 £1.50, 2&3 £13.40 CSF £9.18 TOTE £2.00: £1.80, £3.50; EX 8.10.
Owner David Brownlow **Bred** Dermot Brennan And Associates Ltd **Trained** Kingsclere, Hants

FOCUS
This ordinary juvenile maiden was the first race run on turf here this year and once again the stands' rail proved the place to be. Nevertheless, the winner was impressive.

NOTEBOOK
Stargaze(IRE) ◆ made all to open his account at the third time of asking. The worry was whether this would be sharp enough for him, but he had clearly learned again for his second outing at Bath and ultimately scored with plenty left up his sleeve. He should relish being faced with a stiffer test in due course and looks one to follow. (op 11-8 tchd 11-10)
I'Malwaysright(IRE) cost £14,000 and is precociously bred. He lacked anything like the pace of the winner, but left the impression he would come on nicely for the run and has a future. (tchd 6-1)
Diamond Affair(IRE) ◆, disappointing on debut last month, still showed distinct signs of inexperience through the first half of the race. She still showed enough to suggest she will come on again for the run and is one to keep an eye on. (op 4-1 tchd 7-1)
Khanivorous, for whom there was solid support, is bred to make his mark at two and is already a gelding. He walked out of the gates, however, and lacked the early pace to get seriously involved. He got the hang of things late on and has plenty of size about him, so looks one to become more interested in as he becomes more streetwise. (op 13-2)
Jackie Danny showed early pace and the benefit of her debut 11 days earlier, but was readily shaken off as the race got serious. Official explanation: jockey said filly hung right closing stages
Strike Shot has a speedy pedigree, but he was one of the first off the bridle and the initial experience appeared much needed. (tchd 6-1)

1836 HINDLEAP WALK H'CAP — 5f
3:10 (3:11) (Class 4) (0-85,85) 4-Y-0+ **£6,476** (£1,927; £963; £481) **Stalls** High

Form RPR

4-23 **1** **Our Piccadilly (IRE)**17 1425 4-8-4 **76**........ Louis-PhilippeBeuzelin(5) 11 83
(W S Kittow) *hld up in midfield on stands' rail: hdwy and swtchd lft over 1f out: rdn and r.o wl to ld on post* **9/21**

00-6 **2** nse **Ocean Blaze**17 1425 5-8-7 **74**.. ChrisCatlin 8 81
(B R Millman) *led and racd on stands' rail: rdn over 1f out: r.o wl tl hdd on post* **15/2**

-436 **3** 1 1/4 **Merlin's Dancer**16 1457 9-9-1 **82**.. ShaneKelly 7 84
(S Dow) *hld up towards rr: hdwy over 1f out: swtchd lft 1f out: drvn and r.o fnl f: nt rch ldrs* **13/23**

0-04 **4** 3/4 **Golden Dixie (USA)**11 1565 10-8-5 **72**.................... FrankieMcDonald 5 72
(R A Harris) *awkward leaving stalls: bhd: hdwy and rdn over 1f out: edgd rt and r.o wl ins fnl f: wnt 4th nr fin: nvr trbld ldrs* **10/1**

00-0 **5** 1/2 **Best One**17 1418 5-8-5 **75**..(p) KevinGhunowa(3) 6 73
(R A Harris) *chsd ldrs: effrt over 1f out: ev ch ent fnl f: hrd rdn and wknd fnl 100yds* **25/1**

025- **6** nk **Lochstar**209 6650 5-8-13 **80**... LPKeniry 1 77
(A M Balding) *chsd ldr but off the rail: ev ch and rdn over 1f out: wknd ins fnl f* **13/23**

65-0 **7** 1 3/4 **Bertoliver**16 1457 5-9-4 **85**.. RichardKingscote 3 75+
(Tom Dascombe) *sn pushed along in midfield: nvr pce to rch ldrs* **5/12**

2400 **8** 3/4 **Whiskey Creek**16 1457 4-8-12 **79**................................(b) JimCrowley 10 67
(C A Dwyer) *hld up bhd: rdn and effrt over 1f out: nvr trbld ldrs* **11/1**

33-3 **9** 1 1/2 **Even Bolder**14 1494 6-8-13 **80**...................................... StephenCarson 9 62
(E A Wheeler) *hld up in midfield: effrt and rdn wl over 1f out: drvn and wknd ent fnl f* **7/1**

4110 **10** 1 1/4 **Princess Rose Anne (IRE)**6 1672 4-8-6 **76**............... MarcHalford(3) 2 54+
(J R Best) *racd in midfield on outer: rdn and wknd wl over 1f out* **11/1**

10-0 **11** 1/2 **Choreography**6 1668 6-8-6 **80**... JustinHeath(7) 4 56
(Jim Best) *v.s.a: a bhd* **33/1**

56.87 secs (-1.33) **Going Correction** -0.125s/f (Firm) **11** Ran SP% **118.3**
Speed ratings (Par 105): **105,104,102,101,100 100,97,96,94,92 91**
toteswinger: 1&2 £13.00, 1&3 £10.90, 2&3 £15.30 CSF £38.45 CT £221.46 TOTE £5.20: £1.90, £2.90, £2.00; EX 50.50 Trifecta £190.40 Part won. Pool: £257.32 - 0.60 winning units..
Owner S Kittow, R Perry, B Hopkins **Bred** Mrs Hopkins, Kittow And Mrs Perry **Trained** Blackborough, Devon

■ Stewards' Enquiry : Justin Heath fourteen-day ban: in breach of Rule 158 (May 22-Jun 4)

FOCUS
A fair sprint handicap and another wide-open contest. It was certainly no coincidence that the first pair raced nearest to the stands' rail. As expected there was a strong pace on. The form looks sound enough rated through the winner to a personal best.
Choreography Official explanation: jockey said, regarding running and riding, that his orders were to jump out and be handy, but the gelding missed the break and was outpaced; trainer confirmed but was not satisfied with the way the gelding had been ridden, as it had missed the break and was not ridden to make up the ground.

1837 THREE BRIDGES MAIDEN STKS (DIV I) — 7f
3:45 (3:46) (Class 5) 3-Y-0 **£2,388** (£705; £352) **Stalls** High

Form RPR

3 **1** **Arrivederla (IRE)**37 1066 3-8-12 0.................................. JamesDoyle 8 76+
(H J L Dunlop) *in tch: rdn over 2f out: hdwy wl over 1f out: led jst over 1f out: styd on fnl f* **8/1**

00P- **2** 1 1/2 **Arteus**237 5905 3-9-3 0.. PatCosgrave 2 77
(Jane Chapple-Hyam) *chsd ldr tl led over 2f out: rdn 2f out: hdd over 1f out: kpt on same pce fnl f* **66/1**

625- **3** 1 **Sparkling Crystal (IRE)**220 6362 3-8-12 71..................... ChrisCatlin 5 69
(B W Hills) *led and grad crossed to stands' rail: hdd and rdn over 2f out: outpcd wl over 1f out: styd on again ins fnl f to snatch 3rd on post* **6/12**

24- **4** nse **Winged Harriet (IRE)**216 6473 3-8-12 0............................ LiamJones 4 69
(W J Haggas) *stdd s: t.k.h: chsd ldrs on outer: ev ch and rdn over 1f out: sn hld hd high and hung lft: fnd nil and btn ins fnl f* **5/61**

00- **5** 7 **Play It Sam**206 6715 3-9-3 0... AdamKirby 9 55
(W R Swinburn) *wnt rt s: sn outpcd in rr: plugged on steadily fnl 2f: nvr nr ldrs* **15/2**

6 4 1/2 **Quasi Congaree (GER)** 3-9-3 0....................................(t) JimCrowley 7 43
(I A Wood) *t.k.h: chsd ldrs: ev ch 2f out: wknd rapidly over 1f out* **20/1**

00 **7** 6 **Royal Adelaide (IRE)**11 1563 3-8-12 0................... FrankieMcDonald 3 22
(J A Osborne) *sn outpcd in rr: hanging lft 4f out: wl bhd fr 1/2-way* **100/1**

5- **8** 3 1/2 **Fat Chance**199 6885 3-8-12 0... NickyMackay 10 12
(Rae Guest) *hmpd s: a wl outpcd in rr: lost tch 1/2-way* **20/1**

9 2 1/2 **La Belle Dane** 3-8-12 0.. ShaneKelly 1 6
(J Noseda) *wnt lft s: a bhd: lost tch 1/2-way* **7/13**

1m 21.92s (-1.38) **Going Correction** -0.125s/f (Firm) **9** Ran SP% **116.2**
Speed ratings (Par 99): **102,100,99,99,91 85,79,75,72**
toteswinger: 1&2 £38.20, 2&3 £38.20 1&3 8.50 CSF £428.12 TOTE £6.40: £2.00, £21.90, £2.10; EX 407.50 TRIFECTA Not won..
Owner William Armitage **Bred** Roundhill Stud & Gleadhill House Stud Ltd **Trained** Lambourn, Berks

FOCUS
The winning time was over a second faster than the second division and it has been rated around the third.

Play It Sam Official explanation: jockey said colt jumped right

1838 THREE BRIDGES MAIDEN STKS (DIV II) 7f
4:20 (4:21) (Class 5) 3-Y-O **£2,388** (£705; £352) **Stalls** High

Form RPR

3 **1** **Mackten**[17] 1423 3-9-3 0 ShaneKelly 9 70+
(W J Knight) *chsd ldr: rdn to chal wl over 1f out: led jst ins fnl f: drew clr ins fnl f: eased towards fin* **11/10**[1]

44- **2** 2 ½ **Little Calla (IRE)**[130] 7810 3-8-12 0 DO'Donohoe 10 59
(E A L Dunlop) *led: hrd pressed and rdn over 1f out: hdd jst ins fnl f: wknd fnl 100yds* **7/2**[3]

00- **3** 1 ¾ **Theologist (IRE)**[217] 6443 3-9-3 0 JimCrowley 2 59+
(Mrs A J Perrett) *wnt lft s: bhd: outpcd and lost tch over 4f out: nudged along over 2f out: swtchd lft over 1f out: kpt on to go 3rd last strides: nvr threatened ldrs* **3/1**[2]

60 **4** *hd* **Crystal B Good (USA)**[19] 1379 3-8-9 0 MarcHalford(3) 4 53
(J R Best) *chsd ldng pair: rdn and outpcd by ldng pair jst over 2f out: plugged on fnl f: lost 3rd last strides* **14/1**

0-0 **5** ¾ **Peak (IRE)**[7] 1638 3-9-3 0 TravisBlock 7 56
(H Morrison) *racd off the pce in midfield: rdn and struggling 4f out: styd on ins fnl f: nvr trbld ldrs* **14/1**

6 1 ¼ **Diamond Dee** 3-8-7 0 GabrielHannon(5) 1 48
(M D I Usher) *wnt lft s: sn outpcd in rr: styd on steadily fr over 1f out: nvr trbld ldrs* **66/1**

00-0 **7** 7 **Risky Lady (IRE)**[14] 1490 3-8-5 35 RyanPowell(7) 6 29
(J Ryan) *stdd s: sn chsd ldrs on outer: rdn and struggling over 2f out: wknd wl over 1f out* **66/1**

0 **8** *nk* **Vigorosa (IRE)**[53] 849 3-8-12 0 PaulDoe 8 28
(P Howling) *stdd and swtchd rt s: a bhd* **20/1**

0- **9** ¾ **Richardlionheart (USA)**[284] 4480 3-9-3 0 SamHitchcott 3 31
(B Gubby) *chsd ldrs: rdn and struggling 3f out: no ch fnl 2f* **50/1**

0 **10** *dist* **Supreme Glimpse**[17] 1419 3-8-12 0 ChrisCatlin 5 —
(Mrs N Smith) *sn hopelessly t.o* **50/1**

1m 22.95s (-0.35) **Going Correction** -0.125s/f (Firm) **10** Ran SP% **119.8**
Speed ratings (Par 99): **97,94,92,91,91 89,81,81,80,—**
CSF £5.18 TOTE £2.10: £1.20, £1.30, £1.40; EX 6.30 Trifecta £12.80 Pool: £623.14 - 35.93 winning units..
Owner Mrs Felicity Ashfield **Bred** Mr And Mrs P Ashfield **Trained** Patching, W Sussex

FOCUS
This second division of the maiden looked the weakest of the pair and the winning time was over a second slower. The form looks muddling and there's a good chance one or two are flattered by their performances.
Theologist(IRE) ◆ Official explanation: jockey said colt was unsuited by the good to firm ground

1839 BET 1% IN RUNNING - BETDAQ H'CAP 7f
4:55 (4:56) (Class 5) (0-70,70) 3-Y-O **£4,857** (£1,445; £722; £360) **Stalls** High

Form RPR

24 **1** **Lighthearted (FR)**[21] 1322 3-8-12 **64** AdamKirby 17 68+
(C G Cox) *in tch: nt clr run and swtchd lft over 1f out: hdwy on outer u.p 1f out: r.o wl to ld on post* **7/2**[1]

30-2 **2** *nse* **Safari Guide**[17] 1423 3-9-4 **70** JimCrowley 3 74
(P Winkworth) *t.k.h: hld up in tch: hdwy to join ldr jst over 2f out: led wl over 1f out: rdn ent fnl f: r.o tl hdd post* **12/1**

40-2 **3** 1 **Fly By Nelly**[8] 1620 3-8-8 **60** RobertHavlin 11 61
(H Morrison) *t.k.h: chsd ldrs: rdn 2f out: hdwy to chse ldng pair jst ins fnl f: kpt on same pce fnl 100yds* **11/2**[2]

20-4 **4** *nse* **Megasecret**[17] 1419 3-9-3 **69** PatDobbs 4 70
(R Hannon) *chsd ldrs tl led over 4f out: hdd wl over 1f out: kpt on u.p fnl f: no ex fnl 100yds* **14/1**

1-01 **5** 1 ½ **Shadow Bay (IRE)**[17] 1424 3-9-4 **70** SamHitchcott 12 67
(Miss Z C Davison) *led tl over 4f out: styd chsng ldrs: drvn over 1f out: one pce fnl f* **12/1**

01- **6** *nk* **Saturn Way (GR)**[213] 6552 3-9-3 **69** LPKeniry 10 65+
(P R Chamings) *t.k.h: hld up in midfield: n.m.r over 1f out: edgd out lft ent fnl f: drvn and styd on ins fnl f: nt rch ldrs* **15/2**[3]

20-3 **7** *nk* **Night Lily (IRE)**[100] 317 3-9-1 **67** LiamJones 13 62
(J Jay) *hld up bhd: switching lft fr wl over 1f out: hdwy on outer ins fnl f: styd on: nt rch ldrs* **8/1**

5-45 **8** 1 **Lady Micklegate (USA)**[17] 1423 3-9-1 **70** MarcHalford(3) 18 63+
(J R Best) *taken down early: t.k.h: hld up in midfield on stands' rail: nt enough room fr 2f out tl swtchd lft ins fnl f: styd on: nvr able to chal* **9/1**

06-1 **9** 1 ¼ **Kings Ace (IRE)**[17] 1437 3-8-7 **59** EdwardCreighton 8 48
(A P Jarvis) *racd freely: pressed ldrs: rdn 2f out: wknd jst over 1f out* **25/1**

1226 **10** ¾ **Imperial Skylight**[44] 960 3-8-10 **67** MCGeran(5) 14 54
(M R Channon) *stdd s: hld up bhd on stands' rail: nt enough room fr 2f out: kpt on ins fnl f: nvr trbld ldrs* **12/1**

31 **11** *shd* **Royal Crest**[58] 810 3-8-13 **65** ShaneKelly 2 52
(J A Osborne) *in tch towards on outer: shkn up jst over 2f out: rdn and no hdwy over 1f out: eased ins fnl f* **12/1**

0-40 **12** 1 ¾ **Sermons Mount (USA)**[10] 1580 3-7-13 **56** oh1 Louis-PhilippeBeuzelin(5) 16 38
(Mouse Hamilton-Fairley) *hld up in midfield: shufled bk and towards rr wl over 1f out: nvr trbld ldrs* **25/1**

-144 **13** 2 **Millway Beach (IRE)**[56] 829 3-9-3 **69** StephenCarson 5 46
(Pat Eddery) *in tch: rdn and unable qck 2f out: wknd over 1f out* **14/1**

-321 **14** 2 ¼ **Kiss A Prince**[56] 826 3-9-4 **70** ChrisCatlin 15 41
(D K Ivory) *hld up towards rr on outer: swtchd lft and bmpd rival 3f out: wknd 2f out:* **10/1**

2400 **15** ¾ **Josiah Bartlett (IRE)**[22] 1311 3-8-6 **58** (t) FrankieMcDonald 7 27
(P S McEntee) *t.k.h: chsd ldrs tl rdn and wknd qckly over 2f out* **50/1**

1165 **16** 9 **Quick Single (USA)**[30] 1180 3-9-4 **70** JerryO'Dwyer 9 15
(P S McEntee) *s.i.s: towards rr: rdn and struggling 1/2-way* **33/1**

0-00 **17** 6 **Thefillyfromepsom**[30] 1183 3-8-5 **57** CatherineGannon 1 —
(P M Phelan) *hld up towards rr on outer: bmpd 3f out: sn struggling* **33/1**

1m 22.19s (-1.11) **Going Correction** -0.125s/f (Firm) **17** Ran SP% **139.2**
Speed ratings (Par 99): **101,100,99,99,98 97,97,96,94,93 93,91,89,86,86 75,68**
toteswinger: 1&2 £16.80, 1&3 £14.40, 2&3 £6.80 CSF £51.50 CT £258.09 TOTE £5.10: £1.60, £4.80, £1.40, £4.20; EX 77.90 Trifecta £383.70 Part won. Pool: £518.59 - 0.10 winning units. Place 6: £45.07 Place 5: £31.16.
Owner H E Sheikh Sultan Bin Khalifa Al Nahyan **Bred** Sheikh Sultan Bin Khalifa Al Nayan **Trained** Lambourn, Berks

FOCUS
A tricky 3yo handicap and unsurprisingly the field came stands' side. The runner-up and fourth were well ridden to come across from their low draws, while the third looks the best guide to the level.
Night Lily(IRE) Official explanation: jockey said filly lost its action 2f out.

T/Plt: £50.60 to a £1 stake. Pool: £41,108.56. 592.02 winning tickets. T/Qpdt: £10.40 to a £1 stake. Pool: £2,473.50. 175.10 winning tickets. SP

[1590]NOTTINGHAM (L-H)
Friday, May 8

OFFICIAL GOING: Good to firm (firm in places) changing to firm (good to firm in places) after race 2 (2.30)
Wind: Fresh against Weather: Cloudy with sunny spells and the odd light shower

1840 TOTEPLACEPOT MEDIAN AUCTION MAIDEN STKS 6f 15y
2:00 (2:03) (Class 5) 3-Y-O **£2,590** (£770; £385; £192) **Stalls** High

Form RPR

4 **1** **Devil You Know (IRE)**[10] 1592 3-9-3 0 RyanMoore 11 78+
(D R C Elsworth) *dwlt: racd keenly: hdwy 4f out: n.m.r 2f out: led 1f out: shkn up and r.o* **1/1**[1]

5- **2** 1 ¼ **Trading Nation (USA)**[286] 4430 3-9-3 0 SteveDrowne 10 74+
(R Charlton) *s.s: hld up: nt clr run 2f out: hdwy over 1f out: r.o: nt rch wnr* **16/1**

3 ½ **Tagseed (IRE)** 3-9-3 0 TPO'Shea 9 72+
(W J Haggas) *chsd ldrs: swtchd lft 2f out: rdn over 1f out: styd on same pce ins fnl f* **4/1**[2]

2-5 **4** 1 ¼ **Doc Jones (IRE)**[14] 1491 3-8-12 0 RichardEvans(5) 7 68
(P D Evans) *chsd ldrs: led over 2f out: rdn and hdd 1f out: no ex* **10/1**[3]

5 1 ½ **Alis Aquilae (IRE)** 3-9-0 0 LeeVickers(3) 8 63+
(T J Etherington) *s.s: sn pushed along in rr: hdwy over 1f out: nt rch ldrs* **80/1**

44- **6** 2 ½ **Rainy Night**[196] 6953 3-9-0 0 RussellKennemore(3) 1 55+
(R Hollinshead) *prom: lost pl over 4f out: styd on fnl f* **40/1**

0-0 **7** *nse* **Brynfa Boy**[6] 1662 3-9-3 0 IanMongan 4 55
(P W D'Arcy) *hld up: hdwy over 2f out: rdn and hung lft over 1f out: styd on same pce* **50/1**

55 **8** 3 ½ **Miss Porky**[16] 1451 3-8-12 0 DarryllHolland 16 39
(R Hollinshead) *sn pushed along in rr: n.d* **20/1**

350- **9** ½ **Peper Harow (IRE)**[218] 6426 3-8-12 65 DaneO'Neill 13 37
(M D I Usher) *prom: rdn over 2f out: wknd over 1f out* **10/1**[3]

00-6 **10** ¾ **Cavitie**[16] 1465 3-9-0 50 JackMitchell(3) 12 40
(Andrew Reid) *chsd ldrs: rdn over 2f out: wknd over 1f out* **66/1**

000- **11** 2 **Davana**[279] 4647 3-8-9 25 KellyHarrison(3) 15 29
(W J H Ratcliffe) *sn pushed along: a in rr* **200/1**

0 **12** *nk* **Bridge Note (USA)**[11] 1563 3-8-12 0 TPQueally 17 28
(J Noseda) *s.i.s: sn prom: rdn: edgd lft and wknd over 1f out* **14/1**

0-4 **13** 1 **Miss Pusey Street**[38] 1045 3-8-12 0 TedDurcan 6 24
(J Gallagher) *prom: lost pl over 4f out: hdwy over 2f out: sn rdn: edgd lft and wknd* **40/1**

500- **14** 2 ¼ **Bold Hawk**[232] 6062 3-9-3 57 FrancisNorton 3 22
(Mrs C A Dunnett) *chsd ldrs: rdn 1/2-way: sn wknd* **100/1**

0-0 **15** 1 **Princess Soraya**[20] 1355 3-8-7 0 WilliamCarson(5) 5 14
(R Dickin) *prom over 3f* **66/1**

00 **16** 17 **Hello Sunshine**[10] 1592 3-9-3 0 J-PGuillambert 2 —
(T J Pitt) *stmbld s: a in rr: wknd 1/2-way* **80/1**

3 **17** 3 ¼ **Island Legend (IRE)**[21] 1317 3-9-3 0 PaulFitzsimons 14 —
(J M Bradley) *mde most over 3f: hmpd and wknd sn after* **20/1**

1m 14.84s (-0.06) **Going Correction** -0.025s/f (Good) **17** Ran SP% **124.0**
Speed ratings (Par 99): **99,97,96,95,93 89,89,84,84,83 80,80,78,75,74 51,47**
toteswinger: 1&2 £5.10, 1&3 £5.60, 2&3 £13.10 CSF £19.11 TOTE £2.10: £1.30, £4.50, £1.60; EX 18.90.
Owner Raymond Tooth **Bred** Joseph Stewart Investments **Trained** Newmarket, Suffolk

FOCUS
The ground had dried up despite rain and watering earlier in the week, probably as a result of the strong headwind. Moderate form amongst those with official ratings but several unexposed sorts headed the market and they dominated the finish. The level looks a bit fluid and could be a little higher.
Bridge Note(USA) Official explanation: jockey said filly was unsuited by the good to firm (firm in places) ground
Hello Sunshine Official explanation: jockey said gelding stumbled leaving stalls

1841 TOTEEXACTA MEDIAN AUCTION MAIDEN FILLIES' STKS 5f 13y
2:30 (2:33) (Class 5) 2-Y-O **£2,590** (£770; £385; £192) **Stalls** High

Form RPR

3 **1** **Habaayib**[22] 1298 2-9-0 0 TPO'Shea 3 80+
(E A L Dunlop) *chsd ldr: shkn up and edgd rt ins fnl f: sn led: hung lft and styd on wl* **1/4**[1]

2 3 ¼ **Fenella Rose** 2-9-0 0 SaleemGolam 2 66
(S C Williams) *hld up: racd keenly: hdwy over 2f out: led over 1f out: rdn and hdd ins fnl f: wknd nr fin* **14/1**[3]

3 1 ¼ **La Fortunata** 2-9-0 0 GregFairley 10 62
(J R Jenkins) *led: rdn and hdd over 1f out: wknd ins fnl f* **50/1**

4 1 ½ **Tartufo Dolce (IRE)** 2-9-0 0 TPQueally 8 57
(J G Given) *wnt lft s: sn pushed along in rr: swtchd lft over 2f out: sn rdn: nt trble ldrs* **10/1**[2]

5 ½ **Monte Mayor One** 2-9-0 0 DaneO'Neill 13 55
(D Haydn Jones) *sn pushed along in rr: n.d* **20/1**

0 **6** *hd* **Pursuit Of Gold**[13] 1511 2-9-0 0 SteveDrowne 15 54
(J R Best) *prom: rdn over 2f out: wknd over 1f out* **20/1**

7 ½ **Let It Rock (IRE)** 2-8-9 0 MartinLane(5) 9 52
(K R Burke) *s.i.s: sn pushed along in rr: rdn over 2f out: n.d* **10/1**[2]

8 2 ¾ **Bookiesindex Girl (IRE)** 2-9-0 0 RichardMullen 5 42
(J R Jenkins) *chsd ldrs tl rdn and wknd over 1f out* **20/1**

9 12 **Micky's Bird** 2-8-9 0 MarkCoumbe(5) 7 —
(R C Guest) *s.i.s and hmpd s: a in rr: wknd over 2f out* **66/1**

63.32 secs (2.32) **Going Correction** -0.025s/f (Good) **9** Ran SP% **122.6**
Speed ratings (Par 90): **80,74,72,70,69 69,68,64,44**
toteswinger: 1&2 £3.20, 1&3 £8.20, 2&3 £25.10 CSF £5.32 TOTE £1.30: £1.02, £3.30, £12.30; EX 6.70.
Owner Hamdan Al Maktoum **Bred** Whitley Stud **Trained** Newmarket, Suffolk

NOTEBOOK
Habaayib had shown plenty of promise on her Newmarket debut and, with two that finished behind her having been successful since, she appeared to have everything in her favour. She travelled well enough but tended to wander when first asked for her effort and, for a brief moment, an upset looked possible. However, once her rider got serious, she pulled away to score decisively. She should be more professional next time, and could be aimed at Royal Ascot. (op 2-5)

Fenella Rose ◆, out of a 6f juvenile winner whose two previous foals also scored at two years old, is certainly bred for the job and moved up looking as if she was going to give the winner a real race. Although she could not sustain her effort in the final furlong, she still showed enough to suggest she can pick up a similar race. (op 16-1 tchd 12-1)
La Fortunata showed good pace on this debut, taking them along until the principals came by. Like the runner-up she can win races if going on from this. (op 40-1 tchd 33-1)
Tartufo Dolce(IRE), a half-sister to a couple of smart juvenile sprinters in Siena Gold and Crazee Mental among others, looked quite green on this debut, missing the break and wandering around under pressure. She should come on a good deal for the experience. (op 17-2 tchd 8-1)
Let It Rock(IRE), another related to several juvenile winners, showed some ability and should do better in time as her stable's juveniles have been needing the outing. (tchd 7-1)

1842 TOTESUPER7 H'CAP — 1m 6f 15y
3:00 (3:00) (Class 5) (0-75,75) 3-Y-O — **£4,857** (£1,445; £722; £360) **Stalls** Low

Form — RPR
40-6 **1** **Darley Sun (IRE)**[16] 1464 3-9-1 **69** .... DarrylHolland 1 77+
(D M Simcock) *hld up: hdwy and hung lft fr over 1f out: rdn to ld wl ins fnl f: sn clr* **16/1**
4-44 **2** *2 ³/₄* **Penang Princess**[18] 1408 3-9-3 **71** .... RyanMoore 5 74
(R M Beckett) *hld up in tch: rdn over 5f out: styng on same pce whn edgd lft and wnt 2nd wl ins fnl f* **9/2**[2]
5203 **3** *1* **Longboat Key**[26] 1231 3-9-5 **73** .... GregFairley 4 75
(M Johnston) *chsd ldrs: rdn over 2f out: led over 1f out: hdd ins fnl f: edgd lft and no ex* **12/1**
-320 **4** *hd* **Strikemaster (IRE)**[44] 953 3-7-9 **56** oh2 .... CharlesEddery(7) 6 58
(J W Hills) *s.s: hld up: hdwy over 2f out: rdn and nt clr run over 1f out: styng on whn hmpd towards fin* **40/1**
0-12 **5** *³/₄* **Ermyn Lodge**[11] 1570 3-8-8 **62** .... TedDurcan 9 63
(P M Phelan) *chsd ldr: pushed along 8f out: reminders 6f out: rdn and ev ch over 1f out: no ex ins fnl f* **11/2**[3]
1-25 **6** *1 ¹/₂* **Canmoss (USA)**[4] 1747 3-8-12 **66** .... FrancisNorton 2 67+
(E J O'Neill) *sn led: rdn over 2f out: hdd over 1f out: no ex fnl f* **7/2**[1]
-124 **7** *1 ³/₄* **Sounds Of Jupiter (IRE)**[18] 1397 3-9-2 **70** .... JamieSpencer 3 66
(D M Simcock) *hld up: hmpd over 5f out: swtchd rt and hdwy over 3f out: sn rdn and edgd lft: wknd and eased ins fnl f* **7/2**[1]
-400 **8** *1 ³/₄* **Tropical Duke (IRE)**[18] 1408 3-8-6 **60** .... TPO'Shea 7 54
(D W P Arbuthnot) *hld up: hdwy over 2f out: sn rdn: edgd lft and wknd fnl f* **100/1**
6-43 **9** *15* **Favours Brave**[23] 1286 3-9-7 **75** .... RichardMullen 10 48
(J H M Gosden) *chsd ldrs: rdn over 2f out: sn wknd* **8/1**
4161 **10** *1 ³/₄* **Good Buy Dubai (USA)**[11] 1570 3-8-9 **63** 6ex .... TPQueally 8 33
(J R Best) *hld up: hdwy over 3f out: rdn and wknd wl over 1f out* **12/1**
0030 **11** *5* **Milemilia (IRE)**[37] 1063 3-8-8 **62** .... SteveDrowne 11 25
(H Morrison) *chsd ldrs: rdn and lost pl over 5f out: wkng whn hung lft wl over 2f out* **40/1**

3m 5.65s (0.65) **Going Correction** -0.025s/f (Good) **11** Ran SP% **116.3**
Speed ratings (Par 99): **97,95,94,94,94 93,92,91,82,81 79**
toteswinger: 1&2 £17.40, 1&3 £25.90, 2&3 £9.90 CSF £85.24 CT £911.61 TOTE £26.50: £5.30, £1.70, £3.70; EX 130.20.
Owner Abdullah Saeed Belhab **Bred** Manfred Hoffer & Ballygrelihan Farm **Trained** Newmarket, Suffolk

FOCUS
The ground was changed to Firm, Good to Firm in places before this race. This ordinary three-year-old handicap presented a number of imponderables, not least the trip. It became something of a war of attrition into the headwind in the straight. The form looks reasonable for the level.
Milemilia(IRE) Official explanation: jockey said filly hung left

1843 TOTESWINGER MAIDEN FILLIES' STKS (DIV I) — 1m 75y
3:35 (3:35) (Class 5) 3-Y-O — **£2,266** (£674; £337; £168) **Stalls** Low

Form — RPR
22- **1** **Say No Now (IRE)**[228] 6166 3-9-0 0 .... TedDurcan 11 83+
(D R Lanigan) *chsd ldr tl led over 2f out: shkn up and clr fnl f: comf* **1/1**[1]
0 **2** *3* **Arabian Pearl (IRE)**[21] 1329 3-9-0 0 .... AdrianMcCarthy 6 73
(P W Chapple-Hyam) *led: rdn and hdd over 2f out: styd on same pce appr fnl f* **12/1**
5 **3** *hd* **Sunceleb (IRE)**[18] 1406 3-9-0 0 .... SteveDrowne 1 73
(H Morrison) *s.i.s: hld up: hdwy over 4f out: rdn over 2f out: wandered over 1f out: styd on* **17/2**
4 *shd* **Olive Green (USA)** 3-9-0 0 .... PaulEddery 4 73+
(Pat Eddery) *hld up: hdwy over 2f out: styd on: nrst fin* **33/1**
5 *6* **I See Nice Sea** 3-9-0 0 .... DaneO'Neill 8 59
(L M Cumani) *hld up: rdn over 2f out: n.d* **8/1**[3]
0- **6** *³/₄* **Charismatic Lady**[288] 4337 3-8-9 0 .... AndreaAtzeni(5) 5 57
(M Botti) *prom: lost pl over 5f out: wknd over 2f out* **33/1**
-0 **7** *1* **Angelica's Art (IRE)**[22] 1302 3-9-0 0 .... JamieSpencer 7 55
(B J Meehan) *chsd ldrs: rdn and wknd 2f out* **12/1**
8 *5* **High Morning** 3-9-0 0 .... DarrylHolland 10 43
(D M Simcock) *hld up: hdwy over 3f out: wknd over 2f out* **9/2**[2]
00-0 **9** *17* **Sharp Discovery**[3] 1772 3-9-0 37 ....(p) PaulFitzsimons 3 4
(J M Bradley) *prom: reminders over 5f out: wknd 3f out* **250/1**

1m 47.08s (1.48) **Going Correction** -0.025s/f (Good) **9** Ran SP% **111.5**
Speed ratings (Par 96): **91,88,87,87,81 80,79,74,57**
toteswinger: 1&2 £4.50, 1&3 £2.80, 2&3 £11.40 CSF £13.79 TOTE £2.00: £1.10, £3.30, £2.60; EX 12.70.
Owner Saif Ali & Saeed H Altayer **Bred** Limetree Stud Ltd **Trained** Newmarket, Suffolk

FOCUS
A couple of well-bred newcomers but the first division of this maiden looked to provide the favourite a good opportunity to get off the mark and she duly took it without any fuss. She did not need to run to her best and the third is the best guide to the form.
High Morning Official explanation: jockey said filly was unsuited by the firm, (good to firm places) ground

1844 TOTESWINGER MAIDEN FILLIES' STKS (DIV II) — 1m 75y
4:10 (4:12) (Class 5) 3-Y-O — **£2,266** (£674; £337; £168) **Stalls** Low

Form — RPR
60 **1** **Queen Martha (USA)**[18] 1406 3-9-0 0 .... SteveDrowne 9 74
(M A Magnusson) *led 7f out: rdn and hdd over 1f out: rallied to ld ins fnl f: jst hld on* **14/1**[3]
2 *hd* **Kinetix** 3-9-0 0 .... RichardMullen 1 73+
(J H M Gosden) *s.i.s: hld up: hdwy over 2f out: swtchd rt and r.o wl ins fnl f* **14/1**[3]
3 **3** *1* **Barynya**[21] 1327 3-9-0 0 .... RyanMoore 11 71
(Sir Michael Stoute) *hld up: hdwy over 3f out: led over 1f out: rdn and hdd ins fnl f: unable qck* **1/4**[1]
0- **4** *2 ¹/₄* **Penzena**[219] 6392 3-9-0 0 .... TPQueally 5 66
(W J Knight) *chsd ldrs: rdn and ev ch over 2f out: styd on same pce fnl f* **12/1**[2]
0 **5** *1 ³/₄* **Soho Secrets**[114] 160 3-9-0 0 .... GregFairley 3 62
(M Johnston) *prom: outpcd 3f out: r.o ins fnl f* **33/1**
6 *¹/₂* **Rockabout (IRE)** 3-9-0 0 .... JamieSpencer 6 61+
(B J Meehan) *s.i.s: hld up: hdwy over 2f out: edgd lft and styd on same pce appr fnl f* **14/1**[3]
00- **7** *hd* **Aine's Delight (IRE)**[228] 6166 3-9-0 0 .... PaulEddery 2 60
(Andrew Turnell) *led 1f: chsd wnr: rdn over 2f out: styd on same pce appr fnl f* **150/1**
8 *1 ¹/₄* **Barter** 3-9-0 0 .... DaneO'Neill 8 57+
(L M Cumani) *mid-div: effrt over 2f out: nt trble ldrs* **12/1**[2]
9 *2 ¹/₂* **Course De Diamante (IRE)** 3-9-0 0 .... TedDurcan 7 52
(D R Lanigan) *s.i.s: hld up: n.d* **50/1**
00- **10** *11* **Ela Gorrie Mou**[217] 6438 3-9-0 0 .... DarrylHolland 10 26
(T T Clement) *hld up: hdwy 5f out: wknd over 2f out* **150/1**
0 **11** *2 ¹/₂* **Court Wing (IRE)**[30] 1185 3-8-7 0 .... MatthewDavies(7) 4 21
(George Baker) *mid-div: wknd 3f out* **150/1**

1m 47.69s (2.09) **Going Correction** -0.025s/f (Good) **11** Ran SP% **122.3**
Speed ratings (Par 96): **88,87,86,84,82 82,82,80,78,67 64**
toteswinger: 1&2 £10.50, 1&3 £3.60, 2&3 £3.40 CSF £193.57 TOTE £18.90: £3.10, £4.20, £1.02; EX 281.00.
Owner Eastwind Racing Ltd and Martha Trussell **Bred** Albert P Coppola Et Al **Trained** Upper Lambourn, Berks

FOCUS
This second division was run in a squall although that had no bearing on the surprise result, and the time was 0.61secs slower than the first leg. The form is rated around the beaten favourite to her debut form.

1845 BET TOTEPOOL AT TOTESPORT.COM H'CAP — 1m 2f 50y
4:45 (4:45) (Class 5) (0-75,72) 4-Y-O+ — **£3,885** (£1,156; £577; £288) **Stalls** Low

Form — RPR
216- **1** **Dream Of Olwyn (IRE)**[184] 7202 4-8-13 **67** .... TPQueally 11 75
(J G Given) *hld up: hdwy over 3f out: rdn over 1f out: r.o u.p to ld ins fnl f: edgd rt towards fin* **9/2**[3]
651- **2** *³/₄* **Miss Pelling (IRE)**[217] 6437 4-8-12 **66** .... JamieSpencer 1 72
(B J Meehan) *led: hdd over 6f out: chsd ldr tl rdn to ld 2f out: sn hung lft: hdd and unable qck ins fnl f* **11/4**[1]
2050 **3** *nk* **General Tufto**[9] 1612 4-8-6 **67** ....(b) RichardRowe(7) 3 72
(C Smith) *hld up: hdwy over 2f out: rdn and hung lft over 1f out: r.o* **33/1**
-120 **4** *¹/₂* **Templetuohy Max (IRE)**[70] 713 4-9-1 **69** ....(v) DarrylHolland 5 73
(J D Bethell) *chsd ldr tl led over 6f out: rdn and hdd 2f out: ev ch ins fnl f: no ex towards fin* **9/1**
0-00 **5** *2* **Dragon Slayer (IRE)**[25] 1261 7-8-10 **64** .... J-PGuillambert 2 64
(John A Harris) *plld hrd and prom: rdn over 3f out: styd on same pce fnl f* **6/1**
00-0 **6** *nk* **Gallego**[10] 1581 7-8-13 **67** .... SaleemGolam 10 67
(R J Price) *stdd s: hld up and bhd: rdn over 1f out: nvr nr to chal* **14/1**
103- **7** *1 ³/₄* **Animator**[219] 6400 4-9-3 **71** .... RyanMoore 8 67
(C Grant) *hld up: rdn over 3f out: n.d* **7/1**
443- **8** *15* **Highland Love**[184] 7202 4-9-0 **68** .... IanMongan 6 34
(J T Stimpson) *chsd ldrs tl wknd over 2f out* **4/1**[2]

2m 10.62s (-1.08) **Going Correction** -0.025s/f (Good) **8** Ran SP% **111.2**
Speed ratings (Par 103): **103,102,102,101,100 99,98,86**
toteswingers: 1&2 £4.60, 1&3 £17.70, 2&3 £7.80 CSF £16.30 CT £342.69 TOTE £6.20: £1.80, £1.60, £5.40; EX 23.50.
Owner Alex Owen **Bred** Crandon Park Stud **Trained** Willoughton, Lincs

FOCUS
An ordinary handicap that produced a good battle up the straight. The form is ordinary and there is a doubt about its solidity.
Highland Love Official explanation: jockey said gelding was unsuited by the firm (good to firm places) ground

1846 BET TOTEPOOL ON 0800 221 221 APPRENTICE H'CAP — 6f 15y
5:20 (5:21) (Class 6) (0-60,60) 4-Y-O+ — **£2,047** (£604; £302) **Stalls** High

Form — RPR
02-0 **1** **Misplaced Fortune**[25] 1244 4-9-0 **58** ....(v[1]) LeeNewnes(3) 2 68
(N Tinkler) *hld up: hdwy over 2f out: rdn to ld over 1f out: edgd rt: r.o* **28/1**
6250 **2** *1 ¹/₂* **Bateleur**[11] 1558 5-8-8 **52** .... MatthewDavies(3) 1 58+
(M R Channon) *s.i.s: hld up: nt clr run over 2f out: hdwy and swtchd rt over 1f out: sn rdn: styd on* **10/1**
5-13 **3** *³/₄* **Many Welcomes**[72] 675 4-8-9 **53** .... BillyCray(3) 9 56
(B P J Baugh) *dwlt: outpcd: hdwy over 1f out: sn rdn: no ex nr fin* **8/1**[3]
0-00 **4** *2 ¹/₄* **Colombard (IRE)**[23] 1285 4-8-10 **54** ....(v[1]) MartinLane(3) 4 50
(Patrick Morris) *chsd ldrs: rdn 1/2-way: hung rt over 1f out: one pce* **66/1**
4000 **5** *2 ¹/₂* **Replicator**[57] 818 4-8-12 **58** .... TobyAtkinson(5) 8 46
(Pat Eddery) *mid-div: hdwy 2f out: sn rdn and hung rt: no ex fnl f* **9/1**
06-0 **6** *nk* **Avoncreek**[11] 1558 5-8-6 **52** .... SoniaEaton(5) 11 39
(B P J Baugh) *sn pushed along in rr: styd on fnl f: nvr trbld ldrs* **28/1**
0-00 **7** *nk* **Party In The Park**[80] 580 4-9-0 **60** .... MJMurphy(5) 5 50+
(Miss J A Camacho) *chsd ldrs: rdn over 2f out: nt clr run over 1f out: sn wknd* **25/1**
2004 **8** *1 ¹/₄* **Davids Mark**[17] 1421 9-8-9 **55** .... DannyBrock(5) 14 37
(J R Jenkins) *sn pushed along in rr: hmpd over 3f out: hdwy over 1f out: wknd fnl f* **7/1**[2]
-620 **9** *1* **Sion Hill (IRE)**[83] 554 8-8-6 **52** ....(p) NSLawes(5) 17 31
(John A Harris) *mid-div: outpcd over 3f out: styd on ins fnl f* **16/1**
0050 **10** *¹/₂* **Gower**[2] 1787 5-8-10 **54** .... SophieDoyle(3) 16 31
(R J Price) *mid-div: rdn 1/2-way: n.d* **12/1**
16 **11** *1* **Great Knight (IRE)**[58] 811 4-8-13 **59** .... MatthewBirch(5) 10 33
(S Kirk) *mid-div: rdn 1/2-way: sn edgd rt and wknd* **8/1**[3]
2062 **12** *nk* **Loose Caboose (IRE)**[11] 1558 4-8-7 **51** ....(v) AmyRyan(3) 6 24
(A J McCabe) *w ldr over 2f: sn rdn: hung rt and wknd over 1f out* **3/1**[1]
4003 **13** *1 ¹/₄* **Realt Na Mara (IRE)**[15] 1477 6-9-0 **60** ....(b[1]) RyanClark(5) 7 29
(H Morrison) *led: rdn: hung rt and hdd over 1f out: sn wknd* **10/1**
2-00 **14** *11* **Little Eden (IRE)**[20] 1360 4-8-13 **54** .... DeanHeslop 13 —
(T D Barron) *mid-div: wknd over 2f out* **9/1**

1m 16.4s (1.50) **Going Correction** -0.025s/f (Good) **14** Ran SP% **123.7**
Speed ratings (Par 101): **89,87,86,83,79 79,78,77,75,75 73,73,71,57**
toteswingers: 1&2 £30.90, 1&3 £28.30, 2&3 £13.60 CSF £287.40 CT £2541.89 TOTE £26.30: £7.00, £2.90, £3.20; EX 294.30 Place 6: £13.85 Place 5: £10.46.
Owner W F Burton **Bred** Adrian Smith **Trained** Langton, N Yorks

FOCUS
A moderate apprentice sprint but the picture changed dramatically in the closing stages. The principals came from off the pace and the form is modest with the placed horses to form.
Great Knight(IRE) Official explanation: vet said gelding lost a front shoe

Little Eden(IRE) Official explanation: jockey said gelding never travelled
T/Plt: £8.50 to a £1 stake. Pool: £36,949.53. 3,141.74 winning tickets. T/Qpdt: £5.30 to a £1 stake. Pool: £2,410.10. 332.50 winning tickets. CR

[1517] RIPON (R-H)
Friday, May 8

OFFICIAL GOING: Good to firm (good in places; 8.7)
Wind: Light, half behind

1847 SIS MAIDEN AUCTION STKS — 5f
5:50 (5:51) (Class 5) 2-Y-O — **£3,238** (£963; £481; £240) **Stalls** Low

Form — RPR

1 **Novay Essjay (IRE)** 2-8-8 .... PatrickDonaghy(5) 4 — 72+
(P C Haslam) *in tch: hdwy 2f out: rdn over 1f out: styd on strly ins fnl f to ld nr fin* **16/1**

2 *shd* **Pepper Lane** 2-8-9 .... PhillipMakin 7 — 68
(T D Barron) *trckd ldrs: effrt 2f out and sn rdn: drvn and styd to chal ins fnl f: ev ch tl no ex nr fin* **10/3[3]**

6 3 *hd* **Pinnacle Lad (IRE)**[10] 1577 2-8-9 .... TolleyDean 3 — 67
(J L Spearing) *led: rdn wl over 1f out: drvn and hdd ins fnl f: hdd and no ex towards fin* **9/4[1]**

4 *5* **Refuse To Wait (IRE)** 2-8-7 .... DavidAllan 6 — 47+
(T D Easterby) *sn outpcd and rdn along in rr: hdwy 2f out: kpt on u.p fnl f* **12/1**

5 *1½* **Sacred Star (IRE)** 2-8-5 .... TWilliams 9 — 40
(M Brittain) *cl up: rdn along 2f out: drvn and wknd appr fnl f* **16/1**

0 6 *hd* **Bring Sweets (IRE)**[8] 1623 2-8-10 .... PJMcDonald 8 — 44
(B Ellison) *sn outpcd and a towards rr* **33/1**

7 *nk* **Ingleby Spirit** 2-8-12 .... FrederikTylicki(5) 1 — 50
(R A Fahey) *a in rr* **11/4[2]**

6 8 *shd* **Miccolo**[35] 1097 2-8-9 .... JamieMoriarty 5 — 41
(P T Midgley) *prom: rdn along 1/2-way: wknd fnl 2f* **20/1**

9 *8* **Sir Christie** 2-8-13 .... RoystonFfrench 2 — 17
(N Tinkler) *a in rr* **12/1**

60.36 secs (-0.34) **Going Correction** -0.175s/f (Firm) — **9 Ran SP% 115.4**
Speed ratings (Par 93): **95,94,94,86,84 83,83,83,70**
toteswinger: 1&2 £9.90, 1&3 £7.20, 2&3 £1.20 CSF £68.88 TOTE £23.30: £3.70, £2.10, £1.10; EX 83.50.
Owner Middleham Park Racing XXXI **Bred** Camogue Stud Ltd **Trained** Middleham Moor, N Yorks

FOCUS
An ordinary juvenile maiden, but the race should produce some winners.

NOTEBOOK
Novay Essjay(IRE), a £12,000 purchase, has a bit of size about him and made a pleasing introduction. He came under pressure at about halfway, but responded well when switched out widest of all and produced a sustained challenge. He should get 6f without a bother and ought to progress. (op 25-1)
Pepper Lane ◆, a £15,000 daughter of Exceed And Excel, did not enjoy the clearest of runs through until about a furlong out, but she was in the clear for long enough if good enough. She only just missed out and is clearly well up to winning a race like this. (op 5-2)
Pinnacle Lad(IRE), well behind a potentially decent type on his debut at Bath, improved on that form with a highly creditable effort in defeat. He was harassed up front for much of the way by Sacred Star, who ultimately dropped away, and it's to his credit he kept on to finish so close. (tchd 2-1 and 5-2)
Refuse To Wait(IRE) ◆, a 13,000 euros buy, missed the break and was outpaced for most of the way, but she was going on nicely at the finish. This should have taught her plenty and she'll be of interest when stepped up to 6f. (op 11-1 tchd 10-1)
Sacred Star(IRE), who cost only 6,500 euros, showed good early speed but did not see her race out. (op 33-1)
Bring Sweets(IRE) improved on his debut performance and might be one for nurseries in due course. (op 28-1)
Ingleby Spirit ◆, a 25,000gns half-brother to 1m3f winner Norman The Great, only seemed to get the idea when the race was as good as over, but he did keep on. There should be much better to come, especially when he steps up in trip. (op 3-1 tchd 7-2)

1848 SIS DISPLAY MANAGEMENT SOLUTIONS (S) STKS — 1m 1f 170y
6:20 (6:20) (Class 6) 3-4-Y-O — **£2,590** (£770; £385; £192) **Stalls** High

Form — RPR

500- 1 **Joinedupwriting**[198] 6905 4-9-10 56 .... TonyHamilton 5 — 63
(R M Whitaker) *trckd ldrs: hdwy 3f out: rdn to ld over 1f out: drvn ins fnl f: hld on gamely* **5/1**

2002 2 *nk* **Dark Oasis**[5] 1691 3-8-9 60 .... (p) JamieMoriarty 1 — 61
(K A Ryan) *hld up towards rr: hdwy over 3f out: rdn over 1f out: drvn to chal ins fnl f and ev ch tl no ex nr fin* **7/2[2]**

0-00 3 *2¾* **Rose Of Coma (IRE)**[8] 1620 3-8-1 54 .... KellyHarrison(3) 7 — 51
(Miss Gay Kelleway) *hld up in rr: hdwy over 4f out: effrt on outer over 2f out: sn rdn and kpt on u.p fnl f: nrst fin* **16/1**

23-5 4 *nk* **Musashi (IRE)**[120] 90 4-9-10 68 .... PJMcDonald 8 — 56
(T P Tate) *prom: led 4f out: rdn along over 2f out: hdd over 1f out: sn drvn and wknd ins fnl f* **9/4[1]**

-020 5 *3* **Rannoch Rose (IRE)**[63] 779 3-8-4 50 .... TWilliams 4 — 44
(J L Spearing) *chsd ldrs: hdwy 3f out: rdn wl over 1f out: drvn and wknd ent fnl f* **9/1**

-002 6 *1¾* **Whaston (IRE)**[13] 1520 4-9-10 56 .... (v) DavidAllan 14 — 47
(J D Bethell) *hld up towards rr: hdwy on inner over 3f out: rdn along 2f out: sn no imp* **9/2[3]**

0 7 *2¼* **Bestowed**[18] 1407 4-9-5 0 .... FrederikTylicki(5) 11 — 42
(M C Chapman) *chsd ldrs: rdn along over 3f out: sn wknd* **66/1**

05-0 8 *18* **Desdamona (IRE)**[5] 1691 3-8-4 0 .... DuranFentiman 6 — —
(A Berry) *a in rr: hung lft and wd bnd over 5f out: bhd after* **33/1**

3/04 9 *¾* **Regal Tradition (IRE)**[13] 1523 4-9-5 60 .... PatrickDonaghy(5) 9 — 5
(G J Smith) *chsd ldrs: rdn along over 4f out: sn wknd* **18/1**

0000 10 *5* **So Sublime**[17] 1438 4-9-7 35 .... (bt) LeeVickers(3) 12 — —
(M C Chapman) *led: rdn along and hdd 4f out: sn wknd* **28/1**

4600 11 *4½* **Miss Understanding**[13] 1520 4-9-5 41 .... PhillipMakin 2 — —
(J R Weymes) *a in rr* **28/1**

3600 12 *9* **Meg Jicaro**[7] 1652 3-8-4 43 .... RoystonFfrench 3 — —
(Mrs L Williamson) *a bhd* **33/1**

2m 6.23s (0.83) **Going Correction** -0.025s/f (Good)
WFA 3 from 4yo 15lb — **12 Ran SP% 123.3**
Speed ratings (Par 101): **95,94,92,92,89 88,86,72,71,67 64,56**
toteswinger: 1&2 £3.90, 1&3 not won, 2&3 £27.80 CSF £22.83 TOTE £7.60: £2.60, £1.70, £2.70; EX 46.60.There was no bid for the winner. Dark Oasis was claimed by M C Chapman for £6,000.
Owner R C Dollar **Bred** Ink Pot Partnership **Trained** Scarcroft, W Yorks

FOCUS
A standard seller run at what looked a decent gallop. The form reads sound enough.

Regal Tradition(IRE) Official explanation: jockey said gelding hung badly right throughout
Meg Jicaro Official explanation: jockey said filly failed to handle the bend

1849 SIS PICTURE SERVICES H'CAP — 6f
6:55 (6:56) (Class 4) (0-85,85) 4-Y-O+ — **£6,476** (£1,927; £963; £481) **Stalls** Low

Form — RPR

0015 1 **Excusez Moi (USA)**[11] 1560 7-9-4 85 .... (p) PJMcDonald 11 — 97
(Mrs R A Carr) *hld up towards rr: hdwy on outer 2f out: rdn and qcknd to ld ins fnl f: edgd lft and styd on strly* **14/1**

0-14 2 *1½* **High Curragh**[6] 1663 6-8-13 80 .... (p) RoystonFfrench 4 — 88
(K A Ryan) *led: rdn along 2f out: drvn over 1f out: edgd rt and hdd ins fnl f: kpt on same pce* **6/1**

03-2 3 *hd* **Solar Spirit (IRE)**[6] 1663 4-8-13 80 .... GrahamGibbons 9 — 87
(J J Quinn) *trckd ldrs: pushed along and hdwy 2f out: swtchd rt and rdn over 1f out: sn ev ch: drvn and nt qckn whn n.m.r wl ins fnl f* **11/2[3]**

0-02 4 *4* **Sunrise Safari (IRE)**[11] 1560 6-8-13 85 .... (v) FrederikTylicki(5) 2 — 79+
(R A Fahey) *sn in rr: rdn along and outpcd 1/2-way: hdwy u.p 2f out: styd on strly ins fnl f: nrst fin* **11/4[1]**

3130 5 *shd* **Blue Tomato**[26] 1227 8-8-6 78 .... WilliamCarson(5) 8 — 72
(D Nicholls) *hld up: hdwy over 3f out: rdn to chse ldrs over 1f out: sn no imp* **14/1**

00-0 6 *shd* **Dazzling Bay**[22] 1309 9-8-8 75 .... (b) JohnEgan 5 — 69
(T D Easterby) *dwlt and towards rr: hdwy 1/2-way: swtchd rt and rdn over 1f out: styd on ins fnl f* **33/1**

0-14 7 *2½* **Malcheek (IRE)**[20] 1365 7-8-13 80 .... DavidAllan 6 — 66
(T D Easterby) *in tch: pushed along 1/2-way: rdn 2f out and no hdwy* **8/1**

0-43 8 *¾* **Indian Trail**[16] 1457 9-8-12 82 .... (v) AhmedAjtebi(3) 13 — 65
(D Nicholls) *prom: effrt and cl up 1/2-way: rdn 2f out and ev ch tl drvn and wknd appr fnl f* **7/2[2]**

00-0 9 *½* **Stevie Gee (IRE)**[16] 1467 5-9-2 83 .... RobertWinston 10 — 65
(G A Swinbank) *prom: rdn along 2over 2f out: drvn and hld whn n.m.r over 1f out: wknd* **14/1**

004- 10 *½* **Steel Blue**[187] 7152 9-8-1 71 oh2 .... KellyHarrison(3) 1 — 51
(R M Whitaker) *chsd ldrs on inner: rdn along 1/2-way: sn wknd* **50/1**

4-00 11 *hd* **Baldemar**[23] 1278 4-9-4 85 .... AndrewElliott 12 — 64
(K R Burke) *midfield: hdwy on outer to chse ldrs 1/2-way: sn rdn and wknd over 2f out* **20/1**

00-0 12 *¾* **Hotham**[23] 1278 6-9-2 83 .... JamieMoriarty 3 — 60
(N Wilson) *a towards rr* **40/1**

430- 13 *½* **Grazeon Gold Blend**[185] 7175 6-8-13 80 .... PhillipMakin 7 — 55
(J J Quinn) *dwlt: a in rr* **25/1**

1m 11.06s (-1.94) **Going Correction** -0.175s/f (Firm) — **13 Ran SP% 125.6**
Speed ratings (Par 105): **105,103,102,97,97 97,93,92,92,91 91,90,89**
toteswinger: 1&2 not won, 1&3 £27.80, 2&3 £8.50 CSF £95.95 CT £552.35 TOTE £15.10: £4.00, £3.10, £2.70; EX 214.30.
Owner S B Clark **Bred** Lyons Demesne **Trained** Huby, N Yorks
■ Stewards' Enquiry : Ahmed Ajtebi one-day ban: careless riding (May 22)
P J McDonald one-day ban: careless riding (May 22)
Graham Gibbons caution: careless riding.

FOCUS
This looked a decent sprint handicap for the grade, although a couple of the more likely types disappointed. The main action took place away from the stands' rail and, just like in the earlier race on the straight track, a low draw did not provide the advantage anticipated by many before racing. The runner-up looks the best guide to the level.

1850 SIS OB SERVICES H'CAP — 1m 1f 170y
7:25 (7:25) (Class 3) (0-90,90) 4-Y-O+ — **£9,714** (£2,890; £1,444; £721) **Stalls** High

Form — RPR

0-22 1 **Granston (IRE)**[20] 1347 8-8-11 83 .... RobertWinston 2 — 91
(J D Bethell) *trckd ldr: cl up 1/2-way: led over 3f out: rdn along 2f out: drvn ent fnl f: styd on gamely* **7/2[2]**

0-36 2 *¾* **Just Lille (IRE)**[9] 1613 6-9-0 86 .... (p) TPQueally 4 — 93
(Mrs A Duffield) *hld up in rr: hdwy over 2f out: swtchd outside and rdn wl over 1f out: styd on ent fnl f: sn drvn to chal and ev ch tl no ex last 50yds* **8/1**

3 *¾* **Rangefinder**[265] 5-8-10 82 .... DaneO'Neill 5 — 87
(L M Cumani) *trckd ldrs: hdwy over 3f out: effrt and n.m.r over 2f out: swtchd lft and rdn over 1f out: drvn and kpt on ins fnl f* **5/2[1]**

660- 4 *2¼* **Snoqualmie Boy**[300] 3974 6-9-4 90 .... JohnEgan 1 — 91
(T P Tate) *trckd ldrs: hdwy 3f out: chal over 2f out: sn rdn and ev ch tl drvn and wknd appr fnl f* **5/1[3]**

0-31 5 *1½* **Demolition**[15] 1473 5-9-2 88 .... (p) LeeEnstone 6 — 86
(N Wilson) *t.k.h: trckd ldrs on inner: hdwy 3f out: rdn over 2f out: drvn and wknd appr fnl f: n.m.r towards fin* **10/1**

6463 6 *1¼* **Veiled Applause**[6] 1660 6-8-11 83 .... GrahamGibbons 3 — 78
(J J Quinn) *hld up in tch: hdwy over 3f out: rdn along over 2f out and sn btn* **11/2**

412- 7 *¾* **Shaloo Diamond**[196] 6949 4-8-6 81 .... MichaelJStainton(3) 7 — 75
(R M Whitaker) *led: rdn along and jnd 4f out: hdd over 3f out: sn drvn and grad wknd* **14/1**

20-0 8 *3¾* **Magic Echo**[20] 1347 5-8-13 85 .... PhillipMakin 8 — 71
(M Dods) *rrd s: reluctant and lost 10 l: hdwy 1/2-way: rdn along 3f out and sn wknd* **14/1**

2m 6.19s (0.79) **Going Correction** -0.025s/f (Good) — **8 Ran SP% 116.4**
Speed ratings (Par 107): **95,94,93,92,90 89,89,86**
toteswinger: 1&2 £5.80, 1&3 £1.70, 2&3 £10.50 CSF £32.01 CT £81.82 TOTE £4.40: £1.70, £2.20, £1.20; EX 31.00.
Owner The Four Players Partnership **Bred** Yeomanstown Stud **Trained** Middleham Moor, N Yorks
■ Stewards' Enquiry : John Egan two-day ban: careless riding (May 22-23)

FOCUS
The bare form looks ordinary for the level, and it has been rated through the runner-up back to his best.

NOTEBOOK
Granston(IRE) has been in good order since reappearing and held a few of these on his recent Doncaster efforts. Given a good, positive ride, he ran on gamely for pressure and earned this success. However, a rise in the weights might just be enough to stop him following up. (op 10-3 tchd 3-1)
Just Lille(IRE), in contrast to the winner was held up, but she was produced with a sustained challenge towards the outside in the straight and had her chance. She finished well and this was an improvement on her recent Pontefract effort. (op 15-2)
Rangefinder ◆, a multiple winner in Italy who was having his first start for Luca Cumani after 265 days off, lacked the required speed when produced with his challenge in the straight, but he kept on gradually. He can be expected to improve considerably on this form in time, particularly on easier ground, and he may also stay 1m4f. (tchd 3-1)

Snoqualmie Boy looked the likeliest winner when produced with his chance in the straight, but he didn't see his race out and almost certainly needed this after 300 days on the sidelines. This was his first start for Tom Tate and he ought to be capable of better when his new yard hits a bit of form. (op 9-1 tchd 10-1)
Demolition was not up to defying a 6lb rise for his recent 1m4f Beverley success, with the drop in trip probably not in his favour. Official explanation: jockey said gelding was denied a clear run in straight and suffered interference final furlong (op 17-2 tchd 7-1)
Veiled Applause, a previous course-and-distance winner, came into this in fair form and could have been expected to fare better. (op 5-1 tchd 6-1)
Magic Echo Official explanation: jockey said mare jumped awkwardly and missed the break

1851 SIS DATA SERVICES H'CAP — 2m
8:00 (8:01) (Class 5) (0-70,70) 4-Y-0+ **£3,238** (£963; £481; £240) **Stalls** Low

Form				RPR
0-20	**1**		**Danzatrice**[26] 1230 7-9-2 **67** ... FrederikTylicki(5) 2 (C W Thornton) *hld up in rr: smooth hdwy 4f out: sn swtchd outside and effrt on bit to trck ldr over 2f out: shkn up to ld ent fnl f: rdn and kpt on towards fin* **4/1**[2]	76
023-	**2**	½	**Unawatuna**[200] 6861 4-8-2 **54** ... KellyHarrison(3) 8 (Mrs K Walton) *hld up in rr: gd hdwy to trck ldng pair 5f out: effrt to ld wl over 2f out and sn rdn: drvn and hdd ent fnl f: rallied u.p and ev ch tl no ex towards fin* **7/1**	62
6434	**3**	16	**Dramatic Solo**[31] 1171 4-9-2 **65** ... (b) AndrewElliott 4 (K R Burke) *trckd ldr: effrt to dispute ldr 3f out and sn rdn: drvn 2f out and sn one pce* **6/1**[3]	54
000-	**4**	4 ½	**Mceldowney**[16] 6838 7-8-12 **61** ... (b) LeeVickers(3) 5 (M C Chapman) *chsd ldrs: rdn along 4f out: drvn and plugged on same pce fr over 2f out* **40/1**	45
6652	**5**	1 ¼	**Lucky Dancer**[9] 1609 4-8-6 **55** ... JohnEgan 6 (D R C Elsworth) *led: rdn along and jnd 3f out: sn hdd and drvn: wknd 2f out* **5/4**[1]	37
600-	**6**	24	**Toboggan Lady**[230] 6115 5-8-10 **56** ... PhillipMakin 7 (Mrs A Duffield) *t.k.h: hld up towards rr: effrt 5f out: sn rdn and nvr a factor* **8/1**	10
006-	**7**	2 ¾	**Fossgate**[191] 7078 8-9-1 **61** ... GrahamGibbons 10 (J D Bethell) *chsd ldrs: rdn along over 4f out: sn wknd and bhd* **10/1**	11
00-	**8**	65	**Revolving World (IRE)**[291] 4261 6-8-5 **51** oh6 ... (t) TWilliams 9 (L R James) *dwlt: sn chsng ldng pair: rdn along over 5f out and sn wknd* **50/1**	—

3m 29.89s (-1.91) **Going Correction** -0.025s/f (Good)
WFA 4 from 5yo+ 3lb — **8** Ran SP% **115.8**
Speed ratings (Par 103): **103,102,94,92,91 79,78,46**
toteswinger: 1&2 £10.60, 1&3 £2.90, 2&3 £10.10 CSF £32.36 CT £166.56 TOTE £5.50: £1.70, £2.00, £2.10; EX 32.40.
Owner 980 Racing **Bred** G G A Gregson **Trained** Middleham Moor, N Yorks

FOCUS
An ordinary staying handicap in which the leaders looked to go off too fast. That suited the winner, who was given a good ride and has been rated as posting a personal best in victory.
Fossgate Official explanation: jockey said gelding had no more to give
Revolving World(IRE) Official explanation: jockey said gelding had no more to give; trainer said gelding finished diressed and was found to have an irregular heartbeat.

1852 SIS LIVE MAIDEN STKS — 6f
8:30 (8:30) (Class 5) 3-Y-O **£3,238** (£963; £481; £240) **Stalls** Low

Form				RPR
023-	**1**		**Midnight Fantasy**[199] 6885 3-8-12 70 ... SaleemGolam 2 (Rae Guest) *prom: effrt 2f out: rdn to ld over 1f out: drvn out* **15/2**[3]	74
6	**2**	3 ¼	**Reject**[18] 1400 3-9-3 0 ... KirstyMilczarek 7 (W J Haggas) *bmpd s: sn trcking ldrs: hdwy 1/2-way: rdn over 1f out: sn edgd lft and kpt on same pce* **9/4**[2]	69
0-2	**3**	3 ¼	**Diamond Blade**[11] 1563 3-9-3 0 ... DavidAllan 1 (T D Easterby) *led 2f: cl up tl led again 2f out: sn rdn and hdd over 1f out: kpt on same pce* **14/1**	58
60	**4**	1	**Cry Of Truth (IRE)**[6] 1683 3-8-12 0 ... TonyHamilton 3 (D W Barker) *dwlt: hdwy 1/2-way: rdn to chse ldrs 2f out: sn drvn and no imp appr fnl f* **66/1**	50
	5	13	**Monsieur Harvey** 3-9-3 0 ... RoystonFfrench 5 (B Smart) *sn outpcd and alway bhd* **28/1**	13
	6	nk	**Choree (IRE)** 3-8-12 0 ... DuranFentiman 8 (T D Easterby) *racd wd: chsd ldrs: rdn along 1/2-way and sn wknd* **66/1**	7
66-2	**7**	shd	**Alpha Tauri (USA)**[25] 1250 3-9-3 76 ... TPQueally 4 (H R A Cecil) *cl up: led after 2f: rdn and hdd 2f out: sn btn and eased over 1f out* **8/13**[1]	12+
00-0	**8**	2 ½	**Pennine Rose**[16] 1455 3-8-12 40 ... PhillipMakin 6 (A Berry) *wnt rt s: a in rr* **150/1**	—

1m 12.05s (-0.95) **Going Correction** -0.175s/f (Firm) — **8** Ran SP% **118.2**
Speed ratings (Par 99): **99,94,90,89,71 71,71,67**
toteswinger: 1&2 £3.00, 1&3 £13.60, 2&3 £6.30 CSF £25.59 TOTE £8.00: £3.10, £2.00, £4.70; EX 26.10 Place 6: £99.08, Place 5: £57.90.
Owner C J Mills **Bred** C J Mills **Trained** Newmarket, Suffolk

FOCUS
An ordinary sprint maiden but the form still looks fair rated around the third to his Southwell effort.
Alpha Tauri(USA) Official explanation: vet said colt returned lame near-hind
T/Plt: £116.80 to a £1 stake. Pool: £46,908.31. 293.06 winning tickets. T/Qpdt: £17.00 to a £1 stake. Pool: £4,245.12. 184.40 winning tickets. JR

1853 - 1857a (Foreign Racing) - See Raceform Interactive

1596 CHANTILLY (R-H)
Friday, May 8

OFFICIAL GOING: Good to soft

1858a PRIX DE GUICHE (GROUP 3) (COLTS) — 1m 1f
2:25 (2:31) 3-Y-O **£38,835** (£15,534; £11,650; £7,767; £3,883)

			RPR
1		**Calvados Blues (FR)**[33] 1145 3-9-2 ... GMosse 6 (P Demercastel, France) *free to post: racd in last: pushed along 2f out: hdwy in centre 1 1/2f out: rdn to ld 100yds out: styd on wl* **7/2**[2]	100
2	nk	**Dovil Boy (IRE)**[28] 3-9-2 ... DBoeuf 4 (S Wattel, France) *hld up: 7th on rail st: hdwy over 1 1/2f out: rdn and ev ch fnl f: styd on: jst hld 2nd* **20/1**	99
3	shd	**Vesuve (IRE)**[29] 3-9-2 ... ACrastus 3 (E Lellouche, France) *mid-div: disputing 5th st: pushed along and r.o over 1f out: rdn fnl f: jst missed 2nd* **37/10**[3]	99
4	2	**Glamstar (FR)**[25] 3-9-2 ... (b) C-PLemaire 1 (J-C Rouget, France) *prom: 3rd st: rdn to chal over 1f out: led 150yds out to 100yds out: one pce* **31/5**	95
5	1 ½	**Polarix**[18] 3-9-2 ... MGuyon 9 (H-A Pantall, France) *hld up: 8th st: sn pushed along: rdn over 1 1/2f out: styd on at one pce down outside* **13/1**	92
6	nk	**Sadiri (FR)**[25] 3-9-2 ... CSoumillon 8 (A De Royer-Dupre, France) *mid-div: disputing 5th st: pushed along 2f out: wknd fnl f* **3/1**[1]	91
7	1	**Take D'Or (FR)**[26] 1238 3-9-2 ... DBonilla 2 (F Head, France) *led: rdn and r.o 2f out: hdd 150yds out: sn eased* **20/1**	89
8	1	**Strike Ballot (USA)**[22] 3-9-2 ... SPasquier 5 (Mme C Head-Maarek, France) *racd in 2nd: pushed along st: sn u.p and wknd* **58/10**	87
9	¾	**Lando Junior (FR)**[361] 3-9-2 ... GBenoist 7 (X Nakkachdji, France) *in tch on outside: 4th st: pushed along 2f out: sn one pce* **37/1**	85

1m 52.3s (1.20) — **9** Ran SP% **116.4**
PARI-MUTUEL: WIN 4.50; PL 1.70, 3.90, 1.80; DF 56.30.
Owner M Parrish **Bred** T, Mme D & A De La Heronniere **Trained** France

1598 ASCOT (R-H)
Saturday, May 9

OFFICIAL GOING: Good to firm (good in places on round course)
Wind: Moderate, against Weather: Mainly cloudy

1859 JOHN DOYLE BUCKHOUNDS STKS (LISTED RACE) — 1m 4f
1:05 (1:06) (Class 1) 4-Y-0+
£22,708 (£8,608; £4,308; £2,148; £1,076; £540) **Stalls** High

Form				RPR
60-1	**1**		**Duncan**[17] 1460 4-8-12 107 ... JimmyFortune 6 (J H M Gosden) *lw: disp 4th and a gng strly: led over 1f out: sn in command: impressive* **11/10**[1]	116+
520-	**2**	3 ¾	**Starfala**[190] 7108 4-8-7 87 ... EddieAhern 2 (P F I Cole) *bit bkwd: disp 4th: hrd rdn over 2f out: styd on to take 2nd nr fin: no ch w wnr* **14/1**	102
2-24	**3**	shd	**Steele Tango (USA)**[14] 1526 4-8-12 110 ... AlanMunro 3 (R A Teal) *b: disp 2nd tl 4f out: outpcd and rdn ent st: kpt on fnl f: wnt 3rd nr fin* **4/1**[2]	107
1-05	**4**	¾	**Charlie Farnsbarns (IRE)**[14] 1526 5-9-4 113 ... MartinDwyer 1 (B J Meehan) *lw: disp 2nd: led 3f out and kicked 2 l ahd: hdd over 1f out: hrd rdn and sn easily outpcd: lost 2nd nr fin* **13/2**[3]	112+
2040	**5**	15	**Baylini**[6] 1696 5-8-7 85 ... JamesDoyle 4 (Ms J S Doyle) *dwlt: hld up in rr: hrd rdn and btn over 2f out* **66/1**	77
/02-	**6**	11	**Zaham (USA)**[385] 1468 5-8-12 112 ... (b1) TPO'Shea 5 (M Johnston) *led tl 3f out: wknd over 2f out* **4/1**[2]	64

2m 31.93s (-0.57) **Going Correction** 0.0s/f (Good) — **6** Ran SP% **109.1**
Speed ratings (Par 111): **111,108,108,107,97 90**
toteswinger: 1&2 £6.40, 1&3 £1.60, 2&3 £12.20 CSF £17.00 TOTE £1.90: £1.50, £3.30; EX 16.70.
Owner Normandie Stud Ltd **Bred** Normandie Stud Ltd **Trained** Newmarket, Suffolk

FOCUS
Jockeys reported that the ground was nearer good than good to firm out in the country, but that it was genuinely good to firm in the straight. Quite a tight Listed race on the figures, with only 5lb separating the four principal runners on adjusted official ratings. However, one horse came into the race with a far more progressive profile than the rest and he was impressive, although there are questions about the form of those behind.

NOTEBOOK
Duncan had impressed on his debut for John Gosden when successful in the City and Suburban, and a return to 1m4f always looked likely to suit. This smaller-field Listed race provided a different test, but he settled quite well held up off the decent pace, was travelling strongly entering the straight, and picked off Charlie Farnsbarns with ease when the button was pressed. His jockey only had to shake him up and he bounded clear for an impressive success, and while the bare form will still leave him with a bit to find with his biggest rivals in the Hardwicke, he will deserve plenty of respect in that Group 2 contest, especially having now proven himself on quick ground at this track. (op Evens tchd 6-5 in places)
Starfala came in for some support at big prices on her seasonal reappearance despite looking to have plenty on at the weights. She did, however, have ground conditions to suit and kept on stoutly for second. It would appear that she has progressed significantly from three to four, and she might be able to win a race of this status against her own sex. (op 16-1)
Steele Tango(USA), with good runs in the Earl of Sefton and Gordon Richards Stakes under his belt already this term, was stepping up 2f in distance, and both the way he has been finishing his races over shorter, and his pedigree, offered hope that he would improve for it. That didn't happen, although he seemed to stay all right, and connections may have to consider going abroad to look for Pattern-race success. (op 9-2)
Charlie Farnsbarns(IRE), one place behind Steel Tango in the Gordon Richards Stakes, was 3lb worse off at the weights with that rival, and the step up to 1m4f for the first time looked less likely to suit him on breeding. He took over the lead at the top of the straight, but weakened from over 1f out and clearly didn't stay. (tchd 6-1 and 7-1)
Baylini is fully exposed and had an impossible task at the weights. (tchd 50-1)
Zaham(USA), edgy beforehand, was restricted to just two starts last year and has clearly had his problems. Blinkered for the first time on his return, he was given a positive ride, but he was easily beaten off from the top of the straight and now has a few questions to answer. Official explanation: jockey said gelding ran too free (tchd 9-2)

1860 BOVIS HOMES FILLIES' STKS (HERITAGE H'CAP) — 1m (S)
1:40 (1:41) (Class 2) 3-Y-0+ **£25,904** (£7,708; £3,852; £1,924) **Stalls** Centre

Form				RPR
3-14	**1**		**Good Again**[7] 1679 3-8-4 **85** ... EddieAhern 2 (G A Butler) *hld up towards rr: hdwy gng wl 3f out: led 2f out: pushed clr fnl f: comf* **7/1**[3]	99
2-13	**2**	3 ¾	**Secret Night**[21] 1343 6-8-9 **77** ... (v1) AlanMunro 4 (C G Cox) *hld up in midfield: smooth hdwy 2f out: wnt 2nd jst over 1f out: nt pce of wnr fnl f* **10/1**	84
00-1	**3**	1 ¾	**Trumpet Lily**[19] 1405 4-9-4 **86** ... RichardHughes 1 (J G Portman) *lw: stdd s: hld up in rr: smooth hdwy to press ldrs 3f out: hrd rdn 2f out: one pce* **8/1**	89
41-4	**4**	1	**Feeling Fab (FR)**[15] 1484 3-8-9 **90** ... JoeFanning 3 (M Johnston) *lw: plld hrd: led after 1f tl 2f out: sn outpcd* **15/2**	88
105-	**5**	2 ¼	**Ballyalla**[219] 6426 3-8-2 **83** ... FrancisNorton 9 (R Hannon) *bhd: sme hdwy and hrd rdn 2f out: styd on same pce: nvr able to chal* **16/1**	76

31-1 **6** *hd* **Supaverdi (USA)**[18] 1417 4-8-8 **76**................................ SteveDrowne 11 71
(H Morrison) *lw: chsd ldrs tl hrd rdn and btn 2f out* **2/1**[1]

604- **7** *4 ½* **Classic Legend**[161] 7492 4-9-8 **90**................................ MartinDwyer 13 75
(B J Meehan) *swtg: towards rr: hdwy 1/2-way: rdn and wknd 2f out* **13/2**[2]

0-10 **8** *2* **Haakima (USA)**[21] 1353 3-7-10 **82**.............. Louis-PhilippeBeuzelin(5) 10 59
(C E Brittain) *chsd ldrs: lost pl and rdn after 3f: n.d after* **28/1**

30-0 **9** *1 ¼* **Summer's Lease**[10] 1613 4-8-7 **78**................................ DavidProbert(3) 5 55
(M L W Bell) *lw: prom over 5f* **14/1**

3062 **10** *6* **Binfield (IRE)**[18] 1417 4-8-0 **68**................................ FrankieMcDonald 8 31
(B G Powell) *led 1f: rdn and lost pl 1/2-way: bhd fnl 2f* **33/1**

000- **11** *1 ¼* **Basque Beauty**[224] 6266 4-9-10 **92**................................ DaneO'Neill 7 53
(W J Haggas) *lw: hld up in midfield: hdwy and prom 1/2-way: rdn and wknd over 2f out* **12/1**

140- **12** *1 ¼* **Izzibizzi**[168] 7419 4-9-1 **83**................................ TGMcLaughlin 12 41
(E A L Dunlop) *bhd: sme hdwy into midfield 3f out: hrd rdn and wknd 2f out* **22/1**

-036 **13** *17* **Flying Valentino**[19] 1405 5-8-4 **75**................................ AhmedAjtebi(3) 6 —
(Ian Williams) *pressed ldrs over 4f: sn lost pl: bhd and eased fnl 2f* **33/1**

1m 43.34s (2.74) **Going Correction** +0.40s/f (Good)
WFA 3 from 4yo+ 13lb **13** Ran SP% **125.1**
Speed ratings (Par 96): **102,98,96,95,93 93,88,86,85,79 78,76,59**
toteswinger: 1&2 £8.90, 1&3 £8.10, 2&3 £14.40 CSF £75.81 CT £430.73 TOTE £9.10: £2.80, £3.20, £2.10; EX 82.00 Trifecta £138.80 Pool: £957.00 - 5.10 winning units..
Owner Future In Mind Partnership **Bred** L A Garfield **Trained** Newmarket, Suffolk

FOCUS
Not that many got into this fillies' handicap but the form seems sound enough rated around the runner-up and fourth.

NOTEBOOK
Good Again, whose trainer won this race last season with Baharah, was ridden by Eddie Ahern, who got down to below his minimum weight to take the ride. The decision proved worthwhile as the filly, who apparently wasn't suited to Newmarket last time, appreciated returning to the scene of her maiden victory. She tracked the pace going nicely before being produced, and although she hung right under pressure, she was sprinting clear at the time. A significant bump up the ratings is now likely, but she's still likely to hold strong claims when returning here for the Listed Sandringham Handicap at the Royal meeting. (op 15-2)
Secret Night, representing an in-form yard, is currently in foal, and ran a fine race considering that she was on her toes beforehand and plenty keen enough in the race itself. She has responded well to changes in headgear before so it shouldn't have been a surprise to see her run well in a first-time visor. (op 8-1)
Trumpet Lily, 4lb higher than when successful at Windsor on her reappearance, was given a patient ride and came through to have every chance. The winner simply had a smarter turn of foot at the finish.
Feeling Fab(FR), the pick of the paddock, used up too much energy early at Sandown on her reappearance, and it was a case of 'same old story' here. She was always wanting to go quicker than her rider would let her, and in the circumstances she did well to keep on for fourth. (op 13-2 tchd 8-1 in places)
Ballyalla, ridden to get the trip, did stay on late, but she is bred to be a sprinter and will be of more interest when dropped back in distance. (op 20-1 tchd 25-1 in places)
Supaverdi(USA) overcame a troubled passage and showed a nice turn of foot to win at Bath on her reappearance, and her Group 2 Windsor Forest Stakes entry suggested connections have a high opinion of her. Edgy beforehand, she saw plenty of daylight towards the outside and perhaps she could have done with getting more cover, but this has to go down as a disappointing effort. (op 9-4 tchd 5-2)
Classic Legend, the other filly in the field with a Windsor Forest entry, was running in a handicap for the first time and looked to hold sound claims dropped in class, but she was well held in the end on her seasonal reappearance. (op 12-1)

1861 TOTESPORT VICTORIA CUP (HERITAGE H'CAP) 7f
2:15 (2:18) (Class 2) 4-Y-O+
£52,963 (£15,861; £7,930; £3,969; £1,980; £994) **Stalls** Centre

Form RPR

465- **1** **Swift Gift**[162] 7470 4-8-5 **85**................................ MartinDwyer 29 101
(B J Meehan) *prom in centre: overall ldr 2f out: drvn out* **25/1**

2-34 **2** *1 ¾* **Nezami (IRE)**[17] 1467 4-8-0 **85**................................ AndreaAtzeni(5) 6 96
(J Akehurst) *chsd stands' side ldr: rdn to chal over 1f out: nt qckn fnl 100yds* **50/1**

040- **3** *1 ½* **Dhaular Dhar (IRE)**[182] 7245 7-9-5 **99**................................ DanielTudhope 27 106
(J S Goldie) *lw: wnt rt s: sn in midfield in centre: hdwy over 2f out: chsd ldrs over 1f out: kpt on same pce* **33/1**

302- **4** *nse* **Signor Peltro**[204] 6783 6-8-12 **92**................................ DaneO'Neill 16 99
(H Candy) *prom in centre: hrd rdn 2f out: one pce* **28/1**

5-51 **5** *¾* **Trafalgar Bay (IRE)**[10] 1603 6-8-5 **90**................................ MartinLane(5) 3 95
(K R Burke) *s.s: bhd stands' side: hdwy and in tch over 2f out: no imp over 1f out* **10/1**[3]

122- **6** *nk* **Markab**[153] 7594 6-9-5 **99**................................ FergusSweeney 5 103
(H Candy) *led stands' side gp: edgd rt fnl 2f: one pce* **25/1**

-511 **7** *2 ¼* **Mr Macattack**[64] 777 4-8-6 **86**................................ FrancisNorton 22 84
(N J Vaughan) *mid-div in centre: effrt over 2f out: styd on same pce: nvr able to chal* **14/1**

304- **8** *nk* **We'll Come**[182] 7245 5-9-0 **94**................................(p) AlanMunro 11 91
(M A Jarvis) *in rr of midfield in centre: drvn along and sme hdwy 2f out: nt pce to chal* **14/1**

-310 **9** *½* **L'Hirondelle (IRE)**[18] 1433 5-8-6 **86**................................ EddieAhern 20 89+
(M J Attwater) *lw: towards rr in centre: rdn and styd on fnl 2f: nvr nrr* **100/1**

3304 **10** *1 ¾* **Majuro (IRE)**[7] 1684 5-9-0 **94**................................ NCallan 13 85
(K A Ryan) *mid-div in centre: drvn along and no hdwy fnl 2f* **12/1**

1-42 **11** *1 ¾* **Arabian Spirit**[21] 1352 4-8-12 **92**................................ TGMcLaughlin 2 78
(E A L Dunlop) *chsd ldng pair stands' side: outpcd fnl 2f* **20/1**

4336 **12** *1 ¾* **Aeroplane**[49] 916 6-9-8 **102**................................ RichardHughes 4 84
(S A Callaghan) *stdd s: sn swtchd to centre gp: hld up in rr: sme hdwy 2f out: nvr nr to chal* **50/1**

00-2 **13** *nk* **Fishforcompliments**[35] 1124 5-8-7 **92**.................... FrederikTylicki(5) 17 73
(R A Fahey) *disp ld in centre tl wknd 2f out* **7/1**[2]

-003 **14** *shd* **Blue Sky Basin**[57] 4-9-4 **101**................................ AhmedAjtebi(3) 24 82
(Saeed Bin Suroor) *lw: pressed ldrs in centre 5f* **14/1**

0-50 **15** *nk* **Giganticus (USA)**[35] 1124 6-8-11 **94**................................ PatrickHills(3) 7 74
(B W Hills) *t.k.h: mid-div stands' side: rdn and btn 2f out* **16/1**

0-31 **16** *1 ½* **Evens And Odds (IRE)**[6] 1699 5-9-2 **96** 6ex............ AdrianTNicholls 23 72
(D Nicholls) *chsd ldrs in centre: rdn 3f out: sn outpcd* **13/2**[1]

3-00 **17** *shd* **Slugger O'Toole**[21] 1352 4-8-10 **90**................................ SteveDrowne 15 65
(S C Williams) *bhd in centre: squeezed for room over 2f out: nvr nr ldrs* **33/1**

0-20 **18** *½* **Zaahid (IRE)**[21] 1352 5-9-4 **98**................................ TPO'Shea 12 72
(B W Hills) *lw: sn towards rr stands' side: jnd centre gp over 4f out: nvr trbld ldrs* **12/1**

56-4 **19** *nk* **Maze (IRE)**[19] 1398 4-8-10 **90**................................ TomEaves 19 63
(B Smart) *prom in centre over 4f* **16/1**

0-51 **20** *hd* **Quest For Success (IRE)**[21] 1365 4-8-10 **90**............ TonyHamilton 28 63
(R A Fahey) *lw: dwlt and carried rt s: sn in midfield in centre: effrt 3f out: wknd 2f out* **25/1**

2364 **21** *shd* **Red Somerset (USA)**[8] 1641 6-8-5 **90**................................ MCGeran(5) 1 62
(R J Hodges) *lw: bhd stands' side fr 1/2-way: n.d whn hung rt fnl 2f* **50/1**

0104 **22** *1 ½* **Beaver Patrol (IRE)**[14] 1513 7-9-5 **104**..................(v) RichardEvans(5) 14 72
(Eve Johnson Houghton) *chsd ldrs in centre 4f* **40/1**

10-3 **23** *2 ½* **Guilded Warrior**[17] 1467 6-8-3 **88**.............. Louis-PhilippeBeuzelin(5) 10 50
(W S Kittow) *jnd centre gp after 1f: disp ld tl wknd over 2f out* **33/1**

-500 **24** *5* **Bomber Command (USA)**[10] 1603 6-7-5 **80** oh3 ow2(v) CharlesEddery(7) 26 26
(J W Hills) *chsd ldrs in centre: drvn along 3f out: sn wknd* **66/1**

2143 **25** *2 ¼* **Trade Centre**[33] 1152 4-7-9 **78** oh3................................ DavidProbert(3) 25 20
(W R Muir) *lw: mid-div in centre: hrd rdn 3f out: sn lost pl* **25/1**

0012 **26** *19* **Opus Maximus (IRE)**[1] 1821 4-8-10 **90**................................ JoeFanning 8 —
(M Johnston) *a bhd stands' side: no ch and eased fnl 2f* **10/1**[3]

06-4 **27** *3 ¾* **Spitfire**[28] 1212 4-9-0 **94**................................ ShaneKelly 21 —
(J R Jenkins) *mid-div in centre: rdn 3f out: sn lost pl: no ch and eased fnl f* **25/1**

1m 29.09s (1.09) **Going Correction** +0.40s/f (Good) **27** Ran SP% **138.2**
Speed ratings (Par 109): **109,107,105,105,104 104,101,101,100,98 96,94,94,94,93 92,91,91,91,90 90,88,86,80,77 56,51**
toteswinger: 1&2 £98.00, 1&3 £203.50, 2&3 £294.00 CSF £969.34 CT £33275.64 TOTE £43.90: £9.10, £19.30, £8.30, £7.50; EX 1340.20 Trifecta £40227.60 Part won. Pool: £54,361.72 - 0.10 winning units..
Owner Social and Affordable Racing Partnership **Bred** Glebe Stud And J F Dean **Trained** Manton, Wilts

FOCUS
A typically competitive renewal of this 7f handicap. They split into three bunches early on, but the far-side group soon drifted over to the centre, and those racing stands' side did likewise inside the final 2f. The form looks pretty sound with the placed horses the best guides.

NOTEBOOK
Swift Gift proved very consistent in handicaps last term, but never actually got his head in front in one of them. He looks to have improved for a winter on his back, though, and won this in good style, coming over from the widest stall and eventually challenging up the centre of the track. He stayed on strongly to see off Nezami and, while he should get a mile in time, it makes sense to keep him to 7f at the moment. His trainer nominated the Bunbury Cup as a likely target, but a return visit here at Royal Ascot will no doubt be hard to resist, with the Buckingham Palace Stakes the obvious race to go for.
Nezami(IRE), who came from the opposite side of the track, stepped up on his Polytrack form returned to turf, but another rise up the weights for this defeat will mean he remains vulnerable. He could come back for the Hunt Cup at the Royal meeting.
Dhaular Dhar(IRE) showed his liking for Ascot last year when placed in three big-field handicaps over the course and distance, so it was no surprise to see him run another cracker. He remains on a pretty stiff mark, though. (op 28-1)
Signor Peltro ran well considering his trainer had expressed concerns about both the fast ground and the straight course. There could be better to come from him this term.
Trafalgar Bay(IRE), who improved for the step up to a mile here at the last meeting, was on his toes beforehand and had an 8lb higher mark to overcome. He was staying on all too late at the finish. (op 14-1)
Markab was always going to struggle to make all in this competitive affair, but he ran a good race on his first start for Henry Candy, especially as a bit of ease in the ground suits him ideally. Official explanation: jockey said gelding hung right
Mr Macattack ◆ didn't get the clearest of runs and wasn't knocked about in the closing stages. This was an eye-catching effort on his return from a two-month break and on only his second start on turf, and there is much better to come from him. He could well be a player in one of the big handicaps back here at the Royal meeting. (op 16-1)
We'll Come, fourth in this race last year, stayed on from off the pace, but he's a difficult horse to win with.
L'Hirondelle(IRE), who has decent form on Polytrack, outran his odds on his first outing on turf. This trip would be on the short side for him and he should do better returned to a mile.
Majuro(IRE) failed to build on the promise of his Thirsk Hunt Cup run. (tchd 14-1)
Arabian Spirit probably found the ground too quick.
Aeroplane travelled well as usual but found little off the bridle. (tchd 40-1)
Fishforcompliments, who was seventh in this race last year, looked better handicapped this time around following his promising return at Newcastle, but he rarely strings two good efforts together, and he proved disappointing, despite looking very fit beforehand. (op 9-1)
Giganticus(USA) was on his toes beforehand. (op 20-1)
Evens And Odds(IRE), an impressive winner over 6f at Newmarket just six days earlier, looked well-in under his 6lb penalty. The longer trip ought not to have been a problem, so perhaps the race just came too soon. Official explanation: jockey said race came too soon for gelding (op 6-1 tchd 7-1 in places)
Zaahid(IRE) won this last year but no horse has ever won this race in successive seasons. Following his down-the-field effort in the Spring Cup, this was another disappointing effort. (op 11-1)
Opus Maximus(IRE) Official explanation: jockey said race came too soon for gelding
Spitfire Official explanation: jockey said gelding lost its action

1862 MCGEE GROUP MAIDEN STKS 5f
2:50 (2:53) (Class 3) 2-Y-O **£7,771** (£2,312; £1,155; £288; £288) **Stalls** Centre

Form RPR

023 **1** **Little Perisher**[10] 1598 2-9-3 0................................ NCallan 6 88+
(A P Jarvis) *disp ld: led over 2f out: drvn clr over 1f out: readily* **7/2**[2]

2 *2 ½* **Absolute Music (USA)** 2-8-12 0................................ EddieAhern 2 74
(R M H Cowell) *w'like: str: bit bkwd: w ldrs: rdn and lost pl 2f out: r.o again to take 2nd nr fin* **5/1**

2 **3** *1* **Monsieur Joe (IRE)**[19] 1404 2-9-3 0................................ DaneO'Neill 1 75
(W R Swinburn) *w'like: disp ld over 2f: 2nd and btn whn edgd lft fnl f* **7/4**[1]

4 *¾* **Key Art (IRE)** 2-9-3 0................................ ShaneKelly 5 73
(J Noseda) *w'like: str: lw: s.i.s: hld up in 5th: rdn 2f out: nvr able to chal* **9/2**[3]

4 *dht* **Jira** 2-8-12 0................................ SebSanders 3 68
(C E Brittain) *tall: scope: hld up in 4th: hrd rdn 2f out: one pce* **16/1**

6 *½* **Master Of Dance (IRE)** 2-9-3 0................................ RichardHughes 4 71+
(R Hannon) *leggy: scope: athletic: hld up in rr: shkn up and no prog fnl 2f* **8/1**

63.00 secs (2.50) **Going Correction** +0.40s/f (Good) **6** Ran SP% **110.4**
Speed ratings (Par 97): **96,92,90,89,89 88**
toteswinger: 1&2 £1.60, 1&3 £1.90, 2&3 £4.80 CSF £20.14 TOTE £4.80: £2.00, £2.70; EX 23.60.
Owner Christopher Shankland **Bred** Mrs Ann Jarvis **Trained** Middleham Moor, N Yorks

FOCUS
Quite a valuable maiden.

NOTEBOOK
Little Perisher was dropping in class following his third to Red Jazz in a conditions race here at the last meeting. Having already had three outings and shown that he handles this track, he had a big edge in experience over his rivals, and that counted for plenty. His trainer is keen to send him to Epsom next for the Listed Woodcote Stakes. (op 5-1 tchd 11-2 and 6-1 in places)
Absolute Music(USA) is a January foal and was the oldest of these by some margin. Representing a stable that sent out another American-bred filly in High Spice to make all on her debut at Newmarket earlier in the week, she rallied well having dropped back to fourth, and there should be better to come from her with this debut under her belt. (tchd 9-2 and 11-2)
Monsieur Joe(IRE) shaped with plenty of promise on his debut at Windsor, but that form has taken a knock or two since, and this run puts another question mark over the value of that form. Hanging left under pressure in the closing stages probably cost him second here, but he has the ability to win an average maiden. Official explanation: jockey said colt hung left (op 5-2)
Key Art(IRE), whose trainer won this race last year with a newcomer, cost 100,000euros at the sales and is one of four entries his stable has in the Group 1 Phoenix Stakes. This colt had been due to run at Windsor earlier in the week but had an infection and came here instead. Wandering about under pressure, he looked as though the experience would bring him on greatly, and he should know more next time. (op 10-3 tchd 5-1)
Jira is a half-sister to King Edward VII winner Plea Bargain so isn't exactly bred to be precocious. She ran green under pressure but put up a promising performance in the circumstances and will naturally appreciate stepping up a furlong in distance. (op 10-3 tchd 5-1)
Master Of Dance(IRE) ◆, the youngest of these, is a May foal. Not at all knocked about on his debut, he should derive plenty from this experience and will be tough to beat in an ordinary maiden next time. (op 11-2 tchd 5-1)

1863 DIAMOND WEDDING H'CAP — 2m
3:25 (3:25) (Class 3) (0-90,88) 4-Y-0+

£7,477 (£2,239; £1,119; £560; £279; £140) **Stalls** High

Form — RPR

66-1 **1** **Judgethemoment (USA)**[18] 1435 4-9-9 **88**................ RichardHughes 6 97
(Jane Chapple-Hyam) *hw: hld up in tch: effrt and swtchd to far rail over 1f out: styd on wl to ld fnl strides* **6/1**[3]
44-2 **2** *nk* **Swingkeel (IRE)**[21] 1356 4-9-2 **81**................ EddieAhern 7 89+
(J L Dunlop) *lw: hld up in rr: hdwy over 3f out: led ins fnl 2f: hrd rdn and kpt on wl fnl f: hdd fnl strides* **5/2**[1]
505/ **3** ½ **Ermine Sea**[66] 6319 6-9-9 **85**................ MartinDwyer 1 93
(Miss H C Knight) *lw: cl up: jnd ldr after 4f: led 7f out tl ins fnl 2f: kpt on: nt qckn fnl 50yds* **20/1**
3024 **4** 1½ **Alnwick**[5] 1732 5-8-13 **75**................ DaneO'Neill 5 81
(P D Cundell) *mid-div: in tch after 6f: wnt 3rd 4f out: hrd rdn over 1f out: kpt on* **7/1**
25-3 **5** 6 **Dolly Penrose**[14] 1519 4-9-1 **80**................ CatherineGannon 9 79
(M R Channon) *dwlt: hld up in rr: hdwy on outside ent st: sn rdn to press ldrs: wknd jst over 1f out* **15/2**
321- **6** 1¼ **Fregate Island (IRE)**[221] 6361 6-9-9 **85**................ FergusSweeney 10 82
(A G Newcombe) *mid-div: sltly lost pl after 6f: effrt into 6th 2f out: nt pce to chal* **12/1**
30-3 **7** 7 **Royal Jet**[11] 1586 7-9-9 **85**................ ShaneKelly 11 74
(Mrs S Leech) *b: hld up in last: rdn over 2f out: nvr trbld ldrs* **25/1**
652- **8** 7 **Absolut Power (GER)**[47] 7110 8-9-4 **80**................(v) SteveDrowne 2 61
(J A Geake) *prom tl wknd 4f out* **20/1**
00-6 **9** *hd* **Wicked Daze (IRE)**[42] 1007 6-9-12 **88**................ StephenDonohoe 3 68
(Ian Williams) *hld up in midfield: hdwy into 4th 4f out: sn rdn: wknd 2f out* **14/1**
0143 **10** 8 **Simonside**[32] 1175 6-8-9 **71**................ NCallan 4 42
(B Ellison) *chsd ldrs tl wknd over 2f out* **16/1**
611- **11** *110* **Casual Garcia**[275] 4775 4-8-11 **76**................(b) SebSanders 8 —
(Sir Mark Prescott) *bit bkwd: led tl 7f out: sn drvn along: wknd qckly 4f out* **11/2**[2]

3m 29.04s (0.04) **Going Correction** 0.0s/f (Good)
WFA 4 from 5yo+ 3lb — 11 Ran SP% **116.1**
Speed ratings (Par 107): **108,107,107,106,103 103,99,96,96,92** —
toteswinger: 1&2 £5.50, 1&3 £15.60, 2&3 £27.90 CSF £20.37 CT £284.39 TOTE £6.10: £1.90, £1.50, £5.30; EX 14.00 Trifecta £188.80 Pool: £969.62 - 3.80 winning units..
Owner Gordon Li **Bred** Todd Graves & Michele Graves **Trained** Newmarket, Suffolk
■ Stewards' Enquiry : Richard Hughes caution: used whip in incorrect place

FOCUS
There were one or two progressive types in this race and the form looks solid.

NOTEBOOK
Judgethemoment(USA) had recorded each of his previous three victories with front-running displays, but there was competition for that role here and his rider was content to track the pace. Switched to the inside, having failed to get a run out wider, he stayed on strongly to get up inside the last and defy a career-high mark. Not only does he stay well but he also clearly likes this track, having finished sixth in the Queen's Vase on his only previous visit. (op 7-1 tchd 5-1)
Swingkeel(IRE) had been narrowly beaten at Newbury on his reappearance and a 3lb higher mark looked far from troublesome, especially given that the quicker conditions promised to suit this son of Singspiel a lot better. However, having hit the front, he thought he'd done enough, and he let the winner, who made his move next to the rail, run him out of it. He looks the type that needs delivering on the line. (op 11-4)
Ermine Sea, third in the 2006 Queen's Vase but absent from the Flat since that season, had showed he retains ability with a couple of placed efforts over hurdles earlier this year. This performance confirms that he's capable of winning off his current mark on the Flat, which is very fair based on his best form. (tchd 25-1)
Alnwick, second behind Judgethemoment at Kempton last time, was unable to reverse the form back on turf. He is largely consistent and the Handicapper seems to have him about right for the time being. (op 9-1)
Dolly Penrose, on her toes beforehand, was left behind inside the final furlong and is ideally suited by softer ground. (tchd 7-1 and 8-1)
Royal Jet travelled well out the back but made no progress in the straight. The step up in trip from 1m4f proved too much for him, but this effort won't do him any harm with the Handicapper and his new stable might be able to get some improvement out of him over a more suitable distance. Official explanation: jockey said gelding moved poorly throughout (tchd 20-1)
Simonside was on his toes beforehand. (tchd 14-1)
Casual Garcia, a highly progressive performer last summer, enjoys bowling along in front. Reappearing off a 14lb higher mark than when last successful, he seemed to resent being taken on by Ermine Sea and spat the dummy out. Official explanation: trainer had no explanation for the poor form shown; jockey said gelding stopped very quickly (op 9-2)

1864 ALFRED FRANKS & BARTLETT SUNGLASSES H'CAP — 6f
4:00 (4:00) (Class 3) (0-95,95) 4-Y-0+ **£7,771** (£2,312; £1,155; £577) **Stalls** Centre

Form — RPR

306- **1** **Striking Spirit**[225] 6239 4-8-8 **88**................ AhmedAjtebi(3) 1 99
(D Nicholls) *lw: mde all: sn 3 l ahd: drvn along and hld on wl fnl 2f* **7/1**[3]
/15- **2** 1 **Jimmy Styles**[357] 2195 5-9-2 **93**................ RichardHughes 8 100+
(C G Cox) *lw: hld up in midfield: hdwy and swtchd lft 2f out: drvn to chse wnr over 1f out: clsd tl hld fnl 100yds* **2/1**[1]
1000 **3** 1¼ **Nightjar (USA)**[19] 1398 4-8-7 **84**................ FrancisNorton 2 87
(M Johnston) *prom: hrd rdn and edgd rt fr 2f out: no ex* **20/1**
0310 **4** 1¼ **Cornus**[7] 1682 7-8-1 **81** oh1................(be) DavidProbert(3) 12 80
(A J McCabe) *s.s: bhd: rdn and hdwy over 1f out: nt rch ldrs* **33/1**
013- **5** *nk* **Seamus Shindig**[259] 5270 7-8-3 **87**................ AmyScott(7) 6 85
(H Candy) *b.hind: mid-div: pushed along 2f out: kpt on same pce: no imp* **12/1**
00-2 **6** 1¼ **Masai Moon**[22] 1321 5-9-1 **95**................ JamesMillman(3) 11 89
(B R Millman) *lw: bhd: mod effrt 2f out: nvr trbld ldrs* **8/1**
1035 **7** 1½ **Ebraam (USA)**[17] 1457 6-8-13 **90**................ TolleyDean 5 80
(P Howling) *b: chsd ldrs 4f* **10/1**
10-0 **8** ½ **Phantom Whisper**[22] 1325 6-9-3 **94**................ TGMcLaughlin 3 82
(B R Millman) *towards rr: rdn over 2f out: n.d* **16/1**
0-05 **9** ½ **Mujood**[9] 1631 6-8-8 **85**................(b) StephenCarson 4 71
(Eve Johnson Houghton) *chsd wnr: hrd rdn 3f out: wknd 2f out* **28/1**
2153 **10** 3¾ **Obe Gold**[19] 1398 7-8-9 **86**................(v) AdrianTNicholls 7 60
(D Nicholls) *blindfold removed after stalls opened: mid-div: sn rdn along: hrd drvn and outpcd fnl 2f* **6/1**[2]
30-0 **11** 1 **Great Charm (IRE)**[28] 1212 4-8-10 **87**................ EddieAhern 9 58
(M L W Bell) *lw: towards rr: rdn 1/2-way: nvr a factor* **16/1**
1363 **12** 6 **Mogok Ruby**[7] 1668 5-8-4 **81** oh1................ MartinDwyer 10 33
(L Montague Hall) *hrd rdn 2f out: a bhd* **20/1**

1m 14.89s (0.49) **Going Correction** +0.40s/f (Good) — **12** Ran SP% **115.7**
Speed ratings (Par 107): **112,110,109,107,106 105,103,102,101,96 95,87**
toteswinger: 1&2 £3.70, 1&3 £24.40, 2&3 £16.00 CSF £19.63 CT £276.16 TOTE £8.10: £2.90, £1.50, £5.00; EX 24.40 Trifecta £164.70 Pool: £1,313,37 - 5.90 winning units. Place 6: £1668.97, Place 5: £875.25..
Owner Bon Accord Racing & D Nicholls **Bred** Juddmonte Farms Ltd **Trained** Sessay, N Yorks

FOCUS
A decent handicap and the form looks reliable with the third setting the standard.

NOTEBOOK
Striking Spirit didn't win for Barry Hills last season but he was picked up at the sales by Dandy Nicholls and his new trainer looks to have a very useful sprinter on his hands. Making every yard under Ahmed Ajtebi, who has an excellent record when riding for Nicholls, he never looked in too much danger, and his trainer is now eyeing the top sprint handicaps of the summer, notably the Wokingham and Stewards' Cup. (op 9-1)
Jimmy Styles, who won this race last year off a mark of 88, only had one more outing afterwards, suggesting he had his problems, but his stable is in cracking form and he was popular in the market on his reappearance off a 5lb higher mark. He ran well and was unlucky to bump into one. (op 15-8 tchd 7-4 and 9-4 in places)
Nightjar(USA), who has recorded his last four wins on Fibresand, has dropped a fair way in the weights on turf and ran one of his better races on the grass.
Cornus, racing from 1lb out of the handicap, was staying on quite nicely at the finish. He has recorded his last seven wins in class 5 races, though, and this competition was tougher.
Seamus Shindig, resuming off a career-high mark, ran a respectable race and should come on for the outing. (tchd 10-1)
Masai Moon is still on a mark 8lb higher than when last successful, and, while 7f suits her better, she looks held by the assessor for the time being. (op 9-1)
Obe Gold, whose jockey failed to get the blindfold off before the stalls opened and, while it didn't appear to cost his mount too much ground, the gelding never really got involved, and perhaps he should be forgiven this. (op 7-1 tchd 11-2)
T/Jkpt: Not won. T/Plt: £4,085.30 to a £1 stake. Pool: £109,128.73. 19.50 winning tickets.
T/Qpdt: £430.80 to a £1 stake. Pool: £7,161.57. 12.30 winning tickets. LM

1504 HAYDOCK (L-H)
Saturday, May 9

OFFICIAL GOING: Good (good to firm in places on jumps course bends; jump 6.3; flat 6.5)
New course configuration on jumps track - no speed figures yet possible.
Wind: Fresh 1/2 against Weather: overcast and breezy with showers

1865 TOTESCOOP6 SPRING TROPHY STKS (LISTED RACE) — 7f 30y
3:05 (3:08) (Class 1) 3-Y-0+

£22,708 (£8,608; £4,308; £2,148; £1,076; £540) **Stalls** Low

Form — RPR

64-0 **1** **Beacon Lodge (IRE)**[42] 996 4-9-7 102................ GeorgeBaker 9 115
(C G Cox) *hld up in rr: hdwy over 2f out: styd on to ld ins fnl f: r.o* **11/2**
30-4 **2** ¾ **Ordnance Row**[10] 1600 6-9-7 112................ TonyCulhane 6 113
(R Hannon) *chsd ldrs: wnt 2nd over 2f out: led over 1f out: hdd and no ex ins fnl f* **9/2**[3]
4-11 **3** 2¼ **City Style (USA)**[65] 769 3-8-13 109................ TedDurcan 3 107
(Saeed Bin Suroor) *mid-div: sn pushed along: hdwy over 2f out: hung lft and rt: kpt on to take modest 3rd ins fnl f* **10/3**[1]
006- **4** 3¾ **Garnica (FR)**[244] 5738 6-9-7 109................ SilvestreDeSousa 5 97
(D Nicholls) *hld up in mid-div: hdwy over 3f out: sn chsng ldrs: edgd lft and wknd fnl f* **8/1**
40- **5** 1½ **Shallal**[325] 3119 4-9-7 98................ RobertWinston 8 93+
(P W Chapple-Hyam) *chsd ldr: hung rt bnd over 5f out: wknd over 1f out* **14/1**
525- **6** 1¼ **Welsh Emperor (IRE)**[182] 7243 10-9-7 110................(b) MickyFenton 2 89
(T P Tate) *drvn to ld: hdd over 1f out: sn wknd* **20/1**
5-24 **7** 3½ **Vitznau (IRE)**[42] 996 5-9-7 104................ PatDobbs 4 80
(R Hannon) *hld up in rr: effrt on ins over 2f out: nvr nr ldrs* **4/1**[2]
440- **8** 7 **Appalachian Trail (IRE)**[231] 6104 8-9-7 105...........(b) PaulMulrennan 1 61
(I Semple) *in rr: nvr gng wl: nvr on terms* **7/1**
1/-5 **9** 22 **Sammy The Snake (IRE)**[10] 1608 4-9-7 0................ JohnEgan 7 2
(B W Duke) *chsd ldr: rdn over 3f out: sn lost pl and bhd: t.o* **33/1**

1m 30.55s (0.35) **Going Correction** +0.325s/f (Good)
WFA 3 from 4yo+ 12lb — 9 Ran SP% **114.6**
Speed ratings (Par 111): **111,110,107,103,101 100,96,88,63**
toteswinger: 1&2 £7.40, 1&3 £6.80, 2&3 £2.10 CSF £30.21 TOTE £7.50: £2.30, £2.00, £1.40; EX 37.10 Trifecta £216.10 Part won. Pool: £292.15 - 0.40 winning units..
Owner Mr And Mrs P Hargreaves **Bred** Mrs Bill O'Neill **Trained** Lambourn, Berks

FOCUS
They went a really good gallop in this Listed contest and Beacon Lodge returned to something like his best to score. The form looks pretty solid rated around the placed horses.

NOTEBOOK
Beacon Lodge(IRE), a Group 3 winner as a juvenile, he only made the track twice last year in what was a very quiet season for the yard, but they have made a fast start to 2009 and this fellow shaped with a good deal of promise when a keeping-on seventh in the Cammidge Trophy at Doncaster on his reappearance. Held up off the pace, he started to close over two out and came up the inside of the runner-up inside the final furlong. This was his first win on a fast surface and there is every chance he will again make his mark at Group level this term. (op 9-1 tchd 10-1)

Ordnance Row is a tough and consistent performer and he did not go down without a fight. Fourth at Ascot on his reappearance (contested same race last year before winning next time), he was ideally positioned to strike and got first run on the winner, but could not repel him late on. He will no doubt find another race or two at this sort of level. (op 4-1)
City Style(USA), who was receiving 8lb from all his rivals, was formerly trained in America (fourth in Breeders´ Cup Juvenile) before joining Godolphin. Twice a winner in Dubai earlier in the year, he had the potential to prove a cut above these, but never looked happy on the ground and could only keep on at the one pace back in third. This was not a bad run and perhaps he deserves another chance on softer going. (op 3-1 tchd 7-2)
Garnica(FR), a four-time Group 3 winner in France, including for this yard, ran well for a long way on this seasonal reappearance and will find more opportunities later in the season when the ground softens in his favour. (op 9-1 tchd 11-1)
Shallal, off since finishing last of 16 in the Jersey Stakes, was faced with a stiff task on this seasonal reappearance and did not shape too badly considering, though he won´t be easy to place this season. (op 12-1)
Welsh Emperor(IRE) needs softer ground than this and he simply did too much early. (op 12-1)
Vitznau(IRE) never got into it having been held up. (op 9-2)
Appalachian Trail(IRE) never got into it having been held up (op 8-1)
Sammy The Snake(IRE) was quickly beaten and is clearly not up to this level. (op 20-1)

1866 TOTESPORT HOME OF POOL BETTING MAIDEN STKS (DIV I) 6f
3:40 (3:43) (Class 5) 2-Y-O **£2,914** (£867; £433; £216) **Stalls** Centre

Form				RPR
2	1		**Kingdom Of Light**[10] 1610 2-9-3 0 PaulMulrennan 3 (J Howard Johnson) *mde all: edgd lft and kpt on strly fnl f* 7/2[2]	86+
	2	2 ¼	**Step In Time (IRE)** 2-9-3 0 RoystonFfrench 6 (M Johnston) *rr-div: hdwy and edgd lft over 1f out: styd on wl to take 2nd ins fnl f* 4/1[3]	79
	3	1 ½	**Reeds Bay (IRE)** 2-9-3 0 TedDurcan 9 (E S McMahon) *rr-div: hdwy over 2f out: kpt on fnl f* 20/1	75
	4	¾	**Kylladdie** 2-9-3 0 MickyFenton 13 (T P Tate) *chsd ldrs: kpt on same pce appr fnl f* 20/1	73
3	5	1 ¼	**Our Dream Queen**[22] 1323 2-8-12 0 RobertWinston 11 (B W Hills) *chsd ldrs: effrt over 2f out: wknd over 1f out* 3/1[1]	64
4	6	2 ¼	**Mal And Dave (IRE)**[8] 1645 2-9-3 0 SilvestreDeSousa 2 (D Nicholls) *chsd ldrs: edgd rt 1f out: sn fdd* 8/1	62
	7	1 ½	**Magic Footsteps** 2-9-3 0 PhillipMakin 7 (Jedd O'Keeffe) *trckd ldrs: wkng whn hmpd appr fnl f* 33/1	58
0	8	5	**Zambuka (FR)**[23] 1298 2-8-12 0 TonyCulhane 8 (R Curtis) *hld up in tch: effrt over 2f out: lost pl over 1f out* 10/1	38
	9	1 ¼	**Mary Celest (IRE)** 2-8-12 0 JohnEgan 5 (K A Ryan) *mid-div: lost pl 2f out* 16/1	34
	10	2 ¼	**Isdaar (IRE)** 2-9-3 0 RobertHavlin 1 (J H M Gosden) *sn outpcd and pushed along in rr: edgd rt over 2f out: nvr in contention* 7/1	32
	11	12	**Antique Diamond (IRE)** 2-8-12 0 NeilChalmers 10 (Lucinda Featherstone) *s.s: in rr: bhd fnl 2f* 100/1	—
	12	1	**Dazeen** 2-9-3 0 JamieMoriarty 12 (P T Midgley) *s.s: hdwy 4f out: hung lft and lost pl over 2f out* 80/1	—
	13	6	**Campaigner** 2-9-3 0 GeorgeBaker 4 (J W Hills) *s.s: sme hdwy over 2f out: sn wknd* 28/1	—

1m 17.51s (3.51) **Going Correction** +0.50s/f (Yiel) **13 Ran SP% 123.9**
Speed ratings (Par 93): **96,93,91,90,88 85,83,76,75,72 56,54,46**
toteswinger: 1&2 £5.60, 1&3 £16.80, 2&3 not won CSF £17.41 TOTE £4.80: £1.70, £2.20, £6.20; EX 27.10.
Owner Transcend Bloodstock LLP **Bred** D M I Simcock **Trained** Billy Row, Co Durham

FOCUS
The race was run in driving rain, which made it tough for these juveniles. Probably no more than an ordinary maiden, though it should produce winners.

NOTEBOOK
Kingdom Of Light, readily brushed aside by a useful-looking prospect over 5f on his debut at Pontefract, was made plenty of use of on this drop in trip and picked up well to race clear over a furlong out. He was always doing enough inside the final furlong and fully deserves to take his chance in something a bit better now, with connections likely to choose between the Coventry and Norfolk Stakes at Royal Ascot. (op 4-1)
Step In Time(IRE), who holds an entry in the Group 1 Phoenix Stakes, got a bit further back than his rider would have liked, but camestrong in the final quarter mile and stayed on well for second. He will have learned from this and winning a standard maiden should prove a formality. (op 9-2)
Reeds Bay(IRE), a speedily-bred colt representing a yard that does well with its juveniles, came under pressure two out and stayed on well, but never posed a serious threat. Normal improvement should see him good enough to win a minor maiden. (op 12-1)
Kylladdie was only a cheap purchase, but there is plenty of speed in the pedigree and he showed more than enough to suggest he will be winning races at the right level. (op 16-1)
Our Dream Queen, third behind a couple of colts in a 5f maiden at Newbury on debut, failed to improve as expected for the extra furlong and faded close home. She was reported to have hung left. (op 7-2)
Mal And Dave(IRE) failed to improve on his debut effort. (op 9-1 tchd 7-1)
Magic Footsteps offered a bit of promise before fading late on. (op 25-1)
Mary Celest(IRE) did not cost a great deal and offered little promise on this racecourse debut. (op 12-1 tchd 10-1)
Isdaar(IRE), who cost 240,000gns and is already gelded, never recovered from a slow start. (op 13-2 tchd 6-1)

1867 TOTESPORT HOME OF POOL BETTING MAIDEN STKS (DIV II) 6f
4:15 (4:19) (Class 5) 2-Y-O **£2,914** (£867; £433; £216) **Stalls** Centre

Form				RPR
	1		**Pycian** 2-9-3 0 TedDurcan 9 (Mrs L Stubbs) *s.s: detached in last: gd hdwy stands' side over 1f out: fin strly to ld nr fin* 25/1	75+
	2	½	**Atacama Crossing (IRE)** 2-9-3 0 RobertWinston 11 (B W Hills) *mid-div stands' side: hdwy over 2f out: styd on ins fnl f to take cl 2nd nr fin* 7/1	74+
	3	nk	**Lucky Rave** 2-9-3 0 PhillipMakin 10 (D H Brown) *mid-div: hdwy over 2f out: hdd jst ins fnl f: hdd and no ex last 50yds* 20/1	73+
	4	2 ¼	**Running Mate (IRE)** 2-9-3 0 RobertHavlin 8 (J H M Gosden) *in tch: hdwy over 2f out: upsides 1f out: fdd fnl 100yds* 5/2[1]	66
04	5	1	**Ginger Ted (IRE)**[11] 1590 2-9-3 0 (b[1]) GeorgeBaker 6 (R C Guest) *trckd ldr: led over 2f out: hdd jst ins fnl f: sn wknd* 12/1	63
	6	1 ½	**Urban Clubber** 2-9-3 0 PaulMulrennan 2 (J Howard Johnson) *chsd ldrs: fdd fnl f* 16/1	58
6	7	shd	**Polly Macho (IRE)**[14] 1511 2-9-3 0 JohnEgan 3 (P D Evans) *led: hdd over 3f out: wknd over 1f out* 13/2	58
	8	1 ½	**Sir Parky (IRE)** 2-9-3 0 PatDobbs 4 (R Hannon) *dwlt: sn bhd: kpt on fnl 2f: nvr on terms* 5/1[2]	54
	9	1 ¾	**Dolphin Rock** 2-9-0 0 DominicFox[(3)] 5 (Mrs G S Rees) *dwlt: hdwy to chse ldrs 2f out: sn wknd* 40/1	48
	10	3 ½	**Tislaam (IRE)** 2-9-3 0 TonyCulhane 13 (M R Channon) *unruly s: sn chsng ldrs: hung lft and wknd 2f out* 6/1[3]	38+
	11	3 ½	**The Midshipmaid** 2-8-12 0 NeilChalmers 12 (Lucinda Featherstone) *chsd ldrs: lost pl over 2f out* 66/1	22
00	12	½	**Whippers Love (IRE)**[23] 1304 2-9-3 0 RoystonFfrench 1 (M Johnston) *chsd ldrs on outside: wknd 2f out* 12/1	26
	13	3 ¼	**Treasury Bond** 2-9-3 0 JamieMoriarty 7 (P T Midgley) *chsd ldrs: edgd lft over 2f out: sn wknd* 100/1	16

1m 17.56s (3.56) **Going Correction** +0.50s/f (Yiel) **13 Ran SP% 120.2**
Speed ratings (Par 93): **96,95,94,91,90 88,88,86,84,79 74,74,69**
toteswinger: 1&2 £35.50, 1&3 £60.10, 2&3 £25.10 CSF £187.03 TOTE £35.80: £7.00, £3.00, £7.10; EX 351.40.
Owner Tyme Partnership **Bred** H Robinson **Trained** Norton, N Yorks

FOCUS
This looked the weaker of the two divisions on paper, and the result seemed to confirm that impression.

NOTEBOOK
Pycian, whose dam came to hand early as a 2yo, did not cost a lot and things didn´t start well as the horse was slowest away. Well adrift in last and looking to be going nowhere at halfway, he sprouted wings in the final quarter mile and stayed on strongly close home to get up. Matched at 1000 in-running on Betfair, it remains to be seen whether this already gelded son of Mark Of Esteem is capable of following up, but connections do expect him to improve for a seventh furlong, so it´s possible there´s more to come. (op 18-1 tchd 16-1)
Atacama Crossing(IRE), a 38,000gns son of 2,000 Guineas winner Footstepsinthesand, came to have every chance and stuck on well, but could do nothing as the winner swept past close home. (op 4-1, tchd 8-1 in places)
Lucky Rave, a half-brother to Hit The Roof who got a bit upset in the stalls, was slowly away and still had plenty of running to do at halfway, but he quickened through to lead inside the final furlong, in the end just getting run out of it. (op 28-1 tchd 18-1)
Running Mate(IRE), a precociously bred colt who is not that big, cost £180,000 at the sales and was well backed to make a winning debut. He showed plenty of speed and had his chance, but could find no extra in the final 100 yards. (op 9-2 tchd 9-4)
Ginger Ted(IRE) showed plenty of speed in the first-time blinkers, but in the end failed to get home. (tchd 15-2)
Urban Clubber, representing connections who provided the winner of the first division, has a nice pedigree and he will be capable of better once faced with an extra furlong. (op 12-1)
Sir Parky(IRE), a half-brother to a multiple-winner in the US, may get a little further in time and he did not look as far forward as some usually are from this yard. (op 6-1 tchd 7-1)
Tislaam(IRE), who is bred to need further than this, played up a bit beforehand and dropped right out in the end, having shown some early speed. (op 9-2 tchd 13-2)

1868 TOTEEXACTA CONDITIONS STKS 6f
4:50 (4:50) (Class 2) 3-Y-O+
£12,462 (£3,732; £1,866; £934; £466; £234) **Stalls** Centre

Form				RPR
/13-	1		**Royal Rock**[357] 2195 5-9-0 98 GeorgeBaker 8 (C F Wall) *hld up in rr: smooth hdwy over 2f out: led over 1f out: pushed clr: v readily* 9/4[1]	113+
0-56	2	4	**Abraham Lincoln (IRE)**[13] 1543 5-9-0 96 TonyCulhane 2 (D Nicholls) *chsd ldrs: n.m.r 2f out: styd on to take 2nd 1f out: no ch w wnr* 11/1	100+
20-0	3	1 ¼	**Zidane**[23] 1299 7-9-0 107 PaulMulrennan 4 (J R Fanshawe) *hld up in rr: nt clr run 2f out: swtchd outside: kpt on same pce fnl f* 6/1	96
164-	4	3 ¼	**Redford (IRE)**[268] 5025 4-9-0 102 JohnEgan 7 (M L W Bell) *hld up: hdwy to chse ldrs after 2f: wknd 1f out* 5/2[2]	86
2301	5	2 ¾	**Tamagin (USA)**[12] 1560 6-9-0 101 (b[1]) TedDurcan 1 (K A Ryan) *led: hung rt and hdd 2f out: sn appr fnl f* 5/1[3]	77
-001	6	shd	**Buachaill Dona (IRE)**[10] 1608 6-9-8 102 SilvestreDeSousa 3 (D Nicholls) *chsd ldr: led 2f out: sn hdd & wknd* 10/1	85
000/	7	14	**Hamoody (USA)**[406] 5-9-0 0 RobertWinston 5 (P W Chapple-Hyam) *hung lft thrght: chsd ldrs: lost pl over 1f out: sn bhd* 14/1	32

1m 15.65s (1.65) **Going Correction** +0.50s/f (Yiel) **7 Ran SP% 114.4**
Speed ratings (Par 109): **109,103,102,97,94 93,75**
toteswinger: 1&2 £5.90, 1&3 £3.90, 2&3 £7.10 CSF £27.21 TOTE £3.30: £2.60, £2.70; EX 33.10.

Owner Ms Aida Fustoq **Bred** Deerfield Farm **Trained** Newmarket, Suffolk

FOCUS
The field raced towards the far rail in this contest. An interesting conditions sprint that could hardly have been won in more impressive fashion, Royal Rock cruising to the front over a furlong out and readily drawing clear. The winner was impressive but there are doubts about the form in behind.

NOTEBOOK
Royal Rock ◆ cruised to the front over a furlong out and readily drawing clear. Always a promising sort in handicaps, he has not taken much racing in three previous seasons, and hadn´t been seen since finishing third at Newbury just under a year ago. However, the strong support for him beforehand suggested he was ready to roll on this seasonal reappearance and the manner of his victory marks him down as an obvious contender for pattern-race honours, assuming he can be kept sound. He does stay 7f, but there is little doubting 6f is his trip and it will be fascinating to see just how high connections aim with him. (op 4-1)
Abraham Lincoln(IRE), unsuited by the soft ground in Ireland last time, had nowhere to go as the winner went for home and stayed on well once in the clear, but it made no difference to his finishing position. There is a decent prize in him at some stage this season. (op 8-1)
Zidane, below his best on fast ground at Newmarket on his reappearance, would have welcomed the earlier downpour the course encountered, but he tends to do his racing in bigger fields and was not really suited to the way things panned out here, being denied a clear run before keeping on at the one pace. (op 9-2 tchd 4-1)
Redford(IRE), who has been gelded over the winter, lacked the speed to make an impact on this first crack at sprinting. He is entitled to come on for the run and will be much better of back up at 7f and maybe even 1m. (op 11-4 tchd 3-1)
Tamagin(USA), back to winning ways in a handicap at Newcastle last time, showed his customary speed in the first-time blinkers, but was readily brushed aside and faded. (op 9-2)
Buachaill Dona(IRE), a winner at Kempton last time, was always going to struggle under the 8lb penalty. (tchd 8-1)

1869 BET TOTEPOOL AT TOTESPORT.COM H'CAP 6f
5:25 (5:26) (Class 4) (0-85,85) 3-Y-O **£5,504** (£1,637; £818; £408) **Stalls** Centre

Form				RPR
512-	1		**Dark Lane**[225] 6247 3-8-13 **80** PhillipMakin 8 (T D Barron) *t.k.h: trckd ldrs: hdwy to ld appr fnl f: all out* 3/1[1]	85
6-02	2	hd	**Metroland**[14] 1505 3-8-5 72 SilvestreDeSousa 12 (D Nicholls) *in tch: hdwy and swtchd stands' side over 1f out: sn upsides: edgd lft ins fnl f: no ex nr fin* 8/1	76

4332 **3** ½ **Mazzola**[14] 1517 3-8-8 **75** TonyCulhane 7 77
(M R Channon) *led tl 2f out: rallied and ev ch 1f out: no ex towards fin* **9/2**[2]

00-0 **4** 5 **Maggie Lou (IRE)**[37] 1078 3-8-13 **80** AdrianMcCarthy 5 66
(K A Ryan) *in rr: hdwy and edgd rt over 1f out: nvr nr ldrs* **20/1**

1-24 **5** 3 **Coleorton Choice**[14] 1517 3-8-12 **84** AmyRyan(5) 10 61
(K A Ryan) *chsd ldrs: led 2f out: hdd appr fnl f: edgd rt and fdd* **13/2**

440- **6** 4 **Fitzolini**[214] 6549 3-8-5 **72** (p) NeilChalmers 9 36
(A D Brown) *w ldrs: outpcd 3f out: no threat after* **50/1**

125- **7** 1¾ **Suzie Quw**[232] 6067 3-8-5 **79** NoraLooby(7) 11 37
(K R Burke) *chsd ldrs: wknd over 1f out* **20/1**

06-0 **8** 1 **Baycat (IRE)**[22] 1324 3-9-4 **85** PatDobbs 1 40
(J G Portman) *w ldrs on outer: wknd over 1f out* **25/1**

03-0 **9** nk **Top Town Girl**[42] 1002 3-9-4 **85** GeorgeBaker 6 39
(R M Beckett) *chsd ldrs: wknd over 1f out* **14/1**

0-54 **10** ½ **Kyllachy Star**[28] 1214 3-8-13 **80** JamieMoriarty 4 33
(R A Fahey) *chsd ldrs: hung lft and lost pl over 1f out* **5/1**[3]

10-4 **11** 2¾ **Dubai Hills**[23] 1305 3-8-12 **79** TedDurcan 2 23
(B Smart) *chsd ldrs: wknd 2f out* **7/1**

102- **12** 1¾ **Kingswinford (IRE)**[182] 7241 3-9-3 **84** JohnEgan 3 22
(P D Evans) *chsd ldrs: wknd 2f out* **12/1**

1m 16.64s (2.64) **Going Correction** +0.50s/f (Yiel) **12** Ran SP% **126.5**
Speed ratings (Par 101): **102,101,101,94,90 85,82,81,81,80 76,74**
toteswinger: 1&2 £9.40, 1&3 £5.30, 2&3 £9.80 CSF £28.47 CT £115.14 TOTE £4.10: £1.70, £3.20, £2.00; EX 31.90 Place 6: £674.18, Place 5: £296.57..
Owner David W Armstrong **Bred** David Jamison Bloodstock **Trained** Maunby, N Yorks
■ Stewards' Enquiry : Silvestre De Sousa three-day ban: used whip with excessive frequency (May 23-25)

FOCUS
Probably no more than a fair sprint handicap but the first three were clear and the third was close to his best.
Kingswinford(IRE) Official explanation: jockey said gelding had no more to give
T/Plt: £443.40 to a £1 stake. Pool: £103,044.31. 169.63 winning tickets. T/Qpdt: £36.50 to a £1 stake. Pool: £3,241.15. 65.70 winning tickets. WG

1833 LINGFIELD (L-H)

Saturday, May 9

OFFICIAL GOING: Good to firm (str 8.5; rnd 8.9)
Wind: Modest, across Weather: overcast, bright spells

1870 TOTESPORTGAMES.COM H'CAP 7f
2:10 (2:11) (Class 3) (0-90,84) 3-Y-O **£9,714** (£2,890; £1,444; £721) **Stalls** High

Form RPR

0-12 **1** **Seek N' Destroy (IRE)**[28] 1214 3-8-13 **79** MichaelHills 8 86
(B W Hills) *mde all: rdn and asserted over 1f out: in command fnl f: comf* **4/1**[3]

05-0 **2** 1¼ **Acquiesced (IRE)**[18] 1434 3-8-11 **77** RyanMoore 9 81
(R Hannon) *trckd ldrs on stands rail: rdn and unable qck over 1f out: drvn and styd on again ins fnl f: wnt 2nd fnl 50yds: no ch w wnr* **14/1**

10 **3** ½ **Kaabari (USA)**[24] 1293 3-9-1 **81** DarryllHolland 4 84
(C E Brittain) *chsd wnr: shkn up wl over 2f out: drvn and unable qck over 1f out: kpt on same pce fnl f* **20/1**

21-1 **4** ½ **Laudatory**[28] 1214 3-9-3 **83** AdamKirby 10 84+
(W R Swinburn) *hld up in rr on stands rail: switching out lft over 1f out: drvn jst ins fnl f: edgd lft u.p and one pce after* **5/4**[1]

4-11 **5** nk **Seek The Fair Land**[18] 1434 3-8-10 **76** JimCrowley 1 76+
(J R Boyle) *restless stalls: chsd ldrs on outer: rdn and tried to chal wl over 1f out: one pce u.p fnl f* **16/1**

513- **6** 1¾ **Greensward**[196] 6970 3-9-1 **81** PJSmullen 5 77
(B J Meehan) *stdd s: hld up towards rr: swtchd lft and drvn over 1f out: keeping on same pce and hld whn carried lft ins fnl f* **7/2**[2]

15-5 **7** 1½ **Silent Hero**[18] 1434 3-8-10 **76** WilliamBuick 3 68
(M A Jarvis) *stdd s: hld up towards rr: effrt and rdn on outer 2f out: no imp over 1f out* **14/1**

1-30 **8** 39 **Miss Chamanda (IRE)**[23] 1305 3-8-11 **77** TolleyDean 7 —
(P D Evans) *a bhd: rdn 4f out: lost tch 2f out: t.o and eased ins fnl f* **50/1**

1m 21.84s (-1.46) **Going Correction** -0.125s/f (Firm) **8** Ran SP% **112.6**
Speed ratings (Par 103): **103,101,101,100,100 98,96,51**
toteswinger: 1&2 £9.40, 1&3 £10.50, 2&3 £10.60 CSF £54.98 CT £993.61 TOTE £4.80: £1.40, £3.40, £3.10; EX 58.70 Trifecta £221.60 Part won. Pool: £299.53 - 0.10 winning units..
Owner R J Arculli **Bred** James Waldron **Trained** Lambourn, Berks

FOCUS
The successful jockey in this opener described the ground as good to firm, but with no jar, and the official description looked spot-on. A good three-year-old handicap, but the bare result needs treating with some caution. The first three home filled the front three places pretty much throughout, and the winner made all against the stands' rail, which is so often favoured on this straight track.

NOTEBOOK
Seek N' Destroy(IRE) was allowed a surprisingly soft lead and, as heh was almost certainly racing on the quickest part of the track, it was no surprise he was able to reverse recent Polytrack placings with Laudatory. However, for all that the winner had plenty go his way, he's a progressive colt and this was only his fifth start, so there ought to be better to come again. The Britannia Stakes at Royal Ascot is apparently now his aim. (op 9-2 tchd 11-2)
Acquiesced(IRE) tracked the winner throughout and improved significantly on the form she showed when well behind Seek The Fair Land at Kempton on her reappearance. Her only win was gained on soft ground, but she seemed to handle these much faster conditions. (tchd 16-1)
Kaabari(USA), off the mark on her debut in a Polytrack maiden here and down the field in the Nell Gwyn, was always close up and kept on for a respectable third. (op 22-1 tchd 25-1)
Laudatory ◆, who had Seek N' Destroy three-quarters of a length behind when successful over this trip at Kempton on his reappearance, had little chance of confirming the form considering how the race developed. Dropped in from his rails draw, he had to be switched four wide with his challenge and could make no telling impression, with the front three having had the race to themselves pretty much from the off. There's no doubt he's better than this result indicates and is likely to benefit considerably from a stronger-run race. (op 6-4 tchd 13-8 in places)
Seek The Fair Land, who has progressed at a lower level on Polytrack, is slightly better than he showed, as he was stuck wide throughout from the lowest stall. (op 17-2)
Greensward is from a stable that houses some nice three-year-olds, and he's done well from two to three, but things didn't go for him this time. Having raced further back than ideal, he was switched wide with his challenge and, like all of those held up, made no impression. He should do better. (op 4-1 tchd 11-4)

Silent Hero didn't travel with any fluency and his knee action suggests the ground might have been quicker than ideal. (op 11-1 tchd 8-1)

1871 TOTESPORTCASINO.COM OAKS TRIAL STKS (LISTED RACE) (FILLIES) 1m 3f 106y
2:40 (2:40) (Class 1) 3-Y-O
£28,385 (£10,760; £5,385; £2,685; £1,345; £675) **Stalls** High

Form RPR

14-2 **1** **Midday**[17] 1459 3-8-12 93 TPQueally 8 106+
(H R A Cecil) *trckd ldrs: effrt over 3f out: rdn to ld over 2f out: clr and in n.d fnl 2f: v easily* **5/2**[1]

1- **2** 6 **July Jasmine (USA)**[214] 6565 3-8-12 81 RyanMoore 3 93+
(Sir Michael Stoute) *t.k.h early: hld up in last trio after 1f: rdn and outpcd over 3f out: rallied over 1f out: styd on wl fnl f: wnt 2nd towards fin: no ch w wnr* **7/2**[2]

415- **3** ¾ **Tottie**[189] 7144 3-8-12 92 JimCrowley 7 92
(Mrs A J Perrett) *hld up in tch in midfield: rdn and effrt 3f out: chsd clr wnr 2f out: no imp: lost 2nd towards fin* **7/1**

00- **4** nk **Spirit Of Dubai (IRE)**[200] 6884 3-8-12 0 AdamKirby 1 91?
(D M Simcock) *hld up in midfield: rdn and unable qck over 3f out: drvn and hdwy over 1f out: styd on fnl f: no ch w wnr* **50/1**

1- **5** 2½ **Anice Stellato (IRE)**[260] 5240 3-8-12 80 PJSmullen 2 87
(R M Beckett) *t.k.h: trckd ldng pair: rdn and outpcd over 2f out: no ch w wnr after: wknd over 1f out* **4/1**[3]

6-1 **6** ¾ **Inhibition**[18] 1430 3-8-12 75 WilliamBuick 9 85+
(A M Balding) *chsd ldr after 1f: tl rn wd bnd over 3f out: sn rdn and outpcd by wnr: wknd ins fnl f* **12/1**

0-10 **7** 1½ **Sanvean (IRE)**[10] 1599 3-8-12 88 DarryllHolland 6 83
(M R Channon) *hld up in last pair: rdn and no prog over 3f out* **33/1**

321 **8** 3¾ **Wadaat**[25] 1269 3-8-12 80 SPasquier 5 77
(C E Brittain) *hld up in last pair: rdn and no prog 3f out* **11/1**

1- **9** 9 **Floodlit**[289] 4339 3-8-12 78 JimmyFortune 4 61
(J H M Gosden) *led tl hdd over 2f out: wknd qckly 2f out: wl bhd and eased fnl f* **8/1**

2m 30.49s (-1.01) **Going Correction** -0.125s/f (Firm) **9** Ran SP% **115.3**
Speed ratings (Par 104): **98,93,93,92,91 90,89,86,80**
toteswinger: 1&2 £2.50, 1&3 £2.30, 2&3 £5.60 CSF £11.19 TOTE £2.90: £1.70, £1.90, £1.70; EX 10.30 Trifecta £33.00 Pool: £312.40 - 7.00 winning units..
Owner K Abdulla **Bred** Juddmonte Farms Ltd **Trained** Newmarket, Suffolk

FOCUS
The last horse successful in this race on the way to winning the Oaks was Ramruma in 1999, but 12 months ago Look Here finished a close second before winning the fillies' Classic at Epsom. It's hard to be sure of the overall quality of this season's race, which was contested largely by maiden race winners, but Midday has been rated among the better winners, although her RPR still leaves her well shy of Oaks standard. The pace seemed no more than fair and the winning time was 0.56 seconds slower than the following Derby Trial.

NOTEBOOK
Midday ran out an impressive winner. Positioned just in behind the leaders for much of the way, she was a little keen through the early stages, but it was nothing to be worried about and she handled both the downhill run and the turn into the straight beautifully. Once in line for home, she extended in taking style without her rider having to be overly vigorous. The further she went, the better she looked, and this represents another step up on her reappearance second against the colts in the 1m2f Blue Riband Trial Stakes at Epsom. Another half a furlong will be no problem, and as she handles undulations and is thriving at just the right time a good case can now be made for her giving Henry Cecil a ninth Oaks winner, for while further improvement is required, that race lacks strength in depth. (op 9-4 tchd 11-4 in a place)
July Jasmine(USA) ◆ had been off the track since winning a 7f Leicester maiden on her debut last October. Set plenty to do, she didn't handle the downhill run into the straight and lost further ground. That cost her any chance she might have had of winning, but there was much to like about the way she stayed on to claim second once balanced. She's in the Oaks, but would be hard to fancy at Epsom and the Ribblesdale could be the race for her. (op 4-1)
Tottie was another who failed to handle the undulations on the bend, but she kept on quite well in the straight to secure some important black type. This was her first start in six months, so she's open to improvement, and a more galloping track is likely to suit. (op 13-2 tchd 6-1)
Spirit Of Dubai(IRE) should not be used to hold the form down. She didn't show much at two, but she's always been well regarded by a trainer who rarely overfaces his horses - she was entered in the Irish Guineas and Oaks at one stage - and it was no surprise she showed much improved form on this step up in trip and switch to better ground.
Anice Stellato(IRE), the winner of a 7f Newmarket maiden (working out well) on her debut last August, represented a trainer with a good record in this race, but she made no impression. (op 11-2)
Inhibition did not handle the final turn and ended up going extremely wide into the straight. She performed creditably in the circumstances. (op 10-1 tchd 9-1 and 14-1)
Floodlit had not been seen since winning a 7f maiden at Kempton in July on her debut and is not in the Oaks. She led early on, but was kept honest by Inhibition and dropped out tamely in the straight. (op 9-1 tchd 10-1)

1872 TOTESPORT.COM DERBY TRIAL STKS (GROUP 3) (C&G) 1m 3f 106y
3:15 (3:15) (Class 1) 3-Y-O **£36,900** (£13,988; £7,000; £3,490; £1,748) **Stalls** High

Form RPR

4- **1** **Age Of Aquarius (IRE)**[178] 7294 3-8-12 0 JMurtagh 1 108
(A P O'Brien, Ire) *sn led: rdn over 2f out: hdd narrowly 2f out: kpt on gamely u.p to ld again fnl 100yds* **8/11**[1]

21- **2** nk **Montaff**[220] 6384 3-8-12 82 DarryllHolland 2 107
(M R Channon) *trckd wnr: rdn to ld narrowly 2f out: hrd drvn ent fnl f: hdd and one pce fnl 100yds* **16/1**

1-3 **3** hd **Father Time**[22] 1326 3-8-12 99 TPQueally 4 107
(H R A Cecil) *hld up in last pl: hdwy and rdn over 2f out: hrd drvn over 1f out: pressed ldrs ins fnl f: nt qckn and one pce fnl 100yds* **11/4**[2]

31- **4** 5 **Alwaary (USA)**[233] 6057 3-8-12 93 RHills 5 99
(J H M Gosden) *hld up in last pair: hdwy to go 3rd over 5f out: rdn 2f out: sn outpcd* **6/1**[3]

6-0 **5** 25 **Sumbe (USA)**[24] 1291 3-8-12 0 RyanMoore 3 72
(M P Tregoning) *trckd ldng pair: rdn and wknd over 3f out: wl bhd fnl 2f* **16/1**

2m 29.93s (-1.57) **Going Correction** -0.125s/f (Firm) **5** Ran SP% **110.6**
Speed ratings (Par 109): **100,99,99,96,77**
CSF £13.58 TOTE £1.70: £1.10, £3.20; EX 14.60.
Owner Mrs Magnier/Tabor/Smith/Mordutchovitch **Bred** Berend Van Dalfsen **Trained** Ballydoyle, Co Tipperary

FOCUS
The last winner of this race to follow up in the big one at Epsom was High-Rise in 1998, and in more recent years it hasn't been a particularly competitive trial. That said, last year's winner Alessandro Volta acquitted himself well at both Epsom and the Curragh (Irish Derby), while Aqlaam, successful in 2007, ran third in the Derby. All five runners held an Epsom entry, but this was not a strong renewal, and the third looks the best guide. Only marginal improvement therefore from Age Of Aquarius, although he looks sure to rate better in due course. The winning time was quite good; 0.56 seconds faster than impressive Oaks Trial winner Midday.

NOTEBOOK
Age Of Aquarius(IRE) had only a couple of starts at two, winning an ordinary Dundalk maiden before running fourth to Fame And Glory in a 1m2f Group 1 in France. He was a well-supported favourite for his return, representing last year's winning trainer, but had to work hard to justify his odds and still looked quite inexperienced. Although enjoying an uncontested lead, the winning time confirms he by no means dawdled in front, and he was briefly headed by Montaff around 2f out, when Father Time was also threatening out wider. However, he gradually got the idea and ground his way back to the front. As far as the track was concerned, he handled the downhill run just fine, but came wide around the final bend, something his rider attributed to an increase in the tempo at that stage of the race. This form is a long way off what will be required at Epsom and he makes limited appeal at around 20-1 for the Derby, particularly in such a strong-looking year for middle-distance three-year-old colts. However, he's a sizeable individual open to a deal of improvement as the year progresses and it would be no surprise to see him develop into a high-class performer in due course. The 10-1 Ladbrokes quoted for the St Leger probably isn't a terrible price - the trip doesn't look a problem on breeding - but it's worth pointing out he showed a fluent, fast-ground action, despite last year's run in France coming on testing going. (op 5-4)
Montaff didn't achieve much when winning a 1m maiden on testing ground at Newcastle in October, but he showed significantly improved form on this step up in trip. He was arguably flattered to finish so close to the winner, but he's clearly a smart colt in his own right. (op 14-1 tchd 20-1)
Father Time was set a lot to do by Tom Queally, and swung wider than ideal into the straight, but he looks quite a free-going type - wears a cross-noseband - so his rider probably had little choice but to try and settle him out the back. After not handling the downhill run all that well, he made up plenty of ground to move into a threatening position on the outside in the closing stages, but he could never quite get on top, with his earlier exertions probably just telling. Although he looks to have the ability to make up into a genuine Group horse, he still appears immature and one would like to see him settle better in future. A stronger pace on a more galloping track is likely to help on that score, and a race like the King Edward VII Stakes at Royal Ascot could be a suitable target. (op 9-4 tchd 3-1 in a place)
Alwaary(USA) had been off since winning a 1m maiden at Yarmouth in September and he never got in a blow at the front three. He had apparently only been working "okay" before this, so it's not unreasonable to assume the race might bring him on a good deal. (op 4-1)
Sumbe(USA) is evidently well regarded, but he was the first beaten. (op 20-1)

1873 TOTESPORTBINGO.COM CHARTWELL FILLIES' STKS (GROUP 3) 7f
3:45 (3:45) (Class 1) 3-Y-O+
£36,900 (£13,988; £7,000; £3,490; £1,748; £877) **Stalls** High

Form				RPR
3-	**1**		**San Sicharia (IRE)**[205] 6767 4-9-3 0 ... PJSmullen 3 (Ms Joanna Morgan, Ire) *wnt lft s: hld up in rr: hdwy on outer over 1f out: led jst ins fnl f: hld on wl: all out* **16/1**	103+
24-0	**2**	*nse*	**Baileys Cacao (IRE)**[21] 1353 3-8-6 103 ow1 ... RyanMoore 10 (R Hannon) *trckd ldrs on stands rail: edging out lft and bmpd rival 2f out: sn swtchd bk to rail and drvn: ev ch 1f out: hung lft ins fnl f: rallied cl home: jst hld* **3/1**[1]	100
50-6	**3**	*1*	**Please Sing**[21] 1353 3-8-5 97 ... EdwardCreighton 9 (M R Channon) *stdd s: hld up in rr: nt clr run 2f out: sn rdn: hdwy ins fnl f: nt clr run and swtchd lft towards fin: running on fin* **12/1**	96
510-	**4**	*hd*	**Royal Confidence**[203] 6814 4-9-3 103 ... MichaelHills 1 (B W Hills) *hld up in tch: rdn and ev ch ent fnl f: unable qck fnl 100yds* **8/1**	99+
21-2	**5**	*shd*	**Damaniyat Girl (USA)**[24] 1293 3-8-5 100 ... RHills 2 (W J Haggas) *bmpd s: sn rcvrd: led after 1f and crossed to stands' rail: hdd and hung lft 2f out: stl ev ch 1f out: no ex ins fnl f* **4/1**[3]	95
0-04	**6**	*shd*	**Infamous Angel**[7] 1667 3-8-5 100 ... WilliamBuick 5 (R Hannon) *stdd and swtchd rt after s: hld up bhd: looking for run wl over 1f out: swtchd rt ent fnl f: r.o but nvr trbld ldrs* **10/1**	95
22-5	**7**	*2*	**Medicea Sidera**[119] 123 5-9-3 95 ... TPQueally 8 (E F Vaughan) *led for 1f: pressed ldr after tl led again 2f out: hdd jst ins fnl f: wknd fnl 100yds* **16/1**	94
20-1	**8**	*¾*	**Select (IRE)**[32] 1173 3-8-5 90 ... AlanMunro 6 (P W Chapple-Hyam) *hld up in tch: shkn up and sltly hmpd 2f out: sn rdn: no imp* **16/1**	87+
	9	*1 ¼*	**Chasing Stars**[185] 7203 4-9-3 0 ... (t) SPasquier 7 (Mme C Head-Maarek, France) *t.k.h: hld up in tch in midfield: bmpd 2f out: rdn and no hdwy over 1f out* **7/2**[2]	88
121-	**10**	*3 ¾*	**Chantilly Tiffany**[195] 7005 5-9-7 108 ... JimmyFortune 4 (E A L Dunlop) *chsd ldrs: rdn over 2f out: wknd wl over 1f out* **10/1**	82

1m 20.6s (-2.70) **Going Correction** -0.125s/f (Firm)
WFA 3 from 4yo+ 12lb **10** Ran SP% **121.9**
Speed ratings (Par 110): **110,109,108,108,108 108,106,105,103,99**
toteswinger: 1&2 £34.70, 1&3 £130.40, 2&3 £12.90 CSF £66.72 TOTE £29.10: £5.60, £1.50, £3.30; EX 174.50 TRIFECTA Not won..
Owner P Twomey **Bred** Mrs Lisa Kelly **Trained** Ballivor, Co Meath

FOCUS
This has been a quality fillies' Group 3 in recent times, with last season's winner Sabana Perdida following up in the Windsor Forest at Royal Ascot, and Echelon, successful in 2006, subsequently landing a Group 1. However, there was a bunched finish to this year's race, with the first six covered by just over a length, and the bare form looks ordinary for the level.

NOTEBOOK
San Sicharia(IRE) deserves extra credit considering she raced well away from the favoured stands' side - stall three gave her rider little choice - whereas the runner-up sat tight against the rail for most of the way. Debuting for her stable after 205 days off, this looked a marked improvement on the form she had shown in Europe (mainly France), despite her rider feeling the ground was quicker than ideal. (op 12-1)
Baileys Cacao(IRE) carried 1lb overweight and lost this Group 3 by just a nose. She had the benefit of the stands' rail for much of the way and got a good lead early on, but she didn't help her chance by edging left in the closing stages. Despite that, she still ran on and would have got up in another stride. (op 11-2 tchd 6-1 in a place)
Please Sing would have been even closer had she not been short of room near the line, but she wasn't unlucky. (tchd 14-1)
Royal Confidence had every chance but did not see her race out as well as some of these on her return from 203 days off. Although she gets the trip well, it would be fascinating to see her back over a sprint trip considering she's by Royal Applause out of a high-class 5f winner. (op 6-1)
Damaniyat Girl(USA), a seven-length runner-up to Fantasia in the Nell Gwyn on her reappearance, bagged the stands' rail position, but in the process she appeared to go off a stride too quick, especially considering she had to cut across from a low stall. (tchd 9-2 in a place)
Infamous Angel, still last two furlongs out, ran on when switched to the stands' rail before being short of room near the line, but she wasn't unlucky. (op 11-1 tchd 12-1)
Chasing Stars, a Listed winner in France on her final start last year, has been kept in training because she is African Rose's lead horse. She was bumped about two furlongs out, but that's no excuse and it might be that this ground was quicker than she cares for. She was reported to have run too free. Official explanation: jockey said filly ran too free (op 4-1 tchd 9-2)
Chantilly Tiffany Official explanation: jockey said mare was unsuited by the good to firm ground

1874 NEIL MUNCEY 50TH BIRTHDAY MAIDEN STKS 1m 2f
4:20 (4:20) (Class 5) 3-Y-O+ **£4,857** (£1,445; £722; £360) **Stalls** Low

Form				RPR
0-	**1**		**Highland Glen**[204] 6778 3-8-11 0 ... RyanMoore 6 (Sir Michael Stoute) *trckd ldng pair: led over 2f out: rdn clr: pushed out fnl f: v easily* **8/11**[1]	88+
0-0	**2**	*7*	**Fisadara**[22] 1329 3-8-6 0 ... TPO'Shea 4 (B W Hills) *led: wde bnd over 3f out: rdn and hdd over 2f out: no ch w wnr after* **14/1**	69
	3	*6*	**Little Prudence** 3-8-6 0 ... WilliamBuick 2 (R M Beckett) *in tch: pushed along 7f out: outpcd over 3f out: rdn and plugged on into modest 3rd over 1f out* **25/1**	57
	4	*3 ¾*	**Buckie Boy (IRE)** 3-8-11 0 ... (b[1]) TPQueally 1 (H R A Cecil) *v.s.a: in tch in last pair: hung rt and wd bnd over 3f out: sn racd awkwardly and lost tch* **12/1**	55
6-	**5**	*7*	**Albaasha (IRE)**[155] 7552 3-8-11 0 ... RHills 7 (Sir Michael Stoute) *hld up in last pair: lost tch downhill over 4f out: no ch fnl 3f* **10/1**[3]	41+
32	**6**	*5*	**Signaller (USA)**[14] 1522 3-8-11 0 ... JMurtagh 3 (M Johnston) *pressed ldr: ev ch over 3f out: wknd qckly over 2f out: eased fr over 1f out* **11/4**[2]	55+

2m 8.69s (-1.81) **Going Correction** -0.125s/f (Firm) **6** Ran SP% **111.9**
Speed ratings (Par 103): **102,96,91,88,83 79**
toteswinger: 1&2 £2.70, 1&3 £6.80, 2&3 £29.30 CSF £12.73 TOTE £1.70: £1.20, £4.60; EX 11.90.
Owner The Queen **Bred** The Queen **Trained** Newmarket, Suffolk

FOCUS
They finished quite strung out and this maiden lacked much depth. They seemed to go a decent pace.
Albaasha(IRE) Official explanation: jockey said colt ran green
Signaller(USA) Official explanation: jockey said colt stopped quickly

1875 WEATHERBYS BANK CONDITIONS STKS 1m 2f
4:55 (4:55) (Class 2) 4-Y-O+ **£12,462** (£3,732; £1,866; £934; £466) **Stalls** Low

Form				RPR
03-2	**1**		**Unnefer (FR)**[21] 1346 4-9-2 110 ... TPQueally 5 (H R A Cecil) *trckd ldr: pushed into ld wl over 1f out: a in command after: comf* **2/1**[1]	114+
6160	**2**	*1 ½*	**Halicarnassus (IRE)**[2] 1799 5-8-12 108 ... SamHitchcott 4 (M R Channon) *hld up in tch: rdn jst over 3f out: hdwy u.p over 1f out: styd on u.p to chse wnr ins fnl f: no ch w wnr* **9/2**	107
604-	**3**	*½*	**Drumfire (IRE)**[189] 7145 5-9-0 106 ... JMurtagh 3 (M Johnston) *hld up off the pce in last pl: rdn and effrt over 3f out: hdwy u.p over 1f out: styd on but no ch w wnr* **5/2**[2]	108
403-	**4**	*2 ½*	**Khateeb (IRE)**[267] 5070 4-8-12 106 ... (t) RHills 1 (M A Jarvis) *led: rdn over 2f out: hdd wl over 1f out: no ch w wnr fnl f: lost 2 pls ins fnl f* **4/1**[3]	101
44-6	**5**	*12*	**Resplendent Light**[6] 1696 4-8-12 96 ... RyanMoore 2 (W R Muir) *chsd ldng pair: rdn and unable qck over 2f out: wknd over 1f out: eased ins fnl f* **15/2**	85

2m 6.47s (-4.03) **Going Correction** -0.125s/f (Firm) **5** Ran SP% **111.9**
Speed ratings (Par 109): **111,109,109,107,97**
toteswinger: 1&2 £7.30, 1&3 £3.60, 2&3 £13.10 CSF £11.38 TOTE £2.20: £1.60, £2.00; EX 5.80.
Owner Niarchos Family **Bred** S Niarchos **Trained** Newmarket, Suffolk

FOCUS
There was not much between these on the figures, and Unnefer left the impression he has improved. Rather muddling form though.

NOTEBOOK
Unnefer(FR) was a class apart. Always nicely placed, he handled the track well and found plenty for pressure in the straight, winning a little more comfortably than the official margin suggests. Already a Listed winner, he deserves a step back up in class. (op 6-5)
Halicarnassus(IRE), down the field at Chester just two days earlier, did well to get up for second, but he only really got going late on and never threatened the winner. (op 11-2 tchd 13-2 and 4-1)
Drumfire(IRE), held up last, ran okay considering the front two had the benefit of race fitness. (op 7-2)
Khateeb(IRE) was entitled to need the outing, having been off since August. (op 9-2)
Resplendent Light had plenty to find with his four rivals at the weights. (op 11-1 tchd 7-1)

1876 "NEIL'S LOVELY LADIES" STKS (H'CAP) (LADY AMATEUR RIDERS) 7f
5:30 (5:30) (Class 5) (0-75,75) 4-Y-O+ **£3,123** (£968; £484; £242) **Stalls** High

Form				RPR
3141	**1**		**Shaded Edge**[6] 1710 5-10-0 **68** 6ex ... MissSBrotherton 1 (D W P Arbuthnot) *in tch: pushed along and sltly outpcd 2f out: rallied ins fnl f: r.o to ld nr fin* **11/4**[1]	75
42-6	**2**	*½*	**Paraguay (USA)**[16] 1479 6-9-13 **74** ... MissDLenge[(7)] 7 (Mrs D J Sanderson) *s.i.s: sn rcvrd and chsng ldrs: edgd lft fr 3f out: rdn to ld jst over 1f out: hdd nr fin* **16/1**	80
-065	**3**	*nse*	**I Confess**[7] 1682 4-10-4 **72** ... (b) MissEFolkes 11 (P D Evans) *led: hdd over 2f out: sn rdn and sltly outpcd: rallied and hung lft u.p over 1f out: kpt on wl fnl f* **11/2**[3]	78
545-	**4**	*½*	**My Learned Friend (IRE)**[192] 7077 5-10-6 **74** GemmaGracey-Davison 3 (A M Balding) *chsd ldr tl led over 2f out: rdn and hdd jst over 1f out: no ex ins fnl f* **5/1**[2]	79
-500	**5**	*½*	**Carlitos Spirit (IRE)**[14] 1524 5-10-7 **75** ... MissEJJones 4 (B R Millman) *chsd ldrs on stands' rail: nt clr run and lost pl wl over 1f out: rallied fnl f: styng on fin* **8/1**	78
0125	**6**	*1*	**Ryedale Ovation (IRE)**[13] 1539 6-9-10 **69** ... MissHayleyMoore[(5)] 10 (G L Moore) *t.k.h: hld up in rr on stands' rail: switching lft fr 2f out: rdn over 1f out: kpt fnl f: nvr trbld ldrs* **13/2**	70
26-6	**7**	*3 ½*	**Wing Play (IRE)**[15] 1493 4-9-10 **69** ... (b[1]) MissVCartmel[(5)] 12 (H Morrison) *rrd s: t.k.h: hld up in rr: rdn over 2f out: no imp tl kpt on u.p ins fnl f* **7/1**	60
6004	**8**	*1 ½*	**Batchworth Blaise**[6] 1710 6-9-0 **61** oh8 ... MissCNosworthy[(7)] 8 (E A Wheeler) *t.k.h: hld up in rr: struggling 3f out* **20/1**	48
0135	**9**	*¾*	**Tuxedo**[71] 708 4-10-0 **68** ... MrsMarieKing 9 (P W Hiatt) *a towards rr: rdn and no prog over 2f out: nvr trbld ldrs* **10/1**	53

0620 **10** *2* **Ishibee (IRE)**[50] 895 5-9-0 **61** oh13..............................(p) MrsNParry(7) 2 41
(J J Bridger) *t.k.h early: hld up in midfield: rdn and struggling whn rdr dropped whip over 2f out: sn wknd* **66/1**

000- **11** *16* **Captain Sirus (FR)**[146] 7678 6-9-0 **61** oh16...............(t) MissKLoftus(7) 6 —
(P Butler) *a bhd: lost tch wl over 2f out* **100/1**

1m 22.48s (-0.82) **Going Correction** -0.125s/f (Firm) **11** Ran SP% **117.9**
Speed ratings (Par 103): **99,98,98,97,97 96,92,90,89,87 68**
CSF £51.15 CT £234.81 TOTE £3.30: £1.20, £3.90, £2.20; EX 70.00 Place 6: £53.77, Place 5: £10.06..
Owner P M Claydon **Bred** Lady Whent **Trained** Compton, Berks
■ Stewards' Enquiry : Miss V Cartmel three-day ban: used whip with excessive frequency and when out of contention (May 23-24, 26)

FOCUS
A routine lady amateur riders' handicap. The third, who made the running up the rail, is probabloy the best guide to the form.
T/Plt: £302.00 to a £1 stake. Pool: £72,676.27. 175.63 winning tickets. T/Qpdt: £16.90 to a £1 stake. Pool: £3,327.57. 145.15 winning tickets. SP

1840 NOTTINGHAM (L-H)
Saturday, May 9

OFFICIAL GOING: Firm (good to firm in places; 8.9)
Wind: Fresh against Weather: Cloudy with sunny spells

1877 BET ON TOTEPLACEPOT AT TOTESPORT.COM H'CAP — 5f 13y
1:50 (1:50) (Class 5) (0-70,70) 4-Y-O+ **£3,885** (£1,156; £577; £288) **Stalls** High

Form RPR

6612 **1** **Tyrannosaurus Rex (IRE)**[44] 971 5-9-0 **66**.......... GrahamGibbons 14 75
(D Shaw) *trckd ldrs: rdn to ld ins fnl f: r.o* **10/3**[1]

54-0 **2** *1* **King Of Swords (IRE)**[7] 1685 5-9-0 **66**.......................... DavidAllan 12 71
(N Tinkler) *prom: lost pl over 3f out: hdwy over 1f out: swtchd lft ins fnl f: hung lft: r.o* **12/1**

00-2 **3** *1* **The History Man (IRE)**[14] 1528 6-8-7 **59**.....................(be) LiamJones 1 61
(M Mullineaux) *chsd ldrs: rdn over 1f out: carried lft ins fnl f: styd on* **16/1**

-020 **4** *nk* **Comptonspirit**[14] 1518 5-9-1 **67**.................................... J-PGuillambert 5 68
(B P J Baugh) *sn pushed along in rr: hdwy over 1f out: sn rdn: styd on* **10/1**

2123 **5** *hd* **Bluebok**[13] 1540 8-9-1 **67**...(bt) LPKeniry 4 67
(J M Bradley) *w ldr: rdn and ev ch ins fnl f: styd on same pce* **8/1**

3-50 **6** *3/4* **Ryedane (IRE)**[11] 1591 7-8-4 **56** oh1..........................(b) DuranFentiman 11 59+
(T D Easterby) *s.i.s: sn pushed along in rr: r.o ins fnl f: nvr nrr* **16/1**

3000 **7** *1/2* **Brandywell Boy (IRE)**[17] 1468 6-8-9 **61**.................... RichardThomas 2 57
(D J S Ffrench Davis) *chsd ldrs: lost pl 1/2-way: rallied over 1f out: n.m.r and no ex ins fnl f* **11/1**

6055 **8** *shd* **Silver Prelude**[18] 1421 8-8-5 **57**............................... RichardKingscote 17 52
(S C Williams) *led: rdn and hdd ins fnl f: no ex* **7/2**[2]

0066 **9** *1/2* **Thoughtsofstardom**[31] 1181 6-8-6 **65**...................... CarolineKelly(7) 16 58
(P S McEntee) *chsd ldrs: rdn over 1f out: wkng whn nt clr run ins fnl f* **50/1**

5034 **10** *3/4* **Ronnie Howe**[11] 1591 5-8-6 **58**.......................................(bt) ChrisCatlin 10 49
(S R Bowring) *plld hrd and prom: rdn over 1f out: wknd ins fnl f* **15/2**[3]

5443 **11** *2 1/2* **Gwilym (GER)**[5] 1748 6-8-9 **68**................................ DebraEngland(7) 3 50
(D Haydn Jones) *dwlt: hld up: sme hdwy 2f out: wknd fnl f* **17/2**

61.00 secs **Going Correction** -0.05s/f (Good) **11** Ran SP% **117.5**
Speed ratings (Par 103): **98,96,94,94,94 92,92,91,91,89 85**
toteswinger: 1&2 £8.60, 1&3 £12.90, 2&3 £27.80 CSF £43.94 CT £575.97 TOTE £3.90: £1.60, £3.50, £4.50; EX 61.90.
Owner Market Avenue Racing Club Ltd **Bred** Limestone And Tara Studs **Trained** Danethorpe, Notts

FOCUS
After the track decided against watering on Friday evening because they felt conditions would become too loose on top, the ground was riding extremely fast all round. There were, therefore, a host of non-runners, six in this modest sprint handicap, which was run at a good clip.

1878 BET ON TOTESCOOP6 AT TOTESPORT.COM H'CAP — 1m 6f 15y
2:25 (2:27) (Class 4) (0-85,82) 4-Y-O+ **£6,476** (£1,927; £963; £481) **Stalls** Low

Form RPR

316- **1** **Colonel Flay**[220] 6403 5-8-10 **70**.................................. JackMitchell(3) 2 78
(Mrs P N Dutfield) *hld up: hdwy u.p and hung lft fr over 1f out: styd on to ld post* **5/1**[3]

411- **2** *nse* **Silk Hall (UAE)**[36] 6934 4-9-10 **82**............................ RichardKingscote 3 90
(A King) *s.i.s: sn prom: rdn over 2f out: led over 1f out: hdd post* **11/8**[1]

1501 **3** *1 1/4* **Zuwaar**[14] 1506 4-8-13 **71**..(tp) RichardMullen 5 77
(Ian Williams) *hld up: rdn over 2f out: hdwy over 1f out: styd on* **9/2**[2]

00-6 **4** *3/4* **Four Miracles**[14] 1519 5-9-10 **81**..................................... SaleemGolam 1 86
(M H Tompkins) *trckd ldrs: racd keenly: rdn over 2f out: sn outpcd: styd on ins fnl f* **13/2**

-443 **5** *3 1/2* **Step This Way (USA)**[16] 1473 4-9-6 **78**........................... GregFairley 8 78
(M Johnston) *led 1f: chsd ldr: rdn over 2f out: wknd fnl f* **8/1**

2241 **6** *shd* **Sri Kuantan (IRE)**[9] 1635 5-9-1 **77**...........................(t) MarkCoumbe(5) 6 77
(R C Guest) *led after 1f: set stdy pce tl qcknd over 3f out: rdn and hdd over 1f out: wknd wl ins fnl f* **8/1**

3m 8.16s (3.16) **Going Correction** -0.05s/f (Good)
WFA 4 from 5yo+ 1lb **6** Ran SP% **112.5**
Speed ratings (Par 105): **88,87,87,86,84 84**
toteswinger: 1&2 £2.00, 1&3 £4.00, 2&3 £1.70 CSF £12.44 CT £31.89 TOTE £4.80: £2.10, £1.60; EX 12.40 Trifecta £48.90 Pool: £79.45 - 1.20 winning units..
Owner John Boswell **Bred** Mrs Nerys Dutfield **Trained** Axmouth, Devon
■ Stewards' Enquiry : Jack Mitchell three-day ban: used whip with excessive frequency (May 23-25)

FOCUS
A fair staying handicap run at a very steady gallop.

1879 BET IN PLAY AT TOTESPORT.COM H'CAP — 6f 15y
2:55 (2:56) (Class 3) (0-95,95) 3-Y-O **£9,714** (£2,890; £1,444; £721) **Stalls** High

Form RPR

10-2 **1** **Bouvardia**[25] 1272 3-8-9 **86**.. IanMongan 3 97+
(H R A Cecil) *trckd ldrs: led and hung rt over 1f out: shkn up and r.o* **1/1**[1]

2-13 **2** *1 3/4* **Servoca (CAN)**[24] 1296 3-8-7 **84**..................................... ChrisCatlin 2 90
(B W Hills) *led: rdn: hdd and hmpd over 1f out: styd on same pce* **11/4**[2]

21- **3** *1 3/4* **All About You (IRE)**[208] 6702 3-8-8 **85**.......................... LiamJones 8 84
(W J Haggas) *chsd ldrs: pushed along 1/2-way: styd on same pce appr fnl f* **7/2**[3]

3006 **4** *1 3/4* **Smokey Ryder**[6] 1705 3-9-1 **95**.............................. KevinGhunowa(3) 1 89
(R A Harris) *chsd ldr tl rdn 2f out: wknd ins fnl f* **20/1**

120- **5** *8* **Olynard (IRE)**[217] 6483 3-8-9 **86**.................................. RichardKingscote 5 64
(R M Beckett) *hld up: rdn 1/2-way: wknd over 1f out: eased* **8/1**

1m 14.6s (-0.30) **Going Correction** -0.05s/f (Good) **5** Ran SP% **114.8**
Speed ratings (Par 103): **100,97,95,93,82**
toteswinger: 1&2 £4.50 CSF £4.31 TOTE £2.40: £1.30, £2.30; EX 5.00 Trifecta £8.10 Pool: £53.73 - 4.90 winning units..
Owner K Abdulla **Bred** Juddmonte Farms Ltd **Trained** Newmarket, Suffolk

FOCUS
A useful handicap and in the end a clear-cut winner.

NOTEBOOK
Bouvardia looked sure to be suited by the step up to 6f and, very well backed beforehand, she got the job done, but showed she is far from straightforward. She played up behind the stalls, refusing to go in for some time, and then she was very keen through the early stages of the race. Switched around runners, she moved up strongly to challenge but once asked to go to win her race, she hung right towards the rail, coming across Servoca and forcing that rival to snatch up and switch wide. To be fair to the winner, she stayed on well once straightened up and probably would have won anyway, but it's clear she isn't without her chinks and it may be that this lightning fast ground isn't ideal. (op 11-8 tchd 6-4)
Servoca(CAN) looks much more straightforward but she doesn't have the natural ability of the winner. She showed good early speed and to her credit she stayed on well again once she was switched out in the final furlong, but given her early pace, 5f might suit her better. (op 5-2 tchd 3-1)
All About You(IRE), having her first start for William Haggas, couldn't get into it but she stayed on nicely enough on her first run of the year and probably needs slightly easier ground to show her best. She remains open to stacks of improvement this term, off what could still turn out to be a very lenient mark, and looks one to keep an eye on. (op 11-4 tchd 9-4)
Smokey Ryder, a prolific all-weather winner, weakened and didn't run her race, maybe because she's had a busy year, or perhaps the ground was too firm. (op 18-1 tchd 16-1)

1880 BIGGER ODDS GUARANTEED AT TOTESPORT.COM KILVINGTON FILLIES' STKS (LISTED RACE) — 6f 15y
3:30 (3:30) (Class 1) 3-Y-O+ **£23,704** (£8,964; £4,480; £2,240) **Stalls** High

Form RPR

116- **1** **Lesson In Humility (IRE)**[223] 6304 4-9-7 105............... AndrewElliott 1 112
(K R Burke) *mde virtually all: rdn over 1f out: swished tail: r.o* **5/2**[1]

2300 **2** *2 1/4* **Carcinetto (IRE)**[3] 1791 7-9-3 95.............................. PaulHanagan 2 101
(P D Evans) *prom: lost pl 4f out: hdwy u.p over 1f out: r.o* **16/1**

24-1 **3** *nk* **Look Busy (IRE)**[11] 1582 4-9-7 103.................................. SladeO'Hara 8 104
(A Berry) *a.p: rdn over 2f out: chsd wnr over 1f out: styd on same pce ins fnl f* **3/1**[2]

0-60 **4** *nk* **Max One Two Three (IRE)**[22] 1325 4-9-3 97.......... RichardKingscote 4 99
(Tom Dascombe) *s.i.s: sn pushed along in rr: hdwy over 1f out: nt rch ldrs* **4/1**[3]

64-0 **5** *2* **Crystany (IRE)**[20] 1394 4-9-3 90.................................. RichardMullen 9 93
(E A L Dunlop) *hld up: hdwy 1/2-way: rdn over 1f out: no ex ins fnl f* **10/1**

26-0 **6** *1 1/2* **Favourite Girl (IRE)**[21] 1353 3-8-7 102.............................. DavidAllan 10 85
(T D Easterby) *chsd ldrs: rdn over 2f out: wknd ins fnl f* **8/1**

5251 **7** *hd* **Princess Valerina**[23] 1313 5-9-3 84.. IanMongan 6 87
(D Haydn Jones) *s.i.s: hld up: rdn over 1f out: nvr trbld ldrs* **25/1**

30-0 **8** *5* **Quiet Elegance**[42] 996 4-9-3 89.............................. GrahamGibbons 11 71
(E J Alston) *chsd wnr tl rdn over 1f out: wknd fnl f* **14/1**

/6-0 **9** *3 1/4* **La Sylvia (IRE)**[11] 1582 4-9-3 83.. ChrisCatlin 3 61
(E J O'Neill) *hld up: a in rr: rdn over 2f out: wknd over 1f out* **50/1**

35-4 **10** *12* **Quaroma**[21] 1367 4-9-3 92.. PatCosgrave 5 65
(Jane Chapple-Hyam) *chsd ldrs: rdn over 2f out: hung lft and wknd over 1f out: eased* **10/1**

1m 13.35s (-1.55) **Going Correction** -0.05s/f (Good)
WFA 3 from 4yo+ 10lb **10** Ran SP% **121.2**
Speed ratings (Par 108): **108,105,104,104,101 99,99,92,88,72**
toteswinger: 1&2 £8.70, 1&3 £3.00, 2&3 £14.40 CSF £47.10 TOTE £3.80: £1.50, £4.30, £1.40; EX 46.00 Trifecta £111.30 Pool: £150.50 - 1.00 winning units..
Owner M Nelmes-Crocker **Bred** Kevin Quinn **Trained** Middleham Moor, N Yorks

FOCUS
Not a bad Listed sprint for fillies and the time was just under a second quicker than the previous handicap, but very few got into it and the plaudits must go to Andrew Elliott.

NOTEBOOK
Lesson In Humility(IRE) was bounced out from her wide draw and tacked right across towards the more favoured stands' rail. Soon in front, she never saw another rival, dominating the race and staying on strongly in the final furlong to keep everything at arm's length. She had every right to go close given she had the highest official rating, but to get the job done with such authority from the worst draw deserves credit and, although she flashes her tail, she is as game as they come. (op 3-1 tchd 7-2)
Carcinetto(IRE) is being worked hard, this being her seventh run since the start of April, but she continues to respond, staying on well out wide to snatch second, and running with credit given she is rated 10lb inferior to the winner. (tchd 14-1)
Look Busy(IRE) is better suited by the minimum trip, but she is a prolific winner at this level and she won a similar contest at Bath on her seasonal return. She moved up to within striking distance approaching the distance but her stamina began to give way close home and she was passed for second. She still acquitted herself very well and the return to 5f will doubtless see her bounce back. (op 10-3 tchd 7-2)
Max One Two Three(IRE) kept on well from some way back and, given she has won on good to soft, will probably do better on easier ground. (tchd 5-1)
Crystany(IRE) never got into it, although she had a tough task on these terms. (op 11-1 tchd 9-1)
Favourite Girl(IRE) held a good early position in behind the speed, but she dropped out and seems to need easier ground to show her best. (op 9-1)
Quiet Elegance Official explanation: jockey said filly was unsuited by the ground
Quaroma Official explanation: jockey said filly was unsuited by the firm (good to firm places) ground

1881 PLAY ROULETTE AT TOTESPORTCASINO.COM H'CAP — 1m 2f 50y
4:05 (4:05) (Class 6) (0-60,60) 4-Y-O+ **£2,047** (£604; £302) **Stalls** Low

Form RPR

106- **1** **Granary Girl**[204] 6775 7-8-8 **57**.................................... SimonPearce(7) 12 62
(J Pearce) *hld up: hdwy over 2f out: led and hung lft fr over 1f out: sn rdn: jst hld on* **12/1**

3602 **2** *nk* **Johnston's Baby (IRE)**[35] 1131 7-9-4 **60**......................... PatCosgrave 9 68+
(E J Alston) *s.i.s: hld up: hdwy 1/2-way: nt clr run and lost pl 3f out: swtchd rt and rallied over 1f out: r.o wl* **12/1**

2-02 **3** *nk* **Cheers For Thea (IRE)**[16] 1472 4-9-2 **58**........................ DavidAllan 11 62
(T D Easterby) *a.p: led over 2f out: rdn and hdd over 1f out: edgd lft: unable qck towards fin* **11/4**[1]

105- **4** *nk* **Astrolibra**[221] 6364 5-9-0 **56**... SaleemGolam 1 59
(M H Tompkins) *chsd ldrs: rdn over 1f out: styd on* **13/2**[3]

6305 **5** *1/2* **Just Observing**[36] 1099 6-8-8 **57**.................................(p) PaulPickard(7) 7 59
(P T Midgley) *chsd ldrs: outpcd over 2f out: rallied over 1f out: edgd lft: styd on* **5/1**[2]

-060 **6** ¾ **Strike Force**[82] 571 5-8-13 **58** JackMitchell(3) 14 59+
(Miss J Feilden) *hld up and bhd: hdwy over 3f out: nt clr run and lost pl over 1f out: r.o ins fnl f: nvr able to chal* **8/1**

-003 **7** ½ **Mayfair's Future**[13] 1538 4-9-2 **58** RichardMullen 8 58
(J R Jenkins) *chsd ldr tl led over 3f out: hdd over 2f out: rdn and hung lft ins fnl f: one pce* **13/2**[3]

6250 **8** ¾ **Spares And Repairs**[19] 1402 6-8-8 **53** AndrewMullen(3) 3 51
(Mrs S Lamyman) *sn led: rdn and hdd over 3f out: edgd lft over 1f out: no ex ins fnl f* **10/1**

-015 **9** 7 **Southern Mistral**[5] 1728 4-9-3 **59** (p) JerryO'Dwyer 4 43
(Miss Gay Kelleway) *prom: rdn over 2f out: wknd fnl f* **9/1**

2-00 **10** 13 **Gala Sunday (USA)**[19] 1402 9-9-2 **58** (bt) DaleGibson 10 16
(M W Easterby) *sn pushed along in rr: lost tch 1/2-way* **20/1**

2m 12.0s (0.30) **Going Correction** -0.05s/f (Good) **10** Ran SP% **120.3**
Speed ratings (Par 101): **96,95,95,95,94 94,93,93,87,77**
toteswinger: 1&2 £23.50, 1&3 £6.20, 2&3 £6.30 CSF £151.14 CT £516.36 TOTE £12.30: £3.40, £3.00, £1.30; EX 76.30.
Owner Mrs P O'Shea **Bred** Barry Minty **Trained** Newmarket, Suffolk

FOCUS
Low grade stuff but competitive nonetheless and something of a bunch finish despite the pace appearing honest enough throughout.
Gala Sunday(USA) Official explanation: jockey said gelding was unsuited by the firm (good to firm places) ground

1882 PLAY BLACKJACK AT TOTESPORTCASINO.COM H'CAP 1m 75y
4:35 (4:37) (Class 5) (0-75,77) 3-Y-O **£3,885** (£1,156; £577; £288) **Stalls** Low

Form RPR

13-4 **1** **Pride Of Kings**[17] 1462 3-9-3 **74** GregFairley 14 81+
(M Johnston) *chsd ldr: led over 2f out: rdn out* **9/2**[2]

306- **2** 1 ¼ **Veroon (IRE)**[182] 7241 3-9-0 **71** (b[1]) PatCosgrave 16 74
(J G Given) *led 1f: chsd ldrs: rdn over 1f out: kpt on* **16/1**

0-00 **3** 1 ¾ **Perfect Affair (USA)**[31] 1185 3-9-0 **71** RichardKingscote 6 70+
(R M Beckett) *hld up: hdwy over 2f out: rdn and hung lft over 1f out: styd on same pce* **9/1**

1-04 **4** nse **Kaolak (USA)**[37] 1082 3-9-4 **75** IanMongan 7 74
(J Ryan) *chsd ldrs: rdn and edgd lft over 1f out: styd on same pce* **10/1**

61-1 **5** ¾ **Roar Of Applause**[4] 1774 3-9-2 **73** 6ex LPKeniry 12 70
(B J Meehan) *hld up in tch: rdn over 2f out: hung lft over 1f out: no ex ins fnl f* **11/8**[1]

32-0 **6** 2 **Cabernet Sauvignon**[26] 1252 3-9-2 **73** J-PGuillambert 10 66
(J W Hills) *s.i.s: hld up: plld hrd: styd on appr fnl f: nt trble ldrs* **16/1**

431- **7** 3 ½ **Three Ducks**[154] 7578 3-9-4 **75** ChrisCatlin 8 60
(L M Cumani) *mid-div: pushed along over 3f out: n.d* **6/1**[3]

0-05 **8** 3 ¾ **Amethyst Dawn (IRE)**[12] 1559 3-8-12 **69** DavidAllan 3 45
(T D Easterby) *led over 7f out: rdn and hdd over 2f out: wknd over 1f out* **12/1**

25-5 **9** nk **What A Day**[22] 1331 3-8-11 **68** GrahamGibbons 4 43
(J J Quinn) *hld up: shkn up over 2f out: a in rr* **20/1**

56-0 **10** 7 **Inside Knowledge (USA)**[72] 686 3-8-0 **62** oh6 ow1 PatrickDonaghy(5) 11 21
(G Woodward) *hld up: rdn and wknd over 3f out* **66/1**

1-06 **11** 14 **Clumber Place**[16] 1471 3-8-11 **73** MarkCoumbe(5) 9 —
(R C Guest) *dwlt: a bhd* **50/1**

1m 44.57s (-1.03) **Going Correction** -0.05s/f (Good) **11** Ran SP% **121.3**
Speed ratings (Par 99): **103,101,100,99,99 97,93,89,89,82 68**
toteswinger: 1&2 £16.60, 1&3 £8.80, 2&3 £24.90 CSF £75.08 CT £644.83 TOTE £5.60: £1.80, £3.70, £2.50; EX 86.70.
Owner Jaber Abdullah **Bred** Floors Farming And Dominic Burke **Trained** Middleham Moor, N Yorks

FOCUS
Quite an interesting little 3yo handicap featuring some unexposed performers and while hotpot Roar Of Applause didn't run to the same level as Chepstow last time, the pace was honest and form still has a decent feel about it.
Roar Of Applause Official explanation: jockey said gelding was unsuited by the firm (good to firm places) ground
Clumber Place Official explanation: jockey said filly reared when stalls opened

1883 £10 FREE PLAY AT TOTESPORTBINGO.COM APPRENTICE H'CAP 1m 75y
5:05 (5:05) (Class 6) (0-60,69) 4-Y-O+ **£1,942** (£578; £288; £144) **Stalls** Low

Form RPR

3126 **1** **Forbidden (IRE)**[15] 1501 6-8-13 **59** (t) JamesPSullivan(5) 4 68
(Daniel Mark Loughnane, Ire) *hld up: hdwy over 2f out: rdn to ld and hung lft fr over 1f out: styd on u.p* **7/1**[2]

3305 **2** nk **Cavalry Guard (USA)**[8] 1641 5-8-5 **49** (b) AmyBaker(3) 2 57
(T D McCarthy) *led 1f: chsd ldrs: rdn over 3f out: led over 2f out: hdd over 1f out: ev ch ins fnl f: styd on* **12/1**

4040 **3** 1 ¾ **Comrade Cotton**[26] 1259 5-8-7 **55** RyanPowell(7) 8 59
(J Ryan) *prom: n.m.r and lost pl over 2f out: rallied over 1f out: r.o* **12/1**

2240 **4** nk **Aggbag**[18] 1438 5-8-10 **51** MichaelJStainton 1 54
(B P J Baugh) *a.p: rdn over 2f out: styd on same pce ins fnl f* **8/1**[3]

25-0 **5** ¾ **Cwm Rhondda (USA)**[10] 1606 4-9-2 **57** JackMitchell 10 59
(P W Chapple-Hyam) *hld up: rdn over 2f out: r.o ins fnl f: nvr nrr* **10/1**

0441 **6** 1 ¼ **Landucci**[10] 1606 8-9-11 **69** (p) WilliamCarson(3) 7 68
(S Curran) *hld up: racd keenly: hdwy over 2f out: rdn over 1f out: no ex fnl f* **6/1**[1]

6305 **7** 4 ½ **Ming Vase**[24] 1276 7-8-4 **50** PaulPickard(5) 16 38
(P T Midgley) *chsd ldrs: rdn over 2f out: wknd fnl f* **11/1**

00-4 **8** 5 **Lady Amberlini**[19] 1413 4-8-6 **54** DavidKenny(7) 13 31
(C R Dore) *mid-div: hdwy over 2f out: rdn and wknd over 1f out* **9/1**

-200 **9** ¾ **Wahoo Sam (USA)**[5] 9-8-12 **56** 6ex RichardEvans(3) 11 31
(P D Evans) *led over 7f out: rdn and hdd over 2f out: wknd over 1f out* **7/1**[2]

400- **10** 2 **Bed Fellow (IRE)**[151] 7613 5-7-13 **47** JanWilson(7) 15 18
(T D Barron) *dwlt: hdwy to chse ldr over 6f out: rdn and ev ch over 2f out: hung lft and wknd sn after* **7/1**[2]

00/1 **11** 12 **Mccormack (IRE)**[12] 1556 7-8-6 **52** DebraEngland(5) 12 —
(Miss T Jackson) *s.i.s: hld up: hdwy over 3f out: wknd over 2f out: eased over 1f out* **7/1**[2]

34-6 **12** 11 **The Wily Woodcock**[47] 344 5-8-12 **60** ow2 JoshWall(7) 17 —
(T Wall) *hld up: wknd over 3f out* **33/1**

1m 44.52s (-1.08) **Going Correction** -0.05s/f (Good) **12** Ran SP% **121.1**
Speed ratings (Par 101): **103,102,100,100,99 98,94,89,88,86 74,63**
toteswinger: 1&2 £18.90, 1&3 £19.70, 2&3 £33.40 CSF £90.25 CT £1005.67 TOTE £8.00: £2.60, £3.90, £3.90; EX 120.20 Place 6: £53.89, Place 5: £18.43..
Owner Lee Suir Syndicate **Bred** Gainsborough Stud Management Ltd **Trained** Trim, Co Meath

FOCUS
Quite a weak apprentice riders' handicap to end the day but a good finish between Cavalry Guard and Forbidden, who came clear in a driving finish.

T/Plt: £42.20 to a £1 stake. Pool: £53,587.06. 926.63 winning tickets. T/Qpdt: £14.30 to a £1 stake. Pool: £2,777.79. 142.90 winning tickets. CR

1680 THIRSK (L-H)
Saturday, May 9

OFFICIAL GOING: Good to firm (11.5)
Wind: Fresh, half-behind Weather: Sunny periods and showers

1884 TURFTV.CO.UK (S) STKS 5f
6:10 (6:11) (Class 5) 2-Y-O **£4,274** (£1,271; £635; £317) **Stalls** High

Form RPR

4 **1** **Gertmegalush (IRE)**[17] 1450 2-8-10 0 PaulHanagan 6 71
(J D Bethell) *chsd ldr: effrt 2f out and sn rdn: styd on u.p ent fnl f: led last 100yds* **9/4**[2]

352 **2** 1 ¾ **Reel Credit Crunch**[2] 1802 2-7-12 0 AndrewHeffernan(7) 2 60
(P D Evans) *led: rdn along 2f out: drvn ent fnl f: edgd lft: hdd and no ex last 100yds* **5/6**[1]

3 5 **On The Piste (IRE)** 2-7-12 0 JamieKyne(7) 5 42
(P T Midgley) *dwlt and hmpd s: hdwy to chse ldrs 1/2-way: sn rdn and hung bdly lft wl over 1f out: sn one pce* **20/1**

4 3 ¾ **Lairy (IRE)** 2-8-10 0 PaulQuinn 3 34
(D Nicholls) *wnt lft s: towards rr on outer: hdwy and swtchd rt wl over 1f out: sn rdn and hung rt appr fnl f: n.d* **15/2**[3]

0 **5** 4 ½ **Pong Ping**[8] 1653 2-8-5 0 DuranFentiman 4 12
(T D Easterby) *wnt rt s: sn rdn along and a in rr* **28/1**

06 **6** ¾ **Mostofitleft (IRE)**[9] 1624 2-8-5 0 DarrenMoffatt 1 10
(A Berry) *chsd ldrs: rdn along after 2f and sn wknd* **100/1**

7 1 ¾ **Francesca Conti (IRE)** 2-7-12 0 DeclanCannon(7) 7 3
(K R Burke) *sn rdn along and outpcd: a bhd* **14/1**

58.97 secs (-0.63) **Going Correction** -0.25s/f (Firm) **7** Ran SP% **113.0**
Speed ratings (Par 93): **95,92,84,78,71 69,67**
toteswinger: 1&2 £1.02, 1&3 £8.50, 2&3 £4.40 CSF £4.32 TOTE £3.10: £1.10, £1.40; EX 4.40.The winner was bought in for 5,800gns. Reel Credit Crunch was claimed by I. W. McInnes for £10,000.
Owner Business Development Consultants Limited **Bred** Kildare Racing Syndicate **Trained** Middleham Moor, N Yorks
■ Stewards' Enquiry : Paul Hanagan one-day ban: excessive use of the whip (May 23)

FOCUS
The first two home finished clear and set a respectable standard for a juvenile seller.

NOTEBOOK
Gertmegalush(IRE) showed promise at selling level on his debut, after which he was claimed, and the benefit of that experience was put to good use here. Racing against the stands' rail almost certainly helped, but it would be no surprise to find him making up into a nursery type. (op 2-1 tchd 11-4)
Reel Credit Crunch again went a good clip in front, only to be mown down late on by a fair sort at this level. She has more pace than most at this level and can win a race. (op Evens)
On The Piste(IRE), a fit-looking Distant Music filly whose dam won over 5f as a juvenile, has plenty of winners in her family and she showed enough on this debut to suggest she can do a bit better. Despite being stranded in the middle of the track, she did well to recover from a slow start, though she was well beaten by the first two in the end. Official explanation: jockey said filly hung left throughout (op 33-1)
Lairy(IRE), a half-brother to 7f and 1m3f winner Staff Nurse, showed a little on this first attempt despite being hampered by the third, but he needs to improve to find a race. (op 13-2)
Pong Ping, a half-sister to winners at 6f and 1m, is a daughter of the Listed juvenile winner Hoh Chi Min. However, the pairing of that mare with the top-class Dr Fong does not seem to have been particularly successful this time. (op 33-1 tchd 20-1)
Mostofitleft(IRE) showed early speed but has now been well beaten in sellers and the fact that she is now eligible to be handicapped is more a technical observation than anything else.

1885 DICK PEACOCK SPRINT H'CAP 6f
6:40 (6:41) (Class 5) (0-75,75) 4-Y-O+ **£4,274** (£1,271; £635; £317) **Stalls** High

Form RPR

531- **1** **Elijah Pepper (USA)**[276] 4745 4-8-1 **63** DeanHeslop(5) 13 74
(T D Barron) *dwlt: sn trcking ldrs: swtchd lft and hdwy wl over 1f out: rdn to ld jst ins fnl f: styd on strly* **5/1**[1]

000- **2** 2 **Sea Rover (IRE)**[334] 2891 5-8-8 **65** TWilliams 11 70
(M Brittain) *cl up: led 1/2-way: rdn wl over 1f out: drvn and hdd jst ins fnl f: kpt onsame pce* **33/1**

-601 **3** 1 ¼ **Guest Connections**[6] 1694 6-8-2 **66** 6ex (v) AdeleMulrennan(7) 7 67+
(D Nicholls) *hld up in rr: hdwy 1/2-way: swtchd lft and rdn wl over 1f out: styd on ins fnl f* **5/1**[1]

136- **4** ½ **Atlantic Beach**[323] 3202 4-8-13 **70** PaulHanagan 4 69
(R A Fahey) *prom: rdn along over 2f out: drvn over 1f out and kpt on same pce* **9/1**[3]

6-40 **5** nse **No Grouse**[22] 1333 9-8-2 **62** AndrewMullen(3) 9 61
(E J Alston) *midfield: hdwy on inner 2f out: sn rdn and styd on wl fnl f: nrst fin* **14/1**

10-2 **6** 2 ½ **Medici Time**[21] 1369 4-8-7 **64** (v) DavidAllan 10 55
(T D Easterby) *sltly hmpdv s: chsd ldrs: rdn along 2f out and sn no imp* **6/1**[2]

425 **7** shd **Secret Dubai (IRE)**[6] 1689 4-8-3 **67** KristinStubbs(7) 5 58
(Mrs L Stubbs) *chsd ldrs: hdwy over 2f out: sn rdn and wknd over 1f out* **12/1**

0-00 **8** 1 **Dorn Dancer (IRE)**[38] 1060 7-8-10 **72** FrederikTylicki(5) 3 60
(D W Barker) *bhd and rdn along 1/2-way: hdwy 2f out: styd on appr last: nt rch ldrs* **10/1**

-000 **9** 1 **Timber Treasure (USA)**[14] 1510 5-9-2 **73** (b) PaulQuinn 6 58
(Paul Green) *a towards rr* **16/1**

0-25 **10** hd **Jack Rackham**[123] 68 5-9-1 **72** (v) TomEaves 1 56
(B Smart) *chsd ldrs on outer: rdn along wl over 2f out: sn wknd* **14/1**

33-6 **11** 2 **Mr Wolf**[14] 1518 8-9-3 **74** (p) TonyHamilton 12 51
(D W Barker) *led: hdd 1/2-way: sn rdn and wknd wl over 1f out* **5/1**[1]

206- **12** 6 **He's A Humbug (IRE)**[141] 7730 5-9-4 **75** (p) JerryO'Dwyer 2 33
(J O'Reilly) *a in rr* **20/1**

69.85 secs (-2.85) **Going Correction** -0.25s/f (Firm) **12** Ran SP% **118.0**
Speed ratings (Par 103): **109,106,104,104,103 100,100,99,97,97 94,86**
toteswinger: 1&2 £36.70, 1&3 £6.40, 2&3 £49.40 CSF £172.51 CT £884.86 TOTE £6.30: £2.20, £10.70, £2.60; EX 97.60.
Owner Harrowgate Bloodstock Ltd **Bred** Liberation Farm & Oratis Thoroughbreds **Trained** Maunby, N Yorks
■ Stewards' Enquiry : Paul Hanagan one-day ban: failed to ride to draw (May 24)

FOCUS
The first pair were the two closest to the stands' rail, suggesting the traditional advantage was intact for this meeting. The race could rate a bit higher but for the draw advantage.
Mr Wolf Official explanation: jockey said gelding hung left final 2f

He's A Humbug(IRE) Official explanation: jockey said gelding never travelled

1886 GT GROUP H'CAP — 1m 4f
7:10 (7:10) (Class 4) (0-80,79) 4-Y-0+ — £5,569 (£1,657; £828; £413) Stalls Low

Form — RPR

216- **1** **Valdan (IRE)**[133] 7791 5-8-0 **68** .... AndrewHeffernan(7) 10 — 80
(P D Evans) *hld up in rr: smooth hdwy over 3f out: trckd ldrs gng wl 2f out: swtchd rt and rdn to ld over 1f out: clr ins fnl f and styd on strly* **8/1**[3]

12-2 **2** 5 **Aleatricis**[16] 1473 4-8-9 **77** .... JamieKyne(7) 9 — 81
(J J Quinn) *hld up towards rr: hdwy 3f out: rdn wl over 1f out: styd on ins fnl f: no ch w wnr* **11/4**[1]

5510 **3** 2 **Masterofceremonies**[10] 1615 6-8-6 **67** ....(v) DarrenMoffatt 8 — 67
(James Moffatt) *s.i.s and bhd: hdwy over 2f out: sn rdn and styd on strly ins fnl f: tk 3rd nr line* **12/1**

450- **4** hd **Inspector Clouseau (IRE)**[208] 6698 4-8-13 **74** .... MickyFenton 6 — 74
(T P Tate) *chsd ldr: hdwy 3f out: rdn over 2f out: led wl over 1f out: sn drvn: edgd lft and hdd over 1f out: one pce* **4/1**[2]

214- **5** 2 1/4 **Woody Waller**[51] 6113 4-8-12 **73** .... PaulMulrennan 4 — 69
(J Howard Johnson) *in tch: hdwy to chse ldrs 1/2-way: rdn along 3f out: drvn over 2f out and sn btn* **4/1**[2]

32-5 **6** shd **Sir Royal (USA)**[16] 1473 4-9-0 **75** .... TomEaves 7 — 71
(G A Swinbank) *plld hrd: chsd ldng pair: effrt on inner over 2f out: sn rdn and wknd over 1f out* **10/1**

-000 **7** 3 1/4 **Oddsmaker (IRE)**[6] 1692 8-8-7 **68** ....(t) TonyHamilton 11 — 59
(M A Barnes) *led and set str gallop: rdn along 3f out: hdd wl over 1f out and sn wknd* **9/1**

00-4 **8** 2 1/2 **Mister Arjay (USA)**[12] 1557 9-8-4 **65** oh1 .... RoystonFfrench 2 — 52
(B Ellison) *in tch: rdn along over 5f out and sn wknd* **12/1**

534- **9** 6 **Border Owl (IRE)**[71] 6675 4-9-4 **79** .... DaleGibson 5 — 56
(P Salmon) *chsd ldrs: rdn along over 3f out and sn wknd* **20/1**

2m 31.66s (-4.54) **Going Correction** -0.25s/f (Firm) — 9 Ran SP% **117.0**
Speed ratings (Par 105): **105,101,100,100,98 98,96,94,90**
toteswinger: 1&2 £8.60, 1&3 £72.00, 2&3 £4.00 CSF £30.74 CT £268.63 TOTE £15.90: £3.80, £1.10, £4.20; EX 56.40.
Owner D Maloney **Bred** Herbertstown Stud Ltd **Trained** Pandy, Monmouths

FOCUS
They went a fast tempo, so it was no surprise to see the finish dominated by horses coming from some way back. The form looks decent with the third the best guide.
Woody Waller Official explanation: jockey said gelding was unsuited by the good to firm ground

1887 CALVERTS CARPETS H'CAP — 1m
7:40 (7:40) (Class 5) (0-75,72) 4-Y-0+ — £4,274 (£1,271; £635; £317) Stalls Low

Form — RPR

-233 **1** **Bere Davis (FR)**[5] 1722 4-8-11 **72** .... AndrewHeffernan(7) 10 — 79
(P D Evans) *mde all: rdn over 2f out: drvn over 1f out: strly pressed ins fnl f: hld on gamely nr fin* **6/1**[3]

1040 **2** shd **Follow The Flag (IRE)**[15] 1493 5-8-11 **70** ....(p) FrederikTylicki(5) 2 — 77
(A J McCabe) *hld up towards rr: hdwy on outer over 2f out: rdn to chal jst ins fnl f and ev ch tl drvn and no ex nr fin* **11/1**

3353 **3** 1 1/2 **Kildare Sun (IRE)**[22] 1332 7-8-9 **63** ....(v) PaulHanagan 1 — 67
(J Mackie) *midfield: effrt on inner 3f out and sn rdn along: drvn 2f out: styd on ins fnl f: nrst fin* **5/2**[1]

5-02 **4** hd **Champain Sands (IRE)**[19] 1401 10-8-2 **59** .... AndrewMullen(3) 3 — 62
(E J Alston) *hld up towards rr: hdwy over 2f out: sn rdn and kpt on fnl f: nrst fin* **6/1**[3]

-524 **5** 1 1/2 **Obezyana (USA)**[38] 1067 7-8-11 **72** ....(v[1]) NatashaEaton(7) 17 — 72
(A Bailey) *sn chsng wnr: rdn over 2f out: drvn over 1f out: wknd ins fnl f* **25/1**

60-0 **6** 1 3/4 **Slip Star**[26] 1244 6-7-11 **58** oh8 .... MarzenaJeziorek(7) 8 — 54
(T J Etherington) *chsd ldng pair: rdn along over 2f out: sn drvn and grad wknd* **100/1**

50-2 **7** nk **Society Music (IRE)**[22] 1332 7-8-13 **67** .... PhillipMakin 11 — 62
(M Dods) *hld up in midfield: hdwy to chse ldrs wl over 2f out: rdn wl over 1f out and sn no imp* **11/2**[2]

4312 **8** 1 1/2 **Dancing Maite**[14] 1510 4-9-3 **71** .... RobertWinston 4 — 65+
(S R Bowring) *hld up towards rr: sme hdwy over 2f out: nvr nr ldrs and eased ent fnl f* **13/2**

2040 **9** nk **Stoic Leader (IRE)**[19] 1401 9-8-13 **67** .... RoystonFfrench 6 — 58
(R F Fisher) *chsd ldrs: rdn along over 3f out: drvn and wknd over 2f out* **20/1**

/00- **10** 1 1/2 **Fyodorovich (USA)**[206] 2674 4-9-2 **70** .... PAspell 14 — 57
(J S Wainwright) *stdd s: hld up and a towards rr* **100/1**

0-00 **11** 1/2 **Violent Velocity (IRE)**[22] 1332 6-8-4 **65** .... JamieKyne(7) 13 — 51
(J J Quinn) *chsd ldng pair: rdn along over 3f out and sn wknd* **16/1**

-605 **12** 30 **Spin Again (IRE)**[26] 1246 4-8-11 **72** .... NSLawes(7) 9 — —
(D Nicholls) *s.i.s: sddle slipped after 2f: sn chsng ldrs tl wd st and sn bhd* **16/1**

1m 38.32s (-1.78) **Going Correction** -0.25s/f (Firm) — 12 Ran SP% **116.5**
Speed ratings (Par 103): **98,97,96,96,94 92,92,91,90,89 88,58**
toteswinger: 1&2 £15.50, 1&3 £6.00, 2&3 £17.80 CSF £66.84 CT £209.49 TOTE £7.70: £2.10, £3.40, £1.50; EX 120.50.
Owner J G White **Bred** Claude Quellier & Mme Svetlana Timon **Trained** Pandy, Monmouths
■ Stewards' Enquiry : Frederik Tylicki twenty-day ban: two-day ban: used whip with excessive frequency; eighteen days under totting-up procedure (May 22-24, May 26-Jun 5)
Andrew Heffernan two-day ban: excessive use of the whip (May 23-24)

FOCUS
An ordinary handicap in which a well-judged front-running ride from Heffernan helped to win the day. The third is the best guide to the level with the 9out of the handicap) sixth limiting things.
Dancing Maite Official explanation: jockey said gelding was unsuited by the good to firm ground
Stoic Leader(IRE) Official explanation: jockey said gelding slipped on bend
Spin Again(IRE) Official explanation: jockey said saddle slipped

1888 ARMY BENEVOLENT FUND MAIDEN STKS — 1m
8:10 (8:12) (Class 5) 3-Y-0+ — £4,274 (£1,271; £635; £317) Stalls Low

Form — RPR

442- **1** **Russian George (IRE)**[232] 6082 3-8-13 75 .... MickyFenton 5 — 61
(T P Tate) *mde all: rdn along 2f out: drvn ent fnl f and styd on strly* **5/4**[1]

03-6 **2** 1 **Monetary Fund (USA)**[24] 1289 3-8-13 83 .... PaulHanagan 12 — 58
(G A Butler) *trckd ldrs: hdwy to chse wnr 3f out: rdn wl over 1f out: drvn ins fnl f and kpt on same pce* **7/4**[2]

30- **3** 1/2 **Starla Dancer (GER)**[201] 6858 3-8-8 0 .... TonyHamilton 6 — 52+
(R A Fahey) *hld up towards rr: stdy hdwy over 2f out: swtchd rt and rdn over 1f out: kpt on fnl f: nrst fin* **16/1**

00 **4** 2 3/4 **Bestowed**[1] 1848 4-9-9 0 .... LeeVickers(3) 9 — 54
(M C Chapman) *s.i.s and bhd: hdwy over 2f out: sn rdn and styd on ins fnl f: nrst fin* **200/1**

50 **5** 1 1/4 **Funky Munky**[27] 1228 4-9-12 0 .... TomEaves 2 — 51
(G A Swinbank) *t.k.h: hld up towards rr: hdwy over 2f out: kpt on same pce ins fnl f* **20/1**

6 1 **Son Of Monsieur** 3-8-13 0 .... DuranFentiman 11 — 46
(G R Oldroyd) *chsd ldrs: rdn along over 2f out: sn one pce* **66/1**

7 1/2 **Blastie** 4-9-12 0 .... GrahamGibbons 7 — 48
(T D Walford) *t.k.h: chsd ldrs: rdn along over 2f out: sn no imp* **28/1**

0 **8** hd **Bobeachway (IRE)**[14] 1508 3-8-13 0 .... PhillipMakin 8 — 44
(M Dods) *hld up and bhd: hdwy on wd outside over 2f out: swtchd lft over 1f out: kpton ins fnl f: nt rch ldrs* **20/1**

00 **9** 2 3/4 **Flynn's Island (IRE)**[7] 1683 3-8-8 0 .... PatrickDonaghy(5) 10 — 38
(M Dods) *hld up: a in rr* **33/1**

040- **10** 1 **Soviet Rhythm**[214] 6547 3-8-8 62 .... RoystonFfrench 4 — 31
(G M Moore) *chsd ldrs: lost pl after 3f and bhd fnl 3f* **16/1**

11 2 1/4 **Upper Key** 3-8-13 0 .... PaulMulrennan 3 — 30
(K A Ryan) *dwlt: sn prom: rdn along over 3f out and sn wknd* **10/1**[3]

/00- **12** 3/4 **Call Of Ktulu (IRE)**[326] 3115 4-9-12 12 .... PAspell 1 — 32
(J S Wainwright) *prom: rdn along over 3f out and sn wknd* **200/1**

1m 40.02s (-0.08) **Going Correction** -0.25s/f (Firm)
WFA 3 from 4yo 13lb — 12 Ran SP% **120.1**
Speed ratings (Par 103): **90,89,88,85,84 83,83,82,80,79 76,76**
toteswinger: 1&2 £1.20, 1&3 £6.20, 2&3 £5.30 CSF £3.29 TOTE £2.40: £1.30, £1.10, £5.20; EX 3.30.
Owner P J Martin **Bred** Martin Walsh **Trained** Tadcaster, N Yorks

FOCUS
Conditions had already been shown to be ideal for front-runners as long as they set a sensible pace like this. The form is modest and somewhat shaky.
Upper Key Official explanation: jockey said gelding hung both ways throughout

1889 TURFTV.CO.UK H'CAP — 7f
8:40 (8:41) (Class 6) (0-55,57) 4-Y-0+ — £2,978 (£886; £442; £221) Stalls Low

Form — RPR

25-0 **1** **Silly Gilly (IRE)**[22] 1332 5-8-6 **54** .... DeclanCannon(7) 4 — 64
(R E Barr) *chsd ldng pair: hdwy over 2f out: rdn over 1f out: styd on to ld ins fnl f: drvn and hld on wl nr fin* **9/2**[1]

6321 **2** nk **Ace Of Spies (IRE)**[12] 1558 4-9-2 **57** ....(p) SilvestreDeSousa 16 — 66+
(G A Harker) *broke wl: sn stdd and hld up in rr: hdwy on outer 2f out: rdn over 1f out: styd on strly ins fnl f: jst hld* **9/2**[1]

00-4 **3** 3/4 **Brother Barry (USA)**[4] 1777 4-9-0 **55** .... RobertWinston 13 — 62
(G A Swinbank) *sn chsng ldr: hdwy over 2f out: rdn to ld wl over 1f out: drvn and hdd ins fnl f: no ex u.p towards fin* **7/1**[3]

3306 **4** nk **Magical Song**[8] 1655 4-8-11 **52** ....(b) PaulMulrennan 7 — 58
(J Balding) *led: rdn along over 2f out: sn hdd and drvn: cl up and rallied u.p ins fnl f: no ex towards fin* **16/1**

4335 **5** 3/4 **Nabeeda**[106] 277 4-8-7 **55** .... JohnCavanagh(7) 5 — 59
(M Brittain) *chsd ldrs: rdn over 2f out: swtchd rt and hdwy over 1f out: drvn and kpt on ins fnl f* **8/1**

3303 **6** 1 3/4 **Kingsmaite**[12] 1558 8-8-11 **52** ....(b) PhillipMakin 6 — 51
(S R Bowring) *hld up towards rr: effrt and hdwy on outer over 2f out: rdn over 1f out and kpt on ins fnl f: nrst fin* **7/1**[3]

-040 **7** 1 1/4 **Cheery Cat (USA)**[16] 1475 5-8-13 **54** ....(p) TonyHamilton 12 — 50
(D W Barker) *in tch: rdn along and sltly outpcd 3f out: kpt on u.p appr fnl f* **12/1**

000- **8** hd **Rowaad**[194] 7021 4-8-11 **52** .... GrahamGibbons 10 — 47
(A E Price) *chadsed ldrs: rdn along wl over 2f out: drvn and wknd over 1f out* **16/1**

0-60 **9** 1 1/2 **Greek Secret**[12] 1558 6-8-11 **52** ....(p) DavidAllan 9 — 43
(J O'Reilly) *a towards rr* **18/1**

-000 **10** 1 1/2 **Wiseman's Diamond (USA)**[8] 1650 4-8-11 **52** ....(p) JamieMoriarty 2 — 39
(P T Midgley) *dwlt: a towards rr* **25/1**

1661 **11** 3 3/4 **Straight Face (IRE)**[5] 1734 5-8-11 **52** ....(v) PaulHanagan 15 — 29
(Miss Gay Kelleway) *hld up: a in rr* **11/2**[2]

5006 **12** 2 1/2 **Johnny Friendly**[14] 1520 4-8-6 **52** .... MartinLane(5) 14 — 22
(K R Burke) *chsd ldrs: rdn along 3f out: sn wknd* **33/1**

00-0 **P** **Pasta Prayer**[17] 1465 4-8-11 **52** ....(b) MickyFenton 3 — —
(D E Cantillon) *dwlt: sn chsng ldrs: pushed along on inner and lost pl 1/2-way: lost action and bhd whn p.u 2f out* **33/1**

1m 25.62s (-1.58) **Going Correction** -0.25s/f (Firm) — 13 Ran SP% **122.3**
Speed ratings (Par 101): **99,98,97,97,96 94,93,92,91,89 85,82,—**
toteswinger: 1&2 £4.60, 1&3 £4.90, 2&3 £5.90 CSF £23.90 CT £146.54 TOTE £5.70: £1.40, £2.40, £3.40; EX 23.60 Place 6: £11.91, Place 5: £11.80..
Owner Malcolm O'Hair **Bred** Barronstown Stud **Trained** Seamer, N Yorks

FOCUS
A decent gallop, but one which gave every runner a chance, and the placed horses came from both ends of the field. The form looks straightforward but modest.
Ace Of Spies(IRE) ◆ Official explanation: jockey said gelding hung right round bend
Straight Face(IRE) Official explanation: jockey said gelding was unsuited by the good to firm ground
Pasta Prayer Official explanation: vet said gelding pulled up lame
T/Plt: £29.80 to a £1 stake. Pool: £50,447.79. 1,235.22 winning tickets. T/Qpdt: £7.10 to a £1 stake. Pool: £3,290.77. 342.18 winning tickets. JR

1741 WARWICK (L-H)
Saturday, May 9

OFFICIAL GOING: Good to firm (firm in places; 9.8)
Wind: Moderate, behind Weather: Cloudy

1890 RACING UK H'CAP — 6f
5:55 (5:56) (Class 6) (0-65,65) 4-Y-0+ — £1,942 (£578; £288; £144) Stalls Low

Form — RPR

0-30 **1** **Hazytoo**[22] 1320 5-9-3 **64** .... FergusSweeney 3 — 76
(P J Makin) *mde all: rdn and edgd rt jst over 1f out: r.o wl* **6/1**[1]

4161 **2** 3 3/4 **Suhayl Star (IRE)**[11] 1587 5-9-3 **64** .... PaulFitzsimons 1 — 64
(P Burgoyne) *a chsng wnr: rdn fnl f: no imp* **8/1**[2]

4006 **3** 3/4 **Fizzlephut (IRE)**[11] 1591 7-8-9 **56** .... WandersonD'Avila 16 — 54
(Miss J R Tooth) *a.p: rdn 2f out: one pce fnl f* **66/1**

-600 **4** hd **Radiator Rooney (IRE)**[6] 1695 6-8-5 **52** .... RichardMullen 10 — 49
(Patrick Morris) *hld up in mid-div: hdwy on ins over 1f out: sn rdn: kpt on ins fnl f* **20/1**

5603 **5** 3/4 **Teen Ager (FR)**[11] 1587 5-8-5 **52** .... AndrewElliott 8 — 47
(P Burgoyne) *a.p: kpt on same pce fnl 2f* **12/1**

6-40 **6** 1 **Gambling Jack**[15] 1495 4-7-13 **51** .... AndreaAtzeni(5) 6 — 42
(A W Carroll) *in rr: rdn 2f out: hdwy 1f out: nvr trbld ldrs* **20/1**

504 **7** 1 **Zars Gold (IRE)**[9] 1634 4-8-13 **60**....................................(p) JimCrowley 4 48
(J Gallagher) *hld up in tch: rdn wl over 1f out: no hdwy* **8/1**[2]

6-05 **8** 1 ¼ **Ingleby Princess**[21] 1369 5-8-6 **60**.............................. AdamCarter(7) 15 44
(T D Barron) *in rr: rdn and sme prog 1f out: n.d* **14/1**

-000 **9** 1 **Ride A White Swan**[10] 1606 4-8-6 **56**..................... KevinGhunowa(3) 12 37
(D Shaw) *towards rr: rdn over 1f out: n.d* **33/1**

304- **10** ½ **Danzili Bay**[226] 6225 7-9-1 **62**.. ShaneKelly 7 41
(A W Carroll) *chsd ldrs: lost pl 2f out: n.d after* **10/1**

50-0 **11** 2 ¼ **Dualagi**[17] 1468 5-8-10 **57**.. TravisBlock 11 29
(M R Bosley) *a towards rr* **16/1**

20-0 **12** nk **Baby Rock**[26] 1248 4-9-4 **65**... SebSanders 13 36
(C F Wall) *in tch: rdn wl over 1f out: wknd ent fnl f* **9/1**[3]

5001 **13** 2 ¼ **Style Award**[5] 1748 4-9-1 **65**....................................(p) KellyHarrison(3) 17 29
(W J H Ratcliffe) *mid-div: edgd lft and wknd wl over 1f out* **8/1**[2]

60-3 **14** 3 ¼ **Sister Moonshine**[17] 1465 4-8-5 **52**................................ DO'Donohoe 2 6
(W R Muir) *outpcd* **12/1**

0-60 **15** 1 **James Pollard (IRE)**[10] 1606 4-8-9 **56**...................... CatherineGannon 9 6
(D R C Elsworth) *prom tl wknd wl over 1f out* **8/1**[2]

69.97 secs (-1.83) **Going Correction** -0.275s/f (Firm) course record **15** Ran SP% **119.7**
Speed ratings (Par 101): **101,96,95,94,93 92,91,89,88,87 84,84,81,76,75**
toteswinger: 1&2 £12.70, 1&3 £64.30, 2&3 £65.90 CSF £48.93 CT £2949.11 TOTE £6.50: £3.00, £2.00, £12.30; EX 45.00.
Owner Wedgewood Estates **Bred** Mrs Liza Judd **Trained** Ogbourne Maisey, Wilts
■ Stewards' Enquiry : Kevin Ghunowa one-day ban: used whip without giving gelding time to respond (May 23)

FOCUS
Virtually all of these can be disappointing, so this did not make much appeal as a betting medium, although many were punted. The first two home were the first two throughout and the rest made very little impression.
Zars Gold(IRE) Official explanation: jockey said filly hung right-handed throughout

1891 NETWORK GROUP HOLDINGS MAIDEN AUCTION STKS 5f 110y
6:25 (6:28) (Class 5) 2-Y-O **£2,729** (£806; £403) **Stalls** Low

Form RPR

1 **Antonius Moris (IRE)** 2-9-2 0.................................. RichardKingscote 9 77
(Tom Dascombe) *a.p: rdn over 1f out: r.o to ld nr fin* **4/1**[2]

0 **2** nk **Reddy To Star (IRE)**[7] 1669 2-8-11 0................................ AdamKirby 2 71
(C G Cox) *led early: prom: rdn to ld jst over 1f out: sn hung rt: hdd nr fin* **11/10**[1]

64 **3** nk **Flapjack**[13] 1534 2-8-6 0... ShaneKelly 7 65
(R Hannon) *sn led: edgd rt over 2f out: rdn and hdd jst over 1f out: r.o* **9/2**[3]

4 1 ½ **Soul Heaven** 2-8-9 0.. RichardMullen 6 67+
(M L W Bell) *s.i.s: hld up: hdwy 2f out: hld whn n.m.r and eased cl home* **14/1**

0 **5** 4 **Perfect Ch'l (IRE)**[12] 1569 2-8-1 0................................ DavidProbert(3) 1 45
(I A Wood) *s.i.s: bhd: rdn 2f out: edgd lft over 1f out: nvr nr ldrs* **9/1**

6 4 ½ **Sweet Baby Jane (IRE)** 2-8-4 0....................................... DO'Donohoe 8 30
(R A Fahey) *w ldr tl n.m.r over 2f out: wknd over 1f out* **14/1**

026 **7** 3 ¼ **Island Express (IRE)**[10] 1610 2-8-9 0 ow5........................ AnnStokell(5) 4 29
(Miss A Stokell) *s.i.s: sn chsng ldrs: wknd over 2f out* **25/1**

66.09 secs (0.19) **Going Correction** -0.275s/f (Firm) 7 Ran SP% **113.0**
Speed ratings (Par 93): **87,86,86,84,78 72,68**
toteswinger: 1&2 £1.50, 1&3 £4.10, 2&3 £1.10 CSF £8.58 TOTE £5.00: £2.50, £1.60; EX 7.80.
Owner Gary And Linnet Woodward **Bred** Miss Alice Fitzgerald **Trained** Lambourn, Berks

FOCUS
An ordinary-looking juvenile maiden that was weakened by the absence of Kaspirit due to the ground. The market moves before the off were virtually spot-on.

NOTEBOOK
Antonius Moris(IRE), a half-brother to Mullaad, who was a useful dual 5f winner at two, had to give away upward of 5lb on his debut but seemed to know his job and rallied really well, despite reportedly looking a bit green in the preliminaries, to be a comfortable winner. The market spoke in his favour, so this success probably did not surprise too many involved with him. (op 7-1 tchd 8-1)
Reddy To Star(IRE) missed the break on his debut after being well backed the previous weekend and was strong in the market again here. Settled in just behind the leaders, the jockey gave him every chance, but he was not quite good enough and hindered his progress by wanting to hang towards the stands' side. (op 11-8 tchd 6-4)
Flapjack was reportedly still in need of experience when a staying-on fourth in a Brighton maiden last time, and she showed a tiny bit of inexperience again about two furlongs out, although this was probably an accurate guide to her ability. Official explanation: jockey said filly hung right-handed (op 4-1 tchd 7-2)
Soul Heaven ◆ was the eyecatcher of the race. He was very green when asked to make his bid for victory and may have proved very troublesome to the winner had he known what was required. Hampered about 50 yards from the line, races will be won with him. (op 7-1)
Perfect Ch'l(IRE) got behind before staying on but this was a big improvement on her debut effort. (op 16-1)
Sweet Baby Jane(IRE) showed up for quite a while, looking a little keen, before weakening over a furlong out. (op 11-1)

1892 JAMES RYAN FAMILY H'CAP 1m 6f 213y
6:55 (6:56) (Class 5) (0-75,73) 4-Y-O+ **£3,238** (£963; £481; £240) **Stalls** Low

Form RPR

23-2 **1** **Wild Rhubarb**[18] 1427 4-9-11 **73**... AdamKirby 7 85+
(C G Cox) *a.p: wnt 2nd after 4f: led 3f out: rdn clr over 1f out: eased cl home* **15/8**[1]

530- **2** 2 ¾ **Sir Sandicliffe (IRE)**[159] 7515 5-9-4 **64**........................ TGMcLaughlin 1 69
(W M Brisbourne) *s.i.s: hld up and bhd: pushed along over 4f out: rdn 2f out: styd on to take 2nd towards fin: no ch w wnr* **18/1**

3-21 **3** nk **Isabelonabicycle**[18] 1426 4-9-7 **69**... LPKeniry 5 74
(A M Balding) *t.k.h in tch: rdn to chse wnr jst over 1f out: no imp: lost 2nd towards fin* **2/1**[2]

-431 **4** 2 **Colourful Move**[10] 1609 4-8-13 **61**................................. RobertHavlin 3 63
(P G Murphy) *led 3f: a.p: rdn over 1f out: no ex wl ins fnl f* **13/2**[3]

0-60 **5** 3 **Kiho**[24] 1287 4-8-11 **59**... StephenCarson 8 57
(Eve Johnson Houghton) *w ldr: led after 3f to 3f out: wknd ins fnl f* **13/2**[3]

2460 **6** 3 ½ **Hammer**[12] 1571 4-9-0 **62**.. SteveDrowne 2 55
(R T Phillips) *prom tl stdd after 3f: pushed along 3f out: rdn and wknd over 1f out* **10/1**

3m 18.27s (-0.73) **Going Correction** -0.05s/f (Good)
WFA 4 from 5yo+ 2lb 6 Ran SP% **109.1**
Speed ratings (Par 103): **99,97,97,96,94 92**
toteswinger: 1&2 £5.90, 1&3 £1.10, 2&3 £6.80 CSF £30.57 CT £65.39 TOTE £2.80: £1.40, £6.80; EX 25.20.
Owner D J Burke **Bred** Whitley Stud **Trained** Lambourn, Berks

FOCUS
Despite the lack of runners, this had looked a competitive staying race for its grade. The gallop was not that strong in the early stages but quickened about half a mile out, which made the winning time look very poor when considering the quick conditions.

1893 PSA PEUGEOT CITROEN LONG SERVICE MAIDEN FILLIES' STKS 1m 2f 188y
7:25 (7:26) (Class 5) 3-Y-O+ **£2,914** (£867; £433; £216) **Stalls** Low

Form RPR

430- **1** **Multiplication**[225] 6240 3-8-11 79...................................... SteveDrowne 1 73+
(R Charlton) *mde all: clr over 1f out: pushed out* **10/11**[1]

0-5 **2** 7 **Silent Act (USA)**[15] 1488 3-8-11 0..................................(t) JimCrowley 9 59+
(Mrs A J Perrett) *a chsng wnr: rdn 2f out: sn btn* **4/1**[3]

00 **3** 1 ¾ **Rosewin (IRE)**[10] 1611 3-8-8 44............................... KevinGhunowa(3) 7 56
(O Brennan) *hld up in tch: rdn and btn over 1f out: tk 3rd nr fin* **66/1**

0 **4** nk **Gold Maha**[25] 1269 3-8-11 0.. DarryllHolland 2 57+
(M R Channon) *a.p: rdn 2f out: sn btn: eased wl ins fnl f: lost 3rd nr fin* **7/2**[2]

- **5** ½ **Penolva (IRE)** 3-8-11 0... AndrewElliott 3 54
(K R Burke) *s.i.s: hld up: rdn over 2f out: no rspnse* **14/1**

6 13 **Straight Laced** 3-8-11 0.. ShaneKelly 6 30
(W J Knight) *s.i.s: rn green in rr: reminders over 4f out: sn struggling* **12/1**

5- **7** 6 **Fleetwood Flame**[253] 5445 4-10-0 0.............................. TGMcLaughlin 8 18
(W M Brisbourne) *a bhd: lost tch fnl 3f* **40/1**

2m 18.8s (-2.30) **Going Correction** -0.05s/f (Good)
WFA 3 from 4yo 17lb 7 Ran SP% **112.9**
Speed ratings (Par 100): **106,100,99,99,99 89,85**
toteswinger: 1&2 £1.10, 1&3 £10.40, 2&3 £18.80 CSF £4.74 TOTE £1.70: £1.20, £2.10; EX 4.40.

Owner D G Hardisty **Bred** Darley **Trained** Beckhampton, Wilts
■ Stewards' Enquiry : Darryll Holland twenty-one day ban: 2nd offence in 12mths, failed to ride out for third place (May 23-Jun 12)

FOCUS
An ordinary maiden in which the early gallop looked modest, which may have helped the winner.

1894 BAM CONSTRUCTION H'CAP 7f 26y
7:55 (7:56) (Class 4) (0-85,85) 4-Y-O+ **£5,180** (£1,541; £770; £384) **Stalls** Low

Form RPR

3220 **1** **Desert Dreamer (IRE)**[5] 1723 8-8-5 **72**..................... CatherineGannon 1 79
(P D Evans) *hld up in rr: hdwy 2f out: rdn over 1f out: r.o u.p to ld towards fin* **11/2**[3]

4/6- **2** nk **Ocean Transit (IRE)**[262] 723 4-8-8 **75**........................... JamesDoyle 2 81
(R J Price) *a.p: pushed along 3f out: rdn wl over 1f out: ev ch wl ins fnl f: r.o* **40/1**

0-60 **3** ½ **Phluke**[14] 1524 8-8-8 **75**..(v) StephenCarson 5 80
(Eve Johnson Houghton) *chsd ldr tl rdn over 1f out: r.o towards fin* **4/1**[1]

00-4 **4** shd **Salient**[19] 1405 5-8-13 **80**... JimCrowley 9 85
(M J Attwater) *led: rdn 1f out: hdd towards fin* **8/1**

2200 **5** 1 ¾ **Compton's Eleven**[7] 1682 8-8-7 **74**........................... EdwardCreighton 4 74
(M R Channon) *hld up in mid-div: carried hd high whn rdn and hdwy over 1f out: one pce ins fnl f* **10/1**

-332 **6** nk **Princely Hero (IRE)**[24] 1288 5-8-11 **83**..................... AndreaAtzeni(5) 10 82
(M Botti) *hld up towards rr: rdn and hdwy over 1f out: no imp ins fnl f* **5/1**[2]

4-33 **7** 1 ½ **Gap Princess (IRE)**[9] 1627 5-8-4 **71** oh2........................ DO'Donohoe 7 66
(R A Fahey) *hld up in tch: rdn over 1f out: wknd fnl f* **6/1**

050- **8** 5 **Barons Spy (IRE)**[194] 7019 8-9-4 **85**................................. SebSanders 8 66
(R J Price) *hld up towards rr: c wd st: rdn over 1f out: no rspnse* **16/1**

2123 **9** 2 ½ **Flores Sea (USA)**[8] 1649 5-8-13 **80**................................(b) DarryllHolland 11 55
(T D Barron) *hld up in mid-div: hung rt bnd over 3f out: wknd over 2f out* **5/1**[2]

040- **10** 1 ¼ **Bellomi (IRE)**[129] 7837 4-9-4 **85**................................... FergusSweeney 6 56
(A G Juckes) *stdd s: t.k.h: a in rr* **40/1**

1m 23.82s (-0.78) **Going Correction** -0.05s/f (Good) **10** Ran SP% **114.0**
Speed ratings (Par 105): **102,101,101,100,98 98,96,91,88,86**
toteswinger: 1&2 £45.00, 1&3 £5.10, 2&3 £23.10 CSF £188.03 CT £770.87 TOTE £8.10: £2.90, £7.50, £1.80; EX 173.40.
Owner R Piff **Bred** Gainsborough Stud Management Ltd **Trained** Pandy, Monmouths

FOCUS
Plenty of well-known handicappers took their chance in this. All of them were exposed but capable of winning when in the mood.
Flores Sea(USA) Official explanation: jockey said gelding was unsuited by the good to firm (firm in places) ground

1895 WARWICKRACECOURSE.CO.UK H'CAP 7f 26y
8:25 (8:26) (Class 5) (0-75,74) 3-Y-O **£2,914** (£867; £433; £216) **Stalls** Low

Form RPR

05-4 **1** **Beautiful Breeze (IRE)**[16] 1471 3-9-2 **72**........................ GregFairley 2 79+
(M Johnston) *w ldrs: hrd rdn to ld over 1f out: r.o wl* **5/2**[1]

35-0 **2** 2 ¼ **Admiral Sandhoe (USA)**[12] 1574 3-9-3 **73**........................ JimCrowley 1 74
(Mrs A J Perrett) *hld up: hdwy 2f out: rdn over 1f out: kpt on to take 2nd towards fin: nt trble wnr* **7/2**[2]

00-0 **3** ½ **Harriet's Girl**[21] 1345 3-9-3 **73**.. AndrewElliott 10 73
(K R Burke) *sn led: rdn and hdd over 1f out: one pce: lost 2nd towards fin* **16/1**

1-0 **4** ½ **Peking Prince**[33] 1155 3-8-13 **72**.................................. DavidProbert(3) 8 70
(A M Balding) *led early: a.p: rdn over 1f out: edgd lft ent fnl f: one pce* **8/1**[3]

2313 **5** 2 ½ **Captainrisk (IRE)**[48] 924 3-8-13 **74**............................ AndreaAtzeni(5) 3 66
(M Botti) *hld up: rdn and hdwy over 1f out: wknd ins fnl f* **7/2**[2]

000- **6** 1 ¾ **Law And Order**[222] 6342 3-8-6 **62**.................................. PaulFitzsimons 9 49
(Miss J R Tooth) *prom: rdn jst over 1f out: wknd ins fnl f* **28/1**

2200 **7** 1 ¼ **Grand Honour (IRE)**[28] 1214 3-9-3 **73**................................. IanMongan 4 56
(P Howling) *hld up in rr: nt clr run over 1f out: sn swtchd lft: n.d* **11/1**

0-04 **8** 9 **Angelo Poliziano**[19] 1400 3-8-13 **69**.................................... DO'Donohoe 5 28
(Mrs A Duffield) *s.i.s: hld up: short-lived effrt over 2f out* **8/1**[3]

1m 24.33s (-0.27) **Going Correction** -0.05s/f (Good) **8** Ran SP% **112.9**
Speed ratings (Par 99): **99,96,95,95,92 90,89,78**
toteswinger: 1&2 £1.10, 1&3 £19.20, 2&3 £21.60 CSF £10.98 CT £110.92 TOTE £3.30: £1.30, £1.40, £3.10; EX 10.70 Place 6: £24.89, Place 5: £8.40..
Owner Crone Stud Farms Ltd **Bred** Patrick M Ryan **Trained** Middleham Moor, N Yorks

FOCUS
A fair-looking handicap full of interesting types. The pace seemed fair.
T/Plt: £22.10 to a £1 stake. Pool: £55,301.58. 1,818.61 winning tickets. T/Qpdt: £7.20 to a £1 stake. Pool: £3,987.92. 404.58 winning tickets. KH

1896 - 1902a (Foreign Racing) - See Raceform Interactive

1659 CAPANNELLE (R-H)

Saturday, May 9

OFFICIAL GOING: Good to firm

1903a PREMIO CARLO D'ALESSIO (GROUP 3) — 1m 4f

2:50 (2:59) 4-Y-0+ **£38,835** (£17,087; £9,320; £4,661)

RPR

1 **Voila Ici (IRE)**[26] 4-8-13 ... MDemuro 1 112
(V Caruso, Italy) *prom: 3rd 1/2-way: shkn up 2f out: rdn to chal over 1f out: led 150yds out: drvn out (exact SP 59/100F)* **3/5**[1]

2 ¾ **Gimmy (IRE)**[27] 5-8-9 ... DVargiu 7 107
(B Grizzetti, Italy) *prom: 2nd 1/2-way: ev ch 1 1/2f out: styd on steadily to line* **2/1**[2]

3 1 **Vol De Nuit**[27] 8-8-9 ... MPasquale 2 105
(G Pucciatti, Italy) *led: 4 l clr 1/2-way: pushed along 3f out: rdn 2f out: hdd 150yds out: no ex* **16/1**

4 1¼ **Tremoto**[174] 4-8-6 ...(b) SDiana 4 100
(F & L Camici, Italy) *in tch: 4th 1/2-way: drvn over 2f out: styd on at one pce to line* **46/1**

5 3½ **Elleno (IRE)**[263] 5-8-9 ...(b) OFancera 5 98
(F & L Camici, Italy) *towards rr: 5th 1/2-way: sme hdwy on ins over 2f out to 1f out: eased fnl 100yds* **56/1**

6 2 **Papetti (ITY)**[13] 1575 4-8-9 ... SMulas 6 95
(B Grizzetti, Italy) *towards rr: 6th 1/2-way: drvn 3f out: sn outpcd* **19/5**[3]

7 3 **Combat Dance (GER)**[27] 5-8-9 ... MMonteriso 3 90
(A Cascio, Italy) *towards rr: last 1/2-way: n.d* **31/1**

2m 30.0s (2.80) **7 Ran SP% 129.6**
(Including 1 Euro stake): WIN 1.59; PL 1.07, 1.32; SF 1.67.
Owner Scuderia Incolinx **Bred** Soc Finanza Locale Consulting Srl **Trained** Italy

1904a DERBY ITALIANO BETTER (GROUP 2) (C&F) — 1m 3f

4:00 (4:13) 3-Y-0 **£359,223** (£158,058; £86,214; £43,107)

RPR

1 **Mastery**[52] 863 3-9-2 ... LDettori 3 107
(Saeed Bin Suroor) *in tch on ins: cl 4th 1/2-way: rdn and hdwy in centre 2f out: chalng fnl f: led 100yds out: r.o wl (exact SP 2.81/1)* **14/5**[2]

2 1½ **Turati**[20] 1393 3-9-2 ... URispoli 15 104
(G Pucciatti, Italy) *in tch: 5th on rail st: u.p 3f out: rallied and styd on wl fr over 1f out: tk 2nd on line* **111/10**

3 hd **Jakkalberry (IRE)** 3-9-2 ... MMonteriso 4 104+
(E Botti, Italy) *hld up in mid-div: 8th and pushed along st: gd hdwy fr 2f out to ld 1f out: jinked into rail 100yds out: hdd and nt rcvr* **43/10**[3]

4 ½ **Apprimus (IRE)** 3-9-2 ... CSoumillon 1 103
(A & G Botti, Italy) *led: rdn over 3f out: hdd over 1 1/2f out: no ex* **19/2**

5 shd **Sottone**[20] 1393 3-9-2 ... SMulas 6 103
(B Grizzetti, Italy) *in tch: 7th and pushed along in centre st: rdn 2 1/2f out: styd on at one pce to line* **108/10**

6 1¼ **Blue Black Jack (IRE)** 3-9-2 ... OPeslier 9 101
(A & G Botti, Italy) *trckd ldrs: 6th st: sn pushed along: rdn 2 1/2f out: kpt on at one pce* **32/5**

7 nk **Abaton**[21] 3-9-2 ... MDemuro 13 100
(V Caruso, Italy) *hld up: styd on fr over 2f out: nrest at fin* **6/5**[1]

8 hd **Apro Lunare (IRE)**[20] 1393 3-9-2 ... CColombi 5 100
(Laura Grizzetti, Italy) *prom: 3rd 1/2-way: rdn to chal 3f out: jnd ldr 2f out: led over 1 1/2f out: hdd 1f out: wknd* **21/1**

9 1 **Masstorm (ITY)**[20] 1392 3-9-2 ... FBranca 10 98
(F Saggiomo, Italy) *towards rr: n.d* **100/1**

10 4 **Open Intent (IRE)**[26] 3-9-2 ... NMurru 14 91
(M Gasparini, Italy) *hld up on ins: hrd rdn 2f out: late hdwy but n.d* **85/1**

11 1 **Damiani**[20] 1392 3-9-2 ... ADMigheli 2 89
(F & L Camici, Italy) *towards rr of mid-div: rdn 2 1/2f out: unable qck* **111/10**

12 1 **Ad Honores (USA)**[20] 1393 3-9-2 ... LManiezzi 7 87
(R Menichetti, Italy) *nvr in contention* **60/1**

13 nk **Galidon (IRE)**[20] 1392 3-9-2 ... GBietolini 22 87
(R Brogi, Italy) *hld up: effrt in centre 3f out: no imp* **157/10**

14 1 **Desert Cry (IRE)**[20] 1393 3-9-2 ... TThulliez 11 85
(B Grizzetti, Italy) *hld up: nvr in chalng position* **108/10**

15 1¼ **Faidibiri (IRE)**[20] 1392 3-9-2 ... MBelli 8 83
(G Ligas, Italy) *bhd: brief hdwy in st to 2f out: one pce after* **112/1**

16 2 **Acero**[26] 3-9-2 ... C-PLemaire 20 79
(V Caruso, Italy) *bhd: nvr a factor* **6/5**[1]

17 1½ **Relco Italy (IRE)**[20] 1393 3-9-2 ... PConvertino 19 76
(B Grizzetti, Italy) *bhd: nvr a factor* **108/10**

18 10 **Capo Malfatano (IRE)**[20] 1392 3-9-2 ... SSulas 17 58
(R Brogi, Italy) *towards rr: rdn 2f out: sn one pce* **123/1**

19 4 **Seminole Shield (ITY)**[21] 3-9-2 ... MSanna 16 51
(G Fois, Italy) *a bhd* **130/1**

20 2 **Falcharge**[21] 3-9-2 ... SUrru 18 48
(B Grizzetti, Italy) *bhd: nvr a factor* **74/10**

21 7 **Renowing (UAE)**[20] 1392 3-9-2 ... DVargiu 21 35
(B Grizzetti, Italy) *towards rr: drvn st: nvr a factor* **74/10**

2m 16.5s (136.50) **21 Ran SP% 241.7**
WIN 3.81; PL 2.30, 3.62, 2.63; DF 40.01.
Owner Godolphin **Bred** Darley **Trained** Newmarket, Suffolk
■ The Italian Derby has been downgraded to Group 2 status.

NOTEBOOK
Mastery, fourth in the Kentucky Derby trial at Kempton on his only previous start this season, has joined Godolphin. Appreciating the step up to 1m3f, he saw it out really well, although his task was made easier by the eventual third jinking into the rail when leading with half a furlong to run. It is possible that he may be supplemented into the Epsom Derby now, but that will be a much tougher assignment.

1905a PREMIO TUDINI (GROUP 3) — 6f

4:35 (4:57) 3-Y-0+ **£38,835** (£17,087; £9,320; £4,661)

RPR

1 **Remarque (IRE)**[62] 4-9-4 ...(b) CSoumillon 8 104
(L Riccardi, Italy) *c across to r on stands' rail: pushed along 2f out: rdn to ld over 1f out: hld on wl cl home (exact SP 5.19/1)* **26/5**[3]

2 1 **Black Mambazo (IRE)**[64] 4-9-4 ... GMarcelli 6 101
(L Riccardi, Italy) *trckd ldrs in centre: hdwy and swtchd to stands' side 1 1/2f out: 2nd and chalng 1f out: ev ch cl home: jst hld* **32/5**

3 snk **Morgan Drive (IRE)** 4-9-4 ... C-PLemaire 7 101
(M Gasparini, Italy) *hld up on stands' side: shkn up 2 1/2f out: fin wl fnl 150yds: tk 3rd cl home* **22/1**

4 1¼ **Anonimo Veneziano**[20] 1393 3-8-8 ... MDemuro 4 97
(V Caruso, Italy) *hld up on far side: r.o wl fr over 1 1/2f out: 3rd 100yds out: jst lost pl cl home* **26/5**[3]

5 2½ **Lui Rei (ITY)**[20] 1393 3-8-11 ... LDettori 11 92
(A Renzoni, Italy) *prom: 3rd 1/2-way: pushed along 2f out: styd on same pce* **6/5**[1]

6 nk **Thinking Robins (IRE)**[174] 7349 6-9-4 ... SSulas 13 88
(I Bugattella, Italy) *a mid-div* **105/1**

7 1 **Titus Shadow (IRE)**[21] 5-9-4 ... DVargiu 5 85
(B Grizzetti, Italy) *racd on stands' rail: nvr in chalng position* **5/2**[2]

8 shd **L'Indiscreta**[20] 1394 4-9-1 ... SUrru 2 82
(B Grizzetti, Italy) *mid-div: pushed along to chse ldrs 2f out: no ex fr 1 1/2f out* **5/2**[2]

9 2½ **Xenes**[21] 5-9-4 ... MMonteriso 12 78
(R Menichetti, Italy) *racd in 2nd in centre: pushed along over 2f out: u.p 1 1/2f out: wknd fnl f* **142/10**

10 shd **Jordan Strada (ITY)**[174] 7349 5-9-4 ... PAragoni 10 77
(S Santella, Italy) *towards rr: pushed along 2 1/2f out: no imp* **85/1**

11 1½ **Docksil**[20] 1394 5-9-1 ... SMulas 9 70
(B Grizzetti, Italy) *led in centre: pushed along 2f out: hdd over 1f out: wknd* **48/1**

12 1¾ **Lady Marmelade (ITY)**[20] 1394 6-9-1 ... PConvertino 1 65
(D Ducci, Italy) *in tch: drvn 2f out: sn outpcd* **50/1**

13 15 **Polar Wind (ITY)**[48] 5-9-4 ... LManiezzi 3 23
(R Menichetti, Italy) *a in rr* **142/10**

67.80 secs (-2.50)
WFA 3 from 4yo+ 10lb **13 Ran SP% 172.0**
WIN 6.19; PL 2.29, 2.59, 4.60; DF 25.30.
Owner Allevamento La Nuova Sbarra **Bred** Fattoria Di Marcianella Di Razza Del Pian Del Lago **Trained** Italy

1906 - 1909a (Foreign Racing) - See Raceform Interactive

1385 LEOPARDSTOWN (L-H)

Sunday, May 10

OFFICIAL GOING: Good

1910a DERRINSTOWN STUD DERBY TRIAL STKS (GROUP 2) — 1m 2f

3:55 (3:55) 3-Y-0 **£75,728** (£22,135; £10,485; £3,495)

RPR

1 **Fame And Glory**[21] 1388 3-9-4 112 ... JAHeffernan 1 120+
(A P O'Brien, Ire) *racd in mod 5th: 4th and clsd st: chal and led over 1f out: qckly clr: swished tail u.p: styd on wl: impressive* **4/7**[1]

2 5 **Mourayan (IRE)**[21] 1388 3-9-1 111 ... MJKinane 4 107
(John M Oxx, Ire) *racd in mod 4th: niggled along fr 5f out: clsd and chal u.p in 2nd 1 1/2f out: no imp and kpt on same pce fr 1f out* **6/4**[2]

3 ½ **Fergus McIver (IRE)**[7] 1714 3-9-1 105 ...(b[1]) DJMoran 5 106
(J S Bolger, Ire) *racd in 3rd: 2nd fr 1/2-way: led u.p 2f out: hdd and kpt on same pce fr over 1f out* **16/1**[3]

4 2½ **Hail Caesar (IRE)**[21] 1388 3-9-1 102 ... CO'Donoghue 7 101
(A P O'Brien, Ire) *wl off pce in rr: mod 5th over 3f out: kpt on same pce u.p st* **33/1**

5 13 **Tarankali (IRE)**[21] 1388 3-9-1 90 ... FMBerry 3 75
(John M Oxx, Ire) *sn 2nd: on terms after 4f and sn led: hdd 2f out: sn wknd* **66/1**

6 29 **Liszt (IRE)**[21] 1388 3-9-1 93 ... SMLevey 6 17
(A P O'Brien, Ire) *sn led: jnd after 4f: sn hdd: rdn in 3rd fr 5f out: dropped to rr over 3f out: sn bhd and eased over 1f out* **66/1**

2m 3.60s (-4.60) **Going Correction** -0.10s/f (Good) **6 Ran SP% 115.5**
Speed ratings: **114,110,109,107,97 74**
CSF £1.76 TOTE £1.30: £1.10, £1.30; DF 1.70.
Owner Derrick Smith **Bred** Ptarmigan Bloodstock & Miss K **Trained** Ballydoyle, Co Tipperary

FOCUS
The principal Irish Derby trial and an impressive winner who looks a major contender for Epsom. The placed horses set the standard on their Ballysax form.

NOTEBOOK
Fame And Glory ◆ did this in a professional and classy manner and showed definite progression from his win in the Ballysax Stakes a couple of weeks previously. He was held up off the very quick pace set by the two pacemakers and picked them up quickly and without fuss. He quickened well and stayed strongly, so stamina would not be in question. One reservation is how he will handle the track at Epsom and another is that he swished his tail when the rider gave him a smack. He very much earns the benefit of the doubt though, for he's a genuine Derby contender and it will take a very good horse to lower his colours. (op 8/11)
Mourayan(IRE), for whom there was plenty to suggest beforehand that he would give the winner a good bit to think about having been a bit unlucky in the Ballysax Stakes, ran quite flat. He was being pushed along from halfway and was hard ridden to even get to the pacemaker. It was a lack-lustre and sluggish effort, and on the back of that he won't be travelling to Epsom. (op 11/8 tchd 13/8)
Fergus McIver(IRE), for whom the fitting of first-time blinkers didn't seem to do any harm, ran his race and this is probably as good as he is. There's no real reason why he shouldn't stay 1m4f as he lacked gears in the closing stages. It's hard to gauge if there's any more improvement in him for the moment, but there is a decent race to be won with him over middle distances. (op 14/1)
Hail Caesar(IRE) is probably thought quite decent judging from the way he was ridden. He was dropped in at the back of the field and definitely struggled to go the pace, but he stayed on reasonably nicely and may develop into a nice staying type.

1911a DERRINSTOWN STUD 1,000 GUINEAS TRIAL (GROUP 3) (FILLIES) — 1m

4:25 (4:25) 3-Y-0 **£50,563** (£14,834; £7,067; £2,407)

RPR

1 **Baliyana (IRE)**[224] 6318 3-9-0 93 ... MJKinane 3 104+
(John M Oxx, Ire) *mde all: wnt clr fr over 1f out: styd on wl: comf* **9/1**

2 2½ **Aaroness (USA)**[241] 5828 3-9-0 102 ... DEMullins 8 98+
(J S Bolger, Ire) *in rr: hdwy and wd into st: wnt mod 2nd u.p wout troubling wnr ins fnl f* **12/1**

3 1¼ **Firey Red (IRE)**[49] 928 3-9-0 ... PJSmullen 4 95
(D K Weld, Ire) *chsd ldrs: pushed along fr 1/2-way: 7th and wd into st: no imp u.p and kpt on same pce wout threatening fr over 1f out* **10/3**[2]

4 *shd* **Monivea (IRE)**[19] 1447 3-9-0 84..(p) CDHayes 6 95
(Brian Nolan, Ire) *sn trckd ldr in 2nd: t.k.h: no imp u.p and kpt on same pce fr over 1f out* **33/1**

5 *1 3/4* **Hallie's Comet (IRE)**[42] 1024 3-9-0 101.............................. ShaneFoley 5 93
(A Kinsella, Ire) *towards rr: hdwy on inner st: kpt on same pce u.p in 5th fr 1f out* **12/1**

6 *1 1/2* **Maidin Maith (IRE)**[170] 7407 3-9-0 .... DJMoran 7 88
(J S Bolger, Ire) *sn 4th: rdn st: no imp and kpt on same pce fr over 1f out* **5/1[3]**

7 *3/4* **Smart Coco (USA)**[42] 1024 3-9-0 102.............................. WMLordan 2 86
(T Stack, Ire) *sn 3rd: t.k.h: no imp u.p fr over 1f out* **7/4[1]**

8 *1 1/2* **Totally Devoted (USA)**[22] 1372 3-9-0 .... JAHeffernan 1 82
(A P O'Brien, Ire) *sn racd in 5th: short of room and no imp fr over 1f out* **6/1**

1m 39.9s (-1.30) **Going Correction** -0.10s/f (Good) **8** Ran SP% **118.7**
Speed ratings: **102,99,98,98,96 94,94,92**
CSF £112.02 TOTE £9.10: £2.40, £2.40, £1.50; DF 77.40.
Owner H H Aga Khan **Bred** Hh The Aga Khans Stud's Sc **Trained** Currabeg, Co Kildare
■ Stewards' Enquiry : D E Mullins severe caution: excessive use of the whip

FOCUS
This isn't a race that will live up to its title, and this is probably best demonstrated in the fact that the winner was taken out of the Irish 1,000 Guineas last autumn.

NOTEBOOK
Baliyana(IRE) was reasonably impressive and at least earned the right to think about supplementing her. Kinane once again showed that there is no better jockey at riding a race from the front as he set a gradually increasing pace and when he asked the filly to quicken over a furlong out she did it very nicely and opened up a gap that wasn't really threatened. It was a reasonable performance and, while she may not be a Group 1 filly, there was plenty to like about it. (op 8/1)

Aaroness(USA) was ridden like a good filly and while she did have plenty of ground to make up in the straight she was probably beaten by a better filly on the day. She was held up in rear and was travelling very well turning in, but was forced to come around the field to make her challenge and as she started to close the winner had kicked. Connections are entitled to be pleased with this effort and she should improve.

Firey Red(IRE) couldn't quite match her seasonal debut effort at the Curragh and is better than this effort would suggest. She lost her place and wasn't travelling at halfway and although she did make progress late on it was of the more laboured variety. One can expect her to do better. (op 11/4)

Monivea(IRE) ran very well, considering she took such a keen hold early on. She had little enough left inside the final furlong but to stay on at the same pace, although that was perfectly respectable.

Hallie's Comet(IRE) justified the decision to run her in this contest as she kept on inside the final furlong with the inside rail to help. (op 12/1 tchd 14/1)

Smart Coco(USA), the well-backed favourite, ruined her chance by taking quite a fierce hold early in the contest. Official explanation: jockey said filly met with interference in running in home straight (op 2/1 tchd 13/8)

Totally Devoted(USA), whose run can be completely forgotten as she had absolutely no racing room in the straight when trying to make her challenge. Official explanation: jockey said filly met with interference in running and had to check (op 5/1)

1913a AMETHYST STKS (GROUP 3) 1m
5:25 (5:25) 3-Y-O+ **£41,019** (£11,990; £5,679; £1,893)

RPR

1 **Summit Surge (IRE)**[35] 1138 5-9-12 110..............................(t) KLatham 4 112
(G M Lyons, Ire) *a.p: mainly 2nd: rdn to chal and ld over 1 1/2f out: clr and styd on wl ins fnl f* **9/1**

2 *1 1/2* **Three Rocks (IRE)**[21] 1387 4-9-9 108.................................. DJMoran 3 106+
(J S Bolger, Ire) *towards rr: hdwy and wd st: rdn in 4th 1 1/2f out: kpt on into 2nd wout troubling wnr fnl f* **3/1[2]**

3 *1 1/4* **Beach Bunny (IRE)**[225] 6298 4-9-6 106.............................. CDHayes 1 100
(Kevin Prendergast, Ire) *sn trckd ldrs in 3rd: dropped to 5th and rdn 1 1/2f out: kpt on wout threatening into 3rd again cl home* **8/1**

4 *nk* **Mad About You (IRE)**[6] 1756 4-9-9 113..........................(b) PJSmullen 7 102
(D K Weld, Ire) *t.k.h: sn 5th: 4th over 3f out: 3rd 1 1/2f out: sn one pce u.p and dropped to 4th cl home* **7/4[1]**

5 *1 3/4* **Windsor Palace (IRE)**[184] 7235 4-9-9 104..................... CO'Donoghue 8 98
(A P O'Brien, Ire) *led: rdn over 2f out: hdd over 1 1/2f out: sn no imp* **25/1**

6 *1* **Red Rock Canyon (IRE)**[14] 1551 5-9-9 110.................... JAHeffernan 2 96
(A P O'Brien, Ire) *chsd ldrs: 6th over 3f out: kpt on same pce u.p fr 1 1/2f out* **7/2[3]**

7 *1 3/4* **Lord Admiral (USA)**[163] 7488 8-9-9 112..........................(b) MJKinane 6 92
(Charles O'Brien, Ire) *towards rr: wd st: kpt on same pce u.p fr under 2f out* **8/1**

8 *24* **Mourinho (IRE)**[42] 1023 4-9-9 87..................................... DPMcDonogh 5 37
(Edward Lynam, Ire) *trckd ldrs: t.k.h: 5th over 3f out: dropped bhd 1 1/2f out: sn eased* **25/1**

1m 40.3s (-0.90) **Going Correction** -0.10s/f (Good) **8** Ran SP% **123.5**
Speed ratings: **100,98,97,96,95 94,92,68**
CSF £39.27 TOTE £11.00: £2.20, £1.50, £1.90; DF 65.00.
Owner W Bellew **Bred** Norelands Bloodstock **Trained** Dunsany, Co. Meath

NOTEBOOK
Summit Surge(IRE) underlined the fact that Ger Lyons has his team in good order by scoring the sixth win of his career, and his second at Group 3 level, the other having come over 7f at this venue last season. A winner in Dubai during the winter, he clearly appreciated improved conditions here after finishing fifth in the Gladness on his return to Irish action. (op 10/1)

Three Rocks(IRE) now boasts a seasonal race-record of three wins and two seconds is a vindication of the positive approach that Jim Bolger has adopted with him. He was a rapid improver in the early part of the season, and ridden from off the pace in a manner that has been a feature of all his races this season, he consolidated his reputation as a horse who can go on to win a Pattern race with another smart effort here. (op 3/1 tchd 11/4)

Beach Bunny(IRE) lost her place in the straight before running on again for third. This marked a satisfactory start to the season for the filly who was a Listed winner over 7f at the Curragh last August. (op 8/1 tchd 9/1)

Mad About You(IRE), a multiple Group 1-placed filly whose record now reads one from four this term, with three instances of being beaten when favourite. Conditions had been against her when she was beaten at the Curragh last week, but she seemed to have no excuse this time. (op 7/4 tchd 2/1)

Mourinho(IRE) Official explanation: jockey said gelding lost its action

T/Jkpt: @8,658.00. Pool of @11,544.00 - 1 winning unit. T/Plt: @36.20. Pool of @14,131.00 - 292 winning units. II

1912 - 1913a (Foreign Racing) - See Raceform Interactive

1549 COLOGNE (R-H)
Sunday, May 10

OFFICIAL GOING: Soft

1914a SCHWARZGOLD-RENNEN (GROUP 3) (FILLIES) 1m
3:05 (3:24) 3-Y-O **£38,835** (£14,563; £5,825; £3,883)

RPR

1 **Addicted (GER)**[273] 3-9-2 .... ASuborics 11 99
(T Mundry, Germany) *cl up: 3rd st: led 100yds out: jst hld on* **79/10**

2 *shd* **Lukrecia (IRE)** 3-9-2 .... FilipMinarik 6 98
(P Schiergen, Germany) *cl up: 4th st: wnt 3rd over 1f out: styd on wl fnl f: jst failed* **156/10**

3 *1 1/2* **Novita (FR)**[28] 1240 3-9-2 .... AStarke 9 95
(P Schiergen, Germany) *pressed ldr: led over 2f out: wnt 2 l clr: hdd 100yds out: wknd* **17/10[1]**

4 *hd* **All Annalena (IRE)**[196] 7006 3-9-2 .... AHelfenbein 4 95
(Andreas Lowe, Germany) *hld up in rr: styd on wl fnl 2f* **23/1**

5 *1/2* **Fabiana** 3-9-2 .... THellier 3 93
(Andreas Lowe, Germany) *hld up in last: swtchd outside and hdwy 2f out: kpt on* **78/10**

6 *3* **Anjella (GER)**[182] 7264 3-9-2 .... ShaneKelly 1 86
(J Hirschberger, Germany) *in tch: 6th st: rdn and one pce fnl 2f* **31/10[2]**

7 *nk* **Jambalaya (GER)**[224] 3-9-2 .... EPedroza 10 86
(A Wohler, Germany) *hld up: 7th st: nvr a factor* **37/10[3]**

8 *1 1/2* **Turfliebe (GER)** 3-9-2 .... DPorcu 8 82
(M Rulec, Germany) *led to over 2f out* **12/1**

9 *3/4* **Lautenspielerin (GER)**[196] 7006 3-9-2 .... JiriPalik 7 81
(Frau Marion Rotering, Germany) *midfield on ins: 5th st: sn rdn and no imp* **18/1**

10 *8* **Classic Summer (GER)**[28] 1240 3-9-2 .... NCallan 5 62
(M Trybuhl, Germany) *a in rr* **43/1**

1m 38.03s (-0.36) **10** Ran SP% **130.7**
(including 10 euro stakes): WIN 89; PL 26, 25, 17; SF 1166.
Owner Gestut Brummerhof **Bred** Gestut Brummerhof **Trained** Germany

1915a MEHL-MULHENS-RENNEN (GERMAN 2,000 GUINEAS) (GROUP 2) (C&F) 1m
4:15 (4:40) 3-Y-O **£97,087** (£36,893; £17,476; £8,738)

RPR

1 **Irian (GER)**[21] 1395 3-9-2 .... FilipMinarik 2 114
(J Hirschberger, Germany) *6th early: 4th st: hdwy on outside to ld 1 1/2f out: maintained narrow ld tl drew away fnl 100yds* **6/4[1]**

2 *1 1/2* **Zafisio (IRE)**[179] 7294 3-9-2 .... DarryllHolland 6 111
(R Curtis) *led: ducked lft under 3f out and again whn jnd under 2f out: hdd 1 1/2f out: styd pressing wnr tl no ex last 100yds* **39/10[3]**

3 *3 1/2* **Globus (GER)**[21] 1395 3-9-2 .... WMongil 3 103
(Uwe Ostmann, Germany) *racd in 5th: hdwy to press ldrs 2f out: styd on at one pce u.p* **18/5[2]**

4 *3/4* **Mantoro (GER)**[42] 3-9-2 .... AHelfenbein 1 101
(Mario Hofer, Germany) *cl up: 2nd st: disp ld towards ins under 2f out: hdd 1 1/2f out: one pce* **14/1**

5 *3* **Sri Putra**[22] 1354 3-9-2 .... NCallan 5 94
(M A Jarvis) *prom: 3rd st: rdn and one pce fr over 2f out* **47/10**

6 *3/4* **Running Home (GER)**[203] 6853 3-9-2 .... EPedroza 8 93
(A Wohler, Germany) *racd in 7th: nvr a factor* **19/1**

7 *1* **King Of Sydney (USA)**[21] 1395 3-9-2 .... ASuborics 4 90
(Mario Hofer, Germany) *missed break: last to over 2f out* **78/10**

8 *15* **Next Vision (IRE)**[203] 6853 3-9-2 .... ShaneKelly 7 56
(J Hirschberger, Germany) *prom on outside racing freely: lost pl and 6th st: sn btn* **103/10**

1m 35.87s (-2.52) **8** Ran SP% **131.6**
WIN 25; PL 13, 14, 15; SF 103.
Owner Gestut Schlenderhan **Bred** *unknown **Trained** Germany

NOTEBOOK
Irian(GER) scored well to give his trainer a second success in this race in the last three years. He may well take his chance in the Prix du Jockey-Club next.
Zafisio(IRE), who won the Criterium International at Saint-Cloud on heavy ground last season, put up a fine effort on this seasonal debut. He made the running but wandered about in the straight, although when headed he kept battling and was only held late on. He can win more good races when the ground is in his favour.
Sri Putra, who finished fourth in the Greenham on his seasonal debut, was reportedly unable to handle the sticky ground this time. He may be prove more effective back on good ground.

1819 LONGCHAMP (R-H)
Sunday, May 10

OFFICIAL GOING: Good

1917a POULE D'ESSAI DES POULAINS (GROUP 1) (COLTS) 1m
2:25 (2:27) 3-Y-O **£221,903** (£88,777; £44,388; £22,175; £11,107)

RPR

1 **Silver Frost (IRE)**[28] 1238 3-9-2 .... CSoumillon 7 119
(Y De Nicolay, France) *hld up: 9th st: smooth hdwy on outside fr wl over 1f out: drvn to ld 150yds out: r.o wl* **7/1[3]**

2 *2* **Le Havre (IRE)**[30] 1207 3-9-2 .... C-PLemaire 2 114
(J-C Rouget, France) *midfield: 5th st: rdn wl over 1f out: r.o wl to take 2nd cl home* **15/2**

3 *3/4* **Westphalia (IRE)**[28] 1238 3-9-2 .... JMurtagh 3 114+
(A P O'Brien, Ire) *midfield: 6th st: rdn and outpcd 2f out: running on whn nt clr run and snatched up over 1f out: 6th 1f out: r.o: fin 4th: plcd 3rd* **3/1[1]**

4 *1 1/2* **Oiseau De Feu (USA)**[28] 1238 3-9-2 .... IMendizabal 5 109
(J-C Rouget, France) *hld up: 8th st: hdwy on ins 2f out: hrd rdn 1 1/2f out: kpt on same pce: fin 5th: plcd 4th* **12/1**

5 *hd* **Handsome Maestro (IRE)**[38] 3-9-2 .... OPeslier 8 109+
(D Smaga, France) *led after 2f: set str pce: hdd over 1f out: disputing 3rd on rail whn hmpd 100yds out: nt rcvr: fin 6th: plcd 5th* **14/1**

6 *snk* **Naaqoos**[30] 1207 3-9-2 .... DBonilla 1 113
(F Head, France) *first to show: settled in 3rd: led over 1f out: sn drvn: hdd 150yds out: hung rt: lost 2nd cl home: fin 3rd: disqualified and plcd 6th* **4/1**[2]

7 *1 1/2* **Shaweel**[22] 1354 3-9-2 .... LDettori 9 105
(Saeed Bin Suroor) *led after 1f: hdd after 2f: settled in 4th: disp 2nd 2f out: sn rdn and one pce* **10/1**

8 *nk* **Diableside (FR)**[30] 1207 3-9-2 .... J-BEyquem 10 104
(Y Durepaire, Spain) *last to st: sme hdwy fnl f* **50/1**

9 *2* **Roi Des Sables (FR)**[23] 3-9-2 ....(b) TJarnet 4 100
(B De Montzey, France) *7th st: hrd rdn wl over 1f out: one pce* **100/1**

10 *15* **Vocalised (USA)**[6] 1755 3-9-2 .... KJManning 6 65
(J S Bolger, Ire) *hld up: 10th st: btn 2f out: eased* **4/1**[2]

11 *6* **Born To Be King (USA)**[42] 1022 3-9-2 ....(b) JamieSpencer 11 51
(A P O'Brien, Ire) *wnt 2nd after 2f: pressed ldr: 2nd st: sn wknd: eased* **33/1**

1m 35.43s (-2.97) **Going Correction** -0.075s/f (Good) **11 Ran SP% 118.6**
Speed ratings: **113,111,110,108,108 110,106,106,104,89 83**
PARI-MUTUEL: WIN 5.30; PL 1.80, 2.70, 1.70; DF 27.50.
Owner J D Cotton **Bred** Skymarc Farm **Trained** France
■ Stewards' Enquiry : D Bonilla two-day ban: careless riding (May 24-25)

FOCUS
Potential stars were thin on the ground, but this was a solid enough renewal and it was run at an unusually brisk pace for a French Group race.

NOTEBOOK
Silver Frost(IRE), winner of the Prix de Fontainebleau, followed up here in a smart time. He only had two behind him at the halfway point, but they had gone pretty quick and he was travelling strongly as he made headway over 350 yards before leading inside the final 150 yards and before being eased near the line. This was a solid performance, particularly as he may be suited by ground with a bit of ease in it. He could step up to 1m2f for the French Derby next or stay at 1m and head to Royal Ascot for the St James's Palace Stakes. He is a tough and consistent individual with a smart turn of foot, and he must be respected wherever he runs.
Le Havre(IRE) claimed the scalp of Naaqoos in the Prix Djebel at Maisons-Laffitte last month, and he proved that result was no fluke as he once again finished in front of his more high-profile rival. He responded well to his rider's urgings when he got more serious, but did not have the change of gears of the winner late on.
Westphalia(IRE), having raced in mid-division, was inconvenienced by not getting a clear run approaching the furlong marker, but with the winner going so much better at the time, only the wildest optimist could seriously suggest it cost him the race. There will be other days for him.
Oiseau De Feu(USA) may appreciate a bit further over time.
Handsome Maestro(IRE) looked to have gone off at an unsustainable gallop. Although he was dropping back at the time he was hampered, the interference looked to have cost him at least one position and possibly even more.
Naaqoos would not have done his chances any favours by pulling hard early on. He settled better in the second half of the race and took it up briefly a furlong from home. It was no surprise to see him demoted to sixth after hanging in towards the rail when coming under pressure and interfering with Handsome Maestro. While a top-class juvenile, questions can now be reasonably asked as to whether he has trained on. However, he looks and runs like a sprinter, and it would be be no surprise if he found his vocation dropped back in trip.
Shaweel was another who raced plenty keen enough. He has yet to recapture the form he showed as a two-year-old. A drop back in trip may bring about a reversal in fortune and perhaps even a drop in company for something like the Jersey Stakes.
Diableside(FR) looked to have plenty on his plate here. Fluffing the start would not have helped him either.
Vocalised(USA), who was racing here instead of his more fancied stablemate Intense Focus, was bitterly disappointing. He was the first horse beaten and his recent exertions may just have caught up with him.

1918a POULE D'ESSAI DES POULICHES (GROUP 1) (FILLIES) 1m
3:00 (3:00) 3-Y-O **£221,903** (£88,777; £44,388; £22,175; £11,107)

RPR

1 **Elusive Wave (IRE)**[30] 1208 3-9-0 .... C-PLemaire 5 117
(J-C Rouget, France) *mde all: drvn out* **5/1**[3]

2 *1/2* **Tamazirte (IRE)**[28] 1237 3-9-0 .... IMendizabal 1 116+
(J-C Rouget, France) *a cl up: 4th st: drvn to take 2nd 110yds out: r.o* **10/1**

3 *1 1/2* **Fantasia**[25] 1293 3-9-0 .... LDettori 2 113
(L M Cumani) *trckd wnr: rdn 2f out: styd on at one pce u.p* **8/11**[1]

4 *3/4* **Proportional**[28] 1237 3-9-0 .... SPasquier 10 111
(Mme C Head-Maarek, France) *5th st: styd on down outside fnl 2f: nvr able to chal* **9/2**[2]

5 *nk* **Soneva (USA)**[28] 1237 3-9-0 .... CSoumillon 9 110
(Y De Nicolay, France) *hld up: 9th st: hdwy towards ins fr over 2f out: disp 4th over 1f out: kpt on same pce* **12/1**

6 *1 1/2* **Entre Deux Eaux (FR)**[30] 1208 3-9-0 .... JMurtagh 3 107
(Robert Collet, France) *3rd st: hrd rdn 2f out: one pce* **33/1**

7 *1 1/2* **Providanza (FR)**[19] 3-9-0 .... GMosse 4 103
(M Delzangles, France) *hld up: 8th st: kpt on at one pce on outside fnl 2f* **100/1**

8 *2 1/2* **Doriana (FR)**[12] 1596 3-9-0 .... TThulliez 7 98
(A De Royer-Dupre, France) *midfield: 6th st: disputing 4th on ins 2f out: one pce* **40/1**

9 *2* **Oh Goodness Me**[49] 928 3-9-0 .... KJManning 11 93
(J S Bolger, Ire) *hld up in rr: 10th st: nvr a factor* **16/1**

10 *3/4* **Queen America (FR)**[16] 3-9-0 .... DBoeuf 8 91
(Robert Collet, France) *7th st: nvr a factor* **150/1**

11 *1* **Undaunted Affair (IRE)**[42] 1024 3-9-0 .... OPeslier 6 89
(K A Ryan) *a in rr: c wd and last st* **66/1**

1m 36.87s (-1.53) **Going Correction** -0.075s/f (Good) **11 Ran SP% 123.9**
Speed ratings: **106,105,104,103,102 101,99,97,95,94 93**
PARI-MUTUEL: WIN 6.40; PL 1.60, 1.70, 1.40; DF 16.50.
Owner Martin S Schwartz **Bred** Pier House Stud **Trained** Pau, France

NOTEBOOK
Elusive Wave(IRE), posting a time almost one and a half seconds slower than Silver Frost earlier in the day, was allowed to dictate the pace from the front and quickened up nicely in the final 2f. This is not the first time she has executed these tactics successfully and she is not one one to gift an easy lead. A step up to 1m2f for the French Oaks or the Coronation Stakes over this trip are next on the agenda, and with a couple of lofty reputations taking a knock over the last week, she could be a major player in those races, particularly if things go her way again.
Tamazirte(IRE), a stablemate of the winner, was nearest at the finish after making gradual headway in the last quarter-mile. She looks to be continuing on an upward curve.
Fantasia was always well positioned. She simply could not get to the winner, showing none of the sparkle she did when lighting up the Nell Gwyn Stakes last time. A step up to 1m4f could happen in time, but it is likely to be gradual, so the French Oaks is her possible next target.
Proportional stayed on without doing anything spectacular. This was disappointing again, but a stronger gallop would have helped.
Soneva(USA), who spilt Tamazirite and Proportional last time, was the only one who made any sort of progress from out the back, although she never looked like troubling those who finished in front of her.
Oh Goodness Me seemed to find a mile on ground like this plenty sharp enough. She has been racing over further already - and with cut in the ground - so it was no surprise that she was unable to quicken in the closing stages.
Undaunted Affair(IRE) had a lot on her plate and could not get involved.

1919a PRIX DE SAINT-GEORGES (GROUP 3) 5f (S)
3:35 (3:35) 3-Y-O+ **£38,835** (£15,534; £11,650; £7,767; £3,883)

RPR

1 *3/4* **Mood Music**[22] 5-9-0 ....(b) MGuyon 2 109
(Mario Hofer, Germany) *outpcd early: r.o wl fr over 1f out to take 2nd last stride: awrdd r* **25/1**

2 *shd* **Benbaun (IRE)**[22] 1374 8-9-2 ....(v) JMurtagh 3 108
(K A Ryan) *broke v fast: hdd over 3f out: rallying and a nk down whn squeezed up appr fnl f: lost 2nd last stride: fin 3rd: plcd 2nd* **14/1**

3 **Inxile (IRE)**[22] 1374 4-9-2 .... AdrianTNicholls 6 111
(D Nicholls) *led over 3f out: wnt lft appr fnl f: drvn out: fin 1st: disqualified and plcd 3rd* **9/2**[2]

4 *4* **Marchand D'Or (FR)**[43] 1010 6-9-11 .... DBonilla 7 103
(F Head, France) *in rr tl sme hdwy 2f out: sn rdn and nvr nr to chal* **8/11**[1]

5 *hd* **Tayseer**[206] 4-9-0 .... GMosse 5 91
(J E Hammond, France) *disp 3rd: def 3rd after 2f: one pce fnl 1 1/2f* **6/1**[3]

6 *1/2* **Chausson Dore (IRE)**[12] 1596 3-8-2 .... TJarnet 4 86
(A De Royer-Dupre, France) *outpcd tl sme prog fnl f* **16/1**

7 *6* **Contest (IRE)**[17] 1576 5-9-0 ....(b) FBlondel 1 67
(C Theodorakis, Greece) *disp 3rd: btn 1/2-way* **7/1**

55.78 secs (-0.52) **Going Correction** +0.15s/f (Good)
WFA 3 from 4yo+ 9lb **7 Ran SP% 119.3**
Speed ratings: **111,111,113,105,104 104,94**
PARI-MUTUEL: WIN 16.40; PL 6.20, 5.80; SF 192.10.
Owner WH Sport International **Bred** R T And Mrs Watson **Trained** Germany

NOTEBOOK
Mood Music was awarded the race after a stewards' enquiry. Not too quickly into stride, he still had plenty to do at the halfway stage and then came rattling along at the end to take second place virtually on the line. He may well come back to France for the Prix du Gros-Chene at the end of the month.
Benbaun(IRE), smartly into stride, was the leader until the halfway stage. He was then joined by the eventual first past the post who leant on him at the furlong marker. Despite being checked, he ran on again but was then just pipped by Mood Music. He was moved up to second place after the enquiry.
Inxile(IRE), quickly into his stride, looked to have the race at his mercy over a furlong out, but he edged left and caused an incident which eventually led to him being demoted. He was the winner on merit, but the French rules are different to those across the Channel. No doubt he will have his opportunity to take his revenge in the Gros-Chene.
Marchand D'Or(FR) ran way below expectations and never looked like taking a hand in the finish. Slowly into stride, the writing was on the wall shortly after the start. He did make some late progress, but was a remote fourth in the end and had no zip on this occasion. This race is best forgotten and it's worth remembering that he was giving 11lb to the promoted winner. He won the Gros-Chene a year ago and maybe he will find his true form again in that race.

1623 REDCAR (L-H)
Monday, May 11

OFFICIAL GOING: Firm (good to firm in places; 10.3)
Wind: Fresh 1/2 against Weather: Fine and sunny but breezy

1920 BUY YOUR TICKETS ON-LINE @ REDCARRACING.CO.UK MEDIAN AUCTION MAIDEN STKS 5f
2:20 (2:20) (Class 6) 2-Y-O **£2,047** (£604; £302) **Stalls** Centre

Form RPR

5 1 **Whozthecat (IRE)**[9] 1661 2-9-3 0 .... DNolan 4 80+
(D Carroll) *chsd ldrs: led appr fnl f: sn clr: heavily eased towards fin* **20/1**

2 *3* **Orpen Arms (IRE)** 2-8-12 0 .... PaulHanagan 7 61+
(R A Fahey) *mid-div: effrt over 2f out: styd on wl ins fnl f to take 2nd nr line* **16/1**

62 3 *1/2* **Farmer Giles (IRE)**[16] 1511 2-9-3 0 .... JamieSpencer 1 64
(M L W Bell) *w ldr: hrd drvn appr fnl f: kpt on same pce* **8/11**[1]

552 4 *1* **Ignatieff (IRE)**[11] 1623 2-9-3 0 ....(p) TomEaves 5 60
(Mrs L Stubbs) *swvd rt s: led tl appr fnl f: wknd towards fin* **9/2**[2]

5 *1* **Jupiter Fidius** 2-9-3 0 .... TonyHamilton 8 57
(Mrs K Walton) *s.i.s: kpt on fnl 2f: nvr rchd ldrs* **66/1**

6 *2* **Makbullet** 2-9-3 0 .... PaulMulrennan 3 49
(J Howard Johnson) *chsd ldrs: wknd over 1f out* **22/1**

7 *1 1/2* **Kakapuka** 2-9-3 0 .... KirstyMilczarek 6 44
(Mrs A L M King) *towards rr: hdwy and hung lft over 2f out: wknd over 1f out* **66/1**

8 *nk* **Avonrose** 2-8-12 0 .... GregFairley 2 38
(M Johnston) *chsd ldrs: edgd rt and lost pl over 1f out* **12/1**

0 9 *4* **Burtondale Boy (IRE)**[44] 994 2-9-3 0 .... JamieMoriarty 9 28
(P T Midgley) *a outpcd and bhd* **13/2**[3]

58.61 secs (0.01) **Going Correction** +0.05s/f (Good) **9 Ran SP% 115.1**
Speed ratings (Par 91): **101,96,95,93,92 89,86,86,79**
toteswinger: 1&2 £14.40, 1&3 £5.10, 2&3 £5.90 CSF £282.14 TOTE £25.90: £4.70, £5.10, £1.02; EX 122.80.
Owner Ninerus **Bred** Liam Queally **Trained** Sledmere, E Yorks

FOCUS
An ordinary juvenile maiden but a clear-cut winner.

NOTEBOOK
Whozthecat(IRE) was always poised just behind the pace, sprinted clear approaching the final furlong and won eased down. The form is a bit suspect because the two market leaders were both disappointing, but the style of victory was quite impressive. He looked much wiser for his promising four lengths fifth in a 5f Doncaster maiden on debut, seems to have taken a significant step forward and should go on to better things. (op 14-1)
Orpen Arms(IRE) never got into a threatening position but did stay on steadily and has shaped with a a fair amount of promise on her debut. She is a half-sister to the one-time useful and prolific sprint winner Fromsong, and was picked up for what looks a bargain price of 5,000 euros.
Farmer Giles(IRE) set the standard on his narrow defeat in a fair 5f Leicester maiden last month, and held some high-profile entries, including the Phoenix Stakes. He travelled smoothly in the early stages but failed to pick up when asked for an effort and was very disappointing at odds-on. (op 4-6 tchd 4-5 in a place)

Ignatieff(IRE) improved with each of his first three runs, although he did possibly throw it away when hanging left in the closing stages of a course-and-distance maiden last time. He had fair form claims with first-time cheekpieces applied to sharpen up his concentration, but put in a laboured effort and did not look entirely willing when pressure was applied. (op 4-1)
Kakapuka Official explanation: jockey said colt hung left-handed throughout
Burtondale Boy(IRE) was the springer in the market but he started slowly and was in trouble at a very early stage. Official explanation: trainer said gelding was unsuited by the firm (good to firm places) ground (op 16-1)

1921 BOOK YOUR HOSPITALITY AT REDCAR RACECOURSE (S) STKS 5f

2:50 (2:50) (Class 6) 3-Y-O+ **£2,047** (£604; £302) **Stalls** Centre

Form RPR
2104 **1** **Northern Empire (IRE)**[14] 1564 6-9-7 70...................(p) JamieSpencer 2 60+
(K A Ryan) *dwlt: hdwy and swtchd rt over 1f out: nt clr run: burst through to ld ins fnl f: readily* **4/1**[3]
0-00 **2** *1 ½* **Distant Vision (IRE)**[8] 1689 6-8-11 43.......................(b[1]) GaryBartley(5) 3 50
(H A McWilliams) *in rr: hdwy stands' side over 1f out: kpt on wl ins fnl f* **80/1**
1102 **3** *¾* **Swinbrook (USA)**[18] 1477 8-9-7 73..............................(v) PaulHanagan 9 52
(R A Fahey) *bmpd s: sn outpcd and bhd: hdwy 2f out: styd on wl ins fnl f* **5/2**[2]
0000 **4** *½* **Mandelieu (IRE)**[13] 1591 4-9-7 53..................................... TomEaves 10 51
(Ollie Pears) *chsd ldrs: kpt on same pce fnl f* **20/1**
00-0 **5** *nk* **Valiant Romeo**[28] 1243 9-9-7 44...............................(v) DanielTudhope 12 49
(R Bastiman) *led tl hdd and no ex ins fnl f* **50/1**
-005 **6** *½* **Brut**[19] 1456 7-9-7 62...(p) TonyHamilton 13 48
(D W Barker) *w ldrs: kpt on same pce fnl f* **14/1**
660- **7** *¾* **Strensall**[216] 6546 12-9-2 50....................................... FrederikTylicki(5) 11 45
(R E Barr) *hld up in tch: effrt over 1f out: kpt on one pce* **8/1**
200- **8** *hd* **Cranworth Blaze**[187] 7196 5-9-2 45................................ GregFairley 5 39
(T J Etherington) *chsd ldrs: edgd lft over 1f out: one pce* **25/1**
006- **9** *2 ½* **Cool Fashion (IRE)**[205] 6822 4-9-2 43.....................(be) JamieMoriarty 4 30
(Ollie Pears) *w ldrs: wknd over 1f out* **40/1**
50-6 **10** *2 ¼* **Gelert (IRE)**[102] 328 4-9-0 43...........................(b) AndrewHeffernan(7) 8 27
(Peter Grayson) *wnt rt s: w ldrs: wknd over 1f out* **66/1**
00-0 **11** *1 ½* **Howards Prince**[38] 1096 6-9-7 43.. DNolan 1 22
(D A Nolan) *chsd ldrs: lost pl over 1f out* **250/1**
-032 **12** *16* **Dream Theme**[8] 1689 6-9-7 78................................(v[1]) AdrianTNicholls 7 —
(D Nicholls) *s.v.s: completed in own time* **15/8**[1]
00-0 **13** *25* **Neo's Mate (IRE)**[103] 308 3-8-4 42 ow4................. KrishGundowry(7) 6 —
(Paul Green) *in rr: hung bdly lft and virtually p.u over 2f out: t.o: lame* **200/1**

58.67 secs (0.07) **Going Correction** +0.05s/f (Good)
WFA 3 from 4yo+ 9lb **13 Ran SP% 117.8**
Speed ratings (Par 101): **101,98,97,96,96 95,94,93,89,86 83,58,18**
toteswinger: 1&2 £37.50, 1&3 £2.40, 2&3 £49.00 CSF £301.39 TOTE £4.10: £1.60, £13.00, £1.40; EX 317.50.There was no bid for the winner.
Owner Sunpak Potatoes **Bred** Denis McDonnell **Trained** Hambleton, N Yorks

FOCUS
A muddling seller which is limited by the proximity of the lowly rated runner-up and fourth and therefore has been rated negatively.
Neo's Mate(IRE) Official explanation: vet said filly returned lame

1922 REDCAR RACECOURSE CONFERENCE & EVENTS VENUE MAIDEN FILLIES' STKS 6f

3:20 (3:21) (Class 5) 3-Y-O+ **£2,590** (£770; £385; £192) **Stalls** Centre

Form RPR
1 **Laura's Lady (IRE)** 3-8-12 0.. TomEaves 7 57
(G A Swinbank) *s.s: hdwy over 2f out: hung lft and styd on to ld ins fnl f: hld on towards fin* **7/2**[3]
060- **2** *½* **Who's Shirl**[217] 6524 3-8-12 45...................................... PaulMulrennan 1 55
(C W Fairhurst) *w ldr: led over 1f out: hdd ins fnl f: no ex* **11/1**
00- **3** *8* **Alacity (IRE)**[209] 6722 3-8-12 0.. TonyHamilton 6 30
(N Bycroft) *chsd ldrs: rdn 2f out: one pce* **7/1**
0 **4** *¾* **Josphiel (IRE)**[11] 1627 4-9-3 60................................... SladeO'Hara(5) 2 30
(A Berry) *led tl hdd over 1f out: sn wknd* **9/4**[1]
-56 **5** *2 ¾* **Scotch And Soda (IRE)**[11] 1625 3-8-12 0................. AndrewElliott 5 19
(Jedd O'Keeffe) *chsd ldrs: rdn and edgd lft 2f out: sn wknd* **3/1**[2]
6 *26* **Gurtavallig (IRE)** 4-9-5 0.. LeeVickers(3) 4 —
(T J Pitt) *dwlt and sn virtually ref to r: a t.o* **13/2**

1m 12.1s (0.30) **Going Correction** +0.05s/f (Good)
WFA 3 from 4yo 10lb **6 Ran SP% 112.2**
Speed ratings (Par 100): **100,99,88,87,84 49**
toteswinger: 1&2 £5.10, 1&3 £5.20, 2&3 £2.80 CSF £37.99 TOTE £3.70: £1.40, £4.60; EX 29.60.
Owner R H Hall **Bred** Joe Dolan **Trained** Melsonby, N Yorks

FOCUS
A poor race in which all of the runners were pushed along some way out. The winner deserves credit for scoring despite looking in need if the experience.
Gurtavallig(IRE) Official explanation: jockey said filly jumped awkwardly and was never going thereafter.

1923 THE COMMITMENTS PERFORMING HERE ON 29TH AUGUST FILLIES' H'CAP 7f

3:50 (3:50) (Class 4) (0-85,80) 3-Y-O+ **£4,857** (£1,445; £722; £360) **Stalls** Centre

Form RPR
131- **1** **Strawberry Moon (IRE)**[206] 6792 4-9-5 71......................... TomEaves 1 79
(B Smart) *led after 1f: set modest pce: hdd 3f out: led over 1f out: hrd rdn ins fnl f: hld on towards fin* **15/8**[2]
-330 **2** *nk* **Gap Princess (IRE)**[2] 1894 5-8-12 69........................ FrederikTylicki(5) 4 76
(R A Fahey) *trckd ldrs: effrt over 2f out: edgd lft: kpt on wl fnl f: jst hld* **6/5**[1]
22-0 **3** *½* **Sam's Secret**[9] 1682 7-10-0 80.. PaulMulrennan 2 86
(G A Swinbank) *hld up: effrt over 2f out: styd on ins fnl f* **9/1**
334- **4** *3 ¼* **Leftontheshelf (IRE)**[194] 7065 3-9-2 80....................... AdrianTNicholls 3 73?
(J L Spearing) *led 1f: led and qckdnd 3f out: hdd over 1f out: edgd lft: wknd and eased ins fnl f* **9/2**[3]

1m 27.06s (2.56) **Going Correction** +0.05s/f (Good)
WFA 3 from 4yo+ 12lb **4 Ran SP% 108.4**
Speed ratings (Par 102): **87,86,86,82**
CSF £4.53 TOTE £2.60; EX 4.70.
Owner Mrs Julie Martin **Bred** Gerrardstown House Stud **Trained** Hambleton, N Yorks
■ Stewards' Enquiry : Frederik Tylicki one-day ban: used whip with excessive frequency (May 25)

FOCUS
Just four runners but there was an exciting finish to this tactical affair. The form looks reasonable with the second and third to their marks.

1924 WIN A VIP DAY @ REDCARRACING.CO.UK CLAIMING STKS 6f

4:20 (4:21) (Class 6) 3-Y-O+ **£2,047** (£604; £302) **Stalls** Centre

Form RPR
2231 **1** **Stonecrabstomorrow (IRE)**[8] 1689 6-9-3 73.....(b) FrederikTylicki(5) 16 73
(R A Fahey) *trckd ldrs: led over 2f out: hld on towards fin* **7/4**[1]
1305 **2** *½* **Blue Tomato**[3] 1849 8-9-7 78.................................... AdrianTNicholls 19 70
(D Nicholls) *hld up: hdwy over 2f out: styd on wl appr fnl f: no ex towards fin* **7/2**[2]
5-06 **3** *1 ¼* **Soto**[23] 1369 6-9-2 60..(b) PaulMulrennan 17 61
(M W Easterby) *chsd ldrs stands' side: hung lft and kpt on same pce fnl f* **28/1**
3425 **4** *1 ¼* **Wiltshire (IRE)**[28] 1243 7-9-1 55.................................... JamieMoriarty 15 56
(P T Midgley) *s.i.s: hdwy over 2f out: kpt on fnl f* **28/1**
50-3 **5** *1* **Makshoof (IRE)**[8] 1689 5-9-8 78.................................... JamieSpencer 10 60
(K A Ryan) *s.i.s: hdwy over 2f out: edgd rt: kpt on wl fnl f* **4/1**[3]
0-04 **6** *½* **Sheik'N'Knotsterd**[18] 1477 4-9-3 40.................................... DavidAllan 12 53
(J F Coupland) *mid-div: kpt on fnl 2f: nvr nr ldrs* **200/1**
-536 **7** *1 ¾* **Baronovici (IRE)**[10] 1650 4-9-1 55.............................(v) TonyHamilton 14 46
(D W Barker) *led tl over 2f out: fdd appr fnl f* **14/1**
3-00 **8** *5* **Rainbow Bay**[14] 1558 6-8-9 48.................................(p) PaulPickard(7) 18 31
(Miss Tracy Waggott) *mid-div stands' side: nvr a factor* **100/1**
0-00 **9** *shd* **Lifetime Endeavour**[8] 1689 5-8-12 43............................ SladeO'Hara(5) 8 31
(R E Barr) *chsd ldrs: wknd over 2f out* **200/1**
24-0 **10** *1* **Jojesse**[129] 14 5-9-1 47.. TWilliams 5 26
(W Storey) *a towards rr: nvr a factor* **100/1**
40-0 **11** *¾* **Polish World (USA)**[62] 794 5-9-0 57.........................(b[1]) LeeVickers(3) 7 26
(T J Etherington) *chsd ldrs towards far side: lost pl over 2f out* **40/1**
-006 **12** *nse* **Fyodor (IRE)**[14] 1564 8-9-10 84.. PaulHanagan 3 33
(C R Dore) *hld up towards rr: effrt towards far side over 2f out: hung lft and rt: sn wknd* **8/1**
0-00 **13** *¾* **Moonage Daydream (IRE)**[7] 1737 4-9-8 67...........(bt) DuranFentiman 6 28
(T D Easterby) *w ldrs far side: lost pl over 2f out* **28/1**
0-00 **14** *¾* **Seafield Towers**[10] 1647 9-9-4 41..(b) DNolan 1 22
(D A Nolan) *s.s: a bhd* **200/1**
000- **15** *3* **Sea Salt**[143] 7727 6-9-2 66... AndrewElliott 9 10
(A J McCabe) *only one eye: chsd ldrs: lost pl 3f out* **25/1**
210- **16** *1 ½* **Digit**[166] 7451 3-8-7 64 ow1... TomEaves 11 6
(B Smart) *chsd ldrs towards far side: hung bdly lft and lost pl over 2f out* **16/1**
/00- **17** *8* **Bold Haze**[319] 3404 7-8-13 47...............................(v) MichaelJStainton(3) 4 —
(Miss S E Hall) *mid-div: lost pl over 3f out: sn bhd* **125/1**

1m 11.2s (-0.60) **Going Correction** +0.05s/f (Good)
WFA 3 from 4yo+ 10lb **17 Ran SP% 123.1**
Speed ratings (Par 101): **106,105,103,102,100 100,97,91,90,89 88,88,87,86,82 80,69**
toteswinger: 1&2 £4.40, 1&3 £13.90, 2&3 £26.20 CSF £7.08 TOTE £3.00: £1.20, £2.40, £5.50; EX 10.80.Makshoof was claimed by Ian McInnes for £10,000.
Owner Miss S Bowles **Bred** P Dillon **Trained** Musley Bank, N Yorks

FOCUS
An interesting claimer. The field grouped towards the centre of the track. The first two home were officially rated 73 and 78 but the proximity of the next two home limits things.
Fyodor(IRE) Official explanation: jockey said gelding hung both ways
Digit Official explanation: jockey said filly hung left final furlong

1925 RACING UK ON CHANNEL 432 H'CAP 1m 1f

4:50 (4:52) (Class 5) (0-75,75) 3-Y-O **£2,590** (£770; £385; £192) **Stalls** Low

Form RPR
4-42 **1** **Tarzan (IRE)**[11] 1626 3-9-4 75... GregFairley 2 79+
(M Johnston) *trckd ldrs: led over 2f out: rdn and edgd lft over 1f out: kpt on wl* **11/8**[1]
00-3 **2** *1 ¾* **Avitus**[16] 1522 3-8-4 61 oh1.. PaulHanagan 3 61
(Micky Hammond) *led: hdd over 2f out: kpt on same pce fnl f* **16/1**
36-3 **3** *nk* **Justonefortheroad**[16] 1508 3-9-1 72............................... JamieSpencer 1 71
(N J Vaughan) *hld up: stdy hdwy over 2f out: chal 1f out: edgd rt and lft: no ex ins fnl f* **2/1**[2]
0-11 **4** *3 ¾* **Postman**[13] 1595 3-9-4 75... TomEaves 5 66
(B Smart) *trckd ldrs: effrt 3f out: sn hrd drvn and wl outpcd* **7/2**[3]
40-0 **5** *¾* **Bandanaman (IRE)**[19] 1466 3-8-13 70........................ PaulMulrennan 4 60
(G A Swinbank) *hld up: sme hdwy on inner 4f out: shkn up over 2f out: no threat* **18/1**

1m 55.38s (2.38) **Going Correction** +0.05s/f (Good) **5 Ran SP% 108.8**
Speed ratings (Par 99): **91,89,89,85,85**
CSF £20.79 TOTE £2.20: £1.10, £5.80; EX 15.20.
Owner Highclere Thoroughbred Racing(Persimmon) **Bred** Pat Fullam **Trained** Middleham Moor, N Yorks

FOCUS
A fair three-year-old handicap that makes sense at face value, although not necessarily the most solid form.

1926 BODDINGTONS REDCAR STRAIGHT-MILE CHAMPIONSHIP (H'CAP) (QUALIFIER) 1m

5:20 (5:21) (Class 6) (0-60,60) 3-Y-O **£2,047** (£604; £302) **Stalls** Centre

Form RPR
00-0 **1** **Night Knight (IRE)**[18] 1470 3-9-3 59........................(v[1]) JamieSpencer 12 69+
(M L W Bell) *stmbld s: swtchd lft sn after s: hld up in rr: stdy hdwy over 2f out: led over 1f out: heavily eased nr fin* **6/1**[2]
50-6 **2** *2 ¾* **Royal Premium**[10] 1652 3-8-5 50............................... AndrewMullen(3) 10 53
(Mrs G S Rees) *w ldr: led centre over 2f out: hung lft: hdd over 1f out: kpt on same pce* **50/1**
3303 **3** *¾* **Paint Splash**[8] 1691 3-8-3 50..................................... DeanHeslop(5) 18 51
(T D Barron) *hld up in rr: hdwy over 2f out: edgd lft: styd on fnl f* **8/1**
0-05 **4** *2 ½* **Tilerium's Dream (IRE)**[11] 1625 3-8-13 55............. SilvestreDeSousa 3 51
(K A Ryan) *chsd ldrs towards far side: edgd lft 2f out: one pce* **16/1**
0-40 **5** *1* **Ivor Novello (IRE)**[19] 1465 3-8-11 53............................... PaulHanagan 8 47
(G A Swinbank) *hmpd s: kpt on fnl 2f: nt rch ldrs* **25/1**
0051 **6** *2 ¼* **Dante Deo (USA)**[7] 1725 3-9-4 60 6ex............................. PhillipMakin 2 54+
(T D Barron) *hld up in midfield towards far side: hdwy whn hmpd 2f out: nvr nr ldrs* **7/2**[1]
05-0 **7** *1 ¼* **Nut Hand (IRE)**[26] 1281 3-9-0 56... DNolan 17 42
(T D Easterby) *in rr-div stands' side: hrd rdn over 3f out: kpt on fnl 2f: nvr nrr* **18/1**
4-00 **8** *nk* **Bold Bomber**[25] 1308 3-8-4 53 ow1............................ KrishGundowry(7) 7 38
(Paul Green) *swvd rt s: led: t.k.h: hdd over 2f out: wknd over 1f out* **16/1**

The Form Book, Raceform Ltd, Compton, RG20 6NL

00-0 **9** *2 1/4* **Oneofthesedayz (IRE)**[7] 1725 3-8-13 **55**...............(p) AdrianTNicholls 4 35
(Mrs D J Sanderson) *chsd ldrs towards far side: wknd 2f out* **50/1**
00-4 **10** *1 1/4* **Ask Dan (IRE)**[7] 1725 3-9-4 **60**.......................... TomEaves 1 38
(B Smart) *mid-div far side: reminders 4f out: nvr a factor* **13/2**[3]
000- **11** *3 3/4* **Pattern Mark**[194] 7080 3-8-13 **55**.......................... PaulMulrennan 13 24
(Ollie Pears) *mid-div: nvr a factor* **28/1**
-000 **12** *hd* **Irish Saint (IRE)**[7] 1725 3-9-0 **56**.......................... GregFairley 19 25
(T J Pitt) *in rr-div stands' side: nvr on terms* **12/1**
6-05 **13** *hd* **Hawkleaf Flier (IRE)**[13] 1594 3-8-10 **52**.......................... DavidAllan 9 20
(T D Easterby) *chsd ldrs stands' side: rdn and hung lft over 2f out: sn wknd* **11/1**
000- **14** *1* **Rioja Ruby (IRE)**[236] 6009 3-8-1 **48**...................(p) PatrickDonaghy(5) 15 14
(S G West) *chsd ldrs stands' side: lost pl over 2f out* **66/1**
40-0 **15** *6* **Scarth Hill (IRE)**[25] 1308 3-8-7 **49**.......................... TonyHamilton 14 —
(G M Moore) *chsd ldrs towards stands' side: lost pl over 2f out* **16/1**
556 **16** *1 1/4* **Destinationunknown (USA)**[58] 839 3-8-13 **55**.........(p) AndrewElliott 6 —
(A J McCabe) *sn bhd* **14/1**
6-00 **17** *1 1/4* **Ryedon Bye**[11] 1625 3-8-10 **52**.......................... DuranFentiman 5 —
(T D Easterby) *mid-div: rdn 3f out: sn lost pl and bhd* **25/1**
006- **18** *1 1/4* **Another Luke (IRE)**[292] 4292 3-9-0 **59**.......................... LeeVickers(3) 16 —
(T J Etherington) *mid-div: lost pl over 2f out: eased* **28/1**

1m 38.65s (0.65) **Going Correction** +0.05s/f (Good) 18 Ran SP% **126.6**
Speed ratings (Par 97): **98,95,94,92,91 88,87,87,84,83 79,79,79,78,72 71,70,68**
toteswinger: 1&2 £54.00, 1&3 £12.70, 2&3 £33.30 CSF £300.88 CT £2518.03 TOTE £7.10: £2.00, £6.20, £2.30, £3.90; EX 343.10 Place 6: £119.41, Place 5: £74.65..
Owner Scotney,Asplin,Symonds,Ball,Chelingworth **Bred** John Lyons **Trained** Newmarket, Suffolk

FOCUS
A weak handicap in which they finished quite well strung out. Spencer rode an interesting tactical race on the winner, navigating a path from stall 12 over towards the far rail.
Night Knight(IRE) Official explanation: trainer's rep said, regarding apparent improvement in form, that the gelding was better suited by the fitting of a first-time visor.
Bold Bomber Official explanation: jockey said colt ran too free and had no more to give
T/Plt: £70.80 to a £1 stake. Pool: £38,339.32. 395.12 winning tickets. T/Qpdt: £21.60 to a £1 stake. Pool: £1,993.40. 68.15 winning tickets. WG

1810 WINDSOR (R-H)
Monday, May 11

OFFICIAL GOING: Good to firm (8.3)
Wind: Strong, against Weather: Sunny

1927 MAPIS MODELLING ACADEMY NOVICE STKS 5f 10y
5:50 (5:50) (Class 4) 2-Y-O **£4,857** (£1,445; £722; £360) **Stalls** High

Form RPR
501 **1** **Crown (IRE)**[7] 1749 2-9-0 0.......................... RichardHughes 1 86
(R Hannon) *hld up in last: shkn up on outer 2f out: hung rt but prog to ld ins fnl f: bmpd runner-up and sn clr* **2/1**[2]
021 **2** *1 1/4* **Red Avalanche (IRE)**[13] 1590 2-9-5 0.......................... EddieAhern 3 87
(P F I Cole) *trckd ldr: shkn up 2f out: led narrowly over 1f out: jst hdd whn bmpd ins fnl f: no ex* **4/6**[1]
1 **3** *5* **Art Jewel (IRE)**[10] 1637 2-9-0 0.......................... JimmyFortune 4 64
(S A Callaghan) *trckd ldng pair w tail swishing: shkn up 2f out: wl outpcd fr jst over 1f out* **8/1**[3]
01 **4** *5* **Lucky Mellor**[10] 1653 2-9-0 0.......................... IanMongan 2 46+
(D K Ivory) *led: hung bdly lft wl over 1f out: sn hdd & wknd: eased* **20/1**

61.94 secs (1.64) **Going Correction** +0.225s/f (Good) 4 Ran SP% **109.2**
Speed ratings (Par 95): **95,93,85,77**
CSF £3.78 TOTE £2.70; EX 4.50.
Owner Mrs J Wood **Bred** Shortgrove Manor Stud **Trained** East Everleigh, Wilts

FOCUS
A strong wind against contributed to a time well above standard and this was a messy race.

NOTEBOOK
Crown(IRE) used her experience to beat a field of newcomers over this course and distance the previous week, but she still showed signs of greeness this time (possibly due to the wind) when edging sharply to her right inside the last furlong and giving the second a bump. She won with a bit of authority and her dam line suggests she will have no trouble getting 6f. Connections are now considering the Hilary Needler at Beverley next time then a Royal Ascot appearance in either the Queen Mary or Albany Stakes. (tchd 9-4)
Red Avalanche(IRE) was preferred in the market having won easily at Nottingham last time but didn't have much fortune despite the small field. His momentum was checked when he was crossed well over a furlong out and when he got the rail and found his stride well inside the last he was bumped by the winner and again lost momentum. It is hard to say this cost him the race but he couldn't reel in the winner in the time available. He is another bred to benefit from another furlong although he has plenty of pace for 5f. Connections ruled out fast ground as an excuse and sighted lack of pace in the race as a bigger problem. (op 4-5 tchd 5-6)
Art Jewel(IRE) again flashed her tail throughout as she had done when winning on her debut so that is not an excuse and she was beaten on merit here. (op 15-2 tchd 7-1 and 9-1)
Lucky Mellor ran about in the wind when veering up the home stretch but this was a significant step up in class from her Southwell win last time. Official explanation: jockey said colt hung left-handed (op 16-1)

1928 SPORTINGBET.COM H'CAP 1m 2f 7y
6:20 (6:22) (Class 5) (0-75,74) 3-Y-O **£3,070** (£906; £453) **Stalls** Centre

Form RPR
2540 **1** **Tinshu (IRE)**[20] 1431 3-9-2 **72**.......................... AdamKirby 7 77
(D Haydn Jones) *trckd ldrs: prog to ld wl over 1f out: hanging u.p but kpt on wl fnl f* **20/1**
044- **2** *3/4* **Hawk's Eye**[182] 7268 3-8-10 **66**.......................... DarryllHolland 8 70
(E F Vaughan) *stdd s: hld up in detached last: prog on inner whn nt clr run over 2f out: swtchd to wd outside over 1f out: hanging and hd in air but styd on to take 2nd nr fin* **20/1**
0-50 **3** *nk* **Hip Hip Hooray**[7] 1751 3-8-8 **64**.......................... SteveDrowne 1 67
(L A Dace) *trckd ldrs: prog to chal wl over 2f out and upsides: pressed wnr over 1f out: hld ins fnl f and lost 2nd nr fin* **25/1**
000- **4** *hd* **Granski (IRE)**[203] 6865 3-8-9 **65**.......................... RichardHughes 9 68
(R Hannon) *hld up in last pair: prog fr 4f out to chse ldrs 2f out: hanging u.p after: styd on ins fnl f: nvr quite got there* **10/1**
2646 **5** *2 1/4* **Diamond Twister (USA)**[10] 1643 3-9-4 **74**...............(t) RobertWinston 6 72
(J R Best) *hld up in rr: gd prog over 3f out to chal over 2f out: sn upsides: nt qckn over 1f out* **18/1**
323 **6** *3* **Carbon Hoofprint**[33] 1176 3-9-3 **73**.......................... FergusSweeney 5 65
(P J Makin) *trckd ldrs: shkn up 3f out: cl enough 2f out: hanging and fdd* **7/1**
0-15 **7** *1 1/2* **Strong Storm (USA)**[21] 1408 3-9-1 **71**.......................... ShaneKelly 2 60
(J Noseda) *hld up towards rr: effrt on outer over 3f out: no prog u.p over 2f out: no ch after* **3/1**[1]
50-0 **8** *1/2* **Howard**[17] 1489 3-9-3 **73**.......................... EddieAhern 14 61
(J L Dunlop) *trckd ldng pair after 4f: effrt to ld on inner over 2f out: hanging and hdd wl over 1f out: wknd* **6/1**[3]
3-30 **9** *3 1/2* **Duar Mapel (USA)**[14] 1574 3-8-8 **69**...............(b) MCGeran(5) 13 50
(Paul Mason) *towards rr: u.p and struggling over 4f out: n.d fnl 2f* **50/1**
520- **10** *3 3/4* **Cool Strike (UAE)**[194] 7073 3-8-12 **68**.......................... WilliamBuick 10 42
(A M Balding) *hld up in last trio: pushed along and no prog over 3f out: wl btn after* **16/1**
60-5 **11** *3 1/2* **Manolito Montoya (IRE)**[20] 1429 3-8-6 **67** ow2....(v) GabrielHannon(5) 4 34
(J W Hills) *hld up in midfield: gng wl 4f out: pushed along and fdd 3f out* **40/1**
045- **12** *1 3/4* **Silk Cotton (USA)**[252] 5571 3-9-2 **72**.......................... LDettori 3 35
(E A L Dunlop) *led 3f: lost pl: shkn up over 4f out: wknd over 2f out: eased* **14/1**
4-44 **13** *12* **Dhania (IRE)**[19] 1461 3-9-3 **73**.......................... JimCrowley 15 12
(R A Teal) *led after 3f to over 2f out: hanging: wknd and eased* **11/2**[2]
-214 **14** *2 1/2* **Best In Class**[14] 1574 3-9-1 **71**.......................... RichardKingscote 11 5
(Tom Dascombe) *pressed ldr after 3f: upsides 3f out: sn wknd and eased* **17/2**

2m 7.78s (-0.92) **Going Correction** -0.10s/f (Good) 14 Ran SP% **122.4**
Speed ratings (Par 99): **99,98,98,98,96 93,92,92,89,86 83,82,72,70**
toteswinger: 1&2 £24.10, 1&3 not won, 2&3 not won CSF £359.40 CT £9628.88 TOTE £33.00: £5.30, £4.00, £8.10; EX 735.50.
Owner Llewelyn, Runeckles **Bred** Mrs M L Parry & P Steele-Mortimer **Trained** Efail Isaf, Rhondda C Taff

FOCUS
A competitive handicap but the form is nothing out of the ordinary.
Silk Cotton(USA) Official explanation: jockey said filly lost its action

1929 SPORTINGBET.COM STKS (REGISTERED AS THE ROYAL WINDSOR STAKES) (LISTED RACE) (C&G) 1m 67y
6:50 (6:50) (Class 1) 3-Y-O+
£22,708 (£8,608; £4,308; £2,148; £1,076; £540) **Stalls** High

Form RPR
0-42 **1** **Ordnance Row**[2] 1865 6-9-2 112.......................... RichardHughes 7 114
(R Hannon) *trckd ldrs: prog on inner to ld jst over 2f out: hrd rdn over 1f out: in command fnl f* **15/8**[1]
264- **2** *2* **Pinpoint (IRE)**[229] 6201 7-9-2 107.......................... AdamKirby 5 109
(W R Swinburn) *wl in tch: effrt over 2f out: hanging fnl 2f but kpt on to take 2nd ins fnl f* **9/2**[3]
-033 **3** *nk* **Icesolator (IRE)**[23] 1354 3-8-3 105.......................... FrancisNorton 4 105
(R Hannon) *hld up in 6th: effrt on outer over 2f out: kpt on ins fnl f: nvr able to chal* **16/1**
2111 **4** *2* **Abbondanza (IRE)**[10] 1640 6-9-2 108...............(p) RobertWinston 6 104
(I Semple) *drvn to ld: tried to kick on over 3f out: hdd jst over 2f out: wandered over 1f out: lost 2nd ins fnl f* **11/1**
0010 **5** *nse* **Dijeerr (USA)**[44] 1008 5-9-2 111.......................(vt) LDettori 8 104
(Saeed Bin Suroor) *t.k.h early: trckd ldr to over 2f out: nt qckn and sn lost pl* **13/2**
30-3 **6** *shd* **Laa Rayb (USA)**[12] 1600 5-9-2 114.......................... RoystonFfrench 2 103
(M Johnston) *pushed along in last early: nvr really gng: struggling u.p over 3f out: plugged on* **10/3**[2]
5-10 **7** *1* **Manassas (IRE)**[23] 1352 4-9-2 97.......................... JimmyFortune 3 101
(B J Meehan) *trckd ldng pair: effrt on outer over 3f out: sn nt qckn and btn: fdd fnl f* **10/1**

1m 42.72s (-1.98) **Going Correction** -0.10s/f (Good)
WFA 3 from 4yo+ 13lb 7 Ran SP% **112.7**
Speed ratings (Par 111): **105,103,102,100,100 100,99**
toteswinger: 1&2 £14.10, 1&3 £5.30, 2&3 £7.60 CSF £10.25 TOTE £3.00: £2.00, £3.00; EX 10.90.
Owner Mrs P Good **Bred** Mrs P Good **Trained** East Everleigh, Wilts

FOCUS
A decent Listed race and straightforward form with the winner the best guide.

NOTEBOOK
Ordnance Row avoided a penalty for his Group 3 win over 1m at Salisbury last season. Second top rated on official figures at 112, he underlined his durability having been second over a now inadequate 7f at Haydock on Saturday. He is now faced with a severe upgrade in the Eclipse at Sandown and he has been well beaten on the two occasions he has tried 1m2f, admitedly back in 2007. (op 7-4, tchd 2-1 in places)
Pinpoint(IRE) ran a fine race on his comeback having done most of his racing in top-class 1m2f handicaps last season and was meeting the winner 5lb 'wrong' on official figures. He needs to go up in trip and made things difficult by hanging but stayed on well to take second. He looks up to winning a Listed event over further. (op 7-1)
Icesolator(IRE), a stablemate of the winner, still hasn't won beyond 5f since he was a two-year-old last season, but got home better than last time at Lingfield over this distance and looks capable in the right company although a mark of 105 makes him hard to place. (tchd 20-1)
Abbondanza(IRE) forced his way to the front and kept up a good gallop. However, his improvement from 85 to 108 since December has been on the All-Weather and while he did nothing wrong here, he is meeting a better class of opponent on turf. (op 10-1 tchd 12-1)
Dijeerr(USA) could never get to dictate from the front as he did when last successful. (op 7-1)
Laa Rayb(USA), like the winner, got into this with no Group penalty and was best on official figures by 2lb at 114 and had the winner behind when they met at Ascot last time but found it impossible to come from off the pace. (op 11-4 tchd 7-2)
Manassas(IRE) was 15lb 'wrong' with the winner on official figures. (tchd 11-1)

1930 SPORTINGBET.COM H'CAP 1m 3f 135y
7:20 (7:21) (Class 5) (0-75,75) 3-Y-O **£3,070** (£906; £453) **Stalls** Centre

Form RPR
565- **1** **Non Dom (IRE)**[170] 7422 3-8-8 **65**.......................... SteveDrowne 9 74+
(H Morrison) *s.i.s and pushed up to go prom: effrt to ld wl over 1f out and gng best: styd on wl* **3/1**[1]
-002 **2** *2 1/4* **Salybia Bay**[13] 1580 3-8-8 **65**.......................... RichardHughes 1 70
(R Hannon) *hld up in last: prog over 2f out: chsd wnr ins fnl f: no imp* **12/1**
56-2 **3** *3/4* **Sherman McCoy**[20] 1416 3-8-10 **67**.......................... DarryllHolland 5 71
(B R Millman) *mostly chsd ldr to 2f out: chsd wnr over 1f out: no imp: lost 2nd ins fnl f* **15/2**[3]
6630 **4** *4 1/2* **Orsippus (USA)**[10] 1643 3-8-8 **70**...............(v[1]) MCGeran(5) 8 66
(M R Channon) *plld hrd: hld up bhd ldrs: drvn and nt qckn wl over 2f out: plugged on fr over 1f out* **12/1**
6613 **5** *5* **Urban Space**[12] 1614 3-8-13 **70**.......................... SebSanders 4 58
(B G Powell) *trckd ldrs: rdn wl over 3f out: effrt to chal and upsides over 2f out: wknd wl over 1f out* **11/1**

-643 **6** *2 1/4* **Cayman Sky**[14] 1570 3-8-12 **69**.................................(b) JimmyFortune 10 53
(R Hannon) *mde most: drvn 3f out: hdd & wknd wl over 1f out: hanging fnl f* **9/1**

20-5 **7** *8* **Parc Des Princes (USA)**[13] 1580 3-8-4 **61**..................(b) WilliamBuick 6 31
(A M Balding) *t.k.h: hld up in rr: rdn and no rspnse 3f out: wl btn fnl 2f* **17/2**

0-21 **8** *3 1/4* **Lake Kalamalka (IRE)**[13] 1580 3-9-1 **72**.......................... EddieAhern 11 37
(J L Dunlop) *lost midfield position after 4f: effrt on wd outside 3f out: no prog over 2f out: wknd and eased* **10/3**[2]

-223 **9** *5* **Black N Brew (USA)**[47] 962 3-9-3 **74**.......................... RobertWinston 7 30
(J R Best) *wl in tch: drvn and hanging over 3f out: sn btn: eased fnl 2f* **14/1**

53-0 **10** *13* **Play To Win (IRE)**[7] 1747 3-8-0 **62**................................(p) AmyBaker[(5)] 2 —
(D R C Elsworth) *hld up: plld hrd bnd 6f out: dropped out qckly 4f out: t.o* **20/1**

2m 28.12s (-1.38) **Going Correction** -0.10s/f (Good) **10** Ran SP% **115.5**
Speed ratings (Par 99): **100,98,98,95,91 90,84,82,79,70**
toteswinger: 1&2 £23.10, 1&3 £12.70, 2&3 £7.70 CSF £39.42 CT £248.10 TOTE £4.00: £1.80, £3.00, £3.00; EX 37.40.
Owner Raymond Tooth **Bred** Mrs Ann Kennedy **Trained** East Ilsley, Berks

FOCUS
A modest three-year-old handicap rated around the placed horses to recent form.
Non Dom(IRE) Official explanation: trainer said, regarding apparent improvement in form, since its last run, it had been gelded, appreciated the step up in trip and the better ground.
Black N Brew(USA) Official explanation: jockey said colt lost its action

1931 SPORTINGBET.COM MEDIAN AUCTION MAIDEN STKS 1m 2f 7y
7:50 (7:52) (Class 5) 3-5-Y-O **£2,729** (£806; £403) **Stalls** Centre

Form RPR

353- **1** **Featherweight (IRE)**[168] 7438 3-8-8 **72**.......................... MichaelHills 12 77
(B W Hills) *trckd ldrs: wnt 2nd 1/2-way: led wl over 2f out: clr over 1f out: all out nr fin* **5/1**[3]

2- **2** *1/2* **Times Up**[206] 6778 3-8-13 **0**.. EddieAhern 3 81
(J L Dunlop) *trckd ldrs: rdn over 2f out: chsd wnr over 1f out: clsd ins fnl f: nvr quite able to chal* **5/2**[1]

2-02 **3** *3 3/4* **Formula (USA)**[7] 1752 3-8-13 **79**................................. RichardHughes 4 74
(R Hannon) *trckd ldrs: rdn over 2f out: disp 2nd u.p over 1f out: one pce* **5/2**[1]

3-33 **4** *hd* **Bagber**[23] 1362 3-8-13 **75**.. SebSanders 11 73
(H J L Dunlop) *led after 3f: hung lft bnd 6f out: hung bdly lft bnd 5f out: hdd wl over 2f out: continued to hang lft: lost 2nd over 1f out: fdd* **14/1**

00- **5** *1* **Bernie The Bolt (IRE)**[172] 7397 3-8-13 **0**.................. WilliamBuick 16 71+
(A M Balding) *hld up in last quartet and off the pce: pushed along over 3f out: styd on steadily fr over 2f out: nvr nr ldrs* **33/1**

6 *3/4* **Tribal Rule** 3-8-13 **0**.. JimCrowley 8 70+
(Mrs A J Perrett) *dwlt: hld up bhd ldrs: rn green and n.m.r over 2f out: one pce fr over 1f out* **9/2**[2]

0-0 **7** *3/4* **Flannel (IRE)**[28] 1260 3-8-13 **0**... AdamKirby 7 68
(J R Fanshawe) *hld up in midfield: outpcd by ldrs 3f out: pushed along and kpt on fnl 2f: nvr nrr* **66/1**

8 *3 3/4* **La Polka** 3-8-8 **0**.. TravisBlock 1 56
(H Morrison) *trckd ldrs: effrt 3f out: no prog 2f out: fdd* **100/1**

9 *1/2* **Boffin**[117] 4-10-0 **0**.. StephenCarson 13 60
(Eve Johnson Houghton) *sn last: rdn and struggling 1/2-way: plugged on fnl 2f* **100/1**

322- **10** *3 3/4* **Zebrano**[229] 6198 3-8-13 **77**... MickyFenton 10 52
(Miss E C Lavelle) *t.k.h: led: hdd after 3f: carried lft bnd 6f out: rdn 4f out: wknd 3f out* **6/1**

0-0 **11** *2 1/4* **Gaelic Rose (IRE)**[13] 1579 3-8-8 **0**................................. JamesDoyle 14 43
(S Kirk) *hld up in last quartet: pushed along over 3f out: wknd over 2f out* **66/1**

50- **12** *1/2* **Premier Superstar**[277] 4776 3-8-8 **0**.............................. DarryllHolland 6 42
(M H Tompkins) *a in last quartet: rdn and no prog over 3f out* **125/1**

2m 8.46s (-0.24) **Going Correction** -0.10s/f (Good)
WFA 3 from 4yo+ 15lb **12** Ran SP% **121.6**
Speed ratings (Par 103): **96,95,92,92,91 91,90,87,87,84 82,81**
toteswinger: 1&2 £3.80, 1&3 £5.30, 2&3 £3.60 CSF £18.36 TOTE £5.90: £2.10, £1.50, £1.80; EX 22.30.
Owner Jeremy Gompertz & Patrick Milmo **Bred** Jeremy Gompertz **Trained** Lambourn, Berks

FOCUS
An ordinary maiden.
Bernie The Bolt(IRE) Official explanation: jockey said gelding was unsuited by the good to firm ground

1932 MAPISMODELLINGACADEMY.CO.UK H'CAP 1m 67y
8:20 (8:20) (Class 5) (0-70,73) 3-Y-O **£2,729** (£806; £403) **Stalls** High

Form RPR

1-15 **1** **Roar Of Applause**[2] 1882 3-9-7 **73** 6ex.............................. EddieAhern 9 79+
(B J Meehan) *hld up in midfield: gd prog against nr side rail to ld wl over 1f out: shkn up sn after: pushed out fnl 100yds* **11/4**[1]

03-6 **2** *3/4* **Mytivil (IRE)**[119] 136 3-8-8 **65**.................................. RossAtkinson[(5)] 11 69
(M Salaman) *hld up in rr: prog against nr side rail over 2f out: chsd wnr over 1f out: n.m.r sn after: styd on but a hld* **100/1**

365- **3** *1 1/4* **Getcarter**[184] 7240 3-9-2 **68**.. RichardHughes 1 69+
(R Hannon) *t.k.h early and hld up in midfield: prog whn nt clr run briefly 2f out: chsd ldng pair jst over 1f out: styd on but readily hld* **7/2**[2]

65-0 **4** *5* **Wellesley**[28] 1252 3-8-12 **64**... AdamKirby 13 54
(W R Swinburn) *prom: upsides over 2f out: outpcd over 1f out* **8/1**

64-0 **5** *3/4* **Fromthebeginning**[51] 914 3-9-2 **68**................................ RobertHavlin 7 56
(D R C Elsworth) *taken down early and v free to post: hld up towards rr: nt qckn over 2f out: hanging but plugged on fr over 1f out* **33/1**

4212 **6** *1/2* **Wunder Strike (USA)**[13] 1595 3-8-12 **64**....................(p) PatCosgrave 12 51
(J R Boyle) *t.k.h: hld up bhd ldrs: effrt 3f out: wl on terms over 2f out: wknd over 1f out* **4/1**[3]

6-00 **7** *nk* **General Zhukov**[13] 1585 3-8-7 **64**............................ WilliamCarson[(5)] 10 50
(J M P Eustace) *dwlt: hld up in last pair: prog on wd outside 3f out: no hdwy 2f out: wknd* **20/1**

4243 **8** *nse* **Edgeworth (IRE)**[23] 1361 3-9-0 **66**.............................. RobertWinston 3 52
(B G Powell) *t.k.h in midfield: effrt and cl up over 2f out: sn wknd* **14/1**

00-4 **9** *1/2* **Transformer (IRE)**[13] 1585 3-8-13 **65**................................ ShaneKelly 4 50
(W J Knight) *dwlt: hld up in last pair: reminders 2f out: sme prog over 1f out: nvr nr ldrs* **20/1**

36-6 **10** *2 3/4* **Charlie Smirke (USA)**[42] 1034 3-9-0 **66**.................. FergusSweeney 14 45
(G L Moore) *lft in ld after 2f: hdd & wknd wl over 1f out* **25/1**

021- **11** *2 3/4* **Mykingdomforahorse**[202] 6886 3-9-2 **68**....................(v) DarryllHolland 2 40
(M R Channon) *led: hung wildly lft bnd after 2f and hdd: rcvrd to press ldr to 3f out: sn btn* **12/1**

004- **12** *1/2* **Foxtrot Charlie**[202] 6886 3-9-2 **68**..................................... JimCrowley 6 39
(P Winkworth) *hld up in rr: rdn and struggling sn after 1/2-way* **10/1**

1m 44.82s (0.12) **Going Correction** -0.10s/f (Good) **12** Ran SP% **120.8**
Speed ratings (Par 99): **95,94,93,88,87 86,86,86,85,83 80,79**
toteswinger: 1&2 £40.40, 1&3 £4.70, 2&3 £40.40 CSF £346.41 CT £1034.28 TOTE £4.10: £1.40, £12.20, £2.20; EX 165.10 Place 6: £549.37, Place 5: £116.12.
Owner Raymond Tooth **Bred** Southcourt Stud **Trained** Manton, Wilts

FOCUS
Six of the 12 runners were making their handicap debuts but this looks fair form for the grade.
Mykingdomforahorse Official explanation: jockey said colt failed to handle the bend
T/Jkpt: Not won. T/Plt: £557.00 to a £1 stake. Pool: £74,628.06. 97.79 winning tickets. T/Qpdt: £6.10 to a £1 stake. Pool: £7,595.51. 910.00 winning tickets. JN

1528 WOLVERHAMPTON (A.W) (L-H)
Monday, May 11

OFFICIAL GOING: Standard
Wind: Fresh half against Weather: Sunny

1933 BET MULTIPLES - BETDAQ MAIDEN AUCTION FILLIES' STKS 5f 20y(P)
2:10 (2:10) (Class 4) 2-Y-O **£4,209** (£1,252; £625; £312) **Stalls** Low

Form RPR

22 **1** **Diamond Laura**[14] 1569 2-8-6 **0**.............................. CatherineGannon 9 78
(P D Evans) *mde all: edgd rt over 1f out: rdn and hld on towards fin* **9/4**[1]

32 **2** *nk* **Avonvalley**[13] 1577 2-8-5 **0**.. FrancisNorton 5 76
(M S Saunders) *hld up: hdwy over 2f out: c wd st: edgd rt ins fnl f: rdn and r.o towards fin* **11/2**[2]

3 *1 1/4* **Above Limits (IRE)** 2-8-9 **0**.................................. RichardKingscote 10 75+
(Tom Dascombe) *chsd wnr: edgd lft wl over 1f out: sn rdn: nt qckn ins fnl f* **9/4**[1]

032 **4** *3 3/4* **Anjomarba (IRE)**[21] 1396 2-8-4 **0**...................................... LiamJones 3 57
(W G M Turner) *a.p: rdn over 1f out: wknd ins fnl f* **17/2**

3 **5** *1 1/2* **Victorian Art (IRE)**[42] 1031 2-8-7 **0**............................. WilliamBuick 6 55
(M A Magnusson) *chsd ldrs tl wknd 2f out* **8/1**

6 **6** *3 1/2* **Ice Cool Lady (IRE)**[14] 1569 2-8-9 **0**................................. ChrisCatlin 1 44
(W R Swinburn) *sltly hmpd over 3f out: a bhd* **7/1**[3]

06 **7** *13* **Saachi's Vision (IRE)**[10] 1637 2-8-5 **0**....................... FrankieMcDonald 8 —
(D K Ivory) *s.i.s: hung lft thrght: a bhd* **100/1**

0 **8** *6* **Nuts About You (IRE)**[16] 1504 2-7-11 **0**.......................... BillyCray[(7)] 2 —
(A Berry) *s.i.s: outpcd* **200/1**

62.12 secs (-0.18) **Going Correction** +0.125s/f (Slow) **8** Ran SP% **112.5**
Speed ratings (Par 92): **106,105,103,97,95 89,68,59**
toteswinger: 1&2 £1.70, 1&3 £1.60, 2&3 £4.10 CSF £14.90 TOTE £3.30: £1.20, £1.90, £1.40; EX 16.90.
Owner Diamond Racing Ltd **Bred** Paul Sweeting **Trained** Pandy, Monmouths
■ Stewards' Enquiry : Francis Norton three-day ban: used whip with excessive frequency without giving filly time to respond (May 25-27)

FOCUS
A reasonable maiden run at a sound pace in which the runners faced a fairly strong headwind in the straight. This form looks reliable and the first three, who pulled clear, raced centre to stands' side in the straight.

NOTEBOOK
Diamond Laura, who shaped well in race that threw up winners on turf, matched those efforts and showed a good attitude on this all-weather debut. Life will be tougher under a penalty as the better juveniles start to appear but she may be capable of a little better for this yard. She reportedly now goes for a Listed event at York on Friday. (tchd 11-4)
Avonvalley had also run well in races that had worked out well on turf and she showed more than enough on this all-weather debut to suggest a similar event can be found. She should have no problems with the step up to 6f. (op 9-2)
Above Limits(IRE) ◆, who attracted support, is a half-sister to several winners up to middle distances and she shaped with plenty of credit against more experienced rivals from the widest draw on this racecourse debut. She may turn out to be the best of these and looks sure to win a race. (op 5-2)
Anjomarba(IRE) had improved with each of her three previous turf runs but failed to match the pick of these efforts on this all-weather debut. Nevertheless she was far from disgraced and is capable of picking up an uncompetitive event. (op 11-1 tchd 8-1)
Victorian Art(IRE), who showed ability in a race that threw up a couple of winners on her debut, failed to build on that in what looked a stronger event. She may do better in ordinary nursery company in due course. (op 11-2)
Ice Cool Lady(IRE) finished further behind the winner than she had on her debut on turf but she should do better granted more of a test of stamina back on grass. (op 8-1 tchd 9-1)

1934 STAY AT THE WOLVERHAMPTON HOLIDAY INN CLAIMING STKS 5f 20y(P)
2:40 (2:40) (Class 5) 2-Y-O **£2,729** (£806; £403) **Stalls** Low

Form RPR

63 **1** **Six Wives**[7] 1742 2-8-11 **0**.. LiamJones 7 66
(W J Haggas) *t.k.h: sn chsng ldrs: edgd lft over 1f out: led jst ins fnl f: r.o* **13/8**[2]

232 **2** *hd* **Out The Ring (IRE)**[11] 1624 2-8-12 **0**................................... NCallan 4 66
(K A Ryan) *bmpd s: bmpd again sn after s: t.k.h: sn prom: led 2f out: rdn and hdd jst ins fnl f: r.o* **6/5**[1]

02 **3** *5* **Bond Together**[35] 1158 2-8-9 **0**.......................(v[1]) RichardEvans[(5)] 6 50
(P D Evans) *hung lft thrght: hld up: hmpd sn after s: hdwy over 2f out: wkng whn rdr dropped whip 1f out* **13/2**[3]

060 **4** *4 1/2* **Needwood Dancer**[4] 1802 2-8-6 **0** ow4......................... PatrickMathers 2 26+
(Peter Grayson) *s.i.s: sn chsng ldrs: nt clr run on ins over 2f out: wknd wl over 1f out* **100/1**

015 **5** *1 1/2* **Lady Lion**[8] 1706 2-8-2 **0**.. WilliamCarson[(5)] 1 21
(W G M Turner) *wnt rt s: sn w ldr: led over 3f out: rdn and hdd over 2f out: wknd over 1f out* **12/1**

0 **6** *8* **Dinky Deb**[10] 1637 2-8-3 **0**.. ChrisCatlin 8 —
(D K Ivory) *led over 1f: wknd 2f out* **33/1**

64.97 secs (2.67) **Going Correction** +0.125s/f (Slow) **6** Ran SP% **108.5**
Speed ratings (Par 93): **83,82,74,67,65 52**
toteswinger: 1&2 £1.10, 1&3 £2.60, 2&3 £2.50 CSF £3.60 TOTE £2.90: £1.80, £1.10; EX 5.10.Six Wives was claimed by James S Kennerley for £14,000.
Owner Cheveley Park Stud **Bred** Cheveley Park Stud Ltd **Trained** Newmarket, Suffolk

FOCUS
An uncompetitive event in which the two market leaders, who raced towards the far rail in the straight, pulled clear in the closing stages. The pace was only fair and the time was nearly 3secs slower than the opener.

NOTEBOOK

Six Wives avoided the early scrimmaging and bettered her turf form to beat a reliable yardstick on this all-weather debut. While it is a bit of a worry she has been downgraded at such an early stage of her career, she may well be capable of a little better. She was subsequently claimed. (op 7-4 tchd 15-8)

Out The Ring(IRE), who has now been turned over at single-figure odds on each of his four runs, did look a shade unlucky as he took a few hefty bumps early on but it was hard to fault his attitude in the closing stages. He can make amends in similar company granted more luck in running. (op 6-4 tchd Evens)

Bond Together, easy to back tried in the first-time visor, had a bit to find at the weights and, although an early couple of bumps did his chance no favours, he had his limitations exposed against a couple of fair sorts. There will be easier opportunities than this one. (op 4-1)

Needwood Dancer, whose rider posted 4lb overweight, was not totally disgraced in the face of a very stiff task for a yard that has struggled for winners for some time, but she will have to show a fair bit more before she is a solid betting proposition.

Lady Lion, who caused the early inteference when diving right leaving the stalls, was nibbled at in the market for this all-weather debut but proved disappointing after having the run of the race.
Official explanation: jockey said filly jumped right leaving stalls (op 14-1)

Dinky Deb Official explanation: jockey said filly hung right

1935 DINE IN THE HORIZONS RESTAURANT CLAIMING STKS — 5f 20y(P)

3:10 (3:10) (Class 6) 3-Y-O+ — £2,729 (£806; £403) Stalls Low

Form — RPR

4521 **1** — **Harry Up**[21] 1412 8-9-12 82 — (p) NCallan 1 — 83
(K A Ryan) *mde all: rdn 1f out: r.o* — **4/5**[1]

1122 **2** *1 1/2* — **Desperate Dan**[17] 1494 8-9-6 78 — (v) TPQueally 8 — 72
(A B Haynes) *a.p: wnt 2nd over 2f out: sn pressed wnr: rdn and kpt on one pce ins fnl f* — **5/2**[2]

5030 **3** *1 1/4* — **Green Lagonda (AUS)**[5] 1784 7-9-0 55 — MickyFenton 3 — 61
(Stef Liddiard) *bhd: pushed along over 3f out: hdwy 2f out: rdn over 1f out: kpt on ins fnl f* — **16/1**

6643 **4** *3 1/4* — **Pepin (IRE)**[10] 1652 3-8-3 52 — FrankieMcDonald 7 — 43
(D Haydn Jones) *sn outpcd and bhd: kpt on to take 4th ins fnl f: nvr nr ldrs* — **33/1**

04-0 **5** *2 3/4* — **Rapid Flow**[125] 62 7-8-7 44 — AlexEdwards(7) 4 — 39
(J W Unett) *outpcd* — **100/1**

3-34 **6** *1* — **Yungaburra (IRE)**[75] 676 5-9-8 84 — (bt) PatDobbs 6 — 44
(J Balding) *prom tl wknd wl over 1f out* — **11/2**[3]

-200 **7** *2* — **Wicksy Creek**[11] 1617 4-8-8 48 ow1 — (p) MarkFlynn(5) 9 — 28
(G C Bravery) *w wnr tl wknd over 2f out* — **50/1**

63.01 secs (0.71) **Going Correction** +0.125s/f (Slow)
WFA 3 from 4yo+ 9lb — 7 Ran SP% **111.3**
Speed ratings (Par 101): **99,96,94,89,85 83,80**
toteswinger: 1&2 £1.02, 1&3 £3.10, 2&3 £9.60 CSF £2.76 TOTE £1.40: £1.40, £1.80; EX 2.80.Harry Up was claimed by A S Reid for £12,000.
Owner The Fishermen **Bred** J E Rose **Trained** Hambleton, N Yorks

FOCUS

Another uncompetitive event but one run at a fair pace (nearly a second slower than the opening maiden). The winner came down the centre in the straight but the third is the best guide to the level.

1936 BET ASIAN H'CAPS - BETDAQ HANDICAP — 1m 5f 194y(P)

3:40 (3:40) (Class 6) (0-65,65) 4-Y-O+ — £2,729 (£806; £403) Stalls Low

Form — RPR

03-2 **1** — **Kings Maiden (IRE)**[14] 1556 6-8-9 52 — DarrenMoffatt 10 — 65
(James Moffatt) *hld up towards rr: hdwy over 3f out: swtchd rt 2f out and over 1f out: rdn to ld cl home* — **13/2**[3]

23-1 **2** *1* — **Saloon (USA)**[19] 1463 5-9-3 60 — (p) GeorgeBaker 11 — 72
(Jane Chapple-Hyam) *hld up towards rr: smooth prog 5f out: led on bit wl over 1f out: rdn and hung lft ins fnl f: hdd cl home* — **11/2**[1]

21U **3** *5* — **Calculating (IRE)**[20] 1426 5-9-8 65 — NCallan 2 — 70
(M D I Usher) *a.p: chsd ldr over 5f out tl over 3f out: rdn wl over 1f out: wknd ins fnl f* — **6/1**[2]

6164 **4** *5* — **Thorny Mandate**[16] 1506 7-9-1 58 — LiamJones 9 — 56
(W M Brisbourne) *hld up in mid-div: hdwy over 5f out: wnt 2nd over 3f out: led over 2f out: rdn and hdd wl over 1f out: wknd ins fnl f* — **11/2**[1]

5266 **5** *1 1/4* — **Wester Lodge (IRE)**[35] 1153 7-8-9 57 — WilliamCarson(5) 6 — 53
(J M P Eustace) *hld up towards rr: pushed along over 3f out: hdwy over 2f out: rdn over 1f out: nvr nr ldrs* — **10/1**

2126 **6** *7* — **Bold Adventure**[12] 1609 5-9-8 65 — ChrisCatlin 4 — 51
(W J Musson) *in rr: sme prog over 1f out: n.d* — **6/1**[2]

052- **7** *3 1/4* — **Black Or Red (IRE)**[235] 6044 4-8-9 53 — (bt) GrahamGibbons 13 — 35
(I A Wood) *sn prom: rdn over 5f out: wknd 4f out* — **12/1**

4-30 **8** *7* — **Torrens (IRE)**[6] 1770 7-8-10 58 — (t) RichardEvans(5) 1 — 30
(P D Evans) *hld up towards rr: hdwy on outside over 4f out: rdn over 2f out: sn wknd* — **12/1**

/00- **9** *2 1/2* — **Stagecoach Emerald**[242] 5833 7-8-12 55 — MickyFenton 3 — 24
(R W Price) *hld up in tch: pushed along over 6f out: sn lost pl* — **66/1**

420 **10** *3 1/4* — **Zaffeu**[20] 1439 8-8-10 60 — DavidKenny(7) 12 — 24
(A G Juckes) *mid-div: lost pl over 7f out: sn in rr* — **16/1**

0-32 **11** *2 1/4* — **Pertemps Power**[49] 935 5-8-12 55 — StephenDonohoe 8 — 16
(B G Powell) *led 1f: w ldr: led over 6f out tl over 2f out: sn wknd* — **12/1**

1014 **12** *4* — **Almahaza (IRE)**[13] 1589 5-9-3 60 — NeilChalmers 5 — 15
(A J Chamberlain) *hld up in mid-div: wknd 4f out* — **20/1**

4604 **13** *4 1/2* — **Blue Hills**[20] 1442 8-8-8 58 — (b) MatthewDavies(7) 7 — 7
(P W Hiatt) *led after 1f tl over 6f out: wknd over 5f out* — **28/1**

3m 3.68s (-2.32) **Going Correction** +0.125s/f (Slow)
WFA 4 from 5yo+ 1lb — 13 Ran SP% **120.4**
Speed ratings (Par 101): **111,110,107,104,104 100,98,94,92,90 89,87,84**
toteswinger: 1&2 £12.20, 1&3 £25.80, 2&3 £4.60 CSF £41.71 CT £230.89 TOTE £9.30: £2.10, £2.60, £3.50; EX 61.70.
Owner Mrs S C Huntley **Bred** Sweetmans Stud **Trained** Cartmel, Cumbria

FOCUS

A modest handicap in which the pace was decent and the form looks fair. The winner came down the centre in the straight and the first two pulled clear in the closing stages.

Pertemps Power Official explanation: jockey said gelding pulled up stressed.

Almahaza(IRE) Official explanation: jockey said gelding never travelled

1937 BETDAQ.CO.UK FILLIES' H'CAP — 1m 141y(P)

4:10 (4:10) (Class 5) (0-70,70) 3-Y-O

£3,738 (£1,119; £559; £280; £139; £70) Stalls Low

Form — RPR

00-3 **1** — **Inis Boffin**[17] 1491 3-8-13 65 — CatherineGannon 9 — 74+
(S Kirk) *hld up in rr: rdn and swtchd rt over 2f out: c wd st: gd hdwy over 1f out: r.o to ld towards fin* — **6/1**[3]

0-20 **2** *hd* — **Implication**[21] 1406 3-9-2 68 — StephenDonohoe 5 — 77
(E A L Dunlop) *s.i.s: hld up towards rr: hdwy over 3f out: rdn to ld over 1f out: sn hung rt: edgd lft ins fnl f: hdd towards fin* — **10/3**[1]

03-0 **3** *3* — **Punch Drunk**[18] 1470 3-9-0 66 — TPQueally 2 — 71+
(J G Given) *led early: hld up in tch: nt clr run on ins over 1f out: rdn and kpt on ins fnl f* — **9/1**

0-30 **4** *2 1/2* — **Order Order**[23] 1361 3-8-10 62 — FrancisNorton 8 — 58
(H J L Dunlop) *a.p: rdn and hung lft over 1f out: wknd ins fnl f* — **16/1**

1 **5** *1/2* — **Burza**[73] 716 3-9-2 68 — GeorgeBaker 1 — 63
(J Mackie) *hld up in mid-div: pushed along over 3f out: hdwy over 2f out: rdn over 1f out: wknd ins fnl f* — **9/1**

500- **6** *3 1/4* — **Black Nun**[216] 6555 3-8-10 62 — GrahamGibbons 3 — 50
(S Wynne) *hld up in mid-div: pushed along and lost pl whn nt clr run 3f out: c v wd st: kpt on fnl f: n.d* — **33/1**

033- **7** *2* — **Sussex Dancer (IRE)**[143] 7726 3-9-4 70 — SamHitchcott 6 — 53
(J A Osborne) *sn led: hdd over 4f out: led over 2f out: sn rdn: hdd over 1f out: sn wknd* — **12/1**

1012 **8** *1* — **Foreign Investment (IRE)**[19] 1452 3-8-10 67 — RichardEvans(5) 12 — 48
(P D Evans) *stdd s: nvr nr ldrs* — **6/1**[3]

531- **9** *nk* — **Inconspicuous Miss (USA)**[171] 7402 3-8-9 68 — MatthewDavies(7) 10 — 48
(George Baker) *hld up in mid-div: hdwy 4f out: ev ch over 2f out: rdn and wknd wl over 1f out* — **18/1**

452- **10** *nse* — **Leelu**[145] 7708 3-9-1 67 — NCallan 4 — 47
(D W P Arbuthnot) *hld up in tch: rdn and wknd wl over 1f out* — **5/1**[2]

600- **11** *13* — **Sley (FR)**[164] 7467 3-8-5 62 — Louis-PhilippeBeuzelin(5) 11 — 12
(B J Meehan) *chsd ldr: led over 4f out tl over 2f out: sn wknd* — **40/1**

26-3 **12** *4 1/2* — **Chadwell Spring (IRE)**[16] 1531 3-9-2 68 — ChrisCatlin 13 — 8
(Miss J Feilden) *a in rr* — **16/1**

1m 51.49s (0.99) **Going Correction** +0.125s/f (Slow) — 12 Ran SP% **118.4**
Speed ratings (Par 96): **100,99,97,94,94 91,89,88,88,88 77,73**
toteswinger: 1&2 £5.10, 1&3 £13.20, 2&3 £7.50 CSF £26.18 CT £185.29 TOTE £8.50: £2.30, £2.00, £2.50; EX 27.70.
Owner M G White **Bred** C C And Mrs D J Buckley **Trained** Upper Lambourn, Berks

FOCUS

An ordinary handicap in which two progressive sorts pulled clear in the closing stages. The gallop was fair and the winner raced centre to far side in the straight.

1938 HOTEL & CONFERENCING AT WOLVERHAMPTON RACECOURSE AMATEUR RIDERS' H'CAP — 1m 4f 50y(P)

4:40 (4:40) (Class 6) (0-55,55) 4-Y-O+ — £2,307 (£709; £354) Stalls Low

Form — RPR

-610 **1** — **Barbirolli**[19] 1463 7-10-13 50 — MrBenBrisbourne(3) 11 — 60
(W M Brisbourne) *hld up and bhd: smooth prog over 3f out: wnt 2nd over 1f out: led ins fnl f: r.o wl* — **6/1**

5-06 **2** *3 1/4* — **Wizard Looking**[10] 1654 8-11-4 52 — MrSWalker 12 — 57
(P T Midgley) *hld up: stdy hdwy over 6f out: led over 2f out: sn rdn: clr over 1f out: hdd and no ex ins fnl f* — **3/1**[1]

1650 **3** *2* — **Desert Hawk**[46] 969 8-10-11 50 — MrHarryChalloner(5) 6 — 52
(W M Brisbourne) *hld up in mid-div: hdwy over 2f out: rdn over 1f out: kpt on to take 3rd ins fnl f* — **12/1**

150- **4** *3/4* — **Front Rank (IRE)**[115] 6727 9-10-12 51 — MissECSayer(5) 7 — 52+
(Mrs Dianne Sayer) *hld up towards rr: hdwy over 1f out: nvr nr to chal* — **10/1**

-500 **5** *hd* — **Sixth Zak**[35] 1154 4-11-4 52 — (b[1]) MissSBrotherton 4 — 52
(M W Easterby) *hld up in tch: lost pl over 3f out: nt clr run on ins over 2f out: kpt on ins fnl f* — **9/2**[2]

030 **6** *1/2* — **Kirstys Lad**[17] 1495 7-11-2 55 — MissMMullineaux(5) 8 — 55
(M Mullineaux) *hld up in rr: c wd st: nvr nrr* — **20/1**

50/4 **7** *1/2* — **Tilly Shilling (IRE)**[12] 704 5-10-9 50 — MrTJCannon(7) 2 — 49
(Norma Twomey) *prom: pushed along over 2f out: wknd wl over 1f out* — **14/1**

/3-0 **8** *nk* — **Gallantian (IRE)**[16] 1533 7-11-4 52 — (t) DonalDevereux 9 — 50
(David Anthony O'Brien, Ire) *led: rdn and hdd over 2f out: wknd over 1f out* — **5/1**[3]

5600 **9** *4* — **Hurricane Coast**[16] 1528 10-10-11 52 — MissAHeath(7) 5 — 44
(D Flood) *a in rr* — **33/1**

/6-0 **10** *2 1/2* — **Red River Rebel**[20] 1442 11-10-11 52 — MrPHardy(7) 3 — 40
(J R Norton) *chsd ldr to 4f out: wknd over 2f out* — **25/1**

/20- **11** *43* — **Rightful Ruler**[197] 5385 7-10-12 53 — MrAJParker(7) 1 — —
(N Wilson) *bhd fnl 7f: t.o* — **12/1**

-200 **12** *9* — **Fortunella**[14] 1568 4-11-5 53 — (v) MissEJJones 10 — —
(Miss Gay Kelleway) *prom tl lost pl wl over 3f out: t.o* — **12/1**

2m 46.85s (5.75) **Going Correction** +0.125s/f (Slow) — 12 Ran SP% **124.5**
Speed ratings (Par 101): **85,82,81,81,80 80,80,80,77,75 47,41**
toteswinger: 1&2 £6.70, 1&3 £6.70, 2&3 £9.40 CSF £25.02 CT £220.38 TOTE £7.10: £2.40, £1.60, £3.40; EX 20.50 Place 6: £7.05, Place 5: £5.74.
Owner Mark Brisbourne **Bred** Gainsborough Stud Management Ltd **Trained** Great Ness, Shropshire
■ Stewards' Enquiry : Donal Devereux one-day ban: failed to keep straight from stalls (May 25)

FOCUS

A low-grade handicap run at a decent gallop and the winner looks the best guide to the form. The winner raced centre to far side in the straight.

T/Plt: £10.40 to a £1 stake. Pool: £53,292.67. 3,736.78 winning tickets. T/Qpdt: £5.70 to a £1 stake. Pool: £3,292.35. 423.00 winning tickets. KH

1630 YARMOUTH (L-H)

Monday, May 11

OFFICIAL GOING: Good to firm (8.4)

Wind: Strong, behind Weather: Bright, very breezy

1939 WEATHERBYS BLOODSTOCK INSURANCE MAIDEN AUCTION STKS — 5f 43y

2:30 (2:34) (Class 5) 2-Y-O — £3,784 (£1,132; £566; £283; £141) Stalls High

Form — RPR

2 **1** — **Kaspirit (IRE)**[11] 1616 2-8-8 0 — DarryllHolland 5 — 79+
(M Wigham) *wnt lft s: mde all: rdn over 1f out: clr fnl f: comf* — **6/4**[1]

2 *2 1/4* — **Danzoe (IRE)** 2-8-9 0 — JimmyQuinn 1 — 72
(D Donovan) *in tch: effrt on outer 2f out: chsd wnr 1f out: kpt on same pce and no imp fnl f* — **16/1**

3 *3/4* — **Shibhan** 2-8-2 0 — AhmedAjtebi(3) 2 — 65
(C E Brittain) *chsd ldrs: wnt 2nd 1/2-way tl 1f out: kpt on same pce fnl f* — **11/1**

4 **4** *nk* — **Daniella De Bruijn (IRE)**[5] 1782 2-8-9 0 — DaneO'Neill 9 — 68
(A B Haynes) *outpcd in rr: pushed along 3f out: hdwy and swtchd lft ins fnl f: styd on wl: nt rch ldrs* — **6/1**[3]

5 1 **Fasilight** 2-8-7 0 .... JohnEgan 7 63
(M Botti) *in tch in midfield: effrt 2f out: rdn and hung rt over 1f out: one pce fnl f* **12/1**

5 6 2 3/4 **Mahiki**[8] 1700 2-8-8 0 .... RyanMoore 6 55+
(S A Callaghan) *in tch: rdn over 2f out: drvn and no hdwy over 1f out: btn whn n.m.r and eased ins fnl f* **3/1**[2]

0 7 1/2 **Southwark Newshawk**[11] 1630 2-8-1 0 .... DavidProbert[(3)] 3 48
(Mrs C A Dunnett) *chsd wnr tl 1/2-way: rdn 2f out: wknd over 1f out: btn and edgd lft ins fnl f* **100/1**

8 30 **Minnie Rocket** 2-8-4 0 .... NickyMackay 8 —
(R C Guest) *sonn outpcd: t.o fr 1/2-way* **66/1**

5 9 dist **Last Orders (IRE)**[11] 1616 2-9-1 0 .... AlanMunro 4 —
(M G Quinlan) *hmpd s: bhd: lost tch after 2f: sn eased and t.o* **8/1**

62.18 secs (-0.02) **Going Correction** -0.225s/f (Firm) **9** Ran SP% **114.8**
Speed ratings (Par 93): **91,87,86,85,84 79,78,30,—**
toteswinger: 1&2 £8.00, 1&3 £5.70, 2&3 £17.50 CSF £29.05 TOTE £2.30: £1.10, £4.70, £3.30; EX 28.30 Trifecta £217.20 Pool: £525.58 - 1.79 winning units..
Owner J M Cullinan **Bred** Riccioni Giuseppe **Trained** Newmarket, Suffolk

FOCUS
An average maiden, run at a solid pace.

NOTEBOOK
Kaspirit(IRE) finished second on debut to a subsequent winner 11 days earlier and went one better by readily making all. She broke a lot better this time and her rider's decision to track over to the stands' side proved decisive. Well on top at the finish, her life will be tougher from now on but her confidence will be high after this. Her trainer will reportedly now look for a Listed race abroad for her. (tchd 7-4)
Danzoe(IRE) has plenty of speed in his pedigree and is out of a dam who was a multiple winner from 5f-1m. He knew his job as he broke well and kept to his task when put under pressure. There should be more to come from him. (tchd 20-1)
Shibhan, whose breeding suggests speed and stamina, was a market drifter ahead of her racecourse debut. She was another well away and showed enough to suggest she will improve now she has this initial experience behind her. (op 7-1 tchd 14-1)
Daniella De Bruijn(IRE)w as slow to break on her debut five days earlier and again got behind. She was picking up well towards the final furlong when short of room and having to be switched wide with her effort. That cost her vital momentum and she is better than the bare form, but really looks in need of a stiffer test. Official explanation: jockey said filly was denied a clear run (op 11-1 tchd 12-1 and 4-1)
Fasilight Official explanation: trainer said filly was unsuited by the good to firm ground
Mahiki was down in grade after fading on her debut at Newmarket eight days previously. She ran respectably, but again failed to see it out and probably needs more time. (tchd 5-2 and 10-3)
Last Orders(IRE) finished last behind the winner on debut at Folkestone yet was the subject of a gamble. He got a bump at the start, but was never looking happy and supporters knew their fate from halfway. Something presumably went amiss (op 20-1 tchd 7-1)

1940 GREAT YARMOUTH GREYHOUND HOMEFINDERS CLASSIFIED STKS 7f 3y
3:00 (3:08) (Class 6) 3-Y-0+ **£2,590** (£770; £385; £192) **Stalls** High

Form RPR

0-00 1 **Ocean Countess (IRE)**[27] 1269 3-8-10 54 .... JerryO'Dwyer 10 55+
(Miss J Feilden) *s.i.s: bhd and sn rdn along: hdwy 4f out: rdn to ld 1f out: drvn and forged ahd fnl f: eased towards fin* **4/1**[2]

/00- 2 1 1/4 **Chinese Profit**[192] 7111 4-9-8 55 .... PatCosgrave 11 56
(G C Bravery) *chsd ldrs: hdwy to ld ent fnl 2f: sn rdn: hdd 1f out: no ex ins fnl f* **8/1**

60-0 3 3/4 **Bussell Along (IRE)**[11] 1620 3-8-10 55 .... SaleemGolam 16 50
(M L W Bell) *bhd: rdn over 3f out: hdwy u.p over 1f out: styd on fnl f to go 3rd nr fin* **20/1**

044 4 nk **Kings On The Roof**[19] 1465 3-8-10 52 .... AlanMunro 2 49
(G C Bravery) *pressed ldr: ev ch fr 2f out: tl one pce ins fnl f: lost 3rd nr fin* **11/2**[3]

-060 5 2 **Buail Isteach (IRE)**[54] 874 4-9-8 47 .... EdwardCreighton 14 47
(E J Creighton) *in tch in midfield: effrt u.p wl over 1f out: no imp fnl f* **16/1**

-500 6 3/4 **Wicklewood**[19] 1452 3-8-10 49 .... JohnEgan 8 41
(Mrs C A Dunnett) *in tch in midfield: lost pl 3f out: rallied u.p over 1f out: rdr dropped reins jst ins fnl f: styd on* **20/1**

0-23 7 2 **Gun For Sale (USA)**[20] 1420 4-9-8 51 .... TravisBlock 7 40
(P J Makin) *in tch: lost pl and hung lft fr 3f out: no ch w ldrs after* **7/2**[1]

000- 8 nse **Duchess Of Doom (IRE)**[314] 3584 3-8-10 52 .... RyanMoore 1 36
(S A Callaghan) *hld up in midfield: rdn jst over 2f out: drvn and no hdwy over 1f out* **7/2**[1]

210- 9 2 1/4 **Station Place**[168] 7433 4-9-1 55 .... PNolan[(7)] 9 37
(A B Haynes) *led: hung lft fr 4f out: hdd ent fnl 2f: sn wknd: eased ins fnl f* **16/1**

0-00 10 1 1/2 **Yughanni**[22] 1379 3-8-10 54 .... J-PGuillambert 5 33
(C E Brittain) *stdd s: a bhd: nvr a factor* **25/1**

00-0 11 1/2 **Alyseve**[9] 1662 4-9-3 30 ....(p) AndreaAtzeni[(5)] 6 28
(Mrs C A Dunnett) *chsd ldrs tl 1/2-way: sn wknd* **66/1**

040- 12 9 **Myttons Maid**[191] 7141 3-8-3 46 ....(p) NatashaEaton[(7)] 4 —
(A Bailey) *sn rdn along: wl bhd fr 1/2-way* **20/1**

050- 13 5 **Sunley Smiles**[415] 976 4-9-8 52 .... JimmyQuinn 3 —
(P Howling) *stdd s: a bhd* **20/1**

1m 26.74s (0.14) **Going Correction** -0.225s/f (Firm)
WFA 3 from 4yo+ 12lb **13** Ran SP% **127.1**
Speed ratings (Par 101): **90,88,87,87,85 84,81,81,79,77 77,66,61**
toteswinger: 1&2 £18.80, 1&3 £23.60, 2&3 £36.30 CSF £34.49 TOTE £6.20: £2.40, £4.70, £5.10; EX 77.40 Trifecta £124.40 Part won. Pool: £168.15 - 0.20 winning units..
Owner Ocean Trailers Ltd **Bred** Don Commins **Trained** Exning, Suffolk

FOCUS
A typically weak classified event and not form to be positive about.
Ocean Countess(IRE) Official explanation: trainer said, regarding apparent improvement in form, that the filly benefited from a drop in class and trip.
Station Place Official explanation: jockey said filly hung badly left

1941 WEATHERBYS BETTRENDS.CO.UK MAIDEN STKS 1m 3y
3:30 (3:37) (Class 5) 3-Y-0+ **£3,784** (£1,132; £566; £283; £141) **Stalls** High

Form RPR

4-2 1 **Ithbaat (USA)**[11] 1632 3-9-0 0 .... RHills 12 76+
(J H M Gosden) *chsd ldrs: led on bit jst over 2f out: shkn up wl over 1f out: rdn ent fnl f: kpt on* **4/9**[1]

2 2 **Luc Jordan** 3-9-0 0 .... DaneO'Neill 9 68+
(L M Cumani) *racd off the pce in midfield: hdwy over 3f out: pressed ldrs and rdn 2f out: kpt on same pce fnl f: wnt 2nd last stride* **22/1**

0- 3 shd **Papyrian**[192] 7104 3-9-0 0 .... AlanMunro 3 68+
(W Jarvis) *chsd ldrs: rdn 4f out: swtchd lft and hdwy over 3f out: ev ch u.p wl over 1f out: one pce fnl f: lost 2nd last stride* **5/1**[2]

0 4 1 1/4 **Prince Of Johanne (IRE)**[10] 1638 3-9-0 0 .... RyanMoore 10 65+
(J Noseda) *bhd: swtchd rt 3f out: rdn and hdwy over 2f out: kpt on steadily fnl f: nvr trbld ldrs* **9/1**[3]

5 2 1/2 **Sirjosh** 3-9-0 0 .... JimmyQuinn 2 60
(D Donovan) *s.i.s: bhd: hdwy 3f out: kpt on same pce fnl f: nvr trbld ldrs* **100/1**

6 4 1/2 **Black Stocking** 4-9-5 0 .... GilmarPereira[(3)] 8 47
(M Wigham) *s.i.s: bhd: rdn and sme hdwy 3f out: nvr trbld ldrs* **100/1**

P-0 7 3 1/4 **Wild By Nature**[75] 670 4-9-3 0 .... MarkCoumbe[(5)] 1 40
(P Leech) *led tl jst over 2f out: wknd rapidly wl over 1f out* **200/1**

04 8 nk **Mac Wolf**[11] 1622 3-8-9 0 .... NicolPolli[(5)] 11 41
(M G Quinlan) *a wl bhd* **33/1**

9 11 **Mulazem (USA)** 3-9-0 0 .... TPO'Shea 5 16
(W J Haggas) *s.i.s: rn green and a bhd* **12/1**

00 10 1 **Would I Lie To You**[100] 356 5-9-6 0 .... DannyBrock[(7)] 7 16
(J R Jenkins) *chsd ldr tl over 4f out: wknd rapidly over 3f out* **250/1**

0-0 11 dist **Soldier Soldier**[20] 1422 3-9-0 0 .... NickyMackay 4 —
(J R Jenkins) *chsd ldrs: wnt 2nd over 4f out tl over 3f out: wknd rapidly: t.o* **200/1**

1m 38.48s (-2.12) **Going Correction** -0.225s/f (Firm)
WFA 3 from 4yo+ 13lb **11** Ran SP% **114.3**
Speed ratings (Par 103): **101,99,98,97,95 90,87,87,76,75 —**
toteswinger: 1&2 £4.50, 1&3 £1.90, 2&3 £7.00 CSF £17.47 TOTE £1.40: £1.02, £4.70, £2.00; EX 8.20 Trifecta £35.30 Pool: £649.31 - 13.61 winning units..
Owner Hamdan Al Maktoum **Bred** Catherine J Parke & Oakbrook Farm **Trained** Newmarket, Suffolk

FOCUS
This could work out to be a fair maiden and the winner could prove better than the bare form.
Sirjosh Official explanation: jockey said gelding lost its action
Soldier Soldier Official explanation: jockey said colt stopped very quickly

1942 YARMOUTH STADIUM H'CAP 1m 3y
4:00 (4:01) (Class 3) (0-95,95) 4-Y-0 **£7,477** (£2,239; £1,119; £560; £279) **Stalls** High

Form RPR

/1-0 1 **Cadre (IRE)**[37] 1116 4-8-9 86 .... RobertHavlin 1 103+
(J H M Gosden) *w ldrs: rdn to ld over 1f out: edgd rt but drew clr ins fnl f: easily* **8/1**

6201 2 3 1/4 **Tartan Gigha (IRE)**[7] 1722 4-8-10 87 6ex .... JoeFanning 6 94
(M Johnston) *hld up in tch: effrt 2f out: ev ch over 1f out: nt pce of wnr fnl f* **1/1**[1]

4210 3 1 1/4 **Saltagioo (ITY)**[30] 1209 5-8-10 87 .... JohnEgan 2 91
(M Botti) *t.k.h: led untl hdd and rdn 2f out: one pce fnl f* **4/1**[3]

110- 4 3/4 **Stalking Shadow (USA)**[57] 4-9-1 95 ....(t) AhmedAjtebi[(3)] 3 97
(Saeed Bin Suroor) *t.k.h: chsd ldr tl led 2f out: sn rdn: hdd over 1f out: wknd ins fnl f* **3/1**[2]

1160 5 14 **Gallantry**[23] 1365 7-8-10 87 .... TolleyDean 5 73
(P Howling) *stdd s: hld up in last pl: rdn over 2f out wknd wl over 1f out: eased ins fnl f* **16/1**

1m 37.35s (-3.25) **Going Correction** -0.225s/f (Firm) **5** Ran SP% **112.0**
Speed ratings (Par 107): **107,103,102,101,87**
toteswinger: 1&2 £7.60 CSF £17.08 TOTE £7.50: £2.60, £1.30; EX 22.40.
Owner H R H Princess Haya Of Jordan **Bred** Mrs Eithne Hamilton **Trained** Newmarket, Suffolk

FOCUS
A good-quality little handicap, run at an average pace. The form appears sound but not that strong a race for the grade.

NOTEBOOK
Cadre(IRE) ◆ was an expensive failure on his comeback at Lingfield last month, but had returned slightly lame that day and showed his true colours here with a taking success. He was tackling the extra furlong for the first time and travelled sweetly before being asked to seal the race. He drifted right when under pressure inside the final furlong, but was always in control and is clearly talented. This was just his fourth outing to date, so providing he remains sound there could be a deal of further improvement to come. (op 9-2)
Tartan Gigha(IRE) was penalised for his Beverley success a week earlier and unsurprisingly proved very popular. He came through with every chance over this longer trip, but simply found the winner too classy. (op 6-5)
Saltagioo(ITY) was having his first outing away from the all-weather since switching from Italy. He had the run of the race and sets the level, but probably found the ground lively enough. (op 11-2)
Stalking Shadow(USA) was returning to a British racecourse after winning his last two races in Dubai earlier this year. Back up in trip, he proved too free through the early parts and paid at the business end. (op 7-2)

1943 REBECCA ALSLE HILLS MEMORIAL H'CAP 6f 3y
4:30 (4:33) (Class 4) (0-80,80) 4-Y-0+ **£5,180** (£1,541; £770; £384) **Stalls** High

Form RPR

00-5 1 **Earlsmedic**[25] 1309 4-9-4 80 ....(v) SaleemGolam 6 90
(S C Williams) *mde virtually: drvn over 1f out: styd on wl fnl f* **2/1**[1]

0-00 2 1 **Mut'Ab (USA)**[16] 1527 4-8-12 77 ....(b) AhmedAjtebi[(3)] 1 84
(C E Brittain) *w wnr: ev ch and rdn over 1f out: edgd rt 1f out: one pce fnl f* **16/1**

1012 3 1 1/4 **Street Power (USA)**[68] 757 4-8-12 74 .... RyanMoore 7 77
(J R Gask) *stdd s: t.k.h: hld up in tch: hdwy 2f out: drvn and hung lft 1f out: one pce fnl f* **9/4**[2]

3632 4 3/4 **The Tatling (IRE)**[4] 1806 12-8-12 79 .... JackDean[(5)] 3 80
(J M Bradley) *stdd s: hld up towards rr: hdwy over 2f out: sn rdn: swtchd lft 1f out: styd on same pce fnl f* **9/2**[3]

2256 5 3/4 **Dvinsky (USA)**[12] 1607 8-8-8 70 ....(b) JimmyQuinn 4 68+
(P Howling) *chsd ldrs: rdn 2f out: keeping on same pce whn squeezed 1f out: no ch after* **15/2**

2116 6 5 **Imprimis Tagula (IRE)**[9] 1663 5-8-7 76 ....(v) LeeNewnes[(7)] 8 58
(A Bailey) *in tch: rdn over 2f out: wknd over 1f out* **7/1**

06-0 7 9 **Namir (IRE)**[6] 1776 7-9-0 76 ....(vt) TedDurcan 2 29
(D Shaw) *stdd s: plld hrd early: hld up in rr: rdn and no hdwy jst over 2f out: wl btn and eased fnl f* **33/1**

1m 11.91s (-2.49) **Going Correction** -0.225s/f (Firm) **7** Ran SP% **115.4**
Speed ratings (Par 105): **107,105,104,103,102 95,83**
toteswinger: 1&2 £8.20, 1&3 £2.10, 2&3 £4.50 CSF £34.46 CT £77.79 TOTE £3.10: £2.40, £4.40; EX 33.70 Trifecta £273.10 Pool: £494.63 - 1.34 winning units..
Owner Mad Man Plus One **Bred** W N Greig **Trained** Newmarket, Suffolk
■ Stewards' Enquiry : Ahmed Ajtebi two-day ban: careless riding (May 25-26)

FOCUS
A tight sprint handicap, run at a fair pace and the form looks straightforward, if not the most solid.
Street Power(USA) Official explanation: trainer said gelding was unsuited by the track

Namir(IRE) Official explanation: jockey said gelding never travelled

1944 FIRSTBET.COM 0800 230 0800 £50 MATCHED BET H'CAP 1m 3f 101y
5:00 (5:00) (Class 3) (0-90,86) 4-Y-O+ **£7,477** (£2,239; £1,119; £560) **Stalls** Low

Form RPR
311- **1** **Falcativ**[196] 7025 4-9-4 **86** ... DaneO'Neill 3 101+
(L M Cumani) *trckd ldng pair: plld out and hdwy over 2f out: led over 1f out: edgd lft but pushed clr fnl f: comf* **8/13**[1]
0100 **2** *1 3/4* **Sgt Schultz (IRE)**[14] 1571 6-8-8 **76** ... LPKeniry 1 79
(J S Moore) *led for 2f: chsd ldr after tl 2f out: sn drvn: chsd wnr ins fnl f: no imp* **4/1**[2]
2416 **3** *2* **Sri Kuantan (IRE)**[2] 1878 5-8-5 **78** ow1 ... (t) MarkCoumbe(5) 2 78
(R C Guest) *chsd ldr tl led after 2f out: rdn over 2f out: hdd over 1f out: one pce fnl f* **4/1**[2]
00 **4** *2* **Valmari (IRE)**[22] 1383 6-8-11 **86** ... DebraEngland(7) 4 83
(C E Brittain) *stdd and dropped in bhd s: t.k.h: hld up in last pl: rdn and struggling over 3f out: kpt on fnl f* **22/1**[3]

2m 27.95s (-0.75) **Going Correction** -0.175s/f (Firm) 4 Ran SP% 106.3
Speed ratings (Par 107): **95,93,92,90**
CSF £3.24 TOTE £1.60; EX 3.00.
Owner Scuderia Rencati Srl **Bred** Az Agr Francesca **Trained** Newmarket, Suffolk

FOCUS
This was run at a fair pace and the progressive winner is value for further. The third looks the best guide to the form.

NOTEBOOK
Falcativ ◆ made light of a 196-day break to land the hat-trick. 7lb higher, it was his first success on turf and he could have been called the winner shortly after making his move around 3f out. The ground looked to be as fast as he wants it and he was not doing a lot when in front, so rates value for better than the bare margin. The Duke Of Edinburgh Stakes at Royal Ascot next month could well be next. (op 8-11 tchd 4-7)
Sgt Schultz(IRE), whose yard took this last season, bounced back from a poor run at Windsor a fortnight previously, but was firmly put in his place by the winner. He is very well handicapped on turf due to all of his previous wins coming on the all-weather and, on this showing, can be found a race in this sphere. (op 10-3)
Sri Kuantan(IRE), down in trip, eventually made his way to the front and again had very much the run of things. He lost a bandage inside the final furlong, but was done with at that stage. (op 9-2)
Valmari(IRE), 3lb lower, was going without the blinkers for this drop back in trip and looked very one-paced. (op 14-1)

1945 NORFOLK NELSON MUSEUM H'CAP 1m 2f 21y
5:30 (5:30) (Class 5) (0-70,70) 4-Y-O+ **£3,238** (£963; £481; £240) **Stalls** Low

Form RPR
224- **1** **Locum**[154] 7604 4-8-11 **63** ... RyanMoore 3 72
(M H Tompkins) *hld up in last trio: swtchd rt and effrt over 2f out: drvn to ld ins fnl f: r.o wl* **3/1**[1]
23-0 **2** *1 1/2* **Dancing Jest (IRE)**[11] 1633 5-8-8 **60** ... NickyMackay 5 66
(Rae Guest) *led: rdn jst over 2f out: hdd and no ex ins fnl f* **25/1**
0503 **3** *1* **General Tufto**[3] 1845 4-8-3 **62** ... (b) RichardRowe(7) 2 66
(C Smith) *stdd s: hld up in rr: hdwy on outer over 3f out: drvn 2f out: edgd lft and chsd ldng pair ins fnl f: kpt on* **7/1**
623- **4** *1 1/2* **Streets Apart (USA)**[207] 6762 4-9-0 **66** ... TedDurcan 7 67
(W R Swinburn) *chsd ldr: rdn over 3f out: drvn and unable qck wl over 1f out: plugged on same pce fnl f* **7/2**[3]
3440 **5** *3/4* **Iceman George**[19] 1463 5-8-1 **56** oh4 ... (p) KellyHarrison(3) 9 56
(D Morris) *chsd ldrs on outer: rdn 3f out: wknd u.p ent fnl f* **16/1**
023- **6** *hd* **Agente Romano (USA)**[222] 6379 4-9-4 **70** ... DaneO'Neill 8 69
(G A Butler) *hld up in last trio: hdwy on outer over 3f out: chsd ldrs and rdn wl over 1f out: wknd fnl f* **5/1**
0-01 **7** *1 1/4* **Director's Chair**[43] 1014 4-8-13 **65** ... JerryO'Dwyer 4 62+
(Miss J Feilden) *hld up in tch: rdn and unable qck 2f out: no imp after* **10/3**[2]
4000 **8** *2 1/4* **Dinner Date**[28] 1261 7-8-8 **60** ... LPKeniry 6 52
(T Keddy) *hld up in tch: effrt and rdn jst over 2f out: no prog and wl hld fnl f* **20/1**

2m 7.85s (-2.65) **Going Correction** -0.175s/f (Firm) 8 Ran SP% 114.0
Speed ratings (Par 103): **103,101,101,99,99 99,98,96**
toteswinger: 1&2 £8.10, 1&3 £4.40, 2&3 £13.00 CSF £73.74 CT £484.22 TOTE £3.60: £1.50, £4.70, £2.00; EX 51.00 Trifecta £343.20 Part won. Pool: £463.91 - 0.65 winning units. Place 6: £31.04, Place 5: £15.52..
Owner Ray Smith and Partners **Bred** Cheveley Park Stud Ltd **Trained** Newmarket, Suffolk

FOCUS
An ordinary handicap.
T/Plt: £83.40 to a £1 stake. Pool: £44,149.39. 386.06 winning tickets. T/Qpdt: £5.20 to a £1 stake. Pool: £3,010.30. 421.70 winning tickets. SP

1946 - 1948a (Foreign Racing) - See Raceform Interactive

[1719]BEVERLEY (R-H)
Tuesday, May 12

OFFICIAL GOING: Good to firm (firm in places;10.4)
Wind: Fresh behind Weather: Sunny periods, breezy

1949 TURFTV (S) STKS 5f
2:00 (2:00) (Class 6) 3-Y-O **£2,428** (£722; £361; £180) **Stalls** High

Form RPR
-460 **1** **Noodles Blue Boy**[8] 1736 3-8-11 70 ... TonyHamilton 14 71
(Ollie Pears) *trckd ldrs: swtchd lft and hdwy 2f out: sn cl up: rdn to ld ent fnl f and styd on wl* **15/8**[1]
3020 **2** *2 1/4* **Simple Rhythm**[29] 1247 3-8-8 58 ow2 ... PaulMulrennan 9 59
(J G Given) *led: rdn jnd and rdn along wl over 1f out: drvn and hdd ent fnl f: one pce* **14/1**
3223 **3** *4* **Billy Beetroot (USA)**[12] 1617 3-8-6 62 ... (t) WilliamCarson(5) 11 48
(S C Williams) *in tch: hdwy on inner 2f out: sn rdn and kpt on ins fnl f: nt rch ldng pair* **3/1**[2]
4220 **4** *6* **Fashion Icon (USA)**[29] 1247 3-8-6 59 ... (b[1]) FrancisNorton 6 21
(T D Barron) *chsd ldrs: rdn 2f out: sn drvn and wknd over 1f out* **5/1**[3]
5060 **5** *1/2* **Chimbonda**[9] 1691 3-8-11 50 ... (p) RobertWinston 7 25
(S Parr) *towards rr: pushed along after 2f: sme hdwy u.p appr last: nvr a factor* **20/1**
0-55 **6** *2 1/4* **Time Loup**[40] 1084 3-8-6 44 ... (bt[1]) MartinLane(5) 10 17
(S R Bowring) *;prom: rdn along over 2f out: sn drvn and grad wknd* **40/1**
-000 **7** *1* **Waltzing Buddy**[21] 1437 3-8-0 55 ow1 ... PaulPickard(7) 5 9
(P T Midgley) *a towards rr* **40/1**
3452 **8** *1 1/2* **You Avin A Laugh**[17] 1529 3-8-6 60 ... PatrickDonaghy(5) 12 8
(C A Dwyer) *a towards rr* **6/1**
06-0 **9** *4 1/2* **Chipolini (IRE)**[29] 1247 3-8-11 56 ... DNolan 1 —
(D Carroll) *chsd ldrs: rdn along 1/2-way: sn drvn and wknd* **100/1**
00-0 **10** *4* **Madame Jourdain (IRE)**[19] 1469 3-7-13 57 ... CharlotteKerton(7) 15 —
(N Wilson) *dwlt: a in rr* **16/1**
00-0 **11** *2* **Marygate (IRE)**[20] 1455 3-8-0 48 ow1 ... JohnCavanagh(7) 4 —
(M Brittain) *rrd and veered bdly rt s: a bhd* **66/1**

60.56 secs (-2.94) **Going Correction** -0.425s/f (Firm) 11 Ran SP% 115.4
Speed ratings (Par 97): **106,102,96,86,85 82,80,78,70,64 61**
toteswinger: 1&2 £7.20, 1&3 £2.40, 2&3 £7.40 CSF £28.91 TOTE £3.00: £1.20, £2.60, £1.50; EX 36.50.There was no bid for the winner.
Owner Ian Bishop **Bred** Fifehead Farms M C Denning **Trained** Norton, N Yorks

FOCUS
The ground was fast and there was a strong tail wind in the straight, which helps explain why the time was so quick in this uncompetitive seller. The form is rated around the first two to this year's marks.
You Avin A Laugh Official explanation: jockey said gelding was unsuited by the good to firm (firm in places) ground
Marygate(IRE) Official explanation: jockey said filly stumbled on leaving stalls

1950 JOCKEYS LOFT FOR GREAT FOOD MAIDEN STKS 7f 100y
2:30 (2:35) (Class 5) 3-Y-O **£2,590** (£770; £385; £192) **Stalls** High

Form RPR
24-3 **1** **Dr Jameson (IRE)**[19] 1474 3-9-3 75 ... PaulHanagan 4 76
(R A Fahey) *mde all: pushed along 2f out: rdn and edgd lft over 1f out: drvn and hung bdly lft ins fnl f: kpt on* **4/11**[1]
65 **2** *nk* **Steel Trade**[10] 1683 3-8-10 0 ... JohnCavanagh(7) 7 75+
(M Brittain) *dwlt: swtchd outside and hdwy to chse ldrs after 2f: cl up 2f out: sn rdn and ev ch whn hmpd ins fnl f: drvn and kpt on towards fin* **9/1**[2]
04 **3** *8* **Aldaado (IRE)**[8] 1739 3-9-3 0 ... PhillipMakin 6 55
(M Dods) *trckd ldrs on inner: hdwy 2f out: sn rdn: edgd lft and kpt on same pce ent fnl f* **16/1**
6 **4** *1 1/2* **Catch Key (IRE)**[10] 1683 3-8-12 0 ... DuranFentiman 8 47
(T D Easterby) *hld up: hdwy 3f out: rdn over 2f out and sn no imp* **10/1**[3]
5 *1 3/4* **George Adamson (IRE)** 3-9-3 0 ... RobertWinston 2 47
(G A Swinbank) *dwlt: t.k.h and sn chsng ldrs: rdn along over 2f out: sn btn* **16/1**
0 **6** *14* **Kentucky Lakes**[12] 1625 3-9-3 0 ... TonyHamilton 3 12
(Jedd O'Keeffe) *a in rr: bhd fnl 3f* **50/1**
06- **7** *4 1/2* **Fifer (IRE)**[192] 7126 3-8-12 0 ... PaulMulrennan 5 —
(Patrick Morris) *t.k.h: chsd wnr: rdn along over 2f out and sn wknd* **150/1**
6-5 **P** **Liberty Lodge (IRE)**[21] 1440 3-9-3 0 ... TomEaves 1 —
(G A Swinbank) *t.k.h: chsd ldrs 2f: sn lost pl and bhd whn p.u 3f out: lame* **80/1**

1m 32.93s (-0.87) **Going Correction** -0.425s/f (Firm) 8 Ran SP% 108.0
Speed ratings (Par 99): **87,86,77,75,73 57,52,—**
toteswinger: 1&2 £2.10, 1&3 £2.50, 2&3 £9.30 CSF £3.60 TOTE £1.40: £1.02, £2.10, £2.90; EX 3.90.
Owner Black Velvet Racing **Bred** Peter McCutcheon **Trained** Musley Bank, N Yorks

FOCUS
A weak maiden and the form is a bit shaky but the first two were clear and the winner is rated to near his mark.
Kentucky Lakes Official explanation: jockey said gelding ran too free early stages and failed to handle the bend
Liberty Lodge(IRE) Official explanation: vet said gelding pulled up lame behind

1951 SUBSCRIBE ONLINE AT RACINGUK.COM H'CAP 5f
3:00 (3:05) (Class 5) (0-75,75) 4-Y-O+ **£3,238** (£963; £481; £240) **Stalls** High

Form RPR
0-00 **1** **Pacific Pride**[17] 1518 6-8-6 **70** ... (p) JamieKyne(7) 10 78
(J J Quinn) *mde all: rdn over 1f out: drvn ins fnl f and hld on gamely* **5/1**[1]
20-0 **2** *nse* **Baybshambles (IRE)**[7] 1768 5-8-8 **68** ... KellyHarrison(3) 11 76
(R E Barr) *hld up towards rr: hdwy wl over 1f out: swtchd rt and rdn ent fnl f: fin strly: jst hld* **5/1**[1]
534- **3** *3/4* **Tangerine Trees**[150] 7671 4-8-7 **64** ow1 ... TomEaves 8 69
(B Smart) *chsd ldrs: hdwy wl over 1f out: rdne to chse ldng pair ent fnl f: swtchd lft and sn drvn: nt qckn towards fin* **7/1**[3]
1222 **4** *1/2* **Desperate Dan**[1] 1935 8-9-1 **72** ... (v) PhillipMakin 5 75
(A B Haynes) *towards rr: hdwy 2f out: sn rdn and kpt on ins fnl f: nrst fin* **6/1**[2]
0-55 **5** *1/2* **Mambo Spirit (IRE)**[10] 1685 5-9-3 **74** ... PaulMulrennan 3 75+
(J G Given) *in tch: swtchd lft and hdwy wl over 1f out: sn rdn and kpt on same pce ins fnl f* **10/1**
100- **6** *2 1/4* **First Swallow**[210] 6724 4-8-4 **61** ... PaulHanagan 2 54+
(R A Fahey) *chsd ldrs: effrt 2f out and sn rdn: drvn and wknd appr fnl f* **14/1**
-023 **7** *2 1/4* **Buy On The Red**[9] 1694 8-8-12 **69** ... (v) AdrianTNicholls 7 54
(D Nicholls) *stmbld s and sn swtchd rt to ins rail: rdn along in midfield 1/2-way: sn no imp* **7/1**[3]
56-4 **8** *3/4* **Royal Composer (IRE)**[24] 1369 6-8-4 **61** oh3 ... (p) DuranFentiman 9 44
(T D Easterby) *wnt rt s: a towards rr* **14/1**
0-00 **9** *1/2* **Angle Of Attack (IRE)**[7] 1768 4-8-11 **68** ... (b[1]) SilvestreDeSousa 12 49
(A D Brown) *cl up: rdn along 2f out: drvn over 1f out and ev ch tl wknd ent fnl f* **8/1**
-600 **10** *1 3/4* **Highland Warrior**[10] 1685 10-8-13 **70** ... JamieMoriarty 4 44
(P T Midgley) *s.i.s: a in rr* **80/1**
06-0 **11** *1 3/4* **He's A Humbug (IRE)**[3] 1885 5-9-4 **75** ... (b) JoeFanning 1 43
(J O'Reilly) *chsd ldrs on outer: rdn along over 2f out: sn drvn and wknd* **50/1**
360- **12** *2 3/4* **Lake Chini (IRE)**[208] 6766 7-8-7 **64** ... (b) DaleGibson 13 22
(M W Easterby) *chsd ldrs on inner: rdn along over 2f out: sn drvn and wknd* **16/1**
333- **13** *2 1/4* **Monte Cassino (IRE)**[149] 7679 4-8-4 **61** oh14 ... FrancisNorton 6 11
(J O'Reilly) *a in rr* **80/1**

60.91 secs (-2.59) **Going Correction** -0.425s/f (Firm) 13 Ran SP% 116.5
Speed ratings (Par 103): **103,102,101,100,100 96,92,91,90,88 85,80,77**
toteswinger: 1&2 £7.20, 1&3 £7.10, 2&3 £10.00 CSF £28.02 CT £174.98 TOTE £6.20: £2.20, £2.30, £2.40; EX 29.90.
Owner The New Century Partnership **Bred** Whitsbury Manor Stud **Trained** Settrington, N Yorks

FOCUS
A modest but competitive sprint handicap, although the winning time was 0.35 seconds slower than the earlier seller, suggesting the tail wind in the straight had died down somewhat. The first two home were drawn in double-figure stalls but the form looks sound enough with the first four all close to their marks.

1952 WILLIAMHILL.COM RICHARD HORNE TESTIMONIAL H'CAP 1m 100y
3:30 (3:30) (Class 4) (0-85,85) 4-Y-0+ £5,180 (£1,541; £770; £384) Stalls High

Form RPR
60-1 1 **Billy Dane (IRE)**[17] 1507 5-9-0 81 PhillipMakin 8 90
(F P Murtagh) *mde all: pushed along over 2f out: rdn over 1f out: styd on strly* 14/1
6-52 2 1 1/2 **Handsome Falcon**[8] 1722 5-8-6 73 PaulHanagan 6 79
(R A Fahey) *trckd ldrs: hdwy over 2f out: rdn to chse wnr over 1f out: sn drvn and no imp ins fnl f* 9/4[1]
1601 3 2 **Captain Macarry (IRE)**[8] 1723 4-8-12 79 6ex (v) TomEaves 11 80
(B Smart) *trckd ldrs on inner: hdwy over 2f out and sn rdn along: swtchd lft and drvn over 1f out: kpt on ins fnl f* 9/4[1]
5413 4 1/2 **Jebel Tara**[13] 1612 4-8-4 71 oh2 (bt) SilvestreDeSousa 10 71
(A D Brown) *prom: effrt 3f out: rdn along 2f out: sn drvn and one pce fr over 1f out* 6/1[2]
015- 5 1 **Observatory Star (IRE)**[236] 6052 6-8-12 79 (p) RobertWinston 9 77
(T D Easterby) *hld up towards rr: hdwy 2f out: swtchd outside and rdn to chse ldrs over 1f out: drvn and edgd rt ins fnl f: one pce* 10/1[3]
4044 6 1 3/4 **Exit Smiling**[8] 1722 7-9-2 83 JamieMoriarty 4 77
(P T Midgley) *towards rr: rdn along over 3f out: kpt on u.p fnl 2f: nrst fin* 25/1
6050 7 1 1/2 **Spin Again (IRE)**[3] 1887 4-8-5 72 AdrianTNicholls 7 62
(D Nicholls) *chsd wnr: rdn along over 2f out: drvn and wknd wl over 1f out* 33/1
020- 8 3/4 **Traphalgar (IRE)**[159] 7551 4-9-4 85 JoeFanning 2 74
(P F I Cole) *in tch: rdn along 3f out: drvn 2f out and sn btn* 20/1
00-0 9 1 3/4 **Blue Spinnaker (IRE)**[14] 1593 10-9-0 81 DaleGibson 12 66
(M W Easterby) *a towards rr* 40/1
432- 10 1/2 **Nevada Desert (IRE)**[205] 6841 9-8-8 78 MichaelJStainton(3) 5 62
(R M Whitaker) *hld up: nvr bttr than midfield* 22/1
00-3 11 2 3/4 **Bustan (IRE)**[17] 1524 10-8-12 79 J-PGuillambert 1 56
(G C Bravery) *v s.i.s: a bhd* 14/1
316- 12 1 **Riley Boys (IRE)**[298] 4167 8-8-10 77 PaulMulrennan 3 52
(J G Given) *dwlt: hld up: a bhd* 25/1
1m 43.06s (-4.54) **Going Correction** -0.425s/f (Firm) 12 Ran SP% **120.4**
Speed ratings (Par 105): **105,103,101,101,100 98,96,96,94,93 91,90**
totewinger: 1&2 £7.50, 1&3 £9.00, 2&3 £2.10 CSF £42.74 CT £104.57 TOTE £18.30: £4.30, £1.60, £1.40; EX 68.50.
Owner James Callow **Bred** Brian Killeen **Trained** Low Braithwaite, Cumbria

FOCUS
A fair handicap on paper with the winner getting back to his best and the runner-up close to his previous course form.
Nevada Desert(IRE) Official explanation: jockey said gelding was unsuited by the good to firm (firm in places) ground
Bustan(IRE) Official explanation: jockey said gelding missed the break

1953 BEST UK RACECOURSES ON TURFTV H'CAP 1m 1f 207y
4:00 (4:02) (Class 5) (0-70,70) 3-Y-O £2,914 (£867; £433; £216) Stalls High

Form RPR
0-04 1 **Mons Calpe (IRE)**[13] 1614 3-8-10 62 (b[1]) JoeFanning 8 73
(P F I Cole) *trckd ldrs: smooth hdwy 3f out: led over 2f out: rdn over 1f out: styd on strly ins fnl f* 3/1[3]
25-3 2 1 **High Office**[29] 1245 3-9-4 70 PaulHanagan 7 79
(R A Fahey) *dwlt: hld up in rr: n.m.r bnd over 4f out: gd hdwy 3f out: effrt 2f out and sn chsng wnr: drvn ent fnl f and kpt on* 11/4[2]
064- 3 11 **Royal Trooper (IRE)**[223] 6384 3-9-0 66 PaulMulrennan 5 53+
(J G Given) *hld up in rr: hdwy over 2f out: nt clr run over 1f out: swtchd lft and rdn: styd on strly ins fnl f to take 3rd nr line* 9/2
04-4 4 1/2 **Veronicas Boy**[12] 1629 3-8-10 62 TomEaves 1 48
(G M Moore) *chsd ldrs: rdn along over 2f out: sn rdn and outpcd over 1f out: lost 3rd nr line* 14/1
65-4 5 3 1/2 **Susurrayshaan**[24] 1363 3-8-4 56 oh5 (p) DaleGibson 2 35
(Mrs G S Rees) *chsd ldrs: rdn along wl over 2f out: sn drvn and wknd* 33/1
00-0 6 1 3/4 **Luckette**[10] 1683 3-8-4 56 oh11 TWilliams 6 32
(M Brittain) *chsd ldrs on inner: rdn along 3f out and sn wknd* 80/1
-0 7 2 **Zepnove (IRE)**[15] 1574 3-8-12 64 FrancisNorton 4 36
(M Wigham) *hld up: a bhd* 40/1
3663 8 1 1/4 **Antipodean (UAE)**[12] 1629 3-8-0 59 oh1 ow3 PaulPickard(7) 3 28
(P T Midgley) *led: rdn along 3f out: sn hdd & wknd* 18/1
302- 9 38 **Petsas Pleasure**[191] 7148 3-9-2 68 DuranFentiman 9 —
(Ollie Pears) *trckd ldr: hdwy and cl up 3f out: sn rdn and wkng whn n.m.r on inner 2f out: sn bhd and eased* 5/2[1]
2m 4.01s (-2.99) **Going Correction** -0.425s/f (Firm) 9 Ran SP% **117.0**
Speed ratings (Par 99): **94,93,84,84,81 79,78,77,46**
totewinger: 1&2 £2.90, 1&3 £3.50, 2&3 £3.80 CSF £11.79 CT £36.21 TOTE £4.30: £1.30, £1.30, £2.20; EX 9.80.
Owner H R H Sultan Ahmad Shah **Bred** Swettenham Stud **Trained** Whatcombe, Oxon

FOCUS
This looked a reasonable three-year-old handicap for the grade on paper, but something was seemingly amiss with the favourite, and the front pair pulled a long way clear. Despite that it is not a race to be too positive about.
Luckette Official explanation: jockey said filly stumbled on bend leaving back straight
Petsas Pleasure Official explanation: jockey said gelding ran too free

1954 RICHARD HORNE TESTIMONIAL DAY H'CAP 1m 4f 16y
4:30 (4:31) (Class 6) (0-60,66) 3-Y-O £2,590 (£770; £385; £192) Stalls High

Form RPR
-051 1 **Classic Contours (USA)**[4] 1829 3-9-3 66 6ex JamieKyne(7) 6 71+
(J J Quinn) *trckd ldrs: hdwy on outer 3f out: rdn to ld over 1f out: drvn ins fnl f: hld on gamely* 13/8[1]
333 2 hd **Tae Kwon Do (USA)**[21] 1441 3-8-12 54 TomEaves 7 59
(Miss J A Camacho) *hld up in tch: smooth hdwy 3f out: rdn over 1f out: drvn to chal ins fnl f and ev ch tl no ex nr fin* 11/1
00-1 3 1 3/4 **Loulou (USA)**[14] 1594 3-9-4 60 PaulMulrennan 1 62
(S A Callaghan) *sn led: rdn along wl over 2f out: drvn and hdd over 1f out: one pce ins fnl f* 11/2[2]
0-02 4 1 3/4 **Addison De Witt**[22] 1397 3-8-11 58 PatrickDonaghy(5) 8 57
(Micky Hammond) *prom: effrt 3f out and sn rdn along: drvn over 1f out: kpt on same pce fnl f* 22/1
000- 5 1 1/2 **Astrobrava**[178] 7332 3-9-2 58 RobertWinston 12 55
(M H Tompkins) *trckd ldrs on inner: effrt over 2f out: rdn and n.m.r over 1f out: drvn and wknd fnl f* 13/2[3]
-002 6 nk **Rebel Prince (IRE)**[14] 1594 3-8-12 54 EdwardCreighton 5 50+
(M G Quinlan) *dwlt and rr: hdwy on outer over 2f out: rdn wl over 1f out: kpt on ins fnl f: nrst fin* 8/1
-000 7 nse **Best Bidder (USA)**[14] 1580 3-8-8 55 FrederikTylicki(5) 3 51
(Patrick Morris) *towards rr: hdwy 4f out: rdn along wl over 2f out: drvn and styd on appr fnl f: nrst fin* 10/1
0-00 8 5 **Hassadin**[49] 943 3-8-13 55 PhillipMakin 11 43
(A B Haynes) *a towards rr* 25/1
000- 9 3 1/4 **Hill Cross (IRE)**[197] 7016 3-8-13 55 PaulHanagan 2 38
(K G Reveley) *a towards rr* 40/1
006- 10 3 1/2 **Imperial Angel (IRE)**[280] 4697 3-9-0 56 DNolan 9 33
(D Carroll) *in tch: rdn along wl over 2f out and sn wknd* 33/1
-006 11 1 1/4 **Saffron's Son (IRE)**[15] 1562 3-8-13 55 JamieMoriarty 10 30
(P T Midgley) *a towards rr* 25/1
4503 12 8 **Alittlemoreflair**[41] 1070 3-9-3 59 JerryO'Dwyer 4 21
(J Pearce) *prom: hdwy and cl up 1/2-way: rdn along 3f out: wknd qckly over 2f out* 12/1
2m 39.16s (-1.74) **Going Correction** -0.425s/f (Firm) 12 Ran SP% **120.5**
Speed ratings (Par 97): **88,87,86,85,84 84,84,80,78,76 75,70**
totewinger: 1&2 £4.30, 1&3 £2.50, 2&3 £6.20 CSF £19.95 CT £86.02 TOTE £2.30: £1.50, £2.50, £2.00; EX 22.90.
Owner Elsa Crankshaw Gordon Allan **Bred** Hopewell Investments LLC **Trained** Settrington, N Yorks

FOCUS
A reasonable handicap, but they went just an ordinary pace. The form looks sound with those in the frame behind the winner close to their recent marks.
Alittlemoreflair Official explanation: jockey said filly was unsuited by the good to firm (firm in places) ground

1955 TURFTV BETTING SHOP SERVICE H'CAP 1m 100y
5:00 (5:01) (Class 6) (0-60,60) 4-Y-O+ £2,729 (£806; £403) Stalls High

Form RPR
-001 1 **Sarwin (USA)**[18] 1495 6-8-13 55 RobertWinston 9 68
(G A Swinbank) *trckd ldrs: smooth hdwy 3f out: led over 1f out: rdn ins fnl f: drvn and hld on gamely towards fin* 8/1
-040 2 nse **Shadowtime**[13] 1612 4-9-3 59 PhillipMakin 12 72
(Miss Tracy Waggott) *hld up towards rr: gd hdwy 2f out: rdn to chse wnr ins fnl f: sn drvn and styd on strly: jst failed* 5/1[3]
00-5 3 4 **Umverti**[19] 1472 4-8-13 55 (p) FrancisNorton 5 59
(N Bycroft) *led: hdd 3f out: rdn and sltly outpcd 2f out: styd on u.p ins fnl f* 20/1
05- 4 1/2 **Carpe Diem**[225] 6336 4-9-0 56 TonyHamilton 13 59
(R A Fahey) *midfield: hdwy 3f out: rdn to chse ldrs over 1f out: drvn and hung lft ins fnl f kpt on same pce* 8/1
1360 5 1 3/4 **General Feeling (IRE)**[34] 1194 8-9-3 59 AdrianTNicholls 2 58+
(D Nicholls) *stdd and swtchd rt s: rr tl hdwy wl over 2f out: swtchd rt and rdn over 1f out: styd on ins fnl f: nrst fin* 20/1
6-14 6 1/2 **Rossini's Dancer**[19] 1475 4-9-4 60 PaulHanagan 17 57
(R A Fahey) *trckd ldrs on inner: hdwy 2f out and sn rdn: drvn appr fnl f and no imp* 4/1[1]
0-23 7 1 1/2 **Just Sam (IRE)**[8] 1734 4-8-12 57 KellyHarrison(3) 8 51
(R E Barr) *towards rr: hdwy over 2f: sn rdn and kpt on ins fnl f: nt rch ldrs* 25/1
3212 8 3/4 **Ace Of Spies (IRE)**[3] 1889 4-9-1 57 (p) SilvestreDeSousa 1 49+
(G A Harker) *chsd ldrs: effrt on outer over 2f out: sn rdn and wknd over 1f out* 9/2[2]
6-00 9 3/4 **Aussie Blue (IRE)**[25] 1332 5-8-11 56 MichaelJStainton(3) 16 47
(R M Whitaker) *cl up on inner: led 3f out: rdn over 2f out: hdd over 1f out and sn wknd* 12/1
0-05 10 1 **Heart Of Dubai (USA)**[17] 1520 4-8-9 56 FrederikTylicki(5) 6 44
(Micky Hammond) *a towards rr* 33/1
0-00 11 1 3/4 **Emperor's Well**[13] 1612 10-8-13 55 DaleGibson 10 39
(M W Easterby) *midfield: rdn along over 2f out and sn wknd* 66/1
360- 12 1 3/4 **Cullybackey (IRE)**[227] 6275 4-9-1 57 TomEaves 4 37
(G A Swinbank) *a towards rr* 50/1
-006 13 2 **Thompsons Walls (IRE)**[12] 1628 4-8-12 57 (b) AndrewMullen(3) 3 33
(D Nicholls) *cl up: rdn 3f out: drvn over 2f out and sn wknd* 33/1
60-0 14 2 3/4 **Royal Applord**[13] 1612 4-9-2 58 PaulMulrennan 11 27
(P T Midgley) *a towards rr* 20/1
0-65 15 1 **High Profit (IRE)**[13] 1612 5-9-2 58 (v) DarrenMoffatt 14 25
(James Moffatt) *a in rr* 10/1
040- 16 14 **Shosolosa (IRE)**[296] 4219 7-8-11 53 JoeFanning 7 —
(R C Guest) *a in rr* 40/1
1m 43.97s (-3.63) **Going Correction** -0.425s/f (Firm) 16 Ran SP% **123.8**
Speed ratings (Par 101): **101,100,96,96,94 94,92,91,91,90 88,86,84,81,80 66**
totewinger: 1&2 £13.90, 1&3 £41.50, 2&3 £53.30 CSF £42.76 CT £825.79 TOTE £8.00: £2.10, £1.60, £4.10, £3.10; EX 75.30 Place 6: £6.03 Place 5: £4.19.
Owner S Rudolf **Bred** Cynthia Knight **Trained** Melsonby, N Yorks

FOCUS
A moderate but quite competitive handicap and the form looks sound.
Rossini's Dancer Official explanation: jockey said gelding was unsuited by the good to firm (firm in places) ground
Royal Applord Official explanation: jockey said gelding was unsuited by the good to firm (firm in places) ground
T/Plt: £9.20 to a £1 stake. Pool: £49,968.86. 3,942.09 winning tickets. T/Qpdt: £5.20 to a £1 stake. Pool: £3,080.34. 432.80 winning tickets. JR

1534 BRIGHTON (L-H)
Tuesday, May 12

OFFICIAL GOING: Firm (good to firm in places)
Rail realignment added 15yards to advertised distances.
Wind: Strong, behind Weather: Cloudy

1956 BET365.COM MAIDEN STKS 5f 213y
2:10 (2:10) (Class 5) 3-Y-O+ £3,784 (£1,132; £566; £283; £141) Stalls Low

Form RPR
1 **Cleisthenes (USA)** 3-9-0 0 LiamJones 10 87+
(W J Haggas) *settled in 5th: shkn up and r.o to ld 1f out: sn clr: easily* 1/2[1]
43- 2 6 **Celestial Dream (IRE)**[187] 7207 3-8-9 0 WilliamBuick 8 60+
(A M Balding) *chsd ldrs: rdn to chal over 1f out: nt pce of wnr* 15/8[2]

3 3 1/4 **Madhal** 3-8-9 0 .... RossAtkinson(5) 1 55
(M Salaman) *dwlt: sn pushed along in rr: styd on appr fnl f: nt trble ldng pair* **33/1**

600- 4 shd **Blackwater Fort (USA)**[159] 7542 3-9-0 61 .... (b[1]) FergusSweeney 4 54
(J Gallagher) *sn led: rdn and hdd 1f out: wknd fnl f* **20/1**

4630 5 2 1/4 **Tightrope (IRE)**[12] 1617 3-8-9 51 .... AmyBaker(5) 3 47
(T D McCarthy) *chsd ldng pair: rdn 3f out: wknd wl over 1f out* **25/1**

50- 6 1 **State Function (IRE)**[267] 5160 4-9-10 0 .... AdrianMcCarthy 5 47
(G Prodromou) *w ldr tl hung lft and wknd fnl 2f* **16/1**[3]

0250 7 12 **Lois Darlin (IRE)**[71] 736 3-8-6 50 .... (b) KevinGhunowa(3) 7 —
(R A Harris) *bhd fnl 3f* **40/1**

8 6 **Rare Bet** 3-8-4 0 .... JackDean(5) 6 —
(W G M Turner) *outpcd: sn wl bhd* **40/1**

67.61 secs (-2.59) **Going Correction** -0.275s/f (Firm)
WFA 3 from 4yo 10lb **8** Ran SP% **123.8**
Speed ratings (Par 103): **106,98,93,93,90 89,73,65**
toteswingers: 1&2 £1.02, 1&3 £17.40, 2&3 £13.30 CSF £1.77 TOTE £1.90: £1.02, £1.10, £12.30; EX 2.20 Trifecta £54.90 Pool: £189.37 - 2.55 winning units..
Owner Findlay & Bloom **Bred** Clovelly Farms **Trained** Newmarket, Suffolk

FOCUS
There was a strong wind following the runners in the home straight and as a result the ground had dried out slightly to Firm, Good to Firm in places. The runners stayed towards the inside of the track throughout. A very moderate maiden in which only two counted according to the betting and the market got it right. The winner was impressive and the fourth and fifth set the standard.

1957 RADIO REVERB H'CAP — 5f 59y
2:40 (2:40) (Class 5) (0-70,68) 4-Y-O+ **£3,154** (£944; £472; £236; £117) **Stalls** Low

Form RPR

0630 1 **Orpen's Art (IRE)**[24] 1360 4-8-7 57 .... KirstyMilczarek 2 63
(S A Callaghan) *chsd ldrs: n.m.r on rail and swtchd rt jst over 1f out: r.o u.p to ld fnl strides* **6/1**

6002 2 shd **Billy Red**[16] 1540 5-9-3 67 .... (b) FergusSweeney 10 73
(J R Jenkins) *sn led: rdn and edgd lft over 1f out: kpt on u.p: hdd fnl strides* **4/1**[3]

5-30 3 2 1/2 **Multahab**[16] 1540 10-8-12 62 .... (t) JimmyQuinn 3 59
(M Wigham) *hld up in 5th: effrt and hung rt to centre over 2f out: hrd rdn over 1f out: r.o to snatch 3rd on line* **7/2**[2]

0433 4 hd **Hart Of Gold**[12] 1619 5-8-13 66 .... (p) KevinGhunowa(3) 5 62
(R A Harris) *chsd ldrs: sn pushed along: hrd rdn and kpt on same pce fnl 2f* **6/4**[1]

0660 5 nse **Thoughtsofstardom**[3] 1877 6-8-8 65 .... CarolineKelly(7) 8 61
(P S McEntee) *chsd ldr tl jst ins fnl 2f: one pce* **16/1**

2006 6 3 **Peopleton Brook**[12] 1619 7-8-7 57 .... (t) StephenCarson 6 42
(B G Powell) *bhd: rdn into mod 4th 2f out: fdd fnl f* **12/1**

0500 7 4 **Gone'N'Dunnett (IRE)**[12] 1634 10-7-13 54 oh9 .... (v) AmyBaker(5) 9 25
(Mrs C A Dunnett) *sn drvn along towards rr: n.d fnl 2f* **40/1**

60.54 secs (-1.76) **Going Correction** -0.275s/f (Firm) **7** Ran SP% **112.5**
Speed ratings (Par 103): **103,102,98,98,98 93,87**
totewinger: 1&2 £4.70, 1&3 £4.50, 2&3 £1.90 CSF £29.03 CT £95.58 TOTE £5.80: £3.10, £2.60; EX 19.70 Trifecta £122.70 Part won. Pool: £165.86 - 0.66 winning units..
Owner S A Callaghan & N A Callaghan **Bred** Fin A Co S R L **Trained** Newmarket, Suffolk

FOCUS
A modest sprint handicap run at a fair pace and not many got into it. The form looks straightforward rated around the runner-up.
Multahab Official explanation: jockey said gelding hung right

1958 AD:TECH (S) STKS — 6f 209y
3:10 (3:10) (Class 6) 3-Y-O+ **£1,942** (£578; £288; £144) **Stalls** Low

Form RPR

6210 1 **Seneschal**[16] 1539 8-9-7 67 .... GeorgeBaker 5 78
(A B Haynes) *in tch: wnt 4 l 2nd 2f out: rdn to ld ins fnl f: sn clr: comf* **5/2**[1]

5-62 2 5 **Spit And Polish**[14] 1584 3-8-3 66 .... (b) JimmyQuinn 14 55
(J L Dunlop) *led: wnt 4 l clr 2f out: hrd rdn and hdd ins fnl f: no ex* **7/2**[3]

1306 3 2 1/4 **True Britannia**[36] 1148 3-8-4 63 .... LiamJones 4 49+
(A M Hales) *towards rr: lost action on crossing after 1f: rdn 1/2-way: styd on fnl 2f: nvr nrr* **12/1**

0460 4 1 3/4 **Young Ivanhoe**[7] 1781 4-9-1 50 .... (v[1]) WilliamBuick 12 48
(C A Dwyer) *t.k.h: chsd ldr tl over 2f out: sn outpcd* **16/1**

2-0 5 2 1/2 **Come On Buckers (IRE)**[71] 736 3-8-4 60 ow1 .... TPO'Shea 8 38
(E J Creighton) *t.k.h: chsd ldrs tl rdn and btn 2f out* **20/1**

000- 6 hd **Canary Girl**[37] 2374 6-8-10 32 .... AdrianMcCarthy 7 35
(G Prodromou) *sn pushed along towards rr: hrd rdn 3f out: sme late hdwy* **100/1**

20-0 7 1 1/4 **Polmaily**[8] 1748 4-9-1 72 .... DaneO'Neill 11 37
(J Akehurst) *dwlt: towards rr: mod effrt 3f out: nvr trbld ldrs* **12/1**

4500 8 hd **Titus Gent**[29] 1259 4-8-12 46 .... MarcHalford(3) 10 36
(J Ryan) *sn pushed into midfield: outpcd fnl 3f* **66/1**

00-0 9 2 **Rindless**[83] 592 4-8-10 40 .... FergusSweeney 2 26
(J F Panvert) *bhd: rdn 3f out: nvr a factor* **100/1**

-306 10 nse **Mannello**[16] 1536 6-8-5 50 .... (b) AmyBaker(5) 9 26
(S W Hall) *in tch tl wknd over 2f out* **20/1**

1444 11 2 1/2 **Bromhead (USA)**[21] 1429 3-8-9 66 .... SebSanders 1 26+
(B J Meehan) *chsd ldrs over 3f: allowed to coast in after: bit slipped* **3/1**[2]

0045 12 11 **Sorrel Ridge (IRE)**[21] 1424 3-7-12 48 .... NicolPolli(5) 13 —
(M G Quinlan) *s.s: sn prom on outside: hrd rdn and wknd over 2f out* **50/1**

3000 13 26 **Kamanja (UAE)**[12] 1620 3-7-12 53 .... NickyMackay 3 —
(M J Attwater) *chsd ldrs: hmpd and lost pl after 1f: sn in rr and allowed to coast rnd: fin lame* **40/1**

406- S **Border Artist**[208] 6751 10-8-8 49 .... SimonPearce(7) 6 —
(J Pearce) *hld up in last: stmbld bdly and slipped up heavily over 3f out* **33/1**

1m 21.15s (-1.95) **Going Correction** -0.275s/f (Firm)
WFA 3 from 4yo+ 12lb **14** Ran SP% **117.4**
Speed ratings (Par 101): **100,94,91,89,86 86,85,84,82,82 79,67,37,—**
.There was no bid for the winner. Bromhead was claimed by C Dunnett for £5000. Spit And Polish was claimed by C. A. Dwyer for £5000.\n\x\x
Owner P Cook **Bred** Michael E Broughton **Trained** Limpley Stoke, Bath

FOCUS
A moderate seller, but again not that many ever looked like winning. The winner is solid and is rated to his best recent form.
True Britannia Official explanation: jockey said filly jumped the crossing, then lost its action
Come On Buckers(IRE) Official explanation: vet said gelding had been struck into right-hind
Bromhead(USA) Official explanation: jockey said bit pulled through and was unable to ride the gelding out

Kamanja(UAE) Official explanation: jockey said filly suffered interference soon after start; trainer said filly was unsuited by the firm (good to firm in places) ground; vet said filly returned lame

1959 IMEDIA H'CAP — 7f 214y
3:40 (3:48) (Class 6) (0-60,60) 4-Y-O+ **£2,460** (£732; £365; £182) **Stalls** Low

Form RPR

06-0 1 **Mr Fantozzi (IRE)**[14] 1589 4-8-13 55 .... (p) JimmyQuinn 3 63
(D Donovan) *mde virtually all: hrd drvn and jnd by runner-up fnl f: jst on top fnl strides* **7/1**

0006 2 nk **Yakama (IRE)**[12] 1632 4-8-12 54 .... LiamJones 2 61
(Mrs C A Dunnett) *hld up in midfield: hdwy over 2f out: drvn level w wnr fnl f: jst outpcd fnl strides* **20/1**

-400 3 2 1/4 **Wrighty Almighty (IRE)**[48] 959 7-9-4 60 .... GeorgeBaker 13 62
(P R Chamings) *towards rr: rdn and styd on in centre fnl 2f: wnt 3rd ins fnl f* **11/4**[1]

3030 4 1 3/4 **Simpsons Gamble (IRE)**[14] 1587 6-8-4 46 oh1 .... (p) KirstyMilczarek 9 44
(R A Teal) *towards rr on rail: hdwy and hung lft fr 2f out: one pce fnl f* **9/1**

-261 5 1 1/4 **My Flame**[16] 1535 4-9-2 58 .... FergusSweeney 7 53
(J R Jenkins) *prom tl wknd over 1f out* **15/2**

0665 6 1 1/2 **Red Current**[7] 1770 5-8-8 53 .... KevinGhunowa(3) 1 45
(R A Harris) *prom: hrd rdn 2f out: sn btn* **10/1**

1056 7 11 **Djalalabad (FR)**[16] 1535 5-8-11 53 .... (tp) SebSanders 12 19
(Mrs C A Dunnett) *chsd ldrs on outer tl hung lft and wknd fnl 2f* **16/1**

00-2 8 1 3/4 **Your Golf Travel**[110] 247 4-8-4 46 oh1 .... NickyMackay 6 8
(M Wigham) *chsd ldrs over 5f* **5/1**[2]

4530 9 1 1/4 **Moyoko (IRE)**[16] 1537 6-8-3 50 .... RossAtkinson(5) 4 10
(M Salaman) *s.s: hrd rdn 3f out: a bhd* **13/2**[3]

0000 10 3 **Lake Sabina**[16] 1536 4-8-4 46 oh1 .... WilliamBuick 5 —
(M R Hoad) *drvn along 3f out: a bhd* **33/1**

1m 34.04s (-1.96) **Going Correction** -0.275s/f (Firm) **10** Ran SP% **113.6**
Speed ratings (Par 101): **98,97,95,93,92 90,79,78,76,73**
totewinger: 1&2 £45.30, 1&3 £3.90, 2&3 £13.60 CSF £131.85 CT £485.28 TOTE £5.80: £2.50, £6.20, £1.50; EX 152.40 Trifecta £168.30 Part won. Pool: £227.52 - 0.90 winnning units..
Owner Mrs Rita Cioffi **Bred** David Commins **Trained** Newmarket, Suffolk

FOCUS
A very moderate handicap and the early pace didn't look that strong. The winner is rated to his old turf form.
Your Golf Travel Official explanation: vet said filly returned distressed

1960 BRAKES H'CAP — 1m 3f 196y
4:10 (4:15) (Class 5) (0-70,66) 4-Y-O+ **£3,154** (£944; £472; £236; £117) **Stalls** High

Form RPR

000- 1 **Harlequinn Danseur (IRE)**[7] 5377 4-7-13 52 oh7 .... AmyBaker(5) 3 57
(N B King) *in tch in rr: hrd rdn over 2f out: wnt 3rd over 1f out: styd on to ld fnl 50yds* **7/1**[3]

1425 2 1 **Star Choice**[25] 1319 4-9-4 66 .... SebSanders 2 69
(J Pearce) *led: rdn and jnd 3f out: disp ld after tl hdd and outpcd fnl 50yds* **10/11**[1]

-513 3 nk **Nassar (IRE)**[14] 1589 6-8-8 63 .... (p) HollyHall(7) 1 66
(G Prodromou) *t.k.h early: wnt 2nd after 3f: disp ld fnl 3f: kpt on u.p: outpcd fnl 50yds* **5/2**[2]

006- 4 3 1/2 **Robbmaa (FR)**[12] 4930 4-8-4 52 oh4 .... KirstyMilczarek 5 49?
(A W Carroll) *in tch: rdn 3f out: wknd over 1f out* **25/1**

-264 5 25 **Ice Bellini**[8] 1738 4-9-0 62 .... (b) WilliamBuick 4 19
(Miss Gay Kelleway) *dwlt: on and off the bridle: in tch on outer: effrt 4f out: wknd over 2f out* **8/1**

2m 34.22s (1.52) **Going Correction** -0.275s/f (Firm) **5** Ran SP% **108.4**
Speed ratings (Par 103): **83,82,82,79,63**
CSF £13.65 TOTE £10.60: £3.80, £1.40; EX 30.00.
Owner Neil King **Bred** C J Foy **Trained** Newmarket, Suffolk
■ Stewards' Enquiry : Holly Hall one-day ban: used whip with excessive frequency (May 26)

FOCUS
A small field for this handicap and the early pace was modest which turned this into a rather tactical affair. The form is weak with the winner racing from out of the handicap.
Harlequinn Danseur(IRE) Official explanation: trainer said, regarding apparent improvement in form, that the gelding had benefited from a change of trainer, step up in trip and being in form over hurdles.

1961 "HANDS AND HEELS" APPRENTICE H'CAP — 1m 1f 209y
4:40 (4:42) (Class 6) (0-60,60) 4-Y-O+ **£2,331** (£693; £346; £173) **Stalls** High

Form RPR

1262 1 **Chalice Welcome**[8] 1728 6-9-5 60 .... DavidKenny 12 66
(N B King) *stdd s: hld up in rr: rdn and hdwy over 1f out: r.o to ld nr fin* **15/2**

-000 2 hd **Rosy Dawn**[8] 1728 4-8-5 46 oh1 .... DebraEngland 5 52
(J J Bridger) *led: kpt on gamely whn chal fnl 2f: hdd nr fin* **20/1**

0403 3 3 1/4 **Comrade Cotton**[3] 1883 5-8-6 55 .... RyanPowell(8) 1 55
(J Ryan) *hld up in rr: effrt whn n.m.r on rail over 4f out: gd hdwy over 1f out: one pce fnl f* **17/2**

1320 4 1 3/4 **Mystic Art (IRE)**[14] 1578 4-9-2 57 .... RichardRowe 8 53
(C R Egerton) *chsd ldrs tl no ex ent fnl f* **7/2**[2]

0020 5 3/4 **Generous Lad (IRE)**[16] 1537 6-8-10 51 .... (p) NSLawes 2 46
(A B Haynes) *plld hrd in rr: hdwy whn n.m.r over 4f out: sn rdn: no imp whn hmpd ins fnl f* **9/2**[3]

5050 6 shd **Keen As Mustard**[21] 1420 4-8-5 46 oh1 .... GemmaElford 7 40
(M D I Usher) *chsd ldr 7f: prom tl wknd 1f out* **66/1**

05-4 7 3/4 **Astrolibra**[3] 1881 5-8-12 56 .... ThomasBubb(3) 3 49
(M H Tompkins) *t.k.h in rr: rdn 3f out: sme hdwy whn nt clr run over 1f out: unable to chal* **15/8**[1]

000- 8 1 1/2 **Ubiquitous**[202] 6896 4-8-5 46 oh1 .... NathanAlison 9 36
(S Dow) *in tch on outer: wnt cl 2nd 3f out: wknd over 1f out* **16/1**

4000 9 1 3/4 **Dynamo Dave (USA)**[14] 1578 4-8-2 46 .... SeanPalmer(3) 4 32
(M D I Usher) *chsd ldrs tl wknd 2f out* **28/1**

2m 3.60s **Going Correction** -0.275s/f (Firm) **9** Ran SP% **113.1**
Speed ratings (Par 101): **89,88,86,84,84 84,83,82,80**
totewinger: 1&2 £2.90, 1&3 £7.70, 2&3 £19.70 CSF £137.50 CT £1290.02 TOTE £7.30: £1.60, £3.60, £3.10; EX 71.80 Trifecta £114.10 Pool: £415.10 - 2.69 winning units. Place 6: £111.72 Place 5: £102.39.
Owner The Dyball Partnership **Bred** The Dyball Partnership **Trained** Newmarket, Suffolk

FOCUS
A very moderate "hands and heels" apprentice handicap to close the card and again the early pace was modest with a few inclined to take a grip. The form is rated around the placed horses.
T/Plt: £41.70 to a £1 stake. Pool: £46,508.41. 813.98 winning tickets. T/Qpdt: £16.70 to a £1 stake. Pool: £2,949.95. 130.00 winning tickets. LM

[1870]LINGFIELD (L-H)

Tuesday, May 12

OFFICIAL GOING: Standard

Wind: Strong, half against Weather: Bright, breezy

1962 TREECREEPER CLAIMING STKS 1m 2f (P)

5:50 (5:50) (Class 6) 4-Y-O+ **£1,942** (£578; £288; £144) **Stalls** Low

Form RPR

0015 **1** **Polish Power (GER)**[10] 1660 9-8-9 82................................ LPKeniry 5 71
(J S Moore) *hld up in tch: hdwy over 2f out: led jst over 2f out: clr ins fnl f: r.o and a holding on* **5/2**[1]

-60-0 **2** *shd* **Clipperdown (IRE)**[12] 1621 8-8-7 69..........................(t) WilliamBuick 8 69
(E J Creighton) *stdd s: hld up in last pl: plld wd and hdwy ent fnl f: chsd wnr fnl 100yds: r.o wl but nvr quite gng to rch wnr* **12/1**

0556 **3** *2* **Alpes Maritimes**[8] 1750 5-9-7 75..................................(p) GeorgeBaker 7 79
(G L Moore) *hld up in last trio: hdwy on outer over 2f out: rdn and hung lft over 1f out: chsd wnr 1f out: no imp and lost 2nd fnl 100yds* **7/2**[2]

20-2 **4** *1 3/4* **Moonlight Man**[7] 1777 8-8-10 75 ow1..........................(t) SebSanders 2 65
(C R Dore) *led: rdn and hdd jst over 2f out: stl ev ch tl wknd jst ins fnl f* **9/2**[3]

150- **5** *hd* **Jebel Ali (IRE)**[277] 4829 6-9-2 73...................................... JamesDoyle 1 70
(B Gubby) *chsd ldr tl 6f out: styd trcking ldrs on inner: n.m.r ent fnl 2f: effrt and rdn over 1f out: kpt on same pce* **25/1**

-503 **6** *nse* **Cactus King**[34] 1177 6-8-9 70...(b[1]) IanMongan 3 63
(P M Phelan) *t.k.h: hld up in tch in midfield: rdn and nt qckn over 1f out: plugged on fnl f* **15/2**

4 **7** *1 3/4* **Tried And True (FR)**[17] 1515 4-8-11 65............................ TPQueally 6 62
(H R A Cecil) *chsd ldr tl wnt 2nd 6f out tl over 2f out: sn rdn: wknd ent fnl f* **15/2**

5/2 **8** *1* **Castellina**[7] 1770 5-8-6 94.. JimmyQuinn 4 55
(E J Creighton) *hld up in last trio: rdn and effrt over 1f out: kpt on one pce* **12/1**

2m 7.07s (0.47) **Going Correction** +0.125s/f (Slow) **8** Ran SP% **111.7**

Speed ratings (Par 101): **103,102,101,99,99 99,98,97**

toteswinger: 1&2 £11.10, 1&3 £2.50, 2&3 £8.60 CSF £32.03 TOTE £4.00: £1.90, £3.10, £2.10; EX 42.10.

Owner John Wells **Bred** Gestut Hofgut Mappen **Trained** Upper Lambourn, Berks

FOCUS

Exposed sorts in a fair claimer and not a race to be too positive about. The modest gallop only picked up turning for home and the first three raced in the centre in the straight.

1963 NIGHTJAR MEDIAN AUCTION MAIDEN STKS 1m (P)

6:20 (6:22) (Class 5) 3-5-Y-O **£2,590** (£770; £385; £192) **Stalls** High

Form RPR

3-3 **1** **Spring Adventure**[26] 1302 3-8-8 0................................ RyanMoore 9 74+
(E A L Dunlop) *trckd ldr tl rdn to ld jst over 2f out: rdn clr over 1f out: r.o strly: easily* **4/5**[1]

33-5 **2** *3 1/4* **Bennelong**[24] 1355 3-8-13 84... SebSanders 6 72+
(R M Beckett) *stdd after s: hld up towards rr: hdwy over 1f out: 6th ent fnl f: r.o strly to go 2nd last strides: no ch w wnr* **7/2**[2]

5 **3** *hd* **Chicora (USA)**[26] 1302 3-8-8 0....................................... RobertHavlin 8 66
(J H M Gosden) *t.k.h: chsd ldrs: rdn and unable qckn 2f out: styd on again ins fnl f: wnt 3rd last strides* **6/1**[3]

64- **4** *hd* **Zulu Moon**[197] 7023 3-8-13 0.. WilliamBuick 5 71
(A M Balding) *sn led: rdn and hdd jst over 2f out: outpcd by wnr over 1f out: kpt on: lost 2 pls nr fin* **12/1**

0 **5** *1 1/4* **Illusive Spirit (IRE)**[26] 1297 3-8-13 0........................... JimmyFortune 7 68
(J H M Gosden) *s.i.s: towards rr: hdwy into midfield 4f out: rdn jst over 2f out kpt on steadily fnl f: nvr nr wnr* **7/1**

5 **6** *nk* **Some Sunny Day**[14] 1585 3-8-8 0...................................... TravisBlock 4 62
(H Morrison) *chsd ldrs: rdn over 2f out: 3rd and outpcd over 1f out: kpt on same pce: lost 3 pls wl ins fnl f* **33/1**

60 **7** *3 3/4* **The Last Don (IRE)**[14] 1585 3-8-13 0................................ TedDurcan 12 59+
(D R Lanigan) *racd wd: a towards rr: c v wd bnd 2f out: nvr nr ldrs* **80/1**

8 *shd* **Twist Again (IRE)** 3-8-8 0.. JimmyQuinn 3 54
(P Howling) *s.i.s: hld up bhd: sme hdwy over 1f out: nvr nr ldrs* **66/1**

9 *3 1/2* **Any Given Moment (IRE)** 3-8-13 0.................................... LPKeniry 1 51
(D M Simcock) *s.i.s: hld up bhd: rdn and struggling 3f out* **66/1**

10 *2* **Cyber Space** 5-9-7 0.. NicolPolli[(5)] 2 49
(B J McMath) *s.i.s: sn in tch in midfield: rdn and struggling over 2f out* **100/1**

06 **11** *1 1/2* **Poca A Poca (IRE)**[8] 1745 5-9-2 0................................ MarkFlynn[(5)] 11 40
(G C Bravery) *chsd ldrs tl rdn and wknd qckly over 2f out* **100/1**

1m 39.47s (1.27) **Going Correction** +0.125s/f (Slow)

WFA 3 from 5yo 13lb **11** Ran SP% **121.4**

Speed ratings (Par 103): **98,94,94,94,93 92,89,88,85,83 81**

toteswinger: 1&2 £1.50, 1&3 £2.20, 2&3 £3.60 CSF £3.92 TOTE £1.70: £1.10, £1.20, £1.70; EX 5.30.

Owner Mrs Susan Roy **Bred** Mrs S M Roy **Trained** Newmarket, Suffolk

FOCUS

A race lacking strength in depth and just an ordinary gallop but a decisive winner, who raced in the centre in the straight, and may be capable of better. There is some doubt about how solid this form is, with the third to fifth the best guides.

1964 PHIL & DEBBY DICKMAN 30TH WEDDING ANNIVERSARY H'CAP 1m (P)

6:50 (6:50) (Class 4) (0-80,80) 4-Y-O+ **£4,857** (£1,445; £722; £360) **Stalls** High

Form RPR

1110 **1** **More Time Tim (IRE)**[70] 747 4-9-2 78............................... TPQueally 7 89+
(J R Boyle) *chsd ldr for 2f: styd handy: chsd ldr again over 3f out: rdn to ld jst over 2f out: drvn and kpt on wl fnl f: nt trble ldrs* **14/1**

0-04 **2** *1 1/2* **Fiefdom (IRE)**[8] 1723 7-8-11 73.................................. PatrickMathers 5 80
(I W McInnes) *hld up in tch in midfield: rdn and effrt 2f out: chsd wnr 1f out: kpt on same pce u.p* **14/1**

6-26 **3** *1 3/4* **Astrodonna**[12] 1633 4-8-8 70... RyanMoore 3 73
(M H Tompkins) *hld up bhd: hdwy 2f out: drvn to chse ldng trio 1f out: kpt on to go 3rd last stride: nvr nr ldng pair* **15/2**[3]

1-2 **4** *shd* **The Galloping Shoe**[36] 1149 4-9-4 80............................. SebSanders 8 83+
(J Noseda) *in rr: hdwy over 3f out: chsd ldrs jst over 2f out: rdn and outpcd 2f out: kpt on again fnl f* **8/11**[1]

35-2 **5** *1/2* **Barricado (FR)**[7] 1766 4-8-10 72.................................. ChrisCatlin 4 74
(E J O'Neill) *in tch: hdwy to ld after 2f: rdn and hdd jst over 2f out: wknd ins fnl f: lost 2 pls towards fin* **9/2**[2]

44-0 **6** *1 1/4* **La Coveta (IRE)**[22] 1405 4-9-2 78.................................. JimmyFortune 1 77
(B J Meehan) *s.i.s: sn chsng ldrs: rdn and lost pl 3f out: kpt on again fnl f* **12/1**

60-4 **7** *1* **Justcallmehandsome**[26] 1316 7-8-6 75.........................(v) BillyCray[(7)] 2 72
(D J S Ffrench Davis) *bhd: hdwy on outer 3f out: no prog fnl 2f* **25/1**

-305 **8** *9* **Fools Gold**[7] 1777 4-8-10 72... PaulEddery 6 48
(Paul Mason) *led for 2f: chsd ldr tl over 3f out: lost pl and rdn over 2f out: sn bhd* **66/1**

1m 37.51s (-0.69) **Going Correction** +0.125s/f (Slow) **8** Ran SP% **114.2**

Speed ratings (Par 105): **108,106,104,104,104 102,101,92**

toteswinger: 1&2 £13.30, 1&3 £6.70, 2&3 £11.10 CSF £185.80 CT £1591.88 TOTE £16.50: £2.70, £3.00, £2.20; EX 83.50.

Owner M Khan X2 **Bred** Glending Bloodstock **Trained** Epsom, Surrey

■ Stewards' Enquiry : Paul Eddery one-day ban: used whip with excessive frequency (May 26)

FOCUS

A fair handicap but, with the market leader disappointing, it did not take as much winning as seemed likely. The gallop was an ordinary one and the winner raced in the centre in the straight, while the second sets the standard.

La Coveta(IRE) Official explanation: jockey said filly hung right turning for home

1965 AVOCET FILLIES' H'CAP 6f (P)

7:20 (7:21) (Class 4) (0-85,85) 3-Y-O+ **£4,857** (£1,445; £722; £360) **Stalls** Low

Form RPR

2064 **1** **Artistic License (IRE)**[5] 1806 4-10-0 81......................... TonyCulhane 5 94
(M R Channon) *sn niggled along and outpcd in rr: hdwy to chse ldrs 3f out: hdwy between horses to ld ent fnl f: sn clr* **15/2**

01-6 **2** *3 3/4* **Cut The Cackle (IRE)**[18] 1486 3-9-6 83.......................... JimCrowley 2 81
(P Winkworth) *chsd ldr: rdn and ev ch 2f out: led over 1f out: sn hdd: no ch w wnr fnl f* **9/2**

02-1 **3** *3/4* **Lemon N Sugar (USA)**[128] 36 4-9-2 69........................... ShaneKelly 1 68+
(J Noseda) *hld up in tch: nt clr run inner fr 2f out: lost pl and swtchd rt jst over 1f out: kpt on to go 3rd ins fnl f: no ch w wnr* **5/2**[1]

0-34 **4** *1 1/2* **Happy Forever (FR)**[22] 1414 3-8-11 74......................... DarryllHolland 3 65
(M Botti) *sn led: hrd pressed and rdn 2f out: hdd over 1f out: wknd ins fnl f* **11/4**[2]

660- **5** *1 1/2* **Requisite**[214] 6623 4-9-8 75.. NCallan 7 64
(I A Wood) *chsd ldng pair: rdn and effrt over 2f out: ev ch 2f out tl 1f out: wknd fnl f* **20/1**

515- **6** *2 1/2* **Rioliina (IRE)**[232] 6172 3-9-8 85... RyanMoore 6 63
(J G Portman) *sn outpcd in last pl: nvr on terms* **4/1**[3]

1m 11.5s (-0.40) **Going Correction** +0.125s/f (Slow)

WFA 3 from 4yo 10lb **6** Ran SP% **109.9**

Speed ratings (Par 102): **107,102,101,99,97 93**

toteswinger: 1&2 £4.00, 1&3 £3.20, 2&3 £3.60 CSF £38.46 TOTE £7.70: £2.60, £2.30; EX 24.10.

Owner Wood Street Syndicate IV **Bred** Mountarmstrong Stud **Trained** West Ilsley, Berks

FOCUS

Not the strongest of races for the money on offer but the gallop was sound. Tthe winner raced towards the far rail in the straight and recorded a personal best but there are doubts over what else ran its race.

Rioliina(IRE) Official explanation: jockey said filly resented the kickback

1966 HAWFINCH H'CAP 1m 5f (P)

7:50 (7:50) (Class 4) (0-80,80) 4-Y-O+ **£4,857** (£1,445; £722; £360) **Stalls** Low

Form RPR

6043 **1** **Art Man**[23] 1382 6-9-5 78... RyanMoore 10 84
(G L Moore) *stdd and dropped in bhd after s: hld up in last trio: rdn and hdwy over 1f out: str run u.p to ld towards fin* **5/1**[3]

5100 **2** *nk* **Bassinet (USA)**[25] 1319 5-9-3 76....................................... JimCrowley 8 82
(J A R Toller) *stdd and dropped in bhd after s: hld up in last pl: hdwy on outer over 1f out: r.o strly fnl f to go 2nd wl ins fnl f: hld nr fin* **20/1**

04-3 **3** *3/4* **Valvigneres (IRE)**[27] 1287 4-8-12 71........................ StephenDonohoe 5 76
(E A L Dunlop) *hld up in tch: pushed along and hdwy over 3f out: rdn and ev ch 2f out: drvn to ld over 1f out: hdd ins fnl f: no ex towards fin* **6/1**

11 **4** *shd* **Manshoor (IRE)**[23] 1382 4-9-7 80................................... WilliamBuick 9 85
(Mrs L Wadham) *hld up in midfield: hdwy 3f out: rdn to chse ldng pair 2f out: drvn and ev ch over 1f out: led narrowly ins fnl f: hdd and no ex towards fin* **9/4**[1]

004- **5** *1/2* **Jadalee (IRE)**[222] 6424 6-9-3 76.. NCallan 7 80
(G A Butler) *taken down early: stdd and dropped in bhd after s: t.k.h: hld up in rr: hdwy over 2f out: rdn over 1f out: r.o fnl f: nt quite rch ldrs* **3/1**[2]

00-2 **6** *2 1/2* **Invention (USA)**[14] 1581 6-8-6 65.............................(t) ChrisCatlin 2 65
(Miss E C Lavelle) *led: rdn and hrd pressed 2f out: hdd over 1f out: wknd ins fnl f* **16/1**

1255 **7** *1 1/4* **William's Way**[15] 1571 7-8-9 68 ow1.................................. SebSanders 6 66
(I A Wood) *hld up towards rr: shuffled bk and last over 2f out: swtchd rt wl over 1f out: nvr trbld ldrs* **14/1**

624- **8** *3/4* **Bushy Dell (IRE)**[160] 7539 4-8-7 73......................... MatthewCosham[(7)] 3 70
(Miss J Feilden) *chsd ldr tl 7f out: styd chsng ldrs tl rdn and wknd over 1f out* **33/1**

3344 **9** *nk* **Ruff Diamond (USA)**[12] 1635 4-8-13 72...................(p) JimmyFortune 4 69
(J S Moore) *chsd ldrs tl wnt 2nd 7f out tl over 2f out: wknd wl over 1f out* **12/1**

3640 **10** *15* **Apache Fort**[27] 1287 6-8-4 63...(b) NickyMackay 1 37
(T Keddy) *hld up in tch: rdn whn n.m.r and lost pl wl over 1f out: no ch after: eased ins fnl f* **25/1**

2m 45.99s (-0.01) **Going Correction** +0.125s/f (Slow) **10** Ran SP% **118.5**

Speed ratings (Par 105): **105,104,104,104,103 102,101,101,101,91**

toteswinger: 1&2 £12.20, 1&3 £5.70, 2&3 £24.10 CSF £102.19 CT £619.32 TOTE £5.50: £1.60, £4.70, £2.50; EX 65.00.

Owner Matthew Green **Bred** Lady Lonsdale **Trained** Lower Beeding, W Sussex

FOCUS

Not many progressive sorts in another fair handicap in which the gallop was a moderate one and several finished in a heap. The winner raced in the centre in the straight and the form looks sound.

Apache Fort Official explanation: jockey said gelding had no more to give

1967 CROSSBILL CLASSIFIED STKS 1m 2f (P)

8:20 (8:21) (Class 6) 3-Y-O+ **£1,942** (£578; £288; £144) **Stalls** Low

Form RPR

3133 **1** **Dark Ranger**[14] 1594 3-8-6 55.. RobertHavlin 10 57+
(T J Pitt) *hld up towards rr: gd hdwy over 2f out: led ent fnl f: sn clr: r.o strly* **5/2**[1]

50-4 **2** *3 1/4* **On Cue (IRE)**[19] 1481 3-8-6 53................................... KirstyMilczarek 12 50
(J M P Eustace) *t.k.h: chsd ldrs: rdn and clsd on ldr 2f out: led over 1f out: sn hdd: nt pce of wnr fnl f: kpt on to hold 2nd* **8/1**

00-0 **3** *1 ¼* **Arlene Phillips**[10] 1671 3-8-6 55 .... JimmyQuinn 9 48
(R Hannon) *t.k.h: hld up in tch: rdn and unable qck jst over 2f out: edgd rt u.p 1f out: styd on fnl f to go 3rd towards fin* **10/1**

0-60 **4** *nk* **Wightgold**[21] 1420 3-8-1 45 .... SophieDoyle(5) 1 47
(H J L Dunlop) *led tl 7f out: chsd clr ldr after: rdn and clsd 2f out: ev ch over 1f out: outpcd fnl f: lost 3rd towards fin* **66/1**

00-1 **5** *nk* **Blessing Belle (IRE)**[9] 1691 3-8-12 45 .... RyanMoore 4 52+
(M H Tompkins) *hld up in midfield: lost pl and towards rr over 3f out: c wd bnd 2f out: r.o wl u.p fnl f: nvr trbld ldrs* **4/1[3]**

5-33 **6** *nse* **Crystal Feather**[19] 1476 3-8-6 53 .... LPKeniry 11 46+
(E F Vaughan) *stdd s: t.k.h: hld up wl bhd: stl plenty to do wl over 1f out: r.o wl fnl f: nt rch ldrs* **12/1**

0-00 **7** *nk* **Guilin (IRE)**[36] 1148 3-8-6 52 .... (b) ChrisCatlin 3 46
(P F I Cole) *prom in main gp: rdn over 2f out: chsd ldrs and drvn over 1f out: one pce after* **33/1**

0-00 **8** *¾* **Red Dagger (IRE)**[20] 1461 3-8-1 40 .... AmyBaker(5) 14 44
(T D McCarthy) *hld up bhd: c wd and hdwy over 1f out: styd on: nvr trbld ldrs* **66/1**

00-3 **9** *1* **Primo Dilettante**[5] 1811 3-8-6 55 .... ShaneKelly 5 42+
(W J Knight) *hld up bhd: hdwy towards inner over 2f out: nt clr run over 1f out: swtchd rt 1f out: nvr able to chal* **7/2[2]**

0-00 **10** *hd* **Bari Bay**[29] 1250 3-8-6 50 .... (p) RichardKingscote 2 42
(R M Beckett) *in tch in main gp: rdn and struggling over 2f out: no ch fr over 1f out* **20/1**

0-40 **11** *shd* **Bright Wire (IRE)**[21] 1420 3-8-6 48 .... NeilPollard 7 42
(M Madgwick) *hld up towards rr: c v wd bnd 2f out: styd on but nvr trbld ldrs* **66/1**

-040 **12** *3 ¼* **Rubbinghousedotcom (IRE)**[5] 1811 3-8-6 51 .... (b[1]) DO'Donohoe 8 35
(P M Phelan) *stdd after s: t.k.h: hdwy on outer to ld 7f out: sn clr: stl clr 2f out: sn rdn and tiring: hdd over 1f out: sn wknd* **25/1**

4000 **13** *10* **Aegean Rose**[20] 1463 4-9-7 50 .... NCallan 13 15
(M Blanshard) *racd wd: racd in midfield: hdwy to go prom in main gp over 2f out: wkng whn sltly hmpd ent fnl f* **50/1**

500- **14** *dist* **Trireme (IRE)**[262] 5262 5-9-7 49 .... TPQueally 6 —
(K A Morgan) *t.k.h: hld up in midfield: dropped to rr and rdn over 4f out: lost tch rapidly over 3f out: virtually p.u fnl 2f* **16/1**

2m 8.91s (2.31) **Going Correction** +0.125s/f (Slow)
WFA 3 from 4yo+ 15lb 14 Ran SP% **122.6**
Speed ratings (Par 101): **95,92,91,91,90 90,90,90,89,89 89,86,78,—**
toteswinger: 1&2 £5.30, 1&3 £10.70, 2&3 £23.90 CSF £22.58 TOTE £3.80: £1.60, £3.70, £3.30; EX 28.20 Place 6 £375.77, Place 5 £224.89..
Owner Recycled Products Limited **Bred** Thomas G N Burrage **Trained** Norton, N Yorks

FOCUS
A modest event in which an ordinary pace increased around halfway. The winner, who edged towards the far side late on, made his ground in the centre but did not have to improve to score, and the form looks weak.
Primo Dilettante Official explanation: jockey said gelding had been denied a clear run
Trireme(IRE) Official explanation: vet said gelding bled
T/Plt: £289.30 to a £1 stake. Pool: £54,968.30. 138.70 winning tickets. T/Qpdt: £104.60 to a £1 stake. Pool: £4,942.08. 34.95 winning tickets. SP

1890 WARWICK (L-H)
Tuesday, May 12

OFFICIAL GOING: Good to firm changing to firm (good to firm in places) after race 1(2.20)
Wind: Fresh against Weather: Fine and sunny

1968 WEATHERBYS BANK EBF MAIDEN FILLIES' STKS — 5f 110y
2:20 (2:21) (Class 5) 2-Y-O **£3,885** (£1,156; £577; £288) **Stalls** Low

Form RPR

0 **1** **Quaker Parrot**[14] 1577 2-9-0 0 .... RichardKingscote 9 71
(Tom Dascombe) *s.i.s: sn chsng ldrs: led 3f out: rdn: hung rt and hdd over 1f out: rallied to ld ins fnl f: r.o* **9/1**

2 *¾* **Baileys Vision** 2-9-0 0 .... RoystonFfrench 4 69
(M Johnston) *broke wl sn lost pl: hdwy 1/2-way: rdn and edgd lft over 1f out: hung rt ins fnl f: r.o* **16/1**

3 **3** *hd* **Deal (IRE)**[8] 1749 2-9-0 0 .... RichardHughes 1 68
(R Hannon) *edgd rt s: chsd ldrs: rdn to ld and hung rt over 1f out: hdd ins fnl f: styd on* **15/8[2]**

02 **4** *nse* **Angel Of Fashion (IRE)**[8] 1742 2-9-0 0 .... MichaelHills 3 68
(B W Hills) *trckd ldrs: racd keenly: nt clr run and lost pl over 2f out: hdwy over 1f out: sn rdn and hung rt: styd on* **13/8[1]**

5 *5* **Gulf Punch** 2-8-11 0 .... PatrickHills(3) 5 51
(R Hannon) *hld up: pushed along 1/2-way: nvr trbld ldrs* **33/1**

6 *¾* **Acting Elegant** 2-9-0 0 .... CatherineGannon 2 49
(P D Evans) *dwlt: outpcd: nvr nrr* **50/1**

3 **7** *1* **Forget (IRE)**[11] 1637 2-9-0 0 .... RyanMoore 6 45+
(C E Brittain) *chsd ldrs: rdn whn n.m.r over 1f out: sn wknd* **11/2[3]**

8 *4 ½* **The Two G'S** 2-9-0 0 .... JohnEgan 7 31+
(P D Evans) *sn led: hdd 3f out: rdn and wknd wl over 1f out: eased* **33/1**

68.56 secs (2.66) **Going Correction** +0.25s/f (Good) 8 Ran SP% **112.0**
Speed ratings (Par 90): **92,91,90,90,84 83,81,75**
toteswinger: 1&2 £11.90, 1&3 £7.30, 2&3 £4.40 CSF £125.56 TOTE £11.20: £2.60, £3.10, £1.30; EX 256.60.
Owner Timeform Betfair Racing Club Partnership **Bred** Mrs D Du Feu And Trickledown Stud **Trained** Lambourn, Berks

FOCUS
An average juvenile fillies' maiden.

NOTEBOOK
Quaker Parrot proved game in getting her head in front at the business end and opened her account at the second time of asking. She had needed the run on debut a fortnight previously, but was much more professional here despite another tardy start and acted without fuss on the quicker surface. In time she ought to get another furlong and there could still be improvement to come, but things will be tougher from now on. (op 14-1 tchd 18-1)
Baileys Vision ran a big debut race considering she played up in the preliminaries. She looked to need all of the trip and ought to learn a deal for the experience, so should prove hard to beat next time. (op 12-1)
Deal(IRE) made her move 2f out and kept to her task under pressure. This was an improvement on her debut and there ought to be a small race in her before long. (op 2-1 tchd 13-8)
Angel Of Fashion(IRE) was the most experienced in the field, but still showed definite signs of greenness and met a little trouble 2f out. She was not beaten at all far and sets the standard, but already looks in need of a stiffer test. (op 9-4)

1969 BENTLEY HOUSE LTD H'CAP — 6f
2:50 (2:53) (Class 6) (0-65,65) 3-Y-O **£2,047** (£604; £302) **Stalls** Low

Form RPR

0060 **1** **Bold Ring**[7] 1772 3-8-6 53 .... CatherineGannon 4 61
(E J Creighton) *hld up: rdn over out: hdwy over 1f out: r.o to ld wl ins fnl f* **80/1**

04-0 **2** *¾* **Corton Charlemagne (IRE)**[14] 1588 3-8-13 60 .... RyanMoore 3 66
(Rae Guest) *w ldr tl led 4f out: rdn and hung rt over 1f out: hdd wl ins fnl f* **10/3[1]**

45-0 **3** *1 ¼* **Hand Painted**[111] 229 3-9-4 65 .... TravisBlock 13 67
(P J Makin) *chsd ldrs: rdn over 2f out: edgd rt over 1f out: styd on same pce ins fnl f* **11/1**

3450 **4** *1* **Volito**[14] 1583 3-9-1 62 .... RichardKingscote 1 61
(Jonjo O'Neill) *chsd ldrs: rdn and hung rt over 1f out: styd on same pce* **20/1**

6-32 **5** *1 ¼* **Captain Kallis (IRE)**[7] 1772 3-8-11 58 .... FrankieMcDonald 5 53+
(D J S Ffrench Davis) *trckd ldrs: plld hrd: nt clr run and lost pl 1/2-way: hdwy over 1f out: no imp ins fnl f* **5/1[3]**

260- **6** *1 ¾* **Green Poppy**[232] 6172 3-9-3 64 .... RichardHughes 2 53
(Eve Johnson Houghton) *slipped s: hld up: racd keenly: hdwy over 1f out: edgd rt and wknd ins fnl f* **4/1[2]**

-442 **7** *½* **Minturno (USA)**[12] 1625 3-9-2 63 .... DO'Donohoe 8 51
(Mrs A Duffield) *prom: lost pl after 1f: hdwy over 2f out: rdn over 1f out: wkng whn nt clr run ins fnl f* **14/1**

5-53 **8** *¾* **Lucky Buddha**[8] 1736 3-8-11 58 .... PatCosgrave 12 43
(Jedd O'Keeffe) *led 2f: chsd ldrs: rdn over 2f out: wknd fnl f* **11/1**

-323 **9** *1 ¾* **Vamos (IRE)**[14] 1583 3-8-13 60 .... ChrisCatlin 6 40+
(J R Gask) *prom: nt clr run and lost pl 4f out: n.d after* **6/1**

45-0 **10** *11* **Transcentral**[17] 1529 3-9-1 62 .... GrahamGibbons 14 6
(W M Brisbourne) *chsd ldrs tl rdn and wknd over 1f out* **33/1**

4-40 **11** *½* **Handcuff**[14] 1583 3-8-8 55 .... (v[1]) AlanMunro 15 —
(J Gallagher) *s.s: outpcd* **66/1**

0312 **12** *68* **Pipers Piping (IRE)**[15] 1567 3-9-4 65 .... ShaneKelly 11 —
(J A Osborne) *hld up: wknd 4f out: eased* **12/1**

1m 13.61s (1.81) **Going Correction** +0.25s/f (Good) 12 Ran SP% **115.5**
Speed ratings (Par 97): **97,96,94,93,91 89,88,87,85,70 69,—**
toteswinger: 1&2 £48.40, 1&3 £70.60, 2&3 £10.10 CSF £322.94 CT £3294.47 TOTE £67.00: £8.20, £1.80, £4.70; EX 454.40.
Owner Daniel Creighton **Bred** J A Pickering & T Pears **Trained** Mill Hill, London NW7

FOCUS
A moderate handicap, run at a fair pace and, as with the preceding maiden, the far side was shunned down the home straight. The form is ordinary rated around the placed horses.
Captain Kallis(IRE) Official explanation: jockey said gelding was unsuited by the firm (good to firm in places) ground
Green Poppy Official explanation: jockey said filly hung right
Vamos(IRE) Official explanation: jockey said gelding was unsuited by the firm (good to firm in places) ground
Pipers Piping(IRE) Official explanation: jockey said, regarding running and riding, that his orders were to ride the colt as he found him, as he had ridden it on its previous three starts on the all-weather and it being heavy and thickset, was unable to go the pace, was not letting itself down and hating the firm ground, in the interest of its welfare he decided to ease down.

1970 HASLEHURSTS CHARTERED ACCOUNTANTS H'CAP — 5f
3:20 (3:22) (Class 5) (0-70,70) 4-Y-O+ **£3,070** (£906; £453) **Stalls** Low

Form RPR

20-0 **1** **Sands Crooner (IRE)**[131] 2 6-8-13 62 .... (v) PatCosgrave 4 79
(J G Given) *hld up: hdwy 1/2-way: led ins fnl f: shkn up and sn clr* **14/1**

5-44 **2** *3 ¾* **Make My Dream**[21] 1418 6-9-7 70 .... AlanMunro 11 73
(J Gallagher) *hld up: hdwy over 1f out: r.o to go 2nd nr fin: no ch w wnr* **8/1**

3040 **3** *nse* **Ask Jenny (IRE)**[24] 1360 7-8-7 56 .... SaleemGolam 15 59
(Patrick Morris) *s.i.s: hld up: hdwy over 1f out: rdn and ev ch ins fnl f: styd on same pce* **28/1**

0063 **4** *½* **Fizzlephut (IRE)**[3] 1890 7-8-7 56 .... PaulFitzsimons 1 57
(Miss J R Tooth) *w ldrs: led 3f out: rdn and edgd rt over 1f out: hung lft and hdd ins fnl f: no ex* **6/1[2]**

0254 **5** *1* **Sherjawy (IRE)**[8] 1748 5-8-6 55 ow1 .... (b) SamHitchcott 2 53
(Miss Z C Davison) *s.i.s: sn pushed along in rr: r.o ins fnl f: nvr nrr* **25/1**

0-05 **6** *nk* **Minimum Fuss (IRE)**[19] 1477 5-7-11 53 oh6 ow2 AndrewHeffernan(7) 10 50
(M C Chapman) *hld up: hdwy over 1f out: rdn and hung lft ins fnl f: nt rch ldrs* **100/1**

1-00 **7** *hd* **Helping Hand (IRE)**[117] 177 4-8-3 57 .... AndreaAtzeni(5) 14 53
(R Hollinshead) *plld hrd and prom: rdn whn rdr dropped whip over 1f out: styd on same pce* **25/1**

060- **8** *¾* **Monsieur Reynard**[153] 7621 4-9-0 63 .... AdamKirby 9 56
(J M Bradley) *hld up: plld hrd: hdwy over 1f out: hung rt and wknd ins fnl f* **25/1**

60-6 **9** *¾* **Lunces Lad (IRE)**[8] 1748 5-9-0 70 .... LeeNewnes(7) 7 60
(G Brown) *sn pushed along in rr: hdwy 1f out: wknd towards fin* **40/1**

00-0 **10** *1 ½* **Mr Funshine**[7] 1775 4-7-11 51 oh3 .... Louis-PhilippeBeuzelin(5) 5 36
(R J Hodges) *chsd ldrs: rdn over 1f out: wknd ins fnl f* **40/1**

00-0 **11** *1 ½* **Dalarossie**[17] 1518 4-8-11 60 .... DavidAllan 6 40
(E J Alston) *unruly in stalls: chsd ldrs: rdn over 1f out: wknd fnl f* **8/1**

0-11 **12** *1 ¾* **The Magic Blanket (IRE)**[48] 956 4-9-3 66 .... MickyFenton 17 39
(Stef Liddiard) *prom: rdn over 1f out: wknd fnl f* **8/1**

4320 **13** *½* **Affirmatively**[38] 1134 4-8-2 51 oh5 .... CatherineGannon 16 23
(A W Carroll) *s.i.s and hmpd s: a in rr* **33/1**

5036 **14** *2* **Bollin Franny**[41] 1076 5-8-2 51 .... RichardThomas 3 15
(J E Long) *chsd ldrs tl rdn and wknd over 1f out* **14/1**

1114 **15** *2* **What Katie Did (IRE)**[21] 1425 4-9-6 69 .... (p) RyanMoore 12 26
(J M Bradley) *led 2f: rdn and wknd over 1f out* **13/2[3]**

0005 **16** *¾* **Dancing Rhythm**[9] 1704 4-8-2 51 oh1 .... ChrisCatlin 8 5
(M S Saunders) *hld up: n.d* **5/1[1]**

5214 **17** *1* **Ten Down**[36] 1150 4-9-6 69 .... ShaneKelly 13 20
(M Quinn) *w ldrs to 1/2-way: wknd over 1f out* **11/1**

61.06 secs (1.46) **Going Correction** +0.25s/f (Good) 17 Ran SP% **123.1**
Speed ratings (Par 103): **98,92,91,91,89 89,88,87,86,83 81,78,77,74,71 70,68**
toteswinger: 1&2 £28.80, 1&3 £89.70, 2&3 £63.10 CSF £112.65 CT £3217.34 TOTE £19.70: £3.60, £2.40, £5.30, £2.70; EX 177.00.
Owner Danethorpe Racing Partnership **Bred** Peter Molony **Trained** Willoughton, Lincs

FOCUS
An open sprint, run at a solid pace and the placed horses were close to recent marks, although the proximity of the sixth raises doubts.
The Magic Blanket(IRE) Official explanation: jockey said gelding was unsuited by the firm (good to firm in places) ground

1971 STAVERTON WEALTH MANAGEMENT LTD H'CAP 1m 22y
3:50 (3:53) (Class 4) (0-85,83) 3-Y-O **£6,476** (£1,927; £963; £481) **Stalls** Low

Form RPR
26-1 **1** **Mister Dee Bee (IRE)**[26] 1308 3-9-0 **79** MichaelHills 5 85
(B W Hills) *chsd ldr 7f out: led 2f out: rdn out* **5/2**[2]
1225 **2** *1 1/4* **Gaily Noble (IRE)**[10] 1679 3-9-4 **83** SteveDrowne 2 86
(A B Haynes) *a.p: rdn to chse wnr and edgd lft over 1f out: styd on* **7/2**[3]
1-03 **3** *2* **Yellow Printer**[7] 1774 3-8-13 **78** (v[1]) RichardKingscote 3 77
(Tom Dascombe) *led: edgd lft 7f out: rdn and hdd 2f out: styng on same pce whn hung rt towards fin* **9/4**[1]
106- **4** *1 1/4* **Inheritor (IRE)**[217] 6549 3-9-0 **79** RoystonFfrench 1 75
(B Smart) *chsd ldr tl hmpd 7f out: remained handy: rdn over 3f out: no ex fnl f* **11/2**
1-50 **5** *2 1/4* **Geneva Geyser (GER)**[15] 1559 3-8-10 **75** (b[1]) MickyFenton 4 66
(J M P Eustace) *pushed along early: hld up and racd keenly sn after: rdn and hung lft over 2f out: n.d* **25/1**
0-40 **6** *1/2* **Roly Boy**[8] 1751 3-9-4 **83** (b[1]) RichardHughes 6 73
(R Hannon) *hld up: rdn over 1f out: sn hung lft and nt run on* **8/1**
1m 38.65s (-2.35) **Going Correction** -0.20s/f (Firm) **6** Ran SP% **111.9**
Speed ratings (Par 101): **103,101,99,98,96 95**
toteswinger: 1&2 £2.40, 1&3 £2.20, 2&3 £2.10 CSF £11.56 CT £20.76 TOTE £2.40: £1.70, £2.70; EX 12.90.
Owner South Bank Thoroughbred Racing **Bred** Denis McDonnell **Trained** Lambourn, Berks
■ Stewards' Enquiry : Richard Kingscote one-day ban: careless riding (May 26)
FOCUS
This was weakened by non-runners, but the form still looks sound enough.

1972 PREMIER PENSIONS ACTUARIES LTD MAIDEN STKS 7f 26y
4:20 (4:23) (Class 5) 3-Y-O+ **£3,070** (£906; £453) **Stalls** Low

Form RPR
42-2 **1** **Standpoint**[22] 1400 3-9-0 73 RyanMoore 11 71
(Sir Michael Stoute) *trckd ldrs: rdn to ld wl over 1f out: edgd lft ins fnl f: r.o wl* **11/4**[2]
2-54 **2** *3 1/2* **Doc Jones (IRE)**[4] 1840 3-8-9 0 RichardEvans[(5)] 6 61+
(P D Evans) *stdd s: hld up: swtchd rt over 1f out: rdn: hung lft and r.o ins fnl f: wnt 2nd post: no ch w wnr* **14/1**[3]
3 *nse* **Falcon Rock (IRE)**[173] 4-9-12 0 PatDobbs 8 65+
(S A Callaghan) *s.i.s: hld up: hdwy over 1f out: r.o* **20/1**
326- **4** *nse* **Roman Glory (IRE)**[199] 6973 3-9-0 95 JamieSpencer 7 61
(B J Meehan) *sn w ldr: led 2f out: sn rdn: hdd and edgd rt: hung lft and no ex ins fnl f: lost 2nd post* **4/9**[1]
00-5 **5** *4* **Just Oscar (GER)**[47] 963 5-9-12 48 JohnEgan 4 54
(W M Brisbourne) *prom: rdn over 1f out: wknd fnl f* **100/1**
6 *1/2* **Bertie's Birthday (IRE)** 3-8-9 0 SteveDrowne 1 44
(Jonjo O'Neill) *s.s: hld up: plld hrd: hdwy over 2f out: wknd fnl f* **28/1**
0 **7** *1/2* **Paul's Pet**[11] 1638 4-9-12 0 TGMcLaughlin 5 51
(Karen George) *s.i.s: plld hrd and hdwy 5f out: rdn over 2f out: wkng whn hmpd ins fnl f* **150/1**
30 **8** *2* **Love In The Park**[41] 1066 4-9-7 0 RoystonFfrench 2 41
(R Brotherton) *mid-div: rdn over 2f out: wknd over 1f out* **66/1**
0030 **9** *1* **Plaka (FR)**[8] 1741 4-9-7 49 GrahamGibbons 9 38
(W M Brisbourne) *led tl rdn and hdd 2f out: wkng whn hung lft fnl f* **125/1**
0 **10** *7* **Nouailhas**[22] 1410 3-8-11 0 RussellKennemore[(3)] 3 20
(R Hollinshead) *hld up: racd keenly: wknd 2f out* **100/1**
1m 24.37s (-0.23) **Going Correction** -0.20s/f (Firm)
WFA 3 from 4yo+ 12lb **10** Ran SP% **115.7**
Speed ratings (Par 103): **93,89,88,88,84 83,83,80,79,71**
toteswinger: 1&2 £2.00, 1&3 £3.00, 2&3 £4.10 CSF £35.70 TOTE £3.20: £1.70, £3.70, £5.00; EX 27.50.
Owner K Abdulla **Bred** Juddmonte Farms Ltd **Trained** Newmarket, Suffolk
FOCUS
An average maiden. The winner won well. but the race was most notable for the flop of the odds-on favourite and the proximity of the very moderate fifth limits things..
Roman Glory(IRE) Official explanation: jockey said gelding was unsuited by the firm (good to firm in places) ground

1973 WEATHERBYS BLOODSTOCK INSURANCE FILLIES' H'CAP 7f 26y
4:50 (4:51) (Class 5) (0-70,69) 3-Y-O **£3,238** (£963; £361; £361) **Stalls** Low

Form RPR
2-22 **1** **Labisa (IRE)**[27] 1281 3-9-3 **68** SteveDrowne 14 76+
(H Morrison) *stdd and swtchd lft sn after s: bhd: hdwy 2f out: led over 1f out: sn rdn and hung rt: jst hld on* **6/1**[3]
3-13 **2** *hd* **Cheap Thrills**[104] 313 3-9-3 **68** ShaneKelly 3 75
(J A Osborne) *trckd ldrs: ev ch fr over 1f out: hrd rdn ins fnl f: r.o* **16/1**
1250 **3** *1* **Perfect Class**[33] 1196 3-8-12 **63** AdamKirby 2 67
(C G Cox) *chsd ldrs: led 2f out: rdn: hung rt and hdd over 1f out: styd on* **3/1**[1]
1652 **3** *dht* **Kheskianto (IRE)**[8] 1725 3-8-1 **59** AndrewHeffernan[(7)] 5 63
(M C Chapman) *dwlt: hld up: racd keenly: hdwy 2f out: sn rdn: running on whn hung lft and nt clr run wl ins fnl f: nt rch ldrs* **15/2**
00-3 **5** *2* **Russian Rave**[14] 1588 3-9-4 **69** PatCosgrave 4 68
(J G Portman) *chsd ldr: rdn and ev ch 2f out: sn hung rt: no ex fnl f* **4/1**[2]
4-40 **6** *4* **Feet Of Fury**[14] 1588 3-9-1 **66** JohnEgan 6 54
(W M Brisbourne) *hld up: hung rt fr over 3f out: sn rdn: n.d* **12/1**
006- **7** *3/4* **Dark Velvet (IRE)**[297] 4202 3-9-2 **67** DavidAllan 1 53
(E J Alston) *mid-div: lost pl over 3f out: n.d after* **8/1**
-045 **8** *1 3/4* **Nun Today (USA)**[18] 1492 3-7-13 **55** (v) Louis-PhilippeBeuzelin[(5)] 8 36
(Karen George) *mid-div: lost pl 5f out: in rr whn hmpd over 3f out: n.d after* **33/1**
40-5 **9** *1 1/4* **Our Day Will Come**[34] 1176 3-9-2 **67** RichardHughes 7 45
(R Hannon) *prom: rdn over 2f out: wknd over 1f out* **14/1**
6-06 **10** *2* **Deyas Dream**[20] 1461 3-8-9 **63** DavidProbert[(3)] 13 36
(A M Balding) *sn pushed along to ld: hung rt fr 3f out: hdd & wknd 2f out* **8/1**
1m 24.3s (-0.30) **Going Correction** -0.20s/f (Firm) **10** Ran SP% **116.5**
Speed ratings (Par 96): **93,92,91,91,89 84,83,81,80,78**
PL: Perfect Class £1.00 Kheskianto £1.20 TRI: Labisa/Cheap Thrills/PC £176.10, L/CT/K £373.51. toteswinger: 1&2 £28.80, L & PC £1.90, L& K £1.80, L & CT £8.90, CT & PC £8.90, CT&K £8.20 CSF £96.50 TOTE £4.40: £1.20, £5.90; EX 86.80.
Owner Michael Kerr-Dineen **Bred** Illuminatus Investments **Trained** East Ilsley, Berks

FOCUS
A modest fillies' handicap, run at a decent pace and the form looks pretty solid.
Feet Of Fury Official explanation: jockey said filly was unsuited by the firm (good to firm in places) ground
Deyas Dream Official explanation: jockey said filly hung right

1974 G & G FINANCIAL SERVICES LTD H'CAP 1m 2f 188y
5:20 (5:20) (Class 6) (0-55,55) 4-Y-O+ **£2,047** (£604; £302) **Stalls** Low

Form RPR
5554 **1** **Coral Shores**[16] 1537 4-9-1 **54** (v) DavidAllan 7 67
(P W Hiatt) *sn chsng ldr: led over 6f out: rdn clr and hung lft fr over 1f out: eased wl ins fnl f* **7/2**[1]
/00- **2** *5* **Stateside (CAN)**[225] 6337 4-8-7 **46** oh1 SaleemGolam 3 50
(R A Fahey) *chsd ldrs: rdn over 2f out: styd on to go 2nd ins fnl f: no ch w wnr* **20/1**
00-0 **3** *1* **Dr McFab**[76] 679 5-8-11 **50** (p) RichardHughes 16 52
(Miss Tor Sturgis) *led: hdd over 6f out: rdn over 2f out: styd on same pce appr fnl f* **6/1**[3]
6101 **4** *1* **Barbirolli**[1] 1938 7-9-3 **50** 6ex JohnEgan 11 56
(W M Brisbourne) *prom: rdn over 2f out: no imp* **4/1**[2]
0453 **5** *3 1/4* **Jackie Kiely**[15] 1568 8-9-2 **55** (t) RoystonFfrench 9 50
(R Brotherton) *hld up: rdn over 2f out: n.d* **7/1**
34-0 **6** *2 3/4* **Oronsay**[16] 1538 4-8-10 **49** (t) TGMcLaughlin 10 39
(B R Millman) *s.i.s: hld up: plld hrd: rdn over 2f out: nvr nrr* **20/1**
0/40 **7** *1/2* **Irish Stream (USA)**[7] 1770 11-8-11 **50** (v) CatherineGannon 4 39
(B G Powell) *stmbld s: hld up: rdn over 3f out: n.d* **16/1**
000- **8** *3/4* **Goose Green (IRE)**[193] 7114 5-8-3 **47** ow1 MCGeran[(5)] 8 34
(R J Hodges) *hld up in tch: rdn over 3f out: wknd 2f out* **14/1**
00-5 **9** *2* **Bianca Capello**[107] 290 4-9-1 **54** AdamKirby 15 38
(J R Fanshawe) *broke wl: racd keenly: stdd and lost pl after 1f: dropped in rr over 6f out: rdn over 2f out: n.d* **7/1**
0-05 **10** *hd* **Naledi**[84] 581 5-8-0 **46** oh1 AndrewHeffernan[(7)] 14 29
(J R Norton) *plld hrd and prom: rdn and wknd 2f out* **66/1**
00-5 **11** *4* **Janshe Gold**[21] 1420 4-8-10 **49** TolleyDean 5 25
(J G Portman) *hld up: sme hdwy over 3f out: sn wknd* **20/1**
006 **12** *24* **Hill Of Lujain**[76] 682 5-8-9 **48** (p) StephenDonohoe 17 —
(Ian Williams) *plld hrd and prom: wknd over 3f out* **20/1**
0020 **P** **Magic Warrior**[8] 1728 9-8-0 **46** CharlesEddery[(7)] 6 —
(J C Fox) *s.s: hld up: plld hrd: bhd and rdn 7f out: t.o whn p.u and dismntd over 3f out* **16/1**
2m 18.59s (-2.51) **Going Correction** -0.20s/f (Firm) **13** Ran SP% **120.5**
Speed ratings (Par 101): **101,97,96,95,93 91,91,90,89,89 86,68,—**
toteswinger: 1&2 £34.20, 1&3 £7.20, 2&3 £31.60 CSF £81.54 CT £417.96 TOTE £4.00: £1.50, £9.30, £2.70; EX 112.30 Place 6: £171.64 Place 5: £77.65.
Owner P W Hiatt & Charlotte Bird **Bred** Cheveley Park Stud Ltd **Trained** Hook Norton, Oxon
FOCUS
This weak handicap appeared to be run at a strong early pace, but it proved hard to make up ground from behind.
Jackie Kiely Official explanation: jockey said gelding was unsuited by the firm (good to firm in places) ground
Bianca Capello Official explanation: jockey said filly hung left
Naledi Official explanation: jockey said gelding ran too freely and was unsuited by the firm (good to firm in places) ground
Magic Warrior Official explanation: jockey said gelding bled from the nose
T/Jkpt: Not won. T/Plt: £363.70 to a £1 stake. Pool: £66,673.43. 133.80 winning tickets. T/Qpdt: £17.40 to a £1 stake. Pool: £4,558.66. 193.10 winning tickets. CR

1975 - 1978a (Foreign Racing) - See Raceform Interactive

1657 SAINT-CLOUD (L-H)
Tuesday, May 12

OFFICIAL GOING: Heavy

1979a PRIX GREFFULHE (GROUP 2) (C&F) 1m 2f
2:20 (2:19) 3-Y-O **£71,942** (£27,767; £13,252; £8,835; £4,417)

RPR
1 **Cutlass Bay (UAE)**[43] 3-9-2 LDettori 7 114+
(A Fabre, France) *racd in 6th: hdwy on outside to go cl 4th ent st: led under 1 1/2f out: rdn and edgd lft ins fnl f: r.o wl* **7/5**[1]
2 *1/2* **Cavalryman**[44] 1028 3-9-2 JVictoire 6 113
(A Fabre, France) *racd in 4th: 3rd st: led briefly 1 1/2f out: sn hdd but kpt on wl* **7/5**[1]
3 *1 1/2* **Allybar (IRE)**[44] 1028 3-9-2 OPeslier 8 110
(C Laffon-Parias, France) *hld up in last: hdwy down outside fr 2f out: wnt 4th under 1 1/2f out: kpt on steadily to take 3rd fnl 100yds* **29/10**[2]
4 *nk* **Topclas (FR)**[19] 1483 3-9-2 SPasquier 5 109
(P Demercastel, France) *racd in 7th: wnt 3rd under 1 1/2f out: lost 3rd fnl 100yds* **42/10**[3]
5 *3* **Validor (FR)**[37] 1145 3-9-2 (b) GMosse 4 103
(H-A Pantall, France) *racd in 5th: 6th st: outpcd by ldrs fr 1 12/f out* **11/1**
6 *4* **Rolling Bag (FR)**[18] 3-9-2 CSoumillon 2 95
(M Roussel, France) *racd in 2nd: led briefly over 1 1/2f out: sn hdd & wknd* **69/10**
7 *1 1/2* **Wind Of Victory (FR)**[7] 3-9-2 DBonilla 1 92
(J E Hammond, France) *racd keenly in 3rd: 5th st: sn btn* **35/1**
8 *10* **Sokar (FR)**[30] 1239 3-9-2 MAndrouin 3 72
(J Boisnard, France) *set stdy pce to over 1 1/2f out: wknd qckly* **13/1**
2m 14.5s (-1.50) **Going Correction** +0.125s/f (Good) **8** Ran SP% **159.1**
Speed ratings: **111,110,109,109,106 103,102,94**
PARI-MUTUEL: WIN 2.40 (coupled with Cavalryman); PL 1.50, 3.10, 1.70;DF 9.20.
Owner Sheikh Mohammed **Bred** Darley Stud Management Co Ltd **Trained** Chantilly, France

NOTEBOOK
Cutlass Bay(UAE) was brought with a progressive run up the centre of the track and passed his stablemate inside the final furlong. He won with something in hand and considerable improvement can be expected. There are no plans for the moment but races like the Prix Eugene Adam at the end of July and the Prix Guillaume d'Ornano at the end of the following month could come into the reckoning.
Cavalryman went into the lead halfway up the straight and battled on well but was unable to hold his stablemate inside the final furlong. He has been entered in the Prix du Jockey Club and Grand Prix de Paris.
Allybar(IRE) was given quite a lot to do but ran on in the final stages. This was rather a disappointing effort as he was well fancied before the race. His pedigree suggests this distance might be a little long, particularly on testing ground.
Topclas(FR) ran below expectations. He appeared to be outpaced in the straight and then ran on again inside the final furlong.

[1782]**BATH** (L-H)

Wednesday, May 13

OFFICIAL GOING: Firm (10.9) (8.10 abandoned due to unsafe ground)

Wind: Brisk, across Weather: Dull

1980 FREEBETS.CO.UK FREE ONLINE BINGO MONEY H'CAP — 1m 3f 144y

6:10 (6:11) (Class 6) (0-65,65) 4-Y-0+ **£2,072** (£616; £308; £153) **Stalls** Low

Form RPR

2202 **1** **Terminate (GER)**[7] 1786 7-8-7 **54**............(t) TPO'Shea 13 60
(Ian Williams) *s.i.s: hld up in rr: stdy hdwy 3f out: chal ins fnl 2f: led ins fnl f: sn hrd drvn: hld on wl* **7/2**[1]

5462 **2** *1* **Piper's Song (IRE)**[9] 1738 6-9-3 **64**............ SJCraine 1 68
(Patrick Morris) *s.i.s: hld up in rr: gd hdwy on ins fr 3f out to ld jst ins fnl 2f: hdd ins fnl f: styd on u.p but no ex cl home* **8/1**

05-3 **3** *3/4* **Party Palace**[7] 1786 5-8-4 **51** oh6............ CatherineGannon 11 54
(H S Howe) *chsd ldrs: rdn fr over 3f out: kpt on thrght fnl f but nvr quite gng pce of ldng duo* **7/1**

0000 **4** *1/2* **Speagle (IRE)**[7] 1786 7-8-1 **51** oh4............ KellyHarrison(3) 2 53
(A J Chamberlain) *t.k.h: in tch: outpcd over 3f out: sn drvn: styd on again fr 2f out: kpt on ins fnl f but nt rch ldrs* **50/1**

2065 **5** *1/2* **Hatch A Plan (IRE)**[15] 1578 8-8-4 **51** oh1............ ChrisCatlin 10 53
(Mouse Hamilton-Fairley) *s.i.s: in rr: hdwy over 2f out: styd on u.p fnl f but nvr in contention* **20/1**

46U4 **6** *2* **Up In Arms (IRE)**[22] 1426 5-8-8 **55**............ JimCrowley 14 53
(P Winkworth) *chsd ldrs: rdn 3f out: wknd fnl f* **4/1**[2]

0-64 **7** *1* **Corrib (IRE)**[12] 1651 6-8-1 **51** oh1............ DavidProbert(3) 9 48
(B Palling) *t.k.h: chsd ldrs: swtchd rt to outside over 2f out: sn rdn and one pce* **11/2**[3]

0-00 **8** *1* **Gracechurch (IRE)**[8] 1773 6-8-8 **60**............ Louis-PhilippeBeuzelin(5) 12 55
(R J Hodges) *chsd ldrs: rdn 3f out: wknd fr 2f out* **9/1**

500- **9** *1 1/2* **Muffett's Dream**[23] 7707 5-8-6 **53** oh6 ow2............ NeilChalmers 8 46
(J J Bridger) *led tl hdd ins fnl 2f: sn wknd* **100/1**

0300 **10** *4* **Good Effect (USA)**[17] 1537 5-8-4 **51** oh1............ FrankieMcDonald 4 37
(C P Morlock) *s.i.s: wd 5f out: a in rr* **16/1**

0-36 **11** *12* **Double Spectre (IRE)**[7] 1786 7-9-4 **65**............ DaneO'Neill 15 32
(Jean-Rene Auvray) *chsd ldrs tl rn wd 5f out: nvr in contention after* **15/2**

1460 **12** *14* **Gamesters Lady**[21] 1454 6-8-13 **60**............ TGMcLaughlin 5 5
(W M Brisbourne) *chsd ldrs: rdn 3f out: wknd fr 2f out* **33/1**

2m 29.72s (-0.88) **Going Correction** -0.05s/f (Good) **12** Ran SP% **119.5**
Speed ratings (Par 101): **100,99,98,98,98 96,96,95,94,91 83,74**
toteswinger: 1&2 £1.10, 1&3 £1.30, 2&3 £7.00. CSF £31.33 CT £190.06 TOTE £3.70: £1.50, £2.20, £3.00; EX 22.00.
Owner Macable Partnership **Bred** Gestut Hofgut Mappen **Trained** Portway, Worcs

FOCUS
Low-grade handicap form but the fractions looked fairly honest and the finish was dominated by horses who came from off the pace. The form looks straightforward with the winner confirming recent course form with the third.
Corrib(IRE) Official explanation: jockey said mare was denied a clear run
Gracechurch(IRE) Official explanation: jockey said gelding hung right
Double Spectre(IRE) Official explanation: jockey said gelding was unable to handle bend

1981 FREEBETS.CO.UK NEW WEBSITE/EUROPEAN BREEDERS' FUND MEDIAN AUCTION MAIDEN STKS — 5f 11y

6:40 (6:41) (Class 5) 2-Y-0 **£3,885** (£1,156; £577; £288) **Stalls** Centre

Form RPR

1 **Don't Tell Mary (IRE)** 2-8-12 0............ RichardKingscote 6 85+
(Tom Dascombe) *sn trcking ldr: led wl over 1f out: qcknd clr ins fnl f: easily* **9/2**[2]

3 **2** *3 1/4* **Toga Tiger (IRE)**[15] 1577 2-9-3 0............ DarryllHolland 3 74+
(M R Channon) *chsd ldrs: rdn 2f out: chsd wnr fr 1f out: kpt on but nvr any ch* **4/11**[1]

3 *2 1/4* **The Cardinal's Hat (FR)** 2-9-3 0............(t) JimCrowley 7 66
(P Winkworth) *sn chsng ldrs: rdn 1/2-way: wknd and edgd lft fnl f* **12/1**[3]

0 **4** *3/4* **Moonlight Serenade**[9] 1742 2-8-7 0............ JackDean(5) 5 58
(W G M Turner) *led tl hdd wl over 1f out: wknd fnl f* **40/1**

5 *3/4* **Nepotism** 2-9-3 0............ TGMcLaughlin 2 61
(M S Saunders) *s.i.s: rdn and hdwy 1/2-way: chsd ldrs wl over 1f out: wknd qckly fnl f* **16/1**

6 *7* **Highcliffe Bridge (IRE)** 2-8-12 0............ CatherineGannon 4 30
(P D Evans) *outpcd* **25/1**

61.98 secs (-0.52) **Going Correction** -0.275s/f (Firm) **6** Ran SP% **111.4**
Speed ratings (Par 93): **93,87,84,83,81 70**
toteswinger: 1&2 £2.30, 1&3 £8.60, 2&3 £1.10. CSF £6.43 TOTE £4.50: £1.70, £1.10; EX 7.40.
Owner K P Trowbridge **Bred** Mascalls Stud **Trained** Lambourn, Berks

FOCUS
Probably a fair maiden and a nice prospect in the winner.

NOTEBOOK
Don't Tell Mary(IRE) ◆, despite displaying distinct signs of greenness early in the contest and racing with quite a high head carriage, travelled with real zest close to the pace before showing a smart turn of foot to quicken clear over a furlong out and win in pretty taking style. A half-sister to juvenile winner Exceptional Art, she took the eye as a nice type in the paddock and an entry in the big juvenile sales race at Ascot later in the season suggest connections think a bit of her. (op 4-1 tchd 11-2)
Toga Tiger(IRE), all the rage after his very promising debut over the same course and distance, set a fair standard on what he did on debut but he was very fractious in the paddock beforehand, showing signs of greenness, and it's hard to know whether he has shown any kind of improvement. It may be that he has bumped into something above-average though, and he has still shown enough to suggest he can win a maiden. (op 8-13 tchd 4-6 in places)
The Cardinal's Hat(FR), whose dam won over 5f at two, was under pressure quite early but he stayed on quite well in the closing stages, shaping as though he'd come on a good deal for the run. (op 15-2)
Moonlight Serenade was dropped out having led before keeping on again and she looks fairly modest. (op 80-1 tchd 33-1)
Nepotism's trainer felt that he would come on a good deal for this first run and he shaped with some minor promise, keeping on up the rail without ever having the pace to get involved, and he already looks to need a slightly longer trip. (op 12-1)

1982 WINTERSTOKE DECORATORS CLAIMING STKS — 5f 161y

7:10 (7:11) (Class 6) 3-Y-O **£1,942** (£578; £288; £144) **Stalls** Centre

Form RPR

4055 **1** **White Shift (IRE)**[18] 1505 3-8-9 68............ RichardEvans(5) 12 76
(P D Evans) *hld up in tch: smooth hdwy on outside to ld wl over 1f out: sn clr: easily* **10/3**[1]

00-3 **2** *4 1/2* **Mythical Blue (IRE)**[22] 1424 3-8-9 68............ ChrisCatlin 5 56
(J M Bradley) *pressed ldrs: led over 2f out: sn rdn: hdd wl over 1f out: sn no ch w wnr but kpt on wl for 2nd* **7/2**[2]

56-6 **3** *nk* **Ba Globetrotter**[29] 1270 3-8-5 49............ CatherineGannon 10 51
(M R Channon) *in rr: rdn over 3f out: styd on fr 2f out: clsd on 2nd wl ins fnl f but nvr any ch w wnr* **16/1**

355 **4** *nk* **Vegas Baby (IRE)**[15] 1584 3-9-0 77............(b[1]) ShaneKelly 2 59
(J A Osborne) *sn chsng ldrs: ev ch over 2f out: sn hrd drvn and styd on same pce fr over 1f out* **11/2**

1-00 **5** *1 1/2* **Creshendo**[15] 1584 3-8-9 70............(b[1]) JimCrowley 6 49
(R M Beckett) *s.i.s: sn in tch: chsd ldrs and rdn over 2f out: one pce fnl f* **9/2**[3]

0-03 **6** *hd* **Pressed For Time (IRE)**[20] 1469 3-8-10 57............ EdwardCreighton 4 49
(E J Creighton) *chsd ldrs: rdn and swtchd rt 2f out: nvr any danger* **14/1**

-306 **7** *1* **You've Been Mowed**[15] 1583 3-8-0 57............ NickyMackay 13 36
(R J Price) *slowly away: in rr tl kpt on fr over 1f out: nvr in contention* **9/1**

0-30 **8** *2 1/4* **Avrilo**[29] 1270 3-8-10 35............ TGMcLaughlin 7 38
(M S Saunders) *in tch: rdn and effrt over 2f out: nvr gng pce to be competitive and sn wknd* **100/1**

0300 **9** *2 3/4* **Kneesy Earsy Nosey**[70] 759 3-8-9 49............ AnnStokell(5) 8 33
(Miss A Stokell) *s.i.s: outpcd* **50/1**

05-0 **10** *2 1/4* **Louie's Lad**[13] 1617 3-8-9 50............ NeilChalmers 3 20
(J J Bridger) *sn led: hdd over 2f out: sn wknd* **33/1**

-540 **11** *11* **Piccaso's Sky**[30] 1247 3-8-9 47............ FergusSweeney 9 —
(A B Haynes) *chsd ldrs over 3f* **14/1**

00-5 **12** *1 3/4* **Lucky Bid**[21] 1465 3-8-5 35............ TPO'Shea 11 —
(J M Bradley) *a in rr* **66/1**

360 **13** *34* **Christmascametwice**[39] 1129 3-8-0 59............ FrankieMcDonald 1 —
(J A Osborne) *s.i.s: sn in tch: wknd qckly over 2f out: virtually p.u fnl f* **40/1**

69.66 secs (-1.54) **Going Correction** -0.275s/f (Firm) **13** Ran SP% **117.9**
Speed ratings (Par 97): **99,93,92,92,90 89,88,85,81,78 64,61,16**
toteswinger: 1&2 £2.30, 1&3 £11.60, 2&3 Not won. CSF £14.43 TOTE £4.20: £1.80, £1.50, £2.80; EX 17.20.The winner was claimed by Paul Howling for £12,000.
Owner Mrs I M Folkes **Bred** Grange Stud **Trained** Pandy, Monmouths

FOCUS
A weak claimer that was turned into a one-horse race but the form is not strong with doubts about most of the others.
You've Been Mowed Official explanation: jockey said filly was denied a clear run
Christmascametwice Official explanation: jockey said saddle slipped

1983 FREEBETS.CO.UK ONLINE BETTING FORUM H'CAP — 1m 2f 46y

7:40 (7:40) (Class 5) (0-70,73) 4-Y-0+ **£2,914** (£867; £433; £216) **Stalls** Low

Form RPR

2211 **1** **Pelham Crescent (IRE)**[7] 1786 6-9-4 **73** 6ex............ DavidProbert(3) 2 80
(B Palling) *stdd s: hld up in rr: stdy hdwy on outside fr 3f out: rdn to ld wl over 1f out: drvn clr ins fnl f* **9/4**[1]

-330 **2** *2 3/4* **Bramalea**[14] 1604 4-9-0 **66**............ JimCrowley 3 67
(B W Duke) *in tch: hdwy 3f out to chal fr 2f out tl over 1f out: outpcd by wnr ins fnl f but kpt on wl for 2nd* **10/1**

6012 **3** *1* **Siena Star (IRE)**[7] 1785 11-8-10 **62**............ TPQueally 4 61
(Stef Liddiard) *chsd ldr: rdn to ld over 2f out: kpt slt advantage tl hdd wl over 1f out: styd on same pce* **4/1**[2]

000- **4** *10* **Uig**[198] 7009 8-8-8 **60**............ DarryllHolland 1 39
(H S Howe) *t.k.h: led: slipped and rn wd bnd over 5f out: hdd over 2f out and sn wknd* **13/2**

1022 **5** *7* **My Shadow**[24] 1382 4-9-4 **70**............ IanMongan 5 35
(S Dow) *chsd ldrs: rdn and slipped bnd over 5f out: styd wl there tl wknd qckly over 2f out* **6/1**

2242 **6** *11* **Noah Jameel**[30] 1254 7-8-6 **58**............ FergusSweeney 7 1
(A G Newcombe) *chsd ldrs: pushed wd bnd over 5f out: styd wl there tl wknd wl over 2f out* **9/2**[3]

6604 **7** *10* **Lady Aspen (IRE)**[17] 1538 6-8-4 **56** oh2............(t) ChrisCatlin 6 —
(Ian Williams) *a towards rr* **11/1**

2m 9.05s (-1.95) **Going Correction** -0.05s/f (Good) **7** Ran SP% **114.0**
Speed ratings (Par 103): **105,102,102,94,88 79,71**
toteswinger: 1&2 £6.00, 1&3 £1.10, 2&3 £4.30. CSF £25.57 TOTE £3.70: £1.80, £4.40; EX 33.30.
Owner Wayne Devine **Bred** Cathal M Ryan **Trained** Tredodridge, Vale Of Glamorgan

FOCUS
Uig and Noah Jameel both blew the home bend but all of the jockeys who rode in this race came in after saying that part of the track was unraceable, calling it a skating rink, so it was little surprise that the following 1m race was abandoned. Bearing in mind the conditions this form may not be reliable, although the winner is in good heart.

1984 FREEBETS.CO.UK FREE BETS BE HOPEFUL H'CAP — 1m 5y

() (Class 5) (0-75,) 4-Y-0+ £

1985 FREEBETS.CO.UK FREE BETS EVERY DAY FILLIES' H'CAP — 5f 161y

8:40 (8:41) (Class 5) (0-70,70) 3-Y-0+ **£2,914** (£867; £433; £216) **Stalls** Centre

Form RPR

346 **1** **Pinball (IRE)**[18] 1529 3-8-1 **55**............(v[1]) KellyHarrison(3) 3 63
(Patrick Morris) *in rr tl rapid hdwy wl over 1f out to ld ins fnl f: pushed out* **16/1**

0-00 **2** *1* **Dualagi**[4] 1890 5-9-2 **57**............ JimCrowley 6 64
(M R Bosley) *hld up in rr: stdy hdwy fr 2f out: qcknd to chse wnr wl ins fnl f but a hld* **10/3**[2]

0-43 **3** *1 1/4* **Bahamian Ceilidh**[13] 1618 3-9-5 **70**............ RichardKingscote 9 70
(Tom Dascombe) *sn led: rdn 2f out: hdd and edgd rt appr fnl f: styd on again cl home* **2/1**[1]

010- **4** *1 1/2* **Blushing Maid**[251] 5642 3-9-5 **70**............ KirstyMilczarek 1 65
(H S Howe) *chsd ldrs: slt ld appr fnl f: hdd & wknd ins fnl f* **14/1**

30-4 **5** *nk* **Matterofact (IRE)**[17] 1540 6-9-12 **67**............ TGMcLaughlin 8 64
(M S Saunders) *chsd ldrs: rdn to chal ins fnl 2f: wknd fnl f* **9/2**[3]

0300 **6** *nk* **Berrymead**[10] 1695 4-8-11 **57**............(b) AnnStokell(5) 13 53
(Miss A Stokell) *chsd ldrs: rdn over 2f out: wknd appr fnl f* **18/1**

0046 **7** *2 1/2* **Dancing Welcome**[8] 1772 3-8-2 **53**............(b) CatherineGannon 5 37
(J M Bradley) *chsd ldrs: rdn 1/2-way: wknd over 1f out* **22/1**

0-05 **8** *1 3/4* **Zaftil (IRE)**[8] 1772 3-8-0 **56** oh8 ow3............ SophieDoyle(5) 11 31
(H S Howe) *in rr: rdn and sme prog over 2f out: nvr in contention* **40/1**

5-05 **9** *1 1/4* **Twenty Score**[60] 842 3-8-9 **60**............ PaulFitzsimons 10 34
(Miss J R Tooth) *outpcd fr 1/2-way* **18/1**

5020 **10** *2 3/4* **Rapanui Belle**[18] 1529 3-7-13 **53** oh4............ DavidProbert(3) 2 18
(G L Moore) *chsd ldrs to 1/2-way* **20/1**

062- **11** 7 **Final Rhapsody**[180] 7308 3-8-13 **64**.............................. RichardThomas 7 5
(J A Geake) *chsd ldrs to 1/2-way* **17/2**

1m 10.07s (-1.13) **Going Correction** -0.275s/f (Firm)
WFA 3 from 4yo+ 10lb 11 Ran SP% **119.7**
Speed ratings (Par 100): **96,94,93,91,90 90,86,84,82,79 69**
toteswinger: 1&2 £10.70, 1&3 £2.50, 2&3 Not won. CSF £68.70 CT £162.65 TOTE £15.30: £3.10, £1.40, £1.50; EX 99.10 Place 6 £10.30, Place 5 £4.34.
Owner Miss Sharron Pettigrew **Bred** John Morris **Trained** Tarporley, Cheshire

FOCUS
A modest fillies' sprint handicap in which the front two both came from well back, suggesting the leaders might have gone a tad hard early, but the pace didn't look overly strong. The third sets the standard.
T/Plt: £6.80 to a £1 stake. Pool: £58,514.06. 6,207.19 winning tickets. T/Qpdt: £4.60 to a £1 stake. Pool: £3,926.60. 625.89 winning tickets. ST

YORK (L-H)

Wednesday, May 13

OFFICIAL GOING: Good to firm (8.7)

The first meeting since drainage work was undertaken following the abandonment of last season's Ebor festival.

Wind: Fresh, half behind Weather: Overcast, very cool and breezy, showers last 2 races

1986 BLUE SQUARE CASINO STKS (H'CAP) 1m 2f 88y
1:40 (1:40) (Class 2) (0-100,98) 4-Y-0+ **£12,952** (£3,854; £1,926; £962) **Stalls** Low

Form RPR

0-26 **1** **Moonquake (USA)**[61] 4-9-4 **95**................................ LDettori 5 105
(Saeed Bin Suroor) *trckd ldrs on inner: hdwy 4f out: led over 2f out: rdn over 1f out: styd on strly ins fnl f* **8/1[2]**

0-25 **2** 1/2 **Checklow (USA)**[22] 1433 4-8-12 **89**.............................. ShaneKelly 3 98
(J Noseda) *hld up in tch: hdwy on inner over 2f out: swtchd rt and effrt wl over 1f out: rdn to chse wnr ins fnl f: drvn and nt qckn towards fin* **9/1[3]**

61-1 **3** 1 3/4 **Stone Of Scone**[15] 1593 4-9-6 **97**.............................. RyanMoore 6 103+
(E A L Dunlop) *lw: scope: rangy: hld up towards rr: hdwy on wd outside 3f out: rdn and edgd lft wl over 1f out: kpt on same pce u.p ins fnl f* **5/1[1]**

0-53 **4** 1 3/4 **Albaqaa**[36] 1172 4-9-0 **91**.............................. PaulHanagan 10 93
(R A Fahey) *trckd ldrs: smooth hdwy 4f out: cl up 3f out rdn 2f out and ev ch tl drvn and wknd appr fnl f* **9/1[3]**

212- **5** 1 1/2 **Rose Street (IRE)**[235] 6120 5-9-4 **95**.............................. PhilipRobinson 11 94
(M A Jarvis) *in tch: hdwy 3f out: rdn to chse ldrs over 1f out: keeping on same pce whn n.m.r ins fnl f* **5/1[1]**

21- **6** 2 3/4 **Meethaaq (USA)**[345] 2668 4-8-13 **90**.............................. RHills 14 84+
(Sir Michael Stoute) *hld up towards rr: hdwy on outer 3f out: rdn along and hld whn n.m.r over 1f out* **5/1[1]**

31- **7** 1/2 **Red Kestrel (USA)**[274] 4941 4-9-4 **95**.............................. NCallan 8 88
(K A Ryan) *in tch: hdwy over 3f out: rdn along 2f out: sn drvn and grad wknd* **14/1**

/3-0 **8** 1 **Road To Love (IRE)**[11] 1673 6-9-4 **95**.............................. JoeFanning 1 86
(M Johnston) *led: rdn along over 3f out: hdd over 2f out: sn drvn and wknd* **11/1**

1-40 **9** 1 1/4 **Best Prospect (IRE)**[15] 1593 7-8-10 **87**..............................(t) PhillipMakin 7 75
(M Dods) *a towards rr* **66/1**

-203 **10** 1 1/2 **Bencoolen (IRE)**[11] 1684 4-9-0 **91**.............................. AdrianTNicholls 9 76
(D Nicholls) *prom: rdn along over 3f out and sn wknd* **12/1**

0512 **11** 13 **Royal Amnesty**[12] 1646 6-8-0 **84** oh3..............................(b) JamieKyne(7) 12 43
(I Semple) *lw: hld up and bhd: sme hdwy on inner 3f out: rdn along over 2f out and sn wknd* **25/1**

30-2 **12** 44 **Slam**[27] 1306 4-9-4 **95**.............................. MichaelHills 2 —
(B W Hills) *dwlt and shkn up s: rapid hdwy to trck ldr after 1f: rdn along over 3f out: hung rt and sn wknd: bhd and eased over 1f out* **11/1**

2m 10.21s (-2.29) **Going Correction** +0.05s/f (Good) 12 Ran SP% **117.5**
Speed ratings (Par 109): **111,110,109,107,106 104,104,103,102,101 90,55**
toteswinger: 1&2 £14.90, 1&3 £7.50, 2&3 £8.30. CSF £77.42 CT £400.42 TOTE £9.00: £2.80, £3.60, £2.20; EX 117.80 Trifecta £161.60 Pool: £655.20 - 3.00 winning units..
Owner Godolphin **Bred** Stonestreet Mares Llc **Trained** Newmarket, Suffolk

FOCUS
This intriguing handicap has been won by a mixture of improving four-year-olds and exposed handicappers in recent years, and offered a similar mix this season. The pace was decent and the form looks sound, rated through the runner-up.

NOTEBOOK
Moonquake(USA) provided Godolphin with their thrid straight success in this race on his debut for the stable. A winner over this trip on easy ground when with John Gosden, he had handled faster conditions in Dubai earlier in the spring. He was 5lb higher than for the best of those efforts but, under an astute ride from Frankie Dettori, kicked for home halfway up the straight and kept on well to hold off the runner-up. There are no plans but, already rated 95, he will not have that many options with regard to handicaps now, and may need to step up to Listed company. (op 10-1)
Checklow(USA) got a good lead into the race and followed the winner through before being ridden to deliver his challenge going into the last furlong. However, he could never reduce the winner's advantage more than a fraction. (op 10-1)
Stone Of Scone ◆, a winner over this trip on his seasonal debut, was encountering fast ground for the first time, was up in grade and had been raised 7lb. Nevertheless, he went off joint favourite and ran with plenty of credit, being forced to come from the rear and down the wide outside, which meant he never got close enough to land a blow. He remains a decent prospect, though. (op 9-2)
Albaqaa, representing a yard that had won this twice in the previous ten years, ran a fine race having raced close to the pace. He had every chance halfway up the straight before fading. (op 12-1)
Rose Street(IRE) ◆, lightly raced but a consistent, progressive sort, ran second to the subsequent Group 1 winner Presvis last September but was racing off a mark 3lb higher. She ran well but did not look particularly comfortable on this first try on fast ground. (op 6-1 tchd 7-1)
Meethaaq(USA), lightly raced and off for the best part of a year since his maiden win due to a bad case of colic, was well backed but never got involved having been held up. He stays beyond this trip and may be seen to better effect under a more positive ride over further. (tchd 9-2)
Red Kestrel(USA) did not perform badly on his debut for a new stable after a spell on the sidelines but may need to drop in the ratings to be competitive. (op 12-1)
Road To Love(IRE) made the running from his inside stall but dropped away once the winner took his measure and remains on a long losing run. Also, he has never scored going left-handed. (op 12-1)
Bencoolen(IRE) was the subject of market support and has won at around this trip on fast ground. However, his best recent runs have been at 1m. (op 16-1 tchd 11-1)
Slam was far too keen early on and dropped out quickly in the straight. Official explanation: jockey said colt hung right-handed throughout (op 10-1)

1987 BLUE SQUARE STKS (H'CAP) 7f
2:10 (2:13) (Class 2) (0-100,95) 3-Y-O **£16,190** (£3,612; £3,612; £1,202) **Stalls** Low

Form RPR

21-6 **1** **Brief Encounter (IRE)**[26] 1324 3-8-9 **83**.............................. WilliamBuick 9 94+
(A M Balding) *bmpd s and hld up in rr: effrt whn n.m.r and swtchd lft wl over 1f out: swtchd rt to outer over 1f out and sn rdn: drvn and str run ins fnl f to ld on line* **5/1[2]**

010- **2** nk **Hartley**[200] 6972 3-9-4 **92**.............................. PhilipRobinson 5 102
(J D Bethell) *cl up: led over 2f out: rdn: edgd lft and hdd over 1f out: rallied u.pto ld again ins fnl f: drvn and no ex nr fin* **33/1**

11 **2** dht **Photographic**[11] 1679 3-9-1 **89**.............................. MichaelHills 7 99+
(B W Hills) *lw: t.k.h early: hld up towards rr: hdwy 1/2-way: swtchd outside and effrt 2f out: rdn to ld over 1f out: drvn: edgd lft and hdd ins fnl f: rallied nr fin* **9/4[1]**

402- **4** 2 1/2 **Satwa Laird**[200] 6970 3-8-13 **87**.............................. LDettori 10 90
(E A L Dunlop) *hld up in rr: gd hdwy over 2f out: rdn to chse ldrs over 1f out: kpt on same pce* **8/1**

1312 **5** 1 3/4 **Tartan Gunna**[6] 1801 3-9-0 **88**.............................. JoeFanning 12 87
(M Johnston) *lw: midfield: hdwy wl over 2f out: rdn to chse ldrs wl over 1f out: sn hung lft and btn* **11/1**

20-1 **6** 4 **Ishe Mac**[11] 1683 3-8-7 **81** oh4.............................. FrancisNorton 11 69+
(N Bycroft) *chsd ldrs: rdn along and outpcd over 2f out: plugged on u.p fr over 1f out* **40/1**

5-01 **7** 3/4 **Johnmanderville**[16] 1559 3-8-7 **81** oh2.............................. AndrewElliott 14 67
(K R Burke) *chsd ldrs: hdwy and prom 1/2-way: rdn over 2f out and grad wknd* **25/1**

10-2 **8** 3/4 **Enact**[28] 1296 3-9-0 **88**.............................. RyanMoore 8 72+
(Sir Michael Stoute) *lw: dwlt and in rr: effrt whn nt clr run 2f out: nvr a factor* **5/1[2]**

140- **9** hd **Come And Go (UAE)**[245] 5791 3-8-12 **86**.............................. PJMcDonald 1 69
(G A Swinbank) *led: rdn along 1/2-way: hdd wl over 2f out and sn wknd* **66/1**

1-66 **10** 1/2 **Tobond (IRE)**[28] 1296 3-9-2 **95**.............................. AndreaAtzeni(5) 3 77
(M Botti) *hld up in midfield: effrt whn nt clr run 2f out: n.d after* **25/1**

200- **11** 1/2 **Deadly Secret (USA)**[221] 6483 3-9-5 **93**.............................. PaulHanagan 2 73+
(R A Fahey) *chsd ldrs on inner: effrt over 2f out: sn rdn and wknd* **16/1**

10- **12** 3 **North East Corner (USA)**[223] 6428 3-8-11 **85**.............................. RobertWinston 4 57
(B W Hills) *cl up: rdn along wl over 2f out: sn wknd* **6/1[3]**

05-0 **13** 14 **Polish Pride**[25] 1345 3-8-12 **86**.............................. NCallan 13 21
(M Brittain) *a in rr* **40/1**

161- **P** **Knavesmire (IRE)**[350] 2497 3-9-6 **94**.............................. AlanMunro 6 —
(M Brittain) *in rr: wl bhd whn lost action and p.u over 1f out* **50/1**

1m 24.76s (-0.54) **Going Correction** +0.05s/f (Good) 14 Ran SP% **122.7**
Speed ratings (Par 105): **105,104,104,101,99 95,94,93,93,92 92,88,72,—**PL: Hartley £5.70, Photographic £1.60; CSF: BE-H £85.25, BE-P £7.99; EX: BE-H £126.70, BE-P £9.90; TRICAST: BE-H-P £240.26, BE-P-H £175.48; toteswinger: 1&2 (H) £50.70, 1&2 (P) £5.10, 2&3 £21.70. TOTE £6.20: £2.50 TRIFECTA 12-427 Owner.

FOCUS
A very good three-year-old handicap and they seemed to go a fair enough pace from the off. The form has been rated fairly positively with the fifth, sixth and seventh in good form and the winner should rate higher.

NOTEBOOK
Brief Encounter(IRE) improved on the form he showed when an encouraging sixth in a similar race over this trip at Newbury on his reappearance. The plan had apparently been to sit handy, but he soon found himself well back after being bumped at the start. He still had only one behind passing the 2f pole, but he produced a sustained effort when switched to the outside and got up in the final strides, despite edging slightly left. His connections are confident he will get 1m, and the Britannia Stakes is his main aim. There's a chance he could go for the Silver Bowl at Haydock en-route, but Andrew Balding thinks the gelding is better with time between his races, and is favouring going straight to Royal Ascot. (op 11-2 tchd 6-1)
Photographic, bidding for a third straight win off just a 5lb higher mark than when successful over 1m at the Newmarket Guineas meeting, was produced with every chance on the outside over 2f out, but was just held. On breeding this drop in trip should have suited, and she displayed sufficient speed to move into a threatening position in the straight, but the evidence of the last furlong suggests a return to further will suit. She still deserves her chance in the Listed Sandringham at Royal Ascot. (op 11-4)
Hartley, returning from 200 days off, was given a positive ride and kept on most gamely when strongly challenged by Photographic, only to be picked off late on by the winner. He handled the quick ground well and looks a decent handicapper in the making. (op 11-4)
Satwa Laird simply didn't look good enough, although he is entitled to come on for this first start in 200 days and should find opportunities in lesser races. (op 10-1 tchd 15-2)
Tartan Gunna lacked the pace of some of these and gave the impression he'll be suited by a step up to 1m. (op 10-1)
Ishe Mac was badly hampered over 2f out and could never really recover her momentum thereafter. A decent effort from 4lb out the handicap.
Enact started sluggishly and was in an unpromising position for most of the straight, looking for an ambitious gap towards the inside rail. She didn't see much daylight, but that said, it would be hard to describe her as really unlucky. Official explanation: jockey said filly was denied a clear run (op 10-3)
Come And Go(UAE)'s trainer predicted this one would improve for the run, having had 245 days off, and the gelding ran accordingly. There should be better to come. (op 50-1)
Tobond(IRE) was stopped in his run in the straight and is a little better than he showed. (op 20-1)
Deadly Secret(USA) was another denied a clear run. Official explanation: jockey said colt was denied a clear run (op 25-1)
North East Corner(USA) was quite well backed but he offered little after 223 days off, dropping out tamely in the straight after showing early speed. (op 14-1)
Polish Pride Official explanation: jockey said filly was unsuited by the good to firm ground
Knavesmire(IRE) Official explanation: jockey said filly lost its action

1988 TATTERSALLS MUSIDORA STKS (GROUP 3) (FILLIES) 1m 2f 88y
2:40 (2:43) (Class 1) 3-Y-O
£36,900 (£13,988; £7,000; £3,490; £1,748; £877) **Stalls** Low

Form RPR

1-4 **1** **Sariska**[25] 1353 3-8-12 **99**.............................. JamieSpencer 6 117
(M L W Bell) *lw: trckd ldrs: hdwy to chse ldr 3f out: rdn to ld 2f out: styd on strly ins fnl f* **3/1[2]**

1 **2** 3 3/4 **Star Ruby (IRE)**[19] 1488 3-8-12 0.............................. AlanMunro 5 109
(P W Chapple-Hyam) *trckd ldr: hdwy to ld over 3f out: rdn along and hdd 2f out: sn drvn and one pce* **10/3[3]**

11- **3** 3 1/2 **Enticement**[193] 7144 3-8-12 **97**.............................. RyanMoore 1 102
(Sir Michael Stoute) *lw: trckd ldrs: hdwy over 3f out: rdn along to chse ldng pair wl over 2f out and sn no imp* **7/4[1]**

16-1 **4** *3¼* **High Heeled (IRE)**[26] 1326 3-8-12 99 .... MichaelHills 3 96
(B W Hills) *trckd ldrs: hdwy over 3f out: rdn along wl over 2f out and sn btn* **5/1**

04-5 **5** *16* **Pachattack (USA)**[10] 1701 3-8-12 98 .... LDettori 4 64
(G A Butler) *set stdy pce: rdn and qcknd 4f out: sn hdd & wknd 3f out* **11/1**

0033 **6** *32* **Dancing Wave**[9] 1725 3-8-12 57 .... LeeVickers 2 —
(M C Chapman) *sn outpcd and wl bhd fnl 4f* **250/1**

2m 11.41s (-1.09) **Going Correction** +0.05s/f (Good) **6** Ran SP% **109.8**
Speed ratings (Par 106): **106,103,100,97,84 59**
toteswinger: 1&2 £2.30, 1&3 £1.70, 2&3 £1.50. CSF £12.73 TOTE £4.10: £1.90, £2.30; EX 14.80.
Owner Lady Bamford **Bred** Lady Bamford **Trained** Newmarket, Suffolk

FOCUS
The major Oaks trial but none of the previous ten winners had gone on to score at Epsom, although Kalypso Katie finished runner-up and Short Skirt, Secret History and Punctilious all finished third. That said, Alexandrova was beaten by Short Skirt before reversing form in the Oaks. A small field this season but it featured several who had the potential to develop into major contenders for the fillies' Classic. The one note of caution is that the time was 1.2secs slower than the opening handicap. The winner is entitled to Oaks favouritism though with the third setting the level.

NOTEBOOK
Sariska took the race in decisive fashion. She had beaten several subsequent winners on debut over 7f at Newmarket and then looked a little unlucky when fourth in the Fred Darling on her seasonal return. She had looked sure to be suited by a longer trip, especially as her half-sister Gull Wing stayed 1m6f, and that proved to be the case. There was some doubt about her ability to handle the ground, as both her sire's stock and her sibling seemed to prefer cut, but she coped with it without a problem and looks a major contender for the Oaks now, for which she is a best-priced 5/1. (tchd 10-3)
Star Ruby(IRE) ◆, who was quite impressive when taking a Sandown maiden over this trip on her debut, ran really well on this step up in grade, kicking on early in the straight and keeping on well once headed. She beat the rest well enough and it could be worth taking on the winner again at Epsom, although she will have to be supplemented. (op 9-2)
Enticement, unbeaten in two runs over 1m on easy ground at two, including beating Guineas third Super Sleuth and Lingfield Oaks Trial-winner Midday in a Newmarket Listed race, had questions to answer regarding trip and ground. However, she was sent off favourite and appeared to have every chance, but could not pick up well enough to trouble the first two. It may be that she needs some cut in the ground to produce her best and she will not go to Epsom. (op 15-8 tchd 13-8)
High Heeled(IRE) had beaten several useful colts when scoring over this trip at Newbury on good to soft and had her chance, but failed to pick up. Like the third, she may not be as effective on this fast surface. (op 4-1 tchd 11-2)
Pachattack(USA) looked promising on her first two starts, including winning on fast ground at Goodwood, but has been held since in Group and Listed company and the front-running tactics did not bring about any improvement. A return to Listed company will be her best chance of earning black type. Official explanation: jockey said filly lost its action (tchd 10-1)

1989 DUKE OF YORK BLUE SQUARE STKS (GROUP 2) 6f
3:10 (3:13) (Class 1) 3-Y-O+
£60,545 (£22,951; £11,486; £5,727; £2,868; £1,439) **Stalls** Low

Form RPR

361- **1** **Utmost Respect**[190] 7187 5-9-7 111 .... PaulHanagan 3 118
(R A Fahey) *chsd ldrs: drvn over 2f out: kpt on gamely to ld wl ins fnl f* **16/1**

01-0 **2** *¾* **King's Apostle (IRE)**[11] 1676 5-9-10 112 .... LiamJones 11 119
(W J Haggas) *in rr: hdwy on outside over 2f out: styd on strly fnl f: nt quite rch wnr* **16/1**

11-1 **3** *nk* **Tax Free (IRE)**[27] 1299 7-9-7 112 .... AdrianTNicholls 6 115
(D Nicholls) *chsd ldr: led after 2f: edgd rt fnl f: hdd and no ex fnl 50yds* **7/2**[1]

05-4 **4** *½* **Strike The Deal (USA)**[11] 1676 4-9-7 109 ....(v) RyanMoore 7 113
(J Noseda) *chsd ldrs: drvn over 2f out: styd on same pce fnl f* **13/2**[3]

142- **5** *¾* **Rock Of Rochelle (USA)**[199] 7005 4-9-7 108 .... ShaneFoley 4 111
(A Kinsella, Ire) *mid-div: drvn over 2f out: styd on fnl f: nt rch ldrs* **100/1**

6120 **6** *¾* **Hatta Fort**[27] 1299 4-9-7 112 ....(t) LDettori 16 108
(Saeed Bin Suroor) *hld up off pce on outer: hdwy over 2f out: kpt on wl fnl f* **16/1**

0-40 **7** *nk* **Intrepid Jack**[76] 700 7-9-7 110 .... GeorgeBaker 13 107
(H Morrison) *hld up in rr: hdwy over 2f out: kpt on fnl f: nt rch ldrs* **28/1**

11-2 **8** *shd* **Duff (IRE)**[81] 633 6-9-7 109 .... TedDurcan 14 107
(Edward Lynam, Ire) *lw: hld up in mid-div on outer: hdwy over 2f out: kpt on: nvr rchd ldrs* **20/1**

-332 **9** *1* **Knot In Wood (IRE)**[25] 1367 7-9-7 107 .... JamieMoriarty 2 104
(R A Fahey) *chsd ldrs far side: outpcd over 1f out* **25/1**

3332 **10** *1¼* **Dohasa (IRE)**[38] 1138 4-9-7 109 .... KLatham 8 100
(G M Lyons, Ire) *stmbld s: sn drvn along: kpt on fnl 2f: nvr on terms* **20/1**

40-2 **11** *hd* **Equiano (FR)**[27] 1299 4-9-7 116 .... MichaelHills 1 99
(B W Hills) *lw: led overall on far side 2f: wknd appr fnl f* **9/2**[2]

033- **12** *2¼* **Sir Gerry (USA)**[214] 6645 4-9-7 111 .... JamieSpencer 15 92
(J R Fanshawe) *hld up way off pce on outer: kpt on fnl 2f: nvr on terms* **11/1**

400- **13** *¾* **Captain Gerrard (IRE)**[220] 6518 4-9-7 110 .... TomEaves 10 90
(B Smart) *w ldrs on outer: lost pl over 1f out* **33/1**

1-11 **14** *½* **Arganil (USA)**[53] 911 4-9-7 108 .... NCallan 12 88
(K A Ryan) *mid-div: effrt over 2f out: sn chsng ldrs: wknd appr fnl f* **20/1**

03-1 **15** *1¼* **Hitchens (IRE)**[25] 1367 4-9-7 110 .... PhillipMakin 5 84
(T D Barron) *chsd ldrs: rdn over 2f out: sn btn* **17/2**

10-0 **16** *6* **Edge Closer**[27] 1299 5-9-7 112 .... RichardHughes 9 65
(R Hannon) *lw: chsd ldrs: lost pl over 1f out: bhd whn eased ins fnl f* **12/1**

1m 10.7s (-1.20) **Going Correction** +0.05s/f (Good) **16** Ran SP% **123.4**
Speed ratings (Par 115): **110,109,108,107,106 105,105,105,104,102 102,99,98,97,95 87**
toteswinger: 1&2 £61.60, 1&3 £14.40, 2&3 £14.70. CSF £232.25 TOTE £21.50: £5.20, £5.10, £1.80; EX 350.70 Trifecta £1616.90 Pool: £2185.10 - 1.00 winning units..
Owner The Rumpole Partnership **Bred** Heather Raw **Trained** Musley Bank, N Yorks
■ Stewards' Enquiry : Adrian T Nicholls caution: used whip down shoulder in forehand position
Paul Hanagan two-day ban: used whip with excessive frequency (May 27-28)

FOCUS
This looked a really competitive renewal of the Duke Of York, with just 9lb separating all 16 runners on official figures. The pace was predictably frantic throughout and the field were well strung out from an early stage. Four of the first five finishers were drawn in single-figure stalls but the form looks sound rated around the third and fourth.

NOTEBOOK
Utmost Respect ◆ had shown all his best previous form on going good or softer, and he had been off for over six months, but he produced a terrific effort. His rider said afterwards the gelding had become slightly unbalanced, and only just got away with the ground, suggesting there will be even better to come when he gets more suitable conditions. Back on an easier surface, he can win a Group 1 sprint this year. (op 14-1 tchd 20-1)
King's Apostle(IRE) ◆ improved on the form he showed when mid-division in the Palace House on his reappearance, appreciating the step up in trip, and he shaped as though he can do better again. Conceding weight all round, he was outpaced for most of the way, but rattled home in the closing stages, easily faring best of those drawn in double figures, and might have got up in another 50 yards or so. Last season's success in the Group 2 Diadem Stakes was gained in a visor and he very much gives the impression he will benefit from the reapplication of some headgear. He looks one of the more likely winners of this year's Golden Jubilee, particularly given he has already shown a liking for Ascot, and the 16/1 on offer with Stan James and William Hill appeals as worth taking. (op 18-1)
Tax Free(IRE) looked to improve on the form he showed when successful in the Abernant Stakes at Newmarket on his reappearance, but still found a couple too good after going off at a strong pace. (op 5-1)
Strike The Deal(USA) had absolutely every chance if good enough, and he ran a solid race, but he usually comes up short in this sort of company. (op 8-1)
Rock Of Rochelle(USA) lacked the sharpness of some of these and never looked like winning, but he kept on to post a most respectable effort. (tchd 80-1)
Hatta Fort didn't look to be striding out all that fluently early on and soon found himself far too far back, before only running on when the race was all over.
Intrepid Jack was another to run on from a long way back, but he's not really up to this level. (tchd 25-1)
Duff(IRE) briefly looked a big threat inside the final 2f, but he didn't go through with his effort and looked to find the ground quicker than ideal. (op 22-1)
Knot In Wood(IRE) didn't look right in his coat beforehand, but can do better on easier ground. (op 20-1)
Dohasa(IRE) who had something to find at this level, was on his toes beforehand and was never sighted after an awkward start. (op 25-1)
Equiano(FR) is ideally suited by 5f, but he should still have fared better considering he had finished a close second behind today's third-placed horse, Tax Free, over this trip at Newmarket on his reappearance. He'll surely now return to the minimum distance and try to repeat last season's success in the King's Stand at Royal Ascot, but it was no surprise to see William Hill push him out to 16/1 for that race. (tchd 4-1 and 5-1)
Sir Gerry(USA), who looked fit enough despite returning from 214 days off, was set an impossible task, but it was still disappointing he found so little when coming under pressure over 2f out. He might do better when his yard hits full stride. (op 8-1)
Arganil(USA) failed to prove himself on fast turf. (op 16-1)
Hitchens(IRE) looks best caught fresh. (op 9-1 tchd 10-1)

1990 BLUE SQUARE SP GUARANTEE STKS (H'CAP) 1m 4f
3:45 (3:45) (Class 4) (0-85,85) 4-Y-O+ **£7,123** (£2,119; £1,059; £529) **Stalls** Centre

Form RPR

0/16 **1** **Spring Jim**[25] 1347 8-9-5 **83** .... WilliamBuick 5 93+
(J R Fanshawe) *hld up in midfield: stdy hdwy on outer over 2f out: r.o to ld last 75yds* **10/1**

-323 **2** *½* **Dazzling Light (UAE)**[10] 1693 4-8-8 **72** .... PJMcDonald 9 81
(J S Goldie) *chsd ldrs: hdwy on ins to ld appr fnl f: hdd and no ex wl ins fnl f* **25/1**

0-1 **3** *1¼* **Serious Impact (USA)**[18] 1515 4-9-4 **82** .... LDettori 19 89+
(J H M Gosden) *sn trcking ldrs: effrt over 2f out: rdn over 1f out: no ex ins fnl f* **7/2**[1]

601- **4** *1½* **King Fingal (IRE)**[205] 6862 4-9-2 **80** .... GrahamGibbons 7 85
(J J Quinn) *b: prom: nt clr run over 2f out: styd on fnl f* **5/1**[2]

30-4 **5** *nse* **Cyborg**[16] 1571 5-8-13 **77** .... RobertHavlin 3 82
(D R C Elsworth) *lw: trckd ldrs: led over 2f out tl appr fnl f: wknd towards fin* **10/1**

55-5 **6** *¾* **Dzesmin (POL)**[43] 1051 7-9-4 **82** .... PaulHanagan 18 85
(R A Fahey) *hld up in midfield: effrt on outer 3f out: kpt on: nvr a threat* **20/1**

0105 **7** *2¼* **All In The Red (IRE)**[8] 1779 4-8-7 **71** ....(p) JoeFanning 6 71
(A Crook) *mid-div: hdwy on ins 3f out: nvr trbld ldrs* **40/1**

04-5 **8** *2* **Birkside**[5] 1826 6-9-4 **82** .... DavidAllan 12 79+
(Ollie Pears) *hld up in rr: hdwy on ins whn nt clr run over 2f out: nvr trbld ldrs* **10/1**

2-14 **9** *shd* **Overrule (USA)**[11] 1665 5-9-1 **79** .... RichardHughes 11 77+
(B Ellison) *in rr: hdwy whn nt clr run over 2f out tl over 1f out: n.d* **7/1**

55-5 **10** *nk* **Gifted Leader (USA)**[23] 1407 4-8-9 **73** ow2 .... StephenDonohoe 17 69+
(Ian Williams) *in rr: sme hdwy on outside over 2f out: nvr a factor* **28/1**

000- **11** *8* **Mesbaah (IRE)**[197] 7047 5-8-11 **75** .... TonyHamilton 1 58
(R A Fahey) *lw: led tl hdd & wknd over 2f out* **33/1**

-630 **12** *½* **Kingsdale Orion (IRE)**[36] 1170 5-9-3 **81** .... TomEaves 8 63
(B Ellison) *chsd ldrs: wknd appr fnl f* **28/1**

115- **13** *3½* **Wellington Square**[143] 7753 4-9-3 **81** .... GeorgeBaker 16 58
(H Morrison) *swtchd lft s: a in rr* **10/1**

35-2 **14** *2¾* **Rosbay (IRE)**[16] 1557 5-9-1 **84** .... FrederikTylicki(5) 4 56
(T D Easterby) *lw: chsd ldrs: wknd over 2f out* **13/2**[3]

15 *20* **Tres Froide (FR)**[174] 4-8-13 **77** .... RoystonFfrench 14 17
(N Tinkler) *in rr: bhd fnl 3f: t.o* **50/1**

1100 **16** *5* **Stand Guard**[21] 1460 5-9-7 **85** .... TolleyDean 10 17
(P Howling) *b: chsd ldrs: lost pl over 2f out: bhd whn eased: t.o* **66/1**

2m 31.88s (-1.32) **Going Correction** +0.05s/f (Good) **16** Ran SP% **125.4**
Speed ratings (Par 105): **106,105,104,103,103 103,101,100,100,100 94,94,92,90,77 73**
toteswinger: 1&2 £48.70, 1&3 £7.60, 2&3 £19.30. CSF £249.36 CT £1065.44 TOTE £11.80: £2.90, £4.60, £1.50, £1.70; EX 334.30.
Owner Andrew & Julia Turner **Bred** C I T Racing Ltd **Trained** Newmarket, Suffolk
■ Stewards' Enquiry : Robert Havlin caution: used whip down shoulder in forehand position

FOCUS
This good handicap is often won by a battle-hardened performer but in the recent past a low draw has been essential. However, with the drainage work having taken place the advantage was less pronounced, although it paid to not race too far off the pace. The form looks sound rated around the fourth and fifth.
Spring Jim Official explanation: trainer said, regarding apparent improvement in form, that the gelding was suited by the better ground and that it had possibly bounced following its previous win
Birkside Official explanation: jockey said gelding was denied a clear run

1991 BLUE SQUARE EBF NOVICE STKS 5f
4:20 (4:21) (Class 3) 2-Y-O **£8,418** (£2,505; £1,251; £625) **Stalls** Low

Form RPR

140 **1** **Fratellino**[7] 1788 2-9-2 0 .... RobertWinston 5 92+
(A J McCabe) *mde all: rdn and kpt on strly fnl 2f* **14/1**

2 **2** *3* **Ventura Cove (IRE)**[12] 1645 2-8-12 0 .... PaulHanagan 4 77+
(R A Fahey) *str: lw: trckd ldrs: drvn and edgd lft over 1f out: no imp* **5/4**[1]

2 **3** *6* **Paradise Dream**[9] 1726 2-8-12 0 .... LDettori 3 56
(J Noseda) *lw: w'like: swtchd lft to chse ldrs over 2f out: sn hrd drvn: fdd over 1f out* **7/2**[3]

1 **4** *1½* **King Of Axum (IRE)**[11] 1661 2-9-5 0 .... RoystonFfrench 6 57
(M Johnston) *lw: w'like: swvd rt s: drvn to chse ldrs: lost pl over 1f out* **7/1**

4 5 2 1/4 **Starburst Excel**[27] 1298 2-8-7 0 .... AlanMunro 1 37
(M G Quinlan) *hood removed v late: sn chsng ldrs: wknd over 1f out* **11/4**[2]

59.38 secs (0.08) **Going Correction** +0.05s/f (Good) **5** Ran SP% **112.5**
Speed ratings (Par 97): **101,96,86,84,80**
toteswinger: 1&2 £8.80. CSF £33.17 TOTE £15.00: £2.60, £1.50; EX 34.70.
Owner Sale Of The Century **Bred** Llety Stud **Trained** Averham Park, Notts

FOCUS
An ordinary juvenile novice event and the winner was clear for most of the way. The runner-up is rated to his previous form.

NOTEBOOK
Fratellino was allowed to dominate and looked to produce a much-improved performance. Unlucky not to finish closer in the Lily Agnes last time, Alan McCabe's charge boosted the form of Coventry Stakes-bound Red Jazz, who thrashed him at Ascot two starts back. He's very quick and deserves his chance in something better over this trip, but things are likely to get much tougher before long. There's a chance he'll now take his chance at Royal Ascot, presumably in the Windsor Castle, and in the longer term his connections are eyeing a tilt at the Molecomb.
Ventura Cove(IRE) didn't really build on the form he showed when runner-up on his debut at Musselburgh. He edged left when coming under pressure, and could make no impression on the winner, although in fairness he did pull a long way clear of the remainder. (op 13-8 tchd 15-8)
Paradise Dream's debut second on the Polytrack at Kempton came in a pretty ordinary race and he found this tougher. (op 3-1)
King Of Axum(IRE) looked a nice prospect when winning on his debut, and the fifth home franked that form earlier in the week, so this was a bitterly disappointing effort, even though he was conceding weight all round. He went right as the stalls opened and never travelled with any fluency. (op 6-1)
Starburst Excel ran nowhere near the form she showed when fourth on her debut in a fillies' maiden at Newmarket. (op 3-1 tchd 9-4)

1992 MOORTOWN GOLF CLUB CENTENARY STKS (H'CAP) 1m 2f 88y
4:55 (4:58) (Class 4) (0-85,85) 3-Y-O **£6,476** (£1,927; £963; £481) **Stalls** Low

Form RPR
2212 **1** **Barwell Bridge**[10] 1707 3-9-5 **83** .... JamesDoyle 11 90
(S Kirk) *sn chsng ldrs: styd on to ld towards fin* **12/1**
32-1 **2** 1/2 **Union Island (IRE)**[40] 1101 3-9-1 **79** .... NCallan 12 85
(K A Ryan) *hld up in mid-div: hdwy on outer over 2f out: ev ch ins fnl f: no ex* **33/1**
61- **3** *hd* **Raaeidd (IRE)**[180] 7312 3-9-2 **80** .... LDettori 9 86+
(M A Jarvis) *lw: hld up in mid-div: hdwy on outside 3f out: edgd lft: led over 1f out: hdd and no ex wl ins fnl f* **9/2**[1]
3-1 **4** *hd* **Bin End**[41] 1087 3-9-5 **83** .... JamieSpencer 5 89
(M L W Bell) *lw: w ldrs: led after 2f: hdd over 2f out: kpt on wl: no ex wl ins fnl f* **10/1**
5-14 **5** 1 1/2 **Muraweg (IRE)**[27] 1303 3-9-7 **85** .... RHills 15 88+
(J H M Gosden) *s.i.s: in rr: hdwy and swtchd to wd outside 2f out: styd on: nt rch ldrs* **8/1**[3]
610- **6** *nk* **Marching Time**[200] 6973 3-9-5 **83** .... RyanMoore 13 85+
(Sir Michael Stoute) *lw: hld up towards rr: hdwy whn nt clr run over 2f out: hit on hd by rival rdr's whip over 1f out: kpt on same pce* **9/2**[1]
66-1 **7** 1/2 **Puzzlemaster**[39] 1130 3-9-2 **80** .... JimmyQuinn 2 81
(M Botti) *s.i.s: hdwy whn hmpd over 2f out: c outside and styd on* **20/1**
21-0 **8** *nk* **Fastnet Storm (IRE)**[16] 1559 3-9-1 **79** .... AlanMunro 10 83+
(T P Tate) *w ldrs: led over 2f out tl over 1f out: one pce whn hmpd nr fin* **50/1**
041- **9** 1 3/4 **Call It On (IRE)**[219] 6539 3-9-4 **82** .... GeorgeBaker 6 79
(M H Tompkins) *t.k.h: trckd ldrs: one pce whn hmpd over 2f out* **13/2**[2]
024- **10** 3/4 **Cosmic Sun**[214] 6655 3-8-13 **82** .... FrederikTylicki(5) 4 77
(R A Fahey) *in tch: stmbld over 5f out: hmpd over 2f out: no threat after* **16/1**
201- **11** *nk* **Mannlichen**[174] 7397 3-9-0 **78** .... JoeFanning 8 73+
(M Johnston) *chsd ldrs: one pce whn hmpd 2f out* **12/1**
4-11 **12** 3/4 **Topolski (IRE)**[13] 1629 3-9-7 **85** .... RoystonFfrench 3 78
(M Johnston) *led 2f: chsd ldrs: wkng whn hmpd 2f out* **8/1**[3]
2-6 **13** 1 1/4 **Equipe De Nuit**[35] 1185 3-9-2 **80** .... SaleemGolam 18 71
(S C Williams) *t.k.h in rr: sme hdwy on ins whn hmpd over 2f out: no ch after* **33/1**
514- **14** 1 **Warrior One**[242] 5895 3-9-4 **82** .... PaulMulrennan 1 71+
(J Howard Johnson) *chsd ldrs: one pce on ins whn hmpd over 2f out* **20/1**
51-0 **15** 8 **Trumpstoo (USA)**[27] 1307 3-8-13 **77** .... PaulHanagan 20 50
(R A Fahey) *swtchd lft after star: t.k.h in rr: bhd fnl 3f* **40/1**
20-0 **16** 15 **Fol Liam**[45] 1019 3-8-13 **77** .... WilliamBuick 16 20
(Ian Williams) *in rr: bhd fnl 3f: t.o* **100/1**

2m 12.95s (0.45) **Going Correction** +0.05s/f (Good) **16** Ran SP% **123.1**
Speed ratings (Par 101): **100,99,99,99,98 97,97,97,95,95 94,94,93,92,86 74**
toteswinger: 1&2 £33.50, 1&3 £14.00, 2&3 £24.60. CSF £347.14 CT £1795.64 TOTE £16.30: £2.90, £4.00, £2.00, £2.00; EX 327.80 Place 6 £57.52, Place 5 £23.96.
Owner N Pickett **Bred** Dominic J Burke **Trained** Upper Lambourn, Berks
■ Stewards' Enquiry : L Dettori two-day ban:careless riding (May 27-28)

FOCUS
A very strong three-year-old handicap and a race that should produce lots of winners this season. However, it's worth noting Bin End set a muddling gallop, resulting in a time much slower than the other two races over this trip, and there was also some bunching in the straight, so the bare form needs treating with caution. as a result the form has not been rated as positively as it might have been.
Marching Time ◆ Official explanation: jockey said colt was denied a clear run
Puzzlemaster ◆ Official explanation: jockey said colt was denied a clear run
T/Jkpt: Not won. T/Plt: £132.50 to a £1 stake. Pool: £177,029.94. 974.63 winning tickets. T/Qpdt: £30.20 to a £1 stake. Pool: £7,203.59. 176.20 winning tickets. JR

1370 NAAS (L-H)
Wednesday, May 13
OFFICIAL GOING: Good to yielding

1993a CURRAGH LAWNS NURSING HOME EUROPEAN BREEDERS FUND FILLIES MAIDEN 6f
5:50 (5:51) 2-Y-O **£9,392** (£2,188; £965; £557)

RPR
1 **Kitty Kiernan** 2-9-0 .... KJManning 4 87+
(J S Bolger, Ire) *mde most: wnt clr fr under 2f out: rdn and styd on wl fr over 1f out: eased cl home* **7/4**[1]
2 2 1/2 **Lillie Langtry (IRE)** 2-9-0 .... JMurtagh 11 80
(A P O'Brien, Ire) *in tch towards rr: wnt mod 5th over 1f out: r.o wl into 2nd wout threatening wnr ins fnl f* **10/3**[2]
3 3 **A Mind Of Her Own (IRE)** 2-9-0 .... WMLordan 5 71
(David Wachman, Ire) *sn prom: t.k.h: 2nd fr 2f out: no imp fr over 1f out: dropped to 3rd and kpt on same pce ins fnl f* **7/2**[3]
4 1/2 **Diva Dolce (IRE)** 2-9-0 .... CDHayes 9 69
(Kevin Prendergast, Ire) *trckd ldrs: 3rd fr 2f out: no imp and kpt on same pce fr over 1f out* **12/1**
5 *nk* **Whipitydooda (IRE)** 2-9-0 .... PShanahan 10 68
(Tracey Collins, Ire) *trckd ldrs: 4th fr 2f out: no imp and kpt on same pce fr over 1f out* **10/1**
6 1 1/2 **Perino (IRE)** 2-9-0 .... JAHeffernan 13 64
(W McCreery, Ire) *s.i.s: towards rr: hdwy 2f out: rdn to go mod 6th and kpt on wout threatening fr over 1f out* **14/1**
7 1 3/4 **Bewitched (IRE)** 2-9-0 .... FMBerry 3 58
(Charles O'Brien, Ire) *in tch towards rr: clsr in 5th fr 2f out: sn no imp and kpt on same pce fr over 1f out* **12/1**
8 1 1/4 **Pink Lemonade (IRE)** 2-8-9 .... BACurtis(5) 14 55
(John Joseph Murphy, Ire) *trckd ldrs: 6th fr 2f out: sn no imp* **33/1**
9 1/2 **Cinnamon Tart (IRE)** 2-9-0 .... WJLee 12 53
(John Joseph Murphy, Ire) *sn off pce towards rr: n.d and kpt on fr 2f out* **40/1**
10 2 1/2 **Intapeace (IRE)** 2-9-0 .... RPCleary 1 46
(Francis Ennis, Ire) *trckd ldrs: cl 7th bef 1/2-way: no ex fr under 2f out* **20/1**
11 13 **Suas An Staire (IRE)**[10] 1711 2-8-7 .... KTO'Neill(7) 7 7
(Adrian Sexton, Ire) *cl up: rdn bef 1/2-way: lost pl and wknd fr 2f out* **20/1**
12 10 **Lukes Desire (IRE)**[19] 1497 2-9-0 .... CO'Donoghue 6 —
(F Costello, Ire) *cl up and sn disp ld briefly: wknd fr 2f out: eased fr over 1f out* **33/1**
13 10 **Seven Gifts** 2-8-11 .... DJMoran(3) 2 —
(Lee Smyth, Ire) *s.i.s and a bhd* **50/1**

1m 12.39s (-0.81) **13** Ran SP% **132.6**
CSF £7.77 TOTE £2.40: £1.60, £2.40, £1.90; DF 10.80.
Owner Ennistown Stud **Bred** Mrs C Regalado-Gonzalez **Trained** Coolcullen, Co Carlow

NOTEBOOK
Kitty Kiernan broke smartly to dispute the running, and entering the final furlong was a couple clear. She stuck to her task well and looks a decent sort. Her trainer won this corresponding race last year with Cuis Ghaire, who went on to land the Group 3 Swordlestown Stud Sprint back at this track before winning the Albany at the Royal meeting. A similar path wasn't ruled out for the winner, who is out of Alstemeria, a Danehill filly who won over 6f and finished fourth in the Irish 1,000 Guineas. She is a sister to Group 1 winner Spartacus and her offspring here look set for better things to come over the months ahead. (op 9/4)
Lillie Langtry(IRE) raced off the pace before doing her best work in the closing stages. The manner in which she quickened up inside the final furlong was impressive and she looks a surefire future winner with this initial run behind her, especially over a little further. (op 3/1 tchd 4/1)

1994a PAT DUNLEA MEMORIAL RACE 6f
6:20 (6:21) 2-Y-O **£11,740** (£2,735; £1,206; £696)

RPR
1 **Steinbeck (IRE)** 2-9-0 .... JMurtagh 5 99+
(A P O'Brien, Ire) *sn disp ld: in front over 1f out: rdn clr and styd on wl: eased nr fin* **9/4**[2]
2 2 1/2 **Gold Bubbles (USA)**[24] 1385 2-9-1 .... KJManning 4 90
(J S Bolger, Ire) *sn disp ld: jst hdd over 1f out whn bmpd rival and briefly unbalanced: sn no imp: kpt on same pce* **1/1**[1]
3 3 **Rockymountainhigh (IRE)**[9] 1754 2-9-0 .... WMLordan 3 80
(David Wachman, Ire) *trckd ldrs in 4th: rdn to go 3rd and no imp fr 1f out: kpt on same pce* **20/1**
4 4 **King Ledley (USA)**[52] 925 2-9-6 .... DPMcDonogh 1 74
(Kevin Prendergast, Ire) *sn disp ld: jst hdd over 1f out whn bdly hmpd: no ex after* **10/3**[3]
5 3 **Rockin N Reelin (USA)** 2-9-0 .... CDHayes 6 59
(J T Gorman, Ire) *dwlt: in rr: rdn bef 1/2-way: sn 5th and no imp* **25/1**
6 5 **Diamondgeezer Luke (IRE)** 2-9-0 .... JAHeffernan 2 44
(F Costello, Ire) *chsd ldrs in 5th: dropped to rr u.p 1/2-way: sn no imp* **50/1**

1m 12.1s (-1.10) **6** Ran SP% **114.4**
CSF £4.95 TOTE £2.70: £1.80, £1.10; DF 5.70.
Owner Michael Tabor **Bred** Dr D Harron **Trained** Ballydoyle, Co Tipperary
■ Stewards' Enquiry : K J Manning caution: careless riding

NOTEBOOK
Steinbeck(IRE) took advantage of the penalties carried by the two previous winners, but he clearly looked the best of this bunch. It was a muddling enough little race early on as the jockeys on the three market principals were wondering what each were going to do, but once they sorted that out it turned into a proper race. When the winner quickened on over a furlong out he soon had everything in trouble and just one crack of the whip was required as he only had to be nursed home. It was clearly a performance of some quality from a horse that can only improve. (op 9/4 tchd 2/1)
Gold Bubbles(USA) didn't appear to lose a whole lot in defeat. She was up there the whole way but couldn't match the turn of foot of the winner over a furlong out and she did proceed to lean in on King Ledley, but that aside she did pick up again inside the last. There was probably no disgrace in being beaten by Steinbeck, especially with a winner's penalty on her back, and she looks like another furlong won't trouble her. (op 4/5 tchd 11/10)

1996a BLUE WIND STKS (GROUP 3) (F&M) 1m 2f
7:20 (7:20) 3-Y-O+ **£53,640** (£15,679; £7,427; £2,475)

RPR
1 **Beauty O' Gwaun (IRE)**[205] 6869 3-8-9 .... MJKinane 7 105+
(John M Oxx, Ire) *racd in 6th: hdwy st: chal u.p and gained slt ld over 1f out: strly pressed and styd on wl fnl f: jst in front at line* **13/8**[1]
2 *hd* **Festival Princess (IRE)**[242] 5923 4-9-9 87 .... RPCleary 6 104
(Mrs John Harrington, Ire) *racd in 7th: gd hdwy on outer st: rdn in cl 2nd and ev ch fr over 1f out: styd on wl fnl f: jst failed* **33/1**
3 4 1/2 **Chinese White (IRE)**[10] 1715 4-9-9 108 .... PJSmullen 1 95
(D K Weld, Ire) *trckd ldrs in 4th: pushed along st: ev ch over 1f out: sn no imp in 3rd and kpt on same pce* **2/1**[2]
4 2 **Jakarta Jazz (IRE)**[25] 1370 3-8-9 89 .... CDHayes 4 92
(Kevin Prendergast, Ire) *dwlt: towards rr: rdn st: swtchd to chal fr 2f out: sn ev ch: no imp and kpt on same pce fr over 1f out* **12/1**
5 3 1/2 **Tamarind (IRE)**[10] 1716 3-8-9 .... JAHeffernan 3 85
(A P O'Brien, Ire) *racd in 5th: 6th st: sn rdn: no imp and kpt on fr over 1f out* **14/1**

6	*nk*	**Les Fazzani (IRE)**[165] 7491 5-9-9 .... DPMcDonogh 8	83
		(K A Ryan) *trckd ldr: led st: hdd and no ex u.p fr over 1f out* **7/2**[3]	
7	5	**Marina Of Venice (IRE)**[25] 1372 3-8-9 90....................(b[1]) KJManning 2	74
		(J S Bolger, Ire) *trckd ldrs in 3rd: rdn in 2nd st: lost pl and no ex fr over 1f out* **16/1**	
8	½	**Dollar Chick (IRE)**[213] 6689 5-9-9 88........................ WMLordan 5	72
		(Noel Meade, Ire) *racd towards rr in 8th: rdn st: no ex fr wl over 1f out* **50/1**	
9	2½	**Timabiyra (IRE)**[32] 1222 3-8-10 93 ow1............................ FMBerry 9	69
		(John M Oxx, Ire) *led: hdd st: sn lost pl and wknd fr over 1f out* **14/1**	

2m 14.9s (-0.70)
WFA 3 from 4yo+ 15lb **9** Ran SP% **125.5**
CSF £63.70 TOTE £2.40: £1.40, £10.90, £1.70; DF 117.90.
Owner Neil Jones **Bred** Abergwaun Farms **Trained** Currabeg, Co Kildare

FOCUS
The winning time was slow in comparison with the maiden on the card, and the runner-up rates a big improver, but the form could be okay rated around the fourth.

NOTEBOOK
Beauty O' Gwaun(IRE) did just enough on her seasonal reappearance to keep her unbeaten record intact, despite showing signs of inexperience. She looked green when battle commenced against the four-year-old Festival Princess and she rolled across to the far rail, but under a power-packed drive from Mick Kinane she came out on top by a head. She had looked a decent sort when she accounted for the above-average The Bull Hayes in a backend Curragh 7f maiden last October, and looks a good prospect this season. She is in the Epsom Oaks, but is not certain to go there as her trainer thinks she might need more racing and likes some cut in the ground. (op 7/4 tchd 2/1)
Festival Princess(IRE) ran a cracker on her first start since last September and only gave way in the final strides after galloping all the way to the line with the winner. She has a preference for some cut and under similar conditions could add to her sole success, recorded over 1m here last August.
Chinese White(IRE), fourth to Moonstone in last season's Irish Oaks, had the benefit of a previous run at Gowran Park this month and was tackling this trip for the first time. She held every chance after turning for home but was unable to raise her game in this ground. (op 9/4 tchd 7/4)
Jakarta Jazz(IRE) was not helped when she was slightly impeded inside the final furlong, but it made little difference. (op 8/1)
Tamarind(IRE) showed some improvement on her Gowran Park debut and looks to be going the right way. She can win her maiden before long on this evidence.
Les Fazzani(IRE) tracked the leader in second from the outset before taking over briefly into the straight, but she was soon fighting a losing battle. (op 7/2 tchd 3/1)
Marina Of Venice(IRE) was eased when her chance was gone after racing prominently.
Dollar Chick(IRE) travelled well into the straight but once the tempo increased she was another struggling to keep in touch. Given that this was her first start of the season, she should be open to some improvement on a sounder surface.
Timabiyra(IRE), stablemate of the winner, carried 1lb overweight. She set a good pace up front but once headed began to retreat. Official explanation: trainer said filly finished lame

1995 - 1999a (Foreign Racing) - See Raceform Interactive

1696 NEWMARKET (R-H)

Thursday, May 14

OFFICIAL GOING: Good to firm (8.6)
Wind: Light, across Weather: Overcast

2000 IFF CHARITY TRUST MEDIAN AUCTION MAIDEN STKS — 5f

5:45 (5:45) (Class 5) 2-Y-O **£3,885** (£1,156; £577; £288) **Stalls** High

Form				RPR
2	1		**The Hermitage (IRE)**[10] 1719 2-8-12 0............................ JoeFanning 4	84+
			(M Johnston) *mde all: shkn up over 1f out: r.o wl* **1/2**[1]	
	2	3¼	**Social Grace** 2-8-12 0.. PaulMulrennan 1	68
			(D H Brown) *swvd lft s: sn pushed along in rr: hdwy to chse wnr over 1f out: edgd lft and no imp* **28/1**	
	3	¾	**Audacity Of Hope** 2-9-3 0.. DaneO'Neill 3	71
			(P J McBride) *edgd lft s: chsd wnr tl rdn over 1f out: hung lft: styd on same pce* **11/2**[3]	
4	4	2¾	**Marosh (FR)**[21] 1482 2-9-3 0.. ShaneKelly 5	61
			(R M H Cowell) *wnt lft s: prom: racd keenly: rdn: hung lft and wknd over 1f out* **4/1**[2]	
0	5	¾	**Rosedale**[17] 1569 2-8-12 0.. JimCrowley 2	53
			(J A R Toller) *wnt lft s: prom: rdn 2f out: sn hung lft and wknd* **33/1**	

62.19 secs (3.09) **Going Correction** +0.125s/f (Good) **5** Ran SP% **108.4**
Speed ratings (Par 93): **80,74,73,69,68**
CSF £15.58 TOTE £1.40: £1.10, £8.60; EX 9.30.
Owner Sheikh Hamdan Bin Mohammed Al Maktoum **Bred** Lodge Park Stud **Trained** Middleham Moor, N Yorks

FOCUS
A fair maiden despite the small field and the winner built on his debut effort but the time was slow.

NOTEBOOK
The Hermitage(IRE) had no trouble losing her maiden following a debut second in a race that has subsequently seen the sixth horse, Dispol Kabira, win by a nose. She was able to dictate a modest early pace and won with plenty in hand. She has stamina on her dam's side and, although her sire had a propensity for speed, she should comfortably handle a sixth furlong. (op 2-5 tchd 8-15 in places)
Social Grace comes out of this debut with plenty of credit, showing immaturity at the start and during the race but buckling down well throughout the last furlong. By a fast first-season sire in Pastoral Pursuits, she has pace, too, on the dam's side and produced enough here to be worth a try in auctions, as she cost just £5,000. (op 20-1)
Audacity Of Hope tried to go the pace but is bred to want more than the minimum and should be more at home over 7f in time. Official explanation: jockey said colt hung left (op 6-1 tchd 13-2)
Marosh(FR) was disappointing following his encouraging debut in France and was the first to be ridden along but he is another who is bred to want further than this. Official explanation: jockey said colt was unsuited by the firm ground (op 5-1 tchd 11-2 in places)
Rosedale wasn't given a hard time and the Windsor race in which she was 12 lengths 11th on debut is working out. She has stamina on her dam's side and went through the ring for just £1,000 so an auction event over further might be on her agenda.

2001 ST NICHOLAS HOSPICE CARE FILLIES' H'CAP — 1m

6:15 (6:17) (Class 5) (0-75,75) 3-Y-O **£3,885** (£1,156; £577; £288) **Stalls** High

Form				RPR
10-	1		**Bombina**[194] 7144 3-8-13 70...................................... AdrianMcCarthy 8	77+
			(P W Chapple-Hyam) *hld up: hdwy over 3f out: nt clr run over 2f out: swtchd lft over 1f out: r.o to ld wl ins fnl f* **13/2**	
1-30	2	*nk*	**Victoria Sponge (IRE)**[10] 1744 3-9-2 73........................ RyanMoore 1	79
			(R Hannon) *chsd ldr tl led 3f out: rdn and hdd over 1f out: rallied to ld ins fnl f: sn hdd: r.o* **5/1**[2]	
1-	3	*nk*	**Hermione's Magic**[222] 6488 3-9-4 75.............................. DaneO'Neill 12	80+
			(P J McBride) *s.i.s: hld up: swtchd lft and hdwy over 1f out: r.o* **16/1**	
0-30	4	2¼	**Night Lily (IRE)**[6] 1839 3-8-10 67................................ JoeFanning 14	67
			(J Jay) *chsd ldrs: led over 1f out: rdn and hdd ins fnl f: no ex* **13/2**	
50-5	5	¾	**Surprise Party**[19] 1516 3-8-7 64.................................. RichardMullen 2	62
			(C F Wall) *hld up: rdn over 3f out: r.o ins fnl f: nvr nrr* **25/1**	
0-06	6	*nk*	**Breach Of Peace (USA)**[24] 1406 3-8-12 69................ SteveDrowne 15	67
			(R Charlton) *chsd ldrss: rdn and edgd rt over 1f out: styd on same pce* **12/1**	
21-3	7	1¾	**Miss Beat (IRE)**[28] 1315 3-9-2 73................................ JamieSpencer 10	67
			(B J Meehan) *hld up: racd keenly: hdwy over 4f out: rdn and ev ch 2f out: wknd ins fnl f* **7/2**[1]	
1-	8	6	**Chantilly Pearl (USA)**[161] 7546 3-9-1 72...................... PatCosgrave 13	52
			(J G Given) *s.s: a in rr: rdn over 3f out: sn wknd* **11/2**[3]	
6225	9	1	**Abu Dubai (IRE)**[19] 1531 3-8-9 66.................................. JimCrowley 6	43
			(C A Dwyer) *hld up: sme hdwy over 2f out: rdn and wknd over 1f out* **20/1**	
1-24	10	½	**Luckier (IRE)**[25] 1381 3-9-4 75.................................... JamesDoyle 4	51
			(S Kirk) *hld up: rdn over 2f out: sn wknd* **10/1**	
0-64	11	*nse*	**Novastasia (IRE)**[16] 1588 3-8-6 63.............................. ShaneKelly 9	39
			(W R Swinburn) *led 5f: wkng whn n.m.r over 1f out* **12/1**	
52-0	P		**Slant (IRE)**[36] 1185 3-9-4 75.. StephenCarson 11	—
			(Eve Johnson Houghton) *hld up: plld hrd: lost action over 3f out: sn p.u* **16/1**	

1m 39.41s (0.81) **Going Correction** +0.125s/f (Good) **12** Ran SP% **125.8**
Speed ratings (Par 96): **100,99,99,97,96 96,94,88,87,86 86,—**
toteswinger: 1&2 £4.20, 1&3 £35.60, 2&3 £5.70. CSF £41.56 CT £526.85 TOTE £5.90: £3.30, £2.30, £5.80; EX 54.50.
Owner C G P Wyatt **Bred** Dukes Stud & Overbury Stallions Ltd **Trained** Newmarket, Suffolk

FOCUS
Five of these fillies were making their handicap debuts and it produced a close finish.

2002 ORBITAL FOODS MAIDEN STKS — 1m 2f

6:50 (6:55) (Class 4) 3-Y-O **£5,180** (£1,541; £770; £384) **Stalls** High

Form				RPR
	1		**Gripsholm Castle (USA)** 3-8-12 0................................ IanMongan 9	93+
			(H R A Cecil) *hld up: hdwy over 2f out: led ins fnl f: r.o strly* **20/1**	
	2	4½	**Flame Of Gibraltar (IRE)** 3-8-12 0................................ TPQueally 6	84+
			(H R A Cecil) *a.p: chsd ldr over 2f out: rdn and ev ch ins fnl f: unable qck* **6/1**	
6	3	¾	**Mared (USA)**[10] 1729 3-9-3 0...................................... ShaneKelly 4	87
			(J Noseda) *racd alone tl jnd main gp 1/2-way: led: rdn over 1f out: hdd and no ex ins fnl f* **4/1**[3]	
	4	6	**Xtra Special** 3-8-12 0.. RyanMoore 7	70+
			(Sir Michael Stoute) *in rr and pushed along: bhd 6f out: styd on ins fnl f: n.d* **16/1**	
52	5	3½	**Ottoman Empire (FR)**[15] 1611 3-9-3 0.......................... TedDurcan 3	68
			(D R Lanigan) *prom: rdn over 2f out: wkng whn hung rt over 1f out: eased fnl f* **6/4**[1]	
5	6	3¾	**Golden Rock (IRE)**[29] 1289 3-9-3 0.............................. SteveDrowne 1	61
			(R Charlton) *wnt lft s: hld up: rdn over 2f out: sn wknd* **14/1**	
	7	8	**Danse On Wood** 3-9-3 0.. WilliamBuick 8	45
			(J Noseda) *s.s: a in rr: wknd over 3f out* **33/1**	
25-3	8	1½	**Alhaque (USA)**[42] 1088 3-9-3 81................................. JamieSpencer 2	51
			(P W Chapple-Hyam) *chsd ldr tl rdn and wknd over 2f out: eased* **7/2**[2]	

2m 6.14s (0.34) **Going Correction** +0.125s/f (Good) **8** Ran SP% **116.8**
Speed ratings (Par 101): **103,99,98,94,91 88,81,80**
toteswinger: 1&2 £59.10, 1&3 £23.60, 2&3 £3.90. CSF £136.66 TOTE £22.40: £4.50, £1.60, £1.80; EX 78.50.
Owner Gestut Ammerland **Bred** Aleyrion Bloodstock **Trained** Newmarket, Suffolk

FOCUS
A decent maiden with some very costly purchases.
Ottoman Empire(FR) Official explanation: jockey said colt failed to handle the ground
Alhaque(USA) Official explanation: jockey said colt never travelled

2003 GUARDIAN DIRECT MARKETING PRINT, PACK & POST H'CAP — 1m 2f

7:25 (7:29) (Class 3) (0-90,90) 4-Y-O+ **£7,771** (£2,312; £1,155; £577) **Stalls** High

Form				RPR
210/	1		**Seeking The Buck (USA)**[438] 5543 5-8-8 80.................... TPQueally 5	95
			(R M Beckett) *trckd ldrs: led over 2f out: shkn up over 1f out: styd on wl* **10/1**	
0-40	2	3¼	**Kavachi (IRE)**[22] 1460 6-9-0 86.................................... RyanMoore 4	94
			(G L Moore) *hld up: hdwy over 2f out: rdn to chse wnr fnl f: no imp* **4/1**[2]	
655-	3	2	**Mega Watt (IRE)**[202] 6949 4-8-4 76............................ WilliamBuick 2	80
			(W Jarvis) *chsd ldrs: rdn over 2f out: styd on same pce appr fnl f* **5/1**[3]	
50-3	4	*nk*	**Dona Alba (IRE)**[22] 1460 4-9-4 90................................ TedDurcan 8	93
			(J L Dunlop) *hld up: hdwy over 3f out: chsd wnr over 2f out: sn rdn and ev ch: wknd ins fnl f* **9/4**[1]	
010-	5	6	**Bandama (IRE)**[174] 7404 6-9-3 89................................ JimCrowley 6	80
			(Mrs A J Perrett) *hld up in tch: rdn and wknd over 2f out* **6/1**	
0/60	6	11	**Kaleo**[22] 1460 5-8-8 80.. ShaneKelly 7	49
			(S Dow) *chsd ldr tl led over 3f out: hdd over 2f out: sn rdn and wknd* **10/1**	
25-1	7	20	**Serious Choice (IRE)**[30] 1274 4-8-4 79.......................... JackMitchell(3) 1	8
			(J R Boyle) *hld up: rdn: hung rt and wknd over 2f out* **17/2**	
30-0	8	13	**Goodwood Starlight (IRE)**[22] 1460 4-9-3 89.............. RichardMullen 3	—
			(G L Moore) *led over 6f: sn rdn and wknd* **16/1**	

2m 5.21s (-0.59) **Going Correction** +0.125s/f (Good) **8** Ran SP% **116.3**
Speed ratings (Par 107): **107,104,102,102,97 88,72,62**
toteswinger: 1&2 £11.90, 1&3 £5.60, 2&3 £7.60. CSF £50.61 CT £227.94 TOTE £14.20: £2.80, £2.00, £1.60; EX 51.80.
Owner Malcolm C Denmark **Bred** Flaxman Holdings Ltd **Trained** Whitsbury, Hants

FOCUS
A decent handicap but a clear-cut winner.

NOTEBOOK
Seeking The Buck(USA) won on his first Flat appearance since September 2007, having made an abortive attempt over hurdles in March 2008. Previously trained on the Flat by Michael Magnusson and now without the tongue-tie and blinkers that were once a regular fixture, the winner had dropped 7lb and was back to his last winning mark at a distance over which his two victories have come. He doesn't have many miles on the clock and can only improve if staying in one piece. (tchd 12-1)
Kavachi(IRE) got going late but is still coming down slowly and, despite dropping 3lb since last July, is still 6lb higher than his last winning mark of a year ago. (op 10-3 tchd 3-1)
Mega Watt(IRE) was backed to run well and did so, staying on well after looking tapped for toe and rallying to get third. He will be sharper for this reappearance. (op 10-1)
Dona Alba(IRE), racing off the same mark as at Epsom, had no excuse. (op 2-1 tchd 5-2 in places)
Bandama(IRE) is now three from 29 but will be more tuned in for this seasonal debut and probably needs the extra 2f over which his last success came last October. (tchd 5-1)
Kaleo is dropping down the weights but dropped away quickly. Official explanation: jockey said gelding was unsuited by the firm ground (op 12-1 tchd 16-1)

Serious Choice(IRE) failed to cope with an 8lb rise for an easy win last time. (op 8-1)
Goodwood Starlight(IRE) got very warm. (op 25-1)

2004 SIMON GIBSON CONDITIONS STKS 1m

8:00 (8:02) (Class 3) 3-Y-O **£9,066** (£2,697; £1,348; £673) **Stalls High**

Form RPR

13-2 **1** **Four Winds**[27] 1326 3-8-12 100 JamieSpencer 1 103
(M L W Bell) *racd centre: led that pair but off the pce: jnd main gp over 3f out: led over 2f out: rdn and hung rt over 1f out: styd on* **11/10**[1]

136- **2** *2* **Patrician's Glory (USA)**[229] 6267 3-8-12 103 JohnEgan 10 98
(T P Tate) *racd towards far side: hld up: hdwy over 2f out: rdn to chse wnr and hung lft over 1f out: no imp ins fnl f* **7/2**[2]

-622 **3** *2 1/4* **Shampagne**[12] 1679 3-9-3 103 DTDaSilva(7) 5 105
(P F I Cole) *racd towards far side: chsd ldrs: pushed along over 3f out: rdn over 2f out: styd on same pce fnl f* **6/1**[3]

4-1 **4** *2 1/4* **African Art (USA)**[19] 1508 3-8-12 83 TedDurcan 2 88
(B J Meehan) *chsd ldr centre tl jnd main gp over 3f out: rdn over 2f out: no ex fnl f* **13/2**

-305 **5** *5* **Sohcahtoa (IRE)**[20] 1484 3-8-12 97 RyanMoore 8 77
(R Hannon) *racd towards far side: chsd clr ldr tl rdn over 2f out: wknd over 1f out* **7/1**

1650 **6** *14* **Quick Single (USA)**[6] 1839 3-8-5 70 (v) CarolineKelly(7) 4 44
(P S McEntee) *awkward leaving stalls: racd alone in middle of two gps: sn pushed along towards rr: rdn and wknd over 3f out: sn hung rt* **200/1**

464 **7** *nse* **Rossatron**[26] 1362 3-8-12 72 JoeFanning 9 44
(T T Clement) *racd far side: led and sn wl clr: wknd and hdd over 2f out* **200/1**

1m 39.32s (0.72) **Going Correction** +0.125s/f (Good) **7 Ran SP% 111.0**
Speed ratings (Par 103): **101,99,96,94,89 75,75**
toteswinger: 1&2 £1.10, 1&3 £3.20, 2&3 £4.30. CSF £4.81 TOTE £1.90: £1.40, £1.80; EX 5.90.
Owner The Queen **Bred** The Queen **Trained** Newmarket, Suffolk

FOCUS
A good conditions event but the small field spread out to cover nearly the width of the course in the search for suitable ground but came together from halfway.

NOTEBOOK
Four Winds travelled extremely well and was driven right out close home. He got into this race without a penalty and was only 2lb off the top on adjusted ratings and had the pace to handle this drop back from 1m2f over which he was second to High Heeled on his reappearance at Newbury. Connections considered the very soft ground was against him there and he now goes back to 1m2f for the Hampton Court Stakes at Royal Ascot where he escapes a penalty. (op 10-11 tchd 5-4)
Patrician's Glory(USA) was best on official figures by 2lb but had every chance and appears to lack serious pace when it matters. His placed Group form last season was at 7f and he might be worth a try back over that distance now he has had his first run for a new yard. Official explanation: jockey said colt lost his action and hung left (op 11-2)
Shampagne had a double penalty, so while rated the same as Patricians Glory, was always going to struggle conceding 12lb despite the 7lb claim of his inexperienced rider. (op 7-1 tchd 15-2)
African Art(USA) was facing a big upgrade from winning a Haydock maiden and didn't seem to be striding out when put under pressure. (op 9-2)
Rossatron Official explanation: jockey said colt hung both ways and had no more to give

2005 TAXFREEMONEY.COM H'CAP 5f

8:30 (8:30) (Class 5) (0-75,73) 3-Y-O **£3,885** (£1,156; £577; £288) **Stalls High**

Form RPR

0-62 **1** *1/2* **Kheylide (IRE)**[10] 1720 3-8-10 65 SilvestreDeSousa 7 71+
(Mrs D J Sanderson) *chsd ldrs: sn pushed along: rdn and hung rt wl over 1f out: hmpd sn after tl swtchd lft ins fnl f: r.o wl toward fin: fin 2nd, 1/2l: awrdd r* **5/2**[2]

-601 **2** **Ziggy Lee**[28] 1311 3-8-12 72 WilliamCarson(5) 6 79+
(S C Williams) *hld up: hdwy and hung rt fr over 1f out: rdn to ld wl ins fnl f: r.o: fin 1st: disqualified and plcd 2nd* **2/1**[1]

-401 **3** *shd* **Amosite**[26] 1359 3-9-2 71 (v) ShaneKelly 8 73
(J R Jenkins) *led and sn pushed clr: rdn over 1f out: hdd wl ins fnl f* **20/1**

44-6 **4** *1* **Choisharp (IRE)**[17] 1563 3-8-2 62 AndreaAtzeni(5) 10 60
(M Botti) *sn outpcd: rdn and r.o wl ins fnl f: nt rch ldrs* **15/2**

1131 **5** *1/2* **Speak The Truth (IRE)**[16] 1583 3-9-0 69 (p) PatCosgrave 9 66
(J R Boyle) *s.i.s: sn prom: rdn over 1f out: styd on same pce ins fnl f* **15/2**

1034 **6** *2 1/4* **Green Onions**[77] 685 3-8-11 71 GabrielHannon(5) 2 60
(D J S Ffrench Davis) *chsd clr ldr tl rdn over 1f out: n.m.r ins fnl f: wknd towards fin* **20/1**

2325 **7** *2 1/2* **Flamsteed (IRE)**[24] 1414 3-9-3 72 FrancisNorton 1 52
(M Quinn) *sn pushed along in mid-div: outpcd 1/2-way: n.d after* **11/2**[3]

310- **8** *2 1/4* **Zelos Girl (IRE)**[266] 5204 3-9-4 73 SaleemGolam 5 44
(Rae Guest) *s.i.s: outpcd* **25/1**

4000 **9** *1 1/4* **Josiah Bartlett (IRE)**[6] 1839 3-7-11 59 oh1 (t) CarolineKelly(7) 4 26
(P S McEntee) *s.i.s: outpcd* **100/1**

60.20 secs (1.10) **Going Correction** +0.125s/f (Good) **9 Ran SP% 115.2**
Speed ratings (Par 99): **95,96,95,93,92 89,85,81,79**
toteswinger: 1&2 £5.20, 1&3 £8.80, 2&3 £6.10. CSF £7.49 CT £76.67 TOTE £3.00: £1.60, £1.20, £4.20; EX 8.30 Place 6 £61.03, Place 5 £43.11. .
Owner R J Budge **Bred** Ged O'Leary **Trained** Wiseton, Notts
■ Stewards' Enquiry : William Carson three-day ban: careless riding (May 28 -30)

FOCUS
A rough race when it began in earnest, with Ziggy Lee passing the post first but demoted after a stewards' inquiry for causing serious interference to Kheylide a furlong out.
Zelos Girl(IRE) Official explanation: jockey said filly never travelled
T/Plt: £107.80 to a £1 stake. Pool: £52,811.67. 357.61 winning tickets. T/Qpdt: £17.10 to a £1 stake. Pool: £4,798.44. 207.30 winning tickets. CR

1703 SALISBURY (R-H)

Thursday, May 14

OFFICIAL GOING: Firm (good to firm in places; 9.9)
Wind: Moderate, against Weather: overcast, steady rain from 2nd race

2006 SPORTINGBET.COM MAIDEN FILLIES' STKS 1m 1f 198y

1:50 (1:50) (Class 5) 3-Y-O+ **£3,885** (£1,156; £577; £288) **Stalls High**

Form RPR

5- **1** **Aromatic**[237] 6081 3-8-12 0 RichardMullen 12 82
(J H M Gosden) *mde all: hung lft fr wl over 1f out: kpt on: pushed out: hld on* **7/4**[1]

0 **2** *hd* **Lady Artemisia (IRE)**[17] 1573 3-8-12 0 IanMongan 10 82+
(M L W Bell) *mid-div: hdwy over 3f out: rdn to chse wnr 2f out: kpt on ins fnl f: clsng at fin* **28/1**

6-3 **3** *4 1/2* **Entreat**[20] 1488 3-8-12 0 RobertWinston 14 73
(Sir Michael Stoute) *trckd ldrs: effrt over 2f out: styd on same pce fr over 1f out* **2/1**[2]

0- **4** *1* **Beauchamp Xiara**[194] 7140 3-8-12 0 DaneO'Neill 2 71
(H Candy) *wnt lft s: sn mid-div: hdwy in centre fr over 3f out: styd on fr over 1f out but nvr threatened ldrs* **25/1**

0-4 **5** *1 1/2* **Silken Promise (USA)**[20] 1488 3-8-12 0 AdamKirby 9 68
(W R Swinburn) *trckd ldr: rdn to chal over 2f out: fdd ent fnl f* **17/2**

0- **6** *1* **You Say I Say (USA)**[194] 7140 3-8-7 0 Louis-PhilippeBeuzelin(5) 5 66
(Sir Michael Stoute) *chsd ldrs: rdn over 3f out: drifted lft 2f out: fdd fnl f* **7/1**[3]

00- **7** *1/2* **Morning Calm**[202] 6945 3-8-12 0 SteveDrowne 3 65
(R Charlton) *hld up towards rr: rdn 3f out: sme late prog: nvr a danger* **33/1**

50- **8** *7* **Jumaana (IRE)**[219] 6565 3-8-12 0 TPO'Shea 7 51
(J L Dunlop) *awkward leaving stalls: a towards rr* **12/1**

0-0 **9** *4* **Rocky Heights (IRE)**[24] 1407 3-8-12 0 TedDurcan 11 43
(J L Dunlop) *a towards rr* **50/1**

4-5 **10** *2* **Luthien (IRE)**[19] 1532 3-8-12 0 ChrisCatlin 1 39
(W R Swinburn) *a bhd* **25/1**

0-6 **11** *30* **Vella**[16] 1579 3-8-12 0 JamesDoyle 13 —
(H J L Dunlop) *mid-div: rdn over 3f out: sn wknd* **66/1**

2m 6.69s (-3.21) **Going Correction** -0.05s/f (Good) **11 Ran SP% 118.0**
Speed ratings (Par 100): **110,109,106,105,104 103,103,97,94,92 68**toteswinger: 1&2 £31.70, 1&3 £1.50, 2&3 £24.30 CSF £toteswinger: 1&2 £31.70, 1&3 £1.50, 2&3 £24.30 .
Owner Cheveley Park Stud **Bred** Cheveley Park Stud Ltd **Trained** Newmarket, Suffolk

FOCUS
This was probably a decent fillies' maiden and the third looks the best guide to the level.
Vella Official explanation: jockey said filly swerved left-handed

2007 SPORTINGBET.COM MAIDEN STKS 5f

2:20 (2:25) (Class 4) 2-Y-O **£6,476** (£1,927; £963; £481) **Stalls High**

Form RPR

5 **1** **Russian Rock (IRE)**[12] 1669 2-9-3 0 LPKeniry 2 78
(R A Teal) *racd keenly: trckd ldrs: led over 1f out: kpt on: drvn out* **3/1**[2]

0 **2** *1/2* **Spanish Acclaim**[27] 1323 2-9-3 0 TolleyDean 8 76
(J G Portman) *uns rdr and galloped loose to s: s.i.s: in tch: sltly keen after 1f: swtchd lft 2f out: sn rdn: r.o wl fnl f* **16/1**

3 *shd* **Kalam Daleel (IRE)** 2-9-3 0 DarryllHolland 7 76+
(M R Channon) *got rid of rdr ent stalls and cantered loose but sn ct: chsd ldr: rdn to ld over 2f out: hdd over 1f out: kpt on* **4/1**[3]

4 *2 1/4* **Warning Song (USA)** 2-9-3 0 AdamKirby 3 70+
(Mrs A J Perrett) *hld up: outpcd over 2f out: styd on wl fnl f: wnt 4th towards fin* **10/1**

2 **5** *1* **Tiradito (USA)**[14] 1630 2-9-3 0 TedDurcan 9 64+
(M Botti) *led tl over 2f out: sn rdn: hld whn nt clr run on rails over 1f out: edgd lft and one pce fnl f* **15/8**[1]

6 *1* **Palisades Park** 2-9-3 0 RichardHughes 6 60
(R Hannon) *trckd ldrs: nt clr run wl over 1f out: swtchd lft: sn rdn: fdd fnl 70yds* **9/2**

7 *8* **Vadition (IRE)** 2-8-12 0 NeilChalmers 4 25
(J J Bridger) *s.i.s: last of bunch: wknd 2f out* **100/1**

62.21 secs (1.21) **Going Correction** -0.05s/f (Good) **7 Ran SP% 113.9**
Speed ratings (Par 95): **86,85,85,81,79 78,65**
toteswinger: 1&2 £6.00, 1&3 £3.20, 2&3 £11.10 CSF £46.39 TOTE £3.50: £1.80, £7.30; EX 47.70 Trifecta £118.40 Pool: £240.16 - 1.50 winning units..
Owner M Vickers **Bred** Barronstown Stud And Mrs T Stack **Trained** Ashtead, Surrey

FOCUS
An ordinary juvenile maiden with the form rated slightly below average for the race.

NOTEBOOK
Russian Rock(IRE), who came in for good support beforehand, stuck on well for pressure to get the job done. He showed plenty of speed before fading on his debut at Goodwood and showed the benefit of that experience here,leading over a furlong out and knuckling down under a strong ride. He will stay further than this and should have more to offer. (op 11-2)
Spanish Acclaim, who unshipped his rider going to the start and played up in stalls, was also slowly away and he did remarkably well to finish as close as he did, staying on well for pressure and just nicking second. This was a big step up on his initial effort. (op 12-1)
Kalam Daleel(IRE), another to play up and unship his rider down at the start, was soon caught and expended little energy. He was a bit keen in the race and, having gone to the front over two out, couldn´t see it out as well as the winner. This was a pleasing start and natural improvement should see him winning a maiden. (op 3-1 tchd 9-2)
Warning Song(USA), who very much has a US dirt sprinter´s pedigree, kept on nicely having been outpaced and should learn a good deal from this initial experience. Official explanation: jockey said colt hung left-handed (op 9-1 tchd 17-2)
Tiradito(USA), a well-beaten second on his debut at Yarmouth, showed good early speed, but was already headed and beaten when a bit short of room. (op 9-4)
Palisades Park, whose yard had won this for the previous two years, was the selected of six stable entries, but he failed to get home having travelled strongly. He should be able to improve on this. (op 4-1 tchd 5-1)

2008 EUROPEAN BREEDERS' FUND FILLIES' H'CAP 1m 1f 198y

2:50 (2:55) (Class 4) (0-85,81) 3-Y-O **£7,447** (£2,216; £1,107; £553) **Stalls High**

Form RPR

3-1 **1** **Rosika**[16] 1579 3-8-12 77 Louis-PhilippeBeuzelin(5) 9 85+
(Sir Michael Stoute) *hld up: stdy prog fr over 5f out: rdn to ld 2f out: pushed out fnl f: styd on wl* **10/3**[1]

6-1 **2** *1* **Coming Back**[56] 876 3-9-7 81 RobertHavlin 7 87+
(J H M Gosden) *trckd ldrs: swtchd lft over 2f out: sn rdn and ev ch: kpt on but edgd lft fnl f: a being hld* **4/1**[2]

34-1 **3** *2 3/4* **Ballet Dancer (IRE)**[19] 1532 3-9-0 74 PhilipRobinson 6 74
(M A Jarvis) *led for over 1f out: trckd ldr: led over 3f out: rdn and hdd over 2f out: styd on same pce fr over 1f out* **4/1**[2]

400- **4** *1* **Full Of Nature**[246] 5791 3-9-1 75 GeorgeBaker 4 73+
(S Kirk) *v.s.a: bhd: stl last whn nt clr run jst over 2f out: rdn and styd on fr over 1f out: nrst fin* **16/1**

656- **5** *1* **Capitelli (IRE)**[180] 7337 3-9-4 78 RichardHughes 1 74
(R Hannon) *led after 1f tl over 3f out: sn rdn: kpt on same pce fnl 2f* **8/1**

15-0 **6** *shd* **Zaaqya**[28] 1303 3-9-4 78 TPO'Shea 12 74
(J L Dunlop) *trckd ldrs: rdn over 3f out: one pce fnl 2f* **9/1**

021- **7** *shd* **Sri Kandi**[239] 6013 3-9-3 77 ChrisCatlin 13 73
(P F I Cole) *taken v steadily to s: hld up: rdn and prog to chse ldrs: over 3f out: one pce fnl 2f* **18/1**

-232 **8** *nse* **Light Dubai (IRE)**[14] 1622 3-8-13 73 DarryllHolland 5 69
(M R Channon) *trckd ldrs: rdn to ld briefly over 2f out: sn hld: fdd ins fnl f* **6/1**[3]

061- **9** *3 ½* **Red Reef**^{258} [5460] 3-8-5 **65**................................... LiamJones 11 54
(D J Coakley) *t.k.h: hld up: effrt to chse ldrs over 2f out: wknd over 1f out* **12/1**

2m 10.41s (0.51) **Going Correction** -0.05s/f (Good) **9** Ran SP% **117.3**
Speed ratings (Par 98): **95,94,92,91,90 90,90,90,87**
toteswinger: 1&2 £3.70, 1&3 £4.10, 2&3 £3.80 CSF £16.96 CT £55.06 TOTE £4.10: £1.60, £1.50, £1.90; EX 17.00 Trifecta £74.80 Pool: £353.90 - 3.50 winning units..
Owner Sir Evelyn De Rothschild **Bred** Southcourt Stud **Trained** Newmarket, Suffolk

FOCUS
They didn´t go much of a gallop in what looked a fair fillies´ handicap. The front pair pulled clear with the fourth to sixth setting the level.
Ballet Dancer(IRE) Official explanation: jockey said filly was unsuited by the firm (good to firm places) ground
Full Of Nature ◆ Official explanation: jockey said filly missed the break

2009 MATTHEW CLARK CLAIMING STKS 6f 212y
3:25 (3:25) (Class 5) 3-Y-O **£3,238** (£963; £481; £240) **Stalls** High

Form RPR
433 **1** **Danies Boy (IRE)**^{31} [1250] 3-8-11 72................................ RichardHughes 10 66+
(R Hannon) *racd keenly: led for 1f: remained prom: shkn up to ld 1f out: r.o wl* **11/10**^{1}
3-06 **2** *1 ¼* **Mr Flannegan**^{19} [1516] 3-8-0 60.. AmyScott$^{(7)}$ 7 58
(H Candy) *prom: led over 2f out: rdn and hdd ent fnl f: nt pce of wnr* **25/1**
24 **3** *1* **Swans A Swimming (IRE)**^{48} [982] 3-8-11 0................(t) ChrisCatlin 5 60
(J A Osborne) *chsd ldrs: rdn over 2f out: drifted rt but r.o ins fnl f* **10/1**
-640 **4** *1 ½* **Cwmni**^{79} [662] 3-8-2 44.. CatherineGannon 17 47
(B Palling) *trckd ldrs: rdn and ev ch over 2f out: one pce whn hung lft over 1f out* **40/1**
1160 **5** *1* **Swiss Art (IRE)**^{7} [1811] 3-8-9 70.................................. RobertWinston 13 51
(R A Harris) *racd keenly: hung lft most of way: led after 1f tl over 2f out: sn rdn and drifted lft: one pce fr over 1f out* **7/2**^{2}
-040 **6** *¾* **Abhainn (IRE)**^{20} [1492] 3-8-5 49................................ FrankieMcDonald 2 45
(B Palling) *plld hrd in mid-div: rdn over 2f out: swtchd rt and hdwy over 1f out: no further imp ins fnl f* **33/1**
0-51 **7** *4* **Taste Of Honey (IRE)**^{16} [1584] 3-8-6 65...................... KirstyMilczarek 8 39
(D W P Arbuthnot) *mid-div: rdn whn swtchd rt 2f out: wknd 1f out* **9/2**^{3}
8 *1* **Steamer (IRE)** 3-8-5 0.. SaleemGolam 11 32
(P Winkworth) *trckd ldrs: rdn 3f out: wknd jst over 1f out* **20/1**
6P-0 **9** *1 ¾* **Miss Kadee**^{9} [1772] 3-8-4 58 ow2................................ SimonWhitworth 6 26
(J S Moore) *hld up: effrt 3f out but nt pce to get on terms: wknd ent fnl f* **33/1**
1454 **10** *14* **Cognac Boy (USA)**^{62} [827] 3-8-5 60 ow1........................(b) PNolan$^{(7)}$ 3 —
(A B Haynes) *s.i.s: squeezed out after 1f: a in rr* **20/1**
430- **11** *4* **Benetti (IRE)**^{279} [4827] 3-8-9 47.................................. EdwardCreighton 1 —
(M Madgwick) *bhd whn struggling 3f out* **66/1**

1m 28.73s (-0.27) **Going Correction** -0.05s/f (Good) **11** Ran SP% **120.3**
Speed ratings (Par 99): **99,97,96,94,93 92,88,87,85,69 64**
toteswinger: 1&2 £8.00, 1&3 £3.80, 2&3 £15.50 CSF £41.38 TOTE £2.10: £1.30, £3.40, £2.40; EX 34.40.Danies Boy was claimed by Debbie Mountain for £8000.
Owner Simon Leech **Bred** J K Thoroughbreds **Trained** East Everleigh, Wilts

FOCUS
This was not much of a claimer although the majority of the first six ran close to their marks.
Swiss Art(IRE) Official explanation: jockey said gelding hung left-handed
Abhainn(IRE) Official explanation: jockey said gelding ran too free
Taste Of Honey(IRE) Official explanation: jockey said filly lost its action

2010 BEGBIES TRAYNOR H'CAP 6f
4:00 (4:02) (Class 5) (0-75,75) 3-Y-O **£3,238** (£963; £481; £240) **Stalls** High

Form RPR
-305 **1** **Rio Royale (IRE)**^{62} [829] 3-9-1 **72**................................ AdamKirby 5 78
(Mrs A J Perrett) *in tch: tk clsr order over 2f out: led over 1f out: r.o wl: rdn out* **10/1**
061 **2** *1 ¾* **Taurus Twins**^{13} [1644] 3-8-7 **64**..........................(b) RobertWinston 17 64
(R J Price) *hld up on far rails: nt clr run whn swtchd lft over 2f out: hdwy u.p over 1f out: r.o ins fnl f* **8/1**
50-6 **3** *nk* **Red Rossini (IRE)**^{35} [1196] 3-8-13 **70**.......................... RichardHughes 15 69
(R Hannon) *chsd ldrs: rdn over 3f out: swtchd lft over 1f out: r.o* **5/1**^{2}
3201 **4** *nk* **Riflessione**^{16} [1583] 3-9-2 **73**...............................(b) ChrisCatlin 8 71
(R A Harris) *wnt sltly lft s: hld up: rdn over 3f out: edgd rt and hdwy over 1f out: r.o fnl f* **12/1**
2100 **5** *¾* **True Decision**^{16} [1583] 3-8-7 **64**................................ CatherineGannon 4 62+
(S Kirk) *hld up: nt clr run over 2f out: sn rdn: hdwy whn bmpd 1f out: r.o* **16/1**
21-0 **6** *shd* **Hillside Lad**^{24} [1414] 3-8-13 **70**................................ RichardKingscote 12 65
(R M Beckett) *trckd ldrs: rdn to ld briefly over 1f out: no ex fnl f* **14/1**
2-55 **7** *½* **Ben's Dream (IRE)**^{23} [1419] 3-8-12 **69**.............................. LPKeniry 16 63
(A M Balding) *prom: rdn over 2f out: one pce fnl f* **7/1**^{3}
4200 **8** *nk* **Jeremiah (IRE)**^{7} [1814] 3-9-1 **72**................................ PatDobbs 13 65
(J G Portman) *hld up: rdn whn swtchd lft over 2f out: hdwy and edgd further lft over 1f out: kpt on same pce* **16/1**
4112 **9** *1* **Song Of Praise**^{27} [1322] 3-9-2 **73**................................ FergusSweeney 3 63
(M Blanshard) *in tch: effrt over 2f out: wknd ins fnl f* **14/1**
60-6 **10** *nk* **Day In Dubai**^{14} [1618] 3-8-6 **63** oh9 ow2......................... NeilChalmers 14 52
(J J Bridger) *a mid-div* **100/1**
2136 **11** *½* **Auld Arty (FR)**^{45} [1033] 3-9-4 **75**..............................(p) RobertHavlin 9 62
(T G Mills) *nvr bttr than mid-div* **14/1**
00-3 **12** *¾* **Cheam Forever (USA)**^{43} [1075] 3-8-9 **66**........................ TravisBlock 6 51
(R Charlton) *towards rr: struggling over 3f out: nvr a factor* **9/2**^{1}
0-16 **13** *¾* **Hi Shinko**^{28} [1305] 3-9-0 **71**..................................(b^{1}) TGMcLaughlin 2 53
(B R Millman) *wnt lft s: sn chsng ldrs: rdn over 2f out: hld whn bmpd 1f out: wknd* **14/1**
-355 **14** *¾* **Bees River (IRE)**^{16} [1583] 3-8-5 **62**............................. NickyMackay 10 42
(A P Jarvis) *led: rdn and hdd over 1f out: sn wknd* **33/1**
20-0 **15** *2 ¼* **Flute Magic**^{20} [1491] 3-8-12 **72**.............................. JamesMillman$^{(3)}$ 1 45
(W S Kittow) *carried lft s: drifted bdly lft fr over 3f out: a towards rr* **16/1**
60-0 **16** *48* **Bermondsey Bob (IRE)**^{12} [1686] 3-8-8 **65**...................(p) TolleyDean 7 —
(J L Spearing) *hmpd s: sn struggling: virtually p.u wl over 3f out* **16/1**

1m 14.63s (-0.17) **Going Correction** -0.05s/f (Good) **16** Ran SP% **129.4**
Speed ratings (Par 99): **99,96,96,95,94 94,94,93,92,91 91,90,89,88,85 21**
toteswinger: 1&2 £23.60, 1&3 £24.60, 2&3 £6.90 CSF £93.02 CT £481.29 TOTE £17.10: £3.30, £2.30, £1.60, £3.00; EX 139.70.
Owner Mrs Amanda Perrett **Bred** Glending Bloodstock **Trained** Pulborough, W Sussex
■ Stewards' Enquiry : Adam Kirby caution: used whip with excessive frequency.

FOCUS
This was a competitive sprint handicap but the form is modest rated around the placed horses.
Hillside Lad Official explanation: jockey said gelding had no more to give
Flute Magic Official explanation: jockey said gelding hung left-handed

2011 AXMINSTER CARPETS APPRENTICE H'CAP (WHIPS SHALL BE CARRIED BUT NOT USED) 6f 212y
4:35 (4:35) (Class 5) (0-70,74) 4-Y-O+ **£3,238** (£963; £481; £240) **Stalls** High

Form RPR
2101 **1** **Seneschal**^{2} [1958] 8-9-8 **73** 6ex...................................... PNolan 8 81
(A B Haynes) *mde all: drifted lft fr over 2f out: jst hld on* **4/1**^{3}
41 **2** *nse* **Miss Glitters (IRE)**^{21} [1476] 4-9-0 **70**............................ RyanClark$^{(5)}$ 14 78
(H Morrison) *mid-div: hdwy to chse ldrs 4f out: r.o ins fnl f: jst failed* **5/2**^{1}
0-14 **3** *nse* **Hobson**^{9} [1773] 4-8-6 **64**.. DanielBlackett$^{(7)}$ 2 72
(Eve Johnson Houghton) *sn pressing wnr: kpt on and ev ch thrght fnl f: jst hld* **7/2**^{2}
660- **4** *4* **Fifty (IRE)**^{297} [4252] 4-9-2 **70**................................ CharlesEddery$^{(3)}$ 4 67
(R Hannon) *mid-div: hdwy 3f out: swtchd lft 2f out: styd on fnl f* **14/1**
6200 **5** *¾* **Ishibee (IRE)**^{5} [1876] 5-8-0 **56** oh8..........................(p) DannyBrock$^{(5)}$ 11 51
(J J Bridger) *mid-div: outpcd 3f out: styd on fr 2f out: no further imp fnl f* **33/1**
1011 **6** *6* **Super Frank (IRE)**^{14} [1619] 6-8-12 **68**.......................(p) BarryAdams$^{(5)}$ 9 47
(J Akehurst) *awkward leaving stalls: chsd ldrs: effrt over 2f out: wknd over 1f out* **11/2**
-660 **7** *2* **Trivia (IRE)**^{31} [1248] 5-8-5 **56** oh1................................ SimonPearce 5 30
(J J Bridger) *chsd ldrs tl wknd over 1f out* **25/1**
4006 **8** *4 ½* **Stark Contrast (USA)**^{20} [1495] 5-8-0 **56** oh4..................... SeanPalmer$^{(5)}$ 10 17
(M D I Usher) *mid-div tl wknd 2f out* **25/1**
100- **9** *shd* **Hey Presto**^{323} [3371] 9-8-2 **56** oh11.............................. RichardRowe$^{(3)}$ 12 17
(R Rowe) *a towards rr* **66/1**
3043 **10** *nse* **Salt Of The Earth (IRE)**^{32} [1080] 4-8-11 **65**......... AndrewHeffernan$^{(3)}$ 3 26
(T G Mills) *chsd ldrs for over 2f* **9/1**
-546 **11** *6* **Upstairs**^{36} [1187] 5-8-2 **60**.. RichardFelton$^{(7)}$ 15 5
(P Henderson) *slowly away: a bhd* **20/1**

1m 28.2s (-0.80) **Going Correction** -0.05s/f (Good) **11** Ran SP% **119.7**
Speed ratings (Par 103): **102,101,101,97,96 89,87,82,82,82 75**
toteswinger: 1&2 £3.10, 1&3 £4.60, 2&3 £4.00 CSF £13.81 CT £39.70 TOTE £5.30: £2.20, £1.60, £1.50; EX 17.80 Place 6: £34.29 Place 5: £25.47.
Owner P Cook **Bred** Michael E Broughton **Trained** Limpley Stoke, Bath
■ Stewards' Enquiry : Danny Brock seven-day ban: used whip in contravention of race conditions (May29-30, Jun 1, 3, 6, 9-10)

FOCUS
A moderate handicap that produced a good finish. The form is sound rated around the placed horses.
T/Plt: £61.60 to a £1 stake. Pool: £45,195.21. 535.42 winning tickets. T/Qpdt: £6.10 to a £1 stake. Pool: £3,107.78. 374.20 winning tickets. TM

1986 YORK (L-H)
Thursday, May 14

OFFICIAL GOING: Good (good to firm in places; 7.9)
Wind: moderate 1/2 behind Weather: overcast

2012 TOTESUPER7 STKS (H'CAP) 5f
1:40 (1:41) (Class 2) (0-100,100) 4-Y-O+ **£12,952** (£3,854; £1,926; £962) **Stalls** Low

Form RPR
0005 **1** **Internationaldebut (IRE)**^{6} [1821] 4-8-10 **89**....................... JohnEgan 3 98
(S Parr) *lw: midfield: rdn along 1/2-way: hdwy wl over 1f out: swtchd lft and drvn ent fnl f: styd on to ld nr line* **16/1**
0-03 **2** *shd* **Everymanforhimself (IRE)**^{29} [1278] 5-8-11 **90**.................(b) NCallan 1 99
(K A Ryan) *lw: trckd ldrs: hdwy 2f out: rdn to ld over 1f out: drvn ins fnl f: hdd and no ex nr line* **13/2**^{2}
-152 **3** *¾* **Cheveton**^{13} [1647] 5-9-3 **96**.. JimCrowley 12 102
(R J Price) *hld up in tch: hdwy on outer 2f out: rdn and styng on to chal whn edgd lft ent fnl f: sn drvn and nt qckn* **5/1**^{1}
10-4 **4** *nk* **Hamish McGonagall**^{13} [1647] 4-9-6 **99**.............................. DavidAllan 7 104
(T D Easterby) *trckd ldrs: hdwy 2f out and sn ev ch rdn over 1f out and drvn: edgd rt fnl 100yds and sn no ex* **15/2**^{3}
/5-3 **5** *nk* **Osterhase (IRE)**^{26} [1375] 10-9-2 **95**.............................(v) MJKinane 8 99
(J E Mulhern, Ire) *led: rdn along 2f out: hdd over 1f out and sn drvn: no ex wl ins fnl f* **14/1**
0442 **6** *1 ½* **Strike Up The Band**^{8} [1791] 6-9-7 **100**.......................... AdrianTNicholls 11 98
(D Nicholls) *trckd ldrs: hdwy over 2f out: rdn to chal and ev ch over 1f out: drvn and edgd lft ent fnl f: carried rt and one pce fnl 100yds* **12/1**
60-4 **7** *1* **Sonny Red (IRE)**^{27} [1325] 5-9-4 **97**.............................. FrancisNorton 5 92
(D Nicholls) *lw: chsd ldrs: effrt over 2f out: sn rdn and wknd ent fnl f* **8/1**
024- **8** *shd* **Kaldoun Kingdom (IRE)**^{195} [7109] 4-9-2 **95**.................... PaulHanagan 9 92+
(R A Fahey) *hld up in tch: hdwy 2f out: rdn and styng on whn hmpd jst ins fnl f: nt rcvr* **14/1**
0065 **9** *1* **Stoneacre Lad (IRE)**^{25} [1384] 6-8-7 **86** oh1............(b) PatrickMathers 14 77
(Peter Grayson) *racd wd: in tch: sme hdwy wl over 1f out: sn rdn and edgd lft: nvr nr ldrs* **50/1**
0400 **10** *½* **Northern Fling**^{29} [1278] 5-9-0 **93**................................ PhillipMakin 6 82
(D Nicholls) *midfield: effrt over 2f out: sn rdn and no imp* **10/1**
3-14 **11** *1* **Dazed And Amazed**^{12} [1668] 5-8-7 **86** oh4........................ RyanMoore 13 71
(R Hannon) *a in rr* **12/1**
0-04 **12** *½* **Tournedos (IRE)**^{8} [1791] 7-9-5 **98**.............................. SilvestreDeSousa 10 82
(D Nicholls) *swtg: sn rdn along and a in rr* **10/1**
2-60 **13** *6* **Supermassive Muse (IRE)**^{22} [1457] 4-8-7 **86**........(p) GrahamGibbons 4 48
(E S McMahon) *lw: chsd ldrs: rdn along 1/2-way: sn wknd* **16/1**
/0-0 **14** *¾* **Group Therapy**^{12} [1676] 4-9-4 **97**.................................... TPQueally 15 56
(N P Littmoden) *a in rr* **40/1**
525- **15** *3* **Stolt (IRE)**^{307} [3931] 5-8-5 **87**................................ KellyHarrison$^{(3)}$ 2 36
(N Wilson) *cl up: rdn over 2f out: sn drvn and wknd* **16/1**

59.38 secs (0.08) **Going Correction** +0.25s/f (Good) **15** Ran SP% **121.8**
Speed ratings (Par 109): **109,108,107,107,106 104,102,102,100,100 98,97,88,86,82**
toteswinger: 1&2 £29.70, 1&3 £30.80, 2&3 £8.40 CSF £117.08 CT £624.53 TOTE £21.60: £5.30, £2.50, £2.10; EX 204.70 Trifecta £1025.10 Part won. Pool: £1385.40 - 0.10 winning units..
Owner W McKay, J Barton **Bred** Ennistown Stud **Trained**
■ Stewards' Enquiry : N Callan three-day ban: used whip with excessive frequency withrout giving horse time to respond (May 28-30)

FOCUS
A competitive handicap, and the field tended to congregate middle to far side, with the first two racing nearest the far-side rail. the form looks solid with the placed horses close to form.

NOTEBOOK

Internationaldebut(IRE) had been far from disgraced from impossible draws in two outings at Chester the previous week. Despite being a son of High Chaparral and having done his winning over further, he had no trouble chasing the decent gallop and, with the rail to help in the closing stages, stayed on strongly to get up close home. He takes his racing very well, is versatile with regard to trip, and now looks just as effective on turf as he is on the Polytrack. One would imagine that he'll continue to be kept busy. (op 22-1 tchd 25-1)

Everymanforhimself(IRE) has done all his winning over this trip at Beverley, but two of his better efforts last term came over this course and distance, and with the blinkers back on he again showed his liking for the track. He showed good speed throughout and looks a likely candidate for the Dash at Epsom. (op 7-1 tchd 11-2)

Cheveton would have appreciated the overnight rain as he ideally likes to get his toe in a bit. A consistent performer, he confirmed Musselburgh form with Hamish McGonagall on 3lb better terms while challenging more towards the centre of the track. (op 13-2 tchd 7-1)

Hamish McGonagall, successful over this trip at this meeting last year, is at his best over a sharp 5f and he promised to improve for his reappearance. Up there all the way, he wasn't quite able to reverse Musselburgh form with Cheveton on worse terms, but it was a solid effort. (op 8-1)

Osterhase(IRE), who showed good pace to take them along, was a Group 3 winner back in the day, but he didn't look particularly well treated off a mark of 95 judged on his previous two efforts this term. (op 11-1)

Strike Up The Band had a big draw advantage when runner-up at Chester last time but, despite a good record at this track, he was always going to struggle to dominate in this field. (op 11-1)

Sonny Red(IRE) ran a fine race on his debut for Dandy Nicholls at Newbury, and he got to race off the same mark this time, a rating which was 11lb lower than when he ran in the Group 2 Duke of York Stakes at this meeting last year. He needs more cut in the ground to be seen at his best, though, and remains one to be interested in when getting his conditions. (op 17-2 tchd 13-2)

Kaldoun Kingdom(IRE), running over the minimum trip for the first time, was squeezed up inside the last and deserves rating a bit better than the bare form. He looks to need a return to 6f, or at least a stiffer track than this, though. (tchd 16-1)

Stoneacre Lad(IRE), who won this race last year off a 2lb lower mark, couldn't build on his solid effort from a tough draw at Chester the previous week

Northern Fling failed to get involved and it would not be a surprise to see blinkers on next time. (op 14-1)

Tournedos(IRE), who won this race last year off a 2lb lower mark, couldn't build on his solid effort from a tough draw at Chester the previous week Official explanation: jockey said gelding ran flat (op 9-1 tchd 12-1)

2013 TOTEPOOL MIDDLETON STKS (GROUP 3) (F&M) 1m 2f 88y

2:10 (2:10) (Class 1) 4-Y-0+ **£36,900** (£13,988; £7,000; £3,490; £1,748) **Stalls** Low

Form				RPR
111-	1		**Crystal Capella**[208] 6819 4-9-2 108 RyanMoore 5	116
			(Sir Michael Stoute) *h.d.w: lw: trckd ldrs: gd hdwy to ld over 2f out and sn rdn: drvn and hdd ins fnl f: rallied gamely u.p to ld again nr fin* **15/8**[2]	
223-	2	shd	**Dar Re Mi**[222] 6495 4-8-12 114 LDettori 1	112
			(J H M Gosden) *lw: trckd ldng pair: rapid hdwy on inner to join ldr 1/2-way: led 4f out: hdd and rdn over 2f out: drvn over 1f out: styd on gamely to take narrow advantage ins fnl f: hdd and no ex nr line* **4/5**[1]	
6-52	3	8	**Princess Taylor**[15] 1613 5-8-12 87 AlanMunro 3	96
			(M Botti) *cl up: rdn along over 4f out and sn outpcd* **22/1**	
253-	4	2 1/2	**Changing Skies (IRE)**[219] 6567 4-8-12 107 JamieSpencer 2	91
			(B J Meehan) *set stdy pce: jnd 1/2-way: sn rdn and hdd 4f out: sn outpcd* **13/2**[3]	
2-40	5	9	**Rio Guru (IRE)**[15] 1613 4-8-12 74 TonyCulhane 4	73
			(M R Channon) *a in rr: bhd fnl 3f* **100/1**	

2m 15.03s (2.53) **Going Correction** +0.25s/f (Good) 5 Ran SP% **109.0**

Speed ratings (Par 113): **99,98,92,90,83**

CSF £3.63 TOTE £2.70: £1.40, £1.20; EX 3.60.

Owner Sir Evelyn De Rothschild **Bred** Southcourt Stud **Trained** Newmarket, Suffolk

FOCUS

A race that has been won by some high-class fillies in recent years. There was just a modest pace on and the form looks straightforward with the two market leaders coming clear in a real battle. The early pace was moderate but the form should prove sound.

NOTEBOOK

Crystal Capella did nothing but improve last season, completing a five-timer on varying ground which included a win over this course and distance and a narrow defeat of the St Leger runner-up Unsung Heroine in a Newmarket Group 3 on her final start in October. Conceding 4lb to her four rivals and back down in trip for this return to action, she was content to sit off the pace early and briefly came off the bridle when the two leaders were going for it passing the 4f pole. However, she was soon right back on terms and engaged in a nip-and-tuck battle with Dar Re Mi throughout the last 2f. Despite being carried away to her right by her rival, she answered her rider's every call and managed to force her head in front right on the line. The Pretty Polly Stakes at the Curragh at the end of next month is likely next for her, where she will bid to complete the same double achieved by her stable-companion Promising Lead last year. (op 2-1 tchd 9-4)

Dar Re Mi, the highest rated of these having finished runner-up to Lush Lashes in the Yorkshire Oaks and to the great Zarkava in the Prix Vermeille last season, was racing over this shorter trip for the first time since finishing third behind the aforementioned Lush Lashes in the Musidora at this meeting a year ago. She was inclined to take a grip in the middle of the field in the early stages here, but Frankie Dettori allowed her to stride on up the inside of Changing Skies when that one edged off the rail rounding the home bend. She kept on finding for pressure despite edging away to her right over the last couple of furlongs, but ran into a rival who doesn't know the meaning of defeat. A return to further will probably suit her and she should win a decent race or two this year. (tchd 8-11 and 5-6 in places)

Princess Taylor loves quick ground, but she was just beaten in a fillies' handicap at Pontefract last time off a mark of 85 and had a huge amount to find at this level. She seemed likely to be totally left behind by the three leaders starting up the home straight, but her fitness came into play and she stayed on to finish third albeit it a very long way behind the front pair. (op 25-1)

Changing Skies(IRE), who ran some fine races in Pattern company both here and abroad last season but had only a solitary victory in a Leicester maiden to her name, was ridden straight into the lead here and set a modest pace, but the runner-up crept up her inside on the home bend and it wasn't long before she was struggling to keep in touch. She then dropped right out and, although she would probably have preferred easier ground, this was still a modest return effort and she has plenty to prove now. (tchd 7-1)

Rio Guru(IRE), a long way behind Princess Taylor off a mark of 76 in a Pontefract fillies' handicap last time, had no chance in this company and was trailing throughout. (op 80-1 tchd 66-1)

2014 TOTESPORT.COM DANTE STKS (GROUP 2) 1m 2f 88y

2:40 (2:42) (Class 1) 3-Y-0

£85,155 (£32,280; £16,155; £8,055; £4,035; £2,025) **Stalls** Low

Form				RPR
3	1		**Black Bear Island (IRE)**[32] 1239 3-9-0 0 CO'Donoghue 7	113
			(A P O'Brien, Ire) *str: lw: hld up in rr: hdwy wl over 2f out: rdn over 1f out: styd on strly ins fnl f to ld nr fin* **12/1**	
	2	hd	**Freemantle**[221] 6515 3-9-0 0 JMurtagh 6	113
			(A P O'Brien, Ire) *w'like: scope: tall: lengthy: led after 1f: pushed clr over 2f out: rdn wl over 1f out: drvn ins fnl f: hdd and no ex nr fin* **13/2**[3]	
1-2	3	3/4	**Sans Frontieres (IRE)**[28] 1300 3-9-0 107 MJKinane 8	111
			(J Noseda) *lw: hld up in rr: hdwy on wd outside over 2f out: rdn wl over 1f out: kpt on u.p ins fnl f: nrst fin* **16/1**	
1-20	4	1	**Monitor Closely (IRE)**[12] 1675 3-9-0 106 AlanMunro 10	109
			(P W Chapple-Hyam) *lw: trckd ldrs: hdwy over 3f out: rdn 2f out: drvn and ev ch over 1f out: one pce ins fnl f* **16/1**	
211-	5	shd	**Kite Wood (IRE)**[215] 6648 3-9-0 108 LDettori 4	109
			(Saeed Bin Suroor) *t.k.h: led 1f: trckd ldr: effrt over 2f out and sn rdn: drvn over 1f out: kpt on same pce ins fnl f* **9/2**[2]	
01-5	6	hd	**Glass Harmonium (IRE)**[28] 1300 3-9-0 98 RyanMoore 1	109
			(Sir Michael Stoute) *dwlt and towards rr: hdwy over 2f out: rdn to chse ldrs over 1f out: drvn and one pce ins fnl f* **25/1**	
21	7	2	**Native Ruler**[15] 1611 3-9-0 96 TPQueally 2	105
			(H R A Cecil) *lw: trckd ldrs: effrt wl over 2f out and sn rdn along: n.m.r over 1f out: sn no imp* **20/1**	
121-	8	nk	**Crowded House**[201] 6973 3-9-0 120 JamieSpencer 9	104
			(B J Meehan) *hld up towards rr: hdwy on inner 3f out: rdn wl over 1f out and sn btn* **2/1**[1]	
1-1	9	2 1/2	**Redwood**[29] 1294 3-9-0 107 MichaelHills 3	99
			(B W Hills) *lw: in tch: effrt and sme hdwy over 2f out: sn rdn: edgd lft and wknd wl over 1f out* **7/1**	
1-1	10	13	**Nehaam**[29] 1291 3-9-0 103 RHills 5	73
			(J H M Gosden) *chsd ldrs: rdn along over 2f out: sn drvn and wknd* **8/1**	

2m 11.64s (-0.86) **Going Correction** +0.25s/f (Good) **10** Ran SP% **116.5**

Speed ratings (Par 111): **113,112,112,111,111 111,109,109,107,96**

totewinger: 1&2 £9.20, 1&3 £18.40, 2&3 £19.80 CSF £87.79 TOTE £14.80: £3.90, £2.70, £2.40; EX 51.50 Trifecta £1101.40 Part won. Pool: £1488.48 - 0.80 winning units..

Owner Mrs John Magnier & M Tabor **Bred** Tower Bloodstock **Trained** Ballydoyle, Co Tipperary

■ Stewards' Enquiry : C O'Donoghue two-day ban: used whip with excessive frequency and without giving colt time to respond (May 28-29)

FOCUS

Three of the last five Derby winners took the Dante en route to Epsom glory, and Tartan Bearer went close to making it four last year. This looked a strong trial on paper and it was run at a solid gallop, but there is a slight doubt over the form. The first pair are big improvers, but Fame And Glory still appears by some way to be the stable's main hope for Epsom.

NOTEBOOK

Black Bear Island(IRE) may have been rejected by Murtagh, but he had the stronger form of the Ballydoyle pair. He was unlucky in running in the Prix La Force, but very much had the race run to suit this time and picked up well between horses to run down his stablemate close home. It was a pleasing performance and, as a brother to High Chaparral, he looks sure to appreciate the step up to 1m4f at Epsom (cut to 10-1 for the Derby), but only two lengths covered the first six home and his rider was given a whip ban, so he had a hard enough race. It's doubtful he's achieved as much as Fame And Glory so far in his career and one gets the impression that the Derrinstown winner remains by some margin the stable's strongest candidate for the Derby. (tchd 9-1)

Freemantle took three starts to get off the mark at two, but when he eventually won his maiden he routed his rivals. Soon taken to the front, he set a strong pace and found extra when challenged, but he wasn't quite able to hold off his stablemate Black Bear Island, who in contrast was given a patient ride. It was his reappearance, while the winner had had a run, and if he follows the trend, he should come on a good deal for this outing. He's a half-brother to Mashaahed, who was at his best over 1m2f, though, and there has to be a chance that this will turn out to be his best distance rather than 1m4f. He was cut to 20-1 for the Derby. (op 11-2 tchd 7-1)

Sans Frontieres(IRE), second in the Craven on his reappearance, was staying on at the finish in the manner of a horse that promised to be suited by the step up to 1m2f. That was backed up by his pedigree as he's by Galileo out of a Shirley Heights mare. A keen-going sort, it was to his benefit that the pace was generous, and he made good late headway down the centre of the track to take third. He was cut to 20-1 for the Derby, but he's seen as a galloper who wouldn't necessarily be suited by the course at Epsom, and he's likely to head to Royal Ascot instead for the King Edward VII Stakes.

Monitor Closely(IRE) represented the Guineas form, having finished eighth in the Classic. The return to 1m2f promised to suit - he was second in the Tattersalls Timeform 3yo Trophy on his reappearance - and his performance won't have disappointed supporters of Sea The Stars and Gan Amhras for the Derby. A tough sort who clearly takes his racing well, the son of Oasis Dream should be well up to winning in Group 3 company at this trip. (op 28-1)

Kite Wood(IRE), making his eagerly anticipated debut for Godolphin, looked a very promising colt for Michael Jarvis last year, making all to win the Autumn Stakes on his final start, and his pedigree promised much better to come over middle distances this term. Perhaps significantly, he did not spend the winter in Dubai but was kept in Newmarket instead. He got warm beforehand at Ascot, and the same happened here, but it doesn't seem to affect his performance, and connections, who expected him to need the run, were pleased with his effort. The plan remains to go for the Derby, but he isn't guaranteed to stay 1m4f on pedigree and he's drifted out to 25-1 for the Epsom Classic. (op 11-2 tchd 6-1 in places)

Glass Harmonium(IRE), who was only fifth in the Craven on his reappearance, had a good deal to find at this level. The step up to 1m2f was expected to suit, though and, although he was a bit keen early, being held up at the back of the field off the good gallop eventually played into his hands as he stayed on late. He looks the type to keep improving as the season progresses, and softer ground won't inconvenience him. (op 16-1)

Native Ruler has always been well regarded, but this race demanded a great deal more from him than the Pontefract maiden he won last time. He is bred for the job, though, and certainly travelled well for a long way. This competition proved all too much for him at this stage of his career, but he still has the potential to make his mark in Pattern company in time.

Crowded House had produced a devastating turn of foot to win the Racing Post Trophy last term, and, while the form could have worked out better, the manner of his success suggested he might still be something special over middle distances this year. With the Guineas assignment handed to stablemate Delegator, he was free to take the traditional Derby route, and his pedigree suggested he would relish the step up to 1m2f for the first time. The vibes were not great, though, and he was weak in the market beforehand. Held up off the pace, he travelled well enough into contention 2f out, but found nothing under pressure. His rider reported that he ran flat, and his trainer reiterated that this was simply a stepping stone to the Derby and that he might have needed the run more than expected, but the bookmakers understandably gave those excuses short shrift and shunted him out to 16-1 for the Derby. It was later reported that he returned home with a dirty scope and plans are currently on hold for him. (tchd 15-8 and 9-4 in a place)

Redwood won the Feilden Stakes on his reappearance, but, despite the runner-up going on to finish a close third in the Dee Stakes subsequently, that form still left him with a bit to find at this level. His rider said he ran very flat, and he deserves a chance to prove this run all wrong. Official explanation: jockey said colt never travelled (op 8-1)

Nehaam came into the race unbeaten, with a verdict over Monitor Closely to his name on his reappearance. He promised to come on for that outing as he'd been held up in his work prior to that success, but, having entered the straight alongside Kite Wood, he dropped right out with over 2f to run. (tchd 9-1)

2015 TOTESWINGER HAMBLETON STKS (H'CAP) (LISTED RACE) 1m

3:10 (3:13) (Class 1) (0-110,110) 4-Y-0+**£23,704** (£8,964; £4,480; £2,240) **Stalls** Low

Form				RPR
-212	1		**Yamal (IRE)**[84] 615 4-9-1 **104** LDettori 4	115+
			(Saeed Bin Suroor) *lw: hld up in midfield: smooth hdwy over 2f out: rdn to ld ins fnl f: hld on wl* **5/1**[1]	

2560 **2** ½ **Philario (IRE)**[26] 1346 4-8-7 **96** oh1 .... MartinLane 5 106
(K R Burke) *chsd ldrs: led over 1f out: hdd ins fnl f: no ex* **33/1**

-462 **3** nk **Mia's Boy**[14] 1631 5-8-12 **101** .... JimmyQuinn 8 110
(C A Dwyer) *lw: hld up in rr: hdwy and nt clr run over 2f out untl jst ins fnl f: fin strly* **5/1**[1]

0-46 **4** 2 ¾ **Lovelace**[19] 1525 5-9-7 **110** .... RoystonFfrench 13 113+
(M Johnston) *s.i.s: hdwy on ins whn nt clr run over 2f out and over 1f out: kpt on: nt rch ldrs* **12/1**

-206 **5** nk **Blythe Knight (IRE)**[26] 1346 9-9-1 **104** .... GrahamGibbons 7 106
(J J Quinn) *lw: trckd ldrs: hdwy over 3f out: styd on same pce appr fnl f* **18/1**

2134 **6** hd **Flipando (IRE)**[12] 1673 8-8-9 **98** .... PhillipMakin 9 100+
(T D Barron) *dwlt: hld up in rr: effrt and nt clr run over 2f out: kpt on wl fnl f* **10/1**

-030 **7** 2 **Medici Pearl**[12] 1684 5-8-7 **96** oh4 .... DavidAllan 2 93
(T D Easterby) *lw: dwlt: hdwy whn n.m.r over 2f out: kpt on fnl f: nvr rchd ldrs* **28/1**

0231 **8** 1 ¾ **Extraterrestrial**[26] 1352 5-8-10 **99** .... PaulHanagan 10 92
(R A Fahey) *hld up towards rr: hdwy over 2f out: nvr nr ldrs* **8/1**[3]

206- **9** 9 **Lang Shining (IRE)**[194] 7145 5-8-13 **102** .... RyanMoore 11 75
(Sir Michael Stoute) *lw: hld up in rr: sme hdwy on outside 3f out: sn rdn and hung lft: wknd* **6/1**[2]

201 **10** 2 ½ **Furnace (IRE)**[62] 5-9-1 **104** .... AhmedAjtebi 12 71
(Saeed Bin Suroor) *mde most tl over 2f out: wknd over 1f out* **16/1**

300- **11** hd **Lizard Island (USA)**[218] 6576 4-8-13 **102** .... JohnEgan 1 68
(P F I Cole) *mid-div: hdwy and pushed along over 4f out: wknd over 1f out* **33/1**

-001 **12** 4 **Joseph Henry**[26] 1376 7-8-10 **99** .... AdrianTNicholls 3 56
(D Nicholls) *w ldr: led over 2f out: hdd and lost pl over 1f out* **20/1**

101- **13** 2 **Wasan**[245] 5830 4-8-12 **101** .... (b[1]) RHills 15 54
(E A L Dunlop) *hld up in rr: sme hdwy 3f out: sn wknd* **12/1**

-030 **14** 2 ¼ **Dream Lodge (IRE)**[12] 1673 5-8-10 **99** .... J-PGuillambert 14 46
(J G Given) *lw: prom: drvn over 5f out: lost pl over 3f out* **22/1**

234- **15** 2 **Moynahan (USA)**[159] 7579 4-8-8 **97** .... AlanMunro 6 40
(P F I Cole) *prom: drvn over 3f out: lost pl 2f out* **9/1**

1m 39.23s (0.43) **Going Correction** +0.25s/f (Good) **15** Ran SP% **122.8**
Speed ratings (Par 111): **107,106,106,103,103 102,100,99,90,87 87,83,81,79,77**
toteswinger: 1&2 £52.20, 1&3 £4.90, 2&3 £63.10 CSF £186.58 CT £878.15 TOTE £5.50: £2.20, £11.30, £2.50; EX 231.60 Trifecta £1351.10 Pool: £1825.94 - 1.00 winning units..
Owner Godolphin **Bred** Gainsborough Stud Management Ltd **Trained** Newmarket, Suffolk

FOCUS
A very competitive Listed handicap which included the last two winners of the race in Blythe Knight and Mia's Boy. They went a searching pace and the form looks solid, rated around the placed horses.

NOTEBOOK
Yamal(IRE), who ran three good races for Godolphin in Dubai earlier this year, found himself off a stone higher mark than when winning a Goodwood handicap for Mark Johnston last July, but it made little difference as he travelled very nicely behind the leading quartet before being produced with his effort, and sustained it to hit the front well inside the last furlong. Having won this off a mark of 104, opportunities in handicaps will be limited and he is likely to be stepped up into Listed company now. (op 11-2)
Philario(IRE), without a win since landing the Group 3 Sirenia Stakes on Polytrack as a two-year-old, led the main group adrift of the two leaders until taking over passing the 2f pole and was unfortunate to be mugged in the latter stages. It had seemed in the past as though he needed a sharp track in order to see out this trip, but it's hard to crab this effort and he deserved to get his head in front again.
Mia's Boy, 5lb higher than when beating a much smaller field in this race last year, was settled off the pace early. He tried to weave his way through the field and finished in good style when out in the clear, but he could never quite get to the front two. This was another fine effort. (op 13-2 tchd 9-2)
Lovelace, having his first start in a handicap since beaten a head off 2lb lower in last season's Bunbury Cup, was the unlucky horse of the race. Settled last early, he kept on meeting traffic problems when trying to get closer and by the time he saw daylight it was far too late. This effort shows that he is very capable of winning a big handicap off this sort of mark when things go his way. (op 14-1)
Blythe Knight(IRE), running in this race for the fourth year in a row having won it in 2007 and finishing third last year, hasn't been at his very best so far this year but he ran well having raced close to the pace throughout. (op 16-1 tchd 20-1)
Flipando(IRE), who didn't look right in his coat, put in his usual strong finish from off the pace without being able to land an effective blow. He has been running consistently well on both turf and Polytrack in recent months, but the Handicapper seems to have him where he wants him. (tchd 11-1)
Medici Pearl was another to stay on late and wasn't disgraced considering she was 4lb wrong and racing on ground faster than ideal. (tchd 33-1)
Extraterrestrial, raised 4lb for his win in last month's Newbury Spring Cup, could never get involved from off the pace (tchd 10-1)
Lang Shining(IRE) has mainly been disappointing since finishing runner-up to Mia's Boy in this race last year off 6lb lower. Having his first start in six months, he did see rather a lot of daylight on the wide outside and couldn't pick up when asked. (tchd 13-2)
Joseph Henry Official explanation: jockey said gelding had no more to give
Wasan, winner of four of his previous six outings, had blinkers on for the first time on this return from seven months off. He had won first time out in his two previous seasons so fitness shouldn't have been a worry, though there was some doubt over his participation on account of the quick ground and the way he ran here suggests connections were right to be concerned. (op 11-1)
Moynahan(USA), whose only previous win came here as a juvenile, was having his first start since December having been gelded in the meantime. Dropping back from 1m2f, he attracted some market support but having been very edgy and sweating beforehand he ultimately dropped away most disappointingly. (op 11-1)

2016 EUROPEAN BREEDERS' FUND CONDITIONS STKS 5f
3:45 (3:46) (Class 2) 3-Y-O **£12,952** (£3,854; £1,926; £962) **Stalls** Low

Form RPR

254- **1** **Anglezarke (IRE)**[215] 6644 3-8-11 102 .... DavidAllan 3 97
(T D Easterby) *chsd ldrs: styd on fnl 2f to ld last 75yds: hld on wl* **9/1**

4-65 **2** 1 **Rievaulx World**[12] 1676 3-9-2 102 .... NCallan 7 98
(K A Ryan) *set str pce: rdn over 1f out: hdd wl ins fnl f: no ex* **4/1**[3]

3-16 **3** nk **Fault**[6] 1824 3-9-2 90 .... (t) TPQueally 1 97?
(Stef Liddiard) *chsd ldrs: drvn over 2f out: nt clr run and swtchd rt over 1f out: styd on ins fnl f* **33/1**

1-33 **4** 1 ¾ **City Dancer (IRE)**[6] 1824 3-8-11 90 .... PaulHanagan 2 86
(A Berry) *t.k.h: effrt 2f out: styd on fnl f* **7/2**[2]

522- **5** 4 **Waffle (IRE)**[215] 6644 3-9-2 108 .... LDettori 6 76
(J Noseda) *lw: hld up in rr: effrt 2f out: edgd lft and wknd fnl f* **3/1**[1]

5-10 **6** ½ **Brenin Taran**[20] 1486 3-9-2 89 .... AdrianTNicholls 4 74
(D M Simcock) *dwlt: hld up in rr: hdwy 2f out: hrd rdn: nvr nr ldrs* **33/1**

022- **7** 1 ¼ **Thunderous Mood (USA)**[245] 5850 3-9-2 104 .... JohnEgan 8 70
(P F I Cole) *lw: in rr: drvn over 2f out: nvr a factor* **14/1**

21-4 **8** 1 **Aldermoor (USA)**[29] 1296 3-9-2 98 .... GrahamGibbons 5 66
(S C Williams) *lw: dwlt: hld up in rr: nvr a factor* **3/1**[1]

59.97 secs (0.67) **Going Correction** +0.25s/f (Good) **8** Ran SP% **114.8**
Speed ratings (Par 105): **104,102,101,99,92 91,89,88**
toteswinger: 1&2 £5.80, 1&3 £18.60, 2&3 £19.10 CSF £45.03 TOTE £11.10: £2.20, £2.00, £3.80; EX 43.20.
Owner David W Armstrong **Bred** Mount Coote Stud **Trained** Great Habton, N Yorks

FOCUS
A decent contest for the grade, run at a strong pace. The form looks open to question though, with nothing getting nto the race from off the pace, but the first two set the level.

NOTEBOOK
Anglezarke(IRE) won a fast-ground nursery over this course and distance last summer but her best effort came when second in the Group 2 Flying Childers in soft conditions. Clearly adaptable with regard to ground conditions, she won this quite tidily, and she deserves to return to Pattern company now. A 5f specialist, her trainer is sweet on her and, while this bare form will need improving on, she's entitled to come on for her reappearance, and the Temple Stakes and/or King's Stand will now be targeted. (op 17-2 tchd 8-1)
Rievaulx World, who has bags of early speed, didn't run at all badly when fifth in the Palace House Stakes last time. This track was always going to suit his style of running, but the overnight rain would not have been welcome as he cannot have the ground too fast. It was a fine effort in the circumstances. (op 9-2)
Fault kept on for third. His performance appears to hold the form down somewhat, as he came into the race rated only 90 and seemingly exposed. (tchd 28-1)
City Dancer(IRE), who was well drawn but didn't make the most of it at Chester last time, got away on terms here but was a little keen early. A sharp track looks likely to continue to see her at her best. (op 4-1)
Waffle(IRE), the highest rated of these, only found the rapidly improving Amour Propre too strong for him in the Cornwallis last autumn, but that race came on good to soft ground and he was down in the paper as only likely to run if there had been sufficient rain. He took his chance, but he didn't stride out on this ground and one has to suspect that conditions were too quick for him. He is not one to write off back on his favoured surface. (op 11-4 tchd 7-2)
Brenin Taran had a stiff task at the weights and was never in the hunt. (op 25-1)
Thunderous Mood(USA) was missing the blinkers he wore when closing out his two-year-old campaign with a good second in a French Group 3. (op 12-1 tchd 10-1)
Aldermoor(USA) pulled hard and did not see his race out over 6f at Newmarket on his reappearance, so the drop back to 5f looked likely to suit him. He had a bit to find at the weights, but was fancied and this has to go down as a disappointing effort. (op 4-1)

2017 STRATFORD PLACE STUD FOR BREEDERS CUP WINNERS E B F MAIDEN STKS 6f
4:20 (4:20) (Class 3) 2-Y-O **£7,835** (£2,331; £1,165; £582) **Stalls** Low

Form RPR

1 **No Hubris (USA)** 2-9-3 0 .... JohnEgan 3 91+
(P F I Cole) *w'like: scope lengthy: lw: mde virtually all: qcknd clr over 1f out: rdn out* **7/2**[2]

2 2 ¼ **Flying Statesman (USA)** 2-9-3 0 .... PaulHanagan 1 84+
(R A Fahey) *str: bit bkwd: dwlt: sn trcking ldrs: styd on to take 2nd wl ins fnl f* **10/1**

3 ½ **Beethoven (IRE)** 2-9-3 0 .... JMurtagh 4 83
(A P O'Brien, Ire) *athletic: medium-sized: trckd ldrs: effrt and edgd rt over 1f out: styd on to take 2nd ins fnl f: lost 2nd nr fin* **9/4**[1]

42 **4** 4 **Trade Secret**[40] 1126 2-9-3 0 .... AlanMunro 5 71
(M Brittain) *w wnr: wknd jst ins fnl f* **7/1**[3]

5 5 **Hasty (IRE)** 2-8-12 0 .... MichaelHills 10 51
(B W Hills) *unf: scope: dwlt: stdy hdwy over 2f out: nvr nr ldrs* **10/1**

6 2 ¼ **Fine Sight** 2-9-3 0 .... RyanMoore 8 49
(R Hannon) *w'like: mid-div: sn pushed along: nvr rchd ldrs* **10/1**

04 **7** hd **Tagula Pearl (IRE)**[19] 1504 2-8-12 0 .... PatrickMathers 2 43
(I W McInnes) *chsd ldrs: wknd wl over 1f out* **50/1**

8 1 ½ **Original Dancer (IRE)** 2-9-3 0 .... RoystonFfrench 7 44
(M Johnston) *w'like: scope: bit bkwd: lw: dwlt: a wl outpcd and in rr* **9/1**

9 2 **Almadaa** 2-9-3 0 .... RHills 6 38+
(E A L Dunlop) *str: bit bkwd: wnt rt s: keen in rr: hdwy over 2f out: edgd rt: hung lft and sn wknd* **7/1**[3]

10 14 **Kerolad (IRE)** 2-9-3 0 .... PaulQuinn 9 —
(N Wilson) *str: lw: sn outpcd and in rr: bhd fnl 2f* **50/1**

1m 13.94s (2.04) **Going Correction** +0.25s/f (Good) **10** Ran SP% **119.2**
Speed ratings (Par 97): **96,93,92,87,80 77,77,75,72,53**
toteswinger: 1&2 £9.20, 1&3 £3.00, 2&3 £8.80 CSF £39.52 TOTE £5.30: £1.70, £3.40, £1.50; EX 41.00.
Owner Mrs Fitri Hay **Bred** Brereton C Jones **Trained** Whatcombe, Oxon

FOCUS
A decent maiden, won last year by the subsequent Mill Reef-winner Lord Shanakill, and this looked a good renewal. The runners stayed against the inside rail, they finished well spread out, and winners should emerge from this.

NOTEBOOK
No Hubris(USA) ◆, an 85,000gns half-brother to a couple of winners at up to 1m in the US, could hardly have made a more impressive debut. Always up with the pace, he gradually forged clear of his rivals from the 2f pole and the race was soon in the bag. He should go on from here and is likely to go for the Coventry Stakes. (op 6-1)
Flying Statesman(USA) ◆, a $50,000 colt, raced close to the pace from the start and though he took a while to hit top gear, he was doing some pleasing late work up the inside rail. He has a dirt pedigree and could be very interesting on sand, but on this evidence he should win races on turf. (op 16-1 tchd 9-1)
Beethoven(IRE), a 260,000euros colt out of a dual winner over 1m, was representing the stable that took this in 2005 with Marcus Andronicus. He was another to race handily from the start and he had every chance, but couldn't stop the winner from running away from him. Entries for the Phoenix Stakes and next year's Derby suggest he is thought a bit of and he has a future. (op 7-4 tchd 13-8 and 5-2 in a place)
Trade Secret, fourth in the Brocklesby and runner-up to the useful Archers Road at Newcastle last time, helped take them along for a long way before fading and his performance sets the standard. (op 8-1 tchd 13-2)
Hasty(IRE), a 95,000euros sister to the winning plater Invincible Miss and a half-sister to the winning stayer Rajeh, was representing the stable that took this race two years ago with Feared In Flight. Not best away, she saw plenty of daylight on the wide outside and although a mid-race move ultimately amounted to little, she showed enough to suggest there are races to be won with her. (op 15-2 tchd 12-1)
Fine Sight, edgy beforehand: proved too green to do himself justice on this debut, but his dam won over 1m4f so he may be one for later on. (op 7-1)
Original Dancer(IRE) ◆, a 40,000euros brother to the high-class juvenile Barbajuan and a half-brother to two other winners at up to 1m2f, was another to miss the break before looking clueless and is another likely to leave this debut effort well behind as he gains experience. (op 14-1)

Almadaa, out of a winning half-sister to the top-class Hayil and smart Tamid, never got involved but he was keen enough early and is surely capable of better. Richards Hills reported that he had hung left throughout. Official explanation: jockey said colt hung left-handed throughout (op 6-1 tchd 8-1)

2018 THERIPLEYCOLLECTION.COM STKS (H'CAP) 2m 2f
4:55 (4:55) (Class 4) (0-80,78) 4-Y-0+ **£6,476** (£1,927; £963; £481) **Stalls** Low

Form RPR
440- **1** **Kayf Aramis**[28] 3250 7-9-6 **71** JMurtagh 14 94+
(Miss Venetia Williams) *lw: sn w ldr: led over 4f out: sn pushed wl clr: eased ins fnl f* **2/1**[1]
-360 **2** *13* **Rose Bien**[15] 1609 7-8-3 **59** (p) AndreaAtzeni(5) 8 62
(P J McBride) *sn chsng ldrs: wnt modest 2nd 2f out* **12/1**
10-0 **3** *1 ¾* **Go Amwell**[23] 1426 6-8-5 **59** oh1 DavidProbert(3) 13 60+
(J R Jenkins) *lw: mid-div: hdwy over 4f out: kpt on to take modest 3rd 1f out* **33/1**
00-6 **4** *4* **Inchpast**[14] 1635 8-9-1 **66** (b) MichaelHills 12 63
(M H Tompkins) *sn prom: one pce fnl 3f* **10/1**
41-3 **5** *5* **Legion D'Honneur (UAE)**[11] 1692 4-9-6 **75** TomEaves 15 66
(L Lungo) *led tl over 4f out: wknd over 1f out* **6/1**[2]
-606 **6** *½* **Wannarock (IRE)**[10] 1724 4-8-1 **59** oh4 KellyHarrison(3) 1 50
(M C Chapman) *s.i.s: hld up in rr: hdwy 5f out: nvr nr ldrs* **28/1**
13-6 **7** *6* **Kiribati King (IRE)**[26] 1356 4-9-6 **75** TonyCulhane 7 59
(M R Channon) *in rr div: hdwy 5f out: nvr nr ldrs* **7/1**[3]
0-60 **8** *¾* **Criterion**[26] 1356 4-9-5 **74** (p) StephenDonohoe 3 57
(Ian Williams) *prom: drvn 4f out: wknd fnl 2f* **33/1**
0-23 **9** *19* **Sonny Sam (IRE)**[13] 1648 4-8-4 **59** oh4 PaulHanagan 5 21
(R A Fahey) *prom: effrt over 4f out: nvr threatened: heavily eased ins fnl f* **6/1**[2]
00-4 **10** *27* **Winged D'Argent (IRE)**[26] 1356 8-9-13 **78** (p) GrahamGibbons 10 11
(B J Llewellyn) *in rr: drvn along 12f out: bhd fnl 4f: eased whn no ch* **22/1**
2202 **11** *1 ½* **Bridgewater Boys**[11] 1692 8-9-2 **67** (b) J-PGuillambert 9 —
(T J Pitt) *b: hld up in last: nvr on terms: eased* **25/1**
-333 **12** *5* **Soundbyte**[14] 1635 4-9-4 **73** LDettori 11 —
(J Gallagher) *lw: hld up in mid-div: hdwy 6f out: nvr nr ldrs: eased over 1f out* **7/1**[3]
00-4 **13** *5* **Mceldowney**[6] 1851 7-8-3 **61** (b) DavidKenny(7) 2 —
(M C Chapman) *chsd ldrs: lost pl over 5f out: sn bhd: eased* **66/1**

3m 58.16s (-0.24) **Going Correction** +0.25s/f (Good)
WFA 4 from 5yo+ 4lb **13** Ran SP% **122.7**
Speed ratings (Par 105): **110,104,103,101,99 99,96,96,87,75 75,72,70**
toteswinger: 1&2 £8.80, 1&3 £22.00, 2&3 £59.30 CSF £27.23 CT £641.26 TOTE £3.30: £1.30, £4.30, £8.40; EX 28.50 Place 6: £197.98 Place 5: £79.73.
Owner Mrs Isobel Phipps Coltman **Bred** Mrs Isobel Phipps Coltman **Trained** Kings Caple, H'fords

FOCUS
A proper test of stamina. Kayf Aramis has now taken this race three times and did the job with ridiculous ease. He is value for further.
Soundbyte Official explanation: jockey said gelding ran flat
T/Jkpt: Not won. T/Plt: £284.60 to a £1 stake. Pool: £166,039.05. 425.85 winning tickets. T/Qpdt: £119.80 to a £1 stake. Pool: £7,012.70. 43.30 winning tickets. JR

2019 - 2026a (Foreign Racing) - See Raceform Interactive

1827 HAMILTON (R-H)
Friday, May 15

OFFICIAL GOING: Good to firm (good in places; 9.3) changing to good after race 3 (7.30)
Rail realignment around the loop added 25yards to advertised distances on the round course.
Wind: Breezy, across Weather: Overcast

2027 EUROPEAN BREEDERS' FUND MAIDEN STKS 5f 4y
6:20 (6:20) (Class 5) 2-Y-0 **£3,885** (£1,156; £577; £288) **Stalls** Low

Form RPR
4 **1** **Corporal Maddox**[37] 1188 2-9-3 0 JimCrowley 3 74+
(K R Burke) *trckd ldrs gng wl: rdn to ld over 1f out: r.o strly fnl f* **4/6**[1]
2 *1* **Trinder** 2-9-0 0 TonyHamilton 1 67+
(R A Fahey) *prom: pushed along 1/2-way: hdwy to chse wnr ent fnl f: r.o* **11/2**[3]
5 **3** *3 ½* **Cambuslang (IRE)**[14] 1645 2-9-0 0 NeilBrown(3) 5 56
(I Semple) *bhd and sn outpcd: hung rt thrght: hdwy on outside 1/2-way: no ex fnl f* **5/2**[2]
6 **4** *¾* **Lord's Seat**[14] 1645 2-8-12 0 SladeO'Hara(5) 4 53
(A Berry) *led to over 1f out: sn outpcd* **16/1**
5 *10* **Ariel Bender** 2-8-7 0 AndrewHeffernan(7) 2 14
(Peter Grayson) *w ldr to 2f out: sn rdn and wknd* **50/1**

60.92 secs (0.92) **Going Correction** +0.075s/f (Good) **5** Ran SP% **111.8**
Speed ratings (Par 93): **95,93,87,86,70**
CSF £5.13 TOTE £1.80: £1.10, £2.40; EX 4.70.
Owner Mogeely Stud & Mrs Maura Gittins **Bred** Theobalds Stud **Trained** Middleham Moor, N Yorks

FOCUS
Just an ordinary maiden but the winner did it readily enough and the first two can rate higher.

NOTEBOOK
Corporal Maddox is a striking individual and looked to have learned a good deal from his encouraging Nottingham debut, where he attracted significant market support. Always travelling strongly in behind the pace, he picked up nicely when asked to go about his business and although he had to work fairly hard to shake off promising newcomer Trinder, he was well in control at the finish and displayed quite a professional attitude. His trainer is keen not to overface him too soon, so he will likely take in a conditions race in the north before connections decide whether he is Royal Ascot material. Being by Royal Applause, he is sure to appreciate another furlong in time. (op 5-6)
Trinder, who is blind in his near eye, ran an excellent race on debut, keeping straight all the way home and shaping with a deal of promise. He is very speedily bred, and with this under his belt, he ought to be tough to beat in similar company next time. (op 9-2)
Cambuslang(IRE) was again outpaced early but kept on well enough to suggest he has a future, especially when stepped up to 6f. (op 3-1)
Lord's Seat showed good speed early, and although brushed aside over a furlong out, he looks to have stepped up on his modest debut. (op 18-1 tchd 14-1)

Ariel Bender, a very late foal, also showed bright early speed before dropping away and can probably do better in time. (op 33-1)

2028 BRANDON HOMES WILLIAM WALLACE H'CAP 6f 5y
6:55 (6:56) (Class 4) (0-80,77) 3-Y-0 **£6,476** (£1,927; £963; £481) **Stalls** Low

Form RPR
0-61 **1** **All The Nines (IRE)**[18] 1563 3-9-5 **73** SebSanders 8 79
(Mrs D J Sanderson) *mde all: rdn over 2f out: r.o fnl f* **4/1**[2]
3-10 **2** *1 ½* **Al Mugtareb (IRE)**[18] 1561 3-9-4 **72** JoeFanning 6 73
(M Johnston) *prom: effrt and chsd wnr over 1f out: kpt on ins fnl f* **6/1**[3]
-000 **3** *1 ¾* **Red Kyte**[14] 1639 3-9-9 **77** DO'Donohoe 4 72
(K A Ryan) *dwlt: plld hrd in rr: hdwy 2f out: kpt on fnl f* **12/1**
303- **4** *nk* **Exceedingly Good (IRE)**[273] 5043 3-8-13 **67** JimCrowley 7 61
(B Smart) *dwlt: hld up outside: hdwy 2f out: hung lft and no ex fnl f* **6/1**[3]
3351 **5** *¾* **Where's Reiley (USA)**[11] 1736 3-8-11 **68** 6ex NeilBrown(3) 2 60
(T D Barron) *hld up in tch: smooth hdwy over 2f out: rdn and kpt on same pce fnl f* **15/8**[1]
5-01 **6** *1 ¾* **Agent Stone (IRE)**[13] 1662 3-9-3 **74** (v) AndrewMullen(3) 1 60
(D Nicholls) *prom: drvn and outpcd 2f out: n.d after* **6/1**[3]
004 **7** *2* **Cool Art (IRE)**[17] 1584 3-9-9 **77** PatrickMathers 3 57
(Peter Grayson) *in tch: rdn and wkng whn hung rt over 1f out* **25/1**
22-0 **8** *¾* **Liberty Diamond**[13] 1686 3-8-13 **72** MartinLane(5) 5 50
(K R Burke) *cl up tl rdn and wknd over 1f out* **16/1**

1m 12.83s (0.63) **Going Correction** +0.075s/f (Good) **8** Ran SP% **115.1**
Speed ratings (Par 101): **98,96,93,93,92 89,87,86**
toteswinger: 1&2 £5.60, 1&3 £7.50, 2&3 £17.20 CSF £28.32 CT £264.69 TOTE £5.00: £1.70, £2.10, £3.20; EX 29.00.
Owner R J Budge **Bred** Deerpark Stud **Trained** Wiseton, Notts

FOCUS
Not a strong handicap by any means.

2029 TOTEPOOL GLASGOW STKS (LISTED RACE) (C&G) 1m 3f 16y
7:30 (7:30) (Class 1) 3-Y-0 **£30,815** (£11,653; £5,824; £2,912) **Stalls** High

Form RPR
43-1 **1** **Parthenon**[21] 1487 3-9-0 97 GregFairley 5 105
(M Johnston) *mde all: rdn and edgd lft over 2f out: kpt on strly fnl f* **5/2**[2]
2 *2 ½* **Stately Home (IRE)**[26] 1389 3-9-0 0 JMurtagh 6 100
(A P O'Brien, Ire) *trckd wnr: effrt over 2f out: edgd rt: kpt on same pce fnl f* **11/8**[1]
11-1 **3** *¾* **Holberg (UAE)**[20] 1512 3-9-0 90 JoeFanning 4 99
(M Johnston) *dwlt: sn trcking ldrs: effrt over 2f out: kpt on u.p fnl f* **20/1**
13 **4** *6* **Popmurphy**[23] 1459 3-9-0 97 JimCrowley 1 88
(K R Burke) *prom: drvn and outpcd over 3f out: n.d after* **5/1**[3]
1- **5** *2 ½* **Emirates Champion**[190] 7209 3-9-0 85 DO'Donohoe 3 84
(Saeed Bin Suroor) *prom: drvn over 3f out: wknd fr 2f out* **12/1**
2-1 **6** *34* **Bothy**[23] 1461 3-9-0 87 SebSanders 2 23
(R M Beckett) *hld up: shortlived effrt over 3f out: sn btn: eased whn no ch fnl f* **15/2**

2m 22.07s (-3.53) **Going Correction** -0.125s/f (Firm) **6** Ran SP% **111.6**
Speed ratings (Par 107): **107,105,104,100,98 73**
toteswinger: 1&2 £1.10, 1&3 £5.20, 2&3 £6.10 CSF £6.25 TOTE £4.20: £1.70, £1.40; EX 9.10.
Owner Sheikh Hamdan Bin Mohammed Al Maktoum **Bred** Darley **Trained** Middleham Moor, N Yorks
■ Stewards' Enquiry : Greg Fairley caution: used whip without giving colt time to respond

FOCUS
A quality field, probably the strongest assembled for this Listed prize, but in the end very little got into it.

NOTEBOOK
Parthenon went straight to the front and never saw another rival, completing a hat-trick of wins in the race for Mark Johnston. His rider was allowed to set just even fractions without being pestered and this relentless galloper gradually wound things up in the straight, knuckling down to see this out really strongly and confirm that he is a colt very much on the upgrade. He relished the step up in trip having slammed three rivals in a 1m conditions race at Sandown last time, to post a significantly better effort and his mark of 97 is sure to rise on the back of this. A tilt at a decent Group prize must be on the agenda now. (op 7-2 tchd 9-4)
Stately Home(IRE) came into this after his impressive Leopardstown maiden win, and he has a stack of big-race entries. However, although beaten fair and square by a more experienced rival, the big concern has to be his head carriage, which got higher the more pressure Johnny Murtagh applied. He still ran a nice race in defeat, behind a smart horse, but he can't be considered a realistic Derby contender on this evidence. (op 6-4)
Holberg(UAE), who is most progressive despite being rated 7lb inferior to his winning stablemate, was third turning in and couldn't improve on that, although he did see the rest off fairly comprehensively. (op 22-1 tchd 25-1)
Popmurphy is still very green and babyish, and he pulled quite hard early. He came under pressure 4f out and soon lost touch with the leaders, but he clearly has the potential to do much better in time and we might not see the best of him until next season. (op 11-4 tchd 11-2)
Emirates Champion was never on terms, but he is very lightly raced and it is far too soon to be writing him off. (op 16-1 tchd 13-2)
Bothy couldn't cope with the steep rise in class so soon in his career and is another who will doubtless do better in time. Official explanation: trainer had no explanation for the poor form shown (op 10-1 tchd 7-1)

2030 LUDDON CONSTRUCTION MAIDEN STKS 1m 1f 36y
8:05 (8:07) (Class 5) 3-Y-0+ **£3,238** (£963; £481; £240) **Stalls** High

Form RPR
1 **Hillview Boy (IRE)**[41] 5-9-13 0 MickyFenton 11 86
(J S Goldie) *s.i.s: t.k.h in rr: hdwy and hung lft fr 3f out: str run fnl f to ld nr fin* **22/1**
0-2 **2** *1 ¼* **Matraash (USA)**[20] 1508 3-8-13 0 JoeFanning 9 82
(M Johnston) *led: clr whn rdr dropped whip over 1f out: kpt on wl: hdd nr fin* **7/4**[2]
0 **3** *5* **High Severa (IRE)**[28] 1328 3-8-13 0 JimCrowley 4 71
(K R Burke) *in tch: effrt over 2f out: kpt on same pce over 1f out* **20/1**
04-2 **4** *1 ¾* **Dubai Echo (USA)**[25] 1407 3-8-13 83 SebSanders 1 67
(Sir Michael Stoute) *prom: effrt and cl up 3f out: no ex over 1f out* **4/6**[1]
5 *3 ½* **Par Avion**[86] 4-9-5 0 NeilBrown(3) 6 56
(Paul Murphy) *s.i.s: bhd tl styd on fnl 2f: nrst fin* **80/1**
64- **6** *1* **Quick Gourmet**[189] 7221 3-8-3 0 MartinLane(5) 2 52
(J A McShane) *t.k.h: hld up: hdwy 3f out: no imp fnl 2f* **80/1**
4 **7** *8* **Black River Falls (USA)**[18] 1562 3-8-13 0 TonyHamilton 10 40
(I Semple) *prom tl rdn and wknd over 2f out* **8/1**[3]
05 **8** *3* **Baligha**[42] 1101 4-9-8 0 DaleGibson 8 30
(G A Swinbank) *trckd ldrs: rdn over 3f out: wknd over 2f out* **100/1**
06 **9** *2 ¼* **Bumble Rose (IRE)**[11] 1739 6-9-8 0 GregFairley 7 25
(A G Foster) *towards rr: drvn over 3f out: sn wknd* **100/1**

000- **10** 2 3/4 **Sydney Cove (IRE)**200 7011 3-8-8 50 SladeO'Hara(5) 5 22
(R Allan) *bolted bef s: in tch tl wknd over 3f out* **100/1**
11 17 **Moscow Ali (IRE)**1208 9-9-6 0 SFeeney(7) 3 —
(J A McShane) *s.i.s: a bhd* **100/1**
1m 58.73s (-0.97) **Going Correction** -0.025s/f (Good)
WFA 3 from 4yo+ 14lb 11 Ran SP% **123.0**
Speed ratings (Par 103): **103,101,97,95,92 91,84,82,80,77 62**
toteswinger: 1&2 £9.80, 1&3 £68.90, 2&3 £8.10 CSF £63.23 TOTE £17.60: £4.60, £1.30, £5.90; EX 88.50.
Owner Connor & Dunne **Bred** John Coleman **Trained** Uplawmoor, E Renfrews
FOCUS
A fair maiden but the favourite was well below par. Other than that the form looks pretty sound.

2031 MCGRATTAN PILING BRAVEHEART STKS (H'CAP) (LISTED RACE) 1m 4f 17y
8:35 (8:35) (Class 1) (0-110,101) 4-Y-O+
£23,843 (£9,038; £4,523; £2,255; £1,129; £567) **Stalls** High

Form RPR
10-0 **1** **Allied Powers (IRE)**23 1460 4-9-0 **97** MickyFenton 1 112
(M L W Bell) *hld up last: smooth hdwy to ld over 2f out: shkn up and r.o strly* **5/2**2
1251 **2** 4 1/2 **Lady Jane Digby**14 1642 4-8-12 **95** GregFairley 5 103
(M Johnston) *t.k.h early: hld up: hdwy and ev ch over 2f out: kpt on fnl f: no ch w wnr* **8/1**
0203 **3** 4 1/2 **Drill Sergeant**13 1674 4-9-4 **101** JoeFanning 9 102
(M Johnston) *trckd ldrs: rdn 3f out: outpcd fr 2f out* **11/2**3
0-14 **4** 4 **Ladies Best**23 1460 5-8-12 **95** SebSanders 6 89
(B Ellison) *hld up in tch: stdy hdwy 4f out: outpcd over 2f out: n.d after* **9/1**
4-40 **5** 4 **Dunaskin (IRE)**9 1790 9-8-10 **93** TonyHamilton 8 81
(B Ellison) *led 2f: cl up: rdn and lost pl 4f out: sn n.d* **25/1**
1-13 **6** 1 1/2 **Cape Express (IRE)**48 1003 4-9-0 **97** PhilipRobinson 2 83
(M A Jarvis) *prom: lost pl 1/2-way: rallied and prom over 3f out: wknd over 2f out* **13/8**1
00-0 **7** 3 **Lancetto (FR)**23 1458 4-8-4 **87** oh1 MartinLane 4 68
(K R Burke) *led after 2f: hdd over 2f out: sn wknd* **40/1**
50-3 **8** 9 **Amanda Carter**16 1613 5-8-4 **87** oh4 SilvestreDeSousa 3 53
(R A Fahey) *hld up: outpcd 1/2-way: rallied over 3f out: wknd over 2f out* **14/1**
20-0 **9** 5 **Bogside Theatre (IRE)**20 1519 5-8-10 **93** JimCrowley 7 51
(G M Moore) *prom tl lost pl qckly over 3f out* **50/1**
2m 35.02s (-3.58) **Going Correction** -0.025s/f (Good) 9 Ran SP% **118.1**
Speed ratings (Par 111): **110,107,104,101,98 97,95,89,86**
toteswinger: 1&2 £9.40, 1&3 £6.00, 2&3 £9.10 CSF £23.12 CT £103.01 TOTE £3.80: £1.80, £1.90, £2.20; EX 27.40.
Owner David Fish And Edward Ware **Bred** Saad Bin Mishrif **Trained** Newmarket, Suffolk
FOCUS
This had the feel of quite a competitive Listed event on paper and it was run at what looked a decent clip, but it was turned into a rout.
NOTEBOOK
Allied Powers(IRE) absolutely hosed up on his first try in Listed company. He was a huge improver last year, rising 30lb in the ratings and winning four races, and having shaped with plenty of encouragement over a shorter trip at Epsom on his seasonal return, he stepped up significantly on that to confirm that he is a colt still going forward. Given a very patient ride, he was always travelling strongly off the pace and, having moved smoothly through to challenge over 2f out, he quickly went clear in a manner that suggests he is probably ready to tackle Group company now. (op 11-4 tchd 3-1 in a place)
Lady Jane Digby had shaped as though she was well worth a try at this trip, but she raced very keenly in the early stages, suggesting she might be better suited by the pace of a 1m2f contest. She did, though, stay on well to come clear of stablemate. (tchd 15-2)
Drill Sergeant was readily brushed aside, although he faced quite a stiff task conceding weight all round. (op 13-2)
Ladies Best was in front of Allied Powers at Epsom last time on similar terms to these, but he was put firmly in his place here, being readily outspeeded when the pace quickened. (op 8-1 tchd 10-1)
Dunaskin(IRE) finds winning difficult these days and he was left trailing.
Cape Express(IRE) was in trouble a long way out and is surely better than this. Official explanation: jockey said colt never travelled (op 15-8)
Amanda Carter Official explanation: jockey said mare hung left-handed throughout

2032 CHARD CONSTRUCTION H'CAP 5f 4y
9:05 (9:07) (Class 5) (0-75,74) 4-Y-O+ **£3,238** (£963; £481; £240) **Stalls** Low

Form RPR
-500 **1** **Andrasta**12 1689 4-7-11 **55** oh5 CharlotteKerton(7) 5 61
(A Berry) *in tch: rdn 1/2-way: kpt on wl fnl f to ld nr fin* **50/1**
0220 **2** 1/2 **Sandwith**13 1685 6-9-9 **74** GregFairley 10 78
(A G Foster) *cl up: rdn and led over 1f out: kpt on: hdd cl home* **15/2**
-242 **3** hd **Rothesay Dancer**15 1627 6-9-5 **73** KellyHarrison(3) 1 76
(J S Goldie) *hld up: smooth hdwy over 1f out: kpt on fnl f* **9/4**1
00-0 **4** 1/2 **Joyeaux**10 1768 7-9-2 **67** JoeFanning 8 68
(Ollie Pears) *in tch: rdn and hdwy over 1f out: r.o fnl f: no ex towards fin* **16/1**
353- **5** nk **Select Committee**199 7043 4-8-8 **59** (p) TonyHamilton 6 59
(J J Quinn) *in tch: effrt over 1f out: kpt on: no ex wl ins fnl f* **15/2**
0220 **6** 1 **Strathmore (IRE)**20 1518 5-8-5 **63** TimothyAyres(7) 4 60
(R A Fahey) *bhd and outpcd: hdwy over 1f out: one pce wl ins fnl f* **15/2**
0654 **7** 1 3/4 **Silvanus (IRE)**12 1689 4-9-4 **72** NeilBrown(3) 3 63
(I Semple) *stdd s: hld up: hdwy over 1f out: nvr rchd ldrs* **13/2**3
3033 **8** 3/4 **Regal Royale**10 1776 6-9-0 **65** (v) PatrickMathers 7 53
(Peter Grayson) *bhd and outpcd: sme hdwy appr fnl f: nvr rchd ldrs* **14/1**
621 **9** 2 1/2 **Rocketball (IRE)**12 1695 4-8-6 **62** 6ex MartinLane(5) 12 41
(Patrick Morris) *led to over 1f out: sn rdn and wknd* **11/4**2
0-50 **10** 3 1/4 **Stoneacre Donny (IRE)**121 153 5-7-11 **55** oh10 AndrewHeffernan(7) 9 22
(Peter Grayson) *bhd and outpcd: nvr on terms* **100/1**
006/ **11** 7 **Davaye**570 6402 5-7-11 **55** oh8 DeclanCannon(7) 11 —
(K R Burke) *chsd ldrs tl hung rt and wknd fr 2f out* **20/1**
60.49 secs (0.49) **Going Correction** +0.175s/f (Good) 11 Ran SP% **126.3**
Speed ratings (Par 103): **103,102,101,101,100 99,96,95,91,85 74**
toteswinger: 1&2 £65.90, 1&3 £48.10, 2&3 £5.80 CSF £414.62 CT £1246.63 TOTE £91.50: £11.60, £2.80, £1.60; EX 1642.40 Place 6: £59.07, Place 5: £40.55.
Owner A B Parr **Bred** Peter Barclay **Trained** Cockerham, Lancs
■ Stewards' Enquiry : Charlotte Kerton caution: used whip down shoulder in forehand position.
FOCUS
Ordinary sprint handicap form.
T/Plt: £82.50 to a £1 stake. Pool: £48,524.88. 429.01 winning tickets. T/Qpdt: £21.10 to a £1 stake. Pool: £4,010.19. 140.60 winning tickets. RY

1350 NEWBURY (L-H)
Friday, May 15

OFFICIAL GOING: Good (good to soft in places) changing to good to soft after race 5 (3.25)
Rails moved in around 7f and 5f bends but impact on distances not notified.
Wind: Virtually nil Weather: Overcast

2033 ABSOLUTE HOSPITALITY MAIDEN STKS (DIV I) 6f 8y
1:20 (1:20) (Class 4) 2-Y-O **£4,857** (£1,445; £722; £360) **Stalls** Centre

Form RPR
1 **Canford Cliffs (IRE)** 2-9-3 0 RichardHughes 10 97+
(R Hannon) *sn trcking ldrs: wnt 2nd 3f out: led on bit appr fnl f: shkn up and qckn d clr: v easily* **11/8**1
2 7 **Rakaan (IRE)** 2-9-3 0 JamieSpencer 2 78+
(B J Meehan) *outpcd in rr: gd hdwy over 2f out: styd on to go 2nd wl ins fnl f but nvr any ch w wnr* **6/1**3
3 1 1/4 **Barzan (IRE)** 2-9-3 0 RichardKingscote 1 70
(Tom Dascombe) *led: rdn 2f out: hdd appr oaching fnl f: sn no ch w wnr: wknd and lost 2nd wl ins fnl f* **3/1**2
6 **4** 4 **Ant Music (IRE)**30 1290 2-9-3 0 GeorgeBaker 8 58
(J S Moore) *chsd ldrs: rdn over 2f out: sn outpcd* **8/1**
5 1/2 **Jehu** 2-9-3 0 EdwardCreighton 3 57
(M R Channon) *towards rr: hdwy over 2f out: nvr anywhere nr ldrs and kpt on same pce fr over 1f out* **16/1**
6 3 1/4 **Listillo (USA)** 2-9-3 0 SteveDrowne 5 47+
(H J L Dunlop) *s.i.s: sn rcvrd to chse ldrs and wnt 3rd 1/2-way: sn rdn: wknd ins fnl 2f* **22/1**
7 7 **Fantastic Prince** 2-9-3 0 ChrisCatlin 9 26
(P F I Cole) *sn rdn along and a outpcd* **8/1**
8 3/4 **Welsh Legacy (IRE)** 2-8-12 0 GabrielHannon(5) 7 24
(B W Duke) *w ldr early: wknd ins fnl 2f* **100/1**
1m 13.97s (0.97) **Going Correction** +0.225s/f (Good) 8 Ran SP% **114.8**
Speed ratings (Par 95): **102,92,91,85,85 80,71,70**
toteswinger: 1&2 £2.00, 1&3 £2.50, 2&3 £3.70 CSF £10.36 TOTE £2.40: £1.10, £1.90, £1.10; EX 8.10.
Owner The Heffer Syndicate **Bred** S And S Hubbard Rodwell **Trained** East Everleigh, Wilts
FOCUS
Significant rain had changed the ground from "good to firm" overnight and many of these inexperienced juveniles struggled to get going at any stage. The winner impressed but the form is not easy to pin down.
NOTEBOOK
Canford Cliffs(IRE) ◆, a £50,000 son of Tagula out of an unraced half-sister to four winners up to middle distances, arrived with a lofty reputation and made a highly impressive debut. Always travelling well, he settled it in a couple of strides and looks set for an immediate step up in class. While Richard Hannon does not intend to over-race him, the Coventry Stakes, for which he is now 16-1, is an obvious target. (tchd 7-4)
Rakaan(IRE) was a more expensive yearling than the winner, at 140,000gns, but is not as precocious. Green in the rear early, he was shaping better in the final two furlongs, but this son of Bahamian Bounty is bred for speed so he should find this trip suitable with this first outing behind him. (op 13-2)
Barzan(IRE), the only one to make a race of it with the winner, is capable of finding a routine maiden. A son of Danehill Dancer out of an unraced half-sister to Gold Splash, he has already changed hands four times, with a top price of 100,000gns. He should win races, but needs to improve to justify the price-tag. (op 2-1 tchd 15-8)
Ant Music(IRE) showed more speed than he had on his debut, but he was beaten soon after halfway and already he looks a nursery sort in the making. (op 14-1)
Jehu is by the miler Antonius Pius, but there is plenty of stamina in the family and he should appreciate another furlong or two. (op 20-1)
Listillo(USA) Official explanation: jockey said saddle slipped

2034 KINGWOOD STUD GOLDEN SILCA FILLIES' CONDITIONS STKS 5f 34y
1:50 (1:50) (Class 3) 2-Y-O
£6,542 (£1,959; £979; £490; £244; £122) **Stalls** Centre

Form RPR
2 **1** **Kurtanella**12 1706 2-8-10 0 RichardHughes 2 80+
(R Hannon) *t.k.h: hld up in tch: swtchd lft and hdwy over 1f out: drvn to ld fnl 110yds: styd on wl* **7/4**1
25 **2** 1/2 **Mijas Playa**9 1788 2-8-10 0 TPQueally 6 77
(C A Dwyer) *led: rdn over 1f out: hdd and no ex fnl 110yds* **10/3**2
3 1 1/2 **Ailsa Carmel (IRE)** 2-8-7 0 SamHitchcott 7 69
(M R Channon) *s.i.s: sn rcvrd to chse ldrs: rdn along 1/2-way: kpt on same pce ins fnl f* **5/1**3
4 2 1/2 **Guesswork** 2-8-7 0 LiamJones 5 60
(W Jarvis) *chsd ldrs: rdn along 1/2-way: wknd ins fnl f* **20/1**
5 hd **Fly Silca Fly (IRE)** 2-8-7 0 EdwardCreighton 1 59
(M R Channon) *towards rr and sn pushed along: hdwy fnl f: kpt on but nvr a threat* **14/1**
6 shd **Astarta (IRE)** 2-8-8 0 ow1 JamieSpencer 3 60
(P F I Cole) *chsd ldrs: rdn 1/2-way: wknd over 1f out* **5/1**3
7 1 1/4 **More Lashes (USA)** 2-8-7 0 WilliamBuick 4 56+
(M G Quinlan) *hld up in tch: shkn up and outpcd 1/2-way* **11/1**
63.02 secs (1.62) **Going Correction** +0.225s/f (Good) 7 Ran SP% **112.5**
Speed ratings (Par 94): **96,95,92,88,88 88,86**
toteswinger: 1&2 £1.50, 1&3 £2.90, 2&3 £3.40 CSF £7.41 TOTE £2.60: £1.20, £2.30; EX 7.50.
Owner Mrs Philip Snow **Bred** The National Stud **Trained** East Everleigh, Wilts
FOCUS
A quick juvenile double for the stable. This looked far from a vintage renewal but the winner should have more to offer.
NOTEBOOK
Kurtanella had shown promise on her debut in a good race at Salisbury. Though she had to work to get on top, she did it well in the end, with Richard Hannon expecting her to stay 6f, and probably even 7f, in due course. In the meantime she is 25-1 for the Queen Mary. (tchd 6-4 and 15-8 in a place)
Mijas Playa, the most experienced in the field with two races behind her, put in another good effort without being quite good enough to win. She is obviously capable of winning a maiden, but connections appear to have higher aspirations and this sound effort justified their optimism. (op 11-4)
Ailsa Carmel(IRE), a daughter of Antonius Pius and a juvenile winner at 5f, changed hands for 16,000gns earlier this year. She made an encouraging debut, battling on gamely in the final furlong, and should be off the mark soon. (op 9-1 tchd 9-2)
Guesswork, by Rock Of Gibraltar out of a maiden sprinter, is a half-sister to three winners at 6f and 7f. She made a satisfactory debut and should appreciate an extra furlong. (op 16-1)

Fly Silca Fly(IRE), a Hawk Wing debutante, is out of an unraced mare but there is speed in the family and she should sharpen up with experience. (op 12-1)
Astarta(IRE), a 50,000gns Green Desert half-sister to five winners up to 2m, will not need that far to find a race but she does already look as if she will be suited by 6f. (op 7-1 tchd 8-1)
More Lashes(USA) Official explanation: jockey said filly was unsuited by the good (good to soft places) ground

2035 CARNARVON STKS (LISTED RACE) 6f 8y
2:20 (2:20) (Class 1) 3-Y-O
£22,708 (£8,608; £4,308; £2,148; £1,076; £540) **Stalls** Centre

Form RPR
3-1 **1** **Border Patrol**[27] 1350 3-9-0 92 SteveDrowne 3 111
(R Charlton) *towards rr tl gd hdwy over 2f out: stdy on strly fnl f to ld fnl 75yds: won gng away* **9/2**[2]
111- **2** 1 1/4 **Triple Aspect (IRE)**[246] 5850 3-9-5 107 LiamJones 2 112
(W J Haggas) *chsd ldrs: chal over 1f out: rdn and edgd led sn after: led jst ins fnl f: hdd and nt qcknd fnl 75yds* **8/1**[3]
16-2 **3** 1 1/2 **Awinnersgame (IRE)**[30] 1292 3-9-0 107 WilliamBuick 9 102
(J Noseda) *hld up in rr but in tch: rdn over 2f out: styd on thrght fnl f to tale 3rd nr fin but nvr gng pce of ldng duo* **9/4**[1]
5-50 **4** 3/4 **Marine Boy (IRE)**[16] 1602 3-9-0 105 RichardKingscote 5 100
(Tom Dascombe) *chsd ldrs: rdn over 2f out: styd on same pced fnl f* **8/1**[3]
1-25 **5** shd **Elnawin**[16] 1602 3-9-5 105 RichardHughes 4 104
(R Hannon) *led: rdn fr 2f out: hdd jst ins fnl f: wknd nr fnl 100yds* **10/1**
2-42 **6** hd **Enderby Spirit (GR)**[16] 1602 3-9-0 100 RoystonFfrench 10 99
(B Smart) *chsd ldrs: rdn over 2f out: outpcd fnl f* **9/1**
321- **7** 4 **Run For The Hills**[210] 6776 3-9-0 92 RHills 6 86
(J H M Gosden) *sn chsng ldr: rdn over 2f out: wknd fnl f* **9/2**[2]
1-00 **8** 2 1/4 **Imperial Guest**[13] 1675 3-9-3 98 ChrisCatlin 1 82
(G G Margarson) *a outpcd* **50/1**
42-0 **9** 9 **Saxford**[30] 1292 3-9-3 104 TPQueally 7 53
(Mrs L Stubbs) *sn bhd* **20/1**

1m 13.49s (0.49) **Going Correction** +0.225s/f (Good) **9** Ran SP% **115.2**
Speed ratings (Par 107): **105,103,101,100,100 99,94,91,79**
toteswinger: 1&2 £8.70, 1&3 £3.40, 2&3 £4.70 CSF £40.08 TOTE £6.20: £2.10, £2.80, £1.10; EX 38.50.
Owner Elite Racing Club **Bred** Elite Racing Club **Trained** Beckhampton, Wilts
■ Stewards' Enquiry : William Buick caution: used whip with excessive ferquency.

FOCUS
A classy race of its type contested by some proven sorts and potential improvers, the winner in the latter category.

NOTEBOOK
Border Patrol's two previous races had both been over two furlongs farther, but he would have been better suited by the rain than some of his rivals and looks a horse of some potential up to 1m. Connections, who were somewhat surprised by his ability to do this over 6f, reported that he needs good ground or softer, and that he would not be suited by an undulating or downhill track, which limits them to some extent. The original plan was to run him in Heritage handicaps, but they may be forced to concentrate on Listed and Group 3 events now. (op 4-1 tchd 5-1)
Triple Aspect(IRE) ◆, unbeaten in three races last year around 5f, made a bold bid over this extra furlong and cannot be said to have been beaten for lack of stamina. That said, he has enough speed to drop back in trip again, so connections will have a choice of engagements. He should have a good season, with part-owner Harry Findlay expecting him to peak on fast ground. (op 13-2)
Awinnersgame(IRE), already a winner on soft ground, ran a solid race in defeat but gave the impression that he would appreciate a return to 7f. (op 3-1 tchd 2-1)
Marine Boy(IRE) should have been suited by the drop in trip. Away on level terms this time, he showed early speed and is worth another try at 6f on faster ground. (op 10-1)
Elnawin's connections were unsure that he would be suited by the rain-softened ground. While he showed plenty of "early", he did not quite get home, so it may be that he is more at home on quicker conditions, but he has not yet recaptured his winning juvenile form anyway. (op 11-1 tchd 12-1)
Enderby Spirit(GR) faded late on and, while he won his maiden on good to soft, he is probably most effective on better ground than this. (op 8-1)

2036 SWETTENHAM STUD FILLIES' TRIAL STKS (LISTED RACE) 1m 2f 6y
2:50 (2:50) (Class 1) 3-Y-O
£22,708 (£8,608; £4,308; £2,148; £1,076; £540) **Stalls** Low

Form RPR
1-1 **1** **Apple Charlotte**[16] 1599 3-8-12 106 TPQueally 1 101+
(H R A Cecil) *trckd ldr off mod early pce: slt ld ins fnl 3f: drvn clr ins fnl f* **13/8**[1]
3-44 **2** 2 1/4 **The Miniver Rose (IRE)**[12] 1701 3-8-12 93 RichardHughes 5 96
(R Hannon) *hld up in tch off mod early pce: hdwy to chse ldrs 4f out: styd on u.p to go 2nd fnl f but no imp on wnr* **5/1**[3]
51-4 **3** 1/2 **Uvinza**[16] 1599 3-8-12 95 JamieSpencer 6 95
(W J Knight) *led at mod early pce: drvn and narrowly hdd ins fnl 3f: styd chsng wnr tl outpcd fnl f* **16/1**
1- **4** 1/2 **Mooakada (IRE)**[210] 6778 3-8-12 80 RHills 7 94
(J H M Gosden) *trckd ldrs: pushed along over 2f out: no imp and no ex ins fnl f* **9/4**[2]
1 **5** 1 1/2 **Danehill's Pearl (IRE)**[28] 1327 3-8-12 0 RichardKingscote 8 91
(Tom Dascombe) *hld up in rr but in tch off mod early pce: rdn and styd on fnl 2f but nvr gng pce to get into contention* **15/2**
60-1 **6** 7 **King's Starlet**[16] 1605 3-8-12 86 SteveDrowne 3 84+
(H Morrison) *heavily restrained to rr off mod early pce: bit c through mouth 5f out: hdwy over 2f out: nvr quite gng pce to trble ldrs: hung rt and wknd ins fnl f* **14/1**

2m 9.92s (1.12) **Going Correction** +0.225s/f (Good) **6** Ran SP% **109.8**
Speed ratings (Par 104): **104,102,101,101,100 94**
toteswinger: 1&2 £2.40, 1&3 £7.30, 2&3 £7.40 CSF £9.70 TOTE £2.00: £1.20, £2.80; EX 6.90 Trifecta £23.30 Pool: £160.79 - 5.10 winning units.
Owner De La Warr Racing **Bred** Hascombe And Valiant Studs **Trained** Newmarket, Suffolk

FOCUS
Plenty of previous winning form on show here, but the early pace was not taxing. The overall form is only average for the grade, the winner not needing to improve much on her Ascot win.

NOTEBOOK
Apple Charlotte, a daughter of the speedy Royal Applause, had been keen over 1m last time and wore a crossed noseband here, but any concerns about her ability to stay were dispelled by a gritty performance. Henry Cecil, who reported that she is in the Coronation Stakes but not the Ribblesdale, will now have to decide over which trip to campaign her. With that in mind, Tom Queally, who noted how genuine she is, feels she would be better going up in distance rather than down. (op 6-4 tchd 11-8 and 7-4 in a place)
The Miniver Rose(IRE), whose only win was on soft ground, ran her best race to date. Though she will not be easy to place, she has trained on well and it is worth persisting in Listed company for now.
Uvinza promised to be suited by the longer trip, and could probably win over it in lesser company, but in the end she was put in her place by better rivals. (tchd 14-1)
Mooakada(IRE), a Montjeu filly who had two handlers in the paddock, came into the race as a dark horse for the Oaks. Despite being too headstrong, she saw the trip out well enough and, while not quickening in the style of a potential star, she looks the sort who will improve with racing. (tchd 5-2)
Danehill's Pearl(IRE) made a creditable effort in this better company despite hanging across from mid-track to the stands' side rail. Official explanation: jockey said filly hung right-handed (op 14-1)
King's Starlet and her rider never looked happy, apparently having some streering problems from halfway, and from then on she was only making up the numbers. Official explanation: jockey said filly hung right-handed (op 12-1)

2037 ABSOLUTE HOSPITALITY MAIDEN STKS (DIV II) 6f 8y
3:25 (3:32) (Class 4) 2-Y-O **£4,857** (£1,445; £722; £360) **Stalls** Centre

Form RPR
1 **Meglio Ancora** 2-9-3 0 TPQueally 2 81
(J G Portman) *trckd ldrs: led appr fnl 2f: hdd briefly 1f out: sn rdn to ld again: styd on wl* **16/1**
2 1/2 **Alrasm (IRE)** 2-9-3 0 RHills 1 80+
(M A Jarvis) *trckd ldrs: drvn and qcknd to ld briefly 1f out: sn hdd: kpt on same pce* **5/2**[1]
00 **3** 8 **Lofthouse**[16] 1610 2-9-3 0 SamHitchcott 6 56
(M R Channon) *led: rdn and hdd appr fnl 2f: wknd fnl f* **10/1**
4 nk **Brisbane (IRE)** 2-9-3 0 RobertHavlin 3 55+
(J H M Gosden) *trckd ldrs: shkn up over 2f out: sn outpcdm wknd fnl f* **10/3**[2]
5 1 1/2 **Rakhine (IRE)** 2-9-3 0 JamieSpencer 7 50+
(P F I Cole) *wnt rt s: sn rcvrd to chse ldrs: rdn 1/2-way: wknd appr fnl f* **9/2**
6 5 **Calypso Star (IRE)** 2-9-3 0 RichardHughes 4 35
(R Hannon) *s.i.s: outpcd* **7/2**[3]
7 nk **Volatilis (IRE)** 2-9-3 0 SimonWhitworth 8 34
(J W Hills) *bmpd s: a outpcd* **40/1**

1m 15.05s (2.05) **Going Correction** +0.225s/f (Good) **7** Ran SP% **109.5**
Speed ratings (Par 95): **95,94,83,83,81 74,74**
toteswinger: 1&2 £6.70, 1&3 £15.20, 2&3 £5.50 CSF £51.37 TOTE £26.00: £6.80, £1.70; EX 90.90.
Owner Anthony Boswood **Bred** Mrs R Pease **Trained** Compton, Berks
■ First Cat was withdrawn (12/1, bolted bef s). Deduct 5p in the £ under R4. New market formed.

FOCUS
Proof that money and breeding don't count for everything, even in horse racing. Decent form from the first two, who came well clear.

NOTEBOOK
Meglio Ancora does not have the most glamorous of backgrounds, being a bargain-basement gelded son of Best Of The Bests out of an unraced half-sister to a 2m winner. However it would be unfair to underrate him, since he won on merit and the pair finished a long way clear. He is highly rated at home and connections hope to have a lot of fun with him. (old market op 16-1 new market op 20-1)
Alrasm(IRE) ◆ cost £150,000 as a yearling. A well-grown Acclamation colt out of a winner at 1m in France, he was reported to have done plenty of work and looked to be going best entering the final two furlongs, only to be run out of it. He is a long-term prospect and should win his maiden before going on to better things. (old market op 9-4)
Lofthouse, racing over an extra furlong this time, made the running for a change but was left standing by the first two. However he is showing signs of improvement and will be an ideal sort for nurseries. (old market op 12-1 tchd 9-1 new market op 11-1)
Brisbane(IRE), a Kheleyf half-brother to two winning sprinters, showed some early pace and can improve on this on better ground. (old market tchd 3-1 and 4-1 new market op 7-2)
Rakhine(IRE), an Arakan colt whose once-raced dam was a half-sister to two speedy types, was restless in the stalls and can also come on for the experience. (old market op 5-1 tchd 13-2)

2038 HENNESSY RESTAURANT 25 MILE MENU H'CAP 1m 3f 5y
4:00 (4:00) (Class 4) (0-80,80) 3-Y-O **£5,180** (£1,541; £770; £384) **Stalls** Low

Form RPR
65-1 **1** **Simon Gray**[20] 1509 3-9-4 80 RichardHughes 2 87
(R Hannon) *t.k.h after 1f tl over 7f out: styd trcking ldr: rdn 2f out: led jst ins fnl f: hld on wl u.p* **7/1**[3]
51- **2** hd **Alanbrooke**[219] 6580 3-9-2 78 RoystonFfrench 10 84+
(M Johnston) *hld up in rr: rdn and hdwy on outside fr 3f out: styd on str u.p thrght fnl f: nt quite rch wnr* **6/4**[1]
64-3 **3** 1 **Decorum (USA)**[41] 1127 3-9-0 76 (t) RobertHavlin 12 80
(J H M Gosden) *mid-div: rdn along fr 3f out: hdwy over 1f out: kpt on wl cl home but nt rch ldng duo* **16/1**
3-15 **4** hd **Ultimate**[12] 1707 3-9-0 76 SteveDrowne 3 80
(H Morrison) *led 1f: led again over 7f out: rdn along 3f out: kpt slt advantage tl hdd jst ins fnl f: no ex cl home* **16/1**
0-21 **5** hd **Brunston**[12] 1707 3-9-4 80 6ex JamieSpencer 6 84+
(R Charlton) *hld up in rr: stdy hdwy on outside over 2f out: sn rdn: kpt on fnl f but nvr gng pce to rch ldrs* **3/1**[2]
2312 **6** 3 **El Bravo**[25] 1408 3-9-1 77 GeorgeBaker 5 75
(G L Moore) *hld up on ins: pushed along 2f out: styd on fnl f but nvr gng pce to get into contention* **15/2**
-422 **7** 1/2 **Divinatore**[20] 1516 3-8-6 68 EdwardCreighton 1 65
(D Haydn Jones) *chsd ldrs: rdn fr 4f out: wknd over 1f out* **33/1**
5-34 **8** 1/2 **Gulf President**[46] 1034 3-8-6 68 SamHitchcott 4 64
(M R Channon) *t.k.h: chsd ldrs: rdn and ev ch over 2f out: wknd over 1f out* **33/1**
0-14 **9** 3/4 **Peter Grimes (IRE)**[24] 1428 3-8-7 69 FergusSweeney 8 64
(H J L Dunlop) *chsd ldrs: rdn 3f out: wknd ins fnl 2f* **50/1**
04-0 **10** 7 **Sixties Swinger (USA)**[24] 1431 3-8-12 74 WilliamBuick 9 68
(M A Jarvis) *in tch: hdwy on outside to chse ldrs 3f out: sn rdn: wknd wl over 1f out* **12/1**
0-00 **11** 8 **Hilbre Point (USA)**[23] 1461 3-7-13 66 oh6 Louis-PhilippeBeuzelin(5) 11 34
(B J Meehan) *a in rr* **66/1**

2m 26.19s (4.99) **Going Correction** +0.225s/f (Good) **11** Ran SP% **118.1**
Speed ratings (Par 101): **90,89,89,88,88 86,86,85,85,80 74**
toteswinger: 1&2 £3.70, 1&3 £14.60, 2&3 £8.20 CSF £17.61 CT £168.73 TOTE £8.60: £2.10, £1.10, £3.80; EX 18.10.
Owner Mrs James Wigan **Bred** Mrs James Wigan **Trained** East Everleigh, Wilts

FOCUS
There was a weak pace until the tempo increased off the home turn. This looks like a race which will work out well. A lot of these came here as potential improvers and the seventh, eighth and ninth are the best guides.

2039 CLASS1 PERSONNEL H'CAP — 1m 2f 6y
4:35 (4:36) (Class 5) (0-70,70) 4-Y-0+ — £3,238 (£963; £481; £240) Stalls Low

Form — RPR

004- **1** **Beau Fighter**[340] 2885 4-9-0 66 .... GeorgeBaker 8 — 80
(C F Wall) *in tch: hdwy over 2f: led appr fnl f: rdn and hung rt u.p cl home* **11/1**

5014 **2** 1 ¾ **Apotheosis**[37] 1192 4-8-11 63 .... JamieSpencer 10 — 73
(W R Swinburn) *hld up in rr: swtchd towards outside and stdy hdwy on bit over 2f out: chsd wnr fnl f: sn fnd no ex and hld whn carried rt cl home* **7/2**[1]

0-01 **3** 4 ½ **Megalala (IRE)**[11] 1728 8-8-4 56 6ex .... NeilChalmers 12 — 57
(J J Bridger) *led 7f out: rdn and kpt slt advantage fr over 3f out tl hdd appr fnl f: wknd ins fnl f* **12/1**

000- **4** nse **Turjuman (USA)**[202] 6991 4-8-7 59 .... ChrisCatlin 7 — 60
(W J Musson) *hld up in rr: pushed along fr 3f out: styd on thrght fnl 2f: gng on cl home* **16/1**

3643 **5** 2 ¾ **Hucking Hero (IRE)**[8] 1812 4-8-13 68 .... (b[1]) MarcHalford(3) 6 — 63
(J R Best) *s.i.s: rr: rdn 3f out: sme hdwy to chse ldrs 2f out: wknd ins fnl f* **10/1**

244- **6** ½ **Seventh Cavalry (IRE)**[216] 6660 4-9-2 68 .... RichardHughes 5 — 62
(A King) *hld up in rr: pushed and hdwy over 2f out: kpt on ins fnl f but nvr in contention* **7/1**[2]

0004 **7** 1 ¾ **Jago (SWI)**[46] 1042 6-8-9 61 .... (p) LiamJones 11 — 52
(A M Hales) *hld up in rr: rdn and sme prog 3f out: nvr gng pce to chal and wknd over 1f out* **20/1**

05-1 **8** 2 **Balnagore**[16] 1604 5-9-4 70 .... TPQueally 4 — 57
(J L Dunlop) *chsd ldrs: travelling ok 3f out: sn rdn: wknd ins fnl 2f* **10/1**

00-6 **9** 2 **Sinbad The Sailor**[13] 1660 4-9-0 66 .... RHills 1 — 49
(J W Hills) *chsd ldrs: rdn over 3f out: wknd over 2f out* **15/2**[3]

0-61 **10** 2 ½ **Lunar River (FR)**[7] 1834 6-8-11 63 6ex .... (t) FergusSweeney 3 — 41
(David Pinder) *trckd ldrs: rdn 3f out: wknd 2f out* **15/2**[3]

5-33 **11** 6 **Seventh Hill**[17] 1581 4-8-11 63 .... SteveDrowne 2 — 29
(M Blanshard) *a towards rr* **10/1**

5-65 **12** 10 **Burnbrake**[85] 597 4-8-10 62 .... RobertHavlin 14 — 8
(L Montague Hall) *a in rr* **25/1**

-214 **13** 5 **Watchmaker**[16] 1604 6-9-2 68 .... RichardKingscote 9 — 4
(Miss Tor Sturgis) *led tl hdd over 7f out: chal and rdn over 3f out: sn btn* **16/1**

00-4 **14** dist **Lunar Limelight**[119] 186 4-8-4 56 oh7 .... WilliamBuick 15 — —
(P J Makin) *a bhd: virtually p.u fnl 2f: t.o* **50/1**

2m 9.67s (0.87) **Going Correction** +0.225s/f (Good) — **14** Ran SP% **123.9**
Speed ratings (Par 103): **105,103,100,99,97 97,95,94,92,90 85,77,73,—**
toteswinger: 1&2 £8.40, 1&3 £24.90, 2&3 £8.80 CSF £49.69 CT £492.24 TOTE £12.50: £4.00, £1.80, £2.60; EX 76.00.
Owner P G Kingston And P T Kingston **Bred** Mrs P G Kingston **Trained** Newmarket, Suffolk

FOCUS
With the ground easing further following more rain, they went a good gallop in the conditions. Big improvement from the winner, who may do better still.
Burnbrake Official explanation: jockey said gelding was unsuited by the good to soft ground
Watchmaker Official explanation: jockey said gelding had no more to give
Lunar Limelight Official explanation: jockey said gelding was unsuited by the good to soft ground

2040 BETFAIR APPRENTICE TRAINING SERIES STKS (H'CAP) — 1m 4f 5y
5:10 (5:11) (Class 5) (0-75,75) 4-Y-0+ — £2,590 (£770; £385; £192) Stalls Low

Form — RPR

3064 **1** **Corriolanus (GER)**[17] 1578 9-8-1 61 oh1 .... (p) RichardRowe(3) 11 — 73
(A M Balding) *hld up in rr: stdy hdwy over 3f out: trckd ldr 2f out: shkn up and styd on fnl f: drvn to ld fnl 30yds* **17/2**

60-0 **2** ½ **Coyote Creek**[31] 1274 5-9-4 75 .... (v) JPHamblett 9 — 86
(E F Vaughan) *in tch: hdwy 4f out: led wl over 2f out: hrd drvn fnl f: hdd fnl 30yds* **8/1**

320- **3** 11 **Babilu**[216] 6662 4-8-10 72 .... DavidKenny(5) 1 — 65
(A G Newcombe) *chsd ldrs: drvn to chal 3f out: wknd fr 2f out* **16/1**

-005 **4** 6 **Another Bottle (IRE)**[15] 1621 8-9-1 72 .... PNolan 3 — 56
(Mrs S Leech) *in rr tl hdwy 4f out: chsd ldrs and rdn 3f out: wknd 2f out* **25/1**

000- **5** 1 ¾ **Beautiful Lady (IRE)**[194] 7149 4-8-3 63 .... DTDaSilva(3) 2 — 44
(P F I Cole) *hld up in rr: shkn up 3f out: mod prog fnl f* **20/1**

0506 **6** hd **Princess Flame (GER)**[16] 1615 7-8-12 69 .... KylieManser 4 — 50
(B G Powell) *in tch: hdd 5f out: led ins fnl 4f: hdd wl over 2f out and sn wknd* **8/1**

5506 **7** 1 ½ **Ben Bacchus (IRE)**[32] 669 7-7-13 61 oh16 .... KierenFox(5) 8 — 39
(P W Hiatt) *in rr: rdn over 3f out: mod prog through btn horses fnl f* **28/1**

-210 **8** 1 ¾ **Filun**[43] 1081 4-8-10 67 .... SimonPearce 7 — 42
(A Middleton) *stdd towards rr after 3f: sme hdwy over 3f out: nvr in contention and sn wknd* **12/1**

P-33 **9** 1 ½ **Solas Alainn (IRE)**[20] 1506 4-9-1 72 .... MatthewDavies 12 — 45
(M Johnston) *chsd ldrs tl wknd 3f out* **7/2**[1]

0/66 **10** ¾ **King's Revenge**[8] 1815 6-8-10 67 .... LeeNewnes 10 — 39
(A King) *chsd ldrs over a m* **13/2**[2]

-605 **11** 11 **Kiho**[6] 1892 4-7-11 61 oh2 .... (b[1]) DanielBlackett(7) 13 — 15
(Eve Johnson Houghton) *sn led: hdd ins fnl 4f: sn wknd* **7/1**[3]

556- **12** 21 **Marie Louise**[310] 3835 4-8-8 65 .... JemmaMarshall 6 — —
(L A Dace) *chsd ldr over 7f* **25/1**

6130 **13** 30 **Wabbraan (USA)**[27] 1356 4-8-8 70 .... SPRyan(5) 5 — —
(M Hill) *chsd ldrs over a m* **15/2**

2m 38.24s (2.74) **Going Correction** +0.225s/f (Good) — **13** Ran SP% **122.0**
Speed ratings (Par 103): **99,98,91,87,86 86,85,83,82,82 75,61,41**
toteswinger: 1&2 £15.30, 1&3 £26.70, 2&3 £18.10 CSF £72.82 CT £1087.06 TOTE £11.70: £3.80, £3.80, £5.30; EX 100.80 Place 6: £9.39 Place 5: £7.82.
Owner Kingsclere Racing CLub **Bred** Gestut Schlenderhan **Trained** Kingsclere, Hants

FOCUS
The two leaders were soon going faster than ideal, eventually finishing a long way behind, and setting the race up for two hold-up horses. The winner has come down a long way in the weights but this was even so a fair step up on his recent form.
T/Plt: £6.50 to a £1 stake. Pool: £46,375.87. 5,157.84 winning tickets. T/Qpdt: £4.70 to a £1 stake. Pool: £2,791.80. 437.55 winning tickets. ST

1734 NEWCASTLE (L-H)
Friday, May 15

OFFICIAL GOING: Good to soft (7.0)
Rail moved in 2yards from 10f to 5f to provide fresh ground but impact on distances not notified.
Wind: moderate, half behind Weather: rain, becoming overcast and very cool

2041 HOLYSTONE NOVICE STKS — 6f
6:10 (6:10) (Class 4) 2-Y-0 — £4,209 (£1,252; £625; £312) Stalls Low

Form — RPR

31 **1** **Jack My Boy (IRE)**[30] 1275 2-9-2 0 .... CatherineGannon 5 — 75
(P D Evans) *led tl over 2f out: led 1f out: jst hld on* **15/8**[1]

31 **2** nse **Tres Coronas (IRE)**[11] 1735 2-8-11 0 .... DeanHeslop(5) 3 — 75
(T D Barron) *w ldr: led over 2f out tl hdd 1f out: kpt on wl: jst hld* **2/1**[2]

41 **3** ½ **Boga (IRE)**[9] 1783 2-8-7 0 .... TonyCulhane 7 — 64
(M R Channon) *t.k.h: hdwy to trck ldrs over 2f out: chal 1f out: no ex wl ins fnl f* **13/2**

4 1 ¼ **Leopard Hills (IRE)** 2-8-12 0 .... PaulMulrennan 4 — 66+
(J Howard Johnson) *outpcd and lost pl over 3f out: kpt on wl fnl f* **14/1**

1 **5** 1 ¼ **Novay Essjay (IRE)**[7] 1847 2-8-11 0 .... PatrickDonaghy(5) 2 — 66
(P C Haslam) *trckd ldrs: effrt over 2f out: wknd over 1f out* **4/1**[3]

4 **6** 3 **Marchin Star (IRE)**[28] 1330 2-8-12 0 .... TWilliams 6 — 53
(M Brittain) *t.k.h: hdwy over 2f out: wknd over 1f out* **33/1**

7 25 **War Wolf** 2-8-12 0 .... TomEaves 1 — —
(T D Easterby) *wl outpcd and lost pl after 2f: sn wl bhd: t.o* **25/1**

1m 16.84s (1.64) **Going Correction** +0.30s/f (Good) — **7** Ran SP% **114.9**
Speed ratings (Par 95): **101,100,100,98,96 92,59**
toteswinger: 1&2 £1.60, 1&3 £4.50, 2&3 £9.80 CSF £6.01 TOTE £3.00: £1.90, £2.30; EX 8.20.
Owner Terry Earle **Bred** Mrs Sheila Walker **Trained** Pandy, Monmouths
■ Stewards' Enquiry : Catherine Gannon one-day ban: failed to keep straight from stalls; two-day ban: excessive use of the whip (May 29-31)
Dean Heslop one-day ban: failed to keep straight from stalls (May 29)
Patrick Donaghy one-day ban: failed to keep straight from stalls (May 29)

FOCUS
Overnight, the ground was good to firm, but after 15mm of rain during the day the official going was changed to good to soft. This opening event involved four previous winners who were closely matched on form, and three of them fought out a tight finish. This form has been rated around the first two and the time and could be worth more.

NOTEBOOK
Jack My Boy(IRE), who dominated from a high draw at Beverley last time, had solid form claims and did well to muscle his way to the front and hang on. He is a half-brother to a prolific 1m4f winner in Italy, out of a multiple 6f-1m4f scorer, so should stay quite a bit further and looks a decent sort. (op 2-1 tchd 11-4)
Tres Coronas(IRE) improved on his debut third behind Jack My Boy when leading close home in a 5f maiden here last time. He ran another creditable race and showed tenacity to rally and almost steal it in the dying strides. He is out of a 1m4f winner at three, so it is very encouraging that he is showing so much at sprint trips in this early stage of his career. (op 3-1, tchd 7-2 in places)
Boga(IRE) was bought in for 15,000gns after readily winning a 5f Bath seller last week on her second start. She had a bit to find hiked in grade, but saw out the extra furlong well and took another fair step forward. (op 11-2)
Leopard Hills(IRE) looked very inexperienced and appeared to be going nowhere at halfway, but something seemed to click and he stayed on strongly almost to latch on to the leading group close home. This was a promising debut by the £90,000 gelded half-brother to two winners in Greece. His dam was placed at 9.5f-12.5f in France and he should improve with experience and a step up in trip. (op 11-1)
Novay Essjay(IRE) pounced late when making a winning debut in a Ripon auction maiden the previous week. He showed a good cruising speed for quite a long way here but could not quicken when asked for an effort and may have found the step up in trip on taxing ground against him. (op 7-2 tchd 11-4)

2042 WARD HADAWAY MEDIAN AUCTION MAIDEN STKS — 1m 2f 32y
6:45 (6:47) (Class 5) 3-Y-0 — £3,561 (£1,059; £529; £264) Stalls Centre

Form — RPR

63- **1** **Leceile (USA)**[172] 7434 3-8-12 0 .... KirstyMilczarek 1 — 76+
(W J Haggas) *led: qcknd over 4f out: fdd ins fnl f: jst hld on* **7/2**[3]

04-2 **2** nse **Stanstill (IRE)**[12] 1693 3-9-3 0 .... PJMcDonald 3 — 79
(G A Swinbank) *chsd ldrs: drvn 4f out: styd on ins fnl f: jst hld* **11/4**[2]

3 5 **Sanctuary** 3-9-3 0 .... TomEaves 2 — 69+
(B Smart) *s.i.s: in rr: hdwy 3f out: styd on fnl f* **40/1**

6-0 **4** 2 ¾ **Red China Blues (USA)**[16] 1611 3-9-3 0 .... PaulMulrennan 10 — 64
(J Howard Johnson) *t.k.h in midfield: drvn and outpcd over 4f out: hdwy over 2f out: kpt on same pce* **50/1**

06 **5** ½ **The Quiet Genius**[20] 1522 3-8-12 0 .... PatrickDonaghy(5) 4 — 63
(Jedd O'Keeffe) *in tch: drvn over 3f out: one pce fnl 2f* **150/1**

20- **6** 2 ¾ **Drop The Hammer**[191] 7200 3-8-12 0 .... DNolan 5 — 52
(T P Tate) *prom: outpcd over 3f out: no threat after* **25/1**

4 **6** dht **Sana Abel (IRE)**[31] 1269 3-8-12 0 .... NCallan 11 — 52
(M A Jarvis) *chsd ldrs: shkn up over 4f out: wknd over 1f out* **1/1**[1]

8 9 **Gwyre (IRE)** 3-8-12 0 .... DarrenMoffatt 7 — 34
(T D Easterby) *s.v.s: a bhd* **33/1**

00 **9** 7 **Kendalewood**[16] 1611 3-9-3 0 .... JamieMoriarty 9 — 25
(T D Walford) *hld up in midfield: lost pl 3f out* **100/1**

10 8 **Noor Al Bahar (IRE)** 3-8-12 0 .... TonyCulhane 8 — 4
(M R Channon) *in rr: bhd fnl 3f* **33/1**

00-6 **11** 8 **Indigo Belle (IRE)**[24] 1440 3-8-12 40 .... CatherineGannon 6 — —
(Mrs A Duffield) *t.k.h in rr: bhd fnl 3f* **150/1**

2m 17.15s (5.25) **Going Correction** +0.55s/f (Yiel) — **11** Ran SP% **115.3**
Speed ratings (Par 99): **101,100,96,94,94 92,92,84,79,72 66**
toteswinger: 1&2 £1.70, 1&3 £21.30, 2&3 £13.20 CSF £12.71 TOTE £5.30: £1.50, £1.10, £7.80; EX 18.40.
Owner Brian Wallace **Bred** Aaron U Jones & Marie D Jones **Trained** Newmarket, Suffolk

FOCUS
Much of the interest in this maiden centred around Sana Abel, but she may not have handled the ground. Muddling form, rated around the runner-up.

2043 CAMPERDOWN CONTRACTS H'CAP — 1m 2f 32y
7:20 (7:20) (Class 4) (0-80,79) 4-Y-0+ — £4,727 (£1,406; £702; £351) Stalls Centre

Form — RPR

51-4 **1** **Wind Star**[14] 1646 6-9-4 79 .... PJMcDonald 10 — 86
(G A Swinbank) *hld up in tch on outside: smooth hdwy over 2f out: led appr fnl f: hld on wl* **7/2**[1]

020- **2** *1* **Harry The Hawk**[73] 6983 5-8-9 **70** JamieMoriarty 8 75
(T D Walford) *hld up in rr: hdwy on outer over 2f out: hrd rdn and kpt on ins fnl f: a hld* **7/2**[1]

60-5 **3** *1 1/4* **Shy Glance (USA)**[12] 1690 7-8-7 **68** ow1 PaulMulrennan 11 71
(P Monteith) *t.k.h in rr: swtchd ins after 2f: hdwy on inner 3f out: sn chsng ldrs: kpt on same pce fnl f* **14/1**

50-0 **4** *hd* **Desert Destiny**[12] 1690 9-8-8 **69** TonyCulhane 4 71
(C Grant) *hld up in midfield: hdwy over 2f out: kpt on same pce ins fnl f* **25/1**

50-2 **5** *5* **Tufton**[13] 1660 6-8-9 **77** LeeTopliss(7) 7 69
(R A Fahey) *s.i.s: t.k.h in midfield: rdn and nt clr run over 2f out: no ch after* **7/2**[1]

4414 **6** *7* **Destinys Dream (IRE)**[16] 1615 4-8-10 **71** PhillipMakin 2 49
(Miss Tracy Waggott) *led: qcknd over 3f out: hdd appr fnl f: sn wknd* **10/1**

2203 **7** *nk* **Snow Dancer (IRE)**[22] 1472 5-8-2 **68** (p) PatrickDonaghy(5) 3 46
(H A McWilliams) *dwlt: sn trcking ldrs: wknd over 1f out* **14/1**

00-0 **8** *1 1/2* **Grey Command (USA)**[11] 1737 4-8-8 **69** TWilliams 5 44
(M Brittain) *chsd ldrs: wknd over 2f out* **66/1**

150- **9** *11* **Reel Buddy Star**[223] 6482 4-9-0 **75** TomEaves 6 28
(G M Moore) *t.k.h: sn trcking ldrs on outer: lost pl over 3f out: sn bhd* **7/1**[2]

12/ **10** *15* **Call Of Duty (IRE)**[510] 7222 4-9-0 **75** DarrenMoffatt 1 —
(Mrs Dianne Sayer) *t.k.h: trckd ldr: wknd 3f out: sn bhd* **9/1**[3]

2m 15.99s (4.09) **Going Correction** +0.55s/f (Yiel) **10** Ran SP% **116.9**
Speed ratings (Par 105): **105,104,103,103,99 93,93,92,83,71**
toteswinger: 1&2 £2.40, 1&3 £10.10, 2&3 £31.10 CSF £14.91 CT £152.43 TOTE £5.30: £1.10, £1.60, £4.80; EX 15.10.
Owner B Harker, R Hall & Dr C Emmerson **Bred** Mrs N F M Sampson **Trained** Melsonby, N Yorks
■ Stewards' Enquiry : Jamie Moriarty one-day ban: excessive use of the whip (May 29)

FOCUS
An open handicap in which the pace was steady and they were tightly grouped in the early stages. Most of the runners drifted towards the centre of the track in search of better ground in the straight.
Tufton Official explanation: jockey said gelding ran too free

2044 CERAMIC TILE DISTRIBUTORS H'CAP 2m 19y
7:55 (7:56) (Class 5) (0-70,70) 4-Y-0+ **£4,144** (£1,233; £616; £307) **Stalls** Low

Form RPR

/3- **1** **Summer Soul (IRE)**[13] 3198 7-9-11 **70** (p) RobertWinston 3 77
(Miss Lucinda V Russell) *reminders s: led tl over 3f out: hrd rdn and kpt on to ld ins fnl f: all out* **22/1**

0-00 **2** *nk* **Border Tale**[62] 679 9-8-2 **52** oh6 ow1 LanceBetts(5) 5 59
(James Moffatt) *trckd ldrs: led over 1f out: hdd ins fnl f: no ex* **40/1**

2-66 **3** *2* **Mister Pete (IRE)**[32] 1242 6-8-8 **60** JohnCavanagh(7) 7 64
(W Storey) *trckd ldrs: led over 3f out tl over 1f out: one pce* **7/1**

005/ **4** *2 1/4* **Presque Perdre**[16] 4283 5-8-6 **51** oh6 PJMcDonald 14 53
(G M Moore) *chsd ldrs: chal over 3f out: hmpd and one pce fnl 2f* **7/2**[2]

-460 **5** *nk* **Los Nadis (GER)**[14] 1648 5-9-3 PhillipMakin 4 63
(P Monteith) *prom: kpt on same pce fnl 2f* **9/1**

000/ **6** *3/4* **Celtic Carisma**[776] 5960 7-8-6 **51** oh6 PaulQuinn 1 51
(K G Reveley) *stdd s: hld up in rr: hdwy on ins over 2f out: kpt on: nvr nr ldrs* **33/1**

0-5 **7** *3 1/4* **Smugglers Bay (IRE)**[11] 1721 5-9-11 **70** (b) TomEaves 12 66
(T D Easterby) *t.k.h in rr: hdwy over 2f out: kpt on: nvr nr ldrs* **14/1**

6-03 **8** *1 3/4* **Thunderwing (IRE)**[10] 1767 7-8-10 **55** DarrenMoffatt 6 49
(James Moffatt) *t.k.h in midfield: kerpt on fnl 2f: nvr a threat* **9/1**

-551 **9** *1/2* **Dechiper (IRE)**[11] 1738 7-8-12 **62** 6ex PatrickDonaghy(5) 11 56
(R Johnson) *hld up in midfield: hdwy over 3f out: wknd over 1f out* **5/1**[3]

600- **10** *1/2* **Mirjan (IRE)**[40] 7128 13-9-11 **70** (b) PaulHanagan 2 63
(L Lungo) *trckd ldrs: wknd 2f out* **14/1**

00-0 **11** *15* **Byron Bay**[24] 1442 7-7-13 **51** oh2 JamieKyne(7) 17 26
(R Johnson) *t.k.h in rr: hdwy over 4f out: wknd over 2f out: bhd whn eased* **33/1**

1102 **12** *28* **Merrion Tiger (IRE)**[14] 1648 4-9-3 **65** NCallan 10 6
(A G Foster) *trckd ldrs: wknd over 2f out: sn bhd: eased* **3/1**[1]

33-0 **13** *3* **River Danube**[24] 1439 6-9-2 **61** JamieMoriarty 15 —
(T J Fitzgerald) *in rr: bhd fnl 4f: eased* **33/1**

3m 47.5s (8.10) **Going Correction** +0.55s/f (Yiel)
WFA 4 from 5yo+ 3lb **13** Ran SP% **125.3**
Speed ratings (Par 103): **93,92,91,90,90 90,88,87,87,87 79,65,64**
toteswinger: 1&2 £56.70, 1&3 £56.70, 2&3 £56.70 CSF £712.19 CT £6645.25 TOTE £30.30: £3.10, £11.60, £3.30; EX 757.90.
Owner Tay Valley Chasers Racing Club **Bred** Moyglare Stud Farm Ltd **Trained** Arlary, Perth & Kinross
■ Lucinda Russell's first Flat winner.
■ Stewards' Enquiry : Robert Winston seven-day ban: excessive use of the whip (May 29-Jun 4)
John Cavanagh one-day ban: careless riding (May 29)

FOCUS
They went a steady gallop for this staying handicap and the form is further limited by the proximity of the second and fourth from out of the weights. The race is rated around the third.
Merrion Tiger(IRE) Official explanation: jockey said gelding hung right in home straight
River Danube Official explanation: jockey said gelding lost its action

2045 JOHN N DUNN GROUP LTD H'CAP 7f
8:25 (8:27) (Class 3) (0-90,87) 4-Y-0 **£7,443** (£2,227; £1,113; £556; £277) **Stalls** Low

Form RPR

2-00 **1** **The Osteopath (IRE)**[13] 1684 6-9-2 **85** PJMcDonald 13 98
(M Dods) *stdd s: hld up in rr: gd hdwy over 1f out: r.o strly to ld fnl strides* **5/1**[3]

20-1 **2** *hd* **Horatio Carter**[13] 1682 4-9-4 **87** (p) NCallan 12 99+
(K A Ryan) *trckd ldrs: led 2f out: hung rt appr fnl f: hdd nr fin* **4/1**[2]

21- **3** *shd* **Eton Rifles (IRE)**[237] 6114 4-8-8 **77** PaulMulrennan 10 89+
(J Howard Johnson) *tk fierce hold: sn trcking ldrs: styd on to chal ins fnl f: jst hld* **9/4**[1]

00-0 **4** *7* **Game Lad**[13] 1682 7-8-13 **82** (t) DavidAllan 9 75
(T D Easterby) *hld up in rr: hdwy 2f out: one pce fnl f* **25/1**

15-5 **5** *2 1/4* **Borasco (USA)**[94] 491 4-8-13 **82** PhillipMakin 1 69
(T D Barron) *trckd ldr: led 3f out tl 2f out: wknd appr fnl f* **5/1**[3]

5506 **6** *6* **Memphis Man**[18] 1572 6-8-7 **76** CatherineGannon 3 47
(P D Evans) *dwlt: outpcd and lost pl over 2f out: no ch after* **28/1**

-004 **7** *3* **Dabbers Ridge (IRE)**[14] 1649 7-8-13 **82** RobertWinston 6 45
(I W McInnes) *mid-div: hdwy to chse ldrs 3f out: wknd over 1f out* **8/1**

0-40 **8** *2 3/4* **Sir Xaar (IRE)**[14] 1649 6-9-1 **84** (v) TomEaves 8 39
(B Smart) *hld up in rr: effrt over 2f out: wknd over 1f out* **28/1**

1230 **9** *12* **Strabinios King**[14] 1649 5-7-13 **75** BillyCray(7) 11 —
(A Berry) *led tl 3f out: sn lost pl and bhd* **25/1**

55-0 **10** *61* **Hinton Admiral**[14] 1649 5-8-11 **80** PaulHanagan 2 —
(R A Fahey) *chsd ldrs: effrt over 2f out: eased over 1f out: virtually p.u ins fnl f: wl t.o* **9/1**

1m 28.23s (-0.47) **Going Correction** +0.30s/f (Good) **10** Ran SP% **119.8**
Speed ratings (Par 107): **107,106,106,98,96 89,85,82,68,6**
toteswinger: 1&2 £7.20, 1&3 £5.40, 2&3 £1.30 CSF £24.93 CT £57.20 TOTE £5.60: £2.20, £1.80, £1.40; EX 27.10.
Owner Kevin Kirkup **Bred** Joe Rogers **Trained** Denton, Co Durham

FOCUS
A decent handicap that produced a thrilling finish. The first three were a long way clear and the form should work out.

NOTEBOOK
The Osteopath(IRE) started slowly, as he often does, and had about five lengths to find approaching the furlong marker but produced a strong finishing burst and just reeled in the leader. He is a likeable type who should continue to run well, but this win could force him up a grade and he may find it tough to get to grips with classier rivals. (op 6-1)
Horatio Carter was driven clear at Thirsk on his reappearance this month. He coasted into the lead some way out off 7lb higher here and it looked like he was going to register his fourth win in his last seven starts, but he tired in the closing stages and had nothing left to repel the late raider. This was still a highly creditable run and he could gain compensation under a more patient ride next time. (op 5-1 tchd 6-1)
Eton Rifles(IRE) ◆ was second to the highly progressive subsequent Listed winner Arganil in a Hamilton maiden in September before cruising clear at Catterick later that month. He took a fierce hold on his handicap debut back from 237 days off but did incredibly well to go so close. He should be more relaxed next time and should have little trouble winning off a similar mark. (op 3-1, tchd 7-2 in places)
Game Lad plugged on quite well but never got into a threatening position. He is capable of this sort of mark but is an in-and-out performer who is an infrequent winner these days. (op 33-1 tchd 22-1)
Borasco(USA) made an encouraging return over an inadequate 6f at Southwell in February but could not sustain her effort under a positive ride on suitable ground here. (op 7-2)
Hinton Admiral Official explanation: vet said gelding finished lame

2046 PERSIMMON HOMES NORTH EAST FILLIES' H'CAP 5f
8:55 (9:06) (Class 5) (0-70,70) 3-Y-0+ **£3,561** (£1,059; £529; £264) **Stalls** Low

Form RPR

00-0 **1** **Revue Princess (IRE)**[32] 1241 4-9-4 **62** (b) DavidAllan 14 72
(T D Easterby) *hdwy to ld over 3f out: edgd lft ins fnl f: kpt on wl* **22/1**

00-4 **2** *1 1/2* **Twosheetstothewind**[42] 1096 5-8-7 **56** oh1 FrederikTylicki(5) 13 61+
(M Dods) *hld up in rr: hdwy 2f out: chsng wnr 1f out: keeping on same pce whn carried lft fnl 75yds* **3/1**[2]

00-4 **3** *1 1/2* **Speedy Senorita (IRE)**[20] 1518 4-9-5 **70** JamieKyne(7) 9 70
(J J Quinn) *chsd ldrs: kpt on same pce ins fnl f* **6/1**[3]

-502 **4** *3 1/4* **Feelin Foxy**[10] 1768 5-9-7 **65** PaulMulrennan 8 53
(J G Given) *chsd ldrs: wknd fnl f* **6/1**[3]

6-04 **5** *1 3/4* **Miss Daawe**[25] 1411 5-9-2 **65** LanceBetts(5) 1 47
(B Ellison) *racd alone far side: w ldrs: wknd appr fnl f* **10/1**

5620 **6** *3* **Cheshire Rose**[29] 1310 4-9-5 **63** PhillipMakin 3 34
(T D Barron) *outpcd and lost pl after 2f: no threat after* **9/1**

06-0 **7** *1* **Morristown Music (IRE)**[11] 1734 5-8-12 **56** oh11 (p) JamieMoriarty 5 23
(J S Wainwright) *outpcd and lost pl after 2f* **28/1**

00-0 **8** *2 1/4* **Toy Top (USA)**[32] 1241 6-8-8 **57** (b) PatrickDonaghy(5) 2 16
(M Dods) *chsd ldrs: wknd over 1f out* **16/1**

05-1 **9** *4 1/2* **Molly Two**[17] 1591 4-9-6 **64** PaulHanagan 4 7
(L A Mullaney) *led over 1f: wknd over 1f out* **11/4**[1]

064- **10** *14* **Positivity**[191] 7198 3-9-1 **68** TomEaves 11 —
(B Smart) *outpcd and lost pl after 2f: sn wl bhd* **9/1**

61.71 secs (1.01) **Going Correction** +0.30s/f (Good)
WFA 3 from 4yo+ 9lb **10** Ran SP% **123.0**
Speed ratings (Par 100): **103,100,98,93,90 85,83,80,73,50**
toteswinger: 1&2 £17.40, 1&3 £25.50, 2&3 £2.30 CSF £92.20 CT £402.59 TOTE £33.50: £5.30, £2.30, £3.20; EX 29.90 Place 6: £142.07, Place 5: £105.49..
Owner S A Heley **Bred** Raymond Shanahan **Trained** Great Habton, N Yorks
■ Stewards' Enquiry : David Allan three-day ban: careless riding (May 29-31)

FOCUS
A modest sprint handicap in which they finished quite well strung out. There was a dramatic incident before the race when Miacarla got under the stalls, broke free and was withdrawn (28/1, no R4).
T/Plt: £276.50 to a £1 stake. Pool: £58,067.67. 153.30 winning tickets. T/Qpdt: £166.20 to a £1 stake. Pool: £3,593.90. 16.00 winning tickets. WG

2000 NEWMARKET (R-H)
Friday, May 15

OFFICIAL GOING: Good to firm (good in places; 8.1)
Wind: Fresh across Weather: Cloudy with sunny spells

2047 BETINTERNET.COM EBF MAIDEN FILLIES' STKS 6f
2:00 (2:01) (Class 4) 2-Y-O **£5,180** (£1,541; £770; £384) **Stalls** Low

Form RPR

1 **Electric Feel** 2-8-9 0 AndreaAtzeni(5) 8 77+
(M Botti) *s.i.s: hld up: hdwy over 1f out: rdn to ld wl ins fnl f: r.o* **15/2**

4 **2** *3/4* **Angelena Ballerina (IRE)**[8] 1802 2-9-0 0 JimmyQuinn 4 75
(A Bailey) *hmpd s: sn chsng ldrs: rdn over 1f out: r.o: wnt 2nd nr fin* **5/1**[3]

3 *hd* **Bella Swan** 2-9-0 0 AdamKirby 5 74
(W R Swinburn) *hld up: hdwy and nt clr run over 2f out: led over 1f out: rdn and hdd wl ins fnl f* **7/1**

0 **4** *3/4* **Silver Symphony (IRE)**[29] 1298 2-9-0 0 TedDurcan 9 72
(P F I Cole) *chsd ldrs: rdn and ev ch over 1f out: edgd lft and styd on same pce ins fnl f* **12/1**

2 **5** *2 1/4* **Bell's Ocean (USA)**[8] 1810 2-9-0 0 JerryO'Dwyer 11 65
(J Ryan) *prom on outer: rdn over 2f out: no ex ins fnl f* **9/2**[2]

5 **6** *nk* **Two Kisses (IRE)**[11] 1742 2-9-0 0 StephenCarson 3 64
(B G Powell) *edgd rt s: sn chsng ldr: rdn over 1f out: styd on same pce* **28/1**

7 *3/4* **Gallic Star (IRE)** 2-9-0 0 DarryllHolland 10 62
(M R Channon) *hld up: rdn over 1f out: nt trble ldrs* **11/4**[1]

0 **8** *3/4* **Sixpenny Moon (USA)**[18] 1569 2-9-0 0 PatDobbs 7 60
(R Hannon) *mid-div: pushed along 1/2-way: sn outpcd: styd on ins fnl f* **33/1**

9 *1 1/2* **Sarmad (USA)** 2-9-0 0 J-PGuillambert 6 55
(C E Brittain) *s.i.s: sn pushed along in rr: sme hdwy over 2f out: wknd over 1f out* **20/1**

04 **10** *8* **Country Princess (FR)**[8] 1810 2-9-0 0 SebSanders 12 31
(R M Beckett) *hld up: plld hrd: rdn over 2f out: bec unbalanced and wknd over 1f out* **11/1**

11 *nk* **Audrinna (IRE)** 2-9-0 0 AlanMunro 2 30
(M G Quinlan) *led: rdn and hdd over 1f out: wknd qckly* **25/1**

1m 14.37s (2.17) **Going Correction** +0.30s/f (Good) **11** Ran SP% **116.8**
Speed ratings (Par 92): **97,96,95,94,91 91,90,89,87,76 76**
toteswinger: 1&2 £10.60, 1&3 £13.10, 2&3 £12.30 CSF £42.41 TOTE £9.00: £2.30, £2.20, £2.40; EX 65.10.
Owner Joseph Barton **Bred** Bearstone Stud **Trained** Newmarket, Suffolk

FOCUS
The form of this fair maiden has been rated tentatively.

NOTEBOOK
Electric Feel, a £36,000 purchase out of a winning two-year-old, attracted interesting market support and justified it in good style. She was slow to start and ran green throughout but despite hanging right inside the final furlong she finshed best of all. She is on the small side but will have learned a lot from the experience and her very shrewd trainer will surely place her to to win again. (op 25-1)
Angelena Ballerina(IRE) is a well-grown, lengthy filly with scope, but looks a bit weak. She stayed on well inside the final furlong but could not reach the winner. She ran well enough from a bad draw at Chester last week and is certainly going the right way. She should have little difficulty going one better. (op 10-3 tchd 6-1 and 13-2 in places)
Bella Swan was another to attract plenty of market support. A half-sister to six winners including Barolo, she impressed physically (looked as if she would come on for the run) and, considering that she will eventually stay much further, this was a highly encouraging debut. (op 13-2 tchd 9-1)
Silver Symphony(IRE), who is tall and rangy (a typical Paul Cole type), did not really improve on her debut which was over a furlong less. (op 17-2 tchd 8-1)
Bell's Ocean(USA) ran well on her debut but seemed to have her limitations exposed here by a few potentially decent fillies. (op 3-1)
Gallic Star(IRE) was backed down to favouritism and, although she seemed to know her job, she never really looked like winning. She is possibly worth another look. (op 13-2)

2048 BEST ODDS GUARANTEED AT BETINTERNET.COM H'CAP 1m
2:30 (2:34) (Class 5) (0-75,75) 3-Y-O **£3,885** (£1,156; £577; £288) **Stalls** Low

Form RPR

1 **1** **Open Sesame (IRE)**[122] 144 3-9-1 72 AlanMunro 9 92+
(P W Chapple-Hyam) *racd centre: s.i.s: sn mid-div: led over 1f out: r.o wl* **17/2**

55-6 **2** *3 ½* **Cloudesley (IRE)**[93] 503 3-8-6 63 ow1 LPKeniry 13 74+
(A M Balding) *racd centre: hld up: swtchd lft and hdwy over 1f out: r.o wl: nt trble wnr* **25/1**

453- **3** *2 ¾* **Mr Udagawa**[215] 6673 3-8-9 69 JackMitchell(3) 5 73
(R M Beckett) *racd centre: chsd ldrs tl led 2f out: sn rdn and hdd: no ex ins fnl f* **14/1**

-044 **4** *1* **Kaolak (USA)**[6] 1882 3-9-4 75 (v[1]) PatCosgrave 15 77
(J Ryan) *overall ldr in centre: hdd 2f out: no ex fnl f* **14/1**

65-3 **5** *2* **Getcarter**[4] 1932 3-8-11 68 PatDobbs 4 65
(R Hannon) *racd stands' side: hld up: jnd centre gp 5f out: hdwy 3f out: sn rdn: wknd over 1f out* **5/1**[1]

30-6 **6** *1* **Incendo**[17] 1595 3-8-7 64 TravisBlock 2 59
(J R Fanshawe) *racd stands' side: chsd ldrs: jnd centre 5f out: rdn over 2f out: hung rt over 1f out: sn wknd* **11/2**[2]

5-50 **7** *½* **Ponting (IRE)**[17] 1595 3-8-5 62 AdrianMcCarthy 10 56
(R M Beckett) *racd centre: s.i.s: sn chsng ldrs: rdn over 2f out: wknd over 1f out* **12/1**

00-1 **8** *1 ¼* **Bob Stock (IRE)**[11] 1746 3-8-4 61 oh1 NickyMackay 17 52
(W J Musson) *racd centre: prom: rdn over 2f out: hung lft and wknd over 1f out* **15/2**[3]

5-1 **9** *3 ¾* **Echo Dancer**[108] 306 3-8-7 71 HollyHall(7) 7 53+
(S A Callaghan) *racd centre: hld up: nvr trbld ldrs* **25/1**

540- **10** *1 ¾* **River Dee (IRE)**[215] 6673 3-8-11 68 JimmyQuinn 6 46
(D Donovan) *racd centre: hld up: hdwy 3f out: sn rdn: wknd over 1f out* **9/1**

00-4 **11** *nse* **Sham Sheer**[21] 1491 3-8-13 70 DaneO'Neill 14 48
(L M Cumani) *racd centre: hld up: rdn 1/2-way: lost pl over 3f out: n.d after* **9/1**

540- **12** *hd* **Itlaaq**[207] 6857 3-9-2 73 TedDurcan 19 51
(J L Dunlop) *racd centre: dwlt: hld up: rdn over 3f out: a in rr* **20/1**

33-0 **13** *½* **Darwin's Dragon**[11] 1752 3-9-0 71 JosedeSouza 12 48
(P F I Cole) *racd centre: chsd ldr tl rdn 3f out: wknd over 2f out* **100/1**

663- **14** *2 ¼* **Whisky Galore**[205] 6893 3-9-3 74 AdamKirby 3 46
(C G Cox) *racd stands' side: chsd ldr: jnd centre 5f out: rdn and wknd over 2f out* **14/1**

0220 **15** *4* **Esteem Lord**[30] 1295 3-9-0 71 FrancisNorton 11 33
(Jamie Poulton) *racd centre: mid-div: rdn over 3f out: wknd over 2f out* **50/1**

0 **16** *½* **Hard Ball**[46] 1034 3-8-13 70 DarryllHolland 1 31
(M Quinn) *led stands' side: chsd ldrs tl jnd centre 5f out: wknd over 2f out* **33/1**

-300 **17** *1 ¼* **The Bully Wee**[24] 1440 3-8-4 64 DominicFox(3) 16 22
(J Jay) *racd centre: hld up: rdn and hung lft over 3f out: n.d* **100/1**

22-3 **18** *18* **Piccolo Mondo**[17] 1585 3-9-0 71 StephenCarson 8 —
(P Winkworth) *racd centre: s.s: hld up: wknd 3f out* **25/1**

002- **19** *1* **Royal Willy (IRE)**[196] 7106 3-8-13 70 J-PGuillambert 18 —
(W Jarvis) *racd centre: hld up in tch: wknd over 2f out: eased* **16/1**

1m 39.2s (0.60) **Going Correction** +0.30s/f (Good) **19** Ran SP% **131.1**
Speed ratings (Par 99): **109,105,102,101,99 98,98,97,93,91 91,91,90,88,84 84,82,64,63**
toteswinger: 1&2 £25.80, 1&3 £30.30, 2&3 £67.00 CSF £222.42 CT £3039.19 TOTE £6.70: £2.20, £3.90, £3.70, £3.90; EX 152.30.
Owner Joy And Valentine Feerick **Bred** Glending Bloodstock **Trained** Newmarket, Suffolk

FOCUS
A wide open handicap on paper, but a very ready and emphatic winner. There were only three previous winners in the 19-runner race, but the time was good and this looks strong form for the grade, rated around the third.

2049 FOOTBALL IN-RUNNING AT BETINTERNET.COM H'CAP 6f
3:00 (3:07) (Class 3) (0-95,95) 3-Y-O **£9,714** (£2,890; £1,444; £721) **Stalls** Low

Form RPR

01- **1** **Shamwari Lodge (IRE)**[231] 6244 3-8-9 86 PatDobbs 4 95
(R Hannon) *plld hrd and prom: rdn to ld ins fnl f: r.o* **10/1**

41- **2** *nk* **Macdillon**[336] 2999 3-8-11 88 LPKeniry 3 96
(W S Kittow) *led: rdn and hung lft over 1f out: hdd ins fnl f: r.o* **7/1**

1-31 **3** *1 ½* **Swiss Diva**[14] 1639 3-9-0 91 DaneO'Neill 1 94+
(D R C Elsworth) *s.i.s: hld up: nt clr run over 2f out: hdwy over 1f out: r.o* **11/4**[1]

00-5 **4** *1 ¼* **Tagula Breeze (IRE)**[27] 1345 3-8-4 81 FrancisNorton 7 80
(I W McInnes) *hld up: hdwy over 1f out: sn rdn: styd on same pce ins fnl f* **12/1**

60-0 **5** *2* **Kerrys Requiem (IRE)**[16] 1602 3-8-13 90 DarryllHolland 2 83
(M R Channon) *hung rt thrght: chsd ldr: rdn over 2f out: styd on same pce appr fnl f* **16/1**

3-21 **6** *1 ¼* **Invincible Heart (GR)**[8] 1803 3-9-1 92 6ex PatCosgrave 9 81
(Jane Chapple-Hyam) *broke wl: stdd and lost pl 5f out: rdn over 1f out: no imp* **3/1**[2]

230- **7** *3 ½* **Brae Hill (IRE)**[223] 6483 3-8-13 90 TedDurcan 5 67
(M L W Bell) *chsd ldrs tl wknd over 1f out* **12/1**

516- **8** *8* **Archie Rice (USA)**[216] 6644 3-9-4 95 AlanMunro 6 47
(W Jarvis) *s.i.s: sn chsg ldrs: wknd wl over 1f out* **9/2**[3]

1m 14.22s (2.02) **Going Correction** +0.30s/f (Good) **8** Ran SP% **112.7**
Speed ratings (Par 103): **98,97,95,93,91 89,84,74**
toteswinger: 1&2 £17.60, 1&3 £5.10, 2&3 £6.00 CSF £74.98 CT £245.07 TOTE £10.10: £2.00, £3.00, £1.20; EX 95.60.
Owner Andrew Russell **Bred** Pier House Stud **Trained** East Everleigh, Wilts
■ Tropical Paradise (28/1) was withdrawn after breaking out of the stalls.

FOCUS
The front pair were always well placed, but a positive view has been taken of the form with both of them unexposed.

NOTEBOOK
Shamwari Lodge(IRE) won a fast-ground maiden at Haydock and the second and third have scored since, and is clearly on the upgrade as this handicap debut showed. The action developed under the stands' rails and she drew clear with the runner-up, but took quite a while to master her rival. She got on top inside the final 50 yards when getting a clear run against the rail. Connections think a lot of her. (op 7-1 tchd 12-1)
Macdillon was resuming after a 336-day absence but this west country challenger from a small yard almost followed up with another win after his admirable Sandown success last June. He could turn into quite a moneyspinner for connections. (op 16-1 tchd 20-1)
Swiss Diva did not help her cause by pulling hard and gave the impression that she might have been hanging fire in the closing stages. Diva she may be. (op 10-3)
Tagula Breeze(IRE) was taken down early and the delay at the start did not help, but he is probably capable of winning against lesser opposition. (op 16-1 tchd 9-1)
Kerrys Requiem(IRE) confirmed that she is an awkward ride who pulls hard and she kept wanting to hang right, giving her rider big problems. Official explanation: jockey said filly hung right (op 11-1 tchd 10-1)
Brae Hill(IRE) sweated up beforehand. (op 10-1 tchd 8-1)
Archie Rice(USA) Official explanation: trainer said colt never travelled

2050 BETINTERNET.COM H'CAP 7f
3:35 (3:38) (Class 3) (0-95,90) 4-Y-O+ **£6,302** (£6,302; £1,444; £721) **Stalls** Low

Form RPR

5054 **1** **Hustle (IRE)**[13] 1682 4-8-10 82 (t) JimmyQuinn 8 91
(Miss Gay Kelleway) *hld up in tch: racd keenly: rdn and hung lft ins fnl f: r.o to dead-heat post* **13/2**[3]

-404 **1** *dht* **Pravda Street**[20] 1510 4-8-13 85 (b[1]) DarryllHolland 2 94
(P F I Cole) *mde all: rdn over 1f out: jnd post* **8/1**

0-00 **3** *2 ¾* **Brassini**[13] 1663 4-8-13 85 AlanMunro 1 87
(B R Millman) *a.p: chsd wnr 3f out: sn rdn: no ex ins fnl f* **14/1**

1323 **4** *2 ¼* **Autumn Blades (IRE)**[24] 1436 4-8-8 80 FrancisNorton 6 76
(A Bailey) *stdd s: hld up: hdwy and hung rt fr over 1f out: nt run on* **9/1**

10-0 **5** *1 ¼* **Countdown**[12] 1699 7-8-11 83 SaleemGolam 5 75
(M D Squance) *hld up: pushed along 1/2-way: styd on u.p ins fnl f: nvr nrr* **33/1**

2-35 **6** *nk* **Silaah**[13] 1663 5-8-9 81 TGMcLaughlin 10 72
(E A L Dunlop) *hld up: rdn 1/2-way: hdwy over 1f out: hung lft and wknd ins fnl f* **5/1**[1]

31-0 **7** *½* **Aflaam (IRE)**[24] 1433 4-8-10 82 TolleyDean 3 72
(P Howling) *hld up: hdwy 3f out: sn rdn: wknd over 1f out* **28/1**

31-3 **8** *1 ½* **Romany Princess (IRE)**[11] 1733 4-8-12 84 DaneO'Neill 4 70
(R Hannon) *chsd wnr tl rdn 3f out: wknd over 1f out: n.m.r ins fnl f* **9/1**

/10- **9** *3 ½* **Classic Descent**[342] 2819 4-9-2 88 PatCosgrave 9 64
(P J Makin) *dwlt: hld up: rdn and wknd over 1f out:* **11/2**[2]

200- **10** *¾* **Dingaan (IRE)**[168] 7470 6-8-8 80 LPKeniry 12 54
(A M Balding) *chsd ldrs: rdn over 2f out: wknd over 1f out* **15/2**

65-5 **11** *4 ½* **Mountain Pride (IRE)**[25] 1405 4-8-11 83 (b[1]) TedDurcan 11 45
(J L Dunlop) *trckd ldrs: plld hrd: rdn over 2f out: wandered and wknd over 1f out* **5/1**[1]

1m 26.31s (0.91) **Going Correction** +0.30s/f (Good) **11** Ran SP% **118.0**
Speed ratings (Par 107): **106,106,102,100,98 98,97,96,92,91 86**WIN: Pravda Street £3.50, Hustle £4.30 PL: PS £2.70, H £2.50 B £4.30. EX: PS, H £24.30 H, PS £22.90 CSF: PS, H £29.73 H, PS £28.96 TRICAST: PS, H, Brassini £368.16 H, PS, B £360.53 toteswinger: PS&H £12.40, PS&B £27.20, H&B £24.20 , £027, £Owner, £J Thompson,Bill Hinge,KingsClubSyndicateBred Gigginstown House Stud Trifecta £Trained Exning, Suffolk.
Owner R A Instone **Bred** R A Instone **Trained** Whatcombe, Oxon

FOCUS
A decent handicap which resulted in a dead-heat.

NOTEBOOK
Hustle(IRE) often races keenly and gets going too late, but has been running well since joining this yard, and would have scored outright but for hanging in both directions in the closing stages. He claimed a dead-heat in the final stride. (tchd 5-1)
Pravda Street has had his problems, but just hung on for a dead-heat in first-time blinkers, with the jockey working furiously in the final furlong after leading throughout. He created a good impression on his first starts but had not built on them in a few tries since and does not look progressive. (tchd 5-1)
Brassini has been dropped 5lb since his last run but still looks unappealingly handicapped and he could not quicken in the final furlong, although doing little wrong, unlike some of the rest. (op 12-1)
Autumn Blades(IRE), always quirky, pulled hard and hung right. (tchd 10-1)
Countdown was never travelling but did stay on late in the day.
Aflaam(IRE) has clearly declined and was sold inexpensively out of John Gosden's yard after an easy Thirsk maiden win. He had to be driven along from a very early stage here. (op 25-1, tchd 33-1 in places)
Mountain Pride(IRE) was tried in blinkers but looked ungenuine and seemed to hate them. (tchd 6-1)

2051 MILL REEF CLUB (ANTIGUA) MAIDEN FILLIES' STKS 1m 4f
4:10 (4:13) (Class 4) 3-Y-O **£5,180** (£1,541; £770; £384) **Stalls** Centre

Form RPR

3 **1** **Crimson Ribbon (USA)**[20] 1532 3-9-0 0 NickyMackay 1 73
(J H M Gosden) *chsd ldrs: led over 1f out: rdn ins fnl f: edgd lft towards fin: styd on* **9/4**[1]

4- **2** *nk* **Sweet Hollow**[203] 6945 3-9-0 0 AdamKirby 8 72
(C G Cox) *hld up in tch: nt clr run over 2f out: outpcd over 1f out: rallied and nt clr run ins fnl f: r.o wl towards ifnish* **3/1**[2]

3 *nk* **Ramora (USA)** 3-9-0 0 .... JimmyQuinn 6 71
(H R A Cecil) *hld up: swtchd lft over 2f out: hdwy over 1f out: r.o wl nr fin* **7/1**[3]

0 4 *nk* **Dark Quest**[28] 1329 3-9-0 0 .... TedDurcan 3 71
(J L Dunlop) *hld up: hdwy and hung rt fr 2f out: sn rdn: unable qck towards fin* **3/1**[2]

0-0 5 *1 1/4* **Beauchamp Xenia**[18] 1573 3-9-0 0 .... DaneO'Neill 4 69
(H Candy) *chsd ldrs tl led over 3f out: rdn and hdd over 1f out: edgd lft ins fnl f: no ex nr fin* **16/1**

0 6 *8* **Possibly A Ten (USA)**[21] 1488 3-9-0 0 .... PatCosgrave 10 56
(J H M Gosden) *chsd ldr: chal 4f out: rdn over 2f out: wknd over 1f out* **16/1**

0 7 *3 1/4* **Manarah (USA)**[21] 1488 3-9-0 0 .... PatDobbs 2 51
(J H M Gosden) *sn led: hdd over 3f out: rdn and wknd over 1f out* **25/1**

8 *29* **Far 'n Wide** 3-9-0 0 .... FrancisNorton 7 5
(W J Haggas) *s.i.s: hld up: wknd 4f out* **20/1**

35 P **Stormy's Prelude**[36] 1198 3-9-0 0 .... StephenCarson 11 —
(P Winkworth) *prom: hmpd and lost pl 10f out: p.u over 8f out: lame* **33/1**

2m 35.9s (2.40) **Going Correction** +0.30s/f (Good) **9** Ran SP% **116.6**
Speed ratings (Par 98): **104,103,103,103,102 97,95,75,—**
toteswinger: 1&2 £2.70, 1&3 £3.70, 2&3 £4.80 CSF £8.96 TOTE £2.60: £1.20, £1.60, £2.00; EX 12.30.

Owner A E Oppenheimer **Bred** Hascombe And Valiant Studs **Trained** Newmarket, Suffolk

FOCUS
A fair fillies' maiden. The winner had to survive an objection from the second.
Crimson Ribbon(USA) Official explanation: vet said filly returned distressed

2052 BET ON THE PLAY-OFFS AT BETINTERNET.COM H'CAP 1m 2f
4:45 (4:47) (Class 5) (0-75,75) 4-Y-0+ **£3,885** (£1,156; £577; £288) **Stalls** Low

Form RPR

2-24 1 **Summer Winds**[104] 361 4-8-11 **75** .... (b[1]) DToole(7) 9 83
(T G Mills) *chsd ldr: led 1f out: rdn out* **12/1**

40-3 2 *1 1/4* **Gaia Prince (USA)**[15] 1621 4-9-4 **75** .... DarryllHolland 5 81
(Mrs A J Perrett) *led: rdn over 2f out: hdd 1f out: styd on same pce* **8/1**

03-5 3 *1 3/4* **King Columbo (IRE)**[15] 1633 4-8-12 **69** .... JerryO'Dwyer 3 71
(Miss J Feilden) *chsd ldrs: hrd rdn over 1f out: styd on same pce* **10/1**

2-52 4 *1/2* **Indy Driver**[37] 1192 4-9-0 **71** .... (v[1]) FrancisNorton 1 72
(J R Fanshawe) *hld up: swtchd lft and hdwy over 1f out: sn rdn: styd on same pce* **9/2**[2]

25-3 5 *2* **Plaisterer**[18] 1571 4-9-1 **72** .... AlanMunro 6 69
(C F Wall) *s.i.s: hld up: hdwy over 3f out: outpcd 2f out: styd on ins fnl f* **4/1**[1]

066- 6 *1 1/2* **Northern Jem**[343] 2799 5-9-4 **75** .... PatCosgrave 10 69
(Jane Chapple-Hyam) *w ldr: rdn and ev ch over 1f out: hung lft and wknd fnl f* **7/1**

5040 7 *hd* **Magnitude**[17] 1578 4-8-13 **70** .... DaneO'Neill 4 64
(M E Rimmer) *hld up: effrt over 1f out: nvr trbld ldrs* **33/1**

2224 8 *3/4* **Old Romney**[16] 1615 5-9-2 **73** .... JimmyQuinn 8 65
(M Wigham) *stdd s: hld up: nvr nr ldrs* **8/1**

50-1 9 *3/4* **Madam President**[28] 1318 4-8-13 **70** .... AdamKirby 11 61
(W R Swinburn) *chsd ldrs: rdn over 2f out: hung lft and wknd over 1f out* **6/1**[3]

60-1 10 *3 1/4* **Paint The Town Red**[20] 1514 4-9-0 **74** .... JackMitchell(3) 7 58
(H J Collingridge) *hld up: rdn over 2f out: wknd over 1f out* **13/2**

60- 11 *16* **Rosy Alexander**[241] 6007 4-8-10 **67** .... TedDurcan 2 19
(G G Margarson) *prom: rdn over 3f out: sn wknd* **33/1**

2m 8.64s (2.84) **Going Correction** +0.30s/f (Good) **11** Ran SP% **123.2**
Speed ratings (Par 103): **100,99,97,97,95 94,94,93,93,90 77**
toteswinger: 1&2 £15.20, 1&3 £23.60, 2&3 £13.90 CSF £109.59 CT £1011.54 TOTE £10.90: £4.00, £3.10, £3.50; EX 102.40.

Owner John Humphreys **Bred** Beechgrove Stud **Trained** Headley, Surrey
■ Winning rider Dominic Toole is 38, and rode the last of his six previous winners back in 1996.

FOCUS
Just a fair handicap.
Magnitude Official explanation: trainer said gelding had a breathing problem

2053 PLAY LIVE CASINO AT BETINTERNET.COM H'CAP 5f
5:20 (5:20) (Class 4) (0-80,80) 4-Y-0+ **£5,180** (£1,541; £770; £384) **Stalls** Low

Form RPR

2363 1 **Canadian Danehill (IRE)**[49] 985 7-9-3 **79** .... (p) PatCosgrave 9 90
(R M H Cowell) *led 1f: chsd ldr: rdn over 1f out: r.o to ld wl ins fnl f* **9/2**[3]

4455 2 *1* **First Order**[21] 1494 8-8-13 **80** .... (v) AnnStokell(5) 6 87
(Miss A Stokell) *racd keenly: led 4f out: clr 1/2-way: rdn and hdd wl ins fnl f* **14/1**

6-00 3 *2 1/4* **Zowington**[18] 1572 7-8-6 **73** .... WilliamCarson(5) 8 72
(S C Williams) *hld up: hdwy over 1f out: sn rdn: nt trble ldrs* **3/1**[1]

4000 4 *nk* **Whiskey Creek**[7] 1836 4-8-10 **79** .... (v[1]) BMcHugh(7) 11 77
(C A Dwyer) *s.s: sn chsng ldrs: rdn 1/2-way: styd on same pce fnl f* **4/1**[2]

4-02 5 *2 1/4* **Hereford Boy**[24] 1425 5-8-11 **73** .... (b) AlanMunro 1 63
(D K Ivory) *chsd ldrs: rdn over 1f out: wknd ins fnl f* **3/1**[1]

6605 6 *nk* **Thoughtsofstardom**[3] 1957 6-7-11 **66** oh1 .... CarolineKelly(7) 5 55
(P S McEntee) *hld up in tch: plld hrd: pushed along 1/2-way: sn outpcd* **14/1**

660- 7 *1 1/4* **Heaven**[217] 6623 4-9-0 **76** .... DarryllHolland 7 60
(P J Makin) *hld up: racd keenly: rdn and wknd over 1f out* **13/2**

60.03 secs (0.93) **Going Correction** +0.30s/f (Good) **7** Ran SP% **114.8**
Speed ratings (Par 105): **104,102,98,98,94 94,92**
toteswinger: 1&2 £3.70, 1&3 £3.20, 2&3 £8.10 CSF £61.70 CT £217.51 TOTE £3.40: £2.10, £5.90; EX 28.80 Place 6: £1569.44 Place 5: £599.53.

Owner T W Morley **Bred** Skymarc Farm Inc And Dr A J O'Reilly **Trained** Six Mile Bottom, Cambs

FOCUS
Five withdrawals because of the ground left seven sprinters with a combined age of 41 and 347 runs and 47 victories behind them. Fair form.

T/Plt: £420.20 to a £1 stake. Pool: £67,850.06. 117.85 winning tickets. T/Qpdt: £23.40 to a £1 stake. Pool: £4,651.40. 147.00 winning tickets. CR

2012 YORK (L-H)
Friday, May 15

OFFICIAL GOING: Good to soft (7.6) changing to soft after race 5 (3.45)
Wind: Virtually nil Weather: Overcast and raining - heavy at times

2054 LANGLEYS SOLICITORS EBF MARYGATE STKS (LISTED RACE) (FILLIES) 5f
1:40 (1:40) (Class 1) 2-Y-O **£17,778** (£6,723; £3,360; £1,680) **Stalls** Low

Form RPR

1 1 **Misheer**[15] 1630 2-8-12 0 .... NCallan 9 95+
(C E Brittain) *athletic: trckd ldrs: swtchd lft 2f out: effrt and swtchd to ins rail over 1f out: rdn told 1f out: hdd ins fnl f: styd on u.p to ld again last 50yds* **7/2**[1]

3 2 *hd* **Aalsmeer**[20] 1504 2-8-12 0 .... RichardMullen 11 93
(E S McMahon) *w'like: lw: hld up in tch: hdwy 2f out: swtchd rt and hdwy on outer whn bmpd 1f out: sn rdn and led ins fnl f: drvn: hdd and no ex last 50yds* **15/2**[3]

2 3 *3/4* **Little Scotland**[13] 1661 2-8-12 0 .... DavidAllan 12 91
(T D Easterby) *unf: scope: chsd ldrs: hdwy on outer 2f out: rdn to chal and edgd rt and then hunglft 1f out: sn drvn and ever ch tl no ex last 75yds* **16/1**

221 4 *4 1/2* **Diamond Laura**[4] 1933 2-8-12 0 .... CatherineGannon 8 74
(P D Evans) *w'like: str: chsd ldr: rdn along 2f out: cl up whn n.m.r appr fnl f: sn wknd* **8/1**

51 5 *1 1/4* **Azif**[18] 1569 2-8-12 0 .... DavidProbert 10 70
(Miss Gay Kelleway) *prom: effrt 2f out: sn rdn and cl up whn n.m.r and sltly hmpd appr last: sn wknd* **17/2**

21 6 *1 3/4* **Dispol Keasha**[14] 1645 2-8-12 0 .... PhillipMakin 6 64
(T D Barron) *cmpt: lw: qckly away and led: rdn along 2f out: drvn and hdd 1f out: wknd* **7/2**[1]

03 7 *3/4* **Mrs Boss**[12] 1706 2-8-12 0 .... JamesMillman 7 61
(B R Millman) *w'like: str: s.i.s and rdn along in rr: nvr a factor* **33/1**

1 8 *1 1/4* **Eternal Instinct**[20] 1504 2-8-12 0 .... DanielTudhope 3 56
(J S Goldie) *lengthy: chsd ldr: rdn along after 2f out: sn wknd* **6/1**[2]

012 9 *3* **Chicita Banana**[28] 1330 2-8-12 0 .... DO'Donohoe 4 46
(George Baker) *lw: midfield: rdn along 1/2-way: n.d* **20/1**

64 10 *3/4* **Goodbye Earl (IRE)**[9] 1788 2-8-12 0 .... SladeO'Hara 2 43
(A Berry) *a towards rr* **66/1**

13 11 *1/2* **Art Jewel (IRE)**[4] 1927 2-8-12 0 .... (v[1]) RyanMoore 1 41
(S A Callaghan) *in tch on inner: rdn along 1/2-way and sn wknd* **33/1**

11 12 *2 1/4* **Leleyf (IRE)**[12] 1706 2-8-12 0 .... TonyCulhane 5 33
(M R Channon) *unf: midfield: pushed along whn hmpd 2f out: sn rdn and btn* **10/1**

61.94 secs (2.64) **Going Correction** +0.50s/f (Yiel) **12** Ran SP% **119.2**
Speed ratings (Par 98): **98,97,96,89,87 84,83,81,76,75 74,70**
toteswinger: 1&2 £6.10, 1&3 £10.50, 2&3 £21.90 CSF £29.30 TOTE £4.20: £1.80, £2.80, £4.00; EX 37.90 Trifecta £367.80 Part won. Pool: £497.08 - 0.60 winning units..

Owner Saeed Manana **Bred** New England Stud And Partners **Trained** Newmarket, Suffolk

FOCUS
The first Listed event this season for juveniles. All bar four of the runners had previously won and it was a competitive renewal. It was run at a strong early pace and, in keeping with the previous sprint races at the meeting so far, the field congregated more towards the far side. The first three came clear in a tight finish so the form looks sound.

NOTEBOOK
Misheer created a very good impression when hacking up on her debut at Yarmouth 15 days earlier and that form was superior to anything any of her rivals had yet achieved. She was faced with contrasting underfoot conditions, but that was also the case for the rest of the runners. The early pace played into her hands, but she failed to travel with the same fluency as was the case last time and she appeared to take a false step just after 3f out, which caused her to go left. She hampered Leleyf in the process and was immediately then taken over to the fair rail, which cost her some ground. The manoeuvre proved a winning one, however, and she showed a really good attitude to come out on top. It is most likely she will prove happier when reverting to a sounder surface and the Queen Mary at Royal Ascot next month is now on her agenda. She will have decent claims there as this experience should really bring her on once more, and the ground should be more in her favour again. Longer term, her trainer is eyeing the Group 1 Moyglare Stud Stakes at the Curragh in August. (op 3-1 tchd 4-1)
Aalsmeer ◆ ran a blinder. She finished third on her debut behind Eternal Instinct last month, but was backed to reverse that form on this easier surface and did so comprehensively. She made her challenge more towards the middle of the track and looked likely to prevail nearing the finish, but found the winner too resolute. This was clearly a big improvement and, although she obviously has a deal of speed, she is bred to appreciate a stiffer test in due course. Winning a maiden in the coming weeks should prove a formality. (op 12-1 tchd 7-1)
Little Scotland was just denied on her debut at Doncaster 13 days previously. That form was let down when the winner flopped here earlier in the week, but she showed herself to be fast-improving and handled the different surface without fuss. She is another who should win a maiden with little trouble in the coming weeks, but it would not be a surprise to see her head for the Hilary Needler at Beverley later this month, a race her trainer tends to target. (tchd 18-1)
Diamond Laura, narrowly off the mark at Wolverhampton four days previously, kept on respectably on this much stiffer assignment and reversed previous Windsor form with Azif. She was not really helped when the third drifted to her left at the furlong pole and is a likeable sort, but will not be the easiest to place from now on. (tchd 15-2)
Azif had proven herself with a little cut underfoot when scoring at Windsor last month. She did not look to have any real excuses. (op 11-1)
Dispol Keasha displayed abundant early pace when winning at Musselburgh a fortnight earlier and unsurprisingly led the pack here. She was a sitting duck at the furlong pole and her action suggested a return to quicker ground is what she really needs. This was no disgrace. (op 5-1)
Mrs Boss again got taken off her feet early doors, but was keeping on nicely towards the finish and looks sure to be placed to strike when faced with an extra furlong. (op 25-1)
Eternal Instinct clearly ran below par when looking at Aalsmeer's performance, but in contrast to that rival she proved unsuited by the softer surface. (op 13-2 tchd 7-1)
Leleyf(IRE) came here unbeaten in two previous runs and had won the same race at Salisbury that Gilded did before winning three years ago. She was done no favours by the winner around 3f out, but she was beaten too far for this to be her true running and she is worth another chance back on quicker ground. (op 15-2)

2055 SPORTINGBET.COM JORVIK STKS (HERITAGE H'CAP) 1m 4f
2:10 (2:13) (Class 2) (0-105,100) 4-Y-0+
£24,924 (£7,464; £3,732; £1,868; £932; £468) **Stalls** Centre

Form RPR

45-3 1 **Furmigadelagiusta**[47] 1017 5-9-8 **98** .... NCallan 15 111+
(K R Burke) *trckd ldrs on outer: smooth hdwy 4f out: led over 2f out and sn clr: rdnand edgd lft thrght fnl f: kpt on strly* **12/1**

00-2 **2** 3¾ **Sahrati**[28] 1319 5-8-11 **87**....(p) PaulHanagan 11 93
(D R C Elsworth) *in tch: hdwy over 4f out: rdn to chse ldrs over 2f out: drvn to chse wnr wl over 1f out: kpt on: no imp* **18/1**

2-00 **3** ¾ **Tilt**[9] 1790 7-9-0 **90**.... TomEaves 20 95
(B Ellison) *bhd: hdwy over 3f out: sn rdn and styd on strly fnl 2f: nrst fin* **40/1**

210- **4** ½ **Electrolyser (IRE)**[188] 7244 4-9-5 **95**.... PhilipRobinson 8 99
(C G Cox) *h.d.w: chsd ldrs: rdn along and outpcd over 4f out: hdwy 3f out: kpt on u.p fnl 2f* **9/2**[1]

03-5 **5** 2½ **Bollin Felix**[20] 1519 5-8-12 **88**....(b) DavidAllan 3 88
(T D Easterby) *hld up in tch: smooth hdwy on inner over 4f out: cl up 3f out: sn rdn and ev ch tl drvn 2f out and grad wknd* **12/1**

00-6 **6** 4 **King Charles**[13] 1673 5-9-5 **95**.... JimmyFortune 9 89
(E A L Dunlop) *hld up towards rr: stdy hdwy over 3f out: rdn wl over 2f out: kpt on: nvrnr ldrs* **10/1**

33-5 **7** 3¾ **Walking Talking**[27] 1351 5-9-8 **98**.... IanMongan 1 86
(H R A Cecil) *lw: trckd ldrs: hdwy 5f out: led 3f out: sn rdn and hdd over 2f out and grad wknd* **7/1**[3]

6300 **8** 1¼ **Kingsdale Orion (IRE)**[2] 1990 5-8-5 **81**.... RichardMullen 14 67
(B Ellison) *s.i.s and bhd: hdwy over 4f out: sn rdn along and styd on fnl 2f: nvr nr ldrs* **40/1**

600- **9** 7 **Charlie Tokyo (IRE)**[262] 5382 6-8-12 **88**....(v) JamieMoriarty 19 62
(R A Fahey) *hld up towards rr: hdwy 4f out: rdn along over 2f out and sn no imp* **50/1**

4003 **10** 5 **Robby Bobby**[8] 1798 4-8-10 **86**.... GregFairley 18 52
(M Johnston) *lw: midfield: effrt over 3f out: sn rdn and nvr a factor* **16/1**

120- **11** 1¾ **Warringah**[244] 5892 4-9-3 **93**.... RyanMoore 13 57+
(Sir Michael Stoute) *bit bkwd: nvr bttr than midfield* **5/1**[2]

104- **12** *nse* **Laterly (IRE)**[154] 6445 4-9-5 **95**.... MickyFenton 16 59
(T P Tate) *cl up: led over 5f out: rdn along and hdd 3f out: sn drvn and wknd* **33/1**

22-1 **13** 1¾ **Gordonsville**[33] 1230 6-8-9 **85**.... PJMcDonald 7 46
(J S Goldie) *a towards rr* **14/1**

232- **14** 20 **Doubnov (FR)**[442] 740 6-9-8 **98**.... StephenDonohoe 5 27
(Ian Williams) *a in rr* **40/1**

2-12 **15** ¾ **Redesignation (IRE)**[12] 1696 4-9-7 **97**.... RobertWinston 4 25
(R Hannon) *chsd ldrs: hdwy over 4f out: rdn along over 3f out and sn wknd* **7/1**[3]

-410 **16** 23 **Greylami (IRE)**[23] 1460 4-9-1 **91**.... MichaelHills 6 —
(T G Mills) *a towards rr* **14/1**

220/ **17** 2¾ **Aaim To Prosper (IRE)**[915] 6456 5-8-11 **87**.... TonyCulhane 10 —
(M R Channon) *a in rr* **33/1**

50 **18** 17 **Logic Way (USA)**[8] 1799 5-9-7 **100**....(bt) AhmedAjtebi(3) 2 —
(Miss D Mountain) *led: rdn along and hdd over 5f out: sn wknd* **66/1**

2m 37.21s (4.01) **Going Correction** +0.575s/f (Yiel) **18** Ran SP% **125.5**
Speed ratings (Par 109): **109,106,106,105,104 101,98,98,93,90 88,88,87,74,73 58,56,45**
toteswinger: 1&2 £35.50, 1&3 £89.40, 2&3 £119.00 CSF £206.33 CT £8142.43 TOTE £11.60: £2.40, £4.30, £12.40, £2.00; EX 352.40 TRIFECTA Not won..
Owner Keep Racing **Bred** Azienda Agricola Francesca **Trained** Middleham Moor, N Yorks

FOCUS
They came down the middle of the track in the straight and finished quite well strung out in what was a good middle-distance handicap. A few ran disappointingly in the ground and the winner could be a touch flattered at face value.

NOTEBOOK
Furmigadelagiusta showed himself to be a decent handicapper last season, running several big races in defeat (including when fourth in this contest), and the softer ground this time round was always going to be in his favour. Racing off the same mark as last year, he travelled kindly in behind the leaders and went to the front full of running approaching two out. Quickly clear, he stayed on right the way to the line and was good value for the win. The Ebor had been the plan last year, until he got injured at Royal Ascot, and that race will once again be the main aim this term. (op 11-1 tchd 10-1)
Sahrati, back on his last winning mark, finished second at Kempton on his reappearance (rated much lower on the AW), and he ran a fine race on this return to turf. He too travelled strongly just off the leaders and always looked to be holding second, but couldn't match the winner. (op 22-1)
Tilt, a horse who has his quirks, having to be walked to the start, was virtually last turning in, but started to run on really strongly from three out and got up for third inside the final 100 yards. He hasn't won for over three years, though, and despite being on a fair mark at present he is not a horse to back with much confidence. (op 50-1)
Electrolyser(IRE) progressed well at three (first season to race), and could be forgiven his last effort when well beaten in the November Handicap as a result of the very testing conditions. There was plenty of interest in him beforehand and, having been outpaced when the winner kicked, he kept on well for moderate pressure. This was a pleasing comeback and he could have a say in some decent handicaps this term, especially over further. (op 5-1)
Bollin Felix, another progressive sort last season, is ideally suited by further than this, but the softening ground was in his favour and he ran a good race back in fifth. There is more to come from this 5yo once he goes back up in distance, though it remains to be seen how often he gets his ground through the summer. (op 10-1)
King Charles has run well off similar marks in the past and he came with a challenge up the inside of runners, but couldn't get near to the principals.
Walking Talking, backed beforehand, went on three out but he was soon brushed aside by the winner and slowly faded. (op 10-1 tchd 13-2)
Kingsdale Orion(IRE), unplaced here earlier in the week, stayed on late past beaten horses after making a tardy start.
Warringah, 18lb higher than when winning on his handicap debut at Newbury last season, had not been seen since finishing tailed off in the St Leger and he never threatened to get into this. Official explanation: jockey said gelding had no more to give (op 9-2)
Laterly(IRE) showed up well for a long way before weakening. (op 40-1)
Aaim To Prosper(IRE) Official explanation: jockey said gelding had no more to give

2056 EMIRATES AIRLINE YORKSHIRE CUP (GROUP 2) 1m 6f
2:40 (2:44) (Class 1) 4-Y-0+

£79,478 (£30,128; £15,078; £7,518; £3,766; £1,890) **Stalls** Low

Form RPR

560- **1** **Ask**[202] 6980 6-8-13 119.... RyanMoore 6 121+
(Sir Michael Stoute) *lw: hld up in rr: tk clsr order 1/2-way: hdwy 4f out: led wl over 2f out: sn rdn and clr over 1f out: edgd lft ins fnl f: kpt on* **2/1**[1]

530/ **2** 6 **Blue Bajan (IRE)**[27] 3974 7-8-13 111.... MichaelHills 8 113
(Andrew Turnell) *hld up in rr: hdwy over 5f out: effrt on outer to chse wnr wl over 1f out: sn drvn and kpt on same pce* **33/1**

3-21 **3** *hd* **Veracity**[78] 699 5-8-13 117.... LDettori 5 113
(Saeed Bin Suroor) *trckd ldrs: hdwy 5f out: effrt over 3f out: sn rdn and ev ch tl drvnand outpcd 2f out: kpt on u.p ins fnl f* **5/1**[3]

026- **4** 6 **Washington Irving (IRE)**[219] 6592 4-8-12 112.... PaulMulrennan 7 104
(J Howard Johnson) *chsd ldr: rdn along over 4f out: drvn 3f out and sn one pce* **16/1**

23-1 **5** 5 **Fiulin**[37] 1191 4-8-12 106.... JohnEgan 4 97
(M Botti) *lw: trckd ldrs: rdn along 4f out: drvn and edgd lft 3f out: sn wknd* **9/2**[2]

33-2 **6** 30 **Centennial (IRE)**[27] 1351 4-8-12 113....(b) JimmyFortune 3 55
(J H M Gosden) *hld up: effrt over 3f out: sn rdn along and nvr a factor* **5/1**[3]

046/ **7** 1¾ **Percussionist (IRE)**[40] 4691 8-8-13 106.... TomEaves 2 53
(J Howard Johnson) *trckd ldrs: rdn along 6f out and sn wknd* **40/1**

03-4 **8** 2 **Royal And Regal (IRE)**[27] 1351 5-8-13 110.... NCallan 1 50
(M A Jarvis) *led: rdn along 4f out: hdd wl over 2f out: sn drvn and wknd qckly: eased* **5/1**[3]

3m 5.36s (5.16) **Going Correction** +0.575s/f (Yiel)
WFA 4 from 5yo+ 1lb **8** Ran SP% **112.8**
Speed ratings (Par 115): **108,104,104,101,98 81,80,78**
toteswinger: 1&2 £13.10, 1&3 £2.50, 2&3 £19.20 CSF £72.46 TOTE £2.70: £1.40, £4.60, £1.50; EX 51.80 Trifecta £230.10 Pool: £964.11 -3.10 winning units.
Owner Patrick J Fahey **Bred** Side Hill Stud **Trained** Newmarket, Suffolk

FOCUS
On paper it was a fairly open renewal of this staying test. Ask outclassed his rivals, however, and the race is likely to have little bearing on the Gold Cup next month. The winner did not need to run to his Arc form, with a couple of his main rivals not giving their running.

NOTEBOOK
Ask has long been well regarded, but his performances were somewhat hit and miss last season after landing the Gordon Richards Stakes at Sandown on his reappearance. That said, he was an excellent sixth in the Arc and that form was by far the best on offer here. The question was how he would handle the return to a course and distance over which he finished second in the Melrose as a 3yo and then a solid fourth in the St Leger behind Sixties Icon. He got a patient ride before making his move around 3f out and then found the best turn of foot to settle the issue. The fact he drifted over to the far side inside the final furlong would suggest this is as far as he wants to go, plus the burst he displayed 2f out also advertises the speed he possesses. The easing of the ground was to his liking, despite connections' fears it may have gone against him, and he has now been successful first time up for the last three seasons. He is now likely to head to the Coronation Cup over 1m4f on Oaks Day at Epsom next month and, in his final season, his big target is the Irish St Leger in September. (tchd 15-8)
Blue Bajan(IRE), fourth in the Grade 2 Scottish Champion Hurdle on his previous outing, turned in an excellent return to the Flat, over a trip he was far from certain to get on such ground. He travelled kindly into the home straight and, while lacking the turn of foot of the winner, performed right up to his best. He is now due a break and richly deserves to find another winning turn in this sphere.
Veracity drifted in the betting on this return from a 73-day break, probably on account of the deteriorating surface. He had his chance, but found the winner far too speedy on this drop back in trip. This was certainly no disgrace and if there is one horse from the race to take for the Gold Cup it is him, though he will need to raise his game to figure. The extra distance and likely quicker ground there will be right up his street and the 20/1 offered after this by Blue Square looks fair each-way value. (op 10-3)
Washington Irving(IRE) has been gelded since being snapped up by his new connections for 300,000gns last autumn. He raced handily, but hit a flat spot after turning for home. He kept on again for pressure and shaped like a horse in need of the run. However, he still has to prove he is up to this sort of class and could be difficult to place. (op 18-1 tchd 14-1)
Fiulin took the Listed Further Flight Stakes in good style from the front on his seasonal bow last month, but was ridden with greater restraint here. He was in trouble soon after turning into the home straight and looked uneasy on the softer surface. Official explanation: jockey said colt hung left (op 5-1 tchd 11-2)
Centennial(IRE) was well supported with the blinkers back on, but he was one of the first of the market principals in trouble and he ran a long way below his previous level. Although his reappearance second was on a deep surface, perhaps this ground was to blame, but he is evidently not one to completely trust. Official explanation: jockey said colt had no more to give (op 6-1 tchd 13-2)
Percussionist(IRE)'s previous form figures in this race read 214, but he has markedly regressed over jumps in the past two years and ran about as well as could have been expected. Official explanation: jockey said gelding had no more to give (op 33-1)
Royal And Regal(IRE) was given a soft lead when just losing out to Geordieland in this last season and again had his own way out in front this time. He was unable to raise his game when the race got serious and has now disappointed on both his outings this term. His rider appeared to ease him down very quickly after his chance had evaporated and that caught the attention of the Stewards. However, it was later reported by his jockey and the racecourse vet that he had finished distressed. (op 6-1)

2057 MICHAEL SEELY MEMORIAL FILLIES' STKS (LISTED RACE) 1m
3:10 (3:13) (Class 1) 3-Y-0

£22,708 (£8,608; £4,308; £2,148; £1,076; £540) **Stalls** Low

Form RPR

3-10 **1** **Nashmiah (IRE)**[12] 1698 3-9-1 103.... RyanMoore 10 100
(C E Brittain) *hld up in rr: hdwy on inner 3f out: chal 2f out: rdn to ld over 1f out: drvn ins fnl f and kpt on gamely* **2/1**[1]

125- **2** *hd* **Moonlife (IRE)**[209] 6818 3-8-12 101.... LDettori 7 97+
(Saeed Bin Suroor) *hld up in rr: hdwy whn nt clr run and swtchd lfta nds rt over 2f out: effrt on outer wl over 1f out: rdn to chal ins fnl f: sn drvn: edgd lft and nt qckn towards fin* **2/1**[1]

41-0 **3** 1 **Seradim**[12] 1698 3-8-12 99.... JimmyFortune 1 95
(P F I Cole) *trckd ldng pair: hdwy 3f out: swtchd rt and rdn wl over 1f out: drvn and ev ch ent fnl f tl no ex last 75yds* **11/2**[2]

510- **4** 1½ **Isabella Grey**[295] 4348 3-8-12 92.... NCallan 9 91
(K A Ryan) *trckd ldrs: hdwy on outer over 3f out: rdn and edgd lft 2f out: drvn and one pce ins fnl f* **16/1**

60-2 **5** 3 **Ahla Wasahl**[16] 1599 3-8-12 99.... AhmedAjtebi 5 84
(D M Simcock) *set stdy pce: qcknd over 3f out: rdn over 2f out: drvn and hdd over 1f out: wknd* **8/1**[3]

1362 **6** 7 **Common Diva**[18] 1559 3-8-12 77.... AndrewElliott 8 68
(A J McCabe) *t.k.h: chsd ldr: hung rt bnd over 4f out: rdn along over 3f out: hld whn hmpd wl over 1f out* **33/1**

31-3 **7** 5 **Greenisland (IRE)**[33] 1240 3-8-12 91.... RobertWinston 2 57
(H Morrison) *lw: t.k.h: chsd ldrs: rdn along 3f out: hld whn hmpd wl over 1f out* **9/1**

1m 43.46s (4.66) **Going Correction** +0.575s/f (Yiel) **7** Ran SP% **112.0**
Speed ratings (Par 104): **99,98,97,96,93 86,81**
toteswinger: 1&2 £1.90, 1&3 £2.80, 2&3 £2.80 CSF £5.55 TOTE £3.10: £2.00, £1.70; EX 5.70 Trifecta £21.60 Pool: £160.79 - 5.10 winning units.
Owner Saeed Manana **Bred** Deerpark Stud **Trained** Newmarket, Suffolk

FOCUS
As with the preceding two races on the round course the runners in this fillies' Listed event came down the middle of the home straight after turning in. Average fillies' listed form, rated around the first two.

NOTEBOOK

Nashmiah(IRE) had disappointed in the 1000 Guineas 12 days earlier, but had been found to have had a blind abscess afterwards and she proved popular here to make amends. She did so in game fashion and fully proved her effectiveness for the trip. She got niggled along with around 3f to run, but kept finding for her rider's urgings and was all out to score at the finish. She took her maiden on quick ground at two, but was reported to have hated the ground at Newmarket last time and this softer surface looked more up her street, despite connections stating afterwards it was plenty soft enough for her. That would have to be of some concern were she to take in the Coronation Stakes at Royal Ascot next month, as it is often quick at the meeting, but she still has an awful lot to find anyway in order to figure there. Her trainer is hoping to take in the Irish 1000 Guineas next weekend beforehand, however, providing she come out of this well enough. She became the third winner in the last four years to defy a penalty in this event. (op 9-4 tchd 5-2)

Moonlife(IRE) was fourth in the Rockfel on her final outing last year and had finished just in front of the winner in the Oh So Sharp Stakes on her penultimate start. She travelled like the best horse in the race, but found no room when initially attempting to make her challenge and had to be switched right over to the near side to get a run. The ground she lost with that manoeuvre was a lot more than she was eventually beaten and she rates an unfortunate loser. However, while she no doubt has the talent to win races of this nature, there was little to like about the way she carried her head when put under maximum pressure late on. (op 6-4 tchd 9-4)

Seradim held every chance and finished closer to the winner than had been the case in the 1000 Guineas on her seasonal debut. She likes cut underfoot and can build on this, but may now appreciate stepping up in trip. (op 6-1)

Isabella Grey was having her first run since finishing last in this class at Sandown last year. She showed that form to be all wrong with a pleasing effort over this extra furlong and appreciated the easier surface. There should be a deal of improvement in her for the run. (op 28-1 tchd 14-1)

Ahla Wasahl was officially raised 11lb for her second behind Apple Charlotte at Ascot on her seasonal return. She again got an easy lead and set just an ordinary pace. She had the run of the race and does look somewhat flattered by her new mark, but likely found the ground softer than she cares for. (tchd 7-1 and 9-1)

Common Diva faced a very tall order at the weights and, after taking time to settle, was beaten before being hampered.

Greenisland(IRE) had finished third on similar ground in this class in Germany on her return last month. She was eased off soon after and can be rated better than the bare form, but she must learn to settle better. (tchd 17-2 and 10-1)

2058 RALPH RAPER MEMORIAL STKS (H'CAP) 5f

3:45 (3:45) (Class 4) (0-80,80) 3-Y-O £6,476 (£1,927; £963; £481) **Stalls** Low

Form RPR

0-21 **1** **Sloop Johnb**[11] 1720 3-9-3 **79** 6ex PaulHanagan 15 89
(R A Fahey) *in tch: hdwy 2f out and sn rdn along: styd on u.p to ld ins fnl f: edgd lft and kpt on wl towards fin* **8/1**

0-31 **2** *1* **Champagne Future**[24] 1419 3-9-1 **77** RyanMoore 3 86+
(W R Swinburn) *lw: in tch: rdn along 2f out: drvn over 1f out: styd on ins fnl f: tk 2nd nr fin* **13/2**[2]

1-21 **3** *nk* **Impressible**[20] 1505 3-8-8 **70** DavidAllan 5 75
(E J Alston) *lw: prom: effrt 2f out and sn ev ch tl drvn and nt qckn wl ins fnl f* **10/1**

3-45 **4** *nk* **Peninsular War**[31] 1272 3-8-11 **73** AndrewElliott 16 77
(K R Burke) *dwlt: sn chsng ldrs on wd outside: rdn over 1f out: ch ent fnl f: sn drvn and one pce towards fin* **20/1**

51-1 **5** *1* **Titus Andronicus (IRE)**[33] 1232 3-9-4 **80** NCallan 12 80
(K A Ryan) *lw: cl up: led 1/2-way: rdn over 1f out: drvn and edgd lft ent fnl f: sn hdd & wknd* **4/1**[1]

0503 **6** *4* **Sir Geoffrey (IRE)**[27] 1368 3-9-2 **78** (t) JamesDoyle 10 64
(A J McCabe) *sn led: pushed along and hdd 1/2-way: rdn wl over 1f out and sn wknd* **12/1**

05-1 **7** *nk* **Mattamia (IRE)**[37] 1190 3-8-13 **78** JamesMillman(3) 1 63
(B R Millman) *hld up in rr tl sme late hdwy* **9/1**

0-53 **8** *½* **Sweet Applause (IRE)**[11] 1727 3-8-12 **74** LDettori 9 57
(A P Jarvis) *dwlt: sn in tch: rdn along 2f out and sn wknd* **16/1**

21 **9** *3* **Seldom (IRE)**[15] 1625 3-8-8 **70** RobertWinston 13 42
(M Brittain) *a in rr* **20/1**

10-6 **10** *½* **Mullglen**[20] 1517 3-9-4 **80** DuranFentiman 6 50
(T D Easterby) *sn rdn along and a towards rr* **14/1**

3323 **11** *¾* **Mazzola**[6] 1869 3-8-13 **75** TonyCulhane 8 43
(M R Channon) *chsd ldrs: rdn along 1/2-way: sn wknd* **7/1**[3]

1-43 **12** *hd* **Grissom (IRE)**[20] 1505 3-8-8 **70** TomEaves 4 37
(A Berry) *a towards rr* **7/1**[3]

00-0 **13** *3 ¼* **Glorious Dreams (USA)**[25] 1414 3-8-9 **71** ow1 StephenDonohoe 2 26
(T J Pitt) *a towards rr* **50/1**

60.88 secs (1.58) **Going Correction** +0.50s/f (Yiel) **13** Ran SP% **120.3**
Speed ratings (Par 101): **107,105,104,104,102 96,95,95,90,89 88,88,82**
toteswinger: 1&2 £10.90, 1&3 £16.10, 2&3 £14.90 CSF £58.27 CT £552.17 TOTE £10.00: £2.40, £2.30, £3.20; EX 46.20.
Owner Jonathan Gill **Bred** Manor Farm Stud (rutland) **Trained** Musley Bank, N Yorks

FOCUS

All the pace was towards the stands' side in what was a wide-open 3yo sprint handicap. Decent form for the grade overall with the front three boasting progressive profiles.

2059 SPORTINGBET.COM STKS (H'CAP) 6f

4:20 (4:21) (Class 2) (0-105,100) 4-Y-O+ £11,527 (£3,430; £1,714; £856) **Stalls** Low

Form RPR

-004 **1** **Valery Borzov (IRE)**[18] 1560 5-9-4 **97** (v) AdrianTNicholls 15 111
(D Nicholls) *led and sn clr towards stands rail: rdn over 1f out: kpt on strly* **6/1**[2]

22-4 **2** *2 ¾* **Harrison George (IRE)**[47] 1018 4-8-11 **90** PaulHanagan 13 95
(R A Fahey) *lw: hld up towards stands rail: hdwy 2f out: sn rdn and kpt on u.p ins fnl f: nt rch wnr* **85/40**[1]

-562 **3** *¾* **Abraham Lincoln (IRE)**[6] 1868 5-9-3 **96** StephenDonohoe 17 99
(D Nicholls) *hld up in rr towards stands rail: hdwy wl over 1f out: sn rdn and styd on ins fnl f: nrst fin* **12/1**

50-0 **4** *hd* **Barons Spy (IRE)**[6] 1894 8-8-3 **85** DavidProbert(3) 16 87
(R J Price) *chsd wnr towards stands rail: rdn 2f out: sn drvn and kpt on same pce ent fnl f* **40/1**

4-05 **5** *3 ¾* **River Falcon**[14] 1647 9-9-2 **95** DanielTudhope 9 85+
(J S Goldie) *hld up and bhd: hdwy wl over 1f out: styd on strly ins fnl f: nrst fin* **9/1**[3]

010- **6** *½* **Skhilling Spirit**[188] 7243 6-9-4 **97** PhillipMakin 12 86+
(T D Barron) *swtchd lft s and towards rr: hdwy wl over 1f out: sn rdn and kpt on ins fnl f: nrst fin* **22/1**

500- **7** *nk* **Bond City (IRE)**[188] 7245 7-8-13 **92** RyanMoore 4 80
(G R Oldroyd) *prom toewards far side: rdn along 2f out: drvn over 1f out and sn one pce* **20/1**

0151 **8** *2 ¼* **Excusez Moi (USA)**[7] 1849 7-8-12 **91** 6ex (p) PJMcDonald 7 71
(Mrs R A Carr) *lw: in tch: hdwy towards far side 2f out: sn rdn and no imp* **9/1**[3]

03-2 **9** *3 ¾* **Pavershooz**[29] 1309 4-8-4 **83** PaulQuinn 6 51
(N Wilson) *in tch towards far side: rdn along 2f out: no hdwy* **10/1**

-000 **10** *1 ¼* **Ajigolo**[13] 1676 6-9-1 **94** TPO'Shea 14 58
(N Wilson) *chsd wnr towards stands rail: rdn along 2f out: sn wknd* **40/1**

00-5 **11** *3* **Ishetoo**[25] 1398 5-9-2 **95** SilvestreDeSousa 3 50
(A Dickman) *prom towards far side: rdn along 2f out and grad wknd* **16/1**

20/0 **12** *3* **Commando Scott (IRE)**[14] 1649 8-8-9 **88** RichardMullen 11 33
(I W McInnes) *nvr nr ldrs* **25/1**

001- **13** *1* **Roker Park (IRE)**[189] 7222 4-8-10 **89** NCallan 2 31
(K A Ryan) *prom towards far side: rdn along over 2f out and sn wknd* **20/1**

6-00 **14** *nk* **He's A Humbug (IRE)**[3] 1951 5-8-4 **83** oh6 ow2 (p) AndrewElliott 10 24
(J O'Reilly) *prom towards far side: rdn along 1/2-way and sn wknd* **100/1**

000- **15** *½* **Rising Shadow (IRE)**[192] 7187 8-8-12 **91** RobertWinston 8 30
(C W Thornton) *a towards rr* **10/1**

22-3 **16** *48* **Diriculous**[16] 1608 5-9-7 **100** JimmyFortune 1 —
(T G Mills) *in tch far rail: rdn along 1/2-way and sn wknd* **16/1**

1m 12.8s (0.90) **Going Correction** +0.50s/f (Yiel) **16** Ran SP% **127.5**
Speed ratings (Par 109): **114,110,109,109,104 103,103,100,95,93 89,85,84,83,82 18**
toteswinger: 1&2 £5.30, 1&3 £12.60, 2&3 £7.80 CSF £18.33 CT £150.88 TOTE £8.00: £1.80, £1.40, £3.50, £8.80; EX 23.90.
Owner D Kilburn/I Hewitson/D Nicholls **Bred** Vincent Harrington **Trained** Sessay, N Yorks

FOCUS

A typically competitive sprint, but the winner made all and never looked in serious danger. He showed improved form at face value.

NOTEBOOK

Valery Borzov(IRE) blasted off in front of four other horses on the near side and never allowed those on the far side to be in with a sniff. A horse with plenty of soft-ground form, he remained 5lb higher than when last winning, but showed blistering speed and had virtually everything in trouble at halfway. This is a tough course to make ground up on and he showed no sign of wilting, running on right the way to the line. The change of tactics clearly worked a treat on the 5yo and he will go for all the top handicap sprints this season. (op 15-2 tchd 8-1)

Harrison George(IRE) was one of those chasing the winner in the near-side group. A heavy-ground course winner last season, he was unable to quicken when initially asked to close and didn't get going until it was too late. He stays further than this and the winner simply had too much speed on the day. (op 11-4 tchd 2-1)

Abraham Lincoln(IRE), a stablemate of the winner who bumped into a classy sort at Haydock last weekend, would have been better off had the rain stayed away, but he does handle some juice and he kept on well back in third.

Barons Spy(IRE), in need of his recent reappearance at Warwick, is back on a decent mark and ran well on ground that suits. He is due to be dropped 2lb now, so there is every chance he will be winning again before long. (op 50-1)

River Falcon often goes well here and the rain was in his favour. Last and ridden along at halfway, he came out best of those to have raced on the far side, but he didn't get going until the race was over. (op 8-1 tchd 10-1)

Skhilling Spirit, who can be slowly away/has refused to race, jumped off okay and showed enough on this seasonal reappearance to suggest he will again be winning in his turn this season (op 25-1)

Bond City(IRE) showed bright speed on the far side and may be weighted to win again in another run or two. (op 22-1)

2060 CONSTANT SECURITY STKS (H'CAP) 1m 4f

4:55 (4:55) (Class 4) (0-80,78) 3-Y-O £6,476 (£1,927; £963; £481) **Stalls** Centre

Form RPR

2-33 **1** **Antigua Sunrise (IRE)**[22] 1470 3-8-10 **67** PaulHanagan 2 74
(R A Fahey) *hld up in tch: hdwy 4f out: rdn to chse ldrs over 2f out: drvn over 1f out: styd on u.p ins fnl f to ld nr fin* **6/1**[3]

01-2 **2** *1* **Tepmokea (IRE)**[47] 1019 3-9-6 **77** AndrewElliott 5 82
(K R Burke) *led and sn clr: rdn along wl over 2f out: hung bdly rt to stands rail over 1f out: sn drvn: hdd and no ex towards fin* **5/1**[2]

0-05 **3** *nk* **Tapis Wizard**[11] 1740 3-8-10 **67** LeeEnstone 8 72
(M W Easterby) *hld up: hdwy over 4f out: rdn to chse ldrs 3f out: drvn over 1f out and evch tl no ex wl ins fnl f* **20/1**

410- **4** *3 ½* **Kudu Country (IRE)**[203] 6946 3-9-7 **78** JohnEgan 3 77
(T P Tate) *chsd ldr: hdwy on stands rail over 3f out: sn rdn and ev ch whn n.m.r and hmpd over 1f out: swtchd lft and drvn: kpt on same pce* **8/1**

0-53 **5** *3 ¾* **Tropical Bachelor (IRE)**[23] 1451 3-8-13 **70** StephenDonohoe 7 63
(T J Pitt) *lw: midfield: hdwy over 4f out: rdn along over 3f out: kpt on same pce* **25/1**

462 **6** *1 ¼* **Gosforth Park**[18] 1562 3-8-8 **65** AdrianTNicholls 1 56
(M Brittain) *bhd and rdn along after 2f: drvn and hdwy 3f out: styd on fnl 2f: nvr nr ldrs* **16/1**

31 **7** *14* **Off Chance**[20] 1522 3-8-10 **67** DuranFentiman 13 36
(T D Easterby) *towards rr: sme hdwy 4f out: sn rdn and nvr a factor* **14/1**

21-0 **8** *5* **Madamlily (IRE)**[47] 1019 3-9-0 **76** FrederikTylicki(5) 10 37
(J J Quinn) *towards rr: sme hdwy 4f out: sn rdn and nvr a factor* **15/2**

3341 **9** *2 ½* **Haljaferia (UAE)**[13] 1681 3-9-3 **74** JimmyFortune 4 31
(D R C Elsworth) *chsd ldrs: rdn along 4df out: sn wknd* **8/1**

-604 **10** *27* **Nawaadi (USA)**[12] 1707 3-9-5 **76** TPO'Shea 14 —
(J H M Gosden) *prom: rdn along 5f out: sn wknd* **9/1**

521 **11** *5* **Gilded Age**[18] 1562 3-9-5 **76** RobertWinston 6 —
(M Johnston) *lw: chsd ldrs: rdn along over 4f out and sn wknd* **7/2**[1]

564- **12** *40* **Bigalo's Star (IRE)**[210] 6789 3-9-3 **77** AhmedAjtebi(3) 9 —
(L A Mullaney) *plld hrd: prom tl wknd qckly 1/2-way and sn wl bhd* **25/1**

2m 39.61s (6.41) **Going Correction** +0.575s/f (Yiel) **12** Ran SP% **122.2**
Speed ratings (Par 101): **101,100,100,97,95 94,85,81,80,62 58,32**
toteswinger: 1&2 £5.80, 1&3 £31.70, 2&3 £20.10 CSF £36.30 CT £571.28 TOTE £8.50: £2.40, £2.30, £6.10; EX 29.60 Place 6: £84.19 Place 5: £35.15.
Owner David And Jackie Knaggs **Bred** Michael Morrin **Trained** Musley Bank, N Yorks

■ Stewards' Enquiry : Lee Enstone one-day ban: used whip with excessive frequency (May 29)
Paul Hanagan three-day ban: used whip with excessive frequency (May 29-31)
T P O'Shea £140 fine: failed to pass stands' before going to start

FOCUS

A modest handicap, run at a sound gallop. Pretty solid form.

Haljaferia(UAE) Official explanation: jockey said gelding ran too free

Nawaadi(USA) Official explanation: jockey said colt was unsuited by the soft ground

T/Jkpt: Not won. T/Plt: £62.20 to a £1 stake. Pool: £159,499.91. 1,869.20 winning tickets. T/Qpdt: £7.60 to a £1 stake. Pool: £8,942.21. 869.37 winning tickets. JR

2061 - 2067a (Foreign Racing) - See Raceform Interactive

1660 DONCASTER (L-H)

Saturday, May 16

OFFICIAL GOING: Good to soft (7.6)

Wind: fresh 1/2 against Weather: breezy with heavy showers

2068 CROWNHOTEL-BAWTRY.COM APPRENTICE H'CAP 1m 4f

6:00 (6:01) (Class 5) (0-70,70) 4-Y-0+ £3,238 (£963; £481; £240) Stalls Low

Form RPR

0242 1 **Red Wine**[14] 1665 10-8-13 **69**.................... DeclanCannon(5) 9 81
(A J McCabe) *s.s: bhd: stdy hdwy on outside over 3f out: styd on wl fnl f: led post* **5/1**[1]

2312 2 *shd* **Safebreaker**[19] 1568 4-8-10 **64**....................(p) SladeO'Hara(3) 16 76
(K A Ryan) *mid-div: hdwy on outer over 3f out: led over 1f out: edgd rt: jst ct* **8/1**

0-61 3 *7* **Grand Art (IRE)**[11] 1765 5-8-11 **67**.................... PaulPickard(5) 14 67
(P T Midgley) *in tch: effrt over 3f out: one pce fnl 2f* **20/1**

4 *1 1/2* **Ciara Eile (IRE)**[105] 6263 9-7-12 **56** oh11.................... NeilFarley(7) 1 54
(D Carroll) *in rr div: t.k.h: hdwy and swtchd outside over 2f out: kpt on: nrst fin* **33/1**

03-2 5 *3/4* **Sudden Impulse**[17] 1615 8-8-4 **62**.................... AnthonyBetts(7) 4 59
(A D Brown) *hld up in mid-div: smooth hdwy on outer over 3f out: led 2f out: sn hdd: one pce* **15/2**

00-0 6 *1 1/2* **Cripsey Brook**[26] 1402 11-8-7 **61** ow1.................... GaryBartley(3) 5 55
(K G Reveley) *hld up in rr: styd on fnl 3f: nt rch ldrs* **25/1**

0250 7 *shd* **Monfils Monfils (USA)**[14] 1665 7-9-5 **70**.................... AndrewMullen 2 64
(A J McCabe) *trckd ldrs: chal 2f out: kpt on same pce* **7/1**[3]

00-3 8 *1* **Cote D'Argent**[12] 1738 6-8-9 **65**.................... SimonPearce(5) 10 58
(L Lungo) *led 4f: chsd ldrs: one pce fnl 2f* **13/2**[2]

3312 9 *nk* **New England**[21] 1533 7-8-5 **59**.................... DeanHeslop(3) 12 51
(W M Brisbourne) *s.i.s: t.k.h in rr: kpt on fnl 3f: nvr nr ldrs* **17/2**

0-60 10 *nk* **Sporting Gesture**[15] 1654 12-8-4 **60**.................... LanceBetts(5) 8 52
(M W Easterby) *trckd ldrs: one pce fnl 2f* **28/1**

000- 11 *13* **Polish Red**[337] 3010 5-9-2 **70**.................... Louis-PhilippeBeuzelin(3) 13 41
(Jane Chapple-Hyam) *in tch: effrt over 3f out: wknd 2f out* **17/2**

5033 12 *1* **General Tufto**[5] 1945 4-8-11 **67**....................(b) RichardRowe(5) 6 36
(C Smith) *trckd ldrs: led over 3f out: hdd 2f out: wknd* **12/1**

00-4 13 *6* **Crimson Mitre**[23] 1478 4-8-10 **68**.................... LeeTopliss(7) 3 28
(J Jay) *trckd ldrs: lost pl 3f out: sn bhd* **20/1**

231- 14 *10* **Eijaaz (IRE)**[193] 7177 8-9-0 **65**.................... NeilBrown 15 9
(G A Harker) *t.k.h in rr: bhd fnl 3f* **14/1**

250/ 15 *14* **Bernix**[715] 2201 7-8-6 **60**.................... PatrickDonaghy(3) 7 —
(N Tinkler) *mid-div: lost pl over 3f out: sn bhd* **25/1**

6-00 16 *dist* **Rain And Shade**[24] 1454 5-8-2 **60**.................... AdamCarter(7) 11 —
(E W Tuer) *w ldr: led after 4f: hdd over 3f out: wknd qckly: t.o 2f out: virtually p.u* **66/1**

2m 35.98s (0.88) **Going Correction** +0.15s/f (Good) **16** Ran SP% **125.9**

Speed ratings (Par 103): **103,102,98,97,96 95,95,95,94,94 85,85,81,74,65** —

toteswinger: 1&2 £4.20, 1&3 £22.80, 2&3 not won. CSF £41.48 CT £764.03 TOTE £5.20: £1.80, £2.00, £5.30, £9.00; EX 26.60.

Owner Paul J Dixon **Bred** Genesis Green Stud Ltd **Trained** Averham Park, Notts

FOCUS

Even though the strong winds throughout the day had made conditions less testing they still made it hard enough. This was a competitive heat, with plenty in with a chance, and run at just a fair pace. The first two came clear.

Rain And Shade Official explanation: jockey said gelding had a breathing problem

2069 SAN ROSSORE MAIDEN AUCTION STKS 5f

6:35 (6:35) (Class 5) 2-Y-0 £3,238 (£963; £481; £240) Stalls High

Form RPR

1 **On The Bounty** 2-8-11 0.................... PaulHanagan 2 73
(R A Fahey) *towards rr: swtchd stands' side after 1f: hdwy on ins 2f out: led 1f out: styd on wl towards fin* **7/1**

5 2 *1/2* **Rio Caribe (IRE)**[16] 1623 2-8-11 0.................... GrahamGibbons 1 71
(T D Walford) *chsd ldrs on outside: outpcd over 2f out: hdwy over 1f out: kpt on same pce wl ins fnl f* **14/1**

23 3 *nk* **Gower Sophia**[21] 1521 2-8-4 0.................... TWilliams 6 63
(M Brittain) *chsd ldrs: chal 1f out: no ex towards fin* **10/3**[2]

4 *1 1/2* **Whispered Times (USA)** 2-8-13 0.................... PaulMulrennan 7 67+
(P C Haslam) *dwlt: trckd ldrs: nt clr run over 2f out: kpt on same pce fnl f* **16/1**

45 5 *nk* **Masked Dance (IRE)**[15] 1653 2-8-11 0.................... RichardMullen 8 64
(K A Ryan) *led tl 1f out: styd on same pce* **4/1**[3]

6 *3/4* **True Loves Kiss** 2-8-4 0.................... AndrewElliott 9 55+
(A J McCabe) *s.i.s: bhd tl styd on fnl 2f* **25/1**

542 7 *1 1/2* **Bronze Beau**[12] 1735 2-8-9 0.................... TomEaves 4 53
(Mrs L Stubbs) *t.k.h: w ldrs on outer: wknd over 1f out* **2/1**[1]

0 8 *2 1/2* **Daft Lad**[12] 1719 2-8-9 0.................... DuranFentiman 10 45+
(L A Mullaney) *w ldrs: wknd 1f out* **33/1**

05 9 *62* **Bossy Kitty**[9] 1802 2-8-4 0.................... DO'Donohoe 5 —
(N Tinkler) *swvd bdly lft s: rdr briefly lost irons: sn detached and bhd: virtually p.u 2f out: t.o last* **20/1**

62.24 secs (1.74) **Going Correction** +0.15s/f (Good) **9** Ran SP% **113.0**

Speed ratings (Par 93): **92,91,90,88,87 86,84,80,**—

toteswinger: 1&2 £10.90, 1&3 £7.80, 2&3 £10.90 CSF £92.30 TOTE £8.30: £2.50, £3.90, £1.80; EX 122.40.

Owner S W Knowles **Bred** Kingwood Bloodstock & Mrs M Gutkin **Trained** Musley Bank, N Yorks

FOCUS

This was run at a good pace and they finished in a heap as the leaders came back to the closers. Probably modest form.

NOTEBOOK

On The Bounty hails from the yard that won this heat last year and their juveniles have been in good form of late. The Bahamian Bounty-bred colt was settled in behind the leaders and moved to challenge a furlong out before taking it up and keeping on well. (op 13-2 tchd 6-1 and 8-1)

Rio Caribe(IRE) was doing his best work at the end of the race and this was a marked improvement on his encouraging debut run, where he never got involved after missing the break. (op 16-1)

Gower Sophia ◆ yet again put in a spirited effort, but could not muster the pace to sustain her challenge inside the furlong marker. She should be found a little race to get her head in front before long. (op 7-2 tchd 4-1)

Whispered Times(USA) made an encouraging debut after travelling well for most of the way alongside the winner, before encountering traffic problems a furlong out. (op 20-1)

Masked Dance(IRE) cut out most of the running before relenting and finding little entering the final furlong, but he showed enough to suggest he can be found an opportunity. (op 9-2 tchd 7-2)

Bronze Beau did himself few favours by racing keenly early and didn't get home as a result. (tchd 9-4)

Bossy Kitty Official explanation: jockey said filly ducked left at start and lost his iron

2070 NORTHERN RACING COLLEGE MEDIAN AUCTION MAIDEN STKS 6f

7:05 (7:06) (Class 5) 3-4-Y-0 £3,238 (£963; £481; £240) Stalls High

Form RPR

2-2 1 **Strictly**[18] 1592 3-8-7 0.................... Louis-PhilippeBeuzelin(5) 1 75+
(Sir Michael Stoute) *chsd ldrs on outer: styd on to ld ins fnl f: hld on towards fin* **4/5**[1]

- 2 *1/2* **Lochan Mor** 3-9-3 0.................... AndrewElliott 12 78
(M L W Bell) *led on stands' side tl hdd and no ex ins fnl f* **7/1**[3]

6 3 *2 1/2* **Badge**[25] 1419 3-9-3 0.................... RichardMullen 4 70+
(R Charlton) *mid-div on outer: hdwy over 2f out: kpt on same pce fnl f* **14/1**

4 4 *1* **Cheyenne Red (IRE)**[19] 1563 3-8-12 0.................... PatrickDonaghy(5) 13 67
(M Dods) *dwlt: sn chsng ldrs on ins: styd on same pce fnl f* **7/1**[3]

5 *3 1/4* **Qualitas** 3-9-3 0.................... DaleGibson 5 57
(M W Easterby) *dwlt: hdwy over 2f out: kpt on fnl f* **80/1**

6 *3/4* **New Leyf (IRE)** 3-9-3 0.................... ChrisCatlin 6 54
(J R Gask) *t.k.h in rr: hdwy over 2f out: nvr trbld ldrs* **33/1**

3- 7 *nk* **Say You Say Me**[308] 3949 3-8-12 0.................... GregFairley 10 48
(N J Vaughan) *w ldrs: wknd appr fnl f* **8/1**

8 *2 1/4* **Whisper Softly (IRE)** 3-8-12 0.................... GrahamGibbons 3 41
(T D Walford) *dwlt: in rr: sme hdwy over 2f out: nvr on terms* **33/1**

00-3 9 *1* **Jimwil (IRE)**[26] 1400 3-9-3 **69**.................... PhillipMakin 2 43
(M Dods) *trckd ldrs: lost pl over 1f out* **11/2**[2]

0-5 10 *3 1/2* **Iron Max (IRE)**[14] 1662 3-9-3 0.................... RoystonFfrench 8 32
(N J Vaughan) *hld up in rr: nvr a factor* **66/1**

5 11 *2 1/2* **Monsieur Harvey**[8] 1852 3-9-3 0.................... TomEaves 7 24
(B Smart) *chsd ldrs: lost pl over 1f out* **66/1**

0505 12 *1/2* **Rightcar Lewis**[16] 1617 4-9-7 **47**....................(b) PatrickMathers 9 17
(Peter Grayson) *sn drvn along in rr: bhd fnl 2f* **100/1**

0- 13 *61* **Jung (USA)**[224] 6488 3-9-3 0....................(t) PaulHanagan 11 —
(J R Gask) *w ldrs: lost pl 3f out: sn bhd: virtually p.u: t.o* **66/1**

1m 14.5s (0.90) **Going Correction** +0.15s/f (Good)

WFA 3 from 4yo 9lb **13** Ran SP% **126.3**

Speed ratings (Par 103): **100,99,96,94,90 89,88,85,84,79 76,75,**—

toteswinger: 1&2 £1.90, 1&3 £2.50, 2&3 £26.90 CSF £7.56 TOTE £1.90: £1.10, £2.50, £3.70; EX 9.60.

Owner Cheveley Park Stud **Bred** Cheveley Park Stud Ltd **Trained** Newmarket, Suffolk

FOCUS

Not a particularly competitive maiden and it is doubtful the winner had to get too close to her reappearance form.

Jung(USA) Official explanation: jockey said colt lost its action

2071 DONCASTER RACECOURSE SPONSORSHIP CLUB H'CAP 6f

7:40 (7:41) (Class 4) (0-80,83) 4-Y-0+ £4,857 (£1,445; £722; £360) Stalls High

Form RPR

0060 1 **Methaaly (IRE)**[14] 1682 6-8-13 **75**....................(be) AlanMunro 18 84
(M Mullineaux) *dwlt: mid-div stands' side: hdwy over 2f out: led appr fnl f: hld on towards fin* **16/1**

4-00 2 *nk* **Gift Horse**[21] 1510 9-8-13 **75**....................(v) AdrianTNicholls 14 83
(D Nicholls) *trckd ldrs: effrt over 1f out: sn rdn and hung lft: chal jst ins fnl f: no ex cl home* **7/2**[1]

4-00 3 *1 1/4* **Leonid Glow**[14] 1682 4-8-13 **75**.................... PJMcDonald 2 79
(M Dods) *in rr div: hdwy on outer over 3f out: styd on same pce fnl f* **22/1**

33-0 4 *nse* **Artsu**[14] 1685 4-8-12 **74**.................... PhillipMakin 11 78
(M Dods) *chsd ldrs: kpt on same pce fnl f* **8/1**[3]

1400 5 *1 1/4* **Ingleby Arch (USA)**[14] 1663 6-8-9 **74**.................... NeilBrown(3) 8 74
(T D Barron) *mid-div: hdwy 2f out: styd on wl ins fnl f* **18/1**

4-40 6 *nk* **Stanley Goodspeed**[38] 1186 6-9-1 **77**.................... LiamJones 4 76
(J W Hills) *mid-div on wd outside: hdwy over 2f out: sn chsng ldrs: kpt on same pce* **18/1**

-000 7 *nse* **Dorn Dancer (IRE)**[7] 1885 7-8-8 **70**.................... TonyHamilton 10 69
(D W Barker) *hld up in rr: hdwy 2f out: styd on wl ins fnl f* **18/1**

110- 8 *1 1/2* **Chosen One (IRE)**[200] 7040 4-8-5 **67**.................... RoystonFfrench 19 61
(B Smart) *w ldrs stands' side: led over 1f out: sn hdd & wknd* **12/1**

2446 9 *1 1/2* **Bo McGinty (IRE)**[14] 1685 8-8-9 **78**.................... LeeTopliss(7) 7 67
(R A Fahey) *chsd ldrs: rdn and outpcd over 2f out: kpt on fnl f* **28/1**

30-5 10 *hd* **Carleton**[19] 1572 4-9-2 **78**.................... ChrisCatlin 3 66
(W J Musson) *in rr on outside: hdwy 2f out: nvr nr ldrs* **9/1**

46-0 11 *nk* **Al Wasef (USA)**[12] 1737 4-8-8 **70**.................... PaulHanagan 20 58
(J S Goldie) *in rr: sme hdwy on inner 2f out: nvr a factor* **12/1**

-142 12 *1* **High Curragh**[8] 1849 6-9-7 **83**....................(p) PaulMulrennan 12 67
(K A Ryan) *w ldr: led over 2f out: hdd & wknd over 1f out* **7/1**[2]

00-5 13 *3/4* **Sparton Duke (IRE)**[21] 1510 4-8-13 **75**....................(p) RichardMullen 15 57
(K A Ryan) *s.s: sme hdwy over 1f out: nvr a factor* **9/1**

5130 14 *4* **Kipchak (IRE)**[11] 1766 4-8-10 **75**....................(p) AndrewMullen(3) 17 44
(A J McCabe) *led: hung lft and hdd over 2f out: sn lost pl* **10/1**

0-16 15 *3/4* **Sir Nod**[30] 1313 7-8-13 **75**.................... TomEaves 6 42
(Miss J A Camacho) *dwlt: hdwy on outer to trck ldrs over 2f out: wknd over 1f out* **28/1**

0-06 16 *1/2* **Nacho Libre**[13] 1689 4-8-8 **70**.................... DaleGibson 5 35
(M W Easterby) *chsd ldrs on outside: rdn over 2f out: sn lost pl* **50/1**

1m 13.26s (-0.34) **Going Correction** +0.15s/f (Good) **16** Ran SP% **125.2**

Speed ratings (Par 105): **108,107,105,105,104 103,103,101,99,99 99,97,96,91,90 89**

toteswinger: 1&2 £35.40, 1&3 not won, 2&3 £18.70 CSF £70.46 CT £1342.93 TOTE £16.10: £3.00, £2.00, £7.10, £2.50; EX 76.20.

Owner A Jones **Bred** Scuderia Golden Horse S R L **Trained** Alpraham, Cheshire

FOCUS

An open event run at a decent pace with plenty of exposed horses. Sound form.

Carleton Official explanation: jockey said, regarding running and riding, that his orders were to get the gelding organised and into a rhythm early, and not ask for an effort too soon as it had a history of breathing problems, adding that it was outpaced early, but asked for an effort from 2f out, after which it stayed on at the same pace.

High Curragh Official explanation: jockey said gelding hung right

2072 MOSS PROPERTIES H'CAP 7f

8:10 (8:12) (Class 4) (0-85,84) 3-Y-0 £4,857 (£1,445; £722; £360) Stalls High

Form RPR

210- 1 **Magaling (IRE)**[226] 6426 3-9-4 **84**.................... DaneO'Neill 13 92
(L M Cumani) *hld up in rr: gd hdwy over 2f out: edgd rt appr fnl f: styd on to ld nr fin* **7/1**[2]

61-1 2 *nk* **Floor Show**[19] 1561 3-8-13 **79**.................... RichardMullen 3 86
(E S McMahon) *trckd ldrs on ouside: hdwy to ld appr fnl f: hdd nr fin* **8/1**[3]

223- **3** ½ **Clerk's Choice (IRE)**[157] 7627 3-8-4 **75**...... Louis-PhilippeBeuzelin(5) 11 80
(W Jarvis) *dwlt: hdwy over 2f out: styd on wl ins fnl f* **50/1**

4-12 **4** 1 ¼ **Rising Kheleyf (IRE)**[16] 1626 3-8-4 **70** oh1.................. PJMcDonald 4 72
(G A Swinbank) *w ldrs towards outside: styd on same pce fnl f* **7/1**[2]

2-1 **5** ¾ **Respite**[45] 1066 3-8-6 **72**.. LiamJones 10 72+
(W J Haggas) *t.k.h: trckd ldrs stands' side: nt clr run over 2f out: squeezed through appr fnl f: bdly hmpd jst ins fnl f: nt rcvr* **5/2**[1]

22-5 **6** 2 ½ **Striker Torres (IRE)**[34] 1228 3-9-0 **80**.......................... TomEaves 9 73
(B Smart) *led on stands' side: hdd appr fnl f: sn hmpd and wknd* **14/1**

012- **7** nse **Brierty (IRE)**[224] 6477 3-9-2 **82**.. DNolan 14 75
(D Carroll) *in rr: nt clr run over 2f out: kpt on: nvr nr ldrs* **50/1**

30-0 **8** 1 ¼ **Cook's Endeavour (USA)**[30] 1307 3-8-10 **76**.................. DO'Donohoe 6 66
(K A Ryan) *chsd ldrs: wknd appr fnl f* **16/1**

5-1 **9** nse **Maxwell Hawke (IRE)**[33] 1252 3-9-0 **80**.......................... AlanMunro 7 70
(P W Chapple-Hyam) *chsd ldrs: one pce whn hmpd appr fnl f* **8/1**[3]

-032 **10** 1 ½ **Thunderball**[12] 1744 3-8-12 **78**.......................................(p) AndrewElliott 8 64
(A J McCabe) *chsd ldrs: wkng whn hmpd appr fnl f* **9/1**

010- **11** 5 **Bravo Echo**[203] 6979 3-9-4 **84**.. RobertHavlin 5 56
(J H M Gosden) *mid-div: lost pl over 2f out* **8/1**[3]

15-4 **12** 3 ¾ **Whatyouwoodwishfor (USA)**[28] 1345 3-8-12 **78**........ PaulHanagan 2 40
(R A Fahey) *w ldrs on wd outside: lost pl over 1f out* **16/1**

1-0 **13** 27 **Elusive Fame (USA)**[31] 1296 3-9-3 **83**.............................. JoeFanning 12 —
(M Johnston) *in rr stands' side: bhd and eased fnl 2f: t.o* **14/1**

1m 27.96s (1.66) **Going Correction** +0.15s/f (Good) **13** Ran SP% **125.9**
Speed ratings (Par 101): **96,95,95,93,92 89,89,88,88,86 80,76,45**
toteswinger: 1&2 £16.90, 1&3 not won, 2&3 £32.40 CSF £65.66 CT £2717.13 TOTE £8.80: £2.60, £2.50, £7.60; EX 79.80.
Owner Sheikh Mohammed Obaid Al Maktoum **Bred** J Young **Trained** Newmarket, Suffolk
■ Stewards' Enquiry : Dane O'Neill three-day ban: careless riding (May 30-31, Jun 1)
Liam Jones two-day ban: careless riding (May 30-31)

FOCUS
A very competitive three-year-old handicap run at a good clip. Pretty sound form despite the improved effort of the third.

2073 BAWTRY H'CAP 1m (R)
8:40 (8:42) (Class 4) (0-85,85) 3-Y-O+ **£4,857** (£1,445; £722; £360) **Stalls** Low

Form RPR

-110 **1** **Wovoka (IRE)**[21] 1507 6-9-9 **80**.. TonyHamilton 6 86
(D W Barker) *hld up towards rr on inner: nt clr run over 2f out: burst through jst ins fnl f: r.o to ld nr fin* **12/1**

0-00 **2** ½ **Magic Echo**[8] 1850 5-10-0 **85**.. TomEaves 12 90
(M Dods) *hld up towards rr: hdwy on wd outside over 2f out: styd on wl ins fnl f: tk 2nd nr fin* **20/1**

-120 **3** hd **Last Sovereign**[26] 1405 5-9-6 **82**..............(p) Louis-PhilippeBeuzelin(5) 10 86
(Jane Chapple-Hyam) *mid-div: nt clr run over 2f out: chsng ldrs appr fnl f: styd on ins fnl f: no ex towards fin* **5/1**[3]

0-53 **4** ½ **Boy Blue**[21] 1507 4-9-11 **82**.. DaleGibson 15 85
(P Salmon) *trckd ldrs: led over 2f out: hdd and no ex last 50yds* **10/1**

4-60 **5** 1 ½ **Esoterica (IRE)**[15] 1649 6-8-13 **75**...........................(v) GaryBartley(5) 4 75
(J S Goldie) *mid-div: hdwy on ins to trck ldrs over 3f out: one pce appr fnl f* **16/1**

5-45 **6** 1 ½ **Moheebb (IRE)**[12] 1722 5-9-1 **72**...............................(b) AndrewElliott 11 68
(Mrs R A Carr) *mid-div: hdwy to chse ldrs over 2f out: one pce* **8/1**

21-3 **7** 2 ¼ **Allformary**[21] 1509 3-8-4 **73** ow1.................................... RoystonFfrench 9 61
(B Smart) *trckd ldrs: nt clr run over 2f out: wkng whn hmpd over 1f out* **10/1**

0-23 **8** 2 **Pegasus Lad (USA)**[44] 1082 3-9-0 **83**.............................. JoeFanning 1 66
(M Johnston) *sn chsng ldr: wknd over 1f out* **7/2**[1]

0-00 **9** nk **Major Magpie (IRE)**[12] 1722 7-9-10 **81**.......................... PhillipMakin 16 67
(M Dods) *mid-div on outside: lost pl over 3f out: kpt on fnl 2f: nvr on terms* **20/1**

60-4 **10** ¾ **Last Three Minutes (IRE)**[17] 1603 4-9-11 **82**........... TGMcLaughlin 17 66+
(E A L Dunlop) *in rr on outer: hdwy over 2f out: hung bdly lft and wknd 1f out* **4/1**[2]

21-0 **11** 1 **French Art**[17] 1603 4-9-9 **80**.. DO'Donohoe 7 62
(N Tinkler) *hld up in rr: hdwy and nt clr 3f out and over 1f out: nvr trbld ldrs* **20/1**

424- **12** 1 **Applaude**[212] 6762 4-9-2 **73**.. PJMcDonald 14 52
(G A Swinbank) *mde most tl over 2f out: wknd over 1f out* **12/1**

201- **13** 9 **Eastern Hills**[345] 2761 4-9-7 **78**.. PAspell 3 37
(J S Wainwright) *s.i.s: sme hdwy over 3f out: sn wknd* **40/1**

1m 41.11s (0.11) **Going Correction** +0.15s/f (Good)
WFA 3 from 4yo+ 12lb **13** Ran SP% **126.2**
Speed ratings (Par 105): **105,104,104,103,102 100,98,96,96,95 94,93,84**
toteswinger: 1&2 not won, 1&3 £20.80 2&3 £20.80 CSF £242.96 CT £1377.05 TOTE £10.30: £2.80, £7.90, £2.80; EX 371.90 Place 6: £511.61 Place 5: £161.86.
Owner Dales Homes Ltd **Bred** Rathasker Stud **Trained** Scorton, N Yorks

FOCUS
Another competitive affair run with plenty of pace. Sound if ordinary form.
Allformary Official explanation: jockey said filly was denied a clear run
Last Three Minutes(IRE) Official explanation: jockey said gelding hung both ways
French Art Official explanation: jockey said gelding was denied a clear run
T/Plt: £433.80 to a £1 stake. Pool: £88,939.14. 149.65 winning tickets. T/Qpdt: £95.30 to a £1 stake. Pool: £7,213.98. 56.00 winning tickets. WG

2033 NEWBURY (L-H)
Saturday, May 16

OFFICIAL GOING: Soft changing to good to soft (soft in places) after race 4 (3.10)
Rails moved in around 7f and 5f bends but impact on distances not notified.
Wind: Strong ahead Weather: Cloudy

2074 BATHWICK TYRES MAIDEN STKS 1m 2f 6y
1:30 (1:31) (Class 4) 3-Y-O **£6,476** (£1,927; £963; £481) **Stalls** Low

Form RPR

0-2 **1** **Sam Sharp (USA)**[12] 1730 3-9-3 0.. TPQueally 9 83+
(H R A Cecil) *swtg: trckd ldr: led 3f out: drvn clr fr 2f out: comf* **5/1**

2 1 ¼ **Cotillion** 3-9-3 0.. NCallan 11 78
(W J Haggas) *w'like: in rr: stdy hdwy over 3f out: styd on to go 2nd fnl 110yds and gng on cl home but a readily hld by wnr* **13/2**

5- **3** ¾ **Twisted**[239] 6083 3-9-3 0.. JimmyFortune 15 76
(J H M Gosden) *h.d.w: lw: s.i.s: in rr: stdy hdwy fr 3f out: styd on wl fnl f to go 3rd fnl 50yds but a readily hld by wnr* **4/1**[2]

4 1 ¾ **Queen Of Pentacles (IRE)** 3-8-12 0................................ AlanMunro 3 68
(J Noseda) *w'like: str: slowly inbto stride: in rr tl stdy hdwy fr 3f out and kpt on wl thrght fnl f but nvr gng pce to rch wnr* **14/1**

5 1 **Stellar Cause (USA)** 3-9-3 0.. JohnEgan 10 71
(P F I Cole) *w'like: scope: led tl hdd 3f out: styd chsng wnr but no ch fr 2f out: wknd into 5th fnl 110yds* **14/1**

6 ¾ **Pictorial (USA)** 3-9-3 0.. RyanMoore 12 69
(Sir Michael Stoute) *lengthy: scope: mid-div: pushed along over 3f out: styd on fnl 2f but nvr gng pce to be competitive* **7/2**[1]

7 5 **Amroth** 3-8-12 0.. RichardHughes 7 54
(P D Evans) *unf: in rr: pushed along 4f out: styd on fr over 2f out but nvr anywhere nr ldrs* **25/1**

8 nk **Brave Dealer** 3-9-3 0.. SteveDrowne 4 58+
(R Charlton) *w'like: scope: in rr: drvn along and sme prog fnl 3f but nvr in contention* **20/1**

9 4 ½ **Born Romantic** 3-8-12 0.. PhilipRobinson 1 44
(H J L Dunlop) *unf: scope: in rr: hdwy over 3f out and chsd ldrs sn after but nvr in contention: wknd ins fnl 2f* **16/1**

0- **10** 10 **Bathwick Pursuit**[177] 7397 3-9-3 0.................................. CatherineGannon 2 29
(P D Evans) *w'like: in tch: rdn 4f out and sn wknd* **66/1**

0 **11** ¾ **Cridda Boy**[21] 1508 3-9-3 0.. FergusSweeney 8 28
(A G Newcombe) *w'like: lengthy: nvr bttr than mid-div: bhd fnl 4f* **100/1**

00- **12** 1 ¾ **Mystic Prince**[203] 6978 3-9-3 0.. MartinDwyer 14 24
(Miss Tor Sturgis) *chsd ldrs over 6f* **40/1**

05 **13** 23 **The Boat Shed (IRE)**[11] 1780 3-9-3 0.......................... RichardKingscote 13 —
(B W Duke) *chsd ldrs over 6f* **100/1**

04- **14** 20 **Directorship**[219] 6602 3-9-3 0.. GeorgeBaker 5 —
(P R Chamings) *chsd ldrs tl wknd 4f out: virtually p.u fnl f: dismntd after line* **9/2**[3]

2m 11.81s (3.01) **Going Correction** +0.35s/f (Good) **14** Ran SP% **124.1**
Speed ratings (Par 101): **101,100,99,98,97 96,92,92,88,80 80,78,60,44**
toteswinger: 1&2 £7.30, 1&3 £3.10, 2&3 £6.70 CSF £37.08 TOTE £4.10: £1.70, £2.60, £1.90; EX 38.70.
Owner N Martin **Bred** Michael Cahan Thoroughbreds **Trained** Newmarket, Suffolk

FOCUS
The winner slipped the field in this decent maiden. There should be winners coming from the race.
Twisted Official explanation: jockey said colt ran too free
Bathwick Pursuit Official explanation: jockey said colt ran too free
Directorship Official explanation: jockey said colt finished distressed

2075 AON STKS (REGISTERED AS THE ASTON PARK) (LISTED RACE) 1m 5f 61y
2:05 (2:05) (Class 1) 4-Y-O+
£22,708 (£8,608; £4,308; £2,148; £1,076; £540) **Stalls** Low

Form RPR

3-13 **1** **Tastahil (IRE)**[28] 1351 5-8-12 105.. RHills 1 114
(B W Hills) *lw: led: drvn along over 2f out: narrowly hdd ins fnl f: styd on gamely to ld again cl home* **9/2**[2]

124- **2** ½ **All The Aces (IRE)**[330] 3193 4-8-12 111.......................... PhilipRobinson 10 113
(M A Jarvis) *chsd wnr: drvn to chal over 1f out: slt ld ins fnl f: hdd and no ex cl home* **9/4**[1]

2-23 **3** 8 **The Betchworth Kid**[20] 1546 4-8-12 103.......................... JamieSpencer 5 101
(M L W Bell) *in rr: rdn and styd on fr 3f out: nvr nr ldrs and lft wl hld 3rd cl home* **5/1**[3]

013- **4** nk **Tropical Strait (IRE)**[168] 7491 6-8-12 106........................ MartinDwyer 6 106
(D W P Arbuthnot) *chsd ldrs: rdn and styd on to press ldrs ins fnl 2f: outpcd fnl f but clr 3rd whn broke leg cl home: destroyed* **11/2**

100- **5** 7 **Magicalmysterytour (IRE)**[189] 7244 6-8-12 99.................. AlanMunro 7 90
(W J Musson) *in rr: sme prog 3f out: nvr anywhere nr ldrs and wknd over 2f out* **16/1**

130- **6** 3 ¾ **Yellowstone (IRE)**[245] 5921 5-8-12 110.............................. JohnEgan 2 85
(P F I Cole) *in rr: rdn and sme prog over 3f out: nvr anywhere nr ldrs and wknd over 2f out* **9/2**[2]

04-0 **7** 6 **Unleashed (IRE)**[28] 1351 4-8-12 106.................................. TPQueally 8 76
(H R A Cecil) *in tch: sme hdwy 5f out: nvr nr ldrs and wknd ins fnl 3f* **20/1**

20-3 **P** **Spanish Hidalgo (IRE)**[21] 1523 5-8-12 102.................(t) RyanMoore 3 —
(J L Dunlop) *in tch tl wknd qckly over 5f out: p.u over 3f out* **22/1**

2m 52.42s (0.42) **Going Correction** +0.35s/f (Good) **8** Ran SP% **114.2**
Speed ratings (Par 111): **112,111,106,106,102 99,96,—**
toteswinger: 1&2 £2.900, 1&3 £3.70, 2&3 £3.00 CSF £15.01 TOTE £5.20: £1.90, £1.40, £1.50; EX 16.80 Trifecta £69.60 Pool £555.09 - 5.90 winning units..
Owner Hamdan Al Maktoum **Bred** Darley **Trained** Lambourn, Berks

FOCUS
A decent Listed event. The first pair came clear as it proved hard work to make up ground from behind. The winner stepped up on his John Porter form and looks to have improved this year.

NOTEBOOK
Tastahil(IRE) got back to winning ways on this step up in trip with a really brave effort from the front. He had set out to make all when third in the John Porter at this course last month on similar ground, but the extra distance made the difference and there was a lot to like about his attitude when headed by the All The Aces. He has resumed this term an improved performer, indeed he comfortably reversed last season's November Handicap form with the third and fourth, and has become a very consistent performer. No doubt he held a fitness edge over the runner-up, but this was a deserved first success in this class and there could still be a little more to come as he steps up further in distance. There was no real suggestion from connections that he was heading to the Gold Cup next month and he would be ground dependant, but a quote of 25/1 from 50-1 was given for that by William Hill. (op 5-1 tchd 11-2)
All The Aces(IRE) ◆ was having his first outing since finishing fourth in the King Edward VII Stakes at Royal Ascot last year and didn't look 100% fit. He stood out in the paddock though and unsurprisingly got well backed with the easy ground expected to suit. He tracked the winner into the home straight and responded to pressure, just getting his head in front around the furlong pole. As that rival rallied his stride began to shorten nearing the business end, however, and he was ultimately just held. This was a promising return and he would have definite claims of reversing the form now he has the run behind him. His connections may opt to go abroad with him at some stage this season. (op 3-1 tchd 10-3 and 7-2 in a place)
The Betchworth Kid had ground conditions to suit. He made laboured progress down the home straight and is flattered to have finished third, but still ran his race. He helps to set the standard. (op 10-3)
Tropical Strait(IRE) was in the process of running a solid race and booked for third, before breaking down nearing the finish, sadly with tragic consequences. (op 6-1 tchd 5-1)
Magicalmysterytour(IRE) was never in the hunt from off the pace, but ran close enough to his November Handicap form with the winner. He is entitled to come on a deal for the run.
Yellowstone(IRE) was another who struggled to make an impact from off the pace and ran some way below the level of his third over C&D when behind Tropical Strait on his penultimate outing, despite being on much better terms. He too should improve for the run, but has a little to prove now. (op 5-1)
Unleashed(IRE) was bidding to give his stable a third win in this in the last ten years, but was treading water from 4f out and never looked like reversing course form with the winner. (op 14-1)

Spanish Hidalgo(IRE) Official explanation: jockey said gelding bled from the nose

2076 JUDDMONTE LOCKINGE STKS (GROUP 1) 1m (S)
2:40 (2:42) (Class 1) 4-Y-0+

£141,925 (£53,800; £26,925; £13,425; £6,725; £3,375) **Stalls** Centre

Form RPR

11-3 **1** **Virtual**[21] 1525 4-9-0 113 JimmyFortune 10 119
(J H M Gosden) *trckd ldrs: drvn to chal fnl f: styd on gamely u.p to ld last stride* **6/1**[2]

1130 **2** *nse* **Alexandros**[20] 1553 4-9-0 115 LDettori 6 119
(Saeed Bin Suroor) *chsd ldrs: rdn over 1f out: rdr lost whip 1f out: styd on wl to ld fnl 110yds: ct last strides* **16/1**

02-3 **3** *½* **Twice Over**[30] 1301 4-9-0 119 TPQueally 2 118
(H R A Cecil) *sn led: drvn fr 2f out: hrd rdn and narrowly hdd fnl 110yds: kpt on* **15/2**[3]

1-01 **4** *1 ¼* **Paco Boy (IRE)**[21] 1525 4-9-0 124 RichardHughes 7 115
(R Hannon) *lw: t.k.h: hld up in tch: n.m.r 2f out: qcknd over 1f out and str chal ins fnl f: no ex fnl 110yds: wknd cl home* **11/8**[1]

200- **5** *1 ½* **Major Cadeaux**[153] 7684 5-9-0 115 RyanMoore 12 112
(R Hannon) *in rr: hdwy fr 2f out: styd on to chse ldrs ins fnl f but nvr quite gng pce to chal* **12/1**

305- **6** *nk* **Tariq**[290] 4518 5-9-0 115 JamieSpencer 1 111
(P W Chapple-Hyam) *in rr: swtchd rt and hdwy ins fnl 2f: hung lft ins fnl f: kpt on but nvr gng pce to rch ldrs* **33/1**

31-4 **7** *2 ¾* **Atlantic Sport (USA)**[28] 1346 4-9-0 107 DarryllHolland 5 105
(M R Channon) *in rr but in tch: hdwy fr 3f out: styd on but nvr gng pce to chal: outpcd fnl f* **40/1**

110- **8** *3 ½* **Pressing (IRE)**[153] 7684 6-9-0 117 NCallan 8 97
(M A Jarvis) *chsd ldrs: rdn over 2f out: wknd wl over 1f out* **8/1**

3-22 **9** *1 ¾* **Dream Eater (IRE)**[21] 1525 4-9-0 114 (t) FrancisNorton 11 93
(A M Balding) *lw: t.k.h rr but in tch: rdn over 2f out: no imp and sn wknd* **20/1**

/11- **10** *3 ¼* **Aqlaam**[332] 3119 4-9-0 113 RHills 3 85
(W J Haggas) *lw: t.k.h early: rdn and sme hdwy over 2f out: nvr rchd ldrs and sn wknd* **15/2**[3]

05-4 **11** *15* **Winker Watson**[33] 1251 4-9-0 112 AlanMunro 4 51
(P W Chapple-Hyam) *chsd ldrs: rdn ins fnl 3f: wknd qckly fr 2f out* **33/1**

1m 40.32s (0.62) **Going Correction** +0.35s/f (Good) **11** Ran SP% **117.7**
Speed ratings (Par 117): **110,109,109,108,106 106,103,100,98,95 80**
toteswinger: 1&2 £8.70, 1&3 £8.00, 2&3 £15.90 CSF £91.89 TOTE £8.10: £2.60, £2.20, £2.60; EX 98.10 Trifecta £1121.80 Pool: £158,884.91 - 104.80.
Owner Cheveley Park Stud **Bred** Cheveley Park Stud Ltd **Trained** Newmarket, Suffolk
■ Stewards' Enquiry : T P Queally three-day ban: excessive use of the whip (May 30-Jun 1)

FOCUS
By no means a vintage Lockinge, which featured only one other Group 1 winner and no challengers from abroad. It is difficult to rate the form highly as Group 1 standard, but there was a terrific finish and the first three were very closely covered at the line. Virtual carried over his progress from last year, reversing Sandown form with Paco Boy.

NOTEBOOK
Virtual was highly progressive on soft ground last autumn and had resumed with a promising third to Paco Boy in the Sandown Mile, where he was ultimately found out by lack of a recent race. The rain that had fallen in the preceding 36 hours was very much to his advantage, and the strong wind, which was blowing half into their faces, made it quite a test. He looked terrific in the preliminaries, and he was never far away in a race in which they raced up the middle of the track. However, having been right in the thick of it throughout the last 2f, he was lucky perhaps that he had his head down at the right time in a driving finish, as Fortune reckones he was beaten just before the line and beaten again just after it. He will now step back up in trip for the Coral Eclipse. He will need to improve again, but that is eminently possible. (op 15-2 tchd 11-2)
Alexandros, successful in two classy handicaps at Nad Al Sheba early in the year, is a tough colt who is getting better all the time. He had no previous form that entitled him to win a Group 1, but he would probably have won this one but for Dettori having his whip accidentally knocked out of his hand by Queally on Twice Over at the furlong pole. Connections were delighted with his effort, and perhaps he will win at this level one day. However, their immediate target is the Diadem Stakes at Epsom, which is only a Group 3. (op 14-1)
Twice Over ran a big race in third, especially as it probably was not to his advantage that he had to make his own running into the wind. He had not raced on ground this soft before, but it clearly suited him better than the quick surface at Newmarket on his reappearance and he looked much happier on it. This was a step back in the right direction, and he has a nice prize in him, although the Prince Of Wales's at Royal Ascot, which is his next intended target, will be flying high again, and he will not want it too quick underfoot. (tchd 8-1)
Paco Boy(IRE) was unbeaten previously at Newbury but he was a 7f specialist at three, when successful in the Foret, and the burning question here was whether the combination of 1m and soft ground might blunt his finishing speed, for the Sandown Mile in which he beat Virtual, and also Dream Eater, had not been a proper test. He ultimately failed to get home, although he would have been a length or so closer but for his rider easing him in the closing stages when clearly held by the first three. However, while he got upsides, at least, just inside the final furlong Hughes said he had never been that happy with him and he would not have won at any trip. He might not be the easiest to place now in the short term, but a return for the Foret is very much on the cards later on. (op 7-4 tchd 15-8 in places)
Major Cadeaux enjoys this ground and flattered briefly when making an effort from off the pace up the stands' side of the pack. Connections had warned beforehand that the race might have come a week too soon for him, and his effort flattened out, but he should come on for the race. (tchd 11-1)
Tariq, third in the corresponding race 12 months previously, was never on terms this time but was going on at the finish, despite hanging, and he ran very respectably. (op 28-1)
Atlantic Sport(USA) lacked the pace to get involved and perhaps is not quite up to this grade.
Pressing(IRE) weakened in the last 2f and was found out by the conditions perhaps on this first run since Hong Kong in December, where he failed to run his race. (op 17-2 tchd 9-1)
Dream Eater(IRE) was a long way below Sandown form, but his trainer had no hesitation in blaming the ground. (op 22-1 tchd 25-1)
Aqlaam was very disappointing and connections could not account for it. He suffered a stress fracture after impressing in the Jersey last year, but he had the benefit of a racecourse gallop at Kempton and his trainer had him as fit as he could get him. He looked a colt of massive potential at Royal Ascot, but he had to prove himself on the ground, and that may well have been a factor. It will be interesting to see if something else emerges however. (op 6-1)
Winker Watson has had his problems, and at present he seems unable to reproduce his home form on the track, although this 1m may have stretched him on the ground. He could benefit from returning to sprinting.

2077 AON LONDON GOLD CUP (HERITAGE H'CAP) 1m 2f 6y
3:10 (3:12) (Class 2) (0-105,98) 3-Y-0

£24,924 (£7,464; £3,732; £1,868; £932; £468) **Stalls** Low

Form RPR

31-1 **1** **Aqwaal (IRE)**[22] 1489 3-8-8 85 RHills 12 94
(E A L Dunlop) *lw: trckd ldrs: drvn to chse ldr wl over 1f out: styd on dourly thrght fnl f to ld last strides* **6/4**[1]

53-2 **2** *hd* **Decision**[11] 1771 3-7-13 79 DavidProbert(3) 9 88
(C G Cox) *led: drvn and styd on wl fr over 2f out: kpt on fnl f: ct last strides* **14/1**

03-1 **3** *3 ¼* **Holyrood**[33] 1260 3-8-8 85 RyanMoore 11 87
(Sir Michael Stoute) *lw: chsd ldrs wnt 2nd over 2f out and sn hrd drvn and no imp outpcd fr over 1f out* **6/1**[2]

4-02 **4** *1* **Lasso The Moon**[14] 1681 3-8-3 80 CatherineGannon 14 80
(M R Channon) *in rr: rdn 3f out: hdwy fr 2f out and hung lft: styd on wl to take 4th ins fnl f but nvr gng pce to rch ldrs* **14/1**

26-6 **5** *1* **Aurorian (IRE)**[29] 1326 3-8-13 90 RichardHughes 13 88
(R Hannon) *hld up in rr: hdwy over 2f out: styd on to chse ldrs but hung lft ins fnl f: nvr in contention and wknd nr fin* **40/1**

0-31 **6** *½* **River Captain (IRE)**[24] 1462 3-8-6 83 JamesDoyle 6 80
(S Kirk) *towards rr: rdn 3f out: styd on fr over 1f out and kpt on cl home but nvr a threat* **11/1**

3-13 **7** *1* **Legislate**[30] 1303 3-8-9 86 RobertWinston 2 81
(B W Hills) *chsd ldrs: hmpd after 3f: styd prom: rdn 3f out: wknd over 1f out* **6/1**[2]

13-5 **8** *2 ¼* **Alazeyab (USA)**[14] 1678 3-9-7 98 TPO'Shea 5 89
(M A Jarvis) *chsd ldrs: rdn over 3f out: wknd fr 2f out* **33/1**

2131 **9** *¾* **Eastern Aria (UAE)**[52] 962 3-8-3 80 FrancisNorton 3 69
(M Johnston) *in rr: rdn and hung lft over 2f out and nvr in contention* **25/1**

0-12 **10** *7* **Sehoy (USA)**[15] 1643 3-8-8 85 NickyMackay 4 60
(J H M Gosden) *towards rr: rdn and sme hdwy over 3f out: nvr nr ldrs and sn wknd* **9/1**[3]

011- **11** *1* **Dialogue**[155] 7655 3-8-11 88 GregFairley 1 61
(M Johnston) *chsd ldrs: rdn 3f out: wknd qckly 2f out* **14/1**

0-50 **12** *½* **Weald Park (USA)**[31] 1291 3-9-6 97 JimmyFortune 7 69
(R Hannon) *towards rr: sme hdwy over 3f out: nvr any danger and wknd sn after* **16/1**

2m 9.81s (1.01) **Going Correction** +0.35s/f (Good) **12** Ran SP% **122.0**
Speed ratings (Par 105): **109,108,106,105,104 104,103,101,101,95 94,94**
toteswinger: 1&2 £9.10, 1&3 £3.50, 2&3 £16.10 CSF £25.95 CT £108.92 TOTE £2.50: £1.30, £4.40, £2.30; EX 35.80 Trifecta £181.90 Pool: £860.70 - 3.50 winning units..
Owner Hamdan Al Maktoum **Bred** Shadwell Estate Company Limited **Trained** Newmarket, Suffolk

FOCUS
This was perhaps not the strongest running of this traditionally strong 3yo handicap, but it was still typically competitive and littered with potential improvers. The winner maintained his progress to beat the seemingly unexposed runner-up. There was just an average pace on.

NOTEBOOK
Aqwaal(IRE) was all the rage to land the hat-trick and rewarded his supporters with a narrow success. Raised 9lb for his comeback win at Sandown, he was forced to race wide through the early parts, but was never that far away. He took time to master the second throughout the final furlong and drifted across to that rival under pressure, but it always looked as though he would just get there.He clearly acts on most ground and has done enough in his last two runs to suggest a stiffer test should suit ideally. He holds an entry in the King Edward VII over 1m4f at Royal Ascot, but it would not be surprising to see him in the Hampton Court over this trip. He will still have something to find with the principals in either of those, but is clearly still improving (op 2-1 tchd 9-4 in places)
Decision ◆ got a well-judged ride from the front and refused to go down without a fight. He had evidently come on a deal for his seasonal return at Chester 11 days earlier and is another who acts on most ground. However, after a likely rise for this his best short-term opportunity to go one better will likely be in maiden company. (op 16-1 tchd 20-1)
Holyrood was making his handicap debut after winning a modest Yarmouth maiden last month. He got out well from his wide stall and raced handily, which suited. He came under pressure after 4f out, but stuck gamely to his task and it is likely the best of him has still to be seen. (tchd 13-2)
Lasso The Moon stayed on with purpose when the race was all but over and again looked less than straightforward. This was a career-best effort and he should find a race or two, but now looks the time to reach for some headgear. (op 16-1)
Aurorian(IRE), while never seriously threatening, proved he stays the trip well enough and ran more encouragingly for the return to softer ground. He just looks high enough in the weights though.
River Captain(IRE) has form on soft ground, but was ridden more patiently than when scoring at Epsom 24 days earlier and the 8lb rise for that appeared to find him out. (op 10-1 tchd 17-2)
Legislate, 5lb higher, was made to look very one paced and probably wants a return to quicker ground. (tchd 13-2)
Alazeyab(USA) was well held under top weight on this drop down from Listed company and is not going to prove simple to place. (tchd 25-1)
Sehoy(USA) was reported to have been unsuited by the going. Official explanation: jockey said colt was unsuited by the soft ground (op 6-1)
Weald Park(USA) Official explanation: jockey said colt ran too free

2078 BERRY BROS & RUDD H'CAP 6f 8y
3:45 (3:46) (Class 2) (0-100,100) 4-Y-0+

£12,462 (£3,732; £1,866; £934; £466; £234) **Stalls** Centre

Form RPR

100- **1** **Main Aim**[189] 7243 4-9-3 99 RyanMoore 14 119+
(Sir Michael Stoute) *lw: sn in tch: drvn and hdwy over 2f out: led appr fnl f: sn clr: easily* **2/1**[1]

0-31 **2** *7* **Aye Aye Digby (IRE)**[14] 1668 4-8-6 88 FergusSweeney 13 86+
(H Candy) *w ldrs tl def advantage over 3f out: rdn over 2f out: hdd appr fnl f: sn no ch w wnr: hung rt u.p fnl 75yds* **4/1**[3]

0003 **3** *nk* **Nightjar (USA)**[7] 1864 4-8-4 86 oh2 FrancisNorton 11 83
(M Johnston) *in rr: rdn over 2f out: hdwy over 1f out and squeezed through on rails fnl 75yds to get 3rd: gng on fin but nvr any ch w wnr* **12/1**

100- **4** *nk* **Perfect Flight**[189] 7243 4-8-9 91 KirstyMilczarek 10 87
(M Blanshard) *towards rr: rdn 3f out: hdwy fr 2f out: styd on fnl f but nvr any ch w wnr* **14/1**

0-00 **5** *hd* **Phantom Whisper**[7] 1864 6-8-10 92 AlanMunro 4 87
(B R Millman) *chsd ldrs: rdn and one pce 2f out: kpt on again fnl f* **16/1**

0-60 **6** *2* **Spanish Bounty**[13] 1699 4-8-10 92 TPQueally 1 81
(J G Portman) *pressed ldrs: stl upsides 2f out: wknd ins fnl f* **20/1**

0-06 **7** *1* **Good Gorsoon (USA)**[10] 1791 4-8-6 88 RobertWinston 12 83+
(B W Hills) *s.i.s: t.k.h: sn in tch and trckd ldrs over 2f out: wknd fnl f and n.d whn hmpd fnl 75yds* **18/1**

50/4 **8** *3 ½* **Drawnfromthepast (IRE)**[17] 1608 4-9-4 100 (t) SteveDrowne 7 74
(J A Osborne) *s.i.s: outpcd* **40/1**

0-43 **9** *9* **Exclamation**[13] 1699 4-9-4 100 JamieSpencer 3 45
(B J Meehan) *slt ld tl hdd over 3f out: wknd qckly 2f out* **10/3**[2]

0-05 **10** *2* **Esteem Machine (USA)**[24] 1467 5-8-2 87 DavidProbert(3) 9 26
(R A Teal) *plld hrd: chsd ldrs tl wknd over 2f out* **25/1**

000- 11 20 **Sundae**[244] 5930 5-8-8 **90** .... MartinDwyer 5 —
(C F Wall) *plunged s: t.k.h and chsd ldrs over 2f: sn wknd: eased fnl 2f* **12/1**

1m 13.66s (0.66) **Going Correction** +0.35s/f (Good) **11** Ran SP% **120.7**
Speed ratings (Par 109): **109,99,99,98,98 95,94,89,77,75 48**
toteswinger: 1&2 £3.20, 1&3 £8.90, 2&3 £9.80 CSF £9.91 CT £78.73 TOTE £3.10: £1.60, £1.80, £3.50; EX 14.50 Trifecta £198.80 Pool: £ 833.18 - 3.10 winning units..
Owner K Abdulla **Bred** Juddmonte Farms Ltd **Trained** Newmarket, Suffolk
■ Stewards' Enquiry : Fergus Sweeney three-day ban: careless riding (May 30-Jun 1)

FOCUS
The ground was officially changed to good to soft, soft in places prior to this decent sprint handicap. It was run at a good pace and the main action developed more towards the stands' side. The winner was most impressive and will have to step back up in grade.

NOTEBOOK
Main Aim ◆ took this field apart and ran out a very impressive winner on his return from a 189-day break. He took time to settle, but the turn of foot he displayed when asked to win the race was in a different class to his rivals. The trip and ground were ideal, though he did land his first two races on a quick surface so is versatile. He has started favourite on each of his seven career starts, of which he has now won four, and he appears to have improved markedly from three to four. Where he goes from here is not certain, but his handicap days are now behind him. He has been given entries in the Golden Jubilee next month (slashed from 50s to 14-1 with William Hill) and the July Cup, a race his sire won. While it may be a little too soon for him to be thinking about the top level, there is little doubt he is up to winning in Pattern class. The sprint division has also been notable in recent years for former handicappers progressing to the top of the tree, Kyllachy, Pastorial Pursuits and Sahkee's Secret the most notable examples. (op 5-2 tchd 11-4)
Aye Aye Digby(IRE) got a positive ride, but was made to look ordinary by the winner. Time will likely tell this was certainly no disgrace, however, and it was another improved run from his 5lb higher mark. (op 5-1)
Nightjar(USA) was doing his best work at the finish on the stands' rail and posted a career-best display. He was 2lb out of the weights here, but is currently rated 10lb higher on the All-Weather and is a likeable performer. (tchd 16-1)
Perfect Flight, making her seasonal debut, was drawn nearer the stands' side yet ended up having to make her challenge wide of the pack. She ran a respectable race. (op 16-1)
Phantom Whisper had dropped to a mark just 1lb higher than his last win and is versatile as regards underfoot conditions. He lacked a gear change, but was not disgraced. (tchd 20-1)
Spanish Bounty performed sufficiently well considering he was drawn in stall 1. (op 16-1)
Good Gorsoon(USA) would have been closer had he not had to be snatched up near the furlong marker. He was again slow to break though and once more refused to settle. (op 20-1 tchd 22-1)
Exclamation had turned in two solid efforts since resuming this term and was popular on ground that suits. After showing decent early speed he dropped out quickly nearing the final furlong and something may have gone amiss. (op 3-1 tchd 5-2)
Esteem Machine(USA) Official explanation: jockey said gelding hung right-handed
Sundae looked interesting for this seasonal bow, but was never going well and was later reported to have run flat. Official explanation: jockey said gelding moved poorly

2079 CATRIDGE FARM STUD FILLIES' H'CAP 7f (S)
4:20 (4:21) (Class 4) (0-85,85) 3-Y-O **£6,476** (£1,927; £963; £481) **Stalls** Centre

Form RPR
1004 **1** **Never Lose**[15] 1639 3-9-1 **82** .... NCallan 11 92
(C E Brittain) *in tch: hdwy over 2f out: led 1f out: drvn out* **25/1**
21-3 **2** *1* **Glen Molly (IRE)**[12] 1744 3-8-11 **78** .... RobertWinston 13 85+
(B W Hills) *lw: in rr: hdwy over 2f out: n.m.r over 1f out: hung rt and styd on fnl f: kpt on cl home but no imp on wnr* **7/2**[1]
61-1 **3** *1 ¼* **Lovely Thought**[32] 1271 3-9-1 **82** ....(b) RHills 1 86
(W J Haggas) *lw: chsd ldrs: led ins fnl 2f: sn drvn: hdd 1f out: oupced ins fnl f* **4/1**[2]
120- **4** *2* **Belle Des Airs (IRE)**[246] 5855 3-8-13 **80** .... RichardKingscote 7 78
(R M Beckett) *chsd ldrs: rdn over 2f out: wknd ins fnl f* **25/1**
5-02 **5** *1 ¼* **Acquiesced (IRE)**[7] 1870 3-8-12 **79** .... RichardHughes 8 74
(R Hannon) *hld up towards rr: gd hdwy over 2f out: nvr quite gng pce to rch ldrs: wknd ins fnl f* **9/1**[3]
21-0 **6** *¾* **Efficiency**[35] 1214 3-8-13 **80** .... SteveDrowne 16 73
(M Blanshard) *in rr: rdn and hdwy fr 2f out: kpt on fnl f but nvr gng pce to be competitive* **28/1**
-331 **7** *hd* **My Best Bet**[108] 313 3-8-10 **77** .... EdwardCreighton 4 69
(M R Channon) *mid-div: pushed along and hdwy ins fnl 2f: styd on same pce fr over 1f out and nvr rchd ldrs* **28/1**
24-0 **8** *hd* **Key Signature**[29] 1324 3-9-2 **83** .... PaulEddery 2 75
(Pat Eddery) *chsd ldrs: rdn over 2f out: wknd fnl f* **11/1**
2-61 **9** *1 ½* **Volochkova (USA)**[18] 1588 3-8-7 **74** .... FrancisNorton 17 62+
(J R Fanshawe) *towards rr whn hmpd ins fnl 2f: kpt on ins fnl f but nt revover* **14/1**
16- **10** *¾* **Miss Eze**[197] 7107 3-9-2 **83** .... JamieSpencer 15 69+
(M L W Bell) *s.i.s: hld up: hdwy whn bdly hmpd ins fnl 2f: nvr any ch after but kpt on ins fnl f* **4/1**[2]
10-0 **11** *4 ½* **Accede**[9] 1808 3-8-13 **80** .... TPQueally 10 54
(J G Portman) *chsd ldrs: rdn whn n.m.r ins fnl 2f: nvr in contention after* **33/1**
14-0 **12** *½* **Caledonia Princess**[31] 1296 3-8-8 **75** .... DarryllHolland 20 47+
(R Curtis) *towards rr on ins: sme prog whn bdly hmpd ins fnl 2f: nt rcvr* **33/1**
5-52 **13** *½* **Forward Feline (IRE)**[26] 1414 3-8-5 **72** ....(p) CatherineGannon 3 43
(B Palling) *sn led: rdn over 3f out: hdd ins fnl 2f: wknd over 1f out* **14/1**
15-6 **14** *3* **Rioliina (IRE)**[4] 1965 3-9-4 **85** .... TPO'Shea 9 48
(J G Portman) *chsd ldrs: rdn and edgd rt fr 2f out: sn wknd* **33/1**
234- **15** *7* **Bea Menace (USA)**[207] 6877 3-8-4 **71** oh3 .... MartinDwyer 12 15
(P F I Cole) *chsd ldrs: rdn 3f out: wknd over 2f out* **33/1**
21-1 **16** *1 ¼* **Aroundthebay**[61] 852 3-9-1 **82** .... JamesDoyle 18 22
(H J L Dunlop) *chsd ldrs: rdn 3f out: hung rt and weakenbed ins fnl 2f* **12/1**
330- **17** *7* **Golden Destiny (IRE)**[219] 6603 3-8-13 **80** .... JimmyFortune 6 —
(P J Makin) *bhd most of way* **16/1**
03-1 **18** *hd* **Beautiful Filly**[27] 1379 3-8-1 **71** .... AhmedAjtebi(3) 14 —
(D M Simcock) *chsd ldrs tl wknd and hmpd ins fnl 2f* **25/1**

1m 27.79s (2.09) **Going Correction** +0.35s/f (Good) **18** Ran SP% **137.7**
Speed ratings (Par 98): **102,100,99,97,95 94,94,94,92,91 86,86,85,82,74 72,64,64**
toteswinger: 1&2 £29.70, 1&3 £29.60, 2&3 £5.00 CSF £113.26 CT £463.31 TOTE £38.90: £6.40, £1.70, £1.80, £7.20; EX 236.50.
Owner Saeed Manana **Bred** Susan J Jensen **Trained** Newmarket, Suffolk
■ Stewards' Enquiry : James Doyle four-day ban: careless riding (May 30-Jun 2)

FOCUS
Plenty of potential improvers lurking in this 3yo fillies' handicap, which had five last-time-out winners in attendance. The race was run at a fair pace and as with the preceding 6f race the principals ended up towards the stands' side. It was most notable for some hard-luck stories and the form is tricky to assess.
Miss Eze ◆ Official explanation: jockey said filly suffered interference in running
Caledonia Princess Official explanation: jockey said filly suffered interference in running
Forward Feline(IRE) Official explanation: jockey said filly ran too free
Rioliina(IRE) Official explanation: jockey said filly suffered interference in running
Aroundthebay Official explanation: jockey said filly hung right-handed
Golden Destiny(IRE) Official explanation: jockey said filly never travelled

2080 OLYMPIC COACH BUILDERS/CONSTABLE CREDIT MAIDEN STKS (DIV I) 7f (S)
4:55 (4:56) (Class 4) 3-Y-O **£6,152** (£1,830; £914; £456) **Stalls** Centre

Form RPR
1 **Prince Of Dance** 3-9-3 0 .... RichardKingscote 7 97+
(Tom Dascombe) *w'like: str: s.i.s: in rr: gd hdwy over 2f out: led over 1f out: sn pushed clr and edgd rt fnl 110yds* **7/4**[2]
40 **2** *4* **Ermine And Velvet**[17] 1605 3-8-12 0 .... NCallan 2 77
(C E Brittain) *chsd ldrs: led and edgd rt ins fnl 2f: hdd over 1f out: sn no ch w wnr but kpt on for clr 2nd* **11/1**
2- **3** *4* **Broad Cairn**[302] 4150 3-9-3 0 .... SteveDrowne 9 71
(R Charlton) *lw: s.i.s: in rr: hdwy over 3f out: styd on to go 3rd over 1f out but nvr any threat to ldng duo* **6/4**[1]
06- **4** *1 ¼* **Durgan**[238] 6117 3-9-3 0 .... GeorgeBaker 6 68
(Mrs L C Jewell) *plld hrd: chsd ldrs: shkn up and one pce whn hmpd over 1f out* **16/1**
5 *1* **Bermondsey Girl** 3-8-12 0 .... MartinDwyer 10 60+
(C F Wall) *unf: in rr: shkn up 2f out: mod prog fnl f* **16/1**
00 **6** *4 ½* **Secret Hero**[28] 1355 3-9-3 0 .... RichardHughes 5 53
(R Hannon) *sn led: hdd ins fnl 2f and wknd qckly* **20/1**
7 *3* **Regal Blush** 3-8-9 0 .... DavidProbert(3) 8 40
(A M Balding) *w'like: scope: chsd ldrs over 4f* **11/1**
00 **8** *11* **Captain Peachey**[13] 1704 3-9-0 0 .... JamesMillman(3) 11 15
(B R Millman) *chsd ldrs: rdn 3f out: wknd 2f out* **40/1**
0-4 **9** *10* **Francis Walsingham (IRE)**[15] 1636 3-9-3 0 .... RobertWinston 4 —
(H Morrison) *lw: chsd ldrs: ev ch over 2f out: wkng whn bmpd wl over 1f out* **9/1**[3]

1m 27.71s (2.01) **Going Correction** +0.35s/f (Good) **9** Ran SP% **122.0**
Speed ratings (Par 101): **102,97,92,91,90 85,81,69,57**
toteswinger: 1&2 £7.40, 1&3 £1.90, 2&3 £3.70 CSF £23.47 TOTE £3.20: £1.50, £2.90, £1.20; EX 34.70.
Owner Five Horses Ltd **Bred** Five Horses Ltd **Trained** Lambourn, Berks

FOCUS
An ordinary maiden, but the winner looks above average. It was much the faster of the two divisions.
Francis Walsingham(IRE) Official explanation: jockey said colt ran too free

2081 OLYMPIC COACH BUILDERS/CONSTABLE CREDIT MAIDEN STKS (DIV II) 7f (S)
5:30 (5:35) (Class 4) 3-Y-O **£6,152** (£1,830; £914; £456) **Stalls** Centre

Form RPR
04 **1** **Prince Of Johanne (IRE)**[5] 1941 3-9-3 0 .... TPQueally 3 71+
(J Noseda) *s.i.s: sn in tch: drvn and qcknd to ld fnl 110yds: jst hld on* **13/2**[3]
2 *nse* **Criticize (USA)** 3-9-3 0 .... SteveDrowne 5 71+
(R Charlton) *lengthy: scope: lw: s.i.s: hld up in tch: gd hdwy fr 2f: qcknd to chal ins fnl f: kpt on: jst failed* **9/1**
0-4 **3** *1* **Dreamcoat**[28] 1350 3-9-3 0 .... JimmyFortune 2 68
(J H M Gosden) *lw: w ldr: led 2f out: hdd fnl 110yds: one pce* **5/6**[1]
4 *¾* **Truly Asia (IRE)** 3-9-3 0 .... RichardKingscote 4 66
(R Charlton) *w'like: chsd ldrs: rdn over 2f out: styd on same pce fr over 1f out* **14/1**
- **5** *½* **Almuktahem** 3-9-3 0 .... RHills 9 65
(Sir Michael Stoute) *w'like: scope: bit bkwd: chsd ldrs: chal fr 2f out: rdn and hung lft 1f out: sn outpcd* **5/1**[2]
6 *2 ½* **Missrepresentation** 3-8-12 0 .... RichardSmith 10 53
(J C Fox) *leggy: chsd ldrs: rdn over 2f out: outpcd fnl f* **25/1**
7 *nk* **Cottonfields (USA)** 3-9-3 0 .... SimonWhitworth 1 57
(Mrs H S Main) *w'like: bit bkwd: green and sn rdn in rr: styd on fnl f: nvr a threat* **33/1**
8 *shd* **Ryker (IRE)** 3-9-3 0 .... RobertWinston 11 57
(J W Hills) *w'like: athletic: in tch: rdn fr 3f out: wknd over 1f out* **12/1**
56 **9** *hd* **Highgate Cat**[59] 869 3-9-0 0 .... JamesMillman(3) 6 56
(B R Millman) *slt ld to 2f out: sn wknd* **25/1**

1m 30.76s (5.06) **Going Correction** +0.35s/f (Good) **9** Ran SP% **119.5**
Speed ratings (Par 101): **85,84,83,82,82 79,79,79,78**
toteswinger: 1&2 £6.90, 1&3 £2.50, 2&3 £4.30 CSF £63.53 TOTE £7.10: £2.10, £2.20, £1.10; EX 49.30 Place 6: £47.54, Place 5: £14.29.
Owner M Tabor, Mrs Susan Roy, M Green **Bred** T J Rooney And Corduff Stud **Trained** Newmarket, Suffolk

FOCUS
This second division of the maiden was run in a significantly slower time than the first. Muddling form but the winner stepped forward again.
T/Jkpt: Not won. T/Plt: £42.70 to a £1 stake. Pool: £154,378.42. 2,637.66 winning tickets.
T/Qpdt: £18.20 to a £1 stake. Pool: £6,773.62. 275.10 winning tickets. ST

2047 NEWMARKET (R-H)
Saturday, May 16
OFFICIAL GOING: Good to firm (good in places; 7.6)
Wind: Strong half-against Weather: Overcast

2082 SIGN UP BONUS AT BETINTERNET.COM MAIDEN STKS 1m
1:50 (1:50) (Class 4) 3-Y-O **£5,180** (£1,541; £770; £384) **Stalls** Low

Form RPR
3-44 **1** **Invisible Man**[12] 1729 3-9-3 85 .... RichardMullen 10 86
(J H M Gosden) *mde all: rdn and hung lft ins fnl f: styd on* **5/4**[1]
0-3 **2** *2 ¼* **Merdaam**[28] 1355 3-9-3 0 .... TedDurcan 6 81
(J L Dunlop) *a.p: chsd wnr over 3f out: rdn over 1f out: styd on same pce ins fnl f* **7/2**[2]
5- **3** *3 ½* **Kapsiliat (IRE)**[295] 4359 3-8-12 0 .... ShaneKelly 3 67
(J Noseda) *hld up in tch: racd keenly: rdn 2f out: styd on same pce fnl f* **14/1**
4 *3 ¼* **Bourne** 3-9-3 0 .... DaneO'Neill 13 65+
(L M Cumani) *hld up: hdwy over 2f out: no imp fnl f* **12/1**
0-0 **5** *4 ½* **Cake Stand**[25] 1422 3-9-3 0 .... RobertHavlin 16 55
(J A R Toller) *chsd ldrs: rdn over 2f out: wknd over 1f out* **80/1**
0 **6** *2* **Inside Trade (IRE)**[28] 1350 3-9-0 0 ....(t) JackMitchell(3) 8 50
(R M Beckett) *chsd ldrs: rdn over 3f out: hung lft and wknd over 1f out* **40/1**

7 *7* **Bengal Tiger** 3-9-3 0 WilliamBuick 5 34
(A M Balding) *s.i.s: sn mid-div: rdn and wknd over 2f out* 5/1[3]

30- **8** *3 1/4* **Kilkenny Bay**[137] 7823 3-8-12 0 LPKeniry 14 21
(W Jarvis) *s.i.s: hld up: a in rr* 40/1

50 **9** *3/4* **Laminka**[61] 849 3-8-12 0 JimCrowley 9 20
(G C Bravery) *chsd ldr tl rdn over 3f out: wknd over 2f out* 80/1

00- **10** *2 1/4* **Supera (IRE)**[207] 6885 3-8-12 0 PaulHanagan 11 15
(M H Tompkins) *hld up: rdn over 3f out: wknd over 2f out* 40/1

11 *hd* **Secret Life** 3-9-3 0 RoystonFfrench 12 19
(J Noseda) *hld up: a in rr: bhd fr 1/2-way* 12/1

P **Kimberley Rocks (IRE)** 3-8-12 0 SebSanders 4 —
(R M Beckett) *s.i.s: hld up: wknd over 2f out: bhd whn p.u over 1f out: b.b.v* 20/1

1m 40.29s (1.69) **Going Correction** +0.125s/f (Good) 12 Ran SP% **119.9**
Speed ratings (Par 101): **96,93,90,87,82 80,73,70,69,67 67,—**
toteswinger: 1&2 £1.50, 1&3 £5.80, 2&3 £8.20 CSF £5.17 TOTE £2.30: £1.10, £1.50, £4.20; EX 7.40.
Owner H R H Princess Haya Of Jordan **Bred** Darley **Trained** Newmarket, Suffolk

FOCUS
Despite 3mm of overnight rain and watering, the ground remained good to firm, good in places and there was a strong wind meeting the horses at an angle in the straight. A fair-looking maiden in which debutants have a decent record but a three-horse race according to the market, and the field came up the centre of the track. The winner set a good standard and the form seems sound.
Kimberley Rocks(IRE) Official explanation: jockey said filly bled from the nose

2083 PLAY LIVE CASINO AT BETINTERNET.COM H'CAP 1m
2:20 (2:22) (Class 3) (0-95,95) 4-Y-O+ **£9,714** (£2,890; £1,444; £721) **Stalls** Low

Form RPR

5220 **1** **Ace Of Hearts**[49] 997 10-9-1 **95** JackMitchell(3) 14 106
(C F Wall) *racd centre: led that gp 1f: chsd ldr tl led overall over 2f out: sn rdn and hung lft: r.o* 12/1

523- **2** *1/2* **Final Verse**[185] 7291 6-8-12 **89** LPKeniry 1 99
(M Salaman) *racd stands' side: hld up: hdwy over 2f out: rdn over 1f out: r.o* 16/1

104- **3** *3* **Habshan (USA)**[226] 6431 9-8-10 **87** TedDurcan 8 90
(C F Wall) *racd centre: hld up: hdwy over 2f out: sn edgd lft: rdn and ev ch over 1f out: styd on same pce ins fnl f* 33/1

14-0 **4** *1/2* **Priti Fabulous (IRE)**[17] 1603 4-8-5 **82** PaulHanagan 15 84
(W J Haggas) *racd centre: prom: rdn over 2f out: edgd lft over 1f out: styng on same pce whn hung rt nr fin* 25/1

54-4 **5** *2 1/2* **Ellemujie**[21] 1527 4-8-12 **89** JimCrowley 12 85
(D K Ivory) *racd centre: chsd ldrs: rdn and edgd lft over 2f out: wknd ins fnl f* 7/1[2]

40-1 **6** *1 1/4* **Twilight Star (IRE)**[21] 1524 5-8-4 **81** oh1 RoystonFfrench 2 74
(R A Teal) *racd stands' side: chsd ldrs: rdn and ev ch over 2f out: wknd fnl f* 20/1

-252 **7** *1/2* **Viva Vettori**[14] 1673 5-8-12 **89** RobertHavlin 6 81
(D R C Elsworth) *racd stands' side: led overall tl rdn and hdd over 2f out: wknd fnl f* 7/1[2]

1/1- **8** *hd* **Riggins (IRE)**[262] 5405 5-8-12 **89** DaneO'Neill 5 81+
(L M Cumani) *racd stands' side: s.i.s: hld up: nt clr run over 2f out: rdn whn nt clr run over 1f out: hmpd ins fnl f: swtchd rt: nvr able to chal* 5/4[1]

1-50 **9** *5* **Cordell (IRE)**[28] 1352 4-8-13 **90** PatDobbs 3 70
(R Hannon) *racd stands' side: prom: rdn over 2f out: sn wknd* 33/1

02-0 **10** *1 3/4* **Resurge (IRE)**[21] 1527 4-8-8 **85** ShaneKelly 4 61
(W S Kittow) *racd stands' side: chsd ldrs: rdn over 3f out: wknd 2f out* 16/1

0-10 **11** *1 3/4* **Dubai Dynamo**[12] 1731 4-8-13 **90** EddieAhern 9 62
(P F I Cole) *swtchd to r stands' side over 6f out: hld up: hdwy over 2f out: rdn and wknd over 1f out* 14/1

21-6 **12** *3 1/2* **Isphahan**[21] 1527 6-8-13 **90** WilliamBuick 7 54
(A M Balding) *racd centre: led that gp 7f out tl rdn and hung lft over 3f out: wknd over 2f out* 10/1[3]

1m 38.08s (-0.52) **Going Correction** +0.125s/f (Good) 12 Ran SP% **119.1**
Speed ratings (Par 107): **107,106,103,103,100 99,98,98,93,91 90,86**
toteswinger: 1&2 £30.10, 1&3 £43.20, 2&3 £53.10 CSF £180.37 CT £6122.11 TOTE £13.40: £2.80, £3.80, £6.40; EX 189.90 TRIFECTA Not won..
Owner Archangels 1 **Bred** Whitsbury Manor Stud **Trained** Newmarket, Suffolk

FOCUS
A decent, competitive handicap but unlike the first race the field raced in two groups until converging in the final quarter-mile; the time was 2.21secs faster than the opening maiden. Sound form, if ordinary for the grade.

NOTEBOOK
Ace Of Hearts, despite seeing plenty of daylight on the wide outside of his field, found plenty under pressure in the closing stages and ran on gamely to score. He looked high enough in the handicap beforehand, being 5lb above his last winning mark, but despite his age he is still able to hold his own in these good handicaps. (op 10-1)
Final Verse, a dual Listed winner in past, was only 1lb above his last winning mark and ran well on this seasonal debut. His current trainer clearly has him in good heart.
Habshan(USA), a stable companion of the winner who is best suited by fast ground, ran well on this seasonal debut and only faded up the hill. As with the winner, his trainer has done a good job in maintaining his ability and enthusiasm. (tchd 25-1)
Priti Fabulous(IRE), who gained both her wins on Polytrack but acts on fast turf, was 6lb above her last winning mark but performed creditably against some battle-hardened rivals and looks capable of picking up a race or two on turf this summer. (op 16-1)
Ellemujie is a consistent performer and was backed against the favourite. He has not won for nearly two years though and had his chance before fading. (op 10-1)
Twilight Star(IRE), who made all to score last time, was 5lb higher and was again ridden prominently. He can win more races but may be best suited by running on a turning track and slightly easier ground. (op 16-1 tchd 25-1 in a place)
Viva Vettori, a dual Polytrack winner at 1m and 1m2f, had produced his best effort on turf over 1m1f here last time. He made the running but, when taken on running into the dip, capitulated fairly tamely. (op 15-2 tchd 13-2)
Riggins(IRE) was backed to maintain his unbeaten record. However, he was held up and, when he needed openings towards the stands' side, they did not come for him and he was unable to get a clear passage. This run can be ignored. (op 6-4 tchd 11-10)

2084 BEST ODDS AT BETINTERNET.COM H'CAP 1m 4f
2:55 (2:55) (Class 3) (0-95,86) 3-Y-O **£9,714** (£2,890; £1,444; £721) **Stalls** Centre

Form RPR

06-1 **1** **Chiberta King**[26] 1408 3-8-10 **73** WilliamBuick 6 89
(A M Balding) *chsd ldr over 4f: remained handy: wnt 2nd again over 4f out: rdn to ld and edgd lft over 1f out: styd on u.p* 3/1[2]

1-11 **2** *1/2* **Petrovsky**[101] 389 3-9-9 **86** RoystonFfrench 7 101
(M Johnston) *led: rdn and hdd over 1f out: styd on u.p* 6/1

3-31 **3** *1 1/4* **Clowance House**[13] 1708 3-9-2 **79** TedDurcan 8 92+
(R Charlton) *chsd ldrs: rdn over 3f out: sn edgd lft and outpcd: r.o ins fnl f* 7/4[1]

-410 **4** *10* **Headline Act**[10] 1792 3-9-4 **81** RichardMullen 1 78
(J H M Gosden) *hld up: hdwy over 3f out: rdn and wknd 2f out* 9/2[3]

525- **5** *nk* **Orthology (IRE)**[196] 7142 3-9-5 **82** EddieAhern 5 79
(M H Tompkins) *hld up: hdwy over 3f out: rdn and wknd 2f out* 16/1

500- **6** *53* **Highway Magic (IRE)**[191] 7209 3-7-13 **67** MartinLane(5) 3 —
(A P Jarvis) *plld hrd and prom: trckd ldr 8f out to over 4f out: wknd over 3f out: t.o* 40/1

0-31 **7** *1/2* **Admirable Duque (IRE)**[12] 1747 3-9-3 **80** StephenDonohoe 4 —
(D J S Ffrench Davis) *s.i.s: hld up: pushed along 6f out: wknd 4f out: t.o* 8/1

2m 31.22s (-2.28) **Going Correction** +0.125s/f (Good) 7 Ran SP% **113.3**
Speed ratings (Par 103): **112,111,110,104,103 68,68**
toteswinger: 1&2 £3.50, 1&3 £2.20, 2&3 £2.20 CSF £20.72 CT £39.19 TOTE £4.20: £2.70, £2.10; EX 18.80 Trifecta £66.00 Pool: 196.49 - 2.20 winning units..
Owner The Pink Hat Racing Partnership **Bred** Watership Down Stud **Trained** Kingsclere, Hants
■ Stewards' Enquiry : William Buick caution: used whip with excessive frequency

FOCUS
A high-class handicap that has produced subsequent Group winners in its two previous runnings, although this time the top weight was 9lb below the race ceiling. It developed into a real war of attrition up front. Decent form from the first three, who finished clear.

NOTEBOOK
Chiberta King ◆ took on long-time leader Petrovsky well over 3f out and the pair battled away hammer and tongs until he asserted up the hill. He was 6lb higher than when scoring at this trip on his handicap debut but is clearly a progressive performer and tough to boot, so it will be no surprise if he is able to complete the hat-trick. (op 9-2)
Petrovsky lost very little in defeat after making the running into the wind for most of the trip. He had won his previous three starts on Polytrack at up to 1m3f but answered the questions about his ability to handle turf and this longer trip. He is another that looks worth keeping on the right side. (op 15-2 tchd 8-1)
Clowance House ran a strange race, being one of the first under pressure as the principals joined issue but, once his rider put his whip down over a furlong out, he ran on again, staying on really well up the hill so that he finished right on the heels of the first two. On this evidence he will appreciate an even longer distance. (op 15-8 tchd 2-1)
Headline Act was a drifter in the betting but that market signal looked far from justified as he moved into contention at around the half-mile pole. However, from that point he could not produce any more and was beaten in the dip. The trainer's representative later reported the colt was unsuited by the ground. Official explanation: trainer's rep said colt was unsuited by the good to firm (good in places) ground (op 11-4 tchd 5-1)
Orthology(IRE), a maiden with form at up to 1m2f, had questions to answer over this longer trip, and did not appear to get home, having been held up early. (op 20-1)

2085 BETINTERNET.COM STKS (HERITAGE H'CAP) 1m 6f
3:30 (3:30) (Class 2) (0-105,100) 4-Y-O+
£24,924 (£7,464; £3,732; £1,868; £932; £468) **Stalls** Centre

Form RPR

055- **1** **Victoria Montoya**[231] 6272 4-8-2 **78** WilliamBuick 11 92
(A M Balding) *a.p: chsd ldr over 3f out: led over 2f out: sn rdn: styd on* 11/2

5-00 **2** *4 1/2* **Record Breaker (IRE)**[13] 1696 5-8-12 **88** (b[1]) RoystonFfrench 4 96
(M Johnston) *mid-div: hdwy over 8f out: chsd ldr over 5f out: led 4f out: rdn and hdd over 2f out: no ex fnl f* 7/2[2]

1004 **3** *3 1/4* **Young Mick**[17] 1601 7-9-10 **100** (v) SebSanders 1 103
(G G Margarson) *hld up: hdwy over 3f out: rdn over 1f out: hung rt and no imp fnl f* 14/1

01-3 **4** *2 3/4* **Boz**[13] 1696 5-9-2 **92** DaneO'Neill 6 92
(L M Cumani) *hld up: hdwy over 6f out: rdn and wknd over 1f out* 3/1[1]

134- **5** *4 1/2* **Neve Lieve (IRE)**[13] 4-8-9 **85** TedDurcan 2 78
(M Botti) *chsd ldr tl over 7f out: rdn and wknd over 2f out: eased fnl f* 10/1

2-01 **6** *3 1/4* **Mighty Moon**[28] 1356 6-8-4 **80** PaulHanagan 12 69
(R A Fahey) *prom: rdn over 3f out: wknd over 2f out* 7/1

00-5 **7** *3* **Night Crescendo (USA)**[13] 1696 6-9-4 **94** JimCrowley 9 79
(Mrs A J Perrett) *hld up: rdn and wknd over 2f out* 5/1[3]

1-00 **8** *1* **Sereth (IRE)**[13] 1696 6-9-8 **98** MickyFenton 13 81
(B J Curley) *led: rdn: hdd and hung lft 4f out: sn wknd* 33/1

3202 **9** *76* **Wine 'n Dine**[27] 1383 4-9-0 **90** ShaneKelly 5 —
(G L Moore) *s.i.s: hld up: a in rr: bhd fnl 6f: t.o* 14/1

2m 57.01s (-1.49) **Going Correction** +0.125s/f (Good) 9 Ran SP% **117.1**
Speed ratings (Par 109): **109,106,104,103,100 98,96,96,52**
toteswinger: 1&2 £4.50, 1&3 £6.80, 2&3 £11.50 CSF £25.49 CT £258.52 TOTE £7.60: £2.50, £1.80, £2.40; EX 28.80 Trifecta £360.20 Part won. Pool: £486.88 - 0.50 winning units..
Owner Kingsclere Racing CLub **Bred** Kingsclere Stud **Trained** Kingsclere, Hants

FOCUS
A decent line-up for this valuable stayers' handicap although the field was reduced by almost a third due to withdrawals and a number of these had questions to answer. Again it developed into a battle between runners representing the trainers who contested the finish of the preceding race and the outcome was the same. Big improvement from the winner but some of her opponents were disappointing.

NOTEBOOK
Victoria Montoya ran on the better to give trainer and jockey a double. This was her third win at this distance and the cheekpieces no longer seem to be a requirement. Her trainer thought she may need this race having had a minor hold up and hopes she will make up into a Cesarewitch filly. (op 15-2 tchd 8-1)
Record Breaker(IRE) had dropped back to his last winning mark having been held since off higher and had blinkers on for the first time. He was quite keen in the headgear and came through to lead over a half a mile from home. He kept battling on but the filly always had the upper hand in the last 2f. (op 5-1)
Young Mick appears to stay this trip despite having never won beyond 1m4f. He was settled out the back but came through to chase the first two from the bushes without ever looking likely to reel them in. (tchd 11-1)
Boz is best known as a Polytrack performer but has won on a sound surface on turf. He stayed on at one pace in the closing stages and may be most effective at 1m4f. (tchd 7-2)
Neve Lieve(IRE) looks in the Handicapper's grip, being 10lb higher than when last seen in this company. That said, she ran creditably and a return to 2m should be in her favour. (op 9-1 tchd 14-1 and 16-1 in places)
Mighty Moon is a thorough stayer and lost his place soon after halfway over this shorter trip. He was keeping on at the end and this was clearly not a sufficient test for him. Races like the Ascot Stakes will be more his cup of tea. (op 5-1)

Night Crescendo(USA) had been well beaten on two previous attempts at this trip and his record suggested than easier ground would suit. However, this was still a disappointing effort as on previous course form he should have finished within a couple of lengths of Boz. (op 6-1 tchd 13-2)

2086 SPORTS BETTING AT BETINTERNET.COM H'CAP 7f
4:05 (4:06) (Class 4) (0-80,80) 4-Y-0+ **£5,180** (£1,541; £770; £384) **Stalls** Low

Form RPR
6-54 **1** **Oceana Blue**[12] 1733 4-8-12 **74**.....................................(t) WilliamBuick 4 85
(A M Balding) *a.p: rdn over 1f out: r.o to ld wl ins fnl f: edgd rt towards fin* **11/1**
0-24 **2** ½ **Purus (IRE)**[31] 1288 7-8-13 **75**.. DaneO'Neill 1 85+
(R A Teal) *hld up: hdwy and hmpd over 1f out: r.o wl ins fnl f: nt rch wnr* **14/1**
60-3 **3** 1 **Novellen Lad (IRE)**[14] 1682 4-9-0 **76**............................... EddieAhern 12 83
(E J Alston) *led: hdd over 4f out: remained w ldr tl rdn to ld over 1f out: hdd wl ins fnl f* **5/1[1]**
0-64 **4** nse **Pippbrook Gold**[46] 1048 4-8-4 **69**........................... JackMitchell(3) 3 76
(J R Boyle) *chsd ldrs: rdn and ev ch ins fnl f: styd on same pce* **20/1**
1411 **5** ½ **Shaded Edge**[7] 1876 5-8-3 **70**........................... SophieDoyle(5) 15 76
(D W P Arbuthnot) *a.p: rdn over 1f out: styd on same pce ins fnl f* **13/2[3]**
1401 **6** ¾ **Smarty Socks (IRE)**[28] 1343 5-9-4 **80**....................... JamieMoriarty 10 84
(P T Midgley) *s.i.s: hld up: r.o ins fnl f: nrst fin* **9/1**
1-60 **7** hd **Gold Express**[17] 1607 6-8-9 **71**.. TedDurcan 5 74
(P J O'Gorman) *s.i.s: hld up: racd keenly: r.o ins fnl f: nvr nrr* **33/1**
5-00 **8** hd **Lodi (IRE)**[19] 1572 4-8-13 **75**..(t) IanMongan 2 78
(J Akehurst) *prom: rdn: swtchd lft and hmpd rival over 1f out: styd on same pce* **16/1**
4200 **9** hd **Xpres Maite**[17] 1612 6-8-1 **68**.......................................(b) MartinLane(5) 13 70
(S R Bowring) *w ldr tl led over 4f out: rdn and hdd over 1f out: no ex ins fnl f* **14/1**
-500 **10** 1½ **Eastern Gift**[8] 1821 4-8-8 **77**.......................................(p) KylieManser(7) 9 75
(Miss Gay Kelleway) *hld up: sme hdwy fnl f: nvr trbld ldrs* **25/1**
010- **11** ½ **Without Prejudice (USA)**[204] 6952 4-9-4 **80**.................... ShaneKelly 8 77+
(J Noseda) *hld up in tch: lost pl whn hmpd over 2f out: n.d after* **8/1**
3234 **12** shd **Autumn Blades (IRE)**[1] 2050 4-8-11 **80**.................. NatashaEaton(7) 17 77
(A Bailey) *swtchd lft sn after s: hld up: racd keenly: nt clr run over 1f out: swtchd rt: n.d* **12/1**
6466 **13** 3½ **Count Ceprano (IRE)**[79] 691 5-9-1 **77**................................ LPKeniry 18 64
(C R Dore) *hld up: n.d* **25/1**
120/ **14** 2¾ **High Ambition**[615] 5253 6-8-7 **69**...................................(v) PaulHanagan 14 49
(R A Fahey) *hld up: hdwy 1/2-way: n.m.r and wknd over 1f out* **6/1[2]**
-603 **15** 1¾ **Papillio (IRE)**[22] 1493 4-8-11 **73**.................................... PatCosgrave 7 48
(J R Fanshawe) *prom: rdn and wknd fnl f* **11/1**
310- **16** 18 **Sadeek**[189] 7239 5-9-4 **80**.. RoystonFfrench 6 6
(B Smart) *chsd ldrs: rdn 1/2-way: wknd over 2f out* **14/1**

1m 26.29s (0.89) **Going Correction** +0.125s/f (Good) **16** Ran SP% **131.0**
Speed ratings (Par 105): **99,98,97,97,96 95,95,95,95,93 92,92,88,85,83 63**
toteswinger: 1&2 £21.80, 1&3 £9.40, 2&3 £13.00 CSF £160.90 CT £924.75 TOTE £10.10: £2.00, £4.00, £1.80, £4.50; EX 124.70.
Owner The C H F Partnership **Bred** The C H F Partnership **Trained** Kingsclere, Hants

FOCUS
A big field of mainly exposed handicappers and plenty were in with a chance in the dip. Sound if ordinary form.
Sadeek Official explanation: jockey said gelding had no more to give

2087 BETINTERNET.COM NOVICE STKS 6f
4:40 (4:40) (Class 4) 2-Y-O **£6,476** (£1,927; £963; £481) **Stalls** Low

Form RPR
1 **Niran (IRE)** 2-8-12 0.. SebSanders 4 75+
(C E Brittain) *chsd ldrs: rdn and ev ch fr over 1f out: r.o to ld wl ins fnl f* **8/1**
521 **2** nk **Shark Man (IRE)**[30] 1312 2-8-13 0.................................. JackMitchell(3) 2 78
(P J McBride) *w ldr: rdn over 1f out: led 1f out: sn edgd lft: hdd wl ins fnl f* **7/2[2]**
31 **3** 4 **King's Approach (IRE)**[21] 1511 2-9-2 0................................ PatDobbs 1 66
(R Hannon) *led: rdn 2f out: hdd 1f out: hmpd and no ex sn after* **11/8[1]**
4 1¾ **Gold Crusher (USA)** 2-8-12 0... EddieAhern 3 57
(R M H Cowell) *chsd ldrs: nt clr run over 2f out: sn swtchd rt: wknd over 1f out* **9/2[3]**
5 2 **Ginger Grey (IRE)** 2-8-12 0.. TedDurcan 6 54+
(S A Callaghan) *hld up: effrt over 2f out: wknd over 1f out* **13/2**
6 5 **Bubbly Bellini (IRE)** 2-8-12 0.. MickyFenton 5 36
(A Bailey) *dwlt: hld up: wknd over 1f out* **20/1**

1m 15.73s (3.53) **Going Correction** +0.125s/f (Good) **6** Ran SP% **111.7**
Speed ratings (Par 95): **81,80,75,72,70 63**
toteswinger: 1&2 £4.70, 1&3 £2.80, 2&3 £1.80 CSF £35.26 TOTE £10.80: £3.00, £2.20; EX 35.70.
Owner Saeed Manana **Bred** Miss Audrey F Thompson **Trained** Newmarket, Suffolk

FOCUS
A couple of sharp sorts set the standard in this novice stakes and they disputed the running for much of the way. The form has been rated at face value despite the slow time.

NOTEBOOK
Niran(IRE) overcame a jink at the start to join in on the run into the dip and proved just the strongest up the hill. A 40,000gns half-brother to several winners, he was a market drifter on this debut but his yard is going well at present and he should be able to go on from this, with a novice race likely to be next on the agenda. (op 9-2)
Shark Man(IRE) had made his debut in the Brocklesby but his two runs since (including a win) had been on Polytrack. He ran his race on this return to turf but, after getting the better of the favourite and slightly squeezing him out, he could not hold on near the finish. (op 4-1 tchd 9-2)
King's Approach(IRE) made the running up against the rail but he was struggling in the dip and looked held when slightly hampered by the runner-up. It did not appear to affect the result. (op 6-4 tchd 13-8, 5-4 and 7-4 in a place)
Gold Crusher(USA) was well backed for this debut and got a good lead from the principals. He could not pick up in the last 2f but will be better for the experience. (op 13-2 tchd 7-1 in a place)
Ginger Grey(IRE), a 52,000gns half-brother to winners at a mile, showed some ability but may be seen to better effect when qualified for nurseries later on. (op 6-1 tchd 11-2)

2088 BETINTERNET.COM APPRENTICE H'CAP 6f
5:15 (5:16) (Class 5) (0-75,75) 4-Y-0+ **£3,885** (£1,156; £577; £288) **Stalls** Low

Form RPR
3120 **1** **Dancing Maite**[7] 1887 4-9-1 **71**.............................. RussellKennemore 10 83
(S R Bowring) *chsd ldrs: rdn over 1f out: led ins fnl f: r.o* **16/1**
1653 **2** 1¾ **Milne Bay (IRE)**[30] 1313 4-8-8 **71**.....................................(t) LauraPike(7) 8 78
(D M Simcock) *led: rdn over 1f out: hdd ins fnl f: styd on* **11/1**
0323 **3** ¾ **Onceaponatime (IRE)**[19] 1572 4-8-9 **68**.......................... AmyBaker(3) 2 73
(M D Squance) *chsd ldrs: rdn and hung lft fr over 1f out: r.o* **17/2**
00-2 **4** ½ **Millfields Dreams**[11] 1775 10-8-3 **66**..............................(p) HollyHall(7) 13 69
(G C Bravery) *chsd ldrs: rdn over 1f out: styd on same pce ins fnl f* **14/1**
2223 **5** nk **War And Peace (IRE)**[33] 1248 5-9-0 **73**........................ AndreaAtzeni(3) 1 75
(Jane Chapple-Hyam) *hld up: hdwy over 2f out: rdn and edgd lft over 1f out: styd on* **9/2[2]**
6-36 **6** 1¼ **Mango Music**[16] 1627 6-9-5 **75**.. JackMitchell 6 73
(M Quinn) *swtchd lft sn after s: chsd ldrs: rdn over 2f out: no ex fnl f* **10/1**
03-5 **7** shd **Kingsgate Castle**[94] 499 4-8-6 **67** ow1........................ KylieManser(5) 7 65
(Miss Gay Kelleway) *hld up: hdwy fnl f: nt trble ldrs* **33/1**
4-42 **8** 1½ **Our Blessing (IRE)**[12] 1748 5-8-3 **64**.................... MatthewDavies(5) 15 57
(A P Jarvis) *chsd ldr: rdn over 1f out: wknd ins fnl f* **12/1**
00-0 **9** ¾ **Fantasy Believer**[21] 1518 11-8-9 **70**............................ JamieKyne(5) 10 61
(J J Quinn) *hld up: hdwy over 2f out: rdn and wknd fnl f* **8/1[3]**
-111 **10** 1 **Brunelleschi**[26] 1403 6-8-11 **74**.........................(b) JosephineBruning(7) 4 74+
(P L Gilligan) *s.i.s: hld up: racd keenly: hdwy whn hmpd over 1f out: nt rcvr* **4/1[1]**
1-34 **11** ¾ **Johnston's Glory (IRE)**[13] 1694 5-8-4 **65**..................(p) MartinLane(5) 9 50
(E J Alston) *hld up: rdn over 1f out: n.d* **8/1[3]**
-00 **12** 2 **Averoo**[33] 1258 4-7-13 **62**..(p) CarolineKelly(7) 5 41
(M D Squance) *s.i.s and edgd rt s: a bhd* **66/1**
30-4 **13** 3½ **Bahamian Bliss**[18] 1587 4-8-1 **62**.............................. DebraEngland(5) 16 30
(J A R Toller) *hld up: rdn over 1f out: a in rr* **14/1**
1-40 **14** 4½ **Kelamon**[26] 1403 5-8-13 **72**... WilliamCarson(3) 14 25
(S C Williams) *racd alone centre: w ldrs: rdn over 2f out: wknd over 1f out* **14/1**

1m 13.28s (1.08) **Going Correction** +0.125s/f (Good) **14** Ran SP% **126.4**
Speed ratings (Par 103): **97,94,93,93,92 90,90,88,87,86 85,82,78,72**
toteswinger: 1&2 £27.60, 1&3 £25.40, 2&3 £21.70 CSF £190.67 CT £1665.17 TOTE £19.10: £5.20, £5.50, £2.90; EX 303.90 Place 6: £985.48, Place 5: £702.85..
Owner Stuart Burgan **Bred** S R Bowring **Trained** Edwinstowe, Notts

FOCUS
An ordinary apprentice sprint handicap and the field were spread across half of the track. The form is rated around the third, with the first two boh better known as AW performers.
Onceaponatime(IRE) Official explanation: jockey said gelding hung left throughout
Mango Music Official explanation: trainer's rep said the mare was unsuited by the good to firm (good in places) ground
T/Plt: £1,147.10 to a £1 stake. Pool: £102,692.88. 65.35 winning tickets. T/Qpdt: £75.00 to a £1 stake. Pool: £4,728.54. 46.60 winning tickets. CR

1884 THIRSK (L-H)
Saturday, May 16

OFFICIAL GOING: Good (good to soft in places; 10.0)
Wind: Light across Weather: Overcast and showers

2089 EBF MARION GIBSON BROWN MEMORIAL MAIDEN FILLIES' STKS 5f
2:00 (2:05) (Class 4) 2-Y-O **£5,569** (£1,657; £828; £413) **Stalls** High

Form RPR
54 **1** **Tillys Tale**[11] 1764 2-8-7 0.. PaulPickard(7) 9 73
(P T Midgley) *chsd ldng pair: hdwy 1/2-way: rdn to chal 2f out: drvn to ld over 1f out: kpt on wl* **12/1**
5 **2** 1½ **Parbold Hill**[17] 1610 2-9-0 0.. PhillipMakin 12 68
(T D Barron) *wnt lft s: sn cl up: led 1/2-way: rdn along 2f out: drvn and hdd over 1f out: kpt on same pce* **5/2[1]**
0 **3** 1 **Lewyn**[21] 1504 2-9-0 0.. PaulMulrennan 7 64+
(K A Ryan) *swtchd rt s and sn chsng ldrs: effrt 2f out: rdn over 1f out: kpt on ins fnl f* **7/1[3]**
4 3 **Burnt Cream** 2-9-0 0.. TomEaves 4 53
(B Smart) *midfield: hdwy to chse ldrs after 2f: rdn along wl over 1f out and kpt on samepce* **10/1**
5 ¾ **Hathaway (IRE)** 2-9-0 0.. GrahamGibbons 10 51+
(W M Brisbourne) *sn outpcd in rr: hdwy 2f out: styd on wl appr last: nrst fin* **16/1**
6 3¼ **Silver In The Sand** 2-9-0 0... JoeFanning 5 39
(J D Bethell) *in tch: pushed along and edgd lft 1/2-way: sn wknd* **9/2[2]**
5 **7** hd **Sacred Star (IRE)**[8] 1847 2-8-7 0.................................. JohnCavanagh(7) 2 38
(M Brittain) *wnt lft s: racd wd and towards rr tl sme late hdwy* **20/1**
8 1¼ **Silver Linnet (IRE)** 2-9-0 0.. DavidAllan 1 34
(T D Easterby) *sltly hmpd s and sn swtchd rt: in rr tl hdwy 2f out: sn rdn and n.d* **14/1**
9 3 **Cygnet Committee (IRE)** 2-9-0 0.................................. TonyHamilton 8 23
(J S Wainwright) *s.i.s: a towards rr* **50/1**
0 **10** 2½ **Santas Pal**[21] 1521 2-8-11 0.. KellyHarrison(3) 14 14
(C J Teague) *led: rdn along and hdd 1/2-way: sn wknd* **33/1**
11 1½ **Chardonnay Star (IRE)** 2-9-0 0.. DanielTudhope 6 8
(C J Teague) *a bhd* **66/1**
00 **12** 1¾ **Amoureuse**[11] 1764 2-9-0 0.. PatrickMathers 13 2
(I W McInnes) *a in rr* **100/1**

60.65 secs (1.05) **Going Correction** +0.10s/f (Good) **12** Ran SP% **100.7**
Speed ratings (Par 92): **95,92,91,86,85 79,79,77,72,68 66,63**
toteswinger: 1&2 £7.90, 1&3 £27.60, 2&3 £4.20 CSF £28.51 TOTE £11.00: £1.80, £1.20, £2.20; EX 37.10.
Owner Mrs M Hills **Bred** M & S Hills **Trained** Westow, N Yorks

FOCUS
Following 11 millimetres of rain overnight the ground had eased to Good, Good to Soft in places. A modest fillies' maiden, despite a few being backed beforehand, and weakened further by the withdrawal of the second-favourite Fenella Rose who refused to enter the stalls (7/2, deduct 20p in the £ under R4). The higher-drawn horses held sway with all the action unfolding towards the stands' rail and not that many ever got involved. Not easy form to pin down, but the first three all look to have improved.

NOTEBOOK
Tillys Tale, who had shown some ability in her first two starts on quicker ground, was a springer in the market and those that supported her were proved right. Always up with the pace, she responded well to pressure to score and it may be that the easier ground brought about some improvement, but she isn't the biggest and may not have much in the way of scope. (op 20-1)
Parbold Hill, a promising fifth against the boys in a Pontefract maiden last month which has already produced a winner, was also handy from the start and did little wrong, but she couldn't match the winner late on. An ordinary maiden should come her way in due course. (op 11-4)
Lewyn, reportedly unsuited by the fast ground when a well-beaten second-favourite on her Haydock debut last month, was another to go off well backed and she was close enough if good enough for a long way, but she tended to hang about under pressure and although staying on at the line, was never doing quite enough. She couldn't have been feeling the ground this time and it may be that she was still a bit green. (op 10-1 tchd 11-1)

Burnt Cream ◆, who fetched £60,000 at the breeze-ups, is a half-sister to the useful Albaqaa. She deserves plenty for credit for this effort, as not only did she fare best of the newcomers but she also saw plenty of daylight on the outside from her low draw. (op 11-1 tchd 9-1)
Hathaway(IRE), a sister to the winning juvenile-sprinter Ocean Glory, was doing some fair late work from off the pace and looks sure to improve with experience. (op 33-1)
Silver In The Sand did show a bit of early pace before running green and dropping away. Out of a very useful performer at up to 1m2f, she looks one for later on. (op 4-1)
Cygnet Committee(IRE) Official explanation: jockey said filly hung left-handed throughout

2090 WHITBY MAIDEN STKS — 1m 4f
2:30 (2:32) (Class 5) 3-Y-O+ **£4,274** (£1,271; £635; £317) **Stalls** Low

Form				RPR
6	1		**Autumn Harvest**[14] 1681 5-9-13 0 ....(t) AndrewElliott 5 (A J McCabe) *dwlt and in rr: pushed along and hdwy 5f out: effrt on wd outside over 2f out: rdn to ld ent fnl f: sn drvn and edgd lft: kpt on strly towards fin* **66/1**	78
60-3	2	3/4	**Ruud Revenge (USA)**[14] 1681 3-8-10 72 .... SilvestreDeSousa 12 (Mrs D J Sanderson) *trckd ldrs: hdwy over 3f out: rdn to ld and edgd lft wl over 1f out: drvnand hdd ent fnl f: no ex last 75yds* **8/1**[3]	76
0-22	3	5	**Shemoli**[28] 1349 3-8-10 77 .... J-PGuillambert 7 (M A Jarvis) *cl up on inner: led after 1f: rdn along over 2f out: drvn and hdd wl over 1f out: sn one pce* **2/1**[1]	68
64-3	4	2 1/4	**Coiled Spring**[18] 1579 3-8-10 80 .... JoeFanning 8 (Mrs A J Perrett) *led 1f: cl up: rdn and ev ch over 2f out: drvn and wknd wl over 1f out* **2/1**[1]	64
2-2	5	2 3/4	**Taarab**[12] 1739 3-8-10 0 .... DO'Donohoe 10 (Saeed Bin Suroor) *chsd ldrs: rdn along 3f out: n.m.r 2f out: sn drvn and one pce* **11/2**[2]	60
54	6	1 3/4	**Jenny Potts**[23] 1474 5-9-8 0 .... PaulMulrennan 3 (L Lungo) *hld up in rr: gd hdwy over 5f out: chsd ldrs 3f out: rdn over 2f out and sn wknd* **12/1**	53
	7	7	**Lady Anne Nevill**[47] 5-9-5 0 .... KellyHarrison(3) 2 (C W Fairhurst) *a in rr* **200/1**	41
0-5	8	7	**Eborbrav**[12] 1739 3-8-10 0 .... DavidAllan 1 (T D Easterby) *a towards rr* **50/1**	35
3	9	1 3/4	**Johnny Rocket (IRE)**[12] 1739 4-9-10 0 .... NeilBrown(3) 4 (K A Ryan) *a in rr* **33/1**	33
0-	10	21	**Harvest Song (IRE)**[192] 7200 3-8-10 0 .... TomEaves 11 (Sir Michael Stoute) *in tch on inner: pushed along 1/2-way: rdn along over 4f out and sn wknd* **11/1**	—
00-0	11	10	**Kaikoura**[24] 1451 3-8-5 45 .... DuranFentiman 9 (T D Easterby) *midfield: hdwy and in tch 4f out: sn rdn and wknd* **100/1**	—
0	12	102	**My Bodyguard (FR)**[19] 1573 3-8-10 0 ....(t) ChrisCatlin 6 (H J L Dunlop) *s.i.s: a in rr: wl bhd fnl 4f* **80/1**	—

2m 37.03s (0.83) **Going Correction** +0.15s/f (Good)
WFA 3 from 4yo+ 17lb **12 Ran SP% 118.3**
Speed ratings (Par 103): **103,102,99,97,95 94,90,85,84,70 63,—**
toteswinger: 1&2 £66.40, 1&3 £66.40, 2&3 £7.00 CSF £529.35 TOTE £54.30: £8.10, £2.10, £1.40; EX 1170.80.
Owner C H McGhie **Bred** Juddmonte Farms Ltd **Trained** Averham Park, Notts

FOCUS
An ordinary maiden, but they went a decent enough pace. Despite the shock resut the level of the form seems fairly sound. The runner-up looks the best guide.
Autumn Harvest Official explanation: trainer had no explanation for the apparent improvement in form
Harvest Song(IRE) Official explanation: jockey said gelding was unsuited by the good (good to soft places) ground

2091 SANDS END H'CAP — 1m
3:05 (3:08) (Class 6) (0-65,65) 3-Y-O **£2,978** (£886; £442; £221) **Stalls** Low

Form				RPR
323-	1		**Hel's Angel (IRE)**[241] 6008 3-9-4 65 .... DO'Donohoe 18 (Mrs A Duffield) *bhd: gd hdwy on wd outside 3f out: rdn wl over 1f out: stron run to chal ent fnl f: drvn and styd on to ld last 50yds* **16/1**	71+
00-0	2	nk	**Mohawk Ridge**[23] 1470 3-8-10 57 .... PhillipMakin 14 (M Dods) *in tch: hdwy to chse ldrs 1/2-way: rdn to ld 2f out: sn edgd lft: drvn ent fnl f: hdd and no ex last 50yds* **12/1**	62
0-22	3	hd	**Diamond Daisy (IRE)**[21] 1531 3-9-1 62 .... PaulMulrennan 11 (Mrs A Duffield) *in tch: hdwy 3f out: chsd ldrs 2f out: rdn to chal over 1f out and evch tl drvn ins fnl f and no ex towards fin* **6/1**[2]	67
-366	4	1 3/4	**Steel Stockholder**[12] 1736 3-9-2 63 .... TWilliams 10 (M Brittain) *midfield: hdwy on outer 3f out: jnd ldrs 2f out: rdn to chal over 1f out and ev ch tl drvn and wknd wl ins fnl f* **14/1**	64
6-06	5	1 3/4	**Evening Sunset (GER)**[11] 1774 3-8-13 60 .... TonyCulhane 2 (M R Channon) *chsd ldrs on inner: effrt 3f out and sn rdn along: drvn wl over 1f out and kpt on same pce* **16/1**	57
004-	6	nk	**Eurotanz (IRE)**[161] 7577 3-9-3 64 .... TravisBlock 8 (H Morrison) *chsd ldrs: rdn along 3f out: drvn 2f out and kpt on same pce appr last* **8/1**[3]	60
40-0	7	nk	**Musical Maze**[21] 1531 3-8-11 65 .... PaulPickard(7) 12 (W M Brisbourne) *towards rr: hdwy over 2f out: sn rdn and kpt on wl fnl f: nrst fin* **20/1**	61
5-00	8	2 1/4	**Woteva**[21] 1531 3-9-3 64 ....(p) GrahamGibbons 3 (B Ellison) *midfield: hdwy and in tch 3f out: rdn to chse ldrs 2f out: sn drvn and no imp appr last* **14/1**	54
66-6	9	1/2	**Dreamonandon (IRE)**[23] 1470 3-9-2 63 .... PJMcDonald 13 (G A Swinbank) *bhd: hdwy wl over 2f out: styd on appr last: nt rch ldrs* **12/1**	52
0-05	10	2 1/4	**Wabi Sabi (IRE)**[32] 1270 3-8-13 60 .... DavidAllan 16 (N Tinkler) *stdd and swtchd to inner s: hld up and bhd tl sme late hdwy* **33/1**	44
00-5	11	1 3/4	**Billy Smart (IRE)**[28] 1363 3-8-6 58 ow2 .... GabrielHannon(5) 1 (D J S Ffrench Davis) *chsd ldrs: rdn along wl over 2f out and grad wknd* **14/1**	38
2-24	12	1/2	**Victorian Tycoon (IRE)**[23] 1470 3-9-4 65 .... ChrisCatlin 9 (E J O'Neill) *cl up on inner: led 1/2-way: rdn along 3f out: hdd 2f out and sn wknd* **3/1**[1]	44
561-	13	8	**Sampower Rose (IRE)**[238] 6112 3-9-4 65 .... DNolan 17 (D Carroll) *a towards rr* **25/1**	26
06-0	14	11	**Le Reve Royal**[12] 1736 3-8-10 57 .... DuranFentiman 6 (G R Oldroyd) *nvr bttr than midfield* **18/1**	—
055-	15	1 3/4	**Cobos**[190] 7227 3-8-11 65 .... AndrewHeffernan(7) 15 (Ms E L McWilliam) *led: pushed along and hdd 1/2-way: wknd wl over 2f out* **33/1**	—
50-6	16	19	**Kladester (USA)**[24] 1452 3-8-13 60 ....(t) TomEaves 7 (B Smart) *chsd ldrs: rdn along over 3f out and sn wknd* **33/1**	—
00-5	17	1	**Dark Echoes**[18] 1595 3-8-12 59 .... TonyHamilton 5 (Jedd O'Keeffe) *chsd ldrs: rdn along over 3f out and sn wknd* **12/1**	—
024-	18	4 1/2	**Miss Scarlet**[267] 5219 3-9-3 64 .... SilvestreDeSousa 4 (K A Ryan) *s.i.s: a bhd* **20/1**	—

1m 41.9s (1.80) **Going Correction** +0.15s/f (Good) **18 Ran SP% 132.7**
Speed ratings (Par 97): **97,96,96,94,93 92,92,90,89,87 85,85,77,66,64 45,44,39**
toteswinger: 1&2 £39.10, 1&3 £8.90, 2&3 £49.90 CSF £193.97 CT £1347.55 TOTE £13.80: £2.80, £4.60, £1.70, £5.10; EX 211.40.
Owner Mrs H Baines & Middleham Park Racing VII **Bred** S White **Trained** Constable Burton, N Yorks
■ Stewards' Enquiry : Paul Mulrennan one-day ban: used whip with excessive frequency (May 30)

FOCUS
A moderate, but very competitive handicap run at a good pace and there were virtually four in a line across the track half a furlong from home. Fairly sound form.
Victorian Tycoon(IRE) Official explanation: jockey said colt was unsuited by the good (good to soft places) ground
Miss Scarlet Official explanation: jockey said filly lost its action

2092 RUNSWICK BAY H'CAP — 1m
3:40 (3:40) (Class 4) (0-85,84) 3-Y-O **£5,569** (£1,657; £828; £413) **Stalls** Low

Form				RPR
1	1		**Mull Of Killough (IRE)**[33] 1250 3-9-0 80 .... LiamJones 5 (J L Spearing) *trckd ldrs: hdwy on outer 3f out: rdn to chal wl: over 1f out: drvn to ld ent fnl f: styd on wl towards fin* **9/4**[1]	86
13-4	2	2	**Big Apple Boy (IRE)**[19] 1559 3-9-4 84 .... AndrewElliott 4 (Jedd O'Keeffe) *led: rdn along over 2f out: drvn and edgd rt over 1f out: hdd ent fnl f: kpton same pce last 100yds* **11/4**[2]	85
03-4	3	3/4	**Makhaaleb (IRE)**[56] 914 3-8-8 74 .... ChrisCatlin 6 (B W Hills) *sn trcking ldr: effrt to chal over 2f out: sn rdn and ev ch: drvn appr fnl f and kpt on same pce* **4/1**[3]	73
1320	4	1	**Fesko**[12] 1744 3-9-0 80 .... JoeFanning 3 (M Johnston) *trckd ldrs on inner: shkn up wl over 2f out: rdn and sltly outpcd wl over 1f out: drvn and kpt on same pce fnl f* **11/4**[2]	77
-116	5	33	**Bickersten**[29] 1331 3-8-7 73 ow1 .... TonyCulhane 2 (M R Channon) *a in rr: rdn along and outpcd 3f out: sn eased* **10/1**	—

1m 41.39s (1.29) **Going Correction** +0.15s/f (Good) **5 Ran SP% 113.2**
Speed ratings (Par 101): **99,97,96,95,62**
toteswinger: 1&2 £5.10. CSF £9.03 TOTE £2.70: £2.00, £1.90; EX 8.60.
Owner Noel B Lawless **Bred** Owenstown Stud **Trained** Kinnersley, Worcs

FOCUS
The complexion of this race was changed by the non-participation of Roman Republic, who would probably have gone off a very short-priced favourite. The remaining quintet contested a very modestly run race, but in a race where a few took a grip the winning time was still over half a second quicker than the preceding three-year-old handicap. The winner stepped forward on his debut form.
Bickersten Official explanation: jockey said gelding hung right-handed throughout

2093 ROBIN HOODS BAY H'CAP — 6f
4:15 (4:15) (Class 3) (0-90,90) 4-Y-O+ **£8,159** (£2,428; £1,213; £606) **Stalls** High

Form				RPR
4-00	1		**Machinist (IRE)**[19] 1560 9-9-4 90 .... SilvestreDeSousa 1 (D Nicholls) *chsd ldrs on outer: rdn along 2f out: drvn and hdwy over 1f out: led ins fnl f: kpt on* **6/1**	98
0-22	2	1/2	**Legal Eagle (IRE)**[14] 1685 4-8-8 80 .... PaulQuinn 2 (D Nicholls) *cl up: led after 1f: rdn along 2f out: drvn over 1f out: hdd and nt qckn ins fnl f* **9/2**[3]	86
0600	3	3/4	**Osteopathic Remedy (IRE)**[14] 1684 5-9-0 86 .... PhillipMakin 9 (M Dods) *hld up in rr: effrt whn n.m.r wl over 1f out: hdwy appr last: nt clr run and swtchd lft ins fnl f: fin wl* **3/1**[1]	90
00-0	4	hd	**Cape Vale (IRE)**[34] 1227 4-8-11 83 .... AdrianTNicholls 7 (D Nicholls) *led 1f: cl up: effrt to chal 2f out: sn rdn and ev ch tl drvnand wknd ins fnl f* **7/2**[2]	86
5-00	5	1 1/4	**Kiwi Bay**[14] 1663 4-8-8 80 .... TomEaves 5 (M Dods) *trckd ldrs: effrt 2f out: sn rdn: kpt on u.p ins fnl f* **14/1**	79
00-3	6	hd	**Wyatt Earp (IRE)**[14] 1663 8-8-13 85 .... DaleGibson 4 (P Salmon) *chsd ldrs: rdn along 2f out: sn drvn and grad wknd* **10/1**	83
12-0	7	shd	**Speed Song**[18] 1582 4-8-13 85 .... LiamJones 10 (W J Haggas) *dwlt: sn chsng ldrs: rdn along 2f out: edgd lft over 1f out and sn wknd* **9/1**	83
3104	8	3/4	**Cornus**[7] 1864 7-8-5 80 ....(be) AndrewMullen(3) 6 (A J McCabe) *dwlt and in rr: swtchd outside and effrt 2f out: sn rdn and no imp ent fnl f* **15/2**	76

1m 12.02s (-0.68) **Going Correction** +0.10s/f (Good) **8 Ran SP% 117.2**
Speed ratings (Par 107): **108,107,106,106,104 104,104,103**
toteswinger: 1&2 £5.20, 1&3 £5.00, 2&3 £4.50 CSF £33.97 CT £98.19 TOTE £7.60: £2.30, £1.40, £1.70; EX 31.00.
Owner Berry & Gould Partnership **Bred** Ballymacoll Stud Farm Ltd **Trained** Sessay, N Yorks
■ Stewards' Enquiry : Paul Quinn two-day ban: used whip with excessive frequency (May 30-31)

FOCUS
A tight little sprint handicap, but despite what looked an honest pace the field finished in a bit of a heap and it resulted in a one-two-four for David Nicholls. The winner is rated to last year's form.

NOTEBOOK
Machinist(IRE) was always seeing plenty of daylight in a handy position on the outside of the field after having started from the number one stall, but he really knuckled down when asked and actually scored a shade comfortably. He hadn't won since July 2007, but had crept down the weights as a result and now that he has got his head in front again it wouldn't be a surprise to see him add to this in the near future. Official explanation: trainer said, regarding the apparent improvement in form shown, that the gelding had come to himself over the last three weeks. (op 8-1 tchd 5-1)
Legal Eagle(IRE), who 'won' the race on his side when runner-up over an inadequate 5f here earlier this month, soon tacked across from his low draw to take them along and he never stopped trying even after his stable companion had headed him. He deserves to go one better before too long. (tchd 4-1)
Osteopathic Remedy(IRE) had been well beaten in his first four starts this season and was racing over a trip this short for the first time since July 2007, but he was down to a mark 1lb lower than for his last win and significant market support suggested that much better was expected. Having raced in last place for most of the way, he found his stride from the furlong pole and may have finished even closer had he not had to change course well inside the last furlong. It would be pushing things to say he was unlucky, however. (op 5-1 tchd 11-2)
Cape Vale(IRE), less exposed than most and proven on soft ground, would have been suited by the easing conditions and appeared to run his race having been handy from the start against the stands' rail. (op 9-2 tchd 10-3)
Kiwi Bay ◆, well beaten dropped back to this trip in his first two starts this season, never got into it but he was staying on at the line and he will be interesting when put back over an extra furlong. (op 16-1)

Wyatt Earp(IRE), an encouraging third on his debut for the yard and return to action at Doncaster earlier this month, had every chance but didn't really step up from that previous effort and he is still 5lb above his last winning mark. (op 7-1 tchd 11-1)
Speed Song, well beaten in her only previous try over this trip, was very weak in the market and never got into the race. (op 9-2 tchd 10-1)
Cornus, who is still 5lb higher than when successful on much quicker ground over course and distance last month, could never make his presence felt following a tardy start. (tchd 8-1)

2094 SCARBOROUGH H'CAP 5f
4:50 (4:51) (Class 2) (0-100,100) 4-Y-0+ **£12,045** (£3,584; £1,791; £894) **Stalls** High

Form RPR
025- **1** **Biniou (IRE)**[161] 7576 6-8-8 **90** .... GrahamGibbons 8 101
(R M H Cowell) *trckd ldrs: effrt and nt clr run over 1f out: swtchd rt and rdn ent fnl f: qcknd to ld nr fin* **14/1**
30-0 **2** *nk* **Captain Dunne (IRE)**[19] 1560 4-8-13 **95** .... DavidAllan 4 105
(T D Easterby) *sn led on stands rail: rdn along wl over 1f out and sn edgd lft: drvn and hungbdly lft ins fnl f: hdd and nt qckn nr fin* **7/2**[2]
0-34 **3** *1 ½* **Wi Dud**[20] 1543 5-8-13 **100** ....(b) AmyRyan(5) 9 105
(K A Ryan) *swtchd lft after s: trckd ldrs: effrt and hdwy 2f out: rdn over 1f out: one pce and hld whn n.m.r ins fnl f* **11/8**[1]
0650 **4** *2 ¼* **Stoneacre Lad (IRE)**[2] 2012 6-8-4 **86** oh1 ....(b) PatrickMathers 2 82
(Peter Grayson) *wnt lft s and towards rr: hdwy on wd outside 2f out: sn rdn and kpton ins fnl f: nvr nr ldrs* **14/1**
154- **5** *hd* **Kay Two (IRE)**[185] 7290 7-8-7 **89** ....(p) SaleemGolam 6 85
(R J Price) *cl up: rdn along 2f out: drvn over 1f out and grad wknd* **10/1**
505 **6** *1 ¼* **Haajes**[38] 1189 5-8-5 **87** ....(t) JoeFanning 5 78
(J Balding) *a towards rr* **7/1**[3]
600- **7** *5* **Inter Vision (USA)**[238] 6104 9-8-11 **93** .... DanielTudhope 10 66
(A Dickman) *a in rr* **16/1**
000- **8** *3 ¼* **Desert Lord**[248] 5793 9-9-4 **100** ....(b) DO'Donohoe 3 62
(K A Ryan) *prom: rdn along over 2f out: sn wknd and eased* **16/1**

58.86 secs (-0.74) **Going Correction** +0.10s/f (Good) **8** Ran SP% **111.0**
Speed ratings (Par 109): **109,108,106,102,102 100,92,87**
toteswinger: 1&2 £8.30, 1&3 £4.50, 2&3 £2.60 CSF £58.98 CT £109.25 TOTE £15.40: £3.00, £1.60, £1.10; EX 67.20.
Owner Stennett, Dasmal, Rix, Barr, Mrs Penney **Bred** Kilfrush And Knocktoran Studs **Trained** Six Mile Bottom, Cambs
■ Stewards' Enquiry : Graham Gibbons one-day ban: used whip with excessive frequency (June 15th)

FOCUS
A solid pace for this hot sprint handicap, as it should be for the money. The winner is rated to his best form over the last couple of years, with the second one of the few progressive runners in the race.

NOTEBOOK
Biniou(IRE), having his first start since December, is probably better over an extra furlong but the recent rain would have been in his favour as would the strong pace. After having sat in the slipstream of the leader for most of the way, once switched and asked to pick up a furlong from home he produced plenty and managed to wear down the runner-up in the shadow of the post. (op 17-2)
Captain Dunne(IRE), a long last of nine on his Newcastle return last month, performed much better this time. Having set the strong gallop, he eventually edged away from the stands' rail, thereby giving the winner a gap to aim for, and was very unfortunate to have the prize snatched from him late on. He is obviously very speedy and may go for the big 5f handicap at Epsom on Derby Day, where the track ought to suit him. (op 9-2 tchd 5-1)
Wi Dud, back down to probably his optimum trip, raced in mid-division early. Produced to hold every chance, he did his best but couldn't match the front pair in the closing stages. As game and consistent as he is, he is still without a win since the 2006 Flying Childers and is beginning to look a bit of a 'twilight' horse. (op 6-4)
Stoneacre Lad(IRE), well held since winning on the Kempton Polytrack last June and reappearing just two days after finishing ninth in a handicap at York, ran a blinder from 1lb wrong especially as he was rather marooned down the wide outside, but his stable's ongoing lack of winners is an obvious concern. (op 16-1)
Kay Two(IRE), having his first start since November, wouldn't have minded the rain at all and he showed up for a long way. He should come on for this. (tchd 9-1)
Haajes, not at his best lately but down to a mark just 2lb higher than for his last two wins, could never land a blow this time. (op 8-1 tchd 6-1)
Inter Vision(USA) was always struggling and almost certainly needed this first run in eight months. (tchd 20-1)
Desert Lord, running in his first handicap since winning the Vodafone Dash off 8lb lower in June 2006, was also returning from eight months off but he dropped right away after showing early speed. (op 11-1)

2095 FILEY H'CAP 5f
5:25 (5:25) (Class 4) (0-85,84) 4-Y-0+ **£5,569** (£1,657; £828; £413) **Stalls** High

Form RPR
20-2 **1** **Rasaman (IRE)**[29] 1334 5-8-10 **81** .... AmyRyan(5) 5 88
(K A Ryan) *cl up: effrt 2f out: rdn to ld ent: rdr lost irons ins fnl f: edgd lft and kpt on gamely* **5/1**[3]
00-0 **2** *hd* **Divine Spirit**[14] 1685 8-8-7 **73** .... DaleGibson 3 79
(M Dods) *chsd ldrs: hdwy 2f out: rdn over 1f out: styd on to chal ins fnl f and ev ch tl nt qckn nr fin* **20/1**
-315 **3** *¾* **Steelcut**[14] 1672 5-8-9 **80** .... FrederikTylicki(5) 4 84
(R A Fahey) *in tch: hdwy 2f out: sn rdn and kpt on ins fnl f* **7/2**[1]
30-0 **4** *¾* **Equuleus Pictor**[14] 1685 5-8-7 **78** .... JackDean(5) 10 79
(J L Spearing) *led: rdn along 2f out: drvn and hdd ent fnl f: wknd towards fin* **4/1**[2]
3621 **5** *1 ½* **Liberty Ship**[11] 1768 4-8-4 **70** oh1 ....(bt) JoeFanning 1 65
(J D Bethell) *wnt lft s and in rr: rdn along and hdwy 1/2-way: styd on appr fnl f: nrst fin* **6/1**
44-0 **6** *¾* **Glasshoughton**[14] 1685 6-8-7 **73** .... PJMcDonald 11 66
(M Dods) *hld up in tch: nvr able to chal* **12/1**
3-36 **7** *1* **Discanti (IRE)**[19] 1565 4-8-13 **79** ....(t) DavidAllan 9 68
(T D Easterby) *hld up: a in rr* **5/1**[3]
60-0 **8** *nk* **Green Park (IRE)**[14] 1684 6-9-4 **84** .... DNolan 6 72
(D Carroll) *chsd ldrs: rdn along 1/2-way: sn wknd* **7/1**
3264 **9** *½* **Woodcote (IRE)**[22] 1494 7-8-4 **70** ....(vt) PatrickMathers 2 56
(Peter Grayson) *s.i.s: a towards rr* **20/1**

59.73 secs (0.13) **Going Correction** +0.10s/f (Good) **9** Ran SP% **119.6**
Speed ratings (Par 105): **102,101,100,99,96 95,94,93,92**
toteswinger: 1&2 £19.60, 1&3 £5.20, 2&3 £8.60 CSF £100.15 CT £393.65 TOTE £6.40: £2.10, £4.40, £1.80; EX 85.40 Place 6: £30.26, Place 5: £18.40..
Owner Royston Vasey **Bred** Rasana Partnership **Trained** Hambleton, N Yorks

FOCUS
A fair sprint handicap and although the winning time was 0.87 seconds slower than the preceding 86-100 handicap, there was a downpour before this contest which may have had an effect. It proved to be a dramatic event too. Sound form, the winner turning around recent C/D form with the second.

Discanti(IRE) Official explanation: jockey said gelding was denied a clear run
T/Plt: £22.10 to a £1 stake. Pool: £58,674.64. 1,935.08 winning tickets. T/Qpdt: £8.90 to a £1 stake. Pool: £2,797.00. 231.75 winning tickets. JR

1207 MAISONS-LAFFITTE (R-H)
Saturday, May 16

OFFICIAL GOING: Soft

2096a PRIX DE MESNIL LE ROI (PRIX PONTARME) (LISTED RACE) (C&G) (STRAIGHT) 1m (S)
3:20 (3:22) 3-Y-0 **£26,699** (£10,680; £8,010; £5,340; £2,670)

RPR
1 **Fuisse (FR)**[48] 1028 3-9-2 .... DBoeuf 4 113+
(Mme C Head-Maarek, France)
2 *6* **Diableside (FR)**[6] 1917 3-9-2 .... OPeslier 1 99
(Y Durepaire, Spain)
3 *1 ½* **Faylan (FR)**[22] 3-8-12 ....(b) JVictoire 6 92
(C Baillet, France)
4 *3* **Principe Uromonte (IRE)** 3-9-2 .... MGuyon 5 89
(Mario Hofer, Germany)
5 *snk* **Thousand Miles (IRE)**[33] 1257 3-8-12 .... CSoumillon 3 85
(P W Chapple-Hyam) *led to 2f out: sn btn (3/1)* **3/1**[1]

1m 36.2s (-6.10) **5** Ran SP% **25.0**
PARI-MUTUEL: WIN 2.10; PL 1.10, 1.70; SF 5.60.
Owner Alec Head **Bred** Alec & Mme Ghislaine Head **Trained** Chantilly, France

NOTEBOOK
Thousand Miles(IRE), who was smartly into his stride, was soon at the head of affairs. Struggling by the two-furlong marker, he gradually fell back to finish last.

BADEN-BADEN (L-H)
Saturday, May 16

OFFICIAL GOING: Good to soft

2097a BENAZET-RENNEN (GROUP 3) 6f
5:05 (5:25) 3-Y-0+ **£29,126** (£12,136; £4,854; £2,427)

RPR
1 **Contat (GER)**[36] 6-9-6 .... RJuracek 10 105
(P Vovcenko, Germany) *racd on outside: 6th st: hdwy 2f out: hrd rdn over 1f out: drvn to ld on line* **43/10**[2]
2 *nse* **Etoile Nocturne (FR)**[20] 5-8-13 .... WMongil 3 98
(W Baltromei, Germany) *pressed ldr: 2nd st: drvn to ld over 1f out: ct on line* **106/10**
3 *1 ½* **Key To Pleasure (GER)**[20] 9-9-6 .... HGrewe 8 101
(Mario Hofer, Germany) *hld up: last to st: swtchd outside and hdwy fr wl over 1f out: one pce fnl 100yds* **15/1**
4 *½* **Smooth Operator (GER)**[193] 7186 3-8-11 .... AHelfenbein 2 99
(Mario Hofer, Germany) *rrd up in stall bef r: 7th st: rdn 2f out: kpt on u.p to take 4th wl ins fnl f* **1/1**[1]
5 *½* **Florentiner (GER)**[20] 6-9-6 .... AGoritz 5 98
(A Trybuhl, Germany) *trckd ldr: 3rd st: 2nd appr fnl f: one pce* **18/1**
6 *3 ½* **Aturo (FR)**[20] 5-9-6 .... FilipMinarik 9 87
(C Sprengel, Germany) *chsd ldrs: 4th st: one pce fnl 2f* **97/10**
7 *1 ½* **New Fan**[20] 5-9-6 .... ADeVries 7 83
(D Baltromei, Germany) *5th st: sn btn* **83/10**
8 *1 ¼* **Best Joking (GER)**[23] 1576 4-9-3 .... DPorcu 1 76
(W Hefter, Germany) *led to over 1f out* **15/1**
9 *8* **Lips Arrow (GER)**[27] 1394 4-9-3 .... ASuborics 4 52
(Andreas Lowe, Germany) *8th st: a bhd* **26/5**[3]

69.97 secs (-0.32)
WFA 3 from 4yo+ 9lb **9** Ran SP% **131.5**
(including ten euro stakes): WIN 53; PL 23, 36, 37; SF 701.
Owner Stall Sunny **Bred** Klaus Laakman **Trained** Germany

PIMLICO (L-H)
Saturday, May 16

OFFICIAL GOING: Dirt course - fast; turf course - firm

2098a BLACKBERRY PREAKNESS STKS (GRADE 1) (DIRT) 1m 1f 110y(D)
11:15 (11:19) 3-Y-0 **£458,333** (£152,778; £84,028; £45,833; £22,917)

RPR
1 **Rachel Alexandra (USA)**[15] 1763 3-8-9 .... CHBorel 13 118+
(Steven Asmussen, U.S.A) **9/5**[1]
2 *1* **Mine That Bird (USA)**[14] 1688 3-9-0 .... MESmith 2 121
(Bennie L Woolley Jr, U.S.A) **66/10**[3]
3 *½* **Musket Man (USA)**[14] 1688 3-9-0 .... ECoa 3 120
(Derek S Ryan, U.S.A) **111/10**
4 *2 ½* **Flying Private (USA)**[14] 1688 3-9-0 ....(b) AGarcia 10 115
(D Wayne Lukas, U.S.A) **25/1**
5 *1 ½* **Big Drama (USA)**[49] 3-9-0 .... JRVelazquez 1 112
(David Fawkes, U.S.A) **104/10**
6 *2 ¼* **Papa Clem (USA)**[14] 1688 3-9-0 .... RBejarano 7 108
(Gary Stute, U.S.A) **141/10**
7 *nk* **Terrain (USA)**[35] 1225 3-9-0 .... JRose 6 108
(Albert Stall Jr, U.S.A) **26/1**
8 *¾* **Luv Gov (USA)**[14] 3-9-0 ....(b) HJTheriotII 4 106
(D Wayne Lukas, U.S.A) **241/10**
9 *2 ¼* **General Quarters (USA)**[14] 1688 3-9-0 .... JRLeparoux 8 102
(Thomas R McCarthy, U.S.A) **163/10**
10 *7 ¾* **Friesan Fire (USA)**[14] 1688 3-9-0 ....(b) GSaez 5 87
(J Larry Jones, U.S.A) **9/1**
11 *7 ¼* **Pioneerof The Nile (USA)**[14] 1688 3-9-0 .... GKGomez 9 73
(Bob Baffert, U.S.A) **61/10**[2]
12 *6 ¼* **Tone It Down (USA)**[14] 3-9-0 ....(b) KDesormeaux 12 62
(William Komlo, U.S.A) **239/10**

13 ½ **Take The Points (USA)**[42] 3-9-0 ....(b) EPrado 11 61
(Todd Pletcher, U.S.A) **18/1**
1m 55.08s (-0.51) **13** Ran SP% **123.2**
PARI-MUTUEL (Including $2 stake): WIN 5.60; PL (1-2) 4.60, 6.60;SHOW (1-2-3) 3.60, 4.80, 5.00; SF 39.20.
Owner Stonestreet Stables LLC & Harold McCormick **Bred** Dolphus C Morrison **Trained** USA
■ Rachel Alexandra became the first filly to win this since 1924, and only the fifth in the race's history.

NOTEBOOK
Rachel Alexandra(USA), the brilliant Kentucky Oaks winner, was allowed her chance against the colts after being sold to the same owner/trainer combination as Curlin, and she duly confirmed herself a special talent. Given a no-nonsense ride by Borel, who chose her over the runner-up, she displayed good early speed to get across from the outside post and helped force a strong pace. She had to work hard to hold on, but it's to her credit that she was able to sustain her effort, not least considering her rider felt she didn't really act on the track. One cannot help but think she will be vulnerable if taking her chance in the Belmont Stakes, considering she has been kept so busy and her stamina for 1m4f is questionable, but no decision regarding her participation has yet been made.
Mine That Bird(USA), just as when causing a major shock in the Kentucky Derby, was given an exaggerated hold-up ride, only this time he was unable to hug the inside rail. Once again he benefited greatly from many of the pace horses faltering, and he might even have won had he not been slightly checked and forced to switch wide at the top of the lane, although it's hard to argue he was unlucky considering how fast the winner was forced to go early. While this proves his win in the first leg of the Triple Crown was no fluke, one cannot help but think his achievements over the past fortnight flatter him somewhat, for the classic generation has been depleted by injury and, the filly apart, it's a division currently lacking real stars. Everything about him - run style/breeding - suggests he'll relish the stamina test of the Belmont Stakes, but he will still have something to prove if the race is run at an even gallop, as opposed to the mad dash he's encountered the last twice.
Musket Man(USA), the Kentucky Derby third, confirmed himself a very decent colt with another solid run in defeat. He is likely to skip the Belmont and wait for the $1million Haskell Invitational at his home base of Monmouth Park.
Flying Private(USA) appeared a no-hoper on all known form, but he justified his legendary trainer's high opinion of him with a superb effort. He'll now be pointed at the Belmont Stakes, a race Lukas claims "has been our goal since day one".
Big Drama(USA), who got cast in his box the night before the race, and was upset in the stalls just before the off, ran very well over a trip that was always likely to stretch him. It would be no surprise were he to make up into a high-class sprinter.
Friesan Fire(USA) was seemingly not over his Kentucky Derby troubles and has had a nightmare couple of weeks. He's a very talented colt and it is to be hoped that he will bounce back after a break.
Pioneerof The Nile(USA), the Derby second, seemed to run flat.

1847 RIPON (R-H)
Sunday, May 17

OFFICIAL GOING: Good to soft (7.2)
The rail round the bend from the back straight to the home straight was moved out 5 metres, but the impact on advertised distances was not notified.
Wind: Light, half behind Weather: Sunny periods

2099 LEYBURN MAIDEN STKS 6f
2:10 (2:13) (Class 5) 2-Y-O **£3,885** (£1,156; £577; £288) **Stalls** Low

Form RPR
4 1 **Kylladdie**[8] 1866 2-9-3 0 .... MickyFenton 15 78+
(T P Tate) *wnt rt s: racd far side: mde all: rdn clr over 1f out and styd on strly: 1st of 6 in gp* **7/2**[2]
2 2 ¾ **We'll Deal Again** 2-9-3 0 .... DaleGibson 3 70+
(M W Easterby) *dwlt and in rr stands' side: hdwy 2f out: swtchd rt and rdn wl over 1f out: styd on strly ins fnl f: 1st of 10 in gp* **66/1**
3 ½ **Yeadon** 2-8-12 0 .... FrederikTylicki(5) 16 68+
(R A Fahey) *slttly hmpd s: chsd ldrs far side: rdn along 2f out: kpt on same pce 2nd of 6 in gp* **15/2**
0 4 1 ¼ **Bluie**[12] 1764 2-9-3 0 .... AdrianTNicholls 5 65
(D Nicholls) *prom stands' side: effrt 2f out: rdn to ld that gp wl over 1f out: kpt on same pce: 1st of 10 in gp* **16/1**
5 4 **Durham Reflection (IRE)** 2-9-3 0 .... TomEaves 13 53
(J Howard Johnson) *swtchd to far side: chsd wnr: rdn along 2f out and sn one pce: 3rd of 6 in gp* **11/1**
6 5 **Venture Girl (IRE)** 2-8-12 0 .... DavidAllan 4 33
(T D Easterby) *dwlt: sn in tch stands' side: hdwy 1/2-way: swtchd rt and rdn 2f out: sn no imp: 3rd of 10 in gp* **40/1**
0 7 ½ **Bateau Bleu**[32] 1277 2-9-3 0 .... GregFairley 17 36
(P C Haslam) *slttly hmpd s and a towards rr far side: 4th of 6 in gp* **25/1**
60 8 1 ¼ **Polly Macho (IRE)**[8] 1867 2-8-12 0 .... RichardEvans(5) 8 32
(P D Evans) *wnt rt s: towards rr stands' side: hdwy 2f out: sn rdn and n.d: 4th of 10 in gp* **7/1**[3]
9 ¾ **Mighty Clarets (IRE)** 2-9-3 0 .... PaulHanagan 11 30
(R A Fahey) *in tch stands' side: rdn along 2f out: n.d: 5th of 10 in gp* **8/1**
53 10 1 ½ **Sharp Eclipse**[13] 1735 2-9-3 0 .... NCallan 1 26
(K A Ryan) *led stands' side gp: rdn along over 2f out: sn drvn: hdd & wknd over 1f out: 6th of 10 in gp* **5/2**[1]
11 5 **Suzys Dream (IRE)** 2-8-12 0 .... JamieMoriarty 7 6
(P T Midgley) *chsd ldrs stands' side: rdn along 1/2-way: sn wknd: 7th of 10 in gp* **50/1**
0 12 shd **Fairys In A Storm (IRE)**[32] 1275 2-8-12 0 .... LeeEnstone 2 5
(P T Midgley) *cl up stands' side: rdn along 1/2-way: sn wknd: 8th of 10 in gp* **66/1**
13 2 **Powerful Pierre** 2-9-3 0 .... TonyHamilton 18 4
(Jedd O'Keeffe) *chsd ldng pair far side: rdn along 1/2-way: sn wknd: last of 6 in gp* **33/1**
14 10 **Reel Love** 2-9-3 0 .... JerryO'Dwyer 14 —
(J R Holt) *a in rr far side: 5th of 6 in gp* **66/1**
15 3 ¾ **Dispol Antonio (IRE)** 2-9-3 0 .... PhillipMakin 12 —
(P T Midgley) *s.i.s and a bhd stands' side: 9th of 10 in gp* **16/1**
16 6 **Foricherforpoorer** 2-8-12 0 .... JoeFanning 9 —
(N Tinkler) *a bhd stands' side: 10th of 10 in gp* **50/1**
1m 15.41s (2.41) **Going Correction** +0.30s/f (Good) **16** Ran SP% **123.9**
Speed ratings (Par 93): **95,91,90,89,83 77,76,74,73,71 65,64,62,48,43 35**
toteswinger: 1&2 £55.50, 1&3 £10.20, 2&3 £58.30 CSF £245.67 TOTE £4.60: £1.80, £15.80, £2.70; EX 285.60 TRIFECTA Not won..
Owner P J Martin **Bred** Horizon Bloodstock Limited **Trained** Tadcaster, N Yorks
■ Stewards' Enquiry : Greg Fairley
Richard Evans two-day ban: used whip when out of contention (May 31, Jun 11)

FOCUS
The field split into two groups, the smaller on the far side but eventually containing the comfortable winner who built on his debut effort. Many of the field looked green in the paddock.
NOTEBOOK
Kylladdie had the benefit of a run and he confirmed the promise of that debut. Bolting clear in the last furlong, he probably handled the ground better than most but still looks a fair sort for the time of year. (op 3-1, tchd 4-1 in a place)
We'll Deal Again ◆, a first runner for the smart Polytrack performer Gentleman's Deal, is a half-brother to three winners up to 7f. Having done some excellent work to lead home the stands' side group, he looks sure to win a similar event and, if he takes after his sire, he will improve with age too.
Yeadon, a £20,000 Fraam newcomer whose dam won twice over 5f as a juvenile, is a half-brother to three winners up to 1m2f. He chased home the winner on the far side, eventually drifting towards the stands' side group as he tired, but there was plenty to like about this first effort. (op 17-2 tchd 6-1)
Bluie, who cost only £5,000 as a yearling but is bred to sprint, showed a lot more speed than on his debut. He is heading in the right direction and would not be unsuited by a drop to 5f. (op 12-1)
Durham Reflection(IRE), a Pastoral Pursuits gelding out of a sprinter, is bred to win over this trip and should do better next time. (op 14-1 tchd 9-1)
Venture Girl(IRE), a 33,000 euros yearling, is by the 2,000 Guineas winner Footstepsinthesand but there is stamina on her dam's side and she is one for the longer term. (op 33-1)
Sharp Eclipse did not get home over the extra furlong on softer ground under front-running tactics, but he has enough pace to make his mark in nurseries. Official explanation: jockey said colt had no more to give (tchd 3-1)

2100 WOODEN SPOON STIRRING CHILDREN'S SMILES CHARITY (S) STKS 6f
2:40 (2:41) (Class 6) 2-Y-O **£2,590** (£770; £385; £192) **Stalls** Low

Form RPR
123 1 **Transfixed (IRE)**[11] 1783 2-8-9 0 .... RichardEvans(5) 10 58
(P D Evans) *trckd ldrs: hdwy to chal 2f out: rdn to ld over 1f out: drvn ins fnl f: kpt on* **5/2**[1]
3 2 nk **Cassidy K**[15] 1680 2-8-9 0 .... TomEaves 2 55+
(J Howard Johnson) *hld up: hdwy 2f out: effrt whn nt clr run over 1f out: rdn and styng on whn hmpd ins fnl f: styd on strly towards fin* **12/1**
4 3 ½ **Lairy (IRE)**[8] 1884 2-9-0 0 .... AdrianTNicholls 1 56
(D Nicholls) *chsd ldrs: swtchd rt and hdwy over 1f out: sn rdn and wandered: drvn and hung lft ins fnl f: kpt on u.p towards fin* **9/1**
0 4 1 ¼ **Mary Helen**[22] 1504 2-8-9 0 .... TGMcLaughlin 8 47
(W M Brisbourne) *towards rr: hdwy on outer 2f out and sn rdn: drvn to chse ldrs ent fnl f: sn one pce* **5/1**[3]
34 5 1 ¼ **Blue Rum (IRE)**[17] 1624 2-8-9 0 ....(p) PatrickDonaghy(5) 9 48
(P C Haslam) *cl up: rdn to ld over 2f out: drvn and hdd over 1f out: wknd ins fnl f* **7/1**
061 6 1 ¾ **Dispol Kabira**[9] 1827 2-9-0 0 .... PhillipMakin 5 43
(P T Midgley) *s.i.s: sn in tch: hdwy 2f out: swtchd rt and rdn over 1f out: drvn and wknd ins fnl f* **11/4**[2]
4632 7 10 **Musiara**[15] 1680 2-8-9 0 .... TonyCulhane 3 8
(M R Channon) *led: rdn along 3f out: hdd over 2f out and sn wknd* **13/2**
8 17 **Bertie Black** 2-9-0 0 ....(v[1]) DavidAllan 7 —
(N Tinkler) *s.i.s: a wl bhd* **33/1**
1m 17.13s (4.13) **Going Correction** +0.30s/f (Good) **8** Ran SP% **118.4**
Speed ratings (Par 91): **84,83,82,81,79 77,63,41**
toteswinger: 1&2 £11.40, 1&3 £6.30, 2&3 £20.30 CSF £34.48 TOTE £3.30: £1.70, £2.50, £2.60; EX 35.10 Trifecta £124.00 Pool: £316.92 - 1.89 winning units..The winner was bought in for 6,500gns. Lairy was claimed buy Mr M. Harris for £6,000.
Owner Mrs I M Folkes **Bred** Rathasker Stud **Trained** Pandy, Monmouths
■ Stewards' Enquiry : Richard Evans three-day ban: used whip with excessive frequency (Jun 1-3)
FOCUS
A smaller field than the first, and they all stayed close to the stands' rail.
NOTEBOOK
Transfixed(IRE) again put her speed to good use and stuck it out really well over the extra furlong on the softer ground. She is pretty handy for a plater and, although essentially an early sort, she may yet make a successful switch to nurseries. (op 3-1)
Cassidy K, dropped to selling class after only one run, was far more effective at this level but she could not go the early pace and already looks as if 7f will suit. (op 17-2 tchd 8-1)
Lairy(IRE) also ran much better than on his debut and would have to be considered in similar company. He was unable to use his position against the rail, and then did not get the best of runs through, so can be rated a little better than this. (op 7-1)
Mary Helen, a half-sister to several winners up to 1m4f, cost only £1,000 as a yearling but she had run respectably in a maiden on her debut and this was another satisfactory effort. (op 13-2 tchd 9-2)
Blue Rum(IRE), stepping up from 5f, again showed early pace in first-time cheekpieces and is not without hope at this level if dropped back in trip. (op 10-1)
Dispol Kabira was the paddock pick but she could not repeat the big finish she summoned up when landing a 66-1 shock at Hamilton, reverting to the modest form she had shown in both races before then. (op 7-2 tchd 9-2)

2101 RIPON, YORKSHIRE'S GARDEN RACECOURSE H'CAP 1m
3:10 (3:11) (Class 2) (0-100,92) 4-Y-O£11,354 (£3,398; £1,699; £849; £423) **Stalls** High

Form RPR
50-0 1 ½ **Toto Skyllachy**[13] 1722 4-8-8 **82** ow2 .... MickyFenton 14 89
(T P Tate) *chsd ldr: hdwy 3f out: led over 2f out and sn rdn: drvn appr fnl f: kpt on gamely tl hdd and no ex last 50yds: fin 2nd, ½l, awrdd r* **16/1**
0446 2 2 ¼ **Exit Smiling**[5] 1952 7-8-8 **82** .... JamieMoriarty 8 84
(P T Midgley) *hld up: stdy hdwy 3f out: rdn to chse ldng pair ent fnl f: sn drvn and one pce: fin 3rd, ½l & 2¼l: plcd 2nd* **10/1**
20-2 3 3 ¾ **Webbow (IRE)**[15] 1684 7-8-12 **91** .... Louis-PhilippeBeuzelin(5) 1 84
(N Tinkler) *hld up in rr: hdwy on wd outside over 2f out: rdn over 1f out: kpt on ins fnl f: nrst fin: fin 4th, plcd 3rd* **10/1**
45-3 4 2 **Stevie Thunder**[22] 1527 4-9-1 **89** .... StephenDonohoe 7 78
(Ian Williams) *in tch: hdwy 3f out: rdn to chse ldrs 2f out: sn drvn and wknd appr fnl f: fin 5th, plcd 4th* **5/1**[2]
0-52 5 4 **Jewelled Dagger (IRE)**[16] 1649 5-8-12 **86** ....(b) LeeEnstone 13 65
(I Semple) *led: rdn along over 3f out: drvn and hdd over 2f out: grad wknd: fin 6th, plcd 5th* **7/1**
2-00 6 3 ¼ **Mangham (IRE)**[15] 1684 4-9-4 **92** .... PhillipMakin 6 64
(D H Brown) *prom: rdn along 3f out: sn drvn and wknd* **11/2**[3]
1-25 7 2 ¼ **Charlie Tipple**[15] 1684 5-8-10 **84** ....(p) TomEaves 12 51
(T D Easterby) *t.k.h: chsd ldrs: rdn along wl over 2f out and sn wknd* **10/1**
2012 8 4 **Tartan Gigha (IRE)**[6] 1942 4-9-0 **88** .... JoeFanning 5 46
(M Johnston) *midfield: effrt on outer over 3f out: sn rdn and wknd* **8/1**
20-5 9 7 **Mujaadel (USA)**[16] 1649 4-8-10 **84** .... AdrianTNicholls 11 25
(D Nicholls) *s.i.s: a in rr* **9/1**
0/P- 10 12 **Runswick Bay**[395] 1428 4-8-6 **80** .... GregFairley 4 —
(G M Moore) *a towards rr* **50/1**

355- **D** **Tanto Faz (IRE)**[226] 6445 4-8-9 **83**........................ LiamJones 10 91
(W J Haggas) *in tch: hdwy on outer 3f out: rdn along and edgd rt 2f out: drvn to chal and put hd in air over 1f out: kpt on u.p to ld last 50yds* **4/1**[1]

1m 41.84s (0.44) **Going Correction** +0.30s/f (Good) **11** Ran SP% **120.8**
Speed ratings (Par 109): **108,106,102,100,96 93,91,87,80,68 109**
toteswinger: 1&2 £13.40, 1&3 £18.60, 2&3 £21.80 CSF £72.45 CT £623.43 TOTE £4.90: £2.10, £5.40, £4.10; EX 100.40 Trifecta £209.60 Part won. Pool: £283.27 - 0.10 winning units..
Owner P J Martin **Bred** Mrs G Slater **Trained** Tadcaster, N Yorks

FOCUS
A decent handicap run in a good pace in the conditions thanks to Jewelled Dagger, but as so often here it proved hard to come from too far back. Tanto Faz was subs. disq. due to a positive sample.

NOTEBOOK
Toto Skyllachy is on a handier mark these days after a disappointing 2008. This looks to be his trip and he is capable of winning a similar event if keeping up the good work.
Exit Smiling has struggled off higher marks since winning at Southwell in February, but he appreciated the give in the ground and is coming down to a more realistic weight granted similar conditions. (op 8-1)
Webbow(IRE) did reasonably well from his low stall, which left him to make his effort wide, but this mark seems a little harsh. He can win again if dropped a few pounds. (op 17-2 tchd 10-1)
Stevie Thunder is able enough but could do with a little help from the handicapper. (tchd 9-2 and 11-2)
Jewelled Dagger(IRE) took them along at a good gallop as usual but he did not see it out as well as he often does. Official explanation: jockey said gelding became unbalanced in the final furlong (op 6-1)
Mujaadel(USA) Official explanation: jockey said gelding missed the break
Tanto Faz(IRE), a market springer, had been headstrong in many of his previous races, and connections said the original intention had been to make the running, but that would have been inadvisable given the speed they were already going. As things turned out, the strong pace played into his hands. There were hopes that he might stay 1m4f this year, but that is probably best revised downwards to 1m2f now and, given his slightly crooked head carriage, he may be even more effective on a flatter track. He was subsequently disqualified. (op 11-1 tchd 12-1)

2102 C. B. HUTCHINSON MEMORIAL CHALLENGE CUP (FILLIES' H'CAP) 6f
3:40 (3:40) (Class 3) (0-95,95) 3-Y-O+ **£9,462** (£2,832; £1,416; £708; £352) **Stalls** Low

Form RPR
0-66 **1** **Ponty Rossa (IRE)**[15] 1682 5-9-0 **81**........................ DavidAllan 8 92
(T D Easterby) *prom on outer: hdwy over 2f out: rdn to chal over 1f out: sn drvn and kpt on to ld wl ins fnl f* **3/1**[1]
32-5 **2** *½* **Wise Melody**[14] 1699 4-9-6 **87**........................ LiamJones 5 97
(W J Haggas) *cl up: effrt wl over 2f out: rdn to ld 2f out: drvn over 1f out: hdd and no ex wl ins fnl f* **4/1**[2]
0-01 **3** *1 ½* **Pretty Bonnie**[13] 1733 4-9-4 **85**........................ KirstyMilczarek 4 90
(A E Price) *trckd ldrs: hdwy 2f out: rdn to chse ldng pair ent fnl f: kpt on* **14/1**
3002 **4** *5* **Carcinetto (IRE)**[8] 1880 7-9-9 **95**........................ RichardEvans(5) 1 84
(P D Evans) *chsd ldrs on inner: rdn along 2f out: drvn and no impression appr fnl f* **9/1**
-043 **5** *1 ½* **Angus Newz**[11] 1791 6-9-12 **93**........................ DarryllHolland 3 77
(M Quinn) *led: rdn along over 2f out: sn hdd: drvn over 1f out and sn wknd* **7/1**
50-6 **6** *2 ¼* **Caranbola**[29] 1368 3-8-11 **87**........................ AlanMunro 9 64
(M Brittain) *chsd ldrs on outer: effrt 2f out: sn rdn and no imp* **6/1**[3]
13-4 **7** *1 ¼* **Aunt Nicola**[15] 1677 3-8-11 **87**........................ TPQueally 10 60
(M L W Bell) *a towards rr* **7/1**
160- **8** *1 ¾* **Oriental Rose**[240] 6082 3-8-0 **85** oh15........................ PaulHanagan 6 43
(G M Moore) *a towards rr* **50/1**
0641 **9** *3* **Artistic License (IRE)**[5] 1965 4-9-2 **83** 6ex........................ TonyCulhane 2 41
(M R Channon) *midfield: rdn along 1/2-way: sn wknd* **12/1**
021- **10** *1 ½* **Misphire**[190] 7239 6-8-13 **80**........................ PhillipMakin 7 33
(M Dods) *a towards rr* **16/1**

1m 14.2s (1.20) **Going Correction** +0.30s/f (Good)
WFA 3 from 4yo+ 9lb **10** Ran SP% **116.5**
Speed ratings (Par 104): **104,103,101,94,92 89,88,85,81,79**
toteswinger: 1&2 £3.40, 1&3 £12.70, 2&3 £10.60 CSF £14.70 CT £144.53 TOTE £4.70: £1.50, £2.30, £4.10; EX 28.90 Trifecta £147.80 Pool: £219.74 - 1.10 winning units..
Owner The Lapin Blanc Racing Partnership **Bred** Jim McDonald **Trained** Great Habton, N Yorks
■ Stewards' Enquiry : David Allan caution: careless riding.

FOCUS
As with the second race, they all stayed near the stands' rail.

NOTEBOOK
Ponty Rossa(IRE), who was well backed, was operated on for a sinus problem last season, when she had just three low-key runs, but she has hinted at a return to form in two races this year. She took the eye beforehand and, on a handy mark, duly took full advantage on ground that connections expected to suit her. Lightly raced but now back in peak health, she will be interesting in similar races even off a higher mark. (op 4-1)
Wise Melody showed she can handle this sort of mark towards the end of last season and on this evidence she should find a race over this trip soon. (tchd 11-2)
Pretty Bonnie has been raised to a testing mark since winning at Kempton, but she goes well with cut in the ground and put in a solid effort in this better company. (op 11-1 tchd 16-1)
Carcinetto(IRE) brought some decent Listed form into the race, but she is better on fast ground or Polytrack. (op 11-1 tchd 8-1)
Angus Newz is a prolific and capable sprinter but she was 5lb above her highest winning mark. (op 9-2)
Caranbola, nowhere near the form she showed last year, continues to edge down the weights with little positive effect. (op 16-1 tchd 11-2)

2103 MIDDLEHAM TRAINERS ASSOCIATION H'CAP 1m 1f 170y
4:10 (4:10) (Class 4) (0-85,88) 4-Y-O+ **£5,180** (£1,541; £770; £384) **Stalls** High

Form RPR
2-11 **1** **Sirvino**[16] 1646 4-8-11 **78**........................ PhillipMakin 5 96+
(T D Barron) *hld up in tch: hdwy 3f out: effrt 2f out and nt clr run: swtchd rt and rdn to chse ldr ent fnl f: sn drvn and styd on: rdr dropped whip ins fnl 50yds: led last stride* **15/8**[1]
3-06 **2** *shd* **Wigwam Willie (IRE)**[13] 1722 7-8-11 **78**........................(tp) NCallan 4 96
(K A Ryan) *trckd ldrs: hdwy over 2f out: rdn to ld 1f out: drvn ins fnl f: hdd on line* **7/1**
00-4 **3** *9* **Dear Maurice**[15] 1666 5-8-13 **80**........................ SebSanders 3 80
(E A L Dunlop) *hld up in rr: stdy hdwy on outer 3f out: rdn to chal and ch 2f out: sn drvn and wknd ent fnl f* **15/2**
-362 **4** *nk* **Just Lille (IRE)**[9] 1850 6-9-7 **88**........................(p) TPQueally 7 87
(Mrs A Duffield) *prom: effrt 3f out: rdn to ld over 2f out: hdd and drvn wl over 1f out: wknd ent fnl f* **8/1**
4636 **5** *3 ¼* **Veiled Applause**[9] 1850 6-8-8 **82**........................ JamieKyne(7) 1 75
(J J Quinn) *hld up in tch: hdwy 4f out: rdn and ch 2f out: sn drvn and wknd* **6/1**[3]
0-61 **6** *1 ¾* **Arctic Cape**[9] 1830 4-8-9 **76**........................ JoeFanning 8 65
(M Johnston) *prom: hdwy 4f out: led over 3f out: sn rdn and hdd over 2f out: woon wknd* **9/2**[2]
520- **7** *30* **Coole Dodger (IRE)**[168] 7506 4-8-2 **74** ow1........................ LanceBetts(5) 6 —
(B Ellison) *led: rdn along 4f out: hdd over 3f out and sn wknd* **50/1**
6-00 **8** *59* **Goodbye Mr Bond**[22] 1507 9-8-10 **77**........................ DavidAllan 10 —
(E J Alston) *a in rr: outpcd and bhd fnl 3f* **8/1**

2m 6.89s (1.49) **Going Correction** +0.30s/f (Good) **8** Ran SP% **115.7**
Speed ratings (Par 105): **106,105,98,98,95 94,70,23**
toteswinger: 1&2 £4.60, 1&3 £4.60, 2&3 £8.80 CSF £15.96 CT £80.83 TOTE £2.70: £1.10, £2.10, £2.40; EX 17.60 Trifecta £74.00 Pool: £418.39 - 4.18 winning units..
Owner Theo Williams and Charles Mocatta **Bred** A W J Perry **Trained** Maunby, N Yorks

FOCUS
A lively pace set by Coole Dodger did not last long into the straight, following which there were several changes of leader.
Goodbye Mr Bond Official explanation: vet said gelding finished distressed

2104 RIPON-RACES.CO.UK MAIDEN STKS (DIV I) 1m 1f
4:40 (4:42) (Class 5) 3-Y-O **£3,561** (£1,059; £529; £264) **Stalls** High

Form RPR
4 **1** **Lady Luachmhar (IRE)**[18] 1611 3-8-12 0........................ SebSanders 11 76+
(Mrs A Duffield) *cl up: led over 3f out: jnd and rdn over 2f out: drvn ent fnl f and styd on gamely* **3/1**[2]
2 *¾* **French Applause (IRE)** 3-9-3 0........................ MickyFenton 2 79
(T P Tate) *chsd ldng pair: hdwy 4f out: cl up over 2f out: sn rdn and evefry ch tl drvn ins fnl f and no ex last 100yds* **25/1**
60 **3** *hd* **Red Cadeaux**[13] 1730 3-9-3 0........................ TGMcLaughlin 7 79+
(E A L Dunlop) *hld up and bhd: hdwy over 3f out: swtchd outside and rdn 2f out: styd on strly ins fnl f* **12/1**
4 *8* **Merchant Man** 3-9-3 0........................ DarryllHolland 12 60
(J D Bethell) *in rr: hdwy 4f out: rdn to chse ldrs over 2f out: sn drvn and no imp* **20/1**
6-5 **5** *12* **Albaasha (IRE)**[8] 1874 3-9-3 0........................ TPO'Shea 3 33
(Sir Michael Stoute) *towards rr and rdn along 1/2-way: hdwy over 3f out sn: drvn: edgd rt and nvr nr ldrs* **7/1**[3]
0 **6** *4* **Terrymene Prince**[15] 1681 3-8-10 0........................ GihanArnolda(7) 8 24
(L A Mullaney) *chsd ldrs: rdn along over 3f out: sn drvn and wknd* **125/1**
0-65 **7** *½* **Knock Three Times (IRE)**[14] 1691 3-8-5 49........................ JohnCavanagh(7) 1 17
(W Storey) *towards rr: hdwy over 3f out: sn rdn and wknd* **100/1**
5 **8** *4 ½* **Goswick**[22] 1522 3-8-12 0........................ PaulHanagan 6 7
(Micky Hammond) *a towards rr* **66/1**
9 *4 ½* **Willent** 3-9-3 0........................ TomEaves 10 —
(Miss J A Camacho) *chsd ldrs: rdn along 3f out: sn wknd* **100/1**
0-0 **10** *1 ½* **Winterfell**[27] 1406 3-8-12 0........................ AlanMunro 4 —
(C F Wall) *in tch: rdn along 4f out: wknd 3f out* **14/1**
6 **11** *3 ¾* **Flaming Blaze**[24] 1476 3-9-0 0........................ AndrewMullen(3) 13 —
(P C Haslam) *sn led: rdn along 4f out: hdd over 3f out and sn wknd* **100/1**
000- **12** *2 ¾* **Moon Warrior**[152] 7694 3-8-10 30........................ RichardRowe(7) 9 —
(C Smith) *a in rr* **200/1**
43-2 **13** *dist* **Akbabend**[44] 1101 3-9-3 78........................ JoeFanning 5 —
(M Johnston) *midfield: rdn along 4f out: wknd over 3f out and sn bhd: virtually p.u fnl 2f: dismntd after line* **4/5**[1]

1m 57.74s (3.04) **Going Correction** +0.30s/f (Good) **13** Ran SP% **121.8**
Speed ratings (Par 99): **98,97,97,90,79 75,75,71,67,66 62,60,—**
toteswinger: 1&2 £11.10, 1&3 £7.10, 2&3 £13.90 CSF £81.41 TOTE £4.80: £1.60, £3.30, £2.90; EX 84.80 TRIFECTA Not won..
Owner Mrs H Steel **Bred** Stone Ridge Farm **Trained** Constable Burton, N Yorks

FOCUS
A solid gallop soon had the field well strung out, but two of the three pacemakers filled the first two places.
Akbabend Official explanation: trainer said colt was unsuited by the good to soft ground

2105 RIPON-RACES.CO.UK MAIDEN STKS (DIV II) 1m 1f
5:10 (5:12) (Class 5) 3-Y-O **£3,561** (£1,059; £529; £264) **Stalls** High

Form RPR
-04 **1** **Highkingofireland**[22] 1522 3-8-12 0........................ MartinLane(5) 9 71
(K R Burke) *trckd ldrs: hdwy over 2f out: swtchd lft and rdn to ld wl over 1f out: drvn ins fnl f and kpt on gamely* **7/1**[3]
2-6 **2** *1 ¾* **Hukba (IRE)**[30] 1329 3-8-12 0........................ TPO'Shea 6 62
(E A L Dunlop) *prom: effrt over 2f out: rdn and ev ch over 1f out tl drvn and nt qckn wl ins fnl f* **8/11**[1]
0 **3** *6* **Countenance**[45] 1087 3-9-3 0........................ DarryllHolland 3 53
(W J Haggas) *led: rdn along 3f out: drvn 2f out: hdd wl over 1f out and grad wknd* **3/1**[2]
00- **4** *nk* **Maybeme**[247] 5859 3-8-5 0........................ JamieKyne(7) 10 48
(N Bycroft) *in tch: hdwy 3f out: sn rdn: drvn and kpt on fnl f: nrst fin* **25/1**
00 **5** *¾* **Bobeachway (IRE)**[8] 1888 3-9-3 0........................ PhillipMakin 12 51
(M Dods) *prom: rdn along and sltly outpcd 2f out: kpt on u.p ins fnl f* **25/1**
00-5 **6** *1 ¼* **Katie Girl**[27] 1410 3-8-12 45........................ LiamJones 5 43
(Mrs G S Rees) *chsd ldrs: hdwy on outer over 3f out: rdn over 2f out and ch tl drvn and wknd wl over 1f out* **66/1**
0-0 **7** *3 ¾* **Royal Bet (IRE)**[22] 1515 3-9-3 0........................ TPQueally 11 39
(M L W Bell) *bhd tl sme late hdwy* **20/1**
0 **8** *nk* **Go Alone (IRE)**[23] 1490 3-9-3 0........................ TomEaves 1 39
(G A Swinbank) *nvr bttr than midfield* **66/1**
9 *1* **Waltzalong (IRE)** 3-8-12 0........................ DavidAllan 7 31
(T D Easterby) *bhd tl sme late hdwy* **33/1**
0 **10** *28* **Callis Wood**[17] 1625 3-8-12 0........................ JamieMoriarty 8 —
(Ollie Pears) *a bhd* **100/1**
5-0 **11** *24* **Golden Kiss**[15] 1683 3-8-12 0........................ LeeEnstone 2 —
(Paul Murphy) *a bhd* **100/1**

1m 59.48s (4.78) **Going Correction** +0.30s/f (Good) **11** Ran SP% **115.8**
Speed ratings (Par 99): **90,88,83,82,82 81,77,77,76,51 30**
toteswinger: 1&2 £1.80, 1&3 £3.60, 2&3 £2.00 CSF £11.75 TOTE £8.60: £1.60, £1.10, £1.40; EX 16.80 Trifecta £58.50 Pool: £507.83 - 6.42 winning units. Place 6 £205.44, Place 5 £48.61.
Owner Cyril Wall **Bred** Cranford Stud **Trained** Middleham Moor, N Yorks

FOCUS
Just a fair gallop for the second division, so it was no surprise that yet again it paid not to be too far back.
T/Jkpt: £7,756.60 to a £1 stake. Pool: £136,561.22. 12.50 winning tickets. T/Plt: £436.50 to a £1 stake. Pool: £76,691.79. 128.24 winning tickets. T/Qpdt: £72.90 to a £1 stake. Pool: £5,157.08. 52.30 winning tickets. JR

2097 BADEN-BADEN (L-H)

Sunday, May 17

OFFICIAL GOING: Good

2113a BHF-BANK-MEILE (EX BADENER MEILE) (GROUP 3) 1m

5:05 (5:20) 3-Y-O+ **£29,126** (£12,136; £4,854; £2,427)

RPR

1 **Aspectus (IRE)**298 4320 6-9-0 ... AStarke 6 112
(T Mundry, Germany) *in tch: 5th st towards outside: rdn to ld over 1f out: strly pressed 100yds out: jst hld on* **49/10**3

2 *shd* **Konig Turf (GER)**31 7-9-0 ... FilipMinarik 8 112
(C Sprengel, Germany) *in rr early: hdwy on ins to go 4th st: hrd rdn over 1f out: virtually jnd wnr on ins 100yds out: jst hld* **89/10**

3 *2* **Liang Kay (GER)**21 4-9-6 ... WMongil 1 113
(Uwe Ostmann, Germany) *hld up: last st: styd on down outside u.p fr over 1f out: tk 3rd on line* **3/5**1

4 *hd* **Earl Of Fire (GER)**24 1576 4-9-2 ... JLermyte 2 109
(W Baltromei, Germany) *led: stdd pce after 3f: hdd over 1f out: kpt on at same pce: lost 3rd on line* **142/10**

5 *2* **Wiesenpfad (FR)**217 6692 6-9-4 ... ASuborics 7 106
(W Hickst, Germany) *in rr: 7th st on outside: kpt on fnl 1 1/2f: nt rch ldrs* **22/5**2

6 *7* **Abbashiva (GER)**21 4-9-4 ... THellier 3 90
(T Mundry, Germany) *towards rr early: hdwy on ins over 3f out: 2nd st: rdn and wknd over 1f out* **146/10**

7 *2* **Idolino (GER)**21 4-9-2 ... ADeVries 5 84
(J Hirschberger, Germany) *prom pulling hrd early: 3rd st: sn rdn and btn* **20/1**

8 *1 1/2* **Molly Max (GER)**37 5-9-0 ... DPorcu 4 78
(M Rulec, Germany) *4th early: 6th and rdn st: sn wknd* **166/10**

1m 40.71s (1.60) **8 Ran SP% 131.5**
(including 10 Euro stake): WIN 59; PL 18, 15, 12; SF 628.
Owner Gestut Roettgen **Bred** Gestut Rottgen **Trained** Germany

1903 CAPANNELLE (R-H)

Sunday, May 17

OFFICIAL GOING: Good to firm

2114a PREMIO TULLIO RIGHETTI SHADWELL STUD (LISTED RACE) 1m

3:45 (3:50) 3-Y-O **£27,184** (£11,961; £6,524; £3,262)

RPR

1 **Tray My Force (ITY)** 3-8-11 ... MDemuro 3 98
(V Caruso, Italy)

2 *snk* **Corioliss (IRE)**42 3-8-11 ... MBelli 4 97
(R Menichetti, Italy)

3 *1 1/2* **Royal Force (ITY)**273 3-8-11 ... GMarcelli 2 94
(A Renzoni, Italy)

4 *3* **Ad Honores (USA)**8 1904 3-9-2 ... CFiocchi 9 92
(R Menichetti, Italy)

5 *3* **Kiai** 3-8-11 ... GTemperini 1 80
(D Camuffo, Italy)

6 *3/4* **Khor Dubai (IRE)**198 7109 3-8-11 ... TedDurcan 10 78
(Saeed Bin Suroor) *hld up in 6th or 7th: hdwy to dispute 2nd 2f out: hung bdly lft: eased ins fnl f* **3/4**1

7 *nk* **Fontana (GER)** 3-8-11 ... URispoli 5 78
(F Boccardelli, Italy)

8 *2 1/2* **Ragtimeband (IRE)**49 3-8-11 ... FBranca 8 72
(S Onofrio, Italy)

9 *1 1/2* **Exilissi (IRE)** 3-8-11 ... MMonteriso 7 68
(P Meniconi, Italy)

10 *1 3/4* **Desert Cry (IRE)**8 1904 3-9-2 ... DVargiu 6 69
(B Grizzetti, Italy)

1m 37.5s (-2.30) **10 Ran SP% 57.1**
(including 1 Euro stake): WIN 5.03; PL 2.06, 3.87, 3.44; DF 35.78.
Owner Scuderia Incolinx **Bred** Azienda Agricola Loreto Luciani **Trained** Italy

NOTEBOOK
Khor Dubai(IRE), who was sent off at odds-on, hung violently left, right across the course, as he was about to take up the running. He was eased down afterwards.

2115a PREMIO PRESIDENTE DELLA REPUBBLICA AT THE RACES (GROUP 1) 1m 2f

4:55 (5:03) 4-Y-O+ **£131,068** (£57,670; £31,456; £15,728)

RPR

1 **Selmis**21 1575 5-9-2 ... MDemuro 7 115
(V Caruso, Italy) *cl up: 3rd st: rdn to ld over 1 1/2f out: r.o wl (361/100)* **18/5**2

2 *3/4* **Trincot (FR)**42 1144 4-9-2 ... (p) TedDurcan 1 113
(Saeed Bin Suroor) *hld up in rr: last st: rdn on outside over 2 1/2f out: 7th and no imp over 1f out: styd on wl fnl f to take 2nd on line (66-100F)* **7/10**1

3 *shd* **Freemusic (IRE)**14 5-9-2 ... GMarcelli 2 113
(L Riccardi, Italy) *hld up: 7th st: hdwy between rivals to go 2nd 1f out: lost 2nd on line* **57/10**3

4 *3/4* **Gimmy (IRE)**8 1903 5-9-2 ... SUrru 4 111
(B Grizzetti, Italy) *racd in 4th: n.m.r on ins over 2f out: swtchd lft 1 1/2f out: styd on wl fnl 150yds* **138/10**

5 *nk* **Prince Flori (GER)**182 7350 6-9-2 ... HGrewe 6 111
(S Smrczek, Germany) *midfield: 5th st: hrd rdn to go 4th 1f out: one pce* **81/10**

6 *3/4* **Estejo (GER)**154 7685 5-9-2 ... MTellini 3 109
(R Rohne, Germany) *led to over 1 1/2f out: one pce* **123/10**

7 *nk* **Storm Mountain (IRE)**14 6-9-2 ... DVargiu 8 109
(B Grizzetti, Italy) *racd in 6th: dropped to detached last over 2f out: nvr a factor* **78/10**

8 *nk* **Permesso**14 4-9-2 ... URispoli 5 108
(F & L Camici, Italy) *racd in 2nd: rdn and one pce fr 2f out: eased cl home* **57/10**3

2m 2.90s (-0.40) **8 Ran SP% 147.0**
WIN 4.61; PL 1.48, 1.16, 2.64; DF 8.72.
Owner Scuderia Incolinx **Bred** Scuderia Vittadini Srl **Trained** Italy

NOTEBOOK
Selmis, who gave his trainer his third win in this race, is now likely to head for the Eclipse Stakes at Sandown, a race his trainer has saddled two runners in before. Misil was sent off at 25-1 when beaten a short head by Opera House back in 1993, while Altieri was a 22-1 shot when taking third behind Oratorio in 2005, so his raiders should always be respected.
Trincot(FR), having his first start for Godolphin following success in the Group 2 Prix d'Harcourt, got going far too late and could only take second place right on the line.

KRANJI (L-H)

Sunday, May 17

OFFICIAL GOING: Good

2116a KRISFLYER INTERNATIONAL SPRINT (GROUP 1) 6f

12:50 (12:52) 3-Y-O+

£275,362 (£97,826; £49,517; £24,155; £9,662; £4,831)

RPR

1 **Sacred Kingdom (AUS)**16 6-9-0 ... (t) BrettPrebble 1 125+
(P F Yiu, Hong Kong) *prom: cl 4th on ins st: sn hdwy to chal: rdn and 2nd 1 1/2f out: r.o to ld 100yds out: drvn out* **23/5**2

2 *nk* **Rocket Man (AUS)**23 4-8-10 ... RFradd 9 121
(P Shaw, Singapore) *led 1 1/2f: cl 2nd st: led over 1 1/2f out: hdd 100yds out: kpt on* **1/1**1

3 *3 1/2* **Diabolical (USA)**50 1010 6-9-0 ... LDettori 7 113
(Saeed Bin Suroor) *midfield: disputing 6th st: pushed along and hdwy over 1 1/2f out: rdn to go 3rd 1f out: kpt on* **158/10**3

4 *3/4* **Waikato (NZ)**23 6-9-0 ... (b) JSaimee 13 111
(L Laxon, Singapore) *towards rr: 9th st: rdn and hdwy through field fr 1 1/2f out: wnt 4th 100yds out: nrst fin* **45/1**

5 *2 1/2* **Capablanca (AUS)**23 8-9-0 ... JohnPowell 5 104
(D Baertschiger, Singapore) *hld up: 11th and drvn st: wnt 4th briefly over 100yds out: one pce* **113/1**

6 *nk* **Mythical Flight (SAF)**154 7683 6-9-0 ... KShea 11 103
(S g Tarry, South Africa) *led after 1 1/2f: hdd over 1 1/2f out: sn rdn and one pce* **196/10**

7 *nk* **Fantastic Owners (AUS)**23 6-9-0 ... MGallagher 4 102
(B Dean, Singapore) *towards rr: 8th st: nvr in chalng position* **123/1**

8 *hd* **Takeover Target (AUS)**15 10-9-0 ... (p) JayFord 3 101
(Joe Janiak, Australia) *prom: 5th on outside st: rdn 1 1/2f out: sn one pce* **23/5**2

9 *1 3/4* **Inspiration (AUS)**16 6-9-0 ... (t) DarrenBeadman 12 96
(J Moore, Hong Kong) *prom: 3rd and pushed along st: rdn 1 1/2f out: sn one pce* **174/10**

10 *3/4* **Beau Brummell (NZ)**86 5-9-0 ... MichaelCahill 10 94
(D Hill, Singapore) *a towards rr* **51/1**

11 *1 1/4* **Madame Trop Vite (IRE)**247 5852 3-8-2 ... JimmyQuinn 2 85
(K A Ryan) *midfield: pushed along 1/2-way: disputing 6th st: sn rdn: wknd appr fnl f* **27/1**

12 *nk* **Lim's Fighter (AUS)**23 7-9-0 ... (b) DAzis 6 89
(J Meagher, Singapore) *first to show: settled in tch: 6th 1/2-way: no imp fr appr st* **80/1**

13 *3 1/2* **Prime Defender**50 996 5-9-0 ... MichaelHills 14 78
(B W Hills) *pushed along s fr wdst draw: a towards rr* **70/1**

67.80 secs (67.80)
WFA 3 from 4yo+ 9lb **13 Ran SP% 114.0**
(including S$5 stake): WIN 28.00; PL 9.00, 5.00, 16.00; DF 11.00.
Owner Sin Kang Yuk **Bred** Mrs N F Calvert & Estate Of The Late A M Calvert **Trained** Hong Kong

NOTEBOOK
Sacred Kingdom(AUS), racing outside Hong Kong for the first time, had the best of the draw and travelled well in behind the pace-setting Mythical Flight. He just got the better of local hero Rocket Man following a prolonged duel, and his rider actually said that the six-year-old was idling close home. It is possible that he might come over to Ascot for the Golden Jubilee, but he will need supplementing at a cost of £45,000 for that race.
Rocket Man(AUS), unbeaten in in seven previous starts over the course and distance, ran a super race but just bumped into a champion sprinter who looked back to his best.
Diabolical(USA), third in the Golden Shaheen on his last start, ran well back on turf but couldn't cope with the first two.
Takeover Target(AUS), who won this race last year, was disappointing, failing to pick up when his rider pulled him out to challenge. It's worth noting the gelding was off his food only a few days before the race.
Madame Trop Vite(IRE) had a good draw but faced a very stiff task on her first outing of the season.
Prime Defender, who has yet to win in Group company, had the worst of the draw here.

2117a SINGAPORE AIRLINES INTERNATIONAL CUP (GROUP 1) 1m 2f

1:40 (1:42) 3-Y-O+

£826,087 (£293,478; £148,551; £72,464; £28,986; £14,493)

RPR

1 **Gloria De Campeao (BRZ)**50 1013 6-9-0 ... TJPereira 6 120
(P Bary, France) *cl 2nd tl led 4f out: rdn 1 1/2f out: jst hld on* **24/1**

2 *hd* **Presvis**21 1554 5-9-0 ... RyanMoore 12 120+
(L M Cumani) *hld up in last: pushed along and hdwy 3f out: 8th on ins st: rdn and swtchd to centre 1 1/2f out: fin strly* **8/5**1

3 *2 3/4* **Bankable (IRE)**50 1011 5-9-0 ... (t) KShea 3 114
(M F De Kock, South Africa) *towards rr: hdwy 4f out: 4th st: pushed along to go 3rd 1 1/2f out: styd on steadily* **98/10**

4 *1 1/2* **Pompeii Ruler (AUS)**22 7-9-0 ... CraigNewitt 2 111
(Mick Price, Australia) *prom: 4th 1/2-way: 2nd st: drvn to chal over 1f out: nt pce of wnr: no ex fnl 150yds* **36/5**

5 *nk* **Tascata Sorte (JPN)**85 5-9-0 ... YIwata 10 110
(H Fujiwara, Japan) *in tch: 5th st: drvn over 1 1/2f out: styd on at one pce: jst missed 4th* **92/10**

6 *1 1/2* **Sarrera (AUS)**22 9-9-0 ... (t) CraigAWilliams 1 107
(Michael Moroney, Australia) *prom: 3rd st: sn rdn: styd on u.p tl no ex fr 1f out* **25/1**

7 *3 1/2* **Balius (IRE)**50 1011 6-9-0 ... (b) LDettori 8 100
(Saeed Bin Suroor) *midfield: disputing 6th st: rdn over 1 1/2f out: no imp* **16/5**2

8 *2* **The Hornet (AUS)**28 5-9-0 ... JMoreira 4 96
(D Dragon, Australia) *towards rr: 9th st: nvr a factor* **33/1**

9 ½ **El Dorado (JPN)**[28] 5-9-0 ....(tp) RonnieStewart 7 95
(H Takaoka, Singapore) *towards rr: 11th and rdn st: nvr a factor* **95/1**
10 ½ **Top Spin (AUS)**[23] 6-9-0 .... JohnPowell 11 94
(L Laxon, Singapore) *towards rr: 10th st: n.d* **58/1**
11 16 ½ **Ricoco (BRZ)**[28] 5-9-0 ....(b) RFradd 9 61
(P Shaw, Singapore) *prom: 3rd 1/2-way: pushed along on outside over 3f out: disputing 6th and no imp st* **28/1**
12 *dist* **Jay Peg (SAF)**[50] 1011 6-9-0 ....(v) AntonMarcus 5 —
(H J Brown, South Africa) *led to 4f out: wknd: last and eased appr st* **58/10**[3]

1m 59.2s (119.20) **12** Ran SP% **125.2**
WIN 125.00; PL 28.00, 7.00, 14.00; DF 77.00.
Owner Stefan Friborg **Bred** Haras Santarem **Trained** Chantilly, France

NOTEBOOK
Gloria De Campeao(BRZ), runner-up in the Dubai World Cup on his previous start, showed he is just as effective on turf. Given a positive ride and kicked on as they turned out of the back straight, he just held on from the fast-finishing runner-up.
Presvis, successful in the QEII Cup in Hong Kong last time out, had the widest draw to contend with and was always going to need a little luck in running. Held up out the back as usual, his rider initially tried to challenge up the rail, but was forced to switch wide when his path was blocked. He came with a strong late run up the straight, but the line came just too soon. He is now likely to be given a nice break and brought back for either the Breeders' Cup or an autumn campaign in the Far East.
Balius(IRE) never really threatened and was very disappointing.

2026 LONGCHAMP (R-H)
Sunday, May 17

OFFICIAL GOING: Soft

2118a PRIX VICOMTESSE VIGIER (GROUP 2) 1m 7f 110y
2:20 (2:22) 4-Y-0+ **£71,942** (£27,767; £13,252; £8,835; £4,417)

RPR
1 **Americain (USA)**[21] 1552 4-8-11 .... OPeslier 6 109
(A Fabre, France) *racd in 2nd: rdn 1 1/2f out: drvn to ld jst ins fnl f: r.o wl* **14/1**
2 1 **Pointilliste (USA)**[21] 1552 6-8-11 .... ACrastus 7 106
(E Lellouche, France) *led tl hdd jst ins fnl f: kpt on gamely tl no ex fnl 60yds* **5/2**[2]
3 *hd* **Bannaby (FR)**[28] 6-9-2 .... JGrosjean 8 110+
(M Delcher-Sanchez, Spain) *hld up in rr: 6th st: hdwy down outside to go 4th under 2f out: r.o steadily* **5/1**[3]
4 2 **La Boum (GER)**[21] 1552 6-8-8 .... TJarnet 3 100
(Robert Collet, France) *racd in 3rd or 4th on ins: 4th st: 3rd whn n.m.r on ins 1 1/2f out: one pce appr fnl f* **12/1**
5 6 **Emporio (GER)**[17] 5-8-11 .... DBoeuf 1 97
(F Vermeulen, France) *hld up: 5th st: sn rdn and outpcd* **66/1**
6 15 **Mores Wells**[23] 5-8-11 .... CSoumillon 4 86+
(R Gibson, France) *racd in 5th: 7th st: sn rdn and btn* **14/1**
7 1 ½ **Coastal Path**[13] 1762 5-9-0 .... SPasquier 5 86+
(A Fabre, France) *in tch: cl 3rd on outside st: rdn and btn 2f out: sn wknd and eased* **5/6**[1]
8 20 **Perdiccas (FR)**[21] 4-8-11 .... AlexisBadel 2 64+
(J-C Bertin, France) *last thrght: t.o fr over 4f out* **250/1**

3m 28.78s (7.28) **Going Correction** +0.65s/f (Yiel)
WFA 4 from 5yo+ 1lb **8** Ran SP% **122.7**
Speed ratings: **107,106,106,105,102 94,94,84**
PARI-MUTUEL: WIN 7.60; PL 2.70, 2.00; DF 13.70.
Owner Wertheimer Et Frere **Bred** Wertheimer Et Frere **Trained** Chantilly, France

NOTEBOOK
Americain(USA) benefited from a change of tactics and completely reversed last month's form with the runner-up, clearly appreciating the cut in the ground. On this occasion he was well up from the start before going into the lead at the furlong marker and running on well. He will not be going to Ascot for the Gold Cup, but will be campaigned over similar distances in France. Races like the Prix Maurice de Nieuil and the Prix Kergorlay at Deauville are both possible targets.
Pointilliste(USA) tried to make all the running and was at the head of affairs until the furlong marker, but although he battled on well this testing ground did not see him at his best. He could still be sent to Ascot for the Gold Cup, and his owner's colours were carried to success in the race at York in 2005.
Bannaby(FR), last year's Cadran winner, put up an excellent performance in defeat as he was giving two kilos to the winner and runner-up. Given a very patient and gentle ride towards the tail of the field early on, he came with a progressive late run up the centre of the track and was staying on well at the finish. This outing must have brought him on and the target is the Ascot Gold Cup, when hopefully there will be a little cut in the ground.
La Boum(GER) is a consistent filly and she ran another good race here. Settled just off the pace, she ran on bravely in the final two furlongs without ever threatening the first three.
Coastal Path Official explanation: jockey said horse was unsuited by the soft ground

2119a MONTJEU COOLMORE PRIX SAINT-ALARY (GROUP 1) (FILLIES) 1m 2f
2:50 (2:54) 3-Y-0 **£138,689** (£55,485; £27,743; £13,859; £6,942)

RPR
1 **Stacelita (FR)**[64] 3-9-0 .... C-PLemaire 3 117+
(J-C Rouget, France) *mde all: clr fr 2f out: unchal* **5/4**[1]
2 6 **Article Rare (USA)**[35] 1237 3-9-0 .... ACrastus 1 105
(E Lellouche, France) *racd in 3rd: pushed along to go 2nd over 2f out: drvn over 1 1/2f out: no imp* **8/1**[3]
3 2 ½ **Ana Americana (FR)**[21] 1550 3-9-0 .... GMosse 6 100+
(P Demercastel, France) *hld up in last: rdn and hdwy fr over 1 1/2f out to go 3rd 1f out* **12/1**
4 6 **Excellent Girl**[16] 1657 3-9-0 .... CSoumillon 7 88
(Y De Nicolay, France) *racd in 5th: pushed along 2f out: sn rdn: tk 4th but n.d* **16/1**
5 1 **Plumania**[34] 1267 3-9-0 .... OPeslier 4 86
(A Fabre, France) *racd in 2nd: pushed along ent st: rdn and 3rd over 2f out: sn no ex* **7/4**[2]
6 10 **Just Pegasus (USA)**[45] 3-9-0 .... SPasquier 5 66
(S Wattel, France) *racd in 6th: nvr a factor* **33/1**
7 5 **Villa Molitor (FR)**[34] 1267 3-9-0 .... TJarnet 2 56
(F Rohaut, France) *racd in 4th: drvn st: sn btn* **14/1**

2m 10.66s (6.66) **Going Correction** +0.65s/f (Yiel) **7** Ran SP% **115.1**
Speed ratings: **110,105,103,98,97 89,85**
PARI-MUTUEL: WIN 2.30; PL 1.80, 3.30; SF 18.00.
Owner Ecurie Monastic **Bred** J -P Dubois **Trained** Pau, France

NOTEBOOK
Stacelita(FR), given a confident ride from the start, put up the most impressive performance of the season to date, but conditions were very much in her favour as she loves to get her toe in. Immediately taken into the lead, she had this Group 1 event at her mercy even before the straight, and she simply drew further and further away from her struggling opponents. Now unbeaten in four starts, she will be difficult to topple from her pedestal in testing conditions. She now goes for the Prix de Diane and connections will be hoping that Chantilly lives up to its reputation of being the chamber pot of Paris.
Article Rare(USA), equipped with cheekpieces, had absolutely no chance with the winner but still ran a decent race. She liked the cut in the ground and there is a possibility of her turning up for the Diane.
Ana Americana(FR), last in the early stages, began to make a forward move early in the straight and was never challenged for third place.
Excellent Girl stayed on one-paced on the rail in the straight and took fourth position at the furlong marker.

2120a PRIX D'ISPAHAN (GROUP 1) 1m 1f 55y
3:20 (3:25) 4-Y-0+ **£138,689** (£55,485; £27,743; £13,859; £6,942)

RPR
1 **Never On Sunday (FR)**[42] 1144 4-9-2 .... C-PLemaire 2 118+
(J-C Rouget, France) *towards rr: 7th st: pushed along and hdwy on rail 2f out: led 1f out: styd on wl* **7/1**
2 1 **Gris De Gris (IRE)**[16] 1658 5-9-2 .... GMosse 3 116+
(A De Royer-Dupre, France) *in tch: 4th 1/2-way: pushed along to go 2nd 2f out: ev ch appr fnl f: kpt on but a hld* **14/1**
3 2 ½ **Runaway**[64] 846 7-9-2 .... TJarnet 4 111
(R Pritchard-Gordon, France) *in tch: 6th 1/2-way: disputing 5th st: hrd rdn and hdwy 2f out: tk 3rd fnl 50yds* **50/1**
4 ½ **Celebrissime (IRE)**[10] 1819 4-9-2 .... DBonilla 8 110
(F Head, France) *led after 2f: 2 l clr 2f out: hdd 1f out: one pce* **150/1**
5 2 **Proviso**[27] 4-8-13 .... SPasquier 7 103
(A Fabre, France) *hld up: 8th st: rdn 2f out: nvr in chalng position* **9/1**
6 2 ½ **Curtain Call (FR)**[13] 1758 4-9-2 .... FMBerry 1 100
(L M Cumani) *led 2f: 2nd 1/2-way: drvn ent st: btn 1 1/2f out* **5/1**[3]
7 2 **Goldikova (IRE)**[204] 6996 4-8-13 .... OPeslier 6 93
(F Head, France) *prom: 3rd 1/2-way: effrt 1 1/2f out: sn btn* **5/4**[1]
8 5 **Loup Breton (IRE)**[21] 1551 5-9-2 .... ACrastus 5 86
(E Lellouche, France) *hld up in last: rdn over 2f out: no imp* **4/1**[2]
9 8 **Tazeez (USA)**[31] 1301 5-9-2 .... RHills 9 77
(J H M Gosden) *midfield: 5th 1/2-way: disputing 5th st: pushed along 2f out: sn btn* **13/2**

1m 57.2s (0.90) **Going Correction** +0.65s/f (Yiel) **9** Ran SP% **126.2**
Speed ratings: **122,121,118,118,116 114,112,108,101**
PARI-MUTUEL: WIN 7.10; PL 1.90, 2.50, 1.40; DF 29.80.
Owner D-Y Treves **Bred** S C E A Des Prairies **Trained** Pau, France
■ Stewards' Enquiry : D Bonilla 400euro fine: whip abuse

NOTEBOOK
Never On Sunday(FR), highly rated but unlucky in his previous race, was given a patient ride towards the tail of the field in the early stages. He still had plenty to do at the entrance to the straight and was brought with a progressive late run up the far rail, taking the advantage running into the final furlong and staying on well. He has been entered in the Prince of Wales's Stakes, which is his likely next target, the Coral Eclipse and the Arlington Million.
Gris De Gris(IRE) put up a fine performance considering he is at his best on a left-handed track. Settled behind the pace in the early stages, he quickened well to take the lead before the furlong marker and then battled on gamely to the line. This soft-ground specialist is considered a spring and autumn horse so he is unlikely to be seen out again until much later in the year.
Runaway, held up in the early stages, began to run on from halfway up the straight and took third place well inside the final furlong. He certainly enjoyed the testing ground, and this three-time Listed race winner has been entered in the Arlington Million later in the season.
Celebrissime(IRE) was pacemaking for his fancied stablemate Goldikova, who ran way below her best. He set a fair gallop early on, was still going strongly halfway up the straight and only lost his lead at the furlong marker. He still battled on gamely right to the line, though.
Proviso is another Listed winner who has fallen short at Group level. Held up, she was keeping on when it was all over suggesting further at this sort of level will suit this season.
Curtain Call(FR), smartly out of the stalls, was up with the leader early on and stayed there until the straight, where he quickly dropped out of contention. His jockey felt that this race came a little quickly after his win in Ireland and that he was never going well.
Goldikova(IRE) again showed her petulance at the stalls but deigned to load after a few stomps. She looked well for this reappearance, but was also fairly fresh and keen through the early stages despite a good pace. She didn't stride out on the ground – her one blip was when beaten at a much lower level on heavy ground last year as her other two defeats were at the hand of Zarkava – and was beaten before the final furlong. Official explanation: jockey said filly was unsuited by the soft ground
Loup Breton(IRE) was a big disappointment as well, failing to pick up from the back.
Tazeez(USA) was a beaten horse even before the straight and trailed in last. Connections felt the testing ground played a role in this disappointing effort.

1980 BATH (L-H)
Monday, May 18

OFFICIAL GOING: Good (good to soft in places) changing to good to soft after race 1 (2.00)
Wind: Winds strong and variable Weather: Overcast

2121 FREEBETS.CO.UK NEW ONLINE BETTING FORUM EBF NOVICE STKS 5f 11y
2:00 (2:00) (Class 5) 2-Y-0 **£3,561** (£1,059; £529; £264) **Stalls** Centre

Form RPR
2 1 **Radiohead**[15] 1700 2-8-12 ○.......... JamieSpencer 2 88+
(B J Meehan) *trckd ldr: c wd to r alone into st and led 2f out: sn clr: canter* **1/10**[1]
2 4 **Ragsta (IRE)** 2-8-7 ○.......... PatDobbs 4 64+
(R Hannon) *chsd ldrs: wnt 2nd ins fnl 2f but nvr the remotest ch w extremely easy wnr* **12/1**[2]
3 12 **Trelawny Wells** 2-8-12 ○.......... SamHitchcott 1 25+
(M R Channon) *rdn fr s and towards rr: tk poor 3rd wl ins fnl f* **16/1**[3]
4 1 ½ **Ishipink** 2-8-7 ○.......... SteveDrowne 5 15+
(R J Hodges) *led tl hdd 2f out: sn wknd: lost poor 3rd wl ins fnl f* **33/1**

63.26 secs (0.76) **Going Correction** +0.075s/f (Good) **4** Ran SP% **107.4**
Speed ratings (Par 93): **96,89,70,68**
toteswinger: 1&2 £2.30. CSF £2.30 TOTE £1.10; EX 2.10.
Owner Mrs Carmen Burrell & Jonathan Harvey **Bred** Redmyre Bloodstock And S Hillen **Trained** Manton, Wilts

FOCUS
After 10.5mm of rain in the previous 24 hours the ground was on the easy side of good. Fair form, and the winner could be plenty better than this.

NOTEBOOK
Radiohead looked inexperienced but shaped with plenty of promise and finished clear of the rest when second as favourite in a 5f Newmarket maiden on debut earlier this month. He set a decent standard on that form, raced wide for most of the way and had no trouble in converting a straightforward opportunity and justifying 1-10 favouritism against three newcomers. The 78,000gns son of Johannesburg holds several entries in valuable two-year-old events, including the Timeform Million. He looks a potentially useful type who should stay an extra furlong or two this season. (op 1-7 tchd 1-6 in places)
Ragsta(IRE) stayed on nicely and showed quite a bit of promise under an educational ride on her debut. She is out of a very useful multiple winner at 5f-7f and looks a good addition to a yard which is very powerful in the two-year-old division. (op 10-1)
Trelawny Wells ran green and was pushed along at an early stage but showed a bit of ability, staying on very late. He is out of a 7f winner at two who later stayed 1m3f, so should do better when faced with a stiffer test. (op 14-1)
Ishipink blasted into the lead and showed plenty of natural pace before weakening on the approach to the final furlong on this debut. (op 22-1)

2122 GREEN'S OF ST JAMES MEDIAN AUCTION MAIDEN STKS 5f 11y
2:30 (2:31) (Class 6) 3-4-Y-O £2,266 (£674; £337; £168) Stalls Centre

Form RPR
0-0 **1** **Spring Green**[15] 1703 3-8-9 0 SteveDrowne 9 65+
(H Morrison) *in tch: rdn and swtchd lft over 1f out: led jst ins fnl f towards centre crse: drvn out* **9/1**
620- **2** *1* **Musical Bridge**[205] 6987 3-9-0 78 JamieSpencer 2 67
(Mrs L Williamson) *led tl hdd over 2f out: styd chalng and stl upsides wnr ins fnl f: outpcd nr fin* **9/2**[3]
3-36 **3** *1 ¼* **Keep Dancing (IRE)**[30] 1359 3-8-6 67 (p) DavidProbert(3) 7 57
(A M Balding) *trckd ldr: led over 2f out: sn rdn: fnd little whn hdd jst ins fnl f and sn one pce* **7/4**[1]
- **4** *1* **Intolerable (IRE)** 3-9-0 0 SebSanders 1 59+
(R M Beckett) *s.i.s: sn drvn along: styd on fnl 2f: kpt on ins fnl f but nvr gng pce to be competitive* **8/1**
00- **5** *½* **Morning Queen (IRE)**[217] 6697 3-8-9 0 IanMongan 5 52
(C G Cox) *chsd ldrs: rdn 2f out: edgd rt over 1f out: outpcd ins fnl f* **14/1**
-004 **6** *hd* **Sandy Par**[18] 1617 4-9-8 52 (b) LPKeniry 12 53
(J M Bradley) *s.i.s: towards rr and sn rdn: styd on fr over 1f out and kpt on cl home but nvr in contention* **25/1**
000- **7** *6* **Filemot**[154] 7692 4-9-3 55 KirstyMilczarek 8 26
(John Berry) *stmbld in stalls: sn chsng ldrs: rdn 3f out: wknd fnl f* **10/1**
50-0 **8** *¾* **Bilboa**[18] 1617 4-9-8 39 (p) AdamKirby 3 29
(J M Bradley) *outpcd most of way* **66/1**
06-5 **9** *2 ½* **Ariadnes Filly (IRE)**[15] 1703 3-8-9 65 JimCrowley 4 18
(Mrs A J Perrett) *chsd ldrs: rdn and wkng whn hmpd appr fnl f* **4/1**[2]
0-50 **10** *1* **Buckle Up**[75] 753 3-9-0 42 (p) DaneO'Neill 6 19
(D K Ivory) *spd for 3f* **66/1**
0 **11** *13* **Steeple Caster**[27] 1419 3-9-0 0 TPO'Shea 11 —
(J M Bradley) *stmbld whn n.m.r after 1f: a in rr* **50/1**

63.69 secs (1.19) **Going Correction** +0.075s/f (Good)
WFA 3 from 4yo 8lb **11 Ran SP% 120.2**
Speed ratings (Par 101): **93,91,89,87,87 86,77,75,71,70 49**
toteswinger: 1&2 £6.70, 1&3 £5.30, 2&3 £2.40. CSF £49.62 TOTE £12.20: £2.80, £1.10, £1.20; EX 67.00 Trifecta £245.10 Pool: £331.34 - 1.00 winning units..
Owner Nicholas Jones **Bred** Coln Valley Stud **Trained** East Ilsley, Berks

FOCUS
The ground was changed to good to soft. There was not a great deal of strength in depth in this maiden, but two of the three market leaders finished second and third and the form looks solid enough, although the sixth does hold it own..
Filemot Official explanation: jockey said the filly slipped leaving the stalls; trainer said filly was subsequently found to have pulled muscles in its hindquarters
Ariadnes Filly(IRE) Official explanation: jockey said the filly slipped a furlong and a half out

2123 HSBC FILLIES' H'CAP 1m 5f 22y
3:00 (3:00) (Class 5) (0-70,70) 4-Y-0+ £2,719 (£809; £404; £202) Stalls High

Form RPR
000- **1** **Where's Susie**[25] 6868 4-8-8 60 RobertHavlin 2 67
(M Madgwick) *in rr tl hdwy 6f out: rdn over 3f out: styd on to chse ldr ins fnl 2f: led ins fnl f: kpt on wl* **15/2**
423- **2** *1 ½* **Shy**[228] 6413 4-9-4 70 JimCrowley 8 75
(P Winkworth) *led: rdn and kpt on fr 3f out: hdd and no ex ins fnl f* **11/4**[1]
203- **3** *5* **Act Three**[61] 6558 5-8-13 65 WilliamBuick 5 63
(Mouse Hamilton-Fairley) *chsd ldr: rdn and effrt ins fnl 3f: nvr quite on terms: lost 2nd ins fnl 2f: wknd fnl f* **8/1**
3026 **4** *5* **Make Amends (IRE)**[12] 1785 4-8-8 60 ow2 SteveDrowne 3 50
(R J Hodges) *in rr: mod prog fr over 3f out but nvr anywhere nr ldrs* **6/1**
056- **5** *6* **Seedless**[326] 3393 4-8-12 67 DavidProbert(3) 4 48
(A M Balding) *in rr: rdn over 4f out and mod improvement: nvr anywhere nr ldrs and wknd ins fnl 3f* **4/1**[2]
1456 **6** *1 ¾* **Little Carmela**[47] 1069 5-8-11 63 KirstyMilczarek 1 41
(S C Williams) *in rr: sme prog after 5f: nvr in contention and wknd over 3f out* **5/1**[3]
00-5 **7** *8* **Beautiful Lady (IRE)**[3] 2040 4-8-11 63 DarryllHolland 7 29
(P F I Cole) *impr fr rr to chse ldrs after 5f: rdn 6f out: wknd 3f out* **15/2**

2m 55.2s (3.20) **Going Correction** +0.075s/f (Good) **7 Ran SP% 112.3**
Speed ratings (Par 100): **93,92,89,85,82 81,76**
toteswinger: 1&2 £5.90, 1&3 £10.60, 2&3 £4.10. CSF £27.36 CT £168.80 TOTE £9.70: £4.60, £1.20; EX 33.40 Trifecta £138.60 Pool: £342.99 - 1.83 winning units..
Owner Recycled Products Limited **Bred** Mrs L R Burrage **Trained** Denmead, Hants
■ Stewards' Enquiry : Robert Havlin one-day ban: used whip with excessive frequency (June 1)

FOCUS
A modest handicap. It was run at a solid pace but not many of them got into it from behind and the form looks a bit questionable. Improvement from the winner over this longer trip.
Seedless Official explanation: jockey said that the filly had no more to give
Little Carmela Official explanation: jockey said the mare was never travelling

2124 R&R ICES H'CAP 5f 161y
3:30 (3:33) (Class 5) (0-70,70) 4-Y-0+ £2,719 (£809; £404; £202) Stalls Centre

Form RPR
0-31 **1** **Kyllachy Storm**[12] 1787 5-8-11 68 Louis-PhilippeBeuzelin(5) 2 77+
(R J Hodges) *trckd ldrs: rdn to ld 1f out: styd on wl: readily* **10/11**[1]
0403 **2** *nk* **Ask Jenny (IRE)**[6] 1970 7-8-1 56 KellyHarrison(3) 5 64
(Patrick Morris) *in rr: rdn and hdwy over 1f out: chsd wnr ins fnl f: styd on wl cl home but a hld* **7/1**[2]
000 **3** *3 ¼* **Music Box Express**[15] 1694 5-8-3 62 MatthewDavies(7) 4 59
(George Baker) *led: rdn over 2f out: hdd 1f out: outpcd by ldng duo ins fnl f* **16/1**
3055 **4** *3* **Fromsong (IRE)**[28] 1403 11-9-4 70 StephenCarson 7 57
(D K Ivory) *chsd ldrs: rdn 3f out: wknd fnl f* **16/1**
400- **5** *½* **Diane's Choice**[219] 6650 6-8-13 68 (b) DavidProbert(3) 12 53
(Miss Gay Kelleway) *reluctant to post: stdd s: in rr: rdn and styd on fr 2f out: nvr in contention* **10/1**
0-65 **6** *1* **Who's Winning (IRE)**[12] 1787 8-7-11 56 oh3 (t) GemmaElford(7) 13 38
(B G Powell) *chsd ldrs: rdn 1/2-way: one pce fnl 2f* **20/1**
0006 **7** *1* **Towy Boy (IRE)**[23] 1528 4-8-6 58 (b[1]) WilliamBuick 11 36
(I A Wood) *chsd ldr: c to stands' side to r alone 3f out: wknd over 1f out* **9/1**
050- **8** *nk* **Boldinor**[203] 7012 6-8-4 56 oh2 NeilChalmers 6 33
(M R Bosley) *in tch: rdn 3f out: wknd fr 2f out* **12/1**
60-0 **9** *2 ½* **Monsieur Reynard**[6] 1970 4-8-11 63 AdamKirby 10 32
(J M Bradley) *sn outpcd* **8/1**[3]
00-3 **10** *5* **Mr Forthright**[12] 1787 5-8-4 56 oh9 TPO'Shea 1 8
(J M Bradley) *sn outpcd* **20/1**

1m 12.8s (1.60) **Going Correction** +0.075s/f (Good) **10 Ran SP% 124.1**
Speed ratings (Par 103): **92,91,87,83,82 81,79,79,76,69**
toteswinger: 1&2 £2.10, 1&3 £8.70, 2&3 £7.00. CSF £8.53 CT £66.42 TOTE £2.00: £1.10, £2.10, £4.50; EX 10.30 Trifecta £84.20 Pool: £405.49 - 3.56 winning units..
Owner Mrs Angela Hart **Bred** Sir Eric Parker **Trained** Charlton Mackrell, Somerset
■ Stewards' Enquiry : Gemma Elford three-day ban: careless riding (Jun 1-3)
Adam Kirby one-day ban: used whip when out of contention (June 1)

FOCUS
A fair handicap. The first two pulled clear of the rest and although not many came here in top form, the winner took another step forward.

2125 FREEBETS.CO.UK FREE BETS H'CAP 1m 5y
4:00 (4:00) (Class 5) (0-70,69) 4-Y-0+ £2,719 (£809; £404; £202) Stalls Low

Form RPR
06-5 **1** **Full Victory (IRE)**[13] 1775 7-8-13 64 DaneO'Neill 11 75+
(R A Farrant) *stdd s and hld up in rr tl smooth hdwy over 2f out: rdn to ld 1f out: hld on wl cl home* **3/1**[1]
2265 **2** *nk* **Rock Anthem (IRE)**[81] 683 5-8-8 59 LPKeniry 9 69
(Mike Murphy) *hld up towards rr: stdy hdwy whn nt clr run ins fnl 2f: squeezed through to chse wnr 1f out: styd on wl and gng on cl home but a jst hld* **8/1**
62-0 **3** *2 ½* **Tignello (IRE)**[22] 1538 4-8-8 59 PatDobbs 6 63
(G L Moore) *in tch: hdwy fr 3f out: chsd ldrs and ridder 2f out: kpt on fnl f but nt pce of ldng duo* **10/1**
6050 **4** *1 ½* **Master Mahogany**[12] 1785 8-8-8 59 JimCrowley 2 60
(R J Hodges) *sn chsng ldr: rdn to take slt advantage 2f out: hdd 1f out: wknd ins fnl f* **7/1**[3]
30-6 **5** *1 ¾* **April Fool**[10] 1833 5-9-3 68 (v) RichardThomas 5 65
(J A Geake) *led: awkward bnd 5f out: rdn 3f out: hdd 2f out: sn wknd fnl f* **8/1**
12-0 **6** *1* **Croeso Cusan**[13] 1773 4-8-13 64 SteveDrowne 4 58
(J L Spearing) *in rr: rdn over 3f out: sme prog over 2f out: nvr rchd ldrs: wknd fnl f* **11/1**
23-1 **7** *3* **Fancy Footsteps (IRE)**[124] 157 4-9-4 69 AdamKirby 8 57
(C G Cox) *chsd ldrs: rdn 3f out: wknd over 1f out* **3/1**[1]
0603 **8** *2* **Amber Ridge**[13] 1773 4-8-4 55 oh6 TPO'Shea 3 38
(B P J Baugh) *chsd ldrs: styd on outside and rdn 3f out: wknd ins fnl 2f* **33/1**
4004 **9** *30* **Wavertree Warrior (IRE)**[14] 1741 7-8-6 57 (b) WilliamBuick 7 —
(N P Littmoden) *a in rr: eased whn no ch fnl 3f* **11/2**[2]

1m 42.42s (1.62) **Going Correction** +0.075s/f (Good) **9 Ran SP% 120.5**
Speed ratings (Par 103): **94,93,91,89,87 86,83,81,51**
toteswinger: 1&2 £6.50, 1&3 £6.50, 2&3 £13.20. CSF £29.61 CT £220.65 TOTE £3.50: £1.80, £2.30, £2.70; EX 30.90 Trifecta £233.60 Part won. Pool: £315.81 - 0.44 winning units..
Owner Friends of Saunton Sands **Bred** Larry Ryan **Trained** East Garston, Berks
■ Stewards' Enquiry : L P Keniry one-day ban: careless riding (Jun 1)

FOCUS
A modest handicap. The winner only had to match last summer's form, aand the race is rated around the second.
Wavertree Warrior(IRE) Official explanation: jockey said that the gelding was never travelling

2126 BET365.COM H'CAP 1m 2f 46y
4:30 (4:31) (Class 5) (0-75,75) 3-Y-O £2,914 (£867; £433; £216) Stalls Low

Form RPR
3-30 **1** **Rumble Of Thunder (IRE)**[12] 1792 3-9-0 71 WilliamBuick 4 81
(D W P Arbuthnot) *mde all: rdn over 2f out: drvn clr fr over 1f out: unchal* **4/1**[2]
55-2 **2** *3 ¾* **Mabuya (UAE)**[16] 1671 3-9-3 74 SebSanders 10 76
(P J Makin) *mid-div: hrd drvn and hdwy fr 3f out: styd on to chse wnr ins fnl 2f: kpt on but a readily hld* **6/1**[3]
305- **3** *½* **Rockfella**[207] 6926 3-8-10 67 TPO'Shea 12 68
(D J Coakley) *chsd ldrs: rdn and styd on wl fnl 2f to press for 2nd cl home but no ch w wnr* **14/1**
000- **4** *4* **Highland Storm**[226] 6474 3-8-11 75 (p) MatthewDavies(7) 13 68
(George Baker) *in rr: rdn over 3f out: styd on fr 2f out but nvr gng pce to get into contention* **16/1**
232- **5** *1* **Wake Me Now (IRE)**[218] 6682 3-8-12 72 JackMitchell(3) 7 63
(R M Beckett) *prom: chse ldrs on outside over 3f out: styd on same pce fnl 2f* **10/1**
220 **6** *3 ¾* **Mellow Mixture**[86] 630 3-9-3 74 PatDobbs 8 58
(R Hannon) *chsd ldrs: rdn 3f out: wknd over 1f out* **50/1**
03-2 **7** *¾* **Dice (IRE)**[27] 1422 3-8-13 70 DaneO'Neill 6 52
(L M Cumani) *chsd ldrs: rdn over 3f out: wknd ins fnl 2f* **7/2**[1]
4650 **8** *hd* **Sgt Roberts (IRE)**[28] 1408 3-8-13 70 LPKeniry 15 52
(J S Moore) *sn rr: rdn over 3f out: mod prog fnl f* **33/1**
435- **9** *1* **Perception (IRE)**[229] 6391 3-9-0 71 SteveDrowne 16 51
(R Charlton) *t.k.h: in tch: rdn 3f out: hung lft and sn wknd* **10/1**
02-5 **10** *1 ½* **Threestepstoheaven**[21] 1573 3-9-1 72 DarryllHolland 3 49
(B W Hills) *chsd ldrs: rdn over 3f out: wknd over 2f out* **7/1**
6-35 **11** *¾* **King's La Mont (IRE)**[11] 1809 3-9-3 74 JimCrowley 5 49
(Mrs A J Perrett) *mid-div: rdn over 3f out: wknd rapidly over 2f out* **9/1**
-000 **12** *½* **Hilbre Point (USA)**[3] 2038 3-8-4 61 oh1 (b[1]) RichardThomas 11 35
(B J Meehan) *a towards rr* **33/1**
2655 **13** *1* **It's A Mans World**[24] 1490 3-8-8 68 ow3 RussellKennemore(3) 2 40
(K M Prendergast) *in rr: sme prog 3f out: nvr bttr than mid-div: sn wknd* **80/1**

00-4 **14** 1 3/4 **Sir Freddie**[20] 1579 3-8-13 **70** ..... IanMongan 14 39
(Lady Herries) *nvr in contention* **14/1**
420- **15** 7 **Noordhoek Kid**[208] 6893 3-9-2 **73** ..... RobertHavlin 1 28
(C R Egerton) *chsd ldrs tl wknd rapidly over 2f out* **33/1**
2m 11.89s (0.89) **Going Correction** +0.075s/f (Good) **15** Ran SP% **128.4**
Speed ratings (Par 99): **99,96,95,92,91 88,88,87,87,85 85,84,84,82,77**
toteswinger: 1&2 £7.10, 1&3 £20.60, 2&3 £18.00. CSF £29.27 CT £324.45 TOTE £5.50: £2.70, £2.10, £6.10; EX 37.90 TRIFECTA Not won..
Owner Francis Ward and Anthony Ward **Bred** Rathasker Stud **Trained** Compton, Berks
FOCUS
An interesting handicap involving plenty of progressive types. The winner had been dropped 4lb since last time and the form is rated around the third.
Dice(IRE) Official explanation: jockey said that the colt was never travelling

2127 FREEBETS.CO.UK FREE BETS & BETTING FORUM H'CAP (FOR AMATEUR RIDERS) 2m 1f 34y
5:00 (5:01) (Class 6) (0-65,65) 4-Y-0+ **£2,109** (£648; £324) **Stalls** Centre

Form RPR
3-00 **1** **Corking (IRE)**[77] 735 4-9-13 **50** ..... MrDGPrichard(5) 4 59
(J L Flint) *mde all: drvn 5 l clr over 3f out: styd on wl: all out cl home* **20/1**
52-0 **2** 1 **Black Or Red (IRE)**[7] 1936 4-10-2 **53** ..... (b) MrCMartin(5) 2 61
(I A Wood) *hld up in rr: gd hdwy 6f out: chsd ldrs and shkn up whn wnr qcknd 3f out: styd on to go 2nd 1f out: fin wl but a jst hld* **20/1**
23/5 **3** 5 **Dansimar**[16] 1665 5-11-1 **59** ..... WilliamBiddick 1 61
(Miss Venetia Williams) *chsd ldrs: wnt 2nd over 6f out: one pce whn wnr qcknd over 3f out: styd on fr 2f out but nvr on terms: lost 2nd 1f out and sn outpcd* **7/4**[1]
5003 **4** 3/4 **Sand Repeal (IRE)**[39] 1200 7-10-11 **60** ..... MrRBirkett(5) 7 61
(Miss J Feilden) *chsd ldrs: rdn and one pce over 3f out: kpt on again fnl f* **8/1**
440- **5** nse **Brave Bugsy (IRE)**[257] 5613 6-10-9 **53** ..... GemmaGracey-Davison 8 54
(A M Balding) *in rr tl rapid hdwy to chse ldrs 6f out: rdn 3f out and one pce: styd on again fnl f* **7/2**[2]
1-20 **6** nk **Munlochy Bay**[27] 1435 5-11-7 **65** ..... MrSWalker 16 65
(W S Kittow) *in rr: hdwy 5f out: rdn and one pce over 3f out: kpt on again fnl f but nvr in contention* **4/1**[3]
-000 **7** 1 3/4 **Mr Mischief**[19] 1609 9-9-13 **46** oh1 ..... BrianToomey(3) 10 44
(C Gordon) *chsd ldrs: rdn 4f out: sn one pce: kpt on again fnl 2f* **16/1**
0/40 **8** 1 1/4 **Tilly Shilling (IRE)**[7] 1938 5-9-13 **50** ..... MrTJCannon(7) 11 47
(Norma Twomey) *in tch: rdn and lost plcd 4f out: styd again fnl 2f* **20/1**
/0-5 **9** 5 **Openide**[20] 627 8-10-2 **46** ..... (t) MissEJJones 15 37
(B W Duke) *chsd ldrs: rdn fr 1/2-way: no ch fnl 4f* **8/1**
5-05 **10** 12 **Lilac Wine**[20] 1586 6-10-4 **48** ..... (p) MissFayeBramley 13 24
(D J S Ffrench Davis) *chsd ldrs tl over 3f out* **25/1**
005- **11** 13 **Arabian Sun**[35] 6594 5-9-9 **46** ..... (b) MrMTStanley(7) 3 7
(C P Morlock) *chsd ldrs to 4f out* **33/1**
0445 **12** 14 **Summer Bounty**[39] 1200 13-9-11 **48** oh1 ow2 ..... MrBBrackenbury(7) 6 —
(F Jordan) *bhd fr 1/2-way* **33/1**
000- **13** 50 **Promised Gold**[269] 5218 4-9-11 **48** ..... MrJPFeatherstone(5) 17 —
(J A Geake) *in tch to 1/2-way: t.o* **100/1**
/0-0 **14** 54 **Doonigan (IRE)**[17] 1651 5-10-2 **46** oh1 ..... (b1) IanPopham 9 —
(G Brown) *s.i.s: a in rr: virtually p.u fnl 3f: t.o* **66/1**
3m 58.63s (6.73) **Going Correction** +0.075s/f (Good)
WFA 4 from 5yo+ 2lb **14** Ran SP% **133.2**
Speed ratings (Par 101): **87,86,84,83,83 83,82,82,79,74 68,61,38,12**
toteswinger: 1&2 £35.50, 1&3 £12.40, 2&3 £15.50. CSF £374.37 CT £1080.65 TOTE £26.80: £3.90, £6.50, £1.20; EX 600.00 TRIFECTA Not won. Place 6: £22.73, Place 5: £18.93..
Owner T A Jones **Bred** Rosemary McManus And Aerial Bloodstock **Trained** Kenfig Hill, Bridgend
■ David Prichard's first Flat winner.
FOCUS
A modest marathon handicap but it produced an exciting finish and another all-the-way winner. The time was slow and it is doubtful if the winner had to improve.
Lilac Wine Official explanation: trainer said the mare was unsuited by the good to soft going
T/Plt: £50.40 to a £1 stake. Pool: £50,407.91. 729.90 winning tickets. T/Qpdt: £40.40 to a £1 stake. Pool: £2,956.90. 54.10 winning tickets. ST

1776 SOUTHWELL (L-H)
Monday, May 18

OFFICIAL GOING: Standard
Wind: Light across Weather: Sunn periods & showers

2128 WILL YOU MARRY ME "JODIE BAKER" MAIDEN AUCTION STKS 5f (F)
2:10 (2:12) (Class 6) 2-Y-O **£2,729** (£806; £403) **Stalls** High

Form RPR
02 **1** **Koo And The Gang (IRE)**[17] 1653 2-8-12 0 ..... TomEaves 10 68+
(B Ellison) *mde all: rdn over 1f out: kpt on u.p ins fnl f* **9/4**[1]
2 3/4 **Singeur (IRE)** 2-9-1 0 ..... PatCosgrave 7 68
(R Bastiman) *dwlt and swtchd lft after 1f: hdwy 2f out: sn rdn and styd on to chsewnr ins fnl f: drvn and no ex towards fin* **14/1**
00 **3** 2 1/2 **Southwark Newshawk**[7] 1939 2-8-4 0 ..... LiamJones 2 48
(Mrs C A Dunnett) *prom: rdn along 2f out: drvn over 1f out: kpt on same pce ins fnl f* **25/1**
4 shd **Janeiro (IRE)** 2-8-12 0 ..... RichardKingscote 3 56
(Tom Dascombe) *s.i.s: swtchd lft to far rail and bhd: hdwy 1/2-way: rdn to chse ldrs over 1f out: drvn and kpt on ins fnl f: nrst fin* **3/1**[2]
5 hd **Go To Dubai** 2-8-4 0 ..... DaleGibson 8 47
(M W Easterby) *s.i.s: swtchd lft after 1f: hdwy 1/2-way: rdn wl over 1f out: kpt on ins fnl f: nrst fin* **66/1**
05 **6** 1 1/2 **Agent Boo**[13] 1764 2-9-1 0 ..... GrahamGibbons 4 53
(E S McMahon) *prom: rdn along 2f out: grad wknd* **8/1**
045 **7** 3 3/4 **Ginger Ted (IRE)**[9] 1867 2-8-5 0 ow1 ..... (b) MarkCoumbe(5) 6 34
(R C Guest) *in tch: rdn along over 2f out: no imp* **5/1**[3]
0 **8** 1/2 **London Girl (IRE)**[13] 1764 2-8-4 0 ..... AndrewElliott 1 27
(A J McCabe) *a in rr* **18/1**
9 3 3/4 **Vested Interest** 2-8-9 0 ..... DO'Donohoe 13 18
(George Baker) *wnt lft s: a towards rr* **14/1**
0 **10** 3/4 **Magneto (IRE)**[17] 1653 2-8-12 0 ..... EdwardCreighton 5 18
(E J Creighton) *a in rr* **50/1**
11 1 1/4 **Blade Of Class** 2-8-4 0 ..... CatherineGannon 11 6+
(P D Evans) *hmpd s: a in rr* **50/1**
0 **12** nk **Micky's Bird**[10] 1841 2-8-6 0 ow2 ..... SimonWhitworth 12 7+
(R C Guest) *hmpd s: a in rr* **100/1**
0 **13** 3 1/4 **Countrywide Ice (IRE)**[18] 1623 2-8-9 0 ..... NCallan 14 —
(K A Ryan) *racd alone stands' rail: in tch to 1/2-way: sn wknd* **16/1**

0 **14** 8 **Minnie Rocket**[7] 1939 2-8-4 0 ..... SilvestreDeSousa 9 —
(R C Guest) *a bhd* **100/1**
60.24 secs (0.54) **Going Correction** -0.025s/f (Stan) **14** Ran SP% **119.3**
Speed ratings (Par 91): **94,92,88,88,88 85,79,79,73,71 69,69,64,51**
toteswinger: 1&2 £11.60, 1&3 £13.60, 2&3 £75.00 CSF £35.05 TOTE £2.90: £1.10, £5.60, £3.30; EX 46.20.
Owner Koo's Racing Club **Bred** Vincent Howley **Trained** Norton, N Yorks
■ Stewards' Enquiry : Pat Cosgrave caution: used whip with excessive frequency
FOCUS
This looked a moderate juvenile maiden. It was run at a sound pace and those drawn more towards the far side were at an advantage. The winner looks the best guide to the form.
NOTEBOOK
Koo And The Gang(IRE) finished a narrow second over C&D 17 days earlier and went one better in determined style. He again showed decent early dash and knuckled down well inside the final furlong. His effort is all the better considering he was housed in stall ten and his trainer believes he can hold his own in better company, but will want some cut when reverting to turf. (op 5-2)
Singeur(IRE) cost 15,000gns and is bred to appreciate a little further on his dam's side, but his sire injects a speed influence. He turned in a pleasing debut run and should come on a bundle for the run. (tchd 16-1)
Southwark Newshawk had cut little ice in two Yarmouth maidens coming into this AW debut. She lasted a lot longer for the switch to this deeper surface, but her proximity does little for the form. (op 40-1 tchd 50-1)
Janeiro(IRE) is bred to stay further on his dam's side, but his speedy sire has a great record on this surface and he is from a yard doing well. He lost out with a sluggish start and ultimately left the impression another furlong would suit ideally. (op 15-8 tchd 7-4)
Go To Dubai's dam was a speedy sort at two. She kept on in game fashion without seriously threatening and did enough to suggest she can pick up a small race or two in due course. (op 80-1)

2129 TETLEY BITTER AMATEUR RIDERS' CLAIMING STKS 1m 4f (F)
2:40 (2:40) (Class 6) 4-Y-O+ **£1,977** (£608; £304) **Stalls** Low

Form RPR
3106 **1** **Aureate**[10] 1826 5-11-7 89 ..... MissLEllison 13 83
(B Ellison) *trckd ldrs: rapid hdwy to ld after 4f: rdn along 3f out: drvn over 1f out: kpt on gamely ins fnl f* **2/1**[1]
0/0- **2** hd **Realism (FR)**[24] 6974 9-11-3 86 ..... MrOGreenall 10 79
(M W Easterby) *hld up in rr: stdy hdwy on outer 1/2-way: trckd ldrs 4f out: effrt over 2f out: rdn to chal over 1f out: sn drvn and ev ch tl no ex nr fin* **14/1**
2020 **3** 1/2 **Rawdon (IRE)**[11] 1815 8-10-6 72 ..... (bt) MrOJMurphy(7) 6 74
(Miss Gay Kelleway) *hld up in tch: stdy hdwy 4f out: chsd ldrs over 2f out: rdn over 1f out: drvn and ev ch ins fnl f: kpt on same pce last 100yds* **10/1**
5420 **4** 1 1/4 **Nawamees (IRE)**[12] 1786 11-10-9 69 ..... (p) MissEFolkes 11 68
(P D Evans) *trckd ldrs: hdwy and cl up 1/2-way: rdn along 3f out: drvn wl over 1f out and ev ch tl one pce ent fnl f* **7/1**[3]
-043 **5** 10 **Keisha Kayleigh (IRE)**[36] 1226 6-9-13 64 ..... (p) MrDaleSwift(5) 9 47
(B Ellison) *hld up in midfield: hdwy over 4f out: rdn along to chse ldrs 3f out: drvn wl over 1f out and sn wknd* **14/1**
3-54 **6** 7 **Musashi (IRE)**[10] 1848 4-10-0 64 ..... MissKECooper(7) 1 39
(T P Tate) *a towards rr* **11/1**
/3-0 **7** 5 **Dovedon Hero**[50] 1014 9-10-8 60 ..... MrPCollington(3) 14 44
(P J McBride) *hld up in rr: hdwy 5f out: pushed along 4f out: rdn wl over 2f out: nvr nr ldrs* **16/1**
0410 **8** 25 **My Friend Fritz**[14] 1732 9-10-11 70 ..... MrsMarieKing 3 —
(P W Hiatt) *chsd ldrs: rdn along over 4f out and sn wknd* **10/1**
0151 **9** 8 **Polish Power (GER)**[6] 1962 9-10-13 82 ..... MrsSMoore 5 —
(J S Moore) *hld up: pushed along 1/2-way: a bhd* **7/2**[2]
04/0 **10** 5 **Tivers Song (USA)**[136] 11 5-10-2 50 ..... (b1) MissABevan(5) 7 —
(John A Harris) *prom: lost pl 1/2-way and sn bhd* **80/1**
/040 **11** 31 **Regal Tradition (IRE)**[10] 1848 4-10-2 55 ..... (b1) MrHarryChalloner(5) 8 —
(G J Smith) *cl up: rdn along 1/2-way and sn wknd* **100/1**
0 **12** 5 **Newby Abbey (IRE)**[23] 1530 8-10-0 0 ..... MissAHeath(7) 2 —
(D Flood) *led 4f: sn wknd and bhd fr 1/2-way* **125/1**
2m 40.54s (-0.46) **Going Correction** -0.025s/f (Stan) **12** Ran SP% **116.8**
Speed ratings (Par 101): **100,99,99,98,92 87,84,67,62,58 38,34**
toteswinger: 1&2 £11.50, 1&3 £8.50, 2&3 £21.00. CSF £32.73 TOTE £3.00: £1.20, £5.40, £3.10; EX 43.10.
Owner The Seasiders Again **Bred** Darley **Trained** Norton, N Yorks
FOCUS
Not a bad claimer, confined to amateur riders. There was a solid pace on and the first four came well clear. The third and fourth are the best guides to the form.
My Friend Fritz Official explanation: jockey said gelding hung right
Polish Power(GER) Official explanation: vet said horse lost a front shoe

2130 BET AFTER THE OFF AT LADBROKES.COM H'CAP 5f (F)
3:10 (3:10) (Class 6) (0-60,63) 4-Y-0+ **£2,388** (£705; £352) **Stalls** High

Form RPR
0620 **1** **Loose Caboose (IRE)**[10] 1846 4-9-1 **60** ..... (b) AndrewMullen(3) 6 73
(A J McCabe) *prom: effrt 2f out: rdn to ld over 1f out: qcknd clr ins fnl f* **8/1**[3]
000- **2** 4 **Bertbrand**[212] 6821 4-8-13 **60** ..... AndreaAtzeni(5) 1 59
(D Flood) *chsd ldrs: swtchd rt and hdwy wl over 1f out: sn rdn: drvn and kpt on ins fnl f* **17/2**
6301 **3** hd **Orpen's Art (IRE)**[6] 1957 4-9-0 **63** 6ex ..... HollyHall(7) 10 61
(S A Callaghan) *led: rdn along 2f out: drvn and hdd over 1f out: kpt on same pce* **9/1**
0500 **4** nse **Dickie Le Davoir**[23] 1510 5-8-10 **57** ..... MarkCoumbe(5) 12 55+
(John A Harris) *dwlt and towards rr: hdwy on outer wl over 1f out: sn rdn and styd on ins fnl f: nrst fin* **12/1**
1165 **5** 1 1/4 **Handsinthemist (IRE)**[21] 1564 4-8-7 **56** ..... PaulPickard(7) 7 50
(P T Midgley) *in tch: rdn along 1/2-way: styd on appr fnl f: nvr rch ldrs* **5/1**[1]
-212 **6** 2 1/4 **The Geester**[94] 535 5-9-4 **60** ..... (b) NCallan 13 45
(S R Bowring) *cl up: effrt 2f out: sn rdn and wknd wl over 1f out* **5/1**[1]
1-00 **7** 1 **Tenancy (IRE)**[15] 1695 5-8-8 **50** ..... SilvestreDeSousa 5 32
(R C Guest) *in tch: rdn along 2f out: no imp* **10/1**
-600 **8** 1 3/4 **Whinhill House**[20] 1587 9-9-3 **59** ..... (v) JerryO'Dwyer 3 35
(T T Clement) *chsd ldrs: rdn along 1/2-way: sn wknd* **20/1**
360 **9** nk **The Lord**[26] 1468 9-8-10 **57** ..... JackDean(5) 4 31
(W G M Turner) *cl up: rdn along over 2f out and grad wknd* **8/1**[3]
400- **10** 1 3/4 **Egyptian Lord**[138] 7836 6-8-6 **48** ..... (b) FrankieMcDonald 8 16
(Peter Grayson) *a towards rr* **40/1**
4240 **11** shd **Decider (USA)**[21] 1564 6-9-0 **59** ..... KevinGhunowa(3) 14 27
(R A Harris) *cl up: rdn along 1/2-way: sn bhd* **16/1**

000 **12** *1 1/4* **Bishopbriggs (USA)**[61] 861 4-9-1 **57**.............. TravisBlock 9 20
(J Ryan) *a towards rr* **16/1**

00-0 **13** *9* **Black Moma (IRE)**[18] 1619 5-9-2 **58**.............. PatCosgrave 2 —
(J R Boyle) *a in rr: bhd fr 1/2-way* **7/1**[2]

59.53 secs (-0.17) **Going Correction** -0.025s/f (Stan) **13** Ran SP% **124.3**
Speed ratings (Par 101): **100,93,93,93,91 87,86,83,82,79 79,77,63**
toteswinger: 1&2 £29.50, 1&3 £9.80, 2&3 £31.80. CSF £77.62 CT £661.13 TOTE £11.30: £3.20, £3.70, £2.70; EX 125.90.
Owner Dixon, McCabe and Timms **Bred** Paradime Ltd **Trained** Averham Park, Notts

FOCUS
An open sprint handicap in which the main action developed down the middle of the track. Modest form.
Tenancy(IRE) Official explanation: jockey said that the gelding was slow away
Egyptian Lord Official explanation: jockey said gelding hung right and left

2131 BET WITH LADBROKES ON 0800 777 888 H'CAP 1m 3f (F)
3:40 (3:40) (Class 6) (0-60,60) 3-Y-O **£2,047** (£604; £302) **Stalls** Low

Form RPR

06-4 **1** **Lucky Punt**[20] 1580 3-9-3 **59**.............. FergusSweeney 12 68
(B G Powell) *trckd ldng pair: led after 3f: rdn clr wl over 1f out: edgd lft ins fnl f: styd on strly* **9/1**

0-61 **2** *3 1/2* **Eightdaysaweek**[27] 1441 3-9-1 **57**.............. JamesDoyle 10 60
(S Kirk) *in tch: hdwy over 4f out: rdn along 3f out: drvn 2f out: styd on appr fnl f* **9/2**[1]

5330 **3** *shd* **Spring Quartet**[47] 1070 3-8-4 **53** ow1..............(v) TobyAtkinson(7) 5 56
(Pat Eddery) *hld up in rr: hdwy 4f out: effrt over 2f out: rdn to chse ldrs over 1f out: drvn ins fnl f and kpt on same pce* **14/1**

0-20 **4** *1 1/2* **Mekong Miss**[47] 1070 3-9-4 **60**.............. PaulHanagan 3 60
(J Jay) *cl up: rdn along 3f out: drvn wl over 1f out: sn wknd and edgd lft* **25/1**

20-0 **5** *5* **Kristopher James (IRE)**[25] 1481 3-8-13 **55**.............. TGMcLaughlin 9 47
(W M Brisbourne) *midfield hdwy on outer 1/2-way: rdn to chse ldrs over 3f out: drvn and no imp fnl 2f* **18/1**

-605 **6** *2 3/4* **Valkyrie (IRE)**[25] 1481 3-8-10 **52**.............. RichardKingscote 6 39
(N P Littmoden) *in tch: hdwy on outer to chse ldrs over 4f out: rdn along 3f out and sn wknd* **25/1**

60-5 **7** *nk* **Shadows Lengthen**[27] 1441 3-9-2 **58**.............. DaleGibson 2 45
(M W Easterby) *led 3f: cl up on inner tl rdn along over 3f out and grad wknd* **12/1**

000- **8** *1 1/2* **Outland (IRE)**[223] 6553 3-8-8 **50**.............. LiamJones 14 34
(M H Tompkins) *hld up: a towards rr* **8/1**

40-0 **9** *4* **Lomica**[118] 228 3-8-13 **55**.............. TomEaves 8 32
(Miss J A Camacho) *hld up: a towards rr* **50/1**

00-0 **10** *hd* **Castle Myth (USA)**[45] 1098 3-8-3 **50**.............. LanceBetts(5) 4 27
(B Ellison) *a in rr* **40/1**

0235 **11** *7* **Kochanski (IRE)**[10] 1829 3-9-2 **58**.............. JoeFanning 7 23
(M Johnston) *a towards rr* **15/2**[3]

0-04 **12** *1 1/4* **Taste The Wine (IRE)**[20] 1594 3-9-0 **56**.............. PatCosgrave 13 19
(J S Moore) *hld up: hdwy and pushed along 5f out: rdn 4f out and sn btn* **9/2**[1]

0-00 **13** *10* **Romantic Interlude (IRE)**[30] 1363 3-8-12 **54**.............. TPQueally 11 —
(A P Jarvis) *a in rr* **33/1**

0062 **14** *11* **Wahan (USA)**[47] 1070 3-8-13 **55**.............. NCallan 1 —
(C E Brittain) *cl up on inner: rdn along over 3f out: drvn over 2f out and sn wknd: bhdand eased over 1f out* **6/1**[2]

2m 26.22s (-1.78) **Going Correction** -0.025s/f (Stan) **14** Ran SP% **118.2**
Speed ratings (Par 97): **105,102,102,101,97 95,95,94,91,91 86,85,78,70**
toteswinger: 1&2 £9.20, 1&3 £23.50, 2&3 £14.80. CSF £45.86 CT £573.73 TOTE £9.10: £2.00, £2.00, £4.90; EX 75.30.
Owner I S Smith **Bred** S A Douch **Trained** Upper Lambourn, Berks

FOCUS
This was a very ordinary 3yo handicap run at a fair pace in a relatively decent time. The form is best rated around the third and fourth.
Taste The Wine(IRE) Official explanation: jockey said the gelding was unsuited by the fibresand surface
Romantic Interlude(IRE) Official explanation: jockey said that the filly hung right
Wahan(USA) Official explanation: jockey said colt was never travelling

2132 PLAY POKER AT LADBROKES.COM H'CAP 6f (F)
4:10 (4:10) (Class 6) (0-60,59) 3-Y-O **£2,047** (£604; £302) **Stalls** Low

Form RPR

6434 **1** **Pepin (IRE)**[7] 1935 3-8-11 **52**.............. FrankieMcDonald 4 58
(D Haydn Jones) *led tl hung rt bnd after 2f: hdwy over 2f out: rdn and qckd to ld wl over 1f out: kpt on u.p ins fnl f* **15/2**

04-4 **2** *1 1/4* **Top Flight Splash**[26] 1452 3-8-11 **52**..............(v1) DaleGibson 3 54
(Mrs G S Rees) *cl up: effrt 2f out: sn rdn to chse wnr: drvn ins fnl f and kpt on* **6/1**[3]

000- **3** *5* **Lady Zena**[210] 6858 3-8-4 **45**.............. DuranFentiman 8 31
(M W Easterby) *s.i.s and bhd: hdwy on inner 2f out: rdn and styd on strly ins fnl f: nrst fin* **33/1**

0-00 **4** *3/4* **Feeling Stylish (IRE)**[14] 1725 3-8-9 **50**.............. JoeFanning 9 34
(N Tinkler) *chsd ldrs: n.m.r bnd after 2f: hdwy 2f out: sn rdn and no imp appr fnl f* **12/1**

3054 **5** *nse* **If Only**[27] 1437 3-9-3 **58**..............(b1) PaulHanagan 2 41
(J Jay) *wnt rt s: cl up on inner tl hld after 2f: rdn along over 2f out: drvn and hdd wl over 1f out: sn wknd* **7/2**[2]

-500 **6** *1* **Missed Mondays**[26] 1465 3-8-2 **48**.............. AndreaAtzeni(5) 10 28+
(Patrick Morris) *towards rr and carried wd bnd after 2f: hdwy 2f out: sn rdn and no imp* **10/1**

6-10 **7** *4* **Kings Ace (IRE)**[10] 1839 3-9-4 **59**.............. NCallan 11 36+
(A P Jarvis) *in tch on outer whn carried wd bnd after 2f: sn rdn and sme hdwy over 2f out: sn wknd and eased ent fnl f* **7/4**[1]

4040 **8** *1 1/4* **Hint Of Honey**[26] 1465 3-8-12 **53**.............. SimonWhitworth 1 16
(A G Newcombe) *s.i.s: a in rr* **20/1**

0-00 **9** *6* **Risky Lady (IRE)**[10] 1838 3-7-11 **45**.............. RyanPowell(7) 7 —
(J Ryan) *towards rr whn carried wd bnd after 2f: bhd after* **66/1**

40-0 **10** *3/4* **Eden Park**[30] 1359 3-9-3 **58**.............. TomEaves 5 —
(M Dods) *t.k.h: chsd ldrs on inner: rdn along over 2f out: sn wknd* **16/1**

06-0 **11** *5* **Princess Rebecca**[18] 1620 3-8-11 **52**.............. TPQueally 6 —
(H J Collingridge) *a in rr* **25/1**

1m 17.1s (0.60) **Going Correction** -0.025s/f (Stan) **11** Ran SP% **120.3**
Speed ratings (Par 97): **95,93,86,85,85 84,78,77,69,68 61**
toteswinger: 1&2 £4.70, 1&3 £43.00, 2&3 £28.50. CSF £51.30 CT £1437.61 TOTE £8.70: £1.80, £2.00, £7.20; EX 41.00.
Owner Merry Llewelyn And Runeckles **Bred** D Llewelyn & J Runeckles **Trained** Efail Isaf, Rhondda C Taff

FOCUS
A weak 3yo sprint. The first two finished clear and their form might have been rated a bit higher.
If Only Official explanation: jockey said the colt ran too free
Kings Ace(IRE) Official explanation: jockey said gelding hung left in the straight

2133 BETTER PRICES, BIGGER WINS AT LADBROKES.COM H'CAP 7f (F)
4:40 (4:41) (Class 5) (0-70,70) 4-Y-O+ **£3,070** (£906; £453) **Stalls** Low

Form RPR

412 **1** **Miss Glitters (IRE)**[4] 2011 4-9-4 **70**.............. TravisBlock 8 84+
(H Morrison) *midfield: pushed along 1/2-way: hdwy to trck ldrs whn n.m.r wl over 2f out: rdn to ld wl over 1f out: edgd lft ins fnl f: drvn out* **5/4**[1]

-634 **2** *2* **Ancient Cross**[14] 1737 5-9-1 **67**.............. DaleGibson 12 73+
(M W Easterby) *s.i.s and lost 8 l at s: bhd tl hdwy over 2f out: sn rdn and styd on to chse wnr ins fnl f: drvn and no imp towards fin* **7/2**[2]

00-3 **3** *2* **Mafasina (USA)**[13] 1778 4-8-10 **62**.............. TomEaves 11 63
(B Smart) *towards rr: wd st: hdwy on outer wl over 1f out: sn rdn and styd on strly ins fnl f: nrst fin* **20/1**

6460 **4** *1 1/4* **Montiboli (IRE)**[31] 1332 4-8-10 **62**.............. NCallan 10 59
(K A Ryan) *chsd ldrs: rdn along over 2f out: styd on u.p appr fnl f* **20/1**

40-0 **5** *nk* **Cool Sands (IRE)**[136] 13 7-9-2 **68**..............(v) TPQueally 14 64
(J G Given) *cl up on outer: hdwy to ld wl over 2f out: sn rdn and edgd lft: hdd wl over 1f out and grad wknd* **33/1**

20-0 **6** *nk* **Marvo**[15] 1690 5-9-0 **66**.............. LiamJones 5 62+
(M H Tompkins) *bhd tl styd on fnl 2f: nrst fin* **15/2**

-344 **7** *3/4* **Elusive Warrior (USA)**[27] 1438 6-8-11 **63**..............(p) JamesDoyle 13 57
(A J McCabe) *cl up: rdn along 3f out: drvn 2f out and sn one pce* **7/1**[3]

3036 **8** *2 3/4* **Kingsmaite**[9] 1889 8-8-3 **60**..............(b) MartinLane(5) 9 46
(S R Bowring) *cl up: rdn along over 2f out: drvn wl over 1f out: grad wknd* **33/1**

3005 **9** *2 3/4* **Boss Hog**[27] 1438 4-8-11 **63**.............. JamieMoriarty 3 42
(P T Midgley) *led: rdn along 3f out: sn hdd & wknd* **33/1**

00-0 **10** *2 1/2* **Bid For Gold**[41] 1169 5-8-12 **64**.............. PaulHanagan 1 36
(Jedd O'Keeffe) *a in rr* **40/1**

321- **11** *3 1/2* **Lujano**[151] 7725 4-8-13 **65**.............. TonyHamilton 2 28
(Ollie Pears) *cl up on inner: rdn along 3f out and sn wknd* **20/1**

40-4 **12** *2 1/4* **Turfwolke (GER)**[14] 1743 4-8-10 **62**.............. SimonWhitworth 4 18
(Mrs H S Main) *in tch on inner: rdn along 1/2-way: sn wknd* **16/1**

3-06 **13** *1 1/2* **Danish Art (IRE)**[25] 1477 4-8-13 **70**.............. FrederikTylicki(5) 6 22
(M W Easterby) *a in rr* **50/1**

0-00 **14** *2* **Western Art (USA)**[25] 1477 4-8-13 **70**.............. PatrickDonaghy(5) 7 17
(M W Easterby) *a in rr* **100/1**

1m 29.42s (-0.88) **Going Correction** -0.025s/f (Stan) **14** Ran SP% **125.3**
Speed ratings (Par 103): **104,101,99,98,97 97,96,93,90,87 83,80,79,76**
toteswinger: 1&2 £3.20, 1&3 £9.70, 2&3 £15.20. CSF £4.78 CT £64.20 TOTE £2.60: £1.20, £2.00, £5.30; EX 6.80.
Owner Mrs M D W Morrison **Bred** Roger And Henry O'Callaghan **Trained** East Ilsley, Berks

FOCUS
As expected there was plenty of competition for the lead here and the race was run at suit the closers. The winner was well on top at the end against some exposed performers.
Ancient Cross Official explanation: jockey said that the gelding was slow away

2134 LIVE MUSIC AFTER RACING 27TH MAY H'CAP 6f (F)
5:10 (5:13) (Class 6) (0-55,55) 4-Y-O+ **£2,047** (£604; £302) **Stalls** Low

Form RPR

4-00 **1** **Another Try (IRE)**[19] 1606 4-8-13 **54**.............. TPQueally 10 65
(A P Jarvis) *cl up: effrt 2f out and sn led: rdn over 1f out: drvn and edgd lft ins fnl f: kpt on wl towards fin* **18/1**

4254 **2** *1* **Wiltshire (IRE)**[7] 1924 7-9-0 **55**..............(v) JamieMoriarty 9 63
(P T Midgley) *midfield: hdwy over 2f out: sn rdn: drvn and ev ch ent fnl f: one pce towards fin* **5/1**[2]

3462 **3** *3* **Bold Diva**[17] 1655 4-8-13 **54**..............(v) TolleyDean 12 52
(A W Carroll) *towards rr: hdwy on outer 2f out: sn rdn: chsd ldng pair ins fnl f: no imp* **7/2**[1]

0450 **4** *2 1/2* **Blakeshall Quest**[82] 675 9-8-11 **52**..............(b) TomEaves 6 42
(R Brotherton) *chsd ldrs on inner: hdwy over 2f out: sn rdn and ch tl drvn and wknd over 1f out* **16/1**

0-64 **5** *1/2* **City For Conquest (IRE)**[26] 1456 6-8-7 **53**.............. MarkCoumbe(5) 2 42
(John A Harris) *s.i.s and bhd: hdwy over 2f out: sn rdn and kpt on wl fnl f: nrst fin* **20/1**

6000 **6** *1/2* **Hurricane Coast**[7] 1938 10-8-6 **52**..............(b) AndreaAtzeni(5) 5 39
(D Flood) *s.i.s and bhd tl styd on fnl 2f: nrst fin* **12/1**

00-2 **7** *1 1/2* **Bohobe (IRE)**[27] 1421 4-9-0 **55**.............. NCallan 7 37
(Rae Guest) *trckd ldrs: hdwy 1/2-way: effrt 2f out: sn rdn and wknd appr fnl f* **9/1**

0-00 **8** *1/2* **Owed**[52] 975 7-9-0 **55**..............(tp) PatCosgrave 11 36
(R Bastiman) *cl up: rdn along over 2f out: sn drvn and grad wknd* **11/1**

-522 **9** *1* **Creative (IRE)**[15] 1695 4-8-12 **53**.............. LiamJones 14 31
(M H Tompkins) *cl up on wd outside: rdn over 2f out and sn wknd* **7/2**[1]

440 **10** *3/4* **Trinculo (IRE)**[52] 976 12-8-8 **52**..............(b) KevinGhunowa(3) 8 27
(R A Harris) *led: rdn along wl over 2f out: sn jnd and hdd wl over 1f out: wknd* **20/1**

340- **11** *4* **Half A Crown (IRE)**[213] 6792 4-9-0 **55**.............. TonyHamilton 13 17
(D W Barker) *cl up on outer: rdn along over 2f out: sn wknd* **6/1**[3]

-302 **12** *nk* **Divine White**[57] 920 6-8-12 **53**.............. JoeFanning 4 14
(G P Enright) *a in rr* **16/1**

1m 16.42s (-0.08) **Going Correction** -0.025s/f (Stan) **12** Ran SP% **128.0**
Speed ratings (Par 101): **99,97,93,90,89 89,87,86,85,84 78,78**
toteswinger: 1&2 £18.50, 1&3 £19.50, 2&3 £4.40. CSF £114.06 CT £403.04 TOTE £20.40: £5.00, £2.60, £1.80; EX 185.00 Place 6: £314.53, Place 5: £131.05..
Owner The Twyford Partnership **Bred** Jarvis Associates **Trained** Middleham Moor, N Yorks

FOCUS
A wide-open sprint and there were plenty of chances at the two-furlong pole. The first two came clear.

T/Jkpt: Not won. T/Plt: £296.40 to a £1 stake. Pool: £54,168.40. 133.41 winning tickets. T/Qpdt: £48.00 to a £1 stake. Pool: £3,075.68. 47.40 winning tickets. JR

1927 WINDSOR (R-H)

Monday, May 18

OFFICIAL GOING: Good (good to soft in places; 7.7)

Wind: Fresh, half behind Weather: Fine

2135 E B F TERRY DOYLE RETIREMENT MAIDEN FILLIES' STKS 5f 10y

6:10 (6:11) (Class 5) 2-Y-O £3,885 (£1,156; £577; £288) Stalls High

Form RPR

2 **1** **Yer Woman (IRE)**[12] 1782 2-9-0 0 RyanMoore 7 74+
(R Hannon) *wl in rr: pushed along bef 1/2-way: gd prog against nr side rail fr 2f out: led last 150yds: sn clr* **5/2**[2]

4 **2** 1 1/4 **White Daffodil (IRE)**[15] 1706 2-9-0 0 RichardHughes 11 70
(R Hannon) *mde most and racd nr side: edgd lft 2f out: hdd and outpcd last 150yds* **2/1**[1]

5 **3** 1 1/2 **Miss Lesley**[42] 1147 2-8-9 0 RossAtkinson(5) 2 64
(D K Ivory) *dwlt and carried lft s: wl in rr: prog on wd outside fr 1/2-way: rn green but kpt on fnl f* **50/1**

4 hd **Bramshill Lady (IRE)** 2-9-0 0 PaulEddery 12 63
(Pat Eddery) *dwlt: rcvrd and sn in tch: shkn up 2f out: swtchd to r against rail ins fnl f and kpt on* **16/1**

06 **5** 1/2 **Pursuit Of Gold**[10] 1841 2-9-0 0 RobertWinston 3 62
(J R Best) *wnt lft s: w ldng pair to jst over 2f out: plugged on fr over 1f out* **33/1**

5 **6** 1 1/2 **Monte Mayor One**[10] 1841 2-9-0 0 TedDurcan 9 56
(D Haydn Jones) *w ldr to 2f out: steadily fdd u.p fr over 1f out* **12/1**

0 **7** 3 1/4 **Angie's Nap (USA)**[11] 1810 2-9-0 0 DO'Donohoe 6 44
(E A L Dunlop) *t.k.h: cl up: rdn 1/2-way: sn struggling: hanging lft whn wl btn fnl f* **33/1**

0 **8** 1/2 **Lutine Lady**[15] 1706 2-9-0 0 EddieAhern 5 43
(P Winkworth) *chsd ldrs on outer: rdn 1/2-way: in tch over 1f out: sn wknd* **9/2**[3]

6 **9** 2 1/2 **Riffelalp (IRE)**[16] 1669 2-9-0 0 StephenCarson 10 34
(Eve Johnson Houghton) *dwlt: cl up 2f: sn rdn and struggling in rr* **8/1**

10 7 **Ellmollell** 2-9-0 0 AdamKirby 1 8
(S Kirk) *dwlt and carried lft s: detached in last: a bhd* **33/1**

61.51 secs (1.21) **Going Correction** 0.0s/f (Good) 10 Ran SP% **115.6**

Speed ratings (Par 90): **90,88,85,85,84 82,76,76,72,60**

toteswinger: 1&2 £2.20, 1&3 not won, 2&3 £33.10. CSF £7.56 TOTE £3.50: £1.60, £1.20, £5.20; EX 5.00.

Owner Mrs R McArdle **Bred** Mrs Clodagh McStay **Trained** East Everleigh, Wilts

FOCUS

A 1-2 for trainer Richard Hannon and, while the market suggested they would finish the other way round, there was not much between them in the betting. However, the field looked an average bunch in the paddock and this is only fair form.

NOTEBOOK

Yer Woman(IRE) was unable to go the pace but found a dream run along the stands' rail to win going away. She looks sure to be suited by 6f. (op 9-4 tchd 11-4)

White Daffodil(IRE) showed much more early dash than her stablemate, only to be run out of it in the last furlong. She is related to several speedy sorts and ought to win a similar race. (op 9-4)

Miss Lesley would have gone close to winning had she not swerved left leaving the stalls. She then tried to go the same way throughout the last two furlongs when disputing the lead. That left her stranded in the middle of the track, but this was a much better effort than her debut and she has the ability to win races if her steering can be sorted out.

Bramshill Lady(IRE), a £20,000 Verglas newcomer from a prolific family up to 1m, made a promising debut. Despite being keen to post, her best work was done late on and she ought to be suited by 6f, but she will be sharper for the experience. (tchd 20-1)

Pursuit Of Gold has shown progressively more speed in her three races to date and will be a likely sort in nurseries. (op 40-1)

Monte Mayor One was much pacier than on her debut and will be able to make the switch to handicaps after one more run. (tchd 11-1 and 14-1)

Ellmollell Official explanation: jockey said that the filly was slowly away

2136 WEATHERBYS BANK CONDITIONS STKS 5f 10y

6:40 (6:40) (Class 2) 2-Y-O £11,656 (£3,468; £1,733) Stalls High

Form RPR

11 **1** **Monsieur Chevalier (IRE)**[33] 1290 2-9-3 0 RichardHughes 2 100
(R Hannon) *stdd s: trckd ldng pair: pushed into ld 1f out: comf* **2/7**[1]

1122 **2** 1 3/4 **Archers Road (IRE)**[12] 1788 2-9-0 0 SamHitchcott 4 91
(M R Channon) *racd keenly and hanging lft: led: rdn and hdd 1f out: hung lft and no ch w wnr* **10/3**[2]

01 **3** 6 **Kirsty's Boy (IRE)**[16] 1669 2-9-0 0 LPKeniry 3 69
(J S Moore) *hanging lft and nvr gng that wl: chsd ldr: u.str.p over 2f out: wknd and eased fnl f* **18/1**[3]

60.78 secs (0.48) **Going Correction** 0.0s/f (Good) 3 Ran SP% **106.1**

Speed ratings (Par 99): **96,93,83**

CSF £1.50 TOTE £1.20; EX 1.30.

Owner Mrs Valerie Hubbard & Ian Higginson **Bred** Tally-Ho Stud **Trained** East Everleigh, Wilts

FOCUS

With two of the better early juveniles in the field, this had a classy look despite the low turnout.

NOTEBOOK

Monsieur Chevalier(IRE) completed the hat-trick in workmanlike style and, while not as impressive as he had been the previous twice, the ground was softer and he did have to concede 3lb to his rivals. With the other two both drifting left into the centre of the course, he had to do little to finish the job off and he is now likely to take his chance in the Norfolk Stakes at Royal Ascot. (op 3-10 tchd 1-3 in places)

Archers Road(IRE) had yet to finish out of the first two in five outings prior to this. He again showed a tendency to go left-handed and that drew the sting out of his finishing effort. Although smart for the time of year, he falls just short of the best but would probably be most effective running with a rail to his left. (op 7-2)

Kirsty's Boy(IRE) sprang a surprise in a Goodwood maiden last time, but he was taking on two speedy sorts here and was soon being pushed along to keep up with the leader. He is useful at his level, but on this occasion he was outclassed. (op 14-1)

2137 A C BECK CLAIMING STKS 6f

7:10 (7:12) (Class 5) 3-Y-O+ £2,729 (£806; £403) Stalls High

Form RPR

3554 **1** **Vegas Baby (IRE)**[5] 1982 3-8-12 77 (b) RyanMoore 1 61
(J A Osborne) *led and sn swtchd fr wdst draw to r against nr side rail: hrd rdn over 1f out: kpt on wl* **4/1**[1]

4002 **2** 1 **Caribbean Coral**[12] 1784 10-9-4 63 GeorgeBaker 8 56
(A B Haynes) *hld up in last pair: stdy prog on outer fr 2f out: rdn to chse wnr fnl f: kpt on but nvr quite able to chal* **15/2**

046- **3** 3/4 **Castano**[156] 7665 5-9-2 62 (p) JamesMillman(3) 2 55
(B R Millman) *s.i.s: hld up gng wl: effrt to dispute 2nd wl over 1f out: sn rdn and fnd nil: plugged on* **8/1**

00-0 **4** 3/4 **Rough Rock (IRE)**[47] 1074 4-9-12 48 DaneO'Neill 5 60
(C A Dwyer) *mostly chsd wnr to over 1f out: one pce fnl f* **66/1**

1325 **5** nk **Don Pele (IRE)**[47] 1072 7-8-11 72 (p) SimonPearce(7) 9 51
(J Pearce) *hld up towards rr: chsd ldrs 2f out: nt qckn over 1f out: pushed along and kpt on: nt pce to threaten* **9/2**[2]

600- **6** nk **Caustic Wit (IRE)**[169] 7508 11-8-7 55 JakePayne(7) 7 46
(M S Saunders) *rrd s: hld up: trckd ldrs 2f out: nt clr run over 1f out: pushed along and no prog fnl f* **40/1**

2100 **7** 1 1/2 **Dontuwishitwereso**[17] 1656 3-8-7 63 (v[1]) EddieAhern 3 43
(P W D'Arcy) *prom: rdn over 2f out: lost pl over 1f out and hanging lft: n.d fnl f: eased* **15/2**

00-5 **8** nk **Sun Catcher (IRE)**[22] 1535 6-9-2 55 (p) RobertHavlin 14 42
(P G Murphy) *hld up in rr: taken towards outer fr 1/2-way: shkn up and no real prog 2f out* **12/1**

0303 **9** shd **Green Lagonda (AUS)**[7] 1935 7-9-0 55 DO'Donohoe 4 40
(Stef Liddiard) *taken down early: v awkward s: wl in rr: prog on outer and disp 2nd 2f out: wknd fnl f* **20/1**

1510 **10** 1/2 **Mocha Java**[15] 1710 6-8-9 58 RossAtkinson(5) 12 46+
(M Salaman) *prom 2f: lost pl: struggling in rr over 2f out: trying to keep on against nr side rail whn hmpd ins fnl f* **8/1**

430- **11** 3 **Dr Wintringham (IRE)**[396] 1419 3-8-0 74 FrankieMcDonald 10 21
(J S Moore) *dwlt: v keen and sn prom: lost pl fr 1/2-way: sn btn* **7/1**[3]

1m 14.2s (1.20) **Going Correction** 0.0s/f (Good)

WFA 3 from 4yo+ 9lb 11 Ran SP% **112.8**

Speed ratings (Par 103): **92,90,89,88,88 87,85,85,85,84 80**

toteswinger: 1&2 £4.20, 1&3 £11.70, 2&3 £9.60. CSF £31.91 TOTE £4.70: £1.60, £1.90, £3.10; EX 30.00.Don Pele was claimed by R C Guest for £8,000.

Owner William Durkan **Bred** Mrs Mary Gallagher **Trained** Upper Lambourn, Berks

FOCUS

A fine ride by Moore to get from stall one across to the stands' rail and make all on the winner. Dubious form.

Castano Official explanation: jockey said that the gelding hung right

2138 YES EVENTS H'CAP 1m 3f 135y

7:40 (7:41) (Class 4) (0-80,78) 3-Y-O £4,857 (£1,445; £722; £360) Stalls Centre

Form RPR

411- **1** **Lethal Glaze (IRE)**[229] 6394 3-9-4 **78** RichardHughes 4 86
(R Hannon) *hld up in 5th: prog to go 2nd 7f out to 3f out: sn drvn: kpt on fr 2f out to ld ins fnl f* **4/1**[3]

23-0 **2** 3/4 **Perfect Shot (IRE)**[24] 1489 3-9-2 **76** EddieAhern 2 83
(J L Dunlop) *hld up in tch: rdn and effrt 3f out: tried to cl on outer 2f out: kpt on to take 2nd ins fnl f* **3/1**[1]

31-0 **3** 1 3/4 **Calaloo (IRE)**[14] 1751 3-9-4 **78** SteveDrowne 6 82
(C R Egerton) *cl up: rdn to go 2nd 3f out: led u.p wl over 1f out: hdd & wknd ins fnl f* **7/2**[2]

02-5 **4** 3 1/4 **Cosimo**[23] 1515 3-8-12 **72** RyanMoore 1 70
(Sir Michael Stoute) *dwlt: pushed up to ld: hrd rdn over 2f out: hdd wl over 1f out: steadily wknd* **4/1**[3]

133- **5** 3 **Recession Proof (FR)**[206] 6954 3-9-3 **77** PatDobbs 3 70
(S A Callaghan) *hld up in last: wnt 5th 4f out: pushed along and sn lost tch w ldrs* **5/1**

23-0 **6** 17 **Miss Sophisticat**[27] 1430 3-9-1 **75** JimCrowley 5 39
(W J Knight) *chsd ldr to 7f out: last and rdn 4f out: t.o* **10/1**

2m 31.06s (1.56) **Going Correction** +0.075s/f (Good) 6 Ran SP% **113.0**

Speed ratings (Par 101): **97,96,95,93,91 79**

toteswinger: 1&2 £14.80, 1&3 £6.20, 2&3 £3.30. CSF £16.55 TOTE £4.80: £2.40, £2.10; EX 20.60.

Owner Nigel Morris **Bred** B Kennedy **Trained** East Everleigh, Wilts

FOCUS

With no obvious front-runner in the field, there was just a medium pace, and there were four still battling for the lead on the run to the final furlong. Despite the muddling nature of the race it is worth being positive about the form though.

2139 FRENCH BROTHERS MAIDEN FILLIES' STKS 1m 67y

8:10 (8:12) (Class 5) 3-Y-O+ £2,729 (£806; £403) Stalls High

Form RPR

2 **1** **Strawberrydaiquiri**[28] 1406 3-8-12 0 RyanMoore 10 87+
(Sir Michael Stoute) *trckd ldrs: plld out over 2f out: led wl over 1f out: pushed along and sn drew rt away* **10/11**[1]

5 **2** 6 **Candy Ride (IRE)**[31] 1327 3-8-12 0 JimmyFortune 13 73
(E A L Dunlop) *trckd ldr after 3f: rdn to chal over 3f out: upsides 2f out: nt qckn and sn lft bhd by wnr* **5/1**[2]

2- **3** 3/4 **Silk Trail**[200] 7095 3-8-12 0 TedDurcan 1 71
(Saeed Bin Suroor) *led after 2f: drvn and hdd wl over 1f out: sn outpcd* **6/1**[3]

4 3/4 **Silent Oasis** 3-8-12 0 RobertWinston 11 70
(B J Meehan) *s.i.s: towards rr: prog over 3f out to chse ldng quartet over 2f out: sn outpcd: kpt on fnl f* **33/1**

0 **5** hd **Kindest**[28] 1406 3-8-9 0 JackMitchell(3) 12 69+
(C F Wall) *settled towards rr: outpcd fr 3f out: sme prog over 2f out: pushed along and kpt on fr over 1f out* **50/1**

4-4 **6** 2 1/4 **Piquante**[31] 1329 3-8-12 0 EddieAhern 2 64
(M L W Bell) *trckd ldrs gng wl: shkn up 3f out: wknd wl over 1f out* **6/1**[3]

-0 **7** 3/4 **Polemica (IRE)**[19] 1605 3-8-12 0 SebSanders 8 62
(E A L Dunlop) *nvr bttr than midfield: outpcd by ldrs fr 3f out: no imp after* **50/1**

8 2 1/4 **Red Zoe (USA)** 3-8-12 0 MartinDwyer 6 57+
(M L W Bell) *s.s: wl in rr: urged along fr 1/2-way: modest late prog* **33/1**

0 **9** nk **Dolores Ortiz (IRE)**[32] 1297 3-8-12 0 J-PGuillambert 4 56
(S C Williams) *chsd ldrs: rdn over 3f out: wknd over 2f out: eased* **100/1**

10 3 **Mediterranean Sea (IRE)** 3-8-12 0 SimonWhitworth 7 49
(J R Jenkins) *s.s: mostly in last pair: rn v green fr 3f out: nvr on terms* **100/1**

0- **11** 4 1/2 **Royal Bloom (IRE)**[391] 1535 4-9-10 0 DaneO'Neill 3 42
(J R Fanshawe) *nvr beyond midfield: pushed along 1/2-way: wknd 3f out* **100/1**

12 7 **She's Pivotal (IRE)** 3-8-12 0 SteveDrowne 5 23
(J A Osborne) *s.s: a wl in rr: struggling sn after 1/2-way* **50/1**

13 11 **Mission Lodge** 3-8-12 0 RichardHughes 14 —
(B J Meehan) *v keen early: led 2f: prom tl wknd rapidly over 3f out: t.o* **20/1**

1m 45.14s (0.44) **Going Correction** +0.075s/f (Good)
WFA 3 from 4yo 12lb **13** Ran SP% **117.1**
Speed ratings (Par 100): **100,94,93,92,92 90,89,87,86,83 79,72,61**
toteswinger: 1&2 £2.10, 1&3 £1.30, 2&3 £2.40. CSF £4.95 TOTE £1.90: £1.40, £1.80, £1.70; EX 5.10.
Owner Mrs R J Jacobs **Bred** Newsells Park Stud Limited **Trained** Newmarket, Suffolk

FOCUS
Some potentially interesting late-developing types were on show and they went a decent gallop, but one of them left all the others standing. She looks useful, and the next two were close to their marks.
Mission Lodge Official explanation: jockey that the filly lost action

2140 OUR STAFF MAKE US A BETTERBET H'CAP 5f 10y
8:40 (8:41) (Class 4) (0-85,85) 3-Y-O **£5,180** (£1,541; £770; £384) **Stalls** High

Form RPR
1-23 **1** **Affluent**[24] 1486 3-8-13 **80** SteveDrowne 12 94
(R Charlton) *trckd ldng pair: plld out 2f out: rdn over 1f out: led ent fnl f: sn in command* **2/1**[2]
0116 **2** 1 1/4 **Captain Carey**[34] 1272 3-8-9 **76** TGMcLaughlin 8 86
(M S Saunders) *pressed ldr: rdn to ld over 1f out: hdd ent fnl f: sn hld by wnr but wl clr of rest* **20/1**
4-15 **3** 5 **Desert Strike**[14] 1727 3-8-8 **75** RichardHughes 3 67
(P F I Cole) *chsd ldng trio: shkn up over 1f out: sn outpcd: kpt on to take 3rd ins fnl f* **11/1**
1- **4** 1 **Sharp Bullet (IRE)**[278] 4980 3-9-2 **83** AdamKirby 5 71+
(W R Swinburn) *hld up in 6th: sn sme way off the pce: effrt 2f out: kpt on to take 4th nr fin: no ch* **15/8**[1]
230 **5** nk **Satwa Street (IRE)**[10] 1824 3-8-13 **80** RichardMullen 9 67
(D M Simcock) *led to over 1f out: wknd* **15/2**
-000 **6** 1 1/4 **Joe Caster**[17] 1639 3-9-3 **84** RyanMoore 4 66
(J M P Eustace) *sn pushed along in last pair: nvr on terms: modest late prog* **7/1**[3]
600- **7** 2 3/4 **Finnegan McCool**[213] 6769 3-9-2 **83** SebSanders 6 55
(R M Beckett) *settled in last pair and wl off the pce: no prog 2f out* **12/1**
6015 **8** 1 1/2 **Love You Louis**[81] 685 3-8-10 **77** SimonWhitworth 10 44
(J R Jenkins) *hld up in 5th: pushed along 2f out: steadily lost pl* **33/1**

60.07 secs (-0.23) **Going Correction** 0.0s/f (Good) **8** Ran SP% **116.1**
Speed ratings (Par 101): **101,99,91,89,88 86,82,80**
toteswinger: 1&2 £9.90, 1&3 £7.40, 2&3 £32.10. CSF £41.25 CT £362.94 TOTE £3.10: £1.40, £4.20, £3.00; EX 30.20 Place 6: £17.38, Place 5: £11.57..
Owner K Abdulla **Bred** Juddmonte Farms Ltd **Trained** Beckhampton, Wilts

FOCUS
A strong pace and an improving winner who should be able to build on this. The runner-up beat the rest convincingly and nothing got into the race from the rear.
T/Plt: £11.10 to a £1 stake. Pool: £73,051.19. 4,768.12 winning tickets. T/Qpdt: £11.30 to a £1 stake. Pool: £5,119.00. 332.80 winning tickets. JN

1933 WOLVERHAMPTON (A.W) (L-H)
Monday, May 18

OFFICIAL GOING: Standard
Wind: Fresh behind Weather: Overcast

2141 BET UEFA CUP - BETDAQ H'CAP 7f 32y(P)
6:50 (6:51) (Class 6) (0-60,60) 3-Y-O **£2,388** (£705; £352) **Stalls** High

Form RPR
-065 **1** **Crystallize**[18] 1620 3-9-1 **57** StephenDonohoe 6 62
(A B Haynes) *hld up in tch: rdn over 1f out: led and rdr dropped whip ins fnl f: r.o* **13/2**[3]
0-00 **2** shd **Hold The Star**[23] 1532 3-9-4 **60** JamieSpencer 9 65
(E F Vaughan) *hld up: swtchd rt and hdwy over 1f out: hrd rdn and ev ch ins fnl f: r.o* **9/4**[1]
0450 **3** 1 1/2 **Nun Today (USA)**[6] 1973 3-8-13 **55** (v) JerryO'Dwyer 3 56+
(Karen George) *hld up: nt clr run 2f out: hdwy over 1f out: sn rdn: r.o* **9/1**
5440 **4** 3/4 **Ridgeway Silver**[13] 1772 3-8-11 **60** LeeNewnes(7) 8 59
(M D I Usher) *hld up: hdwy to ld 2f out: sn rdn: hdd and unable qck ins fnl f* **14/1**
40-0 **5** 6 **Venetian Lady**[14] 1725 3-8-13 **55** FrancisNorton 5 38
(Mrs A Duffield) *prom: rdn over 2f out: wknd over 1f over 1f out* **10/1**
5-04 **6** nk **Nimmy's Special**[45] 1106 3-8-11 **58** DeanHeslop(5) 12 40
(M Mullineaux) *s.i.s: bhd: rdn over 3f out: sme late prog* **40/1**
60-4 **7** 2 **Mount Ella**[18] 1620 3-9-1 **57** ShaneKelly 1 34
(J A Osborne) *mde most 5f: sn rdn: wknd fnl f* **14/1**
3-60 **8** 3/4 **Captain Cavendish (IRE)**[24] 1492 3-9-0 **56** (b) MickyFenton 2 31
(A Bailey) *sn pushed along and prom: lost pl over 5f out: n.d after* **20/1**
3454 **9** 3/4 **La Gifted**[14] 1746 3-9-3 **59** TonyCulhane 4 32+
(M R Channon) *chsd ldrs: rdn whn nt clr run over 1f out: sn wknd* **11/2**[2]
605- **10** 3/4 **Join Up**[222] 6573 3-9-0 **56** GrahamGibbons 10 26
(W M Brisbourne) *chsd ldrs: ev ch over 2f out: sn rdn: wknd fnl f* **12/1**
25-0 **11** 5 **Lily Jicaro (IRE)**[36] 1228 3-9-4 **60** RoystonFfrench 7 17
(Mrs L Williamson) *chsd ldrs: rdn and ev ch over 2f out: wknd over 1f out* **22/1**
4-50 **12** 23 **Lagan Handout**[14] 1746 3-8-13 **55** FergusSweeney 11 —
(C Gordon) *s.s: hdwy over 5f out: rdn and hung rt fr over 2f out: sn wknd* **22/1**

1m 30.33s (0.73) **Going Correction** +0.025s/f (Slow) **12** Ran SP% **115.5**
Speed ratings (Par 97): **96,95,94,93,86 86,83,82,82,81 75,49**
toteswinger: 1&2 £1.02, 1&3 £30.90, 2&3 £30.90. CSF £19.70 CT £134.97 TOTE £7.60: £2.80, £2.10, £2.80; EX 39.70.
Owner Mrs A De Weck & P De Weck **Bred** Aiden Murphy **Trained** Limpley Stoke, Bath

FOCUS
A modest handicap run at a fair gallop. The first two raced in the centre in the straight and the first four pulled clear.
La Gifted Official explanation: jockey said that the filly was denied a clear run
Lagan Handout Official explanation: jockey said the gelding hung badly right-handed on the bend

2142 DINE IN THE HORIZONS RESTAURANT MAIDEN STKS 7f 32y(P)
7:20 (7:20) (Class 5) 3-Y-O+ **£2,729** (£806; £403) **Stalls** High

Form RPR
1 **Sunshine Always (IRE)** 3-9-0 0 TonyCulhane 10 78+
(W J Haggas) *hld up: hdwy over 2f out: edgd lft over 1f out: led ins fnl f: shkn up and r.o wl* **12/1**
2 4 **Expressive** 3-8-4 0 Louis-PhilippeBeuzelin(5) 3 62+
(Sir Michael Stoute) *mid-div: hdwy over 2f out: rdn to chse ldr over 1f out: styd on same pce ins fnl f* **5/1**[3]
24 **3** nk **Fortunate Flame**[26] 1451 3-9-0 0 FrancisNorton 1 67
(K A Ryan) *led: rdn over 1f out: hdd and no ex ins fnl f* **4/1**[2]
4 1 1/4 **Dom Polski** 3-9-0 0 ShaneKelly 2 63
(W R Swinburn) *a.p: rdn over 2f out: styd on same pce fnl f* **16/1**
2-2 **5** 3 **Kammaan**[29] 1379 3-8-9 0 PhilipRobinson 6 50
(M A Jarvis) *trckd ldrs: racd keenly: rdn and hung lft over 1f out: sn wknd* **11/4**[1]
2- **6** nk **Istiqdaam**[331] 3262 4-9-11 0 DaleGibson 8 58
(M W Easterby) *mid-div: rdn 1/2-way: wknd over 1f out* **14/1**
-32 **7** hd **Know By Now**[103] 386 3-9-0 0 MickyFenton 7 54
(T P Tate) *prom: hung lft and wknd over 1f out* **6/1**
20 **8** nk **Charlietoo**[24] 1492 3-9-0 0 PaulFitzsimons 5 53
(E G Bevan) *chsd ldr tl rdn over 1f out: wknd fnl f* **66/1**
9 5 **Betony (USA)** 3-8-10 0 ow1 JamieSpencer 12 36
(M L W Bell) *s.s: reminders sn after s: a in rr* **9/1**
0 **10** 2 **Cyber Space**[6] 1963 5-9-11 0 FergusSweeney 11 38
(B J McMath) *mid-div: rdn and wknd over 2f out* **100/1**
4- **11** 1 3/4 **Sixties Gift (UAE)**[151] 7720 3-8-6 0 PatrickHills(3) 4 24
(Rae Guest) *s.i.s: hld up: rdn 1/2-way: a in rr* **25/1**
12 3/4 **Panceltica** 4-9-11 0 JerryO'Dwyer 9 31
(Karen George) *sn pushed along: a in rr* **100/1**

1m 29.4s (-0.20) **Going Correction** +0.025s/f (Slow)
WFA 3 from 4yo+ 11lb **12** Ran SP% **115.2**
Speed ratings (Par 103): **102,97,97,95,92 91,91,91,85,83 81,80**
toteswinger: 1&2 £12.20, 1&3 £12.20, 2&3 £4.60. CSF £68.28 TOTE £17.10: £5.30, £2.20, £1.70; EX 67.30.
Owner Cheveley Park Stud **Bred** Moyglare Stud Farm Ltd **Trained** Newmarket, Suffolk

FOCUS
Despite the below-par run of the market leader, this looked a fair maiden for the track and it threw up an impressive winner, who looks the sort to go on to better things.
Kammaan Official explanation: jockey said the filly moved poorly

2143 BET MULTIPLES - BETDAQ CLASSIFIED STKS 1m 141y(P)
7:50 (7:51) (Class 6) 3-Y-O+ **£2,047** (£604; £302) **Stalls** Low

Form RPR
-336 **1** **Crystal Feather**[6] 1967 3-8-2 53 ow1 FrancisNorton 10 59
(E F Vaughan) *hld up: hdwy over 2f out: led 1f out: rdn and r.o* **15/2**
00-0 **2** nk **Superstitious Me (IRE)**[20] 1594 3-8-1 52 CatherineGannon 8 57
(B Palling) *hld up: nt clr run over 2f out: hdwy over 1f out: rdn and ev ch ins fnl f: r.o* **40/1**
56-4 **3** 4 **Hawkeyethenoo (IRE)**[14] 1740 3-8-1 54 (t) DaleGibson 4 48
(M W Easterby) *trckd ldrs: wnt 2nd 3f out: led over 1f out: sn rdn: hung rt: lft and hdd sn after: nt run on* **11/4**[1]
6-06 **4** 3/4 **Georgie Bee**[14] 1725 3-8-1 54 PaulQuinn 1 46
(D Carroll) *prom: pushed along 6f out: rdn and hung lft over 1f out: no ex fnl f* **14/1**
0-05 **5** 4 **Topcroft**[18] 1632 3-8-3 55 ow2 LiamJones 12 39
(Mrs C A Dunnett) *prom: led 6f out: rdn and hdd over 1f out: wknd fnl f* **40/1**
062- **6** 1 3/4 **Gwerthybyd**[161] 7607 3-7-12 54 DavidProbert(3) 3 33
(B Palling) *chsd ldr over 5f: sn rdn: wknd fnl f* **8/1**
00-5 **7** 2 **Sardan Dansar (IRE)**[14] 1725 3-8-1 53 AdrianMcCarthy 5 28
(Mrs A Duffield) *prom: rdn over 2f out: sn wknd* **18/1**
0-42 **8** 1/2 **On Cue (IRE)**[6] 1967 3-7-10 53 Louis-PhilippeBeuzelin(5) 6 27
(J M P Eustace) *hld up: hdwy u.p over 2f out: wknd over 1f out* **5/1**[3]
00-0 **9** 3 1/2 **Duchess Of Doom (IRE)**[7] 1940 3-7-8 52 RichardRowe(7) 2 19
(S A Callaghan) *s.s: a in rr* **25/1**
-400 **10** 7 **Sermons Mount (USA)**[10] 1839 3-8-1 53 RichardThomas 13 3
(Mouse Hamilton-Fairley) *hld up: rdn and wknd over 2f out* **66/1**
-001 **11** 14 **Ocean Countess (IRE)**[7] 1940 3-8-7 54 JerryO'Dwyer 7 —
(Miss J Feilden) *dwlt: hld up: rdn and wknd over 2f out: eased over 1f out* **7/2**[2]
60-0 **12** hd **Sofonisba**[25] 1481 3-7-10 54 AndreaAtzeni(5) 11 —
(M L W Bell) *prom: rdn over 3f out: wknd over 2f out* **20/1**
6040 **13** 8 **Benozzo Gozzoli**[48] 1050 3-8-1 53 NickyMackay 9 —
(H Morrison) *trckd ldrs: racd keenly: rdn and wknd over 2f out* **16/1**

1m 49.26s (-1.24) **Going Correction** +0.025s/f (Slow) **13** Ran SP% **121.2**
Speed ratings (Par 101): **106,105,102,101,97 96,94,94,91,84 72,72,65**
toteswinger: 1&2 not won, 1&3 £11.50, 2&3 not won. CSF £291.90 TOTE £8.10: £3.40, £5.50, £2.00; EX 265.90.
Owner Featherbed Ladies **Bred** Whitsbury Manor Stud **Trained** Newmarket, Suffolk

FOCUS
A low-grade event, but a tightly-knit one with only 3lb covering the whole field on official ratings. The gallop was reasonable and the first two, who raced in the centre, pulled clear in the closing stages.
Ocean Countess(IRE) Official explanation: jockey said the filly was never travelling

2144 BET 1% IN RUNNING - BETDAQ H'CAP 1m 141y(P)
8:20 (8:20) (Class 4) (0-80,84) 4-Y-O+ **£5,046** (£1,510; £755; £377; £188) **Stalls** Low

Form RPR
00-4 **1** **Luck Will Come (IRE)**[18] 1633 5-8-6 **68** KirstyMilczarek 4 75
(H J Collingridge) *chsd ldrs: led over 1f out: rdn out* **8/1**
0-40 **2** 1 1/2 **Justcallmehandsome**[6] 1964 7-8-6 **75** (v) DebraEngland(7) 6 79
(D J S Ffrench Davis) *chsd ldr: rdn and ev ch over 1f out: edgd lft and styd on same pce ins fnl f* **9/1**
5026 **3** 1/2 **Tourist**[14] 1731 4-9-3 **79** GrahamGibbons 1 81
(D Shaw) *trckd ldrs: rdn and ev ch over 1f out: styd on same pce ins fnl f* **11/4**[1]
210- **4** nk **Ogre (USA)**[206] 6949 4-9-0 **76** CatherineGannon 8 78
(P D Evans) *hld up: rdn over 2f out: styd on ins fnl f: nt trble ldrs* **16/1**
15-2 **5** 3/4 **Im Ova Ere Dad (IRE)**[28] 1405 6-9-4 **80** StephenDonohoe 5 80
(D E Cantillon) *hld up: racd keenly: hdwy over 2f out: rdn and hung lft fr over 1f out: no ex ins fnl f* **4/1**[2]
60-1 **6** 1 1/4 **Bold Cross (IRE)**[13] 1775 6-8-7 **69** PaulFitzsimons 2 66
(E G Bevan) *s.s: hld up: racd keenly: rdn over 2f out: n.d* **9/2**[3]
210- **7** 3/4 **Arthur's Edge**[364] 2262 5-8-9 **74** DavidProbert(3) 3 69
(B Palling) *led: rdn and hdd over 1f out: nt clr run ins fnl f: sn hung lft and wknd* **4/1**[2]

1m 49.83s (-0.67) **Going Correction** +0.025s/f (Slow) **7** Ran SP% **111.8**
Speed ratings (Par 105): **103,101,101,100,100 99,98**
toteswinger: 1&2 £12.00, 1&3 not won, 2&3 £1.50. CSF £71.30 CT £245.36 TOTE £8.90: £3.70, £3.00; EX 58.10.
Owner Greenstead Hall Racing Ltd **Bred** Mull Enterprises Ltd **Trained** Exning, Suffolk

FOCUS
Mainly exposed performers in this ordinary handicap. The steady gallop means this bare form is not reliable and the winner came down the centre.

2145 WOLVERHAMPTON-RACECOURSE.CO.UK H'CAP 5f 216y(P)
8:50 (8:52) (Class 6) (0-65,65) 4-Y-O+ **£2,388** (£705; £352) **Stalls Low**

Form RPR

-266 **1** **Restless Genius (IRE)**[13] 1768 4-9-4 **65**.......... TomEaves 7 73
(B Ellison) *hld up in tch: hmpd over 4f out: led over 1f out: rdn out* **4/1**[1]

200- **2** 1 ¼ **Plumage**[214] 6746 4-8-13 **60**.......... KirstyMilczarek 5 64
(M Salaman) *hld up: hdwy over 1f out: hung lft and ev ch ins fnl f: no ex towards fin* **5/1**[2]

5344 **3** ½ **Muktasb (USA)**[23] 1528 8-8-12 **59**..........(v) GrahamGibbons 4 61
(D Shaw) *s.i.s: hld up: hdwy 2f out: sn rdn: no ex ins fnl f* **7/1**

523- **4** 1 **Rosie Says No**[185] 7320 4-8-12 **59**.......... ShaneKelly 2 58+
(R M H Cowell) *hld up: hdwy and hung lft fr over 1f out: r.o: nt rch ldrs* **13/2**[3]

6004 **5** 1 ½ **Radiator Rooney (IRE)**[9] 1890 6-9-0 **61**.......... JamieSpencer 1 63+
(Patrick Morris) *hld up: hmpd over 4f out: nt clr run over 1f out: swtchd rt and hdwy sn after: hung rt and r.o ins fnl f: eased towards fin: nt rch ldrs* **7/1**

60-0 **6** 1 ¾ **Mayoman (IRE)**[84] 654 4-8-13 **60**.......... LiamJones 8 49
(M Mullineaux) *hld up: hdwy fr over 1f out: hmpd sn after: nvr trbld ldrs* **12/1**

0000 **7** nk **Only A Game (IRE)**[69] 793 4-8-12 **59**..........(p) SilvestreDeSousa 6 47
(I W McInnes) *chsd ldrs: rdn whn nt clr run wl over 1f out: no ex fnl f* **33/1**

0 **8** 1 ¼ **Double Carpet (IRE)**[32] 1313 6-9-3 **64**.......... AdrianMcCarthy 9 48
(G Woodward) *chsd ldr: hmpd over 4f out: led over 2f out: rdn and hdd over 1f out: wknd ins fnl f* **9/1**

0-34 **9** 1 ½ **Desert Pride**[13] 1775 4-9-0 **61**.......... FergusSweeney 11 40
(W S Kittow) *chsd ldrs: ev ch over 2f out: sn rdn: wknd fnl f* **7/1**

03-0 **10** nk **Bentley**[35] 1244 5-8-13 **60**..........(v) PatCosgrave 10 38
(J G Given) *chsd ldrs: rdn over 2f out: wknd fnl f* **11/1**

640- **11** ¾ **Tito (IRE)**[213] 6792 4-9-1 **65**.......... RussellKennemore(3) 3 41
(Paul Mason) *dwlt: outpcd* **33/1**

0-06 **12** 7 **Lieutenant Pigeon**[52] 975 4-9-2 **63**..........(b) PaulEddery 13 16
(Paul Mason) *sn led: swtchd lft over 4f out: hdd over 2f out: sn hrd rdn: wknd over 1f out* **16/1**

1m 14.38s (-0.62) **Going Correction** +0.025s/f (Slow) **12** Ran SP% **125.3**
Speed ratings (Par 101): **105,103,102,101,99 97,96,94,92,92 91,82**
toteswinger: 1&2 £23.00, 1&3 £5.40, 2&3 £28.10. CSF £24.87 CT £140.53 TOTE £5.30: £1.80, £2.60, £2.90; EX 22.00.
Owner Koo's Racing Club **Bred** Sunland Holdings Sc **Trained** Norton, N Yorks
■ Stewards' Enquiry : Paul Eddery three-day ban: careless riding (June 1-3)
Kirsty Milczarek caution: entered wrong stall

FOCUS
A moderate handicap run at a sound gallop throughout. The winner raced centre to far side in the straight.

2146 SPONSOR A RACE BY CALLING 01902 390009 H'CAP 1m 4f 50y(P)
9:20 (9:20) (Class 4) (0-85,85) 4-Y-O+ **£5,046** (£1,510; £755; £377; £188) **Stalls Low**

Form RPR

22-2 **1** **Mezzanisi (IRE)**[26] 1458 4-9-4 **85**.......... JamieSpencer 8 94
(M L W Bell) *chsd clr ldr to over 7f out: racd in 3rd tl rdn to chse ldr and hung lft over 1f out: led 1f out: drvn out* **11/10**[1]

1452 **2** 2 **Wind Flow**[27] 1432 5-8-8 **75**..........(v) CatherineGannon 3 81
(C A Dwyer) *led and sn clr: stdd pce 9f out: hdd over 7f out: chsd clr ldr then tl led wl over 1f out: sn rdn and hung lft: hdd 1f out: styd on same pce* **8/1**[3]

3453 **3** 1 ¼ **Teasing**[11] 1815 5-8-5 **72**..........(v) LiamJones 1 76
(J Pearce) *s.i.s and hmpd s: hld up: hdwy 2f out: sn rdn: styd on: nt rch ldrs* **16/1**

1220 **4** ½ **Distinctive Image (USA)**[15] 1696 4-9-4 **85**.......... FergusSweeney 6 88
(R Hollinshead) *hld up and bhd: hdwway over 4f out: rdn 3f out: hung lft over 1f out: styd on same pce* **5/2**[2]

3-65 **5** nk **Jagger**[15] 1709 9-9-2 **83**..........(p) KirstyMilczarek 4 86
(G A Butler) *hld up and bhd: rdn over 1f out: styd on ins fnl f: nt rch ldrs* **8/1**[3]

01-2 **6** hd **Aegean Prince**[18] 1635 5-9-2 **83**.......... StephenDonohoe 5 85
(P Howling) *hld up: hdwy over 1f out: wknd towards fin* **16/1**

06-6 **7** 13 **Crossbow Creek**[37] 1215 11-8-13 **80**.......... TravisBlock 2 62
(M G Rimell) *wnt lft s: trckd ldrs: racd keenly: led over 7f out: sn clr: rdn: hdd and edgd lft wl over 1f out: sn wknd and eased* **28/1**

2m 40.93s (-0.17) **Going Correction** +0.025s/f (Slow) **7** Ran SP% **113.6**
Speed ratings (Par 105): **101,99,98,98,98 98,89**
toteswinger: 1&2 £3.50, 1&3 £4.70, 2&3 £3.40. CSF £10.87 CT £90.15 TOTE £2.40: £1.30, £2.80; EX 12.50 Place 6: £333.76, Place 5: £195.23..
Owner T Redman And P Philipps **Bred** Knocklong House Stud **Trained** Newmarket, Suffolk

FOCUS
Exposed performers in a fair handicap. A fair gallop eased briefly after around 3f and the winner edged towards the far rail in the closing stages.
T/Plt: £597.30 to a £1 stake. Pool: £90,132.14. 110.14 winning tickets. T/Qpdt: £66.70 to a £1 stake. Pool: £6,323.94. 70.10 winning tickets. CR

1510 LEICESTER (R-H)
Tuesday, May 19

OFFICIAL GOING: Good (good to firm in places in straight)
Wind: Light behind Weather: Showery

2147 EBF EMIL ADAM MAIDEN STKS 5f 2y
6:10 (6:10) (Class 4) 2-Y-O **£4,857** (£1,445; £722; £360) **Stalls Low**

Form RPR

2 **1** **Tawaabb**[15] 1749 2-9-3 0.......... RyanMoore 7 87+
(M R Channon) *chsd ldr tl led wl over 1f out: rdn clr fnl f* **8/13**[1]

5 **2** 3 ½ **State Fair**[32] 1323 2-9-3 0.......... JamieSpencer 3 74+
(P F I Cole) *sn pushed along and prom: rdn to chse wnr over 1f out: styd on same pce fnl f* **7/4**[2]

0 **3** nk **George Baker (IRE)**[24] 1511 2-9-3 0.......... GeorgeBaker 8 73+
(George Baker) *mid-div: swtchd rt and hdwy over 1f out: styd on same pce fnl f* **33/1**[3]

4 9 **Yeah** 2-9-3 0.......... EddieAhern 2 41
(Patrick Morris) *hld up: hung rt over 1f out: nvr trbld ldrs* **125/1**

6 **5** 2 **Knightfire (IRE)**[15] 1726 2-9-3 0.......... AdamKirby 9 34
(W R Swinburn) *chsd ldrs: rdn over 1f out: wknd fnl f* **33/1**[3]

440 **6** 4 ½ **Bebenine (IRE)**[12] 1802 2-8-12 0.......... JamesDoyle 1 13
(Patrick Morris) *led: rdn: hung rt and hdd wl over 1f out: sn wknd* **66/1**

7 1 ¼ **Baby Judge (IRE)** 2-9-0 0.......... KevinGhunowa(3) 5 13
(R A Harris) *s.s: outpcd* **66/1**

8 6 **Sandy Toes** 2-9-3 0.......... RobertWinston 6 —
(A J McCabe) *s.i.s: sn pushed along in rr: wknd 1/2-way* **50/1**

59.57 secs (-0.43) **Going Correction** -0.225s/f (Firm) **8** Ran SP% **109.9**
Speed ratings (Par 95): **94,88,87,73,70 63,61,51**
toteswinger: 1&2 £1.02, 1&3 £6.70, 2&3 £4.50. CSF £1.66 TOTE £1.80: £1.02, £1.10, £3.80; EX 1.90.
Owner Sheikh Ahmed Al Maktoum **Bred** D P And Mrs J A Martin **Trained** West Ilsley, Berks

FOCUS
Despite a couple of hefty afternoon showers the ground was left at good, good to firm in places in the straight. The time was just under half a second under the Racing Post standard and the winning rider reported it to be "good" ground. An uncompetitive event in which the pace was reasonable and the first three pulled clear. The winner looks a decent recruit.

NOTEBOOK
Tawaabb ◆, who shaped with plenty of promise when second to a subsequent winner on his debut, kept straighter this time and did not have to improve too much to register a fluent victory after having the run of the race. He should have no problems with 6f and should be able to hold his own in stronger company. (op 8-11)
State Fair, who got loose and pulled hard on his debut, was more professional this time but, although running creditably on this quicker ground, had his limitations exposed against a potentially decent sort. He should be able to pick up a run-of-the-mill event. (tchd 15-8)
George Baker(IRE), taken off his feet on his debut, shaped much better this time, despite edging off a true line in the closing stages. He should be suited by the step up to 6f and is sure to win a race. (op 20-1)
Yeah, a gelding and late foal who has stamina in his pedigree, hinted at ability on this racecourse debut without being knocked about and looks the sort to do better over further in the longer term. (op 100-1)
Knightfire(IRE), who hinted at ability on his debut, showed up well for a long way on this turf debut and he should do better in low-grade nurseries in due course. (tchd 40-1)
Sandy Toes Official explanation: jockey said gelding stumbled and was eased

2148 JOHN FERNELEY H'CAP 5f 218y
6:40 (6:41) (Class 4) (0-80,80) 3-Y-O **£4,857** (£1,445; £722; £360) **Stalls High**

Form RPR

1116 **1** **Esprit De Midas**[22] 1567 3-9-3 **79**.......... NCallan 10 93
(K A Ryan) *chsd ldr tl led over 1f out: sn rdn: r.o wl* **20/1**

3-61 **2** 2 ¼ **Time Medicean**[29] 1400 3-9-3 **79**.......... SamHitchcott 3 85
(M R Channon) *chsd ldrs: rdn over 2f out: r.o to go 2nd ins fnl f: no ch w wnr* **12/1**[3]

2-40 **3** 2 ½ **Evelyn May (IRE)**[25] 1486 3-9-0 **76**.......... WilliamBuick 9 74
(B W Hills) *led: rdn and hdd over 1f out: no ex ins fnl f* **22/1**

41 **4** 2 ¼ **Devil You Know (IRE)**[11] 1840 3-9-3 **79**.......... RyanMoore 11 70
(D R C Elsworth) *dwlt: hdwy over 2f out: rdn and hung lft over 1f out: wknd ins fnl f* **2/1**[1]

0-1 **5** ½ **Rapid Water**[16] 1704 3-8-13 **75**.......... LPKeniry 7 64
(A M Balding) *chsd ldrs: rdn over 2f out: wknd over 1f out* **2/1**[1]

21- **6** 1 **Audemar (IRE)**[215] 6755 3-9-1 **77**.......... JamieSpencer 8 63
(E F Vaughan) *s.i.s: hld up: swtchd rt over 2f out: sn rdn: nvr trbld ldrs* **15/2**[2]

2-55 **7** nk **Rocket Rob (IRE)**[15] 1720 3-8-5 **67**.......... SimonWhitworth 6 52
(S A Callaghan) *s.i.s: sn pushed along in rr: rdn over 2f out: n.d* **33/1**

41-4 **8** ¾ **Saif Al Fahad (IRE)**[11] 1824 3-8-13 **75**.......... MartinDwyer 5 58
(E J O'Neill) *chsd ldrs: rdn over 2f out: wknd wl over 1f out* **16/1**

40-0 **9** 1 ¼ **Turkish Lokum**[21] 1588 3-8-4 **66** ow1.......... LukeMorris 4 45
(J M P Eustace) *s.i.s: hld up: sme hdwy over 2f out: sn rdn and wknd* **50/1**

-622 **10** 8 **Spit And Polish**[7] 1958 3-8-4 **66**..........(b) JimmyQuinn 1 19
(C A Dwyer) *hld up: hdwy 1/2-way: rdn and wknd 2f out* **20/1**

4- **11** 3 ¼ **Kate The Great**[271] 5204 3-9-4 **80**.......... PhilipRobinson 2 23
(C G Cox) *mid-div: rdn over 2f out: sn wknd* **14/1**

1m 10.79s (-2.21) **Going Correction** -0.225s/f (Firm) **11** Ran SP% **117.4**
Speed ratings (Par 101): **105,102,98,95,95 93,93,92,90,79 75**
toteswinger: 1&2 not won, 1&3 £8.70, 2&3 not won. CSF £224.64 CT £5346.49 TOTE £21.50: £5.50, £3.00, £3.40; EX 589.70.
Owner Joseph Ogden, J Hanson, John Ogden **Bred** Jeremy Green And Sons **Trained** Hambleton, N Yorks

FOCUS
This looked a competitive handicap featuring several unexposed sorts but, with the two market leaders failing to progress as anticipated, it did not take as much winning as seemed likely. The gallop was sound but nothing got into it from off the pace.
Rocket Rob(IRE) Official explanation: jockey said gelding stumbled 4f out

2149 JAMES WARD (S) STKS 1m 60y
7:10 (7:11) (Class 6) 3-Y-O+ **£1,942** (£578; £288; £144) **Stalls High**

Form RPR

-601 **1** **Sign Of The Cross**[24] 1530 5-9-12 72.......... RyanMoore 10 72
(G L Moore) *hld up in tch: plld hrd: led over 1f out: rdn and hung rt ins fnl f: r.o* **13/8**[1]

-000 **2** 1 ¾ **Sularno**[28] 1442 5-9-0 51.......... PNolan(7) 4 63
(H Morrison) *w ldr: racd keenly: led over 3f out: rdn and hdd over 1f out: styd on* **25/1**

6430 **3** 2 ¼ **Maddy**[18] 1651 4-8-9 49..........(p) MatthewDavies(7) 8 53
(George Baker) *hld up: rdn over 2f out: hdwy over 1f out: edgd rt: r.o: nt rch ldrs* **28/1**

2540 **4** ½ **Autumn Morning (IRE)**[74] 776 3-8-4 55.......... CatherineGannon 1 49
(P D Evans) *prom: racd keenly: rdn over 2f out: hung rt over 1f out: styd on* **16/1**

3444 **5** ¾ **Herecomesbella**[12] 1811 3-8-4 52..........(b) JimmyQuinn 2 47
(Stef Liddiard) *chsd ldrs: rdn over 2f out: styd on same pce fr over 1f out* **22/1**

6010 **6** nk **Flying Applause**[24] 1514 4-9-12 66..........(bt) RobertWinston 5 59
(S R Bowring) *led: rdn and hdd over 3f out: styd on same pce fr over 1f out* **3/1**[2]

244- **7** 2 ½ **Lady Valentino**[36] 6768 5-8-13 52.......... RussellKennemore(3) 9 44
(B D Leavy) *hld up: rdn over 3f out: nvr trbld ldrs* **33/1**

3302 **8** 8 **Lytham (IRE)**[20] 1604 8-9-12 62.......... TolleyDean 11 35
(A W Carroll) *hld up: rdn over 3f out: n.d* **17/2**

40-0 **9** 1 ¼ **Bellomi (IRE)**[10] 1894 4-9-7 83.......... EddieAhern 14 27
(A G Juckes) *prom: rdn over 2f out: wknd over 1f out* **8/1**[3]

6/0 **10** 3 ½ **Dazzling Colours**[18] 1638 4-9-7 0.......... LukeMorris 13 19
(T T Clement) *stdd s: hld up: rdn 1/2-way: a in rr* **28/1**

40 **11** 2 **Strategic Knight (USA)**[23] 1538 4-9-2 55..........(t) MarkCoumbe(5) 7 15
(R C Guest) *hld up: rdn over 3f out: a in rr* **16/1**

0 **12** *68* **Ei Tanniola (IRE)**28 1438 4-8-13 0........................(p) KevinGhunowa(3) 6 —
(G J Smith) *hld up: racd keenly: bhd fr 1/2-way* **200/1**

1m 44.76s (-0.34) **Going Correction** 0.0s/f (Good)
WFA 3 from 4yo+ 12lb 12 Ran SP% **115.0**
Speed ratings (Par 101): **101,99,97,96,95 95,92,84,83,80 78,10**
toteswinger: 1&2 £11.60, 1&3 £7.70, 2&3 not won. CSF £55.09 TOTE £4.00: £1.10, £4.60, £3.90; EX 40.10.The winner was sold to Ron Harris for 7,200gns. Sularno was claimed by Jeff Pearce for £7,000.
Owner J L B Racing **Bred** T R G Vestey **Trained** Lower Beeding, W Sussex

FOCUS
Not a competitive claimer and one run at just an ordinary gallop.
Ei Tanniola(IRE) Official explanation: jockey said filly hung left and had no more to give

2150 G.D. GILES H'CAP — 1m 1f 218y
7:40 (7:40) (Class 4) (0-80,80) 4-Y-O+ **£4,857** (£1,445; £722; £360) **Stalls** High

Form RPR

22-0 **1** **Dark Prospect**35 1274 4-9-1 **77**.................................... PhilipRobinson 12 91
(M A Jarvis) *led: rdn over 2f out: hdd and n.m.r ins fnl f: rallied to ld and hung lft towards fin* **8/1**

1531 **2** *nk* **Annabelle's Charm (IRE)**19 1621 4-9-2 **78**.................. JamieSpencer 6 92
(L M Cumani) *trckd ldrs: racd keenly: jnd wnr on bit over 2f out: stl travelling best over 1f out: rdn: edgd rt and led ins fnl f: hdd and styng on same pce whn carried lft nr fin* **3/1**1

0-00 **3** *2 3/4* **Danetime Panther (IRE)**31 1357 5-8-6 **68**..................(p) JimmyQuinn 4 76
(Ian Williams) *hld up: hdwy over 2f out: hung rt and styd on ins fnl f: nt rch ldrs* **9/1**

3544 **4** *3* **Can Can Star**15 1750 6-9-2 **78**... ShaneKelly 5 80
(A W Carroll) *hld up in tch: rdn over 2f out: styd on same pce appr* **8/1**

31/2 **5** *nk* **La Rosa Nostra**31 1348 4-8-12 **74**.................................... AdamKirby 11 75
(W R Swinburn) *trckd ldrs: racd keenly: n.m.r and lost pl over 2f out: rallied over 1f out: no ex fnl f* **6/1**3

21-0 **6** *shd* **Prairie Storm**21 1593 4-9-4 **80**... LPKeniry 1 81
(A M Balding) *trckd ldrs: plld hrd: rdn whn hung rt over 1f out: no ex* **9/2**2

2163 **7** *2 1/4* **Quince (IRE)**20 1615 6-8-12 **74**...................................(v) PatCosgrave 10 71
(J Pearce) *hld up in tch: rdn over 2f out: wknd over 1f out* **16/1**

3060 **8** *2* **Folio (IRE)**12 1812 9-8-8 **70**... AlanMunro 7 63
(W J Musson) *mid-div: rdn over 2f out: sn wknd* **16/1**

430- **9** *5* **Thunderstruck**32 6950 4-8-7 **69**.................................... RobertWinston 8 52
(A J McCabe) *hld up: rdn over 3f out: a in rr* **50/1**

00-1 **10** *7* **Snowed Under**15 1721 8-9-4 **80**...................................... FrancisNorton 2 49
(J D Bethell) *chsd ldrs: rdn over 2f out: hmpd and wknd sn after* **14/1**

11 *4 1/2* **Inchando (FR)**332 5-8-8 **70**.. TolleyDean 9 30
(A W Carroll) *hld up: rdn 1/2-way: bhd fnl 3f* **100/1**

2040 **12** *21* **Millie's Rock (IRE)**51 1020 4-8-10 **72**.............................. NCallan 3 —
(K A Ryan) *s.i.s: hld up: rdn and wknd 3f out* **18/1**

2m 7.00s (-0.90) **Going Correction** 0.0s/f (Good) 12 Ran SP% **116.3**
Speed ratings (Par 105): **103,102,100,98,97 97,96,94,90,84 81,64**
toteswinger: 1&2 £4.40, 1&3 not won, 2&3 not won. CSF £31.46 CT £224.37 TOTE £11.40: £4.00, £1.10, £3.10; EX 20.10.
Owner Michael Hill **Bred** Bearstone Stud **Trained** Newmarket, Suffolk

FOCUS
An ordinary handicap but only a moderate gallop and those held up were again at a disadvantage.

2151 SARTORIUS MAIDEN STKS — 5f 218y
8:10 (8:12) (Class 5) 3-Y-O **£2,590** (£770; £385; £192) **Stalls** Low

Form RPR

3- **1** **Zero Money (IRE)**279 4973 3-9-3 0.................................... SteveDrowne 9 79+
(R Charlton) *chsd ldrs: rdn to ld over 1f out: shkn up and r.o wl* **3/1**2

06 **2** *2 1/2* **Wotasparkler**16 1704 3-8-12 0... MickyFenton 7 66
(W S Kittow) *led: rdn and hdd over 1f out: styd on same pce ins fnl f* **20/1**

2 **3** *1/2* **Steel Free (IRE)**32 1327 3-8-12 0..................................... JamieSpencer 4 64
(M L W Bell) *trckd ldrs: rdn over 1f out: styd on same pce ins fnl f* **8/11**1

66- **4** *4* **Flying Silks (IRE)**195 7191 3-9-3 0...................................... NCallan 8 57
(J R Gask) *mid-div: hdwy over 2f out: edgd rt and wknd over 1f out* **10/1**3

405- **5** *nse* **Majestic Lady (IRE)**218 6702 3-8-12 60............................. RobertWinston 5 51
(B W Hills) *chsd ldr tl rdn and wknd over 1f out* **12/1**

0- **6** *7* **Der Rosenkavalier (IRE)**330 3331 3-9-3 0.......................... WilliamBuick 6 34
(A M Balding) *s.i.s: hld up: hdwy over 2f out: rdn and wknd over 1f out* **16/1**

0-0 **7** *2 1/4* **Houdella**15 1745 3-8-12 0.. RyanMoore 3 22
(B W Hills) *hld up: racd keenly: shkn up over 2f out: sn wknd* **40/1**

8 *2* **Exceed Elegance (IRE)**235 6259 3-8-12 0.......................... FrancisNorton 1 15
(D Shaw) *hld up in tch: rdn and wknd over 2f out* **200/1**

9 *33* **Athaakeel (IRE)** 3-8-9 0... KevinGhunowa(3) 2 —
(R A Harris) *s.s: outpcd: hdwy u.p 1/2-way: sn wknd* **33/1**

1m 11.73s (-1.27) **Going Correction** -0.225s/f (Firm) 9 Ran SP% **116.2**
Speed ratings (Par 99): **99,95,95,89,89 80,77,74,30**
toteswinger: 1&2 £3.70, 1&3 £1.10, 2&3 £1.80. CSF £61.29 TOTE £5.10: £1.30, £6.40, £1.02; EX 84.90.
Owner Ms Gillian Khosla **Bred** Carrigbeg Stud **Trained** Beckhampton, Wilts

FOCUS
Very little strength in depth and a race that did not take as much winning as seemed likely with the market leader disappointing. The pace was fair.

2152 HENRY ALKEN H'CAP — 1m 3f 183y
8:40 (8:41) (Class 5) (0-70,70) 3-Y-O **£2,590** (£770; £385; £192) **Stalls** High

Form RPR

6155 **1** **Citizenship**13 1792 3-9-2 **67**....................................... StephenDonohoe 3 78
(Ian Williams) *a.p: rdn to ld 1f out: styd on u.p: hung rt nr fin* **6/1**3

65-1 **2** *3/4* **Non Dom (IRE)**8 1930 3-9-5 **70** 5ex................................ SteveDrowne 1 80
(H Morrison) *a.p: chsd ldr over 2f out: rdn to ld over 1f out: sn hdd: styd on* **1/1**1

-100 **3** *6* **Shifting Gold (IRE)**48 1063 3-8-9 **60**...............................(b) NCallan 10 60
(K A Ryan) *sn led: set stdy pce: qcknd over 3f out: rdn and hdd over 1f out: wknd fnl f* **28/1**

0-32 **4** *3 3/4* **Saborido (USA)**15 1747 3-9-4 **69**...................................... JimCrowley 9 63
(Mrs A J Perrett) *chsd ldrs: rdn over 3f out: wknd over 1f out* **9/2**2

0-56 **5** *3* **Lombok**20 1611 3-9-4 **69**.. JamieSpencer 5 58
(M L W Bell) *hld up: rdn over 2f out: n.d* **10/1**

-510 **6** *2 1/2* **Scottish Affair**21 1580 3-8-12 **63**...................................... EddieAhern 7 48
(E A L Dunlop) *hld up: rdn over 2f out: n.d* **18/1**

546 **7** *12* **Atacama Sunrise**22 1573 3-8-11 **62**................................... PatCosgrave 2 28
(J Pearce) *hld up: hdwy 3f out: sn rdn: wknd 2f out* **14/1**

6103 **8** *nk* **Graycliffe (IRE)**28 1431 3-8-11 **62**.................................... RyanMoore 4 28
(Patrick Morris) *chsd ldr: rdn over 3f out: wknd over 2f out* **20/1**

0000 **9** *shd* **Best Bidder (USA)**7 1954 3-8-1 **55**.............................. DavidProbert(3) 8 21
(Patrick Morris) *hld up: rdn over 3f out: sn wknd* **33/1**

2m 33.49s (-0.41) **Going Correction** 0.0s/f (Good) 9 Ran SP% **114.6**
Speed ratings (Par 99): **101,100,96,94,92 90,82,82,82**
toteswinger: 1&2 £5.20, 1&3 £24.90, 2&3 £4.00. CSF £12.01 CT £156.05 TOTE £8.10: £2.80, £1.10, £6.10; EX 19.50 Place 6 £63.33, Place 5 £63.12..
Owner Dr Marwan Koukash **Bred** Juddmonte Farms Ltd **Trained** Portway, Worcs

FOCUS
An ordinary handicap run at an ordinary gallop and one in which the two progressive sorts pulled clear.
T/Plt: £44.90 to a £1 stake. Pool: £58,062.72. 943.45 winning tickets. T/Qpdt: £3.00 to a £1 stake. Pool: £5,955.50. 1,424.60 winning tickets. CR

1644 MUSSELBURGH (R-H)
Tuesday, May 19
OFFICIAL GOING: Good to firm (good in places; 7.9)
Wind: Light across Weather: Overcast

2153 EUROPEAN BREEDERS' FUND MAIDEN STKS — 5f
2:20 (2:21) (Class 5) 2-Y-O **£3,885** (£1,156; £577; £288) **Stalls** Low

Form RPR

5 **1** **Reignier**21 1590 2-9-3 0.. AndrewElliott 10 80+
(K R Burke) *cl up: effrt 2f out: rdn to ld over 1f out: styd on strly ins fnl f* **5/1**3

4 **2** *2 1/4* **Final Ovation (IRE)**17 1661 2-9-3 0.............................. GrahamGibbons 3 71
(J J Quinn) *led: rdn along over 2f out: drvn and hdd over 1f out: kpt on same pce u.p ins fnl f* **5/2**2

3 *1 1/4* **Maison Brillet (IRE)** 2-9-3 0... TonyHamilton 11 67
(J Howard Johnson) *towards rr: hdwy over 2f out: rdn to chse ldrs over 1f out: kpt on ins fnl f* **25/1**

4 *1* **Commanche Raider (IRE)** 2-9-3 0..................................... PhillipMakin 7 63+
(M Dods) *outpcd and green towards rr: hdwy on outer 1/2-way: styd on ins fnl f: nrst fin* **16/1**

42 **5** *1/2* **Military Call**21 1590 2-9-3 0.. RichardMullen 9 61
(E S McMahon) *cl up: rdn 2f out and ev ch tl drvn and wknd ent fnl f* **6/4**1

6 *2 3/4* **Rightcar** 2-9-3 0.. PatrickMathers 8 51
(Peter Grayson) *in tch: rdn along 2f out: sn one pce* **100/1**

0 **7** *1/2* **Weetentherty**18 1645 2-9-3 0... DanielTudhope 5 49
(J S Goldie) *t.k.h: towards rr: hdwy 2f out: sn rdn and no imp* **50/1**

60 **8** *1* **Miccolo**11 1847 2-9-3 0.. JamieMoriarty 6 46
(P T Midgley) *cl up: rdn along 2f out: sn drvn and wknd* **66/1**

6 **9** *3 1/4* **Sweet Baby Jane (IRE)**10 1891 2-8-12 0........................... PaulHanagan 2 29
(R A Fahey) *dwlt: a towards rr* **12/1**

10 *2 1/4* **Magical Macey (USA)** 2-9-3 0.. TomEaves 1 26
(T D Barron) *dwlt: a in rr* **16/1**

11 *hd* **Stanley Bridge** 2-8-12 0.. SladeO'Hara(5) 4 25
(A Berry) *a in rr* **50/1**

59.79 secs (-0.61) **Going Correction** -0.275s/f (Firm) 11 Ran SP% **114.9**
Speed ratings (Par 93): **93,89,87,85,85 80,79,78,73,69 69**
toteswinger: 1&2 £4.20, 1&3 £17.00, 2&3 £13.10. CSF £17.06 TOTE £5.60: £1.30, £1.30, £5.90; EX 22.10.
Owner Philip Richards **Bred** Sean Gollogly **Trained** Middleham Moor, N Yorks

FOCUS
1.5mm of rain overnight did not make much difference to the ground. With little of interest amongst the newcomers on paper this ordinary maiden looked to involve those with previous experience and the market reflected that.

NOTEBOOK
Reignier was making his debut when behind the favourite at Nottingham, but was well backed in the morning and the support was justified with a decisive success. He had clearly come on a good deal for the run and this victory could be the prelude to further success. (op 4-1)
Final Ovation(IRE) had been well backed on his debut and built on that under a positive ride. He made the most of his low draw but found the winner too strong in the last furlong. He should be up to winning a similar contest. (op 2-1 tchd 11-4)
Maison Brillet(IRE) ◆ is probably the one to take out of the race. A fairly cheap purchase and already gelded, he ran really well from the outside stall on this debut, particularly as he missed the break. If able to build on this he should also win races. (op 20-1)
Commanche Raider(IRE), another gelding, was another to put up a promising effort on this debut, having also been slowly into stride. He will appreciate further and is the sort who can make his mark in handicaps in due course. (op 20-1)
Military Call was sent off favourite on the strength of his good effort at Nottingham on easy ground on his previous start. He appeared to have every chance here but faded out of contention in the last furlong, and the only excuse can be that the faster ground did not suit him as much. (op 15-8)
Sweet Baby Jane(IRE), the only filly in the race, was a market springer but never looked likely to justify the support after missing the kick. (op 25-1)

2154 RACING UK UK'S THE BEST RACECOURSES LIVE H'CAP — 7f 30y
2:50 (2:50) (Class 6) (0-65,65) 3-Y-O **£2,266** (£674; £337; £168) **Stalls** High

Form RPR

55-4 **1** **Legal Legacy**17 1686 3-8-13 **60**.. PhillipMakin 7 71+
(M Dods) *hld up in midfield: swtchd outside and hdwy 2f out: rdn ent fnl f: styd on strly to ld nr fin* **3/1**2

33-0 **2** *1/2* **Island Chief**15 1740 3-8-12 **59**....................................(b) TonyHamilton 6 69
(K A Ryan) *led: rdn clr over 2f out: drvn ent fnl f: hdd and no ex nr fin* **20/1**

-612 **3** *1 1/2* **Solis**15 1736 3-8-8 **62**.. JamieKyne(7) 4 68
(J J Quinn) *trckd ldrs: hdwy 3f out: rdn 2f out: drvn to chse wnr and edgd rt ent fnl f: one pce* **5/2**1

0-00 **4** *8* **Nchike**48 1057 3-9-2 **63**...(v) AdrianTNicholls 9 47
(D Nicholls) *in tch: hdwy on inner over 2f out: sn rdn and kpt on same pce appr fnl f* **25/1**

00-4 **5** *2* **What A Fella**19 1628 3-8-4 **51** oh1.. WJSupple 11 30
(Mrs A Duffield) *chsd ldrs: pushed along 3f out: rdn over 2f out: sn drvn and grad wknd* **12/1**

4060 **6** *2 3/4* **Wee Bizzom**18 1644 3-7-11 **51** oh6.............................. CharlotteKerton(7) 2 23
(A Berry) *prom: rdn along wl over 2f out: sn drvn and grad wknd* **100/1**

40-2 **7** *nse* **Asserting**11 1831 3-8-10 **57**.. PJMcDonald 3 28
(J A McShane) *chsd ldrs: effrt over 2f out: sn rdn and wknd wl over 1f out* **12/1**

06-0 **8** *4* **Another Luke (IRE)**8 1926 3-8-12 **59**................................. GregFairley 10 20
(T J Etherington) *a towards rr* **33/1**

30-4 **9** *5* **Breakevie (IRE)**17 1662 3-8-11 **58**.................................... PaulHanagan 5 —
(R A Fahey) *hld up: a towards rr* **6/1**3

0-40 **10** *1 1/2* **Ask Dan (IRE)**8 1926 3-8-13 **60**....................................(b1) TomEaves 8 —
(B Smart) *s.i.s: a in rr* **10/1**

0-03 **11** 2¾ **Manana Manana**[17] 1662 3-9-4 **65**..............................(b) RichardMullen 1 —
(S Parr) *s.i.s: a in rr* **9/1**

1m 28.98s (-1.32) **Going Correction** -0.175s/f (Firm) **11** Ran SP% **114.9**
Speed ratings (Par 97): **100,99,97,88,86 83,83,78,72,71 67**
toteswinger: 1&2 £14.10, 1&3 £3.50, 2&3 £7.70. CSF £65.50 CT £170.34 TOTE £3.60: £1.60, £6.70, £1.20; EX 78.00.
Owner D Vic Roper **Bred** D Dowling **Trained** Denton, Co Durham

FOCUS
A moderate handicap for three-year-olds and the market suggested it was a three-horse race. One of that trio did eventually win but it did not turn out quite as expected.
Wee Bizzom Official explanation: vet said filly finished distressed
Breakevie(IRE) Official explanation: jockey said filly never travelled
Manana Manana Official explanation: jockey said gelding never travelled

2155 SCOTTISH RACING YOUR BETTER BET (S) STKS 1m 1f
3:20 (3:20) (Class 6) 3-Y-O+ **£1,942** (£578; £288; £144) **Stalls** High

Form RPR
6202 **1** **Lucayan Dancer**[14] 1765 9-9-4 70.............................. AdrianTNicholls 2 60+
(D Nicholls) *hld up and bhd: swtchd outside and hdwy wl over 2f out: sn rdn: drvn ent fnl f and styd on strly to ld nr line* **7/4**[1]
-301 **2** *1* **Rowan Lodge (IRE)**[34] 1276 7-9-9 63......................(b) JamieMoriarty 12 63
(Ollie Pears) *midfield: hdwy over 2f out: sn rdn to chse ldrs over 1f out: drvn to chal and ev ch ins fnl f tl no ex nr fin* **10/1**
6022 **3** *shd* **Johnston's Baby (IRE)**[10] 1881 7-8-13 62.......................... WJSupple 8 53
(E J Alston) *hld up: hdwy 3f out: rdn 2f out: styd on to ld ent fnl f: sn drvn: hdd and no ex nr fin* **5/2**[2]
060- **4** 2¾ **Beaumont Boy**[224] 6546 5-9-4 50....................................(b) PhillipMakin 5 52
(J A McShane) *trckd ldrs: hdwy 3f out: rdn to chse ldr wl over 1f out: sn drvn and wknd ent fnl f* **16/1**
0262 **5** 1¼ **Dancing Lyra**[77] 744 8-9-4 60.............................. PaulHanagan 10 49
(R A Fahey) *hld up and bhd: hdwy 3f out: rdn tio chse ldrs wl over 1f out: drvn and no imp ins fnl f* **6/1**[3]
000- **6** *nse* **Defi (IRE)**[193] 7224 7-8-11 47.......................................(bt) RossSmith(7) 1 49
(D A Nolan) *led: clr 1/2-way: rdn over 2f out: drvn over 1f out: hdd & wknd ent fnl f* **66/1**
00-0 **7** *8* **Complete Frontline (GER)**[32] 1332 4-9-4 52................ AndrewElliott 7 31
(K R Burke) *chsd ldrs: hdwy on inner 3f out: rdn over 2f out and sn wknd* **16/1**
-450 **8** *3* **Sparky Vixen**[14] 1777 5-8-10 47.................................... KellyHarrison(3) 3 20
(C J Teague) *chsd clr ldr: rdn along 3f out: drvn and wknd over 2f out* **16/1**
4-00 **9** ¾ **Jojesse**[8] 1924 5-9-4 47.. TWilliams 11 23
(W Storey) *s.i.s: a in rr* **66/1**
0004 **10** 2½ **Victory Spirit**[22] 1558 5-9-4 47.. TomEaves 6 18
(D A Nolan) *chsd ldng pair: rdn along 3f out: drvn over 2f out and sn wknd* **20/1**
/0-0 **11** *30* **Optical Seclusion (IRE)**[91] 574 6-8-13 41................. SladeO'Hara(5) 4 —
(K W Hogg) *chsd ldrs: rdn along over 3f out: sn wknd* **150/1**

1m 53.85s (-0.85) **Going Correction** -0.175s/f (Firm) **11** Ran SP% **114.4**
Speed ratings (Par 101): **96,95,95,92,91 91,84,81,80,78 52**
toteswinger: 1&2 £3.20, 1&3 £2.30, 2&3 £4.20. CSF £19.63 TOTE £2.80: £1.10, £2.50, £1.10; EX 17.20.There was no bid for the winner.
Owner James E Greaves **Bred** The National Stud Owner Breeders Club Ltd **Trained** Sessay, N Yorks

FOCUS
An uncompetitive seller but quite a close finish.
Jojesse Official explanation: trainer's rep said gelding lost an off-fore shoe; jockey said gelding stumbled on bend going into straight and lost its action in the final furlong

2156 HOMECOMINGEASTLOTHIAN.COM H'CAP 7f 30y
3:50 (3:50) (Class 5) (0-70,67) 4-Y-O+ **£3,238** (£963; £481; £240) **Stalls** High

Form RPR
56-6 **1** **Stellite**[15] 1734 9-8-8 **62**.. GaryBartley(5) 4 70
(J S Goldie) *hld up in rr: swtchd outside and hdwy over 2f out: rdn over 1f out: drvn and styd on strly ins fnl f to ld nr fin* **13/2**[2]
1350 **2** *nk* **Kabis Amigos**[29] 1413 7-9-0 **63**.....................................(b) PaulHanagan 8 70
(Ollie Pears) *t.k.h: hld up towards rr: hdwy 3f out: rdn along 2f: styd on strly ins fnl f and ev ch tl nt qckn nr fin* **14/1**
3004 **3** *nk* **Red Cape (FR)**[33] 1313 6-8-13 **62**.............................. AndrewElliott 9 68
(Mrs R A Carr) *chsd ldr: effrt on inner 2f out: rdn to chal ent fnl f: sn drvn and ev ch tl no ex nr fin* **11/1**
14-0 **4** *nk* **Infinity Bond**[15] 1737 4-8-13 **62**.. PJMcDonald 6 67
(G R Oldroyd) *trckd ldrs: hdwy over 2f out: rdn over 1f out: drvn to ld ent fnl f: hdd and no ex last 50yds* **16/1**
34-5 **5** ¾ **Grand Diamond (IRE)**[18] 1650 5-9-0 **63**..................(p) DanielTudhope 1 66
(J S Goldie) *in tch on wd outside: hdwy 3f out: rdn to chse ldrs 2f out: drvn and kpt onsame pce ins fnl f* **15/2**[3]
0-06 **6** *1* **Summer Dancer (IRE)**[20] 1612 5-9-1 **64**...................... JamieMoriarty 3 64
(P T Midgley) *s.i.s and bhd: hdwy wl over 2f out: rdn and kpt on ins fnl f: nrst fin* **13/2**[2]
5010 **7** ¾ **Splash The Cash**[16] 1694 4-8-13 **67**................................ AmyRyan(5) 5 65
(K A Ryan) *prom: hdwy 3f out: cl up 2f out: rdn to ld over 1f out: drvn and hdd ent fnl f: wknd* **11/2**[1]
-031 **8** 1¾ **Angaric (IRE)**[18] 1650 6-9-3 **66**.. TomEaves 2 60
(B Smart) *in tch: hdwy 3f out: rdn to chse ldrs over 2f out: drvn and wknd over 1f out* **15/2**[3]
2660 **9** 1¼ **Royal Challenge**[26] 1480 8-9-4 **67**............................ PatrickMathers 10 57
(I W McInnes) *s.i.s: a in rr* **33/1**
42-5 **10** ½ **Heureux (USA)**[11] 1832 6-9-0 **63**................................(p) TonyHamilton 11 52
(J Howard Johnson) *in tch: hdwy 3f out: rdn over 2f out: sn drvn and wknd* **11/2**[1]
0506 **11** *6* **H Harrison (IRE)**[14] 1766 9-8-13 **65**.............................. KellyHarrison(3) 7 38
(I W McInnes) *led: rdn wl over 2f out: drvn and hdd over 1f out: sn wknd* **11/1**
10-0 **12** *46* **Mr Toshiwonka**[53] 980 5-9-3 **66**.............................. AdrianTNicholls 12 —
(D Nicholls) *a towards rr* **22/1**

1m 28.39s (-1.91) **Going Correction** -0.175s/f (Firm) **12** Ran SP% **117.5**
Speed ratings (Par 103): **103,102,102,101,101 99,99,97,95,95 88,35**
toteswinger: 1&2 £21.60, 1&3 £18.60, 2&3 £22.40. CSF £93.18 CT £1001.71 TOTE £9.40: £2.60, £4.10, £4.70; EX 130.90.
Owner M Mackay, S Bruce, J S Goldie **Bred** Cheveley Park Stud Ltd **Trained** Uplawmoor, E Renfrews

FOCUS
This modest older-horse handicap was run 0.59sec faster than the earlier contest for three-year-olds. It produced another good finish with four virtually in a line.
Mr Toshiwonka Official explanation: jockey said gelding lost its action

2157 TURFTV MAIDEN STKS 5f
4:20 (4:23) (Class 5) 3-Y-O+ **£2,590** (£770; £385; £192) **Stalls** Low

Form RPR
32 **1** **La Zamora**[17] 1662 3-8-9 0.. PhillipMakin 14 74+
(T D Barron) *prom on wd outside: hdwy 2f out and sn led: rdn and qcknd clr appr fnl f: easily* **13/8**[1]
6- **2** 2½ **Glenlini**[382] 1770 3-8-9 0... DanielTudhope 12 62
(J S Goldie) *towards rr: hdwy 1/2-way: rdn wl over 1f out: styd on ins fnl f* **11/1**[3]
3-33 **3** *nk* **Mo Mhuirnin (IRE)**[11] 1831 3-8-9 65.............................. PaulHanagan 10 61
(R A Fahey) *towards rr: hdwy on outer 2f out: sn rdn and kpt on ins fnl f: nrst fin* **3/1**[2]
4 **4** 1½ **Fatal Attraction**[56] 947 4-9-3 0............................ RichardMullen 6 59
(Rae Guest) *towards rr: hdwy 2f out: rdn whn n.m.r over 1f out: kpt on ins fnl f: nrst fin* **3/1**[2]
-66 **5** 1½ **Aegean King**[19] 1617 3-8-9 0.. SladeO'Hara(5) 2 55
(M Wigham) *s.i.s and bhd: hdwy 2f out: swtchd rt to wd outside over 1f out: kpt on ins fnl f: nrst fin* **11/1**[3]
005- **6** *hd* **Ballarina**[325] 3470 3-8-9 35.. WJSupple 13 49
(E J Alston) *qckly away and led: rdn and edgd lft 2f out: sn hdd and grad wknd* **66/1**
2200 **7** 1¾ **Princess Charlmane (IRE)**[14] 1781 6-9-3 48..............(t) AndrewElliott 5 46
(C J Teague) *cl up: rdn wl over 1f out: drvn and wknd ent fnl f* **25/1**
000 **8** *3* **Stoneacre Baby (USA)**[61] 884 4-9-3 36.................... PatrickMathers 4 35
(Peter Grayson) *in tch: rdn along 2f out: sn wknd* **200/1**
450 **9** 2¼ **Singapore Girl**[105] 381 3-8-9 53.. PJMcDonald 1 24
(G R Oldroyd) *a towards rr* **25/1**
00-0 **10** *4* **Cranworth Blaze**[8] 1921 5-9-3 45.. GregFairley 9 13
(T J Etherington) *in tch: rdn 1/2-way: sn wknd* **28/1**
00 **11** 4½ **Chenin (IRE)**[47] 1077 3-8-6 0.................................... KellyHarrison(3) 8 —
(Peter Grayson) *chsd ldrs: rdn 2f out and sn wknd* **100/1**
06 **12** *hd* **Your True Love (IRE)**[11] 1831 3-8-9 0.............................. TomEaves 11 —
(A Berry) *a in rr* **100/1**
0- **13** ¾ **Petite Rocket (IRE)**[214] 6787 3-8-4 0...................... PatrickDonaghy(5) 7 —
(J A McShane) *a in rr* **100/1**
000- **14** *18* **Compton Lad**[309] 4013 6-9-1 36..................................(bt[1]) RossSmith(7) 3 —
(D A Nolan) *prom: rdn 1/2-way: sn wknd* **100/1**

58.84 secs (-1.56) **Going Correction** -0.275s/f (Firm)
WFA 3 from 4yo+ 8lb **14** Ran SP% **121.9**
Speed ratings (Par 103): **101,97,96,94,91 91,88,83,80,73 66,66,65,36**
toteswinger: 1&2 £7.60, 1&3 £2.40, 2&3 £6.30. CSF £21.85 TOTE £2.70: £1.20, £3.10, £1.60; EX 27.50.
Owner J G Brown **Bred** Miss S J Smith **Trained** Maunby, N Yorks

FOCUS
Those with official marks in this sprint maiden were no better than platers, with the exception of Mo Mhuirnin, so the less exposed runners were of most interest. They bet 25/1 bar five, and that quintet dominated in the end.

2158 BEST HORSERACING ON SKY CHANNEL 432 H'CAP 5f
4:50 (4:51) (Class 6) (0-65,62) 4-Y-O+ **£2,266** (£674; £337; £168) **Stalls** Low

Form RPR
0-00 **1** **Thunder Bay**[16] 1694 4-9-2 **57**.. PaulHanagan 7 65
(R A Fahey) *led to 1/2-way: cl up: rdn to chal appr fnl f: drvn and led last 100yds* **6/1**[2]
2205 **2** ½ **Ridley Didley (IRE)**[46] 1096 4-8-13 **54**...................(t) AdrianTNicholls 12 60
(N Wilson) *cl up: rdn to ld 1f out: sn drvn: hdd and nt qckn last 100yds* **11/2**[1]
60-0 **3** *shd* **Strensall**[8] 1921 12-8-9 **50**.. PhillipMakin 6 56
(R E Barr) *chsd ldrs: rdn over 1f out: n.m.r and swtchd rt ins fnl f: kpt on wl towards fin* **12/1**
-002 **4** *1* **Distant Vision (IRE)**[8] 1921 6-7-11 **45**........................(b) JamieKyne(7) 11 47
(H A McWilliams) *dwlt and in rr: hdwy on wd outside wl over 1f out: sn rdn and styd on ins fnl f: nrst fin* **14/1**
10-5 **5** ¾ **Red River Boy**[19] 1628 4-8-9 **53**.............................. KellyHarrison(3) 14 52
(C W Fairhurst) *chsd ldrs: rdn wl over 1f out: drvn and one pce ent fnl f* **11/1**
54-0 **6** ½ **Angelofthenorth**[22] 1558 7-8-6 **47**.................................. AndrewElliott 3 45
(C J Teague) *in tch: effrt 2f out and sn rdn: drvn over 1f out: kpt on ins fnl f: nrst fin* **20/1**
3330 **7** ¾ **Spirit Of Coniston**[24] 1528 6-8-13 **54**.......................... JamieMoriarty 8 49
(P T Midgley) *chsd ldrs: rdn along 2f out: sn drvn and one pce appr fnl f* **7/1**[3]
0056 **8** *hd* **Brut**[8] 1921 7-9-7 **62**...(p) TonyHamilton 10 56
(D W Barker) *cl up: led 2f over out: drvn and hdd 1f out: wknd* **12/1**
236- **9** *1* **Almost Married (IRE)**[229] 6411 5-9-3 **58**.................. DanielTudhope 9 49
(J S Goldie) *midfield: effrt 2f out: sn rdn and no imp* **11/2**[1]
354- **10** 1¼ **Botham (USA)**[229] 6409 5-8-8 **49**.. PJMcDonald 5 35
(J S Goldie) *a towards rr* **7/1**[3]
00-0 **11** 2¼ **Coconut Moon**[14] 1768 7-8-11 **57**.............................. SladeO'Hara(5) 1 35
(A Berry) *chsd ldrs: rdn along 2f out: sn drvn and wknd* **28/1**
0-00 **12** *2* **Nusoor (IRE)**[14] 1768 6-9-3 **58**.................................(v) DuranFentiman 13 29
(Peter Grayson) *wnt rt s: in tch on wd outside tl lost pl 1/2-way and bhd* **16/1**
0062 **13** *2* **Lady Hopeful (IRE)**[68] 812 7-8-5 **46** ow1................(b) PatrickMathers 2 10
(Peter Grayson) *s.i.s: a in rr* **50/1**

59.44 secs (-0.96) **Going Correction** -0.275s/f (Firm) **13** Ran SP% **116.5**
Speed ratings (Par 101): **96,95,95,93,92 91,90,89,88,86 82,79,76**
toteswinger: 1&2 £7.20, 1&3 £15.80, 2&3 £9.40. CSF £37.10 CT £400.46 TOTE £7.30: £2.80, £1.60, £4.30; EX 34.00.
Owner R A Fahey **Bred** A C M Spalding **Trained** Musley Bank, N Yorks

FOCUS
Another plating-class sprint and the time was 0.6sec slower than the preceding maiden over the trip.

2159 TURFTV.CO.UK APPRENTICE H'CAP 1m 6f
5:20 (5:20) (Class 6) (0-65,62) 4-Y-O+ **£2,590** (£770; £385; £192) **Stalls** High

Form RPR
0-54 **1** **Monte Pattino (USA)**[14] 1780 5-8-11 **54**......................(vt) LanceBetts(5) 6 64
(C J Teague) *reminders s and sn led: clr after 4f: rdn along 3f out: jnd over 2f out: rdr dropped rein and hung lft over 1f out: sn drvn and styd on strly ins fnl f* **25/1**
132- **2** 3¼ **Master Nimbus**[199] 5305 9-9-3 **60**.................................... JamieKyne(5) 8 65
(J J Quinn) *trckd ldrs: hdwy 5f out: chsd wnr 3f out: chal 2f out and sn rdn: drvn over 1f out and ev ch: kpt on same pce ins fnl f* **5/2**[1]

5-06 **3** *1 1/4* **Grandad Bill (IRE)**[16] 1692 6-9-10 **62**.............................. KellyHarrison 2 65
(J S Goldie) *hld up in rr: stdy hdwy 5f out: chsd ldrs over 2f out: sn rdn and kpton same pce* **4/1**[2]

00-0 **4** *3/4* **Wulimaster (USA)**[14] 1767 6-8-8 **46**.............................. MichaelJStainton 10 48
(D W Barker) *in tch: hdwy 5f out: rdn to chse ldrs 3f out: drvn and edgd lft wl over 1f out: wknd ins fnl f* **13/2**

6-06 **5** *3 3/4* **Dimashq**[46] 1102 7-8-2 **45**.............................. PaulPickard(5) 7 42
(P T Midgley) *hld up and bhd: hdwy 3f out: rdn over 2f out: kpt on u.p appr fnl f: nvr rch ldrs* **11/2**

060/ **6** *3 1/4* **Montchara (IRE)**[172] 5280 6-9-0 **55**.............................. SladeO'Hara(3) 9 47
(M Todhunter) *chsd wnr: rdn along over 3f out: sn drvn and wknd over 2f out* **40/1**

350- **7** *1 1/2* **Dance Sauvage**[24] 4556 6-8-4 **45**.............................. DeanHeslop(3) 4 35
(B Storey) *a towards rr* **25/1**

00/- **8** *13* **Countrywide Sun**[176] 4975 7-8-2 **45**.............................. (p) DeclanCannon(5) 1 17
(A C Whillans) *midfield: rdn along 1/2-way: sn lost pl and bhd* **25/1**

6-60 **9** *50* **Grail Knight**[18] 1648 4-8-9 **47**.............................. NeilBrown 3 —
(A G Foster) *in tch: rdn along over 5f out and sn bhd* **14/1**

030/ **P** **Patavium (IRE)**[17] 4493 6-8-6 **47**.............................. PatrickDonaghy(3) 5 —
(E W Tuer) *prom: t.k.h and sddle slipped after 3f: p.u over 9f out* **5/1**[3]

3m 4.81s (-0.49) **Going Correction** -0.175s/f (Firm) **10** Ran SP% **114.6**
Speed ratings (Par 101): **94,92,91,91,88 87,86,78,50,—**
toteswinger: 1&2 £11.30, 1&3 £22.30, 2&3 £2.90. CSF £83.27 CT £315.03 TOTE £25.50: £6.20, £1.30, £1.70; EX 136.30 Place 6: £56.94, Place 5: £18.25..
Owner Collins Chauffeur Driven Executive Cars **Bred** Gainsborough Farm Llc **Trained** Station Town, Co Durham
■ Stewards' Enquiry : Declan Cannon one-day ban: careless riding (Jun 11)

FOCUS
A very moderate apprentice handicap in which a number were better known as jumpers. It produced a surprise result.
Grail Knight Official explanation: trainer said gelding was unsuited by the track
Patavium(IRE) Official explanation: jockey said saddle slipped
T/Plt: £81.60 to a £1 stake. Pool: £51,956.30. 464.32 winning tickets. T/Qpdt: £23.40 to a £1 stake. Pool: £3,306.14. 104.48 winning tickets. JR

1877 NOTTINGHAM (L-H)

Tuesday, May 19

OFFICIAL GOING: Good to firm (good in places; 8.1) changing to good after race 2 (2.30)
Meeting on Outer course. There was a significant bias towards the stands' rail on the straight track.
Wind: fresh, half against Weather: changeable, occasional showers

2160 NOTTINGHAMRACECOURSE.CO.UK H'CAP — 6f 15y

2:00 (2:01) (Class 5) (0-70,70) 3-Y-O £2,590 (£770; £385; £192) Stalls High

Form RPR

612 **1** **Taurus Twins**[5] 2010 3-8-12 **64**.............................. (b) RobertWinston 11 72
(R J Price) *mde all: clr over 2f out: rdn out: unchal* **7/1**[3]

44-6 **2** *1 3/4* **Rainy Night**[11] 1840 3-8-12 **67**.............................. RussellKennemore(3) 8 70
(R Hollinshead) *chsd ldrs: kpt on fnl f: nt rch wnr* **18/1**

3-61 **3** *nse* **West Leake (IRE)**[22] 1567 3-8-11 **63**.............................. MichaelHills 10 66
(B W Hills) *chsd ldrs: kpt on wl fnl f* **9/1**

0-26 **4** *1/2* **Assent (IRE)**[21] 1588 3-8-11 **66**.............................. JamesMillman(3) 5 67
(B R Millman) *mid-div: hdwy on outside 2f out: styd on ins fnl f* **18/1**

23-1 **5** *shd* **Midnight Fantasy**[11] 1852 3-9-4 **70**.............................. SaleemGolam 7 71+
(Rae Guest) *hld up towards rr: effrt and nt clr run 2f out: r.o fnl f* **4/1**[2]

0-63 **6** *3/4* **Red Rossini (IRE)**[5] 2010 3-9-4 **70**.............................. (v[1]) RichardHughes 9 68
(R Hannon) *chsd ldrs: kpt on same pce fnl 2f* **8/1**

035- **7** *nk* **Integria**[188] 7289 3-9-3 **69**.............................. LukeMorris 1 66+
(J M P Eustace) *prom on outer: one pce fnl 2f* **25/1**

04-0 **8** *3/4* **Print (IRE)**[16] 1704 3-9-3 **69**.............................. TonyCulhane 2 64+
(M R Channon) *rrd s: in rr: kpt on fnl 2f: nvr a factor* **12/1**

00-0 **9** *1/2* **The Scorching Wind (IRE)**[28] 1422 3-8-8 **60**.............................. J-PGuillambert 6 53+
(S C Williams) *in rr on outer and sn drvn along: kpt on fnl 2f: nt rch ldrs* **10/3**[1]

400 **10** *1/2* **Hit The Switch**[15] 1740 3-8-10 **62**.............................. CatherineGannon 15 54
(Patrick Morris) *chsd ldrs: one pce fnl 2f* **33/1**

3-10 **11** *1/2* **Yanza**[24] 1505 3-9-3 **69**.............................. SteveDrowne 17 59+
(J R Gask) *in rr: nt clr run on inner over 2f out: nvr on terms* **40/1**

0-0 **12** *nse* **Alexander Loyalty (IRE)**[47] 1077 3-8-13 **65**.............................. LPKeniry 13 55+
(E F Vaughan) *hld up in rr: nt clr run over 2f out: nvr on terms* **33/1**

0-50 **13** *hd* **Rio Cobolo (IRE)**[24] 1505 3-8-10 **62**.............................. (v) NCallan 3 51
(Paul Green) *md-div: drvn over 2f out: lost pl over 1f out* **100/1**

546- **14** *hd* **Pansy Potter**[148] 7760 3-8-11 **63**.............................. RyanMoore 16 52+
(B J Meehan) *hmpd s: towards rr: nt clr run over 2f out: nvr a factor* **12/1**

0101 **15** *3/4* **Bold Rose**[14] 1772 3-8-13 **65**.............................. (p) DaneO'Neill 14 51
(M D I Usher) *s.i.s: a in rr* **18/1**

164- **16** *5* **Cocktail Party (IRE)**[195] 7199 3-8-10 **62**.............................. EddieAhern 12 32
(J W Hills) *prom: rdn over 2f out: sn lost pl* **33/1**

1m 14.81s (-0.09) **Going Correction** -0.025s/f (Good) **16** Ran SP% **124.0**
Speed ratings (Par 99): **99,96,96,95,95 94,94,93,92,92 91,91,91,90,89 83**
toteswinger: 1&2 £17.40, 1&3 £10.90, 2&3 £40.60. CSF £121.22 CT £1164.32 TOTE £7.60: £1.60, £4.80, £2.60, £5.20; EX 162.20.
Owner G E Amey **Bred** G E Amey **Trained** Ullingswick, H'fords

FOCUS
This was a modest three-year-old sprint handicap in which it proved difficult to make up significant amounts of ground. They all raced stands' side and a high draw was an advantage.
Midnight Fantasy Official explanation: jockey said filly was denied a clear run
Yanza Official explanation: jockey said filly was denied a clear run
Alexander Loyalty(IRE) Official explanation: jockey said gelding was denied a clear run
Pansy Potter Official explanation: jockey said filly was hampered leaving stalls and was subsequently denied a clear run

2161 EUROPEAN BREEDERS' FUND MAIDEN STKS — 5f 13y

2:30 (2:31) (Class 5) 2-Y-O £3,885 (£1,156; £577; £288) Stalls High

Form RPR

22 **1** **Dancing Freddy (IRE)**[14] 1764 2-9-3 0.............................. PatCosgrave 5 75+
(J G Given) *mde all: jst hld on* **6/4**[2]

4 **2** *1/2* **Key Art (IRE)**[10] 1862 2-9-3 0.............................. RyanMoore 1 73+
(J Noseda) *w wnr: rdn over 1f out: kpt on wl towards fin* **5/6**[1]

40 **3** *6* **Elegant Dancer (IRE)**[24] 1504 2-8-12 0.............................. EddieAhern 3 47+
(Paul Green) *chsd ldrs: outpcd over 2f out: wknd over 1f out* **33/1**

0 **4** *5* **Lady Bucket**[24] 1504 2-8-12 0.............................. J-PGuillambert 6 29+
(Paul Green) *sn drvn along and outpcd: wknd over 2f out* **100/1**

5 *3 1/2* **Miss Lauz** 2-8-12 0.............................. RichardHughes 7 16+
(R Hannon) *s.s and swvd lft s: a detached in last* **7/1**[3]

62.18 secs (1.18) **Going Correction** -0.025s/f (Good) **5** Ran SP% **111.0**
Speed ratings (Par 93): **89,88,78,70,65**
toteswinger: 1&2 £1.90. CSF £3.10 TOTE £2.30: £1.10, £1.10; EX 3.50.
Owner Danethorpe Racing Partnership **Bred** Vincent Duignan **Trained** Willoughton, Lincs

FOCUS
This maiden only concerned two of the five runners, but both look fair enough types.

NOTEBOOK
Dancing Freddy(IRE) had the benefit of the favoured stands' rail, whereas Key Art was stuck out slightly wider than ideal, and that probably made the difference. He has improved with every run so far, but everything went his way this time. (op 7-4 tchd 15-8)
Key Art(IRE) cannot really be faulted considering the winner benefited from a track bias, and this looked a slight improvement on the form he showed on his debut at Ascot. (op 10-11 tchd Evens)
Elegant Dancer(IRE) showed good early speed and this was a step up on her two previous efforts. (op 25-1)
Lady Bucket was outpaced throughout and looks very moderate (op 66-1)
Miss Lauz, the only newcomer in the line-up, started slowly and showed nothing. (tchd 11-2 and 15-2)

2162 "BOOK YOUR SUMMER HOSPITALITY NOW" H'CAP — 5f 13y

3:00 (3:01) (Class 6) (0-60,61) 3-Y-O £2,047 (£604; £302) Stalls High

Form RPR

0500 **1** **Baby Queen (IRE)**[31] 1359 3-8-11 **53**.............................. J-PGuillambert 17 63
(B P J Baugh) *led stands' side gp: clr that side over 1f out: overall ldr ins fnl f: kpt on wl* **33/1**

5244 **2** *1 3/4* **Rocket Ruby**[53] 986 3-8-10 **52**.............................. FrancisNorton 6 56
(D Shaw) *led 6 others far side: clr that gp over 1f out: hdd overall and no ex ins fnl f* **14/1**

461 **3** *1 1/4* **Pinball (IRE)**[6] 1985 3-9-5 **61** 6ex.............................. (v) RichardHughes 14 61+
(Patrick Morris) *racd stands' side: hld up: hdwy over 2f out: wnt 2nd that side 1f out: kpt on same pce* **8/1**

0202 **4** *2* **Simple Rhythm**[7] 1949 3-9-2 **58**.............................. PatCosgrave 3 50
(J G Given) *racd far side: chsd ldr: kpt on same pce fnl 2f: 2nd of 7 that gp* **13/2**[2]

50-0 **5** *2* **Peper Harow (IRE)**[11] 1840 3-9-4 **60**.............................. DaneO'Neill 8 45
(M D I Usher) *swtchd lft s to r far side: in rr: kpt on fnl 2f: nvr nrr: 3rd of 7 that gp* **10/1**

1223 **6** *nse* **Fasliyanne (IRE)**[18] 1644 3-9-4 **60**.............................. NCallan 12 45
(K A Ryan) *racd stands' side: chsd ldrs: one pce fnl 2f* **11/2**[1]

6305 **7** *1/2* **Tightrope (IRE)**[7] 1956 3-8-4 **51**.............................. AmyBaker(5) 13 34
(T D McCarthy) *racd stands' side: chsd ldrs: one pce fnl 2f* **20/1**

0405 **8** *nk* **Thumberlina**[27] 1455 3-8-6 **48**.............................. (p) CatherineGannon 4 30
(Mrs C A Dunnett) *racd far side: chsd ldrs: wknd appr fnl f: 4th of 7 that gp* **25/1**

0-00 **9** *hd* **Brynfa Boy**[11] 1840 3-9-4 **60**.............................. IanMongan 15 41
(P W D'Arcy) *dwlt: racd stands' side: mid-div: hdwy and hung lft 2f out: nvr nr ldrs* **7/1**[3]

006- **10** *3/4* **Kayceebee**[209] 6906 3-8-8 **50**.............................. (b[1]) RichardKingscote 2 29
(R M Beckett) *racd far side: in rr: nvr a factor: 5th of 7 that gp* **7/1**[3]

550- **11** *1/2* **Rio Pomba (IRE)**[232] 6341 3-9-0 **56**.............................. DNolan 5 33
(D Carroll) *racd far side: towards rr: nvr a factor: 6th of 7 that gp* **33/1**

60-0 **12** *nk* **Red Max (IRE)**[15] 1736 3-8-11 **53**.............................. (p) RobertWinston 7 29
(T D Easterby) *swtchd lft s to r far side: sn chsng ldrs: lost pl over 1f out: last of 7 that gp* **8/1**

6-10 **13** *3/4* **Iachimo**[43] 1157 3-8-13 **55**.............................. JimCrowley 11 28
(K R Burke) *racd stands' side: mid-div: hung lft and lost pl over 2f out* **8/1**

600 **14** *nse* **Carrazara (IRE)**[15] 1745 3-8-1 **48** ow1.............................. MartinLane(5) 10 21
(Edgar Byrne) *s.i.s: racd stands' side: sn outpcd and in rr* **50/1**

-640 **15** *3 3/4* **Cindy Incidentally**[60] 889 3-8-7 **49**.............................. AlanMunro 16 8
(Miss Gay Kelleway) *racd stands' side: chsd ldrs: lost pl over 2f out* **40/1**

-036 **16** *8* **Pressed For Time (IRE)**[6] 1982 3-9-1 **57**.............................. (t) EdwardCreighton 9 —
(E J Creighton) *racd stands' side: chsd ldrs: lost pl 2f out: bhd whn eased ins fnl f* **18/1**

61.38 secs (0.38) **Going Correction** -0.025s/f (Good) **16** Ran SP% **127.0**
Speed ratings (Par 97): **95,92,90,87,83 83,82,82,82,80 80,79,78,78,72 59**
toteswinger: 1&2 £76.30, 1&3 £44.50, 2&3 £8.90. CSF £436.50 CT £4204.06 TOTE £49.70: £7.20, £3.00, £1.80, £2.10; EX 1075.30.
Owner G B Hignett **Bred** Gainsborough Stud Management Ltd **Trained** Audley, Staffs

FOCUS
The field split and there wasn't much between the two groups, but just as in the previous couple of races on the straight course, the winner raced tight against the stands' rail.
Baby Queen(IRE) Official explanation: trainer said, regarding apparent improvement in form, that the filly may have been inconvenienced by the draw last time but this race developed to suit ideally.
Tightrope(IRE) Official explanation: jockey said gelding was unsuited by the good ground
Pressed For Time(IRE) Official explanation: trainer said filly returned in season

2163 PADDOCKS CONFERENCE CENTRE H'CAP — 2m 9y

3:30 (3:30) (Class 5) (0-70,69) 4-Y-0+ £2,590 (£770; £385; £192) Stalls Low

Form RPR

1 **Caoba**[33] 5-9-1 **59**.............................. RyanMoore 4 68+
(V R A Dartnall) *chsd ldrs: drvn 6f out: led 4f out: hld on wl* **11/10**[1]

060- **2** *3/4* **Rare Ruby (IRE)**[211] 6861 5-8-13 **57**.............................. JoeFanning 6 65+
(Jennie Candlish) *led 1f: chsd ldrs: styd on to take 2nd ins fnl f: no ex* **10/1**

1U3 **3** *1/2* **Calculating (IRE)**[8] 1936 5-8-11 **55**.............................. NCallan 2 63
(M D I Usher) *chsd ldrs: drvn 7f out: wnt 2nd over 2f out: styd on same pce fnl f* **6/1**[2]

34-6 **4** *6* **Whitcombe Spirit**[28] 1426 4-8-12 **58**.............................. RobertHavlin 11 58
(Jamie Poulton) *mid-div: hrd drvn over 3f out: one pce* **16/1**

/10- **5** *nk* **Elaala (USA)**[13] 7455 7-8-7 **51**.............................. RobertWinston 5 51
(B D Leavy) *mid-div: pushed along 7f out: one pce fnl 3f* **25/1**

2-54 **6** *3 1/2* **Adage**[30] 1378 6-8-4 **48** oh2.............................. (t) FrankieMcDonald 9 44
(David Pinder) *swtchd lft s: hld up in rr: effrt over 4f out: nvr nr ldrs* **28/1**

2035 **7** *1/2* **Russian Invader (IRE)**[17] 1439 5-9-2 **65**.............................. (be) MarkCoumbe(5) 8 60
(R C Guest) *led after 1f: hdd over 6f out: sn lost pl* **33/1**

4622 **8** *1/2* **Piper's Song (IRE)**[6] 1980 6-9-6 **64**.............................. RichardHughes 3 59
(Patrick Morris) *hld up in rr: sme hdwy on ins 3f out: nvr nr ldrs: eased ins fnl f* **7/1**[3]

21-5 **9** *9* **Art Exhibition (IRE)**[18] 1654 4-8-13 **62**.............................. (b[1]) JamesMillman(3) 10 46
(B R Millman) *chsd ldrs: led over 6f out: hdd 4f out: lost pl over 1f out* **11/1**

60-0 **10** 7 **Flame Creek (IRE)**[70] 790 13-8-4 **48**........................ CatherineGannon 1 23
(E J Creighton) *stmbld s: in rr: bhd fnl 4f* **50/1**

-545 **11** 7 **Miss Serena**[38] 1215 4-9-9 **69**........................ MickyFenton 7 36
(Mrs P Sly) *mid-div: lost pl bnd after 4f: pushed along and hdwy to chse ldrs 7f out: wknd 2f out: eased* **12/1**

3m 34.71s (4.41) **Going Correction** -0.025s/f (Good)
WFA 4 from 5yo+ 2lb **11** Ran SP% **117.6**
Speed ratings (Par 103): **87,86,86,83,83 81,81,80,76,72 69**
toteswinger: 1&2 £6.60, 1&3 £2.40, 2&3 £12.20. CSF £12.54 CT £49.82 TOTE £2.00: £1.10, £3.70, £1.80; EX 17.60.
Owner Exe Valley Racing **Bred** Plantation Stud **Trained** Brayford, Devon

FOCUS
A modest staying handicap.
Art Exhibition(IRE) Official explanation: jockey said gelding had no more to give
Miss Serena Official explanation: jockey said filly lost its action

2164 RACING UK ON CHANNEL 432 FILLIES' H'CAP 1m 2f 50y
4:00 (4:00) (Class 4) (0-80,80) 3-Y-O **£5,828** (£1,734; £866; £432) **Stalls** Low

Form RPR

2-32 **1** **Polly's Mark (IRE)**[25] 1489 3-9-7 **80**........................ PhilipRobinson 7 90
(C G Cox) *sn chsng ldrs: drvn 6f out: led 2f out: drew clr ins fnl f* **13/8**[1]

30-3 **2** 5 **Lonely Star (IRE)**[35] 1269 3-9-5 **78**........................ TedDurcan 1 78
(D R Lanigan) *trckd ldrs: chal over 3f out: kpt on same pce appr fnl f* **9/1**

051- **3** 2 1/2 **Act Green**[219] 6682 3-9-4 **77**........................ JamieSpencer 6 72
(M L W Bell) *led: hdd 2f out: one pce* **5/2**[2]

-221 **4** 3/4 **Onemix**[46] 1092 3-9-7 **80**........................ MichaelHills 8 74
(B W Hills) *trckd ldr: effrt 4f out: edgd lft and one pce fnl 2f* **3/1**[3]

56-4 **5** 6 **Petella**[24] 1509 3-8-4 **63**........................ JoeFanning 3 45
(C W Thornton) *dwlt: in rr: drvn and lost tch over 4f out* **12/1**

-060 **6** 12 **Clumber Place**[10] 1882 3-8-6 **65**........................ FrancisNorton 4 23
(R C Guest) *hld up in tch: effrt 4f out: sn lost pl* **50/1**

2m 11.35s (-0.35) **Going Correction** -0.025s/f (Good) **6** Ran SP% **111.3**
Speed ratings (Par 98): **100,96,94,93,88 79**
toteswinger: 1&2 £3.30, 1&3 £1.80, 2&3 £2.80. CSF £16.67 CT £33.70 TOTE £2.60: £1.60, £3.30; EX 14.70.
Owner Wickham Stud **Bred** Glashare House Stud **Trained** Lambourn, Berks

FOCUS
A fair fillies' handicap.

2165 "SHIELS 50TH WEDDING ANNIVERSARY" MAIDEN STKS 1m 75y
4:30 (4:31) (Class 5) 3-Y-O **£2,590** (£770; £385; £192) **Stalls** Low

Form RPR

-2 **1** **Sovereign Remedy (USA)**[15] 1729 3-9-3 0........................ TedDurcan 12 78+
(Saeed Bin Suroor) *trckd ldrs: led 2f out: styd on wl ins fnl f* **3/1**[2]

0-5 **2** 1 1/2 **Ithinkbest**[27] 1461 3-9-3 0........................ RyanMoore 1 74
(Sir Michael Stoute) *chsd ldrs: chal over 2f out: kpt on same pce ins fnl f* **5/1**[3]

3 **3** 1/2 **Mohtashem (IRE)**[15] 1729 3-9-3 0........................ RHills 9 73+
(Sir Michael Stoute) *trckd ldrs: t.k.h: effrt and hung lft over 2f out: kpt on wl fnl f* **8/11**[1]

2-4 **4** 2 3/4 **Royal Defence (IRE)**[17] 1683 3-9-3 0........................ FrancisNorton 10 67
(D Nicholls) *trckd ldrs: outpcd 2f out: styd on fnl f* **12/1**

45- **5** 2 1/4 **Montmartre (USA)**[287] 4697 3-8-12 0........................ GabrielHannon(5) 13 62
(B J Meehan) *led tl hdd 2f out: sn wknd* **100/1**

0 **6** 1/2 **Peace Corps**[15] 1730 3-9-3 0........................ DaneO'Neill 11 61+
(J R Fanshawe) *dwlt: carried wd bnd after 2f: kpt on fnl 2f: nvr nr ldrs* **50/1**

7 1/2 **Sahaal (USA)** 3-9-3 0........................ MartinDwyer 7 60
(M P Tregoning) *hld up in midfield: drvn over 3f out: one pce* **20/1**

0- **8** 2 1/4 **Choral Service**[203] 7054 3-9-0 0........................ GilmarPereira(3) 2 54
(W J Haggas) *dwlt: sn prom: drvn on ins over 3f out: edgd rt: wknd 2f out* **16/1**

9 *hd* **Alpha Vega (IRE)** 3-8-12 0........................ AdamKirby 4 49
(J R Fanshawe) *s.i.s: kpt on fnl 2f: nvr a factor* **80/1**

0 **10** 3/4 **Singbella**[29] 1406 3-8-12 0........................ PhilipRobinson 8 47
(C G Cox) *in rr-div: effrt 4f out: nvr on terms* **33/1**

11 2 **Picturethatmoment (USA)** 3-8-12 0........................ JimCrowley 6 43
(K R Burke) *hld up towards rr: nvr on terms* **66/1**

0-6 **12** 24 **Cruise Control**[118] 236 3-9-3 0........................ JamesDoyle 5 —
(R J Price) *s.i.s: rn wd bnd after 2f: bhd fnl 3f: t.o* **100/1**

1m 46.95s (1.35) **Going Correction** -0.025s/f (Good) **12** Ran SP% **127.5**
Speed ratings (Par 99): **92,90,90,87,85 84,84,81,81,80 78,54**
toteswinger: 1&2 £2.50, 1&3 £1.80, 2&3 £3.00. CSF £19.56 TOTE £4.00: £1.10, £1.80, £1.20; EX 23.50.
Owner Godolphin **Bred** Gainsborough Farm Llc **Trained** Newmarket, Suffolk

FOCUS
A fair three-year-old maiden, but they went a modest pace, resulting in a time 1.93 seconds slower than the following 51-65 handicap for older horses.
Mohtashem(IRE) Official explanation: jockey said colt ran too free
Cruise Control Official explanation: jockey said colt hung right

2166 "COME RACING ON WEDNESDAY 3RD JUNE" H'CAP 1m 75y
5:00 (5:00) (Class 6) (0-65,65) 4-Y-O+ **£2,047** (£604; £302) **Stalls** Low

Form RPR

0400 **1** **West End Lad**[26] 1479 6-9-3 **64**........................(b) DaneO'Neill 8 74
(S R Bowring) *trckd ldrs: effrt on ins 2f out: styd on to ld towards fin* **16/1**

3533 **2** *hd* **Kildare Sun (IRE)**[10] 1887 7-8-11 **63**........................(v) FrederikTylicki(5) 7 73
(J Mackie) *chsd ldrs: led over 1f out: hdd and no ex nr fin* **9/4**[1]

5150 **3** 2 **Inside Story (IRE)**[34] 1279 7-9-2 **63**........................(b) LPKeniry 14 68
(C R Dore) *in rr-div: t.k.h: hdwy over 2f out: styd on fnl f: tk 3rd nr fin* **14/1**

6-02 **4** *nk* **Resentful Angel**[15] 1743 4-9-3 **64**........................ PaulEddery 12 68
(Pat Eddery) *chsd ldrs: kpt on same pce appr fnl f* **8/1**[3]

0062 **5** *nk* **Yakama (IRE)**[7] 1959 4-8-7 **54**........................ CatherineGannon 6 58
(Mrs C A Dunnett) *in tch on inner: hdwy over 2f out: kpt on: nvr a real threat* **9/1**

-353 **6** 1 1/4 **King Of The Moors (USA)**[11] 1830 6-8-13 **65**........(p) MarkCoumbe(5) 9 66
(R C Guest) *lerd tl over 1f out: wknd towards fin* **11/1**

4-00 **7** 3 **Tanforan**[20] 1612 7-8-10 **57**........................ DavidAllan 11 51
(B P J Baugh) *s.i.s: hdwy over 2f out: nvr nr ldrs* **22/1**

000- **8** 1 1/4 **King Of Rhythm (IRE)**[206] 6989 6-9-4 **65**........................ DNolan 15 56
(D Carroll) *chsd ldrs: wknd over 1f out* **14/1**

-060 **9** 2 **The Grey One (IRE)**[16] 1710 6-9-0 **61**........................(p) TedDurcan 13 47
(J M Bradley) *in rr: nvr nrr* **20/1**

5040 **10** 2 1/2 **Prince Golan (IRE)**[61] 885 5-9-3 **64**........................(p) RichardKingscote 1 45
(J W Unett) *dwlt: nvr on terms* **10/1**

0-06 **11** 1/2 **Registrar**[19] 1634 7-8-7 **54**........................(p) SaleemGolam 3 33
(Mrs C A Dunnett) *in rr: nvr a factor* **22/1**

066- **12** 33 **Pinewood Lulu**[260] 5565 4-8-8 **55**........................ FrancisNorton 2 —
(R C Guest) *t.k.h in midfield: lost pl over 3f out: sn bhd: t.o* **40/1**

252- **13** 11 **Navene (IRE)**[231] 6363 5-9-4 **65**........................ AlanMunro 10 —
(C F Wall) *trckd ldrs: tk fierce hold: wknd over 2f out: sn bhd: t.o* **5/1**[2]

1m 45.02s (-0.58) **Going Correction** -0.025s/f (Good) **13** Ran SP% **121.1**
Speed ratings (Par 101): **101,100,98,98,98 96,93,92,90,88 87,54,43**
toteswinger: 1&2 £11.00, 1&3 £37.70, 2&3 £10.00. CSF £50.30 CT £566.35 TOTE £22.30: £4.70, £1.40, £4.80; EX 81.10 Place 6: £30.93, Place 5: £6.45..
Owner K Nicholls **Bred** Keith Nicholls **Trained** Edwinstowe, Notts

FOCUS
A modest handicap run at a solid gallop.
West End Lad Official explanation: trainer said, regarding apparent improvement in form, that the gelding appeared to greatly benefit from a return to turf.
Navene(IRE) Official explanation: jockey said mare finished distressed
T/Jkpt: Not won. T/Plt: £28.80 to a £1 stake. Pool: £65,211.28. 1,650.33 winning tickets. T/Qpdt: £8.60 to a £1 stake. Pool: £3,652.46. 313.08 winning tickets. WG

1939 YARMOUTH (L-H)
Tuesday, May 19

OFFICIAL GOING: Good to firm (7.8)
Wind: modest but gusty at times, against Weather: showery

2167 EBF/GB DIGGER HIRE MAIDEN STKS 6f 3y
2:10 (2:12) (Class 5) 2-Y-O **£3,784** (£1,132; £566; £283; £141) **Stalls** High

Form RPR

3 **1** **Izaaj (USA)**[16] 1700 2-9-3 0........................(t) LDettori 3 78+
(Saeed Bin Suroor) *stdd s: hld up in tch: rdn and effrt wl over 1f out: led ins fnl f: styd on wl u.p* **1/2**[1]

44 **2** 1 **Rock Of Love (IRE)**[11] 1827 2-9-3 0........................ RoystonFfrench 1 74
(M Johnston) *w ldr tl led after 1f out: rdn over 2f out: drvn over 1f out: hdd ins fnl f: kpt on same pce* **11/1**[3]

3 7 **Fonterutoli (IRE)** 2-8-12 0........................ AndreaAtzeni(5) 4 53+
(M Botti) *t.k.h: led for 1f: stdd to trck ldrs: edgd rt and outpcd 2f out: no ch w ldng pair fnl f: kpt on again to go modest 3rd fnl 100yds* **25/1**

0 **4** 2 3/4 **Clan Piper**[32] 1323 2-9-3 0........................ JimmyFortune 5 45
(J H M Gosden) *chsd ldr after 1f: rdn 2f out: outpcd over 1f out: no ch w ldng pair fnl f: lost modest 3rd fnl 100yds* **5/2**[2]

5 10 **Prince Fortune** 2-9-3 0........................ TPQueally 2 15+
(Mrs L Stubbs) *v.s.a: hdwy to chse ldrs after 2f: shkn up 2f out: wknd qckly wl over 1f out: eased ins fnl f* **80/1**

003 **6** 6 **Usquaebach**[18] 1653 2-8-12 0........................(v) DarrylHolland 6 —
(H J Collingridge) *a in rr: sn pushed along: rdn 1/2-way: lost tch over 2f out: t.o* **80/1**

1m 16.07s (1.67) **Going Correction** +0.125s/f (Good) **6** Ran SP% **109.9**
Speed ratings (Par 93): **93,91,82,78,65 57**
toteswinger: 1&2 £1.90, 1&3 £4.50, 2&3 £12.50. CSF £6.91 TOTE £1.40: £1.10, £3.40; EX 5.00.
Owner Godolphin **Bred** Stoneside Stable **Trained** Newmarket, Suffolk

FOCUS
The going was changed to good to firm all over following a dry night. Two drew clear in what was an just an ordinary maiden. The winner came out of what looked a good race at Newmarket.

NOTEBOOK
Izaaj(USA) shaped with plenty of promise when third on his racecourse debut at Newmarket and the step up to 6f was expected to suit. Chasing the early speed, he was asked for his effort inside the two and eventually got on top. This was just a workmanlike performance, but there may be more to come as he goes up another furlong. He is Godolphin's first winning juvenile this season. (op 8-15 tchd 4-7)
Rock Of Love(IRE), another stepping up to 6f for the first time, was a costly failure at Hamilton last time, but the extra yardage of this contest was always going to suit and he showed markedly improved form. Clear of the third, it should not be long before he wins a standard maiden. (op 12-1 tchd 8-1)
Fonterutoli(IRE), a half-brother to a couple of winners in Italy, kept on at the one pace back in third and shaped as though the experience will do him good. Improvement should be forthcoming. (op 20-1 tchd 18-1)
Clan Piper, a disappointment on his debut at Newbury, again failed to meet with market expectations on this step up in trip, fading right out late on. (op 11-4 tchd 3-1)
Prince Fortune, a 5,000gns purchase from a yard that can get the odd decent juvenile, recovered from a slow start to show plenty of dash, but faded from over a furlong out. (tchd 66-1)
Usquaebach, third in a first-time visor at Southwell last time, was always going to struggle against these and she was beaten a long way. (op 100-1 tchd 66-1)

2168 LADDERLESSWINDOWS.CO.UK H'CAP 7f 3y
2:40 (2:42) (Class 5) (0-75,74) 4-Y-O+ **£2,719** (£809; £404; £202) **Stalls** High

Form RPR

1-24 **1** **To Be Or Not To Be**[25] 1493 4-8-13 **69**........................ TGMcLaughlin 1 81
(John Berry) *v.s.a: bhd: hdwy 4f out: rdn to ld wl over 1f out: rdn clr jst over 1f out: r.o wl: comf* **7/2**[2]

0022 **2** 3 3/4 **Mudhish (IRE)**[21] 1587 4-8-11 **67**........................(b) SebSanders 2 69
(C E Brittain) *t.k.h: trckd ldrs: rdn wl over 1f out: chsd wnr over 1f out: no imp* **11/2**

0410 **3** 1/2 **Grey Boy (GER)**[20] 1603 8-9-4 **74**........................ ShaneKelly 7 75
(A W Carroll) *stdd after s: hld up in tch: rdn and effrt wl over 1f out: drvn and kpt on same pce fr over 1f out* **2/1**[1]

-300 **4** 3 1/2 **Pension Policy (USA)**[11] 1833 4-8-13 **69**........................ JimmyQuinn 8 61
(J M P Eustace) *stdd s: bhd: pushed along 1/2-way: rdn over 2f out: nvr trbld ldrs* **9/1**

0-00 **5** 1 3/4 **Greystoke Prince**[25] 1493 4-8-6 **65**........................(p) DavidProbert(3) 3 52
(W R Swinburn) *led: hdd wl over 1f out: sn rdn: wknd over 1f out: no ch fnl f* **10/1**

5-22 **6** 4 **Elusive Hawk (IRE)**[36] 1258 5-8-12 **68**........................ TPQueally 9 44
(B J Curley) *restless in stalls: chsd ldr: ev ch and drvn 2f out: wknd qckly over 1f out: no ch fnl f* **4/1**[3]

00-0 **7** 16 **Applesnap (IRE)**[29] 1403 4-8-9 **65**........................(v[1]) DO'Donohoe 5 —
(Miss Amy Weaver) *in tch tl lost pl and rdn 4f out: wl bhd fnl 2f: eased ins fnl f* **33/1**

1m 28.3s (1.70) **Going Correction** +0.125s/f (Good) **7** Ran SP% **113.0**
Speed ratings (Par 103): **95,90,90,86,84 79,61**
toteswinger: 1&2 £3.40, 1&3 £1.90, 2&3 £3.30. CSF £22.26 CT £47.02 TOTE £5.10: £2.50, £1.80; EX 24.20 Trifecta £28.50 Pool: £265.83 - 6.88 winning units..
Owner W Thomas **Bred** J M Greetham **Trained** Newmarket, Suffolk

FOCUS
A low-grade handicap.
Pension Policy(USA) Official explanation: jockey said filly stumbled on leaving stalls

Greystoke Prince Official explanation: jockey said gelding hung left

2169 MANORHOTELMUNDESLEY.CO.UK (S) STKS — 1m 3y
3:10 (3:11) (Class 6) 3-Y-O £1,942 (£578; £288; £144) Stalls High

Form RPR

5232 **1** **Why Nee Amy**[35] 1270 3-8-4 52 (p) DavidProbert(3) 7 55
(Miss Gay Kelleway) *hld up towards rr: swtchd lft and hdwy over 2f out: rdn to chse ldrs over 1f out: carried lft fr 1f out led fnl 100yds: hld on gamely nr fin* **4/1**[2]

0-00 **2** *hd* **Kirkson**[29] 1407 3-8-12 23 (b[1]) AdrianMcCarthy 11 60
(P W Chapple-Hyam) *early reminder: towards rr: hdwy 5f out: rdn and lost pl 1/2-way: drvn over 3f out: hdwy u.p 2f out: drvn to ld over 1f out: hung lft fr over 1f out: hdd fnl 100yds: kpt on again nr fin* **40/1**

3063 **3** *2* **True Britannia**[7] 1958 3-8-7 63 AndreaAtzeni(5) 4 55
(A M Hales) *hld up off the pce towards rr: swtchd rt over 2f and hdwy over 2f out: ev ch and carried lft ent fnl f: no ex fnl 100yds* **5/2**[1]

0200 **4** *nk* **Dead Cat Bounce (IRE)**[24] 1520 3-8-12 56 (tp) TGMcLaughlin 9 54
(J Pearce) *v.s.a: wl bhd: hdwy on stands rail over 1f out: r.o wl u.p fnl f: nt rch ldrs* **33/1**

6604 **5** *1/2* **Chantilly Dancer (IRE)**[35] 1270 3-8-6 48 ow2 JackMitchell(3) 8 50
(M Quinn) *led for 1f: chsd ldrs: rdn wl over 2f out: one pce u.p ent fnl f* **14/1**

2550 **6** *2 1/2* **Whotsit (IRE)**[15] 1746 3-8-10 55 (b) LauraPike(7) 1 52
(Miss Amy Weaver) *hld up in rr: rdn and hdwy 3f out: plugged on fr over 1f out: nvr trbld ldrs* **40/1**

4500 **7** *4 1/2* **Lady Salama**[24] 1531 3-8-12 56 RoystonFfrench 6 37
(K R Burke) *v.s.a: bhd: rdn wl over 2f out: nvr trbld ldrs* **14/1**

-00 **8** *8* **Zepnove (IRE)**[7] 1953 3-8-12 64 (b) SebSanders 5 19
(M Wigham) *s.i.s: in tch: rdn over 2f out: sn btn: no ch fnl 2f* **11/1**

0-00 **9** *1/2* **Asakusa**[24] 1532 3-8-7 59 TPQueally 10 12
(H R A Cecil) *chsd ldr over 6f out: led over 2f out: rdn and hung rt wl over 1f out: sn hdd & wknd qckly* **9/2**[3]

3000 **10** *14* **Derringbay (IRE)**[12] 1811 3-8-12 55 (b[1]) LiamJones 12 —
(M H Tompkins) *racd freely: led after 1f: sn clr: hdd over 2f out: sn dropped out: t.o* **25/1**

1m 43.74s (3.14) **Going Correction** +0.125s/f (Good) **10** Ran SP% **100.1**
Speed ratings (Par 97): **89,88,86,86,86 83,79,71,70,56**
toteswinger: 1&2 £35.00, 1&3 £1.90, 2&3 £26.20. CSF £117.69 TOTE £4.70: £1.80, £5.30, £1.10; EX 222.10 TRIFECTA Not won..The winner was bought in for £5,000.
Owner David Jenkins **Bred** D E Jenkins **Trained** Exning, Suffolk
■ Timbaa was withdrawn (5/1, broke out of stalls.) Deduct 15p in the £ under R4.

FOCUS
This was a wide-open seller.
Kirkson Official explanation: jockey said gelding hung left
Derringbay(IRE) Official explanation: jockey said gelding ran too freely

2170 EASY REACH LADDERLESS WINDOW CLEANING MEDIAN AUCTION MAIDEN STKS — 1m 2f 21y
3:40 (3:41) (Class 6) 3-Y-O £2,590 (£770; £385; £192) Stalls Low

Form RPR

60-2 **1** **Dreamwalk (IRE)**[21] 1579 3-9-3 79 SebSanders 8 74+
(R M Beckett) *stdd after s: hld up in last trio: hdwy over 3f out: jnd ldr on bit jst over 2f out: rdn to ld ins fnl f: drew clr towards fin* **11/10**[1]

04-3 **2** *2 3/4* **Andhaar**[28] 1428 3-9-3 78 TPO'Shea 2 68
(E A L Dunlop) *chsd ldr: hdwy to join ldr 3f out: rdn to ld 2f out: hdd ins fnl f: nt pce of wnr fnl 100yds* **11/8**[2]

0-3 **3** *1 1/2* **Daredevil Dan**[36] 1260 3-9-3 0 LiamJones 6 65+
(M H Tompkins) *hld up in last trio: rdn and unable qck 3f out: hdwy ent fnl f: kpt on to 3rd wl ins fnl f: no ch w ldrs* **8/1**[3]

0-3 **4** *nk* **Cluny**[19] 1622 3-8-12 0 TPQueally 1 59
(J R Fanshawe) *chsd ldrs: rdn and unable qck jst over 2f out: kpt on fnl f: nvr pce to threaten ldrs* **14/1**

0-6 **5** *1 1/4* **Charismatic Lady**[11] 1843 3-8-7 0 AndreaAtzeni(5) 4 57
(M Botti) *t.k.h: chsd ldrs: rdn and unable qck over 2f out: no imp after* **33/1**

6 *1 3/4* **Arashi** 3-9-3 0 TGMcLaughlin 3 58
(Lucinda Featherstone) *s.i.s: hld up in last pl: rdn and no prog over 3f out: sme hdwy over 1f out: edgd lft and one pce fnl f: nvr nr ldrs* **66/1**

4-50 **7** *hd* **Count On Guest**[22] 1570 3-9-0 64 JackMitchell(3) 5 58
(G G Margarson) *led: jnd and rdn 3f: hdd 2f out: wknd fnl f* **33/1**

2m 12.26s (1.76) **Going Correction** +0.125s/f (Good) **7** Ran SP% **114.9**
Speed ratings (Par 97): **97,94,93,93,92 90,90**
toteswinger: 1&2 £1.02. 1&3 £1.80, 2&3 £3.10. CSF £2.87 TOTE £2.00: £1.10, £1.10; EX 2.60 Trifecta £12.10 Pool: £536.91 - 32.72 winning units..
Owner P D Savill **Bred** Peter Savill **Trained** Whitsbury, Hants

FOCUS
An uncompetitive maiden.

2171 EASY REACH LADDERLESSWINDOWS.CO.UK H'CAP — 1m 2f 21y
4:10 (4:10) (Class 6) (0-60,60) 4-Y-O+ £2,072 (£616; £308; £153) Stalls Low

Form RPR

5-05 **1** **Cwm Rhondda (USA)**[10] 1883 4-8-10 55 JackMitchell(3) 1 71
(P W Chapple-Hyam) *hld up in tch: trckd ldrs 3f out: rdn to ld ent fnl f: rdn clr: comf* **7/2**[1]

3-02 **2** *5* **Dancing Jest (IRE)**[8] 1945 5-9-4 60 NickyMackay 8 66
(Rae Guest) *led: rdn jst over 2f out: hdd ent fnl f: nt pce of wnr: kpt on* **9/2**[2]

-041 **3** *1/2* **King Of Connacht**[13] 1785 6-9-2 58 (p) LiamJones 2 63
(M Wellings) *t.k.h: hld up towards rr: hdwy over 2f out: rdn over 1f out: kpt on to go 3rd ins fnl f: no ch w wnr* **13/2**[3]

04/4 **4** *1* **Murrumbidgee (IRE)**[40] 1199 6-8-8 50 DarryllHolland 10 53
(Mike Murphy) *in tch: rdn over 2f out: kpt on same pce u.p fr over 1f out* **9/1**

2-0 **5** *nk* **Mick Is Back**[40] 1199 5-9-1 57 (vt) TPQueally 3 59
(G G Margarson) *t.k.h: chsd ldrs: rdn and nt qckn over 2f out: kpt on same pce fnl f* **14/1**

2050 **6** *nk* **Fantasy Ride**[40] 1199 7-8-8 50 TGMcLaughlin 5 52
(J Pearce) *stdd s: hld up wl bhd: hdwy on outer over 3f out: no prog u.p tl kpt on ins fnl f: nvr trbld ldrs* **9/1**

2500 **7** *2 1/2* **Spares And Repairs**[10] 1881 6-8-9 51 RoystonFfrench 9 48
(Mrs S Lamyman) *racd keenly: chsd ldr: rdn over 2f out: wknd over 1f out: no ch fnl f* **25/1**

6-00 **8** *1* **Le Corvee (IRE)**[28] 1415 7-9-1 57 ShaneKelly 11 52
(A W Carroll) *hld up towards rr: hdwy 3f out: wknd u.p over 1f out* **8/1**

4405 **9** *1 3/4* **Iceman George**[8] 1945 5-8-10 52 (p) StephenDonohoe 6 43
(D Morris) *hld up bhd: n.d* **8/1**

0053 **10** *3 3/4* **Maybe I Wont**[29] 1402 4-8-13 55 SebSanders 7 39
(Lucinda Featherstone) *t.k.h: hld up in midfield: rdn and wknd over 2f out: wl bhd fnl f* **8/1**

50-0 **11** *2 1/4* **Oops Another Act**[21] 1589 4-8-6 51 (p) DavidProbert(3) 4 30
(W R Swinburn) *hld up towards rr: hdwy over 3f out: rdn and wknd wl over 1f out* **16/1**

2m 9.37s (-1.13) **Going Correction** +0.125s/f (Good) **11** Ran SP% **123.5**
Speed ratings (Par 101): **109,105,104,103,103 103,101,100,99,96 94**
toteswinger: 1&2 £4.90, 1&3 £7.20, 2&3 £2.80. CSF £19.87 CT £102.37 TOTE £5.60: £2.40, £2.00, £2.40; EX 28.60 Trifecta £50.40 Pool: £246.33 - 3.61 winning units..
Owner Hintlesham Thoroughbreds **Bred** David Allan **Trained** Newmarket, Suffolk

FOCUS
This was a moderate handicap.

2172 JULIE BYRNE 40TH BIRTHDAY SURPRISE H'CAP — 1m 6f 17y
4:40 (4:40) (Class 5) (0-70,70) 4-Y-O+ £2,719 (£809; £404; £202) Stalls High

Form RPR

0030 **1** **Al Azy (IRE)**[14] 1767 4-7-11 51 oh1 AndreaAtzeni(5) 4 56
(D M Simcock) *mde all: set stdy gallop: pushed along and qcknd over 1f out: in command fnl f: r.o wl* **8/1**

31-4 **2** *2 1/4* **Lady Pilot**[14] 1767 7-8-10 59 PaulDoe 6 61+
(Jim Best) *t.k.h: hld up in midfield: n.m.r on inner and shuffled bk over 2f out: rdn and hdwy over 1f out: r.o to go 2nd wl ins fnl f: nvr gng to rch wnr* **7/4**[1]

62/0 **3** *1 1/4* **Annambo**[12] 1815 9-9-0 63 TravisBlock 1 63
(Andrew Reid) *t.k.h: chsd wnr tl 10f out: rdn and effrt 2f out: drvn to chse wnr ent fnl f: no imp: lost 2nd wl ins fnl f* **10/1**

36-4 **4** *nk* **Sphere (IRE)**[49] 1049 4-9-5 68 TPQueally 2 68
(J R Fanshawe) *chsd ldrs: wnt 2nd 10f out: rdn to press wnr 2f out: unable qck over 1f out: lost 2nd ent fnl f: one pce after* **9/2**[3]

23-6 **5** *hd* **Agente Romano (USA)**[8] 1945 4-9-7 70 (t) SebSanders 10 69+
(G A Butler) *stdd s: hld up in last pair: hdwy 3f out: n.m.r fr over 2f out: nt clr run over 1f out tl jst ins fnl f: kpt on u.p: nvr nr wnr* **7/2**[2]

440- **6** *1 1/4* **Faith And Reason (USA)**[36] 7715 6-9-0 63 JerryO'Dwyer 7 61
(B J Curley) *t.k.h: hld up in midfield: hdwy to chse ldrs and shkn up over 3f out: wknd u.p over 1f out* **16/1**

50-0 **7** *2 1/4* **Fourth Dimension (IRE)**[13] 1786 10-8-12 61 LiamJones 3 55
(Miss T Spearing) *hld up in last pair: hdwy on outer over 3f out: rdn 2f out: wknd over 1f out* **6/1**

3m 18.74s (11.14) **Going Correction** +0.125s/f (Good) **7** Ran SP% **117.1**
Speed ratings (Par 103): **73,71,71,70,70 70,68**
toteswinger: 1&2 £5.10, 1&3 £10.30, 2&3 £5.80. CSF £23.40 CT £146.49 TOTE £10.00: £4.70, £1.60; EX 29.30 Trifecta £126.60 Pool: £374.69 - 2.19 winning units. Place 6: £13.57, Place 5: £9.69..
Owner Dr Marwan Koukash **Bred** Shadwell Estate Company Limited **Trained** Newmarket, Suffolk

FOCUS
They went a steady gallop in this staying handicap.
Fourth Dimension(IRE) Official explanation: vet said gelding returned lame
T/Plt: £20.40 to a £1 stake. Pool: £57,838.99. 2,065.75 winning tickets. T/Qpdt: £2.80 to a £1 stake. Pool: £3,771.86. 979.38 winning tickets. SP

2173 - (Foreign Racing) - See Raceform Interactive

1804 GOODWOOD (R-H)
Wednesday, May 20

OFFICIAL GOING: Good
Rail realignment added circa 24yards to races on the mile course and 8 yards to races incorporating the top bend.
Wind: Light, across Weather: Fine but cloudy

2174 RACING UK STKS (H'CAP) — 1m 1f
2:15 (2:17) (Class 4) (0-85,83) 3-Y-O £4,673 (£1,399; £699; £350; £174; £87) Stalls High

Form RPR

004- **1** **Forte Dei Marmi**[245] 6029 3-8-8 73 WilliamBuick 7 87+
(L M Cumani) *lw: trckd ldng trio: trapped bhd rivals fr 3f out: stl trapped and 6th whn hmpd over 1f out: gap appeared sn after: r.o strly fnl f to ld last strides* **4/1**[2]

23-1 **2** *shd* **Sandor**[22] 1585 3-9-1 80 PatCosgrave 8 87
(P J Makin) *swtg: cl up and mostly in 3rd: effrt 2f out: drvn ahd jst ins fnl f: edgd rt then lft: hdd last strides* **10/1**

-004 **3** *nk* **Silver Games (IRE)**[13] 1808 3-9-4 83 TonyCulhane 10 89
(M R Channon) *hld up in 7th: gd prog on inner 2f out to chal 1f out: upsides ins fnl 100yds: r.o but jst outpcd* **20/1**

421- **4** *2 1/4* **Star Links (USA)**[202] 7098 3-9-2 81 RichardHughes 4 82
(R Hannon) *lw: led at mod pce: rdn 2f out: hdd and fdd jst ins fnl f* **12/1**

31-3 **5** *hd* **December Draw (IRE)**[16] 1751 3-9-3 82 ShaneKelly 5 83
(W J Knight) *hld up in abt 6th: prog on outer 3f out: disp 2nd 2f out: drvn and nt qckn over 1f out: fdd fnl f* **10/3**[1]

5-51 **6** *1/2* **Advisor (FR)**[23] 1574 3-8-13 78 JamieSpencer 6 78
(M L W Bell) *lw: hld up in 8th: effrt on outer over 2f out: hrd rdn and nt qckn over 1f out: no ch after: plugged on* **9/2**[3]

314- **7** *1/2* **Lady Rusty (IRE)**[233] 6344 3-8-7 72 SaleemGolam 3 70
(P Winkworth) *hld up in last pair: rdn over 2f out: tried to cl on ldrs over 1f out: one pce* **25/1**

41-0 **8** *nk* **Herschel (IRE)**[35] 1284 3-8-10 75 RichardMullen 2 73
(G L Moore) *t.k.h: mostly trckd ldr to over 1f out: wknd tamely* **40/1**

413- **9** *3 1/4* **Retro (IRE)**[174] 7460 3-8-11 76 RyanMoore 1 67
(R Hannon) *bit bkwd: dropped in fr wd draw and hld up last: rdn over 2f out: no prog* **16/1**

103 **10** *dist* **Kaabari (USA)**[11] 1870 3-9-3 82 DarryllHolland 11 —
(C E Brittain) *trckd ldrs tl wknd rapidly 3f out: t.o* **8/1**

1m 57.97s (1.67) **Going Correction** -0.05s/f (Good) **10** Ran SP% **106.1**
Speed ratings (Par 101): **90,89,89,87,87 87,86,86,83,—**
toteswinger: 1&2 £7.40, 1&3 £11.20, 2&3 £24.40 CSF £34.65 CT £408.12 TOTE £4.50: £1.90, £3.20, £4.50; EX 41.30.
Owner Fittocks Stud **Bred** Fittocks Stud **Trained** Newmarket, Suffolk
■ Becausewecan (9/1) was withdrawn on vet's advice. Deduct 10p in the £ under R4.
■ Stewards' Enquiry : Pat Cosgrave one-day ban: careless riding (Jun 7); £290 fine: failed to stay required time on course after weighed-in signal

FOCUS
This looked quite a good 3yo handicap, although the pace was just ordinary early on, before appearing to slow before the straight. The form is a bit muddling but the winner is the type to rate higher.

Kaabari(USA) Official explanation: jockey said filly stopped quickly

2175 EBF CUCUMBER MAIDEN FILLIES' STKS — 6f
2:50 (2:52) (Class 5) 2-Y-O — £3,561 (£1,059; £529; £264) Stalls Low

Form — RPR

3 **1** **La Pantera**[13] 1810 2-9-0 0 ..... RichardHughes 6 83+
(R Hannon) *w'like: trckd ldrs in 5th: asked for effrt 2f out: shkn up over 1f out: styd on wl to ld ins fnl f: sn clr* **11/4**[1]

2 2 1/4 **Falling Angel** 2-9-0 0 ..... EddieAhern 8 75+
(P F I Cole) *unf: scope: led narrowly to over 2f out: shkn up wl over 1f out: kpt on to chal fnl f: upsides after tl outpcd last 100yds* **7/1**[3]

3 1 3/4 **Velvet Band** 2-9-0 0 ..... NCallan 10 70+
(P F I Cole) *leggy: w ldr: led over 2f out: hdd & wknd ins fnl f* **5/1**[2]

4 1 1/4 **Flyinflyout** 2-9-0 0 ..... SamHitchcott 9 66
(M R Channon) *leggy: w ldng pair: rdn and nt qckn 2f out: outpcd sn after: kpt on again ins fnl f* **16/1**

0324 **5** shd **Anjomarba (IRE)**[9] 1933 2-8-9 0 ..... JackDean(5) 5 66
(W G M Turner) *pressed ldng trio: rdn 2f out: outpcd over 1f out: plugged on last 100yds* **5/1**[2]

6 2 3/4 **Agony And Ecstasy** 2-9-0 0 ..... JimCrowley 11 58
(R M Beckett) *str: bit bkwd: a in same pl: chsng ldrs tl outpcd fr 2f out: no prog after* **10/1**

7 1 1/4 **Easy Terms** 2-8-11 0 ..... JamesMillman(3) 4 54
(B R Millman) *w'like: sn pushed along in 9th and nvr on terms w ldrs: hanging fr 1/2-way: sme modest late prog* **11/1**

8 1 3/4 **Hot Pursuits** 2-9-0 0 ..... SteveDrowne 2 49
(H Morrison) *w'like: scope: bit bkwd: b.hind: s.s: outpcd in 11th and sn rdn: nvr on terms: plugged on* **20/1**

9 2 1/4 **Princess Podge** 2-9-0 0 ..... IanMongan 12 42
(M D I Usher) *w'like: leggy: bit bkwd: s.s: wl off the pce in 10th: sme prog to midfield 1/2-way: 7th and no imp 2f out: wknd fnl f* **100/1**

10 3/4 **Ashkalara** 2-9-0 0 ..... DarryllHolland 1 40+
(H S Howe) *w'like: str: dwlt: veered rt sn after s: v green and detached in last: kpt on fnl f* **25/1**

11 2 **It's A Deal (IRE)** 2-9-0 0 ..... SaleemGolam 7 34
(P Winkworth) *unf: scope: racd in 7th and nt on terms w ldrs: no imp fr 1/2-way: wknd rapidly over 1f out* **16/1**

12 3 **Baoli** 2-9-0 0 ..... RyanMoore 3 25
(R Hannon) *unf: green to post: sn pushed along in 8th and nvr on terms w ldrs: wknd 2f out* **7/1**[3]

1m 12.47s (0.27) **Going Correction** -0.05s/f (Good) — **12** Ran SP% **123.8**
Speed ratings (Par 90): **96,93,90,89,88 85,83,81,78,77 74,70**
toteswinger: 1&2 £5.40, 1&3 £3.00, 2&3 £8.40 CSF £22.88 TOTE £3.50: £1.50, £3.00, £1.90; EX 28.50.
Owner Ms V O'Sullivan **Bred** Howard Barton Stud **Trained** East Everleigh, Wilts

FOCUS
A decent maiden and a progressive winner. The time and the fifth help with the level.

NOTEBOOK
La Pantera, whose stable had won this fillies' maiden four times in the last ten years, including with subsequent French Guineas winner (for a different stable) Elusive Wave 12 months ago, was the better fancied of the pair according to the market and ran out a ready winner, improving significantly on the form she showed when third over 5f on her debut at Windsor. She deserves her chance in something better now. (op 2-1 tchd 15-8 and 3-1 in places)
Falling Angel, a half-sister to among others 1m winner Wooly Bully, who was also successful over hurdles, shaped nicely on her racecourse debut. For a horse bred to appreciate further in time, she showed a surprising amount of early speed and has plenty of ability. (op 12-1 tchd 14-1)
Velvet Band ◆, a half-sister to among others useful 1m winner Jazz Jam, out of a Cherry Hinton winner, travelled as well as anything for much of the way but didn't see her race out. She should be well suited by a drop back to 5f and can make her mark. (op 7-1 tchd 8-1)
Flyinflyout, a 2,000gns purchase, showed early speed and this was a respectable introduction. (op 12-1 tchd 20-1)
Anjomarba(IRE) has some fair form to her name, but she simply didn't look good enough this time. (op 9-1)
Easy Terms Official explanation: jockey said filly hung right-handed throughout

2176 COCKED HAT STKS (LISTED RACE) (C&G) — 1m 3f
3:25 (3:26) (Class 1) 3-Y-O — £22,708 (£8,608; £4,308; £2,148; £1,076) Stalls Low

Form — RPR

31-4 **1** **Alwaary (USA)**[11] 1872 3-9-0 93 ..... RHills 5 106+
(J H M Gosden) *hld up in 4th: gap appeared 2f out: decisive move to ld over 1f out: shkn up and sn wl in command* **5/1**[3]

44 **2** 3 **Beauchamp Xerxes**[14] 1793 3-9-0 0 ..... RyanMoore 2 101
(G A Butler) *lw: hld up in rr: rdn and effrt on outer over 2f out: kpt on to take 2nd nr fin: no ch w wnr* **9/1**

14 **3** 3/4 **Sight Unseen**[13] 1800 3-9-0 100 ..... (t) TPQueally 3 100
(H R A Cecil) *dwlt: sn trckd ldng pair: shkn up to chal over 2f out: hanging rt and nt qckn: stl upsides over 1f out: easily outpcd after* **7/4**[1]

11- **4** nse **Free Agent**[333] 3245 3-9-3 0 ..... RichardHughes 4 103
(R Hannon) *trckd ldr: led wl over 2f out: sn u.p: hdd over 1f out: easily outpcd* **5/1**[3]

5 18 **Chock A Block (IRE)**[206] 3-9-0 0 ..... LDettori 6 69
(Saeed Bin Suroor) *str: lw: led: kicked on 5f out: hdd wl over 2f out: wknd rapidly: t.o* **9/4**[2]

2m 27.98s (-0.32) **Going Correction** -0.05s/f (Good) — **5** Ran SP% **110.5**
Speed ratings (Par 107): **99,96,96,96,83**
CSF £42.27 TOTE £6.50: £2.70, £3.10; EX 61.20.
Owner Hamdan Al Maktoum **Bred** Shadwell Farm LLC **Trained** Newmarket, Suffolk

FOCUS
An interesting Listed race for 3yos - known as the Predominate until 2007 - and seen by many as a late Derby trial, but the standard of this year's race looked some way short of what will be required at Epsom. The winner improved on his Lingfield form. The pace seemed just fair at best.

NOTEBOOK
Alwaary(USA) was comfortably held on his reappearance in the Lingfield Derby Trial, but he improved considerably on that form and was a ready winner. He had to wait for a gap early in the straight, but found a nice opening towards the inside at the cutaway well over a furlong out and picked up in smart style. There could be further improvement to come and he is now likely to be aimed at the King Edward VII Stakes at Royal Ascot. (op 7-2)
Beauchamp Xerxes was outpaced when first coming under pressure in the straight, having been held up last of all in this small field, and never threatened the winner, but he kept on well enough for second. He runs as though he'll get 1m4f and he could re-oppose the winner in the King Edward VII Stakes. (op 16-1)
Sight Unseen ◆ has yet to confirm the immense promise he showed when a taking winner of a decent maiden at Newbury on his debut, but he can be excused this below-par showing considering he looked ill at ease on the track. He remains a horse of Group-class potential and will be suited by easier ground and a flatter track. Like a few of these, he's in the King Edward VII Stakes, but his stable also has Father Time for that race. (op 5-2)
Free Agent had been off the track since winning last year's Chesham Stakes at Royal Ascot and missed the Dee Stakes with a bruised foot. Although comfortably held, he was by no means given a hard time once his winning chance had passed and he should improve a good deal for the run. Richard Hughes thinks the colt will get at least 1m6f and there's a chance he'll be aimed at the Queen's Vase. (op 7-2 tchd 3-1)
Chock A Block(IRE), sold out of Robert Collet's yard after winning his sole start as a juvenile over 1m1f in France, ran an abysmal race on his debut for Godolphin. He took them along early, but offered nothing under pressure. Perhaps he wants a flatter track and easier ground. Official explanation: jockey said colt lost its left-fore shoe (op 11-4 tchd 3-1 in places)

2177 SUSSEX STAYERS STKS (H'CAP) — 2m
4:00 (4:00) (Class 4) (0-80,80) 4-Y-O+ — £4,857 (£1,445; £722; £360) Stalls Low

Form — RPR

0/0- **1** **Sweetheart**[47] 1017 5-8-8 65 ..... NCallan 6 73
(Jamie Poulton) *cl up: wnt 3rd 5f out: rdn 3f out: styd on fr 2f out to ld 1f out: hung lft fnl f: kpt on* **7/1**[3]

20-3 **2** 1 1/4 **Cleaver**[32] 1356 8-9-9 80 ..... RichardHughes 1 86
(Lady Herries) *dropped out s: hld up in last: stl hld together at bk of main gp over 2f out: shkn up and effrt wl over 1f out: styd on fnl f to take 2nd nr fin* **16/1**

03-0 **3** nk **Ned Ludd (IRE)**[32] 1356 6-8-13 70 ..... EddieAhern 9 76
(J G Portman) *dwlt: hld up towards rr: rdn over 3f out: prog over 1f out: styd on ins fnl f to take 3rd nr fin* **20/1**

650/ **4** nk **Takafu (USA)**[578] 6335 7-9-1 75 ..... JamesMillman(3) 2 80
(W S Kittow) *in tch: prog to go 3rd 10f out to 5f out: cl up and drvn 3f out: stl wl there over 1f out: kpt on same pce* **14/1**

40-1 **5** shd **Kayf Aramis**[6] 2018 7-9-6 77 6ex ..... JamieSpencer 11 82
(Miss Venetia Williams) *lw: rousted along fr stalls to press ldr: rdn over 4f out: upsides under maximum press fr 3f out: nt qckn over 1f out: hld whn crossed last 50yds and lost 3 pls* **4/7**[1]

-213 **6** 2 1/2 **Isabelonabicycle**[11] 1892 4-8-10 69 ..... LPKeniry 4 71
(A M Balding) *led: pressed 4f out but gng wl enough: rdn over 2f out: hdd & wknd 1f out* **6/1**[2]

22-0 **7** 2 1/4 **Epsom Salts**[29] 1426 4-8-11 70 ..... IanMongan 5 69
(P M Phelan) *dwlt: sn in tch: chsd ldrs u.p 3f out: stl there wl over 1f out: wknd fnl f* **33/1**

-124 **8** shd **American Spin**[95] 549 5-9-5 76 ..... AdamKirby 3 75
(L A Dace) *plld hrd early in 3rd: restrained to midfield bef 1/2-way: hrd rdn on outer 3f out: no imp wl over 1f out: wknd* **25/1**

00-3 **9** 62 **Look To This Day**[16] 1753 4-9-2 75 ..... SteveDrowne 7 —
(R Charlton) *in tch: rdn 6f out: wknd rapidly over 3f out: sn eased: t.o* **20/1**

3m 29.02s (0.02) **Going Correction** -0.05s/f (Good)
WFA 4 from 5yo+ 2lb — **9** Ran SP% **119.3**
Speed ratings (Par 105): **107,106,106,106,106 104,103,103,72**
toteswinger: 1&2 £8.50, 1&3 £13.40, 2&3 £19.20 CSF £101.74 CT £2140.45 TOTE £7.20: £2.10, £2.50, £5.70; EX 66.10.
Owner R W Huggins **Bred** Darley **Trained** Lewes, E Sussex

FOCUS
A decent staying handicap run at a good pace. The winner only had to match her old form to score, with the favourite well below his York level.
American Spin Official explanation: jockey said gelding ran too free
Look To This Day Official explanation: jockey said filly lost its action

2178 TOTEEXACTA MEDIAN AUCTION MAIDEN STKS — 1m 1f 192y
4:35 (4:35) (Class 5) 3-4-Y-O — £3,238 (£963; £481; £240) Stalls High

Form — RPR

53- **1** **Elliptical (USA)**[179] 7424 3-8-12 0 ..... RichardHughes 3 82+
(G A Butler) *lw: w ldrs: led over 6f out and dictated stdy pce: rdn 2f out and sn at least 2 l clr: in n.d after: eased nr fin* **12/1**

2 1 1/4 **Sabotage (UAE)** 3-8-12 0 ..... GregFairley 8 80+
(M Johnston) *scope: dwlt: wl in rr: 10th over 4f out: prog on inner after: drvn and r.o over 1f out to take 2nd ins fnl f: clsd on eased down wnr* **4/1**[1]

5- **3** 1 3/4 **Kris Kin Line (IRE)**[210] 6893 3-8-12 0 ..... RyanMoore 13 76
(Sir Michael Stoute) *w'like: str: trckd ldrs: 6th 4f out: prog to press ldng pair 3f out: hrd rdn and nt qckn 2f out: plugged on same pce* **4/1**[1]

22-5 **4** nk **Dome Rocket**[28] 1464 3-8-12 76 ..... ShaneKelly 7 76
(W J Knight) *led after 1f to over 6f out: cl 2nd after: chal and upsides over 3f out: drvn and fnd nil 2f out: btn after: lost 2 pls fnl 100yds* **9/2**[2]

5 1/2 **Jewelled** 3-8-7 0 ..... JamesDoyle 12 70
(J W Hills) *w'like: settled midfield: 8th 4f out: plld out and effrt 3f out: prog 2f out: kpt on one pce fr over 1f out* **33/1**

53 **6** 3 3/4 **Chicora (USA)**[8] 1963 3-8-7 0 ..... RichardMullen 10 62
(J H M Gosden) *trckd ldrs: 5th 4f out: rdn and cl enough 3f out: fdd fnl 2f* **11/2**[3]

0- **7** 1 **Sitwell**[182] 7380 3-8-12 0 ..... AdamKirby 2 65+
(J R Fanshawe) *dwlt: dropped in fr wd draw in abt 9th: effrt over 3f out: nt clr run briefly over 2f out: plugged on but nt pce to threaten* **33/1**

6 **8** 8 **Pallaton**[15] 1771 3-8-12 0 ..... JimCrowley 14 49
(R M Beckett) *w'like: str: led 1f: styd handy: 4th 4f out: rdn 3f out: sn wknd* **14/1**

0 **9** 3/4 **Barter**[12] 1844 3-8-7 0 ..... WilliamBuick 6 43
(L M Cumani) *lengthy: lw: mostly in midfield: 7th 4f out: wknd 3f out* **7/1**

0-00 **10** nk **Princess Soraya**[12] 1840 3-8-8 44 ow1 ..... SteveDrowne 4 43
(R Dickin) *dwlt: mostly in last trio: no prog u.p 3f out: wl bhd after* **100/1**

11 3 1/4 **Aasifa (USA)** 3-8-8 0 ow1 ..... NCallan 5 37
(C E Brittain) *leggy: prom: chsd ldng pair over 6f out: drvn and wknd over 3f out* **12/1**

0 **12** 2 1/2 **Scarlett Angel (IRE)**[16] 1752 3-8-7 0 ..... PaulDoe 11 31
(W J Knight) *leggy: dwlt: a in last pair: t.o* **66/1**

13 14 **Double Moon** 3-8-12 0 ..... TonyCulhane 9 8
(George Baker) *w'like: dwlt: a in last pair: wl bhd fnl 3f* **66/1**

2m 10.16s (2.16) **Going Correction** -0.05s/f (Good) — **13** Ran SP% **118.0**
Speed ratings (Par 103): **89,88,86,86,85 82,82,75,75,74 72,70,59**
toteswinger: 1&2 £11.90, 1&3 £9.10, 2&3 £5.50 CSF £57.74 TOTE £16.50: £4.40, £2.20, £1.50; EX 92.60.
Owner Keen As Mustard **Bred** Lavin Bloodstock **Trained** Newmarket, Suffolk

FOCUS
A reasonable maiden that should produce winners, but the early pace was pretty steady. The form is rated through the fourth.

2179 GOLDRING SECURITY SERVICES MAIDEN FILLIES' STKS 7f
5:10 (5:10) (Class 5) 3-Y-O

£3,115 (£933; £466; £233; £116; £58) Stalls High

Form RPR

6 **1** **So Blissful (IRE)**[102] 440 3-9-0 0 .... TPQueally 5 74
(T G Mills) *trckd ldrs on outer gng wl: wnt 2nd 2f out: clsd to ld jst over 1f out: rdn and styd on wl* **33/1**

4- **2** *nk* **Visite Royale (USA)**[187] 7312 3-9-0 0 .... RyanMoore 2 73
(Sir Michael Stoute) *hld up in last pair: prog on outer 2f out: sn rdn: wnt 2nd ins fnl f: drvn to press wnr: a jst hld* **15/8**[2]

03 **3** *1* **Fantasy Land (IRE)**[18] 1683 3-9-0 0 .... (t) LDettori 4 71
(B J Meehan) *lw: hld up in tch: prog on inner wl over 1f out: wnt 2nd briefly ins fnl f: styd on but nt pce of ldng pair* **8/1**[3]

23- **4** *1* **Aurora Sky (IRE)**[165] 7577 3-9-0 0 .... AlanMunro 8 68
(J Akehurst) *lw: t.k.h: hld up bhd ldrs: pushed along 2f out: reminder over 1f out: kpt on steadily but nt pce to chal* **9/1**

0- **5** *½* **Margarita (IRE)**[243] 6080 3-9-0 0 .... EddieAhern 1 67+
(J R Fanshawe) *t.k.h early: hld up in last: stl there 2f out but gng wl: cajoled along over 1f out: styd on steadily: nvr rchd ldrs* **12/1**

02-2 **6** *3* **Miss Tango Hotel**[12] 1825 3-9-0 79 .... JimmyFortune 7 59
(J H M Gosden) *lw: led at stdy pce w plenty of tail swishing: kicked on 2f out: hdd jst over 1f out: folded tamely* **13/8**[1]

0-0 **7** *hd* **Baheeya**[53] 998 3-9-0 0 .... NCallan 6 58
(C E Brittain) *chsd ldr to 2f out: sn u.p and btn* **33/1**

0-6 **8** *11* **Aphrodite's Rock**[12] 1825 3-9-0 0 .... RichardHughes 9 40
(Miss Gay Kelleway) *b: b.hind: t.k.h early: cl up: lost pl 2f out: wknd rapidly and eased* **10/1**

1m 29.85s (2.45) **Going Correction** -0.05s/f (Good) **8 Ran SP% 116.7**
Speed ratings (Par 96): **84,83,82,81,80 77,77,64**
toteswinger: 1&2 £20.90, 1&3 £18.50, 2&3 £3.20 CSF £97.28 TOTE £36.40: £6.80, £1.40, £2.00; EX 177.60.

Owner Mrs Johnny Eddis **Bred** Gigginstown House Stud **Trained** Headley, Surrey

FOCUS
They went a steady pace early and the bare form of this fillies' maiden looks ordinary.

2180 TURFTV.CO.UK APPRENTICE STKS (H'CAP) 5f
5:45 (5:45) (Class 6) (0-65,68) 4-Y-0+ £2,590 (£770; £385; £192) Stalls Low

Form RPR

0066 **1** **Peopleton Brook**[8] 1957 7-8-8 57 .... (t) RossAtkinson(3) 13 67
(B G Powell) *hld up on outer: prog on wd outside 1/2-way: led over 1f out: sn in command: pushed out* **16/1**

00-0 **2** *1 ½* **Miss Firefly**[14] 1787 4-8-7 53 .... MCGeran 7 58
(R J Hodges) *mounted on crse and taken down early: prom: lost pl 1/2-way: struggling 2f out: swtchd rt over 1f out: rdn and r.o to take 2nd ins fnl f: no imp wnr* **14/1**

2223 **3** *shd* **Step It Up (IRE)**[82] 710 5-8-12 63 .... NathanAlison(5) 15 67
(J R Boyle) *lw: heavily reastrained s: hld up and detached in last: gd prog on outer fr 2f out: chal for 2nd ins fnl f: too much to do* **7/1**[3]

0000 **4** *¾* **Brandywell Boy (IRE)**[11] 1877 6-8-10 59 .... PNolan(3) 14 61
(D J S Ffrench Davis) *chsd ldrs on outer: grad c towards nr side: cl up whn nt clr run over 1f out: styd on* **10/1**

0005 **5** *½* **Cosmic Destiny (IRE)**[24] 1540 7-9-1 64 .... JPHamblett(3) 5 64+
(E F Vaughan) *hld up wl in rr: gng easily fr 1/2-way but weaving to find a clr run: swtchd to nr side rail and r.o fnl f: no ch* **14/1**

00- **6** *nse* **Pic Up Sticks**[182] 7377 10-8-12 61 .... SophieDoyle(3) 18 61
(B G Powell) *prom on outer: clsd to chal over 1f out: sn outpcd: no ex* **20/1**

006- **7** *¾* **Solemn**[169] 7528 4-8-5 51 oh6 .... (b) Louis-PhilippeBeuzelin 4 48
(J M Bradley) *pressed ldrs: u.p 2f out: nt qckn over 1f out: fdd fnl f* **33/1**

-246 **8** *¾* **Sofinella (IRE)**[14] 1787 6-8-5 51 oh2 .... AndreaAtzeni 10 45
(A W Carroll) *pressed ldrs: cl enough 2f out: wknd jst over 1f out* **16/1**

1235 **9** *2 ½* **Bluebok**[11] 1877 8-9-5 65 .... (bt) JackDean 12 50
(J M Bradley) *chsd ldrs on outer: no imp over 1f out: wknd fnl f* **10/1**

0100 **10** *1 ½* **Ramblin Bob**[49] 1076 4-8-2 51 oh4 .... MatthewDavies(3) 9 31
(W J Musson) *s.i.s: sn rdn: a in rr: kpt on fnl f* **50/1**

1222 **11** *nse* **Spic 'n Span**[15] 1776 4-8-9 60 .... (b) SPRyan(5) 17 40
(R A Harris) *taken down early: dwlt: rcvrd and sn led: hdd & wknd over 1f out* **9/2**[2]

0000 **12** *½* **Maggie Kate**[14] 1787 4-8-1 52 .... (p) DebraEngland(5) 1 30
(R Ingram) *prom against nr side rail: lost pl fr 2f out* **14/1**

2000 **13** *1* **Wicksy Creek**[9] 1935 4-8-4 55 oh3 ow4 .... (b[1]) HollyHall(5) 2 29
(G C Bravery) *chsd ldrs to 1/2-way: sn lost pl and btn* **40/1**

0006 **14** *1 ¾* **Brazilian Brush (IRE)**[56] 956 4-8-9 55 .... WilliamCarson 11 23
(J M Bradley) *a struggling in rr* **16/1**

-600 **15** *1* **Pegasus Dancer (FR)**[14] 1787 5-8-3 52 .... (p) SimonPearce(3) 8 16
(R H York) *outpcd and a struggling* **22/1**

0-01 **R** **Sands Crooner (IRE)**[8] 1970 6-9-5 68 6ex .... (v) RosieJessop(3) 6 —
(J G Given) *reluctant to go to post: ref to r* **10/3**[1]

58.85 secs (0.45) **Going Correction** -0.05s/f (Good) **16 Ran SP% 126.0**
Speed ratings (Par 101): **94,91,91,90,89 89,88,86,82,80 80,79,78,75,73 —**
toteswinger: 1&2 £86.60, 1&3 £34.40, 2&3 £31.00 CSF £219.09 CT £1795.75 TOTE £24.40: £3.20, £3.90, £2.80, £3.40; EX 282.20 Place 6: £872.87 Place 5: £292.15.

Owner G S Thompson & P Banfield **Bred** Lower Hill Farm Stud **Trained** Upper Lambourn, Berks

■ Stewards' Enquiry : J P Hamblett one-day ban: careless riding (Jun 3)
P Nolan one-day ban: careless riding (Jun 3)

FOCUS
A moderate sprint handicap restricted to apprentices who had not ridden more than 50 winners. They raced middle to stands' side and if anything a high draw looked advantageous. The pace was predictably strong. The winner looked the best guide to the form.

Miss Firefly ◆ Official explanation: jockey said filly was denied a clear run

Cosmic Destiny(IRE) Official explanation: jockey said mare was denied a clear run

T/Jkpt: Not won. T/Plt: £924.10 to a £1 stake. Pool: £84,668.74. 66.88 winning tickets. T/Qpdt: £160.50 to a £1 stake. Pool: £4,554.82. 21.00 winning tickets. JN

1962

LINGFIELD (L-H)
Wednesday, May 20

OFFICIAL GOING: Turf course - good (good to firm in places; 8.7) all-weather - standard
Wind: medium across Weather: cloudy, brighter spells

2181 BET UEFA CUP FINAL - BETDAQ MAIDEN STKS 1m 3f 106y
2:00 (2:00) (Class 5) 3-Y-0+ £2,729 (£806; £403) Stalls High

Form RPR

0-23 **1** **Akmal**[32] 1349 3-8-11 77 .... TPO'Shea 11 74
(J L Dunlop) *dwlt: hdwy to chse ldr after 2f: clr w runner up fr over 3f out: ev ch u.p 2f out: led 1f out: styd on wl* **15/8**[1]

03- **2** *2 ¾* **Silvador**[218] 6715 3-8-11 0 .... DO'Donohoe 2 70
(W R Muir) *t.k.h: chsd ldr tl led after 2f out: drew clr w wnr over 3f out: drvn over 1f out: hdd 1f out: no ex ins fnl f* **7/2**[3]

6-0 **3** *2 ½* **Warrior Conquest**[13] 1809 4-9-12 0 .... GeorgeBaker 5 65
(W J Knight) *t.k.h: chsd ldrs: 3rd and rdn over 3f out: sn wl outpcd by ldng pair: kpt on* **33/1**

2 **4** *¾* **Talimos (IRE)**[17] 1708 3-8-11 0 .... RichardKingscote 7 64+
(R M Beckett) *nvr travelling wl: racd in last pair and niggled along: stl last 3f out: swtchd rt over 2f out: kpt on fr over 1f out: nvr trbld ldrs* **2/1**[2]

5 *1* **Tesserae** 3-8-6 0 .... FergusSweeney 4 57
(A B Haynes) *stdd s: hld up in tch in midfield: outpcd over 3f out: kpt on steadily fr 2f out: nvr rchd ldrs* **66/1**

6 **6** *1 ½* **Straight Laced**[11] 1893 3-8-6 0 .... PaulDoe 1 55
(W J Knight) *led for 2f: chsd ldrs after: unbalanced on downhill run 4f out: outpcd over 3f out: no ch w ldrs after: lost 2 pls wl ins fnl f* **33/1**

0 **7** *6* **Giant Sequoia (USA)**[15] 1771 5-9-12 0 .... PatDobbs 9 49
(K J Burke) *rrd s and v.s.a: bhd: effrt and hanging lft fr 3f out: nvr nr ldrs* **33/1**

0-0 **8** *nk* **Little Sark (IRE)**[15] 1771 4-9-7 0 .... RichardEvans(5) 10 48
(P D Evans) *hld up towards rr: hmpd over 2f out: n.d* **25/1**

0- **9** *7* **Hallingdal Blue (UAE)**[165] 7578 3-8-6 0 .... JimmyQuinn 8 31
(H R A Cecil) *towards rr: rdn along 8f out: rdn and no prog over 3f out: wl bhd whn hmpd wl over 1f out* **10/1**

05 **10** *½* **Roman The Emperor (IRE)**[20] 1622 3-8-11 0 .... JerryO'Dwyer 12 35
(S W Hall) *stdd s: t.k.h: hld up in tch in midfield: rdn over 3f out: sn struggling: bhd fnl 2f* **66/1**

2m 31.93s (0.43) **Going Correction** +0.05s/f (Good)
WFA 3 from 4yo+ 15lb **10 Ran SP% 115.1**
Speed ratings (Par 103): **100,98,96,95,94 93,89,89,84,83**
toteswinger: 1&2 £2.30, 1&3 £13.00, 2&3 £21.80 CSF £8.15 TOTE £2.80: £1.30, £1.50, £6.50; EX 9.30 Trifecta £151.30 Pool: £449.85 - 2.20 winning units..

Owner Hamdan Al Maktoum **Bred** Shadwell Estate Company Limited **Trained** Arundel, W Sussex

FOCUS
A maiden lacking in any depth and run at a moderate early pace with the only rated runner winning with little to spare.

Talimos(IRE) Official explanation: jockey said gelding never travelled

Giant Sequoia(USA) Official explanation: jockey said horse missed the break and hung left

2182 BET ASIAN H'CAPS - BETDAQ HANDICAP 1m 3f 106y
2:35 (2:36) (Class 6) (0-60,58) 4-Y-0+ £2,047 (£604; £302) Stalls High

Form RPR

00/0 **1** **Mossmann Gorge**[25] 1533 7-8-5 48 .... (p) KevinGhunowa(3) 10 56
(A Middleton) *hld up in midfield: hdwy over 2f out: rdn over 1f out: led 1f out: r.o wl* **28/1**

5600 **2** *1 ¼* **Debdene Bank (IRE)**[37] 1254 6-9-3 57 .... GeorgeBaker 4 63
(Mrs Mary Hambro) *chsd ldrs: squeezed through on inner over 3f out: rdn and ev ch 3f out: led wl over 1f out: hdd 1f out: edgd rt u.p ins fnl f: one pce* **12/1**

6354 **3** *1 ¼* **Penang Cinta**[16] 6-9-3 57 .... (p) CatherineGannon 12 61
(P D Evans) *chsd ldrs: rdn and ev ch over 2f out: unable qck ent fnl f: wknd wl ins fnl f* **4/1**[2]

0004 **4** *2 ¾* **Speagle (IRE)**[7] 1980 7-8-3 46 .... KellyHarrison(3) 11 45
(A J Chamberlain) *led for 1f: chsd ldr after: rdn to ld over 2f out: hdd wl over 1f out: wknd ins fnl f* **12/1**

0040 **5** *nse* **Mixing**[35] 1287 7-8-5 45 .... KirstyMilczarek 13 44
(M J Attwater) *dwlt: sn in tch in midfield: rdn and unable qck over 2f out: drvn over 1f out: styd on again ins fnl f: nvr pce to threaten ldrs* **12/1**

-062 **6** *hd* **Wizard Looking**[9] 1938 8-8-5 45 .... JimmyQuinn 14 44
(P T Midgley) *taken down early: hld up in tch: hdwy gng wl over 3f out: rdn 2f out: kpt on same pce* **11/4**[1]

660 **7** *¾* **Follow The Dream**[35] 1286 6-8-8 48 .... JerryO'Dwyer 6 46+
(Karen George) *t.k.h: hld up in rr: c wd 3f out: r.o wl u.p fnl f: nvr trbld ldrs* **66/1**

3006 **8** *¾* **Dazzling Begum**[24] 1537 4-8-6 46 .... DO'Donohoe 5 42
(J Pearce) *hld up towards rr: rdn and hdwy towards inner over 3f out: switching out rt fr over 2f out: nt clr run and swtchd lft over 1f out: no imp after* **14/1**

0205 **9** *1* **Generous Lad (IRE)**[8] 1961 6-8-11 51 .... (p) StephenDonohoe 15 46
(A B Haynes) *hld up in midfield: rdn and effrt over 3f out: drvn and no prog fr wl over 1f out* **10/1**

4535 **10** *1 ¼* **Jackie Kiely**[8] 1974 8-9-1 55 .... (t) PhillipMakin 9 47
(R Brotherton) *hld up in midfield: hdwy jst over 3f out: nt clr run and swtchd lft over 1f out: nvr nr ldrs* **8/1**[3]

-500 **11** *1* **Barton Sands (IRE)**[22] 1589 12-8-12 52 .... (t) TravisBlock 2 43
(Andrew Reid) *stdd s: hld up towards rr: hdwy on outer 4f out: rdn 3f out: wknd wl over 1f out* **20/1**

-300 **12** *6* **Karmei**[77] 760 4-8-7 47 .... TPO'Shea 16 28
(R Curtis) *dwlt: sn bustled along and hdwy to ld after 1f: rdn and hrd pressed 3f out: hdd over 2f out: wknd wl over 1f out: eased ins fnl f* **66/1**

0000 **13** *nk* **Dynamo Dave (USA)**[8] 1961 4-8-6 46 .... LukeMorris 1 26
(M D I Usher) *stdd after s: hld up in rr: nvr on terms* **40/1**

44-0 **14** *4 ½* **The Composer**[21] 1609 7-8-12 52 .... FrancisNorton 8 24
(M Blanshard) *dwlt: bustled along early: a in rr: rdn and toiling over 3f out* **33/1**

00-0 **15** *¾* **Platoche (IRE)**[31] 1378 4-9-2 56 .... (b[1]) DaneO'Neill 7 27
(G A Butler) *in tch: pushed along 4f out: drvn and struggling 3f out: wknd 2f out* **11/1**

-540 **16** ½ **Cash On (IRE)**13 1069 7-9-4 **58**.....(v) TGMcLaughlin 3 28
(Karen George) *rel to r and v.s.a: a bhd* **33/1**

2m 32.35s (0.85) **Going Correction** +0.05s/f (Good) **16** Ran SP% **124.5**
Speed ratings (Par 101): **98,97,96,94,94 94,93,92,92,91 90,86,85,82,82 81**
toteswinger: 1&2 £100.60, 1&3 £42.00, 2&3 £11.80 CSF £327.25 CT £1653.51 TOTE £45.40: £8.50, £3.90, £1.40, £2.70; EX 448.40 TRIFECTA Not won..
Owner Mrs C Middleton **Bred** R S Cockerill (farms) Ltd **Trained** Granborough, Bucks

FOCUS
A very moderate handicap, a seller in all but name.
Cash On(IRE) Official explanation: jockey said gelding missed the break and was reluctant to race

2183 BET IN RUNNING - BETDAQ H'CAP 1m 2f
3:10 (3:11) (Class 5) (0-70,70) 4-Y-O+ **£3,238** (£963; £481; £240) **Stalls** Low

Form RPR
3260 **1** **Samurai Warrior**15 1773 4-8-7 **59**.....(p) CatherineGannon 1 67
(P D Evans) *chsd ldng pair: rdn to chse ldr 3f out: kpt on u.p to ld ins fnl f: styd on wl* **14/1**

500 **2** ¾ **Ross Moor**21 1604 7-8-6 **58**..... FergusSweeney 4 65
(Mike Murphy) *dwlt: sn rcvrd to chse ldrs: rdn 3f out: no hdwy tl r.o u.p ins fnl f: wnt 2nd nr fin* **8/1**

3302 **3** nk **Bramalea**7 1983 4-9-0 **66**..... DaneO'Neill 6 72
(B W Duke) *led: rdn over 2f out: drvn wl over 1f out: hdd ins fnl f: no ex: lost 2nd nr fin* **4/1**3

40-1 **4** 3 **Run For Ede's**23 1571 5-9-1 **70**..... JackMitchell(3) 10 70
(P M Phelan) *stdd s and dropped in bhd after s: t.k.h: hld up in rr: effrt 3f out: rdn 2f out: plugged on to go 4th ins fnl f: nvr pce to threaten ldrs* **7/2**2

00-5 **5** nk **Colour Trooper (IRE)**22 1581 4-9-4 **70**.....(b1) LukeMorris 8 69
(P Winkworth) *chsd ldr: rdn over 3f out: lost 2nd 3f out: wknd u.p over 1f out* **9/1**

0-64 **6** 1 ½ **Classical Rhythm (IRE)**22 1581 4-8-10 **62**..... TGMcLaughlin 2 58
(J R Boyle) *racd in midfield: rdn along 1/2-way: plugged on same pce fnl 2f* **9/1**

2-26 **7** ¾ **Mick's Dancer**13 1812 4-9-1 **67**..... DO'Donohoe 7 62
(W R Muir) *t.k.h: hld up in rr: effrt 3f out: edging lft and no prog fnl 2f* **9/4**1

2120 **8** 28 **Pab Special (IRE)**24 1539 6-9-0 **66**..... SimonWhitworth 3 5
(B R Johnson) *t.k.h: hld up in rr: lost tch 3f out: virtually p.u ins fnl f: t.o* **12/1**

2m 10.13s (-0.37) **Going Correction** +0.05s/f (Good) **8** Ran SP% **118.5**
Speed ratings (Par 103): **103,102,102,99,99 98,97,75**
toteswinger: 1&2 £16.70, 1&3 £9.10, 2&3 £8.20 CSF £123.16 CT £540.23 TOTE £16.10: £3.40, £2.40, £1.80; EX 144.90 Trifecta £265.40 Part won. Pool: £358.70 - 0.50 winning units..
Owner Mrs I M Folkes **Bred** Lady Lonsdale **Trained** Pandy, Monmouths

FOCUS
A modest handicap but run at a sound gallop.

2184 140TH DAY (S) STKS 6f (P)
3:45 (3:48) (Class 6) 3-Y-O+ **£2,047** (£604; £302) **Stalls** Low

Form RPR
1023 **1** **Swinbrook (USA)**9 1921 8-9-7 73.....(v) FrederikTylicki(5) 10 76
(R A Fahey) *chsd ldrs: wnt 2nd over 3f out: rdn to ld over 1f out: kpt on u.p fnl f: hld on* **5/6**1

0060 **2** shd **Fyodor (IRE)**9 1924 8-9-6 90.....(v) FergusSweeney 8 69
(C R Dore) *taken down early: hld up in rr of main gp: smooth hdwy 2f out: trckd ldrs gng wl ent fnl f: rdn to press wnr ins fnl f: nt quite get up* **4/1**2

4500 **3** 2 ¼ **Avoca Dancer (IRE)**29 1421 6-9-1 52.....(v) TGMcLaughlin 9 57
(Karen George) *wnt lft s: in tch: rdn and unable qck jst over 2f out: kpt on u.p fnl f: wnt 3rd towards fin: nvr pce to threaten ldng pair* **20/1**

4140 **4** ¾ **One More Round (USA)**34 1313 11-9-7 67.....(b) RichardEvans(5) 1 66
(P D Evans) *hld up in tch: rdn and effrt on inner over 1f out: keeping on same pce whn n.m.r jst ins fnl f* **4/1**2

0360 **5** ½ **Bollin Franny**8 1970 5-9-6 51..... RichardThomas 6 58
(J E Long) *led: rdn and hdd over 1f out: wknd ins fnl f: lost 2 pls towards fin* **14/1**3

0 **6** 3 **Summer Capers (USA)**16 1743 4-9-1 50..... TPO'Shea 11 43
(J Gallagher) *t.k.h: chsd ldrs on outer: rdn jst over 2f out: wknd over 1f out* **20/1**

06-0 **7** 8 **Kappalyn (IRE)**19 1636 4-9-1 50..... PatCosgrave 5 18
(J R Boyle) *reluctant to go to post: chsd ldr tl over 3f out: sn rdn: bhd fnl 2f* **20/1**

0/ **8** 4 **Kilmeena Dream**532 7029 5-9-1 0..... RichardSmith 12 5
(J C Fox) *s.i.s: a outpcd in last pl* **66/1**

1m 12.21s (0.31) **Going Correction** +0.075s/f (Slow) **8** Ran SP% **117.0**
Speed ratings (Par 101): **100,99,96,95,95 91,80,75**
toteswinger: 1&2 £2.30, 1&3 £4.20, 2&3 £7.00 CSF £4.28 TOTE £1.70: £1.10, £1.70, £2.70; EX 5.80 Trifecta £34.80 Pool: £551.27 - 11.69 winning units..There was no bid for the winner. Fyodor was claimed by P. D. Evans for £6000.
Owner Mark A Leatham **Bred** Bill Bronstad **Trained** Musley Bank, N Yorks

FOCUS
Five of these were in selling grade for the first time.

2185 THE SAW DOCTORS HERE JUNE 20TH CLAIMING STKS 7f (P)
4:20 (4:22) (Class 6) 3-Y-O+ **£2,047** (£604; £302) **Stalls** Low

Form RPR
1300 **1** **Kipchak (IRE)**4 2071 4-9-7 75.....(p) RobertWinston 13 74
(A J McCabe) *mde all: 3l clr and rdn 2f out: edgd rt fr over 1f out: pressed ins fnl f: fnd ex and gng away nr fin* **9/4**1

1166 **2** 1 ¼ **Imprimis Tagula (IRE)**9 1943 5-9-2 76.....(v) LeeNewnes(7) 6 72
(A Bailey) *chsd ldrs: rdn to chse wnr 2f out: pressed wnr ins fnl f: no ex fnl 50yds* **13/2**

3052 **3** ½ **Blue Tomato**9 1924 8-9-6 78..... AdrianTNicholls 11 68
(D Nicholls) *hld up in rr of main gp: gd hdwy on inner over 1f out: chsd ldng pair and drvn jst ins fnl f: no imp fnl 100yds* **5/1**3

6035 **4** nk **Teen Ager (FR)**11 1890 5-9-6 58..... JimmyQuinn 10 67
(P Burgoyne) *hld up in midfield: effrt and rdn 2f out: chsd ldrs ent fnl f: one pce after* **25/1**

4416 **5** 1 ¾ **Landucci**11 1883 8-9-3 69.....(p) GeorgeBaker 5 59
(S Curran) *hld up in midfield hdwy and rdn jst over 2f out: chsd ldrs and drvn ent fnl f: wknd jst ins fnl f* **11/2**

254- **6** 1 **Carmenero (GER)**158 7668 6-9-6 74..... DO'Donohoe 14 60
(W R Muir) *hld up in rr of main gp: hdwy 2f out: nt clr run over 1f out tl jst ins fnl f: no prog after* **9/2**2

5040 **7** 1 ½ **Zars Gold (IRE)**11 1890 4-8-12 57..... TPO'Shea 7 48
(J Gallagher) *chsd wnr tl 5f out: wknd u.p jst over 2f out* **25/1**

0/0- **8** 2 ¼ **Petomic (IRE)**333 3268 4-9-5 0.....(t) EdwardCreighton 2 48
(Christian Wroe) *a outpcd in rr* **66/1**

10 **9** 1 **Sendreni (FR)**16 1734 5-9-7 73.....(t) FrancisNorton 1 48
(M Wigham) *chsd ldrs: chsd wnr 5f out tl 2f out: wknd qckly over 1f out* **10/1**

10 shd **Isitcozimcool (IRE)**25 4-9-12 0..... StephenDonohoe 8 52
(D E Cantillon) *s.i.s: a outpcd in rr* **40/1**

06-0 **11** nk **Chief Exec**37 1258 7-9-4 69.....(b) PatCosgrave 3 44
(J R Gask) *s.i.s: a outpcd in rr* **20/1**

12 24 **Rony Dony (IRE)** 5-9-12 0..... DaneO'Neill 12 —
(M E Rimmer) *v.s.a: a detached in last pl: t.o fnl 2f* **100/1**

1m 24.68s (-0.12) **Going Correction** +0.075s/f (Slow) **12** Ran SP% **120.8**
Speed ratings (Par 101): **103,101,101,100,98 97,95,93,92,91 91,64**
toteswinger: 1&2 £6.40, 1&3 £4.10, 2&3 £7.20 CSF £16.56 TOTE £2.70: £1.40, £2.50, £1.60; EX 25.70 Trifecta £74.10 Pool: £264.67 - 2.64 winning units..Kipchak was claimed by C. R. Dore for £10000.
Owner Timms, Lane, Baker & McCabe **Bred** Miss Mary Davidson & Mrs Steffi Von Schilcher **Trained** Averham Park, Notts

FOCUS
A tight claimer run at a sound pace.
Sendreni(FR) Official explanation: jockey said gelding ran flat
Isitcozimcool(IRE) Official explanation: jockey said gelding hung right

2186 RACING HERE MAY 27TH/28TH H'CAP 1m (P)
4:55 (4:55) (Class 5) (0-75,75) 4-Y-O+ **£3,238** (£963; £481; £240) **Stalls** High

Form RPR
0653 **1** **I Confess**11 1876 4-8-11 **73**.....(b) RichardEvans(5) 5 83
(P D Evans) *chsd ldr: rdn to ld over 2f out: drvn clr over 1f out: a holding runner up: rdn out* **6/1**2

536- **2** ½ **Uncle Fred**246 5995 4-9-1 **72**..... NeilChalmers 6 81
(P R Chamings) *s.i.s: hld up towards rr: rdn and hdwy jost over 1f out: chsd wnr ins fnl f: r.o wl but nvr quite gng to rch wnr* **16/1**

0331 **3** 1 ¾ **Pha Mai Blue**12 1833 4-8-9 **66**.....(v) PatCosgrave 2 71
(J R Boyle) *in tch: rdn to chse ldng pair over 2f out: chsd clr wnr over 1f out: no imp: lost 2nd ins fnl f* **4/1**1

3605 **4** ¾ **General Feeling (IRE)**8 1955 8-8-13 **70**..... AdrianTNicholls 12 73
(D Nicholls) *stdd and dropped in bhd after s: c wd and rdn wl over 1f out: r.o fnl f: nvr trbld ldrs* **7/1**3

5304 **5** 1 **Ocean Legend (IRE)**25 1524 4-9-4 **75**..... JerryO'Dwyer 10 76
(Miss J Feilden) *stdd after s: hld up towards rr on outer: rdn and effrt over 2f out: kpt on but nvr gng to rch ldrs* **9/1**

5245 **6** ½ **Obezyana (USA)**11 1887 7-8-13 **70**.....(v) RobertWinston 1 70
(A Bailey) *chsd ldrs: rdn over 2f out: drvn and carried rt over 1f out: plugged on same pce fnl f* **4/1**1

551- **7** ½ **Sarah Park (IRE)**211 6889 4-8-13 **70**..... DaneO'Neill 8 69
(B J Meehan) *hld up towards rr: drvn and effrt towards inner over 1f out: no imp fnl f* **10/1**

300- **8** 2 ¼ **Cool Ebony**210 6899 6-9-2 **73**..... PhillipMakin 7 67
(P J Makin) *chsd ldrs: rdn over 4f out: drvn and struggling over 2f out: no ch fnl f* **15/2**

2605 **9** 1 ½ **Millfield (IRE)**56 950 6-9-2 **73**..... GeorgeBaker 3 63
(P R Chamings) *s.i.s: hld up in rr: short lived effrt on inner wl over 1f out: n.d* **16/1**

3410 **10** shd **Solent Ridge (IRE)**20 1633 4-9-4 **75**.....(p) LukeMorris 4 65
(J S Moore) *led: rdn and hdd over 2f out: edgd rt u.p over 1f out: wknd ent fnl f* **10/1**

1m 38.13s (-0.07) **Going Correction** +0.075s/f (Slow) **10** Ran SP% **118.5**
Speed ratings (Par 103): **103,102,100,100,99 98,98,95,94,94**
toteswinger: 1&2 £11.40, 1&3 £3.50, 2&3 £22.40 CSF £98.24 CT £433.47 TOTE £7.90: £3.20, £5.40, £1.90; EX 195.20 TRIFECTA Not won. Place 6: £64.20 Place 5: £42.76..
Owner M&R Refurbishments Ltd **Bred** Gestut Sohrenhof **Trained** Pandy, Monmouths

FOCUS
A fair handicap run at a fair gallop.
T/Plt: £41.80 to a £1 stake. Pool: £51,137.43. 891.30 winning tickets. T/Qpdt: £7.70 to a £1 stake. Pool: £3,678.38. 353.20 winning tickets. SP

2174 GOODWOOD (R-H)
Thursday, May 21

OFFICIAL GOING: Good to firm (good in places; 8.9)
Rail realignment added circa 24yards to races on the mile course and 8 yards to races incorporating the top bend.
Wind: fairly modest, half against Weather: bright, partly cloudy

2187 E B F RACING TO SCHOOL MEDIAN AUCTION MAIDEN STKS 6f
2:15 (2:16) (Class 5) 2-Y-O **£3,561** (£1,059; £529; £264) **Stalls** Low

Form RPR
1 **Goodwood Maestro** 2-9-3 0..... EddieAhern 5 84+
(J L Dunlop) *w'like: str: in tch in midfield: hdwy over 2f out: chsd ldr over 1f out: shkn up ent fnl f: led fnl 100yds: pushed out: readily* **11/1**

6 **2** ¾ **Footstepsofspring (FR)**18 1700 2-9-3 0..... DaneO'Neill 2 82+
(R Hannon) *led: rdn wl over 1f out: clr w wnr 1f out: hdd and no ex fnl 100yds* **11/2**3

0 **3** 5 **Timelord (IRE)**23 1577 2-9-3 0..... LPKeniry 12 67
(S Kirk) *w'like: chsd ldrs: wnt 2nd wl over 2f out tl over 1f out: sn rdn: outpcd by ldng pair fnl f* **4/1**1

4 shd **Big Audio (IRE)** 2-9-3 0..... RichardHughes 9 66+
(R Hannon) *athletic: lw: swtchd lft after s: bhd: swtchd rt over 2f out: kpt on steadily fnl f to press for 3rd nr fin: nvr nr ldrs* **4/1**1

45 **5** 6 **Master Mylo (IRE)**31 1404 2-9-3 0..... GeorgeBaker 11 48
(Mrs L C Jewell) *hld up towards rr: hdwy on outer over 2f out: rdn and no prog over 1f out: wl hld fnl f* **10/1**

6 1 ¼ **Imperial Warrior** 2-9-3 0..... SteveDrowne 7 45+
(H Morrison) *w'like: tall: bit bwkd: v.s.a: bhd: sme hdwy and rdn jst over 2f out: no prog and wl btn fr over 1f out* **20/1**

7 4 **Smicker Smacker** 2-8-5 0..... MatthewDavies(7) 3 28
(George Baker) *leggy: in tch: rn green and lost pl 4f out: bhd whn n.m.r 3f out: wl btn fnl 2f* **50/1**

8 shd **Aattash (IRE)** 2-9-3 0..... EdwardCreighton 10 32+
(M R Channon) *leggy: v.s.a: rdn along and hdwy into midfield over 3f out: wknd over 2f out: wl bhd fnl 2f* **9/2**2

0 **9** 2 ½ **Welsh Legacy (IRE)**6 2033 2-8-12 0..... GabrielHannon(5) 8 25
(B W Duke) *chsd ldrs tl wl over 2f out: sn wknd: wl bhd fr over 1f out* **80/1**

10 1 ¾ **Stef And Stelio** 2-9-3 0..... KirstyMilczarek 1 20
(G A Butler) *lengthy: bit bkwd: in tch: rdn and struggling 1/2-way: wl bhd fnl 2f* **11/1**

00 **11** *1* **Kings Aphrodite**[25] 1534 2-9-3 0.. JimmyQuinn 4 17
(Miss Gay Kelleway) *neat: t.k.h: hld up in tch: rdn and wknd over 2f out: wl btn whn hung rt over 1f out: eased ins fnl f* **40/1**

12 *6* **Foxtrot Foxtrot** 2-9-3 0.. JimCrowley 6 —
(P Winkworth) *w'like: chsd ldr tl wl over 2f out: sn wknd: bhd whn edgd rt u.p over 2f out: eased fnl f* **14/1**

1m 12.5s (0.30) **Going Correction** 0.0s/f (Good) **12** Ran SP% **116.4**
Speed ratings (Par 93): **98,97,90,90,82 80,75,75,71,69 68,60**
toteswinger: 1&2 £10.50, 1&3 £10.20, 2&3 £7.00 CSF £67.43 TOTE £8.30: £2.50, £2.30, £2.00; EX 84.60.

Owner Goodwood Racehorse Owners Group(Fifteen) **Bred** J Dunlop **Trained** Arundel, W Sussex

FOCUS
The rail alignment was exactly the same as for the previous day, but the ground was drying out all the time and was officially described as Good to Firm, Good in places. This was probably quite a good maiden as the pace was solid and they finished well spread out. The form looks solid enough rated around the front two.

NOTEBOOK
Goodwood Maestro, his trainer's first two-year-old runner of the season, looked as though the run would bring him on and wasn't particularly strong in the market, but he could be seen travelling like a dream behind the leaders from a very long way out. When eventually asked for his effort, he responded in fine style to hit the front well inside the last furlong. A brother to a winning juvenile sprinter and a half-brother to a multiple winner at up to 1m4f in the Czech Republic, the way he saw his race out suggests he will get further and he has a future. (op 8-1)

Footstepsofspring(FR), who showed early speed before fading to finish last of six over 5f on his Newmarket debut, used his experience to good effect and, having quickly bagged the stands' rail, he lasted much longer this time. He wasn't worn down until late on and pulled a long way clear of the rest, so shouldn't take long in going one better. (op 5-1 tchd 6-1)

Timelord(IRE), ninth in a Bath maiden on debut that has already produced three winners, had to do a bit of running early in order to take a handy position from the outside stall and this was a step up. He too should win races. (tchd 9-2 in places)

Big Audio(IRE) ◆, an £87,000 half-brother to a winner over 6f and a stable companion of the runner-up, was weak in the market beforehand but he can be rated a bit better than his final position. Having been at the back of the field in the early stages he had to switch around the entire field in order to see daylight, but he stayed on in pleasing style late on down the middle of the track. (op 3-1 tchd 11-4)

Master Mylo(IRE), not disgraced in a couple of 5f maidens, was bred to be suited by this extra furlong. He was another to make his effort very wide and there should be a small race in him in due course. (op 17-2 tchd 8-1)

Imperial Warrior ◆ completely blew his chance at the start, but still showed definite signs of ability as he was noted doing some good late work and comes from a stable not normally associated with winning debutants. (op 14-1)

Smicker Smacker Official explanation: jockey said filly was denied a clear run

Aattash(IRE), well backed, also lost all chance at the start. (op 17-2 tchd 9-1)

Stef And Stelio Official explanation: jockey said colt ran very green

Kings Aphrodite Official explanation: jockey said saddle slipped

2188 O'SULLEVANS CAFE STKS (H'CAP) 7f
2:50 (2:51) (Class 4) (0-80,80) 4-Y-0+ **£4,857** (£1,445; £722; £360) **Stalls** High

Form RPR

2-02 **1** **Woodcote Place**[22] 1607 6-9-3 79.. JimCrowley 11 89
(P R Chamings) *s.i.s: hld up towards rr: hdwy over 2f out: chsd ldr over 1f out: rdn to ld jst over 1f out: styd on wl u.p fnl 100yds* **8/1**[2]

/0-6 **2** *½* **Kirk Michael**[36] 1288 5-9-1 77.. DaneO'Neill 6 86
(H Candy) *towards rr: edgd out lft and rdn 3f out: gd hdwy on outer jst over 1f out: pressed wnr wl ins fnl f: kpt on* **10/1**

0-00 **3** *hd* **Ivory Lace**[25] 1539 8-8-6 68.. JimmyQuinn 9 76+
(S Woodman) *hld up in last trio: hdwy and n.m.r over 2f out: swtchd ins 2f out: rdn and gd hdwy ent fnl f: r.o wl: nt quite rch ldrs* **16/1**

61-0 **4** *1 ½* **Koraleva Tectona (IRE)**[53] 1016 4-8-13 75.. PatDobbs 15 79
(Pat Eddery) *lw: hld up in midfield: hdwy towards inner over 1f out: rdn jst over 1f out: chsd ldrs ins fnl f: no imp towards fin* **14/1**

042- **5** *¾* **Lekita**[169] 7540 4-8-8 70.. TedDurcan 13 72
(W R Swinburn) *lw: chsd ldrs: effrt and rdn jst over 2f out: chsd wnr and drvn over 1f out tl fnl 100yds: wknd towards fin* **8/1**[2]

5400 **6** *½* **Councellor (FR)**[22] 1603 7-8-13 75..(t) MickyFenton 14 76
(Stef Liddiard) *sn pushed up to ld: rdn and hung lft 2f out: hdd jst over 1f out: wknd ins fnl f* **13/2**[1]

00-2 **7** *5* **Folly Lodge**[24] 1566 5-9-4 80.. SebSanders 5 67
(R M Beckett) *lw: hld up in rr: sltly hmpd 3f out: edging rt and looking for run whn nt clr run wl over 1f out: plugged on fnl f but nvr nr ldrs* **14/1**

130- **8** *2* **Support Fund (IRE)**[189] 7307 5-8-11 73.. StephenCarson 2 55
(Eve Johnson Houghton) *taken down early: hld up towards rr: drvn and effrt on outer over 3f out: plugged on past btn horses fnl f: nvr nr ldrs* **40/1**

221- **9** *shd* **Oh So Saucy**[303] 4284 5-9-1 77.. GeorgeBaker 16 58
(C F Wall) *hld up in tch: hdwy on inner 3f out: rdn wl over 1f out: little rspnse and btn jst over 1f out* **13/2**[1]

0-44 **10** *hd* **Salient**[12] 1894 5-9-4 80.. KirstyMilczarek 3 61
(M J Attwater) *chsd ldrs: rdn to chse ldr 2f out tl over 1f out: sn wknd* **9/1**[3]

050- **11** *1 ½* **Idle Power (IRE)**[201] 7143 11-9-1 80.. JackMitchell(3) 8 57
(J R Boyle) *t.k.h: hld up in tch: rdn jst over 2f out: wknd over 1f out* **25/1**

-242 **12** *nk* **Gazboolou**[27] 1493 5-8-10 72.. FergusSweeney 12 48
(David Pinder) *lw: w.w in tch in midfield: rdn and effrt over 2f out: wknd over 1f out* **14/1**

2005 **13** *½* **Compton's Eleven**[12] 1894 8-8-11 73.. SamHitchcott 4 48
(M R Channon) *in tch in midfield: rdn on outer 3f out: no prog: wknd 2f out* **25/1**

0-00 **14** *¾* **Choreography**[13] 1836 6-9-1 77.. PaulDoe 1 50
(Jim Best) *stdd and dropped in bhd after s: rdn and effrt over 2f out: no hdwy* **50/1**

3-20 **15** *2 ½* **Buxton**[24] 1572 5-9-3 79..(t) SteveDrowne 10 45
(R Ingram) *stdd s: t.k.h: hld up in midfield: rdn and lost pl wl over 2f out: no ch fnl 2f* **16/1**

10-0 **16** *1 ½* **Mister Ross**[22] 1603 4-9-2 78.. RichardHughes 7 51
(G L Moore) *pressed ldr tl 2f out: sn wknd: wl btn and eased ins fnl f* **8/1**[2]

1m 26.39s (-1.01) **Going Correction** 0.0s/f (Good) **16** Ran SP% **122.9**
Speed ratings (Par 105): **105,104,104,102,101 101,95,93,92,92 91,90,90,89,86 84**
toteswinger: 1&2 £20.60, 1&3 £41.70, 2&3 £51.00 CSF £83.54 CT £1271.48 TOTE £9.60: £2.40, £2.60, £3.60, £3.60; EX 120.10.

Owner The Foxford House Partnership **Bred** Mrs Ann Jenkins **Trained** Baughurst, Hants

FOCUS
A competitive handicap run at a decent pace and the front six pulled clear. It has been rated around the fourth to last year's course and distance win.

2189 M-REAL STKS (H'CAP) 1m 3f
3:25 (3:25) (Class 4) (0-85,83) 3-Y-O **£6,476** (£1,927; £963; £481) **Stalls** Low

Form RPR

-215 **1** **Brunston**[6] 2038 3-9-0 79.. SebSanders 3 90+
(R Charlton) *hld up in tch in rr: hdwy over 4f out: rdn to chse ldr over 2f out: ev ch 2f out: drvn to ld over 1f out: styd on wl to forge clr ins fnl f* **9/2**[2]

3-14 **2** *2 ¾* **Bin End**[8] 1992 3-9-4 83.. JamieSpencer 5 89
(M L W Bell) *lw: t.k.h: hld up in tch in rr: rdn and gd hdwy on outer to ld and edgd rt over 2f out: hrd pressed 2f out: drvn and hdd over 1f out: wknd fnl 100yds* **2/1**[1]

06-1 **3** *hd* **Solar Graphite (IRE)**[30] 1428 3-8-6 71.. EddieAhern 4 81+
(J L Dunlop) *hld up in tch in rr: hdwy on inner over 2f out: swtchd lft and rdn over 1f out: styd on u.p fnl f: pressing for 2nd nr fin* **6/1**[3]

0-1 **4** *3 ¼* **At A Great Rate (USA)**[33] 1362 3-9-0 79.. TPQueally 8 79
(H R A Cecil) *scope: lw: trckd ldrs: short of room briefly over 2f out: chsd ldng pair and rdn over 1f out: little rspnse and no hdwy* **6/1**[3]

6-23 **5** *2 ¾* **Curacao**[20] 1643 3-8-8 73.. JimCrowley 6 68
(Mrs A J Perrett) *hld up in tch towards rr: hdwy 3f out: swtchd lft and rdn 2f out: sn btn* **6/1**[3]

4-50 **6** *¾* **Latin Tinge (USA)**[22] 1613 3-9-3 82.. RichardHughes 1 75
(P F I Cole) *hdwy to ld after 1f: hdd over 2f out: sn rdn: wknd over 1f out* **28/1**

20-4 **7** *2 ¾* **Guestofthenation (USA)**[18] 1702 3-9-3 82.. GregFairley 2 71
(M Johnston) *lw: chsd ldrs: pushed along 4f out: lost pl and rdn 3f out: no ch fnl 2f* **14/1**

-336 **8** *12* **Princability (IRE)**[18] 1707 3-8-10 75.. SamHitchcott 7 50
(M R Channon) *led for 1f: chsd ldr tl over 2f out: sn wknd: eased ins fnl f* **10/1**

2m 25.96s (-2.34) **Going Correction** 0.0s/f (Good) **8** Ran SP% **113.6**
Speed ratings (Par 101): **108,106,105,103,101 100,98,90**
toteswinger: 1&2 £1.90, 1&3 £5.90, 2&3 £3.00 CSF £13.72 CT £53.00 TOTE £4.80: £1.90, £1.40, £1.80; EX 13.70.

Owner Seasons Holidays **Bred** Seasons Holidays **Trained** Beckhampton, Wilts

FOCUS
A good three-year-old handicap, but the early pace was nothing special and it developed into a something of a sprint. The first two were both officially well in and the race has been rated around the runner-up to his York form.

2190 HEIGHT OF FASHION STKS (LISTED RACE) (FILLIES) 1m 1f 192y
4:00 (4:01) (Class 1) 3-Y-O **£23,704** (£8,964; £4,480; £2,240) **Stalls** High

Form RPR

4-53 **1** **Moneycantbuymelove (IRE)**[18] 1701 3-9-0 93.......... JamieSpencer 5 99+
(M L W Bell) *t.k.h: hld up in last pair: swtchd lft and rdn over 1f out: drvn and qcknd to ld ins fnl f: r.o wl* **13/2**[3]

31- **2** *1 ½* **Fallen In Love**[236] 6291 3-9-0 77.. EddieAhern 7 96
(J L Dunlop) *t.k.h: trckd ldrs after 2f: rdn 3f out: chsd ldr wl over 1f out: ev ch over 1f out tl nt pce of wnr fnl 100yds* **12/1**

22-1 **3** *1 ¼* **Say No Now (IRE)**[13] 1843 3-9-0 85.. TedDurcan 1 93
(D R Lanigan) *led for 1f: chsd ldr after tl ld again over 2f out: sn rdn: hrd pressed over 1f out: hdd and no ex ins fnl f* **10/1**

13- **4** *hd* **Splashdown**[201] 7144 3-9-0 94.. DaneO'Neill 8 93
(L M Cumani) *lw: t.k.h: hld up in tch towards rr: hdwy on outer 3f out: rdn wl over 1f out: pressed ldrs ent fnl f: one pce after* **5/2**[2]

1-30 **5** *2* **Miss Beat (IRE)**[7] 2001 3-9-0 73.. RichardHughes 3 89?
(B J Meehan) *lw: stdd s: hld up in last pl: swtchd ins and effrt 2f out: no imp u.p fr over 1f out* **40/1**

3- **6** *2 ¾* **Copperbeech (IRE)**[228] 6519 3-9-0 108.. LDettori 6 83
(Saeed Bin Suroor) *trckd ldng pair: rdn 3f out: drvn to chse wnr briefly 2f out: wknd over 1f out* **7/4**[1]

51-1 **7** *½* **Faldal**[22] 1613 3-9-0 84.. RichardKingscote 9 82
(Tom Dascombe) *lw: led after 1f: rdn and hdd over 2f out: wknd u.p over 1f out* **8/1**

01- **8** *9* **Dulcie**[221] 6674 3-9-0 77.. LiamJones 2 64
(M H Tompkins) *t.k.h: hld up in tch in midfield: effrt on outer 3f out: sn struggling: wl btn fnl 2f* **20/1**

2m 7.91s (-0.09) **Going Correction** 0.0s/f (Good) **8** Ran SP% **113.4**
Speed ratings (Par 104): **100,98,97,97,96 93,93,86**
toteswinger: 1&2 £7.00, 1&3 £6.40, 2&3 £9.60 CSF £77.80 TOTE £7.50: £2.00, £1.90, £2.30; EX 42.50.

Owner Wright,Stanley,Marsh,Lascelles & Harris **Bred** Eurostrait Ltd **Trained** Newmarket, Suffolk

FOCUS
Formerly known as the Lupe, the last filly to win this and then go on to land the Oaks was Love Divine in 2000. Three of these were entered for next month's Epsom classic, but with the early pace only modest and a filly rated just 73 not beaten very far, it seems very unlikely that this year's renewal contained a superstar. Ordinary and dubious form for the grade.

NOTEBOOK
Moneycantbuymelove(IRE) did well to lose her maiden tag at the sixth attempt and was given a well-judged ride by Jamie Spencer, who had her well off the pace early before making his ground gradually. Once switched to the wide outside, she produced a smart turn of foot to cut down her rivals, and she shapes as though she will get a bit further. She is likely to go in search of more black type on the continent now. (op 7-1 tchd 15-2)

Fallen In Love, progressive in three outings at two and bred to appreciate this sort of trip, came from the middle of the field and stuck to her task well, but she couldn't match the winner's turn of foot. She is entitled to come on for this first start in eight months and, whilst she has no big-race entries, she looks well up to winning a Pattern race at some stage this season. (op 14-1 tchd 10-1)

Say No Now(IRE), just in front of the 1000 Guineas-winner Ghanaati at Kempton in her second start at two and an easy winner of a Nottingham maiden on her return earlier this month, was up in trip here but was nonetheless up with the pace from the start. She had every chance and ultimately did best of the three Oaks entries, but just gave the impression late on that this trip stretches her. (op 11-1 tchd 17-2)

Splashdown ◆, last seen splitting Super Sleuth and Midday when third behind Enticement in a Newmarket Listed event last November, was well backed earlier in the day and was produced to hold every chance before her effort flattened out. Her connections had warned that this race may have come a week too soon, so she can be expected to step up a fair amount from this. (op 2-1 tchd 15-8 and 11-4 in places)

Miss Beat(IRE), held in two handicaps so far this season, had a mountain to climb on these terms and plugged on late having been held up well off the pace alongside the winner early. Connections will be hoping that she hasn't blown her handicap mark with this performance.

Copperbeech(IRE), trained by Andre Fabre at two and last seen finishing third in the Prix Marcel Boussac, looked very fit and had every chance but she found little off the bridle. This was a bitterly disappointing debut for Goldolphin. (op 15-8 tchd 5-2 and 11-4 in places)

Faldal, narrow winner of a Pontefract fillies' handicap off a mark of 80 on her return to action last month, had plenty to find at this level but still faded rather tamely once headed considering she had the run of the race out in front. (tchd 6-1)
Dulcie, proven on this track having won a 1m1f maiden here on her second start at two, was backed at fancy prices but eventually dropped right out. (op 40-1)

2191 TURFTV STKS (H'CAP) 5f
4:35 (4:35) (Class 2) (0-105,105) 4-Y-O+ **£11,656** (£3,468; £1,733; £865) **Stalls** Low

Form RPR
102- **1** **Piscean (USA)**[204] 7066 4-8-2 **86** oh1 .... JimmyQuinn 8 97
(T Keddy) *lw: s.i.s: hld up in rr: hdwy 2f out: rdn to chse ldrs 1f out: led fnl 100yds: r.o strly* **12/1**
2-01 **2** *2* **Cake (IRE)**[19] 1672 4-8-9 **93** .... DaneO'Neill 5 97
(R Hannon) *lw: t.k.h: hld up in tch: hdwy and rdn 2f out: led 1f out: edgd lft ins fnl f: hdd and nt pce of wnr fnl 100yds* **15/2**
4-02 **3** *nk* **Little Pete (IRE)**[19] 1672 4-8-6 **90** ....(p) FrancisNorton 1 93+
(A M Balding) *t.k.h: hld up in tch on stands' rail: effrt and hanging rt fr over 2f out: r.o ins fnl f: no ch w wnr* **13/2**[3]
431- **4** *2¼* **Safari Mischief**[223] 6624 6-8-9 **93** .... LukeMorris 9 88
(P Winkworth) *chsd ldrs: rdn ent fnl 2f: drvn and wknd jst over 1f out* **7/2**[2]
2010 **5** *½* **Little Edward**[34] 1321 11-8-4 **93** .... MCGeran(5) 2 86
(R J Hodges) *t.k.h: hld up in tch: rdn and no hdwy 2f out: kpt on same pce fnl f* **25/1**
-502 **6** *nk* **Crimson Fern (IRE)**[23] 1582 5-8-9 **93** .... RichardHughes 6 85
(M S Saunders) *lw: racd freely: chsd ldr tl led over 1f out: sn rdn: hdd 1f out: wknd ins fnl f* **13/8**[1]
3650 **7** *nk* **Judge 'n Jury**[19] 1676 5-9-4 **105** ....(t) KevinGhunowa(3) 3 96
(R A Harris) *led: rdn and hdd over 1f out: wknd fnl f* **8/1**
/14- **8** *7* **Silver Guest**[432] 905 4-8-11 **95** .... EdwardCreighton 7 61
(M R Channon) *swtg: in tch on outer: rdn jst over 2f out: wknd qckly wl over 1f out: wl bhd fnl f* **16/1**

58.56 secs (0.16) **Going Correction** 0.0s/f (Good) **8** Ran SP% **113.9**
Speed ratings (Par 109): **98,94,94,90,89 89,88,77**
CSF £96.68 CT £646.87 TOTE £13.00: £2.90, £2.00, £1.70; EX 88.70 Trifecta £235.20 Pool: £699.29 - 2.20 winning units..
Owner Andrew Duffield **Bred** Connie And John Iacuone **Trained** Newmarket, Suffolk

FOCUS
A decent sprint handicap, but the leaders may have gone off too quick as those held up came to the fore at the finish. The race has been rated around the second and third.

NOTEBOOK
Piscean(USA) was returning from seven months off, but he was only beaten a short head on his reappearance last season, so he had proved that he can go well fresh, and he had gained two of his three previous victories over this course and distance. Despite being a bit of a lad beforehand and then giving his rivals a three-length start, he travelled powerfully off the pace and, when delivered with his effort down the outside, flew home and was well on top at the line. He is likely to reappear at Lingfield next week and if he wins there then the Wokingham may be considered. (tchd 14-1)
Cake(IRE), raised 3lb for her course-and-distance victory earlier this month and therefore 2lb worse off with the runner-up Little Pete, raced keenly behind the leaders and had every chance, but she could do nothing about the winner's turn of foot. (op 7-1 tchd 13-2)
Little Pete(IRE), who had cheekpieces on for the first time, failed to turn that recent course form around with Cake on the revised terms, but having been another to take a keen hold early he saw very little daylight against the stands' rail and had to be switched out wide for his effort, so can be rated a length or so closer. Official explanation: jockey said gelding hung right (op 9-2)
Safari Mischief, very consistent last season and a dual winner here, was on a career-high mark on this return from seven months off. Well backed earlier in the day, he was never far away, was by no means disgraced, and is entitled to come on for it. (op 5-1)
Little Edward, kept very busy on Polytrack since his most recent outing on turf last October, stayed on towards the end but it was too little too late. Official explanation: jockey said gelding was denied a clear run (op 16-1)
Crimson Fern(IRE), beaten a whisker in a Bath fillies' Listed event last time and 3lb lower than when last in a handicap, was up with the pace from the start but she was a bit too keen and probably did too much too soon. Official explanation: jockey said mare stopped quickly (op 15-8 tchd 2-1)
Judge 'n Jury, who has found Pattern company just beyond him in recent months, was off the same mark as when successful in his most recent outing in a handicap at Doncaster last October, but having taken them along against the stands' rail for a long way he didn't get home and doesn't seem at his best at present. (tchd 9-1)
Silver Guest, not seen since finishing fourth behind Paco Boy in a Listed event on the Lingfield Polytrack 14 months ago, was making his handicap debut. He made a brief effort down the wide outside at halfway, but it came to nothing and he has plenty to prove now. (tchd 14-1)

2192 NEW HORSEWALK RESTAURANT MAIDEN FILLIES' STKS 1m 1f 192y
5:10 (5:10) (Class 5) 3-Y-O **£3,238** (£963; £481; £240) **Stalls** High

Form RPR
00 **1** **Saa'lda (IRE)**[36] 1291 3-9-0 0 .... JamieSpencer 6 74
(C E Brittain) *lw: bhd: rdn 4f out: swtchd ins over 3f out: styd on u.p to chse ldrs over 1f out: drvn between horses to ld wl ins fnl f: all out* **15/8**[1]
03- **2** *¾* **Honours Stride (IRE)**[233] 6360 3-8-9 0 .... Louis-PhilippeBeuzelin(5) 8 72
(Sir Michael Stoute) *racd in midfield: rdn fr 6f out: edgd rt u.p 2f out: chsd ldrs over 1f out: plugged on u.p to go 2nd nr fin: nvr gng to rch wnr* **4/1**[3]
6 **3** *½* **Repetischa (IRE)**[35] 1297 3-9-0 0 .... JimmyQuinn 9 71
(E A L Dunlop) *lw: s.i.s: rcvrd to trck ldrs after 2f: gng wl over 2f out: plld out and rdn to chal wl over 1f out: hrd drvn jst over 1f out: plugged on same pce fnl f* **3/1**[2]
0-0 **4** *nk* **My Chestnut Girl (USA)**[27] 1488 3-9-0 0 .... TPQueally 4 71
(H R A Cecil) *lw: led: hrd pressed and rdn wl over 1f out: kpt battling on tl hdd and lost 3 pls wl ins fnl f* **8/1**
6 **5** *2¼* **Dubai Gem**[14] 1804 3-9-0 0 .... FrancisNorton 2 66
(Jamie Poulton) *w'like: bhd: rdn and hdwy on inner 2f out: chsd ldrs ent fnl f: kpt on but nvr pce to rch ldrs* **12/1**
0 **6** *2½* **Course De Diamante (IRE)**[13] 1844 3-9-0 0 .... NeilPollard 1 61
(D R Lanigan) *unf: chsd ldrs: rdn 3f out: drvn and unable qck 2f out: wknd over 1f out* **25/1**
-00 **7** *3¾* **Angelica's Art (IRE)**[13] 1843 3-9-0 0 .... DaneO'Neill 7 54
(B J Meehan) *s.i.s: hld up in rr: rdn and no hdwy jst over 2f out* **20/1**
030- **8** *¾* **Phoenix Enforcer**[217] 6745 3-9-0 74 .... DO'Donohoe 3 52
(George Baker) *chsd ldr: ev ch and rdn over 2f out tl wl over 1f out: wknd qckly over 1f out* **16/1**
00 **9** *18* **Court Wing (IRE)**[13] 1844 3-8-7 0 .... MatthewDavies(7) 5 16
(George Baker) *a towards rr: rdn and lost tch qckly 3f out: t.o* **66/1**

2m 9.63s (1.63) **Going Correction** 0.0s/f (Good) **9** Ran SP% **114.6**
Speed ratings (Par 96): **93,92,92,91,89 87,84,84,69**
toteswinger: 1&2 £2.90, 1&3 £2.40, 2&3 £3.20 CSF £9.22 TOTE £2.90: £1.30, £2.00, £1.40; EX 10.50.
Owner Saeed Manana **Bred** John Gunter & Royal Amber **Trained** Newmarket, Suffolk
■ Stewards' Enquiry : Jamie Spencer one-day ban: careless riding (June 4)

FOCUS
A weak fillies' maiden in which only a handful had previously shown much in the way of ability. Despite an ordinary pace, several of these, including the first two home, were on and off the bridle throughout, but there were still four fillies in a line across the track inside the last half-furlong. The winning time was 1.72 seconds slower than the earlier Listed race. It has been rated around the second and third.

2193 DOUBLE TRIGGER RESTAURANT STKS (H'CAP) 1m
5:40 (5:41) (Class 4) (0-85,85) 4-Y-O+ **£4,857** (£1,445; £722; £360) **Stalls** High

Form RPR
-050 **1** **Mujood**[12] 1864 6-8-12 **82** .... KevinGhunowa(3) 10 91
(Eve Johnson Houghton) *lw: mde all: rdn wl over 1f out: styd on wl fnl f: all out nr fin* **9/1**
6136 **2** *nk* **Marajaa (IRE)**[22] 1603 7-8-10 **77** .... JamieSpencer 5 86
(W J Musson) *t.k.h: hld up in last trio: swtchd lft and hdwy 2f out: trcking ldrs over 1f out: swtchd rt ent fnl f sn drvn: wnt 2nd wl ins fnl f: r.o wl: nt quite rch wnr* **7/2**[1]
0-00 **3** *½* **Cape Hawk (IRE)**[26] 1527 5-9-1 **85** .... PatrickHills(3) 1 92
(R Hannon) *lw: in tch in midfield: rdn and effrt on outer 2f out: drvn to chse ldrs jst over 1f out: kpt on* **6/1**[2]
032- **4** *1½* **Rambling Light**[178] 7439 5-8-8 **75** ....(p) LPKeniry 8 79
(A M Balding) *trckd ldng pair: wnt 2nd on bit 2f out: rdn to chal jst over 1f out: drvn and nt qckn ins fnl f: wknd towards fin* **7/2**[1]
121- **5** *3½* **Suzi Spends (IRE)**[189] 7305 4-9-3 **84** .... JimmyQuinn 6 80
(H J Collingridge) *t.k.h: hld up in midfield: hdwy on inner over 2f out: rdn 2f out: btn over 1f out: wknd ins fnl f* **8/1**
0-56 **6** *1½* **Beauchamp Viceroy**[20] 1642 5-9-4 **85** .... LiamJones 3 78
(G A Butler) *t.k.h: hld up towards rr: rdn and effrt on outer over 2f out: wknd wl over 1f out* **7/1**[3]
3505 **7** *1¼* **Sofia's Star**[14] 1813 4-8-0 **72** .... Louis-PhilippeBeuzelin(5) 2 62
(S Dow) *stdd s: hld up in rr: shkn up over 3f out: rdn and no hdwy over 2f out* **9/1**
43-0 **8** *¾* **Highland Harvest**[22] 1603 5-8-8 **75** .... FrancisNorton 9 63
(Jamie Poulton) *taken down early: t.k.h: chsd wnr tl 2f out: wknd qckly over 1f out* **18/1**
-113 **9** *2¼* **Trafalgar Square**[106] 388 7-9-3 **84** .... KirstyMilczarek 7 67
(M J Attwater) *stdd s: t.k.h: hld up in last trio: rdn and effrt over 2f out: unable qck and sltly hmpd 2f out: wl btn after* **8/1**

1m 40.53s (0.63) **Going Correction** 0.0s/f (Good) **9** Ran SP% **118.7**
Speed ratings (Par 105): **96,95,95,93,90 88,87,86,84**
toteswinger: 1&2 £9.10, 1&3 £11.70, 2&3 £6.00. CSF £41.78 CT £211.31 TOTE £8.80: £1.90, £1.90, £2.60; EX 50.20 Place 6: £205.38 Place 5: £89.78.
Owner Eden Racing **Bred** Bloomsbury Stud & The Hon Sir David Sieff **Trained** Blewbury, Oxon
■ Stewards' Enquiry : Jamie Spencer one-day ban: careless riding (Jun 4)

FOCUS
A fair handicap, but the pace was very modest and that very much played into the hands of the winner. The winner had slipped to a good mark and was seen at his best from the front and from a good draw.
Highland Harvest Official explanation: jockey said gelding ran too free
T/Jkpt: Not won. T/Plt: £208.80 to a £1 stake. Pool: £80,082.27. 279.90 winning tickets. T/Qpdt: £18.30 to a £1 stake. Pool: £5,694.18. 229.80 winning tickets. SP

1865 HAYDOCK (L-H)
Thursday, May 21

OFFICIAL GOING: Soft (5.6) changing to soft (heavy in places) after race 3 (3.00)
Rail realignent reduced the advertised distance of this race by about 22yards and all other races on the Round course were increased in distance by 10yards.
Wind: Moderate, against Weather: Fine

2194 BIG TICKET H'CAP 1m 6f
1:50 (1:50) (Class 4) (0-80,79) 4-Y-O+ **£5,504** (£1,637; £818; £408) **Stalls** Low

Form RPR
5453 **1** **Clear Reef**[30] 1432 5-9-2 **79** ....(p) AndreaAtzeni(5) 4 88
(Jane Chapple-Hyam) *chsd ldrs: led over 2f out: rdn clr over 1f out: styd on wl: pushed out towards fin* **10/1**
002- **2** *2* **Ursis (FR)**[235] 5993 8-8-12 **70** .... WilliamBuick 7 76
(S Gollings) *bustled along leaving stalls to go prom: led after 4f: rdn and hdd over 2f out: kpt on u.p after but no imp on wnr* **6/1**[3]
30-2 **3** *3* **Sir Sandicliffe (IRE)**[12] 1892 5-8-6 **64** .... JohnEgan 9 66+
(W M Brisbourne) *hld up: rdn and hdwy 3f out: sn chsd ldrs: edgd lft u.p fr over 1f out: kpt on one pce fnl f* **14/1**
-404 **4** *2¼* **Puy D'Arnac (FR)**[18] 1692 6-9-0 **77** .... FrederikTylicki(5) 5 76
(G A Swinbank) *chsd ldrs: rdn over 2f out: plugged on at one pce after* **3/1**[1]
33-5 **5** *¾* **Murcar**[36] 1287 4-8-10 **68** .... PhilipRobinson 6 66
(C G Cox) *led early: remained prom: rdn over 2f out: plugged on at one pce after* **4/1**[2]
50-6 **6** *8* **Hawridge King**[24] 1571 7-9-2 **77** .... JamesMillman(3) 12 64
(W S Kittow) *hld up: hdwy 5f out: rdn over 4f out: no imp on ldrs: wknd over 1f out* **22/1**
4-25 **7** *4* **Dart**[112] 325 5-8-10 **68** ....(t) NCallan 1 49
(J R Fanshawe) *midfield: rdn over 3f out: wknd over 1f out: eased fnl f* **11/1**
-301 **8** *½* **Bijou Dan**[16] 1767 8-8-8 **66** .... TomEaves 13 46
(G M Moore) *midfield: pushed along and lost pl 6f out: n.d after* **16/1**
04-5 **9** *2¾* **Jadalee (IRE)**[9] 1966 6-9-4 **76** .... ShaneKelly 3 52
(G A Butler) *hld up: hdwy 7f out: rdn 3f out: wknd over 2f out* **8/1**
5013 **10** *shd* **Zuwaar**[12] 1878 4-8-13 **71** ....(tp) StephenDonohoe 2 47
(Ian Williams) *midfield: pushed along 5f out: sn wknd* **14/1**
1-24 **11** *8* **Spirit Of Adjisa (IRE)**[84] 693 5-9-6 **78** ....(b) PaulEddery 10 43
(Pat Eddery) *sn led: hdd after 4f: remained prom tl rdn and wknd 3f out* **20/1**
1355 **12** *11* **They All Laughed**[21] 1635 6-8-13 **71** ....(b) PaulHanagan 11 21
(P W Hiatt) *a bhd* **33/1**

3m 12.27s (7.97) **Going Correction** +0.70s/f (Yiel) **12** Ran SP% **119.1**
Speed ratings (Par 105): **105,103,102,100,100 95,93,93,91,91 87,80**
toteswinger: 1&2 £11.70, 1&3 £39.90, 2&3 £20.90 CSF £67.54 CT £854.15 TOTE £11.50: £3.20, £2.50, £3.60; EX 101.10.
Owner Chapple-Hyam Tegel Ward **Bred** Hesmonds Stud Ltd **Trained** Newmarket, Suffolk

FOCUS
An open staying handicap, run at an average pace. It proved hard work down the home straight and the form is rated around the second and fourth.

2195 GAMEONBINGO.COM MAIDEN AUCTION STKS (DIV I) 6f
2:25 (2:25) (Class 5) 2-Y-O £2,914 (£867; £433; £216) Stalls Centre

Form				RPR
0	1		**Ingleby Spirit**[13] 1847 2-8-11 0 PaulHanagan 9 (R A Fahey) *towards rr: hdwy over 3f out: led over 1f out: drew clr and wl in command ins fnl f* 3/1[1]	80+
	2	8	**Rjeef (IRE)** 2-8-9 0 WilliamBuick 11 (C E Brittain) *towards rr: hdwy 1/2-way: hung lft fr 2f out: wnt 2nd ins fnl f: no ch w wnr* 4/1[2]	54
5	3	1 3/4	**Brinscall**[31] 1396 2-8-7 0 ow1 DavidAllan 10 (T D Easterby) *racd keenly: hld up: hdwy over 3f: rdn over 2f out: kpt on fnl f but nt pce to chal* 10/1	47
	4	3/4	**Turf Trivia** 2-8-11 0 PJMcDonald 4 (G M Moore) *towards rr: hdwy 1/2-way: effrt over 2f out: outpcd over 1f out: swtchd rt whn nt clr run ins fnl f: kpt on towards fin: nt pce of ldrs* 40/1	49
	5	1	**Diman Waters (IRE)** 2-8-11 0 AdrianTNicholls 7 (E J Alston) *hld up: gd hdwy to chse ldrs over 3f out: chal over 2f out: wknd fnl f* 18/1	46
	6	3/4	**Merseyside Star (IRE)** 2-9-2 0 AndrewElliott 5 (K R Burke) *prom: rdn 2f out: sn outpcd* 11/1	48+
	7	2 3/4	**Tarrants Way** 2-8-4 0 JackDean(5) 1 (Jennie Candlish) *broek wl: prom to 1/2-way: sn wknd* 66/1	33
	8	nse	**Nave (USA)** 2-9-2 0 JoeFanning 2 (M Johnston) *broke wl: w ldr tl wknd 1/2-way* 9/2[3]	40
	9	5	**Whelkeen Rock (IRE)** 2-8-9 0 NCallan 3 (K A Ryan) *led: rdn and hdd over 1f out: wknd qckly fnl f* 9/2[3]	18+
0	10	6	**Johnnyleary (IRE)**[14] 1802 2-8-10 0 ow1 StephenDonohoe 6 (D Nicholls) *chsd ldrs tl pushed along and wknd over 3f out* 11/1	1

1m 21.27s (7.27) **Going Correction** +0.90s/f (Soft) 10 Ran SP% **116.3**
Speed ratings (Par 93): **87,76,74,73,71 70,67,66,60,52**
toteswinger: 1&2 £5.00, 1&3 £8.60, 2&3 £9.30 CSF £14.81 TOTE £3.60: £1.70, £1.40, £2.50; EX 19.00.
Owner Percy/Green Racing **Bred** Barton Stud And Peter Botham **Trained** Musley Bank, N Yorks

FOCUS
Probably just an ordinary first division of the juvenile maiden. The first three home were drawn high and the winner handled the ground best of all. The value of the form is hard to gauge but the winner scored in emphatic style.

NOTEBOOK
Ingleby Spirit stormed clear down the middle inside the final furlong and routed his rivals. He proved too green on his debut on quick ground 13 days earlier, but relished this extra furlong and obviously handled the going best of all. He is in very good hands and, while this form may not work out, is worthy of his chance in something more valuable now. (op 7-2 tchd 4-1 in a place)
Rjeef(IRE), whose stable is doing well with its juveniles so far, is a half-brother to numerous winners, most notably high-class middle-distance winner Housemaster. He showed his inexperience through the early parts, but got the hang of things from halfway and should last longer when faced with less demanding ground. Official explanation: jockey said colt hung left (op 13-2)
Brinscall, along with the winner, was one of only three in attendance with a previous run and that was probably significant to her placing. She got ridden more patiently on this much more taxing surface and should come on again for the experience. (tchd 14-1)
Turf Trivia is bred to stay further in due course so it was unsurprising to see him staying on at the death. He should be all the sharper for this initial experience. (tchd 50-1)
Diman Waters(IRE) did more than enough to suggest he has a future and ought to improve for the run. (op 16-1 tchd 14-1)
Whelkeen Rock(IRE) ◆ is from a stable whose juveniles should always be given a second look at this venue. Speedily-bred, he displayed plenty of pace and looked to be going easily 2f out. He fell in a hole once push came to shove, however, and looked to find it all too testing. It would not be at all surprising to see him fare much better on quicker ground and probably when dropped to the minimum trip. (op 9-4 tchd 5-1)

2196 GAMEONBINGO.COM MAIDEN AUCTION STKS (DIV II) 6f
3:00 (3:02) (Class 5) 2-Y-O £2,914 (£867; £433; £216) Stalls Centre

Form				RPR
44	1		**Daniella De Bruijn (IRE)**[10] 1939 2-8-6 0 JamesDoyle 5 (A B Haynes) *midfield: hdwy 2f out: r.o to ld ent fnl f: pushed clr towards fin* 3/1[1]	74
	2	2 1/4	**Coloursoftheglen (IRE)** 2-8-4 0 RossAtkinson(5) 4 (Tom Dascombe) *chsd ldrs: rdn over 2f out: led wl over 1f out: hdd ent fnl f: sn carried lft: nt pce of wnr* 7/1	70+
00	3	1 3/4	**Take It To The Max**[35] 1304 2-8-9 0 PJMcDonald 2 (G M Moore) *w ldr: led over 3f out: hdd over 2f out: hung lft u.p fr over 1f out whn stl chalng: one pce ins fnl f* 13/2	65
	4	3/4	**Contract Caterer (IRE)** 2-8-11 0 PaulEddery 7 (Pat Eddery) *hld up: pushed along over 2f out: styd on ins fnl f: nt pce to chal* 15/2	65+
0	5	1 1/4	**Flaneur**[33] 1358 2-8-9 0 (b[1]) DavidAllan 1 (T D Easterby) *wnt lft s: led: hdd over 3f out: led over 2f out: hdd wl over 1f out: u.p but stl cl up whn bmpd appr fnl f: sn wknd* 16/1	59
	6	3 1/2	**Sejanus** 2-8-11 0 NCallan 11 (K A Ryan) *midfield: outpcd fr 1/2-way* 5/1[2]	51
	7	12	**Keen Bidder** 2-8-11 0 JohnEgan 3 (D M Simcock) *dwlt: towards rr: rn v green: nvr on terms* 14/1	15
	8	6	**Alfalasteeni** 2-8-11 0 StephenDonohoe 8 (Ian Williams) *bhd: hung bdly rt and toiling over 3f out: lost tch* 16/1	—
	9	3/4	**Royal Blade (IRE)** 2-8-4 0 MartinLane(5) 6 (A P Jarvis) *chsd ldrs tl wknd 2f out* 25/1	—
	10	13	**Pallantes Cross** 2-8-11 0 JoeFanning 10 (M Johnston) *a bhd* 6/1[3]	—

1m 20.57s (6.57) **Going Correction** +0.90s/f (Soft) 10 Ran SP% **115.8**
Speed ratings (Par 93): **92,89,86,85,84 79,63,55,54,37**
toteswinger: 1&2 £3.90, 1&3 £5.80, 2&3 £15.00 CSF £23.96 TOTE £3.40: £1.20, £2.20, £3.10; EX 25.10.
Owner Ms J Loylert **Bred** Manister House Stud **Trained** Limpley Stoke, Bath
■ Stewards' Enquiry : P J McDonald one-day ban: careless riding (Jun 4)

FOCUS
This second division was run in a quicker time and the form is rated around the winner.

NOTEBOOK
Daniella De Bruijn(IRE) gained compensation for an unlucky run at Yarmouth ten days previously and opened her account at the third attempt. She was faced with a contrasting surface, but handled it really well and the step up to 6f was right up her street. Things will be tougher for her now and she did have bottom weight here, but she is a likeable juvenile. (tchd 4-1)
Coloursoftheglen(IRE) ◆ showed early speed and fared best of the newcomers. This half-brother to fair sprinter Discanti should benefit a deal for the experience and looks well up to winning a race or two this term. (op 9-2)
Take It To The Max posted his best effort to date, but appeared to lose his action somewhat when hanging left at the furlong pole and did show a slightly awkward head carriage thereafter. His action looked suited to this softer surface. (op 14-1)
Contract Caterer(IRE) ◆ was the first runner to date from his first-season sire. He got outpaced through the early parts and never looked like winning, but stayed on nicely under a considerate ride late on. A stiffer test will suit in due course, but he is certainly one to take from the race. (op 11-1)
Flaneur, who blew the start on his debut over 5f last month, showed quirks, and it is not hard to see why connections reached for the first-time blinkers. He still posted an improved effort on this deeper surface and ought to find his level in due course. (op 50-1)
Alfalasteeni Official explanation: jockey said colt hung right

2197 PLAY PREMIER 10 AT FOOTBALLPOOLS.COM STKS (H'CAP) 1m 30y
3:35 (3:35) (Class 3) (0-90,92) 4-Y-0+ £9,066 (£2,697; £1,348; £673) Stalls Low

Form				RPR
01-0	1		**Angel Rock (IRE)**[33] 1357 4-8-9 83 AndreaAtzeni(5) 5 (M Botti) *trckd ldrs: rdn to ld wl over 1f out: all out to jst hold on* 6/1[2]	89
56-0	2	hd	**Rattan (USA)**[44] 1170 4-9-1 84 JohnEgan 9 (Rae Guest) *in rr: hdwy 2f out: r.o strly ins fnl f: clsd rapidly on wnr fin* 14/1	90
0-00	3	3/4	**Raptor (GER)**[54] 995 6-9-2 85 NCallan 10 (K R Burke) *midfield: hdwy 2f out: rdn to chal over 1f out: kpt on: hld clsng stages* 17/2	89
2-00	4	hd	**Ilie Nastase (FR)**[13] 1821 5-9-3 86 StephenDonohoe 6 (D Nicholls) *hld up: hdwy over 2f out: sn rdn: hungl lft whn chsd ldrs over 1f out: nt qckn ins fnl f* 7/1[3]	90
145-	5	6	**Visions Of Johanna (USA)**[167] 7556 4-9-0 83 PaulHanagan 7 (R A Fahey) *midfield: outpcd over 4f out: styd on fr over 1f out but nt pce to get competitive* 10/1	73
56-5	6	1	**Mr Hichens**[17] 1731 4-9-2 85 PhilipRobinson 2 (Karen George) *led: rdn over 2f out: hdd wl over 1f out: wknd ins fnl f* 11/1	73
521-	7	3 1/4	**Cara's Request (AUS)**[204] 7084 4-8-11 82 ShaneKelly 1 (L M Cumani) *trckd ldrs: rdn to chal fr over 2f out: wknd ins fnl f* 2/1[1]	60
12-0	8	2 1/4	**Shaloo Diamond**[13] 1850 4-8-8 80 MichaelJStainton(3) 11 (R M Whitaker) *towards rr: pushed along over 4f out: nvr on terms* 9/1	55
0-00	9	3 1/2	**Quiet Elegance**[12] 1880 4-9-4 87 DavidAllan 4 (E J Alston) *hld up: rdn over 2f out: no imp: eased whn btn ins fnl f* 28/1	54
0-11	10	15	**Billy Dane (IRE)**[9] 1952 5-9-4 87 6ex PhillipMakin 3 (F P Murtagh) *prom tl rdn and wknd over 2f out: eased whn btn 1f out* 11/1	20

1m 49.41s (5.61) **Going Correction** +0.90s/f (Soft) 10 Ran SP% **116.5**
Speed ratings (Par 107): **107,106,106,105,99 98,95,93,89,74**
toteswinger: 1&2 £17.20, 1&3 £11.80, 2&3 £13.40 CSF £86.06 CT £715.64 TOTE £7.80: £2.70, £4.50, £2.90; EX 104.40.
Owner Tenuta Dorna Di Montaltuzzo SRL **Bred** Ascagnano S P A **Trained** Newmarket, Suffolk

FOCUS
A good handicap. The first four came clear in a tight finish and the form is rated around the runner-up to his three-year-old best.

NOTEBOOK
Angel Rock(IRE) bounced right back to form on the drop back from 1m2f and won gamely. He had evidently come on a bundle for his disappointing seasonal return last month and has now scored on four of his nine career starts. This appears to be his optimum trip and he needs soft ground, but he had little to spare at the line so would probably not want to be going up much. (op 8-1)
Rattan(USA) ◆ was having just his second outing for current connections and showed much-improved form, only just missing out. He was near last turning into the home straight, but picked up strongly when asked to improve and was closing strongly on the winner near the finish. The line came slightly too soon, but he will still look fairly treated after going up for this and can gain compensation.
Raptor(GER) moved nicely into contention and, while his finishing effort was somewhat one-paced, this was an improvement on his previous two outings this season. He has now dropped to a workable mark. (op 9-1)
Ilie Nastase(FR) really caught the eye at Chester 13 days earlier. He made his effort on the outside of runners down the home straight here and found this more conventional track more to his liking. The softer ground also suited and his turn is probably not far off. (tchd 6-1)
Visions Of Johanna(USA) had won on his only previous outing on turf and was making his debut for the stable. He looks to need a sounder surface and should come on nicely for this first run for 167 days. (op 9-1 tchd 8-1)
Cara's Request(AUS) made all to land a weak maiden on his final outing last term and had no ground worries. He was not asked to get to the front on this seasonal bow and the manner in which he folded when the race became serious would suggest he could well be happiest from the front. (tchd 15-8 and 5-2 in a place)

2198 ENTERPRISE H'CAP 7f 30y
4:10 (4:12) (Class 4) (0-80,78) 3-Y-O £5,504 (£1,637; £818; £408) Stalls Low

Form				RPR
31	1		**Arrivederla (IRE)**[13] 1837 3-9-2 76 JamesDoyle 14 (H J L Dunlop) *midfield: hdwy over 3f out: rdn to ld over 1f out: edgd lft ins fnl f: styd on wl and in full control towards fin* 14/1	85
40-2	2	2 1/2	**Eastern Warrior**[26] 1509 3-9-2 76 PhilipRobinson 4 (J W Hills) *chsd ldrs: rdn over 2f out: kpt on u.p ins fnl f: a hld: tk 2nd nr fin* 4/1[2]	79
41-	3	hd	**Ursula (IRE)**[247] 5988 3-8-13 73 AndrewElliott 1 (K R Burke) *midfield: hdwy over 3f out: led over 2f out: rdn and hdd over 1f out: no ex fnl 75yds* 12/1	75
0-04	4	1	**Maggie Lou (IRE)**[12] 1869 3-9-3 77 NCallan 3 (K A Ryan) *midfield: rdn over 2f out: hdwy over 1f out: styd on ins fnl f: nt quite pce to get to ldrs* 18/1	76
500-	5	nk	**Deadly Encounter (IRE)**[268] 5381 3-9-4 78 TonyHamilton 10 (R A Fahey) *dwlt: swtchd lft sn after s: in rr: hdwy over 2f out: kpt on ins fnl f: nvr nrr* 40/1	76+
-443	6	3	**Belated Silver (IRE)**[20] 1656 3-8-6 71 RossAtkinson(5) 9 (Tom Dascombe) *chsd ldr: led over 4f out: hdd over 2f out: wknd over 1f out* 8/1	61
120-	7	1 3/4	**Diggeratt (USA)**[272] 5228 3-9-3 77 PaulHanagan 2 (R A Fahey) *in rr: rdn and hdwy over 1f out: one pce ins fnl f: nvr able to chal* 16/1	63
51-5	8	1 1/2	**Major Phil (IRE)**[20] 1639 3-9-4 78 WilliamBuick 5 (L M Cumani) *towards rr: pushed along 4f out: nvr rchd chalng position* 9/2[3]	60
20-4	9	3/4	**The Desert Saint**[18] 1703 3-8-13 73 RichardMullen 6 (A M Balding) *in tch: rdn over 2f out: sn wknd* 12/1	53
0-46	10	1	**Athania (IRE)**[14] 1808 3-8-7 72 MartinLane(5) 13 (A P Jarvis) *led: hdd over 4f out: rdn and wknd 2f out* 20/1	49

1 11 3/4 **Secret Witness**[20] 1638 3-9-3 77 ShaneKelly 7 52
(J Noseda) *dwlt: towards rr: pushed along and nvr bttr than midfield over 3f out: no imp on ldrs: wl btn over 1f out* 11/4[1]
10-0 12 3 3/4 **Daisy Moses (IRE)**[26] 1505 3-8-12 72 AdrianTNicholls 12 37
(D Nicholls) *sn pushed along: a bhd* 33/1
0P-2 13 2 **Arteus**[13] 1837 3-8-13 78 AndreaAtzeni(5) 8 37+
(Jane Chapple-Hyam) *chsd ldrs: pushed along 3f out: wknd over 2f out* 16/1

1m 37.47s (7.27) **Going Correction** +0.90s/f (Soft) 13 Ran SP% 125.2
Speed ratings (Par 101): **94,91,90,89,89 86,84,82,81,80 79,75,72**
toteswinger: 1&2 £14.10, 1&3 £17.00, 2&3 £9.80 CSF £71.36 CT £748.53 TOTE £19.60: £5.30, £1.60, £3.50; EX 95.70.
Owner William Armitage **Bred** Roundhill Stud & Gleadhill House Stud Ltd **Trained** Lambourn, Berks

FOCUS
An interesting 3yo handicap. It was run at a solid early pace, but it proved hard work to make up ground from behind.

2199 MOONDARRA MAIDEN STKS 1m 2f 95y
4:45 (4:49) (Class 5) 3-Y-O+ £3,238 (£963; £481; £240) Stalls Low

Form RPR
6-5 1 **Grey Granite (IRE)**[19] 1681 3-8-13 0 JoeFanning 10 84+
(W Jarvis) *mde all: pressed briefly over 2f out: shkn up over 1f out: styd on wl to draw clr fnl f* 1/1[1]
6 2 7 **Cry Alot Boy**[32] 1380 6-10-0 0 SJCraine 7 70
(K A Morgan) *racd keenly in midfield: hdwy over 4f out: rdn to chal over 2f out: n.d to wnr fnl f* 25/1
6/ 3 2 3/4 **Nayef Star**[566] 6618 4-10-0 0 ShaneKelly 1 64
(J Noseda) *prom: chal over 2f out: dropped off ldrs and one pce fr over 1f out* 6/1[2]
0 4 2 3/4 **Final Son**[17] 1752 4-9-9 0 MartinLane(5) 4 58
(A P Jarvis) *prom: pushed along over 3f out: one pce fr over 1f out* 50/1
5 3/4 **East Of The Sun (IRE)** 3-8-13 0 DNolan 13 55
(T P Tate) *trckd ldrs: pushed along and outpcd over 2f out: no imp after* 14/1
0-0 6 1 3/4 **Thegirlsgonewild (USA)**[22] 1605 3-8-8 0 JamesDoyle 12 47
(H J L Dunlop) *trckd ldrs: rdn over 2f out: btn whn wnt lft over 1f out* 12/1[3]
00 7 5 **Paddy Partridge**[15] 1793 3-8-13 0 StephenDonohoe 5 42
(N J Vaughan) *midfield: rdn over 2f out: nvr able to chal* 14/1
5 8 1/2 **George Adamson (IRE)**[9] 1950 3-8-13 0 PJMcDonald 8 41
(G A Swinbank) *hld up: sme hdwy over 2f out: no imp on ldrs* 16/1
0- 9 4 1/2 **Riptide**[272] 5246 3-8-13 0 JohnEgan 3 32
(C F Wall) *midfield: pushed along 4f out: sn wknd* 14/1
6 10 4 **Flora's Pride**[18] 1693 5-9-9 0 PaulHanagan 15 20
(K G Reveley) *hld up: rdn over 2f out: nvr on terms w ldrs* 25/1
0- 11 27 **Stanley Rigby**[272] 5246 3-8-13 0 TomEaves 11 —
(C F Wall) *in rr: rdn 4f out: lost tch over 3f out* 28/1
-5 12 25 **It Must Be Love**[19] 1664 3-8-3 0 AndreaAtzeni(5) 14 —
(D Flood) *midfield early: pushed along in rr over 5f out: lost tch over 3f out* 33/1

2m 23.3s (10.30) **Going Correction** +0.90s/f (Soft)
WFA 3 from 4yo+ 14lb 12 Ran SP% 113.9
Speed ratings (Par 103): **103,97,95,93,92 91,87,86,83,79 58,38**
toteswinger: 1&2 £7.90, 1&3 £2.30, 2&3 £10.00 CSF £37.08 TOTE £2.00: £1.30, £5.00, £1.90; EX 24.50.
Owner Dr J Walker **Bred** Tower Bloodstock **Trained** Newmarket, Suffolk

FOCUS
This was a modest maiden and another race in which it paid to race prominently. Tricky form to pin down with the field well strung out on bad ground. It has been rated around the runner-up improving on his All-Weather debut and the third being a few pounds off his two-year-old debut form.

2200 BLACKPOOL TOWER & CIRCUS H'CAP 1m 2f 95y
5:20 (5:20) (Class 5) (0-75,74) 4-Y-O+ £3,238 (£963; £481; £240) Stalls Low

Form RPR
22-0 1 **Princess Rainbow (FR)**[22] 1615 4-8-6 67 JackDean(5) 14 73
(Jennie Candlish) *midfieled: rdn and hdwy 2f out: styd on to ld wl ins fnl f* 11/2[2]
1050 2 nk **All In The Red (IRE)**[8] 1990 4-9-0 70 (p) JoeFanning 9 75
(A Crook) *missed break: in rr: rdn and hdwy 2f out: swtchd lft ins fnl f: r.o to chal sn after: hld fnl strides* 9/1
4-00 3 3/4 **Kalasam**[22] 1615 5-8-8 64 (b[1]) DaleGibson 6 68
(M W Easterby) *racd keenly: a.p: led over 2f out: rdn 1f out: hdd wl ins fnl f: hld fnl strides* 5/1[1]
2354 4 1/2 **Supercast (IRE)**[19] 1660 6-8-11 74 JosephineBruning(7) 15 77
(N J Vaughan) *w ldr: led over 3f out: hdd over 2f out: continued to chal: no ex cl home* 16/1
00-0 5 2 1/2 **Baizically (IRE)**[18] 1690 6-8-9 65 PJMcDonald 7 63
(G A Swinbank) *towards rr: rdn over 2f out: styd on appr fnl f: nvr able to chal* 14/1
611 6 2 1/2 **Mustajed**[105] 406 8-9-1 74 JamesMillman(3) 3 67
(B R Millman) *midfield: pushed along 2f out: nvr able to land a blow* 9/1
2222 7 1/2 **Benedict Spirit (IRE)**[17] 1721 4-9-2 72 NCallan 1 64
(M H Tompkins) *dwlt: sn trckd ldrs: effrt to chal fr 3f out: wknd ins fnl f* 5/1[1]
5254 8 nk **North Parade**[14] 1812 4-9-2 72 (t) ShaneKelly 8 63
(A W Carroll) *racd keenly in midfield on outside: rdn 2f out: one pce* 8/1[3]
0/ 9 7 **Paint The Town (IRE)**[545] 6917 4-8-9 65 RichardMullen 12 42
(J G Given) *midfield: rdn and wknd over 2f out* 10/1
305- 10 4 1/2 **Vicious Warrior**[198] 7184 10-9-2 72 TonyHamilton 4 40
(R M Whitaker) *led: hdd over 3f out: wknd over 2f out* 16/1
010 11 13 **Uncle Bertie**[22] 1615 4-9-0 70 StephenDonohoe 5 12
(N J Vaughan) *towards rr: pushed along briefly over 6f out: nvr on terms* 12/1
03-0 12 38 **Animator**[13] 1845 4-8-13 69 TomEaves 11 —
(C Grant) *a bhd: pushed along over 5f out: t.o* 16/1

2m 24.52s (11.52) **Going Correction** +0.90s/f (Soft) 12 Ran SP% 120.9
Speed ratings (Par 103): **98,97,97,96,94 92,92,92,86,82 72,42**
toteswinger: 1&2 £10.70, 1&3 £7.20, 2&3 £8.30 CSF £55.63 CT £268.65 TOTE £7.50: £2.70, £2.50, £1.80; EX 77.60 Place 6: £180.38 Place 5: £43.96.
Owner P and Mrs G A Clarke **Bred** Societe Sogir **Trained** Basford Green, Staffs

FOCUS
A moderate handicap, run at a fair pace, and once again it proved an advantage to race handily. The third and fourth help set the level.
Mustajed Official explanation: jockey said gelding was unsuited by the soft, heavy in places ground
T/Plt: £269.60 to a £1 stake. Pool: £68,369.91. 185.10 winning tickets. T/Qpdt: £53.30 to a £1 stake. Pool: £3,918.72. 54.40 winning tickets. DO

2006 SALISBURY (R-H)
Thursday, May 21

OFFICIAL GOING: Good to firm (firm in places)
Wind: Virtually nil. Weather: bright and sunny

2201 E B F BATHWICK TYRES MAIDEN STKS 5f
6:00 (6:01) (Class 4) 2-Y-O £4,695 (£1,397; £698; £348) Stalls High

Form RPR
0 1 **Sir Parky (IRE)**[12] 1867 2-9-3 0 RichardHughes 8 84+
(R Hannon) *a.p: shkn up to ld jst over 1f out: r.o wl: readily* 1/1[1]
0 2 3 1/4 **Tucker's Law**[23] 1577 2-9-3 0 FergusSweeney 1 70
(B R Millman) *prom: rdn over 2f out: kpt on fnl 75yds to snatch 2nd towards fin* 25/1
4 3 1 **Radio City**[17] 1726 2-9-3 0 SebSanders 11 67
(R M Beckett) *led: rdn and hdd jst over 1f out: nt pce of wnr: lost 2nd towards fin* 10/3[2]
0 4 1 3/4 **The Shuffler**[31] 1404 2-9-3 0 GeorgeBaker 4 60
(G L Moore) *chsd ldrs: rdn over 2f out: sn one pce* 12/1
0 5 4 1/2 **Hachi**[31] 1404 2-8-12 0 TolleyDean 2 39
(J L Spearing) *mid-div: rdn whn swtchd lft over 2f out but no imp* 9/2[3]
6 1 **Abandagold (IRE)** 2-8-12 0 CatherineGannon 9 36+
(A B Haynes) *broke wl enough: bhd ldrs whn squeezed out and lost pl sn after s: towards rr whn hmpd again after 1f: nvr any ch after* 16/1
7 nk **Coralamber (IRE)** 2-8-5 0 AndrewHeffernan(7) 5 35
(Garry Moss) *s.i.s: a towards rr* 50/1
05 8 1/2 **Dolly Will Do**[15] 1782 2-8-12 0 FrankieMcDonald 10 33
(N P Mulholland) *chsd ldrs tl wknd over 2f out* 33/1
9 1 **Mactrac** 2-9-3 0 RichardSmith 7 34
(R Hannon) *s.i.s: a towards rr* 14/1

61.82 secs (0.82) **Going Correction** -0.125s/f (Firm) 9 Ran SP% 120.2
Speed ratings (Par 95): **86,80,79,76,69 67,67,66,64**
toteswinger: 1&2 £16.90, 1&3 £1.10, 2&3 £7.20. CSF £36.98 TOTE £2.00: £1.10, £5.80, £1.60; EX 36.50.
Owner Sir David Seale **Bred** Swordlestown Stud **Trained** East Everleigh, Wilts

FOCUS
A modest juvenile maiden with a lively pre-race market. The winner was value for a bit more and the time helps with the standard.

NOTEBOOK
Sir Parky(IRE) looked as though the experience would do him good when eighth of 13 in a 6f Haydock maiden on debut. He is bred to be suited by further, but it was interesting that he was dropped in trip here, with Richard Hughes preferring him to his stablemate. He sat just behind the pace, took the advantage inside the two furlong pole and pulled clear to justify strong support. This form is only modest, but it does represent a significant step forward by the winner. He has plenty of substance about him and his strong galloping style suggests a return to 6f will suit. He is a possible for the Woodcote Stakes at Epsom, a race in which Richard Hannon trained the second and fourth last year. (tchd 8-11 and 11-10 after early 6-5)
Tucker's Law was unfancied and outpaced in an above average 5f Windsor maiden on debut. He was sent off at a big price again here, but stayed on steadily down the outside and shaped with some promise.
Radio City showed up well for a long way under a forcing ride but probably did not improve on his dead-heat for fourth in a moderately run six-runner Kempton maiden on debut. (tchd 4-1)
The Shuffler was never going the pace when 14th of 15 in a 5f Windsor maiden on debut. He travelled with a bit more zest here but was ultimately well held. (op 9-1)
Hachi was backed from 16-1 into 9-2. She was shuffled along at an early stage and never looked like landing the gamble. (op 16-1)
Mactrac Official explanation: jockey said colt was slowly away and ran green

2202 BATHWICK TYRES BOURNEMOUTH H'CAP 6f
6:30 (6:30) (Class 6) (0-65,65) 4-Y-O+ £3,043 (£905; £452; £226) Stalls High

Form RPR
-002 1 **Dualagi**[8] 1985 5-8-7 54 FergusSweeney 14 64
(M R Bosley) *mid-div: hdwy whn nt clr run over 2f out: qcknd up wl whn gap appeared over 1f out: led ins fnl f: drvn out* 6/1[2]
502 2 nk **Bateleur**[13] 1846 5-8-5 52 EdwardCreighton 16 61
(M R Channon) *s.i.s: towards rr: hdwy 3f out: rdn to ld over 1f out: hdd ins fnl f: kpt on* 9/1
1-00 3 1 **Bold Argument (IRE)**[24] 1572 6-9-1 65 JackMitchell(3) 3 74+
(Mrs P N Dutfield) *s.i.s: sn pushed along in rr: nt clr run and hrd rdn whn swtchd lft 2f out: styd on fr over 1f out: drifted rt: fin wl* 7/1[3]
0-00 4 1/2 **Tiger Trail (GER)**[18] 1704 5-8-8 55 TonyCulhane 12 59
(Mrs N Smith) *towards rr: pushed along over 3f out: stdy prog u.p fr 2f out: styd on: nrst fin* 16/1
335- 5 1 **Rhapsilian**[193] 7255 5-8-10 57 RichardThomas 11 58
(J A Geake) *mid-div: hdwy whn nt clr run over 2f out: nt best of runs after but styd on fnl f* 12/1
0-25 6 nk **Conjecture**[18] 1694 7-9-1 62 RichardHughes 10 62
(R Bastiman) *led: rdn and hdd 2f out: kpt on tl no ex ins fnl f* 6/1[2]
0342 7 shd **Manchestermaverick (USA)**[18] 1710 4-8-11 58 (vt) SteveDrowne 2 58
(H Morrison) *chsd ldrs: led 2f out: sn rdn and hdd: edgd rt and fdd wl ins fnl f* 11/2[1]
000- 8 2 1/2 **Goodbye Cash (IRE)**[17] 5-8-11 58 CatherineGannon 9 50
(P D Evans) *chsd ldrs: rdn over 2f out: wknd fnl f* 16/1
0-66 9 1/2 **Stamford Blue**[25] 1540 8-8-11 65 (b) SPRyan(7) 5 55
(R A Harris) *chsd ldrs: struggling whn short of room 2f out: wknd fnl f* 9/1
4005 10 2 1/2 **Golden Prospect**[17] 1748 5-8-11 58 ow1 SebSanders 7 40
(J W Hills) *nvr bttr than mid-div on outer* 8/1
5460 11 2 **Upstairs**[7] 2011 5-8-8 60 AmyBaker(5) 6 36
(P Henderson) *s.i.s: sn outpcd: a in rr* 18/1
0-00 12 1 1/2 **Compton Rose**[15] 1787 4-8-1 55 AmyScott(7) 8 26
(H Candy) *prom whn squeezed out after 1f and lost pl: swtchd lft over 2f out: wknd fnl f* 12/1
000- 13 2 1/2 **Blessed Place**[204] 7081 9-9-4 65 FrankieMcDonald 4 28
(D J S Ffrench Davis) *prom: rdn over 2f out: sn wknd* 50/1

1m 14.43s (-0.37) **Going Correction** -0.125s/f (Firm) 13 Ran SP% 121.9
Speed ratings (Par 101): **97,96,95,94,93 92,92,89,88,85 82,80,77**
toteswinger: 1&2 £7.40, 1&3 £6.30, 2&3 £32.60. CSF £60.56 CT £407.20 TOTE £6.30: £1.70, £3.80, £2.40; EX 39.20.
Owner Inca Financial Services **Bred** B Burrough **Trained** Chalfont St Giles, Bucks

FOCUS
A modest sprint handicap. The winner only had to match her Bath running to score.

Compton Rose Official explanation: jockey said filly suffered interference a furlong after the start

2203 BATHWICK TYRES H'CAP 6f

7:05 (7:05) (Class 4) (0-85,84) 4-Y-0+ £4,857 (£1,445; £722; £360) Stalls High

Form RPR

4440 1 **Vhujon (IRE)**26 1510 4-9-1 81 RichardHughes 3 94
(P D Evans) *slowly away: bhd: smooth prog fr over 2f out: swtchd rt over 1f out: r.o strly to ld ins fnl f: comf* 5/2[1]

-044 2 3 **Golden Dixie (USA)**13 1836 10-8-5 71 LukeMorris 5 74
(R A Harris) *trckd ldrs: rdn and ev ch ent fnl f: kpt on but nt pce of wnr* 9/2[3]

3251 3 nk **Caprio (IRE)**14 1806 4-9-0 80 SebSanders 7 82
(J R Boyle) *slowly away: bhd: rdn and stdy hdwy fr over 2f out: kpt on same pce fnl f* 7/2[2]

0-00 4 nk **Misaro (GER)**19 1672 8-8-9 82 (b) SPRyan(7) 2 83
(R A Harris) *led: rdn and edgd lft over 1f out: hdd ins fnl f: kpt on same pce* 14/1

065- 5 2 ½ **Berbice (IRE)**17 1757 4-8-7 73 RichardSmith 9 66+
(S Donohoe, Ire) *in tch: travelling ok whn swtchd lft over 1f out: sn short of room and snatched up: nt rcvr* 14/1

-055 6 3 ½ **Whiskey Junction**30 1418 5-9-1 81 RobertWinston 11 63
(M Quinn) *trckd ldrs: rdn over 2f out: wknd 1f out* 8/1

60-4 7 3 ½ **Fifty (IRE)**7 2011 4-7-11 70 CharlesEddery(7) 12 41
(R Hannon) *hung rt and struggling 4f out: a in rr* 13/2

-060 8 ½ **Bel Cantor**19 1663 6-8-13 82 (p) KellyHarrison(3) 4 51
(W J H Ratcliffe) *w ldr: rdn over 2f out: wknd over 1f out* 10/1

1m 13.24s (-1.56) **Going Correction** -0.125s/f (Firm) 8 Ran SP% 115.8
Speed ratings (Par 105): **105,101,100,100,96 92,87,86**
toteswinger: 1&2 £3.10, 1&3 £2.70, 2&3 £4.90. CSF £14.17 CT £38.92 TOTE £4.10: £1.50, £1.90, £1.10; EX 16.90.

Owner Nick Shutts **Bred** Robert Berns **Trained** Pandy, Monmouths

■ Stewards' Enquiry : Richard Hughes one-day ban: careless riding (June 4)

FOCUS
A decent handicap won in good style by Vhujon who is rated back to last season's form.

2204 BATHWICK TYRES SALISBURY H'CAP 1m 4f

7:40 (7:41) (Class 6) (0-65,65) 3-Y-0 £3,043 (£905; £452; £226) Stalls High

Form RPR

50-4 1 **Strathcal**17 1747 3-9-4 65 SteveDrowne 7 73
(H Morrison) *trckd ldrs: led 2f out: sn rdn and edgd lft: styd on strly* 9/2[2]

0022 2 4 **Salybia Bay**10 1930 3-9-4 65 RichardHughes 6 67
(R Hannon) *in tch: nt clr run on rails over 3f out: rdn over 2f out: styd on to go 2nd ins fnl f: no ch w wnr* 5/2[1]

1610 3 2 ¼ **Good Buy Dubai (USA)**13 1842 3-8-13 60 RobertWinston 14 58
(J R Best) *stdd s: sn swtchd lft: bhd: rdn and stdy hdwy fr 3f out: chsd wnr over 1f out: no ex and lost 2nd ins fnl f* 15/2[3]

60-2 4 ½ **Beaubrav**43 1183 3-9-4 65 SebSanders 1 63
(P W D'Arcy) *t.k.h early: in tch: hdwy over 3f out: effrt over 2f out: styd on same pce* 15/2[3]

-010 5 nk **Melange (USA)**17 1747 3-9-4 65 JamieSpencer 4 62
(P F I Cole) *led: rdn and hdd 2f out: sn one pce* 14/1

00-6 6 ½ **Money Money Money**23 1580 3-9-4 65 LukeMorris 12 62
(P Winkworth) *s.i.s: sn chsng ldr: nt clr run on rails over 2f out: sn rdn: one pce fr over 1f out* 8/1

0443 7 1 **Squad**23 1580 3-9-2 63 NickyMackay 13 58
(S Dow) *rdn over 4f out: nvr bttr than mid-div* 11/1

0560 8 hd **First Spirit**24 1570 3-8-11 58 LPKeniry 3 52
(J S Moore) *sme prog u.p over 2f out: mainly towards rr* 50/1

00-1 9 5 **Hollow Green (IRE)**14 1811 3-8-13 60 CatherineGannon 5 46
(P D Evans) *a towards rr* 16/1

04-5 10 nk **Heart Of Tuscany**16 1771 3-9-4 65 GeorgeBaker 11 51
(W J Knight) *hld up towards rr: rdn whn swtchd lft over 2f out: no imp* 8/1

60-0 11 2 ½ **Diktalina**24 1570 3-8-13 60 TPO'Shea 9 42
(W R Muir) *mid-div tl wknd over 4f out* 28/1

2m 36.34s (-1.66) **Going Correction** -0.125s/f (Firm) 11 Ran SP% 118.8
Speed ratings (Par 97): **100,97,95,95,95 94,94,94,90,90 88**
toteswinger: 1&2 £2.00, 1&3 £7.60, 2&3 £3.70. CSF £16.28 CT £84.02 TOTE £5.20: £1.90, £1.60, £2.30; EX 12.80.

Owner The Caledonian Racing Society **Bred** Mrs R F Johnson Houghton **Trained** East Ilsley, Berks

FOCUS
An ordinary handicap in which the pace was fairly steady. Sound form, the runner-up the best guide.

2205 BATHWICK TYRES ANDOVER MAIDEN FILLIES' STKS 6f

8:15 (8:16) (Class 5) 3-Y-0+ £3,885 (£1,156; £577; £288) Stalls High

Form RPR

250- 1 **Dubai Legend**229 6473 3-8-9 79 AhmedAjtebi(3) 12 73
(D M Simcock) *stmbld leaving stalls: sn rcvrd into mid-div: hdwy over 2f out: sn rdn and edgd lft: led ent fnl f: rdn out* 9/4[2]

2 ½ **Global Conquest (IRE)** 3-8-12 0 RichardHughes 3 72
(Pat Eddery) *s.i.s: bhd: shkn up and hdwy fr 2f out: fin strly: wnt 2nd nr fin* 28/1

3-0 3 1 **Sharpened Edge**33 1353 3-8-12 0 CatherineGannon 9 68
(B Palling) *t.k.h: prom: led 2f out: rdn and hdd ent fnl f: kpt on but no ex: lost 2nd nr fin* 6/1[3]

022 4 ¾ **Cape Melody**18 1703 3-8-12 70 SteveDrowne 6 66
(H Morrison) *chsd ldrs: rdn over 2f out: kpt on same pce fnl f* 7/4[1]

5 1 ¼ **Dilli Dancer** 4-9-2 0 GabrielHannon(5) 10 64
(G D Blake) *chsd ldrs: rdn over 2f out: kpt on same pce fnl f* 66/1

6 hd **Milldown Story** 3-8-12 0 RobertWinston 5 61
(B R Millman) *mid-div: effrt 3f out: sn hung lft: kpt on same pce fnl f* 28/1

7 2 ¼ **Chandika** 3-8-12 0 SebSanders 8 54+
(C G Cox) *t.k.h: bmpd s: mid-div: rdn and hdwy whn swtchd lft 2f out: fdd ins fnl f* 7/1

00-0 8 3 ½ **Shybutwilling (IRE)**18 1703 4-9-4 45 JackMitchell(3) 14 45
(Mrs P N Dutfield) *led: rdn and hdd 2f out: sn wknd* 100/1

6 9 1 ¾ **Garter Star**20 1638 4-9-7 0 JamieSpencer 2 39
(H Morrison) *mid-div for 3f* 14/1

00- 10 ¾ **Rest By The River**244 6077 3-8-12 0 SimonWhitworth 4 35
(A G Newcombe) *sn restrained towards rr: wknd wl over 1f out* 28/1

11 11 **Rosie Two** 3-8-12 0 FergusSweeney 13 —
(W S Kittow) *s.i.s: a struggling in rr* 16/1

1m 14.58s (-0.22) **Going Correction** -0.125s/f (Firm)
WFA 3 from 4yo 9lb 11 Ran SP% 119.3
Speed ratings (Par 100): **96,95,94,93,91 91,88,83,81,80 65**
toteswinger: 1&2 £11.30, 1&3 £4.00, 2&3 £9.70. CSF £73.18 TOTE £3.40: £1.60, £3.50, £1.70; EX 74.30.

Owner Ahmad Al Shaikh **Bred** Bearstone Stud **Trained** Newmarket, Suffolk

FOCUS
A modest fillies' maiden run at a furious pace, but there was not much separating the first six who were spread across the track. The winner and fourth set a fair standard but were probably not at their best.

Milldown Story Official explanation: jockey said filly hung left handed from halfway
Rosie Two Official explanation: jockey said filly suffered interference in running

2206 BATHWICK TYRES SUPPORTS "HEROS" REHOMING EX-RACEHORSES H'CAP 1m 1f 198y

8:45 (8:45) (Class 5) (0-70,70) 3-Y-0 £3,238 (£963; £481; £240) Stalls Low

Form RPR

10-4 1 **Global**50 1075 3-9-0 69 PatrickHills(3) 11 74
(R Hannon) *mde all: drifted lft fr wl over 1f out: kpt on gamely: drvn out* 20/1

6-53 2 1 **North Cape (USA)**23 1595 3-9-2 68 FergusSweeney 5 71
(H Candy) *t.k.h early: chsd wnr thrght: rdn over 2f out: kpt on but unable to get to wnr: jst hld on for 2nd* 12/1

000- 3 hd **Ja One (IRE)**226 6565 3-8-12 64 RobertWinston 3 67+
(B W Hills) *mid-div: hdwy over 2f out: sn rdn to chse ldrs: styd on fnl f: snatched 3rd fnl strides* 14/1

00-3 4 shd **Theologist (IRE)**13 1838 3-9-1 67 GeorgeBaker 4 69+
(Mrs A J Perrett) *chsd ldrs: rdn over 3f out: styd on fnl f: snatched 4th fnl strides* 6/1[3]

05-3 5 ½ **Lucky Score (IRE)**19 1670 3-9-1 67 LPKeniry 14 68
(Mouse Hamilton-Fairley) *trckd wnr: rdn and drifted lft fr 2f out: disp 2nd tl no ex and lost 2 pls fnl strides* 22/1

50-0 6 1 ½ **Mejala (IRE)**14 1804 3-9-1 67 TPO'Shea 10 65
(J L Dunlop) *mid-div: hrd rdn to chse ldrs over 1f out: one pce fnl f* 20/1

-003 7 ¾ **Perfect Affair (USA)**12 1882 3-9-4 70 SebSanders 7 67
(R M Beckett) *mid-div: rdn 3f out: no imp* 6/1[3]

06-0 8 ¾ **Hi Fling**17 1730 3-8-13 65 NickyMackay 12 60
(B J Meehan) *trckd ldrs: rdn over 3f out: fdd fnl f* 20/1

44-2 9 hd **Hawk's Eye**10 1928 3-8-13 65 JamieSpencer 13 60
(E F Vaughan) *hld up last: hdwy over 2f out: swtchd rt and rdn over 1f out: nt pce to get on terms* 5/2[1]

35-2 10 2 ¼ **Breadstick**19 1670 3-9-4 70 SteveDrowne 6 61
(H Morrison) *mid-div: rdn 3f out: wknd fnl f* 10/1

00-4 11 3 **Granski (IRE)**10 1928 3-8-13 65 RichardHughes 9 50
(R Hannon) *hld up towards rr: rdn and hdwy over 2f out: chsd ldrs over 1f out: wknd fnl f* 9/2[2]

020- 12 1 ½ **Winterbrook King**172 7505 3-8-9 61 LukeMorris 1 43
(J R Best) *a towards rr* 80/1

-450 13 4 ½ **Lady Micklegate (USA)**13 1839 3-9-1 70 MarcHalford(3) 8 43
(J R Best) *a towards rr* 50/1

2m 10.16s (0.26) **Going Correction** -0.125s/f (Firm) 13 Ran SP% 120.6
Speed ratings (Par 99): **93,92,92,91,91 90,89,89,89,87 84,83,80**
toteswinger: 1&2 £24.30, 1&3 £30.80, 2&3 £20.40. CSF £226.62 CT £3465.12 TOTE £25.80: £6.20, £4.70, £5.50; EX 244.20 Place 6 £252.02, Place 5 £181.13..

Owner A J Ilsley & G Battocchi **Bred** Lt-Col And Mrs R Bromley Gardner **Trained** East Everleigh, Wilts

FOCUS
A modest handicap run at a muddling pace. They finished in a heap and the form looks suspect, although it does make some sense.

Lucky Score(IRE) Official explanation: jockey said filly hung left handed
Hawk's Eye Official explanation: jockey said gelding was denied a clear run

T/Plt: £318.70 to a £1 stake. Pool: £61,920.61. 141.80 winning tickets. T/Qpdt: £87.00 to a £1 stake. Pool: £5,211.69. 44.30 winning tickets. TM

1524 SANDOWN (R-H)

Thursday, May 21

OFFICIAL GOING: Good to firm (sprint 8.7, round 9.0)

Races on the Round course were increased by around 8yards due to rail realignment.

Wind: Moderate, across. Weather: Bright, getting dark

2207 PANMURE GORDON SMALL COMPANIES E B F MAIDEN FILLIES' STKS 5f 6y

5:50 (5:54) (Class 4) 2-Y-0 £5,180 (£1,541; £770; £384) Stalls Centre

Form RPR

3 1 **Above Limits (IRE)**10 1933 2-9-0 0 RichardKingscote 1 82
(Tom Dascombe) *mde all: rdn over 1f out and j. path jst ins fnl f: sn persistently chal but a jst pulling out enough* 8/11[1]

5 2 hd **Itwasonlyakiss (IRE)**14 1810 2-9-0 0 MichaelHills 9 81
(J W Hills) *chsd wnr: rdn and str chal thrght fnl f but a jst hld* 7/1[3]

3 3 ¼ **Exotic Beauty** 2-9-0 0 DarryllHolland 5 70+
(M R Channon) *s.i.s but sn chsng ldrs: rdn 1/2-way: outpcd by ldng duo fr over 1f out* 9/2[2]

4 4 2 ¼ **Mind The Monarch**17 1726 2-9-0 0 EddieAhern 3 61
(R A Teal) *t.k.h: chsd ldrs: rdn 1/2-way: wknd over 1f out* 20/1

5 2 ¼ **Fleeting Echo** 2-9-0 0 PatDobbs 2 53
(R Hannon) *s.i.s: sn rcvrd: sme hdwy 1/2-way but nvr any threat to ldrs and sn one pce* 16/1

6 1 ½ **She's Ok (IRE)** 2-9-0 0 LDettori 7 48
(C E Brittain) *outpcd* 10/1

7 8 **Gooseberry Bush** 2-9-0 0 TravisBlock 6 19
(P J Makin) *s.i.s: sme hdwy to get in tch w main gp 1/2-way: nvr anywhere nr ldrs and wknd sn after* 25/1

8 83 **Princess Shamal** 2-9-0 0 AlanMunro 4 —
(J R Jenkins) *unruly paddock: extremely slowly away and t.o thrght* 22/1

62.08 secs (0.48) **Going Correction** 0.0s/f (Good) 8 Ran SP% 116.5
Speed ratings (Par 92): **96,95,90,86,83 80,68,—**
toteswinger: 1&2 £2.20, 1&3 £2.10, 2&3 £3.70. CSF £6.39 TOTE £1.80: £1.10, £1.80, £1.60; EX 7.80.

Owner Findlay & Bloom **Bred** Simba Holdings **Trained** Lambourn, Berks

■ Stewards' Enquiry : Richard KingscoteC one-day ban: failed to keep straight from stalls (Jun 4)

FOCUS
A fair fillies' maiden in which a couple with previous experience dominated. The winner stepped forward on her debut effort.

NOTEBOOK
Above Limits(IRE), extremely well backed, didn't have to improve a great deal on the form she showed when third in a reasonable race at Wolverhampton on her debut, but there's good reason to believe she's can do better. Best away from the stalls, she soon cut to the far rail and showed plenty of natural speed. However, sporting front bandages, her action couldn't be described as fluent, as she was climbing from an early stage and hitting the ground quite hard, and she continually changed her legs, most noticeably when crossing the path in the closing stages. It's possible this ground was quicker than she cares for and she ought to rate higher when connections establish her optimum conditions. (op 4-5 tchd 5-6 and 10-11 in places)
Itwasonlyakiss(IRE) made the favourite work hard and improved significantly on the form she showed when fifth on her debut at Windsor. She was a little keen early, before keeping on well when placed under pressure, and gave the impression she will benefit from being allowed to bowl along in front. (op 9-1)
Exotic Beauty ◆, a 75,000euros half-sister to smart 5f winner Janina, out of a high-class sprinter, recovered well from a sluggish start and fared best of the newcomers. She looked as though the run would do her good and she might be worth following if turned out in similar company next time. (op 6-1 tchd 7-1)
Mind The Monarch didn't seem to improve on her debut fourth in an ordinary Kempton maiden. (op 25-1)
Fleeting Echo was never seen with a chance after starting slowly but will know a lot more next time and can do better as she goes up in trip. (op 14-1 tchd 12-1)
She's Ok(IRE) was outpaced throughout but showed ability and can improve considerably on this, especially when stepped up in trip. (op 6-1)
Princess Shamal Official explanation: jockey said filly missed the break

2208 PANMURE GORDON CORPORATE FINANCE H'CAP 1m 6f
6:20 (6:25) (Class 4) (0-85,85) 3-Y-O **£5,180** (£1,541; £770; £384) **Stalls** High

Form				RPR
-442	1		**Penang Princess**[13] 1842 3-8-9 71 ... TedDurcan 4 (R M Beckett) *led 5f: styd chsng ldrs: rdn and swtchd lft wl over 1f out: str run to ld and edgd rt ins fnl f: drvn out* **8/1**	77
43-1	2	½	**King Of Wands**[30] 1427 3-9-4 80 ... EddieAhern 9 (J L Dunlop) *t.k.h trckd ldrs: rdn to chal 2f out: led 1f out: hdd ins fnl f and edgd lft: no ex nr fin* **7/2**[1]	86
03-1	3	1 ½	**Cry For The Moon (USA)**[22] 1614 3-9-4 80 ... JimCrowley 11 (Mrs A J Perrett) *t.k.h: in tch: hmpd over 2f out: styd on wl fr over 1f out to chse ldng duo ins fnl f but no imp* **15/2**[3]	84+
0-61	4	2 ¼	**Darley Sun (IRE)**[13] 1842 3-8-13 75 ... DarryllHolland 10 (D M Simcock) *chsd ldrs tl drvn: outpcd and dropped to rr over 3f out: styd on again fr over 1f out: gng on cl home* **9/2**[2]	75+
3126	5	1	**El Bravo**[6] 2038 3-9-1 77 ... PatDobbs 7 (G L Moore) *in rr: swtchd lft to outside over 2f out and sme hdwy: nvr gng pce to rch ldrs and sn one pce* **10/1**	76
11-5	6	hd	**Atabaas Allure (FR)**[22] 1613 3-9-5 81 ... RoystonFfrench 2 (M Johnston) *chsd ldrs: led over 3f out: hdd u.p 2f out: wknd fnl f* **16/1**	80
-310	7	2	**Admirable Duque (IRE)**[5] 2084 3-9-4 80 ...(b[1]) AdamKirby 8 (D J S Ffrench Davis) *in rr tl hdwy over 5f out: led 2f out: hdd 1f out: wkng whn hmpd sn after* **20/1**	76
0-12	8	hd	**Lively Fling (USA)**[26] 1512 3-9-9 85 ... JimmyFortune 6 (J H M Gosden) *chsd ldrs: led after 5f: hdd over 3f out: wknd 2f out* **7/2**[1]	81
0-53	9	1 ¾	**Excelsior Academy**[17] 1747 3-8-6 68 ... AlanMunro 5 (B J Meehan) *in tch: hdwy to chse ldrs 6f out: rdn and effrt fr 3f out: chsd ldrs 2f out: btn sn after* **9/1**	61

3m 8.34s (1.74) **Going Correction** 0.0s/f (Good) 9 Ran SP% 115.2
Speed ratings (Par 101): **95,94,93,92,92 91,90,90,89**
toteswinger: 1&2 £10.90, 1&3 £5.30, 2&3 £4.20. CSF £36.08 CT £220.91 TOTE £7.80: £1.90, £1.80, £2.20; EX 45.60.
Owner Mrs A K H Ooi **Bred** Mrs A K H Ooi **Trained** Whitsbury, Hants

FOCUS
This looked like a fair three-year-old staying handicap, but they went a stop-start gallop and the bare form needs treating with some caution. The principals are progressive though.

2209 PANMURE GORDON INSTITUTIONAL EQUITIES H'CAP 1m 14y
6:50 (6:57) (Class 4) (0-85,85) 3-Y-O **£5,180** (£1,541; £770; £384) **Stalls** High

Form				RPR
43-1	1		**Mirrored**[29] 1466 3-9-6 82 ... LDettori 11 (Sir Michael Stoute) *chsd ldrs: rdn to go 2nd over 1f out: str chal and edgd rt ins fnl f: led fnl 75yds: hld on wl* **11/8**[1]	86
3-05	2	½	**Al Sabaheya**[18] 1702 3-9-5 81 ... DarryllHolland 10 (C E Brittain) *led: rdn and qcknd over 2f out: hdd and n.m.r fnl 75yds: no ex cl home* **12/1**	84
151	3	1 ¾	**Roar Of Applause**[10] 1932 3-9-4 80 6ex ... EddieAhern 13 (B J Meehan) *hld up in tch on ins: nvr seeing much daylight whn rdn fr 2f out: kpt on but no imp on ldng duo ins fnl f* **6/1**[2]	79
10-2	4	¾	**Fanditha (IRE)**[32] 1381 3-9-9 85 ... PatDobbs 5 (R Hannon) *chsd ldr: rdn and effrt to press ldr 2f out: lost 2nd over 1f out and styd on same pce ins fnl f* **8/1**[3]	82
1-04	5	nk	**Peking Prince**[12] 1895 3-8-1 70 ... RichardRowe[(7)] 7 (A M Balding) *in rr: stl plenty to do fr 2f out: hdwy over 1f out and pushed rt jst ins fnl f: fin wl* **14/1**	66+
054-	6	nk	**Davids Matador**[232] 6398 3-8-11 73 ... StephenCarson 2 (Eve Johnson Houghton) *in rr: hdwy on outside whn bmpd ins fnl 3f: hdwy over 1f out and edgd rt jst ins fnl f: gng on cl home* **33/1**	69
01-4	7	2 ¼	**Thin Red Line (IRE)**[48] 1105 3-9-4 80 ... JimmyFortune 12 (E A L Dunlop) *in rr: hdwy fr 2f out: styng on whn hmpd jst ins fnl f: kpt on again cl home* **12/1**	70+
001-	8	2	**Moon Lightning (IRE)**[188] 7318 3-9-2 78 ... TedDurcan 9 (M H Tompkins) *in rr: hdwy and hmpd ins fnl 3f: hung rt: wknd over 1f out* **16/1**	64
2-22	9	2 ½	**Barbarian**[24] 1574 3-8-9 71 ...(b[1]) MichaelHills 8 (B W Hills) *chsd ldrs: bmpd ins fnl 3f: styd prom tl wknd over 1f out: dropping away whn hmpd jst ins fnl f* **6/1**[2]	51
50-6	10	1 ½	**Fajita**[17] 1752 3-8-2 71 ... JemmaMarshall[(7)] 4 (G L Moore) *chsd ldrs to 3f out: sn wknd* **50/1**	48
000-	11	3 ¼	**Queen Of Thebes (IRE)**[231] 6426 3-9-2 78 ... JimCrowley 1 (G L Moore) *s.i.s: in rr: hdwy to get into mid-div ins fnl 3f: sn wknd* **16/1**	47

1m 44.07s (0.77) **Going Correction** 0.0s/f (Good) 11 Ran SP% 120.5
Speed ratings (Par 101): **96,95,93,93,92 92,90,88,85,84 80**
toteswinger: 1&2 £6.60, 1&3 £2.20, 2&3 £15.10. CSF £20.65 CT £82.49 TOTE £2.30: £1.30, £4.30, £1.40; EX 23.10.
Owner K Abdulla **Bred** Millsec Limited **Trained** Newmarket, Suffolk
■ Stewards' Enquiry : Richard Rowe four-day ban: careless riding (Jun 4, 7-9)

FOCUS
A reasonable three-year-old handicap, but with Al Sabaheya allowed to dominate under Darryll Holland, few were able to get involved from off the pace. The third looks the best guide to the form.

2210 HARRY PANMURE GORDON MEMORIAL H'CAP 1m 2f 7y
7:25 (7:27) (Class 4) (0-85,85) 3-Y-O **£5,180** (£1,541; £770; £384) **Stalls** High

Form				RPR
2-23	1		**Antinori (IRE)**[27] 1489 3-9-4 85 ... AdamKirby 3 (W R Swinburn) *mde all: drvn along and kpt finding ex fr over 2f out: unchal* **10/3**[2]	94
1-	2	2 ½	**State Banquet (USA)**[232] 6397 3-9-1 82 ... TravisBlock 1 (H Morrison) *chsd wnr thrght: rdn and effrt fr 3f out: nvr quite on terms and nt pce of wnr fr over 1f out* **11/4**[1]	86
34-1	3	1 ¼	**The Fonz**[28] 1474 3-8-12 79 ... LDettori 5 (Sir Michael Stoute) *in tch: hdwy to chse ldrs 5f out: rdn and effrt 3f out: no imp on wnr and outpcd fr over 1f out* **11/4**[1]	81
3-64	4	1	**Fazbee (IRE)**[19] 1664 3-9-4 85 ... DarryllHolland 4 (P W D'Arcy) *in rr: rdn over 3f out: styd on fr 2f out and kpt on ins fnl f but nvr in contention* **20/1**	85?
1-	5	3	**Battle Planner (USA)**[162] 7627 3-9-4 85 ... RoystonFfrench 2 (M Johnston) *rn in snatches and rdn in rr thrght: tl styd on fr over 1f out* **11/2**[3]	79
32-2	6	6	**Wilfred Pickles (IRE)**[28] 1474 3-8-11 78 ... JimCrowley 6 (Mrs A J Perrett) *in tch: rdn 3f out: wknd qckly 2f out* **15/2**	60
1363	7	1 ½	**Doncosaque (IRE)**[18] 1707 3-9-0 81 ... IanMongan 7 (P Howling) *chsd ldrs tl wknd qckly over 2f out* **20/1**	60

2m 10.01s (-0.49) **Going Correction** 0.0s/f (Good) 7 Ran SP% 113.1
Speed ratings (Par 101): **101,99,98,97,94 90,88**
toteswinger: 1&2 £1.40, 1&3 £5.70, 2&3 £7.10. CSF £12.64 TOTE £4.30: £2.00, £2.20; EX 16.40.
Owner P W Harris **Bred** Peter Harris **Trained** Aldbury, Herts

FOCUS
A decent three-year-old handicap in which the winner was allowed his own way in front. The winning time was good, significantly faster than a good-looking maiden and the form has been rated fairly positively.

2211 PANMURE GORDON LIVERPOOL MAIDEN STKS 1m 2f 7y
8:00 (8:02) (Class 5) 3-4-Y-O **£3,885** (£1,156; £577; £288) **Stalls** High

Form				RPR
0/	1		**Bugaku**[572] 6494 4-9-7 0 ... Louis-PhilippeBeuzelin[(5)] 4 (Sir Michael Stoute) *chsd ldrs: led wl over 1f out: drvn out* **4/1**[3]	86+
	2	¾	**Spiekeroog** 3-8-12 0 ... TPQueally 3 (H R A Cecil) *s.i.s: hrd rdn 3f out and no imp on ldrs: drvn again and hdwy appr fnl f: fin wl to take 2nd cl home but nt rch wnr* **10/1**	79+
	3	1 ¼	**Racing Hero (IRE)** 3-8-12 0 ... LDettori 9 (J Noseda) *chsd ldr: rdn: rn green and led over 2f out: hung rt u.p sn after and hdd wl over 1f out: no imp on wnr ins fnl f and lost 2nd nr fin* **9/2**	77
	4	3 ¼	**Count Lucien** 3-8-12 0 ... JimmyFortune 8 (J H M Gosden) *chsd ldrs: drvn to chal over 2f out: wknd fnl f* **11/4**[1]	70
0-	5	1 ½	**Chanrossa (IRE)**[232] 6391 3-8-7 0 ... EddieAhern 1 (E A L Dunlop) *led tl hdd over 2f out: wknd over 1f out* **7/2**[2]	62
-00	6	7	**Refuse Toulouse (IRE)**[33] 1350 3-8-12 0 ...(t) AdamKirby 5 (C G Cox) *a towards rr* **7/1**	53
	7	8	**Iron Master** 3-8-12 0 ...(t) NeilChalmers 6 (J J Bridger) *rdn and rn green 3f out: a towards rr* **50/1**	37

2m 14.04s (3.54) **Going Correction** 0.0s/f (Good)
WFA 3 from 4yo 14lb 7 Ran SP% 110.6
Speed ratings (Par 103): **85,84,83,80,79 74,67**
toteswinger: 1&2 £4.30, 1&3 £3.00, 2&3 £3.20. CSF £39.09 TOTE £5.10: £3.40, £3.30; EX 30.70.
Owner Mrs Denis Haynes **Bred** Wretham Stud **Trained** Newmarket, Suffolk

FOCUS
The winning time was 4.03 seconds slower than the earlier 71-85 handicap for 3yos, but that shouldn't detract from the quality of this contest. A smallish field lined up, but this was an informative maiden and it looked a race that will produce some nice horses over the coming months. The winner was value for extra.
Racing Hero(IRE) ◆ Official explanation: jockey said colt ran green

2212 PANMURE GORDON STOCKBROKING FILLIES' H'CAP 1m 1f
8:35 (8:35) (Class 4) (0-80,80) 3-Y-O+ **£5,180** (£1,541; £770; £384) **Stalls** Centre

Form				RPR
1-	1		**Leocorno (IRE)**[209] 6945 3-8-12 78 ... LDettori 3 (Sir Michael Stoute) *stdd in mid-div: shkn up and hdwy 3f out: led jst ins fnl 2f: pushed 9 l clr 1f out: eased cl home* **8/11**[1]	104+
-503	2	5	**Hip Hip Hooray**[10] 1928 3-7-7 66 oh2 ... RichardRowe[(7)] 5 (L A Dace) *in rr tl hdwy on outside fr 3f out: rdn: edgd rt and chsd wnr 1f out but nvr the remotest ch* **14/1**	69
10-0	3	3 ½	**Maybe I Will (IRE)**[14] 1812 4-9-1 68 ... DarryllHolland 6 (S Dow) *in rr: hdwy over 2f out: styd on fr over 1f to take wl hld 3rd ins fnl f* **40/1**	65
0620	4	1 ½	**Binfield (IRE)**[12] 1860 4-8-13 66 ... JimCrowley 8 (B G Powell) *chsd ldrs: rdn 3f out: no ch w wnr fr ins fnl 2f: wkng whn bmpd and lost 2nd 1f out* **33/1**	60
00-4	5	½	**Uig**[8] 1983 8-8-13 66 oh6 ... TedDurcan 2 (H S Howe) *in rr tl mod last prog fr over 1f out* **33/1**	59
01-1	6	1	**Lyra's Daemon**[30] 1416 3-8-8 74 ... EddieAhern 9 (W R Muir) *led tl hdd 3f out: styd w ldr to 2f out: sn no ch w wnr: wknd and hung rt over 1f out* **11/2**[2]	63
6411	7	½	**Bookiebasher Babe (IRE)**[16] 1778 4-9-3 70 ... FrancisNorton 4 (M Quinn) *chsd ldrs: rdn 3f out: wknd fr 2f out* **20/1**	59
21-4	8	1	**Dakiyah (IRE)**[17] 1753 5-9-13 80 ...(p) IanMongan 1 (Mrs L J Mongan) *chsd ldr: led 3f out: hdd jst ins fnl 2f: sn wknd* **8/1**	67
4-32	9	1	**Lady Brora**[16] 1778 4-9-7 74 ... WilliamBuick 7 (A M Balding) *in rr: hdwy on ins whn nt clr run wl over 1f out: n.m.r after and nt rcvr* **7/1**[3]	67+

1m 54.51s (-1.79) **Going Correction** 0.0s/f (Good)
WFA 3 from 4yo+ 13lb 9 Ran SP% 116.6
Speed ratings (Par 102): **107,102,99,98,97 96,96,95,94**
toteswinger: 1&2 £5.40, 1&3 £11.80, 2&3 £24.30. CSF £12.42 CT £238.74 TOTE £1.70: £1.10, £3.50, £5.30; EX 15.60 Place 6 £29.40, Place 5 £26.11..
Owner Ballymacoll Stud **Bred** Ballymacoll Stud Farm Ltd **Trained** Newmarket, Suffolk

FOCUS
This fillies' handicap was all about the winner, who won easily and is sure to rate higher. The pace was sound but the fifth limits the form.
Lyra's Daemon Official explanation: jockey said regarding riding, that he had run out of room on a long-striding filly and was fearful of clipping heels
Lady Brora Official explanation: jockey said filly was denied a clear run

T/Plt: £45.60 to a £1 stake. Pool: £72,454.03. 1,159.31 winning tickets. T/Qpdt: £21.20 to a £1 stake. Pool: £4,851.52. 169.20 winning tickets. ST

2113 BADEN-BADEN (L-H)

Thursday, May 21

OFFICIAL GOING: Good

2216a BETTY BARCLAY-RENNEN (GROUP 3) 2m

3:55 (4:07) 4-Y-O+ **£29,126** (£12,136; £4,854; £2,427)

RPR

1 **Flamingo Fantasy (GER)**[20] 4-9-0 .... ASuborics 4 106
(W Hickst, Germany) *hld up: 8th 1/2-way: hdwy ent st: led 1f out: r.o to line: drvn out* **47/10**[3]

2 ½ **Ruten (USA)**[20] 4-9-0 .... JiriPalik 8 105
(Andreas Lowe, Germany) *towards rr: 6th 1/2-way: 4th st: led briefly over 1f out to 1f out: r.o fnl f to press wnr to line* **105/10**

3 3 **Shawnee Saga (FR)**[25] 1549 4-9-0 .... DBoeuf 3 102
(W Baltromei, Germany) *prom: 2nd 1/2-way: pushed along st: styd on steadily fr over 1f out* **115/10**

4 1 **Caudillo (GER)**[25] 1552 6-9-2 .... ADeVries 6 101
(Dr A Bolte, Germany) *hld up: 7th 1/2-way: styd on fr over 1f out: wnt 4th ins fnl 100yds* **49/10**

5 1 **Ryan (IRE)**[18] 6-9-0 ....(b) RJuracek 5 98
(J Hanacek, Slovakia) *mid-div: 4th 1/2-way: cl 6th and running on st: r.o tl no ex fnl 150yds* **143/10**

6 3½ **Valdino (GER)**[20] 4-9-2 .... WMongil 9 98
(Uwe Ostmann, Germany) *prom: 3rd 1/2-way: pushed along st: unable qck* **5/2**[1]

7 3 **Limatus (GER)**[226] 6569 8-9-0 .... HGrewe 7 90
(P Vovcenko, Germany) *led: pushed along st: hdd over 1f out: one pce after* **21/1**

8 3 **Ostland (GER)**[25] 1549 4-9-2 .... AStarke 1 91
(P Schiergen, Germany) *racd in last: drvn ent st: no imp* **11/2**

9 ¾ **Mischief Making (USA)**[22] 1601 4-8-11 .... TGMcLaughlin 2 85
(E A L Dunlop) *broke wl: 5th 1/2-way: pushed along 3 1/2f out: drvn ent st: no imp: eased fnl f* **16/5**[2]

3m 29.25s (5.66)
WFA 4 from 6yo+ 2lb **9 Ran SP% 130.0**
(Including 10 Euro stake): WIN 57; PL 22, 25, 34; SF 519.
Owner Gestut Park Wiedingen **Bred** Gestut Park Wiedlingen **Trained** Germany

NOTEBOOK
Mischief Making(USA), who handles most ground, was struggling from some way out and finished off being eased down. She is better than this.

1956 BRIGHTON (L-H)

Friday, May 22

OFFICIAL GOING: Good to firm (firm in places; 8.3)
Dolling out of 3metres between 6f and 2.5f added circa 20yards to advertised distances.
Wind: Fresh, against Weather: Sunny

2218 BET ON TOTEPLACEPOT AT TOTESPORT.COM EBF MAIDEN STKS 5f 213y

2:00 (2:00) (Class 5) 2-Y-O **£3,784** (£1,132; £566; £283; £141) **Stalls Low**

Form RPR

3 1 **Barzan (IRE)**[7] 2033 2-8-12 0 .... RossAtkinson(5) 4 71+
(Tom Dascombe) *in tch: led 2f out: pushed along and a jst holding runner-up fnl f* **4/9**[1]

2 ½ **Going French (IRE)** 2-9-3 0 .... J-PGuillambert 5 69
(R Curtis) *t.k.h in rr: hdwy 2f out: rdn to chal over 1f out: kpt on wl but a readily hld* **16/1**

43 3 6 **Midnight Uno**[14] 1827 2-8-12 0 .... WilliamCarson(5) 6 51
(W G M Turner) *led 100yds: chsd ldrs: hrd rdn and edgd lft 2f out: wknd over 1f out* **10/1**[3]

4 1¼ **Hairspray** 2-8-12 0 .... SamHitchcott 2 42
(M R Channon) *prom: rdn to chal over 2f out: wknd over 1f out* **14/1**

5 1 **Dubawi Phantom** 2-9-3 0 .... StephenDonohoe 1 44
(D M Simcock) *s.s: in rr tl effrt on outside over 3f out: wknd 2f out* **5/1**[2]

6 1¾ **Split The Pot (IRE)** 2-9-0 0 .... DavidProbert(3) 3 39
(P R Chamings) *plld hrd: chsd ldrs: squeezed out after 1f: effrt on rail 2f out: sn edgd lft and wknd* **33/1**

7 1¾ **D'Urberville** 2-9-3 0 .... FergusSweeney 7 33
(R Ingram) *dwlt: hdwy to ld after 100yds: hdd & wknd 2f out* **66/1**

1m 11.93s (1.73) **Going Correction** +0.05s/f (Good) **7 Ran SP% 112.0**
Speed ratings (Par 93): **90,89,81,79,78 76,73**
toteswinger: 1&2 £5.70, 1&3 £2.10, 2&3 £18.50 CSF £9.25 TOTE £1.50: £1.40, £6.40; EX 13.80.

Owner M A Al-Attiyah **Bred** Le Montrachet Syndicate **Trained** Lambourn, Berks
■ Stewards' Enquiry : William Carson three-day ban: careless riding (Jun 7-9)

FOCUS
With at least four of the seven runners looking certain to need considerably further in time the overall form of this race is questionable. The winner was always in command and helps set the level with the third.

NOTEBOOK
Barzan(IRE) is out of a daughter of Nashwan, so he gets his pace from sire Danehill Dancer. He had learned from his Newbury debut over a more testing 6f than this won by a horse with Royal Ascot aspirations in Canford Cliffs. He was value for considerably more than his winning margin, having received the most confident of rides from his 5lb apprentice with only one tap of the whip applied. He will be interesting over at least another furlong. (tchd 1-2 tchd 4-7 in a place)
Going French(IRE), from the first crop of a decent miler, has plenty of pace in his bottom line but took time to get balanced. He will be sharper next time and showed a good attitude. (op 20-1 tchd 22-1)
Midnight Uno, upped in distance for this third run, ran the same style of race as before and lacked pace when it mattered. His rider was banned by three days for allowing his mount to edge left. (op 9-1 tchd 17-2)
Hairspray has pace from the sire and stamina from the dam but it was the former that showed here. She got tired and like most of her juvenile stablemates, will be better for this. (op 12-1)
Dubawi Phantom comes out of this with plenty of credit after a slow start and looking immature. From the first crop of Irish 2000 Guineas winner Dubawi, his dam has a definite stamina influence. He was right in behind them after halfway and would be of interest over a furlong further on a more galloping track. (op 9-1)
Split The Pot(IRE) got over being hampered early, but his immaturity wasn't helped by the track camber to the left throughout the last furlong. Official explanation: jockey said gelding suffered interference in running (op 22-1)
D'Urberville, who should get further, simply ran himself into the ground on debut. (op 40-1)

2219 BIGGER ODDS GUARANTEED AT TOTESPORT.COM H'CAP 5f 59y

2:30 (2:36) (Class 5) (0-75,74) 3-Y-O+ **£3,532** (£1,057; £528; £264; £131) **Stalls Low**

Form RPR

6011 1 **Ziggy Lee**[8] 2005 3-8-11 72 .... WilliamCarson(5) 12 82+
(S C Williams) *bhd: gd hdwy over 1f out: drvn to ld fnl 100yds: sn clr* **7/2**[1]

4401 2 2 **Drifting Gold**[26] 1540 5-9-12 74 ....(b) AdamKirby 6 80
(C G Cox) *in tch: rdn to ld ins fnl f: hdd and one pce fnl 100yds* **6/1**[3]

0055 3 1¾ **Cosmic Destiny (IRE)**[2] 2180 7-8-11 64 .... JPHamblett(5) 1 64+
(E F Vaughan) *hld up in tch: chal on rail 2f out: disputing 2nd and jst hld whn hmpd over 1f out: eased out and kpt on fnl f* **5/1**[2]

-545 4 shd **Digital**[20] 1668 12-9-8 70 ....(v) SamHitchcott 9 69
(M R Channon) *t.k.h in rr of midfield: outpcd and struggling over 2f out: hung lft over 1f out: r.o fnl f* **16/1**

3013 5 ½ **Orpen's Art (IRE)**[4] 2130 4-8-8 63 6ex .... HollyHall(7) 10 61
(S A Callaghan) *w ldrs: led over 2f out: hung lft and hdd ins fnl f: no ex* **10/1**

220- 6 1¼ **Sonhador**[162] 7640 3-9-0 70 .... AdrianMcCarthy 3 60
(G Prodromou) *chsd ldrs tl hung lft and wknd over 1f out* **12/1**

0-10 7 ½ **Magical Speedfit (IRE)**[31] 1418 4-9-12 74 .... GeorgeBaker 2 65+
(G G Margarson) *hld up in rr: hdwy into midfield whn passage blocked over 1f out: nt rcvr* **7/1**

510- 8 3½ **Cape Royal**[196] 7222 9-9-12 74 ....(bt) LukeMorris 5 53
(J M Bradley) *led tl over 2f out: wknd over 1f out* **33/1**

0-36 9 2¼ **Firenza Bond**[28] 1494 4-9-3 65 ....(p) NickyMackay 7 36+
(D Flood) *awkward bef s: towards rr: effrt and nt clr run 2f out: swtchd lft: midfield and styng on whn hmpd over 1f out: eased* **50/1**

0-05 10 hd **Best One**[14] 1836 5-9-8 73 ....(b) KevinGhunowa(3) 8 43
(R A Harris) *prom tl hrd rdn and wknd over 2f out* **8/1**

62.73 secs (0.43) **Going Correction** +0.05s/f (Good)
WFA 3 from 4yo+ 8lb **10 Ran SP% 104.4**
Speed ratings (Par 103): **98,94,92,91,91 89,88,82,79,78**
toteswinger: 1&2 £6.10, 1&3 £6.00, 2&3 £45.60 CSF £19.52 CT £76.76 TOTE £3.40: £1.30, £2.20, £1.80; EX 16.60.
Owner Rothmere Racing Limited **Bred** Ian Allan **Trained** Newmarket, Suffolk
■ Matteroffact was withdrawn (7/1, broke out of stalls). R4 applies, deduct 10p in the £.
■ Stewards' Enquiry : Holly Hall two-day ban: careless riding (Jun 7-8)

FOCUS
A modest handicap.
Magical Speedfit(IRE) Official explanation: jockey said gelding was denied a clear run
Firenza Bond Official explanation: jockey said gelding hung left

2220 BET IN-PLAY AT TOTESPORT.COM (S) STKS 1m 1f 209y

3:05 (3:06) (Class 6) 3-5-Y-O **£1,942** (£578; £288; £144) **Stalls High**

Form RPR

06 1 **Theocritus (USA)**[18] 1753 4-9-8 80 .... StephenDonohoe 4 68+
(D M Simcock) *hld up disputing 5th: hdwy on rail over 2f out: drvn to ld over 1f out: sn clr: eased nr fin: b.b.v* **5/2**[2]

4204 2 5 **Solo River**[14] 1834 4-9-3 64 .... FergusSweeney 5 51
(P J Makin) *sn trcking ldr: led over 2f out tl over 1f out: nt pce of wnr* **13/8**[1]

0066 3 ¾ **King's Chorister**[24] 1594 3-8-8 53 ....(t) KirstyMilczarek 8 53
(Miss Gay Kelleway) *hld up disputing 5th: hdwy to chse ldrs over 2f out: rdn and hung lft over 1f out: one pce* **11/2**[3]

-560 4 2¾ **Forty Thirty (IRE)**[77] 776 3-8-8 61 .... SamHitchcott 1 48
(M R Channon) *led tl over 2f out: wknd over 1f out* **15/2**

-000 5 3¼ **Red Dagger (IRE)**[10] 1967 3-8-3 40 .... AmyBaker(5) 9 41
(T D McCarthy) *towards rr: sme hdwy into 5th over 3f out: edgd lft 2f out: nt pce to chal* **20/1**

005- 6 13 **Scar Tissue**[23] 7463 5-9-3 35 .... EdwardCreighton 10 11
(E J Creighton) *bhd: rdn after 4f: no ch fnl 3f* **80/1**

-050 7 13 **Calling Birds (IRE)**[24] 1578 3-8-3 51 ....(v) FrankieMcDonald 2 —
(Karen George) *s.i.s: sn chsng ldrs: wknd over 4f out: bhd fnl 3f* **25/1**

0060 8 5 **Commandingpresence (USA)**[15] 1811 3-8-3 53 ....(vt[1]) LukeMorris 3 —
(Ms J S Doyle) *prom tl drvn along and wknd over 3f out: sn bhd* **8/1**

2m 4.48s (0.88) **Going Correction** +0.05s/f (Good)
WFA 3 from 4yo+ 14lb **8 Ran SP% 114.8**
Speed ratings (Par 101): **98,94,93,91,88 78,67,63**
toteswinger: 1&2 £1.10, 1&3 £3.10, 2&3 £2.10 CSF £6.85 TOTE £2.70: £1.60, £1.10, £1.90; EX 8.50.The winner was bought in for 8,500gns.
Owner Dr Marwan Koukash **Bred** Allen E Paulson Living Trust **Trained** Newmarket, Suffolk

FOCUS
An ordinary seller and five of the eight starters were in this grade for the first time including the winner.
Commandingpresence(USA) Official explanation: trainer said filly lost both hind shoes

2221 BET ON TOTESUPER7 AT TOTESPORT.COM H'CAP 1m 1f 209y

3:40 (3:41) (Class 6) (0-60,60) 4-Y-O+ **£2,460** (£732; £365; £182) **Stalls High**

Form RPR

00-0 1 **Goose Green (IRE)**[10] 1974 5-7-13 46 .... Louis-PhilippeBeuzelin(5) 2 57+
(R J Hodges) *trckd ldrs: led 2f out: clr over 1f out: comf* **16/1**

/00- 2 2¼ **Shavoulin (USA)**[256] 5748 5-8-6 48 .... LukeMorris 16 53
(P W Hiatt) *hld up in midfield: hdwy 4f out: chal over 2f out: wnt clr 2nd 1f out: nt pce of wnr* **10/1**

3-00 3 1 **Son Of My Heart (USA)**[17] 1780 4-9-4 60 ....(b[1]) GeorgeBaker 11 63
(P F I Cole) *prom: led after 3f tl 2f out: one pce* **5/1**[3]

620- 4 1 **Daring Racer (GER)**[31] 7831 6-8-12 54 ....(p) IanMongan 14 55
(Mrs L J Mongan) *in rr of midfield: rdn over 3f out: swtchd lft and hdwy to chse ldrs ins fnl 2f: one pce* **6/1**

5-40 5 3¼ **Astrolibra**[10] 1961 5-9-1 57 .... NickyMackay 10 51
(M H Tompkins) *chsd ldrs tl outpcd fnl 2f* **4/1**[2]

020P 6 3½ **Magic Warrior**[10] 1974 9-8-4 46 .... KirstyMilczarek 9 33
(J C Fox) *wnt rt s and missed break: bhd tl rdn and styd on fnl 2f: nvr nrr* **25/1**

0030 7 ½ **Mayfair's Future**[13] 1881 4-9-1 57 ....(v[1]) AdrianMcCarthy 12 43
(J R Jenkins) *pressed ldrs tl wknd over 2f out* **14/1**

4-60 8 3½ **Marie Tempest**[102] 469 4-8-5 47 .... SimonWhitworth 8 26
(M R Bosley) *chsd ldrs tl wknd wl over 1f out* **18/1**

20-3 9 2 **Lady Florence**[39] 1065 4-7-12 47 .... RosieJessop(7) 6 22
(A B Coogan) *led 3f: prom tl nt handle hill and lost pl over 3f out: rdn and wknd over 2f out* **22/1**

0-00 **10** *nk* **Space Pirate**[131] 132 4-8-1 **46** oh1..........................(p) DavidProbert[(3)] 13 20
(J Pearce) *mid-div: drvn along on outside 3f out: sn btn* **16/1**
00-0 **11** *3 1/2* **Smart Tazz**[17] 1771 4-8-6 **51** oh1 ow5.......................... KevinGhunowa[(3)] 1 18
(H J Evans) *towards rr: rdn and n.d fnl 3f* **16/1**
64-0 **12** *2 1/4* **Felicia**[18] 1728 4-8-6 **48**.. RichardThomas 3 11
(J E Long) *mid-div: hrd rdn 3f out: sn wknd* **20/1**
000 **13** *14* **Living The Dream**[37] 1286 7-8-8 **50**............................ TGMcLaughlin 4 —
(Karen George) *t.k.h towards rr: rdn 4f out: sn bhd* **25/1**
-315 **P** **Trifti**[33] 1382 8-9-3 **59**.. FergusSweeney 15 —
(Miss Jo Crowley) *towards rr: rdn over 3f out: no rspnse and sn bhd: t.o whn p.u ins fnl f: b.b.v* **7/2**[1]

2m 3.63s (0.03) **Going Correction** +0.05s/f (Good) **14** Ran SP% **128.6**
Speed ratings (Par 101): **101,99,98,97,95 92,91,89,87,87 84,82,71,—**
toteswinger: 1&2 £41.00, 1&3 £23.20, 2&3 £21.20 CSF £170.33 CT £936.74 TOTE £17.30: £4.90, £4.00, £1.80; EX 330.10.
Owner Mrs S G Clapp **Bred** Liam Queally **Trained** Charlton Mackrell, Somerset

FOCUS
Another modest handicap and seven of the 14 runners were maidens.
Shavoulin(USA) ◆ Official explanation: jockey said gelding hung right
Magic Warrior Official explanation: jockey said gelding never travelled
Trifti Official explanation: jockey said gelding bled from the nose

2222 PLAY ROULETTE AT TOTESPORTCASINO.COM H'CAP 1m 3f 196y
4:15 (4:15) (Class 6) (0-55,60) 4-Y-0+ **£2,590** (£770; £385; £192) **Stalls** High

Form RPR
04-3 **1** **Jafaru**[33] 1378 5-8-10 **50**..........................(b) FergusSweeney 10 60
(G L Moore) *in tch: led over 2f out and rdn 2 l ahd: hld on wl whn chal over 1f out* **11/4**[1]
0-02 **2** *2* **Medieval Maiden**[26] 1537 6-8-7 **47**.................................. PaulDoe 14 54
(Mrs L J Mongan) *mid-div on outer: hdwy 4f out: rdn to chal over 1f out: hung lft: nt find enough to pass wnr* **13/2**
5541 **3** *3* **Coral Shores**[10] 1974 4-9-6 **60** 6ex..........................(v) LukeMorris 1 62
(P W Hiatt) *prom: led over 3f out tl over 2f out: no ex over 1f out* **9/2**[2]
0-20 **4** *shd* **Art Value**[24] 1589 4-8-13 **53**.. TGMcLaughlin 13 55+
(M Wigham) *bhd: rdn and styd on fnl 2f: nvr nrr* **16/1**
00-1 **5** *6* **Harlequinn Danseur (IRE)**[10] 1960 4-8-6 **51** 6ex........... AmyBaker[(5)] 8 43
(N B King) *mid-div: hdwy to chse ldrs 4f out: hrd rdn and btn over 2f out* **6/1**[3]
1014 **6** *nk* **Barbirolli**[10] 1974 7-9-2 **56** 6ex.................................... GeorgeBaker 11 48
(W M Brisbourne) *hld up towards rr: gd hdwy on bit 4f out: rdn 3f out: wknd 2f out* **8/1**
00-0 **7** *1 1/2* **Muffett's Dream**[9] 1980 5-8-3 **46** oh1............................ DavidProbert[(3)] 6 36
(J J Bridger) *chsd ldr: led 5f out tl over 3f out: wknd over 2f out* **12/1**
10-0 **8** *2 1/4* **Lady Jinks**[16] 1786 4-8-10 **55**...................................... MCGeran[(5)] 3 41
(R J Hodges) *chsd ldrs: outpcd 3f out: sn btn* **18/1**
4000 **9** *3/4* **Mid Valley**[18] 1728 6-8-6 **46** oh1.................................... AdrianMcCarthy 2 31
(J R Jenkins) *dwlt: sn in midfield: rdn and no hdwy fnl 3f* **33/1**
5060 **10** *2 1/4* **Ben Bacchus (IRE)**[7] 2040 7-7-13 **46** oh1........................ KierenFox[(7)] 9 27
(P W Hiatt) *hld up and bhd: hdwy into midfield 1/2-way: rdn and lost pl 4f out: n.d after* **16/1**
5006 **11** *4 1/2* **Comeintothespace (IRE)**[17] 1770 7-8-1 **46** oh1............. SophieDoyle[(5)] 7 20
(R A Farrant) *chsd ldrs tl wknd 4f out* **50/1**
0002 **12** *16* **Rosy Dawn**[10] 1961 4-7-13 **46** oh1............................... DebraEngland[(7)] 12 —
(J J Bridger) *led tl 5f out: wknd 3f out* **14/1**
303- **13** *10* **My Legal Eagle (IRE)**[289] 4722 15-8-6 **49** oh1 ow3. KevinGhunowa[(3)] 5 —
(E G Bevan) *a bhd: rdn 3f out: no ch and eased over 1f out* **25/1**

2m 32.56s (-0.14) **Going Correction** +0.05s/f (Good) **13** Ran SP% **123.7**
Speed ratings (Par 101): **102,100,98,98,94 94,93,91,91,89 86,76,69**
toteswinger: 1&2 £8.20, 1&3 £4.30, 2&3 £5.20 CSF £20.84 CT £82.09 TOTE £4.50: £2.30, £2.40, £2.30; EX 19.50.
Owner Miss S Bowles **Bred** Nawara Stud Co Ltd **Trained** Lower Beeding, W Sussex

FOCUS
Another moderate handicap.
Comeintothespace(IRE) Official explanation: jockey said gelding had no more to give
My Legal Eagle(IRE) Official explanation: jockey said gelding suffered interference leaving stalls

2223 PLAY BLACKJACK AT TOTESPORTCASINO.COM H'CAP 6f 209y
4:50 (4:50) (Class 6) (0-60,60) 4-Y-0+ **£2,460** (£732; £365; £182) **Stalls** Low

Form RPR
6621 **1** **Annes Rocket (IRE)**[18] 1741 4-8-4 **53**.......................... GemmaElford[(7)] 11 62
(J C Fox) *hld up in rr: hdwy and hung lft fr 2f out: led 1f out: pushed out* **15/2**
0-55 **2** *1* **Just Oscar (GER)**[10] 1972 5-8-2 **49** ow1..................... RossAtkinson[(5)] 6 55
(W M Brisbourne) *hld up in rr: rdn and gd hdwy over 1f out: r.o to take 2nd nr fin* **7/1**[3]
0-55 **3** *3/4* **Iguacu**[17] 1781 5-8-1 **50**.. MatthewDavies[(7)] 13 53
(George Baker) *chsd ldrs: hrd rdn over 1f out: one pce: fin 4th, plcd 3rd* **12/1**
5443 **4** *3 1/2* **Mr Rev**[16] 1784 6-8-8 **50**..(b) PaulFitzsimons 3 44
(J M Bradley) *chsd ldrs: led on rail jst ins fnl 2f tl 1f out: wknd fnl f* **14/1**
-004 **5** *nse* **Colombard (IRE)**[14] 1846 4-8-3 **50**..........(v) Louis-PhilippeBeuzelin[(5)] 16 44
(Patrick Morris) *mid-div on outer: effrt over 2f out: kpt on same pce: nvr able to chal* **14/1**
2005 **6** *1 1/2* **Ishibee (IRE)**[8] 2011 5-8-6 **48**..(p) NeilChalmers 8 38
(J J Bridger) *in tch: pushed along and n.m.r fr over 1f out: no imp* **14/1**
-050 **7** *1 1/4* **Supreme Speedster**[25] 1558 5-8-8 **50**........................ SimonWhitworth 1 36
(A G Newcombe) *w ldrs: hrd rdn 2f out: wknd over 1f out* **25/1**
0401 **8** *1* **Outer Hebrides**[17] 1781 8-8-4 **51**..........................(v) AmyBaker[(5)] 12 35
(J M Bradley) *w ldrs tl wknd wl over 1f out* **20/1**
2615 **9** *3 3/4* **My Flame**[10] 1959 4-9-2 **58**.. FergusSweeney 2 32
(J R Jenkins) *led tl jst ins fnl 2f: wknd over 1f out* **4/1**[2]
0560 **10** *4* **Djalalabad (FR)**[10] 1959 5-8-11 **53**..........................(tp) TGMcLaughlin 5 16
(Mrs C A Dunnett) *hld up towards rr: sme hdwy on rail 2f out: wknd 1f out* **16/1**
4003 **D** *nk* **Wrighty Almighty (IRE)**[10] 1959 7-9-4 **60**........................ GeorgeBaker 15 65
(P R Chamings) *t.k.h towards rr: hdwy to press ldrs ins fnl 2f: kpt on* **2/1**[1]

1m 23.35s (0.25) **Going Correction** +0.05s/f (Good) **11** Ran SP% **119.8**
Speed ratings (Par 101): **100,98,97,93,93 91,90,89,85,80 98**
toteswinger: 1&2 £19.50, 1&3 £4.50, 2&3 £3.30 CSF £60.38 CT £149.05 TOTE £5.90: £2.20, £3.30, £1.10; EX 61.20.
Owner The Cross Keys Racing Club **Bred** S Coughlan **Trained** Collingbourne Ducis, Wilts

FOCUS
An uninspiring bunch of Class 6 handicappers won by one of the few in winning form.

2224 100% NEW PLAYER BONUS AT TOTESPORTCASINO.COM H'CAP 5f 213y
5:25 (5:25) (Class 5) (0-70,68) 4-Y-0+ **£3,154** (£944; £472; £236; £117) **Stalls** Low

Form RPR
2005 **1** **Louphole**[22] 1619 7-8-13 **63**.. AdrianMcCarthy 8 70
(J R Jenkins) *dwlt: hld up and bhd: hdwy 2f out: led jst ins fnl f: rdn out: hld on wl* **7/1**[3]
6-50 **2** *nk* **What Do You Know**[14] 1833 6-8-10 **65**............................ NicolPolli[(5)] 2 71
(A M Hales) *prom: hrd rdn over 2f out: drvn level whn hung lft 1f out: kpt on* **7/1**[3]
0045 **3** *3/4* **Radiator Rooney (IRE)**[4] 2145 6-7-13 **54** oh4
Louis-PhilippeBeuzelin[(5)] 9 58
(Patrick Morris) *chsd ldrs: rdn over 2f out: kpt on wl fnl f* **3/1**[1]
000- **4** *nse* **Jonny Ebeneezer**[212] 6895 10-8-4 **54** oh3..................(be) NickyMackay 4 59+
(D Flood) *in tch: promising effrt to press ldrs whn boxed in on rail fr wl over 1f out: swtchd rt ins fnl f: r.o wl nr fin* **25/1**
00-6 **5** *1* **Caustic Wit (IRE)**[4] 2137 11-8-5 **55**.......................... CatherineGannon 6 55
(M S Saunders) *bhd: rdn and hung lft fnl 2f: nrst fin* **9/2**[2]
4604 **6** *1 1/4* **Young Ivanhoe**[10] 1958 4-7-13 **54** oh6..........................(v) AmyBaker[(5)] 3 50
(C A Dwyer) *led at str pce tl wknd jst ins fnl f* **10/1**
2545 **7** *1 1/2* **Sherjawy (IRE)**[10] 1970 5-8-5 **55**..........................(b) SimonWhitworth 1 46
(Miss Z C Davison) *bhd: sme hdwy 2f out: shkn up and no imp over 1f out* **8/1**
-000 **8** *1 1/2* **Fern House (IRE)**[18] 1723 7-7-11 **54** oh9........................ SeanPalmer[(7)] 7 41
(Bruce Hellier) *dwlt: bhd: rdn over 2f out: nvr a factor* **25/1**
30-0 **9** *3 3/4* **Charlie Delta**[17] 1775 6-9-1 **68**..........................(b) KevinGhunowa[(3)] 10 43
(R A Harris) *w ldrs tl hrd rdn and wknd 2f out* **9/2**[2]
0-60 **10** *2 1/2* **Lunces Lad (IRE)**[10] 1970 5-9-4 **68**..........................(v) GeorgeBaker 5 35
(G Brown) *mid-div: outpcd fr 1/2-way: rdn and n.d fnl 2f* **16/1**

1m 10.87s (0.67) **Going Correction** +0.05s/f (Good) **10** Ran SP% **120.1**
Speed ratings (Par 103): **97,96,95,95,94 92,90,88,83,80**
toteswinger: 1&2 £30.50, 1&3 £30.50, 2&3 £8.00 CSF £57.07 CT £183.13 TOTE £6.90: £2.00, £2.70, £1.50; EX 76.40 Place 6: £12.30 Place 5: £9.23.
Owner Miss K McManus **Bred** Mrs P Harford **Trained** Royston, Herts

FOCUS
A moderate race contested by horses largely out of form or deteriorating.
Lunces Lad(IRE) Official explanation: jockey said gelding had no more to give
T/Jkpt: £12,706.90 to a £1 stake. Pool: £35,794.21. 2.00 winning tickets. T/Plt: £26.00 to a £1 stake. Pool: £67,303.30. 1,884.80 winning tickets. T/Qpdt: £21.90 to a £1 stake. Pool: £3,194.40. 107.60 winning tickets. LM

2194 HAYDOCK (L-H)
Friday, May 22

OFFICIAL GOING: Heavy (soft in places; 5.6)
Rail realignment added 16yards to advertsied distances on the Round course.
Wind: Light 1/2 behind Weather: Overcast and damp

2225 TURFTV.CO.UK APPRENTICE H'CAP 5f
6:20 (6:21) (Class 5) (0-70,68) 4-Y-0+ **£3,238** (£963; £481; £240) **Stalls** Centre

Form RPR
0124 **1** **Imperial Sword**[14] 1832 6-8-9 **63**..........................(b) JanWilson[(5)] 16 73+
(T D Barron) *detached in last: gd hdwy and nt clr run over 1f out: burst through to ld ins fnl f: kpt on wl* **7/1**[3]
-000 **2** *2* **Tenancy (IRE)**[4] 2130 5-8-5 **54** oh4.............................. AdeleMulrennan 7 57
(R C Guest) *wnt lft s: sn chsng ldrs: kpt on to take 2nd wl ins fnl f* **16/1**
06-0 **3** *1 1/4* **Tartatartufata**[141] 2 7-9-1 **64**..........................(v) JamieKyne 11 62
(J G Given) *chsd ldrs stands' side: led over 2f out: hdd and fdd ins fnl f* **11/2**[2]
0-65 **4** *3/4* **Weet A Surprise**[64] 882 4-8-4 **58** ow1..........................(v[1]) DavidKenny[(5)] 9 53+
(J W Unett) *mid-div: hdwy on wd outside 2f out: kpt on same pce* **20/1**
0204 **5** *1 3/4* **Comptonspirit**[13] 1877 5-8-13 **65**.................................. PaulPickard[(3)] 17 54
(B P J Baugh) *chsd ldrs stands' side: kpt on same pce fnl 2f* **10/1**
4016 **6** *1/2* **Guto**[17] 1776 6-8-7 **59**.. RichardRowe[(3)] 2 46
(W J H Ratcliffe) *led over 2f: wknd over 1f out* **7/1**[3]
4-02 **7** *3/4* **King Of Swords (IRE)**[13] 1877 5-9-4 **67**............................ LeeNewnes 15 52
(N Tinkler) *chsd ldrs stands' side: effrt 2f out: no imp* **5/1**[1]
010- **8** *1/2* **Ingleby Star (IRE)**[236] 6308 4-8-9 **61**................................ NSLawes[(3)] 1 44
(N Wilson) *chsd ldrs on outside: wknd ins fnl f* **20/1**
5001 **9** *1/2* **Andrasta**[7] 2032 4-8-7 **56** 6ex.. BillyCray 13 37
(A Berry) *mid-div: drvn along over 2f out: wknd over 1f out* **11/1**
50-4 **10** *3 1/2* **Blazing Heights**[20] 1685 6-9-2 **68**............................ GarryWhillans[(3)] 10 36
(J S Goldie) *hld up: hdwy on outside over 2f out: wknd over 1f out: eased ins fnl f* **15/2**
6-00 **11** *3 1/2* **Town House**[86] 681 7-8-2 **54** oh9.................................. SoniaEaton[(3)] 3 10
(B P J Baugh) *wnt rt s: sn chsng ldrs: lost pl over 2f out* **66/1**
2460 **12** *hd* **Sofinella (IRE)**[2] 2180 6-8-2 **54** oh5............................ MatthewLawson[(3)] 5 9
(A W Carroll) *bmpd s: sn chsng ldrs: hun g lft and wknd 2f out* **12/1**
-000 **13** *4 1/2* **Angle Of Attack (IRE)**[10] 1951 4-9-2 **65**.............................. LanceBetts 14 4
(A D Brown) *w ldrs stands' side: lost pl 2f out* **12/1**

64.42 secs (3.92) **Going Correction** +0.875s/f (Soft) **13** Ran SP% **118.5**
Speed ratings (Par 103): **103,99,97,96,93 93,91,91,90,84 79,78,71**
toteswinger: 1&2 £31.30, 1&3 £9.90, 2&3 £30.10 CSF £110.11 CT £688.44 TOTE £6.70: £2.10, £5.90, £2.30; EX 188.00.
Owner Mrs Margaret Wilson **Bred** David John Brown **Trained** Maunby, N Yorks

FOCUS
They went off at a fast pace in this apprentice handicap.

2226 EUROPEAN BREEDERS' FUND MAIDEN FILLIES' STKS 6f
6:50 (6:50) (Class 5) 2-Y-O **£3,885** (£1,156; £577; £288) **Stalls** Centre

Form RPR
0 **1** **Ananda Kanda (USA)**[37] 1275 2-8-9 0.............................. LanceBetts[(5)] 4 70
(B Ellison) *dwlt: sn trcking ldrs: led 1f out: kpt on wl* **25/1**
2 *1 1/2* **Jeanie Johnston (IRE)** 2-8-9 0.................................. MartinLane[(5)] 9 66+
(K R Burke) *trckd ldrs: effrt over 2f out: hung lft: kpt on to take 2nd wl ins fnl f* **9/2**
4 **3** *1* **Refuse To Wait (IRE)**[14] 1847 2-9-0 0.............................. DavidAllan 7 63
(T D Easterby) *trckd ldrs: upsides over 1f out: kpt on same pce* **15/8**[1]
4 *nk* **Bitter Honey** 2-8-11 0.. AndrewMullen[(3)] 5 62
(Mrs G S Rees) *w ldr: edgd lft and led over 1f out: sn hdd and no ex* **14/1**
5 *5* **Ambrogina** 2-8-9 0.. JackDean[(5)] 10 47
(M Botti) *swvd rt s: mid-div: wknd over 1f out* **4/1**[3]

6 3 3/4 **Sweet Mirasol (IRE)** 2-9-0 0 ... RichardMullen 2 35
(K A Ryan) *chsd ldrs: lost pl over 2f out* **7/2**[2]

50 7 3/4 **Cariad Coch**[21] 1653 2-9-0 0 ... JamieMoriarty 6 33
(Mrs L Stubbs) *led tl over 1f out: sn wknd* **20/1**

0 8 15 **Chardonnay Star (IRE)**[6] 2089 2-9-0 0 ... PatrickMathers 1 —
(C J Teague) *sn wl outpcd and drvn along: wl bhd fnl 2f* **40/1**

1m 21.12s (7.12) **Going Correction** +0.95s/f (Soft) **8 Ran SP% 112.9**
Speed ratings (Par 90): **90,88,86,86,79 74,73,53**
toteswinger: 1&2 £13.50, 1&3 £7.50, 2&3 £3.30 CSF £129.50 TOTE £30.50: £4.50, £1.70, £1.30; EX 290.10.
Owner Koo's Racing Club **Bred** Lowell T Stevens **Trained** Norton, N Yorks

FOCUS
A maiden that was severely weakened by the withdrawal of the main form contender Baileys Vision. They went a fair pace considering the conditions. The winner was much improved on this different ground.

NOTEBOOK
Ananda Kanda(USA) sprang a 25-1 surprise. She was always in rear in a 5f Beverley maiden on debut but put in a much improved display up in trip on testing ground. It was fairly hard work, but she kept finding for pressure, and eventually won with some authority. Not much separated the first four and the form may not amount to much. However, the winner is a half-sister to seven winners, including the high-class 1m2f-1m6f winner and useful hurdler Red Moloney. She seems to have a resilient attitude, should stay further in time and could go on to better things. (op 16-1 tchd 14-1)
Jeanie Johnston(IRE) was having her first start. She looked inexperienced, but kept grinding away and showed some promise. She is a sister to the useful Marine Boy, a 6f winner at two who has produced his best form on a sound surface. (tchd 6-1)
Refuse To Wait(IRE) set the standard on her staying on fourth of nine in a 5f Ripon maiden auction this month. She was well backed and moved smoothly for a long way but failed to pick up. She may have got stuck in the sapping ground. (op 5-2 tchd 11-4 in places)
Bitter Honey has a sprinting pedigree and showed natural pace and some raw ability on her debut run. She should improve for the experience. (op 12-1 tchd 11-1)
Ambrogina is a 22,000gns half-sister to two three year-old winners in Italy at around 7f-1m. She was prominent in the market, but started slowly and faced an uphill struggle on her debut. She should know a lot more next time. (op 7-2 tchd 10-3)

2227 DRESSING ROOM 33 SCHOOL LANE H'CAP 6f
7:20 (7:22) (Class 4) (0-80,80) 3-Y-O **£5,504** (£1,637; £818; £408) **Stalls** Centre

Form RPR

25-0 1 **Suzie Quw**[13] 1869 3-8-10 77 ... MartinLane(5) 12 80
(K R Burke) *trckd ldrs: led over 2f out: hld on wl* **16/1**

10-6 2 1 1/4 **Moonlight Affair (IRE)**[20] 1686 3-8-10 72 ... TedDurcan 9 71
(E S McMahon) *trckd ldrs: chal over 1f out: kpt on same pce* **7/1**

1-60 3 shd **On Offer (IRE)**[25] 1561 3-8-11 73 ... DavidAllan 6 72+
(T D Easterby) *dwlt: effrt and swtchd far side 2f out: upsides 1f out: no ex* **8/1**

0-33 4 3 **Captain Scooby**[20] 1686 3-8-12 74 ... TonyCulhane 10 64
(R M Whitaker) *in tch on outer: effrt over 2f out: kpt on: nvr trbld ldrs* **3/1**[1]

35-0 5 4 **Soul Sista (IRE)**[34] 1345 3-8-8 75 ... JackDean(5) 13 53
(J L Spearing) *dwlt: kpt on fnl 2f: nvr nr ldrs* **10/1**

20-0 6 4 **Miss Hollybell**[15] 1814 3-8-10 72 ... DO'Donohoe 4 38
(J Gallagher) *led tl over 2f out: wknd over 1f out* **25/1**

000 7 2 1/4 **Hit The Switch**[3] 2160 3-8-1 66 oh4 ... (p) KellyHarrison(3) 3 25
(Patrick Morris) *w ldrs: wknd 2f out* **16/1**

3051 8 1/2 **Rio Royale (IRE)**[8] 2010 3-9-2 78 6ex ... AlanMunro 5 35
(Mrs A J Perrett) *chsd ldrs: lost pl over 1f out* **4/1**[2]

-622 9 8 **Kheylide (IRE)**[8] 2005 3-9-0 76 6ex ... SilvestreDeSousa 2 9
(Mrs D J Sanderson) *mid-div: lost pl over 2f out: sn bhd* **13/2**[3]

0-10 10 1 1/4 **Mister Laurel**[27] 1517 3-9-3 79 ... JamieMoriarty 8 9
(R A Fahey) *trckd ldrs: lost pl after 2f: bhd fnl 2f* **8/1**

1m 19.54s (5.54) **Going Correction** +0.95s/f (Soft) **10 Ran SP% 117.8**
Speed ratings (Par 101): **101,99,99,95,89 84,81,80,70,68**
toteswinger: 1&2 £24.00, 1&3 £24.30, 2&3 £10.00 CSF £124.75 CT £977.10 TOTE £14.80: £3.10, £2.70, £3.90; EX 109.70.
Owner Aricabeau Racing Limited **Bred** The National Stud **Trained** Middleham Moor, N Yorks

FOCUS
A decent handicap, involving a couple of last-time-out winners. The first three pulled clear of the fourth and there was an even bigger gap back to the rest.
Suzie Quw Official explanation: trainer had no explanation for the apparent improvement in form
Kheylide(IRE) Official explanation: jockey said gelding was unsuited by the heavy (soft in places) ground

2228 SUBSCRIBE ONLINE AT RACINGUK.COM H'CAP 5f
7:50 (7:51) (Class 4) (0-85,84) 4-Y-O+ **£6,476** (£1,927; £963; £481) **Stalls** Centre

Form RPR

0-04 1 **Equuleus Pictor**[6] 2095 5-8-7 78 ... JackDean(5) 13 93
(J L Spearing) *chsd ldrs: nt clr run and swtchd lft 2f out: led over 1f out: kpt on wl* **4/1**[1]

0030 2 3 **Luscivious**[36] 1313 5-8-0 73 ... (b) DeclanCannon(7) 11 77
(A J McCabe) *bmpd s: in rr: hdwy 2f out: styd on to take 2nd ins fnl f* **13/2**[3]

12-3 3 1 **Rocker**[20] 1672 5-8-11 77 ... RichardMullen 1 78
(G L Moore) *mid-div: hdwy over 2f out: kpt on fnl f* **8/1**

4-60 4 nse **Foxy Music**[52] 1052 5-8-13 79 ... EddieAhern 2 79
(E J Alston) *led: edgd rt over 2f out: hdd over f out: kpt on same pce* **8/1**

2-00 5 1 1/4 **The Jobber (IRE)**[30] 1457 8-9-4 84 ... TedDurcan 6 80
(M Blanshard) *chsd ldrs: outpcd over 2f out: kpt on fnl f* **22/1**

2423 6 1 **Rothesay Dancer**[7] 2032 6-8-4 73 ... KellyHarrison(3) 4 65
(J S Goldie) *sn outpcd and bhd: kpt on fnl f: nvr a factor* **6/1**[2]

5-00 7 1 1/4 **Bertoliver**[14] 1836 5-9-2 82 ... RichardSmith 12 70
(Tom Dascombe) *wnt lft s: chsd ldrs: edgd rt and wknd over f out* **14/1**

0-00 8 2 **Hotham**[14] 1849 6-9-1 81 ... JamieMoriarty 7 62
(N Wilson) *sn outpcd and in rr* **20/1**

0-00 9 3 1/2 **Lord Of The Reins (IRE)**[20] 1672 5-9-0 80 ... AlanMunro 8 48
(J G Given) *wnt rt s: chsd ldrs: outpcd over 2f out: sn wknd* **18/1**

230 10 2 1/4 **After The Show**[17] 1776 8-8-4 70 ... DO'Donohoe 14 30
(Rae Guest) *a in rr* **11/1**

0-02 11 hd **Divine Spirit**[6] 2095 8-8-7 73 ... RoystonFfrench 10 32
(M Dods) *hood removed v late: bmpd s: in rr: rdn and wknd 2f out* **4/1**[1]

64.87 secs (4.37) **Going Correction** +1.00s/f (Soft) **11 Ran SP% 119.2**
Speed ratings (Par 105): **105,100,98,98,96 94,92,89,84,80 80**
toteswinger: 1&2 £7.90, 1&3 £5.90, 2&3 £9.40 CSF £30.13 CT £205.51 TOTE £4.60: £1.90, £2.60, £2.90; EX 41.30.
Owner Masonaires **Bred** A J And Mrs L Brazier **Trained** Kinnersley, Worcs
■ Stewards' Enquiry : Eddie Ahern four-day ban: careless riding (Jun 7-10)

FOCUS
This sprint handicap was run at a blistering pace, but nothing really got into it from behind.
Foxy Music Official explanation: jockey said gelding hung right
Divine Spirit Official explanation: jockey said gelding never travelled

2229 GET RACING UK IN YOUR PUB 0870 351 8834 MAIDEN STKS 1m 30y
8:20 (8:21) (Class 5) 3-Y-O+ **£3,238** (£963; £481; £240) **Stalls** Low

Form RPR

03 1 **High Severa (IRE)**[7] 2030 3-8-9 0 ... MartinLane(5) 13 78
(K R Burke) *in tch: effrt over 3f out: led 1f out: hld on wl* **8/1**

2-2 2 1/2 **Proud Times (USA)**[17] 1769 3-9-0 0 ... AlanMunro 6 77
(G A Swinbank) *trckd ldrs: chal 1f out: no ex wl ins fnl f* **5/1**

23- 3 4 **Yirga**[189] 7311 3-9-0 0 ... (t) TedDurcan 12 68
(Saeed Bin Suroor) *hld up towards rr: hdwy over 3f out: kpt on one pce fnl 2f* **9/4**[1]

53 4 nse **Una Pelota (IRE)**[16] 1793 3-9-0 0 ... FrancisNorton 15 68+
(N J Vaughan) *t.k.h towards rr: drvn over 3f out: styd on wl fnl f* **11/4**[2]

6 5 1 3/4 **Present Alchemy**[34] 1355 3-9-0 0 ... EddieAhern 2 64+
(H Morrison) *trckd ldrs: smooth hdwy 3f out: led over 1f out: sn hdd: wknd* **7/2**[3]

0- 6 7 **Elements (IRE)**[154] 7735 3-8-9 0 ... DavidAllan 16 43
(E J Alston) *in rr: hdwy on wd outside over 3f out: chsng ldrs 2f out: edgd lft and sn wknd* **50/1**

0 7 6 **Red Chieftain (FR)**[21] 1636 4-9-5 0 ... DTDaSilva(7) 4 34
(Mrs H S Main) *led tl hdd & wknd over 1f out* **50/1**

8 4 1/2 **Shame The Devil (IRE)**[12] 4-9-12 0 ... JamieMoriarty 10 23
(Jonjo O'Neill) *s.i.s: reminders after s: sn chsng ldrs: edgd rt over 3f out: sn lost pl* **50/1**

9 3 **Anacot Steel (IRE)**[45] 4-9-12 0 ... SJCraine 14 17
(Patrick Morris) *s.i.s: a in rr* **100/1**

0 10 13 **Ellies Inspiration**[32] 1400 4-9-7 0 ... SilvestreDeSousa 7 —
(M Mullineaux) *chsd ldrs: lost pl over 3f out: sn bhd* **50/1**

5- 11 20 **Da Bomber (IRE)**[361] 2455 4-9-12 0 ... PatrickMathers 5 —
(J W Unett) *t.k.h in midfield: effrt 4f out: sn wknd: bhd whn eased ins fnl f: t.o* **40/1**

0 12 1/2 **Domada**[73] 793 4-9-4 0 ... (t) KellyHarrison(3) 11 —
(W J H Ratcliffe) *s.i.s: in rr: bhd whn eased ins fnl f* **125/1**

1m 53.68s (9.88) **Going Correction** +1.225s/f (Soft)
WFA 3 from 4yo 12lb **12 Ran SP% 119.5**
Speed ratings (Par 103): **99,98,94,94,92 85,79,75,72,59 39,38**
toteswinger: 1&2 £7.00, 1&3 £7.30, 2&3 £3.00 CSF £47.24 TOTE £10.40: £3.00, £2.10, £1.80; EX 55.60.
Owner Mogeely Stud & Mrs Maura Gittins **Bred** Crone Stud Farms Ltd **Trained** Middleham Moor, N Yorks
■ Stewards' Enquiry : Martin Lane four-day ban: used whip with excessive frequency (Jun 7-10)

FOCUS
A reasonable maiden run at a steady pace. The five market leaders filled the first five positions and the first two finished clear of the rest.
Ellies Inspiration Official explanation: jockey said filly ran too free

2230 THE CHARLATANS HERE ON 20TH JUNE STKS (H'CAP) 1m 2f 95y
8:50 (8:51) (Class 5) (0-75,78) 3-Y-O **£3,238** (£963; £481; £240) **Stalls** High

Form RPR

11 1 **Open Sesame (IRE)**[7] 2048 3-9-7 78 6ex ... AlanMunro 2 84+
(P W Chapple-Hyam) *trckd ldrs: t.k.h: led over 2f out: edgd rt: drvn out* **6/5**[1]

262- 2 3 3/4 **Tropical Blue**[216] 6808 3-8-13 75 ... JackDean(5) 8 74
(Jennie Candlish) *trckd ldrs: kpt on same pce appr fnl furlong* **16/1**

000- 3 1 1/4 **Sergeant Pink (IRE)**[214] 6857 3-8-9 66 ... EddieAhern 4 63
(S Gollings) *led tl over 2f out: sn hmpd: kpt on same pce* **33/1**

006- 4 1 3/4 **Brad's Luck (IRE)**[237] 6292 3-8-5 62 ... FrancisNorton 1 56
(M Blanshard) *t.k.h in midfield: hdwy whn hmpd bnd over 4f out: sn chsng ldrs: one pce fnl 2f* **16/1**

24-2 5 3/4 **Oriental Cavalier**[29] 1470 3-8-12 69 ... TedDurcan 14 61+
(R Hollinshead) *chsd ldrs: effrt over 3f out: wandered and n.m.r 2f out: wknd over 1f out* **4/1**[3]

34-5 6 3 1/2 **Hector's House**[22] 1629 3-8-11 68 ... JamieMoriarty 7 54
(M Dods) *s.i.s: hld up in rr: effrt over 3f out: edgd lft 2f out: sn wknd* **16/1**

31-5 7 4 **Hey Up Dad**[27] 1509 3-9-2 73 ... PhillipMakin 9 52
(M Dods) *hld up in rr: effrt over 3f out: edgd lft and sn wknd* **3/1**[2]

006- 8 1 3/4 **Short Sharp Shock**[182] 7402 3-8-5 62 ... SilvestreDeSousa 11 38
(J Mackie) *prominent: effrt over 3f out: wkng whn hmpd over 2f out* **33/1**

00-0 9 13 **Shanavaz**[24] 1595 3-8-8 65 ... DavidAllan 3 17
(Mrs G S Rees) *t.k.h in rr: hdwy whn hmpd bnd over 4f out: wknd 2f out: sn bhd and eased* **50/1**

2m 29.71s (16.71) **Going Correction** +1.225s/f (Soft) **9 Ran SP% 115.9**
Speed ratings (Par 99): **90,87,86,84,84 81,78,76,66**
Place 6: £217.57 Place 5: £50.54 toteswinger: 1&2 £6.00, 1&3 £11.40, 2&3 £28.20 CSF £24.07 CT £430.22 TOTE £2.20: £1.40, £3.20, £4.60; EX 20.60.
Owner Joy And Valentine Feerick **Bred** Glending Bloodstock **Trained** Newmarket, Suffolk
■ Stewards' Enquiry : Alan Munro two-day ban: careless riding (Jun 7-8)

FOCUS
A fair handicap run at a very steady pace.
Short Sharp Shock Official explanation: jockey said colt suffered interference in home straight
T/Plt: £229.30 to a £1 stake. Pool: £72,344.12. 230.30 winning tickets. T/Qpdt: £49.10 to a £1 stake. Pool: £4,601.36. 69.30 winning tickets. WG

2041 NEWCASTLE (L-H)
Friday, May 22

OFFICIAL GOING: Good to soft (soft in places; 6.7)
Wind: Fresh, half against Weather: Cloudy

2231 TARMAC MEDIAN AUCTION MAIDEN STKS 6f
2:10 (2:10) (Class 6) 2-Y-O **£2,590** (£770; £385; £192) **Stalls** Low

Form RPR

1 **Kaptain Kirkup (IRE)** 2-9-3 0 ... PhillipMakin 13 79
(M Dods) *trckd ldrs: led over 1f out: sn rdn: r.o strly fnl f* **16/1**

2 1 3/4 **Count Bertoni (IRE)** 2-9-3 0 ... MickyFenton 7 74+
(T P Tate) *dwlt: sn midfield: gd hdwy and ev ch over 1f out: rdn and one pce ins fnl f* **13/2**[3]

3 1 3/4 **Arabian Pride** 2-9-3 0 ... JamieSpencer 11 69+
(D M Simcock) *dwlt: hld up: gd hdwy and ev ch over 1f out: sn rdn and nt qckn* **3/1**[2]

4 4 1 1/4 **Hairs Vital (IRE)**[15] 1805 2-9-3 0 ... FrancisNorton 10 65
(E J O'Neill) *prom early: led over 2f out to over 1f out: sn one pce* **12/1**

3 5 4 1/2 **Reeds Bay (IRE)**[13] 1866 2-9-3 0 ... RichardMullen 12 51
(E S McMahon) *in tch: effrt and edgd lft over 2f out: sn outpcd* **5/4**[1]

	6	6	**Gold Story** 2-9-3 0 TomEaves 9	33
			(B Ellison) *missed break bhd tl styd on fnl 2f: nvr nrr* **28/1**	
5	7	½	**Valantino Oyster (IRE)**^{14} 1827 2-9-3 0 PaulMulrennan 4	32
			(J Howard Johnson) *midfield: drvn over 2f out: sn outpcd* **12/1**	
	8	½	**Bothwell Castle (IRE)** 2-9-0 0 KellyHarrison(3) 2	30
			(P C Haslam) *sn pushed along towards rr: nvr rchd ldrs* **50/1**	
	9	7	**Another Grand (IRE)** 2-9-3 0 JoeFanning 8	9
			(Mrs R A Carr) *led to over 2f out: sn rdn and btn* **33/1**	
0	10	shd	**Treasury Bond**^{13} 1867 2-9-3 0 JamieMoriarty 6	9
			(P T Midgley) *sn pushed along towards rr: outpcd fr 1/2-way* **150/1**	
6	11	7	**Arctic Destiny (IRE)**^{22} 1623 2-9-3 0 AndrewElliott 1	—
			(K R Burke) *racd alone far side tl wknd fr over 2f out* **22/1**	
04	12	2	**A Touch Of Luck**^{18} 1735 2-9-3 0 DuranFentiman 3	—
			(T D Easterby) *t.k.h early: cl up tl edgd lft and wknd over 2f out* **28/1**	

1m 17.06s (1.86) **Going Correction** +0.225s/f (Good) **12** Ran SP% **120.9**
Speed ratings (Par 91): **96,93,91,89,83 75,75,74,65,64 55,52**
toteswinger: 1&2 £41.80, 1&3 £7.60, 2&3 £4.80 CSF £111.62 TOTE £18.00: £4.20, £2.20, £1.70; EX 159.30 Trifecta £147.70 Part won. Pool: £199.70 - 0.20 winning units..
Owner Kevin Kirkup **Bred** David Barry **Trained** Denton, Co Durham
■ Stewards' Enquiry : Micky Fenton one-day ban: careless riding (Jun 7)

FOCUS
Probably a modest juvenile maiden. The main action was down the middle of the track and the first four finished clear.

NOTEBOOK
Kaptain Kirkup(IRE) went some way to repaying his £15,000 price tag by getting off the mark at the very first attempt. He showed a turn of foot on the easy surface and saw out the trip very well. His sire injects speed, but his dam is a middle-distance influence and so he ought to stay another furlong in due course. The market suggested the run would be of benefit, so there should be improvement to come.
Count Bertoni(IRE) showed up respectably on this racecourse bow and looked at home on the ground. His connections recently sent out a juvenile to score at the second attempt and he will hold decent claims on his next assignment. (op 7-1 tchd 9-1)
Arabian Pride, who cost 110,000gns purchase, is a half-brother to five previous winners, most notably Dubai's Touch and Grantley Adams. He was fancied to go close and looked big player when making up his ground from off the pace after 2f out. He ran green, however, when the gun was put to his head and that cost him. It is fair to expect him to go close next time out. (tchd 11-4 and 7-2)
Hairs Vital(IRE), representing the yard that won this last season, showed the benefit of his Goodwood debut 15 days earlier and is going the right way. A drop back to a stiff 5f may prove ideal in the short term, however. (op 10-1)
Reeds Bay(IRE) was very well backed to better his debut third at Haydock. His fate was sealed a fair way out and it may have been the different ground to blame, but he does now have something to prove. (op 6-4 tchd 11-10)
Gold Story, already gelded, hinted at ability considering he fell out of the gates and proved clueless early on. This initial experience should teach him plenty. (op 22-1)

2232 WARD HADAWAY MEDIAN AUCTION MAIDEN STKS 1m 4f 93y
2:45 (2:45) (Class 6) 3-4-Y-O **£2,590** (£770; £385; £192) **Stalls** Low

Form				RPR
5-3	1		**Final Victory**^{31} 1427 3-8-10 0 LPKeniry 3	80+
			(A M Balding) *led 4f: cl up: led and hung rt over 2f out: clr whn wandered ins fnl f: eased fnl 50yds* **6/4**^{1}	
-334	2	7	**Bagber**^{11} 1931 3-8-10 74 JimmyQuinn 5	66
			(H J L Dunlop) *prom: smooth hdwy and cl up 3f out: rdn: carried hd high and edgd lft 2f out: sn chsng wnr: r.o: no imp* **7/2**^{3}	
0/0-	3	6	**One Tou Many**^{299} 4461 4-9-5 0 KellyHarrison(3) 6	52
			(C W Fairhurst) *towards rr: pushed along over 5f out: styd on fr 2f out: nvr rchd ldrs* **150/1**	
325-	4	½	**Kaloni (IRE)**^{218} 6756 3-8-8 80 ow3 MickyFenton 1	52
			(Mrs P Sly) *midfield: hdwy to ld over 4f out: hdd over 2f out: lost 2nd and wknd over 1f out* **9/2**	
25-5	5	5	**Orthology (IRE)**^{6} 2084 3-8-10 82 (b^{1}) JamieSpencer 7	47
			(M H Tompkins) *t.k.h: sn pressing wnr: led after 4f to over 4f out: wknd over 2f out* **11/4**^{2}	
30	6	29	**Johnny Rocket (IRE)**^{6} 2090 4-9-13 0 PaulMulrennan 8	—
			(K A Ryan) *prom tl rdn and wknd fr 4f out* **50/1**	
	7	16	**Thornton George**^{47} 4-9-13 0 JamieMoriarty 2	—
			(T J Fitzgerald) *dwlt: bhd: pushed along over 5f out: sn struggling* **125/1**	

2m 46.83s (1.23) **Going Correction** +0.15s/f (Good)
WFA 3 from 4yo 17lb **7** Ran SP% **110.5**
Speed ratings (Par 101): **101,96,92,92,88 69,58**
toteswinger: 1&2 £3.50, 1&3 £18.40, 2&3 £11.40 CSF £6.62 TOTE £2.50: £1.30, £2.00; EX 6.10 Trifecta £220.90 Pool: £612.22 - 2.05 winning units.
Owner Sir Gordon Brunton **Bred** Sir Gordon Brunton **Trained** Kingsclere, Hants

FOCUS
An uncompetitive maiden.
Orthology(IRE) Official explanation: jockey said colt would not face first time blinkers

2233 CROFT TECHNOLOGY H'CAP 1m 4f 93y
3:20 (3:20) (Class 6) (0-60,58) 4-Y-0+ **£2,331** (£693; £346; £173) **Stalls** Low

Form				RPR
32-5	1		**Forrest Flyer (IRE)**^{27} 1506 5-9-1 55 PhillipMakin 10	67
			(I Semple) *in tch: hdwy to ld over 2f out: hld on wl fnl f* **5/1**^{1}	
3-21	2	1 ¼	**Kings Maiden (IRE)**^{11} 1936 6-9-4 58 6ex DarrenMoffatt 1	68+
			(James Moffatt) *hld up: hdwy over 2f out: ev ch ins fnl f: hld towards fin* **11/2**^{2}	
0043	3	2 ¾	**Holoko Heights**^{30} 1463 4-9-4 58 JamieSpencer 12	64+
			(N J Vaughan) *hld up in last: hdwy over 2f out: chsd ldrs ent fnl f: no further imp last 100yds* **6/1**^{3}	
0626	4	1 ½	**Wizard Looking**^{2} 2182 8-8-5 45 DuranFentiman 11	48
			(P T Midgley) *prom: effrt and ev ch over 2f out: one pce fnl f* **10/1**	
-000	5	2 ¼	**Altos Reales**^{86} 669 5-8-8 48 JimmyQuinn 9	48
			(J G Given) *in tch: effrt and ev ch over 2f out: outpcd fnl f* **18/1**	
530-	6	1 ¼	**Top Man Dan (IRE)**^{206} 7039 4-8-12 52 (t) GrahamGibbons 3	50
			(T D Walford) *midfield: effrt and rdn over 2f out: nvr able to chal* **9/1**	
325-	7	¾	**Piverina (IRE)**^{158} 7688 4-8-11 51 PaulMulrennan 8	47
			(Miss J A Camacho) *hld up: rdn 3f out: hdwy over 1f out: nvr able to chal* **16/1**	
315-	8	¾	**Sorrento Moon (IRE)**^{178} 6185 5-8-7 47 SilvestreDeSousa 7	42
			(G A Harker) *midfield: effrt and swtchd lft over 2f out: sn no imp* **22/1**	
154-	9	1	**Bollin Freddie**^{189} 7322 5-8-8 48 TonyHamilton 17	42
			(A J Lockwood) *cl up: ev ch over 2f out: edgd lft and wknd appr fnl f* **18/1**	
0/10	10	nk	**Mccormack (IRE)**^{13} 1883 7-8-7 52 PatrickDonaghy(5) 5	45
			(Miss T Jackson) *midfield: effrt 3f out: wknd over 1f out* **25/1**	
0-32	11	¾	**Greenbelt**^{21} 1654 8-9-1 55 TomEaves 6	47
			(G M Moore) *midfield: rdn 3f out: outpcd fnl 2f* **11/1**	
444-	12	nk	**Aston Lad**^{68} 7042 8-8-5 45 PaulHanagan 2	36
			(Micky Hammond) *hmpd sn after s: a bhd* **8/1**	
6134	13	8	**Elliwan**^{25} 1568 4-9-3 57 (b) DaleGibson 16	36
			(M W Easterby) *hld up: drvn 5f out: wknd over 3f out* **10/1**	
0-00	14	5	**Byron Bay**^{7} 2044 7-8-9 49 GregFairley 14	20
			(R Johnson) *plld hrd: trckd ldrs tl wknd over 2f out* **33/1**	
550-	15	20	**Orpen Bid (IRE)**^{264} 5544 4-8-5 45 AdrianTNicholls 15	—
			(A M Crow) *led to over 2f out: sn wknd* **66/1**	
52/0	16	4 ½	**Majestic Chief**^{18} 1738 5-9-2 56 (tp) JoeFanning 4	—
			(Miss Lucinda V Russell) *hld up: drvn 5f out: sn wknd* **50/1**	

2m 46.72s (1.12) **Going Correction** +0.15s/f (Good) **16** Ran SP% **125.0**
Speed ratings (Par 101): **102,101,99,98,96 96,95,95,94,94 93,93,88,84,71 68**
toteswinger: 1&2 £6.20, 1&3 £4.80, 2&3 £4.10 CSF £30.75 CT £175.78 TOTE £8.00: £2.10, £1.90, £1.90, £2.70; EX 27.40 Trifecta £85.00 Pool: £326.46 - 2.84 winning units.
Owner Mrs Camille Macdonald **Bred** Philip Lau **Trained** Carluke, S Lanarks

FOCUS
This weak handicap was wide open. It was run at a sound gallop and the form should work out.
Elliwan Official explanation: jockey said gelding never travelled

2234 MITIE CLAIMING STKS 6f
3:55 (3:55) (Class 6) 3-Y-O **£2,072** (£616; £308; £153) **Stalls** Low

Form				RPR
0335	1		**Blue Noodles**^{20} 1686 3-8-11 64 TonyHamilton 7	66
			(D W Barker) *mde all: rdn 2f out: hld on wl fnl f* **5/2**^{1}	
-004	2	1 ¾	**Nchike**^{3} 2154 3-8-11 63 (v) AdrianTNicholls 3	60
			(D Nicholls) *trckd ldrs: outpcd over 2f out: rallied to chse wnr ins fnl f: kpt on: no imp* **7/2**^{2}	
4204	3	¾	**Denton Diva**^{21} 1652 3-8-5 63 (v^{1}) PatrickDonaghy(5) 6	57
			(M Dods) *pressed wnr to ins fnl f: kpt on same pce* **9/2**^{3}	
-000	4	2 ¼	**Off Hand**^{18} 1725 3-8-2 50 DuranFentiman 5	42
			(T D Easterby) *bhd and sn drvn along: styd on fnl f: nvr rchd ldrs* **20/1**	
-033	5	½	**Aahaygirl (IRE)**^{52} 1045 3-9-4 70 AndrewElliott 1	56
			(K R Burke) *cl up tl edgd lft and outpcd wl over 1f out: n.d after* **6/1**	
-034	6	nse	**York Key Bar**^{29} 1469 3-9-5 61 TomEaves 2	57
			(B Ellison) *hld up: hdwy over 2f out: no imp fnl f* **14/1**	
0-66	7	4	**Meydan Groove**^{49} 1098 3-8-8 50 GrahamGibbons 4	33
			(R Johnson) *in tch: drvn and outpcd 1/2-way: btn over 1f out* **22/1**	
0	8	15	**Upper Key**^{13} 1888 3-9-1 0 JamieSpencer 8	—
			(K A Ryan) *cl up tl wknd over 2f out: eased whn no ch fnl f* **15/2**	

1m 16.45s (1.25) **Going Correction** +0.225s/f (Good) **8** Ran SP% **110.8**
Speed ratings (Par 97): **100,97,96,93,93 92,87,67**
toteswinger: 1&2 £2.90, 1&3 £2.00, 2&3 £3.60 CSF £10.48 TOTE £3.80: £1.30, £1.80, £1.70; EX 11.90 Trifecta £65.20 Pool: £611.44 - 6.93 winning units.
Owner Ian Bishop **Bred** P And Mrs A G Venner **Trained** Scorton, N Yorks

FOCUS
A poor 3yo claimer. There was no more than a fair pace on and the form appears straightforward enough.

2235 EMIRATES NEWCASTLE TO DUBAI H'CAP 7f
4:30 (4:31) (Class 5) (0-75,73) 4-Y-0+ **£3,238** (£963; £481; £240) **Stalls** Low

Form				RPR
4-06	1		**Golden Penny**^{21} 1646 4-9-0 72 NeilBrown(3) 11	81
			(A G Foster) *hld up: hdwy over 1f out: shkn up ins fnl f: styd on wl to ld nr fin* **14/1**	
3-34	2	½	**Bravely (IRE)**^{35} 1333 5-9-4 73 DuranFentiman 13	81
			(T D Easterby) *midfield: smooth hdwy to ld over 1f out: sn rdn: kpt on fnl f: hdd nr fin* **6/1**^{2}	
-560	3	1 ¼	**Navajo Joe (IRE)**^{18} 1737 4-9-1 70 LPKeniry 7	75
			(R Johnson) *hld up: gd hdwy over 1f out: edgd lft ins fnl f: nrst fin* **66/1**	
6342	4	2 ¼	**Ancient Cross**^{4} 2133 5-8-12 67 (b) DaleGibson 4	69+
			(M W Easterby) *dwlt: hld up: effrt whn nt clr run 2f out: kpt on fnl f: nvr rchd ldrs* **5/2**^{1}	
32-3	5	¾	**Mark Of Meydan**^{25} 1563 4-9-3 72 TomEaves 9	69
			(M Dods) *t.k.h: hld up: hdwy over 2f out: rdn and one pce fnl f* **7/1**^{3}	
60-0	6	1 ½	**Kalhan Sands (IRE)**^{17} 1766 4-9-3 72 GrahamGibbons 15	64
			(J J Quinn) *in tch: effrt over 2f out: nt qckn appr fnl f* **25/1**	
6-00	7	2	**Mr Lu**^{21} 1650 4-8-7 62 GregFairley 10	49
			(A G Foster) *taken early to post: t.k.h: prom: led and hung lft over 2f out: hdd over 1f out: wknd fnl f* **20/1**	
-000	8	hd	**He's A Humbug (IRE)**^{7} 2059 5-9-3 72 (v^{1}) JoeFanning 8	59
			(J O'Reilly) *towards rr: effrt over 2f out: sn no imp* **66/1**	
03-0	9	2	**Primo Way**^{19} 1690 8-8-4 66 ow5 (t) RossSmith(7) 12	47
			(D A Nolan) *cl up tl rdn and wknd over 2f out* **66/1**	
5600	10	¾	**Redwater River**^{32} 1413 5-8-5 60 FrancisNorton 14	39
			(Mrs R A Carr) *led to over 2f out: sn rdn and wknd* **9/1**	
-003	11	11	**Dream Express (IRE)**^{18} 1737 4-9-3 72 PhillipMakin 2	21
			(M Dods) *taken early to post: midfield: drvn 3f out: sn btn* **9/1**	
1224	12	1 ¾	**Ballycroy Boy (IRE)**^{29} 1480 4-8-9 67 (b) RussellKennemore(3) 5	12
			(Miss M E Rowland) *prom tl wknd over 3f out* **22/1**	
60-0	13	6	**Musca (IRE)**^{19} 1694 5-8-7 67 PatrickDonaghy(5) 6	—
			(J Wade) *s.s: a bhd* **16/1**	
3-33	14	9	**Business Class (BRZ)**^{17} 1769 4-8-6 62 AdrianTNicholls 3	—
			(D Nicholls) *chsd ldrs tl wknd over 3f out* **6/1**^{2}	

1m 29.68s (0.98) **Going Correction** +0.225s/f (Good) **14** Ran SP% **119.6**
Speed ratings (Par 103): **103,102,101,98,97 95,93,93,91,90 77,75,68,58**
CSF £89.58 CT £5424.35 TOTE £17.30: £5.30, £2.20, £4.70; EX 102.40 TRIFECTA Not won..
Owner J Ross **Bred** Mrs B D Oppenheimer **Trained** Haddington, East Lothian

FOCUS
There was a solid pace on in this modest handicap and the first six came from off the pace.
Golden Penny Official explanation: trainer said, regarding the apparent improvement in form, that the gelding was better suited by the softer ground.
Mr Lu Official explanation: jockey said gelding hung left-handed throughout
Musca(IRE) Official explanation: jockey said gelding was slow away
Business Class(BRZ) Official explanation: jockey said colt was unsuited by the good (good to soft places) ground

2236 DELOITTE NATIONAL H'CAP 1m 3y(S)
5:05 (5:07) (Class 6) (0-65,65) 3-Y-O **£2,331** (£693; £346; £173) **Stalls** Low

Form				RPR
1412	1		**Just Five (IRE)**^{21} 1656 3-8-12 64 PatrickDonaghy(5) 11	77
			(M Dods) *hld up: hdwy to ld over 2f out: pushed clr over 1f out: r.o strly* **9/1**^{3}	
5-62	2	2	**Cloudesley (IRE)**^{7} 2048 3-9-1 62 LPKeniry 13	70+
			(A M Balding) *towards rr: rdn 1/2-way: hdwy and edgd lft over 2f out: edgd rt and chsd wnr ins fnl f: r.o* **6/5**^{1}	

0-56 **3** *2* **Northern Flyer (GER)**29 1481 3-8-5 52 GrahamGibbons 9 56
(J J Quinn) *prom: effot over 2f out: no ex and lost 2nd ins fnl f* **20/1**

340- **4** *6* **Whispering Spirit (IRE)**234 6362 3-8-11 65 BMcHugh(7) 16 55
(Mrs A Duffield) *prom: effrt whn bmpd over 2f out: outpcd over 1f out* **33/1**

0-50 **5** *5* **Dark Echoes**6 2091 3-8-12 59 GregFairley 4 38
(Jedd O'Keeffe) *in tch: effrt 3f out: no imp fnl 2f* **40/1**

3-03 **6** *2 1/2* **Enhancing**28 1490 3-8-13 65 AmyRyan(5) 8 38
(A J McCabe) *sn prom: rdn 3f out: outpcd fr over 2f out* **16/1**

3262 **7** *nk* **Amazing Blue Sky**31 1441 3-8-10 60 (b) RussellKennemore(3) 14 32
(Mrs R A Carr) *led tl bdly bmpd and hdd over 2f out: sn no ex* **22/1**

0516 **8** *3/4* **Dante Deo (USA)**11 1926 3-8-11 58 JoeFanning 1 28
(T D Barron) *in tch: drvn whn n.m.r over 2f out: sn outpcd* **25/1**

060 **9** *1 1/4* **The Last Alzao (IRE)**32 1400 3-8-8 55 TonyHamilton 15 22+
(R A Fahey) *missed break: towards rr: hdwy whn hmpd over 3f out: n.m.r over 2f out: n.d* **9/1**3

0-60 **10** *nk* **Marillos Proterras**18 1724 3-8-4 51 oh3 (v1) FrancisNorton 17 18
(Mrs A Duffield) *prom: losing pl whn n.m.r over 2f out: n.d after* **28/1**

000 **11** *1/2* **Flynn's Island (IRE)**13 1888 3-8-6 53 DaleGibson 2 19
(M Dods) *bhd: drvn 1/2-way: nvr rchd ldrs* **33/1**

3-02 **12** *nk* **Island Chief**3 2154 3-8-12 59 (b) JamieSpencer 6 24
(K A Ryan) *cl up: ev ch whn dived bdly rt and bmpd over 2f out: sn btn* **8/1**2

00-0 **13** *2 1/4* **Sydney Cove (IRE)**7 2030 3-8-4 51 oh1 TWilliams 12 11
(R Allan) *bhd: drvn 1/2-way: nvr on terms* **50/1**

006- **14** *9* **Strevelyn**216 6811 3-8-4 51 oh3 DuranFentiman 3 —
(Mrs A Duffield) *bhd: rdn over 3f out: nvr on terms* **40/1**

443- **15** *2 3/4* **Royal Keva (IRE)**155 7720 3-9-1 65 NeilBrown(3) 7 —
(A D Brown) *prom tl wknd over 3f out* **33/1**

-000 **16** *2 1/4* **Woteva**6 2091 3-9-3 64 (p) TomEaves 5 —
(B Ellison) *bhd: rdn over 3f out: sn btn* **14/1**

4-6 **17** *8* **Haulage Lady (IRE)**18 1740 3-8-13 60 AdrianTNicholls 10 —
(Karen McLintock) *hld up: rdn and effrt whn hmpd over 2f out: sn btn* **22/1**

1m 45.77s (2.37) **Going Correction** +0.225s/f (Good) **17** Ran SP% **125.5**
Speed ratings (Par 97): **97,95,93,87,82 79,79,78,77,76 76,76,73,64,62 59,51**
CSF £17.77 CT £237.17 TOTE £11.50: £2.00, £1.10, £3.50, £8.70; EX 27.50 Trifecta £239.20 Part won. Pool: £323.39 - 0.63 winning units..

Owner Just Five Racing Partners **Bred** Rathbarry Stud **Trained** Denton, Co Durham

FOCUS
An already tricky-looking 3yo handicap was further complicated by the majority of the riders following early leader Jamie Spencer on the fair rail, before congregating to the middle of the track when became apparent that the two who had elected to race more towards the near side were at an advantage. The form is a bit dubious.

Island Chief Official explanation: jockey said colt hung badly both ways

Royal Keva(IRE) Official explanation: jockey said gelding was unsuited by the good (good to soft places) ground

Haulage Lady(IRE) Official explanation: jockey said filly lost its action

2237 SUPERBREAK MINI HOLIDAYS H'CAP — 1m 2f 32y
5:35 (5:36) (Class 6) (0-65,64) 4-Y-0+ **£2,331** (£693; £346; £173) **Stalls** Centre

Form RPR

0-54 **1** **Fell Pack**18 1724 5-8-9 55 DuranFentiman 2 63
(J J Quinn) *hld up in midfield: hdwy to ld ins fnl f: r.o wl* **14/1**

0-33 **2** *3/4* **Society Venue**18 1721 4-9-4 64 TonyHamilton 11 71
(Jedd O'Keeffe) *led: rdn 2f out: hdd ins fnl f: r.o* **12/1**

3122 **3** *1 1/4* **Safebreaker**6 2068 4-8-13 64 (p) AmyRyan(5) 13 68
(K A Ryan) *hld up: hdwy and prom over 1f out: kpt on same pce fnl 100yds* **7/4**1

03-4 **4** *nse* **Tour D'Amour (IRE)**106 399 6-8-4 50 (b) AdrianTNicholls 8 54
(R Craggs) *hld up: hdwy over 1f out: edgd lft and r.o fnl f* **50/1**

3-25 **5** *1 1/4* **Sudden Impulse**6 2068 8-8-13 62 NeilBrown(3) 12 64
(A D Brown) *bhd tl hdwy over 1f out: nrst fin* **11/1**3

606- **6** *1 1/4* **Shaylee**216 6806 4-8-7 53 GrahamGibbons 16 52
(T D Walford) *prom: effrt over 2f out: no ex ins fnl f* **12/1**

2246 **7** *2 1/4* **Quick Off The Mark**63 897 4-8-5 58 BMcHugh(7) 7 53
(J G Given) *prom: drvn over 2f out: btn fnl f* **20/1**

602- **8** *1/2* **Moscow Oznick**161 7656 4-9-0 60 JamieSpencer 3 54
(N J Vaughan) *dwlt: hld up: hdwy u.p over 1f out: n.d* **15/2**2

06-0 **9** *1/2* **Trouble Mountain (USA)**37 1279 12-8-12 58 (t) DaleGibson 1 51
(M W Easterby) *cl up: rdn over 2f out: wknd ent fnl f* **33/1**

2330 **10** *1/2* **Colonel Sherman (USA)**19 1690 4-8-13 62 RussellKennemore(3) 9 54
(P A Kirby) *prom tl wknd over 2f out* **25/1**

052- **11** *nk* **Tender Moments**271 5308 5-8-9 55 TomEaves 15 46
(B Smart) *midfield: drvn 3f out: no imp fnl 2f* **14/1**

5-60 **12** *1/2* **Moonstreaker**23 1615 6-8-13 62 MichaelJStainton(3) 14 52
(R M Whitaker) *t.k.h: midfield: hdwy after 4f: rdn and wknd over 2f out* **12/1**

4655 **13** *1 1/4* **Bourse (IRE)**21 1646 4-9-3 63 GregFairley 4 50
(A G Foster) *in tch tl rdn and wknd fr 3f out* **12/1**

4-31 **14** *5* **Agglestone Rock**77 485 4-9-1 64 LeeVickers(3) 6 41
(P A Kirby) *hld up: pushed along over 2f out: nvr on terms* **16/1**

00-5 **15** *2 1/2* **Three Gold Leaves**48 1127 4-8-11 57 (t) LPKeniry 5 29
(D W Thompson) *racd keenly in midfield: wknd 3f out: eased whn nt ch* **66/1**

-050 **16** *1 1/4* **Heart Of Dubai (USA)**10 1955 4-8-5 56 PatrickDonaghy(5) 10 26
(Micky Hammond) *bhd: rdn 4f out: sn btn* **50/1**

2m 15.35s (3.45) **Going Correction** +0.15s/f (Good) **16** Ran SP% **123.4**
Speed ratings (Par 101): **92,91,90,90,89 88,86,86,85,85 85,84,83,79,77 76**
toteswinger: 1&2 £27.00, 1&3 £10.40, 2&3 £5.50 CSF £164.46 CT £447.53 TOTE £22.50: £3.10, £2.50, £1.10, £11.40; EX 243.40 Trifecta £206.60 Part won. Pool: £323.39 - 0.50 winning units. Place 6: £57.85 Place 5: £18.74.

Owner N Hetherton **Bred** N Hetherton **Trained** Settrington, N Yorks

FOCUS
A moderate handicap, run at a good early pace before it was slowed up going into the home turn.
T/Plt: £81.80 to a £1 stake. Pool: £61,276.95. 546.74 winning tickets. T/Qpdt: £20.80 to a £1 stake. Pool: £4,331.70. 153.60 winning tickets. RY

2082 NEWMARKET (R-H)
Friday, May 22

OFFICIAL GOING: Good to firm (8.1)
Wind: Light half-behind Weather: Overcast

2238 EUROPEAN BREEDERS' FUND MAIDEN FILLIES' STKS — 6f
2:20 (2:20) (Class 4) 2-Y-O **£5,180** (£1,541; £770; £384) **Stalls** Low

Form RPR

25 **1** **Bell's Ocean (USA)**7 2047 2-9-0 0 JerryO'Dwyer 3 75
(J Ryan) *mde all: shkn up over 1f out: r.o wl* **11/4**1

5 **2** *2* **Fasilight**11 1939 2-8-9 0 AndreaAtzeni(5) 6 69
(M Botti) *chsd ldrs: ev ch over 1f out: sn rdn and hung lft: styd on same pce ins fnl f* **11/4**1

3 *3/4* **I'mneverwrong (IRE)** 2-9-0 0 MartinDwyer 4 67+
(D R C Elsworth) *dwlt: in rr: pushed along over 2f out: hdwy over 1f out: styd on: nt trble ldrs* **7/1**

4 *1 1/2* **Tarita (IRE)** 2-9-0 0 RichardHughes 2 62
(R Hannon) *s.i.s: sn prom: shkn up over 2f out: ev ch over 1f out: sn rdn: hung rt and no ex ins fnl f* **3/1**2

5 **5** *1/2* **Gulf Punch**10 1968 2-9-0 0 RyanMoore 5 61
(R Hannon) *chsd wnr: rdn 1/2-way: wknd fnl f* **9/2**3

1m 13.06s (0.86) **Going Correction** -0.10s/f (Good) **5** Ran SP% **109.0**
Speed ratings (Par 92): **90,87,86,84,83**
toteswinger: 1&2 £7.20 CSF £10.33 TOTE £2.90: £1.70, £1.40; EX 8.70.

Owner Ocean Trailers Ltd **Bred** Brereton C Jones **Trained** Newmarket, Suffolk

FOCUS
This was not a strong maiden for Newmarket, but there was an open betting market with three fillies vying for favouritism. The winner and third should improve for the run.

NOTEBOOK
Bell's Ocean(USA), runner-up on her debut at Windsor before finishing fifth in a decent race here next time, was the most experienced filly on show and she put her know how to good use. Breaking smartly from the stalls and making all, she showed a likeable attitude to see off the runner-up and was pulling away late on. Her trainer thinks a bit of her and she could go for the Queen Mary at Ascot, where the stiff 5f would not be a problem, although that Group 2 event would surely be flying too high. (op 3-1 tchd 5-2)
Fasilight, a place behind Thursday's Haydock winner Daniella De Bruijn when fifth on her debut at Yarmouth, travelled strongly on the outside of the bunch but perhaps could have done with a bit of cover. She had her chance but gave best well inside the final furlong to what looked a tougher filly. Easier ground should see her off the mark. (op 7-2)
I'mneverwrong(IRE) ◆ stood still as the stalls opened before coming through nicely for third under a fairly considerate ride. Quite a scopey filly, she will get a bit further than this and will have definitely learned from this debut run. (op 8-1)
Tarita(IRE), a sprint-bred newcomer whose sales price halved as a yearling, tracked the pace on the rail and briefly threatened to play a part in the finish before fading. She may be worth another chance on an easier surface. (op 11-4 tchd 5-2)
Gulf Punch, a stablemate of the fourth who was never nearer on her debut over an extended 5f at Warwick, came under pressure at around halfway and dropped away to finish last. (op 10-3)

2239 PETERS ELWORTHY & MOORE CHARTERED ACCOUNTANTS H'CAP — 1m 2f
2:55 (2:56) (Class 4) (0-85,85) 4-Y-0+ **£5,828** (£1,734; £866; £432) **Stalls** Low

Form RPR

1-66 **1** **Bullet Man (USA)**24 1593 4-8-13 80 RyanMoore 6 89+
(L M Cumani) *s.i.s: sn rcvrd to ld: set stdy pce tl qcknd 3f out: rdn out* **15/8**1

0405 **2** *1 3/4* **Baylini**13 1859 5-8-13 80 JamesDoyle 4 85
(Ms J S Doyle) *dwlt: sn prom: nt clr run over 1f out: swtchd rt and r.o wl ins fnl f: nt rch wnr* **11/2**

4-21 **3** *hd* **Special Reserve (IRE)**15 1812 4-9-1 82 RichardHughes 2 87
(R Hannon) *chsd wnr tl nt clr run over 1f out: sn rdn: styd on* **11/4**2

215- **4** *2 1/4* **Spell Caster**244 6128 4-9-3 84 SebSanders 5 85
(R M Beckett) *hld up: swtchd rt and hdwy over 2f out: rdn to chse wnr over 1f out: sn hung lft: wknd ins fnl f* **6/1**

1540 **5** *7* **Wasp (AUS)**20 1684 7-9-4 85 RobertHavlin 7 72
(W Jarvis) *chsd ldrs: rdn over 2f out: wknd over 1f out* **9/2**3

456- **6** *3 1/2* **Regional Counsel**429 929 5-9-1 82 WilliamBuick 1 62
(A M Hales) *hld up: a in rr: wknd 2f out* **16/1**

2m 6.40s (0.60) **Going Correction** -0.10s/f (Good) **6** Ran SP% **115.2**
Speed ratings (Par 105): **93,91,91,89,84 81**
toteswinger: 1&2 £4.00, 1&3 £2.30, 2&3 £2.90 CSF £13.17 TOTE £2.70: £1.50, £3.20; EX 12.10.

Owner Kevin Bailey & Ms Nicola Mahoney **Bred** Stillmeadow Farm Llc **Trained** Newmarket, Suffolk

FOCUS
A fair handicap but there were doubts over most of the field coming into the race. It turned into a tactical affair and the form looks a little dubious, but the winner is the type to rate higher.

2240 LIAM SHERIDAN RACING MAIDEN STKS — 1m 2f
3:30 (3:31) (Class 4) 3-Y-O **£5,180** (£1,541; £770; £384) **Stalls** Low

Form RPR

2-4 **1** **London Bridge**55 998 3-9-3 0 JimmyFortune 3 82+
(J H M Gosden) *led 9f out: rdn and hung lft over 1f out: drvn out* **11/10**1

6 **2** *2 1/2* **Senses (USA)**18 1730 3-9-3 0 WilliamBuick 8 77
(J Noseda) *a.p: chsd wnr over 3f out: sn rdn: edgd lft over 1f out: styd on same pce* **3/1**2

00 **3** *9* **Bicksta**14 1825 3-8-12 0 RichardHughes 4 54
(E F Vaughan) *led 1f: chsd wnr tl over 3f out: rdn 2f out: wknd and hung rt fnl f* **66/1**

4 *1/2* **Best Tune** 3-8-12 0 ShaneKelly 5 53
(J Noseda) *prom: rdn over 2f out: sn wknd* **16/1**

0 **5** *4* **Twist Again (IRE)**10 1963 3-8-12 0 JimCrowley 6 45
(P Howling) *hld up: rdn: edgd rt and wknd over 2f out* **28/1**

6 *9* **Galiotto (IRE)** 3-9-0 0 JackMitchell(3) 1 32
(C F Wall) *s.s: a in rr: rdn and wknd over 3f out* **10/1**

0 **7** *16* **Golden Ring**37 1289 3-9-3 0 RobertHavlin 2 —
(P J O'Gorman) *prom: rdn over 3f out: sn hung rt and wknd* **100/1**

8 *6* **Madison Park (IRE)** 3-9-3 0 TPQueally 7 —
(H R A Cecil) *dwlt: sn pushed along in rr: rdn and wknd over 3f out: eased* **4/1**3

2m 5.86s (0.06) **Going Correction** -0.10s/f (Good) **8** Ran SP% **113.5**
Speed ratings (Par 101): **95,93,85,85,82 75,62,57**
toteswinger: 1&2 £1.80, 1&3 £11.00, 2&3 £25.50 CSF £4.43 TOTE £1.80: £1.10, £1.50, £5.00; EX 5.50.

Owner K Abdulla **Bred** Juddmonte Farms Ltd **Trained** Newmarket, Suffolk

FOCUS
A weakish maiden for the track, and only steadily run. There is little depth in this although the first two are rated slight improvers.
Madison Park(IRE) Official explanation: jockey said colt ran green

2241 EDMONDSON HALL SOLICITORS & SPORTS LAWYERS H'CAP 7f
4:05 (4:05) (Class 3) (0-95,93) 4-Y-O+ **£9,066** (£2,697; £1,348; £673) **Stalls** Low

Form RPR
221- **1** **Roaring Forte (IRE)**[237] 6283 4-9-4 **93** LiamJones 3 107
(W J Haggas) *mde all: shkn up and edgd rt over 1f out: r.o wl* **5/2**[2]
2-1 **2** 2 ½ **Tryst**[21] 1636 4-8-12 **87** RyanMoore 2 98+
(Sir Michael Stoute) *hld up: rdn over 1f out: r.o to go 2nd ins fnl f: nt rch wnr* **5/6**[1]
050- **3** 3 **Golden Desert (IRE)**[230] 6478 5-9-0 **89** WilliamBuick 5 89
(T G Mills) *chsd wnr: rdn and edgd rt over 1f out: wknd ins fnl f* **15/2**
-500 **4** 1 **Giganticus (USA)**[13] 1861 6-9-0 **92** PatrickHills(3) 6 89
(B W Hills) *stdd and dropped in sn after s: racd keenly: hdwy over 2f out: rdn over 1f out: wknd ins fnl f* **11/2**[3]
0-04 **5** ¾ **Barons Spy (IRE)**[7] 2059 8-8-8 **83** JamesDoyle 7 78
(R J Price) *chsd ldrs: rdn over 2f out: wknd fnl f* **16/1**
000- **6** 14 **Binanti**[281] 5030 9-8-11 **86** JimCrowley 1 43
(P R Chamings) *prom: rdn and wknd over 1f out* **50/1**

1m 22.82s (-2.58) **Going Correction** -0.10s/f (Good) **6 Ran SP% 118.1**
Speed ratings (Par 107): **110,107,103,102,101 85**
toteswinger: 1&2 £1.50, 1&3 £2.50, 2&3 £2.40 CSF £5.31 CT £12.25 TOTE £3.10: £1.70, £1.30; EX 5.60.
Owner Flying Tiger Partnership **Bred** Grangecon Stud **Trained** Newmarket, Suffolk

FOCUS
A decent handicap which saw the fourth winner from as many races to make just about all, but this time there was a true gallop on. The winner proved he is just as effective on turf but the runner-up looks sure to do better.

NOTEBOOK
Roaring Forte(IRE) had successfully adopted front-running tactics when winning at Great Leighs on his last start back in September, and raced off a 7lb higher mark on this return to turf. Down a furlong in trip, he set a sound pace and it was apparent some way out that he had his pursuers in trouble. On the upgrade, he may go to Royal Ascot next month, either for the Buckingham Palace Handicap over this trip or the Hunt Cup back at a mile. (op 10-3 tchd 4-1)
Tryst ♦, a Polytrack maiden winner, was well supported ahead of this handicap debut. Held up, and still at the back of the field with a quarter of a mile to run, a clear passage soon opened up for him and he came through to go after the winner, but he was never going to get to him. He beat the rest well enough and should not be written off on a more forgiving surface, particularly bearing in mind the apparent bias on the day against hold-up horses. (tchd 8-11 and 10-11, 1-1 in places and 11-10 in places)
Golden Desert(IRE), whose best turf efforts last term came at Ascot, could not find a change of gear on this seasonal bow and looks high enough in the weights. (op 8-1 tchd 7-1)
Giganticus(USA) had his optimum conditions of 7f on fast ground and ran respectably, racing on the outer and keeping on willingly, but no match for a couple of progressive types in the end. (op 7-1 tchd 8-1)
Barons Spy(IRE) was officially a pound well in after a good effort over 6f at York last week but was found wanting on this very different ground.
Binanti has not won since taking the Buckingham Palace Handicap at Ascot two years ago and was the first beaten on this seasonal debut. (op 33-1)

2242 NEWMARKETRACECOURSES.CO.UK H'CAP 1m 4f
4:40 (4:41) (Class 3) (0-90,87) 4-Y-O+ **£9,066** (£2,697; £1,348; £673) **Stalls** Centre

Form RPR
6-01 **1** **Martyr**[18] 1750 4-9-2 **85** RichardHughes 4 93+
(R Hannon) *led 2f: chsd ldrs: shkn up over 2f out: rdn to ld wl ins fnl f* **4/1**[2]
6026 **2** ¾ **John Terry (IRE)**[72] 801 6-9-4 **87** JimCrowley 5 93
(Mrs A J Perrett) *led 10f out: hdd over 8f out: chsd ldr tl led over 1f out: rdn and hdd wl ins fnl f* **17/2**
43-0 **3** ¾ **Relative Strength (IRE)**[25] 1571 4-8-8 **77** (v[1]) WilliamBuick 8 82
(A M Balding) *prom: pushed along over 4f out: rdn and hung rt 2f out: styd on ins fnl f: nt rch ldrs* **8/1**
1002 **4** 1 **Sgt Schultz (IRE)**[11] 1944 6-8-7 **76** MartinDwyer 6 79
(J S Moore) *trckd ldrs: plld hrd: led over 8f out: rdn and hdd over 1f out: no ex ins fnl f* **14/1**
12-4 **5** ½ **Lochiel**[111] 360 5-9-4 **87** JimmyFortune 1 90
(G A Swinbank) *wnt lft s: hld up: racd keenly: hdwy and nt clr run 2f out: swtchd rt and sn rdn: styd on same pce ins fnl f* **11/2**[3]
6 1 ½ **War Party**[207] 5-9-2 **85** DarryllHolland 3 85+
(Dr R D P Newland) *hld up: racd keenly: outpcd 3f out: r.o ins fnl f* **20/1**
3 **7** 1 ¼ **Rangefinder**[14] 1850 5-9-0 **83** RyanMoore 7 81
(L M Cumani) *chsd ldrs: rdn and hung rt over 2f out: wknd fnl f* **7/4**[1]
1202 **8** 2 ½ **King Olav (UAE)**[20] 1666 4-9-3 **86** ShaneKelly 2 80+
(A W Carroll) *hld up: rdn over 3f out: a in rr* **10/1**

2m 30.09s (-3.41) **Going Correction** -0.10s/f (Good) **8 Ran SP% 113.9**
Speed ratings (Par 107): **107,106,106,105,105 104,103,101**
toteswinger: 1&2 £21.00, 1&3 £58.40, 2&3 £31.40 CSF £37.12 CT £257.74 TOTE £5.00: £2.10, £2.40, £2.80; EX 35.00.
Owner Highclere Thoroughbred Racing (Delilah) **Bred** D Maroun **Trained** East Everleigh, Wilts

FOCUS
A fair handicap which was run at only an ordinary pace and resulted in something of a bunch finish. The race is rated athrough the fourth to recent form.

NOTEBOOK
Martyr, stepped up to this trip for the first time and raised 4lb for his win at Windsor, secured the early lead, but he was soon headed and his jockey had to be content with tracking the pace in about fourth. He produced a good run to snatch the race in the last half-furlong and remains progressive. Future plans are fluid but he is likely to continue over 1m4f. (tchd 5-1)
John Terry(IRE) has been freshened up by a break following an all-weather campaign. He was back in front going to the final furlong only to succumb to the winner's late charge, and remains frustrating. (op 8-1 tchd 7-1)
Relative Strength(IRE) had disappointed on his return at Windsor but ran a better race on this faster ground with the visor fitted for the first time, without giving the impression that he was putting it all in. (tchd 9-1)
Sgt Schultz(IRE), runner-up to the promising Falcativ in a four-horse race last time, went on with over a mile to go but could not hold on approaching the last. This was a fair run but he is still awaiting his first win on turf. (op 11-1 tchd 9-1)
Lochiel, off since January, was 10lb higher than when last seen on grass and has shown a liking for cut in the ground in the past, so this was a pleasing effort. (op 7-1 tchd 8-1)
War Party ♦, a winner over this trip for Ellie Lellouche at Longchamp last year, was keen early on before staying steadily from the rear in the latter stages. This was a pleasing debut for connections and he is one to keep an eye on when tackling easier ground. Official explanation: jockey said gelding was unsuited by the good to firm ground (op 22-1 tchd 16-1)
Rangefinder dropped away disappointingly after showing prominently. It could have been the fast ground that was to blame rather than the longer trip, which he had promised to stay. (op 15-8 tchd 2-1)
King Olav(UAE) made the running when second at Goodwood but adopted different tactics and was below par. (tchd 8-1)

2243 NEWMARKETEXPERIENCE.CO.UK H'CAP 1m
5:15 (5:16) (Class 5) (0-75,75) 4-Y-O+ **£3,885** (£1,156; £577; £288) **Stalls** Low

Form RPR
0-50 **1** **Thunder Gorge (USA)**[23] 1603 4-9-0 **71** WilliamBuick 10 78
(Mouse Hamilton-Fairley) *racd centre: mde all: rdn over 1f out: styd on* **7/1**
63-2 **2** 1 **Indian Skipper (IRE)**[15] 1812 4-9-4 **75** LiamJones 11 80
(M H Tompkins) *racd centre: chsd wnr: rdn and hung over to stands' side over 1f out: led that gp ins fnl f: styd on* **4/1**[2]
0-26 **3** 1 ¼ **Steig (IRE)**[19] 1690 6-8-12 **69** JamesDoyle 7 71
(George Baker) *led stands' side gp and up w the pce in the centre: rdn and hdd in his gp ins fnl f: styd on same pce* **10/1**
0-51 **4** nk **Charlevoix (IRE)**[22] 1633 4-9-0 **71** TPQueally 4 72+
(C F Wall) *racd stands' side: hld up in tch: rdn over 1f out: styd on* **11/2**[3]
6-12 **5** 3 ¼ **Driven (IRE)**[14] 1833 4-9-4 **75** JimCrowley 5 69
(Mrs A J Perrett) *racd stands' side: chsd ldr: rdn over 2f out: no ex fnl f* **7/2**[1]
004- **6** 2 ¾ **Sonny Parkin**[231] 6446 7-8-7 **71** SimonPearce(7) 9 59+
(J Pearce) *racd stands' side: hld up: rdn whn nt clr run and swtchd lft over 1f out: n.d* **12/1**
0-50 **7** 1 ½ **Bahiano (IRE)**[51] 1067 8-8-13 **70** RyanMoore 2 54
(C E Brittain) *racd stands' side: mid-div: rdn over 2f out: edgd rt and wknd over 1f out* **7/1**
-530 **8** 1 ½ **Marning Star**[18] 1750 4-9-0 **71** ShaneKelly 8 52
(Ian Williams) *racd stands' side: chsd ldrs: rdn 1/2-way: wknd 2f out* **9/1**
3- **9** 17 **Crystal Crown (IRE)**[21] 7374 5-8-10 **67** (t) MartinDwyer 3 9
(B G Powell) *racd stands' side: chsd ldrs tl rdn and wknd over 2f out* **28/1**
5-00 **10** 1 ½ **Hennessy Island (USA)**[86] 669 4-7-12 **62** oh11 ow1 DToole(7) 6 —
(T G Mills) *s.i.s: racd stands' side: a in rr: rdn and wknd 1/2-way* **33/1**

1m 37.73s (-0.87) **Going Correction** -0.10s/f (Good) **10 Ran SP% 115.8**
Speed ratings (Par 103): **100,99,97,97,94 91,89,88,71,69**
toteswinger: 1&2 £4.30, 1&3 £4.40, 2&3 £15.80 CSF £34.88 CT £282.02 TOTE £8.50: £2.20, £1.40, £3.40; EX 43.50.
Owner Bramshill Racing **Bred** Camelia Casby **Trained** Bramshill, Hants

FOCUS
A modest handicap and another all-the-way winner. The two highest-drawn runners raced down the centre, away from the others, and ended up finishing first and second although the runner-up tacked over to the main group late on. The third home led the main body of the field. The runner-up is the best guide to the level.

2244 BOLLINGER CHAMPAGNE CHALLENGE SERIES H'CAP (FOR GENTLEMAN AMATEUR RIDERS) 1m 2f
5:50 (5:52) (Class 5) (0-70,70) 4-Y-O+ **£3,123** (£968; £484; £242) **Stalls** Low

Form RPR
4-04 **1** **Jo'Burg (USA)**[16] 1785 5-11-0 **63** MrSWalker 3 71
(Lady Herries) *hld up: pushed along 1/2-way: hdwy over 3f out: rdn to ld over 1f out: hung lft ins fnl f: styd on* **7/2**[2]
4033 **2** 1 ½ **Comrade Cotton**[10] 1961 5-10-2 **56** oh1 MrJohnEnnis(5) 12 62+
(J Ryan) *hld up: hdwy over 3f out: nt clr run and swtchd lft over 1f out: r.o: nt rch wnr* **20/1**
663- **3** 2 ¼ **Sir Boss (IRE)**[266] 5458 4-11-0 **70** MrOJMurphy(7) 10 71
(D E Cantillon) *s.i.s: sn mid-div: hdwy 1/2-way: rdn and ev ch over 1f out: styd on same pce ins fnl f* **6/1**[3]
3-53 **4** 2 ½ **King Columbo (IRE)**[7] 2052 4-11-1 **69** MrRBirkett(5) 8 65
(Miss J Feilden) *chsd ldrs: led over 2f out: rdn and hdd over 1f out: wknd towards fin* **11/4**[1]
0-06 **5** ½ **Gallego**[14] 1845 7-10-10 **64** MrMPrice(5) 4 59+
(R J Price) *s.s: bhd: hdwy over 1f out: wknd ins fnl f* **12/1**
5240 **6** 4 ½ **Cragganmore Creek**[31] 1442 6-10-2 **56** oh11 (p) MrBMMorris(5) 1 42
(D Morris) *chsd clr ldr tl rdn 1/2-way: wknd 2f out* **33/1**
60-0 **7** ¾ **Stormy Summer**[39] 1260 4-10-4 **60** (t) MrJMQuinlan(7) 6 44
(R W Price) *chsd ldrs: rdn over 3f out: wknd over 2f out* **14/1**
2665 **8** nse **Wester Lodge (IRE)**[11] 1936 7-10-1 **57** MrDJEustace(7) 2 41
(J M P Eustace) *chsd ldrs: lost pl 1/2-way: in rr whn nt clr run and swtchd rt over 1f out* **11/1**
2621 **9** 3 ¾ **Chalice Welcome**[10] 1961 6-11-1 **64** MrRHFowler 9 40
(N B King) *hld up: hdwy u.p over 2f out: wknd over 1f out* **10/1**
6330 **10** 4 **Bavarica**[14] 1834 7-10-9 **63** MrJPFeatherstone(5) 11 31
(Miss J Feilden) *s.i.s: hld up: a in rr: wknd and eased wl over 1f out* **16/1**
3004 **11** 2 **Cape Of Luck (IRE)**[15] 1807 6-10-5 **57** (b) BrianToomey(3) 7 21
(P M Phelan) *chsd ldrs: rdn over 3f out: hung lft and wknd over 1f out* **14/1**
000/ **12** 21 **Neboisha**[569] 6587 5-10-2 **56** oh11 (b[1]) MrSRees(5) 5 —
(M Wigham) *led and sn wl clr: wknd and hdd over 2f out* **50/1**

2m 6.37s (0.57) **Going Correction** -0.10s/f (Good) **12 Ran SP% 117.2**
Speed ratings (Par 103): **93,91,90,88,87 84,83,83,80,77 75,58**
toteswinger: 1&2 £27.00, 1&3 £10.40, 2&3 £5.50 CSF £74.38 CT £411.95 TOTE £3.80: £2.00, £4.00, £2.80; EX 97.00 Place 6: £32.50 Place 5: £20.53.
Owner Seymour Bloodstock (uk) Ltd **Bred** Tim Cooper **Trained** Patching, W Sussex

FOCUS
A moderate handicap for amateurs. The rest of the field ignored the tearaway leader Neboisha. The form is rated around the placed horses.

T/Plt: £75.60 to a £1 stake. Pool: £71,464.10. 689.36 winning tickets. T/Qpdt: £20.20 to a £1 stake. Pool: £4,764.28. 173.84 winning tickets. CR

[1610]PONTEFRACT (L-H)

Friday, May 22

OFFICIAL GOING: Good (8.4)

A false rail was in plcae from 6f to the finish to provide fresh ground but impact on distances not notified.

Wind: Virtually nil Weather: Overcast

2245 ST. JOHN AMBULANCE H'CAP — 1m 4y

6:30 (6:30) (Class 5) (0-70,70) 4-Y-0+ — **£3,238** (£963; £481; £240) **Stalls** Low

Form — RPR

0-06 **1** **Marvo**[4] 2133 5-9-0 **66**.......... SebSanders 3 — 79
(M H Tompkins) *hld up towards rr: hdwy 3f out: swtchd outside and rdn over 1f out: styd on to ld jst ins fnl f: kpt on wl* **4/1**[1]

440- **2** *3* **Tamasou (IRE)**[237] 6287 4-8-13 **65**.......... RichardKingscote 6 — 71
(Garry Moss) *trckd ldrs: hdwy over 2f out: rdn to ld over 1f out: drvn and hdd jst ins fnl f: kpt on same pce* **22/1**

0500 **3** *2¾* **Direct Debit (IRE)**[31] 1415 6-9-1 **67**.......... SteveDrowne 5 — 66
(M Wellings) *trckd ldrs: hdwy over 2f out: rdn to chal over 1f out and ev ch tl drvn and one pce ins fnl f* **16/1**

0540 **4** *½* **Singora Lady (IRE)**[57] 969 4-8-4 **56** oh9.......... JimmyQuinn 14 — 54
(P T Midgley) *s.i.s and bhd: pushed along and hdwy over 2f out: rdn over 1f out: styd on wl fnl f: nrst fin* **40/1**

05 **5** *½* **Golden Future**[29] 1480 6-7-13 **56** oh5.......... AndreaAtzeni(5) 4 — 53
(P D Niven) *in tch: hdwy to chse ldrs 2f out: sn rdn and kpt on same pce* **14/1**

322- **6** *2¼* **Distant Pleasure**[202] 7131 5-8-6 **58**.......... PaulHanagan 10 — 50
(M Dods) *towards rr: hdwy over 2f out and sn rdn: swtchd lft ent fnl f and kpt on: nrst fin* **13/2**

5-45 **7** *¾* **Castlebury (IRE)**[14] 1830 4-8-13 **65**.......... RobertWinston 1 — 55
(G A Swinbank) *trckd ldrs: effrt 2f out: sn rdn and wknd over 1f out* **10/1**

0-33 **8** *hd* **Aggravation**[14] 1833 7-9-2 **68**.......... PaulMulrennan 2 — 58
(D R C Elsworth) *s.i.s and bhd: stdy hdwy on inner 3f out: swtchd rt and rdn over 1f out: swtchd lft and drvn ent fnl f: sn no imp* **11/2**[3]

0-00 **9** *½* **Spirit Of France (IRE)**[20] 1682 7-9-4 **70**.......... DNolan 15 — 58
(D Carroll) *chsd ldr: hdwy to ld over 2f out: sn rdn and hdd over 1f out: wknd ins fnl f* **33/1**

-000 **10** *½* **Aussie Blue (IRE)**[10] 1955 5-8-4 **56**.......... PaulQuinn 7 — 46+
(R M Whitaker) *hld up in rr: hdwy on inner: 2f out: rdn and styng on whn hmpd ent fnl f: nt rcvr* **8/1**

00-0 **11** *1* **San Silvestro (IRE)**[44] 1194 4-8-9 **61**.......... MickyFenton 12 — 46
(Mrs A Duffield) *chsd ldrs: rdn along over 2f out: grad wknd* **28/1**

2341 **12** *1¼* **Blue Charm**[23] 1612 5-9-4 **70**.......... DanielTudhope 11 — 52
(I W McInnes) *hld up: a in rr* **5/1**[2]

3600 **13** *4* **Hunt The Bottle (IRE)**[17] 1781 4-7-11 **56** oh9... JosephineBruning(7) 13 — 29
(M Mullineaux) *midfield: rdn along over 3f out: sn wknd* **66/1**

544- **14** *6* **Wednesdays Boy (IRE)**[114] 7132 6-8-5 **57**..........(p) DarrenMoffatt 9 — 16
(P D Niven) *a towards rr* **20/1**

50-0 **15** *2¾* **Natural Rhythm (IRE)**[44] 1194 4-8-0 **57**..........(b) DeanHeslop(5) 16 — 10
(Mrs R A Carr) *t.k.h: led: rdn along and hdd over 2f out: sn wknd* **40/1**

1m 45.63s (-0.27) **Going Correction** +0.10s/f (Good) — **15** Ran SP% **120.0**

Speed ratings (Par 103): **105,102,99,98,98 96,95,95,94,94 93,91,87,81,79**

toteswinger: 1&2 £19.50, 1&3 £24.50, 2&3 £84.10 CSF £98.56 CT £1291.11 TOTE £4.80: £2.30, £7.00, £6.10; EX 114.10.

Owner M P Bowring **Bred** Mystic Meg Limited **Trained** Newmarket, Suffolk

■ Stewards' Enquiry : Paul Mulrennan caution: careless riding.

FOCUS

This had looked quite a competitive handicap, but the well-backed Marvo ran out quite a cosy winner.

Singora Lady(IRE) Official explanation: jockey said filly missed the break

2246 MSK FILLIES' H'CAP — 1m 2f 6y

7:00 (7:01) (Class 5) (0-70,70) 3-Y-0+ — **£3,238** (£963; £481; £240) **Stalls** Low

Form — RPR

0-53 **1** **Umverti**[10] 1955 4-9-0 **56** oh1.......... SteveDrowne 2 — 67
(N Bycroft) *t.k.h early: hld up in tch: pushed along and sltly outpcd 4f out: hdwy over 2f out: swtchd rt and rdn wl over 1f out: styd on to ld jst ins fnl f: drvn out* **13/2**[3]

0144 **2** *1¾* **Location**[27] 1531 3-7-9 **56**.......... AndreaAtzeni(5) 3 — 63
(Ian Williams) *hld up in rr: tk clsr order 3f out: rdn and hdwy on inner over 1f out: styd on u.p ins fnl f* **6/1**[2]

40-1 **3** *2¾* **Shekan Star**[29] 1472 7-9-0 **56**.......... PaulHanagan 7 — 58
(K G Reveley) *hld up in rr: hdwy over 4f out: rdn to chse ldr 2f out: sn drvn and kpt on same pce ent fnl f* **12/1**

-350 **4** *¾* **Black Dahlia**[34] 1348 4-10-0 **70**.......... MickyFenton 8 — 71
(A J McCabe) *trckd ldng pair: hdwy to ld wl over 2f out: wd st and sn rdn: drvn and hdd jst ins fnl f: wknd* **12/1**

-023 **5** *12* **Cheers For Thea (IRE)**[13] 1881 4-9-3 **59**.......... PaulMulrennan 4 — 36
(T D Easterby) *midfield: hdwy 3f out: rdn to chse ldrs wl over 1f out: sn drvn and no imp* **5/1**[1]

-600 **6** *3½* **Grethel (IRE)**[19] 1690 5-8-9 **56** oh4.......... SladeO'Hara(5) 13 — 26
(A Berry) *towards rr tl sme hdwy fnl 2f: nvr a factor* **40/1**

40-0 **7** *7* **Shosolosa (IRE)**[10] 1955 7-9-0 **56** oh3.......... DarrenMoffatt 9 — 12
(R C Guest) *a towards rr* **40/1**

00-4 **8** *¾* **Playful Asset (IRE)**[39] 1252 3-8-10 **66** ow1.......... SebSanders 1 — 19
(R M Beckett) *chsd ldrs on inner: rdn along 3f out: sn drvn and wknd* **6/1**[2]

30-5 **9** *10* **Wogan's Sister**[15] 1812 4-9-9 **65**.......... MichaelHills 11 — —
(D R C Elsworth) *cl up: led after 1f: rdn along 3f out: sn hdd & wknd* **15/2**

226 **10** *26* **Calling Victory (FR)**[39] 1260 3-8-6 **62**..........(b[1]) JimmyQuinn 6 — —
(M Botti) *chsd ldrs: rdn along wl over 3f out and sn wknd* **17/2**

000- **11** *15* **April's Daughter**[273] 5232 4-8-13 **58**.......... JamesMillman(3) 12 — —
(B R Millman) *chsd ldrs on outer: rdn along over 3f out and sn wknd* **20/1**

5043 **12** *54* **If You Knew Suzy**[17] 1777 4-9-5 **61**.......... RobertWinston 5 — —
(G A Swinbank) *led 1f: cl up: effrt to chal 4f out and ev ch tl rdn and wknd qckly over 2f out: sn bhd and eased* **7/1**

2m 14.9s (1.20) **Going Correction** +0.10s/f (Good)

WFA 3 from 4yo+ 14lb — **12** Ran SP% **118.4**

Speed ratings (Par 100): **99,97,95,94,85 82,76,76,68,47 35,—**

toteswinger: 1&2 £11.30, 1&3 £16.50, 2&3 £19.50 CSF £44.39 CT £459.29 TOTE £10.00: £3.30, £2.50, £2.60; EX 77.50.

Owner Mrs C M Whatley **Bred** N Bycroft **Trained** Brandsby, N Yorks

FOCUS

Not that many seemed to get home in what was a modest fillies' handicap.

Playful Asset(IRE) Official explanation: jockey said filly had no more to give

Wogan's Sister Official explanation: jockey said filly lost its action

Calling Victory(FR) Official explanation: jockey said filly did not face the blinkers

If You Knew Suzy Official explanation: jockey said filly lost its action

2247 DRURY PSM YOUNGSTERS CONDITIONS STKS — 6f

7:30 (7:31) (Class 2) 2-Y-0 — **£9,346** (£2,799; £1,399; £700; £349; £175) **Stalls** Low

Form — RPR

01 **1** **Roi De Vitesse (IRE)**[34] 1358 2-9-0 0.......... JamesMillman 4 — 93
(B R Millman) *trckd ldr on inner: hdwy 2f out: rdn to ld ins fnl f: kpt on wl* **9/1**

15 **2** *1* **Walkingonthemoon**[23] 1598 2-9-0 0.......... RichardKingscote 9 — 90
(Tom Dascombe) *wnt bdly rt s but sn led: rdn and qcknd 2f out: drvn and hdd ins fnl f: kpt on wl u.p towards fin* **5/1**[2]

1 **3** *2½* **Be Invincible (IRE)**[32] 1404 2-9-0 0.......... MichaelHills 3 — 83
(B W Hills) *trckd ldrs: effrt over 2f out: swtchd wd and rdn wl over 1f outy: edgd lft and one pce ins fnl f* **7/4**[1]

4 *1¼* **Music Of The Moor (IRE)** 2-8-8 0.......... MickyFenton 2 — 73+
(T P Tate) *s.i.s and bhd: hdwy on inner 2f out: sn rdn and kpt on ins fnl f: nrst fin* **25/1**

6 **5** *2* **Urban Clubber**[13] 1867 2-8-11 0.......... PaulMulrennan 5 — 70
(J Howard Johnson) *chsd ldrs tl outpcd and lost pl 1/2-way: rdn and kpt on fnl 2f* **22/1**

6 *2¼* **Silenceofthewind (USA)** 2-8-8 0.......... AndrewElliott 6 — 66+
(K R Burke) *dwlt: t.k.h and plld hrd: hld up in rr: effrt whn nt clr run and stmbld 2f out: nt rcvr* **8/1**

51 **7** *2¾* **Maidtorun (IRE)**[18] 1719 2-8-6 0.......... PaulHanagan 7 — 50
(R A Fahey) *chsd ldrs: rdn along over 2f out: sn drvn and wknd* **5/1**[2]

5212 **8** *nk* **Shark Man (IRE)**[6] 2087 2-8-11 0.......... SebSanders 8 — 54
(P J McBride) *cl up: rdn along over 2f out: sn drvn and wknd* **11/2**[3]

1m 18.16s (1.26) **Going Correction** +0.10s/f (Good) — **8** Ran SP% **114.4**

Speed ratings (Par 99): **95,93,90,88,86 83,79,78**

toteswinger: 1&2 £13.60, 1&3 £6.30, 2&3 £2.40 CSF £53.31 TOTE £12.70: £2.30, £2.00, £1.40; EX 88.40.

Owner Mustajed Partnership **Bred** Tally-Ho Stud **Trained** Kentisbeare, Devon

FOCUS

This is a race than can throw up the odd smart 2yo but it seems rather unlikely that any of these will be making their mark at pattern level this season. The front three were always prominent.

NOTEBOOK

Roi De Vitesse(IRE), whose yard won this back in 2003, needed every yard of the 5f when springing a 25/1 surprise in a maiden at Nottingham last time and he showed marked improvement for the extra furlong. Nicely positioned just in behind the lead, he stuck tight to the rail in the straight and ran on well to lead inside the final furlong. There may well be more to come and he should stay another furlong, but things will get tougher now and the Woodcote Stakes at Epsom on Derby Day may well be his next outing. (op 12-1)

Walkingonthemoon, who went to his right at the start, failed to build on his promising debut success (easy ground) when last of five behind a useful sort at Ascot on fast going, but this surface was more to his liking and he ran a good race in defeat. (op 4-1)

Be Invincible(IRE) was a shade disappointing. He created a good impression when winning over 5f on his debut at Windsor and the combination of a step up to 6f on slower ground was not expected to be a problem. However, he was under pressure approaching two out and could raise his game in the straight, just keeping on at the one pace. (tchd 13-8 and 15-8 in a place)

Music Of The Moor(IRE) ◆ shaped with a good deal of promise back in fourth. A son of Rock Of Gibraltar who is going to require further in time, he stayed on nicely for hands and heels riding and should learn a good deal from the experience. Winning a standard maiden should prove a formality. (tchd 20-1)

Urban Clubber, who showed some ability when sixth in a Haydock maiden on debut, improved on that initial effort and clearly has it in him to win races. (tchd 20-1)

Silenceofthewind(USA), a $310,000 purchase who had been spoken of as a potential Royal Ascot colt by his trainer, failed to settle early and seemed to stumble having been denied a clear run when trying to close. He stayed on all too late, but should improve a good deal on this debut effort. (op 11-1 tchd 15-2)

Maidtorun(IRE), narrow winner of a Beverley maiden earlier in the month, struggled on this slower ground and proved most disappointing. (op 7-1)

Shark Man(IRE) also failed to run his race on what was the slowest ground he has encountered to date. (tchd 5-1)

2248 CONSTANT SECURITY SERVICES H'CAP — 1m 4y

8:00 (8:00) (Class 4) (0-85,82) 3-Y-0 — **£5,180** (£1,541; £770; £384) **Stalls** Low

Form — RPR

20-3 **1** **Spinners End (IRE)**[44] 1193 3-8-5 **69**.......... AndrewElliott 2 — 76
(K R Burke) *t.k.h: trckd ldrs: smooth hdwy over 2f out: rdn to ld appr fnl f: drvn and hng rt last 100yds: jst hld on* **4/1**[2]

0-11 **2** *shd* **Full Of Love (IRE)**[27] 1531 3-8-13 **77**.......... MichaelHills 4 — 84
(B W Hills) *trckd ldrs: swtchd outside and hdwy 2f out: rdn over 1f out: styd on to chal ins fnl f and ev ch whn carried rt last 100yds: jst failed* **11/2**

41-0 **3** *1¾* **Call It On (IRE)**[9] 1992 3-9-4 **82**.......... SebSanders 1 — 85+
(M H Tompkins) *hld up in rr: hdwy over 2f out: sn rdn and styd on appr fnl f: nrestfin* **6/4**[1]

2114 **4** *¾* **Green Agenda**[30] 1466 3-9-0 **78**.......... JoeFanning 6 — 79
(M Johnston) *chsd ldrs: effrt on inner 3f out: rdn along wl over 1f out: drvn and kpt on same pce ins fnl f* **9/2**[3]

3626 **5** *nk* **Common Diva**[7] 2057 3-8-13 **77**.......... RobertWinston 7 — 77
(A J McCabe) *led: rdn along 2f out: drvn and hdd appr fnl f: wknd* **16/1**

0-54 **6** *4½* **Olympic Dream**[40] 1228 3-8-8 **72**.......... PaulHanagan 3 — 62
(R A Fahey) *t.k.h: chsd ldrs: rdn along over 2f out: sn drvn and btn* **10/1**

1-0 **7** *3¼* **Charging Indian (IRE)**[41] 1214 3-9-3 **81**.......... SteveDrowne 8 — 63
(D R Lanigan) *cl up: rdn along wl over 2f out and sn wknd* **20/1**

20-5 **8** *hd* **Lakeman (IRE)**[29] 1471 3-9-2 **80**.......... TomEaves 5 — 62
(B Ellison) *hld up: a in rr* **33/1**

1m 46.41s (0.51) **Going Correction** +0.10s/f (Good) — **8** Ran SP% **116.2**

Speed ratings (Par 101): **101,100,99,98,98 93,90,90**

toteswinger: 1&2 £4.00, 1&3 £3.30, 2&3 £4.30 CSF £26.71 CT £46.79 TOTE £6.30: £1.90, £2.10, £1.10; EX 31.90.

Owner Mogeely Stud & Mrs Maura Gittins **Bred** P D Savill **Trained** Middleham Moor, N Yorks

■ Stewards' Enquiry : Andrew Elliott caution: careless riding

FOCUS
This was a decent 3yo handicap and it produced a tight finish, Spinners End just holding on from the hat-trick seeking Full Of Love.

2249 CONSTANT SECURITY SERVING YORKSHIRE RACECOURSES H'CAP — 1m 4f 8y
8:30 (8:30) (Class 4) (0-85,85) 4-Y-0+ — **£5,180** (£1,541; £770; £384) **Stalls** Low

Form — RPR

2-22 **1** **Aleatricis**[13] 1886 4-8-10 **77** .... MickyFenton 10 — 86
(J J Quinn) *hld up towards rr: stdy hdwy 4f out: chsd ldrs over 2f out: rdn and styng on on outer whn hmpd appr fnl f: sn drvn and styd on gamely to ld nr fin* **6/1**

1-42 **2** *nk* **Taikoo**[17] 1779 4-8-12 **79** .... SteveDrowne 9 — 88
(H Morrison) *led: rdn along over 2f out: drvn and edgd rt ent fnl f: hdd and no ex nr fin* **8/1**

51 **3** *2 1/4* **Caerlaverock (IRE)**[19] 1693 4-8-13 **80** .... TomEaves 6 — 85
(G A Swinbank) *trckd ldrs: hdwy 3f out: rdn to chse ldng pair 2f out: drvn over 1f out and ev ch tl no ex ins fnl f* **5/1**[3]

45-3 **4** *1* **Buddy Holly**[17] 1779 4-8-11 **78** .... RobertWinston 3 — 81
(Pat Eddery) *chsd ldr: effrt 3f out: rdn to chal wl over 1f out and ev ch whn hung rt appr last: sn drvn and wknd* **9/1**

604- **5** *shd* **Conquisto**[218] 6763 4-9-4 **85** .... SebSanders 4 — 88+
(C G Cox) *hld up in rr: hdwy to chse ldrs 3f out: rdn 2f out: drvn over 1f out: kpt on: nrst fin* **7/2**[1]

6-04 **6** *6* **Hurlingham**[24] 1593 5-8-12 **79** .... PaulMulrennan 8 — 73
(M W Easterby) *hld up and bhd: sme hdwy 3f out: sn rdn and nvr a factor* **11/1**

660- **7** *16* **Sadler's Kingdom (IRE)**[328] 3493 5-8-8 **75** .... PaulHanagan 1 — 43
(R A Fahey) *in tch: pushed along 4f out: rdn 3f out and sn wknd* **6/1**

100- **8** *12* **Island Vista**[203] 7108 4-9-0 **81** .... PhilipRobinson 7 — 30
(M A Jarvis) *prom: rdn along over 3f out and sn wknd* **4/1**[2]

2m 41.0s (0.20) **Going Correction** +0.10s/f (Good) — **8** Ran SP% **116.9**
Speed ratings (Par 105): **103,102,101,100,100 96,85,77**
toteswinger: 1&2 £10.10, 1&3 £2.40, 2&3 £4.90 CSF £53.75 CT £259.47 TOTE £6.70: £1.90, £1.70, £2.50; EX 28.00.

Owner Exors Of The Late Lady Anne Bentinck **Bred** Miss K Rausing **Trained** Settrington, N Yorks

FOCUS
This was an interesting handicap and the remarkably consistent Aleatricis registered win number six.

Island Vista Official explanation: trainer's rep said filly scoped dirty on return

2250 CASTLE RECRUITMENT MAIDEN STKS — 6f
9:00 (9:05) (Class 5) 3-Y-O — **£3,238** (£963; £481; £240) **Stalls** Low

Form — RPR

0- **1** **Sioux Rising (IRE)**[272] 5271 3-8-12 0 .... PaulHanagan 4 — 83+
(R A Fahey) *prom: effrt over 2f out: rdn to ld wl over 1f out: and sn jnd: drvn ins fnl f and styd on gamely towards fin* **5/2**[2]

2 *1/2* **Avertor** 3-9-3 0 .... SteveDrowne 1 — 86+
(R Charlton) *trckd ldrs on inner: hdwy over 2f out: rdn to chal over 1f out and ev ch tl drvn and no ex last 100yds* **13/8**[1]

0-0 **3** *6* **Rogalt (IRE)**[18] 1739 3-9-3 0 .... TomEaves 15 — 67
(B Smart) *racd wd: cl up: rdn along and edgd rt wl over 1f out: drvn and one pce ent fnl f* **66/1**

44 **4** *1 1/2* **Cheyenne Red (IRE)**[6] 2070 3-8-12 0 .... PatrickDonaghy(5) 17 — 62+
(M Dods) *s.i.s and bhd: hdwy on outer and hung rt bnd 2f out: sn rdn and kpt on ins fnl f: nrst fin* **7/1**

02- **5** *1/2* **Al Qeddaaf (IRE)**[195] 7240 3-9-3 0 .... TPO'Shea 8 — 60
(W J Haggas) *chsd ldrs: rdn along 2f out: drvn over 1f out and sn one pce* **5/1**[3]

6 *1 3/4* **Freya's Flight (IRE)** 3-8-12 0 .... PaulMulrennan 10 — 50+
(K A Ryan) *uns rdr and bolted to s: s.i.s and bhd: hdwy wl over 1f out: swtchd rt ent fnl f and kpt on: nrst fin* **20/1**

0 **7** *1 1/4* **Two Turtle Doves (IRE)**[20] 1683 3-8-12 0 .... MickyFenton 7 — 46+
(M Mullineaux) *bhd tl styd on fnl 2f: nvr nr ldrs* **66/1**

060- **8** *nk* **Our Apolonia (IRE)**[216] 6809 3-8-7 47 .... SladeO'Hara(5) 13 — 45
(A Berry) *in tch: rdn along over 2f out: sn drvn and grad wknd* **100/1**

9 *1/2* **Akabar** 3-9-3 0 .... SebSanders 14 — 48
(R M Beckett) *chsd ldrs: rdn along 2f out: wknd wl over 1f out* **16/1**

0-5 **10** *4* **Jillolini**[35] 1335 3-8-12 0 .... JimmyQuinn 6 — 30
(T D Easterby) *a towards rr* **33/1**

6406 **11** *1 1/2* **Field Fantasy**[35] 1335 3-8-12 52 .... AndrewElliott 2 — 26
(Garry Moss) *a towards rr* **66/1**

050- **12** *4* **Pollish**[198] 7199 3-8-7 42 .... DanielleMcCreery(5) 3 — 13
(A Berry) *led: rdn along over 2f out: hdd wl over 1f out and sn wknd* **100/1**

53- **13** *1 3/4* **Grand Stitch (USA)**[337] 3170 3-9-3 0 .... DNolan 5 — 12
(D Carroll) *midfield: rdn along wl over 2f out and sn wknd* **20/1**

14 *15* **Mrs Medley** 3-8-12 0 .... DanielTudhope 11 — —
(D Shaw) *s.i.s: a in rr* **66/1**

1m 18.74s (1.84) **Going Correction** +0.10s/f (Good) — **14** Ran SP% **122.1**
Speed ratings (Par 99): **91,90,82,80,79 77,75,75,74,69 67,61,59,39**
Place 6: £74.23 Place 5: £24.01 toteswinger: 1&2 £8.60, 1&3 £48.90, 2&3 £32.00 CSF £6.56 TOTE £4.30: £1.50, £1.50, £10.90; EX 9.10.

Owner Mrs Una Towell **Bred** N And Mrs N Nugent **Trained** Musley Bank, N Yorks

FOCUS
Two potentially useful sprinters drew clear in what was a modest maiden.

Cheyenne Red(IRE) ◆ Official explanation: jockey said, regarding running and riding, that the gelding was slow away, became unbalanced approaching 2f out and only began to stay on when it was too late.

Two Turtle Doves(IRE) Official explanation: jockey said filly was denied a clear run

T/Plt: £113.90 to a £1 stake. Pool: £62,246.85. 398.92 winning tickets. T/Qpdt: £14.10 to a £1 stake. Pool: £4,291.50. 224.43 winning tickets. JR

2251 - 2256a (Foreign Racing) - See Raceform Interactive

1949 BEVERLEY (R-H)
Saturday, May 23

OFFICIAL GOING: Good (8.6)
Rail around top bend moved in a metre but effect on distances not notified.
Wind: Light, across Weather: Overcast

2257 RACING AGAIN ON WEDNESDAY EVENING STKS (H'CAP) — 7f 100y
2:15 (2:17) (Class 4) (0-80,77) 4-Y-0+ — **£4,727** (£1,406; £702; £351) **Stalls** High

Form — RPR

2-62 **1** **Paraguay (USA)**[14] 1876 6-9-2 **75** .... EdwardCreighton 10 — 82
(Mrs D J Sanderson) *hld up in tch: hdwy over 2f out: rdn over 1f out: led jst ins fnl f: drvn out* **4/1**[2]

-603 **2** *1/2* **Phluke**[14] 1894 8-9-2 **75** ....(v) StephenCarson 2 — 81
(Eve Johnson Houghton) *trckd ldr: cl up 3f out: shkn up to ld wl over 1f out and sn rdn: edgd lft and hdd jst ins fnl f: sn drvn and one pce* **8/1**

0006 **3** *3/4* **Daaweitza**[28] 1524 6-8-10 **74** .... LanceBetts(5) 5 — 78
(B Ellison) *chsd ldrs: hdwy over 2f out: drvn over 1f out: kpt on u.p ins fnl f* **7/1**

40-0 **4** *1/2* **Ubenkor (IRE)**[19] 1737 4-8-7 **69** .... AhmedAjtebi(3) 11 — 72
(B Smart) *hld up towards rr: swtchd outside and gd hdwy 2f out: sn rdn and styd on ins fnl f: nrst fin* **12/1**

-060 **5** *1* **Arizona John (IRE)**[18] 1766 4-9-2 **75** .... DuranFentiman 3 — 75
(N Wilson) *hld up in rr: swtchd lft and hdwy over 2f out: rdn over 1f out: kpt on ins fnl f: nrst fin* **33/1**

5-66 **6** *2* **Jonny Lesters Hair (IRE)**[22] 1649 4-9-0 **73** .... DNolan 7 — 68
(T D Easterby) *j. awkwardly: t.k.h: trckd ldrs: effrt over 2f out: sn rdn and no imp fr over 1f out* **5/1**[3]

0-1 **7** *hd* **Cotswolds**[18] 1769 4-9-3 **76** .... JoeFanning 6 — 71
(M Johnston) *led: rdn along 3f out: drvn and hdd wl over 1f out: sn wknd* **3/1**[1]

00-6 **8** *3/4* **Danehillsundance (IRE)**[78] 780 5-9-4 **77** .... PaulMulrennan 1 — 75+
(D H Brown) *hld up in rr: effrt and nt clr run over 1f out: nvr a factor* **10/1**

00-0 **9** *1/2* **Mesbaah (IRE)**[10] 1990 5-9-0 **73** .... JamieMoriarty 8 — 65
(R A Fahey) *chsd ldrs: rdn along 2f out: sn drvn and wknd* **8/1**

0-50 **10** *8* **Fitzwarren**[18] 1766 8-8-4 **63** oh13 ....(v) JimmyQuinn 9 — 35
(A D Brown) *chsd ldrs on inner: rdn along over 2f out: sn wknd* **100/1**

1m 34.85s (1.05) **Going Correction** +0.20s/f (Good) — **10** Ran SP% **117.1**
Speed ratings (Par 105): **102,101,100,100,98 96,96,95,94,85**
toteswinger: 1&2 £2.90, 1&3 £1.40, 2&3 £8.20 CSF £36.28 CT £225.28 TOTE £5.70: £1.40, £2.30, £2.90; EX 31.60.

Owner R J Budge **Bred** Nutbush Farm **Trained** Wiseton, Notts

FOCUS
This opener was a reasonable handicap run at a fair pace. With the favourite disappointing this is ordinary form.

Ubenkor(IRE) Official explanation: jockey said colt hung left throughout
Danehillsundance(IRE) Official explanation: jockey said gelding was denied a clear run

2258 BERYL & JOE TURNER MEMORIAL MEDIAN AUCTION MAIDEN STKS — 5f
2:45 (2:53) (Class 4) 2-Y-O — **£3,885** (£1,156; £577; £288) **Stalls** High

Form — RPR

1 **Mon Brav** 2-9-3 0 .... DNolan 9 — 71
(D Carroll) *trckd ldrs: n.m.r over 1f out: rdn ent fnl f: styd on to ld last 50yds* **8/1**

63 **2** *3/4* **Pinnacle Lad (IRE)**[15] 1847 2-9-3 0 .... TolleyDean 5 — 68
(J L Spearing) *led: rdn along wl over 1f out: drvn and edgd lft ins fnl f: hdd and no ex last 50yds* **9/2**[2]

2 **3** *1* **Orpen Arms (IRE)**[12] 1920 2-8-12 0 .... JamieMoriarty 4 — 59
(R A Fahey) *cl up: effrt 2f out: sn rdn and ev ch tl drvn and nt qckn wl ins fnl f* **13/8**[1]

4 *nk* **Midnight Martini** 2-8-12 0 .... DuranFentiman 10 — 60+
(T D Easterby) *in tch: hdwy over 2f out: effrt whn nt clr run ent fnl f: swtchd rt and kpt on towards fin* **14/1**

52 **5** *1 1/2* **Rio Caribe (IRE)**[7] 2069 2-9-0 0 .... KellyHarrison(3) 2 — 58+
(T D Walford) *chsd ldrs: rdn along and sltly outpcd 2f out: kpt on ins fnl f* **5/1**[3]

0 **6** *3/4* **Sir Christie**[15] 1847 2-9-3 0 .... JimmyQuinn 12 — 55
(N Tinkler) *towards rr tl sme late hdwy* **16/1**

00 **7** *1/2* **Camacho Flyer (IRE)**[37] 1304 2-8-10 0 .... PaulPickard(7) 11 — 53
(P T Midgley) *cl up on inner: effrt to chal 2f out: sn rdn and ev ch tl wknd ins fnl f* **25/1**

8 *1* **Bubbelas** 2-8-12 0 .... JoeFanning 6 — 45
(J J Quinn) *racd wd: a towards rr* **11/1**

65 **9** *9* **Ytartfawn (IRE)**[36] 1330 2-9-3 0 .... LeeEnstone 7 — 17
(P T Midgley) *chsd ldrs: rdn along over 2f out and sn wknd* **50/1**

10 *13* **As Brave As You (IRE)** 2-8-10 0 .... AnthonyBetts(7) 8 — —
(B Ellison) *s.i.s: a bhd* **25/1**

65.53 secs (2.03) **Going Correction** +0.20s/f (Good) — **10** Ran SP% **114.6**
Speed ratings (Par 95): **91,89,88,87,85 84,83,81,67,46**
toteswinger: 1&2 £5.80, 1&3 £11.20, 2&3 £1.80 CSF £42.32 TOTE £10.80: £2.80, £1.10, £1.20; EX 61.10.

Owner D Wallis **Bred** J D Graham **Trained** Sledmere, E Yorks

FOCUS
A fair juvenile maiden and, despite the principals finishing in a bit of a heap, a few look to have a decent future. The second and third help with the fairly ordinary standard.

NOTEBOOK
Mon Brav ◆, a half-brother to the winning sprinter Bahamian Lad and making his racecourse debut, tracked the leaders towards the inside. He was fortunate that the gap appeared between the runner-up and Camacho Flyer when it did. To his credit, he made good use of it and quickened well to hit the front inside the final furlong and win going away. This was a decent effort - he beat two horses that had already made the frame - and the way he saw his race out suggests an extra furlong won't be a problem. (op 15-2 tchd 7-1)
Pinnacle Lad(IRE), a narrowly beaten third at Ripon last time when trying to make all, attempted the same tactics and again wasn't caught until late. There should be a maiden in him on an easier track. (op 7-2 tchd 5-1)
Orpen Arms(IRE), a staying-on second of nine at Redcar on her debut earlier this month, was ridden more prominently this time and kept on. She should find a maiden in due course and may also appreciate another furlong. (op 11-4 tchd 3-1 and 6-4 in a place)
Midnight Martini ◆, a £20,000 filly out of a half-sister to three winners at up to 1m2f, can be considered unlucky not to have finished closer. She was putting in an effort between Pinnacle Lad and Orpen Arms entering the last furlong when the gap closed, and there was no way back. She is likely to come on for this and shouldn't take long to find a race. Official explanation: jockey said filly was denied a clear run (tchd 10-1)

Rio Caribe(IRE) shaped as though this stiffer track would suit when a strong finishing second at Doncaster seven days earlier. He held a good position for much of the way from his moderate draw but could never land a blow. He may need more of a test. (tchd 9-2 and 11-2)
Sir Christie, a long way behind Pinnacle Lad on his Ripon debut but backed at long odds here, lacked the pace to make use of the plum draw. He did make a little late headway. (op 25-1 tchd 14-1)
Bubbelas, a half-sister to a winning juvenile sprinter, was soon outpaced. She saw plenty of daylight on the wide outside, but did hint at some ability, and looks sure to improve with experience. (op 8-1 tchd 12-1)

2259 BRANTINGHAM CONDITIONS STKS 5f

3:20 (3:25) (Class 2) 3-Y-O+

£11,215 (£3,358; £1,679; £840; £419; £210) **Stalls** High

Form RPR

1510 **1** **Excusez Moi (USA)**[8] 2059 7-8-12 92........................(p) DuranFentiman 8 100
(Mrs R A Carr) *hld up in rr: pushed along 1/2-way: smooth hdwy over 1f out: rdn and styd on ins fnl f to ld last 50yds* **10/1**

0-30 **2** *½* **Fullandby (IRE)**[20] 1699 7-9-5 100.................................... JoeFanning 11 105+
(T J Etherington) *dwlt and towards rr: hdwy and in tch 1/2-way: trckd ldrs over 1f out: rdn to chal ins fnl f and ev ch tl nt qckn nr fin* **6/1**[2]

4-21 **3** *nk* **Advanced**[33] 1398 6-8-12 99..(p) JamieMoriarty 2 97+
(K A Ryan) *trckd ldrs: effrt wl over 1f out: sn rdn and ev ch ent fnl f tl drvn and nt qckn last 50yds* **3/1**[1]

1623 **4** *1 ½* **Judd Street**[45] 1189 7-8-12 105..................................(b) StephenCarson 7 92
(Eve Johnson Houghton) *trckd ldrs: smooth hdwy to ld over 1f out and sn rdn: drvn and hdd wl ins fnl f: no ex* **3/1**[1]

0051 **5** *hd* **Internationaldebut (IRE)**[9] 2012 4-8-12 92................. KirstyMilczarek 6 91
(S Parr) *towards rr: hdwy on outer over 1f out: sn rdn and styd on ins fnl f: nrst fin* **7/1**[3]

0-06 **6** *2 ¼* **Spirit Of Sharjah (IRE)**[21] 1672 4-8-12 87............ FrankieMcDonald 12 83+
(Miss J Feilden) *in tch on inner: effrt whn nt clr run 2f out and again over 1f out: swtchd lft and kpt on ins fnl f: nrst fin* **16/1**

640- **7** *¾* **Damika (IRE)**[218] 6783 6-9-7 100... PaulEddery 1 89
(R M Whitaker) *towards rr and pushed along on outer after 2f: hdwy 2f out: sn rdn and no imp appr fnl f* **28/1**

114- **8** *nse* **Go Go Green (IRE)**[206] 7075 3-8-4 83............................. JimmyQuinn 5 80
(D H Brown) *dwlt and towards rr: effrt and sme hdwy wl over 1f out: sn rdn and no imp* **17/2**

4552 **9** *hd* **First Order**[8] 2053 8-8-12 80...(v) AnnStokell 9 79
(Miss A Stokell) *cl up: rdn along 2f out: wknd appr fnl f* **66/1**

056 **10** *1 ½* **Haajes**[7] 2094 5-8-12 85..(t) LeeEnstone 10 74
(J Balding) *chsd ldrs on inner: rdn along 2f out: grad wknd* **22/1**

14-3 **11** *1 ¼* **Peace Offering (IRE)**[34] 1384 9-10-0 105....................... AhmedAjtebi 4 86
(D Nicholls) *sn led: rdn along 2f out: hdd over 1f out and wknd qckly* **10/1**

63.29 secs (-0.21) **Going Correction** +0.20s/f (Good)
WFA 3 from 4yo+ 8lb **11** Ran SP% **120.7**
Speed ratings (Par 109): **109,108,107,105,105 101,100,100,99,97 95**
toteswinger: 1&2 £13.30, 1&3 £7.30, 2&3 £6.20 CSF £69.61 TOTE £13.60: £2.80, £2.50, £1.60; EX 88.90.
Owner S B Clark **Bred** Lyons Demesne **Trained** Huby, N Yorks
■ Stewards' Enquiry : Ann Stokell two-day ban: careless riding (Jun 7-8)

FOCUS
A decent conditions event run at a good pace. Few appeared to hold much chance on official ratings and, in a sprint like this, racing room was always likely to be at a premium. The form is rated around the second.

NOTEBOOK
Excusez Moi(USA), rather inconsistent of late, had a bit to find at the weights. He proved awkward to load, but was backed to return to his best form and won well. A gelding who stays further, the decent tempo on a stiff track proved ideal, and he found plenty when the gaps appeared. He seems likely to be aimed at the Wokingham. (op 16-1)
Fullandby(IRE)'s only success last season came over course and distance in September on much softer ground. Although he has won on fast ground, he had a bit to prove following his poor effort at Newmarket last time and was very easy to back. He missed the break and his rider had to nudge him along for a few strides, but he appeared to travel well in midfield. However, he had to wait for the gaps to appear and, as the winner got first run, he could never quite get there. (op 3-1 after early 11-4 in a place)
Advanced, in good form this season and with cheekpieces on for the first time, was one of those most favoured at these weights. He was always up with the pace from his low draw and seemed to have every chance with few excuses. (op 10-3 tchd 7-2)
Judd Street, best in at the weights, was always in a good position and travelled well enough. Having ranged alongside the leaders passing the furlong pole, he couldn't stamp his authority on the race, and was beaten when running out of room near the finish. (op 4-1 tchd 9-2)
Internationaldebut(IRE), who showed himself effective over the minimum trip when scraping home in a handicap at the York Dante meeting, stayed on all too late. Official explanation: jockey said gelding was denied a clear run (tchd 13-2 and 15-2)
Spirit Of Sharjah(IRE), out of form since his juvenile days and with plenty to find on these terms, ran better than his finishing position suggests as he met trouble against the inside rail.
Damika(IRE), racing over the minimum trip for the first time in his 34th race, was returning from seven months off. He never got into it, having seen plenty of daylight on the wide outside. (op 40-1 tchd 25-1)
Go Go Green(IRE), the only three-year-old in the field, faced a stiff task on his debut for this yard. He was a notable springer in the market despite his absence of secen months. However, he gave himself plenty to do and a mid-race move down the outside came to nothing. (op 25-1)
Haajes Official explanation: jockey said gelding was denied a clear run
Peace Offering(IRE), who faced a stiff task under his cumulative penalties, did plenty of running to set the pace from his low draw. It was still disappointing that he capitulated so easily. (tchd 8-1)

2260 BRIAN YEARDLEY CONTINENTAL TWO YEAR OLD TROPHY (CONDITIONS STKS) (C&G) 5f

3:50 (3:53) (Class 2) 2-Y-O

£9,346 (£2,799; £1,399; £700; £349; £175) **Stalls** High

Form RPR

1222 **1** **Archers Road (IRE)**[5] 2136 2-9-4 0......................... EdwardCreighton 4 93
(M R Channon) *chsd ldrs: hdwy 2f out: rdn over 1f out: styd on wl to ld ins fnl f* **9/4**[1]

14 **2** *1* **Hearts Of Fire**[38] 1290 2-9-2 0.. PaulEddery 8 87
(Pat Eddery) *trckd ldr: effrt wl over 1f out and sn rdn: led briefly 1f out: sn drvn: hdd and kpt on same pce* **7/2**[3]

4 **3** *¾* **Janeiro (IRE)**[5] 2128 2-8-12 0... RichardSmith 3 81+
(Tom Dascombe) *s.i.s and towards rr: hdwy on inner 2f out: swtchd lft and rdn over 1f out: styd on wl fnl f: nrst fin* **12/1**

1401 **4** *2 ¼* **Fratellino**[10] 1991 2-9-4 0.. JoeFanning 9 79
(A J McCabe) *led: rdn along wl over 1f out: drvn and hdd 1f out: wknd* **11/4**[2]

22 **5** *nk* **Ventura Cove (IRE)**[10] 1991 2-8-12 0.......................... JamieMoriarty 7 72
(R A Fahey) *chsd ldrs: rdn along 2f out: drvn and wknd over 1f out* **7/2**[3]

0260 **6** *4* **Island Express (IRE)**[14] 1891 2-8-12 0................................ AnnStokell 2 57
(Miss A Stokell) *midfield: rdn along 1/2-way: drvn over 1f out and nvr nr ldrs* **200/1**

03 **7** *1 ½* **Lees Anthem**[21] 1661 2-8-12 0.............................. PatrickMathers 6 52
(C J Teague) *chsd ldrs: rdn along 2f out: sn hung rt and wknd* **20/1**

8 *12* **Eeny Mac (IRE)** 2-8-9 0... JimmyQuinn 1 6
(N Bycroft) *sn outpcd and a bhd* **100/1**

0 **9** *26* **Ron The Don**[19] 1735 2-8-12 0...................................... KrishGundowry 5 —
(A Berry) *dwlt and hmpd s: a outpcd and bhd* **150/1**

64.43 secs (0.93) **Going Correction** +0.20s/f (Good) **9** Ran SP% **116.5**
Speed ratings (Par 99): **100,98,97,93,93 86,84,65,23**
toteswinger: 1&2 £2.10, 1&3 £6.60, 2&3 £11.80 CSF £10.56 TOTE £2.90: £1.10, £1.50, £2.80; EX 11.70 Trifecta £110.90 Pool: £404.94 - 2.70 winning units..
Owner John & Zoe Webster **Bred** John Fielding **Trained** West Ilsley, Berks

FOCUS
A decent juvenile conditions event, although only four had chances according to the market. Seven of the nine previous winners of this contest had already won a race; only three of these nine runners had previously tasted victory and they finished first, second and fourth. The Brocklesby form was also boosted, the front pair from Doncaster filling the first two places here, albeit the other way round. The ultra tough Archers Road ran right up to form.

NOTEBOOK
Archers Road(IRE) has been consistent, having never finished outside the first two in six previous starts, and his last three defeats have been against some of the best juveniles seen this season. Never far away here, he responded in game fashion when asked to hit the front inside the last furlong and won going away. He is a credit to connections and will surely be seen at Royal Ascot, although for which race is unclear. (op 15-8 tchd 7-4)
Hearts Of Fire was rather disappointing behind the smart Monsieur Chevalier at Newmarket on his only start since winning the Brocklesby, but this was much better. Content to track the leader early, he picked that rival up when asked a furlong out, but the winner was produced at the same time and he couldn't match him late on. There are more races to be won with him. (op 10-3)
Janeiro(IRE) ◆, who blew the start before running on into fourth in a maiden on the Southwell Fibresand on debut five days earlier, ran a blinder in this much better contest, as he missed the break again. He stayed on very strongly in the latter stages, however, and was still going forward at the line. On this evidence, a maiden is a formality. (op 18-1)
Fratellino, who had already finished twice behind Archers Road, came into this in good form following his all-the-way win at York. He had the ideal draw from which to attack again. He blazed off into a clear lead, but this stiffer track found him out. He had nothing left once headed over a furlong from home. Official explanation: trainer said colt lost a front shoe (op 3-1 tchd 4-1)
Ventura Cove(IRE), three lengths behind Fratellino at York last time and 2lb better off, had his chance, but looked beaten when hanging markedly inside the final furlong. He is worth another chance to break his duck on a less-demanding track. (op 9-2)
Island Express(IRE) Official explanation: jockey said colt hung left
Lees Anthem, who might have beaten Archers Road before running out on his Newcastle debut, threw it away again at Doncaster last time. Although he looked awkward again here, he was already well beaten and couldn't even get the better of plater Island Express. (op 25-1 tchd 16-1)

2261 BEVERLEY ELECTRIC H'CAP 1m 100y

4:25 (4:26) (Class 5) (0-70,70) 4-Y-O+ **£2,914** (£867; £433; £216) **Stalls** High

Form RPR

4-62 **1** **Salerosa (IRE)**[19] 1723 4-8-8 **60**...................................... JimmyQuinn 8 69
(Mrs A Duffield) *midfield: hdwy over 3f out and sn trcking ldrs: effrt over 1f out and sn rdn: drvn ins fnl f and styd on to ld last 100yds: jst hld on* **5/1**[1]

0304 **2** *shd* **Networker**[29] 1495 6-8-10 **62**................................... EdwardCreighton 7 71
(P J McBride) *trckd ldrs: hdwy 3f out: rdn to chse ldr over 1f out: sn drvn and ev ch tl nt qckn nr fin* **14/1**

0402 **3** *1 ½* **Shadowtime**[11] 1955 4-8-6 **65**.. PaulPickard(7) 4 71
(Miss Tracy Waggott) *prom: hdwy to ld 3f out: rdn clr wl over 1f out: drvn ent fnl f: hdd and no ex last 100yds* **7/1**[3]

2000 **4** *½* **Casino Night**[22] 1646 4-8-12 **69**.................................. DeanHeslop(5) 10 73
(R Johnson) *hld up towards rr: hdwy wl over 2f out: rdn over 1f out: styd on ins fnl f: nrst fin* **14/1**

4-55 **5** *½* **Ermine Grey**[36] 1318 8-8-8 **60**................................... KirstyMilczarek 1 63+
(S Gollings) *hld up in rr: hdwy wl over 2f out: swtchd outside and rdn over 1f out: kpt on u.p ins fnl f: nrst fin* **14/1**

3410 **6** *¾* **Blue Charm**[1] 2245 5-8-11 **70**... BMcHugh(7) 11 72+
(I W McInnes) *in tch on inner: n.m.r and lost pl over 5f out: rdn along and hdwy 3f out: nt clr run on inner 2f out: swtchd lft and drvn over 1f out: kpt on ins fnl f: nrst fin* **5/1**[1]

0530 **7** *4* **Maybe I Wont**[4] 2171 4-8-4 **56** oh1.................................. NeilChalmers 15 48
(Lucinda Featherstone) *bhd: rdn along over 2f out: hdwy over 1f out: kpt on ins fnl f: nvr nr ldrs* **11/1**

-146 **8** *½* **Rossini's Dancer**[11] 1955 4-8-0 **59**............................ TimothyAyres(7) 2 50
(R A Fahey) *chsd ldrs: rdn along over 2f out and grad wknd* **14/1**

0-20 **9** *hd* **Society Music (IRE)**[14] 1887 7-9-1 **67**........................(p) JoeFanning 12 58
(M Dods) *in tch: rdn along over 3f out: drvn 2f out and sn wknd* **6/1**[2]

30-0 **10** *hd* **Thunderstruck**[4] 2150 4-8-10 **69**........................... JonathanHinch(7) 14 59
(A J McCabe) *a towards rr* **20/1**

1140 **11** *1* **Very Well Red**[24] 1612 6-8-9 **66**.............................. WilliamCarson(5) 3 54
(P W Hiatt) *led: rdn along and hdd 3f out: sn wknd* **16/1**

-640 **12** *¾* **Mister Maq**[26] 1556 6-8-1 **56** oh10.........................(v) KellyHarrison(3) 13 42
(A Crook) *a towards rr* **66/1**

3-22 **13** *1* **Oskari**[30] 1476 4-8-13 **65**.. JamieMoriarty 9 49
(P T Midgley) *s.i.s: a in rr* **14/1**

4-06 **14** *7* **Glenridding**[36] 1332 5-8-8 **67**..................................... RosieJessop(7) 5 35
(J G Given) *chsd ldrs to 1/2-way: sn rdn along and wknd over 2f out* **8/1**

1m 47.8s (0.20) **Going Correction** +0.20s/f (Good) **14** Ran SP% **125.0**
Speed ratings (Par 103): **107,106,105,104,104 103,99,99,98,98 97,97,96,89**
toteswinger: 1&2 £18.80, 1&3 £8.80, 2&3 £34.00 CSF £79.36 CT £506.43 TOTE £6.00: £2.30, £4.40, £3.50; EX 93.70.
Owner David K Barker **Bred** Pedro Rosas **Trained** Constable Burton, N Yorks

FOCUS
A modest if competitive handicap in which the pace seemed reasonable. Sound form.

2262 MARATHON STAYERS H'CAP 2m 35y

5:00 (5:00) (Class 5) (0-75,71) 4-Y-O+ **£2,914** (£867; £433; £216) **Stalls** High

Form RPR

0-10 **1** **Herrera (IRE)**[35] 1366 4-9-9 **70**...................................... JamieMoriarty 5 75
(R A Fahey) *hld up: hdwy to trck ldrs over 5f out: cl up 3f out: rdn to ld ent fnl f: sn drvn and hld on wl* **6/1**[3]

01/4 **2** *hd* **Pagan Starprincess**[32] 1439 5-8-6 **56**.................... PatrickDonaghy(5) 3 61
(G M Moore) *hld up in rr: stdy hdwy 3f out: effrt on outer over 1f out: rdn to chal ins fnl f: ev ch tl drvn and no ex nr fin* **11/4**[1]

140- **3** ½ **Jackday (IRE)**[270] 5385 4-8-10 **57**............................ DuranFentiman 6 61
(T D Easterby) *hld up in rr: swtchd outside and hdwy over 2f out: rdn over 1f out: drvn ins fnl f: styd on wl towards fin* **14/1**

-330 **4** nk **Solas Alainn (IRE)**[8] 2040 4-9-10 **71**.............................(b[1]) JoeFanning 9 75
(M Johnston) *trckd ldrs: hdwy to ld wl over 2f out: sn jnd and rdn: drvn and hdd ent fnl f: wknd towards fin* **9/2**[2]

3-02 **5** 2¼ **Aleron (IRE)**[8] 1767 11-9-1 **60**...(p) DNolan 2 61
(J J Quinn) *hld up in midfield: stdy hdwy over 4f out: effrt to chse ldrs 2f out and sn rdn: drvn ent fnl f and kpt on same pce* **7/1**

0-6 **6** 2¾ **Toboggan Lady**[15] 1851 5-8-7 **59** ow7............................ BMcHugh[(7)] 10 57
(Mrs A Duffield) *trckd ldrs: rdn along on inner over 2f out: drvn over 1f out: sn wknd* **25/1**

2062 **7** 3 **Snowberry Hill (USA)**[46] 1171 6-9-0 **59**.......................... JimmyQuinn 8 53
(Lucinda Featherstone) *hld up in tch on inner: effrt and n.m.r over 2f out: rdn and n.m.r over 1f out: sn no imp* **7/1**

0-40 **8** 7 **Mister Arjay (USA)**[14] 1886 9-8-11 **61**............................ LanceBetts[(5)] 4 47
(B Ellison) *sn pushed along and led after 1f: rdn along after 5f: hdd 1/2-way: cl up tl drvn along over 3f out and wknd over 2f out* **8/1**

323- **9** 4 **Moonshine Beach**[252] 5917 11-8-10 **60**................... WilliamCarson[(5)] 7 41
(P W Hiatt) *hld up: a towards rr* **11/1**

400 **10** 10 **Admiral (IRE)**[15] 1826 8-9-11 **70**................................. KirstyMilczarek 1 39
(S Parr) *led 1f: cl up tl led again 1/2-way: rdn along 3f out: sn hdd & wknd qckly* **25/1**

3m 41.46s (1.66) **Going Correction** +0.20s/f (Good)
WFA 4 from 5yo+ 2lb 10 Ran SP% **117.9**
Speed ratings (Par 103): **103,102,102,102,101 100,98,95,93,88**
toteswinger: 1&2 £8.20, 1&3 £19.50, 2&3 £11.50 CSF £23.13 CT £220.65 TOTE £7.30: £2.30, £1.50, £3.50; EX 24.60.
Owner Dr Anne J F Gillespie **Bred** Dr A J F Gillespie **Trained** Musley Bank, N Yorks
■ Stewards' Enquiry : Kirsty Milczarek two-day ban: careless riding (Jun 7-8)

FOCUS
An ordinary staying handicap and the first four home finished in a bunch. The pair that set the early tempo eventually dropped out and the finish was dominated by hold-up horses. The form looks sound.

2263 WHITE ROSE SADDLERY CELEBRATING 25 YEARS LADY AMATEUR RIDERS' H'CAP 1m 1f 207y
5:30 (5:33) (Class 5) (0-70,69) 4-Y-0+ **£2,654** (£823; £411; £205) **Stalls High**

Form RPR
0330 **1** **General Tufto**[7] 2068 4-10-5 **64**.....................................(b) MissEJJones 2 68
(C Smith) *in rr: pushed along over 2f out: hdwy and rdn over 1f out: swtchd rt ent fnl f: styd on strly to chal whn hung lft last 100yds: kpt on to ld nr line* **12/1**

306 **2** shd **Kirstys Lad**[12] 1938 7-9-5 **55** oh9......................... MissMMullineaux[(5)] 5 59
(M Mullineaux) *hld up in rr: hdwy on wd outside 2f out: rdn over 1f out: styd on strly ent fnl f to ld last 100yds: hdd nr line* **25/1**

-000 **3** ½ **Coronado's Gold (USA)**[18] 1767 8-9-3 **55** oh8.......... MissVCoates[(7)] 7 58
(B Ellison) *hld up towards rr: stdy hdwy 1/2-way: chal on outer 2f out: rdn to ld 1f out: sn drvn: hdd and no ex last 100yds* **22/1**

550- **4** 2¼ **Hurricane Thomas (IRE)**[218] 6786 5-9-3 **55** oh1. MissPhillipaTutty[(7)] 3 53
(R A Fahey) *hld up: hdwy 3f out: rdn to chse ldrs over 1f out: edgd rt and kpt on same pce wl ins fnl f* **12/1**

0435 **5** ½ **Keisha Kayleigh (IRE)**[5] 2129 6-10-5 **64**......................(p) MissLEllison 8 61
(B Ellison) *slowly away and in rr tl hdwy over 2f out: sn rdn and styng on whn n.m.r and swtchd rt ins fnl f: kpt on* **11/4**[1]

-143 **6** nse **Street Devil (USA)**[30] 1479 4-10-3 **69**......................... MissCBoxall[(7)] 12 66
(R Curtis) *led: rdn along 2f out: drvn and hung rt over 1f out: hdd ent fnl f and wknd* **11/2**[2]

353- **7** 1¼ **Proficiency**[206] 7085 4-9-13 **58**..................................... MrsCBartley 6 53
(T D Walford) *trckd ldrs: hdwy 3f out: cl up 2f out: sn rdn and ev ch whn hmpd appr fnl f: sn wknd* **8/1**

041- **8** shd **Amazing King (IRE)**[111] 7427 5-9-10 **62**............... MissSMStaveley[(7)] 9 57
(P A Kirby) *hld up towards rr: hdwy 2f out: rdn to chse ldrs over 1f out: wknd ins fnl f* **11/2**[2]

3050 **9** 3 **Ming Vase**[14] 1883 7-9-5 **55** oh5................................. MissWGibson[(5)] 4 44
(P T Midgley) *trckd ldrs: n.m.r over 4f out: sn lost pl and rr fnl 2f* **14/1**

6/30 **10** 1 **Diamond Lass (IRE)**[18] 1778 4-9-12 **62**....................... MrsVFahey[(5)] 11 49
(R A Fahey) *chsd ldr: hdwy 3f out and sn cl up: rdn 2f out: hmpd over 1f out and wknd* **6/1**[3]

-000 **11** 4½ **Gala Sunday (USA)**[14] 1881 9-9-10 **55**......................(bt) MissSBrotherton 1 33
(M W Easterby) *trckd ldrs: hdwy 3f out: rdn 2f out: sn drvn and wknd* **9/1**

060- **12** 10 **Scotty's Future (IRE)**[186] 7373 11-9-10 **55** oh8............ MissADeniel 10 13
(A Berry) *a towards rr: bhd fnl 2f* **25/1**

2m 10.22s (3.22) **Going Correction** +0.20s/f (Good) 12 Ran SP% **126.9**
Speed ratings (Par 103): **95,94,94,92,92 92,91,91,88,88 84,76**
toteswinger: 1&2 £39.60, 1&3 £61.60, 2&3 £59.90 CSF £296.10 CT £6379.05 TOTE £15.20: £3.20, £8.60, £8.80; EX 326.80 Place 6: £44.74, Place 5: £12.85.
Owner Phil Martin & Trev Sleath **Bred** Hascombe And Valiant Studs **Trained** Temple Bruer, Lincs

FOCUS
A modest event with almost half the field out of the weights including the second and third. Two horses raced into a clear lead early, but they had slowed by the time the runners rounded the home bend, and the first three came from the rear. This was a messy contest.
T/Plt: £71.00 to a £1 stake. Pool: £68,865.74. 707.60 winning tickets. T/Qpdt: £25.10 to a £1 stake. Pool: £3,166.65. 93.20 winning tickets. JR

1764 CATTERICK (L-H)
Saturday, May 23

OFFICIAL GOING: Good (8.2)
Wind: Light, half behind Weather: Cloudy

2264 TOTEPLACEPOT (S) STKS 1m 3f 214y
2:30 (2:30) (Class 6) 4-Y-0+ **£2,047** (£604; £302) **Stalls Low**

Form RPR
4204 **1** **Nawamees (IRE)**[5] 2129 11-8-12 69........................(p) RichardEvans[(5)] 11 70
(P D Evans) *chsd ldrs: effrt over 2f out: led ins fnl f: r.o wl* **10/3**[2]

1323 **2** ¾ **Edas**[21] 1099 7-9-3 68.. GrahamGibbons 3 69
(J J Quinn) *prom: rdn to ld over 1f out: hdd ins fnl f: kpt on same pce nr fin* **7/4**[1]

2021 **3** 7 **Terminate (GER)**[10] 1980 7-9-3 58............................(t) J-PGuillambert 6 58
(Ian Williams) *racd keenly: hld up: hdwy 2f out: kpt on fnl f: nt rch first two* **11/2**[3]

-403 **4** 3¼ **Titinius (IRE)**[31] 1454 9-8-11 55..............................(p) PhillipMakin 10 46
(Micky Hammond) *led 1f: prom tl rdn and wknd over 1f out* **9/1**

20- **5** 1 **Evelith Regent (IRE)**[183] 7405 6-8-11 61......................... PJMcDonald 12 45
(G A Swinbank) *t.k.h: led after 1f to over 1f out: sn wknd* **10/1**

2500 **6** 4½ **Epidaurian King (IRE)**[9] 1475 6-8-11 57......................... DanielTudhope 8 38
(D Shaw) *hld up: hmpd 5f out: effrt on outside over 2f out: edgd lft and sn no imp* **25/1**

435/ **7** 2¾ **Campbells Lad**[642] 4670 8-8-4 54.................................. BillyCray[(7)] 13 33
(A Berry) *s.i.s: bhd: rdn 3f out: nvr on terms* **40/1**

0-40 **8** 1 **Mayadeen (IRE)**[116] 300 7-8-11 55............................(v) DaleGibson 1 32
(R A Fahey) *hld up on ins: drvn 3f out: n.d* **18/1**

50-0 **9** 9 **Five Wishes**[20] 1690 5-8-7 60 ow1.......................................(e) DavidAllan 5 13
(G A Harker) *hld up: hdwy and prom over 4f out: wknd over 2f out* **20/1**

40/- **10** 13 **Tip Top Style**[27] 243 6-8-11 45..(p) PaulQuinn 9 —
(A Crook) *hld up: struggling over 3f out: nvr on terms* **150/1**

/00- **P** **Aura Of Calm (IRE)**[25] 6708 7-8-11 44.......................(t) DarrenMoffatt 7 —
(Ronald O'Leary, Ire) *in tch: lost pl qckly 5f out: sn p.u* **28/1**

2m 37.97s (-0.93) **Going Correction** 0.0s/f (Good) 11 Ran SP% **114.3**
Speed ratings (Par 101): **103,102,97,95,95 92,90,89,83,74** —
toteswinger: 1&2 £1.80, 1&3 £3.40, 2&3 £1.50 CSF £8.69 TOTE £4.40: £1.80, £1.10, £2.20; EX 12.50.There was no bid for the winner. Edas was claimed by R. C. Guest for £6,000.
Owner Jeremiah Coffey **Bred** Kilfrush Stud Ltd **Trained** Pandy, Monmouths

FOCUS
Very little strength in depth and the two that spearheaded the market dominated the finish.
Aura Of Calm(IRE) Official explanation: vet said gelding was struck into

2265 TOTESWINGER RACING MEDIAN AUCTION MAIDEN STKS 5f
3:00 (3:00) (Class 6) 3-Y-0 **£2,388** (£705; £352) **Stalls Low**

Form RPR
3-00 **1** **Future Gem**[23] 1628 3-8-12 40.. DanielTudhope 3 55
(A Dickman) *mde all: rdn and hld on wl fnl f* **25/1**

0-60 **2** 1½ **Cavitie**[15] 1840 3-9-3 50.. J-PGuillambert 5 55
(Andrew Reid) *prom: effrt 2f out: kpt on fnl f* **14/1**

0-23 **3** ½ **Diamond Blade**[15] 1852 3-9-3 65..................................... DavidAllan 2 53
(T D Easterby) *prom: drvn over 2f out: effrt over 1f out: kpt on same pce fnl f* **4/5**[1]

2204 **4** 3¾ **Fashion Icon (USA)**[11] 1949 3-8-9 57............................ NeilBrown[(3)] 9 34
(T D Barron) *cl up tl rdn and no ex over 1f out* **6/1**[3]

64-0 **5** 1 **Positivity**[8] 2046 3-8-12 63.. PhillipMakin 7 31
(B Smart) *prom: drvn 1/2-way: edgd lft and no ex over 1f out* **9/2**[2]

600 **6** ¾ **Honey Berry (IRE)**[33] 1400 3-8-12 46...................(v[1]) CatherineGannon 1 28
(Patrick Morris) *dwlt: drvn along in rr 1/2-way: nvr on terms* **50/1**

02-0 **7** 5 **Fifth Amendment**[36] 1335 3-9-3 69................................. MickyFenton 8 15
(A Berry) *dwlt: rdn in rr 1/2-way: sn btn* **11/1**

6 **8** 2¾ **Our Girl Ally (IRE)**[15] 1828 3-8-5 0.............................. BillyCray[(7)] 6 —
(A Berry) *prom to 1/2-way: sn wknd* **33/1**

60.92 secs (1.12) **Going Correction** 0.0s/f (Good) 8 Ran SP% **111.8**
Speed ratings (Par 97): **91,88,87,81,80 79,71,66**
toteswinger: 1&2 £18.00, 1&3 £7.40, 2&3 £7.70 CSF £308.42 TOTE £44.80: £2.70, £3.40, £1.10; EX 683.30.
Owner Coast To Coast **Bred** Genesis Green Stud Ltd **Trained** Sandhutton, N Yorks

FOCUS
A truly awful maiden.
Future Gem Official explanation: trainer said, regarding the apparent improvement in form, that the filly appreciated being able to dominate.

2266 TOTEQUADPOT H'CAP 7f
3:35 (3:35) (Class 3) (0-90,90) 4-Y-0+ **£7,771** (£2,312; £1,155; £577) **Stalls Low**

Form RPR
0-00 **1** **Celtic Sultan (IRE)**[15] 1821 5-8-13 **85**............................. MickyFenton 11 96
(T P Tate) *mde all: rdn and drifted rt to stands' side fr over 2f out: hld on wl fnl f* **9/1**

-653 **2** 1½ **Fathsta (IRE)**[15] 1821 4-9-1 **90**................................... AndrewMullen[(3)] 1 97
(D Nicholls) *t.k.h: trckd ldrs: effrt over 2f out: edgd rt over 1f out: kpt on fnl f: wnt 2nd nr fin* **3/1**[2]

0-12 **3** nk **Horatio Carter**[8] 2045 4-8-13 **90**.................................(p) AmyRyan[(5)] 2 96
(K A Ryan) *pressed wnr: effrt and edgd rt fr over 1f out: kpt on fnl f: no ex and lost 2nd nr fin* **5/2**[1]

0-00 **4** ¾ **Zomerlust**[21] 1682 7-8-6 **78**.. GrahamGibbons 5 82
(J J Quinn) *prom: effrt over 2f out: kpt on fnl f: nrst fin* **20/1**

162- **5** 3¼ **Keys Of Cyprus**[217] 6813 7-8-7 **79**..................................... PaulQuinn 4 74+
(D Nicholls) *hld up: rdn ent st: kpt on fnl f: no imp* **10/1**

-024 **6** ½ **Sunrise Safari (IRE)**[15] 1849 6-8-7 **86**.......................(v) LeeTopliss[(7)] 6 80
(R A Fahey) *midfield: drvn over 2f out: outpcd wl over 1f out* **14/1**

/32- **7** ¾ **Lady Rangali (IRE)**[332] 3369 4-8-11 **83**............................... PhillipMakin 7 75+
(Mrs A Duffield) *bhd: sme hdwy over 1f out: nvr rchd ldrs* **8/1**[3]

0-00 **8** 1¼ **Stevie Gee (IRE)**[15] 1849 5-8-8 **80**................................. PJMcDonald 9 69
(G A Swinbank) *prom tl rdn and wknd fr 2f out* **22/1**

2014 **9** 1 **Obe Royal**[32] 1436 5-8-5 **77**......................................(b) CatherineGannon 8 63
(P D Evans) *bhd: pushed along 3f out: nvr on terms* **33/1**

3-11 **10** nk **Turn Me On (IRE)**[18] 1766 6-8-8 **80**.............................. DanielTudhope 3 65
(T D Walford) *hld up: drvn over 2f out: nvr a factor* **8/1**[3]

-140 **11** 2¼ **Malcheek (IRE)**[15] 1849 7-8-7 **79**....................................... DavidAllan 10 58
(T D Easterby) *midfield on outside: rdn over 2f out: wknd wl over 1f out* **25/1**

1m 25.38s (-1.62) **Going Correction** 0.0s/f (Good) 11 Ran SP% **117.4**
Speed ratings (Par 107): **109,107,106,106,102 101,100,99,98,98 95**
toteswinger: 1&2 £7.00, 1&3 £12.60, 2&3 £1.40 CSF £34.38 CT £91.30 TOTE £14.90: £2.90, £1.20, £1.50; EX 50.60.
Owner Mrs Sylvia Clegg and Louise Worthington **Bred** Miss C Lyons **Trained** Tadcaster, N Yorks

FOCUS
A decent handicap.

NOTEBOOK
Celtic Sultan(IRE) managed to get to the front, despite his wide draw, and soon had his field on the stretch. Despite having looked as though he'd probably done too much early and drifting right across to the stands' side in the straight, he kept on gamely to hold off Fathsta. He doesn't have the most appealing of strike-rates, but he had dropped 15lb since winning at Chester 12 months ago and deserves plenty of credit for doing this the hard way. (op 12-1)
Fathsta(IRE) ran a blinder off this mark at Chester last time and he was well drawn to go close, but he could never get to the trailblazer. Still, he ran another fine race in defeat and continues to knock at the door. (op 7-2 tchd 11-4)
Horatio Carter came here after posting a career-best effort at Newcastle and he kept on well having chased the pace throughout, but he looks a shade vulnerable at the weights now. (op 10-3)
Zomerlust prefers much more testing ground than this, so he has shaped with significant promise in third, staying on strongly up the middle of the track and he's slipped to a very handy mark now, so is one to note when getting his favoured conditions. (op 18-1)
Keys Of Cyprus emerged from the pack to shape with some promise despite his career-high mark and he'll be seen to better effect when getting some juice in the ground. (op 9-1 tchd 11-1)

Turn Me On(IRE) Official explanation: jockey said gelding ran flat

2267 TOTEEXACTA RACING H'CAP 5f 212y

4:10 (4:10) (Class 4) (0-85,87) 4-Y-0+ **£5,180** (£1,541; £770; £384) **Stalls** Low

Form RPR

606- **1** **Johannes (IRE)**[185] 7386 6-8-7 **73** DavidAllan 2 83
(R A Fahey) *prom: drvn to ld ins fnl f: kpt on wl* **4/1**[2]

0-36 **2** 3/4 **Wyatt Earp (IRE)**[7] 2093 8-9-4 **84** DaleGibson 4 92
(P Salmon) *trckd ldr: led over 1f out to ins fnl f: kpt on: hld nr fin* **7/1**

420- **3** 2 **Kashimin (IRE)**[287] 4875 4-9-2 **82** PJMcDonald 1 84
(G A Swinbank) *hld up: hdwy fr 2f out: kpt on fnl f: nt rch first two* **7/1**

00-2 **4** 2 **Bonnie Prince Blue**[15] 1832 6-8-6 **75** AndrewMullen(3) 9 70
(D Nicholls) *prom on outside: effrt over 2f out: edgd lft and outpcd over 1f out* **6/1**[3]

4401 **5** nse **Vhujon (IRE)**[2] 2203 4-9-2 **87** 6ex RichardEvans(5) 3 82+
(P D Evans) *hld up: hdwy and swtchd rt over 1f out: r.o fnl f: nrst fin* **2/1**[1]

3-60 **6** 1 1/2 **Mr Wolf**[14] 1885 8-8-6 **72** (p) CatherineGannon 8 62
(D W Barker) *led to over 1f out: sn rdn and wknd* **10/1**

6100 **7** 2 3/4 **El Dececy (USA)**[16] 1798 5-9-1 **81** PaulDoe 5 62
(S Parr) *prom tl wknd wl over 1f out* **25/1**

30-0 **8** 3 1/4 **Grazeon Gold Blend**[15] 1849 6-8-12 **78** MickyFenton 6 49
(J J Quinn) *hld up: drvn over 2f out: sn btn* **25/1**

02-0 **9** nk **Dig Deep (IRE)**[21] 1685 7-8-8 **74** GrahamGibbons 7 44
(J J Quinn) *hld up in midfield: rdn over 2f out: sn wknd* **12/1**

1m 12.72s (-0.88) **Going Correction** 0.0s/f (Good) **9** Ran SP% **117.1**
Speed ratings (Par 105): **105,104,101,98,98 96,92,88,88**
toteswinger: 1&2 £5.80, 1&3 £6.80, 2&3 £10.50 CSF £32.62 CT £187.75 TOTE £4.00: £1.40, £2.20, £2.30; EX 34.60.

Owner John Nicholls Ltd/David Kilburn **Bred** Blue Bloodstock Limited **Trained** Musley Bank, N Yorks

FOCUS
A competitive looking handicap run at a decent clip thanks to Mr Wolf.

2268 TOTEPOOL MEDIAN AUCTION MAIDEN FILLIES' STKS 5f 212y

4:45 (4:46) (Class 6) 3-4-Y-0 **£2,388** (£705; £352) **Stalls** Low

Form RPR

24-4 **1** **Winged Harriet (IRE)**[15] 1837 3-8-10 80 LiamJones 2 58+
(W J Haggas) *stdd s: hld up: smooth hdwy to trck ldr over 1f out: plld out and qcknd to ld nr fin* **4/9**[1]

6-00 **2** 1/2 **Sleepy Valley (IRE)**[21] 1662 3-8-10 52 (p) DanielTudhope 3 57
(A Dickman) *chsd ldr: led over 1f out tl hdd nr fin* **25/1**

04 **3** 3 **Josphiel (IRE)**[12] 1922 4-8-12 54 (b[1]) BillyCray(7) 8 49
(A Berry) *led to over 1f out: sn outpcd* **14/1**[3]

6 **4** 4 **Choree (IRE)**[15] 1852 3-8-10 0 DavidAllan 6 34
(T D Easterby) *chsd ldrs tl rdn and wknd over 1f out* **16/1**

050 **5** nk **Baligha**[8] 2030 4-9-5 55 (t) PJMcDonald 5 35
(G A Swinbank) *hld up in tch: rdn over 2f out: no imp* **25/1**

0-00 **6** 3/4 **Alyseve**[12] 1940 4-8-12 34 (p) KylieManser(7) 1 33
(Mrs C A Dunnett) *prom tl rdn and wknd fr 2f out* **66/1**

7 4 1/2 **Dalmunzie (IRE)** 3-8-10 0 GrahamGibbons 7 16+
(J J Quinn) *s.i.s: sn outpcd: no ch fr 1/2-way* **7/2**[2]

1m 14.54s (0.94) **Going Correction** 0.0s/f (Good)
WFA 3 from 4yo 9lb **7** Ran SP% **113.2**
Speed ratings (Par 98): **93,92,88,83,82 81,75**
toteswinger: 1&2 £3.70, 1&3 £2.20, 2&3 £10.40 CSF £17.69 TOTE £1.30: £1.10, £8.10; EX 12.30.

Owner Exors of the Late F C T Wilson **Bred** Barronstown Stud **Trained** Newmarket, Suffolk

FOCUS
A very weak maiden.

2269 TOTETRIFECTA H'CAP 7f

5:15 (5:15) (Class 5) (0-75,76) 4-Y-0+ **£3,412** (£1,007; £504) **Stalls** Low

Form RPR

0100 **1** **Splash The Cash**[4] 2156 4-8-5 **67** AmyRyan(5) 12 78
(K A Ryan) *hld up: gd hdwy to ld wl over 1f out: sn clr* **6/1**[3]

2201 **2** 2 1/2 **Desert Dreamer (IRE)**[14] 1894 8-8-12 **74** RichardEvans(5) 11 78
(P D Evans) *missed break: bhd: hdwy 2f out: chsd wnr ins fnl f: r.o* **8/1**

-322 **3** 3 **Kargan (IRE)**[22] 1650 4-8-4 **61** oh1 LiamJones 8 57+
(A G Foster) *s.i.s: bhd tl hdwy over 1f out: edgd lft ins fnl f: r.o* **10/1**

3123 **4** nk **This Ones For Eddy**[20] 1690 4-9-0 **71** PaulDoe 6 66
(S Parr) *trckd ldrs: drvn and led briefly 2f out: sn one pce* **5/1**[2]

00-0 **5** 2 **Call For Liberty (IRE)**[29] 1493 4-8-13 **70** (b) PJMcDonald 2 60
(B Smart) *trckd ldrs tl rdn and outpcd fnl 2f* **33/1**

000- **6** 1/2 **Mountain Cat (IRE)**[332] 3376 5-8-4 **61** PaulQuinn 1 50
(G A Swinbank) *w ldr tl no ex fr 2f out* **16/1**

0-35 **7** nk **We'Re Delighted**[19] 1737 4-9-1 **72** GrahamGibbons 10 60
(T D Walford) *in tch: drvn 3f out: no imp fnl 2f* **6/1**[3]

0- **8** nk **Desert Ben (IRE)**[213] 6915 6-8-5 **62** DarrenMoffatt 9 49
(C Grant) *bhd: rdn 1/2-way: sme late hdwy: nvr on terms* **20/1**

1201 **9** 1 3/4 **Dancing Maite**[7] 2088 4-9-2 **76** RussellKennemore(3) 7 58
(S R Bowring) *prom on outside: rdn and outpcd whn hung rt fr 2f out* **6/1**[3]

0500 **10** shd **Spin Again (IRE)**[11] 1952 4-8-9 **69** AndrewMullen(3) 3 51
(D Nicholls) *mde most to 2f out: sn wknd* **11/1**

0-04 **11** hd **Hiccups**[18] 1766 9-9-4 **75** PhillipMakin 4 56
(M Dods) *hld up: rdn over 2f out: sn wknd* **9/2**[1]

1m 26.3s (-0.70) **Going Correction** 0.0s/f (Good) **11** Ran SP% **119.8**
Speed ratings (Par 103): **104,101,97,97,95 94,94,93,91,91 91**
toteswinger: 1&2 £13.50, 1&3 £12.10, 2&3 £18.00 CSF £54.52 CT £480.03 TOTE £5.90: £2.40, £3.20, £3.10; EX 88.40 Place 6 £36.77, Place 5 £30.95.

Owner The Armchair Jockeys **Bred** G B Turnbull Ltd **Trained** Hambleton, N Yorks

FOCUS
Competitive enough for the grade.

Splash The Cash Official explanation: trainer's rep said, regarding the apparent improvement in form, that the gelding settled better off a stronger pace.

Mountain Cat(IRE) Official explanation: jockey said gelding stumbled on the bend

Dancing Maite Official explanation: jockey said gelding failed to handle the track

T/Plt: £39.90 to a £1 stake. Pool: £44,348.14. 809.53 winning tickets. T/Qpdt: £26.80 to a £1 stake. Pool: £2,213.70. 60.90 winning tickets. RY

2225 HAYDOCK (L-H)

Saturday, May 23

OFFICIAL GOING: Heavy (soft in places)
Races on Round course increased in distance by 16yards with the exception of 4.50 race which was reduced by 22yards.
Wind: Almost nil Weather: Fine

2270 BETFRED "THE BONUS KING" H'CAP 7f 30y

2:05 (2:06) (Class 3) (0-95,95) 3-Y-0 **£9,066** (£2,697; £1,348; £673) **Stalls** Low

Form RPR

10-2 **1** **Exceptional Art**[21] 1664 3-9-1 **92** AlanMunro 1 101
(P W Chapple-Hyam) *hld up and bhd: hdwy over 2f out: rdn to ld ins fnl f: r.o* **12/1**

0-1 **2** 1 3/4 **Leahurst (IRE)**[29] 1491 3-8-10 **87** SebSanders 2 92+
(J Noseda) *a.p: rdn to ld over 1f out: hdd ins fnl f: nt qckn* **8/1**

210- **3** 1 **Quanah Parker (IRE)**[231] 6483 3-8-7 **87** MichaelJStainton(3) 11 89
(R M Whitaker) *w ldr: led 5f out: rdn and hdd over 1f out: kpt on ins fnl f* **40/1**

1-26 **4** 2 1/2 **Wannabe King**[19] 1751 3-8-9 **86** DaneO'Neill 12 82
(D R Lanigan) *hld up and bhd: rdn and hdwy wl over 1f out: nvr able to chal* **13/2**[3]

2132 **5** 1 **Changing The Guard**[30] 1471 3-8-7 **84** (v) TonyHamilton 10 77
(R A Fahey) *hld up and bhd: hdwy over 3f out: rdn over 2f out: sn wandered: no further prog* **16/1**

10-0 **6** 3 1/4 **Definightly**[38] 1296 3-9-0 **91** SteveDrowne 8 75
(R Charlton) *hld up in tch: rdn and wknd wl over 1f out* **16/1**

0-20 **7** 1 1/4 **Enact**[10] 1987 3-8-11 **88** RyanMoore 13 69
(Sir Michael Stoute) *hld up in rr: racd alone on far side st: hdwy over 3f out: rdn over 2f out: wknd over 1f out* **8/1**

2-11 **8** 1/2 **Makaamen**[36] 1324 3-9-4 **95** TPO'Shea 5 75
(B W Hills) *t.k.h: hdwy after 2f: rdn over 2f out: hung lft and wknd wl over 1f out* **5/2**[1]

5-00 **9** 1 1/4 **Polish Pride**[10] 1987 3-8-7 **84** FrancisNorton 3 61
(M Brittain) *a bhd* **22/1**

16-0 **10** 3 1/4 **Miss Eze**[7] 2079 3-8-6 **83** MartinDwyer 7 51
(M L W Bell) *led: hdd 5f out: rdn over 2f out: wknd wl over 1f out* **4/1**[2]

213- **11** 3 **Film Set (USA)**[206] 7075 3-9-0 **91** (t) TedDurcan 4 51
(Saeed Bin Suroor) *prom: rdn over 3f out: wknd over 2f out* **14/1**

20-0 **12** 27 **Zaffaan**[29] 1484 3-8-13 **90** (t) WilliamBuick 6 —
(E A L Dunlop) *prom: rdn over 3f out: wknd over 2f out: t.o* **33/1**

1m 36.42s (6.22) **Going Correction** +0.975s/f (Soft) **12** Ran SP% **120.0**
Speed ratings (Par 103): **103,101,99,97,95 92,90,90,88,85 81,50**
toteswinger: 1&2 £10.50, 1&3 £31.50, 2&3 £41.50 CSF £104.11 CT £3777.16 TOTE £10.40: £3.20, £2.40, £8.70; EX 65.30 TRIFECTA Not won..

Owner Matthew Green **Bred** Mascalls Stud **Trained** Newmarket, Suffolk

FOCUS
A quality 3yo handicap, but it was a real slog in testing conditions. The majority of these were taken towards the centre of the track early in the straight, but they finished well spread out and the main action took place just off the far rail. The form looks sound enough amongst the principals.

NOTEBOOK

Exceptional Art was too keen for his own good when turned over at odds-on in a Doncaster conditions race on his reappearance, but he was more relaxed this time, so much so that he missed the break and took a while to pick up in the straight. He ultimately stayed on best, proving his stamina in no uncertain terms, and he also went some way to justifying the regard in which he is held (ran in last year's Prix Morny). There should be more to come - his connections think he wants 1m - although it remains to be seen whether he'll prove as effective on quicker ground. (op 9-1 tchd 8-1)

Leahurst(IRE), off the mark on his reappearance in a Wolverhampton maiden that's working out quite well, was too keen early. After taking a while to pick up when first coming under pressure, he looked the winner over 1f out - touched 1.11 in-running - but was picked off late on, with his earlier exertions just telling. He can do better as he matures. (op 7-1 tchd 9-1)

Quanah Parker(IRE), back up in trip on his return from 231 days off, was given a positive ride and kept on well for third. He was probably suited by the easy ground. (op 50-1)

Wannabe King, who has held some big-race entries in the past, was well supported on course and didn't fare badly on ground that was probably softer than he really cares for. (op 10-1)

Changing The Guard is better than he showed considering he raced wider than ideal pretty much throughout and he should be capable of better. (op 20-1)

Definightly has won on a soft surface, but he didn't look to be striding out all that fluently late on and gave the impression this ground was more testing than he would have liked. (tchd 14-1)

Enact was the only runner to stick to the far rail throughout and it's impossible to know at how much of a disadvantage she was at, if at all. Whatever, though, things haven't really gone right since her second placing on her reappearance at Newmarket, and she's not one to give up on just yet. (op 6-1)

Makaamen, 5lb higher than when winning a similar race at Newbury (from Wannabe King) on his previous start, didn't help his chance by racing keenly early on and offered little under pressure. Official explanation: jockey said colt ran too free (op 7-2)

Miss Eze had looked unlucky at Newbury last time and seemed sure to be suited by the ground, but she was another to disappoint. (op 6-1)

Zaffaan Official explanation: jockey said gelding was unsuited by the heavy (soft in places) ground

2271 BETFREDCASINO CECIL FRAIL STKS (LISTED RACE) (F&M) 6f

2:35 (2:35) (Class 1) 3-Y-0+

£22,708 (£8,608; £4,308; £2,148; £1,076; £540) **Stalls** Centre

Form RPR

30-6 **1** **Festoso (IRE)**[42] 1210 4-9-2 100 SteveDrowne 2 109
(H J L Dunlop) *hld up and bhd: hdwy over 3f out: nt clr run and swtchd rt 2f out: rdn over 1f out: led wl ins fnl f: r.o* **16/1**

U-26 **2** 1 1/4 **Pusey Street Lady**[25] 1582 5-9-2 99 JimCrowley 5 105
(J Gallagher) *w ldr: led 2f out: rdn over 1f out: hdd and no ex wl ins fnl f* **7/1**

0041 **3** 3 1/4 **Never Lose**[7] 2079 3-8-7 87 MartinDwyer 12 93
(C E Brittain) *hld up in rr: rdn and hdwy wl over 1f out: sn hung lft: kpt on to take 3rd towards fin* **12/1**

110- **4** 1 **Zuzu (IRE)**[231] 6483 3-8-8 91 ow1 PhilipRobinson 3 90
(M A Jarvis) *led 4f: rdn and fdd ins fnl f* **9/1**

414- **5** 2 **Adorn**[232] 6441 3-8-7 105 RyanMoore 6 83
(J Noseda) *a.p on far rail: ev ch 2f out: rdn over 1f out: wknd ins fnl f* **7/2**[2]

-604 **6** 5 **Max One Two Three (IRE)**[14] 1880 4-9-2 94 RichardKingscote 10 69
(Tom Dascombe) *hld up towards rr: rdn and effrt over 2f out: nvr trbld ldrs* **6/1**

02-4 **7** 3 **Aine (IRE)**[35] 1374 4-9-2 97 (b[1]) WMLordan 9 59
(T Stack, Ire) *hld up in tch: wknd 2f out* **10/3**[1]

0435 **8** *1 1/4* **Angus Newz**[6] 2102 6-9-6 93....(v) FrancisNorton 11 59
(M Quinn) *prom tl wknd over 2f out* **16/1**

2510 **9** *3 3/4* **Princess Valerina**[14] 1880 5-9-2 84.... DaneO'Neill 13 43
(D Haydn Jones) *hld up towards rr: rdn over 2f out: sn struggling* **40/1**

10-0 **10** *1 1/4* **Gentle Guru**[25] 1582 5-9-2 85.... Louis-PhilippeBeuzelin 8 39
(R T Phillips) *prom 2f* **40/1**

01-1 **11** *24* **Mullein**[36] 1321 4-9-2 96.... SebSanders 7 —
(R M Beckett) *hld up in tch: wknd wl over 1f out: t.o* **11/2**[3]

1m 19.74s (5.74) **Going Correction** +0.975s/f (Soft)
WFA 3 from 4yo+ 9lb **11** Ran SP% **121.8**
Speed ratings (Par 111): **100,98,94,92,90 83,79,77,72,71 39**
toteswinger: 1&2 £32.50, 1&3 £33.00, 2&3 £18.60 CSF £128.19 TOTE £25.40: £4.70, £2.70, £3.20; EX 157.80 TRIFECTA Not won..
Owner Prince A A Faisal **Bred** Nawara Stud Co Ltd **Trained** Lambourn, Berks

FOCUS
An ordinary fillies' Listed race and quite a few of these probably failed to handle the extremely testing conditions. They raced middle to far side, with the main action taking place close to the far rail. The winner is rated up 7lb on her 2yo form.

NOTEBOOK
Festoso(IRE) didn't offer much on her reappearance in a 1m Listed race on the Polytrack, but she proved a different proposition dropped back to sprinting, this being her first start at 6f since finishing third in the 2007 Cheveley Park. The testing surface also seemed to help and she probably wouldn't want the ground any quicker than good. While the bare form is nothing special, this was a smart effort from a filly who has evidently not been the easiest to train (only ran twice last year) and she could do better again. Her connections will now look for a 6f fillies' Group 3. (tchd 18-1)
Pusey Street Lady handles testing ground well and ran a good race in defeat, leaving behind a below-par effort at Bath on her previous outing. She looks an improved mare this year and could find a similar race. (op 8-1 tchd 13-2)
Never Lose, the winner of a 7f handicap at Newbury off only 82 on her previous start, was outpaced for much of the way but produced a sustained effort up the middle of the track, wide of the front two, and picked up some black type. The testing ground brought her stamina into play. (op 16-1)
Zuzu(IRE), carrying 1lb overweight, made a pleasing return from 231 days off. She's entitled to come on for this and looks capable of picking up some black type this season. (op 10-1)
Adorn ◆, having her first start since running fourth in last season's Cheveley Park, made a pleasing return on ground plenty soft enough for her. She understandably got tired late on and is open to significant improvement. (op 4-1 tchd 9-2 tchd 5-1 in places)
Max One Two Three(IRE) never featured and was probably unsuited by the ground. (op 13-2 tchd 11-2)
Aine(IRE) looked to have obvious claims considering she was runner-up in this race last year, and has winning form on heavy ground, but she disappointed in first-time blinkers. It's possible she didn't face the headgear. (op 7-2 tchd 4-1)
Mullein ran as though something was amiss. Official explanation: jockey said filly lost its action (tchd 5-1 and 6-1)

2272 BETFRED.COM TEMPLE STKS (GROUP 2) 5f
3:10 (3:10) (Class 1) 3-Y-O+
£56,770 (£21,520; £10,770; £5,370; £2,690; £1,350) **Stalls** Centre

Form RPR

4-13 **1** **Look Busy (IRE)**[14] 1880 4-9-1 103.... SladeO'Hara 1 108
(A Berry) *outpcd: hdwy over 1f out: rdn to ld cl home* **15/2**

31-3 **2** *nk* **Borderlescott**[21] 1676 7-9-4 116.... PatCosgrave 11 110
(R Bastiman) *a.p: rdn over 1f out: ev ch wl ins fnl f: r.o* **2/1**[1]

-343 **3** *hd* **Wi Dud**[7] 2094 5-9-4 98....(b) AlanMunro 6 109
(K A Ryan) *a.p: led over 1f out: rdn fnl f: hdd cl home* **33/1**

-110 **4** *2 1/4* **Arganil (USA)**[10] 1989 4-9-4 107.... RyanMoore 12 101
(K A Ryan) *s.i.s: bhd: swtchd lft to far side 3f out: hdwy 2f out: rdn over 1f out: one pce ins fnl f* **12/1**

21-1 **5** *2 3/4* **Total Gallery (IRE)**[24] 1602 3-8-10 105.... LPKeniry 4 91
(J S Moore) *hld up in tch: rdn over 1f out: no imp fnl f* **10/3**[2]

4-20 **6** *4 1/2* **Hogmaneigh (IRE)**[21] 1676 6-9-4 104.... JimCrowley 2 75
(S C Williams) *outpcd: nvr nr ldrs* **16/1**

00-0 **7** *nk* **Captain Gerrard (IRE)**[10] 1989 4-9-4 108.... TomEaves 8 74
(B Smart) *led: hdd and rdn over 1f out: wknd fnl f* **8/1**

3-20 **8** *2 1/2* **Masta Plasta (IRE)**[27] 1543 6-9-4 106.... AdrianTNicholls 7 65
(D Nicholls) *chsd ldrs: rdn over 2f out: wknd wl over 1f out* **16/1**

50-2 **9** *11* **Reverence**[35] 1374 8-9-4 103.... WJSupple 10 25
(E J Alston) *w ldr over 2f: wknd wl over 1f out* **7/1**[3]

64.03 secs (3.53) **Going Correction** +0.975s/f (Soft)
WFA 3 from 4yo+ 8lb **9** Ran SP% **114.2**
Speed ratings (Par 115): **110,109,109,105,101 94,93,89,71**
toteswinger: 1&2 £3.70, 1&3 £21.90, 2&3 £9.60 CSF £22.60 TOTE £8.90: £2.00, £1.30, £4.80; EX 25.30 Trifecta £275.60 Pool £1,527.22 - 4.10 winning units..
Owner A Underwood **Bred** Tom And Hazel Russell **Trained** Cockerham, Lancs

FOCUS
By no means a vintage running of this Group 2 contest (Amour Propre and Tax Free notable absentees because of the ground), but there are few tougher horses in training than the front pair. They were spread out across the track in the closing stages but there seemed no significant bias, with the first two racing towards the stands' side, and the third positioned near the far rail. The pace was strong in the conditions.

NOTEBOOK
Look Busy(IRE) stepped up significantly on the form she showed on her first two starts this year and probably produced a lifetime best on the figures. Her previous career highlight came when winning a Group 3 in Ireland last year, and incidentally Wi Dud filled third in that race as well, but both look to have stepped up on that form. The winner was outpaced early, but she really found her stride in the second half of the contest and stayed on best of all when switched wide inside the final 2f, despite being carried slightly right by the runner-up. This filly, who goes on any ground, could have further improvement in her, but she's not entered at Royal Ascot and her big target this year is apparently the Group 1 Nunthorpe Stakes at York. (op 13-2 tchd 8-1 tchd 9-1 in places)
Borderlescott, runner-up in this race last year, ran well without producing his absolute best. He was inclined to edge right once under pressure, suggesting he wasn't totally comfortable on the testing ground, making this effort all the more creditable. He'll apparently now head to Royal Ascot for the King's Stand. (op 9-4 tchd 15-8 tchd 5-2 in places)
Wi Dud has mainly struggled since a juvenile campaign that saw him land the Flying Childers, as well as run second in the Middle Park, but this represented a return to something like his best. His attitude couldn't be faulted, but he's a difficult horse to predict and is no sure thing to confirm this form next time. (op 25-1)
Arganil(USA) was totally unsuited by quick ground in the Duke Of York Stakes, but this was better and he wasn't too far off the pick of his Polytrack efforts. He might be capable of even better on slightly less testing conditions. (op 10-1 tchd 9-1)
Total Gallery(IRE), upped in grade after winning a Listed race at Ascot on his reappearance, had no easy task against his elders on such testing ground but he ran with credit. (op 6-1)
Captain Gerrard(IRE) dropped out tamely after showing loads of natural speed. (op 7-1)
Reverence, winner of this race at Sandown in 2006, offered nothing this time. (op 8-1 tchd 13-2)

2273 BETFRED SILVER BOWL (HERITAGE H'CAP) 1m 30y
3:40 (3:41) (Class 2) 3-Y-O
£52,963 (£15,861; £7,930; £3,969; £1,980; £994) **Stalls** Low

Form RPR

21-1 **1** **Desert Creek (IRE)**[19] 1751 3-7-12 87.... Louis-PhilippeBeuzelin(5) 8 98+
(Sir Michael Stoute) *t.k.h early: chsd ldr: led over 2f out: rdn over 1f out: sn edgd lft: r.o* **5/4**[1]

131 **2** *1 1/4* **Set The Trend**[38] 1284 3-8-3 87.... WilliamBuick 2 96
(A M Balding) *hld up in tch: rdn over 2f out: kpt on u.p to take 2nd wl ins fnl f: nt trble wnr* **8/1**[2]

33-5 **3** *2* **Derbaas (USA)**[38] 1294 3-9-4 102.... RyanMoore 1 106
(E A L Dunlop) *a.p: ev ch 2f out: one pce and lost 2nd wl ins fnl f* **22/1**

-141 **4** *2 1/4* **Good Again**[14] 1860 3-8-11 95.... SebSanders 5 94
(G A Butler) *hld up in rr: hdwy on ins over 2f out: rdn over 1f out: one pce fnl f* **11/1**

2-31 **5** *2 3/4* **Fareer**[16] 1801 3-8-8 92.... TPO'Shea 6 85
(E A L Dunlop) *hld up in mid-div: bmpd bnd over 5f out: n.m.r and hdwy 2f out: sn rdn: no imp whn hung lft ins fnl f* **10/1**[3]

-104 **6** *3/4* **Markyg (USA)**[42] 1211 3-8-11 95....(t) JimCrowley 7 86
(K R Burke) *hld up in rr: rdn 2f out: wknd over 1f out* **33/1**

2122 **7** *1 3/4* **Thief Of Time (IRE)**[29] 1484 3-8-3 87.... AdrianMcCarthy 4 74
(P W Chapple-Hyam) *hld up towards rr: hdwy over 3f out: rdn over 1f out: no further prog* **12/1**

0-66 **8** *1 3/4* **Canwinn (IRE)**[31] 1459 3-8-9 93....(v[1]) SamHitchcott 10 76
(M R Channon) *t.k.h in rr: swtchd lft 2f out: n.d* **33/1**

1-34 **9** *hd* **Sonning Gate**[19] 1751 3-8-4 88.... AlanMunro 13 70
(D R C Elsworth) *in rr: rdn 1f out: nvr nr ldrs* **14/1**

05-6 **10** *nk* **Cruikadyke**[29] 1484 3-8-6 90.... MartinDwyer 17 72
(P F I Cole) *t.k.h: prom tl wknd over 2f out* **40/1**

00-0 **11** *3* **Deadly Secret (USA)**[10] 1987 3-8-9 93.... TomEaves 16 68
(R A Fahey) *hung lft wl over 1f out: a in rr* **33/1**

10-4 **12** *1 1/4* **Isabella Grey**[8] 2057 3-8-12 96.... TedDurcan 14 68
(K A Ryan) *led: hdd over 2f out: sn wknd* **25/1**

0-54 **13** *nk* **Viva Ronaldo (IRE)**[16] 1801 3-8-11 95.... TonyHamilton 15 66
(R A Fahey) *t.k.h on outside in mid-div: hdwy over 2f out: wknd wl over 1f out* **20/1**

06-3 **14** *1/2* **Foundation Room (IRE)**[16] 1801 3-8-1 88.... DavidProbert(3) 9 58+
(A M Balding) *t.k.h early: in tch: hmpd and lost pl bnd over 5f out: sn bhd* **8/1**[2]

26-4 **15** *5* **Roman Glory (IRE)**[11] 1972 3-8-6 90.... RichardKingscote 12 48
(B J Meehan) *hld up in mid-div: bmpd bnd over 5f out: rdn over 2f out: sn wknd* **28/1**

1m 50.29s (6.49) **Going Correction** +0.975s/f (Soft) **15** Ran SP% **126.1**
Speed ratings (Par 105): **106,104,102,100,97 97,95,93,93,93 90,88,88,87,82**
toteswinger: 1&2 £7.40, 1&3 £18.60, 2&3 £42.00 CSF £10.21 CT £172.73 TOTE £2.00: £1.30, £2.60, £7.30; EX 20.90 Trifecta £337.70 Pool: £19,718.60 - 43.20 winning units..
Owner Saeed Suhail **Bred** Mount Coote Stud And M H Dixon **Trained** Newmarket, Suffolk

FOCUS
A typically competitive renewal of this extremely valuable 3yo handicap, and the 'right' horses dominated. The winning time was 0.50 seconds faster than the following 66-80 handicap for older horses and this looks strong form. The progressive winner can rate higher still.

NOTEBOOK
Desert Creek(IRE) ◆'s recent Windsor success in a handicap off 79 was gained on quick ground, but his maiden victory last year was achieved on a soft surface and he handled the testing conditions well. He was 8lb higher this time, but made light of that rise with quite a taking effort, particularly considering he was keener than ideal on the demanding ground. His most promising young claimer had no hesitation in committing him early, rather than fight him, and this son of Refuse To Bend ran on strongly for a convincing success. Although he was getting weight from most of his rivals, he already looks potentially Pattern class and is likely to prove extremely hard to beat in the Britannia Stakes at Royal Ascot, provided, of course, he is not undone by the draw. (op 15-8 tchd 2-1 in places)
Set The Trend ◆ proved every bit as effective on turf as on Polytrack. Ridden with patience towards the inside, he settled well (can be keen) and was in the clear soon enough if good enough in the straight, but he was always being held. He's progressing fast and it would be no surprise to see him reoppose the winner in the Britannia, although it remains to be seen whether he'll be so effective on quick ground. (op 7-1)
Derbaas(USA) was no sure thing to handle this ground, but ran really well considering he was conceding a lot of weight to a couple of highly progressive colts. He's a smart horse when he puts his mind to it. (tchd 20-1)
Good Again's two turf wins so far were gained on quick ground, so this was a creditable effort. She'll be one to keep on side when getting more suitable conditions. (tchd 10-1 and 12-1)
Fareer probably didn't mind the ground but failed to prove his stamina for this most testing 1m. (op 17-2 tchd 8-1)
Markyg(USA) is unlikely to have appreciated this going and did not run too badly considering. He's worth another try in a tongue-tie under more suitable conditions.
Thief Of Time(IRE) probably wants further and better going. (op 10-1 tchd 14-1)
Foundation Room(IRE) gradually dropped out after racing keenly early and then being squeezed out about 5f from the finish. Official explanation: jockey said filly suffered interference early and was unsuited by the heavy (soft in places) ground (op 10-1)

2274 BETFRED "THE PEOPLES BOOKMAKER" H'CAP 1m 30y
4:15 (4:15) (Class 4) (0-80,80) 4-Y-O+ **£6,476** (£1,927; £963; £481) **Stalls** Low

Form RPR

-456 **1** **Moheebb (IRE)**[7] 2073 5-8-8 70....(b) MartinDwyer 2 89+
(Mrs R A Carr) *hld up in rr: rdn and hdwy over 2f out: led 1f out: drew clr ins fnl f: r.o wl* **13/2**[3]

0022 **2** *6* **Tiger Dream**[19] 1737 4-8-12 74....(p) TedDurcan 11 79
(K A Ryan) *chsd ldr: rdn to ld briefly over 1f out: rdr lost whip jst ins fnl f: one pce* **10/1**

00-0 **3** *1/2* **Brasingaman Hifive**[28] 1507 4-9-1 77.... WJSupple 1 81
(Mrs G S Rees) *a.p: rdn over 2f out: one pce fnl f* **8/1**

0-02 **4** *2 1/2* **Bold Marc (IRE)**[21] 1682 7-9-1 77.... AndrewElliott 10 75
(K R Burke) *led: rdn and hdd over 1f out: no ex ins fnl f* **7/2**[1]

34-0 **5** *2 1/2* **Border Owl (IRE)**[14] 1886 4-8-13 75.... SamHitchcott 12 67
(P Salmon) *a.p: rdn over 2f out: wknd ins fnl f* **40/1**

0-16 **6** *3/4* **Bold Cross (IRE)**[5] 2144 6-8-7 69.... PaulFitzsimons 6 60
(E G Bevan) *hld up and bhd: rdn and hdwy over 2f out: no further prog* **22/1**

0-43 **7** *3/4* **Dear Maurice**[6] 2103 5-9-4 80.... RyanMoore 7 69
(E A L Dunlop) *hld up in rr: nvr nr ldrs* **9/1**

3-40 **8** *hd* **Nisaal (IRE)**[28] 1524 4-8-5 74.... JamieKyne(7) 4 62
(J J Quinn) *hld up in mid-div: rdn over 2f out: edgd lft over 1f out: sn wknd* **6/1**[2]

32-0 **9** *11* **Nevada Desert (IRE)**[11] 1952 9-8-12 **77**.............. MichaelJStainton(3) 3 40
(R M Whitaker) *hld up in tch: rdn and wknd over 2f out* **11/1**

3262 **10** *3* **Barataria**[30] 1479 7-8-10 **72**.............................. PatCosgrave 14 28
(R Bastiman) *bhd fnl 3f: eased ins fnl f* **14/1**

1-24 **11** *10* **The Galloping Shoe**[11] 1964 4-9-4 **80**.......................... SebSanders 15 13+
(J Noseda) *hld up in tch: rdn over 3f out: wknd over 2f out: eased fnl f* **6/1**[2]

0201 **12** *9* **Hilbre Court (USA)**[30] 1479 4-8-10 **72**..........................(p) TomEaves 8 —
(B P J Baugh) *bhd fnl 4f* **25/1**

1m 50.79s (6.99) **Going Correction** +0.975s/f (Soft) **12** Ran SP% **120.0**
Speed ratings (Par 105): **104,98,97,95,92 91,91,90,79,76 66,57**
toteswinger: 1&2 £16.50, 1&3 £14.50, 2&3 £19.50 CSF £69.31 CT £542.59 TOTE £7.40: £2.60, £3.10, £3.20; EX 86.10.
Owner Michael Hill **Bred** Hascombe And Valiant Studs **Trained** Huby, N Yorks

FOCUS
This looked competitive beforehand but nothing could live with the winner, who showed improved form in this testing ground.

2275 TEXT BETFRED TO 83080 FOR MOBILE BETTING H'CAP 1m 3f 200y

4:50 (4:51) (Class 2) (0-100,98) 3-Y-O
£12,462 (£3,732; £1,866; £934; £466; £234) **Stalls** Low

Form RPR

01-3 **1** **Opinion Poll (IRE)**[20] 1702 3-8-11 **88**....................... PhilipRobinson 1 101+
(M A Jarvis) *a.p: nt clr run on ins and swtchd rt 2f out: edgd lft jst over 1f out: led ins fnl f: rdn out* **7/1**

61- **2** *1 ½* **Distant Memories (IRE)**[203] 7126 3-8-2 **79**.................. FrancisNorton 4 87
(T P Tate) *led 3f: chsd ldr to 5f out: prom: swtchd rt 2f out: rdn to ld over 1f out: hdd ins fnl f: nt qckn* **11/2**

62- **3** *2 ½* **Stormy Weather (FR)**[179] 7449 3-9-7 **98**.................. PaulMulrennan 11 102
(J Howard Johnson) *hld up in mid-div: hdwy over 5f out: led jst over 2f out: hdd over 1f out: sn rdn: one pce whn edgd lft wl ins fnl f* **20/1**

3-21 **4** *nk* **Tactic**[16] 1809 3-8-9 **86**... TPO'Shea 9 89
(J L Dunlop) *a.p: wnt 2nd 5f out: led 3f out tl jst over 2f out: rdn over 1f out: btn whn bmpd wl ins fnl f* **7/2**[1]

1-20 **5** *5* **Splinter Cell (USA)**[51] 1086 3-8-9 **86**.......................... AlanMunro 7 81
(M Botti) *hld up in tch: rdn 3f out: hung lft over 1f out: wknd fnl f* **16/1**

0-1 **6** *1 ¾* **Highland Glen**[14] 1874 3-8-12 **89**.............................. RyanMoore 3 81
(Sir Michael Stoute) *nvr nr ldrs* **4/1**[2]

11-6 **7** *¾* **Classic Vintage (USA)**[29] 1489 3-8-8 **85**........................ JimCrowley 2 76
(Mrs A J Perrett) *nvr nr ldrs* **8/1**

10-2 **8** *15* **Quai D'Orsay**[17] 1792 3-8-9 **86**......................... RoystonFfrench 10 53
(M Johnston) *prom: led after 3f out: hdd 3f out: sn rdn: wknd 2f out* **9/2**[3]

-100 **9** *26* **Sanvean (IRE)**[14] 1871 3-8-8 **85**......................... SamHitchcott 6 11
(M R Channon) *hld up in mid-div: rdn 4f out: sn bhd: eased fnl f* **50/1**

51-5 **10** *2 ½* **Simple Solution (USA)**[17] 1789 3-8-9 **86**..................... WilliamBuick 8 8
(B W Hills) *hld up in mid-div: wknd over 3f out: eased over 1f out* **12/1**

2m 40.81s (7.61) **Going Correction** +0.775s/f (Yiel) **10** Ran SP% **119.7**
Speed ratings (Par 105): **105,104,102,102,98 97,97,87,69,68**
toteswinger: 1&2 £8.60, 1&3 £24.30, 2&3 £20.60 CSF £46.59 CT £747.69 TOTE £8.50: £2.60, £2.50, £5.30; EX 61.10.
Owner Sheikh Ahmed Al Maktoum **Bred** Darley **Trained** Newmarket, Suffolk

FOCUS
A very good 3yo handicap on paper, although a few of these were obviously unable to produce their best on the demanding going. Despite that this looks form to be positive about. The winner was value for extra. The pace seemed to slow at about halfway, but it was still a good test considering the conditions.

NOTEBOOK
Opinion Poll(IRE) ◆ didn't look comfortable on quick ground in a decent 1m2f handicap at Newmarket on his reappearance and these conditions proved much more suitable. A little keen when the gallop slowed early on, he then had to be switched about five wide off the inside rail over 1f out but found plenty when in the open. He should improve further and ought to stay beyond this trip, but he probably wouldn't want the ground any faster than good. (op 15-2 tchd 11-2)
Distant Memories(IRE), upped significantly in trip on his return from 203 days off, didn't help his chance by racing keenly early on before eventually settling when getting a lead off the Johnston horse. He kept on surprisingly well in the straight considering his earlier exertions, proving well suited by the going, and is clearly useful when there is plenty of ease underfoot. (op 8-1)
Stormy Weather(FR), placed in Listed company over 1m on testing going when trained in France last year, ran a cracker on his debut for new connections. He couldn't sustain his effort after briefly looking a threat about 2f out but had no easy task off a mark of 98 and was entitled to need this after six months off. The ground suited him well and he could have more to offer when getting his conditions, before presumably going hurdling one day. (op 16-1)
Tactic, off the mark in a maiden over this trip at Goodwood, looked one of the more likely winners halfway up the straight, but he didn't see his race out and looked to find conditions too testing. (op 4-1 tchd 9-2)
Splinter Cell(USA) had the ground to suit but failed to prove his stamina. (tchd 12-1)
Highland Glen was seemingly unsuited by the conditions. (tchd 5-1)
Classic Vintage(USA) was disappointing but might have failed to stay.
Quai D'Orsay looked to have plenty going for him but he ran poorly. It's possible he did too much in getting to the front, even though he was able to slow the gallop at halfway. Official explanation: jockey had no explanation for the poor form shown (op 5-1 tchd 11-2 in places)
Simple Solution(USA) did not seem to enjoy the conditions one bit. Official explanation: jockey said filly was unsuited by the heavy (soft in places) ground (op 11-1 tchd 8-1)

2276 BETFREDBINGO H'CAP 6f

5:25 (5:26) (Class 4) (0-80,81) 4-Y-O+ **£6,476** (£1,927; £963; £481) **Stalls** Centre

Form RPR

21-3 **1** **Eton Rifles (IRE)**[8] 2045 4-9-4 **80**........................... PaulMulrennan 10 96+
(J Howard Johnson) *racd far side: clr over 1f out: rdn ins fnl f: hld on* **5/2**[1]

4005 **2** *½* **Ingleby Arch (USA)**[7] 2071 6-8-8 **73**.......................... NeilBrown(3) 3 84
(T D Barron) *chsd ldrs far side: rdn wl over 1f out: r.o ins fnl f: nt rch wnr* **9/1**[3]

36-4 **3** *3 ¼* **Atlantic Beach**[14] 1885 4-8-7 **69**.......................... TonyHamilton 13 70
(R A Fahey) *chsd ldrs stands' side: rdn over 1f out: kpt on one pce* **16/1**

0123 **4** *¾* **Street Power (USA)**[12] 1943 4-8-12 **74**........................ RyanMoore 12 72
(J R Gask) *racd stands' side: hld up and bhd: rdn and hdwy over 1f out: kpt on same pce fnl f* **9/1**[3]

5066 **5** *2 ¾* **Memphis Man**[8] 2045 6-8-12 **74**.......................... TGMcLaughlin 17 63
(P D Evans) *racd stands' side: hld up and bhd: rdn over 2f out: edgd lft over 1f out: nvr trbld ldrs* **22/1**

-406 **6** *¾* **Stanley Goodspeed**[7] 2071 6-8-13 **75**.......................... JamesDoyle 2 62
(J W Hills) *racd far side: in rr: rdn and hdwy on far rail over 2f out: wknd ins fnl f* **16/1**

22-1 **7** *½* **Westwood**[26] 1572 4-8-10 **72**............................... DaneO'Neill 15 57
(D Haydn Jones) *led stands' side gp: rdn over 1f out: wknd fnl f* **9/1**[3]

0-35 **8** *2* **Kyle (IRE)**[26] 1565 5-9-2 **78**.. LPKeniry 4 57
(C R Dore) *racd far side: towards rr: sme hdwy over 2f out: sn rdn: edgd rt over 1f out: wknd fnl f* **18/1**

02-1 **9** *1 ½* **Tudor Prince (IRE)**[31] 1468 5-8-4 **69**...................... DavidProbert(3) 16 43
(A W Carroll) *chsd ldrs stands' side: rdn and wkng whn edgd lft wl over 1f out* **14/1**

-222 **10** *nk* **Legal Eagle (IRE)**[7] 2093 4-9-5 **81**........................ AdrianTNicholls 14 54
(D Nicholls) *w ldr on stands' side: rdn and edgd lft wl over 1f out: wknd fnl f* **5/1**[2]

04-0 **11** *8* **Steel Blue**[15] 1849 9-8-6 **68**.................................. WilliamBuick 1 16
(R M Whitaker) *chsd wnr on far side: rdn over 2f out: wknd wl over 1f out* **33/1**

630- **12** *3 ¾* **Prince Namid**[246] 6066 7-8-7 **69**............................ FrancisNorton 8 5
(D Nicholls) *rdr late removing blindfold: hld up: swtchd to stands' side gp over 3f out: a bhd* **20/1**

000- **13** *½* **John Keats**[197] 7222 6-8-11 **73**.................................. TomEaves 6 7
(J S Goldie) *racd far side: a bhd* **40/1**

-003 **14** *nk* **Harlech Castle**[16] 1806 4-9-3 **79**............................... MartinDwyer 5 12
(P F I Cole) *s.i.s: racd far side: a bhd* **14/1**

-460 **15** *2* **Charles Darwin (IRE)**[28] 1510 6-8-10 **72**........................ TedDurcan 7 —
(M Blanshard) *racd far side: sn chsng ldrs: wknd 2f out* **20/1**

1434 **16** *nk* **Royal Envoy (IRE)**[47] 1152 6-8-8 **70** ow1........................ JimCrowley 11 —
(P Howling) *racd stands' side: a in rr* **33/1**

0-35 **17** *½* **Makshoof (IRE)**[12] 1924 5-8-8 **70**........................(p) RoystonFfrench 9 —
(I W McInnes) *racd far side: mid-div: rdn over 3f out: sn struggling* **10/1**

1m 18.64s (4.64) **Going Correction** +0.975s/f (Soft) **17** Ran SP% **136.9**
Speed ratings (Par 105): **108,107,103,102,98 97,96,94,92,91 80,75,75,74,72 71,71**
toteswinger: 1&2 £13.30, 1&3 £21.90, 2&3 £51.90 CSF £25.91 CT £348.48 TOTE £3.50: £1.60, £2.70, £4.30, £2.90; EX 46.10 Place 6: £2690.91, Place 5: £340.47.
Owner Transcend Bloodstock LLP **Bred** Grangecon Stud **Trained** Billy Row, Co Durham

FOCUS
A fair, competitive sprint handicap. They were spread out all over the track, and the first two finishers raced far side. The time was quicker than that for the Listed race and the winner posted smart form for the grade. Form to view positively despite the ground.
Tudor Prince(IRE) Official explanation: jockey said gelding was unsuited by the heavy (soft in places) ground
Steel Blue Official explanation: jockey said gelding hung right
Prince Namid Official explanation: jockey said gelding missed the break
T/Jkpt: Not won. T/Plt: £5,349.60 to a £1 stake. Pool: £138,870.45. 18.95 winning tickets. T/Qpdt: £164.00 to a £1 stake. Pool: £8,003.05. 36.10 winning tickets. KH

2238 NEWMARKET (R-H)

Saturday, May 23

OFFICIAL GOING: Good to firm (8.7)
Wind: Light, half against Weather: Overcast

2277 SPILLERS HORSE FEEDS FAIRWAY STKS (LISTED RACE) 1m 2f

2:20 (2:23) (Class 1) 3-Y-O **£22,708** (£8,608; £4,308; £2,148; £1,076) **Stalls** High

Form RPR

1-42 **1** **Palavicini (USA)**[21] 1678 3-9-0 107............................ EddieAhern 1 110
(J L Dunlop) *chsd ldr: rdn to ld over 1f out: jst hld on* **7/4**[2]

1-33 **2** *nk* **Father Time**[14] 1872 3-9-0 101.................................. TPQueally 3 110
(H R A Cecil) *hld up in tch: rdn and hung lft over 1f out: chsd wnr ins fnl f: r.o* **13/8**[1]

-125 **3** *3 ¼* **Big Bound (USA)**[15] 1822 3-9-0 102............................ JimmyFortune 4 103
(J H M Gosden) *led: rdn and hdd over 1f out: no ex ins fnl f* **7/1**

1-51 **4** *1* **Your Old Pal**[21] 1678 3-9-5 108.............................. ShaneKelly 6 106
(J Noseda) *hld up: rdn over 2f out: swtchd lft over 1f out: nvr trbld ldrs* **4/1**[3]

1-36 **5** *¾* **Heliodor (USA)**[21] 1678 3-9-3 100............................ PatDobbs 5 103
(R Hannon) *chsd ldrs: rdn over 2f out: wknd ins fnl f* **25/1**

2m 5.30s (-0.50) **Going Correction** +0.125s/f (Good) **5** Ran SP% **110.8**
Speed ratings (Par 107): **107,106,104,103,102**
toteswinger: 1&2 £2.40 CSF £5.03 TOTE £2.80: £1.50, £1.20; EX 5.60.
Owner Windflower Overseas Holdings Inc **Bred** Windflower Overseas Holdings Inc **Trained** Arundel, W Sussex

FOCUS
This race has produced some top performers in recent years, David Junior, Red Rocks and Lucarno all going on to win at Group 1 level later in the season, but it looks most unlikely that any of these will make it at the top level. The pace lifted with around four to run, but it was still a far from satisfactory test at the distance.

NOTEBOOK
Palavicini(USA), who went down fighting to Your Old Pal over this course and distance last time, was widely expected to reverse the form with a 5lb swing at the weights and in winning he also turned around earlier Newbury form with the runner-up. A bit keen through the first half of the race, he didn´t respond immediately to pressure, but was in front over a furlong out and just did enough to hold on. He is a fine-looking sort, with further improvement in him, and is likely to head to Ascot for the Hampton Court Stakes. (op 15-8 tchd 2-1 and 11-5 in a place)
Father Time, whose Lingfield Derby Trial third received a nice boost when the fourth Alwaary won impressively at Goodwood in the week, had earlier finished ahead of both Palavicini and Your Old Pal at Newbury and this return to 1m2f was not expected to present a problem. He could have done with more of a gallop, though, as he was outpaced when first asked for his effort and still looked a bit unsure of what was required, hanging left. He really found his stride once meeting with the rising ground, but the line just came too soon. This brother to connections' high-class filly Passage Of Time remains capable of better and appeals as a likely type for the Hampton Court Stakes at Royal Ascot, with him not looking good enough for the King Edward VII Stakes. (op 15-8 tchd 2-1 and 9-4 in places)
Big Bound(USA), narrowly denied in an average renewal of the Sandown Classic Trial two starts back, failed to get home having raced keenly in the Dee Stakes and needed to bounce back to take this. He dominated the tempo, but was strongly pressed and beaten approaching the furlong pole. This is his level, though he will remain vulnerable to less-exposed types. (tchd 13-2)
Your Old Pal bounced back from a disappointing effort on his reappearance by taking a course-and-distance Listed event earlier in the month, but he needed to have progressed to confirm form with Palavicini under his 5lb penalty. Held up with Father Time, he was outpaced when the pace lifted and, having been switched left with a furlong to run, could only keep on at the one pace. He didn't run up to his best and it would come as no surprise to see him tried over 1m4f at some point. (tchd 7-2)

Heliodor(USA), the lowest-rated runner in the field yet shouldering a 3lb penalty, finished behind a couple of these over course and distance last time and, though closing the gap on Your Old Pal, he was again well held. (tchd 20-1)

2278 KING CHARLES II STKS (LISTED RACE) 7f
2:50 (2:52) (Class 1) 3-Y-O

£22,708 (£8,608; £4,308; £2,148; £1,076; £540) Stalls High

Form				RPR
01-4	1		**Alyarf (USA)**[37] 1300 3-9-0 105 MichaelHills 7 (B W Hills) *chsd ldrs: led over 2f out: rdn over 1f out: edgd rt ins fnl f: r.o* **2/1**[2]	109
30-6	2	1 3/4	**Nasri**[35] 1354 3-9-0 100 JimmyFortune 1 (B J Meehan) *hld up: hdwy over 2f out: sn rdn: edgd rt and r.o ins fnl f: nt trble wnr* **11/2**[3]	104+
25-0	3	2 3/4	**Courageous (IRE)**[38] 1292 3-9-0 101 RichardMullen 4 (B Smart) *chsd ldrs: led over 5f out: rdn and hdd over 2f out: no ex fnl f* **18/1**	97
111-	4	shd	**Donativum**[210] 6998 3-9-4 115 LDettori 6 (Saeed Bin Suroor) *plld hrd and prom: rdn over 2f out: styd on same pce fnl f* **13/8**[1]	100
4-02	5	2	**Baileys Cacao (IRE)**[14] 1873 3-8-13 103 PatDobbs 5 (R Hannon) *broke wl: sn stdd to chse ldrs: rdn over 2f out: wknd fnl f* **11/2**[3]	90
11-0	6	2 3/4	**Captain Ramius (IRE)**[42] 1211 3-9-4 104 EddieAhern 3 (S A Callaghan) *sn led: hdd over 5f out: chsd ldrs tl rdn and wknd 2f out* **20/1**	87
22-0	7	2 1/2	**Thunderous Mood (USA)**[9] 2016 3-9-0 98 TPQueally 2 (P F I Cole) *s.i.s: hld up: rdn and wknd over 2f out* **40/1**	77

1m 24.97s (-0.43) **Going Correction** +0.125s/f (Good) 7 Ran SP% **114.7**
Speed ratings (Par 107): **107,105,101,101,99 96,93**
toteswinger: 1&2 £2.50, 1&3 £9.40, 2&3 £46.40 CSF £13.60 TOTE £2.90: £1.60, £2.70; EX 13.60.
Owner Hamdan Al Maktoum **Bred** Shadwell Farm LLC **Trained** Lambourn, Berks
■ Stewards' Enquiry : Jimmy Fortune caution: used whip with excessive force

FOCUS
Not a particularly strong Listed event, though the participation of Breeders' Cup Juvenile Turf winner Donativum did make it an interesting spectacle. He was below form, and Alyarf did not have to improve much on his Craven form.

NOTEBOOK
Alyarf(USA), who looked a horse with immense potential when impressively winning a 6f maiden at Haydock last season, failed to see out the 1m when fourth in the Craven on his reappearance (form working out well), and the drop to 7f looked certain to be in his favour. Kept away from the main pack for first few furlongs, he was the last one under pressure and skipped clear a furlong out. He began to tire a little as he met the rising ground, but never looked like being caught and was good value for the win. The Jersey Stakes as Royal Ascot looks the obvious target and it would not surprise to see him run a big race there, but speed is his forte and it may well be that the best of him is seen back at 6f. He will be considered for the Golden Jubilee Stakes and quotes range from 25-1 to 16-1 for the Group 1 contest. (tchd 15-8 and 9-4 and 5-2 in a place)
Nasri, third to Donativum in a valuable contest over this course and distance in October, has not been suited by the soft ground on his last couple of starts and he ran a much better race on this return to a fast surface. He kept on well without looking likely to catch the winner and is another who deserves to take his chance in the Jersey Stakes. (op 15-2 tchd 8-1)
Courageous(IRE) pulled hard and failed to get home in the Free Handicap on his reappearance, but he settled a lot better up with the pace this time and ran well back in third. (op 16-1 tchd 25-1)
Donativum progressed markedly once stepped up in trip on fast ground last autumn, springing a surprise in the valuable Timeform Million over this course and distance (beating subsequent Racing Post Trophy winner Crowded House), and seeing the 1m out well at Santa Anita under this rider. Very keen on this debut for Godolphin, he was taken across to track the winner, but Dettori started to ride away over two out and the grey couldn't quicken. He kept on at the one pace, just missing out on third, and is fully expected to improve for this run, but will need to go back up to 1m before long. Connections, though, may let him take his chance in the Jersey first. (op 2-1 tchd 9-4)
Baileys Cacao(IRE) appreciated the return to a fast surface when narrowly denied in a 7f Group 3 at Lingfield last time, but this was tougher against the boys and she simply wasn´t good enough. (op 5-1 tchd 9-2)
Captain Ramius(IRE), a three-time all-weather winner who struggled in a Listed contest at Kempton last time, steadily dropped back through the field and was outclassed. (op 12-1)
Thunderous Mood(USA) had some okay form as a juvenile, but he has struggled in two starts this season and may do better later in the year, once his handicap mark has had a chance to come down. (op 33-1 tchd 25-1)

2279 CORAL.CO.UK SPRINT (HERITAGE H'CAP) 6f
3:25 (3:29) (Class 2) (0-105,96) 3-Y-O

£24,924 (£7,464; £3,732; £1,868; £932; £468) Stalls High

Form				RPR
0-21	1		**Bouvardia**[14] 1879 3-9-3 **92** TPQueally 11 (H R A Cecil) *chsd ldrs: led over 1f out: rdn out* **4/1**[2]	101+
1006	2	1/2	**Akhenaten**[21] 1679 3-9-1 **90** TonyCulhane 14 (M R Channon) *hld up: hdwy 1/2-way: rdn over 1f out: r.o* **25/1**	97
-300	3	3/4	**Parisian Pyramid (IRE)**[15] 1824 3-8-12 **87** StephenDonohoe 8 (D Nicholls) *chsd ldrs: outpcd over 1f out: sn edgd lft: r.o ins fnl f* **11/1**	92
-611	4	1	**Proclaim**[28] 1517 3-9-5 **94** GregFairley 7 (M Johnston) *chsd ldrs: led over 2f out: rdn and hdd over 1f out: no ex ins fnl f* **5/2**[1]	95
61-4	5	nk	**Global City (IRE)**[20] 1705 3-9-5 **94** (t) LDettori 5 (Saeed Bin Suroor) *hld up: rdn 2f out: r.o ins fnl f: nt rch ldrs* **7/1**	94
-222	6	nk	**Shaws Diamond (USA)**[77] 782 3-8-4 **79** LukeMorris 12 (D Shaw) *led: rdn and hd over 2f out: sn outpcd: r.o ins fnl f* **50/1**	78
1-40	7	1/2	**Aldermoor (USA)**[9] 2016 3-9-7 **96** SaleemGolam 6 (S C Williams) *s.i.s: hld up: plld hrd: hdwy 1/2-way: outpcd whn nt clr run over 1f out: r.o ins fnl f* **25/1**	94+
324-	8	1	**Rowayton**[189] 7335 3-8-10 **85** MichaelHills 9 (J D Bethell) *hld up: plld hrd: rdn over 1f out: r.o ins fnl f: nvr trbld ldrs* **25/1**	80
0-42	9	2 1/4	**Able Master (IRE)**[15] 1828 3-9-1 **95** GaryBartley(5) 4 (B Smart) *prom: rdn over 2f out: wknd over 1f out* **9/1**	82
12-1	10	1/2	**Dark Lane**[14] 1869 3-8-9 **84** EddieAhern 13 (T D Barron) *hld up in tch: plld hrd: lost pl over 3f out: n.d after* **6/1**[3]	70
4-02	11	nse	**Timeteam (IRE)**[20] 1705 3-8-11 **86** PatDobbs 2 (S Kirk) *hld up: hdwy 1/2-way: wknd over 1f out* **16/1**	72
514-	12	1	**Calligrapher (USA)**[220] 6739 3-9-3 **92** JimmyFortune 3 (M A Jarvis) *hld up: hdwy 1/2-way: wknd over 1f out* **16/1**	75
3-10	13	28	**Bajan Tryst (USA)**[19] 1727 3-8-3 **78** RichardMullen 10 (K A Ryan) *hld up: rdn and wknd over 2f out: eased* **25/1**	—

1m 13.04s (0.84) **Going Correction** +0.275s/f (Good) **13** Ran SP% **122.8**
Speed ratings (Par 105): **105,104,103,102,101 101,100,99,96,95 95,94,56**
toteswinger: 1&2 £29.70, 1&3 £13.00, 2&3 £63.30 CSF £111.08 CT £1083.65 TOTE £4.80: £2.00, £5.80, £4.10; EX 148.00 Trifecta £665.20 Part won. Pool: £898.96 - 0.20 winning units..
Owner K Abdulla **Bred** Juddmonte Farms Ltd **Trained** Newmarket, Suffolk

FOCUS
This was a good quality three-year-old sprint, featuring several progressive types, and it was Bouvardia that came out on top. Solid form.

NOTEBOOK
Bouvardia, raised 6lb for winning an ordinary race at Nottingham last time, was always travelling well just in behind the speed and quickened to lead well over a furlong out. She briefly looked vulnerable as they began to close inside the final furlong, but kept finding and was always doing enough. She clearly has bags of pace and a soundly run 6f on fast ground seems ideal, so connections may well run her in the Wokingham before going in search of black type. (op 5-1 tchd 11-2 in places)
Akhenaten, who was trying 6f for the first time, ran a cracker. A son of high-class middle-distance performer High Chaparral, he travelled surprisingly well and kept on strongly for pressure, but could not quite get to the winner. He clearly has deceptive speed, but will require a good gallop at this distance for him to be fully effective. (op 33-1)
Parisian Pyramid(IRE), 9lb better off with Proclaim on last month´s Ripon form, ran on consecutive days at Chester´s May meeting, failing to make an impact either time, but the return to a more conventional track suited and he ran really well, staying on up the hill to claim third. (op 12-1)
Proclaim has been a rapid improver since returning to sprint trips this season, winning narrowly at Doncaster and registering quite an impressive victory at Ripon last time. Racing here off a 14lb higher mark than for the first of those victories, he needed to have made another step forward and wasn´t quite up to it, for all that he still ran with credit. He should prove effective back at 7f and can probably win off this mark. (op 7-2)
Global City(IRE), a close-up fourth at Salisbury on his reappearance (short of room in closing stages), again ran well enough to suggest he can win a decent prize this season. Official explanation: jockey said colt hung left (op 8-1 tchd 9-1 in places)
Shaws Diamond(USA), who finished second at Wolverhampton on three consecutive occasions earlier in the season, was dropping in trip for this return to turf and showed plenty of early pace. She kept on again, having been swamped, and can surely be found a race. (tchd 40-1)
Aldermoor(USA), 3lb lower than when fourth in a good course-and-distance handicap at the Craven meeting, bounced back from a disappointing effort over 5f at York and may have been closer had things gone his way. (op 16-1)
Rowayton was far from disgraced on this seasonal return. (tchd 28-1)
Able Master(IRE), who had run well on each of his two previous starts this season, failed to give his best. (op 10-1)
Dark Lane, a progressive sort at two who won despite appearing to blow up on his reappearance at Haydock, seemed fairly treated off a 4lb higher mark, but he was under strong pressure two out and couldn´t pick up. Official explanation: jockey said gelding ran too free (op 11-2 tchd 5-1)
Timeteam(IRE) came under pressure over two out and was quickly beaten.
Calligrapher(USA), whose yard is struggling for form, flopped on his final start at two and has been gelded since then. Making his handicap debut off a stiff enough mark, he could not pick up for pressure and may be one for later in the season. (op 14-1)
Bajan Tryst(USA) Official explanation: jockey said colt stopped quickly; trainer's rep said colt scoped dirty.

2280 E B F ANNE SCRIVEN MAIDEN STKS 6f
4:00 (4:00) (Class 4) 2-Y-O

£5,180 (£1,541; £770; £384) Stalls High

Form				RPR
2	1		**Step In Time (IRE)**[14] 1866 2-9-3 0 GregFairley 1 (M Johnston) *trckd ldr: plld hrd: chal over 1f out: sn rdn: r.o to ld nr fin* **11/10**[1]	75
0	2	nk	**Fantastic Prince**[8] 2033 2-9-3 0 LDettori 2 (P F I Cole) *led: rdn and hung rt ins fnl f: hdd nr fin* **20/1**	75
25	3	3/4	**Tiradito (USA)**[9] 2007 2-8-12 0 AndreaAtzeni(5) 6 (M Botti) *plld hrd and prom: outpcd over 1f out: r.o ins fnl f: wnt 3rd nr fin* **10/1**	72
4	4	3/4	**Running Mate (IRE)**[14] 1867 2-9-3 0 JimmyFortune 5 (J H M Gosden) *chsd ldrs: rdn and ev ch over 1f out: no ex wl ins fnl f* **9/4**[2]	70
	5	1 1/4	**Rumool** 2-9-3 0 MichaelHills 4 (C E Brittain) *s.i.s: hld up: pushed along 1/2-way: hdwy over 1f out: edgd lft and no ex ins fnl f* **11/1**	66
	6	2 3/4	**He's Invincible** 2-9-3 0 EddieAhern 3 (B J Meehan) *dwlt: hld up: rdn over 1f out: wknd ins fnl f* **9/1**[3]	58

1m 15.52s (3.32) **Going Correction** +0.275s/f (Good) **6** Ran SP% **110.6**
Speed ratings (Par 95): **88,87,86,85,83 80**
toteswinger: 1&2 £2.90, 1&3 £2.90, 2&3 £7.20 CSF £23.41 TOTE £1.90: £1.10, £4.60; EX 14.40.
Owner S R Counsell **Bred** Orpendale **Trained** Middleham Moor, N Yorks

FOCUS
An ordinary maiden that favourite Step In Time made very hard work of winning. Modest form on time, but there are grounds for rating the race higher.

NOTEBOOK
Step In Time(IRE) may not have even won had the runner-up not drifted right under pressure, but he had shaped with tons of promise when second at Haydock on his debut and this was very much the performance of a horse who is in need of 7f. He was quite free through the early stages, and will need to settle better when he goes up in trip, but looks the sort to progress. (op 6-5 tchd 6-4 and 13-8 in a place)
Fantastic Prince, who struggled in soft ground on his debut at Newbury, was a completely different horse on this faster surface and may well have won had he run straight under pressure. He should come on again and can find a maiden. (op 12-1)
Tiradito(USA), already beaten when short of room at Salisbury last time, stayed on well up the final hill and was right on the winner´s heels as they crossed the line. He does not do a great deal for the form, but should find a small race at some stage. (tchd 8-1)
Running Mate(IRE), fourth in the other division of Step In Time´s Haydock maiden, again showed plenty of pace, but was already beaten when carried right by the runner-up. He looks worth a try at 5f. (op 5-2 tchd 15-8)
Rumool, a half-brother to useful juvenile Young Pretender, was not the quickest away, but tried to close over a furlong out and showed enough to suggest he has a future. (op 10-1)
He's Invincible, who cost 120,000euros, was also slowly away and ran a bit better than the beaten distance indicates, his rider easing down on him inside the final furlong. He should know more next time. (op 8-1 tchd 15-2)

2281 HOME OF RACING H'CAP 1m
4:35 (4:35) (Class 3) (0-90,88) 3-Y-O

£9,066 (£2,697; £1,348; £673) Stalls High

Form				RPR
3-21	1		**Suruor (IRE)**[19] 1744 3-8-12 **82** StephenDonohoe 1 (D M Simcock) *hld up: hdwy over 1f out: led ins fnl f: rdn out* **4/1**[2]	91+

42-1 **2** 1 ¾ **Russian George (IRE)**[14] 1888 3-8-9 **79**.......................... GregFairley 7 81
(T P Tate) *led: rdn over 1f out: hdd and unable qck ins fnl f* **11/2**[3]

30-3 **3** ½ **Something Perfect (USA)**[34] 1381 3-8-10 **80**.................... TPQueally 4 81
(H R A Cecil) *chsd ldrs: rdn and ev ch ins fnl f: no ex towards fin* **14/1**

62-1 **4** 1 **Secret Society**[52] 1071 3-8-13 **83**.................................. EddieAhern 5 82
(M L W Bell) *chsd ldrs: rdn and ev ch 1f out: no ex ins fnl f* **11/2**[3]

010- **5** ½ **Brief Candle**[238] 6268 3-9-1 **85**..(t) AdamKirby 2 83+
(W R Swinburn) *hld up and bhd: r.o ins fnl f: nvr nr to chal* **8/1**

12 **6** 1 ¼ **Militarist (USA)**[29] 1487 3-9-4 **88**.. JimmyFortune 6 83
(J H M Gosden) *trckd ldr: plld hrd: rdn and ev ch 1f out: wknd wl ins fnl f* **9/4**[1]

01-5 **7** ¾ **Anthology**[37] 1307 3-8-12 **82**... RichardMullen 3 75
(B Smart) *hld up: rdn over 3f out: sn outpcd* **6/1**

1m 40.65s (2.05) **Going Correction** +0.275s/f (Good) **7** Ran SP% **113.6**
Speed ratings (Par 103): **100,98,97,96,96 95,94**
toteswinger: 1&2 £4.00, 1&3 £7.20, 2&3 £7.60 CSF £25.59 TOTE £5.70: £2.60, £3.10; EX 26.60.

Owner Dr Marwan Koukash **Bred** Shadwell Estate Company Limited **Trained** Newmarket, Suffolk

FOCUS

This was a fair handicap, run at just a steady pace, and the progressive Suruor quickened up well to win going away. The second and third set the standard and the form is a little dubious.

NOTEBOOK

Suruor(IRE), raised 7lb for a ready victory over 7f at Warwick earlier in the month, would not have been too inconvenienced by the lack of an early gallop and came between runners with a powerful run a furlong out. Another rise will follow, but he is clearly improving and fully deserves to take his chance in the Britannia at Royal Ascot. (op 9-2 tchd 7-2)

Russian George(IRE) was responsible for setting the modest gallop. He kept finding once challenged and battled on well for second, but proved no match for the winner. (op 9-1 tchd 5-1)

Something Perfect(USA), who has swished her tail in a couple of occasions in the past, finished third off this mark at Lingfield on her handicap debut and she bettered that effort here in what was a stronger race. She should find easier opportunities in fillies´ races. (op 12-1 tchd 16-1)

Secret Society, narrow winner of a 7f Lingfield maiden on his return, travelled well and held every chance, but could find no extra inside the final furlong. (op 9-2)

Brief Candle, last seen finishing eighth in the Fillies´ Mile, would not have been suited by the lack of pace, but she stayed on nicely inside the final furlong and should improve. (tchd 15-2 and 9-1)

Militarist(USA), who beat the smart-looking Harbinger over this course and distance in the Wood Ditton on debut, bumped into another smart sort at Sandown last time and it was easy to see why he was fancied off a mark of 88 on this handicap debut. However, he pulled hard early and, having come under strong pressure, faded tamely inside the final furlong. This was clearly not his best form. Official explanation: jockey said colt ran too free (op 15-8 tchd 7-4)

Anthology is still a shade high in the weights and may be one for later in the season. (op 8-1)

2282 ROB & ANGELA MCKEOWN DOUBLE CELEBRATION MAIDEN STKS 1m

5:10 (5:11) (Class 4) 3-Y-O **£5,180** (£1,541; £770; £384) **Stalls** High

Form RPR

1 **Loch Linnhe (USA)** 3-9-3 0.. JimmyFortune 6 89+
(J H M Gosden) *mde all: shkn up over 1f out: r.o strly* **10/3**[2]

222- **2** 8 **Seaway**[336] 3245 3-9-3 91.. LDettori 1 70
(Saeed Bin Suroor) *s.i.s: sn trcking wnr: plld hrd: rdn over 1f out: wknd ins fnl f* **11/8**[1]

0- **3** ½ **Flame Of Hestia (IRE)**[203] 7140 3-8-12 0.......................... AdamKirby 4 64
(J R Fanshawe) *chsd ldrs: rdn over 2f out: wknd fnl f* **13/2**

4 2 ¼ **Canyon Ranch** 3-9-3 0.. EddieAhern 5 64+
(L M Cumani) *hld up: effrt over 2f out: hung rt and wknd over 1f out* **10/1**

54- **5** 1 ¾ **Baron Otto (IRE)**[229] 6535 3-9-3 0...................................... MichaelHills 2 60
(W J Haggas) *hld up: rdn 3f out: wknd 2f out* **4/1**[3]

0 **6** ¾ **Roar Of The King (USA)**[22] 1636 3-9-3 0.......................... ShaneKelly 3 58
(J Noseda) *hld up: wknd over 2f out* **20/1**

00- **7** 3 ¼ **Pagan Flight (IRE)**[226] 6602 3-9-3 0.............................. TPQueally 7 51
(Mrs A J Perrett) *s.i.s: sn prom: rdn and wknd wl over 1f out* **33/1**

1m 39.93s (1.33) **Going Correction** +0.275s/f (Good) **7** Ran SP% **115.3**
Speed ratings (Par 101): **104,96,95,93,91 90,87**
toteswinger: 1&2 £1.60, 1&3 £3.40, 2&3 £3.00 CSF £8.48 TOTE £4.00: £2.00, £1.30; EX 6.40.
Owner H R H Princess Haya Of Jordan **Bred** Darley **Trained** Newmarket, Suffolk

FOCUS

Not a strong maiden but it was hard not to be taken with the performance of newcomer Loch Linnhe. With the favourite disappointing it is hard to know what he achieved.

2283 COURSE OF CHAMPIONS H'CAP 1m 6f

5:45 (5:46) (Class 4) (0-85,85) 4-Y-0+ **£5,828** (£1,734; £866; £432) **Stalls** Centre

Form RPR

12-1 **1** **Hendersyde (USA)**[32] 1432 4-9-7 **83**..................................(t) AdamKirby 1 96+
(W R Swinburn) *hld up: hdwy over 2f out: led over 1f out: rdn and edgd rt ins fnl f: styd on wl* **10/3**[2]

4435 **2** 2 **Step This Way (USA)**[14] 1878 4-9-0 **76**.......................... GregFairley 6 83
(M Johnston) *chsd ldr: rdn and ev ch over 1f out: styd on same pce ins fnl f* **14/1**

-633 **3** 1 **Buddhist Monk**[15] 1826 4-9-9 **85**............................. StephenDonohoe 7 91
(Ian Williams) *hld up: swtchd rt and hdwy over 1f out: sn rdn: hung lft ins fnl f: styd on* **7/1**

22-1 **4** ½ **Hawk Mountain (UAE)**[21] 1665 4-8-13 **75**........................ LDettori 5 80+
(J J Quinn) *chsd ldrs: outpcd over 3f out: rallied fnl f: r.o* **9/4**[1]

6-12 **5** 1 ½ **Mista Rossa**[16] 1807 4-8-10 **72**.. TravisBlock 4 75
(H Morrison) *hld up in tch: rdn over 2f out: outpcd over 1f out: kpt on towards fin* **12/1**

11-2 **6** ½ **Silk Hall (UAE)**[14] 1878 4-9-8 **84**.................................... JimmyFortune 2 87
(A King) *prom: led over 2f out: rdn and hdd over 1f out: wknd ins fnl f* **4/1**[3]

3153 **7** ¾ **Eton Fable (IRE)**[21] 1665 4-8-10 **77**..............................(p) AndreaAtzeni(5) 8 78
(W J H Ratcliffe) *led: rdn and hdd over 2f out: wknd over 1f out* **8/1**

2421 **8** 9 **Red Wine**[7] 2068 10-8-6 **75**.. DeclanCannon(7) 3 64
(A J McCabe) *s.s: hld up: rdn and hung rt over 2f out: sn wknd* **25/1**

3m 0.19s (1.69) **Going Correction** +0.275s/f (Good) **8** Ran SP% **115.7**
Speed ratings (Par 105): **106,104,104,104,103 102,102,97**
toteswinger: 1&2 £14.70, 1&3 £5.60, 2&3 £17.60 CSF £48.49 CT £308.86 TOTE £4.30: £1.70, £5.00, £2.70; EX 93.30 Place 6 £56.91, Place 5 £47.43.
Owner P W Harris **Bred** Iron County Farms Inc **Trained** Aldbury, Herts

FOCUS

This was a fair staying handicap, featuring several in-form, progressive types. It was soundly run and the form makes sense.

Buddhist Monk Official explanation: jockey said gelding hung left

Silk Hall(UAE) Official explanation: jockey said gelding was unsuited by the good to firm ground

T/Plt: £125.00 to a £1 stake. Pool: £93,325.21. 544.68 winning tickets. T/Qpdt: £41.90 to a £1 stake. Pool: £3,757.18. 66.24 winning tickets. CR

2284 - (Foreign Racing) - See Raceform Interactive

1754 CURRAGH (R-H)

Saturday, May 23

OFFICIAL GOING: Heavy

2285a TRI EQUESTRIAN STKS (GROUP 3) (F&M) 1m

2:10 (2:10) 4-Y-0+ **£44,174** (£12,912; £6,116; £2,038)

RPR

1 **Emily Blake (IRE)**[19] 1756 5-9-1 107...................................... JMurtagh 2 104
(J C Hayden, Ire) *mde all: t.k.h: rdn clr fr over 1f out: strly pressed and drifted rt ins fnl f: hld on gamely* **4/1**[2]

2 ½ **Beach Bunny (IRE)**[13] 1913 4-8-12 106................................. CDHayes 5 100
(Kevin Prendergast, Ire) *sn racd in 6th: pushed along briefly bef 1/2-way: impr to chse wnr fr over 1f out: clsd and chal ins fnl f: kpt on same pce cl home* **7/4**[1]

3 2 ½ **Deauville Vision (IRE)**[62] 929 6-8-12 100.........................(p) RPCleary 1 94
(M Halford, Ire) *sn racd in 4th: 6th over 3f out: rdn 2f out: kpt on wout rching 1st 2 fr over 1f out* **12/1**

4 nk **Girouette (IRE)**[19] 1756 4-8-12 97... PShanahan 3 93
(Tracey Collins, Ire) *towards rr: rdn 2f out: chsd ldrs fr over 1f out: kpt on wout threatening ins fnl f* **7/1**

5 ½ **Dane Blue (IRE)**[17] 1796 7-8-12 83...................................... JAHeffernan 4 92
(S J Treacy, Ire) *prom: 4th over 2f out: sn rdn: no imp fr over 1f out* **33/1**

6 1 **Perfect Star**[21] 1667 5-8-12 .... MJKinane 7 91
(C G Cox) *trckd ldr: rdn in 2nd over 3f out: no imp fr over 1f out* **5/1**[3]

7 1 ½ **Chantilly Tiffany**[14] 1873 5-9-1 .... DPMcDonogh 8 91
(E A L Dunlop) *trckd ldrs: pushed along in 4th over 3f out: 3rd over 2f out: no imp fr over 1f out* **13/2**

8 4 ½ **Russian Empress (IRE)**[19] 1756 5-8-12 95........................... FMBerry 6 76
(David P Myerscough, Ire) *dwlt: in rr: no ex u.p fr under 2f out* **14/1**

1m 47.61s (5.71) **Going Correction** +1.075s/f (Soft) **8** Ran SP% **116.2**
Speed ratings: **114,113,111,110,110 109,107,103**
CSF £11.63 TOTE £3.50: £1.50, £1.50, £2.10; DF 5.60.
Owner Stephen Hayden **Bred** Francis J O'Toole **Trained** Kilcullen, Co Kildare
■ This race was previously known as the Ridgewood Pearl Stakes.

NOTEBOOK

Emily Blake(IRE), a supplementary entry who is in-foal, was unproven over 1m in this sort of company, but she saw it out very well under a fine front-running ride. It was a good performance especially as she was keen enough early on, but she gradually wound up the pace and had all of her rivals in trouble over a furlong out. She did get a bit tired inside the last but she had enough in hand. (op 7/2)

Beach Bunny(IRE) stays well and did that to very good effect here, but she really needs at least an extra furlong on this evidence. She seemed to knuckle down well enough but just couldn't get there and wasn't helped that much by the winner drifting off the rail and carrying her out somewhat into the middle of the track. (op 9/4)

Deauville Vision(IRE), who like Emily Blake, is in foal. She very much appreciates this surface, but just wasn't good enough, although she kept on to reasonable effect inside the last. (op 14/1)

Girouette(IRE) was towards the back of the field most of the way and just stayed on late. She's a nice filly that handles this sort of ground and looks capable of picking up a Listed race.

Perfect Star raced prominently most of the way, but she looked to be a filly that the rider was quite reluctant to take the stick to. She faded inside the last half-furlong.

Chantilly Tiffany came under pressure well over a furlong out and didn't get home in the end. She looked as though the ground was just that bit too soft for her. (op 11/2)

2286a T P WATERS EUROPEAN BREEDERS FUND MARBLE HILL STKS (LISTED RACE) 5f

2:40 (2:40) 2-Y-O **£31,601** (£9,271; £4,417; £1,504)

RPR

1 **Wrong Answer**[29] 1497 2-8-12 .... CDHayes 7 101+
(Kevin Prendergast, Ire) *trckd ldrs: led fr 2f out: clr and styd on wl ins fnl f* **7/1**

2 2 **Foolish Ambition (GER)** 2-8-12 .... JAHeffernan 8 94+
(David Wachman, Ire) *trckd ldrs: 3rd fr 2f out: kpt on wout troubling wnr in 2nd ins fnl f* **20/1**

3 2 ½ **Air Chief Marshal (IRE)**[20] 1711 2-9-1 .... JMurtagh 4 88+
(A P O'Brien, Ire) *mid-div: prog and short of room under 2f out: rdn to go 4th 1f out: sn 3rd and kpt on wout threatening* **9/10**[1]

4 1 ¼ **Royal Infidelity (IRE)**[14] 1896 2-9-1 .... JamieSpencer 11 83
(T Stack, Ire) *towards rr: swtchd to outer and rdn to go 5th 1f out: kpt on same pce wout threatening* **14/1**

5 5 **This Is Real (IRE)**[14] 1896 2-8-12 .... DJMoran 10 62
(Brian Nolan, Ire) *sn trckd ldrs: 2nd fr 2f out: lost pl and no imp fr over 1f out* **50/1**

6 1 ½ **Pilgrim Dancer (IRE)**[35] 1373 2-9-1 .... RPCleary 1 60
(Emmanuel Hughes, Ire) *led: hdd fr 2f out: sn no imp* **13/2**[3]

7 1 **Corcovada (IRE)**[6] 2106 2-8-12 .... FMBerry 9 53
(Edward P Harty, Ire) *trckd ldrs: 3rd and no ex fr 1f out* **14/1**

8 1 ¼ **Rigid Rock (IRE)**[9] 2019 2-9-1 .... PJSmullen 2 52+
(J T Gorman, Ire) *mid-div best: kpt on same pce u.p fr 2f out* **25/1**

9 3 **Aisy (IRE)**[40] 1262 2-8-12 .... MCHussey 5 38
(T Stack, Ire) *towards rr: rdn wl bef 1/2-way: sn no imp* **25/1**

10 hd **Marcus Galerius (IRE)**[13] 1907 2-9-1 .... WJLee 3 40
(T Stack, Ire) *prom: plld hrd early: no ex u.p 1 1/2f out* **33/1**

11 1 **Cinnamon Tart (IRE)**[10] 1993 2-8-12 .... DMGrant 12 34
(John Joseph Murphy, Ire) *towards rr: no imp u.p fr 2f out* **50/1**

12 1 **Atasari (IRE)**[19] 1754 2-8-12 .... KJManning 6 30
(J S Bolger, Ire) *towards rr: rdn 1/2-way: sn no imp* **9/2**[2]

63.92 secs (3.22) **Going Correction** +0.775s/f (Yiel) **12** Ran SP% **129.3**
Speed ratings: **99,95,91,89,81 79,77,75,71,70 69,67**
CSF £147.72 TOTE £5.10: £1.90, £7.60, £1.10; DF 381.20.
Owner Lady O'Reilly **Bred** Sky Marc Farm And Castlemartin **Trained** Friarstown, Co Kildare

NOTEBOOK

Wrong Answer is a filly with plenty of speed that can lie up over this trip, and once she quickened to the front over a furlong out she had the remainder in trouble. It was a good performance by a filly very much at home in these conditions, but who has shown she can handle quicker ground as well. It could be an interesting season for her. (op 6/1)

Foolish Ambition(GER) ◆ showed that the decision to launch her career in this race was fully justified. Her pedigree suggested that she would handle this ground well and so it proved. She did her best work inside the final furlong when keeping on from just off the pace, but showed a professional attitude and kept on well without having any chance with the winner. She's certain to improve and will get at least an extra furlong.

Air Chief Marshal(IRE) was stepping back in trip and it didn't suit, even with the testing ground. His rider just never seemed to be happy as he raced just behind horses, but there was a gap there for him to challenge two furlongs out if he was quick enough to go through it. He wasn't and he got buffeted about when the door closed on him, eventually he kept on inside the last, but could make no impression on the first two. (op 1/1)

Royal Infidelity(IRE) kept on from the back of the field inside the last and may have surprised that he handled this ground at all. He wasn't good enough, but ran pretty well and should see out an extra furlong without too much difficulty.

2287a WEATHERBYS IRELAND GREENLANDS STKS (GROUP 3) 6f

3:10 (3:11) 3-Y-0+ **£45,752** (£13,373; £6,334; £2,111)

RPR

1 **Utmost Respect**[10] 1989 5-10-0 DPMcDonogh 4 121
(R A Fahey) *chsd ldr in 2nd: pushed along fr over 2f out: swished tail ins fnl f: led and styd on best to go clr ins fnl 100yds* **1/1**[1]

2 2 1/2 **Jumbajukiba**[27] 1543 6-9-12 112 (b) FMBerry 6 111
(Mrs John Harrington, Ire) *attempted to make all: clr for much: reduced ld fr over 1f out: hdd and kpt on same pce fnl 100yds* **4/1**[2]

3 3/4 **Icelandic**[34] 1384 7-9-9 (t) MDemuro 5 106
(F Sheridan) *chsd ldrs: 4th over 2f out: sn rdn: 3rd and kpt on same pce wout threatening fr over 1f out* **10/1**

4 2 **Bushranger (IRE)**[210] 6997 3-9-5 121 JMurtagh 1 103
(David Wachman, Ire) *chsd ldrs: 3rd over 2f out: sn rdn: 4th and kpt on same pce fr over 1f out* **6/1**[3]

5 2 1/2 **Snaefell (IRE)**[35] 1374 5-9-12 108 (p) PJSmullen 9 96
(M Halford, Ire) *chsd ldrs: 5th over 2f out: sn rdn: kpt on same pce wout threatening fr over 1f out* **14/1**

6 4 **Three Rocks (IRE)**[13] 1913 4-9-9 108 KJManning 2 81
(J S Bolger, Ire) *s.i.s: towards rr: rdn 2f out: kpt on same pce wout threatening fr over 1f out* **8/1**

7 1 1/2 **Knot In Wood (IRE)**[10] 1989 7-9-9 MCHussey 8 76
(R A Fahey) *chsd ldrs: rdn 2f out: no imp fr over 1f out* **16/1**

8 2 **Senor Benny (USA)**[35] 1374 10-9-9 102 CDHayes 3 70
(M McDonagh, Ire) *chsd ldrs: rdn 2f out: sn no imp* **50/1**

9 7 **Georgebernardshaw (IRE)**[35] 1374 4-9-9 104 JAHeffernan 7 49
(A P O'Brien, Ire) *chsd ldrs: no imp u.p fr 2f out: no ex fr over 1f out* **16/1**

1m 16.9s (2.20) **Going Correction** +0.775s/f (Yiel)
WFA 3 from 4yo+ 9lb **9 Ran SP% 124.9**
Speed ratings: **115,111,110,108,104 99,97,94,85**
CSF £5.78 TOTE £1.90: £1.20, £1.60, £2.80; DF 6.60.
Owner The Rumpole Partnership **Bred** Heather Raw **Trained** Musley Bank, N Yorks

NOTEBOOK

Utmost Respect had shown his adaptability in terms of ground prior to this win, and following his success in the Duke of York Stakes on fast ground on his previous start, he battled well for victory here, giving weight to all his rivals.He was going away at the finish, and afterwards trainer Richard Fahey said that a tilt at the Golden Jubilee Stakes at Royal Ascot will be considered. (op 5/4)

Jumbajukiba, winner of a Listed race over a slightly shorter trip at Navan on his previous start, revels in testing ground and has produced his best efforts at this track, admittedly going a bit further. He set off in front and only gave best inside the final furlong. (op 9/2)

Icelandic, a six-time winner and winner of a Listed event at Doncaster last season, ran a good race, chasing the leaders and having every chance from one and a half furlongs out. He kept on, although was no threat to the winner over the final furlong. (op 10/1 tchd 11/1)

Bushranger(IRE), winner of the Prix Morny and the Middle Park Stakes last season, was making his reappearance. He looked as if the run would bring him on, and considering the ground was far from ideal for him, it was a satisfactory return from a colt who should do well as a sprinter on a better surface. (op 5/1 tchd 13/2)

Snaefell(IRE) goes on the ground and is a winner at this level. Fitted with cheekpieces for the first time, he chased the leaders, but was unable to improve his position from one and a half furlongs out.

Knot In Wood(IRE) acts well on a softish surface but has been busy of late on much faster ground and was below par back on this testing going. (op 14/1)

2288a BOYLESPORTS.COM IRISH 2,000 GUINEAS (GROUP 1) (ENTIRE COLTS & FILLIES) 1m

3:45 (3:45) 3-Y-0

£221,844 (£74,271; £35,436; £12,135; £8,252; £4,368)

RPR

1 **Mastercraftsman (IRE)**[21] 1675 3-9-0 120 JMurtagh 6 124+
(A P O'Brien, Ire) *sn chsd ldrs in 3rd: clsd in 2nd fr 3f out: rdn to ld over 2f out: clr fr over 1f out: styd on wl: impressive* **6/4**[1]

2 4 1/2 **Rayeni (IRE)**[208] 7029 3-9-0 MJKinane 4 114+
(John M Oxx, Ire) *chsd ldrs in 5th: clsd fr 3f out: rdn fr 2f out: wnt mod 2nd and kpt on same pce fr over 1f out* **5/1**[3]

3 1 3/4 **Soul City (IRE)**[217] 6815 3-9-0 RichardHughes 5 109
(R Hannon) *chsd ldr: cl 5th fr 3f out: no imp u.p fr under 2f out: kpt on same pce wout threatening fr over 1f out* **9/1**

4 1 1/2 **Recharge (IRE)**[55] 1022 3-9-0 110 CDHayes 7 107
(Kevin Prendergast, Ire) *sn mod 6th: clsr in 4th fr 3f out: no imp u.p fr under 2f out: mod 3rd and no imp fr over 1f out* **10/1**

5 3 1/2 **Fergus McIver (IRE)**[13] 1910 3-9-0 105 (b) KJManning 2 98
(J S Bolger, Ire) *sn mod 4th: clsd fr 3f out: kpt on same pce u.p fr under 2f out* **20/1**

6 1 1/2 **Drumbeat (IRE)**[15] 1822 3-9-0 107 JAHeffernan 9 94
(A P O'Brien, Ire) *wl off pce towards rr: clsd 3f out: prom 2f out: no imp u.p fr over 1f out* **10/1**

7 1 3/4 **Hail Caesar (IRE)**[13] 1910 3-9-0 101 CO'Donoghue 8 90
(A P O'Brien, Ire) *wl off pce towards rr: clsd 3f out: no imp u.p and kpt on same pce fr 2f out* **40/1**

8 3 **Delegator**[21] 1675 3-9-0 JamieSpencer 1 83
(B J Meehan) *wl off pce towards rr: clsd 3f out: rdn under 2f out: sn no imp and no ex in 4th fr over 1f out* **3/1**[2]

9 30 **Viceroy Of India (USA)**[20] 1713 3-9-0 SMLevey 3 14
(A P O'Brien, Ire) *sn led and clr: reduced ld 3f out: hdd over 2f out: sn bhd and eased* **100/1**

1m 48.16s (6.26) **Going Correction** +1.075s/f (Soft) **9 Ran SP% 118.0**
Speed ratings: **111,106,104,103,99 98,96,93,63**
CSF £9.55 TOTE £3.70: £1.60, £2.70, £3.50; DF 11.30.
Owner Derrick Smith **Bred** Lynch Bages Ltd **Trained** Ballydoyle, Co Tipperary
■ A ninth consecutive Irish Classic for Aidan O'Brien.

FOCUS

The winner is rated an average winner of this Classic, with the placed horses setting the level.

NOTEBOOK

Mastercraftsman(IRE) might be the sole horse among this group that looks capable of further success in Group 1 company. The usual provisos prevail - some of these just didn't give their running on the testing ground. The winner had already proved he handled conditions to some degree with his narrow win in the National Stakes last year, and this was a case of him both handling the ground better than anything else as well as being the best horse in the race. Murtagh had him in the perfect position to challenge with a clear passage just a couple of horse-widths off the rail, and once he quickened to the front a furlong and a half out he had everything off the bridle and just drew further clear. It was a classy performance against horses that basically weren't in his league, did represent some improvement on his run at Newmarket and he looks more ready now to take on the best milers on better ground. (op 7/4)

Rayeni(IRE) fully justified the decision to run and belied the lack of real confidence behind his challenge. He handled the ground very well as expected and stayed on inside the final furlong, while those that finished in his wake mostly floundered. He normally wouldn't appear good enough to take on the best over 1m, but looks the type that might prove effective stepped up to 1m2f. However, the competitiveness, or maybe lack of, in Group 1 contests over this trip might prove tempting enough for them to give him another try. (op 4/1)

Soul City(IRE) was fresher than most of these and showed it as he raced plenty keen enough early on. He eventually did stay on again inside the final furlong or so without threatening. It was a very decent effort on his seasonal bow and connections do have something to look forward to, although as with most of these, his ability to win in Group 1 company looks limited. (op 12/1)

Recharge(IRE) was also quite keen and that probably told against him more than most late in the day, as his ability to handle this surface would also have been in question. He moved into a challenging position on the outside of the field a quarter of a mile from the finish, but his effort did flatten out inside the last. It would be no surprise if he proved better than the two immediately in front of him on better ground.

Fergus McIver(IRE), whose presence in the first five, albeit beaten over 11 lengths by the winner, does not do a lot for the form of the race. On saying that, he's tough and honest and hasn't regressed for what has been a busy campaign to date. He just kept going, but he is a middle-distance horse and deserves to win a stakes race.

Drumbeat(IRE), who travelled well towards the outside of the field around the 2f pole, when let down was quite disappointing in his response. (op 8/1)

Delegator, the Newmarket Guineas runner-up, was held up towards the rear and did make some ground over a furlong out, but he just floundered on the heavy going inside the final furlong and pretty much stopped. Official explanation: jockey said colt never travelled due to the ground conditions (op 3/1 tchd 7/2)

2289a BOYLEPOKER.COM H'CAP (PREMIER HANDICAP) 1m

4:20 (4:21) 3-Y-0+ **£26,861** (£7,881; £3,754; £1,279)

RPR

1 **Philario (IRE)**[9] 2015 4-9-5 98 MartinLane[(5)] 18 108
(K R Burke) *sn prom: led over 2f out: styd on wl u.p* **6/1**[2]

2 1 **Rock And Roll Kid (IRE)**[62] 929 4-8-10 89 DEMullins[(5)] 10 97+
(Anthony Mullins, Ire) *w.w wl off pce towards rr: prog fr over 2f out: rdn into 3rd over 1f out: styd on ins fnl f wout rching wnr* **5/2**[1]

3 1 1/4 **Dedo (IRE)**[13] 1912 4-9-0 88 DPMcDonogh 17 93
(Kevin Prendergast, Ire) *mid-div: impr to chse ldrs fr over 3f out: rdn into 2nd over 1f out: kpt on same pce ins fnl f* **14/1**

4 hd **Imply**[13] 1912 5-7-12 79 (b) GFCarroll[(7)] 1 84
(James Leavy, Ire) *prom: 3rd fr after 1/2-way: 4th and kpt on same pce u.p fr over 1f out* **16/1**

5 10 **Hard Rock City (USA)**[9] 2024 9-9-4 92 JMurtagh 5 75+
(M J Grassick, Ire) *sn mid-div: rdn to go mod 7th over 1f out: kpt on wout threatening ins fnl f* **8/1**[3]

6 1 **Award Ceremony (IRE)**[13] 1912 4-8-13 97 (b) LFRoche[(10)] 4 76
(D K Weld, Ire) *chsd ldrs: 4th over 2f out: sn no imp u.p: kpt on same pce* **14/1**

7 3/4 **Alone He Stands (IRE)**[13] 1912 9-8-13 87 PJSmullen 9 65
(J C Hayden, Ire) *sn wl off pce towards rr: kpt on wout threatening u.p fr over 2f out* **12/1**

8 5 1/2 **Lonesome Maverick (IRE)**[202] 7160 5-8-6 83 DJMoran[(3)] 2 48
(Donal Kinsella, Ire) *sn wl off pce towards rr: rdn to go mod 5th over 1f out: sn no ex* **20/1**

9 3/4 **Crooked Throw (IRE)**[9] 2024 10-9-4 92 WJLee 3 55
(C F Swan, Ire) *sn wl off pce towards rr: kpt on wout threatening u.p fr over 2f out* **12/1**

10 1 1/4 **Nanotech (IRE)**[6] 2108 5-9-6 101 CPHarrison[(7)] 19 61
(Jarlath P Fahey, Ire) *sn led: hdd over 2f out: sn no ex* **14/1**

11 1 3/4 **Tis Mighty (IRE)**[20] 1712 6-9-2 95 EJMcNamara[(5)] 11 51
(P J Prendergast, Ire) *mid-div: kpt on same pce fr over 2f out* **10/1**

12 5 **Quinmaster (USA)**[169] 7568 7-10-0 102 RPCleary 7 47
(M Halford, Ire) *sn wl off pce towards rr: no imp fr over 2f out* **25/1**

13 4 1/2 **Le Citadel (USA)**[42] 1219 4-8-3 84 (bt) KTO'Neill[(7)] 16 18
(P D Deegan, Ire) *sn prom: no ex fr under 3f out* **33/1**

14 1 **Ready To Rocknroll (IRE)**[9] 2022 4-8-9 83 KJManning 15 15
(J T Gorman, Ire) *chsd ldrs early: no ex fr under 3f out* **10/1**

15 18 **Lime Tree Valley (IRE)**[29] 1501 4-8-8 82 CO'Donoghue 8 —
(David Marnane, Ire) *sn wl off pce towards rr: no ex fr under 3f out* **12/1**

16 7 **Sciatin (IRE)**[9] 2022 6-8-11 85 FMBerry 12 —
(David P Myerscough, Ire) *mid-div: no ex fr under 3f out* **14/1**

17 2 1/2 **Shayrazan (IRE)**[9] 2022 8-8-13 87 (t) JAHeffernan 6 —
(James Leavy, Ire) *v s.i.s: a towards rr* **25/1**

18 1 **Orpailleur**[604] 5761 8-8-9 88 AmyKathleenParsons[(5)] 14 —
(Ms Joanna Morgan, Ire) *prom: wknd fr over 3f out* **25/1**

1m 48.65s (6.75) **Going Correction** +1.075s/f (Soft) **18 Ran SP% 147.0**
Speed ratings: **109,108,106,106,96 95,94,89,88,87 85,80,76,75,57 50,47,46**
CSF £23.96 CT £241.13 TOTE £8.40: £2.50, £1.70, £2.50, £4.30; DF 40.90.
Owner Philip Richards **Bred** David Barry **Trained** Middleham Moor, N Yorks

NOTEBOOK

Philario(IRE), without a win since twice successful as a two-year-old, once at Group 3 level, had been caught close home in a valuable handicap over this trip at York on his previous start. The ground was the concern here as his best form had been shown on better ground, but after racing prominently and going to the front over 2f out, he kept on well under pressure for a game win. (op 13/2 tchd 8/1)

2290a BOYLESPORTS FON-A-BET 1800 44 0000 H'CAP 1m 2f

4:50 (4:50) (60-90,88) 3-Y-0+ **£11,740** (£2,735; £1,206; £696)

RPR

1 **Coolcullen Times (IRE)**[36] 1341 3-8-12 86 KJManning 5 89
(J S Bolger, Ire) *towards rr: clsr in 4th into st: chal fr 2f out: narrowly in front fr over 1f out: styd on wl u.p: all out* **8/1**

2 shd **Master Marvel (IRE)**[6] 2112 8-8-8 73 MACleere[(5)] 3 76
(T J O'Mara, Ire) *towards rr: rdn to go 6th over 1f out: swtchd ins fnl f to chal: styd on wl: jst failed* **14/1**

3 *shd* **Designated Decoy (USA)**29 1502 4-9-12 86................(b) PJSmullen 7 89
(D K Weld, Ire) *mid-div: clsr in 3rd into st: 4th under 2f out: 3rd over 1f out: sn ev ch u.p: kpt on wl: jst failed* **8/1**

4 *1* **Dukedom**6 2112 6-8-7 67...(b1) RPCleary 11 68
(T G McCourt, Ire) *mid-div: 6th into st: chal u.p in 2nd over 1f out: dropped to 4th and kpt on same pce cl home* **14/1**

5 *5 1/2* **Nobunaga**6 2112 4-9-0 74.. KLatham 2 64
(Richard Brabazon, Ire) *prom: on terms bef st: hdd and no ex fr over 1f out* **7/1**

6 *5* **Holly Hill (IRE)**6 2111 6-8-1 64 oh1.......................... DJMoran(3) 8 44
(Edward P Harty, Ire) *mid-div: impr to be on terms into st: dropped to 3rd under 2f out: 5th and no ex fr over 1f out* **5/13**

7 *nk* **Red Jade**25 1593 4-10-0 88.................................. DPMcDonogh 1 67
(K R Burke) *trckd ldrs: rdn in 4th bef st: sn 5th: 7th and no ex fr over 1f out* **9/22**

8 *5* **Bricks And Porter (IRE)**19 1759 9-8-1 66...................(bt) BACurtis(5) 9 35
(T G McCourt, Ire) *trckd ldrs: dropped to 7th and rdn into st: no ex in 8th over 1f out* **16/1**

9 *22* **Sassy Gal (IRE)**19 1757 4-9-1 75.. JMurtagh 4 —
(Peter Maher, Ire) *led: jnd bef st: sn hdd and eased* **10/1**

10 *2 1/2* **Invincible Joe (IRE)**6 2108 4-9-13 87.......................... JAHeffernan 10 7
(John Joseph Hanlon, Ire) *towards rr: 8th appr st: sn no imp u.p: eased ins fnl f* **20/1**

11 *17* **Uncle Eric (IRE)**15 1854 4-9-5 79...................................... FMBerry 6 —
(Mrs John Harrington, Ire) *s.i.s: towards rr: no imp into st: eased fr over 2f out* **3/11**

2m 24.86s (15.36) **Going Correction** +1.625s/f (Heav)
WFA 3 from 4yo+ 14lb **11** Ran SP% **127.6**
Speed ratings: **103,102,102,102,97 93,93,89,71,69 56**
CSF £124.03 CT £950.26 TOTE £8.60: £2.90, £5.60, £2.70; DF 166.20.
Owner Mrs J S Bolger **Bred** J S Bolger **Trained** Coolcullen, Co Carlow

NOTEBOOK
Red Jade, withdrawn from a race at York due to the fast ground, has run all his races on a soft surface. However, he seemed to find this testing ground too much. (op 3/1)
Sassy Gal(IRE) Official explanation: jockey said filly ran very keen in this race
Uncle Eric(IRE) Official explanation: vet said gelding was found to be blowing hard post-race
T/Jkpt: @803.40. Pool of @15,000.00 - 14 winning units. T/Plt: @11.70. Pool of @20,235.00 - 1,293 winning units. II

CHATEAUBRIANT (L-H)
Saturday, May 23

OFFICIAL GOING: Good to soft

2293a PRIX BERING (MAIDEN) (C&G) 1m 1f 165y
4:25 (4:30) 3-Y-O **£6,796** (£2,718; £2,039; £1,359; £680)

RPR

1 **Narjan** 3-9-2 .... MPoirier 74
(A De Royer-Dupre, France)

2 *nk* **Follow The Lead** 3-8-8 .... ALemaitre 65
(F Head, France)

3 *snk* **Dr Valentine (FR)**220 6731 3-9-2 .... AlexisBadel 73
(E J O'Neill) *racd in 3rd on outside: 2nd 1/2-way: led and drvn appr st: sn hdd but styd on to ld again 100yds out: hdd cl home* **28/11**

4 *3/4* **Petit Ecuyer (FR)**21 3-9-2 71
(A Couetil, France)

5 *4* **Monetaire (FR)**27 3-8-10 57
(C Laffon-Parias, France)

6 *2* **Maidstone Marble (FR)** 3-9-2 59
(H-A Pantall, France)

7 *shd* **Good Lord (FR)**32 3-9-2 59
(F Doumen, France)

8 *1* **Rodios (FR)** 3-8-10 51
(D Sepulchre, France)

9 *snk* **Chocolat Noir (FR)** 3-9-2 ....(b) 57
(J Boisnard, France)

10 *3/4* **Polidalite (FR)** 3-9-2 55
(C Lotoux, France)

0 **Rain Is Luck (FR)**51 3-9-2 .... —
(F Cohen, France)

0 **Sakhr (FR)** 3-8-12 .... —
(F Doumen, France)

0 **Larmont (FR)** 3-8-12 .... —
(E Libaud, France)

0 **Ocean Terminal (FR)** 3-8-12 .... —
(J Boisnard, France)

0 **Quick Way (FR)** 3-8-12 .... —
(Mme N Madamet, France)

2m 2.30s (122.30) **15** Ran SP% **3.4**
PARI-MUTUEL (Including 1 Euro stake): WIN 6.40; PL 2.30, 1.90, 5.50;DF 10.50.
Owner H H Aga Khan **Bred** H H The Aga Khan's Studs S C **Trained** Chantilly, France

NOTEBOOK
Dr Valentine(FR), who had only shown modest form previously, was up in trip and encountering easy ground for the first time and ran creditably, only being caught near the line.

2277 NEWMARKET (R-H)
Sunday, May 24

OFFICIAL GOING: Good to firm (firm in places; 8.6)
Wind: Light, behind. Weather: Fine and sunny

2294 NEWMARKET COUNTRYSIDE DAY LADIES' H'CAP (AMATEURS) (IN MEMORY OF LUCINDA STOPFORD-SACKVILLE) 1m 4f
2:20 (2:20) (Class 5) (0-70,66) 4-Y-0+ **£3,123** (£968; £484; £242) **Stalls** Centre

Form RPR

-613 1 **Grand Art (IRE)**8 2068 5-10-1 65.......................... MissWGibson(5) 10 74
(P T Midgley) *hld up: swtchd lft over 4f out: hdwy over 2f out: r.o to ld towards fin* **11/23**

0606 2 *3/4* **Strike Force**15 1881 5-9-8 58.......................... MissALHutchinson(5) 3 66
(Miss J Feilden) *hld up and bhd: hdwy over 3f out: led ins fnl f: hdd towards fin* **18/1**

00-6 3 *1 1/2* **Ovthenight (IRE)**32 1454 4-10-3 65.......................(v1) MissGAndrews(3) 2 71
(Mrs P Sly) *chsd ldr 5f: remained handy: wnt 2nd again over 2f out: led over 1f out: sn rdn: hdd and unable qckn ins fnl f* **9/22**

4343 4 *1* **Dramatic Solo**16 1851 4-9-12 62.........................(b) MissKellyBurke(5) 11 66
(K R Burke) *led: rdn: hung lft and hdd over 1f out: styd on same pce* **10/1**

3543 5 *2 3/4* **Penang Cinta**4 2182 6-9-12 57...............................(p) MissEFolkes 1 57
(P D Evans) *prom: chsd ldr 7f out tl rdn over 2f out: wknd wl ins fnl f* **3/11**

0-15 6 *2 1/2* **Harlequinn Danseur (IRE)**2 2222 4-9-9 54.......... MissFayeBramley 5 50
(N B King) *prom: lost pl 8f out: styd on ins fnl f: nt trble ldrs* **13/2**

00-5 7 *2* **Great View (IRE)**18 1786 10-10-2 61..........................(p) MrsCBartley 7 53
(Mrs A L M King) *s.i.s: sn prom: rdn over 3f out: wknd over 1f out* **10/1**

010 8 *16* **Casablanca Minx (IRE)**75 790 6-9-2 52...............(bt) MissMHugo(5) 6 19
(Miss Gay Kelleway) *mid-div: hmpd sn after s: rdn and wknd 3f out: bhd whn hung lft fnl f* **33/1**

-300 9 *6* **Captain Mainwaring**42 871 4-9-7 52..............(b) MrsEmmaLittmoden 8 9
(N P Littmoden) *hld up: racd keenly: hdwy over 3f out: sn rdn and wknd* **40/1**

4252 10 *3 1/4* **Star Choice**12 1960 4-10-7 66.......................................(p) MissEJJones 4 18
(J Pearce) *swtchd rt sn after s: hld up: rdn over 4f out: wknd over 3f out* **11/23**

0/5- 11 *7* **Theflyingscottie**7 220 7-9-7 52 oh7...........................(v) MrsMMorris 9 —
(D Shaw) *mid-div: hmpd sn after s: wknd over 3f out* **33/1**

2m 33.71s (0.21) **Going Correction** +0.075s/f (Good) **11** Ran SP% **119.1**
Speed ratings (Par 103): **102,101,100,99,98 96,95,84,80,78 73**
toteswinger: 1&2 £28.60, 1&3 £10.00, 2&3 £26.30. CSF £98.39 CT £487.93 TOTE £6.80: £2.10, £5.80, £2.20; EX 113.30.
Owner David Mann **Bred** Mrs Teresa Bergin & Mrs Anne Fitzgerald **Trained** Westow, N Yorks
■ Stewards' Enquiry : Miss Faye Bramley one-day ban: used whip when out of contention (Jun 9)

FOCUS
The ground had firmed up a little from the previous day. A moderate handicap for lady amateurs to start proceedings, and ordinary form. The pace was strong and the first two home came from the back of the field, with the three leaders filling the next three places. The runner-up sets the level.

2295 NEWMARKET DAY CENTRE MAIDEN STKS 5f
2:55 (2:55) (Class 4) 2-Y-O **£5,180** (£1,541; £770; £384) **Stalls** High

Form RPR

1 **Angel's Pursuit (IRE)** 2-9-3 0.................................... RichardHughes 4 90+
(R Hannon) *chsd ldrs: swtchd rt over 1f out: led ins fnl f: shkn up: edgd lft and r.o* **11/101**

252 2 *2 1/2* **Mijas Playa**9 2034 2-8-12 0.. TPQueally 5 75
(C A Dwyer) *chsd ldr tl led 3f out: rdn over 1f out: hung lft and hdd ins fnl f: styd on same pce* **7/42**

3 *1/2* **Dahakaa** 2-9-3 0.. PhilipRobinson 1 78
(M A Jarvis) *chsd ldrs: jnd ldr 3f out: rdn and ev ch ins fnl f: edgd lft and unable qckn* **5/13**

4 *9* **Back On** 2-8-12 0.. MarkFlynn(5) 3 46
(G C Bravery) *s.s: outpcd* **50/1**

0 5 *2 1/2* **Papageno**45 1195 2-9-3 0.. JimCrowley 6 37
(J R Jenkins) *led 2f: chsd ldrs tl rdn and wknd over 1f out* **12/1**

60.01 secs (0.91) **Going Correction** +0.075s/f (Good) **5** Ran SP% **110.3**
Speed ratings (Par 95): **95,91,90,75,71**
toteswinger: 1&2 £2.50. CSF £3.29 TOTE £2.10: £1.10, £1.70; EX 4.00.
Owner Malih L Al Basti **Bred** Hong Kong Breeders Club **Trained** East Everleigh, Wilts

FOCUS
A reasonable maiden despite the small field. The winner did it impressively and will surely post better figures than this. The runner-up helps with the level of the form.

NOTEBOOK
Angel's Pursuit(IRE) ◆ produced a taking performance, slipstreaming the three disputing the lead before being switched right to challenge and quickening up to win readily. He showed his inexperience in the preliminaries and was green in the race too, edging to his left once in front, and there is plenty of improvement to come from this £190,000 buy. There is bags of speed in his pedigree, as he is a half-brother to Middle Park Stakes winner Dark Angel, out of an unraced daughter of smart sprinter Night At Sea, and his sire won the July Cup. He could be a Royal Ascot prospect, either in the Norfolk or the Windsor Castle. (op 5-4 tchd Evens)
Mijas Playa set a solid standard and there seems no reason to suggest she did not run her race, but she has now finished second on three of her four starts, finishing fifth when favourite for the Lily Agnes at Chester on the other occasion. Her attitude is not in question and she should soon get off the mark, perhaps back against her own sex. (op 2-1 tchd 9-4 in places)
Dahakaa sweated up beforehand and was loaded into the stalls with the help of a rug. He had every chance and only conceded defeat late on, perhaps finding underfoot conditions a bit faster than he'd have liked. An ordinary maiden will come his way. (op 7-2 tchd 11-2, 6-1 in places and 10-3 in places)
Back On, trainer Giles Bravery's first juvenile runner of the season, was outpaced in last place before picking up a bit late on for fourth. This was a fairly pleasing introduction and he could be the type for ordinary nurseries later in the year.
Papageno, who was well held on his Folkestone debut, broke smartly and showed plenty of pace to shade the lead before dropping away to finish last. His dam's previous five foals all won and he should add to the family record in time. (op 14-1 tchd 16-1)

2296 EAST ANGLIAN AIR AMBULANCE H'CAP 1m 2f
3:30 (3:30) (Class 2) (0-100,91) 3-Y-O **£12,952** (£3,854; £1,926; £962) **Stalls** High

Form RPR

06-4 1 **Doctor Crane (USA)**30 1489 3-9-4 91........................ JimmyFortune 7 98
(J H M Gosden) *racd alone far side: up w the pce: rdn to ld and hung lft ins fnl f: r.o* **9/1**

2-51 2 *3/4* **Hyades (USA)**24 1632 3-9-1 88.. TPQueally 2 94
(H R A Cecil) *chsd ldrs in centre: rdn to ld over 1f out: edgd rt: hdd ins fnl f: styd on* **7/23**

12 3 *2 1/4* **Mutamaashi**38 1307 3-9-1 88.. TPO'Shea 6 89+
(W J Haggas) *chsd ldr in centre: rdn and hung rt over 1f out: styd on same pce* **10/32**

1-31 4 *hd* **Takaatuf (IRE)**21 1702 3-9-1 88..................................... GregFairley 3 89
(M Johnston) *led centre: rdn: edgd rt and hdd over 1f out: no ex ins fnl f* **3/11**

51-5 5 *1/2* **Tudor Key (IRE)**38 1303 3-9-4 91.................................... JimCrowley 1 91
(Mrs A J Perrett) *racd centre: hld up: plld hrd: rdn over 1f out: nt rch ldrs* **14/1**

1 6 *8* **Namibian Orator (IRE)**27 1573 3-9-0 87........................ RyanMoore 4 71
(Sir Michael Stoute) *racd centre: hld up: plld hrd: swtchd rt and hdwy over 2f out: rdn and hung rt over 1f out: sn wknd* **10/32**

2m 6.16s (0.36) **Going Correction** +0.075s/f (Good) **6** Ran SP% **110.0**
Speed ratings (Par 105): **101,100,98,98,98 91**
toteswinger: 1&2 £4.40, 1&3 £3.80, 2&3 £2.90. CSF £38.38 TOTE £10.70: £3.50, £1.90; EX 37.70.
Owner Ms Rachel D S Hood **Bred** Weldon R Johnson Jr **Trained** Newmarket, Suffolk

FOCUS

A interesting handicap featuring some unexposed types, but the form has a slightly dubious look to it. The pace was only steady until picking up inside the last half-mile, and the winner raced on his own on the far rail, away from the other five who came down the centre of the track. A slight personal-best from the winner, the second stepping up, with the third and fourth progressive.

NOTEBOOK

Doctor Crane(USA) was always up with the pace and he knuckled down well for pressure to score despite hanging off the rail and towards the other runners. He further advertised the form of the Sandown handicap in which he had made his seasonal debut, as the three who finished ahead of him, most notably Aqwaal, have all won since. He was found wanting in Listed company last season after a promising start to his career but may have to go back in that grade following a rise for this win, with the Hampton Court Stakes at Ascot a possibility. The likelihood is that he will not be easy to place now. (op 7-1 tchd 10-1)

Hyades(USA), on his handicap debut, travelled up smoothly but could not quite get past the winner, who perhaps showed the greater resolution in the finish. The return to this trip was not a problem and he should continue to progress, but the King Edward VII would be flying too high and it does look as if his appetite for a battle is in question. (tchd 4-1)

Mutamaashi, who sweated up on a warm afternoon, raced freely through the early stages. He lacked the pace to quite land a blow but did keep on for third, appearing to see out the 1m2f albeit in a falsely-run race (tchd 3-1 and 7-2)

Takaatuf(IRE) made all in a slightly weaker event here three weeks ago for which he was raised 3lb. Setting the pace and winding things up, he kept battling when tackled but had no more to offer inside the last. (op 7-2)

Tudor Key(IRE), another a shade keen when held up, was outpaced a little when the pace lifted before keeping on steadily. He did not fully prove his stamina for this trip. (op 12-1)

Namibian Orator(IRE), a King Edward VII Stakes entry, looked potentially well treated for this handicap debut. He came with his effort from the rear but could not quicken up and was eased when beaten in the last half-furlong. He could be worth another chance back on easier ground. Official explanation: trainer's rep had no explanation for the poor form (op 7-2 tchd 11-4)

2297 VICTOR CHANDLER H'CAP 6f

4:05 (4:06) (Class 2) (0-100,96) 4-Y-0+ £12,952 (£3,854; £1,926; £962) Stalls High

Form RPR

15-2 **1** **Jimmy Styles**[15] 1864 5-9-4 **96** PhilipRobinson 5 108+
(C G Cox) *a.p: racd keenly: led over 1f out: rdn out* **3/1**[1]

-032 **2** 1 3/4 **Everymanforhimself (IRE)**[10] 2012 5-9-0 **92** (v[1]) RyanMoore 8 97
(K A Ryan) *hld up: pushed along 1/2-way: hdwy over 1f out: r.o* **15/2**

4326 **3** 1 1/4 **Orpenindeed (IRE)**[32] 1467 6-8-7 **90** (p) AndreaAtzeni[(5)] 1 91
(M Botti) *led early tl swtchd lft to r alone stands' side: up w the pce: rdn and hung rt over 1f out: styd on same pce ins fnl f* **12/1**

0232 **4** 1/2 **Thebes**[21] 1699 4-9-0 **92** GregFairley 4 91
(M Johnston) *chsd ldrs tl led 2f out: sn rdn: edgd rt and hdd: no ex ins fnl f* **5/1**[3]

100- **5** 2 1/2 **Musaalem (USA)**[239] 6289 5-9-1 **93** TPO'Shea 7 84+
(W J Haggas) *hld up: r.o ins fnl f: nvr nr to chal* **9/2**[2]

-415 **6** 1/2 **Silver Wind**[119] 291 4-8-4 **82** (v) CatherineGannon 11 72
(P D Evans) *sn led: rdn and hdd 2f out: edgd lft and bmpd sn after: wknd ins fnl f* **33/1**

0-06 **7** 1 3/4 **Mac Gille Eoin**[21] 1699 5-9-0 **92** JimCrowley 3 76
(J Gallagher) *chsd ldrs: rdn over 2f out: wknd over 1f out* **12/1**

0350 **8** 2 **Ebraam (USA)**[15] 1864 6-8-10 **88** TolleyDean 6 66
(P Howling) *hld up: rdn over 2f out: hung lft and wknd over 1f out* **33/1**

5623 **9** 1 1/4 **Abraham Lincoln (IRE)**[9] 2059 5-9-4 **96** StephenDonohoe 10 80+
(D Nicholls) *hld up: rdn over 2f out: wkng whn hung lft and eased fnl f* **6/1**

06-1 **10** 14 **Striking Spirit**[15] 1864 4-9-3 **95** AdrianTNicholls 2 24+
(D Nicholls) *chsd ldrs tl rdn and wknd over 1f out: eased* **9/1**

1m 11.09s (-1.11) **Going Correction** +0.075s/f (Good) 10 Ran SP% **117.2**
Speed ratings (Par 109): **110,107,106,105,102 101,99,96,94,76**
toteswinger: 1&2 £5.00, 1&3 £8.10, 2&3 £11.60. CSF £26.19 CT £239.53 TOTE £4.00: £1.70, £2.00, £3.80; EX 27.90 Trifecta £137.70 Pool: £669.90 - 3.60 winning units.
Owner Gwyn Powell and Peter Ridgers **Bred** Barry Minty **Trained** Lambourn, Berks
■ Stewards' Enquiry : Catherine Gannon one-day ban: careless riding (Jun 7)
Andrea Atzeni one-day ban: failed to keep straight from stalls (Jun 7)

FOCUS

A good-quality sprint handicap which was truly run. The winner is verging on Pattern class and the runner-up is rated to his latest form.

NOTEBOOK

Jimmy Styles ◆ tracked the pace before leading inside the final furlong and bursting clear for an impressive victory. Lightly raced due to injury, he had finished second to Striking Spirit at Ascot on his recent return from a year off and was 3lb better off here with that horse, who failed to give his running. The winner remains relatively unexposed and should be on the shortlist for the Wokingham at the Royal Meeting. (op 10-3 tchd 7-2)

Everymanforhimself(IRE) came here in good heart and he ran another solid race in the first-time visor, passing three horses inside the final furlong if never promising to catch the winner. He looks equally at home at this trip or 5f, but his general consistency will make things hard for him to get his head in front as the Handicapper will not be dropping him. (op 7-1 tchd 6-1)

Orpenindeed(IRE) raced along the stands' rail, separate from the rest, for the first part of the race. He stuck on for third in the reapplied cheekpieces and is pretty consistent, but has won only a Great Leighs claimer since arriving from Italy. (op 14-1 tchd 16-1)

Thebes ran well over track and trip three weeks ago and produced another sound effort here. He is showing a bit more consistency but is another who is receiving little help from the Handicapper. Official explanation: jockey said colt hung left (op 7-1)

Musaalem(USA) started slowly before making late gains from the rear past weakening rivals on this seasonal reappearance. This was a fairly pleasing effort but he remains 9lb higher than when winning at Doncaster nearly a year ago. Official explanation: jockey said gelding was slowly away (op 11-2 tchd 6-1)

Silver Wind, returning from a break since January, took a bump from Thebes when the pressure was on and could produce no extra. Official explanation: jockey said gelding hung left

Abraham Lincoln(IRE) had run well on his last two starts but he was under pressure on the outside when he was hampered a furlong out and was then allowed to come own in his own time. Official explanation: jockey said horse hung left throughout (op 5-1)

Striking Spirit, 4lb worse off with Jimmy Styles after beating him by a comfortable length at Ascot, failed to find anything when ridden and was eased off. Official explanation: jockey said gelding never travelled (op 8-1)

2298 COUNTRYSIDE ALLIANCE MAIDEN STKS 7f

4:40 (4:40) (Class 4) 3-Y-0 £5,180 (£1,541; £770; £384) Stalls High

Form RPR

1 **Adoring (IRE)** 3-8-12 0 LiamJones 8 82+
(W J Haggas) *a.p: rdn to ld over 1f out: r.o* **16/1**

0- **2** 1 1/2 **Pumpkin**[223] 6696 3-8-12 0 RyanMoore 9 78
(Sir Michael Stoute) *led: rdn and hdd over 1f out: styd on same pce ins fnl f* **5/1**[3]

4-33 **3** 1/2 **Euston Square**[23] 1636 3-9-3 **86** JimmyFortune 11 82
(J H M Gosden) *hld up in tch: hrd rdn over 1f out: nt qckn towards fin* **4/6**[1]

4 9 **Millers Crossing** 3-9-0 0 KellyHarrison[(3)] 2 58
(W J H Ratcliffe) *prom: racd keenly: rdn over 2f out: hung rt and wknd over 1f out* **66/1**

230- **5** 3/4 **Summers Target (USA)**[228] 6575 3-9-3 **87** EddieAhern 7 56
(R M H Cowell) *hld up: plld hrd: rdn: hung lft and wknd over 2f out* **7/2**[2]

6 hd **Diktat Queen** 3-8-12 0 ChrisCatlin 1 50
(Rae Guest) *s.s: outpcd* **33/1**

00- **7** 1 **Rafta (IRE)**[219] 6785 3-8-5 0 JosephineBruning[(7)] 6 47
(T T Clement) *chsd ldr: rdn and ev ch over 2f out: sn hung lft and wknd* **80/1**

1m 25.71s (0.31) **Going Correction** +0.075s/f (Good) 7 Ran SP% **110.4**
Speed ratings (Par 101): **101,99,98,88,87 87,86**
toteswinger: 1&2 £4.80, 1&3 £3.20, 2&3 £1.50. CSF £84.71 TOTE £10.90: £3.20, £2.30; EX 52.70.
Owner Highclere Thoroughbred Racing (Gimcrack) **Bred** W Maxwell Ervine **Trained** Newmarket, Suffolk

FOCUS

A modest maiden with no strength in depth, and the first three came a long way clear. Not an easy race to pin down and best rated through the third to near his best.

Summers Target(USA) Official explanation: jockey said gelding ran too free

2299 EUROPEAN BREEDERS' FUND FILLIES' H'CAP 6f

5:15 (5:17) (Class 4) (0-85,85) 3-Y-0 £5,828 (£1,734; £866; £432) Stalls High

Form RPR

0551 **1** **White Shift (IRE)**[11] 1982 3-8-4 **71** oh1 JimmyQuinn 7 78
(P Howling) *chsd ldrs: led over 1f out: rdn and edgd rt ins fnl f: styd on* **13/2**

1 **2** 1 **Romanticize**[21] 1703 3-8-6 **73** TedDurcan 8 77
(Dr J D Scargill) *sn outpcd: rdn over 1f out: r.o wl ins fnl f: nt rch wnr* **5/1**[2]

2100 **3** 1 1/4 **Daddy's Gift (IRE)**[21] 1705 3-9-3 **84** RichardHughes 4 84
(R Hannon) *hld up: rdn over 2f out: edgd rt and r.o u.p ins fnl f: nvr nrr* **6/1**[3]

-022 **4** 3/4 **Metroland**[15] 1869 3-8-8 **75** StephenDonohoe 3 73
(D Nicholls) *s.i.s: rcvrd to ld 5f out: rdn and hdd over 1f out: styd on same pce* **10/1**

41-0 **5** 1/2 **Calahonda**[36] 1353 3-9-4 **85** PhilipRobinson 5 81
(P W D'Arcy) *led 1f: chsd ldrs: rdn over 1f out: no ex ins fnl f* **13/2**

1 **6** 2 3/4 **Ingleby Lady**[47] 1174 3-8-13 **80** PhillipMakin 6 67
(T D Barron) *free to post: hld up in tch: plld hrd: rdn over 1f out: wknd fnl f* **5/2**[1]

10-0 **7** 1/2 **Cashleen (USA)**[38] 1315 3-8-5 **72** TPO'Shea 1 58
(K A Ryan) *s.i.s: outpcd: bhd whn hung rt over 1f out* **20/1**

02-0 **8** 2 3/4 **Dove Mews**[39] 1296 3-9-0 **81** JamieSpencer 2 58
(M L W Bell) *chsd ldrs: rdn over 2f out: wknd over 1f out* **6/1**[3]

1m 12.41s (0.21) **Going Correction** +0.075s/f (Good) 8 Ran SP% **114.3**
Speed ratings (Par 98): **101,99,98,97,96 92,92,88**
toteswinger: 1&2 £7.20, 1&3 £7.40, 2&3 £5.20. CSF £38.79 CT £206.57 TOTE £8.10: £2.60, £2.20, £1.20; EX 47.80.
Owner Paul Terry **Bred** Grange Stud **Trained** Newmarket, Suffolk

FOCUS

A fair handicap featuring a mixture of seemingly exposed fillies and lightly raced maiden winners. The third looks the best guide to the level.

2300 NCRD.CO.UK H'CAP 7f

5:50 (5:53) (Class 5) (0-70,71) 3-Y-0 £3,885 (£1,156; £577; £288) Stalls High

Form RPR

-132 **1** **Cheap Thrills**[12] 1973 3-9-5 **71** ShaneKelly 9 77
(J A Osborne) *chsd ldr tl led over 2f out: rdn out* **12/1**

2503 **2** 1/2 **Perfect Class**[12] 1973 3-8-12 **64** (v[1]) PhilipRobinson 19 69
(C G Cox) *a.p: rdn over 2f out: chsd wnr fnl f: r.o* **4/1**[1]

10-0 **3** 1 3/4 **Tidal Force (USA)**[39] 1284 3-9-3 **69** (b[1]) JoeFanning 14 69
(P F I Cole) *chsd ldrs: rdn and hung rt over 1f out: styd on same pce ins fnl f* **10/1**

-105 **4** 3/4 **Toby Tyler**[23] 1656 3-9-3 **69** JamieMoriarty 11 67+
(P T Midgley) *hld up: rdn over 1f out: swtchd lft and r.o ins fnl f: nrst fin* **20/1**

5-55 **5** 1/2 **Land Hawk (IRE)**[32] 1466 3-9-4 **70** StephenDonohoe 7 67
(J Pearce) *hld up: plld hrd: hdwy over 2f out: rdn over 1f out: no imp towards fin* **8/1**[3]

0-06 **6** 1/2 **Caerus (USA)**[22] 1662 3-9-2 **68** (v[1]) JimCrowley 5 64
(W J Knight) *hld up: hdwy and hung rt over 1f out: r.o ins fnl f: nvr nrr* **25/1**

6506 **7** 1/2 **Quick Single (USA)**[10] 2004 3-8-9 **68** (vt) CarolineKelly[(7)] 18 62
(P S McEntee) *prom: rdn over 2f out: styd on same pce fnl f* **66/1**

2260 **8** 1/2 **Imperial Skylight**[16] 1839 3-8-13 **65** TonyCulhane 15 58
(M R Channon) *chsd ldrs: rdn over 2f out: no ex fnl f* **20/1**

15 **9** hd **Burza**[13] 1937 3-9-1 **67** TPQueally 16 62+
(J Mackie) *hld up: rdn and hung rt over 1f out: nt clr run and r.o ins fnl f: nvr nrr* **25/1**

51-0 **10** 1/2 **Noble Dictator**[36] 1361 3-8-12 **64** (p) RichardKingscote 17 55+
(E F Vaughan) *sn pushed along in rr: rdn over 1f out: running on whn hmpd ins fnl f: n.d* **11/2**[2]

615 **11** 1/2 **Here Comes Danny**[75] 797 3-9-4 **70** JimmyQuinn 13 60+
(M Wigham) *hld up: hdwy 1/2-way: rdn and wknd over 1f out* **9/1**

23-5 **12** nse **Arctic Freedom (USA)**[41] 1250 3-9-4 **70** RyanMoore 4 59
(E A L Dunlop) *hld up: rdn over 2f out: hung rt over 1f out: n.d* **9/1**

030- **13** 1/2 **Temperence Hall (USA)**[261] 5671 3-8-12 **67** MarcHalford[(3)] 10 55
(J R Best) *hld up: hdwy 1/2-way: sn rdn: wknd ins fnl f* **33/1**

0-00 **14** 3/4 **Motor Home**[19] 1774 3-8-7 **62** DavidProbert[(3)] 6 48
(A M Balding) *sn pushed along in rr: rdn over 1f out: n.d* **16/1**

006- **15** 1/2 **Calypso Girl (IRE)**[211] 6987 3-8-13 **65** CatherineGannon 20 50
(P D Evans) *led over 4f: sn rdn: wknd ins fnl f* **12/1**

461- **16** 21 **Zim Ho**[153] 7767 3-9-2 **68** J-PGuillambert 8 —
(J Akehurst) *chsd ldrs: rdn and wknd over 1f out* **14/1**

403- **17** 9 **Yeoman Of England (IRE)**[211] 6988 3-9-0 **66** AlanMunro 1 —
(C F Wall) *hld up: bhd fr 1/2-way* **16/1**

-405 **18** 12 **Asian Tale (IRE)**[20] 1744 3-8-10 **67** RichardEvans[(5)] 3 —
(P D Evans) *s.s: outpcd* **10/1**

1m 25.58s (0.18) **Going Correction** +0.075s/f (Good) 18 Ran SP% **140.1**
Speed ratings (Par 99): **101,100,98,97,97 96,95,95,95,94 93,93,93,92,91 67,57,43**
toteswinger: 1&2 £6.00, 1&3 £27.70, 2&3 £16.70. CSF £62.57 CT £553.83 TOTE £11.30: £2.60, £1.80, £3.10, £6.60; EX 46.30 Place 6 £705.06, Place 5 £271.47..
Owner Mr And Mrs Christopher Wright **Bred** Stratford Place Stud **Trained** Upper Lambourn, Berks
■ Stewards' Enquiry : Philip Robinson one-day ban: used whip with excessive frequency (Jun 7)
Shane Kelly two-day ban: careless riding (Jun 7-8)

FOCUS
A wide-open if moderate handicap. Not many got into it and the first two home both came from this month's Warwick handicap won by Labisa. The form looks ordinary.
Burza ◆ Official explanation: jockey said filly was denied a clear run
Noble Dictator Official explanation: jockey said gelding was denied a clear run
Here Comes Danny Official explanation: jockey said colt was denied a clear run
Zim Ho Official explanation: jockey said colt stopped quickly
Asian Tale(IRE) Official explanation: jockey said filly never travelled
T/Jkpt: Not won. T/Plt: £513.30 to a £1 stake. Pool: £77,706.05. 110.50 winning tickets. T/Qpdt: £69.00 to a £1 stake. Pool: £4,737.80. 50.80 winning tickets. CR

[2284]CURRAGH (R-H)
Sunday, May 24

OFFICIAL GOING: Heavy

2302a BOYLECASINO.COM EUROPEAN BREEDERS FUND MAIDEN — 6f
2:35 (2:35) 2-Y-O — **£12,075** (£2,813; £1,240; £716)

RPR
1 — **Alshahbaa (IRE)** 2-8-12 .... DPMcDonogh 1 — 89+
(Kevin Prendergast, Ire) *chsd ldrs: 5th 1/2-way: hdwy to chal 1 1/2f out: led over 1f out: rdn clr fnl f: impressive* **7/2**[2]
2 *4* **Grace And Virtue (IRE)** 2-8-12 .... RPCleary 3 — 77
(Andrew Oliver, Ire) *chsd ldrs early: towards rr after 2f: hdwy in 6th 1 1/2f out: 4th 1f out: kpt on to 2nd ins fnl f: no ch w wnr* **33/1**
3 *nk* **Macnas (USA)** 2-8-12 .... KJManning 5 — 76
(J S Bolger, Ire) *prom: 2nd 1/2-way: led 2f out: rdn and chal 1 1/2f out: hdd over 1f out: no ex and kpt on same pce* **5/1**[3]
4 *6* **Black Quartz (FR)** 2-9-3 .... JMurtagh 7 — 63
(A P O'Brien, Ire) *dwlt: towards rr: rdn 2 1/2f out: no imp in 7th 1f out: kpt on same pce fnl f* **2/1**[1]
5 *3 1/2* **Bygone Age (IRE)** 2-9-3 .... PJSmullen 6 — 53+
(D K Weld, Ire) *chsd ldrs: 4th 1/2-way: rdn into 3rd 1 1/2f out: no ex fnl f* **5/1**[3]
6 *1 1/4* **Elusive Gent (IRE)** 2-9-3 .... CDHayes 2 — 49
(J T Gorman, Ire) *chsd ldrs: 6th 1/2-way: rdn 2f out: sn no ex and wknd* **16/1**
7 *nk* **Pixel Power (IRE)**[9] 2061 2-9-3 .... MCHussey 9 — 48
(Liam McAteer, Ire) *prom: 3rd 1/2-way: rdn to chal 2f out: no ex in 4th 1 1/2f out: wknd over 1f out* **50/1**
8 *2 1/2* **Harry Hunt**[7] 2106 2-9-0 .... DJMoran(3) 4 — 40
(Cecil Ross, Ire) *led: rdn and hdd 2f out: no ex and sn wknd* **5/1**[3]

1m 19.3s (4.60) **Going Correction** +0.60s/f (Yiel) — **8** Ran SP% **116.3**
Speed ratings: **92,86,86,78,73 71,71,68**
CSF £98.55 TOTE £4.30: £1.60, £7.20, £1.50; DF 224.30.
Owner Hamdan Al Maktoum **Bred** Shadwell Estate Co Ltd **Trained** Friarstown, Co Kildare

FOCUS
This maiden has produced such as George Washington, Oratorio and Eagle Mountain in recent seasons, with Intense Focus the winner last year. This year's winner has a lot to live up to but this was a promising debut.

NOTEBOOK
Alshahbaa(IRE) was a visually impressive winner of a muddling race, but there is little doubt he can go on to better things. They went no pace for the first half, but this Alhaarth filly always travelled like a winner and quickened up well between horses 1f out. She went away and scored in style, showing an aptitude for the surface and leaving open the question of how she will handle better ground. If she does, connctions have a filly to look forward to. (op 9/2)
Grace And Virtue(IRE) got her act together as the race developed. Racing towards the back, she was trapped behind horses over 1f out, but when pulled out and seeing some daylight ran on strongly. The favourite was just too good and too professional, but there should be plenty of improvement to come and it will be a surprise if she isn't at least able to win her maiden.
Macnas(USA) ran well on her debut and there should be more to come from her as well. She was close to the pace most of the way but when asked for her effort 1f out ran green and rolled about on the heavy ground. She's certain to improve and should appreciate better ground. (op 7/2)
Black Quartz(FR) was never a factor and will appreciate this experience probably more than anything else. He lost a few lengths coming out of the stalls and ran green most of the way, keeping on inside the last without being a danger. (op 2/1 tchd 9/4)

2303a TATTERSALLS GOLD CUP (GROUP 1) — 1m 2f 110y
3:05 (3:05) 4-Y-0+ — **£168,203** (£50,728; £24,029; £8,009; £2,669)

RPR
1 — **Casual Conquest (IRE)**[22] 1674 4-9-0 117 ....(t) PJSmullen 3 — 123
(D K Weld, Ire) *mde all: pressed fr 4f out: rdn clr over 1f out: styd on strly fnl f* **11/4**[3]
2 *5 1/2* **Famous Name**[20] 1758 4-9-0 120 .... MJKinane 4 — 113+
(D K Weld, Ire) *hld up: 4th 1/2-way: rdn into 3rd 2f out: styd on to 2nd over 1 1/2f out: no imp on wnr fnl f* **9/4**[1]
3 *1 3/4* **Lush Lashes**[161] 7685 4-8-11 119 .... KJManning 5 — 107
(J S Bolger, Ire) *chsd ldrs early: dropped to rr after 3f: rdn in 4th 2f out: styd on to 3rd over 1f out: kpt on same pce* **4/1**
4 *1 1/4* **Moiqen (IRE)**[20] 1758 4-9-0 108 .... DPMcDonogh 1 — 107
(Kevin Prendergast, Ire) *s.i.s: towards rr: hdwy to 2nd after 3f: cl up 4f out: rdn in 2nd 2 1/2f out: no ex over 1 1/2f out: kpt on one pce* **14/1**
5 *13* **Thewayyouare (USA)**[28] 1551 4-9-0 115 .... JMurtagh 2 — 83
(A P O'Brien, Ire) *chsd ldrs: 3rd 1/2-way: rdn and dropped to rr 2 1/2f out: sn no imp* **5/2**[2]

2m 26.4s (11.40) **Going Correction** +1.20s/f (Soft) — **5** Ran SP% **112.7**
Speed ratings: **106,102,100,99,90**
CSF £9.59 TOTE £3.50: £1.30, £1.80; DF 6.40.
Owner Moyglare Stud Farm **Bred** Moyglare Stud Farm Ltd **Trained** The Curragh, Co Kildare

NOTEBOOK
Casual Conquest(IRE), untried on this ground, looked far more at home on it than on the firm at Newmarket a few weeks ago and ran out a convincing winner from a stable companion almost guaranteed to act on the surface. Smullen dictated the pace and gradually wound it up and the horse showed his class by quickening in the straight and leaving his rivals for dead inside the final furlong. The Arc is the long-term target and ground conditions in the autumn should suit him. (op 3/1)
Famous Name was the best backed but has failed to build on his unlucky second in last year's Prix du Jockey-Club. Conditions looked to favour him more than his stable companion, but he was left trailing inside the last furlong, having had every chance inside the final quarter. His trainer did feel afterwards that bringing him back in trip may see him return to his midsummer best of 2008, and he is undoubtedly better than this. (op 9/4 tchd 2/1)
Lush Lashes, whose one previous try on heavy ground saw her put in her worst effort on the track, showed a definite improvement on that and, on the face of it, not a bad run, the surface and it being her seasonal bow are valid excuses. She looked ill-at-ease and was rolling about on the ground coming down the hill into the straight. She picked up as well as she could inside the final quarter-mile but floundered. (op 9/2)
Moiqen(IRE) had a mountain to climb to be involved in this but didn't help his chance by being too free and quickly went from travelling to struggling early in the straight.
Thewayyouare(USA) was hugely disappointing on ground that should have suited him, dropping away in the straight, having been covered up early. Official explanation: jockey said colt did not handle today's ground

2304a BOYLESPORTS.COM IRISH 1,000 GUINEAS (GROUP 1) (FILLIES) — 1m
3:40 (3:40) 3-Y-O
£217,961 (£74,271; £35,436; £12,135; £8,252; £4,368)

RPR
1 — **Again (IRE)**[231] 6519 3-9-0 110 .... JMurtagh 3 — 114+
(David Wachman, Ire) *in rr of mid-div: hdwy in 6th 3f out: rdn into 3rd under 2f out: styd on to chal ins fnl f and led cl home* **5/2**[1]
2 *nk* **Lahaleeb (IRE)**[21] 1698 3-9-0 .... DPMcDonogh 13 — 113
(M R Channon) *mid-div on inner: 6th 1/2-way: hdwy in 5th 3f out: 2nd 2 1/2f out: led under 2f out: rdn and kpt on wl fr over 1f out: chal ins fnl f and hdd cl home* **11/2**[3]
3 *3 1/2* **Oh Goodness Me**[14] 1918 3-9-0 101 .... DJMoran 14 — 105
(J S Bolger, Ire) *chsd ldrs: 2nd 1/2-way: impr to ld 3 1/2f out: rdn and hdd under 2f out: no ex in 2nd over 1f out: kpt on same pce* **16/1**
4 *4* **Rare Ransom**[10] 2024 3-9-0 99 .... PShanahan 16 — 96
(D K Weld, Ire) *chsd ldrs: 3rd 1/2-way: rdn in 4th over 2f out: sn no ex and kpt on same pce* **25/1**
5 *4* **Chintz (IRE)**[56] 1024 3-9-0 109 .... WMLordan 9 — 87
(David Wachman, Ire) *chsd ldrs: 4th 1/2-way: hdwy to 2nd 3f out: rdn in 3rd and no ex 2f out: kpt on one pce* **12/1**
6 *1/2* **Hallie's Comet (IRE)**[14] 1911 3-9-0 98 .... ShaneFoley 6 — 85
(A Kinsella, Ire) *mid-div: hdwy to 3rd 3f out: rdn in 6th and no ex 2f out: kpt on one pce* **66/1**
7 *2* **Love Bird (IRE)**[20] 1760 3-9-0 .... JAHeffernan 2 — 81
(David Wachman, Ire) *towards rr: sme hdwy to mod 8th 2f out: rdn and kpt on one pce* **10/1**
8 *5* **Always Be True (IRE)**[18] 1795 3-9-0 .... FMBerry 12 — 69
(David Wachman, Ire) *led: hdd after 2f: styd centre after 3f: rdn in 7th 1/2-way: no imp in 9th 2f out: kpt on one pce* **33/1**
9 *1 1/4* **Luminous Eyes (IRE)**[238] 6319 3-9-0 106 .... MJKinane 1 — 66
(D K Weld, Ire) *in rr of mid-div: sme hdwy to mod 7th 2f out: rdn and kpt on one pce* **14/1**
10 *4 1/2* **Monivea (IRE)**[14] 1911 3-9-0 94 ....(p) CDHayes 7 — 56
(Brian Nolan, Ire) *towards rr for most: sme late hdwy: nvr a factor* **66/1**
11 *4* **Dance Pass (IRE)**[11] 1999 3-9-0 97 .... PJSmullen 10 — 47
(D K Weld, Ire) *mid-div best: rdn and no imp 3f out* **10/1**
12 *7* **Beauthea (IRE)**[11] 1995 3-9-0 75 ....(t) DMGrant 5 — 31
(H Rogers, Ire) *towards rr for most: nvr a factor* **150/1**
13 *5 1/2* **Super Sleuth (IRE)**[21] 1698 3-9-0 .... LDettori 11 — 18
(B J Meehan) *chsd ldrs early: 8th 1/2-way: rdn and no ex 3f out: wknd* **3/1**[2]
14 *1/2* **Totally Devoted (USA)**[14] 1911 3-9-0 .... CO'Donoghue 4 — 17
(A P O'Brien, Ire) *mid-div best: rdn and no imp over 3f out: wknd* **25/1**
15 *10* **Cuis Ghaire (IRE)**[21] 1698 3-9-0 110 .... KJManning 8 — —
(J S Bolger, Ire) *chsd ldrs: 5th 1/2-way: rdn and wknd 3f out: eased fr 2f out* **13/2**
16 *2 1/2* **Duaisbhanna (IRE)**[21] 1715 3-9-0 96 .... DEMullins 15 — —
(J S Bolger, Ire) *prom: led after 2f: rdn and hdd 3 1/2f out: sn wknd: eased over 1f out* **66/1**

1m 46.3s (4.40) **Going Correction** +0.80s/f (Soft) — **16** Ran SP% **136.5**
Speed ratings: **110,109,106,102,98 97,95,90,89,84 80,73,68,67,57 55**
CSF £18.20 TOTE £4.10: £1.30, £2.50, £4.80, £9.20; DF 25.80.
Owner Michael Tabor **Bred** Southern Bloodstock **Trained** Goolds Cross, Co Tipperary
■ David Wachman's first Classic winner, and Johnny Murtagh's first victory in this race.
■ Stewards' Enquiry : D P McDonogh severe caution: excessive use of the whip

FOCUS
They probably went off a shade too quick for the conditions and finished well strung out, having been spread across the track from an early stage.

NOTEBOOK
Again(IRE), held up early on, was dashed up to take a prominent position towards the centre of the track and closed right up inside the final 2f, but when she was asked to race she drifted badly right, then to her left and made heavy weather of going through with her effort. In the end, Murtagh had to be at his persuasive best to get her over the line, but her ears were pricked a couple of strides afterwards. The impression was of a filly who was clearly the best in the race but wanted to do as little as possible. It was her first run of the season and perhaps she didn't stride out on the ground to total effect inside the last. Her trainer feels she'll have little trouble staying the 1m4f of the Oaks but it may come a little quickly. (op 11/4)
Lahaleeb(IRE), after finding the surface too lively at Newmarket, returned to her best, looking the more professional of the first two, which is testament to how much better the winner actually is. She raced just off the pace and ran on well when grabbing the far rail inside the final 2f but was done on the line. Already a Pattern winner on this sort of surface, she is capable of winning another, but the ground looks an essential component. She may well get an extra couple of furlongs as well. (op 13/2 tchd 7/1)
Oh Goodness Me raced prominently towards the far side most of the way, and was just run out of it inside the final furlong. She showed again she is of Pattern standard when underfoot conditions suit and should be capable of stepping up a couple of furlongs.
Rare Ransom has improved a great deal over the winter on this season's evidence and this was a step up again on her win at Gowran earlier this month. She raced prominently but was one-paced when the race hotted up. She'll probably continue to take her chance in similar contests and, although she's unlikely to improve enough to win one, she can continue to hold her own.
Chintz(IRE) produced a disappointing response when let down, having been travelling as well as anything 2f out. She finished only just in front of outsider Hallie's Comet.
Love Bird(IRE) ran respectably on her first run out of maiden company, staying on from out of the pack and giving the impression she'll get a bit further. (op 8/1)
Super Sleuth(IRE), who was supplemented, wasn't travelling well from halfway and dropped right out inside the final quarter-mile. (op 6/1)

Cuis Ghaire(IRE), was disappointing, although her chances of acting on this heavy ground were always going to be slim. She dropped right away inside the final quarter-mile and was eased right down in the finish. Official explanation: jockey said filly never travelled throughout the race (op 13/2 tchd 6/1)

2305a BOYLESPORTS BEST PRICE GUARANTEED H'CAP (PREMIER HANDICAP) 1m 4f

4:15 (4:15) 3-Y-0+ **£41,082** (£12,053; £5,742; £1,956)

RPR

1 **Sesenta (IRE)**[22] 7159 5-8-11 83 .... JMurtagh 6 89+
(W P Mullins, Ire) *mid-div: hdwy in 6th 3f out: 3rd 2f out: rdn to narrow ld over 1f out: strly pressed fnl f: all out* **2/1**[1]

2 *hd* **Speed Ticket**[14] 1909 5-9-2 88 .... FMBerry 10 94
(Mrs John Harrington, Ire) *hld up: hdwy to 4th 2f out: rdn in cl 3rd 1f out: kpt on to chal ins fnl f: jst hld* **6/1**[3]

3 *4 1/2* **Kaprun (IRE)**[22] 1163 4-8-3 78 ....(p) DJMoran(3) 9 77
(Brian Nolan, Ire) *chsd ldrs: 3rd 1/2-way: impr to ld 4f out: rdn and chal 2f out: narrowly hdd over 1f out: no ex fnl f* **14/1**

4 *2 1/2* **Essex (IRE)**[22] 4754 9-8-11 83 ....(tp) RPCleary 1 78
(M J P O'Brien, Ire) *chsd ldrs: 6th 1/2-way: hdwy to 4th 5f out: rdn into 2nd 3f out: chal 2f out: no ex in 4th over 1f out: kpt on same pce* **4/1**[2]

5 *3* **Alhabeeb (IRE)**[18] 1796 4-9-11 97 .... DPMcDonogh 11 87
(Kevin Prendergast, Ire) *chsd ldrs: 5th 1/2-way: rdn in 7th 3f out: u.p in 6th 2f out: kpt on one pce* **14/1**

6 *1* **Daasij (IRE)**[13] 1948 4-9-7 93 ....(b[1]) PJSmullen 2 81
(D K Weld, Ire) *chsd ldrs: 4th 1/2-way: rdn in 5th 3f out: no ex over 2f out: kpt on one pce* **6/1**[3]

7 *14* **Glitter Baby (IRE)**[7] 1909 6-9-8 94 .... MCHussey 5 60
(Paul Cashman, Ire) *led: rdn and hdd 4f out: no ex in 3rd 3f out: sn wknd* **33/1**

8 *11* **Sweet Wake (GER)**[713] 4774 8-10-0 100 ....(t) MJKinane 8 48
(Noel Meade, Ire) *a towards rr* **14/1**

9 *7* **Lancetto (FR)**[9] 2031 4-8-10 82 .... CO'Donoghue 4 19
(K R Burke) *chsd ldr in 2nd: rdn 3f out: sn no ex and wknd* **25/1**

R **Deputy Consort (USA)**[35] 1391 6-8-12 89 .... DEMullins(5) 7 —
(Matthieu Palussiere, Ire) *ref to r* **13/2**

2m 49.2s (11.70) **Going Correction** +1.20s/f (Soft) **10** Ran SP% **122.0**
Speed ratings: **109,108,105,104,102 101,92,84,80,—**
CSF £15.17 CT £139.54 TOTE £2.90: £1.60, £1.90, £2.10; DF 15.60.
Owner Michael F Carroll **Bred** Michael Carroll **Trained** Muine Beag, Co Carlow

NOTEBOOK
Lancetto(FR), who has form on soft ground on the continent, probably did too much too early and paid for it in the closing stages. Official explanation: jockey said gelding hung badly left in the race

2306a AIRLIE STUD GALLINULE STKS (GROUP 3) 1m 2f

4:45 (4:45) 3-Y-0 **£45,822** (£13,444; £6,405; £2,182)

RPR

1 **Grand Ducal (IRE)**[274] 5296 3-9-1 102 .... JMurtagh 3 102
(A P O'Brien, Ire) *mid-div: 7th 1/2-way: 6th 3f out: rdn in 5th over 1f out: styd on to chal ins fnl f and led cl home* **7/1**[3]

2 *hd* **Alaivan (IRE)**[21] 1714 3-9-1 .... MJKinane 5 102
(John M Oxx, Ire) *chsd ldrs: 4th 1/2-way: hdwy to chal 1 1/2f out: led 1f out: strly pressed ins fnl f and hdd cl home* **13/8**[1]

3 *1 1/4* **The Bull Hayes (IRE)**[28] 1547 3-9-1 100 .... FMBerry 6 100
(Mrs John Harrington, Ire) *mid-div: 8th 1/2-way: rdn into 6th 1f out: kpt on wl fnl f to go 3rd* **9/2**[2]

4 *1 3/4* **Enchanted Evening (IRE)**[7] 2110 3-8-12 90 .... PJSmullen 8 93
(D K Weld, Ire) *mid-div: 6th 1/2-way: 5th 3f out: rdn to chal 1 1/2f out: disp over 1f out: 2nd and no ex ins fnl f: kpt on same pce* **9/1**

5 *4* **Nafaath (IRE)**[21] 1714 3-9-1 91 .... DPMcDonogh 7 88
(Kevin Prendergast, Ire) *prom early: sn chsd ldrs: 3rd 1/2-way: impr to narrow ld 2f out: rdn and hdd 1 1/2f out: no ex in 4th 1f out: kpt on one pce* **25/1**

6 *1 1/4* **Wanna (IRE)**[12] 1978 3-8-12 82 ....(b[1]) WMLordan 9 83
(T Stack, Ire) *towards rr: rdn into mod 8th 1f out: kpt on same pce fnl f* **25/1**

7 *1 3/4* **Sirgarfieldsobers (IRE)**[21] 1714 3-9-1 92 .... CO'Donoghue 11 82
(A P O'Brien, Ire) *towards rr for most: rdn and no imp 2f out: kpt on one pce fr over 1f out* **16/1**

8 *shd* **Handsome Batchelor (IRE)**[21] 1713 3-9-1 .... CDHayes 2 82
(Andrew Oliver, Ire) *chsd ldrs: 2nd 1/2-way: rdn to chal 2f out: briefly led 1 1/2f out: hdd over 1f out and wknd* **25/1**

9 *1 1/2* **Aaroness (USA)**[14] 1911 3-8-12 102 .... KJManning 10 76
(J S Bolger, Ire) *nvr a factor* **10/1**

10 *7* **Chirkova (USA)**[21] 1715 3-8-12 95 .... SMLevey 4 62
(A P O'Brien, Ire) *sn led: rdn and hdd 2f out: no ex and wknd* **33/1**

11 *18* **Chief Lone Eagle (USA)**[20] 1755 3-9-1 ....(b[1]) JAHeffernan 1 29
(A P O'Brien, Ire) *chsd ldrs: 5th 1/2-way: rdn 4f out: sn no ex and wknd* **9/2**[2]

2m 19.7s (10.20) **Going Correction** +1.20s/f (Soft) **11** Ran SP% **126.4**
Speed ratings: **107,106,105,104,101 100,98,98,97,91 77**
CSF £19.49 TOTE £8.00: £3.10, £1.50, £1.90; DF 19.20.
Owner Mrs John Magnier **Bred** A Stroud & J Hanly **Trained** Ballydoyle, Co Tipperary
■ Stewards' Enquiry : J Murtagh one-day ban: excessive use of the whip

NOTEBOOK
Grand Ducal(IRE), having his first run of the season, was being ridden along to try to close on the leaders turning for home. He responded for pressure and ran on well inside the final furlong to get on top near the finish. A winner over 7f on fast ground last season and subsequently in the frame over that trip at Group 2 and Group 3 level, he was taking a big step up in trip. He saw the distance out well and gave the impression that on better ground he just may get further. (op 6/1)
Alaivan(IRE), having only his third run, was dropping in trip following his five-length win over 1m4f at Gowran Park three weeks previously. He tracked the leaders and, after coming under pressure 2f out, got to the front entering the final furlong and stayed on, only to be reeled in close home. (op 2/1 tchd 6/4)
The Bull Hayes(IRE), who had some smart form to his credit before landing a maiden over this trip at Navan last month, goes on the ground and usually comes from off the pace, which is what he did here. He made good headway from 2f out and stayed on well, giving the impression 1m4f will suit him well. (op 5/1)
Enchanted Evening(IRE), a seven-length winner of a 1m maiden at Navan a week previously, performed well considering she had plenty more to do here. She tracked the leaders and closed to have every chance over 1f out before finding no extra in the later stages. (op 8/1)
Nafaath(IRE), twice a winner over 7f on testing ground last year, had been well beaten on his two previous starts this season. Always prominent, he was vying for the lead only in the straight but was soon done with.

2307 - 2308a (Foreign Racing) - See Raceform Interactive

2216 BADEN-BADEN (L-H)
Sunday, May 24

OFFICIAL GOING: Good

2309a GROSSER PREIS DER BADISCHEN UNTERNEHMEN (GROUP 2) 1m 3f

3:15 (3:16) 4-Y-0+ **£38,835** (£14,563; £5,825; £3,883)

RPR

1 *shd* **Ambassador (GER)**[28] 1549 5-9-0 .... THellier 1 107
(T Mundry, Germany) *racd in 4th: hdwy to dispute 2nd whn carried rt over 1f out: carried rt again ins fnl f: r.o: fin 2nd: awrdd r* **115/10**

2 **Tres Rapide (IRE)**[26] 1597 4-8-11 .... GMosse 3 104
(H-A Pantall, France) *racd in 6th: hdwy on ins to ld & hung rt appr fnl f: hld on gamely while hanging rt fnl f: fin 1st: disqualified and plcd 3rd* **14/5**[2]

3 *1/2* **Adelar (GER)**[27] 4-9-0 .... DBoeuf 5 107
(W Baltromei, Germany) *hld up in 7th: hdwy towards outside to dispute 2nd whn hmpd over 1f out: kpt on fnl f: fin 3rd: plcd 2nd* **74/10**

4 *3/4* **Sassoaloro (GER)**[168] 7598 5-9-0 .... HGrewe 4 106
(H Blume, Germany) *racd in 3rd: kpt on steadily down outside fnl 2f* **29/1**

5 *1* **Kamsin (GER)**[28] 1549 4-9-7 .... AStarke 2 111
(P Schiergen, Germany) *racd in 2nd: pushed along 2 1/2f out: rdn to press ldr 2f out: cl 5th but looked btn whn hmpd over 1f out: kpt on fnl f* **4/5**[1]

6 *nse* **Zaungast (IRE)**[28] 1575 5-9-0 .... ASuborics 6 104
(W Hickst, Germany) *racd in 5th: sltly outpcd 2f out: kpt on fnl f* **48/10**[3]

7 *1* **Tullamore (USA)**[18] 4-9-0 .... FilipMinarik 7 102
(Z Koplik, Czech Republic) *racd in last: a in rr* **20/1**

8 *1 1/4* **Lord Hill (GER)**[28] 5-9-0 .... DPorcu 8 100
(C Zeitz) *set stdy pce tl hdd and hmpd over 1f out: one pce* **21/1**

2m 20.52s (1.25) **8** Ran SP% **131.7**
(including ten euro stakes): WIN 125; PL 24, 23, 16; SF 770.
Owner John M O'Connor **Bred** Gestut Fahrhof **Trained** Germany

1575 SAN SIRO (R-H)
Sunday, May 24

OFFICIAL GOING: Good to firm

2310a OAKS D'ITALIA (GROUP 2) (FILLIES) 1m 3f

5:00 (5:24) 3-Y-0 **£194,175** (£85,437; £46,602; £23,301)

RPR

1 **Night Of Magic (IRE)**[23] 3-8-11 .... MDemuro 10 107
(H Steinmetz, Germany) *hld up towards rr to st: gd hdwy on outside fr 3f out: drvn ins fnl f: pushed out and r.o to ld on line* **141/10**

2 *nse* **Wadaat**[15] 1871 3-8-11 .... MartinDwyer 12 107
(C E Brittain) *a.p: 5th st: hdwy 3f out: drvn over 2f out: led wl over 1f out: r.o u.p: ct on line* **232/10**

3 *2 1/2* **Quiza Quiza Quiza**[49] 3-8-11 .... OPeslier 5 102
(L Riccardi, Italy) *mid-div: hdwy over 2f out: rchd 3rd wl over 1f out: unable qck last 100yds* **84/10**

4 *hd* **Galana (GER)**[21] 3-8-11 .... JVictoire 16 102
(P Schiergen, Germany) *hld up towards rr: hdwy over 3f out: hrd rdn over 2f out: r.o steadily fr over 1f out: nrest at fin: fin lame: dead* **33/20**[1]

5 *1 1/4* **Galmalea (IRE)** 3-8-11 .... NPinna 8 100
(A & G Botti, Italy) *mid-div: hdwy 3f out: n.m.r over 2f out: swtchd out 1 1/2f out: r.o u.p: nrest at fin* **22/1**

6 *3 1/2* **Diva Cattiva**[14] 3-8-11 .... PConvertino 2 94
(B Grizzetti, Italy) *a.p: 3rd st: led wl over 2f out to wl over 1f out: grad wknd* **35/1**

7 *1/2* **Sakami (ITY)** 3-8-11 ....(b) PSirigu 4 93
(A Prasciolu, Italy) *last st: rdn and hdwy over 3f out on ins: nt clr run wl over 1f out: swtchd lft: r.o fnl f: nrest at fin* **147/1**

8 *3 1/2* **Louise Aron (IRE)**[23] 1659 3-8-11 .... TThulliez 11 87
(Sante Zanardino, Italy) *hdwy 3f out: disp 5th wl over 1f ot: sn btn: eased in clsng stages* **59/10**[3]

9 *3/4* **Fagutela**[14] 3-8-11 .... IRossi 1 86
(A & G Botti, Italy) *4th st: hrd rdn over 2f out: wkng whn hmpd 2f out* **59/1**

10 *1 1/2* **Taurakina**[23] 1659 3-8-11 .... MMonteriso 15 83
(E Borromeo, Italy) *towards rr to st: hdwy on ins over 3f out: rdn and btn over 1f out* **58/1**

11 *1/2* **Permalosa**[21] 3-8-11 .... GMarcelli 13 83
(L Riccardi, Italy) *nvr in contention* **20/1**

12 *1/2* **Queen Sensazione (IRE)**[14] 3-8-11 .... DVargiu 17 82
(B Grizzetti, Italy) *7th st: 4th 2f out: sn wknd* **89/10**

13 *3 1/2* **Spirit Of Dubai (IRE)**[15] 1871 3-8-11 .... RichardMullen 9 76?
(D M Simcock) *prom: 6th st: btn whn hmpd 2f out* **74/10**

14 *1 1/2* **Laguna Salada (IRE)**[28] 3-8-11 .... SLandi 18 73
(R Feligioni, Italy) *trckd ldr: 2nd st: led wl over 3f out to wl over 2f out: sn wknd* **24/1**

15 *2 1/2* **Satisfaction Life (IRE)**[21] 3-8-11 .... PAragoni 6 69
(Giuseppe Chianese, Italy) *a bhd* **86/1**

16 *1/2* **Red Parisi (IRE)** 3-8-11 .... MTellini 3 68
(A & G Botti, Italy) *a bhd* **22/1**

17 *1/2* **My Sweet Baby (USA)**[23] 1659 3-8-11 .... CFiocchi 7 67
(R Menichetti, Italy) *8th on outside st: 6th 3f out: btn 2f out: eased* **51/10**[2]

18 *8* **Altarma (IRE)** 3-8-11 .... URispoli 14 54
(A & G Botti, Italy) *led to wl over 3f out: wknd qckly* **230/1**

2m 14.7s (-3.90) **18** Ran SP% **137.9**
(including one euro stakes): WIN 15.12; PL 4.63, 4.83, 3.37; SF 250.66.
Owner Stall Nizza **Bred** A Pereira **Trained** Germany

NOTEBOOK
Wadaat clearly did not run her race at Lingfield, but showed her true ability here, only getting caught on the line. The Epsom Oaks is now a definite possibility, although the extra furlong is not sure to suit on pedigree.
Spirit Of Dubai(IRE) finished fourth in the Lingfield Oaks Trial, but was unable to build on that form here. Wadaat comprehensively turned that form around with her.

CARLISLE (R-H)

Monday, May 25

OFFICIAL GOING: Good to firm (7.3)

Wind: Slight, half against Weather: Cloudy, fine

2311 EUROPEAN BREEDERS' FUND MAIDEN STKS 5f

2:20 (2:25) (Class 5) 2-Y-O **£3,885** (£1,156; £577; £288) **Stalls** High

Form				RPR
	1		**Ceedwell** 2-8-12 0 .... TomEaves 9 (B Smart) *sn pushed along towards rr: gd hdwy 2f out: led ins fnl f: r.o strly* **6/4**[1]	74+
203	**2**	2 ½	**Mr Smithson (IRE)**[20] 1764 2-8-12 0 .... LanceBetts(5) 3 (B Ellison) *sltl ld to ins fnl f: kpt on: nt pce of wnr* **8/1**	68
0	**3**	*nk*	**Olympic Ceremony**[17] 1827 2-9-3 0 .... TonyHamilton 10 (R A Fahey) *prom: drvn over 2f out: r.o fnl f* **12/1**	67
	4	¾	**Jack Luey** 2-9-3 0 .... DuranFentiman 8 (L A Mullaney) *bhd: pushed along 1/2-way: kpt on fnl f: nrst fin* **66/1**	64
46	**5**	1 ¼	**Mal And Dave (IRE)**[16] 1866 2-9-3 0 .... AdrianTNicholls 5 (D Nicholls) *disp ld: racd w one other far side ent st: one pce over 1f out* **15/2**[3]	60
46	**6**	2 ¾	**Drumpellier (IRE)**[35] 1396 2-8-12 0 .... JamieMoriarty 2 (P T Midgley) *prom: effrt over 2f out: no ex over 1f out* **25/1**	45
	7	½	**Haltela (IRE)** 2-9-0 0 .... NeilBrown(3) 7 (K A Ryan) *colty in paddock: s.i.s: sn outpcd and bhd: sme late hdwy: nvr on terms* **20/1**	48
	8	2 ¼	**Steeley Flyer** 2-8-5 0 .... AndrewHeffernan(7) 1 (P D Evans) *dwlt and wnt lft s: sn cl up: rdn and wknd over 2f out* **66/1**	35
6	**9**	*shd*	**Charity Fair**[17] 1827 2-8-7 0 .... SladeO'Hara(5) 6 (A Berry) *midfield: drvn 1/2-way: btn over 1f out* **100/1**	35
	10	6	**Cian Rooney (IRE)** 2-9-3 0 .... WJSupple 11 (Mrs A Duffield) *towards rr: racd w one other far side ent st: wknd fr 2f out* **12/1**	18
	11	4 ½	**Mandrake (IRE)** 2-9-3 0 .... JoeFanning 4 (M Johnston) *s.i.s: sn drvn in rr: no ch fr 1/2-way* **3/1**[2]	2

61.71 secs (0.91) **Going Correction** 0.0s/f (Good) **11** Ran **SP% 115.8**

Speed ratings (Par 93): **92,88,87,86,84 79,79,75,75,65 58**

toteswinger: 1&2 not won, 1&3 £2.70, 2&3 not won. CSF £13.56 TOTE £1.80: £1.30, £2.40, £2.70; EX 26.20.

Owner Prime Equestrian **Bred** Minster Stud And Bickerton Racing **Trained** Hambleton, N Yorks

FOCUS

An ordinary sprint maiden but it contained one or two interesting newcomers.

NOTEBOOK

Ceedwell, the most expensive of these at public auction having cost £65,000, was heavily backed beforehand. Bryan Smart´s daughter of Exceed And Excel is bred to make a speedy 2yo and it was clear from the amount of market support she was attracting that she had been showing plenty at home. She looked pretty tuned up in the paddock and so it proved as she powered up the middle of the track to lead inside the final furlong and win going away. Her trainer thinks an awful lot of her, describing her as ´the nicest filly he´s had in a long time´ and she is now Queen Mary-bound, for which Cashmans have given her an initial quote of 20-1. (op 3-1)

Mr Smithson(IRE), having his fourth start, showed good speed before keeping on well down towards the stands side of the track and probably improving slightly on his previous runs. He has the ability to win one of these and a sharper track may well suit. (op 13-2 tchd 9-2)

Olympic Ceremony showed the benefit of his initial outing to track the pace early and see his race out well. He looks to be going the right way and a raft of sales race entries suggest connections feel there is more to come. (op 11-1)

Jack Luey is speedily bred and he shaped with real encouragement, staying on well on the heels of the placed horses down the middle. He could be a good purchase having cost just £800. (tchd 80-1)

Mal And Dave(IRE) showed bright speed and his jockey decided to keep to the far rail in the straight but he couldn´t sustain his effort and is another that will be seen to better effect on a sharper track. (op 8-1 tchd 6-1)

2312 RACING UK £12.99 PER MONTH H'CAP 5f 193y

2:55 (2:56) (Class 5) (0-70,70) 4-Y-0+ **£2,590** (£770; £385; £192) **Stalls** High

Form				RPR
2-01	**1**		**Misplaced Fortune**[17] 1846 4-8-10 **62** ....(v) JoeFanning 14 (N Tinkler) *prom: rdn to ld appr fnl f: kpt on strly* **14/1**	78
34-3	**2**	3 ¾	**Tangerine Trees**[13] 1951 4-8-11 **63** .... TomEaves 16 (B Smart) *cl up: effrt and ev ch over 1f out: kpt on fnl f: nt rch wnr* **17/2**[3]	67
-023	**3**	¾	**Maison Dieu**[24] 1650 6-8-8 **60** .... WJSupple 13 (E J Alston) *prom: drvn over 2f out: kpt on ins fnl f* **11/1**	62
4-55	**4**	1 ¾	**Mey Blossom**[20] 1766 4-8-13 **70** .... AmyRyan(5) 10 (R M Whitaker) *in tch: rdn over 2f out: kpt on u.p fnl f* **13/2**[2]	66
00-2	**5**	*shd*	**Sea Rover (IRE)**[16] 1885 5-9-0 **66** .... TonyHamilton 17 (M Brittain) *led to over 2f out: kpt on same pce* **9/2**[1]	62
10-0	**6**	½	**Apollo Shark (IRE)**[21] 1737 4-8-11 **68** .... PatrickDonaghy(5) 7 (J Howard Johnson) *in tch: drvn over 2f out: one pce over 1f out* **14/1**	62
0-00	**7**	½	**Bid For Gold**[7] 2133 5-8-12 **64** .... AndrewElliott 9 (Jedd O'Keeffe) *bhd tl hdwy over 1f out: nvr rchd ldrs* **33/1**	56+
300-	**8**	¾	**Coleorton Dancer**[164] 7653 7-8-5 **60** .... AndrewMullen(3) 8 (K A Ryan) *midfield: rdn and edgd rt over 2f out: sn outpcd* **16/1**	50
0-26	**9**	1	**Medici Time**[16] 1885 4-8-11 **63** ....(v) DuranFentiman 6 (T D Easterby) *prom: drvn over 2f out: wknd ent fnl f* **20/1**	50
2206	**10**	½	**Strathmore (IRE)**[10] 2032 5-8-3 **62** .... TimothyAyres(7) 3 (R A Fahey) *hld up: sme hdwy on outside over 1f out: nvr rchd ldrs* **16/1**	47
4250	**11**	¾	**Secret Dubai (IRE)**[16] 1885 4-8-6 **65** .... KristinStubbs(7) 5 (Mrs L Stubbs) *s.i.s: rdn after 2f: nvr on terms* **20/1**	48
-510	**12**	1	**Mandalay King (IRE)**[24] 1650 4-8-13 **70** .... LanceBetts(5) 11 (Mrs Marjorie Fife) *s.i.s: hdwy into midfield 1/2-way: sn drvn: no imp fnl 2f* **11/1**	50+
0000	**13**	1 ½	**Dorn Dancer (IRE)**[9] 2071 7-8-13 **68** .... NeilBrown(3) 15 (D W Barker) *hld up: pushed along 1/2-way: sn btn* **14/1**	43
31-0	**14**	*shd*	**Embra (IRE)**[30] 1518 4-8-12 **64** .... GrahamGibbons 2 (T J Etherington) *towards rr: drvn after 2f: nvr on terms* **16/1**	39
260-	**15**	1 ½	**Chosen Forever**[170] 7586 4-8-12 **64** .... JamieMoriarty 12 (G R Oldroyd) *bhd: pushed along 1/2-way: n.d* **16/1**	34
6000	**16**	1 ¾	**Redwater River**[3] 2235 5-8-5 **60** ....(b) KellyHarrison(3) 1 (Mrs R A Carr) *racd wd: cl up: c alone towards stands' side ent st: wandered and wknd fr 2f out* **18/1**	24
-340	**R**		**Johnston's Glory (IRE)**[9] 2088 5-8-11 **63** ....(p) AdrianTNicholls 4 (E J Alston) *ref to r* **22/1**	—

1m 12.82s (-0.88) **Going Correction** 0.0s/f (Good) **17** Ran **SP% 124.3**

Speed ratings (Par 103): **105,100,99,96,96 95,95,94,92,92 91,89,87,87,85 83,—**

toteswinger: 1&2 £10.50, 1&3 not won, 2&3 £5.00. CSF £123.14 CT £888.40 TOTE £12.90: £3.30, £2.10, £1.90, £1.90; EX 93.40.

Owner W F Burton **Bred** Adrian Smith **Trained** Langton, N Yorks

■ Stewards' Enquiry : Amy Ryan caution: careless riding

FOCUS

Quite a competitive sprint handicap on paper but a high draw proved crucial, with the first five home all coming from a double figure stall. The form looks reasonanly sound.

2313 LLOYD MOTORS CARLISLE BELL TRIAL H'CAP 7f 200y

3:30 (3:30) (Class 4) (0-80,77) 4-Y-0+ **£5,180** (£1,541; £770; £384) **Stalls** High

Form				RPR
00-6	**1**		**Sunnyside Tom (IRE)**[21] 1737 5-8-10 **69** .... TonyHamilton 6 (R A Fahey) *in tch: hdwy to ld over 1f out: edgd lft and kpt on wl fnl f* **5/1**[2]	80
-024	**2**	1 ¼	**Champain Sands (IRE)**[16] 1887 10-8-1 **63** oh4 ...... AndrewMullen(3) 10 (E J Alston) *hld up: hdwy and ev ch over 1f out: kpt on ins fnl f* **10/1**	71
0-44	**3**	½	**Prince Evelith (GER)**[17] 1830 6-9-0 **73** .... GrahamGibbons 7 (J J Quinn) *hld up: effrt over 2f out: kpt on u.p fnl f* **6/1**[3]	80
31-1	**4**	*hd*	**Strawberry Moon (IRE)**[14] 1923 4-9-0 **73** .... TomEaves 12 (B Smart) *prom: effrt and rdn over 2f out: kpt on same pce fnl f* **7/2**[1]	79
20-0	**5**	¾	**Ezdeyaad (USA)**[26] 1603 5-9-4 **77** .... WJSupple 4 (G A Swinbank) *t.k.h: prom: effrt over 2f out: one pce fnl f* **9/1**	81
2013	**6**	¾	**Campli (IRE)**[20] 1766 7-8-7 **71** .... LanceBetts(5) 8 (B Ellison) *bhd: pushed along 1/2-way: hdwy over 1f out: nrst fin* **10/1**	73
2331	**7**	½	**Bere Davis (FR)**[16] 1887 4-8-9 **75** .... AndrewHeffernan(7) 5 (P D Evans) *pressed ldr: led 1/2-way tl hung lft and hdd 2f out: kpt on same pce* **8/1**	76
4134	**8**	3 ¾	**Jebel Tara**[13] 1952 4-8-10 **69** ....(bt) AndrewElliott 11 (A D Brown) *led to 1/2-way: rallied: led briefly 2f out: sn no ex* **9/1**	61
1234	**9**	2 ¼	**This Ones For Eddy**[2] 2269 4-8-5 **71** .... ThomasWhite(7) 9 (S Parr) *bhd: detached after 2f: no ch fr 1/2-way* **11/1**	57
065-	**10**	2 ¾	**Zabeel Tower**[202] 7175 6-8-10 **72** ....(p) NeilBrown(3) 2 (R Allan) *prom tl rdn and wknd fr 2f out* **12/1**	51
1-66	**11**	8	**Theonebox (USA)**[87] 713 4-9-4 **77** .... JamieMoriarty 3 (N J Vaughan) *hld up: rdn 3f out: sn btn* **18/1**	36

1m 40.26s (0.26) **Going Correction** 0.0s/f (Good) **11** Ran **SP% 123.8**

Speed ratings (Par 105): **98,96,96,96,95 94,94,90,88,85 77**

toteswinger: 1&2 £2.20, 1&3 £11.30, 2&3 £13.10. CSF £57.47 CT £316.16 TOTE £4.50: £2.90, £4.20, £3.70; EX 55.10.

Owner The Sunnyside Racing Partnership **Bred** S W D Mcllveen **Trained** Musley Bank, N Yorks

■ Stewards' Enquiry : Andrew Mullen caution: excessive use of the whip

FOCUS

A competitive handicap run at a strong pace thanks to Jebel Tara and Bere Davis. Sound form despite the runner-up being 4lb wrong.

This Ones For Eddy Official explanation: jockey said he lost his irons

2314 SUMMER FESTIVAL WITH ESCALA 4TH JULY H'CAP 1m 1f 61y

4:05 (4:07) (Class 6) (0-65,65) 4-Y-0+ **£1,942** (£578; £288; £144) **Stalls** High

Form				RPR
-332	**1**		**Society Venue**[3] 2237 4-9-3 **64** .... AndrewElliott 8 (Jedd O'Keeffe) *mde all: hung lft over 2f out: styd on strly fnl f* **15/8**[1]	75
00-1	**2**	2 ½	**Joinedupwriting**[17] 1848 4-8-12 **59** .... TonyHamilton 3 (R M Whitaker) *trckd ldrs: effrt over 2f out: chsd wnr 1f out: r.o* **8/1**	65
00-	**3**	½	**Portrush Storm**[227] 6629 4-9-4 **65** .... DNolan 11 (D Carroll) *trckd ldrs: effrt and edgd rt over 1f out: one pce fnl f* **25/1**	70
0223	**4**	4	**Johnston's Baby (IRE)**[6] 2155 7-9-1 **62** .... WJSupple 13 (E J Alston) *hld up: hdwy over 2f out: rdn wl over 1f out: no further imp ins fnl f* **5/1**[2]	59+
0026	**5**	4 ½	**Whaston (IRE)**[17] 1848 4-8-7 **54** ....(v) JoeFanning 2 (J D Bethell) *chsd ldrs tl rdn and no ex over 1f out* **12/1**	41
20-4	**6**	2 ¾	**Papa's Princess**[22] 1690 5-8-7 **57** .... KellyHarrison(3) 5 (J S Goldie) *hld up on outside: rdn over 2f out: sn btn* **6/1**[3]	38
0-05	**7**	*shd*	**Malinsa Blue (IRE)**[32] 1475 7-8-8 **55** .... TomEaves 1 (B Ellison) *hld up in tch: outpcd 3f out: sn n.d* **8/1**	36
100-	**8**	1 ½	**Actabou**[32] 6219 4-8-10 **62** ....(t) SladeO'Hara(5) 6 (F P Murtagh) *hld up in midfield on ins: drvn over 3f out: wknd fnl 2f* **50/1**	40
40-4	**9**	½	**Oscar Wild**[20] 1769 7-8-5 **52** .... DarrenMoffatt 4 (James Moffatt) *hld up: rdn and hung lft 3f out: sn outpcd* **16/1**	29
130-	**10**	29	**Boy Dancer (IRE)**[222] 6216 6-9-0 **61** .... GrahamGibbons 9 (J J Quinn) *t.k.h early: cl up tl wknd fr over 3f out: t.o* **8/1**	—

1m 57.17s (-0.43) **Going Correction** 0.0s/f (Good) **10** Ran **SP% 118.4**

Speed ratings (Par 101): **101,98,98,94,90 88,88,86,86,60**

toteswinger: 1&2 £3.80, 1&3 not won, 2&3 not won. CSF £18.01 CT £290.79 TOTE £2.80: £1.10, £2.30, £7.80; EX 11.70.

Owner Ken And Delia Shaw-KGS Consulting LLP **Bred** Mrs S Clifford **Trained** Middleham Moor, N Yorks

FOCUS

Very modest handicap form in which not many got into it and the field were pretty well stretched out by half-way. It is doubtful the winner had to improve much on recent form.

Boy Dancer(IRE) Official explanation: jockey said gelding boiled over in preliminaries

2315 CLEANEVENT CUMBERLAND PLATE TRIAL H'CAP 1m 3f 107y

4:40 (4:40) (Class 4) (0-80,78) 4-Y-0+ **£5,180** (£1,541; £770; £384) **Stalls** Low

Form				RPR
2401	**1**		**Chookie Hamilton**[22] 1692 5-8-0 **65** oh2 ow1 .... PatrickDonaghy(5) 7 (I Semple) *chsd ldr: led over 2f out: edgd lft: drvn out fnl f* **4/1**[2]	71
5510	**2**	2 ¼	**Dechiper (IRE)**[10] 2044 7-8-5 **65** oh1 ow1 .... GrahamGibbons 4 (R Johnson) *prom: effrt and edgd rt over 1f out: kpt on fnl f: nt pce of wnr* **9/2**[3]	67
0-56	**3**	*nk*	**Bergonzi (IRE)**[21] 1721 5-9-1 **75** .... JamieMoriarty 1 (J Howard Johnson) *in tch: hdwy over 2f out: rdn over 1f out: kpt on fnl f* **20/1**	77
61	**4**	1	**Autumn Harvest**[9] 2090 5-9-4 **78** ....(t) AndrewElliott 2 (A J McCabe) *t.k.h: hld up: hdwy on outside 2f out: kpt on fnl f: no imp* **8/1**	78
0-00	**5**	½	**Grey Command (USA)**[10] 2043 4-8-5 **65** .... JoeFanning 10 (M Brittain) *led to over 2f out: no ex over 1f out* **40/1**	65
16-1	**6**	2	**Valdan (IRE)**[16] 1886 5-8-9 **76** .... AndrewHeffernan(7) 9 (P D Evans) *hld up: smooth hdwy and prom 2f out: sn rdn and one pce* **11/4**[1]	72
220-	**7**	2	**Annibale Caro**[38] 4419 7-8-8 **73** .... GaryBartley(5) 5 (J S Goldie) *hld up: rdn over 2f out: nvr able to chal* **11/2**	66

0-50 8 5 **Smugglers Bay (IRE)**[10] 2044 5-8-5 65........................ DuranFentiman 8 50
(T D Easterby) *hld up: drvn and outpcd over 3f out: n.d after* **12/1**

1430 9 1 ½ **Simonside**[16] 1863 6-8-7 67........................ TomEaves 3 49
(B Ellison) *hld up: outpcd over 3f out: sn btn* **10/1**

2m 26.71s (3.61) **Going Correction** 0.0s/f (Good) **9** Ran SP% **115.3**
Speed ratings (Par 105): **86,84,84,83,83 81,80,76,75**
toteswinger: 1&2 £2.40, 1&3 not won, 2&3 £9.80. CSF £22.36 CT £318.95 TOTE £6.80: £1.70, £2.80, £3.30; EX 29.80.
Owner Hamilton Park Members Syndicate **Bred** D And J Raeburn **Trained** Carluke, S Lanarks

FOCUS
Just a modest handicap. Muddling form with the favourite disappointing, and the first two both out of the weights.

2316 EDINBURGH WOOLLEN MILL H'CAP 5f
5:15 (5:16) (Class 6) (0-60,62) 3-Y-O+ **£2,047** (£604; £302) **Stalls** High

Form RPR

-506 1 **Ryedane (IRE)**[16] 1877 7-9-4 54........................(b) DuranFentiman 12 62
(T D Easterby) *prom: drvn over 2f out: rallied and led ins fnl f: hld on wl* **14/1**

040- 2 ½ **Bahamian Ballad**[164] 7648 4-8-12 48........................ WJSupple 4 54
(J D Bethell) *prom: drvn to chal ins fnl f: kpt on: hld nr fin* **40/1**

-060 3 ¾ **Rio Sands**[20] 1768 4-9-5 60........................ AmyRyan(5) 1 64
(R M Whitaker) *hld up: hdwy over 1f out: r.o fnl f: nrst fin* **12/1**

4032 4 ¾ **Ask Jenny (IRE)**[7] 2124 7-9-3 56........................ KellyHarrison(3) 8 57+
(Patrick Morris) *hld up: nt clr run over 1f out to ins fnl f: r.o* **13/2**[2]

6201 5 nk **Loose Caboose (IRE)**[7] 2130 4-9-9 62 6ex........................(b) AndrewMullen(3) 5 62
(A J McCabe) *bhd and sn pushed along: hdwy over 1f out: n.m.r briefly ins fnl f: r.o* **8/1**

0004 6 nse **Mandelieu (IRE)**[14] 1921 4-9-2 52........................ DNolan 9 52
(Ollie Pears) *hld up: hdwy over 1f out: kpt on u.p fnl f* **20/1**

40-0 7 ¾ **Half A Crown (IRE)**[7] 2134 4-9-5 55........................(p) JamieMoriarty 2 52
(D W Barker) *bhd: rdn 1/2-way: kpt on fnl f: nrst fin* **33/1**

350- 8 hd **Quicks The Word**[199] 7218 9-9-3 53........................ JoeFanning 6 49
(T A K Cuthbert) *pressed ldr tl rdn and wknd ent fnl f* **16/1**

6554 9 nk **Whozart (IRE)**[22] 1695 6-8-13 54........................ GaryBartley(5) 7 49+
(A Dickman) *in tch: outpcd whn nt clr run over 1f out: n.d after* **8/1**

00-6 10 hd **First Swallow**[13] 1951 4-9-2 59........................ BMcHugh(7) 3 53
(R A Fahey) *hld up: hdwy over 1f out: nrst fin* **7/1**[3]

0-42 11 ½ **Twosheetstothewind**[10] 2046 5-9-10 60........................ TomEaves 16 53
(M Dods) *hld up: hdwy whn nt clr run over 1f out: nvr able to chal* **8/1**

20-5 12 ½ **Paddy Jack**[27] 1591 4-9-4 54........................(b) GrahamGibbons 10 45
(J R Weymes) *led to ins fnl f: sn btn* **20/1**

-006 13 1 **Obe One**[17] 1832 9-8-9 50........................ SladeO'Hara(5) 11 37
(A Berry) *dwlt: sn rdn in rr: nvr on terms* **33/1**

0-43 14 2 ¼ **Brother Barry (USA)**[16] 1889 4-9-2 55........................ NeilBrown(3) 17 34
(G A Swinbank) *midfield: drvn 1/2-way: btn over 1f out* **7/2**[1]

0104 15 nk **Darcy's Pride (IRE)**[20] 1768 5-9-9 59........................ TonyHamilton 14 37
(D W Barker) *chsd ldrs: drvn over 2f out: wknd over 1f out* **14/1**

0620 16 4 ½ **Just Joey**[42] 1241 5-9-4 59........................(b) PatrickDonaghy(5) 15 21
(J R Weymes) *in tch tl rdn and wknd over 2f out* **20/1**

00-0 17 1 ¼ **Adab (IRE)**[54] 1057 4-8-12 55........................ AndrewHeffernan(7) 13 12
(Miss Tracy Waggott) *cl up tl wknd fr 2f out* **66/1**

61.75 secs (0.95) **Going Correction** 0.0s/f (Good) **17** Ran SP% **132.4**
Speed ratings (Par 101): **92,91,90,88,88 88,87,86,86,85 85,84,82,79,78 71,69**
toteswinger: 1&2 not won, 1&3 £25.10, 2&3 not won. CSF £517.95 CT £6998.90 TOTE £14.20: £3.30, £8.60, £3.20, £1.90; EX 614.00 Place 6: £216.90, Place 5: £131.78.
Owner Ryedale Partners No 5 **Bred** Tally-Ho Stud **Trained** Great Habton, N Yorks
■ Stewards' Enquiry : Duran Fentiman one-day ban: used whip with excessive frequency (Jun 8)
Kelly Harrison caution: careless riding

FOCUS
A wide-open sprint handicap in which a whole raft of horses were in with some sort of a chance entering the final furlong as the field bunched up down the middle of the track.
Ask Jenny(IRE) Official explanation: jockey said mare was denied a clear run
T/Plt: £251.40 to a £1 stake. Pool: £40,583.17. 117.80 winning tickets. T/Qpdt: £61.50 to a £1 stake. Pool: £2,279.49. 27.40 winning tickets. RY

1770 CHEPSTOW (L-H)
Monday, May 25

OFFICIAL GOING: Good (good to firm in places; 8.2)
Wind: Nil Weather: Fine

2317 SPORTINGBET.COM DONATES TODAY'S TRADING PROFITS TO HEROS MAIDEN STKS (DIV I) 1m 14y
2:15 (2:15) (Class 5) 3-Y-O+ **£2,396** (£712; £356; £177) **Stalls** High

Form RPR

5 1 **Stravella (IRE)**[18] 1804 4-9-8 0........................ SebSanders 2 77
(R M Beckett) *led: hdd over 2f out: rdn to ld 1f out: drvn out* **10/1**

452- 2 nk **Ainia**[215] 6896 4-9-8 74........................ DaneO'Neill 14 76
(D M Simcock) *w ldrs on stands' rail: led over 2f out: rdn and hdd 1f out: r.o* **7/4**[1]

6 3 2 ¼ **Reportage (USA)**[37] 1350 3-9-1 0........................ RichardMullen 4 73
(J H M Gosden) *s.i.s: hld up: hdwy over 4f out: rdn wl over 1f out: one pce* **15/8**[2]

000- 4 3 ½ **Hilltop Artistry**[207] 7098 3-8-12 47........................ DavidProbert(3) 8 65
(S W James) *hld up in mid-div: hdwy over 2f out: sn rdn: edgd lft over 1f out: one pce* **66/1**

3-62 5 ¾ **Monetary Fund (USA)**[16] 1888 3-9-1 78........................ PatCosgrave 9 63
(G A Butler) *chsd ldrs: rdn 3f out: no hdwy fnl 2f* **9/2**[3]

0- 6 4 **Levitation (IRE)**[276] 5225 3-8-10 0........................ FergusSweeney 12 49
(W S Kittow) *hld up towards rr on stands' rail: rdn 3f out: nvr trbld ldrs* **50/1**

00 7 7 **Paul's Pet**[13] 1972 4-9-13 0........................ TGMcLaughlin 6 41
(Karen George) *hld up and bhd: rdn over 2f out: nt clr run over 1f out: nvr nr ldrs* **100/1**

40-0 8 1 ¼ **Almowj**[27] 1578 6-9-8 37........................ AmyBaker(5) 7 38
(G H Jones) *dwlt: rdn over 3f out: a bhd* **200/1**

9 ¾ **Weekend Away (IRE)** 3-9-1 0........................ PatDobbs 5 33
(S Kirk) *bhd fnl 5f* **25/1**

000- 10 hd **Wivny (USA)**[336] 3326 4-9-8 0........................ TPO'Shea 3 31
(H J Evans) *w ldr: rdn over 4f out: wknd wl over 2f out* **150/1**

-406 11 1 **Gambling Jack**[16] 1890 4-9-8 48........................ MarkCoumbe(5) 10 33
(A W Carroll) *hld up in mid-div: rdn and struggling over 3f out* **50/1**

0- 12 2 ¼ **Improper (USA)**[224] 6702 3-9-1 0........................ NeilChalmers 11 25
(Mouse Hamilton-Fairley) *dwlt: a in rr* **66/1**

3 13 1 ½ **Madhal**[13] 1956 3-8-10 0........................ RossAtkinson(5) 1 22
(M Salaman) *t.k.h: prom on outside: wknd 3f out* **12/1**

1m 34.59s (-1.61) **Going Correction** -0.275s/f (Firm)
WFA 3 from 4yo+ 12lb **13** Ran SP% **119.0**
Speed ratings (Par 103): **97,96,94,90,90 86,79,77,77,77 76,73,72**
toteswinger: 1&2 £5.70, 1&3 £13.30, 2&3 £13.30. CSF £27.50 TOTE £12.60: £3.20, £1.40, £1.20; EX 30.90.
Owner Five Horses Ltd **Bred** Five Horses Ltd **Trained** Whitsbury, Hants

FOCUS
The two main form contenders set a fair standard and the form is sound enough, although this was the slowest of the three races over C/D.

2318 SPORTINGBET.COM DONATES TODAY'S TRADING PROFITS TO HEROS MAIDEN STKS (DIV II) 1m 14y
2:50 (2:50) (Class 5) 3-Y-O+ **£2,396** (£712; £356; £177) **Stalls** High

Form RPR

3-22 1 **Palacefield (IRE)**[23] 1683 3-9-1 76........................ AlanMunro 9 79+
(P W Chapple-Hyam) *hld up in tch: pushed along 3f out: rdn and swtchd lft jst over 1f out: r.o u.p to ld towards fin* **10/11**[1]

2 2 shd **Luc Jordan**[14] 1941 3-9-1 0........................ DaneO'Neill 2 79+
(L M Cumani) *hld up in mid-div: hdwy over 3f out: led over 1f out: hdd towards fin: r.o* **9/4**[2]

0-22 3 1 ¼ **Park Lane**[36] 1380 3-9-1 79........................ PaulFitzsimons 12 76
(B W Hills) *a.p: led over 2f out: sn rdn: hdd over 1f out: nt qckn wl ins fnl f* **7/1**[3]

0- 4 5 **Royal Superlative**[317] 3959 3-8-10 0........................ SebSanders 8 59
(R M Beckett) *t.k.h: prom: led after 2f: hdd over 2f out: rdn over 1f out: wknd ins fnl f* **33/1**

046- 5 3 ¼ **Hambleden Hill**[238] 6344 3-9-1 73........................ PatDobbs 3 57
(R Hannon) *prom tl rdn and wknd 2f out* **16/1**

00/ 6 7 **Arab League (IRE)**[608] 5707 4-9-8 0........................ WilliamCarson(5) 5 44
(R J Price) *prom: lost pl after 3f: n.d after* **66/1**

7 nse **Monagasque (IRE)** 3-8-10 0........................ CatherineGannon 13 36
(S Kirk) *bhd: rdn over 3f out: nvr nr ldrs* **80/1**

0-00 8 ¾ **Jasper Cliff**[22] 1708 3-9-1 2........................(b[1]) NeilChalmers 10 39
(Mark Gillard) *led 2f: prom tl rdn and wknd over 2f out* **200/1**

0 9 1 **High Morning**[17] 1843 3-8-10 0........................ FergusSweeney 7 32
(D M Simcock) *t.k.h in mid-div: pushed along 3f out: wknd over 1f out* **14/1**

10 3 **Mr Kartoffel (IRE)** 4-9-13 0........................ FrankieMcDonald 14 33
(H Candy) *hld up in mid-div: rdn 4f out: sn bhd* **40/1**

000- 11 2 ¾ **Hold Fire**[380] 2003 5-9-3 48........................ MarkCoumbe(5) 11 21
(A W Carroll) *bhd fnl 5f* **125/1**

00-0 12 1 ¼ **Hill Of Clare (IRE)**[20] 1771 7-9-3 40........................ AmyBaker(5) 4 19
(G H Jones) *a bhd* **100/1**

13 8 **Any Secrets** 3-9-1 0........................ TGMcLaughlin 1 2
(Karen George) *s.s: a in rr* **66/1**

1m 34.53s (-1.67) **Going Correction** -0.275s/f (Firm)
WFA 3 from 4yo+ 12lb **13** Ran SP% **120.1**
Speed ratings (Par 103): **97,96,95,90,87 80,80,79,78,75 72,71,63**
toteswinger: 1&2 £2.10, 1&3 £1.10, 2&3 £1.40. CSF £2.90 TOTE £2.50: £1.10, £1.30, £1.50; EX 3.70.
Owner M J McStay **Bred** De Burgh Equine **Trained** Newmarket, Suffolk
■ Stewards' Enquiry : Paul Fitzsimons one-day ban: used whip with excessive frequency (Jun 8)

FOCUS
Three of the four main form contenders pulled clear of the rest. The form looks solid rated around the principals.

2319 SPORTINGBET.COM HEROS CLAIMING STKS 6f 16y
3:25 (3:26) (Class 6) 2-Y-O **£2,047** (£604; £302) **Stalls** High

Form RPR

5 1 **Underworld Dandy**[21] 1749 2-8-0 0........................ RossAtkinson(5) 2 60
(Tom Dascombe) *mde all: rdn and wandered away fr whip fr over 2f out: r.o wl* **5/1**

43 2 2 ¼ **Alphacino**[49] 1158 2-8-9 0........................ TPO'Shea 8 57
(M R Channon) *hld up: hdwy over 3f out: rdn 2f out: carried lft ins fnl f: kpt on to take 2nd towards fin: nt trble wnr* **11/4**[1]

1231 3 hd **Transfixed (IRE)**[8] 2100 2-8-8 0........................ NeilPollard 6 56
(P D Evans) *wnt lft s: t.k.h: a.p: hung lft fr over 1f out: one pce* **3/1**[2]

0255 4 nk **True Red (IRE)**[19] 1783 2-8-4 0........................ AlanMunro 10 51
(B R Millman) *a.p on stands' rail: rdn over 1f out: one pce* **4/1**[3]

6 5 nk **Highcliffe Bridge (IRE)**[12] 1981 2-8-4 0........................ CatherineGannon 4 50
(P D Evans) *s.i.s: hdwy over 3f out: rdn over 2f out: carried lft ins fnl f: one pce* **20/1**

06 6 1 ¾ **Chifah**[24] 1653 2-8-4 0........................ LukeMorris 7 45
(P D Evans) *prom: lost pl after 2f: rdn wl over 1f out: nvr trbld ldrs* **25/1**

0 7 4 **Southern Goddess (IRE)**[19] 1783 2-7-11 0........................ DavidProbert(3) 9 29
(P D Evans) *s.i.s: outpcd: short-lived effrt over 2f out* **7/1**

04 8 ¾ **Moonlight Serenade**[12] 1981 2-8-5 0........................ WilliamCarson(5) 3 36
(W G M Turner) *prom 3f* **14/1**

00 9 30 **Whip Up (IRE)**[19] 1782 2-8-9 0........................(b[1]) PatCosgrave 1 —
(J G Portman) *wnt lft s: sn prom on outside: wknd over 2f out: eased wl over 1f out* **66/1**

1m 12.19s (0.19) **Going Correction** -0.275s/f (Firm) **9** Ran SP% **117.6**
Speed ratings (Par 91): **93,90,89,89,88 86,81,80,40**
toteswinger: 1&2 not won, 1&3 £3.60, 2&3 £1.40. CSF £19.19 TOTE £4.60: £1.30, £1.70, £2.40; EX 31.20.Underworld Dandy was claimed by P. D. Evans for £6000.
Owner Market Avenue Racing Club Ltd **Bred** S & Mrs M Bayless **Trained** Lambourn, Berks

FOCUS
Four of the nine runners in this two year-old claimer were trained by David Evans. Evans later claimed the winner.

NOTEBOOK
Underworld Dandy didn't show much spark when a well beaten fifth of sixth in a 5f Windsor maiden on debut. Swiftly demoted to a claimer, he won with a bit in hand, despite swerving all over the track. He may have a quirk or two, but is still getting the hang of things, and showed a fair bit of ability to see out the trip well here. He is a sprint-bred half-brother to some modest/fair winners and should have more to offer. (op 4-1 tchd 5-2)
Alphacino was third of five at 3-1 in a 5f Wolverhampton maiden last month. The gelding still looked very green and took a long time to pick up but stayed on quite well. (op 7-2 tchd 5-1)
Transfixed(IRE) arrived here with a record of 1231 in 5f/6f sellers in four previous starts. She had claims on the form of her narrow win on good to soft at Ripon last time. She looked the pick of David Evans' runners, moved well for a long way, but did not find as much as expected. Official explanation: jockey said filly hung left-handed (tchd 5-2 and 10-3)
True Red(IRE) set the standard on her runner-up effort in a Bath maiden on her second start. She had failed to come near that in two runs since and put in a laboured effort here. She wanted to hang left in the closing stages. (op 9-2)

Highcliffe Bridge(IRE) was pushed along at an early stage but kept plugging away. She showed a hint of ability up in trip on her second run here. A half-sister to a dual 1m4f-1m6f winner, and also a hurdle winner, she should be suited by another step up in trip. (op 16-1)
Southern Goddess(IRE) Official explanation: jockey said filly missed the break
Whip Up(IRE) Official explanation: jockey said gelding ran too free

2320 SPORTINGBET.COM HEROS H'CAP — 1m 14y
4:00 (4:01) (Class 5) (0-70,75) 3-Y-O — **£2,914** (£867; £433; £216) **Stalls** High

Form — RPR

0-41 **1** — **Global**[4] 2206 3-9-6 **75** 6ex — PatrickHills(3) 5 — 88
(R Hannon) *a.p: led over 6f out: clr whn rdn over 1f out: r.o wl* — **7/1**[3]

30-5 **2** 6 — **West With The Wind (USA)**[27] 1588 3-9-4 **70** — AlanMunro 16 — 69
(P W Chapple-Hyam) *a.p on stands' rail: wnt 2nd over 2f out: sn rdn: no ch w wnr* — **12/1**

3334 **3** 2 — **My Best Man**[20] 1774 3-8-9 **61** — TGMcLaughlin 15 — 56
(B R Millman) *hld up in tch: rdn over 2f out: one pce* — **16/1**

00-5 **4** 1 3/4 — **Golden Flight (IRE)**[23] 1671 3-9-2 **68** — PhilipRobinson 14 — 59+
(J W Hills) *stmbld s: bhd: hdwy over 2f out: nvr able to chal* — **16/1**

0-34 **5** nk — **The Hague**[55] 1054 3-8-13 **65** — RichardMullen 17 — 55
(J H M Gosden) *hld up in mid-div: rdn over 3f out: no real prog fnl 2f* — **8/1**

00-5 **6** 1/2 — **Minder**[37] 1361 3-8-10 **62** — PatCosgrave 4 — 51
(J G Portman) *s.i.s: bhd: prog on outside whn swtchd lft 2f out: sn rdn: no imp* — **20/1**

-340 **7** 1 — **Gulf President**[10] 2038 3-9-0 **66** — TPO'Shea 13 — 52
(M R Channon) *bhd: hdwy whn swtchd lft over 1f out: n.d* — **20/1**

0-05 **8** 1 1/4 — **Peak (IRE)**[17] 1838 3-8-13 **65** — SteveDrowne 12 — 49
(H Morrison) *led over 1f: prom tl rdn and wknd over 2f out* — **25/1**

6-30 **9** 2 3/4 — **Chadwell Spring (IRE)**[14] 1937 3-8-8 **67** — MatthewCosham(7) 11 — 44
(Miss J Feilden) *prom: rdn over 2f out: wknd wl over 1f out* — **66/1**

2320 **10** 4 — **Duke Of Normandy (IRE)**[32] 1470 3-8-10 **62** — CatherineGannon 3 — 30
(B P J Baugh) *hld up in mid-div: rdn and wknd 3f out* — **33/1**

4-54 **11** hd — **Bahkov (IRE)**[22] 1704 3-8-7 **64** — RossAtkinson(5) 7 — 32
(Tom Dascombe) *prom: lost pl 4f out: n.d after* — **11/2**[2]

3-62 **12** 1 1/2 — **Mytivil (IRE)**[14] 1932 3-8-13 **68** — DavidProbert(3) 1 — 32
(M Salaman) *t.k.h in mid-div: lost pl over 3f out* — **12/1**

53-3 **13** 3/4 — **Mr Udagawa**[10] 2048 3-9-3 **69** — SebSanders 6 — 31
(R M Beckett) *prom tl rdn and wknd 2f out* — **4/1**[1]

54-0 **14** 5 — **Kingshill Prince**[42] 1255 3-8-13 **65** — PatDobbs 8 — 16
(W J Musson) *s.i.s: a in rr* — **33/1**

-440 **15** 1 1/4 — **Dhania (IRE)**[14] 1928 3-9-4 **70** — (v[1]) LukeMorris 10 — 18
(R A Teal) *bhd fnl 4f* — **20/1**

330- **16** 1 1/2 — **Dannios**[253] 5939 3-8-13 **65** — DaneO'Neill 9 — 10
(L M Cumani) *s.i.s: a in rr* — **7/1**[3]

00-0 **17** 4 1/2 — **Louidor**[28] 1574 3-9-1 **67** — FergusSweeney 2 — 1
(M R Bosley) *hld up in mid-div: hdwy on outside 4f out: wknd over 2f out* — **66/1**

1m 34.03s (-2.17) **Going Correction** -0.275s/f (Firm) — **17** Ran SP% **125.6**
Speed ratings (Par 99): **99,93,91,89,88 88,87,86,83,79 79,77,77,72,70 69,64**
toteswinger: 1&2 £2.30, 1&3 £16.30, 2&3 £16.30. CSF £81.40 CT £1364.84 TOTE £6.10: £1.10, £2.50, £6.70, £5.70; EX 77.50.
Owner A J Ilsley & G Battocchi **Bred** Lt-Col And Mrs R Bromley Gardner **Trained** East Everleigh, Wilts

FOCUS
A fair handicap. The winner showed his Salisbury win was no fluke, making all at a good pace. The form is rated around the third.
Mytivil(IRE) Official explanation: trainer said filly was in season

2321 SPORTINGBET.COM HEROS FILLIES' STKS (H'CAP) — 6f 16y
4:35 (4:37) (Class 5) (0-70,70) 3-Y-O — **£2,914** (£867; £433; £216) **Stalls** High

Form — RPR

6- **1** — **Dametime (IRE)**[38] 1337 3-8-13 **65** — (t) NickyMackay 10 — 73
(Daniel Mark Loughnane, Ire) *a.p: rdn over 2f out: sustained chal fnl f: led cl home* — **9/1**

-021 **2** nk — **Perfect Friend**[21] 1743 3-9-4 **70** — SebSanders 4 — 77
(S Kirk) *hld up in mid-div: hdwy over 2f out: rdn to ld 1f out: hdd cl home* — **5/1**[1]

200- **3** 3 1/4 — **Caster Sugar (USA)**[176] 7505 3-9-0 **66** — PatDobbs 9 — 63+
(R Hannon) *a chsng ldrs: rdn over 2f out: kpt on to take 3rd cl home* — **16/1**

-264 **4** nk — **Assent (IRE)**[6] 2160 3-8-11 **66** — JamesMillman(3) 5 — 62
(B R Millman) *s.i.s: bhd: hdwy 2f out: sn rdn: r.o one pce fnl f* — **6/1**[2]

1-04 **5** nk — **Freepressionist**[25] 1618 3-8-13 **65** — AlanMunro 7 — 60
(R A Teal) *led: rdn and hdd 1f out: wknd wl ins fnl f* — **16/1**

-520 **6** 1 — **Forward Feline (IRE)**[9] 2079 3-9-4 **70** — CatherineGannon 8 — 62
(B Palling) *mid-div: nt clr run and swtchd lft over 2f out: hdwy and squeezed through wl over 1f out: sn rdn: kpt on ins fnl f* — **7/1**[3]

-363 **7** 3/4 — **Keep Dancing (IRE)**[7] 2122 3-8-12 **67** — (p) DavidProbert(3) 3 — 56
(A M Balding) *hld up in mid-div: hdwy over 2f out: rdn over 1f out: wknd ins fnl f* — **17/2**

6-40 **8** 1 1/2 — **Peninsula Girl (IRE)**[25] 1618 3-8-12 **64** — TPO'Shea 2 — 49
(M R Channon) *bhd: hdwy over 2f out: sn rdn: no further prog* — **25/1**

0-50 **9** 1 1/4 — **Our Day Will Come**[13] 1973 3-8-8 **63** — PatrickHills(3) 6 — 44
(R Hannon) *s.i.s: bhd: pushed along over 3f out: hdwy over 2f out: rdn over 1f out: wknd ins fnl f* — **14/1**

1010 **10** 4 — **Bold Rose**[6] 2160 3-8-13 **65** — (p) DaneO'Neill 13 — 33
(M D I Usher) *s.i.s: bhd: hdwy on stands' rail 3f out: rdn wl over 1f out: wknd fnl f* — **9/1**

10-0 **11** 1 — **Mary Mason**[54] 1068 3-9-4 **70** — FergusSweeney 12 — 35
(M Hill) *dwlt: a bhd* — **20/1**

020- **12** 9 — **Champion Girl (IRE)**[213] 6954 3-8-11 **63** — LukeMorris 16 — —
(D Haydn Jones) *prom: rdn 3f out: wkng whn n.m.r wl over 1f out* — **15/2**

4220 **13** 1 — **River Rye (IRE)**[31] 1492 3-8-0 **57** — (p) RossAtkinson(5) 15 — —
(J S Moore) *prom: rdn over 2f out: wknd wl over 1f out* — **16/1**

5323 **14** nse — **Peanut Girl (IRE)**[20] 1772 3-8-10 **62** — SteveDrowne 1 — —
(B Palling) *a bhd* — **10/1**

50-3 **15** hd — **Straitjacket**[38] 1322 3-8-7 **59** — (b) PaulFitzsimons 17 — —
(Miss J R Tooth) *prom: rdn over 2f out: wknd wl over 1f out* — **16/1**

62-0 **16** 14 — **Final Rhapsody**[12] 1985 3-8-7 **59** — RichardThomas 11 — —
(J A Geake) *mid-div: rdn over 3f out: bhd fnl 2f* — **33/1**

1m 11.15s (-0.85) **Going Correction** -0.275s/f (Firm) — **16** Ran SP% **136.6**
Speed ratings (Par 96): **100,99,95,94,94 93,92,90,88,83 81,69,68,68,68 49**
toteswinger: 1&2 not won, 1&3 not won, 2&3 £10.00. CSF £58.77 CT £757.75 TOTE £17.10: £6.00, £1.20, £5.40, £2.70; EX 76.90.
Owner Brian Forkan **Bred** Tally-Ho Stud **Trained** Trim, Co Meath
■ Stewards' Enquiry : Fergus Sweeney two-day ban: struck filly in annoyance (Jun 8-9)

FOCUS
The field raced centre to stands' side in this sprint handicap which produced an exciting finish. The first two drew clear of the rest and the form could work out. The winner stepped up slightly on the best of her Irish form.
Keep Dancing(IRE) Official explanation: jockey said filly suffered interference in running
Champion Girl(IRE) Official explanation: jockey said filly suffered interference in running
Peanut Girl(IRE) Official explanation: jockey said filly lost its action

2322 EUROPEAN BREEDERS' FUND / SPORTINGBET.COM HEROS FILLIES' H'CAP — 1m 4f 23y
5:10 (5:10) (Class 5) (0-75,70) 4-Y-O+ — **£3,885** (£1,156; £577; £288) **Stalls** Low

Form — RPR

5-33 **1** — **Party Palace**[12] 1980 5-8-4 **53** — CatherineGannon 1 — 57
(H S Howe) *a.p: rdn over 2f out: r.o u.p to ld cl home* — **3/1**[1]

4-06 **2** 3/4 — **Oronsay**[13] 1974 4-8-2 **51** oh3 — (t) NickyMackay 3 — 54
(B R Millman) *t.k.h: hdwy to chse ldr after 3f: led 3f out: rdn over 1f out: hdd cl home* — **10/1**

P0-0 **3** shd — **Stringsofmyheart**[32] 1478 5-9-3 **66** — AlanMunro 6 — 69
(J J Quinn) *hld up in rr: hdwy on ins over 4f out: rdn over 1f out: ev ch wl ins fnl f: nt qckn* — **4/1**[2]

020- **4** 5 — **Lush (IRE)**[225] 6678 4-9-5 **68** — PatDobbs 7 — 63
(R Hannon) *hld up: hdwy over 3f out: rdn over 1f out: wknd ins fnl f* — **6/1**[3]

24-0 **5** 2 1/4 — **Bushy Dell (IRE)**[13] 1966 4-9-2 **70** — RossAtkinson(5) 5 — 61
(Miss J Feilden) *hld up and bhd: hdwy on outside over 2f out: rdn and wknd wl over 1f out* — **4/1**[2]

301- **6** 3 1/4 — **Addiena**[293] 4708 5-9-1 **67** — DavidProbert(3) 4 — 53
(B Palling) *t.k.h: chsd ldr 3f: prom tl rdn and wknd wl over 1f out* — **3/1**[1]

000/ **7** 30 — **Lillie Le Quesne**[1321] 5832 6-8-4 **53** — NeilChalmers 2 — —
(Jane Southcombe) *led: hdd 3f out: wknd qckly over 2f out: eased over 1f out* — **28/1**

2m 40.18s (1.18) **Going Correction** -0.275s/f (Firm) — **7** Ran SP% **116.8**
Speed ratings (Par 100): **85,84,84,81,79 77,57**
CSF £34.75 TOTE £4.10: £1.90, £3.50; EX 46.30.
Owner Horses Away Racing Club **Bred** Llety Stud **Trained** Oakford, Devon

FOCUS
The majority of runners were struggling for form or returning from a long absence. The pace was steady and there was a bunch finish. The form looks suspect.
Lillie Le Quesne Official explanation: trainer said mare was unsuited by the good (good to firm places) ground

2323 SPORTINGBET.COM HEROS MAIDEN STKS — 1m 4f 23y
5:40 (5:40) (Class 5) 3-Y-O — **£2,719** (£809; £404; £202) **Stalls** Low

Form — RPR

4 **1** — **Dhushan**[38] 1328 3-9-3 0 — PhilipRobinson 3 — 88+
(M A Jarvis) *mde all: clr over 1f out: easily* — **8/11**[1]

0-62 **2** 4 1/2 — **Gibb River (IRE)**[18] 1809 3-9-3 83 — AlanMunro 13 — 79
(P W Chapple-Hyam) *a.p: chsd wnr 6f out: no imp fnl 2f* — **11/8**[2]

00-5 **3** 5 — **Bernie The Bolt (IRE)**[14] 1931 3-9-0 0 — DavidProbert(3) 7 — 71
(A M Balding) *stdd s: hld up in rr: hdwy over 3f out: rdn over 2f out: wnt 3rd jst over 1f out: no ch w ldng pair* — **8/1**[3]

06 **4** 7 — **Langford Decoit (IRE)**[18] 1809 3-9-3 0 — CatherineGannon 10 — 60
(M R Channon) *hld up towards rr: hdwy on ins over 4f out: wnt 3rd over 3f out: wknd over 1f out* — **50/1**

0-0 **5** 3 3/4 — **No Sting**[33] 1464 3-8-12 0 — SimonWhitworth 8 — 49
(W S Kittow) *chsd wnr 6f: prom tl wknd 2f out* — **66/1**

0-0 **6** 3 1/4 — **Aspirational (IRE)**[20] 1771 3-9-3 0 — LukeMorris 12 — 49
(B Palling) *s.i.s: towards rr: sme prog over 2f out: n.d* — **66/1**

7 1 1/2 — **Maskateer (IRE)** 3-9-3 0 — SJCraine 5 — 46
(Mrs A M Thorpe) *bhd: sme prog over 4f out: rdn over 3f out: wknd 2f out* — **50/1**

0 **8** 2 — **Brave Beat**[40] 1286 3-9-3 0 — SteveDrowne 11 — 43
(H J L Dunlop) *hld up in mid-div: rdn over 3f out: wknd 2f out* — **33/1**

-0 **9** 1/2 — **Lady Oakesy**[28] 1573 3-8-12 0 — FergusSweeney 2 — 37
(W S Kittow) *hld up in mid-div: rdn over 3f out: sn wknd* — **66/1**

04 **10** 3 — **Lucy's Perfect**[22] 1708 3-8-12 0 — TGMcLaughlin 4 — 32
(B R Millman) *bhd fnl 4f* — **20/1**

00- **11** 3 — **Lily Of The Nile (UAE)**[248] 6081 3-8-12 0 — PatCosgrave 1 — 28
(J G Portman) *bhd fnl 5f* — **66/1**

00-0 **12** 9 — **Highams Park (IRE)**[34] 1440 3-8-12 25 — DaneO'Neill 6 — 13
(J G Portman) *hld up in tch: pushed along over 4f out: rdn over 3f out: sn wknd* — **100/1**

13 18 — **Bedouin Style (IRE)** 3-8-10 0 — JemmaMarshall(7) 9 — —
(Mrs A M Thorpe) *dwlt: a in rr* — **50/1**

2m 36.28s (-2.72) **Going Correction** -0.275s/f (Firm) — **13** Ran SP% **131.7**
Speed ratings (Par 99): **98,95,91,87,84 82,81,80,79,77 75,69,57**
toteswinger: 1&2 £1.10, 1&3 not won 2&3 £9.20 CSF £2.10 TOTE £1.60: £1.02, £1.20, £2.30; EX 1.60 Place 6: £35.72, Place 5: £27.74.
Owner Sheikh Ahmed Al Maktoum **Bred** Darley **Trained** Newmarket, Suffolk

FOCUS
Not much strength in depth but the two market leaders set a useful standard. They were in clear isolation in the straight and the winner confirmed Goodwood form with the second.
T/Plt: £37.70 to a £1 stake. Pool: £45,622.73. 881.35 winning tickets. T/Qpdt: £20.60 to a £1 stake. Pool: £2,492.10. 89.30 winning tickets. KH

2187 GOODWOOD (R-H)
Monday, May 25

OFFICIAL GOING: Good to firm (good in places; 8.8)
Races on mile course run over 24yards further than advertised, races incorporating the top bend run over 8yards more than advertised.
Wind: Virtually nil Weather: Bright

2324 GOLF AT GOODWOOD MAIDEN AUCTION STKS (DIV I) — 6f
1:30 (2:01) (Class 5) 2-Y-O — **£2,914** (£867; £433; £216) **Stalls** Centre

Form — RPR

0 **1** — **Queen's Hawk**[27] 1577 2-8-12 0 — TPQueally 8 — 70
(D J Coakley) *trckd ldrs: led ins fnl 2f: drvn and over 1f out: edgd rt fnl 110yds: kpt on wl* — **14/1**

32 **2** 1 — **Toga Tiger (IRE)**[12] 1981 2-8-12 0 — SamHitchcott 11 — 67
(M R Channon) *sn led towards centre of crse but nt pce of solitary ldr stands' side tl overall 2nd whn merged 3f out: upsides and rdn sn after and edgd rt u.p: kpt on fnl f but a hld by wnr* — **13/8**[1]

4 **3** ¾ **Super Duplex**[51] **1119** 2-8-11 0 .... IanMongan 5 64
(P M Phelan) *racd along stands' side 3f and overall ldr: hdd ins fnl 2f: stl ev ch 1f out: kpt on same pce ins fnl f* **10/1**

6 **4** ¾ **Master Of Dance (IRE)**[16] **1862** 2-9-2 0 .... JimmyFortune 6 67
(R Hannon) *s.i.s: sn rcvrd to press ldrs: rdn and ev ch 2f out: styng on one pce whn n.m.r fnl 110yds* **11/4**[2]

5 2 ¼ **Joe Packet** 2-8-9 0 .... TolleyDean 10 53
(J G Portman) *chsd ldrs: rdn over 2f out: wknd fnl f* **66/1**

6 1 ¾ **Hold Your Colour (IRE)** 2-9-2 0 .... JamieSpencer 3 55
(B J Meehan) *s.i.s: in rr but in tch: hdwy to trck ldrs 2f out: wknd fnl f* **9/1**

50 **7** 1 ¼ **Captain Cool (IRE)**[35] **1404** 2-8-13 0 .... RichardHughes 9 48
(R Hannon) *chsd ldrs: rdn 3f out: wknd over 2f out* **9/1**

8 ¾ **Yawary** 2-8-5 0 .... WilliamBuick 4 38
(C E Brittain) *s.i.s and wnt rt s: rcvrd and qcknd to trck ldrs 1/2-way: nvr on terms and wknd 2f out* **8/1**[3]

9 10 **Zachary Boy (IRE)** 2-8-11 0 .... AdamKirby 2 14
(B G Powell) *a in rr* **66/1**

1m 13.25s (1.05) **Going Correction** +0.05s/f (Good) **9** Ran SP% **114.6**
Speed ratings (Par 93): **95,93,92,91,88 86,84,83,70**
toteswinger: 1&2 £9.00, 1&3 £14.00, 2&3 £3.50. CSF £36.91 TOTE £18.00: £3.40, £1.40, £2.20; EX 58.30.
Owner Keeper's 12 **Bred** Mrs A M Upsdell **Trained** West Ilsley, Berks
■ Stewards' Enquiry : T P Queally caution: careless riding

FOCUS
No more than a fair juvenile maiden.

NOTEBOOK
Queen's Hawk, who shaped with a bit of promise when eighth on his debut at Bath, was happy enough to re-oppose Toga Tiger over this extra furlong and he found enough improvement to reverse form. In front over a furlong out, he responded well to pressure and ran on to win with a bit in hand. (tchd 12-1)
Toga Tiger(IRE), beaten at odds of 4/11 at Bath last time, led the centre group and held every chance, but couldn't quite match the winner and caused some to question his willingness. The way he kept on suggests he will be suited by 7f, but he is already becoming a bit expensive to follow. (tchd 7-4 in places)
Super Duplex, fourth at Lingfield on debut, was brought across to race alone stands' side and he led the field for much of the way. He kept on right the way to the line and is another who will be suited by an extra furlong before long. (op 12-1)
Master Of Dance(IRE), not beaten far despite finishing last of six on his debut at Ascot, was expected to be helped by the extra furlong, but he could find no extra in the final 100 yards. His rider reported he was still green. Official explanation: jockey said colt ran green (tchd 3-1 in places and 10-3 in a place)
Joe Packet, a cheap purchase bred to be suited by further, made a satisfactory debut back in fifth and should find easier opportunities.
Hold Your Colour(IRE), a son of Verglas, showed up well until over a furlong out and should learn from the experience. (tchd 17-2)
Captain Cool(IRE) should fare better in nurseries later in the season. (op 11-1)

2325 GOODWOOD FAMILY FUN DAY (S) STKS 5f
2:00 (2:35) (Class 4) 2-Y-O **£6,476** (£1,927; £963; £481) **Stalls** Centre

Form RPR

1 nk **Do More Business (IRE)** 2-8-12 0 .... IanMongan 6 69
(P M Phelan) *chsd ldrs: rdn over 2f out: led 1f out: hdd fnl 110yds: kpt on but a jst hld by wnr: fin 2nd, nk: subs awrdd r* **20/1**

2322 **2** 5 **Out The Ring (IRE)**[14] **1934** 2-8-12 0 ....(p) JimmyFortune 4 51
(Miss Gay Kelleway) *sn pressing ldrs: rdn over 2f out: wknd ins fnl f* **5/2**[2]

566 **3** 1 ¾ **Safari Camp (IRE)**[19] **1783** 2-8-12 0 ....(t) JimCrowley 1 45
(P Winkworth) *wnt lft s: sn led: rdn 1/2-way: hdd 1f out: sn wknd* **16/1**

413 **4** ½ **Boga (IRE)**[10] **2041** 2-8-7 0 .... MCGeran(5) 2 43
(M R Channon) *chsd ldrs: rdn and hung bdly lft fr ins fnl 2f: sn btn* **1/1**[1]

0155 **5** 60 **Lady Lion**[14] **1934** 2-8-7 0 ....(p) JackDean(5) 3 —
(W G M Turner) *sn rdn and wl bhd after 2f: t.o* **25/1**

602 **D** **Kate Skate**[19] **1783** 2-8-7 0 .... MartinDwyer 5 65
(P F I Cole) *t.k.h: hld up in tch: rdn and hdwy 2f out: styd on to ld fnl 110yds: a jst holding on: fin 1st, nk: subs disq. (positive sample)* **4/1**[3]

59.44 secs (1.04) **Going Correction** +0.05s/f (Good) **6** Ran SP% **113.1**
Speed ratings (Par 95): **92,84,81,80,— 93**
toteswinger: 1&2 £6.30, 1&3 £1.70, 2&3 £5.00. CSF £67.26 TOTE £3.90: £1.90, £5.00; EX 55.60.The winner was sold to Gay Kelleway for £13,000. Boga was claimed by Miss R Dobson for £10,000.
Owner Sutton Business Centre **Bred** Hardys Of Kilkeel Ltd **Trained** Epsom, Surrey

FOCUS
Two drew a few lengths clear in this seller.

NOTEBOOK
Do More Business(IRE), a son of Dubai Destination starting off at the bottom level, seemed to know exactly what was required and showed plenty of early pace. He went on over a furlong out and stuck on well once headed by the winner, but didn't have enough time to try and fight back. This was a pleasing start and he was subsequently awarded the race. (op 18-1 tchd 16-1)
Out The Ring(IRE) has proved a consistent sort without winning so far, but the application of first-time cheekpieces was no help and he probably ran a shade below his best. (tchd 2-1 and 11-4)
Safari Camp(IRE) showed his customary early speed, but once again failed to get home. The first-time tongue tie clearly made little difference. (op 14-1 tchd 12-1)
Boga(IRE) proved bitterly disappointing. She had beaten the winner at Bath and since gone on to finish third in a novice stakes at Newcastle, but started to hang left once coming under pressure and ended up on the stands' rail. This was clearly not her true form. Official explanation: jockey said filly hung badly left (tchd 11-8)
Lady Lion never went a yard and was beaten out of sight. (op 33-1 tchd 20-1)
Kate Skate, who appreciated the drop to this level when runner-up to Boga at Bath last time, was keen through the early stages, but really ran on well for pressure and got up in the final half furlong to deny the newcomer. She was subsequently disqualified due to a positive sample but should prove just as effective at 6f . She was sold to Gay Kelleway for 13,000gns. (op 9-2 tchd 5-1)

2326 CHILDREN UNDER 18 RACE FREE AT GOODWOOD H'CAP 6f
2:35 (3:10) (Class 4) (0-80,80) 4-Y-0+ **£4,857** (£1,445; £722; £360) **Stalls** Centre

Form RPR

-635 **1** **Alfresco**[44] **1213** 5-8-10 **72** ....(b) RobertWinston 12 83
(J R Best) *sn trcking ldr: drvn to chal fr ins fnl 2f: asserted fnl 110yds: kpt on wl* **4/1**[1]

46/0 **2** 1 **Mymumsaysimthebest**[24] **1636** 4-9-2 **78** .... JimmyFortune 10 86
(G L Moore) *swtg: t.k.h and sn led: rdn whn chal fr 2f out: hdd and outpcd fnl 110yds* **11/1**

6324 **3** 1 ½ **The Tatling (IRE)**[14] **1943** 12-8-13 **80** .... JackDean(5) 3 83
(J M Bradley) *in rr: drvn and hdwy over 1f out: kpt on to chse ldng duo ins fnl f but no imp* **9/1**

0-04 **4** hd **Sam's Cross (IRE)**[89] **671** 4-8-8 **70** .... PaulEddery 4 72+
(Pat Eddery) *t.k.h: hld up in rr: stl plenty to do over 1f out: drvn and qcknd jst ins fnl f: fin wl* **10/1**

0-02 **5** ½ **Orange Pip**[21] **1733** 4-9-4 **80** .... RichardHughes 11 81
(R Hannon) *plld hrd: chsd ldrs: rdn over 1f out: styd on same pce ins fnl f* **6/1**[3]

-320 **6** ½ **Blue Jack**[22] **1699** 4-9-2 **78** .... MartinDwyer 8 77+
(W R Muir) *plld hrd in rr: rdn and hdwy over 1f out: kpt on fnl f but nvr gng pce to rch ldrs* **6/1**[3]

2444 **7** 1 ¼ **C'Mon You Irons (IRE)**[85] **721** 4-8-4 **66** oh1 .... JimmyQuinn 6 61
(M R Hoad) *plunged s: pressed ldrs: rdn 2f out: wknd ins fnl f* **20/1**

4660 **8** 1 ¼ **Count Ceprano (IRE)**[9] **2086** 5-9-0 **76** .... LPKeniry 9 67
(C R Dore) *chsd ldrs: rdn over 2f out: wknd qckly 1f out* **14/1**

0-00 **9** 6 **Fantasy Believer**[9] **2088** 11-8-5 **67** .... WilliamBuick 2 39
(J J Quinn) *a outpcd* **10/1**

0442 **10** 1 ¾ **Golden Dixie (USA)**[4] **2203** 10-8-9 **71** .... JamieSpencer 1 37
(R A Harris) *rdn 1/2-way: a outpcd* **5/1**[2]

310- **11** 32 **Willridge**[215] **6899** 4-8-10 **72** .... JimCrowley 7 —
(J M Bradley) *chsd ldrs: rdn 1/2-way: wknd 1/2-way: t.o* **20/1**

1m 11.69s (-0.51) **Going Correction** +0.05s/f (Good) **11** Ran SP% **117.9**
Speed ratings (Par 105): **105,103,101,101,100 100,98,96,88,86 43**
toteswinger: 1&2 £23.50, 1&3 £16.80, 2&3 not won. CSF £48.98 CT £375.45 TOTE £6.90: £4.30, £2.60, £2.10; EX 91.40.
Owner Mrs A M Riney **Bred** Usk Valley Stud **Trained** Hucking, Kent

FOCUS
They went a good gallop in this sprint handicap. The first two were 1-2 throughout with little getting into it from the rear, and the form is best rated through the winner.
C'Mon You Irons(IRE) Official explanation: jockey said gelding stumbled leaving stalls
Fantasy Believer Official explanation: trainer's rep said gelding moved poorly
Willridge Official explanation: trainer said gelding was unsuited by the good to firm (good in places) ground

2327 FESTIVAL STKS (LISTED RACE) 1m 1f 192y
3:10 (3:45) (Class 1) 4-Y-0+
£22,708 (£8,608; £4,308; £2,148; £1,076; £540) **Stalls** High

Form RPR

515- **1** **Tranquil Tiger**[220] **6780** 5-9-1 114 ....(b) TPQueally 6 115+
(H R A Cecil) *trckd ldr: led over 4f out: 5l clr fr over 2f out: shkn up ins fnl f: hld on wl cl home* **11/4**[1]

1602 **2** nk **Halicarnassus (IRE)**[16] **1875** 5-8-12 103 .... SamHitchcott 9 111
(M R Channon) *chsd ldrs: rdn over 2f out: hung rt over 1f out and sn chsng wnr: styd on wl cl home but a jst hld* **16/1**

-054 **3** 2 ¼ **Charlie Farnsbarns (IRE)**[16] **1859** 5-9-4 112 .... MartinDwyer 4 113
(B J Meehan) *hld up in rr: hdwy on ins whn hmpd over 2f out: kpt on again fr over 1f out to take 3rd ins fnl f but no ch w ldng duo* **13/2**[3]

205- **4** 1 **Illustrious Blue**[201] **7193** 6-8-12 107 .... JimCrowley 2 105
(W J Knight) *stdd s: bhd: hdwy over 2f out: hung rt fr over 1f out: kpt on but nvr any ch of rching ldrs* **12/1**

3-53 **5** shd **Once More Dubai (USA)**[88] **703** 4-9-1 110 ....(bt) WilliamBuick 3 107
(Saeed Bin Suroor) *stdd s and hld up in rr: drvn and hdwy over 2f out: kpt on fnl f but nvr in contention* **20/1**

-421 **6** 5 **Ordnance Row**[14] **1929** 6-9-1 111 .... RichardHughes 8 97
(R Hannon) *sn mid-div: rdn and hdwy 3f out: edgd rt over 2f out: sn chsng clr ldr but nvr any ch: wknd fnl f* **7/1**

3/1 **7** 11 **Made To Ransom**[20] **1771** 4-8-12 95 .... JimmyFortune 7 81
(J H M Gosden) *led tl hdd by wnr over 4f out: 5l bhd 3f out and no ch after: wknd 2f out* **3/1**[2]

0200 **8** 6 **Yahrab (IRE)**[18] **1799** 4-9-1 106 .... LDettori 10 63
(Saeed Bin Suroor) *chsd ldrs tl wknd qckly 2f out* **9/1**

64-2 **9** 13 **Pinpoint (IRE)**[14] **1929** 7-8-12 107 .... AdamKirby 1 34
(W R Swinburn) *a towards rr and no ch fnl 3f* **15/2**

2m 5.69s (-2.31) **Going Correction** +0.05s/f (Good) **9** Ran SP% **117.6**
Speed ratings (Par 111): **111,110,108,108,108 104,95,90,80**
toteswinger: 1&2 £10.10, 1&3 £3.20, 2&3 £16.00. CSF £48.38 TOTE £3.50: £1.70, £3.70, £1.50; EX 51.20.
Owner K Abdulla **Bred** Juddmonte Farms Ltd **Trained** Newmarket, Suffolk
■ Stewards' Enquiry : Richard Hughes caution: careless riding

FOCUS
A good Listed event and decent form for the grade, with Tranquil Tiger close to last year's C/D form.

NOTEBOOK
Tranquil Tiger's rider caught the others out with a bold move running down the hill. The pair raced into the lead, quickly opening up a gap, and had the entire field in trouble. He still seemed full of running with two to run, but began to tire approaching the distance and tied up badly in the final 100 yards, only just holding on in the end. Now a five-time winner at this level, he is effective over a variety of distances, but seems quite well suited to this trip, being such a strong traveller. (op 4-1)
Halicarnassus(IRE), runner-up to a stablemate of the winner at Lingfield last time, came under pressure running down the hill and responded well, but despite finishing strongly the line just came too soon. He wins in his turn and will continue to pay his way for connections. (op 20-1)
Charlie Farnsbarns(IRE), conceding weight to all his rivals, was taken to the rail and beginning to stay on when squeezed up by Ordnance Row. He stayed on again, and the incident didn't affect his finishing position, but he would have been a length or so closer. (op 15-2)
Illustrious Blue, without a win in over two years, likes it around here and he stayed on late to just get up for fourth. A horse who ideally likes coming from off a good pace, he is likely to remain difficult to win with, but the ability is clearly still there.
Once More Dubai(USA), the Godolphin second-string who had last been seen finishing third to Presvis at Nad Al Sheba back in February, kept on to record a creditable effort in fifth. Minor Listed contests and conditions events are likely to represent his best chances of winning. (op 16-1)
Ordnance Row, winner of a 1m contest at Windsor earlier in the month, has yet to win over this far and he faded badly from the furlong marker, his rider reporting him to have not handled the track. He is a tough, consistent sort under the right conditions and should return to his best once dropping back in trip. (op 6-1)
Made To Ransom, an easy winner of a Chepstow maiden on his return from over 18 months off, had finished third behind Twice Over on his sole previous start and was fancied by many to run a big race on this step up in grade. He made the early running, but was swept aside by the winner over four out and gradually dropped away. This was clearly not what was expected of him and he was reported to have run too free. Official explanation: jockey said gelding ran too free (op 10-3, tchd 7-2 in places)
Yahrab(IRE) weakened tamely from over two out and failed to run his race. (op 12-1)

Pinpoint(IRE) never got into it and was later reported to have lost both front shoes. Official explanation: trainer said gelding lost both front shoes (op 6-1)

2328 GOLF AT GOODWOOD MAIDEN AUCTION STKS (DIV II) 6f
3:45 (4:20) (Class 5) 2-Y-O £2,914 (£867; £433; £216) **Stalls** Centre

Form RPR

1 **Reach For The Sky (IRE)** 2-8-4 0 .... JimmyQuinn 8 68+
(R Hannon) *hld up in tch: qcknd over 1f out to ld fnl 110yds: readily* **16/1**

004 2 1 **Pullyourfingerout (IRE)**[25] 1616 2-8-12 0 .... AdamKirby 1 73
(B G Powell) *chsd ldrs: drvn to ld 1f out: hdd and outpcd fnl 110yds* **16/1**

3 1 **Just The Tonic** 2-8-6 0 .... SamHitchcott 10 64
(M R Channon) *in tch: drvn to press ldrs fr over 2f out: styd on fnl f but nt pce of ldng duo* **16/1**

03 4 3¼ **Timelord (IRE)**[4] 2187 2-8-10 0 .... LPKeniry 3 58
(S Kirk) *slt ld tl hdd over 2f out: narrow ld again over 1f out: sn hdd: wknd and hung rt ins fnl f* **15/8**[1]

5 ½ **Libertino (IRE)** 2-9-0 0 .... MartinDwyer 5 61
(B J Meehan) *s.i.s: towards rr: hdwy 2f out: kpt on fnl f but nvr in contention* **20/1**

643 6 1¾ **Flapjack**[16] 1891 2-8-7 0 ow1 .... RobertWinston 4 49
(R Hannon) *pressed ldrs: slt ld over 2f out: hdd over 1f out: wkng whn carried rt ins fnl f* **11/2**[3]

7 1¾ **Danger Mulally** 2-8-13 0 .... WilliamBuick 6 49
(A M Balding) *t.k.h: pressed ldrs and stl upsides 2f out: wknd over 1f out* **11/2**[3]

8 hd **Fire And Stone (IRE)** 2-9-0 0 .... RichardKingscote 7 50
(Tom Dascombe) *rdn and green fr s: a in rr* **9/2**[2]

9 ½ **Looks Like Slim** 2-8-12 0 .... LDettori 2 46
(P F I Cole) *rdn over 2f out: a outpcd* **8/1**

4 10 24 **Ballyvonane (USA)**[21] 1749 2-8-10 0 .... JimCrowley 9 —
(L A Dace) *pressed ldrs over 3f: sn wknd* **20/1**

1m 13.06s (0.86) **Going Correction** +0.05s/f (Good) **10** Ran SP% **122.0**
Speed ratings (Par 93): **96,94,93,89,88 86,83,83,82,50**
toteswinger: 1&2 not won, 1&3 £51.80, 2&3 not won. CSF £255.17 TOTE £20.20: £3.70, £3.50, £3.10; EX 273.50.
Owner R Hannon **Bred** Miss Anne Ormsby **Trained** East Everleigh, Wilts

FOCUS
Probably just the weaker of the two divisions.

NOTEBOOK
Reach For The Sky(IRE), a cheap purchase who is related to a winner in Spain, comes from a yard always to be feared in juvenile maidens and she really started to stay on well from over a furlong out. In front with 100 yards to run, she looks a filly with a bright future and is just the sort to take her chance in the Super Sprint at Newbury later in the season.
Pullyourfingerout(IRE) travelled well through the early stages and came to hold every chance over a furlong out, but he couldn't quite match the winner. He has got a bit better with each run and should find a small race before too long.
Just The Tonic, a daughter of Medicean who is related to winners at this distance, came there going well towards the far-side rail and went on over a furlong out, but she could find no extra in the final 100 yards. This was a promising start and natural progress should see her winning a minor maiden.
Timelord(IRE), third over the C&D just four days earlier, came under strong pressure two out and faded soon inside the final furlong. This was a bit disappointing and perhaps he found the race coming too soon. (op 3-1)
Libertino(IRE), half-brother to a smart 2yo winner in Italy, lacked the pace to race on with the principals, but stayed on steadily and should improve for this initial experience. (tchd 16-1)
Flapjack, whose rider put up 1lb overweight, is exposed now and it may take a drop to claiming/selling level for her to get off the mark. (op 5-1 tchd 9-2)
Danger Mulally, whose yard is in good form at present, is bred to appreciate further than this, but showed a bit of speed and should improve. (op 9-1)
Fire And Stone(IRE) was a bit sluggish away from the gate and soon driven. He never got into it, but is with a good yard and should know more next time. Official explanation: jockey said colt never travelled (op 4-1, tchd 5-1 in a place)
Looks Like Slim, who holds a Derby entry, was outpaced once the tempo increased. (op 7-1)

2329 HORSEWALK RESTAURANT H'CAP 1m
4:20 (4:56) (Class 4) (0-85,83) 3-Y-O £4,857 (£1,445; £722; £360) **Stalls** High

Form RPR

0-31 1 **Eastern Empire**[18] 1804 3-9-3 82 .... LDettori 11 91+
(J W Hills) *trckd ldrs: qcknd to ld ins fnl f: comf* **9/2**[2]

21-4 2 2½ **Star Links (USA)**[5] 2174 3-9-2 81 .... RichardHughes 1 84
(R Hannon) *sn led: rdn over 2f out: hdd and outpcd by wnr ins fnl f but kpt on wl to hold 2nd* **13/2**[3]

1-14 3 ¾ **Laudatory**[16] 1870 3-9-4 83 .... AdamKirby 10 84
(W R Swinburn) *hld up in tch: hdwy 2f out: rdn over 1f out and styd on to take 3rd wl ins fnl f but a hld by ldng duo* **5/2**[1]

-033 4 1 **Yellow Printer**[13] 1971 3-8-12 77 .... RichardKingscote 5 76
(Tom Dascombe) *trckd ldr: rdn to chal over 2f out: sn one pce: wknd ins fnl f* **8/1**

-332 5 ½ **Hypnotist (UAE)**[24] 1638 3-8-10 75 .... WilliamBuick 12 73
(C E Brittain) *hld up in rr: hdwy over 2f out: qcknd on ins over 1f out and kpt on but nvr gng pce to be competitive* **9/1**

-102 6 ½ **Dalradian (IRE)**[20] 1774 3-8-13 78 .... JimCrowley 4 75+
(W J Knight) *stdd in rr: rdn and hdwy fr 2f out: kpt on fnl f but nvr in contention* **7/1**

100- 7 2¼ **Sapphire Prince (USA)**[251] 6002 3-9-1 80 .... RobertWinston 2 72
(J R Best) *stdd s: plld hrd: m wd bnd over 3f out: rdn: awkward and sme prog 2f out: nvr rchd ldrs and wknd fnl f* **33/1**

210- 8 ½ **Outofoil (IRE)**[198] 7241 3-9-0 79 .... JimmyFortune 3 69
(R M Beckett) *chsd ldrs: rdn over 2f out: eased whn btn fnl f* **9/1**

01-0 9 5 **Take The Micky**[33] 1466 3-8-10 75 .... TPQueally 6 54
(W J Knight) *chsd ldrs: rdn 3f out: wknd fr 2f out* **20/1**

6-00 10 11 **Baycat (IRE)**[16] 1869 3-9-1 80 .... TolleyDean 7 34
(J G Portman) *rdn over 3f out: a in rr* **50/1**

540- 11 4 **George Rex (USA)**[215] 6910 3-8-10 75 .... MartinDwyer 9 19
(B J Meehan) *in tch: rdn 3f out: wknd over 2f out: eased whn no ch* **20/1**

1m 39.81s (-0.09) **Going Correction** +0.05s/f (Good) **11** Ran SP% **118.1**
Speed ratings (Par 101): **102,99,98,97,97 96,94,94,89,78 74**
toteswinger: 1&2 £14.40, 1&3 £4.00, 2&3 £3.90. CSF £32.40 CT £90.78 TOTE £6.10: £2.10, £2.70, £2.00; EX 30.80.
Owner Wai Kuen Chan **Bred** Rockwell Bloodstock **Trained** Upper Lambourn, Berks

FOCUS
This looked a fair handicap. The winner is progressing and the form is rated around the second. Not many got into it from the rear.

Outofoil(IRE) Official explanation: jockey said gelding ran too free early on

2330 JUNE FRIDAY EVENINGS AT GOODWOOD H'CAP 1m
4:55 (5:33) (Class 6) (0-65,65) 4-Y-O+ £3,238 (£963; £481; £240) **Stalls** High

Form RPR

1503 1 **Inside Story (IRE)**[6] 2166 7-9-2 63 .... (b) LPKeniry 1 74
(C R Dore) *in rr: hrd drvn over 3f out: hdwy and nt clr run over 2f out: qcknd on ins to ld 1f out: drvn out* **10/1**

0-03 2 ½ **Seasonal Cross**[21] 1741 4-8-6 53 .... WilliamBuick 9 63
(S Dow) *in rr: gd hdwy on outside over 2f out: str run fr over 1f out to chse wnr ins fnl f: kpt on but a jst hld* **7/2**[1]

2-03 3 2½ **Tignello (IRE)**[7] 2125 4-8-12 59 .... RichardHughes 5 63+
(G L Moore) *trckd ldrs: faltered and rdr lost iron over 1f out: sn rcvrd and styd on again ins fnl f but no ch w ldng duo* **11/2**[2]

00-0 4 1¼ **Feasible**[19] 1785 4-8-11 58 .... TolleyDean 2 59
(J G Portman) *chsd ldr: rdn over 2f out: led wl over 1f out: hdd sn after: wknd ins fnl f* **16/1**

0040 5 2½ **Batchworth Blaise**[16] 1876 6-8-5 52 .... MartinDwyer 14 47
(E A Wheeler) *in rr: hdwy 3f out: styng on whn nt clr run ins fnl 2f and edgd rt over 1f out: kpt on again ins fnl f but nvr in contention* **14/1**

2220 6 hd **Duke Of Milan (IRE)**[110] 387 6-9-3 64 .... RichardKingscote 13 59
(Tom Dascombe) *hld up in rr: stdy hdwy and grad swtchd lft to trck ldrs ins fnl 2f: sn rdn: wknd fnl f* **13/2**[3]

1303 7 1¾ **Binnion Bay (IRE)**[22] 1710 8-8-4 54 ow1 .... (b) MarcHalford(3) 11 45
(J J Bridger) *in rr: rdn and sme hdwy fr 2f out: styd on fnl f but nvr any ch* **14/1**

0600 8 1¼ **The Grey One (IRE)**[6] 2166 6-9-0 61 .... (b[1]) AdamKirby 8 49
(J M Bradley) *in rr: rdn over 3f out: mod prog 2f out: nvr in contention* **16/1**

560 9 1¼ **Star Strider**[35] 1401 5-9-4 65 .... JamieSpencer 10 50
(Miss Gay Kelleway) *in rr: drvn and mod prog fr over 2f out but nvr any ch* **14/1**

0504 10 ½ **Master Mahogany**[7] 2125 8-8-12 59 .... JimCrowley 16 43
(R J Hodges) *chsd ldrs: rdn 3f out: wknd ins fnl 2f* **15/2**

0-40 11 2¾ **Turfwolke (GER)**[7] 2133 4-8-10 62 .... JackDean(5) 6 40
(Mrs H S Main) *chsd ldrs: rdn over 3f out: wknd over 2f out* **16/1**

-030 12 nse **Fly In Johnny (IRE)**[62] 946 4-8-1 55 oh6 ow4 .... DebraEngland(7) 4 33
(J J Bridger) *t.k.h: chsd ldrs 5f* **50/1**

0025 13 2 **Lend A Grand (IRE)**[31] 1495 5-9-3 64 .... IanMongan 3 37
(Miss Jo Crowley) *a in rr* **16/1**

0430 14 5 **Salt Of The Earth (IRE)**[11] 2011 4-9-1 62 .... JimmyFortune 12 24+
(T G Mills) *in tch: hdwy and n.m.r ins fnl 2f and over 1f out: nt rcvr and sn dropped away* **14/1**

5/0- 15 2¼ **Beauchamp Viking**[18] 6018 5-8-4 51 .... (t) JimmyQuinn 7 7+
(S C Burrough) *in tch tl lost action and eased wl over 2f out* **50/1**

6600 16 3½ **Trivia (IRE)**[11] 2011 5-8-7 54 .... SamHitchcott 15 2
(J J Bridger) *sn led: hdd wl over 1f out: wknd qckly* **25/1**

1m 39.02s (-0.88) **Going Correction** +0.05s/f (Good) **16** Ran SP% **129.8**
Speed ratings (Par 101): **106,105,103,101,99 99,97,96,94,94 91,91,89,84,82 78**
toteswinger: 1&2 £6.20, 1&3 £13.80, 2&3 £1.80. CSF £47.04 CT £234.09 TOTE £14.80: £3.30, £1.60, £1.90, £4.80; EX 78.40.
Owner Chris Marsh **Bred** Arthur S Phelan **Trained** Cowbit, Lincs

FOCUS
They went a fair gallop in this moderate handicap. The form looks pretty sound.
Tignello(IRE) Official explanation: jockey said he lost an iron

2331 TOTEEXACTA H'CAP 1m 4f
5:30 (6:05) (Class 5) (0-70,68) 4-Y-O+ £3,238 (£963; £481; £240) **Stalls** Low

Form RPR

3-12 1 **Saloon (USA)**[14] 1936 5-9-1 65 .... (p) JamieSpencer 2 74+
(Jane Chapple-Hyam) *hld up in rr: stdy hdwy 3f out: shkn up and hdwy high whn qcknd fr 2f out to ld jst ins fnl f: sn in command: pushed out* **9/4**[2]

0101 2 3 **Cossack Prince**[18] 1807 4-9-4 68 .... IanMongan 4 72
(Mrs L J Mongan) *trckd ldrs: wnt 2nd 6f out: led over 3f out: rdn 2f out: hdd jst ins fnl f: sn outpcd by wnr but clr for 2nd* **7/4**[1]

23-4 3 4 **Streets Apart (USA)**[14] 1945 4-9-1 65 .... (v[1]) AdamKirby 8 63
(W R Swinburn) *chsd ldr to 6f out: wnt 2nd again over 2f out: nvr any ch and wknd over 1f out* **3/1**[3]

0335 4 2¼ **Imperium**[21] 1741 8-8-10 60 .... JimCrowley 3 54
(Jean-Rene Auvray) *in tch: rdn and styd on same pce fr over 2f out* **11/1**

0264 5 14 **Make Amends (IRE)**[7] 2123 4-8-8 58 .... MartinDwyer 6 30
(R J Hodges) *led: sn clr: hdd over 3f out: wknd 2f out and eased fnl f* **9/1**

56-0 6 ½ **Marie Louise**[10] 2040 4-8-7 60 .... MarcHalford(3) 5 31
(L A Dace) *in tch: wknd over 3f out* **40/1**

2505 7 17 **Play Up Pompey**[27] 1589 7-8-4 54 oh8 .... JimmyQuinn 7 —
(J J Bridger) *s.i.s: a bhd* **33/1**

2m 37.93s (-0.47) **Going Correction** +0.05s/f (Good) **7** Ran SP% **115.8**
Speed ratings (Par 103): **103,101,98,96,87 87,75**
toteswinger: 1&2 £1.02, 1&3 £1.90, 2&3 £1.20. CSF £6.80 CT £11.04 TOTE £2.90: £2.20, £1.70; EX 4.40 Place 6: £1691.82, Place 5: £781.55.
Owner Mrs Jane Chapple-Hyam **Bred** R D Hubbard & Coolmore **Trained** Newmarket, Suffolk

FOCUS
This was a modest handicap. The winner is generally progressive and this was a slight personal best.
Make Amends(IRE) Official explanation: jockey said filly ran too free
T/Plt: £1,692.50 to a £1 stake. Pool: £71,991.51. 31.05 winning tickets. T/Qpdt: £123.70 to a £1 stake. Pool: £4,497.81. 26.90 winning tickets. ST

2147 LEICESTER (R-H)
Monday, May 25

OFFICIAL GOING: Good to firm (good in places; 7.9)
Wind: Light across Weather: Overcast

2332 FOREST H'CAP 1m 1f 218y
2:05 (2:08) (Class 5) (0-70,68) 4-Y-O+ £3,238 (£963; £481; £240) **Stalls** High

Form RPR

-600 1 **Surprise Pension (IRE)**[42] 1254 5-7-11 54 .... JamieKyne(7) 1 63
(J J Quinn) *hld up: hdwy over 2f out: led and edgd rt over 1f out: r.o u.p* **7/1**

51-2 2 2¼ **Miss Pelling (IRE)**[17] 1845 4-9-2 66 .... EddieAhern 5 70
(B J Meehan) *led: hdd over 8f out: chsd ldrs tl led over 2f out: rdn and hdd whn rdr dropped reins over 1f out: styd on same pce ins fnl f* **11/4**[1]

24-1 **3** *nk* **Locum**[14] 1945 4-9-4 **68** ... SaleemGolam 3 71
(M H Tompkins) *hld up: hdwy 1/2-way: rdn over 1f out: r.o* **11/2**[2]

5133 **4** *hd* **Nassar (IRE)**[13] 1960 6-8-7 **64** ow1 ...(v) HollyHall(7) 4 67+
(G Prodromou) *s.s: bhd: hdwy over 1f out: r.o* **9/1**

0-06 **5** *shd* **Dubburg (USA)**[30] 1514 4-8-13 **63** ... ChrisCatlin 10 66
(W J Musson) *uns rdr in stalls prior to s: hld up: r.o u.p ins fnl f: nt rch ldrs* **11/1**

2023 **6** *½* **Mister Trickster (IRE)**[26] 1606 8-8-7 **57** ow2 ... TonyCulhane 6 59
(R Dickin) *s.s: hld up: hdwy over 1f out: rdn and edgd rt ins fnl f: r.o* **16/1**

0 **7** *4 ½* **Hidden Door (IRE)**[17] 1833 4-9-3 **67** ... KirstyMilczarek 7 60
(Jane Chapple-Hyam) *prom: rdn to chse ldr over 2f out: losing pl whn hmpd over 1f out: wkng whn n.m.r ins fnl f* **9/1**

3122 **8** *nk* **Gasat (IRE)**[27] 1578 8-8-10 **67** ... PNolan(7) 9 59
(A B Haynes) *chsd ldrs: rdn over 2f out: sn wknd* **6/1**[3]

330- **9** *10* **Channel Crossing**[246] 6154 7-9-4 **68** ... StephenDonohoe 8 40
(S Wynne) *chsd ldr 8f out: rdn over 3f out: sn wknd* **10/1**

00 **10** *hd* **Strategic Knight (USA)**[6] 2149 4-8-6 **63** ow8 ...(t) JRoberts(7) 2 35
(R C Guest) *racd keenly: led over 8f out: hdd over 2f out: wkng whn rdr dropped reins wl over 1f out* **50/1**

2m 6.82s (-1.08) **Going Correction** -0.025s/f (Good) **10** Ran SP% **114.1**
Speed ratings (Par 103): **103,101,100,100,100 100,96,96,88,88**
toteswinger: 1&2 £3.60, 1&3 £14.00, 2&3 £1.70. CSF £25.93 CT £114.00 TOTE £8.50: £2.90, £1.50, £1.90; EX 33.50 Trifecta £125.50 Part won. Pool of £169.60 - 0.60 winning units..
Owner Roberts Green Whittall-Williams Savidge **Bred** Gabriel Bell **Trained** Settrington, N Yorks
■ Stewards' Enquiry : Jamie Kyne one-day ban: careless riding (Jun 8)

FOCUS
A modest handicap but pretty competitive and one or two did not get the best of passages. The form is not totally sound but makes sense at face value.
Hidden Door(IRE) Official explanation: jockey said filly suffered interference in final 2f

2333 GILMORTON (S) STKS — 1m 1f 218y
2:40 (2:40) (Class 6) 3-5-Y-O — **£1,942** (£578; £288; £144) **Stalls** High

Form — RPR

-003 **1** **Rose Of Coma (IRE)**[17] 1848 3-8-2 50 ... AdrianMcCarthy 8 54
(Miss Gay Kelleway) *s.s: hld up: hdwy over 2f out: rdn to ld nr fin* **10/1**

44-0 **2** *shd* **Lady Valentino**[6] 2149 5-8-13 52 ... RussellKennemore(3) 10 55
(B D Leavy) *chsd ldrs: rdn over 2f out: led ins fnl f: edgd lft and hdd nr fin* **16/1**

4303 **3** *¾* **Maddy**[6] 2149 4-8-9 49 ...(p) MatthewDavies(7) 11 53
(George Baker) *hld up: hdwy over 1f out: rdn and edgd rt ins fnl f: r.o* **7/1**

4303 **4** *1 ¼* **Watson's Bay**[21] 1728 4-9-12 65 ... ChrisCatlin 7 63+
(Miss Tor Sturgis) *hld up: hdwy over 1f out: styng on whn n.m.r towards fin* **2/1**[1]

40-0 **5** *1* **Sceilin (IRE)**[136] 107 5-9-2 45 ...(t) SaleemGolam 5 49
(J Mackie) *hld up: hdwy u.p over 1f out: r.o: nt rch ldrs* **12/1**

6656 **6** *shd* **Red Current**[13] 1959 5-8-13 49 ... KevinGhunowa(3) 12 49
(R A Harris) *a.p: chsd ldr 6f out: led over 3f out: rdn and edgd lft fr over 1f out: hdd and no ex ins fnl f* **13/2**[3]

0105 **7** *2 ¼* **Dalrymple (IRE)**[18] 1811 3-8-12 62 ... StephenDonohoe 14 53
(Ian Williams) *prom: rdn over 3f out: wknd ins fnl f* **7/2**[2]

0- **8** *5* **Jeronimo Joe**[168] 7602 3-8-7 0 ... DO'Donohoe 2 38
(A B Haynes) *s.i.s: sn prom: rdn over 4f out: wknd fnl f* **25/1**

50 **9** *3 ½* **Beckenham's Secret**[19] 1784 5-9-7 42 ... KirstyMilczarek 13 32
(A W Carroll) *hld up: hdwy 1/2-way: rdn and wknd over 2f out* **20/1**

-645 **10** *1* **Special Chapter (IRE)**[72] 838 4-8-9 35 ... PNolan(7) 4 25
(A B Haynes) *prom: pushed along 4f out: hung lft and wknd over 2f out* **33/1**

0500 **11** *7* **Glan Lady (IRE)**[34] 1437 3-8-2 45 ...(p) WandersonD'Avila 9 11
(G J Smith) *led: rdn and hdd over 3f out: wknd wl over 1f out* **100/1**

000 **12** *3 ¼* **Tapas Lad (IRE)**[35] 1409 4-9-7 46 ...(b1) TravisBlock 1 10
(G J Smith) *hld up: rdn and wknd over 2f out* **50/1**

2m 8.80s (0.90) **Going Correction** -0.025s/f (Good)
WFA 3 from 4yo+ 14lb **12** Ran SP% **118.6**
Speed ratings (Par 101): **95,94,94,93,92 92,90,86,83,83 77,74**
toteswinger: 1&2 £36.50, 1&3 £6.30, 2&3 £11.90. CSF £148.42 TOTE £9.00: £2.50, £4.40, £2.00; EX 131.90 Trifecta £126.70 Part won. Pool of £171.30 - 0.10 winning units..There was no bid for the winner. Watson's Bay was claimed by Paul Howling for £7000.
Owner Whispering Winds **Bred** Pier House Stud **Trained** Exning, Suffolk
■ Stewards' Enquiry : Matthew Davies caution: careless riding

FOCUS
A poor seller in which two stood out on official ratings, despite carrying penalties, but they failed to reach the places. The time was nearly 2secs slower than the preceding handicap and this is low-end form for the grade.

2334 LEICESTER MERCURY FAMILY FUN DAY FILLIES' H'CAP — 5f 218y
3:15 (3:16) (Class 4) (0-80,80) 4-Y-O+
£6,231 (£1,866; £933; £467; £233; £117) **Stalls** High

Form — RPR

31-4 **1** **Doric Lady**[28] 1572 4-8-11 **73** ... KirstyMilczarek 7 85
(J A R Toller) *hld up: hdwy over 2f out: led ins fnl f: rdn out* **7/1**[3]

-366 **2** *nk* **Mango Music**[9] 2088 6-8-11 **73** ... StephenDonohoe 1 84
(M Quinn) *led: rdn over 1f out: hdd ins fnl f: r.o* **10/1**

311- **3** *3* **Perfect Silence**[224] 6706 4-8-12 **74** ... EddieAhern 6 75+
(C G Cox) *trckd ldrs: rdn over 1f out: no ex ins fnl f* **10/11**[1]

6410 **4** *2 ¾* **Artistic License (IRE)**[8] 2102 4-9-1 **77** ... TonyCulhane 2 70
(M R Channon) *sn pushed along in rr: rdn over 1f out: nvr trbld ldrs* **12/1**

/6-2 **5** *3* **Ocean Transit (IRE)**[16] 1894 4-9-0 **76** ... JamesDoyle 3 59
(R J Price) *chsd ldr: rdn over 2f out: wknd over 1f out* **7/1**[3]

42-0 **6** *3* **Filligree (IRE)**[30] 1510 4-9-4 **80** ... ChrisCatlin 4 53
(Rae Guest) *chsd ldrs: rdn 1/2-way: wknd wl over 1f out* **5/1**[2]

1m 11.53s (-1.47) **Going Correction** -0.175s/f (Firm) **6** Ran SP% **110.8**
Speed ratings (Par 102): **102,101,97,93,89 85**
toteswinger: 1&2 £1.10, 1&3 not won, 2&3 £4.20. CSF £66.30 CT £116.27 TOTE £6.60: £2.90, £3.40; EX 43.70 Trifecta £114.90 Part won. Pool of £155.40 - 0.60 winning units..
Owner Buckingham Thoroughbreds I **Bred** Minster Enterprises Ltd **Trained** Newmarket, Suffolk

FOCUS
A fair and competitive fillies' handicap that produced something of a turn-up. The winner picked up the thread again but the form is ordinary for the grade.

2335 ENDERBY MEDIAN AUCTION MAIDEN STKS — 5f 2y
3:50 (3:51) (Class 5) 2-Y-O — **£3,238** (£963; £481; £240) **Stalls** Low

Form — RPR

2 **1** **Absolute Music (USA)**[16] 1862 2-8-12 0 ... EddieAhern 1 72
(R M H Cowell) *sn led: hdd over 1f out: rallied and edgd rt ins fnl f: r.o to ld nr fin* **4/6**[1]

02 **2** *nk* **Reddy To Star (IRE)**[16] 1891 2-9-3 0 ... ChrisCatlin 7 76
(C G Cox) *chsd wnr tl led over 1f out: sn rdn: hdd nr fin* **9/2**[2]

50 **3** *3* **Ever So Bold**[46] 1195 2-9-3 0 ... KirstyMilczarek 3 65
(W R Muir) *prom: rdn over 1f out: no ex ins fnl f* **40/1**

6 **4** *½* **Prettiest Star (IRE)**[30] 1521 2-8-12 0 ... JamesDoyle 2 58
(K A Ryan) *sn pushed along and prom: rdn over 1f out: styd on same pce* **15/2**[3]

5 **5** *7* **Point To Prove**[25] 1630 2-9-3 0 ... DO'Donohoe 8 38
(Miss Amy Weaver) *chsd ldrs: rdn 1/2-way: wknd over 1f out* **33/1**

6 *1 ¼* **Flaxen Lake** 2-9-0 0 ... RussellKennemore(3) 5 34
(R Hollinshead) *s.s: hld up: hdwy 1/2-way: rdn and wknd over 1f out* **25/1**

0 **7** *4* **Duke Of Rainford**[37] 1358 2-9-3 0 ... StephenDonohoe 4 19
(Ian Williams) *chsd ldrs: rdn 1/2-way: sn wknd* **8/1**

60.30 secs (0.30) **Going Correction** -0.175s/f (Firm) **7** Ran SP% **110.3**
Speed ratings (Par 93): **90,89,84,83,72 70,64**
toteswinger: 1&2 £1.10, 1&3 £9.30, 2&3 £9.30. CSF £3.52 TOTE £1.60: £1.10, £3.50; EX 2.40 Trifecta £9.20 Part won. Pool of £95.38 - 7.60 winning units..
Owner Khalifa Dasmal **Bred** Gilbraltar Group Lp **Trained** Six Mile Bottom, Cambs

FOCUS
An uncompetitive juvenile contest but a good finish between the market leaders.

NOTEBOOK
Absolute Music(USA) ran well on her debut behind a fair sort at Ascot and had clearly come on for the run. She jumped quickly from the rail draw and made the running but looked in trouble when narrowly headed over a furlong out. However, she responded well to pressure to prove just the stronger at the line. She should go on from this and connections may step her up to 6f next time, with the Albany Stakes at Royal Ascot a possible target. (op 4-5 tchd 10-11)
Reddy To Star(IRE) improved on his debut by running a speedy sort close at Warwick and put up another decent effort, just being held having got to the front entering the last furlong. He should have no trouble winning a similar contest. (op 11-4 tchd 5-2)
Ever So Bold had been well beaten in a couple of good races for this grade on his first two outings, but appeared to put up an improved effort on this third start, only fading in the last furlong or so. (op 25-1 tchd 22-1)
Prettiest Star(IRE) got a good tow from the principals in the early stages but could not pick up enough to trouble them at the business end. She was clear of the rest, though. (op 9-1)
Duke Of Rainford was backed late but failed to step up from his debut and was the first beaten. He has clearly been showing ability at home but has something to prove on the track now. (op 14-1)

2336 LEICESTERSHIRE AND RUTLAND LIFE H'CAP — 5f 218y
4:25 (4:26) (Class 5) (0-80,78) 3-Y-O — **£4,857** (£1,445; £722; £360) **Stalls** High

Form — RPR

4-22 **1** **Bobbie Soxer (IRE)**[18] 1814 3-9-1 **75** ... EddieAhern 7 83
(J L Dunlop) *hld up: hdwy to ld over 1f out: r.o wl* **15/8**[1]

3-61 **2** *3 ½* **Apache Ridge (IRE)**[17] 1831 3-8-10 **70** ... StephenDonohoe 4 66
(K A Ryan) *led: rdn and hdd over 1f out: styd on same pce: edgd rt towards fin* **3/1**[2]

2014 **3** *¾* **Riflessione**[11] 2010 3-8-10 **73** ...(b) KevinGhunowa(3) 1 67
(R A Harris) *sn pushed along in rr: rdn and outpcd 2f out: hung rt and r.o ins fnl f: nt trble ldrs* **11/1**

402- **4** *1 ¾* **Diddums**[212] 6987 3-9-4 **78** ... ChrisCatlin 5 66
(J W Hills) *hld up: rdn over 2f out: r.o ins fnl f: n.d* **7/1**

25-6 **5** *2* **Learo Dochais (USA)**[24] 1636 3-9-1 **75** ... MichaelHills 8 57
(M A Jarvis) *chsd ldrs: lost pl 1/2-way: n.d after* **11/2**[3]

1326 **6** *nk* **Raimond Ridge (IRE)**[18] 1814 3-9-1 **75** ... TonyCulhane 9 56
(M R Channon) *hld up: hdwy over 1f out: wknd ins fnl f* **14/1**

-040 **7** *1 ¼* **Angelo Poliziano**[16] 1895 3-8-7 **67** ... DO'Donohoe 2 44
(Mrs A Duffield) *trckd ldrs: hung rt thrght: rdn over 2f out: wknd fnl f* **25/1**

5-30 **8** *3 ¼* **Frank Street**[21] 1744 3-8-12 **72** ... StephenCarson 3 39
(Eve Johnson Houghton) *chsd ldr tl rdn and wknd wl over 1f out* **14/1**

1m 11.44s (-1.56) **Going Correction** -0.175s/f (Firm) **8** Ran SP% **113.2**
Speed ratings (Par 99): **103,98,97,95,92 91,90,85**
toteswinger: 1&2 £3.60, 1&3 £8.20, 2&3 £2.70. CSF £7.31 CT £45.52 TOTE £3.30: £1.10, £1.40, £2.80; EX 12.10 Trifecta £39.50 Part won. Pool of £144.48 - 2.70 winning units..
Owner Windflower Overseas Holdings Inc **Bred** Windflower Overseas Holdings Inc **Trained** Arundel, W Sussex

FOCUS
Another fairly competitive sprint run fractionally faster than the earlier fillies' handicap. The winner confirmed her recent improvement and the form is rated through the third.
Frank Street Official explanation: jockey said gelding became unsettled in stalls and stopped quickly in race

2337 TIGERS APPRENTICE H'CAP — 1m 3f 183y
5:00 (5:00) (Class 6) (0-60,60) 4-Y-O+ — **£2,590** (£770; £385; £192) **Stalls** High

Form — RPR

0332 **1** **Comrade Cotton**[3] 2244 5-8-7 **55** ... RyanPowell(7) 6 54
(J Ryan) *prom: lost pl 8f out: hdwy over 2f out: led over 1f out: styd on wl* **3/1**[2]

3365 **2** *½* **Monaadi (IRE)**[48] 1171 4-8-11 **57** ...(p) DavidKenny(5) 9 56
(R Hollinshead) *led: rdn and hdd over 1f out: styng on same pce whn rdr dropped whip towards fin* **13/2**

0600 **3** *3 ½* **Ben Bacchus (IRE)**[3] 2222 7-8-0 **46** oh1 ... KierenFox(5) 3 39
(P W Hiatt) *sn chsng ldr: rdn and ev ch over 2f out: no ex whn rdr dropped whip ins fnl f* **8/1**

6503 **4** *8* **Desert Hawk**[14] 1938 8-8-5 **49** ...(b) MatthewLawson(3) 7 29
(W M Brisbourne) *s.i.s: sn pushed along in rr: hdwy u.p over 3f out: wkng whn hung rt fr over 1f out* **9/1**

5-50 **5** *shd* **Fistral**[21] 1738 5-8-7 **48** ... JamieKyne 1 28
(P D Niven) *hld up: hdwy over 4f out: rdn and wknd over 1f out* **5/2**[1]

300- **6** *3 ¼* **Soviet Sceptre (IRE)**[225] 6668 8-8-12 **53** ...(tp) SimonPearce 4 28
(Tim Vaughan) *hld up: hdwy over 3f out: rdn and wkng whn rdr dropped whip over 1f out* **4/1**[3]

7 *10* **Iron Hague (IRE)**[8] 5697 8-8-5 **46** oh1 ...(v1) PNolan 10 5
(O Brennan) *chsd ldrs tl rdn and wknd over 2f out* **33/1**

600- **F** **Candy Anchor (FR)**[349] 2908 10-8-2 **46** oh1 ... PaulPickard(3) 8 —
(R E Peacock) *hld up: in rr whn slipped and fell 6f out* **25/1**

2m 35.62s (1.72) **Going Correction** -0.025s/f (Good) **8** Ran SP% **114.8**
Speed ratings (Par 101): **93,92,90,85,84 82,76,—**
toteswinger: 1&2 £7.30, 1&3 £3.40, 2&3 £7.30. CSF £22.93 CT £140.62 TOTE £4.20: £1.40, £1.80, £3.10; EX 19.00 Trifecta £55.50 Part won. Pool of £75.02 - 0.30 winning units..
Owner John Ryan Racing Partnership **Bred** Jeremy Gompertz **Trained** Newmarket, Suffolk
■ A first winner for 22-year-old jockey Ryan Powell.

FOCUS
A weak apprentices' handicap in which three of the field were out of the handicap. It is doubtful the winner had to match his recent form, with the second and third better on sand.

2338 KIBWORTH HARCOURT MEDIAN AUCTION MAIDEN STKS 1m 60y
5:35 (5:43) (Class 5) 3-Y-O £3,238 (£963; £481; £240) Stalls High

Form RPR
1 **Russian Jar (IRE)** 3-9-3 0 MichaelHills 14 81+
(M A Jarvis) *chsd ldr tl led over 1f out: shkn up and r.o wl: eased towards fin* **7/2**[2]
56 2 1 ½ **Some Sunny Day**[13] 1963 3-8-12 0 TravisBlock 13 67+
(H Morrison) *hld up: hdwy over 3f out: r.o to go 2nd ins fnl f: no ch w wnr* **14/1**
0 3 1 ¾ **Young Star Gazer**[21] 1752 3-9-3 0 EddieAhern 9 68
(H R A Cecil) *led and set stdy pce: qcknd over 2f out: rdn and hdd over 1f out: styd on same pce* **10/3**[1]
03 4 2 ¾ **Bomber Brown (IRE)**[115] 343 3-9-3 0 AdrianMcCarthy 10 62+
(P W Chapple-Hyam) *rrd s: bhd: r.o ins fnl f: nvr nr to chal* **7/1**[3]
00- 5 nk **Thief**[215] 6892 3-8-10 0 MJMurphy(7) 12 61+
(L M Cumani) *plld hrd and prom: outpcd whn hung rt 2f out: styd on ins fnl f* **12/1**
40-0 6 7 **Viking Awake (IRE)**[21] 1744 3-9-3 69 (t) StephenDonohoe 7 45
(J W Unett) *chsd ldrs: chal 3f out: sn rdn: wknd wl over 1f out* **25/1**
000- 7 3 ¾ **Igotim**[249] 6062 3-9-0 46 KevinGhunowa(3) 4 36
(J Gallagher) *hld up: plld hrd: hdwy and hmpd over 4f out: rdn: hung lft and wknd over 2f out* **200/1**
-000 8 4 ½ **Risky Lady (IRE)**[7] 2132 3-8-5 43 RyanPowell(7) 5 21
(J Ryan) *plld hrd and prom: rdn: hung rt and wknd over 2f out* **100/1**

1m 47.4s (2.30) **Going Correction** -0.025s/f (Good) 8 Ran SP% 77.5
Speed ratings (Par 99): **87,85,83,81,80 73,69,65**
toteswinger: 1&2 £2.50 1&3 £2.80, 2&3 £2.80. CSF £20.63 TOTE £3.60: £1.10, £1.90, £1.10; EX 24.30 TRIFECTA Not won. Place 6: £322.79, Place 5: £195.12.
Owner J A R Partnership **Bred** Barouche Stud Ireland Ltd **Trained** Newmarket, Suffolk
■ Zouk, Elusive Muse, Jenny's Pride, Princess Soraya and Square Of Gold withdrawn at the stalls; Rule 4, deduction 30p in £.

FOCUS
Those with official ratings in this maiden were modest at best but there were several well-bred, unexposed types from major yards and they dominated the market. There were five withdrawals at the stalls including the favourite Zouk (11/4). A slowly run race which has been rated around the second and third.
Bomber Brown(IRE) Official explanation: jockey said colt missed the break and hung left
Igotim Official explanation: jockey said colt was short of room final bend
T/Plt: £46.10 to a £1 stake. Pool: £41,024.49. 649.47 winning tickets. T/Qpdt: £10.30 to a £1 stake. Pool: £2,734.30. 196.40 winning tickets. CR

1920 REDCAR (L-H)
Monday, May 25

OFFICIAL GOING: Good to firm (9.5)
Wind: Light, half behind Weather: Fine and dry

2339 BUY YOUR TICKETS ON-LINE @ REDCARRACING.CO.UK MAIDEN AUCTION STKS 5f
2:10 (2:11) (Class 5) 2-Y-O £2,729 (£806; £403) Stalls Centre

Form RPR
63 1 **Oondiri (IRE)**[25] 1623 2-8-4 0 JohnEgan 2 69
(T D Easterby) *qckly away: mde all: rdn and edgd lft over 1f out: kpt on wl fnl f* **6/1**
2 1 ½ **Itsthursdayalready** 2-9-0 0 PaulMulrennan 13 74
(J G Given) *chsd ldrs: rdn over 1f out: kpt on ins fnl f* **16/1**
0 3 nk **Regardless**[20] 1764 2-8-1 0 AndreaAtzeni(5) 8 65
(Mrs G S Rees) *chsd wnr: rdn along 2f out: kpt on u.p ins fnl f* **12/1**
2 4 hd **Social Grace**[11] 2000 2-8-5 0 RoystonFfrench 3 63
(D H Brown) *prom: effrt to chse wnr 2f out: sn rdn and hung lft over 1f out: drvn and one pce ins fnl f* **7/2**[2]
5 1 ¾ **Tsar Bomba (USA)** 2-8-9 0 DeanHeslop(5) 1 66+
(T D Barron) *dwlt and towards rr: rdn and styd on wl fr over 1f out: nrst fin* **16/1**
6 nse **Melody In The Mist (FR)** 2-8-6 0 LiamJones 6 57
(T D Barron) *in tch: hdwy to chse ldrs 2f out: rdn and hung lft over 1f out: kpt on same pce* **14/1**
233 7 2 ½ **Gower Sophia**[9] 2069 2-8-5 0 TWilliams 10 47
(M Brittain) *chsd ldrs: rdn 2f out: sn wknd* **10/3**[1]
8 1 **Sands Of Dee (USA)** 2-8-13 0 PaulHanagan 7 52
(R A Fahey) *dwlt and wnt lft s: bhd tl sme late hdwy* **4/1**[3]
9 1 **Miami Gator (IRE)** 2-8-7 0 MartinLane(5) 5 47
(K R Burke) *a towards rr* **20/1**
00 10 1 **Countrywide Ice (IRE)**[7] 2128 2-8-10 0 PhillipMakin 14 42
(K A Ryan) *wnt bdly rt s: sn chsng ldrs on outer: rdn along over 2f out and sn wknd* **50/1**
11 2 ¼ **Havelock Flyer** 2-8-10 0 (t) TedDurcan 11 33
(C Grant) *a in rr* **20/1**
0 12 6 **Another Sold**[20] 1764 2-7-11 0 BillyCray(7) 12 6
(A Berry) *a in rr* **100/1**

58.40 secs (-0.20) **Going Correction** -0.15s/f (Firm) 12 Ran SP% 118.2
Speed ratings (Par 93): **95,92,92,91,89 88,84,83,81,80 76,66**
toteswinger: 1&2 £14.50, 1&3 £17.20, 2&3 £32.80. CSF £93.00 TOTE £5.30: £2.10, £5.00, £3.70; EX 126.50.
Owner C H Stevens **Bred** Newlands House Stud **Trained** Great Habton, N Yorks

FOCUS
An ordinary juvenile maiden.

NOTEBOOK
Oondiri(IRE) improved on her two previous efforts with a straightforward success. Making full use of her light weight, she showed loads of early speed and ran on strongly in the closing stages. This progressive filly could be one for nurseries later in the season. (op 13-2 tchd 7-1)
Itsthursdayalready, an 18,000gns half-brother to 7f juvenile winner Starry Sky, out of a smart 1m2f scorer, made a pleasing debut under joint-top weight. He should be well up to winning a similar race. (op 14-1 tchd 12-1)
Regardless showed good speed and this was a big improvement on the form she showed on her debut at Catterick. (tchd 11-1)
Social Grace didn't run up to the form she showed when second in a weak Newmarket maiden on her debut and was disappointing. She was inclined to edge left under pressure and it's possible this ground was quicker than ideal. (op 4-1)
Tsar Bomba(USA), a $12,000 purchase, fared best of those out the back early on. He's open to considerable improvement. (op 14-1)
Melody In The Mist(FR) hinted at ability. (op 10-1)
Gower Sophia ran below the form she showed on her three previous starts. (op 3-1 tchd 4-1)
Sands Of Dee(USA) ran extremely green and was given reminders soon after the start. Presumably he's thought capable of better. (op 13-2 tchd 7-1)

2340 MARKET CROSS JEWELLERS MAIDEN H'CAP 1m 6f 19y
2:45 (2:46) (Class 6) (0-65,64) 3-Y-O £2,047 (£604; £302) Stalls Low

Form RPR
6-43 1 **Bollin Judith**[21] 1724 3-8-12 55 DavidAllan 1 60+
(T D Easterby) *hld up: pushed along and hdwy over 3f out: rdn and n.m.r 2f out: swtchd lft and squeezed through to chal ent fnl f: sn drvn: led last 100yds and kpt on wl* **9/4**[1]
0543 2 1 **Screaming Brave**[40] 1282 3-8-10 53 TedDurcan 16 57
(M R Channon) *stdd and swtchd lft s: hld up in rr: gd hdwy 3f out: rdn to ld wl over 1f out: sn drvn and hung rt ent fnl f: hdd and nt qckn last 100yds* **10/1**
0060 3 ½ **Saffron's Son (IRE)**[13] 1954 3-8-7 50 (v[1]) PJMcDonald 2 53
(P T Midgley) *hld up in rr: hdwy on inner 3f out: n.m.r and swtchd rt over 2f out: rdn to chal and ev ch whn n.m.r ent fnl f: sn drvn and no ex last 100yds* **50/1**
3332 4 ½ **Tae Kwon Do (USA)**[13] 1954 3-9-0 57 RoystonFfrench 9 59
(Miss J A Camacho) *hld up towards rr: stdy hdwy on inner 4f out: swtchd wd and effrt wl over 2f out: sn rdn and ev ch over 1f out tl drvn and one pce last 100yds* **8/1**[3]
0-02 5 ½ **Pure Crystal**[21] 1724 3-8-12 55 (b) JerryO'Dwyer 5 57
(M G Quinlan) *trckd ldrs: hdwy 4f out: rdn along wl over 2f out: drvn and ch over 1f out: kpt on same pce u.p ins fnl f* **10/1**
4626 6 3 ¼ **Gosforth Park**[10] 2060 3-9-0 64 JohnCavanagh(7) 14 61+
(M Brittain) *hld up in rr: stdy hdwy on outer to take clsr order 1/2-way: chsd ldr 5f out: rdn to ld briefly 3f out: sn hdd and drvn: wknd over 1f out* **5/1**[2]
-024 7 hd **Addison De Witt**[13] 1954 3-8-13 56 PaulHanagan 8 53
(Micky Hammond) *midfield: hdwy 5f out and sn chsng ldrs: rdn to ld wl over 2f out: sn drvn and hdd over 1f out: wknd appr fnl f* **16/1**
5-45 8 nk **Susurrayshaan**[13] 1953 3-8-7 50 (p) DaleGibson 15 46
(Mrs G S Rees) *hld up: hdwy towards outer over 3f out: sn rdn to chse ldrs over 2f out: drvn: edgd lft and wknd over 1f out* **33/1**
05-2 9 5 **New Tricks**[17] 1829 3-9-2 59 (p) PaulMulrennan 11 48+
(I Semple) *trckd ldng pair: pushed along over 5f out: rdn along 4f out: drvn wl over 2f out and grad wknd* **8/1**[3]
00-0 10 2 ½ **Top Tinker**[47] 1183 3-8-12 55 (b[1]) LiamJones 6 41
(M H Tompkins) *hld up: a towards rr* **20/1**
00-0 11 11 **Hill Cross (IRE)**[13] 1954 3-8-8 51 ShaneKelly 4 21
(K G Reveley) *cl up: led 4f out: sn rdn and hdd 3f out: sn wknd* **40/1**
06-0 12 12 **Imperial Angel (IRE)**[13] 1954 3-8-9 52 (b[1]) DanielTudhope 7 6
(D Carroll) *t.k.h: sn led: rdn along and hdd 4f out: sn wknd* **40/1**
500 13 107 **Independent James (IRE)**[42] 1255 3-8-7 50 J-PGuillambert 13 —
(S C Williams) *chsd ldrs: rdn along and wknd over 5f out: sn bhd and t.o fnl 2f* **20/1**
0-32 14 10 **Royal Society**[68] 865 3-9-3 60 PhillipMakin 10 —
(A G Foster) *hld up in rr: hdwy on outer and in tch over 6f out: rdn along over 4f out: wknd qckly and t.o fnl 2f* **8/1**[3]

3m 4.48s (-0.22) **Going Correction** -0.15s/f (Firm) 14 Ran SP% 124.1
Speed ratings (Par 97): **94,93,93,92,92 90,90,90,87,86 79,73,—,—**
toteswinger: 1&2 £8.70, 1&3 £44.20, 2&3 £73.10. CSF £24.74 CT £927.45 TOTE £3.90: £1.80, £3.20, £20.30; EX 23.70.
Owner Sir Neil Westbrook **Bred** Sir Neil & Exors Of Late Lady Westbrook **Trained** Great Habton, N Yorks
■ Stewards' Enquiry : Royston Ffrench one-day ban: used whip with excessive frequency (Jun 8)
Ted Durcan one-day ban: careless riding (Jun 8); three-day ban: used whip with excessive frequency (Jun 9-11)

FOCUS
A moderate maiden handicap.
Independent James(IRE) Official explanation: jockey said gelding hung badly right and lost its action in home straight
Royal Society Official explanation: jockey said gelding lost its action

2341 TOTESWINGER H'CAP 1m 2f
3:20 (3:20) (Class 4) (0-85,84) 3-Y-O £6,476 (£1,927; £963; £481) Stalls Low

Form RPR
-505 1 **Geneva Geyser (GER)**[13] 1971 3-8-9 72 MickyFenton 1 82
(J M P Eustace) *reminders s and sn led: sn clr and set str pce: pushed along over 3f out: rdn over 1f out and styd on strly ins fnl f* **14/1**
11 2 5 **Stagecoach Jade (IRE)**[39] 1315 3-8-13 76 RoystonFfrench 5 76
(M Johnston) *chsd wnr: tk clsr order over 3f out: rdn over 2f out: drvn over 1f: sn no imp* **4/1**[3]
300- 3 nk **Omokoroa (IRE)**[222] 6731 3-8-3 66 LiamJones 6 65+
(M H Tompkins) *hld up: hdwy on outer over 3f out: rdn over 2f out: drvn over 1f out: kpt on ins fnl f* **8/1**
3-11 4 1 ¼ **Tiger Reigns**[21] 1740 3-9-0 77 PhillipMakin 7 74
(M Dods) *trckd ldng pair: hdwy over 3f out: rdn over 2f out: drvn over 1f out and sn btn* **7/2**[2]
40-0 5 1 ½ **Come And Go (UAE)**[12] 1987 3-9-7 84 PJMcDonald 8 78
(G A Swinbank) *hld up in rr: hdwy on inner 3f out: rdn to chse ldrs over 2f out: sn drvn and one pce appr fnl f* **10/1**
6-10 6 1 ½ **Puzzlemaster**[12] 1992 3-9-3 80 JohnEgan 2 71
(M Botti) *hld up in tch: hdwy over 3f out: rdn to chse ldng pair over 2f out: sn drvn and btn over 1f out: eased ins fnl f* **2/1**[1]
01- 7 13 **Wee Giant (USA)**[203] 7165 3-9-1 78 TedDurcan 3 43
(K A Ryan) *hld up in rr: hdwy 4f out: pushed along 3f out: sn rdn and btn 2f out* **15/2**

2m 5.09s (-2.01) **Going Correction** -0.15s/f (Firm) 7 Ran SP% 114.2
Speed ratings (Par 101): **102,98,97,96,95 94,83**
toteswinger: 1&2 not won, 1&3 £6.40, 2&3 not won. CSF £68.40 CT £486.26 TOTE £16.60: £4.00, £3.20; EX 74.90.
Owner J C Smith **Bred** Graf And Grafin Von Stauffenberg **Trained** Newmarket, Suffolk

FOCUS
This looked a decent, competitive 3yo handicap beforehand, but rather surprisingly nothing could get anywhere near the front-running Geneva Geyser.
Puzzlemaster Official explanation: jockey said colt was unsuited by the good to firm ground

2342 TOTESUPER7 ZETLAND GOLD CUP (HERITAGE H'CAP) 1m 2f
3:55 (3:56) (Class 2) (0-105,102) 3-Y-O+£32,380 (£9,635; £4,815; £2,405) Stalls Low

Form RPR
33-2 1 **Kingdom Of Fife**[18] 1798 4-9-0 92 (v) RyanMoore 7 104
(Sir Michael Stoute) *mde most: shkn up and qcknd 3f out: rdn clr over 1f out: styd on strly* **9/4**[1]

51-0 **2** 2 1/2 **Nanton (USA)**[58] 995 7-9-0 **92**.................................. DanielTudhope 11 99+
(J S Goldie) *hld up in rr: hdwy 3f out: swtchd lft and rdn wl over 1f out: styd on strly ent fnl f: nt rch wnr* **12/1**

-164 **3** 1 **Re Barolo (IRE)**[58] 1004 6-9-5 **102**.............................. AndreaAtzeni(5) 12 107
(M Botti) *midfield: hdwy 4f out: rdn to chse ldrs over 2f out: drvn wl over 1f out and kpt on* **16/1**

-500 **4** nk **Military Power**[73] 4-9-4 **96**.. TedDurcan 5 100
(Saeed Bin Suroor) *trckd ldng pair on inner: hdwy to chse wnr 3f out: rdn over 2f out: drvn wl over 1f out and one pce* **13/2**[3]

-321 **5** nse **Mystery Star (IRE)**[23] 1666 4-8-8 **91**.............................. MartinLane(5) 3 95+
(M H Tompkins) *hld up in midfield: hdwy 3f out: rdn along over 2f out: sn drvn and kpt on same pce appr fnl f* **14/1**

3-15 **6** nk **Unbreak My Heart (IRE)**[33] 1460 4-9-1 **93**....................... PaulHanagan 1 97
(R A Fahey) *hld up: hdwy over 2f out and sn rdn: drvn on inner and styd on appr fnl f: nrst fin* **8/1**

0-66 **7** 1 1/4 **King Charles**[10] 2055 5-8-9 **92**...................... Louis-PhilippeBeuzelin(5) 8 93
(E A L Dunlop) *hld up: hdwy 3f out: in tch and rdn 2f out: drvn appr fnl f and kpt on same pce* **6/1**[2]

05-0 **8** 3/4 **Heron Bay**[23] 1673 5-9-6 **98**... GeorgeBaker 9 98+
(C F Wall) *hld up in rr: hdwy 3f out: rdn over 2f out: sn drvn and no imp* **40/1**

-252 **9** 1 3/4 **Checklow (USA)**[12] 1986 4-9-3 **95**.................................... ShaneKelly 13 91
(J Noseda) *stdd s: hld up and a towards rr* **11/1**

60-4 **10** 1/2 **Snoqualmie Boy**[17] 1850 6-8-10 **88**.................................... JohnEgan 15 83
(T P Tate) *hld up towards rr: hdwy on outer over 4f out: rdn to chse ldrs 3f out: drvn: and edgd lft over 2f out: sn wknd* **16/1**

1346 **11** 1/2 **Flipando (IRE)**[11] 2015 8-9-5 **97**.. PhillipMakin 6 91
(T D Barron) *t.k.h: chsd ldrs: rdn along over 3f out: sn wknd* **8/1**

00-0 **12** 1 1/2 **Humungous (IRE)**[18] 1798 6-9-4 **96**........................(p) EdwardCreighton 4 87
(C R Egerton) *hld up: a towards rr* **66/1**

60-3 **13** 4 **Kay Gee Be (IRE)**[23] 1673 5-8-12 **90**............................. J-PGuillambert 2 73
(W Jarvis) *in tch on inner: effrt over 3f out: sn rdn along and wknd over 2f out* **16/1**

6610 **14** 5 **Flawed Genius**[17] 1821 4-8-12 **90**..............................(t) PaulMulrennan 14 63
(K A Ryan) *t.k.h: chsd ldrs on outer: rdn along 4f out: sn wknd* **33/1**

00-1 **15** 3 3/4 **Cheshire Prince**[18] 1798 5-8-13 **91**................................... LiamJones 10 57
(W M Brisbourne) *chsd wnr: rdn along over 3f out and sn wknd* **33/1**

2m 3.30s (-3.80) **Going Correction** -0.15s/f (Firm) **15** Ran SP% **130.8**
Speed ratings (Par 109): **109,107,106,105,105 105,104,104,102,102 101,100,97,93,90**
toteswinger: 1&2 £55.80, 1&3 £61.30, 2&3 £61.30. CSF £33.70 CT £387.05 TOTE £2.90: £2.00, £2.70, £5.30; EX 60.10.
Owner The Queen **Bred** The Queen **Trained** Newmarket, Suffolk

FOCUS
This looked a good, competitive renewal of this valuable handicap, but it was all rather straightforward for the winner.

NOTEBOOK
Kingdom Of Fife was allowed a surprisingly easy lead. He had got going too late when runner-up behind Cheshire Prince in a first-time visor at Chester on his previous start, but the change in tactics ensured that wouldn't be repeated and he readily defied a 4lb higher mark. For all that plenty went his way, the time was good and he won this in the style of a smart gelding. The Wolferton Handicap, a Listed race over this trip at Royal Ascot, could be a suitable target. (op 2-1)
Nanton(USA), back up in trip, stayed on from a long way back to grab second and ran about as well as could have been expected considering the winner had the run of things. He's evidently still improving. (tchd 11-1)
Re Barolo(IRE), back on turf, handled the ground well and had every chance. It's not unreasonable to assume he might do better again on an easier surface. (op 28-1)
Military Power, a winner on dirt in Dubai earlier in the year, didn't see his race out on his debut for Godolphin after over two months off. (op 9-1)
Mystery Star(IRE), raised 6lb for winning a Goodwood handicap on his previous start, was produced with every chance and ran with credit. (op 16-1)
Unbreak My Heart(IRE) managed to win on quick ground at Pontefract earlier in the season, but he looks best suited by some give underfoot. (op 12-1)
King Charles continues below his best. (op 13-2 tchd 7-1)
Heron Bay should do better when stepped up in trip. (tchd 33-1)
Checklow(USA) is in danger of becoming disappointing. (tchd 9-1)
Snoqualmie Boy didn't build on the form he showed when fourth at Ripon on his debut for this yard. (op 20-1)

2343 THE COMMITMENTS PERFORMING HERE ON 29TH AUGUST MEDIAN AUCTION MAIDEN STKS 6f
4:30 (4:32) (Class 5) 3-Y-O **£2,590** (£770; £385; £192) **Stalls** Centre

Form RPR
00 **1** **Go Alone (IRE)**[8] 2105 3-9-3 0.. PJMcDonald 2 72+
(G A Swinbank) *hld up in tch: smooth hdwy to trck ldrs 1/2-way: chal on bit wl over 1f out: shkn up to ld jst ins fnl f: sn clr* **12/1**

60-2 **2** 3 1/4 **Who's Shirl**[14] 1922 3-8-12 55.. TedDurcan 11 57
(C W Fairhurst) *hld up towards rr: gd hdwy on wd outside over 2f out: rdn to ld over 1f out: hdd jst ins fnl f and one pce* **5/1**[3]

5-00 **3** 4 **Lily Jicaro (IRE)**[7] 2141 3-8-7 60.............................. DeanHeslop(5) 10 44
(Mrs L Williamson) *towards rr: hdwy over 2f out: sn rdn and kpt on ins fnl f* **14/1**

4 1/2 **Jill Le Brocq** 3-8-12 0.. PhillipMakin 7 43
(M Dods) *trckd ldrs: effrt over 2f out: sn rdn and hung bdly lft over 1f out: no imp after* **9/1**

000- **5** 1 3/4 **Dance Society**[244] 6187 3-9-3 52..................................(b[1]) DavidAllan 5 42
(T D Easterby) *led: rdn along 2f out: hdd over 1f out and sn wknd* **16/1**

2-36 **6** hd **Abu Derby (IRE)**[132] 140 3-9-3 70.............................. PaulMulrennan 3 41
(J G Given) *cl up: rdn along over 2f out: ev ch tl drvn over 1f out and sn wknd* **2/1**[1]

50 **7** 1 1/4 **Monsieur Harvey**[9] 2070 3-9-3 0...................................... GregFairley 9 37
(B Smart) *chsd ldrs: rdn along 1/2-way: sn wknd* **17/2**

8 2 1/2 **Cipher** 3-9-3 0... RoystonFfrench 8 29
(M Johnston) *s.i.s: hdwy and in tch 1/2-way: rdn to chse ldrs over 2f out: sn wknd* **10/3**[2]

000 **9** 6 **April Lady (IRE)**[113] 364 3-8-5 40.................................. BillyCray(7) 4 5
(A Berry) *prom to 1/2-way: sn lost pl and bhd* **80/1**

1m 12.25s (0.45) **Going Correction** -0.15s/f (Firm) **9** Ran SP% **115.1**
Speed ratings (Par 99): **91,86,81,80,78 78,76,73,65**
toteswinger: 1&2 £10.30, 1&3 not won, 2&3 £10.30. CSF £70.63 TOTE £17.40: £3.50, £1.60, £3.20; EX 117.00.
Owner B Valentine **Bred** Moygaddy Stud **Trained** Melsonby, N Yorks

FOCUS
A weak 3yo sprint maiden.

2344 TOTEEXACTA H'CAP 1m 6f 19y
5:05 (5:05) (Class 6) (0-65,61) 4-Y-0+ **£1,942** (£578; £288; £144) **Stalls** Low

Form RPR
/005 **1** **Zefooha (FR)**[24] 1648 5-9-1 **55**.................................... RoystonFfrench 10 64
(T D Walford) *chsd ldr: effrt 3f out: rdn to chal 2f out: drvn and styd on gamely to ld wl ins fnl f* **7/1**

-541 **2** 1 1/4 **Monte Pattino (USA)**[6] 2159 5-9-0 **54**...........................(vt) DavidAllan 1 61
(C J Teague) *reminders s and sn led: rdn along 3f out: drvn wl over 1f out: hdd and no ex wl ins fnl f* **4/1**[1]

5-06 **3** 2 **Blue Jet (USA)**[20] 1765 5-8-5 **45**.. JohnEgan 8 49
(R M Whitaker) *trckd ldrs: hdwy 3f out: sn rdn and sltly outpcd: styd on u.p appr fnl f* **6/1**

32-2 **4** 2 **Master Nimbus**[6] 2159 9-9-6 **60**................................. PaulMulrennan 12 61
(J J Quinn) *trckd ldrs: hdwy over 3f out: rdn to chse ldng pair over 2f out: sn edgd lft and drvn: kpt on same pce* **9/2**[2]

0-06 **5** nse **Cripsey Brook**[9] 2068 11-9-4 **58**....................................... PhillipMakin 3 59+
(K G Reveley) *hld up towards rr: hdwy on outer 3f out: rdn along 2f out: styd on u.p ins fnl f: nrst fin* **11/1**

0/0- **6** shd **Terenzium (IRE)**[32] 4501 7-8-6 **46**..............................(p) PaulHanagan 7 47
(Micky Hammond) *midfield: effrt and rdn 3f out: styd on u.p appr fnl f: n.d* **14/1**

4356 **7** nk **Miss Keck**[24] 1648 5-9-5 **59**.. PJMcDonald 11 60
(G A Swinbank) *midfield: effrt and sme hdwy over 3f out: sn rdn and one pce fnl 2f* **11/2**[3]

00/6 **8** 1 **Celtic Carisma**[10] 2044 7-8-8 **48**...................................... PaulQuinn 13 47
(K G Reveley) *hld up in rr: hdwy 3f out: rdn over 2f out and sn no imp* **10/1**

500- **9** nk **Rocknest Island (IRE)**[149] 7042 6-8-0 **45**................(p) AndreaAtzeni(5) 5 44
(P D Niven) *chsd ldrs: rdn along 3f out: sn drvn and grad wknd* **14/1**

0050 **10** 1 1/4 **Jonquille (IRE)**[19] 1786 4-8-5 **45**..............................(b) GregFairley 15 42
(T J Pitt) *a towards rr* **28/1**

4 **11** 4 **Ciara Eile (IRE)**[9] 2068 9-8-2 **49**.................................... NeilFarley(7) 16 40
(D Carroll) *a in rr* **16/1**

44-0 **12** 14 **Hunting Haze**[20] 1767 6-8-3 **50** ow5.......................... JohnCavanagh(7) 2 22
(A Crook) *in tch: rdn along over 4f out: sn wknd* **50/1**

000/ **13** 33 **Zeydnaa (IRE)**[149] 1556 9-8-5 **45**.................................. DaleGibson 14 —
(C R Wilson) *a towards rr: bhd fnl 3f* **66/1**

3m 6.49s (1.79) **Going Correction** -0.15s/f (Firm) **13** Ran SP% **123.9**
Speed ratings (Par 101): **88,87,86,85,84 84,84,84,84,83 81,73,—**
toteswinger: 1&2 not won, 1&3 not won, 2&3 £10.80. CSF £36.12 CT £185.58 TOTE £9.80: £4.20, £2.30, £1.80; EX 80.30 Place 6: £1315.58, Place 5: £228.67.
Owner Anthony Preston **Bred** Darley Stud Management Co Ltd **Trained** Sheriff Hutton, N Yorks

FOCUS
The pace seemed modest and the winning time was 2.01 seconds slower than the earlier maiden handicap for 3yos. Unsurprisingly it paid to race handy.
Zeydnaa(IRE) Official explanation: jockey said gelding had a breathing problem
T/Jkpt: Not won. T/Plt: £662.50 to a £1 stake. Pool: £5,379.04. 57.71 winning tickets. T/Qpdt: £82.50 to a £1 stake. Pool: £3,190.70. 28.60 winning tickets. JR

2345 - 2347a (Foreign Racing) - See Raceform Interactive

2317 CHEPSTOW (L-H)
Tuesday, May 26

OFFICIAL GOING: Good to firm
Wind: Moderate across Weather: Sunny periods

2348 FREEBETS.CO.UK CHAMPIONS LEAGUE FINAL FREE BETS MAIDEN AUCTION STKS 5f 16y
2:20 (2:20) (Class 5) 2-Y-O **£2,719** (£809; £404; £202) **Stalls** High

Form RPR
322 **1** **Avonvalley**[15] 1933 2-8-5 0.. EddieAhern 1 71+
(M S Saunders) *mde all: pushed out fnl f* **4/7**[1]

2 1 **Silver Grey (IRE)** 2-8-5 0... RobertHavlin 4 67+
(R Ingram) *s.i.s: outpcd in rr: gd late hdwy: tk 2nd towards fin: nt trble wnr* **33/1**

60 **3** 1 **French Connexion (IRE)**[28] 1577 2-8-4 0......................... LukeMorris 6 61
(J S Moore) *chsd ldrs: outpcd over 3f out: rdn over 1f out: r.o wl u.p on stands' rail ins fnl f: tk 3rd cl home* **40/1**

56 **4** 1/2 **Cane Cat (IRE)**[20] 1782 2-8-3 0.................................. DavidProbert(3) 3 61
(A W Carroll) *chsd wnr 3f: rdn wl over 1f out: edgd lft ent fnl f: one pce* **33/1**

3 **5** 3/4 **Safari Special**[26] 1616 2-8-10 0.. JimCrowley 8 62
(P Winkworth) *s.i.s: hdwy to chse wnr 3f out: rdn over 1f out: one pce ins fnl f* **5/2**[2]

6 1 1/4 **Saxby (IRE)** 2-8-13 0... SamHitchcott 2 61
(M R Channon) *prom: rdn over 2f out: fdd fnl f* **11/1**[3]

59.35 secs (0.05) **Going Correction** -0.125s/f (Firm) **6** Ran SP% **108.9**
Speed ratings (Par 93): **94,92,90,90,88 86**
toteswinger: 1&2 £9.00, 1&3 £6.80, 2&3 £18.40. CSF £23.80 TOTE £1.50: £1.02, £11.80; EX 23.30.
Owner Chris Scott **Bred** Ercan Dogan **Trained** Green Ore, Somerset
■ Stewards' Enquiry : Eddie Ahern one-day ban: careless riding (Jun 11)

FOCUS
Very little overnight rain and a stiffish breeze meant ground conditions had dried out through the morning, and the official going description was changed to good to firm.

NOTEBOOK
Avonvalley had shown more than enough in three previous outings to suggest a race like this was a formality and, very well backed to get off the mark, she got the job done with the minimum of fuss and should now go on to better things. Her wide draw proved immaterial as she made good use of her experience to ping out and soon get across to the rail and, always travelling strongly, she only had to be pushed out to score. (op 5-6)
Silver Grey(IRE) ◆ shaped with real promise on her first racecourse start, and is probably the one to take from the race given she looks sure to come on a bundle for this. Green and detached at half way, she looked odds-on to finish stone last approaching the two pole but she was nursed into contention and she finished best of all through the pack to close in on the winner. (op 25-1)
French Connexion(IRE), who was a long way behind Avonvalley at Bath on her second start, shaped better here, finishing quite nicely and shaping as though there was more to come upped in trip now qualified for a mark (her dam won over a mile as a 3yo). (op 50-1)
Cane Cat(IRE) threatened briefly but was soon on the retreat and has shown only minor promise so far. (tchd 25-1)

Safari Special was the biggest disappointment of the race having shaped so well at Folkestone on his debut, a race that has already thrown up two subsequent winners from three runners. He compromised his chance by breaking slowly from his rail draw and, although he bustled his way up the rail to track the pace by halfway, he was soon being ridden and he dropped away in the final furlong. It is too early to write him off. (op 2-1)

2349 FREEBETS.CO.UK MAN UTD V BARCELONA FREE BETS CLAIMING STKS 5f 16y

2:50 (2:52) (Class 6) 3-Y-0+ **£1,942** (£578; £288; £144) **Stalls** High

Form RPR

0-32 **1** **Mythical Blue (IRE)**[13] 1982 3-8-7 65 ChrisCatlin 2 61
(J M Bradley) *mde all: hrd rdn fnl f: all out* **7/2**[1]

3030 **2** *hd* **Green Lagonda (AUS)**[8] 2137 7-8-13 55 MickyFenton 14 61
(Stef Liddiard) *hld up in tch on stands' rail: chsd wnr wl over 1f out: rdn fnl f: r.o* **14/1**

30-0 **3** *½* **Dr Wintringham (IRE)**[8] 2137 3-8-0 74 ow2 LukeMorris 15 51
(J S Moore) *mid-div: rdn wl over 1f out: hdwy fnl f: tk 3rd cl home* **18/1**

0022 **4** *1 ¼* **Caribbean Coral**[8] 2137 10-9-3 63 GeorgeBaker 1 59
(A B Haynes) *hld up and bhd: hdwy on outside 2f out: rdn 1f out: nt qckn towards fin* **9/2**[2]

2024 **5** *shd* **Joss Stick**[20] 1787 4-8-11 57 (p) LPKeniry 11 52+
(R A Harris) *hld up in mid-div: rdn over 2f out: hdwy 1f out: n.m.r ins fnl f: kpt on* **14/1**

0-66 **6** *nse* **Rockfield Lodge (IRE)**[20] 1784 4-9-0 64 (b) KevinGhunowa(3) 7 58
(R A Harris) *wnt lft and bmpd s: sn prom: rdn over 1f out: one pce ins fnl f* **9/1**

00-5 **7** *¾* **Diane's Choice**[8] 2124 6-8-13 68 (p) DavidProbert(3) 17 54
(Miss Gay Kelleway) *reluctant to go bhd stalls: stmbld sltly s: hld up and bhd on stands' rail: rdn 2f out: late hdwy: nrst fin* **9/1**

00-0 **8** *shd* **Triumphant Welcome**[31] 1528 4-9-0 57 FergusSweeney 16 52+
(H J Evans) *t.k.h early: sn bhd: sme hdwy whn nt clr run and swtchd lft ins fnl f: n.d* **25/1**

0634 **9** *¾* **Fizzlephut (IRE)**[14] 1970 7-8-13 55 (p) WandersonD'Avila 10 48
(Miss J R Tooth) *chsd wnr: rdn over 2f out: wknd ins fnl f* **14/1**

-005 **10** *nk* **Creshendo**[13] 1982 3-8-7 65 ow3 (v[1]) JackMitchell(3) 13 49
(R M Beckett) *prom: rdn over 2f out: wknd 1f out* **13/2**[3]

060- **11** *½* **Walragnek**[154] 7774 5-9-7 47 CatherineGannon 5 54
(J G M O'Shea) *bmpd s: a towards rr* **100/1**

512- **12** *1* **Like For Like (IRE)**[276] 5287 3-7-13 61 ow1 FrankieMcDonald 3 33
(R J Hodges) *prom tl wknd 2f out* **9/1**

4-00 **13** *2* **Our Acquaintance**[29] 1564 4-8-11 49 (b) DO'Donohoe 6 44
(W R Muir) *s.i.s and hmpd s: in rr: nt clr run jst over 1f out: eased ins fnl f* **25/1**

59.13 secs (-0.17) **Going Correction** -0.125s/f (Firm)
WFA 3 from 4yo+ 8lb **13** Ran SP% **117.7**
Speed ratings (Par 101): **96,95,94,92,92 92,91,91,90,89 88,87,84**
toteswinger: 1&2 £18.20, 1&3 £33.00, 2&3 £54.40 CSF £52.59 TOTE £3.90: £2.40, £4.30, £5.20; EX 63.10.
Owner Clifton Hunt **Bred** John O'Dowd **Trained** Sedbury, Gloucs
■ Stewards' Enquiry : Chris Catlin one-day ban: used whip with excessive frequency (Jun 9)

FOCUS
Most of these had something to prove on one count or another and not really form to be dwelling on for too long.
Triumphant Welcome Official explanation: jockey said gelding hung left-handed
Our Acquaintance Official explanation: jockey said gelding was denied a clear run

2350 FREEBETS.CO.UK EUROPEAN FOOTBALL FREE BETS H'CAP 1m 4f 23y

3:20 (3:23) (Class 6) (0-60,60) 3-Y-0 **£2,266** (£674; £337; £168) **Stalls** Low

Form RPR

-040 **1** **Taste The Wine (IRE)**[8] 2131 3-9-0 56 LukeMorris 16 64
(J S Moore) *s.i.s: sn hld up in tch: rdn 2f out: led ins fnl f: r.o wl* **12/1**

00-4 **2** *2 ¼* **Tinkerbelle (IRE)**[48] 1183 3-8-11 53 EddieAhern 17 56
(J L Dunlop) *hld up in tch: led on bit over 2f out: rdn over 1f out: hdd ins fnl f: nt qckn* **6/1**[1]

3204 **3** *½* **Strikemaster (IRE)**[18] 1842 3-8-13 55 JamesDoyle 7 58+
(J W Hills) *hld up towards rr: rdn and hdwy 2f out: hung lft over 1f out: styd on wl to take 3rd cl home* **7/1**[2]

00-5 **4** *½* **Googoobarabajagal (IRE)**[23] 1708 3-8-10 52 FergusSweeney 11 54
(W S Kittow) *hld up towards rr: hdwy 3f out: rdn 2f out: edgd lft 1f out: one pce* **16/1**

03-3 **5** *1* **Peintre D'Argent (IRE)**[104] 506 3-9-1 60 DavidProbert(3) 9 60
(N J Vaughan) *hld up in mid-div: hdwy 3f out: rdn and ev ch over 1f out: no ex ins fnl f* **10/1**

50-5 **6** *2 ¾* **Rebel Swing**[29] 1570 3-9-4 60 DO'Donohoe 15 56
(W R Muir) *a.p: ev ch over 2f out: wknd over 1f out* **8/1**[3]

000- **7** *4 ½* **Lambourn Genie (UAE)**[202] 7191 3-8-9 56 RossAtkinson(5) 4 45+
(Tom Dascombe) *hld up and bhd: hdwy 4f out: rdn over 2f out: wknd wl over 1f out* **8/1**[3]

0026 **8** *hd* **Rebel Prince (IRE)**[14] 1954 3-8-11 53 RobertWinston 2 41+
(M G Quinlan) *dwlt: sn hld up in mid-div: hdwy whn nt clr run over 3f out: wknd over 1f out* **10/1**

0-20 **9** *¾* **Mr Prolific**[28] 1580 3-8-10 55 PatrickHills(3) 5 42
(B W Hills) *hld up in tch: rdn 2f out: wknd over 1f out* **12/1**

6505 **10** *¾* **Key Of Fortune (IRE)**[22] 1724 3-8-13 55 JimCrowley 3 41
(Jennie Candlish) *chsd ldr: led over 3f out: rdn and hdd over 2f out: wknd over 1f out* **18/1**

0-10 **11** *2 ¼* **Hollow Green (IRE)**[5] 2204 3-8-13 60 RichardEvans(5) 10 42
(P D Evans) *nvr nr ldrs* **14/1**

3303 **12** *¾* **Spring Quartet**[8] 2131 3-8-3 52 (v) TobyAtkinson(7) 13 33
(Pat Eddery) *s.i.s: a bhd* **16/1**

0-60 **13** *1 ½* **Vella**[12] 2006 3-8-12 54 DaneO'Neill 6 33
(H J L Dunlop) *hld up in mid-div: wknd over 1f out* **50/1**

0- **14** *nk* **Native Dame (IRE)**[39] 1337 3-8-11 58 MartinLane(5) 8 36
(Edgar Byrne) *wnt rt s: a in rr* **33/1**

000- **15** *21* **New Adventure**[222] 6745 3-8-11 53 ChrisCatlin 14 —
(P F I Cole) *wnt rt s: a in rr* **20/1**

06-0 **16** *½* **Spring Secret**[22] 1746 3-9-3 59 MickyFenton 1 3
(B Palling) *led: hdd over 3f out: wknd qckly over 2f out* **16/1**

00-6 **17** *49* **Gibson Square (USA)**[52] 1130 3-8-13 55 J-PGuillambert 12 —
(S C Williams) *mid-div: pushed along 7f out: bhd 5f out: eased whn lost tch over 2f out* **33/1**

2m 38.24s (-0.76) **Going Correction** -0.125s/f (Firm) **17** Ran SP% **124.8**
Speed ratings (Par 97): **97,95,95,94,94 92,89,89,88,88 86,86,85,85,71 70,38**
toteswinger: 1&2 £26.50, 1&3 £15.30, 2&3 £11.50 CSF £80.69 CT £561.34 TOTE £16.50: £3.80, £1.70, £2.10, £5.10; EX 126.30.
Owner Jimmy & Susie Wenman **Bred** Trevor Reilly **Trained** Upper Lambourn, Berks

FOCUS
Low grade handicap form but plenty of these are lightly-raced sorts open to further improvement and winners should emerge from this race in time. The pace was even enough and a whole host were in with some sort of chance approaching the final couple of furlongs.
Hollow Green(IRE) Official explanation: jockey said, regarding running and riding, that his orders were to jump out and sit midfield, adding that the filly was slightly interferred with early, became detached and felt uncomfortable on the good to firm ground going downhill and that it would prefer more cut in the ground; vet said filly was slightly lame.
Gibson Square(USA) Official explanation: jockey said gelding never travelled

2351 FREEBETS.CO.UK FA CUP FINAL FREE BETS H'CAP 1m 2f 36y

3:50 (3:50) (Class 5) (0-75,75) 4-Y-0+ **£3,885** (£1,156; £577; £288) **Stalls** Low

Form RPR

2500 **1** **Kidlat**[19] 1812 4-9-1 72 (t) JimCrowley 10 78
(B G Powell) *hld up: nt clr run 2f out: hdwy and swtchd lft jst over 1f out: rdn to ld wl ins fnl f: r.o* **8/1**

044- **2** *1* **Finney Hill**[312] 4166 4-9-3 74 DaneO'Neill 13 78+
(H Candy) *hld up in mid-div: hdwy on outside over 2f out: sn rdn: r.o to take 2nd last strides* **5/2**[1]

03-0 **3** *hd* **Holden Eagle**[38] 1357 4-9-3 74 SteveDrowne 11 78
(A G Newcombe) *t.k.h: sn in tch: rdn and ev ch ins fnl f: kpt on* **11/1**

010- **4** *¾* **Laish Ya Hajar (IRE)**[169] 7606 5-8-12 69 TolleyDean 12 71
(P R Webber) *led: rdn over 1f out: hdd and no ex wl ins fnl f* **25/1**

0-45 **5** *1 ¼* **Uig**[5] 2212 8-8-4 61 oh4 LukeMorris 4 61
(H S Howe) *hld up in tch: rdn over 1f out: one pce ins fnl f* **8/1**

043 **6** *½* **I'm In The Pink (FR)**[21] 1771 5-8-10 67 CatherineGannon 3 66
(P D Evans) *hld up in tch: one pce fnl 2f* **8/1**

5013 **7** *nk* **Becuille (IRE)**[18] 1834 4-8-9 66 EddieAhern 2 64
(B J Meehan) *chsd ldr 5f: prom: rdn 2f out: fdd ins fnl f* **7/1**[3]

5000 **8** *1 ¼* **Eastern Gift**[10] 2086 4-8-11 75 KylieManser(7) 1 71+
(Miss Gay Kelleway) *hld up in rr: nt clr run on ins over 2f out: plld out over 1f out: nvr trbld ldrs* **33/1**

01 **9** *½* **Majehar**[56] 1051 7-8-7 64 RobertWinston 7 62+
(A G Newcombe) *hld up towards rr: pushed along over 1f out: nvr trbld ldrs* **10/1**

2- **10** *shd* **Jubilant Note (IRE)**[176] 7512 7-8-7 64 (v) LPKeniry 9 58
(Michael David Murphy, Ire) *prom: chsd ldr 5f out tl 2f out: wknd over 1f out* **13/2**[2]

6/ **11** *44* **Salontiger (GER)**[648] 7-8-13 70 VinceSlattery 8 —
(P J Hobbs) *in rr: lost tch 3f out: eased over 1f out* **50/1**

2m 9.95s (-0.65) **Going Correction** -0.125s/f (Firm) **11** Ran SP% **113.9**
Speed ratings (Par 103): **97,96,95,94 94,93,92,92,92 57**
toteswinger: 1&2 £10.40, 1&3 £23.70, 2&3 £6.50 CSF £26.89 CT £222.13 TOTE £12.30: £3.90, £2.00, £4.20; EX 49.30.
Owner John Stocker **Bred** Darley **Trained** Upper Lambourn, Berks

FOCUS
Laish Ya Hajar was allowed to dictate at just steady fractions, prompting a few of these to race a bit keenly, but the finish was dominated by horses who came from off the pace.
Kidlat Official explanation: trainer's rep said, regarding the apparent improvement in form, that the colt was better suited by being ridden off the pace.
Eastern Gift Official explanation: jockey said gelding was denied a clear run

2352 FREEBETS.CO.UK FREE BETS H'CAP 1m 14y

4:20 (4:21) (Class 5) (0-70,70) 4-Y-0+ **£3,238** (£963; £481; £240) **Stalls** High

Form RPR

1151 **1** **Prince Rossi (IRE)**[21] 1773 5-8-6 57 (v) EddieAhern 2 67
(A E Price) *mde all: crossed to stands' rail after 1f: rdn over 1f out: r.o* **6/1**[2]

000 **2** *½* **Tanforan**[7] 2166 7-7-13 57 BillyCray(7) 9 66
(B P J Baugh) *chsd wnr after 1f: rdn 2f out: r.o ins fnl f* **20/1**

0-24 **3** *1* **Millfields Dreams**[10] 2088 10-8-10 66 (p) MarkCoumbe(5) 15 73
(G C Bravery) *hld up in rr: hdwy 2f out: rdn over 1f out: r.o ins fnl f* **12/1**

00-6 **4** *1* **Oriental Girl**[18] 1834 4-8-13 64 (p) SteveDrowne 13 68
(J A Geake) *hld up in mid-div: hdwy on stands' rail over 3f out: rdn 2f out: kpt on ins fnl f* **11/1**

3-06 **5** *1* **Dancing Storm**[21] 1773 6-8-8 59 FergusSweeney 10 61
(W S Kittow) *hld up in mid-div: hdwy over 3f out: rdn 2f out: no ex ins fnl f* **11/1**

00-0 **6** *½* **Magroom**[30] 1539 5-9-0 65 JimCrowley 16 66
(R J Hodges) *hld up in rr on stands' rail: hdwy over 2f out: rdn over 1f out: one pce fnl f* **20/1**

1261 **7** *nk* **Forbidden (IRE)**[17] 1883 6-8-12 63 (t) JerryO'Dwyer 8 63
(Daniel Mark Loughnane, Ire) *hld up in rr: hdwy on outside over 2f out: rdn over 1f out: no imp* **6/1**[2]

32-4 **8** *nse* **Desert Kiss**[43] 1256 4-9-4 69 RobertWinston 7 69
(W R Swinburn) *sltly hmpd sn after s: sn hld up in tch: rdn over 2f out: hung lft wl over 1f out: fdd fnl f* **6/1**[2]

5000 **9** *3 ¼* **Just Jimmy (IRE)**[22] 1741 4-8-4 55 oh5 CatherineGannon 3 48
(P D Evans) *prom: rdn over 3f out: wknd wl over 1f out* **33/1**

0206 **10** *¾* **Mountain Pass (USA)**[21] 1775 7-8-2 56 (p) DavidProbert(3) 12 47
(B J Llewellyn) *hld up in tch: rdn 2f out: wknd ins fnl f* **16/1**

300 **11** *2 ¾* **Love In The Park**[14] 1972 4-8-1 57 oh1 ow2 RossAtkinson(5) 5 41
(R Brotherton) *a towards rr* **66/1**

6-51 **12** *6* **Full Victory (IRE)**[8] 2125 7-9-5 70 6ex DaneO'Neill 14 41
(R A Farrant) *hld up towards rr: rdn over 2f out: no rspnse* **4/1**[1]

5-26 **13** *¾* **The Staffy (IRE)**[82] 767 4-9-1 66 LukeMorris 1 35
(N J Vaughan) *a in rr* **8/1**[3]

004- **14** *30* **Lordship (IRE)**[215] 6928 5-8-0 58 ow1 JakePayne(7) 6 —
(A W Carroll) *t.k.h in tch: pushed along and wknd over 3f out: t.o* **33/1**

6000 **15** *3 ½* **Cyfrwys (IRE)**[21] 1775 8-8-4 55 oh9 FrankieMcDonald 4 —
(B Palling) *prom: rdn over 3f out: wkng whn hmpd wl over 1f out: t.o* **100/1**

1m 34.17s (-2.03) **Going Correction** -0.125s/f (Firm) **15** Ran SP% **122.1**
Speed ratings (Par 103): **105,104,103,102,101 101,100,100,97,96 93,87,87,57,53**
toteswinger: 1&2 £31.40, 1&3 £18.80, 2&3 £81.50 CSF £130.33 CT £1444.70 TOTE £6.60: £3.20, £4.10, £4.40; EX 128.60.
Owner Business Development Consultants Limited **Bred** Sir Eric Parker **Trained** Leominster, H'fords
■ Stewards' Enquiry : Billy Cray one-day ban: used whip with excessive frequency (Jun 9)

FOCUS
Not a strong handicap by any means.
Desert Kiss Official explanation: jockey said filly hung left-handed
Love In The Park Official explanation: trainer said filly was unsuited by the track

Full Victory(IRE) Official explanation: jockey said gelding never travelled; vet said gelding returned lame behind

2353 FREEBETS.CO.UK NEW HORSE RACING SYNDICATE APPRENTICE H'CAP 6f 16y
4:50 (4:50) (Class 6) (0-65,65) 4-Y-0+ **£2,266** (£674; £337; £168) **Stalls** High

Form RPR
0-65 **1** **Caustic Wit (IRE)**[4] 2224 11-8-2 **55**................ JakePayne(7) 3 63
(M S Saunders) *hld up: hdwy 2f out: wnt 2nd jst over 1f out: led wl ins fnl f: r.o* **10/1**
1-00 **2** *1* **Wooden King (IRE)**[111] 395 4-8-4 **53**................ AndrewHeffernan(3) 1 58
(P D Evans) *led: sn clr: hrd rdn over 1f out: sn hung lft to far rail: hdd wl ins fnl f: kpt on* **14/1**
6-3 **3** *1* **Castano**[8] 2137 5-8-11 **62**................(p) MJMurphy(5) 16 64
(B R Millman) *hld up: rdn and hdwy over 2f out: edgd lft over 1f out: kpt on to take 3rd towards fin* **9/2**[2]
260- **4** *¾* **Gioacchino (IRE)**[167] 7624 4-8-2 **53**................ TobyAtkinson(5) 14 52
(R A Harris) *hld up: rdn and hdwy whn hung lft over 1f out: kpt on u.p on far rail ins fnl f* **10/1**
-133 **5** *hd* **Many Welcomes**[18] 1846 4-8-6 **52**................ BillyCray 4 51
(B P J Baugh) *outpcd in rr: rdn over 2f out: hdwy on stands' side over 1f out: kpt on towards fin* **4/1**[1]
-554 **6** *hd* **Iguacu**[4] 2223 5-8-5 **51** oh1................ MatthewDavies 12 49
(George Baker) *chsd ldrs: rdn over 2f out: kpt on same pce ins fnl f* **13/2**
600- **7** *2* **Pappoose**[232] 6543 4-8-2 **51** oh1................ AmyScott(3) 6 43
(H Candy) *hld up: hdwy over 2f out: rdn over 1f out: wknd wl ins fnl f* **13/2**
3020 **8** *shd* **Divine White**[8] 2134 6-8-5 **54** ow1................ DTDaSilva(3) 11 45
(G P Enright) *nvr nrr* **33/1**
50-0 **9** *nk* **Boldinor**[8] 2124 6-8-3 **54**................ GemmaElford(5) 15 44
(M R Bosley) *a bhd* **14/1**
-660 **10** *½* **Stamford Blue**[5] 2202 8-9-5 **65**................(b) PNolan 8 54
(R A Harris) *rdr lost rein briefly sn after s: chsd clr ldr: hung lft fr over 2f out: rdn and lost 2nd jst over 1f out: wknd ins fnl f* **5/1**[3]

1m 11.86s (-0.14) **Going Correction** -0.125s/f (Firm) **10 Ran SP% 116.0**
Speed ratings (Par 101): **101,99,98,97,97 96,94,94,93,92**
toteswinger: 1&2 £24.40, 1&3 £9.50, 2&3 £15.10 CSF £139.51 CT £736.06 TOTE £10.90: £2.90, £4.20, £1.50; EX 187.00 Place 6: £328.60 Place 5: £216.86.
Owner Mrs Sandra Jones **Bred** Gainsborough Stud Management Ltd **Trained** Green Ore, Somerset
■ Jake Payne's first winner.

FOCUS
Mostly exposed sorts here but it was turned into a real test by Wooden King. There were six absentees because of the ground.
T/Jkpt: Not won. T/Plt: £749.10 to a £1 stake. Pool: £57,622.98. 56.15 winning tickets. T/Qpdt: £109.60 to a £1 stake. Pool: £3,792.56. 25.60 winning tickets. KH

2332 LEICESTER (R-H)
Tuesday, May 26

OFFICIAL GOING: Good to firm (good in places; 7.8)
Wind: Fresh behind Weather: Cloudy with sunny spells

2354 EBF LADBROKES.COM MAIDEN FILLIES' STKS 5f 2y
2:00 (2:01) (Class 4) 2-Y-0 **£4,857** (£1,445; £722; £360) **Stalls** Low

Form RPR
1 **Lady Of The Desert (USA)** 2-9-0 0................ MartinDwyer 5 82+
(B J Meehan) *s.i.s: sn pushed along in rr: hdwy 1/2-way: shkn up to ld ins fnl f: r.o wl* **3/1**[2]
2 *1 ¾* **Tomintoul Singer (IRE)** 2-9-0 0................ TPQueally 6 75+
(H R A Cecil) *a.p: led over 1f out: sn edgd lft: hdd and unable qck ins fnl f* **3/1**[2]
3 **3** *1 ¾* **La Fortunata**[18] 1841 2-9-0 0................ AdrianMcCarthy 3 69
(J R Jenkins) *led: hung rt thrght: rdn and hdd over 1f out: styd on same pce* **33/1**
4 *1* **Vanishing Grey (IRE)** 2-9-0 0................ JamieSpencer 10 65
(B J Meehan) *rr green and sn outpcd: r.o ins fnl f: nrst fin* **16/1**
024 **5** *1 ½* **Angel Of Fashion (IRE)**[14] 1968 2-9-0 0................ MichaelHills 4 60
(B W Hills) *hld up: nt clr run 1/2-way: swtchd rt: styd on ins fnl f: nvr trbld ldrs* **8/1**[3]
3 **6** *nk* **Ailsa Carmel (IRE)**[11] 2034 2-9-0 0................ TonyCulhane 7 59
(M R Channon) *chsd ldr tl rdn over 1f out: wknd fnl f* **9/4**[1]
2 **7** *2 ¼* **Fenella Rose**[18] 1841 2-9-0 0................ SaleemGolam 2 51
(S C Williams) *chsd ldrs: rdn and hung rt fr over 1f out: wknd fnl f* **9/1**
8 *2 ¼* **Totally Invincible (IRE)** 2-9-0 0................ RichardMullen 1 43
(E S McMahon) *chsd ldrs: rdn and wknd over 1f out* **25/1**
9 *5* **Carries Lass** 2-9-0 0................ ShaneKelly 8 25
(J A Osborne) *s.i.s: sn outpcd* **66/1**
10 *16* **Gessabelle** 2-9-0 0................(t) KirstyMilczarek 9 —
(P S McEntee) *prom: lost pl over 3f out: sn bhd* **80/1**

60.52 secs (0.52) **Going Correction** -0.05s/f (Good) **10 Ran SP% 117.3**
Speed ratings (Par 92): **93,90,87,85,83 82,79,75,67,42**
toteswinger: 1&2 £4.20, 1&3 £49.10, 2&3 £49.10. CSF £12.27 TOTE £4.70: £1.10, £1.50, £6.30; EX 20.20 Trifecta £172.80 Pool: £308.36 - 1.32 winning units..
Owner Jaber Abdullah **Bred** Rabbah Bloodstock Llc **Trained** Manton, Wilts

FOCUS
A fair fillies' maiden.

NOTEBOOK
Lady Of The Desert(USA), a daughter of high-class juvenile Queen's Logic, showed her inexperience by staring slowest of all, but she gradually got the idea. After squeezing through a narrow gap around 1f out, she picked up in fine style to quickly settle masters, despite edging right. She looks potentially decent and it would be no surprise were she to try and emulate her dam by winning the Queen Mary (Cashmans gave her a quote of 16-1), although the Albany Stakes could also be an option. (op 4-1 tchd 9-2)
Tomintoul Singer(IRE) ◆, a 25,000gns first foal of a 6f winner, travelled better than anything but did not quite see her race out. She should be extremely hard to beat in a similar race over this trip next time. (op 7-2)
La Fortunata built on her debut effort at Nottingham, but she was inclined to hang right for most of the way and might have found the ground quicker than ideal.
Vanishing Grey(IRE) ◆, a 220,000euros half-sister to Nunthorpe and Golden Jubilee winner Kingsgate Native, was outpaced for much of the way and raced wide, but she showed ability. She's open to significant improvement. (op 10-1)
Angel Of Fashion(IRE) is not progressing. Official explanation: jockey said filly suffered interference in running (op 6-1 tchd 11-2 and 17-2)
Ailsa Carmel(IRE) was well below the form she showed when third on her debut at Newbury, dropping out tamely after showing speed. (tchd 2-1 and 5-2)
Fenella Rose was another to disappoint, but she might be more of a nursery type. (op 14-1 tchd 16-1 and 8-1)

2355 LADBROKES.COM CLAIMING STKS 5f 218y
2:30 (2:32) (Class 6) 3-Y-O **£2,590** (£770; £385; £192) **Stalls** High

Form RPR
1313 **1** **Chocolicious (IRE)**[18] 1832 3-8-6 70................(v) GaryBartley(5) 8 71
(B Smart) *hld up: hdwy 1/2-way: led over 1f out: styd on* **7/2**[2]
2233 **2** *1 ¼* **Billy Beetroot (USA)**[14] 1949 3-8-4 62................(t) SaleemGolam 10 60
(S C Williams) *a.p: rdn to chse wnr fnl f: r.o* **18/1**
3060 **3** *hd* **You've Been Mowed**[13] 1982 3-7-11 53 ow3................ AndreaAtzeni(5) 3 57
(R J Price) *hld up in tch: plld hrd: outpcd over 2f out: rallied over 1f out: r.o* **7/1**
15-3 **4** *1 ¾* **Prize Point**[29] 1559 3-9-4 77................ RichardMullen 2 67
(K A Ryan) *hung rt thrght: prom: outpcd 2f out: r.o ins fnl f* **85/40**[1]
06-0 **5** *½* **Calypso Girl (IRE)**[2] 2300 3-8-9 65................ JohnEgan 5 57
(P D Evans) *sn pushed along in rr: hdwy u.p over 1f out: styd on same pce ins fnl f* **10/1**
036- **6** *1* **All Spin (IRE)**[174] 7538 3-9-4 73................(v[1]) NCallan 12 63
(A P Jarvis) *led and sn clr: rdn: edgd lft and hdd over 1f out: no ex* **12/1**
0 **7** *8* **Steamer (IRE)**[12] 2009 3-8-4 0................ LiamJones 4 23
(P Winkworth) *sn pushed along in rr: nvr nrr* **40/1**
-510 **8** *½* **Taste Of Honey (IRE)**[12] 2009 3-8-4 65 ow1................ MartinDwyer 11 21
(D W P Arbuthnot) *chsd ldr to 1/2-way: rdn and wknd over 1f out* **12/1**
4060 **9** *3 ¼* **Field Fantasy**[4] 2250 3-8-2 52................ AndrewMullen(3) 1 12
(Garry Moss) *sn outpcd* **150/1**
5541 **10** *1 ¼* **Vegas Baby (IRE)**[8] 2137 3-8-9 70................(b) ShaneKelly 7 12
(J A Osborne) *sn pushed along in rr: eased whn no ch over 1f out* **11/2**[3]
0405 **11** *5* **Bold Account (IRE)**[25] 1652 3-8-4 60................(p) JimmyQuinn 6 —
(Garry Moss) *chsd ldrs tl wknd over 2f out* **66/1**

1m 12.9s (-0.10) **Going Correction** -0.05s/f (Good) **11 Ran SP% 116.4**
Speed ratings (Par 97): **98,96,96,93,93 91,81,80,76,74 67**
toteswinger: 1&2 £5.20, 1&3 £8.80, 2&3 £24.50 CSF £63.45 TOTE £5.50: £1.80, £3.30, £2.80; EX 37.40 Trifecta £358.30 Part won. Pool: £484.19 - 0.94 winning units..Prize Point was claimed by J. R. Boyle for £12000.
Owner Mrs Trisha Laughton **Bred** Ballyhane Stud **Trained** Hambleton, N Yorks

FOCUS
A fair claimer run at a furious pace.

2356 LADBROKES.COM ABBEY PARK H'CAP 1m 1f 218y
3:00 (3:01) (Class 4) (0-80,79) 3-Y-O **£4,857** (£1,445; £722; £360) **Stalls** High

Form RPR
03-1 **1** **Larkham (USA)**[36] 1410 3-9-4 **79**................ SebSanders 8 85
(R M Beckett) *a.p: led 2f out: sn rdn: styd on gamely* **15/2**
5401 **2** *1 ¼* **Tinshu (IRE)**[15] 1928 3-9-1 **76**................ AdamKirby 6 79
(D Haydn Jones) *hld up: hdwy over 2f out: rdn over 1f out: r.o* **6/1**[3]
23-3 **3** *nk* **Clerk's Choice (IRE)**[10] 2072 3-8-11 **77**....... Louis-PhilippeBeuzelin(5) 1 79
(W Jarvis) *hld up: rdn over 3f out: hdwy over 2f out: edgd rt: r.o* **8/1**
516 **4** *nse* **Hatta Diamond (IRE)**[35] 1428 3-8-12 **73**................ JoeFanning 7 76+
(M Johnston) *hld up: rdn over 3f out: swtchd rt and hdwy over 1f out: nrst fin* **16/1**
63-0 **5** *2 ¼* **Whisky Galore**[11] 2048 3-8-12 **73**................ PhilipRobinson 3 71
(C G Cox) *s.i.s: in rr and pushed along 1/2-way: hung rt and r.o ins fnl f: nvr nrr* **14/1**
53-1 **6** *¾* **Featherweight (IRE)**[15] 1931 3-9-1 **76**................ MichaelHills 10 72
(B W Hills) *chsd ldrs: chal 2f out: sn rdn: no ex wl ins fnl f* **9/2**[2]
56-5 **7** *8* **Capitelli (IRE)**[12] 2008 3-9-0 **75**................ RichardHughes 4 55
(R Hannon) *chsd ldrs: led over 8f out: rdn and hdd 2f out: wknd and eased fnl f* **12/1**
-230 **8** *6* **Sawab**[24] 1667 3-8-13 **74**................ NCallan 2 42
(C E Brittain) *prom: rdn over 2f out: wknd over 1f out* **20/1**
-211 **9** *10* **Miss Christophene (IRE)**[89] 689 3-8-11 **72**................ RoystonFfrench 9 20
(Mrs S Lamyman) *s.s: a bhd* **28/1**
42-0 **10** *2 ¾* **Mehendi (IRE)**[34] 1461 3-9-0 **75**................ LDettori 11 18
(B J Meehan) *led: hdd over 8f out: chsd ldrs tl rdn and wknd over 2f out* **12/1**
53-5 **11** *1 ¼* **Norwegian Dancer (UAE)**[20] 1793 3-9-0 **75**................ RichardMullen 5 15+
(E S McMahon) *hld up in tch: plld hrd: sddle slipped and trckd ldr 6f out: rdr tried to ease fr over 3f out* **3/1**[1]

2m 7.79s (-0.11) **Going Correction** +0.025s/f (Good) **11 Ran SP% 116.5**
Speed ratings (Par 101): **101,100,99,99,97 97,90,86,78,75 74**
toteswinger: 1&2 £12.30, 1&3 £17.20, 2&3 £8.40 CSF £51.54 CT £373.20 TOTE £10.50: £3.10, £2.20, £2.80; EX 62.80 Trifecta £356.20 Pool: £616.14 - 1.28 winning units..
Owner R A Pegum **Bred** Elk Manor Farm **Trained** Whitsbury, Hants

FOCUS
A fair 3yo handicap. The winning time was 1.56 seconds faster than the following 51-65 handicap for the same age group.
Whisky Galore Official explanation: jockey said colt jumped awkwardly leaving stalls
Capitelli(IRE) Official explanation: jockey said filly kept changing legs
Sawab Official explanation: trainer's rep said filly was unsuited by the track
Norwegian Dancer(UAE) Official explanation: jockey said saddle slipped

2357 LADBROKESCASINO.COM H'CAP 1m 1f 218y
3:30 (3:35) (Class 6) (0-65,65) 3-Y-O **£2,590** (£770; £385; £192) **Stalls** High

Form RPR
-000 **1** **General Zhukov**[15] 1932 3-8-10 **62**................ WilliamCarson(5) 1 70
(J M P Eustace) *s.s: hld up: hdwy over 1f out: led ins fnl f: sn clr* **20/1**
03-0 **2** *1 ¾* **Venture Capitalist**[28] 1595 3-9-1 **62**................ NCallan 2 66
(L M Cumani) *hld up in tch: rdn and hung rt over 1f out: ev ch ins fnl f: unable qck* **11/2**[2]
003 **3** *½* **Toujours Souriante**[22] 1745 3-9-4 **65**................ RoystonFfrench 9 68
(M Johnston) *a.p: chsd ldr over 6f out: edgd rt over 5f out: rdn and ev ch fr over 1f out: unable qck ins fnl f* **25/1**
0-50 **4** *1* **Parc Des Princes (USA)**[15] 1930 3-8-11 **58**................ WilliamBuick 8 59
(A M Balding) *hld up: pushed along over 2f out: hung rt and r.o ins fnl f: nt rch ldrs* **11/2**[2]
50-0 **5** *1 ¼* **Sairaam (IRE)**[34] 1462 3-9-2 **63**................ RHills 7 62
(J L Dunlop) *sn led: rdn over 1f out: hdd and no ex ins fnl f* **15/2**[3]
1442 **6** *1* **Location**[4] 2246 3-8-9 **56**................ StephenDonohoe 13 53+
(Ian Williams) *chsd ldrs: nt clr run over 1f out: styd on same pce* **9/2**[1]
50-0 **7** *½* **Halfway House**[29] 1570 3-9-0 **61**................ JamieSpencer 12 57
(M L W Bell) *hld up: hdwy over 3f out: rdn over 1f out: hung rt and styd on ins fnl f* **9/1**
0-50 **8** *1 ¾* **Manolito Montoya (IRE)**[15] 1928 3-8-11 **63**........(b) GabrielHannon(5) 3 55
(J W Hills) *hld up: rdn over 2f out: n.d* **50/1**

05-0 **9** 3/4 **The Saucy Snipe**[35] 1428 3-9-3 **64**.............................. SaleemGolam 14 55
(P Winkworth) *prom: rdn over 3f out: wknd over 1f out* **66/1**
140- **10** *nse* **Bounty Reef**[198] 7257 3-8-11 **58**.................................. JohnEgan 4 48
(P D Evans) *hld up: hdwy over 4f out: rdn over 2f out: wknd over 1f out* **20/1**
3200 **11** 3 1/2 **Kingaroo (IRE)**[38] 1361 3-9-1 **62**.............................. AdamKirby 11 45
(Garry Moss) *hld up: rdn over 3f out: n.d* **14/1**
-244 **12** 3/4 **Iron Out (USA)**[80] 782 3-9-2 **63**.............................. PaulMulrennan 5 45
(R Hollinshead) *hld up: racd keenly: swtchd rt over 1f out: n.d* **25/1**
60-0 **13** *hd* **Mymateeric**[35] 1428 3-9-2 **63**..............................(p) TPQueally 15 45
(J Pearce) *prom: rdn over 3f out: wknd over 1f out* **33/1**
6540 **14** *13* **Green Dynasty (IRE)**[28] 1595 3-9-2 **63**.............................. JoeFanning 16 19
(M Johnston) *chsd ldr over 3f: remained handy: rdn and hung rt fr over 3f out: wknd and eased fnl 2f* **16/1**
-046 **15** *25* **Nimmy's Special**[8] 2141 3-8-11 **58**.............................. LiamJones 6 —
(M Mullineaux) *s.s: hld up: rdn over 4f out: wknd fnl 3f: eased* **100/1**

2m 9.35s (1.45) **Going Correction** +0.025s/f (Good) 15 Ran SP% **107.9**
Speed ratings (Par 97): **95,93,93,92,91 90,90,88,88,88 85,84,84,74,54**
toteswinger: 1&2 £22.90, 1&3 £58.70, 2&3 £34.20 CSF £95.36 CT £2045.83 TOTE £20.10: £6.50, £1.70, £4.40; EX 236.60 Trifecta £181.20 Part won. Pool: £244.88 - 0.20 winning units..
Owner Mrs Rosemary Moszkowicz **Bred** Henry And Mrs Rosemary Moszkowicz **Trained** Newmarket, Suffolk
■ Eurotanz was withdrawn (8/1, refused to enter stalls.) R4 applies, deduct 10p in the £.

FOCUS
A modest but competitive 3yo handicap. The winning time was 1.56 seconds slower than the earlier 66-80 handicap for the same age group.
General Zhukov Official explanation: trainer said, regarding the apparent improvement in form, that the gelding was suited by waiting tactics over an extended trip.
Sairaam(IRE) Official explanation: jockey said filly slipped going into bend
Manolito Montoya(IRE) Official explanation: jockey said gelding had a breathing problem
Nimmy's Special Official explanation: jockey said filly never travelled

2358 LADBROKES.COM MAIDEN STKS 5f 218y
4:00 (4:02) (Class 4) 2-Y-O £3,885 (£1,156; £577; £288) **Stalls** High

Form RPR
2 **1** **Atacama Crossing (IRE)**[17] 1867 2-9-3 0.............................. MichaelHills 10 77
(B W Hills) *led 5f out: rdn ins fnl f: styd on gamely* **7/4**[1]
2 **2** *shd* **Danzoe (IRE)**[15] 1939 2-9-3 0.............................. JimmyQuinn 9 77+
(D Donovan) *led 1f: trckd ldrs: jnd wnr gng wl ins fnl f: sn rdn: styd on* **11/2**[2]
3 *3* **Motivational (IRE)** 2-9-3 0.............................. TedDurcan 4 68
(D R Lanigan) *in rr and pushed along: hdwy over 2f out: rdn over 1f out: edgd rt and styd on ins fnl f* **25/1**
4 2 3/4 **Lamh Albasser (USA)** 2-9-3 0.............................. LDettori 5 59+
(Saeed Bin Suroor) *rn green in rr and hung rt at various stages: hdwy 1/2-way: rdn over 1f out: no ex* **7/4**[1]
43 **5** 1 1/4 **Petrocelli**[22] 1719 2-9-3 0.............................. PaulFitzsimons 6 56
(A J McCabe) *chsd ldrs: rdn over 1f out: wknd fnl f* **18/1**
6 4 1/2 **Motty's Gift** 2-9-3 0.............................. AdamKirby 1 42
(W R Swinburn) *sn outpcd* **50/1**
62 **7** 1 1/4 **Mind Of Her Own**[38] 1364 2-8-12 0.............................. JohnEgan 3 33
(P D Evans) *prom: rdn over 3f out: wknd 2f out* **22/1**
0 **8** *1* **Zero Seven**[41] 1290 2-9-3 0.............................. NCallan 7 35
(C E Brittain) *plld hrd: trckd wnr 5f out: rdn over 2f out: wknd over 1f out* **11/1**[3]

1m 13.8s (0.80) **Going Correction** -0.05s/f (Good) 8 Ran SP% **111.9**
Speed ratings (Par 95): **92,91,87,84,82 76,74,73**
toteswinger: 1&2 £2.30, 1&3 £10.60, 2&3 £14.80 CSF £11.56 TOTE £2.80: £1.02, £1.40, £6.00; EX 8.40 Trifecta £71.80 Pool: £1018.53 - 10.49 winning units..
Owner Paul Moulton **Bred** Lynn Lodge Stud **Trained** Lambourn, Berks

FOCUS
A reasonable juvenile maiden.

NOTEBOOK
Atacama Crossing(IRE) stepped up on the form he showed when runner-up on his debut at Haydock and displayed a terrific attitude. He looked vulnerable when strongly challenged by Danzoe, but found plenty for pressure and is clearly a tough sort. He might be vulnerable in a better grade in the short term, but looks the type to do well in nurseries later in the season. (op 11-8 tchd 5-4 and 2-1)
Danzoe(IRE) stepped up on his debut effort at Yarmouth, but didn't find as much as had looked likely. Having raced keenly in the winner's slipstream, he looked sure to win when switched out about 1f out, but his rider didn't go for the whip until late on (possibly didn't have the room) and he was just held. On this evidence he'll be well suited by a drop back to 5f. (op 13-2 tchd 9-2)
Motivational(IRE), a 75,000gns first foal of a quite useful 6f winner at two, was outpaced when first coming under pressure before running on quite nicely. He'll probably want 7f before long, but does look to have a fair amount of ability. (op 28-1 tchd 20-1)
Lamh Albasser(USA), who is out of a quite useful triple 6f-7f winner, ran extremely green and should come on a bundle for this experience. (op 2-1 tchd 11-4 and 13-8)
Petrocelli ran a respectable race but simply didn't look good enough and is vulnerable in this sort of company. (op 12-1 tchd 20-1)

2359 LADBROKES.COM H'CAP 5f 2y
4:30 (4:32) (Class 5) (0-75,75) 4-Y-O+ £3,238 (£963; £481; £240) **Stalls** Low

Form RPR
11-0 **1** **Invincible Lad (IRE)**[24] 1685 5-9-4 **75**.............................. RichardHughes 10 90+
(E J Alston) *trckd ldrs: led and edgd lft over 1f out: shkn up and r.o wl: hung rt towards fin* **3/1**[1]
4012 **2** *2* **Drifting Gold**[4] 2219 5-9-3 **74**..............................(b) AdamKirby 3 81
(C G Cox) *hld up: swtchd lft and hdwy over 1f out: rdn and hung rt ins fnl f: nt rch wnr* **8/1**
0-20 **3** *1* **Bahamian Ballet**[24] 1685 7-9-1 **72**.............................. RichardMullen 11 75
(E S McMahon) *trckd ldrs: rdn and ev ch over 1f out: hung rt and no ex ins fnl f* **15/2**
-555 **4** 1/2 **Mambo Spirit (IRE)**[14] 1951 5-9-1 **72**.............................. PaulMulrennan 6 73
(J G Given) *trckd ldr: rdn over 1f out: styd on same pce fnl f* **4/1**[2]
1041 **5** 2 1/2 **Northern Empire (IRE)**[15] 1921 6-8-13 **70**..............................(p) NCallan 8 62
(K A Ryan) *s.i.s: racd keenly and sn trcking ldrs: rdn over 1f out: hung rt and wknd ins fnl f* **7/1**[3]
-000 **6** 1 3/4 **Espy**[19] 1806 4-9-3 **74**.............................. WilliamBuick 9 59
(S Kirk) *prom: rdn over 1f out: wknd ins fnl f* **14/1**
3651 **7** *1* **Circle Dance (IRE)**[83] 758 4-8-7 **64**..............................(v) TedDurcan 5 45
(D Shaw) *s.i.s: outpcd* **25/1**
-442 **8** *1* **Make My Dream**[14] 1970 6-8-13 **70**.............................. AlanMunro 2 48
(J Gallagher) *sn outpcd* **10/1**
2140 **9** *3* **Ten Down**[14] 1970 4-8-11 **68**.............................. MartinDwyer 7 34
(M Quinn) *led: hdd whn hmpd over 1f out: sn wknd* **25/1**
30-0 **10** 1/2 **Shakespeare's Son**[130] 191 4-8-11 **68**.............................. JohnEgan 4 32
(H J Evans) *chsd ldrs: pushed along 1/2-way: wknd wl over 1f out* **16/1**
5454 **11** 1 1/4 **Digital**[4] 2219 12-8-13 **70**..............................(v) TonyCulhane 1 30
(M R Channon) *dwlt: outpcd* **20/1**

59.34 secs (-0.66) **Going Correction** -0.05s/f (Good) 11 Ran SP% **114.5**
Speed ratings (Par 103): **103,99,98,97,93 90,89,87,82,81 79**
toteswinger: 1&2 £5.00, 1&3 £7.10, 2&3 £19.10 CSF £25.63 CT £163.71 TOTE £4.10: £1.80, £2.20, £2.60; EX 33.80 Trifecta £176.50 Pool: £617.95 - 2.59 winning units. Place 6: £202.01 Place 5: £104.80.
Owner Con Harrington **Bred** Mrs Chris Harrington **Trained** Longton, Lancs

FOCUS
An ordinary sprint handicap.
T/Plt: £282.50 to a £1 stake. Pool: £51,696.01. 133.55 winning tickets. T/Qpdt: £23.50 to a £1 stake. Pool: £4,691.54. 147.55 winning tickets. CR

2339 REDCAR (L-H)
Tuesday, May 26

OFFICIAL GOING: Good to firm (firm in places in the chute; 9.7)
Wind: Fresh across Weather: Dry, sunny periods, breezy

2360 EUROPEAN BREEDERS' FUND MEDIAN AUCTION MAIDEN FILLIES' STKS 6f
2:10 (2:10) (Class 5) 2-Y-O £3,691 (£1,098; £548; £274) **Stalls** Centre

Form RPR
0 **1** **Avonrose**[15] 1920 2-9-0 0.............................. GregFairley 3 79+
(M Johnston) *cl up: led over 1f out: rdn clr ins fnl f* **16/1**
2 3 1/2 **Gwynedd (IRE)** 2-9-0 0.............................. GrahamGibbons 2 68
(E S McMahon) *led: rdn along 2f out: hdd over 1f out: kpt on same pce u.p ins fnl f* **8/1**[3]
3 *nk* **Dance For Julie (IRE)** 2-8-9 0.............................. PatrickDonaghy(5) 11 68
(P C Haslam) *s.i.s and bhd: hdwy 1/2-way: rdn over 1f out: kpt on wl ins fnl f* **40/1**
4 1/2 **Pure Nostalgia (IRE)** 2-9-0 0.............................. TonyHamilton 7 66
(J Howard Johnson) *chsd ldrs: effrt over 2f out and sn rdn: kpt on same pce: fin 5th: plcd 4th* **18/1**
4 **5** *hd* **Flyinflyout**[6] 2175 2-9-0 0.............................. EdwardCreighton 12 65
(M R Channon) *in tch: stmbld 1/2-way: rdn along 2f out: sn rdn and kpt on fnl f: nrst fin: fin 6th: plcd 5th* **15/8**[1]
6 3/4 **Wigan Lane** 2-9-0 0.............................. PaulHanagan 10 63
(R A Fahey) *chsd ldrs: effrt 2f out: sn rdn and kpt on same pce: fin 7th: plcd 6th* **7/1**[2]
7 *1* **Wood Fair** 2-9-0 0.............................. DaleGibson 5 60
(K R Burke) *towards rr tl sme late hdwy: fin 8th: plcd 7th* **66/1**
6 **8** 1/2 **Belle Eponine**[21] 1764 2-9-0 0.............................. TPO'Shea 8 59
(E J O'Neill) *chsd ldrs: rdn along 1/2-way: wknd wl over 1f out: fin 9th: plcd 8th* **16/1**
0 **9** 1 3/4 **Mary Celest (IRE)**[17] 1866 2-9-0 0.............................. WJSupple 15 53
(K A Ryan) *in tch on outer: rdn along 1/2-way: sn wknd: fin 10th: plcd 9th* **14/1**
35 **10** 1/2 **Victorian Art (IRE)**[15] 1933 2-9-0 0.............................. TomEaves 1 52
(M A Magnusson) *in tch on outer: rdn along over 2f out: sn wknd: fin 11th: plcd 10th* **7/1**[2]
11 *6* **Howdoyalikemenow (IRE)** 2-8-11 0.............................. NeilBrown(3) 6 34
(K A Ryan) *s.i.s: a bhd: fin 12th: plcd 11th* **25/1**
6 **12** 1 3/4 **Wallgate**[22] 1735 2-9-0 0.............................. PhillipMakin 13 29
(Miss J A Camacho) *midfield: rdn along and bhd fr 1/2-way: fin 13th: plcd 12th* **28/1**
0 **13** *4* **Foricherforpoorer**[9] 2099 2-8-11 0.............................. KellyHarrison(3) 9 17
(N Tinkler) *chsd ldrs to 1/2-way: sn lost pl and bhd: fin 14th: plcd 13th* **100/1**
6 **D** 1/2 **True Loves Kiss**[10] 2069 2-9-0 0.............................. AndrewElliott 14 66+
(A J McCabe) *bhd: gd hdwy on outer wl over 1f out: sn rdn and edgd lft ent fnl f: kpt on wl towards fin: fin 4th, 31/2l, nk & 1/2l: disq: jockey failed to weigh in* **8/1**[3]

1m 12.52s (0.72) **Going Correction** +0.05s/f (Good) 14 Ran SP% **117.9**
Speed ratings (Par 90): **97,92,91,90,90 89,88,87,85,84 76,74,68,91**
toteswinger: 1&2 £14.80, 1&3 £67.10, 2&3 £26.90 CSF £131.47 TOTE £18.70: £5.80, £3.30, £13.70; EX 152.90.
Owner Around The World Partnership **Bred** Mrs Mary Taylor **Trained** Middleham Moor, N Yorks
■ Stewards' Enquiry : Andrew Elliott three-day ban: failed to weigh-in (June 9-11)

FOCUS
The ground had dried on slightly from the previous day and was now officially Good to Firm, Firm in places on the straight course, but the jockeys reported that it wasn't that bad and had no jar. As they usually do here, the runners came straight down the centre of the track.

NOTEBOOK
Avonrose had dropped out after showing early speed over the minimum trip on similar ground here earlier this month, but she had obviously learnt from that and, after having raced up with the pace from the start again, she was sent to the front over a furlong from home and went further and further clear. The form may not be anything special, but she is improving and should be able to find other opportunities. (op 14-1)
Gwynedd(IRE) ◆, a £28,000 half-sister to a couple of winning juvenile sprinters, attracted market support. She broke well and took them along although she was keen enough early, and in view of that she did well to hang in there and keep on for second, though she had no answer to the winner. This was a pleasing start and she should win races. (op 11-1)
Dance For Julie(IRE) ◆, a £14,000 yearling from the stable that took this last year, was noted doing some good late work from off the pace and she is one to keep an eye on. (tchd 50-1)
Pure Nostalgia(IRE), by Choisir but out of a multiple winner at up to 1m4f, tracked the leaders throughout and kept staying on to show promise for the future. (op 20-1)
Flyinflyout, who showed ability when fourth on her Goodwood debut six days earlier, was disappointing and a mid-race move came to little. (op 7-4 tchd 13-8)
Wigan Lane, a 28,000gns half-sister to a couple of winning sprinters including the smart Hoh Hoh Hoh, showed early speed and she can be expected to come on from this. (op 13-2 tchd 6-1)
Foricherforpoorer Official explanation: jockey said filly hung left-handed throughout
True Loves Kiss, up a furlong from her debut, stayed on well up the nearside of the track though she did tend to hang about a bit and perhaps she doesn't want the ground as quick as this. Unfortunately her rider failed to weigh in and she was disqualified. (op 10-1)

2361 RACING UK SKY 432 (S) STKS 7f
2:40 (2:41) (Class 6) 3-5-Y-O £2,047 (£604; £302) **Stalls** Centre

Form RPR
1000 **1** **El Dececy (USA)**[3] 2267 5-9-13 **81**..............................(p) GrahamGibbons 6 75
(S Parr) *mde all: rdn over 1f out: edgd rt ins fnl f: styd on* **8/11**[1]

00 **2** 2 ¼ **King Pin**[22] 1734 4-9-7 0 ... PhillipMakin 9 63
(Miss Tracy Waggott) *hld up in rr: hdwy over 3f out: swtchd lft and effrt 2f out: sn rdn and styd on to chse wnr appr fnl f: sn drvn and no imp* **33/1**

0000 **3** 1 ¾ **Wiseman's Diamond (USA)**[17] 1889 4-9-2 47 ... JamieMoriarty 10 53
(P T Midgley) *hld up towards rr: hdwy 3f out: rdn to chse ldrs 2f out: drvn and kpt on same pce appr fnl f* **40/1**

-050 **4** 1 ¾ **Bertie Vista**[22] 1723 4-9-7 60 ... (b) DavidAllan 11 53
(T D Easterby) *midfield: hdwy 3f out: chsd wnr 2f out: sn rdn and one pce* **9/2**[2]

-050 **5** 2 ½ **Wabi Sabi (IRE)**[10] 2091 3-8-5 59 ... AndrewElliott 5 38
(N Tinkler) *in rr: hdwy over 2f out: rdn to chse ldrs and hung bdly lft over 1f out: no imp after* **10/1**

-062 **6** 5 **My Mate Mal**[31] 1530 5-9-7 66 ... TomEaves 4 33
(B Ellison) *chsd ldrs: rdn along over 2f out: drvn wl over 1f out and sn wknd* **6/1**[3]

/0-5 **7** 2 ¼ **Just Crystal**[22] 1734 5-9-2 39 ... TPO'Shea 13 22
(B P J Baugh) *s.i.s and bhd: hdwy 1/2-way: rdn to chse ldrs on outer over 2f out: sn wknd* **50/1**

0605 **8** 2 **Buail Isteach (IRE)**[15] 1940 4-9-2 48 ... (b[1]) EdwardCreighton 12 17
(E J Creighton) *chsd ldrs: rdn along wl over 2f out: sn wknd* **50/1**

000- **9** ¾ **Nufoudh (IRE)**[199] 5501 5-9-7 42 ... GregFairley 7 20
(Miss Tracy Waggott) *t.k.h: cl up: rdn along 3f out: wknd over 2f out* **100/1**

-000 **10** 2 ¼ **Lifetime Endeavour**[15] 1924 5-9-4 42 ... KellyHarrison[(3)] 8 13
(R E Barr) *midfield: lost pl and bhd fr 1/2-way* **100/1**

00-0 **11** ¾ **Raise All In (IRE)**[26] 1628 3-8-5 52 ... AdrianTNicholls 1 —
(N Wilson) *in tch: rdn along over 3f out and sn wknd* **33/1**

-000 **12** 2 ¼ **Party In The Park**[18] 1846 4-9-7 57 ... PaulHanagan 3 —
(Miss J A Camacho) *in tch: rdn along 1/2-way: sn wknd and bhd* **16/1**

500- **13** 10 **Ducal Regancy Duke**[288] 4924 5-9-7 38 ... (p) PatrickMathers 2 —
(C J Teague) *prom: rdn along 1/2-way: sn lost pl and bhd* **150/1**

1m 24.81s (0.31) **Going Correction** +0.05s/f (Good) **13** Ran SP% **120.2**
WFA 3 from 4yo+ 11lb
Speed ratings (Par 101): **100,97,95,93,90 84,82,80,79,76 75,73,61**
toteswinger: 1&2 £12.10, 1&3 £14.70, 2&3 £49.50 CSF £42.38 TOTE £1.60: £1.10, £7.80, £12.20; EX 38.20.The winner was bought in for 7,500gns.
Owner Willie McKay **Bred** Shadwell Farm LLC **Trained**

FOCUS
A moderate seller in which nine of the 13 runners were maidens and several had no chance on official ratings.
Just Crystal Official explanation: jockey said mare was slowly away

2362 WEATHERBYS BLOODSTOCK INSURANCE H'CAP 1m 1f
3:10 (3:11) (Class 5) (0-70,70) 4-Y-0+ **£2,590** (£770; £385; £192) **Stalls** Low

Form RPR

1204 **1** **Templetuohy Max (IRE)**[18] 1845 4-9-2 68 ... (v) GrahamGibbons 11 79
(J D Bethell) *mde most: rdn clr over 2f out: styd on strly fnl f* **7/1**

-000 **2** 4 **Spirit Of France (IRE)**[4] 2245 7-9-4 70 ... DNolan 8 72
(D Carroll) *towards rr: hdwy 3f out: swtchd outside and rdn wl over 1f: styd on to chse wnr ins fnl f: no imp* **16/1**

0011 **3** ¾ **Sarwin (USA)**[14] 1955 6-8-11 63 ... TPO'Shea 7 64
(G A Swinbank) *hld up: hdwy over 3f out: rdn to chse ldng pair 2f out: drvn to chse wnr over 1f out: sn no imp* **7/2**[1]

0100 **4** 1 ¼ **Uncle Bertie**[5] 2200 4-9-4 70 ... GregFairley 14 68
(N J Vaughan) *a.p: effrt to chse wnr over 3f out and sn rdn: drvn wl over 1f out and one pce* **16/1**

0-00 **5** 2 **Efidium**[22] 1723 11-8-3 62 ... GihanArnolda[(7)] 1 55+
(N Bycroft) *hld up towards rr: effrt on inner and nt clr run 3f out: swtchd rt to wd outsideand rdn over 1f out: styd on ins fnl f: nrst fin* **20/1**

3652 **6** hd **Rosko**[23] 1690 5-9-0 66 ... TomEaves 5 59
(B Ellison) *trckd ldrs: hdwy 3f out: swtchd lft and rdn 2f out: sn drvn and no imp* **6/1**[2]

2030 **7** nk **Snow Dancer (IRE)**[11] 2043 5-8-13 68 ... (p) NeilBrown[(3)] 3 60+
(H A McWilliams) *trckd ldrs on inner: effrt and n.m.r over 2f out and sn lost pl: swtchd rt and styd on ent fnl f: nvr a factor* **13/2**[3]

003- **8** shd **Mooted (UAE)**[172] 7559 4-8-5 64 ... BMcHugh[(7)] 12 56
(Miss J A Camacho) *in tch: effrt over 3f out: sn rdn along and n.d* **15/2**

43-0 **9** nk **Island Music (IRE)**[22] 1737 4-8-7 66 ... JamieKyne[(7)] 6 57
(J J Quinn) *he;ld up: hdwy whn nt clr run wl over 2f out: no imp after* **15/2**

1-40 **10** ½ **Neon Blue**[27] 1615 8-8-7 59 ... TonyHamilton 10 49
(R M Whitaker) *hld up in rr: hdwy 3f out: rdn and keeping on whn n.m.r over 1f out: n.d* **20/1**

0-04 **11** 1 ¾ **Desert Destiny**[11] 2043 9-9-2 68 ... (v) WJSupple 13 54
(C Grant) *hld up: a in rr* **14/1**

00-0 **12** 4 ½ **Fyodorovich (USA)**[17] 1887 4-9-1 67 ow5 ... PAspell 4 44
(J S Wainwright) *trckd wnr: rdn along over 3f out and grad wknd* **80/1**

3-44 **13** 10 **Tour D'Amour (IRE)**[4] 2237 6-8-4 56 oh6 ... (b) AdrianTNicholls 9 11
(R Craggs) *in tch: hdwy on outer to chse ldrs 1/2-way: rdn along 4f out and sn wknd* **16/1**

1m 53.34s (0.34) **Going Correction** +0.125s/f (Good) **13** Ran SP% **120.9**
Speed ratings (Par 103): **103,99,98,97,95 95,95,95,95,94 93,89,80**
toteswinger: 1&2 £13.60, 1&3 £13.60, 2&3 £5.40 CSF £112.60 CT £464.47 TOTE £8.10: £3.60, £5.90, £2.00; EX 127.10.
Owner Craig Monty **Bred** Jim Shanahan **Trained** Middleham Moor, N Yorks

FOCUS
An ordinary handicap, but a competitive event on paper.
Snow Dancer(IRE) Official explanation: jockey said mare was denied a clear run
Neon Blue Official explanation: jockey said gelding was denied a clear run

2363 WEATHERBYS BANK H'CAP 5f
3:40 (3:41) (Class 4) (0-85,85) 4-Y-0+ **£4,857** (£1,445; £722; £360) **Stalls** Centre

Form RPR

005- **1** **Total Impact**[210] 7047 6-9-1 82 ... PaulHanagan 9 94
(R A Fahey) *trckd ldrs: hdwy over 1f out: swtchd lft and rdn to chal ent fnl f: kpt on to ld last 50yds* **11/2**

2-53 **2** ½ **Le Toreador**[24] 1685 4-8-12 79 ... WJSupple 8 89
(K A Ryan) *led: rdn along over 1f out: jnd and drvn ins fnl f: hdd and nt qckn fnl 50yds* **7/2**[1]

-360 **3** ¾ **Discanti (IRE)**[10] 2095 4-8-10 77 ... (t) DavidAllan 6 84
(T D Easterby) *cl up: rdn and ev ch over 1f out tl drvn and one pce ins fnl f* **15/2**

-430 **4** ¾ **Indian Trail**[18] 1849 9-9-1 82 ... (b[1]) AdrianTNicholls 5 87
(D Nicholls) *hld up in rr: hdwy wl over 1f out and sn rdn: drvn ent fnl f: kpt on: nrst fin* **5/1**[3]

0-02 **5** nse **Baybshambles (IRE)**[14] 1951 5-8-1 71 oh3 ... KellyHarrison[(3)] 7 75
(R E Barr) *in tch: hdwy on outer to chse ldrs wl over 1f out: sn rdn and kpt on same pce ent fnl f* **17/2**

0-21 **6** 2 ¾ **Rasaman (IRE)**[10] 2095 5-8-13 85 ... AmyRyan[(5)] 1 80
(K A Ryan) *chsd ldrs on outer: rdn and edgd rt 2f out: drvn and hung rt over 1f out: sn wknd* **9/2**[2]

25-0 **7** 1 ¼ **Stolt (IRE)**[12] 2012 5-9-4 85 ... DanielTudhope 3 75
(N Wilson) *chsd ldrs: rdn along 1/2-way: sn wknd* **16/1**

-001 **8** shd **Pacific Pride**[14] 1951 6-7-11 71 ... (p) JamieKyne[(7)] 2 61
(J J Quinn) *cl up: rdn along 2f out: wkng whn hmpd over 1f out* **8/1**

-000 **9** 2 ¼ **Hotham**[4] 2228 6-9-0 81 ... JamieMoriarty 4 63
(N Wilson) *a in rr* **33/1**

58.20 secs (-0.40) **Going Correction** +0.05s/f (Good) **9** Ran SP% **114.7**
Speed ratings (Par 105): **105,104,103,101,101 97,95,95,91**
toteswinger: 1&2 £4.70, 1&3 £7.60, 2&3 £6.70 CSF £24.89 CT £144.61 TOTE £5.80: £2.40, £1.40, £2.90; EX 30.90.
Owner The Wakey Exiles **Bred** C A Cyzer **Trained** Musley Bank, N Yorks
■ Stewards' Enquiry : Amy Ryan caution: careless riding; one-day ban: used whip down shoulder in forehand position (Jun 9)

FOCUS
A fair sprint handicap and, with a few confirmed front-runners in the field, there was never going to be any shortage of pace.

2364 BUY YOUR TICKETS ON-LINE @ REDCARRACING.CO.UK MAIDEN STKS 1m 2f
4:10 (4:11) (Class 5) 3-Y-0+ **£2,590** (£770; £385; £192) **Stalls** Low

Form RPR

1 **Maqaam** 3-8-12 0 ... TPO'Shea 3 74
(M Johnston) *trckd ldng pair: hdwy to chse ldr 1/2-way: rdn along and outpcd 3f out: drvn to chal wl over 1f out: styd on to ld wl ins fnl f: kpt on* **8/11**[1]

2-0 **2** hd **Peaceful Rule (USA)**[34] 1461 3-8-12 0 ... AdrianTNicholls 1 73
(D Nicholls) *set stdy pce: qcknd 3f out: rdn 2f out and sn jnd: drvn and edgd rt ins fnl f: sn hdd and no ex nr fin* **15/8**[2]

0 **3** 8 **Gwyre (IRE)**[11] 2042 3-8-7 0 ... DavidAllan 2 52
(T D Easterby) *hld up in tch: hdwy over 3f out: rdn over 2f out: drvn wl over 1f out and sn no imp* **12/1**

4 1 **Bogula (IRE)** 3-8-7 0 ... WJSupple 4 50
(Mrs A Duffield) *trckd ldr: pushed along over 4f out: rdn 3f out: grad wknd* **11/1**[3]

5 64 **Silvertown Boy** 3-8-5 0 ... IanCraven[(7)] 5 —
(H A McWilliams) *wnt rt s and s.i.s: bhd tl hdwy to join field whn hung bdly rt home turn: sn outpcd and bhd* **40/1**

2m 11.2s (4.10) **Going Correction** +0.125s/f (Good) **5** Ran SP% **111.2**
Speed ratings (Par 103): **88,87,81,80,29**
CSF £2.35 TOTE £1.80: £1.10, £1.20; EX 2.80.
Owner Hamdan Al Maktoum **Bred** R And Mrs Watson And Mrs A J Ralli **Trained** Middleham Moor, N Yorks
■ Stewards' Enquiry : Adrian T Nicholls one-day ban: used whip down shoulder in forehand position (Jun 9)

FOCUS
A very weak maiden in which the pace was slow, and the finish only concerned the two market leaders.
Silvertown Boy Official explanation: jockey said gelding hung right-handed throughout

2365 ANDERSON BARROWCLIFF H'CAP 6f
4:40 (4:43) (Class 5) (0-70,69) 3-Y-O **£2,590** (£770; £385; £192) **Stalls** Centre

Form RPR

4420 **1** **Minturno (USA)**[14] 1969 3-8-9 60 ... WJSupple 9 62
(Mrs A Duffield) *hld up towards rr: hdwy over 2f out: swtchd lft and rdn over 1f out: styd on ins fnl f to ld on line* **11/1**

3515 **2** shd **Where's Reiley (USA)**[11] 2028 3-8-12 66 ... NeilBrown[(3)] 10 68
(T D Barron) *trckd ldrs: hdwy over 2f out: rdn to ld over 1f out: drvn ins fnl f: hdd nr line* **6/1**

210 **3** nk **Seldom (IRE)**[11] 2058 3-8-11 69 ... JohnCavanagh[(7)] 6 70
(M Brittain) *cl up: led 2f out: sn rdn and hdd over 1f out: drvn and nt qckn wl ins fnl f* **8/1**

0601 **4** 1 **Bold Ring**[14] 1969 3-8-7 58 ... EdwardCreighton 8 56
(E J Creighton) *chsd ldrs: rdn 2f out: drvn and cl up whn hung lft ins fnl f: one pce towards fin* **16/1**

1 **5** ¾ **Laura's Lady (IRE)**[15] 1922 3-8-6 57 ... PJMcDonald 11 52+
(G A Swinbank) *dwlt: sn in tch: hdwy to chse ldrs over 2f out: sn rdn and kpt on same pce fr over 1f out* **5/1**[3]

110 **6** 1 **Just Timmy Marcus**[22] 1736 3-9-2 67 ... GrahamGibbons 14 59
(B P J Baugh) *chsd ldrs on outer: rdn along 2f out: sn drvn: edgd lft and one pce appr fnl f* **4/1**[1]

5-00 **7** nse **Port Ronan (USA)**[22] 1736 3-8-4 55 ... AdrianTNicholls 4 47
(J S Wainwright) *cl up: rdn along over 2f out and grad wknd* **50/1**

044- **8** nk **Africa's Star (IRE)**[168] 7612 3-9-2 67 ... PhillipMakin 3 60
(M Dods) *cl up: rdn wl over 1f out: drvn and one pce whn carried lft and hmpd ins fnl f: wknd after* **18/1**

5-44 **9** 2 ¼ **Abbey Steps (IRE)**[22] 1736 3-8-5 56 ... (b) DuranFentiman 2 40
(T D Easterby) *dwlt: a towards rr* **10/1**

03-4 **10** 5 **Exceedingly Good (IRE)**[11] 2028 3-9-1 66 ... TomEaves 13 34
(B Smart) *in tch: rdn along 1/2-way and sn wknd* **9/2**[2]

0-05 **11** ½ **Venetian Lady**[8] 2141 3-8-4 55 ... PaulHanagan 12 21
(Mrs A Duffield) *a towards rr* **16/1**

231- **12** 4 **Real Diamond**[210] 7038 3-9-1 66 ... DanielTudhope 7 19
(A Dickman) *led: rdn along and hdd 2f out: sn wknd* **16/1**

1m 12.28s (0.48) **Going Correction** +0.05s/f (Good) **12** Ran SP% **122.5**
Speed ratings (Par 99): **98,97,97,96,95 93,93,93,90,83 83,77**
toteswinger: 1&2 £18.40, 1&3 £17.40, 2&3 £10.80 CSF £78.26 CT £573.07 TOTE £13.40: £3.50, £2.70, £3.20; EX 114.20.
Owner Trevor Wilson **Bred** Robert C Francis **Trained** Constable Burton, N Yorks
■ Stewards' Enquiry : Edward Creighton one-day ban: careless riding (Jun 9)

FOCUS
A modest sprint handicap, but quite a competitive event.

2366 WEDDING RECEPTIONS @ REDCAR RACECOURSE AMATEUR RIDERS' MAIDEN H'CAP 6f
5:10 (5:10) (Class 6) (0-60,59) 4-Y-0+ **£1,977** (£608; £304) **Stalls** Centre

Form RPR

-230 **1** **Just Sam (IRE)**[14] 1955 4-10-9 54 ... MissVBarr[(7)] 12 62
(R E Barr) *chsd ldrs: hdwy whn nt clr run and hmpd 2f out: sn swtchd rt: rdn and styd on to ld ins fnl f* **7/1**[3]

646- **2** ¾ **Hansomis (IRE)**[206] 7129 5-11-0 **52** .... MrsCBartley 8 57
(B Mactaggart) *prom: hdwy over 2f out: rdn to ld wl over 1f out: drvn and hdd ins fnl f: one pce* **8/1**

4435 **3** ¾ **Mr Rev**[4] 2223 6-10-7 **50** .... (b) MissSBradley(5) 17 53
(J M Bradley) *hld up: hdwy whn n.m.r and swtchd lft 2f out: rdn over 1f out: sndrvn: edgd lft and kpt on ins fnl f* **9/2**[1]

220- **4** *shd* **Park's Prodigy**[206] 3718 5-10-8 **51** .... (tp) MissEStead(5) 7 54+
(P C Haslam) *bhd: hdwy on outer wl over 1f out: sn rdn and styd on wl fnl f: nrst fin* **6/1**[2]

33-0 **5** 3¼ **Monte Cassino (IRE)**[14] 1951 4-10-9 **47** .... MrSWalker 20 39
(J O'Reilly) *in tch: effrt and hdwy over 2f out: sn rdn and styd on ins fnl f: nrst fin* **8/1**

5050 **6** *nk* **Rightcar Lewis**[10] 2070 4-10-2 **47** .... (b) MrCEllingham(7) 5 38
(Peter Grayson) *cl up: rdn along whn bmpd 2f out: sn drvn and one pce appr fnl f* **33/1**

6052 **7** ¾ **Triple Dream**[20] 1787 4-11-0 **59** .... (p) MissHDavies(7) 11 48
(J M Bradley) *chsd ldrs: swtchd lft wl over 1f out: sn rdn and wknd ent fnl f* **9/2**[1]

00-5 **8** *hd* **Call Me Rosy (IRE)**[21] 1769 5-10-2 **47** .... MrJNewman(7) 18 35
(B Smart) *s.i.s and bhd: hdwy 2f out: sn rdn and kpt on ins fnl f: nt rch ldrs* **20/1**

-046 **9** ¾ **Sheik'N'Knotsterd**[15] 1924 4-10-11 **54** .... MissABevan(5) 19 40
(J F Coupland) *hld up towards rr: hdwy 2f out: kpt on ins fnl f: nvr nr ldrs* **20/1**

3460 **10** ½ **Prince Of Delphi**[20] 1787 6-10-12 **57** .... (p) MrOJMurphy(7) 1 41
(Mrs A L M King) *led: rdn 3f out: hung rt 2f out: sn hdd and grad wknd* **12/1**

000- **11** 3¼ **Tump Mac**[182] 7442 5-10-5 **50** .... MrSebSpencer(7) 14 24
(N Bycroft) *nvr bttr than midfield* **25/1**

/00- **12** ¾ **Warners Bay (IRE)**[321] 3834 4-10-12 **55** .... MissRBastiman(5) 15 26
(R Bastiman) *chsd ldrs: rdn along 2f out: sn wknd* **40/1**

6-00 **13** *1* **Billy Bowmore**[60] 979 4-10-8 **51** .... KyleJames(5) 3 19
(P A Kirby) *midfield: swtchd lft and rdn 1/2-way: sn drvn and outpcd* **14/1**

460- **14** *hd* **Hits Only Time**[275] 5307 4-10-10 **53** .... MissDAllman(5) 9 21
(D Carroll) *in tch: rdn along 1/2-way: wknd 2f out* **25/1**

15 2¼ **Maggie Maggie May (IRE)**[979] 3184 7-10-2 **45**(p) MrJPFeatherstone(5) 2 5
(P C Haslam) *a bhd* **33/1**

66-0 **16** *8* **Pinewood Lulu**[7] 2166 4-10-12 **55** .... MrCAHarris(5) 6 —
(R C Guest) *in tch: rdn along 1/2-way: sn wknd* **66/1**

60-0 **17** 1¼ **Dashing Daniel**[26] 1632 4-10-9 **52** .... MrTRDavid(5) 10 —
(N J Vaughan) *v.s.a: a bhd* **16/1**

1m 13.99s (2.19) **Going Correction** +0.05s/f (Good) **17** Ran SP% **132.6**
Speed ratings (Par 101): **87,86,85,84,80 80,79,78,77,77 72,71,70,70,67 56,54**
toteswinger: 1&2 £19.00, 1&3 £7.60, 2&3 £15.10 CSF £61.12 CT £304.27 TOTE £8.60: £2.10, £2.40, £2.20, £2.30; EX 94.80 Place 6 £239.52 Place 5: £23.53.
Owner P Cartmell **Bred** John J Carroll **Trained** Seamer, N Yorks
■ Victoria Barr's first winner.
■ Stewards' Enquiry : Mr J P Featherstone caution: used whip when out of contention
Mr O J Murphy one-day ban: careless riding (Jun 10)

FOCUS
These 17 runners had the dubious distinction of having run in a total of 204 races on the Flat without winning. It was no surprise that the winning time was 1.71 seconds slower than the preceding three-year-old handicap.
T/Plt: £358.10 to a £1 stake. Pool: £37,389.16. 76.20 winning tickets. T/Qpdt: £24.00 to a £1 stake. Pool: £4,288.98. 132.00 winning tickets. JR

2367 - 2369a (Foreign Racing) - See Raceform Interactive

2257 BEVERLEY (R-H)
Wednesday, May 27

OFFICIAL GOING: Good to firm (good in places; 9.3)
Inside rail around top bend moved in one yard but effect on distances not notified.
Wind: Fresh, half against Weather: Overcast

2370 RACING AGAIN ON WEDNESDAY 10 JUNE H'CAP — 1m 100y
6:20 (6:20) (Class 5) (0-70,70) 3-Y-O — **£1,890** (£1,890; £433; £216) **Stalls** High

Form — RPR

0-62 **1** **Mr Freddy (IRE)**[23] 1740 3-9-1 **67** .... TonyHamilton 10 75+
(R A Fahey) *trckd ldrs: hdwy over 2f out: rdn over 1f out: chal ent fnl f: sn drvn and kpt on to join ldr on line* **13/8**[1]

043 **1** *dht* **Aldaado (IRE)**[15] 1950 3-8-13 **65** .... PhillipMakin 16 73+
(M Dods) *in tch on inner: hdwy over 2f out: effrt over 1f out: rdn to ld ent fnl f: sn drvn and hung lft: jnd on line* **12/1**

5332 **3** 1¼ **Everaard (USA)**[23] 1746 3-8-12 **64** .... PaulMulrennan 6 69
(D R C Elsworth) *stdd s and swtchd rt to rails: hdwy on inner 2f out: rdn to chse ldrs over 1f out: styd on u.p ins fnl f: nrst fin* **7/1**[3]

0400 **4** 1¼ **Vita Mia**[23] 1746 3-8-4 **56** oh2 .... CatherineGannon 14 58
(P D Evans) *led: rdn along 2f out: drvn over 1f out: hdd ent fnl f: sn n.m.r and wknd* **22/1**

1-46 **5** *nk* **Embsay Crag**[27] 1626 3-8-11 **66** .... NeilBrown(3) 11 67
(Mrs K Walton) *in tch on outer: gd hdwy 3f out: rdn to chse ldrs wl over 1f out: drvn and ch appr fnl f: sn edgd rt and kpt on same pce* **8/1**

23-1 **6** ½ **Hel's Angel (IRE)**[11] 2091 3-9-4 **70** .... DO'Donohoe 15 70
(Mrs A Duffield) *t.k.h early: chsd ldrs: effrt whn n.m.r and swtchd lft over 1f out: sn rdn and ev ch ent fnl f: sn one pce* **4/1**[2]

6523 **7** ¾ **Kheskianto (IRE)**[15] 1973 3-8-3 **62** .... AndrewHeffernan(7) 1 61
(M C Chapman) *hld up: hdwy over 2f out: trckd ldrs wl over 1f out: rdn and n.m.r ent fnl f: sn one pce* **20/1**

61-0 **8** 1¾ **Sampower Rose (IRE)**[11] 2091 3-8-13 **65** .... DNolan 12 60
(D Carroll) *midfield: hdwy over 2f out: rdn wl over 1f out: sn drvn and no imp* **25/1**

026- **9** ¾ **Markadam**[160] 7720 3-8-11 **63** .... JimmyQuinn 9 56
(Miss S E Hall) *nvr bttr than midfield* **33/1**

062- **10** 1½ **Challenging (UAE)**[201] 7220 3-8-5 **57** .... DaleGibson 7 46
(M W Easterby) *chsd ldrs: effrt on outer over 2f out: sn rdn: edgd rt and wknd over 1f out* **40/1**

2620 **11** *nk* **Amazing Blue Sky**[5] 2236 3-8-8 **60** .... AndrewElliott 4 49
(Mrs R A Carr) *prom on outer: rdn along 2f out: grad wknd* **14/1**

5-50 **12** *nk* **What A Day**[18] 1882 3-8-12 **64** .... GrahamGibbons 5 52
(J J Quinn) *stdd and swtchd rt s: hld up: a in rr* **14/1**

0-00 **13** 2¾ **Pilot Light**[23] 1724 3-8-4 **56** oh7 .... (p) DuranFentiman 2 38
(T D Easterby) *cl up: rdn along over 2f out: sn drvn and wknd* **50/1**

1m 47.3s (-0.30) **Going Correction** -0.025s/f (Good) **13** Ran SP% **123.0**
Speed ratings (Par 99): **100,100,98,97,97 96,95,94,93,91 91,91,88**
toteswinger: MF/A £4.60, MF/E £3.10, A/E £9.00 TRIFECTA WIN: MF £1.30, A £5.30; PL: MF £1.40, A £3.60 E £2.10; EX: MF-A £22.20, A-MF £11.90; CSF: MF-A £11.05, A-MF £15.25; TRICAST: £62.00.
Owner A Wynn-Williams, D Graham, D Neale **Bred** Deer Forest Stud **Trained** Denton, Co Durham
Owner R F White **Bred** Spratstown Stud Gm **Trained** Musley Bank, N Yorks

FOCUS
Ground described as good to firm but the runners were racing into a stiffish headwind in the straight. A competitive handicap to kick off Beverley's big night of the year but a high draw proved crucial with five of the first six home coming from a double-figure stalls position. The finish was dominated by two progressive horses, with an in-form rival back in third, so the form looks pretty good for the grade and very solid.

2371 SUPABED QUALITY PAPER BEDDING H'CAP — 1m 4f 16y
6:50 (6:51) (Class 5) (0-70,70) 3-Y-O — **£2,914** (£867; £433; £216) **Stalls** High

Form — RPR

-331 **1** **Antigua Sunrise (IRE)**[12] 2060 3-9-3 **69** .... TonyHamilton 2 74+
(R A Fahey) *t.k.h early: trckd ldrs: effrt 2f out: sn rdn and n.m.r appr fnl f: swtchd lft and drvn ins fnl f: styd on strly to ld nr line* **9/4**[1]

0511 **2** *hd* **Classic Contours (USA)**[15] 1954 3-8-11 **70** .... JamieKyne(7) 12 75
(J J Quinn) *trckd ldrs on inner: hdwy over 2f out: swtchd lft and rdn over 1f out: drvn to chal ent fnl f: kpt on to ld briefly last 50yds: hdd and no ex nr line* **11/2**[2]

-535 **3** *nk* **Tropical Bachelor (IRE)**[12] 2060 3-9-2 **68** .... J-PGuillambert 7 72
(T J Pitt) *trckd ldr: hdwy 3f out and sn cl up: rdn to ld over 1f out: drvn ent fnl f: hdd and no ex last 50yds* **14/1**

00-3 **4** 1¼ **Northside Prince (IRE)**[28] 1611 3-8-13 **65** .... PJMcDonald 8 67+
(G A Swinbank) *hld up in tch: hdwy on inner whn n.m.r wl over 1f out and sn rdn: swtchd lft and drvn ent fnl f: kpt on: nrst fin* **11/2**[2]

165- **5** *1* **Dazinski**[250] 6086 3-9-3 **69** .... AlanMunro 9 70+
(M H Tompkins) *hld up in rr: pushed along 3f out: hdwy over 2f out: rdn over 1f out: kpt on ins fnl f: nrst fin* **8/1**[3]

2153 **6** *2* **Dispol Diva**[19] 1829 3-9-1 **67** .... (v) JoeFanning 4 64
(P T Midgley) *chsd ldrs: hdwy and cl up over 3f out: rdn along 2f out: drvn over 1f out and sn one pce* **16/1**

0-32 **7** *hd* **Avitus**[16] 1925 3-8-9 **61** .... PaulMulrennan 1 58
(Micky Hammond) *hld up in rr: hdwy 3f out: rdn to chse ldrs 2f out: drvn and one pce appr fnl f* **28/1**

6304 **8** ¾ **Orsippus (USA)**[16] 1930 3-9-1 **67** .... (v) TonyCulhane 10 63
(M R Channon) *led: rdn along over 3f out: drvn 2f out: sn hdd and grad wknd* **14/1**

1240 **9** ¾ **Sounds Of Jupiter (IRE)**[19] 1842 3-9-3 **69** .... StephenDonohoe 3 64
(D M Simcock) *hld up in rr: effrt and sme hdwy over 2f out: sn rdn and no imp* **14/1**

0-64 **10** 3¼ **Sharp Sovereign (USA)**[19] 1829 3-9-1 **67** .... PhillipMakin 6 56
(T D Barron) *hld up towards rr: hdwy 3f out: rdn over 2f out and sn wknd* **8/1**[3]

003- **11** *shd* **Sampower Quin (IRE)**[219] 6857 3-8-12 **64** .... DNolan 11 53
(D Carroll) *a towards rr* **40/1**

20-6 **12** *nk* **Drop The Hammer**[12] 2042 3-8-8 **60** .... TPQueally 5 49
(T P Tate) *hld up towards rr: hdwy on outer to chse ldrs over 5f out: rdn along 3f out: sn wknd* **25/1**

2m 40.79s (-0.11) **Going Correction** -0.025s/f (Good) **12** Ran SP% **119.4**
Speed ratings (Par 99): **99,98,98,97,97 95,95,95,94,92 92,92**
toteswinger: 1&2 £2.10, 1&3 £12.60, 2&3 £19.80 CSF £13.64 CT £144.20 TOTE £3.20: £1.60, £2.20, £5.10; EX 14.00.
Owner David And Jackie Knaggs **Bred** Michael Morrin **Trained** Musley Bank, N Yorks

FOCUS
A steadily run race which got a bit messy early in the straight, as they often do here, and turned into a bit if a sprint from the three pole.but the finish was dominated by progressive horses so the form seems sound enough.
Sharp Sovereign(USA) Official explanation: jockey said gelding ran too free early stages

2372 HILARY NEEDLER TROPHY (LISTED RACE) — 5f
7:20 (7:21) (Class 1) 2-Y-O
£17,031 (£6,456; £3,231; £1,611; £807; £405) **Stalls** High

Form — RPR

1 **1** **Don't Tell Mary (IRE)**[14] 1981 2-8-12 0 .... RichardKingscote 12 99+
(Tom Dascombe) *hld up towards rr: gd hdwy 2f out: swtchd lft and effrt to chse ldr over 1f out: shkn up and qcknd to ld ins fnl f: sn clr* **11/4**[1]

21 **2** *4* **The Hermitage (IRE)**[13] 2000 2-8-12 0 .... JoeFanning 3 84+
(M Johnston) *cl up: rdn to ld over 1f out: drvn and hdd ins fnl f: kpt on same pce* **15/2**[3]

110 **3** *2* **Leleyf (IRE)**[12] 2054 2-8-12 0 .... TonyCulhane 11 77
(M R Channon) *chsd ldrs: rdn along 2f out: drvn over 1f out: kpt on u.p ins fnl f* **16/1**

42 **4** *1* **Angelena Ballerina (IRE)**[12] 2047 2-8-12 0 .... JimmyQuinn 14 73
(A Bailey) *chsd ldrs on inner: rdn along wl over 1f out: styd on ins fnl f: nrestfin* **13/2**[2]

23 **5** ¾ **Little Scotland**[12] 2054 2-8-12 0 .... DavidAllan 5 76+
(T D Easterby) *in tch whn hmpd after 1f: hdwy whn hmpd wl over 1f out: sn swtchd lft and rdn: styd on strly ins fnl f: nrst fin* **13/2**[2]

41 **6** ½ **Sheka**[32] 1521 2-8-12 0 .... DanielTudhope 9 69
(I W McInnes) *in rr: hdwy over 2f out: sn rdn and kpt on ins fnl f: nvr nr ldrs* **66/1**

52 **7** *nse* **Parbold Hill**[11] 2089 2-8-12 0 .... PhillipMakin 16 69
(T D Barron) *cl up: effrt 2f out: sn rdn and ev ch tl drvn over 1f out and sn wknd* **12/1**

52 **8** *nk* **Dower Glen**[19] 1827 2-8-12 0 .... PaulMulrennan 6 67
(I Semple) *chsd ldrs: rdn along and edgd rt wl over 1f out: sn drvn and one pce* **100/1**

01 **9** 1¼ **Patteresa Girl**[39] 1344 2-8-12 0 .... TomEaves 7 63
(Mrs L Stubbs) *dwlt: a towards rr* **22/1**

01 **10** 2¾ **Quaker Parrot**[15] 1968 2-8-12 0 .... RichardSmith 8 53
(Tom Dascombe) *chsd ldrs: rdn along over 2f out: drvn and edgd lft wl over 1f out: grad wknd* **40/1**

631 **11** 1½ **Six Wives**[16] 1934 2-8-12 0 .... AndrewMullen 13 48
(A J McCabe) *a towards rr* **33/1**

541 **12** ¾ **Tillys Tale**[11] 2089 2-8-12 0 .... PaulPickard 17 45
(P T Midgley) *cl up on inner: led after 2f: rdn 2f out: sn drvn: hdd & wknd* **16/1**

041 **13** 1½ **Lady Lube Rye (IRE)**[27] 1623 2-8-12 0 .... PaulQuinn 2 40
(N Wilson) *a towards rr* **100/1**

2214 **14** 1 3/4 **Diamond Laura**[12] 2054 2-8-12 0 CatherineGannon 15 33
(P D Evans) *a towards rr* **15/2**[3]

515 **15** 2 1/2 **Azif**[12] 2054 2-8-12 0 AlanMunro 4 24
(Miss Gay Kelleway) *bhd fr 1/2-way* **22/1**

31 **16** 3/4 **Existentialist**[20] 1810 2-8-12 0 TPQueally 1 22
(J G Portman) *qckly away on wd outside and led for 2f: sn rdn along and wknd* **12/1**

64.17 secs (0.67) **Going Correction** -0.025s/f (Good) **16** Ran SP% **121.6**
Speed ratings (Par 101): **93,86,83,81,80 79,79,79,77,72 70,69,66,64,60 58**
toteswinger: 1&2 £5.90, 1&3 £3.70, 2&3 £36.00 CSF £21.18 TOTE £4.40: £2.50, £2.80, £5.80; EX 31.50.
Owner K P Trowbridge **Bred** Mascalls Stud **Trained** Lambourn, Berks

FOCUS
The 45th and richest running of the this famous prize and an ultra competitive renewal with 12 previous winners in the line-up. Not since Attraction in 2003 has this race thrown up a top class filly but Don't Tell Mary impressed and looks Queen Mary material.

NOTEBOOK
Don't Tell Mary(IRE) ◆ has the potential to go on to big things after blowing this field away with a burst of speed in the final furlong that marks her down as well above average. She looked a touch outpaced early and her head carriage isn't totally convincing, but once switched out approaching the furlong pole she took off and the way she stormed through the final furlong suggests Cashman's quote of 8-1 (from 25-1) for the Queen Mary, which is her next target according to her trainer, may be a touch generous. (tchd 4-1)
The Hermitage(IRE), the only one of the first four home to come from a single-figure stall, has run a blinder and she travelled like a very good filly close to the pace throughout before finding the turn of foot by the winner too hot to handle. She too looks capable of holding her own in Group company. (op 17-2 tchd 7-1)
Leleyf(IRE) appreciated the return to quicker ground. Behind Little Scotland at York last time on good to soft ground, she proved that run all wrong by sticking on really well, albeit from a handy draw, to grab some valuable black type. (op 14-1)
Angelena Ballerina(IRE) stayed on well up the inside rail and the way she saw her race out suggests she is ready to step back up to 6f, where she looks sure to find success. (op 15-2)
Little Scotland's run can be upgraded significantly as she was way off the pace from her wide draw and she didn't have the clearest of runs well over a furlong out, but once in the clear she stayed on really strongly down the outside. She looks capable of winning in this grade. Official explanation: jockey said filly was denied a clear run (tchd 5-1)
Sheka kept on well from towards the back to run above market expectations. (op 50-1)
Parbold Hill dropped away in the final furlong have been on the sharp end early. (tchd 16-1)
Diamond Laura Official explanation: jockey said filly never travelled
Azif Official explanation: jockey said filly lost its action

2373 WEATHERBYS BLOODSTOCK INSURANCE CONDITIONS STKS 5f
7:50 (7:50) (Class 3) 3-Y-O
£7,352 (£2,201; £1,100; £551; £274; £138) **Stalls** High

Form RPR
4-22 **1** **Noble Storm (USA)**[19] 1824 3-8-12 93 GrahamGibbons 1 103
(E S McMahon) *qckly away: mde all: rdn over 1f out and kpt on strly* **5/6**[1]

22-5 **2** 1 3/4 **Waffle (IRE)**[13] 2016 3-8-12 108 TPQueally 4 97
(J Noseda) *trckd ldrs: hdwy 1/2-way: chsd wnr wl over 1f out: sn rdn and no imp ins fnl f* **9/4**[2]

5036 **3** 5 **Sir Geoffrey (IRE)**[12] 2058 3-8-12 77 (t) AndrewElliott 6 79
(A J McCabe) *chsd ldng pair: effrt 2f out: sn rdn and kpt on same pce* **28/1**

-155 **4** 1 3/4 **Dunes Queen (USA)**[19] 1828 3-8-10 90 TonyCulhane 3 70
(M R Channon) *outpcd in rr: sme hdwy 2f out: sn rdn and nvr a factor* **10/1**[3]

2351 **5** 9 **Glamorous Spirit (IRE)**[23] 1727 3-8-7 88 KevinGhunowa(3) 2 38
(R A Harris) *chsd wnr: rdn along 1/2-way: sn drvn and wknd* **16/1**

406- **6** 3 **La Brigitte**[233] 6533 3-8-4 85 AndrewMullen(3) 7 24
(A J McCabe) *a outpcd in rr* **12/1**

62.52 secs (-0.98) **Going Correction** -0.025s/f (Good) **6** Ran SP% **111.4**
Speed ratings (Par 103): **106,103,95,92,78 73**
toteswinger: 1&2 £1.10, 1&3 £5.50, 2&3 £5.90 CSF £2.81 TOTE £1.90: £1.30, £1.50; EX 3.40.
Owner R L Bedding **Bred** Brereton C Jones **Trained** Lichfield, Staffs

FOCUS
The winner posted a good time and looked to improve again here. The runer-up is probably the best guide and is rated 9lb off his one standout run.

NOTEBOOK
Noble Storm(USA) blasted out and never saw another rival. He is rated 15lb inferior to the second, so the handicapper has a conundrum now, but despite having set strong fractions on the sharp end, Noble Storm stayed on strongly in the final furling to draw clear again and mark himself down as a sprinter to follow. Despite the obvious temptation now to have a crack at a Listed contest, connections seem keen to keep him to conditions races confined to his own age group for the time being. Wherever he goes, he looks all about speed and it was no surprise to see him clock the fastest time of the evening. (op 5-4 tchd 11-8)
Waffle(IRE) clearly isn't as good as his current mark indicates and, although he didn't run badly here and slower ground will suit better, he could be tricky to place now. (op 15-8 tchd 13-8)
Sir Geoffrey(IRE) normally likes to force the pace but he could never get anywhere near Noble Storm and was subsequently never a factor. He wasn't entitled to on these terms, though, given his rating of 77, so he is easily forgiven this. (op 25-1 tchd 33-1)
Dunes Queen(USA) found things happening all too quickly and will need stepping back up in trip. (op 8-1 tchd 15-2)

2374 KEVIN DONKIN MEMORIAL H'CAP 1m 1f 207y
8:20 (8:20) (Class 4) (0-85,85) 4-Y-O+ **£4,727** (£1,406; £702; £351) **Stalls** High

Form RPR
1-41 **1** **Wind Star**[12] 2043 6-9-2 83 PJMcDonald 1 91
(G A Swinbank) *trckd ldrs: smooth hdwy over 2f out: rdn to ld appr fnl f: styd on strly* **5/2**[1]

4163 **2** 2 1/4 **Sri Kuantan (IRE)**[16] 1944 5-8-6 78 ow2 (t) MarkCoumbe(5) 8 82
(R C Guest) *sn led: pushed clr over 2f out: rdn wl over 1f out: drvn and hdd appr fnl f: kpt on same pce* **12/1**

5-20 **3** 2 1/2 **Rosbay (IRE)**[14] 1990 5-9-2 83 DavidAllan 6 82
(T D Easterby) *hld up in rr: hdwy over 2f out: rdn to chse ldrs over 1f out: kpt on same pce ins fnl f* **3/1**[2]

530 **4** nk **Man Of Gwent (UAE)**[93] 660 5-8-4 71 CatherineGannon 5 69
(P D Evans) *hld up in rr: hdwy on outer wl over 2f out: rdn wl over 1f out: kpt on same pce u.p fnl f* **9/1**

0-04 **5** 2 3/4 **Gala Casino Star (IRE)**[20] 1798 4-9-4 85 JamieMoriarty 7 77+
(R A Fahey) *trckd ldrs on inner: effrt over 2f out and sn n.m.r: pushed along wl over 1f out: swtchd lft and rdn ent fnl f: no hdwy* **5/2**[1]

0-00 **6** 1 1/2 **Blue Spinnaker (IRE)**[15] 1952 10-8-12 79 DaleGibson 2 68
(M W Easterby) *chsd ldng pair: rdn along wl over 2f out: drvn over 1f out: sn wknd* **25/1**

16-0 **7** 1/2 **Riley Boys (IRE)**[15] 1952 8-8-8 75 PaulMulrennan 4 63
(J G Given) *trckd ldr on inner: effrt over 2f out: sn rdn and wknd over 1f out* **8/1**[3]

2m 7.55s (0.55) **Going Correction** -0.025s/f (Good) **7** Ran SP% **114.8**
Speed ratings (Par 105): **96,94,92,91,89 88,88**
toteswinger: 1&2 £4.50, 1&3 £2.60, 2&3 £5.30 CSF £33.02 CT £93.49 TOTE £4.30: £1.90, £3.30; EX 30.50.
Owner B Harker, R Hall & Dr C Emmerson **Bred** Mrs N F M Sampson **Trained** Melsonby, N Yorks
■ Stewards' Enquiry : Jamie Moriarty one-day ban: careless riding (Jun 10)

FOCUS
Not the most reliable of form as the pace was steadied on the front end by Sri Kuantan and things panned out nicely for the winner. He is rated back to soewhere near his old level of form.
Gala Casino Star(IRE) Official explanation: jockey said gelding was denied a clear run

2375 BEVERLEY-RACECOURSE.CO.UK MAIDEN FILLIES' STKS 7f 100y
8:50 (8:51) (Class 5) 3-Y-O+ **£2,590** (£770; £385; £192) **Stalls** High

Form RPR
02 **1** **Arabian Pearl (IRE)**[19] 1843 3-8-10 74 AlanMunro 3 76
(P W Chapple-Hyam) *trckd ldr: cl up over 3f out: qcknd to ld 1 1/2f out: rdn clr ent fnl f: styd on* **2/1**[1]

30-3 **2** 2 3/4 **Starla Dancer (GER)**[18] 1888 3-8-10 69 TonyHamilton 4 69+
(R A Fahey) *in tch: hdwy over 2f out: rdn and sltly outpcd wl over 1f out: styd on wl fnl f* **12/1**

452- **3** 1 **Mootriba**[193] 7338 3-8-10 71 (b) TonyCulhane 6 67
(W J Haggas) *trckd ldrs: hdwy to chse wnr over 1f out: drvn and one pce ins fnl f* **10/3**[2]

03-4 **4** 1 **Nesayem (IRE)**[23] 1752 3-8-10 74 StephenDonohoe 1 64+
(D M Simcock) *towards rr: hdwy 2f out: sn rdn and kpt on ins fnl f: nrst fin* **6/1**[3]

4- **5** nk **Jeunopse (IRE)**[222] 6788 3-8-10 0 TomEaves 2 63
(B Smart) *t.k.h: chsd ldng pair: effrt on outer over 2f out and sn rdn: drvn over 1f out and sn one pce* **20/1**

6 2 3/4 **Tahayab (ITY)** 3-8-10 0 TPO'Shea 7 57
(M Johnston) *dwlt: in rr tl sme hdwy over 2f out: sn rdn and wknd* **9/1**

6-24 **7** nk **Izzi Mill (USA)**[20] 1814 3-8-10 72 PaulMulrennan 9 56
(D R C Elsworth) *led: rdn along over 2f out: hdd 1 1/2f out: sn wknd* **10/3**[2]

64 **8** 1 3/4 **Catch Key (IRE)**[15] 1950 3-8-10 0 DavidAllan 10 51
(T D Easterby) *dwlt: hld up: a towards rr* **33/1**

600- **9** 8 **Bun Penny**[222] 6788 3-8-10 40 PJMcDonald 5 31
(G M Moore) *t.k.h early: hld up: hdwy and in tch over 2f out: sn rdn and wknd* **200/1**

1m 34.81s (1.01) **Going Correction** -0.025s/f (Good)
WFA 3 from 4yo 11lb **9** Ran SP% **119.7**
Speed ratings (Par 100): **93,89,88,87,87 84,83,81,72**
toteswinger: 1&2 £7.10, 1&3 £4.70, 2&3 £9.80 CSF £29.28 TOTE £2.50: £1.40, £2.10, £1.60; EX 31.30 Place 6 £13.66, Place 5 £8.60.
Owner Arabian Shield 2004 **Bred** Derek Veitch And Eamon McEvoy **Trained** Newmarket, Suffolk

FOCUS
Not a strong fillies' maiden and the pace was fairly pedestrian. The form seems sound with improvement from the first two.
Izzi Mill(USA) Official explanation: jockey said filly ran too free
T/Jkpt: £401.70 to a £1 stake. Pool: £44,135.23. 78.00 winning tickets. T/Plt: £17.40 to a £1 stake. Pool: £70,548.15. 2,943.84 winning tickets. T/Qpdt: £8.60 to a £1 stake. Pool: £4,157.38. 356.94 winning tickets. JR

2218 BRIGHTON (L-H)
Wednesday, May 27

OFFICIAL GOING: Good changing to good to soft after race 3 (3.15)
Dolling out 3yards around bend between 5f to 2.5 furlongs added 15yards to advertised distances.
Wind: Strong, against Weather: Rain

2376 HARDINGS BAR & CATERING SERVICES MEDIAN AUCTION MAIDEN STKS 5f 213y
2:10 (2:10) (Class 5) 2-Y-O **£3,532** (£1,057; £528; £264) **Stalls** Low

Form RPR
3 **1** **Kalam Daleel (IRE)**[13] 2007 2-9-3 0 SamHitchcott 1 90+
(M R Channon) *mde all: rdn clr ins fnl 2f: easily* **4/9**[1]

5 **2** 15 **Ginger Grey (IRE)**[11] 2087 2-9-3 0 JamieSpencer 4 45+
(S A Callaghan) *cl 2nd tl wknd ins fnl 2f* **7/2**[2]

43 **3** 2 **Lairy (IRE)**[10] 2100 2-9-3 0 SteveDrowne 2 39
(M F Harris) *a 3rd: hrd rdn over 2f out: sn wknd* **20/1**

4 12 **Evergreen Dancer (IRE)** 2-9-3 0 RobertWinston 3 —
(J R Best) *s.s: a last: rdn and lost tch ins fnl 3f* **9/1**[3]

1m 12.91s (2.71) **Going Correction** +0.30s/f (Good) **4** Ran SP% **106.2**
Speed ratings (Par 93): **93,73,70,54**
CSF £2.16 TOTE £1.30; EX 1.90.
Owner Jaber Abdullah **Bred** Bloodhorse International Limited **Trained** West Ilsley, Berks

FOCUS
Persistent rain meant the going changed from good to firm to good - riders thought it rode on the softer side - which meant all runners were racing on a different surface to the one on which they had been declared. This was underlined by the small opening field electing to take the usual route on softened conditions moving towards the centre of the course from over three furlongs out. Kalam Daleel slammed his rivals in a fast time and looks pretty useful, although it is difficult to put a figure on this performance.

NOTEBOOK
Kalam Daleel(IRE) disposed of three modest rivals with the minimum of fuss, coming home in his own time. He probably achieved little but the easier conditions than those he met when making an encouraging debut at Salisbury suited him and he clearly has ability. The step up from 5f was fine although he does have plenty of pace in his pedigree. (tchd 1-2, 4-7 in a place and 8-15 in a place)
Ginger Grey(IRE), who dropped in value from his foal price to yearling, had been well beaten on his debut at Newmarket when around ten lengths fifth of six, and was 15 lengths in arrears this time having been left behind when the winner quickened. He also showed a tendency to hang left from over a furlong out. (op 4-1 tchd 10-3)
Lairy(IRE) was claimed for £6,000 out of David Nicholls' yard after finishing a close third in a 6f seller run on good to soft at Ripon but judged on this will need to go back to that grade. (op 16-1 tchd 14-1)

Evergreen Dancer(IRE), whose foal price increased from 20,000gns to £34,000 as a yearling, never gave any indication of ability. (op 8-1 tchd 10-1)

2377 JUICE 107.2 BRIGHTON H'CAP 5f 213y
2:40 (2:40) (Class 5) (0-75,75) 3-Y-O £3,406 (£1,019; £509; £254; £126) Stalls Low

Form RPR

5-03 1 **Hand Painted**[15] 1969 3-8-8 **65** TravisBlock 6 75
(P J Makin) *prom: drvn to chal whn edgd lft over 1f out: led ins fnl f: rdn out* **13/2**

5-12 2 ½ **Fantastic Dubai (USA)**[56] 1075 3-9-1 **72** SamHitchcott 2 80
(M R Channon) *hld up in tch: smooth hdwy to ld 2f out: hrd rdn and hdd ins fnl f: kpt on* **9/4**[2]

40-0 3 6 **River Dee (IRE)**[12] 2048 3-8-4 **66** (b[1]) JackDean(5) 8 55
(D Donovan) *in tch on outer: hrd rdn and outpcd over 2f out: kpt on to take 3rd wl ins fnl f* **5/1**[3]

3250 4 ¾ **Flamsteed (IRE)**[13] 2005 3-8-13 **70** LPKeniry 3 56
(M Quinn) *chsd ldr: rdn over 2f out: wknd over 1f out* **9/1**

40-0 5 2 ¼ **Tarruji (IRE)**[41] 1311 3-8-0 **62** AndreaAtzeni(5) 7 41
(S A Callaghan) *in tch: effrt over 2f out: no imp* **28/1**

0-22 6 1 ¼ **Safari Guide**[19] 1839 3-9-4 **75** JimCrowley 1 50
(P Winkworth) *led tl 2f out: sn wknd* **85/40**[1]

00-4 7 11 **Blackwater Fort (USA)**[15] 1956 3-8-4 **61** oh2 (b) ChrisCatlin 4 —
(J Gallagher) *dwlt: a bhd: no ch fnl 3f* **20/1**

1m 13.43s (3.23) **Going Correction** +0.525s/f (Yiel) 7 Ran SP% **111.0**
Speed ratings (Par 99): **99,98,90,89,86 84,70**
toteswinger: 1&2 £7.70, 1&3 £4.80, 2&3 £2.50 CSF £20.25 CT £75.43 TOTE £7.70: £2.40, £1.20; EX 25.30 Trifecta £228.70 Pool: £587.25 - 1.90 winning units..
Owner D A Poole **Bred** P J Makin **Trained** Ogbourne Maisey, Wilts

FOCUS
Little strength in depth and the favourite disappointed. The first pair might have improved but were probably the only two to run their race.
Blackwater Fort(USA) Official explanation: jockey said gelding missed the break

2378 ON TONIGHT'S FOOTBALL AT TOTESPORT.COM CLAIMING STKS 7f 214y
3:15 (3:15) (Class 6) 4-Y-O+ £1,942 (£578; £288; £144) Stalls Low

Form RPR

500- 1 **Heroes**[31] 7457 5-9-5 75 (p) FergusSweeney 5 81
(Tim Vaughan) *hld up in rr: rdn and hdwy 3f out: led ins fnl f: pushed clr: comf* **4/1**[2]

05 2 4 ½ **Mick Is Back**[8] 2171 5-8-11 57 (vt) DaneO'Neill 4 63
(G G Margarson) *hld up towards rr: wnt prom and rdn 3f out: one pce fnl f* **15/2**

-263 3 ½ **Steig (IRE)**[5] 2243 6-8-11 69 JamesDoyle 2 62
(George Baker) *prom: led after 2f tl ins fnl f: no ex* **11/8**[1]

4165 4 10 **Landucci**[7] 2185 8-8-7 69 (p) SteveDrowne 7 35
(S Curran) *hld up in tch: effrt over 2f out: wknd over 1f out* **9/2**[3]

1530 5 16 **Fairly Honest**[31] 1535 5-8-5 49 ChrisCatlin 6 —
(P W Hiatt) *prom tl wknd 2f out* **33/1**

000- 6 29 **Den's Boy**[44] 454 4-8-7 39 PaulDoe 3 —
(S Curran) *led 2f: rdn and lost pl 4f out: wl bhd fnl 3f* **100/1**

446/ 7 6 **Leoballero**[1017] 4429 9-8-0 66 (t) AndreaAtzeni(5) 1 —
(K M Prendergast) *in tch: hmpd on ins rail and lost pl over 4f out: sn wl bhd* **13/2**

1m 39.99s (3.99) **Going Correction** +0.525s/f (Yiel) 7 Ran SP% **109.3**
Speed ratings (Par 101): **101,96,96,86,70 41,35**
toteswinger: 1&2 £5.00, 1&3 £1.60, 2&3 £3.00 CSF £30.21 TOTE £5.10: £2.40, £3.30; EX 28.20.

Owner M Khan X2 **Bred** Usk Valley Stud **Trained** Aberthin, Vale of Glamorgan

FOCUS
The field came over to the stands' side due to the softening ground. Only the front pair showed their form.

2379 TONIGHT'S SPECIAL OFFERS AT TOTESPORT.COM H'CAP 1m 3f 196y
3:50 (3:50) (Class 5) (0-75,72) 4-Y-O+ £3,406 (£1,019; £509; £254; £126) Stalls High

Form RPR

-013 1 **Megalala (IRE)**[12] 2039 8-8-4 **58** oh1 NeilChalmers 2 64
(J J Bridger) *led: c to stands' rail st: hdd over 2f out: chsd ldr after tl rallied to ld again fnl 75yds: gamely* **4/1**[3]

3023 2 nk **Bramalea**[7] 2183 4-8-11 **65** JimCrowley 4 71
(B W Duke) *chsd ldr: c stands' side st: led over 2f out: hdd and nt qckn fnl 75yds* **9/4**[2]

5-23 3 1 ¾ **Potentiale (IRE)**[20] 1807 5-9-4 **72** (p) ChrisCatlin 3 75
(J W Hills) *hld up in 4th: c stands' side st: effrt over 2f out: hrd rdn over 1f out: one pce* **2/1**[1]

0203 4 12 **Rawdon (IRE)**[9] 2129 8-8-11 **72** (tp) KylieManser(7) 1 56
(Miss Gay Kelleway) *hld up in 3rd: styd alone far side st: wknd over 2f out* **6/1**

500- 5 20 **Silver Blue (IRE)**[184] 7354 6-8-6 **60** FergusSweeney 5 12
(W K Goldsworthy) *s.s: in rr: wnt alone centre st: no ch fnl 2f* **8/1**

2m 39.6s (6.90) **Going Correction** +0.525s/f (Yiel) 5 Ran SP% **109.5**
Speed ratings (Par 103): **98,97,96,88,75**
CSF £13.19 TOTE £4.30: £2.10, £2.00; EX 14.90.
Owner Tommy Ware **Bred** Joseph Gallagher **Trained** Liphook, Hants

FOCUS
The going was changed to good to soft before this contest. Only five runners but a tricky race. The winner looks the best guide.

2380 INSURE YOUR SCORE AT TOTESPORT.COM H'CAP 1m 1f 209y
4:25 (4:26) (Class 6) (0-65,65) 3-Y-O £2,590 (£770; £385; £192) Stalls High

Form RPR

0-30 1 **Primo Dilettante**[15] 1967 3-8-11 **58** JimCrowley 1 61
(W J Knight) *mid-div: hdwy 3f out: drvn to ld over 1f out: styd on wl* **9/1**

56-0 2 2 **Fongoli**[29] 1580 3-8-6 **53** ow1 (v) FergusSweeney 6 52
(B G Powell) *bmpd s: sn prom: led after 3f tl over 1f out: kpt on same pce* **14/1**

4000 3 2 **Fleur De'Lion (IRE)**[36] 1441 3-7-11 **51** oh6 CharlesEddery(7) 4 46
(S Kirk) *chsd ldrs: rdn and lost pl 3f out: styd on u.p to take 3rd ins fnl f* **40/1**

0-03 4 ½ **Arlene Phillips**[15] 1967 3-8-6 **53** SteveDrowne 10 47
(R Hannon) *chsd ldrs: rdn over 2f out: no imp tl styd on fnl f* **4/1**[2]

00-5 5 ½ **Astrobrava**[15] 1954 3-8-10 **57** LiamJones 2 50
(M H Tompkins) *prom: chsd ldr 2f out: one pce appr fnl f* **9/1**

6-60 6 ½ **Charlie Smirke (USA)**[16] 1932 3-9-3 **64** GeorgeBaker 3 56
(G L Moore) *plld hrd early: towards rr: rdn and hung lft fr 2f out: nvr able to chal* **8/1**[3]

0-13 7 nk **Loulou (USA)**[15] 1954 3-8-13 **60** JamieSpencer 5 51
(S A Callaghan) *led 3f: rdn 4f out: prom tl wknd over 1f out* **5/4**[1]

-406 8 ½ **Some Time Good (IRE)**[19] 1829 3-9-4 **65** SamHitchcott 8 55
(M R Channon) *s.i.s and hmpd s: plld hrd early: bhd: rdn 3f out: n.d* **8/1**[3]

0-00 9 12 **Royal Arthur**[25] 1670 3-7-11 **51** oh6 (v[1]) RichardRowe(7) 7 17
(L A Dace) *wnt lft and bmpd s: plld hrd early: a towards rr: detached last 4f out* **100/1**

0-60 10 1 ¾ **Flirty (IRE)**[36] 1422 3-8-4 **51** oh1 ChrisCatlin 9 14
(Rae Guest) *rdn over 3f out: a bhd* **14/1**

2m 9.29s (5.69) **Going Correction** +0.525s/f (Yiel) 10 Ran SP% **123.4**
Speed ratings (Par 97): **98,96,94,94,94 93,93,92,83,81**
toteswinger: 1&2 £23.00, 1&3 £34.00, 2&3 £56.60 CSF £134.12 CT £4767.02 TOTE £11.90: £3.20, £5.70, £7.40; EX 157.10 Trifecta £295.30 Part won. Pool: £399.07 - 0.10 winning units..
Owner O J Williams **Bred** O J Williams **Trained** Patching, W Sussex
■ Stewards' Enquiry : Steve Drowne caution: careless riding

FOCUS
Just one win to show from the combined efforts of this field. Modest form, rated around the third.
Fleur De'Lion(IRE) Official explanation: jockey said filly hung left

2381 BET IN-PLAY AT TOTESPORT.COM H'CAP 6f 209y
4:55 (4:56) (Class 6) (0-65,65) 4-Y-O+ £2,590 (£770; £385; £192) Stalls Low

Form RPR

1314 1 **Convince (USA)**[72] 853 8-7-13 **51** AndreaAtzeni(5) 9 58+
(K M Prendergast) *chsd ldrs: n.m.r on stands' rail and outpcd over 2f out: rallied on rail fnl f: led post* **10/1**

6-01 2 nse **Mr Fantozzi (IRE)**[15] 1959 4-8-13 **60** (p) ChrisCatlin 4 67
(D Donovan) *w ldrs: edgd rt towards stands' rail over 3f out: drvn to ld ins fnl f: kpt on: jst ct* **5/1**[3]

5205 3 1 ¼ **Lord Deevert**[42] 1285 4-8-10 **62** JackDean(5) 6 66
(W G M Turner) *prom: led 2f out tl ins fnl f: one pce* **16/1**

0033 4 ½ **Wrighty Almighty (IRE)**[5] 2223 7-8-10 **60** DavidProbert(3) 8 62+
(P R Chamings) *dwlt: towards rr: hmpd on stands' rail over 3f out: rdn and hdwy 2f out: styd on fnl f* **3/1**[1]

3013 5 1 **Punching**[22] 1775 5-9-4 **65** LPKeniry 10 65
(C R Dore) *hld up in tch: hmpd on stands' rail over 3f out: swtchd lft and rallied over 2f out: one pce appr fnl f* **7/2**[2]

-000 6 2 ¾ **Hennessy Island (USA)**[5] 2243 4-7-11 **51** oh1 DToole(7) 1 43
(T G Mills) *s.s: bhd: rdn and sme hdwy in centre 2f out: hung lft and btn 1f out* **20/1**

040- 7 ½ **Pragmatist**[261] 5755 5-9-2 **63** JimCrowley 5 54
(P Winkworth) *in tch: rdn to chal 2f out: wknd over 1f out* **11/2**

0000 8 6 **Maggie Kate**[7] 2180 4-8-6 **53** ow1 SteveDrowne 7 28
(R Ingram) *in tch tl wknd 2f out* **20/1**

5060 9 10 **H Harrison (IRE)**[8] 2156 9-9-4 **65** (p) GeorgeBaker 2 13
(I W McInnes) *sn led: hdd & wknd 2f out* **11/1**

060 10 2 ¼ **Poca A Poca (IRE)**[15] 1963 5-7-13 **51** oh2 (p) AmyBaker(5) 11 —
(G C Bravery) *wnt rt s: towards rr: rdn 4f out: bdly hmpd on stands' rail over 3f out: no ch after* **66/1**

1m 26.56s (3.46) **Going Correction** +0.525s/f (Yiel) 10 Ran SP% **113.6**
Speed ratings (Par 101): **101,100,99,98,97 94,94,87,75,73**
toteswinger: 1&2 £5.90, 1&3 £10.30, 2&3 £12.80 CSF £56.49 CT £810.87 TOTE £10.20: £2.40, £1.80, £3.80; EX 78.50 TRIFECTA Not won. Place 6: £896.69, Place 5: £609.40.
Owner M Matthews (Mid-Glamorgan) **Bred** Juddmonte Farms Inc **Trained** Sellack, H'fords
■ Stewards' Enquiry : Chris Catlin six-day ban: careless riding (Jun 10-15)

FOCUS
A modest handicap, but sound enough form.
T/Plt: £832.50 to a £1 stake. Pool: £44,023.57. 38.60 winning tickets. T/Qpdt: £72.40 to a £1 stake. Pool: £3,203.40. 32.70 winning tickets. LM

2181 LINGFIELD (L-H)
Wednesday, May 27

OFFICIAL GOING: Standard
Wind: Fairly strong, behind Weather: Raining

2382 SORRAIA HORSE H'CAP 6f (P)
2:30 (2:31) (Class 5) (0-70,70) 4-Y-O+ £3,070 (£906; £453) Stalls Low

Form RPR

2-13 1 **Lemon N Sugar (USA)**[15] 1965 4-9-2 **68** RyanMoore 5 85+
(J Noseda) *hld up in last pair: rdn and effrt on outer over 1f out: str run to ld ins fnl f: sn clr: readily* **4/5**[1]

1612 2 2 ½ **Suhayl Star (IRE)**[18] 1890 5-8-12 **64** LukeMorris 2 70
(P Burgoyne) *stdd s: plld hrd: trckd ldng pair: rdn and ev ch ent fnl f: nt pce of wnr ins fnl f: kpt on to go 2nd towards fin* **9/2**[2]

1-25 3 nk **Atheer Dubai (IRE)**[89] 710 4-8-11 **68** MarkFlynn(5) 1 73
(E F Vaughan) *dwlt: sn led at slow gallop: qcknd over 3f out: rdn wl over 1f out: hdd ins fnl f: no ch w wnr after: lost 2nd pl towards fin* **11/1**

00-5 4 1 **Cativo Cavallino**[53] 1121 6-8-6 **63** NataliaGemelova(5) 6 65
(J E Long) *pressed ldr: ev ch and rdn 2f out: wknd u.p jst ins fnl f* **10/1**[3]

431 5 3 **Figaro Flyer (IRE)**[30] 1565 6-9-4 **70** IanMongan 7 62
(P Howling) *stdd s: hld up in tch: rdn and effrt over 1f out: no hdwy and wl hld fnl f* **9/2**[2]

0-00 6 3 ½ **Mr Funshine**[15] 1970 4-7-13 **56** oh6 Louis-PhilippeBeuzelin(5) 3 37
(R J Hodges) *awkward leaving stalls and s.i.s: t.k.h: hld up in tch in rr: rdn and struggling 2f out: wl bhd fnl f* **33/1**

1m 11.45s (-0.45) **Going Correction** -0.025s/f (Stan) 6 Ran SP% **112.3**
Speed ratings (Par 103): **102,98,98,96,92 88**
toteswinger: 1&2 £1.60, 1&3 £3.20, 2&3 £4.70 CSF £4.79 TOTE £1.80: £1.50, £1.20; EX 4.90.
Owner The Searchers **Bred** Establo Madoca Corp **Trained** Newmarket, Suffolk

FOCUS
An ordinary handicap, but they went no pace at all early and it's unusual for a sprint around here to be run at such a dawdle. They quickened up eventually and the final time wasn't bad.

2383 TIGER HORSE MAIDEN AUCTION STKS 6f (P)
3:00 (3:02) (Class 5) 2-Y-O £3,070 (£906; £453) Stalls Low

Form RPR

4 1 **Soul Heaven**[18] 1891 2-8-9 0 RichardMullen 3 75+
(M L W Bell) *trckd ldrs: effrt wl over 1f out: led jst over 1f out: r.o wl to assert ins fnl f* **9/4**[2]

2 1 ¾ **Cool Valentine** 2-8-13 0 WilliamBuick 2 74+
(A M Balding) *dwlt: sn rcvrd and in midfield: gd hdwy on inner wl over 1f out: ev ch ent fnl f: kpt on same pce fnl 100yds* **10/1**

62 3 1 ¼ **Any Day (IRE)**[26] 1637 2-8-9 0 SebSanders 8 66
(R M Beckett) *trckd ldrs: rdn and ev ch over 1f out: outpcd ins fnl f* **8/1**[3]

05 **4** 2 3/4 **Rosedale**[13] 2000 2-8-4 0 KirstyMilczarek 9 53
(J A R Toller) *s.i.s: towards rr: rdn wl over 1f out: styd on u.p fnl f: nvr nr ldrs* **33/1**

5 1/2 **Dear Mr Fantasy (IRE)** 2-8-9 0 EddieAhern 1 56+
(J W Hills) *s.i.s: bhd: hdwy on inner over 1f out: styd on wl fnl f: nvr nr ldrs* **14/1**

6 hd **Quaestor (IRE)** 2-8-7 0 RossAtkinson(5) 12 59+
(Tom Dascombe) *stdd s: hld up towards rr: swtchd rt wl over 1f out: styd on wl fnl f: nvr nr ldrs* **8/1**[3]

2 **7** 1 1/4 **I'Malwaysright (IRE)**[19] 1835 2-8-13 0 RobertHavlin 5 56
(D R C Elsworth) *v. keen to post: led for 1f: chsd ldr after: ev ch 2 out tl over 1f out: wknd fnl f* **2/1**[1]

003 **8** 1 3/4 **Southwark Newshawk**[9] 2128 2-8-4 0 LiamJones 6 42
(Mrs C A Dunnett) *racd in midfield: rdn over 2f out: rdn and no prog wl over 1f out* **20/1**

9 1 **Lochbroom Sunset** 2-8-11 0 SaleemGolam 4 46+
(S C Williams) *v.s.a: wl bhd: clsd and in tch in rr 2f out: no prog after: nvr trbld ldrs* **40/1**

10 1/2 **Sirri** 2-8-3 0 AhmedAjtebi(3) 10 39
(C E Brittain) *in tch in midfield: lost pl 3f out: bhd and wd bnd 2f out: no ch after* **20/1**

04 **11** 2 1/2 **Avec Moi**[27] 1630 2-8-4 0 JohnEgan 11 30
(Mrs C A Dunnett) *led after 1f: rdn 2f out: hdd jst over 1f out: wknd rapidly fnl f* **40/1**

12 8 **Bubbly Braveheart (IRE)** 2-8-10 0 MickyFenton 7 12
(A Bailey) *v.s.a: a wl bhd: t.o fr over 1f out* **25/1**

1m 12.77s (0.87) **Going Correction** -0.025s/f (Stan) **12** Ran SP% **123.3**
Speed ratings (Par 93): **93,90,89,85,84 84,82,80,79,78 75,64**
toteswinger: 1&2 £9.60, 1&3 £3.90, 2&3 £7.40 CSF £23.69 TOTE £3.50: £1.20, £3.30, £2.70; EX 38.90.
Owner Lady Bamford **Bred** Lady Bamford **Trained** Newmarket, Suffolk

FOCUS
A fair maiden auction event run at a reasonable pace and the first three came nicely clear of the rest.

NOTEBOOK
Soul Heaven had finished a promising fourth on his Warwick debut when looking in need of the experience and appeared much more the finished article here. Always in a handy position, he seized the gap which presented itself soon after turning in and eventually won going away. The form is nothing special, but he should continue to progress and there should be other opportunities for him. (op 15-8 tchd 7-4 and 5-2)
Cool Valentine, a 13,000gns half-brother to the dual 1m2f winner Dark Prospect, moved into contention tight against the inside rail turning for home and kept on to the line. This was promising enough, but he can be expected to improve from it and he will probably appreciate further. (tchd 11-1)
Any Day(IRE), who had already shown ability in a couple of outings over the minimum trip on this track, was weak in the market beforehand. She had every chance having raced up with the pace early and certainly ran her race, but she lacks the scope of the pair that beat her. (op 9-2)
Rosedale, well held in both starts on turf, stayed on from off the pace towards the end and this was an improvement.
Dear Mr Fantasy(IRE), a 3,000gns colt out of a half-sister to three winners including the useful Silver Pivotal, was a springer in the market. He was soon outpaced and, although he never got into the race, he was noted doing some solid late work against the inside rail. Better can be expected. (op 20-1 tchd 25-1 and 12-1)
Quaestor(IRE), a 15,000euros half-brother to a winner on the Flat in Japan and also to a winning hurdler, was another to make some late progress from off the pace and he should have learnt something from this. (tchd 6-1)
I'Malwaysright(IRE), second of six over the minimum trip on the turf track here on debut earlier this month, albeit beaten a long way by the winner, raced prominently early but the way he folded tamely from the furlong pole was very disappointing. (op 4-1)

2384 CLEVELAND BAY FILLIES' H'CAP 1m 2f (P)
3:35 (3:35) (Class 4) (0-85,85) 3-Y-0+ **£5,828** (£1,734; £866; £432) **Stalls** Low

Form RPR
5-1 **1** **Aromatic**[13] 2006 3-8-7 **78** RichardMullen 3 89+
(J H M Gosden) *t.k.h: chsd ldr for 1f: w.w in midfield after: clsd 4f out: swtchd ins and rdn wl over 1f out: sn ev ch: swished tail u.p: led ins fnl f: edgd rt and kpt on fnl f* **11/10**[1]

1310 **2** 1/2 **Eastern Aria (UAE)**[11] 2077 3-8-9 **80** GregFairley 5 87
(M Johnston) *led for 1f: chsd clr ldr after: clsd 4f out: led over 2f out: hrd pressed and rdn wl over 1f out: hdd ins fnl f: unable qck* **9/4**[2]

546- **3** 1 1/4 **Quirina**[208] 7108 4-9-13 **84** SebSanders 2 89
(R M Beckett) *stdd s: hld up in rr: hdwy on outer over 1f out: chsd ldrs 1f out: kpt on same pce fnl 100yds* **15/2**[3]

506 **4** 3 1/4 **Confidentiality (IRE)**[39] 1348 5-10-0 **85** NickyMackay 4 83
(M Wigham) *hld up in midfield: hdwy 4f out: chsd ldrs and rdn 2f out: wknd fnl f* **20/1**

0/0- **5** 7 **King's Kazeem**[377] 2123 4-9-1 **72** RyanMoore 1 56
(G L Moore) *stdd s: hld up in rr: niggled along 5f out: rdn 2f out: sn wknd: eased ins fnl f* **16/1**

21-0 **6** 17 **Sri Kandi**[13] 2008 3-8-4 **75** JohnEgan 6 25
(P F I Cole) *t.k.h: led after 1f and sn clr: rdn 3f out: hdd over 2f out: wknd 2f out: eased fnl f: t.o* **10/1**

2m 5.84s (-0.76) **Going Correction** -0.025s/f (Stan)
WFA 3 from 4yo+ 14lb **6** Ran SP% **109.9**
Speed ratings (Par 102): **102,101,100,98,92 78**
toteswinger: 1&2 £1.02, 1&3 £2.10, 2&3 £3.80 CSF £3.53 TOTE £2.00: £1.70, £1.20; EX 3.30.
Owner Cheveley Park Stud **Bred** Cheveley Park Stud Ltd **Trained** Newmarket, Suffolk

FOCUS
A decent little fillies' handicap. Three-year-olds filled the first two places in this race last year when it was run at Great Leighs and precisely the same happened here.

2385 SKYROS PONY CONDITIONS STKS 6f (P)
4:10 (4:11) (Class 3) 3-Y-0+ **£9,714** (£2,890; £1,444; £721) **Stalls** Low

Form RPR
5-44 **1** **Strike The Deal (USA)**[14] 1989 4-9-4 110 (v) RyanMoore 2 110+
(J Noseda) *chsd ldrs: rdn to chal over 1f out: led jst ins fnl f: drvn out* **10/11**[1]

3015 **2** nk **Tamagin (USA)**[18] 1868 6-9-4 101 (p) NCallan 8 109
(K A Ryan) *chsd ldr: led wl over 1f out: drvn over 1f out: hdd jst ins fnl f: kpt on* **14/1**

1-1 **3** 1 1/4 **Mutheeb (USA)**[27] 1631 4-9-4 102 RHills 4 105+
(Saeed Bin Suroor) *stdd s: hld up in last pl: effrt and n.m.r on inner jst over 2f out: rdn and hdwy over 1f out: chsd ldrs 1f out: kpt on same pce fnl 100yds* **3/1**[2]

-033 **4** 1/2 **Nota Bene**[90] 696 7-9-7 100 RobertHavlin 1 106
(D R C Elsworth) *in tch: hdwy over 2f out: effrt to press ldrs ent fnl f: drvn ins fnl f: wknd fnl 75yds* **20/1**

0041 **5** 3 **Valery Borzov (IRE)**[12] 2059 5-9-4 105 (v) AdrianTNicholls 5 94
(D Nicholls) *led tl hung rt and hdd wl over 1f out: drvn and wknd ent fnl f* **9/1**[3]

2-30 **6** 4 **Diriculous**[12] 2059 5-9-4 100 JohnEgan 3 81
(T G Mills) *dwlt: sn bustled along: in tch towards rr: rdn over 2f out: wknd over 1f out: wl btn fnl f* **25/1**

0000 **7** 2 **Matsunosuke**[25] 1676 7-9-11 109 LukeMorris 6 82
(A B Coogan) *stdd s: t.k.h: hld up in midfield early: lost pl and bhd jst over 2f out: rdn and wknd over 1f out* **16/1**

69.65 secs (-2.25) **Going Correction** -0.025s/f (Stan) course record **7** Ran SP% **108.5**
Speed ratings (Par 107): **114,113,111,111,107 101,99**
toteswinger: 1&2 £2.20, 1&3 £1.10, 2&3 £5.70 CSF £13.88 TOTE £1.80: £1.70, £3.40; EX 14.70.

Owner M Barber **Bred** Five-D Thoroughbreds, Llc **Trained** Newmarket, Suffolk

FOCUS
A decent conditions sprint though the field was reduced by one when Eisteddfod (16/1) broke out of his stall and had to be withdrawn. With a couple of confirmed front-runners in the field there was never likely to be much hanging about and the winning time was just 4/100ths of a second outside the course record.

NOTEBOOK
Strike The Deal(USA) was taking a big drop in class after his decent efforts in the Palace House and Duke Of York Stakes and he was comfortably best in at the weights. He was successful on this surface on his racecourse debut back in June 2007 so there were no doubts over his ability to act on the surface. Settled in third place early whilst the two established pace-setters got on with it, he was produced on reaching the home straight and, although he didn't have that much to spare at the line, he always looked like winning. In theory he hasn't run to his mark as he was 9lb well in with the runner-up, but given the different surface that may not be very relevant and this first win since the 2007 Richmond Stakes should have boosted his confidence. He now goes for the Golden Jubilee. (op 6-5 tchd 5-6)
Tamagin(USA), runner-up to Nota Bene in this race last year when it was run at Great Leighs but disappointing in first-time blinkers at Haydock last time, had the cheekpieces back on in which he has already been successful four times. Normally a real trailblazer, this time he was settled in the slipstream of the leader and that was probably a wise move. Sent to the front off the home bend, he battled all the way to the line and ran a blinder to run a much higher-rated rival close. (op 20-1)
Mutheeb(USA), winner of his first two starts over 7f including one here, was settled in last place and when he was produced it was tight against the inside rail, which is not usually the place to be here. He ran on well despite that, but lacked a decisive turn of foot and he will be stepped back up in trip now. (op 5-2 tchd 9-4)
Nota Bene, not seen since making the frame in a couple of races on turf in Dubai in February, made an effort rounding the home bend and did well to finish where he did considering he was worst in at the weights. (op 33-1)
Valery Borzov(IRE), who has winning form on Polytrack, was taking on better company after his spectacular front-running performance in a hot York handicap earlier this month. Soon in front and setting a serious pace, he lost the advantage when hanging away to his right off the home bend and that was that. Official explanation: jockey said gelding hung right (op 15-2 tchd 11-1)
Diriculous, successful six times on sand last year, had finished a tailed-off last of 16 on soft ground at York earlier this month and he never offered a threat here either. (op 25-1 tchd 33-1)
Matsunosuke, who was in cracking form on Polytrack during the winter including three wins here, likes to be delivered late off a strong pace and had the race run to suit. His 7lb penalty meant that he only had a fair chance at these weights, but even so this was a very below-par effort. (op 16-1)

2386 EXMOOR PONY H'CAP 5f (P)
4:45 (4:46) (Class 5) (0-75,70) 3-Y-0 **£3,070** (£906; £453) **Stalls** High

Form RPR
43-2 **1** **Celestial Dream (IRE)**[15] 1956 3-8-10 **62** WilliamBuick 5 69+
(A M Balding) *stdd s: hld up in rr: hdwy wl over 1f out: rdn to chse ldr ent fnl f: led ins fnl f: rdn clr: eased nr fin* **15/8**[1]

0-00 **2** 1 **Pocket's Pick (IRE)**[20] 1814 3-9-4 **70** RyanMoore 4 73
(G L Moore) *stdd s: bhd: pushed along over 2f out: c v wd bnd 2f out: r.o strly fnl f: wnt 2nd wl ins fnl f: nvr gng to rch wnr* **15/2**

-433 **3** 2 **Bahamian Ceilidh**[14] 1985 3-8-12 **69** RossAtkinson(5) 2 65+
(Tom Dascombe) *led after 1f: hung rt and wd bnd 2f out: rdn over 1f out: hdd ins fnl f: sn no ch w wnr: tired and lost 2nd wl ins fnl f* **5/2**[2]

5-34 **4** 1/2 **Piste**[29] 1583 3-8-9 **66** Louis-PhilippeBeuzelin(5) 3 60
(B J Meehan) *t.k.h: hld up in midfield: effrt over 1f out: drvn ent fnl f: kpt on but nvr pce to threaten ldrs* **12/1**

61-0 **5** 2 1/4 **Rublevka Star (USA)**[32] 1505 3-8-13 **65** ShaneKelly 7 51
(J Noseda) *chsd ldrs: rdn and effrt wl over 1f out: drvn and wknd ent fnl f* **9/2**[3]

6220 **6** 1 **Spit And Polish**[8] 2148 3-8-13 **65** (v[1]) JohnEgan 6 47
(C A Dwyer) *chsd ldr after 1f: carried wd bnd 2f out: sn rdn: wknd ent fnl f* **11/1**

5-00 **7** 5 **Louie's Lad**[14] 1982 3-8-4 **56** oh8 FrankieMcDonald 1 20
(J J Bridger) *hung rt thrght: led for 1f: steadily lost pl bhd fr over 1f out* **50/1**

58.85 secs (0.05) **Going Correction** -0.025s/f (Stan) **7** Ran SP% **111.3**
Speed ratings (Par 99): **98,96,93,92,88 87,79**
toteswinger: 1&2 £3.80, 1&3 £1.80, 2&3 £4.30 CSF £15.70 TOTE £2.10: £1.02, £6.80; EX 13.90.

Owner J C Smith **Bred** Littleton Stud **Trained** Kingsclere, Hants

FOCUS
A moderate sprint handicap in which only two of the seven runners had previously tasted success.
Bahamian Ceilidh Official explanation: jockey said filly hung badly right
Spit And Polish Official explanation: jockey said gelding stumbled on leaving stalls
Louie's Lad Official explanation: jockey said gelding hung badly right

2387 ERISKAY PONY H'CAP 1m (P)
5:15 (5:15) (Class 4) (0-80,80) 4-Y-0+ **£5,828** (£1,734; £866; £432) **Stalls** Low

Form RPR
0-40 **1** **Last Three Minutes (IRE)**[11] 2073 4-9-4 **80** RyanMoore 1 89+
(E A L Dunlop) *stdd s: hld up in rr: pushed along over 2f out: stl last 2f out: c wd over 1f out: str run fnl f to ld last strides* **5/2**[2]

-211 **2** nk **Elisiario (IRE)**[36] 1436 4-8-11 **73** PatCosgrave 7 81
(J R Boyle) *rdn and effrt jst over 2f out: chsd ldr and drvn 1f out: led wl ins fnl f: hdd last strides* **11/2**[3]

-440 **3** 1/2 **Salient**[6] 2188 5-9-4 **80** KirstyMilczarek 8 87
(M J Attwater) *chsd ldr: rdn to ld 2f out: drvn over 1f out: hdd wl ins fnl f: no ex* **12/1**

4-32 **4** 1 1/4 **Halsion Chancer**[123] 283 5-9-4 **80** RobertWinston 5 84
(J R Best) *t.k.h: trckd ldrs: rdn jst over 2f out: drvn and unable qck over 1f out: kpt on same pce fnl f* **7/1**

-042 **5** 3/4 **Fiefdom (IRE)**[15] 1964 7-8-13 **75**.................................. PatrickMathers 10 77
(I W McInnes) *stdd s: t.k.h: hld up towards rr: rdn jst over 2f out: r.o ins fnl f: nt rch ldrs* **20/1**

06-2 **6** 3/4 **Mount Hadley (USA)**[28] 1603 5-9-0 **76**..........................(v) WilliamBuick 6 77
(G A Butler) *led: rdn over 2f out: hdd 2f out: drvn and one pce over 1f out: wknd ins fnl f* **2/1**[1]

3313 **7** *shd* **Pha Mai Blue**[7] 2186 4-7-11 **66**..................................(v) NathanAlison(7) 3 66
(J R Boyle) *s.i.s: t.k.h: hld up towards rr: hdwy 2f out: swtchd lft and effrt over 1f out: hung lft and no imp fnl f* **12/1**

5654 **8** *shd* **Lopinot (IRE)**[19] 1833 6-7-11 **66**..............................(v) GemmaElford(7) 9 66
(M R Bosley) *stdd s: t.k.h: hld up in midfield: rdn and effrt over 1f out: keeping on same pce whn n.m.r fnl f* **33/1**

21-0 **9** *13* **Spotty Muldoon (IRE)**[32] 1524 4-8-9 **71**.......................... SebSanders 4 41
(R M Beckett) *racd in midfield tl dropped to rr and rdn 4f out: lost tch wl over 1f out* **8/1**

1m 37.06s (-1.14) **Going Correction** -0.025s/f (Stan) **9** Ran SP% **124.0**
Speed ratings (Par 105): **104,103,103,101,101 100,100,100,87**
toteswinger: 1&2 £,4.50 1&3 £8.30, 2&3 £21.00 CSF £18.41 CT £147.97 TOTE £3.80: £1.10, £2.40, £4.30; EX 24.20 Place 6: £18.59, Place 5: £14.19.
Owner The Right Angle Club **Bred** Apache Stud Pty Ltd **Trained** Newmarket, Suffolk

FOCUS
A fair handicap run at a reasonable pace and a rather typical Lingfield finish.
Mount Hadley(USA) Official explanation: trainer had no explanation for the poor form shown
Spotty Muldoon(IRE) Official explanation: jockey said gelding resented the kickback
T/Plt: £31.60 to a £1 stake. Pool: £52,394.36. 1,209.64 winning tickets. T/Qpdt: £17.90 to a £1 stake. Pool: £3,273.50. 135.30 winning tickets. SP

AYR (L-H)

Thursday, May 28

OFFICIAL GOING: Good (good to firm in places; 9.0)
Straight course split in two and far side used.
Wind: Breezy, half against Weather: Overcast

2388 BURNS MALL, KILMARNOCK E B F MAIDEN STKS 6f

2:20 (2:22) (Class 4) 2-Y-O **£5,018** (£1,493; £746; £372) **Stalls** Low

Form RPR

3 **1** **Maison Brillet (IRE)**[9] 2153 2-9-3 0.............................. PaulMulrennan 9 74
(J Howard Johnson) *dwlt: sn w ldr: rdn to ld ins fnl f: r.o wl* **11/2**[3]

2 **2** 1/2 **Baileys Vision**[16] 1968 2-8-12 0.............................. JoeFanning 7 67
(M Johnston) *led to ins fnl f: no ex towards fin* **11/4**[2]

3 *2* **Below Zero (IRE)** 2-9-3 0.............................. AdrianTNicholls 6 66
(M Johnston) *prom: effrt and ev ch over 1f out: one pce fnl f* **7/1**

4 2 1/4 **Bradford (IRE)** 2-9-3 0.............................. AndrewElliott 1 62+
(K R Burke) *bhd tl hdwy over 1f out: kpt on fnl f: nrst fin* **20/1**

5 1 1/4 **Clear Ice (IRE)** 2-9-0 0.............................. AndrewMullen(3) 5 56
(D Nicholls) *midfield: rdn and hung lft over 2f out: no imp over 1f out* **16/1**

2 **6** *nk* **Trinder**[13] 2027 2-9-3 0.............................. TonyHamilton 10 55
(R A Fahey) *prom on outside tl edgd rt and wknd appr fnl f* **2/1**[1]

7 3/4 **Sassanian (IRE)** 2-8-12 0.............................. PatrickDonaghy(5) 2 52
(J Howard Johnson) *hld up: pushed along over 2f out: nvr rchd ldrs* **28/1**

00 **8** 1/2 **Weetentherty**[9] 2153 2-9-3 0.............................. DanielTudhope 4 51
(J S Goldie) *t.k.h: hld up: rdn over 2f out: sn outpcd* **50/1**

6 **9** 1 1/4 **Emeralds Spirit (IRE)**[26] 1661 2-8-12 0.............................. JamieMoriarty 3 42
(J R Weymes) *prom: outpcd whn n.m.r over 2f out: sn btn* **12/1**

10 *3* **Mark Carmers** 2-9-3 0.............................. PhillipMakin 8 38
(T D Barron) *prom tl rdn and wknd fr 2f out* **16/1**

1m 13.67s (0.07) **Going Correction** -0.15s/f (Firm) **10** Ran SP% **117.5**
Speed ratings (Par 95): **93,92,89,86,85 84,83,82,81,77**
toteswinger: 1&2 £3.50, 1&3 £4.90, 2&3 £4.80 CSF £20.77 TOTE £5.80: £2.20, £1.70, £2.30; EX 25.40.
Owner J Howard Johnson **Bred** Liam Webb **Trained** Billy Row, Co Durham

FOCUS
Probably a fair juvenile maiden with the runner-up rated to his debut form.

NOTEBOOK
Maison Brillet(IRE), who caught the eye when a running-on third in a 5f Musselburgh maiden on his debut, was always going to improve for the extra furlong and he gradually wore down the runner-up. His yard is doing well with its juveniles and this one looks capable of further progress. (tchd 5-1 and 6-1)
Baileys Vision made a really pleasing debut when second at Warwick and she held obvious claims over the extra half a furlong. Soon in front, she kept finding for pressure and ran on right the way to the line, but couldn't repel the winner. (op 9-4 tchd 3-1)
Below Zero(IRE) will no doubt have delighted connections with this debut effort. A son of Shamardal who is bred to require further than this, he came to challenge against the rail inside the two, but couldn't quicken on inside the final furlong. He should learn from this and winning a standard maiden should prove a formality, especially as he will soon get the chance to race over 7f. (op 10-1)
Bradford(IRE), a half brother to a smart sprinting juvenile, made some good late headway having been outpaced and should learn from the experience. (op 25-1)
Clear Ice(IRE), who has already been gelded, comes from a yard whose juveniles often come on for a run and he showed a bit of ability. (tchd 14-1)
Trinder showed plenty of speed when finishing second at Hamilton on debut and he appeared to not see out the trip on this first try at 6f, fading from a furlong out having held every chance.
Official explanation: jockey said colt became upset in stalls (op 11-4)
Sassanian(IRE), a stablemate of the winner, was green early and got the message all too late. (op 33-1)

2389 TURNBERRY HOLIDAY PARK CLAIMING STKS 6f

2:50 (2:51) (Class 5) 3-Y-O+ **£3,070** (£906; £453) **Stalls** Low

Form RPR

-002 **1** **Gift Horse**[12] 2071 9-9-4 78.............................(p) AdrianTNicholls 4 74
(D Nicholls) *hld up: hdwy to ld over 1f out: drvn out* **7/4**[1]

-063 **2** 3/4 **Soto**[17] 1924 6-9-2 60.............................(b) PaulMulrennan 13 70
(M W Easterby) *prom: hdwy to ld briefly over 1f out: edgd lft: kpt on u.p fnl f* **16/1**

0231 **3** *nk* **Swinbrook (USA)**[8] 2184 8-9-1 70.............................(v) JamieMoriarty 1 68
(R A Fahey) *hld up: pushed along whn nt clr run over 2f out: hdwy over 1f out: r.o* **6/1**[3]

000- **4** *6* **Mormeatmic**[239] 6382 6-8-13 44.............................. PatrickDonaghy(5) 7 52
(M W Easterby) *prom: effrt and ev ch over 1f out: outpcd fnl f* **66/1**

0-55 **5** 1 1/4 **Ice Planet**[107] 489 8-8-9 65.............................. DeanHeslop(5) 11 44
(Mrs R A Carr) *hld up: effrt on outside over 2f out: no imp over 1f out* **8/1**

-000 **6** 1 1/2 **Seafield Towers**[17] 1924 9-8-8 41.............................(p) RossSmith(7) 2 40
(D A Nolan) *prom tl rdn and wknd over 1f out* **100/1**

-000 **7** *shd* **The Bear**[25] 1694 6-9-6 62.............................. TonyHamilton 5 45
(D A Nolan) *led to over 1f out: sn wknd* **33/1**

0400 **8** 1 1/2 **Millie's Rock (IRE)**[9] 2150 4-9-6 72.............................. JoeFanning 8 40
(K A Ryan) *dwlt: sn cl up: ev ch over 1f out: sn wknd* **12/1**

2300 **9** 2 1/4 **Strabinios King**[13] 2045 5-9-5 70.............................. SladeO'Hara(5) 10 37
(A Berry) *hld up: rdn after 2f: nvr on terms* **20/1**

000- **10** *nk* **Talon (IRE)**[190] 7382 4-9-1 55.............................. PJMcDonald 12 27
(G A Swinbank) *prom tl rdn and wknd fr 2f out* **33/1**

-213 **11** 3 1/2 **Epic Odyssey**[63] 973 4-9-3 82.............................(p) PhillipMakin 6 18
(Lee Smyth, Ire) *midfield: drvn over 3f out: wknd fnl 2f* **5/2**[2]

0-60 **12** *12* **Yahwudhee (FR)**[35] 1477 4-9-1 70.............................. DaleGibson 9 —
(N Wilson) *midfield: drvn over 3f out: sn wknd* **50/1**

1m 12.31s (-1.29) **Going Correction** -0.15s/f (Firm) **12** Ran SP% **119.0**
Speed ratings (Par 103): **102,101,100,92,90 88,88,86,83,83 78,62**
toteswinger: 1&2 £5.90, 1&3 £3.70, 2&3 £9.10 CSF £30.91 TOTE £2.60: £1.50, £2.90, £1.70; EX 36.00.Gift Horse was claimed by David Evans for £8,000.
Owner Alfi and Partners **Bred** Theakston Stud **Trained** Sessay, N Yorks

FOCUS
Not many could be given a chance in this claimer but the runner-up sets the level.
The Bear Official explanation: jockey said gelding hung badly right-handed throughout

2390 BELHAVEN HAPPY BIRTHDAY MATTY EVANS H'CAP 1m 1f 20y

3:20 (3:21) (Class 6) (0-60,60) 4-Y-O+ **£2,914** (£867; £433; £216) **Stalls** Low

Form RPR

00-2 **1** **Stateside (CAN)**[16] 1974 4-8-4 **46**.............................. SilvestreDeSousa 3 59+
(R A Fahey) *chsd ldrs: effrt over 2f out: led over 1f out: r.o strly: eased nr fin* **5/1**[3]

00-5 **2** 3 1/4 **Rain Stops Play (IRE)**[13] 254 7-8-7 **49** ow1.............................. PaulMulrennan 12 54
(N G Richards) *hld up: hdwy over 2f out: wnt 2nd ins fnl f: kpt on: no ch w wnr* **20/1**

260- **3** 1 3/4 **Willyn (IRE)**[252] 6042 4-8-10 **52**.............................. DanielTudhope 1 56+
(J S Goldie) *hld up in midfield: hdwy whn nt clr run over 2f out to over 1f out: kpt on fnl f: nrst fin* **12/1**

234/ **4** *hd* **Barndeh (IRE)**[19] 1902 6-7-12 **47**.............................(p) JamieKyne(7) 9 47
(Lee Smyth, Ire) *prom: effrt over 2f out: edgd lft over 1f out: sn one pce* **9/2**[2]

2265 **5** 1 1/4 **Kielty's Folly**[23] 1773 5-8-7 **49** ow1.............................. TonyHamilton 2 48+
(B P J Baugh) *in tch: effrt whn n.m.r wl over 1f out: sn rdn and no imp* **6/1**

60-0 **6** 3/4 **Cullybackey (IRE)**[16] 1955 4-8-13 **55**.............................. PJMcDonald 8 51
(G A Swinbank) *midfield: drvn over 2f out: plugged on fnl f: nvr able to chal* **17/2**

6054 **7** *nk* **General Feeling (IRE)**[8] 2186 8-9-3 **59**.............................. AdrianTNicholls 7 54
(D Nicholls) *missed break: bhd tl hdwy on outside over 1f out: n.d* **7/2**[1]

00- **8** *nk* **Coughlans Locke (IRE)**[180] 7503 6-8-1 **50**.............................. DeclanCannon(7) 11 45
(Kieran P Cotter, Ire) *s.i.s: effrt on outside over 2f out: no imp over 1f out* **14/1**

-650 **9** 1 1/4 **High Profit (IRE)**[16] 1955 5-9-0 **56**.............................. DarrenMoffatt 13 48
(James Moffatt) *hld up: rdn 3f out: n.d* **16/1**

6-06 **10** *nk* **Wilmington**[55] 1101 5-8-4 **51**.............................. PatrickDonaghy(5) 5 42
(Mrs J C McGregor) *towards rr: drvn 3f out: nvr on terms* **33/1**

60/3 **11** 1/2 **Tommy Tobougg**[22] 1556 5-8-8 **50**.............................. JoeFanning 14 40
(Miss Lucinda V Russell) *chsd clr ldr: drvn over 2f out: edgd lft and wknd over 1f out* **9/1**

00-6 **12** 4 1/2 **Defi (IRE)**[9] 2155 7-8-5 **54** ow7.............................(bt) RossSmith(7) 4 34
(D A Nolan) *led and sn clr: hdd over 1f out: sn wknd* **20/1**

1m 54.94s (-3.46) **Going Correction** -0.35s/f (Firm) **12** Ran SP% **124.6**
Speed ratings (Par 101): **101,98,96,96,95 94,94,94,92,92 92,88**
toteswinger: 1&2 £22.30, 1&3 £13.00, 2&3 £33.50 CSF £108.12 CT £1168.29 TOTE £6.80: £1.90, £6.00, £4.50; EX 155.00.
Owner P Timmins **Bred** Yvonne Schwabe & Dagmar Schwabe **Trained** Musley Bank, N Yorks
■ Stewards' Enquiry : Jamie Kyne caution: careless riding.

FOCUS
A low-grade handicap but the winner scored decisively.
Wilmington Official explanation: trainer said gelding lost a front shoe

2391 WILLIAM HILL HOMECOMING H'CAP 1m

3:50 (3:50) (Class 5) (0-75,75) 4-Y-O+ **£3,885** (£1,156; £577; £288) **Stalls** Low

Form RPR

-605 **1** **Esoterica (IRE)**[12] 2073 6-9-3 **74**.............................(v) DanielTudhope 4 81
(J S Goldie) *trckd ldrs: rdn 2f out: led ins fnl f: r.o wl* **11/4**[3]

2-56 **2** *1* **Sir Royal (USA)**[19] 1886 4-9-1 **72**.............................. PJMcDonald 8 77
(G A Swinbank) *pressed ldr: led over 2f out: edgd lft over 1f out: hdd ins fnl f: kpt on* **6/1**

0-61 **3** 3 1/4 **Sunnyside Tom (IRE)**[3] 2313 5-9-4 **75** 6ex.............................. TonyHamilton 3 73
(R A Fahey) *led to over 2f out: one pce fnl f* **9/4**[1]

-000 **4** *nk* **Cigalas**[27] 1646 4-8-13 **70**.............................. PhillipMakin 2 67
(Mrs J C McGregor) *prom: outpcd over 2f out: r.o fnl f* **33/1**

1121 **5** *shd* **Ergo (FR)**[25] 1690 5-9-0 **71**.............................(b) DarrenMoffatt 5 68
(James Moffatt) *s.i.s: hld up: hdwy over 1f out: nvr rchd ldrs* **5/2**[2]

0006 **6** 4 1/2 **Talk Of Saafend (IRE)**[20] 1830 4-8-13 **70**.............................. PaulMulrennan 7 56
(P Monteith) *trckd ldrs tl rdn and wknd fr over 2f out* **25/1**

3-00 **7** 3/4 **Primo Way**[6] 2235 8-8-4 **61**.............................(t) DuranFentiman 6 46
(D A Nolan) *hld up: rdn over 2f out: sn btn* **40/1**

104- **8** *6* **Obe Brave**[220] 6864 6-9-4 **75**.............................. JamieMoriarty 1 46
(Lee Smyth, Ire) *hld up: struggling 1/2-way: nvr on terms* **9/1**

1m 39.61s (-4.19) **Going Correction** -0.35s/f (Firm) **8** Ran SP% **119.5**
Speed ratings (Par 103): **106,105,101,101,101 96,96,90**
toteswinger: 1&2 £5.30, 1&3 £2.90, 2&3 £3.90 CSF £20.23 CT £44.09 TOTE £4.40: £1.40, £1.60, £1.40; EX 22.00.
Owner Mrs S E Bruce **Bred** A Lyons Bloodstock **Trained** Uplawmoor, E Renfrews

FOCUS
This was a modest handicap but the form is rated around the first two.

2392 WILLIAM HILL WANNABET FOOTBALL? H'CAP 1m 2f

4:20 (4:21) (Class 4) (0-80,84) 4-Y-O+ **£5,828** (£1,734; £866; £432) **Stalls** Low

Form RPR

-111 **1** **Sirvino**[11] 2103 4-9-8 **84** 6ex.............................. PhillipMakin 3 96+
(T D Barron) *prom: smooth hdwy to ld over 2f out: shkn up fnl f: comf* **2/1**[1]

1 **2** 1 1/4 **Hillview Boy (IRE)**[13] 2030 5-9-3 **79**.............................. DanielTudhope 9 86
(J S Goldie) *cl up: ev ch 2f out: rdn and edgd lft: kpt on same pce fnl f* **4/1**[2]

0-53 **3** *nk* **Shy Glance (USA)**[13] 2043 7-7-12 **67**.............................. JamieKyne(7) 6 73
(P Monteith) *hld up: hdwy over 2f out: kpt on fnl f: nrst fin* **7/1**

140- **4** 2 1/2 **Summer Gold (IRE)**[238] 6431 5-9-4 **80**.............................. JoeFanning 1 81
(E J Alston) *t.k.h: cl up: rdn over 2f out: one pce over 1f out* **8/1**

The Form Book, Raceform Ltd, Compton, RG20 6NL

5103 5 ½ **Masterofceremonies**[19] 1886 6-8-4 66 DarrenMoffatt 8 66
(James Moffatt) *s.i.s: hld up: hdwy on outside over 1f out: nvr rchd ldrs* 20/1

24-4 6 1 **Fujin Dancer (FR)**[24] 1721 4-8-9 71 (b1) JamieMoriarty 2 69
(R A Fahey) *dwlt: hld up in tch: outpcd over 2f out: n.d after* 14/1

4-0 7 3 **Applaude**[12] 2073 4-8-10 72 PJMcDonald 4 64
(G A Swinbank) *in tch tl wknd over 2f out* 12/1

253 8 1¼ **Scamperdale**[55] 1107 7-8-10 72 DuranFentiman 7 62
(B P J Baugh) *hld up: rdn over 2f out: sn wknd* 33/1

50-4 9 2 **Inspector Clouseau (IRE)**[19] 1886 4-8-11 73 PaulMulrennan 5 59
(T P Tate) *led to 2f out: sn rdn and btn* 9/2[3]

2m 7.01s (-4.99) **Going Correction** -0.35s/f (Firm) 9 Ran SP% 117.2
Speed ratings (Par 105): **105,104,103,101,101 100,98,97,95**
toteswinger: 1&2 £2.90, 1&3 £4.40, 2&3 £8.20 CSF £10.06 CT £46.78 TOTE £2.90: £1.40, £1.80, £1.70; EX 12.20.
Owner Theo Williams and Charles Mocatta **Bred** A W J Perry **Trained** Maunby, N Yorks

FOCUS
A fair handicap won in grand style by the highly-progressive Sirvino. The third sets the level.
Inspector Clouseau(IRE) Official explanation: trainer's rep had no explanation for the poor form shown

2393 WILLIAMHILL.COM BEST FOOTBALL ODDS - FACT! H'CAP 6f
4:50 (4:52) (Class 4) (0-85,85) 3-Y-O £5,828 (£1,734; £866; £432) Stalls Low

Form RPR
-245 1 **Coleorton Choice**[19] 1869 3-9-2 83 SilvestreDeSousa 4 87
(K A Ryan) *mde all: rdn 2f out: kpt on wl fnl f* 4/1[2]

212 2 1 **Lenny Bee**[24] 1727 3-8-12 79 PaulMulrennan 6 80
(D H Brown) *t.k.h: sn cl up: effot 2f out: kpt on ins fnl f* 5/4[1]

03-4 3 1½ **Blown It (USA)**[20] 1828 3-8-8 80 PatrickDonaghy(5) 7 76
(I Semple) *stdd in tch: nt clr run over 2f out: effrt whn carried hd high and hung lft over 1f out: kpt on same pce fnl f* 12/1

16 4 hd **Ingleby Lady**[4] 2299 3-8-13 80 PhillipMakin 3 75
(T D Barron) *taken steadily to post: racd keenly in tch: effrt over 1f out: one pce fnl f* 9/2[3]

-102 5 4½ **Al Mugtareb (IRE)**[13] 2028 3-8-7 74 JoeFanning 1 55
(M Johnston) *cl up tl rdn and wknd fr 2f out* 4/1[2]

040 6 1 **Cool Art (IRE)**[13] 2028 3-8-0 74 (b) AndrewHeffernan(7) 2 52
(Peter Grayson) *t.k.h: chsd ldrs tl wknd wl over 1f out* 33/1

1m 12.46s (-1.14) **Going Correction** -0.15s/f (Firm) 6 Ran SP% 113.3
Speed ratings (Par 101): **101,99,97,97,91 90**
toteswinger: 1&2 £1.70, 1&3 £6.20, 2&3 £4.10 CSF £9.63 TOTE £4.80: £2.60, £1.20; EX 10.10.
Owner Coleorton Moor Racing **Bred** A Holmes **Trained** Hambleton, N Yorks

FOCUS
Not a bad little sprint but the impression was the winner was the only one to run his race.

2394 KERR & SMITH 24/7 RECOVERY H'CAP 5f
5:20 (5:20) (Class 5) (0-70,65) 3-Y-O £2,914 (£867; £433; £216) Stalls Low

Form RPR
6243 1 **Dispol Grand (IRE)**[24] 1720 3-9-4 62 JoeFanning 7 69
(P T Midgley) *chsd ldrs: effrt over 1f out: led ins fnl f: edgd rt: kpt on wl* 7/2[3]

2236 2 nk **Fasliyanne (IRE)**[9] 2162 3-8-11 60 (b) AmyRyan(5) 3 66
(K A Ryan) *cl up: led 2f out: hung bdly rt appr fnl f: hdd ins fnl f: kpt on fin* 15/8[1]

650- 3 2½ **Scrapper Smith (IRE)**[278] 5277 3-8-9 60 JamieKyne(7) 5 57
(A C Whillans) *bhd and outpcd tl styd on wl fnl f: nrst fin* 14/1

3030 4 1 **Badtanman**[27] 1644 3-7-11 48 oh1 ow2 (b) AndrewHeffernan(7) 1 41
(Peter Grayson) *sn drvn along in tch: kpt on fnl f: nvr able to chal* 20/1

-312 5 shd **Compton Ford**[27] 1644 3-9-7 65 PaulMulrennan 6 58
(M Dods) *in tch: effrt over 1f out: kpt on same pce fnl f* 9/4[2]

05-6 6 nk **Ballarina**[9] 2157 3-7-13 46 oh1 AndrewMullen(3) 2 38
(E J Alston) *taken early to post: plld hrd: led to 2f out: sn one pce* 13/2

0000 7 4½ **April Lady (IRE)**[3] 2343 3-8-2 46 oh1 DarrenMoffatt 4 22
(A Berry) *towards rr: struggling 1/2-way: nvr on terms* 33/1

59.64 secs (-0.46) **Going Correction** -0.15s/f (Firm) 7 Ran SP% 115.5
Speed ratings (Par 99): **97,96,92,90,90 90,83**
toteswinger: 1&2 £1.40, 1&3 £5.70, 2&3 £6.40 CSF £10.74 TOTE £4.80: £2.20, £2.10; EX 9.40 Place 6: £37.99, Place 5: £14.16.
Owner W B Imison **Bred** Martyn J McEnery **Trained** Westow, N Yorks
■ Stewards' Enquiry : Amy Ryan two-day ban: careless riding (Jun 11-12)

FOCUS
This was a low-grade sprint handicap and the form is modest. The winner stepped up on recent form and is rated back to his juvenile form.
T/Plt: £15.70 to a £1 stake. Pool: £55,688.94. 2,576.09 winning tickets. T/Qpdt: £10.50 to a £1 stake. Pool: £3,113.54. 218.87 winning tickets. RY

2382 LINGFIELD (L-H)
Thursday, May 28

OFFICIAL GOING: Standard
Wind: Virtually nil Weather: Bright

2395 BET FA CUP FINAL - BETDAQ MEDIAN AUCTION MAIDEN STKS 1m 2f (P)
2:30 (2:33) (Class 5) 3-5-Y-O £3,238 (£963; £481; £240) Stalls Low

Form RPR
1 **Hallstatt (IRE)** 3-8-12 0 RoystonFfrench 11 77+
(M Johnston) *trckd ldr: led ins fnl 3f: drvn along fr 2f out and hld on wl u.p cl home* 3/1[2]

5332 2 nk **Pyrus Time (IRE)**[30] 1585 3-8-12 77 LukeMorris 6 76
(J S Moore) *hld up towards rr: stdy hdwy to trck ldrs fr 4f out: chsd wnr ins fnl 2f: styd on u.p thrght fnl f but a jst hld* 5/2[1]

3 3 2¼ **Lords A Leaping (IRE)**[94] 659 3-8-12 0 ShaneKelly 8 72
(J A Osborne) *in tch: trckd ldrs 1/2-way: wnt 2nd over 2f out but nvr on terms: outpcd into 3rd ins fnl quarter m and kpt on same pce* 12/1

4 4½ **Jabroot (IRE)** 3-8-7 0 TedDurcan 7 58+
(M A Jarvis) *s.i.s and green: hdwy and in tch over 3f out: sn rdn and outpcd: styd on again thrght fnl f but nvr a threat* 8/1

54 5 1 **Extracurricular (USA)**[38] 1410 3-8-2 0 AndreaAtzeni(5) 10 56
(M Botti) *led tl hdd ins fnl 3f: wknd over 1f out* 20/1

6- 6 hd **Whatami**[224] 6759 3-8-8 0 ow1 StephenDonohoe 3 56
(E A L Dunlop) *in tch: chsd ldrs over 4f out: outpcd over 2f out: styd on again ins fnl f* 10/1

7 1¾ **Beat Companion** 3-8-12 0 IanMongan 13 57+
(P Howling) *t.k.h: hld up in rr: stdy hdwy over 3f out: wd into st and one pce: kpt on again fnl f* 33/1

6 8 3 **Diamond Dee**[20] 1838 3-8-7 0 MartinDwyer 14 46
(M D I Usher) *in rr: rdn over 6f out: mod prog fnl 2f* 33/1

9 2½ **Brandy Butter** 3-8-12 0 WilliamBuick 4 46
(A M Balding) *chsd ldrs: rdn 4f out: wknd 3f out* 9/2[3]

0 10 1¼ **La Polka**[17] 1931 3-8-7 0 SteveDrowne 5 38
(H Morrison) *chsd ldrs: rdn over 4f out: wknd 3f out* 25/1

0- 11 2½ **Wolverton (IRE)**[228] 6674 3-8-7 0 NataliaGemelova(5) 12 38
(N P Littmoden) *chsd ldrs: rdn over 4f out: wknd 3f out* 66/1

12 34 **Fidler Bay** 3-8-12 0 FergusSweeney 2 —
(H Candy) *slowly away: v green and immediately drvn along: a bhd: t.o* 16/1

2m 6.53s (-0.07) **Going Correction** 0.0s/f (Stan) 12 Ran SP% 121.5
Speed ratings (Par 103): **100,99,97,94,93 93,92,89,87,86 84,57**
toteswinger: 1&2 £3.40, 1&3 £9.90, 2&3 £3.30 CSF £10.57 TOTE £3.80: £1.30, £1.10, £3.70; EX 12.60.
Owner Sheikh Hamdan Bin Mohammed Al Maktoum **Bred** Darley **Trained** Middleham Moor, N Yorks

FOCUS
A maiden that looked there for the taking for one of the lighter-raced contenders, with Pyrus Time, who set the standard, looking fairly exposed. The runner-up is the best guide to the level.

2396 GRAYBURY LANE H'CAP 6f (P)
3:00 (3:00) (Class 4) (0-85,84) 4-Y-O+ £5,828 (£1,734; £866; £432) Stalls Low

Form RPR
4-0 1 **For Life (IRE)**[49] 1197 7-8-1 72 NataliaGemelova(5) 8 80
(J E Long) *mde all: rdn over 1f out: hld on all out* 20/1

-356 2 hd **Silaah**[13] 2050 5-9-0 80 RHills 3 87
(E A L Dunlop) *trckd ldrs: wnt 2nd over 2f out: hrd drvn over 1f out and styd on to press wnr wl ins fnl f: a jst hld* 7/4[1]

-600 3 nse **Gold Express**[12] 2086 6-8-4 70 WilliamBuick 7 77
(P J O'Gorman) *hld up in rr: stdy hdwy on outside wl over 1f out: str run u.p fnl f: gng on cl home: nt quite get up* 7/2[2]

152- 4 1 **Vintage (IRE)**[230] 6624 5-9-1 81 IanMongan 6 85
(J Akehurst) *t.k.h: hld up in tch: drvn and hdwy to chse ldrs over 1f out: styd on same pce ins fnl f* 4/1[3]

50-0 5 2¼ **Idle Power (IRE)**[7] 2188 11-8-7 73 MartinDwyer 4 70
(J R Boyle) *chsd ldrs: rdn and outpcd over 2f out: styd on again fnl f* 16/1

0556 6 3 **Whiskey Junction**[7] 2203 5-9-1 81 LPKeniry 2 68
(M Quinn) *chsd wnr tl over 2f out: wknd fnl f* 10/1

2513 7 3¼ **Caprio (IRE)**[7] 2203 4-9-0 80 PatCosgrave 5 57
(J R Boyle) *in rr: drvn and mod prog 1/2-way: sn wknd* 15/2

2565 8 3 **Dvinsky (USA)**[17] 1943 8-9-4 84 (b) StephenDonohoe 1 51
(P Howling) *sn outpcd* 12/1

1m 10.78s (-1.12) **Going Correction** 0.0s/f (Stan) 8 Ran SP% 117.8
Speed ratings (Par 105): **107,106,106,105,102 98,94,90**
toteswinger: 1&2 £12.60, 1&3 £18.50, 2&3 £2.90 CSF £57.28 CT £162.92 TOTE £22.50: £4.80, £1.10, £2.20; EX 96.00.
Owner T H Bambridge **Bred** R N Auld **Trained** Caterham, Surrey

FOCUS
A fair handicap and solid form rated around the placed horses.

2397 BETDAQ BETTING EXCHANGE H'CAP 5f (P)
3:30 (3:30) (Class 4) (0-85,84) 3-Y-O+ £5,828 (£1,734; £866; £432) Stalls High

Form RPR
25-6 1 **Lochstar**[20] 1836 5-9-7 79 WilliamBuick 10 92
(A M Balding) *mde all: drvn along fnl f: styd on strly: unchal* 15/8[1]

50-3 2 1¼ **Peak District (IRE)**[31] 1564 5-9-11 83 RyanMoore 1 92
(K A Ryan) *s.i.s: sn rcvrd and t.k.h to chse wnr tl over 2f out: rallied to go 2nd again u.p over 1f out but a readily hld* 3/1[2]

0554 3 1¼ **Fromsong (IRE)**[10] 2124 11-9-5 77 StephenCarson 3 81
(D K Ivory) *chsd ldrs: wnt 2nd over 2f out but nvr any ch w wnr: outpcd into 3rd over 1f out* 25/1

-005 4 ½ **The Jobber (IRE)**[6] 2228 8-9-12 84 TedDurcan 4 86
(M Blanshard) *hld up in tch: hdwy to chse ldrs over 1f out: no imp and styd on same pce* 6/1[3]

0004 5 1 **Whiskey Creek**[13] 2053 4-9-3 82 (v) MatthewDavies(7) 6 81
(C A Dwyer) *chsd ldrs: rdn and edgd lft bnd 2f out: outpcd fnl f* 9/1

01-6 6 1¼ **Rebecca De Winter**[24] 1727 3-9-0 80 FergusSweeney 9 71
(David Pinder) *towards rr: rdn and sme hdwy fr over 1f out but nvr in contention* 33/1

-025 7 1 **Hereford Boy**[13] 2053 5-9-0 72 (b) LukeMorris 2 63
(D K Ivory) *s.i.s: outpcd most of way* 8/1

60-5 8 hd **Requisite**[16] 1965 4-9-0 72 JimCrowley 7 62
(I A Wood) *outpcd most of way* 20/1

5011 9 1¼ **Almaty Express**[34] 1494 7-9-8 80 (b) RobertWinston 5 65
(J R Weymes) *chsd ldrs tl hmpd and snatched up bnd 2f out: nt rcvr and sn wknd* 8/1

58.52 secs (-0.28) **Going Correction** 0.0s/f (Stan)
WFA 3 from 4yo+ 8lb 9 Ran SP% 117.8
Speed ratings (Par 105): **102,100,98,97,95 93,92,91,89**
toteswinger: 1&2 £3.10, 1&3 £4.60, 2&3 £14.30 CSF £7.44 CT £104.33 TOTE £3.10: £1.40, £1.40, £9.30; EX 6.30.
Owner J C Smith **Bred** Littleton Stud **Trained** Kingsclere, Hants

FOCUS
There promised to be a lot of pace on here but actually the winner dominated with relative ease. The first three held those positions throughout.
Almaty Express Official explanation: jockey said gelding hung right on bend

2398 WATERY LANE CONDITIONS STKS 1m 2f (P)
4:00 (4:00) (Class 3) 4-Y-O+ £8,742 (£2,601; £1,300; £649) Stalls Low

Form RPR
01-0 1 **Wasan**[14] 2015 4-8-12 101 RHills 2 111+
(E A L Dunlop) *trckd ldrs: qcknd on ins to ld over 1f out: drvn clr ins fnl f: easily* 11/4[3]

2-44 2 4½ **Fairmile**[21] 1799 7-8-12 107 StephenDonohoe 3 101
(Ian Williams) *s.i.s: in rr but in tch: rdn and hdwy on ins to chse wnr fnl f but nvr any ch* 5/2[2]

2-50 3 ¾ **Alarazi (IRE)**[40] 1352 5-8-12 98 AlanMunro 6 99
(T G Mills) *chsd ldrs: wnt 2nd 7f out: rdn over 2f out: styd on same pce fnl f* 8/1

02-6 4 ½ **Zaham (USA)**[19] 1859 5-8-12 112 RyanMoore 5 98
(M Johnston) *chsd ldrs: rdn over 2f out: outpcd fr over 1f out* 2/1[1]

456/ 5 ¾ **Art Deco (IRE)**[762] 1274 6-9-4 105 SteveDrowne 4 103
(C R Egerton) *in rr: rdn and hung lft over 1f out: nvr in contention* 20/1

3- **6** *1* **Birbone (FR)**206 7171 4-8-9 103 AhmedAjtebi(3) 1 95
(Saeed Bin Suroor) *led: rdn: hd to one side and hdd over 1f out: sn btn* **8/1**

2m 3.87s (-2.73) **Going Correction** 0.0s/f (Stan) **6** Ran SP% **115.6**
Speed ratings (Par 107): **110,106,105,105,104 104**
toteswinger: 1&2 £2.30, 1&3 £5.70, 2&3 £4.10 CSF £10.50 TOTE £3.70: £1.90, £1.80; EX 10.90.

Owner Hamdan Al Maktoum **Bred** Belgrave Bloodstock **Trained** Newmarket, Suffolk

FOCUS

A conditions race made up mostly of horses with a bit to prove based on recent efforts, and they went an ordinary pace. The winner was impressive and the third sets the level, but the form may not be totally solid.

NOTEBOOK

Wasan ran no sort of race at York on his reappearance, where a combination of a drop back to a mile, quick ground and the fitting of blinkers for the first time saw him run well below the form that had seen him progress through handicap company last term. A winner of a maiden on his only previous try on Polytrack, he appreciated this more suitable distance, and, nipping through on the inside as they entered the straight, quickened right away for a thoroughly convincing success. On pedigree another quarter-mile might prove troublesome, but he saw this race out strongly, and the Hardwicke Stakes could well figure in plans now, although the Listed Wolferton Handicap over 1m2f could be more suitable. His trainer is keen to avoid firm ground with him, though. (op 3-1 tchd 7-2)

Fairmile, who ran a perfectly sound race when fourth behind Doctor Fremantle in the Huxley Stakes last time, was held up at the back of the field off the fairly ordinary pace. He followed the winner through on the inside but lacked his gears. A stronger all-round gallop would have suited him. (op 11-4 tchd 9-4)

Alarazi(IRE) was worst in at the weights on adjusted official ratings, but he held a good position alongside the leader for a long way and kept on fairly well in the straight. He might be a little flattered by the way the race was run, but this was still an encouraging effort following a spell in the doldrums. (op 10-1 tchd 12-1)

Zaham(USA) was the best horse in the race on official ratings, but he had been desperately disappointing at Ascot on his reappearance, and, having come there to have every chance early in the straight, he was soon treading water. Clearly all is not well with him. (op 3-1)

Art Deco(IRE) had a stiff task giving 6lb all round on his return from two years on the sidelines. (op 16-1)

Birbone(FR), placed in Listed company in France last year, was having his first start for Godolphin. He enjoyed the run of the race out in front but, once put under pressure in the straight, began to carry his head awkwardly and didn't want to know. He might have issues. (op 9-2)

2399 BETDAQ POKER H'CAP — 1m (P)
4:30 (4:31) (Class 4) (0-85,85) 3-Y-O — £5,828 (£1,734; £866; £432) Stalls High

Form / RPR

1026 **1** **Dalradian (IRE)**3 2329 3-9-4 85 JimCrowley 8 88+
(W J Knight) *hld up in rr: stl last ins fnl 2f: qcknd ins fnl f but nt clr run: qcknd again and squeezed through cl home to ld last stride* **13/2**

034- **2** *shd* **Dancourt (IRE)**194 7333 3-8-6 73 RyanMoore 10 75+
(Sir Michael Stoute) *towards rr but in tch: gd hdwy appr fnl f and str run to take slt ld nr fin: hdd last stride* **3/1**1

3-12 **3** *½* **Royal Executioner (USA)**61 1001 3-8-13 80 StephenDonohoe 5 81
(D M Simcock) *chsd ldrs: rdn and outpcd over 2f out: rdn and rapid hdwy over 1f out: drvn to chal fnl 50yds: no ex claose home* **7/2**2

02-4 **4** *shd* **My Kingdom (IRE)**24 1744 3-8-12 79 (t) TravisBlock 7 80
(H Morrison) *chsd ldrs: rdn to chal ins fnl f: upsides whn edgd lft and no ex cl home* **10/1**

0-10 **5** *nse* **Lastroarofdtiger (USA)**31 1561 3-8-10 77 RobertWinston 2 78
(K R Burke) *chsd ldrs: chal over 1f out: slt ld u.p ins fnl f: hdd and no ex nr fin* **20/1**

31-5 **6** *hd* **Hail Promenader (IRE)**24 1751 3-8-13 80 MichaelHills 11 81
(B W Hills) *chsd ldrs: rdn to chal over 1f out: stl upsides ins fnl f: nt qckn whn carried sltly rt cl home* **5/1**

3-31 **7** *1 ¾* **Spring Adventure**16 1963 3-8-13 80 EddieAhern 9 77
(E A L Dunlop) *in rr but in tch: pushed along over 1f out: styd on fnl f but nvr gng pce to get into contention* **9/2**3

06-0 **8** *nse* **Perfect Citizen (USA)**24 1751 3-9-1 82 (p) AdamKirby 1 78
(W R Swinburn) *led: rdn over 2f out: narrowly hdd ins fnl f: wknd fnl 75yds* **20/1**

31 **9** *nk* **Mackten**20 1838 3-8-9 76 ShaneKelly 4 72
(W J Knight) *t.k.h: towards rr: n.m.r after 1f: hdwy ins fnl f: kpt on cl home but nvr in contention* **12/1**

3-44 **10** *nk* **Dukes Art**28 1632 3-8-8 75 AlanMunro 3 70
(J A R Toller) *chsd ldrs: rdn over 2f out: styd wl there tl wknd ins fnl f* **20/1**

4116 **11** *3 ¾* **Woolston Ferry (IRE)**36 1466 3-8-11 78 FergusSweeney 6 64
(David Pinder) *in rr: sme hdwy over 2f out: nvr gng pce to get into contention* **25/1**

1m 38.67s (0.47) **Going Correction** 0.0s/f (Stan) **11** Ran SP% **130.3**
Speed ratings (Par 101): **97,96,96,96,96 96,94,94,93,93 89**
toteswinger: 1&2 £9.60 1&3 £7.60, 2&3 £5.10 CSF £27.86 CT £86.80 TOTE £6.90: £1.60, £2.30, £1.70; EX 44.10.

Owner Canisbay Bloodstock **Bred** Hesmonds Stud Ltd **Trained** Patching, W Sussex

FOCUS

A number of unexposed horses open to plenty of improvement gave this handicap a tricky look, while a steady early pace followed by a dash to the line resulted in a bunch finish. The form is unreliable but the race should throw up future winners.

Lastroarofdtiger(USA) Official explanation: jockey said colt ran too free

Mackten Official explanation: jockey said colt suffered interference 1f after start

2400 SHERNDAN LANE H'CAP — 1m (P)
5:00 (5:00) (Class 6) (0-65,65) 4-Y-O+ — £2,047 (£604; £302) Stalls High

Form / RPR

0354 **1** **Teen Ager (FR)**8 2185 5-8-11 58 StephenCarson 9 67
(P Burgoyne) *trckd ldrs: led over 2f out: drvn and hld on wl thrght fnl f* **16/1**

002- **2** *½* **One Oi**190 7392 4-8-8 55 WilliamBuick 12 63
(D W P Arbuthnot) *in rr: hdwy on outside over 1f out: str run ins fnl f: kpt on wl cl home: nt quite rch wnr* **9/2**2

054- **3** *shd* **Billberry**179 7507 4-9-4 65 (t) AdamKirby 7 73+
(S C Williams) *hld up in rr: stl plenty to do whn gd hdwy fnl f: fin strly: nt quite get up* **4/1**1

0-15 **4** *½* **Colour Of Money**59 1039 4-8-12 59 StephenDonohoe 6 65
(S A Callaghan) *chsd ldrs: wnt 2nd u.p 1f out: no imp on wnr and outpcd into 4th cl home* **5/1**3

1645 **5** *½* **Barodine**24 6-8-4 56 ow1 MCGeran(5) 4 61
(R J Hodges) *in tch: drvn along 3f out: styd on towards outside fnl f: nvr quite gng pce to get into contention* **16/1**

2355 **6** *1 ¼* **Sew'N'So Character (IRE)**20 1833 8-9-4 65 LPKeniry 2 67
(M Blanshard) *towards rr: rdn and sme hdwy 2f out: nvr gng pce to rch ldrs and wknd ins fnl f* **10/1**

0252 **7** *1 ¾* **Takaamul**23 1773 6-8-4 51 RichardThomas 11 49
(K A Morgan) *s.i.s: in rr: hdwy on ins to chse ldrs over 1f out: wknd ins fnl f* **11/2**

0304 **8** *1 ¾* **Simpsons Gamble (IRE)**16 1959 6-8-4 58 (p) MatthewDavies(7) 3 52
(R A Teal) *chsd ldrs: rdn over 2f out: wknd fnl f* **25/1**

0335 **9** *3 ¾* **Lord Theo**50 1194 5-9-2 63 (b) LukeMorris 8 49
(N P Littmoden) *led: rdn and hdd over 2f out: wknd over 1f out* **11/2**

0060 **10** *7* **Tallulah Sunrise**20 1834 4-8-6 58 ow3 GabrielHannon(5) 5 28
(M D I Usher) *nvr bttr than mid-div* **40/1**

1020 **11** *1 ¾* **Postage (USA)**22 1785 6-8-13 60 PatCosgrave 10 26
(K A Morgan) *chsd ldrs over 5f* **9/1**

1m 37.71s (-0.49) **Going Correction** 0.0s/f (Stan) **11** Ran SP% **122.8**
Speed ratings (Par 101): **102,101,101,100,100 99,97,95,91,84 83**
toteswinger: 1&2 £14.40, 1&3 £16.40, 2&3 £4.70 CSF £90.48 CT £364.74 TOTE £20.30: £3.00, £2.10, £1.80; EX 141.40 Place 6: £15.75, Place 5: £10.09.

Owner L Tomlin **Bred** Haras De Beauvoir **Trained** Shepton Montague, Somerset

■ Stewards' Enquiry : Luke Morris one-day ban plus five-days deferred: careless riding (Jun 12-17)

FOCUS

An ordinary handicap run at a sound pace and the winner is the best guide to the level.

T/Plt: £47.10 to a £1 stake. Pool: £53,458.66. 827.03 winning tickets. T/Qpdt: £16.50 to a £1 stake. Pool: £2,881.71. 129.22 winning tickets. ST

2231 NEWCASTLE (L-H)
Thursday, May 28

OFFICIAL GOING: Good to firm (8.5)

Wind: virtually nil Weather: Fine, warm and dry

2401 BOTOX & FILLERS MAIDEN FILLIES' STKS — 6f
6:25 (6:26) (Class 4) 2-Y-O — £4,921 (£1,464; £731; £365) Stalls Low

Form / RPR

1 **Amary (IRE)** 2-9-0 0 MickyFenton 8 78+
(C E Brittain) *s.i.s and in rr: hdwy over 2f out: swtchd outside and effrt to chse ldr ent fnl f: rdn and kpt on to ld last 100yds* **9/2**3

5 **2** *1* **Fly Silca Fly (IRE)**13 2034 2-9-0 0 EdwardCreighton 9 75
(M R Channon) *chsd ldrs on outer: hdwy 2f out: rdn to ld over 1f out: drvn ins fnl f: hdd and no ex last 100yds* **11/4**2

3 *3 ¼* **Lady Springbank (IRE)** 2-9-0 0 AndrewElliott 2 65
(K R Burke) *wnt rt s: t.k.h early and sn chsng ldng pair: effrt over 2f out: sn rdn and ev ch tl drvn and kpt on same pce ins fnl f* **8/1**

4 *3 ¼* **Seven Of Diamonds (IRE)** 2-9-0 0 DavidAllan 3 56
(T D Easterby) *s.i.s and bhd: hdwy over 2f out: rdn and kpt on ins fnl f: nrst fin* **16/1**

32 **5** *hd* **Cassidy K**11 2100 2-9-0 0 TomEaves 7 55
(J Howard Johnson) *cl up: rdn along over 2f out: drvn and wknd over 1f out* **10/1**

6 *2 ½* **Sarahthecarer (IRE)** 2-9-0 0 TPO'Shea 4 47
(P M Mooney, Ire) *chsd ldrs: rdn along wl over 2f out: sn wknd* **25/1**

7 *¾* **Bikini Babe (IRE)** 2-9-0 0 GregFairley 1 45+
(M Johnston) *sn led: rdn along and hung lft 2f out: sn hdd & wknd* **2/1**1

8 *12* **Sixbox** 2-9-0 0 FrancisNorton 5 —
(D Shaw) *a in rr: outpcd and bhd fr 1/2-way* **20/1**

1m 15.85s (0.65) **Going Correction** -0.175s/f (Firm) **8** Ran SP% **112.9**
Speed ratings (Par 92): **88,86,82,78,77 74,73,57**
toteswinger: 1&2 £8.80, 1&3 £14.00, 2&3 £12.70 CSF £16.82 TOTE £6.80: £2.00, £1.50, £2.80; EX 21.40.

Owner Saeed Manana **Bred** Marie & Mossy Fahy **Trained** Newmarket, Suffolk

FOCUS

Just an ordinary fillies' maiden to kick off with and the two who drew clear came down the centre of the track. The form is probably modest. Jockeys who rode in this first race came back in describing the ground as 'dead'.

NOTEBOOK

Amary(IRE), a 65,000gns daughter of Acclamation, looked pretty forward in the parade ring beforehand and, although she was a bit tardy from the stalls, she travelled nicely through the race before being switched out to make her move over a furlong out. Her rider didn't have to get overly vigorous as the filly picked up nicely and went by Fly Silca Fly to provide her trainer with a third winning juvenile newcomer of the season. She doesn't have any big race entries at this stage, and this form probably isn't anything to get excited about, but she impressed with the way she travelled and quickened, and she might turn out to be pretty useful. (op 15-2)

Fly Silca Fly(IRE), who had the benefit of a run, is by Hawk Wing and she displayed some of the wayward tendencies of her sire by holding her head a bit high on occasions and, although it may seem a bit harsh given this was only her second start, she didn't look the hardiest of battlers despite coming clear in second. She clearly has ability but it will need to be harnessed correctly if she is to go on and win races. (op 4-1)

Lady Springbank(IRE) shaped with plenty of promise, travelling well before keeping on and, given her yard's runners tend to come on a good deal from first to second run, she should soon find a winning opportunity. Also, she displayed quite a bit of knee action so easier ground might suit her better. (op 5-1 tchd 10-1)

Seven Of Diamonds(IRE), was slowly away and green early but she looked to be getting the hang of things entering the final furlong when appearing to take a false step and she weakened after that. Like Lady Springbank, she has quite a high knee action, and her stable's runners always come on a bundle for their initial outing.

Cassidy K, having her third start, wasn't good enough.

Bikini Babe(IRE) looked on the burly side in the paddock and is sure to come on a good deal for this run.

2402 FRAXEL LASER TREATMENT H'CAP — 7f
7:00 (7:00) (Class 4) (0-80,80) 4-Y-O+ — £4,792 (£1,425; £712; £355) Stalls Low

Form / RPR

5-25 **1** **Barricado (FR)**16 1964 4-8-10 72 FrancisNorton 9 84
(E J O'Neill) *hld up towards rr: gd hdwy 2f out: rdn to chse ldrs over 1f out: drvn to ld ins fnl f: kpt on strly* **9/1**

-342 **2** *1 ¾* **Bravely (IRE)**6 2235 5-8-11 73 DavidAllan 4 80
(T D Easterby) *hld up towards rr: gd hdwy 2f out: rdn to chse ldrs over 1f out: kpt on ins fnl f: nt rch wnr* **13/2**2

00-5 **3** *1 ¼* **Middlemarch (IRE)**40 1343 9-8-6 73 (b) GaryBartley(5) 6 77
(J S Goldie) *in rr: swtchd rt and hdwy wl over 1f out: rdn and styd on strly ins fnl f: nrst fin* **20/1**

-024 **4** *¾* **Bold Marc (IRE)**5 2274 7-8-10 77 MartinLane(5) 16 79
(K R Burke) *led: rdn along wl over 1f out: drvn 1f out: hdd and one pce ins fnl f* **5/1**1

20-1 **5** 1 1/4 **Celtic Lynn (IRE)**[24] 1737 4-9-1 **77** TomEaves 7 75
(M Dods) *in tch: hdwy 2f out: rdn to chse ldng pair over 1f out: sn drvn and kpt on same pce* **10/1**

0-50 **6** hd **Sparton Duke (IRE)**[12] 2071 4-8-10 **72** (p) TPO'Shea 8 76+
(K A Ryan) *hld up in rr: hdwy over 2f out: swtchd lft and n.m.r over 1f out: kpt on ins fnl f: nrst fin* **18/1**

2-03 **7** 1 **Sam's Secret**[17] 1923 7-9-4 **80** RobertHavlin 5 75
(G A Swinbank) *t.k.h early: hld up towards rr: hdwy over 2f out: rdn wl over 1f out: no imp ins fnl f* **16/1**

0063 **8** 1/2 **Daaweitza**[5] 2257 6-8-7 **74** LanceBetts(5) 2 68
(B Ellison) *dwlt and sltly hmpd s: midfield: pushed along 1/2-way: rdn 2f out: styd on u.p ins fnl f: nrst fin* **10/1**

0162 **9** 1 3/4 **Carnivore**[24] 1734 7-8-8 **75** DeanHeslop(5) 1 64
(T D Barron) *racd wd: prom: effrt 2f out: sn rdn and ev ch ent fnl f: sn drvn and wknd qckly* **25/1**

5-55 **10** nk **Borasco (USA)**[13] 2045 4-9-1 **80** NeilBrown(3) 15 68
(T D Barron) *chsd ldrs: hdwy over 2f out: rdn wl over 1f out: sn wknd* **7/1**[3]

01-0 **11** 1/2 **Eastern Hills**[12] 2073 4-8-13 **75** PAspell 10 62
(J S Wainwright) *chsd ldrs: rdn along 2f out: grad wknd appr fnl f* **66/1**

5603 **12** 3 3/4 **Navajo Joe (IRE)**[6] 2235 4-8-8 **70** AndrewElliott 12 47
(R Johnson) *hld up: a in rr* **16/1**

2311 **13** 1/2 **Stonecrabstomorrow (IRE)**[17] 1924 6-8-4 **73** (b) BMcHugh(7) 11 48
(R A Fahey) *t.k.h: cl up: rdn along wl over 2f out and sn wknd* **15/2**

-002 **14** nk **Mut'Ab (USA)**[17] 1943 4-9-3 **79** (b) EdwardCreighton 14 53
(C E Brittain) *prom: rdn along over 2f out and sn wknd* **11/1**

1m 27.75s (-0.95) **Going Correction** -0.175s/f (Firm) 14 Ran SP% **117.9**
Speed ratings (Par 105): **98,96,94,93,92 92,90,90,88,88 87,83,82,82**
toteswinger: 1&2 £23.90, 1&3 £33.00, 2&3 £29.50 CSF £63.73 CT £1150.20 TOTE £10.40: £3.60, £2.10, £6.10; EX 70.00.
Owner David Barlow **Bred** Sarl Elevage Du Haras De Bourgeauville **Trained** Southwell, Notts
■ Stewards' Enquiry : Robert Havlin one-day ban: failed to ride to draw (Jun 11)
Dean Heslop one-day ban: failed to keep straight from stalls (Jun 11)

FOCUS
A wide-open handicap featuring mainly exposed performers and the majority of the field came across to the stands' side despite the stalls being positioned on the far side. The finish was ultimately dominated by horses coming from some way back, although entering the final furlong it looked as though little was going to get into it from off the pace, so the picture changed dramatically in the final half furlong. The form is fair for the grade with the runner-up a pretty solid guide.
Bravely(IRE) Official explanation: jockey said gelding ran too free
Sparton Duke(IRE) Official explanation: jockey said gelding was denied a clear run

2403 THERMAGE MAIDEN FILLIES' STKS 1m 2f 32y
7:35 (7:37) (Class 5) 3-Y-O+ **£3,238** (£963; £481; £240) **Stalls** Centre

Form RPR

1 **Charity Belle (USA)** 3-8-10 0 RobertHavlin 9 83
(J H M Gosden) *trckd ldrs tl led after 4f: jnd and rdn over 2f out: qcknd clr ent fnl f and styd on strly* **5/1**[2]

02 **2** 5 **Lady Artemisia (IRE)**[14] 2006 3-8-10 0 MickyFenton 1 72
(M L W Bell) *prom: trckd wnr over 4f out: cl up over 2f out: rdn and ev ch over 1f out: sn drvn and kpt on same pce* **2/5**[1]

3 8 **Mexican Jay (USA)** 3-8-10 0 TomEaves 5 56
(B Smart) *trckd ldrs: hdwy to chse ldng pair over 2f out: sn drvn and no imp* **11/1**[3]

4 1 1/2 **Smarties Party**[41] 6-9-10 0 PAspell 2 53
(C W Thornton) *s.i.s: sn in midfield: effrt to trck ldrs 3f out: sn rdn and kpt on same pce* **25/1**

60 **5** 1 **Flora's Pride**[7] 2199 5-9-10 0 FrancisNorton 10 51
(K G Reveley) *hld up in rr: hdwy on inner 3f out: swtchd rt and rdn wl over 1f out: n.d* **16/1**

6 hd **Yashkur** 3-8-10 0 EdwardCreighton 4 51
(C E Brittain) *chsd ldrs: rdn along 3f out: drvn over 2f out and sn wknd* **20/1**

50 **7** 1 1/2 **Goswick**[11] 2104 3-8-8 0 ow1 NeilBrown(3) 3 49
(Micky Hammond) *led 4f: prom tl rdn over 3f out and sn wknd* **100/1**

0 **8** hd **Waltzalong (IRE)**[11] 2105 3-8-10 0 DavidAllan 7 47
(T D Easterby) *a towards rr* **33/1**

9 3/4 **Flying Phoebe** 3-8-10 0 GregFairley 6 46
(Mrs L Stubbs) *a towards rr* **20/1**

0 **10** 2 1/4 **Lady Anne Nevill**[12] 2090 5-9-10 0 AndrewElliott 8 41
(C W Fairhurst) *a in rr* **80/1**

2m 13.68s (1.78) **Going Correction** +0.075s/f (Good)
WFA 3 from 5yo+ 14lb 10 Ran SP% **120.8**
Speed ratings (Par 100): **95,91,84,83,82 82,81,81,80,78**
toteswinger: 1&2 £2.00, 1&3 £3.20, 2&3 £3.00 CSF £7.25 TOTE £7.40: £1.30, £1.02, £2.60; EX 12.70.
Owner H R H Princess Haya Of Jordan **Bred** Stonerside Stable **Trained** Newmarket, Suffolk

FOCUS
An uncompetitive maiden and probably not that solid.

2404 LIPOSCULPTURE (S) STKS 1m (R)
8:10 (8:11) (Class 6) 3-5-Y-O **£1,942** (£578; £288; £144) **Stalls** Centre

Form RPR

0626 **1** **My Mate Mal**[2] 2361 5-9-0 66 LanceBetts(5) 9 63
(B Ellison) *trckd ldrs: hdwy 3f out: rdn to ld over 1f out: drvn ins fnl f and kpt on gamely* **5/2**[1]

0-00 **2** 1 **San Silvestro (IRE)**[6] 2245 4-8-12 61 (p) BMcHugh(7) 4 61
(Mrs A Duffield) *cl up: rdn to ld over 2f out: drvn and hdd over 1f out: kpt on wl u.p ins fnl f: no ex towards fin* **3/1**[2]

00-5 **3** hd **Not Now Lewis (IRE)**[31] 1558 5-9-5 50 PJMcDonald 8 60
(F P Murtagh) *hld up and bhd: smooth hdwy 4f out: chsd ldrs wl over 1f out: sn rdn and edgd lft ins fnl f: one pce towards fin* **6/1**[3]

0060 **4** 4 **Johnny Friendly**[19] 1889 4-9-0 47 MartinLane(5) 1 51
(K R Burke) *chsd ldrs: rdn along over 2f out: sn drvn and one pce* **12/1**

0-04 **5** 7 **Paint Stripper**[24] 1734 4-8-12 42 JohnCavanagh(7) 2 35
(W Storey) *sn led: rdn along 4f out: hdd over 2f out and grad wknd* **20/1**

0000 **6** hd **Ride A White Swan**[19] 1890 4-9-5 51 GrahamGibbons 3 35
(D Shaw) *dwlt: sn in midfield: effrt and in tch wl over 2f out: sn rdn and no hdwy* **17/2**

205- **7** 1 1/4 **Reddy Ronnie (IRE)**[331] 3593 5-9-5 51 AndrewElliott 6 32
(D W Thompson) *a midfield* **17/2**

0-00 **8** 3/4 **Royal Applord**[16] 1955 4-9-5 56 (p) JamieMoriarty 10 30
(P T Midgley) *a towards rr* **10/1**

-000 **9** 4 1/2 **Jojesse**[9] 2155 5-9-5 45 TWilliams 7 20
(W Storey) *dwlt: hdwy into midfield 1/2-way: rdn along 4f out and sn wknd* **33/1**

00-0 **10** 1 1/4 **Kathanikki Girl (IRE)**[33] 1530 3-7-9 40 BillyCray(7) 13 12
(Mrs L Williamson) *stdd s: a towards rr* **50/1**

006- **11** 16 **Aspendale (IRE)**[307] 4378 4-9-5 35 (b[1]) DNolan 11 —
(D Carroll) *a in rr* **33/1**

00-0 **12** 24 **Call Of Ktulu (IRE)**[19] 1888 4-9-5 12 PAspell 5 —
(J S Wainwright) *a towards rr* **125/1**

1m 43.96s (0.56) **Going Correction** +0.075s/f (Good)
WFA 3 from 4yo+ 12lb 12 Ran SP% **119.1**
Speed ratings (Par 101): **101,100,99,95,88 88,87,86,82,80 64,40**
toteswinger: 1&2 £4.50, 1&3 £5.00, 2&3 £3.40 CSF £9.46 TOTE £3.60: £1.70, £2.30, £2.50; EX 12.50.There was no bid for the winner.
Owner Koo's Racing Club **Bred** Mrs A M Mallinson **Trained** Norton, N Yorks

FOCUS
Basement grade form with the third the best guide to the level.

2405 JADE GOODY FOUNDATION H'CAP 6f
8:40 (8:40) (Class 3) (0-90,90) 4-Y-O **£7,569** (£2,265; £1,132; £566; £282) **Stalls** Low

Form RPR

0-40 **1** **Baby Strange**[25] 1699 5-8-13 **90** MartinLane(5) 6 97
(D Shaw) *dwlt: hdwy 2f out: chsd ldrs over 1f out: rdn to ld jst ins fnl f: sn drvn and kpt on gamely* **5/1**[3]

431- **2** nk **Errigal Lad**[255] 5962 4-8-9 **81** TPO'Shea 7 87
(K A Ryan) *prom: led wl over 2f out: rdn wl over 1f out: drvn and hdd jst ins fnl f: kpt on gamely* **9/1**

3-23 **3** nk **Solar Spirit (IRE)**[20] 1849 4-8-11 **83** GrahamGibbons 8 88
(J J Quinn) *a.p: effrt over 1f out: sn rdn and ev ch tl drvn ins fnl f and nt qckn towards fin* **3/1**[1]

6-40 **4** nk **Maze (IRE)**[19] 1861 4-9-1 **87** TomEaves 9 91
(B Smart) *in tch: hdwy to chse ldrs 2f out: rdn and sltly outpcd over 1f out: kpt on wl u.p ins fnl f* **15/2**

00-0 **5** nse **Bond City (IRE)**[13] 2059 7-9-4 **90** PJMcDonald 5 94
(G R Oldroyd) *trckd ldrs: hdwy wl over 1f out: rdn and ch whn edgd lft ins fnl f: no ex towards fin* **22/1**

6003 **6** 1 **Osteopathic Remedy (IRE)**[12] 2093 5-9-0 **86** PhillipMakin 10 87+
(M Dods) *hld up towards rr: hdwy on outer 2f out: rdn over 1f out: kpt on ins fnl f: nrst fin* **9/2**[2]

-510 **7** 2 1/4 **Quest For Success (IRE)**[19] 1861 4-9-4 **90** TonyHamilton 3 84
(R A Fahey) *trkd ldrs: effrt 2f out: sn rdn and wknd ent fnl f* **9/1**

3-20 **8** 1/2 **Pavershooz**[13] 2059 4-8-10 **82** DavidAllan 1 74
(N Wilson) *cl up: rdn along wl over 1f out: grad wknd* **7/1**

0-00 **9** 4 1/2 **Green Park (IRE)**[12] 2095 6-8-8 **80** DNolan 4 58
(D Carroll) *chsd ldrs: rdn along over 2f out: sn wknd* **40/1**

0-00 **10** 2 1/2 **Great Charm (IRE)**[19] 1864 4-8-12 **84** MickyFenton 2 54
(M L W Bell) *sn led: rdn along and hdd over 2f out: sn wknd* **20/1**

1m 13.1s (-2.10) **Going Correction** -0.175s/f (Firm) 10 Ran SP% **115.7**
Speed ratings (Par 107): **107,106,106,105,105 104,101,100,94,91**
toteswinger: 1&2 £17.30, 1&3 £4.10, 2&3 £2.90 CSF £47.50 CT £157.98 TOTE £5.40: £1.90, £2.90, £1.80; EX 71.50.
Owner Market Avenue Racing Club Ltd **Bred** Michael John Williamson **Trained** Danethorpe, Notts
■ Stewards' Enquiry : Graham Gibbons two-day ban: used whip with excessive frequency (Jun 11-12)

FOCUS
A competitive sprint handicap and a bunch finish. The form looks sound enough rated around the placed horses.

NOTEBOOK
Baby Strange bounced back to something like his best and displayed the battling qualities of his sire Superior Premium to squeeze through a gap and battle on strongly to hold off his rivals. Now back down to a 3lb lower mark than when going close at Goodwood last August, he was totally unsuited by conditions at Newmarket last time but was able to show his true colours here and take advantage of what looked a very handy mark, especially when taking into consideration the 5lb claim of his young rider. (op 6-1)
Errigal Lad has run a blinder on seasonal return, battling away all the way to the line having been front rank throughout. He was 5lb higher than winning his final start of last term so he has clearly wintered well and looks a sprinter on the upgrade. (op 12-1)
Solar Spirit(IRE) was also bang there throughout and he has run his usual honest race, but has been bumped up to a career-high mark of 83 despite being beaten on his last three starts, so the handicapper isn't making life easy. (op 7-2)
Maze(IRE) made little impact in the Victoria Cup last time but, appreciating the drop back to 6f, this was much more like it and the handicapper is beginning to cut him some slack now. (op 10-1)
Bond City(IRE) has been dropped 2lb for his promising York reappearance, and he stayed on strongly up the far side to finish close up. (tchd 25-1)
Osteopathic Remedy(IRE) kept on from off the pace, but he couldn't get into it. (op 3-1)

2406 BREAST AUGMENTATION H'CAP 1m 3y(S)
9:15 (9:15) (Class 4) (0-85,84) 3-Y-O **£5,180** (£1,541; £770; £384) **Stalls** Low

Form RPR

0043 **1** **Silver Games (IRE)**[8] 2174 3-9-3 **83** EdwardCreighton 4 90
(M R Channon) *hld up towards rr: hdwy on outer 2f out: rdn to chse ldr over 1f out: drvn to ld ins fnl f: jst hld on* **7/1**

-421 **2** nse **Tarzan (IRE)**[17] 1925 3-8-13 **79** GregFairley 7 86
(M Johnston) *trckd ldr: hdwy to ld over 2f out: rdn over 1f out: drvn and hdd ins fnl f: rallied gamely towards fin* **5/4**[1]

-222 **3** 4 1/2 **Andean Margin (IRE)**[120] 317 3-8-9 **75** DaleGibson 8 72
(M W Easterby) *trckd ldrs: effrt 2f out: sn rdn: drvn appr fnl f and kpt on same pce* **33/1**

444- **4** shd **Honimiere (IRE)**[253] 6013 3-8-6 **72** PJMcDonald 5 68
(G A Swinbank) *led: rdn along and hdd over 2f out: drvn and one pce fr over 1f out* **33/1**

4-31 **5** 2 1/4 **Dr Jameson (IRE)**[16] 1950 3-8-9 **75** TonyHamilton 3 66
(R A Fahey) *hld up: hdwy over 2f out: rdn to chse ldrs over 1f out: sn drvn and wknd* **12/1**

3-42 **6** nk **Big Apple Boy (IRE)**[12] 2092 3-9-4 **84** AndrewElliott 6 74
(Jedd O'Keeffe) *chsd ldrs: rdn along over 2f out: sn drvn and grad wknd* **11/2**[3]

4-21 **7** 3/4 **Ithbaat (USA)**[17] 1941 3-9-2 **82** TPO'Shea 1 71
(J H M Gosden) *prom: rdn along over 2f out: drvn wl over 1f out and sn wknd* **11/4**[2]

2-56 **8** 22 **Striker Torres (IRE)**[12] 2072 3-8-12 **78** TomEaves 2 16
(B Smart) *trckd ldrs: effrt on outer 3f out: sn rdn and wknd 2f out* **14/1**

1m 40.35s (-3.05) **Going Correction** -0.175s/f (Firm) 8 Ran SP% **119.2**
Speed ratings (Par 101): **108,107,103,103,101 100,100,78**
toteswinger: 1&2 £5.20, 1&3 £19.90, 2&3 £2.20 CSF £16.96 CT £279.68 TOTE £10.20: £1.90, £1.20, £4.30; EX 25.20 Place 6: £26.35, Place 5: £10.18..
Owner Box 41 **Bred** Ceka Ireland Limited **Trained** West Ilsley, Berks

FOCUS
Not the strongest of 0-85 handicaps but a decent time for the grade. The first two are improving and came clear.

T/Plt: £43.90 to a £1 stake. Pool: £53,157.33. 882. 19 winning tickets. T/Qpdt: £4.30 to a £1 stake. Pool: £4,223.14. 722. 40 winning tickets. JR

2207 SANDOWN (R-H)

Thursday, May 28

OFFICIAL GOING: Good (good to firm in places on round course; round 8.5, sprint 8.2)

Wind: modest across Weather: bright but overcast, warm amd muggy

2407 BLUE SQUARE POKER H'CAP — 1m 2f 7y

6:05 (6:06) (Class 4) (0-85,85) 4-Y-O+ **£5,180** (£1,541; £770; £384) **Stalls High**

Form / RPR

5-50 **1** **Mountain Pride (IRE)**13 2050 4-9-0 **81** TedDurcan 6 — 91
(J L Dunlop) *stdd s: hld up towards rr: hdwy on outer over 3f out: rdn to ld over 1f out: edgd rt u.p: drvn and kpt on wl fnl f* **16/1**

103- **2** *1 1/4* **Dr Livingstone (IRE)**212 7056 4-9-3 **84** SteveDrowne 13 — 92
(C R Egerton) *t.k.h: chsd ldng pair: jnd ldr travelling wl over 2f out: rdn wl over 1f out: chsd wnr and one pce after* **16/1**

100- **3** *2* **Kensington Oval**242 6302 4-9-4 **85** RyanMoore 10 — 89
(Sir Michael Stoute) *lw: on toes: dwlt: sn rcvrd and hld up in midfield: hdwy over 3f out: swtchd lft and rdn over 1f out: chsd ldng pair jst ins fnl f: kpt on steadily but nvr pce to rch ldng pair* **7/4**1

4052 **4** *2 1/4* **Baylini**6 2239 5-8-13 **80** JamesDoyle 4 — 79
(Ms J S Doyle) *hld up in rr: rdn and hdwy on inner over 2f out: kpt on u.p: nvr pce to rch ldrs* **8/1**3

00-0 **5** *nk* **By Command**21 1812 4-8-10 **77** RHills 1 — 75
(J W Hills) *led: rdn and qcknd over 2f out: hdd over 1f out: wknd fnl f* **18/1**

60/5 **6** *nk* **Sharpazmax (IRE)**125 271 5-8-13 **80** EddieAhern 5 — 78
(P J Makin) *swtg: chsd ldrs: rdn and unable qckn wl over 2f out: losing pl and sltly hmpd over 2f out: rallied u.p fnl f: kpt on but nvr pce to trble ldrs* **8/1**3

01-3 **7** *1/2* **Wiggy Smith**30 1593 10-9-0 **81** DaneO'Neill 14 — 78
(H Candy) *stdd s: hld up towards rr: rdn and no real hdwy over 2f out: plugged on u.p fnl f: nvr trbld ldrs* **6/1**2

4-6 **8** *shd* **Mafeking (UAE)**134 156 5-9-1 **82** IanMongan 7 — 79
(M R Hoad) *t.k.h: chsd ldr tl over 2f out: wkng whn wandered u.p wl over 1f out: kpt on same pce fnl f* **50/1**

2111 **9** *1/2* **Pelham Crescent (IRE)**15 1983 6-8-7 **77** DavidProbert(3) 8 — 73
(B Palling) *on toes: t.k.h: hld up in midfield: rdn and outpcd 3f out: kpt on again fnl f: nvr pce to trble ldrs* **17/2**

413- **10** *8* **Alfie Tupper (IRE)**215 6989 6-8-6 **73** MartinDwyer 2 — 53
(J R Boyle) *t.k.h: hld up in last pair: rdn and no hdwy over 3f out: wl btn and eased ins fnl f* **16/1**

11-3 **11** *2 1/4* **Moves Goodenough**40 1357 6-9-1 **82** (b) PatDobbs 9 — 57
(Andrew Turnell) *swtg: wnt v freely to post: plld hrd and hld up in rr: rdn and struggling over 3f out: wl bhd and eased ins fnl f* **12/1**

2m 8.87s (-1.63) **Going Correction** -0.05s/f (Good) **11 Ran SP% 116.0**

Speed ratings (Par 105): **104,103,101,99,99 99,98,98,98,91 90**

toteswinger: 1&2 £25.40, 1&3 £10.80, 2&3 £8.40 CSF £244.21 CT £676.34 TOTE £15.80: £5.30, £3.70, £1.20; EX 221.20.

Owner Ian Cameron **Bred** Raymond P Doyle **Trained** Arundel, W Sussex

FOCUS

A competitive mid-rank handicap but ordinary form for the grade, rated through the runner-up.

Moves Goodenough Official explanation: jockey said gelding ran too free

2408 BLUE SQUARE CASINO NATIONAL STKS (LISTED RACE) — 5f 6y

6:35 (6:36) (Class 1) 2-Y-O

£17,031 (£6,456; £3,231; £1,611; £807; £405) **Stalls High**

Form / RPR

111 **1** **Monsieur Chevalier (IRE)**10 2136 2-9-0 0 RichardHughes 3 — 105+
(R Hannon) *racd in midfield: rdn 3f out: hdwy and swtchd lft over 1f out: sn chsng ldng pair: led ins fnl f: styd on strly and sn clr* **5/4**1

1113 **2** *3 1/4* **Star Rover (IRE)**21 1805 2-9-0 0 JohnEgan 5 — 93
(P D Evans) *led: rdn 2f out: hdd ins fnl f: no ch w wnr but kpt on gamely to hold 2nd pl* **8/1**

1 **3** *3/4* **Raine's Cross**30 1577 2-9-0 0 JimCrowley 6 — 91
(P Winkworth) *unf: swtg: towards rr: rdn over 3f out: hdwy u.p over 1f out: styd on fnl f to go 3rd towards fin* **11/4**2

12 **4** *1* **Soccer (USA)**43 1290 2-9-0 0 (t) RichardKingscote 8 — 87
(Tom Dascombe) *chsd ldrs: wnt 2nd over 3f out: pressed ldr gng wl 1/2-way: rdn over 1f out: wknd ins fnl f* **12/1**

4014 **5** *1 1/4* **Fratellino**5 2260 2-9-0 0 RobertWinston 2 — 83
(A J McCabe) *lw: chsd ldr tl over 3f out: rdn and rdr dropped whip 2f out: wkng whn carried sightly lft over 1f out* **33/1**

1 **6** *2 1/2* **High Spice (USA)**25 1700 2-8-9 0 EddieAhern 1 — 69+
(R M H Cowell) *lw: wnt lft s and s.i.s: sn swtchd rt and dropped in bhd: short of room and hmpd over 3f out: sme hdwy 1/2-way: wknd over 1f out* **13/2**3

2522 **7** *18* **Mijas Playa**4 2295 2-8-9 0 RyanMoore 4 — 4
(C A Dwyer) *a towards rr: rdn and effrt 1/2-way: wknd over 1f out: eased fnl f* **33/1**

030 **8** *5* **Lees Anthem**5 2260 2-9-0 0 (v1) PatrickMathers 7 — —
(C J Teague) *chsd ldrs: rdn and struggling 1/2-way: wl bhd and eased fnl f* **100/1**

60.83 secs (-0.77) **Going Correction** -0.05s/f (Good) **8 Ran SP% 110.1**

Speed ratings (Par 101): **104,98,97,96,94 90,61,53**

toteswinger: 1&2 £2.00, 1&3 £1.10, 2&3 £4.80 CSF £11.16 TOTE £2.00: £1.20, £1.60, £1.20; EX 10.30.

Owner Mrs Valerie Hubbard & Ian Higginson **Bred** Tally-Ho Stud **Trained** East Everleigh, Wilts

■ Stewards' Enquiry : Richard Hughes one-day ban: careless riding (Jun 11)

FOCUS

This established juvenile event usually produces a high-class sort and this year's running lived up to its reputation, with a strong gallop providing a good test. The form looks very solid.

NOTEBOOK

Monsieur Chevalier(IRE) made it four from four with a stylish victory, powering clear of his rivals in the final furlong. He gives every impression of being likely to stay 6f, but he has plenty of pace and the fact that he stays 5f so well will be useful for the challenges to come. His next race will be the Norfolk Stakes over this trip at Royal Ascot, for which he has been trimmed a point or two to 5-1 favourite, with Richard Hughes reporting that he intends to employ the same tactics. (op Evens tchd 11-8 in a place)

Star Rover(IRE) has had a splendid time of it so far this season and he put in another spirited effort to chase home the talented winner. He is a very useful juvenile but falls just short of the best so, while he will also go to Royal Ascot, the Windsor Castle looks a sensible target. Official explanation: jockey said colt hung right-handed (op 12-1 tchd 15-2)

Raine's Cross ◆ arrived with a good reputation following his debut win at Bath, but he took too long to get going. However, he confirmed his ability in this higher grade with a strong finish up the final climb and looks likely to be even better over 6f. (tchd 7-2)

Soccer(USA) was comfortably beaten by the winner at Newmarket and, though he travelled well for a long way, he was again firmly put in his place. He can win races against slightly lesser opponents. (op 14-1 tchd 11-1)

Fratellino is smart at his level but was slightly outclassed here. The fact that Winston's whip went flying, and that the winner carried him left-handed for a few strides, did not materially affect his chance. (op 50-1 tchd 25-1)

High Spice(USA) fluffed the start and then ran out of room on the rail, leaving her with too much ground to recover. She looked a speedy sort when making all at Newmarket and deserves another chance. (op 7-1 tchd 15-2)

Mijas Playa Official explanation: jockey said filly lost its action

2409 BLUE SQUARE HENRY II STKS (GROUP 2) — 2m 78y

7:10 (7:11) (Class 1) 4-Y-O+

£56,770 (£21,520; £10,770; £5,370; £2,690; £1,350) **Stalls** Centre

Form / RPR

125- **1** **Geordieland (FR)**285 5094 8-9-2 117 ShaneKelly 3 — 121
(J A Osborne) *hld up in rr: hdwy 3f out: chsd ldr over 2f out: rdn to chal over 1f out: led jst ins fnl f: sn hung rt: rdn out* **5/1**2

14-1 **2** *5* **Patkai (IRE)**29 1601 4-9-0 114 RyanMoore 2 — 118+
(Sir Michael Stoute) *lw: hld up towards rr: plld out and gd hdwy over 3f out: led over 2f out: sn hung rt onto rail: hrd pressed and drvn over 1f out: hdd ins fnl f: btn whn hmpd fnl 100yds and eased after* **1/2**1

-131 **3** *5* **Tastahil (IRE)**12 2075 5-9-2 111 RHills 1 — 109
(B W Hills) *lw: hld up in 4th pl: effrt to press ldrs over 2f out: rdn and sltly hmpd 2f out: sn no ch w ldng pair* **15/2**3

50-5 **4** *16* **Tungsten Strike (USA)**29 1601 8-9-2 106 (v1) JimCrowley 4 — 90
(Mrs A J Perrett) *led tl rdn and hdd over 2f out: sn wknd* **40/1**

3-15 **5** *3/4* **Fiulin**13 2056 4-9-0 105 JimmyFortune 6 — 89
(M Botti) *swtg: chsd ldr: rdn over 4f out: drvn and wknd 3f out* **10/1**

050- **6** *10* **Bulwark (IRE)**9 6817 7-9-2 103 StephenDonohoe 5 — 77
(Ian Williams) *nvr gng wl in last pl: nvr a factor: t.o* **100/1**

11- **7** *58* **Viper**171 7110 7-9-2 92 RichardHughes 7 — 7
(R Hollinshead) *swtg: chsd ldng pair: rdn wl over 4f out: wl bhd fnl 3f: virtually p.u fnl f: t.o* **33/1**

3m 30.07s (-8.63) **Going Correction** -0.05s/f (Good)

WFA 4 from 5yo+ 2lb **7 Ran SP% 110.6**

Speed ratings (Par 115): **119,116,114,106,105 100,71**

toteswinger: 1&2 £1.10, 1&3 £3.30, 2&3 £2.40 CSF £7.39 TOTE £5.10: £2.10, £1.20; EX 8.80.

Owner A Taylor **Bred** Mle Michele Bliard **Trained** Upper Lambourn, Berks

■ Stewards' Enquiry : Shane Kelly three-day ban: careless riding (Jun 11-13)

FOCUS

A quality turnout for this high-class event, run at a searching gallop that left no hiding place for a doubtful stayer. The time was very good for the grade and the front pair are rated as having run personal bests.

NOTEBOOK

Geordieland(FR) was winning his third Group 2, and has also proved himself at Group 1 level, and this victory takes his career winnings through the half-million pound barrier. In the past he has been accused of not finding enough in the finish, but this turned into a severe test and he found plenty, showing that there is nothing wrong with his resolution. Trainer Jamie Osborne, who had expected him to hit the front later than he did, says he is a "happier horse" these days and has even started to pass his galloping companions during his homework. He will have every chance in the Gold Cup at Royal Ascot, in which he was second to Yeats in both 2007 and 2008. (op 11-2 tchd 13-2)

Patkai(IRE) chased the pace and made a sudden dash for home early in the straight which for a while looked like succeeding. Though clearly held when being badly squeezed against the rail by the winner, the manner in which he had seized the initiative was impressive, though in the end it meant he had nothing left for the final battle. He remains a much-improved stayer and would not be out of it if taking on the winner again in the Gold Cup at Royal Ascot. (op 8-15 tchd 4-7 and 8-13 in places)

Tastahil(IRE) was stepping up from 1m5f and looks worth another crack at these longer distances. Though unable to match the first two as they went for home, he was losing no further ground at the finish. (tchd 7-1)

Tungsten Strike(USA) is best when ridden like this, but he went plenty fast enough in the first-time visor and was a sitting duck for these smart stayers in the home straight.

Fiulin, who was very warm in the paddock, was a good winner at Listed level but again found the step into Group company beyond him. (op 11-1)

Bulwark(IRE), a winner over hurdles last week, was on his worst behaviour and showed no interest at all.

Viper, a giant-sized individual, will be more effective back in handicaps. (op 40-1 tchd 50-1 in a place)

2410 BLUE SQUARE BRIGADIER GERARD STKS (GROUP 3) — 1m 2f 7y

7:45 (7:46) (Class 1) 4-Y-O+

£36,900 (£13,988; £7,000; £3,490; £1,748; £877) **Stalls High**

Form / RPR

00-6 **1** **Cima De Triomphe (IRE)**32 1551 4-9-0 116 C-PLemaire 8 — 115
(L M Cumani) *w'like: str: hld up in tch in midfield: rdn 2f out: hdwy 1f out: str run ins fnl f to ld on post* **4/1**3

111- **2** *nse* **Conduit (IRE)**215 7000 4-9-7 125 RyanMoore 12 — 121
(Sir Michael Stoute) *t.k.h: chsd ldr for 1f: styd in tch: rdn and ev ch 2f out: edgd rt ins fnl f: led fnl 100yds tl hdd on post* **11/4**2

01-4 **3** *1* **Stotsfold**33 1525 6-9-0 116 AdamKirby 13 — 112+
(W R Swinburn) *lw: taken down early: stdd s: hld up towards rr: rdn wl over 1f out: r.o wl ins fnl f: wnt 3rd nr fin* **14/1**

04-3 **4** *1/2* **Drumfire (IRE)**19 1875 5-9-0 104 RHills 9 — 111
(M Johnston) *hld up in rr: plld out and rdn 2f out: r.o wl ins fnl f: wnt 4th last strides: nt rch ldrs* **16/1**

40-2 **5** *hd* **Pipedreamer**33 1526 5-9-0 117 JimmyFortune 3 — 111
(J H M Gosden) *lw: hld up in midfield: hdwy 4f out: hdwy on outer 3f out: led over 1f out: edgd rt u.p: rdr dropped whip and hdd fnl 100yds: lost 3 pls nr fin* **15/8**1

0-12 **6** *1/2* **Staying On (IRE)**21 1799 4-9-0 110 (t) EddieAhern 6 — 110
(W R Swinburn) *lw: led: rdn 3f out: hdd over 2f out: keeping on same pce whn short of room and hmpd ins fnl f: kpt on again nr fin* **16/1**

-243 **7** *1/2* **Steele Tango (USA)**19 1859 4-9-0 110 LukeMorris 5 — 109
(R A Teal) *towards rr: rdn and unable qck 3f out: styd on fnl f: nvr pce to rch ldrs* **33/1**

42- **8** ½ **Campanologist (USA)**[306] 4436 4-9-0 116 TedDurcan 1 108
(Saeed Bin Suroor) *t.k.h: chsd ldr after 1f: led over 2f out tl over 1f out: keeping on same pce whn hmpd ins fnl f* **9/1**
-05 **9** nk **Indian Days**[21] 1799 4-9-0 105 AlanMunro 10 107
(J G Given) *t.k.h: hld up in midfield: rdn and effrt to chse ldrs over 2f out: drvn and wknd jst over 1f out* **66/1**
3-5 **10** ½ **Perks (IRE)**[24] 1758 4-9-0 105 JimmyQuinn 4 106+
(J L Dunlop) *s.i.s: bhd: rdn and effrt on inner 3f out: kpt on fnl f but nvr pce to threaten ldrs* **33/1**
0-01 **11** ¾ **Allied Powers (IRE)**[13] 2031 4-9-0 106 JamieSpencer 11 105
(M L W Bell) *t.k.h: chsd ldrs: rdn 3f out: drvn and wknd over 1f out* **25/1**
560- **12** ¾ **Smokey Oakey (IRE)**[208] 7145 5-9-0 110 MichaelHills 7 103
(M H Tompkins) *stdd s: hld up in rr: nvr trbld ldrs* **66/1**

2m 6.60s (-3.90) **Going Correction** -0.05s/f (Good) **12** Ran SP% **122.6**
Speed ratings (Par 113): **113,112,112,111,111 111,110,110,110,109 109,108**
toteswinger: 1&2 £4.30, 1&3 £18.40, 2&3 £13.70 CSF £15.43 TOTE £5.70: £2.10, £1.20, £3.80; EX 24.80.
Owner Teruya Yoshida **Bred** Sofim Srl **Trained** Newmarket, Suffolk

FOCUS
An outstanding renewal of this Group 3 event, in terms of both size and quality. However, the proximity of Drumfire in fourth place lets the form down a bit, as does the fact that the entire field was covered by just six lengths.

NOTEBOOK
Cima De Triomphe(IRE) won last year's Italian Derby and also ran well when finishing a close ninth in the Arc, but this trip looks a minimum for him and he only got there in the nick of time. Trainer Luca Cumani will review the race again before announcing a target, with races at 1m2f and 1m4f under consideration, and a return Group 1 events on the agenda. (op 6-1 tchd 13-2)
Conduit(IRE) ◆ was coltish when he arrived in the parade ring but ran an amazing race, especially considering he won last year's St Leger over a much longer trip. Conceding weight all round to race-fit rivals, he went agonizingly close to winning but he looks better than ever and will be a major player in the big middle distance events this season. (op 5-2 tchd 9-4 and 3-1, and 10-3 in a place)
Stotsfold's six wins have all been around this trip, and he confirmed that he is something of a 1m2f specialist with a return to form after dropping to 1m last time. He has won twice in Group 3 company in the past, but this was a high-class contest for the grade, so it must rate as his best performance to date. (tchd 16-1)
Drumfire(IRE), the lowest-rated of these on official figures, also produced a career-best, running on in manner that suggests he should stay a bit farther. (op 28-1 tchd 33-1)
Pipedreamer looked the winner when taking it up but was again run out of it near the finish, as he had been recently over course and distance. Fortune losing his whip did not help, but he probably needs to be produced a bit later if facing an uphill finish like this. Alternatively a drop back to 1m might be the answer and, although he is not in the Queen Anne, connections have entered him in the Sussex Stakes. (op 2-1 tchd 7-4 and 9-4 in places)
Staying On(IRE) was always going to find it hard to hold off a field of this quality, though he made a bold bid to defy the odds.
Steele Tango(USA) again showed he is not out of place in Group events, if still falling a little short of winning one.
Campanologist(USA) looked particularly well for his return and he was by no means disgraced. He has the option of stepping back up to 1m4f if lacking a bit of finishing pace for this trip these days. (op 10-1 tchd 17-2)
Perks(IRE) Official explanation: jockey said gelding was slowly away
Smokey Oakey(IRE), winner of this race last year, could never get out of the rear, finding the quality of opponents and the faster-than-ideal ground counting against him.

2411 BLUE SQUARE SP GUARANTEE HERON STKS (LISTED RACE) 1m 14y
8:20 (8:23) (Class 1) 3-Y-O
£22,708 (£8,608; £4,308; £2,148; £1,076; £540) **Stalls** High

Form RPR
3-11 **1** **Border Patrol**[13] 2035 3-9-3 108 SteveDrowne 3 110+
(R Charlton) *lw: taken down early: stdd after s: t.k.h: hld up in last pair: plld out and hdwy over 2f out: rdn over 1f out: led ins fnl f: styd on wl* **10/3**[2]
16-0 **2** 1 **Ashram (IRE)**[26] 1675 3-9-3 113 TedDurcan 2 108
(Saeed Bin Suroor) *lw: dwlt: sn rcvrd and trckd ldng pair: rdn to press ldr jst over 2f out: led ent fnl f: tl ins fnl f: no ex* **6/1**[3]
-123 **3** hd **Spring Of Fame (USA)**[26] 1678 3-8-12 101 AhmedAjtebi 4 102+
(Saeed Bin Suroor) *hld up in last pair: rdn 2f out: no hdwy on outer ins fnl f: r.o wl to go 3rd fnl 50yds: gng on fin* **8/1**
1 **4** 1 **Bridge Of Gold (USA)**[40] 1355 3-8-12 90 RyanMoore 1 100
(M A Magnusson) *lw: s.i.s: t.k.h: hld up in tch: rdn and ev ch over 1f out: wknd ins fnl f* **6/1**[3]
21-1 **5** ½ **Racketeer (IRE)**[34] 1484 3-8-12 99 JimmyFortune 7 99
(J H M Gosden) *lw: led: c off rail over 3f out: rdn and hung lft over 1f out: hdd ent fnl f: wknd fnl 100yds* **11/10**[1]
4-10 **6** 2 ¼ **Everynight (IRE)**[42] 1303 3-8-12 81 AlanMunro 5 94?
(M Botti) *chsd ldr tl jst over 2f out: wknd u.p over 1f out* **40/1**

1m 42.63s (-0.67) **Going Correction** -0.05s/f (Good) **6** Ran SP% **112.8**
Speed ratings (Par 107): **101,100,99,98,98 96**
toteswinger: 1&2 £1.90, 1&3 £4.10, 2&3 £6.70 CSF £23.11 TOTE £4.30: £1.30, £3.20; EX 17.70.

Owner Elite Racing Club **Bred** Elite Racing Club **Trained** Beckhampton, Wilts

FOCUS
A decent level of form for this Listed event, and the winner is very obviously going in the right direction. The runner-up is rated close to his Dewhurst form with the winner and third slight improvers.

NOTEBOOK
Border Patrol looks a highly progressive sort, having handled a drop to 6f last time and reverting here to his usual trip to defeat these rivals in the style of a horse who stays 1m well. Given his versatility as regards trip, and his ability to act on varying ground, connections will have a multitude of options to consider. However they do not consider him to be a Royal Ascot horse, so he will now be rested until September. (op 5-2 tchd 9-4 and 7-2 in a place)
Ashram(IRE) bounced back following a weak effort in the 2000 Guineas to show that he has trained on after all. However, he still has to prove that he can fulfil the potential that he showed last season. (tchd 9-1)
Spring Of Fame(USA) found the drop to 1m failing to play to his strengths, and he was in danger of being left behind until coming home well and only just failing to snatch second. He needs at least an extra furlong. (op 9-1 tchd 7-1)
Bridge Of Gold(USA) ran respectably, having won a maiden at Newbury on his only previous outing. However, Border Patrol took the other division of that race and clearly looks the stronger of the two now. (op 8-1 tchd 9-1)
Racketeer(IRE) had to make his own running this time but wanted to drift left-handed in the straight, which made him easier to pass than he might have been. He looked happier in previous races tracking a rival and kicking for home in the last quarter-mile. Official explanation: jockey said colt hung left-handed (op 11-8 tchd 6-4)

Everynight(IRE) was well beaten in a handicap last time and this defeat confirmed that his sights will have to be lowered. (op 33-1)

2412 BLUE SQUARE WHITSUN CUP H'CAP 1m 14y
8:50 (8:53) (Class 3) (0-95,95) 4-Y-O+
£9,346 (£2,799; £1,399; £700; £349; £175) **Stalls** High

Form RPR
-016 **1** **Dunn'o (IRE)**[20] 1821 4-9-1 92 PhilipRobinson 16 102
(C G Cox) *taken down early: racd keenly: mde all: rdn over 2f out: styd on gamely fnl f* **11/2**[3]
015- **2** ½ **Axiom**[201] 7245 5-9-1 92 DaneO'Neill 12 101
(L M Cumani) *lw: hld up in tch: n.m.r 2f out: swtchd rt over 1f out: hdwy ent fnl f: chsd wnr ins fnl f: r.o but a hld* **20/1**
-402 **3** 1 **Kavachi (IRE)**[14] 2003 6-8-9 86 RyanMoore 3 93
(G L Moore) *stdd after s: hld up bhd: hdwy on inner over 1f out: drvn and r.o wl fnl f: wnt 3rd nr fin* **11/1**
0-00 **4** hd **Proponent (IRE)**[26] 1673 5-9-2 93 SteveDrowne 8 99
(R Charlton) *chsd ldrs: rdn and unable qckn jst over 2f out: keeping on same pce whn short of room 1f out: kpt on u.p fnl 100yds* **10/1**
1/3 **5** hd **Wintercast**[37] 1433 4-8-11 88 AdamKirby 10 94+
(W R Swinburn) *lw: hld up towards rr: short of room over 2f out: switching rt after: hdwy towards inner ent fnl f: r.o fnl f: nt rch ldrs* **7/2**[1]
1-01 **6** hd **Cadre (IRE)**[17] 1942 4-9-4 95 JimmyFortune 2 100+
(J H M Gosden) *lw: stdd s: hld up in last pl: rdn over 2f out: hdwy on outer over 1f out: r.o wl fnl f: nt rch ldrs* **13/2**
6-12 **7** ½ **Light From Mars**[33] 1527 4-8-13 93 JamesMillman(3) 4 97
(B R Millman) *hld up towards rr: hdwy and sltly hmpd over 3f out: chsd wnr over 1f out: hung rt 1f out: wknd fnl 100yds* **5/1**[2]
631- **8** 1 ¼ **Shamali**[194] 7344 4-8-8 85 TonyCulhane 14 86
(W J Haggas) *chsd ldrs: rdn to chse wnr over 2f out tl over 1f out: wknd jst ins fnl f* **15/2**
0-13 **9** 1 ¼ **Trumpet Lily**[19] 1860 4-8-9 86 JimCrowley 7 84
(J G Portman) *hld up in last trio: rdn and effrt 2f out: nvr trbld ldrs* **20/1**
50-4 **10** shd **Kinsya**[21] 1813 6-8-5 82 LiamJones 17 80
(M H Tompkins) *hld up towards rr: short of room and swtchd rt over 2f out: hanging rt after: nvr trbld ldrs* **20/1**
-420 **11** 9 **Arabian Spirit**[19] 1861 4-9-1 92 TGMcLaughlin 9 69
(E A L Dunlop) *in tch: swtchd lft and rdn over 3f out: wknd 2f out: wl btn fnl f* **25/1**
000- **12** ¾ **Unshakable (IRE)**[208] 7146 10-9-0 91 PaulEddery 15 67
(Bob Jones) *chsd ldrs: rdn and struggling wl over 2f out: wl btn over 1f out* **40/1**
1-44 **13** 1 ¾ **The Fifth Member (IRE)**[24] 1731 5-8-11 88 PatCosgrave 11 60
(J R Boyle) *chsd wnr tl over 2f out: wknd wl over 1f out: wl btn fnl f* **10/1**

1m 41.31s (-1.99) **Going Correction** -0.05s/f (Good) **13** Ran SP% **126.5**
Speed ratings (Par 107): **107,106,105,105,105 104,104,103,101,101 92,92,90**
toteswinger: 1&2 £23.50, 1&3 £10.70, 2&3 £39.20 CSF £120.65 CT £1240.80 TOTE £6.10: £1.90, £4.90, £3.30; EX 167.90 Place 6: £59.39, Place 5: £29.97..
Owner Dennis Shaw **Bred** R Hodgins **Trained** Lambourn, Berks

FOCUS
A competitive, good-quality handicap run at a lively gallop. The form is rated around the winner, third and seventh.

NOTEBOOK
Dunn'o(IRE), well drawn for these tactics, had already shown that he goes well round here, and deserves extra credit for again making all at such a good pace. He is very game and should not be underestimated when he goes to Ascot for the Royal Hunt Cup, for he showed his effectiveness on a straight track when second there last September. (op 8-1)
Axiom, who looks likely to appreciate at least 1m this year, made an encouraging seasonal debut. He is fairly handicapped and, while he looked effective enough on this good ground, past form suggests he is particularly well suited by soft. He may well be targeted at the Royal Hunt Cup, but will only run in it if there is a bit of cut. (tchd 22-1)
Kavachi(IRE)'s recent wins have all been at least a furlong farther than this. While he is capable enough at 1m given a good gallop, he finished in a style that confirms that he is even better at 1m1f or 1m2f. (op 9-1)
Proponent(IRE) ran his best race for some time and appears to be on the way back, with trainer Roger Charlton feeling that this trip is a bit sharp for him. (op 16-1)
Wintercast ◆, having only his third race, was backed down to favourite and ran well enough to suggest that his turn will come. He looks likely to peak at a slightly longer distance. (tchd 3-1, 4-1 and 9-2 in a place)
Cadre(IRE) looked well suited by this distance when winning at Yarmouth but his stamina kicked in too late in this better class. The higher mark should not be problem over an extra furlong or two. (op 11-2 tchd 5-1)
Light From Mars gave Dunn'o a good race here last month but was run out of the places this time, the winner having made a shade more progress since then. He looked the winner when he arrived on the scene, and perhaps a slight drop in distance or an easier track might see him in a better light. (op 17-2 tchd 9-1)
T/Jkpt: Not won. T/Plt: £55.70 to a £1 stake. Pool: £82,790.64. 1,084.54 winning tickets. T/Qpdt: £22.00 to a £1 stake. Pool: £5,316.64. 178.45 winning tickets. SP

2167 YARMOUTH (L-H)
Thursday, May 28

OFFICIAL GOING: Good (good to firm in places; 7.4)
Wind: Fresh across Weather: Cloudy with sunny spells

2413 EUROPEAN BREEDERS' FUND NOVICE STKS 6f 3y
2:10 (2:13) (Class 5) 2-Y-O **£4,037** (£1,208; £604; £302; £150) **Stalls** High

Form RPR
1 **1** **Niran (IRE)**[12] 2087 2-9-5 0 SebSanders 2 81
(C E Brittain) *chsd ldr tl led over 2f out: rdn and edgd lft fnl f: r.o* **4/5**[1]
4 **2** 1 **Brisbane (IRE)**[13] 2037 2-8-12 0 RichardMullen 4 71
(J H M Gosden) *chsd ldrs: rdn over 2f out: edgd lft and r.o ins fnl f* **7/2**[2]
14 **3** ½ **King Of Axum (IRE)**[15] 1991 2-9-5 0 J-PGuillambert 5 77
(M Johnston) *led: hung lft thrght: rdn and hdd over 2f out: styd on same pce ins fnl f* **4/1**[3]
4 1 ½ **Excellent Guest** 2-8-12 0 TPQueally 1 65
(G G Margarson) *dwlt: sn pushed along in rr: hdwy 1/2-way: rdn over 1f out: hung lft and no ex ins fnl f* **25/1**
5 3 ½ **England (IRE)** 2-8-12 0 JamieSpencer 3 55
(N P Littmoden) *s.i.s: sn pushed along in rr: effrt over 1f out: wknd ins fnl f* **12/1**

1m 15.28s (0.88) **Going Correction** -0.175s/f (Firm) **5** Ran SP% **109.3**
Speed ratings (Par 93): **87,85,85,83,78**
CSF £3.82 TOTE £1.60: £1.10, £2.20; EX 4.10.
Owner Saeed Manana **Bred** Miss Audrey F Thompson **Trained** Newmarket, Suffolk

FOCUS
This novice event has thrown up some decent performers in the past, most notably Asset, Wilko, Membership and Imperial Stride. The winner confirmed the good impression from his debut but the form is somewhat fluid.

NOTEBOOK
Niran(IRE), penalised for his hard-fought debut success in similar company at Newmarket 12 days earlier, met strong support to follow up and did so in workmanlike fashion. He looks the type who only does just enough and in truth he could have been called the winner after passing the furlong pole, so in all likelihood the best of him has still to be seen. The Coventry Stakes could well be next and the stiff finish would be much to his liking, but he will have to raise his game again to trouble the likely principals there. It must also be noted that the winning time was slower than the following seller, where the winner coasted home inside the final furlong. (op 5-4)
Brisbane(IRE) was well backed to step up on the level of his Newbury debut in receipt of 7lb from the winner and duly did so, but still showed distinct signs of greenness. He also played up down at the start so clearly has temperament, but the way he found a turn of foot inside the final furlong suggests he has a definite future when becoming more streetwise. (op 4-1 tchd 9-2 and 10-3)
King Of Axum(IRE), up in trip, showed his York running to be wrong, but had the benefit of the stands' rail and again looked less than straightforward. This was no disgrace under his penalty though and he is in the right hands. (op 11-4 tchd 9-2)
Excellent Guest, whose stable had taken this with their two previous runners in the last ten years, has a pedigree which suggests a mix of speed and stamina. He overcame a tardy start and posted a pleasing debut display. There should be more to come next time up. (op 20-1)
England(IRE), another whose pedigree suggests speed and stamina, was the greenest runner in the field. He should prove a lot wiser for the initial experience and can certainly find easier assignments. (op 15-2 tchd 13-2)

2414 GREAT YARMOUTH ADVERTISER (S) STKS — 6f 3y
2:40 (2:41) (Class 6) 2-Y-O — **£1,942** (£578; £288; £144) **Stalls** High

Form — RPR

3245 **1** **Anjomarba (IRE)**[8] 2175 2-8-6 0 .... TolleyDean 4 68+
(W G M Turner) *mde all: clr fr over 1f out: eased fnl 100yds* **8/13**[1]

00 **2** *3* **Micky's Bird**[10] 2128 2-8-6 0 .... PaulEddery 5 53
(R C Guest) *chsd ldrs: pushed along 1/2-way: sn outpcd: rallied fnl f: wnt 2nd nr fin: no ch w wnr* **40/1**

04 **3** *nk* **Mary Helen**[11] 2100 2-8-6 0 .... LiamJones 10 52
(W M Brisbourne) *chsd wnr: rdn and hung lft fr over 2f out: outpcd over 1f out* **4/1**[2]

4 *1/2* **Scilly Breeze** 2-8-11 0 .... RichardMullen 3 56
(Rae Guest) *mid-div: rdn over 3f out: hdwy over 2f out: styd styd on same pce appr fnl f* **12/1**

00 **5** *2 3/4* **Fairys In A Storm (IRE)**[11] 2099 2-8-6 0 .... FrankieMcDonald 2 42
(P T Midgley) *chsd ldrs: rdn and hung rt fr over 2f out: wknd over 1f out* **33/1**

060 **6** *9* **Saachi's Vision (IRE)**[17] 1933 2-8-6 0 ....(b[1]) ChrisCatlin 6 15
(D K Ivory) *n.m.r sn after s: hld up: racd keenly: shkn up over 2f out: sn wknd* **66/1**

06 **7** *nk* **Our Georgie Girl**[28] 1630 2-8-6 0 .... SaleemGolam 9 14
(G G Margarson) *chsd ldrs: rdn and hung lft over 2f out: sn wknd* **33/1**

00 **8** *6* **Minnie Rocket**[10] 2128 2-8-5 0 ow6 .... JRoberts(7) 1 —
(R C Guest) *wnt lft s: outpcd* **80/1**

0 **9** *5* **Val's Princess**[27] 1653 2-8-6 0 .... AdrianMcCarthy 7 —
(J R Jenkins) *prom: rdn and hung rt over 3f out: sn wknd* **40/1**

P **Arken Lad** 2-8-11 0 .... JimmyQuinn 8 —
(D Donovan) *lost action and p.u sn after s* **13/2**[3]

1m 14.38s (-0.02) **Going Correction** -0.175s/f (Firm) **10** Ran SP% **116.4**
Speed ratings (Par 91): **93,89,88,87,84 72,71,63,57,—**
toteswinger: 1&2 £10.90, 1&3 £1.60, 2&3 £18.20 CSF £45.64 TOTE £1.70: £1.02, £10.50, £1.40; EX 27.40 Trifecta £377.90 Pool: £1,031.81 - 2.02 winning units..The winner was bought in for 5,600 guineas.
Owner Marbary Partnership **Bred** Tally-Ho Stud **Trained** Sigwells, Somerset

FOCUS
A very weak juvenile affair but the winner was in a different league.

NOTEBOOK
Anjomarba(IRE) made all and deservedly shed her maiden tag at the sixth time of asking. She stamped her authority on the race nearing the furlong marker and rates value for a good deal further than her eased-down winning margin. She is evidently a little better than this grade, but the drop in class worked the oracle and there should be more races of this calibre to be won with her. Her trainer bought her back in and now intends to go for a valuable race of this nature at Thirsk on Monday, where she ought to take all the beating. (op 4-7 tchd 4-6 and 8-11 in places)
Micky's Bird, hampered at the start on Fibresand last time, showed her most worthwhile form to date on this first outing in selling company and looked to need all of the extra furlong. She is flattered by her proximity to the winner, however. (op 50-1)
Mary Helen had every chance and ran her race, helping to set the lowly standard. Official explanation: jockey said filly hung left (op 13-2 tchd 7-1 and 7-2)
Scilly Breeze showed his inexperience through the race, but was gradually getting the hang of things late on and shaped as though he already needs a stiffer test. An easier surface may also prove ideal. (op 7-1 tchd 14-1)
Arken Lad Official explanation: vet said gelding pulled up lame

2415 EVENTGUARD STAFF MAIDEN STKS (DIV I) — 1m 3y
3:10 (3:14) (Class 5) 3-Y-O+ — **£2,525** (£751; £375; £187) **Stalls** High

Form — RPR

1 **Lowther**[70] 4-9-12 0 .... NeilChalmers 2 91
(A Bailey) *hld up: hdwy over 3f out: chsd ldr over 2f out: rdn to ld ins fnl f: r.o* **100/1**

33 **2** *hd* **Big Bay (USA)**[24] 1730 3-9-0 0 .... JamieSpencer 11 87
(Jane Chapple-Hyam) *chsd ldrs: led over 2f out: rdn over 1f out: hdd ins fnl f: r.o* **9/4**[1]

4-34 **3** *7* **Maverin (IRE)**[24] 1730 3-9-0 78 .... SebSanders 5 71
(J Noseda) *hld up in tch: plld hrd: rdn over 1f out: no ex fnl f* **7/2**[2]

0-0 **4** *2 3/4* **Choral Service**[9] 2165 3-9-0 0 .... LiamJones 4 65+
(W J Haggas) *s.i.s: hld up: hdwy u.p over 2f out: nt trble ldrs* **14/1**

0-3 **5** *1 1/4* **Papyrian**[17] 1941 3-8-9 0 .... Louis-PhilippeBeuzelin(5) 9 62
(W Jarvis) *s.i.s: sn prom: chsd ldr 6f out: j. path sn after: rdn over 2f out: wknd over 1f out* **9/4**[1]

05 **6** *1* **Illusive Spirit (IRE)**[16] 1963 3-9-0 0 .... RichardMullen 8 60
(J H M Gosden) *hld up: rdn over 3f out: edgd lft: n.d* **12/1**[3]

00-6 **7** *2 3/4* **Toballa**[33] 1515 4-9-7 47 .... JimmyQuinn 7 51
(P Leech) *chsd ldr 2f: remained handy tl rdn and wknd over 2f out* **66/1**

40 **8** *1 1/4* **Fantastical**[30] 1585 3-8-9 0 .... TPQueally 12 45
(C E Brittain) *hld up: hdwy over 3f out: rdn and wknd over 1f out* **33/1**

0- **9** *5* **Silk Star (IRE)**[209] 7117 3-8-6 0 .... KellyHarrison(3) 6 34
(Patrick Morris) *led: rdn and hdd over 2f out: wknd over 1f out* **150/1**

5/5 **10** *1 3/4* **Muzmin (USA)**[37] 1422 4-9-12 0 .... TGMcLaughlin 10 38
(E A L Dunlop) *s.i.s: hld up: a in rr* **20/1**

5 **11** *3 3/4* **I See Nice Sea**[20] 1843 3-8-9 0 .... ChrisCatlin 13 21
(L M Cumani) *hld up: rdn over 3f out: sn edgd lft and wknd* **14/1**

0 **12** *28* **Rony Dony (IRE)**[8] 2185 5-9-12 0 .... NeilPollard 1 —
(M E Rimmer) *s.i.s: a in rr: bhd fnl 3f* **200/1**

1m 38.35s (-2.25) **Going Correction** -0.175s/f (Firm)
WFA 3 from 4yo+ 12lb **12** Ran SP% **116.1**
Speed ratings (Par 103): **104,103,96,94,92 91,89,87,82,81 77,49**
toteswinger: 1&2 £24.80, 1&3 £50.10, 2&3 £2.30 CSF £310.88 TOTE £115.30: £15.00, £1.40, £1.40; EX 265.40 TRIFECTA Not won..
Owner A Bailey **Bred** L J Barratt **Trained** Newmarket, Suffolk

FOCUS
An average maiden run at a routine sort of pace. Despite the shock result the race could rate higher, with the fourth the best guide to the level.

2416 EVENTGUARD STAFF MAIDEN STKS (DIV II) — 1m 3y
3:40 (3:42) (Class 5) 3-Y-O+ — **£2,525** (£751; £375; £187) **Stalls** High

Form — RPR

02- **1** **Class Is Class (IRE)**[204] 7200 3-8-9 0 .... Louis-PhilippeBeuzelin(5) 7 87+
(Sir Michael Stoute) *chsd ldrs: led over 2f out: sn rdn and hung rt: r.o* **15/8**[2]

34-5 **2** *1 3/4* **Espiritu (FR)**[43] 1295 3-9-0 90 .... SebSanders 14 83
(J Noseda) *hld up: racd keenly: hdwy over 2f out: rdn and hung lft over 1f out: hung rt ins fnl f: nt run on* **11/8**[1]

0- **3** *1* **Turning Top (IRE)**[210] 7097 3-8-9 0 .... JamieSpencer 5 76
(S A Callaghan) *hld up: hdwy and swicthed lft over 2f out: sn rdn: styd on same pce ins fnl f* **7/1**[3]

0 **4** *1 3/4* **Mutawarath (IRE)**[21] 1804 3-8-11 0 .... GilmarPereira(3) 8 77+
(W J Haggas) *prom: rdn: rn green and ev ch over 2f out: hmpd over 1f out: no ex ins fnl f* **33/1**

5- **5** *1* **Sabi Star**[309] 4311 3-9-0 0 .... RichardMullen 1 75
(J H M Gosden) *chsd ldr: led over 3f out: wandered over 2f out: sn rdn: hmpd over 1f out: no ex ins fnl f* **12/1**

62 **6** *5* **Cry Alot Boy**[7] 2199 6-9-12 0 .... JimmyQuinn 13 66
(K A Morgan) *s.s: hld up: shkn up over 2f out: styd on fr over 1f out: nvr nr to chal* **16/1**

0- **7** *1 1/2* **Orlando's Tale (USA)**[213] 7026 4-9-12 0 .... GeorgeBaker 12 63
(J R Fanshawe) *s.i.s: hld up: shkn up over 1f out: n.d* **50/1**

0 **8** *1 1/4* **Mister Frosty (IRE)**[30] 1584 3-9-0 0 .... AdrianMcCarthy 11 57
(G Prodromou) *hld up: hdwy over 3f out: rdn and wknd over 1f out* **66/1**

40- **9** *1 3/4* **My Girl Jode**[208] 7141 3-8-9 0 .... SaleemGolam 2 48
(M H Tompkins) *hld up: plld hrd: n.d* **40/1**

10 *2* **Mayolynn (USA)** 3-8-9 0 .... TPQueally 3 43
(H R A Cecil) *prom: hung lft thrght: wknd 3f out* **20/1**

0 **11** *hd* **Any Given Moment (IRE)**[16] 1963 3-8-7 0 .... LauraPike(7) 6 48
(D M Simcock) *prom: rdn over 2f out: sn wknd* **100/1**

12 *1/2* **Yanbu (USA)** 4-9-4 0 .... JackMitchell(3) 9 45
(R W Price) *led over 4f: sn rdn: wknd over 2f out* **100/1**

P-00 **13** *3 1/2* **Wild By Nature**[17] 1941 4-9-7 0 .... DO'Donohoe 10 37
(P Leech) *chsd ldrs: rdn and wknd over 2f out* **100/1**

0- **14** *1 3/4* **Vin De Rose**[212] 7054 3-8-9 0 .... MarkCoumbe(5) 4 35
(John A Harris) *plld hrd and prom: rdn and wknd over 2f out* **150/1**

1m 38.58s (-2.02) **Going Correction** -0.175s/f (Firm)
WFA 3 from 4yo+ 12lb **14** Ran SP% **120.2**
Speed ratings (Par 103): **103,101,100,98,97 92,91,89,88,86 85,85,81,80**
toteswinger: 1&2 £2.00, 1&3 £3.90, 2&3 £3.90 CSF £4.51 TOTE £2.80: £1.20, £1.10, £2.60; EX 5.30 Trifecta £20.80 Pool: £313.20 - 11.09 winning units..
Owner R Ahamad & P Scott **Bred** P And C Scott & Exors Of The Late N Ahamad **Trained** Newmarket, Suffolk

FOCUS
This second division of the maiden looked the strongest of the pair on paper. There was just a modest pace on but the runner-up sets a decent standard.
Cry Alot Boy Official explanation: jockey said gelding was slowly away

2417 FIRSTBET.COM 0800 230 0800 £50 MATCHED BET H'CAP — 7f 3y
4:10 (4:14) (Class 6) (0-60,63) 3-Y-O — **£2,072** (£616; £308; £153) **Stalls** High

Form — RPR

0651 **1** **Crystallize**[10] 2141 3-9-7 63 6ex .... SebSanders 10 69
(A B Haynes) *mid-div: hdwy 1/2-way: chsd ldr over 1f out: rdn to ld ins fnl f: r.o* **6/1**[3]

6-50 **2** *1/2* **Itainteasybeingme**[36] 1462 3-8-11 56 .... JackMitchell(3) 3 61
(J R Boyle) *mid-div: sn pushed along: hdwy over 2f out: led over 1f out: sn rdn: hdd ins fnl f: styd on* **16/1**

-100 **3** *1 1/2* **Kings Ace (IRE)**[10] 2132 3-9-3 59 ....(v) TPQueally 6 60
(A P Jarvis) *led: rdn and hdd over 1f out: styd on same pce fnl f* **12/1**

-135 **4** *3/4* **Baby Josr**[31] 1574 3-9-4 60 ....(vt) GeorgeBaker 1 59
(I A Wood) *s.i.s and swtchd rt sn after s: hld up: hdwy over 1f out: styd on: nt rch ldrs* **7/1**

00-5 **5** *1 1/2* **Almazar**[24] 1746 3-9-3 59 .... RichardMullen 12 54+
(J L Dunlop) *hld up: n.m.r over 2f out: swtchd lft and hdwy over 1f out: sn rdn: nt trble ldrs* **4/1**[1]

3-53 **6** *1* **Itsher**[103] 542 3-9-0 56 .... SaleemGolam 5 48
(S C Williams) *chsd ldrs: rdn over 1f out: wknd ins fnl f* **11/1**

0336 **7** *1* **Dancing Wave**[15] 1988 3-8-12 57 .... LeeVickers(3) 16 46
(M C Chapman) *chsd ldrs: rdn over 1f out: wknd ins fnl f* **25/1**

2334 **8** *1 1/4* **Jonnie Skull (IRE)**[37] 1440 3-8-7 56 ....(vt) CarolineKelly(7) 7 42
(P S McEntee) *chsd ldr to wl over 1f out: wknd fnl f* **14/1**

3300 **9** *2* **L'Arco Baleno (IRE)**[40] 1361 3-9-3 59 .... ChrisCatlin 13 39
(S A Callaghan) *sn pushed along in rr: rdn over 1f out: nvr nrr* **33/1**

605- **10** *2 3/4* **Sister Clement (IRE)**[203] 7205 3-9-2 58 .... JamieSpencer 2 31
(C R Egerton) *hld up: racd keenly: swtchd lft and hdwy over 1f out: wknd ins fnl f* **9/2**[2]

0-00 **11** *nk* **Eye For The Girls**[21] 1804 3-8-13 55 .... SamHitchcott 14 27
(M R Channon) *s.i.s: hld up: sme hdwy over 2f out: wknd over 1f out* **16/1**

530- **12** *2 1/2* **Silent Treatment (IRE)**[240] 6350 3-8-11 60 .... KylieManser(7) 8 25
(Miss Gay Kelleway) *prom: rdn 1/2-way: wknd over 2f out* **16/1**

-050 **13** *1/2* **Twenty Score**[15] 1985 3-9-1 57 ....(p) PaulFitzsimons 4 21
(Miss J R Tooth) *chsd ldrs: rdn 1/2-way: wknd over 2f out* **28/1**

05-0 **14** *2 3/4* **Join Up**[10] 2141 3-9-0 56 .... TGMcLaughlin 11 13
(W M Brisbourne) *hld up: rdn over 2f out: sn wknd* **25/1**

-600 **15** *19* **Captain Cavendish (IRE)**[10] 2141 3-9-0 56 ....(b) NeilChalmers 15 —
(A Bailey) *sn drvn along and reluctant: a bhd* **40/1**

1m 26.0s (-0.60) **Going Correction** -0.175s/f (Firm) **15** Ran SP% **121.8**
Speed ratings (Par 97): **96,95,93,92,91 90,88,87,85,82 81,78,78,75,53**
toteswinger: 1&2 £28.40, 1&3 £16.40, 2&3 £44.80 CSF £92.81 CT £1156.43 TOTE £6.30: £2.10, £4.80, £4.00; EX 140.10 TRIFECTA Not won..
Owner Mrs A De Weck & P De Weck **Bred** Aiden Murphy **Trained** Limpley Stoke, Bath

FOCUS
A big field for this moderate handicap.
Captain Cavendish(IRE) Official explanation: jockey said gelding never travelled

2418 SOUTHDOWNSBETTING.CO.UK H'CAP 6f 3y
4:40 (4:42) (Class 5) (0-70,70) 4-Y-0+ £2,719 (£809; £404; £202) Stalls High

Form RPR
00-0 1 **Luminous Gold**[24] 1748 4-9-1 67 SebSanders 2 79
(C F Wall) *led: hdd over 3f out: led again over 2f out: rdn out* 14/1
00-2 2 ¾ **Plumage**[10] 2145 4-8-5 57 KirstyMilczarek 10 67
(M Salaman) *hmpd s: hld up: hdwy over 2f out: swtchd lft over 1f out: sn rdn to chse wnr: edgd rt ins fnl f: r.o* 6/1[2]
5004 3 1 ¾ **Dickie Le Davoir**[10] 2130 5-8-8 65 MarkCoumbe(5) 15 69
(John A Harris) *s.s: outpcd: hdwy u.p and hung lft fr over 1f out: eased whn hld nr fin* 10/1
006- 4 ½ **Tyfos**[187] 7428 4-9-4 70 TGMcLaughlin 5 73
(W M Brisbourne) *chsd ldrs: rdn over 1f out: styd on same pce ins fnl f* 16/1
0324 5 2 ½ **Ask Jenny (IRE)**[3] 2316 7-8-1 56 KellyHarrison(3) 14 51
(Patrick Morris) *hld up: r.o ins fnl f: nearest fin* 9/2[1]
022 6 ½ **Bateleur**[7] 2202 5-8-4 56 oh4 CatherineGannon 8 49
(M R Channon) *hmpd s: sn mid-div: rdn over 2f out: styd on same pce fnl f* 9/1[3]
-160 7 ½ **Sir Nod**[12] 2071 7-9-4 70 ChrisCatlin 7 62
(Miss J A Camacho) *edgd rt s: chsd ldr tl led over 3f out: hdd over 2f out: wknd ins fnl f* 14/1
2224 8 ¾ **Desperate Dan**[16] 1951 8-9-4 70 (v) TPQueally 16 59
(A B Haynes) *hld up in tch: shkn up over 1f out: wknd ins fnl f* 6/1[2]
3-50 9 1 **Kingsgate Castle**[12] 2088 4-8-12 64 (b) RichardMullen 1 50
(Miss Gay Kelleway) *hld up: rdn over 2f out: nt trble ldrs* 12/1
321 10 nk **Gracie's Gift (IRE)**[27] 1655 7-8-5 57 PaulEddery 13 42
(R C Guest) *sn pushed along in rr: hdwy 1/2-way: rdn and wknd over 1f out* 6/1[2]
0060 11 ½ **Towy Boy (IRE)**[10] 2124 4-8-6 58 DO'Donohoe 12 41
(I A Wood) *hld up: rdn over 1f out: n.d* 33/1
6056 12 2 ¼ **Thoughtsofstardom**[13] 2053 6-8-1 60 TobyAtkinson(7) 3 36
(P S McEntee) *chsd ldrs: rdn and wknd over 1f out* 40/1
-000 13 ½ **Averoo**[12] 2088 4-8-0 59 (p) CarolineKelly(7) 11 34
(M D Squance) *sn pushed along in mid-div: lost pl over 4f out: swtchd lft over 2f out: n.d after* 66/1
002- 14 2 **Mystic Roll**[153] 7782 6-8-4 56 oh3 WandersonD'Avila 4 24
(Jane Chapple-Hyam) *mid-div: rdn and wknd 2f out* 40/1
00 15 6 **Double Carpet (IRE)**[10] 2145 6-8-2 59 RossAtkinson(5) 9 8
(G Woodward) *prom: wknd and eased 2f out* 16/1

1m 13.06s (-1.34) **Going Correction** -0.175s/f (Firm) 15 Ran SP% **122.2**
Speed ratings (Par 103): **101,100,97,97,93 93,92,91,90,89 88,85,85,82,74**
toteswinger: 1&2 £21.80, 1&3 £24.70, 2&3 £20.10 CSF £94.81 CT £919.25 TOTE £17.70: £3.90, £2.80, £4.10; EX 150.20 TRIFECTA Not won..
Owner Dr Philip Brown **Bred** Darley **Trained** Newmarket, Suffolk

FOCUS
This modest handicap was wide open and the form looks straightforward enough.

2419 EASTERN DAILY PRESS H'CAP 1m 3f 101y
5:10 (5:10) (Class 6) (0-65,70) 4-Y-0+ £2,072 (£616; £308; £153) Stalls Low

Form RPR
-056 1 **Graylyn Ruby (FR)**[24] 1738 4-9-4 65 ChrisCatlin 1 73+
(J Jay) *a.p: nt clr run and swicthed rt 2f out: r.o to ld wl ins fnl f* 7/1[3]
06-1 2 1 ¾ **Granary Girl**[19] 1881 7-8-6 60 SimonPearce(7) 3 65
(J Pearce) *hld up: hdwy over 2f out: led over 1f out: rdn and hdd wl ins fnl f* 7/1[3]
-005 3 shd **Dragon Slayer (IRE)**[20] 1845 7-8-9 61 (p) MarkCoumbe(5) 4 66
(John A Harris) *s.i.s: hld up: hdwy over 2f out: rdn and ev ch fr over 1f out tl uanble to qckn wl ins fnl f* 17/2
-060 4 2 ¼ **Lady Sorcerer**[29] 1609 4-8-7 54 (v[1]) RichardMullen 2 55
(A P Jarvis) *led 1f: chsd ldrs: rdn and ev ch over 1f out: styd on same pce fnl f* 13/2[2]
6066 5 1 **Wannarock (IRE)**[14] 2018 4-8-2 52 KellyHarrison(3) 8 51
(M C Chapman) *led after 1f: hung rt almost thrght: rdn and hdd over 2f out: wknd ins fnl f* 12/1
340- 6 1 **Rising Force (IRE)**[162] 7711 6-8-9 61 (b) JackDean(5) 10 59
(J L Spearing) *hld up: hdwy u.p over 1f out: nt rch ldrs* 8/1
3301 7 shd **General Tufto**[5] 2263 4-9-2 70 6ex (b) RichardRowe(7) 9 68
(C Smith) *s.i.s: hld up: hdwy over 3f out: led over 2f out: rdn and hdd over 1f out: wknd ins fnl f* 9/1
3120 8 ½ **New England**[12] 2068 7-8-9 56 TGMcLaughlin 7 53
(W M Brisbourne) *s.i.s: hld up: hdwy over 2f out: sn rdn: edgd lft and no imp fnl f* 4/1[1]
2406 9 1 ¼ **Cragganmore Creek**[6] 2244 6-8-4 51 oh6 (p) CatherineGannon 11 46
(D Morris) *chsd ldrs: rdn over 3f out: outpcd over 2f out: n.d after* 16/1
00-0 10 ½ **Stagecoach Emerald**[17] 1936 7-8-5 52 ow1 (p) SaleemGolam 5 46
(R W Price) *chsd ldrs: rdn and lost pl over 3f out: n.d after* 33/1
0000 11 nk **Josh You Are**[23] 1767 6-8-4 51 oh4 (t) KirstyMilczarek 12 44
(Ian Williams) *s.i.s: hld up: plld hrd: hdwy over 8f out: rdn and wknd over 1f out* 33/1
6210 12 1 ½ **Chalice Welcome**[6] 2244 6-9-0 64 JackMitchell(3) 6 55
(N B King) *hld up: plld hrd: hdwy over 2f out: sn rdn: hung lft and wknd fnl f* 9/1

2m 28.09s (-0.61) **Going Correction** -0.275s/f (Firm) 12 Ran SP% **119.4**
Speed ratings (Par 101): **91,89,89,88,87 86,86,86,85,84 84,83**
toteswinger: 1&2 £11.00, 1&3 £17.70 2&3 £12.50 CSF £55.84 CT £425.54 TOTE £10.50: £3.10, £2.10, £3.30; EX 70.30 Trifecta £232.40 Part won. Pool: £314.14 - 0.43 winning units..
Owner Graham & Lynn Knight **Bred** Jonathan Jay **Trained** Newmarket, Suffolk

FOCUS
A moderate handicap run at a solid early pace. The form looks ordinary rated around the placed horses with little solid about the fourth and fifth.
Wannarock(IRE) Official explanation: jockey said gelding hung right

2420 AVENUE PUBLIC HOUSE H'CAP 1m 2f 21y
5:40 (5:41) (Class 6) (0-55,61) 4-Y-0+ £2,072 (£616; £308; £153) Stalls Low

Form RPR
-051 1 **Cwm Rhondda (USA)**[9] 2171 4-9-3 61 6ex JackMitchell(3) 11 74+
(P W Chapple-Hyam) *hld up in tch: led over 1f out: shkn up and r.o wl* 4/5[1]
4050 2 3 ¾ **Iceman George**[9] 2171 5-8-12 53 (b) RichardMullen 14 58
(D Morris) *a.p: rdn and hung rt over 2f out: styd on* 20/1
00P- 3 ½ **Camera Shy (IRE)**[271] 5489 5-8-8 49 NeilChalmers 8 53
(K A Morgan) *s.i.s: sn prom: led and edgd rt over 2f out: rdn and hdd over 1f out: styd on same pce ins fnl f* 40/1
-000 4 2 **Eagle Nebula**[104] 531 5-9-0 55 SebSanders 10 55
(B R Johnson) *hld up: hdwy over 2f out: rdn over 1f out: styd on same pce* 8/1[2]
2050 5 ½ **Generous Lad (IRE)**[8] 2182 6-8-8 49 (b[1]) DO'Donohoe 9 48
(A B Haynes) *s.i.s: hld up: hdwy over 1f out: nt rch ldrs* 16/1
36-6 6 1 **Pretty Officer (USA)**[27] 1651 4-7-13 47 NoelGarbutt(7) 3 44
(Rae Guest) *s.i.s: hld up: hdwy and nt clr run over 1f out: nt trble ldrs* 25/1
3204 7 1 ¼ **Mystic Art (IRE)**[16] 1961 4-8-7 55 (p) RichardRowe(7) 16 50
(C R Egerton) *hld up: hdwy over 1f out: sn hung lft: wknd fnl f* 16/1
300- 8 4 **Credential**[217] 6930 7-8-6 52 MarkCoumbe(5) 4 39
(John A Harris) *sn led: hdd over 2f out: wknd fnl f* 33/1
/30- 9 1 **Viable**[14] 4797 7-9-0 55 JerryO'Dwyer 15 40
(Mrs P Sly) *prom: lost pl over 5f out: n.d after* 14/1
3261 10 1 **Sir Haydn**[27] 1651 9-8-1 49 (v) DannyBrock(7) 1 32
(J R Jenkins) *hld up: hdwy over 2f out: rdn and wknd over 1f out* 12/1
066- 11 2 ¼ **Zain (IRE)**[314] 4172 5-8-9 50 TPQueally 5 28
(J G Given) *chsd ldrs: rdn over 2f out: wknd fnl f* 9/1[3]
5034 12 5 **Desert Hawk**[3] 2337 8-8-8 49 (b) KirstyMilczarek 12 17
(W M Brisbourne) *rdr unable to remove hood whn stalls opened: s.s: hld up: a in rr* 16/1
00 13 ¾ **Strategic Knight (USA)**[3] 2332 4-8-7 55 GihanArnolda(7) 7 22
(R C Guest) *s.s: a in rr* 50/1
-550 14 11 **Lawyer To World**[44] 1273 5-8-6 47 (p) CatherineGannon 6 —
(Mrs C A Dunnett) *chsd ldr tl rdn and wknd over 2f out* 40/1
0-06 15 5 **Usetheforce (IRE)**[110] 444 4-8-6 47 ChrisCatlin 2 —
(M Quinn) *hld up: wknd over 3f out* 40/1
0-20 16 ¾ **Your Golf Travel**[16] 1959 4-8-5 46 oh1 NickyMackay 13 —
(M Wigham) *s.i.s: sn prom: rdn and wknd over 2f out: eased* 40/1

2m 7.34s (-3.16) **Going Correction** -0.275s/f (Firm) 16 Ran SP% **131.9**
Speed ratings (Par 101): **101,98,97,96,95 94,93,90,89,89 87,83,82,73,69 69**
toteswinger: 1&2 £10.30, 1&3 £34.30, 2&3 £106.10 CSF £27.45 CT £486.23 TOTE £1.70: £1.20, £4.40, £13.40, £2.60; EX 26.60 TRIFECTA Not won. Place 6: £39.01, Place 5: £33.40.
Owner Hintlesham Thoroughbreds **Bred** David Allan **Trained** Newmarket, Suffolk
■ Stewards' Enquiry : Gihan Arnolda one-day ban: used whip when out of contention (Jun 11)

FOCUS
A weak handicap that was run at a decent pace but little in the way of solid opposition to the winner..
Desert Hawk Official explanation: jockey said she was slow to remove blindfold from gelding in stalls
Lawyer To World Official explanation: trainer said gelding was unsuited by the good (good to firm places) ground
T/Plt: £34.10 to a £1 stake. Pool: £49,363.96. 1,056.41 winning tickets. T/Qpdt: £34.90 to a £1 stake. Pool: £2,660.10. 56.30 winning tickets. CR

2421 - 2424a (Foreign Racing) - See Raceform Interactive

1907 LEOPARDSTOWN (L-H)
Thursday, May 28

OFFICIAL GOING: Good (good to firm in places)

2425a SEAMUS & ROSEMARY MCGRATH MEMORIAL SAVAL BEG STKS (LISTED RACE) 1m 6f
8:00 (8:00) 4-Y-0+ £37,922 (£11,126; £5,300; £1,805)

RPR
1 **Hindu Kush (IRE)**[22] 1790 4-9-1 CDHayes 4 108
(D Nicholls) *mde all: rdn and kpt on wl fr over 1f out* 7/1[3]
2 1 **Alandi (IRE)**[32] 1546 4-9-4 MJKinane 5 110+
(John M Oxx, Ire) *chsd ldrs: 3rd early: hdwy to 2nd after 6f: rdn 2f out: 3rd 1 1/2f out: kpt on same pce fr over 1f out: styng on and short of room cl home: grabbed 2nd on line* 8/13[1]
3 shd **Sublimity (FR)**[79] 2406 9-9-1 (t) JAHeffernan 7 106
(Robert Alan Hennessy, Ire) *settled bhd ldrs: impr to 4th after 5f: rdn into 3rd 2f out: styd on to 2nd 1 1/2f out: kpt on fr 1f out: nt rch wnr: lost 2nd on line* 14/1
4 ¾ **Suailce (IRE)**[49] 1204 4-8-12 96 (b) PJSmullen 2 102+
(D K Weld, Ire) *hld up: rr 1/2-way: rdn under 2f out: styd on to 5th 1f out: kpt on same pce fnl f* 8/1
5 1 ¼ **The Betchworth Kid**[12] 2075 4-9-1 JMurtagh 3 104
(M L W Bell) *chsd ldrs: 4th early: 5th after 6f: rdn in 5th 2f out: no imp in 4th over 1f out: kpt on same pce fnl f* 13/2[2]
6 3 ½ **Merveilles**[63] 6100 6-9-1 98 (p) FMBerry 1 100
(Mrs John Harrington, Ire) *s.i.s: hld up towards rr: hdwy to 5th 3f out: rdn in 6th 2f out: sn no ex and kpt on one pce* 20/1
7 ½ **Donegal (USA)**[26] 5685 4-9-4 (b) DPMcDonogh 6 101
(Robert Alan Hennessy, Ire) *chsd ldr: 3rd after 6f: rdn in 4th 2f out: sn no ex* 14/1

3m 4.50s (3.50) **Going Correction** -0.075s/f (Good) 7 Ran SP% **117.0**
Speed ratings: **87,86,86,85,85 83,82**
CSF £12.23 TOTE £8.90: £3.00, £1.50; DF 23.20.
Owner Dr MArwan Koukash & D Nicholls **Bred** Annemarie O'Brien,Jcrowley,Pma **Trained** Sessay, N Yorks

FOCUS
The winner enjoyed the run of the race and he, along with the sixth, have been rated back to their best.

NOTEBOOK
Hindu Kush(IRE) had found Alandi three and a half lengths too good for him when the pair clashed in the Vintage Crop Stakes in testing conditions at Navan last month, but conditions were very different here and this time Hindu Kush, under a fine tactical ride from Chris Hayes, reversed the placings. Hayes slowed the pace after going about four furlongs before quickening the tempo leaving the back-straight and his mount responded keenly, keeping on well in the straight to hold off his rivals. (op 7/1 tchd 6/1)
Alandi(IRE) had won both his previous starts and was encountering quick ground for the first time. Conditions were probably faster than ideal for him, but he appeared to cope with the quicker ground well enough and it was probably the quick-slow-quick pace that told against him more. Pushed along in second place over 3f out, he dropped to third over one and a half furlongs from home before staying on under pressure inside the final furlong to snatch second place virtually on the line, despite appearing to edge right in the closing stages. (op 8/11 tchd 4/5)
Sublimity(FR) was having his first run on the Flat for four years and his first race since having a palate procedure carried out after a disappointing performance in the Champion Hurdle in March. His best Flat form had been shown over shorter distances and he acquitted himself well here, beginning his effort off the final bend and going second over a furlong and a half out. He kept on well without getting to the winner and lost second spot only at the line. He is heading for a long break now and will return over hurdles later in the year. (op 12/1)

Suailce(IRE), winner of the Irish Cesarewitch, was held up before staying on steadily in the straight. She finished out the race well and, in hindsight and because of the way the race was run, she would probably have fared better had more use been made of her. (op 8/1 tchd 9/1)
The Betchworth Kid had lost out narrowly to Hindu Kush when third at Navan. Reported to have had a rough ferry journey from England, the ground was much quicker than he likes and, in the circumstances, he performed creditably, keeping on from over a furlong out without ever posing a serious threat. (op 6/1)

2426 - 2427a (Foreign Racing) - See Raceform Interactive

[1979]SAINT-CLOUD (L-H)

Thursday, May 28

OFFICIAL GOING: Good to soft

2428a PRIX CORRIDA (GROUP 2) (F&M) — 1m 2f 110y

1:05 (1:06) 4-Y-O+ £71,942 (£27,767; £13,252; £8,835; £4,417)

RPR

1 **Alpine Rose (FR)**[22] 4-8-9 .... GMosse 11 107
(A De Royer-Dupre, France) *prom on outside racing keenly tl led 1/2-way: kicked clr over 2f out: 3 l clr appr fnl f: hld on wl* **194/10**

2 ½ **Danse Grecque (USA)**[30] 1597 4-8-9 .... ACrastus 9 106
(E Lellouche, France) *hld up in rr: 10th st: hdwy down outside fr 2f out to go 2nd 1f out: styd on wl: nrst fin* **17/2**[3]

3 1 **La Boum (GER)**[11] 2118 6-8-11 .... TJarnet 4 106
(Robert Collet, France) *hld up: 8th st: disputing 7th jst ins fnl f: r.o wl to take 3rd on line* **29/10**[2]

4 hd **Shemima**[30] 1597 4-8-11 .... CSoumillon 8 106
(A De Royer-Dupre, France) *cl up: pushed along 3f out: 5th st: tk 3rd 150yds out: kpt on but lost 3rd on line* **1/1**[1]

5 ¾ **Rainbow Dancing**[30] 1597 4-8-9 .... DBoeuf 3 102
(Mlle H Van Zuylen, France) *in tch: 4th st: rdn and one pce fnl 1 1/2f* **33/1**

6 nk **Goose Bay (GER)**[30] 1597 4-8-13 .... DBonilla 12 106
(F Head, France) *led to 1/2-way: 3rd st: rdn over 2f out: one pce* **36/1**

7 1½ **Albisola (IRE)**[30] 1597 4-8-11 .... JVictoire 1 101
(Robert Collet, France) *broke on terms: in rr: 9th st: nvr a factor* **29/10**[2]

8 snk **Tubular Bells (USA)**[30] 1597 4-8-9 .... MGuyon 2 98
(H-A Pantall, France) *midfield: 6th st: effrt and n.m.r on ins under 2f out: one pce* **26/1**

9 ½ **Salve Germania (IRE)**[30] 1597 4-8-9 .... ASuborics 5 98
(W Hickst, Germany) *last to ins fnl f* **16/1**

10 ½ **Guantana (GER)**[45] 4-8-9 .... SPasquier 6 97
(J Hirschberger, Germany) *reluctant to enter stalls: 11th st: a towards rr* **13/1**

11 **Stella Di Quattro**[30] 1597 5-8-9 .... AStarke 7 —
(Uwe Ostmann, Germany) *cl up: 2nd st: rdn over 2f out: wknd over 1f out* **52/1**

12 **Diyakalanie (FR)**[30] 1597 5-8-9 .... OPeslier 10 —
(Y De Nicolay, France) *in tch: 7th st: effrt and no imp 2f out* **37/1**

2m 16.0s (-3.60) **12** Ran SP% **143.6**
PARI-MUTUEL: WIN 20.40; PL 4.70, 2.80, 3.50; DF 49.80.
Owner Ecurie Des Monceaux & Skymarc Farm **Bred** H H Aga Khan's Stud's S C **Trained** Chantilly, France

NOTEBOOK
Alpine Rose(FR) was taken to the head of affairs soon after the start and, given a good tactical ride, made every yard of the running. It was only a fair gallop early on but she suddenly quickened things up early in the straight and then fended off challenges throughout the final furlong. This was her first Group success and she will now be aimed at the Grand Prix de Saint-Cloud, which is longer, but she has plenty of stamina on her dam's side.
Danse Grecque(USA) was held up early on in this slowly run race. She still had plenty to do in the straight but came with a run up the centre of the track and looked dangerous at the furlong marker, but she just couldn't peg back the winner.
La Boum(GER), waited with for much of this falsely run race, was another who came with a run up the outside. She has plenty of stamina and was staying on at the end over a distance short of her best.
Shemima was given every possible chance and proved disappointing. However, she has shown some of her best form over longer distances and was probably unsuited by the way this race was run. Raced in mid-division for much of the contest, she couldn't quicken early in the straight and just stayed on one-paced.

[2324]GOODWOOD (R-H)

Friday, May 29

OFFICIAL GOING: Good (8.5)

Races on mile course run over 20yards further than advertised.
Wind: Light, across, 1st 4 races; fresh, half behind, last 2 races Weather: Fine, warm

2429 GOODWOOD AERODROME STKS (H'CAP) — 2m

2:25 (2:25) (Class 5) (0-70,70) 4-Y-O+ £3,238 (£963; £481; £240) Stalls Low

Form RPR

0-64 1 **Inchpast**[15] 2018 8-9-4 63 ....(b) TPQueally 14 74
(M H Tompkins) *rn in snatches in abt 6th: prog u.p on inner 4f out: led over 2f out: drvn and kpt on wl* **10/1**

-206 2 1¼ **Munlochy Bay**[11] 2127 5-9-6 65 .... IanMongan 5 75
(W S Kittow) *rn in snatches in abt 7th: drvn and prog on outer fr 5f out to chal 3f out: chsd wnr jst over 2f out: kpt on but a hld* **7/1**[3]

20-0 3 4 **Bob's Your Uncle**[33] 1537 6-8-9 54 .... TPO'Shea 3 59
(J G Portman) *hld up wl in rr: gd prog on outer fr over 3f out: wnt 3rd 1f out: kpt on but no imp on ldrs* **25/1**

4311 4 1 **Eforetta (GER)**[25] 1732 7-9-2 61 .... RichardHughes 9 65
(A W Carroll) *hld up wl in rr: rdn over 3f out: prog on outer over 2f out: wnt 4th ins fnl f: no ch w ldrs* **12/1**

0-26 5 1¾ **Invention (USA)**[17] 1966 6-9-4 63 ....(t) AlanMunro 6 65
(Miss E C Lavelle) *led tl 1f: trckd ldr: led again over 3f out: to over 2f out: fdd over 1f out* **33/1**

3-03 6 2½ **Ned Ludd (IRE)**[9] 2177 6-9-11 70 .... EddieAhern 2 69
(J G Portman) *chsd clr ldrs in abt 5th: cl up 4f out: lost pl and hmpd 3f out: kpt on one pce after* **10/1**

1 7 3¾ **Caoba**[10] 2163 5-9-6 65 6ex ....(p) RyanMoore 11 59
(V R A Dartnall) *trckd clr ldng pair: cl up over 3f out: hrd rdn and nt qckn sn after: wknd 2f out* **9/4**[1]

2-00 8 ¾ **Salut Saint Cloud**[30] 1609 8-8-7 52 ....(p) FergusSweeney 13 45
(G L Moore) *nvr bttr than midfield: in tch whn nt clr run briefly 3f out: sn outpcd* **25/1**

U33 9 1 **Calculating (IRE)**[10] 2163 5-8-8 53 .... WilliamBuick 4 45
(M D I Usher) *hld up wl in rr: rdn over 3f out: no prog and hanging over 2f out: plugged on* **7/1**[3]

0-03 10 1¼ **Go Amwell**[15] 2018 6-8-8 56 .... DavidProbert[(3)] 8 47
(J R Jenkins) *mostly in midfield: effrt and in tch over 3f out: outpcd fr over 2f out: hanging and wknd over 1f out* **6/1**[2]

4314 11 10 **Colourful Move**[20] 1892 4-8-12 59 .... RobertHavlin 1 38
(P G Murphy) *chsd clr ldng pair: nt qckn and sing to lose pl whn hmpd over 3f out: sn no ch* **12/1**

-546 12 3¾ **Adage**[10] 2163 6-8-6 51 oh5 ....(t) NeilChalmers 15 25
(David Pinder) *wl in rr: drvn and effrt on inner 4f out: wknd wl over 2f out* **40/1**

004- 13 6 **High Point (IRE)**[381] 2091 11-9-3 62 .... AdamKirby 10 29
(G P Enright) *hld up in rr: lost tch and hanging 4f out: bhd after* **100/1**

50 14 3¾ **Tabaran (FR)**[30] 1609 6-8-12 57 ....(b[1]) MartinDwyer 16 19
(L A Dace) *swtg: plld hrd: led after 1f to over 3f out: wknd rapidly* **33/1**

000- 15 66 **Mister Completely (IRE)**[229] 6672 8-8-7 52 ....(v) JamesDoyle 7 —
(Ms J S Doyle) *a last: struggling 6f out: t.o and virtually p.u 2f out* **50/1**

3m 28.81s (-0.19) **Going Correction** -0.075s/f (Good)
WFA 4 from 5yo+ 2lb **15** Ran SP% **122.6**
Speed ratings (Par 103): **107,106,104,103,103 101,99,99,99,98 93,91,88,86,53**
toteswinger: 1&2 £26.40, 1&3 £41.30, 2&3 £58.80 CSF £75.09 CT £1730.56 TOTE £14.50: £3.30, £3.60, £3.70; EX 136.70.
Owner Marcoe Racing Welwyn **Bred** Stanley Estate And Stud Co **Trained** Newmarket, Suffolk

FOCUS
Some exposed and out-of-form stayers here. Ordinary form with the winner rated in line with last autumn's form.
Salut Saint Cloud Official explanation: vet said gelding returned lame on his right-fore
High Point(IRE) Official explanation: vet said gelding returned lame on his right-fore
Mister Completely(IRE) Official explanation: jockey said gelding lost its action

2430 CASCO MAIDEN AUCTION STKS — 6f

3:00 (3:00) (Class 5) 2-Y-O £3,238 (£963; £481; £240) Stalls Low

Form RPR

1 **Xtension (IRE)** 2-8-11 0 .... AdamKirby 6 82+
(C G Cox) *str: lw: trckd ldrs on outer: cl up 2f out: shkn up to ld jst ins fnl f: drifted rt but sn clr* **5/2**[1]

5 2 4 **Jehu**[14] 2033 2-9-1 0 .... TonyCulhane 4 74
(M R Channon) *w'like: w ldr: rdn to ld 2f out: hdd and outpcd jst ins fnl f* **8/1**

3 ¾ **Merchant Of Medici** 2-8-11 0 .... MartinDwyer 1 68+
(W R Muir) *w'like: outpcd in last trio: pushed along fr 1/2-way: prog jst over 1f out: styd on wl to take 3rd clsng stages* **9/2**[3]

4 1 **Folletta (IRE)** 2-8-4 0 .... WilliamBuick 9 58
(R Hannon) *w'like: str: bit bkwd: rn green and sn in last trio: tail swishing whn pushed along fr 1/2-way: styd on fnl f: nrst fin* **7/2**[2]

0 5 ½ **One Cool Buck (IRE)**[42] 1323 2-8-13 0 .... RichardHughes 3 65
(R Hannon) *racd against nr side rail: pressed ldrs: shkn up and on terms 2f out: fdd fnl f* **8/1**

0 6 hd **Volatilis (IRE)**[14] 2037 2-8-11 0 .... RHills 5 63
(J W Hills) *w'like: narrow ld to 2f out: shkn up and grad wknd* **14/1**

7 ¾ **Mnarani (IRE)** 2-8-13 0 .... LPKeniry 2 62
(J S Moore) *unf: bit bkwd: s.i.s: rcvrd to trck ldrs: cl up 2f out: fdd over 1f out* **8/1**

8 4½ **Boquito (IRE)** 2-8-13 0 .... JerryO'Dwyer 7 49
(Miss Amy Weaver) *w'like: athletic: dwlt: rcvrd to chse ldrs: wknd rapidly over 1f out* **25/1**

9 10 **Arkellion** 2-8-11 0 .... TPQueally 8 17
(A B Haynes) *leggy: dwlt: rn green and sn wl bhd in last: t.o* **25/1**

1m 12.87s (0.67) **Going Correction** -0.075s/f (Good) **9** Ran SP% **116.7**
Speed ratings (Par 93): **92,86,85,84,83 83,82,76,63**
toteswinger: 1&2 £5.50, 1&3 £4.20, 2&3 £7.20 CSF £23.67 TOTE £3.70: £1.50, £2.20, £1.70; EX 25.20.
Owner Brighthelm Racing **Bred** Paul McCartan **Trained** Lambourn, Berks

FOCUS
A nice start from the winner, while the second paid another compliment to Canford Cliffs.

NOTEBOOK
Xtension(IRE) won this very easily. His yard isn't renowned for getting two-year-olds ready first time and this one did edge to his right after getting a couple of taps to assert in very good style. The time was 2.57 above standard and, despite having no reliable form in the race, this was a decent performance from a horse that should be okay over another furlong. Connections are keeping options open for a possible run in something at Royal Ascot. (tchd 3-1 and 10-3 in a place)
Jehu was one of three runners with experience and showed signficantly more than on his debut at Newbury when left toiling behind Royal Ascot bound Canford Cliffs. In contrast, here he was on the pace throughout and stayed on well once the winner had gone. Another furlong won't be a problem. (op 7-1 tchd 6-1)
Merchant Of Medici, whose dam won the Chevelely Park Stakes, cost only 13,000gns and made an encouraging debut, staying on better than anything bar the winner having struggled early. His yard has been on the slow side lately but this was an encouraging sign and a race of this type is well within range. Official explanation: vet said colt returned lame on his right-fore (op 4-1)
Folletta(IRE), who cost just £5,000, was getting upwards of 7lb from all contestants. She broke well but flashed her tail when driven. For the moment that can be put down to inexperience, and she should have no trouble winning a race of this grade if she improves from her debut in the usual style of her juvenile stablemates. (op 5-1 tchd 3-1)
One Cool Buck(IRE) showed more pace than on his debut at Newbury but there is some stamina in the pedigree. (tchd 15-2)
Volatilis(IRE) was much more awake than on his debut at Newbury and doesn't look a forlorn hope in this grade. (op 12-1 tchd 16-1)

2431 INTERNATIONAL BUREAU OF AVIATION STKS (H'CAP) — 1m

3:35 (3:36) (Class 5) (0-70,81) 3-Y-O £3,238 (£963; £481; £240) Stalls High

Form RPR

-411 1 **Global**[4] 2320 3-9-12 81 12ex .... PatrickHills[(3)] 4 87
(R Hannon) *lw: t.k.h: hld up in midfield: rdn and prog on outer over 2f out: led over 1f out: drifted lft but kpt on wl enough* **11/10**[1]

01-6 2 1½ **Saturn Way (GR)**[21] 1839 3-9-3 69 .... LPKeniry 11 72
(P R Chamings) *dwlt: t.k.h and sn trckd ldng pair: cl up 2f out: chsd wnr fr over 1f out: kpt on but no imp fnl f* **5/1**[3]

-000 3 1¼ **Ymir**[27] 1671 3-8-6 58 .... PaulDoe 7 58
(M J Attwater) *led: hanging lft and reminders after 2f: sn clr: hung lft fr 2f out: hdd and one pce over 1f out* **100/1**

0-4 **4** ¾ **Flapper (IRE)**[22] 1804 3-8-10 **62** RyanMoore 8 60
(J W Hills) *lw: hld up in midfield: rdn and nt qckn over 2f out: styd on fr over 1f out: nrst fin* **4/1**[2]

0-0 **5** *nk* **Countess Zara (IRE)**[31] 1588 3-8-13 **65** (v[1]) WilliamBuick 1 63
(A M Balding) *hld up in last trio: rdn over 2f out and no prog: styd on u.p jst over 1f out: nrst fin* **33/1**

241 **6** 1 ¾ **Lighthearted (FR)**[21] 1839 3-9-4 **70** AdamKirby 6 64
(C G Cox) *lw: taken down early: chsd ldr: clsd over 2f out: nt qckn wl over 1f out: wknd fnl f* **5/1**[3]

0-6 **7** 2 **Green Poppy**[17] 1969 3-8-9 **61** EddieAhern 3 50
(Eve Johnson Houghton) *t.k.h in midfield: nt qckn over 2f out: nvr on terms after* **16/1**

550 **8** 1 ½ **Lilly Blue (IRE)**[27] 1670 3-8-12 **64** TonyCulhane 10 50
(M R Channon) *hld up in last trio: shkn up 2f out: no prog* **33/1**

504 **9** 1 **Crystal B Good (USA)**[21] 1838 3-8-10 **62** RobertHavlin 5 45
(J R Best) *chsd ldng trio: wknd fr 2f out* **50/1**

-00 **10** 5 **Spinning Joy**[51] 1183 3-8-4 **56** oh4 MartinDwyer 9 28
(J R Boyle) *blindfold removed late and slowly away: plld hrd in last pair: nvr a factor* **66/1**

4-50 **11** 3 ¼ **Silver Salsa**[45] 1271 3-8-1 **56** oh7 DavidProbert[(3)] 2 20
(J R Jenkins) *nvr beyond midfield: urged along bef 1/2-way: wknd over 2f out* **80/1**

1m 41.8s (1.90) **Going Correction** -0.075s/f (Good) **11** Ran SP% **118.4**
Speed ratings (Par 99): **87,85,84,83,83 81,79,77,76,71 68**
toteswinger: 1&2 £2.60, 1&3 £28.20, 2&3 £56.60 CSF £6.84 CT £352.29 TOTE £2.20: £1.10, £1.80, £11.30; EX 8.00.
Owner A J Ilsley & G Battocchi **Bred** Lt-Col And Mrs R Bromley Gardner **Trained** East Everleigh, Wilts

FOCUS
A 56-70 handicap but Global raced off 81 under his penalty. He more or less confirmed his Chepstow win, and this form is rated around the third.
Ymir Official explanation: jockey said colt hung left

2432 GOODWOOD AIRCRAFT ENGINEERING STKS (H'CAP) 1m 1f 192y
4:10 (4:11) (Class 4) (0-80,80) 3-Y-O **£4,857** (£1,445; £722; £360) **Stalls High**

Form RPR

40-0 **1** **Itlaaq**[14] 2048 3-8-8 **70** RHills 1 85+
(J L Dunlop) *hld up in last trio: steaady prog on outer fr 3f out: reminder 2f out: wnt 2nd ins fnl f: shkn up to ld last 100yds: cleverly* **8/1**

0-54 **2** ½ **Just Like Silk (USA)**[28] 1643 3-8-10 **72** EddieAhern 8 86
(G A Butler) *lw: on toes: chsd clr ldng quartet: clsd over 3f out: pressed ldr over 2f out: rdn to ld ent fnl f: hdd and hld last 100yds* **6/1**[3]

5-22 **3** 2 ¼ **Mabuya (UAE)**[11] 2126 3-8-12 **74** FergusSweeney 2 84
(P J Makin) *lw: chsd clr ldng pair: clsd to ld 3f out: drvn over 1f out: hdd and outpcd ent fnl f* **5/1**[2]

10-0 **4** 5 **Sequillo**[37] 1466 3-8-9 **71** RichardHughes 6 71
(R Hannon) *swtg: hld up in rr: 10th 1/2-way: prog on outer fr 3f out: hanging bdly rt fr over 2f out: pressed ldrs wl over 1f out: wknd fnl f* **8/1**

6465 **5** 1 **Diamond Twister (USA)**[18] 1928 3-8-7 **72** (t) MarcHalford[(3)] 14 70+
(J R Best) *taken down early: hld up: 9th 1/2-way: pushed along whn nt clr run briefly 3f out: rdn and sme prog 2f out: nvr on terms* **20/1**

01-6 **6** 1 ½ **Nice Time (IRE)**[27] 1670 3-8-6 **68** AlanMunro 10 66+
(M H Tompkins) *hld up in last trio: nt clr run fr over 3f out and grad taken to outer: kpt on fnl 2f: no ch* **25/1**

1-14 **7** 1 **Blaise Tower**[131] 209 3-9-3 **79** RyanMoore 9 72
(G L Moore) *hld up in last trio: pushed along over 3f out: no prog u.p over 2f out: kpt on fr over 1f out on outer: no ch* **14/1**

54-6 **8** 5 **Davids Matador**[8] 2209 3-8-11 **73** StephenCarson 13 56
(Eve Johnson Houghton) *hld up in midfield: 8th 1/2-way: no prog 3f out: sn btn* **14/1**

31-0 **9** *nk* **Three Ducks**[20] 1882 3-8-10 **72** MartinDwyer 11 54
(L M Cumani) *mostly in midfield: 6th 1/2-way: hanging whn rdn 3f out: no prog and sn btn* **10/1**

065 **10** ½ **Viva La Vida**[21] 1825 3-8-12 **74** KirstyMilczarek 12 55
(Jane Chapple-Hyam) *mostly in midfield: 7th 1/2-way: effrt on inner 3f out: no prog 2f out: wknd* **14/1**

2140 **11** 4 ½ **Best In Class**[18] 1928 3-8-8 **70** RichardKingscote 7 42
(Tom Dascombe) *chsd clr ldng pair: wknd wl over 2f out* **50/1**

-406 **12** ¾ **Roly Boy**[17] 1971 3-9-1 **80** PatrickHills[(3)] 3 50
(R Hannon) *pressed ldr and sn clr of rest: carried wd bnd 5f out: upsides 3f out: sn wknd* **16/1**

-301 **13** 2 **Rumble Of Thunder (IRE)**[11] 2126 3-9-1 **77** 6ex WilliamBuick 5 43
(D W P Arbuthnot) *led at decent pce: rn wd bnd 5f out: hdd & wknd tamely 3f out: eased* **7/2**[1]

2m 6.64s (-1.36) **Going Correction** -0.075s/f (Good) **13** Ran SP% **120.9**
Speed ratings (Par 101): **102,101,99,95,95 93,93,89,88,88 84,84,82**
toteswinger: 1&2 £13.20, 1&3 £10.60, 2&3 £5.90 CSF £54.99 CT £270.90 TOTE £11.10: £3.40, £2.50, £2.10; EX 76.00.
Owner Hamdan Al Maktoum **Bred** Shadwell Estate Company Limited **Trained** Arundel, W Sussex

FOCUS
There was a very strong pace on here and that was the downfall of favourite Rumble Of Thunder, who got an easy lead when winning at Bath last time but was persistently harried by Roly Boy here. In the end both dropped away having set the race up for something with a finishing kick. It is probably worth rating the front three positively.
Rumble Of Thunder(IRE) Official explanation: jockey said gelding ran flat

2433 GOODWOOD FLYING SCHOOL MAIDEN FILLIES' STKS 1m
4:45 (4:48) (Class 5) 3-Y-O **£3,238** (£963; £481; £240) **Stalls High**

Form RPR

0- **1** **Louise Bonne (USA)**[312] 4251 3-9-0 0 AdamKirby 12 79
(C G Cox) *unf: trckd ldrs: rdn and prog to go 3rd 2f out: clsd over 1f out: styd on wl to ld last 75yds* **33/1**

4- **2** ¾ **Aqwaas (USA)**[173] 7593 3-9-0 0 RHills 14 77
(Sir Michael Stoute) *t.k.h: trckd ldng trio: smooth prog to ld 2f out: shkn up fnl f: hdd and nt qckn fnl 75yds* **9/2**[2]

4 **3** 1 **Critical Path (IRE)**[30] 1605 3-9-0 0 WilliamBuick 8 75+
(A M Balding) *sn midfield: pushed along fr 1/2-way: sme prog over 2f out to 4th over 1f out: styd on wl last 150yds to take 3rd nr fin* **4/1**[1]

4 **4** ¾ **Olive Green (USA)**[21] 1843 3-9-0 0 PaulEddery 2 73
(Pat Eddery) *unf: prog to ld after 2f: rdn and hdd 2f out: kpt on wl tl outpcd last 100yds* **13/2**[3]

5 2 ¼ **Halling Gal** 3-8-11 0 DavidProbert[(3)] 7 68+
(W R Muir) *w'like: lengthy: hld up towards rr: sme prog over 2f out: shkn up over 1f out: styd on wl fnl f: nrst fin* **28/1**

4-3 **6** 2 ½ **Welsh Anthem**[39] 1406 3-9-0 0 MartinDwyer 10 62
(W R Muir) *led 2f: chsd ldrs: grad wknd fr 2f out* **4/1**[1]

5- **7** 1 **All For You (IRE)**[191] 7380 3-9-0 0 AlanMunro 11 60
(M Botti) *lw: wl plcd bhd ldrs: plld out over 3f out: stl cl up 2f out: reminder over 1f out: steadily fdd* **7/1**

06- **8** 1 ½ **Arcola (IRE)**[211] 7093 3-9-0 0 RyanMoore 1 57
(D M Simcock) *reluctant to enter stalls: wl in rr: rdn 3f out: kpt on fnl 2f: nrst fin* **16/1**

0-4 **9** ¾ **Penzena**[21] 1844 3-9-0 0 JimCrowley 9 55
(W J Knight) *chsd ldrs: pushed along over 3f out: bmpd sn after: fdd fnl 2f* **14/1**

10 2 ½ **Haling Park (UAE)** 3-9-0 0 FergusSweeney 13 49
(G L Moore) *dwlt: rchd midfield on inner by 1/2-way: no prog over 2f out: sn wknd* **50/1**

11 7 **Platinum Bounty** 3-9-0 0 RobertHavlin 5 33
(J A Geake) *leggy: s.s: mostly wl in rr: no ch over 2f out* **100/1**

0 **12** 2 **Mediterranean Sea (IRE)**[11] 2139 3-9-0 0 SimonWhitworth 3 28
(J R Jenkins) *w'like: a wl in rr: wknd over 2f out* **100/1**

0-0 **13** 5 **Flying Cloud (USA)**[30] 1605 3-8-9 0 GabrielHannon[(5)] 4 17
(B J Meehan) *restless in stalls: a wl in rr: rdn over 3f out: sn bhd* **66/1**

14 2 ¾ **Phantom Ridge (IRE)** 3-9-0 0 RichardHughes 15 11
(R Hannon) *unf: s.s: a wl in rr: wl bhd fnl 2f* **16/1**

6 **15** 22 **Rockabout (IRE)**[21] 1844 3-9-0 0 EddieAhern 6 —
(B J Meehan) *w ldrs to over 3f out: wknd v rapidly and eased: t.o* **9/1**

1m 40.31s (0.41) **Going Correction** -0.075s/f (Good) **15** Ran SP% **124.3**
Speed ratings (Par 96): **94,93,92,91,89 86,85,84,83,81 74,72,67,64,42**
toteswinger: 1&2 £40.60, 1&3 £33.30, 2&3 £5.10 CSF £178.57 TOTE £65.00: £11.80, £2.00, £2.10; EX 405.00.
Owner Old Peartree Stud **Bred** Fasttrack Farms Llc **Trained** Lambourn, Berks

FOCUS
There was a moderate pace for the first two furlongs which resulted in several fighting for their heads and some bunching. Probably ordinary form, rated around the third and fourth.
Rockabout(IRE) Official explanation: jockey said filly lost its action

2434 GOODWOOD AERO CLUB STKS (H'CAP) 7f
5:15 (5:23) (Class 4) (0-85,85) 4-Y-O+ **£4,857** (£1,445; £722; £360) **Stalls High**

Form RPR

120- **1** **King's Wonder**[233] 6576 4-9-3 **84** MartinDwyer 14 97
(W R Muir) *taken down early: w ldr: led 3f out: rdn clr over 1f out: unchal after* **12/1**

4006 **2** 3 ½ **Councellor (FR)**[8] 2188 7-8-8 **75** (t) TPQueally 11 79
(Stef Liddiard) *wl in rr and sn pushed along: prog on outer fr 2f out: styd on wl u.p to take 2nd nr fin* **8/1**

6-10 **3** *nk* **Den's Gift (IRE)**[53] 1149 5-9-1 **82** (b) AdamKirby 9 85
(C G Cox) *prom: chsd wnr over 2f out: no imp and lft bhd over 1f out: lost 2nd nr fin* **7/1**[3]

1011 **4** 1 ¼ **Seneschal**[15] 2011 8-8-9 **76** RichardHughes 4 75
(A B Haynes) *hld up wl in rr: stdy prog on inner fr over 2f out: n.m.r wl over 1f out: pushed along and kpt on to take 4th nr fin* **16/1**

-003 **5** ½ **Brassini**[14] 2050 4-9-3 **84** AlanMunro 5 82
(B R Millman) *pressed ldrs: rdn to dispute 2nd fr 2f out to jst over 1f out: fdd* **9/1**

1203 **6** 1 ½ **Last Sovereign**[13] 2073 5-8-10 **82** (p) Louis-PhilippeBeuzelin[(5)] 13 76
(Jane Chapple-Hyam) *chsd ldrs: rdn over 2f out: nt pce to cl fr over 1f out* **11/4**[1]

3-00 **7** ¾ **Highland Harvest**[8] 2193 5-8-8 **75** RobertHavlin 16 67
(Jamie Poulton) *taken down early: pressed ldrs: disp 2nd on inner 2f out: fdd fnl f* **40/1**

5000 **8** ½ **Hallingdal (UAE)**[39] 1405 4-8-4 **71** oh1 TPO'Shea 8 62
(J J Bridger) *wl in rr: rdn sn after 1/2-way and no prog: kpt on fr over 1f out* **66/1**

0-20 **9** ½ **Folly Lodge**[8] 2188 5-8-13 **80** JimCrowley 15 69
(R M Beckett) *restless in stalls: taken out and put bk in: dwlt: rchd midfield on inner 3f out: n.m.r 2f out: no prog after* **9/1**

-000 **10** *hd* **Choreography**[8] 2188 6-8-10 **77** (p) PaulDoe 10 68+
(Jim Best) *stdd s: wl in rr: shkn up over 2f out: nt clr run after: nvr nr ldrs* **33/1**

1130 **11** *nk* **Trafalgar Square**[8] 2193 7-9-3 **84** EddieAhern 12 72
(M J Attwater) *chsd ldrs: pushed along after 3f: struggling whn taken to outer over 2f out: wknd* **25/1**

00-0 **12** ¾ **King's Caprice**[44] 1288 8-8-8 **75** (t) TravisBlock 1 61
(J A Geake) *led to 3f out: sn lost pl u.p* **50/1**

00-0 **13** 1 ¾ **Dingaan (IRE)**[14] 2050 6-8-10 **77** WilliamBuick 2 58
(A M Balding) *hld up wl in rr: pushed along after 2f and no rspnse: nvr a factor* **10/1**

-500 **14** 6 **Cordell (IRE)**[13] 2083 4-9-4 **85** RyanMoore 7 50
(R Hannon) *taken down early: nvr beyond midfield: wknd over 2f out: wl bhd after* **16/1**

231- **15** 2 ¼ **Rum Jungle**[248] 6194 5-9-0 **81** FergusSweeney 6 40
(H Candy) *in tch on outer: wknd wl over 2f out: sn bhd* **13/2**[2]

1m 25.86s (-1.54) **Going Correction** -0.075s/f (Good) **15** Ran SP% **124.8**
Speed ratings (Par 105): **105,101,100,99,98 96,96,95,94,94 94,93,91,84,82**
toteswinger: 1&2 £20.50, 1&3 £21.80, 2&3 £15.30 CSF £104.44 CT £743.44 TOTE £16.20: £4.70, £2.90, £3.00; EX 156.50 Place 6: £211.67 Place 5: £125.87.
Owner D G Clarke & C L A Edginton **Bred** Bearstone Stud **Trained** Lambourn, Berks

FOCUS
A fair handicap. The form is rated around the second, with a small step up from the winner.
Dingaan(IRE) Official explanation: jockey said gelding was denied a clear run
T/Jkpt: Not won. T/Plt: £991.10 to a £1 stake. Pool: £79,132.51. 58.28 winning tickets. T/Qpdt: £65.00 to a £1 stake. Pool: £6,770.27. 77.00 winning tickets. JN

2027 HAMILTON (R-H)
Friday, May 29

OFFICIAL GOING: Good to firm (good in places)
Due to dolling out of the rail, all races over 1m or further had approximately 25 yards added to the official race distance.
Wind: Light, half behind Weather: Sunny, hot

2435 NEILSLAND AND EARNOCK MAIDEN AUCTION STKS 5f 4y
2:10 (2:10) (Class 6) 2-Y-O **£2,729** (£806; £403) **Stalls Low**

Form RPR

1 **Rose Blossom** 2-8-8 0 TonyHamilton 9 87+
(R A Fahey) *mde virtually all: rdn clr fnl f: readily* **2/1**[1]

0 **2** 4 1/2 **Dazeen**[20] 1866 2-8-9 0 PJMcDonald 3 70+
(P T Midgley) *dwlt: sn wl bhd: hdwy over 1f out: chsd wnr ins fnl f: no imp* **100/1**

05 **3** 2 3/4 **Flaneur**[8] 2196 2-8-10 0 (b) PhillipMakin 7 61
(T D Easterby) *towards rr and sn drvn along: hdwy over 1f out: kpt on: n.d* **8/1**

03 **4** 1 **Lewyn**[13] 2089 2-8-7 0 PaulMulrennan 1 54
(K A Ryan) *w ldrs tl rdn and outpcd appr fnl f* **10/3**[3]

5420 **5** hd **Bronze Beau**[13] 2069 2-8-9 0 TomEaves 2 56
(Mrs L Stubbs) *cl up: drvn 1/2-way: outpcd fnl f* **9/4**[2]

6 **6** 5 **Rightcar**[10] 2153 2-8-10 0 LiamJones 6 39
(Peter Grayson) *midfield: drvn and outpcd 1/2-way: edgd rt over 1f out: n.d* **18/1**

050 **7** 1 **Bossy Kitty**[13] 2069 2-8-5 0 JoeFanning 5 30
(N Tinkler) *cl up tl rdn and wknd over 1f out* **25/1**

64 **8** 1 **Lord's Seat**[14] 2027 2-8-6 0 ow2 SladeO'Hara(5) 4 32
(A Berry) *sn outpcd and bhd: nvr on terms* **28/1**

040 **9** nk **Tagula Pearl (IRE)**[15] 2017 2-8-6 0 PatrickMathers 8 26
(I W McInnes) *midfield: drvn and outpcd 1/2-way: sn btn* **25/1**

57.95 secs (-2.05) **Going Correction** -0.40s/f (Firm) 2y crse rec **9** Ran SP% **115.7**
Speed ratings (Par 91): **100,92,88,86,86 78,76,75,74**
toteswinger: 1&2 £31.20, 1&3 £3.90, 2&3 £31.20 CSF £226.74 TOTE £3.40: £1.40, £14.80, £1.90; EX 197.60.
Owner J J Staunton **Bred** J R Mitchell **Trained** Musley Bank, N Yorks

FOCUS
Those with previous experience didn't look up to much, but it was hard not to be impressed by Rose Blossom, who looks Royal Ascot material.

NOTEBOOK
Rose Blossom ◆ broke an all-age track record which had stood since 1972, and was also 0.67 seconds quicker than the following 51-70 handicap. A £21,000 purchase who's bred for speed, she travelled better than anything under a really positive ride and drew well clear when coming under pressure inside the final 2f. An entry in the Hillary Needler earlier in the week gave a clue as to the regard in which she's held and this victory is all the more creditable considering her trainer was previously only 1-16 with first time out juveniles this season. Richard Fahey apparently thinks she's the best filly he's ever trained and the Queen Mary, for which Cashmans make her a 12/1 shot, is now the target. (tchd 11-4)
Dazeen achieved next to nothing on his debut over 6f at Haydock and this represented significant improvement. He was soon well in rear after a sluggish start, but gradually got the idea and finished well. Evidently still learning, there should be better to come again.
Flaneur might do better over 6f on slightly easier ground, but he looks only modest. (op 11-1 tchd 15-2)
Lewyn looks only selling class. Official explanation: jockey said filly hung right-handed throughout (op 3-1 tchd 5-2)
Bronze Beau is another who probably needs dropping in grade. (op 11-4 tchd 3-1)

2436 WEATHERBYS BLOODSTOCK INSURANCE H'CAP 5f 4y
2:45 (2:47) (Class 5) (0-70,66) 4-Y-0+ **£4,094** (£1,209; £604) **Stalls** Low

Form RPR

00-5 **1** **Sunley Sovereign**[26] 1695 5-8-2 **47** oh1 (b) SilvestreDeSousa 3 56
(Mrs R A Carr) *chsd ldrs: rdn and edgd rt 1/2-way: styd on to ld ins fnl f: drvn out* **12/1**

10-6 **2** 1 **Top Bid**[41] 1360 5-9-0 **59** (b) TomEaves 11 64
(T D Easterby) *cl up: led over 1f out to ins fnl f: r.o* **17/2**

-045 **3** 3/4 **Miss Daawe**[14] 2046 5-8-12 **62** LanceBetts(5) 12 65
(B Ellison) *prom: effrt 2f out: kpt on u.p fnl f* **11/2**[3]

60-0 **4** hd **Lake Chini (IRE)**[17] 1951 7-9-1 **60** (b) DaleGibson 1 62
(M W Easterby) *in tch: drvn over 2f out: r.o fnl f* **25/1**

00-4 **5** 1/2 **Jonny Ebeneezer**[7] 2224 10-8-6 **51** (be) LiamJones 4 51
(D Flood) *towards rr: drvn and hung rt 1/2-way: hdwy over 1f out: r.o fnl f* **5/1**[2]

0-00 **6** 1 1/4 **Dalarossie**[17] 1970 4-8-8 **56** AndrewMullen(3) 6 52
(E J Alston) *midfield: outpcd 1/2-way: sme hdwy over 1f out: nvr rchd ldrs* **9/1**

6000 **7** shd **Highland Warrior**[17] 1951 10-9-6 **65** PaulMulrennan 2 60
(P T Midgley) *bhd tl hdwy over 1f out: nvr rchd ldrs* **40/1**

0-04 **8** 3/4 **Joyeaux**[14] 2032 7-9-7 **66** DuranFentiman 10 59
(Ollie Pears) *towards rr: hdwy 2f out: wknd fnl f* **12/1**

0010 **9** nk **Andrasta**[7] 2225 4-8-6 **58** CharlotteKerton(7) 8 50
(A Berry) *in tch tl hung rt and outpcd over 2f out: n.d after* **25/1**

0-60 **10** 1/2 **Gelert (IRE)**[18] 1921 4-7-10 **48** oh2 ow1 (b) AndrewHeffernan(7) 7 38
(Peter Grayson) *led to over 1f out: sn wknd* **50/1**

1241 **11** 1 1/2 **Imperial Sword**[7] 2225 6-8-11 **63** (b) JanWilson(7) 9 47
(T D Barron) *bhd and outpcd: shkn up fnl f: nvr nr ldrs* **6/4**[1]

0-00 **12** 11 **Howards Prince**[18] 1921 6-8-5 **57** oh2 ow10 RossSmith(7) 5 2
(D A Nolan) *missed break: a bhd* **100/1**

58.62 secs (-1.38) **Going Correction** -0.40s/f (Firm) **12** Ran SP% **121.0**
Speed ratings (Par 103): **95,93,92,91,91 89,88,87,87,86 84,66**
toteswinger: 1&2 £15.20, 1&3 £14.10, 2&3 £9.60 CSF £107.71 CT £643.09 TOTE £12.70: £2.80, £3.10, £2.00; EX 130.10.
Owner David W Chapman **Bred** John B Sunley **Trained** Huby, N Yorks

FOCUS
A modest sprint handicap. The winner is probably the best guide to the form.
Imperial Sword Official explanation: jockey said, regarding running and riding, that her orders were to settle at the back of the field and make a run in the final 1 1/2f, adding that the gelding was outpaced and unable to keep in touch going down the hill.

2437 BOOK NOW FOR CASH FOR KIDS CLAIMING STKS 1m 3f 16y
3:20 (3:20) (Class 5) 4-6-Y-0 **£2,729** (£806; £403) **Stalls** High

Form RPR

4-50 **1** **Birkside**[16] 1990 6-8-13 78 DNolan 3 82
(Ollie Pears) *pressed ldr: led and rdn over 3f out: edgd lft and hld on wl fnl f* **5/4**[1]

45-5 **2** 1 3/4 **Visions Of Johanna (USA)**[8] 2197 4-9-7 83 TonyHamilton 2 87
(R A Fahey) *t.k.h: trckd ldrs: outpcd and rdn 3f out: hung rt: rallied to chse wnr ins fnl f: kpt on same pce* **5/4**[1]

100- **3** 2 1/4 **Ozone Trustee (NZ)**[172] 6288 5-8-11 82 PJMcDonald 1 73
(G A Swinbank) *led to over 3f out: one pce appr fnl f* **9/2**[2]

2m 23.87s (-1.73) **Going Correction** -0.25s/f (Firm) **3** Ran SP% **107.1**
Speed ratings: **96,94,93**
CSF £3.08 TOTE £2.50; EX 3.40.Birkside was claimed by Ken McGarrity for £12,000.
Owner We-Know Partnership **Bred** Pendley Farm **Trained** Norton, N Yorks

FOCUS
A small field, but all three are fair types for the grade. The early pace was predictably steady and this is muddling form, best rated around the winner.

2438 WEATHERBYS BANK H'CAP 6f 5y
3:55 (3:56) (Class 4) (0-80,80) 3-Y-0+ **£7,447** (£2,216; £1,107; £553) **Stalls** Low

Form RPR

-611 **1** **All The Nines (IRE)**[14] 2028 3-9-11 **79** SilvestreDeSousa 10 86
(Mrs D J Sanderson) *mde all: hrd pressed fnl f: hld on gamely* **4/1**[3]

0-06 **2** hd **Dazzling Bay**[21] 1849 9-9-13 **72** (b) DuranFentiman 3 80
(T D Easterby) *in tch: effrt and edgd rt 2f out: disp ld ins fnl f: kpt on: jst hld* **7/1**

0-13 **3** 1 1/4 **Pickering**[43] 1309 5-9-10 **72** (p) AndrewMullen(3) 4 76
(E J Alston) *trckd ldrs: effrt over 1f out: kpt on fnl f: hld towards fin* **11/4**[1]

2661 **4** 2 1/4 **Restless Genius (IRE)**[11] 2145 4-9-12 **71** 6ex TomEaves 6 68
(B Ellison) *t.k.h: trracked ldrs: effrt 2f out: no ex ins fnl f* **8/1**

1-00 **5** 2 1/4 **Elusive Fame (USA)**[13] 2072 3-9-12 **80** GregFairley 8 68
(M Johnston) *cl up: rdn over 2f out: wkng whn n.m.r ins fnl f* **10/1**

0052 **6** nk **Ingleby Arch (USA)**[6] 2276 6-9-11 **73** NeilBrown(3) 2 62
(T D Barron) *bhd: rdn over 2f out: edgd rt and sn no imp* **3/1**[2]

-506 **7** 3/4 **Chookie Heiton (IRE)**[26] 1695 11-8-3 **55** JamieKyne(7) 1 41
(I Semple) *bhd: drvn 1/2-way: n.d* **10/1**

69.91 secs (-2.29) **Going Correction** -0.40s/f (Firm)
WFA 3 from 4yo+ 9lb **7** Ran SP% **113.5**
Speed ratings (Par 105): **99,98,97,94,91 90,89**
toteswinger: 1&2 £4.40, 1&3 £2.90, 2&3 £3.80 CSF £30.92 CT £88.14 TOTE £4.30: £1.80, £3.80; EX 29.80.
Owner R J Budge **Bred** Deerpark Stud **Trained** Wiseton, Notts

FOCUS
A fair sprint handicap run in a decent time for the grade. The winner took another significant step forward.
Chookie Heiton(IRE) Official explanation: jockey said gelding hung right-handed

2439 JOHN HIGGINS "WIZARD OF WISHAW" MAIDEN STKS 6f 5y
4:30 (4:31) (Class 5) 3-Y-0+ **£2,729** (£806; £403) **Stalls** Low

Form RPR

62 **1** **Reject**[21] 1852 3-9-2 0 LiamJones 9 78+
(W J Haggas) *trckd ldrs: rdn to ld over 1f out: drew clr fnl f: readily* **8/13**[1]

0-03 **2** 5 **Rogalt (IRE)**[7] 2250 3-9-2 0 TomEaves 4 62
(B Smart) *w ldr: ev ch over 1f out: kpt on fnl f: no ch w wnr* **9/1**[3]

3 1 3/4 **Crime Writer (USA)** 3-9-2 0 GregFairley 1 56
(M Johnston) *trckd ldrs: effrt over 2f out: kpt on same pce fnl f* **7/2**[2]

50 **4** 2 1/4 **Trade Price (GR)**[29] 1617 3-9-2 0 PhillipMakin 2 49
(I Semple) *trckd ldrs tl rdn and wknd appr fnl f* **22/1**

2-6 **5** 1/2 **Istiqdaam**[11] 2142 4-9-11 0 DaleGibson 8 50
(M W Easterby) *outpcd and bhd: hdwy over 1f out: nvr rchd ldrs* **14/1**

6 10 **Raffanetti (IRE)** 3-9-2 0 PaulMulrennan 10 16
(T D Barron) *unruly in preliminaries: rn green in rr: no ch fr 1/2-way* **20/1**

7 1 **Tarus (IRE)**[310] 4319 5-9-1 46 SladeO'Hara(5) 7 9
(A Berry) *led to over 1f out: sn btn* **66/1**

8 hd **Beaumont Princess (IRE)** 3-8-11 0 PJMcDonald 3 7
(G A Swinbank) *s.i.s: nvr on terms* **33/1**

69.87 secs (-2.33) **Going Correction** -0.40s/f (Firm)
WFA 3 from 4yo+ 9lb **8** Ran SP% **114.4**
Speed ratings (Par 103): **99,92,90,87,86 73,71,71**
toteswinger: 1&2 £2.90, 1&3 £1.30, 2&3 £2.20 CSF £6.71 TOTE £1.50: £1.02, £2.00, £1.40; EX 6.10.
Owner B Haggas **Bred** Darley **Trained** Newmarket, Suffolk

FOCUS
A reasonable sprint maiden but there was little strength in depth. The form is rated through the second.
Beaumont Princess(IRE) Official explanation: jockey said filly was unsuited by the good to firm ground

2440 HAMILTON-PARK.CO.UK H'CAP (QUALIFIER FOR THE SCOTTISH TROPHY HANDICAP SERIES FINAL) 1m 1f 36y
5:05 (5:05) (Class 5) (0-70,76) 4-Y-0+ **£4,094** (£1,209; £604) **Stalls** High

Form RPR

0113 **1** **Sarwin (USA)**[3] 2362 6-8-11 **63** TomEaves 5 71
(G A Swinbank) *trckd ldrs: rdn to ld over 1f out: kpt on strly* **2/1**[1]

4561 **2** 2 3/4 **Moheebb (IRE)**[6] 2274 5-9-10 **76** 6ex (b) LiamJones 3 78
(Mrs R A Carr) *prom: rdn to ld over 2f out: hung lft and hdd over 1f out: kpt on same pce* **5/1**[3]

-003 **3** 2 **Kalasam**[8] 2200 5-8-12 **64** DaleGibson 4 62
(M W Easterby) *sn w ldrs: led over 4f out: passed 2f out: one pce over 1f out* **5/1**[3]

3-06 **4** 1 1/2 **Sarraaf (IRE)**[32] 1556 13-7-11 **56** oh6 JamieKyne(7) 1 51
(I Semple) *dwlt: hld up in tch: effrt over 2f out: edgd rt and no imp over 1f out* **28/1**

/0-0 **5** 11 **Toshi (USA)**[20] 1000 7-8-5 **57** PJMcDonald 2 29
(J S Goldie) *sn cl up: ev ch over 4f out: rdn over 3f out: wknd over 2f out* **9/4**[2]

6 29 **Chesapeake Bay**[91] 719 4-8-11 **63** (t) PaulMulrennan 6 —
(J J Lambe, Ire) *led to over 4f out: sn rdn: wknd over 3f out: t.o* **12/1**

1m 56.77s (-2.93) **Going Correction** -0.25s/f (Firm) **6** Ran SP% **108.6**
Speed ratings (Par 103): **103,100,98,97,87 61**
toteswinger: 1&2 £2.10, 1&3 £2.10, 2&3 £2.50 CSF £11.46 TOTE £2.50: £1.30, £3.00; EX 10.70.
Owner S Rudolf **Bred** Cynthia Knight **Trained** Melsonby, N Yorks

FOCUS
A weak handicap for the grade. It was steadily run and the form does not look that strong.
Chesapeake Bay Official explanation: jockey said gelding was unsuited by the good to firm ground

2441 J&S MONTGOMERY AMATEUR RIDERS' H'CAP 1m 65y
5:35 (5:35) (Class 6) (0-55,55) 4-Y-0+ **£2,307** (£709; £354) **Stalls** High

Form RPR

54-0 **1** **Botham (USA)**[10] 2158 5-10-8 **49** MrPNorton(5) 14 55
(J S Goldie) *hld up: hdwy over 2f out: swtchd lft over 1f out: led ins fnl f: jst hld on* **10/1**

5404 **2** shd **Singora Lady (IRE)**[7] 2245 4-10-6 **47** MissWGibson(5) 5 52+
(P T Midgley) *s.i.s: hld up: plenty to do 1/2-way: hdwy 2f out: styd on wl fnl f: jst failed* **4/1**[2]

-000 **3** 1 **Ninth House (USA)**[43] 1316 7-10-11 **52** (t) MissRachelClark(5) 9 55
(Mrs R A Carr) *hld up: hdwy centre 2f out: kpt on fnl f: nrst fin* **16/1**

0503 **4** 1 **Time To Regret**[35] 1496 9-11-5 **55** (p) MrsCBartley 13 56
(I W McInnes) *cl up: rdn over 2f out: ev ch ins fnl f: one pce* **12/1**

The Form Book, Raceform Ltd, Compton, RG20 6NL

-050 **5** ½ **Malinsa Blue (IRE)**[4] 2314 7-11-5 **55**............................(b) MissLEllison 8 55
(B Ellison) *in tch: rdn over 2f out: hung bdly both ways ins fnl f: kpt on* **17/2**[3]

0-06 **6** ½ **Crux**[24] 1769 7-10-5 **48**.. MissVBarr(7) 15 46
(R E Barr) *prom: effrt over 2f out: kpt on same pce fnl f* **28/1**

00/0 **7** *nk* **Neboisha**[7] 2244 5-10-5 **46** oh1...(b) MrSRees(5) 4 44
(M Wigham) *unruly in preliminaries: led to ins fnl f: no ex* **40/1**

26-0 **8** *1* **Reve Vert (FR)**[25] 1741 4-10-8 **49**.................................. MrTRDavid(5) 11 44
(Tim Vaughan) *prom: effrt over 2f out: one pce whn blkd ins fnl f* **10/1**

5-4 **9** *3* **Carpe Diem**[17] 1955 4-11-0 **55**....................................... MrsVFahey(5) 12 44
(R A Fahey) *towards rr: pushed along 3f out: sme late hdwy: nvr rchd ldrs* **11/4**[1]

0006 **10** 1¾ **Hurricane Coast**[11] 2134 10-10-9 **52**..........................(b) MissAHeath(7) 2 36
(D Flood) *hld up in midfield: rdn and hung rt over 2f out: nvr rchd ldrs* **40/1**

0-00 **11** 4½ **Shosolosa (IRE)**[7] 2246 7-10-10 **51**.............................. MrCAHarris(5) 6 25
(R C Guest) *hld up: rdn along over 3f out: nvr on terms* **25/1**

1320 **12** *2* **King Of Legend (IRE)**[70] 898 5-10-11 **54**...................... MrMEnnis(7) 3 24
(A G Foster) *prom tl rdn and wknd fr 3f out* **9/1**

0 **13** *5* **Call Me Al (IRE)**[98] 627 4-10-11 **52**........................... EJO'Connell(5) 10 10
(J J Lambe, Ire) *midfield: outpcd and hung rt 3f out: sn btn* **11/1**

000- **14** *10* **Grey Gurkha**[366] 2510 8-11-0 **50**... MrSDobson 7 —
(I W McInnes) *prom tl rdn and wknd fr over 3f out* **33/1**

1m 46.81s (-1.59) **Going Correction** -0.25s/f (Firm) **14** Ran SP% **122.4**
Speed ratings (Par 101): **97,96,95,94,94 93,93,92,89,87 83,81,76,66**
toteswinger: 1&2 £11.10, 1&3 £24.70, 2&3 £19.40 CSF £48.25 CT £668.07 TOTE £12.20: £3.40, £1.90, £5.30; EX 65.60 Place 6: £121.96 Place 5: £50.70.
Owner J S Morrison **Bred** France Weiner & Neal Hayias **Trained** Uplawmoor, E Renfrews
■ Stewards' Enquiry : Miss L Ellison two-day ban: careless riding (Jun 13, 15)

FOCUS
A very moderate amateur riders' handicap. It was well run and the first three came from the rear.
T/Plt: £244.90 to a £1 stake. Pool: £42,906.86. 127.85 winning tickets. T/Qpdt: £19.20 to a £1 stake. Pool: £3,299.56. 126.70 winning tickets. RY

2270 HAYDOCK (L-H)
Friday, May 29

OFFICIAL GOING: Good to soft (good in places; 6.7)
Races were run over 21yards further than advertised and the1m 6f race was reduced in distance by 20yards.
Wind: Light 1/2 behind Weather: Fine and sunny

2442 CHAMPAGNE LANSON GOLD LABEL VINTAGE H'CAP (FOR LADY AMATEUR RIDERS) 1m 2f 95y
6:40 (6:40) (Class 5) (0-70,69) 4-Y-0+ **£3,296** (£1,014; £507) **Stalls** High

Form RPR

0436 **1** **I'm In The Pink (FR)**[3] 2351 5-10-5 **67**.............................. MissEFolkes 8 77
(P D Evans) *in tch: effrt over 2f out: styd on to ld ins fnl f: hrd drvn and kpt on* **7/2**[3]

16-1 **2** 1¾ **Dream Of Olwyn (IRE)**[21] 1845 4-10-7 **69**............... MissSBrotherton 6 75
(J G Given) *led early: trckd ldrs: led over 3f out: hdd and no ex ins fnl f* **11/8**[1]

002 **3** *hd* **Ross Moor**[9] 2183 7-9-10 **58**.. MissEJJones 4 64
(Mike Murphy) *dwlt: hdwy on outside over 3f out: chsng ldrs 2f out: kpt on same pce fnl f* **10/3**[2]

6340 **4** *hd* **Hucking Heat (IRE)**[95] 656 5-9-12 **65**..................(p) MissRKneller(5) 1 70
(R Hollinshead) *hld up: hdwy over 3f out: swtchd rt over 1f out: styd on ins fnl f* **6/1**

0400 **5** *10* **Prince Golan (IRE)**[10] 2166 5-9-11 **64**..................(p) MissJCWilliams(5) 2 49
(J W Unett) *t.k.h: led after 3f: hdd over 3f out: wknd over 2f out* **14/1**

6006 **6** *7* **Grethel (IRE)**[7] 2246 5-9-7 **55** oh3...................................... MissADeniel 3 26
(A Berry) *in rr: sme hdwy whn bdly hmpd over 3f out: nt rcvr* **16/1**

0060 **7** *20* **Comeintothespace (IRE)**[7] 2222 7-9-0 **55** oh10......(p) MissCEReid(7) 5 —
(R A Farrant) *t.k.h in rr: lost tch 4f out* **33/1**

000- **8** *5* **Skylarker (USA)**[217] 6950 11-9-5 **58** oh3 ow3........... MissHCuthbert(5) 7 —
(T A K Cuthbert) *sn led: hdd after 3f: lost pl over 3f out: sn bhd* **66/1**

2m 18.48s (5.48) **Going Correction** +0.225s/f (Good) **8** Ran SP% **118.7**
Speed ratings (Par 103): **95,93,93,93,85 79,63,59**
toteswinger: 1&2 £2.10, 1&3 £4.60, 2&3 £2.40 CSF £9.09 CT £17.24 TOTE £4.70: £1.40, £1.20, £1.60; EX 12.90.
Owner S Flook **Bred** Mme Catherine Auniac **Trained** Pandy, Monmouths
■ Stewards' Enquiry : Miss H Cuthbert caution: careless riding.

FOCUS
The good to soft, good in places, going had dried out as a result of the warm, sunny weather. A modest lady amateur riders' handicap and not that competitive, with three of the eight racing from out of the handicap. In the end the race concerned four of the other five. The form looks sound.
Skylarker(USA) Official explanation: trainer said gelding was struck into

2443 RACING UK £12.99 PER MONTH H'CAP 5f
7:10 (7:11) (Class 4) (0-85,85) 3-Y-0 **£5,504** (£1,637; £818; £408) **Stalls** Centre

Form RPR

-054 **1** **Fivefootnumberone (IRE)**[22] 1803 3-8-11 **75**.......... GrahamGibbons 4 81
(J J Quinn) *w ldrs: led over 1f out: edgd lft: kpt on wl ins fnl f* **8/1**[3]

0346 **2** 1¼ **Green Onions**[15] 2005 3-8-2 **66**.. NickyMackay 10 67
(D J S Ffrench Davis) *led tl over 1f out: kpt on wl ins fnl f* **33/1**

-211 **3** *hd* **Gilt Edge Girl**[22] 1814 3-9-7 **85**.. PhilipRobinson 1 85
(C G Cox) *racd far side: chsd ldrs: chal 1f out: kpt on same pce* **7/2**[1]

00-6 **4** *hd* **Spiritofthewest (IRE)**[41] 1345 3-9-2 **80**........................ SteveDrowne 6 80
(D H Brown) *outpcd and lost pl after 2f: hdwy over 1f out: edgd lft: styd on strly towards fin* **16/1**

1162 **5** 1½ **Captain Carey**[11] 2140 3-8-12 **76**.................................... TGMcLaughlin 9 70+
(M S Saunders) *s.s: in rr tl hdwy and hung lft over 1f out: styd on ins fnl f* **9/1**

-454 **6** 1½ **Peninsular War**[14] 2058 3-8-9 **73**.................................... AndrewElliott 7 62
(K R Burke) *chsd ldrs: wknd over 1f out* **8/1**[3]

-132 **7** *5* **Servoca (CAN)**[20] 1879 3-9-7 **85**.................................... MichaelHills 11 56
(B W Hills) *racd stands' side: chsd ldrs: wknd over 1f out* **7/2**[1]

315- **8** ½ **Visterre (IRE)**[203] 7219 3-9-4 **82**................................... RoystonFfrench 2 51
(B Smart) *outpcd and bhd after 2f* **33/1**

41-1 **9** *nk* **Doctor Parkes**[21] 1824 3-9-4 **82**...................................... PatCosgrave 3 50
(E J Alston) *rr-div: hdwy over 2f out: chsng ldrs over 1f out: sn wknd* **9/2**[2]

10-0 **10** 2¼ **Gower Valentine**[35] 1486 3-8-13 **77**............................. AdrianTNicholls 8 37
(D Nicholls) *chsd ldrs: lost pl over 1f out* **20/1**

10-0 **11** 3½ **Blades Princess**[31] 1582 3-9-4 **82**.............................. StephenDonohoe 5 29
(E S McMahon) *chsd ldrs: lost pl over 1f out* **16/1**

61.07 secs (0.57) **Going Correction** +0.15s/f (Good) **11** Ran SP% **117.3**
Speed ratings (Par 101): **101,99,98,98,95 93,85,84,84,80 75**
toteswinger: 1&2 £29.90, 1&3 £8.20, 2&3 £19.80 CSF £247.38 CT £1102.25 TOTE £9.50: £1.70, £6.40, £1.70; EX 239.90.
Owner Maxilead Limited **Bred** Arne Stang **Trained** Settrington, N Yorks
■ Stewards' Enquiry : Graham Gibbons one-day ban: used whip with excessive frequency (Jun 13)

FOCUS
A decent sprint and pretty competitive, but with a tail wind springing up before the race, it proved best to race close to the pace. The winner returned to his easy-ground 2yo form.
Captain Carey ◆ Official explanation: jockey said gelding missed the break
Doctor Parkes Official explanation: trainer said gelding was unsuited by the good to soft (good in places) ground

2444 EBF MHA INT-ELECT MAIDEN STKS 6f
7:40 (7:40) (Class 5) 2-Y-O **£3,885** (£1,156; £577; £288) **Stalls** Centre

Form RPR

1 **Shakespearean (IRE)** 2-9-3 0.................................. RoystonFfrench 3 82+
(M Johnston) *mid-div: drvn and outpcd after 2f: hdwy and edgd lft 2f out: styd on to ld ins fnl f: kpt on strly* **7/1**[3]

2 3¼ **Il Forno** 2-9-3 0.. StephenDonohoe 5 72
(D Nicholls) *s.i.s: sn chsng ldrs: edgd rt and led 3f out: hdd and no ex ins fnl f* **20/1**

3 *hd* **Tamanaco (IRE)** 2-9-3 0.. GrahamGibbons 9 71
(T D Walford) *s.s: hdwy over 2f out: kpt on ins fnl f* **40/1**

6 **4** ½ **Abandagold (IRE)**[8] 2201 2-8-12 0................................. SteveDrowne 4 65
(A B Haynes) *chsd ldrs: n.m.r and swtchd lft over 1f out: kpt on wl ins fnl f* **11/1**

3 **5** *2* **Admin (IRE)**[27] 1669 2-9-3 0.. SebSanders 1 64
(R M Beckett) *trckd ldrs: t.k.h: rdn and edgd rt over 1f out: sn wknd* **5/6**[1]

6 ¾ **Victoire De Lyphar (IRE)** 2-9-3 0.............................. J-PGuillambert 8 64+
(P C Haslam) *sn pushed along and outpcd: rn v green: edgd lft 2f out: kpt on fnl f* **6/1**[2]

7 1¾ **Green For Luck (IRE)** 2-9-3 0....................................... MickyFenton 6 56
(T P Tate) *led 3f: outpcd and lost pl over 1f out* **11/1**

8 *hd* **Confessional** 2-9-3 0... PatCosgrave 2 56
(T D Easterby) *dwlt: sn trcking ldrs: t.k.h: wknd over 1f out* **7/1**[3]

0036 **9** *18* **Usquaebach**[10] 2167 2-8-9 0..(v) JackMitchell(3) 7 —
(H J Collingridge) *w ldrs: lost pl over 12f out: sn bhd: eased* **50/1**

1m 15.81s (1.81) **Going Correction** +0.15s/f (Good) **9** Ran SP% **119.7**
Speed ratings (Par 93): **93,88,88,87,85 84,81,81,57**
toteswinger: 1&2 £7.30, 1&3 £36.50, 2&3 £55.70 CSF £133.05 TOTE £6.10: £2.00, £4.90, £7.50; EX 99.40.
Owner Sheikh Hamdan Bin Mohammed Al Maktoum **Bred** Mrs H Owen **Trained** Middleham Moor, N Yorks

FOCUS
A race which has thrown up the odd good horse in recent years, such as Spinning Queen and Parasol, and several nicely bred newcomers were taking on the form selection, who did not reproduce his debut form. The winner did it well.

NOTEBOOK
Shakespearean(IRE) ◆ making an impressive winning start. An 80,000gns son of Shamardal from a family of Group-class performers, mainly in France, he has plenty of size about him but was a little green in the early stages. However, once his rider got serious he swept into the lead and was clear in no time. The Chesham is a possibility, although Royal Ascot may come too soon, but he looks a decent prospect in any case. (op 11-2 tchd 9-1)
Il Forno ◆, who is bred for speed, although there are middle-distance winners in the family, showed plenty of it on this debut. Picking up a maiden should be a formality and he can go on to better things. (op 14-1)
Tamanaco(IRE) ran a nice race, staying on steadily in the closing stages having missed the break, and looks up to winning races. (op 33-1)
Abandagold(IRE) improved on her debut the previous week and another step forward should see her pick up an ordinary fillies' maiden. (op 20-1)
Admin(IRE) was the disappointment of the race. His Goodwood form has started working out and, although keen early, when he hit the front over a furlong out he looked like scoring. However, when headed inside the last he stopped quickly as if he did not get the trip. (op 11-10 tchd 6-5 in places)
Victoire De Lyphar(IRE) was backed but looked rather green early before staying on to finish on the heels of the favourite. He can be expected to come on a fair amount for the experience. (tchd 5-1 and 13-2)

2445 GEORGE FORMBY BIRTHDAY H'CAP 1m 6f
8:10 (8:11) (Class 5) (0-70,70) 4-Y-0+ **£3,238** (£963; £481; £240) **Stalls** Low

Form RPR

5-50 **1** **Gifted Leader (USA)**[16] 1990 4-9-4 **70**...................... StephenDonohoe 6 85+
(Ian Williams) *hld up towards rr: hdwy 6f out: swtchd rt over 2f out: led on stands' side 1f out: drew readily clr: eased towards fin* **7/1**

02-2 **2** *4* **Ursis (FR)**[8] 2194 8-8-11 **70**.. MatthewDavies(7) 4 77
(S Gollings) *trckd ldrs: led 4f out: hdd 1f out: no ex* **6/1**[3]

00-4 **3** ½ **Twilight Dawn**[36] 1472 5-8-12 **64**................................. RoystonFfrench 13 70
(L Lungo) *s.v.s: hdwy over 3f out: chsng ldrs over 1f out: kpt on same pce: lame* **8/1**

1266 **4** 2¼ **Bold Adventure**[18] 1936 5-8-8 **60**............................... PhilipRobinson 2 63
(W J Musson) *dwlt: t.k.h in rr: hdwy over 3f out: chsng ldrs over 1f out: one pce* **7/1**

1-44 **5** 1¾ **Bollin Greta**[28] 1648 4-9-2 **68**.. SebSanders 3 69
(T D Easterby) *hld up in rr: hdwy over 5f out: chsng ldrs 2f out: one pce* **10/3**[1]

00-6 **6** *5* **Royal Premier (IRE)**[22] 1807 6-8-7 **62**......................(v) JackMitchell(3) 5 56
(H J Collingridge) *chsd ldrs: drvn over 5f out: wknd over 1f out* **66/1**

260- **7** ½ **Mcqueen (IRE)**[250] 5396 9-8-8 **60**................................... PatCosgrave 11 53
(B D Leavy) *led tl 4f out: wknd over 1f out* **28/1**

3652 **8** 1½ **Monaadi (IRE)**[4] 2337 4-8-5 **57**...(p) PaulQuinn 7 48
(R Hollinshead) *mid-div: drvn over 6f out: nvr a factor* **10/1**

06-5 **9** 3¾ **Moonwalking**[20] 1000 5-8-8 **60**.. AndrewElliott 9 46
(Jedd O'Keeffe) *prom: hdwy on outside to join ldrs over 6f out: lost pl over 1f out* **9/2**[2]

105- **10** *3* **Directa's Digger (IRE)**[290] 4955 5-8-13 **70**..............(p) JackDean(5) 10 51
(M J Scudamore) *t.k.h: trckd ldrs: wknd over 2f out: eased ins fnl f* **11/1**

-024 **11** *nk* **Drawn Gold**[37] 1454 5-8-9 **61**.. GrahamGibbons 1 42
(R Hollinshead) *chsd ldrs: hrd drvn over 5f out: lost pl over 1f out* **12/1**

3m 6.33s (2.03) **Going Correction** +0.225s/f (Good) **11** Ran SP% **121.7**
Speed ratings (Par 103): **103,100,100,99,98 95,95,94,92,90 90**
toteswinger: 1&2 £10.00, 1&3 £13.70, 2&3 £13.60 CSF £50.51 CT £352.19 TOTE £9.50: £2.60, £2.20, £3.20; EX 60.30.
Owner Gifted Leader Partners **Bred** Juddmonte Farms Inc **Trained** Portway, Worcs

FOCUS
A fair staying handicap. The winner did it well but overall this is ordinary form, if sound.

Twilight Dawn Official explanation: jockey said mare missed the break; vet said mare returned lame

2446 CHAMPAGNE LANSON ROSE LABEL NV MAIDEN STKS 1m 30y
8:40 (8:43) (Class 5) 3-Y-0+ **£3,238** (£963; £481; £240) **Stalls** Low

Form RPR
2-3 **1** **Broad Cairn**[13] 2080 3-9-2 0 SteveDrowne 4 80
(R Charlton) *trckd ldrs: led over 2f out: drvn rt out* **7/4**[1]
44- **2** *1* **Bessie Lou (IRE)**[234] 6565 3-8-11 0 AdrianTNicholls 13 73+
(K A Ryan) *led tl over 3f out: rallied over 1f out: no ex ins fnl f* **14/1**
2- **3** *3* **Tricky Situation**[240] 6392 3-8-11 0 PatCosgrave 14 66
(J G Given) *in rr: drvn over 4f out: styd on fnl 2f: nt rch ldrs* **4/1**[2]
06 **4** *2 ¾* **Peace Corps**[10] 2165 3-9-2 0 MichaelHills 8 65+
(J R Fanshawe) *s.i.s: sn shkn up: detached over 4f out: styd on fnl 3f: nvr nr to chal* **6/1**
5 *2* **Fernando Torres** 3-9-2 0 SebSanders 12 60+
(D Nicholls) *s.i.s: hdwy over 3f out: chsng ldrs 2f out: sn wknd* **9/2**[3]
6 **6** *½* **Arashi**[10] 2170 3-9-2 0 TGMcLaughlin 7 59
(Lucinda Featherstone) *mid-div: kpt on fnl 2f: nvr nr ldrs* **40/1**
7 *1 ½* **Evna (USA)** 3-8-11 0 StephenDonohoe 16 51+
(R A Fahey) *mid-div: drvn to join ldrs over 3f out: wknd over 1f out* **33/1**
0 **8** *hd* **Red Zoe (USA)**[11] 2139 3-8-11 0 MickyFenton 9 50
(M L W Bell) *s.i.s: mid-div: nvr a factor* **16/1**
9 *2 ¼* **Borromeo (USA)** 3-9-2 0 RoystonFfrench 5 50+
(M Johnston) *s.i.s: rr-div whn hmpd and hit rail 6f out: nvr on terms* **15/2**
6 **10** *3* **Cils Blancs (IRE)**[34] 1508 3-8-11 0 J-PGuillambert 2 38+
(B Smart) *w ldrs: led over 3f out: hdd over 2f out: wknd over 1f out* **33/1**
5-0 **11** *¾* **Da Bomber (IRE)**[7] 2229 4-10-0 0 GrahamGibbons 17 41+
(J W Unett) *hld up in rr: hmpd over 3f out: nvr a factor* **66/1**
0 **12** *6* **Willent**[12] 2104 3-9-2 0 AndrewElliott 10 28
(Miss J A Camacho) *prom: lost pl over 2f out* **100/1**
6- **13** *6* **Fantino**[304] 4497 3-9-2 0 PhilipRobinson 6 14
(J Mackie) *w ldrs: lost pl and eased 2f out* **14/1**
00- **14** *8* **Cool Libby (IRE)**[191] 7380 3-8-4 0 PNolan(7) 11 —
(A B Haynes) *w ldrs: lost pl 3f out* **66/1**
00 **15** *21* **Ellies Inspiration**[7] 2229 4-9-9 0 NickyMackay 15 —
(M Mullineaux) *trckd ldrs: lost pl over 3f out: sn wl bhd* **100/1**

1m 47.45s (3.65) **Going Correction** +0.225s/f (Good)
WFA 3 from 4yo 12lb **15** Ran SP% **133.1**
Speed ratings (Par 103): **90,89,86,83,81 80,79,79,76,73 73,67,61,53,32**
toteswinger: 1&2 £10.00, 1&3 £9.20, 2&3 £22.60 CSF £34.21 TOTE £2.80: £1.50, £3.80, £2.30; EX 37.80.
Owner The Queen **Bred** The Queen **Trained** Beckhampton, Wilts
■ Stewards' Enquiry : Seb Sanders one-day ban: careless riding (Jun 12)

FOCUS
An interesting maiden with very little experience amongst the 15 runners, nothing having run more than twice before. Probably fair maiden form.

2447 MAKE DRESSMAKER MAIDEN STKS 1m 2f 95y
9:10 (9:14) (Class 5) 3-Y-0+ **£3,238** (£963; £481; £240) **Stalls** High

Form RPR
0-40 **1** **Devotion To Duty (IRE)**[21] 1822 3-8-13 87 MichaelHills 2 83
(B W Hills) *chsd ldr: led after 2f: rdn and edgd lft over 1f out: hld on towards fin* **7/2**[2]
3 **2** *nk* **Sanctuary**[14] 2042 3-8-13 0 RoystonFfrench 9 82
(B Smart) *s.i.s: sn trcking ldrs: chal over 2f out: carried lft fnl f: no ex towards fin* **9/1**[3]
00-0 **3** *11* **Oke Bay**[31] 1579 3-8-5 50 (v[1]) JackMitchell(3) 8 55
(R M Beckett) *w ldrs: rdn and outpcd 3f out: kpt on to take modest 3rd jst ins fnl f* **50/1**
3-22 **4** *4 ½* **Decision**[13] 2077 3-8-13 86 PhilipRobinson 5 51
(C G Cox) *led 2f: chsd wnr: rdn over 3f out: wknd over 1f out* **1/2**[1]
04 **5** *1 ¼* **Gold Maha**[20] 1893 3-8-8 0 SamHitchcott 10 44
(M R Channon) *s.i.s: hld up towards rr: effrt over 2f out: sn rdn and no imp* **20/1**
5 **6** *nk* **Tesserae**[9] 2181 3-8-9 0 ow1 SteveDrowne 11 44
(A B Haynes) *in rr: effrt over 3f out: nvr on terms* **40/1**
7 *2* **Carsington**[14] 5-9-9 0 TGMcLaughlin 6 40
(Lucinda Featherstone) *s.i.s: hld up in rr: drvn 4f out: sn btn* **100/1**
00 **8** *4 ½* **Nouailhas**[17] 1972 3-8-10 0 RussellKennemore(3) 3 35
(R Hollinshead) *sn trcking ldrs: rdn and hung lft 3f out: wknd over 1f out* **200/1**
9 *2 ½* **Saxona (IRE)**[18] 5-9-9 0 StephenDonohoe 1 26
(Ian Williams) *s.i.s: sn chsng ldrs: drvn 4f out: sn wknd* **28/1**
10 *35* **Sleepy Silver**[36] 4-9-9 0 PatCosgrave 4 —
(J Mackie) *chsd ldrs 4f: lost pl over 4f out: bhd and eased 2f out: t.o* **50/1**

2m 18.11s (5.11) **Going Correction** +0.225s/f (Good)
WFA 3 from 4yo+ 14lb **10** Ran SP% **114.9**
Speed ratings (Par 103): **97,96,87,84,83 83,81,77,75,47**
toteswinger: 1&2 £5.20, 1&3 £18.60, 2&3 £48.30 CSF £31.08 TOTE £4.70: £1.60, £2.40, £12.10; EX 30.00 Place 6: £324.39, Place 5: £277.23.
Owner J Hanson & Cavendish Investing Ltd **Bred** Sorento Farm **Trained** Lambourn, Berks

FOCUS
An uncompetitive maiden with the market leaders setting the standard, having achieved ratings of 86 and 87 respectively. They went 20-1 bar three and the trio made the frame, although not in the expected order. The favourite ran poorly and the form is rated around the winner.
Decision Official explanation: trainer said gelding was unsuited by the dead ground
T/Plt: £287.20 to a £1 stake. Pool: £60,622.60. 154.07 winning tickets. T/Qpdt: £49.50 to a £1 stake. Pool: £3,462.22. 51.70 winning tickets. WG

[2153]MUSSELBURGH (R-H)
Friday, May 29

OFFICIAL GOING: Good to firm (8.2)
Winning post bend widened by 3 metres but effect on distances not notified.
Wind: Light against Weather: Dry and fine

2448 RACING UK HORSERACING IN YOUR HOME APPRENTICE H'CAP 1m 5f
6:20 (6:21) (Class 6) (0-65,62) 4-Y-0+ **£2,590** (£770; £385; £192) **Stalls** High

Form RPR
3434 **1** **Dramatic Solo**[5] 2294 4-9-7 62 (b) MartinLane(3) 2 70
(K R Burke) *mde all: sn clr: stdd pce 1/2-way: rdn along over 2f out: styd on strly fnl f* **11/10**[1]
-002 **2** *6* **Border Tale**[14] 2044 9-8-11 54 BillyCray(5) 4 53
(James Moffatt) *hld up in rr: pushed along and outpcd over 3f out: hdwy on outer 2f out: rdn and edgd lft ent fnl f: kpt on same pce* **4/1**[2]
600- **3** *¾* **Always Best**[9] 7042 5-8-3 46 AndrewHeffernan(5) 3 44
(R Allan) *chsd ldrs: effrt 3f out: rdn along over 2f out: drvn and outpcd over 1f out: kpt on u.p ins fnl f* **11/1**
0-40 **4** *nk* **Jane Of Arc (FR)**[16] 1648 5-8-8 49 (p) GaryBartley(3) 6 46
(J S Goldie) *chsd wnr: rdn along over 2f out: drvn over 1f out and sn one pce* **9/2**[3]
0-04 **5** *½* **Wulimaster (USA)**[10] 2159 6-8-5 50 ow4 RossSmith(7) 5 47
(D W Barker) *hld up in tch: hdwy over 5f out: chsd wnr wl over 2f out and sn rdn: drvn over 1f out and wknd ent fnl f* **11/2**

2m 50.05s (-1.95) **Going Correction** -0.35s/f (Firm) course record **5** Ran SP% **109.5**
Speed ratings (Par 101): **92,88,87,87,87**
toteswinger: 1&2 £1.60 CSF £5.70 TOTE £1.80: £1.10, £2.10; EX 5.80.
Owner Malih L Al Basti **Bred** Matthews Breeding And Racing Ltd **Trained** Middleham Moor, N Yorks

FOCUS
As weak a handicap as you will see all year and none of the five had a remotely convincing profile, so not form to be dwelling on. The winner is rated back to form.

2449 EUROPEAN BREEDERS' FUND MAIDEN STKS 5f
6:50 (6:50) (Class 5) 2-Y-O **£3,885** (£1,156; £577; £288) **Stalls** Low

Form RPR
1 **Capercaillie (USA)** 2-8-12 0 GregFairley 6 84+
(M Johnston) *prom: hdwy to ld over 2f out: rdn over 1f out: drvn ins fnl f and kpt onwl* **9/4**[2]
2 *nk* **Exgray (IRE)** 2-8-7 0 GaryBartley(5) 4 84+
(B Smart) *s.i.s and in rr: hdwy 1/2-way: swtchd rt and rdn to chse ldrs over 1f out: styd on strly ins fnl f: jst failed* **5/1**
6 **3** *5* **Makbullet**[18] 1920 2-9-0 0 NeilBrown(3) 2 70
(J Howard Johnson) *cl up: led after 1f: rdn along and hdd over 2f out: kpt on same pce appr fnl f* **16/1**
2 **4** *2* **Pepper Lane**[21] 1847 2-8-12 0 PhillipMakin 1 58
(T D Barron) *cl up: rdn to chse wnr 2f out: drvn over 1f out: sn wknd* **2/1**[1]
5 *5* **Ducal Destiny** 2-9-3 0 TonyHamilton 3 45
(J R Weymes) *sn outpcd and a bhd* **50/1**
0 **P** **Whelkeen Rock (IRE)**[8] 2195 2-9-3 0 JoeFanning 7 —
(K A Ryan) *wnt rt s: chsd ldrs tl p.u after 1f: lame* **3/1**[3]

60.46 secs (0.06) **Going Correction** -0.225s/f (Firm) **6** Ran SP% **113.6**
Speed ratings (Par 93): **90,89,81,78,70**
toteswinger: 1&2 £1.40, 1&3 £7.00, 2&3 £12.10 CSF £14.07 TOTE £3.80: £1.90, £3.30; EX 19.10.
Owner Sheikh Hamdan Bin Mohammed Al Maktoum **Bred** R Michael O'Malley **Trained** Middleham Moor, N Yorks

FOCUS
This looked a run-of-the-mill event on paper but it may well have thrown up a couple of above-average fillies. Both the front pair are nice prospects and this is a race to be positive about.

NOTEBOOK
Capercaillie(USA), who cost $375,000 as a yearling, is evidently held in high regard given her Listed-race entries and showed terrific early speed to lay up with two rivals who had the benefit of a run before taking over well over a furlong out and drawing right away. This was a performance of immense promise and connections must surely have to give the Queen Mary serious thought now. (op 5-2 tchd 11-4)
Exgray(IRE) ◆ ran a totally different race to the winner, yet one with almost as much promise. She was outpaced early and got behind, but the further she went the better she picked up and she stormed home down the middle of the track to pull clear of the third. She looks sure to come on a bundle for this and looks one to keep on the right side of. (op 7-2 tchd 6-1)
Makbullet showed up well for over 3f but he was left behind at the business end and his limitations have been exposed here. (op 18-1)
Pepper Lane was the biggest disappointment, having run so well on her debut. She was bang there early but her response from the two-pole was very one-paced and she has taken a step backwards here. (op 5-2)

2450 TURFTV BETTING SHOP SERVICE H'CAP 7f 30y
7:20 (7:20) (Class 5) (0-70,70) 3-Y-O **£3,885** (£1,156; £577; £288) **Stalls** High

Form RPR
-020 **1** **Island Chief**[7] 2236 3-8-10 59 (p) TonyHamilton 3 66
(K A Ryan) *chsd ldr: effrt over 2f out: rdn wl over 1f out: drvn ins fnl f: styd on to ld nr fin* **11/2**[3]
026- **2** *½* **Liberty Trail (IRE)**[253] 6037 3-9-5 68 TomEaves 5 74
(I Semple) *led: rdn over 2f out: drvn ins fnl f: hdd and no ex nr fin* **14/1**
6-04 **3** *2 ¾* **Red China Blues (USA)**[14] 2042 3-9-3 66 PaulMulrennan 7 64
(J Howard Johnson) *chsd ldrs on inner: effrt over 2f out: rdn wl over 1f out: kpt on same pce u.p ins fnl f* **8/1**
-223 **4** *3 ¼* **Diamond Daisy (IRE)**[13] 2091 3-8-8 64 BMcHugh(7) 4 53
(Mrs A Duffield) *hld up towards rr: hdwy 1/2-way: swtchd outside and rdn along 3f out: styd on to chse ldrs wl over 1f out: sn drvn and no imp* **10/3**[2]
-124 **5** *shd* **Rising Kheleyf (IRE)**[13] 2072 3-9-7 70 PJMcDonald 6 59
(G A Swinbank) *hld up in tch: hdwy 3f out: effrt to chse ldrs 2f out: sn rdn and btn* **1/1**[1]
0000 **6** *2* **Hit The Switch**[7] 2227 3-8-10 62 KellyHarrison(3) 2 46
(Patrick Morris) *a in rr* **25/1**
0606 **7** *23* **Wee Bizzom**[10] 2154 3-7-9 51 oh6 CharlotteKerton(7) 1 —
(A Berry) *prom: rdn along 3f out: sn wknd* **80/1**
0-00 **8** *1 ¾* **Pennine Rose**[21] 1852 3-7-9 51 oh6 BillyCray(7) 9 —
(A Berry) *a towards rr* **100/1**

1m 28.0s (-2.30) **Going Correction** -0.35s/f (Firm) **8** Ran SP% **112.3**
Speed ratings (Par 99): **99,98,95,91,91 89,62,60**
toteswinger: 1&2 £7.40, 1&3 £3.40, 2&3 £11.20 CSF £71.37 CT £612.31 TOTE £8.10: £1.70, £2.10, £1.90; EX 26.40.
Owner The C H F Partnership **Bred** The C H F Partnership **Trained** Hambleton, N Yorks

FOCUS
The market had this down as a one-horse race with Rising Kheleyf backed as if defeat were out of the question, yet it proved anything but with the favourite running well below expectations. The pace was strong and nothing got into it from the rear. The form is rated around the third.
Wee Bizzom Official explanation: jockey said filly bled from the nose

2451 SCOTTISH RACING (S) STKS 5f
7:50 (7:50) (Class 6) 3-Y-0+ **£2,590** (£770; £385; £192) **Stalls** Low

Form RPR
0523 **1** **Blue Tomato**[9] 2185 8-9-2 74 (p) JamieKyne(7) 8 71
(D Nicholls) *in tch: pushed along 1/2-way: rdn to chse ldrs whn n.m.r over 1f out: squeezed through ins fnl f and styd on to ld on line* **7/4**[1]

0415 **2** *shd* **Northern Empire (IRE)**[3] 2359 6-9-9 70........................(p) JoeFanning 11 71
(K A Ryan) *s.i.s and bhd: gd hdwy on outer 2f out: rdn over 1f out: styd on strly to ld ins fnl f: hdd and nt qckn on line* **4/1**[3]

2-13 **3** *1 1/4* **Raccoon (IRE)**[24] 1768 9-9-9 68........................ PJMcDonald 4 66
(Mrs R A Carr) *chsd clr ldr: rdn wl over 1f out: drvn to ld briefly ins fnl f: sn hdd and no ex* **7/2**[2]

0-00 **4** *nk* **Dubai To Barnsley**[120] 327 4-8-10 45................ AndrewHeffernan(7) 5 59
(D A Nolan) *chsd ldrs: rdn along wl over 1f out: n.m.r and swtchd lft ent fnl f: kpt on* **66/1**

40-0 **5** *1* **Cayman Fox**[24] 1768 4-8-12 65........................ PhillipMakin 1 50
(James Moffatt) *qckly away and sn clr: rdn along 2f out: jnd and hung rt over 1f out: hdd & wknd ins fnl f* **10/1**

6540 **6** *1/2* **Silvanus (IRE)**[14] 2032 4-9-3 69........................ TomEaves 9 54
(I Semple) *chsd clr ldr: hdwy and cl up wl over 1f out: sn drvn and grad wknd* **9/2**

4-06 **7** *3 1/2* **Angelofthenorth**[10] 2158 7-8-7 47........................ LanceBetts(5) 10 36
(C J Teague) *in rr: sme hdwy on outer 2f out: sn rdn and no imp* **20/1**

000 **8** *3* **Mr Rooney (IRE)**[26] 1695 6-9-4 52........................ SladeO'Hara(5) 3 36
(A Berry) *a towards rr* **25/1**

0006 **9** *1* **Seafield Towers**[1] 2389 9-9-3 41........................(p) GregFairley 6 27
(D A Nolan) *in tch: rdn along and lost pl 1/2-way: sn bhd* **100/1**

000- **10** *1 1/4* **Sokoke**[280] 5220 8-8-10 30........................ RossSmith(7) 7 22
(D A Nolan) *a in rr* **200/1**

500- **11** *3/4* **Mutayam**[289] 4971 9-9-3 41........................(t) PaulMulrennan 2 19
(D A Nolan) *a in rr* **200/1**

58.70 secs (-1.70) **Going Correction** -0.225s/f (Firm)
WFA 3 from 4yo+ 8lb **11** Ran SP% **117.9**
Speed ratings (Par 101): **104,103,101,101,99 98,93,88,86,84 83**
toteswinger: 1&2 £2.80, 1&3 £1.70, 2&3 £3.00 CSF £8.72 TOTE £2.50: £1.50, £2.10, £1.20; EX 11.80.There was no bid for the winner.
Owner Dab Hand Racing **Bred** Bearstone Stud **Trained** Sessay, N Yorks

FOCUS
A scorching pace to this 5f seller set the race up for the finishers. The proximity of the fourth is a bit puzzling.

2452 SCOTTISH RACING YOUR BETTER BET H'CAP 1m 6f
8:20 (8:20) (Class 4) (0-85,80) 4-Y-O+
£6,231 (£1,866; £933; £467; £233; £117) **Stalls** High

Form RPR

3232 **1** **Dazzling Light (UAE)**[16] 1990 4-9-1 **74**........................ DanielTudhope 6 82+
(J S Goldie) *trckd ldrs: effrt 2f out: nt clr run and hmpd over 1f out: sn swtchd lft and drvn: styd on ins fnl f to ld on line* **3/1**[2]

4352 **2** *nse* **Step This Way (USA)**[6] 2283 4-9-3 **76**........................ GregFairley 4 83
(M Johnston) *trckd ldr: cl up over 3f out: led over 2f out: rdn and hdd over 1f out: drvn and rallied to ld again ins fnl f: hdd on line* **4/1**[3]

3131 **3** *nk* **That'll Do Nicely (IRE)**[28] 1648 6-8-7 **66**........................ TomEaves 1 73
(N G Richards) *hld up in rr: smooth hdwy on outer over 2f out: shkn up to ld over 1f out: drvn and hdd ins fnl f: ev ch tl no ex nr fin* **11/4**[1]

30-0 **4** *2 1/2* **Luna Landing**[34] 1519 6-8-13 **72**........................ TonyHamilton 7 75
(Jedd O'Keeffe) *led: rdn along over 3f out: hdd over 2f out: drvn and wknd appr fnl f* **8/1**

20/2 **5** *3/4* **Sonara (IRE)**[58] 1058 5-8-10 **69**........................ PaulMulrennan 3 71
(J Howard Johnson) *trckd ldrs: effrt 3f out: rdn over 2f out: sn drvn and wknd appr fnl f* **14/1**

5-56 **6** *1 1/4* **Dzesmin (POL)**[16] 1990 7-9-0 **80**........................ BMcHugh(7) 2 80
(R A Fahey) *hld up: effrt on inner 3f out: chsd ldrs over 2f out: sn rdn and wknd* **3/1**[2]

3m 2.68s (-2.62) **Going Correction** -0.35s/f (Firm) **6** Ran SP% **114.4**
Speed ratings (Par 105): **93,92,92,91,90 90**
toteswinger: 1&2 £2.20, 1&3 £2.10, 2&3 £2.30 CSF £15.71 TOTE £5.00: £2.40, £2.10; EX 20.30.

Owner M Mackay, S Bruce, J S Goldie **Bred** Darley **Trained** Uplawmoor, E Renfrews

FOCUS
Just an even gallop. The form reads sound enough.

2453 TURFTV H'CAP 7f 30y
8:50 (8:50) (Class 5) (0-70,68) 4-Y-O+ **£3,885** (£1,156; £577; £288) **Stalls** High

Form RPR

-060 **1** **Woodsley House (IRE)**[21] 1832 7-9-1 **68**........................ NeilBrown(3) 1 75
(A G Foster) *t.k.h on outer: led after 1f and sn clr: rdn along over 2f out: drvn and edgd rt ins fnl f: hld on gamely* **20/1**

4-04 **2** *1/2* **Infinity Bond**[10] 2156 4-8-12 **62**........................ PJMcDonald 5 68
(G R Oldroyd) *led 1f: trckd wnr: smooth hdwy and cl up over 2f out: rdn over 1f out: drvn and ev ch ins fnl f tl no ex towards fin* **7/1**

00-4 **3** *1* **Optical Illusion (USA)**[28] 1650 5-7-11 **54** oh1.............. JamieKyne(7) 9 60+
(R A Fahey) *trckd ldng pair on inner: effrt over 2f out: rdn over 1f out: styng on whn n.m.r and hmpd ins fnl f: nt rcvr* **4/1**[1]

3223 **4** *1* **Kargan (IRE)**[6] 2269 4-8-10 **60**........................ TonyHamilton 3 61
(A G Foster) *hld up: hdwy on inner over 2f out: sn rdn and kpt on ins fnl f: n.d* **9/2**[2]

3502 **5** *2* **Kabis Amigos**[10] 2156 7-8-13 **63**........................(b) PaulMulrennan 6 58
(Ollie Pears) *t.k.h: hld up towards rr: hdwy over 2f out: rdn to chse ldrs wl over 1f out: sn drvn and no imp* **6/1**[3]

500- **6** *nk* **Imperial Echo (USA)**[181] 7497 8-8-0 **55** oh1 ow1.......... MartinLane(5) 4 49
(T D Barron) *chsd ldrs: rdn along 2f out: sn drvn and wknd over 1f out* **13/2**

6-61 **7** *4* **Stellite**[10] 2156 9-8-13 **68** 6ex........................ GaryBartley(5) 2 52
(J S Goldie) *hld up in rr: effrt and hdwy on outer 2f over 2f out: rdn over 1f out: sn btn* **4/1**[1]

0310 **8** *2 1/2* **Angaric (IRE)**[10] 2156 6-9-2 **66**........................ TomEaves 7 43
(B Smart) *chsd ldrs: rdn along over 2f out: sn drvn and wknd* **7/1**

1m 31.55s (1.25) **Going Correction** -0.35s/f (Firm) **8** Ran SP% **115.6**
Speed ratings (Par 103): **78,77,76,75,72 72,67,65**
toteswinger: 1&2 £12.60, 1&3 £12.00, 2&3 £8.10 CSF £152.73 CT £687.70 TOTE £23.70: £5.60, £3.00, £1.70; EX 136.90.
Owner Mrs V L Davis **Bred** Roger G English **Trained** Haddington, East Lothian

FOCUS
A farcical early pace meant most pulled hard early and this isn't form to be taking too literally.

2454 RACING UK £12.99 PER MONTH H'CAP 5f
9:20 (9:22) (Class 6) (0-65,68) 3-Y-O **£2,590** (£770; £385; £192) **Stalls** Low

Form RPR

04-0 **1** **Secret Venue**[34] 1505 3-9-4 **62**........................ TonyHamilton 5 64
(Jedd O'Keeffe) *cl up: rdn wl over 1f out: drvn to ld jst ins fnl f: hld on wl* **7/2**[3]

2431 **2** *hd* **Dispol Grand (IRE)**[1] 2394 3-9-10 **68** 6ex........................ PaulMulrennan 3 69
(P T Midgley) *led: rdn along wl over 1f out: drvn and hdd ins fnl f: rallied gamely nr fin* **11/4**[2]

-100 **3** *1/2* **Iachimo**[10] 2162 3-8-6 **55**........................(v[1]) MartinLane(5) 2 54
(K R Burke) *chsd ldrs on inner: effrt and n.m.r over 1f out: swtchd rt and drvn ent fnl f: ev ch tl nt qckn towards fin* **10/1**

3125 **4** *2 1/4* **Compton Ford**[1] 2394 3-9-7 **65**........................ PhillipMakin 6 56
(M Dods) *chsd ldrs: cl up 2f out: sn rdn and one pce ent fnl f* **9/4**[1]

50-0 **5** *5* **Pollish**[7] 2250 3-7-9 **46** oh1........................ BillyCray(7) 8 19
(A Berry) *chsd ldrs on outer: rdn along 1/2-way: sn wknd* **33/1**

5-00 **6** *hd* **Miss Thippawan (USA)**[58] 1064 3-7-9 **46** oh1.............. JamieKyne(7) 4 18
(P T Midgley) *outpcd and bhd fr 1/2-way* **25/1**

4613 **U** **Pinball (IRE)**[10] 2162 3-9-0 **61**........................(v) KellyHarrison(3) 1 —
(Patrick Morris) *rrd and uns rdr s* **4/1**

59.65 secs (-0.75) **Going Correction** -0.225s/f (Firm) **7** Ran SP% **115.5**
Speed ratings (Par 97): **97,96,95,92,84 83,—**
toteswinger: 1&2 £3.00, 1&3 £4.30, 2&3 £5.50 CSF £13.89 CT £86.46 TOTE £5.60: £1.90, £2.30; EX 12.60 Place 6: £96.13, Place 5: £77.81.
Owner Ken And Delia Shaw-KGS Consulting LLP **Bred** Sherwoods Transport Ltd **Trained** Middleham Moor, N Yorks

■ Stewards' Enquiry : Jamie Kyne two-day ban: used whip with excessive frequency without giving filly time to respond (Jun 12-13)

FOCUS
A tight finish to this low-grade sprint handicap. The pace was fast and furious and the front two were always front rank. The winner probably didn't need to improve on last year's nursery form.
T/Plt: £345.10 to a £1 stake. Pool: £49,641.25. 104.99 winning tickets. T/Qpdt: £43.40 to a £1 stake. Pool: £3,516.24. 59.90 winning tickets. JR

2413 YARMOUTH (L-H)
Friday, May 29

OFFICIAL GOING: Good to firm (good in places) changing to good to firm after race 4 (3.45)
Wind: Light half-against Weather: Fine, warm and sunny

2455 YARMOUTH STADIUM MEDIAN AUCTION MAIDEN STKS 6f 3y
2:00 (2:02) (Class 6) 3-5-Y-O **£2,590** (£770; £385; £192) **Stalls** High

Form RPR

-2 **1** **Lochan Mor**[13] 2070 3-9-3 0........................ JamieSpencer 9 75
(M L W Bell) *chsd ldr: hrd rdn fr over 1f out: hung lft and led ins fnl f: styd on* **1/4**[1]

6 **2** *1 3/4* **Quasi Congaree (GER)**[21] 1837 3-9-3 0........................ GeorgeBaker 6 70
(I A Wood) *led: rdn: edgd lft and hdd ins fnl f: styd on same pce* **20/1**[3]

0-40 **3** *2* **Sweet Possession (USA)**[34] 1509 3-8-12 68.............. RichardMullen 8 58
(A P Jarvis) *s.i.s: sn prom: swtchd lft and rdn over 2f out: styd on same pce fnl f* **7/1**[2]

6-00 **4** *4 1/2* **Athboy Auction**[29] 1634 4-9-0 47........................(t) RosieJessop(7) 3 46
(H J Collingridge) *s.s: outpcd: rdn and hung rt over 1f out: styd on ins fnl f: nvr nrr* **33/1**

0455 **5** *3* **Chantilly Jewel (USA)**[40] 1379 4-9-7 59........................(p) ShaneKelly 2 36
(R M H Cowell) *hld up: hdwy 1/2-way: rdn and wknd over 1f out* **33/1**

0- **6** *6* **Expensive Dinner**[287] 5066 3-8-7 0........................ MarkFlynn(5) 1 15
(E F Vaughan) *chsd ldrs: rdn 1/2-way: sn wknd* **40/1**

4360 **7** *4* **Thoosa**[59] 1045 3-8-12 49........................ LukeMorris 7 —
(P S McEntee) *prom: rdn and wkng whn hung rt over 3f out* **125/1**

50-0 **8** *2 1/2* **Shirley High**[114] 390 3-8-12 48........................(t) JimmyQuinn 4 —
(P Howling) *prom: lost pl over 4f out: sn bhd* **66/1**

9 *16* **Ivy The Terrible** 3-8-12 0........................ RichardThomas 5 —
(Dr J D Scargill) *dwlt: outpcd* **22/1**

1m 13.6s (-0.80) **Going Correction** -0.10s/f (Good)
WFA 3 from 4yo 9lb **9** Ran SP% **112.2**
Speed ratings (Par 101): **101,98,96,90,86 78,72,69,48**
toteswinger: 1&2 £2.70, 1&3 £1.10, 2&3 £5.10 CSF £9.12 TOTE £1.20: £1.02, £3.70, £1.50; EX 6.50 Trifecta £17.90 Pool: £478.22 - 19.72winning units.
Owner A Buxton **Bred** Andrew Buxton **Trained** Newmarket, Suffolk

FOCUS
This was a weak maiden and red-hot favourite Lochan Mor made hard work of winning despite a lack of solid opposition.
Thoosa Official explanation: jockey said filly hung right

2456 EAST COAST ENERGY ASSESSORS CLAIMING STKS 6f 3y
2:35 (2:36) (Class 6) 3-Y-O+ **£1,942** (£578; £288; £144) **Stalls** High

Form RPR

5-00 **1** **Hinton Admiral**[14] 2045 5-9-9 77........................ JimmyQuinn 10 77
(R A Fahey) *hmpd sn after s: hdwy 5f out: shkn up to ld over 1f out: r.o wl* **5/1**[3]

34-4 **2** *4* **Leftontheshelf (IRE)**[18] 1923 3-8-7 78........................(p) TolleyDean 6 55
(J L Spearing) *chsd ldrs: rdn and ev ch over 1f out: styd on same pce ins fnl f* **2/1**[1]

0224 **3** *1 1/4* **Caribbean Coral**[3] 2349 10-9-8 63........................ GeorgeBaker 13 59
(A B Haynes) *hld up: hdwy over 2f out: rdn and hung lft over 1f out: styd on same pce: wnt 3rd post* **15/2**

5-35 **4** *nse* **Jack's House (IRE)**[117] 366 3-8-4 51........................(t) AndreaAtzeni(5) 15 53
(Jane Chapple-Hyam) *s.i.s: pushed along thrght: hdwy u.p over 1f out: styd on* **12/1**

-530 **5** *shd* **Sweet Applause (IRE)**[14] 2058 3-8-11 71.............. RichardMullen 14 55
(A P Jarvis) *led: rdn and hdd over 1f out: no ex ins fnl f* **9/2**[2]

5220 **6** *3 1/4* **Creative (IRE)**[11] 2134 4-9-7 53........................ TedDurcan 5 47
(M H Tompkins) *hld up: hdwy over 2f out: rdn over 1f out: wknd fnl f* **12/1**

00-0 **7** *1 1/4* **Goodbye Cash (IRE)**[8] 2202 5-8-8 58........................ RichardEvans(5) 3 35
(P D Evans) *s.i.s: sn mid-div: hdwy over 3f out: rdn and wknd over 1f out* **18/1**

0-04 **8** *hd* **Rough Rock (IRE)**[11] 2137 4-9-1 48........................ CharlesEddery(7) 2 43
(C A Dwyer) *chsd ldrs: rdn over 2f out: wknd over 1f out* **25/1**

00-4 **9** *4 1/2* **Talamahana**[23] 1784 4-9-0 43........................ ChrisCatlin 4 21
(A B Haynes) *chsd ldrs tl wknd 1/2-way* **33/1**

6000 **10** *1 1/4* **Whinhill House**[11] 2130 9-8-10 59........................(v) JosephineBruning(7) 11 20
(T T Clement) *chsd ldrs: rdn over 2f out: wknd over 1f out* **50/1**

20-6 **11** *2 3/4* **Sonhador**[7] 2219 3-8-12 70........................ AdrianMcCarthy 12 13
(G Prodromou) *hld up: rdn 1/2-way: a in rr* **10/1**

6046 **12** *2* **Young Ivanhoe**[7] 2224 4-8-11 52........................(v) AmyBaker(5) 9 4
(C A Dwyer) *chsd ldrs tl rdn and wknd over 2f out* **40/1**

0000 **13** 3 ¾ **So Sublime**[21] 1848 4-8-13 34 ..... LeeVickers(3) 7 —
(M C Chapman) *chsd ldrs: lost pl over 3f out: sn bhd* **100/1**

1m 13.2s (-1.20) **Going Correction** -0.10s/f (Good)
WFA 3 from 4yo+ 9lb **13** Ran SP% **121.9**
Speed ratings (Par 101): **104,98,97,96,96 92,90,90,84,82 79,76,71**
toteswinger: 1&2 £5.40, 1&3 £4.50, 2&3 £5.50 CSF £15.14 TOTE £5.60: £2.00, £1.60, £2.60; EX 21.10 Trifecta £61.90 Pool: £451.14 - 5.39 winning units.Hinton Admiral was claimed by G.F. Bridgwater for £10,000. Jack's House was claimed by Miss Julie Camacho for £5,000.
Owner Aidan J Ryan Racing I **Bred** Gainsborough Stud Management Ltd **Trained** Musley Bank, N Yorks

FOCUS
This claimer was turned into a bit of a rout by Hinton Admiral, who came right back to form on this drop in grade. Ordinary form for the grade.
Goodbye Cash(IRE) Official explanation: trainer's rep said mare was unsuited by the good to firm (good in places) ground
Sonhador Official explanation: jockey said colt lost its action

2457 LINDLEY CATERING - OFFICIAL RACECOURSE CATERERS (S) STKS 5f 43y
3:10 (3:12) (Class 6) 2-Y-O **£1,942** (£578; £288; £144) **Stalls** High

Form RPR
3 **1** **On The Piste (IRE)**[20] 1884 2-8-7 0 ..... FrankieMcDonald 5 57
(P T Midgley) *s.i.s: sn chsng ldrs: rdn to ld and hung lft fr over 1f out: styd on* **3/1**[2]
00 **2** *nse* **Angie's Nap (USA)**[11] 2135 2-8-7 0 ..... DO'Donohoe 8 57
(E A L Dunlop) *s.i.s: sn prom: led 1/2-way: rdn and hdd over 1f out: sn hung lft: styd on* **9/2**[3]
50 **3** *nk* **Michaelmas Daisy**[56] 1090 2-8-2 0 ..... AndreaAtzeni(5) 1 56
(Miss Amy Weaver) *sn outpcd: hdwy over 1f out: rdn and carried lft ins fnl f: r.o* **11/10**[1]
05 **4** 4 ½ **Jackie Danny**[21] 1835 2-8-7 0 ..... SaleemGolam 7 40
(C A Dwyer) *led to 1/2-way: rdn over 1f out: wknd ins fnl f* **9/1**
0604 **5** 3 ¾ **Needwood Dancer**[18] 1934 2-8-7 0 ..... (b[1]) AdrianMcCarthy 3 26
(Peter Grayson) *s.s: in rr and pushed along: hdwy u.p 2f out: hung rt over 1f out: sn wknd* **20/1**
05 **6** 7 **Barton Chancer**[28] 1637 2-8-7 0 ..... TolleyDean 2 —
(W G M Turner) *prom: rdn 1/2-way: wknd over 1f out* **18/1**
06 **7** 12 **Dinky Deb**[18] 1934 2-8-7 0 ..... ChrisCatlin 6 —
(D K Ivory) *chsd ldrs: lost pl whn n.m.r over 3f out: sn wl bhd* **33/1**

64.75 secs (2.55) **Going Correction** -0.10s/f (Good) **7** Ran SP% **113.8**
Speed ratings (Par 91): **75,74,74,67,61 50,30**
toteswinger: 1&2 £2.70, 1&3 £1.60, 2&3 £2.50 CSF £16.69 TOTE £3.70: £2.10, £3.30; EX 14.50 Trifecta £23.00 Pool: £942.08 - 23.63 winning units.The winner was bought in for 4,200 guineas.
Owner Tony Coyle **Bred** C Kelly **Trained** Westow, N Yorks
■ Stewards' Enquiry : D O'Donohoe caution: careless riding.

FOCUS
Three drew clear in what was a weak seller, below average for the grade.

NOTEBOOK
On The Piste(IRE), third in this grade at Thirsk on debut, was again not the quickest away, but soon recovered and was up with the pace. She edged to the front over a furlong out and, despite hanging, kept onwell to just shade it in a tight finish. Se was bought in for 4,200gns. (op 5-2 tchd 9-4)
Angie's Nap(USA) initially came with her challenge against the stands´ rail, but also hung out into the centre of the track and just lost out in a head-bobber. This drop in grade clearly helped. (op 4-1 tchd 5-1)
Michaelmas Daisy, not beaten far on either start in maidens, was soon outpaced on this drop in grade and her rider was at work on her from an early stage. She kept responding, though, and may well have won had she not been carried left by the front pair. (op 7-4 tchd 15-8 in places)
Jackie Danny showed a bit of early speed, but was left behind by the front trio from a furlong out. (op 7-1)

2458 BLOOMBERGOFFSHORERACING.COM H'CAP 1m 3y
3:45 (3:46) (Class 6) (0-60,60) 4-Y-O+ **£2,072** (£616; £308; £153) **Stalls** High

Form RPR
0120 **1** **High Five Society**[80] 792 5-8-12 54 ..... (bt) JimmyQuinn 4 62
(S R Bowring) *s.i.s: sn prom: rdn to ld 1f out: edgd lft: r.o* **16/1**
030- **2** ½ **Confide In Me**[245] 6255 5-8-5 52 ..... (t) AndreaAtzeni(5) 13 59
(G A Butler) *prom: lost pl over 4f out: swtchd lft and hdwy over 1f out: sn rdn: ev ch ins fnl f: styd on* **8/1**[3]
-450 **3** 1 ½ **Daring Dream (GER)**[30] 1606 4-9-1 57 ..... (v) RichardMullen 5 60
(A P Jarvis) *s.i.s: hld up: plld hrd: hdwy over 1f out: rdn and ev ch ins fnl f: no ex towards fin* **14/1**
00-3 **4** *hd* **Hits Only Cash**[35] 1495 7-8-8 57 ..... SimonPearce(7) 8 60+
(J Pearce) *hld up: hdwy over 1f out: r.o: nt rch ldrs* **7/1**[2]
0-00 **5** 2 ½ **Libre**[24] 1773 9-9-0 56 ..... TolleyDean 2 53
(F Jordan) *hld up in tch: led over 1f out: sn rdn: edgd rt and hdd: no ex ins fnl f* **20/1**
350- **6** 1 ¼ **Superior Duchess**[173] 7590 4-8-11 53 ..... WandersonD'Avila 3 47
(Jane Chapple-Hyam) *led: clr 1/2-way: rdn and hdd over 1f out: wknd ins fnl f* **66/1**
353- **7** 1 ¾ **Astroangel**[254] 6036 5-8-11 53 ..... TedDurcan 16 43
(M H Tompkins) *hld up: hdwy over 1f out: sn rdn and edgd lft: wknd ins fnl f* **8/1**[3]
06-0 **8** 1 **Spanish Cross (IRE)**[34] 1533 4-8-12 54 ..... AdrianMcCarthy 15 42
(G Prodromou) *s.i.s: hld up: hdwy over 1f out: wknd ins fnl f* **33/1**
-012 **9** *hd* **Mr Fantozzi (IRE)**[2] 2381 4-9-4 60 ..... (p) FrancisNorton 11 48
(D Donovan) *chsd ldr: rdn over 2f out: wknd fnl f* **10/3**[1]
0040 **10** ¾ **Ugenius**[30] 1606 5-9-1 57 ..... DO'Donohoe 12 43
(Mrs C A Dunnett) *hld up: rdn over 2f out: n.d* **14/1**
5000 **11** *nk* **Spares And Repairs**[10] 2171 6-8-9 51 ..... ChrisCatlin 1 36
(Mrs S Lamyman) *s.i.s: hld up: hdwy over 3f out: rdn and wknd over 1f out* **16/1**
002 **12** 2 **Wooden King (IRE)**[3] 2353 4-8-8 55 ow2 ..... RichardEvans(5) 14 36
(P D Evans) *hld up: hdwy 1/2-way: rdn and wknd wl over 1f out* **9/1**
0-45 **13** ½ **Zeffirelli**[46] 1258 4-9-0 56 ..... ShaneKelly 7 35
(M Quinn) *prom: racd keenly: wknd wl over 1f out* **12/1**
00-2 **14** 2 ¾ **Chinese Profit**[18] 1940 4-8-13 55 ..... LukeMorris 9 28
(G C Bravery) *s.i.s: hld up: a in rr: rdn and wknd over 2f out* **12/1**
004 **15** 4 **Bestowed**[20] 1888 4-9-1 60 ..... LeeVickers(3) 6 24
(M C Chapman) *chsd ldrs tl wknd 2f out* **50/1**

1m 40.25s (-0.35) **Going Correction** -0.10s/f (Good) **15** Ran SP% **119.4**
Speed ratings (Par 101): **97,96,95,94,92 91,89,88,88,87 87,85,84,81,77**
toteswinger: 1&2 £51.00, 1&3 £44.40, 2&3 £29.10 CSF £133.06 CT £1897.96 TOTE £20.60: £6.30, £3.70, £3.60; EX 343.60 Trifecta £231.50 Part won. Pool - 312.94 winning units..
Owner S R Bowring **Bred** A C M Spalding **Trained** Edwinstowe, Notts

FOCUS
This was a low-grade handicap. Modest form, best rated through the third.
Hits Only Cash Official explanation: jockey said gelding stumbled 1f out.

2459 LINDLEY-CATERING.CO.UK H'CAP 7f 3y
4:20 (4:23) (Class 5) (0-70,67) 4-Y-O+ **£2,719** (£809; £404; £202) **Stalls** High

Form RPR
2000 **1** **Xpres Maite**[13] 2086 6-9-4 67 ..... (b) AmirQuinn 4 75
(S R Bowring) *led to 1/2-way: chsd ldr: rallied to ld ins fnl f: r.o* **5/1**[3]
-143 **2** *nk* **Hobson**[15] 2011 4-9-3 66 ..... RichardMullen 6 73
(Eve Johnson Houghton) *chsd ldr tl led 1/2-way rdn over 1f out: edgd lft and hdd wl ins fnl f* **9/4**[1]
0400 **3** ½ **Magnitude**[14] 2052 4-9-4 67 ..... FrancisNorton 8 73
(M E Rimmer) *dwlt and bmpd s: hld up: hdwy over 2f out: rdn over 1f out: r.o* **10/1**
3042 **4** 3 ½ **Networker**[6] 2261 6-8-13 62 ..... EdwardCreighton 7 58
(P J McBride) *hmpd s: sn pushed along in rr: hdwy and nt clr run over 2f out: rdn and hung lft fr over 1f out: no ex ins fnl f* **11/4**[2]
0000 **5** ½ **Party In The Park**[3] 2361 4-8-8 57 ..... (b) ChrisCatlin 1 52
(Miss J A Camacho) *hld up: rdn 1/2-way: nvr trbld ldrs* **20/1**
3630 **6** 1 ¼ **Copperwood**[35] 1495 4-8-4 53 oh3 ..... JimmyQuinn 3 44
(M Blanshard) *hld up: swtchd lft over 2f out: rdn and wkng whn hung rt over 1f out* **9/1**
0222 **7** *hd* **Mudhish (IRE)**[10] 2168 4-9-4 67 ..... (b) ShaneKelly 10 58
(C E Brittain) *chsd ldrs: rdn over 1f out: wknd ins fnl f* **9/1**
0164 **8** 10 **Divertimenti (IRE)**[102] 573 5-9-1 67 ..... (b) KevinGhunowa(3) 9 31
(C R Dore) *chsd ldrs: rdn over 2f out: wknd over 1f out* **16/1**

1m 26.2s (-0.40) **Going Correction** -0.10s/f (Good) **8** Ran SP% **113.8**
Speed ratings (Par 103): **98,97,97,93,92 91,90,79**
toteswinger: 1&2 £3.00, 1&3 £7.10, 2&3 £5.10 CSF £16.52 CT £106.77 TOTE £7.10: £1.70, £1.30, £3.10; EX 21.30 Trifecta £128.80 Pool: £436.93 - 2.51 winning units.
Owner Charterhouse Holdings Plc **Bred** S R Bowring **Trained** Edwinstowe, Notts

FOCUS
A modest handicap, rated around the runner-up.
Divertimenti(IRE) Official explanation: jockey said gelding jumped left on leaving stalls

2460 BETTERBET FREE £50 ON 08000 89 88 87 H'CAP 5f 43y
4:55 (4:56) (Class 5) (0-75,72) 3-Y-O+ **£2,719** (£809; £404; £202) **Stalls** High

Form RPR
15-0 **1** **Dragon Flame (IRE)**[32] 1565 6-9-7 67 ..... ShaneKelly 2 77
(M Quinn) *mde all: rdn over 1f out: edgd rt and r.o wl* **17/2**
0004 **2** 2 ¾ **Brandywell Boy (IRE)**[9] 2180 6-8-13 59 ..... RichardThomas 6 59
(D J S Ffrench Davis) *chsd wnr to 1/2-way: rdn to go 2nd again over 1f out: no ex ins fnl f* **7/1**[3]
042 **3** 1 ¼ **Imaginary Diva**[41] 1359 3-8-12 66 ..... ChrisCatlin 9 59
(G G Margarson) *a.p: chsd wnr 1/2-way tl rdn over 1f out: no ex ins fnl f* **10/1**
5554 **4** *hd* **Mambo Spirit (IRE)**[3] 2359 5-9-9 72 ..... (b[1]) LeeVickers(3) 4 67
(J G Given) *hld up: hdwy over 1f out: rdn and n.m.r ins fnl f: styd on same pce* **5/2**[1]
6220 **5** 1 ¾ **Kheylide (IRE)**[7] 2227 3-9-2 70 ..... EdwardCreighton 3 56
(Mrs D J Sanderson) *trckd ldrs: rdn over 1f out: wknd ins fnl f* **3/1**[2]
0-50 **6** 2 **Diane's Choice**[3] 2349 6-9-8 68 ..... LukeMorris 7 49
(Miss Gay Kelleway) *hld up in tch: rdn 1/2-way: sn outpcd* **10/1**
0010 **7** 1 ¼ **Style Award**[20] 1890 4-9-6 66 ..... (p) JimmyQuinn 8 43
(W J H Ratcliffe) *hld up in tch: racd keenly: rdn and hung lft fr over 2f out: wknd over 1f out* **8/1**
2640 **8** 7 **Woodcote (IRE)**[13] 2095 7-9-5 65 ..... (vt) GeorgeBaker 1 17
(Peter Grayson) *rrd s: a bhd: wknd and eased over 1f out* **14/1**

62.20 secs **Going Correction** -0.10s/f (Good)
WFA 3 from 4yo+ 8lb **8** Ran SP% **112.6**
Speed ratings (Par 103): **96,91,89,89,86 83,81,70**
toteswinger: 1&2 £13.30, 1&3 £14.20, 2&3 £5.00 CSF £63.85 CT £607.60 TOTE £13.30: £2.70, £2.50, £2.00; EX 81.30 Trifecta £301.40 Part won. Pool: £407.30 - 0.74 winning units..
Owner A Newby **Bred** Denis Hackett **Trained** Newmarket, Suffolk

FOCUS
A moderate sprint and Dragon Flame was never headed. He produced a clear personal best but this form is not that solid.
Kheylide(IRE) Official explanation: jockey said gelding hung left
Woodcote(IRE) Official explanation: jockey said gelding was slowly away

2461 LINDLEY CATERING H'CAP 1m 2f 21y
5:25 (5:27) (Class 6) (0-55,59) 3-Y-O **£2,072** (£616; £308; £153) **Stalls** Low

Form RPR
5432 **1** **Screaming Brave**[4] 2340 3-8-12 53 ..... TedDurcan 10 59
(M R Channon) *hld up: hdwy over 3f out: rdn to ld over 1f out: edgd lft: jst hld on* **2/1**[1]
0-60 **2** *nse* **Extremely So**[44] 1282 3-9-0 55 ..... ChrisCatlin 7 61
(P J McBride) *stdd s: hld up: hdwy over 2f out: rdn over 1f out: r.o* **12/1**
6056 **3** 2 ¼ **Valkyrie (IRE)**[11] 2131 3-8-6 52 ..... (p) MarkCoumbe(5) 2 53
(N P Littmoden) *s.i.s: hld up: rdn over 3f out: hdwy over 1f out: r.o: nt rch ldrs* **20/1**
6045 **4** ½ **Chantilly Dancer (IRE)**[10] 2169 3-8-8 49 ow1 ..... ShaneKelly 4 49
(M Quinn) *chsd ldrs: led 3f out: rdn and hdd over 1f out: styd on same pce ins fnl f* **20/1**
4004 **5** *nse* **Vita Mia**[2] 2370 3-8-8 54 ..... RichardEvans(5) 12 54
(P D Evans) *led 1f: chsd ldrs: rdn over 1f out: styd on* **13/2**[3]
3361 **6** ½ **Crystal Feather**[11] 2143 3-9-4 59 6ex ..... FrancisNorton 13 58
(E F Vaughan) *s.i.s: hld up: hdwy over 2f out: rdn over 1f out: styd on* **7/1**
-006 **7** 3 **Red Margarita (IRE)**[32] 1570 3-8-12 53 ..... SaleemGolam 16 46
(D R C Elsworth) *hld up: rdn whn stmbld over 2f out: hdwy and hung lft fr over 1f out: nt rch ldrs* **14/1**
-420 **8** 2 ½ **On Cue (IRE)**[11] 2143 3-8-12 53 ..... LukeMorris 15 41
(J M P Eustace) *chsd ldrs: rdn over 2f out: wknd ins fnl f* **14/1**
0620 **9** 1 ¾ **Wahan (USA)**[11] 2131 3-8-11 55 ..... AhmedAjtebi(3) 3 40
(C E Brittain) *hld up: hdwy over 6f out: rdn over 2f out: wknd fnl f* **9/1**
-000 **10** ¾ **Guilin (IRE)**[17] 1967 3-8-10 51 ..... (b) JimmyQuinn 9 34
(P F I Cole) *prom: rdn over 3f out: wknd 2f out* **25/1**
2321 **11** ½ **Why Nee Amy**[10] 2169 3-8-12 58 6ex ..... (p) AndreaAtzeni(5) 1 40
(Miss Gay Kelleway) *s.i.s: hld up: effrt over 3f out: sn wknd* **6/1**[2]
656- **12** 11 **Baileys Red**[259] 5870 3-8-13 54 ..... DO'Donohoe 11 14
(J G Given) *hld up: a in rr* **20/1**
000- **13** ½ **Welcome Applause (IRE)**[201] 7257 3-8-13 54 ..... EdwardCreighton 14 13
(M G Quinlan) *a in rr: bhd fnl 6f* **50/1**

-000 **14** *nse* **Romantic Interlude (IRE)**[11] 2131 3-8-13 **54**........(v[1]) RichardThomas 6 13
(A P Jarvis) *led after 1f: clr 5f out: hdd 3f out: wknd over 1f out* **50/1**
2m 8.73s (-1.77) **Going Correction** -0.25s/f (Firm) **14** Ran SP% **126.5**
Speed ratings (Par 97): **97,96,95,94,94 94,91,89,88,87 87,78,78,78**
toteswinger: 1&2 £7.90, 1&3 £16.00, 2&3 £70.00 CSF £27.06 CT £401.66 TOTE £2.90: £1.30, £3.00, £8.80; EX 36.80 TRIFECTA Not won. Place 6: £129.68 Place 5: £125.87..
Owner Billy Parish **Bred** Norman Court Stud **Trained** West Ilsley, Berks

FOCUS
This was a low-grade handicap. The fourth looks the best guide, with the winner probably only having to repeat his Redcar form.
T/Plt: £211.50 to a £1 stake. Pool: £50,178.66. 173.13 winning tickets. T/Qpdt: £147.60 to a £1 stake. Pool: £3,191.47. 16.00 winning tickets. CR

2462 - 2466a (Foreign Racing) - See Raceform Interactive

2068 **DONCASTER (L-H)**
Saturday, May 30

OFFICIAL GOING: Good to firm
Wind: Fresh behind Weather: Fine and sunny

2467 TRADE UNION UNISON & THOMPSONS LAWYERS E B F MAIDEN STKS 6f
2:30 (2:33) (Class 5) 2-Y-O **£3,885** (£1,156; £577; £288) **Stalls** High

Form RPR
2 **1** **Alrasm (IRE)**[15] 2037 2-9-3 0.. RHills 3 87+
(M A Jarvis) *chsd ldrs: led over 3f out: rdn and r.o wl fnl f* **5/6**[1]
4 **2** *2 ½* **Big Audio (IRE)**[9] 2187 2-9-3 0.. PatDobbs 8 77+
(R Hannon) *chsd ldrs: rdn over 1f out: styd on same pce ins fnl f* **10/3**[2]
435 **3** *1* **Petrocelli**[4] 2358 2-9-3 0..(b[1]) PaulFitzsimons 15 74
(A J McCabe) *hld up: hdwy over 1f out: rdn and edgd lft ins fnl f: nt rch ldrs* **33/1**
4 *1 ½* **Rigid** 2-9-3 0.. PatCosgrave 14 69+
(J G Given) *prom: rdn over 1f out: edgd lft and styd on same pce fnl f* **100/1**
5 *1* **Key Breeze** 2-9-3 0.. JimmyFortune 1 66
(J H M Gosden) *s.i.s: hdwy 1/2-way: rdn over 1f out: edgd lft and no ex ins fnl f* **10/1**[3]
6 *4 ½* **Branderburgo (IRE)** 2-8-12 0.................................... AndreaAtzeni(5) 12 53
(M Botti) *prom: rdn over 1f out: hung lft and wknd fnl f* **12/1**
2606 **7** *¾* **Island Express (IRE)**[7] 2260 2-8-12 0.......................(p) AnnStokell(5) 10 50
(Miss A Stokell) *led: hdd over 3f out: rdn and wknd over 1f out* **100/1**
8 *2 ¾* **Public Service (IRE)** 2-9-3 0.................................... JoeFanning 2 42
(B J Meehan) *s.i.s: hdwy 1/2-way: rdn and hung lft over 2f out: wknd over 1f out* **25/1**
9 *1 ¼* **Nolecce** 2-8-10 0.. GihanArnolda(7) 9 38
(R C Guest) *prom: rdn 1/2-way: hung lft and wknd 2f out* **150/1**
0 **10** *¾* **Sandy Toes**[11] 2147 2-9-0 0...................................... AndrewMullen(3) 13 36
(A J McCabe) *s.i.s: sn pushed along in rr: n.d* **100/1**
11 *nse* **Desert Forest (IRE)** 2-9-3 0.................................... PhillipMakin 4 36
(J Howard Johnson) *s.i.s: rdn over 2f out: sn hung lft: n.d* **50/1**
12 *3* **Thinking** 2-9-3 0.. DuranFentiman 11 27
(T D Easterby) *mid-div whn hmpd wl over 4f out: sn bhd* **66/1**
000 **13** *¾* **Camacho Flyer (IRE)**[7] 2258 2-9-3 0.............................. JamieMoriarty 5 25
(P T Midgley) *chsd ldrs: rdn over 2f out: sn hung lft and wknd* **100/1**
14 *¾* **The Caped Crusader (IRE)** 2-9-3 0................................ MickyFenton 7 22
(T P Tate) *s.s: in rr whn swvd lft wl over 4f out: sn wl bhd* **14/1**
0 **F** **Another Grand (IRE)**[8] 2231 2-9-3 0................................ LukeMorris 6 —
(Mrs R A Carr) *chsd ldrs: n.m.r and fell wl over 4f out* **100/1**
1m 11.27s (-2.33) **Going Correction** -0.425s/f (Firm) **15** Ran SP% **116.9**
Speed ratings (Par 93): **98,94,93,91,90 84,83,79,77,76 76,72,71,70,—**
toteswinger: 1&2 £1.60, 1&3 £11.00, 2&3 £17.20 CSF £3.09 TOTE £1.80: £1.10, £1.30, £5.40; EX 4.30 Trifecta £40.00 Pool £718.86 - 13.28 winning units..
Owner Hamdan Al Maktoum **Bred** New Deal Partnership **Trained** Newmarket, Suffolk

FOCUS
Warm, sunny weather resulted in the going being changed to Good to Firm before racing, but the rider of the winner reported it was 'Firm'. This maiden has thrown up several decent juveniles in recent years, including Royal Lodge winner Leo and July Stakes winner Meshaheer. This renewal looked uncompetitive beforehand, they bet 25-1 bar five. The winner was value for at least another length.

NOTEBOOK
Alrasm(IRE) finished runner-up on his debut at Newbury and that experience had clearly been of benefit. He was always travelling well before asserting in the final furlong to score in comfortable fashion, breaking the juvenile track record in the process. Connections are likely to have bigger targets in mind now, although they are likely to avoid running him on ground this fast next time. (op 10-11)
Big Audio(IRE) had clearly come on for his debut at Goodwood and, although no match for the winner, beat the rest well enough. He should not be long in getting off the mark. (op 7-2 tchd 4-1 and 3-1)
Petrocelli had failed to build on his promising debut in two subsequent starts, but first-time blinkers had a positive effect, and he stayed on well in the closing stages. (op 25-1)
Rigid ◆ was an eyecatcher. His pedigree suggests longer trips will suit. However, once he got the hang of things, he ran on nicely past tiring rivals and should be a lot wiser next time.
Key Breeze is another bred to stay further than a mile on the dam's side. He showed a fair bit of pace on this debut before fading. (op 13-2 tchd 6-1)
Branderburgo(IRE) was quite well backed on this debut, so had clearly shown something at home. He never really got competitive but should be better for the experience. (op 22-1)

2468 UNISON & FRIZZELL "CAR INSURANCE" H'CAP 1m 2f 60y
3:00 (3:02) (Class 3) (0-95,94) 4-Y-O+ **£7,771** (£2,312; £1,155; £577) **Stalls** Low

Form RPR
03-0 **1** **Jack Dawkins (USA)**[35] 1527 4-9-0 **90**.............................. IanMongan 6 101+
(H R A Cecil) *hld up: hdwy over 2f out: led over 1f out: sn rdn: jst hld on* **10/3**[2]
61- **2** *nse* **Hevelius**[326] 3810 4-8-10 **86**.. TonyCulhane 2 97+
(W R Swinburn) *chsd ldrs: outpcd and nt clr run over 2f out: swtchd rt and rallied over 1f out: r.o wl* **7/1**
5005 **3** *3 ¼* **Bazergan (IRE)**[28] 1673 4-8-10 **86**................................(tp) JoeFanning 3 91
(C E Brittain) *racd keenly: led after 1f: rdn and hdd over 1f out: styd on same pce ins fnl f* **4/1**[3]
-221 **4** *5* **Granston (IRE)**[22] 1850 8-8-6 **87**........................ Louis-PhilippeBeuzelin(5) 10 83
(J D Bethell) *led 1f: chsd ldr: rdn and ev ch over 2f out: wknd fnl f* **9/2**
00-0 **5** *1* **Charlie Tokyo (IRE)**[15] 2055 6-8-10 **86**......................(v) JamieMoriarty 5 80
(R A Fahey) *hld up: rdn over 2f out: n.d* **16/1**
-411 **6** *1* **Wind Star**[3] 2374 6-8-13 **89** 6ex................................... PJMcDonald 7 81
(G A Swinbank) *chsd ldrs: rdn over 2f out: wknd fnl f* **11/4**[1]
53-0 **7** *nk* **St Jean Cap Ferrat**[32] 1593 4-8-10 **86**...............................(v) PatDobbs 1 77
(P J Hobbs) *hld up in tch: rdn over 2f out: wknd over 1f out* **14/1**
2m 6.76s (-4.44) **Going Correction** -0.325s/f (Firm) **7** Ran SP% **113.0**
Speed ratings (Par 107): **104,103,101,97,96 95,95**
toteswinger: 1&2 £7.50, 2&3 £6.70, 1&3 not won CSF £25.77 CT £94.47 TOTE £4.20: £2.50, £3.80; EX 32.70 Trifecta £54.60 Pool £339.07 - 4.59 winning units..
Owner Malih L Al Basti **Bred** Clovelly Farms **Trained** Newmarket, Suffolk

FOCUS
A good handicap weakened by the withdrawal of five of the 12 runners, including the four at the head of the weights. The betting suggested it was an open race and it produced a good finish. The form is rated around the winner and third, with decent efforts from the first two.

NOTEBOOK
Jack Dawkins(USA), twice a winner here in the past, maintained his unbeaten record on the track by the skin of his teeth. He opened up a decisive advantage entering the final furlong, but his rider became increasingly desperate, and he only just held on. This looks as far as he wants to go. (op 7-2 tchd 4-1)
Hevelius who had suffered an injury following his maiden success last July, was quite keen on his return. He found himself behind a wall of horses when the pace increased. However, once switched out into the wake of the winner he found extra and was cutting the winner down all the way to the line. He is unexposed and deserves to pick up a similar race on this evidence. (op 9-2)
Bazergan(IRE) made the running and stuck on well under pressure, but had no answer to the late challengers. (op 5-1)
Granston(IRE) is in good form but was 4lb higher than for his recent success and, although he appeared to have every chance early in the straight, he had nothing extra to give soon afterwards. (op 6-1)
Charlie Tokyo(IRE) has not scored since taking the John Smith's Cup last summer but, as a result, has slipped down the weights. He did not show a great deal here until staying on late, but this may put him right for another crack at the big York handicap. (op 18-1 tchd 20-1)
Wind Star has been in terrific form but had a 6lb penalty to carry. He was also 10lb higher than when scoring the first of his two recent successes, and it may just have been enough to stop him. That said, he was still a little disappointing. Official explanation: jockey said gelding ran flat (op 5-2 tchd 10-3)

2469 UNISON "BEYOND THE BARRIERS" CLASSIFIED STKS 6f
3:30 (3:31) (Class 2) 3-Y-O **£12,952** (£3,854; £1,926; £962) **Stalls** High

Form RPR
6114 **1** **Proclaim**[7] 2279 3-8-10 94.. JoeFanning 1 99+
(M Johnston) *chsd ldrs: led over 1f out: sn rdn and hung rt: r.o* **11/8**[1]
0062 **2** *¾* **Akhenaten**[7] 2279 3-8-10 94.. TonyCulhane 2 97
(M R Channon) *hld up in tch: rdn to chse wnr and edgd rt ins fnl f: r.o* **13/2**[3]
-301 **3** *¾* **Saucy Brown (IRE)**[28] 1664 3-8-10 93.................................. PatDobbs 5 95
(R Hannon) *sn led: rdn: edgd lft and hdd over 1f out: styd on same pce ins fnl f* **4/1**[2]
1524 **4** *2* **Five Star Junior (USA)**[31] 1602 3-8-10 95.................... JamieMoriarty 3 88
(Mrs L Stubbs) *hld up in tch: nt clr run over 1f out: no imp ins fnl f* **7/1**
-000 **5** *¾* **Imperial Guest**[15] 2035 3-8-10 94.. LukeMorris 7 86
(G G Margarson) *sn pushed along in rr: hdwy over 1f out: no ex ins fnl f* **10/1**
010- **6** *2* **Prime Mood (IRE)**[238] 6483 3-8-10 93................................ PhillipMakin 4 79
(B Smart) *w ldr: racd keenly: rdn over 2f out: wknd ins fnl f* **16/1**
10-2 **7** *7* **Crystal Moments**[29] 1639 3-8-7 90.. RHills 6 54+
(E A L Dunlop) *hld up in tch: racd keenly: effrt and hmpd over 1f out: eased* **8/1**
69.56 secs (-4.04) **Going Correction** -0.425s/f (Firm) course record **7** Ran SP% **114.0**
Speed ratings (Par 105): **109,108,107,104,103 100,91**
toteswinger: 1&2 £1.10, 1&3 £1.40, 2&3 £11.10 CSF £10.86 TOTE £2.10: £1.10, £3.20; EX 10.50.
Owner Sheikh Hamdan Bin Mohammed Al Maktoum **Bred** Gainsborough Stud Management Ltd **Trained** Middleham Moor, N Yorks

FOCUS
A tight conditions stakes with only 5lb covering the field on official ratings. Decent for, if not the most solid.

NOTEBOOK
Proclaim had finished behind the runner-up last time but was 4lb better off for less than two lengths. Given a typically no-nonsense ride by Joe Fanning, he travelled close to the pace until picking up well over a furlong out. He ran on strongly to the line, breaking the track record in the process. He looks progressive and can win more decent races. (op 15-8)
Akhenaten had beaten the winner at Newmarket on his first try at 6f, having been campaigned over as far as 1m2f in the past. He tracked the leaders and picked up well to chase his old rival throughout the last furlong but was only gradually reducing the margin. He should win his share of races at around this distance. (tchd 7-1)
Saucy Brown(IRE), who won over an extra furlong here last time, ran a fine race from the front and did not drop away once headed. He is in good form at the moment and his versatility gives connections plenty of options. (op 9-2 tchd 5-1)
Five Star Junior(USA) has been progressive on the all-weather and had been fourth in Listed company on his recent return to turf. He travelled well for much of the way, but wandered when asked for his effort before running on. However, he had given the principals a start and never looked like reeling them in. He did enough to suggest there are races to be won with him on turf. (op 5-1)
Imperial Guest gained his last success in a Listed race over course and distance. He never figured having been held up. (op 12-1)
Prime Mood(IRE) showed plenty of pace on this return to action before fading late. He should be better for the outing. Official explanation: jockey said colt hung left (tchd 18-1)
Crystal Moments got a good lead but was just beginning to make her effort when broadsided by Five Star Junior. That cost her momentum and she was allowed to come home in her own time. This run can be forgotten. (op 6-1)

2470 UNISON "POSITIVELY PUBLIC" H'CAP 7f
4:05 (4:06) (Class 2) (0-100,100) 4-Y-O+
£15,577 (£4,665; £2,332; £1,167; £582; £292) **Stalls** High

Form RPR
02-4 **1** **Signor Peltro**[21] 1861 6-8-7 **92**.................................. AhmedAjtebi(3) 9 102
(H Candy) *sn prom: rdn to ld over 1f out: r.o* **9/2**[1]
-001 **2** *1* **Celtic Sultan (IRE)**[7] 2266 5-8-8 **90**................................ MickyFenton 3 97
(T P Tate) *led: swtchd rt to stands' rail 6f out: edgd lft and hdd over 1f out: styd on* **15/2**[2]
-050 **3** *½* **Lucky Dance (BRZ)**[42] 1352 7-8-9 **91**................................ PatCosgrave 15 97
(A G Foster) *mid-div: sn pushed along: hdwy over 1f out: r.o* **20/1**
5110 **4** *2 ¾* **Mr Macattack**[21] 1861 4-8-4 **86**.. LukeMorris 17 85+
(N J Vaughan) *dwlt: outpcd: swtchd lft 2f out: hdwy over 1f out: r.o: nt rch ldrs* **9/2**[1]
1305 **5** *2* **Al Muheer (IRE)**[29] 1640 4-9-0 **96**..............................(b) JimmyFortune 16 89
(C E Brittain) *prom: rdn over 1f out: styd on same pce* **16/1**

634- **6** *nk* **Lindoro**220 6911 4-8-7 **89** PatDobbs 8 81+
(W R Swinburn) *hld up: carried lft over 3f out: nt clr run over 2f out: swtchd rt over 1f out: sn rdn and hung rt: nvr nrr* **25/1**
0362 **7** *1 1/4* **Capricorn Run (USA)**29 1640 6-9-1 **100** (v) AndrewMullen(3) 13 89
(A J McCabe) *mid-div: sn drvn along: n.d* **20/1**
40-0 **8** *1/2* **Damika (IRE)**7 2259 6-9-0 **99** MichaelJStainton(3) 2 87
(R M Whitaker) *chsd ldrs: rdn over 2f out: wknd fnl f* **25/1**
0-26 **9** *1* **Masai Moon**21 1864 5-8-12 **94** IanMongan 6 79
(B R Millman) *prom: rdn over 2f out: wknd over 1f out* **20/1**
4000 **10** *2* **Northern Fling**7 2012 5-8-7 **89** ow1 GrahamGibbons 18 69
(D Nicholls) *hld up: effrt and hmpd over 1f out: sn wknd* **17/2**3
0010 **11** *3 1/4* **Joseph Henry**16 2015 7-9-1 **97** JoeFanning 4 68
(D Nicholls) *chsd ldr: rdn over 2f out: w eakened over 1f out* **20/1**
66-5 **12** *1/2* **Decameron (USA)**35 1527 4-7-13 **86** oh3(v1) Louis-PhilippeBeuzelin(5) 7 55
(Sir Michael Stoute) *chsd ldrs: rdn and wknd over 2f out* **9/2**1
6-40 **13** *3/4* **Spitfire**21 1861 4-8-10 **92** AdrianMcCarthy 1 59
(J R Jenkins) *wnt lft s: sn prom: rdn and wknd 2f out* **25/1**
4- **14** *30* **Hanoverian Baron**232 6635 4-8-7 **94** AndreaAtzeni(5) 14 —
(D Nicholls) *s.i.s: sn pushed along in rr: hung lft and lost tch over 3f out* **17/2**3

1m 21.81s (-4.49) **Going Correction** -0.425s/f (Firm) **14** Ran SP% **123.8**
Speed ratings (Par 109): **108,106,106,103,100 100,99,98,97,95 91,90,89,55**
toteswinger: 1&2 £6.10, 1&3 £25.80, 2&3 £45.60 CSF £34.57 CT £629.55 TOTE £5.70: £2.40, £3.40, £7.90; EX 53.80 Trifecta £365.60 Part won. Pool £494.15 - 0.10 winning units..
Owner First Of Many Partnership **Bred** R D And J S Chugg & The Overbury Partnership **Trained** Kingston Warren, Oxon
■ Stewards' Enquiry : Pat Dobbs two-day ban: careless riding (Jun 13-14)

FOCUS
A good, competitive handicap but weakened a little by four withdrawals. Solid form, with a slight personal best from the winner.

NOTEBOOK
Signor Peltro, fourth in the Victoria Cup last time out, scored in pretty good style. He got a good lead into the race and, once he hit the front over a furlong out, always looked like holding on. The Buckingham Palace Handicap at Royal Ascot looks an obvious target and, as all ground conditions seem to come alike to him, he looks likely to be a major player in that contest. (op 4-1)
Celtic Sultan(IRE) had been dropped in the handicap before scoring at Catterick but ran well once again from the front, despite being 5lb higher. He is clearly in good heart, but would be of more interest next time if racing on a turning track. (op 7-1 tchd 8-1)
Lucky Dance(BRZ) gained his only win in this country when scoring off 5lb lower on easy ground at Newmarket last season. However, he ran well on this much faster surface, staying on late without ever looking like catching the first two. (op 25-1)
Mr Macattack ◆ was the real eyecatcher. He was backed late, but had to be scrubbed along leaving the stalls, and was still last at halfway. However, he then started to run on and finished strongly to make the frame, beaten not much further by the winner then he was at Ascot. He looks one to bear in mind. (op 5-1 tchd 13-2)
Al Muheer(IRE) is better known for his exploits on Polytrack, but he has won on fast ground and is likely to pop up at some stage this summer. (op 12-1)
Lindoro was another to catch the eye on this seasonal debut, staying on steadily from the rear. He should be better for the outing but will appreciate easier ground than this. (tchd 28-1)
Capricorn Run(USA) was another to stay on late. (op 16-1)
Damika(IRE) showed pace before fading and seems to be gradually finding his form. (tchd 22-1)
Decameron(USA) was a big disappointment in the first-time visor. He raced up with the pace but was on the retreat before the quarter-mile pole. (tchd 7-2 and 5-1)

2471 UNISON & UIA "HOME INSURANCE WITH PRINCIPLES" H'CAP 1m 4f
4:40 (4:40) (Class 2) (0-100,100) 4-Y-O+ **£16,190** (£4,817; £2,407; £1,202) **Stalls** Low

Form RPR
5-34 **1** **Dansili Dancer**27 1696 7-9-3 **99** LukeMorris 5 105
(C G Cox) *hld up: swtchd rt and hdwy to ld over 2f out: rdn and hung lft fr over 1f out: styd on* **5/1**3
21-6 **2** *1 1/2* **Meethaaq (USA)**17 1986 4-8-7 **89** RHills 8 93+
(Sir Michael Stoute) *chsd ldr tl led over 3f out: rdn and hdd over 2f out: sn hung lft: styd on: wnt 2nd towards fin* **3/1**2
2033 **3** *1/2* **Drill Sergeant**15 2031 4-9-4 **100** JoeFanning 3 103
(M Johnston) *led: hdd over 3f out: outpcd 2f out: rallied ins fnl f: wnt 3rd towards fin* **9/1**
300- **4** *nk* **Camps Bay (USA)**281 5229 5-8-9 **96** Louis-PhilippeBeuzelin(5) 4 99
(Mrs A J Perrett) *hld up: hdwy and ev ch over 2f out: rdn over 1f out: hmpd wl ins fnl f and lost 2 pls towards fin* **5/1**3
11-1 **5** *2 1/2* **Falcativ**19 1944 4-8-6 **93** AndreaAtzeni(5) 7 92
(L M Cumani) *hld up in tch: plld hrd: rdn and hung lft over 2f out: no ex fnl f* **9/4**1
52-5 **6** *2 1/4* **Sevenna (FR)**41 1383 4-8-6 **88** DO'Donohoe 6 83
(H R A Cecil) *prom: rdn over 2f out: wknd fnl f* **16/1**
215- **7** *70* **King O'The Gypsies (IRE)**235 6563 4-8-8 **90** PhillipMakin 2 —
(J Howard Johnson) *s.i.s: sn prom: rdn over 3f out: wknd over 2f out: eased* **15/2**

2m 28.28s (-6.82) **Going Correction** -0.325s/f (Firm) **7** Ran SP% **116.7**
Speed ratings (Par 109): **109,108,107,107,105 104,57**
toteswinger: 1&2 £3.60, 1&3 £5.30, 2&3 £4.50 CSF £21.12 CT £132.26 TOTE £6.90: £2.60, £2.10; EX 29.50 Trifecta £101.70 Pool £809.57 - 5.89 winning units..
Owner The Loyal Troupers **Bred** The Magic Slipper Partnership **Trained** Lambourn, Berks
■ Stewards' Enquiry : Luke Morris three-day ban: careless riding (Jun 21-23)

FOCUS
A good handicap featuring a number of twilight horses or horses in the grip of the handicapper. Despite the poor run of the favourite this is sound form.

NOTEBOOK
Dansili Dancer had not scored since winning the Old Newton Cup in August 2007 but was still 4lb higher than for that success. However, his stable is in cracking form at present and he sealed the victory by establishing an advantage going into the final furlong. Presumably, the Haydock race will be on the agenda once again, but it would be no surprise to see him go to Royal Ascot for the Duke of Edinburgh Handicap. (op 7-1)
Meethaaq(USA) is relatively inexperienced and raced quite close to the front, in fact he disputed the lead turning in. He was outpaced when the winner and fourth went for home before staying on again. He looks capable of better, but it will be interesting to see if connections try him over an extra quarter-mile at some stage. (op 7-2)
Drill Sergeant set the pace and his rider stacked his rivals up turning for home, hoping to kick on again. However, his mount could not respond initially and looked like finishing well beaten, only for the gelding to run on to good effect in the closing stages. Royal Ascot could also be on the cards for him, but he could be worth trying over 1m6f. He might not look out of place in the Ebor. (op 13-2)
Camps Bay(USA) was making his seasonal reappearance having had a light season last year. He got a gap halfway up the straight and was in front at the quarter-mile pole. He was then headed by the winner, but looked booked for second when short of room against the rail inside the final furlong, losing two places. He could renew rivalry with the winner at Ascot and Haydock, having contested those races last summer. (op 15-2 tchd 8-1)
Falcativ came into this in good form but was sweating up beforehand and was very keen in the race. Unsurprisingly he had nothing in reserve when things got serious. He was 7lb higher than for his last success and has gone up 20lb in the weights since initiating his hat-trick last autumn. However, he can be given another chance to prove this was just an off-day. (op 2-1 tchd 13-8)
Sevenna(FR) was dropping back in trip and was not suited by the muddling pace. (op 14-1)
King O'The Gypsies(IRE) Official explanation: jockey said colt was unsuited by the good (good to firm) ground

2472 UNISON "YOUR FRIEND AT WORK" H'CAP 5f
5:15 (5:15) (Class 5) (0-75,75) 4-Y-O+ **£3,238** (£963; £481; £240) **Stalls** High

Form RPR
2015 **1** **Loose Caboose (IRE)**5 2316 4-8-1 **61** oh1 (b) AndrewMullen(3) 14 71
(A J McCabe) *a.p: led over 1f out: sn rdn and hung rt: r.o* **9/1**
6-00 **2** *nk* **Namir (IRE)**19 1943 7-9-3 **74** (vt) DuranFentiman 19 83
(D Shaw) *sn pushed along in rr: swtchd lft 1/2-way: hdwy over 1f out: r.o wl* **18/1**
5024 **3** *shd* **Feelin Foxy**15 2046 5-8-9 **66** JamieMoriarty 5 75
(J G Given) *s.i.s: sn prom: rdn over 1f out: r.o* **12/1**
0661 **4** *2* **Peopleton Brook**10 2180 7-7-13 **61** (t) Louis-PhilippeBeuzelin(5) 7 62
(B G Powell) *s.i.s: sn pushed along in rr: swtchd lft and hdwy over 1f out: r.o: nt rch ldrs* **11/1**
0-62 **5** *1* **Ocean Blaze**22 1836 5-9-4 **75** JoeFanning 8 73
(B R Millman) *w ldr: rdn and ev ch over 1f out: n.m.r sn after: styd on same pce* **11/2**2
5-10 **6** *nse* **Molly Two**15 2046 4-8-4 **64** KellyHarrison(3) 1 62
(L A Mullaney) *led: rdn and hdd over 1f out: no ex ins fnl f* **25/1**
020 **7** *1 1/4* **King Of Swords (IRE)**8 2225 5-8-5 **67** AndreaAtzeni(5) 9 60
(N Tinkler) *prom: rdn and hung lft fr over 1f out: wknd ins fnl f* **7/1**
0-05 **8** *nse* **Circuit Dancer (IRE)**25 1768 9-8-9 **66** SilvestreDeSousa 13 59+
(D Nicholls) *sn pushed along and prom: rdn and nt clr run over 1f out: wknd ins fnl f* **11/2**2
0022 **9** *nk* **Billy Red**18 1957 5-8-10 **67** (b) AdrianMcCarthy 17 59
(J R Jenkins) *chsd ldrs: rdn over 1f out: wknd ins fnl f* **6/1**3
0-25 **10** *7* **Sea Rover (IRE)**5 2312 5-8-9 **66** TWilliams 16 33
(M Brittain) *s.i.s: sn pushed along in rr: rdn whn hmpd 1/2-way: sn wknd* **9/2**1
0-00 **11** *5* **Not My Choice (IRE)**96 654 4-8-7 **71** ThomasWhite(7) 6 20
(S Parr) *rrd s: outpcd* **40/1**
0330 **12** *76* **Regal Royale**15 2032 6-8-4 **61** (v) PatrickMathers 15 —
(Peter Grayson) *s.i.s: sn pushed along in rr: rdn and wknd wl over 1f out: virtually p.u fnl f* **16/1**

57.96 secs (-2.54) **Going Correction** -0.425s/f (Firm) **12** Ran SP% **119.2**
Speed ratings (Par 103): **103,102,102,99,97 97,95,95,94,83 75,—**
toteswinger: 1&2 £36.00, 1&3 £13.80, 2&3 £25.50 CSF £160.67 CT £1985.32 TOTE £10.20: £3.30, £5.20, £3.70; EX 225.60 TRIFECTA Not won..
Owner Dixon, McCabe and Timms **Bred** Paradime Ltd **Trained** Averham Park, Notts

FOCUS
An ordinary sprint handicap with plenty of exposed sorts, but seven withdrawals due mainly to the ground reduced the field by over a third. The form looks sound.
Regal Royale Official explanation: vet said gelding bled from the nose

2473 UNISON FAMILY PROTECTION "THERE FOR YOU" APPRENTICE H'CAP 1m (S)
5:50 (5:51) (Class 6) (0-60,63) 4-Y-O+ **£2,914** (£867; £433; £216) **Stalls** High

Form RPR
2353 **1** **Betteras Bertie**104 565 6-8-7 **53** JohnCavanagh(5) 12 69
(M Brittain) *s.s: outpcd: swtchd lft and hdwy over 3f out: led 2f out: sn rdn and hung rt: r.o wl* **11/1**
6030 **2** *7* **Amber Ridge**12 2125 4-8-3 **49** (p) PaulPickard(5) 4 49
(B P J Baugh) *led: rdn and hdd 2f out: sn hung rt: no ex fnl f* **33/1**
5-01 **3** *hd* **Silly Gilly (IRE)**21 1889 5-8-13 **57** DeclanCannon(3) 8 57
(R E Barr) *chsd ldrs: rdn over 2f out: styd on same pce appr fnl f* **15/2**
-621 **4** *shd* **Salerosa (IRE)**7 2261 4-9-8 **63** Louis-PhilippeBeuzelin 1 62
(Mrs A Duffield) *prom: rdn to chse wnr over 1f out: no ex fnl f* **11/4**1
1213 **5** *2 1/2* **Jord (IRE)**33 1566 5-8-7 **48** AndreaAtzeni 15 42
(A J McCabe) *chsd ldrs: rdn over 2f out: wknd over 1f out* **7/2**2
/30- **6** *1 1/2* **Private Soldier**474 521 6-8-9 **50** DeanHeslop 16 40
(N J Vaughan) *dwlt: outpcd: hdwy u.p over 2f out: wknd over 1f out* **14/1**
0-06 **7** *nk* **Slip Star**21 1887 6-8-3 **51** MarzenaJeziorek(7) 17 40
(T J Etherington) *mid-div: sn pushed along: edgd lft over 5f out: n.d* **16/1**
00-0 **8** *1 3/4* **Jay Gee Wigmo**26 1741 4-8-8 **49** AmyBaker 5 34
(A W Carroll) *mid-div: sn drvn along: n.d* **20/1**
0000 **9** *1 1/4* **Pharaohs Justice (USA)**66 961 4-8-7 **55** (b) AlexOwen(7) 20 38
(N P Littmoden) *chsd ldrs: rdn and hung lft over 3f out: wkng whn hung rt over 1f out* **33/1**
6200 **10** *2 3/4* **Sion Hill (IRE)**22 1846 8-8-8 **52** (p) SimonPearce(3) 10 28
(John A Harris) *prom: rdn over 2f out: wkng whn hmpd over 1f out* **25/1**
0000 **11** *1 1/2* **Bright Falcon**27 1690 4-8-4 **52** (bt) ThomasWhite(7) 7 25
(S Parr) *s.s: outpcd* **33/1**
2404 **12** *4 1/2* **Aggbag**21 1883 5-8-6 **50** BillyCray(3) 19 12
(B P J Baugh) *chsd ldrs tl wknd over 2f out* **7/1**3
050 **13** *2* **Carnival Fair**33 1562 4-7-12 **46** oh1 FrazerWilliams(7) 11 4
(R A Fahey) *in rr whn hmpd over 5f out: n.d after* **33/1**
0040 **14** *3 3/4* **Mays Louise**36 760 5-7-13 **47** NoraLooby(7) 13 —
(B P J Baugh) *sn outpcd* **100/1**
00-0 **15** *8* **Flashy Max**37 1475 4-8-9 **50** PatrickDonaghy 9 —
(Jedd O'Keeffe) *s.i.s: sn prom: wknd 1/2-way* **20/1**
-500 **16** *15* **Stoneacre Donny (IRE)**15 2032 5-8-0 **46** oh1 AndrewHeffernan(5) 2 —
(Peter Grayson) *s.s: outpcd* **40/1**

1m 37.21s (-2.09) **Going Correction** -0.425s/f (Firm) **16** Ran SP% **122.6**
Speed ratings (Par 101): **93,86,85,85,83 81,81,79,78,75 74,69,67,63,55 40**
toteswinger: 1&2 £40.00, 1&3 £15.50, 2&3 £27.20 CSF £342.09 CT £2996.62 TOTE £12.50: £2.10, £5.90, £2.00, £1.40; EX 447.60 TRIFECTA Not won. Place 6 £264.40, Place 5 £214.89..
Owner Mrs V C Sugden **Bred** Mrs V C Sugden **Trained** Warthill, N Yorks
■ Stewards' Enquiry : Paul Pickard one-day ban: used whip down shoulder in forehand position (Jun 13)

FOCUS
Another big field for this moderate apprentices' handicap, but it was a one-horse race in the final furlong as Betteras Bertie showed improved form to slam his field.
Aggbag Official explanation: jockey said gelding was unsuited by the good to firm (good in places) ground
Flashy Max Official explanation: jockey said gelding hung left throughout
T/Plt: £1,002.30 to a £1 stake. Pool: £80,460.32. 58.60 winning tickets. T/Qpdt: £156.60 to a £1 stake. Pool: £3,026.38. 14.30 winning tickets. CR

[2429]**GOODWOOD** (R-H)

Saturday, May 30

OFFICIAL GOING: Good (good to firm in places)

Rail repositioning on the one mile course added 20yards to advertised distances.

Wind: Moderate, across Weather: Glorious

2474 TOTESCOOP6 STKS (H'CAP) 6f

2:20 (2:21) (Class 2) (0-100,98) 3-Y-0+

£11,215 (£3,358; £1,679; £840; £419; £210) **Stalls** Low

Form RPR

22-1 **1** **High Standing (USA)**[28] 1663 4-9-4 **91**...................... JamieSpencer 13 107+
(W J Haggas) *taken down early: hld up in rr: swtchd rt over 1f out: gd hdwy ent fnl f: led ins fnl f: sn in command: eased nr fin* **15/8**[1]

0-05 **2** 1 ¼ **Kerrys Requiem (IRE)**[15] 2049 3-8-5 **87**............................ TPO'Shea 6 93
(M R Channon) *awkward s: wl bhd: hanging rt and hdwy fr 2f out: r.o wl fnl f: wnt 2nd nr fin: no ch w wnr* **40/1**

0-12 **3** ½ **Rash Judgement**[28] 1668 4-9-0 **87**.............................. EddieAhern 14 93
(W S Kittow) *t.k.h: hld up in rr: rdn wl over 2f out: hdwy u.p over 1f out: styd on wl fnl f: wnt 3rd nr fin* **6/1**[3]

101- **4** nk **Osiris Way**[230] 6669 7-9-8 **95**............................ JimCrowley 8 100+
(P R Chamings) *chsd ldng pair: rdn 2f out: clsd on ldr ent fnl f: ev ch ins fnl f: one pce fnl 100yds* **10/1**

/50- **5** 1 ¼ **Major Eazy (IRE)**[220] 6903 4-9-11 **98**........................ RichardHughes 11 99
(B J Meehan) *taken down early: stdd s: hld up wl bhd: stl plenty to do 2f out: swtchd rt over 1f out: r.o wl fnl f: nt rch ldrs* **25/1**

0/40 **6** hd **Drawnfromthepast (IRE)**[14] 2078 4-9-8 **95**....................(t) ShaneKelly 9 95
(J A Osborne) *racd off the pce in midfield: rdn over 2f out: no hdwy tl kpt on u.p fnl f: nvr pce to threaten ldrs* **18/1**

0400 **7** hd **Benllech**[63] 1006 5-9-5 **92**.............................. RichardMullen 4 95+
(D M Simcock) *bhd: rdn wl over 2f out: nt clr run and hmpd wl over 1f out: r.o wl ins fnl f: nt rch ldrs* **40/1**

03-0 **8** ½ **Shifting Star (IRE)**[27] 1699 4-9-10 **97**........................ AdamKirby 5 95
(W R Swinburn) *racd off the pce in midfield: rdn wl over 2f out: kpt on same pce and no imp fnl 2f* **11/2**[2]

-005 **9** hd **Phantom Whisper**[14] 2078 6-9-0 **90**........................ JamesMillman(3) 1 87
(B R Millman) *dwlt: sn handy in main gp: rdn and hung rt jst over 2f out: no prog after* **18/1**

-316 **10** ½ **Peter Island (FR)**[28] 1668 6-8-13 **86**..........................(v) ChrisCatlin 10 82
(J Gallagher) *led at fast gallop and sn clr: rdn over 1f out: hdd ins fnl f: fdd fnl 100yds* **16/1**

13-5 **11** nk **Seamus Shindig**[21] 1864 7-8-7 **87**........................ AmyScott(7) 7 82+
(H Candy) *hld up in midfield: shuffled bk towards rr 1/2-way: hmpd 2f out: nt clr run fr over 1f out: no ch* **8/1**

0-51 **12** ¾ **Earlsmedic**[19] 1943 4-8-12 **85**...............................(v) SaleemGolam 2 78
(S C Williams) *chsd clr ldr tl jst over 1f out: sn hrd drvn and wknd fnl f* **9/1**

0105 **13** 3 ¾ **Little Edward**[9] 2191 11-9-0 **92**............................ MCGeran(5) 12 73
(R J Hodges) *taken down early: in tch: rdn over 2f out: sn struggling* **40/1**

1m 10.03s (-2.17) **Going Correction** -0.125s/f (Firm)

WFA 3 from 4yo+ 9lb **13** Ran SP% **122.2**

Speed ratings (Par 109): **109,107,106,106,104 104,104,103,103,102 102,101,96**

toteswinger: 1&2 £18.40, 1&3 £2.80, 2&3 £23.90 CSF £110.35 CT £407.90 TOTE £2.80: £1.40, £8.80, £2.30; EX 107.00 Trifecta £346.00 Part won. Pool £467.58 - 0.40 winning units..

Owner Findlay & Bloom **Bred** Dr Melinda Blue **Trained** Newmarket, Suffolk

FOCUS

A sunny day and the ground had dried up, resulting in a change of the going description to good, good to firm in places. The whole field came up the centre of the track, spearheaded by Peter Island, who set a very strong pace which inevitably resulted in the race being set up for the closers. The winner was always going well and has more to offer.

NOTEBOOK

High Standing(USA) ◆ is a very progressive sprinter and, being a confirmed hold-up performer, could not have hoped for things to pan out any better for him, as the decent gallop proved ideal. Challenging towards the far side of the group, he quickened up well to join the leader and then drew clear inside the final half furlong. The Wokingham, for which he's now disputing favouritism, looks the logical next step as 6f is very much his trip, having now won each of his four starts over the distance. However, connections suggested he wouldn't want the ground any quicker than this. (op 7-4 tchd 2-1)

Kerrys Requiem(IRE) carried the winning owner's second colours. Held up in last position, she hung right, like last time, carrying her head awkwardly and looking far from happy at halfway, but she found her stride in the closing stages and, as the leaders hit the wall, she finished her race off well. She had been dropped 11lb since the beginning of the season so was entitled to respect from a handicapping point of view, but the way the race was run means she is possibly flattered by the bare form.

Rash Judgement, raised 2lb for finishing second here earlier in the month, again showed his liking for the track with a sound effort in third. (op 8-1)

Osiris Way did best of those that chased the strong gallop. Another with a good record at this track (two wins from his previous four starts), this was a good effort off a career-high mark, particularly as he had been lame the previosu day and so his participation had been in doubt. (tchd 9-1)

Major Eazy(IRE), running in a handicap for the first time on his reappearance, was another who was held up towards the rear of the field and passed a number of rivals late on. His finishing position possibly flatters him and he might yet need some help from the handicapper. Official explanation: jockey said gelding jumped awkwardly (op 33-1)

Drawnfromthepast(IRE) was well beaten at Newbury but this sort of ground suits him much better. (op 16-1 tchd 20-1)

Benllech didn't get a clear run and shaped better than his finishing position, but he's still winless on turf.

Shifting Star(IRE)'s wins have all come on good ground or softer and the drying conditions were probably against him. (op 13-2)

Seamus Shindig Official explanation: jockey said gelding was denied a clear run

2475 TOTESWINGER STKS (H'CAP) 1m 4f

2:50 (2:54) (Class 3) (0-90,90) 4-Y-0+ **£9,714** (£2,890; £1,444; £721) **Stalls** Low

Form RPR

-321 **1** **Red Merlin (IRE)**[22] 1826 4-8-13 **85**..............................(v) AdamKirby 3 96
(C G Cox) *hld up in midfield: stdy hdwy 3f out: chsd ldng pair over 1f out: rdn and r.o wl fnl f to ld fnl 75yds* **5/1**[3]

311- **2** ¾ **Crackentorp**[267] 5682 4-9-0 **86**........................... GeorgeBaker 11 96+
(R M Beckett) *trckd ldrs: wnt 2nd 5f out: led gng wl over 3f out: rdn clr 2f out: hdd and no ex fnl 75yds* **10/3**[1]

440- **3** 2 **Manyriverstocross (IRE)**[235] 6563 4-9-0 **86**................ JamieSpencer 13 93
(A King) *t.k.h: hld up in tch: rdn and effrt 3f out: chsd ldr over 2f out: no imp and hld whn hung rt ins fnl f* **5/1**[3]

20/0 **4** 2 **Aaim To Prosper (IRE)**[15] 2055 5-8-10 **82**............ EdwardCreighton 10 86
(M R Channon) *chsd ldrs: rdn over 4f out: drvn and unable qck 3f out: kpt on u.p but nvr pce to rch ldrs* **40/1**

54-0 **5** 1 **Sam Lord**[30] 549 5-8-10 **82**............................... ShaneKelly 9 84
(A King) *hld up towards rr: effrt towards inner over 2f out: swtchd lft over 1f out: r.o fnl f but nvr gng to rch ldrs* **20/1**

-213 **6** ¾ **Special Reserve (IRE)**[8] 2239 4-8-10 **82**.................... RichardHughes 4 83+
(R Hannon) *stdd after s: hld up towards rr: hdwy and n.m.r 2f out: swtchd lft ent fnl f: edgd lft but styd on after: nvr trbld ldrs* **7/1**

0-00 **7** 1 **Goodwood Starlight (IRE)**[16] 2003 4-9-1 **87**.................... LPKeniry 12 88
(G L Moore) *hld up towards rr: hdwy jst over 2f out: nt clr run and hmpd over 1f out: nvr trbld ldrs* **40/1**

0262 **8** 2 ¼ **John Terry (IRE)**[8] 2242 6-9-4 **90**.............................. JimCrowley 7 86
(Mrs A J Perrett) *led tl rdn and hdd over 3f out: drvn and wknd over 2f out* **20/1**

165- **9** 1 **Rowan Rio**[222] 6866 4-8-12 **84**.. LDettori 1 78
(W J Haggas) *hld up in midfield: rdn and effrt jst over 2f out: no prog and edgd rt wl over 1f out* **10/1**

1002 **10** 1 ¾ **Bassinet (USA)**[18] 1966 5-8-5 **77**........................ KirstyMilczarek 8 68
(J A R Toller) *stdd s: hld up in rr: hdwy on outer over 3f out: rdn and wknd over 2f out* **25/1**

0-34 **11** nk **Dona Alba (IRE)**[16] 2003 4-9-4 **90**.............................. EddieAhern 14 81
(J L Dunlop) *chsd ldr tl 5f out: rdn over 3f out: drvn and wknd 2f out* **4/1**[2]

2020 **12** ¾ **Wine 'n Dine**[14] 2085 4-9-0 **86**.............................. RichardMullen 6 76
(G L Moore) *hld up in midfield: rdn 4f out: bhd fr wl over 2f out* **33/1**

4162 **13** 13 **King Supreme (IRE)**[26] 1753 4-8-11 **83**..........................(b) TPO'Shea 5 52
(R Hannon) *hld up in rr: rdn and no rspnse 3f out: t.o fnl f* **40/1**

2m 35.92s (-2.48) **Going Correction** -0.125s/f (Firm) **13** Ran SP% **121.6**

Speed ratings (Par 107): **103,102,101,99,99 98,98,96,95,94 94,93,85**

toteswinger: 1&2 £12.00, 1&3 £17.30, 2&3 £16.50 CSF £20.61 CT £88.18 TOTE £6.30: £1.80, £1.90, £2.80; EX 28.70 Trifecta £482.20 Pool £16,553.84 - 25.40 winning units..

Owner Reid's Allstars **Bred** Keatly Overseas Ltd **Trained** Lambourn, Berks

FOCUS

The early pace was far from frenetic, but the right horses came to the fore at the finish and the form looks solid enough. A clear personal best from the winner, and a highly encouraging reappearance from the second.

NOTEBOOK

Red Merlin(IRE) travelled well and, although the favourite got first run on him, was able to pick up well enough once switched to close him down inside the last. He has a progressive profile - he was 8lb higher here than when dead-heating at Chester last time - and one would imagine that something like the Duke of Edinburgh at Royal Ascot could be on his agenda now. (op 6-1 tchd 9-2)

Crackentorp ◆, making his debut for his new stable. looked the winner when going on with over two furlongs to run but was cut down late by a similarly progressive rival. A Northumberland Plate entry suggests that connections expect him to stay a good deal further, and there should be improvement to come when he does step up in distance. Still only lightly raced, he is probably capable of a much better and is one to keep on the right side of (op 11-4 tchd 4-1)

Manyriverstocross(IRE) was very well backed and ran a sound race on his reappearance. One would expect him to come on for this, and he will have prospects in similar company off his mid-80s mark. (op 10-1)

Aaim To Prosper(IRE) improved for his return from a long absence and posted a respectable effort. (op 33-1)

Sam Lord probably found the ground on the quick side. (op 25-1 tchd 28-1)

Special Reserve(IRE) was continually denied a clear run up the straight and shaped as though he could have finished a lot closer had the gaps arrived earlier. He wasn't knocked about in a lost cause, but he has a poor strike-rate and is not one to go overboard about. Official explanation: jockey said, regarding running and riding, that his orders were to ride the colt as he had done on its last three runs, drop it in and try to arrive in a challenging position on the bridle, adding that that race was run slower than he had anticipated and from 2f out when he wanted to challenge he failed to get a clear run. (op 8-1)

Dona Alba(IRE) didn't settle well enough and could have done with a stronger pace. Her rider also reported that she hung right. Official explanation: jockey said filly hung right (op 11-2 tchd 7-2 and 6-1 in a place)

2476 ON THE HOUSE STKS (LISTED RACE) 1m

3:25 (3:25) (Class 1) 3-Y-0+

£22,708 (£8,608; £4,308; £2,148; £1,076; £540) **Stalls** High

Form RPR

-112 **1** **Premio Loco (USA)**[70] 913 5-9-8 109........................... GeorgeBaker 7 112+
(C F Wall) *taken down early: trckd ldrs: rdn 2f out: nt clr run after tl squeezed between horses wl ins fnl f: qcknd to ld fnl strides* **5/1**

-130 **2** nk **Pure Poetry (IRE)**[28] 1675 3-8-10 107........................ RichardHughes 8 108
(R Hannon) *chsd ldr: rdn to ld narrowly ent fnl 2f: hld on gamely tl hdd fnl strides* **6/1**

2121 **3** hd **Yamal (IRE)**[16] 2015 4-9-8 109.. LDettori 1 110
(Saeed Bin Suroor) *in tch in midfield tl lost pl over 5f out: rdn and effrt on outer over 2f out: hdwy over 1f out: ev ch fnl f: no ex fnl strides* **7/2**[2]

210- **4** nse **Mac Love**[164] 7703 8-9-8 104.. AdamKirby 5 110
(Stef Liddiard) *taken down early: stdd s: hld up in rr: hdwy and edging out lft fr 2f out: drvn and hdwy ent fnl f: str chal ins fnl f: edgd sltly rt fnl 50yds: no ex nr fin* **50/1**

-151 **5** 1 ¾ **King Of Dixie (USA)**[29] 1641 5-9-5 107........................ JimCrowley 3 103+
(W J Knight) *taken down early: hld up in tch: rdn and effrt jst over 2f out: pressed ldrs and hrd drvn over 1f out: wknd ins fnl f* **9/1**

60-2 **6** hd **Perfect Stride**[31] 1600 4-9-5 108.................................. JamieSpencer 2 103+
(Sir Michael Stoute) *stdd s: hld up in last pl: rdn and effrt 2f out: nvr pce to rch ldrs* **9/2**[3]

0-06 **7** ½ **Bushman**[23] 1799 5-9-5 103.. RichardMullen 9 101
(D M Simcock) *led: rdn and hdd ent fnl 2f: kpt on pressing ldr tl wknd ins fnl f* **12/1**

3-21 **8** ½ **Unnefer (FR)**[21] 1875 4-9-5 111.................................... EddieAhern 4 104+
(H R A Cecil) *in tch: rdn and effrt jst over 2f out: drvn and ev ch over 1f out: stl pressing ldr but one pce whn squeezed out wl ins fnl f: eased after* **3/1**[1]

1m 36.58s (-3.32) **Going Correction** -0.125s/f (Firm)

WFA 3 from 4yo+ 12lb **8** Ran SP% **116.0**

Speed ratings (Par 111): **111,110,110,110,108 108,108,107**

toteswinger: 1&2 £7.70, 1&3 £3.70, 2&3 £4.80 CSF £35.40 TOTE £6.80: £2.20, £1.90, £1.50; EX 37.80 Trifecta £94.80 Pool £1,473.25 - 11.50 winning units..

Owner Bernard Westley **Bred** Kidder, Cole & Griggs **Trained** Newmarket, Suffolk

FOCUS

A competitive little Listed contest on paper, and that was borne out in the race itself, but messy form, with just about all of the runners in with a chance a furlong out, and four crossing the line almost The form has been rated around the second running to his Guineas level and the long-priced fourth to the best of last year's AW form.

NOTEBOOK

Premio Loco(USA), last seen being beaten narrowly in the Winter Derby on his favoured Polytrack surface, had to prove he could be as effective on turf - his last outing on grass in the Cambridgeshire still left a few question marks. He showed his trademark turn of foot to quicken up between horses and grab the race close home and, while the bare form of this success would still not be quite as strong as the very best of his all-weather efforts, it shows he can compete successfully at Pattern level on turf. Connections are likely to look for something similar at Listed/Group 3 level next. (op 6-1 tchd 13-2 in a place)

Pure Poetry(IRE), seventh in the 2000 Guineas on his previous start, didn't do that form any harm with a solid effort against these older horses. He is clearly up to winning another race at this level, but Royal Ascot is next up, with the Jersey looking a more attractive option than the St James's Palace Stakes at the moment. (op 7-1)

Yamal(IRE), who won a handicap over this C&D last summer for Mark Johnston, has looked steadily progressive since. He challenged widest of all and had every chance but just couldn't reel in the principals. His pedigree suggests this is as far as he'd need to go. (tchd 4-1 and 9-2 in a place)

Mac Love was restricted to just four starts last year, but managed to take a Listed race on the Polytrack towards the backend. Making his reappearance, he was fully expected to need this, and in the circumstances ran a cracker. One win from his last 31 starts suggests he's not one to be piling into, but he clearly retains the ability to win at Pattern level when things drop right. (op 66-1)

King Of Dixie(USA), comfortable winner of a little conditions race on the Polytrack last time out, was a little one-paced in the closing stages and still looks a better horse on the artificial surface for now. (op 12-1)

Perfect Stride didn't look happy on this track when a beaten favourite in a similar race here last summer, and it looked to be the same again this time. (op 4-1 tchd 5-1)

Bushman needs softer ground to be seen at his best.

Unnefer(FR) also needs more give in the ground, and is probably more effective over 1m2f as well. Official explanation: trainer said colt was unsuited by the good (good to firm places) ground (op 7-2)

2477 NICK BROOKS E B F MAIDEN STKS — 6f

3:55 (3:56) (Class 4) 2-Y-O — **£6,476** (£1,927; £963; £481) **Stalls** Low

Form — RPR

1 **Fremont (IRE)** 2-9-3 0 ... RichardHughes 7 — 78+
(R Hannon) *chsd ldrs: wnt 2nd wl over 1f out: sn outpcd by ldr: rallied ins fnl f: r.o wl to ld last stride* **4/1**[3]

2 2 *shd* **Rakaan (IRE)**[15] 2033 2-9-3 0 ... JamieSpencer 1 — 78
(B J Meehan) *t.k.h: hld up in tch: effrt to ld 2f out: sn rdn clr: tiring fnl 100yds: ct last stride* **11/8**[1]

52 3 1 ¼ **State Fair**[11] 2147 2-9-3 0 ... MartinDwyer 4 — 75+
(P F I Cole) *hld up in tch: rdn and effrt jst over 2f out: chsd ldrs and hung lft jst over 1f out: wnt 3rd ins fnl f: running on fin: nt rch ldng pair* **11/4**[2]

4 4 **Marine Spirit (GER)** 2-9-3 0 ... LDettori 2 — 64+
(Saeed Bin Suroor) *wnt rt s and s.i.s: t.k.h: hld up towards rr: hdwy and rdn 2f out: chsd ldng pair over 1f out: wkng whn hit on nose by rivals whip ins fnl f: eased towards fin* **9/1**

5 3 ¾ **Orpen Grey (IRE)** 2-8-12 0 ... RossAtkinson(5) 5 — 51
(Tom Dascombe) *hmpd s and s.i.s: bhd: kpt on past btn horses fnl f: nvr nr ldrs* **14/1**

00 6 3 ½ **Silvee**[23] 1810 2-8-12 0 ... NeilChalmers 3 — 35
(J J Bridger) *led tl 1/2-way: sn wknd u.p* **100/1**

7 1 ¾ **Wing Of Faith** 2-9-3 0 ... GeorgeBaker 9 — 35
(S Kirk) *w ldr tl led 1/2-way: sn hdd: wknd qckly* **25/1**

3 8 4 ½ **Trelawny Wells**[12] 2121 2-9-3 0 ... EdwardCreighton 6 — 22
(M R Channon) *s.i.s: a bhd* **33/1**

9 8 **Extreme Warrior (IRE)** 2-9-3 0 ... ChrisCatlin 8 — —
(D R Lanigan) *s.i.s: a outpcd in rr* **20/1**

1m 12.24s (0.04) **Going Correction** -0.125s/f (Firm) — **9** Ran SP% **118.0**
Speed ratings (Par 95): **94,93,92,86,81 77,74,68,58**
toteswinger: 1&2 £2.90, 1&3 £4.20, 2&3 £1.10 CSF £9.82 TOTE £5.30: £1.80, £1.20, £1.50; EX 11.40.
Owner Mrs J Wood **Bred** Peter Gibbons And Dermot Forde **Trained** East Everleigh, Wilts

FOCUS

Probably a fair maiden and it was dominated by the market principals. A nice start from Fremont, and the next three all look capable of winning maidens.

NOTEBOOK

Fremont(IRE) ◆, a brother to Listed-class performer Asset, looked the part beforehand and got the job done in good style having looked held by the favourite entering the final furlong. Sure to come on for the outing, his next target has yet to be decided, but he could be useful. (op 9-2 tchd 5-1)

Rakaan(IRE), who had the benefit of experience, looked to have poached a decisive lead when sent to the front two furlongs out, but he idled inside the last and was run out of it close home. Plenty was done on him at 1.01 and no doubt in future his challenge will be delayed a lot longer. Given his pedigree it's possible he won't want the ground any quicker than this. (op Evens tchd 10-11)

State Fair was having his third start but stepping up to 6f for the first time. He is by Marju and, as expected, the longer distance brought about improvement. There should be a maiden for him at one of the lesser tracks before the nursery season kicks off. (op 9-2 tchd 5-1)

Marine Spirit(GER) ◆, who was a bit keen early, briefly threatened to run on for second before his effort flattened out inside the last. A brother to Molly Max, who was champion two-year-old in Germany, he should come on a good deal for this debut effort. Official explanation: jockey said colt ran green (op 8-1 tchd 15-2)

Orpen Grey(IRE), a half-brother to a couple of juvenile winners, showed signs of inexperience but shaped fairly well. He might need a bit more time. (op 16-1 tchd 17-2)

Silvee had clearly learned from her first two starts, when she was slowly away both times, and showed a good deal more early speed here. (op 66-1)

2478 GEMINI JUBILEE STKS (H'CAP) — 5f

4:30 (4:31) (Class 5) (0-70,68) 3-Y-O — **£3,238** (£963; £481; £240) **Stalls** Low

Form — RPR

505- 1 **Silky Way (GR)**[175] 7574 3-8-13 63 ... LPKeniry 8 — 70
(P R Chamings) *mde all: rdn wl over 1f out: edgd lft u.p: hld on wl fnl 100yds* **13/2**

-344 2 *nk* **Piste**[3] 2386 3-9-2 66 ... (b[1]) JamieSpencer 7 — 72
(B J Meehan) *in tch: hdwy and rdn 2f out: chsd wnr over 1f out: edgd lft u.p: pressed wnr ins fnl f: nt qckn and hld towards fin* **3/1**[2]

-000 3 2 ½ **Louie's Lad**[3] 2386 3-8-4 54 oh6 ... (p) FrankieMcDonald 6 — 51+
(J J Bridger) *chsd wnr: rdn jst over 2f out: 4th and btn whn hmpd ent fnl f: kpt on to regain 3rd wl ins fnl f* **25/1**

1-06 4 ½ **Hillside Lad**[16] 2010 3-9-4 68 ... GeorgeBaker 5 — 63
(R M Beckett) *in tch: rdn 1/2-way: drvn to chse ldrs over 1f out: wknd ins fnl f* **9/4**[1]

-325 5 2 ¼ **Captain Kallis (IRE)**[18] 1969 3-8-12 62 ... (v[1]) ChrisCatlin 3 — 49
(D J S Ffrench Davis) *rrd s and hmpd sn after: bhd: rdn and sme hdwy 1/2-way: edgd lft and wknd wl over 1f out* **4/1**[3]

3-14 6 ¾ **Jolly Ranch**[103] 568 3-8-10 60 ... SimonWhitworth 1 — 44
(A G Newcombe) *chsd ldrs: rdn 1/2-way: wknd wl over 1f out* **16/1**

0-05 7 *hd* **Peper Harow (IRE)**[11] 2162 3-8-8 58 ... (v[1]) RichardMullen 2 — 42
(M D I Usher) *towards rr: rdn and effrt jst over 2f out: no prog whn hung rt ent fnl f: wl btn after* **6/1**

0-60 8 8 **Day In Dubai**[16] 2010 3-8-5 55 ... NeilChalmers 4 — 10
(J J Bridger) *wnt lft s: chsd ldrs tl 1/2-way: sn struggling: bhd fnl 2f* **20/1**

57.97 secs (-0.43) **Going Correction** -0.125s/f (Firm) — **8** Ran SP% **117.9**
Speed ratings (Par 99): **98,97,93,92,89 87,87,74**
toteswinger: 1&2 £5.50, 1&3 £21.20, 2&3 £12.10 CSF £27.24 CT £394.57 TOTE £9.20: £2.30, £1.50, £4.20; EX 27.60.
Owner Mrs Alexandra J Chandris **Bred** Ippotour Stud **Trained** Baughurst, Hants
■ Stewards' Enquiry : Jamie Spencer one-day ban: careless riding (Jun 13)

FOCUS

A modest sprint, but the winner was unexposed and hails from a stable that does well with her type. The form is limited by teh third, who was 6lb 'wrong'.

Silky Way(GR) Official explanation: trainer said, regarding apparent improvement in form, that the filly had grown and matured over the winter.

Captain Kallis(IRE) Official explanation: jockey said gelding was hampered start

Day In Dubai Official explanation: jockey said filly jumped left on leaving stalls

2479 "LIFETIME IN RACING" STKS (H'CAP) — 1m 3f

5:05 (5:06) (Class 5) (0-70,70) 3-Y-O — **£3,238** (£963; £481; £240) **Stalls** Low

Form — RPR

6-23 1 **Sherman McCoy**[19] 1930 3-8-12 67 ... JamesMillman(3) 1 — 75+
(B R Millman) *chsd ldr tl led over 4f out: rdn clr over 2f out: in command and pushed out fnl f* **9/2**[2]

20-0 2 1 ½ **Cool Strike (UAE)**[19] 1928 3-8-13 65 ... (v[1]) FrancisNorton 9 — 70
(A M Balding) *hld up towards rr: hdwy and nt clr run over 2f out: rdn to chse ldrs and edgd lft over 1f out: chsd wnr ent fnl f: kpt on but nvr gng to rch wnr* **25/1**

00-0 3 1 **Harlestone Snake**[28] 1670 3-9-0 66 ... ChrisCatlin 12 — 73+
(J L Dunlop) *stdd s: hld up bhd: n.m.r and hmpd over 2f out: hdwy over 1f out: r.o u.p fnl f: nt rch ldrs* **8/1**

6436 4 2 ¾ **Cayman Sky**[19] 1930 3-8-12 67 ... (b) PatrickHills(3) 3 — 66
(R Hannon) *t.k.h: hld up in midfield: hdwy over 3f out: rdn to chse clr wnr over 2f out: no imp: lost 2nd ent fnl f* **14/1**

0-60 5 6 **Abulharith**[40] 1408 3-9-3 69 ... RichardHughes 8 — 57
(P W Chapple-Hyam) *t.k.h: hld up towards rr: rdn and hdwy 3f out: drvn and no prog 2f out: wl btn whn hung lft over 1f out* **11/2**[3]

0-34 6 3 **Theologist (IRE)**[9] 2206 3-9-2 68 ... JimCrowley 7 — 50
(Mrs A J Perrett) *in tch: rdn and effrt over 3f out: hrd drvn and lost pl over 2f out: no ch fnl 2f* **5/2**[1]

0-16 7 2 ½ **Spinning Waters**[26] 1747 3-9-1 67 ... StephenCarson 6 — 45
(Eve Johnson Houghton) *led: rdn and hdd over 4f out: wknd u.p over 2f out* **20/1**

000- 8 *nk* **Kidson (USA)**[270] 5590 3-8-4 56 oh11 ... NeilPollard 2 — 33
(George Baker) *s.i.s and rdn along early: bhd: short lived effrt u.p on outer 3f out: wl btn fnl 2f* **66/1**

0-54 9 8 **Arrogance**[28] 1670 3-9-0 66 ow1 ... GeorgeBaker 11 — 29
(G L Moore) *in tch in midfield: hdwy to trck ldrs wl over 3f out: rdn and edgd rt over 2f out: sn wl btn: eased ins fnl f* **14/1**

0-00 10 3 ¼ **Flannel (IRE)**[19] 1931 3-9-4 70 ... AdamKirby 13 — 27
(J R Fanshawe) *in tch: rdn over 3f out: wkng whn short of room over 2f out: sn bhd: eased ins fnl f* **16/1**

-612 11 9 **Eightdaysaweek**[12] 2131 3-7-12 57 ... CharlesEddery(7) 4 — —
(S Kirk) *t.k.h: hld up in rr: reminders over 4f out: bit slipped through mouth: c wd over 3f out: lost tch over 2f out: t.o and eased fnl f* **12/1**

1- 12 16 **Aboukir**[209] 7148 3-9-4 70 ... LDettori 5 — —
(P F I Cole) *chsd ldr: rdn over 3f out: wkg whn hmpd over 2f out: eased after: t.o* **15/2**

2m 25.71s (-2.59) **Going Correction** -0.125s/f (Firm) — **12** Ran SP% **122.0**
Speed ratings (Par 99): **104,102,102,100,95 93,91,91,85,83 76,65**
toteswinger: 1&2 £25.10, 1&3 £7.60, 2&3 £43.80 CSF £118.47 CT £893.95 TOTE £5.50: £2.00, £7.20, £2.90; EX 151.20.
Owner Mustajed Partnership **Bred** Horizon Bloodstock Limited **Trained** Kentisbeare, Devon

FOCUS

They didn't go a great pace early on in this ordinary middle-distance handicap, and the form looks decidedly modest as there were few progressive types in the line up and the favourite disappointed. The form makes sense overall, however, and there was slight improvement from the first three.

Abulharith Official explanation: trainer said colt bled from the nose

Spinning Waters Official explanation: jockey said gelding hung left

Eightdaysaweek Official explanation: jockey said bit slipped through

Aboukir Official explanation: jockey said gelding lost its action

2480 RACING UK 5TH BIRTHDAY CELEBRATION STKS (H'CAP) — 1m

5:40 (5:41) (Class 3) (0-90,90) 4-Y-O+

£7,477 (£2,239; £1,119; £560; £279; £140) **Stalls** High

Form — RPR

/1-0 1 **Riggins (IRE)**[14] 2083 5-9-3 89 ... LDettori 10 — 104+
(L M Cumani) *t.k.h: chsd ldrs: hdwy on inner over 2f out: ev ch fr over 1f out: drvn to ld ins fnl f: forged ahd towards fin* **4/6**[1]

0501 2 ¾ **Mujood**[9] 2193 6-8-9 84 ... KevinGhunowa(3) 7 — 96
(Eve Johnson Houghton) *led: rdn over 2f out: hrd pressed over 1f out: hdd ins fnl f: no ex towards fin* **12/1**[3]

4-46 3 2 ½ **Vainglory (USA)**[23] 1798 5-8-11 83 ... RichardMullen 5 — 89
(D M Simcock) *chsd ldrs: pushed along over 3f out: rdn and unable qck over 2f out: kpt on u.p on to go 3rd ins fnl f* **7/1**[2]

-003 4 *shd* **Cape Hawk (IRE)**[9] 2193 5-8-10 85 ... PatrickHills(3) 1 — 91
(R Hannon) *t.k.h: hld up in rr: effrt on outer jst over 2f out: hdwy u.p over 1f out: pressing for 3rd nr fin: nvr threatened ldrs* **14/1**

2-00 5 1 ¼ **Resurge (IRE)**[14] 2083 4-8-10 82 ... SimonWhitworth 11 — 85
(W S Kittow) *s.i.s: hld up bhd: rdn and hdwy 3f out: chsd ldrs over 2f out: wknd over 1f out* **50/1**

20-0 6 *hd* **Traphalgar (IRE)**[18] 1952 4-8-3 82 ... DTDaSilva(7) 9 — 85
(P F I Cole) *s.i.s: hld up towards rr: rdn wl over 2f out: nvr pce to trble ldrs* **33/1**

/40- 7 ½ **Overturn (IRE)**[346] 3122 5-9-1 87 ... AdamKirby 6 — 89
(W R Swinburn) *chsd ldr tl over 2f out: wknd u.p over 1f out* **7/1**[2]

04-0 8 ¾ **Classic Legend**[21] 1860 4-8-13 90 ... GabrielHannon(5) 8 — 90
(B J Meehan) *hld up in midfield: rdn and unable qck 3f out: plugged on same pce fnl 2f* **33/1**

-340 9 4 ½ **Prince Of Thebes (IRE)**[23] 1813 8-8-9 81 ... KirstyMilczarek 4 — 70
(M J Attwater) *chsd ldrs: rdn and wknd ent fnl 2f out: wl btn and eased ins fnl f* **20/1**

1-60 10 6 **Isphahan**[14] 2083 6-9-2 88 ... FrancisNorton 3 — 64
(A M Balding) *a bhd: rdn and no prog 3f out: wl btn and eased ins fnl f* **25/1**

-100 **P** **Dubai Dynamo**[14] 2083 4-9-1 **87** .... GeorgeBaker 2 —
(P F I Cole) *wnt lft s: hld up in last pl tl eased and p.u 5f out: sddle slipped* **20/1**

1m 36.68s (-3.22) **Going Correction** -0.125s/f (Firm) **11** Ran SP% **120.6**
Speed ratings (Par 107): **111,110,107,107,106 106,105,104,100,94** —
toteswinger: 1&2 £3.20, 1&3 £2.50, 2&3 £7.30 CSF £8.98 CT £38.87 TOTE £1.70: £1.10, £2.40, £2.10; EX 9.70 Place 6 £57.73, Place 5 £35.67..
Owner Scuderia Rencati Srl **Bred** Compagnia Generale S R L **Trained** Newmarket, Suffolk

FOCUS
A routine handicap in which the interest all centred on Riggins, who was sent here in the hope of picking up a penalty for the Hunt Cup. He was not that impressive, but this is unlikely to be the limit of his improvement. The second has been rated to his level in the same race last year.

NOTEBOOK
Riggins(IRE), who looked so unlucky at Newmarket on his previous start, was running off the same mark and was sent off at odds-on to make amends. Although he did enough to pick up the penalty that will ensure a run in the Royal Hunt Cup, it has to be said that he was no more than workmanlike in victory. Indeed, it was surprising that some bookmakers saw enough to trim his price for the big Ascot handicap to as short as 6-1. On the plus side, he was beating a course specialist here, the pair clear, and a stronger pace in a big field will no doubt suit him better. Also, having been beaten only once - and unluckily at that - so far in his four-race career, there is a suspicion he could yet be a good deal better than this bare form suggests. (op 8-11 tchd 4-5)
Mujood, three times a winner at this track in the past, including last time out, gave the favourite a real race having enjoyed the run of things out in front. He rallied after being headed and is clearly at the top of his game at present. (op 9-1 tchd 8-1)
Vainglory(USA), who had not enjoyed much luck with the draw on his previous two starts, came in for good each-way support and kept on just well enough to hold off Cape Hawk for third. He doesn't have a great strike-rate but is on a fair mark at the moment. (op 10-1 tchd 13-2)
Cape Hawk(IRE) won off a 2lb higher mark last summer, so is fairly weighted these days. Whether he really needs the ground as quick as this is another question, though. (op 12-1)
Resurge(IRE) ran a more encouraging race, but he probably needs to drop a few pounds before becoming of interest. (op 33-1)
Overturn(IRE), returning from a year on the sidelines, raced keenly and dropped out from the two-furlong pole. He might just have needed this. (op 11-1 tchd 12-1)
Dubai Dynamo Official explanation: jockey said saddle slipped
T/Plt: £96.90 to a £1 stake. Pool: £93,066.14. 700.71 winning tickets. T/Qpdt: £24.50 to a £1 stake. Pool: £3,877.67. 116.70 winning tickets. SP

2442 HAYDOCK (L-H)
Saturday, May 30

OFFICIAL GOING: Good (good to soft in places; 7.7)
Races on round course run over 25yards further than advertised except the 4.45 race which was run over 20yards less due to rail realignment.
Wind: Moderate, half-behind Weather: fine, sunny and warm

2481 J. W. LEES ACHILLES STKS (LISTED RACE) 5f
2:05 (2:07) (Class 1) 3-Y-O+
£22,708 (£8,608; £4,308; £2,148; £1,076; £540) **Stalls** Centre

Form RPR
1 **Ialysos (GR)**[103] 5-9-3 0 .... WilliamBuick 10 112+
(L M Cumani) *racd stands' side: in rr: gd hdwy over 1f out: edgd lft and r.o wl to ld overall nr fin* **14/1**
54-1 **2** *nk* **Anglezarke (IRE)**[16] 2016 3-8-4 102 .... AndrewElliott 11 103
(T D Easterby) *swvd rt s: racd stands' side: chsd ldrs: led that gp over 1f out: edgd lft: kpt on wl* **13/2**[2]
0012 **3** *nk* **Hoh Hoh Hoh**[28] 1676 7-9-3 104 .... RyanMoore 1 110
(R J Price) *racd centre: chsd ldrs: led that gp over 1f out: hdd and no ex wl ins fnl f* **7/1**[3]
0-20 **4** *1 ¾* **Reverence**[7] 2272 8-9-3 103 .... WJSupple 8 104
(E J Alston) *racd stands' side: chsd ldrs: hrd rdn and hung rt 1f out: no ex* **28/1**
4-30 **5** *shd* **Peace Offering (IRE)**[7] 2259 9-9-7 103 .... SilvestreDeSousa 5 108
(D Nicholls) *racd centre: chsd ldrs: kpt on same pce appr fnl f* **20/1**
13-1 **6** *1* **Royal Rock**[21] 1868 5-9-3 107 .... AlanMunro 6 100+
(C F Wall) *racd centre: in rr: hdwy over 1f out: nvr trbld ldrs* **6/4**[1]
-302 **7** *1 ¾* **Fullandby (IRE)**[7] 2259 7-9-3 100 .... RoystonFfrench 9 94
(T J Etherington) *racd stands' side: sn outpcd and in rr: kpt on fnl 2f: nvr on terms* **12/1**
120- **8** *¾* **Percolator**[281] 5245 3-8-4 109 .... JimmyQuinn 2 83+
(P F I Cole) *racd centre: w ldr: wknd over 1f out* **18/1**
00-0 **9** *2 ½* **Dandy Man (IRE)**[28] 1676 6-9-3 106 .... (bt[1]) SebSanders 4 82
(Saeed Bin Suroor) *led centre tl hdd & wknd over 1f out* **7/1**[3]
0-00 **10** *3 ½* **Captain Gerrard (IRE)**[7] 2272 4-9-3 105 .... (b[1]) TomEaves 7 69
(B Smart) *led stands' side tl hdd & wknd over 1f out* **11/1**
-604 **11** *1 ½* **Foxy Music**[8] 2228 5-9-3 78 .... PJSmullen 3 64
(E J Alston) *racd centre: outpcd and dropped to rr over 3f out* **80/1**

59.71 secs (-0.79) **Going Correction** -0.10s/f (Good)
WFA 3 from 4yo+ 8lb **11** Ran SP% **115.7**
Speed ratings (Par 111): **102,101,101,98,98 96,93,92,88,82 80**
toteswinger: 1&2 £18.60, 1&3 £12.40, 2&3 £4.90. CSF £98.87 TOTE £15.10: £3.30, £2.50, £2.00; EX 118.90 Trifecta £395.60 Part won. Pool £534.70 - 0.70 winning units..
Owner Mrs M Marinopoulos **Bred** Figaia Stud **Trained** Newmarket, Suffolk

FOCUS
Conditions were drying out and the ground was riding quite quick according to the winning jockey in the opener, a view backed up by the time which was just inside the standard. This was the first running at Haydock of this Listed sprint, which has switched between Kempton and Goodwood in recent years. The first two home both came from a group of five which raced down the stands' side a little away from the others, although the field fanned out across the track in the closing stages. The form looks fair for the grade and sound rated around the placed horses.

NOTEBOOK
Ialysos(GR) came here unbeaten in seven starts at Markopoulou in his native Greece, all of them on sand at 5-7f, and had reportedly put up some very quick times there. Making his debut for Cumani, he stumbled slightly leaving the stalls and took time to find his full stride, but he picked up really well inside the last, while edging into the centre of the track, and finished strongly to get up. A good-looking son of Nunthorpe winner So Factual, he is set to go to Royal Ascot where he is likely to go for the Golden Jubilee Stakes over 6f. He is the only sprinter in Cumani's care and his new trainer is sure to place him to good effect. (op 12-1 tchd 16-1 in places)
Anglezarke(IRE), who made a successful return to action against her own sex at York, enjoyed all the allowances as a three-year-old filly. Racing down the stands' rail, she ran on well inside the last, but Ialysos finished that bit better. She should not be long in getting off the mark in this grade. (op 7-1)
Hoh Hoh Hoh's second to Amour Propre in the Palace House at the beginning of the month arguably represented his best-ever form at the age of seven, and he ran well here down in grade here, improving to lead on the far side but edging right under pressure in front and losing out close home. (op 6-1 tchd 11-2)
Reverence was well held in his favoured heavy ground here in the Temple Stakes a week ago, but he ran respectably on this different surface, sticking on for fourth after coming under pressure. (op 33-1)
Peace Offering(IRE) conceded at least 4lb to each of his rivals and found himself rather isolated racing down the middle, so this was a decent effort, certainly a better effort than he put in at Beverley the previous week.
Royal Rock, who had bolted up over 6f here three weeks ago, was disappointing. Upped in grade, he did not really have anything to race with down the centre of the track and, although staying on, never promised to pick up the leaders. This was his first-ever run over the minimum trip and a return to 6f looks required. He should be given another chance. (op 7-4 tchd 15-8 in places)
Fullandby(IRE) found this on the sharp side and was only getting going when it was as good as over. (tchd 14-1)
Percolator, off the track since taking on her elders last August in the Nunthorpe at York where she sustained a bone chip, showed pace before weakening. (op 12-1 tchd 20-1)
Dandy Man(IRE) was tried in blinkers and was also dropping in grade after some lacklustre efforts. The drying ground should have been in his favour, but after showing decent pace, he was easily taken care of. (op 8-1 tchd 13-2)
Captain Gerrard(IRE), also fitted with first-time headgear, got across to lead against the rail, but was under pressure at halfway and dropped out. He has become disappointing. (op 14-1)

2482 E B F JOAN WESTBROOK PINNACLE STKS (LISTED RACE) (F&M) 1m 3f 200y
2:35 (2:35) (Class 1) 4-Y-O+
£34,062 (£12,912; £6,462; £3,222; £1,614; £810) **Stalls** Low

Form RPR
131- **1** **Suzi's Decision**[300] 4667 4-8-12 100 .... PJSmullen 5 107+
(P W D'Arcy) *hld up in rr: hdwy 3f out: chal over 1f out: led jst ins fnl f: r.o wl* **11/2**[3]
12-6 **2** *2 ½* **Les Fazzani (IRE)**[17] 1996 5-9-1 105 .... StephenDonohoe 9 106
(K A Ryan) *sn chsng ldrs: led over 2f out: hdd jst ins fnl f: no ex* **15/2**
0-0 **3** *nse* **Cassique Lady (IRE)**[28] 1667 4-8-12 93 .... WilliamBuick 3 103
(Mrs L Wadham) *hld up in rr: hdwy over 3f out: kpt on wl fnl f* **22/1**
20-2 **4** *2 ½* **Starfala**[21] 1859 4-8-12 100 .... TomEaves 8 99
(P F I Cole) *s.i.s: hdwy on outside over 7f out: outpcd 3f out: styd on fnl f* **13/2**
-523 **5** *½* **Princess Taylor**[16] 2013 5-8-12 92 .... RoystonFfrench 7 98
(M Botti) *rn in snatches: lost pl over 5f out: kpt on fnl 2f* **16/1**
23-4 **6** *3 ¼* **Montbretia**[29] 1642 4-8-12 92 .... JimmyQuinn 6 93
(H R A Cecil) *sn trcking ldrs: effrt over 3f out: wknd over 1f out: lame* **5/2**[1]
16-4 **7** *1 ¼* **Syvilla**[31] 1613 4-8-12 90 .... SteveDrowne 1 91
(Rae Guest) *hld up in rr: hdwy over 3f out: wknd over 1f out* **16/1**
00/ **8** *1 ½* **Athlone (IRE)**[195] 5-9-1 94 .... RyanMoore 10 92
(L M Cumani) *led tl hdd over 2f out: lost pl over 1f out* **10/1**
214- **9** *1 ¾* **Gravitation**[261] 5826 4-8-12 108 .... AlanMunro 2 86
(W Jarvis) *awkward s: sn chsng ldrs: drvn 4f out: lost pl over 1f out* **9/2**[2]

2m 32.57s (-0.63) **Going Correction** +0.15s/f (Good) **9** Ran SP% **112.4**
Speed ratings (Par 111): **108,106,106,104,104 102,101,100,99**
toteswinger: 1&2 £8.90, 1&3 £18.30, 2&3 £19.70. CSF £44.65 TOTE £5.60: £1.70, £2.10, £5.00; EX 54.20 Trifecta £232.20 Part won. Pool £313.90 - 0.40 winning units..
Owner Greenstead Hall Racing Ltd **Bred** David And Mrs Vicki Fleet **Trained** Newmarket, Suffolk

FOCUS
Just a fair Listed race, run at an even pace and the form is sound, if ordinary for the grade. They raced down the centre of the track in the home straight.

NOTEBOOK
Suzi's Decision made rapid strides at three, beginning the season with an official rating of 69 and ending it on 100 following a win in a similar race to this at Newbury in August, and she looks to have maintained her progression. Running for the first time in ten months, having been given time to strengthen up, she improved from the back of the field down the stands' side of the bunch in the home straight. She had to battle to get the better of the runner-up, but stayed on strongly to be well on top at the line. Quicker ground than this suits her ideally and she has a date in Group 3 company at Cork next month. (op 15-2)
Les Fazzani(IRE), under a penalty for her win in this grade at Doncaster in the autumn, showed ahead in the straight and tried hard when tackled, but she could not hold off the winner inside the last. This was a good run, but she will not mind a drop back to 1m2f. (op 6-1)
Cassique Lady(IRE) travelled strongly but could only keep on at the same pace on this first try at 1m4f. She was the least-experienced runner in the field and deserves credit for a sound effort. (op 25-1 tchd 20-1)
Starfala, runner-up in an Ascot Listed race on her reappearance, for which she was raised 13lb by the official Handicapper, was outpaced by the principals in the straight here but fought on for a never-threatening fourth. (tchd 7-1)
Princess Taylor failed to settle and ran in snatches before plugging on for fifth. Another trying this trip for the first time, she appeared to stay it well enough. (op 18-1 tchd 20-1)
Montbretia, reverting to this trip, was found wanting on this rise in grade and could not turn around last October's autumn form with Starfala despite a 7lb pull. It was subsequently reported that she had finished lame. Official explanation: vet said filly returned lame on off-fore (op 3-1 tchd 9-4)
Athlone(IRE), penalised for her win in this grade in heavy ground back in November, made the running as she often does before fading on this debut in this country. (op 7-1)
Gravitation had a clear chance on official figures, but she was disappointing on her seasonal debut. All her best form has been over further and she needs at least 1m6f these days. (op 4-1 tchd 11-2)

2483 TIMEFORM JURY STKS (REGISTERED AS THE JOHN OF GAUNT STAKES) (GROUP 3) 7f 30y
3:05 (3:09) (Class 1) 4-Y-O+
£39,739 (£15,064; £7,539; £3,759; £1,883; £945) **Stalls** Low

Form RPR
00-1 **1** **Main Aim**[14] 2078 4-9-0 113 .... RyanMoore 1 121+
(Sir Michael Stoute) *trckd ldrs: led over 2f out: styd on strly fnl f: readily* **7/4**[1]
4-01 **2** *2* **Beacon Lodge (IRE)**[21] 1865 4-9-0 112 .... WilliamBuick 8 116
(C G Cox) *t.k.h: trckd ldrs: wnt 2nd over 1f out: no imp* **7/2**[2]
641- **3** *1* **Arabian Gleam**[259] 5893 5-9-5 115 .... (p) SebSanders 9 118
(J Noseda) *mid-div: effrt over 3f out: styd on fnl f* **10/1**
4101 **4** *½* **Asset (IRE)**[35] 1513 6-9-0 108 .... (b) WJSupple 2 112+
(Saeed Bin Suroor) *t.k.h in rr: hdwy on outer 3f out: kpt on fnl f* **11/1**
1-40 **5** *nk* **Atlantic Sport (USA)**[14] 2076 4-9-0 107 .... SamHitchcott 6 111
(M R Channon) *chsd ldrs: styd on same pce fnl 2f* **10/1**
10-4 **6** *¾* **Royal Confidence**[21] 1873 4-8-11 103 .... MichaelHills 5 106
(B W Hills) *hld up in rr: hdwy on wd outsider over 2f out: kpt on: nvr threatened ldrs* **33/1**
05-6 **7** *nk* **Tariq**[14] 2076 5-9-0 112 .... AlanMunro 3 108
(P W Chapple-Hyam) *hld up in rr: hdwy on ins to chse ldrs over 2f out: wknd fnl f* **4/1**[3]
25-6 **8** *1 ¾* **Welsh Emperor (IRE)**[21] 1865 10-9-0 108 .... (b) SteveDrowne 7 103
(T P Tate) *led tl over 2f out: lost pl over 1f out* **50/1**

0-36 **9** 1/2 **Laa Rayb (USA)**[19] 1929 5-9-0 110 .... RoystonFfrench 10 102
(M Johnston) *chsd ldrs: rdn and hung bdly lft over 3f out: wknd over 1f out* **18/1**

06-4 **10** 1 **Garnica (FR)**[21] 1865 6-9-0 109 .... SilvestreDeSousa 4 99
(D Nicholls) *mid-div: effrt over 3f out: wknd 1f out* **40/1**

1m 30.42s (0.22) **Going Correction** +0.15s/f (Good) **10** Ran SP% **117.7**
Speed ratings (Par 113): **104,101,100,100,99 98,98,96,95,94**
toteswinger: 1&2 £2.20, 1&3 £4.20, 2&3 £6.80. CSF £7.73 TOTE £2.60: £1.40, £1.80, £2.80; EX 7.70 Trifecta £91.80 Pool £538.66 - 4.34 winning units..
Owner K Abdulla **Bred** Juddmonte Farms Ltd **Trained** Newmarket, Suffolk

FOCUS
A good renewal of this Group 3 and the form looks solid rated around the placed horses. The pace was strong and again the runners took the centre-course route in the straight.

NOTEBOOK
Main Aim had been most impressive in a 6f handicap at Newbury on his return and was stepping up to this grade for the first time with something to prove, having been beaten twice in Listed company at three. He passed the test in fine style, showing a ready turn of foot to lead and always being in command from then on. It is likely that he will revert to 6f for the Golden Jubilee Stakes at Ascot, for which he was cut from 12-1 to 6-1 by VCbet, but his trainer still has suspicions that he could be a miler and a supplementary entry for the Queen Anne has not been ruled out. Either way he will need to improve again in Group 1 company and he would not want the ground much quicker than it was here. (op 5-4 tchd 2-1)
Beacon Lodge(IRE) was always to the fore and he stuck on willingly for second. His Listed win here three weeks ago (Garnica and Welsh Emperor behind) has been boosted by runner-up Ordnance Row, and he was unfortunate to come up against a progressive opponent this time. (op 11-2)
Arabian Gleam, penalised 5lb for his win in last September's Park Stakes at Doncaster, ran on gamely for third on this ease in grade without quite getting to grips with the principals. (op 14-1 tchd 15-2)
Asset(IRE) could never land a telling blow either, but he did run on having travelled strongly at the rear of the field. (op 20-1)
Atlantic Sport(USA) should have been suited by the drop in grade and trip after finding it all too much in the Lockinge, but while not discredited, he remains a difficult horse to place. (op 12-1)
Royal Confidence performed creditably, but she has now run nine times in Group company without winning.
Tariq, another found wanting in the Lockinge, had not run over 7f since 2007, when he completed the Jersey Stakes-Lennox Stakes double. He gave the impression he might benefit from the application of some headgear. (op 3-1)
Welsh Emperor(IRE), who gave problems at the stalls, found the drying ground against him. He made the running until the winner went past. (op 100-1)
Laa Rayb(USA) held his head at an awkward angle and was one of the first beaten. (op 25-1 tchd 28-1)
Garnica(FR) took time to settle in the race.

2484 EBF TOMBOY CAVANAGH MAIDEN STKS 5f
3:35 (3:38) (Class 5) 2-Y-O
£3,885 (£1,156; £577; £288) **Stalls** Centre

Form RPR

6 **1** **Strike Shot**[22] 1835 2-9-3 0 .... WilliamBuick 1 75
(W R Muir) *racd wd: w ldr: led 1f out: kpt on wl* **5/1**[2]

640 **2** *nk* **Goodbye Earl (IRE)**[15] 2054 2-8-7 0 .... SladeO'Hara(5) 7 69
(A Berry) *swvd rt s: led: hdd 1f out: kpt on wl towards fin* **9/1**

3 2 1/2 **Look Whos Next** 2-9-3 0 .... SebSanders 8 65+
(E S McMahon) *sn chsng ldrs: kpt on same pce fnl f* **6/1**[3]

6 **4** 4 1/2 **Senate Majority**[44] 1304 2-9-3 0 .... AlanMunro 5 49
(T D Easterby) *in tch: one pce fnl 2f* **8/1**

5 1/2 **Take Ten** 2-9-3 0 .... RyanMoore 6 47
(M Johnston) *chsd ldrs: outpcd and edgd rt over 2f out: no threat after* **11/10**[1]

6 3 3/4 **Ibmab** 2-9-3 0 .... (t) TomEaves 9 33
(Mrs L Stubbs) *sn outpcd: nvr on terms* **25/1**

7 2 1/4 **Firetrap** 2-9-3 0 .... RoystonFfrench 4 25
(Mrs A Duffield) *dwlt: sn chsng ldrs: wknd over 1f out* **11/1**

0 **8** 1 **Alfalasteeni**[9] 2196 2-9-3 0 .... StephenDonohoe 3 22
(Ian Williams) *sn outpcd and hung rt: a in rr* **25/1**

5 **9** 4 **Ariel Bender**[15] 2027 2-8-10 0 .... AndrewHeffernan(7) 2 7
(Peter Grayson) *gave problems to s: sn outpcd: bhd fnl 2f* **50/1**

60.73 secs (0.23) **Going Correction** -0.10s/f (Good) **9** Ran SP% **117.7**
Speed ratings (Par 93): **94,93,89,82,81 75,71,70,63**
toteswinger: 1&2 £7.60, 1&3 £6.80, 2&3 £4.10. CSF £48.72 TOTE £5.90: £2.00, £2.10, £2.10; EX 66.30.
Owner The Strike Partnership **Bred** Whitsbury Manor Stud **Trained** Lambourn, Berks

FOCUS
Not much strength in depth to this maiden, but fair form from the principals. Not many were able to get involved.

NOTEBOOK
Strike Shot finished last of six on his debut on Lingfield's Polytrack, but he had clearly learned from that experience. Always towards the fore, he fought off the runner-up before his rider appeared to take things a shade easily close to the line. He is the tenth winner out of his dam, who won the 1990 Ayr Gold Cup, and should have more to offer. (op 11-1)
Goodbye Earl(IRE)'s Lily Agnes fourth at Chester was the best form on offer, although she was out of her depth in a York Listed event next time. She showed bright pace and kept battling away, but was flattered to finish as close as a neck to the winner. Jinking after the line, she unseated her rider with no harm done. (op 5-1)
Look Whos Next is the first foal of a smart sprinter from a family which has served the McMahon yard well, and he should make the grade. He was noticeably green on this debut but stuck on for a clear third. (op 4-1)
Senate Majority made his debut in a Ripon maiden which has been working out well, but after chasing the pace, he faded to finish well held. (tchd 15-2)
Take Ten, a 210,000gns half-brother to amongst others the useful sprinter Aahayson, broke well but was outpaced by the principals from halfway. He is probably worth another chance, perhaps at 6f. (op 11-8 tchd 6-4 in places)
Ibmab, who was retained for just 800gns as a yearling, was fitted with a tongue-tie on his debut. He trailed after a slow start but was getting the hang of things late on. (op 33-1 tchd 20-1)
Firetrap laid up with the leaders until weakening in the last furlong and a half. A half-brother to seven winners, notably the smart and tough sprinter Golden Nun, he should do better with this initial experience behind him. (op 12-1 tchd 9-1)
Alfalasteeni Official explanation: jockey said colt hung right

2485 J.W. LEES SANDY LANE STKS (LISTED RACE) 6f
4:10 (4:10) (Class 1) 3-Y-O
£22,708 (£8,608; £4,308; £2,148; £1,076; £540) **Stalls** Centre

Form RPR

30-3 **1** **Danehill Destiny**[42] 1353 3-8-9 102 .... (t) RyanMoore 5 107
(W J Haggas) *trckd ldrs: t.k.h: hmpd over 4f out: effrt 2f out: hrd rdn and led jst ins fnl f: styd on wl* **15/8**[1]

65-0 **2** 1 1/2 **Doncaster Rover (USA)**[70] 912 3-9-0 101 .... SteveDrowne 7 107
(D H Brown) *in tch: effrt over 2f out: styd on to chse wnr ins fnl f: no imp* **20/1**

0-46 **3** 2 **Damien (IRE)**[31] 1602 3-9-0 105 .... MichaelHills 8 101
(B W Hills) *chsd ldrs: effrt over 2f out: led over 1f out: hdd jst ins fnl f: fdd towards fin* **11/2**

20-1 **4** *hd* **Sayif (IRE)**[58] 1085 3-9-0 118 .... AlanMunro 9 100
(P W Chapple-Hyam) *chsd ldrs: sltly hmpd over 4f out: kpt on same pce appr fnl f* **3/1**[2]

6-23 **5** 3/4 **Awinnersgame (IRE)**[15] 2035 3-9-0 107 .... WilliamBuick 4 98
(J Noseda) *mid-div: plld wd over 3f out: kpt on fnl 2f: nvr really threatened* **7/2**[3]

-031 **6** 3 1/4 **Jobe (USA)**[22] 1828 3-9-0 100 .... WJSupple 3 88
(K A Ryan) *led: swtchd rt over 4f out: hdd & wknd over 1f out* **8/1**

10-0 **7** 13 **Magic Cat**[31] 1602 3-9-3 105 .... AndrewElliott 1 49
(K R Burke) *sn chsng ldrs: hung rt and lost pl 2f out* **18/1**

1m 12.21s (-1.79) **Going Correction** -0.10s/f (Good) **7** Ran SP% **118.5**
Speed ratings (Par 107): **107,105,102,102,101 96,79**
toteswinger: 1&2 £8.80, 1&3 £3.60, 2&3 £15.70. CSF £42.89 TOTE £2.60: £1.80, £6.40; EX 44.90.
Owner Cheveley Park Stud **Bred** T G Mills And J Humphreys **Trained** Newmarket, Suffolk
■ Stewards' Enquiry : W J Supple three-day ban: carelesss riding (Jun 13-15)

FOCUS
Not the strongest edition of this Listed event and not the most solid form, but a good performance from the winner. The whole field tacked over to race on the stands' side.

NOTEBOOK
Danehill Destiny made a fine return to action when third behind Super Sleuth and Lahaleeb, both of whom have boosted the form since, in the 7f Fred Darling Stakes at Newbury, and this drop back in trip was expected to suit her. Equipped with a tongue-tie again, she battled on gamely to fight off the third then held the late challenge of the runner-up. The winner has been found wanting half a dozen times in Group company but is capable of putting that right, perhaps on the continent. (op 9-4 tchd 5-2)
Doncaster Rover(USA) has left Stuart Parr's yard since his seasonal debut on the Polytrack in March. Back down to 6f, he came from the rear to deliver the final challenge to the winner, but was always just being held. (op 33-1)
Damien(IRE) had every chance a furlong out, but the filly wanted it more and he faded inside the last. He could be in need of some headgear now. (op 8-1)
Sayif(IRE), a smart maiden at two when he was runner-up in the Middle Park, was below form despite winning on his reappearance at Leicester and was slightly disappointing here, although he was keeping on at the death after being outpaced by the principals. (op 9-4 tchd 7-2)
Awinnersgame(IRE) was placed in this grade on his first two starts of the season, but the drying ground was against him here. His optimum trip remains a point of debate. (op 3-1)
Jobe(USA)'s rider was anxious to tack across and claim the rail, causing problems for a couple in behind as he did so. The colt, a winner in lesser company at Hamilton last time, faded once headed over a furlong out. (op 12-1 tchd 6-1)
Magic Cat dropped away before halfway and looks to have serious questions to answer now. (op 16-1 tchd 14-1)

2486 TURFTV.CO.UK STKS (H'CAP) 2m 45y
4:45 (4:46) (Class 2) (0-100,100) 4-Y-0+
£12,462 (£3,732; £1,866; £934; £466; £234) **Stalls** Low

Form RPR

105- **1** **Hits Only Vic (USA)**[203] 7244 5-9-5 **94** .... DNolan 10 105
(D Carroll) *in rr: stdy hdwy over 3f out: styd on to ld jst ins fnl f: hld on wl* **28/1**

3-55 **2** 3/4 **Bollin Felix**[15] 2055 5-8-11 **86** .... (v[1]) AlanMunro 3 96
(T D Easterby) *in tch: effrt over 3f out: chsd ldrs over 1f out: kpt on wl ins fnl f: a jst hld* **10/1**

-003 **3** 1/2 **Tilt**[15] 2055 7-9-1 **90** .... (p) TomEaves 5 99
(B Ellison) *s.i.s: reminders after 1f: hdwy over 3f out: narow ld over 1f out: no ex ins fnl f* **20/1**

-002 **4** 3/4 **Record Breaker (IRE)**[14] 2085 5-8-13 **88** .... (b) RoystonFfrench 14 96
(M Johnston) *in rr: hdwy on outside over 3f out: styd on wl fnl f* **20/1**

1-32 **5** 1 1/4 **Dayia (IRE)**[26] 1732 5-8-4 **79** oh3 .... AndrewElliott 1 86
(J Pearce) *prom: ev ch 3f out: hung lft over 1f out: one pce* **25/1**

3-21 **6** 4 1/2 **Wild Rhubarb**[21] 1892 4-8-5 **82** .... WilliamBuick 6 86+
(C G Cox) *chsd ldrs: hmpd 4f out: wkng whn hmpd over 1f out* **3/1**[2]

12-5 **7** 2 **Amerigo (IRE)**[24] 1790 4-9-9 **100** .... PhilipRobinson 4 99
(M A Jarvis) *chsd ldrs: effrt over 3f out: lost pl over 1f out* **11/4**[1]

5-35 **8** *nk* **Dolly Penrose**[21] 1863 4-8-4 **81** oh1 ow2 .... WJSupple 12 79
(M R Channon) *hld up in midfield: hdwy 6f out: led 3f out: hdd over 1f out: sn wknd* **20/1**

64/ **9** 6 **Faasel (IRE)**[21] 6253 8-8-13 **88** .... SteveDrowne 15 79
(N G Richards) *chsd ldrs: drvn 6f out: lost pl over 3f out* **20/1**

000- **10** 1 3/4 **Mudawin (IRE)**[224] 6817 8-8-6 **86** ow4 .... SladeO'Hara(5) 9 75
(James Moffatt) *rrd s: hdwy into midfield over 4f out: wknd 2f out* **100/1**

16-4 **11** 2 1/2 **Nemo Spirit (IRE)**[41] 1383 4-8-13 **90** .... JimmyQuinn 13 76
(W R Muir) *led tl 3f out: sn wknd* **12/1**

63-0 **12** 7 **Double Banded (IRE)**[24] 1790 5-8-12 **87** .... StephenDonohoe 2 65
(Ian Williams) *t.k.h: trckd ldrs: chal 3f out: wknd over 1f out: eased* **14/1**

015- **13** 6 **Cape Tribulation**[56] 6948 5-8-11 **86** .... SebSanders 7 57
(J M Jefferson) *mid-div: hdwy over 4f out: chsd ldrs 3f out: sn wknd: eased over 1f out* **11/2**[3]

000- **14** 4 1/2 **Missoula (IRE)**[91] 6817 6-8-11 **86** .... SamHitchcott 8 51
(Miss Suzy Smith) *sn drvn along in rr: nvr on terms* **40/1**

4531 **15** 2 3/4 **Clear Reef**[9] 2194 5-8-9 **84** .... (p) WandersonD'Avila 11 46
(Jane Chapple-Hyam) *trckd ldrs: t.k.h: edgd lft 4f out: sn lost pl* **25/1**

3m 31.11s (-4.89) **Going Correction** -0.075s/f (Good)
WFA 4 from 5yo+ 2lb **15** Ran SP% **124.1**
Speed ratings (Par 109): **109,108,108,108,107 105,104,103,100,100 98,95,92,90,88**
toteswinger: 1&2 £68.70, 1&3 £38.00, 2&3 £28.70. CSF £261.90 CT £5677.38 TOTE £30.60: £5.80, £2.80, £4.50; EX 505.90 Place 6 £973.46, Place 5 £298.36..
Owner Kell-Stone & Watson **Bred** Peter E Blum **Trained** Sledmere, E Yorks

FOCUS
A competitive staying handicap run at a sound clip and the form should prove solid. The principals came from off the pace.

NOTEBOOK
Hits Only Vic(USA) was one of the success stories of last season and he resumed with his sixth handicap win in the space of 12 months. He has risen 30lb in the ratings in that period and there may yet be more to come from this admirably versatile performer, who was in full control once striking the front. (op 25-1 tchd 22-1)
Bollin Felix, who raced on the stands' side as the field fanned out across the track in the final stages, stayed on for second on this step back up in trip but seemed to lack the resolution of the winner. He was trying a visor for the first time, having been blinkered regularly. (op 9-1)
Tilt was administered early reminders following a sluggish start, but he came through to show briefly ahead in the straight. He is not straightforward and the cheekpieces were back on here. (tchd 18-1)

Record Breaker(IRE), blinkered again, stayed on from the rear without really announcing his presence. He has been running respectably since adopting more patient tactics.
Dayia(IRE) ran a sound race from 3lb out of the weights, just lacking a change of pace late on. (op 22-1)
Wild Rhubarb was slightly hampered early in the home straight and again when held in the latter stages. She went up 9lb for her win at Warwick and a drop of a couple of pounds for this should make her competitive again. (op 7-2 tchd 4-1 in places)
Amerigo(IRE) was well placed turning in, but he lacked a change of pace and was a little disappointing. (op 5-2 tchd 9-4 and 3-1 in places)
Dolly Penrose ◆ travelled well before striking the front, but she did not get home. She looks worth dropping back to 1m6f. (op 16-1)
Double Banded(IRE) Official explanation: jockey said gelding lost its action
Cape Tribulation disappointed on his last two starts over hurdles, albeit in Grade 1 company, and it was a similar story here as he dropped away rather tamely. (op 7-1)
T/Jkpt: Not won. T/Plt: £734.90 to a £1 stake. Pool: £107,324.51. 106.60 winning tickets. T/Qpdt: £53.80 to a £1 stake. Pool: £5,504.11. 75.60 winning tickets. WG

2395 LINGFIELD (L-H)
Saturday, May 30

OFFICIAL GOING: Turf course - good to firm (8.6); all-weather - standard
Wind: Moderate, half against, becoming almost nil Weather: Sunny, warm

2487 MARIAN WILSON-SMITH (S) STKS — 1m 4f (P)
6:00 (6:00) (Class 6) 3-Y-O — £2,047 (£604; £302) Stalls Low

Form				RPR
5600	1		**First Spirit**[9] 2204 3-8-2 55 (p) SophieDoyle(5) 6	56
			(J S Moore) *hld up bhd ldrs: prog to chse clr ldr 3f out: drvn 2f out: styd on to ld last 150yds: sn clr* **3/1**[2]	
-000	2	3 1/4	**Bari Bay**[18] 1967 3-8-4 48 (b[1]) JackMitchell(3) 7	51
			(R M Beckett) *led after 1f tl after 3f: trckd ldr: led again 4f out: drew 5 l clr over 2f out: drvn wl over 1f out: wknd and hdd last 150yds* **10/1**	
0663	3	3 1/2	**King's Chorister**[8] 2220 3-8-12 55 (t) JerryO'Dwyer 1	50
			(Miss Gay Kelleway) *hld up in last pair: sme prog 1/2-way: gng wl but plenty to do over 3f out: chsd clr ldng pair over 2f out: plugged on: nvr able to chal* **6/1**[3]	
-000	4	5	**Zepnove (IRE)**[11] 2169 3-8-8 55 ow1 (b) TGMcLaughlin 2	38
			(M Wigham) *sn rdn to stay in tch: bhd fr 1/2-way: kpt on fr over 2f out: no ch* **20/1**	
50	5	6	**And A Partridge**[23] 1811 3-8-12 0 ShaneKelly 5	33
			(J A Osborne) *led 1f: prom: rdn and outpcd over 3f out: brief effrt over 2f out: sn wknd* **10/1**	
00-0	6	nse	**Peace In Paradise (IRE)**[31] 1605 3-8-7 44 EddieAhern 3	28
			(J A R Toller) *a in last trio: lost tch 5f out: nvr on terms after* **14/1**	
00	7	36	**Scarlett Angel (IRE)**[10] 2178 3-8-0 0 KierenFox(7) 8	—
			(W J Knight) *slowly away: nvr gng wl: lost tch 1/2-way: t.o* **14/1**	
6-46	8	38	**Midnight Bay**[89] 740 3-8-12 65 (v[1]) TPO'Shea 4	—
			(M R Channon) *t.k.h: led after 3f: hdd u.p 4f out: dropped out rapidly: t.o and eased over 1f out* **6/4**[1]	

2m 35.35s (2.35) **Going Correction** +0.125s/f (Slow) 8 Ran SP% **115.6**
Speed ratings (Par 97): **97,94,92,89,85 85,61,35**
toteswinger: 1&2 £7.50, 1&3 £6.50, 2&3 £8.80. CSF £33.09 TOTE £3.30: £1.60, £2.90, £1.40; EX 41.10.There was no bid for the winner.
Owner Bill Wyatt **Bred** W J Wyatt **Trained** Upper Lambourn, Berks

FOCUS
A poor seller, rated around the winner, and unconvincing form.
King's Chorister Official explanation: jockey said gelding hung left
And A Partridge Official explanation: jockey said gelding hung left
Midnight Bay Official explanation: jockey said gelding lost its action

2488 ULTIMATE RACING FRATERNITY MAIDEN STKS — 1m 2f (P)
6:30 (6:40) (Class 5) 3-Y-O — £2,729 (£806; £403) Stalls Low

Form				RPR
50-	1		**Mooteeah (IRE)**[235] 6565 3-8-12 0 TPO'Shea 6	68+
			(M A Jarvis) *cl up on outer: rdn over 2f out: styd on to take 2nd ent fnl f: edgd ahd last 75yds* **9/2**[2]	
2320	2	nk	**Morning Sir Alan**[27] 1707 3-9-3 75 JerryO'Dwyer 2	72
			(S A Callaghan) *led at mod pce: kicked on fr 4f out: hrd rdn over 1f out: worn down last 75yds* **10/1**	
0	3	3 1/4	**M'Lady Rousseur (IRE)**[26] 1729 3-8-12 0 RobertHavlin 7	61+
			(D R C Elsworth) *hld up in rr: pushed along over 4f out: sme prog 3f out but nt on terms w ldrs: rdn and styd on steadily to take 3rd nr fin* **50/1**	
0	4	1/2	**Secret Life**[14] 2082 3-9-3 0 TGMcLaughlin 13	65+
			(J Noseda) *dwlt: rn green early in rr: rchd midfield after 4f: cl up bhd ldrs and pushed along over 3f out: effrt 2f out: kpt on one pce* **16/1**	
0	5	2 1/4	**Dream On Connie**[23] 1804 3-9-3 0 PaulDoe 4	60
			(W J Knight) *trckd ldr: rdn over 2f out: no imp over 1f out: lost 2nd and wknd ent fnl f* **20/1**	
30	6	2	**Calypso Bay (IRE)**[24] 1793 3-9-3 0 ShaneKelly 3	56
			(J Noseda) *dwlt: sn cl up bhd ldr: rdn 3f out: nt qckn and lost pl 2f out: btn whn n.m.r over 1f out* **4/9**[1]	
5	7	3/4	**Sirjosh**[19] 1941 3-9-0 0 MarcHalford(3) 12	55
			(D Donovan) *racd wd: hld up in tch: clsd on ldrs over 2f out gng wl enough: drvn over 1f out: wknd* **9/1**[3]	
	8	shd	**Vivachi (IRE)** 3-8-9 0 JackMitchell(3) 10	49
			(R M Beckett) *s.i.s: hld up last: sme prog over 3f out but nt on terms w ldrs: pushed along and one pce* **20/1**	
	9	6	**Sanctum** 3-8-12 0 RichardThomas 8	37
			(Dr J D Scargill) *a in last trio: wl bhd 3f out* **66/1**	
00-	10	9	**Captain Flack**[225] 6778 3-9-3 0 LPKeniry 9	24
			(J A R Toller) *a in rr: u.p sn after 1/2-way: wl bhd fnl 3f* **100/1**	
	11	21	**Wise Princess** 3-8-7 0 JackDean(5) 5	—
			(W G M Turner) *restless bef ent stalls: chsd ldrs: rdn and wknd 1/2-way: t.o* **66/1**	

2m 8.06s (1.46) **Going Correction** +0.125s/f (Slow) 11 Ran SP% **127.9**
Speed ratings (Par 99): **99,98,96,95,93 92,91,91,86,79 62**
toteswinger: 1&2 £11.90, 1&3 Not won, 2&3 £31.60. CSF £49.13 TOTE £7.50: £2.60, £3.30, £17.10; EX 40.10.
Owner Hamdan Al Maktoum **Bred** Shadwell Estate Company Limited **Trained** Newmarket, Suffolk
■ Stellar Cause was withdrawn after breaking out of the stalls (4/1, deduct 20p in the £ under R4). New market formed.

FOCUS
A maiden that took little winning with the favourite running poorly. Modest form, rated around the runner-up.
Calypso Bay(IRE) Official explanation: trainer had no explanation for the poor form shown

2489 BENGAL VILLAGE H'CAP — 1m 2f (P)
7:00 (7:07) (Class 6) (0-60,64) 3-Y-O — £2,047 (£604; £302) Stalls Low

Form				RPR
-450	1		**Sumani (FR)**[28] 1670 3-9-0 **59** JackMitchell(3) 1	65
			(S Dow) *mde all: set modest pce: wound it up fr over 3f out: drvn 2 l clr over 1f out: jst lasted* **20/1**	
000-	2	1/2	**Broughtons Paradis (IRE)**[246] 6240 3-8-11 **53** TPO'Shea 10	58
			(W J Musson) *hld up in midfield: rdn and in tch over 2f out: prog on outer over 1f out: wnt 2nd last 150yds: clsng on wnr fin* **11/2**[3]	
6103	3	hd	**Good Buy Dubai (USA)**[9] 2204 3-8-13 **58** MarcHalford(3) 2	63+
			(J R Best) *stdd s: hld up in last pair in slowly run r: wl off the pce whn rdn over 2f out: rapid prog on wd outside 1f out: fin best of all* **9/2**[2]	
4-30	4	1 1/2	**Bubses Boy**[39] 1441 3-9-2 **58** JamieSpencer 9	60
			(M L W Bell) *hld up in last quartet in slowly run r: prog into midfield over 2f out: sn rdn: styd on fr over 1f out: nt pce to chal* **7/2**[1]	
00-0	5	nk	**Rowan Tiger**[38] 1461 3-9-4 **60** RobertHavlin 8	61
			(J R Boyle) *trckd ldng pair: rdn to chse wnr over 2f out: no imp over 1f out: wknd last 150yds* **13/2**	
26-0	6	2 1/4	**Chalk Hill Blue**[42] 1363 3-9-1 **57** ShaneKelly 12	54
			(Eve Johnson Houghton) *chsd wnr to over 2f out: hrd rdn and fading whn hmpd last 50yds* **20/1**	
-301	7	hd	**Primo Dilettante**[3] 2380 3-9-1 **64** 6ex KierenFox(7) 4	60
			(W J Knight) *trckd ldrs: gng wl 3f out: lost pl and shkn up over 1f out: nt qckn* **7/1**	
-604	8	3/4	**Wightgold**[18] 1967 3-8-4 **51** SophieDoyle(5) 3	46
			(H J L Dunlop) *hld up in midfield: rdn on inner 3f out: sn outpcd: n.d after* **33/1**	
3600	9	3/4	**Daily Double**[23] 1811 3-9-0 **59** JamesMillman(3) 7	52
			(D K Ivory) *stdd s: hld up in last pair in slowly run r: wl off the pce whn shkn up 2f out: nvr nr ldrs* **22/1**	
45-2	10	3 1/2	**Honorable Endeavor**[134] 196 3-9-0 **56** LPKeniry 5	42
			(E F Vaughan) *trckd ldng pair: drvn over 3f out: wknd over 2f out* **16/1**	
0-00	11	3 1/2	**Pursuit Of Purpose**[51] 1198 3-8-3 **52** JemmaMarshall(7) 13	31
			(G L Moore) *hld up in last quartet in slowly run r: u.p and no prog over 2f out: no ch after* **33/1**	
00-0	12	4	**Free Falling**[35] 1531 3-9-4 **60** EddieAhern 6	31
			(L M Cumani) *hld up in midfield: dropped to rr whn pce lifted 3f out: drvn and no prog: eased fnl f* **9/2**[2]	

2m 8.16s (1.56) **Going Correction** +0.125s/f (Slow) 12 Ran SP% **125.4**
Speed ratings (Par 97): **98,97,97,96,96 94,94,93,92,90 87,84**
toteswinger: 1&2 Not won, 1&3 £28.40, 2&3 £13.10. CSF £126.22 CT £601.37 TOTE £25.50: £6.00, £2.30, £1.60; EX 279.20.
Owner T G Parker **Bred** Christian Wattinne **Trained** Epsom, Surrey

FOCUS
This moderate handicap was run at a fair pace. The first two are less exposed than most and the third looks the best guide.
Wightgold Official explanation: jockey said filly hung right closing stages
Free Falling Official explanation: jockey said filly was unsuited by the polytrack

2490 GEOFF BOORMAN FUELS MAIDEN FILLIES' STKS — 6f
7:35 (7:37) (Class 5) 2-Y-O — £2,729 (£806; £403) Stalls High

Form				RPR
4	1		**Hairspray**[8] 2218 2-9-0 0 TonyCulhane 7	75
			(M R Channon) *pressed ldr: rdn to ld jst over 1f out: edgd lft fnl f: hld on* **14/1**	
33	2	nk	**Curtains**[24] 1782 2-9-0 0 LPKeniry 3	74
			(S Dow) *trckd ldrs: swtchd to nr side rail and drvn over 1f out: wnt 2nd ins fnl f: edgd lft and pressed wnr last 100yds* **8/1**	
	3	1	**Crystal Gale (IRE)** 2-9-0 0 PaulDoe 11	71+
			(W J Knight) *towards rr: pushed along 1/2-way: prog u.p over 1f out: styd on wl to take 3rd nr fin* **33/1**	
2	4	1	**Ragsta (IRE)**[12] 2121 2-9-0 0 RichardSmith 6	68
			(R Hannon) *racd towards centre: pressed ldrs: rdn and nt qckn over 1f out: edgd lft and one pce* **3/1**[1]	
6	5	1/2	**Astarta (IRE)**[15] 2034 2-9-0 0 EddieAhern 8	67
			(P F I Cole) *led and racd against nr side rail: edgd lft u.p fr 2f out: hdd jst over 1f out: fdd* **3/1**[1]	
	6	4 1/2	**Three's A Crowd** 2-9-0 0 RobertHavlin 12	53
			(D R C Elsworth) *dwlt: chsd ldrs and racd against rail: nt pce to threaten fr 2f out: wknd fnl f* **14/1**	
	7	1	**Cool Kitten (IRE)** 2-9-0 0 ShaneKelly 5	50
			(W J Knight) *chsd ldrs: outpcd fr over 2f out: wknd fnl f* **16/1**	
6	8	1/2	**Chinese Democracy (USA)**[26] 1742 2-9-0 0 JosedeSouza 2	49
			(P F I Cole) *t.k.h early: wl on terms w ldrs and racd wd: wknd fr 2f out* **50/1**	
	9	1/2	**Lathaat** 2-9-0 0 TPO'Shea 4	47
			(J L Dunlop) *dwlt: a struggling in rr and in centre* **15/2**[3]	
	10	1	**Brunette (IRE)** 2-9-0 0 FrancisNorton 10	44
			(R Hannon) *s.s: wl outpcd in last: nvr a factor* **6/1**[2]	
	11	2 1/2	**Arabian Jewel** 2-9-0 0 JamieSpencer 9	37+
			(D M Simcock) *s.s: a struggling in rr: racd centre fr over 2f out: wknd over 1f out* **8/1**	

1m 11.4s (0.20) **Going Correction** -0.075s/f (Good) 11 Ran SP% **122.4**
Speed ratings (Par 90): **95,94,93,91,91 85,83,83,82,81 77**
toteswinger: 1&2 £2.60, 1&3 £21.80, 2&3 £43.60. CSF £126.40 TOTE £13.50: £2.20, £2.50, £7.40; EX 82.40.
Owner John Breslin **Bred** J Breslin **Trained** West Ilsley, Berks

FOCUS
An average-looking fillies' maiden. The form should prove reliable enough.

NOTEBOOK
Hairspray, despite drifting, opened her account at the second try and showed a likeable attitude in prevailing. Never far away, she found plenty nearing the final furlong and was not going to be denied at the business end. Clearly going the right way, she stays well and can win again. (op 11-1 tchd 10-1)
Curtains was closing on the winner at the finish yet the line was always coming too soon. She enjoyed this flatter track and got the longer trip well, so her turn should not be too far off. (op 11-2)
Crystal Gale(IRE) ◆, who is bred to stay further, was doing some decent work inside the final furlong. This was a nice debut and she is the one to take from the race. (op 25-1)
Ragsta(IRE) failed to improve on the level of her Bath debut and did not appear to have any obvious excuses. (op 9-4)

Astarta(IRE) was very well backed and bagged the stands' side rail, but failed to see out the extra furlong. (op 13-2)

2491 MILLWOOD DESIGNER HOMES AT DORMANS PARK H'CAP 7f
8:10 (8:10) (Class 5) (0-75,77) 4-Y-0+ **£3,238** (£963; £481; £240) **Stalls** High

Form RPR

-000 **1** **Lodi (IRE)**[14] 2086 4-9-3 **74**....................(t) AdamKirby 10 83+
(J Akehurst) *sn settled in rr: shkn up and prog 2f out: got through to ld over 1f out: in command whn edgd rt last 100yds* **9/2**[2]

0504 **2** ¾ **Credit Swap**[30] 1619 4-9-3 **74**.................... FrancisNorton 7 81
(M Wigham) *settled in rr: pushed along over 2f out: n.m.r but got through 1f out: r.o to take 2nd clsng stages* **13/2**[3]

5005 **3** ¾ **Carlitos Spirit (IRE)**[21] 1876 5-9-0 **74**.................... JamesMillman(3) 5 79+
(B R Millman) *hld up in rr: nt clr run fr over 2f out tl swtchd to wd outside 1f out: r.o wl to take 3rd nr fin* **7/1**

6002 **4** nk **Napoletano (GER)**[34] 1539 8-8-9 **66**....................(p) EddieAhern 9 70
(S Dow) *stdd s but sn cl up nr side: chal 2f out: upsides over 1f out: nt qckn after* **11/1**

6531 **5** ½ **I Confess**[10] 2186 4-9-1 **77**....................(b) RichardEvans(5) 2 80
(P D Evans) *pressed ldr towards outer: u.p over 2f out: stl upsides over 1f out: fdd fnl f* **10/1**

4103 **6** nk **Grey Boy (GER)**[11] 2168 8-9-2 **73**.................... TolleyDean 6 75
(A W Carroll) *hld up in rr: effrt on wd outside over 2f out: drvn and nt qckn over 1f out: one pce* **14/1**

-003 **7** ½ **Ivory Lace**[9] 2188 8-8-13 **70**.................... RobertHavlin 3 71
(S Woodman) *stdd s: hld up in rr on outer: rdn and no imp on ldrs over 1f out: plugging on whn short of room nr fin* **10/1**

0050 **8** nse **Compton's Eleven**[9] 2188 8-9-0 **71**.................... TonyCulhane 8 76+
(M R Channon) *hld up in rr against nr side rail: effrt and nt clr run 2f out: styng on and ch of a pl whn hmpd ins fnl f* **33/1**

45-4 **9** 1¾ **My Learned Friend (IRE)**[21] 1876 5-9-3 **74**.................... LPKeniry 12 70
(A M Balding) *racd against nr side rail: narrow ld: rdn and hdd over 1f out: wknd* **15/8**[1]

6-00 **10** 18 **Ghost Dancer**[25] 1775 5-8-11 **68**.................... TPO'Shea 1 15
(J M Bradley) *t.k.h: pressed ldrs on outer to over 2f out: wknd rapidly over 1f out: t.o* **33/1**

26-0 **11** shd **Stand In Flames**[23] 1806 4-9-1 **72**.................... ShaneKelly 11 19
(Pat Eddery) *pressed ldr to 2f out: wknd rapidly over 1f out: t.o* **25/1**

1m 22.15s (-1.15) **Going Correction** -0.075s/f (Good) **11** Ran SP% **121.7**
Speed ratings (Par 103): **103,102,101,100,100 100,99,99,97,76 76**
toteswinger: 1&2 £14.80, 1&3 £12.10, 2&3 £35.80. CSF £34.59 CT £208.10 TOTE £8.30: £2.40, £3.60, £2.70; EX 50.70.
Owner Tattenham Corner Racing 3 **Bred** Allevamento Gialloblu S R L **Trained** Epsom, Surrey

FOCUS
Sound form to an ordinary handicap. The winner produced his best effort since last summer.
Carlitos Spirit(IRE) Official explanation: jockey said gelding was denied a clear run and hung right
Stand In Flames Official explanation: jockey said filly ran too free

2492 DAVID SANDS MEMORIAL FILLIES' H'CAP 5f
8:40 (8:40) (Class 5) (0-70,69) 3-Y-0+ **£3,070** (£906; £453) **Stalls** High

Form RPR

0-22 **1** **Rathlin Light (USA)**[30] 1617 3-8-11 **62**....................(t) AdamKirby 3 70
(W R Swinburn) *mde virtually all: plenty of tail swishing: drvn over 1f out: kpt on wl* **5/2**[2]

0-45 **2** 1½ **Matterofact (IRE)**[17] 1985 6-9-8 **65**.................... TGMcLaughlin 5 72+
(M S Saunders) *cl up against nr side rail: wnt 2nd over 1f out: hrd rdn and hld whn n.m.r ins fnl f* **9/4**[1]

0553 **3** hd **Cosmic Destiny (IRE)**[8] 2219 7-9-7 **64**.................... LPKeniry 6 69
(E F Vaughan) *hld up in 5th: effrt 2f out: hrd rdn to press ldrs 1f out: kpt on same pce* **5/1**

3110 **4** 1¼ **Green Velvet**[34] 1540 4-9-5 **62**.................... EddieAhern 1 62
(P J Makin) *hld up in 4th: rdn fr 1/2-way: effrt over 1f out: no imp after* **9/2**[3]

5060 **5** 2¼ **Wibbadune (IRE)**[30] 1627 5-9-7 **69**.................... RichardEvans(5) 4 61
(D Shaw) *awkward s: hld up last: gng easily on outer 2f out: reminder and veered rt 1f out: veered lft ins fnl f: fnd nil* **11/2**

40-4 **6** 1½ **Kalligal**[112] 447 4-9-3 **60**.................... RobertHavlin 2 47
(R Ingram) *pressed wnr to over 1f out: wknd* **22/1**

57.62 secs (-0.58) **Going Correction** -0.075s/f (Good)
WFA 3 from 4yo+ 8lb **6** Ran SP% **113.9**
Speed ratings (Par 100): **101,98,98,96,92 90**
toteswinger: 1&2 £1.80, 1&3 £3.20, 2&3 £3.20. CSF £8.79 TOTE £3.30: £2.00, £2.30; EX 10.10 Place 6 £658.04, Place 5 £309.01..
Owner Cricketers Club Racing Group **Bred** Gaines-Gentry Thoroughbreds **Trained** Aldbury, Herts

FOCUS
A modest sprint handicap, run at a routine pace. The winner put a put a disappointing effort behind her but this form is not too solid.
Wibbadune(IRE) Official explanation: jockey said mare was unsuited by the good to firm ground
T/Plt: £771.70 to a £1 stake. Pool: £46,032.28. 43.54 winning tickets. T/Qpdt: £171.70 to a £1 stake. Pool: £5,221.00. 22.50 winning tickets. JN

2074 NEWBURY (L-H)
Saturday, May 30

OFFICIAL GOING: Good to firm (9.6)
Rails on back a straight and around 5f and 7furlong bends moved out but impact on distances not notified.
Wind: Moderate, behind Weather: Sunny getting dark

2493 RIDGEWAY LADY RIDERS' H'CAP 1m 2f 6y
6:10 (6:10) (Class 5) (0-70,70) 4-Y-0+ **£3,123** (£968; £484; £242) **Stalls** Low

Form RPR

0/0- **1** **Norman The Great**[29] 6667 5-10-2 **70**.................... RachelKing(5) 2 79
(A King) *trckd ldrs: led 2f out: drvn out* **8/1**

1200 **2** ½ **New England**[2] 2419 7-9-7 **56**.................... MissSBrotherton 3 65+
(W M Brisbourne) *t.k.h: chsd ldrs: rdn over 2f out: chsd wnr fnl f: kpt on but no imp cl home* **5/1**[2]

4600 **3** ½ **Gamesters Lady**[17] 1980 6-9-7 **56** oh1....................(b[1]) MissADeniel 13 63
(W M Brisbourne) *chsd ldrs: wnt 2nd over 1f out but no imp on wnr: lost 2nd fnl f and kpt on same pce* **33/1**

2652 **4** ½ **Rock Anthem (IRE)**[12] 2125 5-9-13 **62**.................... MissLEllison 14 68
(Mike Murphy) *swtchd lft s: in rr: hdwy fr 3f out: styd on fr over 1f out kpt on but no imp on ldrs ins fnl f* **8/1**

050- **5** nk **Venir Rouge**[20] 7385 5-10-4 **67**.................... MissFayeBramley 12 72+
(M Salaman) *wnt sharply lft s: in tch: rdn: nt clr run and swtchd rt ins fnl 2f: kpt on fnl f but nvr gng pce to be competitive* **10/1**

63-3 **6** nk **Sir Boss (IRE)**[8] 2244 4-10-2 **68**.................... MissMSowerby(3) 11 73+
(D E Cantillon) *s.i.s: in rr: hdwy on outside over 2f out: styd on fnl f but nvr gng pce to rch ldrs* **4/1**[1]

0-60 **7** 1¾ **Sinbad The Sailor**[15] 2039 4-9-8 **62**.................... MissHayleyMoore(5) 1 63
(J W Hills) *hmpd on rails sn after s: in rr: hdwy on ins fr 2f out: nvr gng pce to be competitive* **17/2**

6062 **8** 2½ **Strike Force**[6] 2294 5-9-4 **58**.................... MissALHutchinson(5) 6 54+
(Miss J Feilden) *in rr: swtchd sharply rt to outside fr 3f out: styd on fnl 2f: nvr in contention* **6/1**[3]

030- **9** nse **Chatanoogachoochoo**[257] 5965 4-10-0 **63**.................... MissEJJones 8 59
(M Hill) *in tch: hdwy and nt clr run whn swtchd rt ins fnl 2f: styd on same pce fnl f* **16/1**

-213 **10** ½ **Western Roots**[25] 1770 8-9-13 **67**.................... MissMBryant(5) 7 62
(P Butler) *t.k.h: led: hdd 2f out and sn wknd* **14/1**

5105 **11** 1¼ **Waterside (IRE)**[35] 1530 10-9-10 **66**....................(t) MissLCGriffiths(7) 5 59
(S Curran) *a towards rr* **22/1**

0-00 **12** 1½ **Houri (IRE)**[24] 1785 4-9-5 **57**....................(b) MissZoeLilly(3) 15 47
(J T Stimpson) *c lft after s: t.k.h and chsd ldrs: ev ch over 2f out: wknd over 1f out* **33/1**

5066 **13** 1 **Princess Flame (GER)**[15] 2040 7-9-12 **66**.................... MissCLWills(5) 9 54
(B G Powell) *chsd ldrs: rdn 3f out: wknd over 1f out* **14/1**

0054 **14** 7 **Another Bottle (IRE)**[15] 2040 8-10-2 **70**.................... MissJennyCarr(5) 10 44
(Mrs S Leech) *in rr: hdwy 3f out: nvr rchd ldrs and wknd fr 2f out* **20/1**

/00- **15** 7 **Ghaill Force**[461] 606 7-9-0 **56** oh11.................... MissKLoftus(7) 4 16
(P Butler) *lost 20 l s: effrt to cl on main gp after 3f: wknd 3f out* **100/1**

2m 8.75s (-0.05) **Going Correction** -0.075s/f (Good) **15** Ran SP% **128.0**
Speed ratings (Par 103): **97,96,96,95,95 95,93,91,91,91 90,89,88,82,77**
toteswinger: 1&2 £9.80, 1&3 £125.10, 2&3 £37.60. CSF £47.97 CT £1304.41 TOTE £11.60: £4.00, £2.40, £18.10; EX 84.20.
Owner McNeill Racing **Bred** Barton Stud Partnership **Trained** Barbury Castle, Wilts
■ Rachel King's first Flat win.
■ Stewards' Enquiry : Miss M Bryant three-day ban: careless riding (Jun 13, 15, 22)

FOCUS
Not a strong race, and the early pace seemed only ordinary. Not form to get at all carried away with.

2494 BATHWICK TYRES MAIDEN AUCTION FILLIES' STKS 6f 8y
6:45 (6:47) (Class 5) 2-Y-0 **£3,885** (£1,156; £577; £288) **Stalls** Centre

Form RPR

1 **Bahati (IRE)** 2-8-4 0.................... FrankieMcDonald 1 79+
(J G Portman) *t.k.h early: chsd ldrs: led ins fnl 2f: drvn and green fr over 1f out: idled whn rdn ins fnl f: readily* **25/1**

04 **2** ¾ **Silver Symphony (IRE)**[15] 2047 2-8-6 0.................... MartinDwyer 16 79
(P F I Cole) *led tl hdd ins fnl 2f: rdn and rallied fnl f kpt on cl home but alway hld by wnr* **7/2**[1]

3 2½ **Andina (IRE)** 2-8-7 0 ow1.................... SteveDrowne 11 72
(J W Hills) *s.i.s: bhd: gd hdwy fr over 2f out: styd on wl fnl f but nt rch ldng duo* **33/1**

4 1½ **Bathwick Xaara** 2-8-4 0.................... SaleemGolam 15 65+
(J G Portman) *chsd ldrs: rdn and outpcd 2f out: styd on again ins fnl f but nvr a threat* **66/1**

3 **5** 1 **Just The Tonic**[5] 2328 2-8-6 0.................... SamHitchcott 14 64
(M R Channon) *chsd ldrs: drvn along fr 3f out: styd on same pce u.p fnl 2f* **5/1**[2]

4 **6** ¾ **Pepi Royal (IRE)**[26] 1742 2-8-6 0.................... PaulEddery 4 62
(Pat Eddery) *chsd ldrs: rdn over 2f out: wknd fnl f* **15/2**

7 1 **Flashy Lover (IRE)** 2-8-4 0.................... ChrisCatlin 10 57+
(M R Channon) *in rr: pushed along 3f out: styd on fr 2f out: gng on ins fnl f but nvr in contention* **16/1**

8 1½ **Magic Lantern** 2-8-11 0.................... RichardHughes 9 59
(R Hannon) *chsd ldrs: shkn up 3f out: wknd over 1f out* **11/2**[3]

9 1¼ **Rebecca Romero** 2-8-5 0 ow1.................... EdwardCreighton 2 49
(D J Coakley) *sn in tch: rdn over 2f out: sn chsng ldrs: wknd fnl f* **12/1**

10 6 **Kinky Afro (IRE)** 2-8-6 0.................... StephenCarson 3 32
(J S Moore) *in rr: mod prog fnl f* **16/1**

11 4½ **Wasmi (IRE)** 2-8-4 0.................... NickyMackay 7 17
(C E Brittain) *chsd ldrs: rdn and hung lft over 2f out: sn wknd* **9/1**

12 ½ **Miracle Wish (IRE)** 2-8-6 0.................... PaulFitzsimons 6 17
(R M Beckett) *chsd ldrs: rdn over 2f out: sn wknd* **33/1**

13 4½ **Emma Dora (IRE)** 2-8-10 0 ow2.................... SebSanders 8 8
(D R C Elsworth) *s.i.s: a outpcd* **12/1**

14 1 **Cultured Pride (IRE)** 2-8-8 0.................... TravisBlock 13 3
(R Hannon) *s.i.s: a in rr* **14/1**

03 **15** 2 **Dream Of Gerontius (IRE)**[26] 1726 2-8-8 0.................... J-PGuillambert 5 —
(R Hannon) *sn bhd* **33/1**

1m 11.07s (-1.93) **Going Correction** -0.30s/f (Firm) 2y crse rec **15** Ran SP% **124.0**
Speed ratings (Par 90): **100,99,95,93,92 91,90,88,86,78 72,71,65,64,61**
toteswinger: 1&2 £30.30, 1&3 £64.50, 2&3 £33.70. CSF £109.91 TOTE £36.60: £8.60, £2.00, £11.60; EX 145.50.
Owner Prof C D Green **Bred** Carrigbeg Stud **Trained** Compton, Berks

FOCUS
The standard set by Silver Symphony would suggest the bare form is just fair, even allowing for that one probably stepping up a little on her recent Newmarket effort, but sound and reliable. However, the juvenile track record, previously held by Mixed Blessing, a Group 3 winner in 2005, was lowered by 0.12 seconds, and the time was also fractionally faster than the later older-horse maiden.

NOTEBOOK
Bahati(IRE), a 6,000gns half-sister to six winners, represented last year's successful stable and was able to get off the mark on her debut. She seemed to know her job better than most of the other newcomers and is perhaps not open to as much improvement as some of these, but she broke the juvenile track record and is evidently quite useful. The Albany Stakes at Royal Ascot is a possible target and her performance on the clock suggests she will by no means be out of place. (op 20-1)
Silver Symphony(IRE) seems to be going the right way and had her chance after showing good speed. (op 9-2)
Andina(IRE), an 11,000gns purchase who is out of a useful dual 7f winner, kept on nicely in the closing stages and this was a pleasing debut. She is open to improvement.
Bathwick Xaara, the winner's stablemate, cost only 800gns but she's related to winners and showed ability. She should be suited by a step up to 7f in time.
Just The Tonic's debut third at Goodwood only five days earlier looked to represent only modest form and she was well held this time. (op 11-2)
Pepi Royal(IRE) finished her race tamely and didn't build on her debut performance. (op 8-1)
Flashy Lover(IRE), an 8,000euros purchase, out of a 1m2f winner, ran green for much of the way before gradually getting the idea and looks capable of leaving this form behind. (tchd 14-1)

Magic Lantern ◆ proved easy to back just before the off and looked to both find this trip too short, and need the experience. A 25,000gns half-sister to 1m2f winner Papality, out of a useful miler, she can do better in time. (op 4-1 tchd 7-2)

Rebecca Romero was supported in the market and, hailing from a decent stable, it would be no surprise to see her do better in due course. (op 20-1)

Wasmi(IRE) was very green. (op 14-1)

2495 HENNESSY RESTAURANT 25 MILE MENU H'CAP 1m (S)

7:20 (7:23) (Class 4) (0-80,80) 4-Y-O+ **£5,504** (£1,637; £818; £408) **Stalls** Centre

Form RPR

36-2 **1** **Uncle Fred**[10] 2186 4-8-13 **75** JimCrowley 4 86
(P R Chamings) *in tch: hdwy 3f out: led ins fnl 2f: hrd drvn and hld on wl thrght fnl f* **6/1**[3]

-166 **2** *hd* **Bold Cross (IRE)**[7] 2274 6-8-7 **69** PaulFitzsimons 6 80
(E G Bevan) *in rr but in tch: hdwy over 2f out: hrd drvn and stryd on strly fnl f: nt quite get up* **16/1**

4-02 **3** *shd* **Effigy**[23] 1813 5-8-13 **75** FrankieMcDonald 2 86
(H Candy) *chsd ldrs: rdn to ld 2f out: hdd sn after: styd chalng u.p fnl f: kpt on wl cl home but a jst hld* **4/1**[2]

4-06 **4** *1* **La Coveta (IRE)**[18] 1964 4-9-0 **76** MartinDwyer 9 84
(B J Meehan) *chsd ldrs tl rdn and outpcd 2f out: styd on again u.p fnl f: kpt on cl home* **9/1**

-463 **5** *shd* **The Cayterers**[23] 1813 7-8-7 **74** MCGeran(5) 7 82
(A W Carroll) *towards rr: hdwy over 1f out: styd on u.p ins fnl f but nvr quite gng pce to chal* **12/1**

2130 **6** *2* **Kilburn**[23] 1813 5-8-8 **70** J-PGuillambert 8 74
(A J Lidderdale) *chsd ldrs: rdn to chal 2f out: styd pressing ldrs 1f out: wknd fnl 110yds* **14/1**

3645 **7** *3 1/2* **Count Trevisio (IRE)**[44] 1316 6-8-13 **75** WilliamBuick 1 71
(J R Gask) *led tl rdn and hdd 2f out: wknd over 1f out* **10/1**

1-16 **8** *6* **Supaverdi (USA)**[21] 1860 4-9-0 **76** SteveDrowne 3 58
(H Morrison) *chsd ldrs: drvn along 3f out: hrd rdn over 2f out and no rspnse* **2/1**[1]

002- **9** *15* **Deo Valente (IRE)**[221] 6888 4-8-13 **75** ChrisCatlin 11 22
(J M Bradley) *t.k.h: chsd ldrs: rdn 3f out: wknd qckly over 2f out* **33/1**

11-2 **10** *19* **Hyde Lea Flyer**[134] 199 4-8-13 **75** SebSanders 10 —
(E S McMahon) *slowly away and awkard leaving stalls: plld hrd in rr: rdn 3f out: wknd qckly* **6/1**[3]

1m 36.25s (-3.45) **Going Correction** -0.30s/f (Firm) **10** Ran SP% **124.2**

Speed ratings (Par 105): **105,104,104,103,103 101,98,92,77,58**

toteswinger: 1&2 £13.10, 1&3 £6.10, 2&3 £16.90. CSF £103.07 CT £440.22 TOTE £5.20: £1.70, £4.80, £2.10; EX 126.40.

Owner P R Chamings M A Kirby **Bred** Netherfield House Stud **Trained** Baughurst, Hants

■ Stewards' Enquiry : Paul Fitzsimons two-day ban: used whip with excessive frequency (Jun 13-14)

Frankie McDonald one-day ban: used whip with excessive frequency (Jun 13)

FOCUS

An ordinary handicap for the grade and they finished in a bit of a heap. Nevertheless, it was another step in the right direction from the winner.

Count Trevisio(IRE) Official explanation: jockey said gelding hung right-handed

Deo Valente(IRE) Official explanation: jockey said gelding ran free to post

2496 BATHWICK TYRES MAIDEN STKS 6f 8y

7:50 (7:57) (Class 5) 3-Y-O **£3,885** (£1,156; £577; £288) **Stalls** Centre

Form RPR

0 **1** **Santefisio**[27] 1703 3-9-3 0 TravisBlock 2 77
(P J Makin) *trckd ldrs: styd on u.p fnl f to ld fnl 100yds* **100/1**

2 *hd* **Femme De Fer** 3-8-12 0 IanMongan 5 71
(C G Cox) *plld hrd: sn led: rdn over 1f out: hdd fnl 100yds: kpt on* **33/1**

00 **3** *1 3/4* **Lord Fidelio (IRE)**[26] 1729 3-9-3 0 NeilChalmers 14 70+
(A M Balding) *chsd ldrs: rdn and effrt between horses 1f out: n.m.r ins fnl f and outpcd fnl 100yds* **33/1**

0 **4** *2 1/2* **Quinsman**[42] 1355 3-9-3 0 GeorgeBaker 4 62
(J S Moore) *in tch: pushed along and one pce 2f out: drvn and styd on again fnl f but nvr gng pce to rch ldng trio* **40/1**

0- **5** *nk* **Eyes Like A Hawk (IRE)**[304] 4534 3-8-7 0 (t) RossAtkinson(5) 10 56+
(Tom Dascombe) *in rr: hdwy over 2f out: sn hanging lft: styd on ins fnl f: nt rch ldrs* **10/1**[2]

0 **6** *3/4* **Chandika**[9] 2205 3-8-12 0 PaulFitzsimons 11 54+
(C G Cox) *in tch: pushed long over 2f out: kpt on fnl f but nvr in contention* **12/1**

5-2 **7** *3/4* **Trading Nation (USA)**[22] 1840 3-9-3 0 SteveDrowne 16 57
(R Charlton) *s.i.s: in rr: pushed along 3f out: hrd drvn over 2f out: hung lft: little rspnse and one pce after* **8/13**[1]

60- **8** *2 1/4* **Kuanyao (IRE)**[212] 7098 3-9-3 0 PatCosgrave 3 49
(P J Makin) *chsd ldrs: drvn over 2f out: wknd fnl f* **66/1**

6 **9** *nk* **New Leyf (IRE)**[14] 2070 3-9-3 0 ChrisCatlin 1 48
(J R Gask) *chsd ldrs: rdn over 2f out: wknd over 1f out* **25/1**

0-0 **10** *1/2* **Iron Man Of Mersey (FR)**[32] 1579 3-8-12 0 MCGeran(5) 13 47
(A W Carroll) *in rr: sme hdwy into mid-div over 2f out: wknd over 1f out* **50/1**

11 *1/2* **Medicean Man** 3-9-3 0 MartinDwyer 9 45+
(J R Gask) *s.i.s: green and drvn in rr thrght: mod late prog* **33/1**

6 **12** *1 3/4* **Bertie's Birthday (IRE)**[18] 1972 3-8-12 0 JimCrowley 7 35
(Jonjo O'Neill) *t.k.h: in tch: wknd fr 2f out* **16/1**

13 *3 3/4* **Tarqua (IRE)** 3-8-12 0 RichardHughes 6 23
(R Hannon) *chsd ldrs tl wknd over 2f out* **12/1**

0-6 **14** *3/4* **Der Rosenkavalier (IRE)**[11] 2151 3-9-3 0 WilliamBuick 12 25
(A M Balding) *a in rr* **33/1**

36 **15** *2* **Tender Charm (USA)**[27] 1703 3-9-3 0 SebSanders 15 19
(R M Beckett) *a in rr* **11/1**[3]

16 *9* **Fiftyfourth Street** 3-9-3 0 StephenCarson 8 —
(P J Makin) *s.i.s: sn in mid-div: wknd and eased over 1f out* **66/1**

1m 11.1s (-1.90) **Going Correction** -0.30s/f (Firm) **16** Ran SP% **124.6**

Speed ratings (Par 99): **100,99,97,94,93 92,91,88,88,87 86,84,79,78,75 63**

toteswinger: 1&2 £167.90, 1&3 £46.40, 2&3 £174.60. CSF £2032.84 TOTE £120.40: £22.10, £5.40, £11.10; EX 3921.60.

Owner Weldspec Glasgow Limited **Bred** D Brocklehurst **Trained** Ogbourne Maisey, Wilts

FOCUS

A race dominated by outsiders, and the winning time, although under standard, was fractionally slower than the earlier juvenile maiden. All things considered, the bare form is probably no better than fair, but that said, some nice types lined up and a few of these should step forward considerably in time.

Fiftyfourth Street Official explanation: jockey said colt hung badly right-handed

2497 RELYON CLEANING NEWBURY H'CAP 1m 5f 61y

8:25 (8:26) (Class 5) (0-75,75) 4-Y-O+ **£2,590** (£770; £385; £192) **Stalls** Low

Form RPR

3-55 **1** **Murcar**[9] 2194 4-8-13 **65** (b[1]) IanMongan 5 77+
(C G Cox) *trckd ldrs: led 3f out: rdn clr fr 2f out: eased nr fin* **2/1**[1]

4-40 **2** *3 1/2* **Drum Major (IRE)**[122] 319 4-9-2 **68** GeorgeBaker 9 73
(G L Moore) *in tch: rdn over 2f out: chsd wnr fr 2f out but nvr any ch* **16/1**

1644 **3** *1 1/4* **Thorny Mandate**[19] 1936 7-8-5 **57** MartinDwyer 4 60
(W M Brisbourne) *hld up in tch: n.m.r fr over 3f out: drvn and hdwy fr 2f out: styd on to go 3rd fnl f: kpt on one pce* **11/1**

0115 **4** *3* **Bell Island**[39] 1435 5-9-9 **75** (v) RichardHughes 7 74
(Lady Herries) *s.i.s: in rr: n.m.r 3f out: hdwy and rdn over 2f out: kpt on same pce fr over 1f out* **4/1**[2]

-330 **5** *1 1/2* **Seventh Hill**[15] 2039 4-8-10 **62** SteveDrowne 2 58
(M Blanshard) *mid-div: hdwy 4f out: drvn to chse ldrs over 2f out: nvr in contention: wknd u.p over 1f out* **25/1**

110 **6** *2* **Moonshine Creek**[24] 1786 7-8-12 **64** ChrisCatlin 1 57
(P W Hiatt) *led: hdd 3f out: sn rdn: wknd 2f out* **8/1**[3]

-125 **7** *nk* **Mista Rossa**[7] 2283 4-9-3 **69** TravisBlock 11 62
(H Morrison) *chsd ldr tl over 3f out: n.m.r on ins and lost position ins fnl 2f: kpt on again cl home* **8/1**[3]

03-3 **8** *1/2* **Act Three**[12] 2123 5-8-11 **63** JimCrowley 13 55
(Mouse Hamilton-Fairley) *in rr: hdwy 4f out: effrt u.p on outside 3f out: nvr rchd ldrs and wknd qckly 2f out* **16/1**

00-0 **9** *2 1/2* **Kasban**[35] 1506 5-9-9 **75** StephenDonohoe 6 63
(Ian Williams) *chsd ldrs: rdn over 3f out: wknd qckly 2f out* **14/1**

3-65 **10** *3 3/4* **Agente Romano (USA)**[11] 2172 4-9-5 **71** (t) SebSanders 12 54
(G A Butler) *bhd most of way* **12/1**

0-40 **11** *hd* **Red Twist**[100] 604 4-8-7 **59** SimonWhitworth 3 42
(M Hill) *chsd ldrs: wkng whn hmpd ins fnl 2f* **33/1**

0-00 **12** *11* **Flame Creek (IRE)**[11] 2163 13-7-11 **56** oh11 CharlesEddery(7) 8 22
(E J Creighton) *a in rr* **50/1**

56-5 **13** *1 3/4* **Seedless**[12] 2123 4-8-13 **65** WilliamBuick 10 28
(A M Balding) *bhd most of way* **16/1**

2m 49.76s (-2.24) **Going Correction** -0.075s/f (Good) **13** Ran SP% **124.6**

Speed ratings (Par 103): **103,100,100,98,97 96,95,95,94,91 91,84,83**

toteswinger: 1&2 £9.60, 1&3 £11.90, 2&3 £70.60. CSF £39.89 CT £306.91 TOTE £3.20: £1.70, £3.70, £3.20; EX 53.70.

Owner Peter J Skinner **Bred** John W Ford And Peter J Skinner **Trained** Lambourn, Berks

FOCUS

A modest staying handicap run at an honest pace. The winner was back on a good mark and the rest looked pretty exposed.

Bell Island Official explanation: jockey said gelding missed the break

2498 RACING UK SKY432 FILLIES' H'CAP 7f (S)

8:55 (8:57) (Class 5) (0-75,75) 3-Y-O+ **£2,590** (£770; £385; £192) **Stalls** Centre

Form RPR

5-22 **1** **Cumana Bay**[23] 1808 3-9-2 **74** RichardHughes 6 82+
(R Hannon) *hld up in tch: drvn and qcknd to ld jst ins fnl f: styd on strly* **7/4**[1]

34-0 **2** *3 1/4* **Bea Menace (USA)**[14] 2079 3-8-10 **68** MartinDwyer 11 68
(P F I Cole) *trckd ldrs: led over 3f out: stl travelling wl 2f out: rdn over 1f out: hdd jst ins fnl f: sn no ch w wnr but styd on wl for 2nd* **25/1**

30-0 **3** *hd* **Support Fund (IRE)**[9] 2188 5-9-10 **71** StephenCarson 2 74
(Eve Johnson Houghton) *in tch: rdn and hdwy fr 2f out: styd on u.p to go 3rd ins fnl f: clsng on 2nd cl home but nvr any ch w wnr* **16/1**

21-0 **4** *3/4* **Young Dottie**[38] 1462 3-9-0 **72** IanMongan 4 69
(P M Phelan) *chsd ldrs: rdn and ev ch fr over 2f out tl over 1f out: wknd ins fnl f* **11/2**[2]

10-0 **5** *1 1/4* **Ken's Girl**[26] 1743 5-9-4 **65** ChrisCatlin 15 63
(W S Kittow) *chsd ldrs: rdn over 2f out: styd on fnl f but nvr in contention* **14/1**

0-35 **6** *1 1/2* **Russian Rave**[18] 1973 3-8-10 **68** JimCrowley 7 58
(J G Portman) *in rr but in tch: rdn 2f out: sme prog fnl f but nvr in contention* **8/1**

1-04 **7** *shd* **Koraleva Tectona (IRE)**[9] 2188 4-10-0 **75** PaulEddery 9 68+
(Pat Eddery) *in rr but in tch: rdn ins fnl 2f: no imp: styd on same pce fnl f* **7/1**[3]

46-0 **8** *2 3/4* **Pansy Potter**[11] 2160 3-8-5 **63** NickyMackay 1 45
(B J Meehan) *trckd ldrs: rdn over 3f out to 2f out: wknd over 1f out* **16/1**

41-0 **9** *4 1/2* **King's Siren (IRE)**[23] 1808 3-8-10 **68** WilliamBuick 8 38
(A M Balding) *mid-div: rdn 3f out: nvr gng pce to be competitive: no ch whn n.m.r on rails ins fnl 2f* **7/1**[3]

-240 **10** *6* **Luckier (IRE)**[16] 2001 3-9-2 **74** GeorgeBaker 13 28
(S Kirk) *restless in stalls: s.i.s: a outpcd* **16/1**

52-0 **11** *3 3/4* **Leelu**[19] 1937 3-8-8 **66** SteveDrowne 5 9
(D W P Arbuthnot) *led tl hdd over 3f out: wknd 2f out* **20/1**

0033 **12** *6* **Love Allowed**[39] 1422 3-8-2 **60** FrankieMcDonald 12 —
(Jamie Poulton) *a in rr* **20/1**

1m 23.82s (-1.88) **Going Correction** -0.30s/f (Firm)

WFA 3 from 4yo+ 11lb **12** Ran SP% **125.5**

Speed ratings (Par 100): **98,94,94,93,91 90,89,86,81,74 70,63**

toteswinger: 1&2 £17.30, 1&3 £15.30, 2&3 £22.40. CSF £63.15 CT £596.03 TOTE £2.90: £1.80, £5.60, £4.50; EX 89.10 Place 6 £5,109.96, Place 5 £1,522.67..

Owner J R Shannon **Bred** J R Shannon **Trained** East Everleigh, Wilts

■ Stewards' Enquiry : Stephen Carson two-day ban: used whip with excessive frequency (Jun 13-14)

FOCUS

A modest, uncompetitive fillies' handicap run at a strong pace. Improved form from the winner.

Luckier(IRE) Official explanation: jockey said filly hung right-handed throughout

Love Allowed Official explanation: jockey said filly cut itself in stalls

T/Plt: £17,824.50 to a £1 stake. Pool: £65,926.25. 2.70 winning tickets. T/Qpdt: Part won. £4,362.50 to a £1 stake. Pool: £5,895.40. 0.70 winning tickets. ST

[2054]YORK (L-H)

Saturday, May 30

OFFICIAL GOING: Good to firm (8.3)

Rail realignment added 7yards to advertised distances on the round course.

Wind: Light, across. Weather: Dry and sunny

2499 FUTURE SELECT CLAIMING STKS — 1m 4f

2:10 (2:10) (Class 4) 4-Y-0+ — **£5,828** (£1,734; £866; £432) **Stalls** Centre

Form				RPR
000/	1		**Nosferatu (IRE)**[69] 6169 6-9-1 85........(b1) NeilBrown(3) 1 (J Howard Johnson) *sn chsng clr ldr: hdwy 3f out: led 2f out and sn rdn: styd on strly ins fnl f* **10/1**	84
2220	2	3 ¾	**Benedict Spirit (IRE)**[9] 2200 4-8-9 71........MartinLane(5) 7 (M H Tompkins) *in midfrield: hdwy over 4f out: rdn to chse ldrs over 2f out: drvn and kpt on ins fnl f* **9/1**	74
21-1	3	1	**Gross Prophet**[25] 1770 4-9-0 77........RichardKingscote 14 (Tom Dascombe) *hld up: hdwy on wd outside 4f out: rdn to chse ldrs wl over 2f out: drvn over 1f out: kpt on same pce* **7/2**[1]	73
3232	4	½	**Edas**[7] 2264 7-8-7 68........MarkCoumbe(5) 2 (R C Guest) *towards rr: hdwy 3f out: rdn wl over 1f out: kpt on ins fnl f: nrst fin* **12/1**	70
-016	5	¾	**Trip The Light**[28] 1665 4-9-2 71........(v) TonyHamilton 10 (R A Fahey) *in tch: hdwy to chse ldng pair over 4f out: rdn 3f out: drvn 2f out and kpt on same pce* **10/1**	73
405	6	5	**Dunaskin (IRE)**[15] 2031 9-8-11 87........(v1) LanceBetts(5) 9 (B Ellison) *led and sn clr: pushed along 3f out: rdn and hdd 2f out: sn wknd* **7/2**[1]	65
2041	7	1	**Nawamees (IRE)**[7] 2264 11-8-9 69........(p) JohnEgan 4 (P D Evans) *chsd ldrs: rdn along over 3f out: grad wknd* **7/1**[2]	59
/0-2	8	2 ¼	**Realism (FR)**[12] 2129 9-8-11 75........DaleGibson 3 (M W Easterby) *in rr and hmpd after 1 1/2f: nvr a factor* **8/1**[3]	55
2020	9	15	**Bridgewater Boys**[16] 2018 8-8-2 65........(b) DeclanCannon(7) 12 (T J Pitt) *a towards rr* **25/1**	29
05-0	10	23	**Vicious Warrior**[9] 2200 10-8-11 68........PhilipRobinson 5 (R M Whitaker) *plld hrd in rr: rapid hdwy after 2f to chse ldrs: rdn along 4f out and sn wknd* **20/1**	—
0000	11	1 ¼	**Oddsmaker (IRE)**[21] 1886 8-8-11 64........(t) RichardEvans(5) 13 (M A Barnes) *chsd ldrs: rdn along 4f out and sn wknd* **50/1**	—
4533	F		**Teasing**[12] 2146 5-8-4 71........(v) SimonPearce(7) 11 (J Pearce) *hld up in rr whn bdly hmpd and fell after 1 1/2f* **12/1**	—

2m 32.6s (-0.60) **Going Correction** +0.075s/f (Good) **12 Ran SP% 122.2**

Speed ratings (Par 105): **105,102,101,101,101 97,97,95,85,70 69,—**

toteswinger: 1&2 £29.20, 1&3 £5.20, 2&3 £9.80. CSF £97.95 TOTE £13.50: £3.60, £3.20, £2.00; EX 157.60.Benedict Spirit was claimed by Mr Dai Burchell for £16,000.

Owner Andrea & Graham Wylie **Bred** Newberry Stud Company **Trained** Billy Row, Co Durham

■ Stewards' Enquiry : Mark Coumbe three-day ban: used whip with excessive frequency (Jun 13-15)

Neil Brown two-day ban: used whip with excessive frequency (Jun 13-14)

FOCUS

They went a really good gallop in this fair claimer and it turned into a proper test at the distance. The winner was a stone off his best old form.

Vicious Warrior Official explanation: jockey said gelding ran too free

2500 SPORTINGBET.COM STKS (CONDITIONS RACE) — 7f

2:40 (2:40) (Class 3) 3-Y-0+ — **£8,095** (£2,408; £1,203; £601) **Stalls** Low

Form				RPR
4-62	1		**Regal Parade**[35] 1513 5-9-2 106........AdrianTNicholls 11 (D Nicholls) *in tch: hdwy over 2f out: rdn to chse ldrs over 1f out: drvn ins fnl f: styd on to ld last 75yds: hld on wl* **13/2**	110
4623	2	nk	**Mia's Boy**[16] 2015 5-9-2 103........JohnEgan 6 (C A Dwyer) *towards rr: pushed along and edgd lft over 2f out: swtchd rt and rdn over 1f out: styd on wl u.p ins fnl f* **11/4**[1]	109
005/	3	hd	**Court Masterpiece**[791] 858 9-9-2 114........GrahamGibbons 5 (J J Quinn) *hld up: smooth hdwy 3f out: swtchd rt wl over 1f out: rdn to chal ins fnl f and ev ch tl drvn and nt qckn nr fin* **12/1**	108+
226-	4	½	**Tombi (USA)**[231] 6653 5-9-2 104........TonyHamilton 8 (J Howard Johnson) *chsd ldrs: hdwy 3f out: rdn to ld wl over 1f out: drvn ins fnl f: hdd and no ex last 75yds* **13/2**	107
1-11	5	2 ½	**Taqdeyr**[38] 1467 4-9-2 96........PhilipRobinson 9 (M A Jarvis) *cl up: effrt over 2f out: sn rdn and ev ch tl drvn and wknd over 1f out* **5/1**[2]	100+
2-50	6	3 ¼	**Medicea Sidera**[21] 1873 5-8-8 96........DavidProbert(3) 2 (E F Vaughan) *chsd ldrs: rdn along over 2f out: sn drvn and wknd* **16/1**	86
0/6-	7	1 ¼	**McCartney (GER)**[380] 2131 4-9-2 110........TedDurcan 10 (Saeed Bin Suroor) *hld up: hdwy on wd outside over 2f out: rdn to chse ldrs over 1f out: sn wknd* **6/1**[3]	88
5-03	8	3 ¼	**Courageous (IRE)**[7] 2278 3-8-5 101........GregFairley 7 (B Smart) *t.k.h: led: rdn along over 2f out: drvn and hdd wl over 1f out: sn wknd* **14/1**	79
-504	9	2 ¾	**Marine Boy (IRE)**[15] 2035 3-8-5 102........RichardKingscote 1 (Tom Dascombe) *hld up: hdwy on inner over 2f out: sn rdn and wknd over 1f out* **11/1**	72
600-	10	1 ½	**Alan Devonshire**[230] 6670 4-8-11 94........MartinLane(5) 3 (M H Tompkins) *chsd ldng pair: rdn along 3f out: sn wknd* **33/1**	68

1m 24.11s (-1.19) **Going Correction** -0.05s/f (Good)

WFA 3 from 4yo+ 11lb **10 Ran SP% 115.8**

Speed ratings (Par 107): **104,103,103,102,100 96,94,91,88,86**

toteswinger: 1&2 £4.20, 1&3 £20.10, 2&3 £8.50. CSF £24.51 TOTE £6.10: £1.80, £1.70, £3.40; EX 15.20.

Owner Dab Hand Racing **Bred** Highclere Stud And Harry Herbert **Trained** Sessay, N Yorks

■ Stewards' Enquiry : Adrian T Nicholls one-day ban: used whip down shoulder in forehand position (Jun 13)

FOCUS

This was a decent conditions event, any number looking in with a chance, and it produced a cracking finish. Basically Listed grade form, and pretty solid too.

NOTEBOOK

Regal Parade, winner of last season's Ayr Gold Cup, finished a good second in a 7f Listed contest at Leicester last time and he started to close inside the three. His effort briefly looked to be flattening out inside the final furlong, but he found extra close home and stuck out a willing neck. Effective from 6f-1m and happy on any going, this five-year-old still seems to be progressing and may well land a Listed race at some stage this season. (op 11-2 tchd 7-1)

Mia's Boy has now run well in defeat on all five outings this season. A fast-finishing third in a 1m handicap at the course last time, he took a while to pick up on this drop in trip and, though he stayed on well inside the final furlong, he never quite looked to be getting there. He deserves to find a race at some stage. His rider reported him to have hung left. Official explanation: jockey said horse hung left-handed (op 7-2 tchd 9-2 in a place)

Court Masterpiece, who was returning from a lengthy absence having been in action at stud in Ireland, won the Group 1 Sussex Stakes in his prime with Ed Dunlop. The nine-year-old was having his first start for the John Quinn yard and momentarily looked like winning when challenging between runners inside the final furlong, but he just couldn't pull out that bit extra. There is every reason to believe he will be straighter next time and he could provide connections with some fun in these races. (op 14-1 tchd 10-1)

Tombi(USA) won a decent sprint at this course just over a year ago and later went on to place at Listed level. He ran really well on this seasonal reappearance, especially as all his wins have been over 6f, and only got run out of it in the final 100 yards. (op 11-2 tchd 5-1)

Taqdeyr has progressed well on the AW, winning all three starts since November, including a handicap off 91 last time, but he needed to have improved again for this return to turf and was brushed aside soon after two out. He will find easier opportunities. Philip Robinson reported he was unsuited by the going. Official explanation: jockey said gelding was unsuited by the good to firm ground (op 7-2)

Medicea Sidera, nibbled at beforehand, came up short in a Group 3 at Lingfield last time and she couldn't adopt her usual front-running tactics here. (op 22-1 tchd 14-1)

McCartney(GER), once a smart two-year-old with Mark Johnston, was making only his second visit to the track for Godolphin (last of six in Dante on first run) and, having made a brief forward move with three to run, he gradually dropped away. (op 7-1 tchd 11-2 and 8-1 in a place)

2501 STOWE FAMILY LAW LLP GRAND CUP (LISTED RACE) — 1m 6f

3:15 (3:15) (Class 1) 4-Y-0+

£22,708 (£8,608; £4,308; £2,148; £1,076; £540) **Stalls** Low

Form				RPR
541-	1		**Caracciola (GER)**[42] 6817 12-9-0 105........DaleGibson 7 (N J Henderson) *led: qcknd over 3f out: rdn over 2f out: hdd over 1f out: drvn to ld again ent fnl f: hld on wl towards fin* **7/1**	104
34/1	2	shd	**Friston Forest (IRE)**[113] 437 5-9-3 108........TedDurcan 6 (Saeed Bin Suroor) *trckd ldr: hdwy 3f out: rdn to ld over 1f out: drvn and hdd ent fnl f: rallied u.p towards fin: jst hld* **9/4**[1]	107+
0-03	3	6	**Halla San**[24] 1790 7-9-0 100........TonyHamilton 2 (R A Fahey) *hld up in tch: rdn and outpcd 3f out: styd on u.p appr fnl f: nrst fin* **9/2**[3]	95
30-6	4	½	**Yellowstone (IRE)**[14] 2075 5-9-0 108........JohnEgan 1 (P F I Cole) *t.k.h: hld up in rr: hdwy on outer 3f out: rdn to chse ldrs 2f out: sn drvn and no imp* **3/1**[2]	95
6333	5	nk	**Buddhist Monk**[7] 2283 4-9-0 84........AdrianTNicholls 8 (Ian Williams) *hld up: hdwy over 4f out: rdn along 3f out: sn drvn and no imp* **17/2**	94?
125-	6	3 ½	**Si Belle (IRE)**[269] 5625 4-8-9 95........RichardKingscote 4 (Rae Guest) *trckd ldrs: rdn along 4f out: drvn over 2f out and sn wknd* **10/1**	84
0-	7	5	**Valentino Rossi (BRZ)**[280] 5264 7-9-0 97........GregFairley 3 (A G Foster) *chsd ldrs: rdn along over 3f out: drvn over 2f out and sn wknd* **16/1**	82

3m 2.68s (2.48) **Going Correction** +0.075s/f (Good) **7 Ran SP% 112.0**

Speed ratings (Par 111): **95,94,91,91,91 89,86**

toteswinger: 1&2 £3.50, 1&3 £6.90, 2&3 £1.90. CSF £22.18 TOTE £9.20: £3.50, £1.90; EX 19.50 Trifecta £116.70 Pool £362.94 - 2.30 winning units..

Owner P J D Pottinger **Bred** Frau I U A Brunotte **Trained** Upper Lambourn, Berks

■ Stewards' Enquiry : Ted Durcan four-day ban: used whip with excessive frequency without giving horse time to respond (Jun 13-15 & 21)

FOCUS

The absence of morning favourite Furmigadelagiusta made this more open than it would have been, and veteran Caracciola scored under a fine ride from Dale Gibson. The form is a bit muddling with the fifth finishing close enough.

NOTEBOOK

Caracciola(GER) became the oldest horse ever to win a Listed event. Now aged 12, he caused a 50-1 shock when winning last season's Cesarewitch and has since been out a few times over hurdles, most recently when fifth at Ayr in April. He had a bit to prove on this drop in trip, but Gibson was keen to have him out in front and, although they didn't set much of a gallop, he quickened it up off the home bend and quickly had a few of them in trouble. He looked beaten when passed over two out, but battled back with the rail to run against, and held on well in a tight finish. A good test on fast ground suits him best and he may well be up to running a big race in the Queen Alexandra Stakes at Royal Ascot. (op 8-1 tchd 6-1)

Friston Forest(IRE), a triple Listed winner in France who made a successful debut for connections when narrowly denying classy stablemate Veracity in a 1m6f handicap off 104 at Nad Al Sheba in February, reportedly looked in need of the race in the paddock and got a bit warm beforehand. He travelled like a good horse, though, and edged to the front over two out, but seemed to blow up and, despite battling back gamely, couldn't quite get there. Conceding 3lb to all his rivals, he is the one to take from the race and should be capable of landing a nice prize or two this season. (op 7-4 tchd 5-2)

Halla San, ahead of the winner over hurdles in April and a close third in the Chester Cup last time, was outpaced when the tempo increased and never got going until the race was all over. (tchd 5-1)

Yellowstone(IRE), winner of a decent prize over course and distance for Jane Chapple-Hyam last season (wore cheekpieces), showed little on his first start for this yard at Newbury on his reappearance (should have handled the testing ground), and came into this with a bit to prove. He started to close three out, but couldn't quicken on the ground. This was at least a step back in the right direction. (op 7-2)

Buddhist Monk, the lowest rated of these by some way, has been running well in handicaps and he deserves a good deal of credit for this effort, battling on gamely in the bunch for third. Official explanation: jockey said gelding hung left-handed from four out (op 14-1)

Si Belle(IRE) progressed well last season and is expected to do so again in 2009, being from a good family. The only filly in the field, she was left behind a bit in the end, but will find easier opportunities to gain more black type. Official explanation: jockey said filly had no more to give (op 9-1)

Valentino Rossi(BRZ), a fast-ground winning stayer in Brazil, has yet to prove he is up to this rating on two starts in Britain. (tchd 11-1)

2502 SPORTINGBET.COM SPRINT (HERITAGE H'CAP) — 5f

3:45 (3:45) (Class 2) (0-105,105) 3-Y-0+

£24,924 (£7,464; £3,732; £1,868; £932; £468) **Stalls** High

Form				RPR
0-50	1		**Ishetoo**[15] 2059 5-8-5 93........JamieKyne(7) 15 (A Dickman) *in tch: rdn along 1/2-way: hdwy wl over 1f out: drvn and styd on strly ins fnl f to ld nr fin* **12/1**	102
0-32	2	nk	**Peak District (IRE)**[2] 2397 5-8-6 92 ow4........AmyRyan(5) 8 (K A Ryan) *cl up: led 2f out: rdn and hung rt ent fnl f: sn drvn: hdd and no ex nr fin* **9/1**	100

-055 **3** ½ **River Falcon**[15] 2059 9-8-12 **93**........ DanielTudhope 1 99+
(J S Goldie) *in tch on wd outside: rdn along 2f out: kpt on u.p ins fnl f: nrst fin* **14/1**

0-44 **4** ½ **Hamish McGonagall**[16] 2012 4-9-3 **98**........ TedDurcan 12 102
(T D Easterby) *prom: effrt 2f out: sn rdn and kpt on same pce ins fnl f* **7/1**[2]

0515 **5** *shd* **Internationaldebut (IRE)**[7] 2259 4-8-11 **92**........ JohnEgan 14 96
(S Parr) *tlowards rr: hdwy 2f out: sn rdn and kpt on ins fnl f: nrst fin* **17/2**[3]

3-10 **6** ½ **Hitchens (IRE)**[17] 1989 4-9-7 **105**........ NeilBrown(3) 5 107+
(T D Barron) *hld up and bhd: hdwy 2f out: swtchd rt and rdn over 1f out: styd on ins fnl f: nrst fin* **14/1**

24-0 **7** ½ **Kaldoun Kingdom (IRE)**[16] 2012 4-8-13 **94**........ TonyHamilton 3 94
(R A Fahey) *hld up in rr: hdwy 2f out: rdn and kpt on ins fnl f: nrst fin* **16/1**

20-3 **8** ¾ **Siren's Gift**[32] 1582 5-8-9 **93**........(b) DavidProbert(3) 13 91
(A M Balding) *cl up: effrt wl over 1f out: sn rdn and ev ch tl drvn and wknd enteing fnl f* **5/2**[1]

-060 **9** ½ **Good Gorsoon (USA)**[14] 2078 4-8-5 **86**........ GregFairley 11 82
(B W Hills) *cl up: rdn along 2f out: grad wknd* **10/1**

05-5 **10** ½ **Bahamian Babe**[32] 1582 3-7-7 **89**........ MatthewLawson(7) 10 80
(M L W Bell) *led: rdn along and hdd 2f out: sn swtchd rt: drvn and wknd over 1f out* **10/1**

6504 **11** 1 ¾ **Stoneacre Lad (IRE)**[14] 2094 6-8-3 **84**........(b) PatrickMathers 6 72
(Peter Grayson) *nvr bttr than midfield* **40/1**

0016 **12** 2 ¼ **Buachaill Dona (IRE)**[21] 1868 6-9-7 **102**........ AdrianTNicholls 2 82
(D Nicholls) *chsd ldrs: rdn along 2f out: sn wknd* **16/1**

3/0- **13** *hd* **Copper Dock (IRE)**[49] 1219 5-8-5 **91**........ AmyKathleenParsons(5) 4 70
(T G McCourt, Ire) *t.k.h: hld up towards rr: hdwy 1/2-way: rdn 2f out and sn wknd* **20/1**

004- **14** ½ **Flash McGahon (IRE)**[242] 6367 5-8-7 **95**........ NSLawes(7) 9 72
(D Nicholls) *s.i.s: hdwy and in tch over 2f out: sn rdn and wknd* **28/1**

57.92 secs (-1.38) **Going Correction** -0.05s/f (Good)
WFA 3 from 4yo+ 8lb **14** Ran SP% **123.2**
Speed ratings (Par 109): **109,108,107,106,106 105,105,103,103,102 99,95,95,94**
toteswinger: 1&2 £16.90, 1&3 £21.60, 2&3 £32.40. CSF £116.36 CT £1588.94 TOTE £15.80: £3.70, £3.60, £4.60; EX 183.10 Trifecta £598.80 Pool £1,780.50 - 2.20 winning units..
Owner John H Sissons **Bred** Longdon Stud Ltd **Trained** Sandhutton, N Yorks
■ Stewards' Enquiry : Amy Ryan one-day ban: careless riding (Jun 13)

FOCUS
A fiercely-competitive sprint handicap that was run at a proper gallop. Solid form.

NOTEBOOK
Ishetoo, on the same mark as when third in this a year ago, would not have been suited by the soft ground when beaten a long way in a strange race over 6f here last time, and conditions here were much more in his favour. Under pressure at halfway, he started to run on once switched left and stayed on strongly to get up inside the final 50 yards. He has been most progressive over the past couple of seasons and still looks to be going the right way.
Peak District(IRE), runner-up at Lingfield just two days earlier and carrying 4lb overweight, was 5lb higher for this return to turf and looked all over the winner when going into a nice lead over a furlong out, but he edged right under pressure and was just run out of it late on. He should find a race at some stage. (op 11-1 tchd 12-1)
River Falcon continues to run well despite his advancing years, but you have to go back to August 2007 for his last win, and he's still 1lb higher. He came home well towards the far side and should continue to pay his way. (op 12-1)
Hamish McGonagall, a most progressive sort last season, was 1lb lower than when fourth over this course and distance last time and soon up disputing the lead. He battled away best he could having been headed and just held on for fourth. (op 13-2)
Internationaldebut(IRE), 3lb higher than when winning over course and distance earlier in the month, has since run well in defeat at Beverley and he kept on well late having been outpaced when the runner-up kicked for home. (op 9-1 tchd 8-1)
Hitchens(IRE), outclassed in the Group 2 Duke Of York Stakes last time, got going too late on this drop in trip. (op 12-1)
Kaldoun Kingdom(IRE) again ran well enough to suggest he isn't far from hitting form, for all that he is still quite high in the weights. (op 14-1)
Siren's Gift, who has not won since September 2007, ran several good races in defeat last term and returned with a fine effort when third behind subsequent Temple Stakes winner Looks Busy at Bath. Andrew Balding's runners can do little wrong at present, but this one weakened having been in the early firing line and clearly failed to run her race. (op 10-3)
Bahamian Babe, the only three-year-old in the field, showed good early speed before fading.

2503 YORKSHIRE REGIMENT EBF MAIDEN FILLIES' STKS 6f
4:20 (4:22) (Class 4) 2-Y-O **£6,605** (£1,965; £982; £490) **Stalls** High

Form RPR

1 **Sweet Sonnet (USA)** 2-9-0 0........ TedDurcan 6 76+
(Saeed Bin Suroor) *s.i.s: green and sn outpcd in rr: hdwy wl over 1f out: rdn ins fnl f: str run to ld nr fin* **11/4**[2]

2 **2** *nk* **Falling Angel**[10] 2175 2-9-0 0........ RichardKingscote 8 76+
(P F I Cole) *led: shkn up and edgd lft over 1f out: pushed clr ins fnl f: idled and hdd nr fin* **10/11**[1]

3 3 ¼ **Babylonian** 2-9-0 0........ GregFairley 3 65
(M Johnston) *chsd ldng pair: rdn along over 2f out: drvn and one pce appr fnl f* **4/1**[3]

4 ¾ **Perfect Blossom** 2-9-0 0........ DanielTudhope 2 63
(I W McInnes) *bmpd after s and sn pulling hrd: chsd ldr on outer: hdwy to chal 2f out: sn rdn and wknd appr fnl f* **25/1**

50 **5** 1 ¼ **Mrs Jones And Me (IRE)**[42] 1344 2-9-0 0........ TonyHamilton 4 59
(P T Midgley) *green and hung lft after s: hld up in tch: rdn along 2f out and no imp* **20/1**

6 **6** 2 ¼ **Venture Girl (IRE)**[13] 2099 2-9-0 0........ JohnEgan 7 53
(T D Easterby) *chsd ldr: rdden along over 2f out: drvn wl over 1f out and sn wknd* **12/1**

1m 13.54s (1.64) **Going Correction** -0.05s/f (Good) **6** Ran SP% **115.4**
Speed ratings (Par 92): **87,86,82,81,79 76**
toteswinger: 1&2 £1.70, 1&3 £1.90, 2&3 £1.60. CSF £5.86 TOTE £4.00: £2.00, £1.40; EX 5.80.
Owner Godolphin **Bred** Stonerside Stable **Trained** Newmarket, Suffolk

FOCUS
The outcome of this fillies' maiden changed dramatically late on. This was an interesting race but the time, the fifth and the sixth hold down the form.

NOTEBOOK
Sweet Sonnet(USA) was last and driven along for much of the contest but flew home to sucker-punch the favourite. From a highly successful US dirt family, she was edgy in the stalls and ran green having been slowly away. It looked as though Durcan had accepted the fact she was going to finish last approaching the two, and she was still a long way down at the distance, but everything all of a sudden clicked and she rattled home to get up in the final stride. This was a very pleasing start and the combination of a rise in distance on slightly slower ground should see her in an even better light. (op 3-1 tchd 7-2)
Falling Angel ◆ travelled beautifully on her debut at Goodwood and again showed bags of pace. She drifted more towards the centre of the track, but was still clear and looked to have the race won until the winner pounced on her close home. She would have won had her jockey ridden her right out, but gaining compensation should not prove too difficult. She would have no trouble with a drop to 5f. Official explanation: jockey said, regarding running and riding, that his orders were to bounce out, not to wait and two out kick on and get on with the job, adding that the filly ran green in closing stages and tended to hang left. (op 6-5)
Babylonian, a half-sister to a couple of middle-distance winners, comes from a yard whose juveniles are beginning to roll and she shaped pleasingly on this racecourse debut, staying on again having been outpaced. She should learn a good deal from the experience and winning a standard maiden should prove a formality once she has a chance to race over 7f. (op 9-2 tchd 11-2 in a place)
Perfect Blossom, half-sister to winners at this distance, ran well for a long way and should improve for the experience. She pulled a bit early on and will find easier opportunities. (op 18-1)
Mrs Jones And Me(IRE) should find a race at a lower level. (op 14-1)
Venture Girl(IRE) looks a nursery prospect. (op 11-1 tchd 10-1)

2504 SPORTINGBET.COM STKS (H'CAP) 7f
4:55 (4:56) (Class 3) (0-90,90) 3-Y-O **£7,771** (£2,312; £1,155; £577) **Stalls** Low

Form RPR

-540 **1** **Kyllachy Star**[21] 1869 3-8-11 **80**........ TonyHamilton 5 87
(R A Fahey) *towards rr: hdwy wl over 2f out: rdn wl over 1f out: drvn ins fnl f: styd on u.p to ld on line* **12/1**

10-3 **2** *nse* **Quanah Parker (IRE)**[7] 2270 3-9-4 **87**........ JohnEgan 3 94
(R M Whitaker) *trckd ldrs: hdwy over 2f out: rdn to ld wl over 1f out: drvn ins fnl f: hdd post* **9/2**[2]

06-4 **3** *nk* **Inheritor (IRE)**[18] 1971 3-8-5 **77**........ DavidProbert(3) 2 83
(B Smart) *in tch: hdwy to trck ldrs 3f out: swtchd lft and rdn to chal over 1f out: drvn ins fnl f: ev ch tl no ex nr fin* **6/1**[3]

-121 **4** 8 **Seek N' Destroy (IRE)**[21] 1870 3-9-1 **84**........ RichardKingscote 7 69
(B W Hills) *cl up: led 3f out: rdn and hdd wl over 1f out: grad wknd* **2/1**[1]

515- **5** 2 ¼ **Darcey**[236] 6533 3-8-0 **76** oh1........ TimothyAyres(7) 1 55
(R A Fahey) *towards rr: hdwy on inner 3f out: rdn to chse ldrs over 2f out: sn no imp* **20/1**

0-1 **6** 2 ¼ **Smart Endeavour (USA)**[36] 1490 3-9-2 **85**........ TedDurcan 6 57
(W R Swinburn) *trckd ldrs: hdwy 3f out: rdn along 2f out: sn drvn and wknd* **13/2**

0-16 **7** 3 ¼ **Ishe Mac**[17] 1987 3-8-1 **77**........ MatthewLawson(7) 8 41
(N Bycroft) *t.k.h: sn led: rdn along and hdd 3f out: sn wknd* **12/1**

01-0 **8** 2 ¼ **Moon Lightning (IRE)**[9] 2209 3-8-2 **76**........ MartinLane(5) 4 34
(M H Tompkins) *a in rr* **12/1**

1-44 **9** 5 **Feeling Fab (FR)**[21] 1860 3-9-7 **90**........ GregFairley 9 34
(M Johnston) *chsd ldrs: rdn along 3f out: sn wknd* **7/1**

1m 24.15s (-1.15) **Going Correction** -0.05s/f (Good) **9** Ran SP% **119.5**
Speed ratings (Par 103): **104,103,103,94,91 89,85,83,77**
toteswinger: 1&2 £11.40, 1&3 £14.20, 2&3 £5.60. CSF £67.54 CT £366.33 TOTE £16.30: £3.90, £1.80, £2.10; EX 90.60.
Owner CBWS Partnership **Bred** John James **Trained** Musley Bank, N Yorks
■ Stewards' Enquiry : John Egan two-day ban: excessive use of the whip (Jun 13-14)

FOCUS
A rock-solid sprint handicap for three-year-olds, and decent form for the grade.

NOTEBOOK
Kyllachy Star got there in the final stride, just denying the game runner-up in a bob of the head. Disappointing over 6f at Haydock last time, he needed every yard of this trip to score and if anything shapes as though worth a try at 1m. He reversed April's Kempton for with Search N' Destroy, but will need to progress again if he is to defy much of a rise. (op 10-1 tchd 14-1)
Quanah Parker(IRE), third at 40-1 on her reappearance at Haydock (heavy ground), was off the same mark here and had no problem with the contrasting ground conditions. In front well over a furlong out, he kept finding when challenged on both sides and looked to have held on as they flashed past the post, but his head was just up at the wrong time. He has clearly done well from two to three and can win a nice race at some point. Official explanation: two-day ban: used whip with excessive frequency (Jun 13-14) (op 5-1 tchd 13-2)
Inheritor(IRE), who just seemed to find the 1m beyond him at Warwick on his reappearance, came to challenge against the far rail and stuck on right the way to the line, but couldn't quite do enough. (op 15-2 tchd 5-1)
Seek N' Destroy(IRE), 5lb higher than when winning with the assistance of a bias at Lingfield last time, could find no extra from over a furlong out and was disappointing. (op 3-1)
Darcey kept on late and could be of interest for a small race. (tchd 18-1)
Smart Endeavour(USA), an easy Wolverhampton maiden winner, was nowhere near as effective back on turf and may have been unsuited by the ground. (op 5-1 tchd 7-1)
Feeling Fab(FR) never looked happy and failed to run her race. (tchd 13-2)

2505 BOLLINGER CHAMPAGNE CHALLENGE SERIES FOR GENTLEMAN AMATEUR RIDERS (H'CAP) 1m 4f
5:25 (5:25) (Class 4) (0-80,79) 4-Y-O+ **£6,246** (£1,937; £968; £484) **Stalls** Centre

Form RPR

6131 **1** **Grand Art (IRE)**[6] 2294 5-10-13 **71** 6ex........ MrSWalker 5 79
(P T Midgley) *hld up towards rr: hdwy 3f out: effrt and hung lft 2f out: swtchd rt and rdn to chal ent fnl f: sn led and rdn clr* **11/4**[1]

632- **2** 3 ¼ **It's A Date**[233] 6607 4-10-13 **78**........ MrJBanks(7) 7 81
(A King) *chsd ldrs: hdwy 3f out: rdn to ld wl over 1f out: drvn and hdd jst ins fnl f: kpt on same pce* **5/1**[3]

35-1 **3** 3 **Timocracy**[31] 1615 4-11-4 **79**........ MrMWalford(3) 2 77
(T D Walford) *prom: hdwy to ld 3f out: rdn and hdd wl over 1f out: ev ch tl drvn and one pce ins fnl f* **9/2**[2]

2-45 **4** 2 ¾ **Elite Land**[27] 1692 6-10-2 **65** oh2........(p) MrDaleSwift(5) 3 59
(B Ellison) *hld up: hdwy 4f out: rdn to chse ldrs over 2f out: drvn wl over 1f out and no imp* **10/1**

6116 **5** ¾ **Mustajed**[9] 2200 8-10-11 **74**........ MrPMillman(5) 6 66
(B R Millman) *in tch: hdwy over 3f out: rdn wl over 2f out and sn no imp* **5/1**[3]

2500 **6** 13 **Monfils Monfils (USA)**[14] 2068 7-10-5 **68**........ MrJohnEnnis(5) 1 40
(A J McCabe) *a in rr* **12/1**

0-05 **7** 14 **Film Festival (USA)**[48] 1230 6-10-5 **70**........ MrJohnWilley(7) 8 19
(B Ellison) *set str pce: rdn along 4f out: hdd 3f out and sn wknd* **14/1**

-033 **8** 7 **Karmest**[87] 384 5-10-5 **68**........(b) MrJoshuaMoore(5) 4 6
(A D Brown) *a in rr* **22/1**

020- **9** 12 **Smarterthanuthink (USA)**[185] 7070 4-10-5 **68**........ MrBenHamilton(5) 9 —
(R A Fahey) *cl up: rdn along 4f out: sn wknd* **8/1**

2m 35.83s (2.63) **Going Correction** +0.075s/f (Good) **9** Ran SP% **117.1**
Speed ratings (Par 105): **94,91,89,88,87 78,69,64,56**
toteswinger: 1&2 £4.10, 1&3 £3.70, 2&3 £3.30. CSF £16.75 CT £60.19 TOTE £3.50: £1.30, £2.20, £2.00; EX 17.00 Place 6 £190.07, Place 5 £73.04..
Owner David Mann **Bred** Mrs Teresa Bergin & Mrs Anne Fitzgerald **Trained** Westow, N Yorks

FOCUS
They went a good gallop in this amateur riders' handicap, which meant a hold-up horse was able to prevail. Things went the way of the winner, but he has been rated at face value.

T/Plt: £600.90 to a £1 stake. Pool: £96,769.19. 117.54 winning tickets. T/Qpdt: £56.70 to a £1 stake. Pool: £4,899.27. 63.90 winning tickets. JR

2506 - 2512a (Foreign Racing) - See Raceform Interactive

2369 LONGCHAMP (R-H)

Saturday, May 30

OFFICIAL GOING: Good

2513a PRIX DU PALAIS-ROYAL (GROUP 3) 7f
3:15 (3:21) 3-Y-0+ £38,835 (£15,534; £11,650; £7,767; £3,883)

RPR

1 Dunkerque (FR)[37] 1576 4-9-4 DBoeuf 1 92
(Mme C Head-Maarek, France) *3rd on ins: no room and lost pl 1 1/2f out: bmpd w wnr over 1f out: fnd room last 100yds: fin wl: fin 2nd, hd: awrdd r* **11/5**[1]

2 hd As De Trebol (USA)[27] 3-8-7 IMendizabal 2 92
(G Arizkorreta Elosegui, Spain) *t.k.h in midfield: squeezed through on rail 1 1/2f out: no room over 1f out: swtchd lft ins fnl f: led cl home: fin 1st: disq: plcd 2nd* **11/1**

3 nk **Mariol (FR)**[37] 1576 6-9-6 CSoumillon 4 93
(Robert Collet, France) *racd in 5th: hdwy to dispute ld over 1f out tl hdd cl home* **57/10**[2]

4 snk **Chasing Stars**[21] 1873 4-9-1 SPasquier 3 88
(Mme C Head-Maarek, France) *hld up in 8th: r.o towards outside fr over 1f out to take 4th on line* **9/1**

5 nse **Parfum Des Dieux**[37] 1576 4-9-4 C-PLemaire 6 91
(J-C Rouget, France) *led: jnd over 1f out: hdd & wknd cl home* **10/1**

6 3/4 **Trajano (USA)**[23] 1819 4-9-4 (b) MGuyon 7 89
(T Callejo-Solana, Spain) *hld up: 11th st: hdwy towards outside to chse ldrs 1f out: one pce* **27/1**

7 snk **Ottomax (GER)**[24] 4-9-4 AHelfenbein 5 88
(Andreas Lowe, Germany) *hld up: 9th st: effrt and swished tail on outside under 2f out: kpt on at one pce* **49/1**

8 1/2 **Kenchop (FR)**[20] 5-9-4 VVion 8 87
(Mme C Vergne & D Sicaud, France) *in rr: last st: kpt on fr over 1f out: nrst fin* **23/1**

9 3/4 **Leap Ahead (IRE)**[58] 4-9-4 OPeslier 12 85
(F Rohaut, France) *hld up: 10th st: nvr a factor* **84/10**[3]

10 nk **Salut L'Africain (FR)**[14] 4-9-4 GMosse 14 84
(Robert Collet, France) *a in rr* **29/1**

11 **Up And Coming (IRE)**[20] 5-9-4 THuet 13 —
(J E Pease, France) *hld up in 13th: hdwy whn no room over 1f out: nt rcvr* **13/1**

12 **Contat (GER)**[14] 2097 6-9-6 RJuracek 11 —
(P Vovcenko, Germany) *racd in 4th: ev ch over 2f out to 1 1/2f out: wknd* **12/1**

13 **Isanous (FR)**[141] 110 4-9-1 NCoutreau 10 —
(M Roussel, France) *midfield on outside: outpcd fr over 1f out* **37/1**

14 **New Fan**[14] 2097 5-9-4 TThulliez 9 —
(D Baltromei, Germany) *pressed ldr tl weakeend over 2f out* **60/1**

1m 19.4s (-1.30) **Going Correction** +0.125s/f (Good)
WFA 3 from 4yo+ 11lb **14 Ran SP% 116.4**
Speed ratings: **112,113,112,112,112 111,111,110,109,109 109,109,109,109**
PARI-MUTUEL: WIN 3.20; PL 1.60, 3.00, 2.20; DF 22.90.
Owner Alec Head **Bred** A & Mme A Head **Trained** Chantilly, France

NOTEBOOK

Dunkerque(FR) notched up a well deserved Group success, although he won it after a Stewards' inquiry and an objection by his jockey. Tucked in behind the leaders, he had little room a furlong and a half out and was then hampered by the original winner at the furlong marker. Checked, he then ran on and finally went under by a head. Connections now feel a mile is his best distance so he will probably be aimed at the Prix Messidor at Maisons-Laffitte next time out.

As De Trebol(USA), towards the tail of the field until the straight, had nowhere to go at the furlong marker and was moved to the rail where he interfered with the runner-up. He then produced an impressive turn of foot to be first past the post. He was disqualified as the Stewards felt he had stopped the second obtaining the best possible prize money. His jockey was not suspended and his trainer is considering an appeal. This Spanish colt may well be aimed at the Maurice de Gheest at Deauville.

Mariol(FR), the joint top-weight, put up another fine effort and was only beaten by under half a length at the post. Always well up, he went to the head of affairs at the furlong marker and was just run out of victory in the final 30 yards.

Chasing Stars ran a lot better than at Lingfield earlier in the month over a similar distance. This performance augurs well for the future and she looks capable of winning at this level.

2121 BATH (L-H)

Sunday, May 31

OFFICIAL GOING: Firm (10.9)

Wind: gentle breeze Weather: very warm and sunny

2514 BET ON TOTEPLACEPOT AT TOTESPORT.COM MEDIAN AUCTION MAIDEN FILLIES' STKS 5f 161y
2:10 (2:11) (Class 6) 2-Y-O £2,266 (£674; £337; £168) Stalls Centre

Form RPR

46 1 **Flyinflyout**[5] 2360 2-9-0 0 SamHitchcott 8 74+
(M R Channon) *trckd ldrs: led after 2f: shkn up and r.o wl fnl f* **6/4**[1]

2 1 1/4 **Nina Rose** 2-9-0 0 AdamKirby 2 70+
(C G Cox) *led for over 2f: chsd wnr: rdn whn edgd rt over 1f out: kpt on but no imp on wnr* **4/1**[3]

3 9 **Secret Queen** 2-9-0 0 EddieAhern 4 39
(B J Meehan) *w ldr tl squeezed out after 1f: sn rdn to chse ldng pair but nvr pce to chal: wknd fnl f* **5/2**[2]

4 9 **Perle D'Amour (IRE)** 2-9-0 0 PatDobbs 5 9
(R Hannon) *w ldrs for over 1f: sn struggling: wknd over 1f out* **7/1**

4 5 4 1/2 **Ishipink**[13] 2121 2-9-0 0 LPKeniry 3 —
(R J Hodges) *plld hrd early: hld up: short lived effrt 3f out* **33/1**

0 6 6 **Carries Lass**[5] 2354 2-9-0 0 ChrisCatlin 7 —
(J A Osborne) *unsettled in stalls: sn outpcd and nvr a threat* **18/1**

1m 11.29s (0.09) **Going Correction** -0.125s/f (Firm) **6 Ran SP% 109.3**
Speed ratings (Par 88): **94,92,80,68,62 54**
toteswinger: 1&2 £1.30, 1&3 £1.20, 2&3 £2.90 CSF £7.41 TOTE £2.80: £1.60, £2.10; EX 5.80 Trifecta £37.20 Pool: £321.97 - 6.39 winning units..
Owner Racegoers Club Owners Group **Bred** Norman Court Stud **Trained** West Ilsley, Berks

FOCUS

Flyinflyout had run to just a modest level on her first couple of starts and the bare form of this fillies' maiden looks ordinary, although the front two did at least pull well clear. The winner looks to have improved.

NOTEBOOK

Flyinflyout was given a positive ride on this slight drop in trip and put her experience to good use to readily hold off a fancied newcomer. She's obviously going the right way and looks an ideal type for nurseries later in the season. (op 2-1 tchd 9-4)

Nina Rose, closely related to 1m winner One Upmanship, made a pleasing debut. She showed bright speed, but couldn't quite match the winner's finishing effort and was always being held after being switched off the far rail late on. Open to improvement, it will be a surprise if she doesn't win a similar race in the coming weeks. (op 9-2 tchd 7-2)

Secret Queen, the first foal of a 7f juvenile winner, made a moderate debut but she should be capable of better, particularly when stepped up in trip. (op 15-8)

Perle D'Amour(IRE) , a 7,500gns half-sister to among others triple 7f-1m1f winner Elusive Lady, didn't show much but she's another who really should be capable of better at some point.

Ishipink was too keen early on. (op 28-1)

Carries Lass was outpaced throughout. (tchd 20-1)

2515 BIGGER ODDS AT TOTESPORT.COM H'CAP 1m 5y
2:40 (2:40) (Class 6) (0-60,60) 3-Y-O £2,072 (£616; £308; £153) Stalls Low

Form RPR

06-0 1 **Sapphire Rose**[33] 1594 3-9-2 58 TravisBlock 8 63+
(J G Portman) *in tch: rdn to cl on ldrs fr 3f out: led over 1f out: sn idled: drvn out* **11/1**

0-00 2 1/2 **Jewelled Reef (IRE)**[29] 1670 3-9-3 59 StephenCarson 4 63
(Eve Johnson Houghton) *in tch: rdn and stdy prog fr 2f out: styd on ins fnl f: wnt 2nd towards fin* **10/1**

00-1 3 1 **Second To Nun (IRE)**[40] 1420 3-8-13 60 Louis-PhilippeBeuzelin(5) 2 62
(Jean-Rene Auvray) *mid-div: pushed along 3f out: hdwy 2f out: sn rdn: styd on but nt clrest of runs ins fnl f* **9/4**[1]

4540 4 1 3/4 **La Gifted**[13] 2141 3-9-2 58 TonyCulhane 14 56
(M R Channon) *chsd ldr: rdn over 2f out: hld in 4th whn hung lft ins fnl f* **12/1**

2620 5 shd **Miss Mojito (IRE)**[48] 1253 3-9-1 57 (t) ChrisCatlin 9 55
(J W Hills) *swtchd lft sn after s: t.k.h in rr: rdn over 2f out: hdwy over 1f out: hung lft but styd on fnl f* **12/1**

0-30 6 shd **Heartsease**[29] 1670 3-9-3 59 PatDobbs 6 59+
(J G Portman) *trckd ldrs: rdn 3f out: one pce fnl 2f: edgd lft and nt clr run ins fnl f* **12/1**

00-0 7 1 1/2 **Sley (FR)**[20] 1937 3-9-2 58 (b[1]) EddieAhern 12 52
(B J Meehan) *led: hrd rdn over 2f out: hdd over 1f out: one pce after* **28/1**

0-03 8 3 1/4 **Jobekani (IRE)**[27] 1746 3-9-1 60 RussellKennemore(3) 5 47
(Mrs L Williamson) *t.k.h in rr: rdn and sme prog into midfield 3f out: no further imp* **4/1**[2]

00-0 9 3 3/4 **Aine's Delight (IRE)**[23] 1844 3-9-4 60 PaulEddery 13 38
(Andrew Turnell) *chsd ldrs: rdn 3f out: wknd over 1f out* **22/1**

5404 10 hd **Autumn Morning (IRE)**[12] 2149 3-8-4 53 AndrewHeffernan(7) 3 31
(P D Evans) *s.i.s: a towards rr* **11/1**

-350 11 nk **Tarawa Atoll**[93] 707 3-8-12 54 SamHitchcott 11 31
(M R Channon) *mid-div: rdn over 3f out: wknd 2f out* **40/1**

50-0 12 hd **Call Me Courageous (IRE)**[27] 1746 3-8-12 54 RobertHavlin 7 30
(A B Haynes) *mid-div: rdn over 3f out: wknd wl over 1f out* **40/1**

4000 13 1 3/4 **Hatman Jack (IRE)**[33] 1580 3-9-4 60 StephenDonohoe 1 32
(B G Powell) *hmpd sn after s: a towards rr* **66/1**

56-6 14 1 1/4 **Tricky Trev (USA)**[132] 214 3-8-13 55 AdamKirby 16 24
(S Curran) *broke wl: sn restrained towards rr: rdn 3f out: no imp* **6/1**[3]

1m 39.41s (-1.39) **Going Correction** -0.25s/f (Firm) **14 Ran SP% 128.1**
Speed ratings (Par 97): **96,95,94,92,92 92,91,87,84,83 83,83,81,80**
toteswinger: 1&2 £50.50, 1&3 £27.70, 2&3 £26.80 CSF £118.97 CT £353.59 TOTE £16.80: £4.80, £4.90, £1.40; EX 218.70 TRIFECTA Not won..
Owner P A & M J Reditt **Bred** Manor Farm Packers Ltd **Trained** Compton, Berks
■ Stewards' Enquiry : Chris Catlin three-day ban: careless riding (Jun 21-23)

FOCUS

A moderate but competitive handicap and the pace was good.

Sapphire Rose Official explanation: trainer said, regarding apparent improvement in form, that the filly was better suited by the faster ground, the drop in trip and class.

Second To Nun(IRE) Official explanation: jockey said filly was denied a clear run

2516 BET IN PLAY AT TOTESPORT.COM H'CAP 1m 2f 46y
3:10 (3:10) (Class 6) (0-65,65) 4-Y-O+ £2,266 (£674; £337; £168) Stalls Low

Form RPR

2601 1 **Samurai Warrior**[11] 2183 4-8-9 63 AndrewHeffernan(7) 2 73
(P D Evans) *t.k.h bhd ldrs: smooth run on inner to ld 3f out: styd on wl fnl f:* **4/1**[2]

0655 2 3 1/2 **Hatch A Plan (IRE)**[18] 1980 8-8-4 51 oh1 NeilChalmers 8 54
(Mouse Hamilton-Fairley) *hld up: hdwy 4f out: rdn over 2f out: chsd wnr but edgd lft over 1f out: a being hld* **8/1**

4-00 3 2 1/4 **Ba Dreamflight**[119] 368 4-8-4 51 JimmyQuinn 10 50
(H Morrison) *chsd ldrs: rdn over 2f out: kpt on to dispute 2nd over 1f out: no ex ins fnl f* **5/1**[3]

-000 4 shd **Gracechurch (IRE)**[18] 1980 6-8-5 57 Louis-PhilippeBeuzelin(5) 3 55
(R J Hodges) *hld up: rdn over 2f out: little imp: kpt on ins fnl f but nt pce to get on terms* **5/2**[1]

/0-0 5 7 **Beauchamp Viking**[6] 2330 5-8-4 56 ow5 (t) JackDean(5) 7 40
(S C Burrough) *prom: rdn 3f out: sn hung lft: wknd over 1f out* **28/1**

0123 6 3 **Siena Star (IRE)**[18] 1983 11-9-4 65 MickyFenton 4 50
(Stef Liddiard) *sn pushed into ld: hdd 3f out: sn rdn: wkng whn hmpd over 1f out* **5/2**[1]

500- 7 5 **Ground Patrol**[24] 4664 8-8-4 51 oh6 ChrisCatlin 1 19
(N R Mitchell) *a in rr* **40/1**

2m 8.10s (-2.90) **Going Correction** -0.25s/f (Firm) **7 Ran SP% 110.8**
Speed ratings (Par 101): **101,98,96,96,90 88,84**
toteswinger: 1&2 £8.50, 1&3 £8.00, 2&3 £2.20 CSF £32.75 CT £154.04 TOTE £3.70: £1.60, £2.40; EX 25.00 Trifecta £84.10 Pool: £306.91 -2.70 winning units..
Owner Mrs I M Folkes **Bred** Lady Lonsdale **Trained** Pandy, Monmouths

FOCUS

A really weak handicap.

Gracechurch(IRE) Official explanation: jockey said gelding hung right-handed

Siena Star(IRE) Official explanation: jockey said gelding finished lame

2517 BET ON TOTESUPER7 AT TOTESPORT.COM FILLIES' H'CAP 1m 3f 144y
3:40 (3:40) (Class 6) (0-65,65) 4-Y-0+ £2,266 (£674; £337; £168) Stalls Low

Form RPR
40-3 1 **Auntie Mame**[25] 1785 5-9-3 **64** .... TPO'Shea 3 70
(D J Coakley) *hld up: gd prog fr 3f out: swtchd off rails over 2f out: led ent fnl f: styd on strly: rdn out* **15/8**[1]
0-00 2 1 ¼ **Lady Jinks**[9] 2222 4-8-0 **52** .... Louis-PhilippeBeuzelin(5) 2 56
(R J Hodges) *hld up: rdn 3f out: stdy prog on outer fr 2f out: styd on ins fnl f: wnt 2nd towards fin* **14/1**
5413 3 ½ **Coral Shores**[9] 2222 4-9-1 **62** ....(v) ChrisCatlin 9 65
(P W Hiatt) *w ldr: led after 3f: rdn over 2f out: hdd ent fnl f: no ex and lost 2nd towards fin* **6/1**
00-1 4 1 ¾ **Where's Susie**[13] 2123 4-9-4 **65** .... RobertHavlin 1 65
(M Madgwick) *mid-div: rdn and hdwy over 2f out: one pce fr over 1f out* **4/1**[2]
/0-0 5 ½ **Dee Cee Elle**[19] 1154 5-8-1 **51** ....(p) DavidProbert(3) 6 50
(D Burchell) *mid-div: rdn over 2f out: styd on same pce* **12/1**
6360 6 5 **Encore Belle**[25] 1785 4-8-8 **55** .... WilliamBuick 4 46
(Mouse Hamilton-Fairley) *led for over 3f: chsd ldr: rdn over 2f out: btn whn hmpd over 1f out* **17/2**
-331 7 ½ **Party Palace**[6] 2322 5-8-12 **59** 6ex .... KirstyMilczarek 7 49
(H S Howe) *chsd ldrs: rdn over 2f out: wknd ent fnl f* **9/2**[3]
0060 8 9 **Cross Reef**[26] 1773 4-8-12 **59** .... LPKeniry 5 34
(R A Harris) *plld hrd: hld up in mid-div: rdn over 3f out: sn wknd* **25/1**
0000 9 ½ **Cate Washington**[34] 1556 6-8-4 **51** oh6 .... LukeMorris 8 25
(Mrs L Williamson) *chsd ldrs: rdn wl over 3f out: wknd wl over 2f out* **80/1**

2m 30.5s (-0.10) **Going Correction** -0.25s/f (Firm) 9 Ran SP% **117.2**
Speed ratings (Par 98): **90,89,88,87,87 84,83,77,77**
toteswinger: 1&2 £7.40, 1&3 £3.30, 2&3 £12.90 CSF £32.25 CT £137.17 TOTE £2.90: £1.20, £4.10, £2.20; EX 36.10 Trifecta £92.10 Pool: £249.02 - 2.00 winning units..
Owner Finders Keepers Partnership **Bred** Eclipse-Rogers Partnership **Trained** West Ilsley, Berks

FOCUS
A moderate fillies' handicap run at a decent gallop.
Cross Reef Official explanation: jockey said filly ran too free

2518 100% NEW PLAYER BONUS AT TOTESPORTCASINO.COM H'CAP 1m 5y
4:10 (4:10) (Class 5) (0-70,70) 4-Y-0+ £2,719 (£809; £404; £202) Stalls Low

Form RPR
0-65 1 **April Fool**[13] 2125 5-8-13 **65** ....(v) RichardThomas 7 76
(J A Geake) *mde all: sn clr: unchal* **15/2**
0-06 2 3 ¼ **Magroom**[5] 2352 5-8-8 **65** .... Louis-PhilippeBeuzelin(5) 6 69
(R J Hodges) *led chsng gp in 4th: rdn 3f out: styd on to go 2nd ent fnl f: no ch w wnr* **5/1**[3]
-040 3 ¾ **Never Sold Out (IRE)**[27] 1741 4-8-4 **56** oh7 ....(v) LukeMorris 8 58
(J G M O'Shea) *chsd ldrs: rdn wl over 2f out: styd on same pce: regained 3rd ins fnl f* **40/1**
5040 4 nk **Master Mahogany**[6] 2330 8-8-0 **57** .... MartinLane(5) 3 58
(R J Hodges) *chsd wnr: rdn over 2f out: lost 2nd ent fnl f: no ex* **8/1**
-622 5 3 **Magic Rush**[35] 1538 7-9-2 **68** .... LPKeniry 2 62+
(Norma Twomey) *v awkward leaving stalls: bhd: sme late prog but no ch whn swtchd rt over 1f out* **7/2**[2]
0-03 6 3 ¼ **Maybe I Will (IRE)**[10] 2212 4-9-1 **67** .... WilliamBuick 1 54
(S Dow) *mid-div: rdn wl over 2f out: no imp* **10/3**[1]
6-60 7 ½ **Wing Play (IRE)**[22] 1876 4-9-2 **68** .... GeorgeBaker 5 54
(H Morrison) *rdn wl over 2f out: a towards rr* **13/2**
4423 8 8 **Flamestone**[76] 853 5-8-4 **56** oh8 .... KirstyMilczarek 10 23
(A E Price) *a towards rr* **22/1**
54/4 9 22 **Kickahead (USA)**[32] 1606 7-8-4 **56** .... TPO'Shea 4 —
(Ian Williams) *a in rr: eased whn btn fnl 2f* **15/2**

1m 38.67s (-2.13) **Going Correction** -0.25s/f (Firm) 9 Ran SP% **116.7**
Speed ratings (Par 103): **100,96,96,95,92 89,88,80,58**
toteswinger: 1&2 £10.50, 1&3 £55.30, 2&3 £48.10 CSF £45.29 CT £1413.64 TOTE £11.20: £2.60, £2.50, £8.10; EX 63.30 Trifecta £363.90 Part won. Pool: £491.78 - 0.62 winning units..
Owner Miss B Swire **Bred** Miss B Swire **Trained** Kimpton, Hants

FOCUS
A modest, uncompetitive handicap in which the winner was allowed too big a lead.
Maybe I Will(IRE) Official explanation: jockey said filly was unsuited by the firm ground
Wing Play(IRE) Official explanation: jockey said gelding was unsuited by the firm ground

2519 OVER 50 INSTANT GAMES AT TOTESPORTGAMES.COM H'CAP 2m 1f 34y
4:40 (4:41) (Class 6) (0-60,60) 4-Y-0+ £2,072 (£616; £308; £153) Stalls Centre

Form RPR
/004 1 **Lord Oroko**[25] 1786 5-9-5 **59** .... TGMcLaughlin 1 65
(J G M O'Shea) *hld up towards rr: gd hdwy on outer over 3f out: led 2f out: all out: hld on* **9/2**[3]
40-5 2 nk **Brave Bugsy (IRE)**[13] 2127 6-8-12 **52** ....(v[1]) WilliamBuick 3 58
(A M Balding) *rn in snatches: mid-div: nudged along to chse ldrs 1/2-way: hmpd on rails over 4f out: sn rdn: styng on whn bmpd ins fnl f: fin wl* **3/1**[2]
6050 3 1 ¼ **Kiho**[16] 2040 4-8-12 **54** ....(b) StephenCarson 5 59
(Eve Johnson Houghton) *stdd s: t.k.h towards rr: hdwy over 3f out: effrt 2f out: hung lft and kpt on same pce fnl f* **28/1**
1-42 4 3 **Lady Pilot**[12] 2172 7-9-6 **60** .... PaulDoe 13 61
(Jim Best) *mid-div: smooth hdwy on outer fr over 4f out to trck ldr 3f out: rdn and ev ch over 2f out: no ex ent fnl f* **6/1**
23-2 5 5 **Tobago Bay**[40] 1426 4-9-3 **59** ....(b) ChrisCatlin 7 54
(Miss Sheena West) *led tl 2f out: wknd ent fnl f* **5/2**[1]
201/ 6 2 **Royal Prodigy (USA)**[27] 10-8-10 **55** .... Louis-PhilippeBeuzelin(5) 11 48
(R J Hodges) *in tch: rdn 3f out: wknd fnl f* **25/1**
-001 7 2 ½ **Corking (IRE)**[13] 2127 4-8-9 **54** .... KevinGhunowa(3) 10 44
(J L Flint) *prom tl 3f out: wknd over 1f out* **9/1**
2 8 23 **Roisin's Prince (IRE)**[20] 148 7-8-13 **53** ....(t) MickyFenton 12 15
(M Sheppard) *a bhd* **9/1**
000- 9 nk **Owain James**[12] 4810 4-8-4 **46** oh1 ....(p) KirstyMilczarek 9 8
(M Salaman) *chsd ldrs tl wknd 3f out* **66/1**
05-6 10 9 **Scar Tissue**[9] 2220 5-8-6 **46** oh1 .... EdwardCreighton 4 —
(E J Creighton) *a bhd* **100/1**
00-0 11 2 ¾ **Lupita (IRE)**[14] 1426 5-9-0 **54** ....(p) StephenDonohoe 6 1
(B G Powell) *trckd ldrs tl wknd 3f out* **50/1**

3m 45.72s (-6.18) **Going Correction** -0.25s/f (Firm)
WFA 4 from 5yo+ 2lb 11 Ran SP% **117.8**
Speed ratings (Par 101): **104,103,103,101,99 98,97,86,86,82 80**
toteswinger: 1&2 £4.40, 1&3 £29.30, 2&3 £16.90 CSF £17.87 CT £341.29 TOTE £6.20: £1.90, £1.70, £6.20; EX 21.90 Trifecta £480.00 Pool: £648.76 - 0.50 winning units..
Owner Alan G Craddock **Bred** A M Tombs **Trained** Elton, Gloucs

■ Stewards' Enquiry : William Buick two-day ban: used whip with excessive frequency (Jun 14-15)

FOCUS
Not too bad a race for the grade and quite competitive. The pace seemed good pretty much throughout.
Roisin's Prince(IRE) Official explanation: jockey said gelding hung left-handed throughout

2520 £10 FREE PLAY AT TOTESPORTBINGO.COM H'CAP 5f 161y
5:10 (5:11) (Class 4) (0-85,82) 3-Y-0+ £4,857 (£1,445; £722; £360) Stalls Centre

Form RPR
2240 1 **Desperate Dan**[3] 2418 8-8-6 **70** ....(v) PNolan(7) 2 77
(A B Haynes) *dwlt: sn trcking ldr: led over 2f out: kpt on whn chal ins fnl f: hld on wl* **7/1**
3243 2 nk **The Tatling (IRE)**[6] 2326 12-9-4 **80** .... JackDean(5) 1 86
(J M Bradley) *cl up: wnt 2nd 3f out: str chal ins fnl f: hld towards fin* **9/2**[3]
-004 3 3 **Misaro (GER)**[10] 2203 8-9-9 **80** ....(b) LukeMorris 4 76
(R A Harris) *led: rdn and hdd over 2f out: one pce fnl f* **7/2**[2]
-140 4 3 ¼ **Dazed And Amazed**[17] 2012 5-9-11 **82** .... PatDobbs 5 67
(R Hannon) *cl up: squeezed up after 1f: rdn over 2f out: nt pce to chal: fdd ins fnl f* **5/1**
-311 5 1 **Kyllachy Storm**[13] 2124 5-8-11 **73** .... Louis-PhilippeBeuzelin(5) 8 54
(R J Hodges) *cl up tl outpcd over 2f out: nvr threatened* **3/1**[1]
10-4 6 3 **Blushing Maid**[18] 1985 3-8-2 **68** .... JimmyQuinn 3 37
(H S Howe) *squeezed up after 1f: a towards rr* **11/1**
-050 7 1 ½ **Best One**[9] 2219 5-8-10 **70** ....(p) KevinGhunowa(3) 6 36
(R A Harris) *s.i.s: sn chsng ldrs: rdn over 2f out: hung lft and wknd over 1f out* **22/1**
30-6 8 1 **Polar Annie**[76] 852 4-9-5 **76** .... TGMcLaughlin 9 39
(M S Saunders) *s.i.s: a towards rr* **16/1**
05-0 9 20 **Countrywide City (IRE)**[28] 1705 3-8-9 **75** .... LPKeniry 7 —
(Jane Southcombe) *t.k.h early: trckd ldrs for over 2f: sn btn* **40/1**

69.63 secs (-1.57) **Going Correction** -0.125s/f (Firm)
WFA 3 from 4yo+ 9lb 9 Ran SP% **115.6**
Speed ratings (Par 105): **105,104,100,96,94 90,88,87,60**
toteswinger: 1&2 £5.90, 1&3 £6.90, 2&3 £4.60 CSF £38.55 CT £129.65 TOTE £6.90: £2.50, £1.80, £1.80; EX 37.40 Trifecta £141.70 Pool: £584.36 - 3.05 winning units. Place 6 £215.12, Place 5 £140.89.
Owner Joe McCarthy **Bred** Sheikh Amin Dahlawi **Trained** Limpley Stoke, Bath

FOCUS
An ordinary sprint handicap for the grade and few were ever involved.
Blushing Maid Official explanation: jockey said filly was hampered at start
Countrywide City(IRE) Official explanation: jockey said gelding jumped left out of stalls
T/Jkpt: Not won. T/Plt: £391.20 to a £1 stake. Pool: £76,231.07. 142.23 winning tickets. T/Qpdt: £102.30 to a £1 stake. Pool: £5,035.55. 36.40 winning tickets. TM

2173 CHANTILLY (R-H)
Sunday, May 31

OFFICIAL GOING: Good

2521a PRIX DE SANDRINGHAM (GROUP 2) (FILLIES) 1m
2:30 (2:32) 3-Y-0 £71,942 (£27,767; £13,252; £8,835; £4,417)

RPR
1 **Homebound (USA)**[49] 1237 3-8-11 .... C-PLemaire 8 111
(J-C Rouget, France) *trckd ldrs: 4th st: hdwy 2f out: qcknd to ld 1f out: rdn out: r.o wl* **7/2**[3]
2 ½ **Reggane**[26] 3-8-11 .... GMosse 5 110
(A De Royer-Dupre, France) *hld up: 7th st: hdwy 2f out trcking wnr: swtchd out wl over 1f out: chsd wnr fnl f: r.o* **2/1**[1]
3 3 **Aria Di Festa (IRE)**[30] 1659 3-8-11 .... DVargiu 4 103
(B Grizzetti, Italy) *trckd ldr: 3rd st: ct bhd ldrs ins fnl 2f: got through 1 1/2f out: styd on same pce* **16/1**
4 hd **Ciel Rouge (FR)**[37] 3-8-11 .... IMendizabal 1 103
(J-C Rouget, France) *hld up: 8th st: hdwy 2f out: rdn over 1f out: styd on* **14/1**
5 1 ½ **Only Green (IRE)**[17] 2026 3-8-11 .... DBonilla 7 99
(F Head, France) *disp 2nd on outside: 2nd st: chal over 2f out: sn drvn: ev ch appr fnl f: one pce* **10/1**
6 hd **Entre Deux Eaux (FR)**[21] 1918 3-8-11 .... CSoumillon 6 99
(Robert Collet, France) *led to 1f out: one pce* **8/1**
7 ¾ **Celebra (FR)**[35] 1550 3-8-11 .... OPeslier 2 97
(C Laffon-Parias, France) *mid-div: 5th st on ins: disp 3rd 2f out: sn rdn and one pce* **10/3**[2]
8 2 **First City**[46] 1293 3-8-11 .... AhmedAjtebi 9 92
(D M Simcock) *mid-div: 6th st on outside: kpt on one pce fnl 2f* **20/1**
9 2 ½ **Stefer (USA)**[51] 1208 3-8-11 .... DBoeuf 3 87
(D Smaga, France) *last thrght* **16/1**

1m 38.1s (0.10) **Going Correction** +0.25s/f (Good) 9 Ran SP% **122.0**
Speed ratings: **108,107,104,104,102 102,101,99,97**
PARI-MUTUEL: WIN 5.70; PL 2.00, 1.80, 4.00; SF 8.80.
Owner Joseph Allen **Bred** Joseph Allen **Trained** Pau, France

NOTEBOOK
Homebound(USA), given a fine ride by her jockey, just held off a late challenge from the favourite. In the early stages, she was just behind the leading group before taking up the running at the furlong marker. She then battled on gamely to the line. Her form is excellent and her only bad run came on poor ground last October. It would be no surprise to see her line up for the Falmouth Stakes on July 8th.
Reggane put up a fine effort considering it was just her second run, but her trainer blamed himself for the defeat because in hindsight he felt that she should have been closer to the pace. Following instructions, she was held up for a late run and last but one in the straight. She then made up a lot of ground but couldn't quite get to the winner. There is still scope for further improvement and it would be no surprise to see her line up for the Coronation Stakes at Ascot.
Aria Di Festa(IRE), runner-up in the Italian 1000 Guineas, was tucked in behind the leading group rounding the final turn and wasn't too lucky at the furlong and a half marker. She then ran on well to hold third place by a head. Connections were pleased and her target is now the Prix Rothschild (ex Astarte) at Deauville in August.
Ciel Rouge(FR) was another to be given a waiting race and didn't appear on the scene until the furlong marker. She was brought with a run up the centre of the track and couldn't quite peg back the third.

First City raced on the outside for much of the race and was never seen with a chance. She couldn't quicken in the straight and was beaten a long way out. She apparently didn't like the firmish ground and was also reported in season.

2522a GRAND PRIX DE CHANTILLY (GROUP 2) 1m 4f

3:05 (3:05) 4-Y-O+ **£71,942** (£27,767; £13,252; £8,835; £4,417)

RPR

1 **Scintillo**[23] 1823 4-8-11 RichardHughes 6 115
(R Hannon) *hld up in 6th: last st: hdwy over 1f out: drvn 1f out: led wl ins fnl f: r.o* **10/1**

2 *hd* **Chinchon (IRE)**[35] 1554 4-8-11 GMosse 3 115
(C Laffon-Parias, France) *disp 4th: cl 5th st: hdwy 2f out: disp 2nd over 1f out: drvn and ev ch wl ins fnl f: no ex cl home* **15/2**[3]

3 ½ **Magadan (IRE)**[27] 1762 4-8-11 ACrastus 1 114
(E Lellouche, France) *hld up in rr: 6th st on outside: hdwy 2f out: drvn 1f out: r.o same pce* **4/6**[1]

4 *nk* **Barongo (IRE)**[31] 4-8-11 MGuyon 7 114
(U Suter, France) *led 1f: trckd ldr: led 1 1/2f out to wl ins fnl f: kpt on* **33/1**

5 *hd* **Timos (GER)**[27] 1762 4-8-11 OPeslier 2 113
(T Doumen, France) *disp 4th on outside: 4th st: drvn over 1f out: kpt on same pce* **12/1**

6 *nk* **Ideal World (USA)**[25] 4-8-11 SPasquier 5 113
(A Fabre, France) *racd in 3rd to st: disp 2nd 1 1/2f out: one pce fnl 150yds* **11/4**[2]

7 *10* **Petrograd (IRE)**[27] 1762 8-8-11 YBourgois 4 97
(E Lellouche, France) *led after 1f tl hdd 1 1/2f out* **100/1**

2m 34.6s (3.60) **Going Correction** +0.25s/f (Good) **7** Ran SP% **119.1**
Speed ratings: **96,95,95,95,95 95,88**
PARI-MUTUEL: WIN 13.70; PL 5.50, 3.10; SF 60.20.
Owner White Beech Farm **Bred** Woodcote Stud Ltd **Trained** East Everleigh, Wilts

NOTEBOOK

Scintillo showed the best acceleration at the end of this 1m4f event, which was run at a crawl early on. It was a fine victory and the colt was beautifully ridden. He cantered along at the tail of the field for the early part of the race and was still was one of the last at the turn into the straight. At the furlong and a half marker he really began to fly and held on gamely to hold the runner-up. A Group 1 winner at two, he has many possibilities. These could include the Gran Premio di Milano, the Hardwicke Stakes and the Grand Prix de Saint-Cloud, which is the most likely target now.

Chinchon(IRE) put up a fine effort considering this was his first race since a trip to Hong Kong at the end of April. Fifth rounding the final turn, he began a forward move a furlong and a half out and was slightly hampered by the eventual fourth. He then ran on bravely to the line and was only beaten a head. The Grand Prix de Saint-Cloud is also on the cards for him.

Magadan(IRE)'s pacemaker was ridden in an extremely amateur way and plans went seriously wrong for this odds-on favourite. Still one of the last into the straight, he came with a sweeping late run up the centre of the track but never quite looked likely to get to the head of affairs. This race is best forgotten and he will try and take revenge in the Grand Prix de Saint-Cloud.

Barongo(IRE), second from the start, took up the running two out when the pacemaker dropped out of contention. He battled on bravely and eventually was beaten by under a length.

2523a PRIX DU GROS-CHENE (GROUP 2) 5f

3:40 (3:42) 3-Y-O+ **£71,942** (£27,767; £13,252; £8,835; £4,417)

RPR

1 **Tax Free (IRE)**[18] 1989 7-9-2 AdrianTNicholls 4 117
(D Nicholls) *a cl up: led 2f out: drvn over 1f out: hdd ins fnl f: hung rt and rallied to ld again cl home* **5/2**[1]

2 *nk* **Black Mambazo (IRE)**[22] 1905 4-9-2 CSoumillon 5 116
(L Riccardi, Italy) *hld up: gd hdwy on outside over 2f out: drvn to ld ins fnl f: hdd cl home: carried rt last strides* **20/1**

3 1 ½ **Benbaun (IRE)**[21] 1919 8-9-2 (b) JamieSpencer 9 111
(K A Ryan) *broke out of stalls: rn 1f but sn returned: led 3f: r.o u.p* **10/1**

4 *snk* **African Rose**[239] 6496 4-9-5 SPasquier 1 113
(Mme C Head-Maarek, France) *hld up in rr: hdwy wl over 1f out: kpt on but nvr able to chal* **5/1**[3]

5 *1* **Mood Music**[21] 1919 5-9-2 (b) MGuyon 6 107
(Mario Hofer, Germany) *outpcd: last 2f out: r.o u.p on outside: nrest at fin* **8/1**

6 *nk* **Delvita (FR)**[20] 5-8-13 OPeslier 2 103
(J-V Toux, France) *mid-div: kpt on one pce* **50/1**

7 ¾ **Tayseer**[21] 1919 4-9-2 GMosse 3 103
(J E Hammond, France) *sweating: cl up tl wkng wl over 1f out* **16/1**

8 *1* **Marchand D'Or (FR)**[21] 1919 6-9-8 DBonilla 7 105
(F Head, France) *trckd ldrs tl wkng over 2f out* **3/1**[2]

9 *10* **Equiano (FR)**[18] 1989 4-9-2 MichaelHills 8 63
(B W Hills) *pressed ldr on outside: one pce whn squeezed up 2f out: sn bhd* **5/1**[3]

56.70 secs (-1.40) **Going Correction** +0.10s/f (Good) **9** Ran SP% **119.7**
Speed ratings: **115,114,112,111,110 109,108,107,91**
PARI-MUTUEL: WIN 3.90; PL 1.50, 2.60, 2.60; SF 22.10.
Owner Ian Hewitson **Bred** Denis & Mrs Teresa Bergin **Trained** Sessay, N Yorks

NOTEBOOK

Tax Free(IRE) was smartly away and took control of the race just over a furlong out. He was passed by the runner up 100 yards out and then fought back bravely to retake the lead. The two got very close to each other when tiring at the end and there was a Stewards' Inquiry, followed by an objection, which was one of three after the race. The Stewards left the result unchanged and this tough sprinter will now be heading for the King's Stand Stakes at Royal Ascot.

Black Mambazo(IRE) quickened well from the two-furlong marker and had a small advantage over the winner towards the end of the race, but he just couldn't keep it until the post. If anything, he moved a little to his left as the race came to an end. It was a decent run by this Italian sprinter and he well may well return to France for the Prix de Ris-Oranges.

Benbaun(IRE) broke the stalls and had to go back for a second start. He was quickly into the lead before being passed by the winner and then by the runner-up. He still battled on gamely to the line, and this eight year old still looks capable of winning a race at this level. His jockey objected unsuccessfully to the runner-up.

African Rose, who was giving weight to the first three past the post, put up a fine performance considering that she hadn't been out for eight months. Racing near the stands' rail, she quickened at the furlong marker but couldn't quite make it into third place. Her trainer was delighted and her main target is the Prix Maurice de Gheest at Deauville, a race in which she finished runner-up last year, although the Golden Jubilee at Royal Ascot has not been totally ruled out.

Equiano(FR), smartly into his stride, was a beaten force by the halfway stage and eventually finished last. The ground came up a little fast for him, but he was well below his best form here.

HOPPEGARTEN (R-H)

Sunday, May 31

OFFICIAL GOING: Good

2524a DIANA-TRIAL (GROUP 2) (FILLIES) 1m 2f

3:55 (3:59) 3-Y-O **£38,835** (£14,563; £5,825; £3,883)

RPR

1 **Miss Europa (GER)** 3-9-2 AStarke 3 107
(P Schiergen, Germany) *trckd ldrs tl led 2f out: sn rdn: drvn out* **2/1**[1]

2 ½ **Bolivia (GER)**[30] 3-9-2 ASuborics 9 106
(W Hickst, Germany) *led: sn 4 l clr: hdd 2f out: drvn and ev ch 1f out: one pce* **3/1**[2]

3 *4* **Night Magic (GER)**[28] 1718 3-9-2 KKerekes 8 98
(W Figge, Germany) *hld up in rr: last st: styd on up outside to take 3rd ins fnl f* **54/10**

4 1 ½ **Soberania (GER)**[42] 3-9-2 EPedroza 7 95
(A Wohler, Germany) *disp 4th: 5th st: hdwy to go 3rd wl over 1f out: one pce fnl f* **42/10**[3]

5 *5* **Near Galante (GER)**[28] 3-9-2 JBojko 5 85
(A Wohler, Germany) *racd in 3rd to st: sn one pce* **20/1**

6 *hd* **Sworn Pro (GER)**[217] 7006 3-9-2 AHelfenbein 4 85
(Mario Hofer, Germany) *a towards rr* **78/10**

7 *2* **Wildfahrte (GER)**[21] 3-9-2 ABest 2 81
(T Mundry, Germany) *mid-div: 7th st: sn btn* **12/1**

8 *1* **Dubai (IRE)**[28] 3-9-2 MartinDwyer 6 79
(P Schiergen, Germany) *hld up towards rr: 6th st: btn 2f out* **19/1**

9 *4* **Exotic Dream (FR)**[22] 3-9-2 THellier 1 71
(A Trybuhl, Germany) *s.i.s: sn disputing 4th: 4th st: btn 2f out* **15/1**

2m 5.10s (-1.60) **9** Ran SP% **128.3**
TOTE (including ten euro stake): WIN 30; PL 14, 17, 17; DF 99.
Owner Gestut Hony-Hof **Bred** Gestut Hony-Hof **Trained** Germany

2310 SAN SIRO (R-H)

Sunday, May 31

OFFICIAL GOING: Good

2525a PREMIO CARLO VITTADINI (GROUP 2) 1m

4:00 (4:19) 3-Y-O+ **£67,962** (£29,903; £16,311; £8,155)

RPR

1 **Pressing (IRE)**[15] 2076 6-9-7 NCallan 6 113
(M A Jarvis) *racd in 3rd to st: jnd ldrs on outside 3f out: led 2f out: sn clr: r.o wl (62/100F)* **3/5**[1]

2 3 ¼ **Miles Gloriosus (USA)**[28] 6-9-7 LManiezzi 5 106
(R Menichetti, Italy) *hld up in tch: 5th st: r.o fr over 1f out to take 2nd cl home* **167/10**

3 *snk* **Farrel (IRE)**[15] 4-9-7 URispoli 4 106
(B Grizzetti, Italy) *trckd ldr: chal 3f out: ev ch 2f out: sn one pce: lost 2nd cl home* **23/5**[3]

4 *2* **Integral (GER)**[28] 5-9-7 MDemuro 3 101
(R Rohne, Germany) *led: moved wd appr st and led field into middle: hdd 2f out: one pce* **3/1**[2]

5 *6* **Rockhorse (IRE)**[14] 4-9-7 PConvertino 2 87
(B Grizzetti, Italy) *racd in 4th to st: rdn over 2f out: btn wl over 1f out* **25/1**

6 3 ½ **Senlis (IRE)**[322] 4010 4-9-7 CColombi 1 79
(E Botti, Italy) *last thrght* **51/10**

1m 36.6s (-5.50) **6** Ran SP% **131.2**
(including one euro stakes): WIN 1.62; PL 1.38, 4.24; SF 19.97.
Owner Gary A Tanaka **Bred** Agricola Del Parco **Trained** Newmarket, Suffolk

NOTEBOOK

Pressing(IRE), down the field in the Lockinge on his previous start, had less to do in this company and returned to winning ways with an easy success. He is likely to run in the big mile races this summer before going back to Turkey in September to try and repeat last year's victory in the Topkapi Trophy.

2311 CARLISLE (R-H)

Monday, June 1

OFFICIAL GOING: Good to firm (good on the inside between the 9f and 4f markers; 8.1)

Wind: Almost nil Weather: Hot, sunny

2526 EDINBURGH WOOLLEN MILL MEDIAN AUCTION MAIDEN STKS 5f

2:15 (2:15) (Class 5) 2-Y-O **£3,238** (£963; £481; £240) **Stalls** High

Form RPR

1 **Bow Beaver (USA)** 2-9-3 0 PaulMulrennan 4 79+
(J Howard Johnson) *mde all: pushed along over 1f out: edgd lft ins fnl f: hld on wl* **5/4**[2]

3 2 ¾ **Yeadon**[15] 2099 2-9-3 0 PaulHanagan 2 76
(R A Fahey) *chsd ldrs: outpcd over 2f out: rallied to chse wnr appr fnl f: kpt on fin* **11/10**[1]

6 3 *7* **Silver In The Sand**[16] 2089 2-8-12 0 JoeFanning 6 46
(J D Bethell) *cl up: outpcd over 2f out: plugged on fnl f: no ch w first two* **10/1**[3]

4 1 ¾ **Mercers Row** 2-9-3 0 DanielTudhope 3 45
(A Dickman) *dwlt: sn chsng ldrs: rdn over 2f out: edgd rt and wknd over 1f out* **14/1**

0 5 1 ½ **Countrymans Dream**[27] 1764 2-9-3 0 PhillipMakin 1 39
(J R Weymes) *in tch on outside: drvn and outpcd over 2f out: sn n.d* **40/1**

06 6 *1* **Bring Sweets (IRE)**[24] 1847 2-9-3 0 TomEaves 5 36
(B Ellison) *hld up: rdn over 2f out: sn outpcd* **40/1**

0 7 *7* **Stanley Bridge**[13] 2153 2-9-3 0 FrancisNorton 7 —
(A Berry) *bhd: drvn 1/2-way: sn wknd* **50/1**

62.90 secs (2.10) **Going Correction** +0.20s/f (Good) **7** Ran SP% **114.7**
Speed ratings (Par 93): **91,89,78,75,73 71,60**
toteswinger: 1&2 £1.90, 1&3 £2.00, 2&3 £2.10 CSF £2.95 TOTE £2.40: £1.40, £1.10; EX 3.10.
Owner W M G Black & J Howard Johnson **Bred** Hertrich-McCarthy Livestock **Trained** Billy Row, Co Durham

FOCUS
Two drew clear in what was otherwise a moderate juvenile maiden and they will ultimately to dictate the level.

NOTEBOOK
Bow Beaver(USA), whose stable took this with subsequent Royal Ascot winner South Central a year ago, cost 35,000gns at the breeze-ups and he was heavily-backed throughout the day. He certainly knew his job and, having been clear over a furlong out, he stayed on right the way to line. This was a very pleasing start and it will be interesting to see if he is allowed to take his chance in something like the Norfolk Stakes at the royal meeting. (op 11-10 tchd 11-8 and 6-4 in places)
Yeadon, a promising third over 6f at Ripon on his debut, lacked the speed on this drop in trip and only got going inside the final furlong. It was still a fair effort, pulling clear of the remainder, and he should find a small race before long. (op 11-8 tchd evens in a place)
Silver In The Sand improved on her initial effort when sixth at Thirsk and will appreciate an extra furlong before long. (tchd 9-1)
Mercers Row, who has a blend of speed and stamina in his pedigree, showed plenty of pace and looked a threat two out, but he couldn't race on from a furlong out. He should learn from this initial experience and may well improve for a slower surface. (op 33-1 tchd 40-1)
Countrymans Dream needs further than this and should be seen to better effect once nurseries come into play. (op 50-1)

2527 RACING UK £12.99 PER MONTH CLAIMING STKS 7f 200y
2:45 (2:45) (Class 6) 3-Y-O+ **£2,047** (£604; £302) **Stalls** High

Form RPR
3012 **1** **Rowan Lodge (IRE)**[13] 2155 7-9-5 64........................(b) JamieMoriarty 9 63
(Ollie Pears) *prom: drvn to ld over 1f out: edgd lft ins fnl f: kpt on wl* **7/2**[2]
2021 **2** 1 1/4 **Lucayan Dancer**[13] 2155 9-9-2 68........................ AdeleMulrennan(7) 6 64+
(D Nicholls) *t.k.h: hld up on outside: effrt and shkn up over 2f out: kpt on to go 2nd wl ins fnl f: nt rch wnr* **4/1**[3]
06-6 **3** 1/2 **Shaylee**[10] 2237 4-8-12 51........................ GrahamGibbons 8 52
(T D Walford) *trckd ldrs: outpcd over 2f out: rallied over 1f out: kpt on same pce ins fnl f* **7/2**[2]
-000 **4** 1 **Carnival Dream**[49] 1243 4-9-0 44........................(p) JoeFanning 3 52
(H A McWilliams) *led to over 1f out: kpt on same pce fnl f* **100/1**
-600 **5** 2 1/4 **Moonstreaker**[10] 2237 6-9-4 60........................ MichaelJStainton(3) 10 54
(R M Whitaker) *missed break: t.k.h: bhd tl hdwy 2f out: no imp fnl f* **9/1**
2456 **6** 1 **Obezyana (USA)**[12] 2186 7-9-2 68........................(v) LeeNewnes(7) 2 53
(A Bailey) *w ldr: ev ch 2f out: rdn: hung rt and sn outpcd* **2/1**[1]
20-0 **7** 1 1/4 **Coole Dodger (IRE)**[15] 2103 4-9-4 70........................ TomEaves 5 45
(B Ellison) *bhd: hdwy and hung rt over 2f out: nvr rchd ldrs* **16/1**
0-00 **8** 8 **Rascasse**[29] 1693 4-8-9 40........................ BillyCray(7) 1 25
(Bruce Hellier) *midfield: outpcd 3f out: sn btn* **100/1**
9 28 **Its Beyond Me**[33] 5-8-11 0........................ SladeO'Hara(5) 7 —
(F P Murtagh) *bhd: lost tch fr over 3f out: eased whn no ch* **100/1**

1m 43.02s (3.02) **Going Correction** +0.20s/f (Good)
WFA 3 from 4yo+ 11lb **9** Ran SP% **116.6**
Speed ratings (Par 101): **92,90,90,89,87 86,84,76,48**
toteswinger: 1&2 £2.10, 1&3 £3.20, 2&3 £3.30 CSF £18.22 TOTE £3.80: £1.70, £1.70, £1.20; EX 9.40.
Owner K C West & Venture Racing **Bred** M P B Bloodstock Ltd **Trained** Norton, N Yorks

FOCUS
Not much of a claimer and Fotunate Isle was withdrawn at the start on veterinary advice. The third sets the standard.
Its Beyond Me Official explanation: jockey said geldings saddle slipped

2528 LLOYD MOTOR GROUP FILLIES' H'CAP 1m 1f 61y
3:15 (3:15) (Class 5) (0-70,67) 3-Y-O **£3,238** (£963; £481; £240) **Stalls** High

Form RPR
310 **1** **Off Chance**[17] 2060 3-9-5 65........................ DuranFentiman 4 79+
(T D Easterby) *hld up: smooth hdwy 3f out: chsd ldr over 1f out: led wl ins fnl f: r.o* **11/4**[1]
00-6 **2** hd **Ethics Girl (IRE)**[30] 1671 3-8-9 55........................ AndrewElliott 2 69
(John Berry) *prom: hdwy to ld 2f out: hdd wl ins fnl f: kpt on* **8/1**
0-00 **3** 11 **Musical Maze**[16] 2091 3-8-11 64........................ PaulPickard(7) 9 54
(W M Brisbourne) *chsd ldrs: led briefly over 2f out: sn rdn and outpcd by first two* **7/2**[3]
0-00 **4** 1 **Lomica**[14] 2131 3-7-12 51 ow1........................(p) JamieKyne(7) 3 39
(Miss J A Camacho) *prom: drvn and outpcd over 2f out: n.d after* **10/1**
33-4 **5** 5 **Do The Deal (IRE)**[32] 1625 3-9-5 65........................ GrahamGibbons 10 43
(J J Quinn) *hld up in midfield: hdwy to trck ldrs over 3f out: outpcd fr 2f out* **3/1**[2]
4-60 **6** 4 **Haulage Lady (IRE)**[10] 2236 3-8-10 56........................(p) PaulHanagan 1 25
(Karen McLintock) *pressed ldr: ev ch over 2f out: sn rdn and wknd* **16/1**
040 **7** 14 **Miss Cracklinrosie**[47] 1281 3-8-8 54........................ TonyHamilton 7 —
(J R Weymes) *hld up: rdn over 3f out: sn wknd* **33/1**
5-00 **8** 15 **Kasaa Ed**[42] 1400 3-9-7 67........................ JoeFanning 6 —
(M Johnston) *led to over 2f out: edgd lft and sn wknd* **7/1**
5-00 **9** 38 **Desdamona (IRE)**[24] 1848 3-7-9 48 oh3........................ BillyCray(7) 8 —
(A Berry) *bhd: struggling 1/2-way: t.o* **100/1**

1m 59.5s (1.90) **Going Correction** +0.20s/f (Good) **9** Ran SP% **116.4**
Speed ratings (Par 96): **99,98,89,88,83 80,67,54,20**
toteswinger: 1&2 £4.50, 1&3 £4.10, 2&3 £8.50 CSF £25.76 CT £79.07 TOTE £3.10: £1.20, £2.10, £1.40; EX 18.60.
Owner L B Holliday **Bred** Cleaboy Farms Co **Trained** Great Habton, N Yorks

FOCUS
This was a moderate fillies' handicap and the front pair drew well clear.
Desdamona(IRE) Official explanation: jockey said filly had a breathing problem

2529 SHOP ONLINE@EWM.CO.UK H'CAP 5f 193y
3:45 (3:46) (Class 6) (0-65,59) 4-Y-O+ **£2,047** (£604; £302) **Stalls** High

Form RPR
46-2 **1** **Hansomis (IRE)**[6] 2366 5-8-11 52........................ NeilBrown(3) 9 61
(B Mactaggart) *prom: effrt 2f out: led ins fnl f: r.o wl* **9/1**
605- **2** 1/2 **Finsbury**[201] 7292 6-9-2 59........................ GaryBartley(5) 16 66+
(J S Goldie) *hld up: hdwy 2f out: chsd wnr wl ins fnl f: r.o* **12/1**
0024 **3** 1 1/2 **Distant Vision (IRE)**[13] 2158 6-8-2 47........................(b) JamieKyne(7) 13 50
(H A McWilliams) *mde most to ins fnl f: kpt on same pce* **12/1**
-050 **4** 4 **Ingleby Princess**[23] 1890 5-9-5 57........................ PhillipMakin 14 47+
(T D Barron) *towards rr: drvn and styd on fr over 1f out: n.d* **8/1**[3]
0000 **5** 1 1/2 **Only A Game (IRE)**[14] 2145 4-9-5 57........................(p) DanielTudhope 17 42
(I W McInnes) *in tch: effrt over 2f out: no ex over 1f out* **33/1**
2120 **6** 3/4 **Ace Of Spies (IRE)**[20] 1955 4-9-7 59........................(p) SilvestreDeSousa 5 42
(G A Harker) *cl up tl edgd rt and no ex over 1f out* **9/2**[2]
0046 **7** 3/4 **Mandelieu (IRE)**[7] 2316 4-9-0 52........................ TomEaves 15 32
(Ollie Pears) *in tch: drvn over 2f out: no imp over 1f out* **14/1**
0060 **8** 2 **Obe One**[7] 2316 9-8-7 50........................ SladeO'Hara(5) 12 24
(A Berry) *bhd: rdn over 3f out: sme late hdwy: nvr on terms* **50/1**
54-3 **9** 1 3/4 **Baltimore Jack (IRE)**[49] 1244 5-9-7 59........................ GrahamGibbons 4 27
(T D Walford) *chsd ldrs: drvn and edgd rt over 2f out: outpcd over 1f out* **5/2**[1]
06-0 **10** 1 3/4 **Cool Fashion (IRE)**[21] 1921 4-8-9 47 ow2........................(be) PaulMulrennan 2 10
(Ollie Pears) *in tch tl edgd rt and no ex wl over 1f out* **100/1**
-500 **11** 1 1/2 **Fitzwarren**[9] 2257 8-8-12 50........................(v) FrancisNorton 3 8
(A D Brown) *midfield on outside: drvn 1/2-way: sn outpcd* **66/1**
6-40 **12** 1 1/2 **Royal Composer (IRE)**[20] 1951 6-9-5 57........................ DuranFentiman 11 10
(T D Easterby) *sn rdn towards rr: nvr on terms* **25/1**
0200 **13** 1 1/2 **Rio L'Oren (IRE)**[63] 1039 4-8-8 51........................ Louis-PhilippeBeuzelin(5) 6 —
(N J Vaughan) *trckd ldrs tl wknd over 2f out* **33/1**
0-00 **14** 3/4 **Half A Crown (IRE)**[7] 2316 4-8-12 50........................(p) TonyHamilton 10 —
(D W Barker) *in tch: hmpd and lost pl over 3f out: n.d after* **12/1**
0-50 **15** 1 1/2 **Welcome Approach**[108] 540 6-9-4 56........................ JamieMoriarty 7 —
(J R Weymes) *bhd: drvn over 3f out: nvr on terms* **40/1**
50-0 **16** 1 1/2 **Quicks The Word**[7] 2316 9-8-12 53........................ KellyHarrison(3) 8 —
(T A K Cuthbert) *prom: drvn over 2f out: wknd wl over 1f out* **10/1**

1m 14.67s (0.97) **Going Correction** +0.20s/f (Good) **16** Ran SP% **123.3**
Speed ratings (Par 101): **101,100,98,93,91 90,89,86,84,81 79,77,75,74,72 70**
toteswinger: 1&2 £28.20, 1&3 £16.40, 2&3 £17.20 CSF £108.89 CT £1372.44 TOTE £14.00: £2.90, £4.00, £1.60, £2.50; EX 178.50.
Owner Corsby Racing **Bred** J Beckett **Trained** Hawick, Borders
■ Stewards' Enquiry : Neil Brown one-day ban: used whip with excessive frequency (June 15)

FOCUS
This was a really competitive sprint handicap and the form looks sound for the grade rated around the first three.
Quicks The Word Official explanation: trainer said gelding finished lame behind

2530 JOHN KERR 50TH BIRTHDAY H'CAP 5f
4:15 (4:15) (Class 5) (0-70,70) 3-Y-O **£3,412** (£1,007; £504) **Stalls** High

Form RPR
-213 **1** **Impressible**[17] 2058 3-9-7 70........................ DavidAllan 1 77
(E J Alston) *mde all: rdn over 1f out: kpt on wl fnl f: jst hld on* **4/9**[1]
500 **2** nse **Rio Cobolo (IRE)**[13] 2160 3-8-8 60 ow1........................(v) NeilBrown(3) 7 67
(Paul Green) *hld up in tch: hdwy u.p over 1f out: kpt on fnl f: jst failed* **20/1**
4601 **3** 1 1/4 **Noodles Blue Boy**[20] 1949 3-9-7 70........................ TonyHamilton 2 73
(Ollie Pears) *trckd ldrs: effrt 2f out: kpt on u.p fnl f* **3/1**[2]
5 **4** 10 **Ice Attack (IRE)**[74] 881 3-7-11 51 oh1........................ Louis-PhilippeBeuzelin(5) 3 18
(Patrick Morris) *pressed wnr tl rdn and wknd over 1f out* **50/1**
4-05 **5** 3 1/4 **Positivity**[9] 2265 3-8-9 58........................ TomEaves 4 13
(B Smart) *prom tl rdn and wknd fr 2f out* **14/1**[3]

62.02 secs (1.22) **Going Correction** +0.20s/f (Good) **5** Ran SP% **107.6**
Speed ratings (Par 99): **98,97,95,79,74**
CSF £10.52 TOTE £1.40: £1.20, £4.70; EX 11.30.
Owner Mr & Mrs G Middlebrook **Bred** Mr & Mrs G Middlebrook **Trained** Longton, Lancs
■ Stewards' Enquiry : Neil Brown one-day ban: used whip with excessive frequency (June 21st)

FOCUS
This wasn't much of a race and is best rated around the placed horses.
Ice Attack(IRE) Official explanation: jockey said filly hung left throughout

2531 LEVY BOARD H'CAP 6f 192y
4:45 (4:45) (Class 5) (0-70,70) 4-Y-O+ **£2,590** (£770; £385; £192) **Stalls** High

Form RPR
4-05 **1** **Stonehaugh (IRE)**[28] 1723 6-9-3 66........................ PaulMulrennan 12 81
(J Howard Johnson) *mde all: rdn 2f out: hld on wl fnl f* **10/1**
00-6 **2** 1 1/2 **Mountain Cat (IRE)**[9] 2269 5-8-10 59........................ TomEaves 11 70
(G A Swinbank) *t.k.h: hld up on ins: hdwy to chse wnr ins fnl f: r.o* **8/1**
00-0 **3** 2 3/4 **King Of Rhythm (IRE)**[13] 2166 6-8-13 62........................ DNolan 8 66
(D Carroll) *cl up: effrt over 2f out: kpt on same pce fnl f* **11/2**[2]
00-6 **4** 2 1/4 **Imperial Echo (USA)**[3] 2453 8-7-13 53........................ MartinLane(5) 3 51
(T D Barron) *hld up: hdwy 3f out: one pce appr fnl f* **8/1**
5100 **5** 3/4 **Mandalay King (IRE)**[7] 2312 4-9-2 70........................ LanceBetts(5) 10 65
(Mrs Marjorie Fife) *dwlt: bhd tl hdwy and in tch over 1f out: sn no imp* **12/1**
0-33 **6** nk **Mister Jingles**[28] 1723 6-8-6 58........................ MichaelJStainton(3) 1 53
(R M Whitaker) *trckd ldrs tl rdn and no ex over 1f out* **5/1**[1]
-060 **7** nk **Forzarzi (IRE)**[39] 1475 5-8-9 58........................(p) JoeFanning 4 55+
(H A McWilliams) *hld up: n.m.r over 2f out: nvr rchd ldrs* **18/1**
0004 **8** 3 1/2 **Casino Night**[9] 2261 4-8-12 68........................ JamieKyne(7) 7 52
(R Johnson) *in tch: outpcd 3f out: n.d after* **9/1**
-405 **9** 4 **No Grouse**[23] 1885 9-8-12 61........................ DavidAllan 2 35
(E J Alston) *hld up on outside: rdn over 2f out: n.d* **13/2**[3]
4-00 **10** 2 **Avontuur (FR)**[31] 1655 7-8-3 57........................ DeanHeslop(5) 6 25
(Mrs R A Carr) *midfield: drvn and outpcd over 2f out: sn btn* **12/1**
12/0 **11** 8 **Call Of Duty (IRE)**[17] 2043 4-9-7 70........................ PhillipMakin 5 17
(Mrs Dianne Sayer) *dwlt: bhd: struggling 1/2-way: nvr on terms* **25/1**
21-0 **12** 17 **Lujano**[14] 2133 4-9-1 64........................ TonyHamilton 9 —
(Ollie Pears) *cl up tl rdn and wknd over 2f out* **12/1**

1m 27.74s (0.64) **Going Correction** +0.20s/f (Good) **12** Ran SP% **118.9**
Speed ratings (Par 103): **104,102,99,96,95 95,95,91,86,84 75,55**
toteswinger: 1&2 £20.20, 1&3 £14.70, 2&3 £14.50 CSF £88.00 CT £492.29 TOTE £11.10: £3.00, £3.60, £2.40; EX 82.00.
Owner J Howard Johnson **Bred** Yakup Demir Tokdemir **Trained** Billy Row, Co Durham

FOCUS
This was a moderate handicap and is rated around the winner to last year's best.
Stonehaugh(IRE) Official explanation: trainer said, regarding the apparent improvement of form, that the gelding was better suited by being able to dominate today
No Grouse Official explanation: the trainer was unable to offer any explanation for the poor form shown

2532 EDINBURGH WOOLLEN MILL APPRENTICE H'CAP 7f 200y
5:15 (5:15) (Class 6) (0-65,69) 4-Y-O+ **£2,047** (£604; £302) **Stalls** High

Form RPR
0-00 **1** **Desert Hunter (IRE)**[47] 1276 6-8-3 45........................ JamieKyne(3) 10 57
(Micky Hammond) *prom: rdn to ld over 2f out: edgd rt: kpt on strly fnl f* **12/1**[3]
0000 **2** 3 1/2 **Aussie Blue (IRE)**[10] 2245 5-8-12 54........................ AmyRyan(3) 12 58
(R M Whitaker) *midfield: hdwy and swtchd lft 2f out: sn chsng wnr: kpt on same pce fnl f* **7/2**[2]
5031 **3** 6 **Inside Story (IRE)**[7] 2330 7-10-2 69 6ex........................(b) MichaelJStainton 8 59
(C R Dore) *s.i.s: bhd tl styd on fr 2f out: nt rch first two* **7/2**[2]
10-0 **4** nk **Apache Nation (IRE)**[33] 1612 6-9-4 57........................ PatrickDonaghy 7 46
(M Dods) *hld up: hdwy 2f out: kpt on fnl f: n.d* **12/1**[3]
0000 **5** 1 **Fern House (IRE)**[10] 2224 7-8-3 45........................ BillyCray(3) 5 32
(Bruce Hellier) *bhd tl hdwy over 2f out: no ex ins fnl f* **50/1**

1131 **6** *10* **Sarwin (USA)**[3] 2440 6-10-2 69 6ex.................................... MartinLane 6 33
(G A Swinbank) *hld up: pushed along over 3f out: hdwy over 2f out: wknd ent fnl f* **6/4**[1]

0-60 **7** *3/4* **Defi (IRE)**[4] 2390 7-8-8 52 ow4.......................................(bt) RossSmith(5) 4 14
(D A Nolan) *led 1f: cl up tl wknd fr 2f out* **25/1**

04- **8** *5* **Drumadoon Bay (IRE)**[257] 6015 5-8-6 52.................. JoshuaCrane(7) 13 3
(G A Swinbank) *led after 1f to 2f out: sn wknd* **12/1**[3]

0000 **9** *1* **Jojesse**[4] 2404 5-8-1 45..(b[1]) JohnCavanagh(5) 2 —
(W Storey) *midfield on outside: drvn over 3f out: sn btn* **25/1**

0-50 **10** *7* **Three Gold Leaves**[10] 2237 4-9-0 53.............................(t) DeanHeslop 9 —
(D W Thompson) *prom: drvn over 3f out: wknd over 2f out* **40/1**

1m 42.11s (2.11) **Going Correction** +0.20s/f (Good) **10** Ran SP% **119.6**
Speed ratings (Par 101): **97,93,87,87,86 76,75,70,69,62**
toteswinger: 1&2 £9.80, 1&3 £10.50, 2&3 £4.60 CSF £53.70 CT £184.60 TOTE £12.90: £2.60, £1.70, £1.50; EX 64.80 Place 6: £40.06 place 5: £37.18.
Owner The Rectangle Partnership **Bred** Meridian Stud **Trained** Middleham Moor, N Yorks

FOCUS
This was a weak handicap and it is not form to rate too positively.
Sarwin(USA) Official explanation: jockey said gelding ran flat
T/Jkpt: £13,698.60 to a £1 stake. Pool: £77,175.67. 4.00 winning tickets. T/Plt: £66.80 to a £1 stake. Pool: £60,019.60. 655.70 winning tickets. T/Qpdt: £29.60 to a £1 stake. Pool: £8,199.60. 204.90 winning tickets. RY

[2354]LEICESTER (R-H)

Monday, June 1

OFFICIAL GOING: Good to firm (firm in places; 9.0)
Wind: Light against Weather: Fine and sunny

2533 FEDERATION OF SMALL BUSINESSES "KEEP TRADE LOCAL" MAIDEN STKS 5f 218y

2:00 (2:02) (Class 4) 2-Y-O **£3,885** (£1,156; £577; £288) **Stalls** Low

Form RPR

4 **1** **Jira**[23] 1862 2-8-12 0.. SebSanders 10 81+
(C E Brittain) *a.p: led over 1f out: shkn up and r.o* **9/2**[3]

2 *hd* **Party Doctor** 2-9-3 0.. RichardKingscote 12 85+
(Tom Dascombe) *chsd ldr: led wl over 1f out: sn rdn and hdd: r.o* **10/3**[2]

4 **3** *5* **Warning Song (USA)**[18] 2007 2-9-3 0................................. JimCrowley 2 70
(Mrs A J Perrett) *chsd ldrs: edgd rt over 1f out: styd on same pce fnl f* **5/2**[1]

4 *4* **Capacity (IRE)** 2-9-3 0.. RoystonFfrench 7 58+
(M Johnston) *s.i.s: hdwy 4f out: outpcd 3f out: edgd rt and styd on fr over 1f out* **13/2**

5 *2 1/4* **My Red Kite** 2-8-12 0.. GabrielHannon(5) 1 52
(G D Blake) *s.i.s: hld up: rdn: edgd rt and hdwy over 2f out: wknd over 1f out* **66/1**

00 **6** *1* **Magneto (IRE)**[14] 2128 2-9-3 0.................................. EdwardCreighton 3 49
(E J Creighton) *led: rdn and hdd wl over 1f out: wknd fnl f* **200/1**

7 *3* **Dragonessa (IRE)** 2-8-12 0.. SteveDrowne 4 35
(B Palling) *s.i.s: sn pushed along in rr: n.d* **40/1**

8 *1 1/4* **Rock A Doodle Doo (IRE)** 2-9-3 0.............................. J-PGuillambert 8 36
(W Jarvis) *chsd ldrs tl rdn and wknd over 2f out* **9/1**

9 *1 1/4* **Go Blue Chip** 2-9-3 0.. FrankieMcDonald 13 32
(H Candy) *chsd ldrs: rdn: hung lft and wknd 2f out* **25/1**

0 **10** *6* **Zachary Boy (IRE)**[7] 2324 2-9-3 0.............................. StephenCarson 11 14
(B G Powell) *sn outpcd* **66/1**

11 *nse* **Avongate** 2-9-3 0.. PatDobbs 5 14
(R Hannon) *hld up: a in rr: bhd fr 1/2-way* **12/1**

0 **12** *shd* **The Two G'S**[20] 1968 2-8-12 0.................................. CatherineGannon 6 9
(P D Evans) *chsd ldrs tl rdn and wknd over 2f out* **66/1**

13 *1* **First Cat** 2-9-3 0.. RichardMullen 9 11
(R Hannon) *sn pushed along in rr: bhd fr 1/2-way* **20/1**

1m 13.09s (0.09) **Going Correction** -0.025s/f (Good) **13** Ran SP% **116.9**
Speed ratings (Par 95): **98,97,91,85,82 81,77,75,74,66 66,65,64**
toteswinger: 1&2 £4.20, 1&3 £3.10, 2&3 £3.40 CSF £18.52 TOTE £5.30: £1.70, £1.50, £1.20; EX 28.00 Trifecta £42.90 Pool: £254.10 - 4.38 winning units..
Owner Saeed Manana **Bred** W And R Barnett Ltd **Trained** Newmarket, Suffolk

FOCUS
This looked a decent maiden for the track and the way the first two pulled well clear of the third suggests they are above average and the form is strong for the grade.

NOTEBOOK
Jira, purchased for 110,000gns as a yearling, had not been beaten far on her debut in a small-field Ascot maiden that has already produced a winner. She impressed on paddock inspection and went on to handle the lively ground, although the way she went to post indicated that she may prefer it a little easier. Connections weren't in a hurry to map out her future but she wouldn't be out of place heading to Royal Ascot for the Albany Stakes given the way she won here. (op 5-2)
Party Doctor ◆ was green in the preliminaries, rearing up in the paddock. He soon settled down and went on to run a race full of promise. He looked to hit the ground quite hard and may benefit from an easier surface. He is entitled to come on for this debut, and a maiden looks his for the taking on this evidence before his connections eye loftier targets. (op 7-2 tchd 11-4)
Warning Song(USA) was fourth beaten less than 4l on his debut on very quick ground at Salisbury over 5f. Outpaced on that occasion, this extra furlong seemed likely to see him in a better light. His skimming action showed that the fast ground was to his liking and 2f out he looked sure to play a part in the finish, but he simply didn't possess the gears of the first two home. He is entitled to progress again from here and, if shrewdly placed, can pick up a maiden. (op 7-2)
Capacity(IRE), the second foal of Cheveley Park Stakes winner Carry On Katie, ran an intriguing race. Not particularly a stand-out on paddock inspection, he moved to post well before breaking slowly from the stalls. Having made up some of the lost ground, he seemed to be tapped for toe as the race unfolded before staying on again. (op 7-1 tchd 9-1)
My Red Kite was another to miss the break before going on to make a satisfactory debut. He flattened out in the latter stages and is entitled to improve for a run. (op 100-1)
Magneto(IRE) showed a decent level of speed at the head of affairs before weakening and may be worth dropping back to 5f. (op 100-1)
Rock A Doodle Doo(IRE), well supported in the market, looked a sturdy sort in the preliminaries and should significantly build on this effort. (op 20-1 tchd 25-1)
Avongate Official explanation: vet said colt finished lame

2534 FEDERATION OF SMALL BUSINESSES "WORKING FOR BUSINESS" (S) STKS 5f 218y

2:30 (2:35) (Class 6) 3-5-Y-O **£1,942** (£578; £288; £144) **Stalls** Low

Form RPR

1006 **1** **All You Need (IRE)**[27] 1781 5-9-3 48..........................(p) DavidKenny(7) 4 58
(R Hollinshead) *racd stands' side: hld up: hdwy over 1f out: r.o to ld post* **20/1**

2060 **2** *shd* **Strathmore (IRE)**[7] 2312 5-8-12 62.......................... TimothyAyres(7) 5 53
(R A Fahey) *racd stands' side: sn prom: led overall over 3f out: shkn up over 1f out: hdd nr fin* **1/1**[1]

0406 **3** *2* **Abhainn (IRE)**[18] 2009 3-8-11 49.................................. SteveDrowne 11 44
(B Palling) *racd centre: hld up: hdwy over 2f out: rdn and hung lft fr over 1f out: styd on* **15/2**[3]

0600 **4** *nk* **Stormburst (IRE)**[90] 746 5-8-7 43.............................. RichardRowe(7) 9 40
(A J Chamberlain) *led centre gp: rdn and hung lft fr over 1f out: no ex ins fnl f* **40/1**

66 **5** *4 1/2* **Majestic Cheer**[123] 327 5-9-0 52.................................(p) MarkCoumbe(5) 1 31
(John A Harris) *racd stands' side: hld up: hdwy u.p over 1f out: nt trble ldrs* **33/1**

4060 **6** *1 1/4* **Gambling Jack**[7] 2317 4-9-0 48.................................. AndreaAtzeni(5) 3 27
(A W Carroll) *racd stands' side: sn drvn along in rr: n.d* **10/1**

60-4 **7** *5* **Gioacchino (IRE)**[6] 2353 4-9-2 53.............................. KevinGhunowa(3) 6 11
(R A Harris) *racd stands' side: hung rt thrght: led overall 5f out: hdd over 3f out: rdn and wknd over 1f out* **4/1**[2]

0-60 **8** *1 3/4* **August Days (IRE)**[44] 1359 3-8-6 55.......................... RoystonFfrench 10 —
(J Pearce) *racd centre: chsd ldrs tl rdn and wknd over 2f out* **25/1**

0060 **9** *nk* **Brazilian Brush (IRE)**[12] 2180 4-9-5 49.........................(t) TravisBlock 2 —
(J M Bradley) *racd stands' side: overall ldr 1f: chsd ldrs tl rdn and wknd over 2f out* **16/1**

6-00 **10** *1* **Pintano**[29] 1710 4-9-5 50...(p) LiamJones 12 —
(J M Bradley) *racd centre: chsd ldr: rdn and wknd over 2f out* **28/1**

0-00 **11** *11* **Bilboa**[14] 2122 4-9-5 43...(p) PatCosgrave 7 —
(J M Bradley) *racd stands' side: prom: racd keenly: rdn and wknd over 2f out* **50/1**

-056 **12** *4 1/2* **Minimum Fuss (IRE)**[20] 1970 5-8-7 48.................. AndrewHeffernan(7) 8 —
(M C Chapman) *racd stands' side: s.s: plld hrd and hdwy over 4f out: wknd 1/2-way* **50/1**

1m 14.16s (1.16) **Going Correction** -0.025s/f (Good)
WFA 3 from 4yo+ 8lb **12** Ran SP% **118.1**
Speed ratings (Par 101): **91,90,88,87,81 80,73,71,70,69 54,48**
toteswinger: 1&2 £9.00, 1&3 £19.00, 2&3 £3.00 CSF £38.62 TOTE £25.80: £5.00, £1.10, £2.20; EX 57.80 Trifecta £269.90 Part won. Pool: £364.82 - 0.94 winning units..The winner was bought in for 3,400gns.
Owner N Chapman **Bred** D J Maher **Trained** Upper Longdon, Staffs

FOCUS
A very weak race on paper with over half the field being rated below 50 on official figures. In 46 cumulative starts this year, the 12 runners could only boast one success between them and the winner is rated to his February all-weather mark.
Pintano Official explanation: jockey said gelding was never travelling

2535 FEDERATION OF SMALL BUSINESSES "CUT RED TAPE" H'CAP 1m 1f 218y

3:00 (3:00) (Class 4) (0-85,83) 3-Y-O **£4,857** (£1,445; £722; £360) **Stalls** High

Form RPR

6-11 **1** **Mister Dee Bee (IRE)**[20] 1971 3-9-7 83.......................... MichaelHills 6 91
(B W Hills) *chsd ldrs: rdn over 3f out: sn outpcd: rallied over 1f out: rdn to ld ins fnl f: edgd rt: r.o* **11/4**[2]

3-41 **2** *1 1/4* **Pride Of Kings**[23] 1882 3-9-3 79.................................. GregFairley 3 84
(M Johnston) *chsd ldr tl led over 1f out: hdd and unable qckn ins fnl f* **7/4**[1]

63-0 **3** *2 3/4* **Wee Sonny (IRE)**[45] 1328 3-8-13 75.......................... RichardKingscote 4 75
(Tom Dascombe) *trckd ldrs: racd keenly: rdn over 2f out: sn hung rt: styd on same pce appr fnl f* **16/1**

30-1 **4** *1 1/4* **Multiplication**[23] 1893 3-9-3 79.................................. SteveDrowne 1 76
(R Charlton) *sn led: rdn and hdd over 1f out: wknd towards fin* **3/1**[3]

3630 **5** *10* **Doncosaque (IRE)**[11] 2210 3-9-5 81.............................. IanMongan 2 58
(P Howling) *hld up: plld hrd: rdn and wknd over 2f out* **33/1**

3325 **6** *6* **Hypnotist (UAE)**[7] 2329 3-8-13 75.................................. NCallan 5 40
(C E Brittain) *hld up: hdwy over 3 out: sn rdn: wknd wl over 1f out* **15/2**

2m 5.86s (-2.04) **Going Correction** -0.175s/f (Firm) **6** Ran SP% **108.6**
Speed ratings (Par 101): **101,100,97,96,88 84**
toteswinger: 1&2 £1.80, 1&3 £5.50, 2&3 £4.30 CSF £7.42 TOTE £2.80: £1.30, £1.80; EX 8.50.
Owner South Bank Thoroughbred Racing **Bred** Denis McDonnell **Trained** Lambourn, Berks

FOCUS
A fair contest run at just an ordinary pace with the third and fourth rated close to their maiden form.
Hypnotist(UAE) Official explanation: jockey said colt hung right

2536 FEDERATION OF SMALL BUSINESSES FILLIES' CONDITIONS STKS 7f 9y

3:30 (3:30) (Class 2) 3-Y-O+ **£12,462** (£3,732; £1,866; £934) **Stalls** Centre

Form RPR

024 **1** **Carcinetto (IRE)**[15] 2102 7-8-12 95.......................... CatherineGannon 4 101
(P D Evans) *mde all: rdn and hung lft over 1f out: r.o wl* **13/8**[1]

22-0 **2** *7* **Qalahari (IRE)**[72] 912 3-8-2 90.................................. TPO'Shea 2 78
(D J Coakley) *hld up: hdwy to chse wnr over 2f out: sn rdn: edgd rt and no ex ins fnl f* **5/2**[3]

6046 **3** *1 3/4* **Max One Two Three (IRE)**[9] 2271 4-8-12 94......... RichardKingscote 1 77
(Tom Dascombe) *chsd wnr tl rdn over 2f out: edgd rt and no ex ins fnl f* **2/1**[2]

14- **4** *3 1/4* **Mamlakati (IRE)**[243] 6401 3-8-6 85.............................. RichardMullen 3 69
(R Hannon) *plld hrd and prom: rdn over 1f out: wknd ins fnl f* **12/1**

1m 25.38s (-0.82) **Going Correction** -0.025s/f (Good)
WFA 3 from 4yo+ 10lb **4** Ran SP% **107.7**
Speed ratings (Par 96): **103,95,93,89**
CSF £5.89 TOTE £2.10; EX 5.40.
Owner Mrs Sally Edwards **Bred** M A Doyle **Trained** Pandy, Monmouths

FOCUS
A disappointingly small field for the prizemoney with the winner possibly the only one to have run her race.

NOTEBOOK
Carcinetto(IRE) has been in good heart during her busy campaign. She was given an uncontested lead in this, her return to 7f, as they only went a steady pace on ground that suits her. As her rivals attempted to get to grips with her, she - unsurprisingly given the way the race unfolded - found plenty, although she did hang left from over 1f out. Her jockey did a good job straightening her out and she surged away to prevail. She was duly cut from 33-1 to 20s for the Wokingham by Victor Chandler but isn't guaranteed to beat the cut. Connections stated that if she got in and had her favoured fast ground, they'd certainly give it a crack. (op 7-4 tchd 11-8)
Qalahari(IRE) travelled well but was unable to answer the winner's late kick. She has been Listed-placed with underfoot ease as well as second to the smart Ouqba on a good surface. This, then, may have been plenty fast enough for her and she remains of interest, especially if returned to action against her own age group. (op 3-1)
Max One Two Three(IRE) is becoming a bit disappointing. She was fourth in a 6f Listed race that Carcinetto finished second in last month at Nottingham but wasn't able to get anywhere near as close to her this time. She has not won since October 2007, although admittedly is lightly-raced. (op 13-8)

Mamlakati(IRE) didn't help her chance by running too free on what was her seasonal reappearance but this was only her third career start. (tchd 16-1)

2537 FSB "FAIR BANKING FOR ALL" CLAIMING STKS 1m 1f 218y
4:00 (4:00) (Class 5) 4-Y-O+ **£2,590** (£770; £385; £192) **Stalls** High

Form RPR
2042 **1** **Solo River**[10] 2220 4-8-2 60 JimmyQuinn 9 67
(P J Makin) *led 1f: chsd ldrs: led 3f out: shkn up and styd on wl fnl f* **9/4**[1]
6-00 **2** *6* **Princelywallywogan**[37] 1514 7-8-11 63 PatCosgrave 2 67
(John A Harris) *hld up in tch: rdn over 2f out: chsd wnr fnl f: styd on same pce* **11/2**[2]
3033 **3** *9* **Maddy**[7] 2333 4-8-2 49 (p) FrankieMcDonald 1 37
(George Baker) *hld up: rdn over 2f out: nvr on terms* **14/1**
30-0 **4** *½* **Channel Crossing**[7] 2332 7-9-1 68 LiamJones 7 49
(S Wynne) *chsd ldrs: lost pl 1/2-way: n.d after* **7/1**[3]
40 **5** *29* **Tried And True (FR)**[20] 1962 4-8-10 65 (b[1]) EddieAhern 6 —
(H R A Cecil) *s.s: rcvrd to ld 9f out: rdn and hdd 3f out: sn wknd* **11/2**[2]
0-00 **6** *21* **Admiral Arry**[26] 1784 4-8-5 40 ow1 (p) KevinGhunowa(3) 3 —
(J M Bradley) *hld up: bhd fnl 4f* **125/1**
1220 **7** *12* **Gasat (IRE)**[7] 2332 8-8-11 67 SebSanders 5 54
(A B Haynes) *prom: chsd ldr 6f out: jnd ldr 3f out: rdn over 1f out: 3rd and wkng whn virtually p.u ins fnl f* **9/4**[1]

2m 5.93s (-1.97) **Going Correction** -0.175s/f (Firm) 7 Ran SP% **112.3**
Speed ratings (Par 103): **100,95,88,87,64 47,38**
toteswinger: 1&2 £4.00, 1&3 £4.70, 2&3 £7.50 CSF £14.79 TOTE £2.70: £1.50, £2.90; EX 16.30 Trifecta £127.90 Pool: £423.76 - 2.45 winning units..
Owner Ten Of Hearts II **Bred** D J And Mrs Deer **Trained** Ogbourne Maisey, Wilts

FOCUS
A weak heat with the winner rated to her best form. They went a fair gallop thanks to Tried And True and the time was only fractionally slower than the 1m 2f handicap staged earlier in the card.
Tried And True(FR) Official explanation: jockey said filly was unsuited by the ground (good to firm – firm in places)
Gasat(IRE) Official explanation: vet said horse finished lame

2538 FEDERATION OF SMALL BUSINESSES "SURVIVAL" MAIDEN STKS 1m 3f 183y
4:30 (4:30) (Class 5) 3-Y-O **£2,986** (£939; £508) **Stalls** High

Form RPR
2 **1** **Sabotage (UAE)**[12] 2178 3-9-3 0 GregFairley 2 88+
(M Johnston) *dwlt: rcvrd to ld after 1f: rdn over 1f out: styd on strly: eased nr fin* **10/11**[1]
3 **2** *6* **Birdinthehand (FR)**[27] 1780 3-8-12 0 IanMongan 3 73
(H R A Cecil) *hld up in tch: rdn and edgd rt over 2f out: outpcd fr over 1f out* **15/2**[3]
2-2 **3** *¾* **Times Up**[21] 1931 3-9-3 0 EddieAhern 4 78
(J L Dunlop) *trckd ldrs: rdn and hung rt over 2f out: eased whn hld ins fnl f* **6/4**[2]
P **Spirit Is Needed (IRE)** 3-9-3 0 RoystonFfrench 5 —
(M Johnston) *sn led: hdd after 1f: chsd ldrs tl p.u and dismntd over 7f out* **40/1**

2m 33.61s (-0.29) **Going Correction** -0.175s/f (Firm) 4 Ran SP% **106.6**
Speed ratings (Par 99): **93,89,88,—**
CSF £7.52 TOTE £1.90; EX 6.10.
Owner Sheikh Hamdan Bin Mohammed Al Maktoum **Bred** Darley **Trained** Middleham Moor, N Yorks

FOCUS
The time of this maiden was nothing out of the ordinary. The winner won well though and the third is rated close to his mark.
Times Up Official explanation: jockey said gelding was unsuited by the ground (good to firm – firm in places)
Spirit Is Needed(IRE) Official explanation: trainer's representative said colt pulled up lame behind

2539 FSB "FIRING UP THE BRITISH ECONOMY" FILLIES' H'CAP 7f 9y
5:00 (5:00) (Class 5) (0-70,70) 3-Y-O+ **£3,238** (£963; £481; £240) **Stalls** Centre

Form RPR
4-20 **1** **Tikka Masala (IRE)**[34] 1588 3-9-3 69 (t) RichardKingscote 3 73
(Tom Dascombe) *wnt lft s: hld up in tch: rdn over 2f out: hung rt over 1f out: r.o to ld post* **15/2**
0212 **2** *nk* **Perfect Friend**[7] 2321 3-9-4 70 EddieAhern 5 74
(S Kirk) *trckd ldrs: rdn to ld over 1f out: sn edgd lft: hdd post* **11/10**[1]
-000 **3** *1* **Yughanni**[21] 1940 3-8-0 52 JimmyQuinn 2 53
(C E Brittain) *s.i.s and hmpd s: plld hrd and hdwy to ld 6f out: hdd 1/2-way: rdn and ev ch over 1f out: styd on same pce ins fnl f* **50/1**
0-02 **4** *nk* **Superstitious Me (IRE)**[14] 2143 3-8-5 57 CatherineGannon 8 57
(B Palling) *racd keenly: led 1f trckd ldr tl led 1/2-way: rdn and hdd over 1f out: unable qck wl ins fnl f* **12/1**
0-00 **5** *1* **Applesnap (IRE)**[13] 2168 4-9-6 62 (p) JerryO'Dwyer 9 63
(Miss Amy Weaver) *prom: outpcd over 2f out: styd on u.p fnl f* **33/1**
-645 **6** *3 ¼* **City For Conquest (IRE)**[14] 2134 6-8-6 53 ow1 MarkCoumbe(5) 1 46
(John A Harris) *s.i.s: hld up: rdn 1/2-way: hdwy and hung rt fr over 2f out: wknd ins fnl f* **33/1**
00-3 **7** *2 ¾* **Caster Sugar (USA)**[7] 2321 3-9-0 66 RichardMullen 7 47
(R Hannon) *prom: rdn over 2f out: wknd over 1f out: eased* **9/2**[2]
31-0 **8** *2 ½* **Inconspicuous Miss (USA)**[21] 1937 3-8-12 67 DavidProbert(3) 6 41
(George Baker) *hld up: pushed along over 4f out: nvr trbld ldrs* **16/1**
0300 **9** *9* **Plaka (FR)**[20] 1972 4-8-9 51 LiamJones 11 —
(W M Brisbourne) *s.i.s: hld up: a in rr: rdn and wknd over 2f out* **50/1**
-263 **10** *8* **Astrodonna**[20] 1964 4-10-0 70 MichaelHills 10 —
(M H Tompkins) *chsd ldrs: rdn over 2f out: wknd over 1f out: eased* **13/2**[3]

1m 25.94s (-0.26) **Going Correction** -0.025s/f (Good)
WFA 3 from 4yo+ 10lb 10 Ran SP% **114.3**
Speed ratings (Par 100): **100,99,98,98,97 93,90,87,77,67**
toteswingers: 1&2 £2.90, 1&3 £36.20, 2&3 £19.50 CSF £15.51 CT £383.72 TOTE £8.40: £2.30, £1.20, £8.90; EX 22.10 TRIFECTA Not won..
Owner A Black **Bred** Raysiza Partnership **Trained** Lambourn, Berks

FOCUS
A modest handicap for fillies rated around the fourth.

2540 HORSERACE BETTING LEVY BOARD H'CAP 1m 3f 183y
5:30 (5:30) (Class 5) (0-70,70) 3-Y-O **£2,590** (£770; £385; £192) **Stalls** High

Form RPR
0045 **1** **Vita Mia**[3] 2461 3-8-5 54 CatherineGannon 9 59
(P D Evans) *sn led: hdd over 7f out: chsd ldrs: rdn to ld over 1f out: edgd rt: styd on* **11/2**
04-0 **2** *¾* **Deuce**[42] 1407 3-9-0 63 (b[1]) StephenCarson 10 67
(Eve Johnson Houghton) *prom: outpcd 3f out: rallied and hung rt over 1f out: r.o: wnt 2nd towards fin* **25/1**
4-00 **3** *1 ¼* **Persian Memories (IRE)**[24] 1834 3-9-2 65 RichardMullen 1 67
(J L Dunlop) *hld up: hdwy over 3f out: rdn and edgd rt over 1f out: styd on* **9/2**[3]
2350 **4** *shd* **Kochanski (IRE)**[14] 2131 3-8-7 56 RoystonFfrench 2 58
(M Johnston) *chsd ldrs: led over 7f out: rdn and hdd over 1f out: styd on same pce ins fnl f* **17/2**
600- **5** *4* **Water Hen (IRE)**[234] 6622 3-9-4 67 RichardKingscote 5 62
(R Charlton) *dwlt: hld up: hdwy over 3f out: sn rdn: hung rt over 1f out: styd on same pce* **5/1**
441- **6** *hd* **Blue Dynasty (USA)**[245] 6330 3-9-7 70 JimCrowley 8 65
(Mrs A J Perrett) *chsd ldrs: drvn along at various stages thrght: hung rt and wknd over 1f out* **11/4**[1]
6135 **7** *69* **Urban Space**[21] 1930 3-9-5 68 MichaelHills 4 —
(B G Powell) *hld up: bhd fr 1/2-way* **7/2**[2]

2m 31.79s (-2.11) **Going Correction** -0.175s/f (Firm) 7 Ran SP% **113.5**
Speed ratings (Par 99): **100,99,98,98,95 95,49**
toteswingers: 1&2 £10.60, 1&3 £5.50, 2&3 £13.80 CSF £112.84 CT £665.66 TOTE £6.70: £3.20, £4.20; EX 112.80 Trifecta £208.30 Part won. Pool: £281.51 -0.87 winning units. Place 6: £9.91 Place 5: £8.01.
Owner Countess Of Lonsdale **Bred** Lady Lonsdale **Trained** Pandy, Monmouths

FOCUS
A modest handicap which was dominated by fillies and the winner rated to previous form.
T/Plt: £41.10 to a £1 stake. Pool: £52,921.60. 938.33 winning tickets. T/Qpdt: £20.90 to a £1 stake. Pool: £2,507.64. 88.70 winning tickets. CR

2089 THIRSK (L-H)
Monday, June 1

OFFICIAL GOING: Firm (10.6)
Wind: Virtually nil Weather: Sunny and dry

2541 SCARBOROUGH FAIR (S) STKS 6f
6:10 (6:11) (Class 5) 2-Y-O **£4,274** (£1,271; £635; £317) **Stalls** High

Form RPR
2451 **1** **Anjomarba (IRE)**[4] 2414 2-8-7 0 JackDean(5) 5 71
(W G M Turner) *mde all: rdn clr over 1f out: drifted bdly lft ins fnl f: kpt on* **8/11**[1]
2 *1 ¼* **Inlovingmemory (IRE)** 2-8-7 0 PaulHanagan 7 62+
(R A Fahey) *outpcd and in rr: gd hdwy wl over 1f out: rdn to chse wnr ins fnl f: kpt on towards fin* **12/1**
65 **3** *4 ½* **Highcliffe Bridge (IRE)**[7] 2319 2-8-9 0 ow2 JamieSpencer 10 51
(P D Evans) *towards rr: rdn along 2f out: styd on appr fnl f: nrst fin* **11/2**[3]
50 **4** *1 ¾* **Zaskia (IRE)**[44] 1344 2-8-7 0 GrahamGibbons 1 44
(K A Ryan) *wnt lft s: sn chsng wnr: rdn along over 2f out and sn wknd* **25/1**
432 **5** *2* **Alphacino**[7] 2319 2-8-12 0 SamHitchcott 11 43
(M R Channon) *chsd ldrs: rdn along over 2f out: sn wknd* **10/3**[2]
0 **6** *2* **Coralamber (IRE)**[11] 2201 2-8-0 0 AndrewHeffernan(7) 4 32
(Garry Moss) *chsd ldrs: rdn along over 2f out: sn wknd* **16/1**
0 **7** *14* **Aryacoddinme (IRE)**[40] 1450 2-8-12 0 SilvestreDeSousa 8 —
(G A Harker) *s.i.s: a bhd* **66/1**
00 **8** *9* **Nidamar**[40] 1450 2-8-7 0 AndrewElliott 3 —
(Mrs R A Carr) *cl up: hanging lft thrght: rdn over 2f out: wknd qckly and eased* **80/1**

1m 13.3s (0.60) **Going Correction** -0.075s/f (Good) 8 Ran SP% **116.5**
Speed ratings (Par 93): **93,91,85,83,80 77,59,47**
toteswinger: 1&2 £2.10, 1&3 £1.60, 2&3 £8.70 CSF £11.82 TOTE £1.60: £1.02, £2.80, £2.30; EX 16.50.The winner was bought in for £4,200. Inlovingmemory was claimed by D Maloney for £6,000.
Owner Marbary Partnership **Bred** Tally-Ho Stud **Trained** Sigwells, Somerset

FOCUS
A typically weak event for the class, althoug the winner looks better than this grade.

NOTEBOOK
Anjomarba(IRE) had made short work of the opposition when dropped to selling company at Yarmouth just four days earlier. She soon had them at full stretch and, about four lengths clear when drifting left over a furlong out, she was never in any danger. Connections were able to retain her much cheaper this time and she is useful in this class. (op 10-11)
Inlovingmemory(IRE), a newcomer bred for stamina rather than speed, made up a lot of ground to go in pursuit of the winner. She was closing him down all the way to the line, but was never going to get on terms. She is sure to find a similar event, especially if stepped up to 7f. (op 15-2)
Highcliffe Bridge(IRE), in her first try in plating company, kept on to secure a modest third and posted her best effort yet. (op 6-1)
Zaskia(IRE), who went left leaving the stalls from the number one draw, was soon chasing the winner. This was her third outing and she is looking exposed. (op 18-1)
Alphacino, runner-up in a Chepstow claimer on his third start, looks to be going backwards. (op 7-2 tchd 3-1)
Nidamar Official explanation: jockey said filly hung left

2542 INJURED JOCKEYS FUND H'CAP 1m
6:40 (6:40) (Class 5) (0-75,73) 4-Y-O+ **£4,274** (£1,271; £635; £317) **Stalls** Low

Form RPR
0242 **1** **Champain Sands (IRE)**[7] 2313 10-8-4 59 AndrewMullen(3) 5 65
(E J Alston) *hld up in tch: hdwy over 2f out: effrt and n.m.r over 1f out: swtchd rt and rdn ent fnl f: styd on wl to ld last 75yds* **10/3**[2]
5332 **2** *1* **Kildare Sun (IRE)**[13] 2166 7-9-0 66 (v) PaulHanagan 4 70
(J Mackie) *led: jnd and rdn along 2f out: drvn over 1f out: hdd and no ex last 75yds* **3/1**[1]
4-05 **3** *nk* **Border Owl (IRE)**[9] 2274 4-9-7 73 DaleGibson 6 76
(P Salmon) *chsd ldng pair: hdwy 1/2-way: chal 2f out and sn rdn: drvn and ev ch ent fnl f: no ex last 100yds* **13/2**
4604 **4** *1 ¼* **Montiboli (IRE)**[14] 2133 4-8-9 61 NCallan 3 61
(K A Ryan) *chsd ldrs: hdwy 3f out: rdn along wl over 1f out: drvn ent fnl f and kpt on same pce* **9/1**
301- **5** *shd* **Cherri Fosfate**[18] 7732 5-9-3 69 StephenDonohoe 2 69
(D Carroll) *outpcd and bhd: hdwy over 1f out: styd on strly ins fnl f: nrst fin* **22/1**
0402 **6** *hd* **Follow The Flag (IRE)**[23] 1887 5-9-6 72 (p) JamieSpencer 7 72
(A J McCabe) *hld up: hdwy on outer over 2f out: rdn over 1f out: sn drvn and no imp* **7/2**[3]

4-55 **7** *nk* **Grand Diamond (IRE)**[13] 2156 5-8-11 **63**..................(p) DanielTudhope 1 62
(J S Goldie) *chsd ldr: effrt on inner over 2f out: sn rdn: drvn and wknd ent fnl f* **11/2**

1m 37.93s (-2.17) **Going Correction** -0.175s/f (Firm) 7 Ran SP% **113.4**
Speed ratings (Par 103): **103,102,101,100,100 100,99**
toteswinger: 1&2 £2.90, 1&3 £5.60, 2&3 £3.40 CSF £13.52 TOTE £4.00: £2.80, £2.00; EX 14.80.

Owner Geoff & Astrid Long **Bred** Gerrardstown House Stud **Trained** Longton, Lancs

FOCUS
A modest handicap, run at a sound pace.

2543 BUCK INN THORNTON WATLASS MAIDEN STKS 7f
7:10 (7:11) (Class 5) 3-Y-0+ **£4,274** (£1,271; £635; £317) **Stalls** Low

Form RPR
-542 **1** **Doc Jones (IRE)**[20] 1972 3-9-2 72..................... JamieSpencer 9 72
(P D Evans) *cl up on outer: led after 1f and stdd pce: qcknd over 3f out: rdn and qcknd clr 2f out: drvn ins fnl f: hld on* **4/1**[2]

05- **2** *1 1/4* **Splendorinthegrass (IRE)**[219] 6979 3-9-2 0.................. SteveDrowne 3 69
(R Charlton) *prom: chsd wnrr whn rdn and outpcd 2f out: sn drvn: swtchd rt ent fnl f and kpt on u.p: nt rch wnr* **1/4**[1]

0- **3** *10* **Neva A Mull Moment (IRE)**[227] 6789 3-9-2 0......... SilvestreDeSousa 1 42
(D Nicholls) *cl up on inner: rdn along 3f out: drvn over 2f out and sn one pce* **22/1**

6 **4** *4* **Son Of Monsieur**[23] 1888 3-9-2 0.............................. DuranFentiman 7 31
(G R Oldroyd) *in tch: hdwy 1/2-way: rdn wl over 2f out and n.d* **16/1**[3]

0-0 **5** *1 3/4* **Bathwick Pursuit**[16] 2074 3-9-2 0......................... StephenDonohoe 6 26
(P D Evans) *hld up: a in rr* **66/1**

0- **6** *2 3/4* **Special Adviser**[192] 7402 3-9-2 0........................... GrahamGibbons 4 19
(T J Etherington) *led 1f: cl up whn n.m.r and hmpd bnd over 4f out: rdn along 3f out and sn wknd* **50/1**

7 *1* **Simply Sensational (IRE)** 3-9-2 0.............................. SJCraine 5 16
(Patrick Morris) *s.i.s: a bhd* **100/1**

1m 26.38s (-0.82) **Going Correction** -0.175s/f (Firm)
WFA 3 from 4yo 10lb 7 Ran SP% **114.7**
Speed ratings (Par 103): **97,95,84,79,77 74,73**
toteswinger: 1&2 £1.02, 1&3 £4.80, 2&3 £3.10 CSF £5.48 TOTE £4.60: £1.60, £1.10; EX 6.60.
Owner Barry McCabe **Bred** Holburn Trust Co **Trained** Pandy, Monmouths
■ Stewards' Enquiry : S J Craine caution: used whip out of contention

FOCUS
A weak maiden in which the first pauir came clear.
Splendorinthegrass(IRE) Official explanation: jockey said colt was unsuited by the firm ground

2544 WEATHERBYS FINANCE H'CAP 7f
7:40 (7:40) (Class 4) (0-85,85) 3-Y-O **£5,569** (£1,657; £828; £413) **Stalls** Low

Form RPR
2-14 **1** **Secret Society**[9] 2281 3-9-4 **82**.............................. JamieSpencer 6 98
(M L W Bell) *in rr and sn pushed along: hdwy 3f out: effrt to chse ldrs and hung lft over 1f out: swtchd outside and rdn to ld: hung lft ent fnl f: sn clr* **7/4**[1]

12-0 **2** *5* **Brierty (IRE)**[16] 2072 3-9-3 **81**.................................. DNolan 5 83
(D Carroll) *chsd ldrs: hdwy 3f out: rdn to chal 2f out: drvn and ev ch whn n.m.r ent fnl f: kpt on same pce* **7/1**

0320 **3** *1 1/4* **Thunderball**[16] 2072 3-8-10 **77**.......................(b[1]) AndrewMullen[(3)] 7 76
(A J McCabe) *led and sn clr: rdn along over 1f out: jnd wl over 1f out: sn drvn and hdd ent fnl f: sn wknd* **5/1**[2]

421- **4** *1/2* **Snow Bay**[330] 3754 3-8-10 **74**.................................. TomEaves 8 71
(B Smart) *bhd: hdwy 2f out: sn rdn and kpt on ins fnl f: nrst fin* **20/1**

0003 **5** *1* **Red Kyte**[17] 2028 3-8-12 **76**...................................... NCallan 1 71
(K A Ryan) *chsd ldr on inner: rdn along wl over 2f out: sn drvn and grad wknd* **20/1**

3310 **6** *1/2* **My Best Bet**[16] 2079 3-8-12 **76**.............................. SamHitchcott 3 69
(M R Channon) *chsd ldrs: rdn along wl over 2f out: sn no imp* **20/1**

130- **7** *1 1/4* **Stan's Cool Cat (IRE)**[246] 6319 3-9-7 **85**..................... JoeFanning 10 75
(P F I Cole) *a towards rr* **40/1**

04-2 **8** *3 1/2* **Richo**[35] 1561 3-9-0 **78**.. PaulMulrennan 12 58
(D H Brown) *chsd ldng pair: rdn along 3f out: drvn over 2f out and sn wknd* **8/1**

2103 **9** *2 1/4* **Seldom (IRE)**[6] 2365 3-8-5 **69**............................. SilvestreDeSousa 13 43
(M Brittain) *racd wd: nvr bttr than midfield* **13/2**[3]

00-4 **10** *1/2* **Regal Lyric (IRE)**[35] 1561 3-8-8 **72**............................. MickyFenton 11 45
(T P Tate) *chsd ldrs: rdn along 3f out: sn wknd* **7/1**

1m 24.81s (-2.39) **Going Correction** -0.175s/f (Firm) 10 Ran SP% **119.2**
Speed ratings (Par 101): **106,100,98,98,97 96,95,91,88,88**
toteswinger: 1&2 £5.60, 1&3 £4.20, 2&3 £7.90 CSF £13.95 CT £54.12 TOTE £2.80: £1.40, £2.40, £2.60; EX 20.00.
Owner Sheikh Marwan Al Maktoum **Bred** Darley **Trained** Newmarket, Suffolk

FOCUS
This modest handicap was run at a strong pace.
Seldom(IRE) Official explanation: jockey said colt hung right round the bottom bend
Regal Lyric(IRE) Official explanation: jockey said gelding was never travelling

2545 BOLTBY H'CAP 1m 4f
8:10 (8:10) (Class 4) (0-85,82) 3-Y-O **£5,569** (£1,657; £828; £413) **Stalls** Low

Form RPR
-231 **1** **Akmal**[12] 2181 3-9-5 **80**.. TPO'Shea 5 89
(J L Dunlop) *led 1f: cl up: rdn along 3f out: led 2f out: jnd and drvn over 1f out: kpt on gamely towards fin* **4/1**

-110 **2** *hd* **Topolski (IRE)**[19] 1992 3-9-7 **82**.............................. GregFairley 2 91
(M Johnston) *trckd ldng pair: effrt over 2f out: swtchd rt and rdn to chal over 1f out: drvn and ev ch ins fnl f tl no ex nr fin* **9/4**[1]

5051 **3** *5* **Geneva Geyser (GER)**[7] 2341 3-9-3 **78** 6ex............... MickyFenton 1 79
(J M P Eustace) *rrd s and s.i.s: swtchd outside and rapid hdwy to ld after 1f: rdn 3f out: drvn and hdd 2f out: wknd appr fnl f* **7/2**[3]

0-32 **4** *2 1/4* **Ruud Revenge (USA)**[16] 2090 3-9-0 **75**................... SilvestreDeSousa 3 72
(Mrs D J Sanderson) *in rr and pushed along 1/2-way: hdwy on outer 3f out: sn rdn and no imp* **5/2**[2]

1-50 **5** *6* **Hey Up Dad**[10] 2230 3-8-10 **71**.............................. PhillipMakin 4 58
(M Dods) *hld up in tch: hdwy over 3f out: sn rdn and wknd over 2f out* **17/2**

2m 33.72s (-2.48) **Going Correction** -0.175s/f (Firm) 5 Ran SP% **112.1**
Speed ratings (Par 101): **101,100,97,96,92**
CSF £13.61 TOTE £3.60: £1.90, £2.00; EX 8.70.
Owner Hamdan Al Maktoum **Bred** Shadwell Estate Company Limited **Trained** Arundel, W Sussex

FOCUS
A fair handicap but a muddling race.

2546 YORKSHIRE'S HERRIOT COUNTRY FILLIES' H'CAP 5f
8:40 (8:40) (Class 5) (0-75,75) 3-Y-O+ **£4,274** (£1,271; £635; £317) **Stalls** High

Form RPR
0-00 **1** **Toy Top (USA)**[17] 2046 6-8-11 **52**...........................(b) TomEaves 3 61
(M Dods) *cl up: rdn to ld over 1f out: drvn and hdd ins fnl f: rallied gamely to ld nr line* **11/1**

6-03 **2** *hd* **Tartatartufata**[10] 2225 7-9-9 **64**...........................(v) PaulMulrennan 1 72
(J G Given) *cl up on wd outside: effrt 2f out: rdn to ld ins fnl f: sn drvn: hdd and nt qckn nr fin* **11/1**

0-43 **3** *1* **Speedy Senorita (IRE)**[17] 2046 4-9-7 **69**.................... JamieKyne[(7)] 4 74
(J J Quinn) *trckd ldrs: effrt and n.m.r wl over 1f out: nt clr run and swtchd rt ins fnl f: kpt on* **3/1**[2]

0-40 **4** *hd* **Red Rosanna**[28] 1720 3-9-9 **71**............................. GrahamGibbons 10 72
(R Hollinshead) *led: rdn along 2f out: drvn and wandered over 1f out: sn hdd and kpt on same pce ins fnl f* **11/2**[3]

321 **5** *1/2* **La Zamora**[13] 2157 3-9-13 **75**.................................. PhillipMakin 8 74+
(T D Barron) *trckd ldrs on rail: effrt 2f out and n.m.r: nt clr run over 1f out and ent fnl f: squeezed through and kpt on wl towards fin* **5/2**[1]

0224 **6** *nk* **Metroland**[8] 2299 3-9-13 **75**.................................. StephenDonohoe 6 73
(D Nicholls) *wnt lft s: towards rr tl hdwy 2f out: rdn and n.m.r over 1f out: kpt on same pce ins fnl f* **11/2**[3]

0-01 **7** *2 1/4* **Revue Princess (IRE)**[17] 2046 4-10-0 **69**.....................(b) DavidAllan 7 62
(T D Easterby) *cl up: rdn along and edgd lft 2f out: sn wknd* **15/2**

3006 **8** *2 1/2* **Berrymead**[19] 1985 4-8-9 **55**.................................(b) AnnStokell[(5)] 5 39
(Miss A Stokell) *bmpd s: chsd ldrs: rdn wl over 1f out and sn wknd* **33/1**

58.85 secs (-0.75) **Going Correction** -0.075s/f (Good)
WFA 3 from 4yo+ 7lb 8 Ran SP% **115.7**
Speed ratings (Par 100): **103,102,101,100,99 99,95,91**
toteswinger: 1&2 £10.10, 1&3 £9.90, 2&3 £7.50 CSF £123.42 CT £384.74 TOTE £12.30: £2.60, £3.30, £1.20; EX 74.40 Place 6: £12.52, Place 5: £9.41.
Owner D Vic Roper **Bred** Lajos Kengye **Trained** Denton, Co Durham

FOCUS
A tight fillies' handicap.
Toy Top(USA) Official explanation: trainer said, regarding the apparent imporvement of form, that the mare is unrealiable and takes time to come to hand each season
T/Plt: £20.00 to a £1 stake. Pool: £54,814.06. 1,997.80 winning tickets. T/Qpdt: £7.40 to a £1 stake. Pool: £3,955.40. 395.30 winning tickets. JR

2135 WINDSOR (R-H)
Monday, June 1

OFFICIAL GOING: Good to firm
Wind: Light, against Weather: Fine, very warm

2547 SPORTINGBET.COM EBF NOVICE STKS 5f 10y
6:25 (6:25) (Class 5) 2-Y-O **£3,885** (£1,156; £577; £288) **Stalls** High

Form RPR
1 **Navajo Chief** 2-8-12 0.. AlanMunro 1 82
(A P Jarvis) *chsd ldrs: pushed into ld over 1f out: hrd pressed fnl f: rdn and styd on grittily* **50/1**

62 **2** *1/2* **Footstepsofspring (FR)**[11] 2187 2-8-12 0................... RichardHughes 4 80
(R Hannon) *led against nr side rail: shkn up and hdd over 1f out: pressed wnr fnl f: a hld* **11/10**[1]

1 **3** *hd* **Nadeen (IRE)**[36] 1534 2-9-5 0.................................. RyanMoore 5 86
(M R Channon) *chsd ldrs: pushed along 2f out: rdn to cl 1f out: chal fnl f: a hld* **15/8**[2]

1 **4** *1 1/2* **Antonius Moris (IRE)**[23] 1891 2-8-11 0.................. RossAtkinson[(5)] 6 78
(Tom Dascombe) *hld up bhd ldrs: hanging fr 2f out: hd high and no rspnse whn pushed along fnl f* **6/1**[3]

4 **5** *3/4* **Bramshill Lady (IRE)**[14] 2135 2-8-7 0.......................(t) TedDurcan 2 66
(Pat Eddery) *mostly chsd ldr to 2f out: sn lost pl: no prog fnl f* **12/1**

6 *5* **Ba Jetstream** 2-8-12 0.. TonyCulhane 3 53
(M R Channon) *a last and nvr on terms* **25/1**

62.31 secs (2.01) **Going Correction** +0.125s/f (Good) 6 Ran SP% **110.2**
Speed ratings (Par 93): **88,87,86,84,83 75**
toteswinger: 1&2 £18.50, 1&3 £12.50, 2&3 £1.10 CSF £103.33 TOTE £31.90: £8.10, £1.50; EX 126.10.
Owner Geoffrey Bishop **Bred** Eurostrait Ltd **Trained** Middleham Moor, N Yorks

FOCUS
A novice event capable of throwing up a juvenile with Royal Ascot pretensions. The form is not east to assess, especially with the time ordinary, but the winner is a colt of real potential.

NOTEBOOK
Navajo Chief, one of only two debutants in the line-up, is a colt of considerable potential. Considering the winner is bred to want much further than this trip - by King's Best out of a Rainbow Quest mare - it was no surprise he was sent off a seemingly unconsidered 50-1 shot. However, he knew his job and picked up best of all when coming under pressure in the closing stages, displaying plenty of speed to deny the favourite. He will apparently take his chance in the Coventry Stakes and Cashmans make him a 25-1 chance.
Footstepsofspring(FR), dropped in trip after running an improved second over 6f at Goodwood, never looked totally comfortable, giving the impression he might have been feeling the fast ground a touch. He did keep on for pressure, but could not muster the required speed and might be better suited by another furlong, as well as a more forgiving surface. (op 10-11 tchd 6-5 and 5-4 in places)
Nadeen(IRE) had no easy task conceding weight all round, but his trainer won this in 2007 with Hatta Fort, who was subsequently third in the Windsor Castle before landing the Superlative Stakes. This Bahamian Bounty colt looked to step up a good deal on the bare form of his debut success at Brighton, and gave the impression he can do better again, considering he wasn't helped by having to challenge widest of all. (op 9-4)
Antonius Moris(IRE) had little room to play with in behind the leaders for much of the straight. There is no way of knowing how he would have fared with a clear run, but he would probably have finished closer. He also gave the impression he would not want the ground any faster, and a slightly easier surface, as well as a step up to 6f, might see him in a better light. (op 7-1 tchd 5-1)
Bramshill Lady(IRE)'s debut fourth over course and distance was just modest form and this looked an improved effort, even though she was ultimately well held. (op 16-1)

Ba Jetstream, a 5,000gns half-sister to dual 5f winner Cheshire Rose and multiple sprint scorer Peopleton Brook, was outpaced pretty much throughout and looked to need the experience. (op 33-1 tchd 16-1)

2548 BEST JOB BEN EXPERIENCES QUEENSLAND ISLANDREEFJOB.COM H'CAP 1m 67y

6:55 (6:56) (Class 5) (0-70,70) 3-Y-O £2,729 (£806; £403) **Stalls High**

Form RPR

2430 **1** **Edgeworth (IRE)**[21] 1932 3-9-2 **65**.................................. LukeMorris 5 68
(B G Powell) *hld up in midfield: clsng on ldrs whn nt clr run wl over 1f out: squeezed through fnl f: drvn to ld nr fin* **20/1**

0-60 **2** 1/2 **Fajita**[11] 2209 3-9-4 **67**.. GeorgeBaker 4 69
(G L Moore) *hld up bhd ldrs: effrt over 2f out: led over 1f out: wandered u.p and sn jnd: hdd and nt qckn nr fin* **12/1**

40-0 **3** *nse* **When Doves Cry**[35] 1570 3-8-12 **61**.............................. PhilipRobinson 2 63
(B W Hills) *free to post: hld up towards rr: prog on outer over 2f out: drvn to join ldr 1f out: upsides nr fin: nt qckn* **33/1**

0-00 **4** *nse* **Howard**[21] 1928 3-9-7 **70**.. JimmyFortune 13 72
(J L Dunlop) *t.k.h early: hld up cl bhd ldrs: got through over 1f out: str chal fnl f: nt qckn nr fin* **5/1**[2]

00-5 **5** 3 1/2 **Play It Sam**[24] 1837 3-9-4 **67**.. ChrisCatlin 8 61
(W R Swinburn) *hld up towards rr: rdn wl over 2f out: kpt on fr over 1f out: nvr rchd ldrs* **28/1**

00-5 **6** 3/4 **Murhee (USA)**[43] 1380 3-9-7 **70**.. TedDurcan 10 62+
(D R Lanigan) *hld up in rr: shkn up and no prog over 2f out: styd on fr over 1f out: nrst fin* **14/1**

21 **7** 1 1/4 **Sullenberger (IRE)**[80] 833 3-9-4 **70**.............................. JackMitchell(3) 1 59
(J A Osborne) *pressed ldrs: narrow ld wl over 2f out to over 1f out: wknd tamely fnl f* **25/1**

1-00 **8** 2 1/2 **Noble Dictator**[8] 2300 3-9-1 **64**.................................(p) TonyCulhane 12 47
(E F Vaughan) *stdd s: hld up in last: pushed along over 2f out: plugged on: nvr nr ldrs* **17/2**[3]

04-4 **9** 3/4 **Noverre To Hide (USA)**[27] 1772 3-9-1 **64**...................... SebSanders 11 46
(J R Best) *t.k.h: cl up bhd ldrs: nudged along and steadily lost pl fnl 2f* **12/1**

0-1 **10** *shd* **The Mumbo**[142] 121 3-9-5 **68**.. AlanMunro 9 49
(W Jarvis) *t.k.h: hld up in cl tch: chal and upsides 3f out: wknd over 1f out* **25/1**

531- **11** 1/2 **Super Fourteen**[245] 6333 3-9-0 **63**................................... RichardHughes 6 43
(R Hannon) *led to 4f out: styd w ldrs: upsides and reminders 2f out: lost pl over 1f out: eased* **12/1**

36-3 **12** 1 1/2 **Eddie Boy**[41] 1440 3-9-4 **67**.. MartinDwyer 14 50+
(M L W Bell) *hld up in last pair: shkn up 3f out: trying to cl but no ch whn hmpd jst over 1f out* **10/1**

2126 **13** 8 **Wunder Strike (USA)**[21] 1932 3-9-1 **64**.......................... PatCosgrave 7 22
(J R Boyle) *a wl in rr: u.p and struggling 3f out* **16/1**

1-62 **14** 65 **Saturn Way (GR)**[3] 2431 3-9-6 **69**.................................. RyanMoore 3 —
(P R Chamings) *pressed ldr: led narrowly 4f out: sn rdn: hdd & wknd wl over 2f out: virtually p.u* **2/1**[1]

1m 45.48s (0.78) **Going Correction** 0.0s/f (Good) **14** Ran SP% **124.1**
Speed ratings (Par 99): **96,95,95,95,91 91,89,87,86,86 86,84,76,11**
toteswinger: 1&2 £43.10, 1&3 £83.40, 2&3 £48.70 CSF £236.39 CT £4330.86 TOTE £28.10: £8.00, £4.90, £10.30; EX 513.20.
Owner K Rhatigan **Bred** Yvonne & Gerard Kennedy **Trained** Upper Lambourn, Berks
■ Stewards' Enquiry : George Baker one-day ban: careless riding (june 15)

FOCUS
A modest handicap in which the first four came home in a blanket finish. The form looks modest.
Saturn Way(GR) Official explanation: jockey said colt stopped very quickly

2549 SPORTINGBET.COM H'CAP 6f

7:25 (7:26) (Class 4) (0-80,78) 4-Y-O+ £4,857 (£1,083; £1,083; £360) **Stalls High**

Form RPR

-003 **1** **Bold Argument (IRE)**[11] 2202 6-8-7 **65**......................... JackMitchell(3) 10 74
(Mrs P N Dutfield) *hld up in 7th: prog on wd outside over 2f out: drvn to ld ins fnl f: in command after* **8/1**

-003 **2** 1 1/4 **Zowington**[17] 2053 7-8-11 **71**....................................(v) WilliamCarson(5) 2 76
(S C Williams) *trckd ldrs: cl 3rd over 1f out: nt clr run and swtchd lft ent fnl f: kpt on* **14/1**

6351 **2** *dht* **Alfresco**[7] 2326 5-9-9 **78** 6ex...(p) SebSanders 1 83
(J R Best) *pressed ldrs: led 2f out: hrd rdn over 1f out: hdd and outpcd ins fnl f* **11/2**

0665 **4** *nk* **Memphis Man**[9] 2276 6-9-3 **72**.. PaulDoe 7 76+
(P D Evans) *stdd s: hld up last: stdy prog on outer fr 2f out: jst pushed along and styd on wl fnl f: nvr cl enough to chal* **16/1**

-002 **5** 2 1/4 **We Have A Dream**[32] 1619 4-9-3 **72**............................... MartinDwyer 5 69
(W R Muir) *prom: w ldr 2f out tl edgd rt and fdd jst over 1f out* **8/1**

0-50 **6** *hd* **Carleton**[16] 2071 4-9-7 **76**.. ChrisCatlin 3 72
(W J Musson) *s.i.s: hld up in last trio: effrt over 2f out: kpt on fr over 1f out: nt pce to threaten* **4/1**[2]

2605 **7** *shd* **Resplendent Alpha**[25] 1806 5-9-3 **72**............................ JimmyQuinn 9 68+
(P Howling) *dwlt: hld up in last trio: nudged along fr 2f out: swtchd lft ent fnl f: hanging but kpt on: nvr nr ldrs* **12/1**

0602 **8** 2 **Fyodor (IRE)**[12] 2184 8-9-6 **75**....................................(p) RichardHughes 11 64
(P D Evans) *t.k.h: hld up bhd ldrs: cl up but rdn whn hmpd jst over 1f out: fdd* **9/2**[3]

00-0 **9** 7 **Blessed Place**[11] 2202 9-8-7 **62**..................................... FrankieMcDonald 6 29
(D J S Ffrench Davis) *led to 2f out: sn wknd* **40/1**

-301 **10** 12 **Hazytoo**[23] 1890 5-9-4 **73**.. RyanMoore 4 2
(P J Makin) *w ldrs to 1/2-way: lost pl rapidly 2f out: sn eased* **7/2**[1]

1m 12.93s (-0.07) **Going Correction** +0.125s/f (Good) **10** Ran SP% **120.7**
Speed ratings (Par 105): **105,103,103,102,99 99,99,96,87,71**
PL: A £2.40, Z £3.50. Exacta: BA & A £22.90, BA & Z £43.40, CSF: BA & A £26.75, BA & Z £58.65. Tricast: BA, A & Z £315.59, BA, Z & A £344.71. toteswinger: 1&A £9.70, 1&Z £8.90, A&Z £8.90 TOTE £10.20: £3.00.
Owner Simon Dutfield **Bred** K S Lee **Trained** Axmouth, Devon
■ Stewards' Enquiry : Martin Dwyer caution: careless riding

FOCUS
An ordinary handicap, run at a decent pace and sound form rated around the winner, backed up by the third.
Resplendent Alpha Official explanation: jockey said gelding was denied a clear run
Fyodor(IRE) Official explanation: jockey said gelding lost his action
Hazytoo Official explanation: jockey said gelding lost his action

2550 SPORTINGBET.COM UP UP AND AWAY STKS (LISTED RACE) (REGISTERED AS THE LEISURE STAKES) 6f

7:55 (7:55) (Class 1) 3-Y-O+

£22,708 (£8,608; £4,308; £2,148; £1,076; £540) **Stalls High**

Form RPR

61 **1** **J J The Jet Plane (SAF)**[95] 700 5-9-7 120........................ RyanMoore 1 121+
(M F De Kock, South Africa) *mde all: in command wl over 1f out: rdn out fnl f* **4/7**[1]

-400 **2** 4 **Intrepid Jack**[19] 1989 7-9-0 109.. GeorgeBaker 3 102
(H Morrison) *settled in 4th: effrt to dispute 2nd 2f out: drvn and kpt on: no ch w wnr* **12/1**

0-00 **3** *hd* **Edge Closer**[19] 1989 5-9-0 109....................................(t) RichardHughes 5 102
(R Hannon) *chsd wnr: rdn and no imp 2f out: lost 2nd wl ins fnl f* **5/1**[2]

0-21 **4** 1/2 **Sohraab**[26] 1791 5-9-0 102.. EddieAhern 6 100
(H Morrison) *cl up on inner: rdn 2f out: nt qckn and hld fr over 1f out* **17/2**[3]

/40- **5** 1/2 **Genki (IRE)**[394] 1809 5-9-0 97.. TedDurcan 4 98
(R Charlton) *hld up in last pair: effrt 2f out: hanging and nowhere to go over 1f out: kpt on ins fnl f* **28/1**

1-43 **6** 1 1/2 **Icelandic**[9] 2287 7-9-4 105...(t) SebSanders 2 98
(F Sheridan) *settled in last pair: rdn and effrt on outer 2f out: sn no prog: wknd fnl f* **10/1**

1m 11.28s (-1.72) **Going Correction** +0.125s/f (Good) **6** Ran SP% **111.1**
Speed ratings (Par 111): **116,110,110,109,109 107**
toteswinger: 1&2 £1.90, 1&3 £1.30, 2&3 £4.30 CSF £8.54 TOTE £1.50: £1.10, £2.80; EX 5.90.
Owner H S N Du Preez **Bred** Mrs P J Devine **Trained** South Africa

FOCUS
A classy performance from South Africa's sprinting star, although there are doubts about the form of the opposition. He was conceding 7lb to all bar one of his rivals and is value for further.

NOTEBOOK
J J The Jet Plane(SAF) was using this Listed contest as his prep for a tilt at the Golden Jubilee Stakes, having been off since winning a Group 3 in Dubai earlier in the year. While it is true his rivals are thoroughly exposed as little better, if at all, than this level, this still looked a high-class performance on the figures. For example, both the runner-up and third came into this officially rated 109, and even if they were slightly below form, it was hard not to be taken by winner's 4l success considering he was conceding 7lb to that pair. This performance was all the more creditable considering his trainer expects him to improve for the outing. He seems well primed to run a big race at Royal Ascot, but that said, the Golden Jubilee does look hot this year and the general 5-1 probably offers limited value as an ante-post investment. (op 8-13 tchd 8-11 and 4-5 in places)
Intrepid Jack ran well. However, while a stronger, more contested gallop would have suited better, he was outclassed. (op 8-1)
Edge Closer had every chance but wasn't good enough and is not simple to place. (op 11-2 tchd 6-1)
Sohraab, a Chester handicap winner off 96 last time when well drawn, was not up to this class and will now be aimed at the Wokingham (op 9-1 tchd 10-1)
Genki(IRE)made a pleasing return from over a year off the track and might have been slightly closer had he not been short of room inside the final furlong. He was progressing well when last seen and evidently retains plenty of ability. He was reported to have been denied a clear run and was trimmed in most ante-post lists for the Wokingham. Official explanation: jockey said gelding was denied a clear run (op 22-1 tchd 20-1)
Icelandic failed to seriously compete on ground quicker than he cares for. (op 12-1 tchd 9-1)

2551 SPORTINGBET.COM MAIDEN STKS 1m 2f 7y

8:25 (8:26) (Class 5) 3-Y-O £2,729 (£806; £403) **Stalls Low**

Form RPR

6 **1** **Pictorial (USA)**[16] 2074 3-9-3 0.. RyanMoore 10 83+
(Sir Michael Stoute) *pressed ldr: drvn to ld 3f out: hrd pressed u.p fr 2f out: kpt on wl* **5/4**[1]

2 3/4 **Shakalaka (IRE)**[277] 5442 3-9-3 78................................. GeorgeBaker 4 81
(G L Moore) *trckd ldrs: wnt 2nd over 2f out and gng bttr than wnr: upsides over 1f out: rdn and nt qckn* **8/1**[3]

3 **3** *nk* **Maria Nunziata**[25] 1804 3-8-12 0.................................... EddieAhern 2 75
(J Noseda) *t.k.h early: trckd ldrs: clsd on ldng trio 2f out: swtchd lft over 1f out: tried to chal fnl f: nt qckn* **10/3**[2]

4 *nk* **Acquisition** 3-8-12 0.. JimmyQuinn 3 75+
(H R A Cecil) *dwlt and rousted along to rch midfield: outpcd 3f out: wl adrift of ldrs 2f out: styd on strly fnl f: gaining fast at fin* **8/1**[3]

5- **5** 6 **Pointillist (IRE)**[243] 6398 3-8-12 0................................... SebSanders 8 63
(R M Beckett) *plld hrd: narrow ld to 3f out: wknd 2f out* **11/1**

0- **6** 10 **Mid Wicket (USA)**[241] 6443 3-9-3 0................................ ChrisCatlin 5 48+
(B W Hills) *hld up in last: pushed along and outpcd over 3f out: no ch after: modest late prog* **20/1**

0-0 **7** 3 1/4 **Sitwell**[12] 2178 3-9-3 0.. TravisBlock 9 41
(J R Fanshawe) *wl in rr: pushed along 4f out: lft bhd fr over 3f out* **33/1**

6 **8** *nk* **Galiotto (IRE)**[10] 2240 3-9-3 0.. AlanMunro 1 41+
(C F Wall) *sn restrained to rr: shkn up 4f out: outpcd 3f out and no ch after* **50/1**

9 3 1/4 **Kyllachy King** 3-9-3 0... TedDurcan 12 34
(Mrs A J Perrett) *chsd ldrs: rdn 4f out: wknd 3f out: bhd after* **33/1**

0-0 **10** 3/4 **Improper (USA)**[7] 2317 3-9-3 0.. NeilChalmers 11 33
(Mouse Hamilton-Fairley) *in tch: rdn and outpcd over 3f out: sn no ch* **100/1**

11 36 **Catchmeifyoucan (FR)** 3-9-3 0.. PhilipRobinson 7 —
(C G Cox) *dwlt: sn trckd ldrs: shkn up and wknd rapidly 3f out: eased: t.o* **14/1**

2m 8.82s (0.12) **Going Correction** 0.0s/f (Good) **11** Ran SP% **118.3**
Speed ratings (Par 99): **99,98,98,97,93 85,82,82,79,79 50**
toteswinger: 1&2 £3.60, 1&3 £1.50, 2&3 £4.90 CSF £11.69 TOTE £2.20: £1.10, £2.60, £1.70; EX 10.00.
Owner Highclere Thoroughbred Racing (Gimcrack) **Bred** Samac Ltd , Lynch Bages Ltd & Tim Hyde **Trained** Newmarket, Suffolk

FOCUS
A fair maiden, run at an uneven pace. The runner-up is rated in line with his Irish juvenile form.

2552 A C BECK H'CAP 1m 3f 135y

8:55 (8:55) (Class 5) (0-75,75) 4-Y-O+ £3,070 (£906; £453) **Stalls Low**

Form RPR

00-4 **1** **Gloucester**[39] 597 6-8-12 **66**.. SebSanders 3 77
(M J Scudamore) *hld up in tch: stdy prog gng wl to trck ldr over 2f out: led wl over 1f out: in command and pushed out fnl f* **11/4**[1]

-240 **2** 1 **Spirit Of Adjisa (IRE)**[11] 2194 5-9-4 **75**...................... DavidProbert(3) 8 84
(Pat Eddery) *dwlt: hld up in 7th: prog wl over 2f out: drvn to chse wnr jst over 1f out: styd on but a hld* **15/2**

3034 **3** 2 1/4 **Watson's Bay**[7] 2333 4-8-11 **65** .... JimmyQuinn 10 70
(P Howling) *dwlt: hld up in detached 8th: prog fr over 2f out: reminder and wnt 3rd ins fnl f: styd on but nvr nr ldng pair* **14/1**

31-4 **4** 1 3/4 **Rose Row**[47] 1287 5-9-1 **69** .... RyanMoore 9 71
(Mrs Mary Hambro) *sn led: drvn and hdd wl over 1f out: wknd fnl f* **3/1**[2]

001- **5** 1 1/4 **Sainglend**[24] 6868 4-9-4 **72** .... RichardHughes 1 72
(S Curran) *prom: chsd ldr over 4f out to wl over 2f out: nt qckn u.p: fdd over 1f out* **6/1**[3]

2/03 **6** 4 1/2 **Annambo**[13] 2172 9-8-8 **62** .... TravisBlock 4 54
(Andrew Reid) *mostly chsd ldr to over 4f out: rdn wl over 3f out: wknd fnl 2f* **22/1**

3/52 **7** 6 **Khun John (IRE)**[53] 798 6-9-6 **74** .... ChrisCatlin 5 56
(W J Musson) *hld up in detached last: urged along over 4f out: sn btn* **7/1**

444/ **8** 1 3/4 **Croon**[280] 662 7-9-0 **68** .... GeorgeBaker 2 47
(Andrew Turnell) *chsd ldrs: rdn and struggling 3f out: wknd 2f out* **16/1**

0-55 **9** 2 **Colour Trooper (IRE)**[12] 2183 4-9-1 **69** ....(b) LukeMorris 7 45
(P Winkworth) *prom: rdn 4f out: wknd rapidly u.p over 2f out* **10/1**

2m 27.19s (-2.31) **Going Correction** 0.0s/f (Good) **9** Ran SP% **116.2**
Speed ratings (Par 103): **107,106,104,103,102 99,95,94,93**
toteswinger: 1&2 £11.40, 1&3 £8.90, 2&3 £17.70 CSF £24.12 CT £246.35 TOTE £4.10: £1.70, £2.60, £3.90; EX 33.80 Place 6: £362.75, Place 5: £186.68.
Owner S M Smith & Keith Hunter **Bred** Juddmonte Farms Ltd **Trained** Bromsash, Herefordshire

FOCUS
A modest handicap but a sound gallop and the runner-up sets the level.
T/Plt: £380.40 to a £1 stake. Pool: £65,948.97. 164.90 winning tickets. T/Qpdt: £8.40 to a £1 stake. Pool: £7,775.36. 681.34 winning tickets. JN

2553 - 2554a (Foreign Racing) - See Raceform Interactive

1993 NAAS (L-H)
Monday, June 1

OFFICIAL GOING: Good to firm

2555a NAAS SPRINT STKS (LISTED RACE) 5f
3:40 (3:40) 3-Y-O+ **£26,861** (£7,881; £3,754; £1,279)

RPR

1 **Inxile (IRE)**[22] 1919 4-9-10 .... AdrianTNicholls 6 110
(D Nicholls) *sn led: rdn and drifted to rt away fr rail over 1f out: styd on wl ins fnl f* **2/5**[1]

2 1 **Miss Gorica (IRE)**[95] 700 5-9-4 102 .... DPMcDonogh 1 100
(Ms Joanna Morgan, Ire) *trckd ldrs in 3rd: wnt 2nd u.p ins fnl f: kpt on wout matching wnr* **12/1**

3 nk **Invincible Ash (IRE)**[36] 1543 4-9-4 95 .... JMurtagh 3 99
(M Halford, Ire) *trckd ldr in 2nd: rdn and sltly impeded over 1f out: 3rd and kpt on wout matching wnr ins fnl f* **10/1**[3]

4 1 1/2 **Call Me Alice (USA)**[3] 2466 3-8-11 96 .... WMLordan 5 91
(David Wachman, Ire) *trckd ldrs: sn 4th: kpt on same pce u.p fr over 1f out* **20/1**

5 1 1/2 **Cnocan Gold (IRE)**[19] 1995 3-8-11 91 ....(b) PJSmullen 2 86
(D K Weld, Ire) *sn wl off pce in rr: struggling bef 1/2-way: sn no imp and kpt on wout threatening* **12/1**

6 1 **Dahindar (IRE)**[570] 6783 4-9-7 95 .... MJKinane 4 88
(John M Oxx, Ire) *sn towards rr in mod 6th: kpt on same pce u.p fr 2f out* **5/1**[2]

7 1 1/4 **Senor Benny (USA)**[9] 2287 10-9-10 99 .... FMBerry 7 86
(M McDonagh, Ire) *sn racd in 5th: rdn fr 1/2-way: sn no imp* **40/1**

57.43 secs (-4.57)
WFA 3 from 4yo+ 7lb **7** Ran SP% **119.8**
CSF £7.80 TOTE £1.40: £1.10, £6.10; DF 5.60.
Owner Ian Hewitson **Bred** Denis & Mrs Teresa Bergin **Trained** Sessay, N Yorks

FOCUS
The winner is the most reliable guide to the level of the form.

NOTEBOOK
Inxile(IRE) repeated his course and distance success recorded in April. He was smartly away to establish an early lead and, although wandering around under pressure in the closing stages, did the job well to provide David Nicholls with his third successive win in the race. A stewards' inquiry was called as he forced Miss Gorcia to lose slight momentum when tacking over to the far rail at halfway. When he drifted right inside the final furlong he also slightly hampered the third. Overall though, the best horse won on the day to provide his connections with some compensation for losing a valuable Group 3 event at Deauville last time. (op 4/7)
Miss Gorica(IRE) looked the biggest domestic threat on official ratings, and was reportedly in good shape after her stint in Dubai earlier in the year that yielded a handicap success off 101 in January. She was returning from a short break since her return home so one would expect her to find more next time. (op 12/1 tchd 10/1)
Invincible Ash(IRE) struggled in soft ground last time at Navan but she was certainly more at home on this quicker surface. She showed more like her best form in the process but was always struggling to get to the winner after entering the final furlong. (op 15/2)
Call Me Alice(USA) showed more here than at Down Royal last time. (op 10/1)
Cnocan Gold(IRE) was detached at halfway as things happened a bit quick for her here. After receiving a firm reminder, she stayed on looking like she'll appreciate a return to 6f or even longer. (op 10/1)

2557a COOLMORE STUD FILLIES' SPRINT STKS (GROUP 3) 6f
4:40 (4:40) 2-Y-O **£63,203** (£18,543; £8,834; £3,009)

RPR

1 **Lillie Langtry (IRE)**[19] 1993 2-8-12 .... JMurtagh 1 100+
(A P O'Brien, Ire) *sn settled in 5th: chal and led 1f out: sn rdn clr: styd on wl: comf* **1/1**[1]

2 2 1/2 **Kitty Kiernan**[19] 1993 2-8-12 .... KJManning 7 91+
(J S Bolger, Ire) *sn trckd ldrs in 4th: rdn fr 1/2-way: kpt on wout troubling wnr fr 1f out: wnt 2nd nr fin* **2/1**[2]

3 nk **A Mind Of Her Own (IRE)**[19] 1993 2-8-12 .... WMLordan 5 90
(David Wachman, Ire) *sn led: 2nd 1/2-way: no imp u.p and kpt on wout threatening fr 1f out* **20/1**

4 1 **What About Me (IRE)**[49] 1262 2-8-12 .... DJMoran 6 87
(Brian Nolan, Ire) *in tch towards rr: rdn into 5th and no imp fr over 1f out: kpt on wout threatening* **16/1**

5 1 1/2 **Wrong Answer**[9] 2286 2-8-12 .... CDHayes 4 83
(Kevin Prendergast, Ire) *cl up: in front 1/2-way: hdd and no ex fr 1f out* **6/1**[3]

6 1/2 **Electric Feel**[17] 2047 2-8-12 .... PJSmullen 3 81
(M Botti) *prom: dropped to 6th and no ex u.p fr over 1f out* **8/1**

7 3 **Justaroundmidnight (IRE)**[22] 1907 2-8-12 .... JAHeffernan 2 72
(David Wachman, Ire) *towards rr: no ex u.p in last fr over 1f out* **33/1**

1m 10.34s (-2.86) **7** Ran SP% **122.3**
CSF £3.60 TOTE £1.90: £1.50, £1.70; DF 4.20.
Owner Michael Tabor **Bred** K B Lynch **Trained** Ballydoyle, Co Tipperary

FOCUS
The winner put up a taking effort, but the questions over the form are the poor time and the field finishing fairly compressed.

NOTEBOOK
Lillie Langtry(IRE) ◆, whose good impression first time out over this course and distance behind Kitty Kiernan saw her attract substantial support to reverse that form, duly delivered in the style of a very smart filly. The daughter of Danehill Dancer looks likely to start a warm favourite on this evidence for the Albany Stakes and she was cut to 10-1 for next year's 1000 Guineas with Cashmans. She raced keenly early but the manner in which she quickened when a gap appeared approaching the final furlong was impressive and she won with plenty in hand. She'll be all the rage to follow this up when she heads to Royal Ascot later this month. (op 11/8)
Kitty Kiernan had two-and-a-half lengths to spare when she clashed with Lillie Langtry first time out last month, but it was a totally different story on this quicker surface. The daughter of Pivotal wasn't helped when slightly hampered at halfway and she ran on well inside the final furlong to snatch second close home. She is also a decent filly but was outclassed on this occasion. (op 2/1 tchd 9/4)
A Mind Of Her Own(IRE) was a reluctant leader as nothing was keen to go on and in the circumstances ran a good race to fill the same berth as when the trio clashed last time. She looks more than good enough to win her maiden before long. (op 16/1)
What About Me(IRE) won first time out on contrasting ground at Cork over 5f but these were very different underfoot conditions. Her trainer expressed his concern beforehand but to her credit she ran reasonably well over this furlong longer journey. (op 12/1)
Wrong Answer, who got to the front under 2f from home, was soon fighting a losing battle on this faster surface. (op 4/1)
Electric Feel, a Newmarket debut winner, struggled in this company and will probably be more effective when her sights are lowered. (op 7/1)

2556 - 2559a (Foreign Racing) - See Raceform Interactive

MUNICH (L-H)
Monday, June 1

OFFICIAL GOING: Good

2560a ONEXTWO.COM BAVARIAN CLASSIC (GROUP 3) 1m 2f
3:55 (4:12) 3-Y-O **£31,068** (£9,709; £4,854; £2,913)

RPR

1 **Saphir (GER)**[29] 1718 3-9-2 .... AStarke 6 105
(P Schiergen, Germany) *racd in 4th: 3rd st: rdn to chse ldr under 2f out: styd on u.str.p to ld post* **17/10**[2]

2 shd **Peligroso (FR)**[204] 7264 3-9-2 .... LDettori 5 105
(Saeed Bin Suroor) *sn led: 2 l clr 2f out: stl 1 1/2 l clr 1f out: sn rdn: hdd post* **9/10**[1]

3 1 1/2 **Hansom (GER)** 3-9-2 .... JiriPalik 4 102
(Frau E Mader, Germany) *racd in 2nd to under 2f out: one pce* **97/10**

4 1 **Quo Dubai (GER)**[29] 1718 3-9-2 ....(b) DPorcu 2 100
(Mario Hofer, Germany) *racd keenly in 7th: kpt on u.p fnl 2f* **32/1**

5 1/2 **Glad Panther**[29] 1718 3-9-2 .... WMongil 7 99
(Uwe Ostmann, Germany) *racd in 5th: rdn and one pce fnl 2f* **43/10**[3]

6 3 **Budai (GER)** 3-9-2 .... THellier 1 93
(A Trybuhl, Germany) *racd in 3rd: 4th st: sn rdn and nt qckn* **81/10**

7 4 **Enzio (GER)**[29] 1718 3-9-2 .... JLermyte 8 85
(A Wohler, Germany) *racd in 6th: nvr a factor* **34/1**

8 4 **Schachspieler (GER)** 3-9-2 .... KKerekes 3 77
(W Figge, Germany) *last thrght* **41/1**

2m 6.60s (-2.37) **8** Ran SP% **137.1**
(including 10 Euro stake): WIN 28; PI 10, 12; SF 56.
Owner Frau M Herbert **Bred** Gest Fahrhof Stiftung **Trained** Germany

NOTEBOOK
Peligroso(FR), a winner of a Group 3 on heavy ground at Krefeld for Mario Hofer, tried to make all the running only to be collared on the line. It may be that this longer trip just found him out.

2561 - (Foreign Racing) - See Raceform Interactive

1616 FOLKESTONE (R-H)
Tuesday, June 2

OFFICIAL GOING: Good to firm (firm in places on straight course)
Wind: Light, across Weather: Sunny, very warm

2562 FREEBETS.CO.UK NEW HORSE RACING SYNDICATE H'CAP 5f
6:20 (6:20) (Class 5) (0-75,75) 3-Y-O **£3,070** (£906; £453) **Stalls** Low

Form RPR

-160 **1** **Hi Shinko**[19] 2010 3-9-0 **68** .... TGMcLaughlin 1 73
(B R Millman) *mde all and racd against nr side rail: drvn over 1f out: edgd rt fnl f: hld on wl* **4/1**[3]

-153 **2** 1/2 **Desert Strike**[15] 2140 3-9-6 **74** .... MartinDwyer 4 77
(P F I Cole) *pressed wnr: shkn up to chal over 1f out: nt qckn and a hld fnl f* **3/1**[1]

-403 **3** 3/4 **Evelyn May (IRE)**[14] 2148 3-9-7 **75** .... MichaelHills 8 76
(B W Hills) *chsd ldrs and racd on outer: pressed ldng pair 2f out: nt qckn 1f out: kpt on* **4/1**[3]

-300 **4** 2 **Avrilo**[20] 1982 3-8-2 **56** oh11 .... CatherineGannon 5 49
(M S Saunders) *racd wd: outpcd and struggling bef 1/2-way: kpt on fr over 1f out: n.d* **66/1**

01- **5** shd **Bold Tie**[232] 6701 3-9-7 **75** .... RichardHughes 7 68
(R Hannon) *chsd ldng pair: slt stumble 2f out and outpcd: nvr gng w any fluency after* **7/2**[2]

15 **6** nk **Shadow Bay (IRE)**[25] 1839 3-9-2 **70** .... IanMongan 3 62
(Miss Z C Davison) *bdly outpcd in last: shkn up over 1f out: styd on wl fnl f: nrst fin* **11/2**

00-0 **7** 8 **Queen Of Thebes (IRE)**[12] 2209 3-9-7 **75** .... JimCrowley 2 38
(G L Moore) *wnt rt s: sn pushed along to stay in tch: wknd 1/2-way: bhd after* **8/1**

0-40 **8** 5 **Maigh Eo (IRE)**[31] 1662 3-8-3 **62** .... Louis-PhilippeBeuzelin(5) 9 7
(Patrick Morris) *racd wd early: nvr on terms: struggling 1/2-way: t.o* **40/1**

59.41 secs (-0.59) **Going Correction** -0.125s/f (Firm) **8** Ran SP% **117.6**
Speed ratings (Par 99): **99,98,97,93,93 93,80,72**
toteswinger: 1&2 £3.40, 1&3 £4.00, 2&3 £1.90 CSF £17.00 CT £51.56 TOTE £4.40: £1.70, £1.60, £1.30; EX 20.70.
Owner Always Hopeful Partnership **Bred** Mrs Laura Grasby **Trained** Kentisbeare, Devon

FOCUS
There was a lively market for the opening sprint handicap. The first three were prominent throughout and nothing got into it from behind.

Bold Tie Official explanation: jockey said colt stumbled 2f out

2563 FREEBETS.CO.UK OWN A RACEHORSE SYNDICATE MAIDEN FILLIES' STKS 6f
6:50 (6:51) (Class 5) 2-Y-O £3,070 (£906; £453) Stalls Low

Form RPR
1 **Mudaaraah** 2-9-0 0 RHills 6 84+
(J L Dunlop) *s.s: rn green and hld up towards rr: gd prog on outer fr 2f out: led 1f out: pushed clr* 3/1[2]

3 2 1 1/2 **Exotic Beauty**[12] 2207 2-9-0 0 TonyCulhane 2 78
(M R Channon) *racd against nr side rail: w ldr: led after 2f: drvn and hdd 1f out: one pce* 13/8[1]

0 3 1/2 **Lady Pattern (IRE)**[36] 1569 2-9-0 0 IanMongan 3 76
(P W D'Arcy) *dwlt: hld up in midfield: prog and swtchd rt over 1f out: styd on to chse ldng pair fnl f: nvr able to chal* 8/1

66 4 4 **Ice Cool Lady (IRE)**[22] 1933 2-9-0 0 AdamKirby 10 64
(W R Swinburn) *sn trckd ldrs on outer: pressed ldng pair over 2f out: wknd jst over 1f out* 12/1

56 5 1/2 **Two Kisses (IRE)**[18] 2047 2-9-0 0 StephenCarson 9 63
(B G Powell) *awkward s but led for 2f: pressed ldr tl over 1f out: wknd* 12/1

0 6 2 1/4 **Xaara Star (IRE)**[26] 1810 2-9-0 0 JimmyQuinn 7 56
(Eve Johnson Houghton) *taken down early: dwlt: hld up in last pair: shkn up over 1f out: sme prog fnl f: nvr on terms* 40/1

6 7 hd **Aegean Destiny**[26] 1810 2-9-0 0 RichardHughes 4 55
(R Hannon) *s.s: hld up towards rr: outpcd and shkn up 2f out: nvr on terms* 6/1[3]

8 nk **Exceed Power** 2-9-0 0 MartinDwyer 1 54
(D M Simcock) *dwlt: sn cl up bhd ldrs and racd against rail: rdn and wknd 2f out* 14/1

9 4 **Rosa Gurney (IRE)** 2-8-11 0 MarcHalford(3) 8 42
(J R Best) *dwlt: a in last pair: lft bhd fr over 2f out* 20/1

44 10 3/4 **Mind The Monarch**[12] 2207 2-9-0 0 LPKeniry 5 40
(R A Teal) *chsd ldng pair to over 2f out: wknd rapidly* 22/1

1m 12.01s (-0.69) **Going Correction** -0.125s/f (Firm) 10 Ran SP% **122.1**
Speed ratings (Par 90): **99,97,96,91,90 87,87,86,81,80**
toteswinger: 1&2 £1.02, 1&3 not won, 2&3 £10.30 CSF £8.50 TOTE £4.60: £2.00, £1.40, £1.30; EX 10.40.
Owner Hamdan Al Maktoum **Bred** Shadwell Estate Company Limited **Trained** Arundel, W Sussex

FOCUS
A fair juvenile fillies' maiden.

NOTEBOOK
Mudaaraah moved well to post, travelled smoothly during the race and quickened up down the centre of the track to win with quite a bit in hand and give John Dunlop his second two-year-old winner from three runners this season. The daughter of Cape Cross is closely related to the very useful 6f-1m performers Ethaara and Sudoor, and is out of an unraced sister to the high-class juvenile Bahhare who was later smart over 1m. She looks a useful prospect and could improve significantly for this initial experience. (op 9-4 tchd 2-1 and 7-2 in a place)

Exotic Beauty's proximity in second gives this form a solid look. She set the standard on her third at 9-2 in an eight-runner 5f Sandown fillies' maiden on debut, and has run a solid race from a good draw, but could not cope with the potentially useful winner. She will find easier opportunities to get off the mark. (op 6-4 tchd 15-8)

Lady Pattern(IRE) stumbled and her rider lost an iron when in midfield at Windsor on her debut. She looked more streetwise here and stayed on strongly to reverse recent form with Ice Cool Lady. She is related to several winners at trips ranging from 6f-1m4f, and should continue to progress. (op 12-1)

Ice Cool Lady(IRE) was never competitive on Polytrack last time but the return to turf seems to have encouraged her to run to something like the form of her sixth behind three next-time-out winners at Windsor on her debut. She travelled well for a long way before fading and could be an interesting contender when contesting nurseries back over 5f. (tchd 14-1)

Two Kisses(IRE) raced near the pace but could not sustain her effort and was a bit disappointing because she had a form chance on her promising runs in 5f-6f maidens on her two previous starts. (op 16-1)

Aegean Destiny Official explanation: jockey said filly hung left early on

Mind The Monarch Official explanation: jockey said filly stumbled twice

2564 FREEBETS.CO.UK FREE BETS H'CAP 6f
7:20 (7:20) (Class 5) (0-70,70) 4-Y-O+ £3,070 (£906; £453) Stalls Low

Form RPR
0226 1 **Bateleur**[5] 2418 5-8-6 55 EdwardCreighton 7 71
(M R Channon) *hld up in last trio: smooth prog w plenty of room on nr side 2f out: led over 1f out: sn clr* 7/1

35-5 2 5 **Rhapsilian**[12] 2202 5-8-7 56 RobertHavlin 2 56+
(J A Geake) *hld up bhd ldrs: trapped fr 2f out tl prog against nr side jst over 1f out: hanging but kpt on to take 2nd ins fnl f* 5/1[2]

-656 3 1/2 **Who's Winning (IRE)**[15] 2124 8-8-3 52 (t) LukeMorris 3 50
(B G Powell) *hld up in midfield: drvn 2f out: kpt on to take 3rd wl ins fnl f* 11/2[3]

003 4 2 **Music Box Express**[15] 2124 5-8-4 60 MatthewDavies(7) 9 52
(George Baker) *wnt rt s: led but styd towards outer: drvn 2f out: hdd over 1f out: fdd fnl f* 10/1

-651 5 1 1/2 **Caustic Wit (IRE)**[7] 2353 11-8-5 54 CatherineGannon 1 41
(M S Saunders) *taken down early: trckd ldr but racd off nr side rail: wknd jst over 1f out* 7/2[1]

-532 6 1 1/4 **Forest Dane**[109] 533 9-9-2 70 Louis-PhilippeBeuzelin(5) 5 53
(Mrs N Smith) *racd off nr side rail: prom bhd ldr tl wknd fr 2f out* 5/1[2]

6-03 7 nk **Reigning Monarch (USA)**[113] 472 6-7-11 51 oh4 NicolPolli(5) 4 33
(Miss Z C Davison) *hld up in last trio: rdn over 2f out: nvr on terms* 25/1

0302 8 2 1/4 **Green Lagonda (AUS)**[7] 2349 7-8-6 55 DO'Donohoe 8 30
(Stef Liddiard) *taken down early: hld up in last trio: sme prog on wd outside over 2f out: hanging and wknd over 1f out* 12/1

0453 9 7 **Radiator Rooney (IRE)**[11] 2224 6-8-5 54 WilliamBuick 6 7
(Patrick Morris) *t.k.h early: prom on outer: hanging fr 1/2-way: wknd wl over 1f out* 8/1

1m 11.34s (-1.36) **Going Correction** -0.125s/f (Firm) 9 Ran SP% **115.2**
Speed ratings (Par 103): **104,97,96,94,92 90,89,86,77**
toteswinger: 1&2 £10.50, 1&3 £12.70, 2&3 £5.50 CSF £41.75 CT £208.58 TOTE £9.70: £3.00, £1.60, £1.60; EX 47.00.
Owner Dave and Gill Hedley **Bred** G Hedley & Mike Channon Bloodstock Limited **Trained** West Ilsley, Berks

FOCUS
A moderate sprint handicap, involving several veterans. It was run at a furious pace and the first three came from some way back.

2565 FREEBETS.CO.UK NEW ONLINE BETTING FORUM H'CAP 7f (S)
7:50 (7:50) (Class 4) (0-80,78) 4-Y-O+ £5,828 (£1,734; £866; £432) Stalls Low

Form RPR
21- 1 **Monaadema (IRE)**[348] 3180 4-9-1 72 RHills 5 81+
(W J Haggas) *cl up: trckd ldr 1/2-way: rdn to chal over 1f out: led ins fnl f: grad gained upper hand* 10/11[1]

1432 2 3/4 **Hobson**[4] 2459 4-8-9 66 StephenCarson 4 73
(Eve Johnson Houghton) *led: styd off nr side rail tl over 2f out: drvn over 1f out: hdd ins fnl f: kpt on* 6/1

-242 3 3/4 **Purus (IRE)**[17] 2086 7-9-7 78 LukeMorris 1 83
(R A Teal) *hld up in last trio: effrt 2f out: rdn and nt qckn over 1f out: styd on: nvr able to chal* 9/2[2]

0500 4 1 **Compton's Eleven**[3] 2491 8-8-9 71 MCGeran(5) 2 73
(M R Channon) *stdd s: hld up in last trio: effrt and n.m.r briefly over 1f out: sn rdn and nt qckn: kpt on* 16/1

3310 5 1/2 **Bere Davis (FR)**[8] 2313 4-9-4 75 RichardHughes 3 76
(P D Evans) *racd against nr side rail: chsd ldr to 3f out: sn rdn: plugged on fr over 1f out* 5/1[3]

1350 6 9 **Tuxedo**[24] 1876 4-8-11 68 JimCrowley 6 45
(P W Hiatt) *hld up in last trio: effrt on outer 2f out: sn wknd* 22/1

1m 25.55s (-1.75) **Going Correction** -0.125s/f (Firm) 6 Ran SP% **111.7**
Speed ratings (Par 105): **105,104,103,102,101 91**
toteswinger: 1&2 £4.30, 1&3 £2.60, 2&3 £4.40 CSF £6.87 TOTE £1.70: £1.10, £2.60; EX 4.50.
Owner Hamdan Al Maktoum **Bred** Shadwell Estate Company Limited **Trained** Newmarket, Suffolk

FOCUS
A modest handicap.

Tuxedo Official explanation: jockey said gelding stumbled app f mark

2566 FREEBETS.CO.UK OVER £12000 IN FREE BETTING OFFERS H'CAP 1m 4f
8:20 (8:20) (Class 4) (0-85,83) 4-Y-O+ £5,828 (£1,734; £866; £432) Stalls Low

Form RPR
/42- 1 **Hada Men (USA)**[244] 6403 4-8-10 72 WilliamBuick 5 80+
(L M Cumani) *chsd ldng pair to 3f out: sn rdn: effrt 2f out: wnt 2nd 1f out: styd on u.p to ld post* 13/8[1]

1620 2 hd **King Supreme (IRE)**[3] 2475 4-9-7 83 (b) RichardHughes 3 88
(R Hannon) *hld up in last: swift move on outer over 3f out: rdn to ld 2f out: drvn 2l clr 1f out: collared post* 6/1

0-32 3 3 1/4 **Gaia Prince (USA)**[18] 2052 4-9-1 77 JimCrowley 1 77
(Mrs A J Perrett) *trckd ldr: effrt to ld narrowly 3f out: drvn and hdd 2f out: steadily outpcd fnl f* 11/4[2]

1004 4 3/4 **Profit's Reality (IRE)**[28] 1779 7-9-5 81 PaulDoe 4 80
(M J Attwater) *hld up in 4th: rdn and nt qckn over 2f out: one pce and no imp on ldrs after* 10/1

0024 5 3/4 **Sgt Schultz (IRE)**[11] 2242 6-9-0 76 LPKeniry 6 73
(J S Moore) *hld up in 5th: nt qckn 3f out and sn outpcd: plugged on one pce fnl 2f* 5/1[3]

446- 6 9 **Segal (IRE)**[27] 1919 4-9-2 78 LiamJones 2 61
(A M Hales) *led: rdn and hdd 3f out: cl enough 2f out: wknd* 16/1

2m 37.23s (-3.67) **Going Correction** -0.20s/f (Firm) 6 Ran SP% **110.7**
Speed ratings (Par 105): **104,103,101,101,100 94**
toteswinger: 1&2 £1.30, 1&3 £2.50, 2&3 not won. CSF £11.50 TOTE £2.20: £1.50, £3.00; EX 11.50.
Owner Paul Moulton **Bred** Overbrook Farm **Trained** Newmarket, Suffolk

FOCUS
A decent handicap. It was run at a stop-start gallop but the first two were involved in an exciting finish and pulled clear of the rest.

2567 FREEBETS.CO.UK FREE ONLINE BETTING H'CAP 1m 1f 149y
8:50 (8:53) (Class 5) (0-70,70) 3-Y-O £3,070 (£906; £453) Stalls Centre

Form RPR
-041 1 **Mons Calpe (IRE)**[21] 1953 3-9-6 69 (b) MartinDwyer 4 74
(P F I Cole) *pushed up fr wd draw to ld and set gd pce: hrd pressed and edgd rt over 1f out: hdd ent fnl f: rallied to ld last strides* 11/2[3]

430- 2 hd **Mefraas (IRE)**[312] 4394 3-9-7 70 RHills 13 75+
(E A L Dunlop) *hld up in 7th: prog 3f out: clsd on ldrs over 1f out: drvn to ld ent fnl f: hdd last strides* 4/1[2]

206 3 1 1/4 **Mellow Mixture**[15] 2126 3-9-7 70 RichardHughes 12 72
(R Hannon) *trckd ldng pair tl wnt 2nd 3f out: drvn to chal on inner whn hmpd over 1f out: one pce fnl f* 16/1

1440 4 2 3/4 **Millway Beach (IRE)**[25] 1839 3-9-4 67 JimmyQuinn 5 63
(Pat Eddery) *trckd wnr to 3f out: drvn and nt qckn 2f out: plugged on* 33/1

-066 5 hd **Breach Of Peace (USA)**[19] 2001 3-8-13 67 Louis-PhilippeBeuzelin(5) 11 63
(R Charlton) *trckd ldng quartet: wnt 4th 3f out but sn rdn and outpcd: kpt on one pce after* 7/1

3-20 6 3 1/4 **Dice (IRE)**[15] 2126 3-9-7 70 WilliamBuick 1 59
(L M Cumani) *trckd ldrs in 6th: rdn over 3f out: sn outpcd: no imp fnl 2f* 17/2

-446 7 2 1/4 **Mohanad (IRE)**[34] 1614 3-9-7 70 TonyCulhane 8 54+
(M R Channon) *hld up wl in rr: dropped to last 4f out: sn lft bhd: modest late prog* 28/1

00-3 8 nse **Ja One (IRE)**[12] 2206 3-9-2 65 MichaelHills 10 49+
(B W Hills) *hld up in last: sme prog on wd outside 4f out: wknd wl over 2f out* 7/2[1]

3000 9 1 3/4 **The Bully Wee**[18] 2048 3-8-12 61 LukeMorris 6 41
(J Jay) *hld up in last trio: struggling whn rn wd bnd over 2f out: no real prog* 66/1

25-0 10 1 3/4 **Peace Concluded**[47] 1315 3-9-4 70 JamesMillman(3) 9 47
(B R Millman) *chsd ldng trio tl wknd 3f out* 9/1

30-0 11 1 3/4 **Temperence Hall (USA)**[9] 2300 3-9-1 67 MarcHalford(3) 7 40
(J R Best) *nvr bttr than 8th: wknd and no ch sn after 3f out* 14/1

06-5 12 4 1/2 **Bishop Rock (USA)**[109] 529 3-9-1 64 LiamJones 3 28
(M H Tompkins) *a in rr: wknd 3f out: wl bhd after* 20/1

2m 3.08s (-1.82) **Going Correction** -0.20s/f (Firm) 12 Ran SP% **115.8**
Speed ratings (Par 99): **99,98,97,95,95 92,91,91,89,88 86,83**
toteswinger: 1&2 £6.30, 1&3 £10.10, 2&3 £12.10 CSF £26.01 CT £332.33 TOTE £6.70: £2.80, £2.20, £3.60; EX 36.20 Place 6 £28.62, Place 5 £19.08..
Owner H R H Sultan Ahmad Shah **Bred** Swettenham Stud **Trained** Whatcombe, Oxon

FOCUS
An interesting handicap, involving plenty of unexposed types. There was big turn-up in-running as Mefraas was outbattled after being matched at 1.04 on the exchanges.

T/Plt: £57.00 to a £1 stake. Pool: £69,456.27. 888.79 winning tickets. T/Qpdt: £40.10 to a £1 stake. Pool: £4,284.56. 78.90 winning tickets. JN

2099 RIPON (R-H)

Tuesday, June 2

OFFICIAL GOING: Good to firm (8.9)
Wind: Virtually nil Weather: Fine and dry

2568 EBF SHIRLEY JONES CLINGING TO 49 MAIDEN STKS 5f
2:30 (2:33) (Class 5) 2-Y-O **£4,209** (£1,252; £625; £312) **Stalls** Low

Form RPR
44 1 **Di Stefano**[31] 1669 2-9-3 0 SamHitchcott 10 79+
(M R Channon) *led 1f: cl up: effrt to ld again wl over 1f out: edgd rt ent fnl f: rdn clr* **2/1**[1]
2 2 3/4 **Cherry Bee** 2-8-12 0 RoystonFfrench 3 62+
(M Johnston) *in tch: pushed along 1/2-way: swtchd rt and rdn wl over 1f out: kpt on ins fnl f* **6/1**
0 3 3/4 **Silver Linnet (IRE)**[17] 2089 2-8-12 0 DavidAllan 7 59
(T D Easterby) *trckd ldrs: hdwy 1/2-way: rdn to chse wnr over 1f out: kpt on same pce ins fnl f* **20/1**
4 1 **Crushing (IRE)** 2-9-0 0 NeilBrown(3) 2 61
(T D Barron) *cl up: led after 1f: rdn along 2f out: sn hdd & wknd appr fnl f* **11/4**[2]
5 3 3/4 **Watch Chain (IRE)** 2-9-3 0 TedDurcan 1 47
(M H Tompkins) *towards rr: pushed along over 2f out: swtchd rt and styd on appr fnl f: nvr a factor* **12/1**
4 6 1/2 **Jack Luey**[8] 2311 2-9-3 0 DuranFentiman 4 46
(L A Mullaney) *prom: rdn along over 2f out: grad wknd* **9/2**[3]
7 2 1/2 **Captain Cash** 2-9-3 0 GrahamGibbons 5 37
(T D Easterby) *dwlt: a towards rr* **14/1**
8 shd **William Arnold** 2-9-0 0 KellyHarrison(3) 9 36
(C W Fairhurst) *sn outpcd and bhd* **100/1**
46 9 1 1/4 **Marchin Star (IRE)**[18] 2041 2-8-10 0 JohnCavanagh(7) 6 32
(M Brittain) *midfield: pushed along after 2f: sn rdn and wknd* **33/1**
10 3 1/4 **Twoellies** 2-8-12 0 PaulMulrennan 8 15
(Ollie Pears) *dwlt and hmpd s: hdwy into midfield 1/2-way: sn rdn and wknd* **40/1**

60.20 secs (-0.50) **Going Correction** -0.025s/f (Good) **10** Ran SP% **118.0**
Speed ratings (Par 93): **103,98,97,95,89 89,85,84,82,77**
toteswinger: 1&2 £2.40, 1&3 £8.90, 2&3 £13.40 CSF £14.39 TOTE £3.10: £1.10, £2.50, £5.00; EX 15.50 Trifecta £67.50 Pool: £429.50 - 4.70 winning units..
Owner Jon and Julia Aisbitt **Bred** P V And Mrs J P Jackson **Trained** West Ilsley, Berks

FOCUS
Just an ordinary juvenile maiden.

NOTEBOOK
Di Stefano didn't progress from a promising debut when only fourth at Goodwood on his latest start, but this was better and he was a convincing winner. He still looked a little green in the closing stages and there could be more to come again. A fair type for nurseries later in the season. (op 7-4 tchd 9-4)
Cherry Bee, a 35,000euros half-sister to among others 6f juvenile winner Fragrant Star, out of a 1m winner, gradually got the idea and finished well. This was a pleasing debut and she should have learnt enough to win a similar event next time. (op 3-1 tchd 7-1)
Silver Linnet(IRE) was never involved on her debut at Thirsk after being hampered at the start, but this was much better. She showed plenty of early speed this time and is going the right way. (tchd 16-1)
Crushing(IRE), a £41,000 purchase, took the eye in the paddock and showed plenty of speed against the stands'-side rail, but he didn't see his race out. This run should bring him and there ought to be better to come. (op 8-1)
Watch Chain(IRE), the first foal of 7f winner at three, made some late headway from off the pace and should do better with the benefit of this experience. (op 14-1 tchd 16-1)
Jack Luey didn't build on the form he showed when fourth at Carlisle on his debut. Official explanation: jockey said colt was unsuited by the good to firm ground (op 11-2 tchd 7-2)

2569 NFU MUTUAL CHALLENGE H'CAP 1m 1f 170y
3:00 (3:00) (Class 5) (0-70,65) 4-Y-0+ **£3,238** (£963; £481; £240) **Stalls** High

Form RPR
0-12 1 **Joinedupwriting**[8] 2314 4-9-1 59 PaulMulrennan 2 66
(R M Whitaker) *trckd ldr: hdwy and cl up 3f out: rdn to ld 1f out: drvn ins fnl f and kpt on wl* **5/2**[2]
6-03 2 nk **Andorn (GER)**[38] 1530 5-9-2 63 LeeVickers(3) 1 69
(P A Kirby) *led: jnd and rdn along 3f out: drvn and hdd 1f out: kpt on gamely u.p ins fnl f: no ex nr fin* **22/1**
0002 3 1 **Spirit Of France (IRE)**[7] 2362 7-9-7 65 DNolan 4 69
(D Carroll) *in tch: hdwy to chse ldrs 3f out: effrt over 2f out and sn rdn: drvn over 1f out and ev ch tl kpt on same pce ins fnl f* **9/4**[1]
4034 4 3/4 **Titinius (IRE)**[10] 2264 9-8-4 53 (p) PatrickDonaghy(5) 3 56
(Micky Hammond) *chsd ldng pair on inner: effrt over 2f out and sn rdn: drvn over 1f out: kpt on same pce u.p ins fnl f* **8/1**
/300 5 shd **Diamond Lass (IRE)**[10] 2263 4-9-2 60 PaulHanagan 7 62
(R A Fahey) *chsd ldrs: effrt over 2f out and sn rdn: drvn over 1f out: kpt on same pce ins fnl f* **13/2**[3]
31-0 6 shd **Eijaaz (IRE)**[17] 2068 8-9-0 65 JamieKyne(7) 5 67
(G A Harker) *hld up towards rr: gd hdwy on outer 3f out: rdn wl over 1f out and ev ch tl drvn and one pce ins fnl f* **7/1**
0-00 7 3/4 **Plenilune (IRE)**[59] 1123 4-9-4 62 JoeFanning 6 63
(M Brittain) *in tch: effrt over 2f out: rdn to chse ldrs wl over 1f out: keeping on whn n.m.r ins fnl f* **20/1**
0-00 8 48 **Thunderstruck**[10] 2261 4-9-0 65 JonathanHinch(7) 8 —
(A J McCabe) *hld up: a in rr: bhd fnl 3f* **16/1**

2m 4.74s (-0.66) **Going Correction** -0.175s/f (Firm) **8** Ran SP% **111.3**
Speed ratings (Par 103): **95,94,93,93,93 93,92,54**
toteswinger: 1&2 £6.30, 1&3 £1.30, 2&3 £10.50 CSF £50.52 CT £134.25 TOTE £3.20: £1.10, £5.30, £1.10; EX 41.90 Trifecta £93.20 Pool: £471.10 - 3.74 winning units..
Owner R C Dollar **Bred** Ink Pot Partnership **Trained** Scarcroft, W Yorks
■ Stewards' Enquiry : D Nolan two-day ban: used whip with excessive frequency (Jun 21-22)

FOCUS
The top weight was rated 5lb below the ceiling of 70 and they finished in a bunch. This is weak form.

Plenilune(IRE) Official explanation: trainer said gelding lost its near-fore shoe

2570 NICK WILMOT-SMITH MEMORIAL H'CAP 6f
3:30 (3:31) (Class 3) (0-95,95) 4-Y-O **£8,831** (£2,643; £1,321; £660; £329) **Stalls** Low

Form RPR
0-00 1 **Grazeon Gold Blend**[10] 2267 6-7-9 76 oh1 (p) JamieKyne(7) 5 83
(J J Quinn) *chsd ldrs: pushed along 1/2-way: hdwy wl over 1f out and sn ev ch: drvn ins fnl f and styd on to ld on line* **10/1**
4015 2 nse **Vhujon (IRE)**[10] 2267 4-8-13 87 PaulHanagan 9 94
(P D Evans) *dwlt: hld up towards rr: gd hdwy on outer wl over 1f out: rdn to ld ins fnl f: hdd and no ex nr fin* **5/1**[3]
0600 3 1/2 **Bel Cantor**[12] 2203 6-8-2 79 (p) KellyHarrison(3) 8 84
(W J H Ratcliffe) *cl up: led 1/2-way: rdn wl over 1f out: drvn and hdd ins fnl f: kpt on* **20/1**
5101 4 1 3/4 **Excusez Moi (USA)**[10] 2259 7-9-7 95 (p) PaulMulrennan 2 95+
(Mrs R A Carr) *hld up in tch: smooth hdwy 2f out: n.m.r and swtchd rt over 1f out: sn rdn and one pce* **9/2**[2]
1420 5 1 3/4 **High Curragh**[17] 2071 6-8-9 83 (p) TedDurcan 3 77
(K A Ryan) *led: rdn along and hdd 1/2-way: drvn and wknd over 1f out* **4/1**[1]
-066 6 nk **Spirit Of Sharjah (IRE)**[10] 2259 4-8-13 87 TPO'Shea 1 80
(Miss J Feilden) *dwlt: sn trcking ldrs: effrt 2f out: sn rdn and swtchd rt: no imp* **13/2**
00-0 7 nk **Inter Vision (USA)**[17] 2094 9-9-3 91 DanielTudhope 4 83+
(A Dickman) *chsd ldrs: rdn along 2f out: sn edgd lft and wknd* **12/1**
02-0 8 2 3/4 **Van Bossed (CAN)**[41] 1457 4-9-6 94 AdrianTNicholls 6 77
(D Nicholls) *hld up: a towards rr* **5/1**[3]
030- 9 10 **Burnwynd Boy**[241] 6484 4-9-0 95 NSLawes(7) 7 46
(D Nicholls) *a in rr* **14/1**

1m 11.7s (-1.30) **Going Correction** -0.025s/f (Good) **9** Ran SP% **113.1**
Speed ratings (Par 107): **107,106,106,103,101 101,100,97,83**
toteswinger: 1&2 £11.60, 1&3 £25.60, 2&3 £13.40 CSF £58.02 CT £985.56 TOTE £11.20: £2.90, £2.00, £5.30; EX 55.00 TRIFECTA Not won..
Owner J R Rowbottom **Bred** Mrs E McKee **Trained** Settrington, N Yorks
■ Stewards' Enquiry : Kelly Harrison one-day ban: failed to ride to draw (Jun 21)

FOCUS
A decent sprint handicap.

NOTEBOOK
Grazeon Gold Blend hadn't offered much on his first couple of starts this year but, with a promising 7lb claimer taking over from a professional, he returned to form with a narrow success from 1lb out of the weights. He's no sure thing to build on this, but will remain well handicapped on his best form once reassessed. Official explanation: trainer had no explanation for the apparent improvement in form (op 12-1 tchd 15-2)
Vhujon(IRE) challenged widest of all and had every chance but he was denied on the nod. He had conditions to suit and can have few excuses. (op 6-1 tchd 7-1)
Bel Cantor is not badly handicapped on the pick of his form but, despite showing bright speed, he couldn't dominate and didn't quite see his race out. (op 16-1)
Excusez Moi(USA) ◆ has been in superb form lately but things didn't really fall for him this time off a mark 10lb higher than when successful over course and distance three starts back. He was continually blocked when trying to pick up and didn't have sufficient momentum when finally in the open. He can most certainly be given another chance and remains of interest for the Wokingham. (op 4-1 tchd 5-1)
High Curragh dropped out tamely after being taken on for the lead. (op 5-1)
Spirit Of Sharjah(IRE) never really featured after a sluggish start but hinted he could be on his way back to some sort of form. Official explanation: jockey said gelding was denied a clear run (tchd 5-1)
Inter Vision(USA) Official explanation: jockey said gelding was denied a clear run
Van Bossed(CAN) didn't step up on the form he showed on his reappearance. (op 4-1)

2571 WEATHERBYS FINANCE H'CAP 1m 1f 170y
4:00 (4:00) (Class 4) (0-80,79) 3-Y-O **£5,180** (£1,541; £770; £384) **Stalls** High

Form RPR
1-00 1 **Fastnet Storm (IRE)**[20] 1992 3-9-6 78 MickyFenton 4 89
(T P Tate) *trckd ldr: led over 2f out: rdn clr 1f out* **4/1**[2]
510 2 3 **Sign Of Approval**[48] 1291 3-8-11 74 MartinLane(5) 5 79
(K R Burke) *trckd ldrs: hdwy 6f out: cl up 3f out: rdn and ev ch 2f out tl drvn and one pce ins fnl f* **14/1**
1-50 3 1 1/2 **Anthology**[10] 2281 3-9-7 79 RichardMullen 9 81+
(B Smart) *hld up: stdy hdwy 3f out: swtchd outside and rdn 2f out: drvn and kpt on ins fnl f* **7/1**
5-32 4 1 1/2 **High Office**[21] 1953 3-9-3 75 PaulHanagan 8 74
(R A Fahey) *t.k.h early: trckd ldrs: pushed along and outpcd over 2f out: sn rdn and kpt on ins fnl f* **3/1**[1]
-050 5 1 1/4 **Amethyst Dawn (IRE)**[24] 1882 3-8-6 64 DuranFentiman 7 61
(T D Easterby) *led: rdn along 3f out: sn hdd and grad wknd* **33/1**
5164 6 1 1/4 **Hatta Diamond (IRE)**[7] 2356 3-9-1 73 JoeFanning 2 67+
(M Johnston) *a towards rr* **3/1**[1]
0114 7 4 1/2 **Cornish Castle (USA)**[33] 1626 3-9-2 74 GrahamGibbons 3 59
(T D Walford) *hld up: hdwy and in tch 1/2-way: rdn over 3f out wknd over 2f out* **6/1**[3]
2-44 8 42 **Royal Defence (IRE)**[14] 2165 3-9-5 77 AdrianTNicholls 6 —
(D Nicholls) *in tch: effrt and sme hdwy on outer 1/2-way: sn rdn and wknd* **11/1**

2m 3.20s (-2.20) **Going Correction** -0.175s/f (Firm) **8** Ran SP% **114.7**
Speed ratings (Par 101): **101,98,97,96,95 94,90,57**
toteswinger: 1&2 £13.10, 1&3 £7.00, 2&3 £14.90 CSF £56.99 CT £379.71 TOTE £5.70: £1.70, £3.80, £2.10; EX 64.70 Trifecta £550.70 Part won. Pool: £744.22 - 0.53 winning units..
Owner The Kittywake Partnership **Bred** Norelands Bloodstock **Trained** Tadcaster, N Yorks

FOCUS
A modest handicap run at a solid pace.
Royal Defence(IRE) Official explanation: jockey said gelding had a breathing problem

2572 STUDLEY MAIDEN STKS 1m
4:30 (4:31) (Class 5) 3-Y-O **£3,238** (£963; £481; £240) **Stalls** High

Form RPR
06-2 1 **Veroon (IRE)**[24] 1882 3-9-3 73 PaulMulrennan 1 70
(J G Given) *sn led: rdn along wl over 2f out: drvn over 1f out: kpt on wl u.p ins fnl f* **11/8**[1]
2-06 2 nk **Cabernet Sauvignon**[24] 1882 3-9-3 71 SteveDrowne 3 69
(J W Hills) *chsd wnr: hdwy 3f out: rdn to chal 2f out: drvn over 1f out and ev ch tl no ex wl ins fnl f* **13/8**[2]
3 3/4 **Hajar (USA)** 3-9-3 0 RoystonFfrench 5 68
(M Johnston) *trckd ldrs effrt 3f out: rdn 2f out: swtchd lft and drvn over 1f out: ch tl edgd rt and one pce ins fnl f* **4/1**[3]

4 2 1/4 **Brockfield** 3-9-3 0 ... JoeFanning 4 62
(M Brittain) *t.k.h: trckd ldrs: hdwy 3f out: rdn over 2f out: drvn and wknd over 1f out* **10/1**

0-50 5 8 **Nassau Beach (IRE)**41 1452 3-9-3 49 ... DavidAllan 2 44
(T D Easterby) *dwlt: a in rr* **40/1**

1m 40.79s (-0.61) **Going Correction** -0.175s/f (Firm) **5** Ran SP% **111.7**
Speed ratings (Par 99): **96,95,94,92,84**
CSF £4.00 TOTE £2.40: £1.20, £1.90; EX 4.90.
Owner Danethorpe Racing Partnership **Bred** C M Farrell **Trained** Willoughton, Lincs

FOCUS
A modest maiden and a close finish.

2573 BISHOPTON H'CAP 1m 4f 10y
5:00 (5:00) (Class 5) (0-70,67) 4-Y-0+ **£3,238** (£963; £481; £240) **Stalls** High

Form RPR

311/ 1 **Golden Groom**631 5283 6-8-7 53 ... AndrewElliott 2 61
(P Beaumont) *cl up rdn to ld wl over 2f out: drvn over 1f out: hdd briefly ins fnl f: rallied wl to ld again nr fin* **8/1**

-024 2 *hd* **Summer Lodge**49 1154 6-8-9 55 ... (p) TPO'Shea 7 63
(A J McCabe) *in tch: hdwy to ld after 4f: rdn along 3f out: sn hdd and cl up: drvn over 1f out: rallied ins fnl f: no ex nr fin* **11/2**

3504 3 1/2 **Black Dahlia**11 2246 4-9-7 67 ... SteveDrowne 8 74+
(A J McCabe) *hld up towards rr: hdwy over 3f out: chsd ldng pair 2f out and sn rdn: drvn to ld briefly ins fnl f: sn no ex* **9/2**2

50-4 4 3 1/2 **Hurricane Thomas (IRE)**10 2263 5-8-6 52 ... PaulHanagan 5 53
(R A Fahey) *trckd ldrs: effrt over 3f out: rdn along over 2f out: drvn and no imp over 1f out* **11/4**1

-541 5 1/2 **Fell Pack**11 2237 5-8-13 59 ... DuranFentiman 4 59
(J J Quinn) *hld up in rr: effrt and sme hdwy over 2f out: sn rdn and kpt on ins fnl f: nrst fin* **5/1**3

41-0 6 *nk* **Amazing King (IRE)**10 2263 5-8-12 61 ... LeeVickers(3) 6 61
(P A Kirby) *hld up in rr: hdwy over 3f out: sn rdn and one pce fnl 2f* **16/1**

-600 7 8 **Sporting Gesture**17 2068 12-8-11 57 ... PaulMulrennan 3 44
(M W Easterby) *led 4f: chsd ldrs: rdn along 4f out: grad wknd* **16/1**

06-0 8 49 **Fossgate**25 1851 8-8-12 58 ... TedDurcan 1 —
(J D Bethell) *hld up: hdwy to trck ldrs over 4f out: effrt over 2f out: sn wknd and heavily eased* **7/1**

2m 36.08s (-0.62) **Going Correction** -0.175s/f (Firm) **8** Ran SP% **112.3**
Speed ratings (Par 103): **95,94,94,92,91 91,86,53**
toteswinger: 1&2 £6.30, 1&3 £7.10, 2&3 £5.70 CSF £49.34 CT £221.33 TOTE £10.30: £2.70, £2.10, £1.70; EX 52.20 Trifecta £245.90 Pool: £441.98 - 1.33 winning units..
Owner Colin Stirling **Bred** G H And Simon Leggott **Trained** Stearsby, N Yorks
■ Stewards' Enquiry : Steve Drowne caution: used whip with excessive frequency

FOCUS
A modest handicap and, continuing the theme of the day, it proved hard to make up significant amounts of ground.
Fossgate Official explanation: jockey said gelding had no more to give

2574 LEVY BOARD MAIDEN STKS 6f
5:30 (5:30) (Class 5) 3-4-Y-0 **£2,590** (£770; £385; £192) **Stalls** Low

Form RPR

0-40 1 **Francis Walsingham (IRE)**17 2080 3-9-3 0 ... SteveDrowne 1 74+
(H Morrison) *mde all: rdn clr over 1f out: kpt on* **10/11**1

-233 2 4 1/2 **Diamond Blade**10 2265 3-9-3 60 ... DavidAllan 5 58
(T D Easterby) *chsd ldng pair: hdwy to chse wnr over 2f out: sn rdn and no imp* **7/4**2

5- 3 3/4 **Rascal In The Mix (USA)**210 7179 3-8-9 0 ... MichaelJStainton(3) 6 50
(R M Whitaker) *trckd ldng pair: effrt 2f out: sn rdn and kpt on same pce* **5/1**3

4 5 **Carragold** 3-8-10 0 ... JohnCavanagh(7) 8 39+
(M Brittain) *v s.i.s and a bhd* **33/1**

6 5 7 **Gurtavallig (IRE)**22 1922 4-9-3 0 ... LeeVickers(3) 3 12
(T J Pitt) *cl up: rdn along 1/2-way: sn wknd* **66/1**

1m 14.28s (1.28) **Going Correction** -0.025s/f (Good)
WFA 3 from 4yo 8lb **5** Ran SP% **109.8**
Speed ratings (Par 103): **90,84,83,76,67**
toteswinger: 1&2 £3.00. CSF £2.73 TOTE £2.20: £1.10, £1.60; EX 3.00 Trifecta £3.80 Pool: £363.24 - 3.80 winning units. Place 6: £108.95, Place 5: £50.16.
Owner Mrs M Kerr-Dineen & Partners **Bred** John Yarr **Trained** East Ilsley, Berks

FOCUS
A really weak sprint maiden.
T/Plt: £217.40 to a £1 stake. Pool: £70,416.66. 236.35 winning tickets. T/Qpdt: £33.40 to a £1 stake. Pool: £3,738.46. 82.60 winning tickets. JR

2128 SOUTHWELL (L-H)
Tuesday, June 2

OFFICIAL GOING: Standard
Wind: Almost nil Weather: Sunny

2575 BET WITH LADBROKES ON 0800 777 888 MEDIAN AUCTION MAIDEN STKS 5f (F)
2:15 (2:17) (Class 6) 2-Y-0 **£2,729** (£806; £403) **Stalls** High

Form RPR

2 1 **Singeur (IRE)**15 2128 2-9-3 0 ... PatCosgrave 1 70
(R Bastiman) *a.p: chsd ldr over 3f out: led 2f out: rdn ins fnl f: jst hld on* **5/4**1

53 2 *nk* **Miss Lesley**15 2135 2-8-12 0 ... ChrisCatlin 9 64
(D K Ivory) *outpcd: swtchd rt over 3f out: hdwy u.p over 1f out: r.o wl* **6/1**3

2 3 1 3/4 **Going French (IRE)**11 2218 2-9-3 0 ... J-PGuillambert 8 63
(R Curtis) *chsd ldrs: rdn 1/2-way: sn hung lft: styd on* **2/1**2

0 4 3 1/4 **Tarrants Way**12 2195 2-8-12 0 ... JackDean(5) 5 51
(Jennie Candlish) *chsd ldrs: rdn 1/2-way: no ex ins fnl f* **20/1**

5 1 1/2 **Turf Time** 2-9-0 0 ... AndrewMullen(3) 11 46?
(A J McCabe) *sn outpcd: styd on ins fnl f: nvr nrr* **22/1**

0F 6 2 1/4 **Another Grand (IRE)**3 2467 2-9-3 0 ... SilvestreDeSousa 10 37
(Mrs R A Carr) *led 3f: sn rdn: wknd fnl f* **33/1**

06 7 *hd* **Coralamber (IRE)**1 2541 2-8-5 0 ... AndrewHeffernan(7) 2 32
(Garry Moss) *mid-div: outpcd 3f out: n.d after* **25/1**

8 2 **Brave Ambition (IRE)** 2-9-0 0 ... DominicFox(3) 4 30
(Garry Moss) *dwlt and hmpd s: outpcd* **40/1**

00 9 4 1/2 **Santas Pal**17 2089 2-8-12 0 ... PhillipMakin 6 8
(C J Teague) *chsd ldrs: rdn over 3f out: wknd 1/2-way* **33/1**

000 10 3 **Amoureuse**17 2089 2-8-12 0 ... (p) TomEaves 7 —
(I W McInnes) *sn outpcd* **66/1**

11 3/4 **Beach Boy (IRE)** 2-9-3 0 ... SJCraine 12 —
(S Wynne) *s.s: outpcd* **66/1**

60.72 secs (1.02) **Going Correction** 0.0s/f (Stan) **11** Ran SP% **116.3**
Speed ratings (Par 91): **91,90,87,82,80 76,76,73,65,61 59**
toteswinger: 1&2 £2.60, 1&3 £1.80, 2&3 £2.50 CSF £8.25 TOTE £2.40: £1.10, £1.60, £1.40; EX 8.70.
Owner Ms M Austerfield **Bred** Patrick Cassidy **Trained** Cowthorpe, N Yorks

FOCUS
A modest juvenile maiden in which only three mattered according to the market and it proved to be correct as they were the first three home.

NOTEBOOK
Singeur(IRE), beaten less than a length and clear of the rest when runner-up on his debut over course and distance last month, had the plum draw and made full use of it. Racing up with the pace throughout, he looked like winning easily entering the last furlong, but in the end it was a close-thing. The form is nothing special, but he should be able to find another modest event though he won't be risked on fast ground. (op 13-8)
Miss Lesley, a good third at Windsor last time despite jinking left exiting the stalls and then hanging left throughout, produced a near carbon-copy performance here. Considering she was outpaced early and found herself so far out of her ground, she did incredibly well to almost get up and snatch a highly unlikely victory. An extra furlong will help, but she is obviously not an easy ride. (op 9-2)
Going French(IRE), runner-up over a furlong further on his Brighton debut, was handy from the start but he was always having to be ridden along to stay in touch with the leaders. A return to 6f looks required. (tchd 15-8 and 9-4)
Tarrants Way, who showed a bit of early pace before weakening on his Haydock debut, ran well for a long way again and there should be a small race in him. (op 22-1)
Turf Time ♦, out of a sister to the useful sprinter No Time, wasn't best drawn close to the stands' rail, but he made a little late progress to fare best of the newcomers and is likely to step up on this in due course. (op 18-1)
Santas Pal Official explanation: jockey said filly had no more to give

2576 BET AFTER THE OFF AT LADBROKES.COM CLAIMING STKS 7f (F)
2:45 (2:46) (Class 6) 3-Y-0+ **£2,047** (£604; £302) **Stalls** Low

Form RPR

1662 1 **Imprimis Tagula (IRE)**13 2185 5-9-7 75 ... (v) LeeNewnes(7) 7 87
(A Bailey) *mde virtually all: rdn over 1f out: styd on* **6/1**3

450- 2 1 1/4 **Hits Only Jude (IRE)**365 2679 6-9-6 78 ... AlanMunro 8 76
(D Carroll) *chsd wnr over 3f: rdn to go 2nd again over 1f out: edgd rt: styd on* **11/2**2

2200 3 1 1/4 **Ours (IRE)**40 1479 6-9-10 73 ... (p) ChrisCatlin 12 76
(John A Harris) *s.i.s: outpcd: hdwy u.p and edgd lft over 1f out: r.o: nt rch ldrs* **12/1**

1230 4 1 3/4 **Flores Sea (USA)**24 1894 5-10-0 80 ... PhillipMakin 14 76
(T D Barron) *s.i.s: sn chsng ldrs: rdn over 2f out: edgd lft and no ex fnl f* **7/2**1

0140 5 1/2 **Obe Royal**10 2266 5-9-7 77 ... (b) AndrewHeffernan(7) 11 74
(P D Evans) *s.i.s: sn drvn along in mid-div: hdwy over 1f out: nt trble ldrs* **6/1**3

1160 6 2 3/4 **Lethal**29 1734 6-9-0 65 ... TonyHamilton 10 53
(R A Fahey) *prom: chsd wnr over 4f out tl rdn over 1f out: wknd fnl f* **10/1**

1261 7 1/2 **Cap St Jean (IRE)**42 1438 5-8-9 64 ... (p) DavidKenny(7) 1 53
(R Hollinshead) *s.s: outpcd: styd on fr over 1f out: n.d* **15/2**

0040 8 13 **Dabbers Ridge (IRE)**18 2045 7-9-8 80 ... (b1) TomEaves 2 24
(I W McInnes) *hld up in tch: rdn over 2f out: wknd wl over 1f out* **17/2**

-000 9 3/4 **Western Art (USA)**15 2133 4-9-0 63 ... PJMcDonald 5 14
(M W Easterby) *sn outpcd* **100/1**

0200 10 1 1/4 **Captain Jacksparra (IRE)**32 1649 5-10-0 79 ... NCallan 4 25
(K A Ryan) *chsd ldrs: rdn 1/2-way: wknd over 2f out: eased fnl f* **12/1**

-060 11 4 **Nacho Libre**17 2071 4-10-0 64 ... DaleGibson 3 14
(M W Easterby) *prom: sn drvn along: wknd over 2f out* **66/1**

-060 12 5 **Danish Art (IRE)**15 2133 4-8-13 66 ... BMcHugh(7) 9 —
(M W Easterby) *sn outpcd* **50/1**

0-06 13 2 **Wessex (USA)**112 491 9-10-0 79 ... (v) J-PGuillambert 6 —
(R Curtis) *sn outpcd* **33/1**

1m 29.18s (-1.12) **Going Correction** -0.075s/f (Stan) **13** Ran SP% **120.3**
Speed ratings (Par 101): **103,101,100,98,97 94,93,79,78,76 72,66,64**
toteswinger: 1&2 £9.80, 1&3 £15.40, 2&3 £16.00 CSF £38.85 TOTE £8.80: £3.30, £2.60, £4.50; EX 59.50.Lethal was claimed by Andrew Reid for £5,000.
Owner Middleham Park Racing XLI & Alan Bailey **Bred** Glashare House Stud **Trained** Newmarket, Suffolk

FOCUS
This looked a fair claimer with a couple of 80-rated performers taking part and several of these have plenty of previous winning form here. The early pace was decent too, with five horses vying for the lead across the track starting the turn for home.
Lethal Official explanation: jockey said gelding stumbled
Captain Jacksparra(IRE) Official explanation: jockey said gelding never travelled
Wessex(USA) Official explanation: jockey said gelding had no more to give

2577 PLAY BINGO AT LADBROKES.COM H'CAP 7f (F)
3:15 (3:15) (Class 6) (0-55,55) 3-Y-0 **£2,047** (£604; £302) **Stalls** Low

Form RPR

0603 1 **You've Been Mowed**7 2355 3-8-7 53 ... AndreaAtzeni(5) 2 60
(R J Price) *chsd ldrs: rdn over 2f out: led 1f out: styd on wl* **13/2**2

4-42 2 2 3/4 **Top Flight Splash**15 2132 3-8-12 53 ... (v) DaleGibson 6 53
(Mrs G S Rees) *led: hdd over 3f out: rallied to ld over 1f out: sn hdd: styd on same pce* **9/2**1

200 3 *hd* **Street Spirit (USA)**35 1592 3-8-13 54 ... (t) TomEaves 9 53+
(T D Easterby) *dwlt: outpcd: hdwy over 1f out: r.o: nrst fin* **8/1**

0-50 4 4 1/2 **Billy Smart (IRE)**17 2091 3-8-13 54 ... (b1) ChrisCatlin 14 41
(D J S Ffrench Davis) *prom: hrd rdn over 2f out: styng on same pce whn hung lft over 1f out* **7/1**3

1045 5 1 3/4 **Valdemar**41 1452 3-8-9 50 ... (v) SilvestreDeSousa 7 32+
(A D Brown) *chsd ldr tl led over 3f out: rdn and hdd over 1f out: sn wknd* **9/1**

450- 6 3/4 **Barbeito**180 7547 3-8-7 48 ... KirstyMilczarek 10 28
(M D Squance) *mid-div: sn pushed along: edgd lft over 4f out: rdn over 2f out: n.d* **10/1**

-004 7 1/2 **Feeling Stylish (IRE)**15 2132 3-8-6 47 ... GregFairley 8 26
(N Tinkler) *mid-div: pushed along whn n.m.r over 4f out: n.d* **17/2**

64-6 8 1 **Golden Pool (IRE)**33 1620 3-8-13 54 ... PatCosgrave 3 30
(S A Callaghan) *chsd ldrs: rdn over 3f out: wknd over 2f out* **12/1**

444 9 4 **Kings On The Roof**22 1940 3-8-11 52 ... (p) AlanMunro 4 17
(G C Bravery) *s.i.s: a in rr* **15/2**

4300 10 5 **Private Passion (IRE)**50 1253 3-8-12 53 ... TPQueally 5 5
(Pat Eddery) *sn pushed along in mid-div: n.m.r over 4f out: sn wknd* **8/1**

6-00 **11** 1 ¾ **Chipolini (IRE)**[21] 1949 3-8-6 50 AndrewMullen(3) 1 —
(D Carroll) *prom: rdn over 4f out: wknd 1/2-way* **50/1**
0600 **12** 4 ½ **Field Fantasy**[7] 2355 3-8-2 50 (b¹) AndrewHeffernan(7) 12 —
(Garry Moss) *sn outpcd* **80/1**
000- **13** 5 **Manhattan Sunrise (USA)**[223] 6910 3-8-11 55 RussellKennemore(3) 11 —
(Paul Mason) *s.i.s: outpcd* **40/1**
1m 30.41s (0.11) **Going Correction** -0.075s/f (Stan) 13 Ran SP% **120.9**
Speed ratings (Par 97): **96,92,92,87,85 84,84,82,78,72 70,65,59**
toteswinger: 1&2 £4.80, 1&3 £13.10, 2&3 £6.80 CSF £36.06 CT £252.46 TOTE £7.20: £2.90, £1.40, £3.30; EX 20.60.
Owner Mrs K Oseman **Bred** T E Pocock **Trained** Ullingswick, H'fords
FOCUS
A very moderate handicap in which 11 of the 14 runners were maidens coming into it.

2578 BETTER PRICES, BIGGER WINS AT LADBROKES.COM H'CAP 7f (F)
3:45 (3:46) (Class 5) (0-75,75) 3-Y-O **£3,412** (£1,007; £504) **Stalls** Low

Form RPR
5-50 **1** **Silent Hero**[24] 1870 3-9-6 74 PhilipRobinson 14 85+
(M A Jarvis) *s.i.s: edgd lft 6f out: pushed along and hdwy 1/2-way: rdn to ld 1f out: edgd lft: r.o wl* **3/1**¹
-313 **2** 2 ¾ **Arachnophobia (IRE)**[42] 1434 3-9-3 71 TPQueally 1 74
(Pat Eddery) *chsd ldrs: led over 4f out: rdn and hdd 1f out: styd on same pce* **17/2**
326- **3** 2 **Passage To India (IRE)**[158] 7784 3-9-1 69 PaulFitzsimons 11 67
(Miss J R Tooth) *hld up: hdwy over 2f out: rdn over 1f out: styd on same pce ins fnl f* **33/1**
0-50 **4** ½ **Lakeman (IRE)**[11] 2248 3-9-7 75 TomEaves 9 72
(B Ellison) *hld up: hdwy over 1f out: edgd lft and r.o: nt rch ldrs* **25/1**
243 **5** ¾ **Fortunate Flame**[15] 2142 3-8-13 67 NCallan 4 62
(K A Ryan) *prom: rdn over 2f out: no ex fnl f* **9/2**²
05-3 **6** 1 **Dean Iarracht (IRE)**[36] 1561 3-9-0 68 PhillipMakin 2 60
(M Dods) *mid-div: rdn 1/2-way: styd on same pce fnl 2f* **11/1**
0-1 **7** 1 **Desire To Excel (IRE)**[51] 1228 3-9-6 74 (b¹) GeorgeBaker 10 63
(P F I Cole) *chsd ldrs: rdn over 2f out: wknd over 1f out* **9/1**
40-6 **8** 3 **Fitzolini**[24] 1869 3-9-2 70 (p) SilvestreDeSousa 12 51
(A D Brown) *sn pushed along in rr: effrt and nt clr run over 1f out: n.d* **50/1**
02-6 **9** 2 ¾ **Thurston (IRE)**[32] 1656 3-8-8 67 GabrielHannon(5) 8 41
(D J S Ffrench Davis) *led: hdd over 4f out: chsd ldr: rdn and edgd rt over 3f out: wknd over 1f out* **40/1**
-213 **10** 1 ¾ **Avoir Choisi (IRE)**[46] 1331 3-9-7 75 AlanMunro 7 44
(P W Chapple-Hyam) *dwlt: outpcd* **5/1**³
0-30 **11** ½ **Cheam Forever (USA)**[19] 2010 3-8-12 66 RichardKingscote 3 34
(R Charlton) *chsd ldrs: rdn over 2f out: sn wknd* **14/1**
02-0 **12** ¾ **Petsas Pleasure**[21] 1953 3-9-0 68 TonyHamilton 5 34
(Ollie Pears) *sn pushed along: a in rr* **18/1**
3210 **13** hd **Kiss A Prince**[25] 1839 3-9-2 70 ChrisCatlin 6 35
(D K Ivory) *s.s: outpcd* **20/1**
3-00 **14** 9 **Darwin's Dragon**[18] 2048 3-9-0 68 (b¹) GregFairley 13 9
(P F I Cole) *hmpd 6f out: a in rr* **33/1**
1m 29.59s (-0.71) **Going Correction** -0.075s/f (Stan) 14 Ran SP% **119.5**
Speed ratings (Par 99): **101,97,95,95,94 93,91,88,85,83 82,81,81,71**
toteswinger: 1&2 £5.60, 1&3 £26.50, 2&3 £24.30 CSF £26.33 CT £733.25 TOTE £3.90: £1.80, £2.30, £6.00; EX 31.90.
Owner Mrs P Good **Bred** Mrs P Good **Trained** Newmarket, Suffolk
FOCUS
An ordinary handicap, though the pace was solid enough and the winning time was 0.82 seconds faster than the preceding handicap.
Avoir Choisi(IRE) Official explanation: trainer's rep said colt was not suited by the surface

2579 CARLSBERG H'CAP 6f (F)
4:15 (4:16) (Class 6) (0-60,60) 3-Y-O+ **£2,047** (£604; £302) **Stalls** Low

Form RPR
0360 **1** **Kingsmaite**[15] 2133 8-8-13 58 (b) AndrewYoxall(7) 6 74
(S R Bowring) *a.p: rdn to ld wl over 1f out: drvn clr ins fnl f* **9/1**
4504 **2** 5 **Blakeshall Quest**[15] 2134 9-9-0 52 (b) PhillipMakin 13 52
(R Brotherton) *mid-div: hdwy u.p and hung lft over 1f out: styd on same pce ins fnl f* **12/1**
-000 **3** 2 ¼ **Owed**[15] 2134 7-8-12 50 (bt¹) PatCosgrave 5 43
(R Bastiman) *s.i.s: sn chsng ldrs: led over 4f out: rdn and ev ch wl over 1f out: no ex fnl f* **16/1**
-536 **4** 1 **Spoof Master (IRE)**[35] 1587 5-9-6 58 TPQueally 8 48
(C R Dore) *sn pushed along in rr: styd on u.p fnl f: nvr nrr* **8/1**³
-600 **5** nse **Highly Acclaimed**[29] 1725 3-8-8 57 AndrewMullen(3) 11 44
(Mrs A Duffield) *led: hdd over 4f out: rdn over 2f out: styd on same pce* **16/1**
0000 **6** 3 **Redwater River**[8] 2312 5-8-12 50 (b) SilvestreDeSousa 4 30
(Mrs R A Carr) *chsd ldrs: rdn over 2f out: wknd over 1f out* **17/2**
0600 **7** 2 ¾ **Poca A Poca (IRE)**[6] 2381 5-8-6 49 (p) MarkFlynn(5) 14 20
(G C Bravery) *s.s: outpcd: nvr nrr* **100/1**
3443 **8** ¾ **Muktasb (USA)**[15] 2145 8-9-7 59 (v) NCallan 7 28
(D Shaw) *hld up in tch: rdn over 2f out: wknd over 1f out* **15/2**²
-000 **9** ½ **Captain Royale (IRE)**[29] 1734 4-8-10 48 (v) GregFairley 10 15
(Miss Tracy Waggott) *chsd ldrs: led 3f out: rdn and hdd wl over 1f out: sn wknd* **9/1**
00-2 **10** shd **Bertbrand**[15] 2130 4-9-8 60 SJCraine 3 27
(D Flood) *mid-div: hdwy 1/2-way: rdn over 2f out: wknd over 1f out* **8/1**³
0-50 **11** 2 ¾ **Virtuality (USA)**[30] 1694 4-9-6 58 TomEaves 2 16
(B Smart) *hld up: rdn and wknd over 2f out* **12/1**
-200 **12** 9 **Kaystar Ridge**[114] 461 4-9-6 58 (bt) ChrisCatlin 12 —
(D K Ivory) *sn pushed along in rr: bhd fr 1/2-way* **8/1**³
23-4 **13** 22 **Rosie Says No**[15] 2145 4-9-7 59 (p) ShaneKelly 9 —
(R M H Cowell) *sn outpcd and bhd: eased fnl 3f* **10/3**¹
1m 16.47s (-0.03) **Going Correction** -0.075s/f (Stan)
WFA 3 from 4yo+ 8lb 13 Ran SP% **126.8**
Speed ratings (Par 101): **97,90,87,86,85 81,78,77,76,76 72,60,31**
toteswinger: 1&2 £19.80, 1&3 £29.00, 2&3 £44.10 CSF £119.62 CT £1796.87 TOTE £12.60: £3.40, £5.10, £4.40; EX 152.70.
Owner S R Bowring **Bred** S R Bowring **Trained** Edwinstowe, Notts
FOCUS
A very moderate handicap with recent winning form very much thin on the ground, and it was rendered even less competitive when the favourite Rosie Says No found herself tailed off before reaching the end of the back straight.
Virtuality(USA) Official explanation: vet said filly bled from the nose
Rosie Says No Official explanation: trainer had no explanation for the poor form shown

2580 LADIES DAY AT SOUTHWELL 16 AUGUST H'CAP 1m 4f (F)
4:45 (4:45) (Class 6) (0-60,59) 4-Y-0+ **£2,388** (£705; £352) **Stalls** Low

Form RPR
2625 **1** **Dancing Lyra**[14] 2155 8-9-1 56 TonyHamilton 14 67
(R A Fahey) *hld up: hdwy 1/2-way: led 2f out: rdn clr fnl f* **9/1**
5350 **2** 5 **Jackie Kiely**[13] 2182 8-9-1 56 (t) PhillipMakin 10 59
(R Brotherton) *s.i.s: hld up: hdwy over 3f out: rdn to chse wnr fnl f: no imp* **9/2**²
3 1 ¼ **Champagne Cocktail (IRE)**[13] 4408 8-8-9 50 ShaneKelly 6 51
(R J Price) *chsd ldr tl led 1/2-way: rdn and hdd over 2f out: no ex fnl f* **28/1**
-320 **4** ½ **Greenbelt**[11] 2233 8-8-13 54 ChrisCatlin 9 54
(G M Moore) *prom: led over 2f out: sn rdn and hdd: no ex fnl f* **15/2**
-511 **5** 1 **World Of Choice (USA)**[32] 1654 4-9-4 59 (b) DaleGibson 3 58
(M W Easterby) *hld up: hdwy u.p over 3f out: styd on same pce fnl 2f* **7/2**¹
3204 **6** 5 **Gayanula (USA)**[32] 1654 4-8-7 55 (p) BMcHugh(7) 2 46
(Miss J A Camacho) *chsd ldrs: rdn over 4f out: wknd over 3f out* **11/1**
6002 **7** 1 ½ **Debdene Bank (IRE)**[13] 2182 6-9-4 59 GeorgeBaker 8 47
(Mrs Mary Hambro) *chsd ldrs: rdn and wknd over 3f out* **15/2**
4/0- **8** 6 **Red**[50] 88 5-7-13 45 AmyBaker(5) 11 24
(Mrs S J Humphrey) *s.s: hld up: hdwy over 5f out: wknd 4f out* **40/1**
0044 **9** 11 **Speagle (IRE)**[13] 2182 7-8-2 46 AndrewMullen(3) 5 7
(A J Chamberlain) *hld up: hdwy over 4f out: wknd over 3f out* **14/1**
-646 **10** 2 ½ **Classical Rhythm (IRE)**[13] 2183 4-8-9 50 PatCosgrave 12 7
(J R Boyle) *hld up: rdn and wknd over 3f out* **7/1**
0-66 **11** 8 **Smetana**[91] 744 4-8-4 45 (v¹) SilvestreDeSousa 1 —
(E J Creighton) *led to 1/2-way: wknd 4f out* **66/1**
0/2- **12** 33 **Munching Mike (IRE)**[472] 277 6-8-4 50 AndreaAtzeni(5) 13 —
(K M Prendergast) *sn outpcd and bhd* **6/1**³
2m 40.29s (-0.71) **Going Correction** -0.075s/f (Stan) 12 Ran SP% **123.1**
Speed ratings (Par 101): **99,95,94,94,93 90,89,85,78,76 71,49**
toteswinger: 1&2 £12.00, 1&3 £23.00, 2&3 £21.70 CSF £50.72 CT £1124.13 TOTE £9.20: £2.70, £2.00, £5.50; EX 49.90.
Owner Aidan J Ryan Racing **Bred** Shadwell Estate Company Limited **Trained** Musley Bank, N Yorks
FOCUS
An ordinary middle-distance handicap, but a decent early pace meant that it became a good test of stamina and the front five pulled clear.
World Of Choice(USA) Official explanation: jockey said gelding boiled over in preliminaries

2581 SOUTHWELL RACECOURSE FOR CONFERENCES H'CAP 5f (F)
5:15 (5:15) (Class 6) (0-60,60) 3-Y-O **£2,047** (£604; £302) **Stalls** High

Form RPR
2024 **1** **Simple Rhythm**[14] 2162 3-9-4 60 TPQueally 2 68
(J G Given) *led 1f: chsd ldr tl led 2f out: rdn out* **4/1**²
-602 **2** 1 ½ **Cavitie**[10] 2265 3-8-10 52 TravisBlock 3 55
(Andrew Reid) *hld up: hdwy 1/2-way: rdn to chse wnr over 1f out: r.o* **5/1**³
4050 **3** 7 **Bold Account (IRE)**[7] 2355 3-8-1 50 (p) LauraPike(7) 5 27
(Garry Moss) *sn outpcd: styd on fr over 1f out: nvr trbld ldrs* **20/1**
5-00 **4** 2 ½ **Transcentral**[21] 1969 3-8-10 59 PaulPickard(7) 9 27
(W M Brisbourne) *sn outpcd: rdn and hung lft 1/2-way: nvr nrr* **20/1**
00-3 **5** 1 ½ **Lady Zena**[15] 2132 3-8-4 46 oh1 (b¹) DaleGibson 8 9
(M W Easterby) *s.s: outpcd: nvr nrr* **14/1**
005- **6** hd **Equinity**[180] 7542 3-9-1 57 JerryO'Dwyer 4 19
(J Pearce) *chsd ldrs: rdn 1/2-way: sn wknd* **10/1**
2442 **7** ¾ **Rocket Ruby**[14] 2162 3-8-12 54 NCallan 6 14
(D Shaw) *chsd ldrs: rdn over 3f out: hung lft and wknd over 1f out* **5/2**¹
2044 **8** ¾ **Fashion Icon (USA)**[10] 2265 3-8-13 55 PhillipMakin 7 12
(T D Barron) *sn outpcd* **15/2**
-556 **9** ½ **Time Loup**[21] 1949 3-8-4 46 oh1 (bt) FrankieMcDonald 10 1
(S R Bowring) *prom: rdn 1/2-way: sn wknd* **33/1**
5-66 **10** 5 **Dedante**[125] 316 3-8-13 55 (b) ChrisCatlin 1 —
(D K Ivory) *led 4f out: rdn and hdd 2f out: sn wknd* **8/1**
59.97 secs (0.27) **Going Correction** 0.0s/f (Stan) 10 Ran SP% **116.3**
Speed ratings (Par 97): **97,94,83,79,77 76,75,74,73,65**
toteswinger: 1&2 £4.60, 1&3 £15.70, 2&3 £16.50 CSF £23.59 CT £356.79 TOTE £5.30: £1.80, £1.90, £5.10; EX 28.20 Place 6: £437.18, Place 5: £413.56.
Owner Elite Racing Club **Bred** P Quinlan **Trained** Willoughton, Lincs
FOCUS
A very moderate sprint handicap and only four of these had tasted success before. All the action unfolded down the centre of the track and the early pace was very strong.
T/Jkpt: Not won. T/Plt: £549.50 to a £1 stake. Pool: £71,380.03. 94.82 winning tickets. T/Qpdt: £80.90 to a £1 stake. Pool: £4,407.79. 40.30 winning tickets. CR

2114 CAPANNELLE (R-H)
Tuesday, June 2

OFFICIAL GOING: Soft

2586a PREMIO ALESSANDRO PERRONE (LISTED RACE) (FILLIES) 5f 110y
3:10 (12:00) 2-Y-O **£27,184** (£11,961; £6,524; £3,262)

RPR
1 **Cool Contest (IRE)** 2-8-11 GBietolini 5 94
(R Brogi, Italy)
2 2 **Joanna (IRE)**[16] 2-8-11 DVargiu 4 87
(B Grizzetti, Italy) **11/20**¹
3 1 ¼ **Kaspirit (IRE)**[22] 1939 2-8-11 FrancisNorton 1 83
(M Wigham) *a cl up on rails: 3rd and rdn over 1f out: kpt on steadily* **14/5**²
4 3 **Kadabra (IRE)** 2-8-11 URispoli 7 73
(F & L Camici, Italy)
5 hd **Exotic Girl (IRE)** 2-8-11 PAragoni 6 72
(A Peraino, Italy)
6 dist **Jasmin Noir (USA)** 2-8-11 CFiocchi 3 —
(R Menichetti, Italy)
68.90 secs (68.90) 6 Ran SP% **90.8**
(Including 1 Euro stake): WIN 5.77; PL 1.72, 1.29; SF 12.24.
Owner Locsot **Bred** Locsot S R L **Trained** Italy

NOTEBOOK
Kaspirit(IRE), who got off the mark on fast going at Yarmouth last month, seemed to handle this very different ground and earned black type in the process.

TABY (R-H)

Tuesday, June 2

OFFICIAL GOING: Good

2587a STOCKHOLMS STORA PRIS (GROUP 3) 1m 1f 153y

8:05 (8:05) 4-Y-O+ £48,373 (£21,988; £10,554; £7,036; £4,398)

RPR

1 **Appel Au Maitre (FR)**16 5-9-2 FJohansson 3 101
(Wido Neuroth, Norway) *mid-div: cl 6th on outside st: rdn and hdwy 1 1/2f out: led ins fnl f: rdn clr: r.o (exact SP 56/100)* **11/20**1

2 1 **Peas And Carrots (DEN)**14 6-9-2 MSantos 13 99
(L Reuterskiold Jr, Sweden) *in rr early: mid-div at 1/2-way: hdwy on outside 1 1/2f out: chsd wnr fnl f: kpt on but nvr able to chal* **4/1**2

3 1 **Luca Brasi (FR)**14 5-9-2 (b) ManuelMartinez 2 97
(F Castro, Sweden) *led tl ins fnl f: one pce* **36/5**3

4 1 **Alpacco (IRE)**30 7-9-2 LennartHammer-Hansen 4 95
(F Reuterskiold, Sweden) *chsd ldr: dropped bk to 4th over 3f out: 2nd st on ins: chal wl over 1f out: ev ch 1f out: one pce* **68/1**

5 hd **Smart Enough**326 3921 6-9-2 RSchistl 8 95
(F Reuterskiold, Sweden) *hld up in last pl: gd hdwy fr 1/2-way to go 3rd: 4th st: ev ch appr fnl f: one pce* **15/2**

6 2 **Quilboquet (BRZ)**14 6-9-2 FDiaz 5 91
(L Reuterskiold Jr, Sweden) *cl up in 3rd early: last st: sme late hdwy* **46/1**

7 nk **Dan Tucket**16 4-9-2 JacobJohansen 11 90
(B Olsen, Denmark) *a mid-div* **33/1**

8 ½ **Volo Cat (FR)**16 5-9-2 CarlosLopez 12 89
(B Olsen, Denmark) *mid-div: hdwy to press ldr 4f out: 3rd st: sn btn* **34/1**

9 1 **Fricoteiro (ARG)**16 6-9-2 (b) EspenSki 1 87
(Niels Petersen, Norway) *mid-div: slipped through on ins to be 5th st: sn wknd* **52/1**

10 hd **Maybach**14 8-9-2 P-AGraberg 14 87
(Lars Bexell, Sweden) *a towards rr* **23/1**

11 4 **Hotel Du Cap**256 6073 6-9-2 MadeleineSmith 10 79
(Madeleine Smith, Sweden) *a in last two* **45/1**

2m 1.60s (121.60) 11 Ran SP% **126.1**
(including one krona stakes): WIN 1.56; PL 1.08, 1.22, 1.52; DF 4.54.
Owner Stall Perlen **Bred** Gilles & Aliette Forien **Trained** Norway

2388 AYR (L-H)

Wednesday, June 3

OFFICIAL GOING: Good to firm (10.0) changing to firm (good to firm in places) after race 5 (4.20)

Wind: Breezy, half behind Weather: Hot, sunny

2588 EUROPEAN BREEDERS' FUND VICTOR CHANDLER MAIDEN STKS 6f

2:20 (2:20) (Class 4) 2-Y-O £5,018 (£1,493; £746; £372) Stalls Low

Form RPR

2 1 **Flying Statesman (USA)**20 2017 2-9-3 0 PaulHanagan 3 90+
(R A Fahey) *t.k.h early: mde all: pushed out fnl f: comf* **2/5**1

2 1½ **Layali Al Andalus** 2-9-3 0 GregFairley 1 85+
(M Johnston) *trckd ldrs: effrt over 2f out: kpt on fnl f: improve* **6/1**3

02 3 2¾ **Fantastic Prince**11 2280 2-9-3 0 JoeFanning 4 75
(P F I Cole) *cl up: rdn over 2f out: edgd lft over 1f out: no ex fnl f* **9/2**2

4 4½ **Paradise Spectre** 2-8-12 0 MartinLane(5) 2 62
(K R Burke) *dwlt: sn prom: rdn over 2f out: wknd wl over 1f out* **33/1**

6060 5 38 **Island Express (IRE)**4 2467 2-8-12 0 (p) AnnStokell(5) 5 —
(Miss A Stokell) *in tch: struggling 1/2-way: eased whn no ch* **100/1**

1m 11.6s (-2.00) **Going Correction** -0.30s/f (Firm) 5 Ran SP% **107.8**
Speed ratings (Par 95): **101,99,95,89,38**
CSF £3.14 TOTE £1.30: £1.10, £2.50; EX 2.90.
Owner Hazel Tattersall & G Hyde **Bred** Skymarc Farm And Castlemartin Stud **Trained** Musley Bank, N Yorks

FOCUS
The ground was reported to be very fast and, despite the stalls being placed against the far rail, the runners raced more towards the centre of the track. This race was won last year by the subsequent Gimcrack winner Shaweel and four years ago by Amadeus Wolf, who went on to win the same race at York before taking the Middle Park. Whether any of these will reach those heights remains to be seen, but there is certainly plenty more to come from the front pair.

NOTEBOOK
Flying Statesman(USA) had finished a very promising runner-up in a decent York maiden on debut last month and was sent off a short-priced favourite to go one better. Soon in front though it hadn't been the plan to make the running, he travelled very nicely and only needed to be shaken up entering the last half-furlong in order to assert. His breeding suggests that another furlong won't be a problem and he looks well worth a try in something better now. (tchd 4-9 and 1-2 in a place)
Layali Al Andalus ♦, a 60,000gns colt out of a useful winner at up to 1m2f, represented the yard that had taken two of the last four runnings of this race. Having attracted some market support on-course late on, he was inclined to race rather green once underway, but also showed plenty of ability and made sure that the favourite wasn't allowed to take things easy. With this experience under his belt, he looks a sure-fire winner before too long and should also improve as he goes up in trip. (op 8-1)
Fantastic Prince, who improved for a faster surface when only just beaten at Newmarket last time, was fairly weak in the market and though he was close enough from the start, he could never make much impression on the first two. He was up against a couple of decent prospects, but should be well up to winning an ordinary event. (op 7-2)
Paradise Spectre, despite fluffing the start and ending up well held, did show some ability in the middle of the contest. A 42,000gns half-brother to a winning juvenile sprinter, he ought to improve for the experience and should be able to find an ordinary maiden.
Island Express(IRE), already exposed as moderate, was firmly put in his place from an early stage. Official explanation: jockey said colt hung right throughout and had a breathing problem (op 80-1)

2589 CALL VICTOR CHANDLER 08000 78 78 78 H'CAP 7f 50y

2:50 (2:51) (Class 4) (0-85,85) 4-Y-O+ £4,727 (£1,406; £702; £351) Stalls Low

Form RPR

6051 1 **Esoterica (IRE)**6 2391 6-9-2 80 6ex (v) DanielTudhope 4 96
(J S Goldie) *hld up in tch: hdwy to ld over 1f out: rdn clr* **5/2**1

0-05 2 4½ **Ezdeyaad (USA)**9 2313 5-8-13 77 PJMcDonald 8 81
(G A Swinbank) *prom on outside: hdwy to ld over 2f out: hdd over 1f out: nt pce of wnr* **9/2**3

65-0 3 3½ **Zabeel Tower**9 2313 6-8-1 72 (p) JamieKyne(7) 2 67
(R Allan) *trckd ldrs: rdn over 2f out: no ex over 1f out* **12/1**

-526 4 3¼ **Jewelled Dagger (IRE)**17 2101 5-9-7 85 (b) PhillipMakin 5 71
(I Semple) *led to over 2f out: wknd over 1f out* **3/1**2

6-00 5 2¼ **Al Wasef (USA)**18 2071 4-8-1 68 KellyHarrison(3) 6 48
(J S Goldie) *hld up: rdn 3f out: edgd rt over 1f out: nvr able to chal* **18/1**

3302 6 nk **Gap Princess (IRE)**23 1923 5-8-6 70 PaulHanagan 7 49
(R A Fahey) *t.k.h: in tch: rdn over 2f out: wknd over 1f out* **11/2**

5500 7 7 **My Gacho (IRE)**31 1699 7-9-2 80 (b) GregFairley 3 40
(M Johnston) *rrd in stalls: chsd ldr: rdn over 3f out: wknd over 2f out* **8/1**

1m 28.55s (-4.85) **Going Correction** -0.55s/f (Hard) 7 Ran SP% **111.2**
Speed ratings (Par 105): **105,99,95,92,89 89,81**
CSF £13.22 CT £105.46 TOTE £2.90: £1.30, £3.20; EX 14.60.
Owner Mrs S E Bruce **Bred** A Lyons Bloodstock **Trained** Uplawmoor, E Renfrews

FOCUS
A fair handicap and a demonstration of just how fast the ground was with the winning time only 0.33 seconds outside the course record, despite the early pace not appearing that strong. The runners edged out towards the centre of the track on reaching the home straight. A clear personal best at face value from the winner.

2590 VICTORCHANDLER.COM FILLIES' H'CAP 1m

3:20 (3:23) (Class 5) (0-70,68) 4-Y-O+ £3,238 (£963; £481; £240) Stalls Low

Form RPR

6214 1 **Salerosa (IRE)**4 2473 4-9-2 63 PaulHanagan 3 68+
(Mrs A Duffield) *cl up: led 2f out: kpt on wl fnl f* **6/5**1

603- 2 ½ **Pantherii (USA)**354 3030 4-8-13 60 JoeFanning 6 64
(P F I Cole) *led to 2f out: rallied: kpt on same pce wl ins fnl f* **14/1**

-200 3 1¼ **Society Music (IRE)**11 2261 7-9-4 65 (p) PhillipMakin 2 66
(M Dods) *trckd ldrs: effrt wl over 1f out: kpt on same pce fnl f* **9/2**2

60-3 4 nk **Willyn (IRE)**6 2390 4-8-2 52 KellyHarrison(3) 4 52
(J S Goldie) *hld up: effrt and rdn over 1f out: kpt on fnl f: no imp* **5/1**3

0066 5 ¾ **Grethel (IRE)**5 2442 5-7-12 52 BillyCray(7) 1 51
(A Berry) *prom on ins: stmbld bdly after 3f: outpcd over 2f out: no imp fnl f* **25/1**

0-46 6 ¾ **Papa's Princess**9 2314 5-8-10 57 DanielTudhope 8 54
(J S Goldie) *w ldr: drvn over 2f out: wknd ent fnl f* **8/1**

0000 7 1¼ **Dorn Dancer (IRE)**9 2312 7-9-0 68 JamieKyne(7) 5 62
(D W Barker) *hld up: smooth hdwy on outside and cl up 2f out: rdn and wknd appr fnl f* **14/1**

5-50 8 25 **Milton Of Campsie**130 281 4-8-10 64 ThomasWhite(7) 7 1
(S Parr) *s.s: wl bhd: lost tch fnl 3f* **33/1**

1m 41.58s (-2.22) **Going Correction** -0.30s/f (Firm) 8 Ran SP% **111.5**
Speed ratings (Par 100): **99,98,97,96,96 95,94,69**
toteswinger: 1&2 £2.30, 1&3 £1.90, 2&3 £5.90 CSF £19.38 CT £57.04 TOTE £2.00: £1.30, £1.90, £1.50; EX 14.40.
Owner David K Barker **Bred** Pedro Rosas **Trained** Constable Burton, N Yorks

FOCUS
This moderate fillies' handicap was run at an average pace. The form makes sense and the winner is progressing.
Grethel(IRE) Official explanation: jockey said mare clipped heels on bend leaving back straight
Milton Of Campsie Official explanation: jockey said filly missed the break

2591 VICTOR CHANDLER H'CAP 5f

3:50 (3:52) (Class 3) (0-90,90) 4-Y-O+ £7,641 (£2,273; £1,136; £567) Stalls Low

Form RPR

4236 1 **Rothesay Dancer**12 2228 6-8-1 73 KellyHarrison(3) 6 81
(J S Goldie) *hld up in tch: smooth hdwy to ld ins fnl f: shkn up and r.o strly* **5/1**

050- 2 1¼ **Cute Ass (IRE)**235 6653 4-9-2 90 MartinLane(5) 1 94+
(K R Burke) *dwlt: sn cl up: led 2f out to ins fnl f: kpt on: nt pce of wnr* **10/3**2

0560 3 nk **Haajes**11 2259 5-9-0 83 (t) PJMcDonald 5 85
(J Balding) *prom: effrt and swtchd rt over 1f out: kpt on u.p fnl f* **8/1**

4460 4 1¼ **Bo McGinty (IRE)**18 2071 8-8-7 76 (v) PaulHanagan 2 74
(R A Fahey) *w ldr: rdn over 2f out: kpt on same pce fnl f* **4/1**3

5520 5 ½ **First Order**11 2259 8-8-7 80 ow1 (v) AnnStokell(5) 4 77
(Miss A Stokell) *prom: effrt and edgd lft over 1f out: one pce fnl f* **12/1**

3603 6 nk **Discanti (IRE)**8 2363 4-8-8 77 (t) DavidAllan 7 72
(T D Easterby) *led to 2f out: no ex fnl f* **2/1**1

57.48 secs (-2.62) **Going Correction** -0.30s/f (Firm) 6 Ran SP% **111.9**
Speed ratings (Par 107): **108,106,105,103,102 102**
toteswinger: 1&2 £4.10, 1&3 £8.30, 2&3 £4.50 CSF £21.65 TOTE £5.80: £2.20, £2.10; EX 26.60.

Owner Highland Racing **Bred** Frank Brady **Trained** Uplawmoor, E Renfrews
■ Stewards' Enquiry : David Allan caution: used whip down shoulder in forehand position

FOCUS
A tight and decent handicap and they went a fierce pace with Discanti and Bo McGinty eyeballing each other from the start, but they merely cut each other's throats and set the race up for the winner.

NOTEBOOK
Rothesay Dancer found these conditions much more suitable than the heavy ground she encountered at Haydock last time and for a mare who probably appreciates a stiffer track, the strong early pace was also ideal. Having been held up in a detached last early, she arrived there on the bridle towards the inside of the track as the early leaders folded and was skilfully nursed home from that point. She may turn out again in the Scottish Sprint Consolation event at Musselburgh on Saturday. (tchd 4-1 and 11-2)
Cute Ass(IRE), slipping down the weights having been very highly tried in her younger days, has gone well fresh before so the eight-month absence wouldn't necessarily have been a problem. Close to the pace throughout, she took over in front inside the last 2f as the pace-setters started to feel the heat but had no response to the winner. This was still more like it and she seems to be nearing the sort of mark she can win off. (op 5-1 tchd 3-1)
Haajes, now 2lb lower than for his last two wins, stayed on well from off the pace once switched out wide, but his best turf form has come on easier ground. (tchd 15-2)
Bo McGinty(IRE), 4lb lower than for his last win just under a year ago, didn't help himself by getting involved in the early speed duel, but remains capable off this mark when the race is run to suit. (tchd 7-2 and 9-2)
First Order, out of his depth in a conditions event last time but a decent second off this mark at Newmarket prior to that, had his chance and was close enough entering the last furlong, but couldn't find much when put under maximum pressure. (op 9-1)

Discanti(IRE) was taken on for the lead but remains perfectly capable of winning off this sort of mark on quick ground when able to dominate on his own. (op 15-8 tchd 9-4)

2592 GMC CORSEHILL H'CAP — 1m 7f
4:20 (4:20) (Class 6) (0-60,60) 4-Y-0+ — £2,266 (£674; £337; £168) Stalls Low

Form — RPR

0433 **1** **Holoko Heights**[12] 2233 4-9-2 **58**......(p) GregFairley 7 — 65
(N J Vaughan) *hld up: niggled 1/2-way: gd hdwy to ld over 2f out: hung lft: hld on wl fnl f* — **2/1**[1]

-505 **2** *nk* **Fistral**[9] 2337 5-7-13 **48**...... JamieKyne(7) 8 — 55
(P D Niven) *prom: hdwy and ev ch over 2f out: kpt on ins fnl f* — **7/2**[3]

/000 **3** *9* **Millagros (IRE)**[21] 1738 9-8-10 **52** ow2...... PhillipMakin 5 — 47
(I Semple) *in tch: hdwy to chse ldrs 2f out: outpcd fnl f* — **12/1**

00-3 **4** *1 1/2* **Always Best**[5] 2448 5-8-4 **46**...... PJMcDonald 4 — 39
(R Allan) *pressed ldr: led over 3f out to over 2f out: edgd lft and wknd appr fnl f* — **7/1**

600- **5** *7* **Kyber**[94] 7293 8-8-12 **59**...... GaryBartley(5) 6 — 43
(J S Goldie) *hld up: drvn 3f out: nvr able to chal* — **11/4**[2]

/00- **6** *3 1/2* **Phoenix Nights (IRE)**[11] 4739 9-7-11 **46** oh1...... BillyCray(7) 2 — 26
(A Berry) *bhd: rdn and hung lft 3f out: nvr on terms* — **100/1**

4000 **7** *7* **Admiral (IRE)**[11] 2262 8-8-11 **60**......(tp) ThomasWhite(7) 1 — 31
(S Parr) *led to over 3f out: sn wknd* — **16/1**

000- **8** *11* **Firestorm (IRE)**[208] 4924 5-8-1 **46** oh1......(b) KellyHarrison(3) 3 — 2
(C W Fairhurst) *hld up: hdwy to chse ldrs 1/2-way: wknd over 2f out* — **66/1**

3m 18.68s (-1.72) **Going Correction** -0.30s/f (Firm) — **8** Ran SP% **110.8**
Speed ratings (Par 101): **92,91,87,86,82 80,76,71**
toteswingers: 1&2 £2.90, 1&3 £6.60, 2&3 £8.90 CSF £8.61 CT £59.18 TOTE £3.00: £1.40, £1.80, £2.50; EX 8.50.

Owner Owen Promotions Limited **Bred** Owen Promotions Ltd **Trained** Helshaw Grange, Shropshire

FOCUS
A weak staying handicap containing a couple of complete no-hopers, but with Admiral soon tearing off into a clear lead the pace was solid enough and they finished well spread out. The form is not solid and the winner probably did not have to improve.

Firestorm(IRE) Official explanation: jockey said gelding had a breathing problem

2593 CALL VICTOR CHANDLER 08000 78 78 78 H'CAP — 6f
4:50 (4:53) (Class 6) (0-60,55) 3-Y-0 — £2,266 (£674; £337; £168) Stalls Low

Form — RPR

0-20 **1** **Asserting**[15] 2154 3-8-11 **55**...... BillyCray(7) 1 — 59
(J A McShane) *prom: drvn over 2f out: led over 1f out: styd on wl* — **8/1**

4-0 **2** *1* **Salgrev (IRE)**[38] 1548 3-8-3 **47**...... JamieKyne(7) 5 — 48
(Irene J Monaghan, Ire) *bhd and outpcd: hdwy over 1f out: styd on to go 2nd towards fin: nt rch wnr* — **9/1**

0-45 **3** *1/2* **What A Fella**[15] 2154 3-8-11 **48**...... PhillipMakin 11 — 47
(Mrs A Duffield) *t.k.h early: led tl edgd lft and hdd over 1f out: one pce fnl f* — **4/1**[1]

0536 **4** *3/4* **Pedregal**[33] 1644 3-8-8 **45**...... DanielTudhope 8 — 42
(J S Goldie) *bhd: hdwy over 1f out: kpt on fnl f: nrst fin* — **4/1**[1]

5006 **5** *nse* **Missed Mondays**[16] 2132 3-8-3 **45**...... LanceBetts(5) 10 — 42
(Patrick Morris) *cl up: effrt and ev ch 2f out: one pce fnl f* — **14/1**

6006 **6** *hd* **Honey Berry (IRE)**[11] 2265 3-8-3 **45**......(v) DeanHeslop(5) 3 — 41
(Patrick Morris) *dwlt: in tch: effrt 2f out: one pce fnl f* — **50/1**

604 **7** *3/4* **Cry Of Truth (IRE)**[26] 1852 3-9-0 **51**...... PJMcDonald 2 — 45
(D W Barker) *w ldrs tl no ex over 1f out* — **13/2**[3]

-660 **8** *1* **Meydan Groove**[12] 2234 3-8-3 **45**...... MartinLane(5) 6 — 36
(R Johnson) *prom: outpcd over 1f out: n.d after* — **9/2**[2]

00-0 **9** *9* **Hettie Hubble**[29] 1769 3-8-13 **55**...... AmyRyan(5) 9 — 17
(D W Thompson) *trckd ldrs tl wknd fr 2f out* — **20/1**

0-50 **10** *1/2* **Iron Max (IRE)**[18] 2070 3-8-13 **50**...... GregFairley 7 — 10
(N J Vaughan) *cl up tl wknd over 2f out* — **8/1**

1m 11.08s (-2.52) **Going Correction** -0.30s/f (Firm) — **10** Ran SP% **117.1**
Speed ratings (Par 97): **104,102,102,101,100 100,99,98,86,85**
toteswinger: 1&2 £13.20, 1&3 £7.60, 2&3 £8.50 CSF £78.12 CT £341.60 TOTE £10.20: £3.00, £2.90, £1.60; EX 77.00.

Owner Lothian Recycling Limited **Bred** Bolton Grange **Trained** Dalkeith, Midlothian

■ John McShane's first winner.
■ Stewards' Enquiry : Billy Cray five-day ban: used whip with excessive frequency (June 17-21)

FOCUS
The going was officially changed to firm, good to firm in places prior to this very moderate sprint for 3yos. There was no real bias with the draw and the form looks sound but limited.

Iron Max(IRE) Official explanation: jockey said gelding ran too free

2594 VICTORCHANDLER.COM APPRENTICE H'CAP — 1m 1f 20y
5:20 (5:20) (Class 6) (0-60,60) 4-Y-0+ — £2,266 (£674; £337; £168) Stalls Low

Form — RPR

3-12 **1** **Joe Jo Star**[25] 145 7-8-9 **57**...... LeeTopliss(7) 8 — 71
(R A Fahey) *t.k.h: w ldr: led 1/2-way: edgd lft over 2f out: clr over 1f out: eased nr fin* — **2/5**[1]

656- **2** *5* **Darfour**[298] 4851 5-9-5 **60**...... AmyRyan 4 — 63
(J S Goldie) *led 1f: chsd ldrs: outpcd over 2f out: rallied to chse wnr ins fnl f: no imp* — **7/2**[2]

60-4 **3** *1 1/4* **Beaumont Boy**[15] 2155 5-8-10 **51**......(b) BillyCray 5 — 51
(J A McShane) *trckd ldrs: effrt over 2f out: one pce over 1f out* — **12/1**[3]

0 **4** *1 1/2* **Oh Landino (GER)**[31] 1692 4-8-3 **49**...... AdamCarter(5) 1 — 46
(P Monteith) *hld up: pushed along over 3f out: no imp fr 2f out* — **50/1**

060 **5** *2 1/2* **Bumble Rose (IRE)**[19] 2030 6-8-9 **50**......(p) LanceBetts 6 — 41
(A G Foster) *trckd ldrs: drvn and outpcd 4f out: n.d after* — **50/1**

000- **6** *1/2* **Dolly No Hair**[239] 6560 4-9-0 **55**...... JamieKyne 2 — 45
(D W Barker) *t.k.h: led after 1f: hdd 1/2-way: wknd over 2f out* — **25/1**

1m 56.37s (-2.03) **Going Correction** -0.30s/f (Firm) — **6** Ran SP% **109.1**
Speed ratings (Par 101): **97,92,91,90,87 87**
toteswinger: 1&2 £1.50, 1&3 £2.00, 2&3 £1.60 CSF £1.86 CT £3.71 TOTE £1.50: £1.10, £1.60; EX 2.10 Place 6: £23.67 Place 5: £19.24.

Owner The Ipso Facto Syndicate **Bred** B J And Mrs Crangle **Trained** Musley Bank, N Yorks

■ The first winner for Lee Topliss.

FOCUS
A very moderate contest run at a modest early tempo.

T/Plt: £42.90 to a £1 stake. Pool: £46,643.86. 793.16 winning tickets. T/Qpdt: £16.90 to a £1 stake. Pool: £2,969.60. 129.80 winning tickets. RY

[1726] KEMPTON (A.W) (R-H)
Wednesday, June 3

OFFICIAL GOING: Standard
Wind: Moderate, half against Weather: Cloudy

2595 TURFTV MEDIAN AUCTION MAIDEN STKS — 5f (P)
6:20 (6:22) (Class 6) 2-Y-0 — £2,047 (£604; £302) Stalls High

Form — RPR

5 **1** **Fleeting Echo**[13] 2207 2-8-12 0...... RichardHughes 4 — 68
(R Hannon) *pressed ldr: chal over 1f out: rdn to ld jst ins fnl f: grad asserted* — **11/4**[1]

20 **2** *3/4* **I'Malwaysright (IRE)**[7] 2383 2-9-3 0......(b[1]) RobertHavlin 8 — 70
(D R C Elsworth) *led: clr w wnr fr 1/2-way: hdd jst ins fnl f: hld last 100yds* — **5/1**[2]

00 **3** *7* **Duke Of Rainford**[9] 2335 2-9-3 0......(t) RichardKingscote 11 — 45
(Ian Williams) *in tch: rdn to chse clr ldng pair 2f out: no imp* — **9/1**

4 **4** *2 1/4* **Khanivorous**[26] 1835 2-9-3 0...... PatCosgrave 6 — 37+
(J R Boyle) *dwlt: nvr gng pce of ldrs: struggling fr 1/2-way: kpt on fr over 1f out* — **11/4**[1]

5 *1* **One Hit Wonder** 2-9-3 0...... NeilChalmers 9 — 33
(Mouse Hamilton-Fairley) *s.s: t.o in last pair after 2f: kpt on fr over 1f out: nrst fin* — **12/1**

6 *2 3/4* **Dixi Heights** 2-8-12 0...... AlanMunro 7 — 18
(J R Boyle) *outpcd: t.o in last pair after 2f: modest late prog* — **12/1**

4 **7** *1/2* **Back On**[10] 2295 2-8-12 0...... MarkFlynn(5) 1 — 22
(G C Bravery) *chsd ldrs to 1/2-way: sn struggling: hanging and wknd over 1f out* — **33/1**

0 **8** *1* **Vadition (IRE)**[20] 2007 2-8-12 0...... LPKeniry 10 — 13
(J J Bridger) *a struggling to go the pce: no ch sn after 1/2-way* — **25/1**

9 *5* **Sapphire Spirit (USA)** 2-9-3 0...... SteveDrowne 5 — —
(J R Best) *chsd ldng pair to 2f out: wknd u.p* — **6/1**[3]

61.52 secs (1.02) **Going Correction** +0.075s/f (Slow) — **9** Ran SP% **116.5**
Speed ratings (Par 91): **94,92,81,78,76 72,71,69,61**
toteswinger: 1&2 £3.10, 1&3 £5.90, 2&3 £24.10 CSF £16.82 TOTE £3.50: £1.50, £1.70, £3.00; EX 15.40.

Owner P J & Mrs J P Haycock **Bred** P J Haycock **Trained** East Everleigh, Wilts

FOCUS
Little to get excited about on previous form shown and it was two with experience who soon had this between them.

NOTEBOOK
Fleeting Echo left her previous effort behind when she was tardy at the stalls and had the pace to move over from a moderate draw here. She always had the leader in her sights and given the stamina in her pedigree this was a fair performance over a sharp track and it was only a matter of time before she nosed ahead. (op 5-1)

I'Malwaysright(IRE), in blinkers for the first time, was soon dominating but was a nice target for the winner. He didn't appear to get home last time over six and this sharp five played to his strengths. (op 9-2 tchd 11-2)

Duke Of Rainford was having his third, run but never had the pace to cope with the first two and should be suited by 6f when the nurseries start. (tchd 12-1)

Khanivorous has some scope and gave the impression this quick five isn't what he wants. He was slightly more tuned in than on debut but was beaten further this time by I'malwaysright and is another that might be interesting when 6f nurseries come along. (op 10-3 tchd 5-2)

One Hit Wonder ◆ ran an most encouraging debut. Green and slow from the stalls he was still last inside the final 2f but really quickened and while never a threat will be of interest in a race of this calibre next time. Although there is plenty of pace in his pedigree, another furlong would help.
Official explanation: jockey said colt missed the break (op 14-1)

Dixi Heights was another that got going late but needs a stiffer test. (op 8-1)

2596 DIGIBET.COM H'CAP — 5f (P)
6:50 (6:52) (Class 5) (0-70,70) 3-Y-0+ — £2,590 (£770; £385; £192) Stalls High

Form — RPR

-010 **1** **Garstang**[49] 1285 6-9-10 **65**......(b) GeorgeBaker 7 — 83
(J Balding) *trckd ldr after 1f: pushed into ld jst over 1f out: shkn up and sn drew clr* — **10/1**

0550 **2** *4 1/2* **Silver Prelude**[25] 1877 8-9-9 **64**...... RichardHughes 11 — 65
(S C Williams) *led: clr w wnr 2f out: hdd jst over 1f out: tired but hld on for 2nd* — **7/2**[1]

2350 **3** *3/4* **Bluebok**[14] 2180 8-9-9 **64**......(bt) LPKeniry 2 — 63
(J M Bradley) *chsd ldrs but nvr on terms: pushed along 1/2-way: styd on fnl f to take 3rd nr fin* — **14/1**

4-40 **4** *nk* **Mac's Power (IRE)**[36] 1592 3-9-8 **70**......(t) RobertHavlin 3 — 68
(P J O'Gorman) *chsd ldng pair over 3f out: rdn and nt on terms 2f out: no imp after: lost 3rd nr fin* — **8/1**

0-00 **5** *1* **Monsieur Reynard**[16] 2124 4-9-5 **60**......(p) AdamKirby 12 — 54
(J M Bradley) *hld up in abt 5th: checked 3f out: pushed along over 1f out: nvr nr ldrs: ch of pl last 100yds: fdd* — **7/1**

0135 **6** *3/4* **Orpen's Art (IRE)**[12] 2219 4-9-7 **62**...... WilliamBuick 6 — 53
(S A Callaghan) *wl off the pce towards rr: rdn 2f out: brief effrt over 1f out: one pce* — **9/2**[2]

6510 **7** *nk* **Circle Dance (IRE)**[8] 2359 4-9-9 **64**......(v) JimCrowley 9 — 54
(D Shaw) *nvr on terms w ldrs: abt 8th 1/2-way: plugged on fnl f but no real prog* — **6/1**[3]

300 **8** *nk* **After The Show**[12] 2228 8-9-8 **63**......(b[1]) MartinDwyer 10 — 52
(Rae Guest) *s.i.s: a wl in rr: rdn over 2f out: no real prog* — **13/2**

-303 **9** *1 1/4* **Multahab**[22] 1957 10-9-5 **60**......(t) SaleemGolam 4 — 45
(M Wigham) *dwlt: wl in rr: nvr on terms w ldrs* — **25/1**

6340 **10** *7* **Fizzlephut (IRE)**[8] 2349 7-9-0 **55**......(p) PaulFitzsimons 5 — 14
(Miss J R Tooth) *chsd wnr 1f: sn lost pl and struggling: wknd over 1f out* — **25/1**

-110 **11** *65* **The Magic Blanket (IRE)**[22] 1970 4-9-11 **66**...... MickyFenton 8 — —
(Stef Liddiard) *awkward s: a in last trio: no ch whn lost action over 1f out and virtually p.u* — **8/1**

60.49 secs (-0.01) **Going Correction** +0.075s/f (Slow)
WFA 3 from 4yo+ 7lb — **11** Ran SP% **126.2**
Speed ratings (Par 103): **103,95,94,94,92 91,90,90,88,77** —
toteswinger: 1&2 £10.80, 1&3 £20.50, 2&3 £13.40 CSF £48.37 CT £518.86 TOTE £11.20: £3.70, £1.80, £5.20; EX 70.10.

Owner The Foulrice Twenty **Bred** Mrs S E Barclay **Trained** Scrooby, Notts

FOCUS
Some old sweats in competition here.

The Magic Blanket(IRE) Official explanation: jockey said gelding lost its action

2597 DIGIBET REDFERN H'CAP 1m 2f (P)

7:20 (7:22) (Class 3) (0-95,95) 4-Y-O+

£7,352 (£2,201; £1,100; £551; £274; £138) Stalls High

Form RPR

1- 1 **Covert Ambition**[230] 6762 4-9-6 **94**........................ TedDurcan 1 111+
(Saeed Bin Suroor) *settled in abt 7th: clsd on ldrs over 2f out: drvn ahd jst over 1f out: styd on wl* **9/2**[1]

6-02 2 1 ¾ **Rattan (USA)**[13] 2197 4-8-11 **85**........................ SebSanders 11 96
(Rae Guest) *trckd ldng quartet: effrt on inner wl over 1f out: styd on to take 2nd jst ins fnl f: no imp on wnr* **15/2**[3]

0/1 3 nk **Bugaku**[13] 2211 4-8-12 **86**........................ RyanMoore 10 96+
(Sir Michael Stoute) *rousted along early to rch midfield early: lost pl and struggling in 10th 3f out: prog over 1f out: styd on to take 3rd fnl f: nrst fin* **9/2**[1]

1-34 4 3 ¼ **Humble Opinion**[60] 1117 7-9-2 **90**........................ RichardHughes 13 94
(A King) *trckd ldng pair: effrt on inner to ld briefly over 1f out: wknd ins fnl f* **8/1**

2-01 5 nk **Dark Prospect**[15] 2150 4-8-11 **85**........................ PhilipRobinson 14 88+
(M A Jarvis) *restless stalls: led at decent pce but pestered thrght: hanging lft bnd 2f out: hdd over 1f out: wknd last 150yds* **11/2**[2]

1010 6 2 ¾ **Brouhaha**[35] 1603 5-8-11 **85**........................ RichardKingscote 5 83
(Tom Dascombe) *trckd ldng quartet: u.p and wdst of all bnd 2f out: wknd over 1f out* **14/1**

-552 7 ¾ **Trans Siberian**[30] 1750 5-8-11 **85**........................ MartinDwyer 4 81
(P F I Cole) *t.k.h early: trckd ldng pair: rdn on outer over 2f out: fdd over 1f out* **9/1**

1-60 8 ½ **Paktolos (FR)**[42] 1458 6-9-3 **91**........................(b) ShaneKelly 2 86
(A King) *stdd s: hld up in last no prog u.p 3f out: passed wkng rivals fnl f* **25/1**

5300 9 nk **Grand Passion (IRE)**[33] 1642 9-9-7 **95**........................ GeorgeBaker 12 90
(C F Wall) *hld up in last pair: nvr a factor: shkn up and no real prog over 2f out* **16/1**

1311 10 2 ½ **Ahlawy (IRE)**[61] 1107 6-9-2 **90**........................(bt) JimmyFortune 9 80
(F Sheridan) *dwlt: wl in rr: off the pce in 9th and rdn 3f out: no prog* **9/1**

-623 11 ½ **Encircled**[46] 1348 5-9-0 **88**........................ AdamKirby 7 77
(J R Jenkins) *hld up in rr: sme prog 3f out: cl enough and gng wl enough over 2f out: rdn over 1f out: wknd tamely* **20/1**

2/0- 12 ½ **Kevkat (IRE)**[37] 6459 8-9-5 **93**........................ ChrisCatlin 3 81
(D E Pipe) *a in rr: rdn in last trio over 3f out: btn after* **66/1**

0-10 13 4 **Invasian (IRE)**[29] 1779 8-8-4 **78**........................ WilliamBuick 8 58
(P W D'Arcy) *pressed ldr fr s: drvn over 2f out: wknd wl over 1f out: eased* **40/1**

2m 7.50s (-0.50) **Going Correction** +0.075s/f (Slow) **13 Ran SP% 119.7**
Speed ratings (Par 107): **105,103,103,100,100 98,97,97,97,95 94,94,91**
toteswinger: 1&2 £4.70, 1&3 £5.30, 2&3 £4.60 CSF £36.68 CT £163.43 TOTE £6.70: £2.60, £2.80, £1.30; EX 33.60.
Owner Godolphin **Bred** Cyril Humphris **Trained** Newmarket, Suffolk

FOCUS
A competitive handicap with several potential improvers.

NOTEBOOK
Covert Ambition was rated 94 after running away with a weak 1m2f maiden at Nottingham last October. He showed immaturity on his debut, but was much more tuned in here, and got himself into the race well. He will benefit from a step up in trip. As befits a Godolphin inmate, he has a fine pedigree. His sire is multiple Group 1 winner Singspiel and his dam won the Yorkshire Oaks. He has precautionary entries for the Hardwicke and Irish St Leger and, while those are light years away from this, he could be interesting in a race like the Duke of Edinburgh Handicap at Royal Ascot. (op 5-1 tchd 11-2)
Rattan(USA) was well-suited by this step up from a mile and was tight for room up the straight. He'll go up for this, having been beaten off 1lb lower last time, but looked well suited by the surface. (op 11-2 tchd 5-1)
Bugaku was struggling to go the pace. He had to do much more than when winning a modest maiden at Sandown last time. This course and distance looked too sharp and another couple of furlongs will help him. (tchd 5-1)
Humble Opinion has been lightly raced since winning a year ago off a 4lb higher mark. He has been off for nearly two months since his last run, but had no excuses. (op 10-1)
Dark Prospect was up 8lb for winning a lesser handicap by a neck at Leicester last time. In this class he couldn't dictate as he was taken on by Invasian. (op 5-1 tchd 6-1)
Brouhaha was happier back on this surface after a dismal turf effort, but the handicapper has his measure. (op 16-1)
Paktolos(FR) came through beaten horses and looks better over an extra 2f. (op 20-1)

2598 DIGIBET CASINO H'CAP 7f (P)

7:50 (7:51) (Class 6) (0-65,65) 4-Y-O+ £2,047 (£604; £302) Stalls High

Form RPR

002 1 **Sweet Gale (IRE)**[44] 1413 5-9-1 **59**........................ FrankieMcDonald 6 73
(Mike Murphy) *dwlt: sn rcvrd to midfield: smooth prog fr 3f out: led over 1f out: rdn and steadily drew away* **14/1**

04-0 2 2 ¾ **Art Market (CAN)**[35] 1606 6-9-0 **58**........................ IanMongan 2 65
(Miss Jo Crowley) *pressed ldr: rdn to ld over 2f out to over 1f out: kpt on but no ch w wnr fnl f* **33/1**

0-54 3 ½ **Cativo Cavallino**[7] 2382 6-9-2 **63**........................ NataliaGemelova(3) 12 68
(J E Long) *hld up towards rr: rdn and prog on outer fr over 2f out: kpt on to take 3rd ins fnl f: no imp after* **10/1**

-002 4 ½ **Munich (IRE)**[35] 1606 5-8-12 **61**........................ AndreaAtzeni(5) 9 65
(Norma Twomey) *hld up in last urged along and prog fr 2f out: rchd 4th ins fnl f: kpt on but nvr able to chal* **4/1**[2]

204 5 1 ¾ **Convallaria (FR)**[47] 1320 6-9-3 **61**........................(b) AlanMunro 13 60
(C F Wall) *settled in last quartet: rdn and prog fr 2f out: chsd ldrs 1f out: one pce after* **9/2**[3]

5255 6 ½ **Takitwo**[35] 1606 6-9-0 **58**........................(v) SimonWhitworth 11 56
(P D Cundell) *hld up wl in rr: effrt against far rail 2f out: kpt on steadily but nt pce to threaten ldrs* **10/1**

0-40 7 nse **Fifty (IRE)**[13] 2203 4-9-4 **62**........................ RichardHughes 8 60
(R Hannon) *chsd ldng pair: u.p over 2f out: stl chsng ldrs over 1f out: 3rd briefly ins fnl f: wknd* **10/1**

05-6 8 6 **Gold Again (USA)**[49] 1285 4-9-3 **61**........................(t) AdamKirby 10 42
(W R Swinburn) *in tch in midfield: hrd rdn and struggling over 2f out: n.d after: wknd fnl f* **11/4**[1]

0-00 9 1 ¾ **Onenightinlisbon (IRE)**[124] 344 5-9-3 **61**........................ PatCosgrave 4 38
(J R Boyle) *trckd ldrs: rdn and lost pl jst over 2f out: wknd over 1f out* **33/1**

3236 10 1 ¾ **Ever Cheerful**[60] 1121 8-9-4 **62**........................(p) SteveDrowne 3 34
(A B Haynes) *led at decent pce to over 2f out: wknd over 1f out* **25/1**

00- 11 1 **Sweet Kiss (USA)**[186] 7490 4-9-0 **58**........................ KirstyMilczarek 14 27
(M J Attwater) *trckd ldrs: rdn and stl cl up 2f out: wknd* **16/1**

4300 12 ¾ **Salt Of The Earth (IRE)**[9] 2330 4-9-7 **65**........................ JimmyFortune 5 32
(T G Mills) *chsd ldrs on outer: rdn 1/2-way: losing pl and struggling over 2f out* **16/1**

6-0 13 3 ¼ **Sawpit Sunshine (IRE)**[29] 1775 4-8-11 **60**........................ JackDean(5) 7 19
(J L Spearing) *a wl in rr and struggling bef 1/2-way: wl bhd fnl 2f* **33/1**

1m 26.5s (0.50) **Going Correction** +0.075s/f (Slow) **13 Ran SP% 123.2**
Speed ratings (Par 101): **100,96,96,95,93 93,93,86,84,82 81,80,76**
toteswinger: 1&2 £89.80, 1&3 £22.90, 2&3 £60.70 CSF £426.54 CT £4896.05 TOTE £12.40: £3.60, £10.80, £3.20; EX 594.50.
Owner Ms L M Bartlett **Bred** Rozelle Bloodstock **Trained** Westoning, Beds

FOCUS
A tight handicap.

2599 EUROPEAN BREEDERS' FUND NOVICE STKS 6f (P)

8:20 (8:23) (Class 4) 2-Y-O £5,018 (£1,493; £746; £372) Stalls High

Form RPR

5 1 **Rumool**[11] 2280 2-8-12 0........................ SebSanders 7 85
(C E Brittain) *uns rdr and bolted bef s: cl up: wnt 2nd 1/2-way: hung lft to nr side rail 2f out: awkward hd carriage but in front by 1f out: drvn out* **3/1**[2]

43 2 1 ½ **Janeiro (IRE)**[11] 2260 2-9-0 0........................ RichardKingscote 6 81
(Tom Dascombe) *dwlt: t.k.h: hld up: trckd ldrs over 2f out: drvn and hanging lft over 1f out: passed original ldr ins fnl f but no imp wnr: hung lft last 100yds* **1/2**[1]

6310 3 4 ½ **Six Wives**[7] 2372 2-8-11 0........................ PatCosgrave 2 66
(A J McCabe) *mounted on crse: led: edgd lft fr over 2f out: lost ld by 1f out: wknd* **14/1**[3]

44 4 10 **Marosh (FR)**[20] 2000 2-8-7 0........................(p) AndreaAtzeni(5) 4 37
(R M H Cowell) *rring bef stalls opened: in tch tl wknd over 2f out* **20/1**

014 5 2 **Lucky Mellor**[23] 1927 2-9-0 0........................ ChrisCatlin 1 33
(D K Ivory) *plld hrd: pressed ldr to 1/2-way: sn wknd* **33/1**

0 6 1 ¼ **Mactrac**[13] 2201 2-8-12 0........................ RichardHughes 5 27
(R Hannon) *in tch tl wknd over 2f out* **16/1**

7 10 **Musical Delight** 2-8-5 0........................ MatthewDavies(7) 3 —
(A P Jarvis) *dwlt: sn t.o* **66/1**

1m 14.43s (1.33) **Going Correction** +0.075s/f (Slow) **7 Ran SP% 113.4**
Speed ratings (Par 95): **94,92,86,72,70 68,55**
toteswinger: 1&2 £1.20, 1&3 £3.40, 2&3 £2.40 CSF £4.74 TOTE £4.00: £1.80, £1.30; EX 6.80.
Owner Saeed Manana **Bred** Carl Holt **Trained** Newmarket, Suffolk

FOCUS
A fair novice event and there is probably plenty more to come from the front pair.

NOTEBOOK
Rumool is clearly a bit of a boy, but has ability. He was truculent coming out of the paddock and, when the race began in earnest, he looked, at the most charitable, to be extremely green. Hanging the full width of the track, he ended up on the stands' rail. He has an extremely awkward head carriage, but still managed to win. By a speedy sire, Exceed And Excel, he has stamina in his dam line, but it remains to be seen which way he goes mentally. (tchd 7-2)
Janeiro(IRE) had twice missed the break over 5f. The extra furlong, tried here for the first time, helped him but he had no chance with the winner. (op 8-13 tchd 8-11 in places)
Six Wives' win came in a claimer and, although this was a drop in class from her latest run when behind in a Listed contest, this first attempt at 6f didn't play to her strengths. She was left behind after making the running. (op 12-1 tchd 8-1)
Lucky Mellor pulls too hard. (op 20-1)
Mactrac still looks immature and needs further. (op 20-1 tchd 22-1)

2600 TURFTV H'CAP (LONDON MILE QUALIFIER) 1m (P)

8:50 (8:50) (Class 4) (0-80,80) 3-Y-O £4,727 (£1,406; £702; £351) Stalls High

Form RPR

64-1 1 **Love Pegasus (USA)**[119] 386 3-9-7 **80**........................ RoystonFfrench 5 96
(M Johnston) *trckd ldr: led over 2f out: shkn up and clr over 1f out: styd on wl: unchal* **5/1**[2]

-202 2 3 **Implication**[23] 1937 3-9-0 **73**........................ RyanMoore 12 82
(E A L Dunlop) *hld up in midfield: prog 3f out: chsd wnr wl over 1f out: styd on wl but no imp* **11/4**[1]

0625 3 6 **Wilbury Star (IRE)**[29] 1774 3-9-2 **75**........................ RichardHughes 2 70
(R Hannon) *pressed ldrs: rdn and outpcd over 2f out: plugged on fr over 1f out to take 3rd nr fin* **10/1**

60-6 4 ¾ **The Happy Hammer (IRE)**[40] 1490 3-8-6 **65**........................ MartinDwyer 14 58
(E V Stanford) *prom on inner: outpcd over 2f out: battled for 3rd fnl f* **66/1**

22-0 5 2 ¾ **Zebrano**[23] 1931 3-9-2 **75**........................ AlanMunro 1 62
(Miss E C Lavelle) *led after 50yds to over 2f out: lft bhd by ldng pair fr wl over 1f out: lost 3rd fnl f* **20/1**

3-52 6 hd **Bennelong**[22] 1963 3-9-7 **80**........................ SebSanders 9 67
(R M Beckett) *hld up last: stmbld over 3f out: prog on inner over 2f out: plugged on but nvr any ch* **15/2**

41- 7 1 **Emeebee**[155] 7823 3-9-1 **74**........................ ChrisCatlin 13 58+
(W J Musson) *led 50yds: t.k.h: heavily restrained and sn wl in rr: prog on inner 2f out: kpt on but nvr in the hunt* **6/1**[3]

00-0 8 1 ¼ **Sapphire Prince (USA)**[9] 2329 3-9-7 **80**........................ SteveDrowne 6 62
(J R Best) *nvr beyond midfield: u.p over 3f out: sn lft bhd by ldrs* **16/1**

1113 9 ¾ **Statute Book (IRE)**[64] 1056 3-9-2 **78**........................ DavidProbert(3) 10 58
(S Kirk) *a in rr: rdn and no prog over 2f out* **6/1**[3]

5-02 10 1 **Admiral Sandhoe (USA)**[25] 1895 3-9-0 **73**........................ JimCrowley 11 50
(Mrs A J Perrett) *t.k.h in midfield: rdn and no prog over 2f out: sn wknd* **16/1**

010- 11 6 **Dustry (IRE)**[237] 6603 3-8-13 **75**........................ PatrickHills(3) 7 39
(R Hannon) *chsd ldrs on outer tl wknd over 2f out* **33/1**

1-06 12 8 **Efficiency**[18] 2079 3-9-6 **79**........................ LPKeniry 4 24
(M Blanshard) *a towards rr: u.p on outer over 3f out: sn no ch* **20/1**

1-00 13 17 **Take The Micky**[9] 2329 3-9-2 **75**........................ ShaneKelly 8 —
(W J Knight) *dwlt: hld up wl in rr: wknd over 2f out: t.o* **20/1**

1m 39.3s (-0.50) **Going Correction** +0.075s/f (Slow) **13 Ran SP% 123.2**
Speed ratings (Par 101): **105,102,96,95,92 92,91,90,89,88 82,74,57**
toteswinger: 1&2 £3.70, 1&3 £7.90, 2&3 £10.60 CSF £18.36 CT £142.63 TOTE £7.80: £2.00, £1.80, £3.60; EX 20.40.
Owner M Doyle **Bred** Eaton Sales **Trained** Middleham Moor, N Yorks

FOCUS
A decent handicap and an impressive winner.

Take The Micky Official explanation: jockey said colt finished distressed

2601 WEATHERBYS BETTRENDS.CO.UK APPRENTICE H'CAP (ROUND 1) — 1m 4f (P)
9:20 (9:20) (Class 6) (0-65,65) 4-Y-O+ **£2,047** (£604; £302) **Stalls** Centre

Form RPR
0405 1 **Mixing**14 2182 7-8-8 **54** KierenFox(5) 8 62
(M J Attwater) *trckd ldng trio: reminder 5f out: prog to ld wl over 2f out: rdn and kpt on wl* 6/1³
0020 2 1 ½ **Rosy Dawn**12 2222 4-8-1 **47** DebraEngland(5) 6 53
(J J Bridger) *led to wl over 2f out: chsd wnr after: kpt on but no imp over 1f out* 28/1
200- 3 hd **Smooth As Silk (IRE)**273 5605 4-9-5 **65** RichardRowe(5) 14 70
(C R Egerton) *stdd s: hld up in last: prog on wl outside fr 5f out: urged along over 2f out: styd on to take 3rd over 1f out: nvr able to chal* 20/1
545 4 ½ **Everyman**28 1785 5-8-11 **52** MCGeran 2 56
(A W Carroll) *hld up towards rr: nt wl plcd on inner 3f out: eased to outer looking for run over 2f out: prog over 1f out: wnt 4th fnl f: nt rch ldrs* 9/1
2401 5 3 **Zalkani (IRE)**39 1533 9-9-3 **61** SimonPearce(3) 12 61
(J Pearce) *hld up towards rr: effrt over 2f out: sme prog over 1f out: bmpd along and nvr rchd ldrs* 5/2¹
050- 6 ¾ **Looping The Loop (USA)**244 6421 4-8-9 **50** JackDean 7 48
(J G Portman) *awkward s: t.k.h: hld up in abt 5th: drvn over 3f out: tried to cl on ldrs over 1f out: fdd ins fnl f* 10/1
-100 7 2 **Sky Quest (IRE)**35 1604 11-9-3 **63** NathanAlison(5) 13 58
(J R Boyle) *hld up in last quartet: effrt on inner 3f out: plugged on one pce: n.d* 12/1
362- 8 ¾ **Stormbeam (USA)**294 4991 4-9-10 **65** (t) AndreaAtzeni 1 59
(G A Butler) *hld up in last quartet: rdn and no prog 3f out: plugged on* 7/2²
0-40 9 ½ **Crimson Mitre**18 2068 4-9-9 **64** WilliamCarson 11 57
(J Jay) *trckd ldng pair to 3f out: stl 3rd wl over 1f out: sn wknd* 13/2
6563 10 1 ¼ **Jiminor Mack**33 1651 6-7-12 **46** oh1 (p) LeonnaMayor(7) 3 37
(W J H Ratcliffe) *dwlt: hld up in last quartet: taken wd in st and no real prog* 20/1
003- 11 2 **Star Of Pompey**384 2125 5-8-9 **55** AndrewHeffernan(5) 9 43
(A B Haynes) *hld up in abt 6th: rdn 3f out: wknd 2f out* 16/1
000- 12 3 **Templet (USA)**255 5415 9-8-2 **48** (b) JosephineBruning(5) 5 31
(T T Clement) *pressed ldr to 3f out: wknd rapidly wl over 1f out* 66/1
-000 13 47 **Sovietta (IRE)**93 734 8-8-2 **46** oh1 (tp) RossAtkinson(3) 4 —
(Ian Williams) *in tch tl wknd rapidly over 3f out: t.o* 20/1

2m 37.68s (3.18) **Going Correction** +0.075s/f (Slow) 13 Ran SP% **130.3**
Speed ratings (Par 101): **92,91,90,90,88 88,86,86,85,85 83,81,50**
toteswinger: 1&2 £39.70, 1&3 £31.60, 2&3 £73.80 CSF £180.11 CT £3222.11 TOTE £7.10: £1.90, £6.10, £10.70; EX 132.40 Place 6: £106.90 Place 5: £58.20.
Owner Canisbay Bloodstock **Bred** Juddmonte Farms **Trained** Epsom, Surrey
■ Stewards' Enquiry : Simon Pearce two-day ban: careless riding (Jun 21-22)

FOCUS
A race where it was difficult to come from off the pace.
T/Plt: £177.50 to a £1 stake. Pool: £62,719.88. 257.88 winning tickets. T/Qpdt: £32.00 to a £1 stake. Pool: £4,951.22. 114.30 winning tickets. JN

2160 NOTTINGHAM (L-H)
Wednesday, June 3
OFFICIAL GOING: Good to firm (firm in places; 8.4)
Wind: Almost nil Weather: Overcast

2602 BEST UK RACECOURSES ON TURFTV H'CAP — 6f 15y
2:10 (2:11) (Class 5) (0-70,70) 3-Y-O **£2,590** (£770; £385; £192) **Stalls** High

Form RPR
4504 1 **Volito**22 1969 3-8-11 **60** RichardKingscote 4 70
(Jonjo O'Neill) *chsd ldr: led over 1f out: sn rdn and hung rt: r.o wl* 10/1
60-0 2 4 **Oriental Rose**17 2102 3-9-7 **70** EddieAhern 6 67
(G M Moore) *led: rdn and hdd over 1f out: no ex ins fnl f* 28/1
060- 3 ¾ **Pure Rhythm**247 6342 3-8-6 **55** (t) SaleemGolam 15 50
(S C Williams) *chsd ldrs: shake up over 2f out: rdn and swtchd lft over 1f out: styd on same pce fnl f* 4/1²
4-62 4 hd **Rainy Night**15 2160 3-9-2 **68** RussellKennemore(3) 7 62
(R Hollinshead) *chsd ldrs: rdn over 1f out: styd on same pce* 9/4¹
-636 5 ½ **Red Rossini (IRE)**15 2160 3-9-7 **70** PatDobbs 11 63
(R Hannon) *hld up in tch: rdn over 1f out: styd on same pce* 6/1³
6014 6 nk **Bold Ring**8 2365 3-8-9 **58** EdwardCreighton 10 50
(E J Creighton) *hld up: rdn over 2f out: nt trble ldrs* 11/1
0-30 7 1 ¼ **Jimwil (IRE)**18 2070 3-9-4 **67** (b¹) TomEaves 12 55
(M Dods) *hld up: racd keenly: rdn over 1f out: swtchd lft ins fnl f: n.d* 10/1
40-6 8 nse **Layer Cake**36 1585 3-9-6 **69** SimonWhitworth 2 57
(J W Hills) *s.i.s: hld up: racd keenly: hdwy over 2f out: sn rdn: wknd ins fnl f* 16/1
05-0 9 2 ½ **Kyle Of Bute**34 1620 3-8-4 **53** DO'Donohoe 8 33
(J L Dunlop) *prom: rdn over 2f out: wknd over 1f out* 18/1
520- 10 16 **Chasing Amy**209 7205 3-9-1 **64** (b¹) ShaneKelly 13 —
(M G Quinlan) *slipped s: a in rr: wknd over 1f out* 20/1

1m 13.53s (-1.37) **Going Correction** -0.25s/f (Firm) 10 Ran SP% **110.9**
Speed ratings (Par 99): **99,93,92,92,91 91,89,89,86,64**
toteswinger: 1&2 £11.10, 1&3 £7.00, 2&3 £21.80 CSF £237.19 CT £1282.09 TOTE £9.60: £2.80, £4.00, £2.20; EX 169.90.
Owner Mrs Liz Brazier **Bred** A J And Mrs L Brazier **Trained** Cheltenham, Gloucs

FOCUS
A modest sprint handicap with the field reduced by five withdrawals and nothing got into the race from behind. A clear personal best from the winner.
Rainy Night Official explanation: jockey said colt was unsuited by the slow early pace
Chasing Amy Official explanation: jockey said filly slipped on leaving stalls and was slowly away

2603 TRENT BRIDGE MEDIAN AUCTION MAIDEN STKS — 5f 13y
2:40 (2:40) (Class 5) 3-4-Y-O **£2,590** (£770; £385; £192) **Stalls** High

Form RPR
20-2 1 **Musical Bridge**16 2122 3-9-0 75 JamieSpencer 4 71
(Mrs L Williamson) *sn led: hung lft thrght: reminders 1/2-way: hdd wl ins fnl f: rallied to ld nr fin* 9/4²
4-64 2 hd **Choisharp (IRE)**20 2005 3-8-9 62 AndreaAtzeni(5) 7 70
(M Botti) *chsd ldrs: pushed along 1/2-way: rdn to ld wl ins fnl f: hdd nr fin* 7/4¹
-4 3 2 ¼ **Intolerable (IRE)**16 2122 3-9-0 0 SebSanders 1 62
(R M Beckett) *chsd ldrs: pushed along 1/2-way: rdn over 1f out: styd on same pce ins fnl f* 9/4²
046 4 3 ¼ **Sandy Par**16 2122 4-9-2 58 (b) JackDean(5) 6 53
(J M Bradley) *dwlt: swtchd lft and hdwy 1/2-way: no ex fnl f* 25/1³
0-00 5 3 ½ **Shybutwilling (IRE)**13 2205 4-8-13 50 JackMitchell(3) 3 36
(Mrs P N Dutfield) *chsd ldrs: rdn 1/2-way: wknd over 1f out* 25/1³
000 6 ½ **Captain Peachey**18 2080 3-9-0 40 TGMcLaughlin 8 36
(B R Millman) *chsd wnr tl rdn 3f out: wknd over 1f out* 25/1³
6400 7 6 **Cindy Incidentally**15 2162 3-8-9 45 TomEaves 5 9
(Miss Gay Kelleway) *plld hrd and prom: stdd and lost pl 4f out: wknd wl over 1f out* 80/1
6-00 8 nk **Lydia's Legacy**34 1628 4-8-13 38 LeeVickers(3) 2 —
(T J Etherington) *dwlt: sn pushed along: a in rr: wknd wl over 1f out* 50/1

59.60 secs (-1.40) **Going Correction** -0.25s/f (Firm)
WFA 3 from 4yo 7lb 8 Ran SP% **112.6**
Speed ratings (Par 103): **101,100,97,91,86 85,75,75**
toteswinger: 1&2 £1.90, 1&3 £1.50, 2&3 £1.40 CSF £6.14 TOTE £2.70: £1.10, £1.10, £1.10; EX 7.40.
Owner John Conway **Bred** John Starbuck **Trained** Saighton, Cheshire

FOCUS
A weak sprint maiden, and sound but limited form.

2604 EUROPEAN BREEDERS' FUND MAIDEN FILLIES' STKS — 5f 13y
3:10 (3:10) (Class 5) 2-Y-O **£3,885** (£1,156; £577; £288) **Stalls** High

Form RPR
42 1 **White Daffodil (IRE)**16 2135 2-9-0 0 PatDobbs 4 68+
(R Hannon) *racd in 4th but off the pce and pushed along: rdn over 1f out: r.o wl ins fnl f to ld post* 11/4²
3 2 hd **Velvet Band**14 2175 2-9-0 0 NCallan 6 67
(P F I Cole) *chsd clr ldr: rdn over 1f out: edgd lft ins fnl f: r.o* 10/11¹
3 nk **Lady Royal Oak (IRE)** 2-8-9 0 AndreaAtzeni(5) 11 66+
(M Botti) *led and sn clr: edgd lft fr over 1f out: hdd post* 6/1³
3522 4 3 **Reel Credit Crunch**25 1884 2-8-7 0 AndrewHeffernan(7) 10 55
(I W McInnes) *chsd ldrs: rdn 1/2-way: hung lft over 1f out: styd on same pce* 12/1
0 5 1 ¼ **The Midshipmaid**25 1867 2-9-0 0 TGMcLaughlin 9 51
(Lucinda Featherstone) *dwlt: outpcd: r.o wl ins fnl f: nt rch ldrs* 100/1
6 shd **Raine Supreme** 2-9-0 0 SebSanders 8 50
(E S McMahon) *s.i.s: outpcd: r.o fnl f: nvr nrr* 20/1
7 1 ¾ **Val C** 2-9-0 0 LukeMorris 7 44
(N P Littmoden) *s.s: outpcd: rdn and hung lft 1/2-way: n.d* 22/1
5 8 2 ¾ **Miss Lauz**15 2161 2-9-0 0 RichardMullen 3 34
(R Hannon) *s.s: outpcd* 40/1
0 9 4 **Antique Diamond (IRE)**25 1866 2-9-0 0 NeilChalmers 2 20
(Lucinda Featherstone) *sn outpcd* 100/1
10 13 **Moonlight Babe (USA)** 2-9-0 0 TomEaves 1 —
(I W McInnes) *swvd lft s: a t.o* 50/1

60.97 secs (-0.03) **Going Correction** -0.25s/f (Firm) 10 Ran SP% **116.5**
Speed ratings (Par 90): **90,89,89,84,82 82,79,75,68,47**
toteswingers: 1&2 £1.70, 1&3 £2.80, 2&3 £2.40 CSF £5.31 TOTE £3.70: £1.10, £1.30, £1.30; EX 7.40.
Owner Knockainey Stud **Bred** Aston Mullins Stud & Knockainey Stud **Trained** East Everleigh, Wilts

FOCUS
Quite an interesting fillies' maiden with a couple hoping to build on earlier promise opposed by several newcomers with decent pedigrees. However, they went 20/1 bar four and that quartet dominated.

NOTEBOOK
White Daffodil(IRE), who made the running last time, could not go the early pace but picked up in the second half of the race and finished well to get to the front close home. A half-sister to four winners, including the smart Lady Links, she looks to be going the right way. (tchd 5-2 and 10-3)
Velvet Band had shown plenty of speed on her debut at Goodwood and as a result went off a hot favourite. She chased the leader from the start this time and gradually reeled her in but the winner got there just ahead of her. She should not be long in winning a race. (op 8-11 tchd evens in places)
Lady Royal Oak(IRE) ◆ showed tremendous early pace and for much of the way looked unlikely to be caught, but she drifted left as she got tired and was collared by the market leaders near the line. If she can repeat this sort of pace in future she should be able to win races. (op 12-1 tchd 14-1)
Reel Credit Crunch, the most experienced runner, was having her first start since being claimed out a seller. She too tried to chase the leaders but had nothing left in the last furlong and a half. (op 10-1)
Val C, out of a dual 6f juvenile winner and from the family of Qadar and Sheikh Albadou, reared as the stalls opened and missed the break but still showed ability despite tiring late on. (op 20-1 tchd 25-1)
Moonlight Babe(USA), Tom Eaves reported the filly hung left leaving the stalls. Official explanation: jockey said filly hung violently left on leaving stalls (op 100-1 tchd 150-1)

2605 RACING UK LIVE IN YOUR HOME H'CAP — 1m 6f 15y
3:40 (3:41) (Class 5) (0-70,70) 3-Y-O **£2,590** (£770; £385; £192) **Stalls** Low

Form RPR
0401 1 **Taste The Wine (IRE)**8 2350 3-8-12 **61** 6ex LukeMorris 1 74
(J S Moore) *dwlt: in rr and rn in snatches: hdwy over 3f out: rdn to chsd ldr over 1f out: styd on u.p to ld wl ins fnl f* 2/1¹
0-00 2 nk **Golden Games (IRE)**30 1747 3-8-6 **55** EddieAhern 11 67
(J L Dunlop) *hld up: hdwy over 4f out: led over 2f out: sn rdn: hdd wl ins fnl f* 6/1³
0603 3 18 **Saffron's Son (IRE)**9 2340 3-8-2 **51** oh1 (v) FrankieMcDonald 7 38
(P T Midgley) *hld up: hdwy over 5f out: rdn and wknd over 2f out: wnt 3rd nr fin* 12/1
-565 4 ½ **Lombok**15 2152 3-9-4 **67** JamieSpencer 8 53+
(M L W Bell) *sn led: rdn over 4f out: hung rt and lft over 3f out: hdd over 2f out: sn wknd* 7/2²
-000 5 9 **Suitably Accoutred (IRE)**30 1724 3-8-2 **51** oh4 FrancisNorton 10 25
(Mrs A Duffield) *chsd ldrs: rdn: edgd lft and wknd over 2f out* 50/1
00-0 6 8 **Mountain Forest (GER)**43 1441 3-8-2 **51** oh2 NickyMackay 3 14
(H Morrison) *led early: chsd ldr: rdn over 3f out: hung rt and wknd over 2f out* 20/1
000- 7 21 **Just Dan**193 7424 3-8-7 **56** GrahamGibbons 9 —
(R Hollinshead) *s.i.s: hld up: last and rdn over 6f out: wknd over 4f out: eased* 33/1
10 8 19 **Clippity Clop (IRE)**43 1416 3-9-5 **68** ShaneKelly 4 —
(J A Osborne) *prom: chsd ldr 10f out: rdn over 5f out: wknd over 3f out: eased* 13/2

0105 9 *19* **Melange (USA)**^{13} [2204] 3-8-13 **62** .... NCallan 2 —
(P F I Cole) *prom: racd keenly: rdn over 6f out: wknd 5f out: eased* **13/2**

3m 4.91s (-0.09) **Going Correction** +0.125s/f (Good) **9** Ran SP% **113.9**
Speed ratings (Par 99): **105,104,94,94,89 84,72,61,50**
toteswinger: 1&2 £4.70, 1&3 £4.50, 2&3 £13.0 CSF £13.88 CT £112.30 TOTE £3.10: £1.10, £2.60, £2.50; EX 15.90.
Owner Jimmy & Susie Wenman **Bred** Trevor Reilly **Trained** Upper Lambourn, Berks

FOCUS
The longer trip in this staying handicap was an unknown for most of the runners and in the end only two truly lasted the trip, and they both came from off the pace. The first pair could have been rated higher.
Lombok Official explanation: jockey said colt hung left and right

2606 WEATHERBYS BLOODSTOCK INSURANCE CONDITIONS STKS 1m 75y
4:10 (4:10) (Class 2) 3-Y-0+
£12,462 (£3,732; £1,866; £934; £466; £234) **Stalls** Low

Form RPR

03-4 **1** **Khateeb (IRE)**^{25} [1875] 4-9-1 102 .... (t) RHills 1 109
(M A Jarvis) *mde all: rdn over 1f out: r.o* **11/4^{2}**

03/2 **2** *1 1/4* **Emmrooz**^{103} [642] 4-9-1 105 .... LDettori 4 106
(Saeed Bin Suroor) *chsd wnr tl over 6f out: wnt 2nd again 3f out: sn rdn: styd on* **6/5^{1}**

0000 **3** *3 3/4* **Docofthebay (IRE)**^{67} [997] 5-9-1 97 .... TPQueally 2 97
(J A Osborne) *s.s: hld up: hdwy over 2f out: rdn and hung lft fr over 1f out: no imp fnl f* **10/1**

460- **4** *8* **Dubai's Touch**^{242} [6476] 5-9-1 102 .... RoystonFfrench 5 79
(M Johnston) *chsd wnr over 6f out tl rdn 3f out: sn wknd* **5/1^{3}**

3160 **5** *1 1/2* **Elna Bright**^{26} [1821] 4-9-9 92 .... JamieSpencer 3 84
(P D Evans) *hld up in tch: rdn and wknd over 2f out* **40/1**

205- **6** *6* **Royal God (USA)**^{213} [7162] 4-9-1 105 .... TedDurcan 6 62
(Saeed Bin Suroor) *hld up: rdn over 3f out: sn wknd and eased* **10/1**

1m 44.75s (-0.85) **Going Correction** +0.125s/f (Good) **6** Ran SP% **109.4**
Speed ratings (Par 109): **109,107,104,96,94 88**
toteswingers: 1&2 £1.40, 2&3 £3.50, 1&3 not won. CSF £6.09 TOTE £3.30: £1.40, £1.40; EX 4.40.
Owner Hamdan Al Maktoum **Bred** Kilfrush Stud **Trained** Newmarket, Suffolk
■ Stewards' Enquiry : L Dettori one-day ban: used whip down shoulder in forehand position (Jun 21)

FOCUS
Often a strong conditions event and this year's running was another decent affair. It was steadily run and the winner looks the best guide.

NOTEBOOK
Khateeb(IRE) opened his account for the season at the second time of asking and registered a first win since scoring on his second outing last season. He pretty much had his own way out in front, which suits ideally, and proved more resolute than the runner-up inside the final furlong. The positive tactics over this sharper test worked the oracle and, while he has been held in Listed company twice before, now looks the time to try him in that grade again as he has improved from three to four. (op 5-2)
Emmrooz was representing a stable that sent out subsequent Group 1 winners Librettist and Dubai Destination to win on their seasonal return in this event in the past six years. An excellent second on his return from injury in Dubai 103 days earlier, he was unsurprisingly popular to go one better. Having raced handily early on, he was taken back going into the home turn, and the manner in which he eventually finished his race suggests he would have got closer under a more positive ride. He lacks any big-race entries and from his current mark events such as this should offer his best opportunity of success, but a stiffer test is likely what he now requires. (op 11-10 tchd 5-4 in a place)
Docofthebay(IRE), who has always looked happiest when racing in large fields, had the blinkers left off and fell out of the gates. The way in which he kept on without seriously threatening was much more encouraging than anything he has done of late, however, and he could have finished a bit closer had his rider been more vigorous in the final furlong. A return to Royal Ascot for the Hunt Cup, in which he finished second last term from a 6lb higher mark, now looks firmly on the cards. (tchd 9-1)
Dubai's Touch raced prominently on this return from his seasonal break and shaped as though the run was needed. He is not simple to place. (op 13-2 tchd 7-1)
Elna Bright made a positive move around 3f out, but his effort was short lived. He faced a nigh on impossible task at the weights, however, so was not disgraced. He holds an entry in a claimer next week. (op 28-1)
Royal God(USA) was making his debut for connections and was very much the stable's second string. He was never in the hunt from off the pace, and all of his best form has been with plenty of cut in the ground. The vet reported that the colt finished lame. Official explanation: vet said colt finished lame (op 18-1 tchd 25-1)

2607 WEATHERBYS BANK E B F FILLIES' H'CAP 1m 75y
4:40 (4:42) (Class 4) (0-85,80) 3-Y-0 **£4,201** (£4,201; £963; £481) **Stalls** Low

Form RPR

302- **1** **Suba (USA)**^{216} [7097] 3-9-3 **76** .... RHills 3 86+
(L M Cumani) *dwlt: hld up: hmpd over 3f out: hdwy over 2f out: rdn over 1f out: edgd lft and r.o u.p to join wnr on line* **6/1**

1-21 **1** *dht* **Charlotte Point (USA)**^{27} [1808] 3-9-7 **80** .... EddieAhern 7 86
(P F I Cole) *sn led: rdn over 1f out: styd on gamely: jnd post* **10/3^{1}**

150 **3** *1 1/2* **Burza**^{10} [2300] 3-8-5 **67** .... DavidProbert$^{(3)}$ 6 70
(J Mackie) *a.p: rdn over 2f out: styd on* **15/2**

0-14 **4** *hd* **At A Great Rate (USA)**^{13} [2189] 3-9-4 **77** .... TPQueally 1 79
(H R A Cecil) *a.p: chsd wnr over 1f out: sn rdn and ev ch: unable qck wl ins fnl f* **7/2^{2}**

6265 **5** *3/4* **Common Diva**^{12} [2248] 3-9-2 **75** .... AndrewMullen 4 75
(A J McCabe) *chsd wnr tl rdn over 1f out: styd on same pce* **12/1**

51-3 **6** *1 3/4* **Act Green**^{15} [2164] 3-9-3 **76** .... JamieSpencer 10 72+
(M L W Bell) *s.i.s hld up: swtchd lft and hdwy over 1f out: nt rch ldrs* **11/2^{3}**

-150 **7** *1 1/2* **Fong's Alibi**^{31} [1707] 3-8-12 **71** .... (p) LukeMorris 9 64
(J S Moore) *s.i.s: hld up: hung lft fr over 3f out: sn rdn: n.d* **40/1**

250- **8** *nse* **Damini (USA)**^{221} [6970] 3-8-8 **72** .... Louis-PhilippeBeuzelin$^{(5)}$ 5 65
(Sir Michael Stoute) *prom: rdn over 2f out: styd on same pce appr fnl f* **13/2**

3204 **9** *2* **Fesko**^{18} [2092] 3-9-6 **79** .... RoystonFfrench 2 67
(M Johnston) *hld up in tch: rdn over 2f out: wknd over 1f out* **14/1**

0-00 **10** *nk* **Cashleen (USA)**^{10} [2299] 3-8-13 **72** .... AdrianTNicholls 8 59
(K A Ryan) *hld up: hdwy over 4f out: sn rdn: wknd over 1f out* **40/1**

1m 46.44s (0.84) **Going Correction** +0.125s/f (Good) **10** Ran SP% **119.3**
Speed ratings (Par 98): **100,100,98,98,97 95,94,94,92,91**WIN: Charlotte Point £1.70, Suba £3.80 PL: CP £1.70 S £2.20 B £2.50.EX: CP/S £12.50, S/CP £10.50 CSF: CP/S £12.18, S/CP £13.49 TRI CP/S/Burza £70.35 S/CP/B £76.94 toteswinger: 1&2 £4.20, 1&3 £10.90, 2&3 £6.00 Trifecta £86.90 Part won. Pool of £235.13 -27 Owner.
Owner Sheikh Mohammed Obaid Al Maktoum **Bred** Darley **Trained** Newmarket, Suffolk

FOCUS
A couple of handicap debutantes from major yards added interest to this fair fillies' contest. It was quite steadily run but the form reads sound enough.
Act Green Official explanation: jockey said filly was denied a clear run

2608 "HANDS AND HEELS" APPRENTICE SERIES H'CAP 1m 2f 50y
5:10 (5:10) (Class 6) (0-60,61) 4-Y-0+ **£2,047** (£604; £302) **Stalls** Low

Form RPR

4/44 **1** **Murrumbidgee (IRE)**^{15} [2171] 6-8-8 **49** .... BarryAdams 11 60
(Mike Murphy) *hld up: hdwy over 2f out: styd on to ld post* **8/1**

6-66 **2** *nse* **Pretty Officer (USA)**^{6} [2420] 4-7-12 **47** .... NoelGarbutt$^{(8)}$ 3 58
(Rae Guest) *led 1f: chsd ldrs tl led again over 6f out: clr 5f out: shkn up over 1f out: hdd post* **4/1^{2}**

4/00 **3** *4* **Tivers Song (USA)**^{16} [2129] 5-8-4 **45** .... (b) SoniaEaton 7 48
(John A Harris) *hld up: hdwy over 3f out: shkn up over 1f out: edgd lft and no ex fnl f* **25/1**

0046 **4** *5* **Ruwain**^{40} [1496] 5-8-10 **51** .... TobyAtkinson 6 44
(P J McBride) *plld hrd: led 9f out: hdd 8f out: chsd ldr tl edgd rt and wknd over 1f out* **8/1**

3000 **5** *1 3/4* **Karmei**^{14} [2182] 4-8-4 **45** .... CharlesEddery 4 35
(R Curtis) *s.i.s: hld up: hdwy over 3f out: wknd wl over 1f out* **25/1**

603/ **6** *4* **Captain Oats (IRE)**^{653} [4660] 6-8-13 **54** .... DebraEngland 12 36
(Mrs P Ford) *s.i.s: hld up: pushed along over 3f out: n.d* **18/1**

3321 **7** *2 3/4* **Comrade Cotton**^{9} [2337] 5-9-3 **61** 6ex .... RyanPowell$^{(3)}$ 1 37
(J Ryan) *chsd ldrs: pushed along over 2f out: sn wknd* **10/3^{1}**

4-02 **8** *nk* **Lady Valentino**^{9} [2333] 5-8-12 **53** ow3 .... MJMurphy 9 28
(B D Leavy) *hld up in tch: wknd over 2f out* **8/1**

0000 **9** *1 1/4* **Dynamo Dave (USA)**^{14} [2182] 4-8-4 **45** .... (p) RichardRowe 13 18
(M D I Usher) *s.s: hld up: last whn stmbld bnd over 4f out: n.d* **25/1**

0000 **10** *hd* **Treetops Hotel (IRE)**^{37} [1556] 10-8-4 **45** .... AndrewHeffernan 5 18
(L R James) *chsd ldrs: pushed along 1/2-way: wknd over 3f out* **66/1**

2426 **11** *1* **Noah Jameel**^{21} [1983] 7-9-3 **58** .... DavidKenny 2 29
(A G Newcombe) *prom over 7f* **11/2^{3}**

0506 **12** *1/2* **Keen As Mustard**^{22} [1961] 4-8-4 **45** .... JohnCavanagh 10 15
(M D I Usher) *w ldrs: led 8f out: hdd over 6f out: wknd over 2f out* **28/1**

50/0 **13** *9* **Bernix**^{18} [2068] 7-8-11 **57** .... NoraLooby$^{(5)}$ 8 9
(N Tinkler) *hld up: a in rr: wknd over 3f out* **25/1**

2m 12.78s (1.08) **Going Correction** +0.125s/f (Good) **13** Ran SP% **117.4**
Speed ratings (Par 101): **100,99,96,92,91 88,85,85,84,84 83,83,76**
toteswinger: 1&2 £9.00, 1&3 £25.60, 2&3 £37.00 CSF £36.05 CT £776.02 TOTE £9.70: £3.20, £2.10, £9.80; EX 41.90 Place 6: £10.36 Place 5: £2.55.
Owner D J Ellis **Bred** R Warren **Trained** Westoning, Beds
■ Stewards' Enquiry : Debra England caution: entered wrong stall

FOCUS
A moderate hands-and-heels contest for apprentices and little better than a seller but another really close finish. The winner probably only had to match this year's form.
Karmei Official explanation: jockey said gelding hung right
T/Jkpt: Not won. T/Plt: £25.70 to a £1 stake. Pool: £53,149.27. 1,508.56 winning tickets. T/Qpdt: £2.80 to a £1 stake. Pool: £4,061.50. 1,054.80 winning tickets. CR

2568 RIPON (R-H)
Wednesday, June 3

OFFICIAL GOING: Good to firm (8.9)
Wind: light 1/2 against Weather: fine but very cool

2609 BOROUGHBRIDGE (S) H'CAP 1m 4f 10y
6:40 (6:40) (Class 6) (0-60,56) 4-5-Y-0 **£2,590** (£770; £385; £192) **Stalls** High

Form RPR

000- **1** **Promise Maker (USA)**^{210} [7189] 4-9-3 **55** .... GrahamGibbons 2 60
(T D Walford) *chsd ldr: led after 3f: qcknd over 3f out: edgd lft over 1f out: hld on wl* **11/2^{3}**

504 **2** *1* **Den Maschine**^{39} [1520] 4-9-2 **54** .... TomEaves 7 57
(Ollie Pears) *hld up in midfield: effrt over 3f out: hung rt and styd on same pce ins fnl f* **11/2^{3}**

00 **3** *3/4* **Beckenham's Secret**^{9} [2333] 5-8-2 **45** .... AmyBaker$^{(5)}$ 3 47
(A W Carroll) *hld up towards rr: effrt 3f out: kpt on wl fnl f* **40/1**

104- **4** *1 1/2* **Follow The Sun (IRE)**^{156} [6726] 5-9-4 **56** .... TonyHamilton 1 56
(Ronald O'Leary, Ire) *t.k.h in midfield: effrt over 3f out: kpt on same pce appr fnl f* **5/1^{2}**

-204 **5** *nk* **Art Value**^{12} [2222] 4-8-11 **49** .... FrancisNorton 4 48
(M Wigham) *trckd ldrs: t.k.h: drvn over 3f out: one pce fnl f* **3/1^{1}**

053- **6** *2 1/4* **Benayoun**^{15} [788] 5-8-10 **48** ow1 .... (b) NCallan 10 44
(B J Llewellyn) *trckd ldrs: drvn 4f out: wknd jst ins fnl f* **7/1**

15-0 **7** *shd* **Sorrento Moon (IRE)**^{12} [2233] 5-8-7 **45** .... SilvestreDeSousa 8 40
(G A Harker) *mid-div: drvn over 3f out: one pce fnl 2f* **11/2^{3}**

0301 **8** *13* **Al Azy (IRE)**^{15} [2172] 4-9-4 **56** .... StephenDonohoe 5 31
(D M Simcock) *led 3f: chsd ldrs: wknd 1f out: eased* **9/1**

4040 **9** *24* **Doctor Delta**^{122} [368] 4-8-7 **45** .... JimmyQuinn 6 —
(M Brittain) *in rr: drvn 6f out: lost pl over 2f out: bhd whn eased fnl f: t.o* **40/1**

2m 37.51s (0.81) **Going Correction** -0.05s/f (Good) **9** Ran SP% **115.2**
Speed ratings: **95,94,93,92,92 91,91,82,66**
toteswinger: 1&2 £54.60, 1&3 £54.60, 2&3 not won. CSF £35.67 CT £1083.03 TOTE £9.40: £2.30, £1.80, £7.60; EX 89.60.There was no bid for the winner. Den Maschine was subject to a friendly claim.
Owner Jamie Smith **Bred** Juddmonte Farms Inc **Trained** Sheriff Hutton, N Yorks
■ Stewards' Enquiry : Francis Norton two-day ban: used whip with excessive frequency and down the shoulder in the forehand position (Jun 21-22)

FOCUS
They went a sensible pace in this modest, if competitive selling handicap. Limited form, with the third out of the handicap.
Promise Maker(USA) Official explanation: trainer said, regarding apparent improvement in form, that the gelding was better suited by the step up in trip and had improved physically over the winter

2610 EURA AUDIT UK YORKSHIRE'S SMALL BUSINESS ACCOUNTANTS MAIDEN STKS 6f
7:10 (7:11) (Class 5) 2-Y-0 **£3,238** (£963; £481; £240) **Stalls** Low

Form RPR

3 **1** **Audacity Of Hope**^{20} [2000] 2-9-3 0 .... EdwardCreighton 8 75+
(P J McBride) *trckd ldrs: led 1f out: r.o strly: readily* **9/2^{3}**

2 **2** *1 1/4* **Rjeef (IRE)**^{13} [2195] 2-9-3 0 .... NCallan 5 69
(C E Brittain) *chsd ldrs: swtchd ins over 1f out: styd on to chse wnr ins fnl f: no imp* **6/4^{1}**

0 **3** 2¼ **Nave (USA)**[13] 2195 2-9-3 0 .... JoeFanning 6 63
(M Johnston) *w ldrs: led over 1f out: sn hdd and no ex* **5/1**
6 **4** ½ **Merseyside Star (IRE)**[13] 2195 2-9-3 0 .... AndrewElliott 1 61+
(K R Burke) *led: hung rt and hdd over 1f out: sn wknd* **7/2**[2]
6 **5** 4½ **Gold Story**[12] 2231 2-8-10 0 .... AnthonyBetts(7) 2 48
(B Ellison) *in rr: hdwy over 2f out: lost pl over 1f out* **25/1**
30 **6** ½ **Gentle Beat (IRE)**[35] 1610 2-9-3 0 .... TomEaves 9 46
(T D Easterby) *chsd ldrs: wknd over 1f out* **8/1**
0 **7** 2½ **As Brave As You (IRE)**[11] 2258 2-9-0 0 .... NeilBrown(3) 7 39
(B Ellison) *dwlt: a outpcd and in rr* **66/1**
8 5 **Meetings Man (IRE)** 2-9-3 0 .... TonyHamilton 3 24
(Micky Hammond) *in rr: bhd fnl 2f* **40/1**
0 **9** 3¾ **Dispol Antonio (IRE)**[17] 2099 2-9-3 0 .... JamieMoriarty 4 12
(P T Midgley) *uns rdr and rn loose to post: chsd ldrs: sn drvn along: lost pl over 2f out* **40/1**

1m 14.65s (1.65) **Going Correction** +0.125s/f (Good) **9** Ran SP% **118.4**
Speed ratings (Par 93): **94,92,89,88,82 82,78,72,67**
toteswinger: 1&2 £1.80, 1&3 £6.30, 2&3 £2.80 CSF £11.77 TOTE £5.20: £1.60, £1.30, £1.70; EX 7.70.
Owner Four Winds Racing **Bred** Wood Farm Stud (Waresley) **Trained** Newmarket, Suffolk
■ Stewards' Enquiry : N Callan one-day ban: failed to ride to draw (Jun 21)

FOCUS
Probably not a strong maiden but it was a truly-run affair and the form should work out.

NOTEBOOK
Audacity Of Hope delivered on the promise he'd shown in a small-field maiden at Newmarket last time with a cosy victory. A powerful-looking individual, he still looked green and wasn't helped by coming up the centre of the track, but having travelled well, he won a shade tidily. This is his trip, but he should get further in time. (op 3-1 tchd 5-1)
Rjeef(IRE) created a good impression on his Haydock debut and had the benefit of the rail this time. He looks one to keep on the right side of, but may have found this ground a bit too lively. (tchd 5-4)
Nave(USA), well backed, travelled well on ground he is bred to appreciate. He looks a promising colt and should win races in the near future. (op 8-1)
Merseyside Star(IRE) did the donkey work up front and just got run out of it in the closing stages. He is worth trying at this trip again. (op 5-1)

2611 RIPON FARM SERVICES H'CAP 6f
7:40 (7:40) (Class 4) (0-85,84) 3-Y-O **£5,180** (£1,541; £770; £384) **Stalls** Low

Form RPR
013- **1** **Mabait**[221] 6987 3-8-13 **76** .... NCallan 3 85+
(L M Cumani) *chsd ldrs: drvn along and outpcd over 3f out: styd on wl to ld 1f out: eased towards fin* **5/1**[3]
5511 **2** 1¼ **White Shift (IRE)**[10] 2299 3-8-13 **76** 6ex .... JimmyQuinn 2 84+
(P Howling) *t.k.h: trckd ldrs: nt clr run and swtchd wd over 1f out: r.o to take 2nd ins fnl f: no real imp* **9/2**[2]
0-54 **3** ½ **Tagula Breeze (IRE)**[19] 2049 3-9-2 **79** .... TomEaves 1 82
(I W McInnes) *hld up in rr: nt clr run over 2f out tl over 1f out: r.o fnl f* **17/2**
-221 **4** 1 **Bobbie Soxer (IRE)**[9] 2336 3-9-4 **81** 6ex .... TPO'Shea 4 81
(J L Dunlop) *chsd ldrs: led 2f out: hdd 1f out: fdd wl ins fnl f* **11/8**[1]
40-5 **5** 2½ **Fathey (IRE)**[30] 1736 3-8-7 **70** .... SilvestreDeSousa 5 62
(R A Fahey) *led over 1f: sn drvn: wknd jst ins fnl f* **5/1**[3]
4-10 **6** ¾ **Paddy Bear**[32] 1686 3-8-8 **71** .... TonyHamilton 7 61
(R A Fahey) *swvd rt s: hdwy and c stands' side to ld over 4f out: clr over 3f out: hdd 2f out: sn wknd* **20/1**
0-66 **7** 7 **Caranbola**[17] 2102 3-9-7 **84** .... JoeFanning 6 51
(M Brittain) *chsd ldrs: lost pl over 1f out* **28/1**

1m 13.52s (0.52) **Going Correction** +0.125s/f (Good) **7** Ran SP% **112.4**
Speed ratings (Par 101): **101,99,98,97,94 93,83**
toteswinger: 1&2 £1.60, 1&3 £3.60, 2&3 £5.50 CSF £26.52 TOTE £6.80: £2.80, £2.20; EX 32.60.
Owner Sheikh Mohammed Obaid Al Maktoum **Bred** L A C Ashby Newhall Estate Farm **Trained** Newmarket, Suffolk

FOCUS
A decent little sprint handicap run at a fair clip. The winner is progressing and the form is rated around the third.

2612 DIRECTORS CUP (HANDICAP STKS) 1m
8:10 (8:10) (Class 3) (0-95,94) 4-Y-O+ **£8,831** (£2,643; £1,321; £660; £329) **Stalls** High

Form RPR
4020 **1** **Benandonner (USA)**[46] 1352 6-9-7 **94** .... PaulHanagan 7 103
(R A Fahey) *trckd ldrs: led over 1f out: hld on wl* **6/1**[3]
400- **2** ½ **City Of The Kings (IRE)**[229] 6783 4-9-0 **87** .... SilvestreDeSousa 1 95
(G A Harker) *in rr: hdwy on outer over 2f out: kpt on wl fnl f* **25/1**
3-65 **3** ½ **Capucci**[39] 1507 4-8-5 **78** ....(t) GrahamGibbons 4 85
(J J Quinn) *in tch: hdwy over 3f out: kpt on wl fnl f* **5/1**[1]
122- **4** 1 **Acrostic**[279] 5425 4-9-7 **94** .... NCallan 5 98+
(L M Cumani) *hld up in midfield: nt clr run over 2f out and over 1f out: kpt on ins fnl f* **11/2**[2]
-004 **5** 1¾ **Ilie Nastase (FR)**[13] 2197 5-8-13 **86** .... StephenDonohoe 9 86
(D Nicholls) *hld up in midfield: effrt on inner and nt clr run over 2f out: swtchd lft over 1f out: kpt on* **6/1**[3]
1101 **6** 2 **Wovoka (IRE)**[18] 2073 6-8-10 **83** .... TonyHamilton 3 79
(D W Barker) *t.k.h in rr: hdwy and nt clr run over 2f out: plld wd over 1f out: kpt on: nvr on terms* **10/1**
4-42 **7** nk **Collateral Damage (IRE)**[39] 1524 6-8-6 **79** ....(t) DuranFentiman 10 74
(T D Easterby) *trckd ldrs: one pce whn nt clr run over 1f out* **8/1**
0064 **8** 1¾ **Kings Point (IRE)**[26] 1821 8-9-3 **90** .... AdrianTNicholls 8 81
(D Nicholls) *led tl over 6f out: chsd ldrs: n.m.r over 1f out: sn wknd* **7/1**
4463 **9** 1½ **Exit Smiling**[17] 2101 7-8-0 **80** .... PaulPickard(7) 6 68
(P T Midgley) *trckd ldrs: led over 6f out: qcknd clr over 3f out: hdd & wknd over 1f out* **17/2**
3050 **10** 1½ **Minority Report**[39] 1507 9-8-3 **76** .... FrancisNorton 2 60
(D Nicholls) *s.i.s: effrt and n.m.r over 2f out: nvr a factor* **17/2**

1m 39.41s (-1.99) **Going Correction** -0.05s/f (Good) **10** Ran SP% **118.2**
Speed ratings (Par 107): **107,106,106,105,103 101,100,99,97,96**
toteswinger: 1&2 £24.90, 1&3 £4.90, 2&3 £59.80 CSF £143.31 CT £828.56 TOTE £8.00: £2.70, £7.40, £2.40; EX 228.70.
Owner J C Parsons & Sinead Parsons **Bred** Gainsborough Farm Llc **Trained** Musley Bank, N Yorks

FOCUS
A competitive handicap, run at a decent pace in which there were a couple of hard-luck stories. Sound form.

NOTEBOOK
Benandonner(USA) justified the confidence under a well-judged ride. Always handy, he showed guts after taking it up on ground that would have been plenty quick enough, to gain his first turf victory for two years. He looks fairly treated on the pick of his form.
City Of The Kings(IRE) poses a question mark over the form. He had to drop into a claimer to win last year and this was a career-best effort. He should come on for the race. (op 28-1)
Capucci was a little one-paced in the closing stages and held every chance. The ground may have been a shade lively for him. (op 6-1)
Acrostic found traffic problems and was more than a shade unlucky. He was still full of running at the death. Progressive last season, he is a lightly-raced gelding who looks capable of landing a nice handicap or two this term. (op 6-1)
Ilie Nastase(FR) was not disgraced and continues to hold his form. (op 13-2 tchd 7-1)
Collateral Damage(IRE) was all dressed up with nowhere to go two furlongs out. His rider had no room on the rail and had to snatch him up, before pulling him wide, but he had lost momentum. This ground would have proved as lively as he wanted and once the ground eases, compensation awaits. (tchd 17-2)
Kings Point(IRE) Official explanation: jockey said horse was unsuited by the track

2613 FISHERGREEN MAIDEN STKS 1m 1f 170y
8:40 (8:44) (Class 5) 3-Y-O+ **£3,238** (£963; £481; £240) **Stalls** High

Form RPR
4-24 **1** **Dubai Echo (USA)**[19] 2030 3-8-11 82 .... NCallan 2 81
(Sir Michael Stoute) *mde all: qcknd over 3f out: drvn out: unchal* **5/2**[2]
2 2 **Interdiamonds** 3-8-6 0 .... JoeFanning 4 72
(M Johnston) *dwlt: t.k.h: sn trcking ldrs: wnt 2nd 4f out: kpt on ins fnl f: no imp* **11/1**[3]
0-32 **3** 4 **Merdaam**[18] 2082 3-8-11 80 .... TPO'Shea 7 69
(J L Dunlop) *chsd ldrs: drvn 4f out: one pce* **4/6**[1]
4 **4** 1½ **Bogula (IRE)**[8] 2364 3-8-6 0 .... JimmyQuinn 6 61
(Mrs A Duffield) *in rr: outpcd over 3f out: kpt on one pce fnl 2f* **50/1**
5 37 **Princess Aliuska**[50] 4-9-5 0 .... PaulMulrennan 1 —
(Mrs S Lamyman) *dwlt: tk fierce hold and sn w wnr: lost pl 3f out: sn bhd: eased: t.o* **100/1**

2m 4.92s (-0.48) **Going Correction** -0.05s/f (Good)
WFA 3 from 4yo 13lb **5** Ran SP% **99.8**
Speed ratings (Par 103): **99,97,94,93,63**
CSF £21.07 TOTE £3.40: £1.60, £2.60; EX 12.30.
Owner Saeed Suhail **Bred** Paradigm Thoroughbreds **Trained** Newmarket, Suffolk
■ Merchant Man and Acquavella were withdrawn (refused to enter stalls). No r4 deduction.

FOCUS
What looked on paper to be a competitive maiden turned into something of a cake-walk for Dubai Echo. He probably only had to match his Windsor form.
Merdaam Official explanation: trainer had no explanation for the poor form shown

2614 URE BANK H'CAP 2m
9:10 (9:11) (Class 5) (0-75,71) 4-Y-O+ **£3,238** (£963; £481; £240) **Stalls** Low

Form RPR
-641 **1** **Inchpast**[5] 2429 8-9-9 **69** 6ex ....(b) NCallan 5 76+
(M H Tompkins) *trckd ldrs: effrt 4f out: burst through to ld over 2f out: drvn rt out* **5/2**[1]
40-3 **2** ¾ **Jackday (IRE)**[11] 2262 4-8-10 **57** .... DuranFentiman 7 61
(T D Easterby) *hld up in rr: stdy hdwy 3f out: styd on wl to take 2nd wl ins fnl f* **4/1**[3]
/0-6 **3** ¾ **Terenzium (IRE)**[9] 2344 7-8-0 **51** oh5 ....(p) PatrickDonaghy(5) 4 54
(Micky Hammond) *trckd ldrs: led over 3f out tl over 2f out: styd on same pce* **20/1**
060- **4** 2½ **Spiders Star**[239] 6550 6-8-0 **53** oh6 ow2 .... PaulPickard(7) 6 53
(S G West) *dwlt: in rr: effrt on outside over 3f out: kpt on fnl 2f: nvr a real threat* **50/1**
-663 **5** ½ **Mister Pete (IRE)**[19] 2044 6-8-7 **60** .... JohnCavanagh(7) 3 59
(W Storey) *hld up in rr div: hdwy over 4f out: one pce fnl 2f* **9/2**
-101 **6** 10 **Herrera (IRE)**[11] 2262 4-9-10 **71** .... PaulHanagan 2 58
(R A Fahey) *hld up in midfield: drvn over 5f out: n.m.r over 3f out: lost pl over 1f out: eased* **7/2**[2]
-600 **7** 3 **Criterion**[20] 2018 4-9-10 **71** ....(p) StephenDonohoe 8 55
(Ian Williams) *led 2f: chsd ldr: lost pl over 2f out* **10/1**
6-45 **8** 3¾ **Harcas (IRE)**[14] 1767 7-9-0 **60** ....(p) PaulMulrennan 1 39
(M Todhunter) *led after 2f: qcknd over 5f out: hdd over 3f out: lost pl 2f out* **8/1**

3m 33.04s (1.24) **Going Correction** -0.05s/f (Good)
WFA 4 from 6yo+ 1lb **8** Ran SP% **115.9**
Speed ratings (Par 103): **94,93,93,92,91 86,85,83**
toteswinger: 1&2 £1.20, 1&3 £11.50, 2&3 £7.50 CSF £12.94 CT £160.78 TOTE £4.00: £1.50, £2.00, £3.60; EX 11.90 Place 6: £143.68 Place 5: £48.01.
Owner Marcoe Racing Welwyn **Bred** Stanley Estate And Stud Co **Trained** Newmarket, Suffolk

FOCUS
A modest staying handicap run at a sensible pace. The winner was well on top in the end but the third and fourth keep the form down.
T/Plt: £268.60 to a £1 stake. Pool: £70,332.43. 191.12 winning tickets. T/Qpdt: £42.90 to a £1 stake. Pool: £6,344.30. 109.30 winning tickets. WG

2615 - 2622a (Foreign Racing) - See Raceform Interactive

2435 HAMILTON (R-H)
Thursday, June 4

OFFICIAL GOING: Good to firm (firm in places; 10.8)
Racing was delayed for an hour due to an accident that led to the nearby M74 being closed. Many runners had their arrival delayed.
Wind: Slight, half against Weather: Cloudy

2623 CASH FOR KIDS RACENIGHT NEXT WEEK MAIDEN AUCTION STKS 6f 5y
2:10 (3:10) (Class 6) 2-Y-O **£2,590** (£770; £385; £192) **Stalls** Low

Form RPR
4 **1** **Whispered Times (USA)**[19] 2069 2-9-3 0 .... PhillipMakin 1 77+
(P C Haslam) *w ldrs: led 2f out: rdn out fnl f* **9/2**[2]
0 **2** 1½ **Magic Footsteps**[26] 1866 2-9-2 0 .... TonyHamilton 4 72
(Jedd O'Keeffe) *blkd s: prom: effrt over 1f out: styd on to go 2nd towards fin: nt rch wnr* **12/1**
442 **3** ½ **Rock Of Love (IRE)**[16] 2167 2-9-3 0 .... GregFairley 2 71
(M Johnston) *t.k.h early: led to 2f out: one pce fnl f* **5/6**[1]
0 **4** 1¼ **Sands Of Dee (USA)**[10] 2339 2-8-13 0 ....(v[1]) PaulHanagan 7 63
(R A Fahey) *wnt lft s: prom: outpcd over 3f out: hrd rdn and rallied over 1f out: kpt on fnl f: no imp* **9/1**
5 nk **Unshakable Will (IRE)** 2-9-3 0 .... TomEaves 5 66
(B Smart) *blkd s: trckd ldrs tl rdn and nt qckn appr fnl f* **25/1**
5 **6** 4 **Durham Reflection (IRE)**[18] 2099 2-9-2 0 .... PaulMulrennan 6 53
(J Howard Johnson) *blkd s: t.k.h: w ldrs tl wknd appr fnl f* **13/2**[3]

7 ½ **Hold On Tiger (IRE)** 2-8-13 0 JamieMoriarty 3 49+
(I Semple) *s.s: bhd and outpcd: nvr on terms* **40/1**

1m 12.25s (0.05) **Going Correction** -0.175s/f (Firm) 7 Ran SP% **110.0**
Speed ratings (Par 91): **92,90,89,87,87 81,81**
toteswinger: 1&2 £5.80, 1&3 £1.90, 2&3 £4.70 CSF £50.08 TOTE £4.40: £2.10, £5.10; EX 45.10.
Owner Mrs E O'Leary **Bred** Hetrich-McCarthy Livestock **Trained** Middleham Moor, N Yorks

FOCUS
This was only a modest maiden.

NOTEBOOK
Whispered Times(USA), a keeping-on fourth having met trouble over 5f on his debut at Doncaster, was always likely to benefit from the extra furlong, and, with the benefit of the rail to run against, he got on top inside the final furlong. There should be more to come from this progressive sort, who reportedly loved the fast ground, and he appeals as the type to do well in nurseries later in the season. (tchd 7-2 and 5-1 in a place)
Magic Footsteps hinted at ability before fading on his debut at Haydock and it was no surprise to see him improve with that outing under his belt. He stayed on well inside the final furlong, having been outpaced, and definitely has races in him. He will want 7f before long and is another likely to do well in nurseries. (op 14-1 tchd 11-1)
Rock Of Love(IRE) showed improved form for the step up to 6f on fast ground when second at Yarmouth last time and hewas soon in the firing line. He held every chance, but couldn´t race on with the winner and was run out of second close home. There are races in him, but he won´t be seen at his best until racing over trips of 7f and beyond. (op 8-11 tchd Evens)
Sands Of Dee(USA) stayed on again in the first-time visor and improved on his debut effort. The extra furlong was clearly a help and he may well progress again. (op 10-1 tchd 17-2)
Unshakable Will(IRE), a half-brother to useful stablemate Inheritor, went left coming out of the gates, but showed early speed and should do better with this outing behind him.
Durham Reflection(IRE), who got a bump at the start, didn´t do much better than when fifth on his debut at Ripon. (op 7-1 tchd 11-2 and 8-1 in a place)
Hold On Tiger(IRE), who cost £16,000 at the breeze-ups, never recovered from a slow start.

2624 HAMILTON-PARK.CO.UK CLAIMING STKS 6f 5y
2:40 (3:40) (Class 6) 3-4-Y-O £2,388 (£705; £352) Stalls Low

Form RPR
2220 1 **Legal Eagle (IRE)**[12] 2276 4-9-4 81 AdrianTNicholls 6 82+
(D Nicholls) *wnt rt s: sn crossed to stands rail: mde all: pushed out fnl f: comf* **2/7**[1]
0335 2 2 **Aahaygirl (IRE)**[13] 2234 3-7-13 65 (b[1]) DaleGibson 3 63
(K R Burke) *cl up: effrt and chsd wnr over 1f out: kpt on u.p fnl f* **13/2**[2]
10-0 3 9 **Digit**[24] 1924 3-8-7 59 TomEaves 2 42
(B Smart) *in tch: outpcd over 3f out: rallied and chsd (clr) ldrs ins fnl f: no imp* **20/1**
2500 4 1 **Secret Dubai (IRE)**[10] 2312 4-8-7 65 KristinStubbs(7) 5 40
(Mrs L Stubbs) *chsd wnr tl rdn and wknd over 1f out* **11/1**[3]
0000 5 ¾ **Waltzing Buddy**[23] 1949 3-8-0 50 ow2 FrankieMcDonald 1 30
(P T Midgley) *in tch tl hung rt and wknd fr 2f out* **80/1**
0-55 6 2 **Smelly Cat**[34] 1644 3-7-9 50 ow4 JamieKyne(7) 4 25
(D W Thompson) *prom: rdn and hung rt over 2f out: sn wknd* **33/1**

1m 10.84s (-1.36) **Going Correction** -0.175s/f (Firm)
WFA 3 from 4yo 8lb 6 Ran SP% **108.4**
Speed ratings (Par 101): **102,99,87,86,85 82**
toteswinger: 1&2 £1.80, 1&3 £2.20, 2&3 £2.60 CSF £2.23 TOTE £1.20: £1.02, £3.50; EX 3.20.Legal Eagle was claimed by Paul Green for £12,000.
Owner Mrs Jackie Love & D Nicholls **Bred** John Cooke **Trained** Sessay, N Yorks

FOCUS
A weak claimer that was won readily by red-hot favourite Legal Eagle who did not need to match his recent success.

2625 FRANK FLYNN & CO ACCOUNTANTS H'CAP 5f 4y
3:10 (4:11) (Class 6) (0-65,64) 3-Y-O+ £2,388 (£705; £352) Stalls Low

Form RPR
1443 1 **Argentine (IRE)**[32] 1695 5-9-5 55 (b) PaulMulrennan 4 65
(J A McShane) *hld up: hdwy over 1f out: edgd lft and led ins fnl f: edgd rt: r.o wl* **5/1**[2]
40-0 2 ¾ **Howards Tipple**[38] 1558 5-9-2 52 TomEaves 1 59
(I Semple) *hld up: hdwy and ev ch ins fnl f: kpt on: hld nr fin* **12/1**
0-23 3 1 **The History Man (IRE)**[26] 1877 6-9-0 57 (be) GarryWhillans(7) 9 61
(M Mullineaux) *chsd ldrs: effrt over 1f out: kpt on same pce ins fnl f* **6/1**
6210 4 ½ **Rocketball (IRE)**[20] 2032 4-9-9 59 PaulHanagan 10 61
(Mrs L Williamson) *led to ins fnl f: kpt on same pce* **8/1**
1655 5 shd **Handsinthemist (IRE)**[17] 2130 4-8-12 55 PaulPickard(7) 3 57
(P T Midgley) *prom: drvn over 2f out: one pce fnl f* **10/1**
2045 6 1 **Comptonspirit**[13] 2225 5-10-0 64 J-PGuillambert 11 62
(B P J Baugh) *in tch: effrt 2f out: kpt on same pce fnl f* **5/1**[2]
0243 7 2 **Distant Vision (IRE)**[3] 2529 6-8-4 47 (b) JamieKyne(7) 6 38
(H A McWilliams) *in tch tl rdn and no ex over 1f out* **11/2**[3]
0-51 8 ¾ **Sunley Sovereign**[6] 2436 5-9-2 52 6ex (b) SilvestreDeSousa 8 40
(Mrs R A Carr) *chsd ldrs: drvn and edgd rt over 2f out: wknd over 1f out* **9/2**[1]
0100 9 1 ½ **Andrasta**[6] 2436 4-9-0 57 BillyCray(7) 2 40
(A Berry) *sn outpcd and drvn along: nvr rchd ldrs* **20/1**
000 10 6 **Stoneacre Baby (USA)**[16] 2157 4-8-9 45 PatrickMathers 7 6
(Peter Grayson) *prom tl rdn and wknd over 2f out* **80/1**

59.33 secs (-0.67) **Going Correction** -0.175s/f (Firm) 10 Ran SP% **115.1**
Speed ratings (Par 101): **98,96,95,94,94 92,89,88,85,76**
toteswinger: 1&2 £18.50, 1&3 £7.10, 2&3 £17.50 CSF £62.45 CT £375.20 TOTE £6.80: £1.90, £4.30, £2.10; EX 88.30.
Owner D Moriarty **Bred** Tony Hirschfeld & L K Piggott **Trained** Dalkeith, Midlothian

FOCUS
This was a low-grade sprint handicap. Ordinary form, the winner turning in his best effort since 2007.

2626 PRESTIGE SCOTLAND H'CAP (A QUALIFIER FOR THE SCOTTISH TROPHY HANDICAP SERIES FINAL) 1m 65y
3:40 (4:40) (Class 5) (0-70,70) 4-Y-O+ £3,561 (£1,059; £529; £264) Stalls High

Form RPR
0-62 1 **Mountain Cat (IRE)**[3] 2531 5-8-10 59 TomEaves 1 69+
(G A Swinbank) *trckd ldr: rdn to ld over 1f out: kpt on wl fnl f* **6/4**[1]
2340 2 2 ¾ **This Ones For Eddy**[10] 2313 4-9-7 70 PaulMulrennan 2 74
(S Parr) *led to over 1f out: kpt on same pce* **6/1**
4042 3 ¾ **Singora Lady (IRE)**[6] 2441 4-8-4 53 FrankieMcDonald 7 55+
(P T Midgley) *hld up: rdn and hdwy centre 2f out: kpt on fnl f: nt rch first two* **13/2**[3]
0600 4 ½ **Forzarzi (IRE)**[3] 2531 5-8-9 58 (p) PaulHanagan 9 59
(H A McWilliams) *hld up: effrt over 2f out: kpt on fnl f: no imp* **25/1**
0-50 5 nk **Bold Indian (IRE)**[125] 353 5-8-0 54 PatrickDonaghy(5) 3 54
(I Semple) *t.k.h: chsd ldrs tl rdn and nt qckn over 1f out* **14/1**
002 6 nk **Tanforan**[9] 2352 7-7-13 55 BillyCray(7) 4 55
(B P J Baugh) *t.k.h: prom tl rdn and no ex over 1f out* **7/1**
520- 7 ½ **Pianoforte (USA)**[277] 5538 7-8-9 58 (b) DavidAllan 6 57
(E J Alston) *t.k.h: in tch: effrt over 2f out: no ex over 1f out* **14/1**
6550 8 1 ¼ **Bourse (IRE)**[13] 2237 4-8-11 60 GregFairley 5 56
(A G Foster) *hld up: drvn 3f out: nvr able to chal* **6/1**[2]
0000 9 1 ½ **Bright Falcon**[5] 2473 4-8-3 52 DaleGibson 8 44
(S Parr) *bhd: drvn over 3f out: nvr on terms* **50/1**

1m 46.6s (-1.80) **Going Correction** -0.425s/f (Firm) 9 Ran SP% **113.5**
Speed ratings (Par 103): **92,89,88,88,87 87,86,85,84**
toteswinger: 1&2 £2.60, 1&3 £2.90, 2&3 £6.20 CSF £10.44 CT £44.61 TOTE £2.20: £1.40, £2.10, £1.50; EX 9.80.
Owner S Rudolf **Bred** Mrs Mary Gallagher **Trained** Melsonby, N Yorks

FOCUS
They didn´t go much of a gallop in this and hardly anything got into it. The winner will still be well handicapped on his old form.

2627 SAM COLLINGWOOD-CAMERON H'CAP 1m 3f 16y
4:10 (5:10) (Class 6) (0-65,63) 3-Y-O £2,388 (£705; £352) Stalls High

Form RPR
5-20 1 **New Tricks**[10] 2340 3-9-3 59 (b[1]) TomEaves 4 71
(I Semple) *mde all: rdn clr over 2f out: unchal* **15/8**[1]
00-0 2 9 **Blackstone Vegas**[27] 1829 3-9-7 63 (b[1]) PaulMulrennan 2 59
(J Howard Johnson) *chsd wnr thrght: rdn and one pce fnl 2f* **6/1**[3]
0-00 3 3 ¼ **Sydney Cove (IRE)**[13] 2236 3-7-12 47 JamieKyne(7) 6 37
(R Allan) *midfield: hdwy over 3f out: rdn and no imp fnl 2f* **14/1**
00-0 4 7 **Step Fast (USA)**[31] 1724 3-8-7 49 GregFairley 7 26
(M Johnston) *prom: outpcd 4f out: n.d after* **6/1**[3]
0-00 5 1 ¼ **Ernies Keep**[40] 1520 3-8-3 45 DarrenMoffatt 5 20
(W Storey) *chsd ldrs tl rdn and wknd over 2f out* **50/1**
60-0 6 hd **Tillietudlem (FR)**[108] 570 3-8-3 45 PaulHanagan 3 20
(J S Goldie) *hld up: drvn over 4f out: nvr on terms* **5/1**[2]
06-0 7 3 **Strevelyn**[13] 2236 3-8-5 47 FrancisNorton 1 16
(Mrs A Duffield) *hld up: rdn 4f out: nvr rchd ldrs* **16/1**
-650 8 2 ¾ **Knock Three Times (IRE)**[18] 2104 3-8-0 49 ow3 JohnCavanagh(7) 9 13
(W Storey) *hld up towards rr: rdn and hung rt over 2f out: sn btn* **11/1**
0 9 6 **Annes Sound (IRE)**[29] 1793 3-9-1 57 PhillipMakin 8 11
(Patrick Morris) *hld up: drvn over 3f out: nvr on terms* **8/1**

2m 21.0s (-4.60) **Going Correction** -0.425s/f (Firm) 9 Ran SP% **114.0**
Speed ratings (Par 97): **99,92,90,85,84 83,81,79,75**
toteswinger: 1&2 £3.80, 1&3 £6.90, 2&3 £19.40 CSF £13.04 CT £119.41 TOTE £2.30: £1.20, £1.80, £3.70; EX 11.90.
Owner David McKenzie **Bred** P And Mrs A G Venner **Trained** Carluke, S Lanarks
■ Stewards' Enquiry : John Cavanagh one-day ban: careless riding (Jun 21)

FOCUS
This was a weak middle-distance handicap and there is some doubt over how much the easy winner needed to improve.
Knock Three Times(IRE) Official explanation: trainer said filly was struck into and returned home lame

2628 SODEXO STOP HUNGER CHARITY H'CAP 6f 5y
4:40 (5:41) (Class 5) (0-70,69) 4-Y-O+ £3,238 (£963; £481; £240) Stalls Low

Form RPR
4-32 1 **Tangerine Trees**[10] 2312 4-9-1 63 TomEaves 1 71
(B Smart) *mde all: edgd rt u.p ins fnl f: drvn out* **6/4**[1]
6-43 2 nk **Atlantic Beach**[12] 2276 4-9-7 69 PaulHanagan 2 76
(R A Fahey) *pressed wnr: drvn over 2f out: rallied over 1f out: kpt on: hld cl home* **7/4**[2]
0233 3 1 ½ **Maison Dieu**[10] 2312 6-8-12 60 DavidAllan 3 65+
(E J Alston) *in tch: effrt over 1f out: keeping on whn n.m.r ins fnl f: one pce* **8/1**
-000 4 ¾ **Mr Lu**[13] 2235 4-8-9 60 NeilBrown(3) 7 60
(A G Foster) *prom: effrt on outside over 1f out: one pce fnl f* **7/1**[3]
0006 5 2 ¼ **Ride A White Swan**[7] 2404 4-8-3 51 FrancisNorton 6 43
(D Shaw) *in tch: effrt over 1f out: nt qckn fnl f* **20/1**
2542 6 3 ¾ **Wiltshire (IRE)**[17] 2134 7-8-7 55 (v) FrankieMcDonald 4 35
(P T Midgley) *cl up tl rdn and wknd over 1f out* **14/1**
0600 7 4 ½ **Obe One**[3] 2529 9-7-9 50 BillyCray(7) 9 16
(A Berry) *dwlt: plld hrd and hld up: rdn over 2f out: sn wknd* **50/1**
-000 8 1 ¾ **Rainbow Bay**[24] 1924 6-8-2 50 oh5 (v) SilvestreDeSousa 8 10
(Miss Tracy Waggott) *cl up on outside tl wknd fr 2f out* **40/1**

1m 10.64s (-1.56) **Going Correction** -0.175s/f (Firm) 8 Ran SP% **115.8**
Speed ratings (Par 103): **103,102,100,99,96 91,85,83**
toteswinger: 1&2 £1.50, 1&3 £3.10, 2&3 £2.70 CSF £4.33 CT £13.79 TOTE £2.70: £1.10, £1.20, £1.80; EX 4.50.
Owner Tangerine Trees Partnership **Bred** Mrs B A Matthews **Trained** Hambleton, N Yorks

FOCUS
This wasn´t the most competitive of sprints and the ´big´ two came home first and second, but whether that would have been the case had Maison Dieu not been squeezed out inside the final furlong remains to be seen. Straightforward form.

2629 TURFTV H'CAP 1m 5f 9y
5:10 (6:15) (Class 5) (0-70,67) 4-Y-O+ £3,238 (£963; £481; £240) Stalls High

Form RPR
0-05 1 **Baizically (IRE)**[14] 2200 6-8-9 62 PaulPickard(7) 8 72
(G A Swinbank) *racd keenly: cl up: led 1/2-way: clr fr 4f out: unchal* **3/1**[2]
40-4 2 4 **Fenners (USA)**[153] 18 6-8-3 49 DaleGibson 3 53
(M W Easterby) *sn bhd: niggled 1/2-way: rdn over 3f out: rallied over 1f out: chsd wnr ins fnl f: no imp* **7/1**
2-51 3 shd **Forrest Flyer (IRE)**[13] 2233 5-9-1 61 PhillipMakin 6 65
(I Semple) *led to 1/2-way: chsd wnr: effrt over 2f out: sn one pce* **6/4**[1]
0-13 4 4 **Shekan Star**[13] 2246 7-8-9 55 PaulHanagan 1 53
(K G Reveley) *sn trcking ldrs: rdn 3f out: one pce fnl 2f* **4/1**[3]
00-5 5 22 **Hill Billy Rock (IRE)**[95] 3 6-9-7 67 PaulMulrennan 7 32
(Mrs S C Bradburne) *hld up in tch: struggling over 4f out: nvr on terms* **14/1**
-065 6 8 **Dimashq**[16] 2159 7-8-2 48 oh3 FrankieMcDonald 2 —
(P T Midgley) *prom tl rdn and wknd fr 3f out* **16/1**

2m 47.38s (-6.52) **Going Correction** -0.425s/f (Firm) 6 Ran SP% **110.0**
Speed ratings (Par 103): **103,100,100,98,84 79**
toteswinger: 1&2 £2.60, 1&3 £2.30, 2&3 £1.90 CSF £22.35 CT £38.66 TOTE £3.90: £2.20, £1.80; EX 21.00 Place 6: £36.12 Place 5: £5.71.
Owner Shropshire Wolves **Bred** G And Mrs Middlebrook **Trained** Melsonby, N Yorks

FOCUS
This was a weak staying handicap. The winner had slipped a long way in the weights and the form is rated around the third.
Hill Billy Rock(IRE) Official explanation: jockey said gelding was unsuited by the good to firm (firm in places) ground
Dimashq Official explanation: jockey said the mare finished distressed
T/Plt: £43.20 to a £1 stake. Pool: £49,125.87. 829.34 winning tickets. T/Qpdt: £4.90 to a £1 stake. Pool: £4,512.80. 671.70 winning tickets. RY

2487 LINGFIELD (L-H)
Thursday, June 4
OFFICIAL GOING: Turf course - good to firm (9.1); all-weather - standard

2630 FELBRIDGE (S) STKS — 7f (P)
2:20 (2:21) (Class 6) 3-Y-O+ — **£2,047** (£604; £302) **Stalls** Low

Form — RPR
0-30 **1** **Straitjacket**[10] 2321 3-8-6 59 ......(p) PaulFitzsimons 8 57
(Miss J R Tooth) *chsd ldrs: rdn to chal over 1f out: led jst ins fnl f: kpt on wl and a holding runner up* **8/1**
2416 **2** *nk* **Northern Desert (IRE)**[97] 706 10-9-13 70 ......(p) JamesDoyle 9 71
(S Curran) *hld up in tch in rr: hdwy to chse ldrs and rdn jst over 2f out: ev ch 1f out: kpt on but a jst hld fnl f* **6/4**[1]
0000 **3** *2 3/4* **Hatman Jack (IRE)**[4] 2515 3-8-11 60 ...... FergusSweeney 5 54
(B G Powell) *trckd ldr: rdn to ld 2f out: hdd jst ins fnl f: wknd fnl 75yds* **9/1**
105 **4** *1 3/4* **Fun In The Sun**[66] 1030 5-9-13 57 ...... StephenDonohoe 3 59
(A B Haynes) *t.k.h: hld up in tch in rr: rdn and nt qckn 3f out: plugged on fnl f to go 4th nr fin* **5/1**[3]
0-00 **5** *3/4* **Polmaily**[23] 1958 4-9-7 65 ......(b) IanMongan 12 51
(J Akehurst) *sn led: hdd and rdn 2f out: wknd ent fnl f* **3/1**[2]
P-00 **6** *5* **Miss Kadee**[21] 2009 3-8-6 50 ...... LukeMorris 11 28
(J S Moore) *dwlt: in tch in rr: rdn and struggling over 2f out: sn bhd* **20/1**
0-00 **7** *5* **Black Draft**[74] 921 7-9-7 35 ...... NeilChalmers 1 24
(B Forsey) *led briefly: chsd ldrs: rdn and wknd qckly 3f out: wl bhd fnl 2f* **100/1**
00-0 **8** *3 3/4* **Igotim**[10] 2338 3-8-11 46 ...... ChrisCatlin 4 10
(J Gallagher) *sn rdn and swtchd to outer: a wl bhd* **25/1**
00-0 **U** **Always The Sun**[121] 383 3-8-1 47 ......(p) AmyBaker(5) 10 —
(P Leech) *rrd and uns rdr as stalls opened* **50/1**
1m 26.09s (1.29) **Going Correction** +0.075s/f (Slow)
WFA 3 from 4yo+ 10lb — **9** Ran SP% **114.3**
Speed ratings (Par 101): **95,94,91,89,88 82,77,72,—**
toteswinger: 1&2 £3.30, 1&3 £9.30, 2&3 £4.10 CSF £19.77 TOTE £9.10: £2.10, £1.30, £2.50; EX 22.80 Trifecta £73.30 Pool: £529.19 - 5.34 winning units.There was no bid for the winner.
Owner Raymond Tooth **Bred** John M Troy **Trained** Upper Lambourn, Berks
FOCUS
An ordinary seller in which the pace was no more than fair. It is doubtful if the winner had to improve on last year's nursery form.
Polmaily Official explanation: trainer said gelding bled from the nose

2631 HENRY STREETER MEDIAN AUCTION MAIDEN STKS — 6f (P)
2:50 (2:53) (Class 6) 2-Y-O — **£2,388** (£705; £352) **Stalls** Low

Form — RPR
33 **1** **Swilly Ferry (USA)**[28] 1802 2-9-3 0 ...... MichaelHills 8 79+
(B W Hills) *sn led: crossed towards inner after 1f: rdn clr over 1f out: styd on strly: comf* **5/4**[1]
2 *3 1/2* **Diamond Johnny G (USA)** 2-9-3 0 ...... SteveDrowne 3 70+
(J R Best) *t.k.h: chsd ldr tl over 4f out: chsd ldrs after: rdn to chse ldng pair wl over 1f out: outpcd over 1f out: kpt on again ins fnl f to go 2nd towards fin: no ch w wnr* **20/1**
0 **3** *3/4* **Almadaa**[21] 2017 2-9-3 0 ...... RHills 11 66
(E A L Dunlop) *s.i.s: rcvrd to chse wnr over 4f out: pressed wnr and rdn 2f out: wknd ent fnl f: lost 2nd towards fin* **11/4**[2]
4 *nse* **Dubai Miracle (USA)** 2-9-3 0 ...... StephenDonohoe 7 66+
(D M Simcock) *in tch: rdn over 2f out: outpcd wl over 1f out: styd on again ins fnl f: no ch w wnr* **8/1**[3]
04 **5** *3/4* **The Shuffler**[14] 2201 2-9-3 0 ...... RyanMoore 6 64+
(G L Moore) *rrd s and s.i.s: sn in tch: rdn and unable qck 2f out: styd on again ins fnl f: nvr trbld wnr* **11/1**
6 *1 3/4* **Amno Dancer (IRE)** 2-9-3 0 ...... SebSanders 12 59
(M H Tompkins) *restless in stalls: s.i.s: swtchd lft after s: hld up in rr of main gp: rdn and outpcd jst over 2f out: plugged on same pce fnl f* **33/1**
7 *2 1/4* **Kyoatee Kilt** 2-9-3 0 ...... MartinDwyer 5 52
(P F I Cole) *t.k.h: prom: hmpd after 1f: chsd ldrs after: rdn over 2f out: wknd wl over 1f out* **12/1**
8 *1* **Al Khimiya (IRE)** 2-8-12 0 ...... EddieAhern 10 44
(S A Callaghan) *stdd s: hld up in tch in main gp: rdn and outpcd jst over 2f out: wknd wl over 1f out* **25/1**
9 *2* **Dashing Doc (IRE)** 2-9-3 0 ...... RobertHavlin 4 43
(D R C Elsworth) *v.s.a: wl bhd: sme hdwy 3f out: no hdwy 2f out: nvr on terms* **16/1**
10 *5* **Rodrigo De Freitas (IRE)** 2-9-3 0 ...... PatCosgrave 2 28
(J R Boyle) *v.s.a: a wl bhd* **33/1**
11 *8* **New Den** 2-9-3 0 ...... TPQueally 1 —
(J R Boyle) *v.s.a: a wl bhd* **66/1**
1m 13.58s (1.68) **Going Correction** +0.075s/f (Slow) — **11** Ran SP% **120.1**
Speed ratings (Par 91): **91,86,85,85,84 81,78,77,74,68 57**
toteswinger: 1&2 £6.30, 1&3 £2.00, 2&3 £8.50 CSF £36.30 TOTE £2.40: £1.20, £3.80, £1.50; EX 27.10 Trifecta £58.10 Pool: £518.07 - 6.59 winning units.
Owner John C Grant **Bred** Kilboy Estate, Inc **Trained** Lambourn, Berks
■ Stewards' Enquiry : Michael Hills two-day ban: careless riding (Jun 21-22)
FOCUS
A pretty ordinary maiden without too much strength in depth.
NOTEBOOK
Swilly Ferry(USA), third in the Brocklesby on day one of the turf season before being beaten at odds-on at Chester, made the most of what looked a straightforward opportunity to shed his maiden tag. Upped in trip and switched to Polytrack, he soon led and stretched out well up the straight to assert. He looks a nice type for when the nurseries start next month. (tchd 6-4 and 13-8 in a place)
Diamond Johnny G(USA) ◆ showed promise on this debut, never far from the pace and running on for second. A big individual who will come on for the outing, he is bred to make his mark at sprint trips on artifical surfaces and a similarly modest race should soon come his way. (tchd 16-1)
Almadaa, who looked green on his debut at York, had a wide draw to overcome here and did not help his cause with a tardy start. He recovered to have his chance, but was left behind by the winner up the straight and was caught for second too late on. (op 4-1 tchd 5-2)
Dubai Miracle(USA), a half-brother to five winners in the USA, came in for a bit of support and did not shape without promise. (op 16-1)
The Shuffler, stepping up in trip and switched from turf, was a little short of room early in the straight but in truth was well held at the time. He is now qualified for nurseries. (op 9-1)
Kyoatee Kilt, who was hampered early on, chased the pace before fading.
Dashing Doc(IRE), a half-brother to Listed juvenile winner Doctor Dash, was clueless on this debut but should leave this running behind in time and when tackling further.

2632 BET MULTIPLES - BETDAQ FILLIES' H'CAP — 6f (P)
3:20 (3:22) (Class 5) (0-75,75) 3-Y-O — **£3,238** (£963; £481; £240) **Stalls** Low

Form — RPR
6-1 **1** **Dametime (IRE)**[10] 2321 3-8-12 71 6ex ......(t) AndreaAtzeni(5) 1 77
(Daniel Mark Loughnane, Ire) *mde all: hrd pressed and rdn 2f out: battled on gamely fnl f: all out* **6/1**[3]
1120 **2** *nk* **Song Of Praise**[21] 2010 3-9-5 73 ...... JimmyQuinn 10 78
(M Blanshard) *t.k.h: trckd ldrs on inner: n.m.r wl over 1f out: squeezed through 1f out: str chal ins fnl f: unable qck nr fin* **14/1**
0-01 **3** *shd* **Spring Green**[17] 2122 3-9-5 73 ...... SteveDrowne 3 78+
(H Morrison) *chsd ldrs tl hmpd and lost pl after 1f: sn pushed along: hdwy over 3f out: drvn over 1f out: hdwy to press ldrs and edgd lft fnl 100yds: r.o but nt quite rch ldng pair* **9/1**
1- **4** *2 1/4* **Night Affair**[167] 7734 3-9-7 75 ...... MartinDwyer 2 72
(D W P Arbuthnot) *chsd wnr: ev ch and rdn 2f out: wknd ins fnl f: btn whn short of room towards fin* **11/2**[2]
4-02 **5** *nk* **Bea Menace (USA)**[5] 2498 3-9-0 68 ...... EddieAhern 4 65+
(P F I Cole) *in tch tl bdly hmpd and dropped to rr of main gp after 1f: rdn over 2f out: styd on u.p fnl f: nt threaten ldrs* **9/2**[1]
0-46 **6** *1/2* **Blushing Maid**[4] 2520 3-9-0 68 ...... KirstyMilczarek 11 63
(H S Howe) *chsd ldrs: ev ch and rdn 2f out: hrd rdn and wknd ins fnl f: btn whn short of room wl ins fnl f* **16/1**
3-10 **7** *3/4* **Beautiful Filly**[19] 2079 3-9-2 70 ...... RichardMullen 9 63
(D M Simcock) *bustled along leaving stalls: rdn and unable qck over 2f out: kpt on u.p fnl f but nvr pce to threaten ldrs* **14/1**
61-0 **8** *nk* **Merry Diva**[28] 1814 3-9-6 74 ...... AlanMunro 12 66
(C F Wall) *racd in midfield tl lost pl over 2f out: sn rdn: kpt on fnl f but nvr pce to threaten ldrs* **14/1**
30-5 **9** *7* **Leadenhall Lass (IRE)**[28] 1814 3-9-3 71 ...... IanMongan 5 40
(P M Phelan) *chsd ldrs tl 2f out: wknd qckly wl over 1f out* **8/1**
2-16 **10** *3/4* **Princess Zohra**[83] 829 3-8-11 65 ...... RyanMoore 8 32
(E A L Dunlop) *s.i.s and hmpd s: a towards rr: swtchd to outer 3f out: n.d* **6/1**[3]
2-00 **11** *3 3/4* **Final Rhapsody**[10] 2321 3-8-10 64 ...... RobertHavlin 6 19
(J A Geake) *in tch in midfield: rdn and struggling 3f out: no ch fnl 2f* **33/1**
-100 **12** *2 1/4* **Yanza**[16] 2160 3-9-1 69 ...... ChrisCatlin 7 17
(J R Gask) *racd wd: a bhd* **16/1**
1m 12.45s (0.55) **Going Correction** +0.075s/f (Slow) — **12** Ran SP% **118.0**
Speed ratings (Par 96): **99,98,98,95,95 94,93,93,83,82 77,74**
toteswinger: 1&2 £20.90, 1&3 £7.70, 2&3 £21.10 CSF £86.69 CT £766.10 TOTE £7.80: £2.60, £4.30, £2.50; EX 97.70 TRIFECTA Not won..
Owner Brian Forkan **Bred** Tally-Ho Stud **Trained** Trim, Co Meath
FOCUS
An open fillies' handicap. Fair form for the grade with the winner stepping up, the second progressing and the next two unexposed.
Princess Zohra Official explanation: jockey said filly did not face the kickback

2633 BET 1% IN RUNNING - BETDAQ MAIDEN FILLIES' STKS — 1m 2f
3:50 (3:53) (Class 5) 3-Y-O+ — **£2,729** (£806; £403) **Stalls** High

Form — RPR
2 **1** **Flame Of Gibraltar (IRE)**[21] 2002 3-8-9 0 ...... TPQueally 1 85+
(H R A Cecil) *in tch and a gng wl: led on bit 2f out: clr over 1f out: eased towards fin* **2/5**[1]
30 **2** *3* **Monaco Dream (IRE)**[28] 1804 3-8-9 0 ...... AlanMunro 11 74
(W Jarvis) *hld up towards rr: hdwy into midfield 6f out: rdn to chse ldng pair 2f out: wnt 2nd ins fnl f: kpt on but no ch w wnr* **17/2**
536 **3** *4* **Chicora (USA)**[15] 2178 3-8-9 70 ...... RichardMullen 12 66
(J H M Gosden) *chsd ldr after 2f: rdn to ld over 2f out: hdd 2f out: wl outpcd by wnr over 1f out: lost 2nd ins fnl f* **13/2**[2]
4 *8* **Maid Of Stone (IRE)** 3-8-9 0 ...... RobertHavlin 7 50+
(D R C Elsworth) *s.i.s: t.k.h: hld up in rr: hdwy 5f out: rdn and rn green over 2f out: wnt modest 4th ent fnl f: nvr nr ldrs* **20/1**
0-0 **5** *4* **Arabian Moonlight**[45] 1406 3-8-9 0 ...... LPKeniry 4 42
(E F Vaughan) *in tch in midfield tl lost pl on downhill run over 3f out: no ch w ldrs fnl 3f* **33/1**
30 **6** *hd* **Sadaska**[71] 951 3-8-9 0 ...... SteveDrowne 9 42
(S C Williams) *in tch in midfield: rdn over 3f out: wknd wl over 2f out* **40/1**
4 **7** *nk* **Tisifone**[31] 1745 3-8-9 0 ...... PhilipRobinson 2 41
(C G Cox) *led for 1f: chsd ldr tl 8f out: rdn 3f out: wknd over 2f out* **8/1**[3]
00- **8** *2 1/2* **Full Blue**[220] 7015 3-8-9 0 ...... SaleemGolam 10 36
(S C Williams) *bhd: struggling 4f out: wl btn after* **100/1**
0000 **9** *1/2* **Risky Lady (IRE)**[10] 2338 3-8-9 43 ...... KirstyMilczarek 5 35
(J Ryan) *dwlt: dashed up to ld after 1f: rdn and hdd over 2f out: sn wknd* **100/1**
10 *9* **She's A Model** 3-8-9 0 ...... PatCosgrave 6 17
(R Ingram) *a towards rr: wl bhd fnl 3f* **100/1**
11 *117* **Urban Bounty** 4-9-8 0 ...... JimmyQuinn 8 —
(M J McGrath) *nvr gng wl in rr: t.o fr 5f out* **66/1**
2m 7.93s (-2.57) **Going Correction** -0.20s/f (Firm)
WFA 3 from 4yo 13lb — **11** Ran SP% **121.0**
Speed ratings (Par 100): **102,99,96,90,86 86,86,84,84,76 —**
toteswinger: 1&2 £2.30, 1&3 £2.30, 2&3 £4.20 CSF £4.73 TOTE £1.40: £1.02, £2.00, £2.20; EX 4.80 Trifecta £25.60 Pool: £622.44 - 17.94 winning units.
Owner Mrs R McKeon **Bred** Kilcarn Stud **Trained** Newmarket, Suffolk
FOCUS
A pretty modest race overall run at an ordinary pace, but the winner did it well and is the type to do much better.
Tisifone Official explanation: jockey said filly was unsuited by the track

2634 BET EPSOM OAKS - BETDAQ H'CAP — 1m 3f 106y
4:20 (4:22) (Class 6) (0-55,55) 4-Y-O+ — **£2,047** (£604; £302) **Stalls** Low

Form — RPR
1 **Newmarket Story (IRE)**[686] 3694 7-8-5 46 oh1 ...... NickyMackay 7 56
(W J Austin, Ire) *in tch: rdn and gd hdwy to ld wl over 2f out: clr 2f out: styd on wl and unchal after* **66/1**

4-31 **2** 2 3/4 **Jafaru**[13] 2222 5-9-0 **55** RyanMoore 12 61
(G L Moore) *chsd ldrs: rdn to chse wnr over 2f out: drvn and hung lft over 1f out: no imp* **11/8**[1]

0146 **3** nk **Barbirolli**[13] 2222 7-8-11 **52** LukeMorris 16 57
(W M Brisbourne) *hld up towards rr: rdn and hdwy over 3f out: chsd ldng pair over 1f out: kpt on u.p but nvr threatened wnr* **10/1**

1305 **4** 3 1/2 **Amwell Brave**[29] 1463 8-8-8 **49** FergusSweeney 15 48
(J R Jenkins) *hld up wl in rr: hdwy 3f out: n.m.r over 1f out: styd on u.p: nvr gng to rch ldrs* **10/1**

0000 **5** 1 **Mid Valley**[13] 2222 6-8-5 **46** oh1 AdrianMcCarthy 9 43
(J R Jenkins) *hld up towards rr: hdwy and rdn on outer 3f out: kpt on same pce fnl 2f* **33/1**

-000 **6** nk **Le Corvee (IRE)**[16] 2171 7-8-8 **54** AndreaAtzeni(5) 13 51
(A W Carroll) *hld up bhd: hdwy and n.m.r 3f out: swtchd towards inner fr over 2f out: kpt on ins fnl f: nvr nr ldrs* **11/1**

100 **7** 1 **Casablanca Minx (IRE)**[11] 2294 6-8-11 **52** (v) StephenDonohoe 5 47
(Miss Gay Kelleway) *hld up in midfield: hdwy over 3f out: drvn and unable qck 2f out: wl btn fnl f* **28/1**

500- **8** 1 1/2 **Looks The Business (IRE)**[226] 6882 8-8-11 **52** SteveDrowne 8 45
(A B Haynes) *prom: chsd ldr 9f out tl led over 5f out: rdn and hdd wl over 2f out: wknd over 1f out* **15/2**[3]

9 1 1/2 **Ridgetime Anna (IRE)**[13] 2251 4-8-5 **46** CatherineGannon 11 36
(Daniel Mark Loughnane, Ire) *hld up bhd: sme hdwy but hanging bdly lft 3f out: swtchd rt over 2f out: stl hanging after: modest late hdwy: n.d* **25/1**

0/0- **10** 5 **Spartan Dance**[292] 5087 5-8-10 **51** RichardThomas 6 33
(J A Geake) *plld hrd early: chsd ldrs tl stdd towards midfield 8f out: pushed along 6f out: rdn and wknd 3f out* **66/1**

021/ **11** 1 3/4 **Hathaal (IRE)**[9] 3795 10-8-5 **46** oh1 JimmyQuinn 4 25
(Jim Best) *broke wl: sn in midfield: rdn and wknd over 3f out* **20/1**

00- **12** 7 **Amarillo Slim (IRE)**[22] 843 5-8-5 **46** (b[1]) KirstyMilczarek 2 13
(S Curran) *led for 1f: chsd ldrs after tl rdn and wknd wl over 2f out* **66/1**

0-03 **13** 10 **Dr McFab**[23] 1974 5-8-8 **49** (v[1]) EddieAhern 14 —
(Miss Tor Sturgis) *led after 1f: sn clr: hdd and rdn over 5f out: wl bhd fnl 2f: t.o* **13/2**[2]

04-0 **14** 9 **Compton Charlie**[56] 1200 5-8-10 **51** TolleyDean 10 —
(J G Portman) *hld up in rr: rdn and no rspnse 3f out: t.o and virtually p.u fnl f* **12/1**

2m 28.99s (-2.51) **Going Correction** -0.20s/f (Firm) **14** Ran SP% **120.9**
Speed ratings (Par 101): **101,99,98,96,95 95,94,93,92,88 87,82,75,68**
toteswinger: 1&2 £33.80, 1&3 £161.10, 2&3 £4.20 CSF £152.89 CT £1085.30 TOTE £115.50: £18.90, £1.20, £3.30; EX 453.10 Trifecta £316.60 Part won. Pool: £427.89 - 0.10 winning units..
Owner W J Austin **Bred** Leo Glennon And Louis Creaven **Trained** Cloughjordan, Co Tipperary

FOCUS
A very moderate handicap run at a sound pace, this produced a real shock winner.
Newmarket Story(IRE) Official explanation: trainer said, regarding apparent improvement in form, that the mare was unable to run in Ireland due to its low rating, and had its first run after a lengthy lay-off.
Amarillo Slim(IRE) Official explanation: jockey said gelding hung left
Compton Charlie Official explanation: trainer's rep said gelding was unsuited by the good to firm ground

2635 MICHAEL WRIGHT RACING H'CAP 1m 3f 106y
4:50 (4:51) (Class 6) (0-60,59) 3-Y-O £2,047 (£604; £302) Stalls Low

Form RPR

4321 **1** **Screaming Brave**[6] 2461 3-9-5 **59** 6ex TedDurcan 1 63+
(M R Channon) *hld up towards rr: hdwy over 3f out: rdn to chse ldrs wl over 1f out: wnt 2nd and edgd lft jst ins fnl f: r.o wl to ld fnl strides* **2/1**[1]

-633 **2** hd **Persian Tomcat (IRE)**[57] 1183 3-8-0 **47** MatthewCosham(7) 3 51
(Miss J Feilden) *t.k.h: chsd ldrs: rdn to chal ent fnl 2f: led over 1f out: hdd fnl strides* **14/1**

0-00 **3** 2 1/4 **Rocky Heights (IRE)**[21] 2006 3-9-0 **54** EddieAhern 11 54+
(J L Dunlop) *hld up bhd: hdwy over 2f out: rn green over 1f out: r.o to chse ldng pair ins fnl f: styng on fin* **4/1**[2]

6-02 **4** 3 1/4 **Fongoli**[8] 2380 3-8-12 **52** (v) FergusSweeney 12 46
(B G Powell) *sn pushed along: hdwy to ld after 1f: hrd pressed and rdn over 2f out: hdd over 1f out: wknd fnl f* **6/1**[3]

-000 **5** 1 1/4 **Hassadin**[23] 1954 3-8-11 **51** StephenDonohoe 9 43
(A B Haynes) *hld up bhd: rdn and effrt on outer 3f out: kpt on fnl f but nvr pce to rch ldrs* **25/1**

-400 **6** 1/2 **Bright Wire (IRE)**[23] 1967 3-8-8 **48** JimmyQuinn 14 40
(M Madgwick) *hld up towards rr: bhd and hmpd over 3f out: hdwy over 1f out: styd on past btn horses fnl f: nvr nr ldrs* **12/1**

6-00 **7** 3 **Very Distinguished**[44] 1428 3-9-4 **58** LiamJones 13 44
(M G Quinlan) *t.k.h: hld up in tch tl hdwy to chse ldr 6f out: ev ch over 2f out: wknd qckly over 1f out* **8/1**

0005 **8** 1 1/4 **Red Dagger (IRE)**[13] 2220 3-8-9 **49** KirstyMilczarek 10 33
(T D McCarthy) *t.k.h: hld up towards rr: hdwy over 5f out: rdn and effrt 3f out: wknd over 1f out* **33/1**

0205 **9** 3 1/2 **Rannoch Rose (IRE)**[27] 1848 3-8-8 **48** (p) TolleyDean 4 26
(J L Spearing) *t.k.h: hld up in midfield: lost pl and racd awkwardly bnd over 3f out: hung lft 3f out: bhd after* **14/1**

0-60 **10** 1/2 **Gibson Square (USA)**[9] 2350 3-9-1 **55** (v[1]) AdamKirby 2 32
(S C Williams) *led for 1f: chsd ldr tl 6f out: reminder over 5f out: wknd 2f out* **40/1**

3-00 **11** 7 **Play To Win (IRE)**[24] 1930 3-9-4 **58** RobertHavlin 7 24
(D R C Elsworth) *hld up in midfield: losing pl and rdn whn hung lft and hmpd over 3f out: n.d* **14/1**

50-0 **12** 44 **Premier Superstar**[24] 1931 3-9-0 **54** SebSanders 5 —
(M H Tompkins) *chsd ldrs tl rdn and wknd 3f out: eased fr over 1f out: t.o* **20/1**

2m 31.78s (0.28) **Going Correction** -0.20s/f (Firm) **12** Ran SP% **120.4**
Speed ratings (Par 97): **90,89,88,85,84 84,82,81,78,78 73,41**
toteswinger: 1&2 £7.80, 1&3 £2.20, 2&3 £10.30 CSF £32.28 CT £108.62 TOTE £2.80: £1.20, £4.00, £1.60; EX 34.30 Trifecta £269.20 Place 6: 17.48 Place 5: £9.69 Pool: £425.65 - 1.174 winning units.
Owner Billy Parish **Bred** Norman Court Stud **Trained** West Ilsley, Berks

FOCUS
A very moderate handicap run in a time the best part of three seconds slower than the previous handicap for older horses. A slight personal best from the winner, the form rated around the third.
Persian Tomcat(IRE) Official explanation: jockey said gelding hung badly left coming down the hill
Premier Superstar Official explanation: jockey said filly was unsuited by the good to firm ground
T/Plt: £5.40 to a £1 stake. Pool: £49,650.76. 6,620.18 winning tickets. T/Qpdt: £5.30 to a £1 stake. Pool: £3,523.80. 489.90 winning tickets.

2407 SANDOWN (R-H)
Thursday, June 4

OFFICIAL GOING: Good to firm (9.1)
Wind: Virtually nil Weather: Bright

2636 JUNE MAIDEN AUCTION STKS 5f 6y
6:10 (6:12) (Class 5) 2-Y-O £3,238 (£963; £481; £240) Stalls High

Form RPR

1 **Treadwell (IRE)** 2-8-13 0 ShaneKelly 1 81+
(J A Osborne) *s.i.s: sn t.k.h and trcking ldrs: qcknd to ld 1f out and j. path sn after: shkn up and styd on strly* **11/1**

6 **2** 3/4 **Palisades Park**[21] 2007 2-8-13 0 RyanMoore 11 78
(R Hannon) *trckd ldrs and keen early: drvn: swtchd lft and qcknd over 1f out: wnt 2nd cl home but a hld by wnr* **6/4**[1]

43 **3** nk **Warning Song (USA)**[3] 2533 2-8-13 0 JimCrowley 3 77
(Mrs A J Perrett) *chsd ldrs: led over 2f out: hdd 1f out: styd chsng wnr but a hld: lost 2nd cl home* **11/4**[2]

6 **4** 7 **Listillo (USA)**[20] 2033 2-8-11 0 TPQueally 8 50
(H J L Dunlop) *green in rr: drvn along over 3f out: stl green but styd on for mod 4th fr over 1f out* **9/2**[3]

5 2 1/4 **Storm Hawk (IRE)** 2-8-11 0 PaulEddery 10 42
(Pat Eddery) *green in rr: drvn along fr 3f out: mod late prog* **20/1**

0 **6** 3 3/4 **Royal Blade (IRE)**[14] 2196 2-8-9 0 AlanMunro 5 26
(A P Jarvis) *led tl hdd over 2f out: sn wknd* **33/1**

7 3/4 **Private Olley** 2-8-10 0 ow1 IanMongan 4 25
(J Akehurst) *s.i.s: in tch tl outpcd fr 1/2-way* **16/1**

8 1/2 **Lucky Flyer** 2-8-4 0 ChrisCatlin 6 17
(Rae Guest) *green and in rr thrght* **33/1**

60.34 secs (-1.26) **Going Correction** -0.275s/f (Firm) **8** Ran SP% **109.7**
Speed ratings (Par 93): **99,97,97,86,82 76,75,74**
toteswinger: 1&2 £2.60, 1&3 £6.00, 2&3 £1.20 CSF £25.77 TOTE £14.30: £3.90, £1.10, £1.20; EX 37.20.
Owner Mrs F Walwyn & A Taylor **Bred** Liberty Road Stables **Trained** Upper Lambourn, Berks

FOCUS
An ordinary sprint maiden which very few got into. The first three pulled clear.

NOTEBOOK
Treadwell(IRE) looked a little burly in the paddock but knew his job, despite running a little green – he jumped a path two furlongs out. He didn't have the best of draws and his breeding suggests he will need further, so it was a pretty smart performance under the circumstances. He looks a colt with plenty of scope and is the first sharp two-year-old to run for the yard this season. He will be stepped up in trip next time and his trainer intimated that he would not rule out the Coventry Stakes at Royal Ascot. (op 14-1 tchd 10-1)
Palisades Park found his path blocked at a crucial stage, just as he did on his Salisbury debut. Again, he ran on strongly at the finish. He looks another who should be able to handle a step up in trip before too long. (op 6-5 tchd 11-10)
Warning Song(USA), who has plenty of scope, showed a willing attitude and ran on well to suggest that a race or two will fall his way. He didn't have the best draw and it may be that two races in the space of four days might have taken their toll. (tchd 5-2 and 7-2)
Listillo(USA) showed promise on his debut, but looked a very hard ride here, through greenness more than anything. He may have found the ground a bit lively. (op 8-1)
Storm Hawk(IRE), related to a couple of very quick juveniles, showed promise, but he needs further. (tchd 22-1)
Private Olley looked as though he would come on a ton for the run and was green. He weakened from the furlong pole. (op 20-1 tchd 14-1)
Lucky Flyer looked the one who would come on most for a run. With experience, she could make her mark in nursery company.

2637 HOMEBUILDING & RENOVATING SHOW H'CAP 5f 6y
6:45 (6:45) (Class 4) (0-85,84) 3-Y-O+ £5,180 (£1,541; £770; £384) Stalls High

Form RPR

3206 **1** **Blue Jack**[10] 2326 4-9-8 **78** (b[1]) MartinDwyer 6 91
(W R Muir) *in tch: hdwy fr 2f out: str run on ins and carried rt ins fnl f: led fnl 110yds: hld on all out* **10/1**

3631 **2** nk **Canadian Danehill (IRE)**[20] 2053 7-9-13 **83** (p) LDettori 9 95
(R M H Cowell) *chsd ldrs: rdn to ld and edgd rt appr fnl f: edgd lft u.p and hdd fnl110yds: styd on but a jst hld* **15/2**[3]

1-01 **3** nse **Invincible Lad (IRE)**[9] 2359 5-9-11 **81** 6ex RyanMoore 4 93+
(E J Alston) *towards rr: str run on outside fr 2f out: drvn to chal ins fnl f: styd upsides: no ex nr fin* **5/4**[1]

-050 **4** 1 1/4 **Esteem Machine (USA)**[19] 2078 5-9-12 **82** (v[1]) LukeMorris 7 91+
(R A Teal) *s.i.s: t.k.h in rr: hdwy fr 2f out: styng on whn hmpd fnl 110yds: nt rcvr and one pce* **16/1**

-025 **5** 3 **Orange Pip**[10] 2326 4-9-10 **80** JimmyFortune 5 77
(R Hannon) *in tch: drvn and hdwy 2f out to chse ldrs over 1f out: nvr gng pce to chal and wknd ins fnl f* **16/1**

0-00 **6** 1 1/2 **Victorian Bounty**[33] 1663 4-10-0 **84** (v[1]) MickyFenton 8 75
(Stef Liddiard) *led tl hdd appr fnl f: wkng whn hmpd sn after* **12/1**

6614 **7** 2 **Peopleton Brook**[5] 2472 7-8-4 **65** oh4 (t) Louis-PhilippeBeuzelin(5) 3 49
(B G Powell) *rdn 1/2-way: nvr gng pce to get into contention* **33/1**

3-30 **8** 1/2 **Even Bolder**[27] 1836 6-9-9 **79** StephenCarson 10 61
(E A Wheeler) *chsd ldr: rdn and wkng whn hmpd appr fnl f* **20/1**

2-33 **9** 1 **Rocker**[13] 2228 5-9-6 **76** GeorgeBaker 11 55
(G L Moore) *in tch: hdwy to chse ldrs 2f out: wknd over 1f out* **8/1**

0031 **10** 1 1/4 **Bold Argument (IRE)**[3] 2549 6-8-12 **71** 6ex JackMitchell(3) 1 45
(Mrs P N Dutfield) *outpcd* **7/1**[2]

4420 **11** 1 **Make My Dream**[9] 2359 6-9-0 **70** TPO'Shea 2 40
(J Gallagher) *outpcd* **33/1**

60.08 secs (-1.52) **Going Correction** -0.275s/f (Firm) **11** Ran SP% **119.0**
Speed ratings (Par 105): **101,100,100,98,93 91,88,87,85,83 82**
toteswinger: 1&2 £6.50, 1&3 £4.00, 2&3 £2.00 CSF £82.17 CT £161.27 TOTE £12.10: £3.00, £2.30, £1.20; EX 65.10.
Owner Martin P Graham **Bred** Miss S N Ralphs **Trained** Lambourn, Berks
■ Stewards' Enquiry : L Dettori three day ban: careless riding (Jun 22-24)

FOCUS
A competitive handicap for the money, only slightly faster than the hand-timed juvenile opener on the card, but truly-run. The form reads sound enough.

Esteem Machine(USA) Official explanation: jockey said gelding hung right.

2638 XL INSURANCE H'CAP 7f 16y

7:15 (7:17) (Class 4) (0-85,83) 3-Y-O £5,180 (£1,541; £770; £384) Stalls High

Form RPR

-104 **1** **Cyflymder (IRE)**[28] 1803 3-9-6 **80** PatDobbs 9 85
(R Hannon) *led for 1f: trckd ldr: led again wl over 1f out: drvn and kpt on wl cl home* **10/1**

321 **2** *1 ¼* **Head Down**[78] 869 3-9-4 **78** RyanMoore 8 80
(R Hannon) *chsd: rdn over 2f out: chsd wnr over 1f out: kpt on u.p but a hld* **7/1**

10-0 **3** *hd* **Bravo Echo**[19] 2072 3-9-9 **83** JimmyFortune 7 84+
(J H M Gosden) *towards rr: hdwy over 2f out: str run u.p fr over 1f out: clsng on 2nd nr fin but nvr gng pce to rch wnr* **9/2**[2]

0-1 **4** *2 ¾* **Sir Isaac**[33] 1671 3-9-1 **75** KirstyMilczarek 10 69+
(W J Haggas) *s.i.s: rr: hdwy on ins over 2f out: styng on whn nt clr run over 1f out: rallied ins fnl f: gng on cl home but nt trble ldng trio* **11/2**[3]

4-00 **5** *¾* **Key Signature**[19] 2079 3-9-8 **82** PaulEddery 5 74
(Pat Eddery) *broke wl: stdd but wl in tch: pushed along ins fnl 2f: kpt on fnl f but nvr gng pce to be competitive* **6/1**

610- **6** *1 ½* **Advertise**[267] 5791 3-8-13 **73** LPKeniry 1 61
(A M Balding) *s.i.s: sn rcvrd to ld after 1f: 4 l clr over 3f out: rdn over 2f out: hdd wl over 1f out: wknd ins fnl f* **16/1**

1-50 **7** *1 ½* **Major Phil (IRE)**[14] 2198 3-9-3 **77** LDettori 6 61
(L M Cumani) *hld up towards rr: drvn and effrt over 2f out: nvr gng pce to be competitive: wknd fnl f* **7/2**[1]

5-41 **8** *1 ½* **Beautiful Breeze (IRE)**[26] 1895 3-9-4 **78** RoystonFfrench 3 57
(M Johnston) *towards rr but in tch: rdn and effrt into mid-div over 3f out: sn fnd no ex and wknd 2f out* **10/1**

010- **9** *nse* **Master Fong (IRE)**[231] 6756 3-9-5 **79** MichaelHills 2 58
(B W Hills) *t.k.h: chsd ldrs: rdn: hung lft and hd high over 2f out: fnd little and sn wknd* **16/1**

06-4 **10** *13* **Durgan**[19] 2080 3-9-1 **75** GeorgeBaker 4 19
(Mrs L C Jewell) *t.k.h: rdn 3f out: a bhd* **20/1**

1m 27.43s (-2.07) **Going Correction** -0.225s/f (Firm) **10** Ran SP% **117.3**
Speed ratings (Par 101): **102,100,100,97,96 94,92,91,91,76**
toteswinger: 1&2 £14.70, 1&3 £4.20, 2&3 £13.30 CSF £78.66 CT £297.55 TOTE £11.90: £3.40, £2.90, £2.40; EX 77.50.
Owner Amblestock Partnership **Bred** Miss Laura G F Ferguson **Trained** East Everleigh, Wilts
■ Stewards' Enquiry : Jimmy Fortune one-day ban: careless riding (June 21)

FOCUS
A fair handicap in which it seemed an advantage to race prominently. The form is rated around the first two.
Durgan Official explanation: jockey said colt ran too free

2639 EXTRABET.COM H'CAP 1m 14y

7:50 (7:51) (Class 3) (0-90,90) 4-Y-O+ £7,771 (£2,312; £1,155; £577) Stalls High

Form RPR

4-45 **1** **Ellemujie**[19] 2083 4-9-6 **87** RyanMoore 2 96
(D K Ivory) *towards rr: rdn and gd hdwy over 2f out: str run to ld 1f out: kpt on wl* **7/2**[1]

5012 **2** *1* **Mujood**[5] 2480 6-9-0 **84** KevinGhunowa[(3)] 9 91
(Eve Johnson Houghton) *led: rdn whn chal fr 2f out: hdd 1f out: styd on wl for 2nd but a hld by wnr* **8/1**

-003 **3** *1 ¼* **Ballinteni**[31] 1750 7-9-4 **85** SebSanders 4 89
(D K Ivory) *in tch: rdn and hdwy fr 2f out: styd on wl fnl f but nvr gng pce to trble ldng duo* **10/1**

5312 **4** *2* **Annabelle's Charm (IRE)**[16] 2150 4-9-4 **85** LDettori 6 84
(L M Cumani) *chsd ldrs: t.k.h: rdn and hdwy to chal fr wl over 1f out: wknd ins fnl f and hung rt nr fin* **9/2**[2]

0-10 **5** *½* **Cotswolds**[12] 2257 4-8-8 **75** RoystonFfrench 5 73
(M Johnston) *chsd ldrs: rdn over 2f out: wknd ins fnl f* **11/1**

04-3 **6** *nk* **Habshan (USA)**[19] 2083 9-9-6 **87** GeorgeBaker 3 84
(C F Wall) *s.i.s: bhd: pushed along and hdwy fr 2f out: kpt on ins fnl f but nvr in contention* **12/1**

201- **7** *1 ¼* **Willow Dancer (IRE)**[245] 6431 5-9-9 **90** (p) AdamKirby 7 85
(W R Swinburn) *chsd ldrs: rdn over 2f out: edgd rt over 1f out: wknd fnl f* **6/1**[3]

4121 **8** *1* **Miss Glitters (IRE)**[17] 2133 4-8-10 **77** SteveDrowne 10 69
(H Morrison) *trckd ldrs: rdn ins fnl 3f: wkng whn n.m.r on rails 1f out* **8/1**

3400 **9** *½* **Prince Of Thebes (IRE)**[5] 2480 8-9-0 **81** PaulDoe 8 72
(M J Attwater) *chsd ldr: rdn over 2f out: sn ev ch: wkng whn hmpd ins fnl f: eased* **33/1**

000- **10** *2 ¼* **Hurricane Hymnbook (USA)**[263] 5942 4-9-9 **90** MickyFenton 11 76
(Stef Liddiard) *t.k.h: rdn and hung rt over 2f out: a in rr* **10/1**

6-25 **11** *4 ½* **Ocean Transit (IRE)**[10] 2334 4-8-9 **76** JamesDoyle 1 52
(R J Price) *a in rr* **50/1**

1m 39.94s (-3.36) **Going Correction** -0.225s/f (Firm) **11** Ran SP% **116.0**
Speed ratings (Par 107): **107,106,104,102,102 101,100,99,99,96 92**
toteswinger: 1&2 £6.60, 1&3 £17.30, 2&3 £24.60 CSF £31.27 CT £261.49 TOTE £4.90: £1.70, £2.30, £4.30; EX 41.90.
Owner Mrs J A Cornwell & John G Smith **Bred** Mrs J A Cornwell **Trained** Radlett, Herts

FOCUS
A fair handicap for the grade, run quicker than the standard time. The winner is rated back to form.

NOTEBOOK
Ellemujie, who was winning for only the second time in 25 starts, landed something of a gamble. Dropped out early on, he came with a rattle up the outside and just found enough, overturning Newmarket form with Habshan. He is a consistent type, who would probably do even better with a bit more cut in the ground. This stiffer track clearly helped and the Royal Hunt Cup is on the agenda. (op 9-2)
Mujood is worth following, despite going up 4lb after this. He is a right battler and came back at Ellemujie when he went past. He is capable of picking up a nice handicap or two. (op 5-1)
Ballinteni followed his stablemate through from the rear and ran an eyecatching race. Sixth in the Hunt Cup last year, he appears to be nearing his peak, though his trainer reported that he has not been easy to train, suffering an overreach in the spring. (op 14-1 tchd 16-1)
Annabelle's Charm(IRE) has been upped 7lb since her last win and gave the impression that she would have preferred a bit further. Official explanation: jockey said filly hung right (op 7-2)
Cotswolds came there with every chance, but he didn't have the easiest passage and his rider was sympathetic after his chance had gone. He will win in his turn. Official explanation: jockey said gelding ran too free (op 12-1 tchd 14-1)
Habshan(USA), who finished in front of today's winner at Newmarket, was well held but left the impression he had more to give. (op 8-1)
Willow Dancer(IRE), racing off a career-high mark, made a promising comeback, despite looking in need of the run. (op 9-1 tchd 10-1)
Prince Of Thebes(IRE) Official explanation: jockey said gelding suffered interference in running
Hurricane Hymnbook(USA) is best when fresh, but he looked burly and ran as though he would come on a ton for the run. (op 12-1)

2640 TAKE A PROFIT IN-RUNNING WITH EXTRABET.COM MAIDEN STKS 1m 2f 7y

8:25 (8:25) (Class 5) 3-Y-O £3,238 (£963; £481; £240) Stalls High

Form RPR

62 **1** **Senses (USA)**[13] 2240 3-9-3 0 RyanMoore 11 79+
(J Noseda) *hld up in mid-div: str run on outside fr over 2f out: chsd wnr over 1f out: styd on to ld fnl 50yds: won gng away* **3/1**[2]

4 **2** *½* **Buckie Boy (IRE)**[26] 1874 3-9-3 0 (b) TPQueally 5 78
(H R A Cecil) *led: 5 l clr ins fnl 3f: kpt on wl whn drvn fnl 2f: hdd and nt qckn fnl 50yds: but wl clr of 3rd* **22/1**

3 *6* **Funday** 3-8-12 0 FergusSweeney 10 61
(G L Moore) *hld up towards rr: hdwy over 1f out: styd on wl fnl f to take 3rd last strides but nt ch w ldng duo* **66/1**

5-3 **4** *hd* **Twisted**[19] 2074 3-9-3 0 JimmyFortune 4 66
(J H M Gosden) *in tch: hdwy 3f out: chsd ldrs 2f out but nvr nr clr ldr: wknd ins fnl f and lost 3rd last strides* **11/10**[1]

05- **5** *1 ¾* **Lady Drac (IRE)**[232] 6731 3-8-12 0 MichaelHills 7 57
(B W Hills) *chsd ldrs: wnt 2nd 3f out: but nvr nr clr ldr: sn drvn and hung rt: lost 2nd over 1f out and wknd ins fnl f* **14/1**

0 **6** *2* **Borromeo (USA)**[6] 2446 3-9-3 0 RoystonFfrench 1 58
(M Johnston) *chsd ldrs: rdn over 3f out: wknd over 1f out* **12/1**

05 **7** *3 ¾* **Twist Again (IRE)**[13] 2240 3-8-12 0 JimCrowley 3 46
(P Howling) *s.i.s: bhd tl styd on fr over 1f out but nvr anywhere nr ldrs* **100/1**

8 *3 ½* **Double Whammy** 3-9-3 0 SteveDrowne 9 44
(Jamie Poulton) *in rr tl mod late prog* **100/1**

00 **9** *2 ¼* **Dolores Ortiz (IRE)**[17] 2139 3-8-12 0 CatherineGannon 2 34
(S C Williams) *chsd ldr tl 3f out: sn btn* **100/1**

00- **10** *19* **Desert Streak (FR)**[217] 7098 3-9-3 0 SebSanders 8 1
(H J L Dunlop) *t.k.h: a in rr* **50/1**

4 **11** *1 ½* **Bourne**[19] 2082 3-9-3 0 LDettori 6 —
(L M Cumani) *trckd ldrs: stmbld and lost action bnd over 3f out: eased fnl 2f* **4/1**[3]

2m 7.76s (-2.74) **Going Correction** -0.225s/f (Firm) **11** Ran SP% **117.7**
Speed ratings (Par 99): **101,100,95,95,94 92,89,86,85,69 68**
toteswinger: 1&2 £19.40, 1&3 £19.80, 2&3 £84.00 CSF £69.64 TOTE £5.30: £1.40, £3.20, £13.40; EX 81.70.
Owner Sir Robert Ogden **Bred** Dr K K Jayaraman Et Al **Trained** Newmarket, Suffolk

FOCUS
What looked on paper to be a reasonable maiden provided more than a few disappointments, though the time was solid enough. The form is rated around the winner but might not prove too solid.
Twisted Official explanation: jockey said colt hung right in the straight
Twist Again(IRE) Official explanation: jockey said filly missed the break
Dolores Ortiz(IRE) Official explanation: jockey said filly hung badly right
Bourne Official explanation: jockey said colt hung badly right

2641 GRAB A FREE BET WITH EXTRABET.COM H'CAP 1m 2f 7y

8:55 (8:55) (Class 4) (0-80,80) 4-Y-O+ £3,361 (£3,361; £770; £384) Stalls High

Form RPR

010- **1** **Shavansky**[192] 7439 5-9-5 **79** JamesMillman[(3)] 11 85
(B R Millman) *trckd ldrs: rdn over 2f out: slt ld over 1f out: narrowly hdd fnl 75yds: rallied to force dead-heat* **13/2**[3]

240- **1** *dht* **Cosmea**[103] 6127 4-9-7 **78** RyanMoore 5 84+
(A King) *hld up in rr: rdn and hdwy on outside fr over 2f out: drvn to take slt advantage fnl 75yds: jnd for dead-heat last stride* **3/1**[1]

5001 **3** *nk* **Kidlat**[9] 2351 4-9-7 **78** 6ex (t) JimCrowley 6 83
(B G Powell) *t.k.h in mid-div: rdn and styd on fnl 2f: styd on wl thrght fnl f: clsng on dead heaters cl home* **15/2**

231- **4** *1* **Barliffey (IRE)**[223] 6956 4-9-2 **73** (v) TPO'Shea 9 76
(D J Coakley) *s.i.s: hld up towards rr: hdwy 3f out: styng on whn n.m.r over 1f out: kpt on ins fnl f: fin wl* **12/1**

1245 **5** *½* **Basra (IRE)**[31] 1750 6-9-9 **80** IanMongan 1 82+
(Miss Jo Crowley) *hld up in rr: stdy hdwy over 2f out: sn nt clr run and stl no room over 1f out: swtchd rt jst ins fnl f: fin strly but nt rcvr* **14/1**

1/25 **6** *2 ¾* **La Rosa Nostra**[16] 2150 4-9-2 **73** (t) AdamKirby 7 70
(W R Swinburn) *sn led: rdn 3f out: hdd over 2f out: wknd over 1f out* **6/1**[2]

00-5 **7** *1* **Northern Spy (USA)**[28] 1815 5-9-2 **73** SebSanders 2 68
(S Dow) *chsd ldr: led over 2f out: hdd & wknd qckly over 1f out* **11/1**

0524 **8** *hd* **Baylini**[7] 2407 5-9-9 **80** JamesDoyle 12 74
(Ms J S Doyle) *chsd ldrs: rdn over 2f out: wknd over 1f out: no ch whn n.m.r sn after* **10/1**

0-30 **9** *1* **Bustan (IRE)**[23] 1952 10-9-3 **79** Louis-PhilippeBeuzelin[(5)] 10 71
(G C Bravery) *chsd ldrs: rdn over 2f out: no ch whn hmpd over 1f out* **14/1**

-065 **10** *½* **Gallego**[13] 2244 7-8-6 **63** SaleemGolam 3 54
(R J Price) *s.i.s: a in rr* **10/1**

-241 **11** *2 ¼* **Summer Winds**[20] 2052 4-9-2 **80** (b) DToole[(7)] 8 67
(T G Mills) *bhd most of way* **14/1**

2m 7.55s (-2.95) **Going Correction** -0.225s/f (Firm) **11** Ran SP% **118.6**
Speed ratings (Par 105): **102,101,101,100,100 98,97,97,96,96 94**WIN: Shavansky £4.70 Cosmea £2.00, PL: S £3.20 C £2.10, Kidlat £2.30. EX: S, C £13.25 C, S £17.50. CSF: S, C £13.25 C, S £11.01. Tricast: S, C, K £76.55 C, S, K £68.07 toteswinger: S&C £19.10, S&K £36.30, C&K £5.70 Pl27 Owner.
Owner John Southway & Andrew Hughes **Bred** George Strawbridge **Trained** Kentisbeare, Devon
■ Stewards' Enquiry : Ian Mongan three-day ban: careless riding (Jun 21-23)

FOCUS
Modest fare and it was steadily run, though the time was up to standard. It produced an enthralling finish as Shavansky and Cosmea dead-heated. Both produced slight personal bests.
Basra(IRE) Official explanation: jockey said gelding was denied a clear run

T/Jkpt: Not won. T/Plt: £78.60 to a £1 stake. Pool: £87,665.18. 814.11 winning tickets. T/Qpdt: £54.20 to a £1 stake. Pool: £5,793.86. 79.10 winning tickets. ST

2642 - (Foreign Racing) - See Raceform Interactive

2421 LEOPARDSTOWN (L-H)

Thursday, June 4

OFFICIAL GOING: Good to firm

2643a **IRISH STALLION FARMS EUROPEAN BREEDERS FUND MAIDEN** 6f
6:30 (6:38) 2-Y-O **£11,740** (£2,735; £1,206; £696)

RPR

1 **Moran Gra (USA)**[39] 1544 2-9-3 .... KJManning 3 84+
(Ms Joanna Morgan, Ire) *dwlt and wnt lft stalls: hld up in rr: hdwy in 3rd 2f out and edgd lft: sn led: rdn and kpt on strly fr over 1f out: comf* **12/1**

2 3 **Mark Twain (IRE)**[21] 2019 2-9-3 .... JMurtagh 6 75+
(A P O'Brien, Ire) *pressed ldr in cl 2nd: impr to ld briefly 2f out: rdn in 2nd 1 1/2f out: no imp wnr over 1f out: kpt on same pce* **4/6**[1]

3 2 1/2 **Waajida** 2-8-12 .... PJSmullen 1 65+
(D K Weld, Ire) *chsd ldrs in 3rd: rdn in 4th whn hmpd under 2f out: 3rd 1 1/2f out: kpt on same pce fr over 1f out* **5/2**[2]

4 2 **Goldarover (IRE)**[21] 2019 2-9-3 .... FMBerry 5 61
(Noel Meade, Ire) *racd mainly 4th: rdn in 5th 2f out: no imp in 4th over 1f out: kpt on same pce* **16/1**

5 7 **One Set (IRE)**[7] 2422 2-9-3 .... (t) KLatham 4 40
(G M Lyons, Ire) *led: strly pressed: rdn and hdd 2f out: no ex and wknd over 1f out* **6/1**[3]

1m 15.3s (1.20) **Going Correction** +0.05s/f (Good) **5 Ran SP% 116.4**
Speed ratings: **94,90,86,84,74**
CSF £22.34 TOTE £8.70: £3.80, £1.10; DF 29.70.
Owner M A Ryan **Bred** Airlie Stud & Robert N Clay **Trained** Ballivor, Co Meath

NOTEBOOK
Moran Gra(USA) quickened up impressively to sweep to the front under Kevin Manning and he stuck to his task well to win very comfortably. In mounting his challenge he forced second favourite Waajida's rider to snatch up, effectively ruining her chance. This was a significant step forward from the colt's debut effort at Navan over the minimum trip and underlined that Joanna Morgan's string are beginning to hit form again after a sluggish start to the Irish campaign. The winning trainer described Moran Gra as "still a baby" and admitted afterwards that he struggled in the testing ground first time out at Navan. Royal Ascot could figure next. (op 10/1)
Mark Twain(IRE) was expected to step up on his Gowran debut sixth and he broke smartly to dispute early before he was settled in second behind leader One Set. He couldn't go with the winner when he quickened the tempo in good style, but this was a better display from the Ballydoyle colt, who'll appreciate further in due course. (op 9/10)
Waajida was easy enough to back in the end and the daughter of the 2005 Irish 2,000 Guineas winner Dubawi wasn't disgraced after meeting with interference at a crucial stage. Her rider accepted the situation and let her come home in her own time inside the final furlong. One would expect this well-bred filly to learn a fair bit from this initial effort. (op 7/4 tchd 3/1)

2644a **BALLYOGAN STKS (GROUP 3) (F&M)** 6f
7:00 (7:08) 3-Y-O+ **£41,019** (£11,990; £5,679; £1,893)

RPR

1 **Lesson In Humility (IRE)**[26] 1880 4-9-6 .... AndrewElliott 3 109+
(K R Burke) *chsd ldr: 2nd 1/2-way: chal ent st: rdn to ld 1 1/2f out: kpt on wl fnl f: flashed tail* **2/1**[1]

2 1 3/4 **San Sicharia (IRE)**[26] 1873 4-9-9 104 .... PJSmullen 5 105
(Ms Joanna Morgan, Ire) *chsd ldrs: 3rd 1/2-way: rdn in 4th 1 1/2f out: kpt on into 2nd ins fnl f: nt rch wnr* **5/1**[3]

3 shd **Maoineach (USA)**[31] 1756 3-9-3 105 .... KJManning 8 105
(J S Bolger, Ire) *chsd ldrs: 6th 1/2-way: rdn into 5th 1 1/2f out: kpt on fnl f to 3rd cl home* **9/1**

4 1/2 **Sugar Free (IRE)**[18] 2107 3-8-12 100 .... WMLordan 1 98
(T Stack, Ire) *chsd ldrs: 4th 1/2-way: rdn in 3rd 2f out: 2nd 1f out: kpt on in 3rd ins fnl f: no ex cl home* **14/1**

5 1 1/4 **Kalidaha (IRE)**[31] 1756 4-9-6 99 .... MJKinane 7 96
(John M Oxx, Ire) *led: rdn and chal ent st: hdd 1 1/2f out: no ex over 1f out: kpt on same pce* **10/1**

6 3/4 **Ohiyesa (IRE)**[31] 1755 3-8-12 93 .... KLatham 2 92
(G M Lyons, Ire) *chsd ldrs: 5th 1/2-way: rdn 2f out: no ex in 6th 1 1/2f out: kpt on same pce* **16/1**

7 1/2 **Aine (IRE)**[12] 2271 4-9-6 97 .... MCHussey 9 93
(T Stack, Ire) *s.i.s: nvr a factor* **20/1**

8 1 **Love Intrigue (IRE)**[251] 4-9-6 101 .... WJLee 6 90
(T Stack, Ire) *a towards rr* **33/1**

9 2 **Aleagueoftheirown (IRE)**[249] 6315 5-9-6 104 .... DPMcDonogh 10 84
(David Wachman, Ire) *a towards rr* **14/1**

10 shd **Pursuit Of Glory (IRE)**[32] 1698 3-8-12 107 .... JMurtagh 4 81
(David Wachman, Ire) *mid-div: 7th 1/2-way: rdn 2f out: no ex fr 1 1/2f out: wknd* **9/4**[2]

1m 12.8s (-1.30) **Going Correction** +0.05s/f (Good)
WFA 3 from 4yo+ 8lb **10 Ran SP% 126.8**
Speed ratings: **110,107,107,106,105 104,103,102,99,99**
CSF £13.99 TOTE £3.00: £1.30, £1.70, £2.20; DF 13.50.
Owner M Nelmes-Crocker **Bred** Kevin Quinn **Trained** Middleham Moor, N Yorks

FOCUS
The runner-up down to the sixth have all been rated close to their marks.

NOTEBOOK
Lesson In Humility(IRE) continued her progression for Karl Burke when landing this Group 3 event under another polished ride from regular pilot Andrew Elliott. The Listed winner at Nottingham on her seasonal debut relishes fast underfoot conditions. Always in front rank, she took over a furlong and a half out and kept on well for her sixth career win. She figures among the market leaders for the Wokingham and, on this evidence, she'll go to Royal Ascot with a live chance. Her trainer will consider a crack at the Group 1 Golden Jubilee on the Saturday of the Royal meeting as a 5lb penalty in the Wokingham does not appeal. (op 2/1 tchd 9/4)
San Sicharia(IRE), successful in a Group 3 contest over a furlong longer at Lingfield last month, proved best of the home challenge. A dual French winner over 7f, she mounted her challenge into the straight but couldn't go with the winner. She might be more effective up in trip, but this was still a fair effort, and she was beaten by a decent filly. (op 6/1 tchd 9/2)
Maoineach(USA) was reluctant to load. She showed more like her best form on her favoured surface over a trip that was short of ideal on this faster ground. (op 11/2)
Sugar Free(IRE) was easy to back. She raced close up from the outset, but was another who couldn't quicken when asked a serious question. She probably found this surface on the lively side. (op 10/1)
Kalidaha(IRE), who raced up front until giving way early in the straight, probably found this shorter trip against her. She handles faster ground but another furlong or two could see her play a more prominent role.
Pursuit Of Glory(IRE), third in last year's Cheveley Park over this trip, and eighth in the 1000 Guineas on her reappearance, was a disappointment. She was pushed along into the straight and her rider accepted the situation and eased her down inside the final furlong. Official explanation: jockey said filly was never travelling (op 5/2 tchd 15/8)

2647a **GLENCAIRN STKS (LISTED RACE)** 1m
8:30 (8:30) 4-Y-O+ **£26,861** (£7,881; £3,754; £1,279)

RPR

1 **Shreyas (IRE)**[31] 1758 4-9-3 108 .... KJManning 4 108
(J S Bolger, Ire) *chsd ldr in 2nd: impr to chal ent st: rdn to ld over 1f out: kpt on strly fnl f* **2/1**[1]

2 3 **Quinmaster (USA)**[12] 2289 7-9-1 102 .... (p) JMurtagh 3 99
(M Halford, Ire) *led: chal ent st: rdn and hdd over 1f out: no ex and kpt on same pce* **4/1**[3]

3 1 1/4 **Indiana Gal (IRE)**[32] 1715 4-9-1 99 .... (p) FMBerry 5 96
(Patrick Martin, Ire) *hld up towards rr: rdn into 3rd 2f out: no imp on ldrs over 1f out: kpt on same pce* **10/1**

4 1/2 **Festival Princess (IRE)**[22] 1996 4-8-12 102 .... RPCleary 6 92
(Mrs John Harrington, Ire) *dwlt: sn chsd ldrs: 4th 1/2-way: rdn 1 1/2f out: kpt on same pce fr over 1f out* **9/4**[2]

5 shd **Finicius (USA)**[46] 1387 5-9-1 106 .... (t) JAHeffernan 7 95
(Eoin Griffin, Ire) *hld up towards rr: 6th 1/2-way: rdn into 5th 2f out: no imp over 1f out* **9/2**

6 3 **Gist (IRE)**[195] 7406 6-8-12 95 .... (b) NGMcCullagh 1 85
(W J Martin, Ire) *chsd ldrs: 3rd 1/2-way: rdn and dropped to 6th 2f out: kpt on one pce* **25/1**

7 2 1/2 **Dane Blue (IRE)**[12] 2285 7-8-12 90 .... PJSmullen 2 79
(S J Treacy, Ire) *chsd ldrs: 5th 1/2-way: rdn and wknd ent st* **20/1**

1m 39.0s (-2.20) **Going Correction** +0.05s/f (Good) **7 Ran SP% 120.0**
Speed ratings: **113,110,108,108,108 105,102**
CSF £11.33 TOTE £2.70: £1.70, £1.70; DF 11.70.
Owner Miss A H Marshall **Bred** Frank Dunne **Trained** Coolcullen, Co Carlow

FOCUS
The race has been rated around the fifth to his previous course and distance form.

NOTEBOOK
Shreyas(IRE), the only Group race winner in the line up, ran out a convincing winner here on the quickest ground she has raced on to date. A half-sister to Youmzain, she was soon in second place and, after being ridden along to begin her effort into the straight, she went to the front over a furlong out and stretched clear in good style inside the final furlong. Going back up in trip will suit her well. (op 9/4)
Quinmaster(USA) had run poorly on heavy ground at the Curragh on his previous start. A seven-time Flat winner who likes fast ground, he won this event two years ago. Front-running tactics were reverted to here and he appeared to be travelling well into the straight as the winner began her effort. Unable to raise his game when Shreyas asserted over a furlong out, he kept on and was always winning the race for second. (op 9/2)
Indiana Gal(IRE) was another back on more suitable ground following a moderate effort on heavy on her previous start. Ridden to try and close from behind early in the straight, she kept on without ever holding a winning chance.
Festival Princess(IRE) missed the break, but was soon close up and had her chance early in the straight before failing to raise her game under pressure. She has shown a liking for at least some ease in the ground and conditions were probably too lively for her here. (op 11/4)
Finicius(USA) was held up and began a forward move two furlongs out. He kept on under pressure but never posed a threat. (op 7/2)

2648 - (Foreign Racing) - See Raceform Interactive

2514 BATH (L-H)

Friday, June 5

OFFICIAL GOING: Firm (11.2)
Wind: Light, across Weather: Light rain 8.35 and 9.05

2649 **E.B.F./GAYMER CIDER COMPANY MAIDEN STKS** 5f 161y
6:25 (6:27) (Class 5) 2-Y-O **£3,885** (£1,156; £577; £288) **Stalls** Centre

Form RPR

3 1 **Below Zero (IRE)**[8] 2388 2-9-3 0 .... RoystonFfrench 4 93+
(M Johnston) *mde all: pushed clr over 1f out: eased towards fin* **7/4**[1]

0 2 8 **Six Diamonds**[39] 1569 2-8-12 0 .... TravisBlock 7 60
(H Morrison) *a chsng wnr: btn over 1f out* **33/1**

23 3 1 3/4 **Going French (IRE)**[3] 2575 2-9-3 0 .... J-PGuillambert 3 59
(R Curtis) *s.i.s: sn prom: pushed along over 3f out: rdn over 1f out: one pce: hld on for 3rd* **9/2**[3]

5 4 hd **Rakhine (IRE)**[21] 2037 2-9-3 0 .... JosedeSouza 5 58
(P F I Cole) *hld up in tch: pushed along and outpcd over 2f out: rdn over 1f out: kpt on same pce fnl f* **12/1**

5 5 **Huygens** 2-9-3 0 .... StephenCarson 9 42
(D J Coakley) *hld up towards rr: sme hdwy on outside over 2f out: wknd over 1f out* **16/1**

6 1 1/4 **Breeze Of The Air** 2-8-10 0 .... MatthewDavies(7) 2 38
(M R Channon) *hld up and bhd: sme hdwy over 2f out: rdn and wknd over 1f out* **25/1**

5 7 1/2 **Nepotism**[23] 1981 2-9-3 0 .... FrankieMcDonald 8 36
(M S Saunders) *prom: rdn over 2f out: wknd over 1f out* **20/1**

65 8 10 **Knightfire (IRE)**[17] 2147 2-9-3 0 .... ChrisCatlin 6 3
(W R Swinburn) *s.i.s: outpcd* **40/1**

02 U **Spanish Acclaim**[22] 2007 2-9-0 0 .... JackMitchell(3) 1 —
(J G Portman) *jinked lft and uns rdr sn after s* **2/1**[2]

1m 10.42s (-0.78) **Going Correction** -0.325s/f (Firm) **9 Ran SP% 115.4**
Speed ratings (Par 93): **92,81,79,78,72 70,69,56,—**
toteswinger: 1&2 £24.20, 1&3 £1.60, 2&3 £24.20. CSF £68.91 TOTE £2.70: £1.40, £5.10, £2.20; EX 68.40.
Owner Sheikh Hamdan Bin Mohammed Al Maktoum **Bred** Darley **Trained** Middleham Moor, N Yorks

FOCUS
An ordinary juvenile contest.

NOTEBOOK
Below Zero(IRE) travelled well out in front before blowing the field away in the final two furlongs. Only time will tell what he achieved here, but he has come on a good deal for his promising Ayr debut, and has plenty of speed for a colt bred to want 1m+. (op 9-4 tchd 11-4)
Six Diamonds, who didn't show a great deal at Windsor on debut, found ground conditions much quicker here and that may have helped her take a step forward. She should continue to improve. (op 20-1)
Going French(IRE)'s limitations are beginning to become apparent. He was left trailing in the winner's wake, having been in touch mid-race. (op 11-2)
Rakhine(IRE) could never get into it. Lightning fast ground may not be ideal for him. (op 14-1 tchd 9-1)

Spanish Acclaim, a leading contender on his latest second, jinked to his right and unseated Jack Mitchell. (op 15-8 tchd 13-8)

2650 BLACK IS BACK BLACKTHORN H'CAP 1m 2f 46y
6:55 (6:55) (Class 5) (0-70,68) 4-Y-0+ £2,719 (£809; £404; £202) Stalls Low

Form RPR
6552 1 **Hatch A Plan (IRE)**[5] 2516 8-8-3 50 ChrisCatlin 4 56
(Mouse Hamilton-Fairley) *a.p: wnt 2nd over 6f out: led on bit 2f out: rdn over 1f out: r.o wl* 11/4[2]
0004 2 3 ¾ **Gracechurch (IRE)**[5] 2516 6-8-5 57 WilliamCarson(5) 2 56
(R J Hodges) *chsd ldr over 3f: rdn over 2f out: kpt on same pce fnl f: tk 2nd towards fin* 4/1[3]
0060 3 ¾ **Stark Contrast (USA)**[22] 2011 5-8-5 52 CatherineGannon 1 49
(M D I Usher) *hld up: pushed along over 3f out: hdwy over 2f out: rdn over 1f out: chsd wnr jst ins fnl f: sn edgd lft: lost 2nd towards fin* 7/1
0232 4 8 **Bramalea**[9] 2379 4-9-7 68 WilliamBuick 3 64
(B W Duke) *set slow pce: qcknd over 4f out: rdn and hdd 2f out: eased whn btn jst ins fnl f* 1/1[1]
2m 18.47s (7.47) **Going Correction** -0.025s/f (Good) 4 Ran SP% 109.2
Speed ratings (Par 103): **69,66,65,59**
CSF £12.91 TOTE £4.00; EX 16.90.
Owner Hamilton-Fairley Racing **Bred** Camogue Stud Ltd **Trained** Bramshill, Hants

FOCUS
There was no pace on here and it developed into a sprint turning for home. The favourite disappointed and the form should not be taken literally.

2651 GAYMERS ORIGINAL CLAIMING STKS 5f 11y
7:30 (7:30) (Class 6) 3-Y-O £1,942 (£578; £288; £144) Stalls Centre

Form RPR
-321 1 **Mythical Blue (IRE)**[10] 2349 3-8-11 65 ChrisCatlin 8 67
(J M Bradley) *sn led: hrd rdn fnl f: all out* 7/4[1]
5305 2 hd **Sweet Applause (IRE)**[7] 2456 3-8-7 71 MatthewDavies(7) 5 69
(A P Jarvis) *led early: chsd wnr to 2f out: nt clr run and swtchd rt over 1f out: rdn and r.o ins fnl f: tk 2nd nr fin* 2/1[2]
0-03 3 nk **Dr Wintringham (IRE)**[10] 2349 3-7-13 70 SophieDoyle(5) 1 58
(J S Moore) *wnt lft s: t.k.h: sn prom: chsd wnr 2f out: rdn and ev ch ins fnl f: nt qckn: lost 2nd nr fin* 9/2[3]
6-63 4 5 **Ba Globetrotter**[23] 1982 3-8-5 49 CatherineGannon 3 41
(M R Channon) *hld up: stmbld after 1f: pushed along over 2f out: hdwy over 1f out: rdn and wknd ins fnl f* 7/1
5400 5 1 **Piccaso's Sky**[23] 1982 3-8-2 39 (b[1]) DavidProbert(3) 4 38
(A B Haynes) *hld up: hdwy on outside over 2f out: rdn and hung lft jst over 1f out: sn wknd* 25/1
06-0 6 2 **Kayceebee**[17] 2162 3-8-7 48 (b) WilliamBuick 6 32
(R M Beckett) *s.i.s: hld up in rr: hdwy on outside wl over 1f out: rdn and wkng whn hung lft ins fnl f* 10/1
00- 7 4 **Boundless Applause**[249] 6327 3-8-6 0 FrankieMcDonald 7 17
(I A Wood) *hld up in tch: rdn and wkng whn hmpd 1f out* 33/1
30-0 8 13 **Benetti (IRE)**[22] 2009 3-8-4 47 (v[1]) MarcHalford(3) 2 —
(M Madgwick) *s.i.s: sn in mid-div: rdn over 2f out: sn bhd* 28/1
61.94 secs (-0.56) **Going Correction** -0.325s/f (Firm) 8 Ran SP% 119.7
Speed ratings (Par 97): **91,90,90,82,80 77,71,50**
toteswinger: 1&2 £1.10, 1&3 £3.00, 2&3 £1.40. CSF £5.72 TOTE £2.50: £1.30, £1.40, £1.90; EX 8.20.
Owner Clifton Hunt **Bred** John O'Dowd **Trained** Sedbury, Gloucs

FOCUS
No strength in depth to this claimer and the first three, who drew clear, filled those positions throughout. The form is fairly sound.
Dr Wintringham(IRE) Official explanation: jockey said filly became unbalanced inside final furlong
Ba Globetrotter Official explanation: jockey said gelding stumbled half furlong out

2652 ADDLESTONES MEDIAN AUCTION MAIDEN STKS 1m 5y
8:00 (8:00) (Class 6) 3-Y-O £2,266 (£674; £337; £168) Stalls Low

Form RPR
36-2 1 **Tilos Gem (IRE)**[46] 1410 3-9-3 78 RoystonFfrench 5 69+
(M Johnston) *chsd ldr: rdn to ld over 2f out: r.o wl* 5/4[1]
3 2 3 **Voortrekker**[32] 1752 3-9-3 0 NickyMackay 6 62+
(D J Coakley) *a.p: chsd wnr over 1f out: rdn jst ins fnl f: no imp* 5/4[1]
-054 3 3 ½ **Piccolo Express**[63] 1108 3-9-3 52 J-PGuillambert 2 54
(B P J Baugh) *hld up in tch: hrd rdn over 1f out: wknd wl ins fnl f* 33/1
26-0 4 1 **Pokfulham (IRE)**[44] 1462 3-8-10 64 (v) MatthewDavies(7) 8 52
(A P Jarvis) *led: hdd over 2f out: sn rdn: wknd ins fnl f* 8/1[2]
05- 5 3 ¾ **Peal Park**[236] 6682 3-8-12 0 CatherineGannon 4 38
(Karen George) *hld up in mid-div: rdn over 2f out: sn wknd* 33/1
0 6 nk **Monagasque (IRE)**[11] 2318 3-8-9 0 DavidProbert(3) 1 37
(S Kirk) *hld up towards rr: rdn over 2f out: sn struggling* 25/1[3]
000- 7 6 **Queens Forester**[261] 6008 3-8-12 45 WilliamBuick 3 24
(P F I Cole) *hld up in rr: rdn over 1f out: no rspnse* 40/1
30 8 3 ¼ **Madhal**[11] 2317 3-9-3 0 ChrisCatlin 7 21
(M Salaman) *stdd s: a in rr* 25/1[3]
1m 41.02s (0.22) **Going Correction** -0.025s/f (Good) 8 Ran SP% 116.0
Speed ratings (Par 97): **97,94,90,89,85 85,79,76**
toteswinger: 1&2 £1.02, 1&3 £29.40, 2&3 £22.50. CSF £2.77 TOTE £2.20: £1.02, £1.10, £8.20; EX 2.80.
Owner Grant Mercer **Bred** South House Stud **Trained** Middleham Moor, N Yorks

FOCUS
A weak maiden, effectively a match between the front pair. Neither were at their best off the modest pace.

2653 OLDE ENGLISH H'CAP 5f 161y
8:35 (8:36) (Class 4) (0-85,83) 3-Y-0+ £4,857 (£1,445; £722; £360) Stalls Centre

Form RPR
2-06 1 **Filligree (IRE)**[11] 2334 4-9-8 80 DavidProbert(3) 5 88
(Rae Guest) *a.p: swtchd rt over 1f out: rdn to ld ins fnl f: drvn out* 3/1[1]
2401 2 1 ½ **Desperate Dan**[5] 2520 8-9-0 76 6ex (v) PNolan(7) 6 79
(A B Haynes) *w ldr: led over 2f out: carried hd high and rdn over 1f out: hdd ins fnl f: nt qckn* 3/1[1]
2-00 3 hd **Speed Song**[20] 2093 4-10-0 83 (b[1]) LiamJones 2 85
(W J Haggas) *s.i.s whn rdr slow to remove blindfold: t.k.h: sn in tch: pushed along 3f out: rdn over 1f out: kpt on ins fnl f* 3/1[1]
2432 4 7 **The Tatling (IRE)**[5] 2520 12-9-6 80 JackDean(5) 4 58
(J M Bradley) *hld up: effrt on outside 2f out: carried sltly rt over 1f out: sn wknd* 3/1[1]

305 5 3 ¾ **Satwa Street (IRE)**[18] 2140 3-8-12 78 MarcHalford(3) 1 44
(D M Simcock) *led: hdd over 2f out: sn rdn: wknd over 1f out* 6/1[2]
69.92 secs (-1.28) **Going Correction** -0.325s/f (Firm)
WFA 3 from 4yo+ 8lb 5 Ran SP% **114.3**
Speed ratings (Par 105): **95,93,92,83,78**
toteswinger: 1&2 £5.60. CSF £12.65 TOTE £5.00: £2.30, £1.30; EX 20.10.
Owner The Filligree Partnership **Bred** T Hirschfeld **Trained** Newmarket, Suffolk
■ Stewards' Enquiry : P Nolan one-day ban: used whip with excessive frequency (Jun 21)
David Probert one-day ban: careless riding (Jun 21)

FOCUS
This looked all over when the runner-up kicked clear around 2f out. However, the picture changed dramatically in the final half-furlong. Ordinary form for the grade.

2654 GAYMERS PEAR FILLIES' H'CAP 5f 11y
9:05 (9:06) (Class 5) (0-70,70) 3-Y-O £2,719 (£809; £404; £202) Stalls Centre

Form RPR
5001 1 **Baby Queen (IRE)**[17] 2162 3-8-11 60 J-PGuillambert 8 68+
(B P J Baugh) *mde all: rdn 1f out: sn clr: eased towards fin* 6/1[2]
3004 2 1 ½ **Avrilo**[3] 2562 3-8-2 51 oh6 NickyMackay 5 52
(M S Saunders) *a.p: rdn and wnt 2nd wl ins fnl f: no ch w wnr* 20/1
3-21 3 1 **Celestial Dream (IRE)**[9] 2386 3-9-5 68 6ex WilliamBuick 10 65
(A M Balding) *hld up in tch: rdn and nt qckn fnl f* 8/13[1]
3550 4 ½ **Bees River (IRE)**[22] 2010 3-8-2 58 MatthewDavies(7) 6 54
(A P Jarvis) *t.k.h: chsd wnr: rdn over 1f out: lost 2nd and no ex wl ins fnl f* 10/1
12-0 5 2 **Like For Like (IRE)**[10] 2349 3-8-12 61 FrankieMcDonald 1 49
(R J Hodges) *sn outpcd and bhd: kpt on fnl f: n.d* 16/1
-214 6 4 **Halaak (USA)**[135] 229 3-9-0 66 (b) MarcHalford(3) 9 40
(D M Simcock) *hld up and bhd: hdwy 2f out: rdn over 1f out: wknd fnl f* 8/1[3]
020- 7 3 ½ **Nativity**[284] 5363 3-9-1 64 LiamJones 4 25
(J L Spearing) *hld up in mid-div: wknd 1f out* 25/1
00-0 8 3 **Fly Butterfly**[31] 1772 3-8-2 51 CatherineGannon 2 2
(M R Channon) *sn pushed along in mid-div: wknd over 2f out* 33/1
9 4 **Brideview**[42] 1498 3-9-0 63 (tp) PaulFitzsimons 7 —
(Edgar Byrne) *s.i.s: a bhd* 50/1
61.30 secs (-1.20) **Going Correction** -0.325s/f (Firm) 9 Ran SP% 115.8
Speed ratings (Par 96): **96,93,92,91,88 81,76,71,64**
toteswinger: 1&2 £12.40, 1&3 £1.02, 2&3 £3.60. CSF £114.53 CT £174.98 TOTE £6.00: £2.10, £3.30, £1.10; EX 121.10 Place 6 £14.46, Place 5 £8.16..
Owner G B Hignett **Bred** Gainsborough Stud Management Ltd **Trained** Audley, Staffs

FOCUS
A modest handicap, but the time was good for the grade and the form has been rated at face value. That said, the runner-up was 10lb wrong.
T/Plt: £22.40 to a £1 stake. Pool: £46,412.91. 1,508.94 winning tickets. T/Qpdt: £4.00 to a £1 stake. Pool: £4,131.21. 749.53 winning tickets. KH

2264 CATTERICK (L-H)
Friday, June 5

OFFICIAL GOING: Good to firm (firm in places; 8.9) changing to good (good to firm in places) after race 4 (3.35) changing to good after race 5 (4.15)
Wind: moderate 1/2 against Weather: persistent rain

2655 EUROPEAN BREEDERS' FUND NOVICE STKS 5f
1:50 (1:51) (Class 5) 2-Y-O £4,094 (£1,209; £604) Stalls Low

Form RPR
1 1 **Ceedwell**[11] 2311 2-9-0 0 GregFairley 4 90+
(B Smart) *sn drvn along: sn chsng ldrs: led over 2f out: hung lft 1f out: forged clr ins fnl f* 1/2[1]
5410 2 5 **Tillys Tale**[9] 2372 2-8-7 0 PaulPickard(7) 2 72
(P T Midgley) *led tl over 2f out: edgd rt and kpt on wl fnl f* 14/1
631 3 ¾ **Oondiri (IRE)**[11] 2339 2-8-11 0 DavidAllan 3 66
(T D Easterby) *w ldr: keeping on same pce whn n.m.r 1f out* 10/3[2]
41 4 3 ¼ **Gertmegalush (IRE)**[27] 1884 2-8-12 0 PaulHanagan 5 56
(J D Bethell) *chsd ldrs: outpcd and lost pl after 2f: styd on fnl f* 9/1[3]
5 8 **Bonasera (IRE)** 2-8-8 0 ow1 TonyHamilton 1 23
(A Berry) *s.s: a detached in fnl f* 125/1
60.54 secs (0.74) **Going Correction** +0.225s/f (Good) 5 Ran SP% 107.2
Speed ratings (Par 93): **103,95,93,88,75**
CSF £8.21 TOTE £1.70: £1.20, £2.50; EX 8.00.
Owner Prime Equestrian **Bred** Minster Stud And Bickerton Racing **Trained** Hambleton, N Yorks
■ Stewards' Enquiry : David Allan caution: used whip down the shoulder in the forehand

FOCUS
The jockeys reported the ground was decent with no jar. Quite an interesting novice stakes with the four that had run having won. The winner is ueful and the type to rate higher.

NOTEBOOK
Ceedwell was a strong favourite having scored well at Carlisle and being considered a possible Queen Mary filly by her trainer. She was not the quickest away but was upsides the leaders by the halfway point and came right away in the last furlong. Handling this undulating track will have made her more street-wise. (op 4-7 tchd 4-6, 8-11 in a place)
Tillys Tale had gained her previous success on easier ground but she ran with credit, getting to the front after a furlong and battling away for the runner-up spot, although no match for the winner. She looks the type for nurseries in due course. (op 12-1)
Oondiri(IRE) made all over Redcar's fast five when scoring on her previous start but could never quite get to the front, and was struggling when slightly short of room as the winner edged left entering the final furlong. Her rider reported that the filly hung left throughout. Official explanation: jockey said filly hung left throughout (op 4-1 tchd 3-1)
Gertmegalush(IRE) got a quicker start than the four fillies but he only stayed in front for about a furlong as he did not have the pace to keep with the principals. (op 6-1)
Bonasera(IRE), a cheaply-bought first foal of an unraced mare, missed the break and was always struggling. (op 66-1)

2656 RACING UK (S) STKS 1m 5f 175y
2:25 (2:26) (Class 6) 4-Y-O+ £2,047 (£604; £302) Stalls Low

Form RPR
-040 1 **Desert Destiny**[10] 2362 9-8-12 68 TonyHamilton 7 63
(C Grant) *trckd ldrs: led over 2f out: carried hd high: drvn out* 5/2[2]
0213 2 3 ¼ **Terminate (GER)**[13] 2264 7-9-4 58 (t) ShaneKelly 10 64
(Ian Williams) *hld up in rr: hdwy to trck ldrs 7f out: wnt 2nd over 1f out: no imp* 2/1[1]
00-0 3 11 **Cecina Marina**[35] 1651 6-8-4 40 KellyHarrison(3) 11 38
(Mrs K Walton) *led 1f: w ldr: led 7f out tl over 2f out: one pce* 33/1

-045 4 1 3/4 **Wulimaster (USA)**[7] 2448 6-8-12 43 PaulMulrennan 4 40
(D W Barker) *hld up in rr: hdwy over 3f out: kpt on same pce: nvr threatened* 5/1

0-40 5 2 1/2 **Mceldowney**[11] 2018 7-8-5 53 (p) DavidKenny(7) 9 37
(M C Chapman) *led after 1f tl 7f out: drvn 5f out: one pce* 12/1

0200 6 2 1/4 **Bridgewater Boys**[6] 2499 8-8-11 65 (v) DeclanCannon(7) 1 40
(T J Pitt) *hld up in rr: effrt over 3f out: sn hrd drvn and no imp* 4/1[3]

0/0- 7 hd **Amjad**[85] 4879 12-9-2 33 ow4 (v) MHNaughton 2 37
(S G West) *in rr: nvr a factor* 150/1

00-0 8 24 **Pennybid (IRE)**[53] 1243 7-8-12 42 (b[1]) PAspell 6 —
(C R Wilson) *t.k.h: trckd ldrs: drvn over 3f out: sn wknd: t.o* 150/1

00-6 9 6 **Phoenix Nights (IRE)**[2] 2592 9-8-5 38 (b) BillyCray(7) 8 —
(A Berry) *t.k.h on outer: sn trcking ldrs: lost pl over 3f out: sn bhd: t.o* 80/1

3m 6.78s (3.18) **Going Correction** +0.20s/f (Good) **9** Ran SP% **111.8**
Speed ratings (Par 101): **98,96,89,88,87 86,86,72,68**
toteswinger: 1&2 £2.50, 1&3 £13.60, 2&3 £7.80 CSF £7.49 TOTE £3.50: £1.30, £1.40, £4.80; EX 9.60.There was no bid for the winner.
Owner Chris Grant **Bred** Pegasus Racing Ltd **Trained** Newton Bewley, Co Durham

FOCUS
The rains arrived before the start of this race. A mixed bunch ability-wise in this seller and not that competitive. In the end the market leaders came right away. The winner did not need to match his recent handicap form.

2657 LIONWELD KENNEDY SPRINT H'CAP 5f
3:00 (3:03) (Class 5) (0-70,69) 3-Y-0+ **£2,914** (£867; £433; £216) **Stalls** Low

Form RPR

-133 1 **Raccoon (IRE)**[7] 2451 9-9-13 68 PJMcDonald 7 78
(Mrs R A Carr) *trckd ldrs: led over 1f out: styd on wl* 7/1

6215 2 2 **Liberty Ship**[20] 2095 4-9-13 68 (bt) GrahamGibbons 10 71
(J D Bethell) *chsd ldrs: edgd lft after 1f: drvn over 2f out: styd on to take 2nd nr fin* 7/2[1]

0560 3 hd **Brut**[17] 2158 7-8-11 57 (p) AmyRyan(5) 6 59
(D W Barker) *chsd ldrs: rallied over 1f out: kpt on ins fnl f* 14/1

1035 4 1 **Nomoreblondes**[36] 1627 5-10-0 69 (p) JamieMoriarty 5 68
(P T Midgley) *led tl over 2f out: kpt on same pce fnl f* 11/1

151 5 1 **Loose Caboose (IRE)**[6] 2472 4-9-11 66 6ex (b) AndrewMullen 1 61
(A J McCabe) *chsd ldrs: hmpd over 3f out: edgd rt 1f out: kpt on ins fnl f* 9/2[3]

0-50 6 1 1/4 **Paddy Jack**[11] 2316 4-8-13 54 (b) TonyHamilton 2 45
(J R Weymes) *w ldrs: wknd jst ins fnl f* 16/1

000 7 2 3/4 **Mr Rooney (IRE)**[7] 2451 6-8-4 52 BillyCray(7) 3 33
(A Berry) *sn drvn along and outpcd in rr: kpt on fnl 2f: nvr on terms* 25/1

2052 8 3/4 **Ridley Didley (IRE)**[17] 2158 4-9-1 56 (bt[1]) DanielTudhope 4 37+
(N Wilson) *tk fierce hold: w ldrs: led over 2f out: hdd over 1f out: sn wknd and sltly hmpd* 4/1[2]

003- 9 2 1/4 **Windjammer**[235] 6711 5-9-4 59 DuranFentiman 11 29
(L A Mullaney) *sn chsng ldrs on outer: lost pl over 1f out* 14/1

0-03 10 10 **Strensall**[17] 2158 12-8-11 52 PaulHanagan 9 —
(R E Barr) *sn outpcd and in rr: bhd whn eased ins fnl f* 12/1

61.03 secs (1.23) **Going Correction** +0.325s/f (Good) **10** Ran SP% **112.0**
Speed ratings (Par 103): **103,99,99,97,96 94,89,88,85,69**
toteswinger: 1&2 £4.80, 1&3 £19.80, 2&3 £12.00 CSF £30.36 CT £330.53 TOTE £8.50: £3.00, £1.50, £3.80; EX 27.40.
Owner P D Savill **Bred** P D Savill **Trained** Huby, N Yorks
■ Stewards' Enquiry : Jamie Moriarty one-day ban: careless riding (Jun 21)

FOCUS
A modest sprint but quite competitive and plenty with chances, and the time was nearly half a second slower than the opening juvenile contest. It was a headlong dash with four upsides most of the way. The form is rated around the winner and second.
Nomoreblondes Official explanation: jockey said mare hung left final two furlongs
Ridley Didley(IRE) Official explanation: jockey said gelding suffered interference in running

2658 ANNE & TONY'S SILVER WEDDING ANNIVERSARY H'CAP 5f 212y
3:35 (3:36) (Class 4) (0-85,85) 4-Y-0+ **£4,857** (£1,445; £722; £360) **Stalls** Low

Form RPR

0-33 1 **Novellen Lad (IRE)**[20] 2086 4-8-13 77 DavidAllan 1 93+
(E J Alston) *trckd ldrs: led appr fnl f: r.o strly: eased towards fin* 9/4[1]

06-1 2 2 **Johannes (IRE)**[13] 2267 6-8-13 77 PaulHanagan 8 84
(R A Fahey) *in rr: effrt on outer over 2f out: styd on to take 2nd wl ins fnl f* 10/3[2]

20-3 3 1 1/2 **Kashimin (IRE)**[13] 2267 4-9-4 82 PJMcDonald 4 85
(G A Swinbank) *trckd ldrs: kpt on same pce fnl f* 7/1

1001 4 2 **Splash The Cash**[13] 2269 4-8-5 74 ow1 AmyRyan(5) 5 70
(K A Ryan) *trckd ldrs: effrt on outside over 2f out: chal over 1f out: kpt on same pce* 13/2[3]

-362 5 hd **Wyatt Earp (IRE)**[13] 2267 8-9-7 85 DaleGibson 2 81
(P Salmon) *sn drvn along: sn chsng ldrs: one pce fnl 2f* 8/1

1530 6 1 3/4 **Obe Gold**[27] 1864 7-9-7 85 (v) PaulQuinn 9 75
(D Nicholls) *hld up in rr: kpt on fnl 2f: nvr a factor* 12/1

3100 7 2 3/4 **Angaric (IRE)**[7] 2453 6-7-9 66 JamieKyne(7) 3 47
(B Smart) *chsd ldrs: wknd appr fnl f* 14/1

-540 8 1 1/4 **Chartist**[34] 1663 4-8-13 77 AndrewMullen 6 54
(D Nicholls) *led: hdd & wknd appr fnl f* 16/1

3000 9 3/4 **Strabinios King**[8] 2389 5-7-13 70 (b[1]) BillyCray(7) 7 45
(A Berry) *s.i.s: hld up in rr: nvr on terms* 50/1

1m 13.66s (0.06) **Going Correction** +0.20s/f (Good) **9** Ran SP% **113.0**
Speed ratings (Par 105): **107,104,102,99,99 97,93,91,90**
toteswinger: 1&2 £3.40, 1&3 £4.40, 2&3 £4.30 CSF £9.33 CT £43.14 TOTE £3.20: £1.30, £1.50, £2.10; EX 14.10.
Owner Con Harrington **Bred** Mrs Chris Harrington **Trained** Longton, Lancs

FOCUS
A decent sprint, and sound form.

2659 BOOK TICKETS ON-LINE @ CATTERICKBRIDGE.CO.UK MAIDEN STKS 1m 3f 214y
4:15 (4:18) (Class 5) 3-Y-0+ **£3,238** (£963; £481; £240) **Stalls** Low

Form RPR

5 1 **Act Of Kalanisi (IRE)**[33] 1693 3-8-11 0 GregFairley 1 81+
(M Johnston) *trckd ldr: jnd ldr 7f out: led 2f out: edgd lft jst ins fnl f: drvn out* 8/11[1]

33 2 5 **Lords A Leaping (IRE)**[8] 2395 3-8-11 0 ShaneKelly 2 69
(J A Osborne) *set modest pce: qcknd over 4f out: hdd 2f out: keeping on same pce whn swtchd rt jst ins fnl f* 6/4[2]

0 3 4 1/2 **California Bright (IRE)**[37] 1611 3-7-13 0 JamieKyne(7) 4 56
(J G Given) *hld up in last: hdwy to chse ldrs over 4f out: outpcd over 2f out: kpt on to take modest 3rd ins fnl f* 25/1[3]

00 4 2 **Waltzalong (IRE)**[8] 2403 3-8-7 0 ow1 DavidAllan 3 54?
(T D Easterby) *trckd ldng pair: drvn over 4f out: outpcd over 2f out: fdd and lost 3rd ins fnl f* 25/1[3]

2m 43.96s (5.06) **Going Correction** +0.30s/f (Good) **4** Ran SP% **105.6**
Speed ratings (Par 103): **95,91,88,87**
CSF £1.94 TOTE £1.90; EX 2.00.
Owner Mrs Joan Keaney **Bred** Mrs Joan Keaney **Trained** Middleham Moor, N Yorks

FOCUS
The going was changed to Good, Good to Firm in places before this race. An uncompetitive maiden that looked a match judged on previous form and very much turned out that way, although the outsiders had shown little before and were not that far behind at the end, which limits the form. The winner progressed significantly.

2660 PEN HILL H'CAP 5f 212y
4:45 (4:45) (Class 6) (0-65,65) 3-Y-0+ **£2,388** (£705; £352) **Stalls** Low

Form RPR

0043 1 **Red Cape (FR)**[17] 2156 6-9-13 63 AndrewElliott 10 76
(Mrs R A Carr) *trckd ldrs: swtchd stands' side over 2f out: r.o strly to ld overall ins fnl f: wnt clr* 8/1

000 2 4 1/2 **Royal Acclamation (IRE)**[33] 1694 4-9-5 55 (v[1]) SilvestreDeSousa 1 54
(G A Harker) *led tl hdd and no ex ins fnl f* 7/2[2]

0-0 3 4 1/2 **Desert Ben (IRE)**[13] 2269 6-9-10 60 JamieMoriarty 4 44
(C Grant) *hld up in rr: hdwy over 2f out: kpt on to take modest 3rd nr fin* 14/1

2333 4 1/2 **Maison Dieu**[1] 2628 6-9-10 60 DavidAllan 3 43
(E J Alston) *in tch: effrt to chse ldrs over 2f out: kpt on same pce* 5/2[1]

3351 5 nse **Blue Noodles**[14] 2234 3-9-7 65 TonyHamilton 8 45
(D W Barker) *chsd ldr: brought stands' side over 2f out: fdd fnl f* 13/2[3]

005- 6 3 1/4 **Only A Splash**[352] 3139 5-8-9 45 DuranFentiman 7 17
(Mrs R A Carr) *in tch: effrt over 2f out: wknd over 1f out* 80/1

0000 7 shd **Nawaaff**[30] 1784 4-8-4 45 MCGeran(5) 2 17
(M R Channon) *chsd ldrs: outpcd over 2f out: wknd over 1f out* 12/1

0 8 1/2 **Listen Carefully (IRE)**[40] 1541 5-8-9 45 PJMcDonald 6 15
(Patrick Morris) *in rr: nvr on terms* 80/1

-256 9 1 1/2 **Conjecture**[15] 2202 7-9-4 61 JamieKyne(7) 5 26
(R Bastiman) *chsd ldrs: rdn and hung rt over 2f out: lost pl over 1f out* 7/2[2]

600- 10 1/2 **Mintoe**[262] 5997 3-9-4 65 NeilBrown(3) 11 27
(K A Ryan) *wnt rt s: a in rr* 40/1

1m 14.88s (1.28) **Going Correction** +0.30s/f (Good)
WFA 3 from 4yo+ 8lb **10** Ran SP% **116.7**
Speed ratings (Par 101): **103,97,91,90,90 85,85,85,83,82**
toteswinger: 1&2 £8.60, 1&3 £7.90, 2&3 £9.30 CSF £36.12 CT £398.80 TOTE £7.10: £2.20, £1.80, £2.90; EX 56.90.
Owner Middleham Park Racing LVI **Bred** Gilles And Mrs Forien **Trained** Huby, N Yorks

FOCUS
The ground was changed again, this time to Good, before this race. The rain had clearly got into the ground and the jockeys had a difference of opinion as to where to race in the straight. The time was 1.22secs slower than the earlier better class contest over the same trip. Modest handicap, with the winner back to last year's turf form.
Conjecture Official explanation: trainer said gelding was unsuited by the rain-softened ground

2661 TURFTV BETTING SHOP SERVICE FILLIES' H'CAP 7f
5:15 (5:16) (Class 5) (0-75,77) 3-Y-0+ **£2,914** (£867; £433; £216) **Stalls** Low

Form RPR

053- 1 **Ykikamoocow**[248] 6362 3-9-2 66 SilvestreDeSousa 3 68
(G A Harker) *t.k.h: trckd ldrs: effrt over 2f out: hrd rdn and styd on fnl f: led towards fin* 9/4[2]

-240 2 nk **Izzi Mill (USA)**[9] 2375 3-9-8 72 RobertHavlin 1 73
(D R C Elsworth) *led: qcknd over 2f out: hdd and no ex nr fin* 3/1[3]

1321 3 3 1/4 **Cheap Thrills**[12] 2300 3-9-13 77 6ex ShaneKelly 4 69
(J A Osborne) *unruly s: w ldr: drvn over 2f out: fdd 1f out* 5/4[1]

516- 4 7 **Devinius (IRE)**[284] 5362 4-9-10 64 PJMcDonald 2 42
(G A Swinbank) *hld up in tch: effrt over 2f out: sn rdn and hung lft: lost pl over 1f out* 8/1

1m 29.76s (2.76) **Going Correction** +0.30s/f (Good)
WFA 3 from 4yo 10lb **4** Ran SP% **111.3**
Speed ratings (Par 100): **96,95,91,83**
CSF £9.23 TOTE £4.00; EX 9.30 Place 6: £23.47 Place 5: £16.75.
Owner Mrs Eve Sweetman & Paul Benson **Bred** Mrs Karen Heath **Trained** Thirkleby, N Yorks

FOCUS
A fair fillies' handicap although all the runners had questions to answer. The favourite was 10lb off her Newmarket form.
Cheap Thrills Official explanation: jockey said filly was unsuited by the rain-softened ground
T/Plt: £45.80 to a £1 stake. Pool: £34,330.70. 546.59 winning tickets. T/Qpdt: £18.20 to a £1 stake. Pool: £2,410.82. 97.50 winning tickets. WG

2467 DONCASTER (L-H)
Friday, June 5

OFFICIAL GOING: Good to firm (8.5)
Wind: Light, half-behind Weather: Overcast

2662 AUTEC CONSTRUCTION TRAINING H'CAP 1m (R)
6:05 (6:06) (Class 5) (0-75,74) 3-Y-0 **£4,209** (£1,252; £625; £312) **Stalls** Low

Form RPR

601 1 **Queen Martha (USA)**[28] 1844 3-9-7 74 PaulHanagan 2 77+
(M A Magnusson) *mde all: qcknd 3f out: rdn and qcknd wl over 1f out: drvn and edgd rt ins fnl f: kpt on wl* 7/1

25-3 2 2 **Sparkling Crystal (IRE)**[28] 1837 3-9-4 71 TPO'Shea 3 69
(B W Hills) *trckd ldng pair: hdwy to chse wnr over 2f out: rdn wl over 1f out: drvn and no imp ins fnl f* 11/2[3]

000- 3 3/4 **Well Of Echoes**[254] 6214 3-8-9 62 AndrewMullen 4 58
(A J McCabe) *hld up in rr: hdwy on outer wl over 2f out: rdn wl over 1f out: kpt on u.p ins fnl f: nrst fin* 33/1

053- 4 shd **Block Party**[225] 6926 3-9-7 74 SteveDrowne 7 70
(R Charlton) *dwlt: hld up in tch: hdwy to trck ldrs 1/2-way: effrt 3f out: rdn 2f out: sn edgd lft and drvn over 1f out: one pce* 4/5[1]

0-05 5 1/2 **Bandanaman (IRE)**[25] 1925 3-9-0 67 PaulMulrennan 6 62
(G A Swinbank) *hld up towards rr: hdwy 3f out: rdn to chse ldrs 2f out: drvn and no imp appr fnl f* 20/1

45-5 **6** *8* **Montmartre (USA)**[17] 2165 3-9-5 72 GrahamGibbons 8 48
(B J Meehan) *chsd wnr: rdn along over 3f out: drvn and wknd over 2f out* **40/1**

3664 **7** *2 1/4* **Steel Stockholder**[20] 2091 3-8-10 63 TomEaves 5 34
(M Brittain) *chsd ldrs: rdn along over 3f out and sn wknd* **5/1**[2]

1m 36.94s (-2.76) **Going Correction** -0.525s/f (Hard) **7 Ran SP% 110.2**
Speed ratings (Par 99): **99,97,96,96,95 87,85**
toteswinger: 1&2 £1.50, 1&3 £21.10, 2&3 £22.90. CSF £40.40 CT £1111.99 TOTE £7.30: £3.10, £2.40; EX 21.70.
Owner Eastwind Racing Ltd and Martha Trussell **Bred** Albert P Coppola Et Al **Trained** Upper Lambourn, Berks

FOCUS
A dry day and only a light tailwind on watered (good to firm) ground. A couple of unexposed performers in an ordinary handicap. The pace was only moderate and those held up were at a disadvantage. The winner is on the upgrade but the placed form is only ordinary.
Sparkling Crystal(IRE) Official explanation: jockey said filly hung right
Steel Stockholder Official explanation: trainer said colt would not let itself down on the fast ground

2663 TOTAL RECLAIMS DEMOLITION MAIDEN AUCTION STKS 6f
6:35 (6:40) (Class 5) 2-Y-O **£4,209** (£1,252; £625; £312) **Stalls High**

Form RPR

6 **1** **Victoire De Lyphar (IRE)**[7] 2444 2-8-12 0 PhillipMakin 3 81+
(P C Haslam) *chsd ldng pair: smooth hdwy 2f out: rdn to ld over 1f out: qcknd clr ent fnl f* **12/1**

3 **2** *3 1/4* **Fonterutoli (IRE)**[17] 2167 2-8-7 0 AndreaAtzeni(5) 2 71
(M Botti) *chsd ldrs: pushed along 2f out: sn rdn: kpt on ins fnl f: no ch w wnr* **8/1**

3 *nk* **Mingun Bell (USA)** 2-8-12 0 IanMongan 10 70
(H R A Cecil) *wnt lft s: sn cl up: effrt to ld 2f out and sn rdn: rn green: stmbld and hdd over 1f out: one pce after* **3/1**[2]

4 *2* **Hoof It** 2-8-9 0 DaleGibson 8 61+
(M W Easterby) *bdly hmpd s and bhd: hdwy 2f out: rdn and styd on wl appr fnl f: nrst fin* **12/1**

6 **5** *1* **Quaestor (IRE)**[9] 2383 2-8-9 0 RichardKingscote 11 58
(Tom Dascombe) *led: rdn along and hdd 2f out: sn drvn and wknd* **6/1**[3]

2 **6** *nk* **Count Bertoni (IRE)**[14] 2231 2-9-1 0 MickyFenton 7 64+
(T P Tate) *carried rt and hmpd s: bhd tl hdwy 1/2-way: swtchd outside wl over 1f out: styd on ins fnl f: nt rch ldrs* **2/1**[1]

0 **7** *1/2* **Mighty Clarets (IRE)**[19] 2099 2-8-12 0 PaulHanagan 4 59
(R A Fahey) *in tch: rdn along over 2f out and sn no imp* **16/1**

8 *shd* **Pat Seamur** 2-9-1 0 SteveDrowne 1 62
(E A L Dunlop) *nvr bttr than midfield* **33/1**

9 *4 1/2* **Colonel Mak** 2-8-9 0 PaulMulrennan 5 42
(D H Brown) *midfield: rdn along over 2f out: sn wknd* **16/1**

10 *5* **French Seventyfive** 2-8-9 0 GrahamGibbons 9 27
(T D Walford) *hmpd s: a bhd* **20/1**

0 **11** *5* **Lady Navara (IRE)**[32] 1735 2-8-4 0 TPO'Shea 6 7
(M Brittain) *wnt rt s: chsd ldrs to 1/2-way: sn wknd* **100/1**

1m 11.43s (-2.17) **Going Correction** -0.525s/f (Hard) **11 Ran SP% 119.6**
Speed ratings (Par 93): **93,88,88,85,84 83,83,83,77,70 63**
toteswinger: 1&2 £6.40, 1&3 £8.20, 2&3 £4.80. CSF £104.65 TOTE £16.00: £3.80, £3.20, £1.50; EX 105.90.
Owner Middleham Park Racing Xviii **Bred** Mrs Monica Hackett **Trained** Middleham Moor, N Yorks

FOCUS
With the market leader disappointing and the second favourite failing to justify market support, this was less informative than it promised to be but it was still a much improved effort from the winner. The pace was sound.

NOTEBOOK
Victoire De Lyphar(IRE) ◆, too green to do himself justice on his debut on easy ground the previous week, was more professional this time and turned in a much improved effort on this quicker surface. He should stay 7f and appeals as the type to win more races. (op 14-1 tchd 11-1)
Fonterutoli(IRE), who showed ability at an ordinary level on a sound surface on his debut, bettered that effort. He left the impression that the step up to 7f would suit and he should be able to win a race away from the more progressive sorts. (op 11-1)
Mingun Bell(USA), well supported prior to this racecourse debut, was the first runner for his sire and he fared the best of the newcomers. He took the eye in the preliminaries, should be all the better for this experience and is likely to be placed to best effect. Official explanation: jockey said colt lost its action (op 7-2 tchd 11-4)
Hoof It ◆, who is related to several winners over sprint distances, shaped with a degree of promise after taking a bump at the start on his racecourse debut. He is sure to be all the wiser for this experience and looks sure to pick up an ordinary event in the north. (op 8-1)
Quaestor(IRE), ridden more positively than on his debut, again showed ability at an ordinary level, but looks the type that should fare best once qualified for a handicap mark. (op 9-2)
Count Bertoni(IRE), shaped with plenty of promise on his debut, again took the eye in the paddock, but was a fair way below that level after taking a bump at the start. However, he is well worth another chance to confirm debut promise in similar company. Official explanation: jockey said colt was slowly away (tchd 15-8)
French Seventyfive Official explanation: jockey said gelding suffered interference shortly after start

2664 REPLAS CONCRETE REPAIR MAIDEN STKS 7f
7:10 (7:12) (Class 5) 3-Y-O **£4,209** (£1,252; £625; £312) **Stalls High**

Form RPR

26 **1** **Invincible Isle (IRE)**[37] 1605 3-8-12 0 IanMongan 6 78
(H R A Cecil) *t.k.h early: in tch: hdwy and swtchd lft over 1f out: sn rdn to chse ldr: drvn to chal ins fnl f: styd on to ld last 100yds* **8/1**

3 **2** *1/2* **Hightime Heroine (IRE)**[33] 1704 3-8-12 0 ShaneKelly 9 77
(J Noseda) *cl up gng wl: effrt 2f out: led over 1f out: rdn ins fnl f: hdd and no ex last 100yds* **13/2**[3]

54- **3** *1 3/4* **Diapason (IRE)**[235] 6702 3-8-12 0 RichardKingscote 12 72
(Tom Dascombe) *led: rdn along over 2f out: hdd and drvn over 1f out: kpt on u.p ins fnl f tl no ex towards fin* **16/1**

-5 **4** *5* **Almuktahem**[20] 2081 3-9-3 0 TPO'Shea 14 64
(Sir Michael Stoute) *cl up: effrt over 2f out and ev ch tl rdn and one pce over 1f out* **2/1**[1]

2- **5** *1/2* **Cross Section (USA)**[233] 6737 3-8-12 0 GrahamGibbons 11 57
(E F Vaughan) *trckd ldrs: effrt over 2f out: sn rdn and no imp appr fnl f* **7/1**

6 *2 1/2* **Burns Night** 3-9-3 0 GregFairley 8 56+
(M Johnston) *s.i.s: rapid hdwy to chse ldrs after 1f out: rdn along 1/2-way: wkng whn hmpd over 2f out* **9/2**[2]

60- **7** *hd* **Age Of Couture**[255] 6187 3-8-12 0 SteveDrowne 4 50
(W Jarvis) *in tch: effrt 1/2-way: sn rdn along and no imp* **66/1**

0 **8** *1/2* **Ryker (IRE)**[20] 2081 3-9-3 0 PhilipRobinson 2 54
(J W Hills) *cl up on outer: rdn along whn hmpd over 2f out: sn rdn and wknd* **20/1**

0-5 **9** *1/2* **Margarita (IRE)**[16] 2179 3-8-12 0 AdamKirby 15 47
(J R Fanshawe) *a towards rr* **12/1**

0-0 **10** *4* **Jack Cool (IRE)**[51] 1289 3-9-3 0 TomEaves 13 42
(P W Chapple-Hyam) *midfield: pushed along 1/2-way: sn towards rr* **10/1**

0 **11** *2 1/2* **Proud Junior (USA)**[53] 1257 3-9-3 0 JamieMoriarty 1 35
(S A Callaghan) *t.k.h: in tch on outer: pushed along bef 1/2-way: sn wknd* **100/1**

00 **12** *1/2* **Vigorosa (IRE)**[28] 1838 3-8-12 0 TolleyDean 3 28
(P Howling) *s.i.s: a in rr* **150/1**

1m 24.76s (-1.54) **Going Correction** -0.25s/f (Firm) **12 Ran SP% 119.0**
Speed ratings (Par 99): **98,97,95,89,89 86,86,85,84,80 77,76**
toteswinger: 1&2 £14.00, 1&3 £45.60, 2&3 £29.70. CSF £58.67 TOTE £10.20: £3.10, £2.60, £5.40; EX 55.50.
Owner H E Sheikh Sultan Bin Khalifa Al Nahyan **Bred** Ascagnano S P A **Trained** Newmarket, Suffolk
■ Stewards' Enquiry : Jamie Moriarty caution: used whip without giving colt time to respond

FOCUS
A few potential improvers and, although the two market leaders disappointed to varying degrees, this race should throw up a few winners. The pace was reasonable after a slow start and the first three pulled clear.
Almuktahem Official explanation: jockey said colt ran green

2665 CONSTRUCTION INDEX H'CAP 1m (S)
7:40 (7:41) (Class 4) (0-80,83) 4-Y-O+ **£6,476** (£1,927; £963; £240; £240) **Stalls High**

Form RPR

46-1 **1** **Alsace Lorraine (IRE)**[53] 1256 4-9-4 76 AdamKirby 10 89+
(J R Fanshawe) *hld up towards rr: gd hdwy 3f out: swtchd lft and effrt to ld wl over 1f out: rdn clr ent fnl f: kpt on* **11/2**[3]

0-41 **2** *2 1/4* **Luck Will Come (IRE)**[18] 2144 5-8-10 68 JimmyQuinn 7 75
(H J Collingridge) *hld up in tch: hdwy to trck ldrs 2f out: rdn to chse wnr ins fnl f: sn drvn and no imp* **12/1**

3322 **3** *1* **Kildare Sun (IRE)**[4] 2542 7-8-1 66 (p) JamieKyne(7) 5 71
(J Mackie) *led: rdn along over 2f out: hdd wl over 1f out and sn drvn: kpt on u.p fnl f* **4/1**[1]

1-00 **4** *hd* **Aflaam (IRE)**[21] 2050 4-9-7 79 TolleyDean 1 84
(P Howling) *prom: rdn along wl over 2f out: drvn over 1f out and kpt on same pce* **20/1**

2041 **4** *dht* **Templetuohy Max (IRE)**[10] 2362 4-9-2 74 6ex (v) GrahamGibbons 12 79
(J D Bethell) *cl up: rdn along 2f out: drvn over 1f out and kpt on same pce appr fnl f* **11/1**

-621 **6** *1/2* **Paraguay (USA)**[13] 2257 6-9-6 78 SilvestreDeSousa 13 86+
(Mrs D J Sanderson) *trckd ldrs: effrt 2f out and sn n.m.r: nt clr run over 1f out and ent fnl f: no ch after* **9/2**[2]

4026 **7** *nk* **Follow The Flag (IRE)**[4] 2542 5-9-0 72 (p) JamesDoyle 8 75
(A J McCabe) *chsd ldrs: rdn along wl over 2f out and no imp* **16/1**

20/0 **8** *nk* **High Ambition**[20] 2086 6-8-11 69 PaulHanagan 11 71
(R A Fahey) *hld up in rr: hdwy 2f out: swtchd lft and rdn over 1f out: kpt on ins fnl f: nrst fin* **18/1**

10-4 **9** *2 1/2* **Ogre (USA)**[18] 2144 4-8-12 75 RichardEvans(5) 4 71
(P D Evans) *chsd ldrs: rdn over 2f out: sn drvn and wknd* **8/1**

0-60 **10** *3* **Danehillsundance (IRE)**[13] 2257 5-9-5 77 PaulMulrennan 3 66
(D H Brown) *in tch: hdwy to chse ldrs over 2f out: sn rdn and wknd* **11/2**[3]

0-53 **11** *15* **Middlemarch (IRE)**[8] 2402 9-8-10 73 (v) GaryBartley(5) 2 28
(J S Goldie) *hld up: a in rr* **16/1**

01 **12** *8* **El Dececy (USA)**[10] 2361 5-9-4 83 6ex (p) ThomasWhite(7) 6 19
(S Parr) *t.k.h: racd wd: chsd ldrs tl rdn 3f out and sn wknd* **40/1**

1m 36.2s (-3.10) **Going Correction** -0.25s/f (Firm) course record **12 Ran SP% 120.3**
Speed ratings (Par 105): **105,102,101,101,101 101,100,100,97,94 79,71**
toteswinger: 1&2 £17.40, 1&3 £12.90, 2&3 £22.40. CSF £71.14 CT £297.46 TOTE £6.60: £2.50, £2.00, £2.10; EX 54.90.
Owner Merry Fox Stud Limited **Bred** 6c Stallions Ltd **Trained** Newmarket, Suffolk

FOCUS
Several previous winners in a fair handicap for the grade. The pace was reasonable but several finished in a heap behind the ready winner. The form looks sound.
Paraguay(USA) Official explanation: jockey said gelding was denied a clear run
Middlemarch(IRE) Official explanation: jockey said gelding never travelled

2666 MULTIFAB METALS ENGINEERING & FABRICATION H'CAP 1m 2f 60y
8:15 (8:16) (Class 4) (0-85,85) 4-Y-O+ **£6,476** (£1,927; £963; £481) **Stalls Low**

Form RPR

50-2 **1** **Never Ending Tale**[50] 1316 4-9-3 81 (p) RichardKingscote 6 89
(E F Vaughan) *trckd ldrs: hdwy on outer over 2f out: rdn to chal ent fnl f: sn drvn and kpt on to ld nr fin* **6/1**

6-00 **2** *nk* **Shady Gloom (IRE)**[49] 1319 4-8-11 75 PaulHanagan 3 82
(K A Ryan) *led: rdn over 2f out: drvn 1f out: hdd and no ex nr fin* **14/1**

-140 **3** *1 1/2* **Overrule (USA)**[23] 1990 5-8-11 78 NeilBrown(3) 2 82+
(B Ellison) *hld up towards rr: hdwy on inner 3f out: swtchd rt and rdn wl over 1f out: drvn and kpt on ins fnl f: tk 3rd nr fin* **4/1**[1]

-004 **4** *1/2* **Ellmau**[48] 1347 4-9-4 82 JamesDoyle 4 85
(A J McCabe) *chsd ldr: rdn along over 2f out: drvn wl over 1f out: one pce ent fnl f* **5/1**[2]

3-00 **5** *3* **Jeer (IRE)**[38] 1593 5-8-13 77 DaleGibson 1 74
(M W Easterby) *chsd ldrs: hdwy on inner 3f out: rdn over 2f out: drvn wl over 1f out and grad wknd* **12/1**

10-0 **6** *1/2* **Bivouac (UAE)**[45] 1436 5-8-2 66 oh1 JimmyQuinn 10 62
(G A Swinbank) *hld up in tch: hdwy to chse ldrs over 3f out: rdn along over 2f out: drvn and one pce fr wl over 1f out* **20/1**

533/ **7** *1 1/4* **Lazy Darren**[21] 6055 5-8-12 76 TonyHamilton 8 70
(C Grant) *hld up towards rr: effrt 3f out and sn rdn along: nvr nr ldrs* **16/1**

5444 **8** *2 1/4* **Can Can Star**[17] 2150 6-8-6 77 JamieKyne(7) 5 66
(A W Carroll) *hld up in rr: effrt and sme hdwy 3f out: sn rdn along and wknd* **11/2**[3]

20-0 **9** *4* **Annibale Caro**[11] 2315 7-8-9 73 DanielTudhope 7 54
(J S Goldie) *trckd ldrs: rdn along 3f out: sn edgd rt and wknd* **11/1**

2103 **10** *3* **Saltagioo (ITY)**[25] 1942 5-9-2 85 AndreaAtzeni(5) 11 60
(M Botti) *hld up: a in rr* **6/1**

2m 9.91s (-1.29) **Going Correction** 0.0s/f (Good) **10 Ran SP% 114.0**
Speed ratings (Par 105): **105,104,103,103,100 100,99,97,94,91**
toteswinger: 1&2 £33.00, 1&3 £5.70, 2&3 £14.90. CSF £84.08 CT £374.25 TOTE £5.30: £2.20, £4.40, £1.70; EX 81.40.
Owner Ali Saeed **Bred** Gainsborough Stud Management Ltd **Trained** Newmarket, Suffolk

FOCUS
Mainly exposed performers in a fair handicap. The pace was on the steady side and those held up were at a disadvantage. Steady rain that had fallen since the second race saw the horses taking the top off the surface. The runner-up looks the best guide.

Can Can Star Official explanation: jockey said horse was denied a clear run

2667 THECONSTRUCTIONINDEX.CO.UK H'CAP — 1m 4f

8:45 (8:45) (Class 5) (0-70,70) 3-Y-O **£4,209** (£1,252; £625; £312) **Stalls** Low

Form — RPR

603 **1** **Deauville Flyer**[39] 1562 3-9-2 **65** .... DavidAllan 10 72+
(T D Easterby) *hld up in tch: hdwy on inner 3f out: rdn to chal 2f out: led 1f out: drvn ins fnl f and kpt on wl* **7/1**

6-55 **2** *nk* **Albaasha (IRE)**[19] 2104 3-8-12 **61** .... (v[1]) TPO'Shea 9 68
(Sir Michael Stoute) *trckd ldr on outer: pushed along 3f out: effrt and cl up 2f out: sn rdn and ev ch: drvn and hung lft ins fnl f: no ex towards fin* **8/1**

5112 **3** *1 ¾* **Classic Contours (USA)**[9] 2371 3-9-0 **70** .... JamieKyne(7) 4 74
(J J Quinn) *hld up towards rr: hdwy over 3f out and sn rdn along: swtchd lft and drvn to chse ldrs over 1f out: n.m.r ins fnl f: kpt on same pce* **5/2**[1]

0-34 **4** *2* **Northside Prince (IRE)**[9] 2371 3-9-2 **65** .... PJMcDonald 2 66+
(G A Swinbank) *trckd ldng pair: smooth hdwy 3f out: led on bit over 2f out: rdn over 1f out: sn hdd and wkng whn n.m.r ins fnl f* **3/1**[2]

-304 **5** *¾* **Night Lily (IRE)**[22] 2001 3-9-3 **66** .... PaulHanagan 6 66
(J Jay) *hld up in rr: hdwy over 3f out: rdn to chse ldrs 2f out: drvn and no imp appr fnl f* **11/1**

0-40 **6** *9* **Sham Sheer**[21] 2048 3-9-0 **70** .... MJMurphy(7) 3 55
(L M Cumani) *trckd ldrs: swtchd rt and rdn to chse ldrs over 3f out: drvn 2f out and sn wknd* **11/2**[3]

040 **7** *hd* **Cooperman**[37] 1611 3-7-13 **55** oh2 ow4 .... PaulPickard(7) 1 40
(P T Midgley) *a towards rr* **40/1**

4102 **8** *hd* **Spartan Prince (USA)**[36] 1629 3-9-5 **68** .... PhillipMakin 7 53
(T D Barron) *led: rdn along over 3f out: drvn and hdd over 2f out: sn wknd* **12/1**

1536 **9** *13* **Dispol Diva**[9] 2371 3-9-4 **67** .... (v) JamieMoriarty 11 31
(P T Midgley) *in tch on outer: rdn along 4f out and sn wknd* **20/1**

000- **10** *7* **Reel Bluff**[241] 6547 3-8-8 **57** .... TonyHamilton 5 10
(D W Barker) *a bhd* **50/1**

2m 35.5s (0.40) **Going Correction** 0.0s/f (Good) **10** Ran SP% **117.8**
Speed ratings (Par 99): **98,97,96,95,94 88,88,88,79,75**
toteswinger: 1&2 £8.10, 1&3 £5.80, 2&3 £5.40. CSF £61.20 CT £179.98 TOTE £8.00: £1.90, £3.10, £1.50; EX 91.40 Place 6 £482.09, Place 5 £94.06..
Owner Mr And Mrs J D Cotton **Bred** Harts Farm And Stud **Trained** Great Habton, N Yorks

FOCUS
An ordinary handicap run at a reasonable gallop. The form looks sound, with more to come from the winner.

T/Plt: £87.60 to a £1 stake. Pool: £59,363.76. 494.69 winning tickets. T/Qpdt: £11.60 to a £1 stake. Pool: £5,104.08. 323.30 winning tickets. JR

1457 EPSOM (L-H)

Friday, June 5

OFFICIAL GOING: Good (good to firm in places; 8.5)
Wind: medium, across Weather: overcast, quite chilly

2668 INVESTEC DIOMED STKS (GROUP 3) — 1m 114y

1:40 (1:43) (Class 1) 3-Y-O+ **£36,900** (£13,988; £7,000; £3,490; £1,748; £877) **Stalls** Low

Form — RPR

10-4 **1** **Mac Love**[6] 2476 8-9-4 104 .... MickyFenton 4 112
(Stef Liddiard) *stdd s: hld up in last pair: hdwy on outer 2f out: led ins fnl f: r.o wl* **14/1**

54-1 **2** *¾* **Confront**[34] 1673 4-9-4 110 .... RyanMoore 8 110+
(Sir Michael Stoute) *lw: s.i.s: sn rcvrd to chse ldr: rdn over 2f out: drvn and ev ch over 1f out: nt pce of wnr fnl 100yds* **6/4**[1]

-024 **3** *1* **Deposer (IRE)**[28] 1822 3-8-7 103 ow1 .... RobertWinston 7 106
(J R Best) *lw: t.k.h: led: rdn jst over 2f out: hrd pressed and drvnn over 1f out: hdd ins fnl f: no ex fnl 100yds* **14/1**

0325 **4** *¾* **Without A Prayer (IRE)**[76] 913 4-9-4 105 .... SebSanders 1 106+
(R M Beckett) *lw: trckd ldng pair: rdn jst over 2f out: nt clr run 2f out tl 1f out: kpt on same pce ins fnl f* **14/1**

-240 **5** *½* **Vitznau (IRE)**[27] 1865 5-9-4 102 .... RichardHughes 3 105
(R Hannon) *t.k.h: hld up in midfield: effrt 3f out: chsd ldrs and drvn 2f out: wknd jst ins fnl f* **25/1**

-464 **6** *1 ½* **Lovelace**[22] 2015 5-9-9 110 .... JamieSpencer 5 107+
(M Johnston) *t.k.h: hld up in last pair: hdwy but hanging lft fr over 3f out: drvn to chse ldrs 2f out: wknd ent fnl f* **9/2**[2]

1206 **7** *1 ¾* **Hatta Fort**[23] 1989 4-9-7 112 .... (t) LDettori 2 101
(Saeed Bin Suroor) *swtg: stdd s: hld up in last pair: rdn and no hdwy jst over 2f out: hung lft ent fnl f* **11/2**[3]

20-1 **8** *hd* **General Eliott (IRE)**[37] 1600 4-9-4 109 .... (b[1]) JimmyFortune 6 97
(P F I Cole) *in tch: rdn and effrt 3f out: jostled jst over 2f out: wknd over 1f out* **8/1**

1m 43.61s (-2.49) **Going Correction** +0.025s/f (Good)
WFA 3 from 4yo+ 12lb **8** Ran SP% **113.0**
Speed ratings (Par 113): **112,111,110,109,109 108,106,106**
toteswinger: 1&2 £5.70, 1&3 £16.40, 2&3 £5.80 CSF £34.71 TOTE £16.90: £2.80, £1.20, £3.50; EX 45.90 Trifecta £135.10 Pool: 1296.50 - 7.10 winning units.
Owner Vimal Khosla **Bred** Kingwood Bloodstock **Trained** Great Shefford, Berks
■ Stef Liddiard's first Group winner.

FOCUS
There was some light rain in the morning, but it appeared to have little impact on the ground. This didn't look a particularly strong Group 3 contest, as has often been the case in the past, and the result only seemed to confirm that impression. They didn't go much of a gallop and the form is a bit messy. The exposed winner has been rated to the best of his form of the last two years, and the second 6lb off his Newmarket handicap form.

NOTEBOOK
Mac Love, given that they didn't go much of a gallop, did well to make up ground the way he did. A classy sort in his prime, he returned with a cracking effort when fourth, beaten just half a length, at 50/1 in a Listed contest at Goodwood the previous weekend, and his trainer reportedly had him bouncing for this quick reappearance. Held up early, he came widest of all with his challenge down the straight, handling the camber better than most, and swept to the front in the final half a furlong under a perfectly-judged ride by Micky Fenton. The 8yo has clearly returned in cracking form and remains capable of paying his way in races at Listed/Group 3 level, though he looks certain to find sterner opposition at this level in future. The Celebration Mile is a likely target. (op 16-1 tchd 12-1)

Confront didn't live up to expectations at three, having looked a top prospect as a juvenile, but he clearly had problems to have only made the course twice, and he looked more the real deal when readily defying a mark of 105 on his handicap debut at Newmarket's Guineas meeting. The step back up to this level wasn't expected to present a problem and he was well placed to counter the lack of pace, but couldn't quicken for strong pressure and only really mastered the pace-setting Deposer in the final half a furlong. The winner had too much speed for him, but this effort confirmed he is going the right way and he should find a race at this level when presented with more of a test. It later emerged he had lost a front shoe, which could have been highly significant. Official explanation: jockey said gelding lost a front shoe (op 5-4)

Deposer(IRE), the only 3yo in the field, registered a much-improved effort when setting his own tempo in the Dee Stakes, being beaten under a length, and he was able to do the same here. He kept finding from the front and was only headed inside the final furlong, in the end holding on well for third. There is a suspicion he was flattered again, though. (op 16-1 tchd 20-1)

Without A Prayer(IRE), twice placed over 1m2f in Dubai earlier in the year, ran a good race in the Winter Derby on his latest start and he looked unlucky not to be even more involved in the finish. He tried to create a gap between the second and third, but Ryan Moore managed to keep him in and in the end he could only stay on once the race was over. Things may have been different had Sanders been able to get him rolling earlier and he can be rated better than the bare form. (op 11-1)

Vitznau(IRE) ran above expectations on this first try at Group level, just getting run out of fourth close home. Most of his best form is at shorter and he seemed to find this half a furlong too far, so could find a race at Listed level over slightly shorter. (op 20-1)

Lovelace, back to form when fourth off a mark of 110 in a Listed handicap at York last time, looked vulnerable to an improver under his Group 2 winners' penalty, but he seemed to have more of a problem with the track than anything, hanging left in the straight and never looking comfortable. Official explanation: jockey said horse hung left (op 11-2 tchd 13-2)

Hatta Fort never got into it having been held up and was another who didn't look at home on the track. (op 13-2)

General Eliott(IRE), narrow winner of a Listed contest at Ascot on his seasonal return, was sporting first-time blinkers and never looked happy. His rider reported he was unsuited by the track. (op 7-1 tchd 13-2)

2669 INVESTEC MILE (H'CAP) — 1m 114y

2:10 (2:12) (Class 2) (0-105,105) 4-Y-O+ **£18,693** (£5,598; £2,799; £1,401; £699; £351) **Stalls** Low

Form — RPR

0120 **1** **Tartan Gigha (IRE)**[19] 2101 4-8-7 **88** .... JoeFanning 1 97
(M Johnston) *chsd ldr: rdn over 2f out: sustained effrt to ld fnl 100yds: styd on wl* **9/2**[2]

10-1 **2** *2 ¼* **Plum Pudding (IRE)**[53] 1251 6-9-10 **105** .... RichardHughes 3 109
(R Hannon) *lw: led: rdn over 2f out: drvn ent fnl f: hdd fnl 100yds: wknd towards fin* **7/1**[3]

6021 **3** *nk* **Philario (IRE)**[13] 2289 4-9-5 **105** .... MartinLane(5) 8 108
(K R Burke) *chsd ldrs: rdn and unable qck u.p 2f out: kpt on same pce after* **3/1**[1]

0400 **4** *½* **Royal Power (IRE)**[69] 997 6-9-0 **95** .... TonyCulhane 6 97
(D Nicholls) *t.k.h: hld up in midfield: rdn and effrt to chse ldrs jst over 2f out: kpt on ins fnl f: nvr gng pce to rch ldrs* **10/1**

-100 **5** *1* **Intabih (USA)**[35] 1642 4-8-0 **86** oh1 .... Louis-PhilippeBeuzelin(5) 4 86
(C E Brittain) *chsd ldrs: rdn and struggling 3f out: kpt on same pce after* **25/1**

101 **6** *3 ¼* **More Time Tim (IRE)**[24] 1964 4-8-5 **86** oh2 .... MartinDwyer 5 78
(J R Boyle) *t.k.h: hld up in last pair: rdn and effrt wl over 2f out: no hdwy fnl 2f* **8/1**

2030 **7** *1 ½* **Bencoolen (IRE)**[23] 1986 4-8-9 **90** .... AdrianTNicholls 2 79
(D Nicholls) *stdd s: hld up in rr: rdn and no hdwy 3f out* **9/2**[2]

056- **8** *2 ¾* **South Cape**[218] 7101 6-8-7 **88** .... RichardMullen 9 71
(G L Moore) *stdd s: hld up towards rr: rdn and sme hdwy 3f out: sn wknd* **9/1**

00-4 **9** *10* **Capable Guest (IRE)**[92] 766 7-8-6 **87** .... (v) SamHitchcott 7 47
(M R Channon) *dwlt: sn rdn along in midfield: rdn and wknd 3f out: eased ins fnl f* **14/1**

1m 44.01s (-2.09) **Going Correction** +0.025s/f (Good) **9** Ran SP% **114.6**
Speed ratings (Par 109): **110,108,107,107,106 103,102,99,90**
toteswinger: 1&2 £6.20, 1&3 £3.10, 2&3 £4.60 CSF £35.63 CT £108.82 TOTE £5.80: £2.00, £1.60, £1.50; EX 36.40 Trifecta £71.60 Pool: 959.06 - 9.90 winning units.
Owner Mrs I Bird **Bred** Gainsborough Stud Management Ltd **Trained** Middleham Moor, N Yorks

FOCUS
Just an ordinary handicap for the grade. The principals were always prominent and it was a clear personal best off a career high mark from the winner.

NOTEBOOK
Tartan Gigha(IRE), 7lb higher than when winning at Beverley last month, ran disappointingly at Ripon last time and had since been freshened-up. Soon tracking the speed, he came with a strong challenge under Joe Fanning and got nicely on top inside the final furlong. He will need to progress further if he is to defy a rise, though, as he will be faced with stiffer opposition in future. Official explanation: trainer said, regarding apparent improvement in form, that he had no explanation for the gelding's last run but had allowed it to freshen up. (op 11-2 tchd 6-1)

Plum Pudding(IRE), who is something of a Newmarket specialist, won away from that track for the first time at Warwick on his reappearance and he ran a cracking race off a mark of 105 on this return to handicap company. Soon in front setting a true pace, he gave it a bold go and had them all off the bridle with three to run, but in the end was just found out by a stronger stayer. (op 11-2 tchd 15-2 and 8-1 in places)

Philario(IRE), 7lb higher than when winning a heavy-ground handicap at the Curragh last time, is fully effective on this quicker surface and he had his chance, but couldn't race on with the winner. He is clearly still progressing, but may continue to be vulnerable off his new mark. (op 10-3 tchd 11-4)

Royal Power(IRE), back to a mark that saw him finish third in last season's Royal Hunt Cup, kept on again, having been outpaced and only just failed to snatch third. (op 14-1 tchd 16-1)

Intabih(USA), racing from 1lb out of the handicap, has recorded all of his wins on the AW and struggled badly in two starts back on turf this year. He was going on close home, though, and this was much better. (op 20-1)

More Time Tim(IRE) has been in cracking form on the AW, winning four of his last five, but he was 6lb higher for his first turf start in this country (2lb out of the handicap) and he never threatened to get involved. (op 10-1)

Bencoolen(IRE), held up in last, was under strong pressure soon after straightening for home and couldn't make any ground down the straight. (op 7-2)

2670 INVESTEC CORONATION CUP (GROUP 1) — 1m 4f 10y

2:45 (2:51) (Class 1) 4-Y-O+ **£137,809** (£52,239; £26,144; £13,035; £6,529; £3,277) **Stalls** Centre

Form — RPR

60-1 **1** **Ask**[21] 2056 6-9-0 119 .... RyanMoore 8 121
(Sir Michael Stoute) *lw: trckd ldng pair: 3rd st: rdn to ld over 2f out: hrd pressed over 1f out: hld on gamely to narrow ld fnl f: all out* **5/1**[3]

32-4 **2** *nse* **Youmzain (IRE)**[69] 1012 6-9-0 125 .... RHills 5 121
(M R Channon) *hld up in midfield: 5th st: hdwy 3f out: ev ch fr wl over 1f out: r.o wl fnl f but a jst hld* **2/1**[1]

213- **3** *nse* **Look Here**[265] 5892 4-8-11 119 .... SebSanders 1 118
(R M Beckett) *hld up in last pair: 7th st: hdwy on outer over 2f out: edgd lft but str chal ins fnl f: r.o but nt quite get up* **9/2**[2]

0-11 **4** *3/4* **Duncan**[27] 1859 4-9-0 113 .... JimmyFortune 3 120
(J H M Gosden) *hld up in last trio: 6th st: hdwy and rdn 3f out: drvn wl over 1f out: pressed ldrs ins fnl f: keeping on same pce whn n.m.r towards fin* **9/2**[2]

10-3 **5** *3 1/4* **Frozen Fire (GER)**[28] 1823 4-9-0 117 .... JMurtagh 7 114
(A P O'Brien, Ire) *swtg: sn led: c off rail ent st: hung lft 3f out: hdd and rdn over 2f out: edgd rt and lft after: wknd ent fnl f* **17/2**

-111 **6** *7* **Eastern Anthem (IRE)**[69] 1012 5-9-0 117 .... (t) LDettori 6 103
(Saeed Bin Suroor) *swtg: stdd s: hld up in last pl: 8th strt: rdn and effrt 3f out: sn btn and hung lft fnl 2f* **12/1**

1-13 **7** *3 1/2* **Expresso Star (USA)**[29] 1799 4-9-0 109 .... RichardMullen 4 98
(J H M Gosden) *lw: led briefly: chsd ldr after: 2nd st: rdn 3f out: lost pl and wknd over 2f out* **25/1**

6-31 **8** *nk* **Buccellati**[28] 1823 5-9-0 115 .... (v) WilliamBuick 2 97+
(A M Balding) *swtg: hld up in midfield: 4th st: rdn and qcknd to press ldr on inner whn bdly hmpd over 2f out: lost all ch and nt rcvr: eased fr over 1f out* **9/1**

2m 37.0s (-1.90) **Going Correction** +0.025s/f (Good) **8** Ran SP% **118.4**
Speed ratings (Par 117): **107,106,106,106,104 99,97,97**
toteswinger: 1&2 £2.70, 1&3 £5.00, 2&3 £3.10 CSF £16.06 TOTE £7.20: £2.20, £1.10, £2.60; EX 17.00 Trifecta £56.70 Pool: £11,611.80 - 151.52 winning units.

Owner Patrick J Fahey **Bred** Side Hill Stud **Trained** Newmarket, Suffolk

■ Stewards' Enquiry : Ryan Moore three-day ban: used whip with excessive frequency without giving horse time to respond (Jun 21-23)

J Murtagh five-day ban: careless riding (Jun 19-23)

FOCUS

This wasn't exactly a vintage renewal, though there is every reason to believe it was up to scratch, with both last year's runner-up Youmzain, and Oaks heroine Look Here, losing out narrowly in a truly gripping finish. The pace was just a routine one. Ask has been rated to his Arc figure, and Youmzain 4lb off his mark in the same race. It was a fine comeback from Look Here and another improved effort from the highly progressive Duncan..

NOTEBOOK

Ask has often come up short at the top level over middle-distances, albeit not being beaten far in some quality events including the Prince Of Wales's Stakes and the Arc, but he again showed himself well suited by staying trips when romping away with the Yorkshire Cup on his reappearance. Solid in the market, he was driven into the lead over two furlongs out, Moore keen to get him going early, and he kept finding more when pressed by the runner-up from a furlong out. With the help of the rail to run against close home, he just managed to hold on in a three-way go and record his first victory at Group 1 level. His future plans will very much depend on the ground, as although it was on the quick side here, it wasn't jarring ground. His trainer has other options for Royal Ascot, so he will instead wait for the Irish St Leger and then have another crack at the Arc before likely retirement. (op 11-2 tchd 13-2)

Youmzain(IRE) achieved yet another near miss in a major contest. Runner-up in the Arc for a second successive year when finding only the brilliant Zarkava too good last October, he reappeared with a slightly unlucky fourth in the Sheema Classic in March and was bidding to go one better than when second to Soldier Of Fortune in this contest last term. A bigger field is preferable, as he is a horse who likes to get plenty of cover, and Hills did his best to kid him past the post in front, but he was unable to get the better of the winner in a prolonged battle. He has won twice at the top level abroad, but time is running out for him to him to plunder an elite Group 1 contest. The King George will be next on the agenda. (op 5-2 tchd 11-4)

Look Here, bidding to become the first filly since Lupe in 1971 to win this contest the year after taking the Oaks, was only seen out once more following that famous victory last season, finishing third to Conduit in the St Leger, and she reportedly looked fit for this return. Held up in rear, she began to close from two out and briefly looked the winner inside the final furlong, but edged left down the camber and couldn't quite get there. This was a smashing effort first time back against the boys and either the Eclipse or King George, or both, will be next on the agenda. (op 11-2 tchd 6-1)

Duncan has improved markedly since joining his current yard, readily winning a 1m2f handicap at this track on his reappearance and then romping away with a Listed contest over this trip at Ascot last month. This represented a big step up, but connections clearly felt he was up to it, having supplemented, and he more than rewarded their faith. He closed up over two out, a length or so ahead of the third, but was unable to quicken on inside the final furlong. This highly-progressive 4yo looks capable of better still and would have to be given plenty of respect if he turns up for the Hardwicke. (op 5-1)

Frozen Fire(GER) was never going to be seen at his best when last of three in the Ormonde Stakes, which was run at a farcical pace. He got very warm beforehand and it was bizarre to see him go off in front, considering what happened at Chester. Brought off the rail in the straight, he soon started to hang left and cut off Buccellati when that one was trying to come with a run. There were some positives to take from this and he will be seen to better effect coming from off a true pace, as he did when winning at the Curragh last season. (op 8-1 tchd 15-2)

Eastern Anthem(IRE) took his form to a new level for another yard in Dubai earlier in the year, rounding off a hat-trick of wins with narrow victory in the Sheema Classic. Back with his original yard, he was relatively weak in the market and never threatened to close in the straight, looking uneasy on the camber. Dettori reported he hung left. Official explanation: jockey said horse hung left (op 10-1)

Expresso Star(USA), a ready winner of the Lincoln who was not beaten far in the Group 3 Huxley Stakes last time, was soon close up, but he quickly retreated in the straight and ended up well held. His rider reported he hung right. Official explanation: jockey said colt hung right

Buccellati has been progressing well over the past year and he ran an excellent race when third behind Tartan Bearer in a Group 3 at Sandown on his reappearance. A ready winner when quickening up best in a farce of a race at Chester last time, he ran well on his one previous visit here and was in the process of coming through with a strong challenge against the rail when badly hampered by Frozen Fire. He lost all chance in the incident and can safely have this run ignored. (op 8-1 tchd 10-1)

2671 INVESTEC CHALLENGE (HERITAGE H'CAP) 1m 2f 18y

3:25 (3:29) (Class 2) 4-Y-0+

£24,924 (£5,598; £5,598; £1,868; £932; £468) **Stalls** Low

Form RPR

10/1 **1** **Seeking The Buck (USA)**[22] 2003 5-9-1 87 .... SebSanders 4 96
(R M Beckett) *chsd ldrs: wnt 2nd 7f out: rdn to ld over 2f out: sn hrd pressed: edgd rt u.p fr over 1f out: asserted wl ins fnl f* **9/2**[2]

-542 **2** *3/4* **Lake Poet (IRE)**[44] 1460 6-9-10 96 .... RyanMoore 11 103+
(C E Brittain) *hld up in tch in midfield: rdn and effrt over 2f out: chsd ldrs and carried rt fr over 1f out: kpt on wl u.p fnl f* **11/4**[1]

3215 **2** *dht* **Mystery Star (IRE)**[11] 2342 4-9-5 91 .... TPQueally 6 98
(M H Tompkins) *lw: chsd ldrs: rdn to chal over 2f out: ev ch after: carried rt fr over 1f out: no ex wl ins fnl f* **12/1**

040- **4** *1/2* **William Blake**[223] 6984 4-8-13 85 .... JoeFanning 1 91
(M Johnston) *chsd ldr tl 7f out: styd chsng ldrs: swtchd rt wl over 1f out: carried rt fr over 1f out: unable qck ins fnl f* **9/1**

-004 **5** *2 1/2* **Charm School**[36] 1631 4-9-7 93 .... JimmyFortune 5 94+
(J H M Gosden) *lw: hld up in rr: swtchd rt and c wd over 3f out: no prog tl styd on ins fnl f: nvr trbld ldrs* **10/1**

-400 **6** *nk* **Ramona Chase**[34] 1673 4-9-5 91 .... JimCrowley 3 91
(M J Attwater) *hld up towards rr: rdn and unable qck over 2f out: kpt on same pce fr wl over 1f out* **14/1**

114 **7** *1 1/4* **Manshoor (IRE)**[24] 1966 4-8-8 80 .... WilliamBuick 10 78
(Mrs L Wadham) *hld up bhd: hdwy on outer 3f out: chsd ldrs and drvn wl over 1f out: wknd ent fnl f* **20/1**

-360 **8** *1* **Dream Desert (IRE)**[29] 1798 4-8-13 85 .... EdwardCreighton 9 81
(M R Channon) *lw: t.k.h: hld up towards rr: rdn and effrt 3f out: sn no imp and wl hld fr over 1f out* **9/2**[2]

5-00 **9** *4 1/2* **Cobo Bay**[48] 1352 4-9-6 92 .... (p) NCallan 7 79
(K A Ryan) *sn led: rdn and hdd over 2f out: wknd wl over 1f out* **33/1**

1/40 **P** **Foolin Myself**[34] 1673 4-9-0 86 .... JamieSpencer 2 —
(M L W Bell) *lw: t.k.h: in tch: rdn and lost action 3f out: sn eased: p.u and dismntd ins fnl f* **6/1**[3]

2m 10.55s (0.85) **Going Correction** +0.025s/f (Good) **10** Ran SP% **118.5**
Speed ratings (Par 109): **97,96,96,96,94 93,92,91,88,**—PL: Lake Poet £1.40 Mystery Star £3.70. Ex: Seeking The Buck-LP £5.80, STB-MS £29.80. CSF: STB-LP £8.79, STB-MS £29.16. Tricast: STB-LP-MS £70.49 STB-LP-MS £88.65. toteswinger: STB&LP £2.40, STB&MS £6.50, LP&MS £7.60 TOTE £5.00: £1.9027 Owner Trifecta £Malcolm C Denmark Bred Flaxman Holdings Ltd.

■ Stewards' Enquiry : Seb Sanders three-day ban: careless riding (Jun 21-23)

FOCUS

This was a decent handicap, though there wasn't much pace on and it produced something of a bunch finish. The principals all raced fairly prominently. Seeking The Buck continues to progress, and Mystery Star is on the up too.

NOTEBOOK

Seeking The Buck(USA) returned from over a year off to win well at Newmarket last month, but was 7lb higher in a stronger race here and needed to have taken a step forward. Nicely positioned just in behind the leader, he went to the front over two out, and, despite edging right under pressure and taking the placed horses with him, he pulled out plenty and always looked to be doing enough inside the final half a furlong. He has clearly returned in top condition and fully deserves to take his chance in something like the Wolferton Handicap at Royal Ascot. (tchd 5-1 in places)

Lake Poet(IRE) likes it around here and was only 1lb higher than when winning this contest in 2007. Runner-up in the City And Suburban over CD last time, he came to have every chance and ran his usual honest race, but couldn't quite get to the winner. (op 7-2)

Mystery Star(IRE), off the same mark as when finishing fifth in the Zetland Gold Cup last time, briefly looked like getting on top of the winner, but he couldn't pull out any extra close home and was joined on the line for second. (op 7-2)

William Blake didn't quite progress as expected having notched a hat-trick early last year, but he still ran several good races in defeat off higher marks than this and he looked interesting here having been gelded over the winter. Sat just in behind the pace, Fanning wanted to go early in the straight, but he had no room to get out and was forced to wait. He was still in the clear in plenty of time, though, and couldn't quicken on inside the final furlong. (op 10-1 tchd 11-1 in places)

Charm School has been falling short off slightly higher marks and failed to improve for the first-time blinkers when only fourth at Yarmouth latest. He was last and being ridden along with three to run, but eventually consented to run on inside the final furlong. (op 8-1)

Ramona Chase was tried in a net muzzle here to help him settle. (op 12-1 tchd 11-1 and 16-1 in places)

Dream Desert(IRE) was a notable disappointment, fading from a furlong out. (op 5-1 tchd 11-2)

Foolin Myself was pulled up and dismounted inside the final furlong, having lost his action. Official explanation: jockey said colt lost its action (op 8-1)

2672 INVESTEC OAKS (GROUP 1) (FILLIES) 1m 4f 10y

4:05 (4:10) (Class 1) 3-Y-O

£198,695 (£75,320; £37,695; £18,795; £9,415; £4,725) **Stalls** Centre

Form RPR

1-41 **1** **Sariska**[23] 1988 3-9-0 115 .... JamieSpencer 5 120+
(M L W Bell) *lw: hld up in midfield: 6th st: gd hdwy and edgd lft 3f out: led over 2f out: rdn ent fnl 2f: edgd rt over 1f out: styd on gamely fnl f* **9/4**[1]

4-21 **2** *hd* **Midday**[27] 1871 3-9-0 105 .... TPQueally 2 119
(H R A Cecil) *lw: in tch in midfield: 5th st: sn swtchd rt: hdwy and carried lft 3f out: chsd ldrs over 2f out: drvn to chse wnr over 1f out: kpt gamely fnl f* **5/1**[3]

6-14 **3** *2 1/2* **High Heeled (IRE)**[23] 1988 3-9-0 100 .... MichaelHills 9 115
(B W Hills) *hld up in last pair: 9th strt: gd hdwy on outer 3f out: chsd wnr jst over 2f out tl sltly hmpd over 1f out: kpt on same pce fnl f* **33/1**

11-5 **4** *4 1/2* **Rainbow View (USA)**[33] 1698 3-9-0 118 .... JimmyFortune 10 110+
(J H M Gosden) *lw: hld up in last trio: 7th st: gd hdwy 3f out: rdn and disputing cl 3rd whn hmpd and snatched up 2f out: no ch w ldrs after: wknd over 1f out* **3/1**[2]

-442 **5** *9* **The Miniver Rose (IRE)**[21] 2036 3-9-0 96 .... RichardHughes 4 94
(R Hannon) *stdd s: hld up towards rr: 8th st: effrt 3f out: sn wl outpcd by ldrs: no ch fnl 2f* **33/1**

0-52 **6** *5* **Phillipina**[30] 1789 3-9-0 103 .... RyanMoore 3 86+
(Sir Michael Stoute) *led for 1f: chsd ldrs after: 4th st: rdn and nt qckning whn hmpd 3f out: nt rcvr and no ch after* **13/2**

-103 **7** *3/4* **Oh Goodness Me**[12] 2304 3-9-0 106 .... KJManning 6 84
(J S Bolger, Ire) *t.k.h: chsd ldrs tl led over 8f out: rdn and hdd over 2f out: sn wknd* **8/1**

15-3 **8** *2 1/4* **Tottie**[27] 1871 3-9-0 92 .... JimCrowley 8 81
(Mrs A J Perrett) *dwlt: hld up in last pair: 10th st: lost tch wl over 2f out* **66/1**

2102 **9** *29* **Wadaat**[12] 2310 3-9-0 80 .... NCallan 7 34+
(C E Brittain) *b: swtg: chsd ldrs: wnt 2nd over 6f out: 2nd st: wkng whn bdly hmpd wl over 2f out: wl bhd after: t.o and eased fnl f* **33/1**

40-1 **10** *86* **Perfect Truth (IRE)**[30] 1789 3-9-0 104 .... JMurtagh 1 —+
(A P O'Brien, Ire) *led after 1f tl over 8f out: 3rd and rdn st: wkng whn bdly hmpd wl over 2f out: virtually p.u after* **10/1**

2m 35.28s (-3.62) **Going Correction** +0.025s/f (Good) **10** Ran SP% **116.3**
Speed ratings (Par 110): **113,112,111,108,102 98,98,96,77,20**
toteswinger: 1&2 £3.30, 1&3 £14.20, 2&3 £21.90 CSF £13.41 CT £288.41 TOTE £3.70: £1.40, £2.00, £5.60; EX 15.80 Trifecta £183.40 Pool: 14,128.24 - 57.00 winning units.

Owner Lady Bamford **Bred** Lady Bamford **Trained** Newmarket, Suffolk

■ There was a lengthy stewards' enquiry before the winner kept the race.

■ Stewards' Enquiry : Jamie Spencer five-day ban: careless riding (Jun 19-23)

FOCUS
In comparison to some recent runnings this may have lacked a little strength in depth, yet any of the three market leaders would have been an entirely credible winner. It was a roughish race, particularly the last 3f of it, but two of the three principals emerged to fight out a superb finish. It has been rated as an up-to-scratch renewal, with Sariska and High Heeled both improving on their Musidora form and Midday stepping up markedly on her Lingfield level too. There was a lengthy stewards' inquiry

NOTEBOOK
Sariska proved herself a most worthy Oaks winner with a performance that incorporated most of the qualities that one would hope to see in a top-class middle-distance filly, albeit in a race in which a fair bit of the trouble could be laid at her door. Held up towards the rear, she was nicely poised in sixth straightening for home, and when Jamie Spencer asked her to close on front runner Oh Goodness Me she quickened smoothly to get there very quickly, although edging left down the camber in the process, doing Phillipina no favours and initiating an unfortunate chain reaction. In front over 2f out, she soon had a fight on her hands, with challenges to either side from Midday and High Heeled, and Rainbow View closing too when squeezed out, but she certainly put her head down and battled under pressure. She and Midday eventually came clear and it was interesting to hear Jamie Spencer say afterwards that he went so early in order to run the finish out of Rainbow View, and to argue she might have been more impressive if he had waited longer. She returned with a nasty cut to a hind leg, but Michael Bell hopes to have her ready for the Irish Oaks. (op 7-2)
Midday brought proven course form to the event, and she had been highly impressive in the Lingfield Oaks Trial. However, she beat a field of maiden winners there and had plenty to find strictly on the figures. Having sat a little handier than the winner on the inner it's fair to say she didn't enjoy an untroubled passage in the straight, for she was carried left in the incident initiated by the winner. However, she was in the clear to make her challenge in plenty of time, and hard though she tried, she simply could not quite get past an equally resolute rival. Clearly a top-class filly, it will be surprising if she is not placed to advantage in a Group 1 before the end of the season. (op 11-2 tchd 9-2 in places)
High Heeled(IRE) had beaten colts at Newbury before finding the fast ground against her when disappointing in the Musidora. Connections thought carefully before running her here, but there is seldom any jar at this meeting and she showed career-best form in third, looking a real threat when starting her effort from the rear on the outside and not out of it until inside the final furlong. Beaten only by two really good fillies here, she could now be supplemented for the Irish Oaks, where easier ground could show her in an even better light.
Rainbow View(USA)'s connections were adamant that firm ground was to blame when she was an odds-on fifth in the Guineas, and they had resolved immediately to aim her here rather than for the Irish 1000 Guineas. Calm again in the preliminaries although brought into the paddock very late, she stood out on the form of her May Hill and Fillies' Mile wins, but she had her stamina to prove and there remained a nagging worry that her Guineas defeat might in part have reflected the possibility that her contemporaries had simply caught up with her. In the event, however, those questions remained unanswered, for she was effectively put out of contention two out when the gap closed as she tried to nose between Sariska and High Heeled and she had to be snatched up. While she looked tired in the final furlong and there is a suspicion she would have been no better than fourth anyway, she would have been a good deal closer. (op 11-4)
The Miniver Rose(IRE), patiently ridden, ran ran respectably enough in the face of a tough task but was not among those hampered significantly.
Phillipina was bidding to become the first maiden to win the Oaks since Sun Princess in 1983, having failed by only a short head to catch Perfect Truth at Chester. She was being pushed along when Sariska edged left and hampered her starting up the straight. While she was not going well enough to suggest she would have been concerned in the finish, we saw at Chester how well she stays and this obviously was not her running. (op 5-1 tchd 7-1)
Oh Goodness Me was racing on a sound surface for the first time and stepping up half a mile after her third to Again in the Irish 1000 Guineas. Her pedigree gave plenty of encouragement for the longer trip, but she was too keen early on, so much so that she was allowed to take over from Perfect Truth in front with around a mile to go. She was in trouble as soon as they straightened up and clearly did not run her race. (op 11-1)
Tottie finished close behind Midday at Newmarket last year, but the margin was much wider at Lingfield and it was wider still here. Jim Crowley felt she did not stay, but she was clearly outclassed too. (tchd 50-1)
Wadaat was badly hampered towards the inner early in the straight. Official explanation: jockey said filly suffered interference
Perfect Truth(IRE) was out of contention when meeting interference. She had been the first off the bridle and was struggling to hold her place coming down the hill, Johnny Murtagh reporting subsequently that she had not handled the track. (op 8-1)

2673 INVESTEC SURREY STKS (LISTED RACE) 7f
4:50 (4:51) (Class 1) 3-Y-O

£22,708 (£8,608; £4,308; £2,148; £1,076; £540) **Stalls** Low

Form RPR
1-10 **1** **Ocean's Minstrel**[34] 1675 3-9-3 102 JerryO'Dwyer 9 100
(J Ryan) *sn led: mde rest: rdn over 2f out: drvn and styd on wl fnl f* **8/1**
402 **2** ¾ **Ermine And Velvet**[20] 2080 3-8-8 77 MartinDwyer 2 88
(C E Brittain) *sn chsng wnr: rdn over 2f out: drvn and kpt on fnl f: a hld* **33/1**
0-62 **3** 1 ½ **Nasri**[13] 2278 3-8-13 105 JamieSpencer 5 89+
(B J Meehan) *lw: stdd s: towards rr: awkward bnd over 3f out: hdwy u.p over 1f out: wnt 3rd and hung lft 1f out: no imp fnl f* **6/4**[1]
0622 **4** ½ **Akhenaten**[6] 2469 3-8-13 94 TonyCulhane 4 88
(M R Channon) *lw: hld up in midfield: effrt and hanging lft 3f out: kpt on u.p fnl f: nvr pce to rch ldr* **8/1**
2-36 **5** nk **Mishrif (USA)**[42] 1485 3-8-13 97 AlanMunro 7 87
(P W Chapple-Hyam) *chsd ldng pair: rdn over 2f out: hrd drvn and one pce fr over 1f out* **25/1**
41-6 **6** nk **Khor Dubai (IRE)**[19] 2114 3-8-13 102 (v[1]) LDettori 1 86
(Saeed Bin Suroor) *t.k.h: hld up towards rr: nt clr run and swtchd rt over 2f out: nt clr run 2f out tl 1f out: one pce after* **15/2**[3]
1 **7** 1 ¼ **Mastoora (IRE)**[45] 1423 3-8-8 82 RHills 6 78+
(W J Haggas) *leggy: s.i.s: bhd: last st: hdwy on outer over 2f out: wanting to hang lft fr 2f out: no hdwy and nt pushed ins fnl f* **5/1**[2]
0-40 **8** 8 **Isabella Grey**[13] 2273 3-8-8 96 NCallan 3 56
(K A Ryan) *t.k.h: in tch: rdn over 2f out: wkng whn hung lft wl over 1f out: eased ins fnl f* **20/1**
2 **9** 21 **Croisultan (IRE)**[19] 2107 3-8-13 100 JMurtagh 8 4
(Liam McAteer, Ire) *in tch: lost pl 3f out: sn hung bdly lft and lost tch: eased fr over 1f out: t.o* **5/1**[2]

1m 22.99s (-0.31) **Going Correction** +0.025s/f (Good) **9** Ran SP% **118.9**
Speed ratings (Par 107): **102,101,99,98,98 98,96,87,63**
toteswinger: 1&2 £22.10, 1&3 £4.60, 2&3 £13.00 CSF £241.87 TOTE £8.20: £2.40, £5.60, £1.20; EX 308.60 TRIFECTA Not won..
Owner Ocean Trailers Ltd **Bred** Black Horse Farm **Trained** Newmarket, Suffolk

FOCUS
Not a strong Listed prize and very few got into it, the front two holding their positions throughout. The time was slower than for the following handicap and there is little solid to go on, so there has to be a doubt over the runner-up's apparent improvement.

NOTEBOOK
Ocean's Minstrel had won in this grade over 1m at Lingfield in April and was far from disgraced when tenth, beaten ten lengths, behind Sea The Stars in the 2000 Guineas. He had an easy time of things on the front end and, having been given a kick in the belly over two out, soon had them all in trouble. He stayed on well for pressure and never looked likely to be caught inside the final furlong. He will head to Ascot for the Jersey Stakes now. (op 9-1 tchd 10-1)
Ermine And Velvet, who has an official rating of just 77, ran a massive race in second. Runner-up in a Newbury maiden last time, she had the run of the race, but kept on right the way to the line and still managed to finish ahead of some much higher-rated rivals. This has given her some valuable black-type and she should find a race at some stage.
Nasri came into this having registered a career-best when second to the smart-looking Alyarf at Newmarket last month and set a strong standard. However, he wasn't the quickest into stride and soon found himself with plenty of ground to make up. He didn't look that in love with the track, being awkward round the bend and hanging under pressure, and in the end could only keep on at the one pace. (op 9-4)
Akhenaten has been a revelation since dropping back in trip, twice finishing second in 3yo sprints, and he ran another good race on this step up to 7f. He got going too late though, having initially hung left under pressure, and this fellow is likely to remain troublesome to win with. (op 17-2 tchd 9-1)
Mishrif(USA), who ran as though something had gone amiss when a tailed-of last of six in the Sandown Classic Trial last time, had earlier been running well in 1m Listed contests and he returned to something like his best by finishing a close-up fifth. (op 20-1 tchd 16-1)
Khor Dubai(IRE) was wearing a first-time visor. Twice he got stopped in his run when trying to close and he can be rated a good bit better than the bare form. (op 13-2 tchd 6-1)
Mastoora(IRE) made light work of weak opposition on her debut at Folkestone and this represented a huge step up. Slowly away and showing signs of greenness, she started to make ground over two out, but was then hanging to her left and could make no further inroads. This was a tough ask and she deserves another chance to show what she is capable of. (op 4-1)
Croisultan(IRE) has improved in Ireland this season, finishing second to Jumbajukiba before winning easily at Navan last time, but those efforts have come in testing ground and he soon began to struggle as they straightened for home, eventually tailing off. His rider reported he hung left. Official explanation: jockey said colt hung badly left (tchd 6-1)

2674 INVESTEC OPPORTUNITY STKS (H'CAP) 7f
5:25 (5:26) (Class 2) (0-100,92) 3-Y-O

£12,462 (£3,732; £1,866; £934; £466; £234) **Stalls** Low

Form RPR
1-03 **1** **Cloudy Start**[36] 1631 3-9-5 88 TPQueally 9 96
(H R A Cecil) *lw: chsd ldrs: rdn to chse ldr 2f out: drvn over 1f out: led fnl 100yds: r.o wl* **10/1**[3]
01-1 **2** ½ **Shamwari Lodge (IRE)**[21] 2049 3-9-8 91 RichardHughes 13 98
(R Hannon) *dwlt: towards rr: rdn and hdwy over 2f out: chsd ldrs ent fnl f: pressed wnr fnl 100yds: r.o but hld after* **11/2**[2]
-612 **3** 1 ½ **Time Medicean**[17] 2148 3-8-13 82 TonyCulhane 5 85
(M R Channon) *chsd ldrs: rdn and effrt 3f out: unable qck 2f out: kpt on u.p ins fnl f: wnt 3rd last strides* **11/2**[2]
3003 **4** hd **Parisian Pyramid (IRE)**[13] 2279 3-9-6 89 AdrianTNicholls 4 91
(D Nicholls) *led: rdn over 2f out: hung rt fr 2f out: hdd fnl 100yds: no ex and lost 2 pls after* **14/1**
3125 **5** hd **Tartan Gunna**[23] 1987 3-9-6 89 JoeFanning 10 91+
(M Johnston) *lw: s.i.s: towards rr: hdwy over 2f out: drvn over 1f out: edgd lft but r.o wl fnl f: nt rch ldrs* **10/1**[3]
-043 **6** ½ **Agente Parmigiano (IRE)**[28] 1828 3-9-7 90 JamieSpencer 12 91+
(G A Butler) *v.s.a: sn swtchd lft: bhd: stl last 2f out: str run on outer ent fnl f: edgd lft but fin wl: nt rch ldrs* **25/1**
2226 **7** ½ **Shaws Diamond (USA)**[13] 2279 3-8-4 78 MartinLane(5) 2 77
(D Shaw) *chsd ldrs: rdn 3f out: hanging lft u.p fr 2f out: wknd ins fnl f* **25/1**
16-0 **8** nk **Archie Rice (USA)**[21] 2049 3-9-9 92 AlanMunro 3 90
(W Jarvis) *hld up in midfield: rdn and unable qck 3f out: drvn and hdwy over 1f out: swtchd rt ins fnl f: styd on* **33/1**
21-3 **9** 2 ¼ **All About You (IRE)**[27] 1879 3-9-1 84 JMurtagh 7 76
(W J Haggas) *hld up in midfield: rdn and unable qck 3f out: sme hdwy over 1f out: swtchd rt jst ins fnl f: kpt on but nvr pce to threaten ldrs* **9/2**[1]
02-4 **10** 2 ¾ **Satwa Laird**[23] 1987 3-9-4 87 JimmyFortune 6 72
(E A L Dunlop) *s.i.s: towards rr: rdn and effrt 3f out: no prog whn n.m.r jst over 1f out* **9/2**[1]
-230 **11** 1 **Pegasus Lad (USA)**[20] 2073 3-8-11 80 NCallan 11 62
(M Johnston) *in tch in midfield: rdn and effrt 3f out: drvn and edging lft wl over 1f out: wknd ent fnl f* **14/1**
-020 **12** ½ **Timeteam (IRE)**[13] 2279 3-9-3 86 PatDobbs 1 67
(S Kirk) *bhd: nvr trbld ldrs* **40/1**
20-4 **13** nk **King's Sabre**[35] 1638 3-9-0 83 MartinDwyer 15 63
(W R Muir) *t.k.h: hld up towards rr: rdn 3f out: no hdwy: hung lft fr over 1f out* **33/1**
05-5 **14** ½ **Ballyalla**[27] 1860 3-9-0 83 RyanMoore 8 62
(R Hannon) *chsd ldr tl 2f out: sn drvn: styd chsng ldrs tl btn and heavily eased ins fnl f: sddle slipped* **10/1**[3]
6-40 **15** ½ **Roman Glory (IRE)**[13] 2273 3-9-2 85 SebSanders 14 62
(B J Meehan) *racd on outer in midfield: rdn over 3f out: wkng whn n.m.r over 1f out: no ch fnl f* **25/1**

1m 22.46s (-0.84) **Going Correction** +0.025s/f (Good) **15** Ran SP% **127.6**
Speed ratings (Par 105): **105,104,102,102,102 101,101,100,98,95 93,93,93,92,91**
toteswinger: 1&2 £13.60, 1&3 £18.30, 2&3 £9.60 CSF £62.92 CT £356.55 TOTE £14.20: £4.30, £2.30, £2.70; EX 96.70 TRIFECTA Not won. Place 6: £14.51 Place 5: £7.23.
Owner K Abdulla **Bred** Juddmonte Farms Ltd **Trained** Newmarket, Suffolk

FOCUS
A race that is usually very competitive and this year's renewal was certainly no different. They went a good gallop and the form looks sound. A race that should produce winners.

NOTEBOOK
Cloudy Start, a progressive sort at two, had been a bit disappointing in a couple of outings this term and the Handicapper had failed to drop him, but he seemed suited to the way this race was run and stayed on strongly inside the final furlong. He probably needs another furlong now, as he took a while to pick up when first asked, and there may well be more to come from him at that distance. Therefore, the Britannia Stakes at Royal Ascot seems the logical target. (op 12-1)
Shamwari Lodge(IRE), raised 5lb having scored narrowly at Newmarket on her seasonal/handicap debut, also seemed suited by the decent gallop up front. She started to close with two to run and looked set to sweep into the lead inside the final furlong, but the winner found more and she was made to settle for second. She travels well and looks capable of further success. (op 7-1 tchd 5-1 and 8-1 in places)
Time Medicean, up 3lb having finished second over 6f on his handicap debut at Leicester, kept on well inside the final furlong to just snatch third. He seems to be going the right way. (op 13-2 tchd 7-1)
Parisian Pyramid(IRE), back to form when third in a competitive sprint handicap at Newmarket last time, was back up to a mark of 89 and also trying 7f for the first time. He was ridden positively and still led inside the distance, but the front pair pulled away close home and he was just run out of third. His rider reported he was unsuited by the track, so all things considered this was a good effort. Official explanation: jockey said gelding was unsuited by the track (op 10-1)

Tartan Gunna, a tough and progressive sort racing off a career-high mark, is proving most consistent and he kept on well late to bustle up the placed horses. He would have been made more use of in an ideal world. (op 12-1 tchd 14-1)
Agente Parmigiano(IRE) has been running creditably outside of handicap company and he may well have gone close to winning had he not missed the break and got too far back. Official explanation: jockey said colt missed the break
Shaws Diamond(USA), sixth in a good sprint at Newmarket on her recent return to turf, again ran well in defeat and she can find a race at a slightly lower level. (op 33-1)
Archie Rice(USA) ran a lot better than he had done at Newmarket last time, though is still rather high in the weights.
All About You(IRE) seemed unsuited by the very firm ground when third to subsequent winner Bouvardia at Nottingham on his seasonal return (also debut for yard), but this extra furlong looked in his favour. He couldn't quicken when initially asked for his effort, though, and despite staying on, he never looked like getting involved. (op 7-2)
Satwa Laird, fourth off this mark at York on his seasonal return, was a bit slow to get going and could only make limited headway in the straight. (op 5-1 tchd 11-2)
Ballyalla was in the process of running a good race when the saddle slipped and she had to be eased right down. Official explanation: jockey said saddle slipped (op 12-1 tchd 14-1 and 16-1 in places)
T/Jkpt: Not won. T/Plt: £11.20 to a £1 stake. Pool: £203,682.91. 13,265.82 winning tickets. T/Qpdt: £4.80 to a £1 stake. Pool: £9,486.71. 1,444.86 winning tickets. SP

2474 GOODWOOD (R-H)

Friday, June 5

OFFICIAL GOING: Good to firm (9.2)
Wind: Almost nil Weather: Cloudy

2675 GOODWOOD FARM SHOP STKS (H'CAP) (FOR AMATEUR RIDERS) — 1m 1f

6:15 (6:15) (Class 5) (0-70,70) 4-Y-0+ — **£3,123** (£968; £484; £242) **Stalls** High

Form — RPR
36-3 **1** **Addwaitya**[41] 1514 4-11-3 **69**........ MissGAndrews(3) 7 — 78
(C F Wall) *hld up in mid-div: gd hdwy over 2f out: led over 1f out: r.o wl* **4/1**[2]
3300 **2** *1* **Bavarica**[14] 2244 7-10-6 **60**........ MrRBirkett(5) 1 — 67
(Miss J Feilden) *sn chsd ldrs: kpt on wl fnl f* **10/1**
00-2 **3** *shd* **Shavoulin (USA)**[14] 2221 5-10-2 **51** oh1........ MrsMarieKing 9 — 58
(P W Hiatt) *s.i.s: sn prom: led 2f out to over 1f out: kpt on one pce fnl f* **11/2**[3]
10-4 **4** *2* **Laish Ya Hajar (IRE)**[10] 2351 5-10-13 **69**........ MrDHannig(7) 12 — 71
(P R Webber) *led after 1f: hdd 2f out: rdn and styd on same pce* **10/1**
20P6 **5** *2 1/2* **Magic Warrior**[14] 2221 9-9-11 **51** oh6........ MissSarah-JaneDurman(5) 4 — 48
(J C Fox) *slowly away: in rr: styd on ins fnl 2f: nvr nrr* **40/1**
400 **6** *3/4* **Dudley Docker (IRE)**[86] 807 7-10-10 **66**........ MrJPearce(7) 3 — 61
(T T Clement) *mid-div: swtchd rt to far side 2f out: no ex fr over 1f out* **33/1**
20-4 **7** *1 1/2* **Lush (IRE)**[11] 2322 4-11-0 **68**........ JimmyDerham(5) 10 — 60
(R Hannon) *towards rr and nvr nr to chal* **12/1**
0040 **8** *nk* **Artreju (GER)**[30] 1785 6-10-3 **57**........ MrJoshuaMoore(5) 14 — 48
(G L Moore) *prom: hit rails over 4f out: led 3f out: hdd 2f out: sn wknd* **11/4**[1]
6050 **9** *2 1/4* **Millfield (IRE)**[16] 2186 6-11-2 **70**........ MrNdeBoinville(5) 13 — 56
(P R Chamings) *slowly away: in rr: hit rails over 5f out: nvr on terms* **12/1**
3030 **10** *1 1/4* **Binnion Bay (IRE)**[11] 2330 8-9-13 **53**........(b) MrAshleyBird(5) 2 — 36
(J J Bridger) *prom tl rdn and wknd 2f out* **14/1**
6566 **11** *12* **Red Current**[11] 2333 5-9-11 **51** oh2........ MrCDThompson(5) 6 — 8
(R A Harris) *a towards rr* **20/1**
2130 **12** *3 3/4* **Western Roots**[6] 2493 8-10-13 **67**........ MissMBryant(5) 11 — 16
(P Butler) *slowly away but sn prom on outside: wknd 3f out* **14/1**
2000 **13** *3 1/4* **I Certainly May**[115] 482 4-9-12 **54** oh6 ow3........ MrAlexBarlow(7) 8 — —
(S Dow) *led for 1f: wknd 1/2-way* **66/1**
0006 **14** *25* **Looter (FR)**[39] 1177 4-9-9 **51** oh6........(tp) MissKLoftus(7) 5 — —
(P Butler) *a bhd: t.o fnl 3f* **100/1**

1m 58.23s (1.93) **Going Correction** +0.10s/f (Good) — **14 Ran SP% 121.6**
Speed ratings (Par 103): **95,94,94,92,90 89,88,87,85,84 73,70,67,45**
toteswinger: 1&2 £12.80, 1&3 £4.60, 2&3 £18.10. CSF £42.63 CT £233.09 TOTE £4.50: £2.00, £3.00, £2.40; EX 47.10.
Owner Les McLaughlin **Bred** L McLaughlin **Trained** Newmarket, Suffolk

FOCUS
Just a modest handicap for amateur riders. It was run at a reasonable pace but the gallop was not as strong as it can be for these races, and the time was the best part of seven seconds outside the Racing Post standard. The form is rated around the second and fourth.

2676 NEW CENTURY MEDIA EUROPEAN BREEDERS' FUND MAIDEN STKS — 6f

6:45 (6:47) (Class 5) 2-Y-0 — **£3,885** (£1,156; £577; £288) **Stalls** Low

Form — RPR
1 **Sabii Sands (IRE)** 2-9-3 0........ RyanMoore 3 — 80+
(R Hannon) *mde all: shkn up and qcknd wl whn chal fr 1f out* **13/8**[2]
3 **2** *1/2* **Arabian Pride**[14] 2231 2-9-3 0........ EddieAhern 2 — 78
(D M Simcock) *hld up in 3rd: hdwy to chal 1f out: nt pce of wnr ins fnl f* **5/4**[1]
3 *4 1/2* **Blue Sparkle (IRE)** 2-8-12 0........ JimCrowley 6 — 60
(Mrs A J Perrett) *trckd wnr to 1f out: readily outpcd* **7/1**[3]
4 *3 1/4* **Call Of The Kings** 2-9-3 0........ LukeMorris 5 — 55
(R A Teal) *s.i.s: in tch tl over 1f out* **14/1**
5 *9* **Rainsborough** 2-9-3 0........ SamHitchcott 1 — 28
(M R Channon) *outpcd thrght* **12/1**

1m 14.14s (1.94) **Going Correction** +0.10s/f (Good) — **5 Ran SP% 109.4**
Speed ratings (Par 93): **91,90,84,80,68**
toteswinger: 1&2 £1.90. CSF £3.96 TOTE £2.70: £1.40, £1.20; EX 3.60.
Owner Andrew Russell **Bred** Mrs Sheila Morrissey **Trained** East Everleigh, Wilts

FOCUS
Only one of the five had seen a racecourse before in what was probably a fair maiden. The first two pulled clear in a good finish.

NOTEBOOK
Sabii Sands(IRE) ◆, whose yard won this a year ago, is not very attractively bred but cost 120,000 euros as a yearling. Well away to claim the lead on the rail, he was tackled by the favourite inside the last but did not wilt and fought him off in the last 50 yards. A strong colt, he was not as wound up first time as a lot of Hannon juveniles and improvement can be expected. He looks one to keep on the right side. (op 11-4)
Arabian Pride was third on his debut on easy ground at Newcastle, a place behind Count Bertoni who was a beaten favourite at Doncaster ten minutes before this race. Covered up in third place, he had to wait until a gap opened for him with a furlong left and looked set to go on and score, but the winner proved too tough late on. He did nothing much wrong and his turn is only delayed. (op 10-11)
Blue Sparkle(IRE), the sole filly in the line-up, travelled well up with the pace but showed signs of greenness when the pressure was on and was left behind by the first two late on. Sprint-bred, she can win a maiden against her own sex. (op 6-1 tchd 11-2)
Call Of The Kings, the first foal of a multiple dirt sprint winner in the USA, was in fourth place all the way after a tardy start. (tchd 16-1)
Rainsborough, who was retained very cheaply as a foal, was slowly away and struggling at an early stage. (tchd 9-1)

2677 WHEB VENTURES AND RUSTON WHEB STKS (REGISTERED AS THE TAPSTER STAKES) (LISTED RACE) — 1m 4f

7:20 (7:20) (Class 1) 4-Y-0+ — **£23,704** (£8,964; £4,480; £2,240) **Stalls** Low

Form — RPR
240- **1** **Mad Rush (USA)**[213] 7188 5-9-0 112........ RyanMoore 1 — 112+
(L M Cumani) *sn led: mde rest: hrd rdn fnl f: jst hld on* **5/4**[1]
6022 **2** *nse* **Halicarnassus (IRE)**[11] 2327 5-9-0 103........ SamHitchcott 2 — 112
(M R Channon) *trckd wnr to over 4f out: outpcd 3f out: rallied to press wnr ins fnl f: jst failed* **7/1**[3]
05-4 **3** *1 3/4* **Illustrious Blue**[11] 2327 6-9-0 107........ JimCrowley 6 — 109
(W J Knight) *hld up in rr: hdwy and r.o to go 3rd ins fnl f* **10/1**
4-00 **4** *2* **Unleashed (IRE)**[20] 2075 4-9-0 103........ TPQueally 3 — 106
(H R A Cecil) *in tch: wnt 2nd over 4f out: rdn and wknd appr fnl f* **20/1**
632- **5** *3* **Sagara (USA)**[230] 6820 5-9-0 109........(v) TedDurcan 5 — 101
(Saeed Bin Suroor) *in rr: kpt on one pce fnl 2f* **10/1**
-102 **6** *57* **Crime Scene (IRE)**[106] 613 6-9-0 113........ LDettori 4 — 10
(Saeed Bin Suroor) *hld up: hdwy over 3f out: wknd wl over 1f out: eased: t.o* **9/4**[2]

2m 36.18s (-2.22) **Going Correction** +0.10s/f (Good) — **6 Ran SP% 110.7**
Speed ratings (Par 111): **111,110,109,108,106 68**
toteswinger: 1&2 £2.20, 1&3 £3.00, 2&3 £4.20. CSF £10.36 TOTE £2.30: £1.40, £2.90; EX 9.50.
Owner The Honorable Earle I Mack **Bred** Avalon Farm **Trained** Newmarket, Suffolk

FOCUS
A decent Listed race run in a time just under two seconds above the standard. Mad Rush was not at his best and the form is rater muddling.

NOTEBOOK
Mad Rush(USA), who was making his reappearance, has been gelded since his trip to Australia last autumn which yielded a Caulfield Cup fourth and a seventh, when favourite, for the Melbourne Cup. Setting his own pace, his rider no doubt mindful that a falsely run affair would be no use to him, he wound things up with 3f to run and had his pursuers in trouble entering the final furlong, but then had to withstand a strong challenge from the second and the line only just came in time. This was his first win in a stakes race although he was just denied in the Prix Kergorlay at Deauville last summer. He will go next for the Group 3 Curragh Cup at the end of the month and the step back up in trip will suit, but connections will be hoping for some easier ground there. (tchd 11-10 and 11-8 in a place)
Halicarnassus(IRE) seemed held in third passing the furlong pole but really found his feet late on and in one more stride would have run down the favourite. Finishing second for the third time in a row, including in a race in this grade over 1m2f here last time, he has never previously shone at this trip but saw it out well. (op 9-1 tchd 13-2)
Illustrious Blue was rather caught in a pocket at the 3f pole just as the race really developed. He ran on inside the last and this was another creditable effort at a track he likes, all bar one of his six British wins having come here. He has now been beaten 18 times since his latest victory though. (op 9-1 tchd 8-1)
Unleashed(IRE) had not shown much on either of his previous two starts this year and this was better. The worst in on official ratings, he went after the winner early in the straight and was only relegated two places inside the final furlong. (op 16-1)
Sagara(USA) started favourite for this last year on his debut for Godolphin only to finish last of ten. He did not fare badly on his seasonal bow this time and will be seen to better effect back over 2m plus, although once again he won't be too easy to place. (op 8-1)
Crime Scene(IRE), off the track since a decent stint for another yard in Dubai earlier in the year, dropped away tamely and was allowed to come home in his own time. Official explanation: jockey said gelding lost its action (op 11-4)

2678 ECOLOGIST STKS (H'CAP) — 1m 1f 192y

7:50 (7:52) (Class 5) (0-75,74) 4-Y-0+ — **£3,885** (£1,156; £577; £288) **Stalls** High

Form — RPR
3544 **1** **Supercast (IRE)**[15] 2200 6-9-5 **72**........ LukeMorris 8 — 82
(N J Vaughan) *trckd ldr: led over 2f out: rdn out fnl f* **9/1**
-041 **2** *1/2* **Jo'Burg (USA)**[14] 2244 5-8-13 **66**........ RyanMoore 4 — 75
(Lady Herries) *v.s.a and dropped out wl in rr: hdwy 2f out: r.o to go 2nd ins fnl f: clsng on wnr but nvr threatened* **11/4**[2]
-233 **3** *3* **Potentiale (IRE)**[9] 2379 5-9-5 **72**........(p) LDettori 7 — 75
(J W Hills) *hld up in tch: hdwy to press wnr 2f out: no ex and lost 2nd ins fnl f* **9/2**[3]
405 **4** *2 1/4* **Rio Guru (IRE)**[22] 2013 4-9-7 **74**........ SamHitchcott 1 — 73
(M R Channon) *hld up: styd on one pce ins fnl 2f* **20/1**
0161 **5** *nk* **Vinces**[62] 1122 5-9-2 **69**........ KirstyMilczarek 3 — 67
(T D McCarthy) *in tch: wnt 3rd 1/2-way: rdn over 2f out: wknd appr fnl f* **14/1**
04-1 **6** *nk* **Beau Fighter**[21] 2039 4-9-5 **72**........ GeorgeBaker 5 — 69
(C F Wall) *hld up: mde sme late hdwy* **7/4**[1]
0131 **7** *3 1/2* **Megalala (IRE)**[9] 2379 8-8-10 **63** 6ex........ NeilChalmers 6 — 53
(J J Bridger) *led tl hdd over 2f out: rdn and wknd over 1f out* **28/1**
-455 **8** *16* **Uig**[10] 2351 8-8-6 **59** ow1........ EddieAhern 2 — 17
(H S Howe) *trckd ldrs to 1/2-way: bhd fr over 2f out: eased* **12/1**

2m 7.40s (-0.60) **Going Correction** +0.10s/f (Good) — **8 Ran SP% 113.8**
Speed ratings (Par 103): **106,105,103,101,101 100,98,85**
toteswinger: 1&2 £3.30, 1&3 £.70, 2&3 £2.60. CSF £33.70 CT £127.45 TOTE £10.70: £2.50, £1.20, £1.70; EX 38.90.
Owner Betfair Club ROA **Bred** J Egan, J Corcoran And J Judd **Trained** Helshaw Grange, Shropshire

FOCUS
Ordinary but straightforward handicap form. The pace was fair and the runner-up was arguably an unlucky loser.
Beau Fighter Official explanation: trainer said gelding was unsuited by the good to firm ground

2679 CLIMATE CHANGE CAPITAL MAIDEN FILLIES' STKS — 1m

8:25 (8:28) (Class 5) 3-Y-0+ — **£3,885** (£1,156; £577; £288) **Stalls** High

Form — RPR
13- **1** **Cosmopolitan**[223] 6981 4-9-9 0........ JimmyFortune 5 — 84+
(J H M Gosden) *mde all: rdn to go clr appr fnl f* **6/4**[1]
4 **2** *3 3/4* **Silent Oasis**[18] 2139 3-8-12 0........ RobertWinston 2 — 72
(B J Meehan) *trckd ldrs: kpt on to chse wnr fnl f* **8/1**[3]

- 3 2 **Toolentidhaar (USA)**[214] 5-9-9 0 GeorgeBaker 9 70
(Andrew Turnell) *a.p: rdn and styd on fnl f* **66/1**
4-2 4 2 1/2 **Visite Royale (USA)**[16] 2179 3-8-12 0 RyanMoore 6 71+
(Sir Michael Stoute) *w.w: styng on whn hmpd over 1f out* **6/4**[1]
65 5 2 1/4 **Dubai Gem**[15] 2192 3-8-12 0 JimCrowley 8 56+
(Jamie Poulton) *hld up: nvr on terms to chal* **20/1**
-00 6 1 **Polemica (IRE)**[18] 2139 3-8-12 0 RichardMullen 1 54
(E A L Dunlop) *hld up: one pce fnl 2f* **50/1**
00- 7 2 **Allexes (IRE)**[239] 6601 3-8-12 0 EddieAhern 3 57+
(J R Boyle) *t.k.h: trckd wnr tl wknd over 1f out* **50/1**
8 12 **Tentears** 3-8-12 0 TPQueally 7 22
(H R A Cecil) *v.s.a and flashed tail: mde sme hdwy over 2f out but sn wknd* **6/1**[2]
00- P **Fine Tolerance**[203] 7311 3-8-5 0 NathanAlison(7) 4 —
(J R Boyle) *sddle slipped sn after s: rdr lost irons and p.u sn after* **66/1**

1m 39.91s (0.01) **Going Correction** +0.10s/f (Good)
WFA 3 from 4yo+ 11lb **9** Ran SP% **117.1**
Speed ratings (Par 100): **103,99,97,94,92 91,89,77,—**
toteswinger: 1&2 £4.10, 1&3 £34.00, 2&3 £41.60. CSF £15.28 TOTE £2.50: £1.40, £1.80, £10.50; EX 17.30.
Owner H R H Princess Haya Of Jordan **Bred** G S Shropshire **Trained** Newmarket, Suffolk
■ Stewards' Enquiry : Robert Winston four-day ban: careless riding (Jun 21-24)

FOCUS
There was plenty of incident in this fillies' maiden. The winner is useful but this was probably an ordinary event overall with the form held down by the third and the winner not needing to run to her best.
Fine Tolerance Official explanation: jockey said saddle slipped

2680 GO GREEN! BELU WATER STKS (H'CAP) 6f
8:55 (8:57) (Class 5) (0-70,70) 4-Y-O+ **£3,885** (£1,156; £577; £288) **Stalls** Low

Form RPR
5450 1 **Sherjawy (IRE)**[14] 2224 5-8-4 **53** (b) KirstyMilczarek 11 62
(Miss Z C Davison) *chsd ldrs: led briefly 2f out: rdn and rallied to ld again towards fin* **18/1**
2261 2 1/2 **Bateleur**[3] 2564 5-8-12 **61** 6ex EdwardCreighton 9 68
(M R Channon) *t.k.h: hld up: hdwy to ld over 1f out: rdn and kpt on: hdd towards fin* **15/8**[1]
-044 3 2 **Sam's Cross (IRE)**[11] 2326 4-9-7 **70** PaulEddery 5 71
(Pat Eddery) *hld up: rdn and hdwy 2f out: nt qckn fnl f* **9/4**[2]
000- 4 1 1/4 **Ile Royale**[314] 4414 4-8-2 **51** oh4 RichardThomas 3 48
(W S Kittow) *v.s.a: hdwy on outside 1/2-way: kpt on one pce fr over 1f out* **33/1**
0050 5 1/2 **Ishibee (IRE)**[14] 2223 5-8-3 **52** oh4 ow1 (p) NeilChalmers 4 47
(J J Bridger) *chsd ldrs: rdn over 2f out: kpt on ins fnl f* **25/1**
2233 6 1/2 **Step It Up (IRE)**[16] 2180 5-8-7 **63** NathanAlison(7) 8 56
(J R Boyle) *led tl hdd 2f out: wknd appr fnl f* **8/1**
4334 7 1 1/4 **Hart Of Gold**[24] 1957 5-9-2 **65** (p) RobertWinston 7 54
(R A Harris) *t.k.h: in tch but hld whn short of room appr fnl f* **15/2**[3]
4420 8 1 **Golden Dixie (USA)**[11] 2326 10-9-7 **70** LukeMorris 1 56
(R A Harris) *in tch tl outpcd 2f out* **14/1**
0051 9 1 3/4 **Louphole**[14] 2224 7-9-3 **66** AdrianMcCarthy 10 47
(J R Jenkins) *a towards rr* **10/1**
6-00 10 6 **Red Amaryllis**[38] 1587 4-8-6 **55** EddieAhern 6 16
(H J L Dunlop) *w ldr tl wknd rapidly 2f out* **25/1**

1m 12.13s (-0.07) **Going Correction** +0.10s/f (Good) **10** Ran SP% **120.1**
Speed ratings (Par 103): **104,103,100,99,98 97,96,94,92,84**
toteswinger: 1&2 £10.90, 1&3 £11.60, 2&3 £2.40. CSF £52.79 CT £115.23 TOTE £23.40: £4.50, £1.40, £1.50; EX 69.60 Place 6 £20.30, Place 5 £ 6.41..
Owner Charlie's Starrs **Bred** Darley **Trained** Hammerwood, E Sussex

FOCUS
A modest sprint handicap. There were no obvious front runners in the line-up so there was a possibility of a falsely run race, but that did not materialise. The winner is rated back to his best.
Ile Royale Official explanation: jockey said filly went right at start
T/Plt: £22.90 to a £1 stake. Pool: £55,534.21. 1,768.32 winning tickets. T/Qpdt: £12.00 to a £1 stake. Pool: £3,612.77. 221.10 winning tickets. JS

2141 WOLVERHAMPTON (A.W) (L-H)
Friday, June 5

OFFICIAL GOING: Standard
Wind: Light against Weather: Overcast

2681 ENJOY EXECUTIVE HOSPITALITY AT WOLVERHAMPTON CLAIMING STKS 1m 1f 103y(P)
2:00 (2:00) (Class 6) 3-Y-O **£2,729** (£806; £403) **Stalls** Low

Form RPR
2-54 1 **Dome Rocket**[16] 2178 3-9-3 75 PaulDoe 2 70
(W J Knight) *trckd ldr: led over 2f out: rdn over 1f out: hung lft ins fnl f: styd on* **13/8**[1]
5500 2 nk **Lilly Blue (IRE)**[7] 2431 3-8-4 64 CatherineGannon 5 56
(M R Channon) *hld up: hdwy 6f out: chsd wnr over 2f out: sn rdn: hung lft ins fnl f: r.o* **10/1**
0-00 3 3 1/2 **Castle Myth (USA)**[18] 2131 3-8-5 45 LanceBetts(5) 9 55
(B Ellison) *hld up: hdwy over 1f out: sn rdn: no imp ins fnl f* **50/1**
54-5 4 6 **Baron Otto (IRE)**[13] 2282 3-9-3 73 (b[1]) LiamJones 1 49
(W J Haggas) *sn led: hdd over 7f out: chsd ldrs: rdn over 2f out: wknd over 1f out* **11/4**[3]
2250 5 1 3/4 **Abu Dubai (IRE)**[22] 2001 3-8-3 66 JimmyQuinn 4 31
(C A Dwyer) *hld up in tch: lost pl 6f out: pushed along 4f out: rdn: hung lft and wknd wl over 1f out* **9/4**[2]
0500 6 1/2 **Twenty Score**[6] 2417 3-8-5 57 WandersonD'Avila 7 32
(Miss J R Tooth) *hld up: plld hrd: hdwy 7f out: rdn over 2f out: sn wknd* **66/1**
62-6 7 1 **Gwerthybyd**[18] 2143 3-8-2 53 DavidProbert(3) 8 30
(B Palling) *hld up: sme hdwy over 2f out: sn rdn and wknd* **18/1**
6000 8 3/4 **Captain Cavendish (IRE)**[8] 2417 3-8-9 52 (p) NeilChalmers 6 33
(A Bailey) *chsd ldrs: led over 7f out: rdn and hdd over 2f out: wknd wl over 1f out* **100/1**

2m 2.78s (1.08) **Going Correction** +0.05s/f (Slow) **8** Ran SP% **114.3**
Speed ratings (Par 97): **97,96,93,88,86 86,85,84**
toteswinger: 1&2 £2.60, 1&3 £17.40, 2&3 £17.40 CSF £19.32 TOTE £2.40: £1.20, £3.00, £18.10; EX 13.20 Trifecta £186.40 Pool: £332.64 - 1.32 winning units.Lily Blue was claimed by Mr. C. R. Dore for £6,000.
Owner Bluehills Racing Limited **Bred** Hesmonds Stud Ltd **Trained** Patching, W Sussex

FOCUS
An ordinary gallop to this modest claimer. It is doutful f the winner had to match her latest form to win.

2682 BET WORLD CUP FOOTBALL - BETDAQ H'CAP 5f 20y(P)
2:35 (2:36) (Class 6) (0-55,55) 3-Y-O+ **£2,729** (£806; £403) **Stalls** Low

Form RPR
-654 1 **Weet A Surprise**[14] 2225 4-9-5 **54** (v) FergusSweeney 2 71
(J W Unett) *trckd ldrs: led 1f out: rdn and edgd lft: r.o wl* **4/1**[1]
2400 2 4 **Decider (USA)**[18] 2130 6-9-2 **54** KevinGhunowa(3) 11 56
(R A Harris) *w ldr: rdn over 1f out: styd on same pce* **9/1**
035 3 hd **Albero Di Giuda (IRE)**[67] 1038 4-9-0 **54** (tp) AndreaAtzeni(5) 7 55
(F Sheridan) *sn led: rdn and hdd 1f out: styd on same pce* **6/1**[3]
23-0 4 3 3/4 **Eleanor Eloise (USA)**[146] 114 5-8-12 **50** DavidProbert(3) 12 38
(J R Gask) *sn pushed along in rr: rdn 1/2-way: edgd lft and r.o ins fnl f: nvr nrr* **5/1**[2]
0-00 5 nse **Sovereignty (JPN)**[33] 1710 7-9-1 **50** PatCosgrave 6 38
(D K Ivory) *sn outpcd: swtchd rt over 1f out: rdn and r.o ins fnl f: nt trble ldrs* **15/2**
3400 6 1 **Fizzlephut (IRE)**[2] 2596 7-9-6 **55** (p) PaulFitzsimons 13 39
(Miss J R Tooth) *chsd ldrs: rdn 1/2-way: wkng whn hung lft fnl f* **20/1**
-000 7 3/4 **Nusoor (IRE)**[17] 2158 6-9-1 **50** (v) PatrickMathers 8 31
(Peter Grayson) *hmpd sn after s: outpcd: nt clr run fr over 1f out tl r.o ins fnl f: nrst fin* **20/1**
-006 8 1 1/2 **Mr Funshine**[9] 2382 4-9-1 **50** NickyMackay 10 26
(R J Hodges) *mid-div: sn pushed along: btn whn n.m.r over 1f out* **50/1**
6540 9 nk **Lithaam (IRE)**[87] 794 5-9-6 **55** (p) LPKeniry 4 30
(J M Bradley) *plld hrd: led early: chsd ldrs: hmpd over 3f out: rdn and wknd over 1f out* **8/1**
0-00 10 2 **Coconut Moon**[17] 2158 7-8-12 **52** SladeO'Hara(5) 3 20
(A Berry) *hld up: rdn 1/2-way: sme hdwy over 1f out: wknd ins fnl f* **20/1**
052- 11 2 **Woqoodd**[156] 7835 5-9-1 **50** AdamKirby 1 11
(D Shaw) *trckd ldrs: lost pl over 3f out: n.d after* **6/1**[3]
000- 12 1 1/2 **Blakeshall Diamond**[156] 7835 4-8-12 **52** MarkCoumbe(5) 9 7
(A J Chamberlain) *chsd ldrs: rdn and hung lft 1/2-way: wknd over 1f out* **28/1**

62.20 secs (-0.10) **Going Correction** +0.05s/f (Slow) **12** Ran SP% **117.8**
Speed ratings (Par 101): **102,95,95,89,89 87,86,84,83,80 77,74**
toteswinger: 1&2 £8.30, 1&3 £4.80, 2&3 £6.90 CSF £36.78 CT £219.19 TOTE £4.90: £1.50, £2.80, £1.70; EX 50.60 TRIFECTA Not won..
Owner J E Price **Bred** Longdon Stud Ltd **Trained** Tedsmore Hall, Shropshire

FOCUS
A moderate sprint handicap. The winner was good-value for her wide-margin win and looks back to soemthing like her 2yo best.
Nusoor(IRE) Official explanation: jockey said gelding hung right on the bend

2683 GREAT OFFERS AT WOLVERHAMPTON-RACECOURSE.CO.UK (S) STKS 5f 216y(P)
3:10 (3:12) (Class 6) 3-Y-O **£2,047** (£604; £302) **Stalls** Low

Form RPR
0 1 **Athaakeel (IRE)**[17] 2151 3-8-6 0 ow2 KevinGhunowa(3) 2 66
(R A Harris) *s.i.s: bhd: hdwy over 1f out: r.o to ld wl ins fnl f: sn clr* **50/1**
34-4 2 3 3/4 **Officer Mor (USA)**[154] 10 3-8-5 57 (b) NoraLooby(7) 8 57
(K R Burke) *chsd ldrs: rdn over 1f out: sn hdd and unable qck* **25/1**
4520 3 1 **You Avin A Laugh**[24] 1949 3-8-12 60 CatherineGannon 12 54
(C A Dwyer) *hld up: rdn over 1f out: r.o wl towards fin: nt rch ldrs* **12/1**
-004 4 1 **Transcentral**[3] 2581 3-8-7 59 LiamJones 13 46
(W M Brisbourne) *sn chsng ldr: rdn 1/2-way: hung lft fr over 1f out: no ex ins fnl f* **16/1**
0346 5 1/2 **York Key Bar**[14] 2234 3-8-7 61 LanceBetts(5) 9 49
(B Ellison) *sn pushed along in rr: r.o ins fnl f: nvr nrr* **8/1**
-301 6 1 1/4 **Straitjacket**[1] 2630 3-8-12 59 PaulFitzsimons 11 45
(Miss J R Tooth) *prom: rdn 1/2-way: edgd lft over 1f out: wknd ins fnl f* **8/1**
4404 7 1/2 **Ridgeway Silver**[18] 2141 3-8-7 59 GabrielHannon(5) 3 43
(M D I Usher) *broke wl: n.m.r and lost pl 5f out: rdn over 1f out: styd on ins fnl f* **4/1**[1]
-420 8 1/2 **Tillers Satisfied (IRE)**[31] 1772 3-8-9 59 DavidProbert(3) 10 42
(R Hollinshead) *hld up in tch: rdn over 1f out: wknd ins fnl f* **6/1**[2]
0-60 9 1 1/4 **Sonhador**[7] 2456 3-8-12 69 NickyMackay 4 38
(G Prodromou) *chsd ldrs: rdn 1/2-way: wknd fnl f* **13/2**[3]
2206 10 1/2 **Spit And Polish**[9] 2386 3-8-12 65 (b) JohnEgan 5 36
(C A Dwyer) *led: rdn clr over 1f out: hdd whn hmpd and wknd ins fnl f* **4/1**[1]
0-00 11 3 3/4 **Louidor**[11] 2320 3-8-12 67 VinceSlattery 6 24
(M R Bosley) *prom: rdn over 2f out: wkng whn hung lft over 1f out* **25/1**
00 12 7 **Rambling Rosie (IRE)**[32] 1729 3-8-4 0 ow2 WilliamCarson(5) 1 —
(C Drew) *n.m.r and lost pl sn after s: n.d after* **100/1**
60 13 2 1/4 **Marzy**[47] 1379 3-8-2 0 AndreaAtzeni(5) 7 —
(M Botti) *mid-div: sn pushed along: rdn over 2f out: sn wknd* **28/1**

1m 15.78s (0.78) **Going Correction** +0.05s/f (Slow) **13** Ran SP% **117.5**
Speed ratings (Par 97): **96,91,89,88,87 86,85,84,83,82 77,68,65**
toteswinger: 1&2 £53.30, 1&3 £51.20, 2&3 £33.70 CSF £947.90 TOTE £75.20: £22.70, £12.60, £3.90; EX 1412.80 TRIFECTA Not won..There was no bid for the winner.
Owner Mrs J Bloomfield **Bred** Shadwell Estate Company Limited **Trained** Earlswood, Monmouths

FOCUS
They went a good gallop here and that set it up for the closers. The winner's victory was a shock but no fluke.

2684 BET EPSOM DERBY - BETDAQ H'CAP 1m 4f 50y(P)
3:45 (3:46) (Class 5) (0-75,73) 4-Y-O+ **£3,885** (£1,156; £577; £288) **Stalls** Low

Form RPR
14- 1 **Rotative**[247] 6379 4-9-7 **73** AdamKirby 3 82
(W R Swinburn) *hld up: drvn along over 4f out: hdwy over 2f out: rdn to ld and hung lft over 1f out: styd on wl* **5/1**[3]
6400 2 3 **Apache Fort**[24] 1966 6-8-7 **59** (b) LPKeniry 8 63
(T Keddy) *hld up: hdwy over 5f out: rdn over 1f out: styd on same pce fnl f* **11/1**
0343 3 nk **Watson's Bay**[4] 2552 4-8-13 **65** JimmyQuinn 5 69
(P Howling) *s.i.s and hmpd s: hld up: hdwy over 5f out: rdn and hung lft fr over 1f out: styd on same pce fnl f* **11/4**[1]
0/0- 4 1 1/2 **Twill (IRE)**[371] 2567 6-8-13 **65** VinceSlattery 2 67
(D Burchell) *hld up: rdn over 3f out: hdwy over 2f out: styd on same pce fnl f* **33/1**
20-4 5 1/2 **Into The Light**[29] 1815 4-9-1 **67** StephenDonohoe 7 68
(E S McMahon) *a.p: rdn and swtchd lft over 1f out: no ex ins fnl f* **13/2**

-524 **6** *2 ½* **Indy Driver**[21] 2052 4-9-4 **70** .... FrancisNorton 10 67
(J R Fanshawe) *prom: chsd ldr over 5f out: led over 2f out: rdn: edgd rt and hdd over 1f out: wknd ins fnl f* **4/1**[2]
4-13 **7** *10* **Locum**[11] 2332 4-9-2 **68** .... SaleemGolam 6 49
(M H Tompkins) *chsd ldrs: rdn over 4f out: wknd over 3f out* **6/1**
6120 **8** *1* **Waldorf (IRE)**[49] 1318 4-8-8 **60** .... DO'Donohoe 12 39
(W R Muir) *chsd clr ldr tl led over 5f out: rdn and hdd over 2f out: sn wknd* **16/1**
01-6 **9** *14* **Addiena**[11] 2322 5-8-12 **67** .... DavidProbert(3) 1 24
(B Palling) *hld up: hdwy over 5f out: wknd 4f out: eased over 1f out* **20/1**
500- **10** *5* **Desert Leader (IRE)**[364] 2804 8-8-5 **57** .... LiamJones 11 6
(W M Brisbourne) *hld up: rdn and wknd 4f out: eased over 1f out* **50/1**
0-00 **11** *109* **Smart Tazz**[14] 2221 4-8-2 **54** oh9 .... (b[1]) NickyMackay 4 —
(H J Evans) *sn led and clr: wknd and hdd over 5f out: eased* **66/1**

2m 39.77s (-1.33) **Going Correction** +0.05s/f (Slow) **11 Ran SP% 116.3**
Speed ratings (Par 103): **106,104,103,102,102 100,94,93,84,80** —
toteswinger: 1&2 £4.80, 1&3 £3.10, 2&3 £5.70 CSF £55.87 CT £181.50 TOTE £6.20: £1.70, £2.30, £1.70; EX 49.30 Trifecta £251.40 Part won. Pool: £339.78 - 0.20 winning units..
Owner Pendley Farm **Bred** Pendley Farm **Trained** Aldbury, Herts

FOCUS
The eventual last raced clear for a long way, ignored by the rest. The winner showed more resolution than the placed horses.
Locum Official explanation: jockey said gelding ran flat
Addiena Official explanation: jockey said mare hung right

2685 CARLSBERG EXPORT H'CAP — 1m 141y(P)
4:25 (4:26) (Class 5) (0-70,70) 3-Y-O — **£3,885** (£1,156; £577; £288) **Stalls Low**

Form — RPR
4-16 **1** **Cool Hand Jake**[58] 1193 3-9-7 **70** .... FergusSweeney 3 78+
(P J Makin) *hld up in tch: rdn over 1f out: r.o u.p to ld wl ins fnl f* **7/2**[1]
04-0 **2** *nk* **Drum Dragon**[59] 1174 3-9-7 **70** .... SaleemGolam 11 78
(M H Tompkins) *chsd ldrs: rdn to ld 1f out: hdd wl ins fnl f* **14/1**
02-0 **3** *1 ¼* **Royal Willy (IRE)**[21] 2048 3-9-6 **69** .... LiamJones 13 74+
(W Jarvis) *stdd s: hld up: hdwy over 1f out: sn rdn: styd on* **33/1**
-240 **4** *2 ½* **Victorian Tycoon (IRE)**[20] 2091 3-9-1 **64** .... FrancisNorton 6 63
(E J O'Neill) *led: rdn and hdd 1f out: no ex* **5/1**[2]
-220 **5** *shd* **Barbarian**[15] 2209 3-9-4 **70** .... PatrickHills(3) 2 69
(B W Hills) *hld up: hdwy on outside over 2f out: r.o ins fnl f: nt rch ldrs* **7/2**[1]
3-50 **6** *3* **Arctic Freedom (USA)**[12] 2300 3-9-7 **70** .... (b[1]) StephenDonohoe 9 62
(E A L Dunlop) *prom: rdn and ev ch over 2f out: wknd ins fnl f* **16/1**
3-03 **7** *1 ¼* **Punch Drunk**[25] 1937 3-9-3 **66** .... PatCosgrave 10 55
(J G Given) *hld up: n.m.r 7f out: hdwy over 4f out: rdn and hung lft over 1f out: sn wknd* **7/1**[3]
0-54 **8** *2 ¾* **Golden Flight (IRE)**[11] 2320 3-9-5 **68** .... JamesDoyle 12 51
(J W Hills) *s.i.s: hld up: rdn over 2f out: n.d* **16/1**
-620 **9** *1* **Mytivil (IRE)**[11] 2320 3-9-0 **68** .... RossAtkinson(5) 1 48
(M Salaman) *hld up: a in rr* **12/1**
20-0 **10** *1 ½* **Champion Girl (IRE)**[11] 2321 3-9-0 **63** .... LPKeniry 8 40
(D Haydn Jones) *hld up in tch: racd keenly: rdn over 3f out: wknd over 2f out* **33/1**
5-10 **11** *1 ¾* **Echo Dancer**[21] 2048 3-9-7 **70** .... DO'Donohoe 5 43
(S A Callaghan) *s.i.s: hld up: plld hrd: nt clr run wl over 1f out: nvr nr to chal* **14/1**
45-0 **12** *2 ¾* **Silk Cotton (USA)**[25] 1928 3-9-7 **70** .... (b[1]) TGMcLaughlin 7 37
(E A L Dunlop) *hld up: rdn over 4f out: a in rr* **33/1**
26-0 **13** *2 ½* **New Beginning (FR)**[45] 1416 3-9-2 **65** .... JimmyQuinn 4 26
(H J L Dunlop) *chsd ldrs tl rdn and wknd over 2f out* **16/1**

1m 51.08s (0.58) **Going Correction** +0.05s/f (Slow) **13 Ran SP% 121.1**
Speed ratings (Par 99): **99,98,97,95,95 92,91,89,88,86 85,82,80**
toteswinger: 1&2 £14.00, 1&3 £26.70, 2&3 £73.70 CSF £55.67 CT £1421.11 TOTE £4.50: £1.50, £4.40, £9.70; EX 84.50 TRIFECTA Not won..
Owner Wedgewood Estates **Bred** Wedgewood Estates **Trained** Ogbourne Maisey, Wilts

FOCUS
An open handicap and fair form for the grade. The pace was strong and the first three all showed improvement.
Silk Cotton(USA) Official explanation: jockey said filly lost its action

2686 BETDAQ.CO.UK H'CAP — 7f 32y(P)
5:00 (5:01) (Class 6) (0-60,60) 4-Y-O+ — **£2,729** (£806; £403) **Stalls High**

Form — RPR
-000 **1** **Avontuur (FR)**[4] 2531 7-8-10 **57** .... DeanHeslop(5) 9 66
(Mrs R A Carr) *s.s: bhd: hdwy over 1f out: led and edgd lft ins fnl f: r.o* **14/1**
020- **2** *1 ¼* **Vanadium**[159] 7803 7-9-4 **60** .... FergusSweeney 12 66
(G L Moore) *hld up: hdwy over 2f out: rdn over 1f out: hung lft ins fnl f: styd on* **15/2**[3]
0056 **3** *½* **Imperial Djay (IRE)**[67] 1039 4-8-10 **52** .... PatCosgrave 6 57
(J R Holt) *prom: pushed along and n.m.r 6f out: rdn and edgd lft over 2f out: led ins fnl f: sn hdd and edgd lft: one pce* **13/2**[2]
5600 **4** *1 ¼* **Djalalabad (FR)**[14] 2223 5-9-0 **56** .... (tp) TGMcLaughlin 3 61+
(Mrs C A Dunnett) *hld up: hmpd over 2f out: running on whn nt clr run wl ins fnl f: nvr able to chal* **12/1**
0 **5** *1 ½* **Great Knight (IRE)**[28] 1846 4-9-2 **58** .... JamesDoyle 4 55
(S Kirk) *led early: trckd ldrs: rdn to ld over 1f out: edgd and hdd ins fnl f: hmpd and no ex sn after* **10/1**
0-40 **6** *¾* **Lady Amberlini**[27] 1883 4-9-0 **56** .... LPKeniry 2 51
(C R Dore) *led over 6f out: hdd over 5f out: rdn and ev ch 1f out: wknd towards fin* **8/1**
4535 **7** *nse* **Jessica Wigmo**[86] 803 6-8-6 **53** .... MarkCoumbe(5) 11 48
(A W Carroll) *s.i.s: hld up: rdn over 1f out: n.d* **14/1**
-154 **8** *3 ½* **Colour Of Money**[8] 2400 4-9-3 **59** .... (p) StephenDonohoe 8 45
(S A Callaghan) *chsd ldrs: rdn over 2f out: ev ch over 1f out: wkng whn n.m.r ins fnl f* **2/1**[1]
2000 **9** *1* **Rio L'Oren (IRE)**[4] 2529 4-8-13 **55** .... (b) FrancisNorton 10 38
(N J Vaughan) *led over 5f out: rdn and hdd over 1f out: wknd ins fnl f* **33/1**
0046 **10** *2* **Colombard (IRE)**[14] 2223 4-8-12 **54** .... (v) SaleemGolam 5 32
(Patrick Morris) *mid-div: hdwy over 3f out: rdn over 1f out: sn wknd* **20/1**
4-60 **11** *6* **The Wily Woodcock**[27] 1883 5-8-9 **56** .... PatrickDonaghy(5) 1 17
(T Wall) *hld up: wknd 1/2-way* **20/1**
0005 **F** **Replicator**[28] 1846 4-8-6 **55** .... TobyAtkinson(7) 7 —
(Pat Eddery) *hld up: hdwy whn hmpd and fell over 2f out* **12/1**

1m 30.58s (0.98) **Going Correction** +0.05s/f (Slow) **12 Ran SP% 119.8**
Speed ratings (Par 101): **96,94,94,92,90 90,89,85,84,82 75,**—
toteswinger: 1&2 £26.00, 1&3 £26.30, 2&3 £9.80 CSF £113.53 CT £774.26 TOTE £17.30: £3.90, £2.20, £3.20; EX 128.70 TRIFECTA Not won. Place 6: £1,421.49, Place 5: £602.38.
Owner J M Chapman **Bred** Haras D'Etreham **Trained** Huby, N Yorks

FOCUS
There was a contested lead here and as a result the early gallop was very strong. The first two came from the rear and the winner is rated back to near his best.
Avontuur(FR) Official explanation: trainer's rep said, regarding apparent improvement in form, that the gelding can be inconsistent but couldn't offer any further explanation.
Jessica Wigmo Official explanation: jockey said mare was hampered in running
T/Plt: £2,311.70 to a £1 stake. Pool: £41,643.10. 13.15 winning tickets. T/Qpdt: £796.50 to a £1 stake. Pool: £3,444.40. 3.20 winning tickets. CR

LYON PARILLY (R-H)
Friday, June 5

OFFICIAL GOING: Good to soft

2694a PRIX DES PERVENCHES (MAIDEN) — 6f
1:05 (1:07) 2-Y-O — **£6,796** (£2,718; £2,039; £1,359; £680)

RPR
1 **Bertie's Best** 2-8-8 .... RonanThomas 75
(F Doumen, France)
2 *1 ½* **Exotica (FR)** 2-8-13 .... ASanglard 75
(B Goudot, France)
3 *½* **Tagar Bere (FR)** 2-9-2 .... FBlondel 77
(M Pimbonnet, France)
4 *2* **Calvero (FR)**[10] 2-9-2 .... THuet 71
(Robert Collet, France)
5 *nk* **Hairs Vital (IRE)**[14] 2231 2-9-2 .... DBonilla 70
(E J O'Neill) *prom: led after 2f: pushed along st: drvn and hdd over 1f out: one pce* **11/4**[1]
6 *shd* **Walistol (FR)**[32] 2-9-2 .... FLefebvre 70
(S Jesus, France)
7 *shd* **Salut Royale (FR)**[32] 2-8-13 .... MSautjeau 66
(S Jesus, France)
8 *snk* **Herbier D'Ecajeul (FR)** 2-9-2 .... LProietti 69
(X Betron, France)

1m 13.87s (73.87) **8 Ran SP% 26.7**
PARI-MUTUEL (Including 1 Euro stake): WIN 6.50; PL 2.00, 1.50, 1.90; DF 11.70.
Owner Robert Jeffcock **Bred** Jenny Hall Bloodstock Ltd **Trained** Bouce, France

NOTEBOOK
Hairs Vital(IRE) went to the head of affairs rounding the final turn but could find only the one pace.

2662 DONCASTER (L-H)
Saturday, June 6

OFFICIAL GOING: Soft (7.1) changing to good to soft (soft in places on round course) after race 2 (2.35)
Wind: Fresh across Weather: Overcast

2695 32RED AWARDED BEST CASINO AGAIN H'CAP — 7f
2:05 (2:07) (Class 3) (0-90,92) 4-Y-O+ — **£9,714** (£2,890; £1,444; £721) **Stalls High**

Form — RPR
-541 **1** **Oceana Blue**[21] 2086 4-8-9 **78** .... (t) WilliamBuick 4 88
(A M Balding) *hld up: hdwy u.p fr over 2f out: styd on to ld post* **5/1**[2]
0-20 **2** *shd* **Fishforcompliments**[28] 1861 5-9-2 **90** .... FrederikTylicki(5) 14 100
(R A Fahey) *a.p: chsd ldr 1/2-way: rdn to ld 1f out: sn hung lft: hdd post* **6/1**[3]
-005 **3** *¾* **Kiwi Bay**[21] 2093 4-8-9 **78** .... TonyHamilton 7 86
(M Dods) *hld up: plld hrd: hdwy over 2f out: sn rdn: edgd lft ins fnl f: styd on* **6/1**[3]
2010 **4** *nk* **Dancing Maite**[14] 2269 4-8-2 **76** .... MartinLane(5) 1 83
(S R Bowring) *led: rdn and hdd 1f out: hung lft and styd on same pce ins fnl f* **20/1**
31-2 **5** *½* **Errigal Lad**[9] 2405 4-8-13 **82** .... TPO'Shea 16 88
(K A Ryan) *chsd ldr tl rdn 4f out: hung lft ins fnl f: styd on same pce* **7/2**[1]
1040 **6** *2 ¾* **Cornus**[21] 2093 7-8-9 **78** .... (be) JamesDoyle 2 76
(A J McCabe) *s.i.s: hld up: hdwy u.p over 1f out: sn hung rt: hung lft and no imp ins fnl f* **25/1**
7 *2 ¾* **One Way Or Another (AUS)**[273] 6-9-5 **88** .... SteveDrowne 12 79
(J R Gask) *hld up: hdwy over 3f out: rdn and wknd over 1f out* **33/1**
6013 **8** *3 ¼* **Captain Macarry (IRE)**[25] 1952 4-8-13 **82** .... (v) RoystonFfrench 15 64
(B Smart) *trckd ldrs: racd keenly: rdn 1/2-way: wknd 2f out: eased fnl f* **7/1**
10-0 **9** *¾* **Without Prejudice (USA)**[21] 2086 4-8-5 **79** Louis-PhilippeBeuzelin(5) 13 59
(J Noseda) *mid-div: rdn 1/2-way: wknd over 2f out* **8/1**
0/00 **10** *1 ¼* **Commando Scott (IRE)**[22] 2059 8-9-1 **84** .... PJMcDonald 10 61
(I W McInnes) *chsd ldrs: rdn 1/2-way: wknd over 2f out* **33/1**
2340 **11** *¾* **Autumn Blades (IRE)**[21] 2086 4-8-9 **78** .... RobertWinston 11 52
(A Bailey) *s.i.s: hld up: a in rr* **14/1**
541 **12** *1 ¾* **Hustle (IRE)**[22] 2050 4-9-3 **86** .... (t) JimmyQuinn 5 56
(Miss Gay Kelleway) *hld up: rdn 1/2-way: hung lft and wknd over 2f out* **10/1**

1m 25.82s (-0.48) **Going Correction** +0.10s/f (Good) **12 Ran SP% 121.3**
Speed ratings (Par 107): **106,105,105,104,104 100,97,94,93,91 90,88**
toteswinger: 1&2 £11.10, 1&3 £3.40, 2&3 £17.20 CSF £34.39 CT £188.48 TOTE £4.70: £1.90, £2.50, £2.30; EX 29.40 Trifecta £236.90 Part won. Pool: £320.24 - 0.50 winning units..
Owner The C H F Partnership **Bred** The C H F Partnership **Trained** Kingsclere, Hants
■ Stewards' Enquiry : Frederik Tylicki one-day ban: careless riding (Jun 21)

FOCUS
Following 26mm of rain overnight and more during the morning the going was officially soft and, with the ground at the 48-hour declaration stage having been good to firm, plenty of non-runners were to be expected. However, the winning time suggested the ground wasn't that soft. A competitive handicap in which the field stuck to the stands' rail and the front five came clear. Sound form.

NOTEBOOK
Oceana Blue was 4lb higher than when beating a big field at Newmarket last month. On that occasion it seemed the further she went, the better she was going and it was a similar story here. Tracking the pace on the wide outside, it seemed for a long time as though her finishing effort wasn't going to be enough, but she kept at it and managed to snatch the prize on the line. She seems to go on any ground and this consistent filly should continue to pay her way. The Bunbury Cup is a possible target. (op 6-1 tchd 9-2)

Fishforcompliments isn't the most consistent, but this was one of his better efforts and having been handy from the off and looking like he had done enough to score, he was unfortunate to have the race snatched from him on the line. Without a win since his second start at two, this effort shows he can win off this mark, but whether he will reproduce it next time is questionable. (tchd 13-2)

Kiwi Bay, down to a mark 3lb higher than for his last win a year ago, was back up to his optimum trip after three outings over 6f this season. Despite coming off the bridle on the outside of the pack some way from home, he kept on well to take third and was closing in on the front pair at the line. There should be a race in him over this sort of trip. (op 11-2)

Dancing Maite, still 5lb above his highest winning mark, had to do a fair amount of running early in order to get across and grab the lead from the outside stall. He kept going for longer than might have been anticipated and emerges with plenty of credit. (op 22-1 tchd 18-1)

Errigal Lad, only just beaten on his return to action at Newcastle last month but well beaten in both previous tries beyond 6f, was handy enough early but it looked another case of his stamina letting him down. (op 5-1)

Cornus, gradually edging back down the weights but still 3lb above his last winning mark, never really threatened. (op 20-1 tchd 18-1)

One Way Or Another(AUS) ◆, a four-time winner in Australia, was making his debut for the yard after a nine-month absence. He appeared to travel well enough behind the leaders until lack of a recent run took its toll and better can be expected, possibly over further.

Autumn Blades(IRE) Official explanation: jockey said gelding ran flat

2696 32RED.COM H'CAP — 1m (S)

2:35 (2:38) (Class 2) (0-100,90) 3-Y-O **£16,190** (£4,817; £2,407; £1,202) **Stalls High**

Form — RPR

01- **1** **Roman Republic (FR)**[225] 6944 3-9-0 **83**.................. RoystonFfrench 9 93+
(M Johnston) *s.i.s: hdwy 1/2-way: rdn to ld and hung rt over 1f out: r.o* **6/1**[3]

0-00 **2** 1 1/4 **Deadly Secret (USA)**[14] 2273 3-9-0 **88**.................. FrederikTylicki(5) 2 95
(R A Fahey) *chsd ldr tl led 5f out: rdn and hdd over 1f out: hung rt ins fnl f: styd on same pce* **8/1**

21-2 **3** 2 1/2 **Emirates Roadshow (USA)**[33] 1751 3-9-3 **86**................ TedDurcan 10 87
(Saeed Bin Suroor) *led: hdd over 6f out: chsd ldrs: rdn over 1f out: styd on same pce* **5/1**[2]

311 **4** *shd* **Arrivederla (IRE)**[16] 2198 3-9-0 **83**................................ JamesDoyle 1 84
(H J L Dunlop) *a.p: rdn over 1f out: no ex ins fnl f* **5/1**[2]

0-05 **5** 1 1/4 **Come And Go (UAE)**[12] 2341 3-8-11 **80**......................... PJMcDonald 8 78
(G A Swinbank) *awkward leaving stalls: hld up: effrt over 2f out: nvr trbld ldrs* **20/1**

2-21 **6** 1 1/4 **Standpoint**[25] 1972 3-8-5 **79**......................... Louis-PhilippeBeuzelin(5) 11 74
(Sir Michael Stoute) *hld up: rdn over 1f out: n.d* **8/1**

01 **7** *nk* **Uniquely Poised (USA)**[33] 1730 3-9-7 **90**..................... RichardMullen 6 84
(J H M Gosden) *hld up: rdn over 3f out: n.d* **11/1**

10-1 **8** 1 3/4 **Magaling (IRE)**[21] 2072 3-9-6 **89**...................................... WilliamBuick 12 79
(L M Cumani) *hld up: hdwy over 2f out: wknd over 1f out* **3/1**[1]

-010 **9** 2 3/4 **Johnmanderville**[24] 1987 3-8-4 **78**................................. MartinLane(5) 3 62
(K R Burke) *led over 6f out: hdd 5f out: rdn and wknd over 2f out* **12/1**

1m 38.75s (-0.55) **Going Correction** +0.10s/f (Good) **9** Ran **SP% 115.6**

Speed ratings (Par 105): **106,104,102,102,100 99,99,97,94**

toteswinger: 1&2 £10.30, 1&3 £8.00, 2&3 £15.40 CSF £53.08 CT £259.40 TOTE £6.90: £2.30, £3.00, £1.80; EX 52.90 Trifecta £321.90 Part won. Pool: £435.10 - 0.44 winning units..

Owner Sheikh Hamdan Bin Mohammed Al Maktoum **Bred** Famille Niarchos **Trained** Middleham Moor, N Yorks

FOCUS

A decent three-year-old handicap containing several unexposed and progressive types and a few were well backed, but they only went a steady early pace and it developed into something of a sprint. Strong form nevertheless.

NOTEBOOK

Roman Republic(FR), making his handicap debut and racing for the first time since winning a maiden here last October, wasn't best away but he was soon back on terms and travelling well on the outside of the field. Set alight passing the 2f pole to hit the front, he dug deep when the runner-up rallied and kept finding what was required. Connections believe he may be even better on quicker ground and the Britannia will be considered. (op 9-2)

Deadly Secret(USA) ◆, representing an in-form yard, had been well beaten in his first two starts this season, but he never got a run at York first time and then may not have handled the heavy ground at Haydock. Dropped 5lb here, he was a springer in the market and duly ran a big race. Always up with the pace, he battled back very gamely after the winner had gone past him and shouldn't take long in going one better. (op 16-1)

Emirates Roadshow(USA), runner-up to the subsequent Betfred Silver Bowl winner Desert Creek on his seasonal reappearance at Windsor last month, broke well but his rider was then content to get a lead. Still apparently travelling well passing the 3f pole, once asked for his effort he didn't find as much as had looked likely and all he could do was plug on for third. (op 9-2 tchd 11-2)

Arrivederla(IRE), trying this trip for the first time and bidding for a hat-trick off a 7lb higher mark, was another of those to attract market support. She had every chance, but couldn't pick up when asked and perhaps a combination of the longer trip and her inflated mark was enough to find her out. (op 13-2)

Come And Go(UAE), back in trip after failing to see out the extra 2f at Redcar last time, was very awkward leaving the stalls but stayed on in the latter stages and is far from a lost cause. (op 25-1)

Standpoint, making his handicap debut after easily winning a weak-looking Warwick maiden last time, could never get into the race but this was his first try on soft ground and perhaps his mark of 79 flatters him. (op 7-1 tchd 13-2)

Uniquely Poised(USA), making his handicap debut after his impressive victory in a maiden on the Kempton Polytrack last month which has already produced a couple of winners, was extremely weak in the market and ran accordingly. His rider reported that he was unsuited by the ground. Official explanation: jockey said colt was unsuited by the soft ground (op 6-1)

Magaling(IRE), upped in trip again and 5lb higher than when making a successful handicap debut on his return to action here last month, was very disappointing and never threatened to get involved from the back of the field. (op 4-1)

2697 £32 FREE AT 32RED.COM FILLIES' H'CAP — 1m 2f 60y

3:05 (3:06) (Class 2) (0-100,96) 4-Y-O+ **£16,190** (£4,817; £2,407; £1,202) **Stalls Low**

Form — RPR

/00- **1** **Short Affair**[209] 4-9-0 **89**.. ShaneKelly 2 99+
(L M Cumani) *hld up: hdwy over 2f out: led over 1f out: rdn and r.o wl* **10/1**

2512 **2** 1 1/2 **Lady Jane Digby**[22] 2031 4-9-7 **96**............................ RoystonFfrench 8 102
(M Johnston) *hld up: hdwy 6f out: led over 2f out: rdn and hdd over 1f out: styd on same pce ins fnl f* **15/8**[1]

21-5 **3** 2 1/4 **Suzi Spends (IRE)**[16] 2193 4-8-9 **84**.............................. JimmyQuinn 7 86
(H J Collingridge) *hld up: hdwy 2f out: rdn and hung lft fr over 1f out: no ex ins fnl f* **9/1**

15-4 **4** 2 1/4 **Tactful (IRE)**[56] 1210 4-9-3 **92**.. GeorgeBaker 1 89
(R M Beckett) *set stdy pce: rdn and hdd over 2f out: wknd ins fnl f* **9/2**[3]

1/0- **5** 3 1/2 **Laughter (IRE)**[395] 1915 4-8-11 **91**................ Louis-PhilippeBeuzelin(5) 3 81
(Sir Michael Stoute) *trckd ldrs: plld hrd: rdn over 2f out: wknd over 1f out* **5/1**

021- **6** 20 **Amanjena**[253] 6238 4-9-1 **90**.. WilliamBuick 5 40
(A M Balding) *trckd ldr: plld hrd: chal over 3f out: rdn over 2f out: wknd over 1f out: eased* **5/2**[2]

2m 15.09s (3.89) **Going Correction** +0.425s/f (Yiel) **6** Ran **SP% 117.3**

Speed ratings (Par 96): **101,99,98,96,93 77**

toteswinger: 1&2 £4.10, 1&3 £43.20, 2&3 £8.30 CSF £30.81 CT £182.51 TOTE £12.80: £4.10, £1.90; EX 31.20 Trifecta £170.20 Part won. Pool: £230.06 - 0.44 winning units..

Owner Aston House Stud **Bred** Aston House Stud **Trained** Newmarket, Suffolk

FOCUS

The ground had dried out a little and was now officially good to soft, soft in places, on the round course. A slightly disappointing turnout for a race of its value and they went no pace early. It didn't quicken noticeably under entering the last half-mile. Muddling form. The winner was on a fair mark on her best Italian form.

NOTEBOOK

Short Affair ◆ had been placed at Group level in Italy as a juvenile and was making her debut for her yard after a seven-month absence. Settled in last place early, she may not have been in the ideal position in a steadily run race, but it made no difference as she made smooth progress down the wide outside up the home straight and quickened up nicely when asked. Connections were pleased to see the rain arrive and she looks yet another smart import for the stable. (op 6-1)

Lady Jane Digby, who probably pulled too hard when runner-up over 1m4f at Hamilton last time, was happier back over this trip, although the steady pace possibly wasn't ideal. Nonetheless, she came to win her race a quarter of a mile from home, but then had no answer to the winner. She does look handicapped up to her best now, but she is tough and further success can't be ruled out. (op 3-1)

Suzi Spends(IRE), all the better for her seasonal reappearance at Goodwood last month and back up to her optimum trip, didn't have much room for part of the home straight, but it didn't affect her final placing. She may be slightly better suited by Polytrack, but has the ability to win more races on turf. (op 10-1 tchd 15-2)

Tactful(IRE), making her turf debut after four runs on Polytrack, the last two in Listed company, enjoyed the run of the race out in front but was comfortably picked off. Apart from this surface being an unknown, she had questions to answer over the trip as well and this performance didn't answer them. (op 6-1)

Laughter(IRE), having her first start since finishing unplaced in last year's Cheshire Oaks, had her chance but found little once switched to the inside rail and she is best watched. (op 10-3)

Amanjena, racing for the first time since winning narrowly off 3lb lower at Ascot last September, could probably have done without the rain but she ruined her chance by taking a strong hold early and gave herself little chance of getting home. Her rider reported that she was unsuited by the ground. Official explanation: jockey said filly was unsuited by the good to soft (soft in places) ground (op 4-1)

2698 SOCIETY LIFESTYLE AND LEISURE MAGAZINE H'CAP — 1m 4f

3:35 (3:35) (Class 4) (0-85,80) 4-Y-O+ **£5,180** (£1,541; £770; £384) **Stalls Low**

Form — RPR

0065 **1** **Cape Colony**[46] 1432 4-9-2 **77**.................................... SteveDrowne 5 84
(R Hannon) *hld up: hdwy over 1f out: sn rdn and edgd lft: r.o to ld nr fin* **14/1**

01-4 **2** 3/4 **King Fingal (IRE)**[24] 1990 4-9-5 **80**........................... GrahamGibbons 3 85
(J J Quinn) *trckd ldr tl led over 2f out: hrd rdn and hung lft ins fnl f: hdd nr fin* **13/8**[1]

513 **3** *hd* **Caerlaverock (IRE)**[15] 2249 4-9-5 **80**.......................(b[1]) RobertWinston 6 85
(G A Swinbank) *chsd ldrs: rdn and ev ch fr over 2f out: hung lft ins fnl f: unable qck nr fin* **5/1**[3]

403- **4** 3 1/4 **Yes Mr President (IRE)**[314] 4448 4-9-5 **80**................. RoystonFfrench 2 80
(M Johnston) *led: rdn and hdd over 2f out: no ex fnl f* **7/1**

442- **5** 2 **Force Group (IRE)**[227] 6898 5-9-3 **78**.............................. TedDurcan 1 75
(M H Tompkins) *chsd ldrs: rdn over 2f out: wknd fnl f* **11/4**[2]

614 **6** 15 **Autumn Harvest**[12] 2315 5-9-2 **77**..................................(t) JamesDoyle 4 50
(A J McCabe) *stdd and awkward leaving stalls: hld up: plld hrd: wknd 2f out* **9/1**

2m 38.43s (3.33) **Going Correction** +0.425s/f (Yiel) **6** Ran **SP% 110.6**

Speed ratings (Par 105): **105,104,104,102,100 90**

toteswinger: 1&2 £8.90, 1&3 £9.70, 2&3 £2.30 CSF £36.33 TOTE £17.90: £5.20, £1.50; EX 58.70.

Owner P D Merritt **Bred** Allan Merritt **Trained** East Everleigh, Wilts

■ Stewards' Enquiry : Steve Drowne one-day ban: excessive use of whip (Jun 21)

FOCUS

Another race run at a very steady early pace and it developed into a 3f sprint, so the form may not be entirely reliable. A slight turf personal best from the winner.

2699 EBF MOSS PROPERTIES MAIDEN FILLIES' STKS — 6f

4:10 (4:12) (Class 4) 2-Y-O **£4,857** (£1,445; £722; £360) **Stalls High**

Form — RPR

1 **She's A Character** 2-8-9 0.. FrederikTylicki(5) 9 85+
(R A Fahey) *s.i.s: hld up: swtchd lft over 2f out: hdwy to ld 1f out: edgd rt and r.o wl* **7/1**[3]

3 **2** 5 **Babylonian**[7] 2503 2-9-0 0.. RoystonFfrench 7 70
(M Johnston) *led: rdn and hdd 1f out: sn outpcd* **10/11**[1]

3 *hd* **Caviar** 2-9-0 0.. WilliamBuick 3 69+
(R Hannon) *prom: pushed along 1/2-way: rdn over 1f out: styd on same pce* **6/1**[2]

4 1/2 **Proper Littlemadam** 2-8-9 0........................ Louis-PhilippeBeuzelin(5) 1 68+
(M Botti) *dwlt: hld up: hdwy 2f out: sn rdn: styd on same pce fnl f* **14/1**

5 1/2 **Love Match** 2-9-0 0.. SteveDrowne 6 66
(R Charlton) *s.i.s: sn prom: rdn: edgd lft and ev ch over 1f out: wknd ins fnl f* **6/1**[2]

53 **6** 1 **Brinscall**[16] 2195 2-9-0 0.. TedDurcan 4 63
(T D Easterby) *trckd ldr: racd keenly: rdn over 2f out: wknd ins fnl f* **20/1**

7 3 1/4 **Raddy 'Ell Pauline (IRE)** 2-9-0 0.................................. TPO'Shea 8 54+
(K A Ryan) *prom: rdn over 2f out: wknd over 1f out* **8/1**

8 3/4 **Fasette** 2-9-0 0.. SaleemGolam 5 51
(M H Tompkins) *s.s: a in rr: wknd 2f out* **33/1**

1m 13.7s (0.10) **Going Correction** 0.0s/f (Good) **8** Ran **SP% 118.9**

Speed ratings (Par 92): **99,92,91,90 89,85,84**

toteswinger: 1&2 £2.40, 1&3 £4.40, 2&3 £2.80 CSF £14.40 TOTE £7.80: £1.90, £1.10, £1.90; EX 12.30 Trifecta £28.30 Pool: £169.83 - 4.44 winning units..

Owner Aykroyd And Sons Ltd **Bred** Genesis Green & Deerpark Stud **Trained** Musley Bank, N Yorks

FOCUS

This looked a modest maiden, with only two having experience, but it went to a newcomer and it's hard not to have been impressed by the way she did it.

NOTEBOOK

She's A Character ◆, a 28,000gns half-sister to three winners at up to 1m4f including the useful Celtic Spirit, didn't have a lot of room on occasions, but once through the gap she produced a devastating turn of foot to leave her rivals for dead. She should stay a bit further and it will be fascinating to see where she goes next. (op 13-2 tchd 5-1)

Babylonian, a promising third at York on her debut seven days earlier, soon bagged the stands' rail in front and had the run of the race, but the winner made her look slow over the last furlong or so. She will appreciate further, but the feeling is that the York race may not have been that strong. (op 11-8)
Caviar, a 45,000gns half-sister to a winning sprinter in the US, saw plenty of daylight on the outside of the field and ran green, but also showed a degree of ability and should have learnt from it.
Proper Littlemadam, a half-sister to the winning sprinter Music Box Express, also showed her inexperience by swerving out to her left as the stalls opened, but did show a degree of promise on the outside of the field and better can be expected with this experience. (op 10-1)
Love Match, a half-sister to a couple of winners at around 1m, was produced to hold every chance inside the last 2f before folding as though the run was needed. She will probably appreciate further. (op 8-1)
Brinscall, third though beaten a long way by the winner in a soft-ground maiden auction event at Haydock last time, showed up for a while but is starting to look exposed and she will have more options when the nurseries start next month. (op 16-1 tchd 14-1)
Raddy 'Ell Pauline(IRE), retained for 140,000gns at the breeze-ups, is a half-sister to four winners including a couple of useful performers at up to 1m in Italy. She met one or two traffic problems on this debut and is probably capable of better. (op 17-2 tchd 15-2)

2700 DONCASTER SPONSORSHIP CLUB MAIDEN STKS 5f
4:45 (4:45) (Class 4) 3-Y-O+ **£5,180** (£1,541; £770; £384) **Stalls** High

Form RPR
2 **1** **Avertor**[15] 2250 3-9-3 0 .... SteveDrowne 11 76+
(R Charlton) *mde all: shkn up over 1f out: sn clr: comf* **30/100**[1]
20 **2** 4 ½ **She's In The Money**[51] 1302 3-8-10 0 ow1 .... LeeVickers(3) 4 56
(J G Given) *w wnr tl rdn over 1f out: edgd rt: styd on same pce ins fnl f* **11/1**[3]
44 **3** ¾ **Fatal Attraction**[18] 2157 4-9-5 0 .... RichardMullen 8 55
(Rae Guest) *hld up in tch: rdn over 1f out: styd on same pce* **6/1**[2]
50 **4** hd **Moneysupermarket (IRE)**[29] 1825 3-8-7 0. Louis-PhilippeBeuzelin(5) 5 51
(Patrick Morris) *chsd ldrs: rdn 1/2-way: no ex ins fnl f* **33/1**
0 **5** hd **Exceed Elegance (IRE)**[18] 2151 3-8-7 0 .... MartinLane(5) 2 51
(D Shaw) *s.i.s: outpcd: styd on fr over 1f out: nvr trbld ldrs* **50/1**
6 nk **Roodee King** 3-9-3 0 .... JamesDoyle 10 55
(Patrick Morris) *chsd ldrs: rdn over 1f out: no ex fnl f* **20/1**
7 ½ **Francis Albert** 3-9-3 0 .... GeorgeBaker 7 53
(M Mullineaux) *s.s: bhd: r.o ins fnl f: nvr nrr* **20/1**
0 **8** 3 **Whisper Softly (IRE)**[21] 2070 3-8-12 0 .... RoystonFfrench 6 37
(T D Walford) *sn pushed along in rr: wknd 2f out* **20/1**

60.30 secs (-0.20) **Going Correction** 0.0s/f (Good)
WFA 3 from 4yo 7lb 8 Ran SP% **118.7**
Speed ratings (Par 105): **101,93,92,92,91 91,90,85**
toteswinger: 1&2 £2.80, 1&3 £1.40, 2&3 £2.70 CSF £4.27 TOTE £1.30: £1.02, £2.30, £1.40; EX 4.70 Trifecta £8.90 Pool: £322.05 - 26.72 winning units. Place 6 £32.76, Place 5 £11.28.
Owner D J Deer **Bred** D J And Mrs Deer **Trained** Beckhampton, Wilts

FOCUS
A moderate older-horse maiden and a very one-sided contest from some way out. It was steadily run and the winner cn rate higher than this. The placed form is probably no better than plating class.
T/Plt: £25.90 to a £1 stake. Pool: £77,752.65. 2,190.79 winning tickets. T/Qpdt: £2.30 to a £1 stake. Pool: £3,265.91. 1,021.20 winning tickets. CR

2668 EPSOM (L-H)
Saturday, June 6

OFFICIAL GOING: Derby course - good (good to firm in places; 8.3) changing to good after race 1 (1.25); 5f course - good to firm (good in places; 8.7)
Wind: Fresh, behind Weather: Showery

2701 INVESTEC SIR CLEMENT FREUD MEMORIAL STKS (HERITAGE H'CAP) 1m 2f 18y
1:25 (1:30) (Class 2) (0-105,89) 3-Y-O
£31,155 (£9,330; £4,665; £2,335; £1,165; £585) **Stalls** Low

Form RPR
-316 **1** **River Captain (IRE)**[21] 2077 3-9-1 83 .... EddieAhern 1 99
(S Kirk) *chsd ldr: rdn to ld 2f out: clr ent fnl f: r.o strly* **16/1**
1-22 **2** 5 **Tepmokea (IRE)**[22] 2060 3-8-10 78 .... FrancisNorton 15 84
(K R Burke) *sn led: clr over 5f out: rdn over 2f out: hdd 2f out: outpcd and no ch w wnr ent fnl f: kpt on for clr 2nd* **8/1**[3]
-024 **3** 2 ½ **Lasso The Moon**[21] 2077 3-8-12 80 .... CatherineGannon 7 81+
(M R Channon) *rrd s and slowly away: bhd: effrt towards outer 3f out: switching lft fr over 2f out: gd hdwy wl over 1f out: wnt 3rd 1f out: kpt on but nvr nr ldrs* **12/1**
22-1 **4** nk **History Lesson**[37] 1622 3-9-2 84 .... RichardHughes 12 84
(R Hannon) *chsd ldng pair: rdn over 2f out: outpcd by ldng pair 2f out: no ch w ldrs after: kpt on* **16/1**
10-6 **5** nk **Marching Time**[24] 1992 3-9-1 83 .... RyanMoore 14 82+
(Sir Michael Stoute) *t.k.h: hld up in midfield on outer: rdn 3f out: hdwy u.p 2f out: pressing for modest 3rd ent fnl f: kpt on same pce after* **3/1**[1]
6-65 **6** 1 **Aurorian (IRE)**[21] 2077 3-9-7 89 .... MJKinane 6 86
(R Hannon) *stdd s: hld up bhd: hdwy on outer 2f out: styd on but nvr gng to rch ldrs* **40/1**
2-41 **7** 2 ¾ **London Bridge**[15] 2240 3-9-0 82 .... JimmyFortune 17 74+
(J H M Gosden) *lw: t.k.h: hld up in midfield: rdn and unable qck 3f out: sme hdwy fnl f: nvr trbld ldrs* **13/2**[2]
2-12 **8** hd **Dubai Crest**[34] 1702 3-9-5 87 .... (b[1]) JimCrowley 10 79
(Mrs A J Perrett) *t.k.h: hld up in tch in midfield: rdn over 2f out: sn edging lft and struggling: no ch fr over 1f out* **14/1**
11-0 **9** shd **Dialogue**[21] 2077 3-9-1 83 .... LDettori 9 74
(M Johnston) *in tch: rdn and unable qck whn bmpd over 2f out: no ch w ldrs fnl 2f* **22/1**
4212 **10** 2 ¾ **Tarzan (IRE)**[9] 2406 3-9-2 84 .... JohnEgan 16 70
(M Johnston) *lw: in tch: rdn and unable qck over 2f out: drvn and wknd wl over 1f out* **16/1**
0-21 **11** ½ **Sam Sharp (USA)**[21] 2074 3-9-1 83 .... TPQueally 3 68
(H R A Cecil) *lw: chsd ldrs: 4th and rdn over 2f out: sn struggling: no ch fr over 1f out* **8/1**[3]
2-12 **12** 3 ½ **Union Island (IRE)**[24] 1992 3-9-0 82 .... NCallan 8 60
(K A Ryan) *taken down early: hld up in midfield: rdn and no hdwy 3f out: sn wknd* **16/1**
14-0 **13** 1 **Goliaths Boy (IRE)**[30] 1801 3-9-5 87 .... StephenDonohoe 13 63
(R A Fahey) *hld up towards rr: nvr trbld ldrs* **50/1**
53-1 **14** nk **Elliptical (USA)**[17] 2178 3-8-13 81 .... PJSmullen 5 56
(G A Butler) *hld up in midfield: rdn and effrt on inner over 2f out: wknd wl over 1f out* **14/1**
001 **15** 15 **Saa'Ida (IRE)**[16] 2192 3-8-12 80 .... JamieSpencer 4 25
(C E Brittain) *hld up in rr: lost tch over 2f out: eased ins fnl f: t.o* **22/1**
0-21 **16** 2 ¼ **Dreamwalk (IRE)**[18] 2170 3-9-0 82 .... SebSanders 11 23
(R M Beckett) *in tch: rdn over 2f out: sn wknd: wl bhd and eased ins fnl f: t.o* **12/1**
60 **17** hd **Equipe De Nuit**[24] 1992 3-8-10 78 .... ChrisCatlin 2 18
(S C Williams) *s.i.s: hld up in last pl: lost tch 3f out: t.o* **33/1**

2m 7.07s (-2.63) **Going Correction** 0.0s/f (Good) **17** Ran SP% **128.8**
Speed ratings (Par 105): **110,106,104,103,103 102,100,100,100,98 97,94,94,93,81 80,79**
toteswinger: 1&2 £39.40, 1&3 £53.90, 2&3 £32.90 CSF £138.52 CT £1633.80 TOTE £17.80: £4.60, £2.90, £4.10, £3.20; EX 255.30 Trifecta £1076.90 Pool: £2,182.94 - 1.50 winning units..
Owner S J McCay **Bred** Sean Finnegan **Trained** Upper Lambourn, Berks
■ Stewards' Enquiry : John Egan caution: entered wrong stall.

FOCUS
Riders involved in the opener said that the rain had made the ground loose on top, but the time was just over a second outside the Racing Post standard suggesting that conditions were still fairly quick at this stage. This was a valuable and competitive handicap, but not a particularly strong renewal with the top weight in this 0-105 race running off only 89. There is unlikely to be anything in the field with the potential to become another Conduit, who won this a year ago before going on to St Leger and Breeders' Cup Turf glory, but plenty of handicap winners should emerge from the race. The pace was sound and not too many got into it, with three of those to fill the frame having been in the first four throughout. The winner showed big improvemnent but has been generally progressive.

NOTEBOOK
River Captain(IRE) ◆ was able to race more prominently than he did on his first try over this trip at Newbury, where he was ridden to conserve his energy, and utilised similar tactics to those which brought him success over the extended 1m at the spring meeting here. He careered away from the runner-up in the final furlong and there looks to be plenty more to come from him. On the evidence of this run he might stay even further, but he is likely to drop back to 1m now for the Britannia at Royal Ascot. (op 20-1)
Tepmokea(IRE) ran a sound race on this drop in trip. Once more attempting to make all, he held a three-length break over the rest of the field on straightening up, and although unable to shake off the winner, he beat the remainder well enough. (op 12-1 tchd 14-1 in places)
Lasso The Moon, in contrast to the first two who were always up there, had to pick his way through horses from the back of the field after losing ground when rearing as the stalls opened. Stil a maiden, he is not straightforward, but has plenty of ability and a return to 1m4f will suit him.
Official explanation: jockey said colt reared as the stalls opened (op 25-1)
History Lesson, winner of a Folkestone maiden at the end of April, was another to race prominently, but he could not go with the front pair in the latter stages and was edged out of third late on. This was a good handicap debut. (op 20-1)
Marching Time represented a yard which sent out last year's winner Conduit as well as two other winners of this in the past five years, and has now supplied the favourite in each of the last five runnings. Well supported after his promising return to the track at York but coltish beforehand, made his effort down the outside in the straight and briefly challenged for third, but he was never going to trouble the first two. He was coltish in the preliminaries and could be worth one more chance. (op 11-4 tchd 7-2)
Aurorian(IRE), the top-weight, made late progress from off the pace and is worth persevering with at this sort of trip, although he is perhaps still high enough in the weights.
London Bridge, winner of a Newmarket maiden from Senses, who won in the week, was not disgraced in his first handicap and may benefit from a stiffer track at this trip. (tchd 6-1 and 7-1)
Dubai Crest, in first-time blinkers, was engaged in a barging match with Dialogue over two furlongs out, already looking in trouble at the time. (tchd 12-1)
Dialogue, dropped 5lb following his reappearance, became involved in a bumping match with Dubai Crest from which he could not recover, although a place in the frame looked out of reach for him at the time. (op 20-1 tchd 25-1 in places)
Tarzan(IRE), who went up 5lb for his narrow defeat at Newcastle, did not race as close to the pace as usual and he did not quite see out this longer trip. (op 14-1 tchd 20-1 in places)
Sam Sharp(USA), a comfortable winner of a maiden in soft ground at Newbury, was well enough placed turning in, but he could not race on in the straight. This track seemed to find him out, and a drop back to 1m may suit him. (tchd 15-2)
Goliaths Boy(IRE) Official explanation: jockey said gelding ran too free

2702 INVESTEC WOODCOTE STKS (LISTED RACE) 6f
1:55 (1:59) (Class 1) 2-Y-O
£17,031 (£6,456; £3,231; £1,611; £807; £405) **Stalls** High

Form RPR
41 **1** **Corporal Maddox**[22] 2027 2-9-0 0 .... JimCrowley 11 96+
(K R Burke) *lw: little slowly away: pushed along briefly towards rr: rdn whn swtchd rt over 2f out: gd hdwy on outer fr wl over 1f out: r.o strly but drifted lft fnl f: led fnl towards fin* **14/1**
152 **2** nk **Walkingonthemoon**[15] 2247 2-9-0 0 .... RichardKingscote 10 95
(Tom Dascombe) *chsd ldrs: rdn and hung lft fr over 1f out: r.o stly to ld ins fnl f: drifted lft to far rails: ct towards fin* **8/1**
0212 **3** 2 ¾ **Red Avalanche (IRE)**[26] 1927 2-9-0 0 .... MartinDwyer 3 87
(P F I Cole) *lw: led at gd pce: rdn and hrd pressed fr over 2f out: kpt on gamely tl hdd ins fnl f: no ex* **5/1**[2]
0145 **4** hd **Fratellino**[9] 2408 2-9-0 0 .... AndrewMullen 8 86
(A J McCabe) *prom: rdn over 2f out: nt pce to mount serious chal but kpt on fnl f* **14/1**
31 **5** ¾ **Barzan (IRE)**[15] 2218 2-9-0 0 .... RichardSmith 5 84+
(Tom Dascombe) *lw: s.i.s: rdn and hdwy whn nt clr run over 1f out: swtchd rt: styd on: nt rch ldrs* **16/1**
0231 **6** nk **Little Perisher**[28] 1862 2-9-0 0 .... NCallan 6 83
(A P Jarvis) *in tch: hdwy 3f out: rdn whn swtchd lft 2f out: one pce fnl f* **7/1**
1 **7** 2 ¼ **Mon Brav**[14] 2258 2-9-0 0 .... DNolan 1 76
(D Carroll) *chsd ldrs: rdn over 2f out: fdd fnl f* **14/1**
313 **8** 2 **King's Approach (IRE)**[21] 2087 2-9-0 0 .... RyanMoore 13 70
(R Hannon) *sn struggling to go pce: a towards rr* **16/1**
01 **9** shd **Avon River**[33] 1726 2-9-0 0 .... JimmyFortune 2 70
(R Hannon) *mid-div: rdn 3f out: little imp whn swtchd and jinked lft over 1f out* **25/1**
631 **10** 3 ½ **Royal Desert**[31] 1782 2-9-0 0 .... TonyCulhane 4 60
(M R Channon) *in tch: rdn over 2f out: wknd over 1f out* **12/1**
3311 **11** 16 **Desert Auction (IRE)**[30] 1805 2-9-0 0 .... RichardHughes 9 12+
(R Hannon) *hmpd on bnd 4f out: a towards rr: eased whn btn fnl 2f* **9/2**[1]
311 **12** 14 **Jack My Boy (IRE)**[22] 2041 2-9-0 0 .... JamieSpencer 7 —
(P D Evans) *nvr travelling: a bhd: eased fnl 2f* **11/2**[3]

69.39 secs (-0.01) **Going Correction** 0.0s/f (Good) **12** Ran SP% **117.1**
Speed ratings (Par 101): **100,99,95,95,94 94,91,88,88,83 62,43**
toteswinger: 1&2 £22.50, 1&3 £28.50, 2&3 £9.50 CSF £120.28 TOTE £18.00: £5.40, £3.10, £2.00; EX 137.40 Trifecta £1031.40 Part won. Pool: £1,393.84 - 0.30 winning units..
Owner Mogeely Stud & Mrs Maura Gittins **Bred** Theobalds Stud **Trained** Middleham Moor, N Yorks
■ Stewards' Enquiry : N Callan two-day ban: careless riding (Jun 22-23)

FOCUS
Another average-looking renewal of a race that could well struggle to hold on to its Listed status. Traditionally a wide draw has been difficult to overcome, but the leaders went a good pace, which suited the winner, who was able to tuck in from stall 11 and come with a late challenge. The winner can do better but this form is limited for the grade, if solid enough.

NOTEBOOK
Corporal Maddox always promised to be suited by the step up to 6f. Short of room early in the straight, he was switched before being brought with a relentless run down the outside. Green on his debut, he picked up his maiden at Hamilton last time and has now followed up in Listed company, which underlines his progressive profile, but the bare form is nothing to get too excited about, and he will face much tougher competition if turning up at Royal Ascot. However, at the moment connections are considering waiting for the July meeting at Newmarket. (op 12-1 tchd 16-1)
Walkingonthemoon had proved his stamina for 6f when second in a conditions event at Pontefract last time, and once again he was keen to get on with things. Crossing over from his wide draw, he got a good prominent pitch and didn't lose too much ground going into the turn, but he never looked entirely happy on the track. He eventually wore down Red Avalanche, only to find the winner finishing fast on his outside, and a return to a more conventional course should suit him. He too could now head for the July meeting. (tchd 7-1 and 17-2)
Red Avalanche(IRE) had a good low draw and was pushed along to lead. Bang there all the way, he certainly got the trip, but his early efforts meant that he got tired in the closing stages. It was a solid effort, but a little more cut in the ground would surely suit him in future. (op 11-2 tchd 9-2)
Fratellino has good early pace and predictably was disputing at the head of affairs early on. Beaten off from two furlongs out, he could only keep on the one pace after that, and he looks the type that could prove hard to place in the coming months.
Barzan(IRE) handled the bend into the straight well, but he was short of room on the inside and rather one-paced once angled towards the outside. He can do better with more experience, and his pedigree suggests he will continue to improve as he steps up in distance. (tchd 20-1)
Little Perisher came into the race with a steadily progressive profile, but he looked uncomfortable on the course and failed to run to his best. He can do better back on a more galloping track. (op 8-1)
Mon Brav had a good draw but a lot more to do in this company than when successful at Beverley on his debut. He got unbalanced on the track. (op 12-1)
King's Approach(IRE) was dropped out from his wide draw and simply never got competitive. (tchd 18-1 and 20-1 in places)
Avon River (op 16-1)
Royal Desert failed to act on the track. (op 11-1)
Desert Auction(IRE) got hampered and shuffled back in the field on the turn into the straight and could not get competitive afterwards. This was not his true running. (op 7-2)
Jack My Boy(IRE) palpably failed to handle this unique track. Official explanation: jockey said colt missed the break and did not handle the track (op 10-1)

2703 PRINCESS ELIZABETH STKS (SPONSORED BY INVESTEC) (GROUP 3) (F&M) — 1m 114y

2:25 (2:27) (Class 1) 3-Y-O+

£36,900 (£13,988; £7,000; £3,490; £1,748; £877) **Stalls** Low

Form	Pos	Dist	Horse	Jockey	RPR
3001	**1**		**Eva's Request (IRE)**[35] 1667 4-9-6 109 (M R Channon) *lw: hld up in last pair: 7th st: hdwy on inner over 2f out: swtchd rt 2f out: rdn to ld over 1f out: hrd pressed jst ins fnl f: kpt on gamely and in command towards fin* **4/1**[2]	EdwardCreighton 5	112
3-25	**2**	*1*	**Alnadana (IRE)**[36] 1658 4-9-6 0 (A De Royer-Dupre, France) *w'like: stdd s: hld up in last pair: 8th st: hdwy on outer jst over 2f out: hanging lft but rdn to chal 1f out: hung lft into wnr ins fnl f: btn and eased towards fin* **4/1**[2]	CSoumillon 8	111+
144-	**3**	*4 1/2*	**Spacious**[232] 6781 4-9-6 110 (J R Fanshawe) *lw: in tch: hdwy and 3rd st: rdn and ev ch 2f out: keeping on same pce whn short room over 1f out: no ch w ldng pair fnl f: wnt 3rd wl ins fnl f* **13/8**[1]	JMurtagh 7	99
-025	**4**	*3/4*	**Baileys Cacao (IRE)**[14] 2278 3-8-8 103 (R Hannon) *led for 1f: chsd ldr after: 2nd st: rdn to ld over 2f out: hdd over 1f out: wknd fnl f* **17/2**	RichardHughes 2	96
4-21	**5**	*3*	**Badiat Alzaman (IRE)**[33] 1745 3-8-8 82 (D M Simcock) *t.k.h: hld up towards rr: 6th st: effrt and jostling match w rival over 2f out: n.d fnl 2f* **16/1**	JimCrowley 4	89
-046	**6**	*6*	**Infamous Angel**[28] 1873 3-8-8 100 (R Hannon) *plld hrd: hld up in tch: 4th st: rdn and sltly hmpd over 2f out: sn wknd* **9/1**	RyanMoore 1	75
-052	**7**	*32*	**Al Sabaheya**[16] 2209 3-8-8 84 (C E Brittain) *t.k.h: chsd ldrs: 5th and wkng st: lost tch 3f out: t.o and eased ins fnl f* **28/1**	NCallan 6	—
444-	**8**	*9*	**Red Dune (IRE)**[232] 6782 4-9-6 100 (M A Jarvis) *t.k.h: led after 1f: rdn and hdd over 2f out: sn wknd: t.o and eased fnl f: b.b.v* **8/1**[3]	LDettori 3	—

1m 43.84s (-2.26) **Going Correction** 0.0s/f (Good)
WFA 3 from 4yo 12lb — **8** Ran SP% **119.1**
Speed ratings (Par 113): **110,109,105,104,101 96,68,60**
toteswinger: 1&2 £3.90, 1&3 £2.30, 2&3 £2.30 CSF £21.37 TOTE £5.30: £1.70, £1.80, £1.20; EX 20.50 Trifecta £23.30 Pool: £1,458.87 - 46.30 winning units..
Owner Liam Mulryan **Bred** Ballylinch Stud **Trained** West Ilsley, Berks
■ Stewards' Enquiry : C Soumillon two-day ban: careless riding (Jun 21-22)

FOCUS
Not a particularly strong edition of this distaff Group 3. The pace was sound and the first two both came from the rear. With Spacious below par there is a bit of doubt over the form, but the winner looks to be improving.

NOTEBOOK
Eva's Request(IRE) had been well beaten into sixth place in this last year, but she came into this in better heart having won a Listed race at Goodwood on her latest start. She has not always been the most consistent, but was able to follow up with a decent effort, coming with a good run along the rail to lead and going a couple of lengths up before holding off the wayward runner-up. Smart on her day, the Windsor Forest at Royal Ascot remains the obvious target. (tchd 7-2)
Alnadana(IRE) was held up at the back and was pushed out by Badiat Alzaman when beginning to improve in the straight. Coming with a sweeping run down the outside, drifting left under a right-hand drive towards the camber as she did so, she looked set to pick up the winner when her jockey switched his stick, only for him to pull it through to his right hand again. She then hung badly into Eva's Request, losing momentum and quite possibly costing her the race. This was a poor ride from Christophe Soumillon, who picked up a two-day ban, but in his defence the filly was clearly ill at ease on the track's undulations. (op 5-1)
Spacious was never quite able to reproduce her second in the 1,000 Guineas during the remainder of last season. Making her reappearance, with soft ground having scuppered a scheduled trip to the Curragh last month, she improved entering the straight but lacked the pace to force her head in front and seemed held when she was slightly inconvenienced by the runner-up approaching the last furlong. She did rally for third and looks worth another try over 1m2f, but is essentially an underachiever. The track did not suit her though, and connections were pleased enough with the run. The Windsor Forest is a possibility now. (op 7-4 tchd 2-1 and 9-4 in places)
Baileys Cacao(IRE) ran well up with the pace and briefly showed in front, but she was stepping up a furlong and a half in trip and her stamina was on the wane late on. (op 12-1)
Badiat Alzaman(IRE) had only a Warwick maiden win to her name and had a lot to find on these terms, but although she was found wanting she was certainly not disgraced. She may prove tricky to place though, with her handicap mark likely to suffer after this. (op 20-1)
Infamous Angel, a stablemate of the fourth, was already in trouble when she was slightly hampered going to the two-pole. This trip stretches her, but she is going to be hard to place this season. (op 12-1)
Red Dune(IRE), on her seasonal debut, made the running as usual and flashed her tail a couple of times early on. She could not hold on when tackled and trailed in well beaten, probably not staying this longer trip, although she was also reported to have broken a blood vessel. Official explanation: vet said filly burst a blood vessel (op 15-2 tchd 7-1)

2704 INVESTEC "DASH" (HERITAGE H'CAP) — 5f

3:00 (3:00) (Class 2) 3-Y-O+

£46,732 (£13,995; £6,997; £3,502; £1,747; £877) **Stalls** High

Form	Pos	Dist	Horse	Jockey	RPR
4304	**1**		**Indian Trail**[11] 2363 9-8-2 **82** (v) (D Nicholls) *hmpd sn after s: hld up in rr on stands' rail: swtchd lft over 1f out: gd hdwy to chse wnr jst ins fnl f: led last stride* **11/1**	PaulQuinn 18	92
0-02	**2**	*shd*	**Captain Dunne (IRE)**[21] 2094 4-9-1 **95** (T D Easterby) *lw: led at fast pce: rdn over 1f out: r.o wl tl hdd last stride* **8/1**[2]	MJKinane 12	105
4426	**3**	*1 3/4*	**Strike Up The Band**[23] 2012 6-9-6 **100** (D Nicholls) *chsd wnr: rdn over 1f out: lost 2nd jst ins fnl f: kpt on same pce* **16/1**	JimCrowley 11	104
6-60	**4**	*nk*	**Oldjoesaid**[34] 1699 5-9-5 **99** (H Candy) *racd in midfield on outer: hdwy 2f out: chsd ldrs and rdn over 1f out: kpt on but nt pce to rch ldrs* **16/1**	FergusSweeney 1	102
0-00	**5**	*1/2*	**Group Therapy**[23] 2012 4-9-3 **97** (N P Littmoden) *in tch: hdwy 1/2-way: chsd ldrs and rdn over 1f out: kpt on same pce fnl f* **50/1**	ChrisCatlin 4	98
0-30	**6**	*1*	**Siren's Gift**[7] 2502 5-8-13 **93** (b) (A M Balding) *lw: trckd ldrs: gng wl: rdn over 1f out: fnd little 1f out: one pce fnl f* **8/1**[2]	LDettori 14	90
3433	**7**	*1/2*	**Wi Dud**[14] 2272 5-9-6 **100** (b) (K A Ryan) *lw: chsd ldrs on stands' rail: rdn 2f out: drvn and no ex ent fnl f* **5/1**[1]	NCallan 20	95
-116	**8**	*1/2*	**Fol Hollow (IRE)**[36] 1647 4-9-1 **95** (D Nicholls) *sn outpcd towards rr and rdn along: hdwy 1/2-way: styd on fnl f: nvr pce to rch ldrs* **14/1**	AndrewMullen 17	89
-206	**9**	*1*	**Hogmaneigh (IRE)**[14] 2272 6-9-5 **104** (S C Williams) *bhd: rdn and hung lft over 1f out: sme modest late hdwy: nvr trbld ldrs* **11/1**	WilliamCarson(5) 13	94
-012	**10**	*3/4*	**Cake (IRE)**[16] 2191 4-8-13 **93** (R Hannon) *lw: in tch in midfield: rdn wl over 1f out: wknd ent fnl f* **17/2**[3]	PatDobbs 19	80
31-4	**11**	*1 1/4*	**Safari Mischief**[16] 2191 6-8-13 **93** (P Winkworth) *sn outpcd in rr: modest late hdwy: nvr a factor* **14/1**	LukeMorris 16	76
222	**12**	*nse*	**Wotashirtfull (IRE)**[45] 1457 4-8-2 **82** (v) (J R Boyle) *s.i.s: hdwy into midfield over 3f out: chsd ldrs 1/2-way: rdn and wknd 2f out* **14/1**	NickyMackay 9	65
-023	**13**	*1 1/2*	**Little Pete (IRE)**[16] 2191 4-8-10 **90** (A M Balding) *lw: sn outpcd in rr: sme hdwy 1/2-way: no prog over 1f out: nvr nr ldrs* **12/1**	FrancisNorton 10	67
-040	**14**	*3/4*	**Tournedos (IRE)**[23] 2012 7-9-4 **98** (D Nicholls) *chsd ldrs tl 1/2-way: wknd 2f out: wl btn whn bmpd 1f out* **50/1**	MartinDwyer 5	73
4363	**15**	*1*	**Merlin's Dancer**[29] 1836 9-8-3 **83** ow1 (S Dow) *chsd ldrs tl 1/2-way: wkng and hanging lft over 1f out: wl btn whn bmpd 1f out* **25/1**	JohnEgan 7	54
-040	**16**	*5*	**Elhamri**[31] 1791 5-8-4 **84** (S Kirk) *a bhd: no ch and hanging rt wl over 1f out: hmpd 1f out* **40/1**	RichardKingscote 2	37
00-0	**17**	*26*	**Desert Lord**[21] 2094 9-9-6 **100** (b) (K A Ryan) *chsd ldrs for 1f: sn lost pl: wl bhd and eased fr wl over 1f out: t.o* **25/1**	JamieSpencer 8	—
5026	**P**		**Crimson Fern (IRE)**[16] 2191 5-8-13 **93** (M S Saunders) *in tch in midfield: hdwy 2f out: rdn whn hung lft and faltered bdly 1f out: sn eased: p.u and dismntd nr fin: burst blood vessel* **16/1**	TGMcLaughlin 15	—

54.67 secs (-1.03) **Going Correction** 0.0s/f (Good) — **18** Ran SP% **125.5**
Speed ratings (Par 109): **108,107,105,104,103 102,101,100,98,97 95,95,93,92,90 82,40,—**
toteswinger: 1&2 £22.90, 1&3 £50.10, 2&3 £30.40 CSF £93.59 CT £1473.20 TOTE £15.70: £3.30, £1.90, £4.50, £5.30; EX 130.90 Trifecta £2757.30 Part won. Pool: £3,726.11 - 0.10 winning units..
Owner Martin Love **Bred** Whitsbury Manor Stud **Trained** Sessay, N Yorks

FOCUS
An ultra-competitive sprint handicap over the quickest 5f track in the country. David Nicholls, who had sent out three of the previous seven winners of this race, had four in the race this time including the winner who produced his best effort since last spring. Solid form.

NOTEBOOK
Indian Trail, who crept in at the bottom of the weights, was one of four runners from the yard and came out narrowly on top. A confirmed hold-up performer who needs the breaks, he has not always had the best of luck at this track, notably two years ago when finishing full of running having been denied a clear passage in the 6f handicap that closes the Derby day card. Things could not have worked out any better this time, though, as the ground was in his favour, he had dropped to a good mark, he had been handed a great draw and, just when he needed the gaps to appear for him, they came, and he was able to burst through with a decisive turn of foot. He idled once he hit the front, and is clearly not an easy ride, but everything fell into place this time. He wouldn't be an obvious choice to follow up, but clearly retains plenty of talent given his conditions.
Captain Dunne(IRE), officially 2lb well in, has plenty of early pace and used it to good effect here to cross over from stall 12 and make the running towards the stands' side rail. Only narrowly denied, a sharp 5f clearly suits his style of running ideally, but another rise in the weights for this could well mean that the handicapper retains a grip on his steady improvement. (tchd 15-2)
Strike Up The Band is another blessed with early speed, and he too showed up well towards the stands' side. He couldn't dominate as he would have liked, though, and once again found a couple too good. The handicapper knows where he is with him. (tchd 20-1 in places)
Oldjoesaid ◆ ran a cracker from the worst draw having raced wide throughout, especially considering that the ground was probably on the quick side for him. He won off a 3lb higher mark last year, so is certainly fairly handicapped, and he should be kept in mind for a similar race over the minimum trip. (op 22-1)
Group Therapy was also burdened with a low draw and ran a fine race in defeat. This was a return to form following three down-the-field efforts since his juvenile campaign, and it was a very encouraging sign. He, too, is on a mark he can win off. (op 66-1)
Siren's Gift, who finds winning difficult, was able to get over and chase the leader towards the favoured stands' rail, and, although not getting the clearest of runs, found little once she saw daylight and didn't look unlucky. (op 9-1 tchd 10-1)

Wi Dud finished third in the Temple Stakes last time and as a result found himself 5lb well in here. He wasn't done any favours when Siren's Gift came across and gave him a hefty bump, but he held on to his position on the rail and was given every chance. His performance underlines how little there is between the top handicappers and the Group-class sprinters in this country. (op 7-1)

Fol Hollow(IRE) had a good draw, but he found things happening a bit quick here and a stiffer 5f probably suits him better. (op 12-1 tchd 16-1 in places)

Hogmaneigh(IRE), who won this race two years ago and was fourth in it last year, didn't get a clear run when trying to stay on from off the pace. The ground was quicker than he would like it, too. (op 12-1)

Cake(IRE) is very effective at Goodwood and promised to be suited by this track, so she was a little disappointing in the circumstances. (op 9-1 tchd 8-1)

Safari Mischief disappointed. Third in this last year, he had run a satisfactory prep race on his reappearance at Goodwood and looked to have been trained for this. Squeezed out early, though, he soon got outpaced and never figured. (op 9-1)

Wotashirtfull(IRE) is a consistent sort, but he normally tackles a lower class of opposition than this. (op 16-1)

Crimson Fern(IRE) Official explanation: vet said mare bled from the nose and was struck into

2705 INVESTEC DERBY (GROUP 1) (ENTIRE COLTS & FILLIES) 1m 4f 10y

3:45 (3:53) (Class 1) 3-Y-O

£709,625 (£269,000; £134,625; £67,125; £33,625; £16,875) **Stalls** Centre

Form				RPR
11-1	**1**		**Sea The Stars (IRE)**[35] 1675 3-9-0 121 .... MJKinane 4 (John M Oxx, Ire) *lw: t.k.h early: handy in main gp: 4th st: wnt 3rd 3f out: chsd ldr gng wl 2f out: rdn to ld ent fnl f: in command and pushed out fnl 100yds* **11/4**[2]	124+
1-11	**2**	1 ¾	**Fame And Glory**[27] 1910 3-9-0 122 .... JAHeffernan 10 (A P O'Brien, Ire) *w'like: scope: hld up in midfield: 5th st: rdn and hdwy 3f out: sn swtchd rt: chsd ldng pair over 1f out: r.o wl fnl f to go 2nd towards fin: nvr gng to rch wnr* **9/4**[1]	121
30-2	**3**	nk	**Masterofthehorse (IRE)**[30] 1800 3-9-0 111 .... RichardHughes 2 (A P O'Brien, Ire) *swtg: stdd s: hld up in last trio: 10th st: rdn and hdwy wl over 2f out: r.o wl fnl f to go 3rd on post: nvr gng to rch wnr* **16/1**	120
10-4	**4**	nse	**Rip Van Winkle (IRE)**[35] 1675 3-9-0 115 .... JMurtagh 9 (A P O'Brien, Ire) *swtg: hld up in midfield: rdn and effrt 3f out: edging lft after: swtchd rt over 1f out: stl edging lft but styd on strly fnl f: wnt 4th last stride: nt pce to rch wnr* **6/1**[3]	120+
5-41	**5**	shd	**Golden Sword**[30] 1800 3-9-0 109 .... CO'Donoghue 7 (A P O'Brien, Ire) *led at stdy pce for 2f: wnt clr over 9f out: rdn wl over 2f out: hdd ent fnl f: no ex u.p: lost 3 pls towards fin* **25/1**	120
21-0	**6**	6	**Crowded House**[23] 2014 3-9-0 120 .... JamieSpencer 12 (B J Meehan) *stdd after s: hld up in rr: 11th st: rdn and hdwy on outer over 2f out out: edgd lft and hmpd 2f out: no hdwy after* **20/1**	110
4-1	**7**	½	**Age Of Aquarius (IRE)**[28] 1872 3-9-0 109 .... PJSmullen 1 (A P O'Brien, Ire) *swtg: chsd ldr: clr of remainder over 8f out: 2nd st: rdn over 2f out: lost 2nd 2f out: wknd u.p over 1f out* **25/1**	109
-113	**8**	nk	**Debussy (IRE)**[30] 1800 3-9-0 103 .... JimmyFortune 5 (J H M Gosden) *t.k.h: hld up in midfield: rdn and effrt on inner 3f out: wknd 2f out* **33/1**	109
11-5	**9**	4 ½	**Kite Wood (IRE)**[23] 2014 3-9-0 108 .... LDettori 8 (Saeed Bin Suroor) *swtg: t.k.h: chsd clr ldng pair: 3rd and pushed along st: wknd over 2f out: wl btn and eased ins fnl f* **28/1**	104
2-31	**10**	hd	**Black Bear Island (IRE)**[23] 2014 3-9-0 112 .... RyanMoore 3 (A P O'Brien, Ire) *stdd s: t.k.h: hld up in last trio: last st: rdn and sme hdwy 3f out: sn struggling and wl hld fnl 2f* **7/1**	101
2-3	**11**	5	**Gan Amhras (IRE)**[35] 1675 3-9-0 115 .... KJManning 6 (J S Bolger, Ire) *t.k.h: hld up in midfield: rdn 4f out: 9th st: sn drvn and wknd: wl bhd fnl 2f* **8/1**	93
21-2	**12**	11	**Montaff**[28] 1872 3-9-0 106 .... RHills 11 (M R Channon) *swtg: in tch in main gp: 8th and losing pl st: wknd and bhd fr wl over 2f out* **40/1**	76

2m 36.74s (-2.16) **Going Correction** 0.0s/f (Good) **12** Ran SP% **122.5**

Speed ratings (Par 113): **107,105,105,105,105 101,101,101,98,97 94,87**

toteswinger: 1&2 £2.20, 1&3 £9.80, 2&3 £10.70 CSF £8.80 TOTE £3.40: £1.50, £1.50, £5.00; EX 11.20 Trifecta £228.30 Pool: £62,008.79 - 200.91 winning units..

Owner Christopher Tsui **Bred** Sunderland Holdings **Trained** Currabeg, Co Kildare

FOCUS

There had not been a smaller field since Nijinsky won in 1970, but it was a quality line-up nevertheless, without any complete no-hopers, and it looked relatively open, too, as the betting confirmed. Its make-up was quite extraordinary, with none of the four home-trained runners trading at less than 20-1 and the remainder of the runners all hailing from Ireland - six from the Aidan O'Brien stable, and all six of them credible contenders in their own right. The Guineas form was very strongly represented, as were most of the main trials. They went very steady for the first two furlongs and at a moderate pace thereafter. Irish-trained runners took the first five places. Sea The Stars probably only had to run to his Guineas form, rating an average Derby-winning performance, but can rate much higher. The second and fourth were close to their marks, with the third and fifth biggish improvers on their Chester form.

NOTEBOOK

Sea The Stars(IRE) ◆ confirmed himself a colt of the very highest class by completing a double last achieved by the great Nashwan 20 years previously. He had his stamina to prove, like all Guineas winners, but while his sire Cape Cross gave cause for some concern, the dam Urban Sea had won the Arc and had already produced a Derby winner in Galileo, so he was a far more likely stayer than most of the eight who had tried and failed to complete the double since Nashwan. In the event, his stamina was not fully tested in a race run at a steady pace. Thoroughly composed and relaxed throughout the preliminaries while plenty of others were sweating up, he was quite keen until the pace picked up but then travelled like a dream, disputing third with Kite Wood behind the two clear leaders. Three out he was clearly going best, and his main rivals were all hard at work. As Age Of Aquarius cracked he was sent in pursuit of Golden Sword, and having readily taken the leader's measure a furlong from home he was not at all hard pressed to win well. The winning margin was not extravagant, but it was a performance of sheer class and one that places him among the sport's true greats. It also promised further major prizes before the year is out, with the Irish Derby the likely next target and the Eclipse an alternative if it came up unsuitably soft at the Curragh. Races like the International at York, the Irish Champion and the Arc could all come into consideration later for this exceptional colt. (tchd 3-1 in places and 5-2 in places)

Fame And Glory had beaten the same horses both times in the Ballysax and the Derrinstown, and though he was impressive in the latter race, there remained a doubt about the strength of the form. Well backed on course, his best chance of beating the favourite appeared to be for stamina rather than speed so it was rather surprising that he took up a position behind him. He acquitted himself extremely well in second, but he could not quicken with the winner and never looked as if he was going to beat him. A more searching test might have suited him better, but one suspects Sea The Stars would always have his measure over this distance or shorter provided the ground was suitable. That said, he is obviously a worthy contender for all the big middle-distance prizes. (op 7-2 tchd 4-1 in places)

Masterofthehorse(IRE) had only a couple behind him into the straight, but he enjoyed a trouble-free run through from the back of the field and challenged for second between his stablemates inside the final furlong. This was a cracking effort from a colt who was said to have thrived since Chester and will merit plenty of respect wherever we see him next. (op 20-1)

Rip Van Winkle(IRE), among those who sweated up, has a lot of speed on his dam's side and was held up to get the trip. He stayed much better than many expected, albeit in a Derby run in slowish time, and he might have been second but for his inclination to edge left down the camber, even once switched right to the outside. Although he has been beaten in all three attempts at Group 1 level, one can see why connections, and Murtagh in particular, rate him so highly. There were no plans forthcoming for any of the O'Brien colts, but one could well see him dropping back two furlongs for races like the Eclipse. (op 13-2 tchd 7-1 in places)

Golden Sword, who beat Masterofthehorse in the Chester Vase, looks a stayer and a galloper. He saw the race out far more strongly than Age Of Aquarius, who had kept him company most of the way, and it was only well inside the final furlong that he lost second. He looks an obvious St Leger type. (op 28-1 tchd 20-1)

Crowded House, who had reportedly scoped badly after York and whose participation was in doubt until the start of the week, did best of the home team in sixth, but he was fully six lengths behind the fifth, having been held up at the back of the field and still virtually last into the straight. Although he made some headway on the outside he never looked happy and was edging left when he ran up the back of Kite Wood two out. It was a step in the right direction, but it bears repeating that the Racing Post form is not as strong as it looked at the time. (op 16-1)

Age Of Aquarius(IRE), winner of the Lingfield Oaks Trial, chased leader Golden Sword but did not see his race out as well as him. (op 20-1 tchd 28-1)

Debussy(IRE), only third in the Chester Vase, was outclassed but by no means disgraced. (op 50-1)

Kite Wood(IRE), who kept Sea The Stars company for so long, was struggling as soon as they reached the straight and dropped out right away. This was disappointing. (tchd 25-1 and 33-1 in places)

Black Bear Island(IRE), the Dante winner, made only limited headway from the back of the field and was going nowhere in the last two furlongs. He could have done with a stronger pace. (tchd 6-1)

Gan Amhras(IRE), third to Sea The Stars at Newmarket, was the biggest disappointment of the race. His pedigree promised improvement over the extra half-mile, but having been edgy beforehand he was keen through the early stages and, having been anchored towards the rear, was no threat at all in the straight. Connections felt the track was against him. (op 7-1 tchd 17-2)

Montaff, the outsider of the party, was in touch to the straight, but dropped away quickly. (tchd 33-1)

2706 INVESTEC SUREFOOTED STKS (H'CAP) 1m 4f 10y

4:30 (4:34) (Class 2) (0-100,100) 4-Y-O+

£12,462 (£3,732; £1,866; £934; £466; £234) **Stalls** Centre

Form				RPR
40-4	**1**		**Coin Of The Realm (IRE)**[22] 1458 4-8-7 **84** .... PatDobbs 3 (G L Moore) *trckd ldrs: pushed along over 2f out to chse ldng pair: rdn over 1f out: str run on far side rails to ld ins fnl f: won gng away* **6/1**[2]	93
0333	**2**	2	**Drill Sergeant**[7] 2471 4-9-9 **100** .... LDettori 8 (M Johnston) *trckd ldrs: rdn to chal fr over 2f out: remained w ev ch ent fnl f: dug deep but unable to match wnr wl ins fnl f* **6/1**[2]	106
-011	**3**	½	**Martyr**[15] 2242 4-9-0 **91** .... RichardHughes 2 (R Hannon) *disp ld tl overall ldr 4f out: sn rdn and hrd pressed: battled on gamely: hdd ins fnl f: kpt on but no ex* **13/2**[3]	96
16-0	**4**	shd	**Storyland (USA)**[34] 1696 4-8-12 **89** .... KirstyMilczarek 9 (W J Haggas) *restrained s: in last pair: rdn and stdy prog fr 3f out: swtchd rt and styd on fnl f: wnt 4th towards fin* **9/1**	94+
6	**5**	¾	**War Party**[15] 2242 5-8-1 **83** .... AndreaAtzeni(5) 6 (Dr R D P Newland) *trckd ldrs: rdn wl over 2f out: kpt on* **14/1**	87
0-05	**6**	¾	**Group Captain**[45] 1458 7-9-0 **91** .... RichardKingscote 16 (H J Collingridge) *lw: mid-div: rdn 4f out: no impreesion tl styd on fnl f* **12/1**	94
100-	**7**	½	**Bureaucrat**[252] 5229 7-8-13 **90** .... JamieSpencer 14 (P J Hobbs) *mid-div: rdn and hung lft fr 3f out: styd on fnl f* **14/1**	92+
4-65	**8**	2 ½	**Resplendent Light**[28] 1875 4-9-1 **92** .... DO'Donohoe 15 (W R Muir) *mid-div: rdn over 3f out: no imp* **33/1**	90
/606	**9**	3 ¾	**Kaleo**[23] 2003 5-8-4 **81** oh3 .... JohnEgan 1 (S Dow) *nvr bttr than mid-div* **66/1**	75
3065	**10**	3 ½	**Love Galore (IRE)**[80] 864 4-9-5 **96** .... JMurtagh 5 (M Johnston) *lw: s.i.s: a towards rr* **10/1**	84
3/5-	**11**	hd	**Hot Diamond**[28] 2202 5-8-4 **81** .... MartinDwyer 4 (P J Hobbs) *lw: a towards rr* **5/1**[1]	67
1-26	**12**	7	**Aegean Prince**[19] 2146 5-8-4 **81** .... FrancisNorton 10 (P Howling) *hld up towards rr: nvr a threat* **50/1**	56
10-5	**13**	5	**Bandama (IRE)**[23] 2003 6-8-10 **87** .... JimCrowley 12 (Mrs A J Perrett) *in tch: rdn 3f out: wknd 2f out: eased* **11/1**	54
31-0	**14**	¾	**Red Kestrel (USA)**[24] 1986 4-9-1 **92** .... NCallan 17 (K A Ryan) *in tch: rdn over 3f out: wknd over 2f out* **16/1**	58
4060	**15**	14	**Pevensey (IRE)**[34] 1696 7-8-13 **90** ....(p) ChrisCatlin 13 (J J Quinn) *hld up towards rr of mid-div: rdn and wknd over 2f out: eased* **33/1**	33
-105	**16**	7	**Press The Button (GER)**[30] 1798 6-8-13 **90** .... PatCosgrave 7 (J R Boyle) *disp ld tl 4f out: grad fdd* **16/1**	22

2m 38.2s (-0.70) **Going Correction** 0.0s/f (Good) **16** Ran SP% **128.1**

Speed ratings (Par 109): **102,100,100,100,99 99,98,97,94,92 92,87,84,83,74 69**

toteswinger: 1&2 £7.70, 1&3 £6.60, 2&3 £4.80 CSF £43.22 CT £253.43 TOTE £7.90: £2.20, £1.80, £1.70, £2.40; EX 48.50 Trifecta £307.30 Pool: £2,051.54 - 4.94 winning units..

Owner B Siddle & B D Haynes **Bred** Grangecon Stud **Trained** Lower Beeding, W Sussex

FOCUS

A competitive enough renewal of this event, which was previously known as the Northern Dancer Handicap. The pace was fairly steady and most of the principals were prominent throughout. The winner is generally progressive and the second looks a good guide.

NOTEBOOK

Coin Of The Realm(IRE) was an arguably unlucky fourth in the Great Metropolitan over course and distance in April, after needing to be switched, and has since finished runner-up in a novice hurdle. Always tracking the pace on the inside, he ran on to lead inside the last and scored readily in the end. There could be more to come from the winner on the Flat, although apparently he is likely to concentrate on a hurdles career now. (op 17-2)

Drill Sergeant ran a solid race under top weight, always at the sharp end if not actually leading this time and battling on well to finally get past Martyr, only for Coin Of The Realm to quickly sweep past the pair of them. He is tough and consistent, as the handicapper well knows. (op 10-1)

Martyr made a bold show on this bid for a hat-trick, having been raised 6lb for his win in a less competitive race at Newmarket. Going for home in the straight, but pressed all the while by Drill Sergeant, he could produce no extra inside the last. This easier ground was not a problem to him. (op 6-1 tchd 5-1)

Storyland(USA) ◆ did very well to finish where she did from off the pace, as the other principals all raced prominently. This was a much better run than she had produced on her reappearance at Newmarket. (op 8-1 tchd 10-1)

War Party was sixth in the Newmarket race won by Martyr, finishing well from the rear, and he ran a good race under these different tactics. The track did not entirely seem to suit him and he remains worth following. (tchd 16-1)
Group Captain, a place behind today's winner in the Great Met here, plugged on from midfield without threatening the leaders. (op 10-1)
Bureaucrat, last year's winner, was only 2lb higher this time round but was never a factor, although he did stay on late. He did not have the benefit of recent hurdles runs this year. (op 16-1)
Resplendent Light has been dropped 4lb since his last handicap appearance, but remains high enough in the weights. (op 25-1)
Kaleo, who was 3lb out of the handicap, was under pressure before the home turn and stuck on surprisingly well until being eased when beaten.
Love Galore(IRE), again rater keen, was another to stay on a bit when it was all over. Official explanation: jockey said gelding ran too free (op 12-1)
Hot Diamond, representing last year's winning stable, was third in the Swinton Handicap Hurdle on his latest start. Held up at the back here, he had no chance the way this race was run, but did make a modicum of late headway. Official explanation: vet said gelding returned lame (tchd 9-2 and 11-2 and 6-1 in a place)
Bandama(IRE), last year's runner-up, was eased when his chance had gone. Official explanation: jockey said horse lost its action (op 10-1 tchd 12-1)
Red Kestrel(USA) was dropped 3lb after his debut for this yard at York but could do with a bit more help from the handicapper. (op 12-1)

2707 INVESTEC DISTINCTIVE STKS (H'CAP) 6f
5:05 (5:11) (Class 2) (0-100,98) 4-Y-0+

£12,462 (£3,732; £1,866; £934; £466; £234) Stalls High

Form					RPR
-000	1		**Baldemar**[29] 1849 4-8-8 **82** LiamJones 17		94
			(K R Burke) *chsd ldrs: rdn and ev ch 2f out: led over 1f out tl ins fnl f: rallied gamely to ld again last strides*	**33/1**	
060	2	hd	**Mac Gille Eoin**[13] 2297 5-9-2 **90** JimCrowley 7		101
			(J Gallagher) *lw: chsd ldrs: effrt over 2f out: rdn and ev ch 2f out: edgd lft and led ins fnl f: kpt on u.p tl hdd last strides*	**5/1**[2]	
04-1	3	1 1/4	**Something (IRE)**[56] 1212 7-9-5 **93** PaulQuinn 4		103+
			(D Nicholls) *lw: stdd s: t.k.h: hld up in midfield: hdwy over 2f out: chsng ldrs 1f out: keeping on whn short of room and snatched up wl ins fnl f: sn swtchd rt: nt rcvr*	**9/1**	
0-10	4	2	**Northern Dare (IRE)**[31] 1791 5-9-0 **88** FrancisNorton 8		89
			(D Nicholls) *stmbld s: sn rcvrd and chsd ldr: rdn to ld 2f out: sn hdd: keeping on same pce whn n.m.r ins fnl f*	**16/1**	
5430	5	1	**Mutamared (USA)**[34] 1699 9-8-10 **84** (t) NCallan 13		82
			(K A Ryan) *in tch: rdn and effrt 2f out: hung lft and kpt on same pce fr over 1f out*	**25/1**	
-312	6	1/2	**Aye Aye Digby (IRE)**[21] 2078 4-9-0 **88** FergusSweeney 11		95+
			(H Candy) *trckd ldrs: gng wl whn nt clr run 2f out tl over 1f out: hung lft and nt clr run again 1f out: styd on fnl 100yds: nvr able to chal*	**10/3**[1]	
6-10	7	2	**Striking Spirit**[13] 2297 4-9-7 **95** AndrewMullen 16		85
			(D Nicholls) *in tch in midfield: rdn and unable qck over 2f out: edgd lft u.p over 1f out: nvr pce to rch ldrs*	**33/1**	
0-04	8	3/4	**Cape Vale (IRE)**[21] 2093 4-8-8 **82** CatherineGannon 10		69
			(D Nicholls) *sn led: rdn and hdd 2f out: wknd and hung lft fnl f: eased towards fin*	**10/1**	
02-1	9	1	**Piscean (USA)**[16] 2191 4-9-4 **92** TonyCulhane 1		76+
			(T Keddy) *t.k.h: stdd to rr after s: plenty to do 3f out: hdwy 2f out: styng on but nvr gng to rch ldrs whn nt clr run ins fnl f*	**10/1**	
5155	10	1	**Internationaldebut (IRE)**[7] 2502 4-9-4 **92** JohnEgan 14		85+
			(S Parr) *stdd and awkward ldng stalls: sn swtchd lft and hld up towards rr: hdwy but hanging lft fr over 1f out: keeping on but no ch w ldrs whn bdly hmpd fnl 100yds: eased after*	**10/1**	
0000	11	1 1/4	**Ajigolo**[22] 2059 6-9-2 **90** DO'Donohoe 5		67
			(N Wilson) *v.s.a: n.d*	**40/1**	
6230	12	1	**Abraham Lincoln (IRE)**[13] 2297 5-9-7 **95** StephenDonohoe 2		91+
			(D Nicholls) *lw: hld up wl bhd: hdwy over 1f out: styng on but no ch w ldrs whn bdly hmpd fnl 100yds: eased after*	**10/1**	
0246	13	1/2	**Sunrise Safari (IRE)**[14] 2266 6-8-10 **84** (v) AlanMunro 12		56
			(R A Fahey) *taken down early: racd in midfield: nt happy on downhill run and lost pl over 4f out: no ch fnl 3f*	**16/1**	
00-0	14	1 1/4	**Rising Shadow (IRE)**[22] 2059 8-9-1 **89** RichardKingscote 6		57
			(C W Thornton) *s.i.s: a bhd*	**40/1**	
2-00	15	1/2	**Van Bossed (CAN)**[4] 2570 4-9-6 **94** JMurtagh 3		61
			(D Nicholls) *racd in midfield on inner: struggling over 2f out: wl bhd fr over 1f out*	**7/1**[3]	
3620	16	1/2	**Capricorn Run (USA)**[7] 2470 6-9-10 **98** (b) PatCosgrave 15		63
			(A J McCabe) *s.i.s: reminders sn after s: n.d*	**25/1**	

68.36 secs (-1.04) **Going Correction** 0.0s/f (Good) **16 Ran SP% 128.8**
Speed ratings (Par 109): **106,105,104,101,100 99,96,95,94,93 91,90,89,87,87 86**
toteswinger: 1&2 £52.50, 1&3 £84.20, 2&3 £8.00 CSF £192.75 CT £1742.24 TOTE £43.80: £7.30, £1.80, £2.40, £5.70; EX 451.30 Trifecta £1611.60 Part won. Pool: £2,177.92 - 0.50 winning units. Place 6 £153.83, Place 5 £43.96.
Owner A Rhodes Haulage And P Timmins **Bred** Hellwood Stud Farm **Trained** Middleham Moor, N Yorks
■ Stewards' Enquiry : Jim Crowley two-day ban: careless riding (Jun 21-22)
Catherine Gannon three-day ban: careless riding (Jul 16-18)
Liam Jones three-day ban: careless riding (Jun 21-23)

FOCUS
Another competitive sprint handicap, run at a sound gallop, but nothing really got into it from off the pace. The form looks solid enough although a few encountered trouble late on.

NOTEBOOK
Baldemar had struggled in his previous three starts this term, but as a result he had been dropped 6lb to a mark 2lb lower than when he won at Ripon last August. Showing early dash to overcome his wide draw, the winner gained a prominent position chasing the leaders, and found plenty under pressure to see his race out strongly. Arguably best with a little more cut in the ground than he had here, he has a good record at Ripon, and the Great St Wilfrid appeals as a likely target for him later in the summer. (tchd 40-1)
Mac Gille Eoin won this race last year, but an unsuccessful run since meant that he had dropped to a mark 3lb lower this time around. He had clearly been primed for a repeat bid and ran a smashing race in defeat, only losing out narrowly in a duel to the line with Baldemar. Each of his wins on turf have come on an undulating track. (tchd 6-1)
Something(IRE) did best of the six runners representing David Nicholls, who had sent out five of the previous ten winners of this race. Off the track since winning at Kempton in April, he raced keenly through the early stages but looked to be travelling well with two furlongs to run only to find his path blocked, and again inside the last. With a clear run he might well have won, and one or two bookmakers saw enough to clip him a few points for the Wokingham, a race in which he finished fourth two years ago. He certainly has the ability to win a nice handicap off his current mark. (op 7-1)
Northern Dare(IRE) was up there throughout disputing the lead and had every chance if good enough, but he simply ran into some better-treated rivals. That is likely to continue to be the case for the time being. (tchd 20-1 and 25-1 in places)

Mutamared(USA), dropped 3lb since his last outing, travelled well enough into contention but got unbalanced under pressure. He retains ability but is likely to remain vulnerable to younger rivals in this type of race.
Aye Aye Digby(IRE) was well placed entering the straight but Mutamared was on his outside and would not let him out of the pocket he had found himself in. After being snatched up, he stayed on well and the impression left was that he would have done a lot better with a clear run. He remains on an upward curve and capable of defying his current mark. (op 11-2 tchd 3-1)
Striking Spirit had a difficult draw to overcome and struggled to land a blow. (op 25-1)
Cape Vale(IRE) showed good speed but would surely have appreciated easier ground. (op 12-1)
Piscean(USA) is a 5f specialist and raced too keenly. (op 9-1)
Abraham Lincoln(IRE) didn't shape too badly despite being beaten a long way. He had plenty of work to do entering the straight and wasn't being given a hard time in a lost cause when running into trouble on the inside. He has hinted on more than one occasion this term that there is a race to be won with him. (op 9-1 tchd 15-2)
T/Jkpt: Not won. T/Plt: £341.40 to a £1 stake. Pool: £278,162.62. 594.69 winning tickets. T/Qpdt: £14.00 to a £1 stake. Pool: £16,094.84. 848.57 winning tickets. SP

2630 LINGFIELD (L-H)
Saturday, June 6

OFFICIAL GOING: Turf course - good to firm (8.6); all-weather- standard
Wind: Almost nil

2708 COWDEN (S) STKS 1m 4f (P)
5:50 (5:50) (Class 6) 3-Y-0+ £2,047 (£604; £302) Stalls Low

Form					RPR
-022	1		**Medieval Maiden**[15] 2222 6-9-9 47 PaulDoe 4		53
			(Mrs L J Mongan) *hld up in rr: hdwy on outside over 2f out: r.o to ld ins fnl f*	**10/1**	
0212	2	3/4	**Sunset Boulevard (IRE)**[66] 1073 6-10-0 61 ChrisCatlin 12		57
			(Miss Tor Sturgis) *a.p: rdn over 1f out: r.o to go 2nd ins fnl f*	**5/2**[1]	
0-02	3	1/2	**Clipperdown (IRE)**[25] 1962 8-10-0 67 (t) EdwardCreighton 9		56
			(E J Creighton) *hld up: hdwy 1/2-way: rdn to ld over 1f out: kpt on but hdd ins fnl f*	**9/1**	
666-	4	1 3/4	**Pinnacle Point**[18] 7010 4-9-10 52 (be[1]) PatDobbs 13		49
			(G L Moore) *t.k.h: trckd ldr: reminders 5f out: rdn and no ex fr over 1f out*	**25/1**	
2034	5	1 3/4	**Rawdon (IRE)**[10] 2379 8-9-7 70 (bt) KylieManser(7) 6		53+
			(Miss Gay Kelleway) *mid-div: hdwy 4f out: rdn and nt qckn fr over 1f out*	**7/2**[2]	
-036	6	1 1/4	**City Stable (IRE)**[39] 1586 4-10-0 65 NickyMackay 1		49
			(M Wigham) *in tch: outpcd 4f out: rdn and r.o ins fnl f*	**16/1**	
3420	7	nk	**Turner's Touch**[39] 1586 7-9-7 55 (b) JemmaMarshall(7) 3		48
			(G L Moore) *mid-div: nvr plcd to chal*	**16/1**	
006/	8	3/4	**Homebred Star**[729] 2412 8-9-7 36 SimonPearce(7) 5		47
			(G P Enright) *slowly away: hld up: nvr on terms*	**66/1**	
5036	9	3/4	**Cactus King**[25] 1962 6-10-0 68 (b) IanMongan 7		46
			(P M Phelan) *led tl hdd over 1f out: sn wknd*	**15/2**	
2040	10	1 1/4	**Mystic Art (IRE)**[9] 2420 4-9-7 52 RichardRowe(7) 8		44
			(C R Egerton) *trckd ldrs tl wknd over 1f out*	**11/2**[3]	
00-0	11	21	**The Slider**[18] 171 5-9-9 29 (v) FrankieMcDonald 2		5
			(Mrs L C Jewell) *trckd ldrs tl wknd 4f out: t.o*	**80/1**	

2m 34.47s (1.47) **Going Correction** -0.10s/f (Stan) **11 Ran SP% 115.4**
Speed ratings (Par 101): **91,90,90,89,87 87,86,86,85,84 70**
toteswinger: 1&2 £2.30, 1&3 £3.00, 2&3 £2.90 CSF £34.24 TOTE £8.60: £2.40, £1.50, £2.70; EX 32.80.There was no bid for the winner
Owner Condover Racing **Bred** Eclipse Bloodstock Ltd **Trained** Epsom, Surrey
■ Stewards' Enquiry : Richard Rowe one-day ban: used whip when out of contention (Jun 21)

FOCUS
Basement grade and a steady pace. Not form to be getting excited about and the winer probably only had to run somewhere near his recent turf form.

2709 BET API - BETDAQ H'CAP 1m 2f (P)
6:20 (6:21) (Class 6) (0-60,60) 3-Y-0 £2,047 (£604; £302) Stalls Low

Form					RPR
0550	1		**Brett Vale (IRE)**[102] 663 3-9-1 **57** SebSanders 1		76+
			(Sir Mark Prescott) *trckd ldr: led over 2f out: rdn clr over 1f out: v easily*	**11/2**[2]	
4-20	2	7	**Litenup (IRE)**[86] 817 3-8-13 **55** WandersonD'Avila 5		57
			(A J Lidderdale) *led tl hdd over 2f out: kpt on to hold 2nd but no ch w wnr fr over 1f out*	**20/1**	
1033	3	3/4	**Good Buy Dubai (USA)**[7] 2489 3-9-1 **60** MarcHalford(3) 10		61
			(J R Best) *slowly away: in rr tl hdwy over 1f out: styd on fnl f: nvr nrr*	**5/2**[1]	
6200	4	3	**Wahan (USA)**[8] 2461 3-8-11 **53** J-PGuillambert 8		48
			(C E Brittain) *chsd ldrs: rdn over 4f out: hld position but one pce fnl 2f*	**8/1**	
0031	5	1/2	**Rose Of Coma (IRE)**[12] 2333 3-8-9 **51** AdrianMcCarthy 13		45
			(Miss Gay Kelleway) *towards rr: mde sme hdwy ins fnl 2f but nvr nr to chal*	**20/1**	
0003	6	1/2	**Fleur De'Lion (IRE)**[10] 2380 3-8-3 **48** DavidProbert(3) 12		41
			(S Kirk) *in tch: rdn over 2f out: sn outpcd*	**10/1**	
20-0	7	3 3/4	**Winterbrook King**[16] 2206 3-9-4 **60** LPKeniry 3		45
			(J R Best) *towards rr: nvr nr to chal*	**25/1**	
3000	8	5	**L'Arco Baleno (IRE)**[9] 2417 3-9-0 **56** PatDobbs 9		31
			(S A Callaghan) *a towards rr*	**18/1**	
0-0	9	1	**Native Dame (IRE)**[11] 2350 3-8-11 **53** PaulFitzsimons 4		26
			(Edgar Byrne) *hld up: rdn over 2f out: nvr got into r*	**22/1**	
000-	10	1/2	**Clear Hand**[248] 6397 3-9-0 **56** TGMcLaughlin 14		28
			(B R Millman) *a in rr*	**33/1**	
2260	11	1/2	**Calling Victory (FR)**[15] 2246 3-8-13 **60** AndreaAtzeni(5) 2		31
			(M Botti) *t.k.h: prom tl wknd wl over 1f out*	**8/1**	
0-06	12	10	**Thegirlsgonewild (USA)**[16] 2199 3-8-13 **55** ChrisCatlin 6		6
			(H J L Dunlop) *mid-div: rdn 3f out: sn btn*	**10/1**	
000-	13	1 1/2	**Caught On Camera**[237] 6682 3-9-4 **60** TPQueally 11		8
			(M L W Bell) *mid-div: dropped to rr fnl 3f*	**13/2**[3]	

2m 6.18s (-0.42) **Going Correction** -0.10s/f (Stan) **13 Ran SP% 123.6**
Speed ratings (Par 97): **97,91,90,88,88 87,84,80,79,79 79,71,69**
toteswinger: 1&2 Not won., 1&3 £5.00, 2&3 £13.50 CSF £119.22 CT £349.66 TOTE £6.50: £2.70, £8.80, £1.50; EX 157.60.
Owner G D Waters **Bred** Mrs O Murtagh **Trained** Newmarket, Suffolk

FOCUS
A moderate handicap won easily by the well-handicapped Brett Vale. He was value for extra and will be hard to beat in the short term. The form behind him is sound enough.

Brett Vale(IRE) ◆ Official explanation: trainer's rep said, regarding apparent improvement in form, that the gelding had benefited from a step up in trip, and that horses from the yard had previously shown signs of being under the weather.

2710 HARTFIELD MAIDEN STKS — 1m (P)
6:50 (6:52) (Class 5) 3-Y-O — **£2,729** (£806; £403) **Stalls High**

Form — RPR

25 **1** **El Loco Uno (USA)**[33] 1729 3-9-3 0 .... TPQueally 9 86+
(H R A Cecil) *mid-div on outside: rdn and hdwy to go 2nd 1f out: led ins fnl f: rdn out* **7/2**[2]

63 **2** *nk* **Mared (USA)**[23] 2002 3-9-3 0 .... ShaneKelly 1 85+
(J Noseda) *led tl rdn and hdd ins fnl f: no ex cl home* **5/1**[3]

3-3 **3** *1 ½* **Ebiayn (FR)**[49] 1350 3-9-3 0 .... RHills 7 82+
(M A Jarvis) *a.p: wnt 2nd over 2f out tl 1f out: kpt on but nt qckn ins fnl f* **10/11**[1]

03 **4** *6* **Countenance**[20] 2105 3-9-3 0 .... LiamJones 5 68
(W J Haggas) *trckd ldr to over 2f out: one pce fr over 1f out* **20/1**

-40 **5** *2* **King's Masque**[33] 1730 3-9-3 0 .... DO'Donohoe 6 64
(W R Muir) *in tch: rdn 2f out: one pce after* **33/1**

0-3 **6** *nse* **Turning Top (IRE)**[9] 2416 3-8-12 0 .... PatDobbs 4 58
(S A Callaghan) *nvr bttr than mid-div* **9/1**

7 *3 ¾* **Moojeh (IRE)** 3-8-12 0 .... StephenDonohoe 10 50
(E A L Dunlop) *in rr: rdn over 2f out: nvr on terms* **33/1**

8 *4* **Pellinore (USA)** 3-8-12 0 .... LPKeniry 12 41
(E F Vaughan) *in tch tl rdn 1/2-way* **20/1**

9 *nk* **Lady Lam** 3-8-5 0 .... MatthewDavies(7) 11 40
(George Baker) *a towards rr* **80/1**

40 **10** *nk* **Gaselee (USA)**[113] 529 3-8-12 0 .... ChrisCatlin 3 39
(Rae Guest) *a struggling in rr* **80/1**

11 *1 ½* **Starkat** 3-8-12 0 .... KirstyMilczarek 8 36
(J A R Toller) *mid-div: outpcd fr 1/2-way* **50/1**

3- **12** *80* **Rapid Light**[182] 7578 3-8-12 0 .... SebSanders 2 —
(E A L Dunlop) *chsd ldrs tl dropped out qckly 1/2-way: t.o* **25/1**

1m 37.42s (-0.78) **Going Correction** -0.10s/f (Stan) **12 Ran SP% 125.0**
Speed ratings (Par 99): **99,98,97,91,89 89,85,81,81,80 79,—**
toteswinger: 1&2 £1.40, 1&3 £2.20, 2&3 £1.60 CSF £20.75 TOTE £4.60: £1.50, £1.60, £1.10; EX 17.40.
Owner H E Sheikh Sultan Bin Khalifa Al Nahyan **Bred** Sultan Bin Khalifa Al Nahyan **Trained** Newmarket, Suffolk

FOCUS
Not much strength in depth to this maiden and the first three, who dominated the market, finished clear. All three looks useful and the first two reproduced their Kempton form from last month.
Countenance Official explanation: jockey said gelding hung right on the bends
Rapid Light Official explanation: jockey said filly stopped quickly

2711 EUROPEAN BREEDERS' FUND MAIDEN FILLIES' STKS — 6f
7:20 (7:20) (Class 5) 2-Y-O — **£3,561** (£1,059; £529; £264) **Stalls High**

Form — RPR

1 **Chachamaidee (IRE)** 2-9-0 0 .... TPQueally 3 79+
(H R A Cecil) *slowly away and t.k.h: picked up to go 2nd over 1f out: r.o wl to ld ins fnl f* **5/4**[1]

5 **2** *1 ¼* **Hasty (IRE)**[23] 2017 2-9-0 0 .... MichaelHills 8 71
(B W Hills) *hld up: swtchd lft over 1f out: kpt on to go 2nd cl home* **9/4**[2]

030 **3** *shd* **Mrs Boss**[22] 2054 2-8-11 0 .... JamesMillman(3) 6 71
(B R Millman) *led tl rdn and hdd ins fnl f: lost 2nd last strides* **9/2**[3]

4 *3* **Pastel Blue (IRE)** 2-9-0 0 .... ChrisCatlin 4 62
(M L W Bell) *t.k.h: trckd ldr tl wknd over 1f out* **14/1**

5 *nk* **Areeda (IRE)** 2-9-0 0 .... SebSanders 7 61
(C E Brittain) *hld up: rdn over 2f out: nvr got into r* **9/1**

1m 10.87s (-0.33) **Going Correction** -0.125s/f (Firm) **5 Ran SP% 110.1**
Speed ratings (Par 90): **97,95,95,91,90**
toteswinger: 1&2 £4.70 CSF £4.29 TOTE £2.40: £1.40, £1.60; EX 4.60.
Owner R A H Evans **Bred** Cheval Court Stud **Trained** Newmarket, Suffolk

FOCUS
A small field but quite an informative little event.

NOTEBOOK
Chachamaidee(IRE), a 135,000gns daughter of 2000 Guineas winner Footstepsinthesand, got off the mark at the first time of asking despite plenty going against her. Slowly away and green as she charted a wider course than her rivals, she proved very difficult to settle, understandable given she saw so much daylight, but displayed an impressive cruising speed. She is bred to want further in time, so may head to the Albany Stakes rather than the Queen Mary. (op 11-8 tchd 6-4)
Hasty(IRE) took a big step forward on her modest debut effort and also looks a nice filly. She had to wait to get a run but, once switched out, she stayed on well. Given her dam won over 1m4f, she will probably be better suited by a stiffer test of stamina. (op 5-2 tchd 11-4 in a place)
Mrs Boss bounced back from a disappointing effort in Listed company at York last time. She's got plenty of speed and the drop back to 5f can see her get off the mark. (op 6-1 tchd 13-2)
Pastel Blue(IRE) shaped with some promise and can improve. (op 10-1 tchd 9-1)
Areeda(IRE) wasn't beaten far and is another who will benefit for this first experience. (op 6-1)

2712 BETDAQ THE BETTING EXCHANGE FILLIES' H'CAP — 5f
7:50 (7:50) (Class 5) (0-70,70) 3-Y-O+ — **£3,070** (£906; £453) **Stalls High**

Form — RPR

0243 **1** **Feelin Foxy**[7] 2472 5-9-11 67 .... TPQueally 8 77
(J G Given) *mde all: r.o strly fnl f* **11/4**[2]

-452 **2** *1* **Matterofact (IRE)**[7] 2492 6-9-9 65 .... TGMcLaughlin 2 71
(M S Saunders) *a.p on on outside: chsd wnr fr over 1f out* **5/1**[3]

3200 **3** *1 ¾* **Affirmatively**[25] 1970 4-8-4 51 oh6 .... (bt) AndreaAtzeni(5) 1 51
(A W Carroll) *in rr: hdwy fr over 1f out to go 3rd ins fnl f* **25/1**

245 **4** *hd* **Ask Jenny (IRE)**[9] 2418 7-9-2 58 .... RobertWinston 5 57
(Patrick Morris) *s.i.s: hdwy fnl f: nvr nrr* **7/1**

-045 **5** *1 ¾* **Freepressionist**[12] 2321 3-9-0 63 .... AlanMunro 6 53
(R A Teal) *in tch: rdn fr 2f out: fdd fnl f* **6/1**

0505 **6** *1* **Ishibee (IRE)**[1] 2680 5-8-9 51 oh4 .... (p) NeilChalmers 7 40
(J J Bridger) *sn rdn: no hdwy ins fnl 2f* **10/1**

-506 **7** *¾* **Diane's Choice**[8] 2460 6-9-2 61 .... (e[1]) DavidProbert(3) 3 48
(Miss Gay Kelleway) *sn pushed along: nvr on terms* **12/1**

5/0- **8** *1 ½* **Littlemisssunshine (IRE)**[227] 6915 4-10-0 70 .... (p) LPKeniry 4 51
(J S Moore) *chsd ldrs: rdn 2f out: sn wknd* **9/4**[1]

57.20 secs (-1.00) **Going Correction** -0.125s/f (Firm)
WFA 3 from 4yo+ 7lb **8 Ran SP% 121.5**
Speed ratings (Par 100): **103,101,98,98,95 93,92,90**
toteswinger: 1&2 £1.10, 1&3 £4.00, 2&3 £8.80 CSF £18.31 CT £296.10 TOTE £4.10: £1.80, £1.50, £7.00; EX 14.00.
Owner Danethorpe Racing Partnership **Bred** Bearstone Stud **Trained** Willoughton, Lincs

FOCUS
Run of the mill, straightforward handicap form featuring mainly exposed types.

2713 BETDAQ ON 0870 178 1221 H'CAP — 7f
8:20 (8:20) (Class 5) (0-70,70) 4-Y-O+ — **£3,238** (£963; £481; £240) **Stalls High**

Form — RPR

-324 **1** **Halsion Chancer**[10] 2387 5-9-5 68 .... RobertWinston 8 78
(J R Best) *t.k.h: a in tch: led over 1f out: rdn clr* **3/1**[1]

1-30 **2** *2 ¼* **Balata**[118] 457 4-9-7 70 .... TGMcLaughlin 10 75
(B R Millman) *in rr on ins: rdn and hdwy fr over 1f out to go 2nd ins fnl f* **7/2**[2]

2420 **3** *1 ¾* **Gazboolou**[16] 2188 5-9-6 69 .... FergusSweeney 7 69+
(David Pinder) *a.p: kpt on but nt qckn fnl f* **4/1**[3]

600 **4** *nk* **Star Strider**[12] 2330 5-8-13 62 .... StephenDonohoe 2 61
(Miss Gay Kelleway) *t.k.h: in tch tl no imp fnl f* **12/1**

-243 **5** *½* **Millfields Dreams**[11] 2352 10-8-12 66 .... (p) MarkCoumbe(5) 3 64
(G C Bravery) *trckd ldr tl wknd appr fnl f* **7/1**

6000 **6** *4 ½* **Trivia (IRE)**[12] 2330 5-7-13 51 oh1 .... DavidProbert(3) 4 37
(J J Bridger) *led tl wknd over 1f out* **20/1**

5000 **7** *4* **Glencalvie (IRE)**[29] 1833 8-9-0 63 .... (v) IanMongan 6 39
(J Akehurst) *awkward leaving stalls: sn rdn and nvr on terms* **7/1**

050- **8** *2 ¾* **Ejeed (USA)**[359] 2982 4-8-10 62 .... KevinGhunowa(3) 5 31
(Miss Z C Davison) *prom on outside tl wknd 2f out* **20/1**

030 **9** *hd* **Reigning Monarch (USA)**[4] 2564 6-8-2 51 oh4 .... CatherineGannon 1 19
(Miss Z C Davison) *trckd ldrs tl outpcd 1/2-way* **12/1**

0300 **10** *3 ¾* **Fly In Johnny (IRE)**[12] 2330 4-8-3 52 oh6 ow1 .... ChrisCatlin 9 10
(J J Bridger) *a bhd* **16/1**

1m 21.82s (-1.48) **Going Correction** -0.125s/f (Firm) **10 Ran SP% 123.0**
Speed ratings (Par 103): **103,100,98,98,97 92,87,84,84,80**
toteswinger: 1&2 £2.50, 1&3 £5.00, 2&3 £4.30 CSF £14.37 CT £42.63 TOTE £3.80: £1.50, £1.60, £1.90; EX 16.70 Place 6 £10.11, Place 5 £4.57.
Owner Halsion Ltd **Bred** Mrs S Hansford **Trained** Hucking, Kent

FOCUS
This didn't look particularly strong on paper with most of these having a bit to prove at present. Slightly suspect form, best rated through the runner-up.
Gazboolou Official explanation: jockey said gelding was denied a clear run
Glencalvie(IRE) Official explanation: jockey said gelding missed the break
T/Plt: £8.80 to a £1 stake. Pool: £61,183.94. 5,042.18 winning tickets. T/Qpdt: £3.20 to a £1 stake. Pool: £4,631.39. 987.70 winning tickets. JS

2448 MUSSELBURGH (R-H)
Saturday, June 6

OFFICIAL GOING: Good (good to firm in places; 7.1)
Wind: Light, half behind Weather: Overcast and showers

2714 TOTEPOOL EDINBURGH CASTLE CONDITIONS STKS — 5f
2:20 (2:21) (Class 2) 2-Y-O
£15,577 (£4,665; £2,332; £1,167; £582; £292) **Stalls Low**

Form — RPR

1 **1** **Capercaillie (USA)**[8] 2449 2-8-9 0 .... GregFairley 1 90+
(M Johnston) *cl up on stands' rail: effrt 2f out: rdn to ld 1f out: styd on wl* **9/4**[1]

51 **2** *2 ¼* **Reignier**[18] 2153 2-9-0 0 .... AndrewElliott 2 87
(K R Burke) *cl up: effrt 2f out: rdn over 1f out and ev ch tl drvn and nt qckn ins fnl f* **8/1**

221 **3** *½* **Dancing Freddy (IRE)**[18] 2161 2-9-0 0 .... PaulHanagan 6 85
(J G Given) *outpcd in rr: hdwy 1/2-way: rdn wl over 1f out: styd on ins fnl f: nrst fin* **12/1**

216 **4** *1 ¼* **Dispol Keasha**[22] 2054 2-8-9 0 .... PhillipMakin 3 76
(T D Barron) *sn led: rdn along 2f out: drvn and hdd 1f out: wknd* **6/1**[3]

2221 **5** *1 ¾* **Archers Road (IRE)**[14] 2260 2-9-9 0 .... SamHitchcott 10 83
(M R Channon) *chsd ldrs: rdn 2f out: edgd lft and no imp appr fnl f* **3/1**[2]

6 *½* **North Central (USA)** 2-8-8 0 .... PaulMulrennan 9 67
(J Howard Johnson) *chsd ldrs: rdn 2f out: sn wknd* **16/1**

10 **7** *shd* **Eternal Instinct**[22] 2054 2-8-9 0 .... DanielTudhope 5 67
(J S Goldie) *in tch: effrt 2f out: sn rdn and no imp* **11/1**

2032 **8** *1* **Mr Smithson (IRE)**[12] 2311 2-8-11 0 .... DavidAllan 4 66
(B Ellison) *a towards rr* **40/1**

021 **9** *¾* **Koo And The Gang (IRE)**[19] 2128 2-8-11 0 .... TomEaves 7 63
(B Ellison) *prom: rdn along over 2f out and sn wknd* **20/1**

6402 **10** *2* **Goodbye Earl (IRE)**[7] 2484 2-8-6 0 .... SladeO'Hara 8 51
(A Berry) *prom on outer whn sddle slipped after 1f: sn edgd bdly rt and bhd* **18/1**

58.19 secs (-2.21) **Going Correction** -0.35s/f (Firm) **10 Ran SP% 115.5**
Speed ratings (Par 99): **103,99,98,96,93 93,92,91,90,86**
toteswinger: 1&2 £3.00, 1&3 £7.30, 2&3 £27.60 CSF £20.83 TOTE £2.70: £1.70, £1.80, £2.10; EX 17.20 Trifecta £83.90 Part won. Pool: £113.40 - 0.30 winning units..
Owner Sheikh Hamdan Bin Mohammed Al Maktoum **Bred** R Michael O'Malley **Trained** Middleham Moor, N Yorks

FOCUS
Despite a little rain overnight, the going remained on the quick side. This looked a decent sprint contest for juveniles and the form should be solid. The first two home were drawn one and two.

NOTEBOOK
Capercaillie(USA) ◆ only just prevailed over course and distance on her previous outing, but is highly regarded and showed that she is going in the right direction by winning with plenty in hand. Always prominent down the stands' rail, she moved clear inside the final furlong to win with authority. The jockey feels as though she will get another furlong without a problem. A trip south for the Queen Mary could be on the agenda and she collected this victory is a quicker time that she recorded on debut. (tchd 3-1)
Reignier, another course-and-distance winner, tried in vain to go with the winner in the final furlong but was readily held. He appears to be progressing though, and can land more races. (tchd 13-2)
Dancing Freddy(IRE) had gone close on all of his previous three starts - winning last time - and liked to make the running. However, he was soon outpaced here before staying on strongly in the final stages. (op 14-1 tchd 16-1)
Dispol Keasha showed tons of pace last time in Listed company and again in this, but was firmly put in her place a furlong out. (tchd 13-2)
Archers Road(IRE) was the most experienced of these and took the Brian Yeardley Continental Two-Year-Old Trophy at Beverley last time. Under the maximum penalty, he struggled to make much impact after sitting off the pace. (op 7-2 tchd 5-2)
North Central(USA), a brother to the stable's 2008 Royal Ascot 2yo winner South Central, made £47,500 at breeze-ups but needs more time on this evidence. (tchd 20-1)
Eternal Instinct, behind Dispol Keasha last time, had every chance but found the company too hot again. (op 10-1 tchd 9-1)

Goodbye Earl(IRE) Official explanation: jockey said saddle slipped

2715 TOTESCOOP6 TRADESMAN'S DERBY H'CAP — 1m 4f 100y

2:50 (2:51) (Class 2) (0-90,86) 3-Y-O

£24,924 (£7,464; £3,732; £1,868; £932; £468) **Stalls** High

Form				RPR
0-20	1		**Quai D'Orsay**[14] 2275 3-9-7 **86** JoeFanning 10	99
			(M Johnston) *mde all: rdn along over 2f out: hrd pressed and drvn over 1f out: slt ld whn hung rt ins fnl f: sn clr and styd on strly* **9/1**	
1-14	2	3 ¾	**Kings Destiny**[31] 1792 3-9-7 **86** PhilipRobinson 9	96+
			(M A Jarvis) *t.k.h: trckd ldrs: cl up fr 1/2-way: effrt on inner to chal 3f out: rdn 2f out and ev ch: drvn whn n.m.r and hmpd jst ins fnl f: nt rcvr* **2/1**[1]	
5-12	3	2	**Non Dom (IRE)**[18] 2152 3-8-3 **75** JamieKyne(7) 11	78
			(H Morrison) *dwlt and towards rr: hdwy into midfield 1/2-way: effrt on outer 3f out: rdn along 2f out: drvn and kpt on fnl f* **11/2**[3]	
1551	4	hd	**Citizenship**[18] 2152 3-8-3 **73** MCGeran(5) 6	76
			(Ian Williams) *prom: rdn along 3f out: drvn 2f out and sn one pce* **20/1**	
2320	5	1	**Light Dubai (IRE)**[23] 2008 3-8-5 **70** SamHitchcott 5	71
			(M R Channon) *hld up towards rr: hdwy over 3f out: rdn over 2f out: drvn and no imp appr fnl f* **50/1**	
51-2	6	nk	**Alanbrooke**[22] 2038 3-9-2 **81** GregFairley 8	82+
			(M Johnston) *s.i.s and bhd: steayed on fnl 3f: nvr nr ldrs* **5/2**[2]	
3120	7	1 ¼	**Fin Vin De Leu (GER)**[36] 1643 3-9-0 **79** AndrewElliott 2	78
			(M Johnston) *in tch: rdn along over 3f out: sn one pce* **50/1**	
5353	8	¾	**Tropical Bachelor (IRE)**[10] 2371 3-7-12 **70** DeclanCannon(7) 1	68
			(T J Pitt) *prom: rdn along 3f out: grad wknd fnl 2f* **40/1**	
24-0	9	1 ½	**Cosmic Sun**[24] 1992 3-9-1 **80** PaulHanagan 12	75+
			(R A Fahey) *midfield whn hung bdly lft and rn wd bnd after 2f: bhd after* **12/1**	
3-13	10	3 ½	**Holyrood**[21] 2077 3-9-7 **86** (v1) TomEaves 3	76
			(Sir Michael Stoute) *trckd ldrs: rdn along wl over 2f out and sn wknd* **7/1**	
2-02	11	1 ¼	**Peaceful Rule (USA)**[11] 2364 3-8-4 **69** AdrianTNicholls 4	57
			(D Nicholls) *a in rr* **40/1**	
0033	12	2 ¼	**Toujours Souriante**[11] 2357 3-7-7 **65** MatthewLawson(7) 7	49+
			(M Johnston) *towards rr whn hmpd bnd after 2f: bhd after* **40/1**	

2m 42.06s (0.06) **12 Ran SP% 123.5**

toteswinger: 1&2 £7.60, 1&3 £9.70, 2&3 £5.40 CSF £27.32 CT £115.10 TOTE £12.10: £3.30, £1.40, £2.50; EX 46.60 Trifecta £154.40 Part won. Pool: £208.77 - 0.60 winning units..

Owner Sheikh Hamdan Bin Mohammed Al Maktoum **Bred** Miss K Rausing **Trained** Middleham Moor, N Yorks

■ Stewards' Enquiry : Joe Fanning three-day ban: careless riding (Jun 21-23)

FOCUS

A useful-looking affair in which two of three topweights dominated the finish. The early gallop did not look anything special. Indeed, the leader seemed to slow it right down at halfway, and the first four were always prominent. The form makes sense and the first two showed improvement.

NOTEBOOK

Quai D'Orsay ◆ could be forgiven his previous effort on heavy ground, as his form before that had looked very sound (he was in front of Kings Destiny at Chester). Allowed a fairly easy lead, he was made to battle as he pressed on up the home straight, but was a clear winner in the end. He may be the type to make his way to Royal Ascot but he and the runner-up paid a handsome compliment to the Sir Mark Prescott-trained Braveheart Move, who comfortably beat them at Chester. Official explanation: trainer had no explanation for the apparent improvement in form (op 12-1)

Kings Destiny was a little unlucky at Chester when chasing his third win in a row, and was again the recipient of bad fortune. The best horse probably won here, but he did badly impede Kings Destiny inside the final furlong, which made his effort come to an abrupt halt. He still managed to finish well clear of the bunch for third. (op 5-2 tchd 11-4)

Non Dom(IRE) won on his handicap debut and then only narrowly failed to follow that up. He lacked the speed of the first two when the tempo increased but stayed on nicely. Official explanation: jockey said gelding missed the break (op 17-2 tchd 10-1)

Citizenship had provided Ian Williams with a couple of wins since joining him and finished in front of Nom Dom, albeit narrowly, last time. The margin was much the same here, although reversed, and he appeared to run to form. (tchd 22-1)

Light Dubai(IRE), raised in trip, was behind early before staying on. It was not easy to know whether she did not stay or was not up to the grade. (op 66-1)

Alanbrooke ◆ had improved with every start but got away slowly here, and lost some ground. However, he was soon back on terms and looked to be undone by the race turning into a bit of a sprint. He was staying on strongly inside the final furlong and is not one to give up on yet. Official explanation: jockey said colt was slowly away (op 7-4)

Cosmic Sun Official explanation: jockey said gelding hung badly left-handed on stands bend

Holyrood, in a visor for the first time, dropped away tamely and cannot be back with any confidence until showing more. (tchd 11-2)

2716 TOTESWINGER SCOTTISH SPRINT CUP STKS (HERITAGE H'CAP) — 5f

3:20 (3:25) (Class 2) (0-105,105) 3-Y-O+

£24,924 (£7,464; £3,732; £1,868; £932; £468) **Stalls** Low

Form				RPR
-200	1		**Pavershooz**[9] 2405 4-7-13 **80** DuranFentiman 5	91
			(N Wilson) *prom: effrt to ld over 1f out: rdn ins fnl f and kpt on strly* **28/1**	
0553	2	1	**River Falcon**[7] 2502 9-8-12 **93** DanielTudhope 14	100
			(J S Goldie) *in rr: swtchd outside and gd hdwy 2f out: rdn to chse ldrs over 1f out: kpt on strly ins fnl f* **12/1**	
-200	3	shd	**Masta Plasta (IRE)**[14] 2272 6-9-10 **105** AdrianTNicholls 2	112
			(D Nicholls) *cl up on stands' rail: effrt 2f out: sn rdn and n.m.r: swtchd rt over 1f and styd on strly ins fnl f* **8/1**	
-444	4	hd	**Hamish McGonagall**[7] 2502 4-9-3 **98** DavidAllan 17	104
			(T D Easterby) *a cl up: effrt 2f out: sn rdn and ev ch tl drvn and nt qckn ins fnl f* **13/2**[2]	
-334	5	hd	**City Dancer (IRE)**[23] 2016 3-8-0 **95** BillyCray(7) 1	98
			(A Berry) *dwlt and in rr: hdwy wl over 1f out: rdn and nt clr run appr fnl f: swtchd lft and styd on strly ins fnl f: nrst fin* **9/1**	
-501	6	shd	**Ishetoo**[7] 2502 5-8-8 **96** JamieKyne(7) 12	101
			(A Dickman) *sn pushed along towards rr: hdwy wl over 1f out: sn rdn and styd on wl fnl f: nrst fin* **17/2**	
1130	7	¾	**Nickel Silver**[55] 1227 4-7-12 **79** (b) SilvestreDeSousa 10	82
			(B Smart) *cl up: rdn wl over 1f out and ev ch tl drvn ent fnl f and wknd* **18/1**	
01	8	½	**Mandurah (IRE)**[35] 1685 5-7-9 **83** oh1 ow4 AdeleMulrennan(7) 9	84
			(D Nicholls) *chsd ldrs: rdn along wl over 1f out: wknd appr fnl f* **16/1**	
05-1	9	nk	**Total Impact**[11] 2363 6-8-4 **85** PaulHanagan 4	85
			(R A Fahey) *chsd ldrs: effrt 2f out: sn rdn and no imp appr fnl f* **6/1**[1]	
-106	10	shd	**Hitchens (IRE)**[7] 2502 4-9-9 **104** PhillipMakin 13	103
			(T D Barron) *dwlt and in rr: hdwy on outer 2f out: rdn over 1f out: no imp ins fnl f* **6/1**[1]	
5-00	11	¾	**Stolt (IRE)**[11] 2363 5-8-2 **83** AndrewElliott 16	80
			(N Wilson) *led: rdn along 1/2-way: drvn and hdd over 1f out: wknd* **66/1**	
2361	12	½	**Rothesay Dancer**[3] 2591 6-7-12 **82** 6ex ow3 KellyHarrison(3) 7	77
			(J S Goldie) *towards rr: effrt and sme hdwy over 1f out: nvr a factor* **16/1**	
3153	13	1 ¼	**Steelcut**[21] 2095 5-7-13 **80** DaleGibson 8	70
			(R A Fahey) *in tch: effrt 2f out: sn rdn: hld whn drvn and n.m.r over 1f out wknd after* **28/1**	
01-0	14	¾	**Roker Park (IRE)**[22] 2059 4-8-8 **89** (b1) PaulMulrennan 3	77
			(K A Ryan) *a in rr* **16/1**	
-111	15	1 ½	**Jaconet (USA)**[37] 1627 4-8-5 **86** (b) JoeFanning 6	68
			(T D Barron) *chsd ldrs: rdn along wl over 1f out and sn wknd* **7/1**[3]	

57.52 secs (-2.88) **Going Correction** -0.35s/f (Firm)

WFA 3 from 4yo+ 7lb **15 Ran SP% 125.0**

Speed ratings (Par 109): **109,107,107,106,106 106,105,104,103,103 102,101,99,98,96**

toteswinger: 1&2 £82.30, 1&3 £56.00, 2&3 £20.20 CSF £340.86 CT £3015.29 TOTE £42.00: £7.70, £4.80, £3.20; EX 423.10 Trifecta £642.30 Part won. Pool: £867.99 - 0.30 winning units..

Owner Mrs Michael John Paver **Bred** Exors Of The Late M J Paver **Trained** Flaxton, N Yorks

FOCUS

This promised to be run at a hectic pace, considering the number of front-runners that took part, and the gallop looked strong. The winner won nicely but those behind finished in a heap. Typically solid form.

NOTEBOOK

Pavershooz, dropping to 5f for the first time in his career, was a fairly easy winner after coming towards the near-side rail late on. This looks a surprising result against so many established speed merchants, so one can only presume he has more to come at this distance. He could run at York next Friday. (op 25-1)

River Falcon is a grand servant but is without a win since August 2007, mainly because his handicap mark rarely changes. He ran another blinder but was never getting to the winner quickly enough after having plenty of horse to pass over a furlong out. (op 10-1 tchd 9-1)

Masta Plasta(IRE) failed to get involved in the Group 2 Temple Stakes last time, but he'd won on his last start in a handicap. His jockey had the chance to bag the stands' rail and get to the front, but dropped him in, which meant his passage did not look that clear in the latter stages. Once out, he finished well but it was too late. It was a fine effort under his big weight. (op 10-1 tchd 13-2)

Hamish McGonagall has made up into a decent sprinter and has been wonderfully consistent. He has a good record at this course and shaped well again, from his high draw, after holding every chance. (op 8-1 tchd 17-2)

City Dancer(IRE) ◆ has quickly made up into a very useful filly. Having only her seventh start, she finished well towards the stands' side after meeting trouble and surely has more to come. (op 8-1 tchd 15-2)

Ishetoo won the York heritage handicap that a few of these ran in last time but could not confirm the form with the second or fourth after getting behind. It was still a decent effort, however. (op 8-1)

Total Impact landed a punt on his return to action last time, but could make no impression when the race took shape. (op 11-1 tchd 12-1)

Hitchens(IRE) finished strongly again but never really got involved. (op 11-1)

Jaconet(USA), chasing a four-timer, had been in tremendous heart since June last year and improved immeasurably, but failed to fire this time after being close up. (op 6-1 tchd 5-1)

2717 JENNERS SCOTTISH SPRINT CONSOLATION H'CAP — 5f

4:05 (4:08) (Class 3) (0-105,82) 3-Y-O+ **£7,771** (£2,312; £1,155; £577) **Stalls** Low

Form				RPR
5231	1		**Blue Tomato**[8] 2451 8-9-5 **72** AdrianTNicholls 11	84
			(D Nicholls) *towards rr and rdn along after 2f: hdwy 2f out: swtchd rt and rdn ent fnl f: qcknd to ld last 100yds* **10/1**	
1-15	2	nk	**Titus Andronicus (IRE)**[22] 2058 3-9-3 **82** AmyRyan(5) 7	90
			(K A Ryan) *led: rdn over 1f out: drvn ins fnl f: hdd and nt qckn last 100yds* **15/8**[1]	
5406	3	1 ½	**Silvanus (IRE)**[8] 2451 4-8-9 **67** (p) PatrickDonaghy(5) 8	73
			(I Semple) *in tch: hdwy wl over 1f out: rdn and styd on ins fnl f: nrst fin* **16/1**	
6614	4	1 ¼	**Restless Genius (IRE)**[8] 2438 4-9-2 **69** TomEaves 9	71
			(B Ellison) *chsd ldrs: rdn along wl over 1f out: drvn and one pce ent fnl f* **20/1**	
06-0	5	hd	**Lucky Art (USA)**[49] 1368 3-9-8 **82** PaulMulrennan 5	80
			(J Howard Johnson) *cl up: rdn and ev ch over 1f out: drvn and wknd ins fnl f* **33/1**	
-000	6	2 ½	**Lord Of The Reins (IRE)**[15] 2228 5-9-3 **77** JamieKyne(7) 2	69
			(J G Given) *dwlt and in rr: hdwy 2f out: swtchd rt and rdn to chse ldrs over 1f out: no imp ins fnl f* **25/1**	
2202	7	1 ½	**Sandwith**[22] 2032 6-9-7 **74** GregFairley 4	60
			(A G Foster) *chsd ldrs: rdn along wl over 1f out: sn wknd* **11/2**[2]	
3-51	8	1 ½	**Kyzer Chief**[42] 1518 4-8-13 **66** PhillipMakin 6	47
			(R E Barr) *chsd ldrs: rdn along 2f out: sn drvn and wknd* **7/1**[3]	
-001	9	½	**Thunder Bay**[18] 2158 4-8-8 **61** PaulHanagan 10	40
			(R A Fahey) *in tch: rdn along 2f out and sn wknd* **10/1**	
0000	10	¾	**Mr Rooney (IRE)**[1] 2657 6-7-9 **55** oh2 ow4 BillyCray(7) 3	31
			(A Berry) *a towards rr* **40/1**	
005-	11	½	**Barraland**[233] 6765 4-8-13 **71** GaryBartley(5) 1	46
			(J S Goldie) *a in rr* **16/1**	
0-40	12	3 ¼	**Blazing Heights**[15] 2225 6-8-12 **65** DanielTudhope 12	28
			(J S Goldie) *dwlt: a bhd* **14/1**	

57.93 secs (-2.47) **Going Correction** -0.35s/f (Firm)

WFA 3 from 4yo+ 7lb **12 Ran SP% 113.3**

Speed ratings (Par 107): **105,104,102,100,99 95,93,91,90,89 88,83**

toteswinger: 1&2 £3.40, 1&3 £18.60, 2&3 £11.90 CSF £26.47 CT £302.65 TOTE £5.40: £2.50, £1.60, £4.50; EX 22.30.

Owner Dab Hand Racing **Bred** Bearstone Stud **Trained** Sessay, N Yorks

FOCUS

This was run in a time only marginally slower than the feature contest, so the form should be reasonably sound. The winner's best turf run since last summer.

NOTEBOOK

Blue Tomato, without the cheekpieces he wore to victory in a seller last time, showed a really good attitude to get on top inside the final furlong. He is a useful sort on his day and could easily complete the hat-trick. (op 7-1)

Titus Andronicus(IRE) ◆, the winner of two of his previous three starts, is in great heart and was possibly unlucky not to win. He had the run of the race up the stands'-side rail before drifting towards the middle late on. (op 5-2 tchd 13-8 and 11-4 in a place)

Silvanus(IRE) ◆, with cheekpieces fitted, finished behind Blue Tomato last time but may have been a little unlucky not to make that rival work harder here. He had nowhere to go between the pair that fought out the finish in the final 50 yards and had a little left in the locker. (tchd 18-1 in places)

Restless Genius(IRE), dropping in trip, did not run too badly but was readily held once the first three had gone on. (op 25-1)

Lucky Art(USA), beaten over ten lengths on his last two outings, went with the second for much of the race but could not find another gear when that horse quickened. Official explanation: jockey said gelding hung right-handed throughout (op 25-1)

Lord Of The Reins(IRE) was only fairly treated on his winning form and kept on repectably after starting slowly. (op 14-1 tchd 12-1)

Sandwith is a consistent type when on his game, but he disappointed in this. (op 13-2 tchd 5-1)

2718 BALFOUR KILPATRICK SUPPLY CHAIN (S) STKS 1m 1f
4:40 (4:40) (Class 5) 3-Y-O+ **£3,238** (£963; £481; £240) **Stalls** High

Form RPR

-002 **1** **San Silvestro (IRE)**[9] 2404 4-8-10 55..........................(p) BMcHugh(7) 1 61
(Mrs A Duffield) *mde most: jnd and rdn 2f out: drvn and edgd lft ins fnl f: kpt on u.p* **6/1**[3]

2304 **2** *1* **Flores Sea (USA)**[4] 2576 5-9-8 78.................................. PhillipMakin 4 63
(T D Barron) *trckd ldrs: hdwy 3f out: rdn wl over 1f out: sn drvn and kpt on same pce* **4/5**[1]

-066 **3** *hd* **Crux**[8] 2441 7-9-0 46.................................. KellyHarrison(3) 5 58
(R E Barr) *cl up: effrt over 2f out: sn rdn and ev ch tl drvn: switchd rt and no ex ins fnl f* **33/1**

0212 **4** *1 ½* **Lucayan Dancer**[5] 2527 9-9-8 68.................................. AdrianTNicholls 2 60+
(D Nicholls) *hld up in tch: effrt over 2f out and sn rdn: drvn and kpt on ins fnl f: nrst fin* **11/4**[2]

46-0 **5** *½* **Red Skipper (IRE)**[36] 1650 4-9-3 60..........................(p) PaulMulrennan 9 54
(N Wilson) *trckd ldng pair: effrt over 2f out: sn rdn and wknd over 1f out* **16/1**

0-43 **6** *2 ½* **Beaumont Boy**[3] 2594 5-8-10 51..........................(b) BillyCray(7) 6 49
(J A McShane) *hld up in tch: hdwy on inner over 2f out: rdn wl over 1f out and sn no imp* **12/1**

60-0 **7** *½* **Hawkit (USA)**[34] 1690 8-9-0 59.................................. NeilBrown(3) 3 48
(P Monteith) *hld up: a in rr* **14/1**

000/ **8** *18* **Cuccinello (IRE)**[10] 2077 6-8-7 21.................................. SladeO'Hara(5) 7 —
(K W Hogg) *a in rr* **125/1**

1m 53.35s (-1.35) **Going Correction** -0.45s/f (Firm)
WFA 3 from 4yo+ 12lb **8** Ran SP% **120.5**
Speed ratings (Par 103): **88,87,86,85,85 82,82,66**
toteswinger: 1&2 £1.90, 1&3 £14.20, 2&3 £10.50 CSF £11.86 TOTE £8.50: £1.50, £1.10, £5.70; EX 31.70.There was no bid for the winner.

Owner Middleham Park Racing Xiv **Bred** Canice M Farrell Jnr **Trained** Constable Burton, N Yorks

FOCUS
A very ordinary seller which was slowly run. The front pair in the market were a fair way below their best.

Red Skipper(IRE) Official explanation: jockey said gelding hung left-handed in the straight

2719 EDINBURGH EVENING NEWS H'CAP 7f 30y
5:15 (5:15) (Class 5) (0-70,72) 3-Y-O **£3,238** (£963; £481; £240) **Stalls** High

Form RPR

5-41 **1** **Legal Legacy**[18] 2154 3-9-2 **65**.................................. PhillipMakin 3 81
(M Dods) *hld up in tch: hdwy 3f out: chsd ldr wl over 1f out and sn rdn: drvn ins fnl f: styd on to ld nr fin* **1/1**[1]

-563 **2** *hd* **Northern Flyer (GER)**[15] 2236 3-7-10 **52**.......................... JamieKyne(7) 8 67
(J J Quinn) *sn led: rdn and qcknd over 2f out: drvn over 1f out: hdd and no ex nr fin* **5/1**[2]

0201 **3** *6* **Island Chief**[8] 2450 3-9-1 **64**..........................(p) PaulMulrennan 6 63+
(K A Ryan) *cl up tl carried wd bnd after 2f: hdwy to chse ldrs wl over 2f out: sn drvn and kpt on same pce* **8/1**

5152 **4** *1 ¾* **Where's Reiley (USA)**[11] 2365 3-9-2 **68**.......................... NeilBrown(3) 7 62
(T D Barron) *cl up: rdn along wl over 2f out: drvn over 1f out and sn wknd* **6/1**[3]

64-6 **5** *3 ¾* **Quick Gourmet**[22] 2030 3-7-9 **51**.................................. BillyCray(7) 9 35
(J A McShane) *dwlt: plld hrd and hdwy on inner whn hung lft and rn v wd bnd after 2f: racd wd in st and chsd ldng pair tl wknd fnl 2f* **12/1**

2600 **6** *hd* **Imperial Skylight**[13] 2300 3-8-9 **63**.................................. MCGeran(5) 2 47
(M R Channon) *prom: rdn along 3f out: wknd over 2f out* **16/1**

26-2 **7** *25* **Liberty Trail (IRE)**[8] 2450 3-9-9 **72**..........................(p) TomEaves 5 —
(I Semple) *chsd ldrs: rdn along 3f out: drvn over 2f out and sn wknd* **6/1**[3]

00-5 **8** *1* **Dance Society**[12] 2343 3-8-2 **51** oh1..........................(b) DuranFentiman 1 —
(T D Easterby) *in tch: rdn along 1/2-way and sn wknd* **40/1**

1m 27.28s (-3.02) **Going Correction** -0.45s/f (Firm) **8** Ran SP% **122.4**
Speed ratings (Par 99): **99,98,91,89,85 85,56,55**
toteswinger: 1&2 £1.90, 1&3 £4.30, 2&3 £5.30 CSF £7.10 CT £29.21 TOTE £2.50: £1.10, £2.10, £2.10; EX 8.60.

Owner D Vic Roper **Bred** D Dowling **Trained** Denton, Co Durham

FOCUS
There did not look a great deal between this lot on recent form, but two came well clear of their rivals.

Quick Gourmet Official explanation: jockey said filly hung left throughout

Liberty Trail(IRE) Official explanation: trainer had no explanation for the poor form shown

2720 STEPHEN HAY AND ASSOCIATES LTD APPRENTICE H'CAP 1m 6f
5:45 (5:45) (Class 4) (0-85,78) 4-Y-O+ **£6,476** (£1,927; £963; £481) **Stalls** High

Form RPR

-051 **1** **Baizically (IRE)**[2] 2629 6-8-9 **68** 6ex.................................. PaulPickard(5) 2 76
(G A Swinbank) *trckd ldr: led 1/2-way: rdn wl over 2f out: drvn ins fnl f and styd on wl* **5/2**[3]

-350 **2** *shd* **Dolly Penrose**[7] 2486 4-9-7 **78**.................................. MCGeran(3) 3 86
(M R Channon) *hld up in rr: stdy hdwy 3f out: rdn to chse wnr wl over 1f out: drvn ins fnl f: edgd lft and rt: r.o towards fin: jst hld* **13/8**[1]

4341 **3** *14* **Dramatic Solo**[8] 2448 4-8-7 **66**..........................(b) DeclanCannon(5) 6 54
(K R Burke) *trckd ldng pair: effrt over 3f out: rdn along over 2f out: sn one pce* **9/4**[2]

10/0 **4** *2 ½* **My Immortal**[55] 1230 7-9-4 **77**.................................. JamieKyne(5) 5 62
(J J Quinn) *led to 1/2-way: rdn along over 3f out and grad wknd* **13/2**

3m 1.73s (-3.57) **Going Correction** -0.45s/f (Firm) **4** Ran SP% **110.8**
Speed ratings (Par 105): **92,91,83,82**
toteswinger: 1&2 £3.70 CSF £7.11 TOTE £3.60; EX 7.00 Place 6 £59.76, Place 5 £31.94.

Owner Shropshire Wolves **Bred** G And Mrs Middlebrook **Trained** Melsonby, N Yorks

FOCUS
A tactical affair was always likely because of the small field at this sort of distance. The pace was fair considering the conditions and the form is sound enough.

T/Plt: £160.40 to a £1 stake. Pool: £68,234.82. 310.50 winning tickets. T/Qpdt: £36.10 to a £1 stake. Pool: £3,404.13. 69.60 winning tickets. JR

2401 NEWCASTLE (L-H)
Saturday, June 6

OFFICIAL GOING: Good (good to soft in places; 7.7)
Wind: moderate 1/2 behind Weather: fine but breezy

2721 NESTLE "FAWDON CHARITY" MAIDEN AUCTION STKS 6f
6:40 (6:40) (Class 5) 2-Y-O **£3,238** (£963; £481; £240) **Stalls** Low

Form RPR

43 **1** **Refuse To Wait (IRE)**[15] 2226 2-8-8 0.................................. DavidAllan 9 69
(T D Easterby) *trckd ldrs: led over 2f out: 4 l clr 1f out: drvn rt out* **10/1**

4 **2** *1 ½* **Bradford (IRE)**[9] 2388 2-9-3 0.................................. AndrewElliott 8 73
(K R Burke) *mid-div: reminders after 2f: hdwy 2f out: kpt on same pce fnl f* **4/1**[2]

3 *hd* **Opus Dei** 2-9-1 0.................................. JamieMoriarty 7 70
(A J McCabe) *s.i.s: hdwy 2f out: kpt on wl fnl f* **25/1**

4 *8* **Saint Sebastian (IRE)** 2-8-11 0.................................. GrahamGibbons 2 42
(E S McMahon) *dwlt: hung lft and hdwy to chse ldrs on far side after 2f: wknd fnl f* **12/1**

322 **5** *4 ½* **Toga Tiger (IRE)**[12] 2324 2-9-1 0.................................. SamHitchcott 1 33
(M R Channon) *chsd ldrs: wknd over 1f out* **6/1**[3]

22 **6** *2* **Danzoe (IRE)**[11] 2358 2-8-9 0.................................. JimmyQuinn 3 21
(D Donovan) *trckd ldrs: edgd lft over 2f out: wknd over 1f out* **4/5**[1]

7 *2 ½* **High Rolling** 2-8-11 0.................................. PJMcDonald 5 15
(T D Easterby) *s.s: sn trcking ldrs: lost pl over 2f out* **50/1**

8 *5* **Mason Hindmarsh** 2-8-13 0.................................. PaulHanagan 6 —
(Karen McLintock) *chsd ldrs: wknd over 2f out* **33/1**

0 **9** *17* **Havelock Flyer**[12] 2339 2-8-11 0..........................(t) TonyHamilton 4 —
(C Grant) *led tl hdd & wknd over 2f out: bhd whn eased ins fnl f* **66/1**

1m 15.8s (0.60) **Going Correction** +0.05s/f (Good) **9** Ran SP% **116.9**
Speed ratings (Par 93): **98,96,95,85,79 76,73,66,43**
toteswinger: 1&2 £7.50, 1&3 Not won, 2&3 Not won CSF £49.10 TOTE £9.80: £1.50, £1.90, £4.40; EX 21.60.

Owner Ryedale Partners No 8 **Bred** Dermot & Catherine Dwan **Trained** Great Habton, N Yorks

■ Stewards' Enquiry : Sam Hitchcott one-day ban: failing to keep straight from stalls (Jun 21)

FOCUS
This looked a weak maiden, and they spread out across the track.

NOTEBOOK
Refuse To Wait(IRE), who shows a high knee action, really grabbed the ground and used the benefit of her experience to draw nicely clear, her rider winding up the pace approaching halfway. She apparently found the ground too testing at Haydock last time in a fillies' maiden, but she looked a totally different proposition here. She will get further on this evidence. (op 8-1)
Bradford(IRE), who made a promising debut at Ayr, looked to have benefited from that in the paddock beforehand, and giving weight to his rivals, took plenty of time to get going. He probably found the ground a bit too testing, but he is another who looked in need of further. (tchd 7-2)
Opus Dei looked fit beforehand and, after breaking slowly, he came home really well. He's a well-built colt who will benefit from faster ground. (op 20-1)
Saint Sebastian(IRE) made a pleasing introduction. He raced up the far rail alone and seemed to handle the ground well enough. He should make his mark in nursery company at least. (op 14-1)
Toga Tiger(IRE), another with previous experience, never really got into it and the ground looked to be the only excuse. His previous form says he's better than this. (op 11-2 tchd 13-2)
Danzoe(IRE) never got into contention. The race may have come a bit too soon after his run at Leicester, and aside for the ground, this was a startlingly poor display. Official explanation: jockey said colt was unsuited by the good (good to soft in places) ground (op Evens tchd 11-10 in places)

2722 SAICA H'CAP 7f
7:10 (7:11) (Class 5) (0-70,70) 4-Y-O+ **£3,238** (£963; £481; £240) **Stalls** Low

Form RPR

50-0 **1** **Young Gladiator (IRE)**[36] 1655 4-8-3 **52**..........................(b[1]) TPO'Shea 7 62
(Miss J A Camacho) *t.k.h: mde all: rdn 4 l clr over 1f out: unchal* **10/1**

002 **2** *1* **King Pin**[11] 2361 4-8-6 **55**.................................. GregFairley 13 62+
(Miss Tracy Waggott) *hld up towards rr: hdwy and nt clr run over 1f out: styd on strly to take 2nd towards fin: nt rch wnr* **11/2**[2]

06-0 **3** *1 ¼* **Big Slick (IRE)**[44] 1480 4-8-7 **56** ow1.................................. DavidAllan 6 60
(M Brittain) *chsd ldrs: sn drvn along: kpt on same pce fnl f* **11/1**

-450 **4** *½* **Castlebury (IRE)**[15] 2245 4-9-0 **63**..........................(b[1]) PJMcDonald 9 65
(G A Swinbank) *chsd ldrs: reminders 4f out: rdn and hung lft over 2f out: styd on same pce fnl f* **15/2**

-066 **5** *¾* **Summer Dancer (IRE)**[18] 2156 5-9-0 **63**.......................... JamieMoriarty 4 63
(P T Midgley) *hld up in rr: hdwy over 2f out: kpt on same pce fnl f* **8/1**

3-00 **6** *3 ¾* **Bentley**[19] 2145 5-8-7 **56**.................................. JoeFanning 10 46
(J G Given) *w ldrs: wknd fnl f* **12/1**

0003 **7** *1* **Ninth House (USA)**[8] 2441 7-7-12 **54**..........................(t) AdeleMulrennan(7) 11 41
(Mrs R A Carr) *dwlt: kpt on fnl 2f: nvr nr ldrs* **8/1**

-045 **8** *½* **Paint Stripper**[9] 2404 4-8-2 **51** oh6.................................. JimmyQuinn 1 37
(W Storey) *chsd ldrs: one pce fnl 2f* **33/1**

0-00 **9** *3 ¼* **Fyodorovich (USA)**[11] 2362 4-8-12 **61** ow1..........................(v) PAspell 5 38
(J S Wainwright) *mid-div: wknd 2f out* **33/1**

1340 **10** *7* **Jebel Tara**[12] 2313 4-9-6 **69**..........................(bt) SilvestreDeSousa 2 27
(A D Brown) *hood removed v late: sn chsng ldrs: wknd over 2f out* **7/2**[1]

0-06 **11** *7* **Kalhan Sands (IRE)**[15] 2235 4-9-7 **70**.................................. GrahamGibbons 14 10
(J J Quinn) *w ldrs: wknd over 2f out: sn bhd* **7/1**[3]

4000 **12** *3 ¾* **Mont Cervin**[94] 760 4-8-2 **51** oh4..........................(b) DarrenMoffatt 8 —
(Mrs R A Carr) *dwlt: in rr: bhd fnl 2f* **18/1**

1m 27.96s (-0.74) **Going Correction** +0.05s/f (Good) **12** Ran SP% **120.4**
Speed ratings (Par 103): **106,104,103,102,102 97,96,96,92,84 76,72**
toteswinger: 1&2 £16.40, 1&3 £20.40, 2&3 £16.40 CSF £65.17 CT £632.68 TOTE £12.70: £3.60, £2.50, £3.70; EX 94.80.

Owner Barrett,Hope,Postill,Adamson,Wainwright **Bred** Edmond And Richard Kent **Trained** Norton, N Yorks

FOCUS
A weak handicap run at an ordinary pace and the form may not be reliable. They all came up the centre of the track. The winner showed his first form for a year, and the second is worth a bit more than the bare form.

Jebel Tara Official explanation: jockey said gelding was unsuited by the good (good to soft in places) ground

2723 NESTLE ROWNTREE RANDOMS MAIDEN STKS 1m 2f 32y
7:40 (7:40) (Class 5) 3-Y-O+ **£3,238** (£963; £481; £240) **Stalls** Centre

Form RPR

0-22 **1** **Matraash (USA)**[22] 2030 3-8-12 78.................................. TPO'Shea 8 79+
(M Johnston) *mde virtually all: qcknd clr over 3f out: 6 l ahd over 1f out: drvn rt out* **5/6**[1]

5-2 **2** 3 3/4 **Astrodiva**[53] 1269 3-8-7 0 TedDurcan 9 66+
(M H Tompkins) *trckd ldrs: wnt 2nd over 2f out: styd on: no imp* **11/8**[2]
3 7 **Rapid Desire (IRE)** 3-8-7 0 TonyHamilton 7 52
(J R Weymes) *in rr: hdwy over 2f out: styd on to take modest 3rd ins fnl f* **66/1**
03 **4** 1 1/2 **Gwyre (IRE)**[11] 2364 3-8-7 0 DavidAllan 12 49
(T D Easterby) *s.i.s: hdwy over 2f out: nvr nr ldrs* **25/1**
43-0 **5** 4 **Royal Keva (IRE)**[15] 2236 3-8-12 60 SilvestreDeSousa 13 46
(A D Brown) *hld up in rr: sme hdwy 3f out: nvr a factor* **33/1**
000- **6** 3/4 **Cape Dancer (IRE)**[200] 5308 5-9-6 39 PAspell 4 41
(J S Wainwright) *t.k.h: sn prom: wnt modest 3rd over 1f out: sn wknd* **100/1**
7 13 **Real Desire** 3-8-12 0 TomEaves 2 19
(I Semple) *s.i.s: in rr: nvr on terms* **18/1**[3]
/00- **8** 1/2 **Recoil (IRE)**[12] 6485 4-9-4 45 JohnCavanagh(7) 1 19
(R Johnson) *hld up in rr: pushed along over 4f out: nvr on terms* **100/1**
06 **9** 1 **Kentucky Lakes**[25] 1950 3-8-12 0 AndrewElliott 10 16
(Jedd O'Keeffe) *w ldrs: drvn along over 5f out: lost pl over 2f out* **100/1**
060/ **10** 1 **Viola Rosa (IRE)**[521] 12 4-9-6 41 PaulMulrennan 6 9
(J G Given) *t.k.h in midfield: wkng whn hmpd over 2f out* **66/1**
6-0 **11** 8 **Fuzzy Cat**[67] 1047 3-8-7 0 DeanHeslop(5) 3 —
(T D Barron) *sn chsng ldrs: edgd rt and wknd over 2f out* **28/1**
06 **12** 7 **Terrymene Prince**[20] 2104 3-8-5 0 GihanArnolda(7) 5 —
(L A Mullaney) *chsd ldrs: drvn over 5f out: lost pl 4f out: sn bhd* **100/1**

2m 14.32s (2.42) **Going Correction** +0.375s/f (Good)
WFA 3 from 4yo+ 13lb **12** Ran SP% **119.1**
Speed ratings (Par 103): **105,102,96,95,92 91,81,80,79,79 72,67**
toteswinger: 1&2 £1.30, 1&3 £19.80, 2&3 £15.40 CSF £2.03 TOTE £2.10: £1.02, £1.60, £9.30; EX 2.20.
Owner Hamdan Al Maktoum **Bred** Shadwell Farm LLC **Trained** Middleham Moor, N Yorks
■ Stewards' Enquiry : Dean Heslop one-day ban: careless riding (Jun 21)

FOCUS
A weak maiden, run at a modest pace. There was plenty of dead wood and the first two pulled clear. The winner did not need to match his Hamilton form.

2724 PMP RECRUITMENT H'CAP — 1m 2f 32y
8:10 (8:10) (Class 5) (0-75,75) 4-Y-O+ **£3,238** (£963; £481; £240) **Stalls** Centre

Form RPR
5102 **1** **Dechiper (IRE)**[12] 2315 7-8-11 65 GrahamGibbons 2 72
(R Johnson) *hld up towards rr: nt clr run over 2f out: plld wd over 1f out: str run to ld last 75yds* **7/2**[2]
005 **2** 1 1/2 **Grey Command (USA)**[12] 2315 4-8-8 62 JoeFanning 5 66
(M Brittain) *set stdy pce: qcknd 3f out: hdd and no ex ins fnl f* **14/1**
3-00 **3** 1 1/4 **Island Music (IRE)**[11] 2362 4-8-10 64 PaulHanagan 6 66
(J J Quinn) *trckd ldrs: lost pl over 4f out: hdwy 2f out: styd on ins fnl f* **6/1**
1215 **4** hd **Ergo (FR)**[9] 2391 5-9-3 71 (v) DarrenMoffatt 10 72
(James Moffatt) *trckd ldr: t.k.h: styd on same pce ins fnl f* **10/1**
0222 **5** 1 1/2 **Tiger Dream**[14] 2274 4-9-1 74 AmyRyan(5) 7 72
(K A Ryan) *hld up in rr: hdwy on wd outside over 4f out: chal 2f out: sn rdn: kpt on same pce* **3/1**[1]
6-00 **6** shd **Trouble Mountain (USA)**[15] 2237 12-8-2 56 oh1 (t) DaleGibson 3 54
(M W Easterby) *s.i.s: kpt on fnl 3f: nvr a factor* **25/1**
0502 **7** hd **All In The Red (IRE)**[16] 2200 4-8-13 72 (p) FrederikTylicki(5) 8 70
(A Crook) *sn chsng ldrs: styd on same pce fnl 2f* **9/2**[3]
-255 **8** nk **Sudden Impulse**[15] 2237 8-8-7 61 SilvestreDeSousa 11 58
(A D Brown) *t.k.h towards rr: hdwy 7f out: sn chsng ldrs: one pce fnl 2f* **8/1**
0 **9** 5 **Tres Froide (FR)**[24] 1990 4-9-7 75 TomEaves 1 62
(N Tinkler) *trckd ldrs: wknd appr fnl f* **40/1**

2m 18.18s (6.28) **Going Correction** +0.375s/f (Good) **9** Ran SP% **112.8**
Speed ratings (Par 103): **89,87,86,86,85 85,85,84,80**
toteswinger: 1&2 £7.10, 1&3 £6.70, 2&3 £27.70 CSF £49.68 CT £282.03 TOTE £3.30: £1.10, £2.70, £2.80; EX 46.10.
Owner L Armstrong **Bred** Tommy Burns **Trained** Newburn, Tyne & Wear
■ Stewards' Enquiry : Darren Moffatt one-day ban: careless riding (Jun 21)

FOCUS
A modest handicap and aside from the winner they finished in a heap. Muddling form, not to be taken at face value.

2725 NESTLE CONFECTIONERY H'CAP — 2m 19y
8:40 (8:41) (Class 6) (0-65,63) 4-Y-O+ **£2,201** (£655; £327; £163) **Stalls** Low

Form RPR
3560 **1** **Miss Keck**[12] 2344 5-9-5 58 PJMcDonald 6 71
(G A Swinbank) *trckd ldrs: hdwy on ins to ld over 1f out: drvn clr ins fnl f* **5/1**[3]
0/60 **2** 6 **Celtic Carisma**[12] 2344 7-8-6 45 PaulHanagan 4 51
(K G Reveley) *hld up in rr: hdwy on outer over 3f out: styd on wl fnl f: tk 2nd nr line* **17/2**
4-64 **3** hd **Whitcombe Spirit**[18] 2163 4-9-1 55 RobertHavlin 5 60
(Jamie Poulton) *led: qcknd 6f out: hdd over 1f out: styd on same pce* **6/1**
0-30 **4** 5 **Cote D'Argent**[21] 2068 6-9-9 62 JoeFanning 12 61
(L Lungo) *sn prom: one pce fnl 2f* **10/1**
432- **5** 1/2 **Wotchalike (IRE)**[16] 4366 7-9-0 53 (p) PAspell 11 52
(Miss S Johnstone) *mid-div: hdwy on outer 6f out: one pce fnl 3f* **14/1**
4-51 **6** 1 1/2 **No Rules**[53] 1273 4-9-0 54 TedDurcan 10 51
(M H Tompkins) *trckd ldrs: one pce fnl 2f* **7/2**[2]
/0-3 **7** 1 1/4 **One Tou Many**[15] 2232 4-8-7 50 KellyHarrison(3) 3 46
(C W Fairhurst) *hld up in rr: hdwy on inner over 2f out: nvr nr ldrs* **20/1**
405/ **8** nk **Uptown Lad (IRE)**[4] 4926 10-7-13 45 (v[1]) MatthewLawson(7) 1 40
(R Johnson) *s.s: detached in rr and drvn 7f out: sme hdwy over 2f out: nvr on terms* **50/1**
046- **9** 1 **Centenary (IRE)**[265] 4879 5-8-6 45 DaleGibson 8 39
(M W Easterby) *t.k.h in mid-div: hdwy 6f out: drvn 4f out: lost pl 2f out* **28/1**
000- **10** 3 1/2 **Risk Runner (IRE)**[29] 6551 6-9-10 63 (b) DarrenMoffatt 9 53
(James Moffatt) *hld up in rr: shkn up 10f out: drvn 3f out: sn btn* **14/1**
0144 **11** 9 **Rough Sketch (USA)**[72] 967 4-9-4 58 PaulMulrennan 2 37
(Sir Mark Prescott) *chsd ldrs: drvn over 3f out: wknd 2f out: eased whn bhd ins fnl f* **10/3**[1]
50-0 **12** 41 **Dance Sauvage**[18] 2159 6-8-7 46 ow1 TonyHamilton 7 —
(B Storey) *t.k.h: hdwy on outside to trck ldrs 10f out: drvn over 5f out: lost pl over 3f out: wl bhd whn eased ins fnl f: virtually p.u: t.o* **40/1**

3m 41.71s (2.31) **Going Correction** +0.375s/f (Good)
WFA 4 from 5yo+ 1lb **12** Ran SP% **121.8**
Speed ratings (Par 101): **101,98,97,95,95 94,93,93,93,91 86,66**
toteswinger: 1&2 Not won, 1&3 £8.80, 2&3 Not won. CSF £46.77 CT £267.24 TOTE £5.90: £2.10, £3.00, £2.80; EX 74.00.
Owner Alan Wright **Bred** The Woodhaven Stud **Trained** Melsonby, N Yorks
■ Stewards' Enquiry : Robert Havlin two-day ban: excessive use of the whip (Jun 21-22)

FOCUS
A poor staying handicap not run at that strong a pace. The winner is on the upgrade.
Rough Sketch(USA) Official explanation: trainer's rep said she had no explanation for the poor form shown
Dance Sauvage Official explanation: jockey said gelding hung badly right throughout

2726 MARIE CURIE H'CAP — 5f
9:10 (9:11) (Class 5) (0-75,74) 3-Y-O **£3,238** (£963; £481; £240) **Stalls** Low

Form RPR
4312 **1** **Dispol Grand (IRE)**[8] 2454 3-9-1 68 JoeFanning 7 72
(P T Midgley) *w ldrs: chal over 1f out: led jst ins fnl f: kpt on wl towards fin* **9/4**[1]
6013 **2** nk **Noodles Blue Boy**[5] 2530 3-9-3 70 TonyHamilton 5 73
(Ollie Pears) *hld up in tch: effrt 2f out: upsides ins fnl f: no ex nr fin* **10/3**[2]
-004 **3** 1 1/2 **Dispol Kylie (IRE)**[37] 1627 3-9-7 74 PhillipMakin 4 72
(P T Midgley) *trckd ldrs: led 2f out: hdd jst ins fnl f: kpt on same pce* **4/1**[3]
200- **4** 1 3/4 **Rossett Rose (IRE)**[172] 7693 3-8-7 60 DavidAllan 6 51
(M Brittain) *hld up in tch: effrt and sltly outpcd 2f out: kpt on fnl f* **8/1**
1003 **5** 6 **Iachimo**[8] 2454 3-7-13 57 oh2 ow2 (v) MartinLane(5) 1 27
(K R Burke) *led tl hdd 2f out: sn wknd* **10/3**[2]
4500 **6** 3 1/4 **Singapore Girl**[18] 2157 3-7-13 55 oh5 NataliaGemelova(3) 3 13
(G R Oldroyd) *s.i.s: sn chsng ldrs: wknd 2f out* **33/1**

61.04 secs (0.34) **Going Correction** +0.05s/f (Good) **6** Ran SP% **111.0**
Speed ratings (Par 99): **99,98,96,93,83 78**
toteswinger: 1&2 £1.02, 1&3 £1.10, 2&3 £1.90 CSF £9.76 TOTE £3.20: £2.10, £2.00; EX 7.00 Place 6 £148.73, Place 5 £44.37.
Owner W B Imison **Bred** Martyn J McEnery **Trained** Westow, N Yorks
■ Stewards' Enquiry : Tony Hamilton caution: used whip with excessive force

FOCUS
A fair sprint handicap and a slight personal best from the winner.
T/Plt: £329.30 to a £1 stake. Pool: £68,817.83. 152.54 winning tickets. T/Qpdt: £13.50 to a £1 stake. Pool: £6,283.55. 343.80 winning tickets. WG

2727 - 2728a (Foreign Racing) - See Raceform Interactive

2301 CURRAGH (R-H)
Saturday, June 6

OFFICIAL GOING: Good changing to soft after race 5 (7.30)

2729a MOGEELY STUD SILVER STKS (LISTED RACE) — 1m 2f
6:30 (6:37) 3-Y-O+ **£26,861** (£7,881; £3,754; £1,279)

RPR
1 **Deauville Vision (IRE)**[14] 2285 6-9-6 99 (p) RPCleary 2 105
(M Halford, Ire) *chsd ldrs: 3rd 1/2-way: hdwy into 2nd 4f out: rdn to ld 1 1/2f out: kpt on wl fnl f* **10/1**
2 2 1/2 **She's Our Mark**[34] 1715 5-9-9 107 DMGrant 4 103+
(Patrick J Flynn, Ire) *hld up bhd ldrs: mod 5th 1/2-way: clsr 4f out: 7th 2f out: hdwy 1 1/2f out: rdn into 2nd under 1f out: kpt on fnl f: nt rch wnr* **7/2**[2]
3 3 **Dance Pass (IRE)**[13] 2304 3-8-7 97 DPMcDonogh 1 93+
(D K Weld, Ire) *hld up towards rr: clsr in 6th 2f out: rdn in 5th 1f out: kpt on same pce fnl f to take 3rd cl home* **8/1**[3]
4 hd **Kargali (IRE)**[33] 1758 4-9-12 109 (t) FMBerry 8 100
(John M Oxx, Ire) *hld up bhd ldrs: mod 6th 1/2-way: clsr 4f out: hdwy into 3rd 2f out: rdn in 4th and no ex 1f out: kpt on same pce in 3rd ins fnl f: lost 3rd cl home* **11/8**[1]
5 3 **Ghimaar**[27] 1909 4-9-9 99 PShanahan 5 91
(D K Weld, Ire) *chsd ldrs: led after 2 1/2f: rdn and hdd 1 1/2f out: no ex and kpt on one pce* **12/1**
6 2 1/2 **Born To Be King (USA)**[27] 1917 3-8-10 100 DavidMcCabe 6 85
(A P O'Brien, Ire) *led: hdd after 2 1/2f: 2nd 1/2-way: 4th 3f out: rdn in 5th 2f out: no ex* **8/1**[3]
7 1/2 **Northgate (IRE)**[28] 1902 4-9-9 95 (b) CDHayes 3 85
(Joseph G Murphy, Ire) *hld up towards rr: clsr in 6th 4f out: rdn into 4th 2f out: no ex fr 1 1/2f out* **16/1**
8 4 1/2 **Byzantine**[34] 1714 3-8-10 SMLevey 10 75
(A P O'Brien, Ire) *chsd ldrs: 4th 1/2-way: rdn in 3rd 3f out: sn no ex and wknd over 2f out* **8/1**[3]

2m 18.03s (8.53) **Going Correction** +1.05s/f (Soft)
WFA 3 from 4yo+ 13lb **8** Ran SP% **120.3**
Speed ratings: **107,105,102,102,100 98,97,94**
CSF £47.41 TOTE £11.00: £2.50, £1.50, £2.90; DF 39.90.
Owner T Kimura **Bred** T Kimura **Trained** the Curragh, Co Kildare

FOCUS
The runner-up and third were not best placed in a slowly run contest and have been rated just off their best.

NOTEBOOK
Deauville Vision(IRE) had not won since landing a similar event over 1m at Tralee in August 2007. Third in a 1m Group 3 event here on her previous start last month, this was her fifth win and her first above 1m. Suited by plenty of ease, she was helped by the rain gradually getting into the ground since the start of the meeting. She got the extra 2f well and, after tracking the leaders and going to the front over a furlong and a half out, she kept on and was well on top in the closing stages. She is in foal to Kheleyf. (op 8/1)
She's Our Mark, winner of a similar race over just short of this trip on heavy ground at Gowran Park last month and also a winner at Group 3 level two years ago, was held up before making steady headway from the back under 2f out. She went early in the final furlong and kept on to the line without seriously troubling the winner. (op 4/1)
Dance Pass(IRE), a maiden winner over 1m at Naas last month before failing to make any impact in the Irish 1,000 Guineas on heavy ground, was held up and began to make progress early in the straight. Fifth and under pressure over 1f out, she kept on steadily and took third spot close home. (op 7/1)
Kargali(IRE), a winner at this level over 1m at Leopardstown in April, had gone on to finish last in a Group 3 event over this course and trip early last month (trainer subsequently reported the colt had suffered a quarter crack). Held up in touch, he was third 2f out but could raise no extra when asked over 1f out. (op 5/4 tchd 6/5)
Ghimaar, winner of a 1m4f handicap at last year's Galway festival, was having his second run of the season and was in front just over 2f out. He led until headed by the winner and was quickly done with. (op 16/1)

2730 - 2733a (Foreign Racing) - See Raceform Interactive

BELMONT PARK (L-H)

Saturday, June 6

OFFICIAL GOING: Turf course - yielding; dirt course - fast

2734a BELMONT STKS (GRADE 1) (DIRT) 1m 4f (D)

11:27 (11:29) 3-Y-O

£416,667 (£138,889; £76,389; £41,667; £20,833; £2,778)

RPR

1 **Summer Bird (USA)**35 1688 3-9-0 ....(b) KDesormeaux 4 123
(Tim Ice, U.S.A) *mid-division on inside, close 8th & edged outside approaching straight, 4th 1 1/2f out, driven to lead 120yds out, ran on* **119/10**

2 2 ¾ **Dunkirk (USA)**35 1688 3-9-0 .... JRVelazquez 2 119
(Todd Pletcher, U.S.A) *led, challenged by 3rd & 4th entering straight, headed just inside final f, driven & every chance 120yds out, kept on one pace* **23/5**2

3 nk **Mine That Bird (USA)**21 2098 3-9-0 .... CHBorel 7 119
(Bennie L Woolley Jr, U.S.A) *held up in rear, headway on outside over 4f out, 3rd & challenging entering straight, took narrow lead just inside final f, headed 120y out, one pace* **5/4**1

4 3 ¾ **Charitable Man (USA)**28 3-9-0 .... AGarcia 6 113
(Kiaran McLaughlin, U.S.A) *disputed 3rd, went 2nd over 2f out, driven & challenged well over 1f out, one pace when squeezed out between 2nd & 3rd just ins fnl f, not recover* **23/5**2

5 3 ¾ **Luv Gov (USA)**21 2098 3-9-0 ....(b) MMena 5 107
(D Wayne Lukas, U.S.A) *towards rear, last 4f out, 9th straight, never a factor* **224/10**

6 4 ½ **Flying Private (USA)**21 2098 3-9-0 ....(b) JRLeparoux 8 101
(D Wayne Lukas, U.S.A) *mid-division, 5th straight, soon beaten* **17/1**

7 2 **Brave Victory (USA)**28 3-9-0 .... RMaragh 10 98
(Nicholas Zito, U.S.A) *mid-division, 7th half-way, headway on outside over 4f out, disputed 3rd over 3f out, carried wide 3f out, soon weakened* **28/1**

8 1 ¼ **Mr. Hot Stuff (USA)**35 1688 3-9-0 .... EPrado 3 96
(Eoin Harty, U.S.A) *disputed 3rd, weakened 3f out, 6th & beaten straight* **23/1**

9 7 **Chocolate Candy (USA)**35 1688 3-9-0 .... GKGomez 1 85
(Jerry Hollendorfer, U.S.A) *held up towards rear, closed up on outside over 3f out, 8th & beaten straight* **19/2**3

10 30 **Miner's Escape (USA)**35 3-9-0 ....(b) JLezcano 9 40
(Nicholas Zito, U.S.A) *pressed leader til weakening quickly 3f out* **22/1**

2m 27.54s (-1.42) **10** Ran SP% **119.2**
PARI-MUTUEL: WIN 25.80; PL (1-2) 9.30, 5.40; SHOW (1-2-3) 4.70, 3.60,2.60; SF 121.00.
Owner Kalarikkal K & Vilasini D Jayaraman **Bred** Dr K Jayaraman & V Jayaraman **Trained** North America

FOCUS
Summer Bird became the first horse since 1933 to win the Belmont Stakes having not been in the first three at the top of the straight, suggesting Dunkirk went too quick, and Mine That Bird went too soon.

NOTEBOOK
Summer Bird(USA), off since a fair effort in the Kentucky Derby and blinkered for the first time, was well ridden considering how the race unfolded. This fine, big horse was also much happier at Belmont than at Churchill Downs and picked up smartly to peg back tiring rivals in the straight. He is likely to be pointed towards the Breeders' Cup for either the Classic or the Turf, but has yet to try synthetics or grass.
Dunkirk(USA) was a surprise leader, and he probably went off a bit too quick. He battled on well to keep second, but unsurprisingly had no answer to the winner's late burst. He'll now be given a short break ahead of a probable return in the Jim Dandy at Saratoga on August 1, before taking in his main target, the Travers at the same venue on August 29.
Mine That Bird(USA), who benefited greatly from being held up well off an overly strong pace in both previous legs of the Triple Crown, rather surprisingly again had a decent gallop to chase, but this time he looked to be given an ill-judged ride. Having been last early as usual, he made a big move out wide around the final turn and simply went much too soon. He briefly looked the winner, but soon faded and gave the impression the more patient tactics employed the last twice would probably have seen him finish closer. His main target now is the Breeders' Cup Classic, but he's likely to have two runs beforehand, ideally against 3yos on dirt.
Charitable Man(USA) was slightly squeezed around 1f out, and that exaggerated the beaten distance, but he wasn't unlucky. A disappointing effort and he'll probably be happier back over shorter.

2376 BRIGHTON (L-H)

Sunday, June 7

OFFICIAL GOING: Good (good to firm in places; 7.9)
Wind: medium, against Weather: bright, partly cloudy

2735 EUROPEAN BREEDERS' FUND MAIDEN STKS 5f 213y

2:30 (2:30) (Class 5) 2-Y-O **£3,565** (£1,090; £561; £297) **Stalls** Low

Form RPR

36 1 1 ¼ **Ailsa Carmel (IRE)**12 2354 2-8-12 0.... SamHitchcott 1 71
(M R Channon) led: rdn ent fnl 2f: hdd and no ex ins fnl f: fin 2nd, awrdd r **3/1**3

2 1 ¼ **Florio Vincitore (IRE)** 2-9-3 0.... EdwardCreighton 4 73
(E J Creighton) *chsd ldr: ev ch 2f out: sn rdn: wknd ins fnl f* **66/1**

52 3 1 ¾ **Ginger Grey (IRE)**11 2376 2-9-3 0.... RyanMoore 2 67
(S A Callaghan) *trckd ldrs: rdn and effrt jst over 2f out: hung lft over 1f out: no hdwy and wl btn fnl f* **14/1**

0042 4 10 **Pullyourfingerout (IRE)**13 2328 2-9-3 0.... JimCrowley 5 37
(B G Powell) *racd in last pair: edgd rt and rdn 3f out: drvn and wknd over 1f out* **9/4**2

332 D **Curtains**8 2490 2-8-12 0.... SebSanders 3 76+
(S Dow) *stdd s: hld up in last pair: hdwy to join ldrs travelling wl 2f out: pushed into ld ins fnl f: pushed out: fin 1st, 1¼l: subs disq* **11/10**1

1m 10.94s (0.74) **Going Correction** +0.075s/f (Good) **5** Ran SP% **111.5**
Speed ratings (Par 93): **96,94,92,79,98**
CSF £4.89 TOTE £1.90: £1.10, £1.80; EX 4.60.
Owner Mrs M Findlay **Bred** F Sheedy **Trained** West Ilsley, Berks

FOCUS
This has the look of very ordinary maiden form.

NOTEBOOK
Ailsa Carmel(IRE) battled on well on the front end and was only worn down in the final half furlong. This was a much more encouraging effort after she disappointed over 5f at Leicester last time and she was subsequently awarded the race. (op 9-2)
Florio Vincitore(IRE), already gelded, shaped with definite promise on debut, especially as he's bred to want further than this in time.
Ginger Grey(IRE) ruined his chance by hanging left into the rail when coming under pressure and it may be that he didn't handle the track too well. (op 12-1)
Pullyourfingerout(IRE) bombed out completely and was way below the level of form he showed last time. This wasn't his running. Official explanation: jockey said colt did not handle the track (op 5-2)
Curtains is progressing well and made the most of what looked on paper her easiest opportunity to date. Brought three or four horse widths wide by Seb Sanders, she didn't pick up immediately, but gradually wound up down the middle of the track to assert in the final half furlong and see this 6f out strongly. He was subsequently disqualified but another furlong looks well within range and she should keep on progressing. (op Evens tchd 5-4)

2736 SUPERJAM FROM WAITROSE BRIGHTON H'CAP 6f 209y

3:00 (3:01) (Class 5) (0-75,72) 4-Y-O+ **£3,280** (£981; £490; £245; £122) **Stalls** Low

Form RPR

0050 1 **Golden Prospect**17 2202 5-8-3 54.... LiamJones 6 61
(J W Hills) *stdd s: hld up in last pl: hdwy ent fnl f: pushed along hands and heels after: r.o wl to ld towards fin* **8/1**

3420 2 ½ **Patavium Prince (IRE)**62 1152 6-9-7 72.... IanMongan 1 78
(Miss Jo Crowley) *dwlt: sn trcking ldrs: swtchd lft and rdn to chal jst over 1f out: led ins fnl f: hdd and no ex towards fin* **5/1**

0030 3 nk **Ivory Lace**8 2491 8-9-5 70.... JimCrowley 5 75
(S Woodman) *hld up in tch: rdn and effrt on outer 2f out: drvn ent fnl f: kpt on but nt quite pce to rch ldrs* **11/4**1

54-6 4 1 **Carmenero (GER)**18 2185 6-9-7 72.... NCallan 4 74
(W R Muir) *t.k.h: chsd ldr: ev ch over 2f out: rdn to ld 2f out: hdd ins fnl f: one pce fnl 100yds* **4/1**3

0024 5 2 **Napoletano (GER)**8 2491 8-9-1 66....(p) SebSanders 3 63
(S Dow) *stdd s: plld hrd: hld up in last pair: swtchd rt and hdwy over 3f out: led 3f out tl 2f out: drvn and btn ent fnl f* **7/2**2

0000 6 12 **Whinhill House**9 2456 9-7-9 53 oh3....(p) JosephineBruning(7) 2 18
(T T Clement) *led at stdy pce: hung rt and hdd 3f out: wknd u.p wl over 1f out* **50/1**

1m 25.46s (2.36) **Going Correction** +0.075s/f (Good) **6** Ran SP% **98.6**
Speed ratings (Par 103): **89,88,88,86,84 70**
toteswinger: 1&2 £6.30, 1&3 £3.90, 2&3 £2.10. CSF £34.81 TOTE £8.50: £4.40, £2.10; EX 44.40.
Owner Michael Wauchope And Partners **Bred** D E And Mrs J Cash **Trained** Upper Lambourn, Berks
■ Fifty (5/1, unruly in stalls) was withdrawn. Deduct 15p in the £ under R4.

FOCUS
They dawdled through the first 3f until Seb Sanders and Napoletano took over, but they didn't last long and were soon on the retreat having pulled very hard early.

2737 SUPERJAM RASPBERRY AND CRANBERRY (S) STKS 6f 209y

3:30 (3:30) (Class 6) 3-Y-O+ **£1,942** (£578; £288; £144) **Stalls** Low

Form RPR

1654 1 **Landucci**11 2378 8-9-13 64....(p) JamesDoyle 5 66
(S Curran) *t.k.h: chsd ldr tl 5f out: trckd ldrs after tl led 3f out: rdn wl over 1f out: drvn out fnl f: styd on wl* **3/1**1

2060 2 1 **Mountain Pass (USA)**12 2352 7-9-7 54....(p) NCallan 8 57
(B J Llewellyn) *t.k.h: hld up in tch: hdwy over 3f out: chsd wnr jst over 2f out: no imp u.p ins fnl f* **5/1**2

-400 3 3 ½ **Lancaster Lad (IRE)**34 1741 4-9-7 47.... SebSanders 6 48
(A B Haynes) *stdd s: t.k.h: hld up in rr: hdwy on outer 3f out: chsd ldng pair 2f out: sn rdn and hung bdly lft fr over 1f out: wl hld fnl f* **8/1**3

0 4 1 **Final Drive (IRE)**55 1260 3-8-11 57.... EdwardCreighton 4 41
(E J Creighton) *stdd s: t.k.h early: hld up bhd: rdn and no hdwy 3f out: plugged on fnl f: nvr trbld ldrs* **16/1**

4445 5 ¾ **Herecomesbella**19 2149 3-8-6 51....(b) JimmyQuinn 1 34
(Stef Liddiard) *in tch: rdn and outpcd over 2f out: hrd drvn and kpt on fnl f: nvr pce to threaten ldrs* **3/1**1

1050 6 1 ¼ **Dalrymple (IRE)**13 2333 3-9-3 59.... JimCrowley 3 41
(Ian Williams) *led tl over 5f out: chsd ldr untl hung rt 3f out: wknd 2f out: wl btn fnl f* **3/1**1

2005 7 14 **Yellow River (USA)**73 964 3-8-1 45....(e1) Louis-PhilippeBeuzelin(5) 7 —
(E J Creighton) *stdd and rrd s: plld hrd: hdwy to chse ldr 5f out: led over 4f out tl 3f out: wknd qckly over 2f out* **33/1**

1m 24.14s (1.04) **Going Correction** +0.075s/f (Good)
WFA 3 from 4yo+ 10lb **7** Ran SP% **111.6**
Speed ratings (Par 101): **97,95,91,90,89 88,72**
toteswinger: 1&2 £4.50, 1&3 £4.30, 2&3 £7.90. CSF £17.48 TOTE £3.70: £1.90, £3.10; EX 14.50 Trifecta £40.70 Pool: £193.26 - 3.51 winning units.There was no bid for the winner. Dalrymple was claimed by Mr. M. Madgwick for £5,000.
Owner L M Power **Bred** D J And Mrs Deer **Trained** Hatford, Oxon

FOCUS
Basement-grade stuff.
Yellow River(USA) Official explanation: jockey said filly ran too free

2738 SUPERJAM CREAM TEA MAIDEN STKS 1m 3f 196y

4:00 (4:01) (Class 5) 3-Y-O+ **£3,406** (£1,019; £509; £254; £126) **Stalls** High

Form RPR

24 1 **Talimos (IRE)**18 2181 3-8-12 0.... SebSanders 4 79+
(R M Beckett) *in tch: reminder over 8f out: rdn and hdwy 4f out: led 2f out: sn drvn clr and in n.d after* **9/2**2

4-00 2 12 **Sixties Swinger (USA)**23 2038 3-8-12 70.... NCallan 6 60
(M A Jarvis) *chsd ldrs tl led over 6f out: hdd over 4f out: led again over 3f out tl 2f out: no ch w wnr after* **5/1**3

56 3 1 ¼ **Tesserae**9 2447 3-8-4 0 ow4.... PNolan(7) 1 57
(A B Haynes) *bhd: reminder 7f out: rdn and outpcd 4f out: hung rt 3f out: plugging on and hung lft 1f out: hmpd and swtchd rt ins fnl f: wnt modest 3rd fnl 100yds* **33/1**

4 4 1 ½ **Best Tune**16 2240 3-8-2 0.... Louis-PhilippeBeuzelin(5) 3 50
(J Noseda) *taken down early: trckd ldrs: rdn whn hmpd on rail over 2f out: 3rd and wl btn after: hung lft fnl f: lost modest 3rd fnl 100yds* **6/1**

6-33 5 20 **Entreat**24 2006 3-8-7 72.... RyanMoore 7 18
(Sir Michael Stoute) *led for 2f: chsd ldr over 6f out tl led over 4f: hdd over 3f out: rdn and hung lft over 2f out: swtchd rt 2f out: sn wl btn: eased ins fnl f* **8/11**1

0 6 23 **Noor Al Bahar (IRE)**23 2042 3-8-7 0.... SamHitchcott 5 —
(M R Channon) *bustled along early: in tch in rr: rdn and struggling 4f out: t.o fnl 2f* **66/1**

7 74 **Shannon Weir (IRE)**364 7-9-10 0 AlanCreighton(3) 2 —
(E J Creighton) *pushed along leaving stalls: led after 2f tl hdd over 6f out: sn dropped out: wl t.o fr 4f out* **100/1**

2m 31.15s (-1.55) **Going Correction** +0.075s/f (Good)
WFA 3 from 7yo 15lb **7 Ran SP% 112.5**
Speed ratings (Par 103): **108,100,99,98,84 69,20**
toteswinger: 1&2 £2.50, 1&3 £10.20, 2&3 £19.70. CSF £25.60 TOTE £5.60: £2.40, £1.90; EX 34.70.
Owner A E Frost **Bred** J Joyce **Trained** Whitsbury, Hants
■ Stewards' Enquiry : Ryan Moore two-day ban: careless riding (Jun 24-25)

FOCUS
With hot favourite Entreat proving bitterly disappointing, this form doesn't have a strong feel to it.

2739 COMMERCIAL CATERING CONTRACTS H'CAP 1m 1f 209y
4:30 (4:30) (Class 6) (0-65,60) 4-Y-O+ £2,460 (£732; £365; £182) Stalls High

Form RPR
-600 1 **Sinbad The Sailor**8 2493 4-9-7 60 (v1) SebSanders 4 66
(J W Hills) *led tl hdd jst over 3f out: rdn over 2f out: drvn to ld again 1f out: kpt on wl fnl f* **7/2**3

052 2 1 1/4 **Mick Is Back**11 2378 5-9-5 58 (vt) RyanMoore 1 62
(G G Margarson) *chsd ldrs: rdn wl over 2f out: hung lft u.p over 1f out: chsd wnr wl ins fnl f: no imp fnl 50yds* **10/3**2

60-6 3 shd **Tevez**138 224 4-9-6 59 (b) JimmyQuinn 3 62
(D Donovan) *in tch: rdn over 2f out: pressed ldrs and drvn ent fnl f: kpt on same pce* **9/2**

0-01 4 shd **Goose Green (IRE)**16 2221 5-8-9 53 Louis-PhilippeBeuzelin(5) 7 56
(R J Hodges) *chsd ldr: led jst over 3f out: sn rdn: drvn 2f out: hdd 1f out: no ex and lost 2 pls wl ins fnl f* **3/1**1

00-0 5 shd **Ubiquitous**26 1961 4-8-6 45 JamesDoyle 8 48
(S Dow) *stdd s: hld up in rr: rdn and effrt wl over 1f out: hung lft over 1f out: kpt on ins fnl f: nt pce to rch ldrs* **25/1**

3354 6 6 **Imperium**13 2331 8-9-5 58 (p) JimCrowley 6 49
(Jean-Rene Auvray) *hld up in rr: rdn over 2f out: sn edging lft and wl btn* **6/1**

4000 7 14 **Shake On It**74 961 5-9-7 60 IanMongan 5 35
(M R Hoad) *stdd s: t.k.h: hld up in last trio: rdn 2f out: wknd over 1f out: wl btn and eased ins fnl f* **12/1**

2m 4.12s (0.52) **Going Correction** +0.075s/f (Good) **7 Ran SP% 114.3**
Speed ratings (Par 101): **100,99,98,98,98 93,82**
toteswinger: 1&2 £2.90, 1&3 £3.30, 2&3 £3.30. CSF £15.58 CT £52.15 TOTE £4.60: £2.50, £2.00; EX 12.80 Trifecta £75.70 Pool: £415.75 - 4.06 winning units.
Owner Wauchope Cottam Sir S Dunning Mrs Caroe **Bred** Sir Eric Parker **Trained** Upper Lambourn, Berks

FOCUS
A low-grade handicap and there were four abreast across the track behind the winner so the form doesn't have much of a feel to it.

2740 LILY FOUNDATION H'CAP 5f 59y
5:00 (5:00) (Class 5) (0-70,68) 3-Y-O £3,154 (£944; £472; £236; £117) Stalls Low

Form RPR
2332 1 **Billy Beetroot (USA)**12 2355 3-8-13 60 (t) RyanMoore 4 67
(S C Williams) *chsd ldrs: effrt and c wd 2f out: led ent fnl f: drvn and r.o wl fnl f* **5/4**1

0003 2 1 1/2 **Louie's Lad**8 2478 3-8-2 49 oh1 (p) FrankieMcDonald 6 51
(J J Bridger) *racd freely: chsd ldr: ev ch 2f out: chsd wnr jst ins fnl f: kpt on* **11/2**

423 3 3 1/4 **Imaginary Diva**9 2460 3-9-0 66 Louis-PhilippeBeuzelin(5) 1 56
(G G Margarson) *led: hrd pressed and rdn 2f out: hdd ent fnl f: wknd ins fnl f* **7/2**2

0200 4 1/2 **Rapanui Belle**25 1985 3-8-2 49 JimmyQuinn 3 38
(G L Moore) *t.k.h: hld up in tch: effrt to chse ldrs over 1f out: wknd u.p ins fnl f* **12/1**

54 5 4 **Ice Attack (IRE)**6 2530 3-8-3 50 (v1) LiamJones 5 24
(Patrick Morris) *a in last pair: rdn and struggling over 2f out: wl btn over 1f out* **25/1**

10-0 6 1 3/4 **Zelos Girl (IRE)**24 2005 3-9-7 68 (e1) SebSanders 2 36
(Rae Guest) *taken down early: stdd s: a last pl: shkn up and hung lft wl over 1f out: sn wl btn* **4/1**3

62.75 secs (0.45) **Going Correction** +0.075s/f (Good) **6 Ran SP% 113.6**
Speed ratings (Par 99): **99,96,91,90,84 81**
toteswinger: 1&2 £2.80, 1&3 £1.70, 2&3 £1.70. CSF £8.94 TOTE £2.00: £1.10, £3.30; EX 7.70 Place 6: 214.94 Place 5: £156.10.
Owner J W Parry **Bred** Cyril Humphris **Trained** Newmarket, Suffolk

FOCUS
A weak handicap.
Zelos Girl(IRE) Official explanation: jockey said filly never travelled
T/Plt: £193.10 to a £1 stake. Pool: £70,508.01. 266.45 winning tickets. T/Qpdt: £26.70 to a £1 stake. Pool: £4,236.97. 117.20 winning tickets. SP

2575 SOUTHWELL (L-H)
Sunday, June 7

OFFICIAL GOING: Standard
Wind: almost nil Weather: persistent heavy rain

2741 BILL, ANNE BRIMSTED'S RUBY WEDDING ANNIVERSARY MAIDEN AUCTION FILLIES' STKS 5f (F)
2:10 (2:10) (Class 5) 2-Y-O £2,729 (£806; £403) Stalls High

Form RPR
0 1 **Three Good Friends (IRE)**68 1044 2-8-6 0 PJMcDonald 1 69
(P T Midgley) *w ldrs: led over 1f out: edgd rt: drvn out* **13/2**3

63 2 1 1/2 **Diamond Affair (IRE)**30 1835 2-7-13 0 NicolPolli(5) 3 62
(M G Quinlan) *t.k.h: led after 1f: hdd over 1f out: kpt on same pce* **10/3**2

03 3 1 1/4 **Regardless**13 2339 2-8-8 0 ow2 GrahamGibbons 2 61
(Mrs G S Rees) *led 1f: chsd ldrs: edgd lft and kpt on same pce fnl f* **10/11**1

4 1 **Zelos Dream (IRE)** 2-8-1 0 DavidProbert(3) 6 53+
(Rae Guest) *dwlt: hdwy over 2f out: kpt on fnl f: nvr trbld ldrs* **14/1**

6 5 3 **China Bay**52 1312 2-8-4 0 AdrianMcCarthy 4 43
(Tom Dascombe) *sn outpcd: hdwy over 2f out: nvr nr ldrs* **10/1**

00 6 hd **London Girl (IRE)**20 2128 2-8-5 0 ow1 AndrewElliott 8 43
(A J McCabe) *racd stands' side: in tch: rdn end edgd lft over 2f out: nvr a threat* **40/1**

7 14 **Sisters Warning** 2-8-4 0 ChrisCatlin 5 —
(J Ryan) *dwlt: wnt lft after s: wl bhd fnl 2f* **16/1**

0 8 3 3/4 **Suzys Dream (IRE)**21 2099 2-8-8 0 PaulMulrennan 7 —
(P T Midgley) *chsd ldrs: wknd 2f out: bhd whn heavily eased ins fnl f* **22/1**

60.21 secs (0.51) **Going Correction** -0.125s/f (Stan) **8 Ran SP% 117.2**
Speed ratings (Par 90): **90,87,85,84,79 78,56,50**
toteswinger: 1&2 £4.60, 1&3 £2.40, 2&3 £1.10. CSF £29.24 TOTE £7.50: £2.30, £1.10, £1.10; EX 32.00.
Owner Anthony D Copley **Bred** C Farrell **Trained** Westow, N Yorks

FOCUS
There looked to be plenty of surface water on the track, putting a question mark on the official going description of standard. 'Sloppy' would have been nearer the mark, and the jockeys described it as 'hard work' and 'testing'. This looked an ordinary maiden.

NOTEBOOK
Three Good Friends(IRE), who was as big as 33-1 in the morning, had a good draw in stall one and was very well supported to improve considerably on her debut effort at Folkestone when beating only one home. There were grounds for expecting her to improve, though, as her stable is in better form now and her pedigree - both her siblings have won on the Fibresand - promised improvement for a switch to this surface. She got the job done well and is likely to appreciate a bit of cut back on turf. (op 16-1)
Diamond Affair(IRE) again raced a touch too keenly. She will have to learn to settle better if she is going to win anything. (op 4-1)
Regardless, whose rider put up 2lb overweight, had run well enough at Redcar last time to suggest a race of this nature was within her ability, but that race was on good to firm ground and she had questions to answer on this very different surface. She deserves another chance back on turf. (op 11-10)
Zelos Dream(IRE), who is out of a half-sister to those smart sprinters Hoh Mike and Hogmaneigh, didn't shape too badly on her debut and can be expected to come on for this debut effort. (op 12-1 tchd 16-1)
China Bay is bred to appreciate further in time. (op 7-1)

2742 SAM BOLDY MEMORIAL H'CAP 1m 4f (F)
2:40 (2:40) (Class 6) (0-65,65) 3-Y-O £2,047 (£604; £302) Stalls Low

Form RPR
6-41 1 **Lucky Punt**20 2131 3-9-7 65 FergusSweeney 10 83+
(B G Powell) *trckd ldrs: led over 4f out: wnt clr over 2f out: abt 15 l clr 1f out: heavily eased* **7/4**1

-204 2 7 **Mekong Miss**20 2131 3-9-0 58 LukeMorris 5 57
(J Jay) *mid-div: drvn 7f out: kpt on fnl 3f: tk modest 2nd over 1f out* **7/1**3

060- 3 2 3/4 **Astroleo**297 5006 3-8-4 48 SaleemGolam 6 42
(M H Tompkins) *in rr: drvn over 3f out: styd on fnl f: snatched 3rd on line* **14/1**

0260 4 shd **Rebel Prince (IRE)**12 2350 3-8-7 51 TPQueally 9 45
(M G Quinlan) *chsd ldrs: one pce fnl 3f: eased nr fin* **7/1**3

6200 5 6 **Amazing Blue Sky**11 2370 3-9-2 60 AndrewElliott 3 45
(Mrs R A Carr) *hld up in rr: hdwy over 3f out: nvr nr ldrs* **10/1**

040 6 2 1/4 **Solo Choice**31 1800 3-9-6 64 (b) SJCraine 7 45
(D Flood) *rr-div: hdwy over 4f out: sn chsng ldrs: wknd 2f out* **13/2**2

1003 7 3 1/2 **Shifting Gold (IRE)**19 2152 3-9-4 62 (b) JoeFanning 8 37
(K A Ryan) *led tl over 4f out: lost pl over 2f out* **10/1**

0300 8 1 1/2 **Milemilia (IRE)**30 1842 3-9-2 60 TravisBlock 2 33
(H Morrison) *mid-div: drvn 8f out: lost pl over 4f out* **22/1**

-530 9 12 **Dulce Domum**31 1811 3-8-3 47 ChrisCatlin 1 1
(A B Haynes) *dwlt: in rr and sn drvn along: bhd fnl 3f* **16/1**

60-0 10 11 **Swing It Ruby (IRE)**34 1724 3-8-7 51 SilvestreDeSousa 4 —
(Mrs D J Sanderson) *chsd ldrs: drvn 8f out: lost pl over 3f out: sn bhd* **14/1**

2m 37.66s (-3.34) **Going Correction** -0.25s/f (Stan) **10 Ran SP% 116.4**
Speed ratings (Par 97): **101,96,94,94,90 88,86,85,77,70**
toteswinger: 1&2 £3.50, 1&3 £9.60, 2&3 £29.90. CSF £14.04 CT £131.66 TOTE £2.60: £1.60, £2.20, £2.90; EX 15.90.
Owner I S Smith **Bred** S A Douch **Trained** Upper Lambourn, Berks

FOCUS
A moderate handicap which was turned into a procession by Lucky Punt.

2743 SHANE W DARBY MEMORIAL CLAIMING STKS 1m 4f (F)
3:10 (3:10) (Class 5) 3-Y-O+ £2,729 (£806; £403) Stalls Low

Form RPR
0-20 1 **Realism (FR)**8 2499 9-9-4 77 FrederikTylicki(5) 5 84
(M W Easterby) *hld up in rr: gd hdwy over 4f out: wnt 2nd over 2f out: drvn to ld over 1f out: sn drew clr: v readily* **5/1**3

1061 2 6 **Aureate**20 2129 5-9-5 85 TomEaves 2 74
(B Ellison) *trckd ldr: led 3f out: hdd over 1f out: sn wl outpcd* **13/8**1

2324 3 6 **Edas**8 2499 7-9-1 67 MarkCoumbe(5) 7 62
(R A Harris) *in rr: hdwy over 3f out: kpt on to take modest 3rd ins fnl f* **6/1**

4522 4 5 **Wind Flow**20 2146 5-9-6 76 (v) MJMurphy(7) 4 61
(C A Dwyer) *sn setting str pce: hdd 3f out: wknd appr fnl f* **9/2**2

0410 5 8 **Nawamees (IRE)**8 2499 11-9-0 68 (p) RichardEvans(5) 6 40
(P D Evans) *chsd ldrs: drvn 6f out: lost pl over 4f out* **8/1**

0-00 6 2 **Top Tinker**13 2340 3-8-4 50 SaleemGolam 3 37
(M H Tompkins) *in rr: nvr on terms* **50/1**

00 7 1 1/2 **My Bodyguard (FR)**22 2090 3-8-3 0 (bt1) ChrisCatlin 9 33
(H J L Dunlop) *chsd ldrs: drvn over 4f out: wknd 3f out* **40/1**

00-3 8 1 3/4 **Ozone Trustee (NZ)**9 2437 5-9-9 78 PJMcDonald 8 36
(G A Swinbank) *mid-div: drvn over 4f out: lost pl over 3f out* **8/1**

6140 9 1/2 **Salute (IRE)**47 1435 10-9-7 77 RobertHavlin 1 33
(P G Murphy) *chsd ldrs: drvn 6f out: lost pl over 4f out: sn bhd* **16/1**

2m 36.6s (-4.40) **Going Correction** -0.25s/f (Stan)
WFA 3 from 5yo+ 15lb **9 Ran SP% 119.7**
Speed ratings (Par 103): **104,100,96,92,87 86,85,83,83**
toteswinger: 1&2 £2.40, 1&3 £5.10, 2&3 £5.40. CSF £14.07 TOTE £5.50: £1.70, £1.10, £2.00; EX 13.80.Edas was claimed by Mr. T. A. K. Cuthbert for £7,000.
Owner S A Hollings **Bred** Darley Stud Management Co Ltd **Trained** Sheriff Hutton, N Yorks

FOCUS
This was not a bad claimer.

2744 BETDAQ.CO.UK (S) STKS 7f (F)
3:40 (3:41) (Class 6) 3-Y-O £2,047 (£604; £302) Stalls Low

Form RPR
605 1 **Swiss Art (IRE)**24 2009 3-9-4 70 JoeFanning 8 78+
(R A Harris) *in rr: hdwy over 3f out: styd on to ld appr fnl f: kpt on wl* **7/4**1

2440 2 1 1/4 **Iron Out (USA)**12 2357 3-8-12 60 GrahamGibbons 11 66
(R Hollinshead) *w ldr: led over 2f out: hdd appr fnl f: kpt on same pce* **11/4**2

0-00 3 6 **Fol Liam**25 1992 3-9-4 74 (b1) StephenDonohoe 2 56
(Ian Williams) *led tl over 2f out: wknd fnl f* **7/1**3

6536 4 1 1/2 **Paymaster In Chief**31 1811 3-8-7 46 (v1) LeeNewnes(5) 6 46
(M D I Usher) *prom: outpcd over 3f out: one pce fnl 2f* **20/1**

5-30 **5** *2* **Kinigi (IRE)**[107] 620 3-8-13 57 .... LukeMorris 10 41
(R A Harris) *rrd s: hdwy and in tch over 4f out: nvr trbld ldrs* **7/1**[3]

-500 **6** *5* **Buckle Up**[20] 2122 3-8-9 42 .... (p) JackMitchell(3) 7 27
(D K Ivory) *chsd ldrs: wknd over 2f out* **40/1**

0-00 **7** *3/4* **Sally's Swansong**[44] 1491 3-8-7 43 .... (p) SaleemGolam 1 20
(M Wellings) *chsd ldrs: lost pl over 3f out* **66/1**

-000 **8** *3/4* **Asakusa**[19] 2169 3-8-7 55 .... (b[1]) TPQueally 3 18
(H R A Cecil) *in rr and sn drvn along: hrd rdn and hung lft over 2f out: nt keen* **8/1**

0-00 **9** *57* **Sharp Discovery**[30] 1843 3-8-7 35 .... (b[1]) FergusSweeney 9 —
(J M Bradley) *s.i.s: reminders after s: sn bhd: t.o whn virtually p.u 3f out* **66/1**

4540 **10** *1 1/2* **Cognac Boy (USA)**[24] 2009 3-9-4 58 .... (v[1]) ChrisCatlin 4 —
(A B Haynes) *sn bhd: t.o whn virtually p.u 3f out* **14/1**

1m 28.75s (-1.55) **Going Correction** -0.25s/f (Stan) **10** Ran SP% **116.0**
Speed ratings (Par 97): **98,96,89,88,85 80,79,78,13,11**
toteswinger: 1&2 £1.50, 1&3 £6.40, 2&3 £3.90. CSF £6.27 TOTE £2.90: £1.10, £1.60, £1.90; EX 8.20.The winner was bought in for 4,000gns. Fol Liam was claimed by A. J. McCabe for £5,500.
Owner W Clifford **Bred** John Yarr **Trained** Earlswood, Monmouths

FOCUS
A moderate seller, with six of the 11 runners trying a new form of headgear for the first time. The market got it right, though, with the first three finishing in betting order. There was a decent gallop on.

2745 JACKSONS WORKWEAR RENTAL H'CAP 6f (F)
4:10 (4:14) (Class 6) (0-60,64) 4-Y-0+ £2,047 (£604; £302) Stalls Low

Form RPR

0-40 **1** **Gioacchino (IRE)**[6] 2534 4-8-8 53 .... KevinGhunowa(3) 1 61
(R A Harris) *mde most: hrd rdn and kpt on wl fnl f* **33/1**

4010 **2** *2* **Outer Hebrides**[16] 2223 8-8-4 51 .... (v) AmyBaker(5) 9 53
(J M Bradley) *in rr: hdwy and edgd lft 2f out: styd on wl fnl f to take 2nd nr fin* **14/1**

0-00 **3** *nk* **Triumphant Welcome**[12] 2349 4-9-1 57 .... FergusSweeney 6 58
(H J Evans) *in tch: stmbld over 4f out: hdwy over 2f out: styd on fnl f* **7/1**[3]

5042 **4** *hd* **Blakeshall Quest**[5] 2579 9-8-10 52 .... (b) PhillipMakin 11 52
(R Brotherton) *hmpd s: mid-div: hdwy on ins over 2f out: kpt on wl fnl f* **7/1**[3]

5364 **5** *1 1/4* **Spoof Master (IRE)**[5] 2579 5-9-2 58 .... (p) TPQueally 12 54
(C R Dore) *wnt lft s: w ldrs on outer: outpcd over 3f out: kpt on fnl 2f* **8/1**

0000 **6** *nk* **Angle Of Attack (IRE)**[16] 2225 4-9-4 60 .... SilvestreDeSousa 2 55
(A D Brown) *chsd ldrs: one pce fnl 2f* **18/1**

3601 **7** *1 1/4* **Kingsmaite**[5] 2579 8-9-1 64 6ex .... (b) AndrewYoxall(7) 13 55
(S R Bowring) *r wd: lost pl over 4f out: sn bhd: styd on fnl 2f: nt rch ldrs* **15/8**[1]

0003 **8** *nk* **Owed**[5] 2579 7-8-5 50 .... (bt) JackMitchell(3) 7 40
(R Bastiman) *in rr: bhd over 3f out: hdwy on outside 2f out: nvr a factor* **13/2**[2]

-005 **9** *3/4* **Sovereignty (JPN)**[2] 2682 7-8-1 50 .... CharlotteKerton(7) 8 38
(D K Ivory) *in rr: hdwy on outer over 2f out: nvr on terms* **14/1**

0-20 **10** *3 1/4* **Bertbrand**[5] 2579 4-8-11 60 .... (b) JamieKyne(7) 5 38
(D Flood) *bmpd s: w ldrs: chal 3f out: hrd rdn and wknd 1f out* **18/1**

3605 **11** *nk* **Bollin Franny**[18] 2184 5-8-8 50 .... RichardThomas 14 27
(J E Long) *reluctant and led to post: in tch on outer: lost pl over 1f out* **20/1**

0460 **12** *2 3/4* **Sheik'N'Knotsterd**[12] 2366 4-8-12 54 .... ChrisCatlin 10 22
(J F Coupland) *chsd ldrs on outer: outpcd 3f out: lost pl over 1f out* **20/1**

600- **13** *1 3/4* **Ledgerwood**[283] 5429 4-8-8 50 .... NeilChalmers 4 12
(A J Chamberlain) *wnt rt s: in tch: lost pl over 3f out* **66/1**

1m 15.97s (-0.53) **Going Correction** -0.25s/f (Stan) **13** Ran SP% **122.0**
Speed ratings (Par 101): **93,90,89,89,88 87,85,85,84,80 79,76,73**
toteswinger: 1&2 £48.90, 1&3 £43.90, 2&3 £17.40. CSF £434.65 CT £3712.95 TOTE £40.20: £4.70, £4.40, £3.00; EX 868.20.
Owner Dream Team Syndicate **Bred** John Cullinan **Trained** Earlswood, Monmouths

FOCUS
Moderate handicap form.
Triumphant Welcome Official explanation: jockey said gelding stumbled in the back straight

2746 BET MULTIPLES-BETDAQ H'CAP 1m (F)
4:40 (4:42) (Class 6) (0-60,60) 4-Y-0+ £2,047 (£604; £302) Stalls Low

Form RPR

-000 **1** **Byron Bay**[16] 2233 7-8-9 51 .... GrahamGibbons 4 62
(R Johnson) *mde virtually all: qcknd clr 3f out: edgd lft fnl f: hld on towards fin* **7/1**

0140 **2** *nk* **Almahaza (IRE)**[27] 1936 5-9-3 59 .... NeilChalmers 1 69+
(A J Chamberlain) *gave problems in stalls: hld up in rr: hdwy on ins over 2f out: wnt 2nd over 1f out: styd on: jst hld* **8/1**

0002 **3** *2 1/4* **Sularno**[19] 2149 5-9-2 58 .... RobertHavlin 10 63
(J Pearce) *prom: outpcd over 2f out: styd on wl fnl f* **15/2**

4200 **4** *3 3/4* **Ten Pole Tudor**[35] 1710 4-9-0 56 .... (p) LukeMorris 3 52+
(R A Harris) *s.s: reminders over 4f out: hdwy over 2f out: kpt on: nvr nr ldrs* **12/1**

00-0 **5** *2 1/2* **Bermacha**[44] 1495 4-9-2 58 .... RichardThomas 14 49
(J E Long) *chsd ldrs: one pce fnl 2f* **33/1**

6023 **6** *1/2* **Haroldini (IRE)**[37] 1655 7-9-1 57 .... (v) PaulMulrennan 8 46
(J Balding) *chsd wnr: wknd over 1f out* **9/2**[1]

3550 **7** *1* **Trans Sonic**[11] 1475 6-8-11 60 .... (v) JamieKyne(7) 6 47
(A J Lockwood) *towards rr: hdwy over 2f out: nvr nr ldrs* **16/1**

52-0 **8** *1/2* **Tender Moments**[16] 2237 5-8-12 54 .... TomEaves 7 40
(B Smart) *chsd ldrs: outpcd over 3f out: one pce fnl 2f* **14/1**

0600 **9** *2* **Cross Reef**[7] 2517 4-9-3 59 .... JoeFanning 5 40
(R A Harris) *s.i.s: in rr: kpt on fnl 2f: nvr a factor* **20/1**

55 **10** *4 1/2* **Ermine Grey**[15] 2261 8-9-3 59 .... (p) ChrisCatlin 2 30
(S Gollings) *in rr: swtchd wd after 2f: nvr on terms* **13/2**[3]

0000 **11** *nk* **Spares And Repairs**[9] 2458 6-8-6 48 .... AndrewMullen 11 18
(Mrs S Lamyman) *racd wd: sn in rr and drvn along: nvr a factor* **12/1**

20/0 **12** *2 1/2* **Legal Lover (IRE)**[37] 1655 7-8-9 54 .... RussellKennemore(3) 9 19
(R Hollinshead) *chsd ldrs: outpcd over 4f out: sn lost pl* **20/1**

0-00 **13** *shd* **Princess Gee**[34] 1728 4-8-3 50 .... NicolPolli(5) 13 14
(B J McMath) *racd wd: chsd ldrs: wknd over 2f out* **20/1**

6-00 **14** *12* **Reve Vert (FR)**[9] 2441 4-8-12 54 .... FergusSweeney 12 —
(Tim Vaughan) *racd wd: in tch: lost pl 3f out: bhd whn eased ins fnl f* **11/2**[2]

1m 42.59s (-1.11) **Going Correction** -0.25s/f (Stan) **14** Ran SP% **127.4**
Speed ratings (Par 101): **95,94,92,88,86 85,84,84,82,77 77,74,74,62**
toteswinger: 1&2 £18.20, 1&3 £17.90, 2&3 £13.40. CSF £62.45 CT £459.57 TOTE £7.80: £2.60, £2.70, £3.20; EX 82.00 Place 6: £67.46 Place 5: £59.41.
Owner James S Kennerley And Miss Jenny Hall **Bred** Ian Murray Tough **Trained** Newburn, Tyne & Wear
■ Stewards' Enquiry : Chris Catlin caution: entered wrong stall

FOCUS
An ordinary handicap.
T/Plt: £90.90 to a £1 stake. Pool: £66,964.08. 537.42 winning tickets. T/Qpdt: £48.60 to a £1 stake. Pool: £3,757.19. 57.10 winning tickets. WG

2747 - 2753a (Foreign Racing) - See Raceform Interactive

[2521]CHANTILLY (R-H)
Sunday, June 7

OFFICIAL GOING: Good

2754a PRIX DE ROYAUMONT (GROUP 3) (FILLIES) 1m 4f
3:15 (3:14) 3-Y-0 £38,835 (£15,534; £11,650; £7,767; £3,883)

RPR

1 **Quetsche (USA)**[44] 3-9-0 .... C-PLemaire 3 96
(J-C Rouget, France) *rrd s: led after 1f: drvn out fnl f* **32/5**

2 *snk* **Shamakiya (IRE)**[42] 3-9-0 .... CSoumillon 4 96
(A De Royer-Dupre, France) *hld up in 4th to st: moved out and pushed along over 2f out: rchd 2nd 1f out: r.o: jst failed* **6/4**[1]

3 *1* **Becqu Adoree (FR)**[31] 1820 3-9-0 .... FBlondel 5 94
(F Rossi, France) *disp 2nd on outside: 2nd st: one pce fnl f* **25/1**

4 *1* **Bahama Bay (GER)**[37] 3-9-0 .... MGuyon 1 93
(A Fabre, France) *first to show: trckd wnr: 3rd st: rdn wl over 1f out: no ex fnl f* **7/2**[2]

5 *1 1/2* **Divine Comedy (FR)**[28] 1916 3-9-0 .... DBoeuf 6 90
(D Smaga, France) *hld up in 6th to st: kpt on one pce u.p to take 5th cl home* **14/1**

6 *nk* **Atlas Silk**[34] 3-9-0 .... SPasquier 2 90
(P Bary, France) *hld up: settled in 5th: nvr able to chal* **69/10**

7 *3* **Landskia (FR)**[28] 1916 3-9-0 .... OPeslier 7 85
(A Fabre, France) *plld hrd and restrained in last: rdn and btn wl over 1f out* **9/2**[3]

2m 33.1s (2.10) **Going Correction** +0.15s/f (Good) **7** Ran SP% **117.1**
Speed ratings: **99,98,98,97,96 96,94**
PARI-MUTUEL: WIN 7.40; PL 2.80, 1.60; SF 21.40.
Owner Ecurie Des Monceaux **Bred** Malibu Farm Llc **Trained** Pau, France

FOCUS
They went an ordinary pace.

NOTEBOOK
Quetsche(USA) was given a fine waiting ride and stayed on bravely. Prior to this outing she had been campaigned mainly in the south west of France and is certainly a horse going the right way. She needs time between races so a tilt at the Prix de Malleret at the end of the month might not be on the cards.
Shamakiya(IRE) was unsuited by a steady pace and was outpaced when things quickened up. Once balanced at the furlong and a half marker she began to cut down the leader and would have won shortly after the post. She is a green filly compared to the winner but certainly looks like to have a bright future in front of her. The Malleret would be an obvious choice now.
Becqu Adoree(FR) was always up with the pace and still there in the entrance to the straight. She battled well to the line and bravely held on to third position.
Bahama Bay(GER) was always well placed but couldn't quicken when the race warmed up.

2755a PRIX PAUL DE MOUSSAC (GROUP 3) (C&G) 1m
3:50 (3:52) 3-Y-0 £38,835 (£15,534; £11,650; £7,767; £3,883)

RPR

1 **Oiseau De Feu (USA)**[28] 1917 3-8-10 .... C-PLemaire 2 109
(J-C Rouget, France) *disp 5th: 5th st: swtchd lft appr fnl f: drvn to ld last strides* **5/2**[1]

2 *snk* **Handsome Maestro (IRE)**[28] 1917 3-8-10 .... CSoumillon 4 109
(D Smaga, France) *racd in 4th: wnt 3rd ent st: led over 1f out: drvn fnl f: ct last strides* **7/2**[2]

3 *2 1/2* **Orizaba (IRE)**[253] 6267 3-8-10 .... LDettori 3 103
(Saeed Bin Suroor) *trckd ldr: 2nd st: drvn 1 1/2f out: ev ch dist: one pce* **9/2**

4 *nse* **Little Dreams (FR)**[44] 3-8-10 .... FBlondel 5 103
(F Rossi, France) *6th st: stl 6th 1f out: drvn and r.o clsng stages* **16/1**

5 *1 1/2* **Sabantuy**[49] 1395 3-8-10 .... IMendizabal 1 100
(C Von Der Recke, Germany) *led to over 1f out* **33/1**

6 *snk* **Broken In Light (FR)**[31] 1820 3-8-10 .... (b) GMillet 10 99
(T Larriviere, France) *hld up: 7th st: hdwy on ins over 1f out: 5th whn nt clr run ins fnl f: no ch after* **24/1**

7 *3/4* **Anco Marzio**[24] 2026 3-8-10 .... GMosse 7 98
(A De Royer-Dupre, France) *last to 1 1/2f out: nvr a factor* **16/1**

8 *shd* **Silverside (USA)**[35] 3-8-10 .... OPeslier 8 97
(C Laffon-Parias, France) *trckd ldrs: 4th st: one pce fr wl over 1f out* **4/1**[3]

9 *shd* **Milanais (FR)**[56] 1238 3-8-10 .... SPasquier 9 97
(M Delzangles, France) *hld up: 8th st: kpt on same pce fnl 2f* **12/1**

10 *10* **Heart Attack (FR)**[21] 3-8-10 .... BClos 6 74
(G Martin, Austria) *9th st: bhd fnl 2f* **33/1**

1m 37.3s (-0.70) **Going Correction** +0.15s/f (Good) **10** Ran SP% **118.3**
Speed ratings: **109,108,106,106,104 104,103,103,103,93**
PARI-MUTUEL: WIN 3.80; PL 1.40, 1.40, 2.20; DF 3.40.
Owner B Weill **Bred** Gallagher's Stud **Trained** Pau, France

NOTEBOOK
Oiseau De Feu(USA), given a waiting ride, was brought with a challenge at exactly the right time and made up at least two lengths from the furlong marker. He is a very consistent individual who had good previous form and no immediate plans were confirmed, but it would be no surprise if he turned out for the Prix Jean Prat at this track in early July.
Handsome Maestro(IRE) was dropped in behind the leading group and made his challenge from one and a half out. He took control at the furlong marker and looked the likely winner before being cut down in the dying stages of the mile.
Orizaba(IRE) quickened well in the straight and began to struggle halfway through the final furlong. He was very brave to the line and held on to third place by inches. This performance augurs very well for the future and he has been entered in several top races including the St. James's Palace Stakes and the Sussex Stakes.

Little Dreams(FR) finished well and only missed third place by a nose.

2756a PRIX DU JOCKEY CLUB (GROUP 1) (C&F) 1m 2f 110y
4:35 (4:36) 3-Y-0 **£832,136** (£332,913; £166,456; £83,155; £41,650)

RPR

1 **Le Havre (IRE)**[28] 1917 3-9-2 .... C-PLemaire 4 121
(J-C Rouget, France) *mid-div: 7th st on ins: swtchd lft jst over 2f out: 2nd 1 1/2f out: led 150yds out: r.o wl* **119/10**

2 1 1/2 **Fuisse (FR)**[22] 2096 3-9-2 .... DBoeuf 3 118
(Mme C Head-Maarek, France) *racd in 3rd to st: led wl over 1f out: drvn and hdd 150yds out: one pce* **10/1**

3 1 1/2 **Westphalia (IRE)**[28] 1917 3-9-2 .... JMurtagh 13 115?
(A P O'Brien, Ire) *mid-div on outside: hdwy over 2f out: 3rd and edgd rt 1 1/2f out: r.o same pce* **6/1**[3]

4 1 1/2 **Beheshtam (FR)**[12] 2369 3-9-2 .... CSoumillon 15 112
(A De Royer-Dupre, France) *hld up towards rr to st: hdwy over 2f out: rdn and one pce fr over 1f out* **9/2**[2]

5 1/2 **Calvados Blues (FR)**[30] 1858 3-9-2 .... GMosse 5 112?
(P Demercastel, France) *hld up in rr: last st: gd hdwy on wd outside fnl 2f: nrest at fin* **40/1**

6 1 1/2 **Silver Frost (IRE)**[28] 1917 3-9-2 .... OPeslier 2 109
(Y De Nicolay, France) *a.p: 4th st: outpcd over 2f out: hrd rdn and kpt on same pce fr over 1f out* **27/10**[1]

7 hd **Vesuve (IRE)**[30] 1858 3-9-2 .... TThulliez 9 108
(E Lellouche, France) *hld up in mid-div: got through on ins wl over 2f out: narrow ldr briefly 2f out: wknd appr fnl f* **33/1**

8 1 1/2 **Drumbeat (IRE)**[15] 2288 3-9-2 .... JimmyFortune 1 105
(A P O'Brien, Ire) *towards rr to st: hdwy over 2f out: kpt on but nvr nr to chal* **33/1**

9 1/2 **Topclas (FR)**[26] 1979 3-9-2 .... SPasquier 8 104
(P Demercastel, France) *mid-div: sme hdwy over 2f out: rchd 6th wl over 1f out: sn btn* **33/1**

10 hd **Glamstar (FR)**[30] 1858 3-9-2 .... FBlondel 12 104?
(J-C Rouget, France) *in rr to st: sme prog fnl 2f: nvr nrr* **66/1**

11 1 1/2 **Guest Ville (FR)**[34] 1761 3-9-2 .... TJarnet 7 101
(Mlle S-V Tarrou, France) *nvr nrr than mid-div* **50/1**

12 snk **Wajir (FR)**[34] 1761 3-9-2 .... ACrastus 10 101
(E Lellouche, France) *hld up: sme prog towards outside whn sltly hmpd 2f out: nvr a factor* **10/1**

13 3 **Zafisio (IRE)**[28] 1915 3-9-2 .... WMLordan 14 95
(R Curtis) *chsd ldrs on outside: 5th st: rdn 2f out: sn btn* **25/1**

14 15 **Parthenon**[23] 2029 3-9-2 .... LDettori 11 67
(Saeed Bin Suroor) *prom: 6th st: btn over 2f out* **14/1**

15 nse **Set Sail (IRE)**[56] 1238 3-9-2 .... JAHeffernan 17 67
(A P O'Brien, Ire) *pressed ldr 2nd st: wknd qckly wl over 1f out* **50/1**

16 2 1/2 **Malibu Bay (USA)**[44] 1485 3-9-2 .... DBonilla 6 62
(A P O'Brien, Ire) *in tch on outside to st: sn wknd* **40/1**

17 20 **Feels All Right (IRE)**[45] 1483 3-9-2 .... IMendizabal 16 24
(E Libaud, France) *led to 2f out* **13/2**

2m 6.80s (-2.00) **Going Correction** +0.15s/f (Good) **17 Ran SP% 128.4**
Speed ratings: **113,111,110,109,109 108,108,107,106,106 105,105,103,92,92 90,75**
PARI-MUTUEL: WIN 12.90; PL 4.40, 3.30, 3.50; DF 60.50.
Owner G Augustin-Normand **Bred** Team Hogdala Ab **Trained** Pau, France

FOCUS
The fifth running of the Jockey Club over its reduced trip once again produced a sizeable field, but it remains a disappointment that such a prestigious Classic has been messed around with and spoiled. This latest running highlighted the increased importance of an inside draw with six of the first eight home having started from stalls four, three, five, two, nine and one.

NOTEBOOK
Le Havre(IRE), representing a sizzling stable, came here having landed the Prix Djebel and finished second in the Poule d'Essai des Poulains, but any doubts about the stamina of a colt with a speedy pedigree were eradicated by an authoritative success. Settled in mid-division near the rail by Christophe Lemaire, the son of Noverre made very easy headway and did not have to be thrashed to put his head in front and extend. Based on his overall profile, it is hard to put him in the same league as Epsom hero Sea The Stars, but he is clearly progressive and, like the Investec Derby winner, could prove best at around 1m2f. That being the case, quotes of between 12-1 and 16-1 for the Arc do not make a great deal of appeal. The main end of year target could be the Champion Stakes at Newmarket, which his trainer took in 2007 with Literato.
Fuisse(FR), a much bigger and scopier individual than the winner, raced closest of all the principals to the frenetic gallop and emerges from the contest with considerable credit. Brought here on the back of a Listed success, he arguably hit the front a shade too soon as he seemed to wander and possibly idle in the lead. That being the case, he could do better in time and Group 1 victories in the future are far from impossible. His connections will now be looking at the Prix Eugene Adam at Maisons-Laffitte at the end of July.
Westphalia(IRE) followed his Poulains third – he was promoted from fourth that day – by filling the same position here, but while in one way he enhanced his reputation, he also left it slightly tarnished. To his credit, he did well to get so close from stall 13, but having been held on to for as long as possible by Johnny Murtagh, he dived violently right when pressure was applied. From there to the line there was much swishing of the tail, all of which suggested that Westphalia is talented but certainly not straightforward.
Beheshtam(FR), who was supplemented, was racing for only the third time and for the first time since sneaking a cheeky Listed win. The fact that his debut came over 1m4f surely highlighted that stamina is one of the horse's strong cards, so it was no surprise that he did not have sufficient toe to land a blow, and he was poorly drawn in 15. He did, however, make impressive if not spectacular headway from the rear, and it would be no surprise to see him prove much better than this come the end of the season. He will be back at 1m4f in the Grand Prix de Paris and his jockey feels he is the perfect sort for the Arc de Triomphe.
Calvados Blues(FR) looked relatively exposed beforehand and a fast-finishing fifth is probably a fair reflection of his ability – indeed, he might have been flattered having been protected from the demanding early pace.
Silver Frost(IRE), who beat Le Havre in the Pouliches, was not certain to stay, and it will now be a surprise if he is not dropped back to 1m. Although far from disgraced, he was given every chance and was simply not good enough on the day. As an insubstantial specimen who was racing for the fourth time this season, he would probably benefit from a break before being brought back for the Jacques le Marois or Moulin.
Vesuve(IRE) ran better than might have been expected.
Drumbeat(IRE) confirmed himself to be shy of Group 1 class by running on for eighth, although but for minor interference up the straight he might have finished slightly closer.
Zafisio(IRE) was in contention for slightly longer but still dropped tamely away.
Parthenon, formerly trained by mark Johnston, was significantly up in class, but it was still disappointing to see him come under a shove a long way from home.
Set Sail(IRE) not surprisingly weakened after trying to follow the front-running Feels All Right.
Malibu Bay(USA) could not land a blow.
Feels All Right(IRE) set off like the clappers and predictably folded quickly once headed.

[1240]DUSSELDORF (R-H)
Sunday, June 7

OFFICIAL GOING: Good

2757a GERMAN 1,000 GUINEAS (GROUP 2) (FILLIES) 1m
3:30 (3:47) 3-Y-0 **£73,786** (£27,184; £13,592; £6,796)

RPR

1 **Penny's Gift**[35] 1698 3-9-2 .... RichardHughes 1 107
(R Hannon) *mde all: rdn over 1f out: drvn out* **9/5**[1]

2 nk **Fabiana**[28] 1914 3-9-2 .... THellier 11 106+
(Andreas Lowe, Germany) *last early: 8th st: hdwy on outside fr wl over 1f out: r.o wl clsng stages* **103/10**

3 hd **Entre Deux Eaux (FR)**[7] 2521 3-9-2 .... GBenoist 4 106
(Robert Collet, France) *a.p: 3rd st: drvn over 1f out: r.o steadily fnl f* **13/1**

4 1 3/4 **Norderney (GER)**[56] 1240 3-9-2 .... FilipMinarik 2 102
(P Schiergen, Germany) *mid-div: 6th st: kpt on fr over 1f out: nrest at fin* **49/10**[2]

5 1 3/4 **Lukrecia (IRE)**[28] 1914 3-9-2 .... AStarke 10 98
(P Schiergen, Germany) *sn trcking wnr: 2nd st: wknd appr fnl f* **73/10**

6 1 1/2 **All Annalena (IRE)**[28] 1914 3-9-2 .... AHelfenbein 9 94
(Andreas Lowe, Germany) *cl up to 1/2-way: 5th st: one pce* **117/10**

7 1 **Pariala (GER)** 3-9-2 .... AGoritz 8 92
(P Schiergen, Germany) *reluctant to load: a in tch: 4th st: btn over 1f out* **29/1**

8 3/4 **Anjella (GER)**[28] 1914 3-9-2 .... ADeVries 12 90
(J Hirschberger, Germany) *mid-div: 7th st: no hdwy* **103/10**

9 1 **Mambo Light (USA)**[252] 6319 3-9-2 .... EPedroza 7 88
(A Wohler, Germany) *nvr a factor* **61/10**[3]

10 1 3/4 **Clarissa Directa** 3-9-2 .... HGrewe 3 84
(C Sprengel, Germany) *a towards rr* **56/1**

11 2 1/2 **Muriel (IRE)**[21] 3-9-2 .... JiriPalik 6 78
(Andreas Lowe, Germany) *a bhd* **31/1**

12 2 **Addicted (GER)**[28] 1914 3-9-2 .... ASuborics 5 74
(T Mundry, Germany) *last st: a bhd* **13/2**

1m 39.29s (-1.87) **12 Ran SP% 133.1**
(including 10 euro stakes): WIN 28; PL 19, 37, 30: SF 378.
Owner Malcolm Brown & Mrs Penny Brown **Bred** Capt A L Smith-Maxwell **Trained** East Everleigh, Wilts

NOTEBOOK
Penny's Gift, sixth in the 1000 Guineas, was left alone in front and took full advantage to make every yard of the running under a fine front-running ride from Hughes. She gamely held off the closers, proving she gets a mile in the process.

[2562]FOLKESTONE (R-H)
Monday, June 8

OFFICIAL GOING: Good to firm (straight course: far side 8.9, stands' side 8.4; round course 8.0)
Wind: virtually nil Weather: mainly overcast

2758 EASTWELL MANOR H'CAP 5f
2:15 (2:16) (Class 6) (0-60,60) 4-Y-0+ **£2,047** (£604; £302) **Stalls Low**

Form RPR

00-6 1 **Pic Up Sticks**[19] 2180 10-9-4 **60** .... GeorgeBaker 1 70
(B G Powell) *trckd ldrs: a gng wl: wnt 2nd 2f out: pushed into ld jst ins fnl f: pushed out* **7/1**[3]

034 2 3/4 **Music Box Express**[6] 2564 5-8-11 **60** .... MatthewDavies(7) 2 67
(George Baker) *led: rdn 2f out: clr w wnr ent fnl f: hdd ins fnl f: kpt on but wl hld by wnr* **9/2**[1]

3020 3 2 3/4 **Green Lagonda (AUS)**[6] 2564 7-8-13 **55** .... TPQueally 3 52
(Stef Liddiard) *taken down early: in tch: drvn jst over 2f out: kpt on u.p to go 3rd ins fnl f: nvr pce to chal ldng pair* **13/2**[2]

0-05 4 3/4 **Valiant Romeo**[28] 1921 9-8-4 **49** ow1 ....(v) JackMitchell(3) 4 44
(R Bastiman) *chsd ldr tl 2f out: drvn and outpcd by ldng pair over 1f out: lost 3rd ins fnl f* **20/1**

0520 5 hd **Triple Dream**[13] 2366 4-9-3 **59** ....(p) SteveDrowne 13 53+
(J M Bradley) *racd towards far side tl 2f out: in tch overall: effrt and drvn jst over 2f out: no imp ent fnl f* **15/2**

0-02 6 3/4 **Miss Firefly**[19] 2180 4-8-6 **53** .... MCGeran(5) 6 44
(R J Hodges) *taken down early: chsd ldrs: rdn 1/2-way: outpcd wl over 1f out: kpt on same pce after* **9/2**[1]

5350 7 1 1/2 **Mr Loire**[95] 762 5-8-4 **46** oh1 ....(b) SimonWhitworth 8 32
(A J Chamberlain) *s.i.s: bhd: sme modest late hdwy: n.d* **33/1**

0506 8 nk **Rightcar Lewis**[13] 2366 4-8-4 **46** oh1 ....(b) PatrickMathers 5 31
(Peter Grayson) *bhd: sme hdwy but hanging rt fr over 1f out: nvr trbld ldrs* **22/1**

60-0 9 1/2 **Walragnek**[13] 2349 5-8-10 **52** .... CatherineGannon 10 35
(J G M O'Shea) *racd in midfield: nvr trbld ldrs* **20/1**

0620 10 nk **Lady Hopeful (IRE)**[20] 2158 7-8-4 **46** oh1 ....(b) FrankieMcDonald 7 28
(Peter Grayson) *s.i.s: a towards rr* **66/1**

464 11 nk **Sandy Par**[5] 2603 4-9-2 **58** ....(b) ChrisCatlin 9 39
(J M Bradley) *a towards rr: nvr nr ldrs* **16/1**

0560 12 1 1/2 **Thoughtsofstardom**[11] 2418 6-9-1 **57** .... LukeMorris 12 32
(P S McEntee) *racd towards far side tl 2f out: a bhd* **9/1**

060 13 11 **Bookiesindex Boy**[41] 1591 5-9-1 **57** ....(b) JimCrowley 11 —
(J R Jenkins) *racd towards far side tl 2f out: led that trio tl over 2f out: sn hung lft and wknd* **9/1**

59.35 secs (-0.65) **Going Correction** -0.10s/f (Good) **13 Ran SP% 118.1**
Speed ratings (Par 101): **101,99,95,94,93 92,90,89,89,88 88,85,68**
toteswinger: 1&2 £5.90, 1&3 £9.20, 2&3 £9.20 CSF £35.40 CT £184.78 TOTE £5.90: £1.80, £2.30, £2.60; EX 19.30 Trifecta £297.40 Pool: £683.22 - 1.70 winning units..
Owner Mrs P Jubert **Bred** J P Coggan **Trained** Upper Lambourn, Berks
■ Stewards' Enquiry : Patrick Mathers one-day ban: used whip down shoulder

FOCUS
Initially four, then three, of the field raced largely in the middle, the rest towards the stands' rail. As is usually the case at this track, the latter bunch held the advantage and the four lowest stalls filled the first four places in the "correct" order. The winner is the best guide to this form.
Triple Dream Official explanation: jockey said that the gelding hung left

Rightcar Lewis Official explanation: jockey said that the filly hung badly right throughout

2759 HYTHE CLAIMING STKS 6f
2:45 (2:45) (Class 6) 3-Y-0+ £2,047 (£604; £302) Stalls Low

Form RPR

3321 **1** **Billy Beetroot (USA)**[1] 2740 3-8-3 60........................(t) AndreaAtzeni(5) 3 59+
(S C Williams) *trckd ldrs: swtchd rt and effrt ent fnl f: rdn and r.o wl to ld wl ins fnl f* **13/8**[1]

6030 **2** *nk* **Papillio (IRE)**[23] 2086 4-9-10 70........................ NCallan 2 68
(J R Fanshawe) *led narrowly: rdn wl over 1f out: edgd rt u.p but kpt on wl tl hdd and no ex wl ins fnl f* **9/4**[2]

2243 **3** *shd* **Caribbean Coral**[10] 2456 10-9-6 63........................ GeorgeBaker 5 64+
(A B Haynes) *hld up in last pair: hdwy and rdn over 1f out: chsd ldrs 1f out: nt clr run ins fnl f tl squeezed between horses to snatch 3rd last strides* **12/1**

2206 **4** *hd* **Creative (IRE)**[10] 2456 4-9-6 52........................(v[1]) SebSanders 1 63
(M H Tompkins) *t.k.h: trckd ldrs: wnt 2nd wl over 1f out: sn ev ch: drvn and unable qck fnl f: lost 2 pls towards fin* **17/2**

4353 **5** *6* **Mr Rev**[13] 2366 6-9-4 50........................(b) AdamKirby 6 42
(J M Bradley) *hld up bhd: rdn and struggling 2f out: no ch after* **16/1**

5410 **6** *3 ¾* **Vegas Baby (IRE)**[13] 2355 3-8-7 69........................(b) TPQueally 4 25
(J A Osborne) *wnt rt and awkward s: hld up in rr: swtchd rt after 2f: hdwy to chse ldr 1/2-way tl wl over 1f out: sn wknd* **11/2**[3]

0600 **7** *2 ½* **Briery Lane (IRE)**[111] 575 8-9-0 45........................(p) ChrisCatlin 7 18
(J M Bradley) *chsd ldr tl 1/2-way: rdn and wknd 2f out: wl bhd fnl f* **66/1**

1m 12.68s (-0.02) **Going Correction** -0.10s/f (Good)
WFA 3 from 4yo+ 8lb 7 Ran SP% **109.8**
Speed ratings (Par 101): **96,95,95,95,87 82,78**
toteswinger: 1&2 £1.40, 1&3 £2.90, 2&3 £4.10 CSF £4.95 TOTE £2.60: £1.50, £1.50; EX 7.60.Billy Beetroot was claimed by R. A. Harris for £6000.
Owner J W Parry **Bred** Cyril Humphris **Trained** Newmarket, Suffolk

FOCUS
A close finish, but the winner appears to be on a slight upward curve, having had to challenge wider than ideal. The pace was modest and the form finished too close for comfort.

2760 BETDAQ THE BETTING EXCHANGE H'CAP 2m 93y
3:15 (3:15) (Class 5) (0-70,70) 4-Y-0+ £2,729 (£806; £403) Stalls Low

Form RPR

/0-1 **1** **Sweetheart**[19] 2177 5-9-10 70........................ NCallan 8 76
(Jamie Poulton) *chsd ldrs: wnt 2nd over 3f out: rdn jst over 2f out: drvn over 1f out: styd on wl to ld wl ins fnl f* **5/2**[1]

046- **2** *½* **Tribe**[11] 6329 7-9-3 63........................ JimmyFortune 6 68+
(P R Webber) *racd in midfield: hdwy to chse ldrs over 2f out: rdn wl over 1f out: hrd drvn and kpt on ins fnl f: wnt 2nd last stride* **7/2**[2]

051/ **3** *shd* **Doubly Guest**[65] 6421 5-9-8 68........................ TonyCulhane 1 73
(N J Henderson) *sn chsng ldr: led 5f out: rdn over 1f out: kpt on tl hdd and no ex wl ins fnl f: lost 2nd last stride* **15/2**

2-00 **4** *¾* **Epsom Salts**[19] 2177 4-9-4 65........................ IanMongan 2 69
(P M Phelan) *in tch: chsd ldng pair 2f out: rdn wl over 1f out: kpt on same pce u.p fnl f* **7/1**

040/ **5** *2 ½* **Swordsman (GER)**[17] 7-9-6 66........................(t) LPKeniry 5 67
(C Gordon) *sn led: hdd and pushed along 5f out: still chsng ldrs and drvn 2f out: wknd over 1f out: eased towards fin* **8/1**

6-44 **6** *7* **Sphere (IRE)**[20] 2172 4-9-6 67........................ AdamKirby 9 60
(J R Fanshawe) *stdd s: hld up in last pl: swtchd lft and hdwy 5f out: rdn wl over 1f out: no prog and wl hld whn flashed tailed over 1f out* **6/1**[3]

/505 **7** *¾* **Eastwell Smiles**[48] 1426 5-8-11 57........................(p) JimCrowley 4 49
(R T Phillips) *in tch in midfield: reminder over 4f out: effrt and rdn 3f out: btn whn edgd rt u.p over 1f out* **14/1**

500- **8** *10* **Synonymy**[32] 7827 6-8-5 51 oh6........................(b) FrankieMcDonald 7 31
(M Blanshard) *hld up in last trio: rdn 5f out: lost tch over 3f out* **33/1**

40-6 **9** *7* **Faith And Reason (USA)**[20] 2172 6-9-1 61........................ TPQueally 10 32
(B J Curley) *t.k.h: hld up in last trio: rdn and struggling over 3f out: sn lost tch: eased ins fnl f* **16/1**

3m 39.72s (2.52) **Going Correction** -0.10s/f (Good)
WFA 4 from 5yo+ 1lb 9 Ran SP% **115.9**
Speed ratings (Par 103): **89,88,88,88,87 83,83,78,74**
toteswinger: 1&2 £2.80, 1&3 £4.00, 2&3 £6.50 CSF £11.19 CT £56.68 TOTE £3.20: £1.20, £1.60, £2.30; EX 12.30 Trifecta £44.30 Pool: £664.90 - 11.10 winning units..
Owner R W Huggins **Bred** Darley **Trained** Lewes, E Sussex

FOCUS
A medium gallop until Doubly Guest kicked ahead and quickened the tempo at the end of the back straight. The race can not be rated too positively due to the lack of pace but the fist three are all entitled to rate higher on jumps/old Flat form.

2761 TRY BETDAQ FOR AN EXCHANGE H'CAP 6f
3:45 (3:45) (Class 4) (0-85,82) 3-Y-0 £5,180 (£1,541; £770; £384) Stalls Low

Form RPR

1-10 **1** **Aroundthebay**[23] 2079 3-9-7 82........................ ChrisCatlin 2 84
(H J L Dunlop) *chsd ldr: chal gng wl over 1f out: pushed into ld 1f out: rdn and edgd lft ins fnl f: r.o wl* **15/8**[2]

0510 **2** *1* **Rio Royale (IRE)**[17] 2227 3-9-3 78........................ JimCrowley 1 77
(Mrs A J Perrett) *led: jnd and rdn over 1f out: hdd 1f out: drvn and nt much too much room fnl 100yds: comf hld after* **5/2**[3]

5-50 **3** *3 ½* **Defector (IRE)**[37] 1671 3-8-13 74........................ SebSanders 3 62
(W R Muir) *stdd s: t.k.h: hld up in last pl: rdn and effrt wl over 1f out: wknd ent fnl f* **13/8**[1]

5060 **4** *1 ¼* **Quick Single (USA)**[15] 2300 3-7-11 65........................(vt) CarolineKelly(7) 6 49
(P S McEntee) *chsd ldrs: rdn 2f out: edgd rt over 1f out: sn wknd* **14/1**

1m 13.56s (0.86) **Going Correction** -0.10s/f (Good) 4 Ran SP% **108.1**
Speed ratings (Par 101): **90,88,84,82**
CSF £6.76 TOTE £2.20; EX 6.90.
Owner The Endeavour Partnership **Bred** R G Levin **Trained** Lambourn, Berks

FOCUS
The first two set a fair standard for the track but the time was slower than the claimer. Modest form, with the runner-up probably the best guide.

2762 BET ASIAN H'CAPS - BETDAQ HANDICAP 1m 4f
4:15 (4:15) (Class 6) (0-60,60) 4-Y-0+ £2,047 (£604; £302) Stalls Low

Form RPR

0-01 **1** **Sagunt (GER)**[56] 1254 6-9-1 57........................ JamesDoyle 3 63+
(S Curran) *hld up in last pair: swtchd lft and gd hdwy 2f out: rdn to ld over 1f out: in command whn edgd rt u.p ins fnl f: r.o wl* **11/4**[1]

1-00 **2** *2 ½* **Carmela Maria**[31] 1834 4-9-4 60........................ SaleemGolam 1 62
(S C Williams) *led at stdy gallop: qcknd wl over 2f out: rdn and hdd over 1f out: keeping on same pce and btn whn swtchd lft ins fnl f* **6/1**

0505 **3** *1 ½* **Generous Lad (IRE)**[11] 2420 6-8-1 46 oh1........................(p) DavidProbert(3) 7 46
(A B Haynes) *chsd ldr tl 8f out: styd chsng ldrs: rdn 2f out: drvn and kpt on same pce fr over 1f out* **10/3**[2]

-320 **4** *1* **Pertemps Power**[28] 1936 5-8-11 53........................ ChrisCatlin 5 51
(B G Powell) *chsd ldrs tl wnt 2nd 8f out: tl 2f out: unable qck u.p wl over 1f out: one pce after* **4/1**[3]

-002 **5** *¾* **Lady Jinks**[8] 2517 4-8-5 52........................ Louis-PhilippeBeuzelin(5) 8 49
(R J Hodges) *t.k.h: hld up in tch in midfield: swtchd lft wl over 1f out: sn rdn and flashed tail u.p: no hdwy and wl hld fnl f* **9/2**

0440 **6** *2* **Speagle (IRE)**[6] 2580 7-8-4 46........................ FrankieMcDonald 2 40
(A J Chamberlain) *hld up in midfield: hdwy on outer to chse ldrs 3f out: rdn and unable qck 2f out: swtchd lft wl over 1f out: sn wknd* **12/1**

4450 **7** *7* **Summer Bounty**[21] 2127 13-8-4 46 oh1........................ LiamJones 6 28
(F Jordan) *stdd s: hld up in last pl: rdn and no reponse 2f out: sn lost tch* **25/1**

2m 44.27s (3.37) **Going Correction** -0.10s/f (Good) 7 Ran SP% **113.8**
Speed ratings (Par 101): **84,82,81,80,80 78,74**
toteswinger: 1&2 £3.80, 1&3 £3.30, 2&3 £5.50 CSF £19.43 CT £55.72 TOTE £4.20: £2.50, £2.20; EX 23.90 Trifecta £71.30 Pool: £857.74 - 8.89 winning units..
Owner L M Power **Bred** Gestut Schlenderhan **Trained** Hatford, Oxon

FOCUS
A weak handicap. The winner was value for a bit extra for coming from off the moderate gallop which only stepped up off the home turn.

2763 LEMOND & GABRIEL FRIENDSHIP ACROSS THE WATER MEDIAN AUCTION MAIDEN STKS 1m 1f 149y
4:45 (4:45) (Class 5) 3-4-Y-0 £2,729 (£806; £403) Stalls Centre

Form RPR

3202 **1** **Morning Sir Alan**[9] 2488 3-8-13 75........................ JerryO'Dwyer 5 78
(S A Callaghan) *mde all: pushed along 2f out: rdn clr wl over 1f out: styd on wl and unchal after* **9/2**[2]

24 **2** *1 ½* **Time Machine (UAE)**[32] 1809 3-8-13 0........................ JimmyFortune 8 75
(J H M Gosden) *bustled along early: hld up towards rr: hdwy jst over 2f out: rdn to chse wnr over 1f out: no imp fnl f* **5/2**[1]

0-04 **3** *6* **My Chestnut Girl (USA)**[18] 2192 3-8-8 74........................ TPQueally 2 57
(H R A Cecil) *chsd wnr: pressed wnr and rdn wl over 2f out: unable qck u.p jst over 2f out: wknd and lost 2nd over 1f out* **6/1**

000- **4** *3 ½* **Fire King**[222] 7080 3-8-13 35........................ RichardThomas 9 55
(J A Geake) *chsd ldrs: rdn and wanting to hang rt fr 2f out: wl btn fr wl over 1f out* **100/1**

5 **5** *1 ½* **Jewelled**[19] 2178 3-8-8 0........................ JamesDoyle 6 47
(J W Hills) *t.k.h: hld up in tch: rdn to chse ldng pair jst over 2f out: wknd qckly wl over 1f out* **5/1**[3]

6 **6** *4* **Tribal Rule**[28] 1931 3-8-13 0........................ JimCrowley 3 43+
(Mrs A J Perrett) *stdd after s: hld up towards rr: rdn and effrt jst over 2f out: hung bdly lft fr 2f out: sn wl btn* **5/2**[1]

00 **7** *2* **Barter**[19] 2178 3-8-8 0........................ WilliamBuick 1 34+
(L M Cumani) *stdd s: hld up in last pair: lost tch over 3f out* **20/1**

006- **8** *½* **D'Artagnans Dream**[250] 6394 3-8-13 65........................ SebSanders 4 38
(G D Blake) *stdd after s: hld up in last pair: lost tch over 3f out* **40/1**

2m 2.90s (-2.00) **Going Correction** -0.10s/f (Good) 8 Ran SP% **114.5**
Speed ratings (Par 103): **104,102,98,95,94 90,89,88**
toteswinger: 1&2 £2.40, 1&3 £3.80, 2&3 £2.80 CSF £16.01 TOTE £5.70: £1.80, £1.20, £1.70; EX 14.80 Trifecta £49.00 Pool: £617.34 - 9.31 winning units..

Owner Gallagher Equine Ltd **Bred** Darley **Trained** Newmarket, Suffolk

FOCUS
The gallop was quite good considering the winner made all, and the time was decent. No better than fair form, the winner the best guide.

Barter Official explanation: jockey said, regarding the running and riding of the filly, that his instructions were that he should drop in and ride his race, that the filly did not handle the track and he had done his best to keep her balanced. Trainer's representative confirmed these instructions, and in the circumstances of the filly not handling the track she was happy with the ride the jockey had given.

D'Artagnans Dream Official explanation: jockey said that the gelding did not handle the bends

2764 LIPSCOMB ABARTH H'CAP 1m 1f 149y
5:15 (5:15) (Class 5) (0-70,67) 4-Y-0+ £3,070 (£906; £453) Stalls Centre

Form RPR

30-2 **1** **Confide In Me**[10] 2458 5-8-4 55........................(t) AndreaAtzeni(5) 1 66+
(G A Butler) *led for 1f: chsd ldr after: shkn up to chal over 1f out: pushed into ld ins fnl f: readily* **7/2**[2]

0412 **2** *1 ¼* **Jo'Burg (USA)**[3] 2678 5-9-7 67........................ SebSanders 6 75
(Lady Herries) *dwlt: rcvrd to ld after 1f: clr 3f out: rdn wl over 1f out: hdd ins fnl f: one pce and no ch w wnr after* **8/11**[1]

3002 **3** *3 ½* **Bavarica**[3] 2675 7-8-7 60........................ MatthewCosham(7) 2 61
(Miss J Feilden) *stdd s: t.k.h: hld up in last pl: sueezed through on inner and hdwy over 2f out: chsd ldng pair and rdn over 1f out: wknd 1f out* **15/2**[3]

6455 **4** *¾* **Barodine**[11] 2400 6-8-4 55........................ MCGeran(5) 4 54
(R J Hodges) *chsd ldng pair: rdn and effrt wl over 1f out: drvn and wknd ent fnl f* **12/1**

400- **5** *nse* **Shesha Bear**[222] 7070 4-9-4 67........................ DavidProbert(3) 3 66
(W R Muir) *hld up in 4th pl: rdn and effrt on outer wl over 1f out: wknd over 1f out* **8/1**

2m 5.02s (0.12) **Going Correction** -0.10s/f (Good) 5 Ran SP% **110.7**
Speed ratings (Par 103): **95,94,91,90,90**
CSF £6.56 TOTE £4.40: £1.90, £1.10; EX 6.60 Place 6: £28.60 Place 5: £14.51 .

Owner A D Spence & Mr And Mrs P Hargreaves **Bred** Cheveley Park Stud Ltd **Trained** Newmarket, Suffolk

FOCUS
A pedestrian gallop set by the runner-up meant it paid to be handy. The winner improved and the beaten favourite is the best guide.

T/Plt: £32.30 to a £1 stake. Pool: £71,299.13. 1,607.49 winning tickets. T/Qpdt: £10.00 to a £1 stake. Pool: £3,999.48. 294.10 winning tickets. SP

2245 PONTEFRACT (L-H)

Monday, June 8

OFFICIAL GOING: Good (8.3)
A false rail was in place for the final 6f.
Wind: Virtually nil Weather: Cloudy

2765 FATHERS DAY FUNDAY ON SUNDAY 21ST JUNE MAIDEN AUCTION FILLIES' STKS 6f
6:50 (6:50) (Class 5) 2-Y-O **£3,238** (£963; £481; £240) **Stalls** Low

Form RPR
0 **1** **Bubbelas**[16] 2258 2-8-4 0 GrahamGibbons 2 73+
(J J Quinn) *towards rr and rdn along 1/2-way: hdwy 2f out: swtchd rt and rdn over 1f out: styd on u.p ins fnl f to ld nr fin* **8/1**
424 **2** *nk* **Angelena Ballerina (IRE)**[12] 2372 2-8-4 0 JimmyQuinn 7 72
(A Bailey) *cl up: effrt to chal over 2f out and sn rdn: drvn to ld 1f out: hdd and no ex nr fin* **6/4**[1]
3 **3** *1 3/4* **Shibhan**[28] 1939 2-8-4 0 MartinDwyer 8 67
(C E Brittain) *led: jnd and pushed along over 2f out: sn rdn: drvn and hdd 1f out: kpt on same pce* **9/2**[3]
4 **4** *nse* **Midnight Martini**[16] 2258 2-8-8 0 DavidAllan 4 71
(T D Easterby) *t.k.h: trckd ldrs: effrt 2f out: rdn wl over 1f out: keeping on whn n.m.r ins fnl f: one pce* **11/4**[2]
5 *3* **Dancing Poppy** 2-8-6 0 SamHitchcott 6 60
(M R Channon) *in tch: hdwy on outer to chse ldng pair 1/2-way: rdn over 2f out: sn drvn and one pce* **25/1**
0 **6** *nse* **Wood Fair**[13] 2360 2-8-8 0 AndrewElliott 3 62
(K R Burke) *chsd ldrs: rdn along over 2f out and sn wknd* **10/1**
0 **7** *1/2* **Smicker Smacker**[18] 2187 2-8-6 0 EdwardCreighton 1 58
(George Baker) *trckd ldr on inner: rdn along over 2f out: sn wknd* **50/1**
8 *7* **Blade Of Glory** 2-8-4 0 AndrewMullen 5 35
(A J McCabe) *dwlt: a in rr* **66/1**

1m 18.64s (1.74) **Going Correction** +0.10s/f (Good) **8 Ran SP% 112.3**
Speed ratings (Par 90): **92,91,89,89,85 85,84,75**
toteswinger: 1&2 £4.00, 1&3 £12.40, 2&3 £1.70 CSF £19.78 TOTE £19.00: £3.70, £1.10, £1.70; EX 50.60.
Owner C D Carr **Bred** D & S Horn **Trained** Settrington, N Yorks
■ Stewards' Enquiry : Andrew Mullen one-day ban: used whip out of contention (June 22)

FOCUS
The ground was reckoned 'near perfect' after watering. The form has been rated very close to the race averages, with more likely to come from the winner.

NOTEBOOK
Bubbelas, who tended to race wide when eighth on her debut at Beverley, was pulled to the outside once in line for home. Only fifth a furlong out, she showed a very willing attitude to get up near the line and become her trainer's third winning juvenile this time from just seven runners. She will be even better suited by 6f and should improve again. (op 14-1)
Angelena Ballerina(IRE), who lacks substance, had finished fourth on her third start in a Listed race at Beverley. She looked the likely winner when getting the better of pacesetter Shiban coming to the final furlong only to miss out near the line and extend her trainer's losing sequence here to 43 runners. (op 10-11)
Shibhan, who was the worst drawn, made her way across to the running rail. She took them along but in the end did not improve on her initial effort when third at Yarmouth in a race working out well. (op 11-2)
Midnight Martini, four places ahead of the winner at Beverley where she met trouble in running, raced very keenly. She was denied a clear run inside the last and looked third best on merit. (op 4-1)
Dancing Poppy tended to race wide and looked very inexperienced. (op 20-1 tchd 16-1)
Wood Fair, a well-made filly, could never go the pace. She needs another outing before waiting for a nursery mark and she looks capable of a fair bit better in due course. (op 14-1)

2766 TONY BETHELL MEMORIAL H'CAP 2m 1f 22y
7:20 (7:20) (Class 4) (0-80,77) 4-Y-O+ **£5,180** (£1,541; £770; £384) **Stalls** Low

Form RPR
52-2 **1** **Tyrrells Wood (IRE)**[57] 631 4-9-7 **75** JoeFanning 5 91+
(T G Mills) *cl up: led 4f out: rdn clr 2f out: styd on strly* **4/1**[1]
51-1 **2** *7* **Mr Crystal (FR)**[49] 1399 5-9-5 **77** FrederikTylicki(5) 10 84
(Micky Hammond) *hld up in tch: hdwy 5f out: chsd wnr 3f out: rdn 2f out: sn drvn and no imp fnl f* **13/2**
0-62 **3** *18* **Haldibari (IRE)**[49] 1399 5-8-6 **59** PaulHanagan 2 44
(S Lycett) *in tch: hdwy over 6f out: rdn to chse ldrs 4f out: drvn along wl over 2f out and plugged on same pce* **14/1**
4044 **4** *8* **Puy D'Arnac (FR)**[18] 2194 6-9-7 **74** RobertWinston 1 49
(G A Swinbank) *hld up: hdwy 6f out: rdn to chse ldng pair over 2f out: sn drvn and plugged on same pce* **5/1**[3]
-250 **5** *10* **Dart**[18] 2194 5-8-12 **65** MartinDwyer 9 28
(J R Fanshawe) *hld up towards rr: hdwy over 5f out: rdn along over 3f out: sn no further prog* **16/1**
3-60 **6** *3 1/2* **Kiribati King (IRE)**[25] 2018 4-9-6 **74** SamHitchcott 3 33
(M R Channon) *s.i.s: in rr tl hdwy over 6f out: rdn along and in tch 4f out: sn wknd* **9/2**[2]
/3-6 **7** *16* **Indonesia**[44] 1506 7-9-10 **77** GrahamGibbons 4 17
(T D Walford) *hld up: a in rr* **11/2**
0620 **8** *nk* **Snowberry Hill (USA)**[16] 2262 6-8-5 **58** oh1 JimmyQuinn 7 —
(Lucinda Featherstone) *a in rr* **14/1**
1530 **9** *3 3/4* **Eton Fable (IRE)**[16] 2283 4-9-1 **76** (p) PaulPickard(7) 8 11
(W J H Ratcliffe) *cl up: led over 7f out: rdn along and hdd 4f out: sn drvn and wknd* **16/1**
56-0 **10** *26* **Keelung (USA)**[36] 1692 8-9-4 **71** MickyFenton 6 —
(R Ford) *led: rdn along and hdd over 7f out: drvn 4f out: sn wknd and bhd* **14/1**

3m 42.97s (-7.03) **Going Correction** -0.175s/f (Firm)
WFA 4 from 5yo+ 1lb **10 Ran SP% 115.3**
Speed ratings (Par 105): **109,105,97,93,88 87,79,79,77,65**
toteswinger: 1&2 £6.00, 1&3 £3.90, 2&3 £9.60 CSF £29.69 CT £330.16 TOTE £5.00: £1.80, £2.20, £3.40; EX 20.50.
Owner P C Ryan **Bred** Kilfrush Stud **Trained** Headley, Surrey

FOCUS
A breakneck pace for this 58-77 stayers' handicap and they were soon well strung out, and in the end the two pacesetters finished well beaten. The winner impressed and can rate higher, although it is hard to know how literally to take this form.

Kiribati King(IRE) Official explanation: jockey said gelding never travelled

2767 BAR LIQUID - PONTEFRACT NUMBER ONE BAR H'CAP 1m 2f 6y
7:50 (7:50) (Class 4) (0-85,83) 3-Y-O **£5,180** (£1,541; £770; £384) **Stalls** Low

Form RPR
1-40 **1** **Thin Red Line (IRE)**[18] 2209 3-9-2 **78** PaulHanagan 3 90
(E A L Dunlop) *trckd ldrs: hdwy on outer 3f out: led 2f out: rdn clr appr fnl f: kpt on strly* **7/1**
4-22 **2** *3 1/2* **Stanstill (IRE)**[24] 2042 3-9-3 **79** PJMcDonald 5 84
(G A Swinbank) *trckd ldrs: effrt 2f out: swtchd rt and rdn to chse wnr over 1f out: drvn ins fnl f and no imp* **3/1**[2]
-205 **3** *1 1/4* **Splinter Cell (USA)**[16] 2275 3-9-6 **82** JimmyQuinn 1 84
(M Botti) *hld up towards rr: hdwy 4f out: rdn to chse ldrs 2f out: drvn over 1f out and kpt on same pce* **4/1**[3]
01-0 **4** *8* **Mannlichen**[26] 1992 3-9-1 **77** JoeFanning 6 63
(M Johnston) *cl up: rdn along wl over 2f out: sn ev ch tl drvn wl over 1f out and sn wknd* **5/2**[1]
14-0 **5** *2 3/4* **Warrior One**[26] 1992 3-9-4 **80** PaulMulrennan 2 61
(J Howard Johnson) *in tch on inner: pushed along over 3f out: sn rdn and wknd fnl 2f* **6/1**
061- **6** *nk* **Sky Gate (USA)**[171] 7726 3-9-7 **83** (b) MartinDwyer 4 63
(B J Meehan) *hld up in rr: effrt 1/2-way: sn rdn along and nvr a factor* **14/1**
102- **7** *4 1/2* **Captain Imperial (IRE)**[195] 7445 3-9-0 **76** MickyFenton 7 47
(T P Tate) *led: rdn along 3f out: drvn and hdd 2f out: wknd qckly* **28/1**

2m 11.5s (-2.20) **Going Correction** -0.175s/f (Firm) **7 Ran SP% 110.5**
Speed ratings (Par 101): **101,98,97,90,88 88,84**
toteswinger: 1&2 £4.00, 1&3 £12.40, 2&3 £1.70 CSF £26.31 TOTE £6.50: £3.70, £2.10; EX 23.90.
Owner Byculla Thoroughbreds **Bred** Peter Jones And G G Jones **Trained** Newmarket, Suffolk

FOCUS
A 76-83 handicap run at a very sound pace. Pretty solid form.

2768 WEATHERBYS BANK PIPALONG STKS (LISTED RACE) (F&M) 1m 4y
8:20 (8:20) (Class 1) 4-Y-O+
£25,236 (£9,607; £4,810; £2,403; £1,201; £603) **Stalls** Low

Form RPR
100- **1** **Rosaleen (IRE)**[254] 6266 4-8-12 98 MartinDwyer 9 92
(B J Meehan) *trckd ldrs: smooth hdwy over 2f out: rdn to ld 1f out: styd on* **10/11**[1]
3624 **2** *2* **Just Lille (IRE)**[22] 2103 6-8-12 87 (p) PaulMulrennan 4 87
(Mrs A Duffield) *led: rdn along and jnd 2f out: drvn and hdd 1f out: kpt on wl u.p ins fnl f* **7/1**
32-0 **3** *1* **Lady Rangali (IRE)**[16] 2266 4-8-12 83 PaulHanagan 7 85
(Mrs A Duffield) *hld up towards rr: hdwy 3f out: rdn to chse ldrs 2f out: drvn over 1f out: kpt on ins fnl f: nrst fin* **13/2**[3]
5043 **4** *3* **Black Dahlia**[6] 2573 4-8-12 67 RobertWinston 3 78
(A J McCabe) *trckd ldr: effrt and cl up 2f out: sn rdn and ev ch tl drvn appr fnl f and sn wknd* **14/1**
4054 **5** *nk* **Rio Guru (IRE)**[3] 2678 4-8-12 74 SamHitchcott 2 77
(M R Channon) *chsd ldng pair: rdn along on inner and outpcd 2f out: drvn and kpt on ins fnl f* **16/1**
-130 **6** *1* **Trumpet Lily**[11] 2412 4-8-12 86 TomEaves 5 75
(J G Portman) *hld up in tch: hdwy 3f out: rdn along 2f out and sn btn* **4/1**[2]
060- **7** *4 1/2* **Nice To Know (FR)**[259] 6170 5-8-12 74 JoeFanning 8 65
(G L Moore) *t.k.h: hld up in rr: hdwy 3f out: rdn wl over 1f out and sn btn* **33/1**
6050 **8** *7* **Amber Moon**[35] 1743 4-8-12 52 (b) AnnStokell 1 49
(Miss A Stokell) *a in rr* **250/1**

1m 44.31s (-1.59) **Going Correction** -0.175s/f (Firm) **8 Ran SP% 114.1**
Speed ratings (Par 111): **100,98,97,94,93 92,88,81**
toteswinger: 1&2 £2.40, 1&3 £1.80, 2&3 £3.60 CSF £8.05 TOTE £2.50: £1.50, £1.70, £2.40; EX 8.80.
Owner Exors of the Late F C T Wilson **Bred** Alan Dargan **Trained** Manton, Wilts

FOCUS
£15,000 more prize money than last year and £5,000 above the BHA bottom limit for a Class 1 race resulted in a disappointing turnout after the withdrawal of Eva's Request, who took a Group 3 at Epsom on Derby day. The top-rated filly Rosaleen is rated 98 and the second highest just 87. Sub-standard form for the grade, the winner not needing to be at her best.

NOTEBOOK
Rosaleen(IRE), successful in this grade at Sandown last year, kept tabs on the leaders. Put about her job going into the final turn, she did more than enough in the end to give her trainer his first success here for 3,899 days - over ten years. She was winning first time out for the first time and this was a golden opportunity grabbed with both hands. (op 5-4 tchd 11-8)
Just Lille(IRE), the second highest-rated filly in the line-up, set a sensible pace. She wound it up going into the final turn but was always going to come off second best. She picked up some valuable black type. (op 5-1 tchd 9-2)
Lady Rangali(IRE), who had just two outings at three, had 4lb to find with her stablemate. She proved well suited by the step back to a mile and she too boosted her stud value. (tchd 6-1 and 7-1)
Black Dahlia, rated just 67, seemed to run above herself in fourth. This trip is her bare minimum and she too managed to pick up some black type. (tchd 12-1)
Rio Guru(IRE), rated 74, is not up to Listed class and is better over further anyway. (tchd 20-1)
Trumpet Lily, backed to upset the favourite even though she had 12lb to find with her, was edgy beforehand and raced keenly early on. Called for an effort turning for home, she never looked like taking a serious hand. (op 11-2)
Amber Moon Official explanation: jockey said that the filly suffered interference shortly after the start

2769 RAYNOR DYSON MEMORIAL H'CAP 6f
8:50 (8:50) (Class 5) (0-70,70) 3-Y-O+ **£3,238** (£963; £481; £240) **Stalls** Low

Form RPR
2313 **1** **Swinbrook (USA)**[11] 2389 8-9-9 **70** (v) FrederikTylicki(5) 11 81
(R A Fahey) *chsd ldrs towards outer: hdwy 1/2-way: cl up 2f out: rdn to ld wl over 1f out: drvn ins fnl f and hld on wl* **10/1**
-000 **2** *1/2* **Bid For Gold**[14] 2312 5-9-6 **62** PaulHanagan 8 71
(Jedd O'Keeffe) *prom: hdwy and cl up whn sltly hmpd by marker bollard 2f out: sn rdn and ev ch tl drvn and no ex last 75yds* **13/2**[3]
213- **3** *1* **Azure Mist**[163] 7790 4-9-9 **65** PaulMulrennan 13 71
(M H Tompkins) *hld up towards rr: hdwy whn sltly hmpd 2f out: sn rdn and styd on ent fnl f: nrst fin* **28/1**
0443 **4** *1/2* **Sam's Cross (IRE)**[3] 2680 4-9-13 **69** PaulEddery 5 74
(Pat Eddery) *chsd ldrs: hdwy 2f out: rdn wl over 1f out: kpt on u.p ins fnl f* **5/1**[1]
0043 **5** *1/2* **Dickie Le Davoir**[11] 2418 5-9-4 **65** MarkCoumbe(5) 15 68+
(John A Harris) *towards rr: hdwy on outer whn j. marker bollard 2f out: sn rdn and kpt on wl fnl f: nrst fin* **9/1**

0-03 **6** *nse* **King Of Rhythm (IRE)**[7] 2531 6-9-6 **62** .... DNolan 4 65
(D Carroll) *hld up in midfield: hdwy whn sltly hmpd 2f out: sn rdn and styd on ins fnl f: nrst fin* **7/1**

5-00 **7** *½* **Poppy's Rose**[38] 1650 5-9-5 **61** .... TomEaves 7 62
(I W McInnes) *prom: rdn along 2f out: sn drvn and grad wknd fnl f* **16/1**

0106 **8** *½* **Flying Applause**[20] 2149 4-9-9 **65** .... (bt) MickyFenton 9 65
(S R Bowring) *led: rdn along 2f out: sn hdd and grad wknd* **16/1**

0431 **9** *shd* **Red Cape (FR)**[3] 2660 6-9-13 **69** 6ex .... AndrewElliott 14 68
(Mrs R A Carr) *trckd ldrs: effrt and hdwy 2f out: sn rdn and no imp ent fnl f* **6/1**[2]

2-35 **10** *1 ½* **Mark Of Meydan**[17] 2235 4-10-0 **70** .... PhillipMakin 1 65+
(M Dods) *nvr bttr than midfield* **8/1**

-260 **11** *1* **Medici Time**[14] 2312 4-9-5 **61** .... (v) GrahamGibbons 16 52
(T D Easterby) *nvr bttr than midfield* **16/1**

6600 **12** *2 ¾* **Royal Challenge**[20] 2156 8-9-8 **64** .... PatrickMathers 3 47
(I W McInnes) *nvr bttr than midfield* **28/1**

0600 **13** *7* **H Harrison (IRE)**[12] 2381 9-9-5 **61** .... GregFairley 6 21
(I W McInnes) *chsd ldr on inner: rdn along 2f out and sn wknd* **40/1**

3-03 **14** *1 ½* **Stellarina (IRE)**[35] 1743 3-9-2 **66** .... RobertWinston 10 21
(G A Swinbank) *s.i.s: a in rr* **14/1**

1m 17.04s (0.14) **Going Correction** +0.10s/f (Good)
WFA 3 from 4yo+ 8lb **14** Ran SP% **120.6**
Speed ratings (Par 103): **103,102,101,100,99 99,98,98,98,96 94,91,81,79**
toteswinger: 1&2 £29.90, 1&3 £2.70, 2&3 £29.90 CSF £72.58 CT £1785.76 TOTE £8.40: £2.50, £1.80, £6.70; EX 108.00.

Owner Mark A Leatham **Bred** Bill Bronstad **Trained** Musley Bank, N Yorks

■ Stewards' Enquiry : Greg Fairley four-day ban plus four days deferred: careless riding (Jul 5-7,9-11,13-14)

FOCUS
A modest 66-70 sprint marred by two traffic cones being left on the track on the home turn. Ordinary but solid form, rated through the third and fourth.

Stellarina(IRE) Official explanation: jockey said that the filly missed the break

2770 HEAVEN LAP DANCING BAR H'CAP 5f
9:20 (9:20) (Class 5) (0-75,75) 4-Y-O+ £3,238 (£963; £481; £240) Stalls Low

Form RPR

-606 **1** **Mr Wolf**[16] 2267 8-9-2 **70** .... (p) TonyHamilton 10 81
(D W Barker) *qckly away and sn clr: rdn wl over 1f out: drvn ins fnl f and kpt on strly* **7/1**[2]

3-04 **2** *1 ¾* **Artsu**[23] 2071 4-9-6 **74** .... PhillipMakin 16 79+
(M Dods) *in tch on outer: hdwy 2f out: rdn and styd on strly to chse wnr ins fnl f: sn edgd lft and nt rch wnr* **11/1**

000- **3** *shd* **Commander Wish**[192] 7471 6-8-8 **67** .... (p) JPHamblett(5) 3 71
(Lucinda Featherstone) *in rr: hdwy 2f out: swtchd rt and rdn wl over 1f out: styd on to chse ldrs whn hung lft ins fnl f: nrst fin* **20/1**

2-00 **4** *½* **Dig Deep (IRE)**[16] 2267 7-9-2 **70** .... (t) GrahamGibbons 11 73
(J J Quinn) *dwlt and bhd: hdwy 2f out: swtchd rt and rdn over 1f out: styd on wl fnl f* **14/1**

-020 **5** *½* **Divine Spirit**[17] 2228 8-9-7 **75** .... TomEaves 14 76
(M Dods) *in rr: hdwy wl over 1f out: sn swtchd rt and rdn: styd on ins fnl f: nrst fin* **33/1**

0200 **6** *½* **King Of Swords (IRE)**[9] 2472 5-8-9 **68** ow2 .... FrederikTylicki(5) 15 67
(N Tinkler) *midfield: effrt 2f out and sn rdn: styd on u.p ins fnl f: nrst fin* **16/1**

0-62 **7** *1* **Top Bid**[10] 2436 5-8-6 **60** .... (b) DavidAllan 13 55
(T D Easterby) *chsd ldrs: rdn wl over 1f out: drvn and one pce ins fnl f* **11/1**

-250 **8** *¾* **Sea Rover (IRE)**[9] 2472 5-8-12 **66** .... JimmyQuinn 8 59
(M Brittain) *chsd ldrs: rdn along 2f out: drvn over 1f out: wknd ins fnl f* **25/1**

0110 **9** *¾* **Almaty Express**[11] 2397 7-8-1 **62** .... (b) PaulPickard(7) 1 52
(J R Weymes) *chsd wnr on inner: rdn along 2f out: grad wknd* **16/1**

0-60 **10** *¾* **First Swallow**[14] 2316 4-8-3 **57** .... PaulHanagan 6 44
(R A Fahey) *chsd ldrs: rdn along 2f out: grad wknd fr over 1f out* **7/1**[2]

11-2 **11** *hd* **Charles Parnell (IRE)**[153] 68 6-9-7 **75** .... DaleGibson 9 62
(M Dods) *midfield: rdn along over 2f out and sn wknd* **10/1**

-002 **12** *1* **Namir (IRE)**[9] 2472 7-9-7 **75** .... (vt) JoeFanning 7 76+
(D Shaw) *chsd ldrs: rdn over 1f out: swtchd ins and styng on whn hmpd ins fnl f and no ch after* **5/1**[1]

0101 **13** *1 ½* **Calmdownmate (IRE)**[34] 1776 4-9-2 **70** .... PaulMulrennan 5 48
(Mrs R A Carr) *a in rr* **7/1**[2]

01-0 **14** *1 ¼* **Braille**[44] 1518 4-8-13 **67** .... JamieMoriarty 12 40
(T D Walford) *chsd ldrs: rdn along wl over 1f out: sn drvn and wknd ent fnl f* **14/1**

302 **15** *½* **Luscivious**[17] 2228 5-8-12 **73** .... (b) DeclanCannon(7) 4 44
(A J McCabe) *dwlt and bhd: gd hdwy on inner 2f out: sn rdn and wknd ent fnl f* **15/2**[3]

63.49 secs (0.19) **Going Correction** +0.10s/f (Good) **15** Ran SP% **128.3**
Speed ratings (Par 103): **102,99,99,98,97 96,95,93,92,91 91,89,87,85,84**
toteswinger: 1&2 £13.00, 1&3 £27.30, 2&3 not won. CSF £85.07 CT £1544.09 TOTE £8.00: £2.60, £3.90, £14.50; EX 139.60 Place 6: £230.70, Place 5: £155.78..

Owner Andrew Turton & David Barker **Bred** P Asquith **Trained** Scorton, N Yorks

■ Stewards' Enquiry : Tony Hamilton one-day ban: failed to ride to draw (Jul 5)

Paul Pickard two-day ban: careless riding (22-23 June)

J P Hamblett two-day ban: careless riding (22-23 June)

FOCUS
The winner got away to a flyer and looks the best guide to this form. The placed form could be rated a length higher.

T/Plt: £124.50 to a £1 stake. Pool: £76,120.11. 446.20 winning tickets. T/Qpdt: £59.40 to a £1 stake. Pool: £5,239.66. 65.27 winning tickets. JR

[2547] WINDSOR (R-H)
Monday, June 8

OFFICIAL GOING: Good to soft (good in places) changing to good (good to soft in places) after race 1 (6.30)
Top bend dolled out 8yds from innermost line, adding 28yds to advertised distances in races of 1m plus.
Wind: Almost nil Weather: Overcast

2771 SPORTINGBET.COM MEDIAN AUCTION MAIDEN STKS 6f
6:30 (6:32) (Class 5) 2-Y-O £2,729 (£806; £403) Stalls High

Form RPR

1 **Dick Turpin (IRE)** 2-9-3 0 .... RichardHughes 8 86+
(R Hannon) *wnt lft s: mde all and racd against nr side rail: clr of all rivals over 2f out: unchal* **3/1**[2]

2 *4 ½* **Missionaire (USA)** 2-9-3 0 .... PaulDoe 3 73+
(W J Knight) *wnt lft s: sn chsd far side ldr: effrt 2f out: styd on to ld gp nr fin: no ch w wnr* **11/1**

2 **3** *½* **Nina Rose**[8] 2514 2-8-12 0 .... AdamKirby 4 66
(C G Cox) *led far side gp: rdn 2f out: no ch w wnr after: hdd by runner-up last strides* **9/4**[1]

4 *2 ½* **Bridge Valley** 2-9-3 0 .... PatDobbs 16 64+
(R Hannon) *cl up on nr side: mostly chsd wnr fr 1/2-way: clr of rest 2f out: no ch* **9/1**[3]

5 *1 ¾* **Larkrise Star** 2-8-12 0 .... ChrisCatlin 1 53
(D K Ivory) *dwlt and carried lft s: rdn to stay in tch far side 1/2-way: no prog fnl 2f* **100/1**

6 *3 ¾* **Fantastic Pick** 2-8-12 0 .... GabrielHannon(5) 5 47
(B J Meehan) *prom on far side: wknd over 1f out* **50/1**

7 *2 ¼* **Barastar** 2-9-3 0 .... PatCosgrave 2 40
(J R Boyle) *carried lft s: racd far side: nvr on terms w ldrs: fin last of gp of 5* **66/1**

8 *1* **Avow (USA)** 2-9-3 0 .... LPKeniry 12 37
(J S Moore) *s.s: wl in rr nr side and outpcd: styd on fr over 1f out: nrst fin* **80/1**

9 *½* **Jessica Hayllar (USA)** 2-8-12 0 .... NCallan 7 31
(M L W Bell) *dwlt: chsd nr side ldrs: lft bhd fr 1/2-way* **12/1**

10 *1* **Astonishment (IRE)** 2-9-3 0 .... GeorgeBaker 9 33
(S Kirk) *dwlt: outpcd in last on nr side and wl bhd: kpt on fnl 2f: no ch* **20/1**

6 **11** *4 ½* **Ba Jetstream**[7] 2547 2-9-3 0 .... CatherineGannon 14 19
(M R Channon) *chsd wnr nr side to 1/2-way: sn wknd* **12/1**

12 *1 ½* **Killusty Fancy (IRE)** 2-9-3 0 .... StephenDonohoe 10 15
(D J S Ffrench Davis) *nvr beyond midfield on nr side: wknd 2f out* **66/1**

13 *2 ½* **Stay On Track (IRE)** 2-9-3 0 .... TPO'Shea 13 7
(E F Vaughan) *prom on nr side to 1/2-way: wknd rapidly* **11/1**

14 *nse* **Miskin Nights** 2-8-12 0 .... RobertHavlin 6 2
(B Palling) *nvr on terms w ldrs nr side: u.p bef 1/2-way: sn no ch* **80/1**

15 *10* **That'Lldonowthen (IRE)** 2-9-3 0 .... JohnEgan 11 —
(J S Moore) *s.s: a in rr nr side: wknd 1/2-way: t.o* **16/1**

1m 14.46s (1.46) **Going Correction** +0.25s/f (Good) **15** Ran SP% **116.9**
Speed ratings (Par 93): **100,94,93,90,87 82,79,78,77,76 70,68,65,64,51**
toteswinger: 1&2 £5.70, 1&3 £1.50, 2&3 £3.80 CSF £33.55 TOTE £3.70: £1.60, £3.50, £1.30; EX 41.40.

Owner John Manley **Bred** John McEnery **Trained** East Everleigh, Wilts

FOCUS
Only two runners with any public form and both were soundly beaten in a race where there was a divergence of opinion about where the best ground was, with the majority favouring the stands' rails despite softened ground historically favouring the far side. The winner created a good impression.

NOTEBOOK
Dick Turpin(IRE) came stands' side but would have won whichever side he had nominated and came away in the style of a progressive colt. He is from the first crop of Arakan who was good from 6f to 1m and there is pace on the dam's side, so this looks the right trip in the short term but 7lb will be better later. Quite simply, he could be anything, although it is worth considering that his stable's runners always improve considerably and the market also spoke in his favour. (op 11-4 tchd 4-1)
Missionaire(USA) raced on the far side and showed plenty of determination to get the better of that group of five. He cost plenty ($320,000) and his sire, El Corredor, has a propensity for dirt winners, so he would be of interest on the all-weather. He was unlucky to bump into a smart one and is sure to improve for this debut. (op 12-1 tchd 10-1)
Nina Rose had the only solid public form and was facing vastly different conditions from when she was second on her debut at Bath. She again showed pace and still did well enough to beat the rest on the stands' side. (tchd 7-4 and 5-2 in places)
Bridge Valley, half brother to the useful Go Nani Go, showed enough to win a race of this description. (op 11-1 tchd 12-1)
Larkrise Star gives the impression that she might be better over another furlong.
Fantastic Pick raced on the far side, and although showing pace will need further than this. (op 66-1)
Avow(USA) was getting the hang of things late on. (op 100-1 tchd 66-1)
Astonishment(IRE) was last at halfway before staying on and will definitely need another furlong or two. (op 16-1 tchd 25-1)

2772 SPORTINGBET.COM CLAIMING STKS 1m 3f 135y
7:00 (7:01) (Class 5) 3-Y-O £2,729 (£806; £403) Stalls Low

Form RPR

-100 **1** **Hollow Green (IRE)**[13] 2350 3-8-9 59 .... CatherineGannon 7 56+
(P D Evans) *hld up in last pair: pushed along 4f out: prog on wd outside 3f out: rdn to ld over 1f out: pushed out and a holding on* **3/1**[2]

1350 **2** *nk* **Urban Space**[7] 2540 3-8-11 68 .... StephenDonohoe 8 57
(B G Powell) *mostly chsd ldr: rdn over 3f out: led over 2f out: hdd over 1f out: kpt on nr fin: a hld* **7/2**[3]

6001 **3** *1 ¼* **First Spirit**[9] 2487 3-8-7 56 .... (p) LPKeniry 9 51
(J S Moore) *hld up in tch: trckd ldrs and poised to chal over 2f out: rdn and no rspnse wl over 1f out: one pce after* **9/2**

0002 **4** *shd* **Bari Bay**[9] 2487 3-8-4 48 .... (b) RichardKingscote 1 48
(R M Beckett) *trckd ldrs: pushed along 4f out: outpcd over 2f out: kpt on one pce fr over 1f out* **11/4**[1]

000- **5** *3 ¼* **Coral Point (IRE)**[198] 7425 3-9-0 45 .... FrankieMcDonald 5 53
(S Curran) *hld up in last pair: reminder after 2f: gng wl enough over 3f out: shkn up and hanging bdly sn after: no real prog* **66/1**

005- **6** 4 ½ **Alderbed**[182] 7607 3-8-5 46........ MatthewDavies(7) 2 43
(George Baker) *pressed ldrs: stl cl up u.p over 2f out: wknd rapidly over 1f out* **50/1**

00-0 **7** 2 **Bertie Smalls**[51] 1363 3-9-2 56........ NCallan 4 44
(M H Tompkins) *led: styd against nr side rail in st: hdd over 2f out: wknd wl over 1f out* **16/1**

1050 **8** 36 **Melange (USA)**[5] 2605 3-9-8 62........(t) RichardHughes 3 —
(P F I Cole) *prom tl wknd 4f out: sn bhd and eased: t.o* **6/1**

2m 33.42s (3.92) **Going Correction** +0.25s/f (Good) 8 Ran SP% **115.7**
Speed ratings (Par 99): **96,95,94,94,92 89,88,64**
toteswinger: 1&2 £2.10, 1&3 £2.30, 2&3 £1.40 CSF £14.18 TOTE £4.10: £1.30, £1.40, £2.10; EX 11.40.
Owner Raymond N R Auld **Bred** R N Auld **Trained** Pandy, Monmouths

FOCUS
A very modest claimer. The winner probably did not have to match her claiming win here last month.
Jeronimo Joe Official explanation: having been unruly in the stalls for the second time within a year, gelding was banned from taking a stalls test for 6 months

2773 EDDIE'S ROBBERS "YOU MAKE ME SMILE" H'CAP 1m 2f 7y
7:30 (7:31) (Class 4) (0-80,80) 4-Y-0+ **£4,857** (£1,445; £722; £360) **Stalls** Low

Form RPR

5-35 **1** **Plaisterer**[24] 2052 4-8-10 72........ JackMitchell(3) 6 89+
(C F Wall) *mostly trckd ldng pair: gap appeared 2f out: cruised through to ld over 1f out: sn clr* **10/3**[1]

0-06 **2** 6 **Traphalgar (IRE)**[9] 2480 4-9-7 80........ JimmyFortune 1 82
(P F I Cole) *hld up in last pair: prog on wd outside 3f out: rdn and kpt on to go 2nd 1f out: no ch w wnr* **9/1**

5-34 **3** 2 **Buddy Holly**[17] 2249 4-9-4 77........ PatDobbs 4 75
(Pat Eddery) *led after 3f: hrd rdn and hdd over 1f out: sn easily outpcd* **4/1**[2]

0-05 **4** hd **By Command**[11] 2407 4-9-4 77........ SebSanders 2 75
(J W Hills) *led 3f: pressed ldr after: hrd rdn over 2f out: sn outpcd* **6/1**

00-1 **5** 2 **Heroes**[12] 2378 5-9-4 77........(p) PatCosgrave 8 71
(Tim Vaughan) *in tch: pushed along over 3f out: cl up and hrd rdn over 2f out: sn outpcd* **9/2**[3]

0600 **6** 6 **Folio (IRE)**[20] 2150 9-8-10 69 ow2........ StephenDonohoe 7 51
(W J Musson) *trckd ldrs: disp 3rd 4f out: pushed along over 3f out: wknd over 2f out* **12/1**

56-6 **7** 3 ¼ **Regional Counsel**[17] 2239 5-9-7 80........ NCallan 5 55
(A M Hales) *cl up: disp 3rd 4f out: rdn 3f out: wknd 2f out* **33/1**

334- **8** 12 **Rehabilitation**[184] 7580 4-8-6 65........(tp) ChrisCatlin 10 16
(W R Swinburn) *a in last pair: lost tch sn after 4f* **5/1**

2m 9.84s (1.14) **Going Correction** +0.25s/f (Good) 8 Ran SP% **112.8**
Speed ratings (Par 105): **105,100,98,98,96 92,89,79**
toteswinger: 1&2 £6.70, 1&3 £4.10, 2&3 £6.30 CSF £32.84 CT £121.79 TOTE £4.00: £1.60, £2.30, £1.80; EX 28.60.
Owner David Andrews Plastering **Bred** Vogue Development Company (kent) Ltd **Trained** Newmarket, Suffolk

FOCUS
A race with some largely out-of-form horses, but won for the third time in four years by trainer Chris Wall. The winner impressed but the form is not strong.

2774 K & L GATES H'CAP 5f 10y
8:00 (8:00) (Class 4) (0-85,82) 3-Y-0 **£5,180** (£1,541; £770; £384) **Stalls** High

Form RPR

1625 **1** **Captain Carey**[10] 2443 3-9-3 78........ TGMcLaughlin 9 91
(M S Saunders) *settled in last pair: taken to outer and prog bef 1/2-way: led 2f out: edgd lft u.p: styd on wl* **7/2**[2]

5-10 **2** ½ **Mattamia (IRE)**[24] 2058 3-9-0 78........ JamesMillman(3) 3 89
(B R Millman) *settled in last pair: effrt on wd outside 1/2-way: pressed wnr fr wl over 1f out: jst hld last 100yds* **7/1**

341- **3** 3 ½ **Bounty Box**[224] 7015 3-9-0 78........ JackMitchell(3) 2 77
(C F Wall) *trckd ldr: upsides 2f out: sn outpcd by ldng pair: fdd* **15/8**[1]

3-00 **4** 5 **Top Town Girl**[30] 1869 3-9-7 82........ SebSanders 6 63
(R M Beckett) *cl up on inner: wknd u.p wl over 1f out* **12/1**

121 **5** 1 **Taurus Twins**[20] 2160 3-8-9 70........(b) ChrisCatlin 5 47
(R J Price) *s.i.s and bustled up to ld: hdd & wknd 2f out* **5/1**[3]

3462 **6** 6 **Green Onions**[10] 2443 3-8-5 66........ NickyMackay 4 21
(D J S Ffrench Davis) *in tch to 1/2-way: sn wknd rapidly* **5/1**[3]

61.26 secs (0.96) **Going Correction** +0.25s/f (Good) 6 Ran SP% **110.5**
Speed ratings (Par 101): **102,101,95,87,86 76**
toteswinger: 1&2 £5.50, 1&3 £1.50, 2&3 £24.20 CSF £26.08 CT £54.51 TOTE £4.70: £2.70, £4.20; EX 33.20.
Owner M S Saunders **Bred** B Walters **Trained** Green Ore, Somerset

FOCUS
A fair handicap. The winner returned to his previous C/D form and the runner-up improved slightly.

2775 SPORTINGBET.COM H'CAP 1m 67y
8:30 (8:30) (Class 5) (0-75,75) 4-Y-0+ **£3,070** (£906; £453) **Stalls** High

Form RPR

51-0 **1** **Sarah Park (IRE)**[19] 2186 4-9-2 70........ RichardHughes 11 81
(B J Meehan) *mde all: pushed clr wl over 1f out: rdn out: in n.d fnl f* **12/1**

3 **2** 2 **Falcon Rock (IRE)**[27] 1972 4-9-4 72........ PatDobbs 10 78+
(S A Callaghan) *dwlt: hld up in last pair: prog over 3f out: chsd ldrs and drvn 2f out: edgd rt over 1f out: styd on to take 2nd nr fin* **4/1**[1]

0000 **3** ½ **Hallingdal (UAE)**[10] 2434 4-9-1 69........ TPO'Shea 9 74
(J J Bridger) *s.s: hld up in last pair: prog fr 1/2-way: rdn and styd on to chse wnr 1f out: no imp: lost 2nd nr fin* **33/1**

0-03 **4** 1 ½ **Support Fund (IRE)**[9] 2498 5-9-3 71........ StephenCarson 8 73+
(Eve Johnson Houghton) *taken down early: hld up in rr: last pair 3f out: tried to make grnd fr over 2f out: drvn and kpt on: nvr able to chal* **10/1**

51 **5** 1 **Stravella (IRE)**[14] 2317 4-9-7 75........ SebSanders 6 74
(R M Beckett) *pressed wnr: rdn and lft bhd fr 2f out: fdd and lost pls fnl f* **6/1**[3]

146 **6** hd **Singleb (IRE)**[89] 806 5-9-4 72........(p) StephenDonohoe 4 71
(Miss Gay Kelleway) *hld up in rr: effrt on outer 3f out: pushed along and kpt on one pce fnl 2f: nvr on terms* **33/1**

6011 **7** ¾ **Sign Of The Cross**[20] 2149 5-9-4 72........ LPKeniry 2 69
(C R Dore) *t.k.h: trckd ldrs: stl cl up 2f out: nt qckn over 1f out: steadily fdd* **10/1**

3045 **8** ¾ **Ocean Legend (IRE)**[19] 2186 4-9-0 73........ RossAtkinson(5) 1 68
(Miss J Feilden) *hld up in midfield: effrt on wd outside 3f out: no imp on ldrs over 1f out: fdd after* **12/1**

560- **9** ¾ **Red Birr (IRE)**[188] 7526 8-9-7 75........(t) JimmyFortune 13 69
(P R Webber) *chsd ldrs: rdn over 3f out and no prog: lost pl over 2f out: n.d after* **16/1**

4434 **10** nk **Mister New York (USA)**[115] 538 4-9-7 75........ GeorgeBaker 12 68
(Noel T Chance) *hld up in midfield: lost pl sn after 1/2-way: last 2f out: shuffled along and nvr nr ldrs after* **18/1**

3-10 **11** 2 ½ **Fancy Footsteps (IRE)**[21] 2125 4-9-1 69........ PhilipRobinson 5 57
(C G Cox) *trckd ldng pair to over 2f out: wkng whn hmpd 1f out* **10/1**

-644 **12** shd **Pippbrook Gold**[23] 2086 4-9-2 70........ PatCosgrave 14 57
(J R Boyle) *stmbld s: rousted along to go prom: drvn over 2f out: wkng whn hmpd 1f out* **11/2**[2]

100- **13** 1 ¾ **Grand Vizier (IRE)**[241] 6625 5-9-1 72........ JackMitchell(3) 7 55
(C F Wall) *hld up in midfield: no prog 3f out: steadily wknd fnl 2f* **6/1**[3]

1m 46.24s (1.54) **Going Correction** +0.25s/f (Good) 13 Ran SP% **123.6**
Speed ratings (Par 103): **102,100,99,98,97 96,96,95,94,94 91,91,89**
toteswinger: 1&2 £10.60, 1&3 not won, 2&3 £15.90 CSF £61.54 CT £1583.06 TOTE £8.40: £3.00, £2.90, £6.70; EX 86.10.
Owner Mrs J & D E Cash **Bred** George S O'Malley **Trained** Manton, Wilts
■ Stewards' Enquiry : Pat Dobbs three-day ban: careless riding (Jun 22-24)

FOCUS
An ordinary handicap but sound form overall.

2776 SPORTINGBET.COM FILLIES' H'CAP 6f
9:00 (9:00) (Class 5) (0-70,70) 3-Y-0 **£2,729** (£806; £403) **Stalls** High

Form RPR

0-06 **1** **Miss Hollybell**[17] 2227 3-9-6 69........ TPO'Shea 10 74
(J Gallagher) *dwlt: wl in rr: prog 2f out: nt clr run briefly over 1f out: str run fnl f: hung lft but led last 100yds* **25/1**

3-13 **2** ¾ **Sarasota Sunshine**[75] 960 3-8-13 62........ JohnEgan 4 65
(N P Littmoden) *trckd ldrs: shkn up 2f out: gd prog jst over 1f out: r.o and hung lft fnl f: jst outpcd by wnr* **8/1**

60-6 **3** nk **Ailsa Craig (IRE)**[35] 1743 3-8-13 62........ RichardHughes 9 64
(R Hannon) *s.s: wl in rr and pushed along: prog and swtchd to outer 2f out: drvn and hung lft to far rail over 1f out: styd on: a hld* **6/1**[2]

-536 **4** ½ **Itsher**[11] 2417 3-8-1 55........ AndreaAtzeni(5) 8 55+
(S C Williams) *pressed ldrs: effrt to ld wl over 1f out: hung lft u.p after: hdd and nt qckn last 100yds* **9/1**

3-15 **5** 1 ½ **Midnight Fantasy**[20] 2160 3-9-7 70........ SaleemGolam 2 68+
(Rae Guest) *prom on outer: edgd lft u.p over 1f out: cl up ent fnl f: hld whn no room nr fin* **7/2**[1]

0100 **6** 6 **Bold Rose**[14] 2321 3-8-10 64........ LeeNewnes(5) 5 40
(M D I Usher) *prom on outer: on terms w ldrs over 1f out: wknd u.p* **33/1**

6-05 **7** 1 ½ **Calypso Girl (IRE)**[13] 2355 3-8-8 62........ RichardEvans(5) 14 33
(P D Evans) *w ldr: led over 3f out: hdd and hanging lft wl over 1f out: wknd fnl f* **12/1**

P40- **8** ½ **Danzadil (IRE)**[168] 7767 3-8-10 59........ LukeMorris 12 29
(R A Teal) *pressed ldrs to wl over 1f out: sn wknd* **40/1**

0-40 **9** nk **Mount Ella**[21] 2141 3-8-7 56........ FrankieMcDonald 7 25
(J A Osborne) *nvr beyond midfield: drvn on outer over 2f out: wl in rr and no ch over 1f out* **50/1**

64-0 **10** ½ **Cocktail Party (IRE)**[20] 2160 3-8-11 60........ SebSanders 15 27
(J W Hills) *prom and racd against nr side rail: on terms 2f out: wknd jst over 1f out* **16/1**

062 **11** 2 ¾ **Wotasparkler**[20] 2151 3-9-2 65........ NCallan 11 23
(W S Kittow) *led to over 3f out: w ldrs to over 2f out: wkng whn squeezed out over 1f out* **7/1**

0146 **12** 1 ¼ **Bold Ring**[5] 2602 3-8-9 58........ CatherineGannon 13 12
(E J Creighton) *cl up on nr side: wknd over 1f out* **20/1**

44-2 **13** 4 ½ **Little Calla (IRE)**[31] 1838 3-8-13 62........ JimmyFortune 3 2
(E A L Dunlop) *stdd s: dropped in towards nr side fr low draw: wl in rr: effrt and taken towards outer 2f out: sn wknd* **13/2**[3]

103 **14** 2 ¼ **May Martin**[55] 1271 3-8-8 57........ ChrisCatlin 16 —
(Rae Guest) *dwlt: a wl in rr and struggling* **8/1**

1m 14.67s (1.67) **Going Correction** +0.25s/f (Good) 14 Ran SP% **124.1**
Speed ratings (Par 96): **98,97,96,95,93 85,83,83,82,82 78,76,70,67**
toteswinger: 1&2 not won, 1&3 £10.50, 2&3 not won CSF £211.65 CT £1386.73 TOTE £44.10: £15.20, £1.90, £2.30; EX 123.00 Place 6: £185.66, Place 5: £129.36..
Owner Gallagher Partnership **Bred** Mrs R J Gallagher **Trained** Chastleton, Oxon
■ Stewards' Enquiry : Andrea Atzeni three-day ban: careless riding (Jun 22-24)

FOCUS
Just an ordinary fillies' handicap in which the front pair were fairly exposed. Probably not form to be too positive about.
Little Calla(IRE) Official explanation: jockey said filly ran too free
T/Jkpt: Not won. T/Plt: £157.70 to a £1 stake. Pool: £89,494.02. 414.17 winning tickets. T/Qpdt: £93.10 to a £1 stake. Pool: £4,947.20. 39.30 winning tickets. JN

2561 SAINT-CLOUD (L-H)
Monday, June 8

OFFICIAL GOING: Soft

2777a PRIX DES LILAS (LISTED RACE) (FILLIES) 1m
2:35 (2:37) 3-Y-0 **£26,699** (£10,680; £8,010; £5,340; £2,670)

RPR

1 **Providanza (FR)**[29] 1918 3-8-12........ GMosse 5 107
(M Delzangles, France)

2 2 ½ **Hallie's Comet (IRE)**[15] 2304 3-8-12........ PJSmullen 11 101
(A Kinsella, Ire) *in tch on outside: 4th 1/2-way: pushed along st: led over 2f out to over 1f out: kpt on: nt pce of wnr cl home* **13/1**[2]

3 3 **Novita (FR)**[29] 1914 3-9-2........ AStarke 3 98
(P Schiergen, Germany)

4 hd **Street Romance (USA)**[19] 3-8-12........ GBenoist 7 94
(D Smaga, France)

5 nk **Seradim**[24] 2057 3-8-12........ DBoeuf 10 93
(P F I Cole) *cl up: 2nd 1/2-way: pushed along st: rdn and u.p 2f out: kpt on: 3rd 50yds out: no ex cl home* **35/4**[1]

6 ¾ **Slap Shade (IRE)**[33] 3-8-12........ C-PLemaire 2 91
(P Bary, France)

7 1 ½ **Prise De Risque (FR)**[56] 3-8-12........ FPrat 1 88
(T Clout, France)

8 snk **Golden Clou (FR)**[38] 1657 3-8-12........ SPasquier 8 87
(P Demercastel, France)

9 3 **Isaonor (FR)**[25] 3-8-12........ TJarnet 9 81
(Mlle S-V Tarrou, France)

10 ½ **Kandalek**[9] 3-8-12 .... OPeslier 6 79
(Rod Collet, France)
11 **Wadjeka (USA)**[20] 2173 3-8-12 .... CSoumillon 4 79
(Y De Nicolay, France)
1m 46.3s (-1.20) **11** Ran SP% **17.4**
PARI-MUTUEL: WIN 4.40; PL 1.70, 3.90, 2.50; DF 20.80.
Owner C Lambert **Bred** C Lambert **Trained** France

NOTEBOOK
Seradim, whose previous visit to France resulted in a win on the Polytrack at Deauville, had been held in five previous attempts at this level and higher but ran well until fading near the finish on ground that may have been softer than ideal.

[1821] CHESTER (L-H)
Tuesday, June 9

OFFICIAL GOING: Good to firm (good in places)
Running rail was out 6yds from 6f marker to 1.5f point, increasing distances by 13yds.
Wind: Light, against Weather: Overcast

2778 RATHBONES EBF MAIDEN STKS 5f 16y
6:45 (6:45) (Class 4) 2-Y-O **£5,504** (£1,637; £818; £408) **Stalls** Low

Form RPR
2 **1** **Itsthursdayalready**[15] 2339 2-9-3 0 .... PaulMulrennan 2 77+
(J G Given) *bmpd s: n.m.r and lost pl sn after s: towards rr: hdwy whn nt clr run 2f out: prog over 1f out: plld out and edgd rt ins fnl f: str run to ld towards fin* **10/11**[1]
022 **2** *nk* **Reddy To Star (IRE)**[15] 2335 2-9-3 0 .... PhilipRobinson 9 76
(C G Cox) *sn led: rdn over 1f out: worn down towards fin* **4/1**[3]
0 **3** *2* **Wigan Lane**[14] 2360 2-8-12 0 .... PaulHanagan 6 64
(R A Fahey) *broke wl: w ldr tl 3f out: rdn over 1f out: lost 2nd and carried sltly rt ins fnl f: nt qckn* **3/1**[2]
4 *1 ¾* **Bazsharani** 2-8-12 0 .... JohnEgan 3 57
(P D Evans) *bmpd s: chsd ldrs: n.m.r and hmpd jst over 2f out: sn lost pl: rallied over 1f out: no imp on ldrs fnl f* **16/1**
60 **5** *3 ¾* **Arctic Destiny (IRE)**[18] 2231 2-9-3 0 .... FrancisNorton 8 49
(K R Burke) *in tch: rdn over 1f out: wknd ins fnl f* **50/1**
6 *hd* **Cheshire Lady (IRE)** 2-8-12 0 .... TGMcLaughlin 4 43
(W M Brisbourne) *s.i.s: towards rr: pushed along and carried wd on bnd wl over 1f out: nvr able to get competitive* **20/1**
50 **7** *¾* **Ariel Bender**[10] 2484 2-9-3 0 .... PatrickMathers 5 46
(Peter Grayson) *in rr: pushed along over 1f out: sn nt clr run: edgd rt ins fnl f: nt pce to get on terms* **100/1**
4 **8** *5* **Bitter Honey**[18] 2226 2-8-12 0 .... GrahamGibbons 12 23
(Mrs G S Rees) *racd on outside: chsd ldrs: hung rt 1/2-way: sn wknd* **20/1**
62.98 secs (1.98) **Going Correction** +0.225s/f (Good) **8** Ran SP% **115.7**
Speed ratings (Par 95): **93,92,89,86,80 80,79,71**
toteswingers: 1&2 £1.10, 1&3 £1.70, 2&3 £3.40 CSF £4.77 TOTE £2.00: £1.10, £1.30, £1.50; EX 3.80.
Owner Danethorpe Racing Partnership **Bred** St Clare Hall Stud **Trained** Willoughton, Lincs
■ Stewards' Enquiry : Paul Mulrennan one-day ban: carless riding (Jun 23)

FOCUS
The finish was dominated by the form horses, and although the time was nearly three seconds outside of standard, winners should emerge from this.

NOTEBOOK
Itsthursdayalready went right as the stalls opened, barging into Bazsharani, and forfeited the advantage of his ideal draw. Short of room along the inside, his rider never really looked happy, but as he turned into the straight he began to make good headway before picking up strongly to nail long-time leader Reddy To Star close home. (op Evens tchd 11-10 in places)
Reddy To Star(IRE) has now finished second on three of his four starts, but he continues to improve and he did absolutely nothing wrong here, showing good speed to get across from his less-than-ideal draw, before kicking a couple of lengths clear turning for home. Although agonisingly collared late on, he's clearly capable of finding one of these soon. (op 7-2 tchd 9-2)
Wigan Lane, who caught the eye in the paddock, also showed up well early, but she couldn't keep tabs on Reddy To Star when he kicked again from the front and she could only keep on at the one speed in the closing stages. She might appreciate stepping back up to 6f. (op 11-2)
Bazsharani, who wasn't done any favours at the start, is bred to make a sprinting two-year-old and she shaped with real encouragement on this racecourse debut, putting in some good late work to close in on the leading trio and put a fair amount of daylight between herself and the remainder. Her stable do well with their two-year-olds and she is quite promising. (op 9-1)

2779 DOUBLETREE BY HILTON CHESTER H'CAP 1m 2f 75y
7:15 (7:16) (Class 5) (0-70,69) 3-Y-O **£4,209** (£1,252; £625; £312) **Stalls** High

Form RPR
-465 **1** **Embsay Crag**[13] 2370 3-9-5 **65** .... PaulMulrennan 11 73
(Mrs K Walton) *mde all: rdn over 1f out: r.o wl and in command fnl f* **11/1**
-003 **2** *3* **Musical Maze**[8] 2528 3-9-4 **64** .... TGMcLaughlin 4 66
(W M Brisbourne) *in tch: rdn over 1f out: styd on to take 2nd wl ins fnl f: nt pce to trble wnr* **9/1**
4-25 **3** *½* **Oriental Cavalier**[18] 2230 3-9-9 **69** .... RobertWinston 3 70
(R Hollinshead) *a.p: rdn over 2f out: kpt on same pce u.p ins fnl f* **11/8**[1]
06-4 **4** *¾* **Brad's Luck (IRE)**[18] 2230 3-9-2 **62** .... FrancisNorton 5 62+
(M Blanshard) *midfield: rdn and hdwy over 1f out: styd on ins fnl f: nt pce to rch ldrs* **8/1**[3]
0-00 **5** *1 ¼* **Shanavaz**[18] 2230 3-9-0 **60** .... JohnEgan 8 57
(Mrs G S Rees) *hld up: rdn over 1f out: kpt on u.p ins fnl f: nvr able to chal* **50/1**
-030 **6** *hd* **Jobekani (IRE)**[9] 2515 3-9-0 **60** .... StephenDonohoe 13 57+
(Mrs L Williamson) *hld up: effrt over 1f out: kpt on wout troubling ldrs* **20/1**
653 **7** *hd* **One Scoop Or Two**[50] 1410 3-9-0 **60** ....(t) JamesDoyle 9 56
(F Sheridan) *in tch: rdn 4f out: outpcd 2f out: wknd over 1f out* **33/1**
055- **8** *nk* **Mister Bombastic (IRE)**[248] 6481 3-9-4 **64** .... PaulHanagan 1 60
(N J Vaughan) *t.k.h: prom: rdn over 1f out: wknd ins fnl f* **11/2**[2]
060 **9** *1 ½* **Winrob**[46] 1490 3-8-8 **59** .... Louis-PhilippeBeuzelin(5) 6 52
(Patrick Morris) *hld up: rdn over 1f out: no imp* **18/1**
03-0 **10** *3* **Sampower Quin (IRE)**[13] 2371 3-9-1 **61** .... DNolan 7 48
(D Carroll) *midfield: rdn 2f out: wknd over 1f out* **11/1**
5400 **11** *4* **Green Dynasty (IRE)**[14] 2357 3-9-0 **60** .... J-PGuillambert 2 39
(M Johnston) *fly-jmpd leaving stalls and slowly away: struggling 3f out: a bhd* **11/1**
2m 13.65s (1.45) **Going Correction** +0.225s/f (Good) **11** Ran SP% **118.5**
Speed ratings (Par 99): **103,100,100,99,98 98,98,98,96,94 91**
toteswingers: 1&2 £10.70, 1&3 £3.80, 2&3 £4.30 CSF £104.89 CT £223.83 TOTE £14.00: £3.30, £2.50, £1.40; EX 81.60.
Owner Keep The Faith Partnership **Bred** Mrs Glenda Swinglehurst **Trained** Middleham Moor, N Yorks

FOCUS
Not strong handicap form but an impressive performance from Embsay Crag who has been rated up 5lb. Overall this is not form to be too positive about.

2780 HIGHSTREETVOUCHERS.COM H'CAP 7f 2y
7:45 (7:46) (Class 3) (0-95,90) 4-Y-O- **£8,831** (£2,643; £1,321; £660; £329) **Stalls** Low

Form RPR
1 **1** **Lowther**[12] 2415 4-9-5 **86** .... NeilChalmers 8 95+
(A Bailey) *midfield: hdwy on outside over 1f out: r.o to ld and edgd lft 100yds out: pushed out cl home* **14/1**
-000 **2** *½* **Stevie Gee (IRE)**[17] 2266 5-8-10 **77** .... RobertWinston 5 85
(G A Swinbank) *led: rdn over 1f out: sn edgd sltly rt: hdd 100yds out: hld after* **11/1**
-132 **3** *¾* **Secret Night**[31] 1860 6-8-13 **80** ....(v) AdamKirby 2 88+
(C G Cox) *midfield: effrt over 1f out: nt clr run and checked ins fnl f: in clr fnl 100yds: rapid prog towards fin* **7/2**[2]
-661 **4** *½* **Ponty Rossa (IRE)**[23] 2102 5-9-5 **86** .... DavidAllan 7 91
(T D Easterby) *w ldr: rdn whn chalng over 1f out: nt qckn fnl 100yds* **8/1**
0511 **5** *shd* **Esoterica (IRE)**[6] 2589 6-9-3 **84** 6ex ....(v) DanielTudhope 1 88
(J S Goldie) *trckd ldrs: effrt over 1f out: styd on: nt pce of ldrs towards fin* **2/1**[1]
0-30 **6** *½* **Guilded Warrior**[31] 1861 6-9-0 **86** .... Louis-PhilippeBeuzelin(5) 6 89
(W S Kittow) *trckd ldrs: rdn whn n.m.r 1f out: styd on tl no ex cl home* **7/1**[3]
-534 **7** *1 ¾* **Boy Blue**[24] 2073 4-9-1 **82** .... DaleGibson 9 80
(P Salmon) *hld up: rdn over 1f out: nvr able to chal* **8/1**
1605 **8** *5* **Gallantry**[29] 1942 7-9-4 **85** .... TGMcLaughlin 10 70
(P Howling) *missed break: pushed along over 2f out: a bhd* **28/1**
/0-0 **9** *hd* **Fireside**[73] 995 4-9-9 **90** .... PhilipRobinson 3 74
(M A Jarvis) *racd keenly: hld up: pushed along over 1f out: nvr on terms* **8/1**
1m 26.73s (0.23) **Going Correction** +0.225s/f (Good) **9** Ran SP% **119.8**
Speed ratings (Par 107): **107,106,105,105,104 104,102,96,96**
toteswingers: 1&2 £37.20, 1&3 £6.80, 2&3 £7.30 CSF £161.92 CT £670.85 TOTE £13.50: £2.60, £2.60, £1.80; EX 215.30.
Owner L J Barratt **Bred** L J Barratt **Trained** Newmarket, Suffolk

FOCUS
A good quality handicap and although they finished in a bit of a heap, the pace was generous and the form quite strong, rated through the third and fourth. There is more to come from the winner.

NOTEBOOK
Lowther, who was sent off at 100-1 when winning at Yarmouth on debut, was beginning life in handicaps off what looked a stiff enough mark of 86, but he is clearly held in quite high regard by Alan Bailey and he landed this in the style of a horse firmly on the upgrade. He travelled well off the pace and, when switched out wide to challenge, he picked up strongly to prove he has the pace for this drop back to 7f. He is an unexposed, improving colt who beat some battle-hardened handicappers on just his second start on the Flat. (op 12-1 tchd 16-1 in places)
Stevie Gee(IRE) had been out of sorts this term but this was much more encouraging and he battled on well from the front. He has slipped back to a handy mark again so now that he's signalled a return to form he should be worth keeping onside. (tchd 12-1 in places)
Secret Night was the unlucky horse of the race for she was making her move when carried into the back of horses by Lowther, and her rider had no choice but to snatch her up. Her chance had gone but she stayed on really well down the outside to snatch third. Although it's hard to be dogmatic about whether she would have won with a clear run, she would definitely have finished much closer. Official explanation: jockey said mare was denied a clear run (tchd 4-1)
Ponty Rossa(IRE), up 5lb for her recent Ripon win, had every chance and kept on well in the closing stages. (op 11-1)
Esoterica(IRE) came into this race in the form of his life but had never raced around this unique circuit. (op 11-4 tchd 3-1)
Guilded Warrior took a step in the right direction after disappointing in the Victoria Cup last month but didn't have enough in the locker to play a major part in the finish. (op 8-1)
Gallantry was never travelling. Official explanation: jockey said gelding never travelled (op 33-1 tchd 25-1)
Fireside Official explanation: trainer's rep had no explanation for the poor form shown

2781 GROWHOW H'CAP 1m 2f 75y
8:15 (8:15) (Class 4) (0-85,84) 4-Y-O+ **£5,504** (£1,637; £818; £408) **Stalls** High

Form RPR
504- **1** **Full Speed (GER)**[227] 6974 4-9-7 **82** .... RobertWinston 8 89
(G A Swinbank) *racd keenly: prom: effrt to ld over 1f out: pushed out and r.o ins fnl f* **15/2**
4361 **2** *1 ¾* **I'm In The Pink (FR)**[11] 2442 5-8-11 **72** .... JohnEgan 3 75
(P D Evans) *racd keenly: prom: rdn and nt qckn over 1f out: styd on ins fnl f: tk 2nd towards fin: nt pce of wnr* **3/1**[2]
0-05 **3** *nk* **Charlie Tokyo (IRE)**[10] 2468 6-9-8 **83** ....(v) PaulHanagan 1 85
(R A Fahey) *led at stdy pce: increased tempo 2f out: hdd over 1f out: no ex towards fin* **7/2**[3]
-203 **4** *nse* **Rosbay (IRE)**[13] 2374 5-9-7 **82** .... DavidAllan 2 84
(T D Easterby) *hld up: rdn over 1f out: styd on ins fnl f: nt quite pce to chal ldrs* **7/2**[3]
5 *1 ¼* **Safari Journey (USA)**[17] 5-8-11 **72** .... PhilipRobinson 5 72
(P J Hobbs) *hld up: effrt on outside over 2f out: outpcd fnl f* **5/2**[1]
2m 18.66s (6.46) **Going Correction** +0.225s/f (Good) **5** Ran SP% **109.8**
Speed ratings (Par 105): **83,81,81,81,80**
toteswingers: 1&2 £12.50 CSF £29.29 TOTE £9.00: £3.30, £1.30; EX 38.30.
Owner P J Carr **Bred** Dr K Schulte **Trained** Melsonby, N Yorks

FOCUS
Unsatisfactory form given the pace was very sedate and it turned into a sprint turning for home. Not the most solid or reliable form.

2782 HAMPDEN UNDERWRITING H'CAP 5f 16y
8:45 (8:45) (Class 4) (0-85,85) 3-Y-O+ **£5,180** (£1,541; £770; £384) **Stalls** Low

Form RPR
6121 **1** **Tyrannosaurus Rex (IRE)**[31] 1877 5-9-1 **71** .... GrahamGibbons 4 84
(D Shaw) *chsd ldrs: rdn and str run against far rail to ld 75yds out: wl on top cl home* **11/1**
-152 **2** *1* **Titus Andronicus (IRE)**[3] 2717 3-9-5 **82** .... RobertWinston 1 88+
(K A Ryan) *led: rdn over 1f out: hdd 75yds out: hld cl home* **5/6**[1]

-000 **3** 2¾ **Bertoliver**[18] 2228 5-9-10 **80** PhilipRobinson 3 79
(Tom Dascombe) *w ldr: rdn over 1f out: no ex fnl 100yds* **9/2**[2]
0601 **4** 2¼ **Methaaly (IRE)**[24] 2071 6-9-5 **80** (be) DeanHeslop(5) 8 71
(M Mullineaux) *outpcd and bhd: prog fnl f: fin wl wout rching ldrs* **14/1**
4604 **5** shd **Bo McGinty (IRE)**[6] 2591 8-9-6 **76** (v) PaulHanagan 7 67
(R A Fahey) *midfield: outpcd 2f out: kpt on ins fnl f: nt pce to chal* **16/1**
6020 **6** nk **Fyodor (IRE)**[8] 2549 8-9-5 **75** JohnEgan 10 65
(P D Evans) *midfield: rdn and prog to chse ldrs over 1f out: no real imp: one pce ins fnl f* **33/1**
-600 **7** 2¼ **Supermassive Muse (IRE)**[26] 2012 4-10-0 **84** (p) StephenDonohoe 6 65
(E S McMahon) *chsd ldrs: pushed along and outpcd 1/2-way: n.d affter* **25/1**
010 **8** 1¾ **Mandurah (IRE)**[3] 2716 5-9-8 **78** FrancisNorton 9 53
(D Nicholls) *a towards rr: nvr on terms* **12/1**
0021 **9** ¾ **Gift Horse**[12] 2389 9-9-3 **78** RichardEvans(5) 2 50
(P D Evans) *midfield: lost pl 3f out: n.m.r and hmpd 2f out: bhd after* **8/1**[3]

61.37 secs (0.37) **Going Correction** +0.225s/f (Good)
WFA 3 from 4yo+ 7lb **9** Ran SP% **119.2**
Speed ratings (Par 105): **106,104,100,96,96 95,92,89,88**
toteswingers: 1&2 £2.20, 1&3 £4.70, 2&3 £2.40 CSF £21.30 CT £53.17 TOTE £11.70: £2.30, £1.10, £1.80; EX 20.40.
Owner Market Avenue Racing Club Ltd **Bred** Limestone And Tara Studs **Trained** Danethorpe, Notts

FOCUS
A blistering gallop to this sprint, as Titus Andronicus blazed the trail with Bertoliver pestering him all the time, but it only set it up for a finisher. A step forward from the winner with the second deserving of a bit of extra credit.
Gift Horse Official explanation: jockey said gelding suffered interference in running

2783 HOLLYOAKS H'CAP (FOR LADY AMATEUR RIDERS) 1m 4f 66y
9:15 (9:16) (Class 5) (0-70,70) 4-Y-0+ £3,903 (£1,210; £605; £302) Stalls Low

Form RPR
0-05 **1** **Toshi (USA)**[11] 2440 7-9-7 **55** MrsCBartley 1 60+
(J S Goldie) *midfield: hdwy and swtchd rt over 1f out: str run ins fnl f to ld fnl stride* **5/1**[3]
0-40 **2** hd **Inspector Clouseau (IRE)**[12] 2392 4-10-1 **70** MissKECooper(7) 12 75+
(T P Tate) *led: hdd 2f out: sn rdn: rallied fnl 75yds: r.o and upsides fnl stride: jst hld* **25/1**
3550 **3** nse **They All Laughed**[19] 2194 6-10-5 **67** MrsMarieKing 4 72
(P W Hiatt) *disp 2nd pl for much of way: chal 2f out: led 1f out: hdd fnl stride* **20/1**
050- **4** ½ **Inspirina (IRE)**[223] 7064 5-9-9 **62** MissHayleyMoore(5) 8 66
(R Ford) *midfield: hdwy on outside 4f out: prom 3f out: led 2f out: sn hrd rdn: hdd 1f out: no ex cl home* **8/1**
000- **5** 1¼ **Prelude**[255] 6279 8-10-4 **66** MissEJJones 13 68
(W M Brisbourne) *disp 2nd pl for much of way: styd on u.p fr over 1f out: edgd sltly rt ins fnl f: one pce cl home* **20/1**
2002 **6** nse **New England**[10] 2493 7-9-10 **58** MissSBrotherton 10 60+
(W M Brisbourne) *missed break: hld up: hdwy over 1f out: sn rdn and edgd lft: styd on: nt quite pce to rch ldrs* **15/2**
6443 **7** nk **Thorny Mandate**[10] 2497 7-9-8 **56** MissADeniel 2 58+
(W M Brisbourne) *hld up: hdwy 1f out: r.o ins fnl f: nrst fin* **4/1**[1]
5435 **8** 2¼ **Penang Cinta**[16] 2294 6-9-8 **56** (v) MissEFolkes 9 54
(P D Evans) *chsd ldrs: rdn over 1f out: sn wknd* **7/1**
6003 **9** 3½ **Gamesters Lady**[10] 2493 6-9-6 **57** (b) MissMSowerby(3) 6 49
(W M Brisbourne) *hld up: pushed along 3f out: nvr a danger* **12/1**
062 **10** 1 **Kirstys Lad**[17] 2263 7-9-2 **55** MissMMullineaux(5) 5 46
(M Mullineaux) *in rr: rdn over 1f out: nvr on terms* **16/1**
6220 **11** shd **Piper's Song (IRE)**[21] 2163 6-10-2 **64** MissNCarberry 11 55
(Patrick Morris) *midfield: rdn over 1f out: no imp: wknd ins fnl f* **9/2**[2]
6520 **12** 2½ **Monaadi (IRE)**[11] 2445 4-9-5 **58** (p) MissRKneller(5) 3 45
(R Hollinshead) *chsd ldrs: lost pl over 3f out: bhd over 1f out* **10/1**

2m 42.4s (2.50) **Going Correction** +0.225s/f (Good) **12** Ran SP% **126.3**
Speed ratings (Par 103): **100,99,99,99,98 98,98,96,94,93 93,92**
toteswingers: 1&2 £67.50, 1&3 £27.70, 2&3 £55.20 CSF £134.37 CT £2353.28 TOTE £7.00: £2.90, £6.70, £3.90; EX 183.00 Place 6 £92.58, Place 5 £85.37.
Owner E Nisbet & Miss L McFadzean **Bred** Tom Wilson **Trained** Uplawmoor, E Renfrews

FOCUS
The early pace was strong but it slackened off mid race and there were a lot of horses getting in each other's way in the pack, so the form is muddling. The second and third are the best guide and the winner is well handicapped.
Piper's Song(IRE) Official explanation: jockey said gelding ran flat
T/Plt: £183.40 to a £1 stake. Pool: £98,381.19. 391.42 winning tickets. T/Qpdt: £138.30 to a £1 stake. Pool: £5,348.39. 28.60 winning tickets. DO

2360 REDCAR (L-H)
Tuesday, June 9

OFFICIAL GOING: Good to firm changing to good (good to firm in places) after race 3 (3.00)
Wind: Fresh against Weather: Overcast and rain

2784 THE COMMITMENTS PERFORMING HERE ON 29TH AUGUST MEDIAN AUCTION MAIDEN STKS 6f
2:00 (2:00) (Class 5) 2-Y-0 £2,590 (£770; £385; £192) Stalls Centre

Form RPR
1 **Marsh Warbler** 2-9-3 0 GregFairley 5 82+
(M Johnston) *cl up: led and hung lft 2f out: pushed clr appr fnl f: r.o* **11/8**[2]
5 **2** 6 **Pure Nostalgia (IRE)**[14] 2360 2-8-5 0 JamieKyne(7) 4 59
(J Howard Johnson) *led: rdn along and hdd 2f out: sn drvn and edgd lft: kpt on same pce* **10/11**[1]
3 12 **Blue Emirate** 2-9-3 0 PhillipMakin 3 28
(P C Haslam) *dwlt: sn chsng ldrs: rdn over 2f out and sn btn* **10/1**[3]
0 **4** 2¼ **War Wolf**[25] 2041 2-9-3 0 DNolan 1 21
(T D Easterby) *cl up: rdn along 1/2-way: sn wknd* **40/1**
5 **5** 18 **Ducal Destiny**[11] 2449 2-9-3 0 TonyHamilton 2 —
(J R Weymes) *cl up: rdn along after 2f: sn wknd and wl bhd fr 1/2-way* **40/1**

1m 13.68s (1.88) **Going Correction** +0.275s/f (Good) **5** Ran SP% **107.3**
Speed ratings (Par 93): **98,90,74,71,47**
CSF £2.74 TOTE £2.40: £1.10, £1.10; EX 3.00.
Owner Sheikh Hamdan Bin Mohammed Al Maktoum **Bred** Darley **Trained** Middleham Moor, N Yorks

FOCUS
A dry night and morning but, after persistent rain on watered ground on the run up to the opener, the jockeys reported the ground to be riding "good" and that the rain was getting in. Little strength in depth for an ordinary maiden and just a fair gallop (into a reasonable headwind) but a decisive debut success from the winner, who looks the sort to improve again.

NOTEBOOK
Marsh Warbler ◆, a brother to 7f juvenile winner Ravi River, was well supported and created a favourable impression on this racecourse debut, despite his apparent greenness. He has physical scope, will be equally at home over 7f and, although this was not a strong race, he appeals as the type to win again. (op 5-4 tchd 11-10)
Pure Nostalgia(IRE), who shaped well over course and distance on her debut when in front of a subsequent winner, was well supported but had her limitations exposed against a potentially useful sort. However she remains capable of picking up an uncompetitive race in this grade. (tchd 11-10)
Blue Emirate, a 23,000gns purchase and the second foal of an unraced half-sister to three winners from 5f to 1m, attracted support and travelled well for a long way on this racecourse debut. His stable had a couple of second-time-out juvenile winners last week and he is likely to improve for this experience. (op 16-1 tchd 9-1)
War Wolf, from a yard in decent form, fared better than on his debut but this again firmly underlined his vulnerability in this type of event. Moderate handicaps will be the way forward with him in due course. (op 66-1 tchd 100-1)
Ducal Destiny again shaped with no immediate promise. (tchd 50-1)

2785 BETFAIR APPRENTICE TRAINING SERIES (S) STKS 1m 6f 19y
2:30 (2:30) (Class 6) 4-6-Y-0 £2,047 (£604; £302) Stalls Low

Form RPR
/06- **1** **Mystified (IRE)**[13] 1972 6-9-0 50 (tp) JamieKyne 1 54
(R F Fisher) *trckd ldr: led 6f out: rdn along and hdd 3f out: led again over 1f out: kpt on wl u.p ins fnl f* **6/1**
-063 **2** 1½ **Blue Jet (USA)**[15] 2344 5-8-11 45 JohnCavanagh(3) 7 52
(R M Whitaker) *trckd ldng pair: hdwy over 4f out: rdn to ld 3f out: drvn and hdd over 1f out: drvn and kpt on same pce* **13/8**[1]
0060 **3** 2¾ **Dazzling Begum**[20] 2182 4-8-9 45 (p) SimonPearce 8 43
(J Pearce) *hld up towards rr: hdwy over 3f out: rdn along wl over 2f out: styd on ins fnl f: nrst fin* **7/2**[3]
4 14 **Nightboat To Cairo (IRE)**[97] 5-8-6 0 ow2 DavidKenny(5) 3 25
(P A Kirby) *in rr: sme hdwy on outer over 3f out: sn rdn along and nvr nr ldrs* **100/1**
5 2½ **Sprinkler**[20] 6-8-7 0 ow1 NSLawes(3) 4 21
(C W Thornton) *in rr: rdn along 4f out: plugged on: nvr a factor* **33/1**
00-0 **6** 6 **Ducal Regancy Duke**[14] 2361 5-9-0 36 (p) LanceBetts 2 17
(C J Teague) *t.k.h: sn led and clr: stdd after 3f: hdd 6f out: rdn along over 3f out: sn wknd* **66/1**
0600 **7** 11 **Lunar Storm (IRE)**[43] 1556 5-9-0 40 PaulPickard 6 1
(Mrs R A Carr) *a bhd* **16/1**
5/20 **8** 2¼ **Castellina**[28] 1962 5-8-9 70 MatthewDavies 5 —
(E J Creighton) *hld up in tch: effrt over 4f out: rdn along wl over 3f out and sn wknd* **11/4**[2]

3m 6.26s (1.56) **Going Correction** +0.15s/f (Good) **8** Ran SP% **112.6**
Speed ratings: **101,100,98,90,89 85,79,78**
toteswingers: 1&2 £3.10, 1&3 £5.20, 2&3 £3.20 CSF £15.70 TOTE £6.20: £2.00, £1.30, £1.60; EX 20.40.The winner was bought in for £6,000.
Owner Great Head House Estates Limited **Bred** Denis And Mrs Teresa Bergin **Trained** Ulverston, Cumbria

FOCUS
A low-grade event in which a fair gallop steadied after 3f. The first three finished clear and the winner probably only had to match last year's form.
Ducal Regancy Duke Official explanation: jockey said gelding hung right-handed throughout
Lunar Storm(IRE) Official explanation: jockey said gelding hung right-handed throughout

2786 WEDDING RECEPTIONS AT REDCAR RACECOURSE H'CAP 7f
3:00 (3:00) (Class 5) (0-75,75) 3-Y-0 £2,590 (£770; £385; £192) Stalls Centre

Form RPR
-300 **1** **Jimwil (IRE)**[6] 2602 3-8-10 **67** (b) NeilBrown(3) 13 77+
(M Dods) *hld up and bhd: smooth hdwy 2f out: led over 1f out: styd on strly ins fnl f* **20/1**
-333 **2** 1½ **Mo Mhuirnin (IRE)**[21] 2157 3-8-11 **65** TonyHamilton 10 68
(R A Fahey) *hld up in rr: stdy hdwy over 2f out: rdn and ev ch over 1f out: edgd lft and one pce u.p ins fnl f* **15/2**
5-36 **3** 6 **Dean Iarracht (IRE)**[7] 2578 3-8-9 **68** FrederikTylicki(5) 1 55+
(M Dods) *hld up in tch: effrt over 2f out and sn rdn along: n.m.r and swtchd rt 1f out: kpt on u.p: nrst fin* **4/1**[1]
44-4 **4** ½ **Honimiere (IRE)**[12] 2406 3-9-4 **72** PJMcDonald 3 57
(G A Swinbank) *prom: rdn along over 2f out: drvn and edgd rt 1f out: sn one pce* **8/1**
50-0 **5** ¾ **Secret City (IRE)**[48] 1452 3-8-4 **58** (b) GregFairley 15 41
(R Bastiman) *prom: rdn along and ev ch 2f out: sn drvn and one pce appr fnl f* **50/1**
3-20 **6** 1 **Mister Tinktastic (IRE)**[36] 1736 3-8-11 **65** (p) PhillipMakin 5 46
(M Dods) *sn led: rdn along over 2f out: drvn and hdd over 1f out: grad wknd* **13/2**[3]
1030 **7** 2 **Seldom (IRE)**[8] 2544 3-8-9 **70** JohnCavanagh(7) 11 45
(M Brittain) *in tch: rdn along wl over 2f out: sn no imp* **14/1**
006- **8** shd **Nino Zachetti (IRE)**[282] 5539 3-8-2 **56** oh6 AndrewMullen 9 31
(E J Alston) *cl up: rdn along wl over 2f out and grad wknd* **100/1**
-005 **9** 1 **Elusive Fame (USA)**[11] 2438 3-9-7 **75** JoeFanning 8 47
(M Johnston) *chsd ldrs: rdn along over 2f out: wkng whn n.m.r wl over 1f out* **10/1**
3-16 **10** 2¾ **Hel's Angel (IRE)**[13] 2370 3-9-1 **69** TPQueally 7 34
(Mrs A Duffield) *nvr bttr than midfield* **5/1**[2]
1-30 **11** 2½ **Allformary**[24] 2073 3-9-3 **71** TomEaves 4 29
(B Smart) *prom: rdn along over 2f out: grad wknd* **15/2**
1360 **12** ½ **Auld Arty (FR)**[26] 2010 3-9-5 **73** (p) RobertHavlin 14 30
(T G Mills) *prom: rdn along 1/2-way: sn wknd* **14/1**
62-0 **13** 1¼ **Dillenda**[36] 1725 3-8-2 **56** DuranFentiman 16 9
(T D Easterby) *a towards rr* **66/1**
40-0 **14** 2 **Soviet Rhythm**[31] 1888 3-8-6 **60** RoystonFfrench 6 8
(G M Moore) *a towards rr* **50/1**
06-0 **15** 9 **Dark Velvet (IRE)**[28] 1973 3-8-8 **65** MichaelJStainton(3) 2 —
(E J Alston) *chsd ldrs on wd ourside: rdn along 1/2-way and sn wknd* **40/1**

1m 26.18s (1.68) **Going Correction** +0.275s/f (Good) **15** Ran SP% **120.7**
Speed ratings (Par 99): **101,99,92,91,91 89,87,87,86,83 80,79,78,76,65**
toteswingers: 1&2 £30.40, 1&3 £20.00, 2&3 £5.40 CSF £158.61 CT £752.94 TOTE £28.50: £6.70, £2.80, £1.50; EX 213.70.
Owner Bill Nelson & Jim Mahony **Bred** Millsec Limited **Trained** Denton, Co Durham

FOCUS
A run-of-the-mill handicap in which the pace was sound. The first two (both held up) pulled clear and the form is rated around the runner-up. This form may not prove as good as it looks.
Hel's Angel(IRE) Official explanation: jockey said filly ran flat
Auld Arty(FR) Official explanation: jockey said gelding hung left throughout

2787 BODDINGTONS REDCAR STRAIGHT-MILE CHAMPIONSHIP H'CAP (QUALIFIER) 1m
3:35 (3:35) (Class 3) (0-95,95) 3-Y-0+

£7,477 (£2,239; £1,119; £560; £279; £140) **Stalls** Centre

Form RPR
0300 **1** **Dream Lodge (IRE)**[26] 2015 5-9-9 **95** FrederikTylicki(5) 7 107
(R A Fahey) *trckd ldrs: hdwy and nt clr run wl over 1f out: sn swtchd rt and rdn to ld 1f out: sn clr* **5/2**[1]
15-5 **2** 3½ **Observatory Star (IRE)**[28] 1952 6-8-11 **78** (tp) RoystonFfrench 3 82
(T D Easterby) *trckd ldrs: hdwy 2f out: rdn over 1f out: and sn ev ch tl drvn andone pce ins fnl f* **4/1**[3]
1144 **3** ½ **Green Agenda**[18] 2248 3-8-0 **78** NickyMackay 5 76
(M Johnston) *stmbld s: sn prom: effrt 2f and sn ev ch tl rdn and one pce ent fnl f* **7/2**[2]
0500 **4** 1 **Minority Report**[6] 2612 9-8-9 **76** AndrewMullen 4 77
(D Nicholls) *hld up in rr: hdwy 2f out: rdn over 1f out and sn no imp* **16/1**
1016 **5** ¾ **Wovoka (IRE)**[6] 2612 6-9-2 **83** TonyHamilton 2 82
(D W Barker) *dwlt: hld up in rr: swtchd outside and hdwy 2f out: rdn over 1f out: sn drvn and btn* **6/1**
-110 **6** 2½ **Billy Dane (IRE)**[19] 2197 5-9-5 **86** PhillipMakin 8 79
(F P Murtagh) *stmbld s: sn led and set stdy pce: qcknd wl over 2f out: rdn wl over 1f out: hdd 1f out and sn wknd* **8/1**
40-4 **7** 4 **Summer Gold (IRE)**[12] 2392 5-8-13 **80** NCallan 6 64
(E J Alston) *t.k.h: trckd ldr: hdwy and cl up 2f out: sn rdn and ev ch tl edgd rt over 1f out and wknd appr fnl f* **8/1**

1m 38.74s (0.74) **Going Correction** +0.275s/f (Good)
WFA 3 from 5yo+ 11lb **7 Ran SP% 113.2**
Speed ratings (Par 107): **107,103,103,102,101 98,94**
toteswingers: 1&2 £3.90, 1&3 £3.50, 2&3 £3.70 CSF £12.42 CT £33.60 TOTE £3.90: £2.80, £2.10; EX 17.70.
Owner The G-Guck Group **Bred** C H Wacker Iii **Trained** Musley Bank, N Yorks
■ Stewards' Enquiry : Nicky Mackay two-day ban: used whip with excessive frequency (Jun 23-24)

FOCUS
The ground was changed to good, good to firm in places after the previous race. Exposed performers in a fair handicap. The gallop was fair and, unlike in the previous race, the field raced towards the stands'-side rail. A clear personal best from the winner.

NOTEBOOK
Dream Lodge(IRE), the subject of plenty of market support, had slipped to a fair mark and returned to something like his best on this first run for in-form Richard Fahey. He has not always looked straightforward or proved consistent but it will be interesting to see if he is able to build on this for this yard. (op 11-4)
Observatory Star(IRE), tried in a tongue-tie, bettered reappearance form and ran creditably against a rival that figured on a decent mark. More of an end-to-end gallop would have suited and he should be able to win again away from progressive sorts when things pan out. (op 9-2)
Green Agenda was not disgraced after enjoying the run of the race and looks a good guide to this form. His improvement in the first half of this year seems to have flattened out but he should continue to give a good account. (op 4-1)
Minority Report has not been at his best this year but he shaped with more encouragement this time. A stronger overall gallop would have suited and he is one to keep an eye on when it looks as though there will be plenty of pace on. (op 12-1)
Wovoka(IRE), an improved performer this year, could have done with a faster pace but, although not totally disgraced, he has little margin for error from his current mark. (op 11-2)
Billy Dane(IRE), back on a sound surface, had the run of the race and had few excuses this time. He is best when able to dominate but is going to have to progress further if he is to win from this rating. Official explanation: jockey said gelding slipped on leaving stalls (tchd 10-1)
Summer Gold(IRE) again failed to settle and failed to reproduce recent reappearance form back in trip. This may have come too quickly, though, and she is worth another chance. (tchd 7-1)

2788 RACING UK CHANNEL 432 MAIDEN CLAIMING STKS 6f
4:10 (4:11) (Class 6) 2-Y-0 **£2,047** (£604; £302) **Stalls** Centre

Form RPR
0 **1** **Miami Gator (IRE)**[15] 2339 2-8-13 0 NCallan 10 59
(K R Burke) *trckd ldrs: hdwy 1/2-way: led jst over 2f out and sn rdn: drvn ins fnl f and kpt on wl* **9/2**[3]
0 **2** ½ **Desert Forest (IRE)**[10] 2467 2-9-2 0 FrederikTylicki(5) 11 66
(J Howard Johnson) *in tch: hdwy on outer 2f out: rdn to chse wnr ins fnl f: kpt on* **8/1**
0 **3** ½ **Bothwell Castle (IRE)**[18] 2231 2-9-0 0 PhillipMakin 3 57
(P C Haslam) *chsd ldrs: hdwy over 2f out: rdn and ev ch whn edgd lft over 1f out: sn drvn and kpt on towards fin* **11/1**
5 **4** ¾ **Go To Dubai**[22] 2128 2-8-6 0 DaleGibson 2 47
(M W Easterby) *cl up: effrt and ev ch over 2f out: sn rdn: drvn appr fnl f and kpt on same pce* **9/4**[1]
650 **5** 4 **Ytartfawn (IRE)**[17] 2258 2-8-0 0 PaulPickard(7) 7 36
(P T Midgley) *chsd ldrs: hdwy on wd outside wl over 1f out: sn rdn: edgd lft and no imp fnl f* **33/1**
6 1½ **Joel The Mole** 2-8-7 0 PaulQuinn 5 31
(D Nicholls) *s.i.s and bhd tl styd on fnl 2f: nrst fin* **14/1**
04 **7** 1½ **Sands Of Dee (USA)**[5] 2623 2-9-7 0 (v) TonyHamilton 1 41
(R A Fahey) *dwlt: sn rdn along and a towards rr* **4/1**[2]
6 **8** 1¼ **Ibmab**[10] 2484 2-8-11 0 (t) TomEaves 4 27
(Mrs L Stubbs) *a in rr* **16/1**
55 **9** 5 **More For Less**[36] 1719 2-8-6 0 DeanHeslop(5) 8 12
(T D Barron) *cl up: rdn along bef 1/2-way and sn wknd* **14/1**
10 1¾ **Fol Wizard** 2-8-7 0 PatrickDonaghy(5) 9 8
(P C Haslam) *a in rr* **33/1**
06 **11** ¾ **Sir Christie**[17] 2258 2-8-11 0 RoystonFfrench 6 5
(N Tinkler) *led: rdn along 1/2-way: hdd over 2f out and sn wknd* **11/1**

1m 14.98s (3.18) **Going Correction** +0.275s/f (Good) **11 Ran SP% 121.8**
Speed ratings (Par 91): **89,88,87,86,81 79,77,75,69,66 65**
toteswingers: 1&2 £13.60, 1&3 £16.70, 2&3 £19.70 CSF £42.15 TOTE £5.90: £1.90, £3.40, £3.80; EX 46.10.
Owner Mrs Elaine M Burke **Bred** Newlands House Stud **Trained** Middleham Moor, N Yorks

FOCUS
A modest event in which the first four finished clear. The gallop was reasonable and the field raced in the centre.

NOTEBOOK
Miami Gator(IRE), who failed to get competitive over 5f at this course on his debut, proved suited by the step up to this trip and the drop in grade and he showed improved form after attracting market support. He may be able to progress again at a modest level. (op 13-2)
Desert Forest(IRE) was nibbled at in the market and bettered debut form dropped in grade. He will be suited by the step up to 7f and should be able to pick up a similar event. (op 14-1)
Bothwell Castle(IRE) had been beaten a fair way on his debut but fared a good deal better in this lesser grade. His stable's juveniles have been running well and he may be capable of a little better. (tchd 8-1)
Go To Dubai, who showed ability at a modest level over 5f on her debut on Fibresand, was far from disgraced over this more suitable trip on this turf debut. She pulled clear of the remainder and should be able to pick up a low-grade event. (op 10-3)
Joel The Mole hinted at ability after a slow start on this racecourse debut and is entitled to improve. (op 12-1)
Sands Of Dee(USA), who looked a tricky ride at Hamilton on his previous start, was never travelling with any fluency and proved disappointing with the visor again fitted. (op 9-2)
Sir Christie Official explanation: jockey said gelding ran too free

2789 LADIES' DAY ON SATURDAY 20TH JUNE MEDIAN AUCTION MAIDEN STKS 1m
4:45 (4:46) (Class 6) 3-5-Y-0 **£2,047** (£604; £302) **Stalls** Centre

Form RPR
0 **1** **Cipher**[15] 2343 3-8-13 0 RoystonFfrench 6 84
(M Johnston) *midfield: hdwy on outer 1/2-way: led wl over 2f out: rdn and hung bdly rt over 1f out: styd on* **25/1**
22 **2** 4½ **Luc Jordan**[15] 2318 3-8-13 0 JoeFanning 13 73
(L M Cumani) *cl up: led briefly 3f out: sn rdn and hdd: drvn and edgd lft over 1f out: kpt on same pce* **8/11**[1]
2-25 **3** *hd* **Kammaan**[22] 2142 3-8-8 70 NCallan 7 68
(M A Jarvis) *trckd ldrs: hdwy and cl up 3f out: rdn over 2f out and ev ch tl drvn and edgd lft over 1f out: sn one pce* **10/1**
56- **4** 6 **Quiquillo (USA)**[231] 6887 3-8-8 0 TPQueally 5 54
(H R A Cecil) *prom: rdn along wl over 2f out and sn one pce* **9/2**[3]
060- **5** ¾ **Noche De Reyes**[325] 4207 4-9-10 45 AndrewMullen 11 60?
(E J Alston) *s.i.s and bhd: hdwy into midfield 1/2-way: rdn and outpcd over 2f out: kpt on ins fnl f: nt rch ldrs* **200/1**
2-22 **6** *nk* **Proud Times (USA)**[18] 2229 3-8-13 79 PJMcDonald 8 57
(G A Swinbank) *led: rdn along and hdd 3f out: sn drvn and wknd* **7/2**[2]
50 **7** 2½ **George Adamson (IRE)**[19] 2199 3-8-13 0 TomEaves 1 51
(G A Swinbank) *hld up and bhd: hdwy wl over 2f out: sn rdn and no imp* **66/1**
0 **8** 11 **Elusive Style (IRE)**[38] 1683 3-8-5 0 MichaelJStainton(3) 9 21
(S P Griffiths) *prom: rdn along 1/2-way: sn wknd* **200/1**
0/6- **9** 1 **Benitez Bond**[223] 7084 4-9-5 0 FrederikTylicki(5) 4 26
(G R Oldroyd) *cl up: rdn along 1/2-way: sn wknd* **66/1**
0 **10** 9 **Dalmunzie (IRE)**[17] 2268 3-8-1 0 JamieKyne(7) 12 —
(J J Quinn) *rdn along 1/2-way: a in rr* **33/1**
11 3½ **Hopeful Lady** 3-8-3 0 LanceBetts(5) 15 —
(I W McInnes) *a towards rr* **100/1**
000- **12** *nk* **Wrecker's Moon (IRE)**[230] 6909 4-8-12 26 MarzenaJeziorek(7) 14 —
(T J Etherington) *in tch: rdn along 1/2-way and sn wknd* **200/1**

1m 39.84s (1.84) **Going Correction** +0.275s/f (Good)
WFA 3 from 4yo+ 11lb **12 Ran SP% 119.7**
Speed ratings (Par 101): **101,96,96,90,89 89,86,75,74,65 62,61**
toteswingers: 1&2 £6.90, 1&3 £7.80, 2&3 £2.40 CSF £44.79 TOTE £16.40: £4.40, £1.10, £2.50; EX 41.90.
Owner Sheikh Hamdan Bin Mohammed Al Maktoum **Bred** Darley **Trained** Middleham Moor, N Yorks

FOCUS
Another maiden lacking much in the way of strength in depth but the winner looks a reasonable prospect. The favourite was probably not too far below his best.
Proud Times(USA) Official explanation: jockey said gelding ran flat

2790 GO RACING IN YORKSHIRE SUMMER FESTIVAL H'CAP 1m 2f
5:15 (5:16) (Class 6) (0-55,55) 3-Y-0 **£2,047** (£604; £302) **Stalls** Low

Form RPR
0600 **1** **The Last Alzao (IRE)**[18] 2236 3-8-12 **53** TonyHamilton 15 58+
(R A Fahey) *trckd ldrs: hdwy over 3f out: rdn to chse ldr wl over 1f out: drvn ins fnl f: styd on to ld last 100yds* **10/1**[3]
2005 **2** 1 **Amazing Blue Sky**[2] 2742 3-9-0 **55** PJMcDonald 3 58
(Mrs R A Carr) *led: rdn clr over 2f out: drvn over 1f out: hdd and no ex last 100yds* **13/2**[2]
00-0 **3** 1 **Pattern Mark**[29] 1926 3-8-12 **53** RoystonFfrench 8 54
(Ollie Pears) *in rr and pushed along 1/2-way: swtchd outside and hdwy 3f out: rdn and hung lft wl over 1f out: styd on strly ins fnl f: nrst fin* **40/1**
00-0 **4** 2½ **Acclaim To Fame (IRE)**[52] 1349 3-8-8 **49** TomEaves 14 45
(K R Burke) *hld up in rr: hdwy on outer 3f out: rdn over 2f out: styd on appr fnl f: nrst fin* **16/1**
0040 **5** 2¼ **Feeling Stylish (IRE)**[7] 2577 3-8-6 **47** JoeFanning 1 39
(N Tinkler) *chsd ldr: rdn along 3f out: drvn over 2f out and grad wknd* **16/1**
-050 **6** 2½ **Hawkleaf Flier (IRE)**[29] 1926 3-8-8 **49** DuranFentiman 12 36
(T D Easterby) *in rr tl styd on fnl 2f: nt rch ldrs* **25/1**
6-00 **7** 1¼ **Miss Gibboa (IRE)**[36] 1724 3-8-5 **51** PatrickDonaghy(5) 6 35
(P C Haslam) *prom: rdn along over 3f out: drvn over 2f out and grad wknd* **16/1**
0-62 **8** *shd* **Ethics Girl (IRE)**[8] 2528 3-9-0 **55** NCallan 13 39
(John Berry) *in tch: hdwy on outer to chse ldrs 3f out: rdn over 2f out and sn btn* **8/13**[1]
0400 **9** 2¾ **Nicky Nutjob (GER)**[42] 1594 3-8-2 **50** (p) SimonPearce(7) 11 28
(J Pearce) *in tch: rdn along 3f out and sn no imp* **20/1**
0000 **10** 1¼ **Flynn's Island (IRE)**[18] 2236 3-8-9 **50** (b[1]) PhillipMakin 4 26
(M Dods) *t.k.h: chsd ldrs: rdn 3f out: wknd 2f out* **16/1**
060- **11** 3½ **Ballade De La Mer**[161] 7824 3-8-3 **47** KellyHarrison(3) 9 16
(A G Foster) *a towards rr* **40/1**
6630 **12** 7 **Antipodean (UAE)**[28] 1953 3-8-13 **54** JamieMoriarty 7 9
(P T Midgley) *midfield: rdn along 1/2-way: sn wknd* **40/1**
00-0 **13** 4 **Rioja Ruby (IRE)**[29] 1926 3-8-7 **51** ow4 (v[1]) RussellKennemore(3) 2 —
(S G West) *midfield: rdn along 4f out: sn wknd* **66/1**

2m 8.40s (1.30) **Going Correction** +0.15s/f (Good) **13 Ran SP% 125.3**
Speed ratings (Par 97): **100,99,98,96,94 92,91,91,89,88 85,79,76**
toteswingers: 1&2 £9.70, 1&3 £54.00, 2&3 £52.30 CSF £72.77 CT £2542.64 TOTE £8.70: £1.90, £1.90, £10.10; EX 45.70.
Owner G Devlin **Bred** G Devlin **Trained** Musley Bank, N Yorks

FOCUS
A weak handicap run at an ordinary gallop and one in which those held up were at a disadvantage. The race did not take as much winning as seemed likely beforehand with the market leader disappointing but the form is sound enough.
The Last Alzao(IRE) ◆ Official explanation: trainer's rep said, regarding apparent improvement in form, that the filly had benefited from being ridden more predominantly and the step up in trip.
Ethics Girl(IRE) Official explanation: trainer said, regarding running, that the race came too soon for the filly
Rioja Ruby(IRE) Official explanation: jockey said filly failed to handle the bend turning out back straight

2791 GO RACING AT BEVERLEY TOMORROW H'CAP 1m
5:45 (5:45) (Class 5) (0-75,74) 4-Y-0+ £2,590 (£770; £385; £192) Stalls Centre

Form RPR
0002 1 **Aussie Blue (IRE)**[8] 2532 5-8-2 55 oh1 PaulQuinn 5 65+
(R M Whitaker) *trckd ldrs: smooth hdwy 2f out: rdn and qcknd to ld 1f out: styd on* **7/2**[2]
-562 2 1 3/4 **Sir Royal (USA)**[12] 2391 4-9-7 74 PJMcDonald 4 78
(G A Swinbank) *trckd ldr: led 2f out and sn rdn: hdd and drvn 1f out: one pce* **5/4**[1]
-005 3 3/4 **Efidium**[14] 2362 11-8-0 60 JamieKyne(7) 2 62
(N Bycroft) *trckd ldrs: hdwy wl over 2f out: rdn wl over 1f out and ch tl drvn and one pce ent fnl f* **9/2**[3]
605 4 2 1/2 **Flora's Pride**[12] 2403 5-8-5 58 DarrenMoffatt 8 55
(K G Reveley) *trckd ldrs: hdwy over 2f out: rdn and ch over 1f out: sn btn* **33/1**
0001 5 1/2 **Xpres Maite**[11] 2459 6-9-4 71 (v) AmirQuinn 1 66
(S R Bowring) *led: rdn along and hdd 2f out: sn drvn and wknd* **13/2**
353- 6 hd **Prince Samos (IRE)**[20] 5961 7-9-1 68 (v) TomEaves 3 63
(C A Mulhall) *dwlt: rdn along in rr 1/2-way: nvr a factor* **33/1**
3531 7 nk **Betteras Bertie**[10] 2473 6-8-3 63 JohnCavanagh(7) 6 57
(M Brittain) *dwlt: hld up in rr: swtchd outside and hdwy over 2f out: rdn to chse ldrs wl over 1f out: sn wknd* **11/2**
1m 40.34s (2.34) **Going Correction** +0.275s/f (Good) 7 Ran SP% **119.4**
Speed ratings (Par 103): **99,97,96,94,93 93,93**
toteswingers: 1&2 £2.20, 1&3 £4.00, 2&3 £3.60 CSF £8.84 CT £19.28 TOTE £5.30: £1.90, £2.20; EX 13.50 Place 6: £20.86, Place 5: £19.16.
Owner G F Pemberton **Bred** T L Adams & G F Pemberton **Trained** Scarcroft, W Yorks

FOCUS
Few progressive sorts in an ordinary event. The pace was just fair and the slowest of the three C/D races. The winner is rated back to something like his best.
T/Plt: £70.60 to a £1 stake. Pool: £60,738.57. 627.23 winning tickets. T/Qpdt: £130.50 to a £1 stake. Pool: £4,076.82. 23.10 winning tickets. JR

2201 SALISBURY (R-H)
Tuesday, June 9

OFFICIAL GOING: Good to firm (9.0)
Wind: Mild breeze Weather: Overcast

2792 GEORGE SMITH HORSEBOXES MAIDEN AUCTION STKS (DIV I) 6f
1:40 (1:41) (Class 5) 2-Y-O £2,914 (£867; £433; £216) Stalls High

Form RPR
1 **Practitioner** 2-8-9 0 RichardHughes 5 71+
(H J L Dunlop) *trckd ldrs: swtchd lft 2f out: carried sltly lft jst over 1f out: led ins fnl f: r.o* **12/1**
64 2 1/2 **Abandagold (IRE)**[11] 2444 2-8-1 0 DavidProbert(3) 12 65
(A B Haynes) *w ldrs: rdn over 2f out: r.o ins fnl f* **5/1**[2]
6 3 nk **Imperial Warrior**[19] 2187 2-8-12 0 SteveDrowne 1 72
(H Morrison) *s.i.s and wnt lft s: bhd: pushed along over 3f out: rdn and hdwy on outside wl over 1f out: kpt on u.p ins fnl f* **7/1**
4 4 nk **Folletta (IRE)**[11] 2430 2-8-4 0 WilliamBuick 8 63
(R Hannon) *sn outpcd in rr: rdn and hdwy on ins over 1f out: kpt on ins fnl f* **5/1**[2]
02 5 1 1/2 **Tucker's Law**[19] 2201 2-8-12 0 AlanMunro 4 66
(B R Millman) *w ldr: led over 2f out: rdn and edgd lft jst over 1f out: hdd ins fnl f: no ex* **13/2**[3]
0 6 nse **Flashy Lover (IRE)**[10] 2494 2-8-4 0 CatherineGannon 9 58
(M R Channon) *led: hdd over 2f out: sn rdn: fdd wl ins fnl f* **9/2**[1]
7 hd **Chairman Pat (USA)** 2-9-2 0 RichardKingscote 10 70+
(Tom Dascombe) *bhd: kpt on ins fnl f: nt rch ldrs* **13/2**[3]
06 8 1/2 **Xaara Star (IRE)**[7] 2563 2-8-4 0 JimmyQuinn 7 56
(Eve Johnson Houghton) *s.i.s: sn hld up in mid-div: rdn 2f out: hdwy 1f out: fdd towards fin* **25/1**
9 3/4 **Madj's Baby** 2-8-7 0 KirstyMilczarek 11 57
(H S Howe) *s.i.s: outpcd and wl in rr: nvr nrr* **40/1**
10 3 **Craicattack (IRE)** 2-8-9 0 LPKeniry 3 50
(J S Moore) *trckd ldrs: rdn over 1f out: wknd fnl f* **100/1**
0 11 2 **Looks Like Slim**[15] 2328 2-8-12 0 MartinDwyer 2 47
(P F I Cole) *wnt lft s: sn chsng ldrs: wknd over 1f out* **50/1**
12 1 3/4 **Many A Slip** 2-8-9 0 SebSanders 6 38
(J L Dunlop) *s.s: outpcd: a in rr* **12/1**
1m 15.07s (0.27) **Going Correction** -0.20s/f (Firm) 12 Ran SP% **115.3**
Speed ratings (Par 93): **90,89,88,88,86 86,86,85,84,80 77,75**
toteswingers: 1&2 £16.40, 1&3 £12.60, 2&3 £18.80 CSF £67.74 TOTE £15.30: £3.20, £2.40, £3.40; EX 129.40.
Owner Here Come The Boys **Bred** Newsells Park Stud Limited **Trained** Lambourn, Berks

FOCUS
A few of these finished in a bit of a bunch and the bare form looks no better than fair, but the winning time was 1.44 seconds faster than the second division won by Decree Absolute.

NOTEBOOK
Practitioner, already gelded, deserves credit for defeating some more experienced rivals on his debut. A £5,500 purchase, out of a 6f-7f winner, he knew his job and kept on best after travelling nicely just in behind the early pace. He looks a nursery type for later in the season. (tchd 11-1 and 14-1)
Abandagold(IRE) showed good speed throughout and had her chance. She looks only modest but is going the right way. (op 7-1)
Imperial Warrior looks a little better than he showed considering he went left on leaving the widest stall and was outpaced for much of the way. This was a big improvement on his debut effort and he very much gave the impression he was still learning. (op 6-1 tchd 11-2)
Folletta(IRE) was outpaced for most of the way and never looked like getting involved, despite keeping on when switched to the far rail. This probably represented slight improvement on her debut performance but she flashed her tail a couple of times when hit with the whip and has yet to really convince. (op 9-2)
Tucker's Law had his chance on this step up in trip but didn't see his race out. (op 6-1 tchd 11-2)
Flashy Lover(IRE) knew much more than when too green on her debut at Newbury and showed good early speed, but despite that, she lacked the required pace inside the final couple of furlongs. (tchd 5-1)
Chairman Pat(USA) ◆, a £24,000 half-brother to a winner at around 1m in the US, as well as a successful sprinting juvenile in the States, out of quite useful miler, ran as though in need of the experience. Conceding weight all round, he was never seen with a winning chance but made some late headway and ought to improve plenty. (op 8-1 tchd 11-2)
Madj's Baby ◆, a 12,000gns first foal of a triple 1m winner, stayed on quite nicely having been badly outpaced for most of the way and has ability. (op 66-1)

2793 GEORGE SMITH HORSEBOXES MAIDEN AUCTION STKS (DIV II) 6f
2:15 (2:15) (Class 5) 2-Y-O £2,914 (£867; £433; £216) Stalls High

Form RPR
1 **Decree Absolute (USA)** 2-8-9 0 PaulFitzsimons 3 69+
(Miss J R Tooth) *trckd ldrs: drifted lft whn rdn over 1f out: r.o wl fnl f: led nr fin* **66/1**
2 1/2 **Pherousa** 2-8-4 0 JimmyQuinn 10 62
(M Blanshard) *in tch: swtchd rt wl over 2f out: r.o to hold ev ch ins fnl f: kpt on: tk 2nd nr fin* **33/1**
3 nk **Newton Circus** 2-8-12 0 RichardHughes 11 69
(R Hannon) *led: hung lft over 1f out: sn rdn: drifted rt ins fnl f: no ex whn hdd nr fin* **5/2**[2]
4 3/4 **Farmers Wish (IRE)** 2-8-4 0 LiamJones 9 59
(J L Spearing) *little slowly away: hld up: rdn over 2f out: styd on fr over 1f out: wnt 4th nr fin* **33/1**
06 5 nk **Volatilis (IRE)**[11] 2430 2-8-9 0 SebSanders 12 63+
(J W Hills) *t.k.h trcking ldrs: rdn whn clr run over 1f out: kpt on but hld whn short of room nr fin* **14/1**
6 6 shd **Saxby (IRE)**[14] 2348 2-8-12 0 SamHitchcott 5 66
(M R Channon) *awkward leaving stalls and wnt rt: hld up bhd: rdn and stdy prog fr 2f out: styd on fnl f* **16/1**
3 7 1 1/4 **Crystal Gale (IRE)**[10] 2490 2-8-7 0 JimCrowley 6 57+
(W J Knight) *rrd leaving stalls: bmpd sn after: sn mid-div: rdn to chse ldrs 2f out: one pce fnl f* **10/11**[1]
0 8 1/2 **Mnarani (IRE)**[11] 2430 2-9-2 0 LPKeniry 8 64+
(J S Moore) *w ldr: rdn whn hung lft 2f out: hld whn hmpd over 1f out* **10/1**[3]
9 4 1/2 **Dudley** 2-8-9 0 PatCosgrave 4 44
(J G Portman) *sn pushed along towards rr of mid-div: wknd fnl f* **33/1**
10 1 3/4 **Atomic Twister** 2-8-4 0 MartinDwyer 7 34
(P F I Cole) *sn pushed along towards rr: wknd 2f out* **33/1**
0 11 2 1/4 **D'Urberville**[18] 2218 2-8-12 0 SteveDrowne 2 35
(R Ingram) *t.k.h in tch: effrt over 2f out: wknd over 1f out* **100/1**
1m 16.51s (1.71) **Going Correction** -0.20s/f (Firm) 11 Ran SP% **116.8**
Speed ratings (Par 93): **80,79,78,77,77 77,75,75,69,66 63**
toteswingers: 1&2 £74.40, 1&3 £21.60, 2&3 £18.10 CSF £1406.64 TOTE £53.40: £8.30, £6.20, £1.30; EX 2297.30.
Owner Miss J R Tooth **Bred** Ladona Hudson & Orientate Syndicate **Trained** Upper Lambourn, Berks
■ Stewards' Enquiry : Richard Hughes two-day ban: careless riding (Jun 23-24)

FOCUS
They went an ordinary pace early on and the winning time was 1.44 seconds slower than the first division won by Practitioner. The bare form looks only modest.

NOTEBOOK
Decree Absolute(USA), a 20,000gns brother to, among others, All-Weather sprint winner Tika Hornet, out of a quite useful sprinter in the States, belied his big odds with a successful racecourse debut. Having travelled quite nicely close to the pace, he picked up well when asked for his effort, despite being carried left by Newton Circus in the closing stages. Although it's hard to rate this form particularly highly, this fair-looking type appeals as the type to do better in a stronger-run race and it would be unwise to underestimate him in nurseries.
Pherousa, a half-sister to Bari Bay, who was placed over 1m4f, made a pleasing introduction, although she was getting weight from most of these and ran to just moderate level.
Newton Circus, the first foal of a 1m winner in France, was allowed an easy lead but ruined his chance by hanging left under pressure. He gives the impression he'll leave this form behind on softer ground. (op 2-1 tchd 3-1)
Farmers Wish(IRE), a half-sister to among others multiple sprint winner Northern Dare, started slowly and was niggled along early, but she finished well after gradually getting the idea. She can be expected to improve a good deal. (op 25-1)
Volatilis(IRE) was too keen for his own good. He might do better in stronger-run nurseries. (tchd 11-1)
Saxby(IRE) ran as though he'll improve considerably on this form in time, keeping on under hands-and-heels riding after staring slowly. He's one to keep in mind for the nursery season. (op 14-1)
Crystal Gale(IRE) was last away from the stalls having been on her heels on the gates opened and, although making up some of the lost ground to move into midfield, she never truly recovered. She had been well backed to confirm the promise of her debut third and can be given another chance. Official explanation: jockey said filly reared as stalls opened (op 11-8)

2794 BATHWICK TYRES CLAIMING STKS 6f 212y
2:45 (2:45) (Class 5) 3-Y-O+ £3,238 (£963; £481; £240) Stalls High

Form RPR
1605 1 **Elna Bright**[6] 2606 4-9-12 92 JamieSpencer 10 82+
(P D Evans) *hld up in mid-div on ins: plld out over 2f out: smooth prog wl over 1f out: edgd rt and rdn to ld 1f out: rdn out* **6/5**[1]
0334 2 1 1/4 **Yellow Printer**[15] 2329 3-9-1 76 RichardKingscote 6 74
(Tom Dascombe) *chsd ldrs: pushed along 4f out: rdn and swtchd lft over 2f out: ev ch 1f out: nt qckn ins fnl f* **85/40**[2]
2556 3 1 1/2 **Takitwo**[6] 2598 6-9-2 58 SimonWhitworth 13 65
(P D Cundell) *hld up and bhd: hdwy on ins over 2f out: rdn wl over 1f out: r.o one pce fnl f* **28/1**
5-00 4 1 **Peace Concluded**[7] 2567 3-8-8 70 AlanMunro 7 60
(B R Millman) *hld up towards rr: hdwy over 2f out: rdn over 1f out: styd on towards fin* **9/1**
3123 5 1/2 **Jake The Snake (IRE)**[41] 1607 8-9-7 78 AmyBaker(5) 15 71
(A W Carroll) *w ldr: led 4f out: sn hdd: led jst over 2f out: rdn and hdd 1f out: wknd wl ins fnl f* **15/2**[3]
33 6 2 3/4 **Castano**[14] 2353 5-9-2 62 (p) JamesMillman(3) 2 57
(B R Millman) *hld up in mid-div: hdwy over 2f out: ev ch over 1f out: sn rdn: wknd fnl f* **20/1**
3420 7 3 1/2 **Manchestermaverick (USA)**[19] 2202 4-9-9 58 (t) SteveDrowne 4 51
(H Morrison) *hld up in tch: lost pl over 4f out: pushed along and sme hdwy 2f out: sn rdn: wknd fnl f* **20/1**
-050 8 3 **Zaftil (IRE)**[27] 1985 3-8-4 40 KirstyMilczarek 9 30
(H S Howe) *in rr: rdn wl over 1f out: nvr nr ldrs* **100/1**
0-60 9 5 **Miracle Baby**[83] 868 7-8-11 43 RichardThomas 11 17
(J A Geake) *prom: rdn over 2f out: wknd wl over 1f out* **100/1**

0-40 **10** *7* **Talamahana**[11] 2456 4-8-11 43....................(v[1]) PatCosgrave 14 —
(A B Haynes) *led: hdd 4f out: rdn over 2f out: wknd wl over 1f out* **80/1**
054 **11** *3 1/2* **Fun In The Sun**[5] 2630 5-9-3 57.................... SebSanders 3 —
(A B Haynes) *prom: led over 3f out: hdd jst over 2f out: wknd qckly wl over 1f out* **33/1**
5-60 **12** *3/4* **Rioliina (IRE)**[24] 2079 3-8-8 82.................... TolleyDean 5 —
(J G Portman) *hld up in mid-div: lost pl and n.m.r 4f out: sn bhd* **20/1**
0-60 **13** *2 1/4* **Frosty's Gift**[138] 254 5-8-12 40.................... RichardSmith 8 —
(J C Fox) *s.i.s: a in rr* **100/1**
0/0 **14** *3/4* **Kilmeena Dream**[20] 2184 5-8-5 0.................... GemmaElford(7) 1 —
(J C Fox) *a towards rr* **200/1**
1m 26.97s (-2.03) **Going Correction** -0.20s/f (Firm) **14** Ran SP% **124.6**
WFA 3 from 4yo+ 10lb
Speed ratings (Par 103): **103,101,99,98,98 95,91,87,81,73 69,69,66,65**
toteswingers: 1&2 £2.20, 1&3 £14.50, 2&3 £19.60 CSF £3.51 TOTE £2.50: £1.30, £1.50, £5.70; EX 6.20.
Owner David Mort **Bred** D R Tucker **Trained** Pandy, Monmouths

FOCUS
A fair claimer, but the leaders went off far too fast, setting this up for the closers. The third was probably the best guide.

2795 BATHWICK TYRES MAIDEN STKS 6f 212y
3:20 (3:20) (Class 5) 3-Y-O **£3,885** (£1,156; £577; £288) **Stalls** High

Form RPR
2- **1** **Shangani**[335] 3848 3-8-5 0.................... AmyScott(7) 12 74+
(H Candy) *trckd ldrs on rails: nt clr run over 2f out: swtchd lft and qcknd up wl to ld ent fnl f: drifted lft: rdn out* **11/2**[3]
440 **2** *1 1/4* **Kloof**[46] 1490 3-9-3 72.................... JimmyFortune 10 74
(J H M Gosden) *prom: led wl over 2f out: rdn whn hdd ent fnl f: kpt on: jst hld on for 2nd* **11/1**
022- **3** *hd* **Burma Rock (IRE)**[245] 6553 3-9-3 77.................... WilliamBuick 5 73+
(L M Cumani) *mid-div: nt clr run briefly over 2f out: hung lft: sn rdn and no immediate imp: styd on wl fnl f: jst failed to snatch 2nd* **3/1**[2]
032- **4** *3* **Poyle Meg**[194] 7458 3-8-12 78.................... SebSanders 1 60
(R M Beckett) *in tch: rdn to chse ldrs 2f out: styd on same pce fnl f* **11/4**[1]
04 **5** *1/2* **Quinsman**[10] 2496 3-9-3 0.................... LPKeniry 4 64
(J S Moore) *in tch: effrt 3f out: swtchd lft ent fnl f: kpt on same pce* **12/1**
6 *hd* **Imperial House** 3-9-3 0.................... TonyCulhane 13 63
(M R Channon) *trckd ldrs: rdn over 2f out: kpt on same pce fnl f* **33/1**
-6 **7** *hd* **Langland Bay**[51] 1379 3-8-9 0.................... DavidProbert(3) 6 58
(W R Muir) *chsd ldrs tl hmpd and lost pl after 3f: rdn and hdwy whn hung bdly lft fr 2f out: one pce fnl f* **16/1**
8 *3* **Tiger Breeze (USA)** 3-9-3 0.................... IanMongan 11 55
(Miss Jo Crowley) *unsettled stalls: slowly away: bhd: rdn and prog into midfield 2f out: no further imp* **66/1**
06 **9** *1/2* **Inside Trade (IRE)**[24] 2082 3-9-3 0....................(t) GeorgeBaker 17 53
(R M Beckett) *led tl wl over 2f out: sn rdn: remained cl up tl wknd fnl f* **33/1**
00 **10** *nk* **Indian Violet (IRE)**[36] 1729 3-9-3 0.................... MartinDwyer 14 53+
(P F I Cole) *towards rr: rdn 3f out: sme late prog: nvr a factor* **33/1**
45-4 **11** *1 1/4* **Casting Couch (IRE)**[54] 1302 3-8-12 72.................... JamieSpencer 3 48
(B W Hills) *trckd ldrs: rdn and ev ch over 2f out tl over 1f out: fading and hanging lft whn squeezed out jst ins fnl f* **8/1**
0 **12** *hd* **Tarqua (IRE)**[10] 2496 3-8-12 0.................... RichardHughes 16 44
(R Hannon) *nvr bttr than mid-div* **20/1**
200- **13** *3/4* **Sunny Future (IRE)**[271] 5827 3-9-3 77.................... TolleyDean 15 47
(M S Saunders) *bmpd s: a towards rr* **10/1**
0 **14** *nse* **Bedarra Boy**[42] 1585 3-9-3 0.................... SimonWhitworth 2 47
(D W P Arbuthnot) *a towards rr* **100/1**
0 **15** *3/4* **Haling Park (UAE)**[11] 2433 3-8-12 0.................... ShaneKelly 7 40
(G L Moore) *mid-div: rdn 3f out: wknd over 1f out* **66/1**
16 *3 3/4* **Public Image** 3-8-12 0.................... SteveDrowne 8 29
(Jamie Poulton) *s.i.s: towards rr: sme hdwy u.p 3f out: wknd 2f out* **66/1**
00 **17** *20* **Cridda Boy**[24] 2074 3-9-3 0.................... RichardThomas 9 —
(A G Newcombe) *struggling over 3f out: a bhd* **100/1**
1m 27.68s (-1.32) **Going Correction** -0.20s/f (Firm) **17** Ran SP% **129.2**
Speed ratings (Par 99): **99,97,97,93,93 93,92,89,88,88 87,86,86,85,85 80,57**
toteswingers: 1&2 £18.70, 1&3 £10.30, 2&3 £7.60 CSF £64.52 TOTE £6.50: £2.50, £2.90, £1.40; EX 92.10.
Owner Henry Candy **Bred** R S A Urquhart **Trained** Kingston Warren, Oxon

FOCUS
A fair 3yo maiden, but the slowest of the three C/D races and the form is a bit muddling. The winner is rated a bit better than the bare form.
Burma Rock(IRE) Official explanation: jockey said colt hung left-handed from 2f out
Casting Couch(IRE) Official explanation: jockey said filly ran flat

2796 EBF MARGADALE FILLIES' H'CAP 1m 1f 198y
3:55 (3:58) (Class 4) (0-85,85) 3-Y-O+ **£6,799** (£2,023; £1,011; £505) **Stalls** High

Form RPR
433 **1** **Cill Rialaig**[33] 1809 4-9-4 73.................... SteveDrowne 1 82
(H Morrison) *s.i.s: hld up towards rr: hdwy 2f out: rdn over 1f out: r.o to ld cl home* **10/1**
15-4 **2** *nk* **Spell Caster**[18] 2239 4-9-11 83.................... JackMitchell(3) 12 91
(R M Beckett) *a.p: swtchd rt to ins rail over 2f out: rdn over 1f out: led ins fnl f: hdd cl home* **8/1**[3]
5-06 **3** *1/2* **Zaaqya**[26] 2008 3-8-7 75.................... TPO'Shea 8 81+
(J L Dunlop) *hld up towards rr: hdwy on ins over 2f out: rdn wl over 1f out: swtchd rt ins fnl f: r.o* **16/1**
223- **4** *1 1/4* **Heritage Coast (USA)**[336] 3813 4-9-9 78.................... TravisBlock 11 83
(H Morrison) *led: rdn jst over 2f out: hdd ins fnl f: no ex towards fin* **25/1**
5-11 **5** *2 1/4* **Aromatic**[13] 2384 3-9-1 83.................... JimmyFortune 10 82
(J H M Gosden) *hld up in tch: chal 2f out: rdn over 1f out: wknd wl ins fnl f* **6/4**[1]
1-4 **6** *1* **Cascata (IRE)**[54] 1315 3-8-8 76.................... WilliamBuick 2 73
(L M Cumani) *hld up towards rr: hdwy on outside over 2f out: rdn over 1f out: wknd ins fnl f* **4/1**[2]
101- **7** *1 1/2* **Maria Di Scozia**[248] 6487 4-9-9 78....................(t) AlanMunro 5 73
(P W Chapple-Hyam) *in rr: pushed along over 3f out: swtchd lft over 1f out: styd on ins fnl f: n.d* **12/1**
0-00 **8** *1/2* **Accede**[24] 2079 3-8-10 78.................... PatCosgrave 7 71
(J G Portman) *hld up and bhd: rdn over 2f out: nvr nr ldrs* **50/1**
4012 **9** *6* **Tinshu (IRE)**[14] 2356 3-8-8 76.................... MartinDwyer 4 57
(D Haydn Jones) *hld up in mid-div: sme hdwy over 3f out: rdn 2f out: wknd 1f out* **11/1**
0-00 **10** *1 1/4* **Shanzu**[45] 1524 4-9-4 73....................(b[1]) GeorgeBaker 6 53
(G L Moore) *chsd ldr tl over 2f out: wknd over 1f out* **66/1**
51- **11** *3/4* **Sampi**[251] 6392 3-9-3 85.................... JimCrowley 9 62
(Mrs A J Perrett) *t.k.h in tch: rdn and wknd over 2f out* **12/1**
31-6 **12** *8* **Brooksby**[55] 1284 3-8-5 73....................(v[1]) JimmyQuinn 3 34
(R Hannon) *hung rt thrght: prom on outside: lost pl bnd after 3f: dropped to rr over 3f out* **16/1**
2m 6.25s (-3.65) **Going Correction** -0.30s/f (Firm)
WFA 3 from 4yo 13lb **12** Ran SP% **123.0**
Speed ratings (Par 102): **102,101,101,100,98 97,96,96,91,90 89,83**
toteswingers: 1&2 £16.10, 1&3 £29.40, 2&3 £22.80 CSF £90.11 CT £1294.40 TOTE £13.50: £3.40, £2.30, £4.50; EX 117.60.
Owner Pangfield Partners **Bred** T J Billington **Trained** East Ilsley, Berks
■ Stewards' Enquiry : Jack Mitchell one-day ban: used whip with excessive frequency (Jun 23)

FOCUS
A decent fillies' handicap for the grade which was well run. The unexposed winner is rated up 5lb.
Zaaqya Official explanation: jockey said filly was denied a clear run

2797 BET AT VICTORCHANDLER.COM H'CAP 6f 212y
4:30 (4:32) (Class 6) (0-65,65) 3-Y-O **£3,043** (£905; £452; £226) **Stalls** High

Form RPR
006 **1** **Secret Hero**[24] 2080 3-9-1 59.................... RichardHughes 4 71+
(R Hannon) *mid-div: rdn 3f out: swtchd lft and hdwy 2f out: r.o to ld ins fnl f: drifted sltly rt: rdn out* **11/4**[1]
0-23 **2** *2* **Fly By Nelly**[32] 1839 3-9-5 63.................... SteveDrowne 10 66
(H Morrison) *in tch: rdn to chal over 2f out: ev ch ent fnl f: kpt on but no ex fnl 100yds* **13/2**[2]
06-4 **3** *1/2* **Mrs Slocombe (IRE)**[146] 158 3-9-6 64.................... IanMongan 8 66
(J Akehurst) *s.i.s: sn pushed along in rr: hdwy 3f out: styd on strly ins fnl f: wnt 3rd nr fin* **40/1**
3-10 **4** *1/2* **Cavendish Road (IRE)**[36] 1746 3-9-3 61.................... MartinDwyer 17 61
(W R Muir) *prom: rdn to ld over 2f out: hdd ins fnl f: no ex* **20/1**
0-05 **5** *1/2* **Countess Zara (IRE)**[11] 2431 3-9-5 63....................(v) WilliamBuick 2 62
(A M Balding) *mid-div: hdwy u.p 2f out: ev ch ent fnl f: edgd rt: fdd towards fin* **14/1**
3343 **6** *1* **My Best Man**[15] 2320 3-8-13 60....................(p) JamesMillman(3) 13 56
(B R Millman) *mid-div: hdwy to chse ldrs 4f out: rdn whn swtchd lft over 1f out: kpt on same pce* **8/1**
310 **7** *3/4* **Royal Crest**[32] 1839 3-9-7 65.................... ShaneKelly 5 59
(J A Osborne) *squeezed out s: towards rr: nt clr run briefly over 2f out: styd on fnl f: nvr nrr* **16/1**
66-4 **8** *shd* **Flying Silks (IRE)**[21] 2151 3-9-7 65.................... PatCosgrave 12 59
(J R Gask) *mid-div: rdn over 3f out: hdwy over 2f out: styd on same pce fnl f* **20/1**
5404 **9** *1 1/2* **La Gifted**[9] 2515 3-9-0 58.................... TonyCulhane 18 48
(M R Channon) *sn prom: led over 3f out tl rdn over 2f out: wknd fnl f* **14/1**
00-3 **10** *3/4* **King Of Defence**[40] 1620 3-9-1 59.................... TPO'Shea 1 47
(M A Jarvis) *hld up towards rr: hdwy over 3f out: rdn whn short of room over 1f out: wknd ins fnl f* **7/1**[3]
00-6 **11** *1/2* **Law And Order**[31] 1895 3-9-2 60.................... PaulFitzsimons 6 47
(Miss J R Tooth) *chsd ldrs: rdn over 2f out: wknd fnl f* **50/1**
-406 **12** *3 3/4* **Feet Of Fury**[28] 1973 3-9-6 64.................... JamieSpencer 14 49+
(W M Brisbourne) *restrained s: bhd and nvr a threat* **11/1**
-062 **13** *7* **Mr Flannegan**[26] 2009 3-8-9 60.................... AmyScott(7) 7 18+
(H Candy) *prom: rdn over 3f out: wknd over 1f out: eased whn btn* **14/1**
-400 **14** *nse* **Peninsula Girl (IRE)**[15] 2321 3-9-2 60.................... SamHitchcott 16 17
(M R Channon) *led tl over 3f out: wknd over 2f out* **16/1**
0-00 **15** *nk* **Conclusive**[55] 1295 3-9-7 65....................(p) SebSanders 3 22
(R M Beckett) *mid-div tl 4f out* **33/1**
-304 **16** *1* **Order Order**[29] 1937 3-9-3 61....................(v[1]) JimmyFortune 15 15
(H J L Dunlop) *prom tl 2f out* **14/1**
1m 27.24s (-1.76) **Going Correction** -0.20s/f (Firm) **16** Ran SP% **127.2**
Speed ratings (Par 97): **102,99,99,98,98 96,96,95,94,93 92,88,80,80,80 78**
toteswingers: 1&2 £7.60, 1&3 £52.50, 2&3 £45.10 CSF £18.58 CT £623.27 TOTE £4.00: £1.50, £1.80, £8.30, £4.80; EX 24.80 TRIFECTA Not won..
Owner Carmel Stud **Bred** Carmel Stud **Trained** East Everleigh, Wilts

FOCUS
A modest 3yo handicap but the pick of the C/D times. The runner-up is probably the best guide.
Secret Hero ◆ Official explanation: trainer said, regarding apparent improvement in form, that the colt had come to himself and appreciated the drop in class
Royal Crest Official explanation: jockey said gelding suffered interference at start
King Of Defence Official explanation: jockey said gelding was unsuited by the good to firm ground
Feet Of Fury Official explanation: jockey said filly was unruly in starting stalls

2798 BATHWICK TYRES H'CAP 1m 4f
5:00 (5:03) (Class 5) (0-75,75) 4-Y-O+ **£3,238** (£963; £481; £240) **Stalls** High

Form RPR
-430 **1** **Yonder**[50] 1399 5-8-6 60.................... SteveDrowne 8 67
(H Morrison) *mde virtually all: rdn over 1f out: r.o wl* **16/1**
2513 **2** *3/4* **Paddy Rielly (IRE)**[39] 1654 4-8-8 62....................(p) JamieSpencer 6 68
(P D Evans) *hld up: hdwy 2f out: sn rdn: chalng whn hung rt ins fnl f: nt qckn* **4/1**[2]
0-45 **3** *6* **Cyborg**[27] 1990 5-9-7 75.................... RichardHughes 7 71
(D R C Elsworth) *w wnr: rdn over 2f out: lost 2nd over 1f out: wknd ins fnl f* **4/5**[1]
3310 **4** *1/2* **Party Palace**[9] 2517 5-8-2 56 oh1.................... CatherineGannon 4 51
(H S Howe) *prom: pushed along over 4f out: wknd over 2f out* **22/1**
-003 **5** *1/2* **Danetime Panther (IRE)**[21] 2150 5-9-2 70....................(p) JimmyQuinn 5 65
(Ian Williams) *hld up and bhd: pushed along over 3f out: effrt on outside over 2f out: sn hrd rdn: wkng whn edgd rt over 1f out* **6/1**[3]
6-03 **6** *nse* **Warrior Conquest**[20] 2181 4-9-2 70.................... GeorgeBaker 2 65
(W J Knight) *prom: nt clr run on ins over 2f out: rdn and wknd over 1f out* **12/1**
-360 **7** *hd* **Double Spectre (IRE)**[27] 1980 7-8-10 64.................... JimCrowley 1 58
(Jean-Rene Auvray) *hld up in rr: hdwy on outside over 3f out: rdn 2f out: wkng whn edgd rt over 1f out* **16/1**
2m 33.33s (-4.67) **Going Correction** -0.30s/f (Firm) **7** Ran SP% **113.6**
Speed ratings (Par 103): **103,102,98,98,97 97,97**
toteswingers: 1&2 £6.80, 1&3 £3.70, 2&3 £1.80 CSF £77.23 CT £112.02 TOTE £14.10: £4.70, £2.10; EX 57.80.
Owner Mrs M D W Morrison **Bred** Peter Storey **Trained** East Ilsley, Berks

FOCUS
A fair handicap but pretty ordinary form for the grade.

2799 AXMINSTER CARPETS APPRENTICE H'CAP (WHIPS SHALL BE CARRIED BUT NOT USED) 6f
5:30 (5:33) (Class 5) (0-75,74) 4-Y-0+ **£3,238** (£963; £481; £240) **Stalls High**

Form RPR
0-20 **1** **Bohobe (IRE)**[22] 2134 4-7-12 **55**........................ NoelGarbutt(7) 4 63
(Rae Guest) *trckd ldrs: chal jst over 1f out: led ins fnl f: hld on wl: pushed out* **7/1**[3]
1110 **2** *nk* **Brunelleschi**[24] 2088 6-9-5 **74**........................(b) JosephineBruning(5) 7 81
(P L Gilligan) *s.i.s: hld up: stdy prgress fr 2f out: ev ch ins fnl f: hld nr fin* **9/1**
2-10 **3** *½* **Tudor Prince (IRE)**[17] 2276 5-9-0 **69**........................ TobyAtkinson(5) 11 74
(A W Carroll) *trckd ldrs: pushed along 2f out: ev ch thrght fnl f: no ex nr fin* **8/1**
00-0 **4** *1* **Royal Intruder**[11] 2464 4-9-0 **69**........................(p) CPHoban(5) 1 71
(S Donohoe, Ire) *trckd ldrs: led 2f out: hdd ins fnl f: no ex* **9/4**[1]
4322 **5** *nk* **Hobson**[7] 2565 4-8-12 **69**........................ DanielBlackett(7) 10 70
(Eve Johnson Houghton) *s.i.s: hld up: styd on ins fnl f: nt pce to get on terms* **5/2**[2]
4600 **6** *hd* **Charles Darwin (IRE)**[17] 2276 6-9-5 **69**........................ PNolan 5 70
(M Blanshard) *prom: pushed along over 2f out: one pce fnl f* **14/1**
6515 **7** *1* **Caustic Wit (IRE)**[7] 2564 11-8-5 **60**........................ JakePayne(5) 6 57
(M S Saunders) *hld up: prog over 1f out: hung sltly rt and one pce fnl f* **22/1**
0-00 **8** *5* **Blessed Place**[8] 2549 9-8-12 **62**........................ DTDaSilva 3 43
(D J S Ffrench Davis) *missed break: sn rcvrd to ld: hdd 2f out: fdd* **50/1**
6122 **9** *4 ½* **Suhayl Star (IRE)**[13] 2382 5-8-9 **64**........................ RyanPowell(5) 8 31
(P Burgoyne) *chsd ldrs tl wknd over 1f out* **8/1**

1m 14.11s (-0.69) **Going Correction** -0.20s/f (Firm) **9 Ran SP% 117.0**
Speed ratings (Par 103): **96,95,94,93,93 92,91,84,78**
toteswingers: 1&2 £8.50, 1&3 £7.70, 2&3 £5.70 CSF £68.83 CT £520.03 TOTE £7.00: £3.00, £2.20, £2.00; EX 79.30 Place 6: £274.89, Place 5: £96.71.
Owner Tremousser Partnership **Bred** Bryan Ryan **Trained** Newmarket, Suffolk
■ Noel Garbutt's first winner.

FOCUS
A modest but competitive sprint handicap in which these apprentices were not allowed to use their whips. The pace was strong and the winner is rated back to her 3yo best.
T/Jkpt: Not won. T/Plt: £561.80 to a £1 stake. Pool: £74,207.11. 96.42 winning tickets. T/Qpdt: £63.00 to a £1 stake. Pool: £6,047.07. 71.00 winning tickets. TM

2370 BEVERLEY (R-H)
Wednesday, June 10

OFFICIAL GOING: Firm (good to firm in places; 10.4)
Wind: Virtually nil Weather: Fine and dry

2800 LACHLAN MCLEAN 65TH CLAIMING STKS 5f
2:00 (2:08) (Class 6) 2-Y-O **£2,266** (£674; £337; £168) **Stalls High**

Form RPR
1 **Midget** 2-8-3 0........................ LanceBetts(5) 7 59
(M A Magnusson) *towards rr: hdwy over 2f out: swtchd lft and rdn over 1f out: styd on strly ins fnl f to ld nr fin* **20/1**
465 **2** *½* **Mal And Dave (IRE)**[16] 2311 2-9-5 0........................ AdrianTNicholls 1 68
(D Nicholls) *qckly away and sn led: rdn wl over 1f out: drvn ins fnl f: hdd and no ex nr fin* **12/1**
35 **3** *1 ¼* **Gasparilla (IRE)**[41] 1624 2-8-2 0........................ AndrewMullen 8 47
(A J McCabe) *a.p: rdn to chse ldr wl over 1f out: drvn and one pce ins fnl f* **33/1**
3223 **4** *1 ¾* **Out The Ring (IRE)**[16] 2325 2-9-1 0........................ JimmyQuinn 12 53
(Miss Gay Kelleway) *chsd ldrs: rdn along 2f out: sn drvn and one pce* **9/2**[2]
31 **5** *¾* **On The Piste (IRE)**[12] 2457 2-8-2 0........................ FrankieMcDonald 13 38
(P T Midgley) *trckd ldrs: effrt 2f out: sn rdn and no imp appr fnl f* **9/1**
5224 **6** *hd* **Reel Credit Crunch**[7] 2604 2-8-3 0........................ AndrewHeffernan(7) 10 45
(I W McInnes) *chsd ldr on inner: rdn along wl over 1f out: drvn and wknd appr fnl f* **6/1**[3]
7 *¾* **Menediva** 2-8-10 0........................ DanielTudhope 9 42
(L A Mullaney) *s.i.s and bhd tl sme late hdwy* **66/1**
8 *2 ½* **Three Sons** 2-8-7 0........................(b[1]) PatrickMathers 2 30
(I W McInnes) *a towards rr* **100/1**
510 **9** *1 ¾* **Maidtorun (IRE)**[19] 2247 2-8-10 0........................ PaulHanagan 11 27
(R A Fahey) *midfield: rdn along 1/2-way: nvr a factor* **4/5**[1]
00 **10** *6* **Suzys Dream (IRE)**[3] 2741 2-7-13 0 ow6........................ PaulPickard(7) 5 —
(P T Midgley) *midfield: rdn along 1/2-way: sn wknd* **100/1**
11 *11* **Dencolstina** 2-8-7 0 ow1........................ TonyHamilton 4 —
(Joss Saville) *dwlt: a in rr* **66/1**

63.73 secs (0.23) **Going Correction** -0.20s/f (Firm) **11 Ran SP% 118.4**
Speed ratings (Par 91): **90,89,87,84,83 82,81,77,74,65 47**
toteswingers: 1&2 £15.30, 1&3 £38.90, 2&3 £30.20 CSF £229.27 TOTE £17.30: £3.90, £3.50, £4.40; EX 263.60.Midget was claimed by Declan Carroll for £9,000.
Owner East Wind Racing Ltd **Bred** Nawara Stud Co Ltd **Trained** Upper Lambourn, Berks

FOCUS
An ordinary-looking claimer.

NOTEBOOK
Midget, making the long journey north for her racecourse debut, took quite a while to fully get going and only just got to the front in time. Representing a shrewd stable, it was surprising that she went off at such long odds, so one can only presume that she is capable of plenty of improvement. However, she will be joining a new stable, as she was claimed by Declan Carroll. (op 16-1)
Mal And Dave(IRE), dropping in grade, led early and did everything right until being headed virtually on the line. (op 20-1 tchd 22-1)
Gasparilla(IRE) got loose before the start and was eventually walked to the stalls by her jockey. Soon prominent during the race, she ran surprisingly well considering her antics. (tchd 40-1)
Out The Ring(IRE), without the cheekpieces he wore last time, had never finished out of the first three previously but was very disappointing here, as he had every chance of playing a part in the finish if good enough. Official explanation: jockey said colt hung left (op 11-2 tchd 6-1)
On The Piste(IRE) lacked a little room at a crucial stage, but when the gaps opened she found very little. (op 8-1 tchd 15-2)
Reel Credit Crunch could only keep on at the one pace after holding every chance up the inside rail. (op 5-1)
Menediva, who became edgy in the paddock, got the idea late on and ran with some promise. (op 80-1)
Maidtorun(IRE), who was heavily supported, got outpaced quite early before making modest late progress. This was a very disappointing effort. Official explanation: jockey said filly hung left (op 10-11 tchd Evens)

2801 BACK A WINNER BY TRAIN H'CAP 5f
2:30 (2:33) (Class 6) (0-65,64) 3-Y-0+ **£2,428** (£722; £361; £180) **Stalls High**

Form RPR
0005 **1** **Only A Game (IRE)**[9] 2529 4-9-7 **57**........................(p) DanielTudhope 14 67
(I W McInnes) *led: stdd and hdd after 1f to trck ldng pair: swtchd lft and effrt over 1f out: qcknd to ld ent fnl f: rdn and hung rt: kpt on* **12/1**
0632 **2** *nk* **Soto**[13] 2389 6-9-5 **60**........................(b) PatrickDonaghy(5) 11 69
(M W Easterby) *chsd ldrs: hdwy 2f out: sn rdn: styd on to chse wnr ins fnl f: drvn and kpt on* **9/2**[1]
5061 **3** *hd* **Ryedane (IRE)**[16] 2316 7-9-8 **58**........................(b) DavidAllan 4 66+
(T D Easterby) *towards rr: effrt 2f out: swtchd outside and rdn wl over 1f out: gd hdwy appr fnl f: fin strly* **12/1**
3300 **4** *2 ½* **Spirit Of Coniston**[22] 2158 6-8-10 **53**........................ PaulPickard(7) 5 52
(P T Midgley) *towards rr: hdwy 2f out: sn rdn and kpt on ins fnl f: nrst fin* **11/1**
3503 **5** *¾* **Bluebok**[7] 2596 8-10-0 **64**........................(bt) PaulHanagan 7 60
(J M Bradley) *cl up: led after 1f: rdn along wl over 1f out: hdd ent fnl f and wknd* **20/1**
0-55 **6** *shd* **Red River Boy**[22] 2158 4-8-13 **52**........................ KellyHarrison(3) 16 48
(C W Fairhurst) *midfield: hdwy 2f out: sn rdn and kpt on ins fnl f: nrst fin* **8/1**
0603 **7** *shd* **Rio Sands**[16] 2316 4-9-5 **60**........................ AmyRyan(5) 13 56
(R M Whitaker) *trckd ldrs: effrt wl over 1f out and sn rdn: wknd ent fnl f* **5/1**[2]
0340 **8** *1* **Ronnie Howe**[32] 1877 5-9-7 **57**........................(b) FrancisNorton 9 49
(S R Bowring) *sn cl up: rdn and ev ch 2f out: sn drvn and grad wknd* **7/1**[3]
-005 **9** *½* **Monsieur Reynard**[7] 2596 4-9-10 **60**........................(b[1]) RichardKingscote 10 50
(J M Bradley) *towards rr: effrt and sme hdwy 2f out: sn rdn and nvr a factor* **14/1**
515 **10** *hd* **Loose Caboose (IRE)**[5] 2657 4-10-0 **64**........................(b) AndrewMullen 17 53
(A J McCabe) *wnt lft s: chsd ldrs on inner: rdn along 1/2-way: sn wknd* **9/2**[1]
01-0 **11** *6* **Sir Don (IRE)**[152] 99 10-9-7 **57**........................(p) StephenDonohoe 2 25
(E S McMahon) *chsd ldrs: rdn along 1/2-way: sn wknd* **66/1**
6/6- **12** *2 ½* **Ocean Glory (IRE)**[502] 298 4-9-7 **57**........................ SJCraine 15 16
(Patrick Morris) *a in rr* **25/1**
6200 **13** *3 ¼* **Just Joey**[16] 2316 5-9-7 **57**........................(b) TonyHamilton 12 4
(J R Weymes) *a in rr* **33/1**

62.28 secs (-1.22) **Going Correction** -0.20s/f (Firm) **13 Ran SP% 120.1**
Speed ratings (Par 101): **101,100,100,96,95 94,94,93,92,91 82,78,73**
toteswingers: 1&2 £16.10, 1&3 £30.10, 2&3 £5.90 CSF £63.33 CT £702.01 TOTE £14.40: £5.20, £2.00, £3.20; EX 124.20.
Owner Ivy House Racing **Bred** Maggie And Eric Hemming **Trained** Catwick, E Yorks

FOCUS
Plenty of runners took part in this modest sprint but, as seems usual, the finish was dominated by horses drawn high. Four non-runners, all drawn in the bottom half, came out.
Red River Boy Official explanation: jockey said gelding missed the break

2802 HEARING DOGS FOR DEAF PEOPLE H'CAP 1m 4f 16y
3:00 (3:02) (Class 6) (0-55,55) 3-Y-0 **£2,428** (£722; £361; £180) **Stalls High**

Form RPR
003 **1** **Rosewin (IRE)**[32] 1893 3-8-4 **52**........................ JamieKyne(7) 11 56
(O Brennan) *trckd ldrs on inner: hdwy over 2f out: rdn along over 1f out: swtchd lft and drvn ins fnl f: styd on strly to ld nr line* **5/1**[2]
5-00 **2** *hd* **Chic Shanique (USA)**[33] 1834 3-9-0 **55**........................ CatherineGannon 8 59
(Tom Dascombe) *led: qcknd 3f out: rdn and qcknd again over 1f out: drvn ins fnl f: hdd and no ex nr line* **15/2**
5-00 **3** *3* **Nut Hand (IRE)**[30] 1926 3-8-13 **54**........................ DavidAllan 3 53
(T D Easterby) *trckd ldr: cl up over 4f out: rdn to chal over 2f out: ev ch tl drvn and one pce appr fnl f* **7/1**
0240 **4** *½* **Addison De Witt**[16] 2340 3-8-13 **54**........................ PaulHanagan 4 52
(Micky Hammond) *hld up in tch: hdwy 3f out: rdn to chse ldrs wl over 1f out: drvn and one pce appr fnl f* **3/1**[1]
5300 **5** *½* **Dulce Domum**[3] 2742 3-8-6 **47**........................ KirstyMilczarek 5 44
(A B Haynes) *in tch: hdwy to chse ldrs 3f out: rdn along over 2f out: sn drvn and kpt on same pce* **12/1**
0-03 **6** *½* **Haafhd Time (IRE)**[38] 1708 3-9-0 **55**........................ RichardKingscote 7 53+
(Tom Dascombe) *midfield: hdwy on inner over 2f out: rdn wl over 1f out: kpt on u.p ins fnl f: nrst fin* **11/2**[3]
6633 **7** *1 ¼* **King's Chorister**[11] 2487 3-8-12 **53**........................(t) StephenDonohoe 9 47
(Miss Gay Kelleway) *hld up: a towards rr* **12/1**
4-60 **8** *5* **Inca Slew (IRE)**[149] 134 3-8-7 **53**........................(v) PatrickDonaghy(5) 2 47+
(P C Haslam) *in tch: hdwy 4f out: rdn along 3f out: sn wknd* **25/1**
500 **9** *3 ¾* **Goswick**[13] 2403 3-9-0 **55**........................ TonyHamilton 12 35
(Micky Hammond) *a in rr* **33/1**
-005 **10** *14* **Ernies Keep**[6] 2627 3-8-1 **49** oh1 ow3........................(p) JohnCavanagh(7) 10 7
(W Storey) *a bhd* **50/1**
0-06 **11** *1 ½* **Luckette**[29] 1953 3-8-5 **46** oh1........................(v[1]) FrancisNorton 1 2
(M Brittain) *chsd ldrs: rdn along 3f out: sn wknd* **25/1**

2m 41.21s (0.31) **Going Correction** -0.325s/f (Firm) **11 Ran SP% 109.3**
Speed ratings (Par 97): **85,84,82,82,82 81,81,77,75,65 64**
toteswingers: 1&2 £9.90, 1&3 £8.80, 2&3 £10.00 CSF £33.99 CT £195.06 TOTE £6.20: £2.20, £3.20, £1.90; EX 57.40.
Owner E Bourke **Bred** E A Bourke M R C V S **Trained** Worksop, Notts
■ Green Endeavour (8/1, ref to ent stalls) was withdrawn. R4 applies, deduct 10p in the £.
■ Stewards' Enquiry : Kirsty Milczarek two-day ban: careless riding (Jun 24-25)

FOCUS
A real mix of ability and experience took part in this contest, so the form may be quite weak.
Nut Hand(IRE) Official explanation: jockey said gelding hung left
Haafhd Time(IRE) Official explanation: jockey said filly was unsuited by the track
Ernies Keep Official explanation: jockey said gelding never travelled

2803 GOODBYE MISS BRADER HELLO MRS LUND H'CAP 1m 1f 207y
3:30 (3:33) (Class 5) (0-70,68) 4-Y-0+ **£4,209** (£1,252; £625; £312) **Stalls High**

Form RPR
54-0 **1** **Bollin Freddie**[19] 2233 5-7-10 **50** oh4 ow1........................ JamieKyne(7) 2 59
(A J Lockwood) *mde most: set stdy pce: jnd: rdn and qcknd 2f out: drvn and edgd lft ins fnl f: styd on gamely* **28/1**
-121 **2** *½* **Joe Jo Star**[7] 2594 7-8-10 **57**........................ PaulHanagan 7 65
(R A Fahey) *trckd ldr: hdwy to chal 2f out: rdn over 1f out and ev ch tl drvn and no ex ins fnl f* **4/9**[1]

0235 **3** 3 1/2 **Cheers For Thea (IRE)**[19] 2246 4-8-11 58 DavidAllan 6 59
(T D Easterby) *hld up: hdwy to trck ldrs 1/2-way: effrt to chse ldng pair over 2f out: rdn wl over 1f out: swtchd rt and drvn ins fnl f: kpt on* **10/1**[3]

6-63 **4** 3 1/2 **Shaylee**[9] 2527 4-8-4 51 SilvestreDeSousa 1 45
(T D Walford) *chsd ldrs: rdn along 3f out: drvn 2f out and grad wknd* **14/1**

3055 **5** 1 3/4 **Just Observing**[32] 1881 6-8-10 57 (p) FrankieMcDonald 5 48
(P T Midgley) *t.k.h: trckd ldrs: effrt over 3f out: rdn along over 2f out and sn btn* **16/1**

-531 **6** 8 **Umverti**[19] 2246 4-9-0 61 FrancisNorton 4 36
(N Bycroft) *plld hrd: trckd ldrs on outer: pushed along over 3f out: sn rdn and btn* **4/1**[2]

2m 5.50s (-1.50) **Going Correction** -0.325s/f (Firm) **6** Ran SP% **114.3**
Speed ratings (Par 103): **93,92,89,87,85 79**
toteswingers: 1&2 £4.60, 1&3 £7.30, 2&3 £2.00 CSF £43.28 CT £162.73 TOTE £26.10: £6.90, £1.10; EX 55.30.

Owner Highgreen Partnership **Bred** Sir Neil & Exors Of Late Lady Westbrook **Trained** Brawby, N Yorks

FOCUS
This looked an uncompetitive event after three came out, but punters that supported the favourite into short odds were in for a nasty shock. The pace looked noticeably slow during the early stages.

2804 CHRISTMAS PARTIES AT BEVERLEY RACECOURSE H'CAP 7f 100y
4:00 (4:01) (Class 5) (0-70,70) 4-Y-0+ **£4,209** (£1,252; £625; £312) **Stalls** High

Form RPR

5025 **1** **Kabis Amigos**[12] 2453 7-9-1 64 (b) TonyHamilton 6 76
(Ollie Pears) *midfield: hdwy on inner: over 2f out: swtchd lft and rdn over 1f out: chal ent fnl f: sn led and kpt on strly* **9/1**

5-40 **2** 3 1/2 **Carpe Diem**[12] 2441 4-8-6 55 (v[1]) PaulHanagan 8 58
(R A Fahey) *trckd ldrs: smooth hdwy 3f out: rdn to ld 1f out: hdd ins fnl f: sn drvn and one pce* **6/1**[3]

0030 **3** 1 3/4 **Ninth House (USA)**[4] 2722 7-8-2 54 (bt) KellyHarrison(3) 4 53
(Mrs R A Carr) *s.i.s and bhd: gd hdwy on outer over 2f out: rdn wl over 1f out: kpt on ins fnl f* **17/2**

0023 **4** 1 3/4 **Spirit Of France (IRE)**[8] 2569 7-9-7 70 DNolan 13 65
(D Carroll) *chsd ldrs: hdwy over 2f out: rdn wl over 1f out: sn no imp* **15/2**

-336 **5** 1/2 **Mister Jingles**[9] 2531 6-8-9 58 J-PGuillambert 2 51
(R M Whitaker) *in rr: rdn along 1/2-way: hdwy u.p 2f out: kpt on ins fnl f: nvr nr ldrs* **13/2**

-000 **6** 1 1/4 **Moonage Daydream (IRE)**[30] 1924 4-8-11 60 (b) DavidAllan 9 50
(T D Easterby) *stdd s: hld up in rr: effrt on inner and nt clr run 2f out: swtchd lft over 1f out: kpt on ins fnl f: nrst fin* **20/1**

-001 **7** 1 3/4 **Desert Hunter (IRE)**[9] 2532 6-7-10 52 oh6 ow1 JamieKyne(7) 3 38
(Micky Hammond) *midfield: effrt over 3f out: rdn over 2f out and n.d* **9/2**[1]

5-26 **8** 2 1/2 **A Big Sky Brewing (USA)**[110] 625 5-8-6 62 AdamCarter(7) 7 42
(T D Barron) *midfield: effrt 3f out: sn rdn and wknd* **8/1**

30-0 **9** 2 3/4 **Boy Dancer (IRE)**[16] 2314 6-8-11 60 StephenDonohoe 14 33
(J J Quinn) *cl up on inner: rdn along 3f out: sn wknd* **33/1**

1206 **10** 2 **Ace Of Spies (IRE)**[9] 2529 4-8-10 59 (v) SilvestreDeSousa 12 27
(G A Harker) *sn led: rdn clr over 2f out: drvn over 1f out: sn hdd & wknd* **5/1**[2]

0-00 **11** 11 **Flashy Max**[11] 2473 4-8-2 51 oh2 AndrewMullen 5 —
(Jedd O'Keeffe) *cl up: rdn along 3f out: sn drvn and wknd* **33/1**

1m 30.93s (-2.87) **Going Correction** -0.325s/f (Firm) **11** Ran SP% **116.5**
Speed ratings (Par 103): **103,99,97,95,94 93,91,88,85,82 70**
toteswingers: 1&2 £7.10, 1&3 £16.20, 2&3 £18.00 CSF £60.26 CT £475.87 TOTE £10.80: £4.00, £2.10, £2.30; EX 39.30.

Owner Ian W Glenton **Bred** Cheveley Park Stud Ltd **Trained** Norton, N Yorks

■ Stewards' Enquiry : Jamie Kyne caution: careless riding.

FOCUS
A modest but competitive contest.

Ninth House(USA) Official explanation: jockey said horse missed the break

Moonage Daydream(IRE) Official explanation: jockey said gelding was denied a clear run

Ace Of Spies(IRE) Official explanation: jockey said gelding had a breathing problem

2805 RACING HERE ON TUESDAY 23 JUNE MAIDEN STKS 7f 100y
4:30 (4:31) (Class 5) 3-Y-0+ **£2,914** (£867; £433; £216) **Stalls** High

Form RPR

4-52 **1** **Espiritu (FR)**[13] 2416 3-8-13 86 (v[1]) TPQueally 1 89+
(J Noseda) *trckd ldrs: smooth hdwy over 2f out: shkn up to ld ent fnl f and sn clr* **10/11**[1]

3 **2** 4 1/2 **Crime Writer (USA)**[12] 2439 3-8-13 0 J-PGuillambert 9 78
(M Johnston) *led: rdn along 2f out: drvn and hdd ent fnl f: sn one pce* **5/4**[2]

- **3** 3 1/4 **Helieorbea** 3-8-13 0 DavidAllan 3 70
(T D Easterby) *hld up in tch: hdwy over 2f out: rdn to chse ldng pair over 1f out: sn drvn and no imp* **40/1**

00- **4** 2 **Chief Red Cloud (USA)**[272] 5825 3-8-13 0 PaulHanagan 5 65
(K R Burke) *t.k.h: stdd s and hld up towards rr: hdwy on inner 2f out: sn rdn and no imp appr fnl f* **20/1**

6 **5** 2 **Freya's Flight (IRE)**[19] 2250 3-8-8 0 SilvestreDeSousa 6 55
(K A Ryan) *chsd ldrs: rdn along 1/2-way: sn wknd* **14/1**[3]

-000 **6** 2 **Billy Bowmore**[15] 2366 4-9-6 45 (b[1]) RussellKennemore(3) 8 58?
(P A Kirby) *cl up: rdn along 3f out: drvn and wknd over 2f out* **100/1**

000/ **7** 51 **Cottam Breeze**[646] 5100 4-9-4 29 (p) PAspell 7 —
(J S Wainwright) *a bhd* **100/1**

1m 30.64s (-3.16) **Going Correction** -0.325s/f (Firm)
WFA 3 from 4yo+ 10lb **7** Ran SP% **112.7**
Speed ratings (Par 103): **105,99,96,93,91 89,31**
toteswingers: 1&2 £1.40, 1&3 £3.90, 2&3 £4.60 CSF £2.18 TOTE £1.80: £1.30, £1.60; EX 2.60 Place 6: £651.09, Place 5: £39.28.

Owner Sir Robert Ogden **Bred** Hubert Honore & Claire Lamotte D'Argy **Trained** Newmarket, Suffolk

FOCUS
An uncompetitive maiden, as the two market leaders dominated the finish.

T/Plt: £2,468.90 to a £1 stake. Pool: £60,201.47. 17.80 winning tickets. T/Qpdt: £14.30 to a £1 stake. Pool: £5,073.20. 260.90 winning tickets. JR

2735 BRIGHTON (L-H)
Wednesday, June 10

OFFICIAL GOING: Good (good to soft in places)
Wind: Fresh, half against Weather: Cloudy

2806 BETDAQ - THE BETTING EXCHANGE H'CAP 6f 209y
2:20 (2:20) (Class 6) (0-65,65) 4-Y-0+ **£2,590** (£770; £385; £192) **Stalls** Low

Form RPR

-621 **1** **Mountain Cat (IRE)**[6] 2626 5-9-7 65 6ex RobertWinston 11 76+
(G A Swinbank) *prom: led 2f out: clr over 1f out: rdn out* **1/1**[1]

0-30 **2** 2 1/2 **Lady Florence**[19] 2221 4-8-4 48 ow2 TPO'Shea 4 49
(A B Coogan) *prom: rdn and lost pl after 2f: sn struggling in midfield: styd on wl fr over 1f out to take 2nd nr fin* **28/1**

2206 **3** 3/4 **Duke Of Milan (IRE)**[16] 2330 6-9-4 62 (p) RichardSmith 10 61
(Tom Dascombe) *hld up and bhd: gd hdwy over 2f out: chsd wnr 1f out: nt qckn: lost 2nd nr fin* **7/1**[3]

3340 **4** 1 3/4 **Hart Of Gold**[5] 2680 5-9-4 65 (p) KevinGhunowa(3) 2 59
(R A Harris) *prom: hrd rdn whn lft 2nd wl over 1f out: one pce* **9/1**

2053 **5** 1 1/2 **Lord Deevert**[14] 2381 4-8-13 62 JackDean(5) 8 52
(W G M Turner) *mid-div: rdn over 2f out: nvr rchd ldrs* **10/1**

-000 **6** 1 1/4 **Harrison's Flyer (IRE)**[121] 480 8-8-3 47 (p) LukeMorris 5 34
(J M Bradley) *mid-div: n.m.r after 2f: effrt over 2f out: no imp* **50/1**

00 **7** 3 3/4 **Listen Carefully (IRE)**[5] 2660 5-7-13 46 oh1 DavidProbert(3) 7 23
(Patrick Morris) *chsd ldrs 2f: sn lost pl* **100/1**

3-60 **8** 17 **Light The Light (IRE)**[133] 309 4-8-11 55 (v[1]) SebSanders 1 —
(M D Squance) *chsd ldrs after 2f tl wknd 2f out* **25/1**

-005 **9** 18 **Applesnap (IRE)**[9] 2539 4-9-4 62 (p) JerryO'Dwyer 3 —
(Miss Amy Weaver) *a bhd: no ch whn hmpd by loose horse and eased over 1f out* **25/1**

6211 **U** **Annes Rocket (IRE)**[19] 2223 4-8-6 57 GemmaElford(7) 9 —
(J C Fox) *s.s: bhd: hmpd after 2f: hdwy over 2f out: disputing 5th whn bmpd and uns rdr wl over 1f out* **11/2**[2]

0/00 **P** **Neboisha**[12] 2441 5-7-11 46 oh1 (b) NicolPolli(5) 6 —
(M Wigham) *led tl 2f out: disputing 2nd and nt pce of wnr whn broke leg and p.u wl over 1f out: dead* **20/1**

1m 24.24s (1.14) **Going Correction** +0.125s/f (Good) **11** Ran SP% **115.8**
Speed ratings (Par 101): **98,95,94,92,90 89,84,65,44,—,—**
toteswingers: 1&2 £11.30, 1&3 £11.60, 2&3 £34.40 CSF £44.13 CT £144.16 TOTE £1.70: £1.10, £7.20, £2.60; EX 49.20 TRIFECTA Not won..

Owner S Rudolf **Bred** Mrs Mary Gallagher **Trained** Melsonby, N Yorks

FOCUS
They went a fair pace for what was an ordinary, if competitive, handicap.

2807 COMMISSION DEALS AVAILABLE AT BETDAQ CLAIMING STKS 7f 214y
2:50 (2:52) (Class 6) 3-Y-0+ **£1,942** (£578; £288; £144) **Stalls** Low

Form RPR

2633 **1** **Steig (IRE)**[14] 2378 6-9-8 67 JamesDoyle 6 67
(George Baker) *trckd ldr: claimed stands' rail and led over 2f out: hrd rdn fnl f: jst hld on* **5/2**[1]

5050 **2** nk **Sofia's Star**[20] 2193 4-9-10 70 JimCrowley 8 69+
(S Dow) *s.s: hld up in rr: nt clr run over 2f out: hdwy and squeezed through over 1f out: clsd on wnr: jst failed* **4/1**[3]

522 **3** 2 1/2 **Mick Is Back**[3] 2739 5-9-10 58 (vt) JohnEgan 3 63
(G G Margarson) *t.k.h: in tch: drvn to chse ldrs 2f out: one pce* **5/1**

3340 **4** 1 1/2 **Jonnie Skull (IRE)**[13] 2417 3-8-6 54 (vt) AndreaAtzeni(5) 5 55
(P S McEntee) *led tl over 2f out: no ex over 1f out* **25/1**

0334 **5** 2 1/4 **Wrighty Almighty (IRE)**[14] 2381 7-9-9 60 DavidProbert(3) 4 56
(P R Chamings) *hld up in 6th: hrd rdn 2f out: no imp* **10/3**[2]

0602 **6** 7 **Mountain Pass (USA)**[3] 2737 7-9-6 54 (p) SteveDrowne 9 34
(B J Llewellyn) *hld up in 5th: rdn and wknd 2f out* **8/1**

0-06 **7** 2 1/4 **Spent**[72] 1030 4-9-7 53 NeilChalmers 7 30
(Mouse Hamilton-Fairley) *a in last pair: rdn 4f out: n.d fnl 2f* **50/1**

1200 **8** 2 **Pab Special (IRE)**[21] 2183 6-9-12 65 IanMongan 2 31
(B R Johnson) *chsd ldrs tl wknd wl over 1f out* **16/1**

1m 37.26s (1.26) **Going Correction** +0.125s/f (Good)
WFA 3 from 4yo+ 11lb **8** Ran SP% **111.1**
Speed ratings (Par 101): **98,97,95,93,91 84,82,80**
toteswingers: 1&2 £2.50, 1&3 £1.90, 2&3 £3.90 CSF £11.91 TOTE £3.90: £1.30, £1.50, £1.60; EX 14.60 Trifecta £51.70 Pool: £552.87 - 7.91 winning units..

Owner Something In The City 2 **Bred** Elisabeth And Neil Draper **Trained** Moreton Morrell, Warwicks

■ Stewards' Enquiry : Jim Crowley caution: used whip without giving gelding time to respond

FOCUS
A modest claimer run at a moderate early pace and they tracked across to the stands' rail.

2808 BET WORLD CUP FOOTBALL - BETDAQ APPRENTICE (S) STKS 1m 1f 209y
3:20 (3:22) (Class 6) 3-5-Y-0 **£1,942** (£578; £288; £144) **Stalls** High

Form RPR

061 **1** **Theocritus (USA)**[19] 2220 4-9-8 77 ChrisHough(6) 8 64
(D M Simcock) *towards rr: hdwy 6f out: led over 1f out: edgd rt: drvn out* **2/1**[1]

0-40 **2** 1/2 **Playful Asset (IRE)**[19] 2246 3-8-4 64 JackMitchell 7 51
(R M Beckett) *chsd ldr: brought v wd st: drvn to chal ins fnl f: r.o: jst hld* **7/2**[2]

0315 **3** 3/4 **Rose Of Coma (IRE)**[4] 2709 3-8-7 51 ow1 KylieManser(4) 11 57
(Miss Gay Kelleway) *plld hrd in rr: brought wd st: gd hdwy over 1f out: drvn to dispute 2nd whn hmpd and swtchd lft ins fnl f: r.o* **8/1**

54-4 **4** 2 1/4 **Ministerofinterior**[20] 59 4-9-4 57 (v[1]) JemmaMarshall(4) 6 51
(G L Moore) *led tl 5f out: hrd rdn over 1f out: one pce* **13/2**[3]

0000 **5** 5 **Dynamo Dave (USA)**[7] 2608 4-9-4 43 (v[1]) LeeNewnes(4) 4 41
(M D I Usher) *chsd ldrs: brought wd st: outpcd and btn 2f out* **80/1**

0333 **6** hd **Maddy**[9] 2537 4-8-13 49 (p) MatthewDavies(4) 3 36
(George Baker) *in tch: led 5f out tl wknd over 1f out* **8/1**

400- **7** hd **Rowan River**[17] 7009 5-8-13 69 (t) SimonPearce(4) 2 35
(A Middleton) *chsd ldrs: hmpd and lost pl over 4f out: hrd rdn and no imp fnl 2f* **8/1**

0603 **8** shd **Stark Contrast (USA)**[5] 2650 5-9-8 52 DavidProbert 5 40
(M D I Usher) *plld hrd in midfield: rdn and outpcd fnl 2f* **11/1**

0 **9** *27* **Wise Princess**^{11} 2488 3-8-4 0 ow2 .... JackDean$^{(2)}$ 9 —
(W G M Turner) *in rr: rdn after 3f: drvn along over 4f out: sn bhd* **100/1**

2m 6.83s (3.23) **Going Correction** +0.125s/f (Good)
WFA 3 from 4yo+ 13lb **9** Ran SP% **112.8**
Speed ratings (Par 101): **92,91,91,89,85 85,84,84,63**
toteswingers: 1&2 £4.30, 1&3 £2.30, 2&3 £9.00 CSF £8.59 TOTE £2.80: £1.20, £1.80, £1.80; EX 9.10 Trifecta £80.70 Pool: £340.36 - 3.12 winning units..The winner was bought in for 6,200gns.
Owner Dr Marwan Koukash **Bred** Allen E Paulson Living Trust **Trained** Newmarket, Suffolk
■ Stewards' Enquiry : Chris Hough caution: careless riding

FOCUS
Moderate horses but a competitive apprentice seller, nonetheless.

2809 BETDAQ SUPPORTS ON-COURSE BOOKMAKERS H'CAP 1m 1f 209y
3:50 (3:51) (Class 6) (0-65,64) 3-Y-O **£2,523** (£755; £377; £188; £94) **Stalls** High

Form RPR

5501 **1** **Brett Vale (IRE)**^{4} 2709 3-9-3 **63** 6ex .... SebSanders 8 78+
(Sir Mark Prescott) *t.k.h: chsd ldr: led after 3f: rdn clr fnl 2f: eased nr fin* **8/15**^{1}

0-24 **2** *5* **Beaubrav**^{20} 2204 3-9-1 **61** .... RobertWinston 4 63
(P W D'Arcy) *t.k.h towards rr: hdwy 6f out: rdn to chse wnr over 2f out: no imp* **5/1**^{2}

3010 **3** *3* **Primo Dilettante**^{11} 2489 3-9-2 **62** .... JimCrowley 9 58
(W J Knight) *in tch: rdn 3f out: styd on same pce* **9/1**^{3}

0-40 **4** *1 1/4* **Transformer (IRE)**^{30} 1932 3-9-3 **63** .... ShaneKelly 10 57
(W J Knight) *in tch: rdn over 4f out: btn 3f out* **10/1**

-050 **5** *shd* **Peak (IRE)**^{16} 2320 3-9-2 **62** .... SteveDrowne 2 55
(H Morrison) *led 3f: drvn and lost pl 4f out: sme hdwy over 1f out: n.d* **16/1**

4430 **6** *1/2* **Squad**^{20} 2204 3-9-0 **60** .... (v^{1}) NickyMackay 7 52
(S Dow) *s.s: t.k.h: prom after 2f: wknd 2f out* **16/1**

-606 **7** *12* **Charlie Smirke (USA)**^{14} 2380 3-9-1 **61** .... (b) GeorgeBaker 6 29
(G L Moore) *a bhd: rdn and n.d fnl 3f: fin lame* **25/1**

3000 **8** *6* **Kneesy Earsy Nosey**^{28} 1982 3-7-13 **50** oh5 .... AmyBaker$^{(5)}$ 1 6
(Miss A Stokell) *chsd ldrs: lost pl qckly 1/2-way: sn bhd* **66/1**

2m 4.54s (0.94) **Going Correction** +0.125s/f (Good) **8** Ran SP% **118.1**
Speed ratings (Par 97): **101,97,94,93,93 93,83,78**
toteswingers: 1&2 £4.30, 1&3 £2.30, 2&3 £9.00 CSF £3.83 CT £12.62 TOTE £1.50: £1.10, £1.60, £2.30; EX 3.40 Trifecta £17.40 Pool: £518.30 - 21.92 winning units..
Owner G D Waters **Bred** Mrs O Murtagh **Trained** Newmarket, Suffolk

FOCUS
A modest handicap run at a sensible pace.

2810 PM-PARTNERS.CO.UK H'CAP 5f 213y
4:20 (4:22) (Class 5) (0-70,70) 3-Y-O **£3,497** (£1,040; £520; £259) **Stalls** Low

Form RPR

-031 **1** **Hand Painted**^{14} 2377 3-9-7 **70** .... TravisBlock 4 74
(P J Makin) *pressed ldr: slt ld fnl 100yds: drvn out* **8/11**^{1}

0032 **2** *nk* **Louie's Lad**^{3} 2740 3-7-13 **51** oh3 .... (p) DavidProbert$^{(3)}$ 1 54
(J J Bridger) *led: hrd rdn and hdd ins fnl f: r.o* **11/4**^{2}

3120 **3** *3* **Pipers Piping (IRE)**^{29} 1969 3-9-2 **65** .... ShaneKelly 3 58
(J A Osborne) *chsd ldng pair: styd alone far rail st: one pce fnl f* **8/1**^{3}

0-40 **4** *3 1/4* **Blackwater Fort (USA)**^{14} 2377 3-8-9 **58** .... (b) TPO'Shea 2 41
(J Gallagher) *mainly 5th: effrt and hrd rdn 2f out: no imp* **10/1**

000 **5** *2 1/4* **Josiah Bartlett (IRE)**^{27} 2005 3-8-2 **51** oh1 .... (bt) LukeMorris 7 27
(P S McEntee) *hmpd s and missed break: bhd: hrd rdn 2f out: n.d whn hung rt fr over 1f out* **12/1**

-500 **6** *11* **Silver Salsa**^{12} 2431 3-8-2 **51** oh4 .... AdrianMcCarthy 6 —
(J R Jenkins) *wnt rt s: 4th tl hrd rdn and wknd 2f out* **40/1**

1m 11.0s (0.80) **Going Correction** +0.125s/f (Good) **6** Ran SP% **114.9**
Speed ratings (Par 99): **99,98,94,90,87 72**
toteswingers: 1&2 £1.40, 1&3 £1.90, 2&3 £3.00 CSF £3.09 TOTE £1.70: £1.40, £1.40; EX 2.70.
Owner D A Poole **Bred** P J Makin **Trained** Ogbourne Maisey, Wilts
■ Stewards' Enquiry : Travis Block one-day ban: used whip with excessive frequency (tba)

FOCUS
A weak handicap but truly-run.

2811 BETDAQ XPRESSBET H'CAP 5f 59y
4:50 (4:50) (Class 6) (0-60,59) 3-Y-O+ **£2,590** (£770; £385; £192) **Stalls** Low

Form RPR

0060 **1** **Berrymead**^{9} 2546 4-9-2 **55** .... AnnStokell$^{(5)}$ 8 61
(Miss A Stokell) *dwlt: hmpd and nrly fell after 150yds: swtchd rt and hdwy 3f out: led jst ins fnl f: drvn out* **7/1**^{3}

0-46 **2** *1* **Kalligal**^{11} 2492 4-9-7 **55** .... (b^{1}) RobertHavlin 4 57
(R Ingram) *dwlt: towards rr: rdn 3f out: hdwy over 1f out: r.o to take 2nd fnl 50yds* **9/1**

5600 **3** *1 1/4* **Thoughtsofstardom**^{2} 2758 6-9-2 **57** .... CarolineKelly$^{(7)}$ 5 55
(P S McEntee) *hld up in tch: rdn to press ldrs over 1f out: one pce fnl f* **9/1**

3300 **4** *1/2* **One Way Ticket**^{35} 1787 9-8-11 **45** .... (tp) SteveDrowne 3 41
(J M Bradley) *pressed ldr: drvn to chal over 1f out: one pce* **14/1**

0400 **5** *1 1/2* **Nordic Light (USA)**^{35} 1784 5-8-11 **45** .... (b) JimCrowley 7 36
(J M Bradley) *chsd ldrs: sn rdn along: no ex over 1f out* **14/1**

000 **6** *1 1/2* **Meikle Barfil**^{35} 1787 7-8-12 **46** .... (tp) LukeMorris 6 31
(J M Bradley) *dwlt: towards rr: hdwy to chse ldrs over 1f out: wknd fnl f* **7/1**^{3}

00-0 **7** *shd* **Blakeshall Diamond**^{5} 2682 4-8-8 **47** .... MarkCoumbe$^{(5)}$ 1 32
(A J Chamberlain) *outpcd and bhd: modest late hdwy* **20/1**

454 **8** *hd* **Ask Jenny (IRE)**^{4} 2712 7-9-10 **58** .... ShaneKelly 9 42
(Patrick Morris) *towards rr whn sltly hmpd after 150yds: hdwy 3f out: effrt on stands' rail 2f out: wknd 1f out* **5/2**^{2}

0245 **9** *1/2* **Joss Stick**^{15} 2349 4-9-6 **57** .... (b^{1}) KevinGhunowa$^{(3)}$ 10 39
(R A Harris) *led tl wknd rapidly jst ins fnl f* **9/4**^{1}

63.75 secs (1.45) **Going Correction** +0.125s/f (Good) **9** Ran SP% **122.4**
Speed ratings (Par 101): **93,91,89,88,86 83,83,83,82**
toteswingers: 1&2 £16.40, 1&3 £11.80, 2&3 £10.60 CSF £72.10 CT £587.83 TOTE £10.80: £3.20, £1.90, £2.10; EX 89.50 Trifecta £197.80 Pool: £801.78 - 3.00 winning units. Place 6: £9.76, Place 5: £6.78.
Owner Ms Caron Stokell **Bred** W T Allgood And M W Easterby **Trained** Brompton-on-Swale, N Yorks
■ Stewards' Enquiry : Kevin Ghunowa four-day ban: careless riding (Jun 24-27)

FOCUS
A moderate sprint.

T/Plt: £27.80 to a £1 stake. Pool: £54,382.54. 1,426.63 winning tickets. T/Qpdt: £9.60 to a £1 stake. Pool: £3,432.22. 262.30 winning tickets. LM

2623 HAMILTON (R-H)
Wednesday, June 10

OFFICIAL GOING: Good to firm (firm in places; 10.6)
Dolling out around loop added circa 25yds to advertised distances on round course.
Wind: Fresh, across Weather: Cloudy, bright

2812 GIVE GENEROUSLY TO CASH FOR KIDS AMATEUR RIDERS' H'CAP 6f 5y
6:40 (6:40) (Class 6) (0-60,61) 4-Y-O+ **£2,637** (£811; £405) **Stalls** Centre

Form RPR

4431 **1** **Argentine (IRE)**^{6} 2625 5-11-8 **61** 6ex .... (b) MrSWalker 9 73+
(J A McShane) *taken early to post: trckd ldrs: led over 2f out: drvn out fnl f* **9/2**^{2}

4-01 **2** *1 1/4* **Botham (USA)**^{12} 2441 5-10-9 **53** .... MrPNorton$^{(5)}$ 4 61
(J S Goldie) *bhd: last and plenty to do over 2f out: gd hdwy to chse wnr ins fnl f: r.o* **6/1**^{3}

05-2 **3** *1* **Finsbury**^{9} 2529 6-11-6 **59** .... MrsCBartley 6 64
(J S Goldie) *bhd tl hdwy over 1f out: kpt on fnl f: nrst fin* **7/2**^{1}

0602 **4** *1* **Strathmore (IRE)**^{9} 2534 5-11-2 **60** .... MrsVFahey$^{(5)}$ 5 62
(R A Fahey) *taken early to post: bhd: swtchd centre and hdwy 1/2-way: kpt on same pce fnl f* **12/1**

5540 **5** *1/2* **Whozart (IRE)**^{16} 2316 6-11-1 **54** .... MrSDobson 3 54
(A Dickman) *cl up: ev ch over 2f out: one pce over 1f out* **14/1**

0061 **5** *dht* **All You Need (IRE)**^{9} 2534 5-10-8 **54** 6ex..(p) MissStefaniaGandola$^{(7)}$ 12 54
(R Hollinshead) *racd centre: towards rr: rdn over 2f out: kpt on fnl f: no imp* **20/1**

00-0 **7** *1/2* **Warners Bay (IRE)**^{15} 2366 4-10-7 **51** .... MissRBastiman$^{(5)}$ 11 49
(R Bastiman) *bhd: effrt centre over 2f out: kpt on fnl f: nvr rchd ldrs* **100/1**

6-06 **8** *nse* **Avoncreek**^{33} 1846 5-10-4 **48** .... MissAWallace$^{(5)}$ 7 46
(B P J Baugh) *prom: rdn and outpcd over 2f out: rallied fnl f: no imp* **25/1**

6000 **9** *3/4* **Obe One**^{6} 2628 9-10-8 **47** .... MissSBrotherton 8 43
(A Berry) *bhd and outpcd tl styd on fnl f: n.d* **50/1**

0-00 **10** *1/2* **Goodbye Cash (IRE)**^{12} 2456 5-10-4 **50** .... MrJEngland$^{(7)}$ 2 44
(P D Evans) *led to over 2f out: wknd over 1f out* **22/1**

-233 **11** *nk* **The History Man (IRE)**^{6} 2625 6-10-13 **57** ....(be) MissMMullineaux$^{(5)}$ 16 50
(M Mullineaux) *racd w one other towards far side: in tch tl outpcd fnl 2f* **7/1**

-510 **12** *nk* **Sunley Sovereign**^{6} 2625 5-10-7 **51** .... (b) MissWGibson$^{(5)}$ 13 43
(Mrs R A Carr) *taken early to post: cl up: ev ch over 2f out: wandered over 1f out: wknd ent fnl f* **16/1**

2301 **13** *1 1/2* **Just Sam (IRE)**^{15} 2366 4-10-13 **57** .... MissVBarr$^{(5)}$ 15 45
(R E Barr) *racd w one other far side: in tch: drvn 1/2-way: wknd over 1f out* **7/1**

00 **14** *3* **Aegean Pride**^{37} 1734 4-10-4 **50** oh1 ow4 .... MrThomasHogg$^{(7)}$ 10 28
(A Berry) *bhd and sn outpcd: nvr on terms* **66/1**

0304 **15** *5* **Tag Team (IRE)**^{36} 1781 8-10-2 **46** oh1 .... (p) MissABevan$^{(5)}$ 14 8
(John A Harris) *prom tl rdn and wknd over 2f out* **33/1**

1m 12.35s (0.15) **Going Correction** -0.15s/f (Firm) **15** Ran SP% **120.3**
Speed ratings (Par 101): **93,91,90,88,88 88,87,87,86,85 85,84,82,78,72**
toteswingers: 1&2 £8.40, 1&3 £6.70, 2&3 £5.80 CSF £29.23 CT £107.32 TOTE £6.00: £2.30, £3.50, £2.40; EX 40.60.
Owner D Moriarty **Bred** Tony Hirschfeld & L K Piggott **Trained** Dalkeith, Midlothian

FOCUS
The opening event was a modest race for amateur riders, but seven of the contenders had won or finished placed on their previous start. Most of the runners moved towards the stands' rail. The pace was fairly steady for a sprint and the time was more than two seconds above standard.
Avoncreek Official explanation: jockey said gelding hung right-handed throughout

2813 IRN BRU MAIDEN STKS 6f 5y
7:10 (7:10) (Class 4) 2-Y-O **£4,533** (£1,348; £674; £336) **Stalls** Low

Form RPR

1 **Leviathan** 2-9-3 0 .... MickyFenton 5 77
(T P Tate) *mde all: pushed along 2f out: hrd pressed fnl f: hld on wl* **11/2**^{3}

2 *1/2* **Loveinthesand (IRE)** 2-9-3 0 .... GregFairley 2 76
(M Johnston) *noisy in paddock: dwlt: sn cl up: rn green thrght: ev ch and hung rt fnl f: kpt on: hld nr fin* **1/1**^{1}

3 *3 1/2* **Irish Jugger (USA)** 2-9-3 0 .... PhillipMakin 4 65
(K R Burke) *w ldrs: reminder over 2f out: one pce over 1f out* **10/3**^{2}

4 *2* **Ya Boy Sir (IRE)** 2-9-3 0 .... TomEaves 6 59
(I Semple) *prom tl rdn and outpcd fr over 2f out* **14/1**

5 *nk* **Dahes (IRE)** 2-9-3 0 .... RoystonFfrench 1 58
(B Smart) *in tch: drvn over 3f out: outpcd over 2f out* **11/2**^{3}

1m 12.6s (0.40) **Going Correction** -0.15s/f (Firm) **5** Ran SP% **110.5**
Speed ratings (Par 95): **91,90,85,83,82**
toteswingers: 1&2 £7.70 CSF £11.68 TOTE £6.90: £2.90, £1.40; EX 17.50.
Owner Paul Moulton **Bred** Laundry Cottage Stud Farm **Trained** Tadcaster, N Yorks

FOCUS
Five newcomers lined up for this two-year-old maiden. The first two pulled clear of the third, who attracted strong support. The form could be decent.

NOTEBOOK
Leviathan moved well for most of the way and showed some fighting qualities to repel the hot favourite in a sustained duel in the final furlong. He is a half-brother to Illustrious Blue, a smart multiple winner over 7f-1m1f, and to Romany Nights, a prolific 6f-7f winner. He could be quite useful, should stay a bit further and looks a bargain at 22,000gns. (op 13-2)
Loveinthesand(IRE) needed to be rousted along in the early stages and kept changing his legs on the uphill climb. He must be given credit for battling on despite looking inexperienced. He holds entries in the Group 1 Phoenix/National Stakes, so is clearly well regarded and should improve significantly. (op 4-5 tchd 8-11)
Irish Jugger(USA) was a bit keen but showed some promise before fading on his debut. He is a $220,000 second foal of a quite useful winner at up to 1m1f on turf and dirt. (op 9-2 tchd 5-1)
Ya Boy Sir(IRE) attracted support, but was intermittently on the bridle and never got into it. He should have learned from this experience and should do better next time. (op 20-1 tchd 25-1)
Dahes(IRE), a £27,000 breeze-up buy, is bred for speed and should build on this debut effort. (op 5-1 tchd 9-2)

2814 HAMILTON-PARK.CO.UK H'CAP 6f 5y
7:40 (7:41) (Class 3) (0-90,90) 4-Y-O+ **£10,361** (£3,083; £1,540; £769) **Stalls** Centre

Form RPR

-202 **1** **Fishforcompliments**^{4} 2695 5-9-4 **90** .... (p) FrederikTylicki$^{(5)}$ 9 102
(R A Fahey) *w ldrs: led over 2f out: edgd rt and kpt on strly fnl f* **9/4**^{1}

0152 **2** 3 **Vhujon (IRE)**[8] 2570 4-9-6 **87**............ PhillipMakin 4 89
(P D Evans) *hld up: hdwy and swtchd rt over 1f out: chsd wnr ins fnl f: kpt on: no imp* **11/2**[2]

-062 **3** 2 ½ **Dazzling Bay**[12] 2438 9-8-8 **75**............(b) DuranFentiman 7 69
(T D Easterby) *in tch: effrt over 2f out: kpt on same pce fnl f* **9/1**

-216 **4** ½ **Rasaman (IRE)**[15] 2363 5-9-1 **85**............ NeilBrown(3) 1 78
(K A Ryan) *chsd ldrs: drvn over 2f out: one pce over 1f out* **20/1**

0-33 **5** 2 ¼ **Kashimin (IRE)**[5] 2658 4-9-1 **82**............ PJMcDonald 8 68
(G A Swinbank) *cl up tl rdn and no ex over 1f out* **15/2**

00-0 **6** 2 **Turnkey**[73] 1018 7-9-2 **90**............ NSLawes(7) 5 69
(D Nicholls) *prom: effrt whn nt clr run over 1f out: no imp whn clr fnl f* **33/1**

-404 **7** nse **Maze (IRE)**[13] 2405 4-9-6 **87**............ TomEaves 6 66
(B Smart) *led to over 2f out: rdn and wknd over 1f out* **6/1**[3]

0033 **8** 1 ¼ **Nightjar (USA)**[25] 2078 4-9-3 **84**............ GregFairley 10 59
(M Johnston) *midfield on outside: rdn over 3f out: wknd fnl 2f* **9/1**

2311 **9** ¾ **Blue Tomato**[4] 2717 8-8-11 **78** 6ex............ AdrianTNicholls 3 51
(D Nicholls) *t.k.h early: hld up: nt clr run over 2f out: rdn over 1f out: sn btn: b.b.v* **11/2**[2]

1m 10.13s (-2.07) **Going Correction** -0.15s/f (Firm) **9** Ran SP% **115.3**
Speed ratings (Par 107): **107,103,99,99,96 93,93,91,90**
toteswingers: 1&2 £3.70, 1&3 £6.90, 2&3 £6.30 CSF £14.51 CT £93.25 TOTE £3.50: £1.20, £2.00, £3.50; EX 20.10.

Owner Mel Roberts and Ms Nicola Meese **Bred** Dunchurch Lodge Stud Co **Trained** Musley Bank, N Yorks

FOCUS
A decent handicap, which was turned into a procession by the well-backed favourite.

NOTEBOOK
Fishforcompliments suffered a last-gasp defeat over 7f on soft ground at Doncaster on Saturday. He was interesting off the same mark, dropped in trip with cheekpieces refitted here, and he absolutely hammered his opponents under a positive ride to register his first success since his second start August 2006. He will get hit hard for this win but was rated 15lb higher in his prime and should not have too much trouble shrugging off a penalty if turned out quickly. (op 11-4 tchd 3-1)
Vhujon(IRE) did not get much luck and had to be switched out wide to find a run before staying on strongly. He just failed off this mark at Ripon last time, is effective on fast turf and Polytrack, and should be able to resume winning ways in the near future. (op 5-1 tchd 4-1)
Dazzling Bay had something of a renaissance on the all-weather before the turn of the year and was just held over course and distance last time. He tracked the winner for most of the way but had no answer to his enterprising move. He was eventually well held but looks a solid benchmark for the form. (tchd 7-1)
Rasaman(IRE) made an early move to the stands' rail and was not disgraced raised in trip and grade, but he has possibly reached a stalemate with the handicapper since a 4lb rise for his brave win at Thirsk last month. (op 25-1)
Kashimin(IRE) was in a good position for most of the way but did not find much when asked for an effort. A switch to an easier track should help but he looks high enough in the weights on recent evidence. (op 9-1)
Blue Tomato Official explanation: vet said gelding bled from the nose

2815 CASH FOR KIDS LANARK SILVER BELL H'CAP — 1m 4f 17y
8:10 (8:11) (Class 2) (0-90,88) 4-Y-0+
£21,808 (£6,531; £3,265; £1,634; £815; £409) **Stalls** High

Form RPR

0024 **1** **Record Breaker (IRE)**[11] 2486 5-9-10 **88**............(b) RoystonFfrench 3 104
(M Johnston) *cl up: led 3f out: sn qcknd clr: unchal* **7/2**[1]

6242 **2** 5 **Just Lille (IRE)**[2] 2768 6-9-9 **87**............(p) PhillipMakin 6 95
(Mrs A Duffield) *chsd ldrs: effrt and chsd wnr over 2f out: no imp fr over 1f out* **8/1**

2-45 **3** 2 ½ **Lochiel**[19] 2242 5-9-6 **87**............ NeilBrown(3) 13 91+
(G A Swinbank) *unruly to post: hld up: nt clr run over 2f out: hdwy over 1f out: nvr rchd ldrs* **8/1**

6-16 **4** 1 ¼ **Valdan (IRE)**[16] 2315 5-8-5 **76**............ AndrewHeffernan(7) 9 78+
(P D Evans) *hld up: nt clr run fr over 2f out to over 1f out: kpt on fnl f: n.d* **16/1**

2-10 **5** 3 ¼ **Gordonsville**[26] 2055 6-9-0 **83**............ GaryBartley(5) 4 80
(J S Goldie) *hld up: effrt over 2f out: hung rt: nvr rchd ldrs* **5/1**[2]

3304 **6** ¾ **Solas Alainn (IRE)**[18] 2262 4-8-6 **70**............(b) JoeFanning 7 66
(M Johnston) *prom: rdn 3f out: outpcd fr 2f out* **10/1**

-563 **7** 1 ¾ **Bergonzi (IRE)**[16] 2315 5-8-11 **75**............ PaulMulrennan 10 68
(J Howard Johnson) *prom: lost pl over 3f out: n.d after* **20/1**

5120 **8** 1 ½ **Royal Amnesty**[28] 1986 6-9-3 **81**............(b) TomEaves 11 71
(I Semple) *hld up: effrt 3f out: wknd over 1f out* **22/1**

-315 **9** 2 **Demolition**[33] 1850 5-9-5 **88**............(p) BMcHugh(5) 12 75
(N Wilson) *in tch tl rdn and wknd over 2f out* **25/1**

0-00 **10** 2 ¾ **Annibale Caro**[5] 2666 7-8-9 **73** ow2............ DanielTudhope 1 56
(J S Goldie) *t.k.h: led to 3f out: wknd 2f out* **25/1**

-501 **11** 1 ½ **Birkside**[12] 2437 6-8-9 **78**............ FrederikTylicki(5) 8 58
(Miss L A Perratt) *hld up: effrt 3f out: wknd wl over 1f out* **9/1**

20-1 **12** 30 **Haarth Sovereign (IRE)**[54] 1319 5-9-2 **80**............ AdamKirby 5 12
(W R Swinburn) *hld up: drvn over 4f out: sn struggling: t.o* **6/1**[3]

2m 30.52s (-8.08) **Going Correction** -0.425s/f (Firm) course record **12** Ran SP% **117.2**
Speed ratings (Par 109): **109,105,104,103,101 100,99,98,97,95 94,74**
toteswingers: 1&2 £9.30, 1&3 £9.80, 2&3 £9.70 CSF £29.21 CT £206.69 TOTE £5.30: £1.90, £3.00, £2.60; EX 41.20.

Owner Triplin Racing **Bred** Sir E J Loder **Trained** Middleham Moor, N Yorks

FOCUS
Dolling out of the rail added approximately 25 yards to the official race distance. A good handicap.

NOTEBOOK
Record Breaker(IRE) justified strong support in tremendous style and recorded a fast time. There was a slight doubt about how he would cope with a drop back from 2m to 1m4f, but he travelled smoothly for most of the way and the result was never in doubt after he seized the initiative early in the straight. The recent application of blinkers seems to have sharpened up his concentration and he may able to win another decent handicap before the handicapper catches up with him. (op 9-2 tchd 5-1)
Just Lille(IRE) was runner-up in a 1m Listed race at Pontefract just two days earlier. This consistent mare ran a fair race up in trip and back in handicap company, and pulled some way clear of the rest. (op 10-1 tchd 7-1)
Lochiel ended 2008 in fine form and had come back just as good this year. She was beaten a long way here but did best of the hold-up horses and should continue to run well. (op 10-1)
Valdan(IRE) could not find a gap when he needed one and the race was over by the time he saw daylight. He is a bit hit and miss, but the smooth traveller looks the type who could strike again when things go his way. (op 12-1)
Gordonsville plugged on out wide from a long way back but never got anywhere near the leaders. (op 7-1)
Demolition Official explanation: jockey said gelding did not come down the hill

Haarth Sovereign(IRE) Official explanation: trainer's rep had no explanation for the poor form shown

2816 PATERSONS OF GREENOAKHILL (S) STKS — 1m 65y
8:40 (8:40) (Class 6) 4-Y-0+ **£2,914** (£867; £433; £108; £108) **Stalls** High

Form RPR

1234 **1** **Fremen (USA)**[56] 1283 9-9-3 83............ AdrianTNicholls 9 79
(D Nicholls) *racd keenly: hld up in tch: shkn up to ld appr fnl f: r.o* **10/11**[1]

102- **2** 1 **Moody Tunes**[138] 6152 6-9-3 72............ PhillipMakin 1 76
(K R Burke) *led: rdn over 2f out: hdd appr fnl f: edgd lft: kpt on ins fnl f* **15/8**[2]

2-50 **3** 4 ½ **Heureux (USA)**[22] 2156 6-9-3 61............ PaulMulrennan 2 66
(J Howard Johnson) *hld up in tch: hdwy 2f out: kpt on fnl f: nt rch first two* **7/1**[3]

-436 **4** 7 **Beaumont Boy**[4] 2718 5-8-5 51............(b) SFeeney(7) 8 45
(J A McShane) *prom: rdn over 3f out: wknd over 2f out* **18/1**

00-0 **4** dht **Actabou**[16] 2314 4-8-12 59............(t) SladeO'Hara(5) 7 50
(F P Murtagh) *chsd ldrs tl rdn and wknd fr 2f out* **33/1**

500- **6** 6 **Borodinsky**[339] 3755 8-9-3 48............ TomEaves 3 36
(R E Barr) *chsd wnr tl wknd over 2f out* **50/1**

50-0 **7** 1 ¼ **Orpen Bid (IRE)**[19] 2233 4-8-7 40............ GregFairley 6 23
(A M Crow) *hld up: rdn on outside 3f out: sn wknd* **50/1**

1m 46.06s (-2.34) **Going Correction** -0.425s/f (Firm) **7** Ran SP% **111.8**
Speed ratings (Par 101): **94,93,88,81,81 75,74**
toteswingers: 1&2 £1.02, 1&3 £2.40, 2&3 £3.20 CSF £2.62 TOTE £1.70: £1.20, £1.50; EX 2.10.There was no bid for the winner.

Owner Miss C King Mrs A Seed Ms Finola Devaney **Bred** Flaxman Holdings Ltd **Trained** Sessay, N Yorks

FOCUS
Dolling out of the rail added approximately 25 yards to the official race distance.

2817 CENTRAL SCAFFOLDING H'CAP — 1m 3f 16y
9:10 (9:10) (Class 5) (0-70,70) 4-Y-0+ **£3,238** (£963; £481; £240) **Stalls** High

Form RPR

/00- **1** **Ifatfirst (IRE)**[242] 6657 6-8-11 **58**............ DanielTudhope 2 70+
(J S Goldie) *trckd ldrs: effrt over 2f out: styd on strly fnl f: led nr fin* **7/2**[3]

265- **2** nk **Wee Charlie Castle (IRE)**[249] 6472 6-9-9 **70**............ TomEaves 4 79
(I Semple) *stdd in tch: hdwy to ld appr fnl f: kpt on: hdd nr fin* **5/2**[2]

4-00 **3** 2 ¾ **Applaude**[13] 2392 4-9-6 **67**............ PJMcDonald 3 72
(G A Swinbank) *trckd ldr: led over 2f out: edgd rt and hdd appr fnl f: one pce* **7/4**[1]

030/ **4** 11 **Patavian (IRE)**[21] 4036 5-8-9 **58** ow1............(p) PaulMulrennan 1 42
(B Storey) *led to over 2f out: sn rdn and outpcd* **25/1**

0/30 **5** hd **Tommy Tobougg**[13] 2390 5-8-4 **51** oh2............ RoystonFfrench 6 37
(Miss Lucinda V Russell) *hld up last: rdn over 2f out: sn btn* **7/2**[3]

2m 23.25s (-2.35) **Going Correction** -0.425s/f (Firm) **5** Ran SP% **113.2**
Speed ratings (Par 103): **91,90,88,80,80**
toteswingers: 1&2 £6.50. CSF £12.96 TOTE £5.90: £2.10, £1.40; EX 17.80 Place 6: £12.68 , Place 5: £8.35.

Owner Mrs Janis Macpherson **Bred** Mrs Belinda Strudwick **Trained** Uplawmoor, E Renfrews

FOCUS
Dolling out of the rail added approximately 25 yards to the official race distance. A modest race, but there was a thrilling finish.
T/Plt: £14.40 to a £1 stake. Pool: £69,351.11. 3,513.31 winning tickets. T/Qpdt: £8.20 to a £1 stake. Pool: £5,017.02. 450.70 winning tickets. RY

2481 HAYDOCK (L-H)
Wednesday, June 10

OFFICIAL GOING: Good to firm (firm in places; 8.5)
Rail realignment added 25yds to distances on round course.
Wind: Light 1/2 against Weather: Fine

2818 WATERAID RACEDAY ON 3RD JULY H'CAP — 1m 3f 200y
2:10 (2:10) (Class 5) (0-75,72) 4-Y-0+ **£3,238** (£963; £481; £240) **Stalls** Low

Form RPR

0-41 **1** **Gloucester**[9] 2552 6-9-2 **72** 6ex............ FrederikTylicki(5) 2 80
(M J Scudamore) *led: drvn over 2f out: crowded fnl f: hld on gamely* **10/11**[1]

121 **2** shd **Saloon (USA)**[16] 2331 5-9-7 **72**............(p) JamieSpencer 3 80
(Jane Chapple-Hyam) *hld up: hdwy to trck ldrs over 5f out: nt clr run over 3f out tl over 1f out: chal and edgd lft: carried hld high: jst hld* **2/1**[2]

5020 **3** 4 ½ **All In The Red (IRE)**[4] 2724 4-9-7 **72**............(p) LDettori 1 73
(A Crook) *dwlt: jnd wnr after 3f: drvn over 4f out: one pce fnl 2f* **6/1**[3]

1035 **4** 7 **Masterofceremonies**[13] 2392 6-9-0 **65**............ DarrenMoffatt 5 54
(James Moffatt) *sn chsng ldrs: pushed along over 5f out: sn outpcd: rallied over 2f out: wandered and wknd over 1f out* **12/1**

2m 33.76s (0.56) **Going Correction** -0.125s/f (Firm) **4** Ran SP% **107.7**
Speed ratings (Par 103): **93,92,89,85**
CSF £2.95 TOTE £2.00; EX 3.70.

Owner S M Smith & Keith Hunter **Bred** Juddmonte Farms Ltd **Trained** Bromsash, Herefordshire
■ Stewards' Enquiry : Jamie Spencer caution: careless riding
L Dettori two-day ban: used whip with erxcessive frequency without giving gelding time to respond (Jun 25-26)

FOCUS
Just the four runners and this was an ordinary handicap for the grade.

2819 CANCER RESEARCH RACEDAY ON 18TH JULY MAIDEN FILLIES' STKS — 6f
2:40 (2:40) (Class 5) 2-Y-0 **£3,238** (£963; £481; £240) **Stalls** Centre

Form RPR

2 **1** **Jeanie Johnston (IRE)**[19] 2226 2-9-0 0............ LiamJones 7 87+
(K R Burke) *mde all: clr over 1f out: v readily* **5/2**[1]

2 3 **Faith Jicaro (IRE)** 2-8-9 0............ DeanHeslop(5) 6 76+
(Mrs L Williamson) *chsd wnr: kpt on same pce appr fnl f* **66/1**

3 4 **Marie De Medici (USA)** 2-9-0 0............ GregFairley 8 64+
(M Johnston) *sn w ldrs: rdn and outpcd over 2f out: styd on ins fnl f: improve* **5/2**[1]

4 1 ¼ **Reallymissgreeley (USA)** 2-9-0 0............ NCallan 3 60+
(K A Ryan) *s.i.s: sn chsng ldrs: wknd ins fnl f* **7/1**[2]

5 4 **Sand Vixen** 2-9-0 0............ LDettori 2 48
(Saeed Bin Suroor) *dwlt: hld up: effrt and swtchd lft over 2f out: wknd over 1f out* **5/2**[1]

6 3 1/2 **Revoltinthedesert** 2-9-0 0 .... RichardMullen 4 38
(E S McMahon) *chsd ldrs: outpcd and lost pl over 3f out* **14/1**[3]

7 2 **Rank Bajin** 2-9-0 0 .... GrahamGibbons 1 32
(E J Alston) *chsd ldrs: lost pl over 3f out* **18/1**

1m 13.09s (-0.91) **Going Correction** -0.125s/f (Firm) **7** Ran SP% **111.6**
Speed ratings (Par 90): **101,97,91,90,84 80,77**
toteswingers: 1&2 £8.10, 1&3 £2.30, 2&3 £28.60 CSF £131.20 TOTE £3.90: £2.20, £10.10; EX 110.90.
Owner Cyril Wall **Bred** Eugene McDermott **Trained** Middleham Moor, N Yorks

FOCUS
Some big stables were represented and this race should produce winners, but the bare form looks no better than fair.

NOTEBOOK
Jeanie Johnston(IRE) improved on the form she showed when runner-up on heavy ground in an ordinary C&D maiden on her debut. Having displayed a good cruising speed, she gradually drew clear for a convincing success and looks a useful filly in the making. Her connections think the Albany Stakes is likely to come too soon and will instead look to step her up in class at Newmarket's July meeting. (op 7-4)
Faith Jicaro(IRE), a 10,000gns purchase, displayed a pronounced knee action. She showed ability in a clear second and might do better again on easier ground. (op 80-1 tchd 100-1)
Marie De Medici(USA), a $340,000 half-sister to 1m winner Hurricane Mist, and 7f scorer Roman Republic, out of a high-class dual 1m1f winner, showed early speed but was left behind late on. This represents only a modest effort but she can be expected to improve a good deal in time. (op 3-1 tchd 10-3)
Reallymissgreeley(USA), a 75,000gns purchase, started slowly and gave the impression she'll come on plenty for the experience. (op 10-1 tchd 12-1)
Sand Vixen, whose sales price increased from 30,000gns as a yearling to 130,000gns this year, is a half-sister to, among others, very useful sprinter So Will I. She didn't show a great deal but looked pretty green. (op 9-4 tchd 11-4)
Revoltinthedesert Official explanation: jockey said filly was unsuited by the good to firm (firm in places) ground

2820 PRINCE'S TRUST RACEDAY ON 15TH SEPTEMBER MAIDEN STKS 6f
3:10 (3:10) (Class 5) 3-Y-O+ **£3,238** (£963; £481; £240) **Stalls** Centre

Form RPR

0 **1** **Sleepy Blue Ocean**[58] 1255 3-9-2 0 .... LDettori 9 68
(J Noseda) *dwlt: chsd ldrs: sn drvn along: edgd lft and styd on to ld over 1f out: drvn out* **9/2**[3]

3-0 **2** 3/4 **Say You Say Me**[25] 2070 3-8-11 0 .... GregFairley 6 61
(N J Vaughan) *chsd ldrs: rdn and hung lft over 2f out: styd on to take 2nd ins fnl f: no ex* **10/3**[2]

043 **3** 1 1/4 **Josphiel (IRE)**[18] 2268 4-8-12 50 ....(b) BillyCray(7) 7 59?
(A Berry) *chsd ldrs: led and edgd rt over 2f out: hdd over 1f out: kpt on towards fin* **14/1**

5 **4** nk **Dilli Dancer**[20] 2205 4-9-0 0 .... GabrielHannon(5) 2 58
(G D Blake) *trckd ldrs: t.k.h: upsides whn sltly hmpd over 1f out: kpt on same pce* **3/1**[1]

5 6 **King Of Eden (IRE)** 3-9-2 0 .... DaleGibson 8 41
(E J Alston) *s.i.s: outpcd and lost pl after 2f* **10/1**

6 8 **Star Addition** 3-9-2 0 .... GrahamGibbons 10 —
(E J Alston) *racd keenly: led tl hdd over 2f out: sn lost pl* **10/3**[2]

6000 **7** 69 **Floods Of Tears**[44] 1573 3-8-11 45 ....(b) LiamJones 4 —
(D Flood) *s.v.s: wl bhd: virtually p.u: hopelessly t.o* **33/1**

1m 14.35s (0.35) **Going Correction** -0.125s/f (Firm)
WFA 3 from 4yo 8lb **7** Ran SP% **108.0**
Speed ratings (Par 103): **92,91,89,88,80 70,—**
toteswingers: 1&2 £2.50, 1&3 £5.70, 2&3 £4.60 CSF £17.58 TOTE £4.00: £1.80, £1.90; EX 12.90.
Owner Five Arrows Racing **Bred** Exors Of The Late N Ahamad & P C Scott **Trained** Newmarket, Suffolk

FOCUS
This looked a really weak maiden and the winning time was over a second slower than the earlier juvenile fillies' contest won by Jeanie Johnston.
Dilli Dancer Official explanation: jockey said filly was unsuited by the good to firm (firm in places) ground

2821 EUROPEAN BREEDERS' FUND H'CAP 6f
3:40 (3:42) (Class 3) (0-95,94) 3-Y-O **£9,066** (£2,697; £1,348; £673) **Stalls** Centre

Form RPR

1-45 **1** **Global City (IRE)**[18] 2279 3-9-7 94 ....(t) LDettori 4 107+
(Saeed Bin Suroor) *trckd ldrs: shkn up to ld over 1f out: r.o strly: v readily* **3/1**[1]

5112 **2** 2 1/4 **White Shift (IRE)**[7] 2611 3-8-4 77 .... RichardMullen 8 81
(P Howling) *hld up: effrt over 2f out: wnt 2nd 1f out: no imp* **10/3**[2]

0-64 **3** 2 1/4 **Spiritofthewest (IRE)**[12] 2443 3-8-7 80 .... PaulMulrennan 5 77
(D H Brown) *hld up in rr: effrt over 2f out: kpt on fnl f* **10/3**[2]

4-40 **4** 1/2 **Desert Falls**[34] 1803 3-8-9 85 .... MichaelJStainton(3) 3 80
(R M Whitaker) *led tl hdd over 1f out: kpt on same pce* **16/1**

20-0 **5** 3/4 **Diggeratt (USA)**[20] 2198 3-8-2 75 .... DaleGibson 5 68
(R A Fahey) *chsd ldrs: one pce fnl 2f* **16/1**

14-0 **6** 1 1/2 **Calligrapher (USA)**[18] 2279 3-9-2 89 .... PhilipRobinson 1 77
(M A Jarvis) *hood removed v late: hld up in rr: effrt over 2f out: wknd over 1f out* **11/1**

055- **7** 2 1/2 **Parisian Art (IRE)**[249] 6466 3-9-2 89 .... NCallan 7 69
(J Noseda) *in rr: effrt over 2f out: hung lft and sn wknd* **15/2**[3]

021- **8** 1 3/4 **Wedding List**[195] 7458 3-8-11 84 .... LiamJones 2 58
(W J Haggas) *w ldr: edgd lft 2f out: sn wknd* **8/1**

1m 12.73s (-1.27) **Going Correction** -0.125s/f (Firm) **8** Ran SP% **114.1**
Speed ratings (Par 103): **103,100,97,96,95 93,90,87**
toteswingers: 1&2 £2.20, 1&3 £5.60, 2&3 £3.80 CSF £13.13 CT £34.21 TOTE £3.90: £1.50, £1.60, £1.80; EX 10.80.
Owner Godolphin **Bred** Mrs Monica Hackett **Trained** Newmarket, Suffolk

FOCUS
A reasonable 3yo sprint handicap.

NOTEBOOK
Global City(IRE) stepped up on his two previous efforts this season with a convincing success. He's evidently very useful, but that said, things are likely to be much tougher in future and he might struggle to follow up. (tchd 11-4 and 7-2)
White Shift(IRE) has been in cracking form since being picked up by her current connections and this was another solid effort. She was clear of the remainder and is one to keep on side for the time being. (op 3-1)
Spiritofthewest(IRE) ran okay but he still looks high enough in the weights. His best form has been achieved on easy ground over 5f. (op 5-1)
Desert Falls had his chance under a positive ride.
Diggeratt(USA) had given the impression she would be suited by the return to quick ground, so this was disappointing. (tchd 20-1)
Calligrapher(USA) started slowly, with his jockey possibly a bit late in removing the blindfold, but that doesn't really excuse this below-par showing. (op 8-1)
Parisian Art(IRE) went without his usual blinkers after 249 days off and offered little. (op 12-1)
Wedding List looked a nice prospect when winning an ordinary Great Leighs maiden on her final start at two, but she was a little keen early after 195 days off and appeared to find the ground plenty quick enough. An easier surface should suit this daughter of Pivotal and it's worth noting she took a couple of runs to find her best form last year. (op 11-2)

2822 RACING WELFARE RACEDAY ON 5TH NOVEMBER H'CAP 1m 30y
4:10 (4:10) (Class 3) (0-90,92) 4-Y-O+ **£9,066** (£2,697; £1,348; £673) **Stalls** Low

Form RPR

-052 **1** **Ezdeyaad (USA)**[7] 2589 5-8-8 77 .... PaulMulrennan 3 87
(G A Swinbank) *mde all: qcknd over 5f out: clr over 3f out: edgd rt: unchal* **8/1**

-045 **2** 2 1/2 **Gala Casino Star (IRE)**[14] 2374 4-8-10 84 .... FrederikTylicki(5) 9 88
(R A Fahey) *swtchd lft s: hld up in rr: hdwy on outside 3f out: hung lft 2f out: sn chsng wnr: no imp* **7/2**[2]

55-1 **3** 2 **Tanto Faz (IRE)**[24] 2101 4-9-4 87 .... LiamJones 1 87
(W J Haggas) *hld up in rr: effrt over 3f out: hmpd 2f out: kpt on same pce* **15/8**[1]

5100 **4** nk **Orpen Wide (IRE)**[31] 1722 7-8-12 84 ....(b) LeeVickers(3) 8 83
(M C Chapman) *chsd ldrs: one pce fnl 2f* **20/1**

50-0 **5** 1 1/4 **Reel Buddy Star**[26] 2043 4-8-5 74 ow1 .... SaleemGolam 5 70
(G M Moore) *chsd ldrs: drvn over 3f out: fdd fnl f* **16/1**

-653 **6** 1/2 **Capucci**[7] 2612 4-8-9 78 ....(t) GrahamGibbons 4 73
(J J Quinn) *trckd ldrs: effrt over 3f out: wknd fnl f* **5/1**[3]

0122 **7** 13 **Mujood**[6] 2639 6-9-5 88 .... StephenCarson 2 53
(Eve Johnson Houghton) *in rr: drvn over 4f out: sn bhd: eased over 1f out* **5/1**[3]

1m 43.34s (-0.46) **Going Correction** -0.125s/f (Firm) **7** Ran SP% **112.1**
Speed ratings (Par 107): **97,94,92,92,90 90,77**
toteswingers: 1&2 £6.00, 1&3 £3.90, 2&3 £3.30 CSF £34.53 CT £73.69 TOTE £7.80: £2.40, £2.40; EX 37.80.
Owner Elsa Crankshaw, G Allan M Wane B Boanson **Bred** Caldara Farm **Trained** Melsonby, N Yorks

FOCUS
Just a fair handicap for the grade.

NOTEBOOK
Ezdeyaad(USA) showed a good attitude under a front-running ride. Although setting a reasonable pace, he was crucially unchallenged and ran on strongly. His strike-rate means he'll make little appeal off a higher mark next time. (op 7-1)
Gala Casino Star(IRE) ruined his chance by hanging left in the closing stages and could make no real impression on the winner. (op 4-1 tchd 9-2)
Tanto Faz(IRE), 4lb higher than when winning on easier ground at Ripon on his previous start, struggled to get involved and probably would have preferred a stronger-run race. Some give underfoot may also have suited better. (op 9-4 tchd 5-2)
Orpen Wide(IRE) didn't seem to have any excuses. (op 25-1 tchd 16-1)
Capucci was disappointing and might have found the ground too quick. (op 9-2 tchd 4-1)
Mujood Official explanation: jockey said gelding ran flat

2823 BEST HORSE RACING SKY CHANNEL 432 H'CAP 1m 2f 95y
4:40 (4:40) (Class 4) (0-85,83) 4-Y-O+ **£5,504** (£1,637; £818; £408) **Stalls** High

Form RPR

-005 **1** **Emperor Court (IRE)**[82] 893 5-9-0 76 .... NCallan 1 89+
(P J Makin) *mde all: qcknd over 4f out: rdn clr 1f out: heavily eased towards fin* **9/4**[2]

0300 **2** 4 1/2 **Snow Dancer (IRE)**[15] 2362 5-8-5 67 ow1 ....(p) GrahamGibbons 5 68
(H A McWilliams) *trckd wnr: chal over 4f out: kpt on same pce fnl 2f* **8/1**

55-3 **3** shd **Mega Watt (IRE)**[27] 2003 4-9-0 76 .... LDettori 2 77
(W Jarvis) *sn chsng ldrs: drvn 4f out: one pce fnl 2f* **5/6**[1]

2-00 **4** 3 1/2 **Shaloo Diamond**[20] 2197 4-9-0 79 .... MichaelJStainton(3) 4 73
(R M Whitaker) *hld up in last: hdwy on outside 4f out: chsng ldrs over 2f out: wknd jst ins fnl f* **7/1**[3]

2m 14.4s (1.40) **Going Correction** -0.125s/f (Firm) **4** Ran SP% **108.9**
Speed ratings (Par 105): **98,94,94,91**
CSF £16.39 TOTE £3.50; EX 18.80 Place 6: £219.38, Place 5: £113.57.
Owner Four Seasons Racing Ltd **Bred** John O'Connor **Trained** Ogbourne Maisey, Wilts

FOCUS
Form to treat with caution as the winner was allowed a very easy lead.
T/Plt: £240.90 to a £1 stake. Pool: £55,528.70. 168.23 winning tickets. T/Qpdt: £37.90 to a £1 stake. Pool: £3,628.82. 70.70 winning tickets. WG

2595 KEMPTON (A.W) (R-H)
Wednesday, June 10

OFFICIAL GOING: Standard
Wind: Moderate behind Weather: Dull

2824 WEATHERBYS PRINTING APPRENTICE H'CAP (ROUND 2) 1m (P)
6:20 (6:21) (Class 5) (0-70,70) 4-Y-O+ **£2,590** (£770; £385; £192) **Stalls** High

Form RPR

2-40 **1** **Desert Kiss**[15] 2352 4-9-7 67 .... AndreaAtzeni 10 80+
(W R Swinburn) *s.i.s: hld up in rr: hdwy on ins fr 3f out: drvn and qcknd to ld ins fnl f: readily* **7/2**[1]

3541 **2** 2 1/4 **Teen Ager (FR)**[13] 2400 5-8-12 61 .... LeeNewnes(3) 7 69
(P Burgoyne) *trckd ldrs: wnt 2nd over 2f out: led appr fnl f: hdd and readily outpcd ins fnl f* **10/1**

0244 **3** 3 **Bold Marc (IRE)**[13] 2402 7-9-7 70 .... DeclanCannon(3) 14 71
(K R Burke) *led: rdn 2f out: hdd appr fnl f: wknd ins fnl f* **4/1**[2]

3234 **4** nk **Murrin (IRE)**[45] 1539 5-9-7 70 .... PNolan(3) 6 70
(T G Mills) *chsd ldrs: rdn over 2f out: styd on fnl f: nvr gng pce to be competitive* **7/1**[3]

4340 **5** 1 1/4 **Royal Envoy (IRE)**[18] 2276 6-9-8 68 .... JackDean 8 66
(P Howling) *broke wl: stdd in rr after 1f: rdn and styd on fnl 2f: nvr in contention* **11/1**

6032 **6** 2 1/4 **Phluke**[18] 2257 8-9-2 69 ....(v) DanielBlackett(7) 12 61
(Eve Johnson Houghton) *chsd ldr tl over 2f out: sn pushed along: hung lft fr over 1f out* **8/1**

3210 **7** 3/4 **Comrade Cotton**[7] 2608 5-8-8 59 ....(p) RyanPowell(5) 3 50
(J Ryan) *in rr: sme hdwy over 2f out: nvr in contention* **20/1**

6524 **8** 1/2 **Rock Anthem (IRE)**[11] 2493 5-8-13 64 .... BarryAdams(5) 2 53
(Mike Murphy) *plld hrd in rr: mod prog fnl 2f* **12/1**

0-00 **9** 2 1/4 **Jay Gee Wigmo**[11] 2473 4-8-5 51 oh3 .... AmyBaker 13 35
(A W Carroll) *chsd ldrs over 5f* **33/1**

2114 **10** *1 3/4* **Agilete**[58] 1261 7-9-4 **67** SimonPearce(3) 4 47
(J Pearce) *c wd 3f out: a towards rr* **15/2**

00-0 **11** *1 1/4* **Hey Presto**[27] 2011 9-8-0 **51** oh6 RichardRowe(5) 9 28
(R Rowe) *in tch over 5f* **66/1**

6540 **12** *10* **Lopinot (IRE)**[14] 2387 6-8-13 **64** (v) GemmaElford(5) 5 18
(M R Bosley) *s.i.s: plld hrd early: a bhd* **12/1**

1m 39.38s (-0.42) **Going Correction** 0.0s/f (Stan) **12** Ran SP% **119.6**
Speed ratings (Par 103): **102,99,96,96,95 92,92,91,89,87 86,76**
toteswingers: 1&2 £9.00, 1&3 £4.50, 2&3 £12.40 CSF £38.83 CT £150.47 TOTE £3.90: £1.30, £3.50, £2.20; EX 40.10.

Owner The Capers **Bred** C R Mason **Trained** Aldbury, Herts

FOCUS
An apprentice handicap which featured plenty with chances. It was run at a reasonable pace with Bold Marc soon taking his customary role at the head of affairs.

2825 KEMPTON FOR OUTDOOR EVENTS MAIDEN AUCTION STKS 6f (P)
6:50 (6:54) (Class 5) 2-Y-0 **£2,590** (£770; £385; £192) **Stalls** High

Form RPR

23 **1** **Iver Bridge Lad**[56] 1290 2-8-6 0 MarcHalford(3) 3 93+
(J Ryan) *sn trcking ldr: led appr fnl 2f: puhed clr over 1f out: easily* **3/1**[2]

2 *5* **Noble Greek (USA)** 2-8-10 0 RobertWinston 12 79+
(J R Best) *chsd ldrs: rdn over 2f out: wnt 2nd over 1f out but nvr any ch w wnr* **5/2**[1]

3 *4 1/2* **King Of Reason** 2-9-0 0 JamieSpencer 2 68+
(D M Simcock) *drvn to chse ldrs fr s then t.k.h: styd in tch: pushed along and green over 2f out: styd on wl fnl f to take 3rd nr fin but nvr any ch w ldng duo* **8/1**

202 **4** *1/2* **I'Malwaysright (IRE)**[7] 2595 2-8-13 0 (b) RobertHavlin 4 65
(D R C Elsworth) *led to s: led: rdn and hdd appr fnl 2f: wknd fnl f and lost 2nd cl home* **6/1**[3]

5 *1* **Marafong** 2-8-11 0 AmirQuinn 9 60
(Miss J Feilden) *chsd ldrs: rdn over 2f out: no imp and wknd over 1f out* **25/1**

5 **6** *1* **One Hit Wonder**[7] 2595 2-8-10 0 NeilChalmers 6 56
(Mouse Hamilton-Fairley) *in tch: rdn 3f out: nvr in contention and wknd over 1f out* **20/1**

7 *4* **Sancho Panza** 2-8-2 0 MatthewCosham(7) 10 43
(Miss J Feilden) *chsd ldrs early: bhd after 2f* **33/1**

8 *8* **Anitra's Dance** 2-8-6 0 JimmyQuinn 1 16
(P Howling) *slowly away: green and a in rr* **50/1**

9 *1 1/2* **Dimaire** 2-8-1 0 ow1 AndreaAtzeni(5) 7 12
(D Haydn Jones) *s.i.s: a in rr* **9/1**

10 *2* **Truly Magic** 2-8-5 0 WilliamBuick 8 5
(H J L Dunlop) *unruly in paddock: a in rr: rdn 1/2-way: eased whn no ch fr over 1f out* **8/1**

11 *1 1/2* **Dunwhinny** 2-8-9 0 IanMongan 11 4
(P W D'Arcy) *a in rr* **14/1**

12 *5* **Mater Mater** 2-8-4 0 MartinDwyer 5 —
(Andrew Reid) *s.i.s: a bhd* **66/1**

1m 12.52s (-0.58) **Going Correction** 0.0s/f (Stan) **12** Ran SP% **121.7**
Speed ratings (Par 93): **103,96,90,89,88 87,81,71,69,66 64,57**
toteswingers: 1&2 £2,40, 1&3 £5.70, 2&3 £4.50 CSF £10.67 TOTE £3.80: £1.50, £1.80, £2.80; EX 11.80.

Owner The Iver Lads **Bred** J C S Wilson Bloodstock **Trained** Newmarket, Suffolk

■ Stewards' Enquiry : Robert Havlin two-day ban: one for failing to ride to draw; one for careless riding (Jun 24-25)

FOCUS
Only three with previous racecourse form. Run at a decent gallop, this could prove to be an above average maiden.

NOTEBOOK
Iver Bridge Lad had been unfortunate to bump into a couple of decent sorts on previous outings over the minimum trip, but confirmed connections belief he would be better when stepped up to 6f. Always travelling up with the pace, he took it up in the straight, and soon powered clear. This was an impressive performance from a nice-looking individual. He is progressing well and the crack at the Coventry Stakes is next on the agenda. (op 15-8 tchd 100-30 in places)
Noble Greek(USA) showed plenty of pace and was always racing up with the principals. Although no match for the winner, this was a very promising debut. If he progresses, he should soon go one better. (op 8-1 tchd 9-4)
King Of Reason was another to make a pleasing debut. He raced just off the pace and did not seem to handle the home bend, but stuck on to snatch third towards the finish. He will benefit from this experience. (op 13-2)
I'Malwaysright(IRE) set a blistering pace and paid the price. He had little to offer after being headed in the straight. (op 9-2)
Marafong ran green early on. He managed to keep tabs on the leaders, although was never a threat. (op 50-1 tchd 22-1)
Truly Magic Official explanation: jockey said filly lost its action

2826 DIGIBET H'CAP 6f (P)
7:20 (7:22) (Class 4) (0-80,79) 3-Y-0 **£4,727** (£1,054; £1,054; £351) **Stalls** High

Form RPR

414 **1** **Devil You Know (IRE)**[22] 2148 3-9-6 **78** JimmyFortune 7 83
(D R C Elsworth) *sn trcking ldrs: rdn: edgd lft and led ins fnl f: hld on wl* **7/2**[2]

2-05 **2** *nk* **Indian Art (IRE)**[39] 1677 3-9-3 **75** PatDobbs 6 79
(R Hannon) *trckd ldrs: rdn 2f out: chal wl ins fnl f: no ex cl home* **7/1**

-21 **2** *dht* **Lochan Mor**[12] 2455 3-9-3 **75** JamieSpencer 2 79
(M L W Bell) *sn led: rdn and edgd lft fr ins fnl 2f: hdd ins fnl f: rallied and kpt on again nr fin* **3/1**[1]

-115 **4** *1/2* **Seek The Fair Land**[32] 1870 3-9-4 **76** PatCosgrave 9 78
(J R Boyle) *sn chsng ldrs: drvn to chal 1f out: no ex cl home* **7/2**[2]

-404 **5** *1 3/4* **Mac's Power (IRE)**[7] 2596 3-8-12 **70** (t) RobertHavlin 1 66
(P J O'Gorman) *s.i.s: sn in tch: pushed along 2f out: kpt on fnl f but nvr gng pce to trble ldrs* **25/1**

4-00 **6** *3/4* **Caledonia Princess**[25] 2079 3-9-3 **75** JimmyQuinn 10 69
(R Curtis) *chsd ldrs: styd towads far rail and ev ch over 1f out: wknd ins fnl f* **9/1**

41P- **7** *1 3/4* **Desert Icon (IRE)**[313] 4588 3-9-7 **79** JimCrowley 5 67
(W J Knight) *towards rr: pushed along fr 3f out: styd on same pce fnl 2f* **12/1**

0363 **8** *8* **Sir Geoffrey (IRE)**[14] 2373 3-9-5 **77** (t) TolleyDean 8 40
(A J McCabe) *plld hrd: a towards rr* **16/1**

02-4 **9** *1* **Diddums**[16] 2336 3-9-5 **77** SebSanders 11 37
(J W Hills) *hmpd on ins after 1f: a in rr* **6/1**[3]

2146 **10** *2* **Trip Switch**[37] 1744 3-8-12 **70** (b[1]) MartinDwyer 3 23
(W R Muir) *a in rr* **16/1**

1m 12.63s (-0.47) **Going Correction** 0.0s/f (Stan) **10** Ran SP% **129.5**
Speed ratings (Par 101): **103,102,102,101,99 98,96,85,84,81**PL Indian Art 2.90, Lochan Mor £1.10. Exacta: DYK & IA £24.10, DYK & LM £11.70. CSF: DYK & IA £16.04, DYK & LM £8.18. Tricast: DYN, IA & LM £43.65, DYK, LM & IA £37.89toteswingers: 1&IA £11.10, 1&LM £4.20, IA&LM £6.70 TOTE £6.00: £2.10 027 Trifecta £Owner Raymond Tooth Bred.

FOCUS
A strong-looking handicap featuring a number of progressive types, which was run at a decent pace.
Lochan Mor Official explanation: jockey said colt hung left

2827 DIGIBET FILLIES' H'CAP 7f (P)
7:50 (7:51) (Class 5) (0-70,70) 3-Y-0 **£2,590** (£770; £385; £192) **Stalls** High

Form RPR

-356 **1** **Russian Rave**[11] 2498 3-9-3 **66** WilliamBuick 14 76
(J G Portman) *hld up in mid-div: swtchd lft to outside over 2f out: sn rdn: styd on wl appr fnl f to ld fnl 110yds: won gng away* **11/2**[2]

03-0 **2** *3* **Foxtrot Alpha (IRE)**[34] 1808 3-9-7 **70** IanMongan 12 71
(P Winkworth) *chsd ldrs: wnt 2nd over 3f out: drvn to ld wl over 1f out: hdd and outpcd fnl 110yds* **16/1**

-460 **3** *3 1/2* **Athania (IRE)**[20] 2198 3-9-0 **70** MatthewDavies(7) 4 62
(A P Jarvis) *led after 1f: rdn over 2f out: hdd wl over 1f out: wknd ins fnl f* **8/1**

0-30 **4** *1/2* **Caster Sugar (USA)**[9] 2539 3-9-2 **65** PatDobbs 8 56
(R Hannon) *towards rr: pushed along over 2f out: styd on ins fnl f but nvr gng pce to rch ldrs* **10/1**

32-0 **5** *1/2* **Penperth**[57] 1269 3-9-4 **67** LukeMorris 1 56
(J M P Eustace) *s.i.s: in rr: hdwy on far side over 2f out: styd on fnl f but nvr gng pce to rch ldrs in centre of crse* **20/1**

0-45 **6** *2* **One Cool Kitty**[41] 1618 3-8-13 **65** JackMitchell(3) 13 49
(M G Quinlan) *led 1f: styd chsng ldrs: rdn over 2f out: wknd fnl f* **10/1**

00-0 **7** *1 3/4* **Barbee (IRE)**[37] 1743 3-9-3 **66** (b[1]) JimmyFortune 11 45
(E A L Dunlop) *s.i.s: sn rcvrd into mid-div: hdwy to chse ldrs 3f out: sn rdn: wknd over 1f out* **20/1**

0-00 **8** *1 3/4* **Alexander Loyalty (IRE)**[22] 2160 3-9-2 **65** LPKeniry 7 39
(E F Vaughan) *n.m.r in rr after 1f: nvr in contention* **10/1**

2416 **9** *2* **Lighthearted (FR)**[12] 2431 3-9-7 **70** PhilipRobinson 10 39
(C G Cox) *chsd ldrs: towards outside 3f out and sn wknd* **5/1**[1]

5100 **10** *2* **Taste Of Honey (IRE)**[15] 2355 3-8-13 **62** MartinDwyer 5 26
(D W P Arbuthnot) *a towards rr* **25/1**

020- **11** *1 3/4* **Timeless Dream**[188] 7546 3-9-7 **70** AlanMunro 2 29
(P W Chapple-Hyam) *a in rr* **7/1**[3]

33-0 **12** *1 3/4* **Sussex Dancer (IRE)**[30] 1937 3-9-5 **68** ShaneKelly 3 22
(J A Osborne) *s.i.s: sn chsng ldrs: rdn and wknd 3f out* **7/1**[3]

6-50 **13** *1 1/4* **Ariadnes Filly (IRE)**[23] 2122 3-9-0 **63** (e[1]) JimCrowley 6 14
(Mrs A J Perrett) *a in rr* **14/1**

004- **14** *5* **Dicey Affair**[190] 7524 3-9-3 **66** GeorgeBaker 9 3
(G L Moore) *in tch over 4f* **14/1**

1m 26.34s (0.34) **Going Correction** 0.0s/f (Stan) **14** Ran SP% **128.0**
Speed ratings (Par 96): **98,94,90,90,89 87,85,83,80,78 76,74,73,67**
toteswingers: 1&2 £21.60, 1&3 £20.40, 2&3 £33.50 CSF £94.06 CT £743.86 TOTE £7.40: £2.30, £7.30, £4.20; EX 81.70.

Owner The Traditionalists **Bred** P A & M J Reditt & Morton Bloodstock **Trained** Compton, Berks

FOCUS
A ready performance from Russian Rave in an open-looking fillies' handicap.
Lighthearted(FR) Official explanation: jockey said filly hung badly left throughout

2828 DIGIBET.COM H'CAP 7f (P)
8:20 (8:21) (Class 4) (0-85,84) 4-Y-0+ **£4,727** (£1,406; £702; £351) **Stalls** High

Form RPR

3562 **1** **Silaah**[13] 2396 5-9-3 **80** TPO'Shea 6 91
(E A L Dunlop) *help up towards rr: hdwy over 2f out: styd on wl fr over 1f out to ld fnl 75yds: in command cl home* **6/1**[3]

-021 **2** *3/4* **Woodcote Place**[20] 2188 6-9-6 **83** JimCrowley 14 92
(P R Chamings) *chsd ldrs: rdn over 2f out: led appr fnl f: hdd and one pce fnl 75yds* **11/2**[2]

1036 **3** *1 1/2* **Grey Boy (GER)**[11] 2491 8-8-13 **76** ShaneKelly 9 81
(A W Carroll) *hld up in tch: swtchd lft 2f out and qcknd to chse ldrs fnl f but no imp fnl 110yds* **12/1**

3001 **4** *nk* **Kipchak (IRE)**[21] 2185 4-8-12 **75** (p) SebSanders 11 79
(C R Dore) *led: rdn over 2f out: hdd wl over 1f out: styd on same pce ins fnl f* **8/1**

1-30 **5** *1* **Romany Princess (IRE)**[26] 2050 4-9-7 **84** PatDobbs 4 85
(R Hannon) *sn chsng ldr: rdn over 2f out: styd wl there tl wknd fnl 110yds* **20/1**

2112 **6** *1/2* **Elisiario (IRE)**[14] 2387 4-8-13 **76** PatCosgrave 13 76
(J R Boyle) *chsd ldrs: drvn to chal 2f out: led briefly wl over 1f out: wknd ins fnl f* **11/2**[2]

5042 **7** *1/2* **Credit Swap**[11] 2491 4-8-13 **76** SteveDrowne 5 75+
(M Wigham) *in rr: pushed along over 2f out: kpt on fnl f but nvr a threat* **12/1**

0-05 **8** *3/4* **Countdown**[26] 2050 7-9-5 **82** AlanMunro 10 81
(M D Squance) *in rr: hung rt whn shkn up 2f: styd on fnl f but nvr in contention* **12/1**

6600 **9** *1 3/4* **Count Ceprano (IRE)**[16] 2326 5-8-9 **72** LukeMorris 12 64
(C R Dore) *in rr: hdwy on ins fr 3f out: effrt 2f out: wknd fnl f* **25/1**

00-6 **10** *hd* **Binanti**[19] 2241 9-9-1 **78** GeorgeBaker 1 69
(P R Chamings) *in rr: mod prog over 1f out* **40/1**

1300 **11** *7* **Trafalgar Square**[12] 2434 7-9-7 **84** PaulDoe 7 57
(M J Attwater) *s.i.s: a towards rr* **20/1**

/04- **12** *nk* **Flashy Photon**[380] 2460 4-8-13 **76** FergusSweeney 8 48
(H Candy) *in tch: hmpd over 3f out and sn bhd* **14/1**

0-16 **13** *1/2* **Twilight Star (IRE)**[25] 2083 5-9-3 **80** LPKeniry 3 50
(R A Teal) *chsd ldrs tl wknd over 2f out* **20/1**

4-04 **14** *4 1/2* **Priti Fabulous (IRE)**[25] 2083 4-9-5 **82** JamieSpencer 2 40
(W J Haggas) *in tch: wknd fr 3f out* **9/2**[1]

1m 25.03s (-0.97) **Going Correction** 0.0s/f (Stan) **14** Ran SP% **124.7**
Speed ratings (Par 105): **105,104,102,102,100 100,99,98,96,96 88,88,87,82**
toteswingers: 1&2 £6.20, 1&3 £10.50, 2&3 £52.80 CSF £37.29 CT £408.02 TOTE £5.20: £1.90, £2.60, £4.70; EX 45.60.

Owner Hamdan Al Maktoum **Bred** Bearstone Stud **Trained** Newmarket, Suffolk

FOCUS
An open-looking heat but with plenty of exposed types which was run at a decent pace.

Priti Fabulous(IRE) Official explanation: jockey said filly never travelled

2829 RENE & BRIAN MITCHELL H'CAP 1m 4f (P)
8:50 (8:52) (Class 4) (0-85,84) 3-Y-O £4,727 (£1,406; £702; £351) Stalls Centre

Form RPR
5-31 1 **Final Victory**[19] 2232 3-9-3 **80** LPKeniry 5 86
(A M Balding) *trckd ldrs in 3rd: drvn to go 2nd 2f out: str chal 1f out: led fnl 110yds: readily* **11/4**[1]
01 2 ½ **Ostaadi**[36] 1780 3-9-1 **78** PhilipRobinson 2 83
(M A Jarvis) *led after 1f: pushed along and qckn d fr over 3f out: hrd drvn whn chal 1f out: hdd fnl 110yds: readily hld by wnr cl home* **3/1**[2]
1-03 3 1¼ **Calaloo (IRE)**[23] 2138 3-9-1 **78** SteveDrowne 7 81
(C R Egerton) *trckd ldrs: drvn along over 2f out: styd on fr over 1f out but nvr gng pce to trble ldng duo* **7/1**
5210 4 2¼ **Gilded Age**[26] 2060 3-8-13 **76** JamieSpencer 3 75
(M Johnston) *sn chsng ldr: rdn over 2f out: lost 2nd 2f out: wknd fnl f* **10/3**[3]
-644 5 nk **Fazbee (IRE)**[20] 2210 3-9-7 **84** (p) AlanMunro 6 83
(P W D'Arcy) *hld up in rr: drvn and hdwy on ins over 2f out: kpt on but nvr gng pce to get into contention* **11/1**
-210 6 ¾ **Lake Kalamalka (IRE)**[30] 1930 3-8-8 **71** JimmyQuinn 4 69
(J L Dunlop) *chsd ldrs: rdn over 2f out: wknd over 1f out* **12/1**
6-10 7 13 **State General (IRE)**[55] 1303 3-9-2 **79** JimCrowley 1 56
(Miss J Feilden) *in rr: rdn 3f out: wknd fr 2f out* **8/1**
2m 36.18s (1.68) **Going Correction** 0.0s/f (Stan) 7 Ran SP% **114.4**
Speed ratings (Par 101): **94,93,92,91,91 90,81**
toteswingers: 1&2 £1.90, 1&3 £2.40, 2&3 £5.40 CSF £11.29 TOTE £3.40: £1.80, £1.70; EX 9.70.

Owner Sir Gordon Brunton **Bred** Sir Gordon Brunton **Trained** Kingsclere, Hants
FOCUS
Although not a big field, there were some progressive types and the front two had a real battle off a steady pace.

2830 BOOK KEMPTON TICKETS ON 0844 579 3008 H'CAP 1m 3f (P)
9:20 (9:20) (Class 6) (0-55,55) 4-Y-0+ £2,047 (£604; £302) Stalls High

Form RPR
00-0 1 **Karky Schultz (GER)**[79] 213 4-9-1 **51** LukeMorris 14 59
(J M P Eustace) *in rr: hdwy on ins and nt clr run over 2f out: str run fr over 1f out and styd on strly u.p to ld last strides* **20/1**
0242 2 hd **Summer Lodge**[8] 2573 6-9-2 **55** (p) DavidProbert(3) 8 62
(A J McCabe) *sn chsng ldr: led appr fnl 2f and pushed along: rdn over 1f out: hdd and no ex last strides* **5/1**[2]
0236 3 ¾ **Mister Trickster (IRE)**[16] 2332 8-9-5 **55** TonyCulhane 12 61
(R Dickin) *in rr: rdn and hdwy over 2f out: styd on wl to cl on ldng duo thrght fnl f but a hld* **16/1**
0604 4 1¼ **Lady Sorcerer**[13] 2419 4-9-2 **52** (v) AlanMunro 3 56
(A P Jarvis) *sn led: rdn 3f out: hdd appr fnl 2f: wknd ins fnl f* **9/1**
-313 5 1¾ **Mix N Match**[52] 494 5-9-4 **54** FrankieMcDonald 11 55
(R M Stronge) *s.i.s: in rr: hdwy fr over 2f out: kpt on fnl f: nt pce to rch ldrs* **10/1**
454 6 2½ **Everyman**[7] 2601 5-8-11 **52** MCGeran(5) 13 49
(A W Carroll) *chsd ldrs: rdn and hung rt pver 2f out: sn btn* **8/1**
05-0 7 ½ **Empire Seeker (USA)**[43] 1589 4-8-13 **54** JackDean(5) 7 50
(Mrs H S Main) *in tch: rdn 3f out: wknd fr 2f out* **16/1**
2610 8 ½ **Sir Haydn**[13] 2420 9-9-3 **53** (v) PatDobbs 2 48
(J R Jenkins) *chsd ldrs: rdn over 2f out: sn wknd* **16/1**
0-00 9 4 **Platoche (IRE)**[21] 2182 4-8-11 **52** (p) AndreaAtzeni(5) 1 40
(G A Butler) *mid-div: pushed along over 3f out and sn wknd* **6/1**[3]
0-23 10 4 **Shavoulin (USA)**[5] 2675 5-9-0 **50** JimCrowley 4 31
(P W Hiatt) *chsd ldrs: rdn and wknd ins fnl 3f* **3/1**[1]
0004 11 dist **Eagle Nebula**[13] 2420 5-9-2 **52** IanMongan 6 —
(B R Johnson) *a bhd: t.o fnl 4f* **15/2**
2m 22.54s (0.64) **Going Correction** 0.0s/f (Stan) 11 Ran SP% **120.3**
Speed ratings (Par 101): **97,96,96,95,94 92,91,91,88,85** —
toteswingers: 1&2 £40.50, 1&3 £80.60, 2&3 £9.30 CSF £119.96 CT £1677.68 TOTE £21.50: £6.40, £1.50, £5.20; EX 170.60 Place 6: £62.22, Place 5: £34.05.
Owner Harold Nass **Bred** B Fassbender **Trained** Newmarket, Suffolk
FOCUS
A steady pace was set for this modest handicap.
Eagle Nebula Official explanation: jockey said gelding was hanging left and heavily eased
T/Jkpt: £8,200.90 to a £1 stake. Pool: £11,550.58. 1.00 winning ticket. T/Plt: £64.70 to a £1 stake. Pool: £73,162.76. 824.57 winning tickets. T/Qpdt: £16.00 to a £1 stake. Pool: £5,008.36. 230.60 winning tickets. ST

2831 - 2837a (Foreign Racing) - See Raceform Interactive

2818 HAYDOCK (L-H)
Thursday, June 11

OFFICIAL GOING: Good to firm (firm in places; 8.1)
Rail realignment added 25yds to distances on round course except for the first race which was reduced by around 20yards.
Wind: Light,half-against Weather: fine and sunny

2838 BET ONLINE AT CORBETTSPORTS.COM P.J.A. APPRENTICE SERIES H'CAP 1m 6f
6:50 (6:50) (Class 5) (0-75,75) 3-Y-O £3,238 (£963; £481; £240) Stalls Low

Form RPR
-614 1 **Darley Sun (IRE)**[21] 2208 3-9-10 **75** JamesMillman 2 83+
(D M Simcock) *trckd ldr: pushed along over 5f out: styd on to ld 1f out: drvn clr* **15/8**[1]
3530 2 4½ **Tropical Bachelor (IRE)**[5] 2715 3-9-0 **70** LanceBetts(5) 6 71
(T J Pitt) *led: qcknd over 5f out: hdd 1f out: no ex* **9/2**[2]
6266 3 4½ **Gosforth Park**[17] 2340 3-8-6 **62** JohnCavanagh(5) 1 57
(M Brittain) *chsd ldrs: pushed along over 5f out: one pce fnl 3f* **9/2**[2]
045 4 10 **Gold Maha**[13] 2447 3-8-5 **59** MCGeran(3) 5 40
(M R Channon) *hld up in last: effrt over 2f out: edgd lft and lost pl over 1f out: eased* **14/1**
3504 5 7 **Kochanski (IRE)**[10] 2540 3-8-0 **56** MatthewLawson(5) 4 27
(M Johnston) *chsd ldrs: drvn over 3f out: wknd 2f out* **13/2**
-501 6 7 **Berriedale**[38] 1724 3-8-1 **57** JamieKyne(5) 3 18
(Mrs A Duffield) *trckd ldrs: effrt over 3f out: edgd lft and lost pl over 2f out* **5/1**[3]
3m 4.19s (-0.11) **Going Correction** -0.025s/f (Good) 6 Ran SP% **107.8**
Speed ratings (Par 99): **99,96,93,88,84 80**
toteswinger: 1&2 £2.70, 1&3 £2.70, 2&3 £3.00. CSF £9.55 TOTE £2.70: £1.60, £2.80; EX 8.40.

Owner Abdullah Saeed Belhab **Bred** Manfred Hoffer & Ballygrelihan Farm **Trained** Newmarket, Suffolk
FOCUS
A dry, breezy day and conditions remained on the quick side. Not a strong handicap but, although the pace was on the steady side, the first two pulled clear in the last quarter mile. The winner is on the upgrade.

2839 WEAVER MAIDEN STKS (C&G) 6f
7:20 (7:21) (Class 5) 2-Y-O £3,238 (£963; £481; £240) Stalls Centre

Form RPR
35 1 **Reeds Bay (IRE)**[20] 2231 2-9-0 0 AdrianTNicholls 2 78
(E S McMahon) *bmpd s: effrt over 2f out: wnt 2nd ins fnl f: led post* **8/1**
2 shd **Chaperno (USA)** 2-9-0 0 LDettori 7 78
(Saeed Bin Suroor) *dwlt: sn trcking ldrs: led over 1f out: edgd lft and hdd post* **5/2**[1]
0 3 2 **Aattash (IRE)**[21] 2187 2-9-0 0 TonyCulhane 5 72
(M R Channon) *t.k.h: trckd ldrs: effrt over 2f out: kpt on same pce appr fnl f* **5/1**
3 4 shd **Lucky Rave**[33] 1867 2-9-0 0 PhillipMakin 1 71
(D H Brown) *wnt rt s: w ldrs: led 3f out: hdd over 1f out: wknd ins fnl f* **3/1**[2]
0 5 2¾ **House Red (IRE)**[52] 1404 2-9-0 0 MichaelHills 4 63
(B W Hills) *led 3f: edgd lft and wknd over 1f out* **12/1**
6 6 **Trailblazing** 2-9-0 0 GregFairley 3 45
(M Johnston) *w ldrs: lost pl 2f out* **4/1**[3]
0 7 7 **Campaigner**[33] 1866 2-8-9 0 GabrielHannon(5) 8 24
(J W Hills) *trckd ldrs: edgd rt over 2f out: sn lost pl* **50/1**
1m 15.43s (1.43) **Going Correction** +0.20s/f (Good) 7 Ran SP% **111.0**
Speed ratings (Par 93): **98,97,95,95,91 83,74**
toteswinger: 1&2 £3.50, 1&3 £5.90, 2&3 £1.30. CSF £26.67 TOTE £10.50: £2.50, £2.00; EX 38.70.
Owner J C Fretwell **Bred** Michael M Byrne **Trained** Lichfield, Staffs
FOCUS
This race has thrown up a few smart sort this decade but it will be a surprise if the winner of this year's renewal goes on to hold his own in either Listed or minor Group company. That said, the form has been rated a shade positively. The pace was reasonable.
NOTEBOOK
Reeds Bay(IRE), the only one in this field to have previously raced more than once, put his experience to good use and turned in his best effort to beat a rival that was noticeably green in front. He shapes as though he'll stay 7f and, while a sound surface clearly suits, he'll have to improve to defy a penalty against the better juveniles. (tchd 13-2)
Chaperno(USA) ◆, a $120,000 yearling out of a half-sister to a smart dirt sprint winner, sported a noseband for this racecourse debut and posted a fair effort against a more experienced rival. He left the impression he would have won had he not run green under pressure and he looks certain to make amends. (op 3-1 tchd 7-2)
Aattash(IRE), well beaten after a slow start on his debut, was much quicker out of the gates this time and turned in a much better effort. He shapes as though the step up to 7f is going to be more to his liking and he is sure to pick up an ordinary event. (op 4-1)
Lucky Rave had shaped well in a race that threw up winners over course and distance on his debut and posted another creditable effort. He should be able to pick up a run-of-the-mill maiden in the north.
House Red(IRE) bettered the form shown over 5f on his debut but his future lies in ordinary nursery company over a bit further and possibly on an easier surface. (op 14-1 tchd 11-1)
Trailblazing, a half-brother to the smart Yamal, attracted a bit of support on this racecourse debut but offered little resistance once pressure was applied. He looks the type to leave this bare form well behind in due course. (op 11-2)

2840 GOWY H'CAP 5f
7:50 (7:51) (Class 4) (0-80,80) 3-Y-O+ £5,180 (£1,541; £770; £384) Stalls Centre

Form RPR
100 1 **Mandurah (IRE)**[2] 2782 5-10-0 **78** AdrianTNicholls 12 90
(D Nicholls) *chsd ldrs: hrd rdn and styd on fnl f: led nr fin* **7/2**[1]
-01R 2 ¾ **Sands Crooner (IRE)**[22] 2180 6-9-9 **73** (v) MickyFenton 3 83
(J G Given) *slowly and sn hmpd: hdwy 2f out: styd on to chal wl ins fnl f: no ex* **18/1**
1331 3 hd **Raccoon (IRE)**[6] 2657 9-9-8 **72** 6ex PJMcDonald 1 81
(Mrs R A Carr) *wnt rt sn after s: led: 2 l clr over 1f out: no ex and hdd towards fin* **8/1**[3]
0020 4 ¾ **Namir (IRE)**[3] 2770 7-9-11 **75** (vt) DuranFentiman 11 81
(D Shaw) *mid-div: hdwy over 2f out: kpt on wl fnl f* **12/1**
-203 5 2¼ **Bahamian Ballet**[16] 2359 7-9-8 **72** RichardMullen 4 70
(E S McMahon) *chsd ldrs: kpt on same pce fnl 2f* **9/1**
10-0 6 1¾ **Cape Royal**[20] 2219 9-9-4 **71** (bt) KevinGhunowa(3) 7 63
(J M Bradley) *chsd ldrs: fdd fnl f* **25/1**
-643 7 1½ **Spiritofthewest (IRE)**[1] 2821 3-9-4 **80** GaryBartley(5) 6 64
(D H Brown) *rrd s: nvr nr ldrs* **9/2**[2]
3230 8 3 **Mazzola**[27] 2058 3-9-5 **76** TonyCulhane 5 49
(M R Channon) *chsd ldrs: edgd lft and wknd over 1f out* **9/1**
36-0 9 1¾ **Jilly Why (IRE)**[47] 1528 8-9-2 **66** (b) GregFairley 2 35
(Paul Green) *hmpd sn after s: sn chsng ldrs: lost pl 2f out* **33/1**
-433 10 9 **Speedy Senorita (IRE)**[10] 2546 4-8-12 **69** JamieKyne(7) 9 6
(J J Quinn) *restless in stalls: sn outpcd and drvn along: lost pl over 2f out: eased* **7/2**[1]
60.82 secs (0.32) **Going Correction** +0.20s/f (Good)
WFA 3 from 4yo+ 7lb 10 Ran SP% **113.5**
Speed ratings (Par 105): **105,103,103,102,98 95,93,88,85,71**
toteswinger: 1&2 £14.50, 1&3 £4.10, 2&3 £19.30. CSF £67.18 CT £479.91 TOTE £4.10: £2.10, £4.90, £2.40; EX 79.80.
Owner Martin Hignett **Bred** Michael Lyons **Trained** Sessay, N Yorks
■ Stewards' Enquiry : P J McDonald two-day ban: careless riding (Jun 25-26)
FOCUS
An ordinary handicap run at a strong gallop. Solid form.
Speedy Senorita(IRE) Official explanation: trainer's rep said, regarding running, that the filly became upset in the stalls and never travelled thereafter.

2841 RIBBLE H'CAP 7f 30y
8:20 (8:20) (Class 4) (0-85,84) 3-Y-O £6,476 (£1,927; £963; £481) Stalls Low

Form RPR
00-5 1 **Deadly Encounter (IRE)**[21] 2198 3-9-0 **77** PaulHanagan 1 80
(R A Fahey) *mde all: qcknd over 3f out: hrd rdn and hung bdly rt wl ins fnl f: all out* **9/2**[3]
1-56 2 nk **Hail Promenader (IRE)**[14] 2399 3-9-3 **80** MichaelHills 2 82
(B W Hills) *w wnr: bmpd and wnt rt wl ins fnl f* **3/1**[2]
4-20 3 ½ **Richo**[10] 2544 3-9-1 **78** (b[1]) PhillipMakin 6 79
(D H Brown) *t.k.h in rr: hdwy over 3f out: upsides over 1f out: keeping on whn bdly hmpd nr fin* **12/1**

1 4 1 1/4 **Sunshine Always (IRE)**[24] 2142 3-9-2 **79** TonyCulhane 4 79+
(W J Haggas) *t.k.h: trckd ldrs: rdn and outpcd over 2f out: styng on whn bdly hmpd wl ins fnl f* **1/1**[1]

315- 5 1 1/4 **Doric Echo**[215] 7241 3-9-4 **81** TomEaves 7 75
(B Smart) *hld up in rr: effrt over 2f out: hrd rdn over 1f out: one pce* **25/1**

0120 6 1 1/4 **Foreign Investment (IRE)**[31] 1937 3-7-12 **68** ow1 JamieKyne(7) 5 64+
(P D Evans) *in rr: hdwy on outside and hrd rdn over 2f out: one pce* **12/1**

1m 32.93s (2.73) **Going Correction** +0.20s/f (Good) **6** Ran SP% **112.4**
Speed ratings (Par 101): **92,91,91,89,88 86**
toteswinger: 1&2 £1.40, 1&3 £6.00, 2&3 £3.70. CSF £18.34 CT £147.58 TOTE £4.50: £2.30, £1.80; EX 18.40.
Owner J J Staunton **Bred** R A Fahey **Trained** Musley Bank, N Yorks
■ Stewards' Enquiry : Paul Hanagan two-day ban: careless riding (Jun 25-26)

FOCUS
Not a strong handicap for a decent prize and a muddling gallop (race run over four and a half seconds outside the Racing Post Standard) coupled with late trouble means this is not a satisfactory contest from a form perspective. The front pair were always 1-2.

2842 WYRE H'CAP 1m 30y
8:50 (8:50) (Class 4) (0-80,80) 4-Y-0+ **£5,180** (£1,541; £770; £384) **Stalls** Low

Form RPR
1662 1 **Bold Cross (IRE)**[12] 2495 6-8-11 **70** PaulFitzsimons 7 76+
(E G Bevan) *hld up: smooth hdwy over 2f out: shkn up to ld appr fnl f: pushed out: readily* **13/8**[1]

-400 2 1 1/4 **Nisaal (IRE)**[19] 2274 4-8-5 **71** (t) JamieKyne(7) 4 74
(J J Quinn) *t.k.h: trckd ldrs: nt clr run fr over 2f out: swtchd outside over 1f out: no imp ins fnl f* **2/1**[2]

0-40 3 1 **Summer Gold (IRE)**[2] 2787 5-9-7 **80** DavidAllan 3 81
(E J Alston) *led: qcknd over 3f out: hdd appr fnl f: kpt on same pce* **85/40**[3]

0-00 4 41 **Mr Toshiwonka**[23] 2156 5-8-6 **65** AdrianTNicholls 6 —
(D Nicholls) *trckd ldr: t.k.h: drvn over 3f out: wknd 2f out: sn bhd and eased: virtually p.u: t.o* **14/1**

1m 46.08s (2.28) **Going Correction** +0.20s/f (Good) **4** Ran SP% **110.1**
Speed ratings (Par 105): **96,94,93,52**
toteswinger: 1&2 £2.20. CSF £5.29 TOTE £2.40; EX 5.20.
Owner E G Bevan **Bred** M Hosokawa **Trained** Ullingswick, H'fords

FOCUS
Four non-runners left an uncompetitive handicap and one that was run at a steady pace. The winner is rated up 3lb.
Mr Toshiwonka Official explanation: jockey said gelding was unsuited by the good to firm (firm in places) ground

2843 MERSEY MAIDEN STKS 1m 2f 95y
9:20 (9:20) (Class 5) 3-Y-0+ **£3,238** (£963; £481; £240) **Stalls** High

Form RPR
32 1 **Sanctuary**[13] 2447 3-9-0 0 TomEaves 3 69
(B Smart) *trckd ldrs: effrt over 2f out: rdn to ld over 1f out: styd on wl* **10/11**[1]

626 2 2 1/4 **Cry Alot Boy**[14] 2416 6-9-13 0 TonyCulhane 4 65
(K A Morgan) *wore net muzzle: hld up detached in last: gd hdwy on outside 3f out: chal 1f out: styd on same pce* **14/1**

2-3 3 3 1/4 **Tricky Situation**[13] 2446 3-8-9 0 PaulHanagan 1 53
(J G Given) *trckd ldrs: chal over 2f out: kpt on same pce fnl f* **9/4**[2]

-450 4 2 3/4 **Susurrayshaan**[17] 2340 3-9-0 47 (p) DaleGibson 6 52
(Mrs G S Rees) *led 2f: chsd ldrs: one pce fnl 2f* **80/1**

5 2 **Gulf Of Aqaba (USA)** 3-9-0 0 GregFairley 2 48
(M Johnston) *s.i.s: sn trcking ldrs: drvn and hung lft over 3f out: lost pl over 1f out* **4/1**[3]

6 3 1/2 **Wandering Minstrel**[35] 6-9-13 0 MickyFenton 5 45
(H J L Dunlop) *s.i.s: hdwy to ld after 2f: qcknd over 3f out: hdd & wknd over 1f out: bdly hmpd nr fin* **50/1**

0400 7 11 **Mays Louise**[12] 2473 5-9-8 45 DuranFentiman 7 15
(B P J Baugh) *hld up in rr: drvn and outpcd 4f out: edgd lft and lost pl over 1f out: eased* **150/1**

2m 17.18s (4.18) **Going Correction** +0.20s/f (Good) **7** Ran SP% **113.7**
WFA 3 from 5yo+ 13lb
Speed ratings (Par 103): **100,98,95,93,91 89,80**
toteswinger: 1&2 £4.50, 1&3 £1.50, 2&3 £1.20. CSF £15.77 TOTE £1.70: £1.10, £2.70; EX 13.80 Place 6 £67.71, Place 5 £48.73..
Owner Mrs Julie Martin **Bred** Bondwood Farm Stud **Trained** Hambleton, N Yorks

FOCUS
A maiden lacking anything in the way of strength in depth and one held down by the proximity of the 47-rated fourth. It was slowly run too.
T/Plt: £152.70 to a £1 stake. Pool: £57,865.67. 276.55 winning tickets. T/Qpdt: £31.10 to a £1 stake. Pool: £4,551.35. 107.95 winning tickets. WG

2493 NEWBURY (L-H)
Thursday, June 11

OFFICIAL GOING: Good to firm (good in places; 9.4)
Running rail around 7f and 5f bends moved but impact on distances not known. A gusty wind also impacted on race times.
Wind: Brisk ahead Weather: Sunny intervals

2844 NEWVOICEMEDIA MAIDEN STKS (C&G) 6f 8y
1:35 (1:38) (Class 4) 2-Y-0 **£5,180** (£1,541; £770; £384) **Stalls** Centre

Form RPR
1 **Arcano (IRE)** 2-9-0 0 MartinDwyer 7 89+
(B J Meehan) *w'like: str: in tch: hdwy to trck ldrs over 2f out: led 1f out: sn drvn: hld on wl cl home* **7/2**[2]

2 hd **Showcasing** 2-9-0 0 JimmyFortune 16 89+
(J H M Gosden) *w'like: t.k.h early: in tch: hdwy 2f out: styd on to chse wnr ins fnl f: gaining cl home but a jst hld* **6/1**[3]

2 3 1 1/4 **Party Doctor**[10] 2533 2-9-0 0 RichardKingscote 3 85
(Tom Dascombe) *str: chsd ldrs: drvn to chal fr 2f out: one pce ins fnl f* **11/8**[1]

4 2 1/4 **Gallant Eagle (IRE)** 2-9-0 0 JamesDoyle 14 78+
(S Kirk) *w'like: bit bkwd: s.i.s: bhd: hdwy fr 2f out: styd on strly fnl f: gng on cl home* **66/1**

5 nk **Lucky General (IRE)** 2-9-0 0 RyanMoore 12 77
(R Hannon) *w'like: scope: chsd ldrs: drvn to chal fr 2f out: wknd fnl 110yds* **12/1**

6 nk **Lord Zenith** 2-9-0 0 WilliamBuick 10 76+
(A M Balding) *tall: scope: bit bkwd: s.i.s: bhd: pushed along over 2f out: hdwy over 1f out: styd on wl fnl f: gng on cl home* **14/1**

7 3 1/4 **Great Intrigue (IRE)** 2-9-0 0 NCallan 11 67
(J S Moore) *in tch: drvn to chse ldrs over 2f out: nvr quite on terms: wknd ins fnl f* **66/1**

8 nse **Sheer Force (IRE)** 2-9-0 0 JimCrowley 13 67
(W J Knight) *w'like: coltish: towards rr: hdwy to get in bhd ldrs over 2f out: sn shkn up: wknd fnl f* **33/1**

9 hd **Fawley Green** 2-9-0 0 SebSanders 1 66
(W R Muir) *w'like: led tl hdd 1f out: wknd qckly ins fnl f* **33/1**

10 1 **Magnus Thrax (USA)** 2-9-0 0 SteveDrowne 6 63
(R Hannon) *w'like: scope: s.i.s: bhd: hdwy over 2f out: nvr gng pce to get into contention* **40/1**

11 1 **Erfaan (USA)** 2-9-0 0 TPO'Shea 2 60
(B W Hills) *w'like: scope: s.i.s: sn in tch: chsd ldrs 1/2-way: wknd ins fnl 2f* **15/2**

12 1 1/4 **Kilmanseck** 2-9-0 0 StephenCarson 8 56
(Eve Johnson Houghton) *str: coltish: s.i.s: a in rr* **66/1**

0 13 nk **New Den**[7] 2631 2-9-0 0 FergusSweeney 5 55
(J R Boyle) *chsd ldrs 4f* **200/1**

1m 16.69s (3.69) **Going Correction** +0.325s/f (Good) **13** Ran SP% **118.0**
Speed ratings (Par 95): **88,87,86,83,82 82,77,77,77,76 74,73,72**
toteswinger: 1&2 £4.80, 1&3 £3.40, 2&3 £3.60 CSF £23.78 TOTE £5.40: £2.00, £2.00, £1.10; EX 30.60.
Owner Brimacombe,McNally,Vinciguerra,Sangster **Bred** Yellow Bird Syndicate **Trained** Manton, Wilts

FOCUS
Only two of these came into this with a run under their belt, so it looked a difficult race to work out, especially as seven of the last nine winners were debutants. The ground was described by one of the jockeys as on the firm side, but the winning time was a little disappointing. Plenty of winners should still come from the race, which has been rated through the third.

NOTEBOOK
Arcano(IRE) ◆, who cost 90,000gns as a yearling, was subject of good reports before the race and attracted market support on his racecourse bow. Nicely away, he sat just behind the leaders, travelling well, before gaining an advantage on his rivals inside the final furlong. There was a late scare as the runner-up made significant ground, but he was value for a bit more than the winning margin and looks set to hold his own in good company. The trainer, who said his horse will improve a ton, hopes to take him to the July Stakes. (tchd 3-1 and 4-1)
Showcasing ◆, a brother to Bouvardia and half-brother to Camacho, represented a stable that had won this race twice since 2001. A real sprinter in make and shape, he sat just off the pace, looking a little green for the most part, and only started to realise what was going on in the final stages. It was an encouraging start to his career and he could be a smart type in time. (tchd 7-1)
Party Doctor, whose trainer said beforehand that he would be gutted if his horse was beaten, got outpaced over a furlong out before staying on again. He was nicely clear of the remainder, which gives the form a decent level. (tchd 6-4 and 5-4 in a place)
Gallant Eagle(IRE), behind early, was given time to find his feet and finished nicely. He should improve on this. (tchd 80-1)
Lucky General(IRE) cost€50,000 as a yearling. He was prominent from the outset and only gave way inside the final furlong. (op 11-1)
Lord Zenith ◆ was doing his best work at the end and should make the grade, although he may need more time. (op 11-1)
Sheer Force(IRE), a half-brother to several winners, shaped with enough promise to suggest races will come his way in time, whether it's in a maiden or handicaps.
Erfaan(USA), a 150,000gns half-brother to a winning sprinter in the US, was nicely supported but dropped away quickly after settling in midfield. One would imagine that he is better than he showed. (op 16-1)

2845 PERTEMPS H'CAP 1m (S)
2:10 (2:11) (Class 5) (0-75,75) 3-Y-0 **£3,238** (£963; £481; £240) **Stalls** Centre

Form RPR
-045 1 **Peking Prince**[21] 2209 3-9-2 **70** WilliamBuick 16 84+
(A M Balding) *hld up in mid-div: hdwy gng wl appr fnl 2f: led 1f out: rdn and edgd lft ins fnl f: styd on strly* **10/1**[3]

3236 2 1 1/2 **Carbon Hoofprint**[31] 1928 3-9-3 **71** FergusSweeney 13 82
(P J Makin) *led after 1f: rdn 2f out: hdd 1f out: no pce of wnr ins fnl f but styd on wl for clr 2nd* **12/1**

0-31 3 3 3/4 **Spinners End (IRE)**[20] 2248 3-9-6 **74** SebSanders 11 76
(K R Burke) *t.k.h towards rr: hdwy fr 3f out: styd on to go 3rd ins fnl f but nvr any ch w ldng duo* **7/1**[2]

3-43 4 2 **Makhaaleb (IRE)**[26] 2092 3-9-5 **73** TPO'Shea 14 71
(B W Hills) *chsd ldrs: rdn over 2f out: no ch w ldng duo fnl f and sn wknd* **18/1**

6-33 5 nk **Justonefortheroad**[31] 1925 3-9-4 **72** RichardKingscote 15 69
(N J Vaughan) *chsd ldrs: rdn over 2f out: wknd fnl f* **12/1**

1-0 6 1 3/4 **Aboukir**[12] 2479 3-9-2 **70** TPQueally 10 63
(P F I Cole) *in rr: rdn 3f out: styd on fnl 2f but nvr gng pce to get into contention* **66/1**

244- 7 1/2 **Too Tall**[266] 6057 3-9-5 **73** NCallan 2 65+
(L M Cumani) *bit bkwd: t.k.h in rr: hdwy over 3f out: chsd ldrs gng ok over 2f out: wknd over 1f out* **10/1**[3]

405- 8 hd **Bouggie Daize**[258] 6240 3-9-5 **73** PhilipRobinson 8 64
(C G Cox) *t.k.h towards rr after 2f: sme prog and rdn 3f out: nvr gng pce to get into contention* **7/1**[2]

4-36 9 1 1/2 **Welsh Anthem**[13] 2433 3-9-4 **72** (b[1]) MartinDwyer 6 60
(W R Muir) *in rr: drvn along over 3f out: mod prog fr over 1f out* **16/1**

4-00 10 1/2 **Jazacosta (USA)**[39] 1707 3-9-4 **72** (b[1]) JimCrowley 3 59
(Mrs A J Perrett) *lw: pressed ldrs over 5f: wknd wl over 1f out* **14/1**

056 11 4 1/2 **Illusive Spirit (IRE)**[14] 2415 3-9-4 **72** JimmyFortune 9 49
(J H M Gosden) *in rr: sme prog 3f out: nver in contention and wknd fr 2f out* **14/1**

33-5 12 2 1/4 **Recession Proof (FR)**[24] 2138 3-9-7 **75** NeilPollard 1 46
(S A Callaghan) *in tch over 5f* **22/1**

2022 13 nse **Implication**[8] 2600 3-9-5 **73** RyanMoore 4 44
(E A L Dunlop) *towards rr after 1f: sme hdwy 3f out: nvr in contention and wknd 2f out* **5/2**[1]

35-3 14 6 **Mister Fantastic**[59] 1252 3-9-4 **72** JamesDoyle 12 29
(N J Vaughan) *led 1f: styd pressing ldrs unti wknd 2f out* **33/1**

033 15 3 **Fantasy Land (IRE)**[22] 2179 3-9-4 **72** (t) RobertWinston 7 23
(B J Meehan) *lw: chsd ldrs over 5f* **20/1**

1m 42.03s (2.33) **Going Correction** +0.325s/f (Good) **15** Ran SP% **125.2**
Speed ratings (Par 99): **101,99,95,93,93 91,91,91,89,89 84,82,82,76,73**
toteswinger: 1&2 £36.00, 1&3 £9.70, 2&3 £29.90 CSF £124.00 CT £914.62 TOTE £10.90: £4.10, £4.80, £2.70; EX 126.00.
Owner Kingsclere Racing CLub **Bred** Kingsclere Stud **Trained** Kingsclere, Hants

FOCUS
This looked no more than a fair 3yo handicap. There was an average pace on and those drawn high were at an advantage. The form among the principals looks sound.
Bouggie Daize Official explanation: jockey said filly ran too free
Implication Official explanation: trainer's rep had no explanation for the poor form shown

2846 LORD WEINSTOCK MEMORIAL STKS (REGISTERED AS THE BALLYMACOLL STUD STAKES) (LISTED RACE) (FILLIES) 1m 2f 6y
2:40 (2:40) (Class 1) 3-Y-O
£22,708 (£8,608; £4,308; £2,148; £1,076; £540) **Stalls** Low

Form RPR
13-4 **1** **Splashdown**[21] 2190 3-8-12 94 RyanMoore 2 105
(L M Cumani) *in tch: hrd drvn fr over 2f out: str run u.p to chse ldr fnl f: led last strides: all out* **9/4[2]**
1-11 **2** *shd* **Apple Charlotte**[27] 2036 3-9-1 106 TPQueally 5 108
(H R A Cecil) *lw: trckd ldrs: wnt 2nd over 3f out: qcknd to ld ins fnl 2f: hrd drvn fnl f: ct last strides* **5/4[1]**
31-2 **3** *1 3/4* **Fallen In Love**[21] 2190 3-8-12 92 SteveDrowne 3 101
(J L Dunlop) *lw: chsd ldrs: rdn over 2f out: styd on fnl f but nt pce of ldng duo* **7/1[3]**
1 **4** *2 3/4* **Charity Belle (USA)**[14] 2403 3-8-12 84 JimmyFortune 1 96
(J H M Gosden) *tall: wl grwn: sn led: rdn along 3f out: hdd isndie fnl 2f: wknd fnl f* **16/1**
0-60 **5** *5* **Snoqualmie Girl (IRE)**[39] 1701 3-9-1 95 MartinDwyer 8 89
(D R C Elsworth) *on toes: t.k.h in rr: pushed along fr 3f out: styd on same pce fnl 2f and nvr in contention* **40/1**
15 **6** *hd* **Danehill's Pearl (IRE)**[27] 2036 3-8-12 92 RichardKingscote 9 85
(Tom Dascombe) *chsd ldr tl rdn over 3f out: wknd ins fnl 2f* **33/1**
204- **7** *1* **Beat Seven**[257] 6268 3-8-12 106 PhilipRobinson 4 83
(Miss Gay Kelleway) *rdn over 3f out: a towards rr* **10/1**
10- **8** *1* **Club Tahiti**[229] 6982 3-8-12 85 WilliamBuick 6 81
(R Charlton) *t.k.h early: rdn and hung lft 3f out: a towards rr* **22/1**
-305 **9** *3* **Miss Beat (IRE)**[21] 2190 3-8-12 87 RobertWinston 7 75
(B J Meehan) *t.k.h early: a towards rr* **66/1**
2m 8.24s (-0.56) **Going Correction** +0.15s/f (Good) **9** Ran SP% **113.9**
Speed ratings (Par 104): **108,107,106,104,100 100,99,98,96**
toteswinger: 1&2 £2.00, 1&3 £3.50, 2&3 £3.60 CSF £5.13 TOTE £3.40: £1.40, £1.10, £1.90; EX 6.50.
Owner Fittocks Stud **Bred** Fittocks Stud Ltd **Trained** Newmarket, Suffolk

FOCUS
It's fair to say this Listed race hasn't produced many stars down the years. However, most of these fillies had shown enough to warrant an outing in this class, so the form looks fair for the grade. It was the quickest of the C/D races.

NOTEBOOK
Splashdown ◆ shaped nicely on her return to the track in late May, especially as her trainer stated that race had come a bit too soon for her. Some of her form at two gave her every chance, and she just denied the favourite close to the line after being involved in a battle royal. One would imagine there is plenty more to come, and connections will give her an entry for the American Oaks at Hollywood Park, which is run over this trip. However, if they feel she definitely wants further, which seemed the immediate reaction, the Lancashire Oaks will come into the equation. (op 11-4)
Apple Charlotte, who took the Swettenham Stud Fillies' Trial Stakes over this course and distance last time, only just failed to defend her unbeaten record. A little keen early, she is a smart sort and can be given another chance. (op 6-5 tchd 11-8)
Fallen In Love was far from disgraced when tried in this grade last time but could not confirm the form with Splashdown. Open to plenty of improvement, a step up in trip will not go amiss. (tchd 8-1)
Charity Belle(USA) didn't make the racetrack until the end of last month but got off the mark straight away when turning over an odds-on shot at Newcastle. Soon in front, she kept on in resolute style once joined and is entitled to come on again for this. (op 14-1)
Beat Seven, off since finishing not far behind Rainbow View and Fantasia in the Fillies' Mile last September, had quite a few runs as a juvenile and only ran in this after the trainer found the ground suitable. A little keen early, she did not show a great deal but should improve for the run. (op 11-1)
Club Tahiti made an impressive debut at this course as a juvenile but proved disappointing in a Listed event, again at Newbury, on her only other start. Having her first outing as a three-year-old, she looked fit but was always towards the rear and may not have acted on the going. (op 20-1)

2847 CHRISTAL MANAGEMENT MAIDEN FILLIES' STKS (DIV I) 1m 2f 6y
3:15 (3:16) (Class 5) 3-Y-O
£3,885 (£1,156; £577; £288) **Stalls** Low

Form RPR
4-24 **1** **Hidden Brief**[36] 1789 3-9-0 95 PhilipRobinson 8 73+
(M A Jarvis) *lw: mde all: drvn along fr 2f out: styd on strly and in command fr over 1f out* **1/3[1]**
2 *1 1/4* **Brief Look** 3-9-0 0 TPQueally 6 70+
(H R A Cecil) *lengthy: scope: trckd ldrs: wnt 2bd 4f out: drvn and effrt fr 2f out: nvr on terms w wnr and kpt on same pce fnl f* **6/1[2]**
00- **3** *3/4* **Going For Gold**[229] 6977 3-9-0 0 SteveDrowne 9 69
(R Charlton) *hld up in rr: hdwy over 2f out: styd on fnl f and tk 3rd cl home but nvr a threat to wnr* **20/1**
06 **4** *nk* **Course De Diamante (IRE)**[21] 2192 3-9-0 0 NeilPollard 2 68
(D R Lanigan) *awkward s: chsd wnr to 4f out: styd wl there: rdn along fr 2f out and styd on same pce: lost 3rd cl home* **66/1**
5 *3 1/2* **Bow To No One (IRE)** 3-9-0 0 NCallan 10 61
(A P Jarvis) *w'like: leggy: in rr: hdwy 4f out: chsd ldrs 3f out: sn drvn: wknd ins fnl 2f* **25/1**
0- **6** *1 1/4* **Crocus Rose**[218] 7200 3-9-0 0 RyanMoore 4 59
(H J L Dunlop) *lengthy: attr: in tch: rdn to chse ldrs 3f out: wknd ins fnl 2f* **20/1**
7 *1/2* **Kenaaya (FR)** 3-9-0 0 TPO'Shea 3 58
(J H M Gosden) *rangy: rdn over 3f out: a in rr* **10/1[3]**
54 **8** *15* **Spirit Of The Glen**[110] 630 3-9-0 0 SimonWhitworth 7 28
(Jamie Poulton) *s.i.s: a in rr* **100/1**
0 **9** *2 3/4* **Mission Lodge**[24] 2139 3-9-0 0 MartinDwyer 1 22
(B J Meehan) *in tch: rdn and effrt 3f: nvr in contention out: sn wknd* **50/1**
2m 10.21s (1.41) **Going Correction** +0.15s/f (Good) **9** Ran SP% **116.2**
Speed ratings (Par 96): **100,99,98,98,95 94,93,81,79**
toteswinger: 1&2 £1.80, 1&3 £4.70, 2&3 £7.40 CSF £2.34 TOTE £1.40: £1.02, £1.60, £3.50; EX 3.00.
Owner Lordship Stud **Bred** R W Russell **Trained** Newmarket, Suffolk

FOCUS
This looked less competitive than the second division, although it did contain the highest rated on RPRs. It is doubtful if she needed to be close to her best of the steady pace and the bare form is pretty ordinary.

2848 CHRISTAL MANAGEMENT MAIDEN FILLIES' STKS (DIV II) 1m 2f 6y
3:50 (3:53) (Class 5) 3-Y-O
£3,885 (£1,156; £577; £288) **Stalls** Low

Form RPR
1 **Whooshka (USA)** 3-9-0 0 WilliamBuick 2 72
(P W Chapple-Hyam) *w'like: scope: hld up in tch: swtchd rt to outside 3f out: shkn up and str run fr 2f out: led jst ins fnl f: drvn and hld on wl* **4/1[2]**
2 **2** *nk* **Kinetix**[34] 1844 3-9-0 0 JimmyFortune 1 71
(J H M Gosden) *unruly in stalls: chsd ldrs: rdn and hung lft fr 2f out: chal 1f out: stl edging lft and no ex ins fnl f* **1/1[1]**
6- **3** *3* **Brilliana**[247] 6565 3-9-0 0 TPQueally 6 65
(D R Lanigan) *str: sn led: rdn and kpt slt advantage fr over 2f out: hdd jst ins fnl f sn wknd* **11/2[3]**
4 *3* **Park Melody (IRE)** 3-9-0 0 MartinDwyer 7 59
(B J Meehan) *str: lengthy: bit bkwd: in rr: drvn along fr 3f out: styd on fnl f but nvr a danger* **17/2**
0-0 **5** *shd* **Carte D'Oro (IRE)**[69] 1092 3-9-0 0 SebSanders 4 59
(R M Beckett) *plld hrd: sn chsng ldrs: wnt 2nd 6f out: stl keen: chal 3f out tl over 2f out: wknd appr fnl f* **20/1**
0-5 **6** *1 1/2* **Chanrossa (IRE)**[21] 2211 3-9-0 0 SteveDrowne 5 56
(E A L Dunlop) *w'like: lengthy: chsd ldr to 6f out: styd trckd ldrs: rdn over 2f out: wknd over 1f out* **7/1**
7 *1 1/2* **Megavista (USA)** 3-8-11 0 RussellKennemore[(3)] 9 53
(Paul Mason) *w'like: b.hind: rdn over 3f out: a towards rr* **66/1**
8 *14* **Red Red Rascal** 3-9-0 0 NeilChalmers 8 25
(A M Balding) *leggy: s.i.s: t.k.h: a in rr* **22/1**
2m 15.07s (6.27) **Going Correction** +0.15s/f (Good) **8** Ran SP% **119.0**
Speed ratings (Par 96): **80,79,77,74,74 73,72,61**
toteswinger: 1&2 £2.30, 1&3 £3.50, 2&3 £2.90 CSF £8.62 TOTE £4.70: £1.60, £1.10, £2.00; EX 13.00.
Owner C G P Wyatt **Bred** Northwest Farms Llc **Trained** Newmarket, Suffolk

FOCUS
This second division of the maiden was slowly run and the slowes of the four C/D races. Not good form for the track, rated through the runner-up.
Red Red Rascal Official explanation: jockey said filly ran too free

2849 BATHWICK TYRES NEWBURY H'CAP 7f (S)
4:25 (4:27) (Class 5) (0-75,75) 3-Y-O
£3,238 (£963; £481; £240) **Stalls** Centre

Form RPR
052- **1** **Maswerte (IRE)**[162] 7830 3-9-7 75 NCallan 3 85+
(L M Cumani) *gd bodied: lw: str: sn mid-div: stdy hdwy fr 3f out to ld ins fnl 2f: rdn and hung rt ins fnl f: drvn but in command whn edgd lft cl home* **9/1**
0-35 **2** *1 1/4* **Papyrian**[14] 2415 3-9-7 75 JimmyFortune 12 82
(W Jarvis) *mid-div: hdwy over 2f out: styng on ins fnl f whn nt clr run and swtchd lft ins fnl f: kpt on but no imp on wnr* **14/1**
426- **3** *3/4* **Equinine (IRE)**[258] 6247 3-9-0 68 RobertWinston 10 73+
(B W Hills) *in rr: wnt sharply lft fr ins fnl 2f: styd on ins fnl f: kpt on cl home* **14/1**
23-4 **4** *hd* **Aurora Sky (IRE)**[22] 2179 3-9-3 71 SebSanders 14 75
(J Akehurst) *s.i.s: in rr: rapid hdwy fr 2f out: styd on wl fnl f* **16/1**
434- **5** *2 1/2* **Lujeanie**[162] 7830 3-9-0 68 FergusSweeney 15 65
(D K Ivory) *in tch 1/2-way: hdwy to chse ldrs over 2f out: wknd ins fnl f* **66/1**
5-35 **6** *5* **Getcarter**[27] 2048 3-9-1 69 RyanMoore 11 53
(R Hannon) *lw: t.k.h: chsd ldrs: rdn over 2f out: wknd fnl f* **11/4[1]**
35-0 **7** *3* **Integria**[23] 2160 3-9-0 68 RichardKingscote 6 44
(J M P Eustace) *towards rr: sme hdwy whn hung lft fr over 2f out: n.d after* **14/1**
0-44 **8** *1* **Megasecret**[34] 1839 3-9-1 72 PatrickHills[(3)] 5 45
(R Hannon) *chsd ldrs: rdn over 2f out: wknd over 1f out* **8/1[3]**
-200 **9** *1* **Bobs Dreamflight**[35] 1814 3-9-4 72 StephenCarson 4 42
(D K Ivory) *chsd ldrs: led over 2f out: hdd ins fnl quarter m: wknd appr fnl f* **28/1**
0-40 **10** *2 1/2* **The Desert Saint**[21] 2198 3-9-4 72 WilliamBuick 7 36
(A M Balding) *in rr: rdn over 2f out: nvr gng pce to get into contention* **12/1**
-020 **11** *2 3/4* **Admiral Sandhoe (USA)**[8] 2600 3-9-5 73 JimCrowley 13 29
(Mrs A J Perrett) *chsd ldrs over 4f* **25/1**
13-0 **12** *1 3/4* **Retro (IRE)**[22] 2174 3-9-5 73 TPO'Shea 8 24
(R Hannon) *pressed ldrs over 4f* **9/1**
2-05 **13** *2* **Zebrano**[8] 2600 3-9-7 75 TPQueally 2 21
(Miss E C Lavelle) *swtg: chsd ldrs over 4f* **28/1**
0-03 **14** *hd* **Tidal Force (USA)**[18] 2300 3-9-1 69 (b) MartinDwyer 1 14
(P F I Cole) *led tl hdd & wknd over 2f out* **12/1**
5-20 **15** *3 3/4* **Trading Nation (USA)**[12] 2496 3-9-6 74 SteveDrowne 16 9
(R Charlton) *towards rr: sme hdwy 3f out: sn rdn: no rspnse and wknd qckly over 2f out* **6/1[2]**
1m 28.08s (2.38) **Going Correction** +0.325s/f (Good) **15** Ran SP% **125.6**
Speed ratings (Par 99): **99,97,96,96,93 87,84,83,82,79 76,74,71,71,67**
toteswinger: 1&2 £18.90, 1&3 £29.30, 2&3 £53.30 CSF £129.40 CT £1820.50 TOTE £12.10: £3.10, £4.00, £6.10; EX 154.60.
Owner Sheikh Mohammed Obaid Al Maktoum **Bred** P D Savill **Trained** Newmarket, Suffolk

FOCUS
Any amount of the exposed types in this could be given a chance on various pieces of form and, with three handicap debutants in the line-up, it was a tricky event to unravel. Probably decent form for the grade and the winner looks sure to do better.

2850 BATHWICK TYRES SWINDON H'CAP 1m 4f 5y
4:55 (4:55) (Class 5) (0-75,75) 3-Y-O
£3,238 (£963; £481; £240) **Stalls** Low

Form RPR
0-41 **1** **Strathcal**[21] 2204 3-9-4 72 SteveDrowne 4 79
(H Morrison) *trckd ldrs: wnt 2nd 6f out: led over 2f out: drvn out* **3/1[1]**
0-01 **2** *1 1/2* **Devil To Pay**[40] 1670 3-9-3 71 SebSanders 10 76
(J L Dunlop) *lw: chsd ldrs: rdn to go 2nd 2f out: styd on same pce u.p ins fnl f and no imp on wnr* **7/2[2]**
0222 **3** *1 1/4* **Salybia Bay**[21] 2204 3-8-11 65 RyanMoore 3 68
(R Hannon) *lw: chsd ldrs: drvn to dispute 2nd fr 2f out: no imression on wnr fnl f and wknd nr fin* **4/1[3]**
1-00 **4** *nk* **Herschel (IRE)**[22] 2174 3-9-5 73 FergusSweeney 6 75
(G L Moore) *in tch: rdn: sme hdwy and hung rt over 1f out: fnd little u.p ins fnl f* **12/1**

3410 **5** 1/2 **Haljaferia (UAE)**[27] 2060 3-9-6 **74** MartinDwyer 7 78+
(D R C Elsworth) *in tch: rdn over 2f out: styng on whn hmpd over 1f out: rallied and styd on again wl ins fnl f* **10/1**
35-0 **6** 1 **Perception (IRE)**[24] 2126 3-9-1 **69** JimCrowley 5 69
(R Charlton) *stdd towards rr: hdwy fr 3f out: rdn and styd on fnl 2f but nvr gng pce to get into contention* **20/1**
00-4 **7** 1 **Highland Storm**[24] 2126 3-8-12 **73** (p) MatthewDavies(7) 1 71
(George Baker) *in rr: hdwy on outside fr 3f out: chsd ldrs 2f out: no imp and wknd ins fnl f* **17/2**
0-40 **8** 10 **Granski (IRE)**[21] 2206 3-8-13 **67** JimmyFortune 11 49
(R Hannon) *sn led: hdd over 2f out: sn wknd* **18/1**
4655 **9** 7 **Diamond Twister (USA)**[13] 2432 3-9-3 **71** (t) RobertWinston 2 42
(J R Best) *plld hrd in rr: brief effrt fr 3f out: nvr in contention and wknd sn after* **11/1**
00-4 **10** 10 **Millharbour (IRE)**[66] 1151 3-9-7 **75** WilliamBuick 9 30
(B W Hills) *in rr: hdwy to chse ldrs over 3f out: sn rdn and hung lft: wknd qckly* **25/1**
3-02 **11** 10 **Horsley Warrior**[37] 1780 3-9-7 **75** NCallan 8 14
(E S McMahon) *lw: in tch: rdn 3f out and sn wknd* **16/1**

2m 38.15s (2.65) **Going Correction** +0.15s/f (Good) **11 Ran SP% 122.6**
Speed ratings (Par 99): **97,96,95,94,94 93,93,86,81,75 68**
toteswinger: 1&2 £3.80, 1&3 £3.40, 2&3 £4.70 CSF £14.02 CT £44.05 TOTE £4.10: £1.50, £2.00, £1.80; EX 6.80.
Owner The Caledonian Racing Society **Bred** Mrs R F Johnson Houghton **Trained** East Ilsley, Berks
■ Stewards' Enquiry : Matthew Davies one-day ban: careless riding (Jun 25)

FOCUS
Some good horses have taken this race in recent years. Last year's winner Warringah went on to run in the St Leger, Hi Calypso landed a Group 2 later in the season, while the winners in 2005 and 2006 (Bauer and Tawqeet) both made up into serious Melbourne Cup contenders. This overall form is quite ordinary but the winner is going the right way.

2851 BOLLINGER CHAMPAGNE CHALLENGE SERIES H'CAP (FOR GENTLEMAN AMATEUR RIDERS) 1m 2f 6y
5:25 (5:25) (Class 5) (0-70,70) 4-Y-0+ **£3,123** (£968; £484; £242) **Stalls** Low

Form RPR
0502 **1** **Iceman George**[14] 2420 5-9-13 **53** (b) MrBMMorris(5) 5 62
(D Morris) *towards rr: hdwy on outside over 2f out: styd on u.p fnl f to ld cl home: won gng away* **6/1**[3]
0400 **2** 1 1/4 **Artreju (GER)**[6] 2675 6-10-3 **57** (p) MrJoshuaMoore(5) 4 63
(G L Moore) *hld up in rr: hdwy 4f out: drvn and qcknd to ld over 1f out: hdd and no ex cl home* **8/1**
0300 **3** 3/4 **Binnion Bay (IRE)**[6] 2675 8-9-12 **52** (p) MrAshleyBird(5) 3 57
(J J Bridger) *stdd in rr: hrd rdn and styd on fr over 2f out: kpt on to take 3rd cl home* **40/1**
-010 **4** 3/4 **Director's Chair**[31] 1945 4-10-11 **65** MrRBirkett(5) 6 68
(Miss J Feilden) *chsd ldrs: led 2f out: sn rdn: hdd over 1f out: styd on same pce* **15/2**
0053 **5** 2 **Dragon Slayer (IRE)**[14] 2419 7-10-12 **61** MrSDobson 10 60
(John A Harris) *sn led: rdn 3f out: hdd 2f out: wknd fnl f* **8/1**
3420 **6** hd **Ghufa (IRE)**[75] 1000 5-11-4 **67** MrSWalker 9 66
(George Baker) *chsd ldrs: rdn 3f out: wknd over 1f out* **10/3**[1]
0650 **7** 6 **Gallego**[7] 2641 7-10-9 **63** MrMPrice(5) 1 50
(R J Price) *s.i.s: bhd: styd on fnl 2f: nvr in contention* **12/1**
2122 **8** 1 **Sunset Boulevard (IRE)**[5] 2708 6-10-7 **61** MrAshleePrice(5) 2 46
(Miss Tor Sturgis) *chsd ldrs: rdn over 3f out: wknd 2f out* **9/1**
1165 **9** shd **Mustajed**[12] 2505 8-11-2 **70** (p) MrPMillman(5) 7 54
(B R Millman) *awkward stalls and slowly away: sn plld hrd and chse ldrs after 3f: wknd 2f out* **11/2**[2]
44-6 **10** nk **Seventh Cavalry (IRE)**[27] 2039 4-10-9 **65** MrJBanks(7) 11 49
(A King) *chsd ldrs tl wknd qckly over 2f out* **8/1**
0 **11** 8 **Inchando (FR)**[23] 2150 5-10-13 **65** MrMJJSmith(3) 12 33
(A W Carroll) *a in rr* **100/1**
00-0 **12** 9 **Hold Fire**[17] 2318 5-9-11 **51** oh6 MrTRDavid(5) 8 1
(A W Carroll) *a in rr* **150/1**

2m 12.78s (3.98) **Going Correction** +0.15s/f (Good) **12 Ran SP% 119.6**
Speed ratings (Par 103): **90,89,88,87,86 86,81,80,80,80 73,66**
toteswinger: 1&2 £11.00, 1&3 £42.40, 2&3 £42.90 CSF £53.89 CT £1777.05 TOTE £7.70: £1.80, £3.70, £10.40; EX 82.20 Place 6: £42.06 Place 5: £35.68.
Owner D & L Racing **Bred** T J And J Wells **Trained** Newmarket, Suffolk
■ Stewards' Enquiry : Mr Ashley Bird two-day ban: used whip with excessive frequency (tbn)
Mr T R David one-day ban: used whip when out of contention and mare showed no response (tbn)

FOCUS
The gallop was really slow, so this is not a result to take seriously for future purposes. A few of the riders used their whips with what seemed excessive frequency, which made the end of the race look a bit ugly. Very ordinary form.
T/Plt: £22.80 to a £1 stake. Pool: £63,314.67. 2,022.49 winning tickets. T/Qpdt: £6.60 to a £1 stake. Pool: £3,748.15. 417.25 winning tickets. ST

2602 NOTTINGHAM (L-H)
Thursday, June 11

OFFICIAL GOING: Good (good to soft in places; 7.2)
Dolling out added 18yds to advertised distances on round course.
Wind: Light across Weather: Cloudy with sunny spells

2852 CHAMPAGNE LANSON BLACK LABEL N.V. H'CAP 6f 15y
1:25 (1:27) (Class 6) (0-65,66) 3-Y-0+ **£2,047** (£604; £302) **Stalls** High

Form RPR
1060 **1** **Flying Applause**[3] 2769 4-9-8 **65** (bt) AndreaAtzeni(5) 9 74
(S R Bowring) *racd stands' side: chsd ldrs: rdn over 2f out: styd on to ld wl ins fnl f* **13/2**[2]
4050 **2** 1 1/2 **No Grouse**[10] 2531 9-9-9 **61** DavidAllan 16 65
(E J Alston) *racd stands' side: prom: rdn and hung lft over 1f out: styd on: 2nd of 9 in gp* **14/1**
-000 **3** nse **Ghost Dancer**[12] 2491 5-9-10 **65** KevinGhunowa(3) 14 69
(J M Bradley) *racd stands' side: chsd ldrs: rdn to ld and hung lft over 1f out: hdd wl ins fnl f: 3rd of 9 in gp* **33/1**
05-0 **4** 3/4 **Compton Blue**[37] 1772 3-9-5 **65** PatDobbs 15 65+
(R Hannon) *racd stands' side: hld up: r.o ins fnl f: nrst fin: 4th of 9 in gp* **25/1**
0-22 **5** 3/4 **Plumage**[14] 2418 4-9-8 **60** AlanMunro 5 59+
(M Salaman) *led far side: rdn over 1f out: styd on: 1st of 7 in gp* **15/2**[3]
-050 **6** 3/4 **Circuit Dancer (IRE)**[12] 2472 9-9-12 **64** AdrianTNicholls 11 61
(D Nicholls) *led stands' side: rdn and hung lft fr over 2f out: hdd over 1f out: no ex fnl f: 5th of 9 in gp* **14/1**
5041 **7** 3/4 **Volito**[8] 2602 3-9-6 **66** 6ex JamieSpencer 3 58+
(Jonjo O'Neill) *racd far side: prom: chsd ldr 1/2-way: rdn over 1f out: styd on same pce: 2nd of 7 in gp* **5/1**[1]
3-30 **8** hd **Elkhorn**[118] 540 7-9-2 **59** (v) BMcHugh(5) 17 53
(Miss J A Camacho) *racd stands' side: s.i.s: hdwy under press out: nt trble ldrs: 6th of 9 in gp* **16/1**
00-0 **9** 2 1/4 **Cross Of Lorraine (IRE)**[39] 1695 6-9-2 **54** (b) PaulMulrennan 6 41
(J Wade) *racd far side: chsd ldrs: rdn and hung lft over 2f out: wknd over 1f out: 3rd of 7 in gp* **50/1**
10-0 **10** 1/2 **Chosen One (IRE)**[26] 2071 4-9-13 **65** TomEaves 13 50
(B Smart) *racd stands' side: s.i.s: sn prom: rdn over 2f out: wknd fnl f: 7th of 9 in gp* **8/1**
0135 **11** hd **Punching**[15] 2381 5-9-13 **65** LPKeniry 8 49
(C R Dore) *racd stands' side: hld up: rdn over 2f out: n.d: 8th of 9 in gp* **17/2**
00-0 **12** 3 **Coleorton Dancer**[17] 2312 7-9-6 **58** JoeFanning 10 33
(K A Ryan) *racd stands' side: chsd ldrs: rdn over 2f out: wknd over 1f out: last of 9 in gp* **12/1**
000 **13** 3 3/4 **Namu**[127] 387 6-9-5 **57** LiamJones 4 20
(Miss T Spearing) *racd far side: prom: rdn over 2f out: wknd over 1f out: 4th of 7 in gp* **33/1**
0-50 **14** 6 **El Potro**[44] 1591 7-9-4 **56** RichardMullen 2 —
(J R Holt) *racd far side: chsd ldrs: rdn over 2f out: wknd over 1f out: 5th of 7 in gp* **33/1**
-613 **15** 2 1/4 **West Leake (IRE)**[23] 2160 3-9-4 **64** MichaelHills 7 —
(B W Hills) *dwlt: racd far side: a in rr: 6th of 7 in gp* **8/1**
050- **16** 18 **Star Acclaim**[291] 5317 4-9-12 **64** (t) PaulHanagan 1 —
(E V Stanford) *racd far side: a in rr: wknd 1/2-way* **50/1**

1m 16.28s (1.38) **Going Correction** +0.25s/f (Good)
WFA 3 from 4yo+ 8lb **16 Ran SP% 118.0**
Speed ratings (Par 101): **100,98,97,96,95 94,93,93,90,90 89,85,80,72,69 45**
toteswinger: 1&2 £44.70, 1&3 £75.50, 2&3 £97.70 CSF £85.14 CT £2766.00 TOTE £8.50: £2.10, £3.90, £7.90, £4.90; EX 208.90.
Owner K Nicholls **Bred** G H Beeby And Viscount Marchwood **Trained** Edwinstowe, Notts

FOCUS
A moderate sprint, but it was typically competitive for the class. Seven of the runners went to the far side but it was those on the near side who filled the first four places. It seemed a plus to race prominently. The winner produced his best effort since last summer.
Punching Official explanation: trainer said gelding was found to be sore behind
West Leake(IRE) Official explanation: jockey said gelding missed the break

2853 EBF CHAMPAGNE LANSON MAIDEN STKS 6f 15y
2:00 (2:00) (Class 5) 2-Y-0 **£3,885** (£1,156; £577; £288) **Stalls** High

Form RPR
1 **Aerodynamic (IRE)** 2-9-3 0 PaulEddery 11 78+
(Pat Eddery) *mid-div: hdwy and nt clr run 2f out: hmpd over 1f out: led ins fnl f: rdn out* **5/1**[2]
2 1 **Ballodair (IRE)** 2-9-3 0 PaulHanagan 9 74
(R A Fahey) *chsd ldrs: rdn and edgd lft over 1f out: led ins fnl f: sn hdd: styd on same pce* **6/1**[3]
3 shd **Kanaf (IRE)** 2-9-3 0 RichardMullen 2 74+
(E A L Dunlop) *dwlt: hld up: hdwy and hmpd over 1f out: styd on* **28/1**
4 **4** 3 **Guesswork**[27] 2034 2-8-12 0 AlanMunro 6 60
(W Jarvis) *led: rdn and hung lft fr over 1f out: hdd and no ex ins fnl f* **8/1**
5 4 **Swiss Cross** 2-8-12 0 AndreaAtzeni(5) 3 53+
(G A Butler) *chsd ldrs: rdn: edegd lft and ev ch whn hmpd over 1f out: wknd ins fnl f* **12/1**
0 **6** 1/2 **Pat Seamur**[6] 2663 2-9-3 0 StephenDonohoe 13 52
(E A L Dunlop) *hld up: pushed along over 2f out: n.d* **20/1**
3 **7** 1 1/4 **Motivational (IRE)**[16] 2358 2-9-3 0 JamieSpencer 10 48
(D R Lanigan) *hld up in tch: rdn over 2f out: wknd over 1f out* **11/4**[1]
8 nse **West Leake Star (IRE)** 2-9-3 0 MichaelHills 4 48
(B W Hills) *s.i.s: a in rr* **16/1**
6 **9** 1 1/4 **He's Invincible**[19] 2280 2-9-3 0 TomEaves 7 44
(B J Meehan) *s.i.s: hld up: hdwy over 2f out: sn rdn and wknd* **15/2**
23 **10** hd **Paradise Dream**[29] 1991 2-9-3 0 LiamJones 5 43+
(J Noseda) *chsd ldr: rdn 1/2-way: hmpd and wknd over 1f out* **8/1**
11 hd **Our Boy Barrington (IRE)** 2-9-3 0 PatDobbs 12 43
(R Hannon) *dwlt: outpcd* **33/1**
0 **12** 3 **Lochbroom Sunset**[15] 2383 2-9-3 0 SaleemGolam 8 34
(S C Williams) *prom: rdn 1/2-way: wknd over 2f out* **125/1**

1m 17.4s (2.50) **Going Correction** +0.25s/f (Good) **12 Ran SP% 117.1**
Speed ratings (Par 93): **93,91,91,87,82 81,79,79,78,77 77,73**
toteswinger: 1&2 £9.20, 1&3 £35.60, 2&3 £34.00 CSF £33.42 TOTE £7.10: £2.50, £2.30, £6.20; EX 49.20.
Owner Mrs Gay Smith **Bred** Swettenham, Carradale, S Cosgrove & T Stack **Trained** Nether Winchendon, Bucks

FOCUS
This was probably a fair juvenile maiden but it was a messy race in many respects. The form makes sense though.

NOTEBOOK
Aerodynamic(IRE), whose price rose to 200,000gns last autumn, is related to several smart performers, mainly over further than this, but he is by Oratorio and looks to have inherited a good deal of that one's speed. In front a furlong out, having met his share of trouble, he ran on nicely to win with a good bit in hand and looks to have a very bright future. He will improve for 7f and is likely to take his chance in the Chesham Stakes at Royal Ascot next week. (op 4-1 tchd 7-2)
Ballodair(IRE), whose dam was a smart sprinting juvenile, chased the early pace and came to hold every chance, but he couldn't race on with the winner. This was a promising start, just managing to hold second, and he should be capable of landing an average maiden. (op 8-1 tchd 11-1)
Kanaf(IRE), an early foal who cost £50,000 as a yearling, kept on nicely in the closing stages to just miss out on second, looking a shade unfortunate as he was hampered. He should learn from this and will be suited by another furlong before long. (op 18-1)
Guesswork shaped with plenty of promise when fourth over 5f at Newbury on debut and she bowled along in front on the rail. However, she hung away to her left under pressure, doing several others no favour, and faded inside the final furlong. (op 10-1)
Swiss Cross, an early foal with plenty of speed on the female side of his pedigree, was backed beforehand and showed plenty of ability before fading having been hampered. He will be of interest next time. (op 25-1)
Pat Seamur stepped up on his debut effort and will be one to look out for in nurseries. (op 16-1)
Motivational(IRE) ailed to improve as much as expected on his debut effort when a promising third at Leicester. He weakened disappointingly having been close enough to challenge and has a bit to prove now. (op 4-1)

He's Invincible looks one for nurseries. (op 6-1 tchd 5-1)

2854 CHAMPAGNE LANSON ROSE LABEL N.V. H'CAP — 1m 6f 15y

2:30 (2:30) (Class 5) (0-75,73) 4-Y-0+ — **£2,590** (£770; £385; £192) — **Stalls** Low

Form — RPR

60-2 **1** — **Rare Ruby (IRE)**[23] 2163 5-8-5 **57** .... JoeFanning 2 — 67
(Jennie Candlish) *chsd ldr tl led over 2f out: clr over 1f out: styd on wl* — **9/2**[2]

0-63 **2** 2 ¾ **Ovthenight (IRE)**[18] 2294 4-8-13 **65** ....(v) MickyFenton 1 — 71
(Mrs P Sly) *broke wl: stdd and lost pl after 1f: hdwy u.p fr over 2f out: hung lft and chsd wnr over 1f out: no imp* — **10/1**[3]

5412 **3** 2 ¼ **Monte Pattino (USA)**[17] 2344 5-8-5 **57** ....(vt) PaulHanagan 6 — 60
(C J Teague) *sn led: rdn and hdld over 2f out: styd on same pce appr fnl f* — **14/1**

0-66 **4** 3 ¾ **Royal Premier (IRE)**[13] 2445 6-7-13 **56** ....(v) SophieDoyle(5) 5 — 54
(H J Collingridge) *s.i.s: hld up: rdn over 3f out: nvr nrr* — **40/1**

3330 **5** 2 ¼ **Soundbyte**[28] 2018 4-9-5 **71** .... LPKeniry 3 — 65
(J Gallagher) *prom: rdn over 3f out: wknd over 1f out* — **11/1**

-551 **6** 1 ½ **Murcar**[12] 2497 4-9-7 **73** ....(b) JamieSpencer 4 — 65
(C G Cox) *hld up: rdn over 2f out: sn hung lft and nt run on* — **8/11**[1]

23-2 **7** 1 **Shy**[24] 2123 4-9-5 **71** .... SaleemGolam 7 — 62
(P Winkworth) *chsd ldrs: rdn over 2f out: wknd over 1f out* — **10/1**[3]

1300 **8** 12 **Wabbraan (USA)**[27] 2040 4-8-6 **63** ....(v[1]) AmyBaker(5) 8 — 37
(M Hill) *prom: racd keenly: rdn over 3f out: sn wknd* — **40/1**

3m 7.36s (2.36) **Going Correction** +0.25s/f (Good) — **8** Ran SP% **114.1**
Speed ratings (Par 103): **103,101,100,98,96 95,95,88**
toteswinger: 1&2 £6.00, 1&3 £4.30, 2&3 £5.60 CSF £47.75 CT £573.78 TOTE £4.80: £1.60, £2.60, £1.70; EX 59.20.
Owner Mrs Judith Ratcliff **Bred** Robert And Michelle Dore **Trained** Basford Green, Staffs

■ Stewards' Enquiry : Sophie Doyle two-day ban: used whip with excessive frequency (Jun 25-26)
Joe Fanning caution: careless riding
L P Keniry two-day ban: careless riding (Jun 25-26)

FOCUS
This was a moderate handicap which took little winning and few got into it. The winner is probably the best guide to the form.

Royal Premier(IRE) Official explanation: trainer said gelding suffered interference at start

2855 CHAMPAGNE LANSON GOLD LABEL VINTAGE 1998 H'CAP — 1m 75y

3:00 (3:01) (Class 3) (0-95,92) 3-Y-0 — **£7,771** (£2,312; £1,155; £577) — **Stalls** Low

Form — RPR

4-22 **1** — **Firebet (IRE)**[40] 1677 3-9-3 **88** .... PaulHanagan 1 — 98
(R A Fahey) *chsd ldrs: rdn over 1f out: led ins fnl f: r.o* — **15/8**[1]

11 **2** ¾ **Mull Of Killough (IRE)**[26] 2092 3-9-0 **85** .... LiamJones 8 — 93
(J L Spearing) *hld up: hdwy over 3f out: led over 2f out: rdn and edgd lft over 1f out: hdd ins fnl f: styd on* — **8/1**[3]

0-03 **3** 1 ¾ **Midnight Cruiser (IRE)**[48] 1484 3-9-5 **90** .... PatDobbs 7 — 94
(R Hannon) *chsd ldr: rdn and ev ch whn rdr dropped reins over 2f out: unable qck ins fnl f* — **12/1**

-106 **4** ½ **Everynight (IRE)**[14] 2411 3-8-10 **81** .... AlanMunro 5 — 84
(M Botti) *hld up: hdwy u.p over 1f out: hung lft: nt rch ldrs* — **8/1**[3]

031 **5** 2 ¾ **High Severa (IRE)**[20] 2229 3-8-9 **80** .... RichardMullen 9 — 77
(K R Burke) *prom: rdn and edgd lft over 1f out: styd on same pce* — **22/1**

-660 **6** 1 ¼ **Tobond (IRE)**[29] 1987 3-9-2 **92** .... AndreaAtzeni(5) 2 — 86
(M Botti) *hld up: racd keenly: rdn and hung lft over 1f out: nvr trbld ldrs* — **16/1**

-224 **7** 2 ¾ **Mt Kintyre (IRE)**[39] 1693 3-8-8 **79** .... JamieSpencer 4 — 66
(M H Tompkins) *hld up: rdn over 1f out: n.d* — **9/1**

5-60 **8** 1 **Cruikadyke**[19] 2273 3-9-0 **85** .... StephenDonohoe 6 — 70
(P F I Cole) *plld hrd and prom: rdn over 2f out: wknd over 1f out* — **33/1**

4-11 **9** hd **Love Pegasus (USA)**[8] 2600 3-9-1 **86** 6ex........ JoeFanning 3 — 71
(M Johnston) *led: rdn and hdd over 2f out: wknd over 1f out* — **11/4**[2]

1m 47.3s (1.70) **Going Correction** +0.25s/f (Good) — **9** Ran SP% **114.5**
Speed ratings (Par 103): **101,100,98,98,95 94,91,90,90**
toteswinger: 1&2 £4.50, 1&3 £7.80, 2&3 £11.40 CSF £17.62 CT £141.01 TOTE £2.90: £1.40, £2.30, £3.60; EX 19.60.
Owner Mrs H Steel **Bred** Derek Veitch And Saleh Ali Hammadi **Trained** Musley Bank, N Yorks

FOCUS
A decent 3yo handicap made up of several progressive types.

NOTEBOOK
Firebet(IRE) came out on top. Making his debut for Richard Fahey, he was always likely to be suited by this step back up in trip and came with a strong challenge between runners from over a furlong out. He always looked to be doing enough once in front and this progressive sort should improve again for a step up to 1m2f. (op 11-4 tchd 7-4)
Mull Of Killough(IRE), also declared to run at Sandown today, had won both previous starts, including a handicap off 80 at Thirsk last time, and he kept finding having been the first one under pressure. He couldn't quite match the winner but is clearly still going the right way. (op 13-2 tchd 9-1)
Midnight Cruiser(IRE), third in what had looked a decent handicap at Sandown last time (winner let down form since), went on inside the final two furlongs but was unable to stick on as strongly as the front pair, with Pat Dobbs dropping the reins doing him few favours. He could do with being dropped a few pounds by the Handicapper. (op 14-1)
Everynight(IRE), last of six, though not beaten far, in a good Listed contest at Sandown last time, ran a lot better than he had done on his previous try in a handicap and could find a small race if building on this. (op 9-1)
High Severa(IRE) progressed with each start in maidens, winning in heavy ground at Haydock last time, but he wasn't good enough to make an impact off a mark of 80 this time. A step up in trip will probably help. (op 25-1 tchd 28-1)
Tobond(IRE) is still too high in the weights. (tchd 22-1)
Love Pegasus(USA) was most disappointing. On a hat-trick following a couple of wins at Kempton, he was making a quick reappearance and looked well treated under a 6lb penalty, but was quickly brushed aside and dropped away tamely. (op 9-4)

2856 CHAMPAGNE LANSON NOBLE CUVEE BRUT 1998 MAIDEN STKS (DIV I) — 1m 75y

3:35 (3:37) (Class 5) 3-Y-0+ — **£2,590** (£770; £385; £192) — **Stalls** Low

Form — RPR

52 **1** — **Candy Ride (IRE)**[24] 2139 3-8-9 0........ StephenDonohoe 5 — 74+
(E A L Dunlop) *chsd ldrs: shkn up over 2f out: led over 1f out: rdn and hung rt ins fnl f: styd on* — **3/1**[2]

0-22 **2** 1 **Eastern Warrior**[21] 2198 3-9-0 77........ MichaelHills 8 — 77
(J W Hills) *chsd ldrs: rdn and ev ch over 1f out: styd on* — **13/8**[1]

5-5 **3** hd **Sabi Star**[14] 2416 3-9-0 0........ RichardMullen 7 — 76
(J H M Gosden) *sn led: rdn and hdd over 1f out: styd on* — **5/1**[3]

05 **4** nk **Kindest**[24] 2139 3-8-9 0........ AlanMunro 2 — 71+
(C F Wall) *prom: rdn over 2f out: sn outpcd: r.o wl ins fnl f* — **8/1**

6-0 **5** 5 **Fantino**[13] 2446 3-9-0 0........ PaulHanagan 10 — 64
(J Mackie) *hld up: hdwy over 1f out: nrst fin* — **100/1**

5 **6** 2 **Pegasus Gold (USA)**[41] 1638 4-9-11 0........ PatDobbs 6 — 59
(W R Swinburn) *hld up: styd on fr over 1f out: nt trble ldrs* — **11/1**

3- **7** 2 ¼ **Nawojka (IRE)**[280] 5650 3-8-9 0........ PaulMulrennan 11 — 49
(J G Given) *s.i.s: rapid hdwy to chse ldr over 6f out: rdn over 2f out: wknd over 1f out* — **40/1**

60- **8** 1 ¼ **Aaman (IRE)**[196] 7458 3-9-0 0........ LPKeniry 9 — 51
(E F Vaughan) *s.i.s: hld up: a in rr* — **125/1**

9 ½ **Lost In The Desert (IRE)**[22] 3-8-9 0........ AndreaAtzeni(5) 3 — 50
(M Botti) *s.i.s: sn pushed along: a in rr* — **16/1**

5- **10** 1 ¼ **Broughtons Silk**[194] 7500 4-9-6 0........ MickyFenton 1 — 42
(W J Musson) *s.i.s: hld up: rdn over 3f out: a in rr* — **40/1**

11 6 **Bolshoi King (IRE)** 3-9-0 0........ JamieSpencer 4 — 34
(B J Meehan) *led early: n.m.r 7f out: chsd ldrs tl rdn and wknd over 2f out* — **22/1**

1m 49.68s (4.08) **Going Correction** +0.25s/f (Good)
WFA 3 from 4yo 11lb — **11** Ran SP% **116.1**
Speed ratings (Par 103): **89,88,87,87,82 80,78,77,76,75 69**
toteswinger: 1&2 £2.70, 1&3 £3.40, 2&3 £3.00 CSF £7.87 TOTE £4.50: £1.40, £1.30, £1.80; EX 10.40.
Owner Rick Barnes **Bred** Grangecon Stud **Trained** Newmarket, Suffolk

FOCUS
Not much of a maiden. It was steadily run and the first four finished in a bit of a heap but the form is sound enough.

2857 CHAMPAGNE LANSON NOBLE CUVEE BRUT 1998 MAIDEN STKS (DIV II) — 1m 75y

4:10 (4:13) (Class 5) 3-Y-0+ — **£2,590** (£770; £385; £192) — **Stalls** Low

Form — RPR

56- **1** — **Gassin**[245] 6597 3-9-0 0........ JamieSpencer 8 — 69
(M L W Bell) *mid-div: hdwy to chse ldr 6f out: led over 2f out: sn rdn: styd on* — **14/1**[3]

5-0 **2** ¾ **All For You (IRE)**[13] 2433 3-8-9 0........ AlanMunro 12 — 62
(M Botti) *hld up: hdwy over 2f out: rdn to chse wnr ins fnl f: styd on* — **20/1**

3 **3** nk **Bolanderi (USA)**[122] 468 4-9-11 0........ PaulEddery 1 — 69
(Andrew Turnell) *dwlt: hld up: swtchd rt and hdwy over 1f out: rdn and edgd lft ins fnl f: r.o: nt rch ldrs* — **66/1**

0- **4** 1 ¾ **Freedom Fire (IRE)**[245] 6600 3-9-0 0........ MickyFenton 2 — 62
(J M P Eustace) *led: rdn and hdd over 2f out: no ex ins fnl f* — **33/1**

5 **5** 2 ¾ **Satwa Star (IRE)**[41] 1636 3-9-0 0........ StephenDonohoe 6 — 56
(E A L Dunlop) *hld up in tch: racd keenly: rdn over 1f out: no ex fnl f* — **6/1**[2]

533- **6** 1 ¾ **Intikama (IRE)**[264] 6110 3-8-9 74........ SaleemGolam 10 — 47
(M H Tompkins) *chsd ldrs: rdn over 2f out: wknd ins fnl f* — **16/1**

0-0 **7** 1 **Royal Bloom (IRE)**[24] 2139 4-9-6 0........ TravisBlock 11 — 48
(J R Fanshawe) *hld up in tch: racd keenly: rdn over 2f out: hung lft and wknd over 1f out* — **80/1**

0-43 **8** ½ **Dreamcoat**[26] 2081 3-9-0 75........ RichardMullen 7 — 48
(J H M Gosden) *chsd ldr 2f: remained handy: rdn over 2f out: wknd over 1f out* — **3/1**[1]

00- **9** 9 **Seminal Moment**[187] 7577 3-8-9 0........ PaulMulrennan 5 — 23
(J G Given) *hld up: a in rr* — **100/1**

1m 52.05s (6.45) **Going Correction** +0.25s/f (Good)
WFA 3 from 4yo 11lb — **9** Ran SP% **63.3**
Speed ratings (Par 103): **77,76,75,74,71 69,68,68,59**
toteswinger: 1&2 £8.60, 1&3 £6.60, 2&3 £14.40 CSF £68.69 TOTE £8.90: £2.30, £2.90, £4.00; EX 75.60.
Owner J L C Pearce **Bred** J L C Pearce **Trained** Newmarket, Suffolk

FOCUS
This already had the look of a weak maiden, and the late withdrawal of hot favourite Criticize (10/11, deduct 50p in the £ under R4), who was unruly in the stalls, further devalued it as a contest. It was almost certainly the lesser of the two divisions.

Bolanderi(USA) Official explanation: jockey said gelding missed the break

2858 CHAMPAGNE LANSON IVORY LABEL DEMISEC N.V. FILLIES' H'CAP — 1m 2f 50y

4:45 (4:51) (Class 5) (0-75,75) 3-Y-0 — **£2,590** (£770; £385; £192) — **Stalls** Low

Form — RPR

32-5 **1** — **Wake Me Now (IRE)**[24] 2126 3-8-13 **70**........ JackMitchell(3) 2 — 77
(R M Beckett) *chsd ldrs: rdn and nt clr run over 1f out: styd on to ld wl ins fnl f* — **9/1**

10-1 **2** 2 **Bombina**[28] 2001 3-9-7 **75**........ AlanMunro 3 — 78+
(P W Chapple-Hyam) *trckd ldrs: racd keenly: rdn to ld over 1f out: hdd wl ins fnl f* — **11/4**[1]

25-4 **3** 1 ½ **Kaloni (IRE)**[20] 2232 3-9-7 **75**........ MickyFenton 6 — 75
(Mrs P Sly) *led: rdn over 2f out: hdd over 1f out: no ex ins fnl f* — **28/1**

4-46 **4** 1 **Piquante**[24] 2139 3-9-2 **70**........ JamieSpencer 15 — 68+
(M L W Bell) *s.i.s: hld up: r.o ins fnl f: nvr nrr* — **4/1**[2]

40-0 **5** ½ **My Girl Jode**[14] 2416 3-8-4 **58**........ LiamJones 9 — 55
(M H Tompkins) *hld up: plld hrd: hdwy over 3f out: sn rdn: edgd lft and styd on: nt trble ldrs* — **16/1**

06-4 **6** 1 ¼ **Triple Cee (IRE)**[84] 876 3-9-1 **69**........ JoeFanning 10 — 64
(M R Channon) *prom: racd keenly: chsd ldr over 3f out: rdn and ev ch wl over 1f out: wknd ins fnl f* — **20/1**

55-2 **7** shd **Teeky**[69] 1092 3-9-1 **69**........ RichardMullen 5 — 64+
(J H M Gosden) *prom: pushed along 7f out: sn lost pl: rdn 1/2-way: swtchd lft and styd on ins fnl f* — **8/1**[3]

0-02 **8** ½ **Fisadara**[33] 1874 3-9-0 **68**........ PatDobbs 7 — 62
(B W Hills) *chsd ldr tl rdn over 3f out: wknd over 1f out* — **9/1**

0-31 **9** 1 **Inis Boffin**[31] 1937 3-9-3 **71**........ LPKeniry 13 — 63
(S Kirk) *hld up: hdwy over 3f out: rdn and hung lft fr over 1f out: wknd ins fnl f* — **11/1**

6200 **10** shd **Mytivil (IRE)**[6] 2685 3-8-9 **68**........ RossAtkinson(5) 11 — 60
(M Salaman) *hld up: rdn over 3f out: n.d* — **33/1**

5460 **11** 24 **Atacama Sunrise**[23] 2152 3-7-13 **60**........ SimonPearce(7) 4 — 6
(J Pearce) *s.i.s: hld up: plld hrd: wknd over 3f out* — **33/1**

2m 14.15s (2.45) **Going Correction** +0.25s/f (Good) — **11** Ran SP% **106.1**
Speed ratings (Par 96): **100,98,97,96,96 95,94,94,93,93 74**
toteswinger: 1&2 £4.80, 1&3 £16.00, 2&3 £8.90 CSF £26.66 CT £483.07 TOTE £7.40: £2.20, £1.40, £5.10; EX 23.30.
Owner Roberts & Pawle **Bred** Liam Ormsby **Trained** Whitsbury, Hants

■ Stewards' Enquiry : Jack Mitchell two-day ban: careless riding (Jun 25-26)

FOCUS
This was a modest fillies' handicap. The first three were always prominent and the winner produced a clear personal best.

2859 CHAMPAGNE LANSON NOBLE CUVEE ROSE H'CAP 1m 2f 50y
5:15 (5:16) (Class 6) (0-60,61) 4-Y-O+ £2,047 (£604; £302) Stalls Low

Form				RPR
5300	1		**Maybe I Wont**[19] 2261 4-8-7 54 ....(p) JPHamblett(5) 16	70
			(Lucinda Featherstone) *hld up: racd keenly: hdwy over 3f out: rdn to ld and hung lft over 1f out: sn clr* **25/1**	
0-21	2	7	**Confide In Me**[3] 2764 5-9-0 61 6ex.................(t) AndreaAtzeni(5) 12	64
			(G A Butler) *prom: rdn over 2f out: chsd wnr over 1f out: styd on same pce* **15/8**[1]	
6-12	3	½	**Granary Girl**[14] 2419 7-8-11 60 .... SimonPearce(7) 4	62+
			(J Pearce) *s.i.s: hld up: last and plenty to do turning for home: r.o fr over 1f out: nt rch ldrs* **12/1**	
2234	4	nk	**Johnston's Baby (IRE)**[17] 2314 7-9-4 60 .... DavidAllan 15	61
			(E J Alston) *hld up: hdwy over 3f out: rdn and hung lft over 2f out: no imp fnl f* **11/1**	
640-	5	hd	**Waterloo Corner**[55] 6786 7-9-0 56 .... AlanMunro 14	57
			(R Craggs) *chsd ldrs: rdn whn nt clr run over 1f out: styd on same pce* **18/1**	
53-0	6	1	**Proficiency**[19] 2263 4-9-1 57 .... JamieMoriarty 11	56
			(T D Walford) *hld up: hdwy and hung lft fr over 1f out: n.d* **12/1**	
02-0	7	nk	**Moscow Oznick**[20] 2237 4-9-3 59.................(v) JamieSpencer 2	57
			(N J Vaughan) *s.s hld up: styd on fr over 1f out: n.d* **9/1**[3]	
055	8	¾	**Golden Future**[20] 2245 6-8-9 51 .... PaulHanagan 3	48
			(P D Niven) *hld up: rdn over 2f out: edgd lft over 1f out: n.d* **8/1**[2]	
2460	9	shd	**Quick Off The Mark**[20] 2237 4-8-13 55 .... PaulMulrennan 5	52
			(J G Given) *led: hdd over 6f out: led again over 2f out: rdn and hdd over 1f out: wknd fnl f* **10/1**	
0040	10	nk	**Bestowed**[13] 2458 4-8-6 55 .... AndrewHeffernan(7) 9	51
			(M C Chapman) *hld up: n.d* **100/1**	
60-0	11	shd	**Tara's Garden**[37] 1773 4-8-8 53 .... JackMitchell(3) 1	49
			(M Blanshard) *hld up: hmpd 1/2-way: hdwy over 3f out: hung lft and wknd over 2f out* **22/1**	
-06	12	1 ½	**Croeso Cusan**[24] 2125 4-8-13 60 .... SophieDoyle(5) 13	53
			(J L Spearing) *plld hrd: trckd ldr tl led over 6f out: rdn and hdd over 2f out: wknd over 1f out* **16/1**	
3000	13	1 ¾	**Our Kes (IRE)**[85] 871 7-9-2 58 .... StephenDonohoe 8	48
			(P Howling) *s.i.s: hld up: a in rr* **25/1**	
6000	14	9	**The Grey One (IRE)**[17] 2330 6-9-0 56.................(b) LPKeniry 6	29
			(J M Bradley) *hld up in tch: plld hrd: rdn over 2f out: sn wknd* **33/1**	
-400	15	14	**Red Twist**[12] 2497 4-8-8 55 .... AmyBaker(5) 10	—
			(M Hill) *racd keenly and sn prom: rdn and wknd over 3f out* **33/1**	
00/0	16	dist	**Mega Dame (IRE)**[52] 1410 5-8-13 55 .... FrankieMcDonald 7	—
			(D Haydn Jones) *prom tl wknd qckly over 3f out* **80/1**	

2m 13.6s (1.90) **Going Correction** +0.25s/f (Good) **16 Ran SP% 120.0**
Speed ratings (Par 101): **102,96,96,95,95 94,94,93,93,93 93,92,90,83,72** —
toteswinger: 1&2 £15.10, 1&3 £27.20, 2&3 £3.50 CSF £67.62 CT £636.31 TOTE £23.00: £4.30, £1.30, £2.70, £1.60; EX 80.70 Place 6: £425.78 Place 5: £96.24.
Owner J Roundtree **Bred** Wheelersland Stud **Trained** Atlow, Derbyshire

FOCUS
This was a low-grade handicap. The winner returned to something like his best from out of the blue, with the placed form sound.
Moscow Oznick Official explanation: jockey said gelding missed the break
Croeso Cusan Official explanation: jockey said filly ran too freely
Mega Dame(IRE) Official explanation: trainer said mare had a breathing problem
T/Jkpt: Not won. T/Plt: £33,233.70 to a £1 stake. Pool: £56,907.08. 1.25 winning tickets. T/Qpdt: £121.00 to a £1 stake. Pool: £3,877.10. 23.70 winning tickets. CR

2455 YARMOUTH (L-H)

Thursday, June 11

OFFICIAL GOING: Good (good to firm in places in back straight; 7.9) changing to soft after race 1 (2.20)
Wind: medium, across Weather: bright but showers threatening

2860 XTRASHINE LTD STAFF DAY OUT MAIDEN AUCTION STKS 6f 3y
2:20 (2:21) (Class 6) 2-Y-O £2,590 (£770; £385; £192) Stalls High

Form				RPR
05	1		**Perfect Ch'I (IRE)**[33] 1891 2-8-4 0 .... FrancisNorton 10	72
			(I A Wood) *mde all: hrd pressed and rdn wl over 1f out: styd on wl to forge ahd fnl 100yds* **20/1**	
2	2	¾	**Tomintoul Singer (IRE)**[16] 2354 2-8-10 0 .... IanMongan 8	76
			(H R A Cecil) *wnt lft s: t.k.h: hld up in tch: effrt to join wnr wl over 1f out: sn rdn and wandered u.p: drvn ent fnl f: no ex fnl 100yds* **2/9**[1]	
	3	2 ¼	**Hill Of Miller (IRE)** 2-8-9 0 .... DavidProbert(3) 9	71
			(Rae Guest) *t.k.h: hld up in midfield: rdn wl over 1f out: chsd ldng pair jst over 1f out: kpt on but nvr pce to threaten ldng pair* **25/1**	
0	4	2 ½	**Yawary**[17] 2324 2-8-5 0 .... EdwardCreighton 3	57+
			(C E Brittain) *s.i.s: bhd and pushed along early: hdwy into midfield 1/2-way: wnt 4th jst ins fnl f: gng on fin but nvr nr ldrs* **12/1**[3]	
0	5	5	**Emma Dora (IRE)**[12] 2494 2-8-8 0 .... NickyMackay 1	45
			(D R C Elsworth) *chsd ldrs tl over 2f out: sn wl outpcd: no ch fnl f* **25/1**	
	6	nk	**Blinka Me** 2-8-11 0 .... RHills 5	47
			(M H Tompkins) *dwely: towards rr: rdn and struggling 1/2-way: wl hld whn sltly hmpd over 1f out* **12/1**[3]	
0	7	hd	**Princess Shamal**[21] 2207 2-8-7 0 .... AdrianMcCarthy 6	42
			(J R Jenkins) *chsd ldr: ev ch 2f out: wknd qckly over 1f out* **100/1**	
0	8	nk	**Keen Bidder**[21] 2196 2-8-13 0 .... PatCosgrave 4	47
			(D M Simcock) *s.i.s: sn pushed along and racd in midfield: rdn and struggling 1/2-way: wl hld whn hung rt over 1f out* **50/1**	
	9	7	**Winston's Lad** 2-8-9 0 .... JimmyQuinn 7	22
			(P Howling) *hld up towards rr: rdn and lost tch 1/2-way* **33/1**	
0	10	5	**Bookiesindex Girl (IRE)**[34] 1841 2-8-6 0 .... JohnEgan 11	4
			(J R Jenkins) *plld hrd: chsd ldrs tl 1/2-way: sn bhd* **50/1**	
	11	nk	**Feisty's Brother** 2-8-12 0 ow1 .... AdamKirby 2	9
			(D M Simcock) *s.i.s: rn green and a bhd: t.o fnl 2f* **10/1**[2]	

1m 13.58s (-0.82) **Going Correction** -0.35s/f (Firm) **11 Ran SP% 126.6**
Speed ratings (Par 91): **91,90,87,83,77 76,76,75,66,59 59**
toteswinger: 1&2 £3.40, 1&3 £26.70, 2&3 £5.40 CSF £26.05 TOTE £22.30: £4.40, £1.02, £5.20; EX 43.00 Trifecta £285.10 Part won. Pool: £385.39 - 0.43 winning units..
Owner Paddy Barrett **Bred** Glencarrig Stud **Trained** Upper Lambourn, Berks
■ Stewards' Enquiry : Francis Norton one-day ban: careless riding (Jun 25)

FOCUS
This looked an ordinary maiden auction contest, but it provided a real turn-up. Massive improvement from the winner with the favourite not far below his debut form.
NOTEBOOK
Perfect Ch'I(IRE), who had hinted at some ability on her second start at Warwick despite missing the break, was sent straight into the lead and, although the favourite may have headed her for a few strides passing the furlong pole, she showed much more resolution to get back in front and saw it out well. There was no fluke about this and she should be able to find another race. She is likely to be given one more run before being given a break, and may then be aimed at the Watership Down Sales race at Ascot in September. (op 25-1)
Tomintoul Singer(IRE), runner-up over the minimum trip on her Leicester debut last month, travelled well enough just behind the leaders and looked likely to win when produced a furlong out, but she was out-battled. She is bred for speed so this extra furlong may not have been ideal, but she didn't prove conclusively that she didn't stay either. (op 2-7 tchd 3-10 in places)
Hill Of Miller(IRE) ◆, a 17,000euros half-brother to a couple of useful performers over 1m to 1m2f, may be the one to take from the race as he raced very green in the middle of the field early, but was doing some decent late work. He is likely to improve with racing and will appreciate further. (op 28-1 tchd 33-1)
Yawary, well beaten on her Goodwood debut, made some late progress from off the pace. This was a bit better and she probably still has some improvement left in her.
Emma Dora(IRE), beaten a very long way on her Newbury debut, showed up for a while before getting left behind and didn't achieve very much here either. (op 28-1)
Bookiesindex Girl(IRE) Official explanation: jockey said filly ran too free

2861 BLP WATERAID (S) STKS 7f 3y
2:50 (3:27) (Class 6) 2-Y-O £1,942 (£578; £288; £144) Stalls High

Form				RPR
043	1		**Mary Helen**[14] 2414 2-8-6 0 .... JohnEgan 2	54
			(W M Brisbourne) *stdd s: bhd: rdn and hdwy over 3f out: led narrowly 2f out: edgd rt u.p ent fnl f: kpt on to forge ahd ins fnl f* **9/2**[2]	
4	2	¾	**Scilly Breeze**[14] 2414 2-8-8 0 .... DavidProbert(3) 3	57
			(Rae Guest) *stdd after s: hld up in tch: rdn and sltly outpcd jst over 2f out: swtchd lft and hdwy u.p ent fnl f: kpt on: unable to rch wnr* **5/2**[1]	
653	3	½	**Highcliffe Bridge (IRE)**[10] 2541 2-8-6 0 .... CatherineGannon 4	51
			(P D Evans) *in tch: rdn 4f out: swtchd lft and hdwy u.p over 2f out: ev ch whn rdr dropped whip over 1f out: no ex ins fnl f* **13/2**	
	4	nk	**Sultan's Choice** 2-8-6 0 .... KirstyMilczarek 1	50
			(J M P Eustace) *chsd ldr: upsides wnr 2f out: rdn and unable qck over 1f out: kpt on one pce ins fnl f* **9/2**[2]	
4325	5	10	**Alphacino**[10] 2541 2-8-11 0 .... SamHitchcott 5	30
			(M R Channon) *t.k.h: chsd ldrs: rdn wl over 2f out: wknd 2f out: wl bhd fnl f* **11/2**[3]	
060	6	5	**Our Georgie Girl**[14] 2414 2-8-6 0.................(b[1]) AdrianMcCarthy 7	13
			(G G Margarson) *racd freely: sn led: hdd 2f out: wknd qckly: wl bhd fnl f* **40/1**	
64	7	18	**Bathwick Gino**[36] 1783 2-8-11 0 .... PatCosgrave 6	—
			(A B Haynes) *restless stalls: sn bhd and nvr gng wl: drvn and hung lft over 4f out: t.o fr over 2f out* **9/2**[2]	

1m 31.83s (5.23) **Going Correction** +0.25s/f (Good) **7 Ran SP% 114.3**
Speed ratings (Par 91): **80,79,78,78,66 61,40**
toteswinger: 1&2 £2.40, 1&3 £3.30, 2&3 £4.10 CSF £16.17 TOTE £6.20: £3.20, £1.90; EX 12.40.The winner was bought in for £3,800. Scilly Breeze was claimed by G. P. Martin for £5000. Sultan's Choice was claimed by P. D. Evans for £5000
Owner P Mort & Mark Brisbourne **Bred** World Racing Network **Trained** Great Ness, Shropshire

FOCUS
Following a 10mm deluge which resulted in some flooding, racing was put back half an hour and the going was changed to Soft. The first 7f race for two-year-olds run in Britain this year wasn't a very good one, but a few of these had shaped as though they would improve for it and/or were bred to appreciate it. However, the change in the ground made this an even greater test of stamina than it would otherwise have been. There wasn't much covering the front four at the line, but they pulled a mile clear of the others.
NOTEBOOK
Mary Helen, who had finished in front of both Scilly Breeze and Our Georgie Girl in a similar event over 6f here last time, was held up early before being produced with her effort down the wide outside at around halfway and then proceeded to battle on very gamely. This is her grade or perhaps she could find a nursery off a modest mark when they start next month. (op 5-1)
Scilly Breeze ran as though he would appreciate this extra furlong on his debut here last month, but he was inclined to race in snatches on this occasion. He was staying on well at the line, giving the impression that he needs an even greater test, so perhaps a stiffer track will help him. (tchd 9-4)
Highcliffe Bridge(IRE), progressive in three outings in moderate company to date, had every chance and kept plugging away to the line. It's hard to say how much of an effect her rider dropping her whip a furlong and a half from home had, but even so a race like this should be within her grasp.
Sultan's Choice, out of a half-sister to a winner over 1m7f, gave plenty of trouble beforehand but ran well for a long way in the race itself. The way she ran here and her breeding suggests that she should be able to win a modest contest given a decent test. (op 5-1)
Alphacino had his chance against the stands' rail but then dropped right out and seems to be going the wrong way.
Our Georgie Girl did far too much too early in the first-time blinkers given the conditions. (op 66-1)
Bathwick Gino had been shaping as though he would relish this sort of test, but ran too badly to be true. Official explanation: jockey said gelding became upset in stalls (op 5-1)

2862 FREE BETTING AT THEBOOKIESOFFERS.CO.UK MAIDEN STKS 6f 3y
3:25 (4:04) (Class 5) 3-Y-O+ £2,901 (£868; £434; £217; £108) Stalls High

Form				RPR
0-2	1		**Pumpkin**[18] 2298 3-8-4 0 .... Louis-PhilippeBeuzelin(5) 4	73
			(Sir Michael Stoute) *mde virtually all: hrd pressed and rdn wl over 1f out: styd on wl u.p fnl f* **7/4**[2]	
-343	2	½	**Maverin (IRE)**[14] 2415 3-9-0 78 .... JohnEgan 1	76
			(J Noseda) *wnt lft s: hld up in tch: hdwy to chse wnr 2f out: sn ev ch and clr w wnr over 1f out: no ex ins fnl f* **7/1**[3]	
	3	2	**River Till (IRE)** 3-8-9 0 .... J-PGuillambert 9	65
			(W Jarvis) *chsd ldrs: wnt 2nd over 2f out tl 2f out: outpcd by ldng pair over 1f out: kpt on again fnl 100yds* **33/1**	
6-	4	1 ¾	**Regeneration (IRE)**[223] 7106 3-9-0 0 .... PatCosgrave 15	64
			(S A Callaghan) *racd alone on stands' side: in tch: rdn and effrt over 2f: chsd ldng trio and drvn wl over 1f out: no imp after* **20/1**	
4	5	2	**Millers Crossing**[18] 2298 3-8-11 0 .... KellyHarrison(3) 11	61+
			(W J H Ratcliffe) *s.i.s: rn green and pushed along: hdwy into midfield 3f out: outpcd over 2f out: styd on again ins fnl f: nvr nr ldrs* **33/1**	
	6	nk	**Eliza Doolittle** 3-8-9 0 .... FrancisNorton 12	52+
			(J R Fanshawe) *s.i.s: in tch in midfield: shkn up an doutpcd over 2f out: plugged on again ins fnl f: nvr pce to threaten ldrs* **12/1**	

	7	1¼	**See Elsie Play** 3-8-9 0............ SamHitchcott 5	48
			(Miss Z C Davison) *s.i.s: towards rr: rdn and hdwy 3f out: modest 5th over 1f out: no prog after* **250/1**	
0	8	3¾	**Isitcozimcool (IRE)**[22] 2185 4-9-3 0............ MarkFlynn(5) 14	41
			(D E Cantillon) *sn bhd: sme modest hdwy fnl f: nvr nr ldrs* **66/1**	
05-	9	1	**Lady Dinsdale (IRE)**[315] 4562 3-8-9 0............ NickyMackay 10	33
			(T Keddy) *s.i.s: in tch in midfield: rdn and wknd over 2f out* **100/1**	
	10	1¼	**Dajen** 3-8-11 0............ MarcHalford(3) 8	34
			(D M Simcock) *in tch tl lost pl and rdn over 3f out: no ch fnl 3f* **66/1**	
22	11	3¼	**Makaam (USA)**[41] 1636 3-9-0 0............ RHills 13	23
			(M P Tregoning) *chsd ldrs tl wknd qckly over 2f out: wl btn and eased fnl f* **5/4**[1]	
3600	12	1¼	**Thoosa**[13] 2455 3-8-9 43............(v[1]) JerryO'Dwyer 7	14
			(P S McEntee) *w wnr tl wl over 2f out: sn lost pl and wandered u.p: wl bhd fnl f* **250/1**	
	13	2	**Yourgolftravel Com** 4-9-1 0............ TobyAtkinson(7) 6	13
			(M Wigham) *wnt rt s and slowly away: a bhd* **150/1**	

1m 16.01s (1.61) **Going Correction** +0.25s/f (Good)
WFA 3 from 4yo 8lb **13 Ran SP% 117.1**
Speed ratings (Par 103): **99,98,95,93,90 90,88,83,82,80 76,74,71**
toteswinger: 1&2 £2.20, 1&3 £21.20, 2&3 £34.10 CSF £13.46 TOTE £3.10: £1.10, £2.10, £7.00; EX 12.70 Trifecta £201.70 Pool: £485.37 - 1.78 winning units..
Owner Cheveley Park Stud **Bred** Cheveley Park Stud Ltd **Trained** Newmarket, Suffolk

FOCUS
This wasn't as competitive as the numbers would suggest and basically it was a two-horse race according to the market. The bulk of the field started off racing down the centre of the track, whilst one raced alone down the stands' rail. The first two home came from the two lowest stalls and the runner-up is the best guide. The slowest of the three C/D races.
Makaam(USA) Official explanation: trainer said colt was unsuited by the soft ground
Yourgolftravel Com Official explanation: trainer said colt was unsuited by the soft ground

2863 WATERAID H'CAP 1m 3y
4:00 (4:35) (Class 6) (0-65,65) 3-Y-O **£2,072** (£616; £308; £153) **Stalls High**

Form				RPR
02-5	1		**Al Qeddaaf (IRE)**[20] 2250 3-9-7 **65**............ RHills 8	83+
			(W J Haggas) *hld up in rr: stdy hdwy 4f out: led over 1f out: edgd rt but rdn clr 1f out: v easily* **15/8**[1]	
0-55	2	4½	**Surprise Party**[28] 2001 3-9-4 **62**............ GeorgeBaker 13	66
			(C F Wall) *hld up in midfield: hdwy 3f out: rdn to chse wnr over 1f out: outpcd and no ch w wnr fnl f but kpt on for clr 2nd* **7/1**	
-065	3	4½	**Evening Sunset (GER)**[26] 2091 3-9-1 **59**............ EdwardCreighton 6	53
			(M R Channon) *in tch: hdwy to chse ldrs 3f out: rdn over 2f out: 3rd and outpcd u.p over 1f out: wknd ent fnl f* **9/1**	
5-04	4	½	**Wellesley**[31] 1932 3-9-5 **63**............ AdamKirby 3	56
			(W R Swinburn) *led: rdn and hdd wl over 1f out: wknd u.p over 1f out* **6/1**[3]	
-502	5	nk	**Itainteasybeingme**[14] 2417 3-9-1 **59**............ PatCosgrave 4	51
			(J R Boyle) *s.i.s: sn in midfield: hdwy to chse ldr 6f out: ev ch and drvn 2f out: led wl over 1f out: hdd over 1f out: sn wknd* **25/1**	
6550	6	nk	**It's A Mans World**[24] 2126 3-9-3 **61**............(v[1]) JimmyQuinn 1	52
			(K M Prendergast) *stdd s: t.k.h: sn hld up in tch: rdn over 2f out: wknd over 1f out* **33/1**	
00	7	5	**Mister Frosty (IRE)**[14] 2416 3-9-2 **60**............ AdrianMcCarthy 5	40
			(G Prodromou) *hld up towards rr: rdn and no hdwy over 2f out: nvr nr ldrs* **33/1**	
3210	8	hd	**Why Nee Amy**[13] 2461 3-8-7 **54**............(p) DavidProbert(3) 10	34
			(Miss Gay Kelleway) *stdd s: in rr: sme hdwy u.p over 2f out: nvr nr ldrs* **25/1**	
3323	9	1¾	**Everaard (USA)**[15] 2370 3-9-7 **65**............ NickyMackay 11	40
			(D R C Elsworth) *chsd ldrs: rdn and struggling over 3f out: no ch fnl 2f* **5/1**[2]	
1354	10	1¾	**Baby Josr**[14] 2417 3-9-2 **60**............(v) TGMcLaughlin 12	31
			(I A Wood) *a in rr: rdn over 3f out: nvr a factor* **20/1**	
00-4	11	1	**Hilltop Artistry**[17] 2317 3-9-7 **65**............ JohnEgan 7	34
			(S W James) *towards rr: rdn 4f out: wl bhd fr over 2f out* **50/1**	
3404	12	9	**Jonnie Skull (IRE)**[1] 2807 3-8-10 **54**............(vt) JerryO'Dwyer 14	—
			(P S McEntee) *racd alone on stands' rail: chsd ldrs tl wknd u.p wl over 2f out: wl bhd and eased fnl f* **16/1**	
0-05	13	3	**Cake Stand**[26] 2082 3-9-0 **58**............ KirstyMilczarek 16	—
			(J A R Toller) *in tch in midfield tl rdn and btn over 3f out* **20/1**	
00	14	hd	**Hard Ball**[27] 2048 3-9-7 **65**............ FrancisNorton 15	6
			(M Quinn) *in tch in midfield: dropped in rr over 3f out: t.o fnl 2f* **33/1**	
040-	15	8	**Musigny (USA)**[176] 7700 3-9-6 **64**............ J-PGuillambert 9	—
			(W Jarvis) *chsd ldr for 2f: styd handy tl wknd qckly over 2f out: t.o and eased fnl f* **16/1**	

1m 42.38s (1.78) **Going Correction** +0.25s/f (Good) **15 Ran SP% 128.0**
Speed ratings (Par 97): **101,96,92,91,91 90,85,85,83,82 81,72,69,69,61**
toteswinger: 1&2 £5.60, 1&3 £10.00, 2&3 £16.00 CSF £14.08 CT £108.07 TOTE £2.50: £1.60, £2.50, £3.90; EX 15.40 Trifecta £112.10 Pool: £194.00 - 1.28 winning units..
Owner Hamdan Al Maktoum **Bred** Gerrardstown House Stud **Trained** Newmarket, Suffolk

FOCUS
A moderate handicap in which the bulk of the field came down the centre whilst a couple came stands' side, but as in the previous contest those that came down the middle seemed to have the advantage. The size of the field suggested that it should have been competitive, but it was turned into a procession by the much improved Al Qeddaaf, who may have raced on the best side.
Hilltop Artistry Official explanation: jockey said colt never travelled
Jonnie Skull(IRE) Official explanation: jockey said gelding ran flat
Musigny(USA) Official explanation: jockey said gelding stopped quickly

2864 ESSEX & SUFFOLK WATER H'CAP 6f 3y
4:35 (5:06) (Class 5) (0-70,69) 3-Y-O+ **£2,719** (£809; £404; £202) **Stalls High**

Form				RPR
06-4	1		**Tyfos**[14] 2418 4-10-0 **69**............ TGMcLaughlin 11	80
			(W M Brisbourne) *hld up in tch: rdn to chal 1f out: drvn to ld fnl 100yds: r.o wl* **9/2**[2]	
50-5	2	½	**Big Boom**[147] 175 4-8-9 **50** oh5............ FrancisNorton 3	59
			(M Quinn) *racd in centre: chsd ldrs: rdn and effrt jst over 2f out: led over 1f out: hrd pressed 1f out: hdd fnl 100yds: no ex* **8/1**	
0-50	3	3¼	**Requisite**[14] 2397 4-10-0 **69**............(v[1]) GeorgeBaker 7	68
			(I A Wood) *slowly away: hmpd sn after s: hld up bhd: hdwy over 2f out: rdn to chse ldrs over 1f out: no hdwy 1f out: wknd fnl 100yds* **11/2**[3]	
-040	4	¾	**Rough Rock (IRE)**[13] 2456 4-9-0 **55**............ JohnEgan 10	52
			(C A Dwyer) *chsd ldrs: rdn over 2f out: drvn and edgd rt u.p over 1f out: plugged on same pce fnl f* **10/1**	
4-60	5	½	**Style Icon**[36] 1787 4-9-5 **63**............ DavidProbert(3) 4	58
			(Rae Guest) *chsd ldrs: rdn to ld jst over 2f out: hdd over 1f out: wknd u.p ent fnl f: btn whn swtchd lft ins fnl f* **11/2**[3]	
-530	6	nse	**Bigfanofthat (IRE)**[42] 1634 4-9-2 **62**............(v[1]) MarkFlynn(5) 9	57
			(M D Squance) *s.i.s: bhd: rdn over 3f out: hdwy but edgd lft fr over 2f out: nvr gng pce to rch ldrs* **14/1**	
6044	7	4½	**Mafaheem**[80] 937 7-9-8 **63**............(b) PatCosgrave 8	43
			(A B Haynes) *awkward leaving stalls and jostled sn after s: in tch in midfield: rdn and fnd little 2f out: wl btn fnl f* **14/1**	
0-14	8	shd	**Efisio Princess**[92] 806 6-9-4 **59**............ RichardThomas 2	39
			(J E Long) *led tl hdd jst over 2f out wknd qckly wl over 1f out* **11/4**[1]	
0000	9	1¼	**Averoo**[14] 2418 4-8-7 **55**............(p) CarolineKelly(7) 12	31
			(M D Squance) *sn bhd: nvr on terms* **33/1**	
4501	10	8	**Sherjawy (IRE)**[6] 2680 5-9-4 **59** 6ex............(b) KirstyMilczarek 6	10
			(Miss Z C Davison) *chsd ldr tl wl over 2f out: sn droped out: t.o fnl f* **8/1**	

1m 15.9s (1.50) **Going Correction** +0.25s/f (Good) **10 Ran SP% 123.2**
Speed ratings (Par 103): **100,99,95,94,93 93,87,87,85,74**
totewinger: 1&2 £5.80, 1&3 £16.50, 2&3 £20.30 CSF £42.98 CT £213.04 TOTE £5.50: £2.10, £3.50, £2.20; EX 83.40 TRIFECTA Not won..
Owner J Tomlinson/G Williams **Bred** J Tomlinson And G Williams **Trained** Great Ness, Shropshire
■ Stewards' Enquiry : John Egan two-day ban: careless riding (Jun 25-26)

FOCUS
An ordinary sprint handicap and the field raced closer to the stands' rail than in the previous contest. The winner was back to his 3yo form but the runner-up was out of the weights.

2865 CHRIS HARRISON "OLDEST STAG IN TOWN" H'CAP 1m 3f 101y
5:05 (5:36) (Class 6) (0-65,69) 3-Y-O **£2,072** (£616; £308; £153) **Stalls Low**

Form				RPR
00-0	1		**Outland (IRE)**[24] 2131 3-8-2 **46**............ AdrianMcCarthy 7	56+
			(M H Tompkins) *racd wl off the pce in midfield: rdn and hdwy over 3f out: chsd ldr 2f out: led over 1f out: sn clr: eased wl ins fnl f* **50/1**	
5011	2	3	**Brett Vale (IRE)**[1] 2809 3-9-4 **69** 12ex............ RosieJessop(7) 2	70
			(Sir Mark Prescott) *led and sn clr: wl clr over 5f out: rdn ent fnl 2f: hdd over 1f out: no ch w wnr after: jst hld on for 2nd* **11/10**[1]	
050-	3	hd	**Windpfeil (IRE)**[183] 7622 3-9-4 **62**............ NickyMackay 6	63
			(J H M Gosden) *hld up wl off the pce towards rr: hdwy on inner over 3f out: swtchd rt over 2f out: chsd ldng pair over 1f out: kpt on to press for 2nd nr fin: no ch w wnr* **12/1**	
50-0	4	1¼	**Jumaana (IRE)**[28] 2006 3-9-4 **62**............ RHills 12	61
			(J L Dunlop) *stdd s: t.k.h: hld up wl off the pce in rr: stl plenty to do 3f out: hdwy u.p over 2f out: chsd ldng trio and wandered u.p over 1f out: kpt on same pce fnl f* **10/1**[3]	
-505	5	7	**Dark Echoes**[20] 2236 3-8-12 **56**............ FrancisNorton 9	43
			(Jedd O'Keeffe) *chsd ldng pair tl 6f out: rdn and effrt wl over 3f out: wknd over 1f out* **66/1**	
0-05	6	½	**Rowan Tiger**[12] 2489 3-9-1 **59**............ PatCosgrave 5	45
			(J R Boyle) *chsd clr ldr: rdn and hung rt over 2f out: lost 2nd 2f out: wknd over 1f out* **10/1**[3]	
6-00	7	3¼	**Hi Fling**[21] 2206 3-8-13 **62**............ Louis-PhilippeBeuzelin(5) 10	43
			(B J Meehan) *racd wl off the pce in midfield: rdn and effrt over 3f out: nvr nr ldrs: wl btn over 1f out* **33/1**	
3302	8	4	**Hector Spectre (IRE)**[35] 1811 3-9-1 **59**............ JimmyQuinn 3	33
			(K M Prendergast) *hld up wl off the pce in midfield: rdn and effrt 4f out: wnt modest 4th over 2f out: no hdwy after: wknd over 1f out* **18/1**	
6332	9	4½	**Persian Tomcat (IRE)**[7] 2635 3-7-10 **47**............ MatthewCosham(7) 13	13
			(Miss J Feilden) *stdd s: hld up wl bhd: effrt on outer over 3f out: sn hung rt and no prog* **20/1**	
3-02	10	5	**Venture Capitalist**[16] 2357 3-9-5 **63**............ AdamKirby 1	21
			(L M Cumani) *chsd ldrs: wnt modest 3rd 6f out: rdn 4f out: no hdwy: wknd over 2f out: wl bhd fnl f* **11/4**[2]	
064	11	35	**Langford Decoit (IRE)**[17] 2323 3-9-7 **65**............ SamHitchcott 4	—
			(M R Channon) *v.s.a: hld up wl bhd: t.o fnl 4f: virtually p.u fnl f* **25/1**	

2m 31.49s (2.79) **Going Correction** +0.25s/f (Good) **11 Ran SP% 120.4**
Speed ratings (Par 97): **99,96,96,95,90 90,87,85,81,78 52**
totewinger: 1&2 £27.60, 1&3 £74.50, 2&3 £7.10 CSF £105.65 CT £803.70 TOTE £64.80: £10.40, £1.20, £3.30; EX 278.20 TRIFECTA Not won..
Owner Rob Douglas **Bred** St Simon Foundation **Trained** Newmarket, Suffolk

FOCUS
A modest handicap. The winner and third stepped forward but the well-in runner-up probably went off too hard.
Outland(IRE) Official explanation: trainer's rep said, regarding apparent improvement in form, that the gelding had strengthened up over the winter and had benefited from running on a turf surface.
Venture Capitalist Official explanation: trainer said colt was unsuited by the soft ground

2866 WATERAID CHARITY H'CAP 1m 6f 17y
5:35 (6:10) (Class 5) (0-70,69) 3-Y-O **£2,719** (£809; £404; £202) **Stalls High**

Form				RPR
-530	1		**Excelsior Academy**[21] 2208 3-8-13 **66**............ Louis-PhilippeBeuzelin(5) 8	74+
			(B J Meehan) *chsd ldr tl 10f out: chsd ldng pair after: rdn and ev ch 4f out: led over 3f out: drvn clr wl over 1f out: eased wl ins fnl f* **4/1**[3]	
00-0	2	3½	**Kidson (USA)**[12] 2479 3-8-2 **50** oh5............ FrancisNorton 2	51
			(George Baker) *prom tl stdd into last pair after 1f: pushed along 5f out: poor 7th 3f out: hdwy and swtchd rt over 1f out: styd on fnl f to go 2nd nr fin: nvr nr wnr* **6/1**	
0-42	3	½	**Tinkerbelle (IRE)**[16] 2350 3-8-7 **55**............ JimmyQuinn 3	55
			(J L Dunlop) *in tch: pushed along and sltly outpcd 5f out: rdn and hdwy over 4f out: ev ch wl over 3f out: chsd wnr 2f out: btn over 1f out: lost 2nd nr fin* **11/4**[1]	
5-20	4	¾	**Honorable Endeavor**[12] 2489 3-8-5 **58** ow3............(v[1]) MarkFlynn(5) 4	57
			(E F Vaughan) *t.k.h early: hld up in rr: hdwy 6f out: rdn and hdwy to press ldrs on outer wl over 3f out: chsd ldng pair and hung lft fr 2f out: wl hld over 1f out: lost 3rd ins fnl f* **33/1**	
-025	5	1½	**Pure Crystal**[17] 2340 3-8-6 **54**............(b) EdwardCreighton 6	51
			(M G Quinlan) *chsd ldrs tl hdwy to go 2nd 10f out: led 5f out: rdn and hdd wl over 3f out: sn outpcd: hung rt over 1f out: one pce after* **17/2**	
0451	6	2	**Vita Mia**[10] 2540 3-8-12 **60** 6ex............ CatherineGannon 7	54
			(P D Evans) *sn led: hdd and rdn 5f out: stl ev ch wl over 3f out: wknd ent fnl 2f* **13/2**	
4011	7	11	**Taste The Wine (IRE)**[8] 2605 3-9-7 **69** 6ex............ JohnEgan 9	48
			(J S Moore) *t.k.h early: in tch: hdwy and ev ch wl over 3f out: wknd jst over 2f out: wl btn and eased fr over 1f out* **3/1**[2]	

5030 **8** 3 1/4 **Alittlemoreflair**[30] 1954 3-8-10 **58** JerryO'Dwyer 5 32
(J Pearce) *hld up in last trio: pushed along over 6f out: lost tch and rdn over 4f out: wl btn after* **25/1**

3m 11.89s (4.29) **Going Correction** +0.25s/f (Good) **8** Ran SP% **116.6**
Speed ratings (Par 99): **97,95,94,94,93 92,86,84**
toteswinger: 1&2 £5.40, 1&3 £4.60, 2&3 £3.40 CSF £28.75 CT £76.75 TOTE £5.20: £1.40, £2.10, £1.10; EX 37.00 Trifecta £96.50 Pool: £249.24 - 1.91 winning units. Place 6: £34.42 Place 5 £26.56.
Owner Lady Laidlaw Of Rothiemay **Bred** Lady Halifax **Trained** Manton, Wilts

FOCUS
A modest staying handicap and a decent test in the ground for these still relatively young horses, but although the early pace was a fair one there were still six horses within a length of each other in a line across the track passing the 3f pole. Probably not form to take too literally with the third the best guide.
Taste The Wine(IRE) Official explanation: jockey said gelding had a breathing problem
Alittlemoreflair Official explanation: jockey said filly never travelled
T/Plt: £92.80 to a £1 stake. Pool: £47,410.27. 372.80 winning tickets. T/Qpdt: £37.10 to a £1 stake. Pool: £3,584.55. 71.40 winning tickets. SP

2867 - 2869a (Foreign Racing) - See Raceform Interactive

2642 LEOPARDSTOWN (L-H)
Thursday, June 11

OFFICIAL GOING: Good (good to firm in places)

2870a BALLYCORUS STKS (GROUP 3) 7f
7:35 (7:37) 3-Y-0+ **£41,019** (£11,990; £5,679; £1,893)

RPR

1 **Duff (IRE)**[29] 1989 6-9-9 109 FMBerry 7 110
(Edward Lynam, Ire) *led: hdd after 2f: impr to ld again 1 1/2f out: rdn and kpt on wl fnl f: all out cl home* **4/1**[2]

2 *nk* **Dohasa (IRE)**[29] 1989 4-9-9 109 JMurtagh 8 109+
(G M Lyons, Ire) *chsd ldrs: 5th 1/2-way: rdn into 3rd 1 1/2f out: kpt on to go 2nd fnl f: pressed wnr cl home: jst hld* **7/2**[1]

3 *1 1/4* **Georgebernardshaw (IRE)**[19] 2287 4-9-9 98 CO'Donoghue 9 106
(A P O'Brien, Ire) *chsd ldrs: impr to ld after 2f: rdn and hdd 1 1/2f out: no ex in 2nd 1f out: kpt on same pce fnl f* **16/1**

4 *1 1/4* **Three Rocks (IRE)**[10] 2554 4-9-9 107 KJManning 1 103+
(J S Bolger, Ire) *in rr of mid-div: dropped to rr 2f out: rdn and kpt on fr over 1f out: styd on fnl f* **7/2**[1]

5 *hd* **Lord Admiral (USA)**[32] 1913 8-9-9 112 (b) MJKinane 6 102+
(Charles O'Brien, Ire) *hld up towards rr: hdwy in 6th 2f out: rdn and no imp 1 1/2f out: 5th 1f out: kpt on same pce* **7/1**[3]

6 *3/4* **San Sicharia (IRE)**[7] 2644 4-9-9 104 PJSmullen 2 100
(Ms Joanna Morgan, Ire) *mid-div: 6th 1/2-way: rdn in 7th 2f out: no imp in 6th 1f out: kpt on one pce* **4/1**[2]

7 *3/4* **Rock Of Rochelle (USA)**[29] 1989 4-9-12 108 ShaneFoley 5 101
(A Kinsella, Ire) *chsd ldrs: 3rd 1/2-way: rdn in 4th 2f out: no ex 1 1/2f out: wknd over 1f out* **8/1**

8 *nk* **Mooretown Lady (IRE)**[230] 6960 6-9-6 99 JAHeffernan 3 94
(H Rogers, Ire) *dwlt: hld up in rr: rdn in 8th 2f out: sn no imp and kpt on one pce* **33/1**

9 *1 3/4* **Gist (IRE)**[7] 2647 6-9-6 95 (b) NGMcCullagh 4 89
(W J Martin, Ire) *chsd ldrs: 4th 1/2-way: rdn in 3rd 2f out: sn no ex and wknd over 1f out* **50/1**

1m 26.37s (-2.33) **Going Correction** -0.20s/f (Firm) **9** Ran SP% **118.8**
Speed ratings: **105,104,103,101,101 100,99,99,97**
CSF £19.06 TOTE £4.50: £1.50, £1.60, £4.20; DF 14.50.
Owner Kilboy Estate **Bred** Kilboy Estate **Trained** Dunshaughlin, Co Meath

FOCUS
This looked a decent Group 3 contest on paper with several decent types among the field. The front-running winner had the run of things and has been rated in line with his turf form from last year.

NOTEBOOK
Duff(IRE) resumed winning ways after taking over early in the straight and holding the staying-on favourite by a diminishing margin under a super ride from Fran Berry. His last two wins were recorded overseas on the all-weather tracks at Kempton and Lingfield and, having won four-times in all in Listed company, this step up was well deserved. Trainer Eddie Lynam intends letting the winner take his chance in the Golden Jubilee at Royal Ascot next Saturday.
Dohasa(IRE) was representing a trainer who was seeking his third win in the last four years in this event. All four of his wins had been recorded over 5f and 6f coming into this, but he ran on well on his favoured ground and was getting there with every stride only for the line to come too soon. (op 3/1)
Georgebernardshaw(IRE) took over at the head of affairs early but he struggled when Duff loomed up travelling much better early in the straight although this was better from the Ballydoyle colt.
Three Rocks(IRE) never looked like imposing his presence despite making some late headway in the straight. Having his eighth start of the season, he raced at the back turning for home and the fact he struggled to settle for Kevin Manning to that point did him no favours. (op 4/1 tchd 9/2)
Lord Admiral(USA) had underfoot conditions in his favour but the 2007 winner was another who never looked like playing a part at the business end. (op 6/1)
San Sicharia(IRE) had a bit to find on official ratings although this trip and ground looked more down her street. The Lingfield Group 3 winner last month made no impression when asked a serious question rounding the home turn. (op 5/1)
Rock Of Rochelle(USA) dropped out when they straightened for home. (op 7/1)

2871 - 2873a (Foreign Racing) - See Raceform Interactive

MULHEIM (R-H)
Thursday, June 11

OFFICIAL GOING: Soft

2874a GROSSER PREIS DER SPARKASSE MULHEIM (LISTED RACE) (FILLIES) 1m 3f
3:55 (4:12) 3-Y-0 **£11,650** (£4,272; £2,330; £1,165)

RPR

1 **Belle Syrienne (GER)** 3-9-0 FilipMinarik 4 100
(P Schiergen, Germany)

2 *1/2* **Andrea (GER)**[59] 3-8-11 FJohansson 1 96
(H Blume, Germany)

3 *4 1/2* **La Poesie (GER)**[26] 3-8-11 THellier 8 89
(W Baltromei, Germany)

4 *2* **Wanna Be (GER)** 3-8-11 ASuborics 5 85
(W Hickst, Germany)

5 *nk* **Jambalaya (GER)**[32] 1914 3-9-2 EPedroza 2 90
(A Wohler, Germany)

6 *1/2* **Cordoba (GER)**[39] 3-9-0 ADeVries 7 87
(H Steinmetz, Germany)

7 *9* **Atabaas Allure (FR)**[21] 2208 3-8-11 RoystonFfrench 3 69
(M Johnston) *disp 3rd to 1/2-way: 5th st: rdn over 2f out: sn btn* **31/5**[1]

2m 28.92s (4.20) **7** Ran SP% **13.9**
(Including 10 Euros stake): WIN 42; PL 17, 22, 16; SF 352.
Owner Stiftung Gestut Fahrhof **Bred** Dr R Wilhelms **Trained** Germany

NOTEBOOK
Atabaas Allure(FR), twice beaten off a mark of 81 this term, was stepping up in grade and probably found the ground too soft.

2348 CHEPSTOW (L-H)
Friday, June 12

OFFICIAL GOING: Good to firm (good in places; 8.9)
Wind: Almost nil Weather: Fine

2875 E.B.F./TOTEPLACEPOT NOVICE STKS 6f 16y
6:30 (6:31) (Class 4) 2-Y-0 **£5,180** (£1,541; £770; £384) **Stalls High**

Form RPR

01 **1** **Sir Parky (IRE)**[22] 2201 2-9-5 0 RichardHughes 4 88+
(R Hannon) *mde all: shkn up 1f out: pushed out* **4/5**[1]

441 **2** *1* **Daniella De Bruijn (IRE)**[22] 2196 2-8-11 0 JamesDoyle 1 74
(A B Haynes) *a chsng wnr: ev ch over 1f out: rdn and nt qckn ins fnl f* **9/2**[3]

3 *2 1/4* **Suffolk Punch (IRE)** 2-8-12 0 LPKeniry 6 68+
(A M Balding) *s.i.s: hld up and bhd: hdwy 2f out: rdn over 1f out: one pce* **16/1**

00 **4** *3/4* **Mnarani (IRE)**[3] 2793 2-8-12 0 CatherineGannon 2 66
(J S Moore) *stdd s: hld up: hdwy 3f out: rdn over 1f out: one pce* **33/1**

61 **5** *nk* **Strike Shot**[13] 2484 2-9-5 0 TedDurcan 5 72
(W R Muir) *a.p: rdn over 1f out: one pce* **7/2**[2]

51 **6** *1 1/4* **Underworld Dandy**[18] 2319 2-9-0 0 (p) FrancisNorton 3 63
(P D Evans) *prom: rdn over 2f out: hung lft and wknd wl over 1f out* **16/1**

1m 12.4s (0.40) **Going Correction** -0.15s/f (Firm) **6** Ran SP% **110.7**
Speed ratings (Par 95): **97,95,92,91,91 89**
toteswinger: 1&2 £1.10, 1&3 £21.30, 2&3 £21.30. CSF £4.63 TOTE £1.60: £1.20; EX 4.20.
Owner Sir David Seale **Bred** Swordlestown Stud **Trained** East Everleigh, Wilts

FOCUS
Four previous winners in this novice stakes, but Sir Parky proved a notch above his rival.

NOTEBOOK
Sir Parky(IRE) proved a notch above his rivals, asserting in a matter of strides in the final furlong, having travelled well in front. He is clearly as effective at 6f having won his maiden over the minimum trip. Entries in some big sales races later in the season suggest connections think he's got plenty more to offer. (op 10-11 tchd 1-1 in a place)
Daniella De Bruijn(IRE) appreciated the step up to 6f and a switch to softer ground when off the mark at Haydock, conditions here were much quicker. She was getting 8lb from the winner, but was beaten fairly comprehensively, but the return to more testing conditions will doubtless see her in a better light. (tchd 5-1)
Suffolk Punch(IRE) shaped with a deal of promise having been slowly away. He displayed a smart cruising speed through the middle of the contest and, although only one-paced in the finish, he looks sure to improve. He is one to keep on-side back in maiden company. (tchd 14-1 and 18-1)
Mnarani(IRE) plugged on and looks the type to do better in handicaps, for which he is now qualified. (op 25-1)
Strike Shot didn't seem to see out the 6f. His trainer said beforehand that he would prefer a bit of cut in the ground, so it appears he would be better suited by easier conditions. (tchd 4-1)
Underworld Dandy Official explanation: jockey said colt hung left

2876 TOTESWINGER (S) STKS 7f 16y
7:00 (7:01) (Class 6) 3-Y-0+ **£1,942** (£578; £288; £144) **Stalls High**

Form RPR

10 **1** **El Dececy (USA)**[7] 2665 5-9-10 77 (p) RichardHughes 14 66
(S Parr) *a.p: led and edgd rt over 1f out: rdn and r.o ins fnl f* **5/4**[1]

0102 **2** *1* **Outer Hebrides**[5] 2745 8-9-5 51 (v) AmyBaker(5) 6 63
(J M Bradley) *hld up towards rr: rdn and hdwy over 2f out: ev ch ins fnl f: nt qckn* **33/1**

6-00 **3** *2 3/4* **Premier Krug (IRE)**[48] 1520 3-8-4 45 CatherineGannon 7 42
(P D Evans) *towards rr: rdn over 2f out: hdwy over 1f out: kpt on to take 3rd wl ins fnl f* **40/1**

5-56 **4** *1 1/4* **Montmartre (USA)**[7] 2662 3-8-9 72 NickyMackay 4 44
(B J Meehan) *a.p: rdn and edgd rt ins fnl f: one pce* **13/2**[3]

40/0 **5** *1* **Picture Frame**[53] 1413 5-9-2 57 KevinGhunowa(3) 16 45
(J T Stimpson) *hld up: rdn and hdwy over 2f out: edgd lft over 1f out: no ex ins fnl f* **25/1**

2004 **6** *3/4* **Ten Pole Tudor**[5] 2746 4-9-0 56 (p) RichardEvans(5) 10 43
(R A Harris) *s.s: in rr: rdn over 2f out: hdwy over 1f out: nvr trbld ldrs* **4/1**[2]

-000 **7** *1/2* **The Jailer**[47] 1535 6-9-0 47 VinceSlattery 9 37
(J G M O'Shea) *prom: rdn and ev ch over 1f out: wknd ins fnl f* **50/1**

5100 **8** *3 1/4* **Mocha Java**[25] 2137 6-9-5 55 RossAtkinson(5) 3 38
(M Salaman) *led: rdn and hdd over 2f out: wknd over 1f out* **16/1**

00 **9** *1 1/2* **Primera Rossa**[90] 839 3-7-13 0 SophieDoyle(5) 8 21
(J S Moore) *s.i.s: a bhd* **100/1**

6404 **10** *1 1/4* **Cwmni**[29] 2009 3-8-4 50 FrancisNorton 12 17
(B Palling) *w ldr: led over 2f out: rdn and hdd over 1f out: wknd ins fnl f* **10/1**

-000 **11** *1/2* **Darwin's Dragon**[10] 2578 3-8-9 68 TedDurcan 15 21
(P F I Cole) *prom tl rdn and wknd 3f out* **9/1**

46/0 **12** *31* **Leoballero**[16] 2378 9-9-5 62 (b[1]) JamesDoyle 17 —
(K M Prendergast) *prom over 3f: eased whn no ch over 1f out* **20/1**

1m 23.4s (0.20) **Going Correction** -0.15s/f (Firm)
WFA 3 from 4yo+ 10lb **12** Ran SP% **119.7**
Speed ratings (Par 101): **92,90,87,86,85 84,83,80,78,76 76,40**
toteswinger: 1&2 £11.20, 1&3 £26.10, 2&3 £26.10. CSF £65.25 TOTE £2.00: £1.20, £2.30, £12.70; EX 18.90.The winner was bought in for 12,500gns.
Owner Willie McKay **Bred** Shadwell Farm LLC **Trained**

FOCUS
A poor race in which El Dececy, who had won three of these events previously this term, had standout claims at the weights. The race could be rated higher but the runner-up limits the form.
Montmartre(USA) Official explanation: jockey said gelding hung right-handed
Primera Rossa Official explanation: jockey said filly was unsuited by the track

Leoballero Official explanation: jockey said gelding stopped very quickly

2877 TOTEQUADPOT MAIDEN FILLIES' STKS 1m 4f 23y
7:35 (7:35) (Class 5) 3-Y-0+ **£3,238** (£963; £481; £240) **Stalls** Low

Form RPR

1 **Alpen Glen** 3-8-12 0 .... J-PGuillambert 10 87+
(M Johnston) *chsd ldr: led over 3f out: clr wl over 1f out: v easily* **14/1**

4-2 2 6 **Sweet Hollow**[28] 2051 3-8-12 0 .... PhilipRobinson 11 74+
(C G Cox) *hld up in tch: wnt 2nd over 2f out: sn rdn: no ch w wnr* **5/6**[1]

6 3 2 ¾ **Galilean Moon**[49] 1488 3-8-12 0 .... RichardHughes 12 68
(Sir Michael Stoute) *a.p: swtchd rt over 2f out: kpt on same pce* **7/1**[3]

3 4 ¾ **Little Prudence**[34] 1874 3-8-9 0 .... JackMitchell(3) 5 66
(R M Beckett) *hld up towards rr: hdwy over 3f out: rdn 2f out: one pce* **16/1**

04 5 shd **Dark Quest**[28] 2051 3-8-12 0 .... TedDurcan 6 66
(J L Dunlop) *hld up in tch: chsd wnr over 3f out tl rdn over 2f out: wknd over 1f out* **9/2**[2]

0- 6 1 ¾ **Theola (IRE)**[226] 7069 3-8-12 0 .... SaleemGolam 3 63+
(M H Tompkins) *sn wl bhd: styd on fr over 2f out: nvr nrr* **50/1**

7 4 **Strategic Princess (IRE)** 3-8-12 0 .... JosedeSouza 7 57
(P F I Cole) *hld up in mid-div: rdn over 3f out: wknd over 2f out* **40/1**

8 6 **Mito**[957] 8-9-13 39 .... NickyMackay 4 47?
(B R Millman) *prom tl rdn and wknd over 3f out* **100/1**

0 9 8 **Saxona (IRE)**[14] 2447 5-9-13 0 .... StephenDonohoe 2 35
(Ian Williams) *hld up in mid-div: rdn over 4f out: wknd over 3f out* **80/1**

02- 10 21 **Bantu**[196] 7474 4-9-13 0 .... RichardMullen 8 1
(J H M Gosden) *led: hdd over 3f out: sn wknd: t.o* **9/1**

66 11 7 **Straight Laced**[23] 2181 3-8-12 0 .... PaulDoe 1 —
(W J Knight) *a in rr: lost tch 6f out: t.o* **80/1**

2m 35.05s (-3.95) **Going Correction** -0.15s/f (Firm)
WFA 3 from 4yo+ 15lb 11 Ran SP% **115.6**
Speed ratings (Par 100): **107,103,101,100,100 99,96,92,87,73 68**
toteswinger: 1&2 £10.30, 1&3 £19.40, 2&3 £6.50. CSF £25.74 TOTE £17.60: £3.10, £1.10, £2.40; EX 29.00.
Owner Sheikh Hamdan Bin Mohammed Al Maktoum **Bred** Darley **Trained** Middleham Moor, N Yorks

FOCUS
Seemingly modest Chepstow maiden form. There were no obvious excuses for the disappointing odds-on favourite, but she may have been unfortunate to bump into an above-average filly and she is rated to her previous mark.
Sweet Hollow Official explanation: jockey said filly was unsuited by the good to firm (good in places) ground
Bantu Official explanation: jockey said filly had no more to give
Straight Laced Official explanation: jockey said filly hung left

2878 TOTETRIFECTA H'CAP 1m 2f 36y
8:10 (8:13) (Class 5) (0-75,72) 4-Y-0+ **£3,367** (£1,002; £500; £250) **Stalls** Low

Form RPR

0-44 1 **Laish Ya Hajar (IRE)**[7] 2675 5-9-4 69 .... RichardHughes 7 79
(P R Webber) *mde all: rdn fnl f: r.o wl* **7/2**[2]

304 2 3 **Man Of Gwent (UAE)**[16] 2374 5-9-0 70 .... RichardEvans(5) 8 74
(P D Evans) *hld up: hdwy over 5f out: chsd wnr 3f out: rdn wl over 1f out: no imp* **3/1**[1]

3305 3 1 ½ **Seventh Hill**[13] 2497 4-8-9 60 .... FrancisNorton 11 61
(M Blanshard) *hld up: hdwy over 3f out: rdn and one pce fnl f* **13/2**

0413 4 ¾ **King Of Connacht**[24] 2171 6-8-7 58 ....(p) LiamJones 6 58
(M Wellings) *hld up: hdwy over 3f out: rdn over 1f out: one pce* **9/2**[3]

4550 5 1 ¼ **Uig**[7] 2678 8-8-8 59 .... CatherineGannon 1 56
(H S Howe) *prom: chsd wnr after 2f to 3f out: sn rdn: fdd ins fnl f* **9/1**

3404 6 ½ **Hucking Heat (IRE)**[14] 2442 5-8-13 67 ....(p) JackMitchell(3) 10 63
(R Hollinshead) *hld up in rr: rdn and hdwy on outside over 2f out: hung lft jst over 1f out: no imp* **15/2**

06-4 7 3 ¼ **Robbmaa (FR)**[20] 1960 4-7-11 53 oh5 .... AmyBaker(5) 9 43
(A W Carroll) *chsd wnr 2f: prom: rdn 3f out: wknd 2f out* **33/1**

1026 8 ¾ **King Of The Beers (USA)**[46] 1568 5-7-11 53 oh2...(p) SophieDoyle(5) 5 41
(R A Harris) *a in rr* **7/1**

2m 10.57s (-0.03) **Going Correction** -0.15s/f (Firm) 8 Ran SP% **115.9**
Speed ratings (Par 103): **94,91,90,89,88 88,85,85**
toteswinger: 1&2 Not won, 1&3 £8.90, 2&3 £6.50. CSF £14.70 CT £64.67 TOTE £4.60: £1.70, £1.60; EX 18.90.
Owner Cream Of The Crop Partnership **Bred** Gainsborough Stud Management Ltd **Trained** Mollington, Oxon
■ Dove Cottage was withdrawn (7/1, uns rdr & bolted bef s). Deduct 10p in the £ under R4. New market formed.

FOCUS
A modest handicap in which the winner dictated from the front. He could be value for a little more but the opposition was generally unreliable.

2879 TOTEEXACTA MAIDEN H'CAP 6f 16y
8:45 (8:46) (Class 5) (0-70,70) 3-Y-0+ **£2,719** (£809; £404; £202) **Stalls** High

Form RPR

0224 1 **Cape Melody**[22] 2205 3-10-0 70 .... TravisBlock 14 77
(H Morrison) *t.k.h early: chsd ldrs: rdn to ld wl ins fnl f: r.o wl* **15/2**

0-63 2 1 ½ **Ailsa Craig (IRE)**[4] 2776 3-9-6 62 .... RichardHughes 17 64
(R Hannon) *w ldr: ev ch over 1f out: rdn and nt qckn ins fnl f* **3/1**[1]

-340 3 shd **Desert Pride**[25] 2145 4-9-12 60 .... FrancisNorton 1 64
(W S Kittow) *a.p on outside: rdn 2f out: led ins fnl f: sn hung rt and hdd: nt qckn* **11/1**

0600 4 nk **Towy Boy (IRE)**[15] 2418 4-9-3 54 ....(v[1]) JackMitchell(3) 8 57
(I A Wood) *chsd ldrs: led wl over 1f out: hdd ins fnl f: sn carried rt: no ex* **20/1**

0065 5 1 ¼ **Ride A White Swan**[8] 2628 4-8-10 47 .... KevinGhunowa(3) 2 46+
(D Shaw) *s.i.s: hld up and bhd: hdwy 2f out: rdn 1f out: one pce* **8/1**

3535 6 ¾ **Mr Rev**[4] 2759 6-9-2 50 ....(b) PaulFitzsimons 9 46
(J M Bradley) *hld up: rdn and hdwy 2f out: one pce fnl f* **33/1**

-025 7 hd **Bea Menace (USA)**[8] 2632 3-9-13 69 .... MartinDwyer 16 70+
(P F I Cole) *led: rdn and hdd wl over 1f out: hld whn hmpd wl ins fnl f* **13/2**[3]

-225 8 nse **Plumage**[1] 2852 4-9-12 60 .... StephenDonohoe 13 56
(M Salaman) *a.p: rdn and one pce fnl 2f* **9/2**[2]

003 9 ½ **Lord Fidelio (IRE)**[13] 2496 3-9-13 69 .... LPKeniry 10 61+
(A M Balding) *bhd: rdn over 2f out: sme prog over 1f out: n.d* **10/1**

5546 10 1 **Iguacu**[17] 2353 5-8-8 49 .... MatthewDavies(7) 7 40
(George Baker) *mid-div: rdn and lost pl 3f out: kpt on ins fnl f* **16/1**

0-00 11 3 ¼ **Walragnek**[4] 2758 5-9-4 52 .... VinceSlattery 4 32
(J G M O'Shea) *s.i.s: a bhd* **50/1**

5206 12 ¾ **Forward Feline (IRE)**[18] 2321 3-9-13 69 .... CatherineGannon 3 45
(B Palling) *prom tl wknd over 2f out* **7/1**

-000 13 8 **Pintano**[11] 2534 4-8-11 50 ....(p) AmyBaker(5) 15 —
(J M Bradley) *s.i.s: outpcd* **80/1**

-000 14 2 **Red Amaryllis**[7] 2680 4-9-7 55 .... TedDurcan 12 —
(H J L Dunlop) *prom 3f* **50/1**

1m 14.56s (2.56) **Going Correction** -0.15s/f (Firm)
WFA 3 from 4yo+ 8lb 14 Ran SP% **128.1**
Speed ratings (Par 103): **82,80,79,79,77 76,76,76,75,74 70,69,58,55**
toteswinger: 1&2 £10.20, 1&3 £41.90, 2&3 £29.20. CSF £31.17 CT £269.18 TOTE £5.30: £2.00, £2.10, £4.00; EX 33.20.
Owner Morrison, Eavis, Usher **Bred** Mrs A Savage **Trained** East Ilsley, Berks

FOCUS
A bunch finish and not form to be getting excited about. The form is somewhat muddling with the runner-up the best guide to the level.

2880 BET TOTEPOOL AT TOTESPORT.COM H'CAP 7f 16y
9:15 (9:16) (Class 5) (0-70,70) 4-Y-0+ **£3,238** (£963; £481; £240) **Stalls** High

Form RPR

523- 1 **Cape Rock**[228] 7026 4-9-7 70 .... PaulDoe 3 80
(W J Knight) *a.p: led over 1f out: sn rdn: r.o* **5/1**[1]

2435 2 shd **Millfields Dreams**[6] 2713 10-8-12 66 ....(p) MarkCoumbe(5) 13 76
(G C Bravery) *bhd: hdwy on stands' rail over 2f out: ev ch ins fnl f: r.o* **11/2**[2]

42-5 3 2 ¼ **Manere Bay**[73] 1048 4-9-2 65 .... TedDurcan 2 69
(J L Dunlop) *s.i.s: bhd: hdwy over 2f out: kpt on ins fnl f* **8/1**

0000 4 nk **Just Jimmy (IRE)**[17] 2352 4-8-2 51 oh1 .... CatherineGannon 16 54
(P D Evans) *a.p: rdn over 1f out: kpt on ins fnl f* **13/2**[3]

3141 5 ½ **Convince (USA)**[16] 2381 8-8-1 55 .... RossAtkinson(5) 9 57
(K M Prendergast) *bhd: hdwy on stands' rail over 1f out: kpt on ins fnl f* **10/1**

0006 6 3 ½ **Harrison's Flyer (IRE)**[2] 2806 8-7-11 51 oh4 ....(p) AmyBaker(5) 15 43
(J M Bradley) *a.p: rdn 3f out: wknd over 1f out* **28/1**

5003 7 ½ **Direct Debit (IRE)**[21] 2245 6-9-2 65 .... LiamJones 5 56
(M Wellings) *prom: lost pl 3f out: n.d after* **7/1**

3402 8 1 **This Ones For Eddy**[8] 2626 4-9-7 70 .... RichardHughes 6 58+
(S Parr) *prom: lost pl over 3f out: n.d after* **5/1**[1]

0-00 9 hd **Shakespeare's Son**[17] 2359 4-9-1 64 .... TolleyDean 12 52
(H J Evans) *led: hdd over 1f out: wknd fnl f* **20/1**

-00 10 ½ **Sawpit Sunshine (IRE)**[9] 2598 4-8-6 60 ....(b[1]) JackDean(5) 11 46
(J L Spearing) *chsd ldrs: wknd over 1f out* **33/1**

00-0 11 2 **Rowaad**[34] 1889 4-8-2 51 oh1 .... NickyMackay 14 32
(A E Price) *s.i.s: a bhd* **16/1**

5260 12 2 ¾ **Loyal Royal (IRE)**[79] 961 6-8-8 57 ....(b) PaulFitzsimons 10 31
(J M Bradley) *s.i.s: a bhd* **28/1**

-000 13 5 **Black Draft**[8] 2630 7-7-12 52 oh6 ow1 .... SophieDoyle(5) 1 12
(B Forsey) *bhd fnl 3f* **100/1**

04-0 14 11 **Lordship (IRE)**[17] 2352 5-8-6 55 .... MartinDwyer 7 —
(A W Carroll) *prom over 3f: eased whn no ch over 1f out* **16/1**

10-0 15 5 **Willridge**[18] 2326 4-9-7 70 .... LPKeniry 8 —
(J M Bradley) *prom 4f: eased whn no ch over 1f out* **66/1**

1m 23.32s (0.12) **Going Correction** -0.15s/f (Firm) 15 Ran SP% **123.6**
Speed ratings (Par 103): **93,92,90,89,89 85,84,83,83,82 80,77,71,59,53**
toteswinger: 1&2 £12.40, 1&3 £13.50, 2&3 £9.10. CSF £30.56 CT £228.60 TOTE £7.70: £2.10, £1.90, £3.20; EX 35.20 Place 6 £13.84, Place 5 £9.90.
Owner Mrs B Sumner **Bred** Bricklow Ltd **Trained** Patching, W Sussex
■ Stewards' Enquiry : Mark Coumbe two-day ban: used whip with excessive frequency (Jun 26-27)

FOCUS
Quantity over quality here, but a good training performance from William Knight. The runner-up is a reliable sort and sets the standard.
T/Plt: £11.60 to a £1 stake. Pool: £55,344.00. 3,468.78 winning tickets. T/Qpdt: £5.70 to a £1 stake. Pool: £4,051.00. 523.10 winning tickets. KH

2675 GOODWOOD (R-H)
Friday, June 12

OFFICIAL GOING: Good (good to firm in places; 8.7)
Races on mile course run over 22yds further than advertised.
Wind: Moderate, half against Weather: Broken cloud but bright

2881 SOUTHERN DAILY ECHO MAIDEN H'CAP 1m 6f
6:20 (6:20) (Class 5) (0-75,75) 3-Y-0 **£3,238** (£963; £481; £240) **Stalls** Low

Form RPR

0-03 1 **Harlestone Snake**[13] 2479 3-9-1 67 .... RyanMoore 11 79+
(J L Dunlop) *mid-div: smooth hdwy to ld over 2f out: drew clr fnl f* **11/8**[1]

4364 2 6 **Cayman Sky**[13] 2479 3-8-13 65 ....(b) PatDobbs 12 66
(R Hannon) *mid-div: hdwy 2f out: wnt 2nd ins fnl f: no ch w wnr* **10/1**

0-53 3 ¾ **Bernie The Bolt (IRE)**[18] 2323 3-9-6 75 .... DavidProbert(3) 1 75
(A M Balding) *in rr: hdwy to press ldrs 4f out: ev ch 3f out: lost 2nd ins fnl f* **4/1**[2]

-430 4 ½ **Favours Brave**[35] 1842 3-9-5 71 .... JimmyFortune 5 70
(J H M Gosden) *sn led: hdd over 2f out: nt qckn fnl f* **8/1**[3]

0-03 5 ¾ **Oke Bay**[14] 2447 3-8-4 56 ....(v) RichardKingscote 6 54
(R M Beckett) *chsd ldrs: rdn over 2f out: styd on one pce after* **25/1**

00-0 6 nk **Morning Calm**[29] 2006 3-8-11 63 .... SteveDrowne 4 60
(R Charlton) *w.w: outpcd over 3f out: mde late prog* **8/1**[3]

4-02 7 nk **Deuce**[11] 2540 3-8-11 63 ....(b) StephenCarson 10 60
(Eve Johnson Houghton) *prom tl rdn and wknd wl over 1f out* **16/1**

6-40 8 7 **Am I Blue**[48] 1532 3-8-12 64 .... AlanMunro 3 51
(H J L Dunlop) *trckd ldrs: rdn and wknd over 2f out* **33/1**

0-05 9 3 ½ **No Sting**[18] 2323 3-8-4 56 oh1 .... RichardThomas 7 37
(W S Kittow) *led for 1f: trckd ldr: wkng whn hmpd over 2f out: eased* **33/1**

00-0 10 18 **Pagan Flight (IRE)**[20] 2282 3-8-8 60 .... TPQueally 8 14
(Mrs A J Perrett) *slowly away: t.k.h: rn wd on bnd after 2f: nvr on terms* **33/1**

-324 11 18 **Saborido (USA)**[24] 2152 3-9-1 67 ....(p) JimCrowley 9 —
(Mrs A J Perrett) *a bhd: lost tch 3f out* **12/1**

3m 4.14s (0.54) **Going Correction** 0.0s/f (Good) 11 Ran SP% **119.7**
Speed ratings (Par 99): **98,94,94,93,93 93,93,89,87,76 66**
toteswinger: 1&2 £4.70, 1&3 £1.30, 2&3 £11.90. CSF £16.26 CT £45.26 TOTE £2.30: £1.30, £3.90, £2.00; EX 20.10.
Owner J L Dunlop **Bred** J L Dunlop **Trained** Arundel, W Sussex

FOCUS
The rail around the lower bend and up the straight were dolled out by six yards, increasing distances by about 22 yards. They went a true pace in this maiden handicap and the form looks sound.

No Sting Official explanation: jockey said filly suffered interference in running

2882 HILDON STKS (H'CAP) 6f
6:50 (6:50) (Class 4) (0-85,83) 3-Y-O £4,857 (£1,445; £722; £360) Stalls Low

Form RPR
210- **1** **Perfect Pride (USA)**274 5827 3-9-5 81 AdamKirby 1 89
(C G Cox) *hld in rr: hdwy over 1f out: led ins all out* 11/1

-122 **2** *nk* **Fantastic Dubai (USA)**16 2377 3-8-13 75 TonyCulhane 6 85+
(M R Channon) *bhd: hdwy whn short of room and swtchd lft over 1f out: kpt on strly for press jst failed* 11/4²

102- **3** *2 ¼* **Pyrrha**253 6426 3-9-7 83 AlanMunro 5 83
(C F Wall) *trck ldr tl rdn and wknd ins fnl f* 7/4¹

5102 **4** *1 ¼* **Rio Royale (IRE)**4 2761 3-8-11 78 Louis-PhilippeBeuzelin(5) 7 74
(Mrs A J Perrett) *led: rdn 2f out: hdd & wknd ins fnl f* 8/1

2146 **5** *hd* **Halaak (USA)**7 2654 3-8-1 66 AhmedAjtebi(3) 4 61
(D M Simcock) *in tch to rdn over 2f out: no hdwy after* 22/1

1-62 **6** *nk* **Cut The Cackle (IRE)**31 1965 3-9-7 83 JimCrowley 8 77
(P Winkworth) *in tch: rdn over 1f out: wknd fnl f* 4/1³

-002 **7** *3* **Pocket's Pick (IRE)**16 2386 3-8-13 75 RyanMoore 2 60
(G L Moore) *t.k.h. on outer: hld up: a in rr* 18/1

1m 11.79s (-0.41) **Going Correction** 0.0s/f (Good) 7 Ran SP% 112.1
Speed ratings (Par 101): **102,101,98,96,96 96,92**
toteswinger: 1&2 £2.90, 1&3 £5.60, 2&3 £1.90. CSF £39.73 CT £78.77 TOTE £12.30: £3.70, £2.00; EX 30.50.

Owner Dr Bridget Drew & E E Dedman **Bred** Camelia Casby **Trained** Lambourn, Berks

■ Stewards' Enquiry : Adam Kirby one-day ban: careless riding (Jun 27)

FOCUS
They didn't go a great pace early on, but the first two home got cover and quickened up from the rear. The form looks reasonable with the front three unexposed.

2883 NO 3 CAR PARK STKS (H'CAP) 7f
7:25 (7:25) (Class 4) (0-80,80) 4-Y-O+ £4,857 (£1,445; £722; £360) Stalls High

Form RPR
15-0 **1** **Wellington Square**30 1990 4-9-6 79 GeorgeBaker 13 89
(H Morrison) *s.i.s: hld up: hdwy and swtchd lft over 1f out: r.o to ld fnl strides* 5/1²

0-62 **2** *hd* **Kirk Michael**22 2188 5-9-7 80 FergusSweeney 6 89
(H Candy) *in tch: swtchd lft 3f out: rdn to ld appr fnl f: hdd fnl strides* 9/2¹

0303 **3** *1 ¼* **Ivory Lace**5 2736 8-8-11 70 JimCrowley 1 76
(S Woodman) *racd on outer: in rr tl hdwy over 2f out: kpt on fnl f* 14/1

-040 **4** *nk* **Koraleva Tectona (IRE)**13 2498 4-9-1 74 PaulEddery 5 79
(Pat Eddery) *prominant: rdn 2f out: kpt on one pce fnl f* 20/1

2012 **5** *½* **Desert Dreamer (IRE)**20 2269 8-9-2 75 RyanMoore 8 79
(P D Evans) *s.i.s: in rr: hdwy on outer 1f out: nvr nrr* 10/1³

0114 **6** *2 ½* **Seneschal**14 2434 8-9-3 76 JamieSpencer 11 73
(A B Haynes) *s.i.s: t.k.h: hdwy whn nt clr run over 2f out: swtchd rt appr fnl f: no further hdwy* 12/1

32-4 **7** *¾* **Rambling Light**22 2193 5-8-12 74 (tp) DavidProbert(3) 4 69
(A M Balding) *trckd ldrs: rdn and ev ch 2f out: fdd 1f out* 9/2¹

0326 **8** *hd* **Phluke**2 2824 8-9-4 77 (v) StephenCarson 14 71
(Eve Johnson Houghton) *trckd ldr: led wl over 2f out: hdd & wknd wl over 1f out* 12/1

0001 **9** *nk* **Lodi (IRE)**13 2491 4-9-5 78 (t) IanMongan 7 72
(J Akehurst) *hld up in rr: rdn over 2f out: nvr on terms* 16/1

0062 **10** *5* **Councellor (FR)**14 2434 7-9-2 75 (t) TPQueally 3 55
(Stef Liddiard) *mid-div: rdn over 3f out: wknd 2f out* 11/1

-241 **11** *nk* **To Be Or Not To Be**24 2168 4-9-3 76 TGMcLaughlin 12 55
(John Berry) *a in rr* 9/2¹

0-00 **12** *2 ½* **King's Caprice**14 2434 8-8-13 72 (t) RichardThomas 10 44
(J A Geake) *led tl hdd wl over 2f out: wknd quickily* 40/1

0-05 **13** *15* **Idle Power (IRE)**15 2396 11-9-2 75 JimmyFortune 2 7
(J R Boyle) *bhd: eased whn btn over 2f out: t.o* 25/1

1m 26.5s (-0.90) **Going Correction** 0.0s/f (Good) 13 Ran SP% 127.6
Speed ratings (Par 105): **105,104,103,103,102 99,98,98,98,92 92,89,72**
toteswinger: 1&2 £11.30, 1&3 £42.80, 2&3 £20.10. CSF £29.23 CT £322.11 TOTE £7.10: £2.80, £2.10, £4.20; EX 51.80.

Owner Roger Barby & Sir T Cassel **Bred** J A Peat **Trained** East Ilsley, Berks

FOCUS
A fair handicap and a successful gamble on the winner. The form looks sound but ordinary for the grade.

2884 CRIMBOURNE STUD STKS (H'CAP) 1m 1f 192y
8:00 (8:01) (Class 4) (0-80,78) 3-Y-O £6,476 (£1,927; £963; £481) Stalls High

Form RPR
3102 **1** **Eastern Aria (UAE)**16 2384 3-9-5 76 GregFairley 1 86
(M Johnston) *mde virtually all: rdn and edgd lft fr over 1f out but in command ins fnl f* 5/1²

-542 **2** *1 ½* **Just Like Silk (USA)**14 2432 3-9-6 77 EddieAhern 6 84
(G A Butler) *in tch: rdn over 1f out and kpt on to go 2nd ins fnl f* 7/4¹

-140 **3** *1 ½* **Blaise Tower**14 2432 3-9-7 78 GeorgeBaker 3 82
(G L Moore) *hld up in rr: rdn and hdwy over 1f out: r.o: nvr nrr* 25/1

-516 **4** *2* **Advisor (FR)**23 2174 3-9-7 78 JamieSpencer 7 78
(M L W Bell) *trckd ldrs: rdn over 1f out: hung rt and wknd fnl f* 6/1³

46-5 **5** *6* **Hambledon Hill**18 2318 3-8-13 70 RyanMoore 4 58
(R Hannon) *trckd wnr to 1/2-way: rdn and wknd ins fnl 2f* 10/1

022 **6** *1* **Red Suede Shoes**111 630 3-8-12 72 JamesMillman(3) 8 58
(B R Millman) *w.w in rr: lost tch wl over 1f out* 16/1

5032 **7** *12* **Hip Hip Hooray**22 2212 3-8-10 67 SteveDrowne 5 29
(L A Dace) *a towards rr: rdn over 2f and sn wl bhd* 12/1

2m 7.18s (-0.82) **Going Correction** 0.0s/f (Good) 7 Ran SP% 93.8
Speed ratings (Par 101): **103,101,100,99,94 93,83**
toteswinger: 1&2 £1.30, 1&3 £8.40, 2&3 £6.40. CSF £9.49 CT £91.03 TOTE £4.90: £2.20, £1.70; EX 9.30.

Owner Sheikh Hamdan Bin Mohammed Al Maktoum **Bred** Darley **Trained** Middleham Moor, N Yorks

FOCUS
a fair contest in which there was little pace on early, so Greg Fairley took the initiative on the winner. The runner-up is the best guide to the form, backed up by the third.

2885 FRANKIE'S 22ND ANNIVERSARY MAIDEN STKS 1m
8:35 (8:36) (Class 5) 3-Y-O £3,238 (£963; £481; £240) Stalls High

Form RPR
33 **1** **Mohtashem (IRE)**24 2165 3-9-3 0 RHills 2 84+
(Sir Michael Stoute) *hld up: swtchd lft 2f out: smooth hdwy to ld 1f out: sn clr* 10/11¹

2 *3 ¾* **Rocky's Pride (IRE)** 3-9-3 0 RyanMoore 7 75+
(J Noseda) *in tch: pushed along over 2f out: r.o to go 2nd ins fnl f: no ch w wnr* 9/2²

0 **3** *1 ¼* **Sahaal (USA)**24 2165 3-9-3 0 TPO'Shea 6 72
(M P Tregoning) *led for 1f: led again over 2f out: rdn and hdd 1f out: lost 2nd ins fnl f* 16/1

-526 **4** *½* **Bennelong**9 2600 3-9-3 80 GeorgeBaker 5 71
(R M Beckett) *in tch: outpcd 2f out: kpt on fnl f* 7/1³

44 **5** *3 ½* **Olive Green (USA)**14 2433 3-8-12 0 PaulEddery 10 58
(Pat Eddery) *plld hrd: led after 1f: rdn and hdd 2f out: one pce fr over 1f out* 7/1³

06- **6** *¾* **Chateauneuf (IRE)**255 6358 3-8-12 0 MichaelHills 9 56
(B W Hills) *in tch: short of room on ins fr over 1f out: rdn and sn btn* 25/1

45 **7** *2 ½* **Zouk**39 1752 3-9-3 0 AdamKirby 1 55+
(W R Swinburn) *c to ins fr wd draw sn after s: a bhd* 16/1

0 **8** *6* **Iron Master**22 2211 3-9-3 0 (t) NeilChalmers 4 42
(J J Bridger) *a bhd* 50/1

5 **9** *6* **Bermondsey Girl**27 2080 3-8-12 0 AlanMunro 3 23
(C F Wall) *t.k.h: prom on outside for 5f* 16/1

1m 42.13s (2.23) **Going Correction** 0.0s/f (Good) 9 Ran SP% 119.0
Speed ratings (Par 99): **88,84,83,82,79 78,75,69,63**
toteswinger: 1&2 £1.40, 1&3 £5.90, 2&3 £7.50. CSF £5.41 TOTE £1.80: £1.10, £1.60, £3.30; EX 6.00.

Owner Hamdan Al Maktoum **Bred** B Wallace And M Lydon **Trained** Newmarket, Suffolk

FOCUS
Probably a decent maiden, although without much depth, but the early pace was steady. The form is muddling and probably best rated through the winner.

Iron Master Official explanation: jockey said colt ran too free

2886 E B F HORSERACING MEMBERS' FILLIES' STKS (H'CAP) 6f
9:05 (9:05) (Class 3) (0-95,90) 3-Y-O+ £9,714 (£2,890; £1,444; £721) Stalls Low

Form RPR
-131 **1** **Lemon N Sugar (USA)**16 2382 4-8-13 75 TPQueally 3 88+
(J Noseda) *w.w: hdwy to ld appr fnl f: qckng clr* 9/2²

20-4 **2** *2 ¼* **Belle Des Airs (IRE)**27 2079 3-8-10 80 RichardKingscote 4 84
(R M Beckett) *led tl hdd appr fnl f: kpt on but nt pce of wnr* 11/2³

11-3 **3** *1 ¼* **Perfect Silence**18 2334 4-8-12 74 AdamKirby 7 76
(C G Cox) *sn trckd ldr: rdn appr fnl f and one pce after* 10/3¹

1-41 **4** *½* **Doric Lady**18 2334 4-9-1 77 KirstyMilczarek 1 77
(J A R Toller) *hld up: hdwy over 1f out: one pce after* 15/2

1003 **5** *hd* **Daddy's Gift (IRE)**19 2299 3-9-0 84 RyanMoore 6 81
(R Hannon) *in tch: rdn 1/2-way: no hdwy fr over 1f out* 11/2³

4-05 **6** *1 ¼* **Crystany (IRE)**34 1880 4-10-0 90 (b¹) JimmyFortune 2 85
(E A L Dunlop) *towards rr: no hdwy fr over 1f out* 11/2³

50-1 **7** *5* **Dubai Legend**22 2205 3-8-6 79 AhmedAjtebi(3) 8 55
(D M Simcock) *s.i.s: racd wd: hung rt and btn fr over 1f out* 15/2

3-40 **8** *24* **Aunt Nicola**26 2102 3-8-13 83 JamieSpencer 5 —
(M L W Bell) *trckd ldrs to 1/2-way: sn struggling and eased wl over 1f out* 12/1

1m 10.93s (-1.27) **Going Correction** 0.0s/f (Good)
WFA 3 from 4yo 8lb 8 Ran SP% 118.6
Speed ratings (Par 104): **108,105,103,102,102 100,94,62**
toteswinger: 1&2 £8.00, 1&3 £2.70, 2&3 £1.80. CSF £30.58 CT £94.53 TOTE £5.20: £1.50, £2.60, £1.60; EX 38.10 Place 6 £19.79, Place 5 £14.27.

Owner The Searchers **Bred** Establo Madoca Corp **Trained** Newmarket, Suffolk

FOCUS
A competitive handicap on paper but an impressive success for the winner. The runner-up and fifth set the level.

NOTEBOOK
Lemon N Sugar(USA) ◆ won in some style and is a filly firmly on the upgrade. She'd been put up 7lb for her latest success on the Polytrack, and had to prove she could be just as effective on turf, but she dispelled any doubts with a commanding performance, going further and further clear as the line approached. A hefty rise in the weights is now on the cards, but she's unexposed on turf, open to plenty of further improvement, and, having proved how well she acts at this track, could well be one for the Stewards' Cup consolation race back over this course and distance at the Glorious meeting. (op 11-2)

Belle Des Airs(IRE) is not short of early speed so the drop back to 6f was not a concern. Up there throughout, she ran a fine race, beating the rest comfortably, and she was simply unlucky to bump into a rapidly improving rival. She should be able to win a similar race. (op 8-1)

Perfect Silence should be competitive off her current mark but she might just need a bit more cut in the ground to be seen at her best. (op 11-4 tchd 7-2 in places)

Doric Lady tracked the winner through the early part of the race but simply couldn't match her turn of foot. A stiffer 6f might be more her cup of tea. (op 6-1 tchd 8-1)

Daddy's Gift(IRE) remains vulnerable to more progressive rivals off her current mark. (op 6-1)

Crystany(IRE), who never looked like landing a blow and is not straightforward, is another who could do with being eased a few pounds. (op 8-1 tchd 9-1)

Dubai Legend's maiden win at Salisbury had been given a boost earlier in the day when the third won at Sandown, and she was well backed beforehand. However, she never looked happy once under pressure, hanging right, then left, then right again, and perhaps she can do better back on a more conventional track. (op 8-1 tchd 13-2)

Aunt Nicola Official explanation: jockey said filly moved poorly throughout

T/Plt: £32.90 to a £1 stake. Pool: £65,789.72. 1,458.57 winning tickets. T/Qpdt: £11.00 to a £1 stake. Pool: £4,188.75. 280.90 winning tickets. JS

2636 SANDOWN (R-H)

Friday, June 12

OFFICIAL GOING: Good (good to soft in places; round 7.9, sprint 7.7)
The course was in its mid-configuration adding 5yds to advertised distances on round course.
Wind: Virtually nil Weather: Bight but a little overcast

2887 BLUEFIN EUROPEAN BREEDERS' FUND MAIDEN STKS 5f 6y
2:10 (2:10) (Class 4) 2-Y-O **£5,180** (£1,541; £770; £384) **Stalls** High

Form RPR
1 **Nosedive** 2-9-3 0 RyanMoore 5 81+
(W J Haggas) *led for 1f: chsd ldr tl 1/2-way: rdn to chal over 1f out: led jst ins fnl f: styd on strly to draw clr fnl 100yds* **15/8**[2]

2 1 3/4 **Swan Wings** 2-8-9 0 DavidProbert(3) 4 70
(A M Balding) *chsd ldrs: pushed into ld jst over 2f out: drvn and hdd jst ins fnl f: edgd lft ins fnl f: wknd fnl 100yds* **13/2**[3]

64 3 nse **Master Of Dance (IRE)**[18] 2324 2-9-3 0 JimmyFortune 2 75
(R Hannon) *bhd: rdn and hdwy to chse ldrs 2f out: hung rt u.p fr wl over 1f out: kpt on fnl f to press for 2nd nr fin: nvr pce to chal wnr* **5/4**[1]

6 4 1/2 **Bubbly Bellini (IRE)**[27] 2087 2-9-3 0 NeilChalmers 1 73
(A Bailey) *hld up and grad crossed to far rail: rdn and effrt 1/2-way: outpcd jst over 1f out: kpt on* **25/1**

5 5 5 **England (IRE)**[15] 2413 2-9-3 0 JamieSpencer 3 55
(N P Littmoden) *dwlt: t.k.h: hld up in tch: swtchd lft and effrt wl over 1f out: sltly hmpd and carried rt over 1f out: wknd ent fnl f* **7/1**

6 61 **Magical Molecule** 2-8-12 0 GabrielHannon(5) 6 —
(G D Blake) *dwlt: hdwy to ld after 1f: hdd 1/2-way: wknd rapidly 2f out: virtually p.u fnl f: t.o: dismntd after fin* **33/1**

63.00 secs (1.40) **Going Correction** +0.025s/f (Good) **6** Ran SP% **111.8**
Speed ratings (Par 95): **89,86,86,85,77** —
toteswinger: 1&2 £3.10, 1&3 £1.10, 2&3 £1.90. CSF £14.14 TOTE £2.40: £1.60, £2.20; EX 9.80.

Owner Duke/Roberts/Netherthorpe/Goddard **Bred** Brook Stud Bloodstock Ltd **Trained** Newmarket, Suffolk

FOCUS
Just an ordinary maiden.

NOTEBOOK
Nosedive, who is out of a frustrating half-sister to smart fillies Silca's Gift and Violette, played up in the preliminaries and eased in the market. He did nothing wrong once under way though and, after displaying a likeable attitude under pressure to get past the runner-up, he was well on top at the line. An entry for the Norfolk Stakes at Ascot, he should build on this debut success and an extra furlong would be no hindrance to him. (op 6-4 tchd 5-4)

Swan Wings ◆, the only filly in the line-up, is closely related to prolific sprinter Texas Gold out of a smart mare. After taking a narrow lead, she edged left when headed and just held on for second. She will benefit considerably from the run and should soon get off the mark, perhaps against her own sex. (op 6-1 tchd 7-1)

Master Of Dance(IRE) held the edge on experience, having already run twice, and this May foal was reportedly still green when fourth at Goodwood last time. He shaped as if this drop back from 6f was not the answer, unable to go after the first two at the two pole but staying on late and nearly snatching second. (op 13-8 tchd 7-4)

Bubbly Bellini(IRE), who finished last in another six-horse race on his debut, broke better this time. After crossing over to the rail from his outside draw he was keeping on without really posing a threat. He looks a nursery type. (op 40-1)

England(IRE), who also beat only one home on his debut, took a bit of a hold and was outpaced by the principals at halfway. He was already in trouble when carried to his right a furlong out and was allowed to come home in his own time. He does not look entirely straightforward, and was reported by Spencer to have hung right under pressure. Official explanation: jockey said colt hung right under pressure (op 8-1 tchd 11-1)

Magical Molecule showed early pace before dropping very quickly to the rear of the field. He was dismounted after the line and was reported lame. Official explanation: vet said gelding returned lame (op 50-1)

2888 TOTESPORTGAMES.COM H'CAP 5f 6y
2:40 (2:42) (Class 5) (0-75,75) 3-Y-O **£3,885** (£1,156; £577; £288) **Stalls** High

Form RPR
3-03 1 **Sharpened Edge**[22] 2205 3-9-6 **72** CatherineGannon 10 85
(B Palling) *mde all: edgd lft 2f out: rdn 2l clr over 1f out: styd on strly: pushed out ins fnl f* **8/1**

2-23 2 3 1/4 **Cawdor (IRE)**[36] 1814 3-9-8 **74** FergusSweeney 6 75+
(H Candy) *sn outpcd towards rr and pushed along: hdwy u.p 2f out: chsd wnr jst ins fnl f: no imp* **6/4**[1]

-064 3 1 3/4 **Hillside Lad**[13] 2478 3-9-1 **67** GeorgeBaker 9 61
(R M Beckett) *chsd wnr: rdn and unable qck over 1f out: lost 2nd jst ins fnl f: plugged on same pce* **11/2**[3]

-550 4 1 1/2 **Ben's Dream (IRE)**[29] 2010 3-8-12 **67** (t) DavidProbert(3) 8 56
(A M Balding) *s.i.s: hdwy to chse ldrs after 1f: rdn wl over 2f out: wknd qckly fnl f* **7/2**[2]

534- 5 1/2 **Fantasy Gladiator**[183] 7640 3-9-4 **70** PatCosgrave 4 57+
(R M H Cowell) *towards rr: rdn and effrt over 2f out: no imp and hung rt ins fnl f* **16/1**

-110 6 hd **Lady Vivien**[55] 1359 3-9-3 **69** SteveDrowne 7 55
(D H Brown) *s.i.s: sn pushed along: chsd ldrs over 3f out tl wknd ent fnl f* **16/1**

1202 7 2 **Song Of Praise**[8] 2632 3-9-4 **70** JimmyQuinn 5 48
(M Blanshard) *sn outpcd in rr: rdn jst over 2f out: no prog* **10/1**

5203 8 4 **You Avin A Laugh**[7] 2683 3-7-11 **56** oh1 AndrewHeffernan(7) 2 19
(C A Dwyer) *chsd ldrs on outer for 2f: sn lost pl and bhd* **33/1**

1-66 9 4 **Rebecca De Winter**[15] 2397 3-9-2 **75** AmyScott(7) 3 23
(David Pinder) *chsd ldrs on outer: wknd and hung lft fr over 2f out: no ch fnl f* **20/1**

61.79 secs (0.19) **Going Correction** +0.025s/f (Good) **9** Ran SP% **117.3**
Speed ratings (Par 99): **99,93,91,88,87 87,84,77,71**
toteswinger: 1&2 £5.40, 1&3 £8.00, 2&3 £3.80. CSF £20.74 CT £75.26 TOTE £9.40: £2.70, £1.10, £2.20; EX 23.70.

Owner Christopher J Mason **Bred** Christopher J Mason **Trained** Tredodridge, Vale Of Glamorgan

FOCUS
A modest sprint handicap best rated around the placed horses.

Lady Vivien Official explanation: jockey said filly jumped the path

2889 EUROPEAN BREEDERS' FUND MAIDEN STKS 7f 16y
3:15 (3:18) (Class 4) 2-Y-O **£5,180** (£1,541; £770; £384) **Stalls** High

Form RPR
0 1 **Bikini Babe (IRE)**[15] 2401 2-8-12 0 GregFairley 11 76+
(M Johnston) *mde all at gd pce: rdn and kicked wl clr over 2f out: unchal after: pushed out fnl f* **4/1**[2]

2 3 1/4 **Liquid Asset (FR)** 2-9-0 0 DavidProbert(3) 10 73
(A M Balding) *t.k.h: racd in midfield: rdn and edgd rt over 2f out: swtchd lft 1f out: kpt on to go 2nd wl ins fnl f: no ch w wnr* **25/1**

3 3/4 **Bitter Man (IRE)** 2-9-3 0 SamHitchcott 2 71
(M R Channon) *chsd ldrs: rdn and edgd lft over 2f out: no ch w wnr fnl 2f: wnt 2nd ins fnl f tl fnl 50yds* **25/1**

4 3/4 **Dream Spinner** 2-9-3 0 TedDurcan 9 69
(J L Dunlop) *chsd wnr: rdn and unable qckn over 2f out: edgd rt u.p 2f out: no ch w wnr after: lost 2 pls ins fnl f* **14/1**

0 5 1 **Bubbly Braveheart (IRE)**[16] 2383 2-9-3 0 NeilChalmers 3 67
(A Bailey) *t.k.h: hld up in midfield: rdn and unable qck over 2f out: kpt on same pce after* **25/1**

5 6 1 1/4 **Dubawi Phantom**[21] 2218 2-9-3 0 MartinDwyer 4 64+
(D M Simcock) *s.i.s: wl off the pce towards rr: rdn and edgd rt wl over 1f out: swtchd lft ent fnl f: styd on steadily after: nvr nr ldrs* **16/1**

7 nse **Deauville Post (FR)** 2-9-3 0 RyanMoore 6 63
(R Hannon) *s.i.s: wl bhd: rdn and rn green 3f out: stl last 2f out: swtchd lft over 1f out: kpt on fnl f: nvr nr ldrs* **6/1**

5 8 1 1/2 **My Red Kite**[11] 2533 2-8-12 0 GabrielHannon(5) 12 60+
(G D Blake) *chsd ldrs: rdn and struggling whn edgd rt jst over 2f out: wl btn over 1f out: wknd fnl f: eased towards fin* **25/1**

0 9 1 1/2 **Desert Aisling (IRE)**[39] 1742 2-8-12 0 PaulFitzsimons 5 51+
(Edgar Byrne) *wnt rt s: sn in midfield: rdn over 2f out: wkng and towards rr whn hmpd wl over 1f out* **100/1**

10 1 **Mass Rally (IRE)** 2-9-3 0 JimmyFortune 8 53
(J H M Gosden) *s.i.s: bhd: hdwy over 3f out: rdn and no prog wl over 1f out: wknd ent fnl f* **11/2**[3]

11 1/2 **Septemberintherain** 2-9-3 0 AlanMunro 13 52
(T G Mills) *s.i.s: rn green and a wl bhd* **4/1**[2]

12 4 **Gumnd (IRE)** 2-9-3 0 JamieSpencer 1 42
(C E Brittain) *s.i.s: wl bhd: sme hdwy over 4f out: nvr a factor: wknd and bhd wl over 1f out* **7/2**[1]

1m 31.27s (1.77) **Going Correction** -0.15s/f (Firm) **12** Ran SP% **120.8**
Speed ratings (Par 95): **83,79,78,77,76 75,74,73,71,70 69,65**
toteswinger: 1&2 £15.40, 1&3 £19.90, 2&3 £38.30. CSF £109.09 TOTE £4.30: £1.90, £4.60, £6.10; EX 96.40.

Owner A D Spence **Bred** Twelve Oaks Stud **Trained** Middleham Moor, N Yorks

FOCUS
The first juvenile maiden over 7f this season, although there was a seller over the trip at Yarmouth earlier in the week. The easy winner made all and few got into the race.

NOTEBOOK
Bikini Babe(IRE) faded after making the running on her debut at Newcastle (favourite) but reportedly pulled a shoe off there. Upped in trip, and soon securing the lead against the rail, she came right away in the last quarter-mile to score more or less unchallenged. A nice prospect, she may take her chance in the Chesham at Royal Ascot and longer term holds an entry in the Group 1 Moyglare Stud Stakes. (op 5-2)

Liquid Asset(FR), who is already gelded, stayed on nicely past a couple of rivals inside the final furlong to chase the filly home. Out of a half-sister to Lingfield Derby Trial winner Linda's Lad, from the family of Arc winner Rail Link, he is bred to need further and this was nice start to his career. (op 50-1)

Bitter Man(IRE), who holds a Derby entry, is another who was never too far from the pace without ever looking like winning. He will get further in time. (op 50-1)

Dream Spinner, whose pedigree is a mixture of speed and stamina, chased the winner for most of the way until fading inside the last. (op 20-1)

Bubbly Braveheart(IRE), whose dam is a half-sister to Champion Stakes winner Pride, was tailed off last on his Polytrack debut but showed more this time. (op 33-1 tchd 40-1)

Dubawi Phantom, having his second outing, was running on nicely when it was all too late over this extra furlong. He will improve. (op 14-1 tchd 12-1)

Deauville Post(FR), a half-brother to four winners in France and the subject of favourable reports prior to this debut. He can do better than this. (op 7-2)

My Red Kite, who showed ability on his debut at Leicester, chased the pace before weakening inside the last. (op 33-1)

Desert Aisling(IRE) might have been a place or two closer had she not been chopped for room on the rail over a furlong out.

Mass Rally(IRE), whose dam was a useful performer at up to 7f, missed the break badly but did improve to dispute sixth at one stage in the straight. (op 4-1 tchd 6-1)

Septemberintherain, a 60,000gns yearling, was very well supported ahead of this debut but started very slowly and showed little. (op 16-1)

Gumnd(IRE), sent off favourite, also failed to make an impact after a tardy start from his outside draw. (op 9-2 tchd 10-3)

2890 MOUSETRAP CHALLENGE CUP H'CAP 1m 14y
3:50 (3:55) (Class 4) (0-85,85) 3-Y-O **£5,180** (£1,541; £770; £384) **Stalls** High

Form RPR
23-3 1 **Yirga**[21] 2229 3-8-12 **74** (t) LDettori 10 86+
(Saeed Bin Suroor) *towards rr: rdn and effrt over 2f out: nt clr run and swtchd lft 2f out: squeezed between horses and over 1f out: drvn and sustained run to ld fnl 100yds: styd on wl* **6/1**

0-14 2 1 **Sir Isaac**[8] 2638 3-8-13 **75** KirstyMilczarek 7 83
(W J Haggas) *chsd ldrs: effrt on inner over 2f out: chsd ldr wl over 1f out: rdn to ld narrowly jst ins fnl f: hdd and no ex fnl 100yds* **6/1**

-412 3 1 **Pride Of Kings**[11] 2535 3-9-3 **79** GregFairley 2 85
(M Johnston) *racd keenly: led: rdn and edgd lft 2f out: hdd narrowly jst ins fnl f: 3rd and hld whn n.m.r fnl 75yds* **7/2**[1]

1513 4 1 3/4 **Roar Of Applause**[22] 2209 3-9-4 **80** EddieAhern 11 82
(B J Meehan) *hld up in tch in midfield: rdn and effrt ent fnl 2f: kpt on u.p fnl f but nvr pce to chal ldrs* **10/1**

24-1 5 1 1/2 **Imaam**[73] 1047 3-9-3 **79** RHills 6 77
(J L Dunlop) *t.k.h: hld up in tch in midfield: rdn over 2f out: unable qck and one pce after* **9/2**[2]

401- 6 hd **Shooting Party (IRE)**[242] 6700 3-9-2 **78** RyanMoore 9 76+
(R Hannon) *stdd after s: hld up off the pce: rdn 2f out: no imp tl hdwy over 1f out: swtchd rt ins fnl f: styd on but nvr gng to rch ldrs* **16/1**

412- 7 hd **Nizhoni Dancer**[234] 6886 3-9-1 **77** AlanMunro 4 74
(C F Wall) *t.k.h: chsd ldrs: rdn and unablen qck jst over 2f out: drvn and wknd ent fnl f* **12/1**

-143 8 3 1/4 **Laudatory**[18] 2329 3-9-7 **83** AdamKirby 3 73
(W R Swinburn) *sn chsng ldr tl wl over 1f out: wknd u.p over 1f out* **11/2**[3]

0261 **9** 3/4 **Dalradian (IRE)**[15] 2399 3-9-2 **78**.............................. JimCrowley 5 66
(W J Knight) *stdd s: hld up towards rr: hdwy on outer over 3f out: rdn and hung rt ent fnl 2f: sn wknd* **10/1**

64-5 **10** 4 1/2 **The Dial House**[70] 1105 3-9-1 **77**.............................. TonyCulhane 8 55
(J A Osborne) *bolted bef s: stdd s: hld up in rr: n.d* **66/1**

1m 42.35s (-0.95) **Going Correction** -0.15s/f (Firm) **10** Ran SP% **117.6**
Speed ratings (Par 101): **98,97,96,94,92 92,92,89,88,83**
toteswinger: 1&2 £7.80, 1&3 £4.80, 2&3 £8.60. CSF £42.29 CT £150.29 TOTE £4.90: £1.90, £2.50, £1.80; EX 24.50.
Owner Godolphin **Bred** Gainsborough Stud Management Ltd **Trained** Newmarket, Suffolk
■ Stewards' Enquiry : L Dettori one-day ban: careless riding (Jun 27)

FOCUS
A decent handicap run at a reasonable pace and the form looks pretty solid rated around the third, fourth and fifth.

2891 TOTESPORTCASINO.COM H'CAP 1m 2f 7y
4:25 (4:25) (Class 3) (0-90,90) 4-Y-0+
£7,477 (£2,239; £1,119; £560; £279; £140) **Stalls** High

Form RPR

22-5 **1** **Australia Day (IRE)**[139] 284 6-9-9 **90**.............................. MartinDwyer 8 104
(P R Webber) *mde all: pushed along and wnt clr over 2f out: unchal after: styd on wl* **14/1**

1/35 **2** 2 1/2 **Wintercast**[15] 2412 4-9-7 **88**.............................. AdamKirby 4 97
(W R Swinburn) *hld up in rr early: stdy hdwy into midfield 1/2-way: rdn over 2f out: drvn to chse wnr over 1f out: hrd rdn and no imp fnl f* **5/2**[1]

31-0 **3** 2 3/4 **Shamali**[15] 2412 4-9-4 **85**.............................. TonyCulhane 11 89
(W J Haggas) *stdd after s: hld up bhd: hdwy on inner over 2f out: chsd ldng pair over 1f out: no imp after* **10/1**

-660 **4** 1/2 **King Charles**[18] 2342 5-9-9 **90**..............................(p) JimmyFortune 9 93+
(E A L Dunlop) *hld up towards rr: rdn and effrt on outer over 2f out: hdwy wl over 1f out: laboured prog fnl f: nvr nr ldrs* **6/1**[3]

46-3 **5** 3 1/2 **Quirina**[16] 2384 4-9-3 **84**.............................. GeorgeBaker 12 80
(R M Beckett) *in tch: hdwy to chse wnr 3f out tl over 1f out: wknd fnl f* **8/1**

03-2 **6** hd **Dr Livingstone (IRE)**[15] 2407 4-9-7 **88**.............................. SteveDrowne 1 83
(C R Egerton) *t.k.h early: rdn and unable qck wl over 2f out: drvn and wknd 2f out* **12/1**

1-00 **7** 2 1/4 **Opera Prince**[51] 1460 4-9-7 **88**.............................. EddieAhern 3 79
(S Kirk) *hld up bhd: rdn and effrt 3f out: no hdwy and wl btn after* **11/1**

0030 **8** 1 1/4 **Robby Bobby**[28] 2055 4-9-5 **86**.............................. GregFairley 7 74
(M Johnston) *hld up bhd: rdn and no prog 3f out: nvr on terms* **14/1**

422- **9** 5 **Mubrook (USA)**[247] 6584 4-9-3 **84**.............................. RHills 5 62
(L M Cumani) *hld up towards rr: rn wd bnd 4f out: sn rdn and struggling: wl bhd fnl 2f* **9/2**[2]

60 **10** shd **Mafeking (UAE)**[15] 2407 5-9-0 **81**.............................. IanMongan 2 59
(M R Hoad) *t.k.h: chsd ldrs on outer: rdn and wanting to hang rt over 2f out: sn wknd* **66/1**

5000 **11** 1 1/4 **Cordell (IRE)**[14] 2434 4-8-13 **80**.............................. RyanMoore 10 55
(R Hannon) *taken down early: in tch tl lost pl and towards rr over 3f out: sn rdn and wl btn* **33/1**

6-56 **12** 1 3/4 **Mr Hichens**[22] 2197 4-9-2 **83**.............................. TGMcLaughlin 6 55
(Karen George) *chsd wnr tl 3f out: wknd qckly ent fnl 2f: eased ins fnl f* **33/1**

2m 6.73s (-3.77) **Going Correction** -0.15s/f (Firm) **12** Ran SP% **118.0**
Speed ratings (Par 107): **109,107,104,104,101 101,99,98,94,94 93,92**
toteswinger: 1&2 £6.80, 1&3 £17.90, 2&3 £8.20. CSF £48.28 CT £381.58 TOTE £12.70: £3.50, £1.50, £2.90; EX 63.90.
Owner Samantha & Emma McQuiston Partnership **Bred** Kenilworth House Stud **Trained** Mollington, Oxon
■ Stewards' Enquiry : Adam Kirby one-day ban: careless riding (Jun 26)

FOCUS
A good handicap in which the winner set a sound pace. The winner recorded a slight personal best and few got into it.

NOTEBOOK
Australia Day(IRE), off the track since a lacklustre effort on the Polytrack back in January, he was expected by his trainer to need the outing but he maintained the gallop to win well and if anything was pulling away at the line. A keen sort who will improve again for faster ground, he may return to hurdles in the near future. (tchd 10-1)
Wintercast went after the winner approaching the final furlong but could make no real inroads. He got the extra quarter mile well enough but just ran into a better one on the day. (op 11-4 tchd 3-1)
Shamali, ridden differently with his stamina for this longer trip in doubt, stayed on against the rail for third and ran close to his earlier course form with Wintercast. (op 8-1 tchd 11-1)
King Charles, who has dropped to a decent mark, stayed on down the outside for fourth but his head carriage in the first-time cheekpieces did not impress. (op 13-2 tchd 15-2)
Quirina, tackling turf for the first time this year, chased the winner for much of the way before fading going to the final furlong. (op 9-1)
Dr Livingstone(IRE) went up 4lb for his second over course and distance last month which must have contributed to this lesser effort, along with his outside draw. (op 9-1)
Mubrook(USA), Dubawi's half-brother, ran up against a couple of smart opponents when second in maidens in the autumn. He looked a likely type on this handicap and seasonal debut, but was always towards the rear and lost any chance of becoming involved after running wide on the home turn. Official explanation: jockey said colt ran wide on bend (op 5-1 tchd 6-1)

2892 TOTESPORTBINGO.COM H'CAP 1m 2f 7y
4:55 (4:56) (Class 5) (0-75,75) 3-Y-0 **£3,885** (£1,156; £577; £288) **Stalls** High

Form RPR

-532 **1** **North Cape (USA)**[22] 2206 3-9-3 **69**.............................. FergusSweeney 11 79+
(H Candy) *hld up in tch: trckd ldrs 4f out: rdn to chse ldr 2f out: drvn to ld over 1f out: kpt on wl fnl f* **4/1**[1]

3342 **2** 2 1/4 **Bagber**[21] 2232 3-9-6 **72**.............................. EddieAhern 7 77
(H J L Dunlop) *led: clr 5f out: rdn 3f out: hdd over 1f out: no ex fnl f: kpt on to hold 2nd* **10/1**

055- **3** 1 1/2 **Nbhan (USA)**[210] 7311 3-9-6 **72**.............................. JimmyFortune 6 74+
(L M Cumani) *t.k.h: hld up in tch: shuffled bk and rdn 3f out: edgd rt u.p 2f out: chsd ldng pair jst ins fnl f: kpt on but nvr pce to rch ldrs* **8/1**[3]

0U1- **4** shd **Worth A King'S**[226] 7067 3-9-7 **73**.............................. RyanMoore 13 75+
(Sir Michael Stoute) *dwlt and pushed along early: racd in last trio: rdn and hdwy wl over 2f out: edgd lft looking for a run u.p over 1f out: styd on fnl f and pressing for 3rd nr fin: nvr pce to chal ldrs* **8/1**[3]

05-3 **5** 3 3/4 **Rockfella**[25] 2126 3-9-1 **67**.............................. TPO'Shea 4 61
(D J Coakley) *t.k.h: hld up in midfield on outer: rdn and wanting to hang rt 3f out: keeping on same pce and wl hld whn hmpd over 1f out* **6/1**[2]

45-6 **6** 1/2 **Mitra Jaan (IRE)**[46] 1574 3-9-4 **70**..............................(t) AdamKirby 10 63
(W R Swinburn) *chsd ldr tl over 1f out: wknd u.p ent fnl f: fdd ins fnl f* **12/1**

2063 **7** 3 **Mellow Mixture**[10] 2567 3-9-4 **70**.............................. JimmyQuinn 1 57
(R Hannon) *dropped to rr and pushed along sn after s: sme hdwy u.p over 2f out: drvn and no hdwy over 1f out: wknd fnl f* **12/1**

-500 **8** 2 1/2 **Manolito Montoya (IRE)**[17] 2357 3-8-6 **63** ow3....(v) GabrielHannon(5) 9 45
(J W Hills) *hld up in midfield: rdn and effrt on inner 3f out: hrd drvn and wknd over 2f out* **40/1**

3-05 **9** 1 **Whisky Galore**[17] 2356 3-9-7 **73**.............................. IanMongan 2 53
(C G Cox) *in tch on outer: rdn and unable qck 3f out: wl btn whn hung rt wl over 1f out* **8/1**[3]

4220 **10** hd **Divinatore**[28] 2038 3-9-1 **67**.............................. AlanMunro 8 47
(D Haydn Jones) *chsd ldrs tl wknd qckly jst over 2f out: wl btn fnl f* **20/1**

4426 **11** nk **Location**[17] 2357 3-8-6 **58**.............................. GregFairley 5 37
(Ian Williams) *hld up towards rr: rdn and no hdwy 3f out: wl btn whn swtchd lft ins fnl f* **12/1**

064 **12** 46 **Peace Corps**[14] 2446 3-9-8 **74**.............................. LDettori 12 —
(J R Fanshawe) *dwlt: hld up in last trio: lost tch qckly 3f out: virtually p.u fr over 1f out: t.o* **6/1**[2]

2m 9.10s (-1.40) **Going Correction** -0.15s/f (Firm) **12** Ran SP% **121.3**
Speed ratings (Par 99): **99,97,96,95,92 92,90,88,87,87 86,50**
toteswinger: 1&2 £8.10, 1&3 £4.50, 2&3 £19.80. CSF £45.81 CT £313.81 TOTE £5.60: £2.10, £3.50, £2.70; EX 61.10 Place 6: £130.68 Place 5: £44.10.
Owner Henry Candy **Bred** W S Farish **Trained** Kingston Warren, Oxon
■ Stewards' Enquiry : Fergus Sweeney caution: used whip down shoulder in forehand position.

FOCUS
An ordinary handicap and not entirely convincing with front runners doing well through the whole card.
Peace Corps Official explanation: jockey said gelding never travelled
T/Plt: £113.30 to a £1 stake. Pool: £64,558.87. 415.94 winning tickets. T/Qpdt: £39.00 to a £1 stake. Pool: £4,717.57. 89.33 winning tickets. SP

2499 YORK (L-H)
Friday, June 12

OFFICIAL GOING: Good to soft (good in places; 6.2)
Wind: Virtually nl Weather: Fine and dry

2893 ACTURIS E.B.F. MAIDEN STKS 5f
2:20 (2:22) (Class 4) 2-Y-0 **£6,929** (£2,061; £1,030; £514) **Stalls** High

Form RPR

1 **Falasteen (IRE)** 2-9-3 0.............................. AdrianTNicholls 5 84+
(D Nicholls) *hld up in tch: hdwy to trckd ldrs 1/2-way: rdn to ld ent fnl f: edgd lft and kpt on strly* **6/1**

424 **2** 3 1/2 **Trade Secret**[29] 2017 2-9-3 0.............................. TomEaves 6 71
(M Brittain) *led: rdn along over 2f out: drvn over 1f out: hdd ent fnl f: kpt on same pce* **9/2**[3]

520 **3** 1 3/4 **Parbold Hill**[16] 2372 2-8-12 0.............................. PhillipMakin 3 60
(T D Barron) *cl up: effrt 2f out and ev ch tl rdn and one pce ent fnl f* **3/1**[2]

2 **4** shd **Cherry Bee**[10] 2568 2-8-12 0.............................. RoystonFfrench 1 59
(M Johnston) *sn rdn along and hanging lft towards rr: hdwy u.p 2f out: chsd ldrs whn hung rt appr fnl f and sn no imp* **11/4**[1]

600 **5** 1 1/2 **Miccolo**[24] 2153 2-9-3 0.............................. JamieMoriarty 4 59
(P T Midgley) *in tch: rdn along over 2f out and sn one pce* **100/1**

5 **6** 1/2 **Fibs And Flannel**[39] 1735 2-9-3 0.............................. DavidAllan 2 57
(T D Easterby) *in rr: pushed along and hdwy 1/2-way: rdn over 2f out and grad wknd* **14/1**

7 2 **Elusive Sue (USA)** 2-8-12 0.............................. PaulHanagan 8 45+
(R A Fahey) *dwlt: sn prom: rdn along 1/2-way and sn wknd* **9/2**[3]

62.35 secs (3.05) **Going Correction** +0.425s/f (Yiel) **7** Ran SP% **110.0**
Speed ratings (Par 95): **92,86,83,83,81 80,77**
toteswinger: 1&2 £8.00, 1&3 £4.90, 2&3 £2.10. CSF £30.27 TOTE £7.70: £3.40, £2.30; EX 38.70.
Owner Dr Marwan Koukash **Bred** Mrs Anne Marie Burns **Trained** Sessay, N Yorks

FOCUS
This looked a modest juvenile maiden and the level of the form is set by the placed horses.

NOTEBOOK
Falasteen(IRE), an already-gelded son of Titus Livius, cost £40,000 and came in for support on this racecourse bow. He showed greenness in the preliminaries and took time to load into the stalls. After jumping well enough he ran a little freely after being asked to adopt a handy position, but was soon travelling with purpose. Once on top of the runner-up, he soon stamped his class on the race and looked better the further he went. He showed a turn of foot on this easy ground, so it clearly suited and he looks a decent acquisition. (tchd 7-1)
Trade Secret set out to make all on this drop back from 6f and had every chance. A stiffer test over this trip is probably what he requires and he deserves to go one better, but is vulnerable to anything with a turn of foot. (op 5-1 tchd 11-2)
Parbold Hill, seventh in the Hilary Needler 16 days earlier, again showed early pace and had her chance. It is possible that this easier ground did not really help her cause and she did nothing wrong, but is now looking exposed. (tchd 10-3 in a place)
Cherry Bee got badly outpaced and, looking uneasy on the ground, eventually stayed on all too late. She has now shown enough in her two outings to suggest she is crying out for a longer trip. (tchd 3-1 and 10-3 in a place)
Miccolo, another who took time to load up, proved free through the early parts yet stuck on to post her most encouraging display to date on this softer surface.
Fibs And Flannel stepped up a little on the level of his Newcastle debut, but again looked in need of a sounder surface. Official explanation: jockey said colt hung left-handed (op 12-1)
Elusive Sue(USA), an $80,000 buy, has a pedigree that is all speed and hails from a yard in tremendous form at present. She was never really in the hunt after a tardy start, but was not given too hard a time from 2f out and it will not be a surprise to see her leave this well behind in time. (op 4-1 tchd 5-1)

2894 BLUE SQUARE CASINO STKS (H'CAP) 1m 208y
2:50 (2:51) (Class 4) (0-80,80) 4-Y-0+ **£5,828** (£1,734; £866; £432) **Stalls** Low

Form RPR

-443 **1** **Prince Evelith (GER)**[18] 2313 6-8-11 **73**.............................. FrederikTylicki(5) 3 87
(J J Quinn) *midfield: hdwy on inner 3f out: led over 2f out: rdn clr over 1f out: kpt on wl* **8/1**[3]

56-0 **2** 4 1/2 **Admiral Dundas (IRE)**[39] 1722 4-9-4 **80**.............................. AndreaAtzeni(5) 10 84
(W Jarvis) *hld up towards rr: gd hdwy 3f out: rdn to chse ldrs over 1f out: styd on u.p ins fnl f* **8/1**[3]

5612 **3** nse **Moheebb (IRE)**[14] 2440 5-9-8 **79**..............................(b) RobertWinston 1 85+
(Mrs R A Carr) *hld up in rr: gd hdwy 4f out: chsd ldrs whn nt clr run over 1f out: sn swtchd rt and rdn: styd on wl fnl f* **9/1**

00- **4** 1 1/2 **Addikt (IRE)**[217] 7224 4-9-6 **77**.............................. MickyFenton 4 78
(G A Harker) *hld up: hdwy 3f out: swtchd rt and rdn over 1f out: styd on strly ins fnl f: nrst fin* **50/1**

0234 **5** 1/2 **Spirit Of France (IRE)**[2] 2804 7-8-13 **70**.............................. DanielTudhope 5 73+
(D Carroll) *midfield: hdwy on inner over 2f out: rdn to chse ldrs whn edgd rt over 1f out: sn drvn and no imp* **16/1**

-616 **6** *nk* **Arctic Cape**[26] 2103 4-9-5 **76**................................ JoeFanning 2 75
(M Johnston) *prom: effrt to chal over 3f out: rdn over 2f out: sn drvn and edgd lft over 1f out: wknd* **16/1**

-006 **7** *1 3/4* **Blue Spinnaker (IRE)**[16] 2374 10-8-13 **77**............ JamesPSullivan(7) 9 72
(M W Easterby) *hld up and bhd: hdwy wl over 2f out: rdn to chse ldrs and edgd rtover 1f out: kpt on ins fnl f: nrst fin* **33/1**

-000 **8** *2* **Plenilune (IRE)**[10] 2569 4-8-5 **62**................................ AdrianTNicholls 6 53
(M Brittain) *bhd: hdwy on inner wl over 2f out: rdn to chse ldrs over 1f out: sn drvn and no imp* **50/1**

-000 **9** *1/2* **Goodbye Mr Bond**[26] 2103 9-9-3 **74**............................ AndrewMullen 16 64
(E J Alston) *midfield: hdwy to chse ldrs 3f out: rdn along over 2f out: sn drvn and no imp* **33/1**

-420 **10** *1 1/4* **Collateral Damage (IRE)**[9] 2612 6-9-8 **79**......................(t) DavidAllan 7 66
(T D Easterby) *midfield: hdwy over 3f out: rdn over 2f out and sn btn* **6/1**[1]

5-20 **11** *nk* **Celtic Change (IRE)**[42] 1646 5-9-3 **74**.........................(p) PhillipMakin 19 60
(M Dods) *cl up: rdn along 3f out: drvn over 2f out and grad wknd* **16/1**

202- **12** *3/4* **Celtic Step**[342] 3716 5-9-6 **77**...................................... PaulMulrennan 15 62
(P D Niven) *sn led: rdn along over 3f out: drvn and hdd over 2f out and grad wknd* **33/1**

-053 **13** *1/2* **Border Owl (IRE)**[11] 2542 4-9-2 **73**................................. DaleGibson 18 56
(P Salmon) *chsd ldrs: effrt 3f out and sn rdn: drvn 2f out and sn wknd* **33/1**

-522 **14** *3 1/4* **Handsome Falcon**[31] 1952 5-9-4 **75**.............................. PaulHanagan 13 51
(R A Fahey) *hld up: hdwy and in tch over 2f out: sn rdn and wknd wl over 1f out* **13/2**[2]

00-3 **15** *3 1/4* **Portrush Storm**[18] 2314 4-8-8 **65**.. DNolan 14 34
(D Carroll) *nvr bttr than midfield* **20/1**

3-22 **16** *11* **Indian Skipper (IRE)**[21] 2243 4-9-4 **75**...........................(b[1]) NCallan 12 20
(M H Tompkins) *chsd ldrs: rdn along 3f out: drvn over 2f out and sn wknd* **9/1**

600- **17** *1* **Royal Fantasy (IRE)**[281] 5635 6-9-3 **74**............................. TomEaves 8 17
(N Tinkler) *a in rr* **66/1**

-501 **18** *10* **Thunder Gorge (USA)**[21] 2243 4-9-3 **74**...................... WilliamBuick 17 —
(Mouse Hamilton-Fairley) *prom: swtchd wd over 3f out: sn rdn along and wknd* **12/1**

321- **19** *9* **Tenjack King**[454] 900 4-9-8 **79**..................................... TonyHamilton 11 —
(Joss Saville) *a towards rr* **28/1**

1m 54.53s (2.53) **Going Correction** +0.425s/f (Yiel) **19** Ran SP% **120.6**
Speed ratings (Par 105): **105,101,100,99,99 98,97,95,95,94 93,93,92,89,86 77,76,67,59**
toteswinger: 1&2 £20.00, 1&3 £18.00, 2&3 £27.40. CSF £61.68 CT £613.04 TOTE £9.00: £2.70, £2.80, £2.90, £12.20; EX 67.10.
Owner Allan Stennett **Bred** Gestut Etzean **Trained** Settrington, N Yorks

FOCUS
This had looked a wide-open handicap but Prince Evelith quickly asserted and had the race won furlong out. The form looks sound and could be rated a little higher.
Spirit Of France(IRE) Official explanation: jockey said gelding was denied a clear run

2895 BLUE SQUARE STKS (H'CAP) 2m 88y
3:25 (3:25) (Class 3) (0-90,88) 4-Y-0+ **£11,009** (£3,275; £1,637; £817) **Stalls** Low

Form RPR

6-40 **1** **Nemo Spirit (IRE)**[13] 2486 4-9-8 **87**................................ WilliamBuick 9 97
(W R Muir) *mde all: pushed along and qcknd 4f out: jnd over 2f out and sn rdn: drvn over 1f out and styd on gamely ins fnl f* **8/1**

2-14 **2** *3/4* **Hawk Mountain (UAE)**[20] 2283 4-8-10 **75**.................... MickyFenton 12 84
(J J Quinn) *trckd ldng pair: hdwy to chse wnr 5f out: effrt to chal over 2f out: sn rdn and ev ch tl drvn and no ex wl ins fnl f* **7/2**[2]

0-32 **3** *3* **Cleaver**[23] 2177 8-8-12 **81**.. FrederikTylicki(5) 4 86
(Lady Herries) *hld up: hdwy 4f out: rdn to chse ldrs wl over 1f out: kpt on same pce ent fnl f* **6/1**[3]

-552 **4** *1 1/2* **Bollin Felix**[13] 2486 5-9-10 **88**...................................(v) DavidAllan 3 91
(T D Easterby) *hld up in rr: hdwy over 6f out: effrt on outer 3f out and sn chsng ldrs: rdn 2f out: sn drvn and no imp* **11/4**[1]

1016 **5** *2 3/4* **Herrera (IRE)**[9] 2614 4-8-6 **71**.. PaulHanagan 2 71
(R A Fahey) *hld up towards rr: hdwy over 3f out: rdn over 2f out: drvn wl over 1f out and kpt on same pce* **12/1**

-201 **6** *nk* **Danzatrice**[35] 1851 7-8-10 **74**...................................... PJMcDonald 5 74
(C W Thornton) *in rr: hdwy 4f out: rdn and in tch 2f out: sn drvn and no imp* **33/1**

3-06 **7** *2 1/4* **Inchnadamph**[37] 1790 9-9-10 **88**...............................(t) RobertWinston 6 85
(T J Fitzgerald) *trckd ldrs: hdwy 3f out: rdn to chse ldng pair 2f out: drvn and wknd over 1f out* **16/1**

5133 **8** *2 1/4* **Caerlaverock (IRE)**[6] 2698 4-9-1 **80**...............................(b) TomEaves 8 74
(G A Swinbank) *trckd ldrs: effrt on inner over 3f out: rdn along over 2f out: wknd wl over 1f out* **9/1**

2131 **9** *32* **Supsonic**[78] 967 6-8-4 **73**.. AndreaAtzeni(5) 10 29
(R J Price) *chsd ldrs: effrt 4f out: rdn along 3f out and sn btn* **16/1**

3522 **10** *9* **Step This Way (USA)**[14] 2452 4-9-1 **80**.................. RoystonFfrench 11 25
(M Johnston) *trckd wnr: pushed along over 4f out: sn rdn and wknd qckly over 3f out: bhd and eased fnl 2f* **14/1**

3m 45.6s (11.10) **Going Correction** +0.425s/f (Yiel)
WFA 4 from 5yo+ 1lb **10** Ran SP% **113.4**
Speed ratings (Par 107): **95,94,93,92,91 90,89,88,72,68**
toteswinger: 1&2 £13.10, 1&3 £9.50, 2&3 £3.90. CSF £35.08 CT £180.41 TOTE £7.90: £2.50, £1.80, £1.80; EX 45.90.
Owner Mrs Monique V Bruce Copp **Bred** Gainsborough Stud Management Ltd **Trained** Lambourn, Berks

FOCUS
A competitive staying handicap, run at an uneven pace. The winner got the run of the race and is rated back to his three-year-old form.

NOTEBOOK
Nemo Spirit(IRE) got off the mark for the season at the third time of asking in most game fashion from the front. The return to softer ground was right up his street and he is always happiest when allowed to dominate. This rates a career-best display and, though he was gifted the run of the race here, should at least remain competitive after a likely rise up the handicap. Official explanation: trainer's rep said, regarding apparent improvement in form, that the colt was better suited by the softer ground. (op 9-1)
Hawk Mountain(UAE) ran a big race on his first attempt over this longer trip on ground probably softer than he truly cares for, but found the winner too resolute at the business end. He remains on an upward curve and is a likeable performer, but one suspects his real future may lie in the jumping sphere. (op 10-3 tchd 4-1)
Cleaver proved somewhat free under restraint and took time to hit top gear down the home straight. A more truly-run race is ideal for him, but for all his consistency he is not one for win-only purposes. (tchd 5-1)
Bollin Felix was 13lb higher than when third in the race last year, but the level of his second at Haydock (off 2lb lower) 13 days earlier gave him every chance. He was also faced with suitably softer ground this time round and was very well backed. The race was not really run to suit him, but this was his second outing in the visor and his attitude is now under scrutiny again. (op 4-1 tchd 5-2)
Herrera(IRE) was very patiently ridden and never looked like winning, but showed her Ripon form nine days earlier to be wrong. She needs a slightly sounder surface and may not be weighted out of winning when things go more her way. (op 10-1)
Danzatrice was 7lb higher and would have enjoyed a stronger overall gallop, so was not disgraced. (op 28-1)
Inchnadamph ran below his recent level, but did not look happy when push came to shove on this contrasting surface. Official explanation: jockey said gelding was unsuited by the good to soft (soft in places) ground
Caerlaverock(IRE) was wearing blinkers for the second occasion, but it was stamina rather than any potential quirks that looked to beat him here. He may also have found it coming too soon. (op 15-2)

2896 SKF ROUS (S) STKS 6f
4:00 (4:00) (Class 4) 2-Y-O **£6,476** (£1,927; £963; £481) **Stalls** High

Form RPR

4511 **1** **Anjomarba (IRE)**[11] 2541 2-8-6 0................................ TolleyDean 2 80
(W G M Turner) *mde all: rdn and qcknd clr wl over 1f out: easily* **11/2**[2]

23 **2** *8* **Orpen Arms (IRE)**[20] 2258 2-8-6 0................................ PaulHanagan 8 56
(R A Fahey) *prom: effrt over 2f out: ev ch and sn rdn: drvn wl over 1f out and kpt on: no ch w wnr* **5/2**[1]

04 **3** *1/2* **Bluie**[26] 2099 2-8-11 0.. AdrianTNicholls 12 60
(D Nicholls) *in tch: hdwy to chse ldrs over 2f out: sn rdn and kpt on same pce* **11/2**[2]

01 **4** *2 1/4* **Miami Gator (IRE)**[3] 2788 2-8-6 0.......................... MartinLane(5) 3 53
(K R Burke) *chsd ldrs: effrt over 2f out and sn rdn: drvn and one pce fr over 1f out* **15/2**

466 **5** *1/2* **Drumpellier (IRE)**[18] 2311 2-7-13 0........................ PaulPickard(7) 10 46
(P T Midgley) *towards rr: hdwy 1/2-way: rdn to chse ldrs 2f out: sn drvn and no imp appr fnl f* **33/1**

505 **6** *1 1/4* **Mrs Jones And Me (IRE)**[13] 2503 2-8-6 0...................... PJMcDonald 1 43
(P T Midgley) *prom on outer: rdn along over 2f out: sn drvn and grad wknd* **22/1**

42 **7** *1* **Final Ovation (IRE)**[24] 2153 2-8-11 0.......................... JamieMoriarty 13 45
(J J Quinn) *prom: rdn along 2f out: sn wknd* **7/1**[3]

54 **8** *3 1/4* **Rakhine (IRE)**[7] 2649 2-8-11 0.................................. JoeFanning 11 35
(P F I Cole) *in tch: rdn along 1/2-way: sn hung lft and wknd* **12/1**

023 **9** *8* **Bond Together**[32] 1934 2-8-11 0..............................(b[1]) TomEaves 4 11
(P D Evans) *in tch: rdn along 1/2-way: sn wknd* **33/1**

414 **10** *7* **Gertmegalush (IRE)**[7] 2655 2-8-11 0........................ RobertWinston 9 —
(J D Bethell) *prom: rdn along 1/2-way: sn wknd* **10/1**

10 *dht* **Willow Mist** 2-8-6 0.. DaleGibson 7 —
(M W Easterby) *dwlt: a in rr* **66/1**

12 *5* **Step To It (IRE)** 2-8-11 0... NCallan 5 —
(K A Ryan) *towards rr: rdn along and bhd fr 1/2-way* **16/1**

13 *5* **Hidden City (IRE)** 2-8-11 0................................(t) SimonWhitworth 14 —
(J S Moore) *dwlt: a in rr* **25/1**

046 **14** *33* **Blue Bond**[55] 1364 2-8-11 0...................................... PaulMulrennan 6 —
(P T Midgley) *a outpcd and bhd fr 1/2-way* **100/1**

1m 14.22s (2.32) **Going Correction** +0.425s/f (Yiel) **14** Ran SP% **122.8**
Speed ratings (Par 95): **101,90,89,86,86 84,83,78,68,58 58,52,45,1**
toteswinger: 1&2 £6.20, 1&3 £5.90, 2&3 £6.50. CSF £18.86 TOTE £6.00: £2.40, £1.90, £2.40; EX 18.40.The winner was bought in for 12,000gns. Orpen Arms was subject to a friendly claim.
Owner Marbary Partnership **Bred** Tally-Ho Stud **Trained** Sigwells, Somerset

FOCUS
This had looked quite a competitive seller but the hat-trick chasing Anjomarba blew her rivals away.

NOTEBOOK
Anjomarba(IRE) blew her rivals away with a performance that suggested she is definitely better than this grade. Soon in front, she was clear inside the two and galloped on relentlessly to win with any amount in hand. She is now three from three at this level and looks fully capable of making her mark in nurseries later in the season. (op 5-1)
Orpen Arms(IRE) kept on to do best of the remainder. Placed in a couple of maidens over 5f, she seemed to appreciate this extra furlong, but the winner never gave her a chance. There is probably a race in her at this level. (op 7-2 tchd 4-1)
Bluie looked a player on the evidence of his fourth at Redcar last time and he came through more towards the stands' rail, but couldn't match the winner and was just run out of second. He can find a small race. (op 7-1 tchd 8-1 in a place)
Miami Gator(IRE), winner of a 6f claimer at Redcar just three days earlier, wasn't disgraced in a stronger heat. (op 6-1)
Drumpellier(IRE) showed enough on this drop in grade to suggest she could find a less-competitive one of these at a minor track. (op 40-1)
Final Ovation(IRE), dropping to this level for the first time, faded rather disappointingly on this first try at 6f and now has a bit to prove. (op 13-2 tchd 6-1 and 8-1 in a place)

2897 BLUESQUARE.COM STKS (H'CAP) 5f
4:35 (4:35) (Class 3) (0-90,87) 3-Y-O+ **£7,641** (£2,273; £1,136; £567) **Stalls** High

Form RPR

-041 **1** **Equuleus Pictor**[21] 2228 5-9-7 **85**................................ JackDean(5) 4 93
(J L Spearing) *sn led: rdn over 1f out: kpt on wl u.p ins fnl f* **7/1**[3]

54-5 **2** *1 1/2* **Kay Two (IRE)**[27] 2094 7-9-9 **87**...............................(p) AndreaAtzeni(5) 9 90
(R J Price) *chsd ldrs: rdn along 2f out: drvn over 1f out: chsd wnr ins fnl f: kpt on* **9/1**

-000 **3** *shd* **Green Park (IRE)**[15] 2405 6-9-4 **77**...............................(b) DNolan 11 80
(D Carroll) *towards rr: hdwy 2f out: sn rdn and kpt on wl fnl f: nrst fin* **22/1**

5040 **4** *hd* **Stoneacre Lad (IRE)**[13] 2502 6-9-7 **80**....................(b) PatrickMathers 2 82
(Peter Grayson) *in tch: hdwy on outer 2f out: rdn to chse ldrs whn hung lft ent fnl f: sn drvn and one pce* **25/1**

1530 **5** *nk* **Steelcut**[6] 2716 5-9-7 **80**.. PaulHanagan 17 81
(R A Fahey) *midfield: rdn along 2f out: kpt on u.p ins fnl f: nrst fin* **16/1**

3041 **6** *nse* **Indian Trail**[6] 2704 9-10-0 **87** 6ex...................................(v) PaulQuinn 5 91+
(D Nicholls) *in rr: hdwy and nt clr run 2f out: swtchd rt and rdn over 1f out: styd on ins fnl f: nrst fin* **15/2**

5-61 **7** *1 1/4* **Lochstar**[15] 2397 5-9-9 **82**.. WilliamBuick 1 78
(A M Balding) *trckd ldrs on outer: effrt 2f out: sn rdn and btn over 1f out* **7/2**[1]

-233 **8** *1 1/2* **Solar Spirit (IRE)**[15] 2405 4-9-5 **83**...................... FrederikTylicki(5) 15 74
(J J Quinn) *s.i.s and in rr tl sme late hdwy* **9/2**[2]

5603 **9** *1/2* **Haajes**[9] 2591 5-9-10 **83**......................................(t) RobertWinston 16 72
(J Balding) *midfield and sn rdn along: outpcd fr 1/2-way* **14/1**

200- **10** *1/2* **The Nifty Fox**[266] 6069 5-9-7 **80**................................ DavidAllan 10 67
(T D Easterby) *chsd ldrs: rdn along 2f out and grad wknd* **25/1**

2006 **11** ½ **King Of Swords (IRE)**[4] 2770 5-8-9 **68** oh2 TomEaves 3 53
(N Tinkler) *nvr nr ldrs* **25/1**
532 **12** 2¾ **Le Toreador**[17] 2363 4-9-7 **80** NCallan 14 56
(K A Ryan) *cl up: rdn along 2f out: drvn over 1f out and wknd qckly ent fnl f* **9/1**
5400 **13** ½ **Chartist**[7] 2658 4-9-4 **77** AdrianTNicholls 6 51
(D Nicholls) *cl up: rdn along over 2f out: sn drvn and wknd* **16/1**

61.08 secs (1.78) **Going Correction** +0.425s/f (Yiel)
WFA 3 from 4yo+ 7lb **13** Ran SP% **119.0**
Speed ratings (Par 107): **102,99,99,99,98 98,96,94,93,92 91,87,86**
toteswinger: 1&2 £11.50, 1&3 £30.40, 2&3 £35.80. CSF £64.78 CT £1299.03 TOTE £8.30: £3.00, £3.00, £5.60; EX 69.80.
Owner Masonaires **Bred** A J And Mrs L Brazier **Trained** Kinnersley, Worcs

FOCUS
A typically wide-open sprint for the grade. As with the preceding two races on the straight track the main action developed down the centre of the track, but the one who drifted to the far side, Stoneacre Lad, fared particularly well. The form looks sound enough overall.

NOTEBOOK
Equuleus Pictor followed up his Haydock win 21 days earlier off a 7lb higher mark and is clearly now back at the top of his game. He was never far away and showed a neat turn of foot when asked for an effort. He looked to be tying up inside the final furlong, but kept finding for pressure and was not for catching. It was his highest winning mark to date and his display would suggest the ground was on the softer side. He could turn out quickly at Salisbury on Sunday, where a penalty for this will ensure he carries topweight and he would want the rain to come there. (op 9-1)
Kay Two(IRE) was bidding to win second time up in consecutive seasons and made a bold effort. He was ridden more conservatively than the winner, which has rarely proved ideal on this course, and is entitled to come on again for the outing. (op 12-1)
Green Park(IRE) bounced back to form with the blinkers re-applied and only just missed out on the runner-up spot. He is well treated at present and is entered again at the track today, where he may just be better offover the extra furlong, provided he is none to worse for this run. (tchd 25-1)
Stoneacre Lad(IRE) has been inconsistent since resuming on turf this year, but has fallen to a decent mark and this was a much better performance. His yard cannot buy a winner at present and he is never one to completely trust, but on this showing he could be the one to end the drought. (op 20-1)
Steelcut was doing his best work towards the finish. (op 20-1)
Indian Trail weaved through the pace when narrowly scoring in Epsom's 'Dash' six days earlier and he ran a solid race in defeat under his penalty, considering the different nature of this track. (op 13-2 tchd 8-1)
Lochstar, 3lb higher than when winning again on Polytrack last time, was ridden with more restraint and never really looked like following up. He has yet to cut the mustard on turf, but probably found the ground softer than he cares for and is still open to some improvement, perhaps back over 6f. (op 10-3 tchd 11-4)
Solar Spirit(IRE) had made the frame in all but one of his outings since registering his one win last term, but he lost all chance on this drop in trip by missing the break. (op 5-1 tchd 11-2 in place)

2898 WEWILLBUYYOURCAR.COM APPRENTICE STKS (H'CAP) 1m 4f
5:05 (5:05) (Class 4) (0-80,79) 4-Y-0+ **£5,180** (£1,541; £770; £384) **Stalls** Centre

Form RPR
1212 **1** **Joe Jo Star**[2] 2803 7-8-7 **65** 6ex ow2 FrederikTylicki(3) 8 81+
(R A Fahey) *cl up: trckd ldr 1/2-way: led over 3f out: rdn clr 2f out: kpt on* **3/1**[1]
-063 **2** 7 **Grandad Bill (IRE)**[24] 2159 6-8-5 **60** oh1 KellyHarrison 9 65
(J S Goldie) *trckd ldrs: hdwy 4f out: rdn along 2f out: drvn to chse wnr and edgd lft appr fnl f: no imp* **13/2**[3]
0546 **3** 1¼ **Maslak (IRE)**[38] 1779 5-9-3 **75** WilliamCarson(3) 5 78
(P W Hiatt) *a.p: effrt to chse wnr over 2f out: sn rdn and no imp* **25/1**
2402 **4** 2¾ **Spirit Of Adjisa (IRE)**[11] 2552 5-9-1 **75** CharlesEddery(5) 1 73
(Pat Eddery) *chsd ldrs on inner: effrt 3f out: rdn along over 2f out: sn drvn and one pce fnl 2f* **7/1**
6-00 **5** 2¾ **Royal Flynn**[10] 1660 7-8-10 **70** (p) PaulPickard(5) 2 64
(Mrs K Walton) *hld up towards rr: hdwy 3f out: sn rdn and kpt on fnl 2f: nvr nr ldrs* **50/1**
42-5 **6** nk **Force Group (IRE)**[6] 2698 5-9-6 **78** MartinLane(3) 11 72
(M H Tompkins) *s.i.s and rr: hdwy over 4f out: rdn along 3f out: drvn 2f out and sn no imp* **9/1**
052 **7** 3 **Grey Command (USA)**[6] 2724 4-8-2 **62** JohnCavanagh(5) 14 51
(M Brittain) *nvr nr ldrs* **20/1**
20-3 **8** 1 **Babilu**[28] 2040 4-8-8 **70** DavidKenny(7) 3 57
(A G Newcombe) *nvr bttr than midfield* **20/1**
0-02 **9** 3 **Coyote Creek**[28] 2040 5-9-5 **79** (v) JPHamblett(5) 6 61
(E F Vaughan) *trckd ldrs: effrt 3f out: sn rdn and wknd 2f out* **13/2**[3]
-032 **10** 8 **Andorn (GER)**[10] 2569 5-8-5 **63** PatrickDonaghy(3) 7 33
(P A Kirby) *led: rdn along 4f out: hdd over 3f out and sn wknd* **25/1**
-201 **11** 2¾ **Realism (FR)**[5] 2743 9-9-4 **78** 6ex JamesPSullivan(5) 12 43
(M W Easterby) *hld up: a in rr* **11/1**
20-2 **12** 16 **Harry The Hawk**[28] 2043 5-9-0 **72** SladeO'Hara(3) 4 12
(T D Walford) *midfield: hdwy and in tch 4f out: sn rdn along and wknd over 2f out* **6/1**[2]
/P-0 **13** 98 **Runswick Bay**[26] 2101 4-9-4 **73** NeilBrown 10 —
(G M Moore) *a towards rr* **66/1**

2m 36.3s (3.10) **Going Correction** +0.425s/f (Yiel) **13** Ran SP% **117.5**
Speed ratings (Par 105): **106,101,100,98,96 96,94,93,91,86 84,74,8**
toteswinger: 1&2 £3.90, 1&3 £12.10, 2&3 £16.30. CSF £19.47 CT £412.95 TOTE £3.40: £1.80, £2.10, £6.80; EX 18.20 Place 6: £271.65 Place 5: £61.01.
Owner The Ipso Facto Syndicate **Bred** B J And Mrs Crangle **Trained** Musley Bank, N Yorks

FOCUS
This apprentices' handicap was turned into a procession by Joe Jo Star. The form is rated through the runner-up to his latest form.
Grey Command(USA) Official explanation: jockey said colt never travelled
Runswick Bay Official explanation: jockey said gelding lost its action
T/Jkpt: Not won. T/Plt: £338.80 to a £1 stake. Pool: £118,516.85. 255.36 winning tickets. T/Qpdt: £56.70 to a £1 stake. Pool: £6,238.04. 81.40 winning tickets. JR

2899 - 2905a (Foreign Racing) - See Raceform Interactive

2649 BATH (L-H)
Saturday, June 13

OFFICIAL GOING: Firm (good to firm in places; 10.4)
Wind: Light against Weather: Fine

2906 BETINTERNET.COM MAIDEN AUCTION STKS 5f 11y
2:15 (2:15) (Class 6) 2-Y-O **£2,072** (£616; £308; £153) **Stalls** Centre

Form RPR
02 **1** **Six Diamonds**[8] 2649 2-8-4 0 NickyMackay 7 73
(H Morrison) *w ldr: led over 3f out: drvn out fnl f* **11/4**[2]
350 **2** hd **Victorian Art (IRE)**[18] 2360 2-8-1 0 (v[1]) DavidProbert(3) 5 72
(M A Magnusson) *chsd ldrs: wnt 2nd over 2f out: rdn over 1f out: chal ins fnl f: r.o* **3/1**[3]
603 **3** 7 **French Connexion (IRE)**[18] 2348 2-7-13 0 SophieDoyle(5) 1 46
(J S Moore) *bhd: edgd rt over 1f out: kpt on to take 3rd last strides: no ch w ldng pair* **10/1**
632 **4** nk **Pinnacle Lad (IRE)**[21] 2258 2-8-9 0 TolleyDean 4 50
(J L Spearing) *led: hdd over 3f out: rdn over 1f out: wknd fnl f* **2/1**[1]
5 hd **Filwa (IRE)** 2-8-8 0 DarryllHolland 3 48
(B J Meehan) *s.i.s: hdwy over 2f out: rdn over 1f out: wknd fnl f* **15/2**
6 1½ **Aintwogrand (IRE)** 2-8-4 0 CatherineGannon 6 38
(M R Channon) *s.s: in rr: n.m.r cl home: n.d* **14/1**
006 **7** 8 **Magneto (IRE)**[12] 2533 2-8-9 0 EdwardCreighton 2 13
(E J Creighton) *sn outpcd* **40/1**

61.57 secs (-0.93) **Going Correction** -0.20s/f (Firm) **7** Ran SP% **115.0**
Speed ratings (Par 91): **99,98,87,87,86 84,71**
toteswinger: 1&2 £7.70, 1&3 £8.20, 2&3 £7.90. CSF £11.61 TOTE £4.30: £2.60, £2.20; EX 20.50.
Owner A J Struthers Mrs J Scott Mrs F Woodd **Bred** Mrs S F Dibben **Trained** East Ilsley, Berks

FOCUS
An ordinary-looking contest that not many got into. The jockeys reported afterwards that the ground was fast.

NOTEBOOK
Six Diamonds showed improved form on her second start, which was here over slightly further, last time and did enough in this to hold off the challengers once in front. This was not a very good race, so she will need to improve to win again. (op 4-1 tchd 9-2)
Victorian Art(IRE), wearing a first-time visor, was never far way and made sure the winner did not have it all her own way in the latter stages. (op 7-2)
French Connexion(IRE) was third behind a fair sort in a similar race at Chepstow last time, but never really figured in this after heading home down the centre of the track. (op 8-1 tchd 7-1)
Pinnacle Lad(IRE) disappointed here after his jockey allowed the winner to go on at about halfway. The horse steadily lost ground about a furlong out. (op 15-8 tchd 9-4)
Filwa(IRE), who cost £20,000 at the sales in April, is speedily bred but ended her chance at the start, where she was slow to break. Official explanation: jockey said filly hung right (op 13-2 tchd 5-1)
Aintwogrand(IRE), a half-sister to a moderate three-year-old 7f winner, was another to start slowly, but she did catch the eye late on, and will be wiser for the run. (tchd 12-1)

2907 E.B.F./PLAY LIVE CASINO AT BETINTERNET.COM NOVICE STKS 5f 11y
2:45 (2:47) (Class 4) 2-Y-O **£5,180** (£1,541; £770; £384) **Stalls** Centre

Form RPR
32 **1** **Exotic Beauty**[11] 2563 2-8-7 0 DarryllHolland 1 79+
(M R Channon) *mde all: rdn and hung rt jst over 1f out: r.o wl* **11/10**[1]
5 **2** 4 **Take Ten**[14] 2484 2-8-12 0 J-PGuillambert 2 69
(M Johnston) *w wnr: rdn over 2f out: no ex ins fnl f* **4/1**[3]
510 **3** ¾ **Kings Of Leo**[38] 1788 2-9-0 0 FergusSweeney 5 68
(R Hannon) *chsd ldrs: rdn over 2f out: one pce fnl f* **2/1**[2]
60 **4** 3½ **Chinese Democracy (USA)**[14] 2490 2-8-1 0 ow1 DTDaSilva(7) 3 49
(P F I Cole) *chsd ldrs: rdn over 2f out: wknd fnl f* **28/1**
4135 **5** 34 **Boga (IRE)**[19] 2325 2-8-4 0 ow2 WilliamCarson(5) 6 —
(R J Hodges) *rrd s: sn wnt lft: a in rr: t.o* **12/1**

61.83 secs (-0.67) **Going Correction** -0.20s/f (Firm) **5** Ran SP% **112.1**
Speed ratings (Par 95): **97,90,89,83,29**
toteswinger: 1&2 £6.00. CSF £6.13 TOTE £2.00: £1.10, £1.70; EX 6.00.
Owner M Al-Qatami & K M Al-Mudhaf **Bred** H G And J R Dutfield **Trained** West Ilsley, Berks

FOCUS
Despite the lack of runners, this was probably a fair race of its type and the winner looks a decent sort for sprints.

NOTEBOOK
Exotic Beauty ♦, who was heavily supported here, broke smartly on this drop in trip and was always holding too many aces for the runner-up. She has some sales-race entries later in the season, and it would be no surprise to see her do well over short trips. (op 6-4 tchd 13-8)
Take Ten ♦, Mark Johnston's only runner on the card, was on his toes at the start and looked green under pressure. He will no doubt be ready to strike next time. (op 2-1)
Kings Of Leo had been given a break since blowing her chance at the start at Chester just two days after winning her maiden at Warwick. She gave the front two an advantage at halfway, which she could not erode until it was all too late. (op 3-1)
Chinese Democracy(USA) once again failed to make any impression and appears a disappointing sort. (op 25-1 tchd 22-1)
Boga(IRE) was claimed for £10,000 out of Mick Channon´s yard last time but he started slowly and finished tailed off. Official explanation: jockey said filly reared and missed the break (tchd 10-1)

2908 JOIN BETINTERNET.COM FOR ROYAL ASCOT (S) STKS 5f 161y
3:20 (3:21) (Class 6) 3-Y-O+ **£1,942** (£578; £288; £144) **Stalls** Centre

Form RPR
2433 **1** **Caribbean Coral**[5] 2759 10-9-4 62 GeorgeBaker 5 70
(A B Haynes) *hld up: hdwy over 2f out: led over 1f out: rdn out* **5/2**[1]
3-20 **2** nk **Piazza San Pietro**[129] 394 3-8-10 78 JerryO'Dwyer 3 67
(J R Gask) *chsd ldrs: rdn and ev ch over 1f out: carried hd high: r.o* **11/4**[2]
0500 **3** 4½ **Best One**[13] 2520 5-9-1 67 (bt) KevinGhunowa(3) 1 54
(R A Harris) *s.i.s: sn led: hdd over 2f out: ev ch over 1f out: sn rdn: wknd wl ins fnl f* **9/2**[3]
5150 **4** 3¼ **Caustic Wit (IRE)**[4] 2799 11-9-4 58 CatherineGannon 2 43
(M S Saunders) *stmbld s: in rr: hdwy 2f out: nvr trbld ldrs* **10/1**
1606 **5** 2½ **Lethal**[11] 2576 6-9-10 67 J-PGuillambert 8 41
(Andrew Reid) *prom: rdn over 2f out: wknd over 1f out* **5/1**
-401 **6** ½ **Gioacchino (IRE)**[6] 2745 4-9-5 53 WilliamCarson(5) 4 40
(R A Harris) *led early: w ldr: led over 2f out: hdd over 1f out: sn rdn and hung lft: wknd ins fnl f* **9/1**
-000 **7** 1 **Our Acquaintance**[18] 2349 4-9-1 49 (b) DavidProbert(3) 7 30
(W R Muir) *a bhd* **22/1**
4403 **8** ¾ **Easy Wonder (GER)**[39] 1781 4-8-13 47 (b) RichardThomas 6 23
(I A Wood) *mid-div: faltered 4f out: bhd fnl 3f* **25/1**
3500 **9** nk **Mr Loire**[5] 2758 5-9-4 45 (b) RichardKingscote 11 27
(A J Chamberlain) *prom tl rdn and wknd over 2f out* **25/1**

1m 10.44s (-0.76) **Going Correction** -0.20s/f (Firm)
WFA 3 from 4yo+ 8lb **9** Ran SP% **121.2**
Speed ratings (Par 101): **97,96,90,86,82 82,80,79,79**
toteswinger: 1&2 £2.50, 1&3 £2.30, 2&3 £4.60. CSF £9.91 TOTE £3.00: £1.30, £1.50, £1.80; EX 13.40 Trifecta £36.00 Pool: £400.53 - 8.23 winning units..There was no bid for the winner. Piazza San Pietro was subject to a friendly claim.
Owner T Hosier **Bred** P And C Scott **Trained** Limpley Stoke, Bath

FOCUS
By selling standards, this did not look a bad contest. The winner is rated to his winter form.
Caustic Wit(IRE) Official explanation: jockey said gelding stumbled leaving the stalls

Easy Wonder(GER) Official explanation: jockey said filly stumbled two furlongs out

2909 50% SIGN UP BONUS AT BETINTERNET.COM H'CAP 1m 3f 144y
3:55 (3:55) (Class 5) (0-70,67) 3-Y-0 £2,719 (£809; £404; £202) Stalls Low

Form RPR
0-02 1 **Cool Strike (UAE)**[14] 2479 3-9-7 67 (v) LPKeniry 2 82+
(A M Balding) *a.p: led 7f out: wl clr over 2f out: rdn over 1f out: eased wl ins fnl f* 11/8[1]
-160 2 5 **Spinning Waters**[14] 2479 3-9-2 65 KevinGhunowa(3) 4 66
(Eve Johnson Houghton) *hld up: hdwy over 2f out: wnt 2nd over 1f out: no ch w wnr* 11/2[2]
040 3 2 1/4 **Lucy's Perfect**[19] 2323 3-7-13 48 oh1 DavidProbert(3) 1 46
(B R Millman) *hld up in tch: rdn to chse wnr over 2f out tl over 1f out: one pce* 8/1
61-0 4 8 **Red Reef**[30] 2008 3-9-4 64 CatherineGannon 6 48
(D J Coakley) *hld up in rr: rdn 2f out: swtchd rt over 1f out: nvr nr ldrs* 9/1
-140 5 4 1/2 **Peter Grimes (IRE)**[29] 2038 3-9-7 67 DarryllHolland 8 44
(H J L Dunlop) *led: hdd 7f out: chsd wnr: rdn over 4f out: lost 2nd over 2f out: wknd over 1f out* 6/1[3]
-300 6 2 3/4 **Duar Mapel (USA)**[33] 1928 3-9-5 65 (v[1]) J-PGuillambert 7 37
(Paul Mason) *rdn along and sn prom: wknd over 2f out* 25/1
0-00 7 31 **Winterbrook King**[7] 2709 3-8-4 53 MarcHalford(3) 3 —
(J R Best) *a bhd: eased whn no ch over 1f out* 12/1
00-0 8 5 **Lambourn Genie (UAE)**[18] 2350 3-8-7 53 RichardKingscote 5 —
(Tom Dascombe) *t.k.h: prom tl wknd over 3f out: eased whn no ch over 1f out* 7/1

2m 27.68s (-2.92) **Going Correction** -0.20s/f (Firm) 8 Ran SP% **116.9**
Speed ratings (Par 99): **101,97,96,90,87 86,65,62**
toteswinger: 1&2 £2.50, 1&3 £4.40, 2&3 £6.40. CSF £9.50 CT £45.19 TOTE £2.00: £1.10, £1.80, £1.80; EX 7.70 Trifecta £67.00 Pool: £564.71 - 6.23 winning units..
Owner Mrs P Hastings **Bred** Darley **Trained** Kingsclere, Hants

FOCUS
A weak-looking contest. The winner was value for 8lb and this form looks sound.
Peter Grimes(IRE) Official explanation: trainer rep said gelding was unsuited by the firm (good to firm in places) ground
Lambourn Genie(UAE) Official explanation: jockey said gelding ran too freely

2910 BETINTERNET.COM FILLIES' H'CAP 1m 5y
4:30 (4:31) (Class 5) (0-70,74) 3-Y-0+ £2,719 (£809; £404; £202) Stalls Low

Form RPR
1400 1 **Very Well Red**[21] 2261 6-9-12 63 DarryllHolland 8 74
(P W Hiatt) *mde all: pushed along over 5f out: r.o wl* 8/1
6031 2 4 **You've Been Mowed**[11] 2577 3-8-9 60 DavidProbert(3) 7 59
(R J Price) *t.k.h: a chsng wnr: rdn over 1f out: no imp* 9/1
6-01 3 2 1/2 **Sapphire Rose**[13] 2515 3-9-0 62 TravisBlock 1 55
(J G Portman) *t.k.h: a.p: rdn jst over 1f out: one pce* 4/1[1]
0-64 4 1 1/2 **Oriental Girl**[18] 2352 4-9-12 63 (p) RichardThomas 2 56
(J A Geake) *hld up in tch: rdn over 1f out: one pce* 9/2[2]
-002 5 1 1/4 **Jewelled Reef (IRE)**[13] 2515 3-8-11 62 KevinGhunowa(3) 6 49
(Eve Johnson Houghton) *hld up in tch: rdn over 2f out: no imp fnl f* 11/2
-201 6 nk **Tikka Masala (IRE)**[12] 2539 3-9-12 74 (t) RichardKingscote 10 60
(Tom Dascombe) *hld up and bhd: pushed wd bnd over 4f out: rdn 2f out: nvr trbld ldrs* 5/1[3]
6204 7 nse **Binfield (IRE)**[23] 2212 4-10-0 65 GeorgeBaker 5 54
(B G Powell) *s.i.s: hung rt bnd over 4f out: rdn wl over 1f out: a bhd* 4/1[1]
-024 8 6 **Superstitious Me (IRE)**[12] 2539 3-8-4 57 JackDean(5) 9 29
(B Palling) *plld hrd: hmpd jst over 3f out: a in rr* 11/1
0-00 9 25 **Fly Butterfly**[8] 2654 3-7-12 46 oh1 CatherineGannon 4 —
(M R Channon) *t.k.h in tch: rdn and wknd over 2f out* 40/1

1m 39.07s (-1.73) **Going Correction** -0.20s/f (Firm)
WFA 3 from 4yo+ 11lb 9 Ran SP% **122.1**
Speed ratings (Par 100): **100,96,93,92,90 90,90,84,59**
toteswinger: 1&2 £14.80, 1&3 £9.40, 2&3 £10.10. CSF £81.72 CT £339.86 TOTE £12.30: £3.90, £3.20, £1.40; EX 149.10 TRIFECTA Not won..
Owner Phil Kelly **Bred** Butts Enterprises Limited **Trained** Hook Norton, Oxon

FOCUS
Not much happened up front in this, but there was some scrimmaging in behind that did not help a few of those well beaten. The first three were always to the fore and this is modest form.
Binfield(IRE) Official explanation: trainer said fillywas unsuited by the firm (good to firm in places) ground

2911 BEST ODDS GUARANTEED AT BETINTERNET.COM H'CAP 5f 161y
5:05 (5:05) (Class 4) (0-80,83) 3-Y-0+ £4,857 (£1,445; £722; £360) Stalls Centre

Form RPR
4104 1 **Artistic License (IRE)**[19] 2334 4-9-9 75 DarryllHolland 10 86+
(M R Channon) *in rr: sn pushed along: hdwy whn nt clr run and swtchd rt over 1f out: led wl ins fnl f: r.o wl* 9/2[2]
3115 2 2 1/4 **Kyllachy Storm**[13] 2520 5-9-6 72 GeorgeBaker 6 76
(R J Hodges) *s.i.s: hdwy on ins over 2f out: rdn jst over 1f out: ev ch ins fnl f: nt qckn* 5/1[3]
4200 3 nk **Golden Dixie (USA)**[8] 2680 10-9-2 68 CatherineGannon 11 71
(R A Harris) *in rr: late hdwy: tk 3rd nr fin* 12/1
5211 4 1 1/2 **Harry Up**[33] 1935 8-9-1 67 (p) J-PGuillambert 5 65+
(Andrew Reid) *led: rdn 1f out: hdd and no ex wl ins fnl f* 7/1
00-0 5 nse **Johnstown Lad (IRE)**[27] 2108 5-9-10 76 (t) RichardKingscote 4 74
(Niall Moran, Ire) *mid-div: hdwy over 2f out: rdn over 1f out: wknd towards fin* 14/1
0043 6 3 1/4 **Misaro (GER)**[13] 2520 8-9-7 78 (b) WilliamCarson(5) 2 65
(R A Harris) *prom tl wknd over 2f out* 8/1
-300 7 1/2 **Even Bolder**[9] 2637 6-9-6 77 LeeNewnes(5) 1 63
(E A Wheeler) *prom: rdn and wknd ins fnl f* 28/1
4012 8 2 **Desperate Dan**[8] 2653 8-9-2 75 (v) PNolan(7) 3 54
(A B Haynes) *prom tl wknd 1f out* 9/2[2]
-061 9 2 1/4 **Filligree (IRE)**[8] 2653 4-10-0 83 DavidProbert(3) 7 54+
(Rae Guest) *towards rr: sddle slipped over 3f out: hdwy on outside over 2f out: rdr lost irons whn nrly uns over 1f out: n.d after* 7/2[1]
1140 10 11 **What Katie Did (IRE)**[32] 1970 4-9-2 68 (p) LPKeniry 9 3
(J M Bradley) *prom tl wknd over 2f out: eased ins fnl f* 14/1

69.56 secs (-1.64) **Going Correction** -0.20s/f (Firm)
WFA 3 from 4yo+ 8lb 10 Ran SP% **123.3**
Speed ratings (Par 105): **102,99,98,96,96 92,91,88,85,71**
toteswinger: 1&2 £7.60 1&3 £14.60, 2&3 £15.40. CSF £29.13 CT £262.14 TOTE £7.00: £2.20, £1.90, £4.70; EX 40.50 TRIFECTA Not won..
Owner Wood Street Syndicate IV **Bred** Mountarmstrong Stud **Trained** West Ilsley, Berks

FOCUS
With quite a few proven front-runners engaged, this was always likely to be run at a generous pace. Those who finished well dominated the final stages. The fourth did best of the prominent runners.
Filligree(IRE) ◆ Official explanation: jockey said saddle slipped

2912 JOIN BETINTERNET.COM FOR "THE US OPEN" H'CAP 1m 2f 46y
5:35 (5:36) (Class 6) (0-55,55) 4-Y-0+ £2,183 (£644; £322) Stalls Low

Form RPR
-014 1 **Goose Green (IRE)**[6] 2739 5-8-12 53 DarryllHolland 9 60
(R J Hodges) *hld up in mid-div: smooth prog on outside 2f out: rdn to ld wl ins fnl f: r.o* 5/1[2]
2645 2 1 1/4 **Make Amends (IRE)**[19] 2331 4-9-0 55 RichardKingscote 5 60
(R J Hodges) *a.p: rdn to ld wl over 1f out: hdd wl ins fnl f: nt qckn* 9/2[1]
5521 3 1 1/2 **Hatch A Plan (IRE)**[8] 2650 8-9-0 55 NeilChalmers 6 57
(Mouse Hamilton-Fairley) *hld up towards rr: hdwy 2f out: n.m.r 1f out: rdn and kpt on ins fnl f* 5/1[2]
-640 4 2 **Corrib (IRE)**[31] 1980 6-8-8 49 CatherineGannon 1 47
(B Palling) *a.p: ev ch 2f out: sn rdn: no ex ins fnl f* 5/1[2]
010- 5 1 **Jelly Mo**[252] 6492 4-8-8 52 MarcHalford(3) 2 48
(W M Brisbourne) *hld up in tch: rdn wl over 1f out: edgd lft ent fnl f: one pce* 10/1
0 6 nk **Thetearsthaticry (IRE)**[55] 216 5-8-5 46 oh1 RichardThomas 12 42
(A E Jones) *chsd ldr: led over 2f out: hdd wl over 1f out: n.m.r ent fnl f: wknd* 33/1
003 7 nk **Beckenham's Secret**[10] 2609 5-8-0 46 oh1 SophieDoyle(5) 10 41
(A W Carroll) *hld up towards rr: rdn over 2f out: styd on ins fnl f: nvr nrr* 16/1
0403 8 nk **Never Sold Out (IRE)**[13] 2518 4-8-7 53 (v) WilliamCarson(5) 3 48
(J G M O'Shea) *hld up: sn mid-div: hdwy on ins 4f out: rdn wl over 1f out: wknd ins fnl f* 8/1[3]
5660 9 1 1/2 **Red Current**[8] 2675 5-8-5 49 ow3 KevinGhunowa(3) 13 41
(R A Harris) *hld up in tch: rdn 2f out: wkng whn n.m.r over 1f out* 16/1
0-05 10 shd **Beauchamp Viking**[13] 2516 5-8-4 50 (t) JackDean(5) 11 42
(S C Burrough) *led: rdn and hdd over 2f out: wknd over 1f out* 33/1
0260 11 10 **King Of The Beers (USA)**[1] 2878 5-8-10 51 (p) LPKeniry 8 24
(R A Harris) *a in rr* 9/2[1]
0/0- 12 3/4 **Monmouthshire**[509] 251 6-8-2 46 (t) DavidProbert(3) 7 —
(R J Price) *a in rr* 18/1

2m 8.58s (-2.42) **Going Correction** -0.20s/f (Firm) 12 Ran SP% **129.5**
Speed ratings (Par 101): **101,100,98,97,96 96,95,95,94,94 86,85**
toteswinger: 1&2 £7.00 1&3 £4.60, 2&3 £7.80. CSF £30.63 CT £124.51 TOTE £5.10: £1.60, £2.50, £2.70; EX 36.00 Trifecta £105.20 Pool: £405.51 - 2.85winning units. Place 6: £45.75, Place 5: £15.99.
Owner Mrs S G Clapp **Bred** Liam Queally **Trained** Charlton Mackrell, Somerset
■ Thi completed a 622/1 four-timer for Darryll Holland.

FOCUS
A modest handicap and muddling form.
Hatch A Plan(IRE) Official explanation: jockey said gelding was denied a clear run
King Of The Beers(USA) Official explanation: trainer said gelding was unsuited by the firm (good to firm places) ground
T/Plt: £158.70 to a £1 stake. Pool: £53,604.00. 246.52 winning tickets. T/Qpdt: £35.10 to a £1 stake. Pool: £4,176.00. 88.00 winning tickets. KH

2533 LEICESTER (R-H)
Saturday, June 13
OFFICIAL GOING: Good to firm (firm in places; 8.7)
Wind: Light behind Weather: Fine and sunny

2913 FENWICK LEICESTER FILLIES' H'CAP 5f 218y
6:40 (6:42) (Class 5) (0-70,65) 3-Y-0+ £3,238 (£963; £481; £240) Stalls Centre

Form RPR
021 1 **Sweet Gale (IRE)**[10] 2598 5-10-0 65 MartinDwyer 9 77+
(Mike Murphy) *chsd ldrs: led over 1f out: sn pushed clr* 11/4[2]
00-5 2 2 1/4 **Morning Queen (IRE)**[26] 2122 3-9-2 61 AdamKirby 3 60
(C G Cox) *led to 1/2-way: outpcd wl over 1f out: rallied and edgd rt ins fnl f: r.o* 11/1
0456 3 3/4 **Comptonspirit**[9] 2625 5-9-12 63 SebSanders 7 62
(B P J Baugh) *chsd ldrs: rdn over 1f out: styd on same pce fnl f* 9/4[1]
3360 4 1/2 **Dancing Wave**[16] 2417 3-8-11 56 AmirQuinn 8 51
(M C Chapman) *chsd ldr tl led 1/2-way: rdn and hdd over 1f out: no ex ins fnl f* 20/1
6456 5 5 **City For Conquest (IRE)**[12] 2539 6-8-13 50 (b) SimonWhitworth 4 31
(John A Harris) *hld up: rdn over 2f out: sme hdwy fr over 1f out: wknd ins fnl f* 14/1
-466 6 1/2 **Blushing Maid**[9] 2632 3-9-6 65 KirstyMilczarek 1 43
(H S Howe) *sn outpcd* 6/1[3]
3540 7 2 3/4 **Azharia**[46] 1588 3-9-2 64 AhmedAjtebi(3) 6 33
(C E Brittain) *chsd ldrs: hung rt: rdn 1/2-way: wknd 2f out: eased ins fnl f* 8/1
-006 8 5 **Alyseve**[21] 2268 4-8-2 46 oh1 (p) RyanPowell(7) 5 1
(Mrs C A Dunnett) *s.i.s: outpcd* 100/1
2003 9 6 **Affirmatively**[7] 2712 4-8-9 46 (bt) SaleemGolam 2 —
(A W Carroll) *awkward leaving stalls: sn prom: rdn and wknd over 2f out* 8/1

1m 11.6s (-1.40) **Going Correction** -0.20s/f (Firm)
WFA 3 from 4yo+ 8lb 9 Ran SP% **114.7**
Speed ratings (Par 100): **101,98,97,96,89 89,85,78,70**
toteswingers: 1&2 £3.40, 2&3 £1.60, 1&3 not won. CSF £32.80 CT £78.26 TOTE £3.60: £1.70, £2.10, £1.40; EX 18.90.
Owner Ms L M Bartlett **Bred** Rozelle Bloodstock **Trained** Westoning, Beds

FOCUS
This was just a modest fillies' handicap. The winner looks back to something like her best form.

2914 VICTORIA CENTRE NOTTINGHAM MAIDEN FILLIES' STKS 5f 218y
7:10 (7:11) (Class 4) 2-Y-O £3,885 (£1,156; £577; £288) Stalls Centre

Form RPR
0 1 **Gallic Star (IRE)**[29] 2047 2-9-0 0 SamHitchcott 4 84
(M R Channon) *a.p: rdn and hung rt fr over 2f out: chsd ldr over 1f out: r.o to ld wl ins fnl f* 7/4[2]
3 2 2 1/4 **Bella Swan**[29] 2047 2-9-0 0 AdamKirby 10 77
(W R Swinburn) *ld: hdd over 4f out: trckd ldr tl led again over 1f out: rdr dropped whip sn after: hdd and unable qck wl ins fnl f* 6/5[1]

0 **3** 3 3/4 **Zinjbar (USA)**[37] 1810 2-8-11 0 AhmedAjtebi(3) 6 66
(C E Brittain) *chsd ldr tl led over 4f out: rdn and hdd over 1f out: no ex fnl f* **16/1**

4 3 1/2 **Ella Grace (USA)** 2-9-0 0 JamieMoriarty 9 56
(R A Fahey) *chsd ldrs: hung rt thrght: rdn and wknd over 1f out* **20/1**

5 8 **Kildangan Girl** 2-9-0 0 MartinDwyer 5 32
(W R Muir) *s.i.s: outpcd* **33/1**

64 **6** 1 3/4 **Prettiest Star (IRE)**[19] 2335 2-9-0 0 NCallan 3 26
(K A Ryan) *chsd ldrs tl rdn and wknd wl over 1f out* **8/1**[3]

7 2 **Botley Bell** 2-9-0 0 PaulMulrennan 7 20
(M R Channon) *s.i.s: outpcd* **33/1**

8 4 1/2 **Ellies Image** 2-8-7 0 RyanPowell(7) 8 7
(B P J Baugh) *dwlt: outpcd* **80/1**

9 1 1/2 **Scintillating (IRE)** 2-9-0 0 MickyFenton 1 2
(R Hollinshead) *mid-div: hung rt thrght: effrt over 2f out: sn wknd* **28/1**

10 25 **Lake Nakuru** 2-9-0 0 KirstyMilczarek 11 —
(H S Howe) *sn outpcd* **66/1**

1m 11.6s (-1.40) **Going Correction** -0.20s/f (Firm) **10** Ran SP% **115.6**
Speed ratings (Par 92): **101,98,93,88,77 75,72,66,64,31**
toteswingers: 1&2 £1.10, 2&3 £12.90 CSF £3.83 TOTE £2.90: £1.10, £1.10, £3.30; EX 3.40.
Owner Jon and Julia Aisbitt **Bred** J M Beever **Trained** West Ilsley, Berks

FOCUS
An uncompetitive fillies´ maiden in which the ´big´ two in the market dominated. Not much strength in depth.

NOTEBOOK
Gallic Star(IRE), well backed when disappointing on her debut at Newmarket, again came in for good support and managed to reverse form with Bella Swan. She was the first of the pair under pressure, but really came good from a furlong out and ran on well to win with a bit in hand. The step up to 7f will suit and she remains capable of better. (op 9-4 tchd 5-2 and 6-4)
Bella Swan travelled much the best and looked all over the winner two out, but in the end proved no match for Gallic Star, Adam Kirby losing his whip probably not affecting the result. Nicely on from the third, she has shown more than enough to pick up a maiden. (tchd Evens and 5-4)
Zinjbar(USA), too green to make an impact over 5f on her debut at Windsor, knew more this time and was up there from the off. She couldn´t race on with the front pair, but is clearly learning and 7f will help before long. (op 14-1)
Ella Grace(USA), half-sister to a middle-distance winner in Germany, comes from a yard going particularly well at present and she made a satisfactory debut. (op 16-1)
Kildangan Girl, very much bred to be suited by further, made a little late headway under an educational ride and should learn from the experience. (op 40-1)
Prettiest Star(IRE) is now qualified for a handicap mark and should fare better in that sphere. (op 9-1)
Scintillating(IRE) Official explanation: jockey said filly was unsuited by the good to firm (firm in places) ground

2915 GEORGE WIMPEY HOMES SUMMER H'CAP 5f 2y
7:40 (7:40) (Class 3) (0-95,89) 3-Y-O
£10,904 (£3,265; £1,632; £817; £407; £204) **Stalls** Centre

Form RPR

5-50 **1** **Bahamian Babe**[14] 2502 3-9-5 **87** NCallan 2 90
(M L W Bell) *chsd ldr: rdn over 1f out: r.o u.p to ld post* **3/1**[2]

2122 **2** nk **Lenny Bee**[16] 2393 3-8-11 **79** PaulMulrennan 3 81
(D H Brown) *chsd ldrs: rdn over 1f out: r.o* **4/1**[3]

10-0 **3** nse **Excellent Show**[49] 1517 3-8-12 **80** TomEaves 5 82
(B Smart) *led: rdn over 1f out: hdd post* **20/1**

1-10 **4** 1 3/4 **Doctor Parkes**[15] 2443 3-9-0 **82** DavidAllan 6 77
(E J Alston) *chsd ldrs: rdn and ev ch over 1f out: no ex wl ins fnl f* **9/4**[1]

-100 **5** 5 **Mister Laurel**[22] 2227 3-8-11 **79** TonyHamilton 1 56
(R A Fahey) *s.i.s: sn pushed along in rr: hdwy unde press and hung rt fr over 1f out: nvr nrr* **16/1**

-052 **6** 3/4 **Kerrys Requiem (IRE)**[14] 2474 3-9-7 **89** SamHitchcott 8 64
(M R Channon) *chsd ldrs: rdn over 1f out: wknd ins fnl f* **13/2**

0 **7** 10 **Kate The Great**[25] 2148 3-8-9 **77** MartinDwyer 4 16
(C G Cox) *prom tl rdn and wknd wl over 1f out* **18/1**

00-0 **8** shd **Finnegan McCool**[26] 2140 3-8-10 **78** SebSanders 7 16
(R M Beckett) *chsd ldrs tl rdn and wknd wl over 1f out* **8/1**

58.59 secs (-1.41) **Going Correction** -0.20s/f (Firm) **8** Ran SP% **116.1**
Speed ratings (Par 103): **103,102,102,99,91 90,74,74**
toteswingers: 1&2 £1.70, 1&3 £11.60, 2&3 £4.90 CSF £15.78 CT £201.72 TOTE £4.50: £1.50, £1.70, £4.00; EX 21.50.
Owner Mrs P D Gray And H J P Farr **Bred** Mrs P D Gray And H Farr **Trained** Newmarket, Suffolk
■ Stewards' Enquiry : Tom Eaves caution: used whip with excessive frequency.

FOCUS
This was a good 3yo sprint and it produced a cracking finish. The winner was back to her 2yo best.

NOTEBOOK
Bahamian Babe just came out on top. A smart sprinting juvenile, she looked a major player on the form shown in two starts this season, in a Listed race at Bath and older-horse handicap at York last time, and the money came in a big way. Down to a mark of 87, she was soon up with the speed and kept finding under strong pressure, just nosing ahead in the final strides. She will go back up the weights now, but should remain capable of paying her way. (op 6-1 tchd 11-4)
Lenny Bee, a beaten favourite on each of his last two starts, was back down to 5f and ran on well inside the final furlong, but again had to make do with second. He is a consistent sort who should find another race before long. (op 11-4)
Excellent Show, never involved over 6f at Ripon on her reappearance, was down in trip and had been eased 5lb, so it was no surprise to see her run well. She didn´t give in without a fight and should come on again. (tchd 16-1 and 25-1)
Doctor Parkes disappointed on slow ground at Haydock last time, but still looked well treated off a mark of 82 judged on his earlier Chester victory. He came to hold every chance over a furlong out, but could find no extra inside the final 100 yards. (tchd 3-1)
Mister Laurel has not gone on from his reappearance win, failing to beat a horse home on each of his last two starts, and he was again well held having been slow away. (op 12-1 tchd 10-1)
Kerrys Requiem(IRE), back to form when second at 40/1 in a good race at Goodwood last time, was beaten two out and failed to reproduce her best. (op 7-1 tchd 6-1)
Kate The Great has shown little in two starts this season. (op 14-1)
Finnegan McCool didn´t pick up for pressure and was eased inside the final furlong. (op 14-1 tchd 16-1)

2916 HAMMONDS FOR FITTED BEDROOMS AND KITCHENS H'CAP 1m 1f 218y
8:10 (8:10) (Class 5) (0-75,75) 4-Y-O+ **£3,885** (£1,156; £577; £288) **Stalls** High

Form RPR

-022 **1** **Dancing Jest (IRE)**[25] 2171 5-8-8 **62** MartinDwyer 3 69
(Rae Guest) *mde all: set stdy pce tl qcknd over 3f out: rdn ins fnl f: r.o* **9/4**[1]

404- **2** 3/4 **Graceful Descent (FR)**[221] 7183 4-8-11 **65** TonyHamilton 1 71
(R A Fahey) *a.p: chsd wnr over 3f out: rdn over 1f out: ev ch ins fnl f: kpt on* **9/2**[2]

0360 **3** nk **Flying Valentino**[35] 1860 5-9-4 **72** NCallan 2 77
(Ian Williams) *hld up in tch: rdn over 1f out: ev ch ins fnl f: unable qck nr fin* **10/1**

5246 **4** 1 3/4 **Indy Driver**[8] 2684 4-9-0 **68** FrancisNorton 7 69
(J R Fanshawe) *hld up in tch: plld hrd: rdn over 1f out: no imp ins fnl f* **9/4**[1]

-222 **5** 1/2 **Will He Wish**[44] 1633 13-9-2 **75** (v) AndreaAtzeni(5) 6 75
(S Gollings) *plld hrd: trckd wnr to over 3f out: sn rdn: edgd lft and styd on same pce fnl f* **5/1**[3]

-350 **6** 1/2 **We'Re Delighted**[21] 2269 4-9-3 **71** JamieMoriarty 4 70
(T D Walford) *hld up: plld hrd: effrt over 2f out: styd on same pce appr fnl f* **11/1**

2m 12.01s (4.11) **Going Correction** -0.20s/f (Firm) **6** Ran SP% **113.8**
Speed ratings (Par 103): **75,74,74,72,72 71**
toteswingers: 1&2 £4.90, 2&3 £6.10, 1&3 not won. CSF £13.07 CT £81.74 TOTE £4.00: £1.60, £2.90; EX 14.80.

Owner Mrs J E Lury and O T Lury **Bred** Knocklong House Stud **Trained** Newmarket, Suffolk

FOCUS
They went no gallop at all in this, the winner making all and recording a slight personal best.

2917 HIGHCROSS LEICESTER H'CAP 7f 9y
8:40 (8:41) (Class 4) (0-80,78) 3-Y-O **£5,180** (£1,541; £770; £384) **Stalls** Centre

Form RPR

10 **1** **Desire To Excel (IRE)**[11] 2578 3-9-1 **72** MartinDwyer 7 77
(P F I Cole) *mde all: rdn over 1f out: hung lft ins fnl f: styd on wl* **9/1**[3]

P-20 **2** 1 1/2 **Arteus**[23] 2198 3-9-0 **76** AndreaAtzeni(5) 1 77
(Jane Chapple-Hyam) *wnt lft s: sn trcking wnr: rdn over 1f out: sn edgd lft: styd on* **11/1**

5032 **3** hd **Perfect Class**[20] 2300 3-8-10 **67** (b[1]) SebSanders 6 67
(C G Cox) *trckd ldrs: racd keenly: rdn over 1f out: no ex towards fin* **9/2**[2]

621 **4** 3 1/2 **Reject**[15] 2439 3-9-4 **75** LiamJones 4 66
(W J Haggas) *plld hrd and prom: shkn up over 2f out: rdn over 1f out: styd on same pce* **4/6**[1]

650- **5** 1/2 **Golden Rosie (IRE)**[274] 5855 3-9-4 **75** MichaelHills 5 65
(B W Hills) *hld up: rdn over 1f out: nvr trbld ldrs* **14/1**

631- **6** 11 **Senor Berti**[238] 6808 3-9-7 **78** TomEaves 2 38
(B Smart) *prom: rdn over 2f out: sn wknd* **14/1**

200 **7** 3/4 **Charlieto**[26] 2142 3-8-13 **70** SaleemGolam 3 28
(E G Bevan) *hld up: bhd fnl 4f* **50/1**

1m 24.53s (-1.67) **Going Correction** -0.20s/f (Firm) **7** Ran SP% **111.8**
Speed ratings (Par 101): **101,99,99,95,94 81,81**
toteswinger: 1&2 £1.70, 1&3 £2.00, 2&3 £2.20 CSF £93.45 TOTE £11.90: £3.60, £6.00; EX 121.80.

Owner H R H Sultan Ahmad Shah **Bred** Glending Bloodstock **Trained** Whatcombe, Oxon

FOCUS
Just a modest handicap. The winner was back to his 2yo best but the favourite disappointed.

2918 POTTERS CARPETS H'CAP 5f 218y
9:10 (9:11) (Class 6) (0-60,61) 3-Y-O **£2,590** (£770; £385; £192) **Stalls** Centre

Form RPR

60-3 **1** **Pure Rhythm**[10] 2602 3-8-12 **54** (t) SaleemGolam 8 59+
(S C Williams) *a.p: chsd ldr 4f out: led 2f out: rdn out* **9/2**[1]

3000 **2** 3/4 **Private Passion (IRE)**[11] 2577 3-8-10 **52** MartinDwyer 16 55
(Pat Eddery) *chsd ldrs: rdn over 1f out: r.o* **16/1**

002 **3** shd **Rio Cobolo (IRE)**[12] 2530 3-9-0 **61** (v) AndreaAtzeni(5) 14 64
(Paul Green) *s.i.s: hdwy over 4f out: rdn over 1f out: r.o* **8/1**

5230 **4** hd **Kheskianto (IRE)**[17] 2370 3-9-1 **60** LeeVickers(3) 11 62
(M C Chapman) *chsd ldr tl led over 4f out: rdn and hdd 2f out: r.o* **11/2**[3]

3-63 **5** nk **Miss Tikitiboo (IRE)**[101] 753 3-9-3 **59** LPKeniry 3 60
(E F Vaughan) *hld up: hdwy 1/2-way: rdn over 1f out: r.o* **20/1**

-634 **6** 1 1/2 **Ba Globetrotter**[8] 2651 3-8-7 **49** SamHitchcott 6 45
(M R Channon) *hld up: hdwy u.p and edgd rt fr over 1f out: nt rch ldrs* **10/1**

-000 **7** 1/2 **Bold Bomber**[33] 1926 3-8-9 **51** PaulMulrennan 12 46
(Paul Green) *hld up: hdwy over 2f out: rdn over 1f out: no ex wl ins fnl f* **14/1**

4402 **8** 1 1/2 **Iron Out (USA)**[6] 2744 3-9-4 **60** MickyFenton 13 50
(R Hollinshead) *mid-div: rdn over 2f out: styd on same pce appr fnl f* **10/1**

000- **9** 2 **Short Cut**[274] 5860 3-8-9 **51** ow1 SebSanders 5 34+
(S Kirk) *hld up: plld hrd: hmpd 1/2-way: n.d* **5/1**[2]

2060 **10** 1/2 **Spit And Polish**[8] 2683 3-8-9 **58** AndrewHeffernan(7) 1 40
(C A Dwyer) *hld up: rdn over 2f out: n.d* **16/1**

5006 **11** 1 3/4 **Wicklewood**[33] 1940 3-7-13 **48** RyanPowell(7) 4 24
(Mrs C A Dunnett) *sn outpcd: no ch whn rdr dropped whip ins fnl f* **50/1**

530- **12** 1/2 **Makaykla**[229] 7015 3-9-4 **60** DavidAllan 15 35
(E J Alston) *led: hdd over 4f out: rdn and wknd over 1f out* **6/1**

5-00 **13** 6 **Join Up**[16] 2417 3-8-11 **53** LiamJones 10 8
(W M Brisbourne) *prom: rdn over 2f out: sn wknd* **40/1**

-000 **14** 5 **Port Ronan (USA)**[18] 2365 3-8-10 **52** (p) TomEaves 9 —
(J S Wainwright) *chsd ldrs tl rdn and wknd over 2f out* **25/1**

00-0 **15** 5 **May Need A Spell**[40] 1746 3-9-0 **56** VinceSlattery 7 —
(J G M O'Shea) *sn outpcd* **100/1**

1m 11.99s (-1.01) **Going Correction** -0.20s/f (Firm) **15** Ran SP% **126.2**
Speed ratings (Par 97): **98,97,96,96,96 94,93,91,88,88 85,85,77,70,63**
toteswingers: 1&2 £23.70, 1&3 £2.40, 2&3 not won. CSF £77.73 CT £593.04 TOTE £6.60: £2.80, £3.40, £2.60; EX 92.50 Place 6: £174.04 Place 5: £115.22.
Owner D A Shekells **Bred** Old Mill Stud And S C Williams **Trained** Newmarket, Suffolk

FOCUS
This was a low-grade handicap. The winne was a bit less exposed than most and built on her Nottingham form.

T/Plt: £356.80 to a £1 stake. Pool: £60,613.00. 124.00 winning tickets. T/Qpdt: £390.40 to a £1 stake. Pool: £4,274.00. 8.10 winning tickets. CR

2708 LINGFIELD (L-H)

Saturday, June 13

OFFICIAL GOING: Turf course - good to firm (8.2); all-weather - standard

Wind: Moderate, behind Weather: Fine but cloudy

2919 LADIES EVENING JULY 25TH MEDIAN AUCTION MAIDEN FILLIES' STKS 5f

5:50 (5:52) (Class 5) 2-Y-O **£2,729** (£806; £403) **Stalls** High

Form RPR

2 **1** **Gwynedd (IRE)**[18] 2360 2-9-0 0 RichardMullen 2 70
(E S McMahon) *racd towards centre: wl on terms: pressed ldr over 1f out: drvn and kpt on wl to ld last stride* **3/1**[1]

2 *nse* **Danny's Choice** 2-8-11 0 JackMitchell(3) 6 70
(R M Beckett) *dwlt: gd spd and sn crossed towards nr side: disp ld: narrow advantage wl over 1f out: kpt on fnl f: pipped on the post* **14/1**

33 **3** *1* **La Fortunata**[18] 2354 2-9-0 0 AdrianMcCarthy 1 66+
(J R Jenkins) *racd virtually alone in centre: wl on terms w ldrs: upsides 1f out: one pce ins fnl f* **8/1**[3]

4 *½* **Mistic Magic (IRE)** 2-9-0 0 EddieAhern 14 64+
(P F I Cole) *trckd ldrs against nr side rail: outpcd 2f out: pushed along and r.o wl last 150yds: gaining at fin* **3/1**[1]

5 *hd* **Athwaab** 2-9-0 0 TPO'Shea 4 64
(E A L Dunlop) *dwlt: sn chsd ldrs: pushed along fr 1/2-way: kpt on fr over 1f out but nvr pce to chal* **8/1**[3]

6 *2 ¾* **Rio Mist** 2-9-0 0 RichardHughes 13 54
(R Hannon) *dwlt: sn rcvrd: racd against nr side rail: w ldr to wl over 1f out: nudged along and fdd* **7/2**[2]

7 *1 ¼* **Take My Hand** 2-9-0 0 EdwardCreighton 5 49
(M R Channon) *s.s: wl off the pce in last gp: modest late prog: n.d* **50/1**

040 **8** *nk* **Avec Moi**[17] 2383 2-9-0 0 TGMcLaughlin 9 48
(Mrs C A Dunnett) *chsd ldrs: rdn 1/2-way: no imp over 1f out: wknd fnl f* **50/1**

564 **9** *1 ¾* **Cane Cat (IRE)**[18] 2348 2-9-0 0 TolleyDean 10 42
(A W Carroll) *nvr on terms: struggling in rr fr 1/2-way* **16/1**

0 **10** *3 ¼* **Ellmollell**[26] 2135 2-9-0 0 JamesDoyle 15 30
(S Kirk) *dwlt: a wl in rr: struggling fr 1/2-way* **40/1**

006 **11** *4 ½* **Silvee**[14] 2477 2-9-0 0 IanMongan 8 14
(J J Bridger) *sweating: wl in rr: nvr a factor* **80/1**

12 *5* **Lilyannabanana** 2-9-0 0 FergusSweeney 11 —
(A B Haynes) *dwlt: outpcd and a wl bhd* **14/1**

57.52 secs (-0.68) **Going Correction** -0.225s/f (Firm) **12** Ran SP% **121.3**

Speed ratings (Par 90): **96,95,94,93,93 88,86,86,83,78 71,63**

toteswinger: 1&2 £1.10, 1&3 £4.70, 2&3 £20.70. CSF £47.87 TOTE £4.20: £1.30, £5.00, £2.80; EX 67.20.

Owner J C Fretwell **Bred** Stanley Estate & Stud Co & Mount Coote Stud **Trained** Lichfield, Staffs

■ Stewards' Enquiry : Fergus Sweeney Fine: £80, vaccination in passport were found to have been altered in contravention of Rule 36 (ii).

FOCUS

Just a fair median auction stakes for juvenile fillies, although it featured a clutch of runners with sound form and a handful of newcomers from stables well capable of turning out first-time winners. They went a decent pace from the start.

NOTEBOOK

Gwynedd(IRE) lined up having finished second over 6f at Redcar on her only previous outing and, although she was taking a drop in distance, she had shown good pace that day and there is enough speed in her pedigree to have suggested this 5f ought not have been a major problem. Getting a good break from stall two and working her way over towards the stands' side, she was always prominent and, when asked for a late thrust under a strong drive, she delivered just enough to secure a narrow victory. She will need to improve on this performance to cope with a step up grade, but, being out of a mare who won at four, she may find some. If not, her connections have the option of going the nursery route, with those races now just around the corner. (op 10-3 tchd 7-2 and 11-4)

Danny's Choice, a newcomer out of a mare successful as a two-year-old, certainly seemed to know her job, as she broke smartly and, despite her stall-six draw, soon gained a prominent position close to the favoured stands' rail. She showed good zip throughout, hitting the front inside the final furlong, but she could not quite sustain her effort and was mugged close home. (op 10-1 tchd 8-1)

La Fortunata seemingly set the standard, based on her third in what had looked a decent contest at Leicester 18 days previously, but that form had taken a knock when the runner-up was turned over at odds-on earlier in the week. She ran well, nonetheless, deserving credit for better than her third place, as, having been drawn in stall 1, she stayed out in the middle of the course, well away from the main action. She tried hard to close as the post approached, but the first two always appeared to have her measure. (op 13-2 tchd 5-1)

Mistic Magic(IRE), another newcomer, in her case out of a mare twice successful as a two-year-old, was among the strongest finishers and, as long as she is not too highly tried, she should be able to find a similar prize. (op 8-1)

Athwaab, whose dam was a 7f winner, is another with prospects in this grade. She was only narrowly pipped for fourth spot and, with a longer trip likely to suit her in time, connections should be able to place her profitably. (op 7-1)

Rio Mist showed early speed, before fading as if the race and the experience were needed, but few of the rest look like imminent future scorers. (op 10-3 tchd 4-1)

Take My Hand was reported unsuited to the ground by her rider.

Ellmollell Official explanation: jockey said filly was unsuited by the good to firm ground

2920 BETDAQ.CO.UK H'CAP 6f

6:20 (6:20) (Class 6) (0-65,65) 3-Y-O+ **£2,047** (£604; £302) **Stalls** High

Form RPR

-001 **1** **Another Try (IRE)**[26] 2134 4-8-13 **58** MatthewDavies(7) 18 67
(A P Jarvis) *racd against nr side rail: pressed ldr: rdn 2f out and nt qckn: styd on fnl f to ld last 75yds* **4/1**[3]

440 **2** *¾* **C'Mon You Irons (IRE)**[19] 2326 4-9-11 **63** IanMongan 4 70
(M R Hoad) *mde most and racd jst off nr side rail: rdn 2f out: kpt on fnl f: hdd and outpcd last 75yds* **12/1**

2612 **3** *½* **Bateleur**[8] 2680 5-9-7 **64** MCGeran(5) 16 69+
(M R Channon) *stdd s: hld up in last pair: swtchd to wd outside over 1f out: drvn and r.o to take 3rd ins fnl f: unable to chal* **10/3**[1]

5-52 **4** *1 ¾* **Rhapsilian**[11] 2564 5-9-4 **56** (v[1]) RobertHavlin 6 56
(J A Geake) *t.k.h early: sn trckd ldrs: disp 2nd over 2f out gng wl: rdn and no rspnse over 1f out: wknd ins fnl f* **9/1**

-050 **5** *1* **Calypso Girl (IRE)**[5] 2776 3-8-11 **62** RichardEvans(5) 11 59
(P D Evans) *trckd ldrs on outer: rdn over 2f out: nt qckn and no imp over 1f out* **7/1**

4115 **6** *¾* **Mr Skipiton (IRE)**[56] 1360 4-9-5 **57** TGMcLaughlin 9 51
(B J McMath) *t.k.h early: w ldrs: lost pl and rdn over 2f out: steadily fdd over 1f out* **7/2**[2]

0021 **7** *shd* **Dualagi**[23] 2202 5-9-7 **59** FergusSweeney 8 53
(M R Bosley) *plld hrd early: hld up bhd ldrs: steadily wknd fnl 2f* **15/2**

50-0 **8** *1 ¼* **Ejeed (USA)**[7] 2713 4-9-8 **60** TPO'Shea 14 50
(Miss Z C Davison) *settled in last pair: shkn up and no prog 2f out: n.d after* **33/1**

050 **9** *hd* **Scruffy Skip (IRE)**[44] 1634 4-9-2 **54** (b) JerryO'Dwyer 12 43
(Mrs C A Dunnett) *racd against nr side rail: in tch: no prog u.p over 2f out: wknd over 1f out* **33/1**

3100 **10** *2* **Hollow Jo**[59] 1285 9-9-5 **57** RichardHughes 7 40
(J R Jenkins) *t.k.h early: trckd ldrs: steadily wknd fr over 2f out* **14/1**

69.62 secs (-1.58) **Going Correction** -0.225s/f (Firm)

WFA 3 from 4yo+ 8lb **10** Ran SP% **119.8**

Speed ratings (Par 101): **101,100,99,97,95 94,94,92,92,89**

toteswingers: 1&2 £0.00, 1&3 £7.00, 2&3 £3.80 CSF £52.82 CT £182.54 TOTE £6.10: £2.80, £3.10, £1.20; EX 130.70.

Owner The Twyford Partnership **Bred** Jarvis Associates **Trained** Middleham Moor, N Yorks

FOCUS

High-number stalls tend to be favoured in sprint handicaps here, particularly when the fields are large and closely matched, but, after a raft of the 48-hour declarations were declared non-runners, this contest might well have confused a few punters. Modest form with the first two the best guide.

Ejeed(USA) Official explanation: jockey said gelding was denied a clear run

Hollow Jo Official explanation: trainer said gelding was unsuited by the good to firm ground

2921 BACK OR LAY AT BETDAQ H'CAP 7f

6:50 (6:51) (Class 6) (0-55,55) 3-Y-O+ **£2,047** (£604; £302) **Stalls** High

Form RPR

5003 **1** **Avoca Dancer (IRE)**[24] 2184 6-9-3 **52** (v) TGMcLaughlin 17 63
(Karen George) *chsd ldrs nr side: prog and rdn wl over 2f out: led wl over 1f out and grabbed nr side rail: styd on wl* **12/1**

3000 **2** *2 ¼* **Love In The Park**[18] 2352 4-9-0 **52** JackMitchell(3) 10 57
(R Brotherton) *trckd ldrs: prog over 2f out: hrd rdn to take 2nd 1f out: styd on but no ch w wnr* **16/1**

-004 **3** *3 ¾* **Athboy Auction**[15] 2455 4-8-9 **51** (t) RosieJessop(7) 13 46
(H J Collingridge) *overall ldr but racd off nr side rail: hdd u.p wl over 1f out: grad fdd* **28/1**

0563 **4** *¾* **Imperial Djay (IRE)**[8] 2686 4-9-3 **52** JerryO'Dwyer 11 45
(J R Holt) *stdd s: hld up in rr: prog over 2f out: kpt on fr over 1f out: nvr rchd ldrs* **7/1**[2]

32-5 **5** *nk* **Dark Camellia**[150] 162 4-9-6 **55** (t) EddieAhern 18 47
(H J L Dunlop) *hld up in rr nr side: effrt against rail over 2f out: prog to chse ldrs over 1f out: nvr on terms and one pce after* **3/1**[1]

-450 **6** *1 ½* **Zeffirelli**[15] 2458 4-9-5 **54** PatCosgrave 3 42
(M Quinn) *led gp in centre: wl on terms to 2f out: sn outpcd* **12/1**

6610 **7** *½* **Straight Face (IRE)**[35] 1889 5-8-10 **52** (v) KylieManser(7) 15 39
(Miss Gay Kelleway) *hld up last nr side: wl off the pce 1/2-way: sme prog over 2f out: kpt on: nvr on terms* **9/1**[3]

3052 **8** *2 ¼* **Cavalry Guard (USA)**[35] 1883 5-8-12 **52** (b) AmyBaker(5) 14 32
(T D McCarthy) *racd against nr side rail: pressed ldr: rdn 1/2-way: wknd fr over 2f out* **7/1**[2]

-565 **9** *1 ¾* **Rydal (USA)**[73] 1065 8-9-5 **54** (v) IanMongan 16 30
(Miss Jo Crowley) *chsd ldrs nr side: u.p and no prog over 2f out: no ch over 1f out* **14/1**

0353 **10** *1* **Albero Di Giuda (IRE)**[8] 2682 4-9-5 **54** (t) NickyMackay 2 27
(F Sheridan) *prom in centre: pressed ldr there 1/2-way: wknd u.p 2f out* **10/1**

0-50 **11** *½* **Sun Catcher (IRE)**[26] 2137 6-9-4 **53** (p) FergusSweeney 8 25
(P G Murphy) *prom in centre to 1/2-way: sn lost pl and no ch* **14/1**

-552 **12** *3 ½* **Just Oscar (GER)**[22] 2223 5-8-11 **51** RossAtkinson(5) 4 13
(W M Brisbourne) *awkward s: wl in rr in centre: nvr a factor* **14/1**

660 **13** *nk* **Mansil**[87] 867 4-9-6 **55** EdwardCreighton 1 16
(P J McBride) *bhd in gp that racd in centre: nvr a factor* **16/1**

3600 **14** *2* **Tamino (IRE)**[41] 1710 6-9-4 **53** JimmyQuinn 6 9
(P Howling) *racd alone towards far side: wl bhd over 2f out* **20/1**

0000 **15** *15* **Pharaohs Justice (USA)**[14] 2473 4-9-4 **53** (b) JamesDoyle 7 —
(N P Littmoden) *chsd ldrs in centre: lost pl by 1/2-way: wl bhd over 2f out: t.o* **14/1**

4-00 **16** *15* **Grizedale (IRE)**[143] 234 10-9-3 **52** (tp) PaulDoe 12 —
(M J Attwater) *prom 3f: sn lost pl: eased 2f out: t.o* **14/1**

1m 21.48s (-1.82) **Going Correction** -0.225s/f (Firm) **16** Ran SP% **137.8**

Speed ratings (Par 101): **101,98,94,93,92 91,90,88,86,84 84,80,80,77,60 43**

toteswingers: 1&2 not won, 1&3 not won, 2&3 not won CSF £215.24 CT £5466.06 TOTE £16.60: £3.70, £4.30, £8.30, £3.00; EX 373.40.

Owner Adam Richard Wilson **Bred** Frank Towey **Trained** Higher Eastington, Devon

FOCUS

A very modest event, contested mainly by disappointing types, and not one of them had scored on his or her latest outing. Those drawn high again seemed to have a distinct advantage. The winner looked back to something like her best.

Sun Catcher(IRE) Official explanation: jockey said gelding hung left

Grizedale(IRE) Official explanation: trainer said gelding was unsuited by the good to firm ground

2922 IRISH NIGHT JUNE 20TH MEDIAN AUCTION MAIDEN STKS 1m 4f (P)

7:20 (7:20) (Class 6) 3-4-Y-0 **£2,729** (£806; £403) **Stalls** Low

Form RPR

5-3 **1** **Kris Kin Line (IRE)**[24] 2178 3-8-6 0 Louis-PhilippeBeuzelin(5) 5 76+
(Sir Michael Stoute) *mde all: stdy pce and rn green: urged along over 2f out: sn jnd: fought on wl to assert ins fnl f* **8/13**[1]

3322 **2** *¾* **Pyrus Time (IRE)**[16] 2395 3-8-11 77 EddieAhern 3 75
(J S Moore) *hld up in 4th: prog to go 2nd over 3f out: jnd wnr 2f out w jockey looking arnd: asked to go and win r jst ins fnl f: fnd nil* **9/4**[2]

6-6 **3** *1 ½* **Whatami**[16] 2395 3-8-6 0 StephenDonohoe 6 68
(E A L Dunlop) *hld up in 5th: prog to chse ldng pair 3f out: shkn up over 1f out: kpt on but nvr nr enough to chal* **12/1**[3]

0 **4** *14* **Boffin**[33] 1931 4-9-12 0 JimmyQuinn 4 50
(Eve Johnson Houghton) *hld up in last: outpcd fr 3f out: bhd after: wnt remote 4th over 1f out* **28/1**

04 **5** *4* **Final Son**[23] 2199 4-9-5 0 MatthewDavies(7) 2 44
(A P Jarvis) *chsd wnr to over 3f out: wknd rapidly over 2f out* **33/1**

60 **6** *hd* **Pallaton**[24] 2178 3-8-11 0 PatCosgrave 7 43
(R M Beckett) *chsd ldng pair tl lost pl u.p 5f out: wknd 3f out: sn bhd* **33/1**

2m 32.76s (-0.24) **Going Correction** +0.025s/f (Slow)

WFA 3 from 4yo 15lb **6** Ran SP% **109.7**

Speed ratings (Par 101): **101,100,99,90,87 87**

toteswingers: 1&2 £1.30, 1&3 £3.60, 2&3 £3.70 CSF £2.02 TOTE £1.50: £1.10, £1.20; EX 1.90.

Owner Saeed Suhail **Bred** Gainsborough Stud Management Ltd **Trained** Newmarket, Suffolk

FOCUS
Not the strongest of Polytrack maidens, despite some big yards being represented by runners with eyecatching pedigrees, and it would be unwise to get carried away with the level of form required to take the honours. The winner built slightly on his reappearance form.
Pyrus Time(IRE) Official explanation: jockey said, regarding running and riding, that his orders were to settle the gelding and ride his race thereafter, it turned for home going very well, disputed the lead approaching final furlong, but when asked to further quicken in the final furlong found nothing under pressure and was decisively beaten, adding that it could be a quirky individual, who would not respond to the whip, hence riding with hands and heels closing stages.

2923 BET ROYAL ASCOT - BETDAQ H'CAP — 1m 2f (P)
7:50 (7:50) (Class 5) (0-70,70) 4-Y-O+ — £3,238 (£963; £481; £240) Stalls Low

Form — RPR

-600 **1** **Wing Play (IRE)**[13] 2518 4-9-3 **66**.........(p) GeorgeBaker 4 — 75
(H Morrison) *hld up in midfield: swift prog jst over 2f out to trck ldr over 1f out: rdn to ld ent fnl f: sn clr: pushed out* — **9/1**

-023 **2** *2 ¾* **Clipperdown (IRE)**[7] 2708 8-9-2 **65**.........(t) EdwardCreighton 6 — 68
(E J Creighton) *trckd ldrs: prog to ld jst over 2f out: edgd rt and hdd ent fnl f: outpcd* — **16/1**

-610 **3** *1 ¼* **Lunar River (FR)**[29] 2039 6-9-5 **68**.........(t) FergusSweeney 13 — 69
(David Pinder) *dwlt: hld up in last quartet: stl there over 2f out: gd prog sn after: drvn to go 3rd ent fnl f: styd on but no imp on ldng pair* — **20/1**

0202 **4** *3 ½* **Rosy Dawn**[10] 2601 4-8-2 **58** oh3 ow7......... DebraEngland(7) 10 — 52
(J J Bridger) *led after 3f: stdd 4f out: rdn and hdd jst over 2f out: fdd over 1f out* — **33/1**

5050 **5** *1* **Play Up Pompey**[19] 2331 7-8-3 **52** oh2 ow1......... TPO'Shea 12 — 44
(J J Bridger) *chsd ldrs: cl up 3f out: rdn to go 3rd briefly 2f out: sn outpcd* — **40/1**

-004 **6** *1* **Resplendent Ace (IRE)**[49] 1533 5-8-12 **61**......... IanMongan 11 — 51
(P Howling) *hld up in rr: effrt on outer 3f out: outpcd 2f out: drvn and kpt on one pce after* — **8/1**[3]

4061 **7** *nk* **Free Tussy (ARG)**[46] 1589 5-8-11 **60**.........(b) RichardMullen 9 — 49
(G L Moore) *hld up in last trio: stl there over 2f out and sn outpcd whn kick for home sed: rdn and kpt on one pce fr over 1f out* — **10/1**

-546 **8** *nk* **Musashi (IRE)**[26] 2129 4-8-11 **60**......... PaulDoe 8 — 48
(Mrs L J Mongan) *s.s: hld up in last trio: sme prog on wd outside over 3f out: sn rdn: outpcd 2f out: n.d after* — **16/1**

0142 **9** *2 ½* **Apotheosis**[29] 2039 4-9-3 **66**......... RichardHughes 7 — 49
(W R Swinburn) *t.k.h early: hld up in rr: last 1/2-way: nvr gng that wl after: taken to wd outside wl over 1f out: no real prog* — **7/4**[1]

5-10 **10** *1 ¼* **Balnagore**[29] 2039 5-9-7 **70**......... EddieAhern 3 — 51
(J L Dunlop) *led at gd pce for 3f: chsd ldr to 4f out: lost pl qckly on inner 2f out* — **10/1**

0530 **11** *1 ¼* **Horseshoe Reef (AUS)**[37] 1815 6-9-2 **70**.... Louis-PhilippeBeuzelin(5) 5 — 48
(J R Gask) *trckd ldrs early: grad lost pl on inner bef 1/2-way: in last trio 2f out: no ch after* — **8/1**[3]

6011 **12** *½* **Samurai Warrior**[13] 2516 4-9-1 **69**......... RichardEvans(5) 2 — 46
(P D Evans) *prom: chsd ldr 4f out to over 2f out: wknd rapidly* — **7/1**[2]

0650 **13** *1 ½* **Bridge Of Fermoy (IRE)**[27] 657 4-8-3 **52**......... AdrianMcCarthy 1 — 26
(D C O'Brien) *cl up on inner tl lost pl rapidly fr 3f out: no ch over 1f out* — **66/1**

2m 5.59s (-1.01) **Going Correction** +0.025s/f (Slow) — **13** Ran SP% **122.7**
Speed ratings (Par 103): **105,102,101,99,98 97,97,96,94,93 92,92,91**
toteswingers: 1&2 £17.30, 2&3 £14.40 CSF £143.17 CT £2813.45 TOTE £12.60: £4.30, £5.60, £6.10; EX 229.30.
Owner Watching Brief **Bred** Churchtown House Stud **Trained** East Ilsley, Berks

FOCUS
No superstars here, but a fair number with sound recent efforts to their name all the same, so it could definitely be described as competitive. They went no great gallop, though, with the stop-start pace clearly counting against some, and the first three came home well clear. Muddling form with the fourth 10lb wrong.
Apotheosis Official explanation: jockey said colt ran too freely
Horseshoe Reef(AUS) Official explanation: jockey said gelding was denied a clear run

2924 SOUL NIGHT AUGUST 1ST H'CAP — 1m (P)
8:20 (8:20) (Class 6) (0-60,60) 4-Y-O+ — £2,047 (£604; £302) Stalls High

Form — RPR

0504 **1** **Copper King**[43] 1655 5-8-5 **47**......... JamesDoyle 4 — 55
(Miss Tor Sturgis) *trckd ldrs: effrt 2f out: drvn between rivals to grab narrow ld jst ins fnl f: hld on* — **14/1**

0-04 **2** *shd* **Feasible**[19] 2330 4-9-0 **56**......... PatCosgrave 10 — 64
(J G Portman) *trckd ldrs: rdn and effrt on outer 2f out: nt qckn over 1f out: styd on ins fnl f: tk 2nd nr fin: jst hld* — **9/2**[3]

-033 **3** *hd* **Tignello (IRE)**[19] 2330 4-9-2 **58**......... GeorgeBaker 1 — 65
(G L Moore) *s.i.s but pushed up to ld: hrd pressed over 2f out: narrowly hdd jst ins fnl f: kpt on but lost 2nd nr fin* — **5/2**[1]

3040 **4** *2* **Simpsons Gamble (IRE)**[16] 2400 6-8-13 **55**.........(p) EddieAhern 7 — 58
(R A Teal) *hld up in midfield: rdn over 2f out: styd on to press ldrs ent fnl f: nt qckn after* — **9/1**

3645 **5** *½* **Spoof Master (IRE)**[6] 2745 5-9-0 **56**......... FergusSweeney 2 — 58
(C R Dore) *t.k.h early: hld up in midfield: effrt 2f out: pressed ldrs 1f out: nt qckn ins fnl f* — **16/1**

0464 **6** *nse* **Ruwain**[10] 2608 5-8-1 **50**......... AshleyMorgan(7) 11 — 51
(P J McBride) *trckd ldr: chal 2f out: upsides ent fnl f: wknd* — **10/1**

02-2 **7** *½* **One Oi**[16] 2400 4-9-1 **57**......... RichardHughes 6 — 57
(D W P Arbuthnot) *dwlt: hld up towards rr: rdn on inner over 2f out: one pce and no real imp* — **11/4**[2]

3003 **8** *nse* **Binnion Bay (IRE)**[2] 2851 8-8-11 **53**.........(v) JerryO'Dwyer 5 — 55+
(J J Bridger) *dwlt: t.k.h early: hld up in rr: shkn up over 3f out: plugged on fr 2f out: grad clsd on ldrs fnl f: n.d* — **17/2**

6004 **9** *19* **Djalalabad (FR)**[8] 2686 5-9-0 **56**.........(tp) TGMcLaughlin 3 — 12
(Mrs C A Dunnett) *taken down early: dwlt: hld up in last: rdn and brief effrt on outer over 2f out: nt keen and wknd rapidly over 1f out: eased: t.o* — **20/1**

0160 **10** *12* **Sharps Gold**[87] 868 4-8-5 **50** ow3.........(t) JackMitchell(3) 8 — —
(D Morris) *hld up in rr: rdn over 2f out: wknd rapidly: t.o* — **50/1**

000 **11** *8* **The Spicer**[42] 1662 4-9-4 **60**.........(bt[1]) NickyMackay 9 — —
(F Sheridan) *s.s: a in last trio: rdn over 3f out: sn wknd: t.o 2f out* — **66/1**

1m 39.11s (0.91) **Going Correction** +0.025s/f (Slow) — **11** Ran SP% **123.8**
Speed ratings (Par 101): **96,95,95,93,93 93,92,92,73,61 53**
toteswingers: 1&2 not won, 1&3 £11.10, 2&3 £5.30 CSF £79.16 CT £222.42 TOTE £18.80: £5.00, £2.10, £1.40; EX 184.90 Place 6: £328.05 Place 5: £134.68.
Owner Paul Reason **Bred** Miss A V Hill **Trained** Lambourn, Berks

FOCUS
This looked a rather downbeat conclusion to the meeting, based on the contestants' overall ability, but a select group could at least claim to have untapped potential - and it resulted in a thrilling finish. The pace was only steady and it is doubtful if the form proves too solid.
Binnion Bay(IRE) Official explanation: jockey said gelding was denied a clear run final furlong
Sharps Gold Official explanation: trainer's rep said filly had a breathing problem
T/Plt: £281.10 to a £1 stake. Pool: £49,540.00. 128.65 winning tickets. T/Qpdt: £73.30 to a £1 stake. Pool: £4,027.00. 40.60 winning tickets. JN

2887 SANDOWN (R-H)
Saturday, June 13

OFFICIAL GOING: Good (good to firm in places on round course; round 8.2, sprint 7.9)
At mid-configuration on the home bend and the home straight, the rail was dolled out, adding about 5yds to advertised race distances.
Wind: Moderate across Weather: Sunny intervals

2925 TOTEPLACEPOT H'CAP — 1m 1f
1:50 (1:52) (Class 3) (0-90,90) 3-Y-O — £7,771 (£2,312; £1,155; £577) Stalls Centre

Form — RPR

3-33 **1** **Clerk's Choice (IRE)**[18] 2356 3-8-10 **77**......... JimCrowley 13 — 89
(W Jarvis) *hld up towards rr: hdwy over 3f out: sn drvn along: led appr fnl f: styd on strly ins fnl f* — **20/1**

34-2 **2** *2 ½* **Dancourt (IRE)**[16] 2399 3-8-3 **75**......... Louis-PhilippeBeuzelin(5) 10 — 82+
(Sir Michael Stoute) *in tch: chsd ldrs 4f out: led over 2f out: sn rdn and hung rt: hdd appr fnl f: kpt on same pce* — **8/1**[3]

-622 **3** *1 ¾* **Cloudesley (IRE)**[22] 2236 3-8-4 **71** oh3......... JimmyQuinn 4 — 74+
(A M Balding) *in rr: drvn and hdwy over 2f out: styd on wl fnl f to take 3rd cl home but no ch w ldng duo* — **11/2**[2]

-210 **4** *nse* **Ithbaat (USA)**[16] 2406 3-9-1 **82**......... TPO'Shea 11 — 85
(J H M Gosden) *sn led: hdd over 2f out and hrd drvn: styd on same pce fr over 1f out: lost 3rd cl home* — **20/1**

1220 **5** *½* **Thief Of Time (IRE)**[21] 2273 3-9-6 **87**......... AlanMunro 3 — 89
(P W Chapple-Hyam) *in tch: rdn and hdwy to chse ldrs over 2f out: styd on same pce fr over 1f out* — **10/1**

51- **6** *3 ½* **Glowing Praise**[250] 6534 3-8-10 **77**......... RichardMullen 9 — 71
(E S McMahon) *hmpd and in rr after 1f: rdn along over 3f out: styd on fr over 1f out but nvr a threat* — **16/1**

04-1 **7** *2 ¾* **Forte Dei Marmi**[24] 2174 3-9-0 **81**......... WilliamBuick 8 — 69
(L M Cumani) *hld up in rr: hdwy on outside fr 3f out: rdn and effrt over 2f out: nvr gng pce to trble ldrs: wknd ins fnl f* — **13/8**[1]

10-5 **8** *1* **Brief Candle**[21] 2281 3-9-4 **85**.........(t) JimmyFortune 2 — 71
(W R Swinburn) *s.i.s: in rr: hrd drvn and hdwy ins fnl 3f: nvr bttr than mid-div: wknd fnl f* — **16/1**

-041 **9** *5* **Highkingofireland**[27] 2105 3-7-13 **71** oh1......... MartinLane(5) 12 — 46
(K R Burke) *chsd ldrs: rdn over 3f out: wknd 2f out* — **14/1**

0-1 **10** *1 ½* **Louise Bonne (USA)**[15] 2433 3-9-1 **82**......... PhilipRobinson 7 — 54
(C G Cox) *plld hrd: in tch early: bhd fnl 4f* — **20/1**

2300 **11** *½* **Pegasus Lad (USA)**[8] 2674 3-8-11 **78**......... GregFairley 1 — 49
(M Johnston) *chsd ldr: chal 4f out: wknd ins fnl 3f* — **12/1**

4111 **12** *12* **Global**[15] 2431 3-9-3 **87**......... PatrickHills(3) 5 — 31
(R Hannon) *racd on outside: pressed ldrs over 4f out: c lft to r alone over 3f out and sn no ch* — **9/1**

1m 52.98s (-3.32) **Going Correction** -0.15s/f (Firm) — **12** Ran SP% **124.1**
Speed ratings (Par 103): **108,105,104,104,103 100,98,97,92,91 91,80**
toteswinger: 1&2 £20.60, 1&3 £17.50, 2&3 £6.10. CSF £175.25 CT £1026.09 TOTE £30.60: £6.30, £2.50, £2.40; EX 281.10.
Owner M C Banks **Bred** N Coman **Trained** Newmarket, Suffolk

FOCUS
They went steady early, meaning those held up out the back were disadvantaged, but the winning time was under standard, confirming the ground was very quick. A good handicap, and sound form overall, rated around the fourth.

NOTEBOOK
Clerk's Choice(IRE) was a maiden after eight starts and beginning to appear exposed prior to this. However, the slight drop in trip clearly suited and he displayed a good turn of foot to reel in the idling runner-up. He evidently has plenty of pace, so the medium early gallop was no inconvenience, and he probably wouldn't mind dropping back to 1m. (tchd 18-1)
Dancourt(IRE), just as on his reappearance when he was narrowly beaten over 1m on the Lingfield Polytrack, was a significant market drifter. He again ran better than many clearly expected, but looked to throw away a winning opportunity. Having been well placed, he quickened up nicely to lead over two furlongs from the finish, but seemed to idle badly, hanging left over to the far rail as well as carrying his head a touch awkwardly. He has plenty of ability, but on reflection, he probably went for home too soon and might do better under more patient tactics. (op 13-2)
Cloudesley(IRE) ◆, who had got going too late in a couple of runs at 1m since switched to handicaps, promised to be suited by this slight step up in trip but he was again left with far too much to do. Racing from 3lb out of the handicap, he was last at the top of the straight and it's to his credit he finished so well off the modest tempo. A rise in the weights is almost inevitable, but he'll still appeal as worth a bet when likely to get a good gallop over 1m2f. Official explanation: jockey said gelding did not handle the final bend (op 10-1)
Ithbaat(USA) had his chance under a positive ride and had no obvious excuses. (op 25-1 tchd 16-1)
Thief Of Time(IRE) probably would have preferred a stronger-run race. (op 12-1)
Glowing Praise had been off for 250 days and can be given another chance. (op 33-1)
Forte Dei Marmi looked much better than the bare form when winning narrowly off 73 on his reappearance over this trip at Goodwood, but he couldn't defy an 8lb rise. A steadily run race was never going to suit a horse bred to appreciate middle-distances, though, and he can be given another chance. (tchd 7-4)
Global has been a revelation in recent weeks, but he was too wayward to give himself any chance of completing the four-timer. After not handling the bend into the straight, he hung badly left and had no chance after ending up against the stands'-side rail. Official explanation: jockey said colt hung badly left in straight (op 8-1)

2926 TOTESCOOP6 H'CAP — 7f 16y
2:20 (2:23) (Class 3) (0-90,84) 3-Y-O — £7,771 (£2,312; £1,155; £577) Stalls High

Form — RPR

5401 **1** **Kyllachy Star**[14] 2504 3-9-9 **84**......... TonyHamilton 8 — 95+
(R A Fahey) *hld up in rr: hdwy whn hmpd and lost position 2f out: hdwy over 1f out: qcknd and edgd lft sn after: str run to ld fnl 100yds: comf* — **3/1**[1]

13-6 **2** *2 ¼* **Greensward**[35] 1870 3-9-5 **80**......... EddieAhern 2 — 83
(B J Meehan) *stdd s and hld up in rr: hdwy over 3f out: swtchd lft 2f out: drvn to ld appr fnl f: hdd and easily outpcd fnl 100yds but kpt on for cl 2nd* — **4/1**[2]

3212 **3** *2 ¼* **Head Down**[9] 2638 3-9-4 **79**......... RichardHughes 9 — 76
(R Hannon) *led: drvn and kpt on wl whn strly chal fr over 3f out: no ex ins fnl f* — **9/2**[3]

1-30 **4** *nk* **All About You (IRE)**[8] 2674 3-9-7 **82**.................................. LiamJones 1 78+
(W J Haggas) *chsd ldrs: rdn and ev ch fr 3f out: one pce and bmpd 1f out* **13/2**

-044 **5** *1 ¾* **Maggie Lou (IRE)**[23] 2198 3-9-2 **77**.................................. AlanMunro 5 68
(K A Ryan) *in rr: rdn over 3f out: styd on ins fnl f but nvr any threat* **16/1**

6-00 **6** *½* **Perfect Citizen (USA)**[16] 2399 3-9-5 **80**....................(tp) RichardMullen 7 70
(W R Swinburn) *towards rr but in tch: hrd drvn on outside fr 3f out: styd on fnl 2f but nvr gng pce to get into contention* **16/1**

2-31 **7** *1 ½* **Broad Cairn**[15] 2446 3-9-8 **83**.. SteveDrowne 4 69
(R Charlton) *sn chsng ldrs: qcknd to chal fr 3f out: rdn 2f out: chsd ldr but u.p over 1f out: wknd qckly ins fnl f* **11/2**

114- **8** *nse* **Portugese Caddy**[263] 6193 3-9-8 **83**.............................. JimCrowley 10 69
(P Winkworth) *chsd ldrs: rdn over 3f out: wknd fr 2f out* **20/1**

-005 **9** *3 ½* **Key Signature**[9] 2638 3-9-5 **80**.................................. PaulEddery 6 56
(Pat Eddery) *sn pressing ldr: ev ch fr over 3f out to 2f out: wknd u.p wl over 1f out* **9/1**

1m 29.66s (0.16) **Going Correction** -0.15s/f (Firm) **9** Ran SP% **118.4**
Speed ratings (Par 103): **93,90,87,87,85 84,83,83,79**
toteswinger: 1&2 £4.30, 1&3 £3.00, 2&3 £4.40 . CSF £15.40 CT £53.97 TOTE £4.00: £1.60, £1.80, £1.80; EX 17.60 Trifecta £191.00 Pool: £387.18 -1.50 winning units..

Owner CBWS Partnership **Bred** John James **Trained** Musley Bank, N Yorks

■ Stewards' Enquiry : Tony Hamilton one-day ban: careless riding (Jun 27)

Eddie Ahern one-day ban: careless riding (Jun 27)

FOCUS

A decent handicap for three-year-olds, but the early pace seemed only modest. The winner is progressing and the third is probably the best guide.

NOTEBOOK

Kyllachy Star ◆ readily defied a 4lb rise for his recent York success, despite being stopped in his run when initially looking to make his move. Having at first struggled in a few outings after winning his maiden, he now looks rapidly progressive and the hat-trick is a distinct possibility, especially if he's turned out under a penalty. (op 7-2 tchd 4-1)

Greensward had his chance after squeezing through a gap inside the final couple of furlongs, but he could not offer any resistance to the winner's late burst. (op 6-1)

Head Down, only 1lb higher than when runner-up over course and distance on his previous start, was joined up front by Key Signature soon after the start, but still went a sensible enough pace and had his chance. (op 5-1)

All About You(IRE) can be given another chance considering he was stuck wide for much of the way. His pedigree is all speed and he could do better back at 6f, the trip over which he won his maiden. (op 4-1)

Maggie Lou(IRE) was driven along and apparently going nowhere at the top of the straight, but she finally ran on when it was all too late, passing beaten rivals. (op 12-1 tchd 11-1)

Perfect Citizen(USA) didn't improve for a first-time tongue-tie. (op 14-1)

Broad Cairn proved disappointing on this drop in trip and switch to quicker ground. (op 6-1 tchd 13-2 and 7-1 in a place)

2927 TOTESWINGER H'CAP 7f 16y

2:50 (2:52) (Class 2) (0-100,92) 3-Y-0+

£11,215 (£3,358; £1,679; £840; £419; £210) **Stalls** High

Form RPR

0035 **1** **Brassini**[15] 2434 4-9-5 **83**.. AlanMunro 4 91
(B R Millman) *chsd ldr: led ins fnl 3f: hrd rdn fnl f: all out* **5/1**[2]

5100 **2** *1* **Quest For Success (IRE)**[16] 2405 4-9-12 **90**................ TonyHamilton 9 95
(R A Fahey) *chsd ldrs: rdn over 2f out: wnt 2nd over 1f out: kpt on u.p but a hld by wnr* **15/2**

0-00 **3** *hd* **Dingaan (IRE)**[15] 2434 6-8-12 **76**..................................(p) WilliamBuick 2 80+
(A M Balding) *t.k.h: hld up in rr: drvn along over 2f out: styd on fr over 1f out and clsng on ldrs nr fin but a looked hld* **14/1**

1-50 **4** *1 ¾* **Dixey**[43] 1640 4-10-0 **92**... PhilipRobinson 10 92
(M A Jarvis) *led tl hdd ins fnl 3f: styd chsng wnr tl outpcd appr fnl f* **16/1**

5405 **5** *1 ¼* **Wasp (AUS)**[22] 2239 7-8-13 **82**.................... Louis-PhilippeBeuzelin(5) 11 78
(W Jarvis) *in rr but in tch: pushed along over 2f out: styd on fnl f but nvr gng pce to rch ldrs* **9/1**

60- **6** *hd* **Jeninsky (USA)**[234] 6911 4-9-5 **83**.................................. SteveDrowne 5 79
(Rae Guest) *in tch: rdn to chse ldrs fr 3f out: nvr on terms and wknd appr fnl f* **11/1**

4066 **7** *1 ¼* **Stanley Goodspeed**[21] 2276 6-8-9 **73**...........................(t) JamesDoyle 6 65
(J W Hills) *in rr but in tch: rdn 3f out: mod prog fr over 1f out* **7/1**[3]

4041 **8** *2 ¼* **Pravda Street**[29] 2050 4-9-11 **89**.................................. JimmyFortune 7 75
(P F I Cole) *t.k.h: chsd ldrs: awkward bnd into st: n.m.r 3f out and lost position: sn rdn and little rspnse* **5/1**[2]

00-0 **9** *2 ¾* **Unshakable (IRE)**[16] 2412 10-9-11 **89**................................ PaulEddery 3 68
(Bob Jones) *chsd ldrs tl wknd fr 2f out* **25/1**

-515 **P** **Trafalgar Bay (IRE)**[35] 1861 6-9-12 **90**.............................. JimCrowley 8 —
(K R Burke) *slowly away: in rr whn p.u 5f out: dismntd* **11/4**[1]

1m 28.83s (-0.67) **Going Correction** -0.15s/f (Firm) **10** Ran SP% **119.0**
Speed ratings (Par 109): **97,95,95,93,92 91,90,87,84,—**
toteswinger: 1&2 £8.80, 1&3 £17.30, 2&3 £20.40. CSF £43.30 CT £511.45 TOTE £6.10: £2.00, £2.60, £3.90; EX 42.50 Trifecta £210.30 Pool: £568.64 - 2.00 winning units..

Owner The Links Partnership **Bred** B N And Mrs Toye **Trained** Kentisbeare, Devon

FOCUS

An ordinary handicap for the grade in which it paid to race handy in a slowly run race. The winner was close to last year's C/D form.

NOTEBOOK

Brassini, soon well placed, looked to nick this when taking a couple of lengths out of the field after early leader Dixey dropped away around two furlongs out. That said, Alan Munro felt the gelding was idling in front, which is understandable. He had dropped to a mark 2lb lower than when winning over course and distance last July, so this was no surprise. (op 8-1)

Quest For Success(IRE) didn't look to have much in hand of the handicapper coming into this, but he was always well placed and ran with credit. (op 7-1)

Dingaan(IRE), with cheekpieces back on, was a little keen early but still fared best of those who raced off the pace.

Dixey looks plenty high enough in the weights. (op 12-1 tchd 18-1)

Wasp(AUS) didn't really have the race run to suit and can be given another chance. (op 14-1)

Pravda Street, without the blinkers he had fitted when winning off a 4lb lower mark at Newmarket on his previous start, looked awkward when short of room around the turn into the straight. He didn't appear to let himself down in the straight and looks to want easy ground. (tchd 11-2)

Trafalgar Bay(IRE) was out the back early on after again starting slowly, before going wrong about five furlongs out. Unfortunately he appeared to have suffered quite a serious injury. (op 5-2)

2928 AGFA HEALTHCARE SCURRY STKS (LISTED RACE) 5f 6y

3:25 (3:27) (Class 1) 3-Y-0

£22,708 (£8,608; £4,308; £2,148; £1,076; £540) **Stalls** High

Form RPR

11-2 **1** **Triple Aspect (IRE)**[29] 2035 3-9-4 **109**.................................. LiamJones 4 116
(W J Haggas) *towards rr: drvn and hdwy fr 2f out: chsd wnr and j. path jst ins fnl f: qcknd to ld fnl 100yds: won gng away: easily* **15/8**[1]

0-45 **2** *2 ¼* **Jargelle (IRE)**[121] 524 3-8-8 **98**.................................. AlanMunro 8 97
(K A Ryan) *led: rdn 2f out: kpt on tl hdd and outpcd fnl 100yds* **14/1**

2- **3** *1 ½* **Rain Delayed (IRE)**[15] 2466 3-8-13 **99**.................................. KLatham 3 97
(G M Lyons, Ire) *chsd ldrs: rdn 2f out: edgd rt u.p 1f out: sn one pce* **11/1**

0413 **4** *nk* **Never Lose**[21] 2271 3-8-8 **92**.................................. RichardHughes 9 91
(C E Brittain) *hld up in rr: hdwy and squeezed through fr 1f out: fin wl but nvr gng pce to rch ldrs* **14/1**

-221 **5** *¾* **Noble Storm (USA)**[17] 2373 3-8-13 **94**................... StephenDonohoe 10 93
(E S McMahon) *chsd ldrs: rdn 2f out: wknd ins fnl f* **5/2**[2]

3345 **6** *hd* **City Dancer (IRE)**[7] 2716 3-8-8 **95**.................................. SladeO'Hara 6 87
(A Berry) *in tch: hdwy to chse ldrs 1/2-way: wknd ins fnl f* **10/1**

-163 **7** *1* **Fault**[30] 2016 3-8-13 **93**..(t) TPQueally 7 88
(Stef Liddiard) *chsd ldr: rdn over 2f out: wkng whn hmpd 1f out* **20/1**

231- **8** *2 ½* **Albertine Rose**[215] 7273 3-8-8 **87**.................................. EddieAhern 2 74
(W R Muir) *outpcd most of way* **33/1**

14-5 **9** *1* **Adorn**[21] 2271 3-8-8 **105**.................................. WilliamBuick 1 70
(J Noseda) *outpcd most of way* **5/1**[3]

20-0 **10** *5* **Lucky Leigh**[46] 1582 3-8-8 **90**.................................. SamHitchcott 5 51
(M R Channon) *rdn 1/2-way: a towards rr* **33/1**

60.77 secs (-0.83) **Going Correction** +0.025s/f (Good) **10** Ran SP% **121.4**
Speed ratings (Par 107): **107,103,101,100,99 99,97,93,91,83**
toteswinger: 1&2 £10.20, 1&3 £6.50, 2&3 £26.50. CSF £31.37 TOTE £2.80: £1.40, £4.60, £2.80; EX 38.20 Trifecta £426.50 Pool: £691.68 - 1.20 winning units..

Owner Findlay & Bloom **Bred** Noel O'Callaghan **Trained** Newmarket, Suffolk

FOCUS

A fair renewal of this Listed sprint and the pace was strong throughout. The winning time was 0.98 seconds faster than the following older-horse 61-80 handicap. A smart effort from the winner to defy a penalty.

NOTEBOOK

Triple Aspect(IRE) was out the back early and surprisingly outpaced through the first half of the contest, but he produced a powerful finish towards the outside in the closing stages. He didn't help his chance by hanging right about a furlong out, and wasn't great over the path at about the same time, but he continued his surge when straightened up to win in convincing fashion; a result not easy to envisage at halfway. This was a very smart effort considering a penalty for last year's Group 3 success in France meant he was conceding upwards of 5lb all round. Although this was an improvement on the form he showed over 6f at Newbury on his reappearance, he shapes as though he will be fully effective back over another furlong. He'll apparently stick to this trip for now, however, with a Group 3 back here on July 4 (Eclipse day) his intended target, and he'll be bidding to extend his unbeaten record at Sandown to three races. (op 11-4 tchd 3-1 in a place)

Jargelle(IRE) was the last to load but she started best of all and soon had most of her rivals on the stretch, setting a fast pace against the far rail. Although ultimately no match for Triple Aspect, she held on well for second and emerges with plenty of credit. Last season's Super Sprint winner, she was poorly placed in a couple of runs in Dubai this year, but this was a decent first start for the Kevin Ryan yard after four months off and she's obviously at her best when the emphasis is on speed. (tchd 16-1)

Rain Delayed(IRE) displayed a fluent, fast-ground action, despite having won on yielding last time, and he can have few excuses. (op 12-1 tchd 14-1)

Never Lose ran on all too late and found this an insufficient test of stamina. (op 12-1)

Noble Storm(USA) was worth a shot at a race like this and looked well positioned after displaying loads of natural speed just in behind the early leader, but he failed to pick up when asked. (op 11-4 tchd 9-4)

City Dancer(IRE) ran a respectable race but wasn't quite up to the task. (op 15-2 tchd 7-1)

Fault was squeezed up inside the final furlong and that exaggerated the beaten distance, but he is another who simply wasn't good enough. Official explanation: jockey said colt suffered interference in running (op 16-1)

Adorn had shaped well under vastly different conditions on her reappearance, but failed to build on that and was disappointing. A return to both 6f and fillies' company will probably help, but she doesn't look anything special. (tchd 11-2)

2929 TOTEEXACTA H'CAP 5f 6y

4:00 (4:01) (Class 4) (0-80,80) 4-Y-0+ **£5,180** (£1,541; £770; £384) **Stalls** High

Form RPR

0-04 **1** **Royal Intruder**[4] 2799 4-8-12 **69**.................................. RichardHughes 3 80
(S Donohoe, Ire) *hld up in rr: gd hdwy over 1f out: squeezed through 1f out: qcknd ins fnl f to ld fnl 75yds: readily* **11/2**[2]

401 **2** *¾* **Efistorm**[68] 1150 8-9-8 **79**.................................. PhilipRobinson 8 87
(C R Dore) *in tch: rdn and qcknd to chse ldrs over 1f out: styd on to take 2nd fnl 75yds but nt pce of wnr* **4/1**[1]

5205 **3** *1* **First Order**[10] 2591 8-9-4 **80**..(v) AnnStokell(5) 14 84
(Miss A Stokell) *chsd ldr: led ins fnl 2f: shkn up over 1f out: hdd and outpcd fnl 75yds* **12/1**

-000 **4** *1 ¼* **Fantasy Believer**[19] 2326 11-8-7 **64**.................................. TonyHamilton 11 70+
(J J Quinn) *towards rr but in tch: n.m.r ins fnl 2f: effrt and nt clr run jst ins fnl f: kpt on wl but nt rch ldrs* **16/1**

315 **5** *¾* **Figaro Flyer (IRE)**[17] 2382 6-8-10 **67**.................................. JimmyQuinn 13 64
(P Howling) *in tch: hdwy on ins to chse ldrs over 1f out: styng on same pce whn n.m.r jst ins fnl f* **14/1**

5-01 **6** *½* **Dragon Flame (IRE)**[15] 2460 6-9-3 **74**.................................. PatCosgrave 9 69
(M Quinn) *chsd ldrs: rdn and effrt u.p whn hung rt jst ins fnl f: sn wknd* **8/1**

0042 **7** *nk* **Brandywell Boy (IRE)**[15] 2460 6-7-13 **61** oh3 Louis-PhilippeBeuzelin(5) 5 55
(D J S Ffrench Davis) *mid-div: rdn and styd on fnl 2f: nvr gng pce to rch ldrs* **8/1**

0250 **8** *¾* **Hereford Boy**[16] 2397 5-8-13 **70**..(p) RobertHavlin 7 61
(D K Ivory) *towards rr: sme prog over 1f out: n.m.r ins fnl f and sn wknd* **12/1**

4540 **9** *½* **Digital**[18] 2359 12-8-10 **67**..(v) TPO'Shea 2 56
(M R Channon) *in rr: sme late prog* **28/1**

3512 **10** *2 ¾* **Alfresco**[12] 2549 5-9-7 **78**..(p) RobertWinston 1 56
(J R Best) *chsd ldrs: rdn 2f out: wkng whn n.m.r jst ins fnl f* **7/1**[3]

0220 **11** *1 ½* **Billy Red**[14] 2472 5-8-10 **67**..(b) TPQueally 10 40
(J R Jenkins) *sn led: hdd ins fnl 2f: wkng whn hmpd jst ins fnl f* **9/1**

2-10 **12** *½* **Westwood**[21] 2276 4-9-1 **72**........ AlanMunro 6 43
(D Haydn Jones) *outpcd most of way* **15/2**

61.75 secs (0.15) **Going Correction** +0.025s/f (Good) **12** Ran SP% **123.3**
Speed ratings (Par 105): **99,97,96,94,93 92,91,90,89,85 82,82**
toteswinger: 1&2 £5.60, 1&3 £17.30, 2&3 £15.10. CSF £28.95 CT £267.19 TOTE £7.30: £2.50, £2.00, £4.40; EX 31.60.
Owner Mrs Anna McDwyer **Bred** Farmers Hill Stud **Trained** Cootehill Road, Co. Cavan

FOCUS
A fair sprint handicap run at a predictably furious pace. The winner used to be a lot better than this and it's hard to know how much ability he retains.
Efistorm Official explanation: jockey said gelding suffered interference in running
Fantasy Believer Official explanation: jockey said gelding was denied a clear run
Figaro Flyer(IRE) Official explanation: jockey said gelding hung right and lost an off-hind shoe

2930 TOTESPORT HOME OF POOL BETTING MAIDEN STKS 1m 2f 7y
4:35 (4:37) (Class 5) 3-Y-O **£3,238** (£963; £481; £240) **Stalls** High

Form RPR
0- **1** **Brooklyn Spirit**[231] 6978 3-9-3 0........ EddieAhern 2 73
(C G Cox) *in tch: hrd drvn fr 3f out: styd on wl fnl 2f to ld fnl 110yds: hld on wl* **33/1**
2 *nk* **Troopingthecolour** 3-9-3 0........ RichardMullen 17 73+
(J H M Gosden) *s.i.s: bhd: hdwy over 2f out: n.m.r and swtchd lft 1f out: fin wl to take 2nd last strides but nt rch wnr* **12/1**
04 **3** *nk* **Secret Life**[14] 2488 3-9-3 0........ RichardHughes 16 76+
(J Noseda) *chsd ldrs: rdn fr over 3f out: n.m.r 1f out appr fnl f and swtchd lft: styd on wl u.p ins fnl f: gng on cl home* **16/1**
4 *¾* **Laughing Boy (IRE)** 3-9-3 0........ TPQueally 14 71+
(L M Cumani) *s.i.s: bhd: rdn over 3f out: hdwy on outside over 2f out: drvn to ld appr fnl f: hdd and no ex fnl 110yds* **7/1**[3]
00- **5** *½* **Marju King (IRE)**[242] 6715 3-9-3 0........ RobertWinston 10 70
(W S Kittow) *chsd ldrs: rdn 3f out: led ins fnl 2f: hdd appr fnl f: no ex ins fnl f* **50/1**
0 **6** *3 ¼* **Brave Dealer**[28] 2074 3-9-3 0........ SteveDrowne 6 63+
(R Charlton) *in rr: pushed along over 3f out: hdwy fr 2f out: swtchd lft appr fnl f: kpt on same pce* **14/1**
4 **7** *2 ½* **Count Lucien**[23] 2211 3-9-3 0........ JimmyFortune 3 58
(J H M Gosden) *prom: rdn to press ldrs ins fnl 2f: wknd fnl f* **10/1**
0 **8** *1* **Spensley (IRE)**[40] 1729 3-8-12 0........ Louis-PhilippeBeuzelin(5) 1 56+
(J R Fanshawe) *in rr: pushed along over 3f out: styd on fr over 1f out: nvr in contention* **28/1**
9 *1 ¾* **Highway Code (USA)** 3-9-3 0........ GregFairley 9 53+
(M Johnston) *w ldr tl def advantage over 5f out: rdn 3f out: hdd ins fnl 2f: sn wknd* **7/1**[3]
2-30 **10** *½* **Classically (IRE)**[59] 1291 3-9-3 80........ JimmyQuinn 8 52
(R Charlton) *chsd ldrs: rdn to chal ins fnl 2f: wknd qckly over 1f out* **4/1**[1]
03- **11** *2 ¾* **All Guns Firing (IRE)**[231] 6977 3-9-3 0........ PhilipRobinson 4 46
(M A Jarvis) *slt ld tl hdd over 5f out: rdn 3f out: n.m.r 2f out and sn wknd* **9/2**[2]
12 *6* **Dangerous Midge (USA)** 3-9-3 0........ AlanMunro 12 34
(B J Meehan) *s.i.s: a towards rr* **9/2**[2]
13 *6* **Warrants Attention (IRE)** 3-9-3 0........ WilliamBuick 15 22
(A M Balding) *s.i.s: a in rr* **22/1**
0 **14** *3 ¾* **Kyllachy King**[12] 2551 3-9-3 0........ JimCrowley 11 15
(Mrs A J Perrett) *mid-div: bhd fnl 4f* **33/1**
00 **15** *8* **Brave Beat**[19] 2323 3-9-3 0........ RobertHavlin 7 —
(H J L Dunlop) *stmbld bnd over 4f out: a in rr* **66/1**

2m 9.04s (-1.46) **Going Correction** -0.15s/f (Firm) **15** Ran SP% **127.8**
Speed ratings (Par 99): **99,98,98,97,97 94,92,92,90,90 88,83,78,75,69**
toteswinger: 1&2 £60.40, 1&3 £35.80, 2&3 £27.70. CSF £391.56 TOTE £35.30: £7.50, £3.80, £4.00; EX 524.80.
Owner Gwyn Powell and Peter Ridgers **Bred** Gainsborough Stud Management Ltd **Trained** Lambourn, Berks

FOCUS
There was a bunch finish, despite the pace appearing strong but still, this looked a decent enough maiden and the race should produce some nice types. Tricky form to pin down with the market leaders disappointing, and it has been rated as an ordinary maiden for the track.

2931 BET ON ROYAL ASCOT AT TOTESPORT.COM H'CAP 1m 6f
5:10 (5:10) (Class 4) (0-85,85) 4-Y-O+ **£5,828** (£1,734; £866; £432) **Stalls** High

Form RPR
4-45 **1** **Callisto Moon**[35] 604 5-8-4 **66**........ GregFairley 6 78
(R Curtis) *trckd ldr: led over 3f out: hrd drvn over 2f out: styd on wl thrght fnl f* **20/1**
55-1 **2** *2 ¼* **Victoria Montoya**[28] 2085 4-9-9 **85**........ WilliamBuick 9 94+
(A M Balding) *trckd ldrs: wnt 2nd and rdn 2f out: styd on u.p but no imp on wnr fr over 1f out* **2/1**[1]
-216 **3** *2 ¼* **Wild Rhubarb**[14] 2486 4-9-4 **80**........ PhilipRobinson 11 86
(C G Cox) *chsd ldrs: drvn along fr 4f out: styd on fnl f but nvr gng pce to rch ldng duo* **11/4**[2]
1154 **4** *2 ¼* **Bell Island**[14] 2497 5-8-7 **74**........(v) MartinLane(5) 4 77
(Lady Herries) *mid-div: hdwy to chse ldrs 4f out: rdn fr 3f out: styd on fnl 2f but nvr gng pce to rch ldng trio* **25/1**
16-1 **5** *¾* **Colonel Flay**[35] 1878 5-8-10 **72**........ RobertHavlin 5 74+
(Mrs P N Dutfield) *hld up in rr: stdy hdwy on outside fr 3f out: clsd on ldrs over 1f out: sn one pce* **16/1**
3-00 **6** *nse* **Double Banded (IRE)**[14] 2486 5-9-9 **85**........ StephenDonohoe 3 86+
(Ian Williams) *hld up in rr: rdn and hdwy fr 3f out: kpt on fnl f but nvr in contention* **20/1**
4-05 **7** *2* **Sam Lord**[14] 2475 5-9-5 **81**........ TPQueally 1 80
(A King) *chsd ldrs: rdn 3f out: wknd over 1f out* **20/1**
50/4 **8** *1* **Takafu (USA)**[24] 2177 7-8-10 **75**........ JamesMillman(3) 2 72
(W S Kittow) *chsd ldrs: rdn 4f out: wknd fr 2f out* **9/1**[3]
65-0 **9** *½* **Rowan Rio**[14] 2475 4-9-6 **82**........ LiamJones 7 79
(W J Haggas) *in rr: sme prog fnl 2f* **16/1**
0651 **10** *1* **Cape Colony**[7] 2698 4-9-4 **80**........ JimmyFortune 14 75
(R Hannon) *in rr: rdn 3f out: mod prog fnl 2f* **16/1**
2062 **11** *½* **Munlochy Bay**[15] 2429 5-8-1 **68**........(p) Louis-PhilippeBeuzelin(5) 12 62
(W S Kittow) *chsd ldrs over 11f* **12/1**
5-10 **12** *hd* **Serious Choice (IRE)**[30] 2003 4-9-2 **78**........ PatCosgrave 8 72
(J R Boyle) *chsd ldrs 11f* **40/1**
-323 **13** *1 ¾* **Gaia Prince (USA)**[11] 2566 4-9-0 **76**........ JimCrowley 15 68
(Mrs A J Perrett) *led tl hdd over 3f out: sn wknd* **25/1**
400- **14** *hd* **Whenever**[238] 6817 5-9-3 **79**........ SteveDrowne 10 70
(R T Phillips) *nvr bttr than mid-div: bhd fnl 4f* **10/1**
110- **15** *½* **Ragdollianna**[260] 6241 5-9-4 **80**........ AlanMunro 13 71
(Norma Twomey) *t.k.h early: a bhd* **20/1**

3m 4.65s (-1.95) **Going Correction** -0.15s/f (Firm) **15** Ran SP% **133.6**
Speed ratings (Par 105): **99,97,96,95,94 94,93,92,92,92 91,91,90,90,90**
toteswinger: 1&2 £24.40, 1&3 £23.90, 2&3 £3.10. CSF £60.89 CT £162.78 TOTE £28.60: £5.00, £1.60, £1.70; EX 105.90 Place 6: £874.75, Place 5: £239.60.
Owner B Bedford & Mrs Gill White **Bred** Barton Stud **Trained** Lambourn, Berks

FOCUS
A fair staying handicap, but they went a modest pace and those who raced handy were at an advantage. The winner is probably the best guide to the form.
Whenever Official explanation: jockey said gelding was denied a clear run
T/Plt: £2,298.30 to a £1 stake. Pool: £122,158.00. 38.80 winning tickets. T/Qpdt: £762.50 to a £1 stake. Pool: £8,141.00. 7.90 winning tickets. ST

2893 YORK (L-H)
Saturday, June 13

OFFICIAL GOING: Good (good to soft in places) changing to good after race 3 (3.10)
Wind: Light 1/2 behind Weather: Fine and sunny

2932 QUEEN MOTHER'S CUP STKS (LADY AMATEUR RIDERS) (H'CAP) 1m 4f
2:05 (2:05) (Class 3) (0-95,90) 3-Y-O+ **£12,492** (£3,874; £1,936; £968) **Stalls** Centre

Form RPR
0-50 **1** **Mull Of Dubai**[37] 1798 6-10-5 **89**........ MissKECooper(6) 4 101
(T P Tate) *hld up and bhd: swtchd outside and hdwy 3f out: rdn and edgd lft 2f out: styd on to chse ldr ins fnl f: led last 100yds* **14/1**
501 **2** *¾* **Gifted Leader (USA)**[15] 2445 4-10-2 **80**........ MissSBrotherton 20 90
(Ian Williams) *lw: trckd ldrs: hdwy 3f out: rdn to ld appr fnl f: hdd and no ex last 100yds* **9/1**[3]
12 **3** *4* **Hillview Boy (IRE)**[16] 2392 5-10-3 **81**........ MrsCBartley 19 85
(J S Goldie) *led: pushed along 4f out: rdn 3f out: drvn and hdd over 1f out: kpt on same pce ins fnl f* **9/1**[3]
-002 **4** *nk* **Shady Gloom (IRE)**[8] 2666 4-10-0 **78**........ MissNCarberry 3 82
(K A Ryan) *lw: trckd ldrs: hdwy 3f out: rdn to chse ldrs 2f out: drvn and one pce appr fnl f* **7/1**[1]
0044 **5** *½* **Profit's Reality (IRE)**[11] 2566 7-10-2 **80**........ MissFayeBramley 1 83
(M J Attwater) *hld up towards rr: swtchd wd and hdwy over 2f out: sn rdn and styng on whn edgd lft ins fnl f: nrst fin* **16/1**
164- **6** *¾* **Dar Es Salaam**[232] 6950 5-10-1 **79**........ MissADeniel 5 81
(J S Goldie) *hld up and bhd: hdwy over 2f out: rdn and n.m.r wl over 1f out: kpt on ins fnl f: nrst fin* **18/1**
40-3 **7** *nk* **Manyriverstocross (IRE)**[14] 2475 4-10-7 **88**........ RachelKing(3) 15 89
(A King) *lw: trckd ldr: cl up 1/2-way: rdn along over 2f out and ev ch tl wknd appr fnl f* **17/2**[2]
4056 **8** *½* **Dunaskin (IRE)**[14] 2499 9-10-7 **85**........ MissJAKidd 16 85
(B Ellison) *trckd ldng pair: hdwy and cl up 4f out: rdn 3f out and ev ch tl drvn wl over 1f out and grad wknd* **25/1**
-053 **8** *dht* **Charlie Tokyo (IRE)**[4] 2781 6-10-2 **83**........(v) MrsVFahey(3) 12 83
(R A Fahey) *in tch on inner: hdwy over 3f out: rdn along 2f out: sn no imp* **16/1**
200/ **10** *¾* **Falpiase (IRE)**[169] 4569 7-10-1 **82**........ MissJennyCarr(3) 7 81
(J Howard Johnson) *chsd ldrs: rdn along 3f out: grad wknd* **33/1**
1311 **11** *1 ½* **Grand Art (IRE)**[14] 2505 5-9-9 **76**........ MissWGibson(3) 13 73
(P T Midgley) *towards rr on inner: hdwy 3f out: sn rdn along and n.d* **11/1**
65 **12** *½* **War Party**[7] 2706 5-10-4 **82**........ MsKWalsh 17 78
(Dr R D P Newland) *midfield: hdwy towards outer 3f out: rdn along whn sltly hmpd 2f out and sn wknd* **9/1**[3]
3000 **13** *½* **Kingsdale Orion (IRE)**[29] 2055 5-9-10 **77**........ MissHayleyMoore(3) 8 72
(B Ellison) *in rr tl sme late hdwy* **16/1**
0245 **14** *1 ¾* **Sgt Schultz (IRE)**[11] 2566 6-9-11 **75**........ MrsSMoore 9 67
(J S Moore) *a towards rr* **33/1**
0-10 **15** *5* **Cheshire Prince**[19] 2342 5-10-12 **90**........ MissEJJones 10 74
(W M Brisbourne) *midfield: rdn along and sme hdwy 3f out: wkng whn sltly hmpd 2f out* **50/1**
-422 **16** *7* **Taikoo**[22] 2249 4-10-2 **83**........ MissVCartmel(3) 2 56
(H Morrison) *hld up: a in rr* **7/1**[1]
3-03 **17** *10* **Holden Eagle**[18] 2351 4-9-11 **75**........ MissCHannaford 6 32
(A G Newcombe) *lw: t.k.h in midfield: effrt and sme hdwy over 4f out: sn rdn and wknd* **20/1**
111 **18** *2 ½* **Riguez Dancer**[130] 384 5-10-8 **89**........(t) MissEStead(3) 14 42
(P C Haslam) *midfield: effrt over 3f out: sn rdn along: edgd lft and wknd* **12/1**
-324 **19** *1* **Ruud Revenge (USA)**[12] 2545 3-8-13 **84** ow10........ MissDLenge(6) 11 35
(Mrs D J Sanderson) *midfield: rdn along on outer over 5f out: sn wknd* **25/1**

2m 36.12s (2.92) **Going Correction** +0.20s/f (Good)
WFA 3 from 4yo+ 15lb **19** Ran SP% **131.4**
Speed ratings (Par 107): **98,97,94,94,94 93,93,93,93,92 91,91,89,86 81,75,73,72**
toteswinger: 1&2 £53.30, 1&3 £47.80, 2&3 £13.30. CSF £132.24 CT £1235.29 TOTE £18.60: £4.10, £3.30, £2.50, £1.80; EX 257.60 Trifecta £495.40 Part won. Pool: £669.50 - 0.20 winning units..
Owner Mrs Fitri Hay **Bred** B Walters **Trained** Tadcaster, N Yorks
■ Katie Cooper's first winner.

FOCUS
The course was at its normal configuration. One of the most prestigious lady riders' races of the season. The betting suggested an open, competitive affair, but the gallop was no more than fair. Sound form with the winner back to something like his best.

NOTEBOOK
Mull Of Dubai had a bad draw at Chester last time, but his previous outing had suggested he retains the ability to win, and he was given a nice, patient ride out the back by Katie Cooper, before being brought with a sustained run up the centre of the track in the straight. The only one to make any significant ground up from off the pace, it was a good effort, and it's possible that there could be more to come from him, despite the fact that he's now a six-year-old.
Gifted Leader(USA)'s rider did well to get some cover for him as he was drawn widest of all. Given every chance from two furlongs down, he stayed on well, only to be mown down late on. This was a good effort off a 10lb higher mark and, as an unexposed sort, he could be open to further improvement. (tchd 10-1)
Hillview Boy(IRE) was also poorly drawn, but Carol Bartley took the initiative and managed to cross over to the inside rail and lead. She eased the pace once there, preserving something for the finish in the process, and the gelding ran a sound race in defeat. (tchd 17-2 and 10-1)
Shady Gloom(IRE) had a good draw and settled well on the rail in behind the pace. This trip probably just stretches him and he will be more effective back over 1m2f. (op 8-1 tchd 9-1)
Profit's Reality(IRE) promised to be suited by the easier ground. He ran okay without suggesting he's about to capitalise on his fair mark. (op 20-1)

Dar Es Salaam ran a bit better than the bare form suggests as he didn't get the clearest of runs. He's entitled to come on for this seasonal reappearance. (op 25-1)
Manyriverstocross(IRE) was another to bag a good prominent position despite being drawn out wide. He raced a bit keenly, though, and could have done with being allowed his own way in front. (op 9-1 tchd 10-1)
Holden Eagle Official explanation: jockey said colt ran flat

2933 LADBROKES.COM STKS (H'CAP) 1m 208y
2:35 (2:36) (Class 2) (0-105,98) 3-Y-O+ **£17,485** (£5,202; £2,600; £1,298) **Stalls Low**

Form RPR
4023 **1** **Kavachi (IRE)**[16] 2412 6-9-2 **86**.......... RyanMoore 4 95
(G L Moore) *hld up in midfield: effrt over 3f out: r.o to ld jst ins fnl f: hld on towards fin* **11/2**[1]
-534 **2** *nk* **Albaqaa**[31] 1986 4-9-7 **91**.......... PaulHanagan 19 100
(R A Fahey) *lw: hld up in rr: gd hdwy over 2f out: chal ins fnl f: no ex* **10/1**[3]
-401 **3** *nk* **Last Three Minutes (IRE)**[17] 2387 4-9-0 **84**.......... RHills 2 96+
(E A L Dunlop) *hld up towards rr: hdwy on ins 3f out: nt clr run tl jst ins fnl f: fin strly* **14/1**
22-4 **4** *2 1/4* **Acrostic**[10] 2612 4-9-10 **94**.......... DaneO'Neill 10 97+
(L M Cumani) *lw: hld up in rr: gd hdwy over 2f out: led over 1f out: hdd jst ins fnl f: fdd* **7/1**[2]
1-01 **5** *1 1/2* **Angel Rock (IRE)**[23] 2197 4-8-10 **85**.......... AndreaAtzeni(5) 12 85
(M Botti) *lw: t.k.h: trckd ldrs: led over 5f out: hdd over 1f out: fdd* **10/1**[3]
0-04 **6** *1 1/2* **Mastership (IRE)**[43] 1640 5-9-5 **89**.......... TomEaves 1 86
(J J Quinn) *hld up in midfield: effrt on ins and n.m.r over 2f out: kpt on same pce appr fnl f* **20/1**
0-40 **7** *2* **Capable Guest (IRE)**[8] 2669 7-9-1 **85**..........(v) TonyCulhane 5 78
(M R Channon) *in rr: kpt on fnl 3f: nvr trbld ldrs* **50/1**
0300 **8** *1/2* **Medici Pearl**[30] 2015 5-9-8 **92**.......... DavidAllan 6 84
(T D Easterby) *in rr: kpt on fnl 3f: nvr nr ldrs* **14/1**
0120 **8** *dht* **Opus Maximus (IRE)**[35] 1861 4-9-6 **90**.......... JoeFanning 7 82
(M Johnston) *trckd ldrs: kpt on same pce fnl 2f* **14/1**
20-4 **10** *1/2* **Moon Sister (IRE)**[41] 1697 4-10-0 **98**.......... LDettori 20 89
(W Jarvis) *sn trcking ldrs: chal over 2f out: fdd appr fnl f* **20/1**
3460 **11** *3/4* **Flipando (IRE)**[19] 2342 8-9-12 **96**.......... PhillipMakin 15 85
(T D Barron) *s.i.s: effrt on ins over 2f out: nvr a factor* **25/1**
1-20 **12** *1/2* **Red Jade**[21] 2290 4-9-1 **85**.......... AndrewElliott 16 73
(K R Burke) *trckd ldrs: drvn 4f out: lost pl 2f out* **11/1**
-400 **13** *2* **Best Prospect (IRE)**[31] 1986 7-9-1 **85**..........(t) DaleGibson 13 69
(M Dods) *hld up in rr: sme hdwy over 2f out: edgd lft: nvr a factor* **50/1**
2520 **14** *1 3/4* **Checklow (USA)**[19] 2342 4-9-11 **95**..........(p) SebSanders 11 75
(J Noseda) *mid-div: hmpd after 2f: drvn over 3f out: chsng ldrs over 1f out: sn wknd* **12/1**
0-02 **15** *shd* **Toto Skyllachy**[27] 2101 4-9-0 **84**.......... MickyFenton 8 64
(T P Tate) *trckd ldrs: upsides over 1f out: sn wknd* **14/1**
-250 **16** *5* **Fanjura (IRE)**[37] 1798 4-9-8 **92**.......... MichaelHills 3 61
(B W Hills) *mid-div: drvn over 3f out: nvr a factor* **14/1**
2214 **17** *8* **Granston (IRE)**[14] 2468 8-9-2 **86**.......... FrancisNorton 17 39
(J D Bethell) *w ldrs: lost pl over 2f out* **33/1**
/40P **18** *3 1/4* **Foolin Myself**[8] 2671 4-9-2 **86**.......... NCallan 9 32
(M L W Bell) *lw: hld up in rr: hdwy 4f out: hmpd and lost pl over 2f out* **16/1**
-440 **19** *3 3/4* **The Fifth Member (IRE)**[16] 2412 5-9-2 **86**.......... MartinDwyer 14 24
(J R Boyle) *led: hdd over 4f out: wknd qckly over 1f out* **33/1**
60-4 **20** *14* **Dubai's Touch**[10] 2606 5-10-0 **98**.......... RoystonFfrench 18 7
(M Johnston) *mid-div: sn drvn along: lost pl over 3f out: sn bhd: virtually p.u* **25/1**

1m 51.97s (-0.03) **Going Correction** +0.20s/f (Good) **20 Ran SP% 128.3**
Speed ratings (Par 109): **108,107,107,105,104 102,101,100,100,100 99,99,97,95,95 91,84,81,77,65**
toteswinger: 1&2 £14.00, 1&3 £15.80, 2&3 £42.90. CSF £53.66 CT £771.30 TOTE £7.70: £2.10, £3.10, £4.00, £2.00; EX 80.80 Trifecta £756.30 Part won. Pool: £1022.11 - 0.10 winning units..
Owner Bryan Pennick & Roy Martin **Bred** Gainsborough Stud Management Ltd **Trained** Lower Beeding, W Sussex

FOCUS
A good-quality handicap open to horses rated up to 105, but the top-weight Moon Sister was rated 7lb below that ceiling. They went a decent gallop and the principals came from well back. Solid form, but the third was unlucky and has been rated a length winner.

NOTEBOOK
Kavachi(IRE) ran well over an inadequate 1m at Sandown last time, but this longer trip, coupled with a decent pace and a bit of cut in the ground, promised to suit him much better. The gap opened up for him two furlongs out and he saw his race out strongly to defy a mark 6lb higher than he had ever won off before. He picks up a 5lb penalty for the Hunt Cup for this but would need a few to come out to get a run there. (op 15-2)
Albaqaa had a poor draw to overcome, but they went fast enough up front and he was able to drop in and get cover. He ran a sound race and will have his supporters in the John Smith's Cup back here next month. (op 14-1)
Last Three Minutes(IRE) ◆ endured a nightmare run up the inside in the straight as he waited for a gap to open up. When it finally came it was too late and the winner had gone beyond recall. Nevertheless, he showed that there is a big handicap in him when things fall right. Official explanation: jockey said gelding was denied a clear run (op 11-1)
Acrostic, racing beyond 1m for the first time, came with a sweeping run down the outside but got there too soon and tied up inside the last. It was still a solid effort and, being relatively lightly raced, there should be better to come from him in the coming weeks. (op 6-1)
Angel Rock(IRE) likes plenty of cut in the ground and so conditions were probably not soft enough for him. Nevertheless, he ran a decent race, especially as he was prominent throughout, and the expectation must be that he's capable of winning off his current mark when conditions allow.
Mastership(IRE) ran a fair race without suggesting that this trip will see him at his best. A strongly run 7f is probably what he wants.
Capable Guest(IRE) has a poor strike-rate and never really threatened. (op 66-1)
Moon Sister(IRE) didn't get home having made her bid for glory with three furlongs to run. (op 25-1)

2934 REG GRIFFIN MEMORIAL TROPHY (HERITAGE H'CAP) 6f
3:10 (3:10) (Class 2) (0-105,97) 3-Y-O **£64,760** (£19,270; £9,630; £4,810) **Stalls High**

Form RPR
-313 **1** **Swiss Diva**[29] 2049 3-9-1 **91**.......... RyanMoore 2 104
(D R C Elsworth) *lw: in tch: hdwy on wd outside 2f out: rdn to chse ldrs over 1f out: drvn to chal ent fnl f: sn led and kpt on* **10/1**
0034 **2** *1 1/4* **Parisian Pyramid (IRE)**[8] 2674 3-8-13 **89**.......... FrancisNorton 6 98
(D Nicholls) *cl up: rdn to ld 2f out: drvn and jnd ent fnl f: sn hdd and nt qckn towards fin* **10/1**
6-06 **3** *2 3/4* **Favourite Girl (IRE)**[35] 1880 3-9-7 **97**.......... DavidAllan 19 97+
(T D Easterby) *prom on outer: rdn 2f out and ev ch tl drvn and nt qckn appr fnl f* **40/1**
24-0 **4** *shd* **Rowayton**[21] 2279 3-8-7 **83**.......... RoystonFfrench 4 83
(J D Bethell) *midfield: hdwy 2f out: sn rdn and styd on strly ins fnl f* **33/1**
0-32 **5** *3/4* **Quanah Parker (IRE)**[14] 2504 3-9-0 **90**.......... MichaelHills 8 87
(R M Whitaker) *closde up: effrt over 2f out and ev ch tl rdn and one pce appr fnl f* **8/1**[2]
5220 **6** *3/4* **Lucky Numbers (IRE)**[36] 1824 3-8-11 **87**.......... PaulMulrennan 16 82
(Paul Green) *towards rr: hdwy and pushed along over 2f out: sn rdn and kpt on ins fnl f: nrst fin* **40/1**
01-1 **7** *1* **Master Of Disguise**[50] 1486 3-9-5 **95**.......... AdamKirby 18 87
(C G Cox) *lw; midfield: hdwy 2f out: sn rdn: edgd lft and no imp appr fnl f* **10/3**[1]
6224 **8** *1/2* **Akhenaten**[8] 2673 3-9-4 **94**.......... TonyCulhane 3 84
(M R Channon) *towards rr: hdwy 2f out: sn rdn and no imp appr fnl f* **18/1**
5-15 **9** *shd* **Dark Mischief**[41] 1705 3-9-4 **94**.......... DaneO'Neill 15 84
(H Candy) *lw: dwlt and towards rr: hdwy 2f out: sn rdn and no imp appr fnl f* **10/1**
41-2 **10** *2* **Macdillon**[29] 2049 3-9-2 **92**.......... LDettori 10 76
(W S Kittow) *led: rdn along and hdd 2f out: sn drvn and wknd* **8/1**[2]
0-06 **11** *hd* **Definightly**[21] 2270 3-8-13 **89**.......... PhillipMakin 20 72
(R Charlton) *hld up: effrt and sme hdwy 2f out: sn rdn and n.d* **18/1**
02-0 **12** *3/4* **Kingswinford (IRE)**[35] 1869 3-8-1 **84**.......... AndrewHeffernan(7) 9 65
(P D Evans) *chsd ldrs: rdn over 2f out: drvn: edgd lft and wknd wl over 1f out* **66/1**
1141 **13** *1 3/4* **Proclaim**[14] 2469 3-9-7 **97**.......... JoeFanning 13 72
(M Johnston) *lw; in tch: rdn along 2f out: no hdwy* **9/1**[3]
2-00 **14** *1 3/4* **Thunderous Mood (USA)**[21] 2278 3-9-5 **95**..........(t) MartinDwyer 5 64
(P F I Cole) *a towards rr* **50/1**
2451 **15** *1* **Coleorton Choice**[16] 2393 3-8-11 **87**.......... NCallan 14 53
(K A Ryan) *prom: effrt over 2f out: sn rdn and ch tl drvn and wknd over 1f out* **28/1**
13-3 **16** *3/4* **The Kyllachy Kid**[37] 1803 3-8-9 **85**.......... MickyFenton 11 49
(T P Tate) *lw: a towards rr* **25/1**
0005 **17** *4 1/2* **Imperial Guest**[14] 2469 3-9-0 **90**.......... SebSanders 17 39
(G G Margarson) *towards rr and sn scrubbed along: rdn 1/2-way: nvr a factor* **40/1**
10-6 **18** *8* **Prime Mood (IRE)**[14] 2469 3-8-13 **89**.......... TomEaves 12 13
(B Smart) *in tch: lost pl and in rr whn stmbld over 2f out: sn rdn: hung lft and lost action: eased* **66/1**
211 **19** *1 1/4* **Sloop Johnb**[29] 2058 3-8-8 **84**.......... PaulHanagan 7 4
(R A Fahey) *dwlt: a in rr* **8/1**[2]
1600 **20** *18* **Gone Hunting**[77] 1002 3-8-7 **83**..........(b[1]) PatrickMathers 1 —
(Peter Grayson) *v.s.a: sn rdn and rel to r* **100/1**

1m 11.6s (-0.30) **Going Correction** +0.20s/f (Good) **20 Ran SP% 127.7**
Speed ratings (Par 105): **110,108,104,104,103 102,101,100,100,97 97,96,94,91,90 89,83,72,71,47**
toteswinger: 1&2 £25.20, 1&3 £85.00, 2&3 £78.50. CSF £101.94 CT £3944.67 TOTE £13.00: £2.70, £3.00, £5.00, £11.00; EX 170.20 Trifecta £9248.60 Pool: £31245.47 - 2.50 winning units..

Owner Lordship Stud **Bred** Lordship Stud **Trained** Newmarket, Suffolk
■ This race was run last year as the Betfair Sprint.

FOCUS
A valuable handicap for three-year-olds, and although perhaps not the strongest of renewals, with the top-weight Proclaim rated 8lb below the ceiling for the race, this is still good, solid form.

NOTEBOOK
Swiss Diva, who is best with a bit of give, boasts a smart turn of foot on her day and this big field always promised to take her along at a pace that would let her display that attribute most effectively. Drawn towards the far side, she raced on the outside of the pack, but got a good lead from Parisian Pyramid, who helped set a sound gallop, and took his measure with a change of pace inside the last. She clearly doesn't need to be ridden with exaggerated waiting tactics to be seen at her best and she might just be finally starting to fulfil the potential she has always had. A crack at some black type now looks the likeliest route. (tchd 11-1)
Parisian Pyramid(IRE), who didn't get home over 7f at Epsom, where the track was also reported to have not suited, showed good early speed but did not go an unsustainable pace. He was a length or two off the field from a furlong and a half out, but Swiss Diva found the better turn of foot to run him down. He deserves a change of luck, but he's tough and will surely win a big pot one of these days. (op 9-1)
Favourite Girl(IRE), who was dropping in class, did best of those drawn high. Back on a fair mark, she was always prominent and kept on stoutly. She seems to go on any ground.
Rowayton settled better than she did at Newmarket last time, and as a result she was able to keep something back for the finish. Quicker ground really ought to suit her better, and there is more to come from her in strongly run handicaps.
Quanah Parker(IRE), beaten narrowly over 7f here last time, was up there throughout, which is a proven advantage at this track. The drop back to 6f didn't seem to inconvenience him at all. (op 9-1)
Lucky Numbers(IRE) didn't run well on his final start at Chester, but his previous form had a solid look to it. This was a return to something like his best.
Master Of Disguise had seen his Sandown form given a number of boosts, and a mark of 95 still left him potentially well handicapped. He did have an extra furlong to travel here, but it was not expected to trouble him. However, he proved disappointing, failing to pick up for pressure, and now has a bit to prove. Official explanation: trainer's rep had no explanation for the poor form shown (op 4-1 tchd 9-2 in a place)
Akhenaten has few secrets from the handicapper now. (tchd 16-1)
Dark Mischief might appreciate a stiffer track. (op 9-1)
Macdillon showed good speed and might be suited by a drop back to 5f. Official explanation: jockey said gelding lost its action (op 10-1)
Prime Mood(IRE) Official explanation: jockey said colt hung left-handed
Sloop Johnb Official explanation: jockey said gelding got upset in stalls and never travelled
Gone Hunting Official explanation: jockey said gelding missed the break

2935 DANIEL PRENN ROYAL YORKSHIRE STKS (H'CAP) 1m 2f 88y
3:45 (3:45) (Class 2) (0-100,92) 3-Y-O **£14,247** (£4,239; £2,118; £1,058) **Stalls Low**

Form RPR
1325 **1** **Changing The Guard**[21] 2270 3-8-10 **84**.......... FrederikTylicki(5) 6 91
(R A Fahey) *in rr: hdwy on ins 3f out: rdn and upsides over 1f out: styd on to ld nr fin* **12/1**
-120 **2** *hd* **Union Island (IRE)**[7] 2701 3-8-13 **82**.......... NCallan 1 89
(K A Ryan) *lw: trckd ldrs: led over 2f out: edgd lft fnl f: hdd nr fin* **25/1**
-231 **3** *2* **Antinori (IRE)**[23] 2210 3-9-9 **92**.......... AdamKirby 9 95
(W R Swinburn) *lw: hld up in tch: effrt over 3f out: swvd rt then lft 2f out: kpt on same pce* **10/1**
0-65 **4** *1 1/4* **Marching Time**[7] 2701 3-8-13 **82**.......... RyanMoore 2 84+
(Sir Michael Stoute) *lw: t.k.h towards rr: hdwy over 3f out: styng on whn hmpd 2f out: edgd lft and kpt on same pce fnl f* **3/1**[1]
1-03 **5** *hd* **Call It On (IRE)**[22] 2248 3-8-13 **82**.......... MichaelHills 4 82
(M H Tompkins) *lw: in rr: drvn 4f out: styd on fnl 2f: gng on wl fin* **8/1**[3]

-21 **6** *hd* **Sovereign Remedy (USA)**[25] 2165 3-9-5 **88**........................ LDettori 3 88
(Saeed Bin Suroor) *lw: trckd ldrs: stdy hdwy over 2f out: ev ch over 1f out: kpt on one pce* **3/1**[1]
61-2 **7** *7* **Distant Memories (IRE)**[21] 2275 3-9-0 **83**..................... MickyFenton 5 69
(T P Tate) *led tl over 2f out: wknd over 1f out* **7/1**[2]
51-0 **8** *7* **Mustaqer (IRE)**[52] 1459 3-9-7 **90**... RHills 10 63
(B W Hills) *s.i.s: hld up towards rr: effrt over 3f out: sn wknd* **14/1**
-222 **9** *1 1/2* **Tepmokea (IRE)**[7] 2701 3-8-12 **81**................................ AndrewElliott 11 51
(K R Burke) *w ldr: drvn over 3f out: wknd over 2f out* **7/1**[2]
4-00 **10** *1 1/2* **Goliaths Boy (IRE)**[7] 2701 3-9-1 **84**............................... PaulHanagan 8 51
(R A Fahey) *t.k.h: trckd ldrs: drvn over 3f out: lost pl over 2f out* **22/1**
3-10 **11** *25* **Rafaan (USA)**[50] 1489 3-9-0 **83**.. JoeFanning 7 3
(M Johnston) *in rr: drvn over 4f out: sn bhd: virtually p.u: t.o* **28/1**

2m 11.93s (-0.57) **Going Correction** +0.20s/f (Good) **11** Ran SP% **121.2**
Speed ratings (Par 105): **110,109,108,107,107 106,101,95,94,93 73**
toteswinger: 1&2 £31.40, 1&3 £15.90, 2&3 £37.60 . CSF £285.12 CT £3101.41 TOTE £12.40: £3.60, £7.10, £3.40; EX 310.00 TRIFECTA Not won..
Owner I L Davies **Bred** R A Bonnycastle And Marston Stud **Trained** Musley Bank, N Yorks
■ Stewards' Enquiry : N Callan caution: used whip down shoulder in forehand position.

FOCUS
The official going was changed to good all round. This was another race in which the top weight came in at 8lb under the ceiling. The early pace was strong, with Tepmokea and Distant Memories taking each other on at the head of affairs and setting it up for a closer. Solid form, with improvement from the winner.

NOTEBOOK
Changing The Guard began his career this season winning over 5f at Great Leighs, but he quickly showed the stamina for further and this step up to 1m2f for the first time brought about a career-best effort from him. Settled out the back off the strong gallop, he certainly had the race run to suit, but still had to get the trip and did so in good style, just getting the better of Union Island in a driving finish. Unexposed at this sort of trip, this Darley cast-off could be capable of further improvement. (tchd 11-1)
Union Island(IRE), who didn't take to Epsom last time, bounced back to form here and answered his rider's every call, only to find the winner, who had been ridden further off the pace, too strong close home. (op 20-1)
Antinori(IRE) came there to have every chance, but he swerved right when hit with the whip. He doesn't look one to trust in a battle and will be better off being ridden from the front in future. (op 12-1)
Marching Time had the race run to suit, but he hung left under pressure and was ultimately disappointing. He has proved an expensive horse to follow so far in his career. (op 7-2 tchd 4-1 in a place)
Call It On(IRE) finished well over 1m last time and promised to be suited by the return to 1m2f, but despite being alongside Changing The Guard early in the straight, he wasn't able to pick up in the same way. It wasn't the trip that beat him, though. (op 7-1)
Sovereign Remedy(USA) travelled well into contention but found little off the bridle. Perhaps he doesn't want to go this far at this stage of his career, so a drop back to 1m might be in order. (op 7-2 tchd 4-1 in a place)
Distant Memories(IRE) Official explanation: jockey said gelding hung right-handed

2936 LEONARD SAINER E B F MAIDEN STKS 6f
4:20 (4:22) (Class 3) 2-Y-O **£6,929** (£2,061; £1,030; £514) **Stalls** High

Form RPR
0 **1** **Haltela (IRE)**[19] 2311 2-9-3 0.. NCallan 2 80+
(K A Ryan) *w'like: scope: cl up: chal 2f out: rdn: edgd lft and led over 1f out: hung bdly lft ins fnl f: kpt on* **20/1**
2 *1* **Summerinthecity (IRE)** 2-9-3 0.................................... RyanMoore 11 77+
(J Noseda) *w'like: athletic: in tch on stands' rail: pushed along over 2f out: hdwy wl over 1f out: rdn to chse ldng pair whn rdr dropped rein ent fnl f: sn drvn and ev ch tl no ex last 75yds* **3/1**[2]
63 **3** *1* **Makbullet**[15] 2449 2-9-3 0.. PaulMulrennan 1 74
(J Howard Johnson) *led: rdn along 2f out: hdd over 1f out: edgd lft and one pce ins fnl f* **9/1**
4 *10* **Tartan Trip** 2-9-3 0.. FrancisNorton 10 44
(A M Balding) *w'like: str: bit bkwd: s.i.s and in rr tl sme late hdwy* **11/2**[3]
4 **5** *nk* **Capacity (IRE)**[12] 2533 2-9-3 0.................................. RoystonFfrench 9 43
(M Johnston) *lengthy: chsd ldrs: rdn along 1/2-way: sn btn* **15/8**[1]
6 *2* **Number One Guy** 2-9-3 0... SebSanders 6 37
(M H Tompkins) *athletic: chsd ldrs: rdn along over 2f out: sn wknd* **9/1**
7 *4* **Fifty Moore** 2-9-3 0.. MickyFenton 8 25
(Jedd O'Keeffe) *str: bit bkwd: s.i.s: a in rr* **10/1**
8 *15* **Rubicon Bay (IRE)** 2-8-12 0... DanielTudhope 4 —
(C J Teague) *w'like: bit bkwd: s.i.s: a in rr* **22/1**
9 *4 1/2* **Woodhouse Mill (IRE)** 2-8-12 0.................................... DavidAllan 3 —
(N Tinkler) *w'like: cl cpld: bit bkwd: dwlt: a in rr* **40/1**
004 **10** *hd* **Lily Lenor (IRE)**[40] 1719 2-8-12 0.................................. TomEaves 7 —
(B Ellison) *on toes: chsd ldrs: rdn along 1/2-way: sn wknd* **22/1**

1m 14.03s (2.13) **Going Correction** +0.20s/f (Good) **10** Ran SP% **120.2**
Speed ratings (Par 97): **93,91,90,77,76 73,68,48,42,42**
toteswinger: 1&2 £12.30, 1&3 £21.00, 2&3 £7.10. CSF £78.89 TOTE £26.00: £5.30, £1.60, £2.70; EX 121.60.
Owner Brendan P Hayes **Bred** Kilfrush Stud **Trained** Hambleton, N Yorks
■ William Morgan was withdrawn (rdr inj in paddock). Deduct 10p in the £ under R4. New market formed.

FOCUS
Previous experience proved the key here in what was a fair maiden. The first three finished a long way clear.

NOTEBOOK
Haltela(IRE), who had been coltish, slowly away and struggled for the most part on his debut, knew a lot more about the game this time and travelled strongly in behind the leader. He quickened up to lead approaching the final furlong, but hung left in the process and continued to hang once in the clear. But once he got over to the far rail he kept on well to hold off the Jeremy Noseda-trained newcomer. The winner can only improve further for this second run and could be a nice type for decent nurseries later in the campaign. (old market op 18-1 tchd 20-1 new market op 20-1 tchd 18-1)
Summerinthecity(IRE) tried to come from off the pace on a track where early pace often holds out. He came to have his chance a furlong out, but his rider dropped his reins and he hung left towards his main two rivals. It was still a promising effort from this half-brother to 7f Listed winner Meydan Princess and he can find a similar race soon enough. (old market op 9-2 new market op 4-1)
Makbullet looks to be improving with racing and put up his best effort to date, showing pace from the off and keeping on well. He looks one for nurseries. (old market op 8-1 tchd 10-1 new market op 10-1)
Tartan Trip, who is by Selkirk out of a 5f winner, shaped as though the experience was very much needed. Slowly away and green, he stayed on to be best of the rest, but looks the type that will need more time. (old market op 9-2 tchd 11-2 new market op 4-1 tchd 6-1 in a place)
Capacity(IRE) failed to justify market confidence that he would improve on his debut effort at Leicester. Scrubbed along from an early stage, this was a step backwards. Official explanation: jockey said colt never travelled (old market op 9-4 tchd 5-2 new market op 2-1)
Number One Guy has the pedigree to suggest that the best of him won't be seen until he tackles middle distances next year. (old market op 12-1 tchd 11-1 new market op 9-1)

2937 MICHAEL SOBELL MAIDEN STKS 1m
4:55 (4:58) (Class 4) 3-Y-O **£6,540** (£1,946; £972; £485) **Stalls** Low

Form RPR
04 **1** **Mutawarath (IRE)**[16] 2416 3-9-3 0...................................... RHills 10 83+
(W J Haggas) *trckd ldng pair: hdwy and cl up 3f out: led over 2f out: sn rdn and hdd appr fnl f: rallied to ld again last 100yds: kpt on wl* **6/1**[2]
2 **2** *1 1/4* **French Applause (IRE)**[27] 2104 3-9-3 0......................... MickyHills 12 80
(T P Tate) *w'like: scope: in tch: hdwy on outer 1/2-way: effrt to chse ldrs over 2f out: sn rdn and led appr fnl f: sn edgd lft: hdd and no ex last 100yds* **6/1**[2]
22-2 **3** *3* **Seaway**[21] 2282 3-9-3 90...(t) LDettori 7 73
(Saeed Bin Suroor) *lw: trckd ldrs: hdwy over 3f out: rdn 2f out and ev ch tl one pce appr fnl f* **9/4**[1]
0- **4** *1* **Aim To Achieve (IRE)**[232] 6945 3-8-12 0........................ MichaelHills 6 65
(B W Hills) *str: in tch: hdwy to trck ldrs 1/2-way: rdn along 3f out: drvn 2f out and sn no imp* **14/1**
00-4 **5** *1 1/2* **Maybeme**[27] 2105 3-8-12 58... PhillipMakin 11 62
(N Bycroft) *hld up: hdwy on outer 3f out: rdn over 2f out: kpt on u.p fnl f: nt rch ldrs* **66/1**
00 **6** *1* **Two Turtle Doves (IRE)**[22] 2250 3-8-7 0........................ DeanHeslop[(5)] 9 60
(M Mullineaux) *in tch: effrt 3f out: rdn along 2f out: sn drvn and no imp appr fnl f* **66/1**
652 **7** *1/2* **Steel Trade**[32] 1950 3-9-3 74... DavidAllan 4 64
(M Brittain) *hld up: hdwy 3f out: rdn along over 2f out: sn no imp* **14/1**
4 **8** *shd* **Canyon Ranch**[21] 2282 3-9-3 0...................................... DaneO'Neill 13 63
(L M Cumani) *w'like: scope: lw: midfield: hdwy and in tch 1/2-way: rdn along and sltly outpcd 3f out: kpt on same pce fnl 2f* **14/1**
9 *5* **Love In The West (IRE)** 3-8-12 0.................................. PJMcDonald 3 47
(G A Swinbank) *w'like: leggy: a towards rr* **50/1**
5 **10** *2* **Fernando Torres**[15] 2446 3-9-3 0..................................... FrancisNorton 1 47
(D Nicholls) *athletic: attr: lw: cl up: led over 5f out: rdn along 3f out: drvn and hdd over 2f out and sn wknd* **10/1**[3]
4 **11** *7* **Brockfield**[11] 2572 3-9-3 0.. TomEaves 8 31
(M Brittain) *w'like: led: hdd over 5f out: cl up tl rdn along 3f out and wkng whn n.m.r over 2f out* **66/1**
0 **12** *8* **Evna (USA)**[15] 2446 3-8-12 0... JoeFanning 5 8
(R A Fahey) *w'like: a in rr* **25/1**

1m 40.8s (2.00) **Going Correction** +0.20s/f (Good) **12** Ran SP% **98.7**
Speed ratings (Par 101): **98,96,93,92,91 90,89,89,84,82 75,67**
toteswinger: 1&2 £3.90, 1&3 £4.20, 2&3 £2.60. CSF £25.58 TOTE £6.60: £2.00, £1.90, £1.30; EX 29.60.
Owner Hamdan Al Maktoum **Bred** Philip Brady **Trained** Newmarket, Suffolk
■ Stewards' Enquiry : Dean Heslop caution: careless riding.

FOCUS
Probably a fair maiden, though mixed messages from the form. The winner has improved with each run.
Fernando Torres Official explanation: jockey said colt hung right-handed

2938 CHARLES HENRY MEMORIAL STKS (H'CAP) 6f
5:25 (5:28) (Class 4) (0-80,80) 3-Y-O+ **£7,123** (£2,119; £1,059; £529) **Stalls** High

Form RPR
0104 **1** **Dancing Maite**[7] 2695 4-9-6 **76**...................................... DaneO'Neill 10 89
(S R Bowring) *mde virtually all: styd on strly fnl f* **9/1**
4156 **2** *3* **Silver Wind**[20] 2297 4-9-3 **80**..........................(v) AndrewHeffernan[(7)] 18 83
(P D Evans) *w ldrs: styd on same pce fnl f* **33/1**
1-00 **3** *3/4* **Eastern Hills**[16] 2402 4-8-12 **73**................................... LanceBetts[(5)] 1 74
(J S Wainwright) *in tch towards far side: kpt on wl fnl f* **50/1**
0003 **4** *nk* **Green Park (IRE)**[1] 2897 6-9-7 **77**...................................(b) DNolan 16 77
(D Carroll) *mid-div: styd on wl fnl f* **20/1**
6014 **5** *1/2* **Methaaly (IRE)**[4] 2782 6-9-10 **80**...........................(be) RyanMoore 6 78
(M Mullineaux) *hld up in mid-div: swtchd lft over 1f out: kpt on: nvr trbld ldrs* **9/2**[2]
0-01 **6** *1 3/4* **Castles In The Air**[36] 1832 4-9-3 **78**.................... FrederikTylicki[(5)] 15 70
(R A Fahey) *chsd ldrs: outpcd over 2f out: kpt on fnl f* **9/4**[1]
10-0 **7** *1/2* **Shotley Mac**[76] 1016 5-9-10 **80**..............................(b) FrancisNorton 17 71
(N Bycroft) *chsd ldrs: kpt on same pce fnl 2f* **33/1**
3422 **8** *nk* **Bravely (IRE)**[16] 2402 5-9-5 **75**.................................. RoystonFfrench 20 65
(T D Easterby) *trckd ldrs: styd on same pce appr fnl f* **12/1**
6003 **9** *3/4* **Bel Cantor**[11] 2570 6-9-6 **79**.................................(p) KellyHarrison[(3)] 19 66
(W J H Ratcliffe) *w ldrs stands' side: fdd appr fnl f* **14/1**
0000 **10** *1/2* **Hotham**[18] 2363 6-9-5 **75**... DanielTudhope 11 61
(N Wilson) *mid-div: nvr a threat* **40/1**
0526 **11** *1/2* **Ingleby Arch (USA)**[15] 2438 6-9-2 **77**......................... DeanHeslop[(5)] 12 61
(T D Barron) *hood removed v late: dwlt: kpt on fnl 2f: nvr on terms* **25/1**
21-0 **12** *2 1/4* **Misphire**[27] 2102 6-9-9 **79**.. PhillipMakin 4 56
(M Dods) *s.s: nvr on terms* **33/1**
0605 **13** *3/4* **Arizona John (IRE)**[21] 2257 4-9-3 **73**........................ DuranFentiman 8 48
(N Wilson) *in tch: drvn over 2f out: sn outpcd* **50/1**
-003 **14** *hd* **Leonid Glow**[28] 2071 4-9-5 **75**.. PJMcDonald 5 49
(M Dods) *in rr: kpt on fnl 2f: nvr a factor* **16/1**
0-24 **15** *2 1/2* **Bonnie Prince Blue**[21] 2267 6-9-5 **75**............................ JoeFanning 2 41
(D Nicholls) *w ldrs far side: wknd over 1f out* **8/1**[3]
00-0 **16** *hd* **Geezers Colours**[129] 388 4-9-10 **80**............................ AndrewElliott 7 45
(K R Burke) *mid-div: sn drvn along: nvr a threat* **50/1**
-110 **17** *8* **River Kirov (IRE)**[146] 212 6-9-10 **80**................................. LDettori 3 20
(M Wigham) *in rr towards far side: bhd fnl 2f* **12/1**
0045 **18** *2 1/4* **Whiskey Creek**[16] 2397 4-8-12 **73**...........................(v) BMcHugh[(5)] 13 6
(C A Dwyer) *dwlt: in rr: bhd fnl 2f* **40/1**
50-2 **19** *hd* **Hits Only Jude (IRE)**[11] 2576 6-8-10 **73**...................... NeilFarley[(7)] 9 5
(D Carroll) *in rr: bhd fnl 2f* **18/1**

1m 12.34s (0.44) **Going Correction** +0.20s/f (Good) **19** Ran SP% **131.5**
Speed ratings (Par 105): **105,101,100,99,98 96,95,95,94,93 93,90,89,88,85 85,74,71,71**
toteswinger: 1&2 £53.80, 1&3 £158.50, 2&3 £127.70. CSF £296.45 CT £13539.36 TOTE £11.30: £2.40, £6.50, £13.50, £4.80; EX 347.50 Place 6: £2131.18, Place 5: £707.53.
Owner Stuart Burgan **Bred** S R Bowring **Trained** Edwinstowe, Notts
■ Stewards' Enquiry : Frederik Tylicki one-day ban: failed to ride to draw (Jun 27)

FOCUS
This looked a more open contest than the betting suggested. Little got into it from off the pace. A clear personal best from the winner but the placed form is not that solid.
T/Jkpt: Not won. T/Plt: £743.30 to a £1 stake. Pool: £179,662.00. 178.60 winning tickets. T/Qpdt: £108.80 to a £1 stake. Pool: £8,432.00. 57.35 winning tickets. JR

The Form Book, Raceform Ltd, Compton, RG20 6NL

[2695] DONCASTER (L-H)

Sunday, June 14

OFFICIAL GOING: Good (good to firm in places) changing to good to firm after race 1 (2.20)

Wind: Almost nil Weather: Fine and sunny

2939 HOWARD HUGHES MEMORIAL HEARTBEAT H'CAP 1m (R)

2:20 (2:24) (Class 4) (0-85,85) 4-Y-0+ £4,857 (£1,445; £722; £360) Stalls Low

Form RPR

-061 1 Marvo[23] 2245 5-8-9 73 TPQueally 12 81
(M H Tompkins) *hld up: swtchd outside over 1f out: styd on wl to ld last 50yds* 5/1

2225 2 1 1/4 Tiger Dream[8] 2724 4-8-10 74 (p) NCallan 2 79
(K A Ryan) *t.k.h: trckd ldr: effrt 3f out: led over 1f out: edgd rt: hdd wl ins fnl f* 5/2[1]

-003 3 1 1/4 Raptor (GER)[24] 2197 6-9-7 85 (vt[1]) JimCrowley 11 87
(K R Burke) *led tl 2f out: kpt on same pce* 4/1[3]

02-2 4 3 1/2 Moody Tunes[4] 2816 6-8-3 72 MartinLane(5) 13 66
(K R Burke) *led: hdd 2f out: wknd ins fnl f* 6/1

4016 5 1 Smarty Socks (IRE)[29] 2086 5-9-2 80 JamieMoriarty 8 72
(P T Midgley) *s.s: hld up in last: drvn 3f out: nvr trbld ldrs* 3/1[2]

00 6 1 1/4 French Art[29] 2073 4-9-2 80 TomEaves 7 69
(N Tinkler) *t.k.h in rr: hdwy on ins over 3f out: chsng ldrs over 1f out: sn wknd* 22/1

1m 39.28s (-0.42) **Going Correction** -0.10s/f (Good) 6 Ran SP% 108.9
Speed ratings (Par 105): **104,102,101,98,97 95**
toteswinger: 1&2 £3.30, 1&3 £3.80, 2&3 £2.10. CSF £16.76 CT £47.74 TOTE £6.50: £2.60, £2.00; EX 18.70 Trifecta £59.90 Pool: £229.24 - 2.83 winning units..
Owner M P Bowring **Bred** Mystic Meg Limited **Trained** Newmarket, Suffolk

FOCUS
The ground, which had dried out significantly since the declaration stage, was changed to good to firm all over after this opener, and there were a host of non-runners throughout the card. Only six took their chance, but this still looked a fair enough handicap for the grade and the pace seemed reasonable. The winner progressed from his Pontefract win.

2940 SOVEREIGN HEALTH CARE HEARTBEAT EBF MEDIAN AUCTION MAIDEN STKS 6f

2:55 (2:58) (Class 4) 2-Y-0 £4,857 (£1,445; £722; £360) Stalls High

Form RPR

3 1 Lady Springbank (IRE)[17] 2401 2-8-12 0 JimCrowley 6 79+
(K R Burke) *trckd ldrs: edgd lft and led over 1f out: edgd rt and styd on strly fnl f* 5/2[1]

003 2 3 Take It To The Max[24] 2196 2-9-3 0 PJMcDonald 13 75
(G M Moore) *w ldrs: styd on fnl f: no imp* 12/1

0 3 1 1/2 Colonel Mak[9] 2663 2-9-3 0 PhillipMakin 4 71
(D H Brown) *w ldrs: led over 2f out: hdd over 1f out: kpt on same pce* 50/1

5 4 1 3/4 Diman Waters (IRE)[24] 2195 2-9-3 0 DavidAllan 12 65
(E J Alston) *t.k.h in rr: hdwy over 2f out: kpt on fnl f* 8/1

02 5 1 3/4 Dazeen[16] 2435 2-9-3 0 JamieMoriarty 10 60
(P T Midgley) *swvd lft s: hld up in rr: kpt on fnl f* 6/1

6 1/2 Lady Lefroy (IRE) 2-8-12 0 TonyHamilton 2 54
(R A Fahey) *chsd ldrs: rdn and edgd lft over 1f out: sn wknd* 14/1

42 7 2 Brisbane (IRE)[17] 2413 2-9-3 0 JimmyFortune 8 53+
(J H M Gosden) *hmpd s: hdwy over 2f out: nvr nr ldrs* 4/1[2]

5 8 2 Dear Mr Fantasy (IRE)[18] 2383 2-9-3 0 RHills 3 47
(J W Hills) *in rr: drvn over 2f out: nvr a factor* 16/1

3 9 2 3/4 Tamanaco (IRE)[16] 2444 2-9-3 0 GrahamGibbons 5 38
(T D Walford) *led tl hdd over 2f out: lost pl over 1f out* 5/1[3]

6 10 8 Polebrook[41] 1749 2-8-12 0 FrederikTylicki(5) 11 14
(J R Jenkins) *sn outpcd and in rr: bhd fnl 2f* 33/1

50 11 5 Valantino Oyster (IRE)[23] 2231 2-9-3 0 PaulMulrennan 7 —
(J Howard Johnson) *w ldrs: lost pl over 2f out: sn bhd* 66/1

1m 13.19s (-0.41) **Going Correction** -0.10s/f (Good) 11 Ran SP% 117.3
Speed ratings (Par 95): **98,94,92,89,87 86,84,81,77,67 60**
toteswinger: 1&2 £8.40, 1&3 £28.20, 2&3 £58.90. CSF £34.49 TOTE £3.70: £1.60, £3.80, £16.10; EX 47.10 TRIFECTA Not won..
Owner Mogeely Stud & Mrs Maura Gittins **Bred** Mrs M Gittins **Trained** Middleham Moor, N Yorks

FOCUS
A fair juvenile maiden won in good style.

NOTEBOOK
Lady Springbank(IRE), who improved on the form she showed when third at Newcastle on her debut. Her trainer has plenty of nice juveniles in his care and this filly looks another useful prospect. (tchd 3-1)
Take It To The Max, back on quicker ground, ran well, but the winner was too good. He should do okay during the nursery season. (op 11-1 tchd 10-1)
Colonel Mak left a moderate debut effort well behind and is evidently going the right way. He's a nice type who very much gives the impression he'll keep improving. (op 66-1)
Diman Waters(IRE) improved on his debut performance but was never a threat having been a little keen early, and a more positive ride might suit better. (op 18-1)
Dazeen was beaten by a good filly at Hamilton last time, but there wasn't much in behind that day and he found this tougher. The step up to 6f promised to suit, but he didn't improve. Official explanation: jockey said gelding ran too free (op 8-1)
Lady Lefroy(IRE) ◆, the only newcomer and a daughter of Oratorio, got tired late on but showed plenty of ability. She should improve enough to win a similar event. (op 20-1 tchd 11-1)
Brisbane(IRE) was left with a bit to do after being hampered at the start and never really recovered. He can be given another chance but looks just ordinary. (op 11-4)
Tamanaco(IRE) didn't run to the form he showed on his debut and it seems his trainer's pre-race worries about this much quicker ground were realised. Official explanation: jockey said gelding was unsuited by the good to firm ground (op 9-2 tchd 6-1)
Valantino Oyster(IRE) Official explanation: jockey said gelding was unsuited by the good to firm ground

2941 SOVEREIGN HEALTH CARE GO-ACTIVE HEARTBEAT H'CAP 6f

3:30 (3:33) (Class 3) (0-95,95) 3-Y-0+ £7,771 (£2,312; £1,155; £577) Stalls High

Form RPR

1-00 1 Roker Park (IRE)[8] 2716 4-9-5 86 (p) NCallan 12 96
(K A Ryan) *chsd ldrs: styd on to ld last 50yds* 14/1

52-5 2 1/2 Barney McGrew (IRE)[77] 1018 6-10-0 95 PhillipMakin 8 103
(M Dods) *trckd ldr: led over 1f out: hdd towards fin* 8/1

1550 3 1 1/4 Internationaldebut (IRE)[8] 2707 4-9-11 92 RobertWinston 9 96
(S Parr) *chsd ldrs: drvn over 2f out: upsides appr fnl f:* 4/1[1]

0666 4 nse Spirit Of Sharjah (IRE)[12] 2570 4-9-4 85 TPO'Shea 17 89
(Miss J Feilden) *mid-div: hdwy over 2f out: kpt on wl fnl f* 14/1

2201 5 1/2 Legal Eagle (IRE)[10] 2624 4-9-0 81 AdrianTNicholls 7 84
(Paul Green) *led tl over 1f out: kpt on same pce* 10/1

-401 6 1 1/2 Baby Strange[17] 2405 5-9-6 92 MartinLane(5) 2 90
(D Shaw) *hld up in mid-div: effrt over 2f out: nvr trbld ldrs* 5/1[2]

3-50 7 nk Seamus Shindig[15] 2474 7-8-13 87 AmyScott(7) 6 84+
(H Candy) *chsd ldrs: one pce fnl 2f* 8/1

0-00 8 1 1/2 Inter Vision (USA)[12] 2570 9-9-8 89 DanielTudhope 4 81+
(A Dickman) *dwlt: hld up in rr: effrt over 2f out: kpt on fnl f* 16/1

2-10 9 4 1/2 Piscean (USA)[8] 2707 4-9-11 92 RHills 16 70
(T Keddy) *t.k.h: trckd ldrs: effrt over 2f out: wknd over 1f out* 15/2

-000 10 1/2 Quiet Elegance[24] 2197 4-9-2 83 DavidAllan 18 59
(E J Alston) *racd stands' side: w ldrs: wknd over 1f out* 10/1

1014 11 3 1/2 Excusez Moi (USA)[12] 2570 7-10-0 95 (p) TomEaves 20 60
(Mrs R A Carr) *restless in stalls: s.s: racd stands' side: effrt over 2f out: hung lft and sn lost pl* 6/1[3]

0-00 12 2 Rising Shadow (IRE)[8] 2707 8-9-4 85 AndrewMullen 15 43
(C W Thornton) *in rr: drvn over 2f out: sn bhd* 40/1

/-50 13 5 Sammy The Snake (IRE)[36] 1865 4-9-9 90 (b[1]) JimCrowley 19 32
(B W Duke) *racd stands' side: chsd ldrs: lost pl over 2f out: sn bhd* 33/1

1m 11.77s (-1.83) **Going Correction** -0.10s/f (Good) 13 Ran SP% 127.7
Speed ratings (Par 107): **108,107,105,105,104 102,102,100,94,93 89,86,79**
toteswinger: 1&2 £30.00, 1&3 £56.90, 2&3 £7.90. CSF £130.12 CT £549.35 TOTE £22.10: £6.10, £3.40, £2.70; EX 290.20 TRIFECTA Not won..
Owner T Alderson **Bred** Dr Dean Harron **Trained** Hambleton, N Yorks
■ Stewards' Enquiry : N Callan caution: used whip with excessive frequency.

FOCUS
A typically competitive sprint handicap despite a depleted field. Fair form for the grade.

NOTEBOOK
Roker Park(IRE) hadn't shown much in a couple of runs since joining this yard, including in blinkers on his latest outing, but with cheekpieces tried this time, he returned to form. This was only his tenth start, so it's possible his new connections will get further improvement out of him, but his overall profile suggests it would be unwise to take a short price about him following up. Official explanation: trainer said, regarding apparent improvement in form, that the gelding was better suited by the application of cheek pieces. (op 20-1 tchd 25-1 and 12-1)
Barney McGrew(IRE) returned from over two months off with a good run in defeat. He looks plenty high enough in the weights, but clearly remains competitive. (op 7-1 tchd 6-1and 9-1 in a place)
Internationaldebut(IRE), really well backed, returned to form after seemingly not taking to Epsom last time. (op 10-1)
Spirit Of Sharjah(IRE) is working his way into form and this was his best effort for some time. (op 9-1)
Legal Eagle(IRE), picked up by these connections after winning a claimer last time, ran well in this tougher heat under a positive ride. (op 12-1 tchd 9-1)
Baby Strange didn't run badly, but he was unable to defy a 2lb rise for his recent Newcastle success. (tchd 13-2)
Piscean(USA) was too keen and is better suited by racing with cover over the minimum trip. (op 7-1 tchd 9-1)
Excusez Moi(USA) was slowly away and ran a mulish race. Official explanation: jockey said gelding became upset in the stalls and missed the break (op 7-1 tchd 11-2)

2942 SIR RODNEY WALKER HEARTBEAT FILLIES' H'CAP 1m 2f 60y

4:05 (4:07) (Class 5) (0-75,75) 3-Y-0 £3,238 (£963; £481; £240) Stalls Low

Form RPR

03-2 1 Honours Stride (IRE)[24] 2192 3-9-7 75 RyanMoore 9 82
(Sir Michael Stoute) *trckd ldrs: effrt over 3f out: led over 1f out: jst hld on* 5/1[2]

1-66 2 shd Nice Time (IRE)[16] 2432 3-9-0 68 NCallan 12 75
(M H Tompkins) *s.i.s: gd hdwy over 1f out: styd on wl ins fnl f: jst failed* 16/1

2-62 3 1 1/4 Hukba (IRE)[28] 2105 3-9-0 68 RHills 6 73
(E A L Dunlop) *mid-div: hdwy over 3f out: sn chsng ldrs: kpt on same pce ins fnl f* 5/2[1]

-030 4 1/2 Punch Drunk[9] 2685 3-8-12 66 TPQueally 7 70+
(J G Given) *s.i.s: nt clr run over 3f out tl over 1f out: plld wd and fin strly* 16/1

06 5 3 1/4 Miss Sophisticat[27] 2138 3-9-3 71 (v[1]) PaulDoe 8 68
(W J Knight) *trckd ldrs: led over 2f out: hdd over 1f out: wknd ins fnl f* 50/1

-602 6 1 1/4 Extremely So[16] 2461 3-8-0 59 JamieKyne(5) 4 54
(P J McBride) *mid-div: swtchd outside over 1f out: nvr nr ldrs* 6/1[3]

0-44 7 1/2 Flapper (IRE)[16] 2431 3-7-13 60 AmyScott(7) 13 54
(J W Hills) *hld up in rr: hdwy on outside 4f out: wknd over 1f out* 14/1

00-3 8 1 1/4 Well Of Echoes[9] 2662 3-8-7 61 AndrewMullen 10 52
(A J McCabe) *hld up in rr: nvr a factor* 7/1

000- 9 3/4 Desert Fairy[245] 6682 3-7-13 56 oh3 DavidProbert(3) 11 46
(J W Unett) *mid-div: lost pl over 1f out* 100/1

5363 10 1 1/4 Chicora (USA)[10] 2633 3-9-2 70 JimmyFortune 3 57
(J H M Gosden) *led tl over 2f out: wknd over 1f out* 9/1

003 11 nk Bicksta[23] 2240 3-8-6 60 RichardMullen 2 46
(E F Vaughan) *chsd ldrs: one pce whn n.m.r over 1f out* 25/1

060- 12 hd Moggy (IRE)[227] 7095 3-8-3 57 AndrewElliott 1 43
(M L W Bell) *chsd ldrs: wknd over 1f out* 8/1

2m 9.92s (-1.28) **Going Correction** -0.10s/f (Good) 12 Ran SP% 118.4
Speed ratings (Par 96): **101,100,99,99,96 95,95,94,93,92 92,92**
toteswinger: 1&2 £14.80, 1&3 £2.70, 2&3 £13.20. CSF £81.05 CT £248.09 TOTE £4.80: £2.00, £5.00, £1.20; EX 116.60 Trifecta £167.30 Pool: £468.26 - 2.07 winning units..
Owner Saeed Suhail **Bred** Swettenham Stud **Trained** Newmarket, Suffolk

FOCUS
A fair, competitive fillies' handicap. Sound form, with improvement from the first two.

2943 ANN AND HOWARD HUGHES HEARTBEAT MAIDEN STKS 1m 4f

4:35 (4:36) (Class 5) 3-Y-0+ £3,238 (£963; £481; £240) Stalls Low

Form RPR

3 1 Racing Hero (IRE)[24] 2211 3-8-12 0 RyanMoore 6 80+
(J Noseda) *hld up in midfield: nt clr run 3f out: plld wd 2f out: sn chsng ldr: led last 100yds: won gng away* 7/2[2]

2 2 2 1/4 Interdiamonds[11] 2613 3-8-7 0 JoeFanning 13 68
(M Johnston) *led: qcknd clr 2f out: hdd and no ex ins fnl f* 3/1[1]

64-3 3 1 3/4 Royal Trooper (IRE)[33] 1953 3-8-12 66 PaulMulrennan 15 71
(J G Given) *trckd ldrs: outpcd over 2f out: styd on same pce fnl 2f* 25/1

0-6 4 4 Khayar (IRE)[69] 1151 3-8-12 0 (t) RHills 19 64+
(M H Tompkins) *in rr: hdwy over 3f out: kpt on fnl f* 40/1

4 5 1 3/4 Jabroot (IRE)[17] 2395 3-8-8 0 ow1 PhilipRobinson 11 57+
(M A Jarvis) *in rr-div: hdwy 3f out: kpt on: nvr nr ldrs* 6/1

6 ¾ **Moon Money (IRE)** 3-8-12 0 NCallan 14 60
(K A Ryan) *in rr: kpt on fnl 3f: nvr nr ldrs* **25/1**

0 7 nk **Danse On Wood**[31] 2002 3-8-12 0 TPQueally 5 60
(J Noseda) *in rr: kpt on fnl 3f: nvr nr ldrs* **33/1**

8 3 **Born To Perform**[70] 4-9-13 0 RobertWinston 1 55
(G A Swinbank) *trckd ldrs: t.k.h: wknd over 1f out* **9/2**[3]

5-34 9 1 ½ **Twisted**[10] 2640 3-8-12 79 JimmyFortune 17 53
(J H M Gosden) *in tch: drvn over 2f out: wknd over 1f out* **9/2**[3]

0 10 ¾ **Real Desire**[8] 2723 3-8-12 0 TomEaves 12 51
(I Semple) *in rr-div: drvn 7f out: rdn over 3f out: kpt on: nvr a factor* **100/1**

5 11 3 ¼ **East Of The Sun (IRE)**[24] 2199 3-8-12 0 MickyFenton 18 46
(T P Tate) *w ldr: lost pl over 2f out* **40/1**

12 2 **Laura Land** 3-8-7 0 TPO'Shea 2 38
(W M Brisbourne) *chsd ldrs: lost pl over 2f out* **28/1**

50- 13 28 **Arch**[22] 2735 6-9-6 0 GarryWhillans(7) 10 —
(A M Crow) *dwlt: hdwy on outside 6f out: lost pl over 3f out: sn bhd: t.o* **100/1**

2m 34.07s (-1.03) **Going Correction** -0.10s/f (Good)
WFA 3 from 4yo+ 15lb **13 Ran SP% 118.8**
Speed ratings (Par 103): **99,97,96,93,92 92,91,89,88,88 86,84,66**
toteswinger: 1&2 £4.50, 1&3 £10.60, 2&3 £10.10. CSF £13.27 TOTE £4.50: £2.00, £1.80, £5.40; EX 12.20 TRIFECTA Not won..
Owner Albert S N Hu **Bred** Lynch Bages Ltd **Trained** Newmarket, Suffolk

FOCUS
Probably just a fair maiden but several shaped better than the bare form. The winner looks a useful prospect and the third seems the best guide.

2944 LADY WALKER HEARTBEAT APPRENTICE H'CAP 1m 6f 132y
5:10 (5:10) (Class 5) (0-70,67) 4-Y-0+ **£3,238** (£963; £481; £240) **Stalls** Low

Form RPR

300- 1 **Markington**[25] 5993 6-8-13 59 (b) WilliamCarson(3) 8 70
(P Bowen) *hld up in rr: hdwy 7f out: wnt 2nd over 1f out: styd on wl to ld last 75yds* **8/1**

2136 2 2 ¼ **Isabelonabicycle**[25] 2177 4-9-10 67 DavidProbert 14 75+
(A M Balding) *t.k.h: trckd ldrs: wnt 2nd over 4f out: led over 2f out: hdd and no ex wl ins fnl f* **9/4**[1]

3 2 ½ **Ticket To Freedom (NZ)**[24] 7-8-12 60 (t) JamieKyne(5) 10 65
(J J Quinn) *hld up in rr: effrt over 2f out: styd on same pce fnl f* **14/1**

-065 4 1 ¼ **Cripsey Brook**[20] 2344 11-8-10 56 GaryBartley(3) 11 59
(K G Reveley) *s.i.s: in rr: rn in snatches: drvn 4f out: styd on fnl 2f* **16/1**

3602 5 2 ¼ **Rose Bien**[31] 2018 7-8-9 57 (p) AshleyMorgan(5) 9 57
(P J McBride) *sn chsng ldrs: drvn over 3f out: fdd over 1f out* **4/1**[2]

0-23 6 ¾ **Sir Sandicliffe (IRE)**[24] 2194 5-9-3 63 DeanHeslop(3) 6 62
(W M Brisbourne) *trckd ldrs: hung lft over 3f out: one pce* **6/1**[3]

5052 7 7 **Fistral**[11] 2592 5-8-8 54 FrederikTylicki(3) 2 44
(P D Niven) *chsd ldrs: lost pl over 1f out* **7/1**

-513 8 ½ **Forrest Flyer (IRE)**[10] 2629 5-9-1 61 PatrickDonaghy(3) 3 51
(I Semple) *led: clr after 3f: hdd over 2f out: sn wknd* **6/1**[3]

300- 9 22 **Extreme Pleasure (IRE)**[200] 7455 4-9-3 63 MCGeran(3) 1 24
(W J Knight) *chsd ldrs: lost pl over 2f out: sn bhd: t.o* **16/1**

3m 7.36s (0.66) **Going Correction** -0.10s/f (Good) **9 Ran SP% 121.4**
Speed ratings (Par 103): **94,92,91,90,89 89,85,85,73**
toteswinger: 1&2 £4.80, 1&3 £12.20, 2&3 £10.50. CSF £27.81 CT £260.82 TOTE £8.20: £3.20, £1.70, £4.80; EX 39.20 Trifecta £278.30 Part won. Pool: £376.11 - 0.93 winning units. Place 6 £56.47, Place 5 £29.41.
Owner Ron Stepney **Bred** Minster Enterprises Ltd **Trained** Little Newcastle, Pembrokes

FOCUS
A modest apprentice handicap.
T/Jkpt: Not won. T/Plt: £39.40 to a £1 stake. Pool: £86,170.12. 1,593.35 winning tickets. T/Qpdt: £9.10 to a £1 stake. Pool: £6,964.10. 564.30 winning tickets. WG

2792 SALISBURY (R-H)
Sunday, June 14

OFFICIAL GOING: Good to firm (good in places)
Course dolled out from the 7f marker to the finish but impact on distances not known.
Wind: Virtually nil Weather: Warm and sunny

2945 ALBERT SAMUEL "CITY BOWL" H'CAP 1m 4f
2:00 (2:00) (Class 4) (0-85,85) 4-Y-0+ **£4,857** (£1,445; £722; £360) **Stalls** High

Form RPR

32-2 1 **It's A Date**[15] 2505 4-9-1 79 DaneO'Neill 5 84
(A King) *led: rdn and narrowly hdd wl over 1f out: rallied to regain ld jst ins fnl f: hld on wl: drvn out* **2/1**[1]

062- 2 nk **Outlandish**[188] 7610 6-8-13 77 SebSanders 2 81
(Miss E C Lavelle) *hld up bhd ldng trio: smooth prog to take narrow advantage wl over 1f out: sn rdn: hdd narrowly jst ins fnl f: edgd sltly lft: kpt on but no ex* **6/1**[3]

6202 3 5 **King Supreme (IRE)**[12] 2566 4-9-7 85 (b) RichardHughes 4 81
(R Hannon) *trckd wnr: rdn over 3f out: lost 2nd 2f out: hld on for 3rd but nt pce to mount chal* **2/1**[1]

0/56 4 nk **Sharpazmax (IRE)**[17] 2407 5-9-2 80 EddieAhern 6 76
(P J Makin) *trckd ldng pair: rdn 3f out: kpt on but nt pce to chal* **11/4**[2]

2m 34.45s (-3.55) **Going Correction** -0.15s/f (Firm) **4 Ran SP% 107.6**
Speed ratings (Par 105): **105,104,101,101**
toteswinger: 1&2 £7.00. CSF £12.61 TOTE £3.00; EX 11.00.
Owner Horace 5 **Bred** Mrs F M Gordon **Trained** Barbury Castle, Wilts

FOCUS
A tight handicap but ordinary form rated arounsd the principals.
Sharpazmax(IRE) Official explanation: trainer said gelding finished distressed

2946 PICADOR CHEVROLET H'CAP 5f
2:30 (2:30) (Class 4) (0-85,91) 3-Y-0+ **£4,857** (£1,445; £722; £360) **Stalls** High

Form RPR

0054 1 **The Jobber (IRE)**[17] 2397 8-9-11 82 DaneO'Neill 9 92
(M Blanshard) *chsd ldrs: swtchd lft 2f out: sn rdn: led jst ins fnl f: jst hld on* **10/1**

11-2 2 hd **Ivory Silk**[150] 170 4-9-4 75 SteveDrowne 12 84
(J R Gask) *mid-div: swtchd lft 2f out: sn rdn and hdwy: r.o wl ins fnl f: jst failed* **4/1**[1]

0-06 3 ½ **Cape Royal**[3] 2840 9-8-11 71 (bt) KevinGhunowa(3) 11 78
(J M Bradley) *led: rdn and hrd pressed fr over 2f out: hdd jst ins fnl f: kpt on but no ex towards fin* **20/1**

20-5 4 1 ¾ **Olynard (IRE)**[36] 1879 3-9-6 84 GeorgeBaker 1 82+
(R M Beckett) *hld up: rdn 2f out: hdwy whn hmpd jst ins fnl f: r.o towards fin* **8/1**

2061 5 nk **Blue Jack**[10] 2637 4-9-10 81 (b) SebSanders 7 81+
(W R Muir) *mid-div: rdn over 2f out: kpt on but nt pce to get on terms* **9/2**[2]

6312 6 shd **Canadian Danehill (IRE)**[10] 2637 7-10-0 85 (p) PatCosgrave 5 85
(R M H Cowell) *chsd ldrs: rdn 2f out: sn hung rt: one pce fnl f* **8/1**

-006 7 ¾ **Victorian Bounty**[10] 2637 4-9-8 82 (v) JackMitchell(3) 3 79
(Stef Liddiard) *wnt rt s: t.k.h: prom: rdn and ev ch over 1f out: fdd ins fnl f* **7/1**

1404 8 3 ¼ **Dazed And Amazed**[14] 2520 5-9-10 81 RichardHughes 6 82+
(R Hannon) *squeezed out s: bhd: rdn and sme prog over 1f out: nt clr run thrght fnl f: eased whn no ch* **5/1**[3]

0504 9 4 **Esteem Machine (USA)**[10] 2637 5-9-11 82 (v) EddieAhern 4 53
(R A Teal) *bmpd leaving stalls: t.k.h in mid-div: stmbld after 1f: rdn 3f out: sn btn: lame* **11/2**

59.84 secs (-1.16) **Going Correction** -0.15s/f (Firm)
WFA 3 from 4yo+ 7lb **9 Ran SP% 118.8**
Speed ratings (Par 105): **101,100,99,97,96 96,95,90,83**
toteswinger: 1&2 £10.30, 1&3 £20.20, 2&3 £11.70. CSF £51.30 CT £618.01 TOTE £13.00: £3.10, £1.60, £6.30; EX 64.10.
Owner Mrs Rosemary Wilkerson & Partners **Bred** Dr T J Molony **Trained** Upper Lambourn, Berks

FOCUS
A messy sprint, despite there being a sound pace on and with the first and third reaching the veteran stage, not a race to treat too positively.
Canadian Danehill(IRE) Official explanation: jockey said gelding hung right and lost a near-fore shoe
Dazed And Amazed Official explanation: jockey sasid gelding was denied a clear run
Esteem Machine(USA) Official explanation: vet said gelding returned lame

2947 EMMA ARBERY MEMORIAL MAIDEN FILLIES' STKS 1m
3:05 (3:05) (Class 5) 3-Y-O **£3,885** (£1,156; £577; £288) **Stalls** High

Form RPR

4- 1 **Mrs Beeton (IRE)**[235] 6910 3-9-0 0 AdamKirby 8 74+
(W R Swinburn) *mid-div tl outpcd over 3f out: stdy prog fr over 2f out: swtchd lft over 1f out: str run fnl f: led towards fin* **7/2**[2]

0-6 2 ½ **Levitation (IRE)**[20] 2317 3-9-0 0 FergusSweeney 2 73
(W S Kittow) *mid-div: hdwy over 2f out: sn rdn into v narrow advantage: kpt on but no ex whn hdd towards fin* **50/1**

2-3 3 nk **Silk Trail**[27] 2139 3-9-0 0 DaneO'Neill 12 72
(Saeed Bin Suroor) *a.p: rdn and ev ch fr over 2f out: kpt on but no ex towards fin* **11/4**[1]

53 4 1 ½ **Sunceleb (IRE)**[37] 1843 3-9-0 0 SteveDrowne 7 69
(H Morrison) *in tch: swtchd rt and rdn over 2f out: little short of room over 1f out: kpt on same pce* **4/1**[3]

5 1 **Insolence (USA)** 3-8-9 0 Louis-PhilippeBeuzelin(5) 10 67+
(Sir Michael Stoute) *mid-div: hdwy 3f out: sn rdn: styd on same pce fnl f* **9/1**

62- 6 1 ¾ **Good For Her**[257] 6360 3-9-0 0 EddieAhern 1 63+
(J L Dunlop) *plld hrd to s and in r: hld up: hdwy into midfield 4f out: rdn over 2f out: swtchd lft over 1f out: styd on same pce* **8/1**

7 hd **Madame Guillotine (USA)** 3-9-0 0 SebSanders 3 62+
(R M Beckett) *s.i.s: towards rr: styd on fr over 1f out: nvr trbld ldrs* **16/1**

0 8 ¾ **Regal Blush**[29] 2080 3-9-0 0 NeilChalmers 4 60
(A M Balding) *hld up: rdn over 2f out: sme late prog: nvr a factor* **33/1**

0- 9 2 ¼ **Rock Art (IRE)**[296] 5240 3-9-0 0 ShaneKelly 14 55
(B J Meehan) *led: rdn and hdd 2f out: sn hung rt: wknd ent fnl f* **10/1**

00 10 nk **Singbella**[26] 2165 3-9-0 0 IanMongan 13 57
(C G Cox) *prom: rdn over 2f out: hld whn hmpd on rails over 1f out: wknd* **33/1**

00 11 9 **Phoenix Rising**[42] 1704 3-9-0 0 TravisBlock 5 34
(H Morrison) *a towards rr* **50/1**

12 ¾ **Highland Lassie (IRE)** 3-9-0 0 RobertHavlin 6 32
(B J Meehan) *s.i.s: a towards rr* **33/1**

6 13 ½ **Missrepresentation**[29] 2081 3-9-0 0 RichardSmith 9 31
(J C Fox) *in tch tl wknd 2f out* **50/1**

00 14 4 ½ **Tarqua (IRE)**[5] 2795 3-9-0 0 RichardHughes 11 21
(R Hannon) *trckd ldrs: rdn over 2f out: sn wknd* **20/1**

1m 41.46s (-2.04) **Going Correction** -0.15s/f (Firm) **14 Ran SP% 124.4**
Speed ratings (Par 96): **104,103,103,101,100 98,98,98,95,95 86,85,85,80**
toteswinger: 1&2 £62.20, 1&3 £4.50, 2&3 £41.30. CSF £186.91 TOTE £6.20: £2.30, £14.40, £1.50; EX 377.10.
Owner Pendley Farm **Bred** Pendley Farm **Trained** Aldbury, Herts

FOCUS
An average fillies' maiden in which the third looks the best guide to the form.
Singbella Official explanation: jockey said filly suffered interference in running

2948 BATHWICK TYRES CATHEDRAL STKS (LISTED RACE) 6f
3:40 (3:40) (Class 1) 3-Y-O+
£22,708 (£8,608; £4,308; £2,148; £1,076; £540) **Stalls** High

Form RPR

6234 1 **Judd Street**[22] 2259 7-9-4 104 (v) DaneO'Neill 5 102
(Eve Johnson Houghton) *t.k.h: hld up: hdwy 2f out: upsides and rdn jst ins fnl f: sn edgd rt: kpt on: won on nod* **11/1**[3]

13-1 2 nse **Palace Moon**[77] 1018 4-9-4 103 SteveDrowne 2 101
(H Morrison) *trckd ldrs: led 2f out: sn rdn: hrd pressed jst ins fnl f: kpt on: lost on nod* **1/2**[1]

-606 3 2 **Spanish Bounty**[29] 2078 4-9-4 90 SebSanders 6 98+
(J G Portman) *led briefly 1st f: trckd ldrs: rdn 2f out: disputing cl 3rd whn sltly hmpd jst ins fnl f: no ex* **16/1**

3114 4 1 ¼ **Diana's Choice (SAF)**[101] 770 5-8-13 110 PatCosgrave 4 94+
(M F De Kock, South Africa) *rrd leaving stalls: racd keenly: sn led: rdn and hdd 2f out: disputing cl 3rd but hld whn hmpd jst ins fnl f* **4/1**[2]

5-50 5 2 **Ballyalla**[9] 2674 3-8-5 80 EddieAhern 3 78
(R Hannon) *hld up: rdn 3f out: nvr pce to get on terms* **16/1**

241 6 ½ **Carcinetto (IRE)**[13] 2536 7-8-13 98 RichardEvans 1 78
(P D Evans) *prom: rdn over 2f out: grad fdd* **16/1**

1m 12.24s (-2.56) **Going Correction** -0.15s/f (Firm)
WFA 3 from 4yo+ 8lb **6 Ran SP% 112.6**
Speed ratings (Par 111): **111,110,108,106,103 103**
toteswinger: 1&2 £2.20, 1&3 £5.70, 2&3 £4.80. CSF £17.41 TOTE £13.90: £3.20, £1.10; EX 21.00.
Owner R F Johnson Houghton **Bred** R F Johnson Houghton **Trained** Blewbury, Oxon
■ Stewards' Enquiry : Dane O'Neill one-day ban, plus three deferred: careless riding (Jun 28-30,Jul 1)
Steve Drowne one-day ban: careless riding (Jun 28)

FOCUS
A competitive Listed prize. The first pair came clear but the form looks muddlign with the 'form' horses not at their best.

NOTEBOOK
Judd Street is a consistent sprinter and fully deserved his place in the line-up. He got into a battle with the runner-up throughout the final furlong and showed grim determination to collect a deserved success. This was a second victory at this level for him, and it will be interesting to see whether he goes for the Wokingham Handicap next week. Connections did not completely rule that race out, but he would have a big weight to carry if asked to run. (op 14-1)
Palace Moon who reportedly lost his edge in April, was bidding to emulate his siblings Sahkee's Secret and Palace Affair in winning this contest. He travelled into the lead going well but his older and wiser challenger just did enough to worry him out of it late on, and he suffered defeat virtually on the line. It is a bit too soon to write him off as a Group horse, as he should be better for this outing after his layoff. (op 4-6 tchd 2-5 and 8-11 in places)
Spanish Bounty has been an in-and-out performer since his last victory, but he ran a blinder here, as he can be rated a bit better than the margin of defeat suggests. He was staying on well when squeezed for room about a furlong out.
Diana's Choice(SAF), who is reportedly being aimed at the Falmouth Stakes, was a disappointment after having her own way out in front. It might be that she was not good enough over this sort of trip against hardened sprinters on home soil, but one would have liked to see a bit more sparkle, even allowing for the fact that Palace Moon came across her inside the final furlong. (op 11-4 tchd 9-2)

2949 HOX BRASSERIE "OUTSTANDING INDIAN FOOD IN SALISBURY" FILLIES' H'CAP — 6f 212y
4:15 (4:15) (Class 5) (0-75,74) 3-Y-O+ **£3,238** (£963; £481; £240) **Stalls** Centre

Form	Pos	Dist	Horse / Details	Jockey	RPR
4-40	1		**Miss Mujanna**[60] 1288 4-9-7 **64** (J Akehurst) *trckd ldr: chal 3f out: sn rdn: tk narrow advantage fnl 100yds: all out* **12/1**	J-PGuillambert 2	73
0-05	2	hd	**Ken's Girl**[15] 2498 5-9-8 **65** (W S Kittow) *led: rdn over 1f out: narrowly hdd fnl 100yds: rallied gamely: jst hld* **12/1**	IanMongan 7	73
-344	3	1 1/4	**Happy Forever (FR)**[33] 1965 3-9-1 **73** (M Botti) *mid-div: rdn over 2f out: no imp tl styd on ins fnl f: wnt 3rd towards fin* **4/1**[3]	AndreaAtzeni(5) 3	74
-034	4	1/2	**Support Fund (IRE)**[6] 2775 5-9-11 **71** (Eve Johnson Houghton) *sn pushed along in tch: styd on fnl f: nvr pce to chal* **6/1**	KevinGhunowa(3) 5	74
-610	5	1	**Volochkova (USA)**[29] 2079 3-9-7 **74** (J R Fanshawe) *in tch: rdn to chse ldrs over 1f out: no ex fnl 100yds* **3/1**[2]	AdamKirby 9	71
-060	6	2 1/4	**Deyas Dream**[33] 1973 3-8-7 **60** (A M Balding) *hld up last: rdn 3f out: little imp* **22/1**	NeilChalmers 1	51
-232	7	3	**Fly By Nelly**[5] 2797 3-8-10 **63** (H Morrison) *trckd ldrs: effrt over 2f out: hld whn squeezed out on rails wl over 1f out: wknd fnl f* **11/4**[1]	SteveDrowne 8	45
2402	8	2 3/4	**Izzi Mill (USA)**[9] 2661 3-9-6 **73** (D R C Elsworth) *trckd ldrs: effrt over 2f out: edgd sltly rt: wknd over 1f out* **7/1**	RobertHavlin 6	48

1m 27.47s (-1.53) **Going Correction** -0.15s/f (Firm)
WFA 3 from 4yo+ 10lb — **8** Ran SP% **118.2**
Speed ratings (Par 100): **102,101,100,99,98 96,92,89**
toteswinger: 1&2 £13.40, 1&3 £10.70, 2&3 £6.80. CSF £146.70 CT £689.43 TOTE £20.20: £4.30, £1.70, £1.70; EX 220.50.
Owner Green Pastures Partnership **Bred** Green Pastures Farm **Trained** Epsom, Surrey
■ Stewards' Enquiry : Robert Havlin caution: careless riding.

FOCUS
A modest fillies' event. It paid to race handily and the form is muddling.
Deyas Dream Official explanation: jockey said filly was slowly away
Izzi Mill(USA) Official explanation: jockey said filly hung right

2950 "HANDS AND HEELS" APPRENTICE SERIES H'CAP — 1m
4:45 (4:48) (Class 6) (0-65,62) 3-Y-O **£3,043** (£905; £452; £226) **Stalls** High

Form	Pos	Dist	Horse / Details	Jockey	RPR
6205	1		**Miss Mojito (IRE)**[14] 2515 3-9-3 **56** (J W Hills) *slowly away: towards rr: swtchd lft and gd hdwy fr over 2f out: led over 1f out: r.o strly: readily* **15/2**	(t) KierenFox 14	66
000-	2	4	**Jachol (IRE)**[218] 7240 3-8-11 **50** (W J Haggas) *chsd ldrs: led over 2f out tl over 1f out: kpt on for clr 2nd but nt pce of wnr* **11/2**[2]	DebraEngland 1	50
00-2	3	5	**Broughtons Paradis (IRE)**[15] 2489 3-9-2 **55** (W J Musson) *prom: rdn and ev ch over 2f out tl wl over 1f out: hung on to 3rd but fdd ins fnl f* **4/1**[1]	DTDaSilva 15	43
0300	4	1/2	**Mystic Touch**[43] 1670 3-9-7 **60** (Miss E C Lavelle) *rrd bdly leaving stalls: towards rr: styd on steadily fnl 2f: nvr trbld ldrs* **16/1**	KrishGundowry 6	47
550	5	1	**Miss Porky**[37] 1840 3-9-6 **62** (R Hollinshead) *mid-div: hdwy 2f out: one pce fnl f* **7/1**[3]	DavidKenny(3) 11	46
5506	6	2	**Whotsit (IRE)**[26] 2169 3-9-1 **54** (Miss Amy Weaver) *s.i.s: towards rr: swtchd lft over 2f out: styd on fr over 1f out: nvr trbld ldrs* **10/1**	(b) LauraPike 8	34
40-0	7	nk	**Bounty Reef**[19] 2357 3-9-3 **56** (P D Evans) *chsd ldrs: effrt over 2f out: wknd over 1f out* **12/1**	JohnCavanagh 5	35
00-0	8	1 1/4	**Suakin Dancer (IRE)**[54] 1416 3-9-8 **61** (H Morrison) *led: rdn and hdd over 2f out: grad fdd* **16/1**	AndrewHeffernan 10	37
0-13	9	3 1/2	**Second To Nun (IRE)**[14] 2515 3-9-8 **61** (Jean-Rene Auvray) *chsd ldrs tl wknd 3f out* **7/1**[3]	GemmaElford 13	28+
00-0	10	hd	**Mystic Prince**[29] 2074 3-9-7 **60** (Miss Tor Sturgis) *chsd ldrs tl wknd 2f out* **17/2**	CharlesEddery 7	27
265-	11	13	**Cherry Belle (IRE)**[228] 7079 3-9-4 **57** (P D Evans) *a towards rr* **14/1**	LeeTopliss 16	—
-360	12	1	**Jaq's Sister**[86] 900 3-9-0 **53** (M Blanshard) *nvr bttr than mid-div: wknd 2f out* **33/1**	RichardRowe 3	—
000-	13	4 1/2	**Saunton Sands**[316] 4625 3-9-2 **55** (A G Newcombe) *racd keenly: prom for 5f* **40/1**	RyanPowell 12	—

1m 42.3s (-1.20) **Going Correction** -0.15s/f (Firm) — **13** Ran SP% **123.3**
Speed ratings (Par 97): **100,96,91,90,89 87,87,85,82,82 69,68,63**
toteswinger: 1&2 £14.40, 1&3 £7.80, 2&3 £6.00. CSF £50.04 CT £200.67 TOTE £10.20: £3.40, £2.60, £2.20; EX 68.50 Place 6 £93.45, Place 5 £35.42.
Owner Gary & Linnet Woodward (2) **Bred** Islanmore Stud **Trained** Upper Lambourn, Berks
■ Stewards' Enquiry : Ryan Powell four-day ban: careless riding (Jun 28-30, Jul 1)

FOCUS
A typically tricky-looking event of its type. The winner won easily and is rated to her best with the runner-up to his maiden form.
T/Plt: £260.40 to a £1 stake. Pool: £56,734.98. 159.00 winning tickets. T/Qpdt: £38.80 to a £1 stake. Pool: £4,490.30. 85.60 winning tickets. TM

2754 CHANTILLY (R-H)
Sunday, June 14

OFFICIAL GOING: Good to soft

2951a PRIX DU LYS (GROUP 3) (C&G) — 1m 4f
2:25 (2:24) 3-Y-O **£38,835** (£15,534; £11,650; £7,767; £3,883)

Pos	Dist	Horse / Details	Jockey	RPR
1		**Claremont (IRE)**[19] 2369 3-8-11 (A Fabre, France) *racd in 2nd: pushed along early st: rdn 1 1/2f out: r.o to chal over 1f out: led 150yds out: styd on wl* **15/8**[1]	MGuyon 6	101
2	1/2	**World Heritage**[19] 2369 3-8-11 (P Bary, France) *in tch: 4th 1/2-way: pushed along over 2f out: wnt 2nd briefly and ev ch over 1f out: regained 2nd ins fnl f: styd on* **7/1**	SPasquier 4	100
3	snk	**Almail (USA)**[37] 3-8-11 (F Head, France) *hld up: last st: effrt over 1 1/2f out: styd on down outside fnl f: wnt 3rd 75yds out: nrest at fin* **7/1**	DBonilla 5	100
4	2	**Gallilei (FR)**[19] 2369 3-8-11 (A De Royer-Dupre, France) *in tch: 3rd 1/2-way: rdn to chse ldrs 1 1/2f out: no ex ins fnl f* **5/2**[2]	GMosse 2	97
5	shd	**Amico Mio (FR)**[24] 2217 3-8-11 (J-M Beguigne, France) *led: pushed along 2f out: rdn over 1f out: r.o tl hdd 150yds out: no ex* **5/1**[3]	OPeslier 1	97
6	5	**Validor (FR)**[22] 2291 3-8-11 (H-A Pantall, France) *settled towards rr: 5th st: drvn over 1 1 1/2f out: unable qck* **9/1**	(b) FVeron 3	89

2m 28.62s (-2.38) **Going Correction** -0.05s/f (Good) — **6** Ran SP% **115.0**
Speed ratings: **105,104,104,103,103 99**
PARI-MUTUEL: WIN 2.80; PL 1.80, 3.40; SF 18.70.
Owner Sheikh Mohammed **Bred** Darley **Trained** Chantilly, France

NOTEBOOK
Claremont(IRE) put up a good effort having previously been second to Beheshtam in the Prix de l'Avre. Always well placed throughout the race, he made his challenge two out and was headed by the runner up at the furlong marker. He then ran on gamely to take the lead 100m from the post. No plans have been finalised, but the obvious choice would be the Grand Prix de Paris.
World Heritage put up a much-improved performance on this better ground. Fourth rounding the final turn behind Claremont, he came with his challenge but just failed by half a length. His trainer thought that he didn't quite stay the distance and will now look at the Prix Eugene Adam at the end of July.
Almail(USA), last round the final bend, was switched to the outside to make his challenge at the beginning of the home straight and carried on gamely to fail by a short neck to catch the runner up.
Gallilei(FR), settled in behind the leaders at the beginning of the home straight, he failed to find a gap on the inside and when he finally made his challenge he accelerated well to the line. It is thought that he will be more suited to longer distances in the future.

2952a PRIX DE DIANE (GROUP 1) (FILLIES) — 1m 2f 110y
3:10 (3:11) 3-Y-O **£443,806** (£177,553; £88,777; £44,350; £22,214)

Pos	Dist	Horse / Details	Jockey	RPR
1		**Stacelita (FR)**[28] 2119 3-9-0 (J-C Rouget, France) *racd in 2nd: led over 2f out: a gng wl: qcknd clr 1 1/2f out: easily* **11/10**[1]	C-PLemaire 4	122+
2	4	**Tamazirte (IRE)**[35] 1918 3-9-0 (J-C Rouget, France) *hld up: disputing 9th on ins st: pushed along over 2f out: hdwy in centre 1 1/2f out: rdn to go 2nd 1f out: r.o: no ch w winnr* **6/1**[3]	IMendizabal 10	114
3	1/2	**Plumania**[28] 2119 3-9-0 (A Fabre, France) *hld up: 11th st: pushed along 2f out: drvn and hdwy on outside 1 1/2f out: styd on to go 3rd cl home: nrest at fin* **25/1**	OPeslier 12	113+
4	1	**Celimene (IRE)**[62] 1267 3-9-0 (C Lerner, France) *racd in last: pushed along early in st: rdn and styd on down outside fr 1 1/2f out: disputing 3rd 1f out: styd on* **9/1**	YLerner 11	111
5	1/2	**Board Meeting (IRE)**[44] 1657 3-9-0 (E Lellouche, France) *prom: disputing 3rd st: pushed along and 2nd over 2f out: rdn 1 1/2f out: kpt on tl no ex fnl 150yds* **11/1**	ACrastus 8	110
6	1/2	**Shediyama (FR)**[17] 3-9-0 (A De Royer-Dupre, France) *in tch: disputing 5th st: effrt over 2f out: rdn and styd on at one pce: nvr in chalng position* **20/1**	CSoumillon 2	109
7	2 1/2	**Fantasia**[35] 1918 3-9-0 (L M Cumani) *in tch: disputing 5th st: pushed along over 2f out: sn u.p: one pce fr over 1f out* **9/2**[2]	SPasquier 7	107
8	1	**Eclair De Lune (GER)**[37] 3-9-0 (Y De Nicolay, France) *prom: disputing 3rd st: drvn over 2f out: wknd fr 1 1/2f out* **20/1**	TThulliez 3	103
9	1/2	**Denomination (USA)**[49] 1550 3-9-0 (Mme C Head-Maarek, France) *mid-div: disputing 7th st: pushed along 2f out: unable qck* **22/1**	DBoeuf 9	102
10	1/2	**Ana Americana (FR)**[28] 2119 3-9-0 (P Demercastel, France) *mid-div: disputing 7th st: effrt 1 1/2f out: no imp* **61/1**	GMosse 6	101
11	10	**Celebra (FR)**[14] 2521 3-9-0 (C Laffon-Parias, France) *towards rr: disputing 9th st: effrt 2f out: n.d* **50/1**	DBonilla 5	82
12	20	**Onega Lake (IRE)**[47] 3-9-0 (E Lellouche, France) *led to over 2f out: eased over 1 1/2f out* **150/1**	SFargeat 1	44

2m 6.23s (-2.57) **Going Correction** -0.05s/f (Good) — **12** Ran SP% **120.4**
Speed ratings: **107,104,103,103,102 102,100,99,99,99 91,77**
PARI-MUTUEL: WIN 2.30; PL 1.40, 2.50, 7.40; DF 6.70.
Owner M Schwartz & Ecurie Monastic **Bred** J -P Dubois **Trained** Pau, France
■ Stewards' Enquiry : C Soumillon 400euro fine: whip abuse
Y Lerner 400euro fine: whip abuse

FOCUS
As well as Stacelita, who came to the contest with an unbeaten record, the race played host to the second and third from the Poule d'Essai des Pouliches, another hitherto undefeated filly in Celimene and fascinating contenders from some of the biggest French stables.

NOTEBOOK
Stacelita(FR) managed to produce a performance that was every bit as breathtaking as Zarkava in the race last year. She did so in a contest that appeared on paper to be well up to scratch and certainly no less than solid than the Investec Oaks. Having stalked the pacemaking Onega Lake, the daughter of Monsun was eased into the lead just over 2f out and, when asked to win her race, responded both immediately and decisively to establish a huge lead that never looked likely to be threatened. Once in front, she galloped with ears pricked all the way to the line, suggestive of a filly idling and with plenty in the tank. Furthermore, although very effective on ground that was considerably quicker than she encountered in the Saint-Alary, she showed a relatively high knee action and would almost certainly be even better on a softer surface. Bookmakers reacted by quoting her at around 7-1 and 8-1 for the Arc, and that looks too big about a horse who will relish being upped to 1m4f. Assuming nothing untoward happens during her summer break, it is inconceivable that connections will not want to aim for the Arc, and she will very possibly be sent off favourite.
Tamazirte(IRE) came from the rear of the field and did not get the clearest passage, but to say she was unlucky would be a huge flight of fantasy. There is no reason, however, to think that she did not run as well as she had in the French Guineas, her stamina appeared to last out and she finished her race in pleasing fashion to confirm herself more than good enough to win a Group 1 race.
Plumania, thumped 15 lengths by Stacelita in the Saint-Alary, produced much more this time. Her tame Longchamp effort had clearly been an inaccurate indication of her ability and she looks like a filly who will improve for 1m4f. Andre Fabre has never been afraid of going for a Curragh Classic and Plumania could be exactly the right type for the Irish Oaks.
Celimene(IRE) highly respectable fourth gives additional strength to the result. In all probability, this is as good as she is.
Board Meeting(IRE) raced with the choke out from an early stage and deserves the chance to show herself in a better light.
Shediyama(FR) connections have done wonderfully in the Diane, but their latest representative is simply not up to Group 1 competition. That said, she can still win Group races in France.
Fantasia, so dazzling in the Nell Gwyn, has failed to fulfil expectations in the French Guineas and was even more disappointing here. Given that her Meon Valley Fillies' Mile conqueror Rainbow View has also been thumped twice this season, it looks a good bet that both have been overrated or the others have caught up with them. Certainly, Fantasia, who was bred to appreciate the trip but seemed to weaken inside the final furlong, now has something to prove.
Denomination(USA), who had twice beaten Ana Americana earlier this season, was hampered in the straight. That said, she looked one-paced and will not blossom until given more of a stamina test.
Ana Americana(FR) ruined her chance by tugging for her head down the back straight.

2953a **PRIX DU CHEMIN DE FER DU NORD (GROUP 3)** **1m**
4:30 (4:33) 4-Y-0+ **£38,835** (£15,534; £11,650; £7,767; £3,883)

RPR

1 **Beacon Lodge (IRE)**[15] 2483 4-8-11 GMosse 6 117
(C G Cox) *hld up disputing last: last st: shkn up and r.o fr over 2f out on outside: drvn to ld 1 1/2f out: r.o wl: drvn out* **4/1**[3]
2 *3* **Sahpresa (USA)**[38] 1819 4-8-8 CSoumillon 5 107
(Rod Collet, France) *hld up: 8th st: hdwy 2f out: rdn to go 2nd 150yds out: kpt on* **6/4**[1]
3 *1* **Precious Boy (GER)**[44] 1658 4-9-2 ASuborics 7 113
(W Hickst, Germany) *hld up disputing last: disputing 6th st: drvn over 1 1/2f out: rdn and r.o fnl f: tk 3rd on line* **3/1**[2]
4 *nk* **Testama (FR)**[24] 5-8-8 SPasquier 9 104
(J De Roualle, France) *hld up disputing 6th st: pushed along in centre 2f out: r.o and 3rd fnl f: snatched up bhd Saphresa 50yds out: lost 3rd on line* **20/1**
5 *1 1/2* **McCartney (GER)**[15] 2500 4-8-11 C-PLemaire 3 104
(Saeed Bin Suroor) *mid-div: 5th st: hdwy 2f out: rdn and chalng 1 1/2f out: r.o tl no ex fnl 100yds* **12/1**
6 *2* **Moyenne Corniche**[254] 6440 4-8-11 (v) IMendizabal 2 99
(M L W Bell) *in tch on rail: 4th st: drvn over 2f out: rdn and one pce fr 1 1/2f out* **16/1**
7 *1/2* **Celebrissime (IRE)**[28] 2120 4-8-11 OPeslier 1 98
(F Head, France) *racd in cl 3rd: led appr st: pushed along 2f out: hdd 1 1/2f out: sn rdn and one pce* **8/1**
8 *20* **Beltanus (GER)**[38] 1819 5-8-11 JLermyte 4 52
(F Willenbrock, Germany) *racd in 2nd: pushed along 2f out: sn outpcd* **20/1**
9 *10* **Setareh (GER)**[29] 4-8-11 DBoeuf 8 29
(P Olsanik, Germany) *led to appr st: 3rd on outside st: rdn over 2f out: sn btn* **33/1**

1m 34.87s (-3.13) **Going Correction** -0.05s/f (Good) **9** Ran SP% **122.2**
Speed ratings: **113,110,109,108,107 105,104,84,74**
PARI-MUTUEL: WIN 8.40; PL 1.50, 1.20, 1.20; DF 6.50.
Owner Mr And Mrs P Hargreaves **Bred** Mrs Bill O'Neill **Trained** Lambourn, Berks

NOTEBOOK
Beacon Lodge(IRE) put up a very fine performance. He was behind for much of the race and came with a sweeping late run from last to first to win by three lengths. His trainer thinks that a mile is now the best distance for him and he has been entered in the Sussex Stakes at Goodwood. There is also talk about coming back to run in the Prix Jacques le Marois at Deauville.
Sahpresa(USA), seventh on the final turn, she found no gap to make her challenge and then eventually ran on well to finish strongly. A Listed winner last time out, she is on the upgrade and can make her mark at this level.
Precious Boy(GER), held up behind early, came with a progressive run on the rail but found no gap. He was then switched to the outside and made a final challenge and just took third place on the line.
Testama(FR), sixth round the final bend, accelerated well on the outside two furlongs out and just lost third place at the end.
McCartney(GER), behind the leading group for much of the race, made his challenge two furlongs out and stayed on one pace in the last fifty yards.
Moyenne Corniche, close up behind the leaders who set a good pace, he could not follow them in the home straight but stayed on well.

1914 COLOGNE (R-H)
Sunday, June 14

OFFICIAL GOING: Good

2954a **OPPENHEIM-UNION-RENNEN (GROUP 2)** **1m 3f**
4:15 (4:23) 3-Y-0 **£58,252** (£22,330; £11,650; £4,854)

RPR

1 **Wiener Walzer (GER)**[65] 3-9-2 ADeVries 2 100
(J Hirschberger, Germany) *led 1f: settled disputing 4th: 4th st: led 2f out: rdn and hung rt 1f out: drvn out* **33/10**[3]
2 *1 1/4* **Oriental Lion**[62] 3-9-2 DPorcu 7 98
(Uwe Ostmann, Germany) *disp 4th after 3f: 5th st: hdwy on ins over 2f out: 3rd wl over 1f out: r.o to take 2nd cl home* **79/10**
3 *hd* **Panyu (GER)**[24] 3-9-2 FilipMinarik 3 98
(P Schiergen, Germany) *hld up in rr: 6th st: 4th over 1f out: r.o one pce to take 3rd cl home* **26/5**
4 *shd* **Egon (IRE)** 3-9-2 EPedroza 5 98
(W Hickst, Germany) *led after 1f: hdd 2f out: drvn and ev ch 1f out: one pce* **15/1**
5 *1 1/4* **Eliot (GER)** 3-9-2 THellier 6 96
(T Mundry, Germany) *hld up in rr: last st: styd on fr over 1f out: nrest at fin* **29/10**[2]
6 *11* **Peligroso (FR)**[13] 2560 3-9-2 LDettori 4 77
(Saeed Bin Suroor) *sn disputing 2nd: 2nd st: rdn and btn 2f out* **6/5**[1]
7 *3 1/2* **Pennyprince (GER)**[24] 3-9-2 RPiechulek 1 71
(Uwe Ostmann, Germany) *broke wl: disp 2nd: 3rd st: sn btn* **29/1**

2m 16.81s (-3.99) **7** Ran SP% **131.3**
(including ten euro stakes): WIN 43; PL 17, 25, 18; SF 262.
Owner Gestut Schlenderhan **Bred** Gestut Schlenderhan **Trained** Germany

NOTEBOOK
Peligroso(FR) had run well on his reappearance, but on his second start for Godolphin he proved very disappointing, being eased right down when beaten.

2525 SAN SIRO (R-H)
Sunday, June 14

OFFICIAL GOING: Good

2955a **GRAN PREMIO DI MILANO SNAI (GROUP 1)** **1m 4f**
5:30 (5:45) 3-Y-0+ **£154,549** (£75,266; £43,187; £21,593)

RPR

1 **Quijano (GER)**[78] 1012 7-9-7 AStarke 5 115
(P Schiergen, Germany) *racd in 3rd to st: drvn to ld 1f out: rdn out (1.78/1)* **7/4**[2]
2 *1* **Age Of Reason (UAE)**[108] 4-9-7 MartinDwyer 4 113
(Saeed Bin Suroor) *trckd ldr to st: tk narrow ld 2f out: sn rdn: hdd 1f out: kpt on same pce u.p (4.08/1)* **41/10**[3]
3 *hd* **Voila Ici (IRE)**[36] 1903 4-9-7 MDemuro 6 113
(V Caruso, Italy) *mid-div: wnt 4th bef half-way: 4th and outpcd over 2f out: r.o wl fnl f to jst miss 2nd (1.63/1F)* **8/5**[1]
4 *2 1/4* **Vol De Nuit**[36] 1903 8-9-7 URispoli 7 109
(G Pucciatti, Italy) *led: set stdy pce: hdd 2f out: drvn and ev ch 1f out: wknd last 150yds (5.94/1 cpld)* **59/10**
5 *nk* **Winkle (IRE)**[41] 1762 4-9-4 MMonteriso 3 106
(M Delzangles, France) *hld up: 6th st: 7th and rdn 2f out: r.o fnl fur;ong: nrest at fin (5.37/1)* **54/10**
6 *3 1/2* **Permesso**[28] 2115 4-9-7 (b) SLandi 9 103
(F & L Camici, Italy) *last st: drvn over 2f out: kpt on one pce (5.94/1 cpld)* **59/10**
7 *7* **Freemusic (IRE)**[28] 2115 5-9-7 GMarcelli 8 92
(L Riccardi, Italy) *7th st: rdn over 2f out: sn btn (5.94/1 cpld)* **59/10**
8 *9* **Gimmy (IRE)**[28] 2115 5-9-7 DVargiu 1 77
(B Grizzetti, Italy) *racd in 5th to st: btn over 2f out: eased (8.58/1)* **17/2**
9 *3/4* **Tremoto**[36] 1903 4-9-4 (b) SDiana 2 73
(F & L Camici, Italy) *8th st: rdn and btn over 2f out: eased (35/1)* **35/1**

2m 29.6s (-1.90) **9** Ran SP% **166.8**
(including one euro stakes): WIN 2.78; PL 1.25, 1.53, 1.26; DF 5.51.
Owner Stiftung Gestut Fahrhof **Bred** Stiftung Gestut Fahrhof **Trained** Germany

NOTEBOOK
Quijano(GER) followed up his win in this last year.
Age Of Reason(UAE), winner of the Qatar International Cup last time out in February, had not tackled this level of opposition before and in the circumstances it was a good effort from the son of Halling. He only found globetrotting Group 1 performer Quijano too strong.

2956 - (Foreign Racing) - See Raceform Interactive

1262 CORK (R-H)
Sunday, June 14

OFFICIAL GOING: Good (good to firm in places on round course)

2957a **KERRY SPRING WATER ROCHESTOWN STKS (LISTED RACE)** **6f**
2:45 (2:46) 2-Y-0 **£30,021** (£8,808; £4,196; £1,429)

RPR

1 **Love Lockdown (IRE)**[13] 2556 2-9-1 KLatham 2 99
(G M Lyons, Ire) *sn led: strly pressed and jnd over 1f out: regained narrow ld and styd on wl ins fnl f* **11/8**[1]
2 *nk* **King Ledley (USA)**[32] 1994 2-9-1 DPMcDonogh 4 98
(Kevin Prendergast, Ire) *in tch towards rr: hdwy into 3rd fr 1f out: styd on wl u.p into 2nd ins fnl f: nt get to wnr* **5/1**[3]
3 *1 1/4* **Roi De Vitesse (IRE)**[23] 2247 2-9-1 JamesMillman 1 94+
(B R Millman) *4th early: dropped in to rr and pushed along bef 1/2-way: wnt 5th fr 1f out: styd on wl wout rching ldrs ins fnl f* **9/2**[2]
4 *3/4* **Dream Deer**[30] 2061 2-9-1 KJManning 5 92
(P D Deegan, Ire) *sn chsd ldrs: clsd into 2nd 2f out: no ex and kpt on same pce ins fnl f* **7/1**
5 *2 1/2* **Avonrose**[19] 2360 2-8-12 GregFairley 3 82
(M Johnston) *trckd ldr: 4th fr 2f out: no ex 1f out* **8/1**
6 *10* **What About Me (IRE)**[13] 2557 2-8-12 DJMoran 6 52
(Brian Nolan, Ire) *trckd ldrs: 3rd for much: dropped to 4th and no ex fr 1f out* **7/1**

1m 10.92s (-1.68) **6** Ran SP% **113.1**
CSF £8.75 TOTE £1.80: £1.80, £2.50; DF 9.80.
Owner Sean Jones **Bred** Moyglare Stud Farm Ltd **Trained** Dunsany, Co. Meath

NOTEBOOK
Love Lockdown(IRE) won his third straight race and handled the step up to Listed company without a problem. Racing in the front rank, he just kept pulling out a bit more when challenged and his rider never had to get serious. It is hard to gauge how good he may be, as he seems to do just enough to win. (op 11/8 tchd 6/4)
King Ledley(USA) showed what grade he belongs in after an unsatisfactory episode at Naas last time against Steinbeck. He came through on the outside to be the last to deliver his challenge but the winner always just had his measure. He looks sure get further and win a nice race. (op 9/2)

Roi De Vitesse(IRE) is another for whom stepping up a furlong would do no harm. Racing prominently on the inner, he was just caught for tactical speed and was ridden to keep his place at halfway. He could not manage that, but ran on well enough inside the last and connections will learn plenty from this. (op 5/1 tchd 4/1)
Dream Deer gives the impression of being a pure sprinter. He quickened to challenge over 1f out but weakened once coming under pressure inside the last. Success in a nice race over the minimum trip is a possibility.
Avonrose needed to improve a good deal to figure, having won an ordinary maiden last time, and while she was not disgraced she was going nowhere inside the final quarter-mile. (op 6/1)
What About Me(IRE) ran well below her best. She was up there for the first half but dropped right out inside the last. (op 8/1 tchd 9/1)

2960a KERRY GROUP NOBLESSE STKS (GROUP 3) (F&M) 1m 4f
4:30 (4:30) 3-Y-0+ £56,796 (£16,601; £7,864; £2,621)

RPR
1 **Grace O'Malley (IRE)**[56] 1388 3-8-9 PJSmullen 12 98+
(D K Weld, Ire) *chsd ldrs: 5th appr st: sn nt clr run tl led 1 1/2f out: strly pressed and styd on wl ins fnl f* 15/2
2 *shd* **Tanoura (IRE)**[42] 1715 3-8-10 94 ow1 FMBerry 7 99+
(John M Oxx, Ire) *dwlt: towards rr: nt clr run and swtchd to outer fr over 2f out: chal u.p in 2nd fnl f: styd on wl: nt quite get to wnr* 7/1
3 *2 1/2* **Jakarta Jazz (IRE)**[32] 1996 3-8-9 92 CDHayes 8 94
(Kevin Prendergast, Ire) *dwlt: in rr of mid-div: short of room briefly appr st: rdn to go 5th over 1f out: kpt on wout threatening* 9/1
4 *shd* **Timabiyra (IRE)**[32] 1996 3-8-9 90 NGMcCullagh 4 94
(John M Oxx, Ire) *towards rr: hdwy st: chal u.p fr over 1f out: sn no imp and kpt on* 16/1
5 *1 3/4* **Roses For The Lady (IRE)**[39] 1789 3-8-9 100 MJKinane 13 91
(John M Oxx, Ire) *prom: 2nd into st: in front over 2f out: hdd and kpt on same pce fr 1 1/2f out* 11/4[1]
6 *5 1/2* **Evening Rushour (IRE)**[28] 2111 5-9-9 85 JAHeffernan 10 81
(A Kinsella, Ire) *mid-div: 6th appr st: kpt on same pce u.p fr 2f out* 14/1
7 *4* **Latin Love (IRE)**[42] 1715 3-8-9 95 WMLordan 6 76
(David Wachman, Ire) *mid-div: clsr in 4th appr st: kpt on same pce u.p fr under 2f out* 11/2[3]
8 *7* **Les Fazzani (IRE)**[15] 2482 5-9-9 StephenDonohoe 9 64
(K A Ryan) *prom: 3rd into st: no ex 1 1/2f out* 9/2[2]
9 *14* **Rory Anna (IRE)**[28] 2111 3-8-9 79 (t) RPCleary 3 42
(John J Walsh, Ire) *dwlt: towards rr: no ex and eased fr over 1f out* 66/1
10 *3* **Silk Mascara (IRE)**[42] 1714 3-8-9 86 (b[1]) CO'Donoghue 2 38
(David Wachman, Ire) *dwlt: sn led: strly pressed and hdd under 3f out: hmpd over 2f out: sn eased* 33/1
P **Always Beautiful (USA)**[64] 1222 4-9-9 97 DPMcDonogh 11 —
(David Wachman, Ire) *stmbld and p.u injured after 4f* 16/1

2m 29.97s (-17.93)
WFA 3 from 4yo+ 15lb 11 Ran SP% 117.4
CSF £59.09 TOTE £9.00: £2.80, £1.90, £2.40; DF 76.00.
Owner Mrs C L Weld **Bred** Hawthorn Villa Stud **Trained** The Curragh, Co Kildare

FOCUS
The first two finished clear and are entitled to build on this, while the fourth and sixth are the guide to the level of the form.

NOTEBOOK
Grace O'Malley(IRE) proved a worthy substitute for the absent Profound Beauty as she battled well to win. She tracked the lead early and did well to avoid disaster when the front-running Always Beautiful broke down after half a mile. She was short of room early in the straight and eventually made her challenge between horses 1f out. Once getting there, she responded admirably just to repel the runner-up. She goes to the Irish Oaks next. (op 13/2)
Tanoura(IRE) carried 1lb overweight and that had to be a factor in her defeat. Held up, she moved up on the outside a furlong and a half out, having been denied a clear passage early in the straight. The winner got first run on her, but she kept going all the way to the line and was a slightly unlucky loser. (op 9/1)
Jakarta Jazz(IRE) justified her place in this company and, with the run of the race, would have been closer. First, she was short of room and lost a few lengths before the turn into the straight and then was squeezed in the straight. She ran on inside the last and was never nearer. She was not an unlucky loser, but would have been closer and looks a Listed-class filly at least.
Timabiyra(IRE) put up a career-best effort. Held up early, she made ground to get into a challenging position 1f out before her effort flattened out. She may get a bit further and should be capable of winning a nice race. (op 20/1)
Roses For The Lady(IRE) was keen early, and when the pace quickened in the straight lost the lead she had briefly held. She lacked the pace to be competitive late on. (op 5/2)
Evening Rushour(IRE) ran well enough upped in class and may prove good enough to get black type. (op 20/1)
Les Fazzani(IRE) was below-par for the second time in Ireland this season. Ridden prominently, she got buffeted around in the straight but was losing her place anyway and dropped out. (op 9/2 tchd 5/1)
Always Beautiful(USA) suffered a broken leg after half a mile. (op 12/1)

2961 - 2962a (Foreign Racing) - See Raceform Interactive

2526 CARLISLE (R-H)
Monday, June 15

OFFICIAL GOING: Good to firm (firm on stands' side home straight; 9.0)
Running rail moved out 2yards on Stable bend but effect on distances not known.
Wind: Breezy, half against Weather: Cloudy, bright, heavy showers

2963 TURFTV.CO.UK MAIDEN AUCTION STKS 5f 193y
2:15 (2:15) (Class 5) 2-Y-0 £2,729 (£806; £403) Stalls High

Form RPR
362 1 **Ailsa Carmel (IRE)**[8] 2735 2-8-7 0 SamHitchcott 4 76+
(M R Channon) *mde all: pushed clr fr over 1f out* 5/2[1]
0 2 *4* **Hold On Tiger (IRE)**[11] 2623 2-8-12 0 TomEaves 3 68
(I Semple) *dwlt: hld up: hdwy 1/2-way: effrt and chsd wnr over 1f out: one pce fnl f* 10/1
3 *4 1/2* **Emerald Girl (IRE)** 2-8-6 0 PaulHanagan 6 48+
(R A Fahey) *towards rr: pushed along 1/2-way: kpt on fnl f: no imp* 9/2
65 4 *nse* **Urban Clubber**[24] 2247 2-9-2 0 PaulMulrennan 1 58
(J Howard Johnson) *pressed wnr: rdn over 1f out: edgd rt and no ex fr over 1f out* 3/1[2]
5 5 *7* **Clear Ice (IRE)**[18] 2388 2-8-11 0 AdrianTNicholls 7 30
(D Nicholls) *chsd ldrs tl rdn and wknd fr 2f out* 7/2[3]
6 *hd* **One Cool Deal (IRE)** 2-8-12 0 DavidAllan 8 31
(T D Easterby) *s.i.s: bhd and green: nvr rchd ldrs* 20/1
05 7 *10* **Countrymans Dream**[14] 2526 2-8-10 0 ow1 PhillipMakin 2 —
(J R Weymes) *prom tl rdn and wknd over 2f out* 80/1
8 *nk* **Kirkby's Gem** 2-7-11 0 BillyCray[(7)] 5 —
(A Berry) *t.k.h: prom to 1/2-way: sn struggling* 66/1

1m 15.42s (1.72) **Going Correction** +0.125s/f (Good) 8 Ran SP% 110.6
Speed ratings (Par 93): **93,87,81,81,72 72,58,58**
toteswinger: 1&2 £6.50, 1&3 £2.90, 2&3 £6.20. CSF £25.94 TOTE £2.90: £1.30, £3.30, £1.70; EX 21.00.
Owner Mrs M Findlay **Bred** F Sheedy **Trained** West Ilsley, Berks

FOCUS
There was hail and torrential rain for around 15 minutes an hour or so before racing, but it had little effect on the ground which remained fast. A moderate juvenile maiden and the winner did it easily.

NOTEBOOK
Ailsa Carmel(IRE) improved for the step up to this trip when second at Brighton last time and appreciated the stiffer test provided by this course. Clear over a furlong out, she stayed on strongly for pressure and should make her mark in nurseries later in the season, with the possibility of more to come over 7f. (op 15-8 tchd 7-4 in places)
Hold On Tiger(IRE), slowly away when last of seven on his debut, was again not the quickest to get going, but he came through to chase the winner at past halfway and stuck on for a clear second. (op 25-1)
Emerald Girl(IRE), bred to be precocious, comes from an in-form yard and she stayed on late to snatch third. She was slightly hampered early on and improvement should be forthcoming. (op 5-1 tchd 4-1)
Urban Clubber is now qualified for a handicap mark and should do better in nurseries (op 4-1)
Clear Ice(IRE) was unable to quicken for pressure and failed to improve on her debut effort. (op 3-1 tchd 11-4)

2964 CARLISLE-RACES.CO.UK H'CAP 5f 193y
2:45 (2:50) (Class 6) (0-60,59) 3-Y-0+ £2,047 (£604; £302) Stalls High

Form RPR
6-21 1 **Hansomis (IRE)**[14] 2529 5-9-5 56 FrederikTylicki[(5)] 1 67
(B Mactaggart) *chsd ldrs: rdn to ld over 1f out: styd on wl fnl f* 9/2[1]
5426 2 *1 1/4* **Wiltshire (IRE)**[11] 2628 7-9-9 55 (v) JamieMoriarty 10 62
(P T Midgley) *midfield: effrt over 2f out: styd on to go 2nd towards fin: nt rch wnr* 20/1
0455 3 *1* **Valdemar**[13] 2577 3-8-8 48 (v) SilvestreDeSousa 3 50
(A D Brown) *led to over 1f out: kpt on same pce fnl f* 16/1
002 4 *hd* **Royal Acclamation (IRE)**[10] 2660 4-9-4 55 (v) PatrickDonaghy[(5)] 12 58+
(G A Harker) *midfield: drvn and outpcd over 2f out: edgd lft and styd on fnl f* 9/1
-201 5 *1* **Asserting**[12] 2593 3-8-12 59 BillyCray[(7)] 8 57
(J A McShane) *trckd ldrs: outpcd over 2f out: hung lft and rallied over 1f out: no imp fnl f* 17/2
0-53 6 *hd* **Not Now Lewis (IRE)**[18] 2404 5-9-2 53 SladeO'Hara[(5)] 9 52+
(F P Murtagh) *bhd: rdn 1/2-way: kpt on fnl f: nrst fin* 12/1
-440 7 *1/2* **Abbey Steps (IRE)**[20] 2365 3-9-1 55 (b) DavidAllan 17 51
(T D Easterby) *cl up tl rdn and no ex over 1f out* 12/1
2430 8 *1/2* **Distant Vision (IRE)**[11] 2625 6-8-10 47 (b) JamieKyne[(5)] 15 43
(H A McWilliams) *trckd ldrs: drvn over 2f out: no ex over 1f out* 14/1
0504 9 *3/4* **Ingleby Princess**[14] 2529 5-9-9 55 PhillipMakin 6 49+
(T D Barron) *bhd: drvn over 2f out: nvr rchd ldrs* 6/1[3]
0-43 10 *2 1/4* **Optical Illusion (USA)**[17] 2453 5-9-8 54 PaulHanagan 14 41+
(R A Fahey) *taken early to post: hmpd and dropped in rr after 1f: nvr rchd ldrs* 5/1[2]
-000 11 *nk* **Fyodorovich (USA)**[9] 2722 4-9-9 55 (b[1]) TonyHamilton 4 41
(J S Wainwright) *s.i.s: sn in tch on outside: drvn and wknd wl over 1f out* 40/1
0-05 12 *2* **Cool Sands (IRE)**[28] 2133 7-9-2 48 (v) PaulMulrennan 16 27
(J G Given) *hld up: pushed along 1/2-way: btn and eased fnl f* 16/1
000- 13 *3 1/2* **Regal Dream (IRE)**[277] 5816 7-8-13 45 RoystonFfrench 2 13
(J W Unett) *prom to 1/2-way: sn lost pl* 20/1
5060 14 *3/4* **Chookie Heiton (IRE)**[17] 2438 11-9-6 52 TomEaves 11 18
(I Semple) *in tch 2f: sn lost pl and struggling* 40/1

1m 15.06s (1.36) **Going Correction** +0.125s/f (Good)
WFA 3 from 4yo+ 8lb 14 Ran SP% 117.9
Speed ratings (Par 101): **95,93,92,91,90 90,89,88,87,84 84,81,77,76**
toteswinger: 1&2 £16.10, 1&3 £20.30, 2&3 £56.50. CSF £92.46 CT £1175.53 TOTE £5.20: £2.20, £6.00, £4.90; EX 86.60.
Owner Corsby Racing **Bred** J Beckett **Trained** Hawick, Borders
■ Just Spike (12/1, ref to ent stalls) & Missed Mondays (40/1, unruly in stalls) were withdrawn. Deduct 5p in the £ under R4.

FOCUS
A poor, but competitive sprint. Little got into it from the rear. The winner is getting back towards the best of her old form.
Fyodorovich(USA) Official explanation: jockey said colt hung left-handed throughout

2965 SUBSCRIBE ONLINE AT RACINGUK.COM CLAIMING STKS 1m 1f 61y
3:15 (3:16) (Class 6) 3-Y-0+ £2,047 (£604; £302) Stalls High

Form RPR
0121 1 **Rowan Lodge (IRE)**[14] 2527 7-9-7 65 (b) JamieMoriarty 4 69
(Ollie Pears) *hld up: hdwy over 3f out: rdn to ld appr fnl f: hld on wl* 5/1[2]
2000 2 *shd* **Captain Jacksparra (IRE)**[13] 2576 5-9-5 78 AmyRyan[(5)] 12 72
(K A Ryan) *hld up in midfield: hdwy and hung lft to ld briefly over 1f out: ev ch fnl f: jst hld* 7/2[1]
4364 3 *10* **Beaumont Boy**[5] 2816 5-9-3 50 (b) PaulMulrennan 1 44
(J A McShane) *led to over 1f out: sn carried lft and outpcd* 25/1
20-0 4 *nse* **Pianoforte (USA)**[11] 2626 7-9-5 56 (b) DavidAllan 5 46
(E J Alston) *t.k.h early: midfield: hdwy and ev ch wl over 1f out: sn outpcd* 17/2
6400 5 *1/2* **Mister Maq**[23] 2261 6-9-3 46 (v) JoeFanning 15 43
(A Crook) *in tch: drvn over 3f out: outpcd fnl 2f: sddle slipped* 40/1
0500 6 *3* **Ming Vase**[23] 2263 7-9-3 49 PJMcDonald 13 36
(P T Midgley) *prom: rdn over 3f out: outpcd fnl 2f* 20/1
0004 7 *hd* **Carnival Dream**[14] 2527 4-8-10 50 (p) JamieKyne[(5)] 8 34
(H A McWilliams) *cl up tl rdn and no ex fr 2f out* 14/1
0-0 8 *3* **Awaken**[53] 1472 8-9-0 48 PhillipMakin 14 27
(Miss Tracy Waggott) *hld up: effrt over 2f out: nvr rchd ldrs* 33/1
-400 9 *1 1/2* **Neon Blue**[20] 2362 8-9-1 57 MichaelJStainton[(3)] 7 27
(R M Whitaker) *s.i.s: rdn in rr 1/2-way: nvr on terms* 11/1
-000 10 *nk* **Fan Club**[130] 399 5-9-13 35 AndrewElliott 6 36
(Mrs R A Carr) *hld up: struggling over 3f out: sn btn* 200/1
0540 11 *4 1/2* **General Feeling (IRE)**[18] 2390 8-9-5 56 AdrianTNicholls 11 18
(D Nicholls) *missed break: bhd: rdn over 3f out: nvr on terms* 7/1[3]
12 *1* **Masters House (IRE)**[78] 6-9-5 0 TonyHamilton 3 16
(Mrs J C McGregor) *s.i.s: nvr on terms* 200/1
13 *3* **Italiano**[51] 10-9-2 0 FrederikTylicki[(5)] 2 12
(P Beaumont) *midfield: rdn over 3f out: sn wknd* 66/1

0-50 **14** *shd* **Fortunate Isle (USA)**[61] 1279 7-9-3 67 PaulHanagan 9 8
(R A Fahey) *bhd: reminders after 2f: nvr on terms* **7/2**[1]

05-0 **15** *½* **Reddy Ronnie (IRE)**[18] 2404 5-9-3 49 RoystonFfrench 10 7
(D W Thompson) *trckd ldrs tl wknd fr 3f out* **28/1**

1m 58.84s (1.24) **Going Correction** +0.125s/f (Good) **15** Ran SP% **119.1**
Speed ratings (Par 101): **99,98,90,89,89 86,86,84,82,82 78,77,74,74,74**
toteswinger: 1&2 £5.70, 1&3 £9.30, 2&3 £24.70. CSF £20.87 TOTE £4.10: £1.60, £1.50, £5.90; EX 22.70.
Owner K C West & Venture Racing **Bred** M P B Bloodstock Ltd **Trained** Norton, N Yorks
■ Stewards' Enquiry : Amy Ryan one-day ban: careless riding (remedial training tbn); one-day ban: used whip with excessive frequency (Jun 29)

FOCUS
Two drew right away in this claimer. Not a race to rate too positively.
Mister Maq Official explanation: jockey said saddle slipped

2966 BELL & PLATE 24TH JUNE H'CAP 5f
3:45 (3:45) (Class 5) (0-70,69) 3-Y-O+ **£2,914** (£867; £433; £216) **Stalls High**

Form RPR

4311 **1** **Argentine (IRE)**[5] 2812 5-9-10 **65** 6ex (b) PaulMulrennan 4 81+
(J A McShane) *trckd ldrs gng wl: smooth hdwy to ld 1f out: rdn out* **3/1**[1]

320- **2** *1¾* **Wicked Wilma (IRE)**[223] 7182 5-8-10 **56** SladeO'Hara(5) 1 66
(A Berry) *mde most to 1f out: kpt on: nt pce of wnr* **16/1**

0613 **3** *3¼* **Ryedane (IRE)**[5] 2801 7-9-3 **58** (b) DavidAllan 10 56
(T D Easterby) *trckd ldrs: drvn and outpcd over 2f out: kpt on fnl f: nt rch first two* **3/1**[1]

40-2 **4** *shd* **Bahamian Ballad**[21] 2316 4-8-9 **50** AlanMunro 12 48
(J D Bethell) *towards rr: drvn 1/2-way: kpt on fnl f: nvr rchd ldrs* **8/1**

6541 **5** *¾* **Weet A Surprise**[10] 2682 4-9-3 **63** (v) JamieKyne(5) 13 58
(J W Unett) *bhd tl edgd rt and hdwy over 1f out: nrst fin* **15/2**

1005 **6** *shd* **Mandalay King (IRE)**[14] 2531 4-9-9 **69** LanceBetts(5) 9 64
(Mrs Marjorie Fife) *missed break: bhd: hdwy 2f out: no imp fnl f* **7/1**[3]

0010 **7** *½* **Thunder Bay**[9] 2717 4-9-1 **61** FrederikTylicki(5) 6 54
(R A Fahey) *midfield: rdn 1/2-way: no imp fr over 1f out* **13/2**[2]

2410 **8** *nk* **Imperial Sword**[17] 2436 6-9-7 **69** (b) JanWilson(7) 8 61
(T D Barron) *s.i.s: bhd tl sme late hdwy: n.d* **16/1**

000- **9** *3¼* **Making Music**[264] 6218 6-8-10 **51** (b) DuranFentiman 2 31
(T D Easterby) *w ldr tl rdn and wknd over 1f out* **50/1**

1040 **10** *7* **Darcy's Pride (IRE)**[21] 2316 5-9-1 **56** TonyHamilton 11 11
(D W Barker) *chsd ldrs to 1/2-way: sn wknd* **18/1**

05-6 **11** *2* **Only A Splash**[10] 2660 5-8-9 **50** oh5 AndrewElliott 5 —
(Mrs R A Carr) *in tch tl wknd fr 1/2-way* **80/1**

2000 **12** *12* **Just Joey**[5] 2801 5-9-2 **57** (b) PhillipMakin 3 —
(J R Weymes) *racd wd in midfield: rdn and wknd fr 1/2-way* **66/1**

61.00 secs (0.20) **Going Correction** +0.125s/f (Good) **12** Ran SP% **120.4**
Speed ratings (Par 103): **103,100,95,94,93 93,92,92,87,75 72,53**
toteswinger: 1&2 £8.80, 1&3 £2.80, 2&3 £12.40. CSF £59.81 CT £162.13 TOTE £4.10: £1.90, £4.50, £1.40; EX 59.00.
Owner D Moriarty **Bred** Tony Hirschfeld & L K Piggott **Trained** Dalkeith, Midlothian

FOCUS
This was not a strong sprint but the time was good and the winner is rated back to the best of his old form. Little got into it from the rear.

2967 CARLISLE CONFERENCE GROUP FILLIES' H'CAP 6f 192y
4:15 (4:15) (Class 4) (0-80,77) 3-Y-O **£6,476** (£1,927; £963; £481) **Stalls High**

Form RPR

3332 **1** **Mo Mhuirnin (IRE)**[6] 2786 3-8-9 **65** PaulHanagan 8 73
(R A Fahey) *in tch: rdn over 2f out: hung lft and led ins fnl f: kpt on strly* **9/4**[2]

021 **2** *2¼* **Arabian Pearl (IRE)**[19] 2375 3-9-7 **77** AlanMunro 2 79
(P W Chapple-Hyam) *trckd ldrs: rdn over 2f out: ev ch 1f out: kpt on same pce ins fnl f* **2/1**[1]

15-5 **3** *1½* **Darcey**[16] 2504 3-8-13 **74** FrederikTylicki(5) 5 72
(R A Fahey) *led to 1f out: kpt on same pce u.p* **4/1**[3]

1-0 **4** *1* **Chantilly Pearl (USA)**[32] 2001 3-9-1 **71** PaulMulrennan 4 66
(J G Given) *stdd in last pl: stdy hdwy whn rdr dropped reins briefly over 1f out: kpt on fnl f: nvr nr ldrs* **16/1**

0-03 **5** *nse* **Harriet's Girl**[37] 1895 3-9-2 **72** AndrewElliott 6 67
(K R Burke) *plld hrd: hld up in tch: effrt over 2f out: one pce over 1f out* **9/1**

0-02 **6** *1* **Oriental Rose**[12] 2602 3-9-0 **70** PJMcDonald 3 62
(G M Moore) *cl up tl rdn and no ex over 1f out* **16/1**

3106 **7** *1½* **My Best Bet**[14] 2544 3-9-3 **73** SamHitchcott 1 61
(M R Channon) *hld up in tch: rdn whn rdr dropped whip over 1f out: no imp fnl f* **14/1**

6600 **8** *2½* **Meydan Groove**[12] 2593 3-7-11 **58** oh13 JamieKyne(5) 7 40
(R Johnson) *t.k.h: chsd ldrs tl rdn and wknd fr 2f out* **100/1**

1m 27.91s (0.81) **Going Correction** +0.125s/f (Good) **8** Ran SP% **113.5**
Speed ratings (Par 98): **100,97,95,94,94 93,91,88**
toteswinger: 1&2 £1.70, 1&3 £2.40, 2&3 £2.90. CSF £7.04 CT £15.58 TOTE £3.30: £1.20, £1.30, £1.60; EX 8.00 Trifecta £43.40 Pool: £182.20 - 3.10 winning units.
Owner Gone West Syndicate **Bred** John McEnery **Trained** Musley Bank, N Yorks

FOCUS
A modestly-run fillies' handicap which probably did not take much winning. The winner stepped up slightly on her previous Redcar run.
Harriet's Girl Official explanation: jockey said filly ran too free
Meydan Groove Official explanation: jockey said filly hung left-handed throughout

2968 ESCALA LIVE HERE ON 4TH JULY H'CAP 7f 200y
4:45 (4:45) (Class 5) (0-70,69) 4-Y-O+ **£2,914** (£867; £433; £216) **Stalls High**

Form RPR

6-06 **1** **Intersky Charm (USA)**[53] 1478 5-8-11 **62** MichaelJStainton(3) 3 71
(R M Whitaker) *midfield: effrt over 2f out: led ins fnl f: rdn out* **9/2**[3]

4023 **2** *1¼* **Shadowtime**[23] 2261 4-9-3 **65** PhillipMakin 2 71
(Miss Tracy Waggott) *prom: hdwy to ld over 1f out: hdd ins fnl f: kpt on same pce* **9/4**[1]

-402 **3** *¾* **Carpe Diem**[5] 2804 4-8-7 **55** (v) PaulHanagan 4 59
(R A Fahey) *led: clr 1/2-way: hdd over 1f out: kpt on same pce* **3/1**[2]

0400 **4** *¾* **Stoic Leader (IRE)**[19] 1887 9-9-3 **65** RoystonFfrench 6 67
(R F Fisher) *midfield: effrt over 2f out: one pce whn flashed tail ins fnl f* **20/1**

6004 **5** *1½* **Forzarzi (IRE)**[11] 2626 5-8-8 **56** (p) TomEaves 9 55
(H A McWilliams) *hld up: nt clr run over 2f out: kpt on u.p fnl f: nvr rchd ldrs* **14/1**

0505 **6** *1* **Malinsa Blue (IRE)**[17] 2441 7-8-7 **55** ow1 (b) TonyHamilton 1 52
(B Ellison) *in tch tl edgd rt and outpcd over 1f out* **12/1**

-060 **7** *3¾* **Wilmington**[18] 2390 5-8-3 **51** DarrenMoffatt 11 39
(Mrs J C McGregor) *chsd clr ldr tl wknd over 2f out* **66/1**

2421 **8** *2½* **Champain Sands (IRE)**[14] 2542 10-9-1 **63** AndrewMullen 8 45
(E J Alston) *s.i.s: hld up: effrt 2f out: btn fnl f* **13/2**

5-00 **9** *17* **Da Bomber (IRE)**[17] 2446 4-8-2 **55** JamieKyne(5) 5 —
(J W Unett) *chsd ldrs tl wknd fr 3f out: t.o* **18/1**

1m 42.22s (2.22) **Going Correction** +0.125s/f (Good) **9** Ran SP% **113.2**
Speed ratings (Par 103): **93,91,91,90,88 87,84,81,64**
toteswinger: 1&2 £3.90, 1&3 £3.7, 2&3 £2.50. CSF £14.68 CT £34.05 TOTE £6.00: £1.90, £1.20, £1.60; EX 22.30.
Owner R M Whitaker **Bred** Phil Booker **Trained** Scarcroft, W Yorks

FOCUS
A modest handicap in which the field came stands' side in the straight. Ordinary but sound form.

2969 EOGHAN QUIGG LIVE HERE 26TH JULY H'CAP 1m 6f 32y
5:15 (5:16) (Class 5) (0-70,64) 4-Y-O+ **£2,914** (£867; £433; £216) **Stalls High**

Form RPR

0051 **1** **Zefooha (FR)**[21] 2344 5-9-3 **60** JamieMoriarty 2 66
(T D Walford) *trckd ldrs: drvn 3f out: rallied and overall ldr ins fnl f: kpt on* **5/2**[1]

06-1 **2** *½* **Mystified (IRE)**[6] 2785 6-8-2 **50** (tp) JamieKyne(5) 5 55
(R F Fisher) *led: styd alone far side ent st: hdd ins fnl f: r.o* **5/1**

-400 **3** *½* **Mayadeen (IRE)**[23] 2264 7-8-8 **51** (v) PaulHanagan 7 56
(R A Fahey) *dwlt: hld up: hdwy and cl up over 5f out: led gp that c stands' side over 2f out: hdd over 1f out: rallied: kpt on ins fnl f* **12/1**

-212 **4** *hd* **Kings Maiden (IRE)**[24] 2233 6-9-5 **62** DarrenMoffatt 6 66
(James Moffatt) *t.k.h: in tch: hdwy to ld stands' side over 1f out to ins fnl f: one pce* **3/1**[2]

3010 **5** *1¼* **Bijou Dan**[25] 2194 8-9-7 **64** PJMcDonald 4 67
(G M Moore) *prom: effrt over 2f out: one pce fnl f* **9/2**[3]

00-0 **6** *16* **Rocknest Island (IRE)**[21] 2344 6-8-2 **45** (p) RoystonFfrench 3 25
(P D Niven) *cl up tl rdn and wknd fr 3f out* **10/1**

-000 **7** *7* **Rascasse**[14] 2527 4-7-9 **45** BillyCray(7) 1 15
(Bruce Hellier) *bhd: drvn over 3f out: sn btn* **100/1**

00-P **8** *11* **Aura Of Calm (IRE)**[23] 2264 7-8-2 **45** (t) AndrewMullen 8 —
(Ronald O'Leary, Ire) *hld up: struggling 3f out: sn btn* **20/1**

3m 12.09s (4.59) **Going Correction** +0.125s/f (Good) **8** Ran SP% **111.0**
Speed ratings (Par 103): **91,90,90,90,89 80,76,70**
toteswinger: 1&2 £2.90, 1&3 £6.80, 2&3 £6.30. CSF £14.40 CT £116.69 TOTE £3.40: £1.50, £2.10, £2.40; EX 17.80.
Owner Anthony Preston **Bred** Darley Stud Management Co Ltd **Trained** Sheriff Hutton, N Yorks

FOCUS
The was not much pace on here, producing a bunch finish and muddling form.

2970 LEVY BOARD H'CAP 5f 193y
5:45 (5:45) (Class 5) (0-75,75) 3-Y-O **£2,590** (£770; £385; £192) **Stalls High**

Form RPR

-206 **1** **Mister Tinktastic (IRE)**[6] 2786 3-8-11 **65** (p) PhillipMakin 3 71
(M Dods) *pressed ldr: led 2f out: edgd rt: hld on wl fnl f* **9/2**[3]

3515 **2** *¾* **Blue Noodles**[10] 2660 3-8-11 **65** TonyHamilton 7 69
(D W Barker) *led to 2f out: rallied: kpt on same pce nr fin* **9/1**

0-22 **3** *1½* **Who's Shirl**[21] 2343 3-7-13 **56** oh1 KellyHarrison(3) 8 55
(C W Fairhurst) *towards rr: hdwy u.p over 1f out: kpt on fnl f: nt rch ldrs* **8/1**

3266 **4** *¾* **Raimond Ridge (IRE)**[21] 2336 3-9-5 **73** SamHitchcott 4 70
(M R Channon) *s.i.s: bhd tl hdwy over 1f out: kpt on: nvr rchd ldrs* **10/1**

3001 **5** *1¾* **Jimwil (IRE)**[6] 2786 3-9-2 **70** 6ex (b) TomEaves 11 61+
(M Dods) *s.s: bhd tl hdwy over 1f out: n.d* **11/4**[1]

0-06 **6** *2¼* **Viking Awake (IRE)**[21] 2338 3-8-8 **62** (t) PaulMulrennan 6 46
(J W Unett) *in tch: drvn and outpcd 2f out: no imp fnl f* **40/1**

0-55 **7** *4½* **Fathey (IRE)**[12] 2611 3-9-0 **68** PaulHanagan 2 38
(R A Fahey) *bhd: shkn up and edgd rt 2f out: sn no imp* **10/3**[2]

0-60 **8** *½* **Fitzolini**[13] 2578 3-9-0 **68** (p) SilvestreDeSousa 1 36
(A D Brown) *prom tl wknd fr 2f out* **16/1**

0-00 **9** *7* **Gower Valentine**[17] 2443 3-9-7 **75** AdrianTNicholls 5 21
(D Nicholls) *midfield: rdn over 2f out: sn btn* **10/1**

00-0 **10** *6* **Bun Penny**[19] 2375 3-8-2 **56** oh11 DuranFentiman 9 —
(G M Moore) *chsd ldrs tl rdn and wknd fr 2f out* **100/1**

0-30 **11** *10* **Gore Hill (IRE)**[54] 1455 3-8-2 **56** oh1 AndrewElliott 10 —
(K R Burke) *chsd ldrs to 1/2-way: sn lost pl* **33/1**

1m 13.66s (-0.04) **Going Correction** +0.125s/f (Good) **11** Ran SP% **119.5**
Speed ratings (Par 99): **105,104,102,101,98 95,89,89,79,71 58**
toteswinger: 1&2 £8.70, 1&3 £10.20, 2&3 £9.10. CSF £45.11 CT £324.87 TOTE £5.10: £2.40, £4.00, £1.60; EX 48.20 Place 6: £15.37 Place 5: £7.59.
Owner Andrew Tinkler **Bred** R G Levin **Trained** Denton, Co Durham

FOCUS
A low-grade sprint handicap in which the front pair were always 1-2. The runner-up is the best guide, with the winner up 5lb.
Jimwil(IRE) Official explanation: jockey said gelding missed the break
T/Plt: £13.90 to a £1 stake. Pool: £53,148.27. 2,777.35 winning tickets. T/Qpdt: £3.60 to a £1 stake. Pool: £5,230.29. 1,069.56 winning tickets. RY

1968 WARWICK (L-H)
Monday, June 15

OFFICIAL GOING: Good to soft
Wind: Almost nil Weather: Showers

2971 RACING UK AMATEUR RIDERS' H'CAP 1m 4f 134y
6:40 (6:40) (Class 6) (0-60,60) 4-Y-O+ **£1,977** (£608; £304) **Stalls Low**

Form RPR

0240 **1** **Drawn Gold**[17] 2445 5-10-13 **57** MrStephenHarrison(5) 4 66
(R Hollinshead) *mde all: pushed along over 3f out: edgd rt towards stands' side over 2f out: rdn wl over 1f out: drvn out* **4/1**[1]

3502 **2** *1¼* **Jackie Kiely**[13] 2580 8-11-0 **53** (t) WilliamBiddick 2 60
(R Brotherton) *hld up towards rr: hdwy on ins over 4f out: carried rt 2f out: sn rdn: ev ch 1f out: nt qckn towards fin* **9/1**

0034 **3** *2* **Sand Repeal (IRE)**[28] 2127 7-11-0 **58** MrRBirkett(5) 12 62
(Miss J Feilden) *w ldrs: rdn over 3f out: kpt on same pce ins fnl f* **7/1**[3]

000- **4** *¾* **Jenny Soba**[222] 7202 6-11-2 **60** MrJPFeatherstone(5) 3 63
(Lucinda Featherstone) *s.i.s: hld up in rr: hdwy on ins 4f out: rdn 2f out: one pce ins fnl f* **16/1**

3204 **5** *¾* **Pertemps Power**[7] 2762 5-11-0 **53** MrSWalker 6 55
(B G Powell) *a.p: chsd wnr 3f out: rdn 2f out: ev ch whn edgd rt over 1f out: wknd ins fnl f* **8/1**

1463 **6** *1* **Barbirolli**[11] 2634 7-10-10 **52** MrBenBrisbourne(3) 1 52
(W M Brisbourne) *hld up in mid-div: sme hdwy over 1f out: rdn and no further prog fnl f* **5/1**[2]

6650 **7** *1 ¼* **Wester Lodge (IRE)**[24] 2244 7-10-8 **54** MrHAEustace(7) 10 53+
(J M P Eustace) *hld up in tch: lost pl over 4f out: rallied on ins over 1f out: wknd wl ins fnl f* **11/1**

00-1 **8** *7* **Promise Maker (USA)**[12] 2609 4-11-0 **60** MrMKing(7) 13 48
(T D Walford) *w wnr tl rdn 3f out: sn wknd* **15/2**

000- **9** *1* **Liberty Seeker (FR)**[29] 7376 10-10-11 **55** (p) MissABevan(5) 11 42
(John A Harris) *hld up in mid-div: wknd 4f out* **100/1**

4-55 **10** *4 ½* **Flowerbud**[55] 1430 4-10-11 **53** MissIsabelTompsett(3) 9 33
(G A Ham) *w ldrs: lost pl over 8f out: bhd fnl 6f* **20/1**

03/6 **11** *14* **Captain Oats (IRE)**[12] 2608 6-10-7 **53** MrKFord(7) 8 12
(Mrs P Ford) *a towards rr: no ch fnl 4f* **33/1**

620 **12** *½* **Kirstys Lad**[6] 2783 7-10-11 **55** MissMMullineaux(5) 7 13
(M Mullineaux) *hld up in mid-div: lost pl over 6f out: no ch fnl 4f* **14/1**

4-40 **13** *8* **Swords**[147] 219 7-10-6 **52** MissSPeacock(7) 5 —
(R E Peacock) *stdd s: a in rr: lost tch 3f out* **22/1**

2m 49.46s (4.86) **Going Correction** +0.05s/f (Good) **13** Ran SP% **116.0**
Speed ratings (Par 101): **87,86,85,84,84 83,82,78,77,75 66,66,61**
toteswinger: 1&2 £7.50, 1&3 £14.20, 2&3 £19.40. CSF £37.06 CT £245.16 TOTE £5.30: £2.10, £2.50, £4.00; EX 47.50.
Owner Tim Leadbeater **Bred** Longdon Stud Ltd **Trained** Upper Longdon, Staffs

FOCUS
A warm, humid evening but a total of 9mm of rain in 12 hours prior to racing changed the going markedly from good to firm (good in places), to good to soft all over. A poor amateur riders' handicap run at a fair early pace, and plenty finished leg-weary. The riders reported it rode as advertised. The winner only needed to match his recent form.

2972 EUROPEAN BREEDERS' FUND MAIDEN FILLIES' STKS 5f
7:10 (7:11) (Class 5) 2-Y-0 **£3,885** (£1,156; £577; £288) **Stalls** Low

Form RPR

33 **1** **Deal (IRE)**[34] 1968 2-9-0 0 EddieAhern 10 81
(R Hannon) *hld up: rdn and hdwy on stands' side 1f out: r.o u.p to ld ins fnl f* **16/1**

32 **2** *1 ¾* **Aalsmeer**[31] 2054 2-9-0 0 RichardMullen 9 75
(E S McMahon) *bhd: swtchd rt 2f out: hdwy and rdn over 1f out: ev ch ins fnl f: nt qckn* **8/11**[1]

0 **3** *2 ¼* **Val C**[12] 2604 2-9-0 0 JohnEgan 7 67
(N P Littmoden) *a.p: rdn and edgd lft over 1f out: ev ch ins fnl f: no ex towards fin* **14/1**

0 **4** *½* **Totally Invincible (IRE)**[20] 2354 2-9-0 0 GregFairley 4 65+
(E S McMahon) *w ldr: led wl over 2f out: rdn whn j. path jst over 1f out: hdd wl ins fnl f: no ex* **33/1**

5 *2 ½* **Excellent Thought** 2-9-0 0 MichaelHills 5 56+
(W J Haggas) *s.i.s: bhd: pushed along over 3f out: hdwy on ins 2f out: j. path jst over 1f out: wknd ins fnl f* **8/1**[3]

32 **6** *2* **Velvet Band**[12] 2604 2-9-0 0 NCallan 6 49+
(P F I Cole) *prom: rdn over 1f out: wknd ins fnl f* **4/1**[2]

56 **7** *1 ¼* **Monte Mayor One**[28] 2135 2-9-0 0 AdamKirby 2 44
(D Haydn Jones) *prom tl wknd ins fnl f* **40/1**

8 *1 ¼* **Satin Princess (IRE)** 2-8-11 0 RussellKennemore(3) 8 40
(Paul Mason) *s.i.s: pushed along and short-lived effrt over 1f out* **66/1**

9 *2 ¼* **Virginia Hall** 2-9-0 0 SebSanders 1 32
(Sir Mark Prescott) *led: hdd wl over 2f out: rdn and wknd over 1f out* **11/1**

61.23 secs (1.63) **Going Correction** +0.20s/f (Good) **9** Ran SP% **116.8**
Speed ratings (Par 90): **94,91,87,86,82 79,77,75,72**
toteswinger: 1&2 £4.70, 1&3 £32.30, 2&3 £4.40. CSF £28.47 TOTE £11.60: £3.60, £1.02, £5.00; EX 26.70.
Owner Mrs Madeleine Mangan **Bred** Mrs M M Mangan **Trained** East Everleigh, Wilts

FOCUS
A good maiden run at a fair pace for the easy ground, where previous experience and the draw played a significant part. As with the first race, the first two came up the stands' rail.

NOTEBOOK
Deal(IRE), who was dropping in trip, having been beaten over half a furlong further here last time, had the benefit of a wide draw and was clearly suited by the softer ground. Though she took her time to get going, her rider never had to get too serious with her and she won a shade cosily. This represented a significant improvement and she is clearly going the right way. A step up in class beckons. (op 14-1)
Aalsmeer, as it turned out, had no excuses with the wide draw. Keen to post and fractious before the start, she missed the break. She still looked a little green and became a little unbalanced when she was produced on the inside of the winner two furlongs out, this looked a regressive display. However, she looks the type to improve with experience and is not one to lose faith with just yet. (tchd 4-5 in places)
Val C finished a little way behind the principals but improved from her Nottingham debut and landed a few hefty each-way bets. She hung left in the closing stages but stuck on well. The ground would probably be soft enough for her. (op 40-1)
Totally Invincible(IRE) helped set the pace and was in front when she jumped the path approaching the furlong marker and became unbalanced. She was eased thereafter but this was an encouraging effort. (op 50-1)
Excellent Thought, on her toes in the paddock, made a promising debut and would have learned plenty. There are certainly races to be won with her. (op 7-1)
Velvet Band set the pace but was eased once her chance had gone. (op 5-1)
Monte Mayor One caught the eye under tender handling. She will be interesting when she runs in nurseries. (op 50-1 tchd 33-1)

2973 TURFTV FILLIES' H'CAP 6f
7:40 (7:41) (Class 6) (0-65,65) 3-Y-0 **£2,047** (£604; £302) **Stalls** Low

Form RPR

-132 **1** **Sarasota Sunshine**[7] 2776 3-9-4 **62** (b[1]) JohnEgan 15 68
(N P Littmoden) *hld up in tch: nt clr run and swtchd lft over 1f out: r.o u.p to ld towards fin: drvn out* **5/1**[1]

5364 **2** *¾* **Itsher**[7] 2776 3-8-6 **55** (b[1]) WilliamCarson(5) 13 58
(S C Williams) *hld up in tch on outside: jnd ldrs whn brought to stands' rail over 2f out: sn rdn: led jst over 1f out: hdd and nt qckn towards fin* **6/1**[2]

3352 **3** *1* **Aahaygirl (IRE)**[11] 2624 3-9-0 **63** (b) MartinLane(5) 7 63
(K R Burke) *wnt rt s: w ldr: led 3f out: hrd rdn whn edgd rt and hdd jst over 1f out: kpt on ins fnl f* **6/1**[2]

2-05 **4** *½* **Like For Like (IRE)**[10] 2654 3-8-11 **55** DarryllHolland 10 53
(R J Hodges) *hmpd s: towards rr: stdy hdwy 3f out: sn pushed along: rdn and kpt on ins fnl f* **12/1**

05-5 **5** *2* **Majestic Lady (IRE)**[27] 2151 3-9-1 **59** MichaelHills 8 51
(B W Hills) *w ldrs: rdn whn hmpd jst over 1f out: one pce* **7/1**[3]

4000 **6** *1 ½* **Peninsula Girl (IRE)**[6] 2797 3-8-13 **57** EdwardCreighton 4 44
(M R Channon) *bhd: pushed along 3f out: rdn and sme hdwy 2f out: nvr trbld ldrs* **16/1**

-422 **7** *½* **Top Flight Splash**[13] 2577 3-8-9 **53** (v) DaleGibson 3 39
(Mrs G S Rees) *prom: pushed along over 1f out: rdn and wknd wl ins fnl f* **10/1**

5504 **8** *2* **Bees River (IRE)**[10] 2654 3-8-12 **56** RichardMullen 1 35
(A P Jarvis) *led 3f: rdn over 1f out: wknd ins fnl f* **10/1**

0455 **9** *¾* **Freepressionist**[9] 2712 3-9-3 **61** EddieAhern 11 38
(R A Teal) *bmpd s: mid-div: pushed along over 2f out: rdn over 1f out: wknd fnl f* **7/1**[3]

0-00 **10** *6* **Glorious Dreams (USA)**[31] 2058 3-9-7 **65** GregFairley 9 23
(T J Pitt) *hmpd s: rdn 2f out: a in rr* **50/1**

4200 **11** *5* **Tillers Satisfied (IRE)**[10] 2683 3-8-6 **57** (p) DavidKenny(7) 5 —
(R Hollinshead) *rdn 2f out: a towards rr* **40/1**

4-60 **12** *1 ¾* **Golden Pool (IRE)**[13] 2577 3-8-8 **52** FrancisNorton 6 —
(S A Callaghan) *a in rr* **11/1**

060- **13** *3 ¼* **Milly Rose**[327] 4304 3-8-7 **58** MatthewDavies(7) 2 —
(George Baker) *mid-div on ins: pushed along after 2f: sn struggling and bhd* **20/1**

1m 13.89s (2.09) **Going Correction** +0.20s/f (Good) **13** Ran SP% **119.5**
Speed ratings (Par 94): **94,93,91,91,88 86,85,83,82,74 67,65,60**
toteswinger: 1&2 £9.30, 1&3 £4.10, 2&3 £8.90. CSF £33.36 CT £193.69 TOTE £5.70: £1.60, £3.80, £2.70; EX 46.40.
Owner Franconson Partners **Bred** London Thoroughbred S'Vces Ltd & West Bl **Trained** Newmarket, Suffolk
■ Stewards' Enquiry : Martin Lane two-day ban: careless riding (Jun 29-30)

FOCUS
A moderate handicap in which, as in the previous two races, the ground again meant there was a draw bias favouring those drawn up the stands' side. The first two ran to their Windsor form.

2974 PRICEWATERHOUSECOOPERS WARWICKSHIRE OAKS STKS (LISTED RACE) (F&M) 1m 2f 188y
8:10 (8:11) (Class 1) 4-Y-0+
£22,708 (£8,608; £4,308; £2,148; £1,076; £540) **Stalls** Low

Form RPR

0-03 **1** **Cassique Lady (IRE)**[16] 2482 4-8-12 102 EddieAhern 5 102
(Mrs L Wadham) *s.i.s: hld up: smooth prog over 4f out: wnt 2nd 3f out: led wl over 1f out: sn rdn: drvn out* **3/1**[2]

5235 **2** *½* **Princess Taylor**[16] 2482 5-8-12 97 AlanMunro 3 101
(M Botti) *hld up: hdwy 2f out: rdn over 1f out: ev ch ins fnl f: r.o* **11/2**[3]

5122 **3** *hd* **Lady Jane Digby**[9] 2697 4-8-12 98 GregFairley 2 101
(M Johnston) *hld up in tch: nt clr run on ins and clipped heels over 3f out: rdn over 2f out: ev ch 1f out: rdr had whip knocked out of his hand wl ins fnl f: r.o* **7/4**[1]

06 **4** *14* **Lady Deauville (FR)**[42] 1758 4-9-3 103 DarryllHolland 6 79
(R Curtis) *a.p: led 4f out: rdn and hdd wl over 1f out: sn wknd* **6/1**

40-2 **5** *3* **Hobby**[51] 1523 4-8-12 98 (p) SebSanders 9 68
(R M Beckett) *t.k.h: led 1f: chsd ldr to 6f out: rdn 3f out: sn wknd* **10/1**

00/0 **6** *6* **Athlone (IRE)**[16] 2482 5-9-1 94 DaneO'Neill 8 60
(L M Cumani) *led after 1f: rdn and hdd wl over 1f out: sn wknd* **16/1**

6-40 **7** *2 ¼* **Syvilla**[16] 2482 4-8-12 90 RichardMullen 7 53
(Rae Guest) *hld up: rdn wl over 2f out: sn bhd* **12/1**

2m 18.84s (-2.26) **Going Correction** +0.05s/f (Good) **7** Ran SP% **113.7**
Speed ratings (Par 111): **110,109,109,99,97 92,91**
toteswinger: 1&2 £4.10, 1&3 £1.60, 2&3 £1.90. CSF £19.50 TOTE £4.10: £2.30, £2.60; EX 24.10.
Owner Mr And Mrs A E Pakenham **Bred** P Syndicate **Trained** Newmarket, Suffolk

FOCUS
This was run at a fair clip for the easy ground, and the front three pulled well clear. Probably not strong Listed form.

NOTEBOOK
Cassique Lady(IRE) clearly appeared to relish this easier test of stamina than she encountered at Haydock last time. Pulling hard early after falling out of the stalls, she eventually settled at the rear and was still last turning in. Her jockey made a dart for the stands' rail and she stayed on doggedly. She is clearly improving and though she would appreciate faster ground, she handled this easy surface well enough. She should be able to handle a step up in class and the Group 3 Lily Langtry at Goodwood looks an obvious target, though connections may head to France. She is still unfurnished and once she fills her frame, she might get further. Long-term plans are to visit Derby winner Sir Percy. (op 10-3 tchd 9-2)
Princess Taylor, considering the ground was as easy as she would want it, produced another fine performance, making up good headway in the straight and only just failing. She has proved vulnerable in handicaps but this was much her best performance and she appears capable of winning at this level, if not at a higher grade. She travels well enough to think she will get further. (op 10-1)
Lady Jane Digby was shuffled back when Athlone back-pedalled approaching the bend, and when she did find daylight, she was forced to come between horses and her rider had his whip knocked out of his hand by Eddie Ahern inside the final furlong. She may have finished closer and arguably would have won. Either way, it was a commendable effort, and she is clearly up to winning races of this nature. (op 2-1 tchd 11-8)
Lady Deauville(FR) helped set the pace but faded approaching a furlong and a half out. She had no excuses in this ground. Official explanation: jockey said filly ran too free (op 11-2 tchd 4-1)
Hobby would have appreciated further and found the principals too sharp and was eased once her chance had gone. (op 11-1 tchd 14-1)
Syvilla Official explanation: jockey said filly had no more to give

2975 WARWICK FOR CONFERENCES H'CAP 1m 2f 188y
8:40 (8:41) (Class 6) (0-65,65) 4-Y-0+ **£2,047** (£604; £302) **Stalls** Low

Form RPR

4133 **1** **Coral Shores**[15] 2517 4-9-3 **61** (v) EddieAhern 1 69
(P W Hiatt) *mde all: c to stands' rail 2f out: sn rdn: r.o wl* **3/1**[1]

00/6 **2** *1 ¼* **Arab League (IRE)**[21] 2318 4-8-4 **48** FrancisNorton 11 53+
(R J Price) *hld up in mid-div: pushed along and lost pl over 7f out: rdn and hdwy wl over 1f out: styd on wl to take 2nd nr fin: nt trble wnr* **33/1**

-002 **3** *½* **Carmela Maria**[7] 2762 4-9-2 **60** SaleemGolam 12 64
(S C Williams) *a.p: chsd wnr 3f out: rdn over 1f out: nt qckn ins fnl f: lost 2nd nr fin* **11/1**

2520 **4** *2* **Star Choice**[22] 2294 4-9-0 **65** (v) SimonPearce(7) 2 65
(J Pearce) *hld up in mid-div: hdwy on ins 3f out: rdn wl over 1f out: sn edgd rt: no ex wl ins fnl f* **9/1**

2550 **5** *8* **Sudden Impulse**[9] 2724 8-9-1 **59** SebSanders 6 44
(A D Brown) *hld up in tch: rdn and wknd 2f out* **9/2**[2]

005 **6** *shd* **Karmei**[12] 2608 4-7-9 **46** oh1 CharlesEddery(7) 4 31
(R Curtis) *s.i.s: hld up in mid-div: rdn 3f out: wknd 2f out* **20/1**

000 **7** 3/4 **Paul's Pet**[21] 2317 4-9-2 **60** .... DarryllHolland 7 44
(Karen George) *s.i.s: hld up in rr: rdn and hdwy 2f out: edgd rt over 1f out: sn wknd* **33/1**

0000 **8** 9 **Autumn Charm**[54] 341 4-8-4 **48** oh1 ow2 ....(v) NeilChalmers 5 14
(Lucinda Featherstone) *a towards rr* **100/1**

0-63 **9** 1 1/4 **Tevez**[8] 2739 4-9-1 **59** ....(b) NCallan 13 23
(D Donovan) *hld up in tch: rdn 3f out: wknd wl over 1f out* **7/1**

3350 **10** 19 **Lord Theo**[18] 2400 5-9-4 **62** ....(v[1]) JohnEgan 9 —
(N P Littmoden) *chsd wnr to 3f out: sn wknd: eased wl over 1f out* **12/1**

-260 **11** 2 1/2 **The Staffy (IRE)**[20] 2352 4-9-5 **63** .... GregFairley 8 —
(N J Vaughan) *hld up in mid-div: rdn over 3f out: sn struggling* **14/1**

4-35 **12** 18 **Dusk**[85] 476 4-9-5 **63** ....(b) DaneO'Neill 14 —
(Mrs S J Humphrey) *a in rr: eased whn no ch fnl 3f* **33/1**

30-6 **13** 1/2 **Top Man Dan (IRE)**[24] 2233 4-8-6 **50** ....(t) EdwardCreighton 10 —
(T D Walford) *a in rr: t.o fnl 3f* **5/1**[3]

2m 21.34s (0.24) **Going Correction** +0.05s/f (Good) **13** Ran SP% **119.6**
Speed ratings (Par 101): **101,100,99,98,92 92,91,85,84,70 68,55,55**
toteswinger: 1&2 £18.70, 1&3 £7.10, 2&3 £27.40. CSF £122.30 CT £985.30 TOTE £3.20: £1.30, £7.10, £2.60; EX 92.70.
Owner P W Hiatt & Charlotte Bird **Bred** Cheveley Park Stud Ltd **Trained** Hook Norton, Oxon

FOCUS
A weak handicap run at a muddling pace and the victory owed much to jockeyship. The winner pretty much repeated last month's win here, and this is modest form.
Lord Theo Official explanation: jockey said gelding ran too free
Top Man Dan(IRE) Official explanation: jockey said gelding hung left and had a breathing problem

2976 CHAMPAGNE LANSON H'CAP 7f 26y

9:10 (9:11) (Class 4) (0-85,83) 4-Y-0+ **£6,476** (£1,927; £963; £481) **Stalls** Low

Form RPR

-250 **1** **Ocean Transit (IRE)**[11] 2639 4-8-12 **74** .... JamesDoyle 4 82
(R J Price) *mde all: wnt rt towards stands' side wl over 1f out: sn rdn: hld on wl* **16/1**

-103 **2** hd **Den's Gift (IRE)**[17] 2434 5-9-6 **82** ....(b) AdamKirby 2 89
(C G Cox) *a.p: wnt 2nd over 2f out: rdn and ev ch fnl f: r.o* **11/4**[1]

6621 **3** 1 1/4 **Bold Cross (IRE)**[4] 2842 6-9-0 **76** 6ex .... PaulFitzsimons 3 80
(E G Bevan) *hld up in mid-div: smooth hdwy over 2f out: rdn and nt qckn ins fnl f* **9/2**[2]

0125 **4** 2 **Desert Dreamer (IRE)**[3] 2883 8-8-8 **75** .... RichardEvans(5) 10 73
(P D Evans) *s.i.s: hld up in rr: hdwy 2f out: rdn over 1f out: one pce ins fnl f* **6/1**[3]

5315 **5** 2 1/2 **I Confess**[16] 2491 4-9-1 **77** ....(b) JohnEgan 7 68
(P D Evans) *w wnr: lost 2nd over 2f out: wknd over 1f out* **8/1**

5004 **6** 1 **Compton's Eleven**[13] 2565 8-8-8 **70** .... EdwardCreighton 11 59
(M R Channon) *hld up in rr: rdn over 2f out: hdwy over 1f out: wknd ins fnl f* **12/1**

045 **7** 3/4 **Barons Spy (IRE)**[24] 2241 8-9-4 **83** .... DavidProbert(3) 6 70
(R J Price) *hld up in mid-div: rdn over 1f out: wknd fnl f* **8/1**

1430 **8** nse **Trade Centre**[37] 1861 4-8-13 **75** .... EddieAhern 9 62
(W R Muir) *prom tl wknd over 2f out* **10/1**

4403 **9** 4 1/2 **Salient**[19] 2387 5-9-6 **82** .... KirstyMilczarek 12 56
(M J Attwater) *a towards rr* **8/1**

2423 **10** 3 1/4 **Purus (IRE)**[13] 2565 7-9-2 **78** .... NCallan 8 44
(R A Teal) *n.m.r s: sn hld up in tch: rdn and wknd wl over 1f out* **10/1**

1m 25.35s (0.75) **Going Correction** +0.05s/f (Good) **10** Ran SP% **124.2**
Speed ratings (Par 105): **97,96,95,93,90 89,88,88,83,79**
toteswinger: 1&2 £15.90 1&3 £36.70, 2&3 £4.80. CSF £63.91 CT £225.73 TOTE £23.80: £7.00, £1.60, £1.90; EX 125.30 Place 6: £42.90 Place 5: £20.07.
Owner G E Amey **Bred** Mike Channon Bloodstock Ltd **Trained** Ullingswick, H'fords
■ Stewards' Enquiry : Adam Kirby two-day ban: used whip with excessive force (Jun 29-30)

FOCUS
A competitive handicap run at a decent clip. Ordinary form. Half the field ran in the C/D race won by Desert Dreamer last month. As with previous races, the runners made for the stands' side.
T/Jkpt: Not won. T/Plt: £90.40 to a £1 stake. Pool: £64,463.27. 520.26 winning tickets. T/Qpdt: £25.20 to a £1 stake. Pool: £5,373.10. 157.75 winning tickets. KH

2771 WINDSOR (R-H)

Monday, June 15

OFFICIAL GOING: Good to firm (good in places; 8.3)
Top bend dolled out 8yards from innermost line adding 28yards to advertised distances of races of a mile plus.
Wind: Blustery, behind Weather: Fine becoming changeable

2977 TOTALLY MEDIA H'CAP 1m 67y

6:00 (6:00) (Class 5) (0-75,78) 4-Y-0+ **£3,070** (£906; £453) **Stalls** High

Form RPR

4635 **1** **The Cayterers**[16] 2495 7-9-2 **74** .... MCGeran(5) 7 85
(A W Carroll) *hld up towards rr: smooth prog against nr side rail to ld jst over 2f out: rdn out fnl f: a in command* **6/1**[3]

-351 **2** 1 1/4 **Plaisterer**[7] 2773 4-9-8 **78** 6ex .... JackMitchell(3) 1 86+
(C F Wall) *trckd ldrs: forced to go v wd in st: effrt and on terms 2f out: rdn and flashed tail over 1f out: chsd wnr ins fnl f: no imp* **5/2**[1]

0003 **3** 1 1/2 **Hallingdal (UAE)**[7] 2775 4-9-2 **69** .... TPO'Shea 2 74
(J J Bridger) *hld up in rr: rdn and sme prog over 2f out: kpt on fr over 1f out: nt pce to chal* **9/1**

-032 **4** 1/2 **Seasonal Cross**[21] 2330 4-8-4 **57** .... NickyMackay 6 61
(S Dow) *hld up in midfield: prog to chal over 2f out: chsd wnr wl over 1f out: no imp: fdd ins fnl f* **8/1**

-330 **5** nk **Aggravation**[24] 2245 7-8-13 **66** .... RyanMoore 11 69
(D R C Elsworth) *hld up in last pair: stl there and pushed along 2f out: reminder 1f out: sn swtchd lft: rdn and r.o nr fin: nvr nr ldrs* **9/2**[2]

-062 **6** 3/4 **Magroom**[15] 2518 5-8-5 **63** .... Louis-PhilippeBeuzelin(5) 4 64
(R J Hodges) *trckd ldrs: effrt and wl on terms 2f out: nt qckn over 1f out: fdd fnl f* **11/1**

10-0 **7** 1 3/4 **Arthur's Edge**[28] 2144 5-9-5 **72** .... CatherineGannon 3 69
(B Palling) *free to post: led at gd pce: steered wd bnd 3f out: hdd jst over 2f out: fdd over 1f out* **20/1**

0500 **8** 4 **Millfield (IRE)**[10] 2675 6-9-1 **68** .... LPKeniry 8 56
(P R Chamings) *taken down early: s.s: mostly last tl effrt u.p over 2f out: wknd over 1f out* **33/1**

-651 **9** 3/4 **April Fool**[15] 2518 5-9-3 **70** ....(v) RichardThomas 10 56
(J A Geake) *taken down early: chsd ldr: forced wd bnd 3f out: lost pl sn after: wknd wl over 1f out* **8/1**

1-00 **10** 5 **Spotty Muldoon (IRE)**[19] 2387 4-9-1 **68** ....(v[1]) JimCrowley 5 43
(R M Beckett) *prom: tried to chal and forced wd 3f out: wknd rapidly 2f out* **25/1**

1m 43.79s (-0.91) **Going Correction** +0.10s/f (Good) **10** Ran SP% **113.1**
Speed ratings (Par 103): **108,106,105,104,104 103,101,97,97,92**
toteswinger: 1&2 £2.20, 1&3 £9.60, 2&3 £82.40. CSF £20.15 CT £135.70 TOTE £7.40: £2.40, £1.50, £3.50; EX 30.70.
Owner R D Willis and M C Watts **Bred** Acrum Lodge Stud **Trained** Cropthorne, Worcs

FOCUS
With the stand-side rails dolled out 14yds at 6f down to 7yds at winning post and the top bend dolled out 8yds, a further 28yds was added to races over a mile. The ground was good to firm with good patches. A modest handicap but with plenty showing signs of returning to form made this a competitive heat with a couple of confirmed front runners making sure the pace was true. The form looks ordinary but sound enough.
Seasonal Cross Official explanation: jockey said filly was denied a clear run
Arthur's Edge Official explanation: jockey said gelding hung left

2978 SPORTINGBET.COM (S) STKS 6f

6:30 (6:30) (Class 6) 2-Y-O **£2,047** (£604; £302) **Stalls** High

Form RPR

24 **1** **Ragsta (IRE)**[16] 2490 2-8-6 0 .... PatDobbs 14 65+
(R Hannon) *settled bhd ldrs: prog to ld over 1f out: sn wl in command: pushed out* **10/11**[1]

05 **2** 2 1/4 **Hachi**[25] 2201 2-8-6 0 .... LiamJones 6 55
(J L Spearing) *pressed ldr: chal 2f out: chsd wnr over 1f out: kpt on but no imp* **13/2**[2]

6 **3** 1 1/4 **Acting Elegant**[34] 1968 2-8-6 0 .... PaulDoe 1 52
(P D Evans) *dwlt: in tch in midfield on outer: prog 2f out: drvn to take 3rd jst over 1f out: one pce fnl f* **14/1**

4 3/4 **Abbi Jicaro** 2-8-1 0 .... DeanHeslop(5) 10 49
(Mrs L Williamson) *sn wl in rr: rdn and sme prog over 2f out: styd on to take 4th ins fnl f: one pce after* **50/1**

5 nk **Chinoise (IRE)** 2-8-6 0 .... JimmyQuinn 11 48
(P M Phelan) *wl in rr: rdn over 2f out: hanging bdly lft fnl 2f but styd on: nrst fin* **20/1**

06 **6** 2 1/2 **Carries Lass**[15] 2514 2-8-7 0 ow1 ....(b[1]) ShaneKelly 3 42
(J A Osborne) *wnt lft s and early reminders: nvr beyond midfield: modest prog over 1f out: no hdwy after* **40/1**

0606 **7** nk **Saachi's Vision (IRE)**[18] 2414 2-8-7 0 ow1 ....(b) StephenCarson 9 41
(D K Ivory) *mde most to over 1f out: wknd fnl f* **80/1**

0606 **8** 2 **Our Georgie Girl**[4] 2861 2-8-6 0 .... AdrianMcCarthy 13 34
(G G Margarson) *trckd ldrs: cl enough 2f out: grad wknd over 1f out* **66/1**

9 1 1/4 **Cecil's Gift** 2-8-1 0 .... RossAtkinson(5) 8 30
(W G M Turner) *chsd ldrs: no prog 2f out: wknd u.p over 1f out* **33/1**

0 **10** 2 1/4 **Atomic Twister**[6] 2793 2-8-6 0 .... MartinDwyer 4 23
(P F I Cole) *sn outpcd and wl in rr: nvr on terms: plugged on* **20/1**

11 5 **Nicosia** 2-8-6 0 .... CatherineGannon 12 8
(M R Channon) *s.v.s: wl bhd in last: modest late prog* **10/1**[3]

65 **12** 1/2 **China Bay**[8] 2741 2-8-6 0 .... RichardKingscote 7 7
(Tom Dascombe) *prom: rdn bef 1/2-way: wknd over 2f out* **10/1**[3]

0 **13** 1 1/4 **Baby Judge (IRE)**[27] 2147 2-8-11 0 .... LPKeniry 2 8
(R A Harris) *dwlt and bmpd s: keen early and sn pressed ldrs and racd on outer: wknd rapidly wl over 1f out* **16/1**

0 **14** 2 **Jasmine Scent (IRE)**[39] 1810 2-8-8 0 ow2 .... TonyCulhane 5 —
(J A Osborne) *nvr on terms w ldrs: wknd u.p 2f out* **18/1**

1m 14.22s (1.22) **Going Correction** +0.10s/f (Good) **14** Ran SP% **121.3**
Speed ratings (Par 91): **95,92,90,89,88 85,85,82,80,77 71,70,68,66**
toteswinger: 1&2 £1.70, 1&3 £3.10, 2&3 £25.80. CSF £6.14 TOTE £2.00: £1.20, £2.30, £3.20; EX 9.40.Baby Judge was claimed by M. C. Chapman for £6,000. Hachi was the subject of a friendly claim.
Owner Fergus Jones **Bred** Fergus Jones **Trained** East Everleigh, Wilts

FOCUS
A clear-cut winner of this run-of-the mill seller.

NOTEBOOK
Ragsta(IRE), dropped in grade following two fair placed efforts in maidens, was settled just off the pace, travelled smoothly through the field to take it up over a furlong out and scored as she liked which she was entitled to do in this company. She was retained by connections for 12,000gns as they think she is better than this grade and is related to a Group 3 winner. (op 5-6 tchd 4-5, 11-10 and evens in places)
Hachi was well backed when disappointing at Salisbury in a maiden last time but seemed to appreciate this drop to selling class. Although no match for the winner she can make her presence felt if kept to this sphere. (op 10-1)
Acting Elegant did not break that well but was soon in touch, she had her chance over 2f out but could only muster the same pace. (op 25-1)
Abbi Jicaro was always going to struggle after being slow away but she did stay on well from over 1f out to snatch fourth near the finish. (op 80-1 tchd 100-1)
Chinoise(IRE) was soon pushed along to hold her position but despite hanging left she did keep on although never going to trouble the principals. (op 16-1)
China Bay Official explanation: jockey said filly had no more to give
Baby Judge(IRE) Official explanation: jockey said colt hung left
Jasmine Scent(IRE) Official explanation: jockey said filly hung right throughout

2979 EBF SPORTINGBET.COM MAIDEN STKS 5f 10y

7:00 (7:01) (Class 4) 2-Y-O **£4,695** (£1,397; £698; £348) **Stalls** High

Form RPR

622 **1** **Footstepsofspring (FR)**[14] 2547 2-9-3 0 .... RichardHughes 7 83+
(R Hannon) *mde virtually all and racd against nr side rail: pressed fr 1/2-way: rdn over 1f out: and edgd lft: asserted ins fnl f* **8/13**[1]

50 **2** 1 1/2 **Nepotism**[10] 2649 2-9-3 0 .... TGMcLaughlin 5 74
(M S Saunders) *w wnr: rdn 1/2-way: persisted and stl chalng over 1f out: no ex ins fnl f* **25/1**

3 2 1/4 **Belinsky (IRE)** 2-9-3 0 .... PatDobbs 3 69+
(S A Callaghan) *mostly chsd ldng pair: nt on terms fr 1/2-way: styd on but no imp after* **10/1**[3]

4 2 1/4 **Almuntaser (IRE)** 2-9-3 0 .... StephenDonohoe 8 57
(Ian Williams) *dwlt: a abt same pl: pushed along and no imp fr 1/2-way: kpt on* **40/1**

6 **5** 2 1/2 **Split The Pot (IRE)**[24] 2218 2-9-3 0 .... LPKeniry 2 48
(P R Chamings) *a abt same pl: outpcd fr 1/2-way: no imp after* **50/1**

0 **6** 1 3/4 **Wing Of Faith**[16] 2477 2-9-3 0 .... RyanMoore 6 42
(S Kirk) *dwlt: wl in rr and sn outpcd: kpt on fnl f: no ch* **9/2**[2]

7 3/4 **Thaliwarru** 2-9-3 0 .... TonyCulhane 1 39
(G G Margarson) *racd on outer: a towards rr: no prog fr 1/2-way* **33/1**

8 1 1/4 **Glass Of Red (IRE)** 2-8-12 0 .... JimCrowley 9 30
(R M Beckett) *sn detached in last and wl outpcd: kpt on fnl f* **11/1**

9 ½ **Be A Devil** 2-9-3 0................................ MartinDwyer 4 33
(W R Muir) *dwlt: sn outpcd in rr: nvr on terms plugged on fnl f* **14/1**

61.45 secs (1.15) **Going Correction** +0.10s/f (Good) 9 Ran SP% **115.4**
Speed ratings (Par 95): **94,91,88,84,80 77,76,74,73**
toteswinger: 1&2 £5.70, 1&3 £1.60, 2&3 £27.70. CSF £25.30 TOTE £1.80: £1.02, £5.30, £2.40; EX 17.90.
Owner Mrs J Wood **Bred** S R L Unitrade **Trained** East Everleigh, Wilts

FOCUS
A fair maiden but not much strength in depth.

NOTEBOOK
Footstepsofspring(FR) was a warm order to lose his maiden tag after some decent runs in defeat of late, most notably when collared late on at Goodwood. Soon taking up the lead at a fair pace, he had to be shaken up to assert in the final furlong but won with enough in hand. It is difficult to gauge what he actually achieved but at least he has now got off the mark. He will now be stepped up to 6f as connections think a bit of him and believe he has a lot more to offer. (op 4-7 tchd 4-6, 8-11 in places and 4-5 in a place)
Nepotism pressed the winner throughout and stuck to his task well, only relenting inside the final furlong. This was a much-improved effort, he is going the right way at present and if reproducing this run he should be found a little opportunity. (op 33-1)
Belinsky(IRE), a 160,000gns purchase as a yearling, chased the leading pair throughout without finding the necessary pace to mount a challenge. He was not given too hard a time once his chance had gone and it was a satisfactory introduction. (tchd 9-1)
Almuntaser(IRE) struggled to hold his position in midfield but did stick to his task and stayed on well enough in the closing stages. (op 33-1)
Split The Pot(IRE) raced a little keenly early on tracking the leaders and hung left from over one furlong out but was already a spent force.
Wing Of Faith, who was hampered by the winner on leaving the stalls, could never find the pace to get on terms. (op 5-1 tchd 11-2)

2980 CLIC SARGENT H'CAP 6f
7:30 (7:30) (Class 4) (0-80,80) 4-Y-O+ **£4,857** (£1,445; £722; £360) **Stalls** High

Form RPR

6654 **1** **Memphis Man**[14] [2549] 6-8-13 **72**................................ PaulDoe 2 79
(P D Evans) *racd wdst of all: hld up: prog over 2f out: hrd rdn and r.o to chal fnl f: led nr fin* **12/1**

0030 **2** *nk* **Harlech Castle**[23] [2276] 4-9-5 **78**................................(b) JamieSpencer 3 84
(P F I Cole) *hld up in midfield and racd on outer: prog over 2f out: rdn to chal fnl f: upsides nr fin: jst outpcd* **16/1**

3255 **3** *nk* **Don Pele (IRE)**[28] [2137] 7-8-11 **70**................................(p) RobertWinston 13 75
(R A Harris) *chsd ldng trio: hrd rdn 2f out: styd on towards nr side fnl f: nt quite on terms w far side ldrs* **33/1**

-506 **4** *hd* **Carleton**[14] [2549] 4-9-1 **74**................................ RichardHughes 5 78
(W J Musson) *stdd s: dropped in to nr side fr low draw: wl in rr: prog and taken to centre fr 2f out: rdn to chal fnl f: upsides nr fin: outpcd* **4/1**[1]

0-25 **5** *nse* **Valatrix (IRE)**[42] [1733] 4-9-5 **78**................................ JimCrowley 16 82
(C F Wall) *hld up bhd ldrs towards nr side: prog 2f out: taken to centre and pressed ldrs ins fnl f: styd on* **15/2**[3]

6/02 **6** ¾ **Mymumsaysimthebest**[21] [2326] 4-9-7 **80**................................ RyanMoore 10 82
(G L Moore) *pressed ldr: led 2f out and sn grabbed nr side rail: hdd & wknd wl ins fnl f* **9/2**[2]

0-60 **7** 1½ **Polar Annie**[15] [2520] 4-8-13 **72**................................ TGMcLaughlin 8 69
(M S Saunders) *led against nr side rail: hdd and nt qckn 2f out: one pce after* **25/1**

2235 **8** ½ **War And Peace (IRE)**[30] [2088] 5-8-7 **72**................................ AndreaAtzeni(5) 15 67
(Jane Chapple-Hyam) *awkward s: sn in tch in midfield: rdn and nt qckn 2f out: kpt on same pce in centre fnl f* **12/1**

-240 **9** *shd* **The Galloping Shoe**[23] [2274] 4-9-6 **79**................................ TPQueally 4 74
(J Noseda) *wl in rr: reminder 2f out and again 1f out: kpt on but nvr on terms w ldrs* **15/2**[3]

5400 **10** ¾ **Digital**[2] [2929] 12-8-8 **67**................................ TonyCulhane 6 60
(M R Channon) *sn outpcd in last pair: racd towards far side and plugged on fr over 1f out* **25/1**

6065 **11** *nk* **Lethal**[2] [2908] 6-8-8 **67**................................ StephenCarson 14 59
(Andrew Reid) *trckd ldng pair to 1/2-way: lost pl and reminders 2f out: no prog 1f out: fdd* **40/1**

5650 **12** 4½ **Dvinsky (USA)**[18] [2396] 8-8-10 **69**................................(b) JimmyQuinn 12 46
(P Howling) *mistimed break: wl in rr: no prog fr 2f out* **20/1**

-200 **13** ½ **Buxton**[25] [2188] 5-9-4 **77**................................(t) RobertHavlin 11 53
(R Ingram) *hld up in midfield: no prog over 2f out: wknd over 1f out* **16/1**

3630 **14** 20 **Mogok Ruby**[37] [1864] 5-9-2 **78**................................ JamesMillman(3) 7 —
(L Montague Hall) *pressed ldrs on outer: rdn over 2f out: wknd over 1f out: eased: t.o* **33/1**

1m 13.08s (0.08) **Going Correction** +0.10s/f (Good) 14 Ran SP% **121.9**
Speed ratings (Par 105): **103,102,102,101,101 100,98,98,98,97 96,90,90,63**
toteswinger: 1&2 £10.70, 1&3 £14.50, 2&3 £40.20. CSF £175.36 CT £6203.49 TOTE £10.80: £3.50, £2.60, £7.40; EX 99.80.
Owner M D Jones **Bred** R T And Mrs Watson **Trained** Pandy, Monmouths

FOCUS
A tricky contest with so many of the runners capable of winning this sprint off their marks, and Polar Annie took them along at a good pace. The form looks ordinary but sound enough.
Don Pele(IRE) Official explanation: vet said gelding was found to be lame
Mymumsaysimthebest Official explanation: jockey said gelding hung right throughout
Lethal Official explanation: jockey said gelding hung badly right
Dvinsky(USA) Official explanation: jockey said gelding hit the gates and was subsequently slowly away
Mogok Ruby Official explanation: jockey said gelding had no more to give

2981 YOU MAKE ME SMILE MAIDEN STKS 1m 2f 7y
8:00 (8:03) (Class 5) 3-Y-O+ **£2,729** (£806; £403) **Stalls** Low

Form RPR

1 **Plymouth Rock (IRE)** 3-9-0 0................................ ShaneKelly 14 79+
(J Noseda) *hld up in chsng gp: gd prog fr 3f out: clsd to dispute ld over 1f out: pushed along and readily asserted fnl f* **15/2**[3]

56 **2** 1 **Golden Rock (IRE)**[32] [2002] 3-9-0 0................................ SteveDrowne 7 77
(R Charlton) *hld up in tch in chsng gp: clsd on ldrs fr 3f out: disp ld and rdn over 1f out: readily hld ins fnl f* **12/1**

3 3½ **Panto Princess** 3-8-9 0................................ FrankieMcDonald 10 65
(H Candy) *dwlt: wl in rr: sme prog on wd outside fr 3f out: r.o wl fr over 1f out: tk 3rd fnl f and clsng at fin* **50/1**

42 **4** 7 **Buckie Boy (IRE)**[11] [2640] 3-9-0 0................................(b) TPQueally 8 56+
(H R A Cecil) *disp ld at furious pce: carried wd bnd over 5f out: led sn after: drew at least 6 l clr 3f out: tired over 2f out: hdd & wknd over 1f out* **7/4**[1]

5 ½ **Monopole (IRE)**[32] 5-9-13 0................................(t) RichardHughes 1 55
(P R Webber) *dwlt: wl in rr: prog fr 3f out: rdn and kpt on: nvr on terms w ldrs* **33/1**

-00 **6** 1½ **Lilleput**[131] [386] 4-9-8 0................................ StephenCarson 3 47
(E A Wheeler) *dwlt: hld up in last pair and wl bhd: sme prog over 3f out: drvn over 2f out: kpt on: nrst fin* **150/1**

0- **7** 1½ **Carbon Print (USA)**[422] [1467] 4-9-13 0................................ JamieSpencer 9 49+
(P R Webber) *dwlt: hld up wl in rr: nudged along and kpt obn steadily fr over 2f out: nrst fin* **17/2**

8 2¼ **Watchoverme** 3-8-9 0................................ JimCrowley 6 40+
(J R Fanshawe) *hld up in rr: stdy prog fr over 2f out: nudged along and rn int trble wl over 1f out: kpt on: nvr nr ldrs* **18/1**

0- **9** 9 **Kaijai (IRE)**[264] [6205] 3-8-9 0................................(t) JerryO'Dwyer 5 22
(Mrs L C Jewell) *t.k.h: chsd clr ldng quartet: wknd over 3f out* **200/1**

0 **10** ½ **Whispered Lands (IRE)**[45] [1638] 3-8-6 0................................ JackMitchell(3) 12 21
(J R Boyle) *prom in chsng gp bhd tearaway ldrs: wknd over 3f out* **200/1**

0/ **11** 8 **Restless Swallow**[641] [5343] 4-9-13 0................................ LPKeniry 13 10
(R A Harris) *t.k.h: hld up in midfield in chsng gp: no prog over 3f out: sn wknd* **200/1**

2-3 **12** 1¾ **Assail**[139] [306] 3-9-0 0................................ TravisBlock 15 6
(H Morrison) *hld up in midfield in chsng gp: no prog 3f out: struggling 2f out: eased fnl f* **15/2**[3]

0 **13** 3 **Mr Kartoffel (IRE)**[21] [2318] 4-9-6 0................................ AmyScott(7) 11 —
(H Candy) *sn last and wl bhd: t.o* **100/1**

5 **14** 2¾ **Stellar Cause (USA)**[30] [2074] 3-9-0 0................................ MartinDwyer 16 —
(P F I Cole) *disp ld at fast pce: hung bdly lft bnd over 5f out: sn hdd: lft bhd by ldr 3f out: sn wknd: t.o* **11/4**[2]

15 8 **Achieved**[153] 6-9-13 0................................ MattieBatchelor 4 —
(D C O'Brien) *chsd clr ldng trio and wl clr of rest: wknd rapidly 1/2-way: t.o* **200/1**

U **Gospel Spirit**[29] 4-9-6 0................................ DannyBrock(7) 2 —
(J R Jenkins) *w ldng pair at frntic pce: hung lft after 3f: crashed into rail and uns rdr over 6f out* **150/1**

2m 9.82s (1.12) **Going Correction** +0.10s/f (Good)
WFA 3 from 4yo+ 13lb 16 Ran SP% **119.2**
Speed ratings (Par 103): **99,98,95,89,89 88,87,85,78,77 71,69,67,65,58** —
toteswinger: 1&2 £42.00, 1&3 not won, 2&3 £75.70. CSF £92.13 TOTE £8.20: £2.10, £4.30, £10.60; EX 53.10.
Owner M Tabor, Mrs J Magnier, D Smith, M Green **Bred** Tullamaine Castle Stud **Trained** Newmarket, Suffolk

FOCUS
A couple of intriguing newcomers against a few with some creditable runs made this an interesting contest on paper, but not many got into it after being set quite a demanding pace. The runner-up is the best guide but the winner can rate a bit higher.
Buckie Boy(IRE) Official explanation: jockey said colt was carried wide on first bend
Carbon Print(USA) Official explanation: jockey said colt pulled too hard early

2982 IRISH EYES ARE SMILING ON 6TH JULY H'CAP 1m 2f 7y
8:30 (8:33) (Class 5) (0-75,74) 3-Y-O **£3,070** (£906; £453) **Stalls** Low

Form RPR

0-04 **1** **Sequillo**[17] [2432] 3-9-3 **70**................................ RichardHughes 11 77+
(R Hannon) *prom: trckd ldr 4f out: led wl over 1f out: jinked rt jst over 1f out: rdn clr ent fnl f: comf* **9/2**[2]

04-0 **2** 2½ **Foxtrot Charlie**[35] [1932] 3-8-13 **66**................................(b) JimCrowley 9 68
(P Winkworth) *trckd ldrs: effrt over 2f out: rdn to take 2nd jst over 1f out: no imp on wnr* **16/1**

30-2 **3** *hd* **Demeanour (USA)**[38] [1834] 3-9-5 **72**................................ RyanMoore 5 74
(E A L Dunlop) *led 3f: chsd ldr to 4f out: taken to outer and effrt over 2f out: rdn and nt qckn over 1f out: kpt on* **5/1**[3]

3230 **4** ¾ **Everaard (USA)**[4] [2863] 3-8-12 **65**................................ JamieSpencer 3 65+
(D R C Elsworth) *hld up in last: pushed along and detached 4f out: sme prog and taken to outer 2f out: kpt on u.p: n.d* **8/1**

3400 **5** *nse* **Gulf President**[21] [2320] 3-8-10 **63**................................(v) TonyCulhane 7 63
(M R Channon) *pushed along early in rr: in tch: hrd rdn and effrt over 2f out: kpt on: nt pce to threaten* **22/1**

-242 **6** 1 **Beaubrav**[5] [2809] 3-8-8 **61**................................ RobertWinston 14 59
(P W D'Arcy) *t.k.h: trckd ldrs: effrt over 2f out: drvn and one pce over 1f out* **7/2**[1]

0-00 **7** 4 **Iron Man Of Mersey (FR)**[16] [2496] 3-8-0 **58**................ AndreaAtzeni(5) 12 48
(A W Carroll) *t.k.h: trckd ldrs: rdn 2f out: nt qckn over 2f out: wknd jst over 1f out* **6/1**

0411 **8** 1 **Mons Calpe (IRE)**[13] [2567] 3-9-7 **74**................................(b) MartinDwyer 10 74+
(P F I Cole) *pressed ldr: led after 3f: hdd wl over 1f out: hld but stl disputing 2nd whn hmpd and stmbld bdly jst over 1f out: nt rcvr* **5/1**[3]

-304 **9** 1½ **Bubses Boy**[16] [2489] 3-8-4 **57**................................ TPO'Shea 2 42
(M L W Bell) *t.k.h: prom: racd wd in st: lost pl 2f out: eased whn no ch fnl f* **16/1**

0-00 **10** 4 **Highland River**[54] [1462] 3-8-7 **60**................................(v[1]) RobertHavlin 1 37
(D R C Elsworth) *a in rr: rdn and struggling wl over 2f out* **25/1**

406 **11** 6 **Solo Choice**[6] [2742] 3-9-1 **68**................................(b) SJCraine 8 33
(D Flood) *hld up in tch: rdn and wknd 3f out* **66/1**

2m 10.15s (1.45) **Going Correction** +0.10s/f (Good) 11 Ran SP% **120.6**
Speed ratings (Par 99): **98,96,95,95,95 94,91,90,89,86 81**
toteswinger: 1&2 £18.40, 1&3 £4.40, 2&3 £24.00. CSF £74.23 CT £380.76 TOTE £5.00: £2.10, £3.90, £2.00; EX 83.50.
Owner White Beech Farm **Bred** Redmyre Bloodstock And S Hillen **Trained** East Everleigh, Wilts

FOCUS
A competitive but ordinary handicap run a fair pace. The form appears sound enough.

2983 SPORTINGBET.COM H'CAP 1m 3f 135y
9:00 (9:07) (Class 5) (0-70,70) 4-Y-O+ **£2,729** (£806; £403) **Stalls** Low

Form RPR

00-4 **1** **Turjuman (USA)**[31] [2039] 4-8-10 **59**................................ TPQueally 1 66
(W J Musson) *hld up in midfield: prog nr side fr 3f out: drvn to ld narrowly against rail ins fnl f: hld on* **11/1**

106 **2** *shd* **Moonshine Creek**[16] [2497] 7-8-13 **62**................................ RobertWinston 2 69
(P W Hiatt) *prom: led over 3f out: edgd lft off rail fr 2f out: hrd pressed over 1f out: narrowly hdd ins fnl f: kpt on wl* **10/1**

3433 **3** *shd* **Watson's Bay**[10] [2684] 4-9-2 **65**................................ JimmyQuinn 6 72
(P Howling) *t.k.h: hld up wl in rr: threaded way through fr over 2f out: c to chal ins fnl f: jst hld* **13/2**[3]

4 3¼ **Kristallo (GER)**[268] 4-8-11 **60**................................ RichardHughes 16 61
(P R Webber) *hld up in midfield: effrt to chse ldrs over 2f out: tried to cl over 1f out: one pce after* **6/1**[2]

-402 **5** *nk* **Drum Major (IRE)**[16] [2497] 4-9-5 **68**................................ RyanMoore 13 69
(G L Moore) *prom: rdn to press ldrs 2f out: nt qckn over 1f out: fdd fnl f* **5/1**[1]

2100 **6** 1 **Filun**[31] [2040] 4-8-11 **65**................................ AndreaAtzeni(5) 4 64
(A Middleton) *trckd ldrs: rdn and effrt over 2f out: cl enough jst over 1f out: wknd ins fnl f* **16/1**

0110 **7** 1 1/2 **Samurai Warrior**[2] 2923 4-8-13 **69** .... AndrewHeffernan(7) 15 66
(P D Evans) *plld hrd: hld up in tch: stl chsng ldrs and rdn over 2f out: fdd jst over 1f out* **10/1**

-004 **8** 4 **Epsom Salts**[7] 2760 4-8-11 **65** .... JackDean(5) 12 55
(P M Phelan) *allowed to s slowly: hld up in last pair: pushed along and modest prog over 2f out: no ch whn rdn over 1f out* **5/1**[1]

-003 **9** 2 1/4 **Ba Dreamflight**[15] 2516 4-8-2 **51** oh1 .... NickyMackay 3 37
(H Morrison) *ldng trio: rdn 4f out: stl pressing 2f out: wknd over 1f out* **16/1**

00-0 **10** 4 1/2 **Polish Red**[30] 2068 5-9-2 **65** .... JamieSpencer 9 43
(Jane Chapple-Hyam) *hld up wl in rr: taken to outer and effrt 3f out: sme prog 2f out: fdd and eased over 1f out* **15/2**

330- **11** 3/4 **Silver Waters**[230] 7060 4-9-2 **65** .... TonyCulhane 11 42
(Tim Vaughan) *hld up in last: detached 4f out: nvr on terms after* **11/1**

000- **12** 2 1/4 **Fantastic Morning**[22] 7461 5-9-1 **64** ....(b[1]) LPKeniry 5 37
(F Jordan) *led to over 3f out: sn wknd* **100/1**

645/ **13** nk **Fixation**[610] 6204 5-8-11 **60** .... SteveDrowne 10 33
(Mrs L C Jewell) *nvr bttr than midfield: rr and struggling 3f out* **66/1**

0 **14** 2 1/4 **Sahara Sunshine**[145] 233 4-9-7 **70** .... IanMongan 7 39
(Mrs L J Mongan) *hld up towards rr: effrt on outer over 3f out: wknd 2f out* **40/1**

045- **15** 3/4 **Crystal Prince**[12] 5630 5-9-7 **70** ....(b) JimCrowley 14 38
(C E Longsdon) *a towards rr: rdn and no prog over 3f out* **50/1**

2m 31.4s (1.90) **Going Correction** +0.10s/f (Good) **15** Ran SP% **126.2**
Speed ratings (Par 103): **97,96,96,94,94 93,92,90,88,85 85,83,83,81,81**
toteswinger: 1&2 £36.70, 1&3 £11.40, 2&3 £18.30. CSF £120.56 CT £793.96 TOTE £16.10: £5.00, £3.40, £3.10; EX 257.90 Place 6: £489.68 Place 5: £282.94.
Owner I Johnson & John D Jacques **Bred** Shadwell Farm LLC **Trained** Newmarket, Suffolk

FOCUS
An open if modest contest run at a an ordinary pace with a lot of the field taking a good hold. The form looks ordinary and muddling.
T/Plt: £263.90 to a £1 stake. Pool: £67,790.75. 187.48 winning tickets. T/Qpdt: £52.10 to a £1 stake. Pool: £5,396.26. 76.60 winning tickets. JN

2984 - 2988a (Foreign Racing) - See Raceform Interactive

LE LION-D'ANGERS (R-H)

Friday, June 12

OFFICIAL GOING: Soft

2989a PRIX URBAN SEA (LISTED RACE) (FILLIES) 1m 3f 110y

2:50 (2:56) 3-Y-O **£26,699** (£10,680; £8,010; £5,340; £2,670)

RPR

1 **Alpine Snow (IRE)**[36] 3-8-11 .... RMarchelli 2 89
(S Wattel, France)

2 1 **Irish Queen (FR)**[22] 2217 3-8-11 .... MGuyon 6 87
(H-A Pantall, France)

3 shd **Liberty Chery**[24] 3-8-11 .... FSpanu 1 87
(J E Hammond, France)

4 1/2 **Inhibition**[34] 1871 3-8-11 .... C-PLemaire 8 86
(A M Balding) *last early bhd slow pce: hdwy on outside to go 3rd 1/2-way: 4th whn hrd rdn over 1f out: kpt on at one pce* **8/1**[2]

5 nse **Satwa Ruby (FR)**[34] 3-8-11 .... TThulliez 7 86
(J De Roualle, France) **9/2**[1]

6 3/4 **Belle Epoch**[68] 3-8-11 .... IMendizabal 4 85
(J-C Rouget, France)

7 3 **Parallel Blossom (FR)**[33] 1916 3-8-11 .... DBonilla 3 80
(P Demercastel, France)

8 1 **Chinese Evergreen (FR)** 3-8-11 .... F-XBertras 5 78
(F Rohaut, France)

2m 29.42s (149.42) **8** Ran SP% **29.3**
PARI-MUTUEL (including 1 Euro stake): WIN 10.40; PL 2.90, 4.00, 2.30; DF 67.40.
Owner Lady O'Reilly & Ecurie De Meautry **Bred** Castlemartin Stud, Skymarc Farm & E De Rothschild **Trained** France

NOTEBOOK
Inhibition, who finished sixth in the Lingfield Oaks Trial following her maiden success, narrowly missed out on earning black type on her first encounter with soft ground. She may be able to earn it on better going.

1859 ASCOT (R-H)

Tuesday, June 16

OFFICIAL GOING: Good to firm (overall 9.4, straight 10.3, round 8.9)
Following 1mm of rain and a further 4mm of watering, the ground was described as Good to firm. Rail alignment on round course dist. inc ny 12yds.
Wind: Light, half behind Weather: Fine

2990 QUEEN ANNE STKS (GROUP 1) 1m (S)

2:30 (2:31) (Class 1) 4-Y-O+
£167,471 (£63,484; £31,771; £15,841; £7,935; £3,982) **Stalls** Centre

Form RPR

-014 **1** **Paco Boy (IRE)**[31] 2076 4-9-0 124 .... RichardHughes 3 125+
(R Hannon) *hld up in midfield: smooth hdwy over 2f out: led wl over 1f out: rdn and edgd rt whn in command ins fnl f: r.o wl* **10/3**[2]

443- **2** 1 1/2 **Cesare**[339] 3940 8-9-0 118 .... JMurtagh 1 121
(J R Fanshawe) *dwlt: hld up: rdn and hdwy on stands' side rail over 2f out: sn led: hdd wl over 1f out: styd on but nt pce of wnr fnl f* **11/1**

11-0 **3** 1/2 **Aqlaam**[31] 2076 4-9-0 113 .... RHills 2 120
(W J Haggas) *lw: sn swtchd lft and handy whn racd alone on stands' rail tl over 5f out: led over 2f out: sn rdn and hdd: styd on u.p: nt qckn ins fnl f* **10/1**

0-11 **4** 1/2 **Main Aim**[17] 2483 4-9-0 116 .... RyanMoore 4 119+
(Sir Michael Stoute) *lw: racd keenly: chsd ldrs: lost pl 3f out: rdn and nt qckn over 2f out: styd on ins fnl f: nt pce to chal ldrs* **5/1**[3]

-220 **5** 4 **Dream Eater (IRE)**[31] 2076 4-9-0 114 ....(t) FrancisNorton 7 110
(A M Balding) *lw: chsd ldr: chal over 2f out: sn rdn: no ex ins fnl f* **20/1**

/111 **6** 13 **Gladiatorus (USA)**[80] 1011 4-9-0 126 .... AhmedAjtebi 9 80
(Saeed Bin Suroor) *lw: led: abt 5l clr over 5f out: pushed along 3f out: hdd over 2f out: losing pl u.p whn bmpd 2f out: sn wl btn* **9/4**[1]

41-3 **7** 3 1/4 **Arabian Gleam**[17] 2483 5-9-0 115 ....(p) SebSanders 6 72
(J Noseda) *swtg: midfield: hung rt and pushed along 1/2-way: effrt to chse ldrs over 2f out: wknd over 1f out* **25/1**

1302 **8** 19 **Alexandros**[31] 2076 4-9-0 116 .... LDettori 8 28
(Saeed Bin Suroor) *in tch: rdn to chal over 2f out: wknd over 1f out: eased fnl f* **13/2**

0-41 **9** 3 3/4 **Mac Love**[11] 2668 8-9-0 110 .... MickyFenton 5 20
(Stef Liddiard) *in rr: pushed along 3f out: nvr on terms w ldrs: eased fnl f* **33/1**

1m 39.31s (-1.29) **Going Correction** +0.20s/f (Good) **9** Ran SP% **112.8**
Speed ratings (Par 117): **114,112,112,111,107 94,91,72,68**
toteswinger: 1&2 £8.40, 1&3 £7.70, 2&3 £12.40. CSF £37.04 CT £271.66 TOTE £4.50: £1.70, £3.10, £3.10; EX 47.20 Trifecta £425.10 Pool: £8,691.61 - 15.13 winning units..
Owner The Calvera Partnership No 2 **Bred** Mrs Joan Browne **Trained** East Everleigh, Wilts

FOCUS
A fascinating Queen Anne to start the meeting, featuring the British debut of Gladiatorus, officially the best horse in the world at present. He was responsible for the rapid early pace which resulted in a winning time 0.49 seconds under Racing Post standard, suggesting the ground was indeed on the quick side. Only Richard Hills aboard Aqlaam came straight over to the stands' rail, but by the time the field reached the 5f pole they had all edged over to the stands' side. A good renewal, and sound form, rated around the placed horses.

NOTEBOOK
Paco Boy(IRE) was already proven at this level and had also proved himself over this trip when beating Dream Eater in the Bet365 Mile at Sandown in April. He also had valid excuses for his two defeats this year, as he had little chance from his high draw and met trouble in running when well behind Gladiatorus and Alexandros in the Dubai Duty Free, and he was found to have an infected off-fore hoof when fourth in the Lockinge. Everything went right for him here, however, as he travelled very nicely in the middle of the field before being produced on the bridle inside the last 2f. As soon as Richard Hughes pressed the button the response was immediate and, though he did hang a little away to his right close to the line, the race was well and truly in the bag by then. The Sussex Stakes is the obvious target, but he is obviously not short of speed and connections are toying with dropping him back to 6f for the July Cup first. (op 7-2)
Cesare has a decent record at the track and was fourth in this last year, but a setback in the spring meant he was returning from an 11-month absence. Connections had been hoping for rain, so this was a smart effort under the circumstances. Having been held up out the back early, he made his move up the fence inside the last 3f and kept on all the way to the line. He is likely to reappear in the Group 2 Summer Mile back here next month, a race he won in 2007 and finished third in last year. (op 10-1 tchd 12-1)
Aqlaam was having his first outing since winning last year's Jersey Stakes when beaten a long way in last month's Lockinge, and he had reportedly been working well since. It was still felt that he would come on again from this, but he was bang there with every chance when the leader dropped out 2f from home, and he kept on well to the line. Connections were rightly delighted by this.
Main Aim was supplemented for this after victories in a Newbury handicap and a Group 3 at Haydock. The form of the latter contest has since been advertised by the runner-up Beacon Lodge, but he still had plenty of questions to answer as not only was this a major step up in class, he was also attempting the trip for the first time. Never far away, he plugged on over the last couple of furlongs and was by no means disgraced, but he didn't really prove his stamina and he may be better over shorter. (op 9-2)
Dream Eater(IRE), who found the ground too soft when beaten a long way in the Lockinge, was beaten less than a length by Paco Boy in the Bet365 Mile at Sandown prior to that but he faced a stiff task in trying to reverse that form on 6lb worse terms. He had his chance until fading inside the last furlong and probably needs to drop back into lesser Group company. (op 25-1)
Gladiatorus(USA) had both Alexandros and Paco Boy behind him when winning the Dubai Duty Free in such devastating style back in March. Representing the stable that had won this seven times since 1996, the big question was whether he would be able to transfer the sort of form he was showing in Dubai earlier this year to this different venue. He was soon ridden into the lead and set a serious pace, but even before reaching the 3f pole his jockey was taking some anxious looks behind him and once headed a furlong later, he folded very tamely. His rider reported that he wasn't half the horse he was in Dubai, but despite this effort he is still to be aimed at the Breeders' Cup in the autumn. Official explanation: jockey said colt ran flat (op 5-2 tchd 11-4)
Arabian Gleam, eighth in this race last year, had a 5lb pull for a three-length beating by Main Aim on his return to action at Haydock last month, but he has still to truly prove that he stays this trip and, although he was close enough on the wide outside passing the 3f pole, he was then left behind. (op 28-1 tchd 33-1 in places)
Alexandros had only just been touched off in last month's Lockinge, finishing ahead of Paco Boy, Dream Eater and Aqlaam, but he was even more disappointing than his stablemate as he stopped very quickly and was eased right off inside the last 2f. He was reported to be lame and will be off until the autumn. Official explanation: jockey said colt lost its action (tchd 7-1 in places)
Mac Love came into this on a high following his victory in the Diomed at Epsom, but this was a much stiffer test and he could never make an impact from off the pace. (op 40-1 tchd 50-1)

2991 KING'S STAND STKS (BRITISH LEG OF THE GLOBAL SPRINT CHALLENGE) (GROUP 1) 5f

3:05 (3:05) (Class 1) 3-Y-O+
£170,310 (£64,560; £32,310; £16,110; £8,070; £4,050) **Stalls** Centre

Form RPR

1 **Scenic Blast (AUS)**[101] 5-9-4 .... StevenArnold 15 127+
(Daniel Morton, Australia) *str: lengthy: lw: patiently rdn towards rr: smooth and rapid hdwy to ld over 1f out: pushed out: impressive* **11/4**[1]

354- **2** 3/4 **Fleeting Spirit (IRE)**[234] 6994 4-9-1 115 .... RyanMoore 1 119
(J Noseda) *lw: dwlt: in rr of main gp tl gd hdwy 2f out: pressed wnr over 1f out: kpt on wl: a hld* **7/2**[2]

4-12 **3** 2 3/4 **Anglezarke (IRE)**[17] 2481 3-8-9 100 .... DavidAllan 2 107
(T D Easterby) *towards rr: sn drvn along: nt clr run and bmpd jst ins fnl 2f: r.o fr over 1f out: nt rch ldng pair* **33/1**

-000 **4** 1/2 **Captain Gerrard (IRE)**[17] 2481 4-9-4 100 .... TomEaves 7 110
(B Smart) *lw: mid-div: rdn and hdwy 2f out: chsd ldrs over 1f out: kpt on* **66/1**

1-32 **5** nk **Borderlescott**[24] 2272 7-9-4 113 .... PatCosgrave 8 109
(R Bastiman) *chsd ldrs: rdn over 2f out: one pce appr fnl f* **10/1**

3/ **6** 1 1/4 **Cannonball (USA)**[46] 4-9-4 ....(t) JRVelazquez 4 104
(Wesley A Ward, U.S.A) *str: swtg: sn outpcd in detached last: hrd rdn 2f out: r.o appr fnl f: nrst fin* **33/1**

0-00 **7** 1/2 **Dandy Man (IRE)**[17] 2481 6-9-4 100 ....(t) LDettori 13 102
(Saeed Bin Suroor) *swtg: in tch: effrt and bdly squeezed over 1f out: kpt on fnl f but nvr able to rcvr* **20/1**

-200 **8** 1/2 **Equiano (FR)**[16] 2523 4-9-4 110 ....(b[1]) MichaelHills 9 100
(B W Hills) *lw: sn led: hdd & wknd over 1f out* **14/1**

4330 **9** 1 1/2 **Wi Dud**[10] 2704 5-9-4 105 ....(b) AlanMunro 11 94
(K A Ryan) *in rr of main gp: nt gng pce 1/2-way: styd on fnl f* **66/1**

11-1 **10** hd **Amour Propre**[45] 1676 3-8-12 114 .... DaneO'Neill 6 92
(H Candy) *lw: chsd ldrs tl wknd over 1f out* **4/1**[3]

0-6 **11** 1/2 **Mythical Flight (SAF)**[30] 2116 6-9-4 .... KShea 3 92
(S g Tarry, South Africa) *in tch: rdn and starting to lose pl whn bmpd jst ins fnl 2f: n.d after* **20/1**

00-1 **12** nk **Spin Cycle (IRE)**[46] 1647 3-8-12 106 .... RichardMullen 14 88
(B Smart) *b: sn pushed along in rr of midfield: n.d fnl 2f* **33/1**

0123 **13** 1 1/2 **Hoh Hoh Hoh**[17] 2481 7-9-4 104 .... RobertWinston 5 85
(R J Price) *lw: dwlt: sn in midfield: rdn 2f out: sn wknd* **33/1**

-131 **14** *4* **Tax Free (IRE)**[16] 2523 7-9-4 111 .... AdrianTNicholls 10 70
(D Nicholls) *chsd ldrs: hrd rdn 2f out: btn whn bdly squeezed over 1f out* **12/1**

-652 **15** *8* **Rievaulx World**[33] 2016 3-8-12 101 .... NCallan 12 37
(K A Ryan) *w ldr: starting to weaken whn bmpd over 1f out: sn bhd* **66/1**

59.54 secs (-0.96) **Going Correction** +0.20s/f (Good)
WFA 3 from 4yo+ 6lb **15** Ran SP% **118.1**
Speed ratings (Par 117): **115,113,109,108,108 106,105,104,102,101 101,100,98,91,78**
toteswinger: 1&2 £3.50, 1&3 £32.40, 2&3 £29.60. CSF £10.29 CT £259.01 TOTE £3.60: £1.70, £2.20, £8.80; EX 15.40 Trifecta £343.70 Pool: £11,266.03 - 24.25 winning units..
Owner Elio Anthony Galante & Partners **Bred** Durham Lodge Thoroughbred Stud **Trained** Australia
■ Australia's third winner of this in four years. Danny Morton and Steven Arnold's first runner/ride in Britain.

FOCUS
The second running of the King's Stand since it was upgraded from Group 2 looked well up to scratch. The pace was predictably furious, which suited the impressive Scenic Blast, whose performance may still be better than the bare result considering he was drawn in stall 15 and the next two finishers emerged from the bottom two boxes. The third and fourth surprised in finishing so close, arguably raising a slight doubt over the form, but Scenic Blast was value for further and rates right up there with compatriots Choisir and Takeover Target.

NOTEBOOK
Scenic Blast(AUS) ◆ had earlier this year completed the same Group 1 Lightning Stakes/Newmarket Handicap double as his compatriots Takeover Target and Miss Andretti before their victories in this, and he duly confirmed himself a top-class sprinter. Not obviously well drawn, he won with more authority than the final margin suggests, travelling very strongly under his usual hold-up ride, effortlessly moving into contention out widest of all inside the final 3f, and looking set to win by upwards of two lengths when hitting the front over a furlong out. He was there plenty soon enough and looked to idle, allowing the runner-up to close near the line, but this was a performance of overwhelming authority. Scenic Blast is equally effective over 6f, but two quick runs wouldn't suit him and he'll wait for the July Cup. It will take a very good one to turn him over. (tchd 3-1 in places)
Fleeting Spirit(IRE), last year's third, came into this without a prep run as she is considered best fresh, and there can be no excuses. Like the winner, she had the race run to suit and, if anything, she's flattered to finish so close to Scenic Blast. Her trainer favours putting her away until the Nunthorpe. (op 4-1 tchd 9-2 in places)
Anglezarke(IRE), whose trainer felt she might just be coming into season, ran a terrific race, confirming herself a rapidly progressive filly. Having been outpaced at halfway, there was much to like about the way she ran on. There could be more to come and she is another for races likes the Nunthorpe.
Captain Gerrard(IRE) finally returned to form, seemingly benefiting from the removal of headgear and, more significantly, the switch to patient tactics.
Borderlescott has been running consistently although below his very best form, achieved in winning last year's Nunthorpe, including when narrowly beaten in the Temple Stakes last time. He again ran creditably but was below his very best. (op 11-1)
Cannonball(USA), a US challenger who had been placed in Grade 3 races at 5f and 5.5f this spring but had won at up to 1m at two, ran on all too late when switched towards the stands' rail, having been well back early.
Dandy Man(IRE) ran better than of late with the headgear left off but still didn't do enough to warrant support in this sort of race. (op 33-1)
Equiano(FR), last year's winner, hasn't been in much form lately and he went off too fast in first-time blinkers. (op 16-1)
Amour Propre appealed as one of the more likely winners, but he proved disappointing, only responding to pressure for about half a furlong, having gone off plenty quick enough and raced quite freely. After winning the Palace House, he missed the Temple Stakes due to unsuitable ground and, on this evidence, he probably could have done with another race to take the freshness out of him. Official explanation: vet said colt lost a front shoe (tchd 9-2)
Mythical Flight(SAF) had won eight times in his native South Africa, including twice in Grade 1 company, but he had been lightly raced in the last 18 months and his last two runs had seen him finish only in mid field in top international races in Hong Kong and Singapore. A front runner who is renowned for his speed, he struggled again here and might not be the force he was. (tchd 22-1 and 25-1 in places)
Tax Free(IRE) was keeping on but still had plenty on his plate when squeezed out over a furlong from the finish and that exaggerated the beaten distance. (op 11-1)

2992 ST JAMES'S PALACE STKS (GROUP 1) (ENTIRE COLTS) 1m (R)
3:45 (3:46) (Class 1) 3-Y-O
£141,925 (£53,800; £26,925; £13,425; £6,725; £3,375) **Stalls** High

Form RPR

4-51 **1** **Mastercraftsman (IRE)**[24] 2288 3-9-0 0 .... JMurtagh 8 124
(A P O'Brien, Ire) *sweating: trckd ldr: kicked into ld over 2f out: sn rdn and pressed: hdd narrowly ins fnl f: battled gamely to regain ld 75yds out: fnd ex fnl strides* **5/6**[1]

-120 **2** *nk* **Delegator**[24] 2288 3-9-0 117 .... JimmyFortune 10 123
(B J Meehan) *lw: hld up: hdwy on inner over 2f out: c between horses to chal over 1f out: wnt abt a hd in front ins fnl f: hdd 75yds out: r.o u.p: hld fnl strides* **4/1**[2]

12-0 **3** *1 ½* **Lord Shanakill (USA)**[45] 1675 3-9-0 116 .... JimCrowley 9 119
(K R Burke) *swtg: in tch: clsd to mount str chal fr over 2f out: sn rdn: styd on same pce fnl 100yds* **20/1**

11-6 **4** *1 ¾* **Evasive**[45] 1675 3-9-0 111 .... RyanMoore 3 115
(Sir Michael Stoute) *lw: hld up in least pl: hdwy over 2f out: swtchd lft to chse ldrs over 1f out: nt quite get to front trio: run flattened out fnl 100yds* **11/2**[3]

31-2 **5** *1 ½* **Intense Focus (USA)**[79] 1022 3-9-0 117 ....(vt) KJManning 4 112
(J S Bolger, Ire) *hld up: rdn and hdwy to chse ldrs whn hung rt over 2f out: one pce fnl f* **12/1**

1302 **6** *1 ¼* **Pure Poetry (IRE)**[17] 2476 3-9-0 109 .... DaneO'Neill 1 109
(R Hannon) *racd keenly: hld up: rdn and sme hdwy over 1f out: nvr able to chal ldrs: kpt on but no imp fnl f* **40/1**

14-3 **7** *7* **Orizaba (IRE)**[9] 2755 3-9-0 116 .... LDettori 7 93
(Saeed Bin Suroor) *swtg: midfield: pushed along over 2f out: no hdwy: wknd over 1f out* **33/1**

10-3 **8** *10* **Soul City (IRE)**[24] 2288 3-9-0 113 .... RichardHughes 5 70
(R Hannon) *broke wl: in tch on outside: pushed along over 2f out: sn wknd* **16/1**

-306 **9** *12* **Born To Be King (USA)**[10] 2729 3-9-0 98 .... CO'Donoghue 6 42
(A P O'Brien, Ire) *bustled along to sn go prom: pushed along 4f out: wknd over 2f out* **200/1**

4-40 **10** *6* **Set Sail (IRE)**[9] 2756 3-9-0 0 .... JAHeffernan 2 29
(A P O'Brien, Ire) *bustled along to sn ld: swtchd rt to run against rail over 5f out: rdn and hdd over 2f out: sn wknd* **100/1**

1m 39.21s (-1.49) **Going Correction** +0.20s/f (Good) **10** Ran SP% **115.1**
Speed ratings (Par 113): **115,114,113,111,109 108,101,91,79,73**
toteswinger: 1&2 £1.70, 1&3 £6.90, 2&3 £11.90. CSF £3.99 CT £35.71 TOTE £1.80: £1.10, £1.60, £5.20; EX 4.60 Trifecta £55.40 Pool: £20,688.12 - 276.07 winning units..
Owner D Smith, Mrs J Magnier, M Tabor **Bred** Lynch Bages Ltd **Trained** Ballydoyle, Co Tipperary
■ Stewards' Enquiry : J Murtagh one-day ban: used whip with excessive frequency (Jun 30)

FOCUS
The inside rail on the round course was positioned three metres out from the inside line from approximately the 1m2f start to where the round course joins the straight. This race has been won by some of the most talented 3yo milers in its history with the likes of Giant's Causeway, Rock Of Gibraltar, Azamour, Shamardal and Henrythenavigator all successful within the past ten years. This year's renewal featured only two previously successful at Group 1 level, however, and the winners of the English and French Guineas were not present, though five of those that ran at Newmarket did line up, including four of the first seven home. With Ballydoyle employing a couple of pacemakers, a strong pace was assured and the final time was almost a second inside Racing Post Standard, just 0.51 seconds outside the course record. The first three all improved on their 2,000 Gineas form, and Mastercraftsman has been rated to a similar level to his Irish Guineas win. The fourth to sixth were close to their marks.

NOTEBOOK
Mastercraftsman(IRE) had gained all five of his previous wins at The Curragh, including the Phoenix Stakes and National Stakes as a juvenile together with a convincing success in very testing ground in the Irish 2000 Guineas last month. Although most of his wins had been on an easy surface, his victory in the Phoenix was on fast ground and these conditions weren't expected to be a problem. He did manage to get himself into a muck sweat beforehand, but it certainly didn't affect him once under way. Content to sit a couple of lengths behind the pacemaker early, he was committed off the final bend but then faced a couple of serious challenges, first from Lord Shanakill and then from Delegator, who narrowly headed him briefly inside the last furlong, but in a manner similar to his predecessor Giant's Causeway, he managed to battle back and force his head in front where it mattered. He has a wide range of options, and stepping up to 1m2f is unlikely to be a problem. (op 8-11 tchd 10-11 in places)
Delegator, around three lengths in front of Mastercraftsman in the 2000 Guineas with Evasive, Pure Poetry and Lord Shanakill further behind, had something to prove again after his moderate performance behind the O'Brien colt in heavy ground at The Curragh, but these conditions suited him much better and he ran a massive race in defeat. Held up off the pace early, he made his move up the inside rail rounding the home bend and looked the likely winner when pulled out to make his effort between the winner and Lord Shanakill. He didn't appear to do anything wrong but, rather like at Newmarket, he was out-battled, or outstayed, by a tip-top colt. It may be that good ground is what he really wants and he deserves to win a Group 1 at some stage. (op 9-2 tchd 5-1 in places)
Lord Shanakill(USA), narrowly beaten by Intense Focus in last season's Dewhurst but a disappointing 12th in the 2000 Guineas following an interrupted preparation, showed his true form this time. Few were travelling better than him turning for home and he had every chance, but couldn't match the front pair inside the last furlong. Already a Group 2 winner as a juvenile, on this evidence he can win again at that level at least and he may now go for the Prix Jean Prat. (tchd 25-1)
Evasive, behind both Delegator and Mastercraftsman when sixth in the 2000 Guineas following a rushed preparation, was held up last early, but although he stayed on well in the home straight, he could never get to the leaders. He was the least-exposed in this field so can probably step up again from this, though he is still to prove that he truly stays 1m. (tchd 6-1)
Intense Focus(USA), a narrow winner from Lord Shanakill in last year's Dewhurst when visored for the first time, missed the Irish Guineas due to the soft ground so hadn't been seen since a beaten favourite in the Leopardstown 2000 Guineas Trial in March. With the visor back on replacing the blinkers, he raced in mid-division early, but when asked to make an effort once into the straight, he was inclined to hang about and didn't find very much. (op 14-1 tchd 11-1 and 16-1 in places)
Pure Poetry(IRE), who had finished runner-up in a Goodwood Listed event against older horses since finishing a fair seventh in the 2000 Guineas, was keen enough at the back of the field early and could only plug on once into the straight. He probably needs to drop back down in grade. (op 50-1)
Orizaba(IRE) had finished a fair third in a Chantilly Group 3 nine days earlier on his debut for Godolphin, but he had a bit to prove on this first try in Group 1 company and was found out.
Soul City(IRE), who enjoyed a very lucrative juvenile campaign, finished a fair third (though comfortably held) behind Mastercraftsman in the Irish 2000 Guineas on his return to action, but his very best form had been achieved with cut and connections were nervous about running him on quick ground. He didn't help himself by doing too much too soon and eventually dropped right out. He is much better than this. Official explanation: jockey said colt was never travelling and hung left (op 20-1)

2993 COVENTRY STKS (GROUP 2) 6f
4:20 (4:21) (Class 1) 2-Y-O
£56,770 (£21,520; £10,770; £5,370; £2,690; £1,350) **Stalls** Centre

Form RPR

1 **1** **Canford Cliffs (IRE)**[32] 2033 2-9-1 0 .... RichardHughes 9 118+
(R Hannon) *w'like: scope: str: lw: racd keenly and restrained in front: mde virtually all: pushed along and qcknd clr fnl 2f: kpt up to work fnl f: impressive* **7/4**[1]

1 **2** *6* **Xtension (IRE)**[18] 2430 2-9-1 0 .... AdamKirby 11 100+
(C G Cox) *lw: sn drvn along in rr: gd hdwy over 1f out: r.o to take 2nd nr fin* **20/1**

22 **3** *¾* **Rakaan (IRE)**[17] 2477 2-9-1 0 .... JamieSpencer 8 98
(B J Meehan) *s.i.s: bhd: swtchd rt and hdwy 2f out: chsd easy wnr 1f out: one pce: lost 2nd nr fin* **28/1**

1 **4** *1 ½* **Moran Gra (USA)**[12] 2643 2-9-1 0 .... KJManning 5 93
(Ms Joanna Morgan, Ire) *str: athletic: in tch: rdn over 2f out: styd on same pce to take 4th ins fnl f* **20/1**

1 **5** *nse* **Treadwell (IRE)**[12] 2636 2-9-1 0 .... ShaneKelly 12 93+
(J A Osborne) *lw: mid-div: rdn 1/2-way: swtchd rt 2f out: nt clr run and swtchd rt wl over 1f out: hrd rdn and styd on: nt pce to rch ldrs* **33/1**

1 **6** *½* **No Hubris (USA)**[33] 2017 2-9-1 0 .... MartinDwyer 2 92
(P F I Cole) *lw: w wnr tl outpcd fnl 2f* **11/2**[2]

11 **7** *¾* **Red Jazz (USA)**[48] 1598 2-9-1 0 .... MichaelHills 3 89
(B W Hills) *w ldrs: rdn over 2f out: wknd 1f out* **11/2**[2]

1 **8** *1 ½* **Fremont (IRE)**[17] 2477 2-9-1 0 .... RyanMoore 6 85
(R Hannon) *mid-div: rdn and no hdwy fnl 2f* **20/1**

21 **9** *1 ¾* **Alrasm (IRE)**[17] 2467 2-9-1 0 .... RHills 4 80
(M A Jarvis) *w'like: scope: str: trckd ldrs: rdn over 2f out: wknd wl over 1f out* **12/1**

21 **10** *2 ¾* **Flying Statesman (USA)**[13] 2588 2-9-1 0 .... PaulHanagan 10 71
(R A Fahey) *lw: trckd ldrs: hrd rdn 2f out: sn wknd* **16/1**

3 **11** *½* **Air Chief Marshal (IRE)**[24] 2286 2-9-1 0 .... JMurtagh 1 70
(A P O'Brien, Ire) *w'like: s.i.s: hdwy and in tch 1/2-way: hrd rdn over 2f out: sn wknd* **11/1**[3]

13 **12** *3 ¾* **Raine's Cross**[19] 2408 2-9-1 0 .... JimCrowley 14 59
(P Winkworth) *swtg: sn rdn along towards rr: n.d fnl 2f* **16/1**

1 **13** *9* **Marsh Warbler**[7] 2784 2-9-1 0 .... LDettori 13 32
(M Johnston) *lengthy: scope: lw: sn outpcd: a in last pair: no ch fr 1/2-way* **16/1**

1m 13.64s (-0.76) **Going Correction** +0.20s/f (Good) **13** Ran SP% **121.5**
Speed ratings (Par 105): **113,105,104,102,101 101,100,98,95,92 91,86,74**
toteswinger: 1&2 £12.30, 1&3 £15.60, 2&3 £64.70. CSF £48.10 CT £773.88 TOTE £2.60: £1.40, £5.20, £8.50; EX 52.90 Trifecta £1325.20 Pool: £7,933.34 - 4.43 winning units..
Owner The Heffer Syndicate **Bred** S And S Hubbard Rodwell **Trained** East Everleigh, Wilts

FOCUS
An outstanding winner - as good as any juvenile we have seen here since the early 90s - and one who is clearly going to take high rank in his division. Much improved form from the next four home too.

NOTEBOOK
Canford Cliffs(IRE) ◆ was plenty keen enough for much of the way and set a gallop that saw many of the other prominent racers in trouble not long after halfway, including the likes of fancied runners No Hubris and Red Jazz. Yet as they dropped back, this Tagula colt visibly quickened from the front, and was ultimately chased home, at a respectful distance, by a couple of rivals who had raced well off the pace for the most part. He's been highly regarded from the moment he did his first bit of work at Richard Hannon's stable and this more than confirmed the impression he made when waltzing in at Newbury first time up. After the race Richard Hughes described him as "by far" the best he's ridden, quite a compliment considering he was aboard Queen Anne winner Paco Boy earlier on the card, and also won a couple of Group 1 sprints on Oasis Dream. He has been rated as good a Royal Ascot juvenile winner as we've seen since the early 90s and looks capable of mopping up the big juvenile races over 6f this year, but whether he will prove as effective over further is questionable, although both his trainer and jockey are confident he'll get 1m. His breeding offers hope (similar pedigree to the stable's recent Easter Stakes winner Pure Poetry), but he'll have to prove he can settle when upped up in distance. His next target is likely to be the Prix Morny. (tchd 15-8 and 2-1 in places)
Xtension(IRE) was badly outpaced before halfway and looked to be going nowhere for much of the contest, but he ran on strongly in the closing stages, confirming the pace set by the winner was very strong. This was a big improvement on the form he showed when successful on his debut at Goodwood and his trainer, who describes him as a lovely horse but lazy at home, will now consider pattern races in the autumn. (op 25-1)
Rakaan(IRE), like the runner-up, stayed on from a long way back, having missed the break and been badly outpaced. He's evidently very useful and should win his maiden next time, but he might not be the easiest to place thereafter. Official explanation: jockey said colt weakened rapidly in the final furlong and had no more to give (op 50-1)
Moran Gra(USA) was worth his place in the line up and ran well, but he wasn't quite good enough. He should stay further. (op 16-1)
Treadwell(IRE) stepped up significantly on the form he showed when winning on his debut over 5f at Sandown and might have been slightly closer with a clearer run. (tchd 40-1 in places)
No Hubris(USA) appeared to pay the price for trying to lay up with the winner and was disappointing. (op 5-1 tchd 6-1)
Red Jazz(USA) appealed as one of the more likely winners but, like No Hubris, he didn't get home after trying to keep tabs on the winner. (op 8-1)
Fremont(IRE), the winner's stablemate, ran okay but seemingly wasn't up to this level. (op 25-1)
Alrasm(IRE), a Doncaster maiden winner, is another who simply wasn't good enough. (op 14-1)
Flying Statesman(USA) could have been expected to fare better. Official explanation: trainer said colt was found to be lame (op 25-1 tchd 33-1 in places)
Air Chief Marshal(IRE) was disappointing, but he might want easier ground - his maiden win came over 7f on testing going. (op 9-1 tchd 12-1)
Raine's Cross got warm and didn't run his race.
Marsh Warbler looked good when winning at Redcar a week earlier, but didn't go a yard this time. Official explanation: jockey said colt was never travelling (op 20-1)

2994 ASCOT STKS (H'CAP) — 2m 4f
4:55 (4:55) (Class 2) (0-95,94) 4-Y-O+

£31,155 (£9,330; £4,665; £2,335; £1,165; £292) Stalls High

Form	Pos	Btn	Horse	Jockey	RPR
6-11	1		**Judgethemoment (USA)**[38] 1863 4-9-5 91 (Jane Chapple-Hyam) *trckd ldrs: pushed along and forced to switch lft over 3f out: swtchd rt 2f out: rdn to ld over 1f out: sn hrd pressed: styd on gamely and on top towards fin* **13/2**[2]	RichardHughes 19	102
2-1	2	½	**Sesenta (IRE)**[23] 2305 5-9-6 90 (W P Mullins, Ire) *swtg: midfield: hdwy over 2f out: rdn to chal over 1f out: upsides wnr ins fnl f: hld towards fin* **10/1**	JAHeffernan 2	100
212/	3	¾	**Royal Rationale (IRE)**[24] 2669 5-8-13 83 (b) (D E Pipe) *hld up: hdwy on wd outside 3f out: rdn and carried sltly lft over 2f out: chal fr over 1f out: styd on u.p ins fnl f: nt quite pce of front 2 towards fin* **20/1**	SebSanders 8	92
6-20	4	3 ¾	**Gala Evening**[41] 1790 7-9-6 90 (J A B Old) *hld up: hdwy 4f out: pushed along 3f out: carried sltly lft over 2f out: chal over 1f out: one pce fnl 100yds* **20/1**	AdamKirby 10	96
50-0	5	4 ½	**Som Tala**[41] 1790 6-9-8 92 (M R Channon) *lw: cl up: rdn over 2f out: wknd over 1f out* **12/1**	LDettori 5	93
0-15	6	2 ¼	**Kayf Aramis**[27] 2177 7-9-1 85 (Miss Venetia Williams) *prom: led 4f out: sn wnt rt: rdn and hdd over 2f out: sn hung lft and regained ld: hdd over 1f out: wknd fnl f* **15/2**[3]	JMurtagh 12	84
02-1	6	dht	**Woolfall Treasure**[44] 1709 4-9-6 92 (G L Moore) *hld up: rdn and stdy hdwy over 2f out: styd on fnl f: nt pce to rch ldrs* **12/1**	RyanMoore 4	91
000-	8	½	**Always Bold (IRE)**[12] 6817 4-9-1 87 (D McCain Jnr) *in tch: pushed along outpcd over 4f out: hdwy over 2f out: edgd rt u.p 1f out: plugged on at one pce wout threatening* **16/1**	PaulHanagan 11	85
10-1	9	1	**Keenes Day (FR)**[58] 1383 4-9-2 93 (M Johnston) *lw: racd in midfield on outside: hdwy 5f out: rdn to ld narrowly over 2f out: sn carried lft and hdd: wknd over 1f out* **6/1**[1]	FrederikTylicki(5) 1	90+
550/	10	3 ¼	**Midas Way**[25] 5800 9-9-6 90 (P R Chamings) *hld up: pushed along 2f out: styd on fr over 1f out: nvr able to trble ldrs* **33/1**	JimCrowley 13	84
0-33	11	5	**Rajeh (IRE)**[44] 1709 6-9-7 91 (J L Spearing) *midfield: u.p 3f out: no hdwy* **25/1**	LiamJones 14	80
0/0-	12	5	**Galient (IRE)**[38] 3104 6-9-3 87 (N J Henderson) *hld up: struggling 3f out: nvr on terms* **20/1**	WilliamBuick 15	71
	13	2 ¾	**Clopf (IRE)**[19] 2427 8-9-0 84 (Andrew Heffernan, Ire) *lw: s.i.s: hld up: hdwy over 5f out: rdn to chse ldrs whn carried lft over 2f out: u.p whn squeezed out over 1f out: wl btn after* **20/1**	WMLordan 6	65+
000/	14	6	**Fire And Rain (FR)**[49] 2182 6-9-4 88 (Miss E C Lavelle) *led: hdd after 2f: remained handy: rdn and wknd over 3f out* **25/1**	AlanMunro 20	63
40-3	15	1 ¾	**Baddam**[27] 1601 7-9-8 92 (Ian Williams) *midfield: hdwy to go handy after 8f: rdn over 3f out: wknd 2f out* **20/1**	IanMongan 18	66
05/3	16	6	**Ermine Sea**[38] 1863 6-9-2 86 (Miss H C Knight) *prom: led after 2f: hdd 4f out: sn n.m.r and hmpd: wknd over 2f out* **10/1**	MartinDwyer 16	54
00-0	17	14	**Missoula (IRE)**[17] 2486 6-8-13 83 (Miss Suzy Smith) *midfield: pushed along 6f out: wknd over 4f out* **25/1**	NCallan 7	37
/30-	18	1	**Liberate**[38] 6817 6-9-3 87 (p) (P J Hobbs) *s.i.s: a bhd* **12/1**	JamieSpencer 3	40
0-0	19	21	**Valentino Rossi (BRZ)**[17] 2501 7-9-10 94 (A G Foster) *prom tl wknd 5f out* **66/1**	GregFairley 9	26
-344	20	8	**Humble Opinion**[13] 2597 7-9-6 90 (A King) *racd keenly: midfield: rdn and wknd 3f out: t.o* **40/1**	DaneO'Neill 17	14

4m 25.55s (4.55) **Going Correction** +0.20s/f (Good)
WFA 4 from 5yo+ 2lb — **20 Ran SP% 128.7**
Speed ratings (Par 109): **98,97,97,96,94 93,93,93,92,91 89,87,86,83,83 80,75,74,66,63**
toteswinger: 1&2 £8.10, 1&3 £29.10, 2&3 £39.10. CSF £59.78 CT £1274.27 TOTE £7.10: £1.90, £2.60, £5.70, £6.40; EX 44.40 Trifecta £716.00 Pool: £9,038.29 - 9.34 winning units..
Owner Gordon Li **Bred** Todd Graves & Michele Graves **Trained** Newmarket, Suffolk
■ Stewards' Enquiry : J Murtagh five-day ban: careless riding (July 1-5); one-day ban: failed to ride out for 6th place (July 6)
Frederik Tylicki three-day ban: careless riding (Jun 30-Jul 2)

FOCUS
As usual a very competitive staying handicap, butthe pace was only a fair one and there were still eight horses almost in a line across the track a furlong and a half from home. Another personal best from the progressive winner, and both the second and third improved in line with their jumps form.

NOTEBOOK
Judgethemoment(USA), bidding for a hat-trick off a 3lb higher mark, was held up in the middle of the field early. Making his move approaching the home turn, he had one anxious moment when he had to take evasive action due to some trouble ahead of him rounding the home bend, but his impetus was barely checked and, once switched inside and produced between horses over a furlong from home, he stayed on very gamely. He doesn't win by far which is handy for his handicap mark, and he is likely to go for the Northumberland Plate later in the month. (op 8-1)
Sesenta(IRE), successful over hurdles and on the Flat last month, had a question mark over her on this ground but after racing in mid-division early, she was produced at just the right time and never stopped battling. She may turn out next in a 2m handicap at The Curragh on Irish Derby day. (tchd 9-1)
Royal Rationale(IRE), having his first outing on the Flat in two years but fit from hurdling, was switched right off out the back early but he put in a powerful late run down the wide outside once into the straight and wasn't beaten at all far. Connections were rightly delighted by this effort and he is likely to return to hurdles now.
Gala Evening, a fair eighth in the Chester Cup last time, is a proven stayer and he was produced to hold every chance in the home straight, but lacked the pace to go with the front trio inside the last furlong. He is 6lb higher than for his last win on the Flat and this effort won't give the handicapper much reason to drop him. (tchd 25-1 in places)
Som Tala, who has gone close in the last two runnings of this, was always up with the pace and he was still there on the inside over a furlong from home before getting left behind. He is without a win since September 2006 and is still 9lb higher.
Kayf Aramis, in fine form over hurdles and on the Flat earlier this year, was a stone higher than when routing the opposition at York last month. Up with the pace from the start, he was committed off the final bend but he could never establish a decisive advantage and, though he battled on for as long as he could, he had nothing left from the furlong pole. (tchd 8-1 and 9-1 in a place)
Woolfall Treasure, fit from hurdling when winning at Salisbury last month, was raised 5lb for that and this was 6f further than he had previously attempted on the Flat. He seemed to be ridden with that in mind, but he made up a lot of ground over the last couple of furlongs and, with his stamina appearing to hold up, it may be worth riding him a bit closer to the pace over extended trips in the future. He has made all over hurdles before now. (tchd 8-1 and 9-1 in a place)
Always Bold(IRE) ◆, a four-time winner on the Flat for Mark Johnston last year, came into this off the back of two recent easy successes over hurdles at up to 3m. He seemed to get shuffled back through the field passing the 5f pole before staying on again too late. He can probably be rated a bit better than the bare result.
Keenes Day(FR), whose last three wins have come on sand, had apparently been laid out for this for a while. He looked likely to win when brought through to lead passing the 2f pole, but once there he tended to hang and his stamina appeared to run out. (op 8-1 tchd 9-1 in places)
Rajeh(IRE) Official explanation: jockey said gelding was denied a clear run
Clopf(IRE), who seemed to be invigorated by a change of stables when successful on his return to the Flat at Leopardstown last month, travelled nicely and had his chance over a furlong from home, but he looked to have run his race when squeezed out soon after.
Ermine Sea, running well on the Flat and over hurdles since returning from over two years off in January, was entitled to go close here. Having made the majority of the running, he was under pressure but not completely done with when badly hampered by Kayf Aramis on the home bend. (op 12-1 tchd 14-1 in places)

2995 WINDSOR CASTLE STKS (LISTED RACE) — 5f
5:30 (5:31) (Class 1) 2-Y-O

£28,385 (£10,760; £5,385; £2,685; £1,345; £675) Stalls Centre

Form	Pos	Btn	Horse	Jockey	RPR
	1		**Strike The Tiger (USA)**[49] 2-9-3 (bt) (Wesley A Ward, U.S.A) *leggy: athletic: mde all: rdn over 2f out: hld on wl fnl f* **33/1**	JRVelazquez 16	101+
1454	2	nk	**Fratellino**[10] 2702 2-9-3 (A J McCabe) *chsd wnr: rdn over 2f out: hung rt over 1f out: kpt on gamely: a jst hld* **33/1**	RobertWinston 2	100
441	3	½	**Di Stefano**[14] 2568 2-9-3 (M R Channon) *lw: sn pushed along towards rr: gd hdwy over 1f out: str run fnl f: clsng fast on ldng pair nr fin* **25/1**	DarryllHolland 4	98+
235	4	1 ¾	**Little Scotland**[20] 2372 2-8-12 (T D Easterby) *lw: in tch: sn rdn along: styd on fnl 2f* **12/1**	DavidAllan 5	87
142	5	1	**Hearts Of Fire**[24] 2260 2-9-3 (Pat Eddery) *sn in mid-div: effrt over 2f out: kpt on fnl f* **25/1**	PaulEddery 18	88
1132	6	1 ½	**Star Rover (IRE)**[19] 2408 2-9-3 (P D Evans) *chsd ldrs: rdn over 2f out: edgd lft over 1f out: one pce* **10/1**	JohnEgan 19	83
03	7	1	**George Baker (IRE)**[28] 2147 2-9-3 (George Baker) *bhd: rdn 1/2-way: hdwy into midfield whn nt clr run and swtchd rt over 1f out: r.o fnl f* **25/1**	GeorgeBaker 6	80+
1	8	hd	**Angel's Pursuit (IRE)**[23] 2295 2-9-3 (R Hannon) *str: lw: dwlt: sn in rr of midfield: rdn over 2f out: hung rt and nt clr run over 1f out: r.o* **4/1**[1]	RichardHughes 8	87+
31	9	½	**Mister Manannan (IRE)**[48] 1610 2-9-3 (D Nicholls) *unf: lw: sn rdn along: prom tl wknd 1f out* **9/2**[2]	AdrianTNicholls 12	77
3110	10	shd	**Desert Auction (IRE)**[10] 2702 2-9-3 (R Hannon) *outpcd in rr: drvn along 1/2-way: sme late hdwy* **25/1**	RyanMoore 3	76
2316	11	shd	**Little Perisher**[10] 2702 2-9-3 (A P Jarvis) *mid-div: effrt and in tch 2f out: hrd rdn and wknd over 1f out* **33/1**	NCallan 21	76
51	12	¾	**Russian Rock (IRE)**[33] 2007 2-9-3 (R A Teal) *chsd ldrs tl hrd rdn and wknd over 1f out* **40/1**	SebSanders 13	73
212	13	2	**The Hermitage (IRE)**[20] 2372 2-8-12 (M Johnston) *w'like: in tch: effrt over 2f out: wknd over 1f out* **15/2**[3]	LDettori 20	61
	14	shd	**Stand And Fight (IRE)**[18] 2465 2-9-3 (Kevin Prendergast, Ire) *leggy: chsd ldrs tl hrd rdn and wknd over 1f out* **16/1**	DPMcDonogh 14	66
	15	hd	**Clashnacree (IRE)**[19] 2421 2-9-3 (T Stack, Ire) *w'like: scope: lw: dwlt: a in rr of midfield: rdn and no prog fnl 2f* **16/1**	WMLordan 22	65

21 **16** *hd* **Itsthursdayalready**[7] 2778 2-9-3 .... AlanMunro 1 64
(J G Given) *swtg: in tch tl rdn and wknd 2f out* **16/1**

5150 **17** *½* **Azif**[20] 2372 2-8-12 .... DavidProbert 7 58
(Miss Gay Kelleway) *b: b.hind: a bhd: drvn along and n.d fr 1/2-way* **100/1**

3221 **18** *hd* **Avonvalley**[21] 2348 2-8-12 .... WilliamBuick 11 57
(M S Saunders) *a towards rr: n.d fr 1/2-way* **40/1**

2213 **19** *½* **Dancing Freddy (IRE)**[10] 2714 2-9-3 .... TPQueally 9 60+
(J G Given) *lw: in tch 3f: btn whn edgd rt and sltly hmpd sn after* **33/1**

14 **20** *¾* **Antonius Moris (IRE)**[15] 2547 2-9-3 .... RichardKingscote 15 57
(Tom Dascombe) *sn outpcd towards rr: drvn along and n.d fr 1/2-way* **66/1**

2123 **21** *½* **Red Avalanche (IRE)**[10] 2702 2-9-3 .... MartinDwyer 10 56
(P F I Cole) *in tch: rdn over 2f out: btn whn n.m.r over 1f out* **33/1**

013 **22** *7* **Kirsty's Boy (IRE)**[29] 2136 2-9-3 ....(b[1]) JimmyFortune 17 30
(J S Moore) *dropped to rr over 3f out: sn wl bhd* **66/1**

61.28 secs (0.78) **Going Correction** +0.20s/f (Good) **22** Ran SP% **123.3**
Speed ratings (Par 101): **101,100,99,96,95 92,91,91,90,90 89,88,85,85,85 84,83,83,82,81 80,69**
toteswinger: 1&2 £122.90, 1&3 £46.60, 2&3 £84.00. CSF £858.94 CT £24466.54 TOTE £20.70: £4.80, £10.20, £8.40; EX 1294.50 Trifecta £5616.10 Part won. Pool: £7,589.40 - 0.62 winning units. Place 6: £1,381.15, Place 5: £435.56..
Owner Mitch Dutko & Ray Sainz **Bred** W Ward, M Dutko & R Sainz **Trained** North America
■ The first ever American-trained Flat winner in Britain.
■ Stewards' Enquiry : Robert Winston one-day ban: used whip with excessive frequency without giving mount time to respond (Jun 30)

FOCUS
A typically competitive Windsor Castle. Just as in the King's Stand, the main action took place stands' side and a low stall looked advantageous, even though the winner was drawn high. The winner is all speed and only just lasted home from the game runner-up, who has been kept busy but showed improved form..

NOTEBOOK
Strike The Tiger(USA), a US challenger who had won his only previous start in a 4.5f maiden on sloppy dirt at Churchill Downs, showed terrific speed and deserves extra credit considering he edged all the way across towards the stands' side from his high draw and was followed home by three rivals drawn low. This was a splendid training performance from Wesley Ward, but it's hard to get too excited by what he actually achieved in terms of figures. He'll apparently head back to the States now, where his trainer is expecting big things from him.
Fratellino displayed blistering pace and to his credit he was coming back at the winner near the line. He's at his best when the emphasis is on pure pace.
Di Stefano, off the mark at the third attempt at Ripon, was badly outpaced early on but ran on strongly once switched towards the stands' rail over a furlong out, although just too late. (op 33-1)
Little Scotland ran okay but couldn't muster the pace to peg back the leaders. Slightly easier ground, or another furlong, might suit her better. (op 16-1)
Hearts Of Fire has struggled since winning the Brocklesby, but this was a respectable effort from his high draw. (op 18-1)
Star Rover(IRE) didn't run badly but looks vulnerable in this sort of race now. Official explanation: jockey said colt hung left (tchd 9-1)
George Baker(IRE) is probably a length or two better than he showed as, having been outpaced for most of the way, he was denied a clear run on a couple of occasions when finally picking up. Official explanation: jockey said gelding was denied a clear run (op 33-1)
Angel's Pursuit(IRE) looked around a couple of lengths better than the bare result. Slow to find his stride, he was blocked in his run a couple of times late on, before finishing well when in the clear. (op 7-2 tchd 9-2 in places)
Mister Manannan(IRE) posted a very useful effort when thrashing a fair field on his second start at Pontefract, but he was able to get his rivals out of their comfort zone that day after enjoying an easy lead, and that was never going to be repeated in this stronger company. Also, he has reportedly suffered from sore shins since that win and might have been feeling the ground. (op 5-1 tchd 4-1)
Desert Auction(IRE) probably wasn't good enough. (op 22-1 tchd 20-1)
Little Perisher was not helped by a wide draw.
The Hermitage(IRE), just like her trainer's runner in the Coventry, ran below expectations. (op 13-2 tchd 6-1 and 8-1 in places and 9-1 in a place)
Stand And Fight(IRE) was well below form and was disappointing. (op 18-1 tchd 20-1)
Clashnacree(IRE) really should have fared much better. (tchd 20-1 in places)
Red Avalanche(IRE) Official explanation: jockey said colt had no more to give
T/Jkpt: £52,306.20 to a £1 stake. Pool: £73,670.82. 1.00 winning ticket. T/Plt: £3,775.30 to a £1 stake. Pool: £454,598.75. 87.90 winning tickets. T/Qpdt: £413.50 to a £1 stake. Pool: £21,848.64. 39.10 winning tickets. DO

2541 THIRSK (L-H)

Tuesday, June 16

OFFICIAL GOING: Good to firm
Wind: Virtually nil Weather: Overcast and warm

2996 TURFTV (S) STKS 6f
2:15 (2:19) (Class 5) 2-Y-O **£4,274** (£1,271; £635; £317) **Stalls** High

Form RPR

66 **1** **Saxby (IRE)**[7] 2793 2-9-0 0 .... SamHitchcott 11 70
(M R Channon) *trckd ldrs: swtchd lft and effrt over 1f out: rdn to ld 1f out: styd on wl* **5/6**[1]

0 **2** *4* **Craicattack (IRE)**[7] 2792 2-9-0 0 .... LPKeniry 13 58
(J S Moore) *cl up on inner: effrt 2f out: sn rdn and ev ch tl drvn and one pce ins fnl f* **3/1**[2]

325 **3** *3* **Cassidy K**[19] 2401 2-8-4 0 .... JamieKyne[(5)] 7 44
(J Howard Johnson) *hld up: hdwy over 2f out: rdn wl over 1f out: kpt on u.p ins fnl f: nrst fin* **7/1**[3]

03 **4** *shd* **Bothwell Castle (IRE)**[7] 2788 2-9-0 0 ....(p) PaulMulrennan 6 49
(P C Haslam) *led: rdn along 2f out: drvn and hdd 1f out: wknd* **11/1**

5 *1½* **Fond** 2-8-9 0 .... SilvestreDeSousa 14 39+
(Ollie Pears) *dwlt: sn chsng ldrs: rdn along and n.m.r and sltly outpcd 2f out: kpt on ins fnl f* **33/1**

0616 **6** *1* **Dispol Kabira**[30] 2100 2-9-2 0 .... JoeFanning 2 43
(P T Midgley) *cl up: rdn along 2f out: grad wknd* **33/1**

0 **7** *nk* **Steeley Flyer**[22] 2311 2-8-2 0 .... AndrewHeffernan[(7)] 5 35
(P D Evans) *dwlt: hdwy and in tch over 2f out: sn rdn and btn* **33/1**

0F6 **8** *½* **Another Grand (IRE)**[14] 2575 2-9-0 0 .... AndrewMullen 12 39
(Mrs R A Carr) *s.i.s: hdwy and in tch over 2f out: sn rdn and n.d* **50/1**

066 **9** *10* **Mostofitleft (IRE)**[38] 1884 2-8-7 0 ow3.......... SladeO'Hara[(5)] 9 7
(A Berry) *a towards rr* **150/1**

0 **10** *2* **Brave Ambition (IRE)**[14] 2575 2-9-0 0 .... DaleGibson 3 3
(Garry Moss) *a in rr* **100/1**

6 **11** *3¾* **Joel The Mole**[7] 2788 2-9-0 0 .... PaulQuinn 4 —
(D Nicholls) *chsd ldrs: rdn along 1/2-way and sn wknd* **28/1**

1m 12.5s (-0.20) **Going Correction** -0.125s/f (Firm) **11** Ran SP% **116.3**
Speed ratings (Par 93): **96,90,86,86,84 83,82,82,68,66 61**
toteswinger: 1&2 £2.20, 1&3 £3.20, 2&3 £4.70. CSF £3.07 TOTE £1.90: £1.10, £1.60, £2.00; EX 4.60.The winner was bought in for 18,000gns.
Owner Mrs M Findlay **Bred** R N Auld **Trained** West Ilsley, Berks
■ Stewards' Enquiry : Sam Hitchcott one-day ban: careless riding (Jun 30)

FOCUS
The track had escaped the heavy, thundery rain and the ground was on the quick side. The winner was too strong for some poor opposition.

NOTEBOOK
Saxby(IRE), who had shown ability in two non-sellers on his previous starts, ran out a wide-margin winner in the end. He will be even better suited by 7f and should be able to hold his own in claiming or nursery company after connections dug deep to retain him at the auction. (op Evens tchd 8-11)
Craicattack(IRE), another dropped in class, came in for plenty of support on his second start. After matching strides with the leader he was left for dead by the winner. He should be able to find a similar event. (op 5-1 tchd 11-2)
Cassidy K, returned to selling company on her fourth start, kept on in her own time to snatch third spot near the line. She already looks fully exposed. (op 9-2)
Bothwell Castle(IRE), set alight by first-time cheekpieces, did too much in front and in the end did not get home. (op 9-1 tchd 12-1)
Fond, on her debut, was tapped for toe at the halfway mark. She was staying on in her own time at the finish and, likely to be suited by a step up to seven, will be wiser next time. (op 18-1)

2997 WHITE SWAN AMPLEFORTH MEDIAN AUCTION MAIDEN STKS 7f
2:50 (2:51) (Class 5) 2-Y-O **£4,274** (£1,271; £635; £317) **Stalls** Low

Form RPR

52 **1** **Jehu**[18] 2430 2-9-3 0 .... SamHitchcott 12 75
(M R Channon) *cl up on outer whn hmpd and pushed wd home turn: effrt over 2f out: rdn to ld over 1f out and sn edgd lft: drvn and hdd wl ins fnl f: rallied gamely to ld on line* **2/1**[1]

0 **2** *nse* **Al Khimiya (IRE)**[12] 2631 2-8-12 0 .... GrahamGibbons 4 70
(S A Callaghan) *cl up on inner: slender advantage 3f out: rdn 2f out: drvn and hdd over 1f out: kpt on u.p to ld again last 75yds: hdd on line* **25/1**

3 *1½* **Bahamian Music (IRE)** 2-8-12 0 .... TonyHamilton 9 66
(R A Fahey) *led: hung rt and edgd out home turn: sn hdd: cl up and rdn over 2f out: drvn wl over 1f out and ev ch tl no ex wl ins fnl f* **7/2**[2]

64 **4** *2¼* **Ant Music (IRE)**[32] 2033 2-9-3 0 .... LPKeniry 14 66
(J S Moore) *prom: sltly hmpd home turn: rdn along over 2f out and kpt on same pce appr last* **6/1**

5 *shd* **Local Hero (GER)** 2-9-3 0 .... DNolan 3 65
(T P Tate) *dwlt and towards rr: hdwy 3f out: rdn 2f out: kpt on ins fnl f: nrst fin* **17/2**

6 *2¼* **New World Symphony (IRE)** 2-9-3 0 .... PaulMulrennan 5 60
(J Howard Johnson) *midfield: hdwy on inner to chse ldrs 3f out: rdn along 2f out and kpt on same pce* **5/1**[3]

7 *2¼* **No Quarter (IRE)** 2-9-3 0 .... DanielTudhope 11 54
(A Dickman) *t.k.h: towards rr: hdwy and n.m.r 2f out: swtchd outside over 1f out: styd on wl fnl f: nrst fin* **25/1**

6 **8** *1* **Fantastic Pick**[8] 2771 2-8-12 0 .... GabrielHannon[(5)] 10 52
(B J Meehan) *chsd ldrs: pushed along over 3f out: sn rdn and wknd* **14/1**

00 **9** *nk* **Dispol Antonio (IRE)**[13] 2610 2-9-3 0 ....(v[1]) PhillipMakin 6 51
(P T Midgley) *s.i.s and a towards rr* **80/1**

00 **10** *1¾* **Bateau Bleu**[30] 2099 2-8-12 0 .... PatrickDonaghy[(5)] 2 46
(P C Haslam) *s.i.s: a in rr* **40/1**

P **11** *7* **Arken Lad**[19] 2414 2-9-3 0 .... JimmyQuinn 8 29
(D Donovan) *t.k.h: chsd ldrs: rdn along over 2f out and sn wknd* **66/1**

12 *1¾* **Star Cruiser (USA)** 2-9-3 0 .... DuranFentiman 13 25
(T D Easterby) *chsd ldrs: rdn along wl over 2f out and sn wknd* **40/1**

0 **13** *67* **Kerolad (IRE)**[33] 2017 2-9-3 0 .... PaulQuinn 7 —
(N Wilson) *a in rr: wl bhd fnl 3f* **80/1**

1m 29.26s (2.06) **Going Correction** -0.125s/f (Firm) **13** Ran SP% **120.2**
Speed ratings (Par 93): **83,82,81,78,78 75,73,72,71,69 61,59,—**
toteswinger: 1&2 £13.30, 1&3 £2.70, 2&3 £17.60. CSF £63.47 TOTE £2.90: £1.20, £5.70, £2.00; EX 76.00.
Owner Box 41 **Bred** W P Churchward And Mrs C Hue-Williams **Trained** West Ilsley, Berks

FOCUS
A 7f race for 2yos and the pace was not particularly strong.

NOTEBOOK
Jehu, no match for Coventry runner-up Xtension on his second start at Goodwood, is a sharp type. He had to overcome a wide draw and showed real battling qualities to get up in the very last stride, to the surprise of many exchange photo-finish punters. (op 7-4 tchd 5-2)
Al Khimiya(IRE), who made her debut on the all-weather, was keen and had two handlers in the paddock. She was left in front turning for home and in the end missed out by a whisker. (tchd 20-1)
Bahamian Music(IRE), out of an unraced half-sister to French 2000 Guineas winner Victory Note, came in for substantial support. She pulled her way to the front after a furlong and showed her inexperience hanging out on the turn for home. She weakened between horses near the line but, clearly well regarded, she will have no difficulty finding a race. (op 9-1)
Ant Music(IRE), just ahead of the winner, who was making his debut, on his second start at Newbury, had the worst of the draw but he does not seem to be progressing. (op 5-1)
Local Hero(GER) ◆, after a tardy start, picked up in encouraging fashion once in line for home and is worth noting. (op 11-2)
New World Symphony(IRE), a breeze-up purchase, showed limited ability on his debut. (op 8-1)
No Quarter(IRE), a gelded son of Refuse To Bend, stayed on nicely under a quiet ride first time. He ought to be able to do a fair bit better in due course. (op 20-1)
Kerolad(IRE) Official explanation: jockey said colt hung right handed

2998 RAMADA YORK AND WETHERBY HOTELS H'CAP 7f
3:25 (3:25) (Class 5) (0-75,75) 3-Y-O+ **£4,274** (£1,271; £635; £317) **Stalls** Low

Form RPR

6240 **1** **White Deer (USA)**[45] 1660 5-10-0 **75** ....(v) SilvestreDeSousa 7 86
(G A Harker) *trckd ldrs: hdwy over 2f out: rdn over 1f out: led ins fnl f and kpt on* **11/2**[1]

-040 **2** *2* **Hiccups**[24] 2269 9-9-12 **73** .... PhillipMakin 13 78+
(M Dods) *j. awkwardly and rr: hdwy over 2f out: n.m.r wl over 1f out: rdn to chse ldrs whn n.m.r ent fnl f: sn swtchd rt and kpt on towards fin* **20/1**

3424 **3** *¾* **Ancient Cross**[25] 2235 5-9-5 **66** ....(b) PaulMulrennan 4 69
(M W Easterby) *trckd ldrs: hdwy over 2f out: rdn to ld over 1f out: drvn and hdd ins fnl f: sn edgd rt and one pce* **7/1**[3]

3105 **4** *½* **Bere Davis (FR)**[14] 2565 4-9-6 **74** .... AndrewHeffernan[(7)] 11 76
(P D Evans) *cl up: led over 2f out: rdn and hdd over 1f out: wknd ins fnl f* **10/1**

-554 **5** *hd* **Mey Blossom**22 2312 4-9-5 **69**............................ MichaelJStainton(3) 3 70
(R M Whitaker) *midfield: hdwy over 2f out: rdn to chse ldrs over 1f out: drvn and one pce ins fnl f* **8/1**

0-06 **6** *nk* **Apollo Shark (IRE)**22 2312 4-9-6 **67**........................ TonyHamilton 1 68
(J Howard Johnson) *hld up towards rr: hdwy over 2f out: sn rdn and edgd lft wl over 1f out: no imp appr fnl f* **12/1**

-600 **7** *3/4* **Danehillsundance (IRE)**11 2665 5-9-7 **73**.................(t) JamieKyne(5) 2 72
(D H Brown) *nvr bttr than midfield* **7/1**3

0014 **8** *1/2* **Kipchak (IRE)**6 2828 4-10-0 **75**..(p) LPKeniry 9 72
(C R Dore) *led: rdn along 3f out: hdd over 2f out: drvn and wknd wl over 1f out* **11/1**

0030 **9** *1* **Dream Express (IRE)**25 2235 4-9-7 **71**.................... NeilBrown(3) 6 66
(M Dods) *t.k.h: chsd ldrs on inner: rdn along over 2f out and grad wknd* **20/1**

01-5 **10** *nk* **Cherri Fosfate**15 2542 5-9-7 **68**... DNolan 10 62+
(D Carroll) *s.i.s: hld up and a in rr* **28/1**

3-22 **11** *9* **Rebel City**153 160 3-9-2 **72**....................................... GrahamGibbons 8 41
(S A Callaghan) *prom: rdn along wl over 2f out and sn wknd* **10/1**

2500 **12** *4 1/2* **Sea Rover (IRE)**8 2770 5-9-5 **66**.................................. JimmyQuinn 12 23
(M Brittain) *a towards rr* **33/1**

31-3 **13** *2 1/2* **Smalljohn**161 64 3-8-9 **72**....................................(v) RichardOliver(7) 14 23
(B Smart) *chsd ldrs on wd outside: rdn along 1/2-way and sn wknd* **14/1**

0014 **P** **Splash The Cash**11 2658 4-9-7 **73**............................... AmyRyan(5) 5 —
(K A Ryan) *midfield: hdwy on outer over 2f out: rdn whn p.u over 1f out: broke leg: dead* **6/1**2

1m 25.66s (-1.54) **Going Correction** -0.125s/f (Firm)
WFA 3 from 4yo+ 9lb **14** Ran SP% **122.6**
Speed ratings (Par 103): **103,100,99,99,99 98,97,97,96,95 85,80,77,—**
toteswinger: 1&2 £25.90, 1&3 £9.70, 2&3 £26.10. CSF £120.78 CT £815.49 TOTE £6.10: £2.50, £4.20, £2.90; EX 122.60.
Owner Ian Bellamy **Bred** Fleetwood Bloodstock Et Al **Trained** Thirkleby, N Yorks

FOCUS
A highly competitive 66-75 handicap run at a strong pace. The winner is rated to the best view of last year's form with the next two close to their marks.
Apollo Shark(IRE) Official explanation: jockey said gelding was denied a clear run
Danehillsundance(IRE) Official explanation: jockey said gelding was denied a clear run
Dream Express(IRE) Official explanation: jockey said gelding hung right throughout
Cherri Fosfate Official explanation: jockey said, regarding riding, that his instructions were to ride the gelding as near to the pace as possible as he may be outpaced, adding that the gelding was outpaced from the start and that in his opinion seven furlongs is too sharp for the gelding, and that he was denied a clear run in the closing stages which was reported following the race.; trainer said, regarding running, that the gelding has returned to his yard after a spell running over hurdles, and is possibly better over a mile and a quarter, but has run well over seven furlongs in the past

2999 EUROPEAN BREEDERS' FUND FILLIES' H'CAP 1m
4:00 (4:01) (Class 3) (0-90,87) 3-Y-0+ **£10,102** (£3,006; £1,502; £750) **Stalls** Low

Form RPR

2040 **1** **Fesko**13 2607 3-8-8 **77**.. JoeFanning 2 82
(M Johnston) *led: pushed along wl over 2f out: rdn and qcknd clr over 1f out: styd on* **12/1**

1-36 **2** *2 1/4* **Act Green**13 2607 3-8-2 **76**... JamieKyne(5) 7 76
(M L W Bell) *stdd s: hld up in rr: swtchd outside and hdwy 2f out: rdn to chse wnr and hung lft ins fnl f: kpt on wl towards fin* **7/2**3

2-03 **3** *1* **Lady Rangali (IRE)**8 2768 4-9-10 **83**........................ PaulMulrennan 4 83
(Mrs A Duffield) *trckd ldrs: hdwy 3f out: rdn to chse wnr wl over 1f out: sn drvn: edgd lft and one pce appr fnl f* **10/3**2

-030 **4** *2 1/4* **Sam's Secret**19 2402 7-9-6 **79**.. PJMcDonald 5 74
(G A Swinbank) *hld up: hdwy wl over 2f out: sn rdn and no imp* **9/1**

4-00 **5** *hd* **Classic Legend**17 2480 4-9-9 **87**......................... GabrielHannon(5) 6 81
(B J Meehan) *cl up on outer: rdn along over 3f out: wknd 2f out* **10/3**2

2-02 **6** *3/4* **Brierty (IRE)**15 2544 3-8-11 **80**.. DNolan 1 70
(D Carroll) *trckd ldrs on inner: effrt over 2f out: sn rdn and ch tl drvn and btn wl over 1f out* **3/1**1

4504 **7** *2* **Mozayada (USA)**42 1778 5-9-0 **73**.................................. JimmyQuinn 3 61
(M Brittain) *t.k.h early: cl up: effrt over 2f out: sn rdn and wkng whn n.m.r wl over 1f out* **20/1**

1m 38.67s (-1.43) **Going Correction** -0.125s/f (Firm)
WFA 3 from 4yo+ 10lb **7** Ran SP% **115.8**
Speed ratings (Par 104): **102,99,98,96,96 95,93**
toteswinger: 1&2 £8.60, 1&3 £5.50, 2&3 £3.50. CSF £54.87 TOTE £15.90: £2.10, £3.00; EX 45.70.
Owner C H Greensit & W A Greensit **Bred** C H And W A Greensit **Trained** Middleham Moor, N Yorks

FOCUS
A 73-87 fillies' handicap, not strong for the money on offer, and the gallop was sound. The winner only had to get back to her winter AW form.

NOTEBOOK
Fesko, back on the same mark as her success on the all-weather at Southwell in February, was allowed to set her own pace. She wound it up once in line for home and never looked in any real danger. Joe Fanning is a master from the front. Official explanation: trainer's representative said, regarding the improved form shown, that he had no explanation for the run last time, but added that the filly was better suited by being able to dominate (op 11-1 tchd 10-1)
Act Green, who made all when taking her maiden at Great Leighs in October, made a slow start for the second time in a row. She made her effort on the wide outside but tended to hang and was never doing anything like enough to trouble the winner. Cheekpieces might aid her cause. (op 3-1 tchd 4-1)
Lady Rangali(IRE), back to form when third in a weak Listed race at Pontefract, had no excuse and this is as good as she is nowadays. (op 11-4 tchd 7-2)
Sam's Secret, suited by fast ground, didn't have the run of the race and had to switch to find racing room. She has struggled to get her head in front since winning five times two years ago. (op 7-1 tchd 5-1)
Classic Legend, dropped 3lb after finishing well beaten in two previous outings this time, has not recovered her smart juvenile form when she won both her starts including a Listed success. (op 5-1 tchd 3-1)
Brierty(IRE), 10lb higher than for her nursery success, has yet to prove herself beyond 7f. (op 5-1)
Mozayada(USA), whose five career wins have been on the Fibresand at Southwell, was on the retreat when squeezed out and she has yet to prove her effectiveness on turf. (tchd 14-1)

3000 BROWNS OF YORK AND HELMSLEY H'CAP 1m 4f
4:35 (4:35) (Class 4) (0-80,79) 4-Y-0+ **£5,569** (£1,657; £828; £413) **Stalls** Low

Form RPR

0165 **1** **Trip The Light**17 2499 4-8-12 **70**...............................(v) JamieMoriarty 4 75
(R A Fahey) *trckd ldng pair: effrt and hdwy whn outpcd 3f out: rdn and edgd lft 2f out: drvn and styng on whn carried rt ins fnl f: kpt on strly u.p to ld last 50yds* **9/2**

-046 **2** *1* **Hurlingham**25 2249 5-9-6 **78**..................................... PaulMulrennan 2 81
(M W Easterby) *trckd ldr: hdwy 3f out: rdn and hung lft over 1f out: n.m.r on inner and swtchd rt ins fnl f: sn drvn and kpt on* **5/1**

123 **3** *nk* **River Ardeche**14 1184 4-9-2 **79**............................ PatrickDonaghy(5) 3 82
(P C Haslam) *led: qcknd 3f out: rdn over 2f out: edgd rt over 1f out: drvn and edgd lft ins fnl f: hdd and no ex last 50yds* **7/2**3

3110 **4** *1/2* **Grand Art (IRE)**3 2932 5-9-4 **76**..................................... JoeFanning 7 78
(P T Midgley) *hld up: hdwy 3f out: nt clr run and hmpd 2f out: swtchd outside and rdn over 1f out: sltly hmpd and swtchd lft ins fnl f: kpt on* **9/4**1

-164 **5** *2 1/4* **Valdan (IRE)**6 2815 5-8-11 **76**............................ AndrewHeffernan(7) 1 75
(P D Evans) *t.k.h: hld up in rr: hdwy on inner 2f out: sn rdn and no imp appr fnl f* **3/1**2

2m 35.48s (-0.72) **Going Correction** -0.125s/f (Firm) **5** Ran SP% **112.8**
Speed ratings (Par 105): **97,96,96,95,94**
toteswinger: 1&2 £14.20. CSF £26.11 TOTE £5.40: £1.80, £2.80; EX 25.40.
Owner The Matthewman One Partnership **Bred** Darley **Trained** Musley Bank, N Yorks

FOCUS
A 69-79 handicap and quite tactical with a steady pace. Modest form.

3001 ADORN HATS H'CAP 6f
5:10 (5:10) (Class 4) (0-85,84) 3-Y-0+ **£5,569** (£1,657; £828; £413) **Stalls** High

Form RPR

4310 **1** **Red Cape (FR)**8 2769 6-9-0 **70**..................................... AndrewElliott 9 81
(Mrs R A Carr) *sn led: rdn along over 2f out: drvn over 1f out: hld on wl u.p ins fnl f* **12/1**

-001 **2** *1/2* **Grazeon Gold Blend**14 2570 6-9-3 **78**........................(p) JamieKyne(5) 5 87
(J J Quinn) *towards rr: pushed along 1/2-way: hdwy 2f out: swtchd lft and rdn over 1f out: styd on u.p and ev ch ins fnl f: nt qckn towards fin* **18/1**

00-0 **3** *3* **John Keats**24 2276 6-9-1 **71**...................................... DanielTudhope 10 71+
(J S Goldie) *in rr: hdwy 2f out: rdn: n.m.r and swtchd lft over 1f out: kpt on u.p ins fnl f: nrst fin* **8/1**

-432 **4** *1/2* **Atlantic Beach**12 2628 4-9-0 **70**................................(v1) TonyHamilton 8 68
(R A Fahey) *trckd ldrs: smooth hdwy over 2f out: effrt and ch wl over 1f out: sn rdn: edgd rt and one pce* **9/2**1

6111 **5** *2* **All The Nines (IRE)**18 2438 3-9-6 **83**..................... SilvestreDeSousa 7 73
(Mrs D J Sanderson) *prom whn n.m.r after 1f and sn pushed along to chse ldrs 1/2-way: rdn 2f out: drvn and no imp over 1f out* **15/2**3

31-1 **6** *hd* **Elijah Pepper (USA)**38 1885 4-8-9 **70**...................... DeanHeslop(5) 11 61
(T D Barron) *sn outpcd and towards rr 1/2-way: hdwy over 2f out: sn rdn and kpt on appr fnl f: nt rch ldrs* **9/2**1

1400 **7** *2* **Malcheek (IRE)**24 2266 7-9-7 **77**.................................. DuranFentiman 2 62
(T D Easterby) *hld up in rr: hdwy on wd outside over 2f out: sn rdn and no imp appr fnl f* **33/1**

0006 **8** *3 3/4* **Lord Of The Reins (IRE)**10 2717 5-9-5 **75**.............. PaulMulrennan 12 48
(J G Given) *prom on stands' rail: rdn 2f out and ev ch tl wknd over 1f out* **20/1**

0002 **9** *hd* **Stevie Gee (IRE)**7 2780 5-9-7 **77**.................................. PJMcDonald 6 49
(G A Swinbank) *prom: rdn along bef 1/2-way: sn wknd* **9/2**1

2164 **10** *6* **Rasaman (IRE)**6 2814 5-9-9 **84**......................................(p) AmyRyan(5) 4 37
(K A Ryan) *cl up: rdn along over 2f out: sn wknd* **16/1**

4205 **11** *1 3/4* **High Curragh**14 2570 6-9-12 **82**..(p) JoeFanning 1 29
(K A Ryan) *cl up on wd outside: rdn along bef 1/2-way and sn wknd* **16/1**

2015 **12** *4* **Legal Eagle (IRE)**2 2941 4-9-11 **81**.............................. PhillipMakin 3 16
(Paul Green) *cl up: rdn along over 2f out: sn drvn and wknd* **7/1**2

1m 11.06s (-1.64) **Going Correction** -0.125s/f (Firm)
WFA 3 from 4yo+ 7lb **12** Ran SP% **122.3**
Speed ratings (Par 105): **105,104,100,99,97 96,94,89,88,80 78,73**
toteswinger: 1&2 £42.70, 1&3 £28.80, 2&3 £40.10. CSF £216.19 CT £1873.94 TOTE £17.10: £3.80, £5.20, £2.40; EX 227.00.
Owner Middleham Park Racing LVI **Bred** Gilles And Mrs Forien **Trained** Huby, N Yorks

FOCUS
A 70-84 sprint handicap run at a furious pace. Ordinary form, rated through the second.
Stevie Gee(IRE) Official explanation: jockey said gelding ran flat

3002 LADIES DAY H'CAP 5f
5:45 (5:45) (Class 6) (0-65,65) 3-Y-0+ **£3,139** (£926; £463) **Stalls** High

Form RPR

-420 **1** **Twosheetstothewind**22 2316 5-9-8 **59**............................ PhillipMakin 19 69
(M Dods) *hld up stands' side: hdwy 2f out: rdn over 1f out: styd on strly to ld ins fnl f: 1st of 12 in gp* **5/1**1

-001 **2** *nk* **Toy Top (USA)**15 2546 6-9-1 **55**................................(b) NeilBrown(3) 15 64
(M Dods) *overall ldr stands' side: rdn 2f out: drvn over 1f out: hdd and no ex ins fnl f: 2nd of 12 in gp* **5/1**1

2600 **3** *3/4* **Medici Time**8 2769 4-9-10 **61**.................................(v) GrahamGibbons 18 67
(T D Easterby) *dwlt and rr stands' side: hdwy 2f out: sn rdn and kpt on wl fnl f: 3rd of 12 in gp* **17/2**

6-00 **4** *1 1/4* **Jilly Why (IRE)**5 2840 8-9-9 **65**................................(b) JPHamblett(5) 7 67
(Paul Green) *prom towards stands' side: rdn 2f out and ev ch tl drvn: edgd lft and one pce ins fnl f: 4th of 12 in gp* **33/1**

-346 **5** *1/2* **Yungaburra (IRE)**36 1935 5-10-0 **65**....................(bt) PaulMulrennan 20 65
(J Balding) *hld up on stands' rail: effrt and hdwy whn nt clr run over 1f out: swtchd lft and rdn: kpt on ins fnl f: 5th of 12 in gp* **12/1**

510 **6** *1/2* **Kyzer Chief**10 2717 4-9-11 **65**.................................... KellyHarrison(3) 3 63+
(R E Barr) *led far side gp: prom and ev ch 2f out: sn rdn and one pce appr fnl f: 1st of 5 in gp* **10/1**

10-0 **7** *nk* **Ingleby Star (IRE)**25 2225 4-9-4 **60**............................ BMcHugh(5) 12 57
(N Wilson) *prom stands' side: rdn along 2f out: sn drvn and wknd over 1f out: 6th of 12 in gp* **16/1**

5405 **8** *1* **Whozart (IRE)**6 2812 6-9-3 **54**..................................... DanielTudhope 16 47
(A Dickman) *in tch stands' side: hdwy 2f out: sn rdn and edgd lft over 1f out: kpt on: nrst fin 7th of 12 in gp* **11/2**2

-000 **9** *nk* **Half A Crown (IRE)**15 2529 4-8-13 **50**........................(p) TonyHamilton 2 42+
(D W Barker) *prom far side: rdn along 2f out: grad wknd: 2nd of 5 in gp* **25/1**

6555 **10** *1 1/2* **Handsinthemist (IRE)**12 2625 4-8-10 **54**..................... PaulPickard(7) 6 41
(P T Midgley) *prom towards stands' side: rdn along 1/2-way: grad wknd: 8th of 12 in gp* **16/1**

1356 **11** *3/4* **Orpen's Art (IRE)**13 2596 4-9-3 **61**................................. HollyHall(7) 4 45+
(S A Callaghan) *chsd ldrs far side: rdn along 2f out: sn drvn and wknd: 3rd of 5 in gp* **25/1**

-000 **12** *3/4* **Coconut Moon**11 2682 7-8-11 **48**...................................... PaulQuinn 14 30
(A Berry) *a towards rr on stands' side: 9th of 12 in gp* **33/1**

-036 **13** *nk* **King Of Rhythm (IRE)**8 2769 6-9-11 **62**............................ DNolan 17 42
(D Carroll) *midfield stands' side: rdn along 1/2-way: sn wknd: 10th of 12 in gp* **6/1**3

2000 **14** 2 **Princess Charlmane (IRE)**[28] 2157 6-8-13 **50**..........(t) PJMcDonald 11 23
(C J Teague) *cl up towards stands' side: rdn along over 2f out: sn wknd: 11th of 12 in gp* **66/1**

-506 **15** 1 1/4 **Paddy Jack**[11] 2657 4-8-10 **52**..........(p) MartinLane(5) 10 21
(J R Weymes) *chsd ldrs towards stands' side: rdn along over 2f out: sn wknd: last of 12 ingp* **25/1**

004- **16** 1 1/4 **Malapropism**[236] 6925 9-10-0 **65**.......... SamHitchcott 1 29
(M R Channon) *racd far side: a in rr: 4th of 5 in gp* **16/1**

00-4 **17** 4 1/2 **Mormeatmic**[19] 2389 6-8-10 **47**..........(b1) DaleGibson 5 —
(M W Easterby) *chsd ldrs far side: rdn along over 2f out: sn wknd 5th of 5 in gp* **25/1**

58.47 secs (-1.13) **Going Correction** -0.125s/f (Firm)
WFA 3 from 4yo+ 6lb **17** Ran SP% **130.7**
Speed ratings (Par 101): **104,103,102,100,99 98,98,96,96,93 92,91,90,87,85 83,76**
toteswinger: 1&2 £11.90, 1&3 £19.10, 2&3 £15.40. CSF £28.83 CT £184.81 TOTE £9.00: £2.10, £1.50, £3.00, £10.10; EX 26.50.
Owner P Taylor **Bred** Mrs R D Peacock **Trained** Denton, Co Durham

FOCUS
Another competitive sprint handicap, a much lower grade though this time, 46-65. The five lowest drawn took a chance and went to the far side, but the stands' rail proved the place to be. A 1-2 for Michael Dods with the winner back to his best.
Whozart(IRE) Official explanation: jockey said gelding hung left throughout

3003 HBLB MAIDEN STKS 5f
6:15 (6:16) (Class 5) 3-4-Y-O **£2,590** (£770; £385; £192) **Stalls** High

Form RPR

1 **Crimea (IRE)** 3-9-3 0.......... JoeFanning 11 81+
(M Johnston) *cl up: led 1/2-way: rdn over 1f out: styd on strly* **11/10**[1]

444 **2** 2 1/2 **Cheyenne Red (IRE)**[25] 2250 3-9-3 0.......... PJMcDonald 12 67
(M Dods) *trckd ldrs: hdwy to chse wnr 2f out: sn rdn and no imp ins fnl f* **8/1**[3]

44-0 **3** hd **Africa's Star (IRE)**[21] 2365 3-8-12 63.......... PhillipMakin 4 61
(M Dods) *chsd ldrs: rdn along 2f out: drvn over 1f out and kpt on same pce* **8/1**[3]

3442 **4** 1 1/2 **Piste**[17] 2478 3-8-7 67.......... Louis-PhilippeBeuzelin(5) 3 56
(B J Meehan) *prom: rdn along 2f out: drvn and one pce over 1f out* **4/1**[2]

2-66 **5** hd **Lucky Dan (IRE)**[120] 572 3-9-3 60.......... SamHitchcott 6 60
(Paul Green) *in tch: hdwy on outer to chse ldrs over 2f out: sn rdn and no imp* **28/1**

6 3 1/2 **Simola** 3-8-12 0.......... TonyHamilton 9 42+
(R A Fahey) *hmpd s: in rr tl sme late hdwy* **10/1**

0- **7** 3 3/4 **Barley Bree (IRE)**[285] 5636 4-9-4 0.......... PaulMulrennan 10 29
(Mrs A Duffield) *wnt lft s: led to 1/2-way: sn rdn along and wknd* **12/1**

6 **8** 5 **Raffanetti (IRE)**[18] 2439 3-9-0 0.......... NeilBrown(3) 5 16
(T D Barron) *wnt bdly lft s: a bhd* **66/1**

64 **9** 1 1/4 **Choree (IRE)**[24] 2268 3-8-12 0.......... DuranFentiman 2 6
(T D Easterby) *sn rdn along and bhd fr 1/2-way* **80/1**

5 **10** 3 1/4 **Alis Aquilae (IRE)**[39] 1840 3-9-0 0.......... LeeVickers(3) 1 —
(T J Etherington) *v.s.a and a bhd* **11/1**

58.68 secs (-0.92) **Going Correction** -0.125s/f (Firm)
WFA 3 from 4yo 6lb **10** Ran SP% **121.1**
Speed ratings (Par 103): **102,98,97,95,94 89,83,75,73,68**
toteswinger: 1&2 £5.40, 1&3 £3.90, 2&3 £6.00. CSF £11.46 TOTE £2.40: £1.30, £2.60, £2.00; EX 13.10 Place 6: £1,584.54, Place 5: £1,484.09..
Owner Sheikh Hamdan Bin Mohammed Al Maktoum **Bred** Lodge Park Stud **Trained** Middleham Moor, N Yorks

FOCUS
A modest sprint maiden but a hitherto unraced winner of real potential. There is a doubt over what he beat.
Barley Bree(IRE) Official explanation: jockey said filly ran too free
Alis Aquilae(IRE) Official explanation: jockey said gelding missed the break
T/Plt: £272.50 to a £1 stake. Pool: £50,154.29. 134.34 winning tickets. T/Qpdt: £228.90 to a £1 stake. Pool: £3,156.08. 10.20 winning tickets. JR

2860 YARMOUTH (L-H)
Tuesday, June 16

OFFICIAL GOING: Good (7.3)
Bottom bend dolled out with drop in at 4f in straight. Effect on distances not quantified.
Wind: Virtually nil Weather: sunny and bright

3004 4HEAD APPRENTICE H'CAP 1m 2f 21y
6:00 (6:01) (Class 6) (0-60,57) 4-Y-O+ **£2,590** (£770; £385; £192) **Stalls** Low

Form RPR

0P-3 **1** **Camera Shy (IRE)**[19] 2420 5-8-13 **49**.......... AndreaAtzeni(3) 10 57
(K A Morgan) *hld up in midfield: hdwy over 3f out: led jst over 2f out: rdn ins fnl f: a doing enough* **11/4**[2]

0506 **2** 3/4 **Fantasy Ride**[28] 2171 7-8-10 **48**.......... SimonPearce(5) 4 55
(J Pearce) *stdd s: hld up in rr: hdwy and rdn over 2f out: 5th ent fnl f: sn swtchd rt and r.o to go 2nd wl ins fnl f: a hld by wnr* **7/2**[3]

-662 **3** 1/2 **Pretty Officer (USA)**[13] 2608 4-8-12 **52**.......... NoelGarbutt(7) 8 58
(Rae Guest) *chsd ldrs: swtchd lft over 4f out: chsd wnr jst over 2f out: rdn and edgd lft ent fnl f: one pce after and lost 2nd wl ins fnl f* **5/2**[1]

00-0 **4** 5 **Credential**[19] 2420 7-8-12 **50**.......... BillyCray(5) 11 46
(John A Harris) *led: c towards centre and racd alone fr over 4f out: rdn and hung rt over 2f out: hdd jst over 2f out: btn ent fnl f: eased towards fin* **20/1**

3000 **5** 2 **Captain Mainwaring**[5] 2294 4-9-0 **47**..........(p) JackMitchell 7 39
(N P Littmoden) *chsd ldr tl over 3f out: sn drvn: styd chsng ldrs tl wknd ent fnl f* **11/1**

0-60 **6** 1 3/4 **Toballa**[19] 2415 4-9-0 **50**.......... AmyBaker(3) 1 38
(P Leech) *hld up towards rr: rdn over 3f out: nvr trbld ldrs* **8/1**

00-0 **7** 3/4 **Templet (USA)**[13] 2601 9-8-5 **45**..........(p) JosephineBruning(7) 3 32
(T T Clement) *a bhd: rdn over 5f out: wl bhd 2f out: sme modest hdwy fnl f: nvr nr ldrs* **50/1**

-200 **8** 3 3/4 **Your Golf Travel**[19] 2420 4-8-5 **45**..........(b1) TobyAtkinson(7) 5 24
(M Wigham) *chsd ldrs: swtchd lft and hdwy over 4f out: chsd ldr over 3f out tl over 2f out: wknd qckly* **28/1**

5630 **9** 6 **Jiminor Mack**[13] 2601 6-8-5 **45**..........(p) LeonnaMayor(7) 6 12
(W J H Ratcliffe) *stdd s: t.k.h: hld up in midfield: struggling 3f out: wl bhd and eased ins fnl f* **12/1**

2m 10.41s (-0.09) **Going Correction** +0.05s/f (Good) **9** Ran SP% **114.8**
Speed ratings (Par 101): **102,101,101,97,95 94,93,90,85**
toteswinger: 1&2 £3.80, 1&3 £1.02, 2&3 £4.00. CSF £12.47 CT £26.02 TOTE £3.30: £1.30, £1.70, £1.60; EX 14.20.
Owner Michael Ogburn **Bred** Haras D'Etreham And Madame Lily Ades **Trained** Little Marcle, H'fords
■ Stewards' Enquiry : Andrea Atzeni one-day ban: careless riding (Jun 30)

FOCUS
After 5mm of rain overnight the going was changed to good. The opening event was a modest handicap, the runners having managed just seven wins between them in a total of 195 starts. It was run at a decent pace and the first three pulled clear of the rest. The winner matched last June's Lingfield form.

3005 DIOMED DEVELOPMENTS (S) STKS 1m 1f
6:30 (6:30) (Class 6) 3-Y-O **£1,942** (£578; £288; £144) **Stalls** Low

Form RPR

0454 **1** **Chantilly Dancer (IRE)**[18] 2461 3-8-2 48.......... AndreaAtzeni(5) 2 51+
(M Quinn) *sn rdn in rr: hdwy and hmpd 3f out: n.m.r ent fnl 2f: swtchd rt over 1f out: r.o wl to ld fnl 50yds* **6/1**[2]

3 **2** 1 **Shared Moment (IRE)**[63] 1270 3-8-7 0..........(p) StephenDonohoe 5 49
(D E Cantillon) *stdd s: hld up in rr: hdwy 4f out: swtchd lft 3f out: n.m.r and swtchd rt 2f out: sn rdn to chse ldrs: led ent fnl f: hld hd high u.p fnl f: hdd and no ex fnl 50yds* **5/2**[1]

0-00 **3** 1 1/4 **Bertie Smalls**[8] 2772 3-8-12 56..........(b1) TedDurcan 6 51
(M H Tompkins) *t.k.h: chsd ldrs: rdn and effrt on inner 3f out: led over 1f out tl hdd and edgd rt ent fnl f: hrd drvn and one pce fnl f* **25/1**

3153 **4** 1 **Rose Of Coma (IRE)**[6] 2808 3-8-13 51.......... RoystonFfrench 8 50+
(Miss Gay Kelleway) *stdd s: t.k.h: hld up in midfield: effrt towards outer 3f out: n.m.r and switching lft whn hit in face by rival's whip 2f out: hdwy over 1f out: styd on wl fnl f: nt rch ldrs* **12/1**

-002 **5** nk **Kirkson**[28] 2169 3-8-12 57..........(b) AdrianMcCarthy 10 48
(P W Chapple-Hyam) *sn rdn along: bhd: hrd rdn 3f out: no hdwy tl swtchd to outer over 1f out: r.o u.p fnl f: nvr rchd ldrs* **12/1**

0-00 **6** 1 1/2 **Terracotta Warrior**[54] 1481 3-8-9 45.......... DominicFox(3) 7 45+
(J Jay) *sn chsng ldr: led 3f out: drvn over 2f out: hdd over 1f out: wknd jst ins fnl f* **80/1**

-600 **7** 1 **Flirty (IRE)**[20] 2380 3-8-7 47.......... ChrisCatlin 1 38
(Rae Guest) *sn detached in last pl: hdwy on inner 2f out: styd on steadily: nvr pce to rch ldrs* **33/1**

-600 **8** 3 3/4 **August Days (IRE)**[15] 2534 3-8-13 52.......... JerryO'Dwyer 13 35
(J Pearce) *bhd: rdn over 2f out: modest late hdwy: nvr nr ldrs* **66/1**

2100 **9** 1 1/4 **Why Nee Amy**[5] 2863 3-8-13 54..........(v1) TGMcLaughlin 12 33
(Miss Gay Kelleway) *chsd ldrs: rdn and effrt 4f out: pressed ldrs and drvn jst over 2f out: hung lft u.p 2f out: wknd over 1f out* **18/1**

5006 **10** 1/2 **Buckle Up**[9] 2744 3-8-12 42.......... SaleemGolam 4 31
(D K Ivory) *t.k.h: hld up in tch: hdwy on outer 4f out: pressed ldrs and rdn over 2f out: wknd qckly over 1f out* **100/1**

2004 **11** nk **Wahan (USA)**[10] 2709 3-8-12 51..........(t) EdwardCreighton 14 30
(C E Brittain) *chsd ldrs: rdn and hanging lft 4f out: wknd ent fnl 2f* **20/1**

50-6 **12** 3/4 **Barbeito**[14] 2577 3-8-7 48.......... CatherineGannon 3 23
(M D Squance) *in tch in midfield: rdn and effrt 4f out: wknd wl over 1f out* **28/1**

-530 **13** 1/2 **Protiva**[39] 1834 3-8-2 60 ow2..........(v) MatthewDavies(7) 11 24
(A P Jarvis) *sn led: clr over 5f out: hdd and drvn 3f out: wknd qckly 2f out* **9/1**[3]

040 **14** nk **Orsippus (USA)**[20] 2371 3-9-4 63..........(v) TonyCulhane 9 32
(M R Channon) *hld up in midfield: hdwy 4f out: chsd ldrs and rdn over 2f out: hrd drvn and wknd qckly 2f out* **5/2**[1]

1m 57.09s (1.29) **Going Correction** +0.05s/f (Good) **14** Ran SP% **120.8**
Speed ratings (Par 97): **96,95,94,93,92 91,90,87,86,85 85,84,84,84**
toteswinger: 1&2 £16.90, 1&3 not won, 2&3 £8.60. CSF £20.20 TOTE £9.00: £2.50, £1.70, £4.70; EX 44.50.There was no bid for the winner. Orsippus was claimed by Michael Smith for £4,500. Shared Moment was claimed by Ollie Pears for £4,500.
Owner John Quorn **Bred** Lynch Bages Ltd & Samac Ltd **Trained** Newmarket, Suffolk
■ Stewards' Enquiry : Stephen Donohoe two-day ban: careless riding (Jun 30, Jul 1)

FOCUS
Quite a tight seller, eight of the runners holding official ratings between 51 and 63. It was run a very fast pace and the winner is probably the best guide to the form.
Shared Moment(IRE) Official explanation: vet said filly was struck into and finished lame
Flirty(IRE) Official explanation: vet said filly lost a front shoe
August Days(IRE) Official explanation: jockey said filly was hampered going into the bend leaving the back straight
Buckle Up Official explanation: jockey said gelding hung right

3006 AEROPAK MAIDEN AUCTION STKS 5f 43y
7:00 (7:02) (Class 5) 2-Y-O **£2,719** (£809; £404; £202) **Stalls** High

Form RPR

1 **Drift And Dream** 2-8-5 0.......... ChrisCatlin 10 65
(C F Wall) *bhd: pushed along and hdwy 1/2-way: chsd ldr over 1f out: r.o wl under hands and heels to ld nr fin* **9/1**

5524 **2** hd **Ignatieff (IRE)**[36] 1920 2-8-12 0.......... RoystonFfrench 4 71
(Mrs L Stubbs) *chsd ldr tl led over 3f out: rdn wl over 1f out: hrd drvn ins fnl f: hdd nr fin* **6/1**

3 1 1/4 **Poppy N'Penny (IRE)** 2-8-2 0.......... GilmarPereira(3) 9 60+
(W J Haggas) *bhd: outpcd 4f out: hdwy wl over 1f out: swtchd rt over 1f out: chsd ldng pair and edgd lft 1f out: kpt on wl: nt pce to rch ldrs* **16/1**

0 **4** 4 1/2 **Wasmi (IRE)**[17] 2494 2-8-5 0.......... EdwardCreighton 7 43
(C E Brittain) *stdd s: outpcd in rr after 1f: hdwy 1/2-way: wknd u.p ent fnl f* **20/1**

3502 **5** shd **Victorian Art (IRE)**[3] 2906 2-8-6 0..........(v) EddieAhern 6 44
(M A Magnusson) *trckd ldrs: shkn up over 2f out: rdn wl over 1f out: fnd nil and btn whn hung lft u.p 1f out* **7/4**[1]

623 **6** 2 1/4 **Any Day (IRE)**[20] 2383 2-8-6 0.......... JackMitchell(3) 8 39
(R M Beckett) *chsd ldrs: rdn and nt qckn 2f out: wl btn fnl f* **11/2**[3]

0030 **7** 1 1/4 **Southwark Newshawk**[20] 2383 2-8-4 0.......... CatherineGannon 2 29
(Mrs C A Dunnett) *led tl over 3f out: chsd prom tl wknd over 1f out: fdd fnl f* **50/1**

2024 **8** 1 **I'Malwaysright (IRE)**[6] 2825 2-8-13 0..........(b) RobertHavlin 5 35
(D R C Elsworth) *dwlt: sn rcvrd and chsd ldrs: rdn 2f out: fnd nil and btn over 1f out* **3/1**[2]

9 6 **Speedyfix** 2-8-10 0 .... TGMcLaughlin 1 10
(Mrs C A Dunnett) *v.s.a: hung lft thrght: sn wl outpcd and detached in last* **66/1**

65.51 secs (3.31) **Going Correction** +0.175s/f (Good) **9** Ran **SP% 115.1**
Speed ratings (Par 93): **80,79,77,70,70 66,64,63,53**
toteswinger: 1&2 £17.00, 1&3 £15.50, 2&3 not won. CSF £60.65 TOTE £12.00: £3.20, £1.90, £3.10; EX 94.40.
Owner Lady Juliet Tadgell **Bred** Lady Juliet Tadgell **Trained** Newmarket, Suffolk

FOCUS
A very modest maiden auction event. The first three finished clear and this is plating-class form, rated through the runner-up.

NOTEBOOK
Drift And Dream did really well to overcome inexperience and shown battling qualities to just get on top in the closing stages. She is a half-sister to Ocean Gift, a quite useful dual 6f/7f winner at three, and holds entries in the Super Sprint and Redcar Two-Year-Old Trophy, so is clearly well regarded and could improve significantly for this initial experience. (op 11-1 tchd 14-1)
Ignatieff(IRE) has shown fair form and some wayward tendencies in four previous starts, but he probably got back near his best and deserves extra credit for going so close because he wasted a bit of energy by taking a keen hold in the early stages. (op 11-2 tchd 9-2)
Poppy N'Penny(IRE) ◆ made a promising debut, looking very green in the early stages before staying on strongly. She looks a potential bargain at 5,500gns and should have learned a lot from this first run. (op 14-1)
Wasmi(IRE) was extremely green and weakened some way out on her debut in a 6f Newbury maiden last month. She looked a bit more professional here, has plenty of winners on the dam's side of her pedigree and should continue to do better with time. (op 25-1)
Victorian Art(IRE) had a fair chance on her much improved effort when narrowly beaten in a first-time visor over 5f at Bath three days earlier, but she put in a very laboured effort as favourite here and this race may have come too soon. (op 11-8)

3007 IGLU GEL H'CAP 7f 3y
7:30 (7:33) (Class 6) (0-60,60) 3-Y-O+ **£2,320** (£685; £342) **Stalls** High

Form RPR
2520 1 **Takaamul**[19] 2400 6-9-2 **51** .... NeilChalmers 6 58
(K A Morgan) *stdd s: hld up towards rr: hdwy over 2f out: jnd ldrs gng wl over 1f out: shkn up to ld 1f out: rdn and hung lft ins fnl f: hld on* **6/1**[3]
465 2 nse **Global Village (IRE)**[49] 1592 4-9-3 **57** .... WilliamCarson(5) 5 64
(Miss D Mountain) *chsd ldrs: rdn wl over 1f out: ev ch over 1f out: pressed wnr fnl f: r.o: jst hld* **6/1**[3]
-005 3 1 ¾ **Libre**[18] 2458 9-9-6 **55** .... TolleyDean 3 57
(F Jordan) *stdd and dropped in bhd after s: hdwy on far side 2f out: rdn to chse ldng pair 1f out: kpt on same pce after* **16/1**
53-0 4 1 ¾ **Astroangel**[18] 2458 5-9-3 **52** .... TedDurcan 13 49
(M H Tompkins) *stdd and dropped in bhd after s: hdwy and edging lft 2f out: chsd ldrs and rdn ent fnl f: nt qckn u.p: wknd fnl 100yds* **5/1**[2]
6004 5 ¾ **Star Strider**[10] 2713 5-9-4 **60** .... KylieManser(7) 16 55
(Miss Gay Kelleway) *stdd after s: hld up bhd: pushed along and effrt 2f out: rdn over 1f out: styd on steadily but nvr gng to rch ldrs* **9/1**
50-6 6 ½ **Superior Duchess**[18] 2458 4-8-11 **51** .... AndreaAtzeni(5) 7 45
(Jane Chapple-Hyam) *led narrowly tl 3f out: styd w ldr: rdn over 2f out: wknd u.p jst ins fnl f* **10/3**[1]
4162 7 3 **Northern Desert (IRE)**[12] 2630 10-9-10 **59** ....(p) JamesDoyle 15 45
(S Curran) *stdd s: hld up in tch in midfield: shkn up and effrt 2f out: drvn and no prog over 1f out* **13/2**
30-0 8 ½ **Morocchius (USA)**[43] 1734 4-9-4 **53** ....(p) RoystonFfrench 9 38
(Miss J A Camacho) *t.k.h: w ldr tl led narrowly 3f out: rdn wl over 1f out: hdd 1f out: wknd qckly* **20/1**
030- 9 5 **Roleplay (IRE)**[200] 7474 4-9-11 **60** ....(b) KirstyMilczarek 8 31
(J M P Eustace) *t.k.h: hld up wl in tch: rdn 2f out: sn hung lft and btn: wl bhd fnl f* **22/1**
500 10 3 ¼ **Scruffy Skip (IRE)**[3] 2920 4-9-5 **54** .... TonyCulhane 11 16
(Mrs C A Dunnett) *t.k.h: chsd ldrs tl 3f out: wknd u.p over 2f out: wl bhd and eased ins fnl f* **28/1**
0400 11 ½ **Ugenius**[18] 2458 5-9-6 **55** .... TGMcLaughlin 12 16
(Mrs C A Dunnett) *taken down early: t.k.h: hld up in rr: short-lived effrt 3f out: sn struggling: wl btn and eased ins fnl f* **11/1**

1m 28.95s (2.35) **Going Correction** +0.175s/f (Good)
WFA 3 from 4yo+ 9lb **11** Ran **SP% 118.4**
Speed ratings (Par 101): **93,92,90,88,88 87,84,83,77,74 73**
toteswinger: 1&2 £12.40, 1&3 £22.50, 2&3 not won. CSF £41.04 CT £424.17 TOTE £7.40: £2.80, £3.20, £5.10; EX 60.10.
Owner K A Morgan **Bred** Shadwell Estate Company Limited **Trained** Little Marcle, H'fords

FOCUS
A modest race, involving five maidens, four infrequent winners and a couple of veterans. The pace was only fair and there was another tight finish. The winner is rated back to his best.

3008 FREEDERM H'CAP 1m 3y
8:00 (8:03) (Class 4) (0-85,85) 3-Y-O+ **£4,667** (£1,397; £698; £349; £173) **Stalls** High

Form RPR
1362 1 **Marajaa (IRE)**[26] 2193 7-9-7 **78** .... ChrisCatlin 2 88+
(W J Musson) *stdd after s: hld up in last pl: clsd 2f out: swtchd rt over 1f out: chal gng wl 1f out: pushed into ld ins fnl f: pushed out: comf* **7/1**
0-40 2 ¾ **Kinsya**[19] 2412 6-9-9 **80** .... SaleemGolam 7 88
(M H Tompkins) *t.k.h: trckd ldrs: effrt and ev ch wl over 1f out: rdn to ld over 1f out: hdd ins fnl f: no ch w wnr but r.o for clr 2nd* **4/1**[2]
-064 3 4 **La Coveta (IRE)**[17] 2495 4-9-5 **76** .... TedDurcan 1 75
(B J Meehan) *chsd ldr: ev ch and rdn 2f out: drvn and outpcd by ldng pair 1f out: plugged on same pce fnl f* **6/1**[3]
-430 4 ¾ **Dear Maurice**[24] 2274 5-9-7 **78** .... TGMcLaughlin 3 75
(E A L Dunlop) *hld up in tch: pushed along and effrt on far side over 2f out: ev ch wl over 1f out: nt pce of ldrs ent fnl f: wknd and lost 3rd ins fnl f* **8/1**
4003 5 ½ **Magnitude**[18] 2459 4-8-12 **69** .... EddieAhern 4 65
(M E Rimmer) *hld up in tch: chsng ldrs whn n.m.r and swtchd lft over 1f out: sn rdn and no hdwy* **9/1**
6-10 6 ½ **Spring Goddess (IRE)**[59] 1348 8-9-4 **82** .... MatthewDavies(7) 5 77
(A P Jarvis) *stdd s: t.k.h: hld up in last pair: rdn and effrt wl over 1f out: wknd over 1f out* **25/1**
6-21 7 3 ½ **Tilos Gem (IRE)**[11] 2652 3-8-11 **78** .... RoystonFfrench 6 65
(M Johnston) *led: rdn over 2f out: hdd over 1f out: wknd qckly ent fnl f* **11/4**[1]
1030 8 2 ¾ **Saltagioo (ITY)**[11] 2666 5-9-9 **85** .... AndreaAtzeni(5) 8 66
(M Botti) *t.k.h: chsd ldrs: rdn over 2f out: wknd u.p over 1f out: wl bhd fnl f* **7/1**

1m 42.2s (1.60) **Going Correction** +0.175s/f (Good)
WFA 3 from 4yo+ 10lb **8** Ran **SP% 110.9**
Speed ratings (Par 105): **99,98,94,93,93 92,89,86**
toteswinger: 1&2 £5.10, 1&3 £26.10, 2&3 £23.90. CSF £32.92 CT £171.31 TOTE £6.00: £2.30, £1.60, £2.20; EX 28.90.
Owner John D Jacques **Bred** Shadwell Estate Company Limited **Trained** Newmarket, Suffolk

FOCUS
A fair handicap. The pace did not appear that stron but the winner came from the rear. The first two finished clear of the rest but the form has not been rated too positvely.

3009 ADIOS RATING RELATED MAIDEN STKS 7f 3y
8:30 (8:31) (Class 5) 3-Y-O **£2,849** (£847; £423; £211) **Stalls** High

Form RPR
0-00 1 **Jack Cool (IRE)**[11] 2664 3-9-3 68 .... AdrianMcCarthy 3 84
(P W Chapple-Hyam) *in tch: hdwy to chse ldrs 4f out: led over 2f out: rdn wl clr over 1f out: rdn out* **28/1**
-602 2 12 **Fajita**[15] 2548 3-9-3 67 .... FergusSweeney 1 52
(G L Moore) *in tch: hdwy 3f out: chsd wnr over 2f out: sn outpcd by wnr: hld hd high u.p but plugged on to hold poor 2nd* **4/1**[2]
-300 3 1 ¼ **Chadwell Spring (IRE)**[22] 2320 3-8-7 62 .... MatthewCosham(7) 10 45
(Miss J Feilden) *hld up towards rr: hdwy 4f out: wnt modest 3rd wl over 1f out: sn edgd rt and flashed tail u.p: plugged on but wl btn after* **25/1**
36-6 4 3 **All Spin (IRE)**[21] 2355 3-8-10 70 .... MatthewDavies(7) 11 40
(A P Jarvis) *stdd s: hld up bhd: hdwy 3f out: swtchd lft over 2f out: chsd ldng pair briefly wl over 2f out: sn outpcd and wl btn* **12/1**
-004 5 6 **Howard**[15] 2548 3-9-3 70 ....(p) EddieAhern 14 24
(J L Dunlop) *hld up towards rr: hdwy and edging lft 3f out: modest 5th and wl btn fr wl over 1f out* **5/2**[1]
-506 6 2 ¼ **Arctic Freedom (USA)**[11] 2685 3-9-0 67 ....(b) KirstyMilczarek 9 15
(E A L Dunlop) *s.i.s: hld up bhd: sme hdwy whn hmpd and swtchd rt 3f out: nvr on terms* **5/1**[3]
2000 7 ¾ **Jeremiah (IRE)**[33] 2010 3-9-0 70 .... JackMitchell(3) 6 16
(J G Portman) *in tch: rdn and edgd rt 3f out: wknd wl over 2f out* **8/1**
3040 8 ¾ **Flamboyant Red (IRE)**[60] 1317 3-9-3 42 ....(t) EdwardCreighton 7 14
(Miss Gay Kelleway) *a towards rr: rdn and struggling 3f out: no ch fnl 2f* **100/1**
055 9 ½ **Topcroft**[29] 2143 3-9-3 53 .... TGMcLaughlin 16 12
(Mrs C A Dunnett) *chsd ldrs wnt 2nd wl over 3f out tl over 2f out: sn wknd and wl btn* **40/1**
40-0 10 2 ¾ **George Rex (USA)**[22] 2329 3-9-3 70 .... ChrisCatlin 12 5
(B J Meehan) *a towards: struggling u.p 3f out* **33/1**
0-00 11 6 **Temperence Hall (USA)**[14] 2567 3-9-0 63 .... MarcHalford(3) 5 —
(J R Best) *chsd ldr tl over 3f out: sn drvn and toiling: t.o fnl 2f* **25/1**
4-54 12 4 **Baron Otto (IRE)**[11] 2681 3-9-3 69 ....(b) TonyCulhane 13 —
(W J Haggas) *led tl over 2f out: sn dropped out: t.o wl over 1f out* **12/1**
40-0 13 2 ½ **Jacobite Prince (IRE)**[55] 1462 3-9-3 68 .... TedDurcan 2 —
(M H Tompkins) *wnt bdly rt s: a in rr: lost tch 3f out: t.o fnl 2f* **10/1**

1m 27.71s (1.11) **Going Correction** +0.175s/f (Good) **13** Ran **SP% 118.3**
Speed ratings (Par 99): **100,86,84,81,74 72,71,70,69,66 59,55,52**
toteswinger: 1&2 £15.90, 1&3 not won, 2&3 £27.30. CSF £130.40 TOTE £18.20: £5.60, £1.80, £8.50; EX 142.50.
Owner Angus McDonnell **Bred** Angus McDonnell **Trained** Newmarket, Suffolk

FOCUS
There was not much between the majority of these on official figures in this maiden restricted to horses with a BHA rating of up to 70, but it was questionable how many were up to their official rating. The race was run at a decent tempo and produced a runaway winner. He is rated a big improver but what he achieved is questionable.
Jack Cool(IRE) Official explanation: trainer's representative said, regarding the apparent improvement in form shown, that the colt may have benefitted from the removal of a drop noseband worn last time, and being able to dominate today's race from the front
Fajita Official explanation: jockey said colt hung right

3010 BAZUKA H'CAP 6f 3y
9:00 (9:03) (Class 6) (0-65,65) 3-Y-O **£2,331** (£693; £346; £173) **Stalls** High

Form RPR
-550 1 **Rocket Rob (IRE)**[28] 2148 3-9-6 **64** .... SimonWhitworth 13 72
(S A Callaghan) *hld up towards rr: n.m.r ent fnl 2f: rdn and hdwy to chse ldng pair jst over 1f out: r.o strly to ld on post* **8/1**
0-00 2 nse **The Scorching Wind (IRE)**[28] 2160 3-9-1 **59** .... SaleemGolam 9 67
(S C Williams) *chsd ldrs: led over 2f out: hdd and rdn over 1f out: rallied to ld again fnl 100yds: hdd on post* **11/4**[1]
-642 3 1 **Choisharp (IRE)**[13] 2603 3-9-2 **65** .... AndreaAtzeni(5) 15 70
(M Botti) *w.w in tch: hdwy over 2f out: led over 1f out: rdn ent fnl f: hdd fnl 100yds: no ex* **7/2**[2]
0-00 4 5 **Winterfell**[30] 2104 3-8-12 **56** .... TedDurcan 1 45+
(C F Wall) *hld up towards rr: hdwy on outer over 2f out: chsd ldrs and rdn wl over 1f out: wknd ent fnl f* **20/1**
-000 5 ½ **Brynfa Boy**[28] 2162 3-9-0 **58** .... TonyCulhane 4 45
(P W D'Arcy) *stdd s: t.k.h: hld up towards rr: hdwy and swtchd lft wl over 1f out: chsd ldrs and rdn over 1f out: wknd fnl f* **16/1**
6022 6 1 **Cavitie**[14] 2581 3-8-9 **53** .... J-PGuillambert 2 37
(Andrew Reid) *in tch in midfield: rdn whn short of room and jostled 2f out: sn outpcd and no ch w ldrs fr over 1f out* **15/2**[3]
6006 7 2 **Imperial Skylight**[10] 2719 3-8-11 **60** .... MCGeran(5) 7 38
(M R Channon) *in tch tl shuffled bk towards rr and n.m.r over 2f out: no ch after* **16/1**
4-40 8 hd **Noverre To Hide (USA)**[15] 2548 3-9-1 **62** .... MarcHalford(3) 5 39
(J R Best) *chsd ldr tl over 2f out: sn edgd rt u.p: wknd over 1f out* **12/1**
1003 9 ½ **Kings Ace (IRE)**[19] 2417 3-8-8 **59** ....(v) MatthewDavies(7) 12 35
(A P Jarvis) *led: edgd lft fr 3f out: hdd over 2f out: drvn and wknd wl over 1f out: no ch whn hung rt ent fnl f* **12/1**
-354 10 1 ¼ **Jack's House (IRE)**[18] 2456 3-8-10 **54** .... RoystonFfrench 10 26
(Miss J A Camacho) *s.i.s and short of room sn after s: a bhd: n.d* **12/1**
6-00 11 1 **Pansy Potter**[17] 2498 3-9-3 **61** ....(b) EddieAhern 3 29
(B J Meehan) *hld up towards rr: hdwy and pushed lft over 2f out: wknd u.p wl over 1f out* **12/1**
00-0 12 4 ½ **Bold Hawk**[39] 1840 3-8-10 **54** ....(p) CatherineGannon 16 8
(Mrs C A Dunnett) *s.i.s: sn bustled along in rr: no ch whn nt clr run ent fnl f: n.d* **50/1**
20-0 13 2 ¼ **Chasing Amy**[13] 2602 3-9-2 **60** ....(b) JerryO'Dwyer 6 7
(M G Quinlan) *chsd ldrs tl lost pl qckly and wandered u.p wl over 3f out: no ch fnl 2f* **50/1**

50-4 **14** *6* **Dahama**[130] 426 3-9-4 62......(t) EdwardCreighton 14 —
(C E Brittain) *half-rrd as stalls opened and v.s.a: a bhd* **40/1**

1m 15.88s (1.48) **Going Correction** +0.175s/f (Good) **14** Ran SP% **125.4**
Speed ratings (Par 97): **97,96,95,88,88 86,84,84,83,81 80,74,71,63**
toteswinger: 1&2 £6.70, 1&3 £5.30, 2&3 £7.90. CSF £30.63 CT £95.89 TOTE £8.20: £2.40, £2.30, £2.30; EX 45.60 Place 6 £229.18, Place 5 £191.99..
Owner Bill Hinge, J Searchfield & N Callaghan **Bred** Mrs Marita Rogers **Trained** Newmarket, Suffolk

FOCUS
An ordinary event. The first three fought out a close finish and there was a long gap back to the rest. The form looks sound.
T/Plt: £572.10 to a £1 stake. Pool: £53,377.47. 68.10 winning tickets. T/Qpdt: £107.40 to a £1 stake. Pool: £5,631.62. 38.80 winning tickets. SP

2990 ASCOT (R-H)
Wednesday, June 17

OFFICIAL GOING: Good to firm (overall 9.8, straight 10.4, round 9.4)
Course set up as on day one with race distances on round course increased by about dozen yards.
Wind: Fresh, across Weather: Cloudy, light showers later

3011 JERSEY STKS (GROUP 3) 7f
2:30 (2:34) (Class 1) 3-Y-O

£45,416 (£17,216; £8,616; £4,296; £2,152; £1,080) **Stalls** Centre

Form RPR

0-10 **1** **Ouqba**[46] 1675 3-9-1 112...... TPO'Shea 3 113
(B W Hills) *lw: stdd in rr s: rdn along and struggling in last over 4f out: gd hdwy over 1f out: styd on wl to ld nr fin* **12/1**

0243 **2** *½* **Deposer (IRE)**[12] 2668 3-9-1 105...... RobertWinston 6 112
(J R Best) *led towards stands' rail: hrd rdn over 1f out: kpt on: hdd nr fin* **16/1**

6-02 **3** *3¼* **Ashram (IRE)**[20] 2411 3-9-4 108......(v[1]) LDettori 9 106
(Saeed Bin Suroor) *lw: hld up towards rr: drvn along and hdwy 2f out: wnt 3rd ent fnl f: styd on same pce* **8/1**[3]

224- **4** *hd* **Gallagher**[257] 6442 3-9-1 118...... MartinDwyer 8 102
(B J Meehan) *dwlt: hld up in rr: gd hdwy to chse ldrs 2f out: one pce fnl f* **9/1**

11-4 **5** *½* **Donativum**[25] 2278 3-9-1 115...... TedDurcan 13 101+
(Saeed Bin Suroor) *dwlt: hld up in rr: gd hdwy 2f out: no imp fnl f* **11/1**

36-2 **6** *1¼* **Patrician's Glory (USA)**[34] 2004 3-9-1 100...... OPeslier 5 98+
(T P Tate) *hld up towards rr: rdn and hdwy over 1f out: kpt on fnl f: nt pce to chal* **20/1**

1 **7** *2* **Loch Linnhe (USA)**[25] 2282 3-9-1 ...... JimmyFortune 7 92
(J H M Gosden) *chsd ldr tl wknd over 1f out* **6/1**[2]

8 *1¾* **Aranel (IRE)**[17] 3-9-1 99...... C-PLemaire 12 87
(M Delcher-Sanchez, Spain) *w'like: mid-div: effrt over 2f out: sn hrd rdn: no imp* **33/1**

-235 **9** *2¼* **Awinnersgame (IRE)**[18] 2485 3-9-1 106......(v[1]) JMurtagh 10 81
(J Noseda) *in tch: rdn over 2f out: sn btn* **12/1**

0316 **10** *3¼* **Jobe (USA)**[18] 2485 3-9-1 97...... NCallan 1 73
(K A Ryan) *t.k.h: sn in midfield: drvn along and wknd 3f out* **66/1**

3013 **11** *nse* **Saucy Brown (IRE)**[18] 2469 3-9-1 93...... RyanMoore 4 73
(R Hannon) *in tch: wknd 4f out: sn bhd* **33/1**

-623 **12** *1* **Nasri**[12] 2673 3-9-1 105...... JamieSpencer 14 70
(B J Meehan) *lw: in tch tl wknd 3f out* **14/1**

02-1 **13** *nse* **Instalment**[45] 1705 3-9-1 101...... RichardHughes 11 70
(R Hannon) *prom tl wknd jst over 2f out* **20/1**

1-15 **14** *1½* **Total Gallery (IRE)**[25] 2272 3-9-1 103...... LPKeniry 15 66
(J S Moore) *hld up in midfield: promising hdwy over 2f out: wknd wl over 1f out* **20/1**

-101 **15** *7* **Ocean's Minstrel**[12] 2673 3-9-1 104...... JerryO'Dwyer 2 47
(J Ryan) *chsd ldrs: rdn over 3f out: sn lost pl* **10/1**

3-11 **16** *12* **Infiraad**[46] 1677 3-9-1 100...... RHills 16 14
(B W Hills) *prom tl wknd jst over 2f out: bhd and eased fnl f* **5/1**[1]

1m 27.65s (-0.35) **Going Correction** +0.20s/f (Good) **16** Ran SP% **119.1**
Speed ratings (Par 109): **110,109,105,105,104 103,101,99,96,92 92,91,91,89,81 68**
toteswinger: 1&2 £41.50, 1&3 £18.00, 2&3 £33.20. CSF £169.58 CT £1635.70 TOTE £15.70: £5.20, £7.00, £2.10; EX 253.80 Trifecta £7025.20 Part won. Pool: £9,493.57 - 0.90 winning units..
Owner Hamdan Al Maktoum **Bred** Highclere Stud **Trained** Lambourn, Berks

FOCUS
There was no rain since the previous day but 2mm of water had been applied overnight. This was an open edition of a race which has featured subsequent Group 1 winners Mozart, Observatory and Proclamation on its roll of honour in the last decade. The runners made their way across to the stands' side and racing near the rail proved a definite advantage. Ouqba probably needed only to reproduce his Free Handicap form, but this was a clear step up from Deposer.

NOTEBOOK
Ouqba failed to shine in the 2000 Guineas, for which he had been supplemented, but the drop in grade enabled the Free Handicap winner to pick up his first Group win. The third highest rated on official figures, but deserted by Richard Hills who opted to ride Infiraad, he raced somewhat lazily in rear on the stands' side of the pack and most were travelling better than him at halfway. Once switched right though, he picked up well and cut down the leader to win in nice style. He may go next for the Lennox Stakes (Betfair Cup) at Glorious Goodwood over this trip but does shape as if worth trying over 1m again further down the line. Official explanation: trainer said, regarding apparent improvement in form, that the colt's previous run had probably come too soon.
Deposer(IRE) was not expected to make the running but broke well to lead and quickly claimed the rail. He was still in command entering the last, but couldn't hold off the winner in the last 50 yards. Another dropping back in trip, this followed similarly good efforts in the Dee Stakes at Chester and Epsom's Diomed Stakes and he deserves extra credit as he was the only one in the first six who did not come from the rear. He deserves to pick up a race at this level but is now likely to be sold, perhaps to Hong Kong. (tchd 18-1)
Ashram(IRE) was conceding 3lb all round, having incurred a penalty for his win in this grade in the Somerville Tattersall Stakes last autumn when trained by John Hills. Having his third run for Godolphin, following a disappointing effort in the Guineas (two places behind Ouqba) and a second in a Sandown Listed race, he came from the back and looked like finishing second at one stage. He was not inconvenienced by the drop back to 7f and was sharpened up by the first-time visor. (op 10-1 tchd 11-1)
Gallagher, the top-rated on BHA figures, made the frame in some top races as a juvenile but his reappearance had been delayed until now. Another to improve from the rear, he was alongside the winner approaching the final furlong but was unable to quicken up from that point. All his previous runs were over 6f and a drop back to that distance should benefit him. (tchd 17-2 and 10-1)
Donativum, the Godolphin second string, settled better than he had on his reappearance at Newmarket and was staying in quite nicely in the end from what proved an unfavourable berth out wide. The return to 1m will suit him and he should pay his way, if to nothing like the same degree as last year's highly lucrative campaign. (op 12-1 tchd 14-1 in a place)
Patrician's Glory(USA) was another who was running on at the end (having briefly had to wait for a run), and he too should benefit from the return to an extra furlong. (op 25-1)
Loch Linnhe(USA) lacked experience for a race like this, having won a Newmarket maiden, albeit by eight lengths, on his only start. He chased the leader before fading over a furlong out and remains a promising colt. (op 8-1 tchd 11-2)
Aranel(IRE), a Spanish challenger whose trainer won last year's King's Stand Stakes with Equiano, has won a couple of races over 1m at home but was flying too high here.
Awinnersgame(IRE), runner-up to Ouqba in the Free Handicap but below that level since, travelled well in the first-time visor but could not pick up when required. He is proving a little frustrating but on this evidence he does look a sprinter. (op 11-1 tchd 9-1)
Instalment, in the Royal colours, had landed a 6f Salisbury handicap on his latest start and could not handle this rise in grade. He was not helped by a high draw and has now been beaten each time he has tackled 7f. (op 16-1)
Ocean's Minstrel is twice a winner at Listed level this year and finished ahead of both Ouqba and Asram when all three were also-rans in the 2000 Guineas. He had a favourable high draw here but his wins this year have come from the front and he was unable to lead this time. Official explanation: jockey said colt was struck into behind (op 14-1)
Infiraad had a good deal to find on official ratings, but he came here on a high and was the choice of the owner's retained jockey. He was well enough placed for 5f but was already on the retreat when he was squeezed out slightly approaching the last. His high draw was no use to him and he might prefer easier ground, for all that his two wins came in fast conditions. Richard Hills reported that the colt was never travelling. Official explanation: jockey said colt never travelled (op 9-2 tchd 11-2 in places)

3012 WINDSOR FOREST STKS (GROUP 2) (F&M) 1m (S)
3:05 (3:08) (Class 1) 4-Y-O+

£70,962 (£26,900; £13,462; £6,712; £3,362; £1,687) **Stalls** Centre

Form RPR

44-3 **1** **Spacious**[11] 2703 4-8-12 107...... JMurtagh 6 115
(J R Fanshawe) *swtg: mde all: shkn up over 2f out: sn strly pressed: rdn over 1f out: r.o gamely and fnd ex towards fin* **10/1**

45-1 **2** *1* **Heaven Sent**[45] 1697 6-8-12 111...... RyanMoore 7 113
(Sir Michael Stoute) *lw: chsd wnr: str chal fr 2f out and upsides: rdn over 1f out: hld fnl strides* **5/2**[2]

0011 **3** *3* **Eva's Request (IRE)**[11] 2703 4-8-12 109...... EdwardCreighton 5 106
(M R Channon) *hld up: hdwy 2f out: chsd front pair over 1f out: edgd rt ins fnl f: styd on: nt pce to threaten ldrs* **8/1**[3]

1-00 **4** *¾* **Chantilly Tiffany**[25] 2285 5-8-12 108...... JimmyFortune 2 104
(E A L Dunlop) *hld up: rdn and hdwy 2f out: styd on ins fnl f: nt pce to get to ldrs* **28/1**

02-2 **5** *½* **She's Our Mark**[11] 2729 5-8-12 106...... JamieSpencer 4 103
(Patrick J Flynn, Ire) *racd keenly: hld up: rdn and nt qckn 2f out: kpt on fnl f: nt pce to chal* **28/1**

20-3 **6** *1½* **Lush Lashes**[24] 2303 4-9-3 119...... KJManning 3 104
(J S Bolger, Ire) *ponied to s: chsd ldrs: rdn over 2f out: wknd over 1f out* **6/4**[1]

00-1 **7** *½* **Rosaleen (IRE)**[9] 2768 4-8-12 98...... MartinDwyer 1 98
(B J Meehan) *in tch: pushed along and outpcd over 2f out: kpt on steadily fnl f: no imp* **33/1**

30-5 **8** *hd* **Proviso**[31] 2120 4-8-12 110...... SPasquier 9 98
(A Fabre, France) *swtg: racd keenly: in tch: effrt to chal over 2f out: wknd over 1f out* **8/1**[3]

0-46 **9** *2¼* **Royal Confidence**[18] 2483 4-8-12 103...... MichaelHills 8 93
(B W Hills) *lw: midfield on outside: clsd 3f out: effrt whn chsng ldrs 2f out: wknd over 1f out* **50/1**

1m 41.07s (0.47) **Going Correction** +0.20s/f (Good) **9** Ran SP% **111.7**
Speed ratings (Par 115): **105,104,101,100,99 98,97,97,95**
toteswinger: 1&2 £5.20, 1&3 £8.30, 2&3 £4.60. CSF £33.15 CT £209.03 TOTE £10.60: £2.60, £1.80, £2.00; EX 40.30 Trifecta £200.10 Pool: £15,092.26 - 55.79 winning units..
Owner Cheveley Park Stud **Bred** Cheveley Park Stud Ltd **Trained** Newmarket, Suffolk
■ A one-two for the Cheveley Park Stud, who have had the winner three times in the race's six-year history.

FOCUS
A somewhat tactical fillies' Group 2. The rail was the place to be and the winner improved for the more positive tactics. The second was close to her best.

NOTEBOOK
Spacious was gifted a soft lead on the favoured stands' rail. She had been comfortably held behind Eva's Request at Epsom on her reappearance, but she got unbalanced on the camber, and this course was far more to her liking. Connections had decided beforehand to let her stride on, and the way things turned out she was always going to be difficult to peg back. Although strongly challenged by Heaven Sent, Murtagh had kept something in reserve and she rallied well. Much had been expected of her following her juvenile campaign, but having come up just short in the Guineas she largely disappointed afterwards. However, she has clearly needed time - her sire Nayef was arguably at his peak as a five-year-old - and there is still a chance she'll finally take a Group 1 race. The Falmouth looks the most obvious target in the short term. (tchd 11-1)
Heaven Sent, whose trainer has a good record in this race was well fancied to improve on her second in this race last year. She ran a very solid race in defeat, but the winner had the run of the race in front, with the added advantage of the rail throughout, and she just could not get by her. There are further Group races to be won with her but she is six now and has her limitations. (tchd 11-4 in places)
Eva's Request(IRE) came here on the back of a career-best win in the Group 3 Princess Elizabeth Stakes at Epsom (Spacious well held in third), and this was probably a better run than it looks, as she was held up in what was a tactical race. She should be a player at this level for the rest of the season, although easier ground arguably suits her better.
Chantilly Tiffany is no better than Listed class really, and her better than expected performance is almost certainly down to having, like the winner, stayed on the favoured stands' rail throughout. (op 33-1 tchd 25-1)
She's Our Mark, for whom the ground was a concern, in the circumstances ran about as well as one could expect, especially as she was on her toes beforehand. Her efforts this season suggests she's as good as ever and it wouldn't be a surprise to see her win another Group 3 race when the mud is flying. (op 33-1 tchd 25-1)
Lush Lashes, despite having to give 5lb all round, was still the one to beat at the weights. Impressive winner of the Coronation Stakes at this meeting last year, her trainer had said that her reappearance in testing ground had been very much needed, and these conditions promised to suit her a lot better. She proved very disappointing, however, weakening right out from the two pole. Having run below her best on both her starts since her unfortunate experience in Hong Kong last term, it remains to be seen whether she retains her sparkling three-year-old ability. (op 13-8)
Rosaleen(IRE) predictably found the competition a bit hot but probably ran her race.
Proviso was expected to be a top three-year-old following a juvenile campaign which culminated in a second place in the Fillies' Mile, but she was ultimately disappointing last year, only scoring towards the backend in Listed company. Tackling ground that was quicker than she'd ever previously encountered, she pulled hard towards the outer, and folded tamely once the pace picked up. (tchd 9-1 in places)

Royal Confidence faced a stiff task in this company and racing widest of all throughout was probably no help. (op 40-1)

3013 PRINCE OF WALES'S STKS (GROUP 1) 1m 2f

3:45 (3:46) (Class 1) 4-Y-0+

£255,465 (£96,840; £48,465; £24,165; £12,105; £6,075) **Stalls** High

Form				RPR
5-31	**1**		**Vision D'Etat (FR)**[52] 1551 4-9-0 122 .... OPeslier 7	124
			(E Libaud, France) *str: hld up in 6th: rdn over 3f out: hdwy over 1f out: styd on wl u.str.p to ld fnl 100yds* **4/1**[3]	
24-1	**2**	½	**Tartan Bearer (IRE)**[53] 1526 4-9-0 122 .... RyanMoore 2	123
			(Sir Michael Stoute) *lw: settled in 4th: drvn to press ldrs whn hung rt over 1f out: r.o fnl f: a jst hld* **6/4**[1]	
1-51	**3**	hd	**Never On Sunday (FR)**[31] 2120 4-9-0 116 .... C-PLemaire 5	123
			(J-C Rouget, France) *w'like: hld up in 7th: rdn and gd hdwy fr over 1f out: r.o wl u.p fnl f: clsng at fin* **7/2**[2]	
2-33	**4**	nk	**Twice Over**[32] 2076 4-9-0 119 .... TPQueally 1	122
			(H R A Cecil) *trckd ldr: rdn 3f out: led 2f out: hung rt: hld on wl tl hdd and lost 3 pls fnl 100yds* **9/1**	
1-10	**5**	3¼	**Tazeez (USA)**[31] 2120 5-9-0 113 .... RHills 8	116
			(J H M Gosden) *led: rdn and hdd 2f out: wknd over 1f out* **16/1**	
1-31	**6**	¾	**Virtual**[32] 2076 4-9-0 117 .... JimmyFortune 3	114
			(J H M Gosden) *lw: trckd ldng pair: rdn to chal whn hung rt on ins rail 2f out: wknd over 1f out* **14/1**	
-012	**7**	4	**Trincot (FR)**[31] 2115 4-9-0 121 ....(p) LDettori 4	106
			(Saeed Bin Suroor) *hld up in last: drvn along and unable to improve over 2f out: nvr trbld ldrs* **16/1**	
10-6	**8**	16	**Estejo (GER)**[31] 2115 5-9-0 112 .... DPorcu 6	74
			(R Rohne, Germany) *lengthy: swtg: t.k.h in 5th: rdn 3f out: wknd over 2f out: sn bhd* **66/1**	

2m 6.90s (-0.10) **Going Correction** +0.20s/f (Good) **8** Ran SP% **112.1**
Speed ratings (Par 117): **108,107,107,107,104 104,100,88**
toteswinger: 1&2 £1.60, 1&3 £2.80, 2&3 £1.70. CSF £9.96 CT £21.49 TOTE £3.30: £1.10, £1.40, £1.50; EX 9.40 Trifecta £24.20 Pool: £21,654.79 - 659.91 winning units..
Owner Jacques Detre **Bred** Gaetan Gilles **Trained** France
■ Stewards' Enquiry : O Peslier one-day ban: used whip in an incorrect position (Jul 1)

FOCUS

With Duke Of Marmalade, Manduro and Ouija Board the last three winners, the Prince Of Wales's is always one of the meeting's highlights and this was another up-to-scratch renewal. The pace, initially sound, then slowed slightly and they stacked up before it became a little bit of a sprint from the two pole, but there were no real excuses and the form looks still solid enough.

NOTEBOOK

Vision D'Etat(FR), with Olivier Peslier replacing the out-of-favour Ioritz Mendizabal, raced in rear on the inside before making rapid progress in the straight. He still had work to do entering the last, but ran on very willingly to force his head in front. This was his eighth win in ten career starts, including last year's Prix du Jockey Club and the Prix Ganay at Longchamp on his latest start, where he idled when in command. There had been controversy before the race when it transpired that his tongue tie had not been declared, but that proved no problem and the aid is obviously not necessary. He was fifth to Zarkava in last year's Arc and that race will be the aim again following the classic French preparation of a prep run in the Prix Foy. He will not mind the return to easier ground. (tchd 5-1)

Tartan Bearer(IRE) won the Gordon Richards Stakes at Sandown first time out but missed an intended run in the Tattersalls Gold Cup because of the testing ground. Racing on the outside of the bunch, he took a little bit of time to pick up when Twice Over went for home, but he was in pursuit of that horse in plenty of time, keeping on strongly but just lacking the pace of the winner who passed him inside the last. His trainer has not won this race since 1991, Opera House, Pilsudski and Fantastic Light among those who have been found wanting, and Tartan Bearer loses nothing in defeat. He has the option of returning to 1m4f and his first Group 1 success should not be too long delayed. (op 13-8 tchd 11-8 and 7-4 in places)

Never On Sunday(FR), the winner's compatriot, was successful in this grade in the Prix D'Ispahan on his latest start and racing for a stable in red-hot form. Not for the first time he became rather stirred up in the preliminaries, though. Held up at the back in company with the winner, he took a little time to get organised but ran on strongly down the outside in the latter stages and would have got up for second in a couple more strides. (tchd 4-1 and 9-2 in places)

Twice Over raced close to the pace before going for home with a quarter of a mile left. It briefly looked like he would last home, but he could not hold the finishers deep inside the last. A versatile colt, he has made the frame on each of his four starts at the top level without quite managing to win one, but that should change with luck. (op 10-1)

Tazeez(USA) had Twice Over behind when winning the Earl Of Sefton first time but had finished last to Never On Sunday in soft ground in the Ispahan. Dull in his coat beforehand, he set the pace and kept on as best he could when headed, but he is not quite up to this level. (op 20-1)

Virtual, the pick of the paddock, has made rapid strides since finishing 17th in the Britannia Handicap a year ago, narrowly winning the Lockinge Stakes last time with Twice Over and Queen Anne winner Paco Boy behind. Tackling this trip for the first time, although he did win a Listed race at 1m1f in soft ground last year, he had every chance up the straight but rather hung to his right against the rail and was not helping his rider. The return to an easier surface should help him get back on track. (op 12-1 tchd 16-1)

Trincot(FR), on his toes beforehand, had both Vision D'Etat and Never On Sunday behind when landing the Prix Harcourt for his previous trainer Peter Demercastel in early April. Having his second run for Godolphin, he was held up with the French pair in rear but did not pick up anything like as well as those two, although in his defence he was slightly hampered at the two marker. (tchd 14-1 and 20-1)

Estejo(GER), the German raider, was on his toes beforehand. He did win a Group 1 in Italy last backend, but had to improve greatly on his best form here and did his chances no good by failing to settle. (op 100-1)

3014 ROYAL HUNT CUP (HERITAGE H'CAP) 1m (S)

4:20 (4:24) (Class 2) 3-Y-0+

£62,310 (£18,660; £9,330; £4,670; £2,330; £1,170) **Stalls** Centre

Form				RPR
1/11	**1**		**Forgotten Voice (IRE)**[44] 1731 4-9-1 101 .... JMurtagh 1	115+
			(J Noseda) *lw: racd on stands' side: in tch: hdwy to ld 2f out: r.o wl fnl f and a in command* **4/1**[1]	
50	**2**	2¼	**Huzzah (IRE)**[60] 1352 4-8-10 96 .... MichaelHills 5	105
			(B W Hills) *lw: racd in midfield on stands' side: hdwy and swtchd rt over 2f out: wnt 2nd over 1f out: styd on ins fnl f: nt pce of wnr: 2nd of 17 in gp* **25/1**	
6232	**3**	¾	**Mia's Boy**[18] 2500 5-9-3 103 .... RyanMoore 4	110
			(C A Dwyer) *racd on stands' side: hld up: rdn and hdwy over 1f out: styd on ins fnl f: nt quite pce to get to front 2: 3rd of 17 in gp* **9/1**[2]	
1-02	**4**	1½	**Nanton (USA)**[23] 2342 7-8-6 92 .... DanielTudhope 21	96+
			(J S Goldie) *sn swtchd lft to r stands' side: hld up: hdwy 2f out: styd on ins fnl f: nt pce of ldrs: 4th of 17 in gp* **16/1**	
206-	**5**	2¾	**Alfathaa**[270] 6123 4-9-3 103 .... RHills 16	101
			(W J Haggas) *missed break: racd stands' side: hld up: hdwy and swtchd rt over 1f out: r.o ins fnl f: nrst fin: 5th of 17 in gp* **25/1**	
15-2	**6**	1¼	**Axiom**[20] 2412 5-8-6 92 .... C-PLemaire 18	87+
			(L M Cumani) *racd on stands' side: midfield: pushed along and hdwy over 2f out: chsd ldrs over 1f out: kpt on same pce fnl f: 6th of 17 in gp* **16/1**	
0640	**7**	1¼	**Kings Point (IRE)**[14] 2612 8-8-4 90 .... TPO'Shea 13	82
			(D Nicholls) *swtg: racd on stands' side: midfield: rdn and carried rt over 1f out: kpt on ins fnl f: 7th of 17 in gp* **100/1**	
0231	**8**	shd	**Kavachi (IRE)**[4] 2933 6-8-5 91 5ex .... FergusSweeney 17	83+
			(G L Moore) *missed break: racd on stands' side: hld up: nt clr run over 2f out: sn swtchd rt: nt clr run over 1f out: styd on ins fnl f: nt get to ldrs: 8th of 17 in gp* **33/1**	
4646	**9**	½	**Lovelace**[12] 2668 5-9-10 110 .... JamieSpencer 24	100+
			(M Johnston) *lw: missed break: racd on far side: hld up: nt clr run whn hdwy and swtchd rt over 2f out: led gp 1f out: no ch w other side: 1st of 8 in gp* **16/1**	
4013	**10**	1¾	**Mahadee (IRE)**[47] 1641 4-9-0 100 ....(b) NCallan 26	86
			(C E Brittain) *racd on far side: chsd ldrs: led gp 2f out tl 1f out but no imp w other side: one pce ins fnl f: 2nd of 8 in gp* **66/1**	
-100	**11**	2¼	**Manassas (IRE)**[37] 1929 4-8-11 97 .... DaneO'Neill 23	78
			(B J Meehan) *lw: racd on far side: chsd ldrs: pushed along 3f out: no ex ins fnl f: 3rd of 8 in gp* **40/1**	
-451	**12**	nk	**Ellemujie**[13] 2639 4-8-6 92 5ex .... MartinDwyer 30	72
			(D K Ivory) *racd on far side: midfield: hdwy over 2f out: sn chsd ldrs: kpt on same pce fnl f: 4th of 8 in gp* **40/1**	
0-11	**13**	nk	**Soccerjackpot (USA)**[83] 974 5-8-8 94 .... IanMongan 8	74
			(C G Cox) *racd on stands' side: prom: rdn and wkng whn bmpd over 1f out: 9th of 17 in gp* **25/1**	
0161	**14**	shd	**Dunn'o (IRE)**[20] 2412 4-8-11 97 5ex .... PhilipRobinson 6	77
			(C G Cox) *racd on satnds' side: overall ldr tl 2f out: wknd fnl f: 10th of 17 in gp* **14/1**	
0-02	**15**	1¾	**Quinmaster (USA)**[13] 2647 7-9-2 102 ....(p) RichardHughes 12	78
			(M Halford, Ire) *missed break: racd on stands' side: in tch: rdn over 2f out: wknd over 1f out: 11th of 17 in gp* **50/1**	
23-2	**16**	1¾	**Final Verse**[32] 2083 6-8-6 92 .... LPKeniry 22	64
			(M Salaman) *racd on far side: towards rr: effrt over 2f out: wknd fnl f: 5th of 8 in gp* **33/1**	
4004	**17**	2¾	**Royal Power (IRE)**[12] 2669 6-8-9 95 .... AdrianTNicholls 25	60
			(D Nicholls) *racd on far side: towards rr: hdwy over 2f out: wknd fnl f: 6th of 8 in gp* **33/1**	
-016	**18**	¾	**Cadre (IRE)**[20] 2412 4-8-9 95 .... RobertHavlin 14	58+
			(J H M Gosden) *swtg: racd on stands' side: midfield: effrt 3f out: sn hung rt: wknd over 1f out: 12th of 17 in gp* **12/1**[3]	
0503	**19**	nk	**Lucky Dance (BRZ)**[18] 2470 7-8-5 91 .... WilliamBuick 10	54
			(A G Foster) *racd on stands' side: prom tl rdn and wknd 3f out: 13th of 17 in gp* **33/1**	
6100	**20**	1	**Flawed Genius**[23] 2342 4-8-4 90 .... PaulHanagan 15	50
			(K A Ryan) *racd on stands' side: in tch: wknd over 2f out: 14th of 17 in gp* **66/1**	
-120	**21**	9	**Light From Mars**[20] 2412 4-8-7 93 .... AlanMunro 9	33
			(B R Millman) *racd on stands' side: chsd ldrs tl rdn and wknd over 1f out: 15th of 17 gp* **20/1**	
355/	**22**	3¼	**Luisant**[38] 1912 6-8-5 91 .... WMLordan 19	23
			(J A Nash, Ire) *racd on stands' side: midfield: wknd over 2f out: 16th of 17 in gp* **80/1**	
4006	**23**	3¼	**Jack Junior (USA)**[67] 1209 5-8-11 97 .... KShea 32	22
			(D Nicholls) *led far-side gp: hdd 2f out: wknd over 1f out: 7th of 8 in gp* **50/1**	
0213	**24**	2¼	**Philario (IRE)**[12] 2669 4-9-0 105 .... MartinLane(5) 33	25
			(K R Burke) *racd on far side: prom: pushed along over 2f out: wknd over 1f out: 8th of 8 in gp* **33/1**	
00-0	**25**	35	**Alan Devonshire**[18] 2500 4-8-8 94 .... TedDurcan 2	—
			(M H Tompkins) *racd on stands' side: chsd ldrs: pshd along and wknd over 3f out: 17th of 17 in gp* **100/1**	

1m 40.41s (-0.19) **Going Correction** +0.20s/f (Good) **25** Ran SP% **108.0**
Speed ratings (Par 109): **108,105,105,103,100 99,98,98,97,95 93,93,93,92,91 89,86,85,85,84 75,72,69,66,31**
toteswinger: 1&2 £29.60, 1&3 £4.40, 2&3 £26.00 . CSF £71.36 CT £367.92 TOTE £3.90: £1.60, £6.20, £1.90, £4.40; EX 160.50 Trifecta £315.50 Pool: £5,203.07 - 12.20 winning units..
Owner Mrs Susan Roy **Bred** Swettenham Stud And Ben Sangster **Trained** Newmarket, Suffolk
■ Bencoolen (80/1), Docofthebay (14/1) and Roaring Forte 11/2 were withdrawn; Rule 4 applies; deduction 20p in the £ (all bets).

FOCUS

As usual this looked a competitive handicap but Soccerjackpot got upset in the stalls, setting off Docofthebay, who was subsequently withdrawn, and with the well fancied Roaring Forte also taken away at the start, the race lost a couple of its main players before the off. The field split into two, with the bigger group heading towards the stands' side, and at the finish that side was well on top. Being on the rail had looked to be favoured in the earlier races on the straight track, and that was confirmed here, with low-drawn horses dominating at the finish.

NOTEBOOK

Forgotten Voice(IRE), the least exposed horse in the line-up, dominated the market and confirmed speculation that he was a Pattern horse in disguise with a comprehensive success. Having said that, he very much had the run of the race as he was drawn in stall one, was never further than one off the favoured stands'-side rail, and got a nice tow through the early part of the race from the likes of Dunn'o. He is clearly just as effective on turf as he is on Polytrack, and plans to go for the John Smith's Cup have apparently now been shelved in favour of going the Pattern-race route. He boasts a fine turn of foot and there should be plenty more to come from him, especially considering he was thought good enough to be aimed at the Guineas after winning his maiden and before a leg injury put an end to that particular ambition. (tchd 7-2, 9-2 in places and 5-1 in a place)

Huzzah(IRE) finished fifth in the Lincoln on his reappearance and has always looked the type that might be able to take one of these major mile handicaps. He was another to benefit from a low draw, racing on the rail through the early parts before being switched to challenge around horses. He was unlucky to bump into a winner who was very well in at the weights.

Mia's Boy was officially 2lb well in at the weights and has been running consistently all season. The strong pace of this cavalry charge promised to bring out the best in him, and, being favourably drawn on the stands' side, he had plenty go his way, although arguably more cut in the ground would suit him ideally. (op 10-1 tchd 17-2 and 12-1 in places)

Nanton(USA) did well considering he raced towards the outer of the stands'-side group and challenged more towards the centre of the track. He's very much at his best coming from off the pace in a strongly run race so this sort of big-field contest suits him down to the ground. (op 20-1)

Alfathaa ◆ also ran well considering he didn't have an ideal draw and this was his seasonal reappearance. A promising juvenile who didn't go on as a three-year-old, he's by Nayef and promises to do better this year. He could be interesting when stepped back up to 1m2f, as he saw this race out strongly. (op 33-1)

Axiom had been well beaten on his only previous start on good to firm ground. In the circumstances he ran a sound race, and the best of him as probably yet to be seen. (op 14-1)
Kings Point(IRE) is at his best on sharper tracks, but he ran quite well, albeit with the advantage of racing towards the stands' rail for a long way.
Kavachi(IRE) was making a quick reappearance after winning at York four days earlier. Connections had expected him to miss the cut, but he got in under his penalty and ended up running a solid race considering he didn't get the clearest of runs and the race was just an afterthought. Official explanation: jockey said gelding missed the break (tchd 28-1)
Lovelace ◆ quite comfortably came out on top from the eight that raced on the far side. Successful in Group company in the past, he won on his only previous visit to Goodwood, and he could be one to look out for at the Glorious meeting there.
Mahadee(IRE), second on the far side, was returning to turf off a 20lb higher mark than when last seen on grass. His improvement in the interim has come on Polytrack, but he is clearly just as effective on both surfaces.
Manassas(IRE), third on the far side, ran a better race back in handicap company on fast ground. These are very much his conditions. (op 33-1)
Ellemujie, another carrying a 5lb penalty, faced a stiff task and wasn't disgraced.
Soccerjackpot(USA), who got stirred up in the stalls beforehand, showed up for a long way but was already on the retreat when hampered. (op 20-1)
Dunn'o(IRE) took them along on the stands' side but he has never won on ground described as quicker than good, and found dominating here a lot more difficult than around Sandown. (op 16-1)
Cadre(IRE) had Robert Havlin, who rode him to success at Yarmouth, back aboard, and appeared to have conditions to suit. He was weak in the betting beforehand, though, and raced on the outer of the stands'-side group. Challenging up the centre of the track, he was pretty soon hanging and going nowhere fast. This was not his true form. His rider reported that the gelding hung right. Official explanation: jockey said gelding hung right (op 10-1 tchd 14-1 in places)

3015 QUEEN MARY STKS (GROUP 2) (FILLIES) 5f

4:55 (4:57) (Class 1) 2-Y-O

£51,093 (£19,368; £9,693; £4,833; £2,421; £1,215) **Stalls** Centre

Form				RPR
	1		**Jealous Again (USA)**[48] 2-8-12 0 ....(bt) JRVelazquez 1 (Wesley A Ward, U.S.A) *rangy: swtg: mde all: easily sprinted 4l clr ins fnl 2f: pushed out: impressive* **13/2**	115+
11	2	5	**Misheer**[33] 2054 2-8-12 0 .... NCallan 4 (C E Brittain) *lw: chsd ldrs: rdn 3f out: kpt on to take 2nd ins fnl f: no ch w wnr* **9/1**	97
11	3	2	**Ceedwell**[12] 2655 2-8-12 0 .... TomEaves 3 (B Smart) *w'like: mid-div: hrd rdn over 2f out: styd on fnl f: snatched 3rd on line* **12/1**	90
11	4	nse	**Capercaillie (USA)**[11] 2714 2-8-12 0 .... LDettori 11 (M Johnston) *w'like: tall: in rr of midfield: rdn and hdwy 2f out: hung lft and wnt 4th over 1f out: kpt on same pce* **4/1**[1]	90
	5	nse	**Chantilly Creme (USA)**[41] 2-8-12 0 .... SPasquier 7 (R Gibson, France) *leggy: in rr of midfield: rdn over 2f out: sme hdwy and swtchd rt over 1f out: styd on fnl f* **16/1**	89
1	6	3 ½	**Lady Of The Desert (USA)**[22] 2354 2-8-12 0 .... MartinDwyer 5 (B J Meehan) *w'like: scope: dwlt: sn prom: wnt 2nd 2f out: sn outpcd by wnr: wknd and lost 2nd ins fnl f* **11/2**[3]	81+
1	7	2	**Rose Blossom**[19] 2435 2-8-12 0 .... PaulHanagan 10 (R A Fahey) *w'like: cl cpld: a abt same pl: rdn over 2f out: nt pce to chal* **5/1**[2]	70
5011	8	¾	**Crown (IRE)**[37] 1927 2-8-12 0 .... RichardHughes 9 (R Hannon) *outpcd in rr: struggling in detached last 1/2-way: sme hdwy whn hung rt over 1f out: nt rch ldrs* **20/1**	67
16	9	nk	**High Spice (USA)**[20] 2408 2-8-12 0 .... EddieAhern 6 (R M H Cowell) *in tch in 5th tl wknd and edgd rt 2f out* **25/1**	66
11	10	3 ¼	**Don't Tell Mary (IRE)**[21] 2372 2-8-12 0 .... RichardKingscote 12 (Tom Dascombe) *str: sn outpcd towards rr: nvr a factor* **11/2**[3]	54
12	11	1 ¼	**Grand Zafeen**[41] 1805 2-8-12 0 .... TonyCulhane 8 (M R Channon) *str: lw: dwlt: a outpcd and bhd* **33/1**	50
52	12	8	**Itwasonlyakiss (IRE)**[27] 2207 2-8-12 0 .... MichaelHills 2 (J W Hills) *mid-div: rdn 3f out: sn wknd: bhd fnl 2f* **40/1**	21
3	13	11	**Lady Royal Oak (IRE)**[14] 2604 2-8-12 0 .... RyanMoore 13 (M Botti) *w'like: racd wd of others towards centre: gd spd to press wnr 3f: wknd qckly* **33/1**	—

60.53 secs (0.03) **Going Correction** +0.20s/f (Good) **13 Ran SP% 121.3**
Speed ratings (Par 102): **107,99,95,95,95 90,86,85,85,79 77,65,47**
toteswinger: 1&2 £14.90, 1&3 £22.90, 2&3 £24.70 . CSF £60.82 CT £504.30 TOTE £7.60: £2.00, £3.40, £4.30; EX 70.50 Trifecta £407.60 Pool: £8.334.19 - 15.13 winning units..
Owner R Abrams,R Brewer,M Dutko,W Ward **Bred** Harold J Plumley **Trained** North America
■ The second American-trained winner of the week, both of them from the stable of Wesley Ward.

FOCUS

This race has suffered since the introduction of the Albany Stakes in 2002, with the last three runnings looking particularly sub-standard, but this looked a strong renewal with seven unbeaten fillies lining up. Again a low draw proved a big plus, with the winner coming out of stall 1 and racing a few yards off the rail, and the next pair home drawn 4 and 3. The winner looks the best since Attraction and the form appears solid with the placed horses rated to their previous marks.

NOTEBOOK

Jealous Again(USA), an American filly who had won over 4.5f at Keeneland, blew her rivals out of the water to give her connections a second juvenile winner at the meeting following Strike The Tiger in the Windsor Castle on day one. Showing tremendous pace from the 1 stall and quickly getting nearly all her rivals in trouble, she maintained the gallop and had the race won entering the final furlong, scoring very impressively. (op 8-1)
Misheer was under pressure at halfway but stayed on to go after the easy winner inside the final furlong. Winner of the Listed Micklegate Stakes at York last time, a race which has had a good bearing on this event recently, she looks ready for a step up to 6f or even 7f now. The Moyglare Stud Stakes may suit her. (op 10-1)
Ceedwell came here two from two and she ran well on this steep rise in grade, although when she came under pressure she looked more likely to finish last than make the frame. To her credit she stuck on well, and she got up for third on the line. Her trainer intends targeting her at the Cheveley Park Stakes, and easier autumn ground will suit her. (op 16-1)
Capercaillie(USA) ◆ is thought by Mark Johnston to be his best juvenile filly since Attraction, who landed this race in 2003 and two Classics the following season. A winner of both her starts, at Musselburgh each time, she never looked like winning this and edged left approaching the final furlong before running on nicely when straightened. She should be kept on the right side. (op 5-1)
Chantilly Creme(USA), a winner on her sole previous start, ran on late to be involved in a three-way photo for third, but never sighted the winner. (op 25-1)
Lady Of The Desert(USA) is a daughter of Queen's Logic, who won this race for the same connections eight years ago. She showed up well for a long way, but her exertions in trying to live with Jealous Again told and she was a tired filly in the latter stages, losing four places from the furlong pole. (op 6-1 tchd 13-2 in places)
Rose Blossom, an impressive Hamilton winner who was sold to Highclere Racing after her debut, could never get into the action but she was running on a bit when it was all over. (op 9-2 tchd 6-1)
Crown(IRE), the most experienced filly on show, could not go the pace at all but made modest late gains. (op 16-1)
High Spice(USA) ran respectably before fading going to the final furlong.
Don't Tell Mary(IRE), on her toes beforehand, looked a leading contender on the strength of her Hilary Needler win at Beverley, but that Listed race has not really been working out; runner-up The Hermitage was well beaten in the Windsor Castle. She was poorly drawn here but even so was disappointing, unable to go the pace and always in rear. Official explanation: jockey said filly never travelled; trainer said filly returned home lame (op 9-2)
Lady Royal Oak(IRE) ◆ finished a long last in the end, but she showed blazing pace down the centre to match strides for a time with the winner, who raced a good way apart from her. One of only two maidens in this field, she should break her duck before long and her natural speed might make her interesting in something like the Molecomb at Goodwood.

3016 SANDRINGHAM H'CAP (LISTED RACE) (FILLIES) 1m (S)

5:30 (5:33) (Class 1) (0-110,106) 3-Y-O

£28,385 (£10,760; £5,385; £2,685; £1,345; £675) **Stalls** Centre

Form				RPR
-531	1		**Moneycantbuymelove (IRE)**[27] 2190 3-8-11 96 .... JamieSpencer 4 (M L W Bell) *hld up: nt clr run and hdwy over 2f out: chsd ldr over 1f out: led 100yds out: r.o wl and in command towards fin* **9/2**[1]	108+
15-6	2	2	**Golden Stream (IRE)**[45] 1701 3-8-9 94 .... RyanMoore 3 (Sir Michael Stoute) *hld up: hdwy 3f out: led and edgd lft wl over 1f out: hdd 100yds out: no ex cl home* **8/1**	101
0-63	3	3	**Please Sing**[39] 1873 3-9-1 100 .... EdwardCreighton 7 (M R Channon) *hld up: pushed along 3f out: hdwy 2f out: hung rt and chsd ldng duo over 1f out: styd on ins fnl f: nt pce to threaten ldrs* **14/1**	100
0431	4	6	**Silver Games (IRE)**[20] 2406 3-8-7 92 oh3 .... TonyCulhane 19 (M R Channon) *s.i.s: hld up: hdwy 1/2-way: rdn 3f out: hung rt fr 2f out: chsd ldrs and styd on same pce fnl f* **25/1**	78+
3-30	5	nse	**First City**[17] 2521 3-8-10 95 .... AhmedAjtebi 11 (D M Simcock) *racd keenly in midfield: pushed along 3f out: carried hd high whn nt clr run over 2f out and over 1f out: fin wl wout getting to ldrs* **66/1**	81
1414	6	½	**Good Again**[25] 2273 3-8-10 95 .... EddieAhern 2 (G A Butler) *lw: chsd ldrs: rdn over 2f out: one pce and no ch fnl f* **11/2**[2]	80
04-0	7	1	**Beat Seven**[6] 2846 3-9-7 106 .... PhilipRobinson 6 (Miss Gay Kelleway) *lw: hld up in midfield: pushed along over 2f out: kpt on fnl f: nt pce to get competitive* **33/1**	89
2-13	8	hd	**Say No Now (IRE)**[27] 2190 3-8-7 92 oh2 .... TedDurcan 14 (D R Lanigan) *lw: chsd ldrs: led over 2f out: rdn and hdd wl over 1f out: sn wknd* **16/1**	74
1-25	9	½	**Damaniyat Girl (USA)**[39] 1873 3-9-1 100 .... JMurtagh 18 (W J Haggas) *chsd ldrs: rdn to chal 2f out: wknd ins fnl f* **12/1**	81
20-0	10	1 ½	**Misdaqeya**[63] 1293 3-9-2 101 .... TPO'Shea 8 (B W Hills) *racd keenly in midfield: effrt 3f out: no imp on ldrs: hung rt and one pce fr over 1f out* **40/1**	79
0-16	11	4 ½	**King's Starlet**[33] 2036 3-8-7 92 oh6 .... RobertHavlin 17 (H Morrison) *prom: led 3f out: hdd over 2f out: wknd wl over 1f out* **33/1**	59
2-02	12	8	**Qalahari (IRE)**[16] 2536 3-8-7 92 oh4 .... RobertWinston 5 (D J Coakley) *prom: pushed along over 3f out: wkng whn n.m.r wl over 1f out* **40/1**	41
0-43	13	2 ¼	**Rose Diamond (IRE)**[49] 1599 3-8-13 98 .... AlanMunro 21 (R Charlton) *midfield: rdn and wknd over 3f out* **20/1**	42
112	14	¾	**Photographic**[35] 1987 3-8-9 94 .... MichaelHills 15 (B W Hills) *swtchd lft s: racd nr side after 2f: hung rt fr 1/2-way: hdwy into midfield over 3f out: wknd 2f out: eased fnl f* **13/2**[3]	36
-215	15	2 ½	**Badiat Alzaman (IRE)**[11] 2703 3-8-7 92 .... JimCrowley 1 (D M Simcock) *midfield: rdn over 3f out: wkng whn n.m.r over 2f out* **16/1**	28
41-4	16	½	**Arabian Mirage**[63] 1293 3-8-8 93 .... MartinDwyer 10 (B J Meehan) *racd keenly: led: hdd 3f out: rdn and stl chalng 2f out: wknd and hung rt over 1f out* **25/1**	28
1-30	17	nk	**Greenisland (IRE)**[33] 2057 3-8-7 92 oh1 .... SteveDrowne 20 (H Morrison) *midfield: rdn over 3f out: wknd over 2f out* **50/1**	26
1-10	18	½	**Wajaha (IRE)**[63] 1293 3-8-8 93 .... RHills 13 (J H M Gosden) *hld up: effrt 3f out: no imp on ldrs: wknd wl over 1f out* **16/1**	26
25-2	19	9	**Moonlife (IRE)**[33] 2057 3-9-2 101 .... LDettori 9 (Saeed Bin Suroor) *swtg: chsd ldrs tl rdn and wknd over 2f out* **8/1**	13

1m 41.81s (1.21) **Going Correction** +0.20s/f (Good) **19 Ran SP% 127.8**
Speed ratings (Par 104): **101,99,96,90,89 89,88,88,87,86 81,73,71,70,68 67,67,66,57**
toteswinger: 1&2 £5.20, 1&3 £11.50, 2&3 £16.70. CSF £36.51 CT £489.78 TOTE £5.90: £1.50, £2.90, £4.10, £6.70; EX 50.50 Trifecta £700.40 Pool: £7,667.01 - 8.10 winning units..
Owner Wright,Stanley,Marsh,Lascelles & Harris **Bred** Eurostrait Ltd **Trained** Newmarket, Suffolk
■ Stewards' Enquiry : Jamie Spencer two-day ban: used whip without giving filly time to respond (Jul 1-2)
Ted Durcan three-day ban: careless riding (Jul 2,3,5)

FOCUS

A tricky Listed handicap featuring a big field of lightly raced three-year-old fillies. The draw was expected to favour those in low stalls, as in the previous races on the card, but although the first three did come from the low numbers, the effect of the draw was not as clear cut as in earlier races. They went a good gallop and the principals came from off the pace, but the final time was the slowest of the three races run over the straight mile on the card.

NOTEBOOK

Moneycantbuymelove(IRE) showed a nice turn of foot to win in Listed company over 1m2f last time, and the drop back to a mile didn't look likely to inconvenience her. Always travelling strongly at the back of the field off a decent gallop, Spencer had to wait for the gaps to appear. When they finally did she quickened up well to take Golden Stream's measure and draw clear. She showed herself to have been let in lightly off a mark of 96, is clearly versatile with regard to trip, and gives the impression that there's more to come from her in better company. (tchd 11-2 tchd 6-1 in places)
Golden Stream(IRE) was once considered an Oaks possible but finished well beaten in the Pretty Polly Stakes on her return. Dropped back to a mile here, like the winner she travelled well out the back, and quickened up nicely between horses. Despite having the benefit of the rail inside the last she still found the winner too strong, but it was a clear personal best in defeat and she should be able to win a race at this level.
Please Sing, third in a Group 3 last time out, was also held up off the pace. Switched to the stands'-side rail with 2f to run, she finished strongly to take third. Having posted solid efforts both this year and last, she is probably the best guide to the level of the form. (op 16-1)
Silver Games(IRE), racing from 3lb out of the handicap, was drawn out wide and, ridden patiently in a race where the early pace failed to hold up, she was able to force her way between horses and throw down a challenge out wide from 2f out. (op 33-1)
First City found Group company too hot on her first two starts this term, but this was more her level. She could have done with settling better, though, and although not getting the clearest of runs, it was also disconcerting to see her put her head in the air when pressure was applied. (tchd 50-1)
Good Again looked an ideal type for this race when scoring impressively over this course and distance last month. The problem was that she had a 10lb higher mark to overcome this time. Her defeat at Haydock was easily excusable on account of the very testing ground and conditions looked to be far more in her favour here, but despite racing towards the favoured stands' side throughout, she was easily put in her place. (op 6-1 tchd 13-2 in places)

Beat Seven had her chance given the way the race was run, but her mark looks too stiff for what she has achieved. (op 40-1 tchd 50-1 in places)
Say No Now(IRE) didn't get home over 1m2f at Goodwood on her reappearance (behind Moneycantbuymelove) and the drop back to a mile promised to be in her favour, but this performance confirmed that she's simply not as good as the Michael Bell-trained filly. (op 12-1)
Damaniyat Girl(USA) was taking a drop in class, having been held in Group 3 company on her previous two starts this season. A mark of 100 proved too high to overcome, though. (op 14-1)
Photographic has improved with every outing, but her latest effort at York over 7f suggested that she'd be suited by this return to a mile. However, she was weak in the market and proved very disappointing in the race itself. Official explanation: jockey said filly hung right (op 6-1 tchd 11-2)
Badiat Alzaman(IRE) was on her toes beforehand. (op 20-1 tchd 22-1)
Wajaha(IRE) two all-weather wins represent a different level of form to that which she has shown on turf. (op 14-1)
Moonlife(IRE) got stirred up beforehand and didn't run her race. Official explanation: jockey said filly ran flat (op 10-1)
T/Jkpt: Not won. T/Plt: £183.80 to a £1 stake. Pool: £480,826.69. 1,909.18 winning tickets. T/Qpdt: £21.90 to a £1 stake. Pool: £29,618.76. 999.64 winning tickets. LM

2812 HAMILTON (R-H)

Wednesday, June 17

OFFICIAL GOING: Good (good to firm in places; 9.5)

Rail realignment around the loop reduced advertised distances on the Round course by around 30yards.

Wind: Fairly strong, across Weather: Overcast

3017 EUROPEAN BREEDERS' FUND MAIDEN STKS — 6f 5y

2:20 (2:21) (Class 5) 2-Y-O £3,885 (£1,156; £577; £288) Stalls Low

Form RPR
1 **Awzaan** 2-9-0 0 .... GregFairley 8 75
(M Johnston) *mde virtually all: rdn over 1f out: edgd rt ins fnl f: r.o wl* 11/4[2]
4 2 1 **Paradise Spectre**[14] 2588 2-9-3 0 .... AndrewElliott 5 75
(K R Burke) *t.k.h: w ldr: rdn over 1f out: kpt on fnl f* 6/4[1]
0 3 shd **Tislaam (IRE)**[39] 1867 2-9-3 0 .... SamHitchcott 6 75
(M R Channon) *trckd ldrs: effrt and ev ch over 1f out: kpt on same pce ins fnl f* 5/1[3]
4 4½ **Layla's Boy** 2-9-0 0 .... TonyHamilton 3 58+
(R A Fahey) *in tch: outpcd over 2f out: edgd rt and kpt on fnl f: no imp* 6/1
6 5 2¼ **Amno Dancer (IRE)**[13] 2631 2-9-3 0 .... SaleemGolam 2 54
(M H Tompkins) *prom tl rdn and wknd fr 2f out* 11/1
4 6 5 **Yeah**[29] 2147 2-9-3 0 .... SJCraine 7 39
(Patrick Morris) *t.k.h: cl up tl edgd rt and wknd fr 2f out* 40/1
1m 14.61s (2.41) **Going Correction** +0.15s/f (Good) 6 Ran SP% **108.4**
Speed ratings (Par 93): **89,87,87,81,78 71**
toteswinger: 1&2 £1.90, 1&3 £2.20, 2&3 £2.80. CSF £6.74 TOTE £3.10: £1.60, £1.40; EX 7.40.
Owner Hamdan Al Maktoum **Bred** Shadwell Estate Company Limited **Trained** Middleham Moor, N Yorks

FOCUS
There was not much pace on in this juvenile maiden. The first three came comfortably clear in a tight finish.

NOTEBOOK
Awzaan got his career off to a perfect start and showed a typically tenacious attitude for one from his yard. There is plenty of speed in his pedigree and considering he was coltish in the preliminaries and somewhat green through the early parts, improvement should be expected for the run. (op 9-4 tchd 10-3)
Paradise Spectre stepped up on his debut fourth at Ayr and had every chance, but perhaps would prefer genuinely quick ground. He ought to be well up to winning a race or two this season. (tchd 11-8 and 7-4)
Tislaam(IRE) had shown distinct inexperience on debut at Haydock and played up before the race here. He took time to find his stride on the outside of runners, but came there with every chance inside the final furlong and this was a clear step in the right direction. He has scope and should go forward again for the experience. (op 9-2 tchd 4-1)
Layla's Boy is bred to enjoy a stiffer test and raced accordingly. He looks the part though and should leave this behind before long. (op 8-1 tchd 5-1)
Amno Dancer(IRE) failed to see out this extra furlong as his breeding suggested he might and looks to need more time. (tchd 10-1 and 16-1)
Yeah proved too keen for his own good and this was a backwards step from his debut fourth at Leicester. (op 50-1)

3018 SUMMER OFFICE PARTY NIGHT H'CAP — 1m 65y

2:55 (2:58) (Class 6) (0-60,60) 3-Y-O £2,266 (£674; £337; £168) Stalls High

Form RPR
06-0 1 **Kiama Bay (IRE)**[44] 1725 3-8-9 56 .... JamieKyne(5) 12 67
(J J Quinn) *midfield: rdn and hung lft over 2f out: edgd rt and hdwy wl over 1f out: led wl ins fnl f: r.o* 4/1[2]
0-62 2 1½ **Royal Premium**[37] 1926 3-8-5 52 ....(v[1]) LanceBetts(5) 11 60
(Mrs G S Rees) *led: rdn over 2f out: hdd wl ins fnl f: edgd lft: one pce* 10/1
0-02 3 ¾ **Mohawk Ridge**[32] 2091 3-9-4 60 .... PhillipMakin 2 66+
(M Dods) *hld up and bhd: hdwy 2f out: kpt on ins fnl f: nrst fin* 5/1[3]
45-0 4 2¼ **Carter**[53] 1509 3-9-3 59 .... PaulMulrennan 14 60
(W M Brisbourne) *t.k.h: trckd ldrs: effrt over 2f out: kpt on same pce fnl f* 25/1
6-43 5 2¾ **Hawkeyethenoo (IRE)**[30] 2143 3-8-4 53 .... JamesPSullivan(7) 4 48
(M W Easterby) *t.k.h in rr: hdwy 2f out: kpt on fnl f: no imp* 17/2
06-0 6 2½ **Nino Zachetti (IRE)**[8] 2786 3-8-8 50 .... AndrewMullen 13 39
(E J Alston) *t.k.h: hld up ins: effrt over 2f out: no imp fnl f* 40/1
3-05 7 5 **Royal Keva (IRE)**[11] 2723 3-9-2 58 .... SilvestreDeSousa 5 36
(A D Brown) *cl up tl rdn and wknd fr 2f out* 22/1
6-60 8 1¼ **Dreamonandon (IRE)**[32] 2091 3-8-13 60 .... FrederikTylicki(5) 1 35
(G A Swinbank) *hld up: drvn over 3f out: nvr able to chal* 10/3[1]
0052 9 1¾ **Amazing Blue Sky**[8] 2790 3-8-13 55 .... AndrewElliott 9 26
(Mrs R A Carr) *towards rr: drvn 1/2-way: nvr able to chal* 13/2
040 10 1½ **La Gifted**[8] 2797 3-9-1 57 .... SamHitchcott 8 24
(M R Channon) *t.k.h: prom: outpcd over 3f out: wknd fr 2f out* 18/1
2003 11 13 **Street Spirit (USA)**[15] 2577 3-8-12 54 ....(t) DuranFentiman 7 —
(T D Easterby) *towards rr: drvn over 3f out: sn struggling* 16/1
6-00 12 12 **Imperial Angel (IRE)**[23] 2340 3-8-5 47 ....(b) PaulQuinn 6 —
(D Carroll) *bhd: struggling 1/2-way: sn btn: eased whn no ch fnl 2f* 66/1
-320 13 79 **Royal Society**[23] 2340 3-9-3 59 .... TonyHamilton 10 —
(A G Foster) *sn chsng ldr: rdn over 3f out: wknd rapidly over 2f out: virtually p.u* 16/1
1m 48.41s (0.01) **Going Correction** -0.025s/f (Good) 13 Ran SP% **121.8**
Speed ratings (Par 97): **98,96,95,93,90 88,83,82,80,78 65,53,—**
toteswinger: 1&2 £12.50, 1&3 £6.60, 2&3 £11.50. CSF £43.29 CT £216.14 TOTE £5.70: £2.40, £2.20, £2.40; EX 57.20.
Owner Mrs S Quinn **Bred** Tipper House Stud **Trained** Settrington, N Yorks
■ Stewards' Enquiry : Lance Betts caution: careless riding

FOCUS
A moderate heat, run at a sound pace. Sound form, with a step up from the winner.
Kiama Bay(IRE) Official explanation: trainer's rep said, regarding apparent improvement in form, that the gelding was better suited by the step up in trip.
Carter Official explanation: jockey said gelding hung left-handed throughout
Imperial Angel(IRE) Official explanation: jockey said filly ran too free
Royal Society Official explanation: jockey said gelding lost its action but returned sound

3019 HAMILTON-PARK.CO.UK FILLIES' H'CAP (QUALIFIER FOR THE SCOTTISH TROPHY HANDICAP SERIES FINAL) — 1m 1f 36y

3:30 (3:31) (Class 5) (0-70,66) 3-Y-O+ £3,885 (£1,156; £577; £288) Stalls High

Form RPR
546 1 **Jenny Potts**[32] 2090 5-9-10 62 .... PaulMulrennan 2 74
(L Lungo) *hld up: hdwy to ld over 1f out: rdn and styd on strly fnl f* 11/2[3]
0665 2 4½ **Grethel (IRE)**[14] 2590 5-8-7 50 .... SladeO'Hara(5) 1 52
(A Berry) *hld up: swtchd lft and hdwy over 2f out: chsd wnr over 1f out: kpt on: no imp* 20/1
141 3 4½ **Salerosa (IRE)**[14] 2590 4-10-0 66 .... PhillipMakin 7 58+
(Mrs A Duffield) *prom: smooth hdwy to chal wl over 1f out: sn rdn and fnd little* 7/4[1]
0032 4 3½ **Musical Maze**[8] 2779 3-8-7 63 .... PaulPickard(7) 6 48
(W M Brisbourne) *cl up: led over 2f out to over 1f out: sn no ex* 3/1[2]
-060 5 4½ **Slip Star**[18] 2473 6-8-13 51 .... GregFairley 9 26
(T J Etherington) *led to over 2f out: sn rdn and btn* 14/1
0066 6 7 **Talk Of Saafend (IRE)**[20] 2391 4-9-8 65 .... FrederikTylicki(5) 3 24
(P Monteith) *cl up: rdn over 2f out: wknd wl over 1f out* 9/1
0-56 7 2½ **Katie Girl**[31] 2105 3-7-11 51 ow1 .... JamieKyne(5) 5 5
(Mrs G S Rees) *hld up: drvn over 3f out: edgd rt and sn wknd* 18/1
0330 8 ¾ **Karmest**[18] 2505 5-9-9 66 .... LanceBetts(5) 4 18
(A D Brown) *s.v.s: nvr on terms* 22/1
450- 9 11 **Mystical Ayr (IRE)**[258] 6408 7-8-10 53 .... PatrickDonaghy(5) 8 —
(Miss L A Perratt) *in tch: rdn over 3f out: hung rt and sn wknd* 18/1
1m 59.44s (-0.26) **Going Correction** -0.025s/f (Good)
WFA 3 from 4yo+ 11lb 9 Ran SP% **113.1**
Speed ratings (Par 100): **100,96,92,88,84 78,76,75,66**
toteswinger: 1&2 £13.40, 1&3 £2.70, 2&3 £8.30. CSF £103.48 CT £266.30 TOTE £6.60: £1.90, £4.20, £1.10; EX 60.20.
Owner Len Lungo Racing Limited **Bred** Ashley House Stud **Trained** Carrutherstown, D'fries & G'way

FOCUS
A weakish fillies' handicap, run at a decent pace. Improvement from the winner on her handicap debut.
Karmest Official explanation: jockey said mare missed the break

3020 LANARKSHIRE CHAMBER OF COMMERCE CLAIMING STKS — 5f 4y

4:10 (4:11) (Class 6) 3-Y-O+ £2,266 (£505; £505; £168) Stalls Centre

Form RPR
0-05 1 **Cayman Fox**[19] 2451 4-8-7 60 ....(e[1]) PJMcDonald 9 64
(James Moffatt) *led and sn clr: rdn over 1f out: kpt on wl fnl f: unchal* 6/1
4152 2 2¼ **Northern Empire (IRE)**[19] 2451 6-9-10 68 ....(p) PaulMulrennan 8 73
(K A Ryan) *chsd wnr: effrt over 1f out: edgd rt and kpt on same pce fnl f* 5/2[1]
2064 2 dht **Creative (IRE)**[9] 2759 4-9-0 52 ....(v) SaleemGolam 2 63
(M H Tompkins) *in tch: effrt over 2f out: edgd rt over 1f out: kpt on ins fnl f* 9/2
0-02 4 ¾ **Howards Tipple**[13] 2625 5-8-5 54 ....(p) PatrickDonaghy(5) 4 56+
(I Semple) *hld up: hdwy over 1f out: kpt on fnl f: no imp* 7/2[2]
5603 5 1¼ **Brut**[12] 2657 7-8-10 56 ....(p) TonyHamilton 7 52
(D W Barker) *towards rr: effrt and rdn 1/2-way: no imp over 1f out* 4/1[3]
0005 6 8 **North South Divide (IRE)**[40] 1831 5-8-10 47 ....(tp) PatrickMathers 6 23
(Peter Grayson) *bhd and sn outpcd: nvr on terms* 33/1
00 7 2¼ **Fire Up The Band**[112] 676 10-8-7 50 .... SladeO'Hara(5) 3 17
(A Berry) *in tch to 1/2-way: sn wknd* 40/1
-000 8 hd **Howards Prince**[19] 2436 6-8-5 41 .... PaulPickard(7) 5 16
(D A Nolan) *chsd ldrs: drvn 1/2-way: sn wknd* 100/1
0605 9 3 **Chimbonda**[36] 1949 3-7-11 45 ....(bt) AndrewHeffernan(7) 1 3
(S Parr) *missed break: nvr on terms* 20/1
60.32 secs (0.32) **Going Correction** +0.15s/f (Good)
WFA 3 from 4yo+ 6lb 9 Ran SP% **114.4**
Speed ratings (Par 101): **103,99,99,98,96 83,79,79,74**
Places: £2.20, NE £1.40, C £1.90. Exacta: CF & NE £12.30, CF & C £14.40. CSF: CF & NE £10.32, CF & C £15.83toteswinger: 1&NE £3.80, 1&C £4.30, NE&C £3.30. TOTE £7.70.North South Divide was claimed by Kevin Ryan for £5,000.
Owner R R Whitton **Bred** R R Whitton **Trained** Cartmel, Cumbria

FOCUS
The field congregated in the middle of the track for this modest claimer and the form looks straightforward enough. The winner reversed Musselburgh form with Northern Empire.

3021 ATISREAL IS NOW BNP PARIBAS REAL ESTATE H'CAP — 6f 5y

4:45 (4:45) (Class 5) (0-75,71) 3-Y-O+ £3,238 (£963; £481; £240) Stalls Centre

Form RPR
0002 1 **Bid For Gold**[9] 2769 5-9-5 62 .... TonyHamilton 1 76
(Jedd O'Keeffe) *led two others stands' side: rdn and r.o strly to draw clr fnl f* 11/4[2]
13-3 2 4½ **Azure Mist**[9] 2769 4-9-8 65 .... SaleemGolam 8 65
(M H Tompkins) *prom centre: led that gp over 2f out: kpt on fnl f: no ch w wnr* 5/2[1]
0001 3 ¾ **Avontuur (FR)**[12] 2686 7-9-4 61 .... AndrewElliott 3 58
(Mrs R A Carr) *trckd stands' side wnr: rdn over 2f out: one pce over 1f out* 12/1
2-65 4 ¾ **Istiqdaam**[19] 2439 4-9-9 66 .... DaleGibson 2 61
(M W Easterby) *in tch stands' side: rdn over 2f out: one pce over 1f out* 16/1
-350 5 nk **Makshoof (IRE)**[25] 2276 5-9-10 67 ....(p) PatrickMathers 5 61
(I W McInnes) *hld up centre: hdwy over 2f out: no imp over 1f out* 14/1
1000 6 2¼ **Andrasta**[13] 2625 4-8-5 55 .... CharlotteKerton(7) 4 42
(A Berry) *cl up centre tl edgd lft and wknd over 1f out* 40/1

0010 **7** *3 3/4* **Pacific Pride**[22] 2363 6-9-9 **71**......(p) JamieKyne(5) 9 46
(J J Quinn) *led centre to over 2f out: edgd rt and wknd over 1f out* **6/1**[3]
240- **8** *19* **Forrest Star**[217] 7288 4-8-12 **55**...... PhillipMakin 6 —
(Miss L A Perratt) *prom in centre tl wknd fr 2f out* **10/1**
600- **9** *15* **The Salwick Flyer (IRE)**[186] 7663 6-8-4 **52**...... PatrickDonaghy(5) 7 —
(I Semple) *cl up in centre tl wknd qckly over 2f out* **8/1**
1m 12.63s (0.43) **Going Correction** +0.15s/f (Good) **9** Ran SP% **112.4**
Speed ratings (Par 103): **103,97,96,95,94 91,86,61,41**
toteswinger: 1&2 £2.30, 1&3 £6.60, 2&3 £5.70 . CSF £9.67 CT £66.41 TOTE £4.20: £1.20, £1.50, £2.10; EX 9.00.
Owner Paul Chapman And Ba'Tat Investments **Bred** B Minty **Trained** Middleham Moor, N Yorks
FOCUS
A moderate sprint which saw the field spread across the track from halfway. Three of the first four places were filled by the group that came stands' side early on. Weakish form.
The Salwick Flyer(IRE) Official explanation: jockey said gelding bled from the nose

3022 CHARLES & EMMA VILLIERS CRYSTAL WEDDING ANNIVERSARY MEDIAN AUCTION MAIDEN STKS 1m 1f 36y
5:20 (5:22) (Class 6) 3-5-Y-O **£2,388** (£705; £352) **Stalls** High

Form RPR
1 **Whispering Gallery** 3-9-1 0...... GregFairley 5 95+
(M Johnston) *chsd ldr: led over 2f out: drvn clr fr over 1f out* **1/1**[1]
5-22 **2** *10* **Astrodiva**[11] 2723 3-8-10 78...... SaleemGolam 6 68
(M H Tompkins) *in tch: outpcd and edgd rt over 2f out: rallied to go 2nd ins fnl f: no ch w wnr* **7/4**[2]
/ **3** *1 1/4* **Whirlijig (IRE)**[75] 4-9-7 0...... PJMcDonald 7 65
(G A Swinbank) *trckd ldrs: rdn over 2f out: sn one pce* **25/1**
3205 **4** *1 1/4* **Light Dubai (IRE)**[11] 2715 3-8-10 69...... SamHitchcott 4 63
(M R Channon) *led to over 2f out: sn rdn and kpt on same pce* **5/1**[3]
66- **5** *25* **Ayrpassionata**[364] 3130 4-9-2 0...... PatrickDonaghy(5) 3 8
(I Semple) *hld up in tch: struggling over 3f out: sn lost tch* **100/1**
6 *16* **Bombie Boy**[10] 4-9-12 0...... SJCraine 2 —
(K W Hogg) *hld up: rdn 4f out: sn lost tch* **200/1**
7 *4 1/2* **Oor Wee Miracle (GER)** 3-8-10 0...... PhillipMakin 1 —
(M Dods) *sn chsng ldrs: rdn over 3f out: sn struggling: t.o* **33/1**
1m 58.57s (-1.13) **Going Correction** -0.025s/f (Good)
WFA 3 from 4yo 11lb **7** Ran SP% **111.3**
Speed ratings (Par 101): **104,95,94,92,70 56,52**
toteswinger: 1&2 £1.10, 1&3 £4.40, 2&3 £3.50. CSF £2.77 TOTE £1.90: £1.10, £1.70; EX 3.10.
Owner Sheikh Hamdan Bin Mohammed Al Maktoum **Bred** Darley **Trained** Middleham Moor, N Yorks
FOCUS
The debut winner came clear in this modest maiden and looks smart, a well above average maiden winner for the track.
Oor Wee Miracle(GER) Official explanation: Fine: £280, 2nd offence within 12mths, vaccinations in passport did not comply with requirements of the Rules of Racing.

3023 TURFTV IN YOUR BETTING SHOP APPRENTICE H'CAP (ROUND 1) 1m 4f 17y
5:50 (5:50) (Class 6) (0-60,60) 4-Y-O+ **£2,388** (£705; £352) **Stalls** High

Form RPR
25-0 **1** **Piverina (IRE)**[26] 2233 4-8-4 **48**...... AndrewHeffernan(3) 7 56
(Miss J A Camacho) *hld up: hdwy over 2f out: disp ld over 1f out: carried rt ins fnl f: kpt on to ld post* **5/1**[3]
0-42 **2** *nse* **Fenners (USA)**[13] 2629 6-8-8 **49**...... JamesPSullivan 11 57
(M W Easterby) *bhd and sn pushed along: hdwy 4f out: led over 1f out: drifted rt ins fnl f: hdd post* **4/1**[1]
4636 **3** *4* **Barbirolli**[2] 2971 7-8-11 **52**...... PaulPickard 3 54
(W M Brisbourne) *hld up in midfield: hdwy over 3f out: effrt over 2f out: one pce fnl f* **9/2**[2]
0-44 **4** *3 1/2* **Hurricane Thomas (IRE)**[15] 2573 5-8-4 **50**...... LeeTopliss(5) 8 46
(R A Fahey) *chsd ldrs: led over 4f out to over 1f out: sn outpcd* **11/2**
00-0 **5** *4* **Bed Fellow (IRE)**[15] 1883 5-7-12 **46** oh1...... TimothyAyres(7) 10 36
(P Monteith) *chsd clr ldr: ev ch 3f out: wknd over 1f out* **40/1**
335- **6** *nk* **Regent's Secret (USA)**[170] 5564 9-9-5 **60**...... JamieKyne 1 49
(J S Goldie) *hld up: hdwy far side over 3f out: rdn and no imp fnl 2f* **9/2**[2]
0-06 **7** *9* **Cullybackey (IRE)**[20] 2390 4-8-4 **52**...... JoshuaCrane(7) 5 27
(G A Swinbank) *in tch tl rdn and wknd over 2f out* **10/1**
0605 **8** *4* **Bumble Rose (IRE)**[14] 2594 6-8-7 **48**......(p) LanceBetts 13 16
(A G Foster) *in tch: struggling 3f out: sn btn* **28/1**
60/6 **9** *8* **Montchara (IRE)**[17] 2159 6-8-9 **50**...... AmyRyan 4 5
(M Todhunter) *midfield: rdn over 3f out: sn wknd* **16/1**
0000 **10** *22* **Admiral (IRE)**[14] 2592 8-8-10 **54** ow4......(b1) KrishGundowry(3) 2 —
(S Parr) *led and sn clr: hdd over 4f out: sn wknd: t.o* **20/1**
500- **11** *17* **Broad Town Girl**[469] 804 6-8-2 **46** oh1...... AmyScott(3) 6 —
(W S Coltherd) *missed break: a wl bhd* **50/1**
2m 37.79s (-0.81) **Going Correction** -0.025s/f (Good) **11** Ran SP% **116.0**
Speed ratings (Par 101): **101,100,98,95,93 93,87,84,79,64 53**
toteswinger: 1&2 £3.70, 1&3 £5.40, 2&3 £4.10. CSF £23.99 CT £96.60 TOTE £6.40: £2.60, £1.90, £2.30; EX 29.10 Place 6: £9.05, Place 5: £6.86.
Owner Miss Julie Camacho **Bred** Gerrardstown House Stud **Trained** Norton, N Yorks
■ Stewards' Enquiry : James P Sullivan four-day ban: careless riding (Jul 1-3,5); two-day ban: used whip with excessive frequency and in incorrect position (Jul 6-7)
FOCUS
A weak handicap for apprentice riders. It was soundly run and the winner produced a sslight personal best.
T/Plt: £7.60 to a £1 stake. Pool: £40,798.30. 3,868.39 winning tickets. T/Qpdt: £3.10 to a £1 stake. Pool: £2,816.54. 660.34 winning tickets. RY

2824 KEMPTON (A.W) (R-H)
Wednesday, June 17

OFFICIAL GOING: Standard
Wind: Brisk, half-behind. Weather: Overcast, drizzly

3024 WEATHERBYS V.A.T. SERVICES APPRENTICE H'CAP (ROUND 3) 1m 2f (P)
6:10 (6:11) (Class 4) (0-80,79) 4-Y-O+ **£4,727** (£1,406; £702; £351) **Stalls** High

Form RPR
-343 **1** **Buddy Holly**[9] 2773 4-9-3 **77**......(v1) CharlesEddery(5) 11 87
(Pat Eddery) *mde all: drew clr fr over 3f out: at least 5 l up wl over 1f out: nvr gng to be ct after: drvn out* **10/1**[3]
32 **2** *1 3/4* **Falcon Rock (IRE)**[9] 2775 4-9-3 **72**...... Louis-PhilippeBeuzelin 13 78+
(S A Callaghan) *hld up in 5th: rdn over 2f out: prog whn nt clr run and swtchd lft over 1f out: r.o to take 2nd nr fin: no ch to chal* **7/4**[1]
1-06 **3** *1* **Prairie Storm**[29] 2150 4-9-5 **79**...... RichardRowe(5) 9 83
(A M Balding) *disp 2nd to over 3f out: sn drvn: effrt to chse clr wnr over 1f out: clsd slowly and no ch: lost 2nd nr fin* **8/1**[2]
336- **4** *1* **Hannicean**[313] 4829 5-8-13 **71**...... LeeNewnes(3) 4 73+
(R W Price) *dwlt: hld up in last trio: prog on wd outside over 2f out: r.o fnl f: nrst fin and only one fr bk of field to fin in tch* **33/1**
56-4 **5** *3/4* **Constant Cheers (IRE)**[48] 1621 6-9-8 **77**......(p) AndreaAtzeni 5 78
(W R Swinburn) *hld up in abt 6th: rdn 3f out: tried to cl fr over 1f out: nvr gng pce to rch ldrs* **8/1**[2]
4440 **6** *1* **Can Can Star**[12] 2666 6-9-6 **75**...... AmyBaker 12 74
(A W Carroll) *hld up in abt 7th: rdn 3f out: plugged on but nvr rchd ldrs* **8/1**[2]
0-50 **7** *3* **Northern Spy (USA)**[13] 2641 5-9-1 **70**...... MCGeran 8 63
(S Dow) *s.s: wl in rr: rchd abt 8th 4f out: nvr on terms: plugged on* **10/1**[3]
5563 **8** *shd* **Alpes Maritimes**[36] 1962 5-9-3 **75**...... JemmaMarshall(3) 10 67
(G L Moore) *chsd ldng trio: nt on terms fr 4f out: no imp 2f out: wknd fnl f* **16/1**
023/ **9** *2* **New World Order (IRE)**[546] 7189 5-9-0 **72**...... PNolan(3) 7 60
(Mrs S Leech) *a abt same pl: outpcd fr 4f out: n.d fnl 2f* **50/1**
-402 **10** *hd* **Justcallmehandsome**[30] 2144 7-9-1 **75**......(v) DebraEngland(5) 14 63
(D J S Ffrench Davis) *disp 2nd tl clr in pursuit of wnr over 3f out: no imp 2f out: wknd over 1f out* **22/1**
1-60 **11** *1/2* **Risque Heights**[98] 798 5-9-4 **73**...... WilliamCarson 3 60
(J R Boyle) *hld up in last quartet: pushed along 1/2-way: no prog and nvr a factor* **16/1**
13-0 **12** *1/2* **Alfie Tupper (IRE)**[20] 2407 6-9-3 **72**...... JackDean 2 58
(J R Boyle) *hld up in last trio: pushed along and outpcd over 4f out: nvr a factor* **22/1**
13 *7* **Martin's Friend (USA)**[31] 4-9-2 **71**......(t) MartinLane 1 43
(Mrs L Wadham) *dwlt: a in last trio: rdn after 3f: struggling remainder: wl bhd over 1f out* **50/1**
2m 7.82s (-0.18) **Going Correction** +0.10s/f (Slow) **13** Ran SP% **115.2**
Speed ratings (Par 105): **104,102,101,101,100 99,97,97,95,95 94,94,88**
toteswinger: 1&2 £5.70, 1&3 £14.10, 2&3 £3.30. CSF £25.30 CT £149.82 TOTE £13.80: £3.80, £1.20, £3.30; EX 26.40.
Owner Hayman, Pearson, Phillips & McGuinness **Bred** R J & S A Carter **Trained** Nether Winchendon, Bucks
■ Stewards' Enquiry : Jemma Marshall caution: used whip when out of contention.
Martin Lane caution: used whip when out of contention.
FOCUS
Just a fair apprentice handicap and with the winner dominating throughout, it proved hard to make up significant amounts of ground. The winner posted a slight personal best.
Falcon Rock(IRE) Official explanation: jockey said gelding was denied a clear run
Northern Spy(USA) Official explanation: jockey said gelding ran too free

3025 ISC MAIDEN FILLIES' STKS 1m 2f (P)
6:40 (6:42) (Class 5) 3-Y-O+ **£2,590** (£770; £385; £192) **Stalls** High

Form RPR
4 **1** **Queen Of Pentacles (IRE)**[32] 2074 3-8-12 0...... EddieAhern 9 81+
(J Noseda) *trckd ldng pair: pushed along 3f out: wnt 2nd sn after: led over 1f out: readily drew clr* **8/11**[1]
0-5 **2** *7* **Zeyadah (IRE)**[49] 1605 3-8-12 0...... ChrisCatlin 4 67
(M A Jarvis) *led: clr w wnr fr 2f out: hdd and brushed aside over 1f out* **9/1**[2]
0- **3** *7* **Samba Mirander**[294] 5404 3-8-12 0...... FrancisNorton 8 53
(C Drew) *racd wd early in abt 6th: swtchd to inner and outpcd fr 3f out: plld out and styd on fr over 1f out to take remote 3rd ins fnl f* **100/1**
0 **4** *3/4* **Moojeh (IRE)**[11] 2710 3-8-12 0...... TPO'Shea 13 52
(E A L Dunlop) *hld up in abt 7th: sme prog over 2f out but already outpcd: chsd clr ldng pair jst over 1f out: no imp: lost 3rd ins fnl f* **9/1**[2]
03 **5** *3 1/2* **M'Lady Rousseur (IRE)**[18] 2488 3-8-12 0...... RobertHavlin 5 45+
(D R C Elsworth) *hld up in last trio: outpcd and pushed along over 2f out: kpt on steadily against rail fnl f: possible improver* **12/1**
6 *1/2* **Celtic Lass** 3-8-12 0...... NCallan 1 44
(M A Jarvis) *chsd ldr to over 2f out: wknd rapidly: lost remote 3rd jst over 1f out* **10/1**[3]
00-P **7** *nk* **Fine Tolerance**[12] 2679 3-8-12 0...... PatCosgrave 7 43
(J R Boyle) *t.k.h early: hld up in 5th: wl outpcd fr over 2f out: no prog after* **100/1**
8 *1 3/4* **Miss Doodle** 3-8-12 0...... StephenCarson 6 39+
(Eve Johnson Houghton) *dwlt: rn green and detached in last: v modest late prog* **50/1**
9 *nse* **Our Last Call (IRE)** 3-8-12 0...... SebSanders 3 39+
(Sir Mark Prescott) *hld up in last trio and racd wd: outpcd over 2f out: no ch after* **14/1**
0 **10** *7* **Sanctum**[18] 2488 3-8-12 0...... RichardThomas 11 25
(Dr J D Scargill) *dwlt: nvr bttr than abt 8th: wl outpcd fr 3f out: sn bhd* **100/1**
0 **11** *1 3/4* **Born Romantic**[32] 2074 3-8-12 0...... SteveDrowne 12 22
(H J L Dunlop) *chsd ldng trio: pushed along 4f out: wknd 2f out: sn wl bhd* **11/1**
2m 8.40s (0.40) **Going Correction** +0.10s/f (Slow) **11** Ran SP% **114.6**
Speed ratings (Par 100): **102,96,90,90,87 87,86,85,85,79 78**
toteswinger: 1&2 £1.50, 1&3 £57.90, 2&3 £104.30. CSF £7.66 TOTE £1.50: £1.10, £2.40, £27.00; EX 8.90.
Owner Normandie Stud Ltd **Bred** Normandie Stud Ltd **Trained** Newmarket, Suffolk
FOCUS
An uncompetitive fillies' maiden and the time was the slowest of the three races over this trip on the card. The winner pulled nicely clear but may not have beaten much, with the runner-up the best guide.

3026 DIGIBET H'CAP 1m 2f (P)
7:10 (7:10) (Class 4) (0-85,84) 3-Y-O **£4,727** (£1,406; £702; £351) **Stalls** High

Form RPR
5-11 **1** **Simon Gray**[33] 2038 3-9-7 **84**...... RichardHughes 4 89
(R Hannon) *led for 1 1/2f: trckd ldr: rdn over 2f out: chal over 1f out: edgd ahd last 100yds: pushed out after* **3/1**[3]
5102 **2** *1/2* **Sign Of Approval**[15] 2571 3-8-7 **75**......(p) MartinLane(5) 2 79
(K R Burke) *s.s: rcvrd to ld after 1 1/2f: drvn over 2f out: kpt on over 1f out: hdd and nt qckn last 100yds* **12/1**
3-12 **3** *3/4* **Sandor**[28] 2174 3-9-7 **84**...... EddieAhern 6 90+
(P J Makin) *trckd ldng pair after 4f: rdn 2f out: trying to cl on ins whn rn short of room and snatched up jst ins fnl f: plld out and r.o nr fin* **11/4**[2]
4-13 **4** *4 1/2* **Ballet Dancer (IRE)**[34] 2008 3-8-11 **74**...... PhilipRobinson 8 68
(M A Jarvis) *hld up in abt 5th: rdn 3f out: no imp on ldng trio 2f out: n.d after* **11/1**

1 **5** 1½ **Hallstatt (IRE)**[20] 2395 3-9-3 **80** RoystonFfrench 5 71+
(M Johnston) *hld up in last trio: pushed along and rn green fr 4f out: outpcd fr 2f out: no imp after* **5/2**[1]

-100 **6** ½ **Echo Dancer**[12] 2685 3-8-6 **69** WilliamBuick 1 59
(S A Callaghan) *chsd ldng pair 4f: rdn 3f out: struggling fnl 2f* **40/1**

01- **7** 16 **Spiritual Treasure (USA)**[233] 7023 3-8-12 **75** PaulHanagan 7 33
(M A Magnusson) *hld up in last: gng wl enough 3f out: shkn up and no rspnse over 2f out: sn bhd: eased fnl f: t.o* **13/2**

2m 8.10s (0.10) **Going Correction** +0.10s/f (Slow) **7** Ran SP% **112.0**
Speed ratings (Par 101): **103,102,102,98,97 96,84**
toteswinger: 1&2 £8.70, 1&3 £1.30, 2&3 £5.90. CSF £35.51 CT £107.25 TOTE £3.30: £1.70, £5.40; EX 32.70.
Owner Mrs James Wigan **Bred** Mrs James Wigan **Trained** East Everleigh, Wilts

FOCUS
A fair 3yo handicap, but yet again on this inner course, it proved hard to make up ground and the first three finishers were always handy. The runner-up looks the best guide to the form.
Sign Of Approval Official explanation: jockey said colt missed the break
Spiritual Treasure(USA) Official explanation: jockey said colt lost its back end leaving stalls

3027 INTEGRATED SECURITY CONSULTANTS EBF MAIDEN FILLIES' STKS 7f (P)
7:40 (7:40) (Class 5) 2-Y-O **£3,885** (£1,156; £577; £288) **Stalls** High

Form RPR

042 **1** **Silver Symphony (IRE)**[18] 2494 2-9-0 0 JamieSpencer 10 82+
(P F I Cole) *mde all: drew clr over 2f out: at least 5 l up over 1f out: urged along and briefly looked vulnerable 1f out: kpt on* **4/6**[1]

0 **2** 2¾ **Brunette (IRE)**[18] 2490 2-9-0 0 RichardHughes 5 75+
(R Hannon) *racd in 5th: pushed along over 4f out: reminder 1/2-way: prog to chse clr wnr 2f out: clsd grad 1f out: no imp last 100yds* **7/2**[2]

3 6 **Lady Valiant** 2-9-0 0 SebSanders 1 60
(R M Beckett) *s.v.s: hld up in last pair: outpcd over 2f out: plugged on to take modest 3rd fnl f* **10/1**[3]

55 **4** 4 **Gulf Punch**[26] 2238 2-9-0 0 PatDobbs 9 50
(R Hannon) *dwlt: disp 2nd to 2f out: sn wl btn* **14/1**

60 **5** 7 **Riffelalp (IRE)**[30] 2135 2-9-0 0 WilliamBuick 3 33
(Eve Johnson Houghton) *disp 2nd for 3f: sn lost pl u.p and btn* **40/1**

6 1¼ **The Frying Pan (IRE)** 2-9-0 0 RichardThomas 2 30
(Dr J D Scargill) *a in last pair: lft bhd fr 3f out* **80/1**

7 32 **Jamary (IRE)** 2-9-0 0 NCallan 7 —
(C E Brittain) *disp 2nd to over 2f out: wknd rapidly: t.o and virtually p.u fnl f* **10/1**[3]

1m 27.98s (1.98) **Going Correction** +0.10s/f (Slow) **7** Ran SP% **110.7**
Speed ratings (Par 90): **92,88,82,77,69 68,31**
toteswinger: 1&2 £1.10, 1&3 £3.40, 2&3 £4.90. CSF £2.94 TOTE £1.40: £1.10, £1.90; EX 3.10.
Owner Manley, Meyrick & Sullivan **Bred** J Jamgotchian **Trained** Whatcombe, Oxon

FOCUS
They finished strung out in this juvenile fillies' maiden and the pace set by the winner seemed strong.

NOTEBOOK
Silver Symphony(IRE), who has improved with each start so far, was much the best, as her odds suggested, but she got tired late on and looked to have a hard enough race. Whatever, though, she got this longer trip well and has the scope to progress again. (op 8-13 tchd 4-7 and 4-5 in places)
Brunette(IRE) stepped up on her debut effort over this longer trip, but still looked green. Under pressure a fair way out, she gradually responded and finished well for a clear second, giving the impression she'll step forward again next time. (op 6-1 tchd 7-1)
Lady Valiant, a half-sister to multiple 1m-1m3f winner Castellina, out of a dual sprint scorer, started slowly and ran green. She can do better. (op 9-1 tchd 8-1)
Gulf Punch is not progressing. (op 16-1)
The Frying Pan(IRE) was extremely green and can improve. (tchd 66-1)
Jamary(IRE) weakened as though something was amiss. Official explanation: trainer said filly finished distressed (op 7-1 tchd 13-2)

3028 DIGIBET CASINO H'CAP 6f (P)
8:10 (8:12) (Class 4) (0-85,85) 3-Y-O **£4,727** (£1,406; £702; £351) **Stalls** High

Form RPR

4045 **1** **Mac's Power (IRE)**[7] 2826 3-8-5 **69** (t) WilliamBuick 12 77
(P J O'Gorman) *mde virtually all: kicked on jst over 2f out and sn 2 l clr: rdn and kpt on fr over 1f out: a holding on* **5/1**[2]

31- **2** ¾ **Fulham Broadway (IRE)**[236] 6953 3-9-4 **82** JamieSpencer 2 91+
(E F Vaughan) *dropped in fr wd draw and hld up in last pair: hmpd over 4f out and wl adrift: gd prog 2f out: drvn and r.o to take 2nd last 75yds: gaining fin* **5/2**[1]

0-10 **3** ½ **Ray Of Joy**[60] 1345 3-9-4 **82** EddieAhern 3 86
(J R Jenkins) *chsd ldng trio: rdn and prog to chse wnr wl over 1f out: kpt on but a hld: lost 2nd last 75yds* **16/1**

-056 **4** 1¾ **Son Of The Cat (USA)**[47] 1639 3-9-7 **85** (t) ChrisCatlin 4 84+
(B Gubby) *off the pce in abt 8th after 2f: pushed along 1/2-way: prog over 1f out: styd on to grab 4th nr fin* **22/1**

055 **5** 2¼ **Satwa Street (IRE)**[12] 2653 3-9-6 **84** RichardMullen 9 75
(D M Simcock) *chsd ldng pair: rdn to go 2nd briefly 2f out: wknd fnl f* **8/1**

1-05 **6** 2 **Calahonda**[24] 2299 3-9-5 **83** RobertWinston 5 68
(P W D'Arcy) *drvn in 6th after 2f: no imp on ldrs: struggling over 2f out* **25/1**

040- **7** nk **Klynch**[254] 6533 3-9-7 **85** (b) RichardHughes 1 69
(B J Meehan) *hld up in last pair: wl off the pce 1/2-way: nvr on terms: kpt on fr over 1f out* **25/1**

3132 **8** 2¾ **Arachnophobia (IRE)**[15] 2578 3-8-9 **73** PaulEddery 8 48
(Pat Eddery) *nvr beyond midfield: rdn sn after 1/2-way: nt on terms after* **6/1**[3]

00-0 **9** 8 **Mister Green (FR)**[41] 1803 3-8-9 **78** (b) AndreaAtzeni[(5)] 6 28
(D Flood) *chsd ldng quartet: no imp u.p over 2f out: wkng rapidly whn hmpd over 1f out* **50/1**

5421 **10** 1 **Doc Jones (IRE)**[16] 2543 3-8-10 **74** JohnEgan 10 20
(P D Evans) *w wnr to over 2f out: wknd rapidly over 1f out* **10/1**

1154 **11** ¾ **Seek The Fair Land**[7] 2826 3-8-12 **76** PatCosgrave 7 20+
(J R Boyle) *dwlt: last pair whn awkward bnd over 4f out: drvn and prog into abt 8th over 3f out: wknd rapidly wl over 1f out* **15/2**

1m 12.74s (-0.36) **Going Correction** +0.10s/f (Slow) **11** Ran SP% **111.4**
Speed ratings (Par 101): **106,105,104,102,99 96,95,92,81,80 79**
toteswinger: 1&2 £2.90, 1&3 £20.30, 2&3 £10.10. CSF £15.42 CT £161.47 TOTE £5.00: £1.80, £1.70, £3.40; EX 16.60.
Owner Michael McDonnell **Bred** Ballyhane Stud **Trained** Newmarket, Suffolk
■ Red Rossini was withdrawn (11/1, unruly in the stalls). Deduct 5p in the £ under R4.
■ Stewards' Enquiry : Andrea Atzeni four-day ban: careless riding (Jul 13-16)
Paul Eddery one-day ban: careless riding (Jul 1)

FOCUS
A fair sprint handicap in which most of the field looked exposed. The winner is rated up 10lb with the third probably the best guide.
Fulham Broadway(IRE) ◆ Official explanation: jockey said colt suffered interference in running
Doc Jones(IRE) Official explanation: jockey said gelding hung both ways

3029 DIGIBET.COM H'CAP 2m (P)
8:40 (8:40) (Class 6) (0-65,63) 4-Y-O+ **£2,047** (£604; £302) **Stalls** High

Form RPR

15-0 **1** **Coda Agency**[83] 112 6-9-7 **63** NCallan 13 71
(D W P Arbuthnot) *trckd ldng pair: wnt 2nd over 3f out: led over 2f out and drvn 2 l clr: kpt on u.p fnl f* **6/1**[3]

-312 **2** 1¼ **Jafaru**[13] 2634 5-9-4 **60** (b) GeorgeBaker 6 67
(G L Moore) *hld up wl in rr: prog fr 3f out: urged along fr over 2f out: wnt 2nd jst over 1f out: kpt on but nvr able to chal* **9/2**[1]

-516 **3** hd **No Rules**[11] 2725 4-8-12 **54** LiamJones 1 60
(M H Tompkins) *hld up wl in rr: rdn in 12th 4f out: gd prog on inner over 2f out: styd on to take 3rd nr fin* **25/1**

330 **4** 1¼ **Calculating (IRE)**[19] 2429 5-9-2 **63** LeeNewnes[(5)] 14 68
(M D I Usher) *hld up in midfield and wl in tch: prog 3f out: disp 2nd u.p wl over 1f out: fdd ins fnl f* **15/2**

00-0 **5** 1 **Mister Completely (IRE)**[19] 2429 8-8-13 **55** (v) JamesDoyle 10 59
(Ms J S Doyle) *settled in midfield: effrt 3f out: drvn to dispute 2nd over 1f out: hld after: wknd ins fnl f: eased nr fin* **66/1**

0-52 **6** 2¾ **Brave Bugsy (IRE)**[17] 2519 6-8-12 **54** (v) WilliamBuick 12 54
(A M Balding) *trckd ldng trio: lost pl and rdn over 3f out: one pce u.p fr over 2f out* **5/1**[2]

6525 **7** 2¾ **Lucky Dancer**[40] 1851 4-9-0 **56** RobertHavlin 8 53
(D R C Elsworth) *led: rdn and hdd over 2f out: chsd wnr to over 1f out: wknd fnl f* **8/1**

545- **8** 1¾ **Mae Cigan (FR)**[100] 6898 6-9-4 **60** SteveDrowne 5 55
(M Blanshard) *t.k.h early: hld up towards rr: effrt over 3f out: no real prog and nt on terms w ldng gp fnl 2f* **12/1**

6-45 **9** 1 **Kokkokila**[41] 1807 5-9-6 **62** RichardHughes 3 56
(Lady Herries) *sn trckd ldrs on outer: wl there 3f out: rdn and wknd over 2f out* **10/1**

0-03 **10** 4½ **Bob's Your Uncle**[19] 2429 6-8-11 **53** TPO'Shea 11 41
(J G Portman) *stdd s: hld up in last: sme prog 1/2-way: taken to outer and drvn over 2f out: nt on terms after* **8/1**

335- **11** 6 **North Walk (IRE)**[14] 7630 6-8-5 **52** (p) MartinLane[(5)] 4 33
(B N Pollock) *wl in tch on outer: rdn 5f out: sn lost pl: bhd fnl 2f* **50/1**

0/0- **12** 10 **Debord (FR)**[100] 7216 6-8-6 **48** FrancisNorton 9 17
(Jamie Poulton) *sn wl in rr and nt gng wl: struggling fr 5f out* **100/1**

3 **13** 12 **Champagne Cocktail (IRE)**[15] 2580 8-8-7 **49** RobertWinston 2 4
(R J Price) *t.k.h early: chsd ldr to over 3f out: wknd rapidly: sn eased: t.o* **10/1**

6-06 **14** 9 **Marie Louise**[23] 2331 4-8-13 **55** PatCosgrave 7 —
(L A Dace) *hld up towards rr: rdn 5f out: wkng whn hmpd on inner 4f out: sn t.o* **40/1**

3m 31.66s (1.56) **Going Correction** +0.10s/f (Slow) **14** Ran SP% **119.7**
Speed ratings (Par 101): **100,99,99,98,98 96,95,94,94,91 88,83,77,73**
toteswinger: 1&2 £9.60, 1&3 £113.50, 2&3 £22.10. CSF £32.05 CT £640.77 TOTE £7.10: £3.00, £1.40, £5.90; EX 39.40.
Owner Banfield, Thompson **Bred** Baydon House Stud **Trained** Compton, Berks
■ Stewards' Enquiry : George Baker three-day ban: careless riding (Jul 1-3)

FOCUS
A moderate staying handicap and the gallop seemed just ordinary. The form seems sound enough with the winner back to his best.
No Rules Official explanation: jockey said gelding was denied a clear run

3030 PANORAMIC BAR & RESTAURANT H'CAP 7f (P)
9:10 (9:10) (Class 4) (0-85,85) 3-Y-O+ **£4,727** (£1,406; £702; £351) **Stalls** High

Form RPR

1234 **1** **Street Power (USA)**[25] 2276 4-9-2 **73** SteveDrowne 7 88+
(J R Gask) *stdd s: hld up in last trio: fnd gap over 1f out and gd burst to go 2nd: rdn to ld ins fnl f: styd on wl* **4/1**[3]

0211 **2** 1½ **Sweet Gale (IRE)**[4] 2913 5-8-9 **71** 6ex Louis-PhilippeBeuzelin[(5)] 2 82
(Mike Murphy) *dwlt: hld up in last trio: rdn and gd prog on outer to ld over 1f out: hdd ins fnl f: styd on but outpcd* **10/3**[2]

1-42 **3** 2¼ **Star Links (USA)**[23] 2329 3-9-2 **82** RichardHughes 4 84
(R Hannon) *w ldr: led over 2f out: hdd and outpcd over 1f out* **2/1**[1]

1405 **4** 1 **Obe Royal**[15] 2576 5-9-4 **75** (v) JohnEgan 5 77
(P D Evans) *settled in 6th: drvn and nt qckn over 2f out: plugged on one pce fr over 1f out* **14/1**

1-60 **5** nk **Brooksby**[8] 2796 3-8-7 **73** (b) PatDobbs 9 71
(R Hannon) *narrow ld to over 2f out: outpcd over 1f out* **33/1**

10-0 **6** ½ **Classic Descent**[33] 2050 4-10-0 **85** SebSanders 6 85
(P J Makin) *cl up: rdn over 2f out: losing pl whn sltly hmpd over 1f out* **7/1**

42-5 **7** 1¾ **Lekita**[27] 2188 4-8-12 **69** AdamKirby 3 64
(W R Swinburn) *w ldrs to over 2f out: wknd fnl f* **12/1**

-350 **8** hd **Kyle (IRE)**[25] 2276 5-9-5 **76** LPKeniry 1 71
(C R Dore) *hld up in last: swtchd to inner and effrt over 2f out: sn no prog and wl btn over 1f out* **33/1**

6500 **9** nk **Dvinsky (USA)**[2] 2980 8-9-11 **82** (b) IanMongan 10 76
(P Howling) *t.k.h: cl up on inner: effrt 2f out: no real prog and wl hld whn nt clr run jst over 1f out* **16/1**

1m 25.84s (-0.16) **Going Correction** +0.10s/f (Slow)
WFA 3 from 4yo+ 9lb **9** Ran SP% **115.0**
Speed ratings (Par 105): **104,102,99,98,98 97,95,95,95**
toteswinger: 1&2 £3.00, 1&3 £3.30, 2&3 £1.20. CSF £17.68 CT £33.13 TOTE £4.90: £1.40, £1.30, £1.40; EX 18.20 Place 6 £25.70, Place 5 £15.88..
Owner Horses First Racing Limited **Bred** John Hawkins **Trained** Sutton Veny, Wilts

FOCUS
A fair handicap for the grade, and solid form. The winner is progressive on the AW.
Dvinsky(USA) Official explanation: jockey said gelding was denied a clear run

T/Plt: £27.50 to a £1 stake. Pool: £62,122.45. 1,644.15 winning tickets. T/Qpdt: £20.80 to a £1 stake. Pool: £4,271.46. 151.54 winning tickets. JN

[2609]RIPON (R-H)

Wednesday, June 17

OFFICIAL GOING: Good (8.5) changing to good to soft after race 2 (7.20)

Course at innermost configuration.

Wind: Light, across Weather: Overcast and showers

3031 HIGH MOOR APPRENTICE (S) STKS 6f

6:50 (6:51) (Class 6) 3-4-Y-0 **£2,590** (£770; £385; £192) **Stalls** Low

Form RPR

0000 **1** **Bright Falcon**[13] 2626 4-9-2 48................................(bt) ThomasWhite(5) 8 55
(S Parr) *s.i.s and in rr: sn swtchd rt to r towards far rail: hdwy 2f out: pushed along over 1f out: styd on ins fnl f to ld last 50yds* **14/1**

4016 **2** 3/4 **Gioacchino (IRE)**[4] 2908 4-9-12 53....................................... SPRyan 14 58
(R A Harris) *prom: chsd ldr 1/2-way: rdn to ld wl over 1f out: edgd rt ins fnl f: hdd and no ex last 50yds* **9/2**[2]

00-0 **3** 1 1/2 **Boundless Applause**[12] 2651 3-8-9 39.................................. HollyHall 3 43
(I A Wood) *towards rr: hdwy over 2f out: rdn wl over 1f out: styd on ins fnl f: nrst fin* **40/1**

4600 **4** nk **Sheik'N'Knotsterd**[10] 2745 4-9-7 54................................. AlexEdwards 4 47
(J F Coupland) *hld up: hdwy over 2f out: rdn wl over 1f out: edgd rt and kpt on ins fnl f: nrst fin* **16/1**

-000 **5** 3/4 **Chipolini (IRE)**[15] 2577 3-8-9 48....................................(v[1]) NeilFarley(5) 2 44
(D Carroll) *prom: chsd ldng pair 2f out: sn rdn and one pce appr fnl f* **33/1**

0006 **6** 2 **Billy Bowmore**[7] 2805 4-9-7 45.....................................(b) DavidKenny 10 38
(P A Kirby) *s.i.s: hdwy and in tch 1/2-way: rdn to chse ldrs over 1f out: sn no imp* **12/1**

0-00 **7** hd **Hettie Hubble**[14] 2593 3-8-9 50.. SeanPalmer 15 32
(D W Thompson) *chsd ldrs: rdn along and edgd lft over 2f out: sn edgd rt and wknd* **40/1**

0650 **8** nse **Know No Fear**[105] 757 4-9-7 72.................................... NathanAlison 13 37
(D Shaw) *bmpd s and towards rr: hdwy 1/2-way: chsd ldrs 2f out: sn rdn and no imp fr over 1f out* **5/2**[1]

0-00 **9** 1/2 **Foreign Rhythm (IRE)**[45] 1695 4-9-2 46....................(v) GemmaElford 1 31
(N Tinkler) *in rr tl sme late hdwy* **20/1**

0503 **10** 1/2 **Bold Account (IRE)**[15] 2581 3-9-0 53................................(p) LauraPike 5 34
(Garry Moss) *in tch: rdn along 1/2-way n.d* **9/1**

0000 **11** 1 1/4 **Piccolo Pete**[23] 1734 4-9-7 41............................ JosephineBruning 16 30
(R Johnson) *prom: rdn along 2f out and sn wknd* **40/1**

4-42 **12** 4 1/2 **Officer Mor (USA)**[12] 2683 3-8-9 57.............................(b) NoraLooby(5) 7 16
(K R Burke) *in tch: rdn along over 2f out: sn wknd* **5/1**[3]

0000 **13** 3 1/4 **Nawaaff**[12] 2660 4-9-7 42... DanielBlackett(5) 6 10
(M R Channon) *a towards rr* **14/1**

0-00 **14** 11 **Adab (IRE)**[23] 2316 4-9-7 50..(v[1]) AnthonyBetts 9 —
(Miss Tracy Waggott) *led and sn clr: rdn along wl over 2f out: hdd wl over 1f out and sn wknd* **40/1**

0066 **15** 6 **The Canny Dove (USA)**[74] 1129 3-9-0 39............................ AdamCarter 11 —
(T D Barron) *chsd ldrs: rdn along 1/2-way and sn wknd* **22/1**

-000 **16** 2 1/2 **Sally's Swansong**[10] 2744 3-8-9 43.................................(p) KierenFox 12 —
(M Wellings) *j. awkwardly and rdr lost irons: chsd ldrs tl wknd over 2f out* **50/1**

1m 17.04s (4.04) **Going Correction** -0.075s/f (Good)

WFA 3 from 4yo 7lb **16** Ran SP% **124.1**

Speed ratings (Par 101): **70,69,67,66,65 62,62,62,61,61 59,53,49,34,26 23**

toteswinger: 1&2 £28.60, 1&3 £46.00, 2&3 £46.00. CSF £71.49 TOTE £24.20: £5.40, £2.50, £10.10; EX 210.10.There was no bid for the winner.

Owner Willie McKay **Bred** A J Coleing **Trained**

■ Thomas White's first winner.

■ Stewards' Enquiry : Gemma Elford caution: used whip above shoulder height

FOCUS

The course had escaped much of the heavy rain falling in the area and after just 4mm the going was reckoned to be 'on the easy side of good'. A rock-bottom opener confined to inexperienced apprentices and they raced over the full width of the track. Weak form, with the winner only having to match his modest recent handicap runs.

Sally's Swansong Official explanation: jockey said he lost his irons leaving stalls

3032 RACING AGAIN TOMORROW MEDIAN AUCTION MAIDEN STKS 5f

7:20 (7:23) (Class 5) 2-Y-0 **£3,238** (£963; £481; £240) **Stalls** Low

Form RPR

623 **1** **Farmer Giles (IRE)**[37] 1920 2-9-3 0.............................. DarryllHolland 13 84+
(M L W Bell) *overall ldr far side: mde all: qcknd clr wl over 1f out: easily: 1st of 8 in gp* **5/4**[1]

2 6 **George Benjamin** 2-8-10 0.. NSLawes(7) 2 60+
(D Nicholls) *hld up stands' side: hdwy over 2f out: rdn over 1f out: kpt on ins fnl f: no ch w wnr on far side: 1st of 7 in gp* **16/1**

0500 **3** nk **Bossy Kitty**[19] 2435 2-8-12 0.. JoeFanning 11 54
(N Tinkler) *chsd wnr far side: rdn along 2f out: sn drvn and kpt on: no ch w wnr: 2nd of 8 in gp* **28/1**

64 **4** 3/4 **Senate Majority**[18] 2484 2-9-3 0... DavidAllan 4 56
(T D Easterby) *cl up stands' side: rdn to ld that gp 2f out: sn drvn and one pce: 2nd of 7 in gp* **9/2**[2]

5 2 **Uddy Mac** 2-8-12 0... JimmyQuinn 9 44
(N Bycroft) *in tch far side: hdwy over 2f out: sn rdn along and kpt on same pce: 3rd of 8 in gp* **66/1**

6 1 1/2 **Lucy Gliters** 2-8-12 0.. MickyFenton 6 39
(T P Tate) *prom stands' side: rdn along over 2f out and grad wknd: 3rd of 7 in gp* **8/1**

7 nk **Star Promise** 2-8-7 0.. DeanHeslop(5) 7 38
(T D Barron) *in tch stands' side: rdn along over 2f out: sn no imp: 4th of 7 in gp* **20/1**

8 1/2 **Russian Davis (IRE)** 2-9-3 0.............................. GrahamGibbons 12 41
(R M H Cowell) *towards rr far side tl sme late hdwy: 4th of 8 in gp* **15/2**[3]

9 1 1/2 **Clever Molly (IRE)** 2-8-12 0.. ShaneKelly 1 30
(E J Alston) *led stands' side gp: rdn along and hdd 2f out: sn wknd: 5th of 7 in gp* **20/1**

0 **10** 3/4 **William Arnold**[15] 2568 2-9-0 0................................... KellyHarrison(3) 17 33
(C W Fairhurst) *chsd ldrs far side: rdn along 1/2-way and sn wknd: 5th of 8 in gp* **66/1**

50 **11** 2 1/4 **Sacred Star (IRE)**[32] 2089 2-8-5 0.............................. JohnCavanagh(7) 16 20
(M Brittain) *chsd ldrs far side: rdn along 1/2-way and sn wknd: 6th of 8 in gp* **33/1**

04 **12** 3 1/4 **War Wolf**[8] 2784 2-9-3 0.. DNolan 3 13
(T D Easterby) *in tch stands' side: rdn along over 2f out and sn wknd: 6th of 7 in gp* **66/1**

13 nk **Rio's Girl** 2-8-9 0.. MichaelJStainton(3) 10 7
(R M Whitaker) *chsd ldrs far side: rdn along 1/2-way: sn wknd: 7th of 8 in gp* **25/1**

5 **14** 5 **Turf Time**[15] 2575 2-9-3 0.. AndrewMullen 8 —
(A J McCabe) *chsd ldrs stands' side to 1/2-way: sn wknd: last of 7 in gp* **9/1**

15 18 **Keithshazel (IRE)** 2-8-9 0.. DominicFox(3) 14 —
(Garry Moss) *wnt bdly rt s and a bhd far side: last of 8 in gp* **80/1**

60.90 secs (0.20) **Going Correction** -0.075s/f (Good) **15** Ran SP% **126.9**

Speed ratings (Par 93): **95,85,84,83,80 78,77,76,74,73 69,64,63,55,27**

toteswinger: 1&2 £1.90, 1&3 £9.00, 2&3 Not won. CSF £24.07 TOTE £2.30: £1.30, £4.70, £5.50; EX 28.80.

Owner R A Green **Bred** Hong Kong Breeders Club **Trained** Newmarket, Suffolk

FOCUS

They split into two groups in this weak-looking median auction maiden race. The winner was value for extra and could go on from here.

NOTEBOOK

Farmer Giles(IRE), narrowly denied at Leicester, failed to run up to expectations when only third when odds-on next time at Redcar. He looked unhappy on the firm ground and was reckoned 'not quite right' afterwards by his trainer. Dominating the far-side group, he came right away to score by a wide margin. Presumably nurseries beckon now, but he can hardly expect a lenient mark. (op 11-8 tchd 6-4)

George Benjamin, a cheaply bought son of first-season sire Trade Fair, stayed on in good style from off the pace to lead home the charge on the stands' side. He will improve and will be suited by a step up to 6f. (op 12-1)

Bossy Kitty, the most experienced in the field, chased the winner throughout on the far side. (tchd 33-1)

Senate Majority took them along on the stands' side. A decent type, he looks a potential nursery horse. (op 8-1)

Uddy Mac, a bargain basement buy, stayed on in good style late on on her debut.

Lucy Gliters, another cheap buy, showed ability first time after giving real problems behind the stalls, unseating her rider twice. (op 15-2 tchd 7-1)

3033 NORMAN WELLS MEMORIAL CHALLENGE TROPHY H'CAP 6f

7:50 (7:50) (Class 3) (0-95,92) 3-Y-O **£8,831** (£2,643; £1,321; £660; £329) **Stalls** Low

Form RPR

1122 **1** **White Shift (IRE)**[7] 2821 3-8-7 **78**..................................... JimmyQuinn 5 84
(P Howling) *trckd ldng pair: hdwy on bit and cl up 2f out: shkn up to ld wl over 1f out: rdn and hung rt ins fnl f: kpt on* **15/2**

3-30 **2** 1/2 **The Kyllachy Kid**[4] 2934 3-9-0 **85**.................................... MickyFenton 7 89
(T P Tate) *hld up: hdwy on outer over 2f out: rdn and ch over 1f out: swtchd lft ent fnl f and styd on strly towards fin* **11/2**[3]

-334 **3** 3 1/4 **Captain Scooby**[26] 2227 3-8-2 **73**.. PaulQuinn 2 67
(R M Whitaker) *hld up towards rr: hdwy 2f out: rdn over 1f out: kpt on ins fnl f* **10/1**

6123 **4** 1/2 **Time Medicean**[12] 2674 3-8-11 **82**.............................. DarryllHolland 10 74
(M R Channon) *led: rdn along over 2f out: hdd wl over 1f out: sn drvn and wknd appr fnl f* **2/1**[1]

-603 **5** 1 **On Offer (IRE)**[26] 2227 3-8-4 **75**.................................... DuranFentiman 3 64
(T D Easterby) *in tch: hdwy over 2f out: sn rdn and one pce ins fnl f* **16/1**

2-00 **6** 5 **Dove Mews**[24] 2299 3-8-6 **77**.. JoeFanning 1 50
(M L W Bell) *chsd ldrs: rdn along and n.m.r over 2f out: sn wknd* **14/1**

1-13 **7** 1 **Lovely Thought**[32] 2079 3-8-11 **82**..........................(b) PaulMulrennan 8 52
(W J Haggas) *cl up on inner: n.m.r and rdn along over 2f out: sn wknd* **5/2**[2]

0064 **8** 1 **Smokey Ryder**[39] 1879 3-9-4 **92**.............................. KevinGhunowa(3) 9 59
(R A Harris) *chsd ldrs: rdn along over 2f out: sn wknd and btn whn rdr dropped whip over 1f out* **40/1**

1m 14.65s (1.65) **Going Correction** +0.375s/f (Good) **8** Ran SP% **113.1**

Speed ratings (Par 103): **104,103,99,98,97 90,89,87**

toteswinger: 1&2 £7.60, 1&3 £8.00, 2&3 £7.10. CSF £47.06 CT £413.21 TOTE £7.40: £2.10, £2.00, £2.00; EX 48.20.

Owner Paul Terry **Bred** Grange Stud **Trained** Newmarket, Suffolk

■ Stewards' Enquiry : Jimmy Quinn caution: careless riding.

FOCUS

The ground was changed to good to soft ahead of this quite valuable 73-92 three-year-olds' sprint handicap. They raced in one group on the stands' side. The winner is probably the best guide to the form.

NOTEBOOK

White Shift(IRE), 7lb higher than her Newmarket success three outings ago, paid a handsome compliment to her Haydock conqueror Global City. Despite fears about how she would handle the easy ground she travelled very strongly. She went right in front, cutting across The Kyllachy Kid, and was all out to keep him at bay at the line. Clearly very tough, she could turn out under a penalty at Newmarket on Saturday. (op 13-2 tchd 8-1)

The Kyllachy Kid, who never fired at York four days earlier, improved on the outer soon after halfway. He was forced to check when the winner went across his bows inside the last and he was fast cutting her back at the line. A stiffer track would play more to his strengths. (op 8-1 tchd 9-1)

Captain Scooby continues to run well without much luck. The handicapper looks to have him in his grip but even softer ground will aid his cause. (op 8-1)

Time Medicean, dropping back to 6f, crossed over to the stands' side rail from his outside draw but had done too much too soon and did not get home. (op 7-2 tchd 15-8)

On Offer(IRE) stayed on in her own time and will appreciate a return to 7f. (op 14-1)

Dove Mews, dropped 4lb after finishing last of eight behind White Shift at Newmarket, was already on the retreat when left short of room. (op 10-1)

Lovely Thought, hoisted 17lb after her wide-margin win at Yarmouth, had two handlers in the paddock and was very weak in the market. Tightened up soon after halfway she dropped right away in most disappointing fashion. Official explanation: jockey said filly never travelled (op 15-8 tchd 7-4 and 11-4)

3034 MIDDLEHAM H'CAP 1m 1f 170y

8:20 (8:20) (Class 4) (0-85,85) 4-Y-O+ **£5,180** (£1,541; £770; £384) **Stalls** High

Form RPR

-062 **1** **Wigwam Willie (IRE)**[31] 2103 7-9-7 **85**.......................(p) PaulMulrennan 6 92+
(K A Ryan) *hld up: pushed along and hdwy on inner over 2f out: nt clr run wl over 1f out: swtchd lft and rdn whn nt clr run ent fnl f: squeezed through and styd on to ld last 100yds* **9/2**[3]

2034 **2** 1 1/4 **Rosbay (IRE)**[8] 2781 5-9-4 **82**... DavidAllan 5 86
(T D Easterby) *hld up: hdwy 4f out: rdn to chse ldr 2f out: drvn over 1f out and ev ch tl edgd lft and one pce wl ins fnl f* **5/1**

5-00 **3** 1/2 **Vicious Warrior**[18] 2499 10-8-2 **66** oh1................................ PaulQuinn 7 69
(R M Whitaker) *led: jnd and rdn along 3f out: drvn wl over 1f out: hdd and no ex last 100yds* **14/1**

11-6 **4** *1¼* **Liberally (IRE)**[60] 1357 4-8-13 **77** .... JoeFanning 8 78
(B J Meehan) *chsd ldrs: rdn along over 2f out: drvn over 1f out: kpt on same pce fnl f* **4/1**[2]

116- **5** *4* **Bavarian Nordic (USA)**[200] 7502 4-9-3 **81** .... AndrewMullen 3 73
(Mrs A Duffield) *chsd ldr: effrt and cl up 4f out: rdn along 3f out: drvn and wknd wl over 1f out* **20/1**

003- **6** *4½* **Coeur De Lionne (IRE)**[223] 7208 5-9-4 **82** .... StephenDonohoe 4 65
(E A L Dunlop) *hld up in tch: hdwy 4f out: rdn along wl over 2f out and sn wknd* **12/1**

4431 **P** **Prince Evelith (GER)**[5] 2894 6-9-1 **79** 6ex .... GrahamGibbons 2 —
(J J Quinn) *cl up on outer tl p.u over 7f out: broke leg: dead* **6/4**[1]

2m 7.79s (2.39) **Going Correction** +0.375s/f (Good) **7** Ran SP% **114.0**
Speed ratings (Par 105): **105,104,103,102,99 95,—**
toteswinger: 1&2 £10.40, 1&3 £18.00, 2&3 £11.90. CSF £26.78 CT £288.52 TOTE £4.50: £2.20, £2.70; EX 24.80.
Owner Neil & Anne Dawson Partnership **Bred** Mrs Margaret Christie **Trained** Hambleton, N Yorks

FOCUS
What looked beforehand an uncompetitive 65-85 handicap was rendered even less informative when the penalised York winner Prince Evelith sadly broke a leg at an early stage. The bare form is only ordinary but the winner could be worth a bit more.

3035 LEYBURN H'CAP — 1m 4f 10y
8:50 (8:51) (Class 5) (0-75,71) 4-Y-0+ **£3,238** (£963; £481; £240) **Stalls** High

Form RPR

2422 **1** **Summer Lodge**[7] 2830 6-8-6 **59** .... (p) DavidProbert[(3)] 2 69
(A J McCabe) *cl up: led over 3f out: rdn 2f out: drvn and qcknd clr ent fnl f: kpt on* **3/1**[2]

03-0 **2** *5* **Mooted (UAE)**[22] 2362 4-8-7 **62** .... BMcHugh[(5)] 1 64
(Miss J A Camacho) *trckd ldrs: hdwy on outer 4f out: cl up 3f out: effrt and ev ch 2f out: sn rdn and ev ch tl drvn and one pce ent fnl f* **7/1**

-445 **3** *1½* **Bollin Greta**[19] 2445 4-9-3 **67** .... DavidAllan 6 67
(T D Easterby) *hld up: hdwy to chse ldrs 3f out: rdn over 2f out: drvn and hung rt over 1f out: kpt on same pce* **11/8**[1]

0520 **4** *2* **Grey Command (USA)**[5] 2898 4-8-13 **63** .... JoeFanning 7 59
(M Brittain) *chsd ldng pair: rdn along 3f out: drvn over 2f out: sn one pce* **11/2**[3]

6-00 **5** *9* **Riley Boys (IRE)**[21] 2374 8-9-7 **71** .... PaulMulrennan 3 53
(J G Given) *hld up in rr: hdwy 3f out: effrt and n.m.r over 2f out: sn swtchd lft and rdn but no imp* **9/1**

060/ **6** *15* **Tranos (USA)**[56] 2254 6-8-2 **52** oh2 .... JimmyQuinn 5 10
(Micky Hammond) *a in rr* **16/1**

0-P0 **7** *33* **Aura Of Calm (IRE)**[2] 2969 7-8-2 **52** oh7 .... (t) AndrewMullen 4 —
(Ronald O'Leary, Ire) *led: rdn along 4f out: hdd over 3f out and sn wknd* **33/1**

2m 41.15s (4.45) **Going Correction** +0.375s/f (Good) **7** Ran SP% **113.8**
Speed ratings (Par 103): **100,96,95,94,88 78,56**
toteswinger: 1&2 £5.20, 1&3 £1.10, 2&3 £7.70. CSF £23.70 CT £39.76 TOTE £4.30: £1.80, £3.10; EX 22.50.
Owner Paul J Dixon **Bred** Seymour Cohn **Trained** Averham Park, Notts

FOCUS
A modest 52-71 handicap run at just a steady pace. The bare form could have been rated a little higher.
Riley Boys(IRE) Official explanation: jockey said gelding ran flat

3036 COVERDALE MAIDEN STKS — 6f
9:20 (9:21) (Class 5) 3-Y-0 **£3,238** (£963; £481; £240) **Stalls** Low

Form RPR

60 **1** **New Leyf (IRE)**[18] 2496 3-9-3 0 .... ShaneKelly 7 77
(J R Gask) *a.p: hdwy and cl up 2f out: rdn over 1f out: styd on ins fnl f to ld last 75yds* **20/1**

62 **2** *1½* **Quasi Congaree (GER)**[19] 2455 3-9-3 0 .... (t) JoeFanning 13 73
(I A Wood) *led on far rail: rdn along 2f out: drvn ent fnl f: hdd and no ex last 75yds* **5/1**[2]

3432 **3** *½* **Maverin (IRE)**[6] 2862 3-9-3 78 .... DarryllHolland 12 71
(J Noseda) *trckd ldrs: effrt 2f out: sn rdn and one pce ent fnl f* **4/7**[1]

0 **4** *½* **Medicean Man**[18] 2496 3-9-3 0 .... StephenDonohoe 5 69
(J R Gask) *in tch: hdwy 2f out: sn rdn and kpt on ins fnl f: nrst fin* **33/1**

5 **5** *5* **Chichen Daawe**[55] 1474 3-8-5 0 .... AnthonyBetts[(7)] 4 48
(B Ellison) *in midfield: rdn along 2f out: kpt on ins fnl f: n.d* **80/1**

4 **6** *1* **Carragold**[15] 2574 3-8-10 0 .... JohnCavanagh[(7)] 14 50
(M Brittain) *s.i.s and sn rdn along in rr: hdwy 2f out: styd on u.p ins fnl f: nrst fin* **66/1**

-003 **7** *shd* **Lily Jicaro (IRE)**[23] 2343 3-8-7 55 .... DeanHeslop[(5)] 8 45
(Mrs L Williamson) *towards rr tl sme late hdwy* **25/1**

8 *½* **Prime Circle** 3-9-3 0 .... GregFairley 11 48
(M Johnston) *nvr bttr than midfield* **6/1**[3]

4 **9** *¾* **Jill Le Brocq**[23] 2343 3-8-12 0 .... PaulMulrennan 15 41
(M Dods) *chsd ldrs: rdn along over 2f out: grad wknd* **33/1**

10 *2* **Crimson Mist** 3-9-3 0 .... JamieMoriarty 1 39
(J J Quinn) *a in rr* **33/1**

04-6 **11** *hd* **Wrens Hope**[65] 1247 3-8-12 48 .... JimmyQuinn 6 34
(N Bycroft) *a towards rr* **80/1**

00 **12** *1¼* **Willent**[19] 2446 3-9-3 0 .... DavidAllan 2 35
(Miss J A Camacho) *hung rt and a towards rr* **125/1**

5 **13** *hd* **Qualitas**[32] 2070 3-9-3 0 .... DaleGibson 10 34
(M W Easterby) *a towards rr* **18/1**

0- **14** *2* **Arriva La Diva**[347] 3707 3-8-12 0 .... GrahamGibbons 9 23
(J J Quinn) *cl up: rdn along wl over 2f out and sn wknd* **22/1**

15 *1* **Arjemis** 3-8-12 0 .... PAspell 3 20
(C R Wilson) *s.i.s: a in rr* **100/1**

1m 14.8s (1.80) **Going Correction** +0.375s/f (Good) **15** Ran SP% **127.4**
Speed ratings (Par 99): **103,101,100,99,93 91,91,90,89,87 86,85,85,82,81**
toteswinger: 1&2 £48.00, 1&3 £9.80, 2&3 £2.10. CSF £116.50 TOTE £23.30: £5.30, £1.90, £1.10; EX 182.50 Place 6 £290.46, Place 5 £72.88..
Owner Horses First Racing Limited **Bred** John Weld **Trained** Sutton Veny, Wilts

FOCUS
A modest sprint maiden and probably ordinary form. Four set off racing towards the stands' side but they were out of contention by halfway.
Willent Official explanation: jockey said gelding hung right throughout
T/Plt: £205.40 to a £1 stake. Pool: £57,399.24. 203.99 winning tickets. T/Qpdt: £19.30 to a £1 stake. Pool: £5,801.54. 222.30 winning tickets. JR

3037 - 3044a (Foreign Racing) - See Raceform Interactive

2096 MAISONS-LAFFITTE (R-H)
Wednesday, June 17

OFFICIAL GOING: Good

3045a PRIX GIRL FRIEND (FEMALE PROFESSIONAL JOCKEYS) (LEFT-HANDED) — 1m (S)
2:40 (2:40) 4-Y-0+ **£10,680** (£4,272; £3,204; £2,136; £1,068)

RPR

1 **Marek (GER)**[65] 6-8-11 .... HanaMouchova 87
(M Weber, Germany)

2 *snk* **Kougouar (FR)**[22] 4-9-2 .... CelineHerissondeBeauvoir 92
(J-M Beguigne, France)

3 *1* **Electric Roi (GER)**[68] 6-8-11 .... DelphineSantiago 84
(H Hiller, Germany)

4 *snk* **Ransom Hope**[267] 4-9-4 .... MichellePayne 91
(P Bary, France)

5 *½* **Barricado (FR)**[20] 2402 4-9-0 .... KirstyMilczarek 86
(E J O'Neill) *hld up in rr: styd on steadily towards ins fr over 2f out: nrst fin* **11/1**[1]

6 *2* **Val d'Espoir (IRE)**[750] 5-8-11 .... KatharinaWerning 78
(H-A Pantall, France)

7 *1* **Gris Tendre (FR)**[234] 4-8-11 .... BrigitteRenk 76
(J-C Rouget, France)

8 *½* **Bleue Doloise (FR)**[22] 5-8-8 .... CarolineBonin 72
(A Bonin, France)

9 *¾* **Bank Guard (IRE)**[102] 788 4-8-13 .... ElodieCristofani[(5)] 80
(Rod Collet, France)

10 *5* **Hello My Lord (FR)**[66] 5-8-11 .... NathalieDesoutter 62
(B Secly, France)

0 **Vantage Point (FR)**[297] 6-8-11 .... ChrystelleCardenne —
(Mlle C Cardenne, France)

0 **Volomist (FR)** 4-8-8 .... KarenBeaumard —
(Mlle I Desagnat, France)

1m 43.8s (1.50) **12** Ran SP% **8.3**
PARI-MUTUEL: WIN 24.40; PL 4.10, 1.20, 2.80; DF 16.00.
Owner Stall Europa **Bred** Gestut Rottgen **Trained** Germany

NOTEBOOK
Barricado(FR), who has looked over 7f on fast ground, was doing his best work late on and only just missed out on a place in the frame.

3011 ASCOT (R-H)
Thursday, June 18

OFFICIAL GOING: Good to firm (overall 10.1, straight 10.9, round 9.6)
Course configured as for days one and two with distances on Round course increased by about 12yards.
Wind: Fresh, against Weather: Cloudy

3046 NORFOLK STKS (GROUP 2) — 5f
2:30 (2:30) (Class 1) 2-Y-0
£51,093 (£19,368; £9,693; £4,833; £2,421; £1,215) **Stalls** Centre

Form RPR

21 **1** **Radiohead**[31] 2121 2-9-1 0 .... (t) JamieSpencer 6 106+
(B J Meehan) *lw: ponied to s: racd keenly and hld up in rr: hdwy whn bdly hmpd wl over 1f out: rcvrd qckly and str run ins fnl f to ld 150yds out: sn edgd rt and r.o wl: in command at fin* **10/1**

512 **2** *2* **Reignier**[12] 2714 2-9-1 0 .... AndrewElliott 5 98
(K R Burke) *w'like: in tch: rdn and c through gap to ld wl over 1f out: hdd 150yds out: nt pce of wnr after* **50/1**

21 **3** *½* **Tawaabb**[30] 2147 2-9-1 0 .... LDettori 11 96+
(M R Channon) *w'like: scope: midfield: hdwy on outside 2f out: chal over 1f out: nt qckn and run flattened out fnl 100yds* **7/1**[3]

1 **4** *2½* **Nosedive**[6] 2887 2-9-1 0 .... RyanMoore 10 87
(W J Haggas) *lw: n.m.r sn after s: towards rr: effrt whn n.m.r and hmpd wl over 1f out: nt clr run and swtchd rt to make prog appr fnl f: r.o but nvr able to fully rcvr* **14/1**

1111 **5** *¾* **Monsieur Chevalier (IRE)**[21] 2408 2-9-1 0 .... RichardHughes 2 84+
(R Hannon) *lw: chsd ldrs: effrt to chal whn bdly hmpd and knocked sideways wl over 1f out: edgd rt whn no ex ins fnl f: allowed to come home under hand ride* **6/4**[1]

2 **6** *2* **Diamond Johnny G (USA)**[14] 2631 2-9-1 0 .... SteveDrowne 4 77
(J R Best) *w'like: towards rr: rdn over 1f out: styd on ins fnl f: nt pce to chal* **16/1**

1326 **7** *1½* **Star Rover (IRE)**[2] 2995 2-9-1 0 .... JohnEgan 12 72
(P D Evans) *showed spd w ldr: rdn over 2f out: wknd fnl f* **28/1**

44 **8** *2¼* **Running Mate (IRE)**[26] 2280 2-9-1 0 .... (v[1]) JimmyFortune 7 64
(J H M Gosden) *missed break: in rr: rdn 2f out: kpt on: nvr able to threaten* **50/1**

9 *1¼* **Yogaroo (USA)**[56] 2-9-1 0 .... (bt) JRVelazquez 3 59
(Wesley A Ward, U.S.A) *w'like: on toes: led: pushed along 2f out: wnt lft and hdd wl over 1f out: sn wknd* **10/3**[2]

21 **10** *3½* **Kingdom Of Light**[40] 1866 2-9-1 0 .... PaulMulrennan 1 47
(J Howard Johnson) *w'like: edgy: chsd ldrs: rdn 2f out: wknd over 1f out* **20/1**

211 **11** *4* **Here Now And Why (IRE)**[47] 1680 2-9-1 0 .... NCallan 9 32
(K A Ryan) *on toes: showed spd w ldrs: rdn 2f out: wknd over 1f out* **18/1**

62.07 secs (1.57) **Going Correction** +0.10s/f (Good) **11** Ran SP% **114.6**
Speed ratings (Par 105): **91,87,87,83,81 78,76,72,70,65 58**
toteswingers: 1&2 £50.60, 1&3 £8.20, 2&3 £42.30 CSF £430.41 CT £3714.71 TOTE £10.00: £2.30, £9.10, £2.20; EX 299.00 Trifecta £7758.80 Pool: £12581.88 - 1.20 winning units..
Owner Mrs Carmen Burrell & Jonathan Harvey **Bred** Redmyre Bloodstock And S Hillen **Trained** Manton, Wilts

FOCUS
A captivating Group 2 juvenile prize with tactics and likely draw bias an intriguing aspect to this year's running. There were only two maidens in attendance and the remainder had accumulated 16 previous wins between them. A last-time-out success has been a pre-requisite in the race in past years and seven of the runners met such criteria. As expected there was a searching early pace, but the closing stages were dramatic and Radiohead did well to win so decisively. He and Reignier are on an upward curve, and the third and fourth can do better again.

NOTEBOOK

Radiohead ◆ was the chief sufferer when Yogaroo bumped into Monsieur Chevalier, losing much momentum and having to be snatched up. That did not stop him from finding a great turn of foot when getting re-organised, though, and he eventually stormed through for a ready success. The fact he won as he did after that incident was very impressive and the strong early fractions played right into his hands, as he took time to warm up through the race. He was unfortunate not to come into this unbeaten as he lost out at Newmarket on his debut through greenness, but his win in a no-contest at Bath next time and the application of a tongue tie were a big help to his cause. He shapes as though another furlong will be ideal for him, but anything beyond that is not certain looking at his breeding. Next up could be the July Stakes at Newmarket, but he would have to carry a penalty in that and also in the Prix Robert Papin over 5.5f at Maisons-Laffitte next month. Perhaps the Group 1 Prix Morny at Deauville in August over 6f would be better, although there would be a concern about the possibility of soft ground. His trainer was also later making noises about a possible Nunthorpe bid. (op 9-1 tchd 8-1)

Reignier looked to have a great deal to find on paper for this big step up in class, but his trainer showed last year with Lord Shanakill that he knows the time of day and made a late decision to enter him for this. He fared best of those to race up with the early pace and showed a likeable attitude under pressure. He would have to be of serious interest if going for the Molecomb at Goodwood next month. (op 40-1)

Tawaabb ◆ won nicely at Leicester second time up and was fancied for this step into Group company. He did very little wrong from what has proved to be a difficult draw so far this week. It would not be a surprise to see him head to the July Stakes now and he should continue to improve. (op 11-1)

Nosedive ◆, allowed to take his chance despte his debut success at Sandown coming just six days earlier, struggled to go the early pace, but he was getting into things when Yogaroo went left and hampered him and he then again met trouble inside the last. He is one to take from the race as the experience should bring him on plenty.

Monsieur Chevalier(IRE) came into this unbeaten in four races, having taken the National Stakes in great fashion last time. He got squeezed at the start, which cannot have helped, and tracked the American runner through the first half of the race. He had just been asked for his effort when that rival hampered him and it is hard to know just how he would have fared without any interference, but this run has to be forgiven. It should be noted that he would almost certainly have taken in the Coventry over 6f had connections not had Canford Cliffs for that and another furlong is likely now what he ideally requires. (op 13-8 tchd 7-4 in places)

Diamond Johnny G(USA) came into this having finished second on Lingfield's Polytrack on his debut a fortnight earlier. It was unsurprising to see him come in for support, though, considering his stable's previous feats with such types at this meeting, and he looked the part in the preliminaries. He was never seriously in the hunt, but was not disgraced and ought to go forward again for the run. (op 33-1)

Star Rover(IRE) had finished sixth in the Windsor Castle and had ground to make up with Monsieur Chevalier on Sandown form. This was also his seventh start of the season and so while he ran his race here, he is now looking exposed. Official explanation: jockey said colt hung left (op 33-1 tchd 40-1)

Running Mate(IRE) was representing a stable, albeit in questionable form at present, that has a good record in the race. He had failed to run up to expectations in two previous runs over another furlong and, equipped with a first-time visor, failed to land a blow after struggling with the early tempo. (op 40-1)

Yogaroo(USA), a US challenger making his turf debut, took them along, not surprisingly for a horse whose two previous races had been over 2.5f and 4.5f, but unlike the two previous winners from this yard earlier in the week he was unable to obtain a clear early lead. He was done with shortly after the 2f pole, but went markedly left when given a smack and initiated a dramatic chain reaction when bumping Monsieur Chevalier, who was just beginning to hit top gear. (op 11-4 tchd 7-2 in places)

Kingdom Of Light, whose yard took this last year and also won it in 2005, showed decent speed on this drop back from 6f but was done with after passing 2f out. He was subsequently reported to have lost his action. Official explanation: jockey said colt lost its action (op 16-1)

Here Now And Why(IRE), successful in two of his three previous starts, dropped right out after showing early dash and is another who needs to drop back in class. (op 20-1)

3047 RIBBLESDALE STKS (GROUP 2) (FILLIES) — 1m 4f

3:05 (3:05) (Class 1) 3-Y-O

£77,173 (£29,254; £14,640; £7,299; £3,656; £1,835) **Stalls** High

Form					RPR
1	**1**		**Flying Cloud (IRE)**[48] 1657 3-8-12 0 (Saeed Bin Suroor) *tall: lengthy: lw: settled in 3rd: led over 2f out: rdn clr over 1f out: comf* **5/1**[3]	LDettori 2	110+
21	**2**	*4*	**Flame Of Gibraltar (IRE)**[14] 2633 3-8-12 88 (H R A Cecil) *str: lw: hld up in midfield: rdn and hdwy 2f out: drvn to chse wnr fnl f: no imp* **12/1**	TPQueally 10	103
1-43	**3**	*1 ¼*	**Uvinza**[34] 2036 3-8-12 95 (W J Knight) *lw: chsd ldr: led briefly ent st: one pce fnl 2f* **28/1**	JamieSpencer 9	101
1-1	**4**	*nk*	**Leocorno (IRE)**[28] 2212 3-8-12 97 (Sir Michael Stoute) *t.k.h in 5th: rdn over 2f out: kpt on fnl f: nt pce to chal* **15/8**[1]	RyanMoore 8	101+
1-2	**5**	*½*	**July Jasmine (USA)**[40] 1871 3-8-12 93 (Sir Michael Stoute) *on toes: chsd ldrs in 4th: rdn 3f out: one pce* **8/1**	MJKinane 3	100
01-1	**6**	*2*	**Take The Hint**[46] 1701 3-8-12 107 (J H M Gosden) *b.hind: swtg: hld up towards rr: rdn 3f out: nvr able to chal* **7/2**[2]	JimmyFortune 7	97
00	**7**	*1*	**Totally Devoted (USA)**[25] 2304 3-8-12 0 (A P O'Brien, Ire) *hld up in last: rdn and mod effrt over 2f out: nvr trbld ldrs* **16/1**	JMurtagh 1	95
1-4	**8**	*25*	**Mooakada (IRE)**[34] 2036 3-8-12 94 (J H M Gosden) *sluggish s: t.k.h: sn in midfield on outer: wknd over 2f out: eased whn no ch over 1f out* **14/1**	RHills 5	55
3-10	**9**	*13*	**It's Dubai Dolly**[48] 1643 3-8-12 73 (A J Lidderdale) *t.k.h in rr: outpcd and lost tch 4f out: eased whn no ch fnl 2f* **80/1**	WandersonD'Avila 6	35
1-5	**10**	*23*	**Anice Stellato (IRE)**[40] 1871 3-8-12 88 (R M Beckett) *racd freely: led and sn 6l clr: hdd ent st: wkng whn squeezed on rail over 2f out: sn bhd and eased* **33/1**	(b[1]) NCallan 4	—

2m 30.67s (-1.83) **Going Correction** +0.025s/f (Good) **10** Ran SP% **112.6**

Speed ratings (Par 108): **107,104,103,103,102 101,100,84,75,60**

toteswinger: 1&2 £7.70, 1&3 £21.00, 2&3 £32.20 CSF £59.69 CT £1500.94 TOTE £4.50: £1.40, £3.50, £8.30; EX 49.90 Trifecta £746.80 Pool: £12110.99 - 12.00 winning units..

Owner Godolphin **Bred** Gainsborough Stud Management Ltd **Trained** Newmarket, Suffolk

FOCUS

This contest is often won by an improving filly but this did not look the strongest renewal. None of the runners had taken part in the Oaks, although several had performed reasonably in trials for that race. The overall time was good though, and the winner looks to have taken another step forward, although the form is somewhat muddling.

NOTEBOOK

Flying Cloud(IRE) ◆, the winner of a Group 3 in France for Andre Fabre, was having her first start for the Godolphin stable. Although stepping up in distance, her breeding suggested the trip should be no problem and she was ridden positively, tracking the eventual third and travelling within herself from a long way out. She took the lead from that rival at the quarter-mile pole and, quickly putting daylight between herself and the others, never looked likely to be caught. She looks a decent prospect and appeals as the sort for a race like the Irish Oaks, although she will have to be supplemented. (op 8-1 tchd 9-1 in a place)

Flame Of Gibraltar(IRE) ◆, a well-bred filly who had built on her debut effort when winning a Lingfield maiden over 1m2f, was stepping up in trip and also taking a big jump in class. She settled nicely in the race before making good headway in the straight but was making no inroads on the winner's advantage in the final furlong. She has sealed her paddock value by earning black type here, but looks capable of winning races at Group level before retiring to the paddocks. (op 14-1 tchd 11-1)

Uvinza, whose only win had come over 1m on Polytrack, had been placed in Listed company at 1m2f and was up in trip. Although not sure to stay on breeding, she got the trip well, going on early in the straight and keeping going under pressure after the leader swept by. She is a credit to connections and is another who can win a pattern race on this evidence. (op 25-1 tchd 40-1 in a place)

Leocorno(IRE), a half-sister to Tartan Bearer and Golan and unbeaten in two starts, headed the market on potential rather than what she had previously achieved (the form of her easy 1m1f handicap win had not worked out). She was stepping up in trip and, although having her chance early in the straight, the effort flattened out. Connections may drop her back to 1m2f in future. (op 2-1 tchd 9-4)

July Jasmine(USA), winner of a soft-ground maiden before finishing a six-lengths second behind the subsequent Oaks runner-up Midday in the Lingfield Oaks Trial, appeared to run her race, and a line through her suggests that today's winner is of a similar level of ability to that filly. (op 6-1)

Take The Hint carried the first colours of her owner and was held up. Bred to stay, she had looked progressive and had won a Listed race at Newmarket with subsequent dual winner Moneycantbuymelove behind. However, she didn't really pick up under pressure and may not be quite up to this level yet. (op 11-4 tchd 4-1 in a place)

Totally Devoted(USA) has yet to pay back much of her $1.6m purchase price but she did not perform too badly and, being a half-sister to the St Leger winner Rule Of Law, she could come into her own over even longer trips, with the Park Hill a possible target later in the season.

Mooakada(IRE) raced wide and much too freely and unsurprisingly did not get home.

Anice Stellato(IRE) went off like a scalded cat in the first-time blinkers, a pace she could not sustain. Official explanation: jockey said filly ran too free (op 25-1 tchd 40-1 in places)

3048 GOLD CUP (GROUP 1) — 2m 4f

3:45 (3:45) (Class 1) 4-Y-O+

£141,925 (£53,800; £26,925; £13,425; £6,725; £3,375) **Stalls** High

Form					RPR
51-6	**1**		**Yeats (IRE)**[53] 1546 8-9-2 122 (A P O'Brien, Ire) *lw: prom: pushed along 4f out: led over 3f out: kicked abt 4l clr over 2f out: styd on gamely: wl in command at fin* **6/4**[1]	JMurtagh 6	125
4-12	**2**	*3 ½*	**Patkai (IRE)**[21] 2409 4-9-0 114 (Sir Michael Stoute) *lw: hld up in midfield: hdwy whn nt clr run 3f out: wnt 2nd over 2f out: styd on but nvr able to chal wnr* **9/2**[3]	RyanMoore 8	121
25-1	**3**	*15*	**Geordieland (FR)**[21] 2409 8-9-2 117 (J A Osborne) *hld up: nt clr run over 2f out: prog to chse ldng duo over 1f out: sn hung rt and no imp* **11/4**[2]	ShaneKelly 3	106
32-5	**4**	*3 ¼*	**Sagara (USA)**[13] 2677 5-9-2 109 (Saeed Bin Suroor) *swtg: in tch: effrt to chse ldrs over 3f out: no imp ent fnl 2f: wl btn after* **50/1**	(v) TedDurcan 5	103
1116	**5**	*1 ¾*	**Eastern Anthem (IRE)**[13] 2670 5-9-2 117 (Saeed Bin Suroor) *lw: stdd s: hld up: pushed along 5f out: hung lft u.p over 2f out: nvr on terms w ldrs* **25/1**	(t) AhmedAjtebi 1	101
5201	**6**	*4*	**Hindu Kush (IRE)**[21] 2425 4-9-0 103 (D Nicholls) *led: pushed along and hdd over 4f out: losing pl whn n.m.r over 3f out: sn wknd* **40/1**	JimCrowley 7	97
3-26	**7**	*12*	**Centennial (IRE)**[34] 2056 4-9-0 112 (J H M Gosden) *trckd ldrs: effrt over 3f out: wknd 2f out* **33/1**	(v[1]) JimmyFortune 9	85
-213	**P**		**Veracity**[34] 2056 5-9-2 116 (Saeed Bin Suroor) *prom: led over 4f out: hdd over 3f out: losing grnd whn wnt wrong over 2f out: sn p.u* **13/2**	LDettori 4	—
26-4	**P**		**Washington Irving (IRE)**[34] 2056 4-9-0 110 (J Howard Johnson) *hld up: struggling 6f out: lost tch 5f out: t.o whn p.u 2f out* **50/1**	PaulMulrennan 2	—

4m 20.73s (-0.27) **Going Correction** +0.025s/f (Good)

WFA 4 from 5yo+ 2lb **9** Ran SP% **111.3**

Speed ratings (Par 117): **101,99,93,92,91 90,85,—,—**

toteswinger: 1&2 £2.10, 1&3 £1.20, 2&3 £2.30 CSF £7.78 CT £15.49 TOTE £2.40: £1.30, £1.80, £1.20; EX 9.10 Trifecta £22.20 Pool: £21394.80 - 712.26 winning units..

Owner Mrs John Magnier & Mrs David Nagle **Bred** Barronstown Stud & Orpendale **Trained** Ballydoyle, Co Tipperary

■ Yeats became the first horse in the 207-year history of the race to win the Gold Cup four times.

FOCUS

A historic renewal, but the pace was ordinary and the first two came right away from the home turn. This can be rated the winner's best effort in the Gold Cup, and it was also a slight personal best from the runner-up.

NOTEBOOK

Yeats(IRE) became the first horse to win this for a fourth time, thus marking himself arguably the greatest stayer in history. He had serious questions to answer, as he had run no sort of race in April at Navan in the Vintage Crop Stakes, albeit on ground verging on heavy, and no eight-year-old had been successful since 1900 when Merman scored, but the vibes from Ballydoyle were positive and there were signs in the preliminaries that he was up for it. Having adopted a handy position early on just off the average pace, he was perfectly positioned as the tempo began to hot up and Murtagh asked him for his initial effort with four to run. He had to get vigorous in the saddle, but Yeats really began to find his stride rounding the home turn and went clear of the field. It momentarily appeared as though he was feeling the pinch as Patkai began to close, but he found extra coming to the furlong pole and once in control he coasted home under hands-and-heels riding. The return to fast ground made the difference, and his pace was a valuable tool, as the early gallop did not appear strong. This was probably his best performance in the race and bodes very well should he return to the Goodwood Cup next month, where he would be bidding for a hat-trick. The King George, for which he would need to be supplemented, the Arc and the Cadran are also all under consideration, but the burning question remains whether he will come back next year and try to win here for a fifth consecutive time. Either way, Ballydoyle is to be highly commended for the handling of this magnificent horse and breathing such life into the staying division that this race has now become the highlight of the week again. (op 7-4 tchd 2-1 in places)

Patkai(IRE), the young pretender, proved the only possible danger to the winner down the home straight and no doubt posted his best effort to date. He too had something to prove after losing out to Geordieland in the Henry II Stakes at Sandown 21 days earlier, but had shown his love for this track by winning on his two previous visits over 2m. He was unsurprisingly ridden with greater restraint here, but he took time to settle and was not well placed coming out of Swinley Bottom. Indeed, he had to snatch up for a stride or two and endured a troubled passage on the home bend. He ran on strongly when in the clear to look a danger coming to 2f out, and though it was apparent at the furlong marker that he was held he has time very much on his side, being only four. (op 7-2 tchd 5-1 in a place)

Geordieland(FR) had found Yeats too strong when second in this the last two years, but he still looked the main danger again after his game success over the runner-up at Sandown, where he had showed a most willing attitude. He raced in a similar position from off the pace as Patkai but found some trouble round the home turn and again coming to 2f out. By the time he was in the clear the race was effectively over, and though he plugged on he lacked Patkai's turn of foot. This was not his form, and he could re-oppose at Goodwood next month, although York's Lonsdale Stakes and the Doncaster Cup are also options. Longer term connections are looking seriously at the Breeders' Cup Marathon at Santa Anita. (op 10-3)

Sagara(USA), one of three runners for Godolphin, finished fifth last year and he stepped up greatly on his disappointing return 13 days earlier to go one place better. He has proved hard to get right after joining his current connections and will likely continue to be hard to place successfully.

Eastern Anthem(IRE) was an interesting contender on this massive step up in trip, being the only other previous Group 1 winner along with Yeats. That came in the Dubai Sheema Classic in March for another trainer and he had failed to fire in the Coronation Cup on his return to Britain last time out. Ridden to get the distance, he first came under pressure 5f out and was cooked when hanging left around 2f out. He needs to drop back in trip, but like Gladiatorus earlier in the week, it remains to be seen whether he can ever return to the sort of form he was in at Nad Al Sheba. (op 20-1)

Hindu Kush(IRE) made all when winning in Ireland 21 days previously and again set out from the front over this much stiffer test. He was responsible for the average gallop and was a sitting duck from 5f out. (op 33-1)

Centennial(IRE) had a first-time visor replacing blinkers and was expected to enjoy the return to quicker ground. He was ridden as though the extra distance would not be a problem, but ultimately failed to get home and is another who is not easy to place. (op 28-1)

Veracity had proved popular as the each-way horse in the race in most ante-post lists, as his profile suggested he would relish this sort of test. The return to quicker ground was also more to his liking and he was ridden just off the early leader for most of the way. He took it up as the race got serious, but was in trouble not long afterwards and appeared to lose his action near the two-furlong pole. He subsequently had to be put down, having broken a cannonbone. Official explanation: vet said horse pulled up lame (op 6-1 tchd 7-1 in places)

3049 BRITANNIA STKS (HERITAGE H'CAP) — 1m (S)

4:20 (4:28) (Class 2) (0-105,103) 3-Y-O

£62,310 (£18,660; £9,330; £4,670; £2,330; £1,170) **Stalls** Centre

Form / RPR

-315 **1** **Fareer**[26] 2273 3-8-10 **92** ... RHills 15 103+
(E A L Dunlop) *bhd stands' side: gd hdwy fr over 2f out: swtchd lft over 1f out: r.o to ld nr fin: 1st of 21 in gp* **20/1**

-141 **2** *hd* **Secret Society**[17] 2544 3-8-8 **90** ... JamieSpencer 13 101
(M L W Bell) *lw: swtchd lft s: bhd stands' side: gd hdwy to ld gp and dispute overall ld over 1f out: r.o: 2nd of 21 in gp* **22/1**

3-11 **3** *shd* **Mirrored**[28] 2209 3-8-7 **89** ow2 ... MJKinane 30 100
(Sir Michael Stoute) *hld up twrds rr far side: hdwy to press ldrs 2f out: disp ld fnl f: r.o: 1st of 9 in gp* **16/1**

-521 **4** *shd* **Espiritu (FR)**[8] 2805 3-8-9 **91** 5ex ... (v) GMosse 29 101
(J Noseda) *bhd far side: hdwy 3f out: led gp and disp overall ld wl over 1f out: kpt on: 2nd of 9 in gp* **20/1**

3161 **5** *1 ¾* **River Captain (IRE)**[12] 2701 3-8-12 **94** ... EddieAhern 2 100
(S Kirk) *chsd ldrs stands' side: chal 2f out: nt qckn fnl f: 3rd of 21 in gp* **14/1**

-512 **6** *1 ½* **Hyades (USA)**[25] 2296 3-8-10 **92** ... TPQueally 17 95+
(H R A Cecil) *lw: in tch centre: jnd stands' side gp after 3f: pressed ldrs 3f out: hrd rdn 2f out: styd on same pce: 4th of 21 in gp* **25/1**

1-23 **7** *¾* **Emirates Roadshow (USA)**[12] 2696 3-8-1 **86** ... AhmedAjtebi(3) 8 87
(Saeed Bin Suroor) *lw: led stands' side gp and disp overall ld tl wknd jst over 1f out: 5th of 21 in gp* **16/1**

2-40 **8** *1* **Satwa Laird**[13] 2674 3-8-4 **86** ... MartinDwyer 3 85
(E A L Dunlop) *lw: hld up twrds rr stands' side: hdwy on rail 3f out: one pce fnl 2f: 6th of 21 in gp* **25/1**

1-61 **9** *1 ¼* **Brief Encounter (IRE)**[36] 1987 3-8-8 **90** ... WilliamBuick 6 86+
(A M Balding) *chsd ldrs stands' side 2f: lost pl: towards rr whn n.m.r 3f out: styd on fnl f: 7th of 21 in gp* **6/1**[1]

660 **10** *½* **Canwinn (IRE)**[26] 2273 3-8-6 **88** ... SamHitchcott 4 83
(M R Channon) *in tch stands' side: drvn along and outpcd fnl 3f: 8th of 21 in gp* **66/1**

01-1 **11** *¾* **Roman Republic (FR)**[12] 2696 3-8-9 **91** ... RoystonFfrench 19 84+
(M Johnston) *edgy: in tch centre: jnd stands' side gp after 3f: hmpd and lost pl over 2f out: kept on fnl f: 9th of 21 in gp* **15/2**[2]

1-55 **12** *1 ¼* **Tudor Key (IRE)**[25] 2296 3-8-8 **90** ... JimCrowley 27 80
(Mrs A J Perrett) *in tch far side: effrt over 2f out: wknd 1f out: 3rd of 9 in gp* **100/1**

441 **13** *¾* **Invisible Man**[33] 2082 3-8-3 **85** ... NickyMackay 32 74
(J H M Gosden) *prom far side: chal over 2f out: wknd over 1f out: 4th of 9 in gp* **25/1**

6223 **14** *1* **Shampagne**[35] 2004 3-9-2 **103** ... Louis-PhilippeBeuzelin(5) 18 89
(P F I Cole) *in tch centre: jnd stands' side gp after 3f: drvn along 3f out: sn outpcd: 10th of 21 in gp* **40/1**

010 **15** *hd* **Uniquely Poised (USA)**[12] 2696 3-8-8 **90** ... RichardMullen 25 76
(J H M Gosden) *towards rr far side: rdn over 2f out: nvr rchd ldrs: 5th of 9 in gp* **50/1**

332 **16** *nk* **Big Bay (USA)**[21] 2415 3-7-12 **85** ... AndreaAtzeni(5) 22 70
(Jane Chapple-Hyam) *lw: towards rr far side: sme hdwy and rdn 2f out: no imp: 6th of 9 in gp* **40/1**

-211 **17** *nk* **Suruor (IRE)**[26] 2281 3-8-6 **88** ... StephenDonohoe 23 72
(D M Simcock) *prom far side: led gp and disp overall ld over 2f out tl wl over 1f out: sn wknd: 7th of 9 in gp* **33/1**

61-1 **18** *shd* **Crackdown (IRE)**[63] 1307 3-9-1 **97** ... LDettori 16 81
(M Johnston) *lw: led centre gp: jnd stands' side gp after 3f and disp overall ld tl wknd over 1f out: 11th of 21 in gp* **16/1**

123 **19** *¾* **Mutamaashi**[25] 2296 3-8-6 **88** ... TPO'Shea 12 71
(W J Haggas) *lw: swtchd lft to stands' gp s: nvr trbld ldrs: 12th of 21 in gp* **16/1**

-365 **20** *½* **Mishrif (USA)**[13] 2673 3-9-0 **96** ... AlanMunro 11 77
(P W Chapple-Hyam) *prom stands' side: hrd rdn over 2f out: sn wknd: 13th of 21 in gp* **80/1**

1-11 **21** *shd* **Desert Creek (IRE)**[26] 2273 3-9-1 **97** ... RyanMoore 26 78+
(Sir Michael Stoute) *swtchd lft to centre after 1f: bhd: jnd stands' side gp after 3f: hdwy 3f out: wknd 2f out: 14th of 21 in gp* **8/1**[3]

-311 **22** *2 ½* **Eastern Empire**[24] 2329 3-8-7 **89** ... MichaelHills 9 64
(J W Hills) *chsd ldrs stands' side over 4f: 15th of 21 in gp* **25/1**

-540 **23** *1 ¼* **Viva Ronaldo (IRE)**[26] 2273 3-8-12 **94** ... PaulMulrennan 24 67
(R A Fahey) *prom far side over 5f: 8th of 9 in gp* **80/1**

-002 **24** *1 ¼* **Deadly Secret (USA)**[12] 2696 3-8-10 **92** ... PaulHanagan 28 62
(R A Fahey) *lw; led far side gp and disp overall ld tl wknd over 2f out: last of 9 in gp* **40/1**

0-10 **25** *3 ¼* **Magaling (IRE)**[12] 2696 3-8-7 **89** ... C-PLemaire 14 51
(L M Cumani) *chsd ldrs centre: jnd stands' side gp after 3f: wknd fr 1/2-way: 16th of 21 in gp* **25/1**

2120 **26** *½* **Tarzan (IRE)**[12] 2701 3-8-2 **84** ... FrancisNorton 5 45
(M Johnston) *prom stands' side over 4f: 17th of 21 in gp* **33/1**

-656 **27** *hd* **Aurorian (IRE)**[12] 2701 3-8-6 **88** ow1 ... SteveDrowne 7 49
(R Hannon) *prom stands' side 5f: 18th of 21 in gp* **40/1**

3 **28** *11* **Rockhampton (IRE)**[34] 2067 3-9-5 **101** ... JMurtagh 20 36
(A P O'Brien, Ire) *chsd ldrs stands' side 3f: rdn and dropped to rr over 3f out: sn bhd: 19th of 21 in gp* **14/1**

1255 **29** *¾* **Tartan Gunna**[13] 2674 3-8-7 **89** ... JoeFanning 21 23
(M Johnston) *prom centre: jnd stands' side gp after 3f: wknd over 3f out: 20th of 21 in gp* **40/1**

1046 **30** *22* **Markyg (USA)**[26] 2273 3-8-10 **92** ... (v[1]) NCallan 10 —
(K R Burke) *lw: chsd ldrs centre: jnd stands' side gp after 3f: wknd over 3f out: midfield and btn whn bmpd over 2f out: sn bhd: last of 21 in gp* **50/1**

1m 40.31s (-0.29) **Going Correction** +0.10s/f (Good) **30** Ran SP% **134.1**
Speed ratings (Par 105): **105,104,104,104,102 101,100,99,98,97 97,95,95,94,93 93,93,93,92,91 91,89,88,86,83 83,82,71,71**
toteswingers: 1&2 £432.20, 1&3 £124.20, 2&3 £54.90 CSF £400.36 CT £7107.06 TOTE £37.10: £7.50, £4.30, £3.70, £7.00; EX 813.50 Trifecta £7983.60 Part won. Pool: £10788.71 - 0.90 winning units..

Owner Hamdan Al Maktoum **Bred** Bishopswood Bloodstock & Trickledown Stud **Trained** Newmarket, Suffolk

FOCUS

Effectively the Hunt Cup for three-year-olds and, like that contest, a strong, competitive handicap that often falls to an improving sort. Unlike the Hunt Cup the previous day where the stands'-side group had a definite advantage, this time the field originally split into three and the principals were spread across the track at the finish, with the first four all coming from the rear. The first four are all rated improvers with the fifth the best guide, the form is solid and should work out.

NOTEBOOK

Fareer, drawn in the middle of the track, was tracked across to the stands'-side group but, along with the runner-up, was one of the last pair at halfway. However, as the front-runners tired he cut through the pack and in a driving finish got to the front in the final strides. He is clearly going the right way and should have more good races in him. (tchd 33-1 in a place and 25-1 in places)

Secret Society was also drawn in the middle. He was held up in the rear towards the centre of the track before sweeping through to lead a furlong or so from the finish. However, despite keeping on under pressure, he could not resist the winner's late challenge. Both his previous wins have been at 7f and he looks the sort who could make his mark in one of the big 7f handicaps back here later in the season. (op 25-1 tchd 20-1)

Mirrored ◆, a dual 1m winner on Polytrack and fast ground but raised 5lb for his last win, ran a fine race from his high draw. He got a good tow into the race and battled on bravely in the final furlong to just get the better of the fourth, but just behind those more towards the stands' side. There is more to come from this lightly raced individual.

Espiritu(FR) had won a maiden over an extended 7f on fast ground in a first-time visor on his previous start and the booking of Gerard Mosse looked significant. Racing in the far-side group, he cut through the pack in much the same way as the first two and appeared to show slightly in front inside the final furlong before his effort flattened out near the finish. The blinkers seem to have been the making of him. (op 25-1 tchd 33-1 in places)

River Captain(IRE) deserves extra credit as he did best of those to race close to the pace most of the way. A progressive sort in handicaps at up to 1m2f but raised 11lb for his most recent success, the ground was a question mark but he handled it well enough and his stamina enabled him to keep going as others faded. A return to further is likely but this performance increases connections' options. (tchd 16-1)

Hyades(USA), a half-brother to Light Shift and Shiva, is progressing with experience and ran well over 1m2f on his handicap debut. This was another decent effort and he was doing his best work late on.

Emirates Roadshow(USA), a 7f winner on easy ground whose form tied in with the market leaders, made the running towards the stands' side and stuck on pretty well when headed. (op 20-1)

Satwa Laird, the winner's stable companion, handles fast ground and was stepping up in trip. He was another to perform with credit although he just faded in the last furlong or so. (tchd 33-1 in places)

Brief Encounter(IRE) was sent off favourite and, like the principals, was held up. However, he was slightly impeded when beginning his run about 3f out and never got into contention. (op 13-2 tchd 7-1 in places)

Canwinn(IRE), Group placed at two, has been struggling this year but this was a better effort from his low draw.

Roman Republic(FR), a dual winner on good and soft ground, was 8lb higher than for the second of those successes and weakened at the business end. (op 8-1 tchd 9-1 in places)

Tudor Key(IRE), whose previous runs this year were at 1m2f, seemed to run his race before fading late on. (tchd 80-1)

Crackdown(IRE), a progressive front-runner with Frankie Dettori on board, showed up well down the centre before weakening late on.

Desert Creek(IRE), a progressive performer with three wins and a second from four starts and the winner of a similar handicap at Haydock last time on heavy ground, when he had the winner and several of his other rivals behind, was 10lb higher. Drawn on the far side, his rider elected to switch across towards the stands' side and came to have his chance at the quarter-mile pole before fading late on. He is clearly better than this performance indicates. (tchd 15-2 and 9-1 in places)

3050 HAMPTON COURT STKS (LISTED RACE) — 1m 2f

4:55 (5:04) (Class 1) 3-Y-O

£28,385 (£10,760; £5,385; £2,685; £1,345; £675) **Stalls** High

Form / RPR

1-56 **1** **Glass Harmonium (IRE)**[35] 2014 3-9-2 108 ... RyanMoore 11 117+
(Sir Michael Stoute) *swtg: midfield: swtchd lft and hdwy over 2f out: str burst of spd on outside and hung rt fr ent fnl 2f: led over 1f out: r.o u.p ins fnl f: looked to be holding runner-up towards fin* **8/1**

2 *½* **Cashelgar (IRE)**[21] 3-9-5 94 ... GMosse 10 119+
(A De Royer-Dupre, France) *w'like: str: attr: lw: racd keenly: trckd ldrs: burst through to chal jst over 2f out: led wl over 1f out: sn hdd: continued to chal and r.o u.p: n.m.r whn looked hld cl home* **20/1**

-204 **3** *4 ½* **Monitor Closely (IRE)**[35] 2014 3-9-2 108 ... AlanMunro 7 107
(P W Chapple-Hyam) *lw: racd keenly: trckd ldrs: rdn 2f out: trying to qckn whn n.m.r jst over 1f out: kpt on same pce ins fnl f* **15/2**[3]

1-16 **4** 2 ½ **Too Much Trouble**[42] 1800 3-9-2 96 TonyCulhane 5 102
(M R Channon) *lw: bustled along in rr early: prog and styd on u.p fr 2f out: nt rch ldrs* **20/1**

3-2 **5** shd **Freemantle**[35] 2014 3-9-2 111 JMurtagh 4 102+
(A P O'Brien, Ire) *lw: w ldr: nosed ahd over 3f out: rdn and hdd wl over 1f out: one pce fnl f* **1/1**[1]

3-21 **6** ¾ **Four Winds**[35] 2004 3-9-2 101 JamieSpencer 13 100
(M L W Bell) *on toes: racd keenly in midfield: hdwy over 2f out: sn rdn and nt qckn: one pce after* **7/1**[2]

1233 **7** 5 **Spring Of Fame (USA)**[21] 2411 3-9-2 102 LDettori 3 95+
(Saeed Bin Suroor) *lw: midfield: clsd over 4f out: pushed along 3f out: rdn whn chsd ldrs over 2f out: wknd over 1f out* **16/1**

-421 **8** 1 **Palavicini (USA)**[26] 2277 3-9-7 108 EddieAhern 1 93+
(J L Dunlop) *lw: hld up: n.m.r on rail over 5f out: rdn over 2f out: nvr able to chal* **16/1**

31-4 **9** 3 ¾ **On Our Way**[64] 1294 3-9-5 103 TPQueally 2 84
(H R A Cecil) *lw: racd keenly w ldrs: rdn over 2f out: wkng whn hung rt over 1f out* **12/1**

0444 **10** 2 **Kaolak (USA)**[34] 2048 3-9-2 74 RichardMullen 6 77
(J Ryan) *towards rr: pushed along over 4f out: nvr on terms* **150/1**

1253 **11** 4 ½ **Big Bound (USA)**[26] 2277 3-9-2 102 JimmyFortune 9 68
(J H M Gosden) *led: hdd over 3f out: rdn over 2f out: wknd over 1f out* **40/1**

5 **12** 3 ¼ **Satwa Ruby (FR)**[6] 2989 3-8-11 93 C-PLemaire 12 56
(J De Roualle, France) *leggy: on toes: rdn over 2f out: a bhd* **50/1**

2m 4.52s (-2.48) **Going Correction** +0.025s/f (Good) **12** Ran SP% **119.4**
Speed ratings (Par 107): **110,109,106,104,103 103,99,98,95,93 90,87**
toteswingers: 1&2 £28.60, 1&3 £9.20, 2&3 £20.70 CSF £161.73 CT £1256.08 TOTE £10.30: £2.80, £3.90, £2.60; EX 156.30 Trifecta £1050.20 Pool: £6244.57 - 4.40 winning units..
Owner Ballymacoll Stud **Bred** Ballymacoll Stud Farm Ltd **Trained** Newmarket, Suffolk
■ The result was confirmed only after a lengthy stewards' enquiry.
■ Stewards' Enquiry : Ryan Moore four-day ban: careless riding (Jul 2,3,5,6)

FOCUS
While this may not have been the hottest three-year-old event of the week, it was still as competitive as ever. The race was run at a frantic early pace as the early leaders cut each other's throats and the first pair eventually came clear in a very tight finish. The form looks good with an unexposed pair clear and the third and fourth setting the level.

NOTEBOOK
Glass Harmonium(IRE) ended a string of near misses at the meeting for his stable and got off the mark for the season at the third time of asking, reversing the key Dante form with both Monitor Closely and Freemantle. He was held up early on and the way the race was run no doubt played into his hands. He began to wind up coming off the home turn and got to the leaders going strongly 2f out. He drifted markedly right when asked to win the race, however, and gave the runner-up little room for manoeuvre against the far rail. That was enough to ensure a lengthy stewards' enquiry, but he always looked to be doing enough inside the final 100yards. He has improved with every outing to date and connections now look to have found his optimum trip. He is the type his trainer does so well with and is versatile as regards underfoot conditions. (op 15-2 tchd 6-1, 9-1 in places)
Cashelgar(IRE) ◆ was allotted an official mark of 94 after narrowly making all over a little further at Saint-Cloud last month on easy ground. Indeed he had only been purchased by Sir Robert Ogden six days previously, but fully justified the decision to come here with an excellent effort in defeat. Well drawn, he travelled easily through the race and got a lovely passage into the home straight. Once asked to hit the front his response was not the quickest, however, and he looked like giving way to the winner when that rival came over to him. The manner in which he rallied when tight for room was very pleasing, though, and he is obviously an improving horse. The step up to 1m4f should prove ideal and he is one to follow. (tchd 22-1 in places)
Monitor Closely(IRE) had finished in front of the winner in the Dante last time and had every chance to confirm the form. He rates the most reliable guide to the form, but the searching test over this trip just looked to stretch his stamina, although his trainer is of the opinion that he might want even further. He richly deserves to find another race. (op 8-1 tchd 10-1)
Too Much Trouble ◆, along with the runner-up, was the most inexperienced in the field and it showed through the early parts. He stayed on strongly when the race was all but over and remains capable of success in this sort of company when stepping back up in trip. (op 40-1)
Freemantle ◆, who had finished ahead of the winner and third when just losing out from the front in the Dante on his seasonal return and avoided the Derby to come here, was a big disappointment. He was considered a banker for many this week with improvement from the run expected, and was backed accordingly. However, his rider's insistence on getting him to the front ultimately cost him as the two that went with him ensured he was not going to have it his own way. The fact those two dropped right out of it and he kept on for fifth is testament to his ability, and surely he would have been seen to much better effect under more patient tactics. He had a hard race this time and could need time to recover sufficiently, but the best of him has likely still to be seen. (tchd 11-10, 11-8 in places)
Four Winds was well backed, with his yard being in decent form, and he had a good draw. He was ridden to get the longer distance and moved nicely enough into the home bend. He had to be switched with his effort down the home straight, but it made little difference and he really paid for running freely early on. Perhaps he is a miler after all. (op 13-2 tchd 6-1)
Spring Of Fame(USA) had his chance, but was another who failed to get home on this step up in trip due to the strong pace. (tchd 18-1)
Palavicini(USA) was bidding to overcome the poor record of penalised winners in this event. He did not look that happy out the back early on and did not get the best of passages, but never rated a serious player.

3051 KING GEORGE V STKS (HERITAGE H'CAP) 1m 4f
5:30 (5:34) (Class 2) (0-105,103) 3-Y-O

£31,155 (£9,330; £4,665; £2,335; £1,165; £585) **Stalls** High

Form RPR
4-00 **1** **Cosmic Sun**[12] 2715 3-7-12 80 oh3 PaulHanagan 14 89
(R A Fahey) *hld up abt 7th: effrt over 2f out: led over 1f out: drvn out* **66/1**

6-11 **2** 1 ¼ **Chiberta King**[33] 2084 3-8-1 83 oh1 ow3 WilliamBuick 11 90
(A M Balding) *chsd ldrs: rdn over 2f out: chal over 1f out: kpt on* **8/1**

2121 **3** nse **Barwell Bridge**[36] 1992 3-8-5 87 JamesDoyle 7 94
(S Kirk) *pressed ldr: led 2f out tl over 1f out: kpt on* **12/1**

4 2 **Zarinski (IRE)**[68] 1224 3-8-4 86 NGMcCullagh 5 90
(John M Oxx, Ire) *lengthy: scope: lw: hld up towards rr: hdwy 5f out: drvn along 3f out: styd on same pce fnl 2f* **9/2**[1]

1102 **5** shd **Topolski (IRE)**[17] 2545 3-8-5 87 JohnEgan 18 91+
(M Johnston) *hld up in midfield: hmpd on rail after 3f: rdn 3f out: hdwy 2f out: styd on fnl f* **33/1**

0-16 **6** 1 ¼ **Highland Glen**[26] 2275 3-8-7 89 ow2 RyanMoore 9 91+
(Sir Michael Stoute) *lw: t.k.h in rr: rdn and styd on wl fnl 2f: nrst fin* **7/1**[3]

1-31 **7** nk **Opinion Poll (IRE)**[26] 2275 3-8-13 95 LDettori 3 96+
(M A Jarvis) *lw: mid-div on outer: sme hdwy and hrd rdn 2f out: no imp* **13/2**[2]

-201 **8** ¾ **Quai D'Orsay**[12] 2715 3-8-12 94 JoeFanning 16 94
(M Johnston) *prom: hrd rdn 2f out: sn btn* **14/1**

2151 **9** nk **Brunston**[28] 2189 3-8-5 87 AlanMunro 13 86+
(R Charlton) *t.k.h in rr of midfield: rdn and no hdwy fnl 3f* **11/1**

-120 **10** 1 **Dubai Crest**[12] 2701 3-8-6 88 ow1 C-PLemaire 10 86
(Mrs A J Perrett) *hld up in midfield: rdn over 2f out: no prog* **20/1**

1200 **11** hd **Fin Vin De Leu (GER)**[12] 2715 3-7-12 80 oh3 AndrewMullen 4 77
(M Johnston) *lw: hld up in rr of midfield: hrd rdn 3f out: sn outpcd* **100/1**

1-16 **12** 1 ¾ **Kimberley Downs (USA)**[43] 1792 3-8-1 83 RoystonFfrench 2 78+
(M Johnston) *in tch tl drvn along and wknd over 3f out* **20/1**

-314 **13** 1 ¼ **Takaatuf (IRE)**[25] 2296 3-8-6 88 RHills 12 84+
(M Johnston) *lw: sn led: hdd 2f out: hrd rdn and wknd over 1f out: eased whn wl btn fnl f* **16/1**

-210 **14** 3 ¾ **Above Average (IRE)**[42] 1800 3-9-7 103 MichaelHills 17 97+
(B W Hills) *bhd: rdn over 3f out: nvr nr ldrs* **40/1**

15 ½ **Johann Zoffany**[21] 2426 3-8-11 100 JPO'Brien(7) 19 86
(A P O'Brien, Ire) *w'like: s.s: bhd: sme hdwy on outer 5f out: drvn along 3f out: sn wknd* **16/1**

-321 **16** 1 ¼ **Polly's Mark (IRE)**[30] 2164 3-8-7 89 PhilipRobinson 1 73+
(C G Cox) *chsd ldrs tl wknd ent st* **12/1**

0243 **17** 1 ¾ **Lasso The Moon**[12] 2701 3-7-12 80 CatherineGannon 6 61
(M R Channon) *lw: s.s: t.k.h in rr: bhd and rdn over 3f out* **12/1**

61-6 **18** 4 ½ **Sky Gate (USA)**[10] 2767 3-8-3 85 ow2 (b) MartinDwyer 15 59
(B J Meehan) *plld hrd towards rr: rdn and struggling over 3f out* **100/1**

-410 **19** 10 **London Bridge**[12] 2701 3-8-0 82 NickyMackay 8 40
(J H M Gosden) *mid-div: drvn along 4f out: sn wknd* **16/1**

2m 31.29s (-1.21) **Going Correction** +0.025s/f (Good) **19** Ran SP% **129.2**
Speed ratings (Par 105): **105,104,104,102,102 101,101,101,101,100 100,99,98,95,95 94,93,90,83**
toteswingers: 1&2 £114.10, 1&3 £154.80, 2&3 £28.60 CSF £544.78 CT £6732.43 TOTE £81.90: £13.30, £2.70, £3.70, £2.00; EX 730.70 TRIFECTA Not won. Place 6: £1255.44 Place 5: £262.87.

Owner The Cosmic Cases **Bred** M Wassall **Trained** Musley Bank, N Yorks
■ Stewards' Enquiry : James Doyle one-day ban: careless riding (Jul 2)

FOCUS
A typically strong renewal of this highly competitive 3yo handicap. Mark Johnston and Sir Michael Stoute had each had three winners in the previous eight runnings and both were represented again but, in what was a rough race early with the hold-up horses getting in each others' way, there was a surprise result. The time was 0.62sec slower than the Ribblesdale earlier in the afternoon and although the race does not give the impression of being as strong as usual, it should throw up plenty of winners.

NOTEBOOK
Cosmic Sun, whose dam Cosmic Case was a middle-distance/stayer on the Flat and won over 3m over hurdles, had done pretty well as a juvenile considering his breeding. However, he came into this as a maiden in ten starts and had been well beaten by two of today's rivals in his previous starts this season. Despite racing from 3lb out of the handicap, he was always going comfortably in the wake of the leaders and picked up well from the home turn to get his head in front entering the final furlong. He was always holding on from that point and is clearly better than he has been showing of late.
Chiberta King had looked a really progressive sort when winning his two previous starts over this trip and confirmed that impression off a 7lb higher mark in a more competitive race, despite not winning. Still a pound out of the handicap, he came through looking as though he might score but had nothing extra to offer in the last furlong. (tchd 9-1 in places)
Barwell Bridge had beaten today's winner over 1m2f at York but was trying this trip for the first time. He was given a positive ride and proved he got the trip, going on early in the straight and battling on after being headed by the winner. He is a consistent sort and remains progressive. (op 14-1)
Zarinski(IRE) was having only his third start on turf and had not been seen since scoring on Dundalk's Polytrack surface in April on his first try at this trip. However, the fact his trainer sent him for this encouraged market support and he was backed in to favouritism. He was held up but made his ground from halfway to be close enough turning in, but from that point he could only stay on at the one pace. (op 5-1 tchd 6-1 in places)
Topolski(IRE) ◆ was held up in rear on the rail and, although he did not seem to suffer much from the scrimmaging, was short of room for much of the way. However, he started to make headway in the last half-mile and finished as well as anything. Despite being 5lb higher than for a narrow defeat at Thirsk, he still seems to be improving and is the one to take from the race with races like the Melrose in mind later in the season.
Highland Glen ◆ was held up in the rear and on the outside. Back on ground that suits, he was doing his best work late and can be given another chance as this was only his fourth start. (op 9-1)
Opinion Poll(IRE) had beaten Highland Glen on heavy ground at Haydock but his two previous defeats had been on fast going and he probably needs more give in the ground to produce his best. (op 8-1 tchd 9-1)
Quai D'Orsay had the winner well behind when scoring at Musselburgh earlier in the month and seemed to have every chance before fading. (op 12-1)
Brunston was much too keen under restraint early on and got involved in the scrimmaging on the run down to Swinley Bottom. Switched outside on the climb to the straight, he could not pick up from that point. He was 8lb higher than for his most recent success and 13lb higher than when scoring on his handicap debut, so perhaps the Handicapper has caught up with him. (op 9-1 tchd 12-1)
Takaatuf(IRE) made the running but could not respond when taken on early in the straight. (tchd 20-1 in places)
Above Average(IRE), the top weight, was possibly the worst sufferer in the early scrimmaging, was last at halfway and can be forgiven this. (tchd 33-1)
Johann Zoffany made all the running last time but missed the break here and then his inexperienced rider made his ground on the outside on the climb to the straight. It was not surprising that he faded once in line for home. (op 14-1)
Polly's Mark(IRE) probably did too much early on this step up in trip (op 14-1)
London Bridge was always in the rear division and was one of the first under pressure. (op 14-1)
T/Jkpt: Not won. T/Plt: £3,521.10 to a £1 stake. Pool: £447,711.72. 92.82 winning tickets.
T/Qpdt: £134.20 to a £1 stake. Pool: £34,234.41. 188.73 winning tickets. DO

2913 LEICESTER (R-H)
Thursday, June 18

OFFICIAL GOING: Good to firm (8.5)
Wind: Light behind Weather: Overcast

3052 BBC RADIO LEICESTER DRIVETIME MAIDEN STKS (C&G) 7f 9y
6:40 (6:41) (Class 4) 2-Y-O **£4,533** (£1,348; £674; £336) **Stalls** Centre

Form RPR
1 **Ishtar Gate (USA)** 2-9-0 0 JosedeSouza 5 76+
(P F I Cole) *a.p: rdn and hung rt over 1f out: r.o wl to ld nr fin* **25/1**

4 **2** hd **Contract Caterer (IRE)**[28] 2196 2-9-0 0 PaulEddery 8 74
(Pat Eddery) *a.p: chsd ldr 1/2-way: rdn to ld and hung lft fr over 1f out: rdr had whip knocked out of his hand wl ins fnl f: hdd nr fin* **3/1**[2]

3 **3** *4½* **Mingun Bell (USA)**[13] 2663 2-9-0 0.................................. IanMongan 7 63+
(H R A Cecil) *led: racd keenly: rdn: hung lft and hdd over 1f out: no ex ins fnl f* **4/6**[1]

4 *4½* **Second Brook (IRE)** 2-9-0 0.................................. ChrisCatlin 1 52
(R Hollinshead) *sn pushed along and rn green in rr: swtchd lft and styd on ins fnl f: wnt 4th nr fin* **33/1**

5 *½* **Comedy Act** 2-9-0 0.................................. SebSanders 4 50
(Sir Mark Prescott) *hld up: hdwy 3f out: rdn and wknd over 1f out* **20/1**

0 **6** *1¼* **The Caped Crusader (IRE)**[19] 2467 2-9-0 0............... MickyFenton 10 47
(T P Tate) *chsd ldr to 1/2-way: rdn and wknd over 1f out* **20/1**

7 *1½* **The Mighty Mod (USA)** 2-9-0 0.................................. AndrewElliott 2 43
(M Johnston) *s.s: hdwy 1/2-way: sn rdn: edgd lft and wknd 2f out* **17/2**[3]

8 *9* **Sir Bruno (FR)** 2-8-11 0.................................. KevinGhunowa(3) 9 21
(B Palling) *dwlt: sn prom: wknd over 2f out* **80/1**

1m 25.51s (-0.69) **Going Correction** -0.225s/f (Firm) **8** Ran SP% **113.1**
Speed ratings (Par 95): **94,93,88,83,82 81,79,69**
toteswingers: 1&2 £10.40, 1&3 £6.80, 2&3 £1.02 CSF £93.05 TOTE £30.50: £6.20, £1.30, £1.02; EX 139.10.
Owner D S Lee **Bred** B P Walden, P Madden Et Al **Trained** Whatcombe, Oxon
■ Jose de Souza's first winner for more than two years, albeit from limited chances.

FOCUS
Just a middle-of-the-road maiden but the placed horses set a decent enough standard. The winner looks capable of better although the initial level of form is fluid.

NOTEBOOK
Ishtar Gate(USA), a $230,000 US-bred yearling who is a half-brother to three multiple winners, looked quite green going to post and in the early stages of the race. He didn't respond instantly when shaken up over a furlong out, but the penny dropped in the final half-furlong and he picked up strongly to run down Contract Caterer close home, with the pair coming clear. Connections were fairly surprised as they felt he would come on a bundle for the run, so he could be a useful colt and another furlong already looks within range. (op 33-1 tchd 22-1)
Contract Caterer(IRE) was tackling much quicker ground than on debut, but he coped with it well and looked for all the world as though he had this in the bag when mastering Mingun Bell on the front end, only to be run out of it by the winner close home. This extra furlong suited and he looks sure to win sooner rather than later. (op 11-4 tchd 9-4)
Mingun Bell(USA) was the disappointment of the race but he spoilt his chance by racing too freely in the early stages. Still, he finished nicely clear of the rest and can do much better if learning to settle. (op 4-5 tchd 10-11)
Second Brook(IRE), a half-brother to the useful Iftitah, amongst others, got going late in the day from a long way back and shaped with promise. (op 20-1 tchd 18-1)
Comedy Act made an encouraging introduction given he is from a family of middle distance performers, notably the same connections' Comic Strip who did well here before developing into a top-class performer in Hong Kong when renamed Viva Pataca. (op 14-1)

3053 NELSON RESTAURANT H'CAP — 5f 2y
7:10 (7:10) (Class 4) (0-80,79) 3-Y-O **£6,308** (£1,888; £944; £472; £235) **Stalls** Centre

Form RPR
-102 **1** **Mattamia (IRE)**[10] 2774 3-9-3 **78**.................................. JamesMillman(3) 5 95
(B R Millman) *mde all: rdn and hung rt ins fnl f: r.o wl* **9/4**[1]

-404 **2** *4½* **Red Rosanna**[17] 2546 3-8-9 **70**.................................. RussellKennemore(3) 7 71
(R Hollinshead) *w wnr tl rdn: hung rt and no ex ins fnl f* **10/1**

0023 **3** *nk* **Rio Cobolo (IRE)**[5] 2918 3-8-3 **61**..................................(v) ChrisCatlin 6 61
(Paul Green) *chsd ldrs: outpcd over 3f out: rallied over 1f out: r.o* **6/1**[3]

-543 **4** *3¼* **Tagula Breeze (IRE)**[15] 2611 3-9-7 **79**.................................. FrancisNorton 4 67
(I W McInnes) *trckd ldrs: plld hrd: rdn and hung rt fr 1/2-way: wknd over 1f out* **10/3**[2]

1532 **5** *11* **Desert Strike**[16] 2562 3-9-3 **75**.................................. SebSanders 2 23
(P F I Cole) *s.i.s: hld up in tch: plld hrd: rdn and wknd wl ins fnl f* **9/4**[1]

20-0 **6** *4* **Nativity**[13] 2654 3-8-2 **60**.................................. LiamJones 1 —
(J L Spearing) *s.i.s: sn chsng ldrs: wknd wl over 1f out* **33/1**

58.70 secs (-1.30) **Going Correction** -0.225s/f (Firm) **6** Ran SP% **110.9**
Speed ratings (Par 101): **101,93,93,88,70 64**
toteswingers: 1&2 £7.30, 1&3 £2.70, 2&3 £27.20 CSF £24.29 TOTE £2.40: £1.90, £2.70; EX 15.90.
Owner C Roper **Bred** H G And J R Dutfield **Trained** Kentisbeare, Devon

FOCUS
Just a modest sprint handicap but fast and furious.
Tagula Breeze(IRE) Official explanation: jockey said gelding hung right
Desert Strike Official explanation: jockey said colt was unsuited by the good to firm ground

3054 TOWN HALL (S) STKS — 1m 1f 218y
7:40 (7:41) (Class 6) 3-Y-O **£1,942** (£578; £288; £144) **Stalls** High

Form RPR
1500 **1** **Fong's Alibi**[15] 2607 3-9-3 68..................................(p) LPKeniry 7 63
(J S Moore) *hld up: hdwy over 4f out: led over 1f out: rdn out* **15/8**[2]

0604 **2** *nk* **Garter Knight**[61] 1361 3-9-3 64.................................. MickyFenton 9 62
(M L W Bell) *hld up: pushed along 1/2-way: sn hung rt: hdwy over 3f out: rdn and ev ch ins fnl f: styd on* **6/4**[1]

000 **3** *4½* **Nouailhas**[20] 2447 3-9-0 46.................................. RussellKennemore(3) 6 53
(R Hollinshead) *led: rdn and hdd wl over 1f out: no ex ins fnl f* **40/1**

00-0 **4** *3* **Welcome Applause (IRE)**[20] 2461 3-8-12 51............... JerryO'Dwyer 1 42
(M G Quinlan) *chsd ldr tl led wl over 1f out: sn rdn and hdd: hung lft and wknd ins fnl f* **25/1**

0505 **5** *4½* **Wabi Sabi (IRE)**[23] 2361 3-8-12 56..................................(p) DO'Donohoe 4 33
(N Tinkler) *prom: racd keenly: rdn over 2f out: wknd over 1f out* **8/1**

05-6 **6** *8* **Alderbed**[10] 2772 3-8-12 46.................................. MatthewDavies(5) 3 22
(George Baker) *chsd ldrs: rdn over 3f out: wknd over 2f out* **12/1**

6-00 **7** *7* **Spring Secret**[23] 2350 3-9-3 54.................................. SteveDrowne 2 8
(B Palling) *hld up: rdn and wknd over 3f out* **15/2**[3]

5000 **R** **Glan Lady (IRE)**[24] 2333 3-8-9 40..................................(b) KevinGhunowa(3) 5 —
(G J Smith) *ref to r: tk no part* **50/1**

2m 9.91s (2.01) **Going Correction** -0.225s/f (Firm) **8** Ran SP% **113.6**
Speed ratings (Par 97): **82,81,78,75,72 65,60,—**
toteswingers: 1&2 £1.10, 1&3 £10.20, 2&3 £20.30 CSF £4.92 TOTE £2.70: £1.20, £1.40, £1.70; EX 4.50.The winner was bought in for 7,600gns.
Owner T & Mrs J Cunningham & R Frost **Bred** Darley **Trained** Upper Lambourn, Berks

FOCUS
A poor race even by selling standards and the pace was very steady, forcing many to race a little too freely in the early stages. The front two, who dominated the market, did so in the race, coming clear, but the future looks bleak for those in behind.

3055 WINDMILL H'CAP — 1m 60y
8:10 (8:11) (Class 4) (0-85,83) 4-Y-O+ **£6,308** (£1,888; £944; £472; £235) **Stalls** High

Form RPR
-463 **1** **Vainglory (USA)**[19] 2480 5-9-7 **83**.................................. SebSanders 7 91
(D M Simcock) *mde all: hrd rdn fnl f: styd on gamely* **11/4**[1]

-023 **2** *hd* **Effigy**[19] 2495 5-9-0 **76**.................................. DaneO'Neill 6 84
(H Candy) *hld up in tch: rdn to chse wnr over 1f out: edgd rt: r.o* **11/4**[1]

-105 **3** *2¾* **Cotswolds**[14] 2639 4-8-12 **74**.................................. GregFairley 5 75
(M Johnston) *chsd wnr 2f: remained handy: rdn and hung rt over 1f out: swtchd lft: r.o* **9/2**[2]

-005 **4** *2* **Resurge (IRE)**[19] 2480 4-9-4 **80**.................................. FergusSweeney 2 77
(W S Kittow) *slipped s: hld up: hdwy over 3f out: outpcd over 2f out: rallied over 1f out: no ex ins fnl f* **6/1**[3]

21-0 **5** *3½* **Cara's Request (AUS)**[28] 2197 4-9-5 **82**.................................. MickyFenton 4 70+
(L M Cumani) *prom: racd keenly: trckd ldr over 6f out: rdn and hung rt fr over 2f out: wknd ins fnl f* **13/2**

40-0 **6** *1¾* **Mount Hermon (IRE)**[54] 1524 5-8-12 **74**.................................. SteveDrowne 9 59
(H Morrison) *chsd ldrs: lost pl 5f out: rdn over 3f out: sn outpcd* **9/1**

6-60 **7** *hd* **Regional Counsel**[10] 2773 5-8-13 **80**..................................(b) MartinLane(5) 3 64
(A M Hales) *s.i.s: hld up: effrt and nt clr run over 3f out: swtchd lft sn after: n.d* **40/1**

0406 **8** *11* **Crocodile Bay (IRE)**[45] 1723 6-8-4 **66**.................................. ChrisCatlin 8 25
(John A Harris) *hld up in tch: plld hrd: lost pl 5f out: wknd over 3f out* **22/1**

1m 41.89s (-3.21) **Going Correction** -0.225s/f (Firm) **8** Ran SP% **115.9**
Speed ratings (Par 105): **107,106,104,102,98 96,96,85**
toteswingers: 1&2 £1.50, 1&3 £2.40, 2&3 £3.50 CSF £10.33 CT £32.15 TOTE £4.10: £1.70, £1.10, £2.00; EX 9.90.
Owner DXB Bloodstock Ltd **Bred** Darley **Trained** Newmarket, Suffolk

FOCUS
Run-of-the-mill handicap form but an even gallop
Cara's Request(AUS) Official explanation: jockey said colt hung right in home straight

3056 LEICESTER RACECOURSE CONFERENCE CENTRE MAIDEN STKS 1m 3f 183y
8:40 (8:40) (Class 5) 3-Y-O+ **£3,238** (£963; £481; £240) **Stalls** High

Form RPR
4 **1** **Acquisition**[17] 2551 3-8-5 0.................................. JimmyQuinn 6 62+
(H R A Cecil) *trckd ldrs: rdn to ld and hung rt fr over 1f out: styd on* **4/7**[1]

0- **2** *1½* **Canton Road**[252] 6602 3-8-10 0.................................. SteveDrowne 2 64
(P F I Cole) *chsd ldrs: rdn over 2f out: r.o: wnt 2nd towards fin* **10/1**[3]

06 **3** *nk* **Borromeo (USA)**[14] 2640 3-8-10 0.................................. GregFairley 3 64
(M Johnston) *led: rdn: hdd and hmpd over 1f out: styd on same pce ins fnl f* **16/1**

302 **4** *2¼* **Monaco Dream (IRE)**[14] 2633 3-8-5 75.................................. LiamJones 4 55
(W Jarvis) *hld up in tch: rdn over 3f out: edgd rt over 1f out: styd on* **10/3**[2]

-5 **5** *½* **Penolva (IRE)**[40] 1893 3-8-5 0.................................. AndrewElliott 7 54
(K R Burke) *s.i.s: plld hrd and sn trcking ldrs: rdn over 3f out: out pced over 2f out: styd on fnl f* **16/1**

60 **6** *15* **Galiotto (IRE)**[17] 2551 3-8-10 0.................................. SebSanders 1 34+
(C F Wall) *hld up: hdwy over 7f out: rdn over 2f out: wknd over 1f out* **66/1**

04 **7** *3¾* **Trempari**[58] 1427 6-9-3 0.................................. BarryAdams(7) 5 27
(Mike Murphy) *s.i.s: a in rr: bhd fr 1/2-way* **100/1**

2m 32.95s (-0.95) **Going Correction** -0.225s/f (Firm)
WFA 3 from 6yo 14lb **7** Ran SP% **110.1**
Speed ratings (Par 103): **94,93,92,91,90 80,78**
toteswingers: 1&2 £1.20, 1&3 £4.20, 2&3 £10.50 CSF £6.90 TOTE £1.50: £1.10, £4.40; EX 6.90.
Owner K Abdulla **Bred** Juddmonte Farms Ltd **Trained** Newmarket, Suffolk

FOCUS
Just an ordinary middle-distance maiden.

3057 WALTHAM-ON-THE-WOLDS H'CAP — 5f 218y
9:10 (9:10) (Class 5) (0-75,74) 3-Y-O+ **£3,238** (£963; £481; £240) **Stalls** Centre

Form RPR
0032 **1** **Zowington**[17] 2549 7-9-7 71..................................(v) WilliamCarson(5) 6 83
(S C Williams) *s.i.s: hld up in tch: racd keenly: rdn to ld wl ins fnl f: r.o* **2/1**[1]

-011 **2** *½* **Misplaced Fortune**[24] 2312 4-9-7 71..................................(v) LeeNewnes(5) 4 81
(N Tinkler) *chsd ldrs: rdn over 1f out: edgd rt and ev ch ins fnl f: styd on* **9/4**[2]

4430 **3** *1½* **Gwilym (GER)**[40] 1877 6-9-7 66.................................. DaneO'Neill 8 72
(D Haydn Jones) *chsd ldrs: led over 1f out: rdn and hdd ins fnl f: styd on same pce* **16/1**

0435 **4** *1½* **Dickie Le Davoir**[10] 2769 5-9-1 65..................................(p) MarkCoumbe(5) 10 68+
(John A Harris) *s.i.s: outpcd: hdwy u.p over 1f out: led ins fnl f: sn hdd: wknd nr fin* **5/1**[3]

5100 **5** *shd* **Circle Dance (IRE)**[15] 2596 4-8-9 59..................................(v) MartinLane(5) 1 59
(D Shaw) *sn pushed along in rr: hdwy 1/2-way: rdn and edgd rt over 1f out: styd on* **18/1**

0-00 **6** *4* **Charlie Delta**[27] 2224 6-9-3 65..................................(b) KevinGhunowa(3) 5 53
(R A Harris) *chsd ldr tl rdn over 2f out: wknd over 1f out* **25/1**

3010 **7** *1¼* **Hazytoo**[17] 2549 5-10-0 73.................................. FergusSweeney 2 57
(P J Makin) *led: rdn and hdd over 1f out: wknd fnl f* **8/1**

0025 **8** *2¼* **We Have A Dream**[17] 2549 4-9-13 72.................................. DO'Donohoe 3 48
(W R Muir) *chsd ldrs: rdn over 2f out: edgd rt and wknd over 1f out* **12/1**

1m 11.83s (-1.17) **Going Correction** -0.225s/f (Firm)
WFA 3 from 4yo+ 7lb **8** Ran SP% **114.6**
Speed ratings (Par 103): **98,97,95,93,93 87,86,83**
toteswingers: 1&2 £1.40, 1&3 £9.00, 2&3 £6.10 CSF £6.71 CT £52.23 TOTE £2.90: £1.80, £1.20, £2.50; EX 13.10 Place 6: £595.69, Place 5: £245.58..
Owner O Pointing **Bred** O Pointing **Trained** Newmarket, Suffolk

FOCUS
The runners were spread across the track here and a strong pace enabled the gambled-on Zowington to pick off the prominent racers close home.
T/Plt: £7.20 to a £1 stake. Pool: £38,465.70. 3,873.16 winning tickets. T/Qpdt: £2.70 to a £1 stake. Pool: £3,112.14. 841.20 winning tickets. CR

2714 MUSSELBURGH (R-H)
Thursday, June 18

OFFICIAL GOING: Good to firm (good in places; 8.0)
Wind: Fresh across Weather: Cloudy and blustery

3058 LINKFIELD MAIDEN AUCTION STKS — 5f
6:30 (6:30) (Class 5) 2-Y-O **£2,729** (£806; £403) **Stalls** Low

Form RPR
43 **1** **Bould Mover**[79] 1044 2-8-9 0.................................. DarrylHolland 6 74+
(R Curtis) *trckd ldrs: hdwy to ld over 1f out: rdn clr ins fnl f: kpt on* **11/4**[3]

2 3 1/4 **Patch Patch** 2-8-10 0 ow1 .... PhillipMakin 7 63
(M Dods) *dwlt: sn in tch: swtchd rt and hdwy wl over 1f out: sn rdn and styd on ins fnl f* **12/1**
520 3 1/2 **Dower Glen**[22] 2372 2-8-8 0 .... TomEaves 5 59
(I Semple) *trckd ldng pair: sltly outpcd over 2f out: swtchd rt and rdn over 1f out: styd on ins fnl f* **11/8**[1]
060 4 1 **Sir Christie**[9] 2788 2-8-13 0 .... PJMcDonald 8 60
(N Tinkler) *towards rr: hdwy on outer 1/2-way: rdn to chse ldrs wl over 1f out: sn drvn and one pce* **50/1**
03 5 3/4 **Silver Linnet (IRE)**[16] 2568 2-8-4 0 .... DuranFentiman 2 49
(T D Easterby) *led: rdn along 2f out: sn drvn: hdd & wknd* **5/2**[2]
640 6 3 1/2 **Lord's Seat**[20] 2435 2-8-7 0 ow3 .... SladeO'Hara(5) 3 44
(A Berry) *prom: rdn along over 2f out and sn wknd* **50/1**
7 1 3/4 **She Knows It All (IRE)** 2-8-6 0 .... PaulQuinn 1 32
(G A Swinbank) *s.i.s: a in rr* **16/1**

60.69 secs (0.29) **Going Correction** -0.225s/f (Firm) **7** Ran SP% **114.8**
Speed ratings (Par 93): **88,82,82,80,79 73,70**
toteswingers: 1&2 £13.70, 1&3 £1.10, 2&3 £8.40 CSF £34.54 TOTE £2.40: £2.10, £6.00; EX 31.10.
Owner H Downs & D Looney **Bred** K W P Engineering **Trained** Lambourn, Berks

FOCUS
A moderate maiden lacking anything in the way of strength in depth. The pace was sound and the form is best rated through the fourth.

NOTEBOOK
Bould Mover looked to have decent claims in an uncompetitive event and he posted his best effort, despite edging off a true line in the closing stages. He should prove equally effective over 6f and may be able to progress further in nursery company. (op 3-1 tchd 5-2)
Patch Patch, the second foal of a heavy-ground turf winner and dual Fibresand scorer, was easy to back but showed ability after running green on this racecourse debut. He should stay 6f and is entitled to improve for this experience. (op 20-1)
Dower Glen was well supported for his return to this much more suitable grade but she proved a shade disappointing. She did not look entirely straightforward and is likely to remain vulnerable in this type of event. (op 2-1 tchd 9-4)
Sir Christie's proximity confirms this bare form is nothing special and low-grade handicaps are likely to provide him of his best chance of success in due course. (op 80-1)
Silver Linnet(IRE) was noticeably easy to back near the off and failed to build on her improved effort at Ripon. She may do better over 6f in modest handicaps when the nursery season begins. (op 13-8)

3059 FISHERROW H'CAP 1m 6f
7:00 (7:00) (Class 5) (0-75,72) 4-Y-O+ **£3,238** (£963; £481; £240) **Stalls** High

Form RPR
-451 1 **Callisto Moon**[5] 2931 5-9-8 **72** 6ex ....(p) DarryllHolland 3 83+
(R Curtis) *trckd ldng pair: hdwy on inner to ld wl over 2f out: rdn clr over 1f out: styd on wl* **6/4**[1]
0401 2 4 **Desert Destiny**[13] 2656 9-8-11 **66** .... AmyRyan(5) 2 70
(C Grant) *hld up: hdwy on outer over 2f out: rdn and hung rt wl over 1f out and thrght fnl f: one pce* **10/1**
1020 3 nse **Merrion Tiger (IRE)**[34] 2044 4-8-13 **63** .... RobertWinston 5 67
(A G Foster) *trckd ldng pair: hdwy over 3f out: rdn to chse wnr over 2f out: sn drvn: keeping on one pce whn n.m.r ins fnl f: lost 2nd nr line* **11/2**[3]
1313 4 1 1/4 **That'll Do Nicely (IRE)**[20] 2452 6-9-5 **69** .... TomEaves 4 71
(N G Richards) *t.k.h: hld up in rr: hdwy 3f out: effrt and nt clr run over 2f out: rdn whn n.m.r and swtchd lft ent fnl f: sn drvn and one pce* **9/4**[2]
6-00 5 7 **Lets Roll**[54] 1506 8-9-7 **71** .... PJMcDonald 6 63
(C W Thornton) *in tch: rdn along 4f out and sn outpcd* **6/1**
100/ 6 8 **Humourous (IRE)**[50] 2940 7-9-1 **65** ....(t) PhillipMakin 1 46
(B Storey) *led: rdn along 3f out: sn hdd & wknd* **66/1**

3m 4.72s (-0.58) **Going Correction** -0.225s/f (Firm) **6** Ran SP% **111.0**
Speed ratings (Par 103): **92,89,89,88,84 80**
toteswinger: 1&2 £3.90, 1&3 £1.80, 2&3 £8.00 CSF £16.78 TOTE £1.90: £1.40, £6.70; EX 11.40.

Owner B Bedford & Mrs Gill White **Bred** Barton Stud **Trained** Lambourn, Berks
■ Stewards' Enquiry : Robert Winston ten-day ban: failed to ride out for 2nd place (Jul 2-11)

FOCUS
An ordinary handicap run at just a moderate gallop and the form is a bit muddling with the runner-up the best guide.

3060 INVERESK FILLIES' H'CAP 1m 1f
7:30 (7:30) (Class 4) (0-85,74) 4-Y-O+ **£5,828** (£1,734; £866; £432) **Stalls** High

Form RPR
52-2 1 **Ainia**[24] 2317 4-9-7 **74** .... DarryllHolland 5 80
(D M Simcock) *mde all: rdn along over 2f out: drvn ent fnl f and kpt on gamely towards fin* **4/5**[1]
3002 2 nk **Snow Dancer (IRE)**[8] 2823 5-8-13 **66** ....(p) TomEaves 3 71
(H A McWilliams) *trckd ldrs: hdwy 3f out: rdn along over 2f out: chal over 1f out and ev ch whn hung lft ent fnl f: sn drvn and styd on wl towards fin* **4/1**[2]
0040 3 1 3/4 **Casino Night**[17] 2531 4-8-7 **67** .... AndrewHeffernan(7) 2 69
(R Johnson) *trckd ldng pair: hdwy 3f out: rdn and ch whn edgd lft wl over 1f out: drvn and one pce fnl f* **15/2**
6652 4 8 **Grethel (IRE)**[1] 3019 5-7-9 **55** oh5 .... CharlotteKerton(7) 4 40
(A Berry) *dwlt: hld up in rr: wd st: hdwy on outer to chse ldrs over 2f out: sn rdn and wknd* **12/1**
4110 5 20 **Bookiebasher Babe (IRE)**[28] 2212 4-8-13 **66** .... RobertWinston 1 9
(M Quinn) *cl up: rdn along 3f out and sn wknd* **5/1**[3]

1m 51.82s (-2.88) **Going Correction** -0.225s/f (Firm) **5** Ran SP% **111.7**
Speed ratings (Par 102): **103,102,101,94,76**
toteswingers: 1&2 £3.80. CSF £4.43 TOTE £2.00: £1.10, £1.50; EX 5.80.
Owner Mrs Julia Annable **Bred** Genesis Green Stud **Trained** Newmarket, Suffolk

FOCUS
Not a strong handicap for the money on offer and a slow pace means this bare form is not entirely reliable; the second is the best guide.

3061 MILLHILL MEDIAN AUCTION MAIDEN STKS 1m
8:00 (8:01) (Class 6) 3-5-Y-O **£2,266** (£674; £337; £168) **Stalls** High

Form RPR
5 1 **Amazing Tiger (GER)**[82] 998 3-8-12 0 .... DarryllHolland 6 73+
(M Johnston) *t.k.h early: trckd ldr: hdwy 3f out: led wl over 2f out: pushed clr apprlast* **1/2**[1]
24-2 2 1 1/2 **Storming Sioux**[45] 1745 3-8-7 73 .... KirstyMilczarek 1 62+
(W J Haggas) *trckd ldng pair: hdwy over 2f out and sn rdn: drvn over 1f out: kpt on ins fnl f: no ch w wnr* **2/1**[2]
0040 3 4 **Carnival Dream**[3] 2965 4-9-3 50 ....(p) PhillipMakin 2 53
(H A McWilliams) *led: rdn along 3f out: hdd wl over 2f out: sn drvn and kpt on same pce* **40/1**
04-0 4 4 **Drumadoon Bay (IRE)**[17] 2532 5-9-8 50 .... RobertWinston 4 49
(G A Swinbank) *hld up: hdwy and in tch over 2f out: sn rdn and no imp* **22/1**[3]
05 5 19 **Soho Secrets**[41] 1844 3-8-7 0 .... TomEaves 3 —
(M Johnston) *in tch: pushed along 4f out: rdn and hung bdly lft wl over 2f out: sn outpcd and bhd* **25/1**

1m 38.76s (-2.44) **Going Correction** -0.225s/f (Firm) course record
WFA 3 from 4yo+ 10lb **5** Ran SP% **110.6**
Speed ratings (Par 101): **103,101,97,93,74**
toteswingers: 1&2 £2.50. CSF £1.69 TOTE £1.40: £1.02, £1.70; EX 2.20.
Owner Sheikh Hamdan Bin Mohammed Al Maktoum **Bred** Gestut Karlshof **Trained** Middleham Moor, N Yorks

FOCUS
A most uncompetitive maiden but, although the early gallop was nothing special, the time was only fractionally outside the course record. The winner scored well but the proximity of the third suggests the runner-up did not run to her mark.

3062 GOOSEGREEN H'CAP 1m
8:30 (8:30) (Class 4) (0-80,80) 3-Y-O **£5,828** (£1,734; £866; £432) **Stalls** High

Form RPR
-313 1 **Spinners End (IRE)**[7] 2845 3-9-1 **74** .... PhillipMakin 4 83
(K R Burke) *mde all: sn led: rdn over 2f out: styd on wl* **7/2**[3]
-142 2 3 1/4 **Sir Isaac**[6] 2890 3-9-2 **75** .... KirstyMilczarek 1 77
(W J Haggas) *chsd wnr: effrt over 2f out: sn rdn and hung rt: drvn ent fnl f and sn no imp* **5/4**[1]
6-43 3 3/4 **Inheritor (IRE)**[19] 2504 3-9-7 **80** .... TomEaves 2 80
(B Smart) *trckd ldng pair: hdwy 3f out: rdn 2f out: drvn over 1f out and kpt on same pce* **3/1**[2]
-363 4 7 **Dean Iarracht (IRE)**[9] 2786 3-8-3 **67** .... JamieKyne(5) 5 51
(M Dods) *dwlt: a bhd* **12/1**
-251 5 nk **Peter's Gift (IRE)**[48] 1656 3-8-8 **72** .... AmyRyan(5) 3 55
(K A Ryan) *in tch: rdn along wl over 2f out and sn outpcd* **7/1**

1m 39.3s (-1.90) **Going Correction** -0.25s/f (Firm) **5** Ran SP% **111.9**
Speed ratings (Par 101): **99,95,95,88,87**
CSF £8.52 TOTE £4.80: £1.50, £1.50; EX 7.80.
Owner Mogeely Stud & Mrs Maura Gittins **Bred** P D Savill **Trained** Middleham Moor, N Yorks

FOCUS
A fair handicap run at a reasonable gallop but not easy form to pin down.
Dean Iarracht(IRE) Official explanation: jockey said gelding was unsuited by the good to firm (good in places) ground

3063 LORETTO H'CAP 5f
9:00 (9:00) (Class 6) (0-65,65) 3-Y-O **£2,266** (£674; £337; £168) **Stalls** Low

Form RPR
4-01 1 **Secret Venue**[20] 2454 3-9-5 **63** .... DarryllHolland 7 69
(Jedd O'Keeffe) *mde all: rdn wl over 1f out: drvn ins fnl f and kpt on gamely* **7/4**[1]
005- 2 hd **Igoyougo**[254] 6548 3-8-13 **57** .... SilvestreDeSousa 1 62
(G A Harker) *cl up: effrt to chal wl over 1f out and sn ev ch tl drvn ins fnl f and no ex towards fin* **11/2**
5364 3 2 1/4 **Pedregal**[15] 2593 3-7-13 **46** oh1 .... KellyHarrison(3) 2 43
(J S Goldie) *in tch: hdwy 2f out: rdn and edgd rt over 1f out: drvn and kpt on ins fnl f: nrst fin* **9/1**
0241 4 1/2 **Simple Rhythm**[16] 2581 3-9-2 **65** .... JamieKyne(5) 8 60
(J G Given) *chsd ldng pair: rdn wl over 1f out: drvn and one pce ent fnl f* **11/4**[2]
304 5 3 3/4 **Badtanman**[21] 2394 3-8-3 **47** oh1 ow1 ....(b) PatrickMathers 6 29
(Peter Grayson) *chsd ldrs: rdn along 1/2-way: sn wknd* **40/1**
1254 6 1 1/4 **Compton Ford**[20] 2454 3-9-7 **65** ....(p) PhillipMakin 4 42+
(M Dods) *j. awkwardly and hmpd s: a in rr* **9/2**[3]
504 7 3 3/4 **Trade Price (GR)**[20] 2439 3-8-10 **54** .... TomEaves 5 18
(I Semple) *chsd ldrs: rdn along 2f out: sn wknd* **14/1**
0-05 8 4 1/2 **Pollish**[20] 2454 3-8-2 **46** oh1 .... PaulQuinn 3 —
(A Berry) *dwlt and wnt bdly rt s: a bhd* **66/1**

59.71 secs (-0.69) **Going Correction** -0.225s/f (Firm) **8** Ran SP% **117.2**
Speed ratings (Par 97): **96,95,92,91,85 83,77,70**
toteswingers: 1&2 £2.20, 1&3 £3.90, 2&3 £9.90 CSF £12.46 CT £69.33 TOTE £2.90: £1.10, £2.00, £2.70; EX 25.50 Place 6: £23.91, Place 5: £3.34..
Owner Ken And Delia Shaw-KGS Consulting LLP **Bred** Sherwoods Transport Ltd **Trained** Middleham Moor, N Yorks
■ This completed a 68/1 five-timer, from five rides, for Darryll Holland.

FOCUS
A moderate handicap run at a sound pace throughout and another race on the card to favour those right up with the pace. The form looks pretty sound rated through the third.
T/Plt: £22.70 to a £1 stake. Pool: £32,025.01. 1,027.28 winning tickets. T/Qpdt: £3.20 to a £1 stake. Pool: £2,650.84. 606.90 winning tickets. JR

3031 RIPON (R-H)
Thursday, June 18

OFFICIAL GOING: Good to soft (7.8)
Course at innermost configuration.
Wind: fresh 1/2 behind Weather: changeable, overcast, cool and very breezy

3064 EBF INGHAM UNDERWRITING MAIDEN STKS 6f
2:10 (2:10) (Class 5) 2-Y-O **£4,209** (£1,252; £625; £312) **Stalls** Low

Form RPR
226 1 **Danzoe (IRE)**[12] 2721 2-9-0 0 .... DavidProbert(3) 7 77
(D Donovan) *racd far side: chsd ldr: led over 1f out: forged clr: 1st of 6 that gp* **6/1**[3]
4 2 3 1/2 **Crushing (IRE)**[16] 2568 2-9-0 0 .... NeilBrown(3) 9 67
(T D Barron) *led far side: hdd over 1f out: kpt on same pce: 2nd of 6 that gp* **7/1**
3 nk **My One Weakness (IRE)** 2-8-12 0 .... LanceBetts(5) 8 66+
(B Ellison) *dwlt: in rr far side: hdwy 2f out: styd on ins fnl f: 3rd of 6 that gp* **40/1**
2 4 3/4 **Il Forno**[20] 2444 2-9-3 0 .... AdrianTNicholls 3 63+
(D Nicholls) *led stands' side gp: clr that side over 1f out: hung rt and kpt on same pce: 1st of 6 that gp* **5/2**[1]
5 5 1 **Storm Hawk (IRE)**[14] 2636 2-9-3 0 .... PaulEddery 10 60
(Pat Eddery) *rrd s: in rr far side: hdwy 2f out: kpt on fnl f: 4th of 6 that gp* **25/1**

5 **6** 4 1/2 **Watch Chain (IRE)**[16] 2568 2-8-12 0............................ MartinLane(5) 12 47
(M H Tompkins) *racd far side: chsd ldrs: wknd over 1f out: 5th of 6 that gp* **14/1**

7 3/4 **Seldom Seen Kid (IRE)** 2-9-3 0............................ GrahamGibbons 6 45+
(T D Easterby) *racd stands' side: chsd ldrs: wknd over 1f out: 2nd of 6 that gp* **25/1**

06 **8** 1/2 **Pat Seamur**[7] 2853 2-9-3 0............................ DO'Donohoe 4 43+
(E A L Dunlop) *in rr and outpcd stands' side: nvr on terms: 3rd of 6 that gp* **40/1**

23 **9** 3/4 **Saucy Girl (IRE)**[48] 1645 2-8-12 0............................ DavidAllan 11 36
(T D Easterby) *racd far side: chsd ldrs: sn drvn along: wknd 2f out: last of 6 that gp* **9/2**[2]

10 3 1/2 **First Instance** 2-9-3 0............................ GregFairley 5 30+
(M Johnston) *swvd rt s: racd stands' side: sn chsng ldrs: rdn and lost pl over 2f out: 4th of 6 that gp* **9/1**

0 **11** 1 3/4 **Great Intrigue (IRE)**[7] 2844 2-9-3 0............................ FergusSweeney 1 25+
(J S Moore) *racd stands' side: w ldr: lost pl over 1f out: 5th of 6 that gp* **6/1**[3]

12 3 1/4 **Sam Jicaro** 2-8-12 0............................ DeanHeslop(5) 2 15+
(Mrs L Williamson) *rrd s: racd stands' side: hdwy to chse ldrs over 2f out: sn lost pl: last of 6 that gp* **100/1**

1m 14.53s (1.53) **Going Correction** +0.10s/f (Good) **12** Ran SP% **118.1**
Speed ratings (Par 93): **93,88,87,86,85 79,78,77,76,72 69,65**
toteswinger: 1&2 £9.40, 1&3 £75.50, 2&3 £88.30. CSF £45.25 TOTE £8.80: £2.30, £2.50, £7.40; EX 60.00.

Owner Philip Mclaughlin **Bred** Miss Anne Ormsby **Trained** Newmarket, Suffolk

■ Stewards' Enquiry : Neil Brown one-day ban: failed to ride to draw (Jul 2)

FOCUS

After the previous evening's rain the wind had picked up in the morning and the ground had dried slightly to be on the soft side of good. A modest maiden which revolved around four with form and an interesting newcomer from the Mark Johnston stable whose two-year-olds had performed well in this particular race over the past few years. Run at a decent pace, the field split into two groups with the far side dominating the closing stages The form looks reasonable although some allowance is made for the draw advantage.

NOTEBOOK

Danzoe(IRE) had solid claims on his first two outings before an odds-on defeat at Newcastle, reportedly due to the ground, which made little difference here. Always racing prominently on the far side, he kicked clear over a furlong out to win in a convincing manner. He looks a tough two-year-old and is progressing well. (tchd 7-1)

Crushing(IRE) had obviously benefited from his initial outing last time when fourth over course and distance, and again put in another satisfactory effort stepped up to six. He took them along on the far side until headed by the winner but was soon outpaced. (op 9-2)

My One Weakness(IRE) broke badly and was soon pushed along in rear and switched to the far side. Once the penny dropped she ran on well from well over a furlong out and this was an encouraging debut. (tchd 28-1)

Il Forno showed plenty of speed on his debut in a fair race at Haydock and again showed the pace to lead the stands'-side group, but he unable to keep tabs on the winner when he kicked clear. He finished well clear of the remainder racing up the stands' side but did not help his cause when hanging to his right in the final furlong. Official explanation: jockey said gelding hung right throughout (op 4-1 tchd 9-4)

Storm Hawk(IRE) was another who was untidily into his stride, but this was an improvement on his debut and he was doing his best work towards the end. His breeding suggests he will be better suited when stepped up in distance. (op 20-1)

Saucy Girl(IRE) raced on the favoured far rail but was always struggling to go the pace and was a beaten horse at halfway. (op 5-1)

First Instance, a half-brother to Windsor Castle winner Holborn, was a drifter in the market and was soon struggling to go the pace on the stands' side. (op 11-2)

3065 BRENTWOOD DESIGN PARTNERSHIP H'CAP 5f

2:45 (2:45) (Class 5) (0-75,75) 3-Y-0+ **£3,238** (£963; £481; £240) **Stalls** Low

Form RPR

-503 **1** **Requisite**[7] 2864 4-9-8 **69**............................(v) TonyHamilton 5 79+
(I A Wood) *chsd ldr stands' side: led over 1f out: kpt on wl to ld overall last strides: 1st of 3 that gp* **14/1**

2152 **2** *hd* **Liberty Ship**[13] 2657 4-9-7 **68**............................(bt) GrahamGibbons 7 77
(J D Bethell) *racd far side: trckd ldr: led that gp 2f out: hdd cl home: 1st of 8 that gp* **4/1**[1]

040- **3** 1 1/4 **Ursus**[225] 7197 4-8-9 **56** oh4............................ SilvestreDeSousa 14 61
(C R Wilson) *racd far side: chsd ldrs: styd on same pce fnl f: 2nd of 8 that gp* **28/1**

53-5 **4** *nk* **Select Committee**[34] 2032 4-8-6 **58**............................(p) JamieKyne(5) 10 61
(J J Quinn) *racd far side: chsd ldrs: styd on same pce fnl f: 3rd of 8 that gp* **6/1**[3]

-025 **5** 1/2 **Baybshambles (IRE)**[23] 2363 5-9-4 **68**............................ KellyHarrison(3) 12 70
(R E Barr) *racd far side: chsd ldrs: kpt on fnl f: 4th of 8 that gp* **5/1**[2]

4100 **6** 1 **Imperial Sword**[3] 2966 6-9-1 **69**............................(b) JanWilson(7) 9 67
(T D Barron) *racd far side: in rr: styd on strly fnl f: 5th of 8 that gp* **16/1**

0-04 **7** 1/2 **Lake Chini (IRE)**[20] 2436 7-8-13 **60**............................(b) DaleGibson 4 56
(M W Easterby) *trckd one other centre: led there over 1f out: kpt on same pce* **16/1**

0060 **8** *nse* **King Of Swords (IRE)**[6] 2897 5-9-5 **66**............................ GregFairley 6 62
(N Tinkler) *racd far side: in tch: hdwy over 1f out: kpt on: 6th of 8 that gp* **8/1**

5544 **9** 1 1/2 **Mambo Spirit (IRE)**[20] 2460 5-9-10 **71**............................ J-PGuillambert 11 62
(J G Given) *led far side tl hdd 2f out: edgd rt and wknd jst ins fnl f: 7th of 8 that gp* **8/1**

0000 **10** *shd* **Highland Warrior**[20] 2436 10-9-2 **63**............................ JamieMoriarty 13 53
(P T Midgley) *chsd ldrs far side: keeping on same pce whn hmpd jst ins fnl f: last of 8 that gp* **25/1**

-010 **11** 3 1/2 **Revue Princess (IRE)**[17] 2546 4-9-7 **68**............................(b) DavidAllan 3 46
(T D Easterby) *led one other centre: wknd over 1f out: last of 2 centre* **22/1**

4000 **12** *shd* **Chartist**[6] 2897 4-10-0 **75**............................(v[1]) AdrianTNicholls 2 52
(D Nicholls) *led trio stands' side: hdd & wknd over 1f out: 2nd of 3 that gp* **16/1**

-106 **13** 5 **Paddy Bear**[15] 2611 3-8-11 **69**............................ FrederikTylicki(5) 1 28
(R A Fahey) *sn last of 3 stands' side: bhd fnl 2f* **8/1**

60.38 secs (-0.32) **Going Correction** +0.10s/f (Good)
WFA 3 from 4yo+ 6lb **13** Ran SP% **120.2**
Speed ratings (Par 103): **106,105,103,103,102 100,100,99,97,97 91,91,83**
toteswinger: 1&2 £7.20, 1&3 £90.50, 2&3 £21.60 CSF £68.12 CT £1641.82 TOTE £14.10: £3.90, £2.10, £8.60; EX 61.20.

Owner Paddy Barrett **Bred** Darley **Trained** Upper Lambourn, Berks

FOCUS

A fairly competitive but modest sprint with a lot of the field having questions to answer and plenty in with a chance if doing so. Again the field split, but this time into three groups, with the main bunch racing up the far side. the wainner is rated back to somewhere near his three-year-old best while the runner-up has improved for blinkers and may do better.

3066 JAMES BRINDLEY OF HARROGATE CLAIMING STKS 6f

3:20 (3:20) (Class 5) 3-Y-0+ **£3,238** (£963; £481; £240) **Stalls** Low

Form RPR

0-06 **1** **Turnkey**[8] 2814 7-9-8 90............................ AdrianTNicholls 11 83
(D Nicholls) *racd far side: towards rr: hdwy and rdn 2f out: styd on to ld nr fin: 1st of 5 that gp* **4/1**[2]

3026 **2** *hd* **Gap Princess (IRE)**[15] 2589 5-8-7 69............................ TonyHamilton 9 67
(R A Fahey) *racd far side: chsd ldr: led 2f out: hdd last strides: 2nd of 5 that gp* **4/1**[2]

-006 **3** 3 3/4 **Dalarossie**[20] 2436 4-8-12 55............................ DavidAllan 10 60
(E J Alston) *led far side: hdd 2f out: one pce fnl f: 3rd of 5 that gp* **16/1**

0600 **4** 1 1/4 **Nacho Libre**[16] 2576 4-8-13 60............................ DaleGibson 8 57
(M W Easterby) *s.i.s: swtchd rt and racd far side: in rr: hdwy 2f out: kpt on fnl f: 4th of 5 that gp* **33/1**

-033 **5** 2 1/2 **Dr Wintringham (IRE)**[13] 2651 3-7-12 60............................ SilvestreDeSousa 12 41
(J S Moore) *racd far side: chsd ldrs: wnt lft and wknd 1f out: last of 5 that gp* **8/1**[3]

52-0 **6** *shd* **Woqoodd**[13] 2682 5-8-5 54............................(v) MartinLane(5) 4 46
(D Shaw) *led stands' side 5: kpt on fnl 2f: no ch w far side: 1st of 5 that gp* **50/1**

4-00 **7** 1 3/4 **Steel Blue**[26] 2276 9-9-0 66............................(p) J-PGuillambert 2 44
(R M Whitaker) *racd stands' side: chsd ldr: hung rt over 1f out: one pce: 2nd of 5 that gp* **20/1**

0450 **8** 1/2 **Paint Stripper**[12] 2722 4-8-3 42............................(p) JohnCavanagh(7) 5 38
(W Storey) *racd stands' side: chsd ldrs: one pce fnl 2f: 3rd of 5 that gp* **66/1**

100- **9** 5 **Uace Mac**[267] 6219 5-9-0 63............................ LeeVickers(3) 7 29
(N Bycroft) *racd towards centre w 1 other: prom: wknd over 1f out: 1st of 2 that gp* **40/1**

0000 **10** *shd* **Western Art (USA)**[16] 2576 4-8-3 58............................ JamesPSullivan(7) 6 22
(M W Easterby) *racd towards centre w 1 other: prom: wknd over 1f out: last of 2 that gp* **66/1**

000- **11** 1 **Union Jack Jackson (IRE)**[212] 7369 7-8-10 38............................(b) DO'Donohoe 3 19
(John A Harris) *racd stands' side: chsd ldrs: wknd over 1f out: 4th of 5 that gp* **100/1**

4305 **12** 4 1/2 **Mutamared (USA)**[12] 2707 9-9-3 82............................(t) FrederikTylicki(5) 1 17
(K A Ryan) *sn last on stands' side: sn drvn along: last of 5 that gp* **11/10**[1]

1m 13.17s (0.17) **Going Correction** +0.10s/f (Good)
WFA 3 from 4yo+ 7lb **12** Ran SP% **120.7**
Speed ratings (Par 103): **102,101,96,95,91 91,89,88,81,81 80,74**
toteswinger: 1&2 £2.90, 1&3 £18.40, 2&3 £13.30 CSF £19.96 TOTE £5.30: £1.60, £1.70, £4.60; EX 14.70.

Owner Middleham Park Racing Xxiii **Bred** Mrs E M Charlton **Trained** Sessay, N Yorks

FOCUS

A claimer that on paper you could only consider a few. They were taken along at a fair pace the far side and totally eclipsed the near-side runners in the later stages. The third looks the best guide to the form.

Mutamared(USA) Official explanation: vet said gelding finished distressed

3067 LADIES DAY H'CAP 1m 1f

4:00 (4:11) (Class 3) (0-90,90) 4-Y-0+

£8,723 (£2,612; £1,306; £653; £326; £163) **Stalls** High

Form RPR

00-2 **1** **City Of The Kings (IRE)**[15] 2612 4-9-6 **89**............................ SilvestreDeSousa 6 96
(G A Harker) *hld up towards rr: drvn and hdwy over 3f out: slt ld over 1f out: hdd jst ins fnl f: kpt on to ld post* **9/4**[2]

4630 **2** *shd* **Exit Smiling**[15] 2612 7-8-3 **79**............................ PaulPickard(7) 8 86+
(P T Midgley) *trckd ldrs: nt clr run on ins fr 3f out: swtchd ins over 1f out: slt ld jst ins fnl f: hdd post* **11/2**[3]

0452 **3** *hd* **Gala Casino Star (IRE)**[8] 2822 4-8-10 **84**............................ FrederikTylicki(5) 7 90
(R A Fahey) *hld up in last: hdwy on wd outside over 3f out: chal over 1f out: no ex towards fin* **15/8**[1]

-000 **4** 4 1/2 **Cobo Bay**[13] 2671 4-9-4 **87**............................(p) TonyHamilton 2 83
(K A Ryan) *led after 1f: edgd lft and hdd over 1f out: fdd* **13/2**

0-00 **5** 3/4 **Humungous (IRE)**[24] 2342 6-9-0 **90**............................(p) RichardRowe(7) 4 85
(C R Egerton) *chsd ldrs: rdn 3f out: outpcd appr fnl f* **16/1**

0-05 **6** *nk* **Reel Buddy Star**[8] 2822 4-8-4 **73**............................ AdrianTNicholls 3 67
(G M Moore) *hld up towards rr: effrt over 3f out: hung rt and one pce: nvr able to chal* **16/1**

2-00 **7** 2 3/4 **Nevada Desert (IRE)**[26] 2274 9-8-3 **75**............................ KellyHarrison(3) 10 63
(R M Whitaker) *t.k.h: led 1f: trckd ldr: wknd over 1f out* **14/1**

1m 54.27s (-0.43) **Going Correction** +0.10s/f (Good) **7** Ran SP% **112.7**
Speed ratings (Par 107): **105,104,104,100,100 99,97**
toteswingers: 1&2 £3.70, 1&3 £1.90, 2&3 £2.60 CSF £14.58 CT £26.07 TOTE £3.60: £2.30, £3.30; EX 22.00.

Owner John J Maguire **Bred** Tom McDonald **Trained** Thirkleby, N Yorks

■ Ben Chorley was withdrawn (9/2, uns rdr and ran loose gng to post, rdr inj). Deduct 15p in the £ under R4. New market formed.

FOCUS

A tricky little handicap that lost some interest with the unfortunate incident that befell Ben Chorley's rider forcing the horse to be withdrawn. It was run at an ordinary pace but the form looks reasonable with the placed horses close to their marks.

NOTEBOOK

City Of The Kings(IRE) put in a game performance to land the spoils. He had scored three times at up to this trip in previous years, albeit on a quicker surface, and had shown he was in good order on his return to action the previous week. Held up in rear before closing to challenge 2f out, he battled on up the hill to get his head in front right on the line in a tight three-way nodding finish. (old market op 3-1, new market op 2-1)

Exit Smiling was racing off a career-high mark but acts well round here and again put in a bold display, being slightly unlucky not to collect. Chasing the leaders from the outset, he was a little short of room when having to switch well over a furlong out but challenged just inside the last, only to just fail on the nod. He should be respected when turning out here again but he likes to have a couple of weeks between his runs. (old market op 8-1, new market op 6-1 tchd 5-1)

Gala Casino Star(IRE) confirmed his yard's cracking form at present and, after being held up off the pace, came there to take a narrow advantage at the furlong marker. He dug deep but could not hold the sustained challenges inside the final furlong, although only went down by a narrow margin. (old market op 3-1 tchd 4-1, new market op 9-4)

Cobo Bay has been on the whole disappointing since scoring over a mile here last year, but he came in for sufficient support during the day. He was soon at the head of affairs but, once headed over 1f out, was soon brushed aside. (old market op 7-1 tchd 15-2 and 11-2, new market op 6-1)

3068 BEAUMONT ROBINSON LADIES' DERBY H'CAP (LADY AMATEUR RIDERS) 1m 4f 10y
4:35 (4:36) (Class 6) (0-65,65) 4-Y-0+ £2,810 (£871; £435; £217) Stalls High

Form RPR
0656 1 **Dimashq**[14] 2629 7-8-13 46 oh1 MissWGibson(5) 14 54
(P T Midgley) *s.i.s: sn trcking ldrs: led over 3f out: edgd rt fnl f: hld on towards fin* **25/1**
500- 2 ¾ **Rudry World (IRE)**[271] 6136 6-9-10 57 MissMMullineaux(5) 1 64
(M Mullineaux) *hld up in rr: hdwy on ins 4f out: sn chsng ldrs: swtchd lft ins fnl f: styd on wl* **18/1**
4300 3 1 ¼ **Simonside**[24] 2315 6-10-8 64 MissLEllison 12 69
(B Ellison) *chsd ldrs: led over 7f out tl over 3f out: kpt on same pce fnl f* **9/1[3]**
0665 4 1 ½ **Wannarock (IRE)**[21] 2419 4-9-3 50 RachelKing(5) 5 53
(M C Chapman) *chsd ldrs: kpt on same pce fnl 2f: hmpd ins fnl f* **10/1**
6251 5 ½ **Dancing Lyra**[16] 2580 8-10-4 65 MrsVFahey(5) 8 67
(R A Fahey) *s.i.s: sn mid-div: hdwy on outside 3f out: kpt on wl fnl f* **7/1[2]**
565- 6 ¾ **Midnite Blews (IRE)**[5] 4580 4-9-5 52 (t) MissAngelaBarnes(5) 4 53
(M A Barnes) *s.i.s: t.k.h in rr: hdwy 7f out: one pce fnl 3f* **20/1**
50-4 7 nse **Front Rank (IRE)**[26] 1938 9-9-4 51 MissECSayer(5) 16 52
(Mrs Dianne Sayer) *chsd ldrs: one pce fnl 3f* **9/1[3]**
5006 8 nk **Monfils Monfils (USA)**[19] 2505 7-10-4 65 MissVBarr(5) 6 65
(R E Barr) *in rr: effrt on outside over 3f out: kpt on: nvr nr ldrs* **10/1**
6635 9 4 ½ **Mister Pete (IRE)**[15] 2614 6-10-2 58 MissPRobson 10 51
(W Storey) *chsd ldrs: hmpd after 1f: chal over 3f out: wknd appr fnl f* **7/2[1]**
10 2 ¼ **King Fernando**[47] 6-9-13 55 (b) MissADeniel 7 44
(P Beaumont) *in rr: drvn over 4f out: nvr on terms* **20/1**
630- 11 4 **Carlton Mac**[220] 7272 4-9-5 47 MissFayeBramley 11 30
(N Bycroft) *drvn to ld: ducked lft after 1f: hdd over 7f out: wknd over 2f out* **20/1**
0-34 12 17 **Always Best**[5] 2592 5-8-13 46 oh1 (v) MissAWallace(5) 2 2
(R Allan) *chsd ldrs on outside: lost pl 3f out: sn bhd* **33/1**
3-43 13 1 ¾ **Streets Apart (USA)**[24] 2331 4-10-5 64 (v) MissGAndrews(3) 15 17
(W R Swinburn) *unruly in stalls: mid-div: rdn and lost pl over 3f out: bhd whn eased over 1f out* **7/2[1]**
5005 14 5 **Sixth Zak**[38] 1938 4-9-10 52 (b) MissSBrotherton 3 —
(M W Easterby) *in rr: bhd fnl 4f: t.o 2f out* **9/1[3]**

2m 40.91s (4.21) **Going Correction** +0.10s/f (Good) 14 Ran SP% **131.5**
Speed ratings (Par 101): **89,88,87,86,86 85,85,85,82,81 78,67,65,62**
toteswingers: 1&2 £166.80, 1&3 £134.70, 2&3 £58.20 CSF £424.81 CT £4354.02 TOTE £56.70: £11.90, £5.40, £3.40; EX 1691.50.
Owner A Bell **Bred** Darley **Trained** Westow, N Yorks

FOCUS
A poor lady riders' amateur handicap run at a fair pace. The form is muddling and the runner-up did not need to match last year's best.
Streets Apart(USA) Official explanation: jockey said filly never travelled

3069 HARROGATE H'CAP 1m 4f 10y
5:10 (5:10) (Class 4) (0-85,81) 3-Y-0 £5,180 (£1,541; £770; £384) Stalls High

Form RPR
3311 1 **Antigua Sunrise (IRE)**[22] 2371 3-8-12 72 TonyHamilton 6 79+
(R A Fahey) *mid-div: effrt over 3f out: hdwy on outer over 2f out: led appr fnl f: kpt on wl* **5/1[2]**
00-3 2 1 ¼ **Omokoroa (IRE)**[24] 2341 3-8-1 66 MartinLane(5) 1 71
(M H Tompkins) *hld up in midfield: hdwy on outside 4f out: led wl over 1f out: hdd and no ex* **20/1**
6031 3 2 ½ **Deauville Flyer**[13] 2667 3-8-10 70 DavidAllan 9 71+
(T D Easterby) *chsd ldrs: effrt over 3f out: kpt on same pce fnl 2f* **8/1**
1-00 4 2 ¼ **Madamlily (IRE)**[34] 2060 3-8-13 73 GrahamGibbons 2 70
(J J Quinn) *dwlt: in rr: drvn over 3f out: hdwy and edgd rt 1f out: kpt on wl* **33/1**
-640 5 1 ½ **Sharp Sovereign (USA)**[22] 2371 3-8-6 66 DaleGibson 4 61
(I Semple) *trckd ldrs: effrt over 3f out: fdd over 1f out* **66/1**
10-4 6 4 ½ **Kudu Country (IRE)**[34] 2060 3-9-3 77 DNolan 7 64
(T P Tate) *led: qcknd 4f out: hdd & wknd wl over 1f out* **15/2[3]**
-411 7 nk **Lucky Punt**[11] 2742 3-8-11 71 6ex FergusSweeney 3 58
(B G Powell) *sn trcking ldr: chal over 3f out: wknd over 1f out* **8/1**
1-26 8 ½ **Alanbrooke**[12] 2715 3-9-7 81 GregFairley 8 67
(M Johnston) *mid-div: drvn 4f out: nvr a threat: hmpd 1f out* **1/1[1]**
053 9 1 **Tapis Wizard**[34] 2060 3-8-2 69 JamesPSullivan(7) 5 54
(M W Easterby) *s.i.s: in rr: effrt on ins over 2f out: nvr a factor* **15/2[3]**

2m 37.35s (0.65) **Going Correction** +0.10s/f (Good) 9 Ran SP% **121.6**
Speed ratings (Par 101): **101,100,98,97,96 93,92,92,91**
toteswinger: 1&2 £11.00, 1&3 £5.50, 2&3 £12.50 CSF £99.44 CT £803.28 TOTE £4.60: £1.70, £5.80, £2.10; EX 83.20.
Owner David And Jackie Knaggs **Bred** Michael Morrin **Trained** Musley Bank, N Yorks

FOCUS
A competitive little handicap ran at just a fair pace until they quickened up over 3f out. The winner is progressive but the proximity of the fourth and fifth limits the form.

3070 RACING AT REDCAR TOMORROW AND SATURDAY H'CAP 1m
5:40 (5:40) (Class 6) (0-65,65) 4-Y-0+ £2,590 (£770; £385; £192) Stalls High

Form RPR
6044 1 **Montiboli (IRE)**[17] 2542 4-8-13 60 (p) NeilBrown(3) 19 70
(K A Ryan) *w ldr: led over 2f out: hld on wl* **7/1[3]**
0-04 2 1 ¾ **Apache Nation (IRE)**[17] 2532 6-8-7 56 FrederikTylicki(5) 13 62+
(M Dods) *mid-div: effrt over 3f out: gd hdwy over 1f out: styd on strly to take 2nd nr line* **9/2[1]**
0663 3 hd **Crux**[12] 2718 7-8-0 51 PaulPickard(7) 5 57
(R E Barr) *in rr: hdwy on outside over 3f out: edgd rt and wnt 2nd over 1f out: kpt on same pce* **25/1**
0-04 4 3 ¼ **Pianoforte (USA)**[3] 2965 7-8-12 56 (b) DavidAllan 7 54+
(E J Alston) *hld up: hdwy on ins over 4f out: hmpd over 2f out: kpt on fnl f* **14/1**
4-30 5 ½ **Baltimore Jack (IRE)**[17] 2529 5-8-13 57 GrahamGibbons 15 54
(T D Walford) *chsd ldrs: one pce fnl 2f* **11/2[2]**
40-0 6 2 ½ **Josephine Malines**[28] 1496 5-8-10 54 ow2 (p) DNolan 17 45
(Mrs A Duffield) *in tch: nt clr run on ins over 1f out: nvr trbld ldrs* **20/1**
2/00 7 ½ **Call Of Duty (IRE)**[17] 2531 4-9-7 65 DarrenMoffatt 11 55
(Mrs Dianne Sayer) *in rr: kpt on fnl 2f: nvr nr ldrs* **50/1**
0130 8 2 **Becuille (IRE)**[23] 2351 4-9-2 65 GabrielHannon(5) 4 50
(B J Meehan) *in rr div: hdwy and hung rt 3f out: nvr nr ldrs* **16/1**
0120 9 ½ **Mr Fantozzi (IRE)**[20] 2458 4-9-1 62 (b) DavidProbert(3) 20 46
(D Donovan) *led: hdd over 2f out: wandered: wknd over 1f out* **8/1**
0-00 10 ½ **Cross Of Lorraine (IRE)**[7] 2852 6-8-3 54 (b) RichardRowe(7) 9 37
(J Wade) *chsd ldrs: wkng whn hmpd over 1f out* **22/1**
001 11 1 ½ **Byron Bay**[11] 2746 7-8-7 51 6ex AdrianTNicholls 18 31
(R Johnson) *chsd ldrs: wkng whn hmpd over 1f out* **9/1**
1460 12 shd **Rossini's Dancer**[26] 2261 4-8-8 57 BMcHugh(5) 10 36
(R A Fahey) *mid-div: effrt over 3f out: one pce whn hmpd jst ins fnl f* **9/1**
44-0 13 2 ¾ **Wednesdays Boy (IRE)**[27] 2245 6-8-4 55 (p) JamesPSullivan(7) 6 28
(P D Niven) *s.i.s: a in rr* **22/1**
0-00 14 nk **Natural Rhythm (IRE)**[27] 2245 4-8-7 54 MichaelJStainton(3) 1 26
(Mrs R A Carr) *in rr: nvr on terms* **50/1**
0400 15 ¾ **Cheery Cat (USA)**[40] 1889 5-8-8 52 (p) TonyHamilton 3 23
(D W Barker) *a towards rr* **20/1**
1-00 16 1 ½ **Lujano**[17] 2531 4-9-4 62 JamieMoriarty 14 29
(Ollie Pears) *prom: lost pl over 2f out* **25/1**
0026 17 shd **Tanforan**[14] 2626 7-9-0 58 J-PGuillambert 8 25
(B P J Baugh) *a in rr: drvn 4f out* **16/1**
6261 18 ½ **My Mate Mal**[21] 2404 5-8-13 62 LanceBetts(5) 2 28
(B Ellison) *in tch: hdwy 4f out: lost pl over 2f out* **14/1**

1m 42.07s (0.67) **Going Correction** +0.10s/f (Good) 18 Ran SP% **132.1**
Speed ratings (Par 101): **100,98,98,94,94 91,91,89,88,88 86,86,83,83,82 81,81,80**
toteswingers: 1&2 £7.20, 1&3 £68.10, 2&3 £29.80 CSF £36.69 CT £808.35 TOTE £9.20: £1.90, £1.80, £6.90, £3.00; EX 26.70 Place 6: £2422.57 Place 5: £576.49.
Owner Dales Homes Ltd **Bred** A Brudenell, James Boughey & Trickledown Stud **Trained** Hambleton, N Yorks

FOCUS
A big field for this open handicap and it was run at a just an ordinary pace. Despite a couple not getting the best of runs the form looks fairly sound with the placed horses close to their marks.
Pianoforte(USA) Official explanation: jockey said gelding was denied a clear run
Josephine Malines Official explanation: jockey said gelding was denied a clear run
T/Plt: £6,086.80 to a £1 stake. Pool: £41,690.96. 5.00 winning tickets. T/Qpdt: £113.80 to a £1 stake. Pool: £3,385.44. 22.00 winning tickets. WG

2971 WARWICK (L-H)
Thursday, June 18

OFFICIAL GOING: Good (good to firm in places)
The rail, from the 1m start to the 2f pole, was out two yards.
Wind: Moderate behind Weather: Cloudy

3071 ARDENCOTE MANOR HOTEL GIRLS NIGHT IN MAIDEN FILLIES' STKS 6f
2:20 (2:22) (Class 5) 3-Y-0+ £2,914 (£867; £433; £216) Stalls Low

Form RPR
0620 1 **Wotasparkler**[10] 2776 3-9-0 65 RobertHavlin 10 61
(W S Kittow) *chsd ldrs: rdn over 1f out: r.o wl to ld wl ins fnl f: drvn out* **8/1[3]**
00- 2 ¾ **Jiggalong**[291] 5530 3-9-0 0 JimmyQuinn 11 59+
(Jane Chapple-Hyam) *wnt rt s: hld up and bhd: rdn and hdwy over 1f out: r.o wl to take 2nd last strides* **50/1**
2 3 shd **Femme De Fer**[19] 2496 3-9-0 0 IanMongan 7 58+
(C G Cox) *t.k.h: w ldr: led 2f out: sn rdn: hung rt 1f out: hdd wl ins fnl f: nt qckn* **10/11[1]**
0-00 4 1 ¾ **Hilltop Legacy**[114] 661 6-9-7 40 ChrisCatlin 4 53
(J R Jenkins) *w ldrs 2f: sn sltly outpcd: rdn and no ex wl ins fnl f* **100/1**
00-4 5 6 **Ile Royale**[13] 2680 4-9-7 47 LPKeniry 13 33
(W S Kittow) *wnt rt s: sn swtchd lft to ins rail: hld up and bhd: swtchd rt over 2f out: rdn over 1f out: nvr nr ldrs* **25/1**
2-5 6 1 ¼ **Cross Section (USA)**[13] 2664 3-9-0 0 DaneO'Neill 2 29
(E F Vaughan) *led: hdd 2f out: rdn over 1f out: wknd ins fnl f* **11/4[2]**
0 7 1 ¼ **Rosie Two**[28] 2205 3-9-0 0 TravisBlock 6 25
(W S Kittow) *chsd ldrs: rdn over 2f out: wknd wl over 1f out* **33/1**
60-4 8 1 ½ **Winterbourne**[54] 1529 3-9-0 47 RichardKingscote 3 21
(M Blanshard) *s.i.s: sn mid-div: pushed along over 2f out: sn wknd* **18/1**
0/00 9 11 **Kilmeena Dream**[9] 2794 5-9-7 0 RichardSmith 8 —
(J C Fox) *a in rr* **66/1**
10 17 **Paris In Mind** 3-9-0 0 FrankieMcDonald 9 —
(C N Kellett) *dwlt: outpcd* **80/1**

1m 11.97s (0.17) **Going Correction** +0.05s/f (Good)
WFA 3 from 4yo+ 7lb 10 Ran SP% **107.9**
Speed ratings (Par 100): **100,99,98,96,88 86,85,83,68,45**
toteswingers: 1&2 £26.20, 1&3 £2.50, 2&3 £9.90 CSF £287.99 TOTE £11.30: £2.30, £9.40, £1.02; EX 562.70.
Owner Miss E J Tanner **Bred** D J Weston **Trained** Blackborough, Devon
■ Accrosstheuniverse, set to be Clare Lindop's first ride in Britain, was withdrawn (11/1, unruly in stalls, deduct 5p in the £ R4).

FOCUS
The two market leaders went off too fast and this was an ordinary sprint maiden. This looks potentially weak form.
Winterbourne Official explanation: jockey said filly was unsuited by the track

3072 RACING UK MEDIAN AUCTION MAIDEN STKS 5f
2:55 (2:55) (Class 5) 2-Y-0 £2,914 (£867; £433; £216) Stalls Low

Form RPR
5 1 **Orpen Grey (IRE)**[19] 2477 2-9-3 0 RichardKingscote 4 89+
(Tom Dascombe) *w ldr: led jst over 1f out: rdn out* **6/1[3]**
35 2 3 ¼ **Admin (IRE)**[20] 2444 2-9-3 0 GeorgeBaker 2 75
(R M Beckett) *led: hdd jst over 1f out: rdn and no ex ins fnl f* **4/5[1]**
3 3 2 ¾ **Look Whos Next**[19] 2484 2-9-3 0 JimmyQuinn 8 65+
(E S McMahon) *dwlt: t.k.h: sn prom: rdn and one pce ins fnl f* **7/2[2]**
503 4 1 ¾ **Ever So Bold**[24] 2335 2-9-3 0 DaneO'Neill 5 59
(W R Muir) *wnt sltly rt s: hld up: rdn over 1f out: nvr nr to chal* **10/1**
56 5 3 **Mahiki**[38] 1939 2-8-12 0 PatCosgrave 6 43
(S A Callaghan) *hld up in tch: pushed along over 2f out: wknd fnl f* **20/1**
6 1 ¾ **Macroy** 2-9-0 0 JamesMillman(3) 1 42
(B R Millman) *hld up: hung lft wl over 1f out: a bhd* **33/1**
7 3 ¾ **Email Exit (IRE)** 2-9-3 0 IanMongan 3 28
(C F Wall) *s.s: a in rr* **16/1**

8 *7* **Chill Out Charley** 2-9-3 0 .... NeilChalmers 7 —
(J J Bridger) *dwlt: pushed along over 3f out: a bhd* **66/1**
60.14 secs (0.54) **Going Correction** +0.05s/f (Good) **8** Ran SP% **116.2**
Speed ratings (Par 93): **97,91,87,84,79 77,71,59**
toteswinger: 1&2 £2.30, 1&3 £3.30, 2&3 £1.60 CSF £11.29 TOTE £8.70: £2.50, £1.10, £1.30; EX 13.50.
Owner The Folly Racers **Bred** John Osborne **Trained** Lambourn, Berks

FOCUS
A fair juvenile maiden and, although the winner was a big improver, the placed horses give it substance.

NOTEBOOK
Orpen Grey(IRE) was a most convincing winner, improving a good deal on the form he showed in a decent maiden at Goodwood first time up. Having got a nice lead off the favourite, he picked that one up readily in the straight and did this comfortably. He looks useful and will now be aimed at a 6f conditions contest at Salisbury, a race his trainer won with subsequent Group 2 winner Classic Blade last year. (op 9-2 tchd 4-1)
Admin(IRE) went off in front but, just the like a couple of fancied runners in the opener who went off quick, he didn't see his race out. He has the ability to win a race like this, but is clearly vulnerable to anything half decent. (op 13-8 tchd 7-4 in places)
Look Whos Next was keen early and never threatened the front two. This probably didn't represent improvement on his debut showing. (op 5-2)
Ever So Bold was never a danger and might be better off in nurseries, or an even lower grade. (op 11-1 tchd 12-1)
Mahiki didn't offer much but will at least soon have the option of nurseries. (op 16-1)

3073 WARWICK RACECOURSE H'CAP — 1m 6f 213y
3:30 (3:30) (Class 5) (0-75,74) 4-Y-O+ **£3,238** (£963; £481; £240) **Stalls** Low

Form RPR
2-55 **1** **Squirtle (IRE)**[147] 249 6-8-3 **56** .... LukeMorris 6 63
(W M Brisbourne) *hld up in tch: wnt 2nd wl over 2f out: sn rdn: led jst over 1f out: styd on* **7/1**
5-02 **2** *1 1/4* **My Mate Max**[54] 1506 4-9-2 **72** ....(p) RussellKennemore(3) 3 77
(R Hollinshead) *led: edgd lft 2f out: sn rdn and hung rt: swvd bdly lft over 1f out: sn hdd: styd on* **6/1**[3]
3224 **3** *3 1/2* **Baan (USA)**[109] 723 6-8-11 **64** .... JimmyQuinn 8 65
(H J Collingridge) *hld up: hdwy 3f out: rdn to take 3rd wl ins fnl f: nt trble ldng pair* **12/1**
2656 **4** *hd* **Lapina (IRE)**[23] 1049 5-8-10 **63** ....(p) IanMongan 1 64
(A Middleton) *hld up in rr: rdn 2f out: hdwy over 1f out: one pce fnl f* **20/1**
0-66 **5** *3/4* **Hawridge King**[28] 2194 7-9-4 **74** .... JamesMillman(3) 4 74
(W S Kittow) *hld up and bhd: hdwy on ins 3f out: rdn and one pce fnl f* **7/2**[2]
-446 **6** *2 1/2* **Sphere (IRE)**[10] 2760 4-8-13 **66** ....(p) PatCosgrave 9 62
(J R Fanshawe) *chsd ldr tl wl over 2f out: sn rdn: edgd rt over 1f out: wknd ins fnl f* **14/1**
-236 **7** *4 1/2* **Sir Sandicliffe (IRE)**[4] 2944 5-8-10 **63** ....(b[1]) TGMcLaughlin 7 53
(W M Brisbourne) *s.i.s: sn hld up in mid-div: rdn and bhd fnl 3f* **8/1**
0244 **8** *2* **Alnwick**[40] 1863 5-9-7 **74** ....(p) DaneO'Neill 10 62
(P D Cundell) *hld up in tch: rdn over 3f out: wknd wl over 2f out* **85/40**[1]
3m 19.06s (0.06) **Going Correction** +0.05s/f (Good) **8** Ran SP% **111.2**
Speed ratings (Par 103): **101,100,98,98,97 96,94,93**
toteswingers: 1&2 £5.00, 2&3 £6.00, 1&3 not won. CSF £45.57 CT £479.79 TOTE £8.50: £2.70, £1.70, £2.60; EX 30.90.
Owner J Jones Racing Ltd **Bred** Ballygallon Stud Limited **Trained** Great Ness, Shropshire

FOCUS
A modest staying handicap and the form is muddling.
Alnwick Official explanation: trainer had no explanation for the poor form shown

3074 TURFTV H'CAP — 1m 2f 188y
4:10 (4:10) (Class 6) (0-55,60) 4-Y-O+ **£2,047** (£604; £302) **Stalls** Low

Form RPR
3001 **1** **Maybe I Wont**[7] 2859 4-9-0 **60** 6ex ....(p) JPHamblett(5) 5 69
(Lucinda Featherstone) *hld up in tch: swtchd rt ent st over 2f out: rdn and edgd lft over 1f out: led ent fnl f: drvn out* **9/2**[2]
0-01 **2** *1 1/4* **Karky Schultz (GER)**[8] 2830 4-9-2 **57** 6ex .... LukeMorris 2 64+
(J M P Eustace) *hld up in rr: c wd st: rdn 2f out: hdwy over 1f out: r.o wl on stands' rail ins fnl f: nt rch wnr* **5/2**[1]
-405 **3** *nk* **Astrolibra**[27] 2221 5-9-0 **55** .... SaleemGolam 9 61
(M H Tompkins) *hld up in mid-div: hdwy 3f out: rdn 1f out: kpt on ins fnl f* **11/1**
0006 **4** *1 1/4* **Le Corvee (IRE)**[14] 2634 7-8-7 **53** .... MarkCoumbe(5) 6 57+
(A W Carroll) *s.i.s: hld up in rr: swtchd rt and hdwy over 1f out: rdn and kpt on ins fnl f* **10/1**
-40 **5** *shd* **Tyrana (GER)**[43] 1785 6-8-12 **53** .... VinceSlattery 1 57
(G F Bridgwater) *hld up in mid-div: hdwy on ins 2f out: sn rdn: no ex towards fin* **7/1**
6452 **6** *1* **Make Amends (IRE)**[5] 2912 4-9-0 **55** .... RichardKingscote 16 57
(R J Hodges) *a.p: wnt 2nd over 8f out: rdn and ev ch 1f out: wknd wl ins fnl f* **9/1**
0/01 **7** *3/4* **Mossmann Gorge**[25] 2182 7-8-9 **53** ....(p) KevinGhunowa(3) 13 54
(A Middleton) *prom: rdn 2f out: edgd lft over 1f out: wknd ins fnl f* **8/1**
0626 **8** *3 1/4* **Ma Ridge**[55] 872 5-8-0 **46** .... AmyBaker(5) 3 41
(T D McCarthy) *t.k.h in tch: hmpd and lost pl over 8f out: rdn over 2f out: wknd fnl f* **80/1**
43-4 **9** *3/4* **Russian Angel**[163] 58 5-8-7 **48** .... LPKeniry 12 42
(Jean-Rene Auvray) *led: rdn 2f out: hdd ent fnl f: wknd* **33/1**
000- **10** *2 1/2* **Marino Prince (FR)**[35] 7560 4-8-2 **48** .... PatrickDonaghy(5) 11 37
(T Wall) *prom: rdn over 2f out: wknd wl over 1f out* **66/1**
0340 **11** *3/4* **Desert Hawk**[21] 2420 8-8-6 **47** .... LiamJones 15 35
(W M Brisbourne) *s.i.s: a bhd* **33/1**
/03- **12** *hd* **Potemkin (USA)**[238] 2719 4-9-0 **55** .... DaneO'Neill 7 42
(A King) *hld up towards rr: rdn wl over 1f out: no rspnse: eased ins fnl f* **6/1**[3]
2024 **P** **Rosy Dawn**[5] 2923 4-8-0 **48** .... DebraEngland(7) 8 —
(J J Bridger) *chsd ldr tl lost action over 8f out: sn p.u* **20/1**
2m 20.16s (-0.94) **Going Correction** +0.05s/f (Good) **13** Ran SP% **125.4**
Speed ratings (Par 101): **105,104,103,102,102 102,101,99,98,96 96,96,—**
toteswinger: 1&2 £5.10, 1&3 £10.30, 2&3 £8.70 CSF £16.36 CT £123.85 TOTE £4.90: £1.90, £1.70, £3.60; EX 19.80.
Owner J Roundtree **Bred** Wheelersland Stud **Trained** Atlow, Derbyshire
■ Stewards' Enquiry : Mark Coumbe one-day ban: used whip with excessive frequency (Jul 2)

FOCUS
A moderate but competitive handicap and the form looks sound rated around the third and fifth.
Make Amends(IRE) Official explanation: jockey said filly had no more to give
Rosy Dawn Official explanation: jockey said filly was struck into

3075 WARWICK FOR CONFERENCES H'CAP — 7f 26y
4:45 (4:45) (Class 5) (0-70,68) 3-Y-O+ **£2,729** (£806; £403) **Stalls** Low

Form RPR
00-0 **1** **Bahamian Kid**[44] 1775 4-10-0 **68** ....(p) GeorgeBaker 12 76
(R Hollinshead) *t.k.h towards rr: hdwy on ins over 2f out: rdn to ld ins fnl f: jst hld on* **9/1**
3506 **2** *hd* **Tuxedo**[16] 2565 4-9-11 **65** .... LukeMorris 7 72
(P W Hiatt) *hld up in mid-div: lost pl over 4f out: sn pushed along: rdn and hdwy on stands' side over 1f out: r.o wl ins fnl f: jst failed* **12/1**
0-00 **3** *nk* **Turkish Lokum**[30] 2148 3-8-6 **60** .... WilliamCarson(5) 1 64
(J M P Eustace) *w ldr: led wl over 1f out: sn edgd rt: rdn and hdd ins fnl f: kpt on* **6/1**[3]
6511 **4** *1 1/2* **Crystallize**[21] 2417 3-9-5 **68** .... DaneO'Neill 5 68
(A B Haynes) *hld up in mid-div: hdwy wl over 1f out: sn rdn: nt qckn ins fnl f* **4/1**[2]
0404 **5** *nk* **Rough Rock (IRE)**[7] 2864 4-8-12 **55** .... KevinGhunowa(3) 11 57
(C A Dwyer) *led 1f: a.p: led over 2f out tl wl over 1f out: one pce ins fnl f* **25/1**
4203 **6** *1/2* **Gazboolou**[12] 2713 5-10-0 **68** .... ChrisCatlin 10 68
(David Pinder) *hld up in rr: hdwy over 1f out: sn rdn: one pce ins fnl f* **6/1**[3]
4010 **7** *nk* **Diego Rivera**[41] 1833 4-9-9 **63** ....(v[1]) PatCosgrave 2 63
(P J Makin) *chsd ldrs: rdn over 1f out: wknd wl ins fnl f* **11/4**[1]
2600 **8** *3* **Loyal Royal (IRE)**[6] 2880 6-9-3 **57** ....(b) LPKeniry 14 49
(J M Bradley) *stdd s: a in rr* **28/1**
60 **9** *2 3/4* **Highgate Cat**[33] 2081 3-8-10 **59** .... TGMcLaughlin 3 40
(B R Millman) *t.k.h: prom tl wknd wl over 1f out* **7/1**
03-0 **10** *4* **Yeoman Of England (IRE)**[25] 2300 3-8-12 **64** .... JackMitchell(3) 13 34
(C F Wall) *hld up in mid-div: rdn and hung lft over 1f out: sn wknd* **22/1**
0-00 **11** *4 1/2* **Flute Magic**[35] 2010 3-9-2 **65** .... IanMongan 4 23
(W S Kittow) *t.k.h: led after 1f: hdd over 2f out: wknd over 1f out* **10/1**
1m 25.27s (0.67) **Going Correction** +0.05s/f (Good)
WFA 3 from 4yo+ 9lb **11** Ran SP% **126.2**
Speed ratings (Par 103): **98,97,97,95,95 94,94,91,87,83 78**
toteswingers: 1&2 £16.40, 1&3 £15.40, 2&3 £16.00 CSF £116.87 CT £730.56 TOTE £17.40: £4.60, £3.80, £2.60; EX 150.20.
Owner Graham Brothers Racing Partnership **Bred** J D Graham **Trained** Upper Longdon, Staffs

FOCUS
A modest handicap but the first four were close to previous marks and the form looks sound.

3076 WARWICKRACECOURSE.CO.UK H'CAP — 1m 22y
5:20 (5:21) (Class 5) (0-75,74) 4-Y-O+ **£3,238** (£963; £481; £240) **Stalls** Low

Form RPR
1-22 **1** **Miss Pelling (IRE)**[24] 2332 4-8-13 **66** .... RobertHavlin 2 73
(B J Meehan) *a.p: hung lft 2f out: rdn ins fnl f: led last stride* **15/8**[1]
214- **2** *shd* **San Antonio**[23] 4895 9-9-7 **74** ....(b) JimmyQuinn 7 81
(Mrs P Sly) *w ldr: led over 6f out: rdn over 1f out: edgd rt ins fnl f: hdd last stride* **16/1**
-660 **3** *1/2* **Theonebox (USA)**[24] 2313 4-9-4 **74** .... PatrickHills(3) 3 80+
(N J Vaughan) *hld up towards rr: hdwy over 1f out: sn rdn: r.o ins fnl f* **16/1**
510 **4** *shd* **Full Victory (IRE)**[23] 2352 7-9-1 **68** .... DaneO'Neill 5 74
(R A Farrant) *hld up in tch: swtchd lft wl over 1f out: sn rdn and edgd lft to ins rail: kpt on ins fnl f* **8/1**
00-0 **5** *1 3/4* **Cool Ebony**[29] 2186 6-9-6 **73** .... TravisBlock 1 75
(P J Makin) *prom: lost pl on ins over 3f out: rdn over 1f out: kpt on one pce ins fnl f* **15/2**[3]
0040 **6** *1/2* **Wavertree Warrior (IRE)**[31] 2125 7-8-2 **55** ....(b) LukeMorris 10 55
(N P Littmoden) *half-rrd s: hld up in rr: c wd st: late hdwy: nrst fin* **20/1**
-514 **7** *3/4* **Charlevoix (IRE)**[27] 2243 4-9-3 **70** .... GeorgeBaker 6 69
(C F Wall) *hld up in mid-div: rdn over 1f out: no hdwy* **3/1**[2]
-060 **8** *1* **Glenridding**[26] 2261 5-8-11 **64** .... PatCosgrave 4 60
(J G Given) *led over 1f: prom: rdn over 1f out: wknd ins fnl f* **14/1**
4566 **9** *7* **Obezyana (USA)**[17] 2527 7-8-13 **66** ....(p) NeilChalmers 9 46
(A Bailey) *hld up in mid-div: hdwy 5f out: wknd wl over 1f out* **9/1**
00-6 **10** *6* **Canary Girl**[37] 1958 6-8-2 **55** oh10 .... AdrianMcCarthy 11 22
(G Prodromou) *a in rr* **100/1**
1m 40.64s (-0.36) **Going Correction** +0.05s/f (Good) **10** Ran SP% **116.8**
Speed ratings (Par 103): **103,102,102,102,100 100,99,98,91,85**
toteswingers: 1&2 £6.70, 1&3 £6.80, 2&3 £24.60 CSF £35.48 CT £390.10 TOTE £2.80: £1.10, £2.80, £3.90; EX 24.30.
Owner Kennet Valley Thoroughbreds Iii **Bred** Epona Bloodstock Ltd **Trained** Manton, Wilts

FOCUS
An ordinary handicap with the runner-up rated to last year's form.
Canary Girl Official explanation: jockey said mare lost its action

3077 TURFTV APPRENTICE H'CAP — 1m 22y
5:50 (5:57) (Class 6) (0-60,60) 4-Y-O+ **£2,047** (£604; £302) **Stalls** Low

Form RPR
4040 **1** **Aggbag**[19] 2473 5-8-4 **50** .... DeclanCannon(5) 3 59
(J Mackie) *a.p: led wl over 1f out: sn rdn and edgd rt: r.o* **10/1**
0-34 **2** *1* **Hits Only Cash**[20] 2458 7-8-11 **57** ....(p) SimonPearce(5) 5 64
(J Pearce) *hld up in rr: hdwy wl over 1f out: rdn and wnt 2nd ins fnl f: kpt on* **4/1**[1]
4554 **3** *1 1/2* **Barodine**[10] 2764 6-8-11 **55** .... AmyBaker(3) 15 58+
(R J Hodges) *hld up in tch: rdn over 2f out: r.o to take 3rd last strides* **11/1**
4-00 **4** *hd* **Lordship (IRE)**[6] 2880 5-8-7 **55** .... JakePayne(7) 4 58+
(A W Carroll) *t.k.h in mid-div: hdwy on ins over 2f out: rdn jst over 1f out: kpt on same pce* **33/1**
1200 **5** *1/2* **Waldorf (IRE)**[13] 2684 4-8-12 **58** .... RossAtkinson(5) 6 60
(W R Muir) *a.p: ev ch over 1f out: sn rdn: fdd towards fin* **10/1**
00-2 **6** *1 1/4* **Al Rayanah**[45] 1741 6-8-10 **56** ....(p) JemmaMarshall(5) 17 55
(G Prodromou) *stdd s: hld up in rr: hdwy over 1f out: sn rdn: no further prog ins fnl f* **11/1**
0000 **7** *1 1/4* **The Grey One (IRE)**[7] 2859 6-8-12 **56** ....(p) MCGeran(3) 10 52+
(J M Bradley) *hld up in rr: rdn over 1f out: styd on ins fnl f: nvr nrr* **11/1**
22-6 **8** *3/4* **Distant Pleasure**[27] 2245 5-9-0 **58** .... PatrickDonaghy(3) 9 52
(M Dods) *hld up towards rr: rdn over 1f out: n.d* **13/2**[2]
250- **9** *3 1/2* **Classic Blue (IRE)**[199] 7516 5-8-12 **53** .... JackMitchell 13 39
(Ian Williams) *hld up in mid-div: rdn and wknd ins fnl f* **17/2**
5-00 **10** *nk* **Empire Seeker (USA)**[8] 2830 4-8-10 **54** .... JackDean(3) 11 39
(Mrs H S Main) *w ldr: led over 6f out: rdn and hdd wl over 1f out: sn wknd* **16/1**

1/0- **11** *1* **My Jeanie (IRE)**[524] [123] 5-8-2 **50**............................ GemmaElford(7) 1 33+
(J C Fox) *led over 1f: w ldr: ev ch 2f out: sltly hmpd over 1f out: wknd ins fnl f* **12/1**

000- **12** *1* **Sorrel Point**[331] [4284] 6-8-1 **47**..................................(t) RosieJessop(5) 16 28
(H J Collingridge) *a in rr* **28/1**

66-0 **13** *nk* **Zain (IRE)**[21] [2420] 5-7-13 **47**.. NoelGarbutt(7) 14 27
(J G Given) *prom tl wknd over 2f out* **9/1**

30-6 **14** *11* **Private Soldier**[19] [2473] 6-8-8 **49**............................ PatrickHills 12 4
(N J Vaughan) *mid-div: c wd to stands' rail ent st: bhd fnl 2f* **8/1**[3]

1m 40.95s (-0.05) **Going Correction** +0.05s/f (Good) **14** Ran SP% **128.1**
Speed ratings (Par 101): **102,101,99,99,98 97,96,95,92,91 90,89,89,78**
toteswingers: 1&2 £10.20, 1&3 £12.40, 2&3 £7.00 CSF £52.90 CT £484.57 TOTE £13.80: £4.30, £1.50, £4.30; EX 93.40 Place 6: £91.02 Place 5: £60.19.
Owner Joe Singh **Bred** D R Tucker **Trained** Church Broughton , Derbys

FOCUS
A moderate apprentice handicap but the form looks pretty sound.
T/Plt: £313.80 to a £1 stake. Pool: £32,801.45. 76.30 winning tickets. T/Qpdt: £206.80 to a £1 stake. Pool: £2,096.84. 7.50 winning tickets. KH

3078 - 3084a (Foreign Racing) - See Raceform Interactive

2513 LONGCHAMP (R-H)
Thursday, June 18

OFFICIAL GOING: Good to soft

3085a LA COUPE (GROUP 3) 1m 2f
2:55 (2:55) 4-Y-O+ £38,835 (£15,534; £11,650; £7,767; £3,883)

RPR

1 **Stotsfold**[21] [2410] 6-8-11 .... AdamKirby 8 113
(W R Swinburn) *racd in 5th: hdwy on outside and 4th st: led jst under 2f out: strly pressed 100yds out: asserted last strides* **12/5**[1]

2 *snk* **Starlish (IRE)**[23] 4-8-11 .... ACrastus 4 113
(E Lellouche, France) *hld up: 8th st: hdwy to take 2nd ins fnl f: pressing wnr on ins 100yds out: no ex last strides* **4/1**[2]

3 *3* **Bon Grain (FR)**[28] 4-8-11 .... FBlondel 9 107
(J J Napoli, France) *hld up in rr: 7th st: hdwy down outside to take 2nd briefly 1f out: sn hdd and one pce* **40/1**

4 *2* **Sans Chichi (FR)**[23] 5-8-8 .... OPeslier 6 100
(Y Barberot, France) *hld up: 5th st: no room over 2f out out tl dropped bk to 7th and swtchd outside 1f out: kpt on wl fnl f* **6/1**

5 *1* **Runaway**[32] [2120] 7-8-11 .... TJarnet 3 101
(R Pritchard-Gordon, France) *cl up: 3rd st: rdn and one pce fnl 2f* **5/1**[3]

6 *shd* **Mr Brock (SAF)**[88] 6-8-11 .... DBoeuf 5 101
(Mme C Head-Maarek, France) *racd in 2nd: pressing ldr ent st: one pce fr over 2f out* **13/1**

7 *2 ½* **Willywell (FR)**[55] 7-8-11 .... IMendizabal 2 96
(J-P Gauvin, France) *racd in 3rd on ins: cl 6th ent st: n.m.r on ins 2f out to 1f out: sn rdn and unable qck* **68/10**

8 *nse* **Goose Bay (GER)**[21] [2428] 4-8-8 .... DBonilla 7 93
(F Head, France) *set gd pce: hdd jst under 2f out: wknd* **17/1**

9 *15* **Torrid Hell (FR)**[19] 4-8-11 .... CSoumillon 1 66
(S Wattel, France) *lost 5 l s: last but jst in tch 5f out: lost tch again under 4f out* **12/1**

2m 5.10s (1.10) **9** Ran SP% **116.0**
PARI-MUTUEL: WIN 3.40; PL 1.60, 1.90, 6.40; DF 9.80.
Owner P W Harris **Bred** Pendley Farm **Trained** Aldbury, Herts

NOTEBOOK
Stotsfold, held up early, started to make a forward move just before the straight and took the lead just over a furlong out. He then battled on bravely to hold off the runner up. There are no immediate plans, but he could come back again to France, possibly to Deauville.
Starlish(IRE), another held up in the early stages, didn't have the clearest run in the straight. Once in the clear he made his challenge up the far rail, but could never peg back the winner in the dying stages.
Bon Grain(FR), last but one on the far side, was putting in his best work inside the final furlong and never looked like losing third place.
Sans Chichi(FR), in mid division down the back straight, had nowhere to go entering the straight and then ran on really well at the end. She must be considered lucky.

3046 ASCOT (R-H)
Friday, June 19

OFFICIAL GOING: Good to firm (overall 10.1; straight 10.1; round 9.6)
The course reverted to its normal configuration and all distances were as advertised.

3086 ALBANY STKS (GROUP 3) (FILLIES) 6f
2:30 (2:32) (Class 1) 2-Y-O
£39,739 (£15,064; £7,539; £3,759; £1,883; £945) **Stalls** Centre

Form RPR

31 **1** **Habaayib**[42] [1841] 2-8-12 0.. RHills 10 105+
(E A L Dunlop) *swtchd lft sn after s and racd on stands' side: hld up: hdwy over 2f out: led jst over 1f out: r.o wl and wl on top at fin* **16/1**

21 **2** *1 ¼* **Lillie Langtry (IRE)**[18] [2557] 2-8-12 0.............................. JAHeffernan 6 101
(A P O'Brien, Ire) *w'like: athletic: hld up bhd ldrs in stands' side gp: chal fr 2f out: r.o u.p ins fnl f: nt pce of wnr towards fin* **11/8**[1]

1 **3** *2 ½* **Chachamaidee (IRE)**[13] [2711] 2-8-12 0.............................. TPQueally 16 93
(H R A Cecil) *w'like: chsd ldrs on far side tl swtchd lft to r in main gp 4f out: led over 3f out: rdn 2f out: hdd jst over 1f out: styd on same pce ins fnl f* **12/1**

1 **4** *2* **She's A Character**[13] [2699] 2-8-12 0.............................. PaulHanagan 5 87
(R A Fahey) *racd stands' side: hld up: wnt rt whn pushed along and hdwy over 2f out: r.o ins fnl f: clsd on ldrs towards fin* **11/1**[3]

3321 **5** *shd* **Curtains**[12] [2735] 2-8-12 0.. C-PLemaire 3 87
(S Dow) *lw: racd on stands' side: led: hdd over 3f out: continued to chse ldrs: rdn 2f out: kpt on same pce fnl f* **100/1**

31 **6** *1* **Above Limits (IRE)**[29] [2207] 2-8-12 0.............................. RichardKingscote 14 84
(Tom Dascombe) *gd spd to ld far side gp: rdn over 2f out: stl in cl contention w main gp over 1f out: edgd lft ins fnl f: no ex fnl 75yds* **33/1**

41 **7** *1 ¾* **Jira**[18] [2533] 2-8-12 0.. SebSanders 20 79
(C E Brittain) *racd on far side: midfield early: chsd gp ldr over 3f out: rdn over 2f out: stl in cl contenion over 1f out: one pce fnl f* **33/1**

1 **8** *2* **Sweet Sonnet (USA)**[20] [2503] 2-8-12 0.............................. LDettori 15 73+
(Saeed Bin Suroor) *w'like: racd on far-side: prom: swtchd lft to r in main gp 4f out: rdn over 2f out: wknd and eased fnl f* **16/1**

9 *¾* **Aegean (USA)**[50] 2-8-12 0..(bt) JRVelazquez 18 71
(Wesley A Ward, U.S.A) *strong: gd spd on far-side: swtchd lft to r in main gp 4f out: handy tl rdn and wknd over 1f out* **11/4**[2]

21 **10** *1 ¾* **Absolute Music (USA)**[25] [2335] 2-8-12 0.............................. EddieAhern 9 65
(R M H Cowell) *racd on stands' side: prom: rdn 3f out: wknd over 1f out* **40/1**

1103 **11** *hd* **Leleyf (IRE)**[23] [2372] 2-8-12 0.. TonyCulhane 12 65
(M R Channon) *hld up: racd towards far-side: swtchd lft to r in main gp 4f out: sme hdwy into midfield over 2f out: no imp on ldrs* **66/1**

461 **12** *1* **Flyinflyout**[19] [2514] 2-8-12 0.. SamHitchcott 17 62
(M R Channon) *towards rr on far-side: swtchd lft to r in main gp 4f out: sme hdwy into midfield and hung rt over 2f out: no imp on ldrs* **100/1**

0120 **13** *½* **Chicita Banana**[35] [2054] 2-8-12 0.. TedDurcan 19 60
(George Baker) *racd on far-side: in midfield: nvr able to chal* **100/1**

22 **14** *1 ¾* **Baileys Vision**[22] [2388] 2-8-12 0.. JoeFanning 1 55
(M Johnston) *w'like: racd on stands' side: chsd ldrs: pushed along and lost pl over 3f out: n.d after* **50/1**

251 **15** *¾* **Bell's Ocean (USA)**[28] [2238] 2-8-12 0.............................. JerryO'Dwyer 4 53
(J Ryan) *racd on stands' side: prom: pushed along 3f out: wknd over 2f out* **100/1**

100 **16** *2* **Eternal Instinct**[13] [2714] 2-8-12 0.............................. DanielTudhope 11 47+
(J S Goldie) *hld up in main gp: gng nowhere whn swvd to avoid uns jockey over 2f out: nvr on terms* **66/1**

6033 **17** *2* **French Connexion (IRE)**[6] [2906] 2-8-12 0.............................. LukeMorris 21 41
(J S Moore) *racd on far-side in midfield: outpcd over 2f out: nvr a danger* **200/1**

6021 **18** *1 ¼* **Kate Skate**[25] [2325] 2-8-12 0.. JimmyQuinn 8 37
(Miss Gay Kelleway) *racd on stands' side: hld up: sme hdwy whn carried rt over 2f out: sn struggling* **150/1**

22 **19** *1* **Falling Angel**[20] [2503] 2-8-12 0.. RyanMoore 7 34+
(P F I Cole) *racd on stands' side: prom: pushed along over 3f out: wknd wl over 1f out: eased fnl f* **20/1**

20 *24* **Core Element (IRE)**[13] [2727] 2-8-12 0.............................. NCallan 2 —
(Adrian Sexton, Ire) *strong: dwlt: stmbld sn after s: racd on stands' side: a bhd and outpcd* **100/1**

010 **21** *18* **Patteresa Girl**[23] [2372] 2-8-12 0.. ShaneKelly 22 —
(Mrs L Stubbs) *leggy: racd on far-side: sn pushed along and outpcd* **100/1**

21 **U** **Kurtanella**[35] [2034] 2-8-12 0.. RichardHughes 13 —
(R Hannon) *racd far-side: swtchd to r in main gp 4f out: midfield: losing pl whn hmpd and uns rdr over 2f out* **28/1**

1m 15.63s (1.23) **Going Correction** +0.15s/f (Good) **22** Ran SP% **125.1**
Speed ratings (Par 100): **97,95,92,89,89 87,85,82,81,79 79,77,77,74,73 71,68,66,65,33 9,—**
toteswinger: 1&2 £25.10, 1&3 £25.40, 2&3 £9.10 CSF £35.69 CT £311.93 TOTE £25.10: £5.00, £1.30, £3.70; EX 68.90 Trifecta £689.20 Pool: £5495.50 - 5.90 winning units..
Owner Hamdan Al Maktoum **Bred** Whitley Stud **Trained** Newmarket, Suffolk

■ Stewards' Enquiry : Paul Hanagan four-day ban: careless riding (Jul 3,5-7)

FOCUS
In its relatively brief history this race has thrown up a number of decent fillies, although as yet none has subsequently scored at above Group 2 level. The betting suggested it was a two-horse race but it did not turn out that way. The winner was quite impressive and the runner-up sets the level which looks up to standard for the race.

NOTEBOOK
Habaayib ◆, third on her Newmarket debut in race that is working out, and then an easy winner of a maiden against ordinary opposition, won this in the style of a juvenile that will be difficult to beat in some of the big 6f fillies' races this summer. The stable had the winner of the Britannia Handicap for the same owner on Thursday and Richard Hills gave this filly a similar ride, switching in behind at the start to join the nearside group. She made her ground very easily and was going best 2f out, then found plenty when asked to hold off the favourite in the final furlong. The Princess Margaret back here or the Lowther look obvious targets. (op 20-1)

Lillie Langtry(IRE) had the best European form coming into this, having won a Group 3 in Ireland. She got a good enough lead into the race and had every chance, but could not match the winner's pace in the closing stages. A step up to 7f looks likely and the Moyglare Stud Stakes could be on the agenda. (tchd 5-4 and 6-4 in places)

Chachamaidee(IRE), the winner of 6f maiden in a reasonable time on her debut at Lingfield, was the best backed outside the two market leaders and showed terrific pace towards the stands' side. She was quite close to the principals entering the final furlong but could only keep on at the one pace. She still looks capable of winning good races on this evidence. (tchd 14-1 and 16-1 in places)

She's A Character, another filly who came into this having won her sole start, struggled to lie up early but made ground from halfway and was keeping on steadily in the closing stages. Although by a speedy sire, she is a half-sister to a couple of middle-distance winners so can be expected to do better at longer trips in time. (op 16-1)

Curtains, one of the rank outsiders, ran a fine race. She had shown decent form in minor maidens and confirmed that she is going the right way by racing in the leading group towards the stands' side throughout. She should give connections plenty more fun and could be up to earning black type. (tchd 80-1)

Above Limits(IRE) deserves extra credit for her effort as she had to race virtually alone towards the far side for much of the way. She had too much speed for the second favourite from the stalls but the race developed more towards the stands' side. This was her first try at 6f and she should get it in time, but she looks capable of dropping back to the minimum if a suitable opportunity arises.
Official explanation: jockey said filly hung left

Jira chased Above Limits from the start and stuck to her task without making any impression. She is a half-sister to King Edward VII winner Plea Bargain so will not mind a step up in trip.

Sweet Sonnet(USA), another who had won her sole start, chased the leaders from the start but could make no inroads in the last quarter-mile. (op 14-1)

Aegean(USA), the second favourite and a dual winner at 4½f and 5f in the USA, had beaten her stable companion and subsequent Queen Mary winner Jealous Again in a Grade 3 last time. She was expected to blast off in front but could not dominate and her rider switched her more towards the stands' side. She raced just off the pace but the writing was on the wall well over a furlong out and connections concluded she better on dirt and Polytrack. (tchd 3-1 and 7-2 in a place)

Eternal Instinct Official explanation: jockey said filly suffered interference in running

Kurtanella, who was racing in the bunch chasing the leaders, was hampered as Kate Skate appeared to go right and she unseated Richard Hughes. Fortunately neither horse nor rider was any the worse, but the blame was apportioned to Paul Hanagan on the fourth, who picked up a four-day ban. (op 33-1)

3087 KING EDWARD VII STKS (GROUP 2) (C&G) 1m 4f

3:05 (3:06) (Class 1) 3-Y-O

£92,946 (£35,233; £17,633; £8,792; £4,404; £2,210) **Stalls** High

Form RPR

-332 **1** **Father Time**27 2277 3-8-12 106 EddieAhern 11 114
(H R A Cecil) *lw: hld up in midfield: hdwy over 3f out: chsd ldr jst over 2f out: rdn to ld wl over 1f out: drvn clr ent fnl f: r.o strly* **9/1**

-514 **2** *4* **Your Old Pal**27 2277 3-8-12 108 RyanMoore 10 107+
(J Noseda) *s.i.s: plld hrd: hld up in rr: hdwy towards inner wl over 2f out: swtchd lft 2f out: squeezed between horses jst over 1f out: chsd wnr fnl 100yds: r.o but no imp* **14/1**

-310 **3** *nk* **Black Bear Island (IRE)**13 2705 3-9-1 112 CO'Donoghue 9 110
(A P O'Brien, Ire) *stdd s: hld up towards rr: hdwy and swtchd lft wl over 2f out: drvn to chse wnr over 1f out: outpcd wnr ent fnl f: lost 2nd fnl 100yds: kpt on* **9/2**2

11-4 **4** *2 1/4* **Free Agent**30 2176 3-8-12 103 RichardHughes 4 103
(R Hannon) *swtg: in tch in midfield: rdn and effrt jst over 3f out: hrd drvn and outpcd over 2f out: plugged on fnl f but nvr pce to threaten ldrs* **14/1**

1-11 **5** *3/4* **Aqwaal (IRE)**34 2077 3-8-12 94 RHills 8 102
(E A L Dunlop) *hld up in tch in midfield: rdn and unable qck wl over 2f out: swtchd lft and drvn 2f out: kpt on same pce* **6/1**3

21 **6** *3* **South Easter (IRE)**42 1822 3-8-12 105 NCallan 12 97
(W J Haggas) *lw: trckd ldrs: rdn and effrt over 2f out: drvn and wknd over 1f out* **7/2**1

210 **7** *1 1/4* **Native Ruler**36 2014 3-8-12 105 TPQueally 1 95+
(H R A Cecil) *lw: t.k.h early: chsd ldrs on outer: pushed along to chse ldr over 3f out: rdn to ld wl over 2f out: hdd wl over 1f out: fdd fnl f* **6/1**3

1-10 **8** *1* **Nehaam**36 2014 3-8-12 103 TPO'Shea 7 94
(J H M Gosden) *lw: t.k.h: hld up in rr: lost tch over 4f out: plugged on past btn horses fnl 2f: nvr nr ldrs* **16/1**

1-20 **9** *9* **Montaff**13 2705 3-8-12 106 DarryllHolland 6 79
(M R Channon) *t.k.h: hld up un rr: hmpd and stmbld after 2f: rdn 5f out: swtchd lft and drvn wl over 2f out: no prog: wl btn fnl 2f* **25/1**

1130 **10** *19* **Debussy (IRE)**13 2705 3-8-12 108 (p) JimmyFortune 2 49+
(J H M Gosden) *racd freely: led and swtchd sharply rt after s: hdd and flashed tail wl over 2f out: sn btn: eased ent fnl f: t.o* **15/2**

4440 **11** *3* **Hail Caesar (IRE)**14 2693 3-8-12 97 JAHeffernan 3 44
(A P O'Brien, Ire) *swtchd sharply rt after s: sn chsng ldr: rdn and lost 2nd over 3f out: wkng whn sltly hmpd wl over 2f out: wl btn and eased ent fnl f: t.o* **50/1**

442 **12** *3* **Beauchamp Xerxes**30 2176 3-8-12 101 DaneO'Neill 5 39
(G A Butler) *lw: plld hrd: hld up in rr: rdn and shortlived effrt 3f out: sn wl btn: eased ent fnl f: t.o* **25/1**

2m 27.37s (-5.13) **Going Correction** -0.10s/f (Good) **12** Ran SP% **119.6**
Speed ratings (Par 111): **113,110,110,108,108 106,105,104,98,85 83,81**
toteswingers: 1&2 £23.70, 1&3 £8.90, 2&3 £16.40 CSF £126.80 CT £648.89 TOTE £12.30: £3.60, £5.40, £1.40; EX 169.30 Trifecta £995.70 Pool: £13496.41 - 10.03 winning units..
Owner K Abdulla **Bred** Juddmonte Farms Ltd **Trained** Newmarket, Suffolk
■ Henry Cecil's first Royal Ascot winner since 2002, but his 71st in all.
■ Stewards' Enquiry : Jimmy Fortune two-day ban: careless riding (Jul 3,5)

FOCUS

This wouldn't have been the strongest running in recent times, the three horses to have come from the Derby all getting well beaten at Epsom, but it was certainly one of the more open renewals. The early pace was just a steady one, but they really began to race leaving Swinley Bottom and the race was ultimately set up nicely for those who had raced off the gallop. The winner looks improved for the longer trip, with the second and fourth to form.

NOTEBOOK

Father Time ◆ was going better than any straightening for home and quickened in the style of a smart performer to go clear over a furlong out. He had shown very useful form in defeat on all three previous starts this season, being beaten just half a length when third in the Lingfield Derby Trial, and twice finishing ahead of today's runner-up on starts either side of that. Still looking green on occasions in those defeats, he was passed over by Queally in favour of Native Ruler, but there was money for him throughout the day and he finally put in the sort of performance many have been expecting all season. His sister Passage Of Time was a classy performer for connections and this one could really thrive in the latter part of the season. The St Leger is a possibility, and Ladbrokes make him a 6/1 chance, but he could make his Group 1 debut in the Grand Prix De Paris at Longchamp. (op 12-1 tchd 17-2)

Your Old Pal was finishing behind Father Time for a third time this season. Winner of a Listed contest at Newmarket in May, he was a bit below his best under a 5lb penalty last time, but this step up to 1m4f was clearly in his favour and he stayed on well for pressure to just take second. He never had that much room to operate in, but didn't get stopped in his run at any point and looks more than capable of winning a Group 3 contest at some stage, with the possibility of more to come. The Gordon Stakes may well be his next target. (op 12-1 tchd 16-1)

Black Bear Island(IRE), penalised for his win in the Dante, had run no sort of race when reportedly failing to handle the track in the Derby, would not have run on ground this fast before and he ran very creditably. He readily made his ground, but had to wait for a run and was then outpaced by the winner. One of the St Leger trials will no doubt be on the agenda. (op 4-1 tchd 11-2 and 6-1 in a place)

Free Agent, last year's Chesham winner, made a satisfactory reappearance when fourth behind an impressive winner in a Listed contest at Goodwood and it was no surprise to see him improve, keeping on right the way to the line having been unable to quicken on. He may come on again for this and looks capable of winning a race at Listed/Group 3 level this term. (op 12-1 tchd 11-1)

Aqwaal(IRE) was up in trip and grade and encountering genuine quick ground for the first time, but he was still going well passing the three and briefly looked set to come with a challenge when pulled out inside the two. He could find no extra and appeared to find the trip too far at this level. (op 13-2)

South Easter(IRE), the Dee Stakes winner, was a late defector from the Derby, having been found to be coughing, and the money came for him before the off. He had a nice position just in behind the pace and held every chance, but couldn't quicken from the two pole and eventually faded. It's possible he still wasn't quite back to his best, and, with this being just his third start, he looks worthy of another chance. (op 5-1)

Native Ruler has quite a reputation, with him being a good worker at home, and he stepped up on his maiden win when beaten just over four lengths in the Dante. He looked interesting on this rise in trip and went to the front on straightening for home, but was readily brushed aside by his stablemate and weakened from over a furlong out. It is unlikely we have seen the best of him and he could be the type to progress later in the season. (op 7-1 tchd 8-1)

Nehaam, who ran dreadfully in the Dante, made some late headway having got himself well behind and finished clear of the remainder. (op 20-1)

Montaff, who got a bit warm beforehand, was always going to struggle having been hampered early. (op 20-1)

Debussy(IRE) dropped out sharply having made a lot of the running, and it was worrying to see him flash his tail in the process. (op 10-1)

Hail Caesar(IRE) was most disappointing last time and struggled on this step back up in grade. (op 66-1 tchd 40-1)

Beauchamp Xerxes, ahead of Free Agent at Goodwood last time, refused to settle and didn't run his race. (op 20-1)

3088 CORONATION STKS (GROUP 1) (FILLIES) 1m (R)

3:45 (3:47) (Class 1) 3-Y-O

£154,698 (£58,642; £29,348; £14,633; £7,330; £3,678) **Stalls** High

Form RPR

31-1 **1** **Ghanaati (USA)**47 1698 3-9-0 114 RHills 6 120+
(B W Hills) *swtg: w'like: strong: trckd ldrs: bmpd jst over 2f out whn displaying explosive turn of foot: sn led: edgd rt ent fnl 2f: r.o powerfully appr fnl f: nvr in danger and wl in command after* **2/1**1

2 **2** *2* **Reggane**19 2521 3-9-0 0 (t) GMosse 7 115
(A De Royer-Dupre, France) *cmpt: hld up in rr: hdwy 2f out: swtchd lft whn nt clr run wl over 1f out: r.o to take 2nd and edgd rt ins fnl f: nt pce to get to wnr* **9/1**

1-54 **3** *2 1/4* **Rainbow View (USA)**14 2672 3-9-0 114 JimmyFortune 3 112+
(J H M Gosden) *hld up in rr: swtchd lft over 2f out: sn n.m.r whn trying to make hdwy: styd on to take 3rd fnl 100yds: nt trble front duo* **13/2**3

2-11 **4** *2* **Elusive Wave (IRE)**40 1918 3-9-0 117 C-PLemaire 1 105
(J-C Rouget, France) *broke wl: led for 1f: chsd ldr: plld out to chal whn bmpd jst over 2f out: sn outpcd by wnr: lost 2nd ins fnl f: wknd fnl 100yds* **4/1**2

-102 **5** *nse* **Lahaleeb (IRE)**26 2304 3-9-0 112 DarryllHolland 5 105
(M R Channon) *drvn jst after s: towards rr: pushed along 3f out: hdwy on outside over 2f out: hung lft whn chsd ldrs over 1f out: kpt on same pce fnl f* **16/1**

2-24 **6** *2 1/2* **Heart Shaped (USA)**47 1698 3-9-0 109 RichardHughes 9 99
(A P O'Brien, Ire) *hld up: hdwy on inner over 2f out: disp 2nd over 1f out but nt pce of wnr: wknd fnl 100yds* **12/1**

10-1 **7** *11* **Again (IRE)**26 2304 3-9-0 113 RyanMoore 10 74
(David Wachman, Ire) *lw: s.i.s: sn in midfield: niggled along at times: pushed along and effrt over 2f out: sn n.m.r and hmpd: wknd wl over 1f out* **8/1**

-101 **8** *3 1/4* **Nashmiah (IRE)**35 2057 3-9-0 105 NCallan 4 67
(C E Brittain) *lw: in tch: pushed along 4f out: wknd 2f out* **50/1**

1-05 **9** *10* **Chintz (IRE)**26 2304 3-9-0 106 JAHeffernan 8 44
(David Wachman, Ire) *led after 1f: set gd gallop after: abt 4 l clr 3f out: pushed along and hdd 2f out: sn wknd* **40/1**

50-1 **10** *13* **Baliyana (IRE)**40 1911 3-9-0 105 MJKinane 2 14
(John M Oxx, Ire) *strong: racd keenly on outside chsng ldrs: pushed along and wknd 3f out: eased whn wl btn over 2f out* **15/2**

1m 38.32s (-2.38) **Going Correction** -0.10s/f (Good) course record **10** Ran SP% **117.5**
Speed ratings (Par 110): **107,105,102,100,100 98,87,83,73,60**
toteswingers: 1&2 £4.90, 1&3 £3.30, 2&3 £12.70 CSF £21.46 CT £101.71 TOTE £3.30: £1.40, £2.30, £2.60; EX 26.50 Trifecta £181.70 Pool: £22721.95 - 92.49 winning units..
Owner Hamdan Al Maktoum **Bred** Shadwell Farm LLC **Trained** Lambourn, Berks

FOCUS

This race is a natural target for horses that have won or run well in the various versions of the 1000 Guineas, with both Russian Rhythm and Attraction following up their Newmarket wins this century. This year's line-up looked well up to standard with the winners of the English, Irish and French Guineas taking each other on and, with Chintz setting off at a strong pace, the track record was broken by 0.38sec. The winner looks capable of rating higher, and so probably is the second, who was showing improved form here, but the fourth was well below form.

NOTEBOOK

Ghanaati(USA) ◆ established herself as easily the best three-year-old miling filly in Europe currently, as she travelled well just behind the strong pace and destroyed her rivals once in line for home. She easily brushed off a bump as the fourth pulled out around the pacemaker, and she opened up a clear advantage which was only reduced once the race was almost over. She has plenty of speed but is from the family of Nashwan and Unfuwain, so can be expected to get another 2f at least if connections decide to step her up in trip. She is in the Falmouth Stakes, although that race is less than three weeks away, and she is also in the Sussex Stakes at the end of next month. (op 9-4 tchd 5-2)

Reggane ◆, the winner of a race for unraced fillies before finishing second in a Group 2 last time, made the step up in grade, running on late for second without ever looking like getting to the winner. She looks more than capable of winning at this level and the Prix D'Astarte at Deauville in August may offer a suitable opportunity. (op 10-1)

Rainbow View(USA), last season's outstanding juvenile filly but only fifth in the 1000 Guineas and fourth in the Oaks, put up a fine effort on ground which may not have entirely been in her favour, especially as she did not get the clearest of runs in the straight and got a bit warm beforehand. She has opportunities at various trips in the next month or so, although connections are keen to re-oppose the principals on easier ground. Official explanation: jockey said filly suffered interference in running (op 15-2 tchd 6-1 and 8-1 in places)

Elusive Wave(IRE), who won the Poule d'Essai des Pouliches from the subsequent Prix de Diane runner-up, got upset in the paddock beforehand and was unable to dominate as she has done of late. She chased the runaway leader into the straight but was beginning to feel the pinch when she bumped into the winner and bounced off as they tackled the pacemaker. To her credit she kept going but did not have things go her way. She is in the Falmouth Stakes but the Prix d'Astarte looks a more likely target. (op 3-1 tchd 9-2 and 5-1 in a place)

Lahaleeb(IRE), the winner of the Fred Darling and narrowly beaten by Again in the Irish Guineas, looks best on good or easier ground and has now been beaten on all four tries on fast. However, this genuine sort ran with credit, especially as she was off the bridle virtually from the start. Connections may opt to give her a break now and hope for more suitable ground in the autumn. (op 18-1 tchd 20-1)

Heart Shaped(USA), fourth in English Guineas and well suited by fast ground was another to come from the back of the field. She followed the winner through but, after getting into second place briefly at about the furlong marker, she weakened out of it in the last furlong. (op 16-1)

Again(IRE), the winner of the Irish 1000 Guineas by a neck from Lahaleeb with Chintz fifth, has looked best on soft ground and she was always struggling to go the pace on this fast surface. She is another who may now be put away for an autumn campaign. (tchd 7-1)

Nashmiah(IRE), the winner of two Listed races this season but only ninth in the English Guineas, had a good deal to find and, despite racing upsides the winner, was struggling before the home turn and is not up to this level. (tchd 40-1)

Baliyana(IRE), another front-runner and winner of Leopardstown 1000 Guineas Trial, had a bit to find on the bare form and, unable to get to the front, was on the retreat soon after halfway. She is likely to be dropped in class next time. (op 9-1 tchd 7-1)

3089 WOLFERTON H'CAP (LISTED RACE) 1m 2f

4:20 (4:22) (Class 1) (0-110,110) 4-Y-O+

£28,385 (£10,760; £5,385; £2,685; £1,345; £675) **Stalls** High

Form RPR

0-26 **1** **Perfect Stride**20 2476 4-9-5 108 RyanMoore 14 115
(Sir Michael Stoute) *t.k.h: chsd ldr for 2f: styd handy: chsd ldr again over 2f out: chal and clr w runner up 2f out: drvn fnl f: led towards fin* **8/1**3

-261 **2** *nk* **Moonquake (USA)**[37] 1986 4-9-0 **103**.................................... LDettori 11 109
(Saeed Bin Suroor) *lw: racd keenly: sn led: rdn and drew clr w wnr 2f out: hld on to narrow ld tl hdd and no ex towards fin* **11/2**[2]

0/0- **3** *½* **Salute Him (IRE)**[14] 2692 6-8-12 **101**............................ RichardHughes 4 106+
(A J Martin, Ire) *hld up towards rr: rdn and effrt 3f out: swtchd lft 2f out: gd hdwy over 1f out: chsd ldng pair jst ins fnl f: r.o and clsng fnl 100yds but nvr quite gng to rch ldrs* **10/1**

1643 **4** *1 ¾* **Re Barolo (IRE)**[25] 2342 6-8-13 **102**.................................. C-PLemaire 2 104+
(M Botti) *hld up wl bhd: stl disputing last pl wl over 2f out: swtchd lft 2f out: gd hdwy on outer over 1f out: wnt 4th ins fnl f: running on wl fin but nvr gng to rch ldrs* **14/1**

40-6 **5** *1* **Mores Wells**[33] 2118 5-9-2 **105**..(bt) GMosse 13 107+
(R Gibson, France) *hld up in rr: shkn up over 3f out: hanging rt but switching lft fr over 2f out: hmpd 2f out: sn swtchd lft to outer: stl hanging rt but styd on fnl f: nt rch ldrs* **12/1**

-050 **6** *nse* **Indian Days**[22] 2410 4-9-3 **106**... AlanMunro 10 105
(J G Given) *lw: w.w in tch: pushed along and effrt 3f out: nt clr run and hmpd 2f out: swtchd lft wl over 1f out: styd on fnl f: nvr gng to rch ldrs* **10/1**

50 **7** *1* **Perks (IRE)**[22] 2410 4-9-2 **105**.. JimmyQuinn 16 102
(J L Dunlop) *in tch on inner: effrt and hdwy wl over 2f out: drvn to chse clr ldng pair 2f out: no imp: one pce and lost 4 pls ins fnl f* **25/1**

3001 **8** *¾* **Dream Lodge (IRE)**[10] 2787 5-8-9 **98** 3ex..................... PaulHanagan 15 94
(R A Fahey) *t.k.h: hld up in midfield: rdn and unable qck 3f out: hdwy u.p over 1f out: kpt on but nvr gng pce to rch ldrs* **8/1**[3]

0222 **9** *2 ½* **Halicarnassus (IRE)**[14] 2677 5-9-7 **110**......................... SamHitchcott 7 101
(M R Channon) *bustled along leaving stalls: chsd ldr after 2f tl over 2f out: hung rt u.p and outpcd over 1f out: wknd fnl f* **9/1**

/6-4 **10** *3 ¾* **Baron De'L (IRE)**[54] 1546 6-9-0 **103**..........................(b) JAHeffernan 6 86
(Edward P Harty, Ire) *s.i.s: a bhd: reminder after 1f: rdn over 3f out: swtchd lft over 2f out: no real prog* **28/1**

-503 **11** *nk* **Alarazi (IRE)**[22] 2398 5-8-11 **100**.................................... TPQueally 8 83
(T G Mills) *in tch in midfield on outer: rdn and unable qck jst over 3f out: btn whn short of room and hmpd 2f out* **40/1**

3-41 **12** *nk* **Khateeb (IRE)**[16] 2606 4-9-5 **108**...(t) RHills 3 90
(M A Jarvis) *lw: t.k.h: hld up towards rr: rdn over 2f out: switching rt ent fnl 2f: nvr trbld ldrs* **16/1**

4-20 **13** *7* **Pinpoint (IRE)**[25] 2327 7-9-3 **106**... AdamKirby 9 74
(W R Swinburn) *w.w in tch in midfield: rdn and unable qck 3f out: wknd over 2f out* **16/1**

4020 **14** *6* **Kandidate**[55] 1525 7-9-3 **106**... SebSanders 5 62
(C E Brittain) *chsd ldrs: rdn jst over 3f out: wkng whn bmpd wl over 1f out: no ch and eased fnl f* **33/1**

1-13 **15** *3* **Stone Of Scone**[37] 1986 4-8-11 **100**.......................... JimmyFortune 12 50
(E A L Dunlop) *lw: chsd ldrs: rdn 3f out: sn struggling: wl btn and eased over 1f out: lame* **7/2**[1]

2m 3.24s (-3.76) **Going Correction** -0.10s/f (Good) **15** Ran SP% **126.8**
Speed ratings (Par 111): **111,110,110,108,108 108,107,106,104,101 101,101,95,90,88**
toteswingers: 1&2 £7.40, 1&3 £12.30, 2&3 £9.40 CSF £52.23 CT £463.46 TOTE £9.70: £2.90, £2.30, £3.60; EX 60.60 Trifecta £304.10 Pool £6966.35 - 16.95 winning units..
Owner Saeed Suhail **Bred** Bloomsbury Stud **Trained** Newmarket, Suffolk

FOCUS
There was a lack of progressive, unexposed runners in this Listed handicap, as can often be the case, but it is always a tough race to win. Not that many got into it, with the early pace being a steady one, and the front pair had it between them from well over a furlong out, both running slight personal bests.

NOTEBOOK
Perfect Stride contested last season's 2000 Guineas and has always been thought a fair bit of. An impressive winner off a 19lb lower mark on his one previous start in handicaps, he looked ready for a go at this trip when staying on late at Goodwood last time and always held a perfect sit under Moore. He was asked for his effort approaching the two and, having been level with Moonquake passing the furlong-marker, just managed to edge ahead in the final strides. He saw the trip out well and will now go back up in grade. (op 9-1 tchd 11-1 in a place)
Moonquake(USA) was 8lb higher than when winning at York last time and managed to set his own tempo. He raced enthusiastically and kicked inside the two, but couldn't shake off the winner and was worn down close home. This was a good effort. (op 8-1 tchd 5-1 and 9-1 in a place)
Salute Him(IRE) ◆ did best of those coming from off the pace, running on well inside the final quarter mile without quite being able to reach the front pair in time. He was 1lb higher than when winning at Navan earlier in the month and is clearly up to winning a decent prize off this sort of mark. (op 8-1 tchd 12-1)
Re Barolo(IRE) was still disputing last turning for home and was another to make up a good deal of ground in the final 2f. He had run well when third off this mark in the Zetland Gold Cup last month and is in the process of proving himself as good on turf as he is the all-weather.
Mores Wells was a really classy performer at three and four, but he had not done much in two starts in France for new connections. That said, his last run had been over 2m and he fared much better on this drop in trip, keeping on despite making things difficult for his rider by hanging. He clearly retains a fair amount of ability. (op 16-1)
Indian Days couldn't quicken sufficiently when asked to race on with the principals, briefly being short of room, and he would have preferred a faster pace. (op 16-1)
Perks(IRE), a stone higher than when last contesting a handicap, has been running well in Group races without suggesting he is quite up to winning one and he didn't fare too badly considering the ground would have been plenty quick enough. Official explanation: jockey said gelding hung left
Dream Lodge(IRE), shouldering a penalty for winning a 1m handicap at Ripon on his recent debut for the yard, kept on late without threatening to get into it.
Halicarnassus(IRE) has been back to something like his best of late, but was always going to do well to take this off top weight and he faded having been up there for a long way. (op 14-1 tchd 16-1 in places)
Baron De'L(IRE) received an early reminder and never got close enough to challenge. (op 20-1 tchd 33-1 in places and 40-1 in a place)
Stone Of Scone looked to have a major chance, but he sustained a serious tendon injury and might not run again. Official explanation: jockey said colt slipped on bend 3f out; vet said colt finished lame in front (op 4-1 tchd 9-2 in places)

3090 QUEEN'S VASE (GROUP 3) 2m
4:55 (4:55) (Class 1) 3-Y-O

£39,739 (£15,064; £7,539; £3,759; £1,883; £945) **Stalls** High

Form RPR

1-13 **1** **Holberg (UAE)**[35] 2029 3-9-1 99.. JoeFanning 9 108+
(M Johnston) *lw: in tch: effrt on inner whn n.m.r over 2f out: prog to ld 1f out: styd on wl to draw clr ins fnl f: fnd plenty* **7/1**[3]

2 *4* **Yankee Doodle**[28] 2252 3-9-1 96................................ RyanMoore 10 101
(A P O'Brien, Ire) *midfield: rdn and hdwy over 2f out: styd on and edgd rt ins fnl f: wnt 2nd fnl 75yds: nt trble wnr* **11/2**[2]

3-41 **3** *¾* **Mastery**[41] 1904 3-9-6 107.. LDettori 12 105
(Saeed Bin Suroor) *lw: trckd ldrs: effrt to ld briefly 2f out: kpt on u.p: one pce fnl 75yds* **7/1**[3]

-214 **4** *½* **Tactic**[27] 2275 3-9-1 86... RHills 1 99
(J L Dunlop) *midfield: hdwy on outer over 3f out: rdn to ld wl over 1f out: hdd 1f out: lugged rt u.p ins fnl f: no ex fnl 75yds* **14/1**

134 **5** *3 ¾* **Popmurphy**[35] 2029 3-9-1 99..........................(v[1]) JimCrowley 14 95
(K R Burke) *lw: racd keenly in midfield: rdn over 2f out: hdwy on outer over 1f out: hung rt and styd on ins fnl f: nt get to front quartet* **14/1**

2 **6** *nk* **Stately Home (IRE)**[35] 2029 3-9-1 0............................. CO'Donoghue 8 95
(A P O'Brien, Ire) *lw: hld up bhd: rdn over 2f out: no imp: swtchd rt over 1f out: styd on ins fnl f: nvr able to get to ldrs* **10/1**

-313 **7** *½* **Clowance House**[34] 2084 3-9-1 81.................................. TedDurcan 3 94+
(R Charlton) *swtg: led for 1f: chsd ldr after: rdn to ld 3f out: hung rt u.p over 2f out: sn hdd and btn: wknd ins fnl f* **12/1**

11-1 **8** *1 ½* **Lethal Glaze (IRE)**[32] 2138 3-9-1 83............................ RichardHughes 6 92
(R Hannon) *trckd ldrs: pushed along and outpcd over 2f out: wknd ins fnl f* **20/1**

21 **9** *1 ¼* **Sabotage (UAE)**[18] 2538 3-9-1 90..................................... EddieAhern 13 91
(M Johnston) *lw: in tch: rdn and nt qckn over 2f out: wknd 1f out* **8/1**

-622 **10** *4 ½* **Gibb River (IRE)**[25] 2323 3-9-1 83.............................. JimmyFortune 11 85
(P W Chapple-Hyam) *b. rrd jst bef s: n.m.r and bmpd sn after s: hld up: pushed along 3f out: no imp* **25/1**

241 **11** *4* **Talimos (IRE)**[12] 2738 3-9-1 0..(b[1]) SebSanders 7 80
(R M Beckett) *hld up: reminder over 9f out: chsd along over 5f out: wl btn over 1f out* **20/1**

41 **12** *16* **Dhushan**[25] 2323 3-9-1 97.. PhilipRobinson 4 61+
(M A Jarvis) *lw: led after 1f: racd freely: hdd 3f out: losing pl whn n.m.r and hmpd over 2f out: sn eased* **4/1**[1]

4105 **13** *12* **Haljaferia (UAE)**[8] 2850 3-9-1 74...................................... MartinDwyer 5 47
(D R C Elsworth) *hld up: rdn over 3f out: nvr a danger* **66/1**

6- **14** *63* **Lord Of The Flame**[273] 6075 3-9-1 0.................................. LukeMorris 2 —
(W De Best-Turner) *a bhd: rdn 6f out: t.o* **100/1**

3m 24.13s (-4.87) **Going Correction** -0.10s/f (Good) **14** Ran SP% **117.5**
Speed ratings (Par 109): **115,113,112,112,110 110,110,109,108,106 104,96,90,58**
toteswingers: 1&2 £8.90, 1&3 £8.10, 2&3 £7.50 CSF £41.58 CT £283.18 TOTE £9.90: £3.00, £2.20, £2.00; EX 60.10 Trifecta £440.10 Pool: £9700.55 - 16.31 winning units..
Owner Sheikh Hamdan Bin Mohammed Al Maktoum **Bred** Darley **Trained** Middleham Moor, N Yorks
■ Stewards' Enquiry : Joe Fanning four-day ban: careless riding (Jul 3,5-7)

FOCUS
A race for three-year-old stayers that Mark Johnston has dominated in the last ten years, having had four winners. He was doubly represented this time in what looked an open contest and recorded another success. The race has been rated on the positive side with the third setting the level.

NOTEBOOK
Holberg(UAE) ◆ overcame a troubled passage in the straight to run out a convincing winner in a time 1.39secs inside the previous course record. A three-time winner at up to 1m4f before finishing third in a 1m3f Hamilton Listed race (behind Stately Home), he proved well suited by the step up in distance and powered up the hill to score in the style of a horse who appreciated every yard of the trip. The St Leger will suit him distance-wise but it is debatable whether he has the class as yet. However, he looks the sort who can make up into a Cup horse next season. (op 8-1 tchd 9-1)
Yankee Doodle, also beaten by Stately Home, albeit on his debut this season, was another that proved well suited by the longer distance. He stayed on well in the last quarter-mile but the winner had already gone beyond recall. (op 7-1 tchd 15-2 in places)
Mastery, clear top on official ratings, having won Italian Derby last time out, was carrying a 5lb penalty for that. He tracked the leaders from the start and briefly got to the front 2f out but was soon overhauled and, although fighting back, was no match for the winner. (op 6-1 tchd 15-2 in places)
Tactic, fourth in a heavy ground handicap, was happier on this fast surface and looked the likely winner when going on inside the final 2f. However, he came to the end of his tether soon after and did not quite get home over this trip. (op 16-1)
Popmurphy, well beaten when fourth behind Stately Home and today's winner in a Hamilton Listed race last time, had a visor on for the first time. He was held up off the pace but could only stay on at the one speed in the straight. (op 12-1 tchd 11-1, 16-1 in places)
Stately Home(IRE) had beaten both of the first two here in their previous meetings but he was settled out the back and never got involved. He did not totally confirm his stamina but kept on and may have been better ridden closer to the pace. (op 7-1 tchd 11-1)
Clowance House had progressed for step up to 1m4f this season, finishing third behind Thursday's King George V Handicap runner-up last time, giving weight. He had given the impression he would stay this longer trip despite his pedigree being that of a middle-distance performer but, after being ridden positively, appeared not to last the trip. Always in the leading trio, he took the lead turning for home but could not go on and was headed at the quarter-mile pole. He hampered the winner as he drifted towards the rail and weakened fairly quickly from that point. 1m6f may prove to be his optimum distance. (tchd 14-1 in places)
Lethal Glaze(IRE), a progressive sort having won his last three races at up to an extended 1m3f, had never raced on fast and his pedigree was not that of a stayer. He tracked the leading group for a long way before tiring. (op 25-1)
Sabotage(UAE), the winner's stable companion, was runner-up in a maiden on his debut and an easy winner of a similar contest next time. He tracked the leading group throughout but was struggling from the home turn and was not given a hard race when his chance had gone. (op 10-1)
Gibb River(IRE) Official explanation: jockey said colt reared as stalls opened
Dhushan made the running but Philip Robinson was keen not to go too fast and his mount took a strong hold for most of the way. He appeared to still be travelling well taking the home turn, but was quickly in trouble when challenged and he was already beaten when badly hampered in the straight. A return to shorter should see him in a better light. Official explanation: jockey said colt ran too free (op 7-2 tchd 9-2 in places)

3091 BUCKINGHAM PALACE STKS (HERITAGE H'CAP) 7f
5:30 (5:33) (Class 2) (0-105,103) 3-Y-O+

£31,155 (£9,330; £4,665; £2,335; £1,165; £585) **Stalls** Centre

Form RPR

5004 **1** **Giganticus (USA)**[28] 2241 6-8-12 **91**................................. MichaelHills 4 106
(B W Hills) *racd stands' side: hld up bhd: stdy hdwy over 2f out: rdn and qcknd to ld ins fnl f: wl in command at fin: 1st of 17 in gp* **12/1**

3055 **2** *1 ¾* **Al Muheer (IRE)**[20] 2470 4-9-2 **95**..................................(b) SebSanders 2 105
(C E Brittain) *racd on stands' side: t.k.h: hld up in midfield: hdwy over 2f out: ev ch 2f out: hrd rdn to ld overall over 1f out: hdd and nt pce of wnr ins fnl f: 2nd of 17 in gp* **33/1**

64-4 **3** *1 ¼* **Redford (IRE)**[41] 1868 4-9-6 **99**................................... RichardHughes 10 106
(M L W Bell) *lw: racd on stands' side: swtchd lft and dropped in bhd after s: t.k.h: hld up in rr: smooth hdwy 2f out: trckd ldrs gng wl over 1f out: rdn and nt qckn ent fnl f: kpt on: 3rd of 17 in gp* **12/1**

1-13 **4** *hd* **Mutheeb (USA)**[23] 2385 4-9-9 **102**... LDettori 7 108
(Saeed Bin Suroor) *lw: racd stands' side: t.k.h: hld up in midfield: hdwy over 3f out: pressed ldrs and carried rt jst over 2f out: ev ch wl over 1f out tl one pce fnl 100yds: 4th of 17 in gp* **13/2**[1]

50-5 **5** *hd* **Racer Forever (USA)**[55] 1513 6-9-10 **103**..............(b) JimmyFortune 30 109+
(J H M Gosden) *racd far side: hld up in rr: hdwy 2f out: rdn and r.o to ld that gp fnl 100yds: unable to chal ldrs: 1st of 12 in gp* **50/1**

50-3 **6** *nk* **Golden Desert (IRE)**[28] 2241 5-8-10 **89**.................... JAHeffernan 12 94
(T G Mills) *racd stands' side: chsd ldrs: effrt u.p and edgd rt jst over 2f out: hrd rdn to ld overall wl over 1f out: sn hdd: no ex ins fnl f: 5th of 17 in gp* **16/1**

0-24 **7** *½* **Webbow (IRE)**[33] 2101 7-8-11 **90**.................................. DO'Donohoe 9 93
(N Tinkler) *mounted on crse and taken down early: racd stands' side: t.k.h: hld up towards rr: rdn 3f out: hdwy and swtchd lft wl over 1f out: pressed ldrs 1f out: one pce u.p after: 6th of 17 in gp* **50/1**

3-00 **8** *hd* **Shifting Star (IRE)**[20] 2474 4-9-2 **95**...............................(t) GMosse 11 98
(W R Swinburn) *racd stands' side: hld up towards rr: rdn and hdwy 3f out: chsd ldrs and drvn 2f out: one pce fr over 1f out: 7th of 17 in gp* **20/1**

-123 **9** *1 ¼* **Horatio Carter**[27] 2266 4-8-11 **90**......................................(p) NCallan 23 89
(K A Ryan) *lw: racd on far side: chsd ldrs: rdn to ld gp over 1f out: kpt on same pce fnl f: 2nd of 12 in gp* **33/1**

4-13 **10** *¾* **Something (IRE)**[13] 2707 7-9-2 **95**................... AdrianTNicholls 31 92
(D Nicholls) *racd far side: hld up in rr: rdn and hdwy on far rail jst over 2f out: no imp u.p fnl f: 3rd of 12 in gp* **12/1**

65-1 **11** *nk* **Swift Gift**[41] 1861 4-8-12 **91**... MartinDwyer 26 88
(B J Meehan) *racd far side: hld up in rr: got hdwy to join ldrs jst over 2f out: hung lft u.p and wknd ent fnl f: 4th of 12 in gp* **8/1**[2]

1104 **12** *1* **Mr Macattack**[20] 2470 4-8-7 **86**...................................... LukeMorris 24 80
(N J Vaughan) *racd on far side: hld up towards rr: hdwy 3f out: drvn and no prog 2f out: wknd ent fnl f: 5th of 12 in gp* **18/1**

5-25 **13** *3* **Wigram's Turn (USA)**[51] 1607 4-8-8 **87**....................(v) WilliamBuick 6 77
(A M Balding) *b. racd satnds' side: hld up towards rr: rdn and hdwy 3f out: pressed ldrs and edgd rt u.p 2f out: btn jst ins fnl f: eased fnl 100yds: 8th of 17 in gp* **40/1**

410 **14** *1 ¼* **Hustle (IRE)**[13] 2695 4-8-7 **86**...(bt[1]) JimmyQuinn 1 68
(Miss Gay Kelleway) *racd stands' side: in tch in midfield: rdn 3f out: hrd rdn and no hdwy 2f out: wknd over 1f out: 9th of 17 in gp* **50/1**

0/3- **15** *1 ¾* **Six Of Hearts**[18] 2553 5-9-3 **96**....................................(p) EddieAhern 29 74
(Cecil Ross, Ire) *racd far side: hld up in midfield: hdwy on far rail over 2f out: rdn 2f out: sn btn: 6th of 12 in gp* **33/1**

2-42 **16** *2* **Harrison George (IRE)**[35] 2059 4-8-12 **91**.................. PaulHanagan 18 63
(R A Fahey) *racd stands' side: in tch in midfield effrt u.p 3f out: wknd wl over 1f out: 10th of 17 in gp* **16/1**

56-0 **17** *nse* **South Cape**[14] 2669 6-8-8 **87**........................... StephenDonohoe 3 59
(G L Moore) *racd stands' side: chsd ldrs: rdn jst over 3f out: hung rt and wknd over 2f out: wl btn fnl f: 11th of 17 in gp* **22/1**

-111 **18** *½* **Mister Hardy**[42] 1821 4-9-1 **97**.................... FrederikTylicki(3) 19 68
(R A Fahey) *racd stands' side: swtchd lft s: in tch in midfield: effrt to chse ldrs and drvn over 2f out wknd wl over 1f out: 12th of 17 in gp* **9/1**[3]

012 **19** *hd* **Celtic Sultan (IRE)**[20] 2470 5-8-13 **92**.................... MickyFenton 25 62
(T P Tate) *racd far side: overall ldr tl 3f out: stl led far side tl over 1f out: sn wknd: 7th of 12 in gp* **22/1**

/406 **20** *3 ½* **Drawnfromthepast (IRE)**[20] 2474 4-9-0 **93**..................(t) ShaneKelly 28 54
(J A Osborne) *racd far side: chsd ldr tl over 2f out: wknd 2f out: wl bhd fnl f:8th of 12 in gp* **33/1**

2/0- **21** *½* **Seasider**[401] 2104 4-8-6 **85**.. RyanMoore 13 45
(Sir Michael Stoute) *racd stands' side: in tch in midfield: wknd and hung rt over 2f out: wl btn over 1f out: 13th of 17 in gp* **10/1**

340- **22** *nk* **Hurricane Spirit (IRE)**[342] 3973 5-8-8 **90**................ MarcHalford(3) 17 49
(J R Best) *swtg: racd stands' side: t.k.h: hld up in midfield rdn 3f out: sn struggling: wl btn over 1f out: 14th of 17 in gp* **66/1**

-000 **23** *hd* **Slugger O'Toole**[41] 1861 4-8-6 **85**.................................. JamesDoyle 21 43
(S C Williams) *racd far side: in tch: pushed along 4f out: drvn 3f out sn struggling: no ch fnl 2f: 9th of 12 in gp* **20/1**

00-5 **24** *nk* **Musaalem (USA)**[26] 2297 5-8-13 **92**.. RHills 14 49
(W J Haggas) *racd stands' side: chsd ldr tl led overall 3f out: hdd wl over 1f out: immediately btn: eased fnl f: 15th of 17 in gp* **14/1**

1201 **25** *¾* **Tartan Gigha (IRE)**[14] 2669 4-9-1 **94**................................. JoeFanning 22 49
(M Johnston) *racd far side: in tch in midfield: rdn 4f out: wknd over 2f out: wl bhd fnl f: 10th of 12 in gp* **33/1**

40-3 **26** *½* **Dhaular Dhar (IRE)**[41] 1861 7-9-6 **99**...................... DanielTudhope 20 53
(J S Goldie) *lw: racd far side: swtchd rt after s: a bhd: nvr on terms: 11th of 12 in gp* **16/1**

0-30 **27** *4 ½* **Clifton Dancer**[134] 416 4-9-2 **95**........................... RichardKingscote 8 37
(Tom Dascombe) *racd stands' side: led tl 3f out: sn rdn and edgd rt: wl bhd fr wl over 1f out: eased ins fnl f: 16th of 17 in gp* **50/1**

4-0 **28** *13* **Hanoverian Baron**[20] 2470 4-8-7 **91**.................... WilliamCarson(5) 27 —
(D Nicholls) *racd far side: chsd ldrs: rdn over 3f out: wknd u.p over 2f out: wl bhd and eased fnl f: t.o:12th of 12 in gp* **100/1**

14-0 **29** *16* **Silver Guest**[29] 2191 4-8-13 **92**.................................... SamHitchcott 15 —
(M R Channon) *racd stands' side: in tch tl lost pl qckly and dropped to rr 3f out: t.o fnl 2f: 17th of 17 in gp* **100/1**

1m 27.44s (-0.56) **Going Correction** +0.15s/f (Good) **29** Ran SP% **142.9**
Speed ratings (Par 109): **109,107,105,105,105 104,104,103,102,101 101,100,96,95,93 91,91,90,90,86 85,85,85,84,83 83,78,**
toteswingers: 1&2 £74.70, 1&3 £42.20, 2&3 £164.10 CSF £389.63 CT £4903.97 TOTE £17.50: £3.90, £11.00, £3.40, £2.60; EX 345.10 Trifecta £7038.80 Part won. Pool: £9511.90 - 0.50 winning units. Place 6: £177.29 Place 5: £109.57.
Owner DM James,Cavendish Inv Ltd,Matthew Green **Bred** Gaines-Gentry Thoroughbreds Et Al **Trained** Lambourn, Berks
■ Stewards' Enquiry : J A Heffernan two-day ban: used whip with excessive frequency (Jul 3,5)

FOCUS
This is always a devilishly difficult handicap and they split into two groups. There was a slightly bigger bunch on the stands' side, and, as had been the case in Thursday's Britannia, the winner came from that group. The form looks solid, with the winner back to something like his best and the placed horses rated close to their best.

NOTEBOOK
Giganticus(USA), 7lb lower than when last winning, is a real 7f specialist and he came right back to form. He made no show from a high draw in the race a year ago, but came with a strong run from over a furlong out and got well on top inside the final half furlong. He is a horse who thrives in the summer and will now bid to win the Bunbury Cup for a second time next month, having taken it in 2007. (op 16-1)
Al Muheer(IRE), twice a winner on the all-weather earlier in the year, has been running respectably back on turf and he produced a massive effort in second, running on right the way to the line for strong pressure. He has yet to win a handicap on turf and is another who looks likely to take his chance in the Bunbury Cup. (op 40-1)
Redford(IRE) ◆ has a touch of class and he was dropped in from the start. He was absolutely cruising with two to run, having been brought right across towards the stands' rail, but couldn't quicken when asked for his effort. He stayed on to just get third, though, and perhaps he was reluctant to fully let himself down on the fast going, as his wins have tended to come with cut in the ground. We have still to see the best of him. (op 14-1)
Mutheeb(USA), who had shown quality form in two starts this season and was making his handicap debut from a mark of 102, held every chance, despite being carried right, but he couldn't race on inside the final furlong. He ran well enough to suggest he is still going the right way. (op 7-1 tchd 6-1)
Racer Forever(USA), 2lb lower than when 11th in the race a year ago, 'won' the race on the far side, but wasn't quite on terms with the first few. He wasn't beaten far in the Bunbury Cup last year and is yet another bound to go to Newmarket again next month.
Golden Desert(IRE), who has a course and distance win to his name, ran reasonably on his reappearance at Newmarket and bettered that effort here. He may need to be dropped a little in the weights before winning again.
Webbow(IRE), a winner on his only previous try at 7f, hasn't really been shaping as though a drop in trip is what was needed and kept on late against the stands' rail. (tchd 66-1)
Shifting Star(IRE) is slowly coming back down the weights and he ran well on this first try at 7f since his juvenile days. (tchd 22-1)
Horatio Carter came through to lead the far-side group over a furlong out and ran well without quite lasting home. (tchd 50-1 in places)
Something(IRE), who had been declared for the Wokingham, made some late headway without ever threatening to challenge. (op 11-1 tchd 10-1)
Swift Gift, 6lb higher than when winning the Victoria Cup over course and distance on his reappearance, hung when put under pressure and was on the wrong side anyway. (op 12-1 tchd 14-1 in places)
Mr Macattack looked an interesting one for this race, following a couple of eye-catching runs, but he couldn't go through with his effort on the far side. (op 16-1 tchd 20-1 in places)
Wigram's Turn(USA) ultimately dropped away having come through for pressure two out. (tchd 50-1 in a place)
Harrison George(IRE) never got into it and was disappointing. (tchd 20-1 in places)
Mister Hardy showed up for a fair way but was under pressure and beaten two out. (op 12-1)
Seasider, returning from well over a year off and having only his fourth start, was never really in it and started to hang under pressure.
Musaalem(USA) was made more use of than may have been expected and stopped quickly once headed. (op 12-1 tchd 16-1)
T/Jkpt: Not won. T/Plt: £256.70 to a £1 stake. Pool: £447,354.91. 1,272.05 winning tickets. T/Qpdt: £37.10 to a £1 stake. Pool: £24,824.82. 495.00 winning tickets. DO

2588 AYR (L-H)
Friday, June 19

OFFICIAL GOING: Good (good to firm in places; 8.4)(both bends moved to minimum width - additional 10yds on all starts over 7f; rail moved across on straight course - racing on 18m fresh ground nearest to stands' rail)
Rail realignment increased distance on the round course by ten yards. races on straight course run on stands' side.
Wind: Fairly strong, half against Weather: Overcast

3092 WOODFORD RESERVE APPRENTICE H'CAP — 1m
6:10 (6:11) (Class 6) (0-55,55) 4-Y-O+ **£2,914** (£867; £433; £216) **Stalls** Low

Form — RPR

3200 **1** **King Of Legend (IRE)**[21] 2441 5-8-6 **52**....................(t) IJBrennan(5) 11 59
(A G Foster) *trckd ldrs: rdn to ld over 1f out: kpt on wl* **7/1**

5034 **2** *1 ¼* **Time To Regret**[21] 2441 9-9-0 **55**........................(p) AndrewHeffernan 4 59
(I W McInnes) *led to 1/2-way: led over 2f out to over 1f out: kpt on fnl f* **9/2**[3]

0600 **3** *1 ¾* **Wilmington**[4] 2968 5-8-5 **51**... JakePayne(5) 9 51
(Mrs J C McGregor) *midfield: effrt over 2f out: hdwy over 1f out: edgd lft and r.o fnl f* **20/1**

0-52 **4** *½* **Rain Stops Play (IRE)**[22] 2390 7-8-7 **48**........................ NSLawes 3 47
(N G Richards) *t.k.h: prom: outpcd over 2f out: rallied fnl f* **7/2**[2]

00-0 **5** *½* **Gifted Heir (IRE)**[163] 78 5-8-0 **46** oh1..................... NatashaEaton(5) 7 44
(A Bailey) *w ldr: led 1/2-way to over 2f out: drifted rt and no ex over 1f out* **16/1**

006- **6** *½* **Phantom Serenade (IRE)**[340] 4019 4-8-9 **50**.............. SoniaEaton 2 47
(M Dods) *t.k.h: hld up ins: rdn over 2f out: edgd lft over 1f out: kpt on fnl f* **13/2**

000- **7** *¾* **Whipma Whopma Gate (IRE)**[275] 6015 4-8-2 **50**........ NeilFarley(7) 12 45
(D Carroll) *bhd: effrt on outside over 2f out: carried rt over 1f out: no imp* **12/1**

8 *1 ¼* **Maranda (IRE)**[41] 1899 5-8-5 **51**............................ AdamCarter(5) 8 43
(Liam P Cusack, Ire) *cl up: ev ch fr 3f out to over 1f out: sn wknd* **14/1**

-012 **9** *2* **Botham (USA)**[9] 2812 5-8-12 **53**................................ MatthewLawson 6 40
(J S Goldie) *bhd: rdn over 3f out: drifted rt 2f out: nvr on terms* **3/1**[1]

-050 **10** *9* **Anduril**[24] 221 8-8-3 **49** ow1...................................(b) AnthonyBetts(5) 10 16
(I W McInnes) *s.s: a detached: c stands' side over 2f out: nvr on terms* **25/1**

1m 43.63s (-0.17) **Going Correction** -0.125s/f (Firm) **10** Ran SP% **120.1**
Speed ratings (Par 101): **95,93,92,91,91 90,89,88,86,77**
toteswingers: 1&2 £4.90, 1&3 £41.80, 2&3 £38.40 CSF £39.79 CT £626.01 TOTE £9.20: £2.80, £1.90, £8.50; EX 36.60.
Owner Joshua Snellings **Bred** Golden Vale Stud **Trained** Haddington, East Lothian

FOCUS
The 4mm of rain earlier in the day had changed the ground to good, good to firm in places, although the track had also been watered. Both bends had been moved to their minimum width, adding ten yards to all starts over 7f, while the stands' rail was moved out on the straight course bringing into play 18m of fresh ground nearest the stands' rail. A weak apprentice riders' handicap in which few had any worthwhile recent form. Weak form, the winner back to something like his old turf best.
Anduril Official explanation: jockey said gelding missed the break

3093 TAYLOR WIMPEY MAIDEN STKS — 7f 50y
6:40 (6:43) (Class 5) 3-Y-O+ **£3,885** (£1,156; £577; £288) **Stalls** Low

Form — RPR

32 **1** **Crime Writer (USA)**[9] 2805 3-9-3 0.............................. RoystonFfrench 6 76+
(M Johnston) *chsd ldrs: led 3f out: pushed clr fr 2f out* **4/5**[1]

6-20 **2** *5* **Liberty Trail (IRE)**[13] 2719 3-9-3 72............................ TonyHamilton 7 61
(I Semple) *led 2f: cl up: effrt and chsd wnr over 2f out: kpt on same pce fnl f* **11/1**

-005 **3** *1 ½* **Al Wasef (USA)**[16] 2589 4-9-7 65............................. GaryBartley(5) 1 59
(J S Goldie) *hld up on ins: hdwy over 1f out: kpt on fnl f: no imp* **12/1**

4 *nk* **Halcyon Dancer** 3-8-12 0.. PhillipMakin 5 51+
(M Dods) *hld up in tch: smooth hdwy to chse ldrs over 2f out: shkn up over 1f out: kpt on same pce* **28/1**

2-00 **5** *1* **Fifth Amendment**[27] 2265 3-8-12 63.......................... SladeO'Hara(5) 2 53
(A Berry) *prom: rdn over 2f out: sn one pce* **33/1**

6 *hd* **Lady Bluesky**[35] 6-9-2 0.. BMcHugh(5) 4 50+
(A C Whillans) *s.i.s: hld up: shkn up and hdwy fnl 2f: nvr nrr* **8/1**[3]

7 10 **Fine Silk (USA)** 3-8-12 0 TomEaves 8 20
(B Smart) *missed break: sn t.o: sme late hdwy to pass btn horses fnl 2f: nvr on terms* 14/1
0 8 2 1/2 **Yes Please**[136] 381 4-9-12 0 PJMcDonald 11 22
(K A Ryan) *s.i.s: hld up: rdn over 2f out: sn btn* 50/1
6 9 3 **Tahayab (ITY)**[23] 2375 3-8-12 0 RobertWinston 10 6
(M Johnston) *hld up: rdn 3f out: nvr on terms* 14/1
0 10 23 **Riley Queen Bee (USA)**[42] 1825 3-8-12 0 AndrewElliott 9 —
(K R Burke) *sddle slipped sn after s: led after 2f: hdd 3f out: sn lost pl* 13/2[2]

1m 32.39s (-1.01) **Going Correction** -0.125s/f (Firm)
WFA 3 from 4yo+ 9lb 10 Ran SP% 117.7
Speed ratings (Par 103): **100,94,92,92,91 90,79,76,73,46**
toteswingers: 1&2 £2.60, 1&3 £3.80, 2&3 £15.90 CSF £10.88 TOTE £1.80: £1.20, £2.20, £2.90; EX 6.60.
Owner Sheikh Hamdan Bin Mohammed Al Maktoum **Bred** Gainsborough Farm Llc **Trained** Middleham Moor, N Yorks

FOCUS
A weak maiden. There are doubts over what the second and third are currently capable of but the winner is progressing.
Riley Queen Bee(USA) Official explanation: jockey said saddle slipped

3094 BULLEIT BOURBON H'CAP 1m
7:15 (7:15) (Class 5) (0-70,67) 4-Y-0+ £3,885 (£1,156; £577; £288) Stalls Low

Form RPR
000- 1 **Tom Tower (IRE)**[295] 5420 5-7-13 50 oh3 ow2 JamieKyne(5) 6 68
(A C Whillans) *mde all: qcknd clr over 2f out: kpt on strly: unchal* 20/1
2610 2 8 **Forbidden (IRE)**[24] 2352 6-8-10 63 (t) JamesPSullivan(7) 5 63
(Daniel Mark Loughnane, Ire) *hld up last: hdwy on outside over 2f out: chsd wnr 1f out: no imp* 2/1[2]
000- 3 2 **Chin Wag (IRE)**[245] 6786 5-8-8 57 KellyHarrison(3) 4 52
(J S Goldie) *chsd wnr: rdn over 2f out: sn one pce* 11/2[3]
56-2 4 nse **Darfour**[16] 2594 5-8-9 60 GaryBartley(5) 1 55
(J S Goldie) *in tch: outpcd over 2f out: rallied fnl f: nvr nr ldrs* 7/4[1]
0004 5 1/2 **Cigalas**[22] 2391 4-9-7 67 PhillipMakin 7 61
(Mrs J C McGregor) *cl up tl rdn and outpcd fr 2f out* 6/1
50-0 6 16 **Mystical Ayr (IRE)**[2] 3019 7-8-7 53 RoystonFfrench 3 10
(Miss L A Perratt) *hld up in tch: rdn over 2f out: sn wknd: t.o* 9/1

1m 41.34s (-2.46) **Going Correction** -0.125s/f (Firm) 6 Ran SP% 114.1
Speed ratings (Par 103): **107,99,97,96,96 80**
toteswingers: 1&2 £11.10, 1&3 £15.70, 2&3 £2.40 CSF £61.70 TOTE £14.50: £3.20, £2.00; EX 132.40.
Owner Play Fair Partnership **Bred** C J Foy **Trained** Newmill-On-Slitrig, Borders

FOCUS
Not hard to pick holes in this form with the winner having shown nothing since he as a 2yo. The time was good for the grade though, and the runner-up came here in decent form.

3095 WALLACES EXPRESS SAINTS & SINNERS H'CAP 1m 5f 13y
7:45 (7:46) (Class 5) (0-75,72) 4-Y-0+ £3,412 (£1,007; £504) Stalls Low

Form RPR
011 1 **Chookie Hamilton**[25] 2315 5-8-13 69 JamieKyne(5) 1 77
(I Semple) *cl up: rdn over 2f out: styd on wl fnl f: led nr fin* 3/1[2]
-304 2 hd **Cote D'Argent**[13] 2725 6-8-9 60 RoystonFfrench 3 68
(L Lungo) *led: qcknd over 3f out: sn rdn: kpt on wl: hdd nr fin* 4/1[3]
/3-1 3 5 **Summer Soul (IRE)**[19] 2044 7-9-7 72 (p) RobertWinston 4 73
(Miss Lucinda V Russell) *prom: pushed along over 4f out: outpcd over 2f out: rallied over 1f out: nt rch first two* 5/1
00-1 4 1 3/4 **Ifatfirst (IRE)**[9] 2817 6-8-8 64 6ex GaryBartley(5) 6 64+
(J S Goldie) *t.k.h: hld up in tch: rdn and no imp whn nt clr run over 1f out: nvr rchd ldrs* 7/4[1]
00-5 5 11 **Kyber**[16] 2592 8-8-3 57 KellyHarrison(3) 5 38
(J S Goldie) *cl up tl edgd lft and wknd wl over 1f out* 17/2
11-0 6 4 1/2 **Orkney (IRE)**[89] 923 4-9-2 67 TomEaves 7 42
(Miss J A Camacho) *prom: rdn and outpcd whn hmpd over 3f out: sn struggling* 10/1

2m 54.67s (0.67) **Going Correction** -0.125s/f (Firm) 6 Ran SP% 117.6
Speed ratings (Par 103): **100,99,96,95,88 86**
toteswingers: 1&2 £3.30, 1&3 £4.00, 2&3 £3.50 CSF £16.23 TOTE £3.50: £1.80, £2.50; EX 15.20.
Owner Hamilton Park Members Syndicate **Bred** D And J Raeburn **Trained** Carluke, S Lanarks

FOCUS
This had quite a competitive look about it on paper but it concerned only two from well over a furlong out. The winner improved in line with his best form of the last couple of years.
Kyber Official explanation: jockey said gelding hung left-handed throughout

3096 SAINTS & SINNERS H'CAP 6f
8:20 (8:20) (Class 4) (0-80,80) 3-Y-O £7,123 (£2,119; £1,059; £529) Stalls High

Form RPR
-430 1 **Grissom (IRE)**[35] 2058 3-8-6 70 ow1 SladeO'Hara(5) 5 75
(A Berry) *mde all: hrd pressed fnl 2f: hld on gamely* 9/1
6-11 2 hd **Dametime (IRE)**[5] 2958 3-8-8 74 (t) JamesPSullivan(7) 8 78
(Daniel Mark Loughnane, Ire) *trckd ldrs against stands' rail: nt clr run fr 1/2-way to over 1f out: ev ch fnl f: jst hld* 7/2[1]
1524 3 4 1/2 **Where's Reiley (USA)**[13] 2719 3-8-9 68 RobertWinston 6 58
(T D Barron) *dwlt: sn prom: nt clr run fr 3f to 2f out: effrt wl over 1f out: outpcd fnl f* 7/2[1]
3-43 4 1 1/4 **Blown It (USA)**[22] 2393 3-9-5 78 PhillipMakin 9 64
(I Semple) *dwlt: hld up: smooth hdwy and cl up 2f out: sn rdn and edgd lft: btn fnl f* 4/1[2]
0-21 5 3 1/4 **Musical Bridge**[16] 2603 3-8-10 74 DeanHeslop(5) 2 49
(Mrs L Williamson) *cl up tl rdn and wknd fr 2f out* 7/1
50-3 6 1 **Scrapper Smith (IRE)**[22] 2394 3-7-13 63 oh1 ow2 JamieKyne(5) 4 35
(A C Whillans) *w wnr tl wknd fr 2f out* 14/1
15-0 7 3 1/4 **Visterre (IRE)**[21] 2443 3-9-7 80 TomEaves 1 42
(B Smart) *in tch: drvn and outpcd over 2f out: sn btn* 12/1
0035 8 2 **Red Kyte**[18] 2544 3-9-2 75 TonyHamilton 3 30
(K A Ryan) *cl up tl wknd over 2f out* 13/2[3]

1m 13.16s (-0.44) **Going Correction** -0.125s/f (Firm) 8 Ran SP% 114.6
Speed ratings (Par 101): **97,96,90,89,84 83,79,76**
toteswingers: 1&2 £6.40, 1&3 £7.00, 2&3 £2.20 CSF £40.68 CT £132.83 TOTE £14.10: £3.40, £1.80, £1.50; EX 74.20.
Owner Jim & Helen Bowers **Bred** Michael McGlynn **Trained** Cockerham, Lancs

FOCUS
An ordinary handicap and the front two came clear. Sound enough form amongst the placed horses.
Grissom(IRE) Official explanation: trainer's rep said, regarding apparent improvement in form, that it had benefited from being gelded.

3097 LA BARRIQUE FINE WINES H'CAP 7f 50y
8:50 (8:50) (Class 4) (0-85,84) 4-Y-0+ £7,123 (£2,119; £1,059; £529) Stalls Low

Form RPR
-610 1 **Stellite**[21] 2453 9-8-0 66 KellyHarrison(3) 5 74
(J S Goldie) *hld up and bhd: smooth hdwy on ins to ld appr fnl f: rdn out* 14/1
0053 2 1/2 **Kiwi Bay**[13] 2695 4-9-1 78 PhillipMakin 4 85+
(M Dods) *prom: effrt and ev ch over 1f out: kpt on fnl f* 15/8[1]
0601 3 1 3/4 **Woodsley House (IRE)**[21] 2453 7-8-8 71 PJMcDonald 3 73
(A G Foster) *hld up: effrt over 2f out: kpt on u.p fnl f* 10/1
621 4 1 1/2 **Imprimis Tagula (IRE)**[17] 2576 5-8-9 72 (v) RobertWinston 2 70
(A Bailey) *chsd ldrs: led over 2f out to over 1f out: no ex ins fnl f* 9/2[3]
5-03 5 7 **Zabeel Tower**[16] 2589 6-8-7 70 (p) TonyHamilton 1 49
(R Allan) *prom: effrt over 2f out: wknd fnl f* 11/2
5264 6 1 **Jewelled Dagger (IRE)**[16] 2589 5-9-2 84 (b) PatrickDonaghy(5) 8 60
(I Semple) *chsd ldr: lft in ld after 3f: hdd over 2f out: wknd wl over 1f out* 10/1
1-25 7 13 **Errigal Lad**[13] 2695 4-9-0 82 (b) AmyRyan(5) 6 23
(K A Ryan) *t.k.h: led: hung bdly rt and hdd after 3f: sn struggling* 7/2[2]

1m 31.62s (-1.78) **Going Correction** -0.125s/f (Firm) 7 Ran SP% 115.4
Speed ratings (Par 105): **105,104,102,100,92 91,76**
toteswingers: 1&2 £6.80, 1&3 £14.40, 2&3 £5.70 CSF £41.53 CT £286.19 TOTE £17.00: £5.30, £1.70; EX 39.10.
Owner M Mackay, S Bruce, J S Goldie **Bred** Cheveley Park Stud Ltd **Trained** Uplawmoor, E Renfrews
■ Stewards' Enquiry : Phillip Makin caution: careless riding

FOCUS
A strongly run handicap with the winner coming from well off the pace. The second did best of those to chase the pace.
Stellite Official explanation: trainer's rep said, regarding apparent improvement in form, that the gelding had been better suited by the truer run race.
Errigal Lad Official explanation: jockey said gelding hung violently right-handed throughout

3098 TENNENTS LAGER H'CAP 1m 2f
9:20 (9:21) (Class 6) (0-65,64) 4-Y-0+ £3,070 (£906; £453) Stalls Low

Form RPR
2160 1 **Ibrox (IRE)**[129] 493 4-9-7 64 SilvestreDeSousa 7 72
(A D Brown) *midfield: rdn along 1/2-way: hdwy 2f out: led ins fnl f: drvn out* 9/2[3]
0-00 2 3/4 **Hawkit (USA)**[13] 2718 8-8-12 55 TomEaves 11 61
(P Monteith) *midfield: hdwy to ld over 1f out: hdd ins fnl f: r.o* 16/1
0-34 3 nk **Willyn (IRE)**[16] 2590 4-8-5 51 KellyHarrison(3) 9 56
(J S Goldie) *hld up: hdwy over 2f out: rdn and r.o fnl f* 15/2
-000 4 3/4 **Primo Way**[22] 2391 8-8-12 55 DuranFentiman 3 59
(D A Nolan) *hld up in midfield: hdwy over 2f out: kpt on same pce fnl f* 28/1
0-06 5 1/2 **Bivouac (UAE)**[14] 2666 5-9-5 62 RobertWinston 6 65
(G A Swinbank) *cl up: led over 2f out to over 1f out: one pce ins fnl f* 4/1[2]
-466 6 hd **Papa's Princess**[16] 2590 5-8-7 55 GaryBartley(5) 12 58
(J S Goldie) *hld up: hdwy over 2f out: kpt on same pce fnl f* 11/2
-003 7 1 1/2 **Island Music (IRE)**[13] 2724 4-9-1 63 JamieKyne(5) 1 63
(J J Quinn) *hld up: effrt over 2f out: kpt on wl fnl f: nvr able to chal* 10/3[1]
0021 8 1 1/4 **San Silvestro (IRE)**[13] 2718 4-8-9 57 (p) BMcHugh(5) 4 54
(Mrs A Duffield) *cl up: drvn over 2f out: wknd appr fnl f* 4/1[2]
0/5- 9 3 **Princess Of Aeneas (IRE)**[17] 2537 6-8-4 47 (p) AndrewElliott 8 38
(A G Foster) *dwlt: sn cl up: rdn and wknd over 2f out* 66/1
04 10 3/4 **Oh Landino (GER)**[16] 2594 4-8-5 48 RoystonFfrench 2 38
(P Monteith) *in tch on ins tl wknd fr 2f out* 28/1
60P- 11 7 **King Of Sparta (USA)**[246] 6753 4-8-5 48 PJMcDonald 10 24
(T J Fitzgerald) *led to over 2f out: sn wknd* 28/1

2m 12.18s (0.18) **Going Correction** -0.125s/f (Firm) 11 Ran SP% 126.1
Speed ratings (Par 101): **94,93,93,92,92 92,90,89,87,86 81**
toteswingers: 1&2 £25.20, 1&3 £9.10, 2&3 £13.10 CSF £75.93 CT £549.05 TOTE £7.40: £2.50, £4.50, £2.90; EX 169.10 Place 6: £99.00, Place 5: £31.06.
Owner sportaracing.com **Bred** Hellwood Stud Farm **Trained** Yedingham, N Yorks

FOCUS
A bunched finish to this low-grade handicap but fairly sound form, with the third the best guide. Ibrox showed himslef to be just as good on turf as Fibresand.
Island Music(IRE) Official explanation: jockey said filly ran flat
T/Plt: £286.50 to a £1 stake. Pool: £33,980.75. 86.58 winning tickets. T/Qpdt: £49.30 to a £1 stake. Pool: £3,443.30. 51.60 winning tickets. RY

2881 GOODWOOD (R-H)
Friday, June 19

OFFICIAL GOING: Good (good to firm in places on round course)
Races on mile course run over 22yards further than advertised.
Wind: Moderate, half against Weather: Mostly sunny

3099 BOOK IN ADVANCE FOR GLORIOUS GOODWOOD STKS (H'CAP) 1m 1f 192y
6:20 (6:22) (Class 5) (0-70,68) 3-Y-O £3,885 (£1,156; £577; £288) Stalls High

Form RPR
0-06 1 **Mejala (IRE)**[29] 2206 3-9-4 65 DaneO'Neill 15 74+
(J L Dunlop) *s.i.s: in rr tl rdn and hdwy 2f out: qcknd to ld ins fnl f: won gng away* 15/2[3]
-345 2 1 1/2 **The Hague**[25] 2320 3-9-2 63 RichardMullen 1 69
(J H M Gosden) *a.p on outside: rdn to ld 2f out: hdd ins fnl f: nt spd of wnr* 8/1
4501 3 1 3/4 **Sumani (FR)**[20] 2489 3-9-2 63 LPKeniry 6 66
(S Dow) *led tl hdd 2f out: kpt on u.p* 10/1
21-0 4 1 1/4 **Mykingdomforahorse**[39] 1932 3-9-7 68 DarryllHolland 13 68
(M R Channon) *a.p on ins: short of room and swtchd lft appr fnl f: kpt on one pce* 6/1[2]
400- 5 1 1/2 **Royal Max (IRE)**[222] 7257 3-8-6 53 RichardThomas 5 50
(C G Cox) *trckd ldr to 2f out: one pce after* 20/1
050- 6 nk **Kayfiar (USA)**[296] 5404 3-9-7 68 JosedeSouza 14 65
(P F I Cole) *in tch on ins: rdn over 2f out: one pce after* 10/1
210 7 1 1/4 **Sullenberger (IRE)**[18] 2548 3-9-6 67 TravisBlock 8 61
(J A Osborne) *hld up: rdn and hdwy over 2f out: sn no imp* 14/1
00-2 8 hd **Jachol (IRE)**[5] 2950 3-8-3 50 KirstyMilczarek 11 44
(W J Haggas) *s.i.s: sn mid-div: no hdwy ins fnl 3f* 9/4[1]

-000 **9** *nk* **Very Distinguished**[15] 2635 3-8-3 **55**........ NicolPolli(5) 4 48
(M G Quinlan) *s.i.s: a bhd* **20/1**

6-30 **10** *3/4* **Eddie Boy**[18] 2548 3-9-3 **64**........ SteveDrowne 16 56
(M L W Bell) *hld up: lost tch fr over 2f out* **6/1**[2]

6-50 **11** *26* **Bishop Rock (USA)**[17] 2567 3-8-13 **60**........(t) AdrianMcCarthy 9 —
(M H Tompkins) *prom: rdn over 3f out: eased sn after* **33/1**

0006 **12** *41* **Hit The Switch**[21] 2450 3-8-7 **57**........ KevinGhunowa(3) 7 —
(Patrick Morris) *t.k.h on outside: lost action over 3f out: eased: t.o: sddle slipped* **25/1**

2m 7.29s (-0.71) **Going Correction** -0.025s/f (Good) 12 Ran SP% **123.4**
Speed ratings (Par 99): **101,99,98,97,96 95,94,94,94,93 73,40**
toteswingers: 1&2 £6.10, 1&3 £8.60, 2&3 £7.00 CSF £65.56 CT £618.36 TOTE £7.80: £2.20, £2.30, £3.10; EX 48.20.
Owner Hamdan Al Maktoum **Bred** Shadwell Estate Company Limited **Trained** Arundel, W Sussex

FOCUS
A moderate handicap, but the form looks reasonable and can work out.
Mejala(IRE) Official explanation: trainer's rep said, regarding apparent improvement in form, that the filly is improving and was unsuited by the slow pace in its earlier race.
Sullenberger(IRE) Official explanation: jockey said gelding was denied a clear run
Jachol(IRE) Official explanation: jockey said gelding ran flat
Hit The Switch Official explanation: jockey said saddle slipped

3100 CHICHESTER CITY MAIDEN FILLIES' STKS — 1m 1f
6:50 (6:53) (Class 5) 3-Y-0+ **£4,533** (£1,348; £674; £336) **Stalls** High

Form RPR

5 **1** **Halling Gal**[21] 2433 3-9-0 0........ DarryllHolland 7 76
(W R Muir) *hld up: rdn whn short of room and swtchd lft over 1f out: drvn to ld cl home* **9/2**[3]

62-3 **2** *hd* **Queen Eleanor**[51] 1605 3-9-0 75........ RichardMullen 6 75
(J H M Gosden) *trckd ldrs: n.m.r over 2f out: led appr fnl f: rdn and hdd nr fin* **5/1**

42 **3** *1 1/2* **Silent Oasis**[14] 2679 3-9-0 0........ DaneO'Neill 8 72
(B J Meehan) *hld up: hdwy whn swtchd lft 2f out: r.o fnl f: nvr nrr* **5/2**[2]

5-3 **4** *1 1/2* **Kapsiliat (IRE)**[34] 2082 3-9-0 0........ TPQueally 2 69
(J Noseda) *t.k.h: hld up: effrt over 2f out: kpt on one pce* **8/1**

0-32 **5** *1 1/2* **Lonely Star (IRE)**[31] 2164 3-9-0 78........ LPKeniry 3 66
(D R Lanigan) *led after 1f: hdd & wknd appr fnl f* **9/4**[1]

6 *1/2* **Ebony Eyes** 3-9-0 0........ JimCrowley 1 65
(W J Knight) *in rr on outside: swtchd to ins over 3f out: nvr on terms* **14/1**

40 **7** *11* **Tisifone**[15] 2633 3-9-0 0........ RichardThomas 9 42
(C G Cox) *led for 1f: trckd ldr tl wknd 2f out* **33/1**

00-0 **8** *2* **Ma Patrice**[58] 1464 3-9-0 44........ KirstyMilczarek 4 38
(T D McCarthy) *s.i.s: sn in tch on outside: bhd fnl 3f* **150/1**

5-0 **9** *1* **Fleetwood Flame**[41] 1893 4-9-11 0........ AdrianMcCarthy 5 35
(W M Brisbourne) *t.k.h: prom tl rdn 3f out: sn wknd* **66/1**

1m 57.33s (1.03) **Going Correction** -0.025s/f (Good)
WFA 3 from 4yo 11lb 9 Ran SP% **117.1**
Speed ratings (Par 100): **94,93,92,91,89 89,79,77,76**
toteswingers: 1&2 £4.90, 1&3 £3.80, 2&3 £3.60 CSF £27.53 TOTE £6.60: £1.60, £1.70, £1.60; EX 26.10.
Owner David & Gwyn Joseph **Bred** Darley **Trained** Lambourn, Berks

FOCUS
A fair fillies' maiden, run at a slow pace but the form appears sound enough with those in the frame behind the winner close to their marks.

3101 GOODWOOD.COM MAIDEN AUCTION FILLIES' STKS — 6f
7:25 (7:27) (Class 4) 2-Y-0 **£5,180** (£1,541; £770; £384) **Stalls** Low

Form RPR

0 **1** **Cultured Pride (IRE)**[20] 2494 2-8-10 0........ SteveDrowne 3 70
(R Hannon) *led to over 2f out: pressed ldr and strly rdn to ld again post* **18/1**

6 **2** *shd* **She's Ok (IRE)**[29] 2207 2-8-8 0........ DarryllHolland 4 68
(C E Brittain) *w ldr: led over 2f out: rdn and hdd post* **5/1**[2]

3 *2 1/4* **Lady Darshaan (IRE)** 2-8-12 0........ LPKeniry 2 65+
(J S Moore) *chsd ldrs: sltly outpcd over 1f out: r.o again towards fin* **6/1**[3]

0 **4** *1 1/2* **Jessica Hayllar (USA)**[11] 2771 2-9-0 0........ TPQueally 5 62
(M L W Bell) *t.k.h: hdwy 2f out: kpt on fnl f* **12/1**

6 **5** *1/2* **Aintwogrand (IRE)**[6] 2906 2-8-6 0........ KirstyMilczarek 10 53
(M R Channon) *prom on outside tl rdn and wknd ent fnl f* **7/1**

6 *1 3/4* **Meer Und Wind (GER)** 2-8-10 0........ DaneO'Neill 6 52
(P R Webber) *outpcd and a towards rr* **7/1**

7 *1* **Goodwood Diva** 2-8-10 0........ JimCrowley 9 49
(J L Dunlop) *wnt rt s: in rr: effrt on outside over 2f out: wknd over 1f out* **9/2**[1]

44 **8** *nk* **Folletta (IRE)**[10] 2792 2-8-7 0........(p) RichardThomas 1 45
(R Hannon) *s.i.s: a bhd* **9/2**[1]

0 **9** *1* **Exceed Power**[17] 2563 2-8-11 0........ RichardMullen 8 46
(D M Simcock) *prom tl wknd appr fnl f* **8/1**

10 *14* **Princess Seren** 2-8-9 0........ AdrianMcCarthy 7 2
(B R Millman) *chsd ldrs to 2f out: wknd qckly* **20/1**

1m 13.42s (1.22) **Going Correction** -0.025s/f (Good) 10 Ran SP% **121.1**
Speed ratings (Par 92): **90,89,86,84,84 81,80,80,78,60**
toteswingers: 1&2 £21.70, 1&3 £19.40, 2&3 £9.40 CSF £109.75 TOTE £24.40: £6.70, £2.50, £2.10; EX 119.90.
Owner D G Churston & R E Greatorex **Bred** Stratford Place Stud **Trained** East Everleigh, Wilts

FOCUS
A modest fillies' maiden that is rated below the average for the grade.

NOTEBOOK
Cultured Pride(IRE) came with a sustained run against the near rail and just prevailed in a very tight finish. She beat only one home after being slow to stride in a Newbury maiden on her debut and looked the stable second string here, but nevertheless did the job in determined style and could go on to better things. (op 14-1 tchd 20-1)
She's Ok(IRE) ◆ was weak in the market and never went the pace when sixth of eight in a Sandown fillies' maiden on her debut. She looked much more professional here and ran an admirable race over this extra furlong. She seems to have a feisty attitude and should not have too much trouble taking a similar race (op 15-2)
Lady Darshaan(IRE) was backed from 20-1 to 6-1. She never really landed a telling blow on this debut but deserves plenty of credit because she took a fierce grip in the early stages, was denied a run when switched wide at a crucial stage, yet still managed to find a powerful finishing burst. (op 20-1 tchd 9-2)
Jessica Hayllar(USA) did well to stay on after pulling hard. She still has a bit to learn but this was a decent step forward from her debut. Official explanation: jockey said filly ran too free (op 11-1 tchd 8-1)
Goodwood Diva proved too green to do herself full justice, but better was clearly expected from her. (op 3-1)
Folletta(IRE) set the target for the others to aim at based on her fourth in a bunch finish at Salisbury last time. She had cheekpieces applied to help her concentrate but was on and off the bridle for most of the way, displayed quite a bit of tail movement and looked a very reluctant character. (op 3-1)
Princess Seren Official explanation: jockey said filly ran green

3102 TAURUS WASTE RECYCLING FILLIES' STKS (H'CAP) — 7f
7:55 (7:56) (Class 4) (0-85,84) 3-Y-0+ **£5,180** (£1,541; £770; £384) **Stalls** High

Form RPR

-302 **1** **Victoria Sponge (IRE)**[36] 2001 3-9-0 **76**........ DaneO'Neill 6 87
(R Hannon) *trckd ldr: led 2f out: in command thrght fnl f* **11/2**[3]

5-21 **2** *1 3/4* **Balaagha (USA)**[42] 1825 3-9-6 **82**........ PhilipRobinson 9 89
(M A Jarvis) *slowly away: hdwy on ins over 2f out: swtchd lft appr fnl f: sn wnt 2nd no imp ins fnl f* **13/8**[1]

2122 **3** *1* **Perfect Friend**[18] 2539 3-8-12 **74**........ LPKeniry 2 78
(S Kirk) *hld up: hdwy on outside 2f out: r.o fnl f: nvr nrr* **10/1**

-221 **4** *1* **Labisa (IRE)**[38] 1973 3-8-10 **72**........ SteveDrowne 7 73
(H Morrison) *t.k.h in mid-div: effrt 2f out: one pce after* **5/1**[2]

0520 **5** *1/2* **Al Sabaheya**[13] 2703 3-9-8 **84**........(b[1]) DarryllHolland 3 84
(C E Brittain) *led tl hdd 2f out: wknd fnl f* **12/1**

01- **6** *3 1/2* **Fleeting Star (USA)**[295] 5430 3-9-0 **76**........ TPQueally 8 67
(J Noseda) *in tch: rdn over 2f out: wknd ent fnl f* **8/1**

05-0 **7** *1/2* **The Jostler**[149] 232 4-9-13 **80**........ RichardMullen 4 72
(Mrs L Wadham) *trckd ldrs: rdn over 2f out: wknd fnl f* **20/1**

60-0 **8** *2 1/2* **Nice To Know (FR)**[11] 2768 5-9-7 **74**........ JimCrowley 5 59
(G L Moore) *slowly away: a bhd* **25/1**

5411 **9** *nk* **Oceana Blue**[13] 2695 4-10-0 **81**........(t) WilliamBuick 1 66
(A M Balding) *in tch on outside tl wknd wl over 1f out* **7/1**

1m 27.05s (-0.35) **Going Correction** -0.025s/f (Good)
WFA 3 from 4yo+ 9lb 9 Ran SP% **119.1**
Speed ratings (Par 102): **101,99,97,96,96 92,91,88,88**
toteswingers: 1&2 £2.20, 1&3 £10.30, 2&3 £5.60 CSF £15.34 CT £90.44 TOTE £6.60: £1.80, £1.30, £2.50; EX 19.10.
Owner Simon Leech **Bred** Corrin Stud & Peter McCutcheon **Trained** East Everleigh, Wilts

FOCUS
A competitive fillies' handicap, involving four last-time-out winners. The third sets the level and the form should work out.

3103 TOTEEXACTA STKS (H'CAP) — 1m 6f
8:30 (8:30) (Class 2) (0-100,95) 4-Y-0+
£11,215 (£3,358; £1,679; £840; £419; £210) **Stalls** Low

Form RPR

03-4 **1** **Yes Mr President (IRE)**[13] 2698 4-8-8 **80**........ JoeFanning 9 93+
(M Johnston) *trckd ldr: led 3f out: wnt clr over 1f out: eased towards fin* **7/1**[3]

2-56 **2** *3 1/2* **Sevenna (FR)**[20] 2471 4-9-0 **86**........ TPQueally 5 92
(H R A Cecil) *chsd ldrs: wnt 2nd 2f out: kpt on but no ch w wnr fr over 1f out* **5/1**[2]

3-03 **3** *1 1/4* **Relative Strength (IRE)**[28] 2242 4-8-6 **78**........(v) WilliamBuick 6 83
(A M Balding) *a abt same pl: rdn over 2f out: kpt on but nt pce to chal* **5/1**[2]

0/04 **4** *2 1/4* **Aaim To Prosper (IRE)**[20] 2475 5-8-10 **82**........ DarryllHolland 3 84
(M R Channon) *mid-div: pushed along over 4f out: effrt over 3f out: one pce after* **8/1**

6-04 **5** *2* **Storyland (USA)**[13] 2706 4-9-3 **89**........ KirstyMilczarek 4 88+
(W J Haggas) *s.i.s: hdwy whn short of room on ins over 3f out: hmpd over 2f out: little ch after* **2/1**[1]

35-3 **6** *1/2* **Presbyterian Nun (IRE)**[72] 1191 4-9-9 **95**........ RichardMullen 2 93
(J L Dunlop) *hld up: t.k.h: nvr on terms* **10/1**

1-13 **7** *3/4* **Greenwich Village**[110] 723 6-8-9 **81**........ JimCrowley 10 78
(W J Knight) *led tl rdn and hdd 3f out: wknd qckly* **8/1**

-000 **8** *12* **Goodwood Starlight (IRE)**[20] 2475 4-8-13 **85**........ LPKeniry 1 65
(G L Moore) *a toiling wl in rr* **12/1**

2m 59.99s (-3.61) **Going Correction** -0.025s/f (Good) 8 Ran SP% **118.2**
Speed ratings (Par 109): **109,107,106,105,103 103,103,96**
toteswinger: 1&2 £6.30, 1&3 £3.40, 2&3 £4.60 CSF £43.20 CT £193.84 TOTE £5.90: £2.10, £2.10, £2.30; EX 46.20.
Owner T J Monaghan **Bred** T J Monaghan **Trained** Middleham Moor, N Yorks

FOCUS
A classy handicap and the form seems sound enough rated around the placed horses.

NOTEBOOK
Yes Mr President(IRE) absolutely slammed his opponents. He was always poised just behind the leader, eased his way to the front halfway up the straight and stormed clear. He had run an encouraging race on his reappearance at Doncaster earlier in the month but found a huge amount of improvement stepped up in trip on quicker ground. He looks a highly progressive type who should be capable of further success and should not have much trouble defying a penalty if turned out quickly. He holds an entry in the Cumberland Plate at Carlisle. (op 11-2)
Sevenna(FR) travelled well for a long way and stayed on gamely, but she was no match for the winner. She had been brushed aside twice since a winter break but probably did not find 1m4f far enough last time, and looked more convincing over this stiffer test. (op 13-2)
Relative Strength(IRE), back to form at Newmarket last time, ran a fair race over this longer trip, but his recent revival has not really gathered momentum. (op 11-2 tchd 6-1)
Aaim To Prosper(IRE) showed that a fair chunk of ability remains over 1m4f here last time but could not muscle his way into contention from off the pace over this more demanding test.
Storyland(USA) was cut off when making a move against the far rail on a couple of occasions and had no chance when she was finally extricated from the pocket. She is worth another chance next time. Official explanation: jockey said filly was denied a clear run (op 9-4 tchd 5-2)

3104 GOODWOOD 0800 018 8191 STKS (H'CAP) — 1m
9:00 (9:02) (Class 5) (0-70,70) 4-Y-0+ **£3,885** (£1,156; £577; £288) **Stalls** High

Form RPR

0225 **1** **My Shadow**[37] 1983 4-9-3 **66**........ DarryllHolland 4 75
(S Dow) *trckd ldrs: n.m.r over 2f out: swtchd lft ent fnl f: rdn to ld towards fin* **5/1**[2]

500- **2** *3/4* **Merrymadcap (IRE)**[61] 5935 7-9-2 **65**........ LPKeniry 8 72
(M Salaman) *trckd ldr: led over 2f out: rdn and hdd towards fin* **12/1**

3033 **3** *nk* **Ivory Lace**[7] 2883 8-9-7 **70**........ JimCrowley 5 76
(S Woodman) *hld up: hdwy on outside over 1f out: kpt on gamely but nt qckn* **5/2**[1]

40-2 **4** *3 1/4* **Tamasou (IRE)**[28] 2245 4-9-4 **67**........ TPQueally 3 66
(Garry Moss) *trckd ldrs: rdn 3f out: wknd fnl f* **5/2**[1]

20-2 **5** *3/4* **Vanadium**[14] 2686 7-8-12 **61**........ ShaneKelly 7 58
(G L Moore) *hld up in tch: rdn 2f out: wknd appr fnl f* **15/2**

5412 **6** *nse* **Teen Ager (FR)**[9] 2824 5-8-3 **52**........ LukeMorris 2 49
(P Burgoyne) *plld hrd: led tl hdd over 2f out: wknd fnl f* **6/1**[3]

0/0- **R** **Path To Glory**[8] 2795 5-8-2 **51** oh6..........................(b) KirstyMilczarek 10 —
(Miss Z C Davison) *ref to r* **11/1**
1m 40.15s (0.25) **Going Correction** -0.025s/f (Good) **7** Ran SP% **115.9**
Speed ratings (Par 103): **97,96,95,92,91 91,—**
toteswinger: 1&2 £13.60, 1&3 £3.80, 2&3 £6.80 CSF £61.38 CT £184.50 TOTE £6.70: £3.00, £4.90; EX 88.50 Place 6: £398.04, Place 5: £97.12.
Owner T G Parker **Bred** Millsec Limited **Trained** Epsom, Surrey

FOCUS
A modest handicap rated through the runner-up to last year's form with the third to her recent best.
Teen Ager(FR) Official explanation: jockey said gelding ran too free
T/Plt: £591.50 to a £1 stake. Pool: £49,428.59. 61.00 winning tickets. T/Qpdt: £247.70 to a £1 stake. Pool: £3,983.55. 11.90 winning tickets. JS

[3058] MUSSELBURGH (R-H)

Friday, June 19

OFFICIAL GOING: Good to firm (8.0)
Wind: Moderate half against Weather: Sunny periods

3105 RACING UK H'CAP 7f 30y
1:50 (1:54) (Class 6) (0-65,65) 4-Y-O+ **£2,590** (£770; £385; £192) **Stalls** High

Form RPR

0665 **1** **Summer Dancer (IRE)**[13] 2722 5-9-4 **62**.......................... PhillipMakin 4 77
(P T Midgley) *hld up in rr: hdwy on inner 2f out: rdn over 1f out: styd on strly to ld wl ins fnl f* **9/2**[1]

006- **2** *2* **Viva Volta**[269] 4875 6-9-2 **65**..................................(b) PatrickDonaghy(5) 11 75
(A C Whillans) *led: rdn over 2f out: drvn over 1f out: hdd and no ex wl ins fnl f* **10/1**

00-0 **3** *2 1/4* **Nufoudh (IRE)**[24] 2361 5-7-13 **46** oh1.......................... KellyHarrison(3) 7 50
(Miss Tracy Waggott) *chsd ldr: hdwy to chal over 2f out and sn rdn: ev ch tl drvn ent fnl f and grad wknd* **40/1**

2234 **4** *1/2* **Kargan (IRE)**[21] 2453 4-9-1 **59**.......................... RobertWinston 9 61
(A G Foster) *s.i.s and towards rr: hdwy on outer over 2f out: rdn to chse ldrs wl over 1f out: drvn and no imp ent fnl f* **11/2**[2]

6000 **5** *shd* **Sands Of Barra (IRE)**[7] 1475 6-8-13 **57**.......................... TomEaves 8 59
(I W McInnes) *chsd ldrs: rdn along wl over 2f out: drvn wl over 1f out: edgd rt and sn no imp* **22/1**

-042 **6** *1 1/2* **Infinity Bond**[21] 2453 4-9-6 **64**.. PJMcDonald 1 62
(G R Oldroyd) *in tch: hdwy to chse ldrs over 2f out and sn rdn: drvn wl over 1f out andsn btn* **11/2**[2]

0040 **7** *6* **Victory Spirit**[31] 2155 5-8-2 **46** oh1.......................... DuranFentiman 6 28
(D A Nolan) *chsd ldng pair: rdn along wl over 2f out: sn drvn and wknd* **50/1**

3643 **8** *1* **Beaumont Boy**[4] 2965 5-8-6 **50**..................................(b) TonyHamilton 5 29
(J A McShane) *a in rr* **7/1**[3]

-600 **9** *1/2* **Defi (IRE)**[18] 2532 7-8-10 **61** ow14..............................(bt) RossSmith(7) 12 39
(D A Nolan) *chsd ldrs to 1/2-way: sn wknd* **66/1**

/305 **10** *shd* **Tommy Tobougg**[9] 2817 5-8-5 **49**.......................... RoystonFfrench 3 26
(Miss Lucinda V Russell) *s.i.s: a bhd* **20/1**

000- **11** *2 3/4* **Mangano**[295] 5420 5-8-2 **46** oh1.......................... DarrenMoffatt 2 16
(A Berry) *sn rdn along and a in rr* **100/1**

1m 27.42s (-2.88) **Going Correction** -0.225s/f (Firm) **11** Ran SP% **86.5**
Speed ratings (Par 101): **107,104,102,101,101 99,92,91,91,91 87**
toteswinger: 1&2 £4.30, 1&3 £14.00, 2&3 £25.20 CSF £22.84 CT £533.30 TOTE £3.60: £1.80, £1.70, £7.90; EX 27.70.
Owner The Howarting's Partnership **Bred** Eddie O'Leary **Trained** Westow, N Yorks
■ Azure Mist (2/1F, ref to ent stalls) was withdrawn. Rule 4 applies to all bets - deduction 30p in the £.

FOCUS
A moderate handicap weakened by the withdrawal of the favourite Azure Mist who refused to enter the stalls. However, they went a good pace and the runner-up sets the level.

3106 SCOTTISH RACING MAIDEN AUCTION STKS 7f 30y
2:20 (2:24) (Class 6) 2-Y-O **£2,266** (£674; £337; £168) **Stalls** High

Form RPR

0 **1** **Pallantes Cross**[29] 2196 2-9-1 0.......................... RobertWinston 2 85+
(M Johnston) *mde all: sn clr: rdn over 1f out: kpt on* **5/1**

2 *1 3/4* **Mister Angry (IRE)** 2-8-13 0.......................... RoystonFfrench 3 79+
(M Johnston) *chsd wnr: effrt over 2f out and sn rdn: drvn and styd on ins fnl f: nt rch wnr* **3/1**[3]

5 **3** *8* **Dancing Poppy**[11] 2765 2-8-8 0.......................... EdwardCreighton 5 53
(M R Channon) *chsd ldng pair: effrt 3f out and sn rdn along: drvn: edgd lft and btn wl over 1f out* **9/4**[2]

4 *2 3/4* **Wing N Prayer (IRE)** 2-8-0 0 ow1.......................... JamieKyne(5) 4 43
(A Berry) *s.i.s and rr: hdwy over 2f out: sn rdn and no imp* **20/1**

5 *nk* **Lutine Bell** 2-9-1 0.......................... TomEaves 1 52
(Sir Mark Prescott) *s.i.s and towards rr: effrt 3f out: sn rdn along and n.d* **2/1**[1]

66 **6** *13* **Rightcar**[21] 2435 2-8-11 0.......................... PatrickMathers 6 14
(Peter Grayson) *t.k.h: chsd ldrs: rdn along wl over 2f out and sn wknd* **18/1**

1m 30.26s (-0.04) **Going Correction** -0.225s/f (Firm) **6** Ran SP% **115.8**
Speed ratings (Par 91): **91,89,79,76,76 61**
toteswinger: 1&2 £3.60, 1&3 £2.00, 2&3 £1.10 CSF £21.08 TOTE £7.70: £3.00, £2.70; EX 15.50.
Owner Mrs R J Jacobs **Bred** Newsells Park Stud **Trained** Middleham Moor, N Yorks

FOCUS
Not a great maiden, though the pace was sound and few ever got into it. In fact the order hardly changed throughout the contest and it resulted in a one-two for Mark Johnston, but it is hard to calculate the true merit of the form.

NOTEBOOK
Pallantes Cross had finished a tailed-off last of ten on soft ground on his Haydock debut, but despite market weakness he was a different proposition this time. Soon in front, his rider kicked him into a clear advantage off the home bend and he was in no danger from that point. Bred to be at his best over trips of around 1m and a colt with some scope, he is entitled to progress again and looks the type for nurseries. (op 3-1 tchd 11-2)
Mister Angry(IRE), a 22,000euros colt out of quite a useful winner at up to 1m2f in France, was always tracking his stable companion but although he did his best to bridge the gap, he could never do so. He should improve from this and may appreciate another furlong in due course. (op 7-2 tchd 5-1)
Dancing Poppy looked in need of the experience on her Pontefract debut and her two winning siblings, including the smart Medicea Sidera, both proved best over this trip, so improvement might have been expected and she was backed to build on that initial effort. However, although she was close enough early she failed to find much when put under pressure and will need to find further improvement if she is to win a race. (op 3-1 tchd 10-3)
Wing N Prayer(IRE), a 4,000euros yearling out of a dual winner at up to 1m, broke slowly and although she passed a couple late on she didn't show enough to suggest she will be winning anytime soon. (op 16-1)
Lutine Bell, a 20,000gns half-brother to three winners at up to 1m4f, was always near the back and looked as green as grass when asked to take closer order. He would hardly be the first juvenile from the stable to need much more time and the best of him is likely to be seen in handicaps over further next term. (op 11-4 tchd 13-8)
Rightcar, unplaced in two previous outings over the minimum, failed to improve for the longer trip and his stable continues to find winners very hard to come by. (op 16-1 tchd 14-1)

3107 RACING UK HORSERACING IN YOUR HOME H'CAP 1m 4f 100y
2:55 (2:55) (Class 5) (0-70,70) 4-Y-O+ **£3,885** (£1,156; £577; £288) **Stalls** High

Form RPR

5130 **1** **Forrest Flyer (IRE)**[5] 2944 5-8-12 **61**.......................... PhillipMakin 3 71
(I Semple) *trckd ldr: hdwy over 2f out and sn rdn: drvn over 1f out: led ent fnl f and styd on wl* **7/2**[3]

0511 **2** *2 1/2* **Baizically (IRE)**[13] 2720 6-9-7 **70**.......................... RobertWinston 1 76
(G A Swinbank) *led: edgd out bnd after 1f: pushed along 3f out: rdn 2f out: drvn over 1f out: hdd ent fnl f: no ex* **2/1**[2]

0632 **3** *1* **Grandad Bill (IRE)**[7] 2898 6-8-7 **59**.......................... KellyHarrison(3) 2 64
(J S Goldie) *stmbld bdly s: trckd ldng pair: hdwy 3f out: rdn and edgd rt 2f out: drvn and hung rt over 1f out: styd on wl towards fin* **11/10**[1]

-404 **4** *5* **Jane Of Arc (FR)**[21] 2448 5-7-9 **51** oh6..............(p) MatthewLawson(7) 4 49
(J S Goldie) *a bhd* **20/1**

2m 41.1s (-0.90) **4** Ran SP% **107.9**
CSF £10.62.
Owner Mrs Camille Macdonald **Bred** Philip Lau **Trained** Carluke, S Lanarks

FOCUS
Just the four runners, the pace was a modest one and the form looks muddling.

3108 MAPEI UK AND SCOTMAT CARPETS H'CAP 7f 30y
3:30 (3:30) (Class 6) (0-65,63) 3-Y-O **£2,590** (£770; £385; £192) **Stalls** High

Form RPR

5632 **1** **Northern Flyer (GER)**[13] 2719 3-8-10 **57**.......................... JamieKyne(5) 6 68+
(J J Quinn) *trckd ldrs: hdwy on inner 2f out: nt clr run and swtchd lft 1f out sn rdn and qcknd to ld ins fnl f: kpt on* **4/5**[1]

4201 **2** *1 1/2* **Minturno (USA)**[24] 2365 3-9-7 **63**.......................... RoystonFfrench 1 67+
(Mrs A Duffield) *dwlt and towards rr whn carried wd bnd after 2f: hdwy over 2f out: effrt and ntclr run over 1f out: swtchd rt and nt clr run ent fnl f: swtchd lft: rdn and r.o* **5/1**[2]

0-50 **3** *3/4* **Lost In Paris (IRE)**[50] 1626 3-9-3 **59**.......................(b[1]) DuranFentiman 4 61
(T D Easterby) *cl up: effrt over 2f out and sn rdn: led over 1f out: drvn and hdd ins fnl f: kpt on same pce* **9/1**

2604 **4** *2 1/2* **Cash In The Attic**[112] 707 3-8-7 **49**.......................... EdwardCreighton 10 44
(M R Channon) *chsd ldrs: rdn along over 2f out: drvn over 1f out and kpt on same pce appr fnl f* **16/1**

-400 **5** *nk* **Ask Dan (IRE)**[31] 2154 3-9-1 **57**..................................(p) TomEaves 8 51
(B Smart) *led: rdn along wl over 2f out: drvn and hdd over 1f out: wknd* **25/1**

4-65 **6** *1/2* **Quick Gourmet**[13] 2719 3-8-6 **53** ow2.......................... GaryBartley(5) 5 46
(J A McShane) *in tch whn rn wd bnd after 2f: effrt and hdwy on wd outside over 2f out: sn rdn and no imp fr over 1f out* **6/1**[3]

00-0 **7** *3/4* **Reel Bluff**[14] 2667 3-8-11 **53**.......................... TonyHamilton 7 44
(D W Barker) *chsd ldrs: rdn along over 2f out: drvn wl over 1f out and sn no imp* **66/1**

6000 **8** *1* **Meydan Groove**[4] 2967 3-8-0 **45**.......................... KellyHarrison(3) 2 33
(R Johnson) *t.k.h: chsd ldrs: hdwy on outer 3f out: rdn along over 2f out and sn wknd* **16/1**

0000 **9** *6* **Flynn's Island (IRE)**[10] 2790 3-8-9 **51** ow1..................(b) PhillipMakin 9 23
(M Dods) *a in rr* **28/1**

60-0 **10** *16* **Our Apolonia (IRE)**[28] 2250 3-8-9 **51**.......................... DarrenMoffatt 3 —
(A Berry) *a bhd* **100/1**

1m 29.24s (-1.06) **Going Correction** -0.225s/f (Firm) **10** Ran SP% **118.0**
Speed ratings (Par 97): **97,95,94,91,91 90,89,88,81,63**
toteswingers: 1&2 £2.40, 1&3 £1.60, 2&3 £11.20 CSF £4.95 CT £23.03 TOTE £2.10: £1.40, £1.30, £2.80; EX 6.40.
Owner N Chapman **Bred** A Pereira **Trained** Settrington, N Yorks

FOCUS
A poor handicap with eight of the ten runners maidens and the early pace was modest, resulting in a winning time 1.82 seconds slower than the older horses in the opener. The third is the best guide to the level.
Quick Gourmet Official explanation: jockey said filly hung left throughout

3109 TURFTV BETTING SHOP SERVICE (S) STKS 5f
4:10 (4:10) (Class 6) 3-Y-O+ **£1,942** (£578; £288; £144) **Stalls** Low

Form RPR

4063 **1** **Silvanus (IRE)**[13] 2717 4-9-4 67.......................... TomEaves 5 62
(I Semple) *cl up: effrt over 1f out: rdn to ld 1f out: drvn ins fnl f: hld on gamely* **11/4**[2]

-004 **2** *nk* **Dubai To Barnsley**[21] 2451 4-8-13 50.......................... GaryBartley(5) 1 61
(D A Nolan) *trckd ldrs on inner: swtchd rt and gd hdwy over 1f out: rdn to chal ent fnl f and ev ch tl drvn and nt qckn nr fin* **16/1**

3313 **3** *1 3/4* **Raccoon (IRE)**[8] 2840 9-9-10 73.......................... PJMcDonald 2 61
(Mrs R A Carr) *led: rdn along wl 2f out: hdd 1f out and kpt on same pce* **5/6**[1]

0642 **4** *1 1/2* **Creative (IRE)**[2] 3020 4-8-13 52..............................(v) JamieKyne(5) 4 49
(M H Tompkins) *chsd ldrs: effrt and cl up wl over 1f out: sn rdn and one pce appr fnl f* **7/2**[3]

0- **5** *9* **Alfie Lee (IRE)**[311] 4950 12-8-13 46..............(t) PatrickDonaghy(5) 3 17
(D A Nolan) *in tch: rdn along 1/2-way: n.d* **150/1**

00-0 **6** *4 1/2* **Mutayam**[21] 2451 9-8-11 36..(t) RossSmith(7) 6 1
(D A Nolan) *s.i.s: a in rr* **200/1**

000- **7** *2 1/2* **Throw The Dice**[294] 5452 7-8-13 40.......................... SladeO'Hara(5) 7 —
(A Berry) *sn outpcd and a in rr* **150/1**

60.15 secs (-0.25) **Going Correction** +0.025s/f (Good) **7** Ran SP% **111.1**
Speed ratings (Par 101): **103,102,99,97,82 75,71**
toteswinger: 1&2 £6.50, 1&3 £1.10, 2&3 £2.70 CSF £38.22 TOTE £3.00: £1.40, £3.80; EX 27.30.There was no bid for the winner.
Owner Kass Racing **Bred** Barronstown Stud And Mrs T Stack **Trained** Carluke, S Lanarks

FOCUS
A moderate seller and form to be sceptical about with the runner-up appearing to have run above himself.

3110 SCOTTISH RACING YOUR BETTER BET H'CAP 1m
4:45 (4:45) (Class 5) (0-70,71) 4-Y-0+ £3,252 (£955; £477; £238) Stalls High

Form RPR
6211 **1** **Mountain Cat (IRE)**[9] 2806 5-9-9 **71** 6ex.................... RobertWinston 3 79+
(G A Swinbank) *trckd ldng pair: hdwy 3f out: rdn to ld over 1f out: edgd rt ins fnl f: drvn out* **10/11**[1]
-550 **2** *1* **Grand Diamond (IRE)**[18] 2542 5-8-9 **62**....................(p) GaryBartley(5) 4 68
(J S Goldie) *trckd ldr: led over 3f out: rdn over 2f out: drvn and hdd over 1f out: n.m.r and swtchd lft ins fnl f: kpt on wl towards fin* **4/1**[2]
0251 **3** *3* **Kabis Amigos**[9] 2804 7-9-8 **70** 6ex..............................(b) TonyHamilton 1 69
(Ollie Pears) *hld up in tch: hdwy over 2f out: rdn to chse ldng pair over 1f out: sn drvn and kpt on* **10/1**
0005 **4** *1 3/4* **Fern House (IRE)**[18] 2532 7-8-2 **50** oh5.................. DarrenMoffatt 6 45
(Bruce Hellier) *chsd ldrs: rdn along and outpcd over 2f out: kpt on same pce u.p ins fnl f* **80/1**
0303 **5** *nk* **Ninth House (USA)**[9] 2804 7-8-5 **53**.......................(bt) PJMcDonald 5 47
(Mrs R A Carr) *s.i.s and bhd: hdwy on outer 3f out: rdn to chse ldrs wl over 1f out: sn drvn and wknd over 1f out* **12/1**
-505 **6** *nk* **Bold Indian (IRE)**[15] 2626 5-8-0 **53** ow1.......................... JamieKyne(5) 8 51+
(I Semple) *hld up: hdwy on inner over 2f out: rdn whn nt clr run and hmpd over 1f out: swtchd lft and styd on u.p ins fnl f: nrst fin* **5/1**[3]
131- **7** *38* **Shunkawakhan (IRE)**[224] 7226 6-9-2 **64**.....................(p) PhillipMakin 7 —
(Miss L A Perratt) *led: rdn along and hdd over 3f out: sn wknd* **10/1**

1m 40.1s (-1.10) **Going Correction** -0.225s/f (Firm) 7 Ran SP% **116.2**
Speed ratings (Par 103): **96,95,92,90,89 89,51**
toteswingers: 1&2 £1.30, 1&3 £1.70, 2&3 £4.40 CSF £5.04 CT £21.73 TOTE £2.10: £1.70, £3.20; EX 6.20.
Owner S Rudolf **Bred** Mrs Mary Gallagher **Trained** Melsonby, N Yorks

FOCUS
An ordinary handicap in which the pace was a fair one, though a couple were still inclined to take a grip early. The form is modest and the proximity of the fourth from out of the handicap limits things.
Bold Indian(IRE) ◆ Official explanation: jockey said gelding was denied a clear run

3111 TURFTV APPRENTICE H'CAP 5f
5:20 (5:21) (Class 6) (0-65,71) 4-Y-0+ £2,590 (£770; £385; £192) Stalls Low

Form RPR
2104 **1** **Rocketball (IRE)**[15] 2625 4-9-1 **58**............................ DeanHeslop(3) 1 66
(Mrs L Williamson) *mde all stands' rail: rdn along over 1f out: drvn ins fnl f and hld on wl* **7/1**[3]
3111 **2** *1/2* **Argentine (IRE)**[4] 2966 5-9-12 **71** 12ex.......................(b) JamieKyne(5) 8 77
(J A McShane) *chsd ldrs: rdn along on outer and edgd rt wl over 1f out: drvn and hdwy to chal ins fnl f: ev ch tl edgd rt and no ex nr fin* **5/6**[1]
3004 **3** *3/4* **Spirit Of Coniston**[9] 2801 6-8-8 **53**.......................... PaulPickard(5) 4 57
(P T Midgley) *trckd ldrs: hdwy 2f out: sn rdn and kpt on ins fnl f: nrst fin* **11/2**[2]
4300 **4** *1* **Distant Vision (IRE)**[4] 2964 6-8-4 **47**..................(b) PatrickDonaghy(3) 2 47
(H A McWilliams) *cl up: effrt over 1f out: sn rdn and ev ch tl drvn and wknd ins fnl f* **20/1**
400 **5** *1 1/2* **Blazing Heights**[13] 2717 6-9-7 **64**.............................. GaryBartley(3) 7 59
(J S Goldie) *in rr: hdwy wl over 1f out: sn rdn and no imp ins fnl f* **8/1**
0000 **6** *nk* **Mr Rooney (IRE)**[13] 2717 6-8-6 **49**............................ SladeO'Hara(3) 3 42
(A Berry) *in tch: rdn along 2f out and sn no hdwy* **40/1**
0520 **6** *dht* **Ridley Didley (IRE)**[14] 2657 4-9-2 **56**...................(t) RussellKennemore 5 49
(N Wilson) *chsd ldrs: rdn along wl over 1f out: sn one pce* **7/1**[3]

60.77 secs (0.37) **Going Correction** +0.025s/f (Good) 7 Ran SP% **113.3**
Speed ratings (Par 101): **98,97,96,94,92 91,91**
toteswingers: 1&2 £1.40, 1&3 £11.40, 2&3 £2.80 CSF £13.05 CT £34.60 TOTE £9.50: £2.50, £1.40; EX 16.50 Place 6: £207.26 Place 5: £75.55.
Owner J Levenson **Bred** John Morris **Trained** Saighton, Cheshire

FOCUS
A modest sprint handicap in which the winning time was 0.62 seconds slower than the seller, but still quite a dramatic contest. A personal best in this country from the winner and the runner-up is rated to his Carlisle form.
T/Plt: £206.50 to a £1 stake. Pool: £33,323.84. 117.80 winning tickets. T/Qpdt: £28.10 to a £1 stake. Pool: £2,476.05. 65.00 winning tickets. JR

2294 NEWMARKET (R-H)
Friday, June 19

OFFICIAL GOING: Good to firm
Wind: Fresh behind Weather: Overcast

3112 NEWMARKET NIGHTS APPRENTICE H'CAP 1m
6:00 (6:00) (Class 5) (0-70,70) 4-Y-0+ £3,885 (£1,156; £577; £288) Stalls Low

Form RPR
04-6 **1** **Sonny Parkin**[28] 2243 7-9-6 **69**..................................(v) SimonPearce(3) 6 74
(J Pearce) *hld up: hdwy over 2f out: swtchd rt over 1f out: rdn to ld nr fin* **11/2**[2]
0302 **2** *hd* **Amber Ridge**[20] 2473 4-8-5 **51** oh2.................................. JackDean 2 56
(B P J Baugh) *chsd ldrs: rdn to ld over 1f out: hdd nr fin* **14/1**
2000 **3** *1* **Sion Hill (IRE)**[20] 2473 8-8-0 **51**.............................(p) TobyAtkinson(5) 14 53
(John A Harris) *led: rdn and hdd over 1f out: no ex nr fin* **33/1**
030 **4** *3/4* **Direct Debit (IRE)**[7] 2880 6-9-2 **65**.............................. JPHamblett(3) 15 66
(M Wellings) *prom: lost pl 6f out: hdwy over 1f out: r.o* **11/2**[2]
3500 **5** *1 1/4* **Lord Theo**[4] 2975 5-8-13 **62**.. LeeNewnes(3) 10 60
(N P Littmoden) *hld up: hdwy over 1f out: r.o* **10/1**[3]
-534 **6** *2 1/4* **King Columbo (IRE)**[28] 2244 4-9-4 **67**.......................... RossAtkinson(3) 1 59
(Miss J Feilden) *chsd ldrs: rdn and ev ch over 1f out: wknd ins fnl f* **11/2**[2]
0000 **7** *nk* **Shake On It**[12] 2739 5-9-0 **60**.......................................(t) MCGeran 3 52
(M R Hoad) *rrd s: hdwy over 5f out: rdn over 2f out: sn edgd rt: styd on same pce fnl f* **33/1**
3300 **8** *1 1/2* **Guildenstern (IRE)**[56] 1493 7-9-4 **69**........................ CharlesEddery(5) 9 57
(P Howling) *hld up: hdwy over 3f out: sn rdn: wknd over 1f out* **33/1**
0-21 **9** *nk* **Focail Eile**[148] 255 4-9-8 **68**.. AndreaAtzeni 13 56
(Miss Gay Kelleway) *prom: rdn over 2f out: wknd over 1f out* **5/1**[1]
0260 **10** *nse* **Follow The Flag (IRE)**[14] 2665 5-9-3 **70**..................... JonathanHinch(7) 5 58
(A J McCabe) *s.i.s: sn pushed along in rr: styd on ins fnl f: nvr nrr* **11/1**
3305 **11** *2* **Aggravation**[4] 2977 7-9-6 **66**.. AmyBaker 16 49
(D R C Elsworth) *s.i.s: hld up: pushed along over 2f out: n.d* **5/1**[1]
0-0 **12** *1/2* **Sweet Kiss (USA)**[16] 2598 4-8-5 **56**..............................(p) KierenFox(5) 4 38
(M J Attwater) *prom: lost pl 1/2-way: n.d after* **25/1**
5603 **13** *1 3/4* **King's Ransom**[82] 1014 6-9-4 **67**................................ MatthewDavies(3) 11 45
(S Gollings) *s.i.s: sn mid-div: wknd over 2f out* **12/1**

1m 38.43s (-1.57) **Going Correction** -0.10s/f (Good) 13 Ran SP% **123.9**
Speed ratings (Par 103): **103,102,101,101,99 97,97,95,95,95 93,92,91**
toteswingers: 1&2 £15.50, 1&3 £62.60, 2&3 £52.20 CSF £80.17 CT £2389.73 TOTE £5.60: £2.10, £4.40, £12.00; EX 85.60.
Owner S & M Supplies (Aylsham) Ltd **Bred** Blenheim Bloodstock **Trained** Newmarket, Suffolk

FOCUS
A modest apprentice handicap and the form looks straightforward. They appeared to go a good, even gallop, although a following wind might have helped the prominent racers. They all raced far side.
Aggravation Official explanation: jockey said gelding never travelled

3113 PERI UP MAIDEN STKS 6f
6:30 (6:30) (Class 4) 2-Y-0 £5,180 (£1,541; £770; £384) Stalls Low

Form RPR
0 **1** **Extreme Warrior (IRE)**[20] 2477 2-9-3 0.........................(b[1]) ChrisCatlin 7 82+
(D R Lanigan) *s.i.s: sn prom: rdn over 1f out: r.o to ld wl ins fnl f* **40/1**
2 *2 1/4* **Black Snowflake (USA)** 2-9-3 0.................................. AhmedAjtebi(3) 10 75
(Saeed Bin Suroor) *chsd ldrs: led over 2f out: rdn and hung lft fr over 1f out: hdd wl ins fnl f* **4/1**[3]
3 *1* **The Human League** 2-9-3 0.. TonyCulhane 9 75+
(M R Channon) *chsd ldrs tl led 1/2-way: rdn and hdd over 2f out: sn hung lft: ev ch whn hmpd 1f out: styd on same pce* **10/1**
4 *hd* **Gunner Lindley (IRE)** 2-9-3 0.. GeorgeBaker 12 71+
(B W Hills) *swvd rt s: in rr: shkn up over 1f out: edgd lft and r.o ins fnl f: nrst fin* **12/1**
5 *1* **Cape D'Or (IRE)** 2-9-3 0.. PatDobbs 1 74+
(R Hannon) *w ldrs: rdn whn hmpd 1f out: nt rcvr* **9/4**[2]
3 **6** *3/4* **Opus Dei**[13] 2721 2-9-3 0.. PatCosgrave 8 66
(A J McCabe) *s.i.s: sn pushed along and prom: rdn over 1f out: styd on same pce* **2/1**[1]
7 *1 1/2* **Right Rave (IRE)** 2-8-9 0.. JackMitchell(3) 11 57
(P J McBride) *sn pushed along in rr: nvr nrr* **28/1**
0 **8** *3/4* **Public Service (IRE)**[20] 2467 2-9-3 0.................................. RobertHavlin 6 59+
(B J Meehan) *led to 1/2-way: hmpd 2f out: wknd fnl f* **16/1**
9 *1 1/4* **Edward Whymper** 2-9-3 0.. SaleemGolam 2 56
(M H Tompkins) *edgd rt s: outpcd* **66/1**
10 *1 3/4* **Kahail (USA)** 2-9-3 0... KShea 3 50
(Miss D Mountain) *hmpd s: sn prom: wknd over 1f out* **20/1**

1m 12.42s (-0.08) **Going Correction** -0.10s/f (Good) 10 Ran SP% **118.9**
Speed ratings (Par 95): **96,93,91,91,90 89,87,86,84,82**
toteswingers: 1&2 £24.40, 1&3 not won, 2&3 £10.10 CSF £193.52 TOTE £28.90: £6.00, £1.90, £2.00; EX 151.10.
Owner Saif Ali **Bred** Rabbah Bloodstock Limited **Trained** Newmarket, Suffolk
■ Stewards' Enquiry : Ahmed Ajtebi five-day ban: careless riding (Jul 3-7)

FOCUS
Quite a rough race for a few of these but this still looked a reasonable maiden and the third and fifth can be rated better than the bare form.

NOTEBOOK
Extreme Warrior(IRE) ◆ avoided all the trouble when produced a little wider than his main dangers and won decisively. He had shown nothing on his debut at Goodwood, but was a different proposition in first-time blinkers. A nice type physically, this colt, who was a very expensive yearling, should not be underestimated in better company. Connections think he might do even better with a bit of cut in the ground. (op 33-1)
Black Snowflake(USA), a $370,000 purchase out of a multiple sprint winner, took the eye on the way to the start and showed plenty of ability, but he wandered under pressure, hampering the third and fifth. Fitted with a sheepskin noseband for this debut, he clearly idled once in front and looks to have a lot of maturing to do before he can fulfil his potential. (op 5-1 tchd 6-1)
The Human League was hampered and is therefore a little better than he was able to show, although it's worth pointing out he didn't appear totally happy, looking to be hanging left and carrying his head at a slight angle for much of the way. This 72,000gns half-brother to 1m winner Noble Dictator is quite a big horse who looked as though the run would do him good, and it's possible slightly easier ground will help his cause. (op 9-1 tchd 8-1)
Gunner Lindley(IRE), a 19,000gns first foal of a 7f winner, was not best away and didn't pose a threat but he finished nicely. (op 11-1 tchd 10-1)
Cape D'Or(IRE), a 100,000gns half-brother to, among others, high-class 1m-1m2f performer Ransom O'War, was keeping on, although possibly just beginning to find one or two too strong when badly hampered against the far rail around a furlong out. Had it not been for that incident he would have finished closer and he's open to a deal of improvement, especially when upped in trip. (op 7-4 tchd 5-2 and 11-4 in places)
Opus Dei was always struggling after starting slowly and didn't build on his debut form, but he finished well enough to be given another chance. (op 11-4 tchd 3-1 in places)
Right Rave(IRE), the only filly in the race, ran green but showed ability. (op 66-1 tchd 25-1)

3114 NGK SPARK PLUGS H'CAP 1m 4f
7:05 (7:06) (Class 5) (0-75,72) 4-Y-0+ £3,885 (£1,156; £577; £288) Stalls Centre

Form RPR
440- **1** **Silent Applause**[222] 7261 6-9-0 **63**.. KShea 5 70
(Dr J D Scargill) *set stdy pce: qcknd over 2f out: rdn and hung lft ins fnl f: styd on* **11/2**[3]
/256 **2** *1 3/4* **La Rosa Nostra**[15] 2641 4-9-8 **71**..................................(t) PatDobbs 3 75
(W R Swinburn) *chsd wnr after 2f: rdn and edgd lft over 1f out: nt clr run ins fnl f: styd on* **7/1**
1212 **3** *3 1/4* **Saloon (USA)**[9] 2818 5-9-4 **72**..............................(p) AndreaAtzeni(5) 4 71+
(Jane Chapple-Hyam) *stdd s: hld up: shkn up over 2f out: rdn and hung lft over 1f out: r.o wl ins fnl f: too much to do* **9/4**[2]
0511 **4** *1* **Cwm Rhondda (USA)**[22] 2420 4-9-3 **69**........................ JackMitchell(3) 1 66
(P W Chapple-Hyam) *stdd s: hld up: hdwy over 2f out: rdn over 1f out: edgd rt and wknd ins fnl f* **15/8**[1]
0561 **5** *2 1/4* **Graylyn Ruby (FR)**[22] 2419 4-9-6 **69**................................... ChrisCatlin 6 63
(J Jay) *chsd wnr 2f: racd in 3rd pl thereafter tl rdn: edgd rt and wknd over 1f out* **8/1**
4002 **6** *8* **Apache Fort**[14] 2684 6-8-10 **59**.................................(b) TonyCulhane 8 40
(T Keddy) *prom: rdn over 2f out: wknd over 1f out* **12/1**
0366 **7** *6* **City Stable (IRE)**[13] 2708 4-8-4 **60**.......................... TobyAtkinson(7) 7 31
(M Wigham) *hld up: plld hrd: wknd wl over 1f out* **25/1**

2m 35.9s (3.00) **Going Correction** -0.10s/f (Good) 7 Ran SP% **116.1**
Speed ratings (Par 103): **86,84,82,82,80 75,71**
toteswingers: 1&2 £6.80, 1&3 £11.20, 2&3 £4.20 CSF £43.84 CT £111.35 TOTE £9.40: £4.20, £2.70; EX 43.50.
Owner J P T Partnership **Bred** R A Dalton **Trained** Newmarket, Suffolk

FOCUS
A modest handicap in which the winner was allowed to set a very steady pace and this is form to treat with caution.

City Stable(IRE) Official explanation: jockey said gelding ran too free

3115 SARAH WALLIS TO BE H'CAP 1m
7:35 (7:38) (Class 5) (0-75,75) 3-Y-O £3,885 (£1,156; £577; £288) Stalls Low

Form RPR

4301 **1** **Edgeworth (IRE)**[18] 2548 3-9-1 **67** GeorgeBaker 6 71
(B G Powell) *a.p: chsd ldr over 2f out: rdn and hung lft over 1f out: styd on u.p to ld towards fin* **14/1**

2362 **2** ¾ **Carbon Hoofprint**[8] 2845 3-9-5 **71** FergusSweeney 1 73
(P J Makin) *led: rdn over 1f out: hdd towards fin* **7/2**[2]

4-20 **3** *nk* **Hawk's Eye**[29] 2206 3-8-12 **69** (p) AndreaAtzeni(5) 2 71+
(E F Vaughan) *hld up: hdwy and nt clr run over 1f out: swtchd lft and carried hd high: nt clr run and swtchd rt ins fnl f: r.o wl nr fin* **12/1**[3]

2-00 **4** *nk* **Petsas Pleasure**[17] 2578 3-8-13 **65** RobertHavlin 11 66
(Ollie Pears) *hld up: hdwy and hung lft fnl f: r.o* **50/1**

0-00 **5** *1* **Sapphire Prince (USA)**[16] 2600 3-9-9 **75** J-PGuillambert 4 74
(J R Best) *chsd ldrs: hrd rdn over 1f out: no ex ins fnl f* **25/1**

-623 **6** *3* **Mutually Mine (USA)**[55] 1516 3-9-2 **68** JerryO'Dwyer 7 60
(Mrs P Sly) *hld up: rdn over 2f out: hdwy over 1f out: styd on same pce fnl f* **18/1**

23-0 **7** *1¼* **Striding Edge (IRE)**[59] 1434 3-9-1 **70** DavidProbert(3) 9 59
(W R Muir) *hld up in tch: rdn over 2f out: hung lft over 1f out: wknd ins fnl f* **25/1**

2-51 **8** *2* **Al Qeddaaf (IRE)**[8] 2863 3-9-5 **71** 6ex TPO'Shea 14 55
(W J Haggas) *stmbld s: hld up: rdn over 2f out: nvr nrr* **5/4**[1]

2130 **9** *hd* **Avoir Choisi (IRE)**[17] 2578 3-9-4 **73** JackMitchell(3) 16 57
(P W Chapple-Hyam) *prom: rdn: hung rt and wknd over 1f out* **12/1**[3]

2000 **10** *1¾* **Grand Honour (IRE)**[41] 1895 3-9-6 **72** PatCosgrave 3 52
(P Howling) *hld up: nt clr run over 2f out: n.d* **66/1**

-066 **11** *nk* **Caerus (USA)**[26] 2300 3-9-1 **67** (v) PaulDoe 8 46
(W J Knight) *chsd ldr tl rdn over 2f out: edgd lft and wknd over 1f out* **40/1**

565- **12** *nk* **Waahej**[310] 4974 3-9-2 **68** TonyCulhane 10 46
(J L Dunlop) *hld up: rdn over 2f out: n.d* **14/1**

160- **13** *1* **Sultans Way (IRE)**[263] 6344 3-8-13 **65** PatDobbs 15 41
(P F I Cole) *hld up in tch: racd keenly: rdn over 2f out: sn edgd lft and wknd* **28/1**

040- **14** ¾ **Big Nige (IRE)**[175] 7784 3-8-8 **67** SimonPearce(7) 12 41
(J Pearce) *hld up: a in rr: bhd whn hung lft over 1f out* **20/1**

0-01 **15** *24* **Night Knight (IRE)**[39] 1926 3-9-2 **68** (v) ChrisCatlin 5 —
(M L W Bell) *prom: rdn and wknd over 2f out: eased* **12/1**[3]

1m 38.59s (-1.41) **Going Correction** -0.10s/f (Good) **15** Ran SP% **130.1**
Speed ratings (Par 99): **103,102,101,101,100 97,96,94,94,92 92,91,90,90,66**
toteswingers: 1&2 £10.80, 1&3 £13.80, 2&3 £15.00 CSF £63.31 CT £645.77 TOTE £17.60: £4.00, £1.90, £4.90; EX 61.70.
Owner K Rhatigan **Bred** Yvonne & Gerard Kennedy **Trained** Upper Lambourn, Berks

FOCUS
A fair, competitive handicap run a decent enough pace. The fourth and fifth help set the level and the race could rate a little higher. They all raced far side.
Al Qeddaaf(IRE) Official explanation: jockey said gelding stumbled on leaving stalls and never travelled thereafter
Night Knight(IRE) Official explanation: jockey said gelding failed to quicken when asked closing stages

3116 INVESCO PERPETUAL H'CAP 7f
8:10 (8:10) (Class 3) (0-95,95) 3-Y-O+ £9,714 (£2,890; £1,444; £721) Stalls Low

Form RPR

21/ **1** **Captain Brilliance (USA)**[686] 4132 4-9-9 **90** AdamKirby 10 105+
(J Noseda) *racd stands' side: hld up: hdwy over 2f out: rdn to ld overall over 1f out: hung lft: r.o wl: eased nr fin* **11/1**

3203 **2** *2¼* **Thunderball**[18] 2544 3-7-12 **77** (v[1]) DavidProbert(3) 15 80
(A J McCabe) *racd stands' side: led those tl over 5f out: rdn to chse wnr over 1f out: hung lft: styd on: 2nd of 4 in gp* **10/1**

0410 **3** *1* **Pravda Street**[6] 2927 4-9-8 **89** (b) GeorgeBaker 13 92
(P F I Cole) *racd stands' side: chsd ldr tl led over 5f out: rdn and hdd over 1f out: hung lft: styd on: 3rd of 4 in gp* **8/1**[3]

-260 **4** *nse* **Masai Moon**[20] 2470 5-9-7 **91** JamesMillman(3) 11 94
(B R Millman) *racd far side: chsd ldrs: rdn to ld that gp and edgd lft over 1f out: styd on: 1st of 10 that side* **7/1**[2]

0420 **5** ½ **Credit Swap**[9] 2828 4-8-2 **76** TobyAtkinson(7) 8 78+
(M Wigham) *racd far side: hld up: hdwy over 1f out: r.o wl: nrst fin: 2nd of 10 in gp* **14/1**

11 **6** *1* **Lowther**[10] 2780 4-9-11 **92** 6ex NeilChalmers 3 91
(A Bailey) *racd far side: chsd ldrs: rdn and edgd lft over 1f out: styd on same pce: 3rd of 10 in gp* **4/1**[1]

-052 **7** ½ **Indian Art (IRE)**[9] 2826 3-8-7 **83** PatDobbs 4 78
(R Hannon) *racd far side: sn drvn along in rr: r.o ins fnl f: nrst fin: 4th of 10 in gp* **10/1**

10-4 **8** *hd* **Stalking Shadow (USA)**[39] 1942 4-9-9 **93** (t) AhmedAjtebi(3) 12 90
(Saeed Bin Suroor) *racd stands' side: chsd ldrs: rdn over 2f out: styd on same pce appr fnl f: last of 4 in gp* **8/1**[3]

1004 **9** ½ **Orpen Wide (IRE)**[9] 2822 7-9-0 **84** (b) LeeVickers(3) 1 80
(M C Chapman) *racd far side: chsd ldrs: rdn over 1f out: styd on same pce: 5th of 10 in gp* **20/1**

0220 **10** *4½* **Noble Citizen (USA)**[42] 1821 4-9-7 **95** (b) LauraPike(7) 5 79
(D M Simcock) *racd far side: overall ldr tl over 1f out: wknd ins fnl f: 6th of 10 in gp* **16/1**

-050 **11** ½ **Countdown**[9] 2828 7-8-13 **80** AlanMunro 6 62
(M D Squance) *racd far side: sn outpcd: no ch whn edgd rt ins fnl f: 7th of 10 in gp* **25/1**

31-0 **12** *3¼* **Rum Jungle**[21] 2434 5-8-13 **80** FrankieMcDonald 7 54
(H Candy) *racd far side: chsd ldr: rdn over 2f out: wknd over 1f out: 8th of 10 in gp* **12/1**

00-0 **13** ¾ **Basque Beauty**[41] 1860 4-9-8 **89** LiamJones 9 61
(W J Haggas) *racd far side: stdd s: a in rr: 9th of 10 in gp* **16/1**

143- **14** *6* **Transcend**[399] 2163 5-9-13 **94** RobertHavlin 2 49
(J H M Gosden) *racd far side: chsd ldrs tl rdn and wknd over 1f out: eased ins fnl f: last of 10 in gp* **8/1**[3]

1m 23.71s (-1.99) **Going Correction** -0.10s/f (Good)
WFA 3 from 4yo+ 9lb **14** Ran SP% **127.1**
Speed ratings (Par 107): **107,104,103,103,102 101,100,100,100,95 94,90,89,83**
toteswingers: 1&2 £54.80, 1&3 £12.50, 2&3 £24.90 CSF £123.23 CT £659.41 TOTE £9.60: £3.30, £5.00, £3.60; EX 191.20.
Owner Bluehills Racing Limited **Bred** John R Penn & John Combs **Trained** Newmarket, Suffolk

FOCUS
The first three home emerged from a group of four who raced towards the stands' side, well away from the others, but even so, Captain Brilliance created quite an impression. The form looks solid rated around those in the frame behind the winner.

NOTEBOOK
Captain Brilliance(USA) ◆ held entries in a host of big juvenile races when successful in a maiden at this track in August 2007, but he's clearly had some problems since then. A powerful individual, he very much took the eye beforehand, but did look as though the run would bring him on and he drifted significantly. However, in the race itself he travelled strongly throughout and displayed smart tactical speed to quickly take command of his small group when asked. He hung left once in front overall, possibly feeling the ground, or maybe just idling and wanting to join the bunch towards the far side of the track, but whatever, it didn't really halt his momentum. In fairness, he stopped hanging once in the middle of the track near the line, and despite his slight waywardness, he recorded a decent time, easily the quickest on the card. He's not too dissimilar in profile to stablemate Forgotten Voice and, like that one, he oozed class, very much looking potentially Group-race material. In the short term, however, his connections will surely look to plunder at least one big handicap, and the Bunbury Cup back over this course and distance next month is an obvious target. Provided he takes this race okay, and does indeed line up at the July meeting, it will take a very well-handicapped rival to stop him. (op 6-1 tchd 12-1)
Thunderball obviously had no chance with the winner but ran well nonetheless. (op 16-1)
Pravda Street ran reasonably, but he might be a slightly better horse with some give underfoot. (tchd 7-1 and 9-1)
Masai Moon elected to race far side, despite being drawn in a double-figure stall, and with the benefit of hindsight he might have been better joining the small group towards the stands' side. Whatever, this was a respectable effort, certainly better than his recent Doncaster showing. (op 9-1)
Credit Swap never got in a telling blow under his 7lb claimer but offered promise. He'll be one to keep on-side when there's money for him. (op 16-1)
Lowther, 2-2 since switching to the Flat, was 1lb wrong under his penalty and, not for the first time, got warm. He ran reasonably, but not quite as well as one might have expected. (tchd 9-2)

3117 NEWMARKETRACECOURSES.CO.UK MAIDEN STKS 1m 2f
8:40 (8:44) (Class 4) 3-Y-O £5,180 (£1,541; £770; £384) Stalls Centre

Form RPR

242 **1** **Time Machine (UAE)**[11] 2763 3-9-3 RobertHavlin 12 80+
(J H M Gosden) *chsd ldrs: rdn to ld wl ins fnl f: edgd lft: r.o* **6/1**

-224 **2** ¾ **Decision**[21] 2447 3-9-0 **86** DavidProbert(3) 5 78
(C G Cox) *led: rdn and edgd lft fr over 1f out: hdd wl ins fnl f* **7/2**[3]

2-23 **3** ½ **Times Up**[18] 2538 3-9-3 **80** TedDurcan 3 77
(J L Dunlop) *chsd ldrs: rdn over 1f out: styd on* **9/1**

4 *1¾* **Charger** 3-9-3 AdamKirby 14 74+
(J Noseda) *hld up in tch: effrt and swtchd lft over 1f out: one pce* **3/1**[1]

00 **5** *3* **Spensley (IRE)**[6] 2930 3-9-3 GeorgeBaker 13 68
(J R Fanshawe) *hld up: hdwy over 2f out: sn rdn: no ex fnl f* **25/1**

2 **6** ½ **Cotillion**[34] 2074 3-9-3 LiamJones 4 67
(W J Haggas) *dwlt: hld up: hdwy u.p over 2f out: nt rch ldrs* **10/3**[2]

0 **7** ¾ **Madison Park (IRE)**[28] 2240 3-9-3 (bt[1]) SebSanders 9 65
(H R A Cecil) *s.i.s: in rr: hrd rdn over 1f out: n.d* **16/1**

0-0 **8** *1* **December**[62] 1350 3-8-12 (t) Louis-PhilippeBeuzelin(5) 8 63
(Sir Michael Stoute) *hld up: hdwy over 1f out: nvr trbld ldrs* **25/1**

05 **9** *1* **Dream On Connie**[20] 2488 3-9-3 PaulDoe 11 61
(W J Knight) *plld hrd and prom: rdn over 1f out: sn wknd* **33/1**

10 *nse* **Laaheb** 3-9-3 TPO'Shea 7 61
(M A Jarvis) *hld up: n.d* **14/1**

0-6 **11** *12* **Desert Fever**[67] 1250 3-9-3 TonyCulhane 6 37
(B W Hills) *prom: rdn and wknd over 1f out* **33/1**

4-0 **12** *nk* **Sixties Gift (UAE)**[32] 2142 3-8-9 PatrickHills(3) 1 31
(Rae Guest) *hld up: rdn over 3f out: sn wknd* **66/1**

0-0 **13** *6* **Wolverton (IRE)**[22] 2395 3-8-12 LeeNewnes(5) 10 24
(N P Littmoden) *chsd ldrs tl wknd 3f out* **100/1**

5-0 **14** *1* **Fat Chance**[42] 1837 3-8-12 ChrisCatlin 2 17
(Rae Guest) *hld up: a in rr: wknd over 2f out* **25/1**

2m 6.37s (0.87) **Going Correction** -0.10s/f (Good) **14** Ran SP% **127.0**
Speed ratings (Par 101): **92,91,91,89,87 86,86,85,84,84 74,74,69,69**
toteswingers: 1&2 £6.90, 1&3 £1.60, 2&3 £12.80 CSF £27.28 TOTE £7.60: £2.60, £2.10, £3.30; EX 42.40.
Owner H R H Princess Haya Of Jordan **Bred** Darley **Trained** Newmarket, Suffolk

FOCUS
Quite an interesting maiden, but the pace was steady and those who raced handy were at an advantage. the placed horses set the standard.

3118 NEWMARKETEXPERIENCE.CO.UK H'CAP 5f
9:10 (9:10) (Class 5) (0-75,74) 3-Y-O £3,885 (£1,156; £577; £288) Stalls Low

Form RPR

4042 **1** **Red Rosanna**[1] 3053 3-9-5 **70** FergusSweeney 6 76
(R Hollinshead) *w ldr tl led over 1f out: edgd lft ins fnl f: r.o* **11/2**[2]

0005 **2** *1½* **Brynfa Boy**[3] 3010 3-8-7 **58** TonyCulhane 9 59
(P W D'Arcy) *hld up: r.o u.p ins fnl f: nt rch wnr* **11/2**[2]

1465 **3** *1* **Halaak (USA)**[7] 2882 3-8-9 **63** (b) AhmedAjtebi(3) 7 60
(D M Simcock) *hld up: hdwy 2f out: sn rdn: styd on* **11/2**[2]

3630 **4** *nk* **Keep Dancing (IRE)**[25] 2321 3-8-11 **65** (p) DavidProbert(3) 2 61
(A M Balding) *led: rdn and hdd over 1f out: styd on same pce ins fnl f* **6/1**[3]

4401 **5** ¾ **Deckchair**[109] 736 3-8-1 **57** (v) AndreaAtzeni(5) 8 51
(H J Collingridge) *sn pushed along in rr: r.o ins fnl f: nvr nrr* **10/1**

1601 **6** *2* **Hi Shinko**[17] 2562 3-9-6 **71** AlanMunro 1 57
(B R Millman) *w ldrs tl rdn over 1f out: wknd ins fnl f* **4/1**[1]

013 **7** *1¼* **Amosite**[36] 2005 3-9-9 **74** (v) TedDurcan 4 56
(J R Jenkins) *chsd ldrs: rdn 1/2-way: wknd fnl f* **8/1**

0011 **8** *nk* **Baby Queen (IRE)**[14] 2654 3-9-1 **66** J-PGuillambert 3 47
(B P J Baugh) *s.i.s: sn prom: rdn 1/2-way: wknd fnl f* **4/1**[1]

58.71 secs (-0.39) **Going Correction** -0.10s/f (Good) **8** Ran SP% **120.6**
Speed ratings (Par 99): **99,96,95,94,93 90,88,87**
toteswingers: 1&2 £31.90, 1&3 £12.80, 2&3 £63.50 CSF £37.74 CT £178.38 TOTE £7.60: £2.20, £3.20, £3.00; EX 49.20 Place 6: £2,511.91, Place 5: £475.14.
Owner Mrs Debbie Hodson **Bred** J R Mitchell **Trained** Upper Longdon, Staffs

FOCUS
A fair sprint handicap run at a predictably strong pace. A personal best from the winner with the runner up matching his maiden form.
Baby Queen(IRE) Official explanation: jockey said filly missed the break, trainer said filly was found to lost a front shoe
T/Plt: £16,096.80 to a £1 stake. Pool: £46,306.03. 2.10 winning tickets. T/Qpdt: £263.00 to a £1 stake. Pool: £4,620.90. 13.00 winning tickets. CR

2784 REDCAR (L-H)
Friday, June 19

OFFICIAL GOING: Good to firm (firm in places; 9.2)

Wind: fresh, half against Weather: overcast and blustery, heavy showers

3119 BUY YOUR TICKETS ON-LINE @ REDCARRACING.CO.UK (S) STKS — 7f
2:10 (2:13) (Class 6) 2-Y-O — £1,942 (£578; £288; £144) Stalls Centre

Form — RPR

60 **1** **Belle Eponine**[24] 2360 2-8-6 0 .... FrancisNorton 8 59
(E J O'Neill) *mde all: drvn rt out* **5/2**[1]

54 **2** 1 ½ **Go To Dubai**[10] 2788 2-8-6 0 .... DaleGibson 1 55
(M W Easterby) *chsd ldrs: rdn to chal over 1f out: styd on same pce ins fnl f* **5/2**[1]

6533 **3** 5 **Highcliffe Bridge (IRE)**[8] 2861 2-8-6 0 .... CatherineGannon 10 42
(P D Evans) *chsd ldrs: one pce appr fnl f* **4/1**[2]

00 **4** 2 **Treasury Bond**[28] 2231 2-8-11 0 .... JamieMoriarty 2 42
(P T Midgley) *in rr: hdwy over 2f out: kpt on fnl f* **20/1**

05 **5** 4 ½ **Pong Ping**[41] 1884 2-8-7 0 ow1 .... DavidAllan 13 26
(T D Easterby) *chsd ldrs: lost pl over 2f out* **14/1**

0 **6** ¾ **Feisty's Brother**[8] 2860 2-8-6 0 .... MartinLane(5) 6 28
(D M Simcock) *in rr div: kpt on fnl 2f: nvr on terms* **7/1**[3]

0 **7** 2 **Cygnet Committee (IRE)**[34] 2089 2-8-12 0 ow6 .... PAspell 11 24
(J S Wainwright) *chsd ldrs: wknd 2f out* **50/1**

8 5 **Moondarra Blade** 2-8-11 0 .... GrahamGibbons 4 10
(J R Weymes) *s.s and swvd lft s: rn green and sn bhd: t.o 3f out: sme late hdwy* **12/1**

0 **9** ½ **Fol Wizard**[10] 2788 2-8-11 0 .... PaulMulrennan 9 9
(P C Haslam) *chsd ldrs: sn drvn along: lost pl over 2f out* **66/1**

00 **10** 37 **Nuts About You (IRE)**[39] 1933 2-7-13 0 .... CharlotteKerton(7) 5 —
(A Berry) *dwlt: in rr: t.o 3f out* **100/1**

1m 26.09s (1.59) **Going Correction** +0.025s/f (Good) **10 Ran SP% 113.2**

Speed ratings (Par 91): **91,89,83,81,76 75,73,67,66,24**

toteswingers: 1&2 £2.10, 1&3 £1.90, 2&3 £2.40 CSF £8.02 TOTE £4.00: £1.50, £1.60, £1.60; EX 11.40.There was no bid for the winner.

Owner Mrs P A L Butler **Bred** P And Mrs A G Venner **Trained** Southwell, Notts

FOCUS

A shower before racing removed any jar from the ground. This was a very moderate seller in which the first three were always to the fore, and nothing else was able to become involved. They finished well spread out and the foirst two showed slight improvement.

NOTEBOOK

Belle Eponine was not disgraced in a couple of maidens over shorter and this drop in class enabled her to get off the mark. Travelling comfortably in front and shrugging off the challenge of the third, she took longer to overcome the runner-up but was nicely on top in the end. (op 9-4)

Go To Dubai, another descending into the bottom grade, finished clear of the rest when fourth over 6f here last time. She kept trying over this extra furlong but could never quite get to the favourite. (op 7-2 tchd 4-1)

Highcliffe Bridge(IRE) was third in this grade at Yarmouth on soft ground and she looks a reasonable guide to this form. (tchd 7-2)

Treasury Bond was beaten a long way in a couple of maidens and this looks more his level. (tchd 16-1 and 22-1)

Pong Ping, stepping up from 5f, was supported at big prices but could never trouble the leaders. (op 50-1)

Feisty's Brother, quicky dropped in grade, was again slow to break. He is related to several winners and should be capable of better. (op 4-1)

3120 REDCAR RACECOURSE FOR YOUR WEDDING VENUE MAIDEN STKS — 1m 2f
2:40 (2:43) (Class 5) 3-Y-O+ — £2,590 (£770; £385; £192) Stalls Low

Form — RPR

20- **1** **Yorgunnabelucky (USA)**[343] 3926 3-9-0 0 .... GregFairley 14 89+
(M Johnston) *w ldr: led on bit over 3f out: clr over 1f out: eased towards fin* **11/10**[1]

5 **2** 16 **Princess Aliuska**[16] 2613 4-9-7 0 .... JamieMoriarty 11 53
(Mrs S Lamyman) *mid-div: hdwy on outer to chse ldrs over 3f out: kpt on to take modest 2nd nr fin* **150/1**

0-52 **3** nse **Ithinkbest**[31] 2165 3-8-9 84 .... Louis-PhilippeBeuzelin(5) 15 58
(Sir Michael Stoute) *chsd ldrs: wnt 2nd over 2f out: one pce* **7/4**[2]

-320 **4** 3 ½ **Know By Now**[32] 2142 3-9-0 71 .... FrancisNorton 4 51
(T P Tate) *chsd ldrs: drvn over 4f out: one pce fnl 3f* **10/1**[3]

5 nk **Big Whitfield** 3-9-0 0 .... DaleGibson 2 51
(M Dods) *dwlt: in rr: hdwy over 3f out: nvr nr ldrs* **50/1**

03 **6** 2 **Young Star Gazer**[25] 2338 3-9-0 0 .... IanMongan 10 47
(H R A Cecil) *in tch: drvn over 3f out: one pce* **10/1**[3]

0 **7** 3 ¾ **Thornton George**[28] 2232 4-9-12 0 .... (b[1]) DavidAllan 7 40
(T J Fitzgerald) *in tch: drvn over 4f out: wknd over 2f out* **150/1**

64 **8** 1 ½ **Son Of Monsieur**[18] 2543 3-9-0 0 .... PaulMulrennan 1 37
(G R Oldroyd) *in rr: kpt on fnl 2f: nvr on terms: sddle slipped* **100/1**

00 **9** ½ **Lady Anne Nevill**[22] 2403 5-9-7 0 .... DNolan 5 31
(C W Fairhurst) *led tl over 3f out: lost pl over 2f out* **200/1**

44 **10** 2 ¾ **Bogula (IRE)**[16] 2613 3-8-9 0 .... AndrewMullen 6 26
(Mrs A Duffield) *in rr: nvr on terms* **33/1**

00- **11** 10 **Are Can (USA)**[321] 4616 3-9-0 0 .... (p) PAspell 12 12
(J S Wainwright) *swtchd lft s: in rr: bhd fnl 2f* **100/1**

0-6 **12** 2 ¾ **Special Adviser**[18] 2543 3-9-0 0 .... GrahamGibbons 3 7
(T J Etherington) *chsd ldrs: drvn over 4f out: sn lost pl* **150/1**

13 36 **Sally O'Riley** 3-8-9 0 .... PaulQuinn 8 —
(F Watson) *s.i.s: sn bhd: t.o 6f out: virtually p.u* **100/1**

2m 5.68s (-1.42) **Going Correction** -0.05s/f (Good)

WFA 3 from 4yo+ 12lb **13 Ran SP% 112.5**

Speed ratings (Par 103): **103,90,90,87,87 85,82,81,80,78 70,68,39**

toteswingers: 1&2 £44.90, 1&3 £1.02, 2&3 £17.90 CSF £237.66 TOTE £1.90: £1.10, £12.20, £1.20; EX 139.00.

Owner Mrs S J Brookhouse **Bred** March Thoroughbreds **Trained** Middleham Moor, N Yorks

FOCUS

This was essentially a match according to the market. The winner impressed and looked smart, though there was a doubt about what he beat with the third and fourth below par. Muddling form, held down by the runner-up.

Son Of Monsieur ◆ Official explanation: jockey said saddle slipped

3121 REDCAR RACECOURSE CONFERENCE & EVENTS VENUE H'CAP — 1m 2f
3:15 (3:15) (Class 5) (0-70,67) 4-Y-O+ — £2,590 (£770; £385; £192) Stalls Low

Form — RPR

-006 **1** **Trouble Mountain (USA)**[13] 2724 12-8-7 53 .... (t) DaleGibson 1 59
(M W Easterby) *sn trcking ldrs: drvn and outpcd over 3f out: styd on to go 2nd over 1f out: kpt on to ld towards fin* **20/1**

1-06 **2** nk **Eijaaz (IRE)**[17] 2569 8-9-4 64 .... SilvestreDeSousa 7 69
(G A Harker) *hld up: hdwy on outer over 3f out: led and edgd lft 2f out: hdd towards fin* **5/1**[3]

/100 **3** 6 **Mccormack (IRE)**[28] 2233 7-8-2 48 .... AndrewMullen 3 41
(Miss T Jackson) *trckd ldrs: led over 2f out: sn hdd: kpt on same pce* **9/1**

0555 **4** ½ **Just Observing**[9] 2803 6-8-11 57 .... (v) GrahamGibbons 2 49
(P T Midgley) *led tl over 2f out: one pce* **7/1**

2345 **5** 1 ¾ **Spirit Of France (IRE)**[7] 2894 7-9-7 67 .... DNolan 6 56
(D Carroll) *in rr: drvn 5f out: nvr a threat* **11/4**[2]

0-00 **6** 1 **Little Sark (IRE)**[30] 2181 4-8-10 56 .... CatherineGannon 8 43
(P D Evans) *w ldr: drvn 6f out: lost pl over 2f out* **20/1**

-121 **7** nk **Joinedupwriting**[17] 2569 4-9-2 62 .... PaulMulrennan 4 48
(R M Whitaker) *hld up: hdwy to trck ldrs 5f out: chal over 2f out: wknd over 1f out* **7/4**[1]

2m 5.81s (-1.29) **Going Correction** -0.05s/f (Good) **7 Ran SP% 111.7**

Speed ratings (Par 103): **103,102,97,97,96 95,95**

toteswingers: 1&2 £7.20, 1&3 £17.10, 2&3 £13.80 CSF £109.76 CT £963.90 TOTE £19.00: £4.30, £2.50; EX 83.70.

Owner Mrs Jean Turpin **Bred** Robert B Berger **Trained** Sheriff Hutton, N Yorks

FOCUS

A moderate handicap and it is hard to be positve about the form even though the first two finished clear. It was the slowest of the three C/D times.

Joinedupwriting Official explanation: trainer had no explanation for the poor form shown

3122 TRY RACE SPONSORSHIP AT REDCAR RACECOURSE H'CAP — 6f
3:55 (3:55) (Class 3) (0-95,94) 3-Y-O+ — £7,771 (£2,312; £1,155; £577) Stalls Centre

Form — RPR

6-12 **1** **Johannes (IRE)**[14] 2658 6-8-12 78 .... JamieMoriarty 9 88
(R A Fahey) *trckd ldrs: str run ins fnl f: led last strides* **11/4**[1]

4000 **2** hd **Benllech**[20] 2474 5-9-5 90 .... MartinLane(5) 5 99
(D M Simcock) *chsd ldrs: sn drvn along: led jst ins fnl f: hdd nr fin* **6/1**

110 **3** 1 **Jaconet (USA)**[13] 2716 4-9-3 86 .... (b) NeilBrown(3) 8 92
(T D Barron) *led tl hdd jst ins fnl f: kpt on same pce* **7/1**

1160 **4** 2 ¼ **Fol Hollow (IRE)**[13] 2704 4-10-0 94 .... PaulQuinn 10 93
(D Nicholls) *w ldrs: fdd jst ins fnl f* **11/2**[3]

3625 **5** 4 **Wyatt Earp (IRE)**[14] 2658 8-9-5 85 .... DaleGibson 4 71
(P Salmon) *chsd ldrs: wknd over 1f out* **15/2**

04-0 **6** 7 **Flash McGahon (IRE)**[20] 2502 5-9-12 92 .... FrancisNorton 2 56
(D Nicholls) *dwlt: in rr: lost pl over 1f out* **16/1**

1522 **7** 4 **Vhujon (IRE)**[9] 2814 4-9-3 88 .... RichardEvans(5) 3 39
(P D Evans) *in rr: rdn over 2f out: sn btn* **4/1**[2]

640- **8** 36 **Tabaret**[240] 6902 6-9-11 91 .... PaulMulrennan 7 —
(R M Whitaker) *stmbld and rdr lost irons s: taken wd to r alone far side: eased fnl 2f: virtually p.u: t.o* **16/1**

1m 10.87s (-0.93) **Going Correction** +0.025s/f (Good) **8 Ran SP% 112.4**

Speed ratings (Par 107): **107,106,105,102,97 87,82,34**

toteswingers: 1&2 £5.20, 1&3 £3.60, 2&3 £12.00 CSF £18.79 CT £101.76 TOTE £3.10: £1.40, £1.60, £2.90; EX 20.10.

Owner John Nicholls Ltd/David Kilburn **Bred** Blue Bloodstock Limited **Trained** Musley Bank, N Yorks

FOCUS

A good little sprint handicap in which the winner built slightly on his recent form.

NOTEBOOK

Johannes(IRE) is enjoying a successful season and he made it two wins and a second from three appearances, running on strongly once switched between horses and nailing the leader on the line. He will still be well handicapped on his old form after this and his yard continues in fine vein. (op 10-3)

Benllech came very close to posting a first turf win to go with his nine on Polytrack, but was just caught. He did nothing wrong. (op 9-2)

Jaconet(USA) disappointed in a hot race at Musselburgh on her bid for a four-timer and she returned to form here to show that she can still be competitive off this elevated mark. (op 6-1 tchd 15-2)

Fol Hollow(IRE), eighth to stablemate Indian Trail in the Epsom Dash last time, set the pace but could not counter when headed. (op 6-1 tchd 13-2)

Wyatt Earp(IRE) came away with a win on both his previous appearances at Redcar, including this race four years ago, but could not enhance that record. He has yet to wear the blinkers this season. Official explanation: trainer said gelding was found to be coughing on return home (op 17-2 tchd 12-1)

Flash McGahon(IRE) was slowly away and never in it. He will be interesting when the handiapper has dropped him a few more pounds and with the headgear back on. Official explanation: jockey said gelding slipped on leaving stalls

Vhujon(IRE) was slightly impeded early on when Tabaret, whose rider had lost his irons, went across him. Official explanation: jockey said gelding ran flat (op 9-2 tchd 7-2)

Tabaret, last year's winner, was effectively out of the race as soon as he had left the stalls. Official explanation: jockey said gelding stumbled and he lost his irons on leaving stalls (op 14-1)

3123 WIN A VIP DAY OUT @ REDCARRACING.CO.UK CLAIMING STKS — 1m 2f
4:30 (4:30) (Class 6) 3-Y-O+ — £2,047 (£604; £302) Stalls Low

Form — RPR

2124 **1** **Lucayan Dancer**[13] 2718 9-10-0 66 .... FrancisNorton 7 68
(D Nicholls) *in rr: hdwy over 3f out: sn rdn: styd on to ld jst ins fnl f: hld on towards fin* **11/2**

5006 **2** ¾ **Ming Vase**[4] 2965 7-9-2 49 .... GrahamGibbons 10 54
(P T Midgley) *prom: upsides 1f out: edgd rt and kpt on same pce* **14/1**

0-25 **3** 3 ¼ **Tufton**[35] 2043 6-9-7 77 .... LeeTopliss(7) 11 60
(R A Fahey) *s.s: gd hdwy on outside to ld over 2f out: edgd lft and hdd jst ins fnl f: sn wknd* **11/4**[1]

330- **4** 1 ¼ **Zaplamation (IRE)**[296] 5399 4-9-2 41 .... GregFairley 4 45
(D W Barker) *led tl over 2f out: one pce fnl f* **25/1**

1211 **5** 1 ¼ **Rowan Lodge (IRE)**[4] 2965 7-9-10 65 .... (b) JamieMoriarty 14 51
(Ollie Pears) *hld up in rr: effrt over 3f out: hung lft over 1f out: nvr rchd ldrs* **7/2**[2]

1001 **6** ¾ **Hollow Green (IRE)**[11] 2772 3-8-9 59 .... CatherineGannon 12 46
(P D Evans) *mid-div: hdwy to chse ldrs over 3f out: fdd over 1f out* **8/1**

0-30 **7** 2 **Ozone Trustee (NZ)**[12] 2743 5-9-8 78 .... DavidAllan 3 43
(G A Swinbank) *trckd ldrs: wknd appr fnl f* **5/1**[3]

-134 **8** 2 ¾ **Shekan Star**[15] 2629 7-9-3 54 .... PaulMulrennan 9 33
(K G Reveley) *in rr: hdwy on outer over 3f out: wknd over 1f out* **11/1**

0-60 **9** *13* **Indigo Belle (IRE)**[35] 2042 3-7-13 37........................(v[1]) AndrewMullen 5 1
(Mrs A Duffield) *chsd ldrs: wknd over 2f out* **100/1**

0000 **10** *9* **Lifetime Endeavour**[24] 2361 5-9-2 40...................................... DNolan 1 —
(R E Barr) *chsd ldrs: lost pl over 2f out: sn bhd* **100/1**

0-00 **11** *9* **Pennybid (IRE)**[14] 2656 7-9-2 36..(b) PAspell 13 —
(C R Wilson) *w ldrs: lost pl over 3f out: sn bhd* **150/1**

40- **12** *18* **Masking Baldini (IRE)**[434] 1304 5-9-12 43............ SilvestreDeSousa 15 —
(J Hetherton) *in rr: rdn over 4f out: sn bhd* **33/1**

2m 5.18s (-1.92) **Going Correction** -0.05s/f (Good)
WFA 3 from 4yo+ 12lb **12** Ran SP% **116.5**
Speed ratings (Par 101): **105,104,101,100,99 99,97,95,85,77 70,56**
toteswingers: 1&2 £12.70, 1&3 £4.70, 2&3 £12.20 CSF £75.49 TOTE £4.50: £1.50, £5.40, £1.30; EX 92.30.Rowan Lodge was subject to a friendly claim.
Owner James E Greaves **Bred** The National Stud Owner Breeders Club Ltd **Trained** Sessay, N Yorks

FOCUS
A routine claimer run at a fair pace and the pick of the C/D times. The second and fourth expose this as modest form for the grade.

3124 BODDINGTONS REDCAR STRAIGHT-MILE CHAMPIONSHIP (H'CAP) (QUALIFIER) 1m
5:05 (5:05) (Class 5) (0-75,74) 3-Y-0+ **£2,590** (£770; £385; £192) **Stalls** Centre

Form RPR

0022 **1** **King Pin**[13] 2722 4-8-11 57.. PaulMulrennan 10 66+
(Miss Tracy Waggott) *hld up: stdy hdwy over 2f out: edgd lft and styd on fnl f: led towards fin* **10/3**[1]

0630 **2** *¾* **Daaweitza**[22] 2402 6-9-11 74.. NeilBrown(3) 5 81
(B Ellison) *trckd ldrs: t.k.h: led over 1f out: edgd lft and hdd towards fin* **7/1**[3]

0033 **3** *1 ¾* **Kalasam**[21] 2440 5-9-4 64.. DaleGibson 6 67
(M W Easterby) *trckd ldrs: styd on same pce fnl f* **7/1**[3]

6526 **4** *¾* **Rosko**[24] 2362 5-9-5 65.. JamieMoriarty 11 66+
(B Ellison) *s.i.s: hdwy over 2f out: kpt on wl fnl f* **17/2**

0021 **5** *nk* **Aussie Blue (IRE)**[10] 2791 5-9-1 61 6ex.............................. PaulQuinn 9 62
(R M Whitaker) *chsd ldrs: one pce fnl 2f* **7/1**[3]

5004 **6** *¾* **Minority Report**[10] 2787 9-10-0 74.............................. AndrewMullen 1 73
(D Nicholls) *s.s: hdwy over 2f out: kpt on fnl f* **6/1**[2]

0006 **7** *1 ¾* **Moonage Daydream (IRE)**[9] 2804 4-9-0 60...................... DavidAllan 8 55
(T D Easterby) *prom: lost pl over 3f out: kpt on fnl f* **12/1**

0053 **8** *1 ¼* **Efidium**[10] 2791 11-8-9 60.. LanceBetts(5) 12 52
(N Bycroft) *t.k.h: w ldrs: led over 3f out: hdd over 1f out: sn wknd* **8/1**

2010 **9** *2* **Hilbre Court (USA)**[27] 2274 4-9-9 69......................(p) GrahamGibbons 4 56
(B P J Baugh) *w ldrs: lost pl over 1f out* **11/1**

0-40 **10** *2 ½* **Regal Lyric (IRE)**[18] 2544 3-9-0 70.............................. FrancisNorton 2 52
(T P Tate) *chsd ldrs: lost pl over 1f out* **9/1**

00-6 **11** *7* **Dolly No Hair**[16] 2594 4-8-9 55 oh2.............................. GregFairley 3 20
(D W Barker) *led tl over 3f out: edgd lft and wknd over 1f out: lame* **28/1**

1m 37.46s (-0.54) **Going Correction** +0.025s/f (Good)
WFA 3 from 4yo+ 10lb **11** Ran SP% **126.0**
Speed ratings (Par 103): **103,102,100,99,99 98,96,95,93,91 84**
toteswingers: 1&2 £6.30, 1&3 £3.50, 2&3 £9.90 CSF £28.78 CT £162.45 TOTE £3.60: £1.70, £2.40, £2.40; EX 43.00.
Owner H Conlon **Bred** Cheveley Park Stud Ltd **Trained** Spennymoor, Co Durham
■ Stewards' Enquiry : Jamie Moriarty one-day ban: used whip with excessive frequency (Jul 3)

FOCUS
Ordinary handicap form, rated around the third, with the winner progressing again. The pace was not particularly strong.
Dolly No Hair Official explanation: vet said gelding finished lame in front

3125 LADIES' DAY TOMORROW MAIDEN H'CAP 5f
5:40 (5:41) (Class 5) (0-70,64) 3-Y-0+ **£2,590** (£770; £385; £192) **Stalls** Centre

Form RPR

060- **1** **Bedloe's Island (IRE)**[244] 6822 4-9-8 53.......................... FrancisNorton 14 68+
(N Bycroft) *chsd ldrs stands' side: led over 1f out: r.o strly: v readily* **12/1**

4555 **2** *2 ¼* **Chantilly Jewel (USA)**[21] 2455 4-9-8 53..............(v[1]) GrahamGibbons 2 60
(R M H Cowell) *dwlt: sn w ldrs on outside: upsides over 1f out: no ex* **8/1**

-453 **3** *2* **What A Fella**[16] 2593 3-8-11 48.............................. PaulMulrennan 7 46
(Mrs A Duffield) *led tl over 1f out: wknd towards fin* **9/4**[1]

3-05 **4** *¾* **Monte Cassino (IRE)**[24] 2366 4-8-13 49 ow3.......... JamesO'Reilly(5) 3 46
(J O'Reilly) *w ldrs on outside: styd on same pce appr fnl f* **15/2**[3]

0-50 **5** *1 ¾* **Jillolini**[28] 2250 3-8-9 46.. DavidAllan 15 35
(T D Easterby) *chsd ldrs stands' side: one pce fnl 2f* **7/1**[2]

0400 **6** *nk* **Angelo Poliziano**[25] 2336 3-9-13 64.............................. AndrewMullen 13 52
(Mrs A Duffield) *hld up: hdwy over 2f out: kpt on same pce: nvr nr ldrs* **8/1**

0 **7** *½* **Tarus (IRE)**[21] 2439 5-9-0 45.. PaulQuinn 1 33
(A Berry) *chsd ldrs on outside: outpcd over 2f out: no threat after* **20/1**

5-60 **8** *¾* **Only A Splash**[3] 2966 5-9-0 45.. AmirQuinn 9 30
(Mrs R A Carr) *chsd ldrs: edgd lft 2f out: sn btn* **16/1**

600 **9** *nk* **Gelert (IRE)**[21] 2436 4-8-7 45.............................. CharlotteKerton(7) 12 29
(A Berry) *chsd ldrs stands' side: rdn and outpcd 2f out* **8/1**

-505 **10** *¾* **Nassau Beach (IRE)**[17] 2572 3-8-12 49.......................... JamieMoriarty 4 28
(T D Easterby) *chsd ldrs: lost pl over 1f out* **20/1**

5060 **11** *1 ¼* **Rightcar Lewis**[11] 2758 4-9-0 45..........................(b) CatherineGannon 5 22
(Peter Grayson) *s.s: nvr a factor* **16/1**

50-0 **12** *1 ¾* **Rio Pomba (IRE)**[31] 2162 3-9-2 53.. DNolan 8 22
(D Carroll) *chsd ldrs: rdn and lost pl over 2f out* **20/1**

58.83 secs (0.23) **Going Correction** +0.025s/f (Good)
WFA 3 from 4yo+ 6lb **12** Ran SP% **122.1**
Speed ratings (Par 103): **99,95,92,91,88 87,86,85,85,84 82,79**
toteswingers: 1&2 £15.50, 1&3 £4.90, 2&3 £3.50 CSF £104.61 CT £299.04 TOTE £18.00: £3.40, £2.90, £1.60; EX 145.30 Place 6: £41.60 Place 5: £34.81.
Owner J G Lumsden & M F Hogan **Bred** Dr Dean Harron **Trained** Brandsby, N Yorks

FOCUS
The dozen-strong field had run a total of 115 times between them previously without success, and this is clearly very moderate form, but the unexposed winner did it well and he has been rated slightly on the positive side.
Bedloe's Island(IRE) ◆ Official explanation: trainer said, regarding apparent improvement in form, that the gelding was having its first run for the yard and had strengthened up since joining him.
T/Plt: £51.10 to a £1 stake. Pool: £37,964.90. 541.54 winning tickets. T/Qpdt: £54.90 to a £1 stake. Pool: £2,318.45. 31.20 winning tickets. WG

3126 - 3137a (Foreign Racing) - See Raceform Interactive

3086 ASCOT (R-H)
Saturday, June 20

OFFICIAL GOING: Good to firm (10.1)
The course was at its normal configuration and all distances were as advertised.
Wind: Modest, across

3138 CHESHAM STKS (LISTED RACE) 7f
2:30 (2:30) (Class 1) 2-Y-O
£28,385 (£10,760; £5,385; £2,685; £1,345; £675) **Stalls** Centre

Form RPR

42 **1** **Big Audio (IRE)**[21] 2467 2-9-3 0.............................. RichardHughes 11 103
(R Hannon) *stdd s: hld up wl in rr: hdwy and switching to outer fr over 2f out: rdn to chal wl over 1f out: drvn to ld jst ins fnl f: length ahd whn wnt sharply lft towards fin: jst lasted* **22/1**

2 *shd* **Emperor Claudius (USA)**[17] 2615 2-9-3 0.......................... RyanMoore 4 103+
(A P O'Brien, Ire) *w'like: athletic: s.i.s and short of room sn after s: bhd: rdn 3f out: swtchd lft and hdwy over 2f out: chsd ldrs over 1f out: r.o wl u.p to go 2nd wl ins fnl f: jst fld* **4/1**[1]

23 **3** *1 ½* **Party Doctor**[9] 2844 2-9-3 0.. RichardKingscote 8 99
(Tom Dascombe) *w'like: chsd ldrs: rdn to ld 2f out: sn hung rt: hdd jst ins fnl f: hung lft ins fnl f: 3rd and keeping on same pce whn hmpd towards fin* **12/1**

3 **4** *1 ¾* **Beethoven (IRE)**[19] 2556 2-9-3 0.............................. JimmyFortune 9 95
(A P O'Brien, Ire) *w'like: scope: in tch: hdwy to chal 2f out: hung rt u.p wl over 1f out: 4th and btn whn sltly hmpd ins fnl f* **4/1**[1]

1 **5** *4 ½* **Shakespearean (IRE)**[22] 2444 2-9-3 0.......................... RoystonFfrench 12 83
(M Johnston) *w'like: strong: in tch in midfield: pushed along 1/2-way: effrt u.p to chse ldrs 2f out: outpcd over 1f out: wl hld fnl f* **8/1**[3]

1 **6** *2 ¾* **Aerodynamic (IRE)**[9] 2853 2-9-3 0.............................. PJSmullen 7 77
(Pat Eddery) *w'like: scope: dwlt: hld up in midfield: lost pl and towards rr 3f out: rdn and hdwy over 2f out: no imp fr wl over 1f out* **15/2**[2]

21 **7** *2 ½* **Step In Time (IRE)**[28] 2280 2-9-3 0.............................. JoeFanning 16 70
(M Johnston) *in tch: effrt over 2f out: ev ch and drvn 2f out: wknd qckly over 1f out* **20/1**

01 **8** *6* **Queen's Hawk**[26] 2324 2-9-3 0.. EddieAhern 10 55
(D J Coakley) *w.w towards rr: pushed along and hdwy 3f out: drvn and wknd ent fnl 2f: wl btn fnl f* **33/1**

01 **9** *1 ¼* **Bikini Babe (IRE)**[8] 2889 2-8-12 0.............................. GregFairley 13 47
(M Johnston) *strong: scope: chsd ldrs: wnt 2nd over 3f out: led 3f out tl 2f out: sn btn: wl bhd fnl f* **12/1**

3 **10** *2 ¼* **Florio Vincitore (IRE)**[13] 2735 2-9-3 0.......................... JamesDoyle 1 47
(E J Creighton) *w'like: chsd ldr tl 1/2-way: wknd u.p jst over 2f out: wl bhd over 1f out* **100/1**

1 **11** *12* **Meglio Ancora**[36] 2037 2-9-3 0.. TPQueally 15 17
(J G Portman) *in tch in midfield: rdn and effrt on outer wl over 2f out: wknd qckly ent fnl 2f: sn wl bhd* **14/1**

0 **12** *2 ¼* **Avow (USA)**[12] 2771 2-9-3 0.. LPKeniry 6 11
(J S Moore) *leggy: sn pushed and struggling: detached last and hung rt u.p over 3f out: t.o fnl 2f* **100/1**

4 **13** *2 ¼* **Rigid**[21] 2467 2-9-3 0.. PatCosgrave 14 5
(J G Given) *leggy: chsd ldrs for 2f out: sn struggling: bhd and rdn 4f out: wl bhd and eased fr over 1f out: t.o* **50/1**

52 **14** *nk* **Fly Silca Fly (IRE)**[23] 2401 2-8-12 0.......................... EdwardCreighton 17 —
(M R Channon) *in tch in midfield on outer: shortlived effrt u.p over 3f out: wknd qckly over 2f out: t.o fnl f* **66/1**

31 **15** *1 ¾* **Izaaj (USA)**[32] 2167 2-9-3 0..(t) LDettori 2 —
(Saeed Bin Suroor) *hld up in midfield: hdwy over 3f out: rdn and hung rt over 2f out: sn wl btn: eased fr over 1f out: t.o* **8/1**[3]

16 *2 ¾* **Honor In Peace (USA)**[38] 2-9-3 0..............................(bt) OPeslier 5 —
(Wesley A Ward, U.S.A) *strong: led at fast gallop: clr early: hdd 3f out: sn rdn: wknd qckly over 2f out: wl bhd and eased fr over 1f out: t.o* **16/1**

1m 30.19s (2.19) **Going Correction** +0.35s/f (Good) **16** Ran SP% **119.4**
Speed ratings (Par 101): **101,100,99,97,92 88,86,79,77,75 61,58,56,55,53 50**
toteswinger: 1&2 £19.20, 1&3 £55.10, 2&3 £13.30. CSF £102.56 CT £1184.70 TOTE £21.80: £4.90, £2.00, £5.60; EX 120.60 Trifecta £2267.60 Pool: £11,644.82 - 3.80 winning units..
Owner Michael Pescod **Bred** Stephen Sullivan **Trained** East Everleigh, Wilts

FOCUS
In addition to 1mm of rain, 4mm of water was added to the track overnight. This race, restricted to the progeny of stallions who won over 1m2f or more, is unlike the other two-year-old races at the Royal meeting in that it caters more for staying types who will come into their own further down the line. Those drawn in the five highest stalls raced a little way apart from the remainder in the early stages before the groups merged. The winner and second delivered their runs on opposing sides of the pack. While this is rarely a strong race there are grounds for thinking this ws the best renewal for a while, and it has been rated as such.

NOTEBOOK
Big Audio(IRE) had been runner-up at Doncaster on his second start three weeks previously and was expected to improve for this extra furlong. Racing lazily in rear and some way off the pace through the first part of the race, he had to be switched to his right to pick up down the outer of the bunch. Coming with a sustained run, he showed ahead inside the last but edged markedly to the left late on and the line came just in time for him. It transpired that he had loosened a tooth after hitting his head in the stalls, which might have accounted for him veering off a true line late on. He also found this ground plenty fast enough. The Superlative Stakes at Newmarket, in which he would incur no penalty, looks an ideal race for him next. (op 16-1)
Emperor Claudius(USA) ◆ found himself at the back of the field after being squeezed out leaving the stalls, but he began to make significant progress once switched left to race nearest to the stands' side. Keeping on determinedly, he would have got up in a couple more strides, and given his problems at the start has to be counted an unlucky loser. By one O'Brien star, Giant's Causeway, out of another, the 1,000 Guineas winner Virginia Waters, he won a 6f maiden at Fairyhouse on his second start and was well suited by this extra yardage. He is a smart prospect. (op 11-2 tchd 6-1 in places)
Party Doctor had every chance but hung slightly to his right and could not hold on to his narrow lead. He was held when the winner went across him just before the line, far too late to affect the outcome. This ground was livelier than he would have liked and he should not be long in getting off the mark. (op 16-1)
Beethoven(IRE), the other O'Brien runner, was beaten by subsequent Listed winner Love Lockdown on his second start at Naas. By the same sire as Big Audio, he challenged at the two pole but was another to hang slightly when the pressure was on. This was a sound effort. (op 5-1 tchd 11-2 in places)
Shakespearean(IRE), one of three runners for Mark Johnston, briefly looked a threat at the two pole but could only stick on at the one pace after, perhaps not truly seeing out the trip at this stage. He should improve as he strengthens up. (op 15-2 tchd 7-1)
Aerodynamic(IRE) made his debut only nine days previously, winning at Nottingham, and he ran respectably without ever threatening the principals. (tchd 7-1 and 8-1)

Step In Time(IRE) ran a creditable race, travelling well for some way, and fared best of the high-drawn runners. (op 16-1)

Queen's Hawk's win came in an ordinary Goodwood maiden auction and he was found out in this better company, if by no means disgraced. (op 50-1 tchd 66-1)

Bikini Babe(IRE), the only runner to have tackled 7f before and one of just two fillies in the field, showed prominently until weakening with over a furlong left. (op 9-1)

Izaaj(USA) finished a place behind Norfolk Stakes winner Radiohead on his debut before landing a little race at Yarmouth in workmanlike fashion. He was expected to step up for this longer trip but was well beaten. He was reported to have a breathing problem. Official explanation: jockey said colt had a breathing problem (op 11-1)

Honor In Peace(USA)'s trainer reported beforehand that he had not had an ideal preparation after becoming 'a little sick' on his arrival in Britain. The colt, unraced beyond 5f, showed plenty of pace but did not last much more than half a mile. (op 9-1)

3139 HARDWICKE STKS (GROUP 2) — 1m 4f

3:05 (3:05) (Class 1) 4-Y-O+

£70,962 (£26,900; £13,462; £6,712; £3,362; £1,687) **Stalls** High

Form				RPR
-331	1		**Bronze Cannon (USA)**[49] [1674] 4-9-3 111 .... JimmyFortune 3 (J H M Gosden) *hld up: rdn and hdwy over 2f out: chsd ldr over 1f out: r.o ins fnl f to ld towards fin* **8/1**[3]	122
42-0	2	½	**Campanologist (USA)**[23] [2410] 4-9-0 115 .... LDettori 9 (Saeed Bin Suroor) *lw: broke wl: chsd ldrs: plld out to ld 2f out: sn edgd rt: r.o u.p: worn down towards fin* **2/1**[1]	118
-261	3	3	**Dansant**[84] [1004] 5-9-0 113 .... EddieAhern 1 (G A Butler) *lw: swtchd rt and dropped in at the bk: swtchd rt and hdwy over 2f out: styd on to take 3rd ins fnl f: nt pce to trble front duo* **8/1**[3]	113
54-1	4	3	**Enroller (IRE)**[63] [1351] 4-9-0 111 .... MartinDwyer 7 (W R Muir) *midfield: pushed along 3f out: kpt on fr over 1f out: nt pce to chal ldrs* **14/1**	108
1-43	5	½	**Barshiba (IRE)**[48] [1697] 5-8-11 105 .... RichardHughes 5 (D R C Elsworth) *led after 2f: racd freely and sn clr: hung lft thrght: at least 8 l ahd 7f out: greatly reduced advantage 3f out: hdd 2f out: kpt on u.p but nt pce of ldrs appr fnl f: wknd fnl 100yds* **25/1**	104
5-43	6	hd	**Illustrious Blue**[15] [2677] 6-9-0 107 .... JimCrowley 4 (W J Knight) *hld up: pushed along 3f out: kpt on u.p fnl f: nvr able to chal ldrs* **20/1**	107
40-1	7	2½	**Doctor Fremantle**[44] [1799] 4-9-0 113 .... RyanMoore 2 (Sir Michael Stoute) *hld up: pushed along 3f out: effrt on outside over 2f out: nvr landed a blow: eased whn no imp fnl 100yds* **5/2**[2]	103
2430	8	2¼	**Steele Tango (USA)**[23] [2410] 4-9-0 110 .... LukeMorris 8 (R A Teal) *b. bustled along s: midfield: pushed along and lost plcd 3f out: bhd after* **11/1**	99
05-0	9	1¼	**Tajaaweed (USA)**[55] [1551] 4-9-0 111 .... RHills 6 (Sir Michael Stoute) *sn led: hdd after 2f: chsd clr ldr after: clsd 3f out: rdn and cl up 2f out: wknd wl over 1f out* **11/1**	97

2m 27.59s (-4.91) **Going Correction** 0.0s/f (Good) **9** Ran SP% **116.1**

Speed ratings (Par 115): **116,115,113,111,111 111,109,108,107**

toteswinger: 1&2 £4.30, 1&3 £10.30, 2&3 £4.60. CSF £24.51 CT £135.54 TOTE £7.60: £2.10, £1.20, £2.70; EX 21.50 Trifecta £58.00 Pool: £10,229.97 - 130.41 winning units..

Owner A E Oppenheimer **Bred** Hascombe And Valiant Studs **Trained** Newmarket, Suffolk

FOCUS

A race that has been won by some high-class performers in recent years including the subsequent King George-winner Doyen in 2004 and the multiple Group-race winner Maraahel in 2006 and 2007. This year's field didn't look the strongest, however, with many of these unproven at this level and/or with doubts over their stamina. They went a furious pace though, with Barshiba soon storming off into a clear early lead from Tajaaweed who in turned race clear of the others, and the winning time was just 0.35 seconds outside the course record. Sound form, rated around the runner-up, with the winner a clear personal best under the penalty.

NOTEBOOK

Bronze Cannon(USA) was at least proven at this level, though his defeat of a below-par Casual Conquest in the three-runner Jockey Club Stakes at Newmarket last month was hard to evaluate. He hadn't run very well in his only previous try here when behind Campanologist in last year's King Edward VII Stakes, though he apparently hurt himself then, but he was able to demonstrate his true ability here. Held up off the furious early pace, he made his move once into the home straight and answered his rider's every call to get up well inside the last furlong. This was a decent effort in conceding upwards of 3lb to his eight rivals, but it seems likely that if he does have a crack at Group 1 company then it will be abroad, with the Grosser Preis von Baden mentioned as a possible target. (op 9-1)

Campanologist(USA), the only other previous Group 2 winner in the field apart from the winner and all the better for his pipe-opener in the Brigadier Gerard last month, had made all when beating Conduit in last season's King Edward VII Stakes, but this time he was happy to let the two trailblazers get on with it and lead the main group. The leaders duly came back to him straightening up for home, and it looked as though he had established a race-winning advantage when going on two out, but despite not stopping he couldn't withstand the winner's late thrust. He has plenty of options with regards to future targets, but nothing specific as yet. (op 9-4 tchd 5-2 and 11-4 in places)

Dansant has winning form on fast ground on turf, but is much better known as a smart performer on Polytrack these days, so this was cracking effort. Dropped right out from his wide draw early, he had plenty to do turning in though he was only a length or so off the winner, but he finished strongly up the inside rail to finish a clear third. His main target remains the Breeders' Cup Marathon in the autumn. (op 9-1)

Enroller(IRE) had looked progressive still when winning the John Porter but came here following an interrupted preparation. Having raced in mid-division early, he came off the bridle a fair way out, but kept responding to pressure to finish a creditable fourth on ground that would have been plenty fast enough for him. His best chance of winning another Group race may be in the autumn. (op 16-1)

Barshiba(IRE), trying this trip for the very first time in her 23rd outing, wasn't ridden as though her stamina was thought to be in doubt, but she surely did far too much too soon and she was hanging noticeably on the run up from Swinley Bottom. It was inevitable that she would be swallowed up, which she was inside the last 2f, but she didn't exactly fall in a heap and there could be another Pattern race in her back over a shorter trip. (op 33-1)

Illustrious Blue keeps on doing his best, but this level looks beyond him and it's over two years since he last won. He could never get involved from off the pace here, but will still be of interest in slightly lesser company back at his beloved Goodwood. (op 28-1)

Doctor Fremantle, whose three previous wins had been on left-handed tracks, two of which have been at Chester including over an inadequate 1m2f on his reappearance last month, got edgy beforehand and proved very weak in the market beforehand. Keen enough at the back of the field early despite the strong gallop, he found very little when switched to the wide outside once into the straight and this wasn't his true running. (op 15-8 tchd 11-4 in places)

Steele Tango(USA), just in front of Campanologist in the Brigadier Gerard last month though he had the advantage of race-fitness there, was the subject of quite a punt here but he never managed to get involved. As admirable as he is, he is yet to prove that he is up to this level or that he truly gets this trip. (op 25-1)

Tajaaweed(USA), lightly raced and disappointing since his victory in the 2008 Dee Stakes, still has to prove his stamina for this trip but like Barshiba he wasn't ridden as though stamina was thought to be an issue. However, once into the straight he dropped right out and obviously still has plenty of questions to answer. (op 12-1)

3140 GOLDEN JUBILEE STKS (BRITISH LEG OF THE GLOBAL SPRINT CHALLENGE) (GROUP 1) — 6f

3:45 (3:45) (Class 1) 3-Y-O+

£278,456 (£105,555; £52,826; £26,339; £13,194; £6,621) **Stalls** Centre

Form				RPR
20-0	1		**Art Connoisseur (IRE)**[66] [1292] 3-8-11 116 .... TPQueally 4 (M L W Bell) *lw: stdd s: hld up in rr: swtchd lft to stands' rail over 2f out: gd hdwy 2f out: led 1f out: drvn and r.o wl fnl f:* **20/1**	120
3/6	2	nk	**Cannonball (USA)**[4] [2991] 4-9-4 107 .... (t) OPeslier 2 (Wesley A Ward, U.S.A) *bhd: rdn and hdwy wl over 1f out: wnt 2nd ins fnl f: r.o wl: clsng at fin* **11/1**	121
6-11	3	2½	**Lesson In Humility (IRE)**[16] [2644] 4-9-1 106 .... AndrewElliott 10 (K R Burke) *sn pressing ldr: rdn to ld 2f out: flashed tail u.p: hdd 1f out: nt pce of ldng pair ins fnl f: kpt on for 3rd* **33/1**	110
611	4	1½	**J J The Jet Plane (SAF)**[19] [2550] 5-9-4 120 .... KShea 9 (M F De Kock, South Africa) *strong: racd keenly: led: hdd 2f out: drvn and unable qck over 1f out: one pce and btn ins fnl f* **5/2**[1]	108
1/1	5	hd	**Sacred Kingdom (AUS)**[34] [2116] 6-9-4 122 .... (t) BrettPrebble 8 (P F Yiu, Hong Kong) *swtg: awkward leaving stalls: sn wl in tch: edging lft looking for gap whn c off best of barging match w rival over 3f out: chal wl over 1f out: led over 1f out: sn hdd: wknd fnl 100yds* **4/1**[2]	108
-333	6	shd	**Diabolical (USA)**[34] [2116] 6-9-4 112 .... LDettori 6 (Saeed Bin Suroor) *b.hind: hld up towards rr: hdwy and swtchd rt 2f out: drvn to chse ldrs over 1f out: one pce fnl f* **12/1**	107+
-441	7	nk	**Strike The Deal (USA)**[24] [2385] 4-9-4 110 .... (v) PhilipRobinson 11 (J Noseda) *w.w wl in tch: n.m.r over 3f out: rdn and effrt 2f out: no imp u.p fnl f* **22/1**	106+
-201	8	¾	**Duff (IRE)**[9] [2870] 6-9-4 109 .... KJManning 1 (Edward Lynam, Ire) *trckd ldrs: effrt and ev ch 2f out: drvn over 1f out: wknd fnl f* **25/1**	104
-621	9	shd	**Regal Parade**[21] [2500] 5-9-4 107 .... AdrianTNicholls 13 (D Nicholls) *stdd after s: hld up in rr: hdwy on outer over 3f out: drvn and effrt over 2f out: hrd rdn and wknd over 1f out* **66/1**	104+
1-02	10	1	**King's Apostle (IRE)**[38] [1989] 5-9-4 115 .... (v) LiamJones 12 (W J Haggas) *lw: towards rr: effrt and rdn over 2f out: chsd ldrs 2f out: drvn and wknd over 1f out* **12/1**	100+
10-4	11	½	**Bushranger (IRE)**[28] [2287] 3-8-11 118 .... (v[1]) PJSmullen 3 (David Wachman, Ire) *swtg: s: in tch: wanting to hang rt fr over 3f out: drvn and hanging rt fr over 2f out: no prog fnl 2f* **12/1**	97
1	12	18	**Ialysos (GR)**[21] [2481] 5-9-4 107 .... WilliamBuick 5 (L M Cumani) *trckd ldrs: c off worse in barging match and lost pl over 3f out: bhd and rdn 2f out: wl btn and eased fr over 1f out* **7/1**[3]	41+
153-	13	3¾	**Kingsgate Native (IRE)**[302] [5245] 4-9-4 118 .... RyanMoore 14 (Sir Michael Stoute) *lw: chsd ldrs: rdn over 2f out: wknd qckly 2f: eased whn no ch over 1f out* **9/1**	29
4002	14	7	**Intrepid Jack**[19] [2550] 7-9-4 109 .... GeorgeBaker 15 (H Morrison) *stdd s: hld up in rr: rdn and lost tch 2f out: eased fr over 1f out: t.o* **50/1**	7

1m 14.9s (0.50) **Going Correction** +0.35s/f (Good)

WFA 3 from 4yo+ 7lb **14** Ran SP% **121.8**

Speed ratings (Par 117): **110,109,106,104,104 103,103,102,102,101 100,76,71,62**

toteswinger: 1&2 £56.10, 1&3 £125.60, 2&3 £77.20. CSF £215.13 CT £7289.64 TOTE £35.50: £8.70, £3.70, £8.00; EX 277.50 Trifecta £9136.80 Pool: £23,459.50 - 1.90 winning units..

Owner R A Green **Bred** D McDonnell **Trained** Newmarket, Suffolk

FOCUS

Another thoroughly international renewal with the home team taken on by representatives from Ireland, Hong Kong, the USA and South Africa, as well as one who has done most of his racing in Greece. There was no Australian challenge though, with connections of brilliant King's Stand winner Scenic Blast opting to wait for the July Cup and Takeover Target, a regular at Ascot for the past three years, being ruled out with a temperature. The pace was fairly modest and the field raced down the stands' side, with a low draw proving beneficial. With the big two foreign raiders J J The Jet Plane and Sacred Kingdom both eclipsed, the form is perhaps not all that strong.

NOTEBOOK

Art Connoisseur(IRE) had been without a victory since last year's Coventry Stakes and it remained to be seen whether he had trained on following a cannonbone injury sustained on his final start last year. After racing too freely in the Free Handicap, in which he was only seventh behind Ouqba, he had been held up by a splint problem and it was touch and go whether he would be ready for this in time. Back down in trip, he was held up in the rear before coming with a devastating run nearest to the stands' rail to strike the front inside the last, a victory reminiscent of his Coventry win. Sprinting on fast ground is his game and the July Cup is the obvious target now. He will have his work cut out against Scenic Blast, but a fast pace there will suit him.

Cannonball(USA) had been taken off his legs in the King's Stand over 5f on Tuesday before finishing well when it was all over, and he was again putting in some good late work down the near flank without quite looking to get to the winner. He will miss the July Cup and return to the States, but connections hope to bring him back to Royal Ascot in 2010. (op 14-1)

Lesson In Humility(IRE), the only filly in the field, ran a blinder from a less favourable draw than the first two and went down fighting. Progressive and admirable though she is, she came here with something to find with the principals on official figures following wins in a Nottingham Listed event and the Group 3 Ballyogan Stakes at Leopardstown, both against her own sex. She ran really well, especially as she was further from the rail than the two principals. (tchd 28-1)

J J The Jet Plane(SAF), on his toes beforehand, made the running, travelling well but not at a breakneck pace. Once headed the South African star dropped out of contention, but he was keeping on again late and shaded fourth on the line. This was only his second defeat on turf at sprint distances and there seemed no obvious excuses. (tchd 11-4, 3-1 in places)

Sacred Kingdom(AUS), supplemented for £45,000 and attempting to emulate his compatriot Cape Of Good Hope who won this for Hong Kong four years ago, became warm at the start and fly-leaped as the stalls opened. After getting the better of a bumping match with Ialysos at around halfway, he came through to show briefly in the lead but could not get away from his pursuers and faded inside the last. His rider reported that the gelding is a pure sprinter who is better suited to a flat track. (op 7-2 tchd 11-2, 6-1 in places)

Diabolical(USA), third to Sacred Kingdom in Singapore last time, regularly performs well in the top sprints around the world and this was no exception. He was slightly checked at halfway, nothing that would have been detrimental to his chances, before running on in the latter stages. (op 16-1 tchd 11-1)

Strike The Deal(USA) won a minor conditions race on Polytrack last time and he ran well on this marked rise in grade without seriously threatening the principals. (op 20-1 tchd 25-1, 40-1 in a place)

Duff(IRE), winner of a Group 3 over 7f last time, had his chance but was unable to capitalise on the prime draw in stall 1. (op 50-1)

Regal Parade, winner of the Buckingham Palace Handicap at the meeting 12 months ago, ran creditably from an unfavourable draw on only his second try in Group company, but is not quite up to this level. (op 50-1)

King's Apostle(IRE) was refitted with the visor he wore to victory in last autumn's Diadem Stakes here. He was not too well drawn near the outside and could never land a blow. (op 11-1)
Bushranger(IRE), who had Art Connoisseur behind when winning the Phoenix Stakes last season, was well held in heavy ground on his reappearance but ran better in the first-time visor. He hung to his right from halfway though and did not look one to trust too much on this evidence. (op 16-1)
Ialysos(GR), upped to 6f after his British debut at Haydock, when he beat King's Stand third Anglezarke, lost his place after being jostled at halfway and was eventually eased right off. He is better than this and may drop down in grade again in a bid to restore his confidence. (op 8-1)
Kingsgate Native(IRE), successful in this for John Best last year, has come back into training after proving infertile at stud. Unable to get much cover, he dropped away in the final two furlongs after becoming tired on this first run for ten months. (op 10-1 tchd 11-1 and 12-1 in places)
Intrepid Jack, who has run in the Wokingham for the past three years, was always in rear and finished much further behind J J The Jet Plane than he had at Windsor. (tchd 40-1)

3141 WOKINGHAM STKS (HERITAGE H'CAP) 6f

4:25 (4:25) (Class 2) (0-110,108) 3-Y-O+

£62,310 (£18,660; £9,330; £4,670; £2,330; £1,170) **Stalls** Centre

Form RPR

2-11 **1** **High Standing (USA)**[21] 2474 4-8-12 **96** 5ex.................. RyanMoore 28 110+
(W J Haggas) *racd on far side: hld up: gd hdwy over 1f out: str run to ld fnl 75yds: r.o* **6/1**[2]

1014 **2** *3/4* **Asset (IRE)**[21] 2483 6-9-10 **108**..(b) LDettori 27 119
(Saeed Bin Suroor) *lw: racd on far side: hld up: hdwy ent fnl 2f: led gp 1f out: tk overall ld ins fnl f: hdd 75yds out: hld cl home: 2nd of 17 in gp* **16/1**

2-50 **3** *2 1/2* **Rock Of Rochelle (USA)**[9] 2870 4-9-10 **108**.................. PJSmullen 25 111
(A Kinsella, Ire) *w'like: racd on far side: midfield: rdn and hdwy over 1f out: r.o ins fnl f: nt get to front pair: 3rd of 17 in gp* **40/1**

22-6 **4** *1/2* **Markab**[42] 1861 6-9-1 **99**.. PatCosgrave 8 101+
(H Candy) *lw: racd on stands' side: overall ld: rdn and hung rt fr 2f out: clr of gp over 1f out: hdd for overall advantage ins fnl f: kpt on but hld: 1st of 9 in gp* **11/1**

0-60 **5** *1 1/4* **Prohibit**[48] 1699 4-9-2 **100**.. JimmyFortune 6 98+
(J H M Gosden) *lw: s.i.s: racd on stands' side: hld up: hdwy over 2f out: sn hung rt: chsd gp (overall) ldr over 1f out: styd on u.p: 2nd of 9 in gp* **14/1**

-213 **6** *1* **Advanced**[28] 2259 6-8-10 **99**.. AmyRyan(5) 26 93
(K A Ryan) *lw: racd on far side: a.p: rdn to chal 2f out: styd on same pce ins fnl f: 4th of 17 in gp* **25/1**

-100 **7** *nk* **Striking Spirit**[14] 2707 4-8-11 **95**.................................. FrancisNorton 20 88
(D Nicholls) *lw: racd on far side: led gp: rdn and hdd 1f out: no ex fnl 100yds: 5th of 17 in gp* **33/1**

0100 **8** *3/4* **Joseph Henry**[21] 2470 7-8-13 **97**.. JoeFanning 31 88
(D Nicholls) *racd on far side: gd spd w gp ldr: rdn 2f out: no ex ent fnl f: 6th of 17 in gp* **50/1**

2454 **9** *1/2* **Orpsie Boy (IRE)**[48] 1699 6-9-0 **98**........................(v[1]) GeorgeBaker 22 87
(N P Littmoden) *racd on far side: towards rr: rdn and hdwy over 1f out: styd on ins fnl f: nt pce to chal ldrs: 7th of 17 in gp* **25/1**

3200 **10** *nk* **Knot In Wood (IRE)**[28] 2287 7-9-1 **102**.................. FrederikTylicki(3) 21 90
(R A Fahey) *racd on far side: chsd ldrs: rdn over 2f out: one pce fnl 100yds: 8th of 17 in gp* **20/1**

-000 **11** *1 1/2* **Van Bossed (CAN)**[14] 2707 4-8-10 **94**........................ RoystonFfrench 3 78
(D Nicholls) *racd on stands' side: chsd gp (overall) ldr tl over 1f out: kpt on same pce fnl f: 3rd of 9 in gp* **25/1**

5-21 **12** *1* **Jimmy Styles**[27] 2297 5-9-3 **101** 5ex.............................. PhilipRobinson 1 81
(C G Cox) *lw: racd on stands' side: chsd ldrs: rdn over 2f out: one pce fr over 1f out: 4th of 9 in gp* **5/1**[1]

0152 **13** *1/2* **Tamagin (USA)**[24] 2385 6-9-3 **101**..(p) NCallan 9 80
(K A Ryan) *swtchd rt to r on far side after 1f: prom: rdn over 1f out: wknd ins fnl f: 9th of 17 in gp* **25/1**

000- **14** *nk* **Brave Prospector**[273] 6121 4-9-4 **102**............................(t) AlanMunro 16 80
(P W Chapple-Hyam) *swtchd rt to r on far side: in tch: edgd rt over 2f out: sn chalng: wknd ins fnl f: 10th of 17 in gp* **25/1**

01-4 **15** *3/4* **Osiris Way**[21] 2474 7-8-11 **95**.. JimCrowley 18 70
(P R Chamings) *swtchd rt to r on far side: towards rr: rdn and hdwy 2f out: chsd ldng bunch: wknd fnl 100yds: 11th of 17 in gp* **40/1**

0334 **16** *nk* **Nota Bene**[24] 2385 7-9-2 **100**.. RichardHughes 13 75
(D R C Elsworth) *s.i.s: swtchd lft to r stands' side after 1f: hld up: rdn 2f out: nvr able to chal: 5th of 9 in gp* **33/1**

4016 **17** *1/2* **Baby Strange**[6] 2941 5-8-6 **95** 5ex................................ MartinLane(5) 15 68
(D Shaw) *swtchd rt to r on far side after 1f: towards rr: pushed along 1/2-way: nvr on terms: 12th of 17 in gp* **40/1**

02- **18** *3/4* **Soap Wars**[70] 1219 4-8-10 **94**.. SebSanders 29 65
(M Halford, Ire) *racd on far side: midfield: rdn 2f out: outpcd fnl f: 13th of 17 in gp* **50/1**

1040 **19** *shd* **Beaver Patrol (IRE)**[42] 1861 7-9-4 **102**........................(v) DaneO'Neill 7 72
(Eve Johnson Houghton) *racd on stands' side: hld up: rdn and outpcd 2f out: 6th of 9 in gp* **12/1**

606- **20** *1/2* **Pearly Wey**[259] 6468 6-8-13 **97**.. AdamKirby 2 66
(C G Cox) *racd on stands' side: hld up: effrt over 1f out: no imp on ldrs: 7th of 9 in gp* **20/1**

-214 **21** *1 1/2* **Sohraab**[19] 2550 5-9-4 **102**.. EddieAhern 17 66
(H Morrison) *swtchd rt to r far side after 1f: in tch: n.m.r and hmpd over 2f out: sn swtchd lft: wknd over 1f out: 14th of 17 in gp* **25/1**

-310 **22** *2 3/4* **Evens And Odds (IRE)**[42] 1861 5-9-1 **99**.................. AdrianTNicholls 19 54
(D Nicholls) *swtchd rt to r on far side after 1f: in tch: rdn 1/2-way: n.m.r and hmpd over 2f out: sn btn: 15th of 17 in gp* **16/1**

2416 **23** *nk* **Carcinetto (IRE)**[6] 2948 7-8-11 **100** 5ex.................. RichardEvans(5) 12 54
(P D Evans) *swtchd to r on far side after 1f: towards rr: nvr gng pce to get competitve: 16th of 17 in gp* **50/1**

-430 **24** *3 1/4* **Exclamation**[35] 2078 4-9-1 **99**.. MartinDwyer 24 43
(B J Meehan) *racd on far side: midfield: pushed along and wknd over 2f out: 17th of 17 in gp* **25/1**

0-03 **25** *5* **Zidane**[42] 1868 7-9-7 **105**.. WilliamBuick 14 33
(J R Fanshawe) *swtchd lft to r stands' side after 1f: hld up: rdn 2f out: nvr on terms: 8th of 9 in gp* **12/1**

40-5 **26** *2* **Genki (IRE)**[19] 2550 5-8-13 **97**.. SteveDrowne 10 18
(R Charlton) *swtchd lft to r stands' side after 1f: chsd ldrs: rdn 2f out: wknd over 1f out: 9th of 9 in gp* **9/1**[3]

1m 14.19s (-0.21) **Going Correction** +0.35s/f (Good) **26** Ran SP% **138.6**
Speed ratings (Par 109): **115,114,110,110,108 107,106,105,104,104 102,101,100,100,99 98,98,97,96,96 94,90,90,85,79 76**
toteswinger: 1&2 £29.00, 1&3 £40.60, 2&3 £77.70. CSF £84.30 CT £2193.05 TOTE £7.50: £2.10, £4.20, £8.00, £4.70; EX 106.50 Trifecta £11917.00 Pool: £75,689.42 - 4.70 winning units..
Owner Floddy & Bloom **Bred** Dr Melinda Blue **Trained** Newmarket, Suffolk

The Form Book, Raceform Ltd, Compton, RG20 6NL

FOCUS
A typically tough and competitive Wokingham featuring the usual bunch of established decent sprint handicappers, plus a couple of useful Pattern-class performers and a handful that had the potential to be a lot better than they had shown so far. The field soon split into two groups with the larger group going far side whilst a smaller group of six soon came over to the stands' side, where they were soon joined by another trio. It became obvious at halfway that the far-side group had the advantage and this is probably decent form as an unexposed improver and two proven Pattern-class sprinters filled the first three places. Five of the past seven winners of this race had started from stall 21 or higher and that trend continued with stalls 28, 27 and 25 filling the first three places. The winning time was 0.71 seconds faster than the Golden Jubilee and the form looks solid, with the winner building on his impressive Goodwood win and the second back to near his best off the strong pace.

NOTEBOOK
High Standing(USA) ◆, who had to be dismounted and walked to the start, was one of those with pretensions of going on to better things. Winner of both starts last month for his new yard, he was 2lb well in compared to his revised mark despite carrying a 5lb penalty and was given a masterful ride by Ryan Moore, who held him up in the far side group before unleashing him to hit the front well inside the last furlong. He is a bit of a character - he had to be blindfolded to get him to complete the last part of the journey down to the start - but he is obviously a very talented sprinter. A horse that apparently needs time between his races, he is in the Stewards' Cup and it is hoped that he will develop into a Listed or Group-class performer in due course. (tchd 7-1 and 15-2 in places)
Asset(IRE), runner-up in the 2006 Jersey Stakes and beaten less than a length into third in the 2007 Golden Jubilee when with Richard Hannon, continues to perform well in Pattern company for his new connections and it looked as though he had timed it just right when switching to the inside rail to hit the front a furlong out, but he was mugged in the very closing stages. His consistency should see him go one better before too long. (op 22-1)
Rock Of Rochelle(USA), another to have spent most of his career contesting Pattern races and only beaten just over two lengths into fifth behind Utmost Respect at 100/1 in the Duke Of York last month, finished well from off the pace to snatch third and earn himself plenty of credit.
Markab ◆ took the smaller stands'-side group along from the start and despite edging away to his right late on, kept going to hold on for fourth and 'win' the race on his side. He was making a rare appearance over a trip this short and had run well for a long way on his first start for the yard in the Victoria Cup last month. He probably needs easier ground, so under the circumstances this was a cracking effort and he is one to watch out for. (op 16-1)
Prohibit, who hasn't really confirmed early promise, was well supported in the market. Held up in the stands' side group early, despite an awkward head-carriage he ran on strongly in the closing stages to finish second in the nearside group and fifth overall. He remains a stone higher than for his last win in a handicap, but on this evidence he can win off this sort of mark when the cards fall right. (op 33-1)
Advanced, running well so far this year and 10lb lower than when winning the 2007 Ayr Gold Cup, had every chance in the far-side group and would be interesting back in the big Ayr sprint off this sort of mark. (tchd 33-1)
Striking Spirit, disappointing in two starts since beating Jimmy Styles off 7lb lower over course and distance last month, performed much better here and showed good speed to lead the main group towards the far side until collared at the furlong pole. His early pace could make him interesting in something like the Great St Wilfrid.
Joseph Henry, well beaten in two starts since winning off 9lb lower at Naas in April, also showed decent pace in the far side group for a long way and this was better.
Orpsie Boy(IRE), over four lengths behind Evens And Odds at Newmarket last time and 9lb better off, had a visor on for the first time and comprehensively turned that form around, but his late effort from well off the pace was never getting him there in time. (tchd 28-1)
Knot In Wood(IRE), who has run some of his best races in the top sprint handicaps including when fourth off 4lb lower in this event last year, was another to race prominently for a long way in the far-side group. His last win came off this mark, but that was on Polytrack and it may be a bit stiff for him on turf now. (op 18-1 tchd 22-1 in places)
Van Bossed(CAN)who was well held in three starts this season but ran very well in defeat off this mark over course and distance in his final outing of last term, ran creditably. For although he was only 11th overall, he was always close to the pace in the stands'-side group and was third home on that side. (op 40-1)
Jimmy Styles has been lightly raced in the past two years, but despite a 5lb penalty for last month's Newmarket win he was still 1lb well in compared to his revised mark. Admittedly he wasn't helped by having to race in the stands'-side group, but this was still a little disappointing. His rider reported that he had hung right throughout. Official explanation: jockey said gelding hung right throughout (op 9-2 tchd 11-2 in places)
Tamagin(USA), a confirmed front-runner and off the same mark as when fifth in this race last year, was taken across to race in the far-side group despite his lowish draw and showed good speed just behind the leaders, but he is much more effective when able to dominate on his own.
Beaver Patrol(IRE), beaten a long way in the Victoria Cup last time and 2lb higher than when runner-up in this race last year, went off well backed but never got involved in the nearside group. (op 25-1 tchd 10-1)
Evens And Odds(IRE) was reported to have lost his action. Official explanation: jockey said gelding lost its action (tchd 20-1 in places)
Zidane, unlucky in this race in 2007 and running in a handicap for the first time since landing that year's Stewards' Cup off 5lb lower, was one of the trio to join the nearside group after a furlong or so but he ran no sort of a race. (op 16-1 tchd 10-1)
Genki(IRE) was two from two here and had been nicely backed following an eye-catching conditions race effort behind JJ The Jet Plane at Windsor on his return from injury. He ran no sort of race but might have bounced. (tchd 8-1)

3142 DUKE OF EDINBURGH STKS (HERITAGE H'CAP) 1m 4f

5:00 (5:01) (Class 2) (0-105,104) 3-Y-O+

£31,155 (£9,330; £4,665; £2,335; £1,165; £585) **Stalls** High

Form RPR

3332 **1** **Drill Sergeant**[14] 2706 4-9-7 **101**.. JoeFanning 4 110
(M Johnston) *chsd ldng pair: wnt 2nd 9f out: clr of remainder 7f out: rdn to ld over 2f out: hrd rdn and styd on gamely fnl f* **14/1**

0241 **2** *1 1/4* **Record Breaker (IRE)**[10] 2815 5-9-4 **98**..................(b) RoystonFfrench 2 105+
(M Johnston) *stdd and swtchd lft after s: hld up bhd: pushed along over 3f out: stl 11th 2f out: sn swtchd lft to wd outside: str run to go 2nd fnl 100yds: nt rch wnr* **14/1**

0113 **3** *1* **Martyr**[14] 2706 4-8-11 **91**.. RichardHughes 1 96
(R Hannon) *chsd ldr tl 9f out: styd chsng ldng pair: clsd and rdn over 2f out: chsd wnr 2f out: kpt on same pce: edgd rt ins fnl f: lost 2nd fnl 100yds* **14/1**

0043 **4** *2 1/2* **Young Mick**[35] 2085 7-9-2 **96**..(v) TPQueally 19 97
(G G Margarson) *chsd ldrs: rdn and effrt 3f out: drvn to chse ldrs over 2f out: hung rt u.p: disp 2nd over 1f out tl wknd fnl 100yds* **8/1**

125/ **5** *3/4* **Pires**[19] 1319 5-8-12 **92**.. JAHeffernan 8 92
(A J Martin, Ire) *t.k.h: hld up in tch: rdn and effrt wl over 2f out: swtchd lft over 1f out: kpt on same pce after* **7/1**[2]

-341 **6** *2 1/2* **Dansili Dancer**[21] 2471 7-9-9 **103**.............................. PhilipRobinson 11 99
(C G Cox) *lw: hld up towards rr: hdwy over 3f out: rdn and effrt on outer over 2f out: no imp fr wl over 1f out* **10/1**

0-50 **7** 1 1/2 **Night Crescendo (USA)**35 2085 6-8-12 92.................(p) JimCrowley 7 86
(Mrs A J Perrett) *hld up in tch: hdwy over 2f out: chsd ldrs and drvn 2f out: nt qckn and no hdwy fr over 1f out* **20/1**

0-5 **8** 2 **Ghimaar**14 2729 4-9-3 97.......................... PJSmullen 14 88
(D K Weld, Ire) *hld up off the pce in midfield: rdn and effrt 3f out: drvn and no prog fr over 2f out* **18/1**

11-2 **9** 1/2 **Crackentorp**21 2475 4-8-11 91.......................... SebSanders 20 81
(R M Beckett) *chsd ldrs: clsd and rdn 3f out: nt clr run and sltly hmpd over 2f out: drvn and wknd over 1f out* **5/1**[1]

004- **10** 1 3/4 **Siberian Tiger (IRE)**27 6649 4-9-7 101.......................... RyanMoore 6 88
(A J Martin, Ire) *hld up wl in rr: rdn and effrt over 2f out: nvr nr ldrs* **11/1**

1-34 **11** 3/4 **Boz**35 2085 5-8-11 91.......................... DaneO'Neill 22 77
(L M Cumani) *racd off the pce in midfield: rdn 4f out: no prog 3f out: wl btn fnl 2f* **14/1**

0-64 **12** hd **Yellowstone (IRE)**21 2501 5-9-10 104.....................(b1) MartinDwyer 13 89
(P F I Cole) *stdd s: hld up wl in rr: rdn and shortlived effrt 3f out: nvr on terms* **25/1**

5-00 **13** 1 1/2 **Heron Bay**26 2342 5-9-2 96.......................... GeorgeBaker 12 79
(C F Wall) *restless stalls: hld up in rr: pushed along 3f out: rdn and no hdwy over 2f out* **10/1**

3-00 **14** 16 **Road To Love (IRE)**38 1986 6-8-11 91.......................... RHills 3 48
(M Johnston) *led: clr 8f out: rdn wl over 2f out: hdd over 2f out: wknd qckly: eased fr over 1f out* **20/1**

5503 **15** 3/4 **Internationaldebut (IRE)**6 2941 4-8-12 92................(t1) AdamKirby 16 48
(S Parr) *lw: t.k.h: hld up in rr: lost tch over 3f out* **50/1**

230- **16** 33 **Strategic Mount**260 6444 6-9-8 102.......................... LDettori 10 5
(P F I Cole) *swtg: hld up in rr: lost tch 3f out: virtually p.u fnl 2f: t.o* **25/1**

-111 **U** **Hatton Flight**48 1696 5-9-5 99..........................(b) WilliamBuick 5 —
(A M Balding) *stmbld and uns rdr sn after s* **15/2**[3]

2m 29.7s (-2.80) **Going Correction** 0.0s/f (Good) **17** Ran SP% **129.7**
Speed ratings (Par 109): **109,108,107,105,105 103,102,101,101,99 99,99,98,87,87 65,—**
toteswinger: 1&2 £24.20, 1&3 £19.60, 2&3 £112.30. CSF £194.80 CT £2827.73 TOTE £17.30: £3.30, £4.40, £3.30, £2.40; EX 87.00 Trifecta £404.30 Pool: £7,436.52 - 13.61 winning units..
Owner J Barson **Bred** Dg Hardisty Bloodstock **Trained** Middleham Moor, N Yorks

FOCUS
A typically competitive Duke Of Edinburgh on paper, but in the event not that many were able to get involved. Mark Johnston trained the winner and second, and although an inside draw had seemed likely to be favoured, the first three came out of stalls 4, 2 and 1. Solid handicap form.

NOTEBOOK
Drill Sergeant did not lead as he likes to but tracked his stablemate Road To Love until taking over in the straight. Getting over to the rail, he galloped on bravely to end a run of placed efforts, including a last of three to Hardwicke winner Bronze Cannon in the Group 2 Jockey Club Stakes. His trainer regards him as just short of Listed class and his admirable consistency has been his downfall as his mark has been largely unchanged since the autumn. The handicapper has been vindicated though, and he will be put up a few pounds for this. (op 16-1)
Record Breaker(IRE) raced freely on the outside from his wide draw before his rider could slot him in towards the rear. He stayed on strongly down the wide outside in the final furlong but his stablemate was in no mood to be caught. This was a big run from a mark 10lb higher than when he won at Hamilton, but he will not mind a return to further.
Martyr finished just behind Drill Sergeant when they were second and third in Coin Of The Realm's race at Epsom on Derby day and put in another sound effort, if not quite able to match that form. Like the winner able to tack over and race prominently, he stuck on willingly and only lost second late on. (op 16-1)
Young Mick won this event three years ago. Given a chance by the handicapper and running off a two-figure mark for the first time since August 2006, he ran a solid race but just lacked a change of gear when one was required. (op 17-2 tchd 12-1 in places)
Pires was never far from the pace and plugged on for fifth. He had never run beyond 1m on the Flat but has been placed over hurdles and saw the trip out well enough. (op 13-2 tchd 8-1 in a place)
Dansili Dancer was raised 4lb to a career-high mark following his Doncaster win. He stayed on from the rear down the outer without troubling the leaders. (op 14-1 tchd 16-1)
Night Crescendo(USA)'s last three wins have come at Ascot and he had the cheekpieces back on for the first time, but he could never really make his presence felt. He needs things to go just right for him. (op 16-1)
Ghimaar, also eighth in last year's King George V Handicap, could never get out of midfield. (op 20-1)
Crackentorp, put up 5lb after finishing second at Goodwood, reportedly bruised a sole on Thursday, which cannot have helped although his trainer was not putting it forward as an excuse. A shade keen through the early stages, he was well placed on the home turn but was slightly checked entering the straight and gradually faded. He may be ready for a step up in trip. (op 11-2 tchd 6-1 in places)
Siberian Tiger(IRE), the second Tony Martin runner, was fit from a hurdles campaign but could make only modest late headway from the back of the field. (op 25-1)
Road To Love(IRE), who has been lightly raced since this meeting two years ago, made the running before fading when the winner passed him. His trainer felt that he had been lit up by the loose horse. (op 25-1)
Hatton Flight's bid for a four-timer ended abruptly as he stumbled and unseated his jockey leaving the stalls. (tchd 7-1)

3143 QUEEN ALEXANDRA STKS (CONDITIONS RACE) 2m 5f 159y
5:35 (5:35) (Class 2) 4-Y-0+

£31,155 (£9,330; £4,665; £2,335; £1,165; £585) **Stalls High**

Form RPR

41-1 **1** **Caracciola (GER)**21 2501 12-9-7 105.......................... EddieAhern 4 99
(N J Henderson) *lw: midfield: hdwy over 3f out: chsd ldr 2f out: led over 1f out: styd on wl and in full control ins fnl f* **6/1**

2-21 **2** 2 1/2 **Tyrrells Wood (IRE)**12 2766 4-9-0 83.......................... JoeFanning 2 93+
(T G Mills) *prom: rdn over 3f out: nt much whn u.p over 2f out: rallied to take 2nd 1f out: nt trble wnr ins fnl f* **9/2**[3]

2-50 **3** 1 **Amerigo (IRE)**21 2486 4-9-0 98.......................... PhilipRobinson 5 90
(M A Jarvis) *lw: racd keenly: hld up: pushed along and hdwy 3f out: hung rt fr over 2f out: styd on to take 3rd ins fnl f: nvr quite able to chal* **4/1**[2]

113- **4** 6 **Tasheba**56 4955 4-9-0 85.......................... RichardHughes 3 84
(N J Henderson) *swtg: trckd ldrs: rdn 5f out: led over 4f out: hdd over 1f out: wknd ins fnl f* **10/3**[1]

1240 **5** 2 1/2 **American Spin**31 2177 5-9-2 73.......................(e1) DaneO'Neill 10 82
(L A Dace) *hld up: pushed along 3f out: hung rt wl over 1f out: nvr able to land a blow* **25/1**

50-6 **6** 1 1/2 **Bulwark (IRE)**23 2409 7-9-2 100..........................(v) JimCrowley 12 80
(Ian Williams) *sn in midfield: hdwy 4f out: chsd ldr over 3f out: rdn to chal 2f out: wknd 1f out* **8/1**

-033 **7** 2 1/4 **Halla San**21 2501 7-9-2 98.......................... PaulHanagan 11 78
(R A Fahey) *trckd ldrs: pushed along 4f out: sn outpcd: wknd over 1f out* **5/1**

3440 **8** 15 **Ruff Diamond (USA)**39 1966 4-9-0 69.......................... LukeMorris 1 63
(J S Moore) *hld up: pushed along 5f out: dropped away 3f out* **14/1**

500/ **9** 12 **Sterling Moll**62 6250 6-8-11 40.......................... KirstyMilczarek 9 46
(W De Best-Turner) *hld up: niggled along 6f out: nvr on terms* **80/1**

422- **10** 2 3/4 **Plane Painter (IRE)**29 3179 5-9-2 72.......................... GeorgeBaker 6 48
(B G Powell) *led: rdn and hdd over 4f out: wkng whn n.m.r over 3f out* **16/1**

4m 53.9s (-2.60) **Going Correction** 0.0s/f (Good)
WFA 4 from 5yo+ 2lb **10** Ran SP% **121.0**
Speed ratings (Par 109): **104,103,102,100,99 99,98,92,88,87**
toteswinger: 1&2 £6.00, 1&3 £4.50, 2&3 £4.40. CSF £34.54 CT £124.14 TOTE £6.00: £2.20, £2.00, £2.00; EX 35.40 Trifecta £148.00 Pool: £6,286.10 - 31.41 winning units. Place 6 £1,383.05, Place 5 £395.59.
Owner P J D Pottinger **Bred** Frau I U A Brunotte **Trained** Upper Lambourn, Berks
■ Caracciola was the oldest ever Royal Ascot winner. Brown Jack had been 10 when gaining his sixth win in this race in 1934.

FOCUS
A wide range of abilities for the longest race of the Flat season with horses rated from 105 down to just 40. Eight of the ten runners had been in action over hurdles this year and as usual stamina was at a premium, even though the pace was only ordinary. Four-year-olds had taken the last three runnings of this, but this was one for the senior citizens.

NOTEBOOK
Caracciola(GER), winner of last season's Cesarewitch and last time a York Listed event, was beaten a long way in this race last year but he was one of those best in at these weights. After travelling well in the middle of the field, he was asked for his effort turning in and as soon as he hit the front inside the last 2f, a historic win was his. Connections are giving greater consideration to a tilt at the Melbourne Cup after this, whilst the Breeders' Cup Marathon may also be considered. (op 9-2 tchd 7-1)
Tyrrells Wood(IRE) ◆, who looked to have stamina in abundance when bolting up off a mark of 75 over the extended 2m1f at Pontefract last time, raced handily but appeared to get slightly outpaced when the tempo increased approaching the home bend. However, he was rallying gamely when running out of room as he tried to squeeze through between Tasheba and the inside rail over 2f from home, and by the time he got through the winner had flown. This was still a fine effort at the weights and he remains a promising young stayer. (op 13-2 tchd 7-1 in places)
Amerigo(IRE) took quite a hold off the pace for much of the way, which wasn't ideal, and when asked to make his effort on the outside once into the straight he never really looked that happy, though he did stay on. Both his wins have come on fast ground, so the surface shouldn't have been a problem. (op 3-1 tchd 9-2 and 5-1 in places)
Tasheba, who developed into a useful staying handicapper for Peter Chapple-Hyam last season, faced a stiff task at the weights but he ran very well in four starts over hurdles for his new yard earlier this year. Trying further than 1m7f for the first time on the Flat, he came seriously off the bridle well before the home bend and was rushed into the lead fully half a mile from home, but he could never get clear and his stamina then seemed to give out. (op 3-1 tchd 7-2 in places)
American Spin, sporting a first-time eyeshield, had a mountain to climb at these weights and had major stamina doubts as well, so he wasn't disgraced though he never looked like winning. (op 40-1)
Bulwark(IRE) is a renowned character and ran a very moody race on his return to the Flat last month, but he was fourth in this race last year and was one of those best treated at these weights. He had every chance starting up the home straight, but didn't get home. (op 12-1)
Halla San, a running-on third in the Chester Cup before finishing over six lengths behind Caracciola at York last month, had a 5lb pull with the Henderson veteran. He was close enough for most of the way, but this extended trip looked beyond him. (tchd 11-2)
T/Jkpt: Not won. T/Plt: £3,055.10 to a £1 stake. Pool: £416,167.78. 99.44 winning tickets.
T/Qpdt: £386.90 to a £1 stake. Pool: £24,626.66. 47.10 winning tickets. SP

3092 AYR (L-H)
Saturday, June 20

OFFICIAL GOING: Good to firm (good in places on round course; 8.5)
Rail realignment increased distances on Round course by ten yards. Races on Straight course run on stands' side.
Wind: Fresh, half against Weather: Overcast

3144 SCOTTISH SUN H'CAP 1m
2:25 (2:25) (Class 2) (0-100,94) 3-Y-O

£15,577 (£4,665; £2,332; £1,167; £582; £292) **Stalls Low**

Form RPR

-221 **1** **Firebet (IRE)**9 2855 3-9-7 94.......................... TonyHamilton 8 109
(R A Fahey) *in tch: pushed along 3f out: led over 1f out: drvn out* **7/2**[2]

-114 **2** 3/4 **Tiger Reigns**26 2341 3-7-13 77.......................... JamieKyne(5) 6 90
(M Dods) *w ldr: ev ch over 1f out: kpt on fnl f* **12/1**

0451 **3** 1 3/4 **Peking Prince**9 2845 3-8-2 78.......................... DavidProbert(3) 4 87+
(A M Balding) *hld up: hdwy over 2f out: kpt on fnl f: nrst fin* **9/4**[1]

-426 **4** 6 **Big Apple Boy (IRE)**23 2406 3-8-11 84.......................... PaulMulrennan 1 79
(Jedd O'Keeffe) *led to over 1f out: sn outpcd* **20/1**

-410 **5** 1/2 **Beautiful Breeze (IRE)**16 2638 3-8-4 77.......................... NickyMackay 2 71
(M Johnston) *dwlt: bhd and pushed along 1/2-way: kpt on fnl f: n.d* **20/1**

-055 **6** 3 **Come And Go (UAE)**14 2696 3-8-5 78.......................... PJMcDonald 3 65
(G A Swinbank) *prom: drvn and outpcd 2f out: sn wknd* **10/1**

1443 **7** 6 **Green Agenda**11 2787 3-8-5 78.......................... AndrewMullen 7 51
(M Johnston) *bhd: pushed along 1/2-way: nvr on terms* **12/1**

4-14 **8** nk **African Art (USA)**37 2004 3-9-0 87.......................... TomEaves 5 60
(B J Meehan) *prom tl hung lft and wknd over 2f out* **8/1**

3131 **9** 1 **Spinners End (IRE)**2 3062 3-8-8 81 6ex ow1.......................... PhillipMakin 9 51
(K R Burke) *cl up tl wknd wl over 1f out* **9/2**[3]

1m 39.8s (-4.00) **Going Correction** -0.25s/f (Firm) **9** Ran SP% **116.3**
Speed ratings (Par 105): **110,109,107,101,101 98,92,91,90**
toteswinger: 1&2 £8.20, 1&3 £1.10, 2&3 £16.10. CSF £45.07 CT £112.47 TOTE £3.80: £1.90, £3.90, £1.60; EX 39.40 Trifecta £105.30 Part won. Pool: £142.38 - 0.10 winning units..
Owner Mrs H Steel **Bred** Derek Veitch And Saleh Ali Hammadi **Trained** Musley Bank, N Yorks

FOCUS
Rail alignments were as the previous evening and a breezy day had dried the track out a touch to good to firm all round. Some progressive sorts on show in this competitive handicap. The first two are progressive and the third sets the level.

NOTEBOOK
Firebet(IRE) ◆ did very well to concede upwards of 7lb to all of his rivals. Allowed a get a lead along the inside, Hamilton just began to nudge away at his mount passing the three pole but the further this horse goes, the stronger he gets and once the gap came over a furlong out, he powered through despite his rider dropping his whip, to continue his rise through the handicap ranks. He looks for all the world as though he'll do even better when stepped up to 1m2f, so he is without doubt open to more improvement yet and he could easily end up a Pattern performer by the end of the season. One point to note, his action suggests he wouldn't want ground any firmer than this. (op 3-1)
Tiger Reigns, dropping back in trip, was ridden close to the pace and has stayed on strongly all the way home to run an excellent race in defeat. He remains one to be interested in. (op 10-1)

Peking Prince was well backed to follow up his Newbury win but he lacked an instant change of gear when switched out to make his challenge. However, he did stay on steadily all the way to the line and given this was a steep rise in class off an 8lb higher mark than last time, this has to go down as a career best and he might benefit from a step up in trip. (op 10-3)

Big Apple Boy(IRE) dropped away after helping to force the pace and was well held by the first three.

Beautiful Breeze(IRE), tackling this trip for the first time, got going late in the day but the race was well and truly over by then and he doesn't have the progressive profile of a few of these. (op 16-1)

Spinners End(IRE) didn't run his race and it may be that this came too quickly after his win at Musselburgh on two days before. Official explanation: jockey said colt had no more to give; trainer's rep said race may have come too soon for colt having run two days earlier (op 13-2)

3145 SCOTTISH NEWS OF THE WORLD EBF LAND O'BURNS FILLIES' STKS (LISTED RACE) 5f

2:55 (2:57) (Class 1) 3-Y-O+

£22,708 (£8,608; £4,308; £2,148; £1,076; £540) **Stalls** High

Form RPR

50-4 **1** **Sugar Free (IRE)**[16] 2644 3-8-11 100 ... WMLordan 5 98
(T Stack, Ire) *prom: hdwy to ld appr fnl f: kpt on strly ins fnl f* **6/1**

3456 **2** ¾ **City Dancer (IRE)**[7] 2928 3-8-11 95 ... PJMcDonald 6 95
(A Berry) *hld up in tch: hdwy 2f out: ev ch ins fnl f: kpt on: hld nr fin* **11/2**

3610 **3** 3 **Rothesay Dancer**[14] 2716 6-9-3 77 ... KellyHarrison 4 86
(J S Goldie) *hld up and bhd: stdy hdwy 2f out: chsd first two ins fnl f: no imp* **33/1**

-306 **4** 1½ **Siren's Gift**[14] 2704 5-9-3 92 ...(b) DavidProbert 3 81
(A M Balding) *midfield: effrt 2f out: no imp fnl f* **9/2**[3]

-231 **5** ½ **Affluent**[33] 2140 3-8-11 90 ... PaulMulrennan 10 77
(R Charlton) *trckd ldrs: effrt 2f out: edgd lft and no ex fnl f* **4/1**[2]

-452 **6** hd **Jargelle (IRE)**[7] 2928 3-8-11 98 ... TonyHamilton 11 76
(K A Ryan) *led to appr fnl f: sn outpcd* **9/4**[1]

-221 **7** 3¼ **Rathlin Light (USA)**[21] 2492 3-8-11 67 ...(t) JamieKyne 7 65
(W R Swinburn) *bhd and sn outpcd: sme late hdwy: nvr on terms* **25/1**

20-0 **8** 1¼ **Percolator**[21] 2481 3-8-11 103 ... TomEaves 1 60
(P F I Cole) *w ldr tl wknd over 1f out* **9/1**

605 **9** 1 **Wibbadune (IRE)**[21] 2492 5-9-3 67 ... DanielTudhope 9 58
(D Shaw) *bhd and outpcd: nvr on terms* **100/1**

0-20 **10** 2½ **Crystal Moments**[21] 2469 3-8-11 90 ... StephenDonohoe 2 47
(E A L Dunlop) *towards rr: outpcd over 3f out: n.d after* **28/1**

57.94 secs (-2.16) **Going Correction** -0.25s/f (Firm)
WFA 3 from 4yo+ 6lb **10** Ran SP% **119.8**
Speed ratings (Par 108): **107,105,101,98,97 97,92,90,88,84**
toteswinger: 1&2 £3.00, 1&3 £28.20, 2&3 £54.60. CSF £38.86 TOTE £6.90: £2.00, £2.20, £2.90; EX 46.50 Trifecta £176.60 Pool: £286.42 - 1.20 winning units..
Owner Rick Barnes **Bred** Grangecon Stud **Trained** Golden, Co Tipperary

FOCUS
A good quality fillies' Listed race that was run at a scorching pace thanks to Jargelle, who blasted off from her high draw and she had Percolator keeping her honest on the front end. That set things up for the closers. The form is rated around the first two with the third appearing to run well above herself.

NOTEBOOK
Sugar Free(IRE), an Irish raider, was always travelling strongly behind the pace before being produced to lead at the furlong pole and stayed on strongly to repel the late thrust of the runner-up, with the pair clear. She was only beaten a length in last year's Queen Mary so she was a classy juvenile, and she has run with credit in two starts this term, both over a stiff 6f, which seems to stretch her. This win will please her breeders, given she is a first foal, and connections are now considering a 6f Group 3 race at York, where the sharp nature of that track should suit. (op 11-2 tchd 5-1)

City Dancer(IRE), whose stable won this race last year, wasn't seen to best effect at Sandown last time but she left that effort way behind here, travelling strongly behind the pace before picking up in good style once switched out to challenge. She is blessed with plenty of natural speed and can make her mark under suitable conditions in this company. (op 6-1 tchd 13-2)

Rothesay Dancer had no right to be anywhere near the first three given her official mark of 77, but she loves to come off a fast pace and she travelled well held up a long way back before picking up nicely. This was a cracking effort but she may be a little flattered given the way things panned out. That will not bother connections though as the black type she earned will boost her value as a broodmare.

Siren's Gift had a bit to find with one or two on these terms and, although she got the perfect tow into the race, she didn't have the change of gear to go with the front two. Her losing run goes back to September 2007. (op 13-2)

Affluent, previously progressive, found this company too hot and couldn't make an impact. Official explanation: jockey said filly was unsuited by the good to firm ground

Jargelle(IRE) probably paid for going to hard early so she deserves to be forgiven this. (op 2-1 tchd 5-2)

Crystal Moments Official explanation: jockey said filly lost it's action in the final furlong

3146 SCOTTISH SUN MISS SCOTLAND H'CAP 1m 5f 13y

3:25 (3:25) (Class 3) (0-95,88) 4-Y-O+ **£11,009** (£3,275; £1,637; £817) **Stalls** Low

Form RPR

-105 **1** **Gordonsville**[10] 2815 6-9-1 82 ... DanielTudhope 3 89
(J S Goldie) *hld up: hdwy to ld after 5f: mde rest: rdn over 2f out: hld on wl whn pressed ins fnl f* **5/1**

3502 **2** 1 **Dolly Penrose**[14] 2720 4-8-13 80 ... TonyCulhane 1 86
(M R Channon) *hld up in tch: hdwy over 2f out: hung lft and chsd wnr over 1f out: ch ins fnl f: hld nr fin* **11/4**[1]

215- **3** 4½ **Master At Arms**[17] 1142 6-8-12 79 ... WMLordan 9 78
(Daniel Mark Loughnane, Ire) *led 5f: chsd ldrs: outpcd over 2f out: kpt on fnl f: no ch w first two* **10/1**

-221 **4** hd **Aleatricis**[29] 2249 4-8-11 83 ... JamieKyne(5) 7 81
(J J Quinn) *prom: outpcd 3f out: rallied over 1f out: no imp* **3/1**[2]

00-0 **5** 2¼ **Mudawin (IRE)**[21] 2486 8-8-9 76 ... DarrenMoffatt 8 71
(James Moffatt) *t.k.h early: trckd ldrs: rdn 3f out: no ex over 1f out* **12/1**

-006 **6** ¾ **Double Banded (IRE)**[7] 2931 5-9-1 82 ... StephenDonohoe 6 76
(Ian Williams) *hld up in tch: effrt 3f out: outpcd fnl 2f* **4/1**[3]

64/0 **7** 5 **Faasel (IRE)**[21] 2486 8-9-3 84 ... TomEaves 2 70
(N G Richards) *in tch: outpcd 1/2-way: struggling fr over 3f out* **11/1**

2m 53.74s (-0.26) **Going Correction** -0.25s/f (Firm) **7** Ran SP% **113.4**
Speed ratings (Par 107): **98,97,94,94,93 92,89**
toteswinger: 1&2 £2.60, 1&3 £12.30, 2&3 £3.30. CSF £18.83 CT £130.44 TOTE £5.80: £2.70, £2.00; EX 24.00.
Owner Mrs Janis Macpherson **Bred** George Strawbridge **Trained** Uplawmoor, E Renfrews

FOCUS
A decent handicap but only two mattered in the later stages and the form is rated around them as it is a bit muddling otherwise.

NOTEBOOK
Gordonsville rider's mid-race move, sweeping around the outside to join the leader, proved a masterstroke because his mount was in front turning for home and he pulled out plenty through the closing stages to bag a third career win.He seemed to relish being out in front and battled on strongly to see off Dolly Penrose in the final furlong to win with his ears pricked. Despite having a stack of placed efforts on his record and having been called plenty of names over the years, this is his second big prize of the season, having won the Musselburgh Gold Cup in April, and it can't be argued that he doesn't pay his way despite his obvious chinks. Connections are planning to run him in the Northumberland Plate if he gets in. (op 6-1)

Dolly Penrose built on her latest Musselburgh second to run right up to her best and, although outbattled by the winner, she kept on really well to come clear of the rest and there are races to be won with her in the north. (op 3-1 tchd 10-3)

Master At Arms, the early pacesetter, looked like dropping away 2f out but he is a winner over hurdles so he stays well and he rallied well in the closing stages. (op 14-1)

Aleatricis kept on steadily but he lacked the gears to challenge, surprisingly given he was stepping up in trip, but he would probably have ideally wanted the early pace to be stronger and remains on an upward curve. Official explanation: jockey said gelding ran flat (op 5-2)

Mudawin(IRE) is undoubtedly well treated nowadays and, although he weakened away in the closing stages, he ran well for a long way and could be slowly working his way back. (op 14-1)

3147 MACBOOKIE EUROPEAN BREEDERS' FUND MAIDEN STKS 6f

4:00 (4:02) (Class 5) 2-Y-O **£3,885** (£1,156; £577; £288) **Stalls** High

Form RPR

3 **1** **Ghostwing**[52] 1610 2-9-3 0 ... TonyHamilton 6 84+
(R A Fahey) *sn cl up: led 2f out: drew clr fnl f* **8/11**[1]

2 6 **Benrish (IRE)** 2-9-3 0 ... TomEaves 1 65+
(B Smart) *t.k.h early: trckd ldrs: smooth hdwy and ev ch over 2f out: one pce over 1f out* **11/2**[2]

3 ¾ **Ask Frank (IRE)** 2-9-3 0 ... PJMcDonald 7 62
(G A Swinbank) *wnt lft s: rn green and outpcd after 2f: hdwy over 1f out: r.o: nvr rchd ldrs* **11/2**[2]

000 **4** 1¾ **Whippers Love (IRE)**[42] 1867 2-9-3 0 ... AndrewMullen 3 57
(M Johnston) *led to 2f out: sn rdn and outpcd* **16/1**

6 **5** 4½ **Sejanus**[30] 2196 2-9-3 0 ... PhillipMakin 2 44
(K A Ryan) *cl up: drvn 1/2-way: sn wknd* **7/1**[3]

6 nse **Jeannie Galloway (IRE)** 2-8-12 0 ... PaulMulrennan 4 38
(A G Foster) *bhd and sn struggling: nvr on terms* **20/1**

1m 13.36s (-0.24) **Going Correction** -0.25s/f (Firm) **6** Ran SP% **111.8**
Speed ratings (Par 93): **91,83,82,79,73 73**
toteswinger: 1&2 £1.30, 1&3 £1.20, 2&3 £2.50. CSF £5.15 TOTE £1.60: £1.10, £2.10; EX 3.80.
Owner Mrs H Steel **Bred** D R Botterill **Trained** Musley Bank, N Yorks
■ Stewards' Enquiry : Andrew Mullen one-day ban: failed to ride to draw (Jul 5)

FOCUS
Not much strength in depth to this maiden, but the first three look nice types and the race could rate a little higher.

NOTEBOOK
Ghostwing ◆ had shaped with promise on his racecourse debut, when trained by Ann Duffield, and he built on that by forging clear in the final furlong to win in very easy fashion. The step up to 6f looked to suit really well and he is a good-looking type who could be above average. (op 5-4)

Benrish(IRE) went left at the start and got detached mid-race as he looked very green, but the penny dropped in the closing stages and he really found his stride to snatch second close home. An £82,000 purchase, he is bred to make a two-year-old, and with the benefit of this outing he should be able to make his mark next time, possibly over another furlong. (op 7-2)

Ask Frank(IRE) also offered plenty of encouragement, travelling eyecatchingly well for a long way before not seeing out the final furlong and he might appreciate the drop back to 5f. He was apparently withdrawn from a race at Hamilton recently because ground conditions were deemed too quick. (tchd 5-1 and 6-1)

Whippers Love(IRE) dropped away after making the running and isn't progressing. Official explanation: one-day ban: failed to ride to draw (Jul 5) (tchd 14-1)

Jeannie Galloway(IRE) might be worth forgiving her effort as she got messed about with in the stalls when Weetentherty played up. (op 16-1)

3148 HELP FOR HEROES H'CAP 6f

4:35 (4:36) (Class 5) (0-70,70) 3-Y-O+ **£2,914** (£867; £433; £216) **Stalls** High

Form RPR

3334 **1** **Maison Dieu**[15] 2660 6-9-3 59 ... AndrewMullen 5 66
(E J Alston) *t.k.h early: hld up in tch: nt clr run over 1f out: squeezed through to ld ins fnl f: r.o* **3/1**[2]

-211 **2** nk **Hansomis (IRE)**[5] 2964 5-9-1 62 6ex ... JamieKyne(5) 3 68
(B Mactaggart) *cl up: led over 1f out to ins fnl f: edgd lft: kpt on fin* **5/2**[1]

4-06 **3** nk **Glasshoughton**[35] 2095 6-10-0 70 ... PhillipMakin 2 75
(M Dods) *stdd in tch: effrt whn n.m.r briefly over 1f out: kpt on fnl f* **9/2**[3]

000- **4** hd **Just For Mary**[14] 2730 5-9-11 67 ... WMLordan 7 71
(Daniel Mark Loughnane, Ire) *trckd ldrs: effrt over 1f out: ev ch ins fnl f: r.o* **6/1**

0000 **5** 3¼ **Obe One**[10] 2812 9-8-9 51 oh6 ... TomEaves 6 45
(A Berry) *trckd ldrs tl rdn and nt qckn over 1f out* **28/1**

0004 **6** 1 **Mr Lu**[16] 2628 4-9-3 59 ...(p) TonyHamilton 4 50
(A G Foster) *prom: outpcd 2f out: no imp fnl f* **5/1**

0060 **7** 9 **Seafield Towers**[22] 2451 9-8-10 59 oh6 ow8 ...(p) RossSmith(7) 8 21
(D A Nolan) *led: hdd and wkng whn hmpd over 1f out* **80/1**

006- **8** 2 **Prospect Court**[360] 3370 7-10-0 70 ... PaulMulrennan 1 26
(A C Whillans) *bhd: outpcd 1/2-way: nvr on terms* **20/1**

1m 12.06s (-1.54) **Going Correction** -0.25s/f (Firm) **8** Ran SP% **112.2**
Speed ratings (Par 103): **100,99,99,98,94 93,81,78**
toteswinger: 1&2 £1.80, 1&3 £3.70, 2&3 £3.60. CSF £10.42 CT £31.25 TOTE £3.40: £1.40, £1.20, £2.00; EX 11.10.
Owner Whitehills Racing Syndicate **Bred** Andy Miller **Trained** Longton, Lancs

FOCUS
A decent sprint handicap run at an even gallop and the front four pulled some way clear. Despite that, the form is a little muddling and the first two off the best guide.

3149 REAL RADIO H'CAP 5f

5:10 (5:10) (Class 4) (0-85,83) 3-Y-O+ **£6,476** (£1,927; £963; £481) **Stalls** High

Form RPR

320 **1** **Le Toreador**[8] 2897 4-9-11 80 ...(t) PaulMulrennan 3 90
(K A Ryan) *cl up: led over 1f out: kpt on wl fnl f* **13/2**

-042 **2** nk **Artsu**[12] 2770 4-9-5 74 ... PhillipMakin 7 83
(M Dods) *hld up: hdwy over 1f out: chsd wnr ins fnl f: r.o* **4/1**[2]

1300 **3** ½ **Nickel Silver**[14] 2716 4-9-9 78 ...(b) TomEaves 8 85
(B Smart) *led to over 1f out: rallied: one pce wl ins fnl f* **9/1**

5305 **4** 3¼ **Steelcut**[8] 2897 5-9-10 79 ...(p) TonyHamilton 9 74
(R A Fahey) *prom: effrt over 1f out: edgd lft and sn no ex* **9/2**[3]

-000 **5** 1¼ **Stolt (IRE)**[14] 2716 5-9-7 81 ... BMcHugh(5) 5 72+
(N Wilson) *blindfold stl on whn put hd down as stalls opened and s.v.s: hdwy 1/2-way: rdn and styd on fnl f: nrst fin* **8/1**

The Form Book, Raceform Ltd, Compton, RG20 6NL

0034 **6** ½ **Green Park (IRE)**[7] 2938 6-9-8 **77**........(b) DNolan 6 66
(D Carroll) *prom tl rdn and wknd over 1f out* **8/1**

-013 **7** 2¾ **Invincible Lad (IRE)**[16] 2637 5-10-0 **83**........ WMLordan 2 62
(E J Alston) *t.k.h: hld up in tch: rdn 2f out: sn wknd* **7/2**[1]

203- **8** 7 **Tadalavil**[257] 6532 4-9-2 **76**........ JamieKyne(5) 4 30
(Miss L A Perratt) *in tch to 1/2-way: sn rdn and wknd* **12/1**

05-0 **9** 18 **Barraland**[14] 2717 4-8-13 **68**........ DanielTudhope 1 —
(J S Goldie) *chsd ldrs on outside to 1/2-way: sn wknd: t.o* **14/1**

58.18 secs (-1.92) **Going Correction** -0.25s/f (Firm) **9** Ran SP% **120.3**
Speed ratings (Par 105): **105,104,103,98,96 95,91,80,51**
toteswinger: 1&2 £3.60, 1&3 £10.10, 2&3 £6.80. CSF £34.17 CT £241.81 TOTE £8.10: £2.40, £1.70, £3.50; EX 26.70.
Owner Guy Reed **Bred** G Reed **Trained** Hambleton, N Yorks

FOCUS
A fair handicap run at a decent gallop and the form looks pretty solid and good for the grade.
Invincible Lad(IRE) Official explanation: jockey said gelding ran flat

3150 ADVANCED WINDOWS H'CAP 1m 2f
5:45 (5:45) (Class 5) (0-75,74) 4-Y-0+ **£3,238** (£963; £481; £240) **Stalls** Low

Form RPR

-533 **1** **Shy Glance (USA)**[23] 2392 7-9-2 **69**........ TonyHamilton 4 74
(P Monteith) *trckd ldrs: led gng wl over 2f out: rdn over 1f out: hld on wl fnl f* **7/4**[1]

6-05 **2** *hd* **Red Skipper (IRE)**[14] 2718 4-8-4 **57**........ AndrewMullen 3 62
(N Wilson) *hld up in tch: hdwy 2f out: chsd wnr ins fnl f: r.o* **14/1**

65-2 **3** *nk* **Wee Charlie Castle (IRE)**[10] 2817 6-9-7 **74**........ TomEaves 6 78
(I Semple) *hld up: hdwy 2f out: kpt on u.p fnl f* **6/1**

5502 **4** ¾ **Grand Diamond (IRE)**[1] 3110 5-8-9 **62**........ DanielTudhope 5 65
(J S Goldie) *chsd ldr: ev ch over 2f out to over 1f out: one pce whn n.m.r nr fin* **3/1**[2]

5/50 **5** 2¼ **Muzmin (USA)**[23] 2415 4-8-9 **62**........ StephenDonohoe 2 60
(E A L Dunlop) *hld up: rdn 3f out: styd on fnl f: nvr able to chal* **10/1**

0030 **6** 29 **Island Music (IRE)**[1] 3098 4-8-5 **63**........ JamieKyne(5) 8 3
(J J Quinn) *led to over 2f out: wknd over 1f out: t.o* **4/1**[3]

000- **7** 13 **Jamieson Gold (IRE)**[225] 7224 6-9-3 **70**........ PhillipMakin 1 —
(Miss L A Perratt) *in tch: struggling 3f out: sn wknd: t.o* **14/1**

2m 9.26s (-2.74) **Going Correction** -0.25s/f (Firm) **7** Ran SP% **118.1**
Speed ratings (Par 103): **100,99,99,99,97 74,63**
toteswinger: 1&2 £6.50, 1&3 £2.90, 2&3 £12.30. CSF £29.45 CT £126.95 TOTE £2.70: £1.60, £6.30; EX 37.80 Place 6 £64.84, Place 5 £45.54.
Owner Walcal Property Development Ltd **Bred** R D Hubbard And Constance Sczesny **Trained** Rosewell, Midlothian

FOCUS
Just an ordinary handicap and muddling form.
Grand Diamond(IRE) Official explanation: jockey said gelding was denied a clear run
T/Plt: £62.70 to a £1 stake. Pool: £54,370.42. 632.62 winning tickets. T/Qpdt: £7.50 to a £1 stake. Pool: £3,245.80. 318.40 winning tickets. RY

2838 HAYDOCK (L-H)
Saturday, June 20

OFFICIAL GOING: Good (good to firm in places; watered; firm from 1m 2f to 1m; goingstick 8.1)
Rail realignment increased distances on round course by 30yards.
Wind: Light, against Weather: Cloudy with sunny periods

3151 BET ONLINE AT CORBETTSPORTS.COM P.J.A. APPRENTICE SERIES H'CAP 1m 2f 95y
6:35 (6:35) (Class 5) (0-75,71) 4-Y-0+ **£3,238** (£963; £481; £240) **Stalls** High

Form RPR

3-0 **1** **Hippolytus**[47] 1737 4-9-4 **68**........ RussellKennemore 6 76
(J J Quinn) *trckd ldrs: hdwy 3f out: chal wl over 1f out: rdn to ld ent fnl f: sn drvn and kpt on wl towards fin* **9/4**[1]

1140 **2** 1¼ **Agilete**[10] 2824 7-8-12 **67**........ SimonPearce(5) 7 72
(J Pearce) *hld up in rr: gd hdwy on outer over 2f out: rdn to chse wnr ent fnl f: sn drvn and kpt on* **6/1**[3]

2-01 **3** 1½ **Princess Rainbow (FR)**[30] 2200 4-9-4 **71**........ JackDean(3) 5 73
(Jennie Candlish) *plld hrd: sn trcking ldng pair: hdwy over 3f out: rdn along over 2f out and sltly outpcd: swtchd lft and drvn over 1f out: kpt on ins fnl f* **9/4**[1]

11-0 **4** 1 **Lilac Moon (GER)**[94] 873 5-8-13 **68**........ RossAtkinson(5) 2 68
(N J Vaughan) *led 2f: trckd ldr tl led 3f out: rdn along and hung lft wl over 1f out: drvn and hdd ent fnl f: sn one pce* **5/1**[2]

600/ **5** 4½ **Astronomical (IRE)**[1066] 3686 7-8-9 **66**........ DavidKenny(7) 4 57
(R Hollinshead) *in tch on inner: effrt 3f out: sn rdn along and no hdwy fnl 2f* **5/1**[2]

00-0 **6** 10 **Royal Fantasy (IRE)**[8] 2894 6-9-0 **71**........ GemmaElford(7) 1 42
(N Tinkler) *plld hrd and rapid hdwy to ld after 2f: rdn and qcknd over 4f out: hdd 3f out and sn wknd* **33/1**

2m 22.66s (9.66) **Going Correction** +0.525s/f (Yiel) **6** Ran SP% **112.1**
Speed ratings (Par 103): **91,90,88,88,84 76**
toteswinger: 1&2 £5.50, 1&3 £1.90, 2&3 £2.10. CSF £16.37 CT £32.08 TOTE £4.10: £1.60, £2.30; EX 17.60.
Owner Lady Legard **Bred** Lady Legard **Trained** Settrington, N Yorks

FOCUS
The form of this apprentices' contest is muddling and should be treated with some caution, as half of the six-strong field either played up before the race, pulled too hard during the moderate early fractions, or both.

3152 LAURA HART 18TH BIRTHDAY MAIDEN AUCTION STKS 5f
7:05 (7:05) (Class 5) 2-Y-0 **£3,238** (£963; £481; £240) **Stalls** Centre

Form RPR

1 **Schoolboy Champ** 2-8-9 0........ JerryO'Dwyer 1 74
(Patrick Morris) *hld up towards rr: stdy hdwy 2f out: rdn to ld jst ins fnl f: pushed out* **33/1**

4652 **2** 2½ **Mal And Dave (IRE)**[10] 2800 2-8-12 0........ J-PGuillambert 10 68
(D Nicholls) *cl up: led 1/2-way: rdn wl over 1f out: drvn and edgd rt over 1f out: hdd jst ins fnl f and one pce* **11/8**[1]

306 **3** *nse* **Gentle Beat (IRE)**[17] 2610 2-9-1 0........ GrahamGibbons 5 71
(T D Easterby) *chsd ldrs: rdn along 2f out: drvn over 1f out: kpt on u.p ins fnl f* **14/1**

4 6 **Brasingaman Eric** 2-8-9 0........ DaleGibson 9 43
(Mrs G S Rees) *dwlt: pushed along 1/2-way: rdn and hdwy whn hung lft wl over 1f out: kpt on ins fnl f: n.d* **28/1**

5 ¾ **Daisy Brown** 2-8-1 0........ NataliaGemelova(3) 4 36
(N Tinkler) *s.i.s and bhd: hung bdly lft 1/2-way: sme late hdwy* **33/1**

4020 **6** 1 **Goodbye Earl (IRE)**[14] 2714 2-7-11 0........ CharlotteKerton(7) 7 32
(A Berry) *t.k.h: led tl rdn and hdd 1/2-way: sn wandered and wknd* **7/2**[3]

24 **7** ½ **Pepper Lane**[22] 2449 2-8-7 0........ RichardMullen 2 33
(T D Barron) *chsd ldrs: rdn along 2f out and sn wknd* **10/3**[2]

8 7 **Sparking** 2-8-2 0........ LanceBetts(5) 8 8
(Mrs G S Rees) *s.i.s: a bhd* **11/1**

62.60 secs (2.10) **Going Correction** +0.40s/f (Good) **8** Ran SP% **111.7**
Speed ratings (Par 93): **99,95,94,85,84 82,81,70**
toteswinger: 1&2 £7.30, 1&3 £19.20, 2&3 £5.10. CSF £75.85 TOTE £22.50: £4.40, £1.10, £3.00; EX 120.00.
Owner Chester Racing Club Ltd **Bred** Stephen Hillen And Hatta Bloodstock **Trained** Tarporley, Cheshire
■ Stewards' Enquiry : Charlotte Kerton one-day ban: used whip without giving filly time to respond (Jul 5)

FOCUS
This looked just a modest maiden beforehand, with none of those already handicapped commanding a mark in excess of 71. The first three finished well clear and the form is assessed through the runner-up.

NOTEBOOK
Schoolboy Champ did not make a lot of appeal as a winning debutant beforehand judged on the achievements of either his half siblings or his trainer (0-11 in juvenile races over the last five seasons before tonight), but this son of Trade Fair still looked full of running two furlongs out after a quiet ride to that point and only needed to be pushed out hands and heels once sent on. He holds entries in the Weatherbys Super Sprint, St Leger Yearling Stakes and Redcar Two-Year-Old Trophy. (op 22-1 tchd 20-1)
Mal And Dave(IRE) showed the same early pace as when denied by only half a length in a Beverley claimer last time out, but once again wasn't quite able to maintain the effort late on. He chased the early pace on his Musselburgh debut, the one race in his career to date around a sharp 5f, and it might be worth sending him back to such a course but attempting to make all instead. (op 5-2)
Gentle Beat(IRE) was already being urged along just before halfway, but he did respond to a degree to press Mal And Dave for second close home. He hadn't seen out either this trip or 6f in his three previous outings, so this represented a step forward in that regard. (op 12-1 tchd 11-1)
Brasingaman Eric ran as well as could have been expected over a trip his breeding suggested would prove well short of his optimum. (tchd 33-1)
Goodbye Earl(IRE) was too free to post and carried that over-exuberance with her into the race early on. (op 9-4 tchd 4-1)
Pepper Lane is starting to look worryingly regressive after a fair debut. (op 3-1 tchd 11-4)

3153 ABACUS SECURITIES FILLIES' H'CAP 6f
7:35 (7:36) (Class 5) (0-75,75) 3-Y-0+ **£3,238** (£963; £481; £240) **Stalls** Centre

Form RPR

3662 **1** **Mango Music**[26] 2334 6-10-0 **75**........ RichardMullen 4 84
(M Quinn) *mde all: rdn wl over 1f out: drvn and edgd lft ins fnl f kpt on* **11/10**[1]

24 **2** 1 **Catalan Bay (AUS)**[115] 680 5-10-0 **75**........ ClareLindop 1 81
(J R Gask) *cl up: effrt 2f out: sn rdn and ev ch tl carried lft and no ex wl ins fnl f* **9/2**[3]

0453 **3** 3½ **Miss Daawe**[22] 2436 5-8-9 **61**........ LanceBetts(5) 2 56
(B Ellison) *trckd ldrs effrt over 2f out sn rdn: drvn and one pce over 1f out* **7/4**[2]

0006 **4** 11 **Andrasta**[3] 3021 4-8-2 **56** oh1........ CharlotteKerton(7) 6 15
(A Berry) *wnt rt s: sn cl up rdn 1/2-way and sn wknd* **14/1**

1m 16.31s (2.31) **Going Correction** +0.40s/f (Good)
WFA 3 from 4yo+ 7lb **4** Ran SP% **108.8**
Speed ratings (Par 100): **100,98,94,79**
toteswinger: 1&2 £2.20. CSF £6.29 TOTE £2.20; EX 4.20.
Owner Brian Morton **Bred** A G Antoniades **Trained** Newmarket, Suffolk
■ Stewards' Enquiry : Clare Lindop two-day ban: used whip with excessive frequency without giving mare time to respond (Jul 5-6)

FOCUS
The defection of half the original eight-strong field (including two of the top five in the betting) denuded this fillies' race of much of its interest. The winner probably only had to match her recent best.

3154 MTB GROUP H'CAP 1m 30y
8:05 (8:05) (Class 3) (0-90,86) 3-Y-0+ **£9,066** (£2,697; £1,348; £673) **Stalls** Low

Form RPR

0 **1** **One Way Or Another (AUS)**[14] 2695 6-10-0 **86**........ ClareLindop 6 94
(J R Gask) *hld up in tch: hdwy over 3f out: rdn to ld 1f out: sn drvn and hld on gamely* **14/1**

-250 **2** *hd* **Charlie Tipple**[34] 2101 5-9-10 **82**........(p) GrahamGibbons 5 90
(T D Easterby) *t.k.h early: chsd ldrs tl outpcd over 3f out and sn rdn along: swtchd rt and hdwy 2f out: drvn to chse wnr ins fnl f: kpt on wl towards fin* **11/4**[2]

0521 **3** 4½ **Ezdeyaad (USA)**[10] 2822 5-9-11 **83**........ PJMcDonald 2 81
(G A Swinbank) *t.k.h: sn led and clr: rdn along wl over 1f out: hdd ent fnl f and sn one pce* **5/2**[1]

363 **4** 2½ **Grey Boy (GER)**[10] 2828 8-9-1 **73**........ TolleyDean 4 65
(A W Carroll) *in rr: rdn along and hdwy 3f out: drvn and no imp wl over 1f out* **13/2**

0-03 **5** 12 **Brasingaman Hifive**[28] 2274 4-9-5 **77**........ DaleGibson 7 41
(Mrs G S Rees) *chsd ldrs: rdn along 3f out and sn wknd* **5/1**

320/ **6** 3½ **King In Waiting (IRE)**[121] 5056 6-9-13 **85**........ JerryO'Dwyer 3 41
(J Hetherton) *sn outpcd and bhd fr 1/2-way* **28/1**

0-21 **7** 1¾ **Never Ending Tale**[15] 2666 4-9-13 **85**........(p) GregFairley 1 37
(E F Vaughan) *t.k.h: chsd ldr: rdn along 3f out and sn wknd* **4/1**[3]

1m 46.49s (2.69) **Going Correction** +0.525s/f (Yiel) **7** Ran SP% **115.4**
Speed ratings (Par 107): **107,106,102,99,87 84,82**
toteswinger: 1&2 £7.40, 1&3 £6.50, 2&3 £1.80. CSF £53.36 TOTE £8.50: £4.00, £2.10; EX 46.80.
Owner Simon Rowlands **Bred** Segenhoe Stud **Trained** Sutton Veny, Wilts
■ The first winner in Britain for Clare Lindop, Australia's leading female jockey.

FOCUS
The first of three consecutive races run over 1m trip was run at a very generous pace, favouring a couple of participants raced more patiently. The winner built on his British debut and may do a bit better.

NOTEBOOK
One Way Or Another(AUS), who looked rippling with health in the paddock, declined the worst excesses of the early pace and found plenty for Clare Lindop's urgings, despite her fears that she had sent him to take closer order a fraction too soon turning in. This strongly run race was almost certainly just what was needed for a gelding successfully campaigned over up to 1m2f in his native Australia this time last year, and he looks fully acclimatised now after two quick runs following a nine-month absence. Plans remain fluid for him. (op 11-1)

Charlie Tipple, plunged in from 7-1 three hours previously, also had the race run to suit, but he didn't enjoy an entirely untrammelled passage entering the final quarter mile. It's a moot point whether the resultant delay to his forward move at that point cost him the race, though, as the winner was in determined mood. He remains of interest at this level, notwithstanding a mark still 4lb above his highest winning one. (op 6-1)
Ezdeyaad(USA) never saw another rival when scoring over course and distance ten days ago, but he was hoisted by his own petard here, setting a pace he couldn't live with himself. (op 2-1 tchd 7-4)
Grey Boy(GER) never threatened on this occasion and would have preferred an easier track. (op 11-2)
Brasingaman Hifive Official explanation: jockey said filly slipped on final bend
Never Ending Tale didn't handle the bend out of the back straight, and the high head carriage of two runs ago resurfaced late on, too. He doesn't appear to be one to trust implicitly. (op 7-2 tchd 9-2)

3155 RACING UK £12.99 PER MONTH MAIDEN STKS 1m 30y
8:35 (8:36) (Class 5) 3-Y-0+ £3,238 (£963; £481; £240) Stalls Low

Form RPR
40- 1 **Royal Destination (IRE)**[337] 4161 4-9-12 0 DaleGibson 6 85+
(J Noseda) *prom: effrt to challlenge 2f out: rdn to ld ent fnl f: kpt on gamely* **9/4**[2]
2 *nk* **Espero (IRE)**[243] 6869 3-9-2 0 GrahamGibbons 8 82?
(R A Farrant) *hld up in rr: hdwy 3f out: switchd rt and rdn over 1f out: drvn to chal ins fnl f and ev ch tl nt qckn nr fin* **16/1**
220- 3 *½* **Captain Ellis (USA)**[259] 6483 3-9-2 85 AndrewElliott 5 81
(K R Burke) *led: rdn along and jnd 2f out: drvn and hdd ent fnl f: kpt on* **7/4**[1]
2- 4 *2½* **Light Sleeper**[289] 5649 3-9-2 0 RichardMullen 1 75
(P W Chapple-Hyam) *in tch: hdwy on inner 3f out chal 2f out and ev ch tl rdn and wknd appr fnl f* **4/1**[3]
0/0- 5 *9* **Perez Prado (USA)**[399] 2199 4-9-12 0 J-PGuillambert 7 56
(W Jarvis) *trckd ldrs hdwy on outer and cl up 1/2-way: rdn 3f and sn wknd* **8/1**
5 6 *7* **Elusive Muse**[65] 1308 3-9-2 0 PJMcDonald 4 40
(M Dods) *chsd ldrs tl rdn and wknd 3f out* **8/1**
6/0- 7 *28* **Becky Quick (IRE)**[343] 3955 4-9-0 0 (b[1]) CharlotteKerton(7) 2 —
(Bruce Hellier) *plld hrd: hased ldrs tl lost pl and bhd fr 1/2-way* **66/1**
1m 48.8s (5.00) **Going Correction** +0.525s/f (Yiel)
WFA 3 from 4yo 10lb 7 Ran SP% **116.7**
Speed ratings (Par 103): **96,95,95,92,83 76,48**
toteswinger: 1&2 £10.70, 1&3 £2.00, 2&3 £10.00. CSF £37.39 TOTE £4.80: £2.40, £5.50; EX 54.10.
Owner Vimal Khosla **Bred** Miss Deirdre Barry **Trained** Newmarket, Suffolk
FOCUS
Six of the seven horses to stand their ground were returning from absences of 243 days or more. The early pace was far gentler than in the preceding 1m contest and the time was the slowest of the three C/D contests. The form is rated around the winner and fourth.

3156 SUBSCRIBE ONLINE AT RACINGUK.COM H'CAP 1m 30y
9:05 (9:06) (Class 4) (0-80,80) 3-Y-0 £5,504 (£1,637; £818; £408) Stalls Low

Form RPR
-123 1 **Royal Executioner (USA)**[23] 2399 3-9-7 80 RichardMullen 7 89
(D M Simcock) *hld up towards rr: hdwy over 2f out: rdn to ld over 1f out: qcknd clr ent fnl f: styd on strly* **3/1**[2]
3135 2 *2½* **Captainrisk (IRE)**[42] 1895 3-9-0 73 (p) JerryO'Dwyer 4 76
(M Botti) *hld up in rr: gd hdwy on outer 2f out: rdn to chse wnr and hung lft ins fnl f: no imp* **20/1**
-621 3 *2½* **Mr Freddy (IRE)**[24] 2370 3-8-12 71 JamieMoriarty 3 77+
(R A Fahey) *hld up: hdwy on inner and nt clr run 2f out: sn swtchd rt and rdn: kpt on u.p ins fnl f* **9/4**[1]
6-21 4 *2¼* **Veroon (IRE)**[18] 2572 3-9-0 73 J-PGuillambert 1 65
(J G Given) *trckd ldrs: effrt over 2f out: sn rdn and one pce* **7/2**[3]
-344 5 *1½* **Hypnotic Gaze (IRE)**[73] 1193 3-8-6 65 GrahamGibbons 6 54
(J Mackie) *trckd ldrs: effrt over 2f out and ch tl rdn and wknd over 1f out* **7/1**
-505 6 *¾* **Hey Up Dad**[19] 2545 3-8-8 67 (b[1]) PJMcDonald 5 54
(M Dods) *t.k.h: led 2f: cl up tl rdn and led wl over 2f out: drvn and hdd over 1f out: wknd* **15/2**
-105 7 *19* **Lastroarofdtiger (USA)**[23] 2399 3-8-13 77 MartinLane(5) 2 20
(K R Burke) *cl up: led after 2f: rdn along 3f out and sn hdd: wknd and eased fnl 2f* **9/1**
1m 45.92s (2.12) **Going Correction** +0.525s/f (Yiel) 7 Ran SP% **117.0**
Speed ratings (Par 101): **110,107,105,102,101 100,81**
toteswinger: 1&2 £9.60, 1&3 £1.20, 2&3 £8.50. CSF £57.82 TOTE £4.10: £2.40, £3.70; EX 36.10 Place 6 £236.24, Place 5 £98.92.
Owner DXB Bloodstock Ltd **Bred** Hot Silks Racing Stable Llc **Trained** Newmarket, Suffolk
FOCUS
This proved to be the quickest of the three 1m contests that ended the card, clocking in half a second quicker than the 0-90 handicap despite a more modest early pace. Fair form.
Mr Freddy(IRE) Official explanation: jockey said colt was denied a clear run
T/Plt: £976.00 to a £1 stake. Pool: £60,900.27. 45.55 winning tickets. T/Qpdt: £236.20 to a £1 stake. Pool: £5,490.24. 17.20 winning tickets. JR

2919 LINGFIELD (L-H)
Saturday, June 20

OFFICIAL GOING: Turf course - good to firm (8.6); all-weather - standard
Wind: Almost nil Weather: Fine but cloudy

3157 SEVENOAKS (S) STKS 1m 4f (P)
5:50 (5:50) (Class 6) 3-Y-0 £2,047 (£604; £302) Stalls Low

Form RPR
00-0 1 **Captain Flack**[21] 2488 3-8-12 50 (b[1]) LPKeniry 10 58
(J A R Toller) *trckd ldr: rdn to ld over 2f out: drvn over 2l clr 1f out: styd on wl* **33/1**
0-00 2 *1¾* **Diktalina**[30] 2204 3-8-7 55 DO'Donohoe 6 50
(W R Muir) *hld up in rr: prog to go 4th 3f out: rdn over 2f out and nt qckn: styd on to take 2nd last 100yds: no imp on wnr nr fin* **5/1**[2]
0013 3 *2½* **First Spirit**[12] 2772 3-8-5 56 (p) AshleyMorgan(7) 8 51
(J S Moore) *racd wd: hld up: trckd ldrs 5f out: wnt 3rd 3f out: nt qckn over 2f out: kpt on same pce u.p* **1/1**[1]
000- 4 *¾* **Timbaa (USA)**[232] 7105 3-8-12 52 RichardKingscote 1 50
(Rae Guest) *led at stdy pce: rdn and hdd over 2f out: w wnr wl over 1f out: sn fdd* **7/1**[3]
0-00 5 *2½* **Gaelic Rose (IRE)**[40] 1931 3-8-7 50 JamesDoyle 9 41
(S Kirk) *hld up in last pair: rdn 5f out: effrt on wd outside 3f out: no imp on ldrs fnl 2f* **12/1**
3005 6 *8* **Dulce Domum**[10] 2802 3-8-4 46 ow4 PNolan(7) 2 32
(A B Haynes) *awkward s and jockey lost iron briefly: in tch in rr tl wknd over 2f out* **12/1**
-006 7 *3* **Top Tinker**[13] 2743 3-8-12 47 SteveDrowne 7 28
(M H Tompkins) *hld up in last pair: pushed along over 3f out: outpcd wl over 2f out: wknd over 1f out* **7/1**[3]
-560 8 *½* **Diktaram**[43] 1829 3-8-12 47 (p) EdwardCreighton 4 28
(J R Weymes) *trckd ldng pair: rdn over 4f out: lost pl 3f out: sn wknd* **22/1**
56-0 9 *23* **Baileys Red**[22] 2461 3-8-12 52 PatCosgrave 5 —
(J G Given) *trckd ldrs tl wknd rapidly over 3f out: t.o* **12/1**
2m 34.92s (1.92) **Going Correction** +0.05s/f (Slow) 9 Ran SP% **122.0**
Speed ratings (Par 97): **95,93,92,91,90 84,82,82,67**
toteswinger: 1&2 £32.10, 1&3 £3.60, 2&3 £1.10. CSF £200.62 TOTE £31.00: £8.20, £2.40, £1.10; EX 375.00.There was no bid for the winner.
Owner M A Whelton **Bred** T R Lock **Trained** Newmarket, Suffolk
■ Stewards' Enquiry : P Nolan two-day ban: used whip when out of contention (Jul 5-6)
FOCUS
This poor seller was run at a fair pace until it steadied for a couple down the back straight.

3158 NSPCC CHILD'S VOICE APPEAL H'CAP 1m 2f (P)
6:20 (6:21) (Class 6) (0-60,60) 4-Y-0+ £2,047 (£604; £302) Stalls Low

Form RPR
0610 1 **Free Tussy (ARG)**[7] 2923 5-9-4 60 (bt) PatCosgrave 9 68
(G L Moore) *hld up towards rr: stdy prog fr 3f out gng wl: rdn on outer to ld over 1f out: jnd ins fnl f: edgd lft but battled on wl* **7/2**[1]
0030 2 *nse* **Binnion Bay (IRE)**[7] 2924 8-8-11 53 (p) NeilChalmers 6 61
(J J Bridger) *stdd s: hld up in rr: stdy prog over 3f out gng wl: drvn on outer wl over 1f out: r.o to join wnr ins fnl f: jst hld* **11/1**
-003 3 *2¾* **Son Of My Heart (USA)**[29] 2221 4-9-4 60 SteveDrowne 3 63
(P F I Cole) *t.k.h early: led 3f: cl up: effrt again to chal over 1f out towards inner: outpcd by ldng pair fnl f* **9/2**[3]
06/0 4 *2¼* **Homebred Star**[14] 2708 8-8-4 46 oh1 FrankieMcDonald 10 44
(G P Enright) *stdd s: hld up in last trio: stl there wl over 1f out: drvn and hanging after: rapid prog ent fnl f: one pce last 100yds* **33/1**
534/ 5 *1* **Henry Holmes**[381] 7256 6-8-4 46 RichardThomas 2 42
(Mrs L Richards) *trckd ldrs: effrt on inner 2f out: prog and cl nough 1f out: sn wl outpcd* **25/1**
6500 6 *1½* **Bridge Of Fermoy (IRE)**[7] 2923 4-8-5 50 (p) KevinGhunowa(3) 4 43
(D C O'Brien) *trckd ldrs: cl up 2f out: rdn and nt qckn over 1f out: sn btn* **20/1**
5460 7 *1¾* **Musashi (IRE)**[7] 2923 4-9-0 56 PaulDoe 14 46
(Mrs L J Mongan) *s.s: rushed up on wd outside to ld after 1f: hdd & wknd over 1f out* **8/1**
0-00 8 *hd* **Stormy Summer**[29] 2244 4-9-0 56 (tp) EdwardCreighton 11 45
(R W Price) *trckd ldrs: prog to go 2nd over 2f out: nt qckn wl over 1f out: wknd fnl f* **9/1**
0-00 9 *1¼* **Abbeygate**[149] 254 8-7-11 46 oh1 TraceyAddey(7) 13 33
(T Keddy) *hld up towards rr: prog on wd outside and wl in tch over 2f out: wknd over 1f out* **25/1**
0505 10 *1* **Play Up Pompey**[7] 2923 7-8-6 48 RichardKingscote 12 33
(J J Bridger) *s.s: sn midfield: lost pl and wl in rr 2f out: no ch after* **4/1**[2]
045- 11 *nk* **Sponge**[306] 5150 4-8-10 52 LPKeniry 7 36
(P R Chamings) *rdn in midfield 1/2-way: sn dropped to rr and btn* **11/1**
-000 12 *nk* **Space Pirate**[29] 2221 4-8-4 46 oh1 (p) DO'Donohoe 5 29
(J Pearce) *s.i.s: hld up in last trio: stl there over 1f out: kpt on against far rail: no imp* **20/1**
434- 13 *1¼* **Dot's Delight**[458] 930 5-8-4 46 oh1 SaleemGolam 8 27
(M G Rimell) *t.k.h: trckd ldr after 3f: losing pl qckly whn n.m.r over 2f out* **9/1**
2m 6.40s (-0.20) **Going Correction** +0.05s/f (Slow) 13 Ran SP% **128.3**
Speed ratings (Par 101): **102,101,99,97,97 95,94,94,93,92 92,92,91**
toteswinger: 1&2 £10.40, 1&3 £6.00, 2&3 £3.70. CSF £43.08 CT £186.97 TOTE £4.80: £1.90, £2.50, £2.30; EX 52.70.
Owner T Bowley **Bred** Antonio Carlos Iguacel Et Al **Trained** Lower Beeding, W Sussex
FOCUS
A modest handicap run at just an ordinary pace until quickening over 3f out. The form is ordinary but the placed horses were close to form.
Tallulah Sunrise Official explanation: vet said filly returned sore and lame

3159 MID-SUMMER H'CAP 7f 140y
6:50 (6:52) (Class 5) (0-75,75) 3-Y-0+ £3,070 (£906; £453) Stalls Centre

Form RPR
0053 1 **Carlitos Spirit (IRE)**[21] 2491 5-9-11 75 JamesMillman(3) 13 84
(B R Millman) *taken down early: mde virtually all and racd against nr side rail: rdn over 1f out: a holding rivals after* **15/8**[1]
6550 2 *1* **Diamond Twister (USA)**[9] 2850 3-8-10 67 (t) RobertWinston 3 72+
(J R Best) *trckd ldrs towards outer: prog to chse wnr wl over 1f out: styd on but a hld* **13/2**
6006 3 *2¼* **Charles Darwin (IRE)**[11] 2799 6-9-6 67 SteveDrowne 8 68
(M Blanshard) *hld up in midfield: swtchd lft to outer 2f out: rdn and prog over 1f out: one pce ins fnl f* **16/1**
31-0 4 *1* **Pressing Matters (IRE)**[59] 1466 3-8-10 72 AndreaAtzeni(5) 12 68
(M Botti) *hld up bhd ldrs against nr side rail: rdn 2f out: nt pce to trble ldrs fnl f* **5/1**[2]
3406 5 *1½* **Comadoir (IRE)**[60] 1434 3-9-4 75 JamesDoyle 6 68
(Miss Jo Crowley) *pressed ldrs: rdn over 2f out: lost pl over 1f out: one pce and n.d after* **16/1**
4-60 6 *nk* **Davids Matador**[22] 2432 3-8-13 70 StephenCarson 5 62
(Eve Johnson Houghton) *trckd ldrs towards outer gng wl: rdn to dispute 2nd over 1f out: fnd nil and sn btn* **12/1**
0245 7 *½* **Napoletano (GER)**[13] 2736 8-9-4 65 (p) SebSanders 11 58+
(S Dow) *stdd s: hld up in rr and racd against nr side rail: eased out over 1f out and sn rn into trble: nvr able to get involved* **13/2**
2-30 8 *nk* **Piccolo Mondo**[36] 2048 3-8-12 69 (t) SaleemGolam 9 59
(P Winkworth) *awkward s: wl in rr: effrt on outer over 2f out: plugged on same pce fr over 1f out: n.d* **16/1**
0-00 9 *6* **Bermondsey Bob (IRE)**[37] 2010 3-8-3 60 LiamJones 2 35
(J L Spearing) *w wnr to 3f out: sn drvn: wknd wl over 1f out* **33/1**
1160 10 *1* **Woolston Ferry (IRE)**[23] 2399 3-9-4 75 FrankieMcDonald 10 47
(David Pinder) *hld up in rr against nr side rail: eased out and effrt over 2f out: no real prog and wl btn whn hmpd 1f out* **20/1**

6-43 **11** *8* **Mrs Slocombe (IRE)**[11] 2797 3-8-7 **64** .... MartinDwyer 7 16
(J Akehurst) *awkward s: towards rr on outer: rdn over 3f out: no prog: wknd wl over 1f out* **6/1**[3]
0000 **12** *2* **Glencalvie (IRE)**[14] 2713 8-8-7 **61** .... (p) BarryAdams(7) 1 10
(J Akehurst) *s.s: racd wd: a in rr: wl bhd fnl 2f* **25/1**
02-0 **13** *½* **Deo Valente (IRE)**[21] 2495 4-9-11 **72** .... LPKeniry 4 20
(J M Bradley) *taken down early: awkward s and slowly away: a wl in rr: bhd fnl 2f* **25/1**

1m 29.84s (-2.46) **Going Correction** -0.225s/f (Firm)
WFA 3 from 4yo+ 10lb **13** Ran SP% **133.1**
Speed ratings (Par 103): **103,102,99,98,97 96,96,96,90,89 81,79,78**
toteswinger: 1&2 £4.90, 1&3 £11.00, 2&3 £51.40. CSF £15.39 CT £177.57 TOTE £3.20: £1.50, £2.70, £2.90; EX 23.20.
Owner Karmaa Racing Limited **Bred** Tally-Ho Stud **Trained** Kentisbeare, Devon
■ Stewards' Enquiry : Robert Winston caution: careless riding.
Andrea Atzeni one-day ban: careless riding (Jul 11)

FOCUS
The turf track was reported to be good to firm and this competitive but modest 7f handicap was run at a fair pace. The form is ordinary rated around the first two.

3160 EDENBRIDGE MAIDEN AUCTION STKS 7f
7:20 (7:25) (Class 6) 2-Y-O **£2,729** (£806; £403) **Stalls** High

Form RPR
3225 **1** **Toga Tiger (IRE)**[14] 2721 2-8-13 0 .... DarryllHolland 8 82
(M R Channon) *trckd ldrs: rdn over 2f out: chal u.p over 1f out: narrow ld ins fnl f: kpt on wl* **6/4**[1]
2 **2** *nk* **Coloursoftheglen (IRE)**[30] 2196 2-8-12 0 .... RichardKingscote 4 80
(Tom Dascombe) *sn led: crossed to nr side rail over 2f out: hrd pressed over 1f out: narrowly hdd ins fnl f: kpt on wl* **6/4**[1]
3 *2½* **Go Forth North (USA)** 2-8-4 0 .... LiamJones 7 66+
(M L W Bell) *in rr of main gp: nt clr run briefly over 2f out: prog sn after: reminder 1f out: pushed along and styd on to take 3rd nr fin* **12/1**[2]
4 *1½* **Heading To First** 2-8-9 0 .... SebSanders 1 67
(C E Brittain) *racd on outer: pressed ldrs gng strly: upsides over 1f out: shkn up and wknd fnl f* **25/1**
5 *6* **Whiepa Snappa (IRE)** 2-8-11 0 .... IanMongan 6 54
(P M Phelan) *wl in tch: outpcd fr over 2f out: sn n.d* **14/1**[3]
6 *2¼* **Orsett Lad (USA)** 2-8-12 0 .... RobertWinston 5 50
(J R Best) *dwlt: wl in rr: prog over 2f out to chse ldrs over 1f out: wknd sn after* **20/1**
7 *1½* **Seeker Rainbow** 2-8-6 0 .... FrankieMcDonald 11 40
(Mrs L C Jewell) *s.i.s: sn prom and racd against nr side rail: fdd fr over 2f out* **50/1**
8 *hd* **Inittowinit** 2-8-4 0 .... MartinDwyer 12 37
(W R Muir) *racd against nr side rail but nt pce to hold prom position: rdn over 2f out: sn btn* **16/1**
9 *5* **Stadium Of Light (IRE)** 2-9-1 0 .... TravisBlock 3 36+
(H Morrison) *dwlt: gd spd to press ldrs: jst beginning to lose pl whn squeezed out 2f out: wknd* **20/1**
433 **10** *1* **Midnight Uno**[29] 2218 2-8-4 0 .... WilliamCarson(5) 9 27
(W G M Turner) *sn struggling in last trio: nvr on terms* **16/1**
11 *2½* **Jinksy Minx** 2-8-6 0 .... SaleemGolam 2 18
(Miss Suzy Smith) *dwlt: rn green and a struggling in last trio* **25/1**
12 *½* **The Great Husk (IRE)** 2-8-9 0 .... LPKeniry 10 20
(J S Moore) *sn pushed along and struggling to go the pce: a wl in rr* **33/1**

1m 23.2s (-0.10) **Going Correction** -0.225s/f (Firm) **12** Ran SP% **128.2**
Speed ratings (Par 91): **91,90,87,86,79 76,74,74,69,67 65,64**
toteswinger: 1&2 £1.30, 1&3 £8.00, 2&3 £8.70. CSF £3.42 TOTE £2.80: £1.10, £1.30, £4.10; EX 5.70.
Owner Ridgeway Downs Racing **Bred** Daniel Spaight **Trained** West Ilsley, Berks

FOCUS
Not a lot to go on but those with form set a fairly solid standard for this 7f maiden auction. They were taken along at a decent pace with the front four finishing well clear of the remainder.

NOTEBOOK
Toga Tiger(IRE) put behind him a rather below-par effort at Newcastle on softish ground on his previous start to land the spoils here. He was settled just behind the leaders but had to dig deep against his market rival to gain the initiative inside the final furlong. (op 5-2 tchd 11-10)
Coloursoftheglen(IRE), from a poor draw, soon tacked across to take over at the head of affairs. He stuck on well when headed inside the final furlong and again should be better for this, as he got rather worked up beforehand. (op 9-4 tchd 5-2, 5-4 in a place)
Go Forth North(USA), the first runner for Derby-winning sire North Light and a tall lengthy filly, was slowly into her stride. She raced slightly green but once sent about her task knuckled down well enough, doing her best work towards the finish to snatch third. It was an encouraging debut and she should build on it. (op 9-1)
Heading To First ◆ took the eye beforehand and travelled well just off the pace. He looked menacing when mounting his effort over a furlong out but tired in the closing stages and lost third towards the finish. He should come on a bundle for the run and is one to note, as he would not have to improve too much to score. (op 14-1)

3161 BATTLE OF THE DIVAS JULY 25TH MAIDEN STKS 6f
7:50 (7:57) (Class 5) 3-Y-O+ **£2,729** (£806; £403) **Stalls** High

Form RPR
-43 **1** **Intolerable (IRE)**[17] 2603 3-9-0 0 .... SebSanders 7 75
(R M Beckett) *racd against nr side rail: mde all: rdn 2f out: drew clr fnl f* **3/1**[2]
243 **2** *2¼* **George Thisby**[48] 1703 3-8-11 75 .... JamesMillman(3) 2 68+
(B R Millman) *wl on terms but racd wd: def 2nd fr 2f out: cl enough 1f out: outpcd fnl f* **5/4**[1]
30-5 **3** *hd* **Summers Target (USA)**[27] 2298 3-9-0 84 .... AdamKirby 4 67
(R M H Cowell) *hld up bhd ldrs: effrt over 2f out: rdn and styd on to press for 2nd ins fnl f* **5/1**[3]
6040 **4** *2* **Crystal B Good (USA)**[22] 2431 3-8-9 59 .... RobertWinston 10 56+
(J R Best) *racd against nr side rail: hld up bhd ldrs: effrt over 2f out: one pce and no imp over 1f out* **12/1**
-000 **5** *3½* **Eye For The Girls**[23] 2417 3-9-0 52 .... DarryllHolland 9 50
(M R Channon) *w wnr to over 2f out: grad wknd fr over 1f out* **14/1**
00 **6** *1¾* **Proud Junior (USA)**[15] 2664 3-9-0 0 .... SteveDrowne 5 44
(S A Callaghan) *hld up wl in rr: reminders sn after 1/2-way and no prog: kpt on fr over 1f out* **33/1**
6- **7** *½* **Hanta Yo (IRE)**[260] 6434 3-9-0 0 .... StephenCarson 6 43
(J R Gask) *stdd s: tk v t.k.h and hld up in rr: sme prog 2f out: wknd fnl f* **12/1**
0 **8** *¾* **See Elsie Play**[9] 2862 3-8-9 0 .... KirstyMilczarek 11 35
(Miss Z C Davison) *s.s and sn ended up marooned in last on wd outside: pushed along and kpt on steadily fr 1/2-way: nrst fin* **14/1**
9 *1½* **Cardenio (USA)** 3-8-9 0 .... PatCosgrave 1 30
(J R Gask) *s.s: sn in tch on wd outside: wknd fr 2f out* **16/1**
3050 **10** *nse* **Tightrope (IRE)**[32] 2162 3-8-9 51 .... AmyBaker(5) 3 35
(T D McCarthy) *w ldrs to 1/2-way: wknd rapidly over 2f out* **50/1**
11 *50* **Blue Warrior (IRE)** 4-9-4 0 .... MarcHalford(3) 8 —
(J R Best) *v green and sn wl adrift: t.o fr 1/2-way* **25/1**

69.91 secs (-1.29) **Going Correction** -0.225s/f (Firm)
WFA 3 from 4yo 7lb **11** Ran SP% **129.5**
Speed ratings (Par 103): **99,96,95,93,88 86,85,84,82,82 15**
toteswinger: 1&2 £1.50, 1&3 £4.50, 2&3 £1.40. CSF £7.82 TOTE £3.90: £1.60, £1.20, £2.00; EX 10.40.
Owner Serpentine Racing **Bred** Austin Lyons **Trained** Whitsbury, Hants

FOCUS
A fair maiden rated around the runner-up but the form is far from solid.
Hanta Yo(IRE) Official explanation: jockey said gelding ran too free
Blue Warrior(IRE) Official explanation: jockey said gelding lost its action

3162 FOREST ROW H'CAP 5f
8:20 (8:21) (Class 5) (0-75,77) 3-Y-O+ **£3,238** (£963; £481; £240) **Stalls** High

Form RPR
01R2 **1** **Sands Crooner (IRE)**[9] 2840 6-9-13 75 .... (v) PatCosgrave 8 85
(J G Given) *a gng wl: hld up bhd ldrs against nr side rail: squeezed through to ld jst ins fnl f: sn clr* **3/1**[2]
-063 **2** *1½* **Cape Royal**[6] 2946 9-9-6 71 .... (bt) KevinGhunowa(3) 9 76
(J M Bradley) *led against nr side rail: rdn wl over 1f out: hdd and outpcd jst ins fnl f* **11/4**[1]
1100 **3** *nk* **Princess Rose Anne (IRE)**[43] 1836 4-9-13 75 .... RobertWinston 4 79
(J R Best) *w ldr: rdn fr 1/2-way: stl chalng 1f out: outpcd after* **11/2**
6140 **4** *1* **Peopleton Brook**[16] 2637 7-8-12 60 .... (t) JimCrowley 1 60
(B G Powell) *sn pushed up to join ldrs but wdst of all: stl on terms jst over 1f out: outpcd after* **10/1**
5533 **5** *1* **Cosmic Destiny (IRE)**[21] 2492 7-9-1 63 .... RichardKingscote 2 59
(E F Vaughan) *hld up bhd ldrs: effrt over 1f out: nt pce to trble ldrs ins fnl f* **4/1**[3]
3000 **6** *nk* **Fly In Johnny (IRE)**[14] 2713 4-8-8 56 oh11 .... (p) LPKeniry 7 51
(J J Bridger) *w ldrs early: unable to hold pl bef 1/2-way: one pce u.p fr over 1f out* **20/1**
5010 **7** *2* **Sherjawy (IRE)**[9] 2864 5-8-10 58 .... (b) KirstyMilczarek 6 46
(Miss Z C Davison) *sn restrained to last: detached 1/2-way: nudged along whn nt clr run briefly 1f out: nvr nr ldrs* **10/1**
335- **8** *7* **Agnes Love**[196] 7575 3-8-4 58 .... FrankieMcDonald 3 21
(J Akehurst) *chsd ldrs and racd wd: wknd over 1f out* **10/1**

57.41 secs (-0.79) **Going Correction** -0.225s/f (Firm)
WFA 3 from 4yo+ 6lb **8** Ran SP% **119.1**
Speed ratings (Par 103): **97,94,94,92,90 90,87,76**
toteswinger: 1&2 £1.50, 1&3 £3.10, 2&3 £2.30. CSF £12.32 CT £43.84 TOTE £3.80: £1.70, £1.70, £2.10; EX 8.30 Place 6 £5.89, Place 5 £3.81.
Owner Danethorpe Racing Partnership **Bred** Peter Molony **Trained** Willoughton, Lincs

FOCUS
An open sprint with all the field fairly exposed with the ones drawn nearest the rail faring best. The form looks sound rated around the first two.
T/Plt: £4.20 to a £1 stake. Pool: £42,390.82. 7,201.72 winning tickets. T/Qpdt: £2.90 to a £1 stake. Pool: £5,386.72. 1,348.62 winning tickets. JN

3112 NEWMARKET (R-H)
Saturday, June 20

OFFICIAL GOING: Good to firm (8.5)
Wind: Light behind Weather: Overcast

3163 INTERCASINO.CO.UK £125 FREE H'CAP 7f
2:10 (2:11) (Class 4) (0-85,85) 3-Y-O **£6,476** (£1,927; £963; £481) **Stalls** High

Form RPR
1041 **1** **Cyflymder (IRE)**[16] 2638 3-9-8 84 .... PatDobbs 11 93
(R Hannon) *led: rdn and edgd lft over 1f out: hdd ins fnl f: rallied to ld post* **11/2**[2]
01 **2** *nse* **Santefisio**[21] 2496 3-8-11 73 .... IanMongan 10 82
(P J Makin) *s.i.s: sn prom: rdn to ld ins fnl f: hdd post* **16/1**
014- **3** *1¾* **Rafiqa (IRE)**[267] 6240 3-9-6 85 .... JackMitchell(3) 7 89
(C F Wall) *hld up: outpcd 3f out: swtchd rt over 1f out: r.o ins fnl f: nt rch ldrs* **7/1**
1-32 **4** *½* **Glen Molly (IRE)**[35] 2079 3-9-5 81 .... MichaelHills 4 84
(B W Hills) *hld up: racd keenly: hdwy over 2f out: rdn and ev ch over 1f out: styd on same pce ins fnl f* **3/1**[1]
0-03 **5** *¾* **Bravo Echo**[16] 2638 3-9-8 84 .... RichardMullen 2 85
(J H M Gosden) *prom: rdn over 2f out: edgd lft and swished tail ins fnl f: styd on same pce* **15/2**
10 **6** *¾* **Mastoora (IRE)**[15] 2673 3-9-8 84 .... TPO'Shea 1 83
(W J Haggas) *s.s: hdwy and swtchd lft 1f out: sn rdn: styd on same pce* **9/1**
2-44 **7** *½* **My Kingdom (IRE)**[23] 2399 3-9-3 79 .... (t) TravisBlock 6 76
(H Morrison) *chsd ldr tl rdn over 1f out: no ex fnl f* **11/1**
12 **8** *½* **Romanticize**[27] 2299 3-9-0 76 .... TedDurcan 9 72
(Dr J D Scargill) *chsd ldrs: rdn over 1f out: no ex fnl f* **6/1**[3]
-203 **9** *1½* **Richo**[9] 2841 3-9-2 78 .... (b) RobertWinston 3 70
(D H Brown) *hld up: rdn over 2f out: nt trble ldrs* **33/1**
-232 **10** *nk* **Cawdor (IRE)**[8] 2888 3-8-12 74 .... FergusSweeney 5 65
(H Candy) *prom: rdn over 2f out: wknd fnl f* **7/1**

1m 24.81s (-0.89) **Going Correction** -0.05s/f (Good) **10** Ran SP% **118.6**
Speed ratings (Par 101): **103,102,100,100,99 98,98,97,95,95**
toteswinger: 1&2 £23.00, 1&3 £17.20, 2&3 £114.50. CSF £90.55 CT £481.01 TOTE £7.20: £2.60, £5.60, £2.30; EX 83.30 Trifecta £178.10 Part won. Pool: £240.74 - 0.20 winning units..
Owner Amblestock Partnership **Bred** Miss Laura G F Ferguson **Trained** East Everleigh, Wilts

FOCUS
The ground was riding slightly faster than it had been for the meeting the previous evening but there was a good covering of grass. An interesting, competitive handicap with 12lb covering the field, and decent form. The early pace was not strong. The first two may have beneifited from racing nearest the rail.

3164 INTERCASINO.CO.UK BLACKJACK H'CAP 6f
2:40 (2:41) (Class 4) (0-80,82) 3-Y-O+ **£6,476** (£1,927; £963; £481) **Stalls** High

Form RPR
1100 **1** **River Kirov (IRE)**[7] 2938 6-9-9 75 .... MichaelHills 7 82
(M Wigham) *led 5f out: rdn and hung lft fnl f: jst hld on* **16/1**

540- **2** *nse* **Baunagain (IRE)**[271] 6169 4-9-12 **78**........................ AdrianMcCarthy 15 85+
(P W Chapple-Hyam) *hld up: plld hrd: nt clr run over 1f out: rdn and r.o wl ins fnl f: jst failed* **6/1**

1041 **3** *½* **Artistic License (IRE)**[7] 2911 4-10-2 **82**...................... DarryllHolland 11 87+
(M R Channon) *prom: rdn and swtchd lft 1f out: r.o wl* **4/1**[1]

103 **4** *½* **Tudor Prince (IRE)**[11] 2799 5-9-3 **69**.............................. TolleyDean 13 73
(A W Carroll) *trckd ldrs: plld hrd: rdn over 1f out: r.o* **9/1**

1-16 **5** *½* **Elijah Pepper (USA)**[4] 3001 4-8-13 **70**.................... DeanHeslop(5) 14 72
(T D Barron) *awkward leaving stalls: sn pushed along in rr: rdn over 2f out: nt clr run and swtchd rt ins fnl f: r.o wl: nt rch ldrs* **9/2**[2]

6-41 **6** *shd* **Tyfos**[9] 2864 4-9-7 **73**.. TGMcLaughlin 1 75
(W M Brisbourne) *chsd ldrs: rdn over 1f out: styd on same pce ins fnl f* **9/1**

1165 **7** *½* **Bahamian Lad**[65] 1313 4-9-10 **76**....................................... TedDurcan 2 76
(R Hollinshead) *led 1f: chsd ldr: rdn over 2f out: styd on same pce fnl f* **16/1**

6050 **8** *nk* **Resplendent Alpha**[19] 2549 5-9-4 **70**............................ JimmyQuinn 3 69+
(P Howling) *hld up: racd keenly: shkn up over 1f out: r.o ins fnl f: nt rch ldrs* **8/1**

6003 **9** *shd* **Gold Express**[23] 2396 6-9-4 **70**.................................... ShaneKelly 5 69
(P J O'Gorman) *hld up: plld hrd: hdwy over 1f out: sn rdn: no ex ins fnl f* **5/1**[3]

-040 **10** *3* **Joyeaux**[22] 2436 7-8-12 **64**... RobertHavlin 4 53
(Ollie Pears) *hld up: hdwy over 1f out: wknd ins fnl f* **25/1**

00-3 **11** *2½* **Commander Wish**[12] 2770 6-8-10 **67**..........................(p) JPHamblett(5) 6 48
(Lucinda Featherstone) *prom: rdn over 1f out: wknd fnl f* **16/1**

1m 12.48s (-0.02) **Going Correction** -0.05s/f (Good)
WFA 3 from 4yo+ 7lb **11** Ran SP% **121.7**
Speed ratings (Par 105): **98,97,97,96,95 95,95,94,94,90 87**
toteswinger: 1&2 £93.10, 1&3 £4.70, 2&3 £9.20. CSF £112.93 CT £471.53 TOTE £15.60: £4.10, £2.90, £1.90; EX 134.30 TRIFECTA Not won..
Owner A Darke T Matthews M Wigham **Bred** Kildaragh Stud **Trained** Newmarket, Suffolk

FOCUS
An ordinary sprint handicap and several with doubts over the trip and surface but it produced another close finish, with the first nine covered by less than three lengths. Muddling form.
River Kirov(IRE) Official explanation: trainer's rep said, regarding apparent improvement in form, that the gelding appeared to benefit from being ridden prominently throughout.

3165 INTERCASINO.CO.UK EBF FILLIES' H'CAP — 1m
3:15 (3:16) (Class 4) (0-85,85) 3-Y-0+ **£6,476** (£1,927; £963; £481) **Stalls** High

Form RPR

13-1 **1** **Cosmopolitan**[15] 2679 4-10-0 **84**.............................. RichardMullen 1 89+
(J H M Gosden) *racd wd but w ldr: led over 4f out: jnd main gp over 3f out: rdn over 1f out: styd on* **6/5**[1]

0-40 **2** *¾* **Penzena**[22] 2433 3-8-0 **66**... JimmyQuinn 6 68
(W J Knight) *led: hdd over 4f out: chsd wnr thereafter: rdn and ev ch over 1f out: styd on* **12/1**

0-33 **3** *nk* **Something Perfect (USA)**[28] 2281 3-9-0 **80**.................... IanMongan 8 81
(H R A Cecil) *a.p: rdn over 2f out: struck over hd by rival's whip ins fnl f: r.o* **3/1**[2]

2630 **4** *1¼* **Astrodonna**[19] 2539 4-8-12 **68**... MichaelHills 7 68
(M H Tompkins) *hld up: hdwy over 3f out: rdn and ev ch over 1f out: styd on same pce ins fnl f* **16/1**

132- **5** *1¼* **Lyceana**[175] 7791 4-9-6 **76**... TedDurcan 3 73
(M A Jarvis) *hld up: shkn up over 1f out: nvr nr to chal* **10/1**

0-24 **6** *2* **Fanditha (IRE)**[30] 2209 3-9-5 **85**..................................... PatDobbs 4 76
(R Hannon) *chsd ldrs: rdn over 2f out: wknd fnl f* **4/1**[3]

1m 39.57s (-0.43) **Going Correction** -0.05s/f (Good)
WFA 3 from 4yo 10lb **6** Ran SP% **113.1**
Speed ratings (Par 102): **100,99,98,97,96 94**
toteswinger: 1&2 £7.60, 1&3 £1.30, 2&3 £3.40. CSF £17.29 CT £36.28 TOTE £2.00: £1.40, £5.00; EX 16.00 Trifecta £93.10 Pool: £213.94 - 1.70 winning units..
Owner H R H Princess Haya Of Jordan **Bred** G S Shropshire **Trained** Newmarket, Suffolk

FOCUS
A fair fillies' handicap. The winner may not have had to improve and may have more to offer.

3166 INTERCASINO.CO.UK VIP GOLD CLUB H'CAP — 5f
3:50 (3:50) (Class 2) (0-100,92) 3-Y-O
£12,462 (£3,732; £1,866; £934; £466; £234) **Stalls** High

Form RPR

3215 **1** **La Zamora**[19] 2546 3-8-6 **75**... ShaneKelly 3 85
(T D Barron) *mde all: crossed to stands' rail over 4f out: rdn over 1f out: r.o* **9/1**

-155 **2** *¾* **Green Beret (IRE)**[43] 1824 3-9-9 **92**.......................... RichardMullen 2 99
(J H M Gosden) *s.i.s: sn prom: chsd wnr 1/2-way: rdn and ev ch over 1f out: styd on* **8/1**

2-21 **3** *1½* **Strictly**[35] 2070 3-8-6 **80**................................ Louis-PhilippeBeuzelin(5) 1 82
(Sir Michael Stoute) *prom: hung rt almost thrght: rdn over 1f out: styd on same pce ins fnl f* **4/1**[2]

-106 **4** *½* **Brenin Taran**[37] 2016 3-9-0 **88**.................................. AndreaAtzeni(5) 4 88
(D M Simcock) *plld hrd: hmpd over 4f out: trckd wnr to 1/2-way: rdn over 1f out: styd on same pce ins fnl f* **14/1**

4-04 **5** *½* **Rowayton**[7] 2934 3-8-13 **82**... RobertWinston 10 80
(J D Bethell) *trckd ldrs: racd keenly: hmpd over 4f out: rdn over 1f out: styd on same pce fnl f* **3/1**[1]

1222 **6** *nk* **Lenny Bee**[7] 2915 3-8-11 **80**.. TedDurcan 5 77
(D H Brown) *sn pushed along in rr: hdwy over 1f out: sn rdn: styng on same pce hmpd ins fnl f* **6/1**

-501 **7** *2* **Bahamian Babe**[7] 2915 3-8-13 **89**.............................. AshleyMorgan(7) 6 79
(M L W Bell) *fly-jmpd s: hld up: effrt and swtchd lft over 1f out: n.d* **6/1**

1221 **8** *nk* **White Shift (IRE)**[3] 3033 3-9-1 **84** 6ex............................ JimmyQuinn 8 73
(P Howling) *chsd ldrs: rdn and wknd over 1f out* **11/2**[3]

2136 **9** *½* **Lesley's Choice**[79] 1078 3-9-1 **84**............................ FrankieMcDonald 7 71
(R Curtis) *in tch whn hmpd and lost pl over 4f out: no ch after* **22/1**

58.18 secs (-0.92) **Going Correction** -0.05s/f (Good) **9** Ran SP% **121.1**
Speed ratings (Par 105): **105,103,101,100,99 99,96,95,94**
toteswinger: 1&2 £10.80, 1&3 £7.80, 2&3 £7.40. CSF £82.29 CT £283.81 TOTE £10.00: £2.50, £3.50, £1.70; EX 94.00 Trifecta £219.70 Part won. Pool: £296.90 - 0.30 winning units..
Owner J G Brown **Bred** Miss S J Smith **Trained** Maunby, N Yorks
■ Stewards' Enquiry : Andrea Atzeni four-day ban: careless riding (July 5-8)

FOCUS
A good handicap over the minimum trip with several relatively unexposed sorts taking part. Another winner with the benefit of the rail, but she is progressive and this is form worth taking at face value.

NOTEBOOK
La Zamora ◆ made all the running. The winner of a maiden at Musselburgh, she got no sort of run on her handicap debut at Thirsk last time. Connections clearly wanted to avoid the same scenario this time and when the gates opened she jumped quickly and her rider quickly came across to the stands' rail, doing a couple of others no favours in the process. Once in front she was always stretching her rivals and ran on strongly to hold off the challenges in the manner of a filly who can win more good races. (op 6-1)
Green Beret(IRE) was also given a prominent ride and, giving the winner 17lb lost little in defeat. He came to challenge over a furlong out but the winner always had his measure. Nevertheless, this was something of a return to form after a couple of slightly below-par efforts. (tchd 9-1)
Strictly was forced to race wide from her outside stall but looked player entering the final furlong. However, she had nothing more to offer and edged right in the closing stages. This was her first try on fast ground and it may not have totally suited, and she may be best on genuinely good going. Official explanation: jockey said filly hung right (op 5-1 tchd 6-1)
Brenin Taran is well suited by fast ground and showed up for a long way, then stuck on under pressure up the hill. Both of his wins have been on flat tracks and he will be worth consideration back on similar courses this summer. His rider picked up a four-day ban for not riding to his draw. (tchd 12-1 and 16-1)
Rowayton tracked the leaders from the rail draw but was rather lit up by the winner going across his bows. He had his chance over a furlong out but could not pick up. (op 4-1 tchd 11-4)
Lenny Bee was slightly unlucky. Settled off the pace, he was making headway when short of room entering the final furlong and the third then leant on him in the last half-furlong. He would not have won but would have made the frame with a clear passage. (tchd 11-2)
Bahamian Babe was held up off the pace and, pulling wide for a run, could never get into a challenging position. (op 13-2 tchd 15-2)
White Shift(IRE) got little room when the winner came across but was in the clear at halfway and could not produce the necessary pace in the last furlong and a half. (op 5-1 tchd 6-1)

3167 INTERCASINO.CO.UK MAIDEN STKS — 7f
4:20 (4:20) (Class 4) 2-Y-O **£5,180** (£1,541; £770; £384) **Stalls** High

Form RPR

1 **Silver Grecian** 2-9-3 0.. MichaelHills 7 85+
(J Ryan) *a prom: led over 1f out: edgd rt: shkn up and r.o wl* **5/1**[3]

2 *4* **Lean Machine** 2-9-3 0.. PatDobbs 1 75
(R Hannon) *s.i.s: hld up: hdwy 1/2-way: rdn over 1f out: styd on same pce* **7/2**[2]

0 **3** *nse* **Dashing Doc (IRE)**[16] 2631 2-9-3 0................................. RobertHavlin 6 75
(D R C Elsworth) *hld up in tch: rdn and hung lft over 2f out: styd on same pce fnl f* **22/1**

4 *2* **Kavak** 2-9-3 0.. TedDurcan 11 70
(M Botti) *prom: rdn and hung lft over 2f out: styd on same pce appr fnl f* **12/1**

64 **5** *1½* **Bubbly Bellini (IRE)**[8] 2887 2-9-3 0.............................. NeilChalmers 4 66
(A Bailey) *trckd ldr: racd keenly: rdn and ev ch over 1f out: wknd ins fnl f* **8/1**

6 *1* **Gold Diamond (USA)** 2-9-3 0...................................... DarryllHolland 10 64
(M Johnston) *led: rdn and hdd over 1f out: wknd fnl f* **11/4**[1]

7 *¾* **Llandovery** 2-9-0 0.. JackMitchell(3) 8 62
(P J McBride) *sn pushed along in rr: hdwy u.p and hung lft over 1f out: wknd fnl f* **50/1**

8 *7* **Multames (IRE)** 2-9-3 0.. TPO'Shea 3 44
(Saeed Bin Suroor) *s.s: sn hung lft: a in rr* **7/1**

9 *½* **Boycott (IRE)** 2-9-3 0.. RichardMullen 5 43
(J H M Gosden) *hld up: rdn 1/2-way: wknd 2f out* **15/2**

10 *10* **The Ducking Stool** 2-8-12 0.. RobertWinston 12 13
(H J Collingridge) *prom: hung lft and bit slipped through mouth sn after s: wknd over 2f out* **33/1**

11 *1* **Lanizza** 2-9-3 0.. TGMcLaughlin 9 16
(E A L Dunlop) *s.s: rn green and a in rr* **22/1**

40 **12** *1½* **Back On**[17] 2595 2-8-12 0.. MarkFlynn(5) 2 12
(G C Bravery) *chsd ldrs: rdn 1/2-way: sn wknd* **66/1**

1m 25.61s (-0.09) **Going Correction** -0.05s/f (Good) **12** Ran SP% **123.7**
Speed ratings (Par 95): **98,93,93,91,89 88,87,79,78,67 66,64**
toteswinger: 1&2 £5.40, 1&3 £16.20, 2&3 £18.90. CSF £22.82 TOTE £6.00: £1.90, £1.90, £5.30; EX 22.10.
Owner Ocean Trailers Ltd **Bred** Deerfield Farm **Trained** Newmarket, Suffolk
■ Stewards' Enquiry : Neil Chalmers one-day ban: failed to ride to draw (Jul 5)
Mark Flynn one-day ban: failed to ride to draw (Jul 5)

FOCUS
Just a fair maiden for the track but quite an impressive winner. He could have been rated up to 7lb better.

NOTEBOOK
Silver Grecian ◆ had been backed at long prices from before racing and ended up third favourite. The 16,000gns breeze-up purchase had clearly been showing something and was from a yard whose juveniles have been going well. Always travelling easily, he picked up really well when asked and had the race in his pocket entering the final furlong. He looks sure to go on to better things and the Superlative Stakes back here next month looks a feasible target. (tchd 9-2)
Lean Machine, whose trainer had won three of the five previous runnings of this maiden, is a half-brother to a couple of juvenile winners. He ran quite promising race on this debut and despite not being helped by having to race on the outside of the field from his outside stall. (op 9-2 tchd 5-1)
Dashing Doc(IRE) had been very green on his debut but had clearly benefited from the outing and ran well, especially as he was another to race wide. (op 12-1)
Kavak, a breeze-up purchase but bred to stay further in time, showed a measure of promise, travelling quite well in the slipstream of the leaders before hitting a flat spot 2f out. He stayed on again up the hill and should be sharper next time. (tchd 14-1)
Bubbly Bellini(IRE), the most experienced runner in the line-up, was stepping up from 5f and showed good pace until fading up the hill. A return to 6f looks sure to be in his favour in the short term. (op 14-1)
Gold Diamond(USA), a half-brother to a middle-distance winner but from a stable whose juveniles are going well, made the most of his high draw by getting the rail early but may have gone too fast, as he had nothing in reserve when taken on by the winner a furlong and a half out. (op 3-1 tchd 7-2)
Llandovery, a cheaply bought half-brother to a middle-distance performer, ran quite well on this debut and should do better over further in time. (op 40-1)
Multames(IRE) Official explanation: jockey said colt was slowly away
The Ducking Stool Official explanation: jockey said filly hung left

3168 INTERCASINO.CO.UK ROULETTE MAIDEN STKS — 1m
4:55 (5:02) (Class 4) 3-Y-O **£5,180** (£1,541; £770; £384) **Stalls** High

Form RPR

1 **In Footlights (USA)** 3-9-3 0... TedDurcan 1 83+
(Saeed Bin Suroor) *chsd ldr: led 3f out: pushed out* **5/2**[1]

2 *2¾* **Wake Up Call** 3-8-12 0.. MichaelHills 10 71
(C F Wall) *difficult to load: hld up: hdwy over 2f out: chsd wnr and hung lft over 1f out: styd on* **7/1**

3 2 1/4 **Miss Kittyhawk (IRE)** 3-8-12 0 .... JimmyQuinn 16 66+
(Rae Guest) *hld up: hdwy over 1f out: edgd lft ins fnl f: nt rch ldrs* **12/1**

4 3/4 **Awesome Surprise (USA)** 3-8-12 0 .... ShaneKelly 4 64
(J Noseda) *chsd ldrs: rdn over 2f out: styd on same pce appr fnl f* **6/1**[2]

5 1 1/4 **Adnams** 3-9-0 0 .... JackMitchell(3) 13 66+
(C F Wall) *hld up: hdwy over 1f out: nt trble ldrs* **10/1**

00 6 8 **Any Given Moment (IRE)**[23] 2416 3-9-3 0 .... DarryllHolland 7 48
(D M Simcock) *hld up: hdwy u.p over 1f out: wknd fnl f* **16/1**

00 7 13 **Golden Ring**[29] 2240 3-9-3 0 .... RobertHavlin 2 18
(P J O'Gorman) *led 5f: sn rdn and wknd* **50/1**

8 nk **Two Tone** 3-9-3 0 .... FergusSweeney 8 17
(G Woodward) *mid-div: rdn over 2f out: sn wknd* **33/1**

9 2 1/4 **A Lot Of Red (IRE)** 3-9-3 0 .... (t) PatDobbs 3 12
(P J O'Gorman) *prom: rdn and wknd over 2f out* **25/1**

10 6 **Primera Vista** 3-9-3 0 .... ChrisCatlin 12 —
(L M Cumani) *outpcd* **13/2**[3]

11 3 **Hilltop Alchemy** 3-9-3 0 .... AdrianMcCarthy 14 —
(J R Jenkins) *swished tail sn after s: outpcd* **50/1**

0 12 27 **Tentears**[15] 2679 3-8-12 0 .... IanMongan 5 —
(H R A Cecil) *swvd lft sn after s and rel to r* **8/1**

1m 39.47s (-0.53) **Going Correction** -0.05s/f (Good) **12 Ran SP% 113.2**
Speed ratings (Par 101): **100,97,95,94,93 85,72,71,69,63 60,33**
toteswinger: 1&2 £5.30, 1&3 £7.80, 2&3 £11.00. CSF £17.89 TOTE £2.60: £1.40, £2.60, £3.20; EX 21.30.
Owner Godolphin **Bred** Darley **Trained** Newmarket, Suffolk

FOCUS
This three-year-olds' maiden has fallen to one of the major Newmarket yards on each of the previous runnings, the best former winner being Multidimensional. Two withdrawals at the start reduced the field and the race was run in a heavy shower. There was little previous form to go on but this was probably just an ordinary race.

3169 INTERCASINO.CO.UK H'CAP 1m 5f
5:30 (5:33) (Class 5) (0-75,74) 4-Y-0+ **£3,885** (£1,156; £577; £288) **Stalls** Centre

Form RPR

/0-1 1 **Norman The Great**[21] 2493 5-9-9 **74** .... FergusSweeney 8 81+
(A King) *a.p: chsd ldr over 2f out: rdn to ld and hung lft fr over 1f out: styd on* **5/1**[3]

-650 2 1/2 **Agente Romano (USA)**[21] 2497 4-9-2 **67** .... (b[1]) ShaneKelly 6 72
(G A Butler) *chsd ldr tl led tl led after 2f out: sn clr: stdd pce over 7f out: qcknd 3f out: rdn and hdd over 1f out: styd on* **14/1**

00-0 3 1 1/2 **Trachonitis (IRE)**[54] 1571 5-9-7 **72** .... AdrianMcCarthy 2 75
(J R Jenkins) *hld up: hdwy 7f out: rdn and ev ch whn hung lft fr over 1f out: hmpd and unable qck ins fnl f* **18/1**

4333 4 nk **Watson's Bay**[5] 2983 4-9-0 **65** .... JimmyQuinn 5 67
(P Howling) *s.i.s: hld up: hmpd over 7f out: hdwy u.p over 1f out: nt rch ldrs* **7/2**[1]

4430 5 2 1/4 **Thorny Mandate**[11] 2783 7-8-5 **56** .... TPO'Shea 1 55+
(W M Brisbourne) *stdd s: hld up: outpcd over 2f out: styd on ins fnl f: nvr trbld ldrs* **8/1**

1544 6 6 **Bell Island**[7] 2931 5-9-2 **72** .... (v) Louis-PhilippeBeuzelin(5) 3 62
(Lady Herries) *prom: chsd ldr 3f out: sn rdn: wknd 2f out* **7/2**[1]

-632 7 hd **Ovthenight (IRE)**[9] 2854 4-9-1 **66** .... (v) ChrisCatlin 7 56
(Mrs P Sly) *led 2f: chsd ldr tl rdn 3f out: wknd 2f out* **4/1**[2]

0020 8 2 1/4 **Bassinet (USA)**[21] 2475 5-9-7 **72** .... TedDurcan 4 58
(J A R Toller) *chsd ldrs: lost pl over 7f out: hdwy over 1f out: sn rdn and wknd* **8/1**

2m 45.77s (1.77) **Going Correction** -0.05s/f (Good) **8 Ran SP% 115.3**
Speed ratings (Par 103): **91,90,89,89,88 84,84,83**
toteswinger: 1&2 £12.50, 1&3 £10.40, 2&3 £12.10. CSF £70.66 CT £1160.76 TOTE £4.60: £2.10, £3.60, £4.40; EX 103.40 Place 6 £193.70, Place 5 £53.76.
Owner McNeill Racing **Bred** Barton Stud Partnership **Trained** Barbury Castle, Wilts
■ Stewards' Enquiry : Fergus Sweeney one-day ban: careless riding (Jul 5)

FOCUS
A modest handicap with a few stepping up in trip and an open betting market. Muddling form, limited by the runner-up.
Bassinet(USA) Official explanation: jockey said mare had no more to give
T/Plt: £319.70 to a £1 stake. Pool: £74,958.67. 171.15 winning tickets. T/Qpdt: £26.20 to a £1 stake. Pool: £4,033.48. 113.60 winning tickets. CR

3119 REDCAR (L-H)
Saturday, June 20

OFFICIAL GOING: Good to firm (firm in places; 9.2)
Wind: light, half behind Weather: changeable, overcast with showers

3170 MARKET CROSS JEWELLERS MAIDEN STKS 7f
2:20 (2:26) (Class 5) 2-Y-0 **£2,590** (£770; £385; £192) **Stalls** Centre

Form RPR

4 1 **Lamh Albasser (USA)**[25] 2358 2-9-0 0 .... AhmedAjtebi(3) 2 79
(Saeed Bin Suroor) *sn chsng ldrs: wnt 2nd over 2f out: styd on fnl f: led post* **7/2**[3]

2 shd **Pytheas (USA)** 2-9-3 0 .... JohnEgan 5 79
(M Johnston) *sn w ldrs: led over 3f out: edgd rt and 4 l clr over 2f out: edgd lft fnl f: jst ct* **6/4**[1]

3 3 1/2 **Tukitinyasok (IRE)** 2-8-12 0 .... SladeO'Hara(5) 6 70
(R F Fisher) *w ldrs: styd on same pce fnl 3f* **50/1**

4 4 1 3/4 **Music Of The Moor (IRE)**[29] 2247 2-9-3 0 .... MickyFenton 8 66
(T P Tate) *drvn to ld: hdd over 3f out: outpcd and edgd lft over 2f out: kpt on same pce* **10/3**[2]

5 4 1/2 **Cosmic Orbit** 2-9-3 0 .... DaleGibson 4 54
(K R Burke) *in rr: drvn over 3f out: kpt on fnl f* **25/1**

4 6 5 **Leopard Hills (IRE)**[36] 2041 2-9-3 0 .... JamieMoriarty 10 42
(J Howard Johnson) *chsd ldrs: rdn over 2f out: sn lost pl* **5/1**

00 7 1 1/2 **As Brave As You (IRE)**[17] 2610 2-9-0 0 .... NeilBrown(3) 3 38
(B Ellison) *sn outpcd and in rr* **100/1**

8 6 **Bollin Rachel** 2-8-12 0 .... GrahamGibbons 9 18
(T D Easterby) *chsd ldrs: drvn and outpcd 3f out: sn wknd* **28/1**

1m 25.35s (0.85) **Going Correction** -0.075s/f (Good) **8 Ran SP% 112.2**
Speed ratings (Par 93): **92,91,87,85,80 75,73,66**
toteswinger: 1&2 £1.40, 1&3 £24.70, 2&3 £40.80. CSF £8.77 TOTE £4.50: £1.80, £1.10, £8.10; EX 14.20.
Owner Godolphin **Bred** Stonestreet Thoroughbred Holdings Llc **Trained** Newmarket, Suffolk

FOCUS
A fair juvenile maiden in which the first two finished clear.

NOTEBOOK
Lamh Albasser(USA) was well backed when fourth on debut at Leicester, but proved too green to do himself justice and again it took time for the penny to drop here. As the runner-up began to wilt late on, however, this son of Mr Greeley began to hit top gear and the extra furlong no doubt suited better. He is no star, but his dam proved useful at two and he should improve again for the run. (op 4-1 tchd 9-2)
Pytheas(USA) ◆ knew his job as he was always on the pace and looked set to justify market confidence when stretching clear. He was tying up at the furlong pole though and eventually got mugged on the line. A more patient ride would have seen him win and this well-bred colt ought to prove very hard to stop next time out. (op 15-8 tchd 2-1)
Tukitinyasok(IRE), an already gelded half-bother to seven winners, broke well and disputed the early lead. He was made to look very one paced when the runner-up kicked on, but kept gamely to his task and this was a pleasing debut. (op 100-1)
Music Of The Moor(IRE) set the standard on the level of his Pontefract debut and looked set to enjoy this step up a furlong, but he was easy to back. Having raced up early, he looked pedestrian when the second went for home and drifted to the middle of the track under pressure. This was disappointing. (op 5-2 tchd 7-2)
Cosmic Orbit cost 35,000gns and is bred to stay further in time. He got markedly outpaced and never figured, but kept on steadily under a considerate ride. (op 16-1 tchd 11-1)
Leopard Hills(IRE) came in for support, but he was in trouble from an early stage and was beaten before stamina for the stiffer test came into question. (op 7-1 tchd 9-2)

3171 BUY YOUR TICKETS ON-LINE @ REDCARRACING.CO.UK H'CAP 1m 6f 19y
2:50 (2:50) (Class 6) (0-60,58) 4-Y-0+ **£1,942** (£578; £288; £144) **Stalls** Low

Form RPR

2-24 1 **Master Nimbus**[8] 2344 9-9-4 **58** .... GrahamGibbons 13 65+
(J J Quinn) *trckd ldrs: t.k.h: led on bit over 2f out: shkn up and edgd lft 1f out: pushed out* **3/1**[1]

6-12 2 1 1/4 **Mystified (IRE)**[5] 2969 6-8-10 **50** .... (tp) JamieMoriarty 9 54
(R F Fisher) *led tl over 2f out: kpt on fnl f: no imp* **4/1**[2]

0654 3 1 3/4 **Cripsey Brook**[6] 2944 11-8-11 **56** .... GaryBartley(5) 4 58+
(K G Reveley) *hld up in rr: hdwy and swtchd outside 2f out: styd on wl to take 3rd nr fin* **4/1**[2]

40-5 4 1 3/4 **Waterloo Corner**[9] 2859 7-9-1 **55** .... DavidAllan 3 54
(R Craggs) *mid-div: effrt 4f out: styd on appr fnl f* **13/2**[3]

2045 5 1 1/4 **Art Value**[17] 2609 4-8-7 **47** .... SamHitchcott 8 45
(M Wigham) *mid-div: hdwy 7f out: rdn over 2f out: one pce* **13/2**[3]

004- 6 hd **Feeling Peckish (USA)**[8] 4899 5-7-12 **45** .... (t) AndrewHeffernan(7) 10 42
(M C Chapman) *chsd ldrs: one pce fnl 3f* **66/1**

0-30 7 1 1/4 **One Tou Many**[14] 2725 4-8-7 **47** .... DuranFentiman 5 43
(C W Fairhurst) *reminders after s: chsd ldrs: drvn 4f out: one pce* **12/1**

46-0 8 3 3/4 **Centenary (IRE)**[14] 2725 5-8-5 **45** .... DaleGibson 11 35+
(M W Easterby) *in rr: drvn over 6f out: slipped bnd over 4f out: kpt on fnl 3f: nvr a factor* **22/1**

06-0 9 3/4 **Able Dara**[66] 1276 6-8-3 **48** ow3 .... PatrickDonaghy(5) 1 37
(N Bycroft) *in rr: nvr on terms* **33/1**

0000 10 4 **Treetops Hotel (IRE)**[17] 2608 10-7-12 **45** .... GemmaElford(7) 7 29
(L R James) *s.s: t.k.h in last: nvr on terms* **100/1**

5-00 11 5 **Sorrento Moon (IRE)**[17] 2609 5-8-5 **45** .... SilvestreDeSousa 14 22
(G A Harker) *mid-div: drvn 4f out: sn wknd* **10/1**

0-03 12 2 1/2 **Cecina Marina**[15] 2656 6-8-5 **45** .... CatherineGannon 6 37
(Mrs K Walton) *prom: drvn over 3f out: wknd and heavily eased over 1f out* **33/1**

0-06 13 65 **Ducal Regancy Duke**[11] 2785 5-8-5 **45** .... (p) PaulQuinn 12 —
(C J Teague) *sn chsng ldrs: slipped bnd and lost pl over 4f out: t.o 3f out* **100/1**

3m 4.67s (-0.03) **Going Correction** -0.075s/f (Good) **13 Ran SP% 122.2**
Speed ratings (Par 101): **97,96,95,94,93 93,92,90,90,87 85,83,46**
toteswinger: 1&2 £2.70, 1&3 £6.40, 2&3 £2.50. CSF £14.54 CT £49.88 TOTE £4.70: £2.10, £1.90, £1.20; EX 10.20.
Owner J H Hewitt **Bred** A H Bennett **Trained** Settrington, N Yorks

FOCUS
A weak staying handicap, with more than half of the field wrong at the weights, run at an uneven pace. The winner only needed to match his recent Flat form.
Centenary(IRE) Official explanation: jockey said gelding slipped on bend
Cecina Marina Official explanation: jockey said mare lost it's action
Ducal Regancy Duke Official explanation: jockey said gelding slipped on bend

3172 WIN A VIP DAY OUT @ REDCARRACING.CO.UK H'CAP 7f
3:30 (3:30) (Class 3) (0-90,90) 4-Y-0+ **£7,771** (£2,312; £1,155; £577) **Stalls** Centre

Form RPR

-331 1 **Novellen Lad (IRE)**[15] 2658 4-9-1 **84** .... DavidAllan 1 93+
(E J Alston) *trckd ldrs: wnt rt and led over 1f out: hld on gamely* **7/2**[2]

0036 2 3/4 **Osteopathic Remedy (IRE)**[23] 2405 5-8-13 **85** .... NeilBrown(3) 2 92+
(M Dods) *trckd ldrs: t.k.h: hmpd over 1f out: no ex wl ins fnl f* **9/2**[3]

-403 3 hd **Atlantic Story (USA)**[63] 1365 7-9-7 **90** .... (bt) JohnEgan 4 96
(M W Easterby) *trckd ldrs: effrt over 2f out: kpt on wl fnl f* **10/3**[1]

-046 4 3/4 **Mastership (IRE)**[7] 2933 5-9-5 **88** .... GrahamGibbons 5 92
(J J Quinn) *trckd ldrs: effrt over 2f out: kpt on same pce ins fnl f* **5/1**

3-61 5 nk **Spinning**[134] 430 6-8-7 **83** .... (b) AdamCarter(7) 8 87
(T D Barron) *hld up: effrt over 2f out: kpt on same pce fnl f* **14/1**

4220 6 1 **Bravely (IRE)**[7] 2938 5-8-6 **75** .... DuranFentiman 3 76
(T D Easterby) *rrd s: tk fierce hold: sn trcking ldrs: kpt on same pce fnl f* **13/2**

0-50 7 nk **Mujaadel (USA)**[34] 2101 4-8-13 **82** .... PaulQuinn 9 82
(D Nicholls) *trckd ldrs: t.k.h: kpt on same pce fnl f* **16/1**

30-0 8 4 **Burnwynd Boy**[18] 2570 4-9-4 **90** .... AhmedAjtebi(3) 6 79
(D Nicholls) *led: drvn over 2f out: hdd and wkng whn sltly hmpd over 1f out* **33/1**

0165 9 4 1/2 **Smarty Socks (IRE)**[6] 2939 5-8-11 **80** .... JamieMoriarty 7 57+
(P T Midgley) *s.v.s: a detached in fnl f* **11/1**

1m 24.51s (0.01) **Going Correction** -0.075s/f (Good) **9 Ran SP% 117.3**
Speed ratings (Par 107): **96,95,94,94,93 92,92,87,82**
toteswinger: 1&2 £3.20, 1&3 £2.90, 2&3 £3.30. CSF £20.07 CT £56.98 TOTE £4.30: £1.30, £2.30, £1.60; EX 21.00 Trifecta £89.80 Pool: £242.84 - 2.00 winning units..
Owner Con Harrington **Bred** Mrs Chris Harrington **Trained** Longton, Lancs

FOCUS
This was wide open and most held a chance passing the furlong pole due to the muddling pace. Ordinary form, but sound enough.

NOTEBOOK
Novellen Lad(IRE) confirmed himself a progressive 4yo and followed up his Catterick success from a 7lb higher mark. He got himself warm beforehand, but it made no difference to his cause and there was a great deal to like about the manner in which he stuck to his task throughout the last furlong. He is obviously versatile as regards trip and appeals as the type to defy another likely higher mark. (op 4-1 tchd 9-2)

Osteopathic Remedy(IRE), stepping back up a furlong, raced upsides the winner for most of the way and failed to find the required gear chance when it really mattered. He was not helped when that rival drifted to him after 2f out, however, and this was a solid effort. A further step back up in trip could do the trick. (tchd 5-1)
Atlantic Story(USA), well backed, hit a flat spot around halfway and then failed to get a clear run when rallying. He could not really be counted as unlucky, but rates a little better than the bare form and his turn is not far off again. (op 9-2)
Mastership(IRE) had his chance, but found just the same pace when push came to shove. The way in which he proved easy to back hints that this may not have been his big day, however, and he should never totally be discounted. (op 9-2)
Spinning, 3lb higher for this return to turf, ran a solid enough race in defeat and remains in good heart. (op 8-1)
Bravely(IRE) proved better off on this return to 7f, but failed to help his cause by refusing to settle and is proving hard to catch right. (op 17-2 tchd 5-1)
Mujaadel(USA) probably needs a searching test to shine over this trip, but is another who is not easy to get right.
Smarty Socks(IRE) Official explanation: jockey said gelding missed the break

3173 H JARVIS 131ST ANNIVERSARY H'CAP — 5f
4:10 (4:11) (Class 4) (0-85,85) 3-Y-O — £4,857 (£1,445; £722; £360) Stalls Centre

Form — RPR
164 1 **Ingley Lady**[23] 2393 3-8-10 **77** .... NeilBrown(3) 2 — 89
(T D Barron) *trckd ldrs: led jst ins fnl f: jst hld on* **13/2[3]**
2131 2 *shd* **Impressible**[19] 2530 3-8-8 **72** .... DavidAllan 6 — 83
(E J Alston) *trckd ldrs: chal 1f out: kpt on wl towards fin: jst hld* **11/2[2]**
1522 3 *3* **Titus Andronicus (IRE)**[11] 2782 3-9-7 **85** .... JamieMoriarty 4 — 85
(K A Ryan) *led tl hdd and no ex jst ins fnl f* **5/2[1]**
0043 4 *1 ½* **Dispol Kylie (IRE)**[14] 2726 3-8-8 **72** .... SamHitchcott 5 — 67
(P T Midgley) *sn chsng ldrs: kpt on same pce fnl f* **14/1**
0-03 5 *nk* **Excellent Show**[7] 2915 3-9-3 **81** .... LeeEnstone 3 — 75
(B Smart) *slowly away: hdwy over 2f out: nvr trbld ldrs* **7/1**
0541 6 *1 ¾* **Fivefootnumberone (IRE)**[22] 2443 3-9-1 **79** .... GrahamGibbons 9 — 73+
(J J Quinn) *sn outpcd and drvn along: edgd lft and sltly hmpd over 1f out: nvr a threat* **11/2[2]**
6430 7 *¾* **Spiritofthewest (IRE)**[9] 2840 3-9-1 **79** .... JohnEgan 7 — 64
(D H Brown) *dwlt: outpcd in rr: sme hdwy 2f out: nvr nr ldrs* **10/1**
3515 8 *2 ¾* **Glamorous Spirit (IRE)**[24] 2373 3-9-0 **85** .... SPRyan(7) 1 — 60
(R A Harris) *w ldrs: edgd lft and wknd over 1f out* **12/1**
6-05 9 *1 ¾* **Lucky Art (USA)**[14] 2717 3-8-11 **80** .... PatrickDonaghy(5) 8 — 49
(J Howard Johnson) *restless in stalls: chsd ldrs: wknd over 1f out* **14/1**

57.34 secs (-1.26) **Going Correction** -0.075s/f (Good) — **9** Ran SP% **115.3**
Speed ratings (Par 101): **107,106,102,99,99 96,95,90,87**
toteswinger: 1&2 £6.50, 1&3 £3.60, 2&3 £2.70. CSF £41.98 CT £114.12 TOTE £9.20: £2.30, £2.00, £1.20; EX 42.50.
Owner Dave Scott **Bred** Hellwood Stud Farm **Trained** Maunby, N Yorks

FOCUS
This was run at a searching pace and two progressive fillies came clear. Fair form for the grade.

3174 REDCAR RACECOURSE FOR YOUR WEDDING VENUE CLAIMING STKS — 7f
4:45 (4:46) (Class 5) 3-Y-O+ — £2,590 (£770; £385; £192) Stalls Centre

Form — RPR
0400 1 **Dabbers Ridge (IRE)**[18] 2576 7-8-13 80 .... NeilBrown(3) 8 — 81
(I W McInnes) *s.i.s: hdwy over 2f out: carried rt to stands' rail over 1f out: r.o wl to ld ins fnl f: sn clr* **7/1**
-101 2 *3 ¼* **Royal Dignitary (USA)**[46] 1777 9-9-4 85 .... NSLawes(7) 7 — 81
(D Nicholls) *led tl hdd and no ex ins fnl f* **9/2[3]**
0003 3 *2* **Wiseman's Diamond (USA)**[25] 2361 4-8-0 47 .... PaulPickard(7) 11 — 58
(P T Midgley) *w ldrs: edgd rt over 1f out: kpt on same pce appr fnl f* **16/1**
6051 4 *4 ½* **Elna Bright**[11] 2794 4-9-9 92 .... JohnEgan 3 — 62
(P D Evans) *swtchd rt after s: t.k.h in midfield: hdwy to chse ldr over 2f out: wknd over 1f out* **15/8[1]**
0304 5 *3 ¼* **Sam's Secret**[4] 2999 7-8-12 79 .... SilvestreDeSousa 6 — 42
(G A Swinbank) *chsd ldrs: drvn over 2f out: wknd over 1f out* **2/1[2]**
-000 6 *nk* **Royal Applord**[23] 2404 4-8-12 51 .... (p) JamieMoriarty 4 — 41
(P T Midgley) *dwlt: in rr: sme hdwy and hung lft 2f out: nvr on terms* **50/1**
360- 7 *shd* **Apres Ski (IRE)**[280] 5916 6-8-8 47 .... MarkCoumbe(5) 10 — 42
(J F Coupland) *t.k.h: trckd ldrs towards stands' side: wknd over 1f out* **66/1**
0/05 8 *2* **Picture Frame**[8] 2876 5-8-11 55 .... SladeO'Hara(5) 2 — 40
(J T Stimpson) *in rr: hdwy on outside over 3f out: rdn and edgd lft over 2f out: sn lost pl* **40/1**
6000 9 *¾* **Carrazara (IRE)**[32] 2162 3-7-5 45 .... (b[1]) JosephineBruning(7) 9 — 29
(Edgar Byrne) *rrd s: sn chsng ldrs: lost pl over 1f out* **100/1**
00-6 10 *1 ½* **Borodinsky**[10] 2816 8-8-12 47 .... DuranFentiman 1 — 30
(R E Barr) *restless in stalls: chsd ldrs: lost pl over 2f out* **80/1**
0600 11 *½* **Danish Art (IRE)**[18] 2576 4-8-10 62 .... JamesPSullivan(7) 5 — 33
(M W Easterby) *a in rr* **50/1**
00-0 12 *1 ½* **Tump Mac**[25] 2366 5-8-12 46 .... PatrickDonaghy(5) 12 — 29
(N Bycroft) *chsd ldrs: outpcd over 3f out: sn lost pl* **100/1**

1m 24.19s (-0.31) **Going Correction** -0.075s/f (Good)
WFA 3 from 4yo+ 9lb — 12 Ran SP% **115.7**
Speed ratings (Par 103): **98,94,92,86,83 82,82,80,79,77 77,75**
toteswinger: 1&2 £6.40, 1&3 £7.10, 2&3 £6.70. CSF £37.03 TOTE £8.30: £2.20, £2.10, £2.80; EX 32.80.
Owner M Shirley **Bred** Franco Castelfranci **Trained** Catwick, E Yorks
■ Stewards' Enquiry : Paul Pickard three-day ban: careless riding (Jul 5-7)

FOCUS
A fair claimer. It has been rated around the winner and both market leaders were disappointing.

3175 THE COMMITMENTS PERFORMING HERE ON SATURDAY 29TH AUGUST MAIDEN STKS — 6f
5:20 (5:21) (Class 5) 3-Y-O+ — £2,590 (£770; £385; £192) Stalls Centre

Form — RPR
6 1 **Imperial House**[11] 2795 3-9-0 0 .... SamHitchcott 4 — 63+
(M R Channon) *chsd ldrs: drvn and outpcd over 3f out: styd on to ld over 1f out: kpt on wl* **2/1[1]**
00- 2 *1* **Exopuntia**[257] 6531 3-8-6 0 .... MichaelJStainton(3) 13 — 55
(R M Whitaker) *in rr: hdwy over 2f out: kpt on fnl f: no real imp* **66/1**
6004 3 *1 ½* **Sheik'N'Knotsterd**[3] 3031 4-9-2 53 .... MarkCoumbe(5) 6 — 57
(J F Coupland) *chsd ldrs: kpt on same pce appr fnl f* **20/1**
0- 4 *½* **Hitches Dubai (BRZ)**[246] 6791 4-9-0 0 .... NSLawes(7) 1 — 56
(D Nicholls) *dwlt: hdwy to chse ldrs on outside after 2f: kpt on same pce appr fnl f* **28/1**
00 5 *1 ¼* **Cardinal**[48] 1703 4-9-0 0 .... SPRyan(7) 5 — 52
(R A Harris) *chsd ldrs: one pce fnl 2f* **16/1**
5-3 6 *nk* **Rascal In The Mix (USA)**[18] 2574 3-8-9 0 .... PaulQuinn 11 — 44
(R M Whitaker) *mid-div: rdn and outpcd over 2f out: kpt on fnl f* **14/1**
7 *2 ¾* **Ms Sophie Eleanor (USA)** 3-8-7 0 ow1 .... NeilBrown(3) 8 — 36
(T D Barron) *chsd ldrs: wknd over 1f out* **10/1**
00 8 *shd* **Isitcozimcool (IRE)**[9] 2862 4-9-7 0 .... (p) JohnEgan 7 — 42
(D E Cantillon) *s.i.s: sme hdwy on outside 2f out: nvr a factor* **20/1**
45 9 *nk* **Millers Crossing**[9] 2862 3-9-0 0 .... JamieMoriarty 9 — 39
(W J H Ratcliffe) *sn outpcd and in rr: kpt on stands' side fnl 2f: nvr on terms* **9/1**
2332 10 *½* **Diamond Blade**[18] 2574 3-9-0 60 .... DavidAllan 2 — 37
(T D Easterby) *led: hdd over 1f out: wknd qckly last 150yds* **6/1[3]**
11 *2 ¼* **Noble Attitude** 3-8-9 0 .... MickyFenton 3 — 25
(N Tinkler) *sn chsng ldrs on outside: wknd 2f out* **50/1**
0433 12 *4* **Josphiel (IRE)**[10] 2820 4-8-11 55 .... (b) SladeO'Hara(5) 12 — —
(A Berry) *chsd ldrs stands' side: lost pl over 2f out* **12/1**
4- U **Sams Lass**[246] 6785 3-8-9 0 .... CatherineGannon 10 — —
(D Nicholls) *rrd s and uns rdr* **10/3[2]**

1m 12.41s (0.61) **Going Correction** -0.075s/f (Good)
WFA 3 from 4yo 7lb — **13** Ran SP% **126.5**
Speed ratings (Par 103): **92,90,88,88,86 85,82,82,81,81 78,72,—**
toteswinger: 1&2 £53.10, 1&3 £11.40, 2&3 £127.10. CSF £199.61 TOTE £3.30: £1.40, £19.20, £5.90; EX 207.80.
Owner Mohammed Jaber **Bred** Imperial & Mike Channon Bloodstock Ltd **Trained** West Ilsley, Berks

FOCUS
A very weak maiden. It is doubtful if the winner had to improve on her recent form.

3176 REDCARRACING.CO.UK H'CAP — 5f
5:55 (5:56) (Class 6) (0-60,65) 3-Y-O — £2,047 (£604; £302) Stalls Centre

Form — RPR
3604 1 **Dancing Wave**[7] 2913 3-8-6 **55** .... AndrewHeffernan(7) 1 — 61
(M C Chapman) *mde all centre: clr over 2f out: jst lasted* **10/1**
-000 2 *nk* **Unbelievable Jeff**[117] 655 3-8-4 **46** oh1 .... CatherineGannon 4 — 51+
(S Parr) *sn outpcd on outside: hrd rdn and hdwy 2f out: edgd rt: styd on ins fnl f: jst hld* **5/1[3]**
060- 3 *1* **Excitable (IRE)**[255] 6579 3-8-8 **50** .... SilvestreDeSousa 8 — 51+
(Mrs D J Sanderson) *led on stands' side: chsd wnr: edgd lft over 1f out: kpt on same pce ins fnl f* **5/2[1]**
3211 4 *½* **Billy Beetroot (USA)**[12] 2759 3-9-2 **65** .... (t) SPRyan(7) 6 — 65
(R A Harris) *mid-div: hdwy 2f out: styd on same pce ins fnl f* **7/2[2]**
001 5 *2 ¾* **Future Gem**[28] 2265 3-8-11 **53** .... DavidAllan 11 — 43
(A Dickman) *chsd ldr stands' side: one pce fnl 2f* **9/1**
00-4 6 *1* **Rossett Rose (IRE)**[14] 2726 3-8-9 **58** .... SeanPalmer(7) 9 — 44
(M Brittain) *wnt rt s: sn chsng wnr: wknd over 1f out* **12/1**
0000 7 *½* **Port Ronan (USA)**[7] 2918 3-8-3 **50** .... (p) PatrickDonaghy(5) 10 — 34
(J S Wainwright) *dwlt and hmpd s: last of 3 stands' side: kpt on fnl 2f: nvr a threat* **28/1**
0003 8 *hd* **Yughanni**[19] 2539 3-8-8 **53** .... AhmedAjtebi(3) 7 — 37
(C E Brittain) *chsd ldrs: wknd over 1f out* **6/1**
650 9 *3* **Red Cell (IRE)**[50] 1644 3-8-10 **55** .... (p) NeilBrown(3) 3 — 28
(I W McInnes) *mid-div: lost pl over 2f out* **20/1**
0035 10 *3 ¾* **Iachimo**[14] 2726 3-8-4 **53** .... (v) DeclanCannon(7) 2 — 12
(K R Burke) *prom: lost pl over 1f out* **9/1**
0 11 *10* **Brideview**[15] 2654 3-9-0 **56** .... AmirQuinn 5 — —
(Edgar Byrne) *s.i.s: in rr: bhd fnl 2f* **33/1**

58.58 secs (-0.02) **Going Correction** -0.075s/f (Good) — **11** Ran SP% **129.7**
Speed ratings (Par 97): **97,96,94,94,89 88,87,87,82,76 60**
toteswinger: 1&2 £15.90, 1&3 £8.50, 2&3 £13.80. CSF £64.46 CT £174.81 TOTE £16.10: £3.70, £1.10, £2.00; EX 122.20 Place 6 £24.65, Place 5 £15.85.
Owner Roy Gowans **Bred** B J Goldsmith **Trained** Market Rasen, Lincs

FOCUS
A moderate 3yo sprint run at a strong pace. Sound if ordinary form for the grade.
Port Ronan(USA) Official explanation: jockey said colt suffered interference shortly after start
T/Plt: £57.60 to a £1 stake. Pool: £44,714.05. 566.04 winning tickets. T/Qpdt: £38.00 to a £1 stake. Pool: £3,057.04. 59.40 winning tickets. WG

3177 - 3184a (Foreign Racing) - See Raceform Interactive

2955 SAN SIRO (R-H)
Saturday, June 20

OFFICIAL GOING: Good to firm

3185a PREMIO PRIMI PASSI (GROUP 3) — 6f
3:05 (3:13) 2-Y-O — £41,631 (£19,184; £10,718; £5,359)

RPR
1 **Orpen Shadow (IRE)**[27] 2-8-11 .... DVargiu 3 — 105
(B Grizzetti, Italy) *led: narrowly hdd under 2f out: hrd rdn ins fnl f: rallied to regain ld fnl 70yds* **23/20[1]**
2 *nk* **Marshade (ITY)** 2-8-11 .... NPinna 1 — 104
(S Botti, Italy) *a.p: led narrowly under 2f out tl hdd 70yds out: no ex* **13/10[2]**
3 *7* **Air Crew (USA)**[27] 2-8-11 .... LManiezzi 5 — 83
(R Menichetti, Italy) *racd in 4th on outside: wnt 3rd under 2f out: outpcd by first two* **26/1**
4 *¾* **Rosendhal (IRE)** 2-8-11 .... GBietolini 4 — 81
(A Renzoni, Italy) *racd in 5th: kpt on at one pce fnl 2f but outpcd by ldrs* **131/10**
5 *2 ½* **Car City (ITY)** 2-8-11 .... URispoli 6 — 73
(L Riccardi, Italy) *racd in 3rd to under 2f out: wknd* **97/10**
6 *¾* **Golden Acclamation (IRE)**[18] 2-8-11 .... MDemuro 2 — 71
(A Renzoni, Italy) *last thrght* **4/1[3]**

1m 10.2s (-1.60) — **6** Ran SP% **130.1**
TOTE (including 1 Euro stake): WIN 2.15; PL 1.36, 2.38; SF 4.51.
Owner Scuderia Blueberry **Bred** Scuderia Blueberry **Trained** Italy

3186a PREMIO MARIO INCISA DELLA ROCHETTA (GROUP 3) (FILLIES) — 1m 2f
4:15 (4:20) 3-Y-O — £44,699 (£21,485; £12,252; £3,063; £3,063)

RPR
1 **Lady Alida**[28] 3-8-11 .... KKerekes 8 — 102
(W Figge, Germany) *hld up towards rr: hdwy towards ins 3f out: drvn to ld under 2f out: drew clr 1f out: comf* **39/20[1]**
2 *3 ½* **Catch Wind (USA)**[55] 3-8-11 .... URispoli 3 — 95
(S Botti, Italy) *midfield: 6th st: rdn over 2f out: responded gamely on ins to take 2nd 1f out: nt pce of wnr* **192/10**

3 ½ **Oh Mambo Girl (USA)** 3-8-11 .... C-PLemaire 1 94
(S Botti, Italy) *led: strly pressed 3f out: hdd under 2f out: nt pce of wnr but kpt on gamely* **108/10**
4 *nk* **Going For Gold (ITY)**[13] 3-8-11 .... PConvertino 5 93
(M Marcialis, Italy) *hld up in rr: hdwy whn n.m.r over 2f out: swtchd rt: kpt on fnl f to join 4th on line* **122/10**
4 *dht* **Lady Sadowa** 3-8-11 .... SUrru 10 93
(B Grizzetti, Italy) *midfield: hdwy to trck ldrs whn n.m.r 2f out: kpt on same pce* **43/1**
6 *snk* **Queen Sensazione (IRE)**[27] 2310 3-8-11 .... DVargiu 14 93
(B Grizzetti, Italy) *hld up: hdwy on outside to dispute 4th 1f out: one pce* **33/10**[2]
7 1 ¼ **Tapioka Express (IRE)**[41] 3-8-11 .... CColombi 11 90
(F & L Camici, Italy) *in rr: disputing last 2 1/2f out: kpt on fnl 2f* **29/1**
8 *nk* **Secret De Vie**[41] 3-8-11 .... SMulas 9 90
(B Grizzetti, Italy) *in rr tl kpt on u.p fnl 2f* **31/5**
9 2 **Fagutela**[27] 2310 3-8-11 .... NPinna 7 86
(S Botti, Italy) *in rr: pushed along 2f out: nvr a factor* **21/1**
10 2 ¼ **Abbotswood (ITY)**[41] 3-8-11 .... MEsposito 13 81
(M Gasparini, Italy) *in tch: rdn to chse ldrs over 2f out: one pce* **29/1**
11 ¾ **Diva Cattiva**[13] 3-8-11 .... MTellini 6 80
(B Grizzetti, Italy) *racd in 2nd: pressed ldr 3f out: wknd 2f out* **71/10**
12 2 ¼ **Garnera (IRE)**[13] 3-8-11 .... GBietolini 2 75
(S Ibido, Italy) *cl up tl wknd 1 1/2f out* **50/1**
13 5 **Flamingo Hill**[41] 3-8-11 .... MKolmarkaj 12 65
(M Gasparini, Italy) *cl up tl wknd 3f out* **42/1**
14 8 **Aloe (IRE)**[41] 3-8-11 .... MDemuro 4 49
(V Caruso, Italy) *cl up tl wknd over 2f out: eased* **57/10**[3]

2m 6.70s 14 Ran SP% **137.1**
TOTE: WIN 2.94; PL 1.80, 4.80, 3.53; DF 41.18.
Owner F W Holtkotter **Bred** Pegasus Europe Ag **Trained** Germany

2765 PONTEFRACT (L-H)

Sunday, June 21

OFFICIAL GOING: Good to firm (8.8)
The course was dolled out from the 6f marker to the finish but impact on distances not known.
Wind: Virtually nil Weather: Sunny and dry

3187 EBF TOTEPLACEPOT MAIDEN FILLIES' STKS 6f
2:10 (2:12) (Class 5) 2-Y-O **£3,885** (£1,156; £577; £288) **Stalls** Low

Form RPR
1 **Hafawa (IRE)** 2-9-0 0 .... TPO'Shea 12 78+
(M Johnston) *dwlt: hld up towards rr: rn geen 1/2-way: swtchd outside wl over 1f out and str run ent fnl f: sn rdn: edgd lft and styd on to ld last 100yds* **6/1**[3]
3 2 1 ¾ **Dance For Julie (IRE)**[26] 2360 2-9-0 0 .... PaulMulrennan 7 71
(P C Haslam) *trckd ldrs: hdwy over 2f out: swtchd lft and rdn to chse ldr over 1f out: styd on to ld ins fnl f: sn drvn: hdd and one pce last 100yds* **13/2**
3 1 ¾ **City Vaults Girl (IRE)** 2-9-0 0 .... PaulHanagan 14 66
(R A Fahey) *in tch: hdwy to chse ldrs 2f out: rdn over 1f out: kpt on: nrst fin* **12/1**
4 1 **Knockenduff** 2-9-0 0 .... TonyCulhane 9 63+
(M R Channon) *hld up towards rr: hdwy on outer wl over 1f out: styd on ins fnl f: nrst fin* **16/1**
5 2 **Sakile** 2-9-0 0 .... AdrianMcCarthy 2 57
(P W Chapple-Hyam) *prom: led over 2f out: rdn over 1f out: drvn and hdd ins fnl f: wknd* **3/1**[1]
6 1 **Asaab (IRE)** 2-9-0 0 .... J-PGuillambert 10 54
(C E Brittain) *dwlt and towards rr: hdwy into midfield 1/2-way: styd on appr last: nrst fin* **33/1**
06 7 ½ **Wood Fair**[13] 2765 2-9-0 0 .... AndrewElliott 6 52
(K R Burke) *hld up: hmpd on inner 1/2-way and sn in rr: swtchd outside wl over 1f out: styd on ins fnl f* **25/1**
3 8 ½ **Caviar**[15] 2699 2-9-0 0 .... DaneO'Neill 13 51
(R Hannon) *cl up on outer: effrt 2f out: sn rdn and wknd over 1f out* **5/1**[2]
52 9 3 **Pure Nostalgia (IRE)**[12] 2784 2-8-9 0 .... JamieKyne(5) 8 42
(J Howard Johnson) *chsd ldrs: rdn along 2f out: sn wknd* **12/1**
10 1 ¾ **Jean Jeannie** 2-9-0 0 .... AlanMunro 4 37
(W J Haggas) *nvr bttr than midfield* **5/1**[2]
11 1 ½ **Walnut Rise** 2-9-0 0 .... SaleemGolam 3 32
(M H Tompkins) *a in rr* **80/1**
12 1 ¼ **Jelly Bean** 2-9-0 0 .... PhillipMakin 5 28
(K A Ryan) *a towards rr* **20/1**
0 13 4 ½ **Menediva**[11] 2800 2-9-0 0 .... DanielTudhope 11 15
(L A Mullaney) *led: rdn along and hdd over 2f out: sn wknd* **100/1**
14 14 **Chilean Fizz** 2-9-0 0 .... MickyFenton 1 —
(Mrs A Duffield) *t.k.h in rr: hmpd 1/2-way and bhd after* **66/1**

1m 17.1s (0.20) **Going Correction** -0.125s/f (Firm) 14 Ran SP% **122.5**
Speed ratings (Par 90): **93,90,88,87,84 83,82,81,77,75 73,71,65,47**
toteswinger: 1&2 £8.80, 1&3 £17.30, 2&3 £19.50. CSF £43.36 TOTE £7.10: £1.90, £2.70, £4.10; EX 51.00.
Owner Hamdan Al Maktoum **Bred** Shadwell Estate Company Limited **Trained** Middleham Moor, N Yorks

FOCUS
This was probably a fair maiden of its type with a couple already having shown promise and some interesting newcomers also lining up. Hafawa took it with something to spare. Winners should come out of this.

NOTEBOOK
Hafawa(IRE) ◆ was one of those making her racecourse debut and it looked like it when she missed the break and then appeared to run green near the back of the field. Still with plenty to do rounding the bend, she produced a telling turn of foot once into the straight and despite hanging away to her left, maintained her effort to hit the front half a furlong out and win going away. She is almost certainly capable of even better and, being a half-sister to two winners at up to 1m2f, she should have no problem getting further. (op 13-2 tchd 11-2)
Dance For Julie(IRE), an eye-catching third on her Redcar debut last month when in front of both Pure Nostalgia and Wood Fair, stepped up from that effort here. Always handy, she hit the front a furlong out but was then swamped by the winner's late swoop. She has probably come up against a potentially nice sort here and it shouldn't be long before she finds a maiden. (tchd 6-1)
City Vaults Girl(IRE) ◆, a 26,000euros half-sister to two winners at up to 1m4f and from a stable still in red-hot form, deserves a lot of credit as she had to do plenty of work to take a handy position from the outside stall early, but kept on going all the way to the line. Better can be expected, especially as she goes up in trip. (op 14-1 tchd 16-1)
Knockenduff ◆, a 130,000gns foal and 75,000gns yearling, is a half-sister to those smart sprinters Sayif and Hunter Street. She stayed on in pleasing style down the wide outside in the home straight despite showing signs of greenness. She should have learnt from this. (op 25-1)
Sakile, out of a winning half-sister to seven minor winners and her trainer's first juvenile runner of the season, was sent off a well-backed favourite. Always handy, she took over in front at halfway but couldn't respond when the eventual runner-up headed her a furlong out and she dropped away. (op 7-2)
Asaab(IRE), whose price fell from 38,000gns as a foal to just 16,000gns as a yearling, kept plugging away on this debut and is bred to appreciate trips of around 1m to 1m2f in due course. (tchd 40-1)
Caviar, green when third behind Friday's Albany Stakes fourth She's A Character on her Doncaster debut, was ominously weak in the market beforehand and dropped tamely way after showing early speed. (op 7-2 tchd 6-1)

3188 TOTEEXACTA FILLIES' H'CAP 1m 4y
2:40 (2:41) (Class 5) (0-70,70) 3-Y-O+ **£3,238** (£963; £481; £240) **Stalls** Low

Form RPR
0423 1 **Singora Lady (IRE)**[17] 2626 4-8-9 51 .... TonyCulhane 7 58
(P T Midgley) *hld up: hdwy on outer 1/2-way: rdn along wl over 1f out: drvn ent fnl f: edgd lft and styd on to ld last 50yds* **4/1**[2]
-412 2 ½ **Luck Will Come (IRE)**[16] 2665 5-9-11 70 .... JackMitchell(3) 9 76
(H J Collingridge) *trckd ldrs: hdwy on outer over 3f out: rdn to chal wl over 1f out: drvn ent fnl f and ev ch: sddle slipped and no ex nr fin* **7/4**[1]
-013 3 *shd* **Silly Gilly (IRE)**[22] 2473 5-8-8 57 .... DeclanCannon(7) 1 63
(R E Barr) *led: rdn along 2f out: drvn over 1f out: kpt on gamely ins fnl f tl hdd and no ex last 50yds* **5/1**[3]
2300 4 3 ¾ **Sawab**[26] 2356 3-9-4 70 .... (b[1]) J-PGuillambert 8 65
(C E Brittain) *t.k.h: chsd ldrs on inner: rdn along 2f out and sn no imp* **20/1**
6054 5 2 ¼ **Flora's Pride**[12] 2791 5-9-0 56 .... PaulHanagan 4 48
(K G Reveley) *trckd ldrs: effrt and hdwy 2f out: sn rdn and no imp* **14/1**
0-30 6 ½ **Portrush Storm**[9] 2894 4-9-8 64 .... (b[1]) DanielTudhope 6 55
(D Carroll) *plld hrd: hld up in rr: hdwy on outer wl over 1f out: sn rdn and nvr a factor* **6/1**
3-45 7 7 **Do The Deal (IRE)**[20] 2528 3-8-11 63 .... (p) GrahamGibbons 5 36
(J J Quinn) *a in rr* **11/1**
0/0 8 20 **Paint The Town (IRE)**[31] 2200 4-9-6 62 .... TPQueally 3 —
(J G Given) *cl up: rdn along 3f out: wknd 2f out* **10/1**

1m 44.93s (-0.97) **Going Correction** -0.125s/f (Firm)
WFA 3 from 4yo+ 10lb 8 Ran SP% **116.2**
Speed ratings (Par 100): **99,98,98,94,92 91,84,64**
toteswinger: 1&2 £2.40, 1&3 £4.30, 2&3 £3.30. CSF £11.63 CT £35.37 TOTE £4.80: £1.50, £1.20, £2.10; EX 13.00.
Owner M McGinn **Bred** Mick McGinn **Trained** Westow, N Yorks

FOCUS
An ordinary fillies' handicap and a couple of them got themselves very warm, but they went a serious pace in this and stamina won the day.
Sawab Official explanation: jockey said filly jumped awkwardly from stalls

3189 TOTEQUADPOT H'CAP 1m 2f 6y
3:10 (3:10) (Class 3) (0-90,85) 3-Y-O+
£9,346 (£2,799; £1,399; £700; £349; £175) **Stalls** Low

Form RPR
-001 1 **Fastnet Storm (IRE)**[19] 2571 3-9-1 84 .... MickyFenton 8 95
(T P Tate) *mde all: rdn along 2f out: drvn ent fnl f: styd on gamely* **11/4**[1]
-661 2 1 **Bullet Man (USA)**[30] 2239 4-10-0 85 .... DaneO'Neill 4 94
(L M Cumani) *midfield: hdwy 3f out: rdn to chse ldrs wl over 1f out: swtchd lft and drvn ent fnl f: styd on strly u.p: nt rch wnr* **7/2**[2]
40-4 3 ¾ **William Blake**[16] 2671 4-10-0 85 .... GregFairley 6 92
(M Johnston) *trckd ldrs: hdwy to chse wnr 2f out: rdn over 1f out: drvn ins fnl f and kpt on* **4/1**[3]
-005 4 3 ¼ **Jeer (IRE)**[16] 2666 5-9-3 74 .... DaleGibson 2 75
(M W Easterby) *hld up in rr: hdwy over 2f out: sn rdn and kpt on appr fnl f: nrst fin* **16/1**
0-30 5 *nk* **Amanda Carter**[37] 2031 5-9-12 83 .... PaulHanagan 5 83
(R A Fahey) *in tch: effrt on outer 3f out: rdn along 2f out and no imp* **7/1**
-400 6 6 **Capable Guest (IRE)**[8] 2933 7-9-13 84 .... (v) TonyCulhane 9 72
(M R Channon) *in rr tl rdn along 3f out and sme late hdwy* **20/1**
0414 7 9 **Templetuohy Max (IRE)**[16] 2665 4-9-4 75 .... (v) GrahamGibbons 1 45
(J D Bethell) *chsd wnr: rdn along over 2f out: sn drvn and wknd* **9/1**
04-1 8 ¾ **Full Speed (GER)**[12] 2781 4-10-0 85 .... PJMcDonald 7 53
(G A Swinbank) *prom: effrt to chse wnr 1/2-way: rdn along over 2f out: sn drvn and wknd* **15/2**

2m 10.41s (-3.29) **Going Correction** -0.125s/f (Firm)
WFA 3 from 4yo+ 12lb 8 Ran SP% **113.8**
Speed ratings (Par 107): **108,107,106,104,103 98,91,91**
toteswinger: 1&2 £2.70, 1&3 £2.80, 2&3 £2.80. CSF £12.31 CT £36.85 TOTE £3.80: £1.40, £1.40, £1.60; EX 15.30.
Owner The Kittywake Partnership **Bred** Norelands Bloodstock **Trained** Tadcaster, N Yorks

FOCUS
A decent and competitive handicap and they went a sensible pace.

NOTEBOOK
Fastnet Storm(IRE) ◆ had been put up 6lb for his comfortable success at Ripon earlier this month, but it made little difference to him. Sent off a well-backed favourite, he travelled very smoothly in front and, sticking to the inside rail throughout, kept on finding more than enough to keep his rivals at bay. He looks a nice, progressive young handicapper and there should be more to come from him. (op 4-1)
Bullet Man(USA), 5lb higher than when benefiting from being allowed a soft lead at Newmarket last month, was held up this time. He stayed on well from off the pace over the last couple of furlongs and was still going forward at the line, but there was also some liberal swishing of the tail so he may not be the most straightforward. (tchd 3-1)
William Blake, a most encouraging fourth despite not enjoying the best of runs on his return from a lengthy layoff at Epsom earlier this month, travelled very nicely just off the pace and had every chance turning in, but he did not find quite as much off the bridle as had looked likely. Perhaps this came soon enough. (op 7-2)
Jeer(IRE) ◆, who ran his best race for his new stable at Doncaster last time, was down to a mark 11lb lower than for his last win just over a year ago. Held up near the back early, he stayed on in the latter stages without landing a blow but still looks one to watch out for off his current mark. (op 12-1)
Amanda Carter, very disappointing at Hamilton last time following a very promising seasonal reappearance here, came seriously off the bridle before the home bend and could only plug on under pressure. She isn't the most consistent. (op 13-2 tchd 6-1)
Capable Guest(IRE), who isn't the easiest to predict, was switched off in a detached last early and merely ran on past a couple of beaten rivals. He hasn't won since taking last season's Zetland Gold Cup off a 7lb higher mark and doesn't look in love with the game these days. (op 18-1 tchd 16-1)
Templetuohy Max(IRE), now on a career-high mark and 7lb higher than when bolting up at Redcar two starts ago, dropped away after tracking the winner early. (op 10-1)

Full Speed(GER), now 3lb higher than when successful on his belated return at Chester earlier this month, folded very disappointingly after showing up for a long way. Perhaps this race came too quick. (op 9-1)

3190 TOTESWINGER PONTEFRACT CASTLE STKS (LISTED RACE) 1m 4f 8y
3:40 (3:40) (Class 1) 4-Y-0+

£25,236 (£9,607; £4,810; £2,403; £1,201; £603) Stalls Low

Form RPR

5-31 1 **Furmigadelagiusta**[37] 2055 5-9-1 106 PhillipMakin 4 112
(K R Burke) *trckd ldng pair gng wl: effrt 2f out: squeezed through to ld wl over 1f out and sn rdn: styd on strly* 9/4[2]

4-34 2 2 ½ **Drumfire (IRE)**[24] 2410 5-9-1 109 DarryllHolland 7 108
(M Johnston) *hld up in rr: hdwy on outer wl over 1f out: rdn and styd on to chse wnr ins fnl f: sn drvn and no imp towards fin* 2/1[1]

-004 3 ¾ **Unleashed (IRE)**[16] 2677 4-9-1 104 TPQueally 3 107
(H R A Cecil) *hld up in tch: hdwy over 2f out: rdn wl over 1f out: drvn and kpt on ins fnl f: nrst fin* 8/1

2-53 4 shd **Sugar Ray (IRE)**[122] 613 5-9-1 105 (t) DaneO'Neill 8 107
(Saeed Bin Suroor) *cl up: rdn along 2f out: sn drvn and ev ch tl wknd ins fnl f* 9/2[3]

-442 5 2 **Fairmile**[24] 2398 7-9-1 107 StephenDonohoe 5 103
(Ian Williams) *trckd ldrs: rdn along 3f out: grad wknd fnl 2f* 11/1

2-64 6 hd **Zaham (USA)**[24] 2398 5-9-1 105 TPO'Shea 1 103
(M Johnston) *led: rdn along over 2f out: drvn and hdd over 1f out: wknd ent fnl f* 9/1

2m 35.75s (-5.05) **Going Correction** -0.125s/f (Firm) 6 Ran SP% 111.7
Speed ratings (Par 111): **111,109,108,108,107 107**
toteswinger: 1&2 £2.20, 1&3 £3.60, 2&3 £2.40. CSF £7.10 TOTE £3.20: £1.80, £1.40; EX 7.70.
Owner Keep Racing **Bred** Azienda Agricola Francesca **Trained** Middleham Moor, N Yorks

FOCUS
This looked an ordinary Listed event on paper, but a tight one with just 5lb covering the six runners on official ratings. They didn't go a great pace either and all six were still within a length or so of each other passing the furlong pole.

NOTEBOOK
Furmigadelagiusta, who was back up in grade after easily defying a mark of 98 in a handicap at York last time, was always travelling extremely well behind the leaders and once the gap appeared between Zaham and Sugar Ray, he was through it and away. He has form on fast ground, but has looked best with some give before now so this uphill finish was probably in his favour. They may be a possibility of him being considered for the Melbourne Cup.
Drumfire(IRE), who ran way above his official mark when a close third behind Cima De Triomphe and Conduit in the Brigadier Gerard at Sandown last time, was tackling this trip for the first time in his 19th outing. Switched off out the back in a detached last, he was given plenty to do in a race run at an ordinary pace and though he finished strongly once switched to the wide outside, the winner had gone beyond recall. His stamina remains unproven. (op 9-4 tchd 5-2)
Unleashed(IRE), whose half-sister also finished third in the opening contest, hadn't shown his best in three previous starts this season following a lengthy absence, though his last run was a bit better. He didn't have a lot of room to play with over a furlong from home, but his chance of winning wasn't affected and it was probably the lack of a decent gallop that proved more of a handicap. (op 10-1)
Sugar Ray(IRE), effective from the front as he showed when winning last year's Duke Of Edinburgh Handicap for Sir Michael Stoute, hadn't been seen since a couple of fair efforts for Godolphin in Dubai at the start of the year. He was always in a handy position, but failed to quicken when asked and the worry is that he has a good record fresh, so is probably unlikely so come on from this. He may therefore be difficult to place.
Fairmile, who wasn't suited by the way the race was run when second in a Polytrack conditions event last time, never really landed a blow and his stamina for the trip remains an issue. (tchd 14-1)
Zaham(USA), well below form in his two previous starts this year following a long absence and behind Fairmile on the Lingfield Polytrack last time, was responsible for the ordinary tempo but had little left to offer once the challengers arrived. (tchd 15-2)

3191 TOTESUPER7 PONTEFRACT CUP H'CAP 2m 1f 216y
4:10 (4:11) (Class 4) (0-85,85) 4-Y-0+ £5,180 (£1,541; £770; £384) Stalls Low

Form RPR

00-1 1 **Markington**[7] 2944 6-8-3 69 oh7 ow3 (b) WilliamCarson[(5)] 7 76
(P Bowen) *s.i.s and in rr: hdwy 4f out: in tch and rdn along 3f out: drvn wl over 1f out: styd on strly on wd outside ins fnl f to ld nr fin* 9/2[2]

1-12 2 nk **Mr Crystal (FR)**[13] 2766 5-8-11 77 JamieKyne[(5)] 2 84
(Micky Hammond) *trckd ldng pair: pushed along and sltly outpcd over 3f out: hdwy on inner wl over 1f out: squeezed through and rdn to ld ins fnl f: sn drvn: hdd and no ex nr fin* 2/1[1]

0-04 3 2 **Luna Landing**[23] 2452 6-8-11 72 TonyHamilton 1 77
(Jedd O'Keeffe) *led: rdn along and jnd over 3f out: drvn wl over 1f out: edgd rt ins fnl f: sn hdd and no ex* 14/1

601 4 ¾ **Miss Keck**[15] 2725 5-8-5 66 PJMcDonald 8 70
(G A Swinbank) *hld up in rr: hdwy over 4f out: rdn to chse ldrs wl over 1f out: drvn and kpt on ins fnl f* 8/1[3]

0/04 5 2 **My Immortal**[15] 2720 7-8-12 73 [1] GrahamGibbons 3 75
(J J Quinn) *in tch: rdn along and outpcd 4f out: drvn and kpt on appr fnl f* 12/1

6411 6 ½ **Inchpast**[18] 2614 8-8-10 71 (b) TPQueally 4 72
(M H Tompkins) *trckd ldrs: hdwy 5f out: cl up 3f out: rdn 2f out and ev ch tl drvn and wknd over 1f out* 9/2[2]

00/1 7 4 ½ **Nosferatu (IRE)**[22] 2499 6-9-10 85 (b) PaulMulrennan 5 81
(J Howard Johnson) *in tch: hdwy and cl up 4f out: rdn along 3f out: drvn 2f out and sn wknd* 8/1[3]

222 8 19 **Dream In Blue**[6] 779 4-8-9 71 ow1 (tp) DarryllHolland 6 46
(Mrs S J Smith) *cl up: rdn along 6f out: sn wknd and bhd: t.o fnl 3f* 16/1

3m 59.59s (-4.31) **Going Correction** -0.125s/f (Firm)
WFA 4 from 5yo+ 1lb 8 Ran SP% 112.2
Speed ratings (Par 105): **104,103,102,102,101 101,99,91**
toteswinger: 1&2 £3.40, 1&3 £11.50, 2&3 £7.40. CSF £13.36 CT £112.10 TOTE £5.20: £1.60, £1.30, £3.10; EX 14.10.
Owner Ron Stepney **Bred** Minster Enterprises Ltd **Trained** Little Newcastle, Pembrokes

FOCUS
A decent handicap with a few in-form stayers in opposition and although the pace wasn't furious, it was still solid enough to make this a proper test. The contest also produced a cracking finish.
Dream In Blue Official explanation: jockey said gelding hung right throughout

3192 BET TOTEPOOL ON ALL UK RACING MAIDEN STKS 1m 4f 8y
4:40 (4:41) (Class 5) 3-Y-0 £3,238 (£963; £481; £240) Stalls Low

Form RPR

-223 1 **Shemoli**[36] 2090 3-9-3 76 PhilipRobinson 2 81+
(M A Jarvis) *mde all: rdn clr wl over 1f out: styd on* 7/4[2]

2 2 2 ¼ **Spiekeroog**[31] 2211 3-9-3 0 TPQueally 4 76+
(H R A Cecil) *midfield: pushed along after 3f: rdn 1/2-way: swtchd outside and hdwy 2f out: sn drvn to chse wnr over 1f out: edgd lft and kpt on u.p ins fnl f: nt rch wnr* 6/5[1]

0-6 3 7 **Theola (IRE)**[9] 2877 3-8-12 0 SaleemGolam 3 59
(M H Tompkins) *chsd ldrs: rdn along 3f out: drvn 2f out: sn one pce* 12/1

0-0 4 ¾ **Riptide**[31] 2199 3-9-3 0 AlanMunro 7 63
(C F Wall) *in rr: rapid hdwy to chse ldng pair after 2f: rdn along over 3f out: drvn 2f out: sn one pce* 40/1

2033 5 4 ½ **Longboat Key**[44] 1842 3-9-3 72 GregFairley 1 56
(M Johnston) *chsd wnr: rdn along over 2f out: sn drvn and wknd wl over 1f out* 9/2[3]

6300 6 24 **Antipodean (UAE)**[12] 2790 3-9-3 50 TonyCulhane 6 18
(P T Midgley) *a in rr: bhd fnl 3f* 66/1

50 P **Sirjosh**[22] 2488 3-9-3 0 MickyFenton 5 —
(D Donovan) *stdd s: hld up in rr: pushed along and outpcd over 3f out: sn bhd and p.u 1f out* 25/1

2m 39.79s (-1.01) **Going Correction** -0.125s/f (Firm) 7 Ran SP% 115.5
Speed ratings (Par 99): **98,96,91,91,88 72,—**
toteswinger: 1&2 £1.10, 1&3 £4.20, 2&3 £4.70. CSF £4.27 TOTE £2.70: £1.50, £1.40; EX 4.60.
Owner Sheikh Ahmed Al Maktoum **Bred** Darley **Trained** Newmarket, Suffolk

FOCUS
Not much strength in depth in this maiden and only a couple seemed to hold a realistic chance.
Sirjosh Official explanation: jockey said gelding lost its action

3193 BET TOTEPOOL AT TOTESPORT.COM H'CAP 6f
5:10 (5:11) (Class 5) (0-75,73) 3-Y-0 £3,238 (£963; £481; £240) Stalls Low

Form RPR

2061 1 **Mister Tinktastic (IRE)**[6] 2970 3-9-3 69 6ex (p) PhillipMakin 6 74
(M Dods) *a.p: effrt to chal 2f out and sn rdn: drvn ins fnl f and kpt on to ld nr line* 5/2[1]

1-00 2 hd **Merry Diva**[17] 2632 3-9-6 72 AlanMunro 4 76
(C F Wall) *led: rdn wl over 1f out: drvn ins fnl f: hdd and no ex nr fin* 10/1

0143 3 hd **Riflessione**[27] 2336 3-9-6 72 (b) DarryllHolland 5 75
(R A Harris) *hld up towards rr: hdwy 2f out: swtchd outside and rdn wl over 1f out: styd on strly ins fnl f* 13/2[2]

2664 4 ¾ **Raimond Ridge (IRE)**[6] 2970 3-9-7 73 TonyCulhane 9 74
(M R Channon) *hld up and bhd: hdwy over 2f out: swtchd outside and rdn over 1f out: styd on wl fnl f* 9/1

0-03 5 1 ¼ **River Dee (IRE)**[25] 2377 3-8-6 63 WilliamCarson[(5)] 7 60
(D Donovan) *towards rr: hdwy 2f out: swtchd rt and rdn over 1f out: styd on ins fnl f: nrst fin* 9/1

-035 6 nse **Harriet's Girl**[6] 2967 3-9-1 72 MartinLane[(5)] 1 69
(K R Burke) *chsd ldrs: rdn along wl over 1f out: sn drvn and kpt on ins fnl f* 13/2[2]

2304 7 nk **Kheskianto (IRE)**[8] 2918 3-8-1 60 AndrewHeffernan[(7)] 2 56
(M C Chapman) *chsd ldrs on inner: rdn along 2f out: sn drvn and one pce appr fnl f* 7/1[3]

2114 8 1 ¾ **Billy Beetroot (USA)**[1] 3176 3-8-10 65 (t) KevinGhunowa[(3)] 11 55
(R A Harris) *chsd ldrs: hdwy to chal 2f out: sn rdn and ev ch tl drvn and wknd ent fnl f* 13/2[2]

600- 9 3 **Gems Star**[338] 4169 3-7-11 54 oh3 JamieKyne[(5)] 3 35
(J J Quinn) *chsd ldrs: rdn along over 2f out and sn wknd* 22/1

0000 10 3 ½ **Derringbay (IRE)**[33] 2169 3-8-2 54 oh4 (b) PaulHanagan 8 23
(M H Tompkins) *midfield: rdn along 1/2-way: sn wknd* 50/1

0050 11 1 ¾ **Elusive Fame (USA)**[12] 2786 3-8-13 72 MarieLussiana[(7)] 10 36
(M Johnston) *a bhd* 16/1

1m 16.14s (-0.76) **Going Correction** -0.125s/f (Firm) 11 Ran SP% 122.4
Speed ratings (Par 99): **100,99,99,98,96 96,96,94,90,85 83**
toteswinger: 1&2 £7.50, 1&3 £6.10, 2&3 £10.90. CSF £30.54 CT £153.11 TOTE £3.70: £1.70, £3.00, £2.50; EX 41.70 Trifecta £269.90 Pool: £510.68 - 1.40 winning units. Place 6 £9.00, Place 5 £1.87..
Owner Andrew Tinkler **Bred** R G Levin **Trained** Denton, Co Durham

FOCUS
A modest sprint handicap, but another cracking finish. The first two home held those positions throughout.
Gems Star Official explanation: jockey said gelding hung right
T/Plt: £13.40 to a £1 stake. Pool: £78,795.72. 4,291.16 winning tickets. T/Qpdt: £2.70 to a £1 stake. Pool: £4,836.86. 1,290.90 winning tickets. JR

3194 - 3200a (Foreign Racing) - See Raceform Interactive

DORTMUND (R-H)
Sunday, June 21

OFFICIAL GOING: Good

3201a GROSSER PREIS DER WIRTSCHAFT (GROUP 3) 1m 2f
4:20 (4:27) 3-Y-0+ £31,068 (£9,709; £4,854; £2,913)

RPR

1 **Zaungast (IRE)**[28] 2309 5-9-5 THellier 4 108
(W Hickst, Germany) *hld up: 8th st: hdwy on outside 2f out: r.o wl to ld 100yds out: drvn out* 31/10[2]

2 1 ¼ **Prince Flori (GER)**[35] 2115 6-9-5 HGrewe 10 106
(S Smrczek, Germany) *mid-div: 4th st: led 2f out to 100yds out: r.o same pce* 17/10[1]

3 ¾ **Il Divo (GER)**[56] 1575 4-9-1 EFrank 7 100
(A Wohler, Germany) *trckd ldrs: 2nd st: led wl over 2f out: hdd 2f out: one pce* 175/10

4 1 **Lord Hill (GER)**[28] 2309 5-9-3 AGoritz 5 100
(C Zeitz) *s.s: last st: hdwy on outside 2f out: styd on* 173/10

5 ¾ **Soberania (GER)**[21] 2524 3-8-1 JBojko 6 95
(A Wohler, Germany) *hld up: 7th st: nvr able to chal* 42/10

6 ¾ **Duellant (IRE)**[56] 1575 4-9-1 AStarke 9 95
(P Schiergen, Germany) *6th st: one pce fnl 2f* 9/2

7 14 **Obelisk (USA)**[281] 7-9-1 DPorcu 2 67
(J Hirschberger, Germany) *racd in 3rd to over 3f out: cl 5th on ins st: sn btn* 4/1[3]

8 shd **Download (GER)**[7] 4-9-1 LydiaLammers 3 67
(R Gross, Germany) *pressed ldr: 3rd st: sn wknd* 72/1

9 18 **Ponticello (GER)**[418] 6-9-1 FXWeissmeier 1 31
(Manfred Turk, Germany) *led to wl over 2f out: wknd qckly* 67/1

2m 4.50s (124.50)
WFA 3 from 4yo+ 12lb 9 Ran SP% 132.6
(including ten euro stakes): WIN 41; PL 15, 18, 28; SF 107.
Owner J Erhardt **Bred** J Erhardt **Trained** Germany

[2951]CHANTILLY (R-H)

Friday, June 19

OFFICIAL GOING: Good

3202a PRIX HAMPTON (LISTED RACE) 5f

1:25 (1:25) 3-Y-O+ **£25,243** (£10,097; £7,573; £5,049; £2,524)

RPR

1 **Delvita (FR)**[19] 2523 5-8-12 .... OPeslier 5 101
(J-V Toux, France)

2 *1* **Masta Plasta (IRE)**[13] 2716 6-9-5 .... TThulliez 9 105
(D Nicholls) *cl 4th on outside: rdn and kpt on fr over 1f out* **2/1**[1]

3 *hd* **Contest (IRE)**[40] 1919 5-9-5 ....(b) CSoumillon 7 104
(C Theodorakis, Greece)

4 *snk* **Skyteam (FR)**[19] 5-9-2 .... DBoeuf 6 100
(Mme C Head-Maarek, France)

5 *nk* **Arc De Triomphe (GER)**[39] 7-9-2 .... MBarzalona 4 99
(F Vermeulen, France)

6 *nk* **Madame Trop Vite (IRE)**[33] 2116 3-8-13 .... SPasquier 8 99
(K A Ryan) *hld up in tch on outside: rdn 2f out: clsd on ldrs over 1f out: one pce fnl f* **9/2**[2]

7 *2* **Derison (USA)**[19] 7-9-2 ....(b) GMasure 1 91
(H De Waele, Belgium)

8 *¾* **Sacho (GER)**[54] 11-9-5 .... MGuyon 3 91
(W Kujath, Germany)

9 *nk* **Best Joking (GER)**[34] 2097 4-9-2 .... JVictoire 2 87
(W Hefter, Germany)

58.50 secs (0.40)
WFA 3 from 4yo+ 6lb **9** Ran SP% **51.5**
PARI-MUTUEL: WIN 10.50; PL 2.20, 1.30, 1.60; DF 18.10.
Owner R Choupeaux **Bred** Raymond Choupeaux **Trained** France

NOTEBOOK
Masta Plasta(IRE), who was touched off in this race in 2008, had subsequently scored at this level back here last autumn. He made another bold bid and seems in good ehart at present.
Madame Trop Vite(IRE), who took the Group 2 Flying Childers last season, had made her seasonal debut against the likes of Sacred Kingdom in Malaysia and this was an easier task. However, she was still taking on her elders and ran her race without ever looking like winning. She might be seen at her best on softer ground later in the season.

[2875]CHEPSTOW (L-H)

Monday, June 22

OFFICIAL GOING: Good (good to firm in places; 8.2)
Wind: Nil Weather: Cloudy

3203 LINDLEY CATERING (S) STKS 5f 16y

6:20 (6:21) (Class 6) 2-Y-O **£1,942** (£578; £288; £144) **Stalls** High

Form RPR

5 **1** **Italian Tom (IRE)**[58] 1511 2-8-11 0........ MartinDwyer 2 68+
(S A Callaghan) *hld up: pushed along and hdwy to ld ins fnl f: readily* **8/15**[1]

2554 **2** *1 ½* **True Red (IRE)**[28] 2319 2-8-6 0........ AlanMunro 4 54
(B R Millman) *wnt sltly rt s: led: hdd over 2f out: ev ch 1f out: rdn and nt qckn ins fnl f* **7/2**[2]

5664 **3** *2 ¾* **Safari Camp (IRE)**[28] 2325 2-8-11 0........(t) SaleemGolam 5 49
(P Winkworth) *bmpd s: plld hrd: sn w ldr: led over 2f out: hung lft and hdd ins fnl f: wknd* **8/1**[3]

60 **4** *nk* **Ba Jetstream**[14] 2771 2-8-11 0........ SamHitchcott 3 48
(M R Channon) *hld up: rdn and effrt 2f out: wknd 1f out* **14/1**

0 **5** *¾* **Cecil's Gift**[7] 2978 2-8-1 0........ RossAtkinson(5) 1 40
(W G M Turner) *prom tl rdn and wknd over 1f out* **25/1**

60.65 secs (1.35) **Going Correction** -0.15s/f (Firm) **5** Ran SP% **109.1**
Speed ratings (Par 91): **83,80,76,75,74**
CSF £2.60 TOTE £1.40: £1.10, £1.70; EX 2.20.The winner was bought in for 16,000 guineas.
Owner Hinge, Searchfield & Tamburro **Bred** Tom Radley **Trained** Newmarket, Suffolk

FOCUS
Even by selling standards a weak contest. Italian Tom won easily on this drop in class.

NOTEBOOK
Italian Tom(IRE) won with consummate ease. The most expensive of the field as a £36,000 two-year-old, he had shown much the best form in one run when just over two lengths fifth in a 5f auction at Leicester in April and once he got a split between horses was soon away for an easy win. He did edge to his left and had gone to his right on debut but it could have been the fast ground. It is impossible to gauge what he achieved but he might be of interest off a low weight when nurseries start. He cost £16,000 to retain at the auction so it seems unlikely that he would be bought back to run in another seller. (op 8-13 tchd 4-6 in places)
True Red(IRE) was the most experienced of these but had been exposed in a seller and a claimer last time. It may be that she was up against a better-than-average winner in this grade. (op 10-3)
Safari Camp(IRE), having his fifth start and behind True Red when they met at Brighton in an April maiden and later in a Bath seller, was much too free and won't be easy to get a result with. Official explanation: jockey said colt hung left (op 10-1 tchd 12-1)
Ba Jetstream ran his best race at the third attempt and first in a seller, but that may be due to the level of the opposition rather than any great improvement. (op 9-1)
Cecil's Gift lasted longer than on debut in a Windsor seller a week earlier. (op 33-1 tchd 20-1)

3204 LINDLEY CATERING CLAIMING STKS 5f 16y

6:50 (6:51) (Class 6) 3-Y-O+ **£2,047** (£604; £302) **Stalls** High

Form RPR

06-0 **1** **Solemn**[33] 2180 4-8-13 45........(b) DavidProbert(3) 4 58
(J M Bradley) *w ldrs: rdn over 1f out: led wl ins fnl f: r.o* **12/1**

4324 **2** *nk* **The Tatling (IRE)**[17] 2653 12-8-13 80........ JackDean(5) 10 59
(J M Bradley) *hld up towards rr: hdwy over 2f out: swtchd lft over 1f out: rdn and ev ch wl ins fnl f: r.o* **1/1**[1]

0203 **3** *1* **Green Lagonda (AUS)**[14] 2758 7-8-13 55........ MickyFenton 1 51
(Stef Liddiard) *w ldrs on outside: led over 2f out: rdn and hdd wl ins fnl f: no ex cl home* **9/2**[2]

3004 **4** *1* **One Way Ticket**[12] 2811 9-9-0 41........(tp) SaleemGolam 12 48
(J M Bradley) *hld up in tch on stands' rail: rdn over 1f out: kpt on same pce ins fnl f* **40/1**

4600 **5** *1 ¼* **Sofinella (IRE)**[31] 2225 6-8-7 47........ CatherineGannon 11 37
(A W Carroll) *led: hdd over 2f out: rdn over 1f out: one pce fnl f* **14/1**

-400 **6** *½* **Talamahana**[13] 2794 4-8-7 43........(v) SamHitchcott 6 35
(A B Haynes) *towards rr: pushed along over 3f out: swtchd rt over 1f out: late prog on stands' rail: nrst fin* **33/1**

640- **7** *1 ½* **The Name Is Frank**[252] 6706 4-8-12 58........ MartinDwyer 2 34
(Mark Gillard) *w ldrs: wknd wl over 1f out* **16/1**

0-30 **8** *¾* **Mr Forthright**[35] 2124 5-9-0 47........ KevinGhunowa(3) 8 37
(J M Bradley) *mid-div: pushed along over 3f out: bhd fnl 2f* **28/1**

6360 **9** *hd* **Spanish Ace**[47] 1784 8-8-12 42........(p) PaulFitzsimons 5 31
(J M Bradley) *prom: rdn jst over 3f out: wknd over 1f out* **33/1**

2220 **10** *½* **Spic 'n Span**[33] 2180 4-8-8 59........(b) SPRyan(7) 9 32+
(R A Harris) *s.s: hdwy 3f out: wknd fnl f* **5/1**[3]

066- **11** *9* **Rose De Rita**[208] 7453 4-8-8 31 ow4........ RussellKennemore(3) 7 —
(L P Grassick) *bhd fnl 3f* **125/1**

0/ **12** *10* **Pitton Justice**[1216] 480 7-8-12 0........ RichardThomas 3 —
(Dr J R J Naylor) *dwlt: outpcd* **100/1**

59.20 secs (-0.10) **Going Correction** -0.15s/f (Firm) **12** Ran SP% **118.6**
Speed ratings (Par 101): **94,93,91,90,88 87,85,83,83,82 68,52**
toteswinger: 1&2 £9.20, 1&3 £10.30, 2&3 £2.80 CSF £23.78 TOTE £14.50: £3.30, £1.50, £1.50; EX 51.80.Green Lagonda was claimed by David Evans for £6,000.
Owner E A Hayward **Bred** Cheveley Park Stud Ltd **Trained** Sedbury, Gloucs

FOCUS
A moderate claimer dominated by the Milton Bradley yard. The Tatling was way below even his recent form with Solemn backt ossoemthing like his best.

3205 LINDLEY CATERING MAIDEN STKS 1m 4f 23y

7:20 (7:21) (Class 5) 3-Y-O+ **£2,719** (£809; £404; £202) **Stalls** Low

Form RPR

3-02 **1** **Perfect Shot (IRE)**[35] 2138 3-8-12 79........ MartinDwyer 8 66+
(J L Dunlop) *chsd ldr: led 2f out: sn rdn and hung lft: clr ins fnl f: eased cl home* **2/11**[1]

00 **2** *4 ½* **Saxona (IRE)**[10] 2877 5-9-7 0........ MickyFenton 9 50
(Ian Williams) *hld up in mid-div: hdwy on outside over 3f out: rdn over 2f out: wnt 2nd towards fin: no ch w wnr* **20/1**

-050 **3** *¾* **No Sting**[10] 2881 3-8-7 51........ RichardThomas 6 49
(W S Kittow) *led: rdn and hung rt over 2f out: sn hdd: btn whn hung rt ins fnl f: lost 2nd towards fin* **16/1**[3]

0000 **4** *1 ¼* **Guilin (IRE)**[24] 2461 3-8-7 49........ JosedeSouza 5 48+
(P F I Cole) *hld up in tch: rdn over 2f out: swtchd rt jst over 1f out: one pce whn nt clr run wl ins fnl f* **25/1**

0 **5** *¾* **Warrants Attention (IRE)**[9] 2930 3-8-5 0........ RichardRowe(7) 4 51
(A M Balding) *s.i.s: hld up and bhd: hdwy 3f out: sn rdn: one pce fnl f* **14/1**[2]

0 **6** *18* **Maskateer (IRE)**[28] 2323 3-8-12 0........ VinceSlattery 7 20
(Mrs A M Thorpe) *s.i.s: a in rr* **33/1**

0/0 **7** *hd* **Restless Swallow**[7] 2981 4-9-5 0........ SPRyan(7) 3 20
(R A Harris) *hld up in tch: rdn and wknd 3f out* **100/1**

00 **8** *2 ¼* **Mr Kartoffel (IRE)**[7] 2981 4-9-5 0........ AmyScott(7) 1 16
(H Candy) *s.i.s: a wl in rr* **50/1**

0- **9** *6* **Sugarbaby Princess (IRE)**[235] 7098 3-8-4 0........ DavidProbert(3) 2 1
(S W James) *prom tl rdn and wknd over 3f out* **50/1**

2m 39.12s (0.12) **Going Correction** +0.05s/f (Good)
WFA 3 from 4yo+ 14lb **9** Ran SP% **113.6**
Speed ratings (Par 103): **101,98,97,96,96 84,84,82,78**
toteswinger: 1&2 £12.80, 1&3 £3.30, 2&3 £3.80 CSF £8.68 TOTE £1.10: £1.02, £5.40, £5.50; EX 6.60.
Owner Sir Philip Wroughton **Bred** David Jamison Bloodstock **Trained** Arundel, W Sussex

FOCUS
A weak maiden in which only the long-odds-on winner had managed to reach a place out of the nine runners. He was value for 6l but still nearly 20lb off his latest form.

3206 WELSH NATIONAL OPERA WORLD PERA H'CAP 1m 2f 36y

7:50 (7:50) (Class 5) (0-75,74) 4-Y-O+ **£3,561** (£1,059; £529; £264) **Stalls** Low

Form RPR

140- **1** **Latin Scholar (IRE)**[59] 6202 4-9-7 **74**........ DaneO'Neill 7 80
(A King) *hld up in tch: rdn over 2f out: led wl over 1f out: drvn out: jst hld on* **10/3**[2]

4352 **2** *nse* **Millfields Dreams**[10] 2880 10-8-12 **70**........(p) MarkCoumbe(5) 3 76
(G C Bravery) *hld up in rr: hdwy on outside over 2f out: rdn wl over 1f out: edgd rt ins fnl f: r.o towards fin: jst failed* **11/1**

60-0 **3** *¾* **Red Birr (IRE)**[14] 2775 8-9-6 **73**........(t) MartinDwyer 6 78
(P R Webber) *hld up and bhd: rdn and hdwy over 2f out: kpt on ins fnl f* **15/2**

3612 **4** *2 ¼* **I'm In The Pink (FR)**[13] 2781 5-9-0 **72**........ RichardEvans(5) 5 72
(P D Evans) *chsd ldr: led 3f out: rdn and hdd wl over 1f out: hld whn eased cl home* **2/1**[1]

5505 **5** *2 ½* **Uig**[10] 2878 8-8-4 **57**........ KirstyMilczarek 1 52
(H S Howe) *prom tl rdn and wknd over 2f out* **9/2**[3]

-054 **6** *hd* **By Command**[14] 2773 4-9-7 **74**........ AlanMunro 4 69
(J W Hills) *led: hdd 3f out: sn rdn: wknd fnl f* **13/2**

-400 **7** *½* **Bespoke Boy**[18] 969 4-7-13 **55** oh2........ DavidProbert(3) 2 49
(Mrs N S Evans) *t.k.h in tch: rdn 2f out: sn wknd* **22/1**

2m 10.23s (-0.37) **Going Correction** +0.05s/f (Good) **7** Ran SP% **112.4**
Speed ratings (Par 103): **103,102,102,100,98 98,98**
toteswinger: 1&2 £2.25, 1&3 £8.80, 2&3 not won CSF £36.74 TOTE £4.80: £2.70, £2.20; EX 60.70.
Owner Let's Live Racing **Bred** David Brickley **Trained** Barbury Castle, Wilts
■ Stewards' Enquiry : Dane O'Neill two-day ban: used whip with excessive frequency without giving gelding time to respond (Jul 6-7)

FOCUS
Modest handicap form off a steady pace. A slight personal best from the winner.

3207 FREEBETS.CO.UK NEW ONLINE BETTING FORUM MAIDEN STKS 1m 14y

8:20 (8:24) (Class 5) 3-Y-O+ **£2,719** (£809; £404; £202) **Stalls** High

Form RPR

0-4 **1** **Royal Superlative**[28] 2318 3-8-8 0........ JackMitchell(3) 2 63+
(R M Beckett) *hld up in tch: led 2f out: rdn out* **3/1**[1]

00-0 **2** *1* **Sunny Future (IRE)**[13] 2795 3-9-2 75........ MickyFenton 10 66
(M S Saunders) *wnt sltly rt s: sn chsng ldr: rdn and ev ch over 1f out: kpt on ins fnl f* **7/2**[2]

0-40 **3** *nk* **Hilltop Artistry**[11] 2863 3-8-13 61........ DavidProbert(3) 3 65
(S W James) *hld up and bhd: rdn and hdwy over 2f out: kpt on ins fnl f* **10/1**

50 **4** *5* **Stellar Cause (USA)**[7] 2981 3-9-2 0........ MartinDwyer 6 54
(P F I Cole) *racd wd: led over 1f: prom: rdn and edgd rt fr over 2f out: wknd ins fnl f* **7/2**[2]

6000 5 1 ¼ **Poca A Poca (IRE)**[20] 2579 5-9-2 45 (p) MarkFlynn(5) 7 48?
(G C Bravery) *mid-div: rdn over 3f out: hdwy 2f out: wknd ins fnl f* **80/1**

6 7 **Square Of Gold (FR)** 3-9-2 0 KirstyMilczarek 12 35+
(A W Carroll) *mid-div: hdwy over 3f out: swtchd lft 2f out: wknd jst over 1f out* **8/1**[3]

000/ 7 ½ **Safari**[406] 3241 6-9-7 35 DaneO'Neill 11 30
(S Curran) *hld up in tch: rdn over 2f out: sn wknd* **40/1**

8 1 ¾ **Flying Gazebo (IRE)** 3-9-2 0 LPKeniry 1 29
(J S Moore) *mid-div: wknd over 3f out* **22/1**

0/6- 9 1 **La Belle Joannie**[497] 523 4-9-7 48 MattieBatchelor 13 24
(S Curran) *led over 6f out: sn clr: hdd 2f out: sn hung lft and wknd* **40/1**

10 ½ **Dramatic Jewel (USA)** 3-9-2 0 AlanMunro 5 26
(J W Hills) *s.i.s: a bhd* **8/1**[3]

0 11 14 **Errol Flynn (IRE)**[67] 1297 3-8-13 0 (b[1]) KevinGhunowa(3) 9 —
(R A Harris) *s.s: hung bdly lft thrght: a in rr* **20/1**

000/ 12 8 **Awe**[18] 6421 5-9-12 42 VinceSlattery 8 —
(Mrs N S Evans) *chsd ldrs 3f* **150/1**

00-6 13 9 **Den's Boy**[26] 2378 4-9-12 38 PaulDoe 4 —
(S Curran) *sn wl in rr* **66/1**

1m 35.75s (-0.45) **Going Correction** -0.15s/f (Firm)
WFA 3 from 4yo+ 10lb **13 Ran SP% 118.1**
Speed ratings (Par 103): **96,95,94,89,88 81,80,79,78,77 63,55,46**
toteswinger: 1&2 £3.40, 1&3 £2.40, 2&3 £14.70 CSF £12.51 TOTE £4.00: £1.50, £2.00, £2.00; EX 16.70.
Owner Prince Of Wales And Duchess Of Cornwall **Bred** The Prince Of Wales & The Duchess Of Cornwall **Trained** Whitsbury, Hants

FOCUS
Not much strength in depth to this maiden. It has been rated through the third and the fifth holds down the level.
Den's Boy Official explanation: jockey said gelding moved poorly

3208 FREEBETS.CO.UK FREE FOOTBALL SHIRT FOR EVERYONE H'CAP 6f 16y
8:50 (8:51) (Class 5) (0-70,70) 3-Y-O+ **£2,914** (£867; £433; £216) **Stalls** High

Form RPR

2003 1 **Golden Dixie (USA)**[9] 2911 10-9-12 68 CatherineGannon 1 76
(R A Harris) *w ldrs: led 2f out: hld on u.p ins fnl f* **6/1**

0004 2 nk **Just Jimmy (IRE)**[10] 2880 4-8-9 51 oh1 (v) PaulDoe 3 58
(P D Evans) *hld up in mid-div: hdwy over 2f out: rdn and r.o ins fnl f* **5/1**[3]

6123 3 2 ¼ **Bateleur**[9] 2920 5-9-8 64 EdwardCreighton 6 64
(M R Channon) *hld up and bhd: hdwy on outside over 2f out: rdn over 1f out: no ex towards fin* **4/1**[1]

6563 4 1 **Who's Winning (IRE)**[20] 2564 8-8-9 51 (t) J-PGuillambert 7 48
(B G Powell) *led 3f: rdn over 1f out: no ex ins fnl f* **9/1**

014- 5 2 ½ **Rondeau (GR)**[252] 6706 4-9-13 69 LPKeniry 12 58
(P R Chamings) *w ldr: led 3f out to 2f out: rdn over 1f out: wknd ins fnl f* **9/2**[2]

0066 6 ½ **Harrison's Flyer (IRE)**[10] 2880 8-8-6 51 oh6 (p) DavidProbert(3) 4 38
(J M Bradley) *hld up in mid-div: rdn wl over 1f out: no hdwy* **20/1**

0-00 7 1 ½ **Rowaad**[10] 2880 4-8-9 51 oh3 (v[1]) KirstyMilczarek 5 33
(A E Price) *hld up in tch: rdn and hung lft over 1f out: wknd ins fnl f* **11/1**

0003 8 1 **Ghost Dancer**[11] 2852 5-9-6 65 KevinGhunowa(3) 2 44
(J M Bradley) *t.k.h: prom: rdn over 1f out: wknd ins fnl f* **8/1**

1504 9 1 ½ **Caustic Wit (IRE)**[9] 2908 11-8-7 56 JakePayne(7) 8 30
(M S Saunders) *a bhd* **14/1**

0-3 10 nk **Signora Frasi (IRE)**[109] 762 4-9-6 62 RichardThomas 13 35
(A G Newcombe) *t.k.h: a in rr* **16/1**

5000 11 2 **Mr Loire**[9] 2908 5-8-9 51 oh6 (b) TravisBlock 9 18
(A J Chamberlain) *s.i.s: a towards rr* **66/1**

1m 11.24s (-0.76) **Going Correction** -0.15s/f (Firm)
WFA 3 from 4yo+ 7lb **11 Ran SP% 117.4**
Speed ratings (Par 103): **105,104,101,100,96 96,94,92,90,90 87**
toteswinger: 1&2 £2.30, 1&3 £6.60, 2&3 £7.80 CSF £36.02 CT £138.29 TOTE £7.30: £2.30, £2.40, £2.10; EX 28.30.
Owner Drag Star On Swan **Bred** George Strawbridge Jr **Trained** Earlswood, Monmouths
■ Stewards' Enquiry : Paul Doe one-day ban: used whip with excessive frequency (Jul 6)

FOCUS
A trappy sprint and modest form.
Rowaad Official explanation: jockey said gelding suffered interference in running

3209 CHEPSTOW RACECOURSE WINE CLUB @ WINEAUX.CO.UK FILLIES' H'CAP 1m 14y
9:20 (9:25) (Class 5) (0-70,70) 3-Y-O **£2,914** (£867; £433; £216) **Stalls** High

Form RPR

0312 1 **You've Been Mowed**[9] 2910 3-8-8 60 DavidProbert(3) 5 63
(R J Price) *mde all: rdn over 1f out: hld on wl u.p ins fnl f* **11/2**[2]

-310 2 nk **Inis Boffin**[11] 2858 3-9-6 69 LPKeniry 15 72
(S Kirk) *in rr: rdn over 3f out: hdwy over 1f out: r.o wl towards fin* **9/1**

1206 3 ¾ **Foreign Investment (IRE)**[11] 2841 3-9-3 66 PaulDoe 13 67
(P D Evans) *hld up in mid-div: hdwy over 2f out: rdn over 1f out: kpt on ins fnl f* **14/1**

0653 4 hd **Evening Sunset (GER)**[11] 2863 3-8-9 58 EdwardCreighton 8 59
(M R Channon) *hld up in tch: rdn over 2f out: kpt on ins fnl f* **11/1**

-304 5 nk **Caster Sugar (USA)**[12] 2827 3-9-0 63 DaneO'Neill 7 63
(R Hannon) *hld up in tch: rdn and edgd lft over 1f out: kpt on ins fnl f* **8/1**[3]

5-20 6 ¾ **Breadstick**[32] 2206 3-9-7 70 TravisBlock 17 68
(H Morrison) *hld up in mid-div: hdwy 3f out: rdn jst over 2f out: nt qckn ins fnl f* **8/1**[3]

0-03 7 nk **When Doves Cry**[21] 2548 3-8-12 61 MartinDwyer 4 58
(B W Hills) *stdd s: hld up and bhd: pushed along 3f out: hdwy whn rdn and edgd rt over 1f out: nvr able to chal* **5/1**[1]

06-0 8 hd **Arcola (IRE)**[24] 2433 3-8-13 62 MickyFenton 11 59
(D M Simcock) *s.s: hld up towards rr: hdwy over 3f out: rdn and ev ch 2f out: fdd towards fin* **12/1**

4040 9 hd **Autumn Morning (IRE)**[22] 2515 3-8-2 51 oh1 CatherineGannon 6 48
(P D Evans) *w wnr: rdn over 2f out: fdd towards fin* **16/1**

-306 10 1 ½ **Heartsease**[22] 2515 3-8-6 58 JackMitchell(3) 14 51
(J G Portman) *hld up in tch: rdn and lost pl over 3f out: n.d after* **8/1**[3]

6-46 11 ¾ **Triple Cee (IRE)**[11] 2858 3-9-2 65 SamHitchcott 2 56
(M R Channon) *hld up towards rr: rdn over 3f out: n.d* **11/1**

6-06 12 8 **Chalk Hill Blue**[23] 2489 3-8-6 55 ow1 (b[1]) StephenCarson 16 28
(Eve Johnson Houghton) *prom: wkng whn n.m.r briefly over 2f out* **28/1**

00-0 13 8 **Now**[48] 1772 3-8-13 62 SaleemGolam 10 17
(P Winkworth) *a in rr* **33/1**

0500 14 ½ **Zaftil (IRE)**[13] 2794 3-8-2 51 oh6 RichardThomas 1 4
(H S Howe) *a in rr* **100/1**

-430 15 6 **Mrs Slocombe (IRE)**[2] 3159 3-9-1 64 J-PGuillambert 12 4
(J Akehurst) *prom tl wknd 4f out* **20/1**

1m 35.78s (-0.42) **Going Correction** -0.15s/f (Firm) **15 Ran SP% 124.4**
Speed ratings (Par 96): **96,95,94,94,94 93,93,93,93,91 90,82,74,74,68**
toteswinger: 1&2 not won, 1&3 not won, 2&3 not won CSF £54.14 CT £691.03 TOTE £8.10: £2.00, £5.00, £6.20; EX 70.70 Place 6: £9.06, Place 5: £8.30.
Owner Mrs K Oseman **Bred** T E Pocock **Trained** Ullingswick, H'fords

FOCUS
A bunch finish to this modest handicap, and it is hard to rate the form positively.
When Doves Cry Official explanation: jockey said filly lost its action
T/Plt: £8.90 to a £1 stake. Pool: £46,568.42. 3,783.42 winning tickets. T/Qpdt: £7.30 to a £1 stake. Pool: £3,219.86. 324.10 winning tickets. KH

3157 LINGFIELD (L-H)
Monday, June 22

OFFICIAL GOING: Turf course - good to firm (9.2); all-weather - standard
Wind: nil Weather: warm, muggy

3210 E B F DEEP HEAT MAIDEN FILLIES' STKS 5f (P)
2:15 (2:15) (Class 5) 2-Y-O **£3,561** (£1,059; £529; £264) **Stalls** High

Form RPR

1 **Brambleberry** 2-9-0 0 RichardKingscote 5 79+
(Tom Dascombe) *chsd ldr: carried wd bnd 2f out: sn led: rdn out and in command fnl f* **7/2**[2]

0 2 1 ¼ **Virginia Hall**[7] 2972 2-9-0 0 StephenDonohoe 7 72
(Sir Mark Prescott) *chsd ldng pair: chsd wnr jst over 1f out: edgd lft u.p: kpt on same pce* **16/1**

0303 3 hd **Mrs Boss**[16] 2711 2-8-11 0 JamesMillman(3) 4 71
(B R Millman) *in rr of main gp: reminder over 2f out: swtchd rt and bmpd rival over 1f out: r.o wl to go 3rd ins fnl f: gng on fin* **11/10**[1]

6 4 4 ½ **Three's A Crowd**[23] 2490 2-9-0 0 RichardHughes 3 55
(D R C Elsworth) *in tch: effrt on inner to chse ldrs 2f out: outpcd jst over 1f out: lost 3rd ins fnl f* **9/1**

440 5 2 **Mind The Monarch**[20] 2563 2-9-0 0 WilliamBuick 1 50+
(R A Teal) *in tch: rdn whn short of room and hmpd bnd 2f out: sn wknd: edging out rt fnl f* **25/1**

00 6 1 ¼ **Princess Shamal**[11] 2860 2-9-0 0 AdrianMcCarthy 2 43
(J R Jenkins) *hung rt thrght: led: hung rt bnd 2f out: sn hdd: wknd over 1f out* **66/1**

44 7 3 ¾ **Guesswork**[11] 2853 2-9-0 0 AlanMunro 8 29
(W Jarvis) *in tch on outer: rdn and struggling whn bmpd over 1f out: no ch after* **4/1**[3]

8 ¾ **Fairywater Grey (IRE)** 2-9-0 0 NeilChalmers 6 27
(J J Bridger) *sn wl outpcd and detached in last pl* **100/1**

60.32 secs (1.52) **Going Correction** +0.15s/f (Slow) **8 Ran SP% 112.1**
Speed ratings (Par 90): **93,91,90,83,80 78,72,71**
toteswingers: 1&2 £14.30, 1&3 £2.30, 2&3 £11.70 CSF £51.64 TOTE £4.30: £1.10, £4.80, £1.10; EX 46.80 Trifecta £360.60 Part won. Pool: £487.33 - 0.92 winning units..
Owner Grant Thornton Racing Club **Bred** Highclere Stud **Trained** Lambourn, Berks

FOCUS
Just a fair juvenile maiden. The winner won with something in hand and can improve on this.

NOTEBOOK
Brambleberry ◆, who is out of the Group 1 winning miler Miss Satamix, knew her job but very much gave the impression the race would bring her on fitness wise. There should be much better to come, particularly as she steps up in trip, and it's not out of the question she could be pattern class in time - some black type would enhance her value considerably. (op 5-2)
Virginia Hall, quite a tall filly, improved significantly on the form she showed on her debut at Warwick. After showing early speed, she kept on but was simply no match for the winner. She looks the type to keep progressing. (tchd 14-1)
Mrs Boss didn't see her race out over 6f on the turf course here last time, yet on this drop in trip she was outpaced for most of the way, only keeping on once switched early in the straight. She's an honest enough type, but is evidently not the easiest to place and might be better suited by a stiffer, or more galloping 5f. (op 5-4 tchd 10-11)
Three's A Crowd improved on her debut form but still looked a little green. (op 17-2 tchd 8-1)
Mind The Monarch was beginning to struggle when badly hampered rounding the final bend. (tchd 33-1)
Princess Shamal Official explanation: jockey said filly hung badly right and the bit went through its mouth
Guesswork raced wider than ideal and was below the form she showed on her first two starts. (op 5-1)

3211 "YOU CAN FEEL IT WORKING" COVONIA H'CAP 7f (P)
2:45 (2:46) (Class 4) (0-80,78) 4-Y-O+ **£5,828** (£1,734; £866; £432) **Stalls** Low

Form RPR

3155 1 **I Confess**[7] 2976 4-9-1 77 (b) RichardEvans(5) 8 85
(P D Evans) *broke wl: led for 1f: chsd ldr tl led again 3f out: drvn and clr over 1f out: hdd fnl 100yds: battled on wl to ld again last strides* **7/2**[1]

54-3 2 shd **Billberry**[25] 2400 4-8-9 66 (t) SaleemGolam 3 74
(S C Williams) *trckd ldrs: rdn to chse wnr jst over 2f out: edging lft 1f out: styd on to ld fnl 100yds tl hdd last strides* **9/2**[2]

235 3 1 **Jake The Snake (IRE)**[13] 2794 8-9-2 78 AmyBaker(5) 12 83
(A W Carroll) *stdd and dropped in bhd after s: hld up in rr: hdwy on inner wl over 1f out: chsd ldng pair 1f out: kpt on* **7/1**

4-64 4 2 **Carmenero (GER)**[15] 2736 6-9-1 72 WilliamBuick 6 72
(W R Muir) *in tch in midfield: hdwy jst over 2f out: chsd ldrs and drvn over 1f out: kpt on same pce fnl f* **9/1**

0425 5 1 ¼ **Fiefdom (IRE)**[26] 2387 7-9-3 74 GeorgeBaker 9 70
(I W McInnes) *hld up in rr: pushed along over 2f out: c wd and rdn over 1f out: styd on fnl f: nvr threatened ldrs* **11/2**[3]

-302 6 1 **Balata**[16] 2713 4-8-13 70 TGMcLaughlin 2 64
(B R Millman) *mounted on crse and taken down early: sn niggled along towards rr: rdn and hdwy over 1f out: kpt on but nvr pce to rch ldrs* **7/1**

500- 7 2 ¾ **Yankee Storm**[196] 7603 4-9-1 72 PatCosgrave 11 58
(M Quinn) *racd in midfield: rdn over 2f out: drvn and no hdwy wl over 1f out: wl hld fnl f* **33/1**

-000 8 hd **Highland Harvest**[24] 2434 5-9-1 72 SteveDrowne 1 58
(Jamie Poulton) *chsd ldrs: rdn to dispute 2nd pl whn jostled bnd ent fnl 2f: sn outpcd: wknd jst over 1f out* **9/1**

2110 9 2 ½ **Dichoh**[19] 1731 6-9-6 77 (vt) RichardHughes 5 56
(M Madgwick) *hld up towards rr: rdn and no hdwy over 1f out: wl btn fnl f* **16/1**

466 10 2 **Singleb (IRE)**[14] 2775 5-9-1 72 (p) StephenDonohoe 7 45
(Miss Gay Kelleway) *in tch in midfield: rdn and unable qck jst over 2f out: wl btn over 1f out* **16/1**

-005 **11** ½ **Greystoke Prince**[34] 2168 4-8-13 **70**..............................(p) AdamKirby 10 42
(W R Swinburn) *chsd ldng pair: rdn and wknd wl over 1f out: wl hld whn hung lft over 1f out* **20/1**

/06- **12** *11* **Beau Jazz**[270] 6225 8-7-11 **59** oh14.................................. NicolPolli(5) 4 1
(W De Best-Turner) *led after 1f tl hdd and rdn 3f out: wknd jst over 2f out: wl bhd over 1f out* **100/1**

1m 24.93s (0.13) **Going Correction** +0.15s/f (Slow) **12** Ran SP% **121.2**
Speed ratings (Par 105): **105,104,103,101,100 98,95,95,92,90 89,77**
toteswinger: 1&2 £3.90, 1&3 £7.70, 2&3 £5.40 CSF £18.91 CT £109.28 TOTE £5.60: £2.20, £1.90, £3.10; EX 23.20 Trifecta £272.30 Pool: £368.10 - 0.20 winning units..
Owner M&R Refurbishments Ltd **Bred** Gestut Sohrenhof **Trained** Pandy, Monmouths

FOCUS
A fair, competitive handicap which was well run. It has been rated through the third.

3212 WINTHROP H'CAP 5f (P)
3:15 (3:15) (Class 3) (0-90,89) 3-Y-O+ **£8,418** (£2,505; £1,251; £625) **Stalls** High

Form RPR

-322 **1** **Peak District (IRE)**[23] 2502 5-9-4 **85**................................ AmyRyan(5) 2 97
(K A Ryan) *sn led: mde rest: pushed clr 2f out: hung rt fr over 1f out: styd on wl* **9/4**[1]

060- **2** *1* **Sir Edwin Landseer (USA)**[253] 6676 9-9-9 **85**.............. GeorgeBaker 1 93
(G L Moore) *taken down early: chsd ldrs: rdn and effrt jst over 2f out: hrd drvn to chse wnr jst over 1f out: kpt on same pce fnl f* **11/1**

0600 **3** ½ **Good Gorsoon (USA)**[23] 2502 4-9-5 **84**........................ PatrickHills(3) 6 91
(B W Hills) *in rr: hdwy towards inner over 1f out: kpt on wl u.p to go 3rd ins fnl f: nvr quite pce to rch ldrs* **6/1**[3]

-610 **4** ½ **Lochstar**[10] 2897 5-9-10 **86**.. WilliamBuick 9 91
(A M Balding) *chsd ldrs: pushed along 2f out: drvn ent fnl f: kpt on same pce* **3/1**[2]

2053 **5** *1 ¼* **First Order**[9] 2929 8-8-13 **80**..(v) AnnStokell(5) 10 80
(Miss A Stokell) *t.k.h: hld up in midfield on outer: rdn and effrt over 1f out: one pce and no imp fnl f* **25/1**

3114 **6** *1 ½* **Chjimes (IRE)**[87] 985 5-9-13 **89**................................... RichardHughes 8 84
(C R Dore) *stdd after s: hld up in rr: pushed along and hdwy over 1f out: no hdwy 1f out and wl hld fnl f* **8/1**

0400 **7** *1 ¼* **Elhamri**[16] 2704 5-9-7 **83**.. JamesDoyle 3 73
(S Kirk) *stdd after s: hld up in last pair: rdn wl over 1f out: no hdwy and nvr nr ldrs* **12/1**

5566 **8** *hd* **Whiskey Junction**[25] 2396 5-9-2 **78**................................ PatCosgrave 7 68
(M Quinn) *sn pushed along in midfield: rdn and losing pl over 2f out: no ch fr over 1f out* **25/1**

0404 **9** *1 ½* **Stoneacre Lad (IRE)**[10] 2897 6-9-13 **89**..........................(b) TPQueally 4 73
(Peter Grayson) *pressed wnr tl rdn and unable qck 2f out: wknd over 1f out* **12/1**

1100 **10** *1 ½* **Almaty Express**[14] 2770 7-9-3 **79**..................................(b) JimmyQuinn 5 58
(J R Weymes) *a in rr: bhd and rdn 2f out: no prog and nvr on terms* **33/1**

58.94 secs (0.14) **Going Correction** +0.15s/f (Slow) **10** Ran SP% **115.5**
Speed ratings (Par 107): **104,102,101,100,98 96,94,94,91,89**
toteswingers: 1&2 £4.50, 1&3 £4.20, 2&3 £31.30 CSF £27.39 CT £135.19 TOTE £3.20: £1.20, £4.40, £2.90; EX 32.90 Trifecta £311.70 Pool: £421.30 - 0.42 winning units..
Owner Sunpak Potatoes **Bred** Western Bloodstock **Trained** Hambleton, N Yorks

FOCUS
An ordinary sprint handicap for the grade, but the winner is progressive and probably just as good on this surface as turf.

NOTEBOOK
Peak District(IRE), having just his fourth start since coming over from Ireland, and only his third since being claimed out of Mick Easterby's yard, confirmed the promise of his recent second placing in a better race at York. He was kept honest up front, but found plenty in the straight and was quite a decisive winner, despite again edging badly right in the closing stages. It seems likely he'll improve again when he has a right-hand rail to run against and he very much looks a sprinter on the up. (op 5-2 tchd 2-1)
Sir Edwin Landseer(USA), now with Gary Moore, looked fit enough for his first run in 253 days and this was a decent effort. His main target is apparently the greys' handicap at the Newmarket July course. (op 16-1 tchd 10-1)
Good Gorsoon(USA) was back on a winning mark but he got quite warm and could only manage third. He ran on late, having been outpaced, and this was a creditable enough effort, but he's not the easiest to win with. (op 8-1 tchd 11-2)
Lochstar had won both his previous starts on the Lingfield Polytrack, including a C&D handicap off a mark of 79 two starts back, but he was comfortably held this time. He came wide into the straight, but it didn't really make much difference. (op 11-4 tchd 7-2)
First Order raced keenly early and never looked like winning. (op 20-1)
Chjimes(IRE) was slow to find his stride and struggled to get involved. (op 6-1)

3213 DUREX PLEASUREMAX H'CAP 1m 2f
3:45 (3:45) (Class 3) (0-95,89) 3-Y-O+ **£9,066** (£2,697; £1,348; £673) **Stalls** Low

Form RPR

10-1 **1** **Shavansky**[18] 2641 5-9-4 **82**.. JamesMillman(3) 1 90
(B R Millman) *t.k.h: chsd ldr: pushed along and hdwy 3f out: rdn to chal over 2f out: led wl over 1f out: hld on wl fnl f* **9/2**[3]

0/11 **2** ½ **Seeking The Buck (USA)**[17] 2671 5-10-0 **89**................ GeorgeBaker 7 96
(R M Beckett) *hld up in last pair: rdn to chse ldng pair 3f out: drvn 2f out: wnt 2nd ins fnl f: edgd lft u.p fnl 100yds: kpt on* **1/1**[1]

40-0 **3** *1 ¼* **Overturn (IRE)**[23] 2480 5-9-10 **85**.................................... AdamKirby 5 90
(W R Swinburn) *racd keenly: led: rdn over 2f out: hdd wl over 1f out: styd pressing wnr tl ins fnl f: keeping on same pce and hld whn short of room fnl 75yds* **3/1**[2]

40-1 **4** *2 ¼* **Cosmea**[18] 2641 4-9-6 **81**.. EddieAhern 6 81
(A King) *stdd s: hld up in last pair: rdn and effrt on inner over 2f out: no imp fr over 1f out* **7/1**

2104 **5** *shd* **Gilded Age**[12] 2829 3-7-9 **75**.................................. MatthewLawson(7) 4 75
(M Johnston) *dwlt: sn rcvrd to chse ldrs: outpcd on downhill run 4f out: rdn 3f out: kpt on same pce fnl 2f* **15/2**

1005 **6** *3 ¼* **Intabih (USA)**[17] 2669 4-9-10 **85**................................. J-PGuillambert 2 78
(C E Brittain) *hld up in tch: rdn and effrot jst over 2f out: unable qck and no hdwy wl over 1f out: eased wl ins fnl f* **16/1**

2m 8.41s (-2.09) **Going Correction** -0.125s/f (Firm)
WFA 3 from 4yo+ 12lb **6** Ran SP% **123.3**
Speed ratings (Par 107): **103,102,101,99,99 97**
toteswingers: 1&2 £1.02, 1&3 £5.30, 2&3 £2.10 CSF £10.62 TOTE £6.50: £2.80, £1.30; EX 14.40.
Owner John Southway & Andrew Hughes **Bred** George Strawbridge **Trained** Kentisbeare, Devon

FOCUS
Quite a decent handicap. The winner improved on his Sandown form, when dead-heating with today's fourth.

NOTEBOOK
Shavansky was apparently not totally wound up when dead-heating with today's fourth-placed finisher after around five months off on his debut for this stable at Sandown and he stepped up on that form to gamely defy a 3lb rise. His connections may now look for an even more valuable handicap. (op 5-1)
Seeking The Buck(USA), bidding for a hat-trick, was left with ground to make up on the winner and third-placed finisher after being dropped in early, and he was forced to try and make ground about three wide around the final bend. He kept on in the straight, but edged slightly left and was just held. This was still a solid effort off a 2lb higher mark than when winning at Epsom on his previous start. (op 6-4 tchd 7-4)
Overturn(IRE), ridden positively from the off, looked set to finish well held when headed in the straight, but he was staying on again near the line and would have finished slightly closer had he not been squeezed for room late on. (op 4-1 tchd 9-2 and 11-4)
Cosmea, the only filly in the line up, had dead-heated with today's winner at Sandown on her latest start, but she was probably unsuited by the way the race unfolded this time and never looked like defying a 3lb rise. (op 5-1)
Gilded Age didn't appear comfortable on the undulations. He should do better on a more galloping track back over 1m4f. (op 10-1 tchd 13-2)

3214 NICORETTE ICY WHITE MAIDEN FILLIES' STKS 1m 2f
4:15 (4:15) (Class 5) 3-Y-O+ **£3,070** (£906; £453) **Stalls** Low

Form RPR

3 **1** **Funday**[18] 2640 3-8-10 0.. FergusSweeney 1 80+
(G L Moore) *trckd ldng pair: rdn to chse ldr 3f out: led 2f out: rdn clr over 1f out: in command fnl f: comf* **14/1**

2 *2 ½* **Doggerbank (IRE)** 3-8-10 0.. JimmyQuinn 4 75+
(H R A Cecil) *dwlt: hld up in last pair: rn green and dropped to last on downhill run 4f out: hdwy over 2f out: swtchd rt over 1f out: kpt on to go 2nd wl ins fnl f: no ch w wnr* **8/1**

33 **3** *nk* **Maria Nunziata**[21] 2551 3-8-10 0...................................... EddieAhern 3 74
(J Noseda) *led: rdn and pressed 3f out: hdd 2f out: btn 1f out: lost 2nd wl ins fnl f* **4/6**[1]

-043 **4** *1* **My Chestnut Girl (USA)**[14] 2763 3-8-10 **70**...................... TPQueally 6 72
(H R A Cecil) *chsd ldr tl 3f out: rdn over 2f out: uanble to qckn and one pce fnl 2f* **11/2**[3]

46 **5** *2 ¾* **Sana Abel (IRE)**[38] 2042 3-8-10 0..................................... TPO'Shea 2 67
(M A Jarvis) *hld up in last pair: rdn and effrt 3f out: no hdwy and wl hld fnl 2f* **5/1**[2]

/ **6** *28* **Action Girl**[115] 4-9-8 0.. PatCosgrave 5 11
(R M H Cowell) *awkward leaving stalls and slowly away: rcvrd to chse ldrs over 8f out: rdn and wknd 3f out: t.o fnl f* **66/1**

2m 9.89s (-0.61) **Going Correction** -0.125s/f (Firm)
WFA 3 from 4yo 12lb **6** Ran SP% **111.3**
Speed ratings (Par 100): **97,95,94,93,91 69**
toteswingers: 1&2 £5.70, 1&3 £2.30, 2&3 £2.50 CSF £110.25 TOTE £10.30: £3.10, £3.00; EX 77.90.
Owner Sir Eric Parker **Bred** Sir Eric Parker **Trained** Lower Beeding, W Sussex

FOCUS
Just a fair fillies' maiden run at a modest early pace. The form makes sense.

3215 BAYER H'CAP 1m 1f
4:45 (4:45) (Class 6) (0-55,53) 3-Y-O+ **£2,388** (£705; £352) **Stalls** Low

Form RPR

0002 **1** **Love In The Park**[9] 2921 4-9-4 **52**................................ JackMitchell(3) 10 65
(R Brotherton) *stdd and dropped in bhd after s: hld up wl in rr: stl plenty to do and swtchd rt 3f out: str run to ld over 1f out: clr ins fnl f: r.o strly* **3/1**[1]

5460 **2** *2 ¾* **Iguacu**[10] 2879 5-8-12 **48**... MatthewDavies(5) 6 55
(George Baker) *stdd s: hld up towards rr: hdwy on outer over 3f out: rdn 3f out: pressed ldrs over 1f out: outpcd by wnr fnl f but kpt on for 2nd* **14/1**

20-4 **3** *1* **Daring Racer (GER)**[31] 2221 6-9-8 **53**................................(p) PaulDoe 3 58
(Mrs L J Mongan) *chsd ldrs: wnt 2nd over 3f out: rdn to ld 2f out: hdd over 1f out: outpcd by wnr fnl f: kpt on same pce* **9/2**[2]

000 **4** *3* **Casablanca Minx (IRE)**[18] 2634 6-9-4 **49**..........(v) StephenDonohoe 12 47
(Miss Gay Kelleway) *stdd after s: hld up in rr: hdwy on inner wl over 2f out: drvn over 1f out: plugged on to go 4th towards fin: nvr nr ldrs* **12/1**

-600 **5** *nk* **Marie Tempest**[31] 2221 4-9-1 **46**..........................(v[1]) RichardKingscote 2 44
(M R Bosley) *led: rdn 3f out: hdd 2f out: wknd u.p over 1f out* **8/1**

6260 **6** *3 ¾* **Ma Ridge**[4] 3074 5-8-10 **46**.. AmyBaker(5) 9 35
(T D McCarthy) *chsd ldrs: wnt 3rd over 3f out: rdn 3f out: wknd qckly over 1f out* **12/1**

4646 **7** *1* **Ruwain**[9] 2924 5-8-11 **49**... AshleyMorgan(7) 1 36
(P J McBride) *rrd s and slowly away: hdwy into midfield 7f out: drvn and effrt over 2f out: no prog and wl btn over 1f out* **10/1**

00-0 **8** *10* **Ledgerwood**[15] 2745 4-9-1 **46**.......................................(p) JamesDoyle 8 11
(A J Chamberlain) *stdd s: plld hrd early: hld up towards rr: rdn and no rspnse over 3f out: wl bhd fnl 2f* **40/1**

0-00 **9** ½ **Royal Bloom (IRE)**[11] 2857 4-9-3 **48**................................... AdamKirby 7 12
(J R Fanshawe) *t.k.h: hld up towards rr: rdn and edgde lft 3f out: sn wl btn* **7/1**[3]

-000 **10** *6* **Jasper Cliff**[28] 2318 3-8-5 **47**...(b) NeilChalmers 11 —
(Mark Gillard) *chsd ldr tl over 3f out: wknd qckly: wl bhd fnl 2f* **50/1**

0050 **11** *1 ¼* **Red Dagger (IRE)**[18] 2635 3-8-4 **46**.................................. TPO'Shea 14 —
(T D McCarthy) *t.k.h: hld up in tch in midfield: rn wd bnd over 7f out: rdn 3f out: sn btn and wl bhd* **14/1**

050- **12** *1 ¼* **Echo Forest**[250] 6737 3-8-5 **47**.. AdrianMcCarthy 5 —
(J R Best) *plld hrd: hld up in midfield: rdn and wknd qckly 3f out: sn wl bhd: t.o* **12/1**

6000 **13** *28* **Maison D'Or**[61] 1461 3-8-5 **47**.. JimmyQuinn 4 —
(R Ingram) *s.i.s: sn bustled up into midfield: rdn 5f out: drvn 3f out: sn btn and eased: t.o* **25/1**

1m 54.1s (-2.50) **Going Correction** -0.125s/f (Firm)
WFA 3 from 4yo+ 11lb **13** Ran SP% **120.5**
Speed ratings (Par 101): **106,103,102,100,99 96,95,86,86,80 79,78,53**
toteswingers: 1&2 £12.40, 1&3 £3.80, 2&3 £16.90 CSF £47.42 CT £198.44 TOTE £4.00: £1.50, £4.90, £2.20; EX 59.80 Trifecta £148.70 Pool: £200.97 - 0.10 winning units..
Owner Arthur Clayton **Bred** New England Stud And Partners **Trained** Elmley Castle, Worcs

FOCUS
A moderate handicap run at a good pace which suited the closers. Sound form.
Ruwain Official explanation: jockey said gelding missed the break
Red Dagger(IRE) Official explanation: jockey said gelding lost its action

Maison D'Or Official explanation: jockey said gelding lost its action

3216 ALL ABOUT HEALTH H'CAP 1m 6f

5:15 (5:15) (Class 5) (0-70,65) 4-Y-0+ **£3,238** (£963; £481; £240) **Stalls** High

Form				RPR
4301	1		**Yonder**13 2798 5-9-7 **65** SteveDrowne 3 (H Morrison) *led to s: mde all: shkn up bnd 11f out: jnd over 3f out: rdn over 2f out: styd on gamely u.p fnl f* **10/11**1	72
0-14	2	*hd*	**Where's Susie**22 2517 4-9-3 **61** GeorgeBaker 2 (M Madgwick) *trckd wnr over 10f out: jnd wnr over 3f out: drvn over 2f out: ev ch after tl no ex and hld towards fin* **11/4**2	68
0503	3	*2 1/4*	**Kiho**22 2519 4-8-10 **54** (b) StephenCarson 4 (Eve Johnson Houghton) *dropped in bhd after s: hld up in last pl: rdn and effrt over 2f out: no imp u.p ins fnl f* **9/2**3	58
00-0	4	*1/2*	**Looks The Business (IRE)**18 2634 8-8-6 **50** FergusSweeney 1 (A B Haynes) *trckd ldr tl over 10f out: rdn and effrt over 2f out: edgd lft and no ex fnl f* **8/1**	53

3m 6.86s (-3.14) **Going Correction** -0.125s/f (Firm) 4 Ran SP% **108.3**
Speed ratings (Par 103): **103,102,101,101**
CSF £3.65 TOTE £1.70; EX 3.40 Place 6: £108.43 Place 5: £79.17.
Owner Mrs M D W Morrison **Bred** Peter Storey **Trained** East Ilsley, Berks
■ Stewards' Enquiry : Steve Drowne three-day ban: used whip with excessive frequency (Jul 6,7,9)

FOCUS
A weak handicap. The winner produced a small personal best.
T/Plt: £88.90 to a £1 stake. Pool: £64,452.23. 528.76 winning tickets. T/Qpdt: £36.40 to a £1 stake. Pool: £3,546.36. 71.90 winning tickets. SP

2977 WINDSOR (R-H)

Monday, June 22

OFFICIAL GOING: Good to firm (8.4)

Top bend dolled out 8yards from innermost line adding 32yards to advertised distances of races of a mile plus.

Wind: Almost nil Weather: Overcast, humid

3217 STARLIGHT CHILDREN'S FOUNDATION FILLIES' H'CAP 1m 2f 7y

6:40 (6:41) (Class 5) (0-70,70) 3-Y-0+ **£2,729** (£806; £403) **Stalls** Centre

Form				RPR
65-0	1		**Kashmina**47 1786 4-9-10 **61** JamesDoyle 10 (Miss Sheena West) *settled in abt 7th: prog 3f out to chal 2f out: drvn to ld over 1f out and edgd rt: hrd pressed fnl f: styd on wl* **6/1**3	70
6103	2	*nk*	**Lunar River (FR)**9 2923 6-9-8 **59** (t) FergusSweeney 4 (David Pinder) *stdd s: hld up wl in rr: smooth prog on outer fr over 2f out: rdn to chal fnl f: nt qckn nr fin* **6/1**3	67
00-0	3	*4*	**April's Daughter**31 2246 4-9-1 **55** JamesMillman(3) 9 (B R Millman) *settled in abt 8th: drvn 3f out: chsd ldrs 2f out: plugged on to snatch 3rd nr fin* **33/1**	55
30-0	4	*1/2*	**Phoenix Enforcer**32 2192 3-9-2 **70** (p) MatthewDavies(5) 5 (George Baker) *led: u.p 3f out: wandering and hdd over 1f out: fdd ins fnl f* **33/1**	69
0023	5	*nk*	**Carmela Maria**7 2975 4-9-10 **61** RichardHughes 8 (S C Williams) *trckd ldng pair: styd against nr side rail in st: upsides over 2f out: nt qckn wl over 1f out: fdd* **10/3**1	59
063-	6	*1/2*	**Yvonne Evelyn (USA)**194 7620 4-9-12 **63** SteveDrowne 2 (J R Gask) *mostly pressed ldr: drvn 3f out: nt qckn 2f out: wknd over 1f out* **9/1**	60
-065	7	*3/4*	**Dancing Storm**27 2352 6-9-6 **57** AdamKirby 11 (W S Kittow) *hld up in last pair: stdy prog 3f out: in tch whn nt clr run 2f out: shuffled along and no hdwy after* **5/1**2	56+
55-0	8	*1 1/2*	**Cobos**37 2091 3-8-11 **60** TonyCulhane 1 (Ms E L McWilliam) *wl in tch in abt 5th: drvn 3f out: stl cl enough 2f out: wknd* **66/1**	53
-034	9	*11*	**Arlene Phillips**26 2380 3-7-9 **51** CharlesEddery(7) 3 (R Hannon) *awkward s: chsd ldng trio: rdn over 3f out: wknd over 2f out* **8/1**	22
0-40	10	*2 1/4*	**Lush (IRE)**17 2675 4-9-10 **64** PatrickHills(3) 12 (R Hannon) *wl in rr: rdn and hung lft over 3f out: no prog and btn after* **8/1**	30
00-5	11	*7*	**Shesha Bear**14 2764 4-10-0 **65** WilliamBuick 7 (W R Muir) *trckd ldrs in abt 6th: rdn over 3f out: no prog and btn over 2f out: wknd* **12/1**	17
0-00	12	*1 1/4*	**Hold Fire**11 2851 5-8-5 **47** oh2 (b1) MCGeran(5) 6 (A W Carroll) *rousted along early: a in rr: struggling over 3f out: sn btn* **66/1**	—

2m 9.59s (0.89) **Going Correction** +0.025s/f (Good)
WFA 3 from 4yo+ 12lb 12 Ran SP% **117.1**
Speed ratings (Par 100): **97,96,93,93,92 92,91,90,81,80 74,73**
toteswinger: 1&2 £32.30, 1&3 £56.90, 2&3 £56.90 CSF £40.53 CT £1094.20 TOTE £6.60: £2.00, £2.40, £5.60; EX 49.90.
Owner Heart Of The South Racing **Bred** B Burrough **Trained** Falmer, E Sussex

FOCUS
The bend was dolled eight yards from the innermost line adding 32 yards to the races at 1m+. The ground was drying out after 24mm of watering last week, and was officially described as good to firm. They went a modest pace for this fillies' handicap. The first two came from some way back and pulled clear of the rest. The winner is rated up 3lb and the form could work out.
Dancing Storm Official explanation: jockey said mare was denied a clear run

3218 DYLAN THOMAS MAIDEN AUCTION STKS 6f

7:10 (7:12) (Class 5) 2-Y-0 **£2,729** (£806; £403) **Stalls** High

Form				RPR
62	1		**Palisades Park**18 2636 2-8-13 0 RichardHughes 1 (R Hannon) *fast away: led and sn crossed to nr side fr wdst draw: in command over 1f out: nvr asked serious question* **4/5**1	76+
0	2	*1 1/2*	**Many A Slip**13 2792 2-8-9 0 RichardMullen 9 (J L Dunlop) *dwlt: settled in rr: pushed along 2f out: prog jst over 1f out: r.o to take 2nd nr fin* **28/1**	64+
0	3	*1/2*	**Fire And Stone (IRE)**28 2328 2-8-13 0 RichardKingscote 4 (Tom Dascombe) *sn rousted along in abt 7th: rdn over 2f out: prog over 1f out: chsd wnr ins fnl f but no ch: lost 2nd nr fin* **9/1**3	65
	4	*1/2*	**Dubai Set** 2-8-9 0 EddieAhern 13 (R Hannon) *hld up in last pair of main gp: swtchd to outer by 1/2-way: sme prog and reminder 1f out: styd on wl* **12/1**	60
	5	*1 1/2*	**Dungannon** 2-8-11 0 WilliamBuick 10 (A M Balding) *s.s: v green and sn t.o: latched on to bk of gp over 1f out: r.o wl fnl 150yds: nrst fin* **16/1**	60+
0	6	*1/2*	**Thaliwarru**7 2979 2-9-2 0 TonyCulhane 14 (G G Margarson) *wl plcd on rail bhd ldrs: hanging lft fr 2f out: outpcd fnl f* **25/1**	61
0	7	*1*	**Gooseberry Bush**32 2207 2-8-4 0 FrankieMcDonald 2 (P J Makin) *t.k.h: w wnr to 2f out: stl 2nd ent fnl f: sn wknd* **16/1**	46
4	8	*1/2*	**Evergreen Dancer (IRE)**26 2376 2-9-2 0 SteveDrowne 8 (J R Best) *towards rr on inner: pushed along firmly over 2f out: eased off rail over 1f out: one pce and no imp* **33/1**	56
	9	*2*	**Rockabilly Rebel** 2-9-2 0 PhilipRobinson 6 (B W Hills) *s.s: gd spd and sn chsd ldng trio: swtchd to rail over 2f out: wknd over 1f out* **15/2**2	50
0	10	*1/2*	**Dudley**13 2793 2-8-9 0 TolleyDean 7 (J G Portman) *a in rr and pushed along bef 1/2-way: nvr a factor* **80/1**	42
00	11	*1*	**Welsh Legacy (IRE)**32 2187 2-8-6 0 ow2 GabrielHannon(5) 3 (B W Duke) *a wl in rr: no prog u.p wl over 1f out* **100/1**	41
	12	*1 1/4*	**Morgans Choice** 2-8-10 0 ow1 StephenDonohoe 5 (J L Spearing) *w ldng pair to over 2f out: wknd over 1f out* **40/1**	36
0	13	*1 1/4*	**Winston's Lad**11 2860 2-8-9 0 JimmyQuinn 12 (P Howling) *chsd ldrs tl wknd 2f out* **66/1**	31
6	14	*1 1/4*	**Motty's Gift**27 2358 2-8-13 0 AdamKirby 11 (W R Swinburn) *a wl in rr: rdn and struggling over 2f out* **14/1**	31

1m 14.35s (1.35) **Going Correction** +0.025s/f (Good) 14 Ran SP% **119.8**
Speed ratings (Par 93): **92,90,89,88,86 86,84,84,81,80 79,77,76,74**
toteswinger: 1&2 £54.90, 1&3 £2.40, 2&3 not won CSF £36.62 TOTE £1.90: £1.30, £8.20, £2.70; EX 48.80.
Owner David F Powell **Bred** Dunchurch Lodge Stud Co **Trained** East Everleigh, Wilts

FOCUS
Just a fair maiden and weak in terms of depth for the track, but the winner did it well.

NOTEBOOK
Palisades Park found only the subsequent Coventry Stakes fifth Treadwell too good in a 5f Sandown maiden auction 18 days ago on his second outing. He set a clear target for the others to aim at, shrugged off the potential perils of stall one by making an early move to the stands' rail and coasted to victory under a positive ride. It is hard to know what the form amounts to, but he was value for much more than the winning margin suggests, seemed to appreciated the step up to 6f and looks a nice prospect. His next target could be the Super Sprint at Newbury next month. (op 5-6 tchd 8-11 after 11-10 in a place and evens in places)
Many A Slip ◆ was picked up for just 2,500gns as a yearling, despite being from a very good family. He was always outpaced when last in a 6f Salisbury maiden on debut but showed plenty of promise here, staying on strongly after finding some trouble in running. (op 33-1 tchd 50-1)
Fire And Stone(IRE) also found a decent finishing effort and improved on his debut effort at Goodwood, where he was sent off as second favourite. (op 8-1 tchd 10-1)
Dubai Set never really got into it but stayed on steadily from an unpromising position and ran an eyecatching race on debut. He is a brother to last year's useful two-year-old sprinter Saxford, and could improve significantly for this first run. (op 17-2)
Dungannon ◆ put up a very promising performance on this debut. He started slowly and was detached at an early stage but flew home under an educational ride. He is a half-brother to three winners, notably Bygone Days, a very smart 6f winner at three-five. (op 12-1 tchd 11-1)

3219 SUNLEY H'CAP 6f

7:40 (7:42) (Class 4) (0-85,85) 3-Y-0 **£5,180** (£1,541; £770; £384) **Stalls** High

Form				RPR
-300	1		**Miss Chamanda (IRE)**44 1870 3-8-11 **75** StephenDonohoe 8 (P D Evans) *chsd ldrs: got through against rail wl over 1f out: drvn to dispute ld ins fnl f: forged ahd nr fin* **33/1**	83
4141	2	*1*	**Devil You Know (IRE)**12 2826 3-9-3 **81** JimmyFortune 4 (D R C Elsworth) *t.k.h: hld up in last: prog and hanging fr 2f out: drvn to chal and upsides ins fnl f: outpcd nr fin* **5/2**2	86
40-0	3	*1*	**Klynch**5 3028 3-8-11 **80** (b) GabrielHannon(5) 5 (B J Meehan) *hld up in rr but in tch: effrt whn hmpd on inner jst over 2f out: swtchd to outer over 1f out: hung lft but styd on u.p* **25/1**	82
-401	4	*nk*	**Francis Walsingham (IRE)**20 2574 3-8-11 **75** SteveDrowne 2 (H Morrison) *trckd ldrs: prog 2f out: rdn to ld over 1f out: hdd and one pce ins fnl f* **7/1**	76
0-15	5	*1/2*	**Rapid Water**34 2148 3-8-9 **73** WilliamBuick 7 (A M Balding) *trckd ldrs: nt clr run over 2f out to over 1f out: rdn and one pce whn in the clr after* **2/1**1	72+
1P-0	6	*1*	**Desert Icon (IRE)**12 2826 3-8-13 **77** ShaneKelly 6 (W J Knight) *mde most to over 1f out: fdd* **17/2**	73
0200	7	*3 1/2*	**Timeteam (IRE)**17 2674 3-9-7 **85** EddieAhern 3 (S Kirk) *hld up in rr but wl in tch: effrt on wd outside over 2f out: rdn and wknd over 1f out* **5/1**3	70
14-4	8	*12*	**Mamlakati (IRE)**21 2536 3-9-4 **82** RichardHughes 1 (R Hannon) *sn w ldr: sing to lose pl but nt u.p whn sltly hmpd over 1f out: eased* **8/1**	28

1m 12.76s (-0.24) **Going Correction** +0.025s/f (Good) 8 Ran SP% **119.5**
Speed ratings (Par 101): **102,100,99,98,98 96,92,76**
toteswinger: 1&2 not won, 1&3 £65.10, 2&3 £5.20 CSF £119.94 CT £2217.01 TOTE £33.00: £4.10, £1.30, £6.30; EX 114.60.
Owner E A R Morgans **Bred** T Molan **Trained** Pandy, Monmouths
■ Stewards' Enquiry : William Buick three-day ban: careless riding (Jul 6,7,9)

FOCUS
A decent sprint handicap, but it was a bit of a messy race. The winner is rated up 5lb with the third the best guide to the form.
Miss Chamanda(IRE) Official explanation: trainer said, regarding apparent improvement in form, that the filly benefited from a break since its last run and appeared to be suited by the track.
Desert Icon(IRE) Official explanation: jockey said gelding hung left

3220 LADBROKES.COM H'CAP 1m 67y

8:10 (8:10) (Class 4) (0-85,84) 3-Y-0 **£5,180** (£1,541; £770; £384) **Stalls** High

Form				RPR
5-32	1		**Sparkling Crystal (IRE)**17 2662 3-8-8 **71** WilliamBuick 2 (B W Hills) *pressed ldr: wl plcd whn pce lifted over 2f out: drvn ahd over 1f out: in command fnl f* **15/2**	78
-221	2	*1*	**Cumana Bay**23 2498 3-9-4 **81** RichardHughes 8 (R Hannon) *led at stdy pce: qcknd over 2f out: hdd over 1f out: kpt on same pce* **15/8**1	85
1-35	3	*1/2*	**December Draw (IRE)**33 2174 3-9-5 **82** ShaneKelly 3 (W J Knight) *hld up in 4th: effrt over 2f out: cl enough whn rdn and hung lft over 1f out: kpt on ins fnl f* **9/4**2	85
0-16	4	*1 1/4*	**Smart Endeavour (USA)**23 2504 3-9-6 **83** AdamKirby 7 (W R Swinburn) *trckd ldng pair: pushed along whn pce qcknd over 2f out: rdn and one pce fr over 1f out* **9/2**3	83

-501 **5** *6* **Silent Hero**[20] 2578 3-9-5 **82**.. PhilipRobinson 6 68
(M A Jarvis) *t.k.h: hld up in 5th: no imp 2f out after pce lifted: crossed by rival sn after: hanging and wknd fnl f* **15/2**

6305 **6** *4* **Doncosaque (IRE)**[21] 2535 3-9-2 **79**.. JimmyQuinn 4 55
(P Howling) *t.k.h: hld up in last: outpcd fr over 2f out: wknd over 1f out* **20/1**

1m 47.47s (2.77) **Going Correction** +0.025s/f (Good) **6** Ran SP% **112.0**
Speed ratings (Par 101): **87,86,85,84,78 74**
toteswinger: 1&2 £2.30, 1&3 £2.90, 2&3 £2.20 CSF £21.97 CT £41.54 TOTE £5.10: £2.10, £1.60; EX 13.30.

Owner Triermore Stud **Bred** Urs Schwarzenbach **Trained** Lambourn, Berks

FOCUS
A decent handicap. It was run at a sedate pace, and those who were held up found it tough to get involved, with the first pair always 1-2. The form is rated through the second and third.

3221 PERTEMPS NETWORK MAIDEN STKS — 1m 67y
8:40 (8:40) (Class 5) 3-Y-O **£2,729** (£806; £403) **Stalls** High

Form RPR

4 **1** **Saturn Girl (IRE)**[63] 1406 3-8-12 0.............................. RichardHughes 3 71+
(S A Callaghan) *mde virtually all: pushed along and looked in command over 1f out: hung lft across crse fnl f: kpt on* **13/8**[1]

2 **2** *¾* **Rocky's Pride (IRE)**[10] 2885 3-9-3 0.............................. ShaneKelly 1 74+
(J Noseda) *trckd wnr after 1f: hrd rdn 2f out: looked hld whn carried across crse fnl f: kpt on* **13/8**[1]

4 **3** *1* **Truly Asia (IRE)**[37] 2081 3-9-3 0.............................. SteveDrowne 6 72
(R Charlton) *t.k.h early: hld up in 5th: pushed along to go 3rd over 1f out: reminder sn after: hmpd ins fnl f: shuffled along and kpt on: eased last strides* **9/2**[2]

60 **4** *3 ½* **Rockabout (IRE)**[24] 2433 3-8-12 0.............................. EddieAhern 7 59
(B J Meehan) *t.k.h early: chsd wnr 1f: cl up after: rdn and nt qckn 2f out: btn whn hung lft fnl f* **14/1**[3]

0- **5** *4 ½* **Major Value**[187] 7699 3-9-3 0.............................. AdamKirby 4 54
(C G Cox) *t.k.h: hld up in 4th: pushed along over 3f out: wknd rapidly over 1f out* **16/1**

00-0 **6** *4 ½* **Davana**[45] 1840 3-8-9 40.............................. KellyHarrison(3) 2 38
(W J H Ratcliffe) *hld up in last: pushed along over 3f out: wknd 2f out* **66/1**

1m 46.44s (1.74) **Going Correction** +0.025s/f (Good) **6** Ran SP% **108.4**
Speed ratings (Par 99): **92,91,90,86,82 77**
toteswinger: 1&2 £1.10, 1&3 £2.20, 2&3 £1.50 CSF £3.96 TOTE £2.60: £1.60, £1.50; EX 5.10.

Owner Michael Tabor **Bred** Lynch Bages Ltd & Samac Ltd **Trained** Newmarket, Suffolk

■ Stewards' Enquiry : Richard Hughes five-day ban (reduced from six days on appeal): careless riding (Jul 6-10)

FOCUS
A few potentially decent types lined up for this maiden, which was steadily run. The three market leaders finished clear of the rest and the form looks fairly solid. The winner had to survive a long stewards' inquiry.

3222 ST JOHN AMBULANCE H'CAP — 1m 3f 135y
9:10 (9:11) (Class 5) (0-75,75) 3-Y-O **£3,070** (£906; £453) **Stalls** Centre

Form RPR

3502 **1** **Urban Space**[14] 2772 3-8-9 **63**.............................. StephenDonohoe 10 71
(B G Powell) *hld up in abt 8th: prog fr 3f out on outer: drvn to ld over 1f out: in command and pushed out last 100yds* **20/1**

-231 **2** *1* **Sherman McCoy**[23] 2479 3-9-3 **74**.............................. JamesMillman(3) 6 80
(B R Millman) *hld up in abt 6th: plld out and prog over 2f out: drvn to chal over 1f out: edgd lft and chsd wnr after: readily hld* **4/1**[1]

-504 **3** *½* **Parc Des Princes (USA)**[27] 2357 3-8-4 **58**.............................. WilliamBuick 7 63+
(A M Balding) *hld up in last: prog fr 3f out: cajoled along over 2f out: drvn and styd on to take 3rd fnl f: nvr able to chal* **11/1**

0-30 **4** *2 ¾* **Ja One (IRE)**[20] 2567 3-8-11 **65**.............................. SteveDrowne 9 66
(B W Hills) *trckd ldng pair to over 2f out: nt qckn against rail after: one pce over 1f out* **16/1**

2021 **5** *3 ½* **Morning Sir Alan**[14] 2763 3-9-7 **75**.............................. JerryO'Dwyer 2 70
(S A Callaghan) *mde most to 5f out: chsd ldr to over 2f out: hrd rdn and grad wknd* **13/2**[2]

0-40 **6** *2* **Highland Storm**[11] 2850 3-8-11 **70**.............................. MatthewDavies(5) 11 61
(George Baker) *s.s: hld up in last trio: rdn on wd outside over 3f out: plugged on but n.d* **7/1**[3]

4-50 **7** *nse* **Luthien (IRE)**[39] 2006 3-8-11 **65**.............................. AdamKirby 1 56
(W R Swinburn) *a abt same pl: rdn and no imp on ldrs over 2f out: grad outpcd* **12/1**

2223 **8** *½* **Salybia Bay**[11] 2850 3-8-11 **65**.............................. RichardHughes 4 55
(R Hannon) *hld up in rr: tried to make prog fr over 3f out: rdn and no imp over 2f out: fdd* **4/1**[1]

3642 **9** *1 ¼* **Cayman Sky**[10] 2881 3-8-8 **65**..............................(b) PatrickHills(3) 12 53
(R Hannon) *pressed ldr: led 5f out to over 1f out: wknd rapidly* **7/1**[3]

0-54 **10** *1 ¾* **Googoobarabajagal (IRE)**[27] 2350 3-8-2 **56** oh4. FrankieMcDonald 13 41
(W S Kittow) *trckd ldng quartet: rdn wl over 2f out: sn lost pl and btn* **16/1**

4404 **11** *¾* **Millway Beach (IRE)**[20] 2567 3-8-11 **65**.............................. PaulEddery 3 49
(Pat Eddery) *towards rr: rdn and struggling over 3f out: sn n.d* **14/1**

000- **12** *43* **Strongarm**[257] 6580 3-8-5 **59**.............................. NeilChalmers 5 —
(A Bailey) *trckd ldrs tl wknd rapidly 3f out: t.o* **50/1**

0640 **13** *21* **Langford Decoit (IRE)**[11] 2865 3-8-7 **61**.............................. TonyCulhane 8 —
(M R Channon) *nvr gng wl: a in last trio: wknd over 3f out: t.o and virtually p.u fnl f* **40/1**

2m 30.02s (0.52) **Going Correction** +0.025s/f (Good) **13** Ran SP% **122.0**
Speed ratings (Par 99): **99,98,98,96,93 92,92,92,91,90 89,60,46**
toteswinger: 1&2 £35.20, 1&3 £54.70, 2&3 £22.60 CSF £99.18 CT £960.83 TOTE £20.70: £4.00, £1.80, £3.60; EX 114.20 Place 6: £90.27, Place 5: £21.13.

Owner Holistic Racing Ltd **Bred** Winterbeck Manor Stud **Trained** Upper Lambourn, Berks

FOCUS
A fair handicap, involving some improvers and several consistent types. The pace was only moderate. The winner is rated back to his early handicap form.

T/Plt: £67.40 to a £1 stake. Pool: £79,989.49. 865.74 winning tickets. T/Qpdt: £11.10 to a £1 stake. Pool: £5,829.34. 387.90 winning tickets. JN

2681 WOLVERHAMPTON (A.W) (L-H)
Monday, June 22

OFFICIAL GOING: Standard
Wind: Light across Weather: Overcast

3223 TETLEY BITTER AMATEUR RIDERS' (S) STKS — 1m 4f 50y(P)
2:30 (2:32) (Class 6) 4-Y-O+ **£1,977** (£608; £304) **Stalls** Low

Form RPR

0612 **1** **Aureate**[15] 2743 5-11-5 82.............................. MissLEllison 1 72
(B Ellison) *led: hdd over 10f out: chsd ldrs: led over 5f out: clr over 2f out: rdn and edgd rt over 1f out: hung lft wl ins fnl f: jst hld on* **8/13**[1]

006- **2** *½* **Gremlin**[76] 6346 5-10-7 70.............................. MissHBethell(7) 12 66
(I W McInnes) *hld up: hdwy over 5f out: chsd wnr over 1f out: r.o: jst failed* **14/1**

2045 **3** *5* **Pertemps Power**[7] 2971 5-10-9 52.............................. MrJeremiahMcGrath(5) 6 58
(B G Powell) *prom: outpcd 4f out: rallied over 1f out: styd on* **10/1**[3]

6500 **4** *4 ½* **High Profit (IRE)**[25] 2390 5-10-7 53.............................. MissRebeccaSparkes(7) 4 51
(James Moffatt) *hld up: styd on ins fnl f: nvr nrr* **33/1**

1050 **5** *5* **Waterside (IRE)**[23] 2493 10-11-5 64..............................(t) MissFayeBramley 11 48
(S Curran) *chsd ldr 10f out: led over 7f out: hdd over 5f out: wknd over 1f out* **25/1**

4200 **6** *2* **Turner's Touch**[16] 2708 7-10-9 52..............................(b) JosephAkehurst(5) 2 40
(G L Moore) *dwlt: sn prom: lost pl 4f out: n.d after* **25/1**

3/1- **7** *7* **Saameq (IRE)**[315] 4932 8-11-0 60.............................. MrSWalker 7 28
(D W Thompson) *hld up: hdwy over 4f out: sn rdn: wknd wl over 1f out* **11/2**[2]

6264 **8** *1 ¼* **Wizard Looking**[31] 2233 8-10-9 51..............................(p) MissWGibson(5) 9 26
(P T Midgley) *plld hrd and prom: wknd over 2f out* **12/1**

320- **9** *14* **Street Crime**[264] 6400 4-11-0 65.............................. WilliamBiddick 10 4
(R Lee) *s.i.s: hld up: sme hdwy 4f out: sn rdn and wknd* **16/1**

300/ **10** *1* **Beauchamp Unique**[1010] 5365 6-10-4 50.............................. MrPJTolman(5) 8 —
(E J Cooper) *hld up: hdwy over 5f out: rdn and wknd over 2f out* **100/1**

0 **11** *21* **Panceltica**[35] 2142 4-10-9 0.............................. MrTRDavid(5) 5 —
(Karen George) *chsd ldrs tl wknd over 4f out* **200/1**

221/ **12** *31* **Masafi (IRE)**[10] 4968 8-10-7 85..............................(t) MrTGarner(7) 3 —
(E J Cooper) *led over 10f out: hdd over 7f out: wknd over 5f out* **16/1**

2m 45.1s (4.00) **Going Correction** +0.05s/f (Slow) **12** Ran SP% **124.6**
Speed ratings (Par 101): **88,87,84,81,78 76,72,71,61,61 47,26**
toteswinger: 1&2 £5.10, 1&3 £4.40, 2&3 £13.00 CSF £11.95 TOTE £1.60: £1.10, £3.20, £2.60; EX 16.90.There was no bid for the winner. Gremlin was claimed by D Burchell for £6000.

Owner The Seasiders Again **Bred** Darley **Trained** Norton, N Yorks

FOCUS
A modest seller, rated through the third. The winner did not need to be at his best.

3224 BETDAQ POKER H'CAP — 7f 32y(P)
3:00 (3:00) (Class 6) (0-60,60) 3-Y-O+ **£2,388** (£705; £352) **Stalls** High

Form RPR

3035 **1** **Ninth House (USA)**[3] 3110 7-9-5 **60**..............................(t) SilvestreDeSousa 7 72
(Mrs R A Carr) *hld up: hdwy over 1f out: sn rdn to chse ldr: r.o u.p to ld wl ins fnl f* **9/2**[1]

-000 **2** *2 ½* **Poppy's Rose**[14] 2769 5-9-1 **59**.............................. FrederikTylicki(3) 4 64
(I W McInnes) *led early: chsd ldrs: led over 2f out: rdn clr over 1f out: hdd wl ins fnl f* **7/1**

0504 **3** *2* **Bertie Vista**[27] 2361 4-9-3 **58**..............................(b) DavidAllan 8 58
(T D Easterby) *a.p: rdn to chse ldr over 2f out tl hung lft over 1f out: styd on* **14/1**

0031 **4** *¾* **Avoca Dancer (IRE)**[9] 2921 6-9-2 **57**..............................(v) JerryO'Dwyer 5 55
(Karen George) *hld up: hdwy u.p over 2f out: styd on* **10/1**

4354 **5** *2 ¼* **Dickie Le Davoir**[4] 3057 5-8-11 **57**..............................(p) MarkCoumbe(5) 9 49
(John A Harris) *s.i.s: outpcd: hdwy on outer over 1f out: sn rdn: no imp fnl f* **13/2**[3]

6000 **6** *¾* **Loyal Royal (IRE)**[4] 3075 6-9-2 **57**..............................(b) LPKeniry 3 47
(J M Bradley) *trckd ldrs: plld hrd: rdn and hung lft over 1f out: sn wknd* **16/1**

0-01 **7** *1* **Young Gladiator (IRE)**[16] 2722 4-9-2 **57**..............................(b) TomEaves 1 44
(Miss J A Camacho) *sn pushed along to ld: rdn and hdd over 2f out: wknd fnl f* **5/1**[2]

4005 **8** *1 ¾* **Prince Golan (IRE)**[24] 2442 5-8-12 **60**..............................(p) AlexEdwards(7) 12 42
(J W Unett) *s.i.s: outpcd: nvr nrr* **33/1**

045 **9** *6* **Convallaria (FR)**[19] 2598 6-9-5 **60**.............................. TedDurcan 6 26
(C F Wall) *sn pushed along in mid-div: rdn 1/2-way: wknd over 2f out* **7/1**

2005 **10** *1 ¾* **Waldorf (IRE)**[4] 3077 4-9-3 **58**.............................. DO'Donohoe 2 19
(W R Muir) *sn pushed along in mid-div: rdn 1/2-way: wknd over 2f out* **7/1**

6010 **11** *6* **The London Gang**[84] 1037 6-8-11 **57**..............................(b) DeanHeslop(5) 11 —
(S Wynne) *sn pushed along in rr: wknd 1/2-way* **66/1**

5-60 **12** *1 ¾* **Gold Again (USA)**[19] 2598 4-9-4 **59**..............................(v[1]) DarryllHolland 10 —
(W R Swinburn) *chsd ldr 6f out to 4f out: sn rdn: wknd over 2f out* **11/1**

1m 28.93s (-0.67) **Going Correction** +0.05s/f (Slow) **12** Ran SP% **120.1**
Speed ratings (Par 101): **105,102,99,99,96 95,94,92,85,83 76,74**
toteswingers: 1&2 £6.00, 1&3 £12.50, 2&3 £25.80 CSF £36.31 CT £416.26 TOTE £4.60: £1.50, £3.60, £5.40; EX 41.50.

Owner David W Chapman **Bred** Juddmonte Farms Inc **Trained** Huby, N Yorks

FOCUS
Modest handicap form, rated around the winner.

Gold Again(USA) Official explanation: jockey said filly was mulish in running

3225 TRY BETDAQ FOR AN EXCHANGE CLAIMING STKS — 5f 216y(P)
3:30 (3:31) (Class 5) 3-Y-O **£2,914** (£867; £433; £216) **Stalls** Low

Form RPR

4436 **1** **Belated Silver (IRE)**[32] 2198 3-9-0 71.............................. RossAtkinson(5) 6 74
(Tom Dascombe) *hld up: hdwy over 1f out: hung lft and r.o to ld wl ins fnl f* **7/2**[2]

0460 **2** *1 ¾* **Dancing Welcome**[40] 1985 3-8-0 50..............................(b) NickyMackay 7 49
(J M Bradley) *chsd ldr: rdn over 1f out: led ins fnl f: sn edgd rt and hdd: unable qck* **25/1**

2000 **3** *½* **Tillers Satisfied (IRE)**[7] 2973 3-8-1 57.............................. JamieKyne(5) 8 54
(R Hollinshead) *s.i.s: hdwy over 4f out: rdn over 1f out: edgd rt ins fnl f: styd on* **20/1**

2030 **4** *hd* **You Avin A Laugh**[10] 2888 3-8-5 60.............................. CatherineGannon 13 52
(C A Dwyer) *outpcd: hdwy over 1f out: r.o: nrst fin* **40/1**

6051 **5** *nk* **Swiss Art (IRE)**[15] 2744 3-8-7 70.............................. SilvestreDeSousa 1 54
(Mrs R A Carr) *mid-div: pushed along 1/2-way: hdwy over 2f out: rdn over 1f out: styng on same pce whn hmpd ins fnl f* **11/4**[1]

0600 **6** 1 1/4 **Spit And Polish**[9] 2918 3-7-12 55......................(v) AndrewHeffernan(7) 11 47
(C A Dwyer) *led: rdn over 1f out: hdd and no ex ins fnl f* **50/1**

0044 **7** shd **Transcentral**[17] 2683 3-8-0 55.. PaulQuinn 2 42
(W M Brisbourne) *s.i.s: bhd: stl last turning for home: r.o ins fnl f: nrst fin* **33/1**

0-00 **8** hd **Daisy Moses (IRE)**[32] 2198 3-8-10 69.............................. DO'Donohoe 3 51
(D Nicholls) *a in rr: no ch whn hmpd ins fnl f* **9/1**

003 **9** 3/4 **Fol Liam**[15] 2744 3-8-11 70...(p) AndrewElliott 5 50
(A J McCabe) *s.i.s: pushed along in rr: n.d* **11/2**[3]

1203 **10** hd **Pipers Piping (IRE)**[12] 2810 3-8-9 65............................... DaneO'Neill 4 47
(J A Osborne) *chsd ldrs: rdn over 2f out: hung lft over 1f out: sn wknd* **13/2**

5400 **11** 6 **Cognac Boy (USA)**[15] 2744 3-8-10 56 ow3................ DarryllHolland 10 29
(A B Haynes) *prom: rdn over 2f out: sn wknd: bhd whn hung lft ins fnl f* **33/1**

0-01 **12** 27 **Capo Regime**[52] 1652 3-9-5 80.................................(v) AdrianTNicholls 9 —
(D Nicholls) *chsd ldrs: rdn and hung rt over 3f out: eased over 2f out* **7/1**

1m 15.27s (0.27) **Going Correction** +0.05s/f (Slow) **12** Ran SP% **119.0**
Speed ratings (Par 99): **100,97,97,96,96 94,94,94,93,93 85,49**
toteswingers: 1&2 £23.40, 1&3 £22.70, 2&3 £82.40 CSF £96.68 TOTE £3.90: £1.50, £8.90, £5.90; EX 113.40.
Owner Findlay & Bloom **Bred** Peter Kelly **Trained** Lambourn, Berks

FOCUS
A very ordinary heat. The winner probably only had to run to his earlier form to win.
Capo Regime Official explanation: jockey said gelding hung violently right

3226 EUROPEAN BREEDERS' FUND MAIDEN STKS 5f 216y(P)
4:00 (4:04) (Class 5) 2-Y-O **£3,885** (£1,156; £577; £288) **Stalls** Low

Form RPR

0 **1** **Dixie Bright (USA)**[54] 1610 2-9-3 0.............................. PaulMulrennan 8 74
(J G Given) *led early: chsd ldrs: rdn over 2f out: edgd lft and r.o to ld wl ins fnl f* **28/1**

64 **2** 1 3/4 **Listillo (USA)**[18] 2636 2-9-3 0.............................. DaneO'Neill 10 69
(H J L Dunlop) *sn led: rdn over 1f out: hdd and unable qck ins fnl f* **4/1**[2]

0 **3** 1 **Dolphin Rock**[44] 1867 2-9-3 0.............................. DaleGibson 12 66
(Mrs G S Rees) *chsd ldr: rdn over 2f out: styd on same pce fnl f* **10/1**

3 **4** 1 **Suffolk Punch (IRE)**[10] 2875 2-9-3 0.............................. LPKeniry 5 63
(A M Balding) *chsd ldrs: rdn over 2f out: no ex ins fnl f* **10/11**[1]

5 3 1/4 **Bond Fastrac** 2-9-3 0.............................. PJMcDonald 13 53+
(G R Oldroyd) *s.i.s: outpcd: r.o ins fnl f: nrst fin* **33/1**

0 **6** 1/2 **Be A Devil**[7] 2979 2-9-3 0.............................. DO'Donohoe 4 52
(W R Muir) *sn pushed along in rr: r.o ins fnl f: nvr nrr* **20/1**

7 3 3/4 **Captain's Paradise (IRE)** 2-8-12 0.............................. DarryllHolland 7 35
(Sir Mark Prescott) *mid-div: sn pushed along hdwy 1/2-way: wknd over 1f out* **8/1**

0 **8** 3 1/2 **Blade Of Glory**[14] 2765 2-8-12 0.............................. AndrewElliott 9 25
(A J McCabe) *hld up: rdn 1/2-way: wknd over 2f out* **50/1**

9 shd **Satwa Crown** 2-9-3 0.............................. TedDurcan 2 29
(E A L Dunlop) *mid-div: pushed along 1/2-way: wknd over 2f out* **7/1**[3]

0 **10** 1 **Beach Boy (IRE)**[20] 2575 2-8-12 0.............................. DeanHeslop(5) 1 26
(S Wynne) *s.i.s: racd keenly and sn prom: rdn over 2f out: sn wknd* **125/1**

11 hd **Thewinnatakesitall** 2-8-12 0.............................. TomEaves 3 21
(H J Evans) *s.s: hld up: effrt over 2 out: sn wkndf* **40/1**

0 **12** 3 **Dragonessa (IRE)**[21] 2533 2-8-12 0.............................. CatherineGannon 11 12
(B Palling) *hld up: a in rr: wknd over 2f out* **40/1**

13 6 **Woodenitbenice** 2-8-7 0.............................. MartinLane(5) 6 —
(D Shaw) *s.i.s: a in rr: wknd over 2f out* **33/1**

1m 15.58s (0.58) **Going Correction** +0.05s/f (Slow) **13** Ran SP% **126.8**
Speed ratings (Par 93): **98,95,94,93,88 88,83,78,78,76 76,72,64**
toteswingers: 1&2 £18.00, 1&3 £40.80, 2&3 £7.00 CSF £138.91 TOTE £32.00: £7.70, £1.50, £1.80; EX 222.20.
Owner Brighton Farm Ltd **Bred** Gainesway Thoroughbreds Ltd **Trained** Willoughton, Lincs

FOCUS
A moderate juvenile maiden rated mainly around the race averages. The winner proved his debut running all wrong.

NOTEBOOK
Dixie Bright(USA) ◆, last of 11 over 5f on his debut at Pontefract, had clearly learned a good deal from that initial effort and relished the extra furlong. Tucked in just behind the speed, he took a while to get on top, but was in front in plenty of time and looks the sort to go on to better in nurseries, with another furlong likely to help before long. Official explanation: trainer's rep said, regarding apparent improvement in form, that the colt has strengthened since its first run, where it suffered an unfavourable draw, and seemed to be well suited by the fibresand surface. (op 16-1)
Listillo(USA) appreciated this step up to 6f and battled right the way to the line. He is now qualified for a handicap mark and should fare better in that sphere. (tchd 7-2 and 9-2)
Dolphin Rock, well backed, did well to get a prominent position from his wide draw and improved markedly on his debut effort, keeping on for pressure and shaping like a horse sure to be suited by 7f. (op 33-1)
Suffolk Punch(IRE) looked a horse to keep on side when a promising third in a novice stakes on his debut at Chepstow and was rightly made favourite. However, he came under pressure before the straight and couldn't pick up against the rail. This was disappointing, but he probably deserves another chance back on turf. (op 6-4)
Bond Fastrac, a son of Monsieur Bond, made some late headway, having been slowly to get going, and should come on a lot for the experience. (op 25-1)

3227 WOLVERHAMPTON-RACECOURSE.CO.UK H'CAP 5f 216y(P)
4:30 (4:32) (Class 6) (0-60,60) 3-Y-O+ **£1,978** (£584; £292) **Stalls** Low

Form RPR

05 **1** **Great Knight (IRE)**[17] 2686 4-9-2 56.............................. LPKeniry 11 63
(S Kirk) *hld up in tch: rdn to chse ldr over 1f out: led ins fnl f: jst hld on* **9/1**

-054 **2** 1/2 **Monte Cassino (IRE)**[3] 3125 4-9-0 59.............................. JamesO'Reilly(5) 9 64
(J O'Reilly) *hld up: hdwy over 1f out: sn rdn: r.o* **14/1**

4652 **3** 3/4 **Global Village (IRE)**[6] 3007 4-8-12 57.............................. WilliamCarson(5) 2 60+
(Miss D Mountain) *chsd ldrs: pushed along over 2f out: rdn and edgd lft over 1f out: r.o* **6/4**[1]

-000 **4** 1 3/4 **Dhhamaan (IRE)**[95] 886 4-9-6 60........................(b) SilvestreDeSousa 13 57
(Mrs R A Carr) *chsd ldrs: rdn over 2f out: styd on* **28/1**

-200 **5** nk **Bertbrand**[15] 2745 4-9-4 58.............................(p) DavidAllan 5 54
(D Flood) *chsd ldrs: led over 2f out: rdn: edgd lft and hdd ins fnl f: no ex* **20/1**

5004 **6** 1 **Secret Dubai (IRE)**[18] 2624 4-8-13 60.....................(bt[1]) KristinStubbs(7) 6 53
(Mrs L Stubbs) *s.s: sn pushed along in rr: r.o ins fnl f: nvr nrr* **12/1**

2000 **7** 1 1/4 **Kaystar Ridge**[20] 2579 4-9-3 57..................................(t) JerryO'Dwyer 12 46
(D K Ivory) *sn pushed along in rr: r.o ins fnl f: nvr nrr* **66/1**

-500 **8** 1 1/2 **Milton Of Campsie**[19] 2590 4-9-3 60.............................. FrederikTylicki(3) 1 44
(S Parr) *chsd ldr: led over 4f out: hdd over 2f out: wknd fnl f* **15/2**[3]

0440 **9** 1/2 **Mafaheem**[11] 2864 7-9-6 60.............................. DarryllHolland 3 43
(A B Haynes) *hld up: rdn over 1f out: n.d* **8/1**

-003 **10** hd **Triumphant Welcome**[15] 2745 4-9-3 57.............................. DuranFentiman 8 39
(H J Evans) *led: hdd over 4f out: chsd ldrs: rdn and wknd over 1f out* **16/1**

-300 **11** 1 3/4 **Elkhorn**[11] 2852 7-9-3 57.......................................(v) TomEaves 7 34
(Miss J A Camacho) *hld up: rdn over 1f out: a in rr* **7/1**[2]

4430 **12** 7 **Muktasb (USA)**[20] 2579 8-9-4 58.......................................(v) TedDurcan 4 12
(D Shaw) *s.i.s: hdwy over 4f out: lost pl over 3f out: wknd over 2f out* **10/1**

1m 14.81s (-0.19) **Going Correction** +0.05s/f (Slow) **12** Ran SP% **124.4**
Speed ratings (Par 101): **103,102,101,99,98 97,95,93,92,92 90,81**
toteswingers: 1&2 £29.00, 1&3 £5.40, 2&3 £7.30 CSF £131.99 CT £301.75 TOTE £11.60: £3.70, £4.50, £1.30; EX 183.30.
Owner Senta Wong **Bred** Max Morris **Trained** Upper Lambourn, Berks

FOCUS
A very modest handicap, run at a sound pace. The winner probably only had to repeat his winter form.
Secret Dubai(IRE) Official explanation: jockey said colt hung right throughout

3228 BETDAQ POKER MEDIAN AUCTION MAIDEN STKS 1m 141y(P)
5:00 (5:01) (Class 5) 3-Y-O **£3,070** (£906; £453) **Stalls** Low

Form RPR

32 **1** **Voortrekker**[17] 2652 3-9-3 0.............................. DarryllHolland 2 71+
(D J Coakley) *s.i.s and stmbld s: sn prom: led over 2f out: rdn and hung lft over 1f out: hung rt ins fnl f: jst hld on* **5/4**[1]

0-60 **2** shd **Layer Cake**[19] 2602 3-9-3 69.............................. SimonWhitworth 6 71
(J W Hills) *hld up: hdwy over 2f out: rdn ins fnl f: sn hung lft: r.o* **9/1**

050- **3** 1 1/4 **Omnium Duke (IRE)**[229] 7190 3-9-3 70........................(v[1]) DaneO'Neill 10 68
(J W Hills) *hld up: hdwy over 2f out: rdn over 1f out: styng on same pce whn n.m.r towards fin* **8/1**

25 **4** 3/4 **Kefalonia (USA)**[70] 1245 3-8-12 0.............................. TedDurcan 13 61+
(B W Hills) *s.i.s and swtchd lft sn after s: hld up: hdwy over 3f out: rdn over 1f out: styd on* **7/2**[2]

5 3 3/4 **Jenny's Pride (IRE)** 3-8-7 0.............................. MartinLane(5) 4 53
(John A Harris) *trckd ldrs: racd keenly: ev ch over 2f out: sn rdn: wknd ins fnl f* **40/1**

06 **6** 8 **Monagasque (IRE)**[17] 2652 3-8-12 0.............................. LPKeniry 5 34+
(S Kirk) *hld up: rdn and wknd over 2f out* **66/1**

00- **7** nse **Blushing Bertie**[357] 3568 3-9-3 0.............................. PaulMulrennan 1 39
(J W Unett) *led: hdd 7f out: chsd ldrs tl rdn and wknd over 2f out* **150/1**

0-0 **8** 3/4 **Vin De Rose**[25] 2416 3-8-12 0.............................. MarkCoumbe(5) 9 37
(John A Harris) *mid-div: plld hrd: hdwy over 5f out: ev ch over 2f out: sn rdn and wknd* **200/1**

0-0 **9** 3/4 **Silk Star (IRE)**[25] 2415 3-8-5 0.............................. MatthewBirch(7) 11 31
(Patrick Morris) *hld up: rdn and wknd over 2f out* **200/1**

0 **10** 2 **Any Secrets**[28] 2318 3-9-3 0.............................. JerryO'Dwyer 7 31
(Karen George) *hld up: sme hdwy over 2f out: sn rdn and wknd* **200/1**

5- **11** 3 3/4 **Devon Diva**[208] 7452 3-8-12 0.............................. TravisBlock 12 17
(C J Down) *hld up: rdn and wknd over 2f out* **16/1**

05- **12** 1 **Dubai Tsunami**[388] 2554 3-8-12 0.............................. KirstyMilczarek 3 15
(E A L Dunlop) *led 7f out: swished tail sn after: hdd over 2f out: wknd wl over 1f out* **14/1**

25- **13** 18 **Izzy Lou (IRE)**[303] 5256 3-8-12 0.............................(p) SilvestreDeSousa 8 —
(K A Ryan) *chsd ldrs: rdn and wknd over 3f out* **15/2**[3]

1m 53.87s (3.37) **Going Correction** +0.05s/f (Slow) **13** Ran SP% **118.2**
Speed ratings (Par 99): **87,86,85,85,81 74,74,73,73,71 68,67,51**
toteswingers: 1&2 £5.70, 1&3 £5.00, 2&3 £10.10 CSF £13.99 TOTE £2.50: £1.10, £3.50, £3.10; EX 16.00.
Owner Chris Van Hoorn **Bred** C T Van Hoorn **Trained** West Ilsley, Berks
■ Stewards' Enquiry : Dane O'Neill caution: careless riding.

FOCUS
A modest and slowly run maiden. Dubious form, rated around the second and third.
Layer Cake Official explanation: jockey said colt suffered interference shortly after start

3229 BETDAQ.CO.UK H'CAP 5f 20y(P)
5:30 (5:31) (Class 5) (0-70,68) 3-Y-O **£3,885** (£1,156; £577; £288) **Stalls** Low

Form RPR

4006 **1** **Angelo Poliziano**[3] 3125 3-9-3 64.............................(p) SilvestreDeSousa 7 74
(Mrs A Duffield) *alwasy prom: rdn 1/2-way: led over 1f out: edgd rt: r.o* **10/1**

2126 **2** 2 1/4 **La Capriosa**[49] 1720 3-9-7 68.............................. AndrewElliott 6 70
(A J McCabe) *hmpd s: hld up: hdwy over 1f out: r.o* **5/1**[2]

3211 **3** 3/4 **Mythical Blue (IRE)**[17] 2651 3-9-4 65.............................. DarryllHolland 1 64
(J M Bradley) *led: rdn and hdd over 1f out: no ex ins fnl f* **7/4**[1]

-633 **4** nk **You'relikemefrank**[145] 316 3-7-11 49 oh4...................(p) JamieKyne(5) 4 47
(J Balding) *chsd ldrs: rdn over 1f out: no ex ins fnl f* **8/1**

05 **5** 1 1/2 **Exceed Elegance (IRE)**[16] 2700 3-8-7 59.............................. MartinLane(5) 3 52+
(D Shaw) *s.i.s and hmpd s: sn pushed along in rr: hdwy u.p and hung lft over 1f out: nt trble ldrs* **7/1**[3]

05-1 **6** 1 3/4 **Silky Way (GR)**[23] 2478 3-9-5 66.............................. LPKeniry 8 52
(P R Chamings) *w ldr: rdn and ev ch over 1f out: hung lft and wknd ins fnl f* **5/1**[2]

-146 **7** 10 **Jolly Ranch**[23] 2478 3-8-11 58.............................. SimonWhitworth 2 8
(A G Newcombe) *edgd rt s: hld up: rdn and wknd over 1f out* **8/1**

000 **8** 6 **Chenin (IRE)**[34] 2157 3-7-9 49 oh4......................(b[1]) AndrewHeffernan(7) 9 —
(Peter Grayson) *prom: rdn and wknd over 1f out* **80/1**

61.96 secs (-0.34) **Going Correction** +0.05s/f (Slow) **8** Ran SP% **114.7**
Speed ratings (Par 99): **104,100,99,98,96 93,77,67**
toteswinger: 1&2 £14.20, 1&3 £4.40, 2&3 £3.50 CSF £59.28 CT £130.48 TOTE £13.20: £3.20, £2.00, £1.10; EX 85.80 Place 6: £132.14 Place 5: £99.08.
Owner Middleham Park Racing XXVIII **Bred** Bumble Bs, C Liesack & Mrs S Nicholls **Trained** Constable Burton, N Yorks

FOCUS
A moderate 3yo sprint, but the form looks sound for the class.
Mythical Blue(IRE) Official explanation: jockey said gelding hung right leaving stalls
Exceed Elegance(IRE) Official explanation: jockey said filly suffered interference immediately after start
Jolly Ranch Official explanation: jockey said filly suffered interference immediately after start
T/Jkpt: £78,696.50 to a £1 stake. Pool: £665,041.25. 6.00 winning tickets. T/Plt: £685.50 to a £1 stake. Pool: £77,196.64. 82.20 winning tickets. T/Qpdt: £150.30 to a £1 stake. Pool: £4,082.84. 20.10 winning tickets. CR

3085 LONGCHAMP (R-H)

Monday, June 22

OFFICIAL GOING: Good

3230a PRIX DAPHNIS (GROUP 3) (C&G) 1m 1f

2:20 (2:25) 3-Y-0 **£38,835** (£15,534; £11,650; £7,767; £3,883)

RPR

1 **Golden Century (USA)**^{23} 3-8-12 .... MGuyon 2 106
(A Fabre, France) *mde all: pushed along and r.o over 1f out: pushed out* **17/10**^{1}

2 *1* **Allybar (IRE)**^{41} 1979 3-8-12 .... OPeslier 7 104
(C Laffon-Parias, France) *racd in 2nd: pushed along early st: rdn 1 1/2f out: styd on: nt pce of wnr* **27/10**^{2}

3 *1/2* **Guest Ville (FR)**^{15} 2756 3-8-12 .... TJarnet 1 103
(Mlle S-V Tarrou, France) *in tch: 3rd 1/2-way: disputing 3rd st: rdn 1 1/2f out: styd on steadily to line* **8/1**

4 *1 1/2* **Dovil Boy (IRE)**^{45} 1858 3-8-12 .... DBoeuf 5 100
(S Wattel, France) *hld up: last 1/2-way: shkn up over 2f out: drvn and styd on to go 4th ins fnl f: n.d* **13/2**

5 *2 1/2* **Globus (GER)**^{43} 1915 3-9-1 .... AStarke 3 98
(Uwe Ostmann, Germany) *hld up: 6th 1/2-way: pushed along over 2f out: rdn to go 4th briefly ins fnl f: n.d* **6/1**

6 *2 1/2* **Milanais (FR)**^{15} 2755 3-8-12 .... GMosse 4 89
(M Delzangles, France) *in tch: disputing 4th 1/2-way: 5th st: drvn to chse ldrs over 1 1/2f out: sn rdn and no ex* **19/1**

7 *snk* **Jukebox Jury (IRE)**^{240} 6973 3-9-3 .... RoystonFfrench 6 94
(M Johnston) *pushed along s: disputing 4th 1/2-way: drvn and disputing 3rd st: sn rdn and no ex* **9/2**^{3}

1m 52.2s (-3.80) **Going Correction** -0.175s/f (Firm) **7 Ran SP% 126.0**
Speed ratings: **109,108,107,106,104 101,101**
PARI-MUTUEL: WIN 2.70; PL 1.60, 1.90; SF 8.30.
Owner Sheikh Mohammed **Bred** Darley **Trained** Chantilly, France

NOTEBOOK

Golden Century(USA) put up a smart performance and was given a professional ride by his young jockey. As there were no takers for the pacemaking role, he was taken into the lead shortly after the start and remained there until the post. He stayed on well, but stamina is not obvious from his pedigree so a longer trip might be avoided, although the Group 2 Prix Eugene Adam over 1m2f might be considered.

Allybar(IRE) chased the winner virtually throughout. He looked dangerous at the furlong marker, but was well held in the latter stages. This trip is probably far enough for him.

Guest Ville(FR), dropped in behind the leaders, was given every possible chance. He quickened when pace was added in the straight, but could never peg back the winner and runner-up.

Dovil Boy(IRE), given a waiting ride, never looked likely to catch the first three. He was putting in his best work at the finish, but this level looks a little out of his reach.

Jukebox Jury(IRE) carried plenty of condition and was a little slow into his stride. He was then settled into fourth position and was well placed to challenge halfway up the straight, but then proved onepaced. This was his first outing for eight months and the race will have done him good.

3231a PRIX DE LA PORTE MAILLOT (GROUP 3) 7f

2:50 (2:53) 3-Y-0+ **£38,835** (£15,534; £11,650; £7,767; £3,883)

RPR

1 **Smooth Operator (GER)**^{37} 2097 3-8-12 .... MGuyon 7 105
(Mario Hofer, Germany) *racd in 3rd or 4th: 4th st trcking ldr on ins: hdwy between rivals ins fnl f to ld cl home* **83/10**

2 *1/2* **Varenar (FR)**^{28} 3-8-7 .... GMosse 1 98
(A De Royer-Dupre, France) *missed break: allowed through on ins to ld after 1f: hdd and no ex cl home* **42/10**^{2}

3 *snk* **Dunkerque (FR)**^{23} 2513 4-9-5 .... DBoeuf 2 104
(Mme C Head-Maarek, France) *led tl restrained in 2nd after 1f: rdn 1f out: kpt on at same pce* **23/10**^{1}

4 *3/4* **Only Green (IRE)**^{22} 2521 3-8-4 .... DBonilla 6 93
(F Head, France) *racd in 3rd or 4th on outside: rdn over 1f out: kpt on at same pce* **59/10**^{3}

5 *1 1/2* **Tertio Bloom (SWE)**^{34} 4-9-2 .... IMendizabal 3 95
(F Reuterskiold, Sweden) *racd in 5th on ins: one pce fr over 1f out* **15/1**

6 *snk* **Mariol (FR)**^{23} 2513 6-9-2 .... C-PLemaire 8 95
(Robert Collet, France) *racd in 6th: one pce fr over 1f out* **42/10**^{2}

7 *1 1/2* **Leap Ahead (IRE)**^{23} 2513 4-9-2 .... OPeslier 9 90
(F Rohaut, France) *dropped out in last: pushed along ent st: reminder over 2f out: hdwy on outside to go 7th 1 1/2f out: no further prog* **12/1**

8 *1 1/2* **Abbashiva (GER)**^{36} 2113 4-9-2 .... AStarke 4 86
(T Mundry, Germany) *hld up: 8th st: nvr a factor* **26/1**

9 *2* **Peace Royale (GER)**^{21} 4-8-12 .... ASuborics 5 77
(Mario Hofer, Germany) *racd in 7th: effrt on outside 1 1/2f out: sn btn* **24/1**

1m 20.0s (-0.70) **Going Correction** +0.20s/f (Good)
WFA 3 from 4yo+ 9lb **9 Ran SP% 115.7**
Speed ratings: **113,112,112,111,109 109,107,106,103**
PARI-MUTUEL: WIN 9.30; PL 2.20, 1.90, 1.30; DF 24.60.
Owner Stall Jenny **Bred** Mario Hofer **Trained** Germany
■ Stewards' Enquiry : G Mosse two-day ban: whip abuse (Jul 12-13)

NOTEBOOK

Smooth Operator(GER), dropped in behind the leaders, found a gap inside the final furlong and quickened impressively to win his third Group race in France. He was carrying a Group 2 penalty and also beat older horses, so his performance merits a lot of credit. He is likely to come back to France again for the Group 1 Prix Jacques le Marois at Deauville in August and a softer surface will be even more of an advantage.

Varenar(FR) attracted plenty of support and came into this on a hat-trick. Smartly into his stride, he was soon at the head of affairs and quickened well when asked halfway up the straight. It was only inside the final furlong that he was outpaced by the winner. He is certainly going the right way and looks sure to make it at this level before the end of the season.

Dunkerque(FR) ran yet another brave race and was always in the font line. He tried vainly to tackle long time leader from one and a half furlongs out, but never managed to hit the front and was then passed by the eventual winner in the latter stages. He lost little in defeat and has been marked down for the Prix Maurice de Gheest at Deauville, where connections hope there will be cut in the ground.

Only Green(IRE) was always thereabouts. She was beautifully placed, but didn't really let herself down on the firm ground when making her challenge. She stayed on at one pace and was game throughout.

2800 BEVERLEY (R-H)

Tuesday, June 23

OFFICIAL GOING: Good to firm (9.8)

Rail around bend moved out a metre but impact on distances not notified.
Wind: Virtually mil Weather: Sunny and dry

3232 RACING AGAIN ON FRIDAY 3 JULY MAIDEN AUCTION STKS 7f 100y

2:15 (2:15) (Class 6) 2-Y-0 **£2,331** (£693; £346; £173) **Stalls High**

Form RPR

4423 1 **Rock Of Love (IRE)**^{19} 2623 2-9-3 0 .... GregFairley 5 87+
(M Johnston) *mde all: rdn clr wl over 1f out: easily* **11/10**^{1}

233 2 *9* **Going French (IRE)**^{18} 2649 2-8-9 0 .... DarryllHolland 3 56
(R Curtis) *tk keen: chsd wnr: rdn along over 2f out: drvn wl over 1f out: sn one pce* **7/4**^{2}

00 3 *1/2* **Mary Celest (IRE)**^{28} 2360 2-8-6 0 .... SilvestreDeSousa 4 52
(K A Ryan) *hld up in rr: hdwy 3f out: rdn 2f out: sn drvn and one pce* **12/1**

42 4 *2 1/2* **Scilly Breeze**^{12} 2861 2-8-4 0 .... JamieKyne$^{(5)}$ 2 49
(A M Hales) *chsd ldng pair: rdn along over 2f out: sn drvn and btn* **9/1**^{3}

0 5 *5* **Billy's Bid**^{64} 1396 2-8-4 0 .... PatrickMathers 6 32
(I W McInnes) *dwlt: a in rr* **66/1**

0 6 *18* **High Rolling**^{17} 2721 2-8-9 0 .... DavidAllan 7 —
(T D Easterby) *t.k.h: trckd ldrs tl hung lft and rn wd bnd at 1/2-way: sn rdn and wknd* **12/1**

1m 33.56s (-0.24) **Going Correction** -0.35s/f (Firm) **6 Ran SP% 110.9**
Speed ratings (Par 91): **87,76,76,73,67 47**
toteswinger: 1&2 £1.10, 1&3 £3.60, 2&3 £4.40 CSF £3.12 TOTE £2.30: £1.20, £1.40; EX 3.50.
Owner Crone Stud Farms Ltd **Bred** Crone Stud Farms Ltd **Trained** Middleham Moor, N Yorks

FOCUS

The ground continued to dry out, described as 'fast', and the rail on the bottom bend had been moved out by a metre. The market suggested a close run thing between the two market leaders, but it did not work out like that as Road Of Love slammed his rivals. The second looks regressive.

NOTEBOOK

Rock Of Love(IRE) had shown a fair level of ability when runner-up over 6f at Yarmouth and third at Hamilton. Stepping up to an extended 7f on his fifth career start, he stepped up the pace once in line for home and was soon out on his own, eased near the line, and was value a dozen lengths. Nurseries are presumably the next step, but after this demolition job he cannot expect a lenient mark. (op 6-5 tchd 5-4)

Going French(IRE), runner up at Brighton first time, did not run to that level of form when third in lesser company at Southwell and Bath in two subsequent starts. He raced keenly on the winner's quarters, but was quickly put in his place. He looks regressive and a claimer might be his best hope now. (op 15-8 tchd 9-4)

Mary Celest(IRE), well beaten on her two previous starts, stuck on from the final turn and was just held for second spot. She looks a likely nursery type now. (op 16-1)

Scilly Breeze, claimed after finishing runner-up in a soft-ground seller at Yarmouth, is only small and was in trouble the moment the winner was sent about his business. (op 15-2)

Billy's Bid has shown little in two starts now. (tchd 50-1)

High Rolling took a fierce hold, failed completely to handle the home turn and was eventually eased right up. Official explanation: jockey said the gelding ran too free and hung left badly on the bend into the back straight (op 11-1)

3233 ST JOHN AMBULANCE CLAIMING STKS 1m 4f 16y

2:45 (2:46) (Class 6) 3-Y-0+ **£2,331** (£693; £346; £173) **Stalls High**

Form RPR

5503 1 **They All Laughed**^{14} 2783 6-9-6 67 .... DarryllHolland 6 63
(P W Hiatt) *hmpd s and bhd: hdwy over 3f out: rdn to chse ldrs over 1f out: drvn and styd on ins fnl f to ld on line* **6/4**^{1}

1340 2 *hd* **Shekan Star**^{4} 3123 7-9-1 54 .... PaulHanagan 8 58
(K G Reveley) *hld up in tch: hdwy to trck ldrs over 4f out: effrt to chse ldr over 2f out: sn rdn and led over 1f out: drvn ins fnl f: hdd and no ex nr line* **4/1**^{3}

0-60 3 *1 3/4* **Drop The Hammer**^{27} 2371 3-7-12 56 .... SilvestreDeSousa 1 52
(T P Tate) *chsd ldng pair: hdwy to ld 3f out and sn rdn: drvn and hdd over 1f out: kpt on u.p ins fnl f* **9/2**

630- 4 *3* **Rawaabet (IRE)**^{12} 7815 7-9-0 45 .... (t) RussellKennemore$^{(3)}$ 12 52
(R Hollinshead) *hld up towards rr: hdwy and n.m.r on inner 3f out: swtchd lft and rdn over 2f out: sn drvn and kpt on: nt rch ldrs* **20/1**

0031 5 *3 3/4* **Rosewin (IRE)**^{13} 2802 3-8-3 57 .... JamieKyne$^{(5)}$ 5 51
(O Brennan) *chsd ldrs on outer: rdn along over 2f out: drvn over 1f out and sn no imp* **7/2**^{2}

0 6 *7* **Italiano**^{8} 2965 10-9-4 0 .... (b) FrederikTylicki$^{(3)}$ 2 39
(P Beaumont) *chsd ldrs: hdwy and cl up 3f out: sn rdn and wknd 2f out* **66/1**

0-06 7 *7* **Peace In Paradise (IRE)**^{24} 2487 3-8-0 40 .... (b^{1}) DaleGibson 7 21
(J A R Toller) *stmbld bdly and wnt lft s: a towards rr* **50/1**

000- 8 *1/2* **Intavac Boy**^{37} 3602 8-9-2 44 .... MichaelJStainton$^{(3)}$ 11 25
(S P Griffiths) *trckd ldrs: effrt over 3f out: sn rdn along and wknd* **66/1**

060 9 *nk* **Terrymene Prince**^{17} 2723 3-8-5 44 .... (v^{1}) DuranFentiman 10 25
(L A Mullaney) *chsd ldr: rdn along over 3f out and sn wknd* **150/1**

30/4 10 *3/4* **Patavian (IRE)**^{13} 2817 5-9-3 52 .... (p) PJMcDonald 4 22
(B Storey) *led: rdn along 3f out: hdd over 2f out and sn wknd* **40/1**

00/5 11 *1* **Monroe Gold**^{8} 712 9-9-3 40 .... (vt) AdrianTNicholls 9 20
(Jennie Candlish) *a bhd* **50/1**

2m 36.39s (-4.51) **Going Correction** -0.35s/f (Firm)
WFA 3 from 5yo+ 14lb **11 Ran SP% 115.2**
Speed ratings (Par 101): **101,100,99,97,95 90,85,85,85,84 84**
toteswinger: 1&2 £2.50, 1&3 £3.50, 2&3 £4.40 CSF £7.22 TOTE £2.50: £1.10, £1.80, £1.80; EX 9.30.They All Laughed was claimed by M. Fife for £8000.
Owner Clive Roberts **Bred** T G And B B Mills **Trained** Hook Norton, Oxon
■ Stewards' Enquiry : Duran Fentiman one-day ban: used whip out of contention (Jul 17)

FOCUS

Plenty of dead wood in this weak claimer and the gallop was not strong.

3234 HAPPY BIRTHDAY YVONNE TURNER H'CAP 7f 100y

3:15 (3:15) (Class 5) (0-70,70) 3-Y-0+ **£2,914** (£867; £433; £216) **Stalls High**

Form RPR

6651 1 **Summer Dancer (IRE)**^{4} 3105 5-9-12 **68** 6ex .... PhillipMakin 7 80+
(P T Midgley) *hld up in midfield: hdwy and n.m.r 2f out: effrt and nt clr run over 1f out: sn swtchd lft and rdn: qckd to ld ins fnl f and sn clr* **7/2**^{1}

0005 2 *2 1/4* **Party In The Park**^{25} 2459 4-8-8 **53** .... (b) FrederikTylicki$^{(3)}$ 9 58
(Miss J A Camacho) *chsd ldrs: hdwy 3f out: rdn to ld 2f out: drvn over 1f out: edgd rt and hdd ins fnl f: one pce* **10/1**

2013 **3** *nse* **Island Chief**[17] 2719 3-8-13 **64**....(p) TonyHamilton 11 66
(K A Ryan) *trckd ldrs: hdwy 3f out: rdn wl over 1f out: drvn and one pce ins fnl f* **7/2**[1]

4106 **4** *1 1/4* **Blue Charm**[31] 2261 5-9-13 **69**.... TomEaves 2 71+
(I W McInnes) *stdd s and hld up in rr: hdwy and n.m.r 2f out: sn rdn: swtchd lft ent fnl f and styd on wl towards fin* **7/1**[2]

6000 **5** *1 1/2* **Count Ceprano (IRE)**[13] 2828 5-9-6 **69**.... DebraEngland(7) 13 67+
(C R Dore) *dwlt and rr: hdwy on inner over 2f out: swtchd lft and rdn whn nt muchroom wl over 1f out: styd on ins fnl f: nrst fin* **8/1**

-000 **6** *1/2* **Cross Of Lorraine (IRE)**[5] 3070 6-8-9 **51**....(b) PJMcDonald 8 48
(J Wade) *towards rr: hdwy over 2f out: sn rdn and no imp appr fnl f* **18/1**

01 **7** *3 1/4* **El Desecy (USA)**[11] 2876 5-10-0 **70**.... GrahamGibbons 4 59
(S Parr) *cl up: led 3f out: sn rdn and hdd 2f out: sn drvn and wknd* **7/1**[2]

0360 **8** *4* **King Of Rhythm (IRE)**[7] 3002 6-9-6 **62**.... DNolan 3 41
(D Carroll) *hld up: a towards rr* **15/2**[3]

-260 **9** *1 1/2* **A Big Sky Brewing (USA)**[13] 2804 5-9-0 **59**.... NeilBrown(3) 6 34
(T D Barron) *led: rdn along and hdd 3f out: sn wknd* **9/1**

5000 **10** *1/2* **Fitzwarren**[22] 2529 8-8-9 **51** oh3....(v) SilvestreDeSousa 12 25
(A D Brown) *cl up: rdn along 3f out: drvn over 2f out and sn wknd* **80/1**

1m 30.68s (-3.12) **Going Correction** -0.35s/f (Firm)
WFA 3 from 4yo+ 9lb **10** Ran SP% **117.9**
Speed ratings (Par 103): **103,100,100,98,97 96,92,88,86,86**
toteswingers: 1&2 £10.90, 1&3 £2.80, 2&3 £6.80 CSF £41.17 CT £132.70 TOTE £4.00: £1.80, £2.30, £1.50; EX 41.80.
Owner The Howarting's Partnership **Bred** Eddie O'Leary **Trained** Westow, N Yorks

FOCUS
A modest 51-70 handicap run at a blistering pace. The winner is rated back to his best.

3235 SIEMENS CHEMICAL SOLUTIONS H'CAP 1m 1f 207y
3:45 (3:45) (Class 4) (0-80,80) 4-Y-0+ **£4,727** (£1,406; £702; £351) **Stalls** High

Form RPR
-062 **1** **Traphalgar (IRE)**[15] 2773 4-9-6 **79**.... GregFairley 5 86
(P F I Cole) *t.k.h: prom: led 3f out: rdn wl over 1f out: kpt on strly u.p ins fnl f* **9/4**[1]

5316 **2** *1 1/4* **Umverti**[13] 2803 4-8-2 **61** oh1.... SilvestreDeSousa 4 66
(N Bycroft) *trckd ldrs: effrt over 2f out: rdn to chse wnr appr fnl f: sn drvn and kpt on* **9/2**[3]

0-10 **3** *1* **Snowed Under**[35] 2150 8-9-7 **80**.... DarryllHolland 6 83
(J D Bethell) *hld up in tch: hdwy 3f out: swtchd lft over 1f out and sn rdn: chsd ldng pair ins fnl f and kpt on* **9/2**[3]

3506 **4** *2 3/4* **We'Re Delighted**[10] 2916 4-8-11 **70**.... GrahamGibbons 1 67
(T D Walford) *hld up in rr: hdwy over 3f out: rdn to chse ldrs 2f out: sn drvn and no imp* **15/2**

0024 **5** *2 1/2* **Shady Gloom (IRE)**[10] 2932 4-9-5 **78**.... TomEaves 3 70
(K A Ryan) *trckd ldrs on outer: hdwy 3f out: rdn along wl over 1f out and grad wknd* **7/2**[2]

20-0 **6** *3 1/4* **Smarterthanuthink (USA)**[24] 2505 4-8-7 **66**....(v[1]) PaulHanagan 8 52
(R A Fahey) *led: rdn along and hdd 3f out: sn wknd* **8/1**

2m 4.09s (-2.91) **Going Correction** -0.35s/f (Firm) **6** Ran SP% **112.2**
Speed ratings (Par 105): **97,96,95,93,91 88**
toteswingers: 1&2 £2.60, 1&3 £1.60, 2&3 £5.50 CSF £12.62 CT £40.23 TOTE £3.00: £1.40, £3.40; EX 15.20.
Owner The Fairy Story Partnership **Bred** Deepwood Farm Stud **Trained** Whatcombe, Oxon

FOCUS
A 61-80 handicap run at a sound pace and a clear-cut, well ridden winner. It is doubtful if he had to improve much on recent efforts though.

3236 LEVY BOARD H'CAP 5f
4:15 (4:17) (Class 3) (0-95,94) 3-Y-0+ **£7,641** (£2,273; £1,136; £567) **Stalls** High

Form RPR
1604 **1** **Fol Hollow (IRE)**[4] 3122 4-9-13 **94**.... AdrianTNicholls 3 103
(D Nicholls) *Soon led: rdn clr over 1f out: drvn ins fnl f and hld on wl towards fin* **3/1**[2]

0322 **2** *3/4* **Everymanforhimself (IRE)**[30] 2297 5-9-11 **92**....(b) DarryllHolland 1 98
(K A Ryan) *Soon pushed along in rr: hdwy on outer 1/2-way: rdn to chse wnr and edgd rt appr fnl f: drvn to chal ins fnl f and ev ch tl no nt qckn towards fin* **7/4**[1]

6045 **3** *2 1/2* **Bo McGinty (IRE)**[14] 2782 8-8-8 **75** oh1....(v) PaulHanagan 6 72
(R A Fahey) *chsd ldrs on inner: rdn along wl over 1f out: kpt on ins fnl f* **7/1**

6036 **4** *1* **Discanti (IRE)**[20] 2591 4-8-9 **76**....(t) DavidAllan 2 70+
(T D Easterby) *chsd ldrs: rdn along whn n.m.r over 1f out: kpt on same pce u.p fnl f* **10/1**

400- **5** *nk* **Hypnosis**[255] 6651 6-8-11 **78**.... TonyHamilton 4 71
(N Wilson) *cl up: rdn along over 2f out: sn drvn and wknd wl over 1f out* **20/1**

0204 **6** *1 3/4* **Namir (IRE)**[12] 2840 7-8-8 **75**....(vt) DuranFentiman 8 61
(D Shaw) *a in rr* **9/2**[3]

60.72 secs (-2.78) **Going Correction** -0.35s/f (Firm) **6** Ran SP% **105.9**
Speed ratings (Par 107): **108,106,102,101,100 97**
toteswingers: 1&2 £1.40, 1&3 £3.30, 2&3 £2.30 CSF £7.63 CT £22.61 TOTE £3.80: £2.00, £1.50; EX 7.40.
Owner Middleham Park Racing Iii **Bred** Dan O'Brien **Trained** Sessay, N Yorks
■ Secret Asset (7/1, ref to ent stalls) was withdrawn. Deduct 10p in the £ under R4.

FOCUS
A 75-94 handicap run at a breakneck pace. The winner made all and improved on the form of his April win here.

NOTEBOOK
Fol Hollow(IRE), who won on his only previous start here in April from a 7lb lower mark, was dropping back to 5f. Soon able to dominate, in the end he did just enough. He could carry a 6lb penalty in the Gosforth Park Cup at Newcastle on Friday night. (op 4-1)
Everymanforhimself(IRE), who took this a year ago from a 2lb lower mark, had the blinkers back on after being tried in a visor when runner-up over 6f at Newmarket. He had the outside draw and again took an age to get going. He looked likely to prevail when moving upsides inside the last, but in the end the winner had the edge. He could re-oppose on much better terms at Newcastle. (op 9-4)
Bo McGinty(IRE), who took this from a 4lb higher mark in 2006, is on a losing run stretching back 21 races now and as usual he showed a marked tendency to hang right. He is a law unto himself nowadays. (op 11-2)
Discanti(IRE), who made all in his two career wins, is hard to predict these days. (op 9-1 tchd 14-1)
Hypnosis, 4lb higher than her last success, had her new trainer at the start with her on her first outing since October. She showed all her old toe to chase the winner until tiring coming to the final furlong. She should be spot on next time. (op 16-1)
Namir(IRE), fourth in this last year, could never go the pace but, only 1lb higher than his last winning mark, he is not one to write off yet. (op 4-1 tchd 7-2)

3237 BEVERLEY ANNUAL BADGEHOLDERS MEDIAN AUCTION MAIDEN STKS 7f 100y
4:45 (4:45) (Class 5) 3-Y-0 **£2,590** (£770; £385; £192) **Stalls** High

Form RPR
4-2 **1** **Aqwaas (USA)**[25] 2433 3-8-12 0.... RHills 2 76+
(Sir Michael Stoute) *trckd ldng pair: smooth hdwy 1/2-way: cl up[over 2f out: led on bit over 1f out: shkn up ins fnl f and kpt on wl* **2/7**[1]

-3 **2** *2 3/4* **Helieorbea**[13] 2805 3-9-3 0.... DavidAllan 4 74
(T D Easterby) *trckd ldr: hdwy to ld wl over 2f out: rdn and hdd over 1f out: drvn ins fnl f and kpt on same pce* **4/1**[2]

46 **3** *15* **Carragold**[6] 3036 3-8-10 0.... JohnCavanagh(7) 6 37
(M Brittain) *bhd tl styd on fnl 2f* **18/1**[3]

0 **4** *2* **Hopeful Lady**[14] 2789 3-8-7 0.... LanceBetts(5) 5 27
(I W McInnes) *led: rdn along 3f out: sn hdd & wknd* **100/1**

5 *1/2* **Rose Avelina** 3-8-12 0.... PatrickMathers 1 25
(I W McInnes) *nvr nr ldrs* **66/1**

6 *3/4* **Admiral Of The Dee (IRE)** 3-9-3 0.... PhillipMakin 3 28
(Patrick Morris) *s.i.s: a in rr* **28/1**

1m 32.19s (-1.61) **Going Correction** -0.35s/f (Firm) **6** Ran SP% **109.0**
Speed ratings (Par 99): **95,91,74,72,71 71**
toteswingers: 1&2 £1.02, 1&3 £2.10, 2&3 £3.60 CSF £1.56 TOTE £1.30: £1.02, £1.70; EX 1.40.
Owner Hamdan Al Maktoum **Bred** Shadwell Farm LLC **Trained** Newmarket, Suffolk

FOCUS
Any price bar two and a big gap to the third. The winner did not have to match her previous form in a better race.
Carragold Official explanation: jockey said the colt hung right

3238 RACING UK ON SKY 432 MAIDEN STKS 1m 100y
5:15 (5:16) (Class 5) 3-Y-0 **£2,590** (£770; £385; £192) **Stalls** High

Form RPR
6 **1** **Burns Night**[18] 2664 3-9-3 0.... GregFairley 1 77+
(M Johnston) *trckd ldrs: hdwy on outer 3f out: rdn to chal over 1f out: drvn to ld ins fnl f: edgd rt and hld on wl towards fin* **13/8**[1]

-54 **2** *nk* **Almuktahem**[18] 2664 3-9-3 0.... RHills 4 76+
(Sir Michael Stoute) *led: rdn along 2f out: drvn and hdd ins fnl f: rallied gamely u.ptowards fin: jst hld* **4/1**[3]

6520 **3** *2 1/4* **Steel Trade**[10] 2937 3-9-3 **72**.... DavidAllan 3 71
(M Brittain) *hld up in rr: hdwy over 2f out: rdn wl over 1f out: kpt on ins fnl f: nrst fin* **9/1**

0-32 **4** *4* **Starla Dancer (GER)**[27] 2375 3-8-12 **71**.... PaulHanagan 5 57
(R A Fahey) *trckd ldrs on inner: effrt 2f out: sn rdn and n.m.r over 1f out: drvn and btn appr fnl f* **11/4**[2]

-062 **5** *1 1/4* **Cabernet Sauvignon**[21] 2572 3-9-3 **71**.... DarryllHolland 2 59
(J W Hills) *cl up: rdn along 3f out: drvn wl over 1f out: n.m.r and wkndappr fnl f* **9/2**

60-0 **6** *25* **Smitain**[52] 1683 3-8-10 **42**.... GihanArnolda(7) 6 —
(Mrs S Lamyman) *a in rr: wl bhd fr 1/2-way* **200/1**

1m 43.76s (-3.84) **Going Correction** -0.35s/f (Firm) **6** Ran SP% **113.4**
Speed ratings (Par 99): **105,104,102,98,97 72**
toteswinger: 1&2 £1.70, 1&3 £3.70, 2&3 £5.50 CSF £8.76 TOTE £3.70: £1.90, £1.50; EX 6.60.
Owner Sheikh Hamdan Bin Mohammed Al Maktoum **Bred** Highclere Stud And Floors Farming **Trained** Middleham Moor, N Yorks
■ Stewards' Enquiry : Gihan Arnolda one-day ban: used whip when out of contention (7 Jul)

FOCUS
An ordinary maiden, run at a sound gallop as a result of the two leaders taking each other on. The front pair can both rate higher.
Cabernet Sauvignon Official explanation: jockey said that the colt hung right-handed in the straight

3239 "HANDS AND HEELS" APPRENTICE H'CAP 5f
5:45 (5:51) (Class 6) (0-55,55) 3-Y-0+ **£2,331** (£693; £346; £173) **Stalls** High

Form RPR
000 **1** **Foreign Rhythm (IRE)**[6] 3031 4-8-10 **46**.... JohnCavanagh 13 53
(N Tinkler) *midfield: hdwy wl over 1f out: swtchd rt and rdn ent fnl f: styd on strly to ld nr fin* **10/1**

0002 **2** *hd* **Unbelievable Jeff**[3] 3176 3-8-4 **46** oh1.... AndrewHeffernan 15 50
(S Parr) *chsd ldrs: hdwy 2f out: rdn and edgd lft ent fnl f: styd on wl towards fin* **2/1**[1]

5400 **3** *hd* **Lithaam (IRE)**[18] 2682 5-9-2 **52**....(p) JamesPSullivan 14 58
(J M Bradley) *cl up: led wl over 1f out and sn rdn: edgd lft ins fnl f: hdd and no ex nr fin* **7/1**[3]

540 **4** *1 3/4* **Ask Jenny (IRE)**[13] 2811 7-9-5 **55**.... JamieKyne 8 54
(Patrick Morris) *hmpd sn after s: in midfield: rdn and hdwy wl over 1f out: swtchd lft and styd on ins fnl f: nrst fin* **11/2**[2]

6003 **5** *1 3/4* **Thoughtsofstardom**[13] 2811 6-9-3 **55**.... TobyAtkinson(2) 7 47
(P S McEntee) *wnt lft s and towards rr: pushed along and in tch 1/2-way: rdn wl over 1f out: swtchd rt over 1f out: kpt on ins fnl f: nrst fin* **9/1**

00-0 **6** *nk* **Making Music**[8] 2966 6-9-1 **51**....(b) MatthewLawson 4 42
(T D Easterby) *cl up: led 1/2-way: rdn and hdd wl over 1f out: kpt on same pce* **22/1**

-000 **7** *1 1/2* **Helping Hand (IRE)**[42] 1970 4-9-3 **55**.... DavidKenny(2) 1 41+
(R Hollinshead) *racd alone nr stands rail: in tch: rdn along 2f out: kpt on ins fnl f* **12/1**

015 **8** *1 1/4* **Future Gem**[3] 3176 3-8-9 **53**.... AlexEdwards(2) 12 32
(A Dickman) *led to 1/2-way: sn rdn along and grad wknd* **14/1**

-556 **9** *nse* **Red River Boy**[13] 2801 4-9-1 **51**.... NSLawes 3 32
(C W Fairhurst) *nvr nr ldrs* **20/1**

2-06 **10** *1* **Woqoodd**[5] 3066 5-9-2 **54**....(v) LeeTopliss(2) 11 31
(D Shaw) *chsd ldrs: rdn along 1/2-way: sn wknd* **18/1**

006 **11** *3 1/2* **Meikle Barfil**[13] 2811 7-8-8 **46** oh1....(tp) IJBrennan(2) 6 9
(J M Bradley) *hmpd s and in rr: hdwy 1/2-way: swtchd rt and rdn to chse ldrs over 1f out: sn wknd* **33/1**

6-60 **12** *3/4* **Tricky Trev (USA)**[23] 2515 3-8-9 **53**....(t) GemmaElford(2) 5 12
(S Curran) *hmpd s: a in rr* **22/1**

-054 **13** *2 3/4* **Valiant Romeo**[15] 2758 9-8-11 **51** ow3....(v) TanyaRedden(4) 9 1
(R Bastiman) *chsd ldrs: rdn along 1/2-way and sn wknd* **28/1**

0-00 **14** *1* **Rio Pomba (IRE)**[4] 3125 3-8-7 **53**....(b[1]) NeilFarley(4) 16 —
(D Carroll) *a towards rr* **25/1**

62.25 secs (-1.25) **Going Correction** -0.35s/f (Firm)
WFA 3 from 4yo+ 6lb **14** Ran SP% **123.6**
Speed ratings (Par 101): **96,95,95,92,89 89,86,84,84,83 77,76,72,70**
toteswingers: 1&2 £8.30, 1&3 £20.30, 2&3 £6.40 CSF £28.13 CT £152.58 TOTE £14.10: £4.80, £1.30, £3.10; EX 54.70 Place 6: £3.28 Place 5: £2.95.
Owner Foreign Rhythm Partnership **Bred** Yeomanstown Stud **Trained** Langton, N Yorks

FOCUS
A 46-55 'hands and heels" apprentice handicap. The first three were all drawn high but the first two raced more towards the centre.
Tricky Trev(USA) Official explanation: jockey said gelding missed the break
T/Plt: £4.00 to a £1 stake. Pool: £59,276.39. 10,629.82 winning tickets. T/Qpdt: £3.00 to a £1 stake. Pool: £3,261.18. 788.28 winning tickets. JR

2806 **BRIGHTON** (L-H)
Tuesday, June 23
OFFICIAL GOING: Good to firm (firm in places; 8.9)
Bends dolled out 4metres to 2.5f marker.
Wind: Fresh, against Weather: Sunny and very warm

3240 HEART 102.4 AND 103.5 FM MAIDEN AUCTION STKS 5f 213y
2:30 (2:30) (Class 5) 2-Y-O **£3,532** (£1,057; £528; £264; £131) **Stalls** Low

Form RPR
02 **1** **Craicattack (IRE)**[7] 2996 2-8-10 0 LPKeniry 1 73+
(J S Moore) *mde all: rdn 3 l clr over 1f out: eased nr fin* **5/2**[2]
04 **2** 1 ¾ **Yawary**[12] 2860 2-8-7 0 EddieAhern 3 64
(C E Brittain) *hld up in handy 4th: drvn to chse wnr over 1f out: no imp* **7/4**[1]
3 2 ½ **Cuthbert (IRE)** 2-8-13 0 MartinDwyer 7 62+
(W Jarvis) *s.s: rn green and rdn along in rr tl r.o fnl f* **7/1**
060 **4** 2 ¾ **Xaara Star (IRE)**[14] 2792 2-8-6 0 StephenCarson 4 47
(Eve Johnson Houghton) *wnt to post v early: pressed wnr: rdn over 2f out: wknd over 1f out* **12/1**
06 **5** 7 **Flashy Lover (IRE)**[14] 2792 2-8-6 0 SamHitchcott 5 26
(M R Channon) *t.k.h: prom on outer tl wknd 2f out: bhd whn hung lft fnl f* **3/1**[3]

1m 10.78s (0.58) **Going Correction** -0.175s/f (Firm) **5** Ran SP% **110.1**
Speed ratings (Par 93): **89,86,83,79,70**
CSF £7.31 TOTE £3.90: £1.80, £1.60; EX 7.90.
Owner W Adams & J S Moore **Bred** A M F Persse **Trained** Upper Lambourn, Berks
FOCUS
An ordinary juvenile maiden. The winner made all to show improved form.
NOTEBOOK
Craicattack(IRE) has improved with each run so far. Although beaten into second in a seller on his latest start, the winner that day looked well above average for the grade and if anything this was easier. Allowed to dominate having displayed sufficient early speed, he found plenty when asked and did this cosily. He looks a fair type for nurseries. (op 3-1)
Yawary had every chance but she looks just modest. A step up in trip is likely to suit. (op 5-2 tchd 11-4)
Cuthbert(IRE), an 11,000gns first foal of a dual 1m-1m2f winner, missed the break and ran green early on before making some late headway. He's likely to come on a good deal for the experience. (op 6-1 tchd 11-2)
Xaara Star(IRE) was below her best form and has something to prove now. (op 17-2)
Flashy Lover(IRE) didn't let herself down under pressure, not looking to handle the quick ground or the track. She had shown some ability in her first two starts and can be given another chance. (op 5-2)

3241 GEN RE CLASSIC H'CAP 7f 214y
3:00 (3:02) (Class 6) (0-55,55) 3-Y-O+ **£2,331** (£693; £346; £173) **Stalls** Low

Form RPR
605- **1** **Hypnotic**[300] 5389 7-9-7 **55** PaulDoe 12 69+
(Jim Best) *mde all: rdn and r.o wl fnl 2f: readily* **4/1**[2]
-302 **2** 2 ½ **Lady Florence**[13] 2806 4-9-0 **48** LPKeniry 2 52
(A B Coogan) *prom: chsd wnr fnl 3f: hung lft fnl 2f: nt qckn* **15/2**
5-00 **3** 2 ½ **Kyle Of Bute**[20] 2602 3-8-6 **50** MartinDwyer 5 46+
(J L Dunlop) *towards rr: n.m.r on rail and dropped to last over 4f out: styd on wl fnl 2f: nrst fin* **7/1**[3]
-003 **4** ¾ **Premier Krug (IRE)**[11] 2876 3-8-2 **46** oh1 CatherineGannon 3 41
(P D Evans) *chsd ldrs: rdn 3f out: wnt 3rd over 1f out: hung lft: one pce* **7/1**[3]
5305 **5** 1 ¾ **Fairly Honest**[27] 2378 5-9-1 **49** EddieAhern 1 42
(P W Hiatt) *chsd wnr tl 3f out: outpcd and btn 2f out* **12/1**
0460 **6** 2 ½ **Colombard (IRE)**[18] 2686 4-8-7 **46** (b) Louis-PhilippeBeuzelin(5) 9 33
(Patrick Morris) *towards rr: rdn and sme hdwy over 2f out: nt pce to chal* **16/1**
640- **7** ½ **Prince Valentine**[243] 6928 8-9-2 **50** (p) GeorgeBaker 10 36
(G L Moore) *plld hrd towards rr: sme hdwy into midfield 3f out: wknd over 1f out* **7/2**[1]
00-0 **8** 15 **Clear Hand**[17] 2709 3-8-8 **52** TGMcLaughlin 8 —
(B R Millman) *in tch: rdn over 2f out: sn wknd* **33/1**
3600 **9** 6 **Isabella's Fancy**[51] 1710 4-9-0 **48** DaneO'Neill 6 —
(A G Newcombe) *mid-div: outpcd and dropped towards rr 1/2-way: n.d fnl 3f* **33/1**
-000 **10** ¾ **Wild By Nature**[26] 2416 4-8-9 **48** MarkCoumbe(5) 11 —
(P Leech) *bhd: hdwy into midfield after 3f: wknd 3f out* **33/1**
4003 **11** hd **Lancaster Lad (IRE)**[16] 2737 4-8-13 **47** (p) FergusSweeney 15 —
(A B Haynes) *dwlt: bhd: mod effrt on outer 3f out: wknd and hung lft over 2f out* **4/1**[2]

1m 34.39s (-1.61) **Going Correction** -0.175s/f (Firm)
WFA 3 from 4yo+ 10lb **11** Ran SP% **121.4**
Speed ratings (Par 101): **101,98,96,95,93 91,90,75,69,68 68**
toteswingers: 1&2 £7.30, 1&3 £9.00, 2&3 £15.90 CSF £34.86 CT £206.08 TOTE £5.80: £2.20, £1.90, £2.30; EX 46.10 Trifecta £197.00 Pool: £359.47 - 1.35 winning units..
Owner Gary Butters **Bred** Cheveley Park Stud Ltd **Trained** Lewes, E Sussex
■ Batchworth Blaise (17/2) was withdrawn on vet's advice. Deduct 10p in the £ unde R4. New market formed.
FOCUS
A moderate, uncompetitive handicap. The winner made all on a card where front runners dominated and should have further improvement to come for his new yard.
Fairly Honest Official explanation: jockey said gelding hung left
Colombard(IRE) Official explanation: jockey said gelding hung left
Lancaster Lad(IRE) Official explanation: jockey said colt ran flat

3242 ON YOUR MARK'S LANE (S) STKS 5f 213y
3:30 (3:31) (Class 6) 3-Y-O+ **£1,942** (£578; £288; £144) **Stalls** Low

Form RPR
4331 **1** **Caribbean Coral**[10] 2908 10-9-10 62 GeorgeBaker 1 68+
(A B Haynes) *hld up in 5th and a gng wl: cruised up to ld jst over 1f out: rdn clr: comf* **2/1**[1]
0500 **2** 2 ½ **Supreme Speedster**[32] 2223 5-9-5 47 SimonWhitworth 7 52
(A G Newcombe) *bhd: shkn up 2f out: gd late hdwy to snatch 2nd on line* **28/1**
2450 **3** nse **Joss Stick**[13] 2811 4-8-12 55 (p) SPRyan(7) 5 52
(R A Harris) *led tl jst over 1f out: comf outpcd by wnr* **8/1**
6541 **4** 2 **Landucci**[16] 2737 8-9-10 64 (p) JamesDoyle 8 50
(S Curran) *prom: jnd ldr 2f out tl outpcd over 1f out* **3/1**[2]
0000 **5** 2 **Nawaaff**[6] 3031 4-9-10 42 CatherineGannon 6 44
(M R Channon) *sltly squeezed s: towards rr: hmpd over 4f out: sn pushed along: nvr able to chal* **50/1**
-666 **6** ¾ **Rockfield Lodge (IRE)**[28] 2349 4-9-2 62 (b) KevinGhunowa(3) 3 37
(R A Harris) *plld hrd: prom tl wknd over 1f out* **4/1**[3]
2005 **7** nk **Arfinnit (IRE)**[48] 1784 8-9-5 45 (v) KirstyMilczarek 4 36
(Mrs A L M King) *prom: drvn along over 2f out: sn btn* **16/1**
4030 **8** 3 **Easy Wonder (GER)**[10] 2908 4-9-0 47 (b) TGMcLaughlin 9 21
(I A Wood) *sn rdn along in 6th: n.d whn hung lft fnl 2f* **25/1**
060- **9** 16 **Place The Duchess**[254] 6666 3-8-7 46 NeilChalmers 2 —
(Miss Sheena West) *plld hrd in rr: lost tch over 2f out: eased* **12/1**

1m 10.3s (0.10) **Going Correction** -0.175s/f (Firm)
WFA 3 from 4yo+ 7lb **9** Ran SP% **112.3**
Speed ratings (Par 101): **92,88,88,85,83 82,81,77,56**
toteswinger: 1&2 £13.70, 1&3 £3.30, 2&3 £30.10 CSF £63.81 TOTE £2.70: £1.30, £5.40, £2.20; EX 71.50 Trifecta £503.50 Pool: £782.60 - 1.15 winning units..The winner was bought in for 6,000gns.
Owner T Hosier **Bred** P And C Scott **Trained** Limpley Stoke, Bath
■ Stewards' Enquiry : Catherine Gannon one-day ban: careless riding (July 7)
FOCUS
An ordinary seller run at a solid pace. The winner should continue to go well in this sort of grade.
Rockfield Lodge(IRE) Official explanation: jockey said gelding ran too free
Place The Duchess Official explanation: jcokey said filly lost its action

3243 WEATHERBYS FINANCE H'CAP 6f 209y
4:00 (4:00) (Class 5) (0-75,75) 3-Y-O+ **£3,280** (£981; £490; £245; £122) **Stalls** Low

Form RPR
4202 **1** **Patavium Prince (IRE)**[16] 2736 6-9-12 **73** DaneO'Neill 2 81
(Miss Jo Crowley) *prom on rail: rdn over 2f out: led jst over 1f out: strly pressed fnl f: all out* **9/2**[3]
5-40 **2** ½ **My Learned Friend (IRE)**[24] 2491 5-9-9 **73** DavidProbert(3) 7 80
(A M Balding) *pressed ldr: str chal over 2f out: drvn and edgd lft fnl f: r.o* **4/1**[2]
0140 **3** nse **Kipchak (IRE)**[7] 2998 4-10-0 **75** (p) LPKeniry 4 82
(C R Dore) *led tl jst over 1f out: hung lft and n.m.r between rivals fnl f: r.o* **9/2**[3]
5114 **4** 6 **Crystallize**[5] 3075 3-8-5 **68** PNolan(7) 5 56
(A B Haynes) *dwlt: bhd: rdn 3f out: styd on to take mod 4th ins fnl f* **9/2**[3]
-220 **5** ½ **Rebel City**[7] 2998 3-9-2 **72** ShaneKelly 6 58
(S A Callaghan) *t.k.h in 4th: hrd rdn 2f out: sn btn* **12/1**
0510 **6** 1 ¾ **Louphole**[18] 2680 7-9-5 **66** AdrianMcCarthy 1 51
(J R Jenkins) *s.s: settled in 5th: effrt over 2f out: sn wknd* **14/1**
2450 **7** ½ **Napoletano (GER)**[3] 3159 8-9-4 **65** (p) TonyCulhane 3 48
(S Dow) *t.k.h in 5th: rdn and dropped to last over 3f out: n.d after* **7/2**[1]

1m 21.21s (-1.89) **Going Correction** -0.175s/f (Firm)
WFA 3 from 4yo+ 9lb **7** Ran SP% **111.1**
Speed ratings (Par 103): **103,102,102,95,94 92,92**
toteswingers: 1&2 £13.70, 1&3 £3.30, 2&3 £30.10 CSF £21.39 CT £81.09 TOTE £3.80: £2.40, £2.00; EX 16.50 Trifecta £93.00 Pool: £586.07 - 4.66 winning units..
Owner Mrs Liz Nelson **Bred** J P Hardiman **Trained** Whitcombe, Dorset
■ Stewards' Enquiry : Dane O'Neill caution: use of whip
FOCUS
A modest handicap in which it paid to race handy. The first three finished clear and the form is sound.

3244 WEATHERBYS BANK H'CAP 1m 3f 196y
4:30 (4:31) (Class 6) (0-65,67) 4-Y-O+ **£2,590** (£770; £385; £192) **Stalls** High

Form RPR
4350 **1** **Penang Cinta**[14] 2783 6-8-10 **54** CatherineGannon 5 64
(P D Evans) *hld up towards rr: hdwy 3f out: styd on to ld ins fnl f: rdn out* **4/1**[3]
0620 **2** 1 ¾ **Strike Force**[24] 2493 5-9-2 **60** JimCrowley 2 67
(Miss J Feilden) *prom: led 3f out tl ins fnl f: nt qckn* **11/2**
3122 **3** nse **Jafaru**[6] 3029 5-8-12 **56** (b) FergusSweeney 8 63
(G L Moore) *hld up in 5th: promising effrt and trckd ldrs over 2f out: one pce fnl f* **11/10**[1]
1331 **4** 8 **Coral Shores**[8] 2975 4-9-9 **67** 6ex (v) EddieAhern 1 61
(P W Hiatt) *led tl 3f out: wknd wl over 1f out* **7/2**[2]
0345 **5** 17 **Rawdon (IRE)**[17] 2708 8-9-0 **65** (bt) KylieManser(7) 6 32
(Miss Gay Kelleway) *hld up in rr: mod effrt on outer 3f out: sn wknd* **16/1**
4406 **6** 10 **Speagle (IRE)**[15] 2762 7-7-13 **46** oh1 KellyHarrison(3) 4 —
(A J Chamberlain) *chsd ldr tl wknd over 3f out* **25/1**
5030 **7** 14 **It's My Day (IRE)**[12] 813 4-9-5 **63** (v[1]) LPKeniry 3 —
(C Gordon) *in tch to 1/2-way: rdn and bhd fnl 5f* **33/1**

2m 29.8s (-2.90) **Going Correction** -0.175s/f (Firm) **7** Ran SP% **117.9**
Speed ratings (Par 101): **102,100,100,95,84 77,68**
toteswinger: 1&2 £4.20, 2&3 £2.20, 1&3 not won. CSF £27.21 CT £39.66 TOTE £5.50: £2.60, £2.40; EX 29.60 Trifecta £105.20 Pool: £514.07 - 3.62 winning units..
Owner Trevor Gallienne **Bred** Mrs A K H Ooi **Trained** Pandy, Monmouths
FOCUS
A moderate handicap run at a strong pace.

3245 SELECT RACING CLAIMING STKS 1m 1f 209y
5:00 (5:03) (Class 6) 3-Y-O+ **£1,942** (£578; £288; £144) **Stalls** High

Form RPR
0341 **1** **What's Up Doc (IRE)**[19] 1314 8-9-4 72 DaneO'Neill 2 76
(Mrs T J Hill) *mde all: rdn and hld on wl fnl 2f* **11/2**
6331 **2** nk **Steig (IRE)**[13] 2807 6-9-2 67 JamesDoyle 1 73
(George Baker) *t.k.h: chsd wnr: chal over 2f out: kpt on u.p fnl f: a jst hld* **7/2**[3]
0-40 **3** 1 ¼ **Ogre (USA)**[18] 2665 4-9-7 74 PaulDoe 6 76
(P D Evans) *hld up in 5th: hdwy to chse frst 2 fnl 2f: hrd rdn over 1f out: styd on same pce* **85/40**[2]
1-13 **4** 2 ½ **Gross Prophet**[24] 2499 4-9-6 76 RossAtkinson(5) 3 75
(Tom Dascombe) *t.k.h in 4th: rdn 4f out: outpcd fnl 2f* **6/4**[1]
0-0U **5** 21 **Always The Sun**[19] 2630 3-8-0 47 (p) DavidProbert(3) 7 23
(P Leech) *prom: rdn 3f out: wknd 2f out* **66/1**

0060 **6** *51* **Alyseve**10 2913 4-8-10 39 TonyCulhane 4 —
(Mrs C A Dunnett) *a last: lost tch 4f out* **100/1**

2m 2.15s (-1.45) **Going Correction** -0.175s/f (Firm)
WFA 3 from 4yo+ 12lb **6** Ran SP% **112.1**
Speed ratings (Par 101): **98,97,96,94,77 37**
toteswinger: 1&2 £3.10, 1&3 £2.60, 2&3 £1.90 CSF £24.67 TOTE £6.40: £2.90, £1.60; EX 18.90 Trifecta £34.50 Pool: £587.53 - 12.57 winning units..
Owner M B Clarke **Bred** James J Monaghan **Trained** Aston Rowant, Oxon

FOCUS
Not a bad claimer, although the winner was allowed the run of the race and set just a steady pace. The front pair were always 1-2.

3246 STANMER HOUSE H'CAP 5f 59y
5:30 (5:31) (Class 6) (0-65,65) 3-Y-O+ **£2,590** (£770; £385; £192) **Stalls** Low

Form RPR
2200 **1** **Billy Red**10 2929 5-9-12 **64** (b) FergusSweeney 4 73
(J R Jenkins) *mde all at gd pce: rdn and hld on gamely fnl 2f* **7/1**
3030 **2** *nk* **Multahab**20 2596 10-9-1 **56** (t) MarcHalford(3) 8 64
(M Wigham) *prom: c alone to stands' rail st: chal fnl f: r.o* **7/1**
0342 **3** *1* **Music Box Express**15 2758 5-9-5 **62** MatthewDavies(5) 7 66
(George Baker) *w ldrs: hrd rdn over 1f out: kpt on* **6/1**3
5335 **4** *½* **Cosmic Destiny (IRE)**3 3162 7-9-8 **63** DavidProbert(3) 2 66
(E F Vaughan) *hld up in tch: promising chal over 1f out: one pce fnl f* **7/2**1
0601 **5** *hd* **Berrymead**13 2811 4-9-0 **57** AnnStokell(5) 1 59
(Miss A Stokell) *outpcd towards rr: rdn and styd on fnl 2f: nvr nrr* **15/2**
5003 **6** *½* **Best One**10 2908 5-9-6 **61** (tp) KevinGhunowa(3) 3 61
(R A Harris) *chsd ldrs: hrd rdn 2f out: one pce appr fnl f* **5/1**2
3560 **7** *1* **Orpen's Art (IRE)**7 3002 4-9-9 **61** JerryO'Dwyer 9 57
(S A Callaghan) *mid-div: effrt over 2f out: no imp fnl f* **14/1**
04-0 **8** *2* **Malapropism**7 3002 9-9-13 **65** SamHitchcott 5 54
(M R Channon) *outpcd in rr: n.d* **14/1**
2004 **9** *2¼* **Rapanui Belle**16 2740 3-8-4 **48** NeilChalmers 11 29
(G L Moore) *outpcd towards rr: nvr a factor* **33/1**
4600 **10** *1½* **Prince Of Delphi**28 2366 6-9-4 **56** (v1) KirstyMilczarek 6 32
(Mrs A L M King) *mid-div: outpcd 2f out: sn btn: eased whn no ch fnl f* **16/1**

61.82 secs (-0.48) **Going Correction** -0.175s/f (Firm)
WFA 3 from 4yo+ 6lb **10** Ran SP% **112.1**
Speed ratings (Par 101): **96,95,93,93,92 92,90,87,83,81**
toteswingers: 1&2 £8.30, 1&3 £8.20, 2&3 £6.60 CSF £53.02 CT £308.92 TOTE £7.20: £2.30, £2.70, £1.90; EX 58.50 TRIFECTA Not won. Place 6: £263.05 Place 5: £185.95.
Owner Mrs Irene Hampson **Bred** D R Tucker **Trained** Royston, Herts

FOCUS
A modest sprint handicap in which the first two finishers were split by the width of the track. The form seems sound enough.
T/Plt: £238.40 to a £1 stake. Pool: £67,609.97. 206.95 winning tickets. T/Qpdt: £35.10 to a £1 stake. Pool: £4,379.48. 92.30 winning tickets. LM

2844 NEWBURY (L-H)
Tuesday, June 23

OFFICIAL GOING: Good to firm
Dolling out added circa 28yards to advertised distances on the round course.
Wind: Moderate behind Weather: Bright getting darker

3247 PUMP TECHNOLOGY APPRENTICE H'CAP 1m 3f 5y
6:20 (6:20) (Class 5) (0-70,70) 4-Y-O+ **£2,590** (£770; £385; £192) **Stalls** Low

Form RPR
50-5 **1** **Venir Rouge**5 2493 5-9-7 **67** MCGeran 2 76
(M Salaman) *hld up in rr: hdwy fr 3f out: drvn to chal 1f out: led ins fnl f: drvn out* **7/2**2
4051 **2** *1½* **Mixing**20 2601 7-8-0 **51** 6h3 KierenFox(5) 7 57
(M J Attwater) *chsd ldrs: led over 2f out: sn rdn: hdd ins fnl f: styd on same pce* **10/1**
6363 **3** *1½* **Barbirolli**6 3023 7-8-6 **52** JackDean 1 55
(W M Brisbourne) *in rr: hdwy 3f out: styd on fr over 1f out but nvr gng pce of ldng duo* **5/1**3
5 **4** *1* **Safari Journey (USA)**14 2781 5-9-10 **70** RPFlint 5 72
(P J Hobbs) *chsd ldrs: rdn and effrt over 2f out: wknd ins fnl f* **10/3**1
6001 **5** *nk* **Sinbad The Sailor**16 2739 4-8-12 **63** (v) AmyScott(5) 8 64
(J W Hills) *chsd ldr: led over 5f out: rdn: edgd lft and hdd over 2f out: styd chsng ldrs tl wknd fnl f* **15/2**
0030 **6** *2½* **Gamesters Lady**14 2783 6-8-9 **55** (p) WilliamCarson 6 51
(W M Brisbourne) *chsd ldrs: rdn over 2f out: wknd fnl f* **16/1**
235/ **7** *hd* **Khanjar (USA)**771 1732 9-8-2 **51** 0h1 (p) SimonPearce(3) 9 47
(J Pearce) *in rr: hdwy on outside over 2f out: nvr gng pce to chal: wknd fnl f* **16/1**
00-3 **8** *1¾* **Smooth As Silk (IRE)**20 2601 4-9-1 **66** RichardRowe(5) 4 59
(C R Egerton) *s.i.s: rr: pushed along and mod prog over 3f out: nvr in contention: wknd 2f out* **10/1**
4134 **9** *4* **King Of Connacht**11 2878 6-8-12 **58** (p) MartinLane 3 44
(M Wellings) *in tch: rdn and sme prog over 2f out: wknd over 1f out* **15/2**
0-00 **10** *6* **Muffett's Dream**32 2222 5-8-5 **51** 0h6 DeanHeslop 10 26
(J J Bridger) *sn led: hdd over 5f out: wknd over 2f out* **40/1**

2m 21.14s (-0.06) **Going Correction** -0.125s/f (Firm) **10** Ran SP% **117.9**
Speed ratings (Par 103): **95,93,92,92,91 90,89,88,85,81**
toteswinger: 1&2 £22.00, 1&3 £5.80, 2&3 £5.90. CSF £39.02 CT £176.88 TOTE £6.00: £2.10, £2.40, £1.90; EX 45.50.
Owner A A Byrne **Bred** Marshalla Salaman **Trained** Upper Lambourn, Berks
■ Stewards' Enquiry : Amy Scott one-day ban: used whip with excessive frequency (July 7)

FOCUS
This was a moderate apprentices' handicap. Straightforward form.

3248 WIN RACES WITH JONATHAN PORTMAN MAIDEN AUCTION FILLIES' STKS 6f 8y
6:50 (6:53) (Class 4) 2-Y-O **£5,180** (£1,541; £770; £384) **Stalls** Centre

Form RPR
03 **1** **Lady Pattern (IRE)**21 2563 2-8-6 0 EddieAhern 9 79+
(P W D'Arcy) *mde virtually all: drvn along 2f out: asserted and r.o strly fnl f* **4/1**1
2 *2¼* **Blue Maiden** 2-8-4 0 CatherineGannon 11 70
(P J McBride) *chsd ldrs: rdn over 2f out: styd on fnl f and hld on wl for 2nd but no ch w wnr* **33/1**
3 *shd* **Snow Fairy (IRE)** 2-8-4 0 DO'Donohoe 5 70
(E A L Dunlop) *s.i.s: in rr: hdwy 2f out: edgd lft and styd on wl fnl f: fin strly to press for 2nd but no ch w wnr* **16/1**
4 **4** *nk* **Bathwick Xaara**24 2494 2-8-4 0 SaleemGolam 4 69
(J G Portman) *chsd ldrs: rdn and edgd lft 2f out: styd on same pce ins fnl f* **9/2**2
33 **5** *2* **Shibhan**15 2765 2-8-4 0 MartinDwyer 8 63
(C E Brittain) *chsd ldrs: rdn over 2f out: wknd ins fnl f* **13/2**3
6 *nk* **Giulietta Da Vinci** 2-8-4 0 RichardSmith 13 62+
(R Hannon) *s.i.s: sn rcvrd to chse ldrs: rdn and outpcd over 2f out: styd on again ins fnl f* **10/1**
7 *6* **My Sister** 2-8-4 0 RichardThomas 10 44
(M D I Usher) *in rr: pushed along 1/2-way: styd on fnl 2f but nvr in contention* **66/1**
8 *1* **Sabatini (IRE)** 2-8-8 0 RichardMullen 14 45
(R Hannon) *in rr: pushed along over 3f out: sme prog fnl 2f* **11/1**
9 *4½* **Gambling Queen** 2-8-4 0 FrankieMcDonald 12 28
(Mrs P Sly) *s.i.s: rr: sn rdn and green: mod late prog* **25/1**
10 *1¼* **Candyfloss Girl** 2-8-8 0 SteveDrowne 7 28
(H J L Dunlop) *s.i.s: sn pushed along and flashed tail: a in rr* **12/1**
11 *1* **Acquaviva** 2-8-6 0 StephenCarson 2 23
(Eve Johnson Houghton) *chsd ldrs 4f* **20/1**
2 **12** *7* **Pherousa**14 2793 2-8-4 0 JimmyQuinn 3 —
(M Blanshard) *t.k.h: chsd ldrs 4f* **7/1**
13 *¾* **Ravens Rose** 2-8-4 0 WilliamBuick 1 —
(J G Portman) *s.i.s: in rr and green: sme prog 1/2-way: sn wknd* **11/1**

1m 11.75s (-1.25) **Going Correction** -0.125s/f (Firm) **13** Ran SP% **116.4**
Speed ratings (Par 92): **103,100,99,99,96 96,88,87,81,79 78,68,67**
toteswinger: 1&2 £26.70, 1&3 £22.70, 2&3 £93.10 CSF £145.48 TOTE £4.40: £1.80, £10.40, £4.60; EX 103.70.
Owner Stapleford Racing Ltd **Bred** Corduff Stud **Trained** Newmarket, Suffolk
■ Show Willing and Fair Nella were withdrawn (ref to ent stalls). No R4.

FOCUS
This was just a modest fillies' maiden, not a strong race for the track. The winner did not need to improve much to win well.

NOTEBOOK
Lady Pattern(IRE) improved on her debut effort when a keeping-on third at Folkestone last time and she stepped forward again to take this. Faster into stride this time, she stayed on well for pressure and always looking to be in control inside the final furlong. She is a progressive filly who will appreciate 7f before long and connections will now try and find her a novice stakes somewhere. (tchd 7-2)
Blue Maiden is bred to need further, being by Eclipse winner Medicean out of a 1m4f winner, so it was very pleasing to see her show up so well on debut. She met a speedier filly on the day, but should learn from the experience and is another who will benefit from a seventh furlong before long. (op 40-1)
Snow Fairy(IRE), whose dam is a half-sister to Big Bad Bob, was disputing last at halfway, but came good in the final furlong and stayed on nicely, despite drifting left, to just take third. She will almost certainly improve for the experience. (tchd 18-1)
Bathwick Xaara, fourth at 66/1 behind a stablemate on her debut over C&D, held every chance from over two out but could find no extra inside the final furlong. (op 5-1)
Shibhan has run to a similar level on all three starts and may find an opening in nurseries. (op 6-1)
Giulietta Da Vinci, who cost just £1,800, was nibbled at beforehand and showed more than enough ability to suggest she can win a small race, keeping on right the way to the line. (op 16-1)
Pherousa failed to build on her debut effort and dropped away. (op 13-2 tchd 8-1)

3249 PUMPMATIC PUMP STATIONS BY PUMP TECHNOLOGY MAIDEN FILLIES' STKS 7f (S)
7:25 (7:28) (Class 4) 2-Y-O **£5,180** (£1,541; £770; £384) **Stalls** Centre

Form RPR
4 **1** **Mistic Magic (IRE)**10 2919 2-9-0 0 MartinDwyer 15 81
(P F I Cole) *trckd ldrs: wnt 2nd over 1f out: hrd drvn ins fnl f to ld fnl 100yds* **7/2**1
3 **2** *¾* **Secret Queen**23 2514 2-9-0 0 EddieAhern 13 79
(B J Meehan) *chsd ldrs: led gng wl 2f out: rdn fnl f: hdd and nt qckn fnl 100yds* **7/1**3
3 *3¼* **Middle Club** 2-9-0 0 JimmyFortune 2 71
(R Hannon) *in tch: pushed along and hdwy over 2f out: wnt 3rd 1f out: outpcd by ldng duo ins fnl f* **7/2**1
4 *¾* **Love Action (IRE)** 2-9-0 0 RichardSmith 14 72+
(R Hannon) *in rr: sme hdwy whn sltly hmpd ins fnl 2f: styd on wl fnl f: gng on nr fin* **28/1**
5 *¾* **Interakt** 2-9-0 0 CatherineGannon 11 68+
(M R Channon) *s.i.s: rr: hdwy whn sltly hmpd ins fnl 2f: styd on fnl f: fin wl* **28/1**
6 *1¼* **Pollenator (IRE)** 2-9-0 0 RichardMullen 1 64
(R Hannon) *s.i.s: sn rcvrd and narrow advantage after 2f: rdn and hdd 2f out: wknd fnl f* **14/1**
7 *1½* **Clarietta** 2-9-0 0 TedDurcan 8 60
(J L Dunlop) *in rr tl styd on fr over 1f out but nvr any danger* **12/1**
8 *¾* **Open Glory (FR)** 2-9-0 0 RichardKingscote 10 59
(Tom Dascombe) *t.k.h and slt ld 2f: styd pressing for ld tl appr fnl 2f: wknd wl over 1f out* **6/1**2
00 **9** *½* **Sixpenny Moon (USA)**39 2047 2-9-0 0 SteveDrowne 3 57
(R Hannon) *chsd ldrs tl wknd fr 2f out* **12/1**
10 *1¼* **Creevy (IRE)** 2-9-0 0 JamesDoyle 6 54
(S Kirk) *outpcd most of way* **33/1**
11 *4* **Universal Circus** 2-9-0 0 EdwardCreighton 4 44
(M R Channon) *chsd ldrs: rdn over 3f out: wknd over 2f out* **66/1**
0 **12** *nk* **Cool Kitten (IRE)**24 2490 2-9-0 0 ShaneKelly 9 43
(W J Knight) *chsd ldrs over 4f* **25/1**
00 **13** *nse* **Vadition (IRE)**20 2595 2-9-0 0 LPKeniry 5 43
(J J Bridger) *in tch tl wknd over 2f out* **100/1**
14 *10* **Amtaar** 2-9-0 0 MichaelHills 7 18
(C E Brittain) *s.i.s: a in rr* **12/1**
6 **U** **Sarahthecarer (IRE)**26 2401 2-8-7 0 RobbieEgan(7) 12 —
(P M Mooney, Ire) *chsd ldrs: rdn over 2f out: wkng whn rdr lost iron and uns ins fnl 2f* **16/1**

1m 25.03s (-0.67) **Going Correction** -0.125s/f (Firm) **15** Ran SP% **123.0**
Speed ratings (Par 92): **98,97,93,92,91 90,88,87,87,85 81,80,80,69,—**
toteswinger: 1&2 £5.60, 1&3 £2.90, 2&3 £6.60 CSF £26.54 TOTE £4.40: £1.70, £2.60, £2.10; EX 28.40.
Owner Stan James Syndicate 2 **Bred** Fiona Craig & S Couldridge **Trained** Whatcombe, Oxon

FOCUS
This was not easy to rate but probably a fair fillies' maiden and it should produce a number of winners. It was fought out by two of those with previous experience, but there were a few in behind who should go on to be the better fillies in time.

NOTEBOOK
Mistic Magic(IRE), a running-on fourth over 5f on her debut at Lingfield, was up two furlongs in trip and relished every yard of it, staying on well inside the final furlong to get nicely on top close home. She may well progress again, connections expecting her to get the 1m, andit will be interesting to see what mark she is given for nurseries. (op 100-30 tchd 4-1)
Secret Queen, who holds a Group 1 Moyglare Stud Stakes entry, improved markedly on her debut effort at Bath and appreciated the extra furlong. This form entitles her to win a maiden. (op 8-1)
Middle Club fared best of the newcomers. A daughter of Fantastic Light who is related to middle-distance winners in France and Germany, she kept on late having been outpaced and will benefit from this initial experience. The step up to 1m willhelp at some stage and she too can win a maiden. (op 100-30 tchd 3-1)
Love Action(IRE) ◆ was one of two to really catch the eye. From the first crop of Derby winner Motivator, she was reportedly the least forward of the Hannon quartet and still had plenty of running to do entering the final quarter-mile. However, she really came home well once the penny dropped, despite being slightly hampered, and was closing with every stride as they passed the line. Improvement is almost certain and she may well appreciate slightly easier conditions at some stage. (op 33-1)
Interakt ◆, a cheap purchase bred to do better over further, really came home well having been outpaced and slightly hampered. She should know more next time and is another who looks capable of winning a maiden. (op 33-1)
Pollenator(IRE), another daughter of Motivator who was backed beforehand, showed up well to a point before fading inside the final furlong. She will be seen to much better effect with this run under her belt and can improve markedly next time. (op 25-1)
Clarietta, who is from a very good family, made some late headway having been outpaced and shown signs of greenness. She is another who should fare better next time. (op 6-1 tchd 14-1)
Open Glory(FR), whose trainer does very well with his juveniles, didn´t get home having raced keenly early on. She is from a successful German family and may well benefit from slower conditions in future. (op 17-2 tchd 9-1)
Sixpenny Moon(USA) is now qualified for a handicap mark and should fare better in that sphere. (op 14-1 tchd 16-1)
Sarahthecarer(IRE) was weakening when her saddle slipped and she unshipped her jockey, causing interference to a couple of the other runners. (op 20-1)

3250 JUNG PUMPEN & PUMP TECHNOLOGY PARTNERSHIP MAIDEN FILLIES' STKS 1m 4f 5y
7:55 (7:57) (Class 4) 3-Y-O+ **£5,180** (£1,541; £770; £384) **Stalls** Low

Form				RPR
022	**1**		**Lady Artemisia (IRE)**[26] 2403 3-8-12 77 EddieAhern 2 (M L W Bell) *trckd ldr: drvn to ld appr fnl 2f: styd on strly thrght fnl f: readily* **5/2**[2]	81
3	**2**	*3*	**Ramora (USA)**[39] 2051 3-8-12 0 TPQueally 4 (H R A Cecil) *sn trcking ldng pair: drvn to chal 2f out: styd chsng wnr but outpcd fnl f* **15/8**[1]	77
23-4	**3**	*3*	**Heritage Coast (USA)**[14] 2796 4-9-12 78 TravisBlock 6 (H Morrison) *towards rr: rdn along 4f out: styd on to take 3rd 2f out but nvr any ch w ldng duo* **5/2**[2]	72
4	**4**	*8*	**Park Melody (IRE)**[12] 2848 3-8-12 0 MartinDwyer 1 (B J Meehan) *led: pushed along over 3f out: hdd appr fnl 2f and edgd lft: sn wknd* **14/1**	59
0	**5**	*1*	**Strategic Princess (IRE)**[11] 2877 3-8-12 0 JosedeSouza 3 (P F I Cole) *chsd ldrs: rdn: green and dropped away 3f out* **25/1**	57
	6	*7*	**Sally Forth** 3-8-12 0 SteveDrowne 5 (R Charlton) *slowly away: sn latched on to main bunch but a last: lost tch 3f out* **12/1**[3]	46

2m 36.1s (0.60) **Going Correction** -0.125s/f (Firm)
WFA 3 from 4yo 14lb **6** Ran SP% **110.1**
Speed ratings (Par 102): **93,91,89,83,83 78**
toteswinger: 1&2 £1.10, 1&3 £1.60, 2&3 £1.60 CSF £7.29 TOTE £3.40: £1.70, £1.60; EX 6.40.
Owner Marco & Sara Moretti **Bred** Old Carhue Stud **Trained** Newmarket, Suffolk

FOCUS
A fair middle-distance maiden for fillies that finally saw Lady Artemisia get off the mark. The winner and fourth look the best guides to the form.

3251 ENJOY THE GAME AT TADLEY RUGBY CLUB FILLIES' H'CAP 1m 2f 6y
8:30 (8:30) (Class 4) (0-85,85) 3-Y-O **£5,180** (£1,541; £770; £384) **Stalls** Low

Form				RPR
1503	**1**		**Burza**[20] 2607 3-8-0 67 DavidProbert(3) 7 (J Mackie) *hld up in 4th: stdy hdwy on outside fr 3f out: trckd ldr 2f out: slt ld 1f out: drvn and hld on thrght fnl f: all out* **4/1**[3]	73
-000	**2**	*shd*	**Accede**[14] 2796 3-8-10 74 TPQueally 6 (J G Portman) *trckd ldrs in 3rd: drvn and qcknd to take slt ld 2f out: narrowly hdd 1f out: styd chalng u.p thrght fnl f: no ex last stride* **16/1**	79
2214	**3**	*3 ¼*	**Onemix**[35] 2164 3-8-13 77 MichaelHills 4 (B W Hills) *trckd ldr: led appr fnl 4f: rdn 3f out: hdd 2f out: wknd fnl f* **5/2**[2]	76
6445	**4**	*2*	**Fazbee (IRE)**[13] 2829 3-9-4 82 (v[1]) ShaneKelly 5 (P W D'Arcy) *hld up in rr but in tch: swtchd rt and shkn up over 1f out: sn no rspnse* **8/1**	77
6-12	**5**	*11*	**Coming Back**[40] 2008 3-9-7 85 JimmyFortune 1 (J H M Gosden) *led tl hdd appr fnl 4f: nt much roon: edgd lft and wknd 2f out* **5/4**[1]	58

2m 7.49s (-1.31) **Going Correction** -0.125s/f (Firm) **5** Ran SP% **110.0**
Speed ratings (Par 98): **100,99,97,95,86**
toteswinger: 1&2 £15.20 CSF £49.64 TOTE £5.40: £2.20, £6.30; EX 84.60.
Owner Norman A Blyth **Bred** Norman A Blyth **Trained** Church Broughton , Derbys

FOCUS
A bit of a surprise in this fillies' handicap, with neither of the front two in the market involved in the finish, and it was Burza who narrowly edged out Accede. Ordinary form, best rated through the third.
Coming Back Official explanation: jockey said filly had no more to give

3252 SHREDDING FOR BEDDING H'CAP 5f 34y
9:00 (9:02) (Class 5) (0-70,74) 3-Y-O+ **£3,238** (£963; £481; £240) **Stalls** Centre

Form				RPR
0420	**1**		**Brandywell Boy (IRE)**[10] 2929 6-9-2 58 RichardThomas 2 (D J S Ffrench Davis) *chsd ldrs: led 2f out: drvn and hld on wl fnl f* **13/2**	67
5205	**2**	*¾*	**Triple Dream**[15] 2758 4-9-3 59 (p) SteveDrowne 11 (J M Bradley) *in rr: hdwy over 1f out: styd on to chse wnr ins fnl f but a hld* **13/2**	65
0-61	**3**	*nk*	**Pic Up Sticks**[15] 2758 10-9-9 65 GeorgeBaker 4 (B G Powell) *in tch: hdwy fr 2f out to chse wnr 1f out: no imp: one pce and outpcd for 2nd ins fnl f* **6/1**[3]	70
0322	**4**	*2*	**Louie's Lad**[13] 2810 3-8-1 52 (p) DavidProbert(3) 12 (J J Bridger) *in tch: rdn and hdwy over 1f out: kpt on fnl f but nvr gng pce to chal* **9/2**[2]	48
0006	**5**	*1 ¼*	**Trivia (IRE)**[17] 2713 5-8-9 51 oh3 NeilChalmers 14 (J J Bridger) *chsd ldrs: rdn 2f out: outpcd fnl f* **33/1**	44
5035	**6**	*2 ½*	**Bluebok**[13] 2801 8-9-7 63 (bt) LPKeniry 1 (J M Bradley) *slt ld tl hdd 2f out: wknd over 1f out* **16/1**	47
2553	**7**	*shd*	**Don Pele (IRE)**[8] 2980 7-9-11 70 (p) KevinGhunowa(3) 13 (R A Harris) *outpcd: rdn 1/2-way: mod late prog* **9/1**	54
6006	**8**	*½*	**Metropolitan Chief**[91] 946 5-8-2 51 oh6 (p) SimonPearce(7) 8 (P Burgoyne) *chsd ldrs: rdn 1/2-way: wknd over 1f out* **33/1**	33
-004	**9**	*2 ½*	**Tiger Trail (GER)**[33] 2202 5-8-12 54 TonyCulhane 5 (Mrs N Smith) *chsd ldrs over 3f* **8/1**	27
5031	**10**	*1 ½*	**Requisite**[5] 3065 4-9-13 74 6ex (v) MartinLane(5) 7 (I A Wood) *chsd ldrs to 1/2-way* **4/1**[1]	42
1100	**11**	*shd*	**The Magic Blanket (IRE)**[20] 2596 4-9-9 65 TPQueally 6 (Stef Liddiard) *pressed ldr 3f* **20/1**	32
00-0	**12**	*9*	**Is It Time (IRE)**[146] 309 5-8-13 55 TGMcLaughlin 3 (Mrs P N Dutfield) *loose bef s: s.i.s: a in rr* **25/1**	—

60.39 secs (-1.01) **Going Correction** -0.125s/f (Firm)
WFA 3 from 4yo+ 6lb **12** Ran SP% **120.6**
Speed ratings (Par 103): **103,101,101,98,96 92,91,91,87,84 84,70**
toteswinger: 1&2 £10.40, 1&3 £10.00, 2&3 £9.90. CSF £47.12 CT £273.28 TOTE £9.00: £2.30, £2.80, £2.00; EX 63.60 Place 6 £ 300.01, Place 5 £146.77..
Owner P B Gallagher **Bred** Mountarmstrong Stud **Trained** Lambourn, Berks

FOCUS
A low-grade sprint handicap. Straightforward form with the third the best guide.
Tiger Trail(GER) Official explanation: jockey said gelding had bled from the nose
T/Plt: £314.70 to a £1 stake. Pool: £59,384.37. 137.75 winning tickets. T/Qpdt: £74.70 to a £1 stake. Pool: £5,158.46. 51.10 winning tickets. ST

3253 - 3255a (Foreign Racing) - See Raceform Interactive

2906 BATH (L-H)
Wednesday, June 24

OFFICIAL GOING: Firm (10.7)
Wind: Light, behind. Weather: Sunny

3256 E.B.F./JOHN SMITH'S MAIDEN STKS 5f 161y
6:40 (6:41) (Class 5) 2-Y-O **£3,561** (£1,059; £529; £264) **Stalls** Centre

Form				RPR
643	**1**		**Master Of Dance (IRE)**[12] 2887 2-9-3 0 DaneO'Neill 1 (R Hannon) *w ldr tl pushed along and sltly outpcd over 2f out: rdn wl over 1f out: rallied to ld ins fnl f: r.o* **11/8**[1]	76+
0	**2**	*½*	**Fawley Green**[13] 2844 2-9-3 0 MartinDwyer 4 (W R Muir) *led: rdn whn bmpd sltly over 1f out: hdd ins fnl f: r.o* **11/2**[3]	72
565	**3**	*½*	**Two Kisses (IRE)**[22] 2563 2-8-12 0 StephenCarson 6 (B G Powell) *a.p: wnt 2nd over 2f out: rdn and ev ch whn bmpd sltly over 1f out: nt qckn wl ins fnl f* **16/1**	66
	4	*2 ¼*	**Electioneer (USA)** 2-9-3 0 RoystonFfrench 5 (M Johnston) *s.i.s: sn pushed along and outpcd: rdn 3f out: kpt on to take 4th wl ins fnl f: nvr nr* **5/2**[2]	63+
	5	*¾*	**Blushing (IRE)** 2-8-12 0 EddieAhern 3 (B J Meehan) *hld up: rdn over 2f out: no hdwy* **9/1**	55+
	6	*2 ¼*	**Mister Hughie (IRE)** 2-9-3 0 TonyCulhane 2 (M R Channon) *dwlt: sn hld up in tch: pushed along over 1f out: wknd fnl f* **17/2**	52

69.99 secs (-1.21) **Going Correction** -0.375s/f (Firm) **6** Ran SP% **112.5**
Speed ratings (Par 93): **93,92,91,88,87 84**
toteswinger: 1&2 £1.60, 1&3 £6.40, 2&3 £32.10. CSF £9.53 TOTE £2.70: £1.80, £4.30; EX 9.80.
Owner P D Merritt **Bred** Mick McGinn **Trained** East Everleigh, Wilts

FOCUS
An ordinary maiden. The three with experience beat the newcomers and the third is the best guide to the level.

NOTEBOOK
Master Of Dance(IRE)'s fair level of form in his three earlier races proved good enough to land this routine maiden. Though he ran respectably over Sandown's stiff 5f last time, he needed most of this trip to get on top and is better at 6f. (op 15-8 tchd 9-4 and 5-2 in a place)
Fawley Green adopted front-running tactics, as he had on his debut, and they appear to suit him well. He looked like holding on for a long way and should find compensation. (op 15-2)
Two Kisses(IRE) has shown plenty of speed in her last three races. Only just short of what it takes to win a maiden, she will use her pace to good effect in nurseries. (op 12-1)
Electioneer(USA), by the smart US sprinter-miler Elusive Quality, was far too green on this debut and got going too late. Improvement can be expected and a slightly longer trip should be in his favour. (tchd 2-1 and 3-1)
Blushing(IRE), a £40,000 Fasliyev half-sister to winners up to 1m who should be suited by this sort of trip for the time being, needed the outing to sharpen her up mentally. (op 15-2 tchd 13-2)
Mister Hughie(IRE), a 60,000euros yearling, is by the top-class juvenile sprinter Elusive City, but his family stayed up to 1m2f in France, so he may need farther than this. Trainer Mick Channon also expects him to come on for the run. (op 7-1 tchd 9-1)

3257 BATHWICK TYRES BRISTOL (S) STKS 1m 5y
7:10 (7:10) (Class 6) 3-Y-O **£1,942** (£578; £288; £144) **Stalls** Low

Form				RPR
-564	**1**		**Montmartre (USA)**[12] 2876 3-8-12 65 EddieAhern 10 (B J Meehan) *mde all: rdn 2f out: edgd rt 1f out: r.o wl* **11/4**[1]	57
6000	**2**	*3*	**Daily Double**[25] 2489 3-9-4 56 DaneO'Neill 16 (D K Ivory) *hld up towards rr: hdwy 2f out: sn rdn: tk 2nd ins fnl f: nt trble wnr* **16/1**	56
2-60	**3**	*nk*	**Gwerthybyd**[19] 2681 3-8-4 51 DavidProbert(3) 8 (B Palling) *a.p: chsd wnr over 2f out: rdn over 1f out: nt qckn and lost 2nd ins fnl f* **14/1**	44
0400	**4**	*¾*	**Autumn Morning (IRE)**[2] 3209 3-8-6 50 AndrewHeffernan(7) 2 (P D Evans) *plld hrd: a.p: swtchd rt over 2f out: sn rdn: edgd lft over 1f out: one pce ins fnl f* **10/1**	49
3020	**5**	*½*	**Hector Spectre (IRE)**[13] 2865 3-8-9 58 RussellKennemore(3) 12 (K M Prendergast) *hld up and bhd: hdwy over 2f out: rdn over 1f out: one pce fnl f* **8/1**[3]	47
00-0	**6**	*1 ¼*	**Cool Libby (IRE)**[26] 2446 3-8-7 50 SamHitchcott 7 (A B Haynes) *stdd s: hld up and bhd: rdn over 3f out: hdwy 2f out: nvr trbld ldrs* **40/1**	39
-460	**7**	*1 ½*	**Midnight Bay**[25] 2487 3-8-12 63 TonyCulhane 14 (M R Channon) *hld up in mid-div: hdwy 2f out: rdn and hung lft over 1f out: wknd ins fnl f* **8/1**[3]	40
-054	**8**	*1*	**Like For Like (IRE)**[9] 2973 3-8-13 55 DarryllHolland 4 (R J Hodges) *s.i.s: bhd: hdwy over 2f out: hung lft over 1f out: n.d* **9/2**[2]	39
5364	**9**	*1 ½*	**Paymaster In Chief**[17] 2744 3-8-7 51 (v) LeeNewnes(5) 9 (M D I Usher) *chsd wnr tl rdn over 2f out: wknd over 1f out* **17/2**	34
000	**10**	*4*	**Primera Rossa**[12] 2876 3-8-7 43 LPKeniry 3 (J S Moore) *mid-div: rdn 3f out: bhd fnl 2f* **66/1**	20

0036 **11** *14* **Fleur De'Lion (IRE)**[18] 2709 3-8-7 47........................(b[1]) MartinDwyer 15 —
(S Kirk) *a bhd* **14/1**

0-00 **12** *½* **Premier Demon (IRE)**[57] 1584 3-8-7 43................. SimonWhitworth 13 —
(P D Evans) *a bhd* **66/1**

0620 **13** *4 ½* **Mr Flannegan**[15] 2797 3-8-5 60.. AmyScott(7) 1 —
(H Candy) *a in rr* **11/1**

6000 **14** *5* **August Days (IRE)**[8] 3005 3-8-13 52............................ JerryO'Dwyer 11 —
(J Pearce) *prom: rdn over 3f out: wknd over 2f out* **28/1**

435- **15** *4* **Percys Corismatic**[344] 4063 3-8-7 52.................................. TPO'Shea 6 —
(J Gallagher) *a bhd* **18/1**

1m 39.52s (-1.28) **Going Correction** -0.10s/f (Good) **15** Ran SP% **128.4**
Speed ratings (Par 97): **102,99,98,97,97 96,94,93,92,88 74,73,69,64,60**
toteswinger: 1&2 £10.20, 1&3 £7.70, 2&3 £43.60. CSF £53.54 TOTE £3.60: £2.10, £7.40, £5.30; EX 53.10.The winner was bought in for 5,000gns. Daily Double was claimed by Mr H. J. Manners for £5,400.
Owner Catesby W Clay **Bred** Runnymede Farm Inc And Catesby W Clay **Trained** Manton, Wilts

FOCUS
A decent gallop in this seller and the winner looked a cut above the rest in making all, with the others finding it impossible to peg him back on this lively ground, with two of the other prominent runners also faring well. The fourth is the best guide to the level.
Fleur De'Lion(IRE) Official explanation: jockey said filly did not face the blinkers
August Days(IRE) Official explanation: jockey said filly had a breathing problem
Percys Corismatic Official explanation: jockey said filly lost its action

3258 BATHWICK TYRES CARDIFF H'CAP — 1m 5y
7:40 (7:40) (Class 5) (0-70,70) 4-Y-0+ **£2,914** (£867; £433; £216) **Stalls** Low

Form RPR

6510 **1** **April Fool**[9] 2977 5-9-0 70...(v) PNolan(7) 5 79
(J A Geake) *mde all: rdn over 2f out: r.o wl* **9/4**[1]

050- **2** *1 ½* **Monashee Rock (IRE)**[221] 7342 4-9-2 65.......................... EddieAhern 1 71
(M Salaman) *sn prom: wnt 2nd over 4f out: chal gng wl over 2f out: rdn wl over 1f out: kpt on same pce* **9/4**[1]

1100 **3** *2* **Samurai Warrior**[9] 2983 4-8-13 69.....................(p) AndrewHeffernan(7) 4 70
(P D Evans) *t.k.h: a.p: rdn over 2f out: no ex ins fnl f* **7/2**[2]

0404 **4** *1 ¾* **Master Mahogany**[24] 2518 8-8-5 54............................ SamHitchcott 6 51
(R J Hodges) *chsd wnr tl over 4f out: rdn over 3f out: wknd fnl f* **8/1**[3]

-540 **5** *1 ¼* **Apache Dawn**[3] 983 5-8-3 52....................................(t) RoystonFfrench 2 46
(A Sadik) *hld up in rr: rdn 3f out: nvr nr ldrs* **8/1**[3]

6030 **6** *hd* **Stark Contrast (USA)**[14] 2808 5-7-13 51 oh1.............. DavidProbert(3) 3 45
(M D I Usher) *prom: stdd and lost pl after 1f: swtchd rt over 2f out: rdn and short-lived effrt on outside over 1f out* **14/1**

1m 39.25s (-1.55) **Going Correction** -0.10s/f (Good) **6** Ran SP% **112.6**
Speed ratings (Par 103): **103,101,99,97,96 96**
toteswinger: 1&2 £2.80, 1&3 £2.20, 2&3 £1.70. CSF £7.51 TOTE £3.00: £2.10, £2.40; EX 9.10.
Owner Miss B Swire **Bred** Miss B Swire **Trained** Kimpton, Hants

FOCUS
A modest handicap in which the winner was the first off the bridle but still managed to make all. The form is rated around the first two.

3259 BATHWICK TYRES BRIDGEND H'CAP — 1m 2f 46y
8:10 (8:13) (Class 6) (0-65,62) 4-Y-0+ **£2,183** (£644; £322) **Stalls** Low

Form RPR

0-05 **1** **Sceilin (IRE)**[30] 2333 5-8-5 46..(t) TPO'Shea 6 56
(J Mackie) *a.p: rdn to ld over 2f out: narrowly hdd wl ins fnl f: led post: all out* **5/2**[2]

5600 **2** *shd* **Clovis**[49] 1785 4-9-6 61..(p) DaneO'Neill 3 71
(N P Mulholland) *s.i.s: hld up in rr: hdwy over 2f out: hrd rdn over 1f out: slt ld wl ins fnl f: hdd post* **11/1**

0042 **3** *6* **Gracechurch (IRE)**[19] 2650 6-9-1 56............................ DarryllHolland 8 54
(R J Hodges) *hld up: hdwy over 4f out: rdn and ev ch 2f out: wknd ins fnl f* **7/2**[3]

0421 **4** *2 ½* **Solo River**[23] 2537 4-9-7 62.. EddieAhern 2 55
(P J Makin) *led: hdd 7f out: chsd clr ldr: lft in ld over 3f out: rdn and hdd over 2f out: wknd jst over 1f out* **7/4**[1]

6-40 **5** *11* **Robbmaa (FR)**[12] 2878 4-7-13 47............................ RosieJessop(7) 5 18
(A W Carroll) *bhd fnl 5f* **25/1**

0005 **6** *15* **Dynamo Dave (USA)**[14] 2808 4-7-11 45.................(v) GemmaElford(7) 4 —
(M D I Usher) *t.k.h: sn prom: sddle slipped and led 7f out: sn clr: rn wd bnd over 4f out: rn v wd ent st and hdd over 3f out: wknd over 2f out* **40/1**

-062 **7** *3* **Oronsay**[30] 2322 4-8-9 50..(t) TGMcLaughlin 7 —
(B R Millman) *prom tl rdn and wknd over 2f out* **7/1**

2m 9.35s (-1.65) **Going Correction** -0.10s/f (Good) **7** Ran SP% **114.3**
Speed ratings (Par 101): **102,101,97,95,86 74,71**
toteswinger: 1&2 £4.50, 1&3 £1.20, 2&3 £8.70. CSF £29.16 CT £95.94 TOTE £3.60: £2.30, £4.40; EX 19.60.
Owner W I Bloomfield **Bred** J S Bolger **Trained** Church Broughton , Derbys
■ Stewards' Enquiry : T P O'Shea five-day ban: used whip with excessive frequency (Jul 8-11, 13)

FOCUS
A very moderate contest which the winner had also won last year. The runner-up is rated to last year's turf form.
Sceilin(IRE) Official explanation: five-day ban: used whip with excessive frequency (July 8 -13)
Dynamo Dave(USA) Official explanation: jockey said saddle slipped

3260 BATHWICK TYRES SWINDON MAIDEN STKS — 1m 3f 144y
8:40 (8:41) (Class 5) 3-Y-O+ **£2,719** (£809; £404; £202) **Stalls** Low

Form RPR

-020 **1** **Fisadara**[13] 2858 3-8-8 65... TPO'Shea 1 62
(B W Hills) *hld up in tch: wnt 2nd 3f out: rdn to ld 1f out: r.o wl* **9/4**[2]

063 **2** *2 ¼* **Borromeo (USA)**[6] 3056 3-8-13 0.............................. RoystonFfrench 2 64
(M Johnston) *w ldr: led over 9f out: rdn and hdd 1f out: nt qckn* **5/4**[1]

563 **3** *11* **Tesserae**[17] 2738 3-8-5 63.. DavidProbert(3) 5 41
(A B Haynes) *led: hdd over 9f out: chsd ldr to 3f out: rdn and wknd over 2f out* **7/1**[3]

-006 **4** *16* **Lilleput**[9] 2981 4-9-8 0.. StephenCarson 4 —
(E A Wheeler) *hld up in last: rdn 2f out: sn struggling* **40/1**

2m 30.29s (-0.31) **Going Correction** -0.10s/f (Good)
WFA 3 from 4yo 14lb **4** Ran SP% **90.2**
Speed ratings (Par 103): **97,95,88,77**
CSF £3.66 TOTE £2.70; EX 2.90.
Owner Hamdan Al Maktoum **Bred** Heather Raw **Trained** Lambourn, Berks
■ Lords A Leaping was withdrawn (4/1, unruly in stalls). Deduct 20p in the £ under R4.

FOCUS
This modest maiden was weakened when Lords A Leaping lived up to his name, reared in the stalls and had to be withdrawn. The gallop was ordinary and the winner sets the standard.
Tesserae Official explanation: jockey said filly was unsuited by the firm ground

3261 BATHWICK TYRES CHIPPENHAM H'CAP — 5f 161y
9:10 (9:10) (Class 5) (0-75,75) 3-Y-0+ **£2,719** (£809; £404; £202) **Stalls** Centre

Form RPR

1233 **1** **Bateleur**[2] 3208 5-8-12 64.. MCGeran(5) 5 72
(M R Channon) *hld up: hdwy 2f out: rdn to ld ins fnl f: pushed out* **7/4**[1]

0006 **2** *¾* **Espy**[29] 2359 4-9-9 70.. EddieAhern 7 75
(S Kirk) *hld up and bhd: hdwy on outside over 1f out: sn rdn: r.o to take 2nd cl home* **13/2**

2355 **3** *1* **Tadlil**[135] 480 7-8-9 56 oh4..(v) LPKeniry 4 58
(J M Bradley) *led: rdn over 1f out: hdd ins fnl f: no ex and lost 2nd cl home* **33/1**

60-0 **4** *½* **Heaven**[40] 2053 4-9-12 73.. DarryllHolland 6 73
(P J Makin) *prom: chsd ldr over 2f out tl no ex ins fnl f* **4/1**[3]

1003 **5** *hd* **Princess Rose Anne (IRE)**[4] 3162 4-10-0 75................... DaneO'Neill 3 75
(J R Best) *hld up and bhd: rdn over 1f out: swtchd rt jst ins fnl f: kpt on towards fin* **10/3**[2]

605 **6** *¾* **Style Icon**[13] 2864 4-8-11 61... DavidProbert(3) 1 58
(Rae Guest) *prom: rdn over 1f out: fdd wl ins fnl f* **6/1**

1405 **7** *1 ¾* **Back In The Red (IRE)**[90] 965 5-9-3 71........................(b) SPRyan(7) 2 62
(R A Harris) *w ldr tl rdn over 2f out: wknd over 1f out* **14/1**

1m 10.13s (-1.07) **Going Correction** -0.375s/f (Firm) **7** Ran SP% **116.7**
Speed ratings (Par 103): **92,91,89,89,88 87,85**
toteswinger: 1&2 £2.60, 1&3 £9.90, 2&3 £8.40. CSF £14.52 TOTE £3.50: £2.00, £3.90; EX 18.70 Place 6 £93.29, Place 5 £55.35..
Owner Dave and Gill Hedley **Bred** G Hedley & Mike Channon Bloodstock Limited **Trained** West Ilsley, Berks

FOCUS
A fair sprint handicap with the winner a slight improver on this year's best but the form limited by the third from 4lb 'wrong'.
T/Plt: £417.30 to a £1 stake. Pool: £62,063.92. 108.55 winning tickets. T/Qpdt: £62.00 to a £1 stake. Pool: £4,622.10. 55.10 winning tickets. KH

2963 CARLISLE (R-H)
Wednesday, June 24

OFFICIAL GOING: Good (good to firm in places; 7.9) changing to good to firm after race 3 (3.05)
Wind: Breezy, across Weather: Sunny

3262 EUROPEAN BREEDERS' FUND MAIDEN STKS — 5f 193y
2:00 (2:01) (Class 5) 2-Y-0 **£4,403** (£1,310; £654; £327) **Stalls** High

Form RPR

64 **1** **Merseyside Star (IRE)**[21] 2610 2-9-3 0............................ PhillipMakin 3 71+
(K R Burke) *in tch: effrt and chsd ldr over 1f out: led ins fnl f: hld on wl* **9/2**[3]

6 **2** *hd* **Trailblazing**[13] 2839 2-9-3 0.. GregFairley 4 70+
(M Johnston) *cl up: led over 2f out to ins fnl f: rallied* **7/2**[2]

3 *3 ½* **Gypsy Jazz (IRE)** 2-8-12 0.. JoeFanning 7 55+
(Jennie Candlish) *s.i.s: bhd and pushed along 1/2-way: hdwy 2f out: kpt on fnl f* **10/1**

4 *2 ½* **William Morgan (IRE)** 2-9-3 0.. PaulHanagan 2 52+
(R A Fahey) *cl up: effrt and ev ch over 2f out: edgd rt and outpcd over 1f out* **9/2**[3]

5 *5* **Lucky Traveller** 2-9-3 0... DavidAllan 5 37
(T D Easterby) *prom: outpcd 1/2-way: n.d after* **20/1**

4 **6** *5* **Ya Boy Sir (IRE)**[14] 2813 2-9-3 0.. TomEaves 6 22
(I Semple) *led to over 2f out: sn wknd* **8/1**

4 **7** *6* **Reallymissgreeley (USA)**[14] 2819 2-8-12 0................ PaulMulrennan 1 —
(K A Ryan) *sn cl up on outside: rdn 1/2-way: wknd fr 2f out* **5/2**[1]

1m 14.82s (1.12) **Going Correction** +0.05s/f (Good) **7** Ran SP% **112.1**
Speed ratings (Par 93): **94,93,89,85,79 72,64**
toteswinger: 1&2 £4.60, 1&3 £7.70, 2&3 £10.00. CSF £19.73 TOTE £5.20: £2.80, £2.60; EX 21.10.
Owner Mogeely Stud & Mrs Maura Gittins **Bred** A M F Persse **Trained** Middleham Moor, N Yorks

FOCUS
No previous winners of this race have emerged to be real stars, so the form will probably be just ordinary in the long term. The fifrst two came clear though and the race has been rated positively.

NOTEBOOK
Merseyside Star(IRE) did not handle the undulations of Ripon last time but travelled sweetly here and just did enough to gain victory. One would imagine connections will look to nurseries for him now. (op 10-3)
Trailblazing looks to have plenty of substance about him and showed a good attitude, despite being headed just inside the final furlong. He has progressed from his first run and can win soon. (op 11-4 tchd 4-1)
Gypsy Jazz(IRE) was making her debut but evidently had been showing something at home, as her price contracted before the off. Slowly away, she took time to get going but was staying nicely in the latter stages. (op 25-1)
William Morgan(IRE), who was withdrawn at the start recently after kicking his rider, showed enough on his first outing to suggest he can take a race at some stage. (op 5-1 tchd 11-2)
Lucky Traveller, who has plenty of size, seemed the greenest of the runners during the race and will improve for the run. (tchd 18-1)
Ya Boy Sir(IRE) attracted market support but weakened in the final stages. A less-demanding track will probably suit him. (op 12-1 tchd 7-1)
Reallymissgreeley(USA) went left at the start (she was slowly into stride on debut) but was soon on an even keel. However, she came under strong pressure well over two furlongs from home and dropped away quickly. She was reported to have been unsuited by the going. Official explanation: jockey said filly was unsuited by the good (good to firm places) ground (op 11-4)

3263 EDMUNDSON ELECTRICAL MAIDEN AUCTION STKS — 5f
2:30 (2:33) (Class 5) 2-Y-0 **£3,238** (£963; £481; £240) **Stalls** High

Form RPR

44 **1** **Midnight Martini**[16] 2765 2-8-8 0... DavidAllan 9 73+
(T D Easterby) *in tch: smooth hdwy to ld over 2f out: clr whn edgd lft ins fnl f: eased nr fin* **5/2**[1]

3 **2** *2 ½* **Emerald Girl (IRE)**[9] 2963 2-8-6 0.................................. PaulHanagan 2 59+
(R A Fahey) *in tch: rdn over 2f out: edgd rt and chsd wnr ins fnl f: r.o* **5/1**[3]

04 **3** *2 ¾* **Tarrants Way**[22] 2575 2-8-9 0.. JoeFanning 3 51
(Jennie Candlish) *w ldrs tl rdn and no ex over 1f out* **25/1**

2330 **4** *1 ¾* **Gower Sophia**[30] 2339 2-8-4 0.................................... AdrianTNicholls 5 40
(M Brittain) *led to over 2f out: no ex over 1f out* **7/2**[2]

605 **5** *shd* **Arctic Destiny (IRE)**[15] 2778 2-8-6 0............................. MartinLane(5) 4 46
(K R Burke) *dwlt: sn in tch: outpcd 2f out: no imp fnl f* **40/1**

6 7 1/2 **Sydney Bridge** 2-8-11 0 .... TomEaves 6 41
(I Semple) *unruly bef s: s.i.s: bhd and rdn: kpt on fnl f: n.d* **8/1**

6 7 1/2 **Raine Supreme**[21] 2604 2-8-4 0 .... GrahamGibbons 8 32
(E S McMahon) *prom tl rdn and wknd over 1f out* **5/1**[3]

8 3 3/4 **Celestial Tryst** 2-8-8 0 .... PJMcDonald 1 23
(G M Moore) *s.s: outpcd and bhd: sme late hdwy: nvr on terms* **50/1**

00 9 2 **Stanley Bridge**[23] 2526 2-8-6 0 .... SladeO'Hara(5) 10 19
(A Berry) *s.i.s: a outpcd* **150/1**

10 2 1/2 **Blue Neptune** 2-8-13 0 .... FrederikTylicki(3) 7 15
(W R Muir) *cl up tl wknd over 1f out* **13/2**

62.32 secs (1.52) **Going Correction** +0.05s/f (Good) **10** Ran SP% **117.5**
Speed ratings (Par 93): **89,85,80,77,77 75,74,68,65,61**
toteswinger: 1&2 £2.30, 1&3 £9.80, 2&3 £10.60. CSF £15.19 TOTE £3.90: £1.10, £1.90, £5.90; EX 12.80.
Owner D A West **Bred** Helescane Stud **Trained** Great Habton, N Yorks

FOCUS
Most of these had racecourse experience, but only a few could be fancied on what they had done. It is unlikely that this will prove to be a strong contest but the winner was value for extra.

NOTEBOOK
Midnight Martini, who ran over 6f last time, ran right away from her rivals in the manner of a decent filly. She has the raw ability but will need to improve again to carry a penalty or be effective in handicaps. (op 3-1 tchd 10-3 in places)
Emerald Girl(IRE), another dropping back in trip after a promising display on her debut at this course, got outpaced but stayed on well to claim second. She may need more time. (op 11-2 tchd 9-2)
Tarrants Way kept on at the one pace to shape with some hope for the future. A sharper 5f will probably help him. (op 20-1)
Gower Sophia, who disappointed last time after a few fair efforts, was fractious in the stalls and weakened fairly quickly once joined. (op 4-1 tchd 10-3)
Arctic Destiny(IRE) kept going for pressure, but never threatened. (op 28-1)
Sydney Bridge, a half-brother to the high-class sprinter Amour Propre, did not cost a great deal at the sales this April considering his sibling, and he got a bit stirred up before loading into the stalls. He started slowly and only showed signs of promise late on, when he passed some rivals. (op 16-1 tchd 20-1)
Blue Neptune looked an interesting contender from a southern stable but he dropped away quickly after showing some early speed. (op 7-1 tchd 8-1)

3264 LLOYD MOTOR GROUP CARLISLE BELL CONSOLATION RACE (H'CAP) 7f 200y
3:05 (3:06) (Class 4) (0-80,80) 3-Y-O+ **£6,476** (£1,927; £963; £481) **Stalls** High

Form RPR
-613 1 **Sunnyside Tom (IRE)**[27] 2391 5-9-9 73 .... PaulHanagan 17 84
(R A Fahey) *mde all: clr over 1f out: r.o wl* **6/1**[2]

6302 2 1 1/2 **Daaweitza**[5] 3124 6-9-10 74 .... J-PGuillambert 11 82
(B Ellison) *midfield: hdwy to chse wnr 1f out: r.o: no imp* **11/2**[1]

-044 3 2 1/2 **Pianoforte (USA)**[6] 3070 7-8-6 56 ....(b) GrahamGibbons 12 58
(E J Alston) *t.k.h: hld up: hdwy 2f out: kpt on fnl f* **9/1**

0136 4 nk **Campli (IRE)**[30] 2313 7-9-7 71 .... TomEaves 10 72+
(B Ellison) *bhd tl hdwy over 1f out: nvr rchd ldrs* **20/1**

-061 5 nk **Intersky Charm (USA)**[9] 2968 5-9-1 68 6ex .... MichaelJStainton(3) 6 68
(R M Whitaker) *midfield: drvn 3f out: hdwy over 1f out: kpt on fnl f* **11/1**

-200 6 3/4 **Celtic Change (IRE)**[12] 2894 5-9-9 73 ....(p) PhillipMakin 1 72
(M Dods) *hld up: effrt on outside over 2f out: no imp over 1f out* **10/1**

4210 7 3/4 **Champain Sands (IRE)**[9] 2968 10-8-13 63 .... AndrewMullen 2 60
(E J Alston) *hld up: hdwy over 1f out: nvr rchd ldrs* **18/1**

0000 8 shd **Goodbye Mr Bond**[12] 2894 9-9-8 72 .... DavidAllan 7 69+
(E J Alston) *bhd tl hdwy and swtchd rt over 1f out: n.d* **9/1**

2620 9 hd **Barataria**[32] 2274 7-9-5 69 .... DanielTudhope 9 65
(R Bastiman) *s.i.s: hdwy over 1f out: nvr on terms* **20/1**

2-24 10 1 3/4 **Moody Tunes**[10] 2939 6-9-3 72 .... MartinLane(5) 15 64
(K R Burke) *prom tl outpcd over 2f out: n.d after* **25/1**

0232 11 1 3/4 **Shadowtime**[9] 2968 4-9-1 65 .... PaulMulrennan 16 53
(Miss Tracy Waggott) *cl up: chsd wnr briefly over 1f out: wknd ent fnl f* **7/1**[3]

3600 12 2 3/4 **King Of Rhythm (IRE)**[1] 3234 6-8-12 62 .... DNolan 14 44
(D Carroll) *midfield: rdn over 2f out: outpcd and edgd rt over 1f out* **25/1**

306 13 7 **Portrush Storm**[3] 3188 4-9-0 64 .... JamieMoriarty 4 30
(D Carroll) *bhd: drvn 3f out: nvr on terms* **22/1**

4146 14 3/4 **Destinys Dream (IRE)**[40] 2043 4-9-1 70 .... JamieKyne(5) 8 34
(Miss Tracy Waggott) *cl up tl wknd fr 2f out* **18/1**

2-12 15 3 1/2 **Russian George (IRE)**[32] 2281 3-9-6 80 .... MickyFenton 3 36
(T P Tate) *in tch: outpcd on outside over 2f out: sn wknd* **8/1**

1620 16 5 **Carnivore**[27] 2402 7-9-6 73 .... NeilBrown(3) 5 18
(T D Barron) *chsd wnr tl wknd fr 2f out* **20/1**

1m 40.4s (0.40) **Going Correction** +0.10s/f (Good)
WFA 3 from 4yo+ 10lb **16** Ran SP% **127.6**
Speed ratings (Par 105): **102,100,98,97,97 96,95,95,95,93 92,89,82,81,78 73**
toteswinger: 1&2 £9.50, 1&3 £14.80, 2&3 £14.30. CSF £36.14 CT £242.18 TOTE £6.10: £1.50, £2.10, £2.10, £5.20; EX 32.60.
Owner The Sunnyside Racing Partnership **Bred** S W D McIlveen **Trained** Musley Bank, N Yorks

FOCUS
The third running of the consolation race for the Carlisle Bell produced another big field chasing some fair prize money. Sound form.

3265 LLOYD MOTOR GROUP CARLISLE BELL (H'CAP) 7f 200y
3:35 (3:37) (Class 4) (0-80,80) 3-Y-O+ **£19,428** (£5,781; £2,889; £721; £721) **Stalls** High

Form RPR
0020 1 **Stevie Gee (IRE)**[8] 3001 5-9-8 80 .... JoeFanning 2 92
(G A Swinbank) *midfield: effrt over 2f out: rdn to ld ins fnl f: r.o wl* **20/1**

240- 2 1/2 **Motafarred (IRE)**[235] 5382 7-9-0 75 .... FrederikTylicki(3) 4 86
(Micky Hammond) *chsd ldrs: effrt over 2f out: ev ch ins fnl f: r.o* **12/1**

2443 3 1/2 **Bold Marc (IRE)**[14] 2824 7-9-4 76 .... AndrewElliott 7 86
(K R Burke) *set decent gallop: hdd ins fnl f: kpt on same pce* **12/1**

5-52 4 1 3/4 **Observatory Star (IRE)**[15] 2787 6-9-6 78 ....(tp) DavidAllan 8 84+
(T D Easterby) *towards rr: effrt whn n.m.r over 1f out: swtchd lft and styd on fnl f: nrst fin* **13/2**[1]

6123 4 dht **Moheebb (IRE)**[12] 2894 5-9-7 79 ....(b) MickyFenton 13 85
(Mrs R A Carr) *bhd tl hdwy 2f out: kpt on fnl f: nrst fin* **9/1**[3]

6216 6 nk **Paraguay (USA)**[19] 2665 6-9-6 78 .... EdwardCreighton 3 83
(Mrs D J Sanderson) *midfield: effrt over 2f out: one pce fnl f* **10/1**

5622 7 1/2 **Sir Royal (USA)**[15] 2791 4-9-2 74 .... PJMcDonald 11 78
(G A Swinbank) *in tch: effrt over 2f out: no ex fnl f* **7/1**[2]

0532 8 1 **Kiwi Bay**[5] 3097 4-9-8 80 .... TomEaves 15 82
(M Dods) *trckd ldrs: rdn over 2f out: no ex over 1f out* **13/2**[1]

-000 9 1/2 **Major Magpie (IRE)**[39] 2073 7-9-6 78 .... PhillipMakin 12 79
(M Dods) *bhd tl sme late hdwy: nvr on terms* **18/1**

4200 10 1 **Collateral Damage (IRE)**[12] 2894 6-9-6 78 ....(t) PaulMulrennan 14 76
(T D Easterby) *towards rr: pushed along over 2f out: n.d* **14/1**

3400 11 1 1/4 **Autumn Blades (IRE)**[18] 2695 4-9-5 77 .... TonyHamilton 10 72
(A Bailey) *n.m.r sn after s: bhd: rdn over 2f out: n.d* **33/1**

-332 12 2 1/2 **Wind Shuffle (GER)**[47] 1830 6-9-8 80 .... DanielTudhope 5 70
(J S Goldie) *chsd ldrs tl wknd over 1f out* **7/1**[2]

000 13 2 3/4 **Commando Scott (IRE)**[18] 2695 8-9-8 80 ....(b[1]) PatrickMathers 16 63
(I W McInnes) *midfield: outpcd over 2f out: sn wknd* **66/1**

62-5 14 1 3/4 **Keys Of Cyprus**[32] 2266 7-9-6 78 .... AdrianTNicholls 1 57
(D Nicholls) *in tch tl edgd rt and wknd fr 2f out* **10/1**

-061 15 1 3/4 **Golden Penny**[33] 2235 4-9-0 77 .... JamieKyne(5) 9 52
(A G Foster) *hld up: pushed along over 2f out: sn wknd* **14/1**

1m 39.77s (-0.23) **Going Correction** +0.10s/f (Good) **15** Ran SP% **123.0**
Speed ratings (Par 105): **105,104,104,102,102 101,101,100,99,98 97,95,92,90,88**
toteswinger: 1&2 £67.60, 1&3 £44.70, 2&3 £29.60. CSF £243.45 CT £3018.65 TOTE £24.80: £5.30, £5.60, £3.10; EX 307.20 TRIFECTA Not won..
Owner Steve Gray **Bred** Irish National Stud **Trained** Melsonby, N Yorks

FOCUS
This race can be traced back to the seventeenth century and the Carlisle Racing Bells are the oldest known horseracing prizes in Britain, so it must be gratifying for all concerned with the contest that it continually draws a big field. Sound form, the winner up a length on this year's best.
Moheebb(IRE) Official explanation: jockey said gelding hung right
Autumn Blades(IRE) Official explanation: jockey said gelding was denied a clear run
Keys Of Cyprus Official explanation: jockey said gelding hung right

3266 GROLSCH CUMBERLAND PLATE (H'CAP) 1m 3f 107y
4:10 (4:10) (Class 4) (0-80,86) 3-Y-O+ **£19,428** (£5,781; £2,889; £1,443) **Stalls** Low

Form RPR
1403 1 **Overrule (USA)**[19] 2666 5-9-6 79 .... NeilBrown(3) 6 95
(B Ellison) *hld up on outside: smooth hdwy over 2f out: led over 1f out: sn clr* **10/1**

3-41 2 5 **Yes Mr President (IRE)**[5] 3103 4-10-2 86 6ex .... JoeFanning 10 94
(M Johnston) *cl up: led over 2f out to over 1f out: kpt on: no ch w wnr* **5/1**[1]

0000 3 2 1/2 **Kingsdale Orion (IRE)**[11] 2932 5-8-12 73 .... LanceBetts(5) 2 77
(B Ellison) *bhd tl styd on fnl 2f: nrst fin* **16/1**

-004 4 1 1/4 **Shaloo Diamond**[14] 2823 4-9-3 76 .... MichaelJStainton(3) 9 78
(R M Whitaker) *midfield: effrt 3f out: kpt on u.p fnl f* **50/1**

2321 5 3/4 **Dazzling Light (UAE)**[26] 2452 4-9-9 79 .... DanielTudhope 16 80
(J S Goldie) *trckd ldrs: effrt over 2f out: edgd rt and no ex over 1f out* **13/2**[3]

5010 6 6 **Birkside**[14] 2815 6-9-7 77 .... TonyHamilton 8 68
(Miss L A Perratt) *towards rr: hdwy over 2f out: nt pce to chal* **33/1**

5112 7 1 1/4 **Baizically (IRE)**[5] 3107 6-8-7 70 .... PaulPickard(7) 17 59
(G A Swinbank) *t.k.h early: mde most to over 2f out: wknd over 1f out* **7/1**

2121 8 nk **Joe Jo Star**[12] 2898 7-9-5 78 .... FrederikTylicki(3) 13 67
(R A Fahey) *in tch: effrt over 2f out: outpcd over 1f out* **6/1**[2]

1-42 9 2 1/4 **King Fingal (IRE)**[18] 2698 4-9-10 80 .... GrahamGibbons 3 65
(J J Quinn) *hld up: pushed along over 3f out: nvr rchd ldrs* **5/1**[1]

0462 10 4 1/2 **Hurlingham**[8] 3000 5-9-8 78 .... PaulMulrennan 1 56
(M W Easterby) *midfield: pushed along 3f out: n.d* **20/1**

021- 11 3 1/2 **West With The Wind**[81] 7446 4-9-5 75 .... MickyFenton 7 47
(T P Tate) *in tch on outside tl wknd over 2f out* **7/1**

6121 12 24 **Aureate**[2] 3223 5-9-5 80 6ex .... JamieKyne(5) 15 14
(B Ellison) *w ldr tl wknd over 3f out: t.o* **12/1**

6-60 13 9 **Crossbow Creek**[37] 2146 11-9-8 78 .... PhillipMakin 14 —
(M G Rimell) *dwlt: bhd: struggling over 4f out: t.o* **50/1**

0203 14 17 **All In The Red (IRE)**[14] 2818 4-9-0 70 ....(p) JamieMoriarty 5 —
(A Crook) *a bhd: t.o fnl 4f* **50/1**

00/6 P **Humourous (IRE)**[6] 3059 7-8-9 65 ....(bt[1]) PJMcDonald 12 —
(B Storey) *towards rr: p.u after 5f* **100/1**

2m 22.25s (-0.85) **Going Correction** +0.10s/f (Good) **15** Ran SP% **123.2**
Speed ratings (Par 105): **107,103,101,100,100 95,94,94,92,89 87,69,63,50,—**
toteswinger: 1&2 £16.80, 1&3 £44.10, 2&3 £26.70. CSF £57.85 CT £818.84 TOTE £14.50: £3.90, £2.00, £6.60; EX 82.10.
Owner The Jury's Out Partnership **Bred** Avalon Farms Inc **Trained** Norton, N Yorks

FOCUS
A valuable contest contested by some in-form and rock-solid handicappers. The form should prove to be reliable, especially as the course record for the distance was lowered. Personal bests from the fron two.
Joe Jo Star Official explanation: trainer had no explanation for the poor form shown
Humourous(IRE) Official explanation: jockey said gelding lost its action

3267 EUROPEAN BREEDERS' FUND FILLIES' H'CAP 1m 1f 61y
4:40 (4:40) (Class 4) (0-85,85) 3-Y-O+ **£6,476** (£1,927; £963; £481) **Stalls** High

Form RPR
4-44 1 **Honimiere (IRE)**[15] 2786 3-8-2 70 .... DaleGibson 5 73
(G A Swinbank) *racd keenly: set stdy pce: rdn over 2f out: hld on wl fnl f* **11/2**[3]

0022 2 1 **Snow Dancer (IRE)**[6] 3060 5-8-9 66 oh1 ....(p) TomEaves 2 68+
(H A McWilliams) *t.k.h early: prom: effrt whn nt clr run 2f out to ent fnl f: r.o wl towards fin* **6/1**

2344 3 shd **Johnston's Baby (IRE)**[13] 2859 7-8-9 66 oh7 .... AndrewMullen 8 68
(E J Alston) *hld up in tch: effrt over 2f out: kpt on u.p fnl f* **8/1**

3101 4 nk **Off Chance**[23] 2528 3-8-6 74 .... DuranFentiman 7 74
(T D Easterby) *prom: effrt 2f out: kpt on u.p fnl f* **13/8**[1]

0666 5 5 **Talk Of Saafend (IRE)**[7] 3019 4-8-9 66 oh1 .... TonyHamilton 3 56
(P Monteith) *hld up: rdn over 2f out: sn no imp* **16/1**

0434 6 1 1/2 **Black Dahlia**[16] 2768 4-8-13 70 .... JamesDoyle 1 57
(A J McCabe) *racd keenly: w wnr: rdn and wkng whn hmpd ins fnl f* **3/1**[2]

2m 1.54s (3.94) **Going Correction** +0.10s/f (Good)
WFA 3 from 4yo+ 11lb **6** Ran SP% **109.8**
Speed ratings (Par 102): **86,85,85,84,80 78**
toteswinger: 1&2 £4.50, 1&3 £5.50, 2&3 £6.10. CSF £35.18 CT £241.60 TOTE £6.20: £2.60, £2.60; EX 31.30.
Owner Mrs J Porter & Mrs David Parkinson **Bred** Peter Collier **Trained** Melsonby, N Yorks
■ Stewards' Enquiry : Tom Eaves one-day ban: careless riding (Jul 9)

FOCUS
Quite a range of abilities on show in this race, and three of them were running from out of the handicap. The early pace was steady and the form is far from reliable. The winner recorded a small personal best.

Black Dahlia Official explanation: jockey said filly lost its action

3268 EDINBURGH WOOLLEN MILL H'CAP 5f
5:15 (5:15) (Class 4) (0-85,83) 3-Y-0+ £5,504 (£1,637; £818; £408) Stalls High

Form RPR
1600 1 Sir Nod[27] 2418 7-8-11 67 PaulHanagan 9 80
(Miss J A Camacho) *trckd ldrs gng wl: n.m.r over 1f out: led ins fnl f: rdn and kpt on wl* 8/1

6040 2 2 Foxy Music[25] 2481 5-9-3 78 GaryBartley(5) 5 84
(E J Alston) *led tl ins fnl f: kpt on same pce u.p* 10/1

5306 3 hd Obe Gold[19] 2658 7-9-13 83 (v) AdrianTNicholls 8 88
(D Nicholls) *s.i.s: bhd and outpcd: swtchd lft and hdwy over 1f out: kpt on fnl f* 13/2

-004 4 ½ Dig Deep (IRE)[16] 2770 7-9-0 70 (t) GrahamGibbons 4 73
(J J Quinn) *towards rr: drvn and hdwy over 1f out: kpt on fnl f: no imp* 4/1[2]

6144 5 1¾ Restless Genius (IRE)[18] 2717 4-8-7 68 LanceBetts(5) 3 65
(B Ellison) *towards rr: rdn after 2f: no imp over 1f out* 5/1[3]

00-0 6 1½ The Nifty Fox[12] 2897 5-9-7 77 DavidAllan 7 69
(T D Easterby) *chsd ldrs tl wknd over 1f out* 8/1

150 7 3½ Loose Caboose (IRE)[14] 2801 4-8-8 64 (b) AndrewMullen 1 43
(A J McCabe) *trckd ldrs tl wknd wl over 1f out* 14/1

3054 8 5 Steelcut[4] 3149 5-9-6 79 (v[1]) FrederikTylicki(3) 2 40
(R A Fahey) *cl up: rdn and hung lft 2f out: sn wknd* 11/4[1]

60.38 secs (-0.42) **Going Correction** +0.05s/f (Good) 8 Ran SP% 114.6
Speed ratings (Par 105): **105,101,101,100,97 95,89,81**
toteswinger: 1&2 £10.70, 1&3 £6.70, 2&3 £8.90. CSF £83.40 CT £551.15 TOTE £11.80: £2.70, £3.20, £2.20; EX 79.60 Place 6: £2,029.50, Place 5: £790.95..
Owner Brian Nordan **Bred** B Nordan And Mrs S Camacho **Trained** Norton, N Yorks
■ Stewards' Enquiry : Andrew Mullen one-day ban: careless riding (Jul 9)

FOCUS
A typically trappy sprint in which any number of them could be given a chance on the best of their form. Sound form.
T/Jkpt: Not won. T/Plt: £746.10 to a £1 stake. Pool: £63,966.72. 62.58 winning tickets. T/Qpdt: £223.10 to a £1 stake. Pool: £5,097.40. 16.90 winning tickets. RY

3024 KEMPTON (A.W) (R-H)
Wednesday, June 24

OFFICIAL GOING: Standard
Wind: Strong, across towards stands Weather: Sunny, warm

3269 WEATHERBYS PRINTING APPRENTICE H'CAP (ROUND 4) 1m (P)
6:20 (6:22) (Class 6) (0-60,60) 4-Y-0+ £2,047 (£604; £302) Stalls High

Form RPR
0050 1 Sovereignty (JPN)[17] 2745 7-8-4 48 SophieDoyle(3) 2 65
(D K Ivory) *a gng wl: prom: wnt 2nd 3f out: clr w runner-up sn after: led over 1f out: pushed clr* 16/1

0003 2 4 Sion Hill (IRE)[5] 3112 8-8-5 51 (p) TobyAtkinson(5) 6 59
(John A Harris) *led: kicked on 3f out: clr w wnr sn after: hung lft 2f out: hdd over 1f out: wl btn whn hung rt fnl f* 4/1[2]

4000 3 ½ Ugenius[8] 3007 5-9-0 55 WilliamCarson 7 62
(Mrs C A Dunnett) *hld up towards rr: rdn and prog to chse clr ldng pair wl over 1f out: steadily gaining on runner-up at fin* 12/1

0050 4 10 Applesnap (IRE)[14] 2806 4-9-0 60 (p) RyanPowell(5) 1 44
(Miss Amy Weaver) *wl away but sn restrained: racd wdst of all in midfield: no ch w ldrs fr over 2f out: plugged on* 28/1

-000 5 2 Abbeygate[4] 3158 8-7-12 46 oh1 (p) TraceyAddey(7) 5 25
(T Keddy) *stdd sn after s: hld up towards rr on outer: outpcd fr 3f out: plugged on* 16/1

1000 6 2 Ramblin Bob[35] 2180 4-8-2 46 MatthewDavies(3) 11 21
(W J Musson) *chsd ldrs: outpcd whn drvn to dispute modest 3rd 2f out: fdd* 33/1

0600 7 nk Comeintothespace (IRE)[26] 2442 7-8-0 46 oh1 CharlesEddery(5) 14 20
(R A Farrant) *chsd ldr 2f: rdn 1/2-way: disp modest 3rd u.p 2f out: fdd* 22/1

0033 8 nk Baba Ghanoush[98] 867 7-8-0 46 oh1 (v) KierenFox(5) 13 19
(M J Attwater) *hld up towards rr on inner: no ch whn effrt over 2f out: no real prog* 16/1

4230 9 2¾ Flamestone[24] 2518 5-8-2 48 RichardRowe(5) 8 15
(A E Price) *s.s: wl in rr: effrt on inner over 2f out: nvr any ch* 10/1

5350 10 ½ Jessica Wigmo[19] 2686 6-8-11 52 MCGeran 3 18
(A W Carroll) *stdd s: t.k.h in rr: no ch whn asked for effrt over 2f out: brief prog over 1f out: sn wknd* 8/1

00-0 11 2½ Wivny (USA)[30] 2317 4-8-6 47 Louis-PhilippeBeuzelin 9 7
(H J Evans) *unruly bef ent stalls: s.s: mostly in last and nvr gng sweetly* 16/1

2305 12 1 Liberty Valance (IRE)[126] 590 4-9-2 57 (t) JackDean 12 15
(P M Phelan) *cl up on inner whn snatched up after 1f: midfield after: rdn and struggling over 2f out: wknd fnl f* 13/2[3]

0-00 13 2¾ Tuning Fork[165] 117 9-8-2 46 oh1 RossAtkinson(3) 4 —
(M J Attwater) *chsd ldr after 2f to 3f out: wknd rapidly 2f out* 40/1

0023 14 nk Sularno[17] 2746 5-9-0 58 (p) SimonPearce(3) 10 9
(J Pearce) *hld up in last trio: nvr any ch: wl off the pce fr over 2f out* 7/2[1]

1m 40.41s (0.61) **Going Correction** +0.125s/f (Slow) 14 Ran SP% 120.2
Speed ratings (Par 101): **101,97,96,86,84 82,82,81,79,78 76,75,72,72**
toteswinger: 1&2 £12.60, 1&3 £52.80, 2&3 £10.90. CSF £76.08 CT £821.60 TOTE £18.70: £7.00, £2.00, £5.90; EX 75.70.
Owner Radlett Racing **Bred** Darley Stud Management, L L C **Trained** Radlett, Herts
■ Stewards' Enquiry : Toby Atkinson three-day ban: careless riding (Jul 9,11,13)

FOCUS
There was a gusty breeze at the backs of the riders entering the home straight for an ordinary apprentices' handicap, run at a modest pace. They finished well strung out. Sovereignty was entitled to win this on his old form.
Wivny(USA) Official explanation: trainer said filly appeared to be in season
Sularno Official explanation: jockey said gelding never travelled

3270 BOOK NOW FOR "BEST OF BRITISH NIGHT" MAIDEN STKS 7f (P)
6:50 (6:50) (Class 5) 2-Y-0 £3,885 (£1,156; £577; £288) Stalls High

Form RPR
1 Invincible Prince (IRE) 2-9-3 0 SebSanders 1 78+
(R M Beckett) *sn trckd ldr: chal over 1f out: edgd ahd last 150yds: on top nr fin* 25/1

52 2 ½ Hasty (IRE)[18] 2711 2-8-12 0 MichaelHills 11 72
(B W Hills) *led: edgd lft over 2f out: hrd pressed over 1f out: narrowly hdd last 150yds: hld nr fin* 7/4[1]

4 3 nk Dubai Miracle (USA)[20] 2631 2-9-3 0 StephenDonohoe 6 76
(D M Simcock) *in tch in 5th: pushed along 1/2-way: effrt to go 3rd over 1f out: grad clsd on ldng pair fnl f* 7/1

4 3½ Duplicity 2-9-3 0 JimmyFortune 5 68+
(R Hannon) *dwlt: sn in tch in 6th on inner: effrt over 2f out: shkn up and kpt on one pce: no imp fnl f* 12/1

0 5 1 Chairman Pat (USA)[15] 2792 2-9-3 0 RichardKingscote 8 65
(Tom Dascombe) *chsd ldng pair: pushed along 1/2-way: lost 3rd and outpcd over 1f out: fdd* 7/2[2]

0 6 ¾ Gumnd (IRE)[12] 2889 2-9-3 0 JamieSpencer 7 63
(C E Brittain) *dwlt: t.k.h and hld up in 7th: rdn and sme prog over 2f out: hung towards nr side and no hdwy after* 4/1[3]

0 7 1½ First Cat[23] 2533 2-9-3 0 RichardMullen 10 59
(R Hannon) *chsd ldng trio: rdn 1/2-way: struggling to stay in tch over 2f out: fdd* 33/1

8 3¾ Rezwaan 2-9-3 0 RHills 3 51+
(E A L Dunlop) *settled in last trio: nudged along and no prog over 2f out* 16/1

04 9 7 Durham Town (IRE)[65] 1404 2-9-3 0 JimCrowley 2 34
(D K Ivory) *rn green in last trio: struggling fr over 2f out* 50/1

10 1 Mountrath 2-9-3 0 IanMongan 4 31
(B R Johnson) *dwlt: rn green and a last: hung lft to nr side rail in st* 28/1

1m 27.82s (1.82) **Going Correction** +0.125s/f (Slow) 10 Ran SP% 116.9
Speed ratings (Par 93): **94,93,93,89,87 87,85,81,73,72**
toteswinger: 1&2 £6.00, 1&3 £22.00, 2&3 £1.800. CSF £67.77 TOTE £15.20: £3.40, £1.10, £2.50; EX 68.50.
Owner R Roberts **Bred** Lady Legard & Sir Tatton Sykes **Trained** Whitsbury, Hants

FOCUS
Probably just a fair maiden, run at a modest pace. The first three came clear.

NOTEBOOK
Invincible Prince(IRE), a scopey individual, looked a little unfurnished in the paddock but travelled well and showed a very willing attitude to wear down the runner-up. It was a very promising introduction, particularly to win from stall 1, and there looked to be a bit more in the tank. His dam, a half-sister to the top-class sprinter Somnus, was a dual 6f winner at two and on this evidence, the colt will get further. Connections said they were surprised by the victory. (op 20-1)
Hasty(IRE), uneasy in the market near the off, set the pace and produced another professional display but was just outbattled. She is a very game filly who is sure to get off the mark sooner rather than later and is worth trying again over this trip. She will get further in time. (op 5-4 tchd 2-1 in a place)
Dubai Miracle(USA) took a while to get going but finished with a flourish and connections were said to be thrilled with his effort. He ran like he may need further. (op 15-2 tchd 8-1)
Duplicity looked well beforehand and stayed on well from a little way back once the penny dropped. He clearly has talent and could pay his way in nursery company shortly.
Chairman Pat(USA) held every chance, but faded down the stretch. The impression remains that he may need further. (op 5-1)
Gumnd(IRE), who came wide, was a little disappointing but probably more through greenness than anything else. Official explanation: jockey said colt ran too freely early (op 7-1 tchd 15-2)
Mountrath Official explanation: jockey said colt did not face the kickback

3271 EUROPEAN BREEDERS' FUND MAIDEN FILLIES' STKS 6f (P)
7:20 (7:21) (Class 5) 2-Y-0 £3,885 (£1,156; £577; £288) Stalls High

Form RPR
0 1 Raddy 'Ell Pauline (IRE)[18] 2699 2-9-0 0 NCallan 4 81+
(K A Ryan) *chsd ldr: followed her by edging lft fr over 2f out: rdn and clsd to ld last 100yds: sn in command* 14/1

2 1¼ Piccadilly Filly (IRE) 2-9-0 0 CatherineGannon 3 77
(E J Creighton) *led: hung bdly lft fr over 2f out and ended up against nr side rail over 1f out: hdd and no ex last 100yds* 50/1

0 3 ½ Hot Pursuits[35] 2175 2-9-0 0 SteveDrowne 5 76
(H Morrison) *dwlt: hld up in last trio: prog 2f out: chsd ldng pair over 1f out: kpt on same pce fnl f* 20/1

4 2½ Mellifera 2-9-0 0 AdamKirby 7 68
(W R Swinburn) *hld up in last trio: prog 2f out: chsd ldrs and in tch over 1f out: fdd fnl f* 12/1

4 5 ¾ Pastel Blue (IRE)[18] 2711 2-9-0 0 JamieSpencer 1 66
(M L W Bell) *hld up in last: swtchd lft over 2f out and ended up on nr side: styd on same pce fr over 1f out: nrst fin* 10/1[3]

0245 6 1½ Angel Of Fashion (IRE)[29] 2354 2-9-0 0 MichaelHills 2 62
(B W Hills) *chsd ldng trio: shkn up over 2f out: sn lost pl: no prog fr over 1f out* 10/1[3]

6 7 1 Rio Mist[11] 2919 2-9-0 0 JimmyFortune 6 59
(R Hannon) *hld up in 6th: shkn up and no real prog over 2f out* 9/2[2]

8 3 Slasl 2-9-0 0 SebSanders 9 50
(C E Brittain) *chsd ldng quartet: shkn up and outpcd 2f out: no imp after: wknd fnl f* 14/1

5 9 ½ Athwaab[11] 2919 2-9-0 0 RHills 8 48
(E A L Dunlop) *t.k.h early: chsd ldng pair: rdn and nt qckn over 2f out: sn lost pl and struggling: wknd fnl f* 1/1[1]

1m 13.87s (0.77) **Going Correction** +0.125s/f (Slow) 9 Ran SP% 114.1
Speed ratings (Par 90): **99,97,96,93,92 90,89,85,84**
toteswinger: 1&2 £77.80, 1&3 £43.40, 2&3 £77.80. CSF £493.67 TOTE £17.20: £3.30, £6.80, £4.70; EX 691.20.
Owner Mike McGeever & Mrs Theresa Marnane **Bred** Fattoria Di Marcianella Di Razza Del Pian Del Lago **Trained** Hambleton, N Yorks

FOCUS
A messy race, but run in a better time than the earlier maiden. A big step up from the promising winner.

NOTEBOOK
Raddy 'Ell Pauline(IRE), a strapping filly with plenty of scope, who beat one home on her Doncaster debut, was a different proposition altogether. Unlike her sire, who wanted to fight everyone when he was a juvenile, she settled well, travelled like a dream and found plenty when asked. She'll improve for this, too. (tchd 12-1 and 16-1)
Piccadilly Filly(IRE), a newcomer bred to do much better as she matures, drifted markedly left and ended up near the stands' rail, and ran on again when the winner went past. She looks a genuine sort and should get further. Official explanation: jockey said filly hung left in straight (op 66-1 tchd 33-1)
Hot Pursuits had one behind her turning in but made up plenty of ground and her run only flattened out late on. She has plenty of scope and looked as though she'd come on a bit for this. She's worth another try at this trip. (tchd 25-1)
Mellifera was nibbled at in the market and although she made a pleasing debut, she ran like she needed further. She is the sort to do better in time. (op 20-1)
Pastel Blue(IRE) confirmed the promise of her Lingfield debut, making a good deal of late headway from a long way back, having found her path blocked entering the straight. She didn't have the best draw here and her turn will come soon, probably over this trip. (op 8-1 tchd 12-1)

Athwaab, the uneasy favourite, pulled hard and failed to settle. She spoiled her chance and her run petered out tamely well before the last furlong and a half. It is worth noting that she shaped with promise on her debut, however, and she is not one to give up on just yet. Official explanation: jockey said filly resented the kickback (op 10-11 tchd 8-11)

3272 DIGIBET FILLIES' H'CAP — 6f (P)

7:50 (7:51) (Class 4) (0-80,80) 3-Y-O+ £4,727 (£1,406; £702; £351) Stalls High

Form / RPR

-155 **1** **Midnight Fantasy**[16] 2776 3-8-10 69 .... SaleemGolam 11 — 76
(Rae Guest) *chsd ldr 2f: styd handy: rdn and clsd on inner to ld over 1f out: hrd pressed fnl f: all out* **5/2**[1]

-100 **2** *shd* **Beautiful Filly**[20] 2632 3-8-8 67 .... (b[1]) RichardMullen 8 — 73
(D M Simcock) *hld up in 5th: prog fr 1/2-way: c wd and wnt 2nd jst over 1f out: persistent chal fnl f: jst failed* **17/2**

0210 **3** *3* **Dualagi**[11] 2920 5-8-9 61 oh2 .... FergusSweeney 9 — 60
(M R Bosley) *t.k.h early: hld up in rr: prog fr 1/2-way: nvr rchd ldrs but styd on to take 3rd ins fnl f* **8/1**

-004 **4** *1 3/4* **Top Town Girl**[16] 2774 3-9-7 80 .... SebSanders 6 — 71
(R M Beckett) *prom on outer: outpcd fr 2f out: plugged on again fnl f* **12/1**

0122 **5** *1/2* **Drifting Gold**[29] 2359 5-9-10 76 .... (b) AdamKirby 2 — 68+
(C G Cox) *tk fierce hold: hld up tl pressed ldr after 2f: upsides 2f out: wknd fr over 1f out* **4/1**[2]

0330 **6** *1 3/4* **Fantasy Land (IRE)**[13] 2845 3-8-11 70 .... (t) JamieSpencer 4 — 54
(B J Meehan) *awkward s: last and off the pce: nt look keen whn rdn 1/2-way: modest late prog* **7/1**[3]

001- **7** *nk* **Nobilissima (IRE)**[293] 5648 5-9-11 80 .... MarcHalford(3) 10 — 65
(Miss Tor Sturgis) *led at fast pce: edgd lft 2f out: hdd & wknd rapidly over 1f out* **10/1**

-406 **8** *1 3/4* **Lady Amberlini**[19] 2686 4-8-9 61 oh7 .... LiamJones 7 — 40
(C R Dore) *fractious bef ent stalls: outpcd in midfield bef 1/2-way: n.d after* **20/1**

40-0 **9** *3/4* **Danzadil (IRE)**[16] 2776 3-8-2 61 oh4 .... LukeMorris 1 — 36
(R A Teal) *a in rr: struggling u.p fr 1/2-way* **40/1**

53 **10** *20* **Deraaya (IRE)**[66] 1379 4-9-4 70 .... JimmyQuinn 5 — —
(K A Morgan) *settled in 6th: outpcd and drvn over 3f out: sn dropped to rr and wl btn: t.o* **9/1**

1m 13.68s (0.58) **Going Correction** +0.125s/f (Slow)
WFA 3 from 4yo+ 7lb — 10 Ran SP% **116.7**
Speed ratings (Par 102): **101,100,96,94,93 91,91,88,87,61**
toteswinger: 1&2 £7.00, 1&3 £6.40, 2&3 £19.20. CSF £24.58 CT £136.96 TOTE £4.10: £1.10, £2.30, £3.70; EX 29.50.
Owner C J Mills **Bred** C J Mills **Trained** Newmarket, Suffolk

FOCUS
An uncompetitive handicap run at a fair pace, and the front two pulled well clear of the remainder. The form looks sound and should hold up. The jockeys reported that the kickback was bad, which meant few horses were coming from off the pace and any that did should be given more credit than the bare form suggested.

3273 DIGIBET.COM H'CAP — 1m 4f (P)

8:20 (8:22) (Class 4) (0-85,84) 4-Y-O+ £4,727 (£1,406; £702; £175; £175) Stalls Centre

Form / RPR

1-40 **1** **Dakiyah (IRE)**[34] 2212 5-9-1 78 .... (p) IanMongan 12 — 86
(Mrs L J Mongan) *hld up in midfield on inner: prog to go 3rd over 3f out: chsd ldr 2f out: sn swtchd lft and drvn: styd on wl to ld last 50yds* **25/1**

4-53 **2** *3/4* **Jabal Tariq**[53] 1666 4-9-7 84 .... MichaelHills 8 — 91
(B W Hills) *mde most at gd pce: hrd rdn fr 2f out: kpt on: hdd last 50yds* **12/1**

0431 **3** *1/2* **Art Man**[43] 1966 6-9-4 81 .... GeorgeBaker 9 — 87
(G L Moore) *hld up towards rr: prog fr 4f out to go 4th jst over 3f out: drvn and nt qckn over 2f out: styd on fnl f* **11/2**[2]

6510 **4** *hd* **Cape Colony**[11] 2931 4-9-1 78 .... JimmyFortune 13 — 84
(R Hannon) *prom: chsd ldr over 3f out to 2f out: nt qckn u.p: styd on again fnl f* **14/1**

3-60 **4** *dht* **Dance The Star (USA)**[52] 1696 4-9-7 84 .... JamieSpencer 3 — 90+
(D M Simcock) *stdd s: hld up last of main gp: stl there 3f out whn nt clr run briefly: rapid prog over 2f out: hrd rdn and clsd on ldrs fnl f: too much to do* **7/1**[3]

0-22 **6** *5* **Sahrati**[40] 2055 5-8-13 76 .... (p) AlanMunro 11 — 74
(D R C Elsworth) *hld up in rr: prog to go 5th briefly 3f out but nt on terms: plugged on but no real imp after* **11/4**[1]

1250 **7** *14* **Mista Rossa**[25] 2497 4-8-8 71 .... SteveDrowne 1 — 46
(H Morrison) *prom: pushed along bef 1/2-way: lft bhd fr over 3f out* **12/1**

5-00 **8** *10* **Rowan Rio**[11] 2931 4-9-2 79 .... LiamJones 5 — 38
(W J Haggas) *hld up in last pair early: nvr on terms: outpcd fr 4f out and bhd after: t.o: pushed out* **20/1**

14-1 **9** *1 1/2* **Rotative**[19] 2684 4-9-2 79 .... AdamKirby 4 — 36
(W R Swinburn) *racd wd: hld up in rr: rdn over 5f out: wknd over 3f out: t.o and eased* **7/1**[3]

5224 **10** *3* **Wind Flow**[17] 2743 5-8-12 75 .... (v) CatherineGannon 2 — 27
(C A Dwyer) *mostly chsd ldr tl wknd rapidly over 3f out: t.o* **16/1**

00-0 **11** *17* **Island Vista**[33] 2249 4-9-4 81 .... PhilipRobinson 7 — 6
(M A Jarvis) *chsd ldrs: rdn bef 1/2-way: wknd 4f out: wl t.o* **20/1**

5-33 **12** *9* **Mega Watt (IRE)**[14] 2823 4-8-11 74 .... (b) WilliamBuick 14 — —
(W Jarvis) *s.v.s: rapid hdwy on outer to go 3rd after 4f: wknd rapidly 4f out: wl t.o* **8/1**

/520 **13** *7* **Khun John (IRE)**[23] 2552 6-8-10 73 .... ChrisCatlin 6 — —
(W J Musson) *sn last and detached: nvr wnt a yard: wl t.o* **20/1**

2m 33.36s (-1.14) **Going Correction** +0.125s/f (Slow) — 13 Ran SP% **124.2**
Speed ratings (Par 105): **108,107,107,107,107 103,94,87,86,84 73,67,62**
toteswinger: 1&2 £96.70, 1&3 £25.40, 2&3 £12.90. CSF £295.88 CT £1913.26 TOTE £33.20: £7.70, £4.70, £2.50; EX 642.70.
Owner Mrs P J Sheen **Bred** His Highness The Aga Khan's Studs S C **Trained** Epsom, Surrey
■ Stewards' Enquiry : William Buick 15-day ban (includes 14 days under "totting up" procedure; three days deferred): careless riding (Jul 10,16-26)

FOCUS
The kickback was significant, with several jockeys opting to sensibly forsake saving ground for a wider route. As such, few got into a muddling race, run at a good pace. Fair form for the grade.
Mista Rossa Official explanation: jockey said gelding suffered interference in running
Wind Flow Official explanation: jockey said gelding did not face the kickback
Island Vista Official explanation: jockey said filly did not face the kickback
Mega Watt(IRE) Official explanation: jockey said gelding missed the break

3274 DIGIBET CASINO H'CAP STKS (LONDON MILE QUALIFIER) — 1m (P)

8:50 (8:50) (Class 4) (0-80,79) 3-Y-O+ £4,727 (£1,406; £702; £351) Stalls High

Form / RPR

-161 **1** **Cool Hand Jake**[19] 2685 3-9-0 75 .... FergusSweeney 1 — 85
(P J Makin) *wl plcd: chsd ldng pair 3f out: rdn and clsd 2f out: led jst over 1f out: styd on wl* **7/2**[1]

6-21 **2** *1 1/4* **Uncle Fred**[25] 2495 4-9-12 77 .... JimCrowley 8 — 86+
(P R Chamings) *hld up in last trio: brought wd ent st and grad edgd to nr side rail: prog u.p 2f out: styd on to take 2nd ins fnl f* **5/1**[2]

4000 **3** *1 1/2* **Prince Of Thebes (IRE)**[20] 2639 8-10-0 79 .... PaulDoe 7 — 85
(M J Attwater) *led: hrd pressed and rdn over 2f out: kpt on tl hdd and no ex jst over 1f out* **6/1**[3]

-506 **4** *3/4* **Sparton Duke (IRE)**[27] 2402 4-9-6 71 .... (p) RichardMullen 11 — 75
(K A Ryan) *v s.i.s: hld up in last pair: sme prog over 2f out but nt on terms: hrd rdn and kpt on: nrst fin* **9/1**

-166 **5** *hd* **Hawaana (IRE)**[48] 1813 4-9-12 77 .... SebSanders 2 — 80+
(Eve Johnson Houghton) *prom: rdn and nt qckn over 2f out: kpt on same pce u.p fr over 1f out* **13/2**

0450 **6** *3/4* **Ocean Legend (IRE)**[16] 2775 4-9-1 71 .... Louis-PhilippeBeuzelin(5) 10 — 73
(Miss J Feilden) *towards rr: rdn sn after: 1/2-way: prog to chse ldng trio 2f out: no imp: fdd fnl f* **8/1**

532/ **7** *1/2* **Apex**[602] 6596 8-9-4 74 .... AmyBaker(5) 6 — 74
(M Hill) *prom: wnt 2nd over 3f out: chal and upsides over 2f out to over 1f out: wknd fnl f* **20/1**

4440 **8** *2 3/4* **Bromhead (USA)**[43] 1958 3-8-5 66 .... (t) LiamJones 3 — 58
(Mrs C A Dunnett) *nvr beyond midfield: outpcd wl over 2f out: plugged on one pce after* **33/1**

26-3 **9** *7* **Passage To India (IRE)**[22] 2578 3-8-8 69 .... PaulFitzsimons 9 — 45
(Miss J R Tooth) *s.i.s: a wl in rr: no prog over 2f out* **22/1**

2200 **10** *3/4* **Esteem Lord**[40] 2048 3-8-8 69 .... SteveDrowne 5 — 43
(Jamie Poulton) *nvr beyond midfield: dropped to rr u.p 3f out: no ch after* **50/1**

-210 **11** *5* **Svindal (IRE)**[51] 1740 3-8-9 70 .... (b) JamieSpencer 4 — 33
(K A Ryan) *chsd ldr to over 3f out: wd bnd after and wknd* **12/1**

2-05 **12** *13* **Penperth**[14] 2827 3-8-4 65 .... LukeMorris 12 — —
(J M P Eustace) *s.i.s: sn chsd ldrs on inner: rdn and wknd over 3f out: t.o* **14/1**

1m 40.04s (0.24) **Going Correction** +0.125s/f (Slow)
WFA 3 from 4yo+ 10lb — 12 Ran SP% **116.0**
Speed ratings (Par 105): **103,101,100,99,99 98,98,95,88,87 82,69**
toteswinger: 1&2 £2.20, 1&3 £4.90, 2&3 £7.00. CSF £18.81 CT £102.92 TOTE £4.60: £1.60, £1.80, £2.50; EX 17.30.
Owner Wedgewood Estates **Bred** Wedgewood Estates **Trained** Ogbourne Maisey, Wilts

FOCUS
A competitive if ordinary handicap run at a modest pace and, as with earlier races, it paid to race prominently owing to the kickback, which jockeys described as severe. The first two stepped forward.
Uncle Fred Official explanation: jockey said colt did not face the kickback
Svindal(IRE) Official explanation: jockey said gelding moved poorly

3275 BOOK KEMPTON TICKETS ON 0844 579 3008 H'CAP — 2m (P)

9:20 (9:20) (Class 6) (0-65,58) 4-Y-O+ £2,047 (£604; £302) Stalls High

Form / RPR

03-0 **1** **Star Of Pompey**[21] 2601 5-9-2 53 .... SebSanders 12 — 62
(A B Haynes) *prom: cl 4th 3f out: rdn to chse ldng pair over 2f out: sustained effrt to ld ins fnl f* **10/1**

3140 **2** *1* **Colourful Move**[26] 2429 4-9-6 57 .... SteveDrowne 3 — 65
(P G Murphy) *sn trckd ldr: led over 3f out: sn rdn and hrd pressed: hdd and one pce ins fnl f* **3/1**[1]

5460 **3** *1/2* **Adage**[26] 2429 6-8-9 46 .... (tp) FergusSweeney 6 — 53
(David Pinder) *hld up in rr: stdy prog on inner fr 3f out: drvn to cl on ldrs fr over 1f out: nvr quite able to chal* **6/1**[3]

-030 **4** *hd* **Go Amwell**[26] 2429 6-9-3 54 .... LiamJones 2 — 61
(J R Jenkins) *hld up in rr: prog on outer over 4f out: wnt 2nd 3f out and sn chalng: upsides over 1f out: nt qckn and lost pl fnl f* **9/2**[2]

-026 **5** *3 1/4* **Home**[13] 1378 4-9-7 58 .... (t) JimCrowley 11 — 61
(C Gordon) *hld up bhd ldrs: effrt 3f out: rdn to go 5th wl over 1f out: no imp after* **13/2**

0/3- **6** *7* **Sparkbridge (IRE)**[481] 751 6-8-1 45 .... (tp) SoniaEaton(7) 9 — 40
(S C Burrough) *t.k.h early: hld up in last: no prog tl shuffled along into modest 6th over 1f out: no ch* **33/1**

05-0 **7** *5* **Arabian Sun**[21] 2127 5-8-8 45 .... (vt) ChrisCatlin 8 — 34
(C P Morlock) *chsd ldrs: rdn 6f out: lost pl and struggling 4f out: n.d after* **33/1**

/2-0 **8** *3/4* **Munching Mike (IRE)**[22] 2580 6-8-9 46 .... (p) StephenDonohoe 5 — 34
(K M Prendergast) *hld up in midfield: rdn and lft bhd by ldrs fr 3f out: wknd over 1f out* **20/1**

-550 **9** *2* **Flowerbud**[9] 2971 4-9-2 53 .... FrankieMcDonald 10 — 39
(G A Ham) *hld up in rr: pushed along over 5f out: struggling over 3f out: sn no ch* **33/1**

060- **10** *3 1/2* **Black Cloud**[210] 3448 6-8-3 45 .... Louis-PhilippeBeuzelin(5) 4 — 26
(G P Enright) *prom: rdn to chal 3f out: wknd rapidly over 2f out* **10/1**

50-6 **11** *5* **Looping The Loop (USA)**[21] 2601 4-8-11 48 .... RichardKingscote 7 — 23
(J G Portman) *led: needed urging to go rnd bnd 9f out: urged again over 5f out: hdd over 3f out: wknd rapidly 2f out* **12/1**

0-26 **P** **My Mate Granite (USA)**[89] 978 5-8-10 47 .... JimmyQuinn 1 — —
(H J Collingridge) *hld up in midfield: rdn 4f out: wknd 3f out: bhd whn p.u ins fnl f: dead* **16/1**

3m 33.84s (3.74) **Going Correction** +0.125s/f (Slow) — 12 Ran SP% **116.1**
Speed ratings (Par 101): **95,94,94,94,92 89,86,86,85,83 80,—**
toteswinger: 1&2 £8.10, 1&3 £13.70, 2&3 £5.50. CSF £37.69 CT £196.74 TOTE £15.60: £3.60, £1.20, £2.50; EX 42.20 Place 6 £2,324.20, Place 5 £655.42..
Owner double-r-racing.com **Bred** Cheveley Park Stud Ltd **Trained** Limpley Stoke, Bath

FOCUS
Those who raced prominently held sway in a very modest handicap, as they had throughout the meeting. Modest from, with a personal best from the winner.
Munching Mike(IRE) Official explanation: jockey said gelding had no more to give

T/Plt: £4,737.00 to a £1 stake. Pool: £61,322.23. 9.45 winning tickets. T/Qpdt: £390.70 to a £1 stake. Pool: £4,646.44. 8.80 winning tickets. JN

[2945]SALISBURY (R-H)

Wednesday, June 24

OFFICIAL GOING: Good to firm (9.1)
Wind: Brisk behind Weather: Bright

3276 LEVY BOARD H'CAP — 1m 6f 21y
1:35 (1:36) (Class 4) (0-85,83) 3-Y-0 £4,727 (£1,406; £702; £351) Stalls Far side

Form RPR
3-12 1 **King Of Wands**[34] 2208 3-9-7 **83** EddieAhern 3 88+
(J L Dunlop) *trckd ldr: led 3f out: drvn along over 1f out: readily* **7/4**[1]
6141 2 ¾ **Darley Sun (IRE)**[13] 2838 3-9-5 **81** DarryllHolland 1 85+
(D M Simcock) *sn led: hdd 3f out: sn rdn: rallied fr over 1f out and kpt on but a hld by wnr* **2/1**[2]
3-13 3 1 **Cry For The Moon (USA)**[34] 2208 3-9-5 **81** JimCrowley 4 84
(Mrs A J Perrett) *trckd ldrs: rdn over 2f out: nvr gng pce to rch wnr and one pce fnl f* **11/2**
-123 4 3½ **Non Dom (IRE)**[18] 2715 3-8-13 **75** SteveDrowne 2 73
(H Morrison) *in tch: rdn over 3f out: no imp on ldrs and wknd over 1f out* **7/2**[3]
3m 5.04s (-2.36) **Going Correction** -0.40s/f (Firm) 4 Ran SP% **107.3**
Speed ratings (Par 101): **90,89,89,87**
CSF £5.46 TOTE £2.40; EX 5.50.
Owner Normandie Stud Ltd **Bred** Normandie Stud Ltd **Trained** Arundel, W Sussex

FOCUS
A small field, but this was still a competitive staying handicap for 3yos. They didn't go much of a gallop. The winner and third were close to their previous Sandown form.

3277 EBF ASHBRITTLE STUD MAIDEN FILLIES' STKS — 5f
2:10 (2:11) (Class 4) 2-Y-0 £4,695 (£1,397; £698; £348) Stalls High

Form RPR
2 1 **Swan Wings**[12] 2887 2-9-0 0 WilliamBuick 6 79+
(A M Balding) *mde all: shkn up 2f out: forged clr fnl f: comf* **10/11**[1]
2 2 **Roodle** 2-9-0 0 StephenCarson 5 72+
(Eve Johnson Houghton) *s.i.s: sn rcvrd to chse ldrs: drvn along 2f out: chsd wnr ins fnl f but a readily hld* **14/1**
3 ¾ **Forest Crown** 2-9-0 0 SebSanders 4 69
(R M Beckett) *trckd wnr: drvn to chal 1/2-way: outpcd appr fnl f and lost 2nd ins fnl f* **7/2**[2]
4 2¾ **Full Mandate (IRE)** 2-9-0 0 JimmyFortune 1 62+
(R Hannon) *wnt lft s: in rr: rcvrd to trck ldrs 3f out: pushed along 2f out: wknd over 1f out* **9/2**[3]
5 1 **Oasis Jade** 2-9-0 0 SteveDrowne 3 56
(G L Moore) *s.i.s: in rr: pushed along and sme prog 2f out: sn green and hung rt: wknd over 1f out* **11/1**
6 10 **Lenkiewicz** 2-8-11 0 JamesMillman[(3)] 7 20
(B R Millman) *chsd ldrs: rdn 3f out: wknd sn after* **14/1**
60.68 secs (-0.32) **Going Correction** -0.40s/f (Firm) 6 Ran SP% **114.5**
Speed ratings (Par 92): **86,82,81,77,75 59**
toteswinger: 1&2 £5.30, 1&3 £1.70, 2&3 £7.60. CSF £16.04 TOTE £1.80: £1.20, £5.50; EX 15.40.
Owner Nicholas Jones **Bred** Coln Valley Stud **Trained** Kingsclere, Hants

FOCUS
Just a modest fillies' maiden. The winner stepped forward from her good debut run and the race is rated through her.

NOTEBOOK
Swan Wings, who showed plenty of speed before being cut down late on by a useful sort on her debut at Sandown, was soon in front and had the race won well over a furlong out. She is evidently a very capable filly and connections will consider the Cherry Hinto for her, with a step up to 6f expected to suit. (op 5-4 tchd 6-4)
Roodle, whose dam was a 5f winner, travelled well in behind the speed and kept on nicely once coming under pressure without being able to match the winner. This was a very pleasing start and she looks capable of landing a minor maiden. (op 9-1)
Forest Crown, whose sister Riotous Applause was a 6f juvenile winner, showed speed and ran well, but the winner was a bit too wise for her first time. (op 4-1 tchd 9-2)
Full Mandate(IRE), half-sister to a couple of juvenile winners, showed signs of greenness on this racecourse debut and should benefit from the experience. (op 4-1 tchd 10-3)
Oasis Jade comes from a successful family and she hinted at ability following a slow start, showing distinct signs of inexperience in the process. (op 9-1 tchd 13-2)
Lenkiewicz, by Oratorio, out of a 1m2f winner, is going to need further than this and she dropped right out. (op 12-1)

3278 SMITH & WILLIAMSON MAIDEN FILLIES' STKS — 6f 212y
2:45 (2:46) (Class 5) 3-Y-0 £3,885 (£1,156; £577; £288) Stalls High

Form RPR
22 1 **Super Academy (USA)**[112] 752 3-9-0 0 ShaneKelly 7 75
(J A Osborne) *trckd ldr: led over 3f out: quickned and over 2 l clr appr fnl f: shkn up ins fnl f: jst hld on* **3/1**[2]
2 2 shd **Global Conquest (IRE)**[34] 2205 3-9-0 0 MartinDwyer 10 75+
(Pat Eddery) *chsd ldrs: rdn over 2f out: swtchd lft then hung lft ins fnl f and styd on strly u.p: fin wl: jst failed* **3/1**[2]
32-4 3 2¼ **Poyle Meg**[15] 2795 3-9-0 76 SebSanders 2 69
(R M Beckett) *sn in tch: rdn and hdwy over 2f out: disp 2nd over 1f out but nvr nr wnr: one pce whn pushed lft ins fnl f* **11/4**[1]
00- 4 3½ **Lucy Brown**[284] 5882 3-9-0 0 JimmyFortune 5 60+
(R Hannon) *t.k.h: led: hdd over 3f out: rdn and green 2f out: wknd and hung lft and rt appr fnl f* **16/1**
0-60 5 1½ **Aphrodite's Rock**[35] 2179 3-9-0 68 JimCrowley 9 56
(Miss Gay Kelleway) *chsd ldrs: rdn along 3f out: sn one pce and no ch ins fnl 2f* **22/1**
60 6 nk **Missrepresentation**[10] 2947 3-9-0 0 RichardSmith 3 55
(J C Fox) *chsd ldrs tl wknd 1f out* **50/1**
7 4 **Early Morning Rain (IRE)** 3-9-0 0 ChrisCatlin 4 44
(Rae Guest) *t.k.h: in tch: rdn over 2f out and sn wknd* **13/2**[3]
00 8 4 **High Morning**[30] 2318 3-9-0 0 (t) FergusSweeney 6 33
(D M Simcock) *slowly away: t.k.h early: a towards rr* **25/1**
9 3¼ **Balzarine** 3-9-0 0 JimmyQuinn 8 24
(M Blanshard) *s.i.s: a towards rr* **50/1**
1m 26.53s (-2.47) **Going Correction** -0.40s/f (Firm) 9 Ran SP% **108.0**
Speed ratings (Par 96): **98,97,95,91,89 89,84,80,76**
toteswinger: 1&2 £1.50, 1&3 £2.10, 2&3 £2.10. CSF £10.20 TOTE £3.40: £1.30, £1.10, £1.30; EX 7.00.
Owner Ben Arbib & Partners **Bred** Airlie Stud **Trained** Upper Lambourn, Berks
■ Highland Starlight was withdrawn (9/1, spread plate.). Deduct 10p in the £ under R4.
■ Stewards' Enquiry : Martin Dwyer caution: careless riding.

FOCUS
Not the strongest of fillies' maidens, and the time was slow. The winner is rated up a stone.
High Morning Official explanation: jockey said filly would not face the tongue strap

3279 RACING HERE ON SUNDAY H'CAP — 1m 1f 198y
3:15 (3:17) (Class 5) (0-75,75) 3-Y-0 £3,238 (£963; £481; £240) Stalls High

Form RPR
-223 1 **Mabuya (UAE)**[26] 2432 3-9-7 **75** NCallan 9 84
(P J Makin) *mde all: rdn and edgd lft fnl f: styd on strly* **2/1**[1]
0640 2 2¾ **Peace Corps**[12] 2892 3-9-2 **70** (v[1]) JimmyFortune 11 74
(J R Fanshawe) *chsd ldrs: rdn and hung lft 2f out: sn chsng wnr: hung rt u.p and no imp fnl f* **25/1**
2304 3 1¾ **Everaard (USA)**[9] 2982 3-8-11 **65** DaneO'Neill 10 65
(D R C Elsworth) *chsd ldrs: rdn along fr 3f out: styd on fnl f but nvr gng pce to rch ldng duo* **15/2**
3-03 4 1½ **Wee Sonny (IRE)**[23] 2535 3-9-6 **74** RichardKingscote 8 71
(Tom Dascombe) *chsd wnr: rdn and hung lft 2f out: lost 2nd sn after: wknd fnl f* **6/1**[3]
0-05 5 4 **Carte D'Oro (IRE)**[13] 2848 3-8-11 **65** SebSanders 4 54
(R M Beckett) *sn in tch: rdn over 3f out: u.p and no ch fnl 2f* **25/1**
6223 6 2½ **Cloudesley (IRE)**[11] 2925 3-9-2 **70** (p) WilliamBuick 3 54
(A M Balding) *in tch: rdn over 3f out and sn btn* **5/2**[2]
6-55 7 hd **Hambledon Hill**[12] 2884 3-8-13 **67** EddieAhern 6 51
(R Hannon) *in rr: rdn over 3f out: n.d* **20/1**
00-5 8 3¼ **Water Hen (IRE)**[23] 2540 3-8-11 **65** SteveDrowne 1 42
(R Charlton) *wnt lft s: nvr bttr than mid-div and bhd fnl 3f* **16/1**
6-44 9 4 **Brad's Luck (IRE)**[15] 2779 3-8-7 **61** JimmyQuinn 5 30
(M Blanshard) *a towards rr* **16/1**
1-06 10 7 **Aboukir**[13] 2845 3-8-13 **67** MartinDwyer 7 22
(P F I Cole) *a towards rr* **18/1**
2-00 11 3¼ **Leelu**[25] 2498 3-8-10 **64** JimCrowley 2 13
(D W P Arbuthnot) *wnt lft s: nvr bttr then mid-div and bhd fnl 3f* **66/1**
2m 7.04s (-2.86) **Going Correction** -0.40s/f (Firm) 11 Ran SP% **118.9**
Speed ratings (Par 99): **95,92,91,90,87 85,84,82,79,73 70**
toteswinger: 1&2 £14.80, 1&3 £3.50, 2&3 £22.20. CSF £62.82 CT £327.63 TOTE £3.20: £1.50, £6.10, £2.10; EX 67.10.
Owner R A Henley **Bred** Darley **Trained** Ogbourne Maisey, Wilts

FOCUS
A fair handicap for the grade with some good formlines on show. The pace was not strong and the first quartet were always to the fore.
Wee Sonny(IRE) Official explanation: jockey said colt hung both ways

3280 ASHBRITTLE STUD BIBURY CUP (H'CAP) — 1m 4f
3:50 (3:51) (Class 3) (0-95,86) 3-Y-0 £7,477 (£2,239; £1,119; £560; £279) Stalls High

Form RPR
1-60 1 **Classic Vintage (USA)**[32] 2275 3-9-4 **85** JimCrowley 1 95+
(Mrs A J Perrett) *in rr but wl in tch: drvn and qcknd to chse ldr 2f out: led appr fnl f: drvn ins fnl f: in command cl home* **13/2**
2311 2 ½ **Akmal**[23] 2545 3-9-5 **86** RHills 4 95
(J L Dunlop) *in rr but wl in tch: hdwy on outside fr 3f out: chal u.p 1f out: styd on but a hld by wnr* **9/4**[1]
-311 3 ¾ **Final Victory**[14] 2829 3-9-4 **85** LPKeniry 3 93
(A M Balding) *chsd ldrs: wnt 2nd 7f out: led over 2f out: sn rdn: hdd appr fnl f: styd on same pce ins fnl f* **7/2**[2]
2-14 4 6 **History Lesson**[18] 2701 3-9-2 **83** JimmyFortune 2 81
(R Hannon) *led 1f: styd chsng ldr to 7f out: rdn 3f out: wknd ins fnl 2f* **4/1**[3]
1-50 5 15 **Simple Solution (USA)**[32] 2275 3-9-5 **86** MichaelHills 5 69
(B W Hills) *led after 1f: hdd over 2f out: sn wknd: eased whn no ch* **16/1**
2m 33.17s (-4.83) **Going Correction** -0.40s/f (Firm) 5 Ran SP% **92.2**
Speed ratings (Par 103): **100,99,99,95,85**
toteswinger: 1&2 £5.50. CSF £14.79 TOTE £6.50: £2.50, £1.10; EX 16.70.
Owner R & P Scott A & J Powell Gallagher Stud **Bred** Gallagher's Stud **Trained** Pulborough, W Sussex
■ Battle Painter was withdrawn on vet's advice (9/2, deduct 15p in the £ under R4.)

FOCUS
This is usually a good handicap, though it was weakened a tad by the late withdrawal of Battle Planner. They went just a steady gallop. The form has been rated on the positive side.

NOTEBOOK
Classic Vintage(USA) had been most progressive at two and didn't have conditions in his favour when unable to cope with the ground at Haydock last time. Back on a faster surface here, he was able to continue his earlier progression, staying on too strongly for a progressive pair. A fine, big sort, he is almost certainly capable of better and may well head to Glorious Goodwood for a 1m4f 3yo handicap before a possible tilt at the Melrose at York later in the season. (op 8-1)
Akmal, a narrow winner at Thirsk on his handicap debut, was up 6lb in a stronger race. He held every chance over a furlong out but was unable to stay on as well as the winner. (op 3-1 tchd 10-3)
Final Victory, up 5lb having won a decent race at Kempton last time, went on two out and held every chance if good enough, but the front pair mastered him in the final furlong. (op 3-1 tchd 11-4)
History Lesson, fourth in what is usually a competitive handicap over 1m2f at Epsom on Derby Day, didn't get home on this first try at 1m4f. (op 3-1 tchd 9-2)
Simple Solution(USA) has done little in three starts this season to suggest she has progressed from two to three and struggled badly off a mark of 86. (op 11-1 tchd 20-1)

3281 NEW FOREST FARM MACHINERY / JOHN DEERE FILLIES' H'CAP — 6f
4:20 (4:20) (Class 5) (0-70,68) 3-Y-0 £3,238 (£963; £481; £240) Stalls High

Form RPR
00-0 1 **Rafta (IRE)**[31] 2298 3-7-12 **52** JosephineBruning[(7)] 2 65
(T T Clement) *s.i.s: in rr tl gd hdwy on outside fr 2f out: str run to ld fnl 100yds: won gng away* **66/1**
3642 2 ½ **Itsher**[9] 2973 3-8-3 **55** (b) WilliamCarson[(5)] 5 66
(S C Williams) *chsd ldrs: rdn over 2f out: led jst ins fnl f: hdd and one pce fnl 100yds* **7/2**[1]
0-50 3 3¼ **Leadenhall Lass (IRE)**[20] 2632 3-9-7 **68** IanMongan 10 69
(P M Phelan) *sn led: rdn over 2f out: hdd jst ins fnl f: wknd fnl 100yds* **7/1**[3]
-055 4 ½ **Countess Zara (IRE)**[15] 2797 3-9-1 **62** (b[1]) WilliamBuick 3 61
(A M Balding) *trckd ldrs: rdn over 2f out and sme prog: nvr on terms and kpt on same pce* **6/1**[2]
0-52 5 2¼ **Morning Queen (IRE)**[11] 2913 3-9-0 **61** AdamKirby 4 53
(C G Cox) *chsd ldrs: rdn over 2f out: styd wl there tl wknd fnl f: eased whn no ch fnl 100yds* **7/2**[1]
4603 6 1 **Athania (IRE)**[14] 2827 3-9-7 **68** NCallan 6 57
(A P Jarvis) *chsd ldrs: rdn 3f out: styd chsng ldrs tl wknd ins fnl f* **7/1**[3]

The Form Book, Raceform Ltd, Compton, RG20 6NL

650 **7** *1 1/2* **Marina Walk**[94] 920 3-8-8 **55**.................................... SteveDrowne 11 39
(H Morrison) *in tch: rdn and outpcd 1/2-way: sme prog and rdn 2f out: wknd appr fnl f* **8/1**

0042 **8** *1/2* **Avrilo**[19] 2654 3-8-3 **50**.................................... CatherineGannon 7 32
(M S Saunders) *in rr: rdn 3f out: sme prog 2f out: nvr gng pce to get into contention and wknd over 1f out* **7/1**[3]

0400 **9** *3 1/2* **Hint Of Honey**[37] 2132 3-8-3 **50**.................................... ChrisCatlin 1 21
(A G Newcombe) *s.i.s: outpcd most of way* **50/1**

00-0 **10** *9* **Rest By The River**[34] 2205 3-8-12 **59**.................................... DaneO'Neill 8 —
(A G Newcombe) *a towards rr* **25/1**

210 **11** *16* **Five Gold Rings (IRE)**[89] 986 3-9-4 **65**.................................... ShaneKelly 9 —
(J A Osborne) *trckd ldr: travelling ok whn lost action and eased 2f out* **18/1**

1m 12.73s (-2.07) **Going Correction** -0.40s/f (Firm) 11 Ran SP% **119.9**
Speed ratings (Par 96): **97,96,92,91,88 87,85,84,79,67 46**
toteswinger: 1&2 £55.10, 1&3 £73.00, 2&3 £6.80. CSF £291.32 CT £1934.10 TOTE £98.80: £13.70, £1.50, £2.50; EX 552.30.
Owner R L Gray **Bred** Thomas And Linda Heffernan **Trained** Newmarket, Suffolk

FOCUS
Quite a shock in this handicap, which was contested by mainly exposed fillies. The runner-up looks the best guide.
Rafta(IRE) Official explanation: trainer said, regarding apparent improvement in form, that this was the filly's 2nd run for him and 1st in a handicap.

3282 MOLSON COORS NOEL CANNON MEMORIAL TROPHY H'CAP 1m
4:55 (4:56) (Class 2) (0-100,97) 3-Y-O+
£11,215 (£3,358; £1,679; £840; £419; £210) **Stalls** High

Form RPR

04-0 **1** **We'll Come**[46] 1861 5-9-11 **94**.................................... (b) DarrylHolland 7 106
(M A Jarvis) *hld up in rr but in tch: stdy hdwy on bit on rails over 1f out: reminder: hld hd sltly high but qcknd to ld ins fnl f: sn in command: easily* **11/4**[1]

1220 **2** *3 1/2* **Mujood**[14] 2822 6-9-5 **88**.................................... StephenCarson 2 92
(Eve Johnson Houghton) *pressed ldr tl rdn to ld ins fnl 2f: hdd ins fnl f: sn no ch w wnr but kpt on wl for 2nd* **9/1**

2520 **3** *2 1/4* **Viva Vettori**[39] 2083 5-9-5 **88**.................................... MartinDwyer 3 87
(D R C Elsworth) *t.k.h early: trckd ldrs: pushed along 3f out: drvn to chal ins fnl 2f: wknd fnl f* **3/1**[2]

3100 **4** *3 1/4* **L'Hirondelle (IRE)**[46] 1861 5-9-2 **85**.................................... (e[1]) PaulDoe 8 76
(M J Attwater) *trckd ldrs: rdn over 2f out: no imp and sn btn* **11/4**[1]

1110 **5** *1 3/4* **Global**[11] 2925 3-8-8 **87**.................................... ChrisCatlin 9 74
(R Hannon) *slt ld tl hdd ins fnl 2f: wknd appr fnl f* **4/1**[3]

060- **6** *6* **Classic Port (FR)**[375] 3040 5-9-11 **97**.................................... MarcHalford(3) 5 71
(J R Best) *chsd ldrs tl wknd qckly over 2f out* **16/1**

1m 38.47s (-5.03) **Going Correction** -0.40s/f (Firm) course record
WFA 3 from 5yo+ 10lb 6 Ran SP% **114.2**
Speed ratings (Par 109): **109,105,103,100,98 92**
toteswinger: 1&2 £3.90, 1&3 £2.30, 2&3 £4.20. CSF £27.40 CT £78.05 TOTE £4.00: £2.10, £2.20; EX 19.90.
Owner Stephen Dartnell **Bred** J A And P Duffy **Trained** Newmarket, Suffolk

FOCUS
An ordinary handicap for the grade. It has been rated around the runner-up.

NOTEBOOK
We'll Come didn't have to work for his victory. He has received no help from the Handicapper, but was able to outclass his rivals on this drop in grade, always travelling strongly under Holland and coming clear, despite carrying his head high under pressure. It would be a surprise, however, were he able to follow up. (op 5-2 tchd 3-1)
Mujood ran no sort of race at Haydock last time, but had earlier been in good form and he fared a lot better here. (op 15-2 tchd 10-1)
Viva Vettori ran one of his better races, but is not the most consistent and remains above his last winning mark. (op 5-1)
L'Hirondelle(IRE) ran well when ninth at 100/1 in the Victoria Cup and was a shade disappointing in the first-time eyeshield. His rider reported he disliked the ground. Official explanation: jockey said gelding was unsuited by the good to firm ground (op 7-2)
Global had been on a roll until hanging badly left and finishing a well-beaten last of 12 at Sandown last time and this effort seemed to confirm he has lost the plot. (op 7-2 tchd 10-3)
Classic Port(FR) was always likely to struggle on this return from a year off. (op 12-1 tchd 11-1)

3283 BOLLINGER CHAMPAGNE CHALLENGE SERIES H'CAP (FOR GENTLEMAN AMATEUR RIDERS) 6f 212y
5:30 (5:30) (Class 6) (0-65,63) 4-Y-0+ **£2,935** (£910; £454; £227) **Stalls** High

Form RPR

6500 **1** **Gallego**[13] 2851 7-10-12 **59**.................................... MrMPrice(5) 12 66
(R J Price) *s.i.s: in rr: stl plenty to do 2f out: str run appr fnl f to ld fnl 30yds: won gng away* **15/2**

6004 **2** *3/4* **Towy Boy (IRE)**[12] 2879 4-10-7 **54**.................................... (v) MrCMartin(5) 9 59
(I A Wood) *chsd ldrs: wnt 2nd 4f out: drvn 2f out: led 1f out: hdd and no ex fnl 30yds* **12/1**

5056 **3** *shd* **Ishibee (IRE)**[18] 2712 5-10-0 **47**.................................... (p) MrAshleyBird(5) 5 52
(J J Bridger) *in rr: hdwy 3f out: drvn to chal ins fnl f: no ex cl home* **20/1**

0-25 **4** *3/4* **Vanadium**[5] 3104 7-11-2 **61**.................................... MrJoshuaMoore(3) 1 64
(G L Moore) *hld up in rr: stdy hdwy over 2f out: rdn: hung rt and ev ch 1f out: one pce ins fnl f* **7/2**[1]

0501 **5** *2* **Golden Prospect**[17] 2736 5-10-10 **57**.................................... MrJSherwood(5) 4 55
(J W Hills) *mid-div: pushed along 3f out: sme prog fnl f: kpt on but nvr in contention* **5/1**[2]

0626 **6** *nk* **Magroom**[9] 2977 5-11-7 **63**.................................... WilliamBiddick 10 63+
(R J Hodges) *mid-div: pushed along 3f out: n.m.r on rail whn continually squeezed through ins fnl f but no imprssion on ldrs fnl 75yds* **5/1**[2]

6600 **7** *5* **Stamford Blue**[29] 2353 8-11-5 **61**.................................... (b) MrSWalker 11 44
(R A Harris) *sn led: rdn over 2f out: hdd 1f out: sn wknd* **7/1**

336 **8** *3/4* **Castano**[15] 2794 5-10-13 **60**.................................... (p) MrPMillman(5) 2 41
(B R Millman) *chsd ldrs: rdn 3f out: wknd 2f out* **11/2**[3]

0000 **9** *2* **Wicksy Creek**[35] 2180 4-9-10 **45**.................................... MrMMarris(7) 8 21
(G C Bravery) *plld hrd: chsd ldrs: rdn 3f out: wknd over 2f out* **50/1**

016- **10** *9* **Connor's Choice**[214] 7416 4-10-10 **59**.................................... MrOJMurphy(7) 7 11
(Andrew Turnell) *a towards rr* **10/1**

0006 **11** *2 1/2* **Whinhill House**[17] 2736 9-9-13 **48**.................................... (b[1]) MrJPearce(7) 6 —
(T T Clement) *chasde ldrs over 4f* **33/1**

1m 27.32s (-1.68) **Going Correction** -0.40s/f (Firm) 11 Ran SP% **121.7**
Speed ratings (Par 101): **93,92,92,91,88 88,82,81,79,69 66**
toteswinger: 1&2 £17.30, 1&3 £22.90, 2&3 £16.70. CSF £95.08 CT £1767.06 TOTE £10.20: £3.50, £4.30, £3.60; EX 137.10 Place 6: £25.97, Place 5: £10.26..
Owner My Left Foot Racing Syndicate **Bred** Mrs C C Regalado-Gonzalez **Trained** Ullingswick, H'fords
■ Stewards' Enquiry : William Biddick two-day ban: careless riding (Jul 16, 24)

FOCUS
This was a low-grade amateur riders' handicap. There was an early dawdle, but the pace soon picked up before collapsing late on. The winner did not need to match this year's best form.
T/Plt: £45.40 to a £1 stake. Pool: £49,622.07. 797.30 winning tickets. T/Qpdt: £9.00 to a £1 stake. Pool: £3,700.60. 303.40 winning tickets. ST

3284 - 3290a (Foreign Racing) - See Raceform Interactive

3017 HAMILTON (R-H)
Thursday, June 25

OFFICIAL GOING: Good to firm (good in places; 10.3)
Rail realignment around the loop reduced advertised distances on the round course by around 30yards.
Wind: Breezy, half against Weather: Cloudy

3291 SUPPORT ANDY MURRAY LADY AMATEUR RIDERS' H'CAP 1m 5f 9y
7:00 (7:00) (Class 6) (0-65,65) 4-Y-0+ **£2,307** (£709; £354) **Stalls** High

Form RPR

0-10 **1** **Hi Dancer**[86] 107 6-10-0 **62**.................................... MissEStead(5) 5 73+
(P C Haslam) *prom: led over 3f out: drew clr over 1f out* **8/1**

0022 **2** *4* **Border Tale**[27] 2448 9-9-0 **50**.................................... MissRebeccaSparkes(7) 11 53
(James Moffatt) *hld up: rdn 4f out: hdwy wl over 1f out: styd on to go 2nd nr fin: no ch w wnr* **10/1**

3243 **3** *hd* **Edas**[18] 2743 7-10-3 **65**.................................... MissHCuthbert(5) 8 68
(T A K Cuthbert) *hld up: hdwy over 3f out: hung rt 2f out: wnt 2nd briefly wl ins fnl f: no imp* **7/1**

0454 **4** *1* **Wulimaster (USA)**[20] 2656 6-9-3 **46** oh1.................................... MissSBrotherton 12 47
(D W Barker) *hld up: hdwy and prom 4f out: chsd wnr over 2f out: one pce fr over 1f out: lost two pls nr fin* **14/1**

4044 **5** *6* **Jane Of Arc (FR)**[6] 3107 5-9-3 **46** oh1.................................... (v[1]) MrsCBartley 2 38
(J S Goldie) *prom: drvn and outpcd over 3f out: plugged on fnl f: no imp* **11/2**[2]

-130 **6** *nse* **Rare Coincidence**[65] 1439 8-10-6 **63**.................................... (p) MissLEllison 10 55
(R F Fisher) *led to 1/2-way: outpcd over 3f out: drifted rt and no imp fnl 2f* **7/2**[1]

414- **7** *1 1/4* **Simple Jim (FR)**[35] 7696 5-9-13 **56**.................................... MissADeniel 9 46
(J Hetherton) *hld up: stdy hdwy over 4f out: outpcd over 2f out: n.d after* **8/1**

65-6 **8** *4* **Midnite Blews (IRE)**[7] 3068 4-9-4 **52**.................................... (t) MissAngelaBarnes(5) 6 36
(M A Barnes) *cl up: led 1/2-way to over 3f out: wknd over 2f out* **9/1**

9 *7* **Sultana (GER)**[27] 1448 7-8-10 **46** oh1.................................... MissPhillipaTutty(7) 3 20
(Mrs L C Jewell) *midfield: outpcd over 3f out: sn btn* **80/1**

00/0 **10** *1 3/4* **Beauchamp Unique**[3] 3223 6-9-0 **50**.................................... MissNVorster(7) 4 21
(E J Cooper) *unruly bef s: t.k.h: hld up in midfield: outpcd over 3f out: sn btn* **66/1**

0-40 **11** *4 1/2* **Front Rank (IRE)**[7] 3068 9-9-3 **51**.................................... MissECSayer(5) 1 15
(Mrs Dianne Sayer) *prom: lost pl over 5f out: n.d after* **6/1**[3]

2m 50.99s (-2.91) **Going Correction** -0.25s/f (Firm) 11 Ran SP% **115.1**
Speed ratings (Par 101): **98,95,95,94,91 91,90,87,83,82 79**
toteswinger: 1&2 £16.30, 1&3 £9.50, 2&3 £5.40 CSF £83.53 CT £588.52 TOTE £7.80: £3.60, £2.90, £2.40; EX 62.50.
Owner Middleham Park Racing & R Tocher **Bred** Mrs E Roberts **Trained** Middleham Moor, N Yorks

FOCUS
A weak lady amateur riders' handicap but run at a fair pace. The form is rated through the runner-up.
Wulimaster(USA) Official explanation: jockey said gelding lost its action
Rare Coincidence Official explanation: jockey said gelding ran too free

3292 RACING UK MAIDEN AUCTION STKS 6f 5y
7:30 (7:30) (Class 6) 2-Y-0 **£2,266** (£674; £337; £168) **Stalls** Low

Form RPR

03 **1** **Colonel Mak**[11] 2940 2-8-10 0.................................... PhillipMakin 1 76+
(D H Brown) *trckd ldrs gng wl: led over 1f out: shkn up and qckd clr fnl f: readily* **11/4**[2]

2 *3 3/4* **Living It Large (FR)** 2-8-9 0.................................... SladeO'Hara(5) 2 69
(R F Fisher) *cl up: rdn over 2f out: kpt on fnl f: no ch w wnr* **40/1**

6 **3** *hd* **Sweet Mirasol (IRE)**[34] 2226 2-8-10 0.................................... SilvestreDeSousa 4 64
(K A Ryan) *led to over 1f out: kpt on same pce* **11/2**[3]

232 **4** *nk* **Orpen Arms (IRE)**[13] 2896 2-8-6 0 ow1.................................... TonyHamilton 6 59
(R A Fahey) *trckd ldrs: outpcd 2f out: kpt on wl towards fin* **11/4**[2]

5 *1 1/2* **Fantastic Strike (IRE)** 2-8-10 0.................................... JoeFanning 5 59
(M Johnston) *dwlt: racd keenly in tch: rdn over 2f out: kpt on same pce fr over 1f out* **2/1**[1]

6 *1/2* **Raleigh Quay (IRE)** 2-8-10 0.................................... NeilBrown(3) 7 60
(Micky Hammond) *in tch: outpcd 1/2-way: rallied and edgd lft over 1f out: no imp* **28/1**

7 *25* **Fleetwoodsands (IRE)** 2-8-10 0.................................... (t) CatherineGannon 3 —
(P C Haslam) *s.i.s: bhd: struggling over 2f out: sn btn* **18/1**

1m 11.8s (-0.40) **Going Correction** -0.125s/f (Firm) 7 Ran SP% **113.2**
Speed ratings (Par 91): **97,92,91,91,89 88,55**
toteswinger: 1&2 £30.50, 1&3 £8.40, 2&3 £40.50 CSF £84.35 TOTE £3.60: £1.90, £5.00; EX 127.00.
Owner Norton Common Farm Racing **Bred** Peter Baldwin **Trained** Maltby, S Yorks

FOCUS
An interesting heat for this maiden auction, but they went very steady until the bottom of the hill where it turned into a sprint.

NOTEBOOK
Colonel Mak ◆ had learnt plenty from his debut run to put in a much-improved performance when third at Doncaster last time and those two efforts held him in good stead to open his account. Settled off the pace, he got a decent split coming up the hill to take the lead entering the final furlong. He looks a lovely looking individual with a very likeable attitude - very laid back - and is the type who will improve as the season progresses, especially when stepped up in distance. He is more likely to go the novice route rather than nurseries. (tchd 7-2)
Living It Large(FR) raced up witht the pace thoughout, and although rather green when asked for his effort he kept on well to regain second near the finish. He ought to build on this encouraging debut. (op 33-1)
Sweet Mirasol(IRE) took them along at a steady pace until quickening up the hill and stuck to the task when headed entering the final furlong, but had no answers to the winner's pace. This was a much better effort than that of his debut where he clearly did not act on the soft ground. (op 8-1 tchd 11-1)
Orpen Arms(IRE) had three runs under her belt and raced to the fore, but when the pace quickened she could not find the required gears. She will probably go for a nursery and looks as though she would also appreciate a step up to 7f. (op 2-1)

Fantastic Strike(IRE), whose breeding suggested that this would be sharp enough for him, made a respectable debut although never having the pace to mount a challenge. (op 5-2 tchd 15-8)

3293 EUROPEAN BREEDERS' FUND FILLIES' CONDITIONS STKS — 1m 65y
8:00 (8:00) (Class 2) 3-Y-O+ **£11,215** (£3,358; £1,679; £840) **Stalls** High

Form RPR

2422 **1** **Just Lille (IRE)**[15] 2815 6-9-0 88........(p) PaulMulrennan 3 93
(Mrs A Duffield) *set mod gallop: rdn whn jnd over 2f out: styd on strly to go clr fr over 1f out* **6/4**[2]

4314 **2** 4 **Silver Games (IRE)**[8] 3016 3-8-4 89........ CatherineGannon 2 86
(M R Channon) *prom: hdwy and ev ch over 2f out: edgd rt and one pce over 1f out* **5/4**[1]

-440 **3** 1 1/4 **Feeling Fab (FR)**[26] 2504 3-8-4 89........ JoeFanning 4 83
(M Johnston) *plld hrd: trckd ldrs: pushed along and outpcd over 2f out: edgd rt over 1f out: no imp* **7/2**[3]

403 **4** 4 **Casino Night**[7] 3060 4-9-0 67........ AndrewHeffernan 1 72?
(R Johnson) *pressed wnr: rdn and outpcd 3f out: sn btn* **50/1**

1m 45.03s (-3.37) **Going Correction** -0.25s/f (Firm)
WFA 3 from 4yo+ 10lb **4 Ran SP% 108.6**
Speed ratings (Par 96): **106,102,100,96**
CSF £3.76 TOTE £2.20; EX 3.80.
Owner Miss Helen Wynne **Bred** Sweetmans Bloodstock **Trained** Constable Burton, N Yorks

FOCUS
Only four runners but a tricky little contest for this fillies' conditions stakes. Fair form for the grade.

NOTEBOOK
Just Lille(IRE) won this in 2007 and she took them along at just a fair pace until quickening when hitting the 3f marker. She proved to be a real tough nut to crack when challenged and although leaning to her left coming down the hill she dug deep to win going away in a decent time just outside standard. This was her 30th race of her career, winning eight of them, including Listed events, and she is a real credit to her connections as she is still producing a decent level of form. It was a deserved success for this game little mare who is in great spirit at present. (op 2-1)
Silver Games(IRE)'s trainer had won with his previous two runners in this and she looked as though she would make it three. Tracking the leaders, she mounted a very strong challenge over 2f out but could not find the resoloution of the winner and was held when hanging in behind the winner entering the final furlong. She had been performing well of late, winning a competitive handicap at Newcastle before running a blinder at Royal Ascot, and should find an opportunity before long to get her head back in front. (op 6-4 tchd 13-8)
Feeling Fab(FR) has won from the front before but she was settled behind the leading pair and when asked for her effort could not find the pace to mount her challenge, although staying on inside the final furlong, she will be better suited to a stronger-run race. (op 5-2 tchd 9-4)
Casino Night had a mountain to climb on official ratings and has not been performing that consistently this season. She sat with the winner at the head of affairs until over 2f out but was soon brushed aside.

3294 TOTESWINGER MAIDEN STKS — 1m 1f 36y
8:30 (8:32) (Class 5) 3-4-Y-O **£2,590** (£770; £385; £192) **Stalls** High

Form RPR

3 **1** **Hajar (USA)**[23] 2572 3-9-0 0........ JoeFanning 8 66+
(M Johnston) *mde all: rdn over 2f out: styd on strly* **4/6**[1]

00 **2** 4 **Real Desire**[11] 2943 3-9-0 0........ TomEaves 1 58
(I Semple) *s.i.s: bhd and outpcd: plenty to do over 3f out: hdwy over 1f out: styd on to go 2nd nr fin: nt rch wnr* **40/1**

040- **3** 1/2 **King's Counsel (IRE)**[274] 6214 3-9-0 55........ CatherineGannon 6 57
(J Hetherton) *w wnr: rdn over 2f out: edgd rt and one pce fr over 1f out* **33/1**

40 **4** nk **Black River Falls (USA)**[41] 2030 3-9-0 0........ PhillipMakin 3 56
(I Semple) *hld up in tch: hdwy to chse wnr over 1f out: one pce fnl f: lost 2nd towards fin* **9/1**[3]

0 **5** 3 3/4 **Born To Perform**[11] 2943 4-9-11 0........ PaulMulrennan 4 48
(G A Swinbank) *t.k.h: trckd ldrs: rdn over 2f out: wknd over 1f out* **2/1**[2]

/06- **6** 29 **Piccolo Pride**[523] 222 4-9-6 30........(t) SladeO'Hara(5) 7 —
(M A Barnes) *prom tl rdn and wknd over 2f out: t.o* **100/1**

1m 57.63s (-2.07) **Going Correction** -0.25s/f (Firm)
WFA 3 from 4yo 11lb **6 Ran SP% 109.7**
Speed ratings (Par 103): **99,95,95,94,91 65**
toteswinger: 1&2 £4.50, 1&3 £6.40, 2&3 £5.70 CSF £29.77 TOTE £1.70: £1.10, £6.40; EX 21.00.Oriental Gem was withdrawn. Price at time of withdrawal 33/1. Rule 4 does not apply.
Owner Sheikh Hamdan Bin Mohammed Al Maktoum **Bred** Darley **Trained** Middleham Moor, N Yorks

FOCUS
A weak maiden in which Hajar had little to beat.
Born To Perform Official explanation: trainer had no explanation for the poor form shown

3295 HAMILTON PARK SUPER SIX SPRINT H'CAP — 5f 4y
9:00 (9:00) (Class 4) (0-80,79) 3-Y-O+ **£5,180** (£1,541; £770; £384) **Stalls** Centre

Form RPR

6103 **1** **Rothesay Dancer**[5] 3145 6-9-7 77........ KellyHarrison(3) 2 84+
(J S Goldie) *hld up in last: niggled 1/2-way: swtchd lft and qcknd to ld wl ins fnl f: comf* **11/4**[2]

4330 **2** 1/2 **Speedy Senorita (IRE)**[14] 2840 4-8-11 69........ JamieKyne(5) 5 74
(J J Quinn) *led: rdn 2f out: hdd wl ins fnl f: no ex* **4/1**[3]

1112 **3** 3/4 **Argentine (IRE)**[6] 3111 5-9-5 72 6ex........(b) PaulMulrennan 3 74
(J A McShane) *trckd ldrs: effrt over 2f out: edgd rt over 1f out: kpt on same pce fnl f* **9/4**[1]

0631 **4** 1/2 **Silvanus (IRE)**[6] 3109 4-9-6 73 6ex........(p) TomEaves 1 74
(I Semple) *t.k.h: cl up: drvn over 2f out: kpt on same pce fnl f* **11/2**

0453 **5** 1 1/2 **Bo McGinty (IRE)**[2] 3236 8-9-0 74........(v) TimothyAyres(7) 6 69
(R A Fahey) *cl up: outpcd and edgd rt 2f out: no imp fnl f* **5/1**

59.38 secs (-0.62) **Going Correction** -0.125s/f (Firm)
WFA 3 from 4yo+ 6lb **5 Ran SP% 109.5**
Speed ratings (Par 105): **99,98,97,96,93**
toteswinger: 1&2 £7.10. CSF £13.55 TOTE £2.80: £1.60, £2.90; EX 14.50.
Owner Highland Racing **Bred** Frank Brady **Trained** Uplawmoor, E Renfrews

FOCUS
A competitive contest with a case for all five for this sprint run at a decent pace. The form is rated around the second and fourth.

3296 QUESTION OF SPORT NEXT TUESDAY H'CAP — 6f 5y
9:30 (9:31) (Class 6) (0-65,65) 4-Y-O+ **£2,388** (£705; £352) **Stalls** Centre

Form RPR

-321 **1** **Tangerine Trees**[21] 2628 4-9-7 65........ TomEaves 8 72
(B Smart) *cl up: rdn over 2f out: led ins fnl f: kpt on wl* **6/4**[1]

3064 **2** nk **Magical Song**[47] 1889 4-8-2 51........(b) JamieKyne(5) 1 57
(J Balding) *led: rdn over 2f out: hdd ins fnl f: kpt on* **6/1**[3]

5040 **3** nk **Ingleby Princess**[10] 2964 5-8-8 55........ NeilBrown(3) 7 60
(T D Barron) *bhd and sn pushed along: hdwy 2f out: kpt on fnl f: nrst fin* **7/2**[2]

0024 **4** 1 3/4 **Royal Acclamation (IRE)**[10] 2964 4-8-11 55........(v) SilvestreDeSousa 4 54
(G A Harker) *trckd ldrs: rdn 1/2-way: kpt on same pce over 1f out* **7/2**[2]

-024 **5** 1/2 **Howards Tipple**[8] 3020 5-8-10 54........ PaulMulrennan 3 52
(I Semple) *hld up in tch: effrt over 2f out: edgd lft and one pce over 1f out* **8/1**

0-04 **6** 9 **Actabou**[15] 2816 4-8-8 57........(t) SladeO'Hara(5) 2 26
(F P Murtagh) *prom: rdn 1/2-way: wknd 2f out* **50/1**

40-0 **7** 20 **Forrest Star**[8] 3021 4-8-11 55........ TonyHamilton 5 —
(Miss L A Perratt) *t.k.h: hld up in tch: rdn and wknd fr 1/2-way: t.o* **33/1**

000- **8** 9 **Madame Rio (IRE)**[308] 5203 4-8-2 46 oh1........ CatherineGannon 6 —
(E J Cooper) *in tch tl wknd over 3f out: t.o* **80/1**

1m 11.19s (-1.01) **Going Correction** -0.125s/f (Firm) **8 Ran SP% 116.0**
Speed ratings (Par 101): **101,100,100,97,97 85,58,46**
toteswinger: 1&2 £2.90, 1&3 £2.00, 2&3 £4.20 CSF £11.48 CT £27.63 TOTE £2.20: £1.10, £2.20, £1.60; EX 9.30 Place 6: £180.78, Place 5: £43.54..
Owner Tangerine Trees Partnership **Bred** Mrs B A Matthews **Trained** Hambleton, N Yorks
■ Stewards' Enquiry : Jamie Kyne one-day ban: failed to ride to draw (Jul 9)

FOCUS
A low-grade contest which was run at a good pace. The winner probably only had to match his previous C&D form.
Forrest Star Official explanation: jockey said filly ran too free
Madame Rio(IRE) Official explanation: jockey said filly bolted to post
T/Plt: £59.40 to a £1 stake. Pool: £64,348.45. 790.37 winning tickets. T/Qpdt: £6.20 to a £1 stake. Pool: £4,007.50. 473.40 winning tickets. RY

3269 KEMPTON (A.W) (R-H)
Thursday, June 25

OFFICIAL GOING: Standard
Wind: fresh, across Weather: warm amd sunny

3297 GARMIN SAT-NAV MAIDEN FILLIES' STKS — 1m (P)
3:10 (3:12) (Class 4) 3-Y-O+ **£4,857** (£1,445; £722; £360) **Stalls** High

Form RPR

0-4 **1** **Aim To Achieve (IRE)**[12] 2937 3-8-12 0........ MichaelHills 2 70
(B W Hills) *trckd ldrs: pushed along and hdwy to ld over 2f out: hdd 1f out: rdn and r.o gamely to ld again fnl 50yds: hld on wl nr fin* **4/1**[2]

-3 **2** shd **Toolentidhaar (USA)**[20] 2679 5-9-8 0........ GeorgeBaker 12 72
(Andrew Turnell) *broke v fast and led for 1f: stdd to trck ldrs after: edgd out lft jst over 2f out: rdn and ev ch fnl f: kpt on wl: jst hld towards fin* **6/1**

63 **3** 3/4 **Repetischa (IRE)**[35] 2192 3-8-12 0........ JimmyFortune 14 68
(E A L Dunlop) *hld up in midfield: hdwy on inner over 2f out: rdn and qckd to ld 1f out: edgd lft u.p: hdd and no ex fnl 50yds* **3/1**[1]

5 **4** 1/2 **Bow To No One (IRE)**[14] 2847 3-8-12 0........ AlanMunro 8 67
(A P Jarvis) *hld up in tch in midfield: swtchd lft and rdn jst over 2f out: chsd ldrs ent fnl f: kpt on wl but nt quite pce to rch ldrs* **6/1**

5 2 1/4 **Valfurva (IRE)** 3-8-12 0........ WilliamBuick 10 62+
(L M Cumani) *sn niggled along in rr: hdwy on inner over 2f out: edgd lft over 1f out: styd on steadily fnl f: nvr threatened ldrs* **14/1**

0 **6** shd **Phantom Ridge (IRE)**[27] 2433 3-8-12 0........ TedDurcan 5 62
(R Hannon) *in tch in midfield: reminder wl over 3f out: drvn and hung rt over 2f out: kpt on fnl f: nt pce to rch ldrs* **33/1**

- **7** nk **One Cool Dream** 3-8-12 0........ AdamKirby 13 61+
(W R Swinburn) *towards rr: pushed along and hdwy on inner over 2f out: chsd ldrs and drvn over 1f out: no imp fnl f: lost 2 pls nr fin* **20/1**

0 **8** 11 **Madame Guillotine (USA)**[11] 2947 3-8-12 0........ J-PGuillambert 7 36
(R M Beckett) *w ldr after 1f: led 4f out tl rdn and hdd over 2f out: wknd qckly wl over 1f out* **5/1**[3]

0 **9** 3 **Sea Lavender**[69] 1327 3-8-12 0........ FergusSweeney 4 29
(R Charlton) *towards rr and sn niggled along: nvr nr ldrs* **20/1**

10 3 1/2 **Catalina Sunrise (USA)** 3-8-12 0........ NCallan 1 21
(L M Cumani) *racd wd: in tch in midfield: hung lft on bnd 4f out: sn lost pl: wl bhd after* **20/1**

0 **11** 9 **Our Last Call (IRE)**[8] 3025 3-8-12 0........ SebSanders 6 —
(Sir Mark Prescott) *sn struggling in last pl: lost tch wl over 2f out: t.o* **33/1**

0 **12** 5 **Red Red Rascal**[14] 2848 3-8-12 0........ NeilChalmers 11 —
(A M Balding) *chsd ldr tl led after 1f: hdd 4f out: chsd ldr tl wknd rapidly over 2f out: wl bhd whn edgd lft 2f out: t.o* **66/1**

1m 41.79s (1.99) **Going Correction** +0.175s/f (Slow)
WFA 3 from 5yo 10lb **12 Ran SP% 118.6**
Speed ratings (Par 102): **97,96,96,95,93 93,93,82,79,75 66,61**
toteswinger: 1&2 £7.20, 1&3 £3.20, 2&3 £4.80 CSF £25.41 TOTE £4.60: £1.90, £1.90, £1.50; EX 36.30.
Owner Jack Hanson & Sir Alex Ferguson **Bred** Gerard & Anne Corry **Trained** Lambourn, Berks

FOCUS
A modest maiden in which it paid to race handily. The first four home all had the benefit of previous experience, but a couple of newcomers also caught the eye. It was the slowest of the four C&D races.

3298 DAY TIME, NIGHT TIME, GREAT TIME CONDITIONS STKS — 1m (P)
3:40 (3:42) (Class 3) 3-Y-O **£7,771** (£2,312; £1,155; £577) **Stalls** High

Form RPR

-031 **1** **Cloudy Start**[20] 2674 3-9-3 93........ EddieAhern 3 108
(H R A Cecil) *mde all: clr over 3f out: rdn and qcknd further clr over 2f out: in n.d after: drvn out: unchal: impressive* **5/1**[3]

1312 **2** 3 3/4 **Set The Trend**[33] 2273 3-9-3 93........ WilliamBuick 4 99
(A M Balding) *hld up in last trio: hdwy on inner over 2f out: qcknd to chse wnr wl over 1f out: r.o but no imp on wnr* **10/3**[1]

602- **3** 4 1/2 **Prince Siegfried (FR)**[235] 7163 3-9-3 111........ TedDurcan 7 89
(Saeed Bin Suroor) *stmbld leaving stalls: t.k.h: hld up in midfield: rdn and effrt over 2f out: no ch w wnr fnl 2f: wnt modest 3rd 1f out* **7/2**[2]

14 **4** 5 **Bridge Of Gold (USA)**[28] 2411 3-9-3 100........ KShea 5 78
(M A Magnusson) *s.i.s: t.k.h: hld up in last pl: effrt and rdn over 2f out: no ch fnl 2f: wnt modest 4th ins fnl f* **7/1**

132- **5** 3/4 **Bonnie Charlie**[243] 6979 3-9-3 106........ JimmyFortune 8 76
(R Hannon) *in tch: rdn over 3f out: drvn to chse clr wnr over 2f out tl wl over 1f out: wknd over 1f out* **6/1**

0-21 **6** 2 **Exceptional Art**[33] 2270 3-9-3 97........ AlanMunro 1 71
(P W Chapple-Hyam) *hld up in last trio: short-lived effrt wl over 2f out: no ch fnl 2f* **11/2**

212- **7** 8 **Full Toss**[279] 6075 3-9-3 100........ SebSanders 6 53
(R Hannon) *t.k.h: chsd wnr tl over 2f out: sn wknd: eased ins fnl f* **12/1**

1- 8 9 **Alkhafif**[397] 2411 3-9-3 98 .... RHills 2 32
(E A L Dunlop) *in tch on outer: rdn over 2f out: sn struggling and bhd: t.o and eased fnl f* **20/1**

1m 38.24s (-1.56) **Going Correction** +0.175s/f (Slow) **8** Ran SP% **116.6**
Speed ratings (Par 103): **114,110,105,100,100 98,90,81**
toteswinger: 1&2 £6.10, 1&3 £4.40, 2&3 £3.10 CSF £22.53 TOTE £5.80: £2.00, £1.40, £1.60; EX 22.90.
Owner K Abdulla **Bred** Juddmonte Farms Ltd **Trained** Newmarket, Suffolk

FOCUS

A decent conditions event, even though only one of these had raced on sand before and half the field were returning from lengthy absences. The pace was unrelenting, however, and the field finished spread out all over Sunbury, with the winning time 3.57 seconds faster than the opening fillies' maiden. The winner impressed and the form is rated fairly positively around the runner-up.

NOTEBOOK

Cloudy Start ◆, successful off a mark of 88 in an Epsom handicap last time, was joint worst in at the weights but he made a complete mockery of that with a devastating display. Sent straight into the lead, he stretched his field starting up the straight and was never in any danger from that point. Again the way the track was riding may well have been helping him, but there is little doubt that he is a colt on the up. (op 8-1 tchd 9-2)

Set The Trend ◆ was the other joint worst in at the weights, but he was the only one of these with previous experience of sand and he was successful over course and distance in April. Given a patient ride, he stayed on well over the last couple of furlongs and tried to bridge the gap to the winner, but he could never get on terms. He can be given credit for this effort though, given how the track appeared to be riding, and he should be winning again before too long. (op 4-1 tchd 9-2 in a place)

Prince Siegfried(FR), last seen going down by just a head in testing ground in the Group 1 Criterium International at Saint-Cloud last November, was making his debut for Godolphin and didn't fare badly in staying on for third, especially as he may have needed it. However, he would have been 18lb worse in with the front pair in a handicap and will need to improve in order to regain the winning thread. (op 3-1 tchd 11-4)

Bridge Of Gold(USA), who probably pulled too hard when fourth of six in a Sandown Listed race last time, is bred to appreciate this surface but he was rather disappointing. Admittedly he did miss the break and gave his rivals a start, but he didn't really take off when put under pressure. Official explanation: jockey said colt missed the break (op 8-1 tchd 9-1)

Bonnie Charlie, never worse than third in six outings at two and placed three times at Group 3 level, raced close to the pace early but didn't find much off the bridle. He was entitled to need this, but may not be the easiest to place. (op 7-2 tchd 3-1)

Exceptional Art, successful off 92 in a heavy-ground Haydock handicap last time, never looked like getting involved from off the pace and perhaps he didn't take to the surface. (op 7-1 tchd 15-2)

Full Toss, never out of the first two in four outings as a juvenile, raced in second place for a long way but came off the bridle on the home bend and dropped away. He has questions to answer now. (tchd 14-1)

Alkhafif, not seen since beating three subsequent winners in a four-runner Newmarket maiden on his debut 13 months ago, dropped out as though something were amiss. Official explanation: jockey said gelding stopped quickly

3299 PANORAMIC BAR & RESTAURANT H'CAP — 6f (P)
4:10 (4:13) (Class 5) (0-70,69) 3-Y-O **£3,469** (£1,038; £519; £259; £129) **Stalls** High

Form / RPR

34-5 **1** **Lujeanie**[14] 2849 3-9-5 **67** .... (p) FergusSweeney 10 78
(D K Ivory) *hmpd s: sn in tch: hdwy on inner jst over 2f out: rdn to ld jst over 1f out: drvn clr fnl f* **7/2**[2]

5506 **2** 3 ¾ **It's A Mans World**[14] 2863 3-8-7 **58** .... (v) RussellKennemore(3) 9 57
(K M Prendergast) *trckd ldrs: wnt 2nd 3f out: led jst over 2f out: drvn and hdd jst over 1f out: no ch w wnr fnl f* **8/1**

6-64 **3** 1 ½ **All Spin (IRE)**[9] 3009 3-9-5 **67** .... AlanMunro 6 61
(A P Jarvis) *dwlt: sn chsng ldrs: rdn to chse ldng pair over 1f out: drvn and one pce ent fnl f* **6/1**[3]

0604 **4** 1 ¼ **Quick Single (USA)**[17] 2761 3-9-6 **68** .... (vt) AdamKirby 8 58
(P S McEntee) *sn outpcd in midfield: rdn over 3f out: hdwy and switching lft over 2f out: kpt on but nvr gng to rch ldrs* **25/1**

3230 **5** ½ **Vamos (IRE)**[44] 1969 3-8-12 **60** .... WilliamBuick 2 48+
(J R Gask) *sn outpcd towards rr: swtchd rt over 2f out: kpt on fnl f: nvr nr ldrs* **8/1**

5-04 **6** 6 **Compton Blue**[14] 2852 3-9-3 **65** .... JimmyFortune 4 34+
(R Hannon) *racd off the pce in midfield: rdn wl over 3f out: nvr nr ldrs* **8/1**

04-0 **7** 5 **Dicey Affair**[15] 2827 3-9-2 **64** .... GeorgeBaker 7 17
(G L Moore) *s.i.s: a in rr: edgd lft over 2f out: n.d* **16/1**

000 **8** 1 ¼ **Pansy Potter**[9] 3010 3-8-13 **61** .... (b) RobertWinston 1 10
(B J Meehan) *sn bustled up to chse ldrs: wknd qckly u.p over 2f out* **25/1**

0643 **9** nk **Hillside Lad**[13] 2888 3-9-4 **66** .... (v[1]) SebSanders 12 14
(R M Beckett) *wnt lft s: sn rcvrd and led: hdd over 2f out: drvn and wknd qckly over 1f out: eased fnl f* **10/3**[1]

05-6 **10** 4 **Equinity**[23] 2581 3-8-7 **55** ow2 .... StephenDonohoe 11 —
(J Pearce) *hmpd and pushed lft s: sn rcvrd to chsd ldr tl 3f out: wknd qckly over 2f out: eased ins fnl f* **14/1**

004- **11** 4 ½ **Miss Perfectionist**[210] 7458 3-9-7 **69** .... JimmyQuinn 3 —
(P Howling) *awkward leaving stalls and slowly away: a wl outpcd in rr: eased ins fnl f: t.o* **25/1**

6 **12** nk **Shadow Bay (IRE)**[23] 2562 3-9-7 **69** .... SamHitchcott 5 —
(Miss Z C Davison) *sn rdn along: a outpcd in last pair: eased ins fnl f: t.o* **16/1**

1m 13.05s (-0.05) **Going Correction** +0.175s/f (Slow) **12** Ran SP% **122.9**
Speed ratings (Par 99): **107,102,100,98,97 89,83,81,80,75 69,69**
toteswinger: 1&2 £13.50, 1&3 £6.00, 2&3 £14.50 CSF £32.38 CT £162.51 TOTE £4.30: £2.00, £2.90, £2.10; EX 44.40.
Owner K T Ivory **Bred** K T Ivory **Trained** Radlett, Herts

FOCUS

A modest handicap with only three of the 12 runners previous winners and those drawn high had the advantage. The first three home were all well backed and the front five pulled well clear, so the form may be alright. It is rated around the third and fourth.

3300 HARRIS CORPORATION H'CAP — 2m (P)
4:40 (4:40) (Class 4) (0-80,80) 3-Y-O **£5,828** (£1,734; £866; £432) **Stalls** High

Form / RPR

4421 **1** **Penang Princess**[35] 2208 3-9-3 **76** .... SebSanders 7 85+
(R M Beckett) *mde all: rdn clr whn swvd bdly lft jst over 2f out: drvn and continued to hang lft: a in command fnl f* **7/4**[1]

012 **2** 3 ¾ **Ostaadi**[15] 2829 3-9-7 **80** .... PhilipRobinson 1 82
(M A Jarvis) *sn chsng wnr: rdn over 3f out: outpcd by wnr jst over 2f out: a hld after* **3/1**[2]

-125 **3** shd **Ermyn Lodge**[48] 1842 3-8-2 **61** .... LukeMorris 5 63
(P M Phelan) *dropped to last pair and rdn after 3f: drvn fr 7f out: styd on fnl f: wnt 3rd nr fin: pressing for 2nd on line: no ch w wnr* **11/2**[3]

5301 **4** ½ **Excelsior Academy**[14] 2866 3-8-10 **74** .... Louis-PhilippeBeuzelin(5) 6 75
(B J Meehan) *hld up in last pair: rdn over 3f out: hdwy and swtchd lft over 2f out: chsd ldng pair and drvn jst over 2f out: kpt on same pce: lost 3rd nr fin* **6/1**

-552 **5** 4 ½ **Albaasha (IRE)**[20] 2667 3-8-6 **65** .... (v) RHills 4 61
(Sir Michael Stoute) *t.k.h: in tch: rdn wl over 3f out: chsd ldrs over 2f out: no prog: wknd over 1f out* **7/1**

2106 **6** 6 **Lake Kalamalka (IRE)**[15] 2829 3-8-10 **69** .... EddieAhern 3 58
(J L Dunlop) *stdd and dropped in bhd after s: rdn over 3f out: no real hdwy: wknd over 2f out* **9/1**

0-05 **7** 37 **Arabian Moonlight**[21] 2633 3-8-2 **61** oh3 .... JimmyQuinn 8 5
(E F Vaughan) *chsd ldrs: pushed along 6f out: rdn 4f out: wknd wl over 2f out: t.o and eased fr wl over 1f out* **40/1**

3m 32.97s (2.87) **Going Correction** +0.175s/f (Slow) **7** Ran SP% **116.0**
Speed ratings (Par 101): **99,97,97,96,94 91,73**
toteswinger: 1&2 £2.30, 2&3 £4.20, 1&3 not won. CSF £7.39 CT £23.11 TOTE £3.10: £1.50, £2.10; EX 7.10.
Owner Mrs A K H Ooi **Bred** Mrs A K H Ooi **Trained** Whitsbury, Hants

FOCUS

A fair staying handicap for three-year-olds, though none of these had tried 2m before. They went a fair pace which made it a good test, and again those who raced at the sharp end were favoured. The winner was probably value for a bit extra.

Excelsior Academy Official explanation: vet said gelding tied up post-race

3301 KEMPTON.CO.UK H'CAP — 1m (P)
5:10 (5:12) (Class 4) (0-85,85) 4-Y-0+ **£5,677** (£1,699; £849; £424; £211) **Stalls** High

Form / RPR

00-0 **1** **Grand Vizier (IRE)**[17] 2775 5-9-7 **85** .... TedDurcan 8 93
(C F Wall) *rdn in snatches: bustled along to chse ldrs early: rdn to chal over 1f out: led ins fnl f: drvn out* **9/2**[2]

0106 **2** ¾ **Brouhaha**[22] 2597 5-9-6 **84** .... RichardKingscote 5 90
(Tom Dascombe) *in tch: effrt u.p jst over 2f out: drvn and styd on wl fnl f: wnt 2nd towards fin* **6/1**[3]

1-01 **3** ½ **Sarah Park (IRE)**[17] 2775 4-8-12 **76** .... EddieAhern 6 81
(B J Meehan) *led for 2f: styd chsng ldr tl led again jst over 2f out: hrd pressed and drvn over 1f out: hdd ins fnl f: no ex and lost 2nd towards fin* **9/2**[2]

-566 **4** ½ **Beauchamp Viceroy**[35] 2193 5-9-2 **85** .... (p) Louis-PhilippeBeuzelin(5) 7 89
(G A Butler) *t.k.h: hld up in rr: hdwy on inner over 2f out: drvn to chse ldrs over 1f out: kpt on same pce fnl f* **6/1**[3]

3/6- **5** 2 ¾ **Quick Release (IRE)**[336] 4345 4-9-2 **80** .... NCallan 1 77
(D M Simcock) *broke wl: t.k.h and grad stdd to rr: pushed along over 3f out: rdn and hdwy over 2f out: one pce and no prog over 1f out* **14/1**

-243 **6** 1 ¾ **Randama Bay (IRE)**[152] 282 4-8-10 **74** .... TGMcLaughlin 10 67
(I A Wood) *sn rdn along to chse ldr: led after 2f: rdn and hdd jst over 2f out: wknd qckly over 1f out* **10/1**

-305 **7** ¾ **Romany Princess (IRE)**[15] 2828 4-9-5 **83** .... JimmyFortune 4 75
(R Hannon) *hld up towards rr on outer: swtchd lft to r v wd over 2f out: sn rdn: no real prog and nvr trbld ldrs* **7/2**[1]

4054 **8** 3 ½ **Obe Royal**[8] 3030 5-8-11 **75** .... (v) StephenDonohoe 2 59
(P D Evans) *hld up in rr: rdn and no rspnse over 2f out: nvr a factor* **10/1**

0 **9** 19 **Pride Of Nation (IRE)**[52] 1731 7-9-4 **82** .... SebSanders 3 22
(J W Hills) *chsd ldrs: hung rt and wknd qckly jst over 2f out: eased ins fnl f* **10/1**

1m 40.63s (0.83) **Going Correction** +0.175s/f (Slow) **9** Ran SP% **121.1**
Speed ratings (Par 105): **102,101,100,100,97 95,95,91,72**
toteswinger: 1&2 £7.50, 1&3 £5.90, 2&3 £6.70 CSF £33.38 CT £131.65 TOTE £6.10: £2.40, £2.90, £2.00; EX 40.80.
Owner Hintlesham SP Partners **Bred** Yeomanstown Stud **Trained** Newmarket, Suffolk

FOCUS

A fair handicap run at an even pace and again it paid to race handily. The winner has a fine AW record and the form is rated through the placed horses.

Pride Of Nation(IRE) Official explanation: jockey said horse stopped quickly

3302 TURFTV H'CAP — 1m (P)
5:40 (5:41) (Class 6) (0-60,60) 3-Y-O **£1,942** (£578; £288; £144) **Stalls** High

Form / RPR

00-4 **1** **Chief Red Cloud (USA)**[15] 2805 3-9-4 **60** .... ShaneKelly 3 67
(K R Burke) *hld up in midfield: hdwy over 3f out: rdn to chal jst over 2f out: drvn to ld over 1f out: edgd lft to stands' rail: hld on wl fnl f* **10/1**

2051 **2** nk **Miss Mojito (IRE)**[11] 2950 3-8-11 **60** .... (t) KierenFox(7) 8 66
(J W Hills) *stdd s: hld up in rr: gd hdwy 2f out: chal wnr jst ins fnl f: edgd lft and flashed tail u.p: hld towards fin* **3/1**[2]

31-0 **3** 2 ½ **Super Fourteen**[24] 2548 3-9-4 **60** .... JimmyFortune 5 60
(R Hannon) *chsd ldrs: rdn 3f out: hrd drvn over 1f out: outpcd by ldng pair ins fnl f: kpt on to snatch 3rd on post* **5/2**[1]

30-0 **4** nse **Silent Treatment (IRE)**[28] 2417 3-9-2 **58** .... JimmyQuinn 12 58
(Miss Gay Kelleway) *hld up towards rr: gd hdwy on inner jst over 2f out: chsd ldng pair and drvn 1f out: outpcd ins fnl f: lost 3rd on post* **25/1**

-000 **5** 4 ½ **Conclusive**[16] 2797 3-9-4 **60** .... GeorgeBaker 7 50
(R M Beckett) *chsd ldr: rdn and ev ch 2f out: hung lft u.p: wknd ent fnl f* **25/1**

0-00 **6** 1 ¾ **Rockson (IRE)**[61] 1532 3-9-2 **58** .... MichaelHills 4 44
(B W Hills) *in tch: hdwy to join ldrs over 2f out: led jst over 2f out: rdn and edgd lft wl over 1f out: hdd over 1f out: wknd fnl f* **16/1**

0000 **7** 1 ½ **Darwin's Dragon**[13] 2876 3-9-4 **60** .... JosedeSouza 9 42
(P F I Cole) *t.k.h: hld up wl in tch: rdn and unable qck jst over 2f out: wknd qckly wl over 1f out* **20/1**

1000 **8** hd **Taste Of Honey (IRE)**[15] 2827 3-9-3 **59** .... EddieAhern 10 41
(D W P Arbuthnot) *hld up towards rr: pushed along 3f out: rdn and no hdwy jst over 2f out: nvr trbld ldrs* **15/2**[3]

360 **9** 1 **Tender Charm (USA)**[26] 2496 3-9-4 **60** .... (v[1]) RichardKingscote 2 40
(R M Beckett) *led: rdn 3f out: hdd jst over 2f out: sn drvn: wknd qckly wl over 1f out* **10/1**

0-00 **10** 1 ¾ **Do Be Brave (IRE)**[55] 1656 3-9-1 **60** .... RussellKennemore(3) 6 36
(Paul Mason) *a towards rr: rdn and no hdwy 3f out* **66/1**

3016 **11** 3 **Straitjacket**[20] 2683 3-9-3 **59** .... (p) PaulFitzsimons 11 28
(Miss J R Tooth) *hld up in tch in midfield: rdn over 2f out: sn wknd and wl btn after* **14/1**

4-00 **12** 2 ½ **Kingshill Prince**[31] 2320 3-9-4 **60** .... TedDurcan 1 23
(W J Musson) *v.s.a: a bhd: rdn and no hdwy wl over 2f out* **20/1**

0-00 **13** nse **Mymateeric**[30] 2357 3-9-3 **59** .... (b[1]) StephenDonohoe 13 22
(J Pearce) *a towards rr: rdn over 3f out: wknd over 2f out and wl bhd fnl 2f* **14/1**

0-00 **14** *14* **Free Falling**[26] 2489 3-9-3 **59** NCallan 14 —
(L M Cumani) *dwlt: sn bustled along: a in rr: rdn and lost tch over 2f out: t.o fnl f* **12/1**

1m 41.53s (1.73) **Going Correction** +0.175s/f (Slow) **14** Ran SP% **129.1**
Speed ratings (Par 97): **98,97,95,95,90 88,87,87,86,84 81,78,78,64**
toteswinger: 1&2 £8.10, 1&3 £8.50, 2&3 £2.60 CSF £40.43 CT £105.33 TOTE £12.40: £2.90, £1.60, £1.90; EX 47.10.
Owner Market Avenue Racing Club Ltd **Bred** Lochlow Farm **Trained** Middleham Moor, N Yorks

FOCUS
A very moderate handicap with just 2lb covering the field, but the form is sound. The pace was ordinary and there were virtually six in a line across the track a furlong out. The winning time was 0.9 seconds slower than the preceding Class 4 handicap.
Miss Mojito(IRE) Official explanation: jockey said filly missed the break

3303 KEMPTON FOR OUTDOOR EVENTS CLASSIFIED STKS 1m 4f (P)
6:10 (6:12) (Class 6) 3-Y-O+ **£1,942** (£578; £288; £144) **Stalls** Centre

Form RPR
-036 **1** **Haafhd Time (IRE)**[15] 2802 3-8-7 54 RichardKingscote 4 58
(Tom Dascombe) *hld up in midfield: rdn and hdwy over 3f out: led jst over 2f out: drvn and forged clr fnl f* **14/1**
0300 **2** *2 ¾* **Mayfair's Future**[34] 2221 4-9-7 55 NCallan 8 54
(J R Jenkins) *hld up towards rr: stdy hdwy over 3f out: swtchd lft 2f out: chsd ldrs and drvn jst over 1f out: wnt 2nd jst ins fnl f: nt pce of wnr after: hld on for 2nd* **5/1**[2]
-423 **3** *hd* **Tinkerbelle (IRE)**[14] 2866 3-8-7 55 EddieAhern 3 53
(J L Dunlop) *hld up in rr: stl pleny to do and rdn wl over 1f out: no prog tl styd on wl fnl f: pressing for 2nd at fin: no ch w wnr* **5/2**[1]
5042 **4** *1 ¾* **Den Maschine**[22] 2609 4-9-7 55 DNolan 9 50
(Ollie Pears) *hld up in midfield: hdwy and rdn over 3f out: drvn to chse wnr 2f out: wknd jst ins fnl f* **11/2**[3]
6600 **5** *nk* **Follow The Dream**[36] 2182 6-9-7 45 TGMcLaughlin 5 50+
(Karen George) *s.i.s: wl bhd: rdn and hung lft 3f out: continued to hang and fin on stands' rail: r.o fnl f: nt rch ldrs* **33/1**
0-05 **6** *2* **Bathwick Pursuit**[24] 2543 3-8-8 55 ow1 StephenDonohoe 1 48
(P D Evans) *stdd s: hld up in rr: rdn and hdwy wl over 2f out: chsd ldrs and drvn wl over 1f out: wknd ent fnl f* **20/1**
0-00 **7** *hd* **Flying Cloud (USA)**[27] 2433 3-8-2 50 Louis-PhilippeBeuzelin(5) 11 48+
(B J Meehan) *hld up in tch in midfield: effrt on inner whn hmpd over 2f out: swtchd lft and trying to rally whn carried lft wl over 1f out: no hdwy fnl f* **25/1**
4006 **8** *1 ¼* **Bright Wire (IRE)**[21] 2635 3-8-7 46 JimmyQuinn 12 44
(M Madgwick) *trckd ldrs: switching rt for ins rail whn barging match w rival over 2f out: drvn and wknd over 1f out* **16/1**
0060 **9** *4 ½* **Red Margarita (IRE)**[27] 2461 3-8-7 50 WilliamBuick 13 37+
(D R C Elsworth) *led for 1f: chsd ldrs after: stl wl in tch whn nt clr run and hmpd over 2f out: nt rcvr and n.d after* **5/1**[2]
000- **10** *½* **Green Endeavour (CAN)**[213] 7438 3-8-7 51 ShaneKelly 14 36
(Mrs A J Perrett) *led: wanting to edge lft fr 8f out: hdd jst over 2f out: hung lft u.p 2f out: sn wknd* **25/1**
000 **11** *12* **Vigorosa (IRE)**[20] 2664 3-8-0 45 KierenFox(7) 6 17
(P Howling) *t.k.h: pressed ldr after 1f: upsides ldr and rdn jst over 3f out: wknd jst over 2f out* **33/1**
-600 **12** *7* **Vella**[30] 2350 3-8-7 50 (b[1]) TedDurcan 10 6
(H J L Dunlop) *hld up towards rr: rdn and struggling wl over 3f out: wl bhd and eased fnl f: t.o* **33/1**
03-0 **13** *nse* **Potemkin (USA)**[7] 3074 4-9-7 55 JimmyFortune 7 6
(A King) *stdd s: a in rr: pushed along 7f out: lost tch wl over 2f out: eased fnl f: t.o* **8/1**
610 **14** *7* **Soul Singer**[92] 953 3-8-7 55 NickyMackay 2 —
(J G Portman) *s.i.s: sn pushed up and chsd ldrs after 1f: rdn over 3f out: lost pl wl over 2f out: wl bhd and eased fnl f: t.o* **16/1**

2m 38.66s (4.16) **Going Correction** +0.175s/f (Slow)
WFA 3 from 4yo+ 14lb **14** Ran SP% **128.1**
Speed ratings (Par 101): **93,91,91,89,89 88,88,87,84,84 76,71,71,66**
toteswinger: 1&2 £13.70, 1&3 £10.00, 2&3 £4.40 CSF £81.51 TOTE £20.60: £3.20, £1.90, £1.60; EX 102.20 Place 6: £16.87 Place 5: £10.75.
Owner Mrs Maureen Coxon **Bred** Gainsborough Stud Management Ltd **Trained** Lambourn, Berks
■ Stewards' Enquiry : Jimmy Quinn two-day ban: careless riding (Jul 9,11)

FOCUS
A poor race with few of these having shown any worthwhile form this season. The winner had had fewer chances than most.
T/Jkpt: Not won. T/Plt: £34.70 to a £1 stake. Pool: £50,580.83. 1,061.72 winning tickets. T/Qpdt: £14.70 to a £1 stake. Pool: £2,953.00. 148.50 winning tickets. SP

3052 LEICESTER (R-H)
Thursday, June 25

OFFICIAL GOING: Good to firm (firm in places; 9.2)
Wind: Light across Weather: Fine and sunny

3304 LANGHAM LADIES' H'CAP (LADY AMATEUR RIDERS) 5f 2y
6:40 (6:41) (Class 5) (0-70,69) 3-Y-O+ **£2,498** (£774; £387; £193) **Stalls** Low

Form RPR
0230 **1** **Buy On The Red**[44] 1951 8-10-5 **67** (b) MissERamstrom(7) 12 78
(D Nicholls) *racd centre: mde all: pushed clr over 1f out: eased towards fin* **8/1**[2]
0255 **2** *1 ¼* **Baybshambles (IRE)**[7] 3065 5-10-8 **68** MissVBarr(5) 14 75
(R E Barr) *racd centre: s.i.s: outpcd: hdwy over 1f out: wnt 2nd ins fnl f: no ch w wnr* **7/1**[1]
0035 **3** *4* **Thoughtsofstardom**[2] 3239 6-10-0 **55** MissEJJones 15 47
(P S McEntee) *racd centre: prom: pushed along 1/2-way: rdn to chse wnr over 1f out: no ex ins fnl f* **12/1**
2205 **4** *2 ¼* **Kheylide (IRE)**[27] 2460 3-10-1 **69** MissDLenge(7) 16 51
(Mrs D J Sanderson) *racd centre: chsd ldrs: rdn whn hmpd: hung lft and lost pl 1/2-way: hung rt over 1f out: styd on* **14/1**
4333 **5** *hd* **Bahamian Ceilidh**[29] 2386 3-10-1 **69** MissALMurphy(7) 10 50
(Tom Dascombe) *racd centre: chsd wnr over 3f: wknd ins fnl f* **12/1**
0030 **6** *hd* **Ghost Dancer**[3] 3208 5-10-3 **65** (p) MissHDavies(7) 8 48
(J M Bradley) *racd stands' side: s.i.s: hld up: nt clr run over 1f out: r.o ins fnl f: nrst fin* **12/1**
0030 **7** *1* **Realt Na Mara (IRE)**[48] 1846 6-10-0 **60** (p) MissVCartmel(5) 7 39
(H Morrison) *racd stands' side: s.i.s: hld up: rdn 1/2-way: n.d* **10/1**[3]
665 **8** *¾* **Lucky Dan (IRE)**[9] 3003 3-9-6 **60** MissACraven(7) 5 34
(Paul Green) *racd stands' side: sn pushed along and prom: hung rt and wknd over 1f out* **33/1**
2330 **9** *¾* **The History Man (IRE)**[15] 2812 6-9-10 **56** (be) MissMMullineaux(5) 11 30
(M Mullineaux) *swtchd to r stands' side: sn pushed along in rr: n.d* **7/1**[1]
4-05 **10** *nk* **Rapid Flow**[45] 1935 7-9-4 **50** oh5 MissJCWilliams(5) 4 22
(J W Unett) *racd stands' side: chsd ldrs: rdn 1/2-way: wknd over 1f out* **66/1**
056- **11** *hd* **Westport**[265] 6448 6-10-9 **69** MissRBastiman(5) 17 41
(R Bastiman) *racd centre: s.i.s: outpcd: nvr nrr* **18/1**
3400 **12** *hd* **Ronnie Howe**[15] 2801 5-9-8 **56** MissJessicaLodge(7) 6 27
(S R Bowring) *racd stands' side: led that gp: rdn: hung rt and wknd over 1f out* **16/1**
00-0 **13** *½* **Union Jack Jackson (IRE)**[7] 3066 7-9-9 **50** oh5 (b) MrsMMorris 13 19
(John A Harris) *racd centre: prom: rdn and hung lft 1/2-way: hung rt and wknd over 1f out* **66/1**
3404 **14** *nk* **Hart Of Gold**[15] 2806 5-10-8 **63** (b) MissFayeBramley 9 31
(R A Harris) *racd stands' side: prom: rdn whn hmpd and wknd 1/2-way* **14/1**
0356 **15** *¾* **Bluebok**[2] 3252 8-10-3 **63** (bt) MissSBradley(5) 2 28
(J M Bradley) *racd stands' side: s.i.s and hmpd s: outpcd* **14/1**
-000 **16** *3 ½* **Town House**[34] 2225 7-9-4 **50** oh5 MissAWallace(5) 3 3
(B P J Baugh) *racd stands' side: chsd ldrs tl wknd 2f out* **25/1**
0354 **U** **Nomoreblondes**[20] 2657 5-10-8 **68** (p) MissWGibson(5) 1 —
(P T Midgley) *stmbld and uns rdr s* **8/1**[2]

60.85 secs (0.85) **Going Correction** -0.05s/f (Good)
WFA 3 from 5yo+ 6lb **17** Ran SP% **120.3**
Speed ratings (Par 103): **91,89,82,79,78 78,76,75,74,73 73,73,72,71,70 65,—**
toteswinger: 1&2 £20.20, 1&3 £25.40, 2&3 £5.20 CSF £60.10 CT £475.55 TOTE £10.60: £3.00, £1.40, £2.70, £4.60; EX 48.10.
Owner R Haim **Bred** J Gittins And Capt J H Wilson **Trained** Sessay, N Yorks
■ Emma Ramstrom's first winner.
■ Stewards' Enquiry : Miss D Lenge caution: careless riding; caution: used whip without giving gelding time to respond.

FOCUS
A collection of modest performers, but they looked closely matched with seemingly just a handful either out of their depth or out of the handicap. Several in the line-up had shown an aptitude for front-running in the past and they went off at a decent pace. The first four home were drawn high. The winner is probably the best guide to the form.
Lucky Dan(IRE) Official explanation: trainer's rep said gelding was struck into and was lame

3305 STAPLEFORD (S) STKS 7f 9y
7:10 (7:40) (Class 6) 3-Y-O **£1,942** (£578; £288; £144) **Stalls** Low

Form RPR
4020 **1** **Iron Out (USA)**[12] 2918 3-9-0 58 MickyFenton 8 63
(R Hollinshead) *racd centre: a.p: chsd ldr 1/2-way: led overall over 1f out: edgd lft ins fnl f: rdn out* **8/1**
-202 **2** *½* **Piazza San Pietro**[12] 2908 3-9-0 72 JamieSpencer 13 62
(J R Gask) *racd centre: stdd s: hld up: hdwy 2f out: rdn ins fnl f: styd on* **7/4**[1]
3524 **3** *1 ¼* **Spinight (IRE)**[92] 960 3-8-9 61 (p) AndreaAtzeni(5) 4 58+
(M Botti) *racd stands' side: chsd ldr tl led that trio over 4f out: rdn over 1f out: hung rt ins fnl f: r.o: nt rch ldrs* **8/1**
6-04 **4** *1 ¼* **Pokfulham (IRE)**[20] 2652 3-9-0 61 (v) ChrisCatlin 14 55
(A P Jarvis) *overall ldr in centre: rdn and hdd over 1f out: no ex ins fnl f* **5/1**[3]
4005 **5** *4 ½* **Ask Dan (IRE)**[6] 3108 3-9-0 57 (p) RichardMullen 1 43
(B Smart) *swtchd to r centre 5f out: mid-div: rdn 1/2-way: styd on u.p fr over 1f out: nvr trbld ldrs* **16/1**
3523 **6** *2 ¾* **Aahaygirl (IRE)**[10] 2973 3-8-4 63 (v[1]) MartinLane(5) 7 30
(K R Burke) *led stands' side trio over 2f: rdn over 2f out: wknd over 1f out* **9/2**[2]
0-00 **7** *5* **Oneofthesedayz (IRE)**[45] 1926 3-8-9 50 (p) EdwardCreighton 9 17
(Mrs D J Sanderson) *racd centre: s.i.s: outpcd* **66/1**
0-00 **8** *4 ½* **Kathanikki Girl (IRE)**[28] 2404 3-8-4 38 DeanHeslop(5) 11 —
(Mrs L Williamson) *racd centre: sn outpcd* **150/1**
6346 **9** *1* **Ba Globetrotter**[12] 2918 3-9-0 49 SamHitchcott 10 7
(M R Channon) *racd centre: mid-div: hdwy u.p over 2f out: wknd over 1f out* **16/1**
00-0 **10** *½* **Pethers Dancer (IRE)**[52] 1729 3-8-11 40 DavidProbert(3) 6 —
(W R Muir) *racd stands' side: chsd ldrs tl hung rt and wknd 3f out* **66/1**
50-0 **11** *4* **Miss Moloney (IRE)**[125] 620 3-8-6 47 ow2 MarkCoumbe(5) 15 —
(Mrs S Lamyman) *s.i.s and unruly leaving stalls: racd alone far side: outpcd: sme hdwy 2f out: sn wknd and eased* **66/1**
24-0 **12** *30* **Miss Scarlet**[40] 2091 3-8-9 62 RobertWinston 12 —
(K A Ryan) *racd centre: chsd ldr tl wknd 1/2-way: eased* **25/1**

1m 26.18s (-0.02) **Going Correction** -0.05s/f (Good) **12** Ran SP% **114.2**
Speed ratings (Par 97): **98,97,96,94,89 86,80,75,74,73 69,34**
toteswinger: 1&2 £4.30, 1&3 £12.80, 2&3 £3.50 CSF £21.16 TOTE £9.70: £2.70, £1.50, £2.10; EX 29.20.The winner was bought in for 3,600gns. Piazza San Pietro was claimed by A. B. Haynes for £7,000.
Owner John L Marriott **Bred** Leslie Hagan **Trained** Upper Longdon, Staffs

FOCUS
This race was delayed more than half an hour following an incident in the first race. Plenty of long-term strugglers tackled this weak seller and none of them had ever notched a victory prior to going to post here. A couple stood out on BHA ratings, though, having recently gone close in better grade, and they were predictably towards the front-end of the betting. The winner is rated close to his AW best.
Oneofthesedayz(IRE) Official explanation: jockey said filly hung left
Miss Moloney(IRE) Official explanation: jockey said filly fly leapt leaving stalls
Miss Scarlet Official explanation: jockey said filly was unsuited by the track and the good to firm (firm in places) ground

3306 OSBASTON MAIDEN AUCTION STKS 5f 218y
7:40 (8:05) (Class 5) 2-Y-O **£3,238** (£963; £481; £240) **Stalls** Low

Form RPR
1 **Jairzihno** 2-9-2 0 TonyCulhane 5 76+
(J R Best) *a.p: chsd ldr over 1f out: shkn up to ld ins fnl f: r.o* **5/1**[3]
4 **2** *1* **Saint Sebastian (IRE)**[19] 2721 2-8-9 0 GrahamGibbons 1 66
(E S McMahon) *chsd ldr: hung rt over 4f out: led 1/2-way: rdn over 1f out: hdd and unable qck ins fnl f* **5/4**[1]
55 **3** *2 ½* **Storm Hawk (IRE)**[7] 3064 2-8-13 0 PaulEddery 2 62
(Pat Eddery) *chsd ldrs: rdn 1/2-way: no ex fnl f* **7/2**[2]
4 *8* **Plutocraft** 2-8-13 0 MartinDwyer 4 38
(J R Fanshawe) *s.i.s: hld up: hdwy over 2f out: wknd over 1f out* **7/2**[2]
5 *12* **Softly Spoken** 2-7-13 0 AndreaAtzeni(5) 3 —
(A W Carroll) *chsd ldrs tl wknd over 1f out* **22/1**

0 **P** **Scintillating (IRE)**[12] 2914 2-8-11 0 .... MickyFenton 6 —
(R Hollinshead) *racd alone in centre: overall ldr tl hung rt and hdd 1/2-way: sn wknd and eased: p.u over 1f out* **20/1**

1m 13.97s (0.97) **Going Correction** -0.05s/f (Good) **6** Ran SP% **114.7**
Speed ratings (Par 93): **91,89,86,75,59** —
toteswinger: 1&2 £4.20, 1&3 £3.20, 2&3 £1.10 CSF £12.13 TOTE £5.00: £2.00, £1.20; EX 7.60.
Owner Findlay & Bloom **Bred** Mrs C Regalado-Gonzalez **Trained** Hucking, Kent

FOCUS
An ordinary median auction event and none of those with previous experience had shown eyecatching form.

NOTEBOOK
Jairzihno, who cost 50,000 euros and is related to the useful sprinter Danehhurst, made a pleasing start to his career, travelling well throughout before making his challenge one off the nearside rail and asserting inside the final furlong. He was easy in the market beforehand, so probably has some improvement in him, and, although he was not the smoothest of movers in his slower paces, he ought now to be able to make some sort of mark in nursery company. (op 4-1)
Saint Sebastian(IRE) had not cut much ice on his first outing, when finishing a well-beaten fourth at Newcastle, but, after a sluggish start, he was always playing catch-up there and appeared to have the potential to improve. He did seem to progress here, too, breaking well, grabbing a position close to the nearside rail and running on well when tackled from the furlong marker. He did not have the finishing pace of his conqueror, but is game enough to find a small prize in the near future. (op 7-4)
Storm Hawk(IRE) had hinted at ability on his 5f debut and showed more on his second start when, despite rearing out of the stalls, he had run on well to take fifth in a fair 6f Ripon maiden. He is probably the marker for the race, as he again performed with credit.
Plutocraft, a son of Starcraft, is bred to appreciate longer distances than this in time, as his dam is related to a useful winner at 1m. He was coltish beforehand and green in the race, making a slow start, never really mounting a challenge and fading in the closing stages.
Softly Spoken, a cheaply bought debutante daughter of Forzando, represented a yard with a moderate first-time-out record with two-year-olds. She made no major impression and will need to find significant improvement to land a similar prize. (op 25-1 tchd 20-1)
Scintillating(IRE), a modest ninth of ten on her debut here 19 days previously, needed to make a considerably leap forward to figure prominently and she failed to do so. She showed early speed, but was soon hanging, as if something was not quite right, and her jockey eventually pulled her up. Official explanation: jockey said filly lost its action (op 25-1)

3307 JON MCGREGOR 60TH BIRTHDAY H'CAP — 1m 1f 218y
8:10 (8:20) (Class 4) (0-85,84) 3-Y-O — **£4,857** (£1,445; £722; £360) **Stalls** High

Form / RPR
-221 **1** **Matraash (USA)**[19] 2723 3-9-7 **84** .... RHills 3 92+
(M Johnston) *mde all: rdn clr fnl f: eased nr fin* **4/5**[1]
2-54 **2** *5* **Cosimo**[38] 2138 3-8-8 **71** .... (v[1]) JamieSpencer 1 69
(Sir Michael Stoute) *chsd wnr: rdn over 1f out: no rspnse: eased whn hld towards fin* **7/2**[2]
-600 **3** *2* **Cruikadyke**[14] 2855 3-9-3 **80** .... MartinDwyer 4 74
(P F I Cole) *prom: rdn over 3f out: wknd fnl f* **11/1**[3]
-210 **4** *5* **Dreamwalk (IRE)**[19] 2701 3-9-2 **79** .... SebSanders 2 63
(R M Beckett) *hld up: outpcd fr over 3f out* **7/2**[2]

2m 5.70s (-2.20) **Going Correction** -0.05s/f (Good) **4** Ran SP% **108.3**
Speed ratings (Par 101): **106,102,100,96**
CSF £3.89 TOTE £1.60; EX 2.50.
Owner Hamdan Al Maktoum **Bred** Shadwell Farm LLC **Trained** Middleham Moor, N Yorks

FOCUS
No better than a fair three-year-old handicap, but interesting nonetheless, as it featured a couple of potential improvers. They went off at a steady pace that did not quicken until the last half-mile. The winner is progressing but he did not have a great deal to beat here.

3308 BRUNTINGTHORPE H'CAP — 1m 3f 183y
8:40 (8:40) (Class 5) (0-75,66) 4-Y-O+ — **£3,885** (£1,156; £577; £288) **Stalls** High

Form / RPR
P-31 **1** **Camera Shy (IRE)**[9] 3004 5-8-0 **49** .... AndreaAtzeni(5) 2 59+
(K A Morgan) *s.i.s: hld up and bhd: hdwy over 3f out: chsd ldr over 2f out: led over 1f out: in command whn idled wl ins fnl f: jst hld on* **1/1**[1]
0-45 **2** *nk* **Into The Light**[20] 2684 4-9-7 **65** .... (b[1]) GrahamGibbons 6 71
(E S McMahon) *led: clr over 7f out: rdn and hdd over 1f out: hung lft ins fnl f: rallied towards fin* **6/4**[2]
0-04 **3** *14* **Channel Crossing**[24] 2537 7-9-4 **62** .... SebSanders 1 46
(S Wynne) *prom: chsd ldr 5f out to over 2f out: wknd over 1f out* **15/2**[3]
101/ **4** *10* **Picky**[49] 6206 5-9-3 **61** .... (b) ChrisCatlin 3 29
(C C Bealby) *chsd ldr 7f: rdn and wknd over 3f out* **25/1**
30-0 **5** *½* **Silver Waters**[10] 2983 4-9-7 **65** .... FrankieMcDonald 7 32
(Tim Vaughan) *sn pushed along in rr: wknd over 3f out* **25/1**

2m 33.52s (-0.38) **Going Correction** -0.05s/f (Good) **5** Ran SP% **109.5**
Speed ratings (Par 103): **99,98,89,82,82**
toteswinger: 1&2 £1.80. CSF £2.70 TOTE £2.10: £1.10, £1.30; EX 3.60.
Owner Michael Ogburn **Bred** Haras D'Etreham And Madame Lily Ades **Trained** Little Marcle, H'fords

FOCUS
A modest enough handicap, weakened by the absence of two penalised recent winners, but the pace was solid. The runner-up is the best guide and the idling winner was value for 2l.
Picky Official explanation: trainer said gelding lost a front shoe

3309 COLD OVERTON H'CAP — 1m 60y
9:10 (9:11) (Class 5) (0-75,75) 3-Y-O — **£3,238** (£963; £481; £240) **Stalls** High

Form / RPR
51-6 **1** **Glowing Praise**[12] 2925 3-9-7 **75** .... RichardMullen 5 82+
(E S McMahon) *trckd ldr: plld hrd: led over 1f out: r.o wl: eased nr fin* **2/1**[2]
30-2 **2** *2* **Mefraas (IRE)**[23] 2567 3-9-6 **74** .... RHills 3 74
(E A L Dunlop) *hld up: hdwy 2f out: rdn to chse wnr and edgd rt ins fnl f: no imp* **11/8**[1]
3342 **3** *nk* **Yellow Printer**[16] 2794 3-9-6 **74** .... SebSanders 4 73
(F J Brennan) *led: rdn and hdd over 1f out: styd on same pce ins fnl f* **9/2**[3]
0226 **4** *½* **Red Suede Shoes**[13] 2884 3-8-13 **70** .... JamesMillman(3) 7 69+
(B R Millman) *a.p: pushed along over 3f out: hmpd and hit over hd by rivals whip over 1f out: n.m.r ins fnl f: styd on* **14/1**
6-05 **5** *½* **Fantino**[14] 2856 3-8-13 **67** .... RobertWinston 2 64
(J Mackie) *chsd ldrs: rdn over 2f out: styd on same pce fnl f* **25/1**
045 **6** *¾* **Quinsman**[16] 2795 3-9-2 **70** .... LukeMorris 6 68+
(J S Moore) *hld up: rdn over 3f out: nt clr run fr over 1f out: nvr able to chal* **12/1**

1m 44.75s (-0.35) **Going Correction** -0.05s/f (Good) **6** Ran SP% **111.8**
Speed ratings (Par 99): **99,97,96,96,95 94**
toteswinger: 1&2 £1.10, 1&3 £1.80, 2&3 £1.02 CSF £5.08 TOTE £3.20: £1.70, £1.20; EX 6.00 Place 6: £9.05, Place 5: £3.31..
Owner J C Fretwell **Bred** Wyck Hall Stud Ltd **Trained** Lichfield, Staffs

FOCUS
No better than a fair-to-middling three-year-old handicap. Despite the small turn-out, however, the presence of several lightly raced contenders made for an interesting conclusion to the meeting and the race was truly run. More than one encountered trouble though and the form is slightly dubious.
Red Suede Shoes Official explanation: jockey said gelding was denied a clear run
Quinsman Official explanation: jockey said colt was denied a clear run
T/Plt: £10.10 to a £1 stake. Pool: £60,904.06. 4,365.86 winning tickets. T/Qpdt: £3.50 to a £1 stake. Pool: £4,040.00. 841.80 winning tickets. CR

2721 NEWCASTLE (L-H)
Thursday, June 25

OFFICIAL GOING: Good to firm (good in places; 7.9)
Rail realignment from 9f to 4.5f increased advertised distances on the round course by about 35yards.
Wind: moderate 1/2 behind Weather: fine and sunny

3310 COOPERS MARQUEES MEDIAN AUCTION MAIDEN STKS — 6f
2:30 (2:31) (Class 5) 2-Y-O — **£3,238** (£963; £481; £240) **Stalls** High

Form / RPR
6 **1** **Silenceofthewind (USA)**[34] 2247 2-9-3 0 .... JimCrowley 9 87+
(K R Burke) *w ldr: led over 3f out: shkn up over 1f out: clr jst ins fnl f: readily* **13/8**[1]
2 *3* **Antoniola (IRE)** 2-9-3 0 .... DavidAllan 13 77+
(T D Easterby) *dwlt: hld up in midfield: effrt 2f out: chsd wnr jst ins fnl f: no imp* **8/1**
0 **3** *3¾* **Powerful Pierre**[39] 2099 2-9-3 0 .... PhillipMakin 12 64
(Jedd O'Keeffe) *chsd ldrs: styd on same pce appr fnl f* **20/1**
3 **4** *¾* **King Of Reason**[15] 2825 2-9-3 0 .... DarryllHolland 7 62+
(D M Simcock) *trckd ldrs: t.k.h: kpt on same pce appr fnl f* **4/1**[3]
5 *2* **Lord Aeryn (IRE)** 2-9-3 0 .... TonyHamilton 6 56+
(R A Fahey) *chsd ldrs: outpcd over 2f out: wknd over 1f out* **3/1**[2]
6 **6** *4½* **North Central (USA)**[19] 2714 2-9-3 0 .... PaulMulrennan 1 42
(J Howard Johnson) *t.k.h: led tl over 3f out: wknd over 1f out* **10/1**
7 *2¼* **Dead Womans Pass (IRE)** 2-8-12 0 .... DanielTudhope 10 31
(N Wilson) *s.i.s: sme hdwy 2f out: nvr a factor* **40/1**
8 *4½* **Moonlight Blaze** 2-9-0 0 .... KellyHarrison(3) 3 22
(C W Fairhurst) *chsd ldrs: lost pl over 2f out* **50/1**
00 **9** *nse* **Kerolad (IRE)**[9] 2997 2-8-12 0 .... BMcHugh(5) 5 22
(N Wilson) *w ldrs: wknd 2f out* **200/1**
0 **10** *1¾* **Twoellies**[23] 2568 2-8-12 0 .... JamieMoriarty 8 12
(Ollie Pears) *s.i.s: bhd fnl 3f* **100/1**
65 **11** *nk* **Gold Story**[22] 2610 2-9-3 0 .... TomEaves 4 16
(B Ellison) *in rr div: sn drvn along: nvr on terms* **40/1**
0 **12** *1¾* **Captain Cash**[23] 2568 2-9-3 0 .... RoystonFfrench 11 10
(T D Easterby) *in rr div: sn pushed along: bhd fnl 3f* **40/1**

1m 13.77s (-1.43) **Going Correction** -0.475s/f (Firm) **12** Ran SP% **118.8**
Speed ratings (Par 93): **90,86,81,80,77 71,68,62,62,59 59,57**
toteswingers: 1&2 £7.10, 1&3 £14.00, 2&3 £15.00 CSF £15.36 TOTE £2.90: £1.10, £2.40, £4.70; EX 17.00 Trifecta £184.90 Pool: £417.45 - 1.67 winning units..
Owner Mogeely Stud & Mrs Maura Gittins **Bred** Lavin Bloodstock & Brereton C Jones **Trained** Middleham Moor, N Yorks

FOCUS
Probably no more than an ordinary maiden.

NOTEBOOK
Silenceofthewind(USA) travelled like an above-average horse before being asked to go and win his race well over a furlong out. He quickly went clear without his rider having to use the whip and he looks a really nice type. Karl Burke, who has him in a couple of big sales races later in the season, thinks a lot of him and this $310,000 yearling colt looks the type to do even better next year over slightly longer trips. Connections are now eyeing a 7f Listed race at Ascot or maybe even the Superlative Stakes at Newmarket. (op 2-1 tchd 9-4 in a place)
Antoniola(IRE) attracted significant support in the market beforehand. He forfeited his good high draw by breaking quite slowly but he travelled well through the race as his rider was forced to wait in behind horses until entering the final furlong. Once in the clear he picked up well to sweep by all bar the winner and he emerged easily the second best horse in the race. (op 20-1 tchd 22-1)
Powerful Pierre was beaten a long way on debut but he fared much better on this quicker ground and shapes as though he can improve again. (op 40-1)
King Of Reason spoilt his chance by racing far too freely in the early stages and he did well to finish fourth. He needs to learn to settle. Official explanation: jockey said colt ran too free (tchd 9-2)
Lord Aeryn(IRE) stayed on late in the day having looked a bit green once shaken up and he looks the type to come on a fair bit for this. (op 5-2 tchd 9-4 and 4-1)
North Central(USA) managed to get across from his wide draw but he raced quite keenly through the first couple of furlongs and dropped away pretty tamely, arguably taking a step backwards from his promising debut run. (op 6-1)

3311 TRADERSBETTINGEXCHANGE.CO.UK NOVICE STKS — 6f
3:00 (3:01) (Class 4) 2-Y-O — **£3,885** (£1,156; £577; £288) **Stalls** High

Form / RPR
1 **1** **Kaptain Kirkup (IRE)**[34] 2231 2-9-0 0 .... PhillipMakin 4 84+
(M Dods) *free to post and uns rdr at s: trckd ldrs: effrt over 2f out: led 1f out: styd on wl* **9/4**[1]
3621 **2** *1¾* **Ailsa Carmel (IRE)**[10] 2963 2-8-11 0 .... DarryllHolland 6 76
(M R Channon) *led hdd 1f out: no ex* **3/1**[3]
01 **3** *¾* **Ingleby Spirit**[35] 2195 2-9-2 0 .... TonyHamilton 5 79+
(R A Fahey) *trckd ldr: drvn over 3f out: hung lft over 1f out: kpt on same pce* **6/1**
32 **4** *nk* **Arabian Pride**[20] 2676 2-8-12 0 .... TPQueally 1 74+
(D M Simcock) *dwlt and carried lft s: swtchd rt sn after s: hld up: effrt and nt clr run 2f out: kpt on same pce* **6/1**
1 **5** *1¾* **Leviathan**[15] 2813 2-9-5 0 .... MickyFenton 2 75+
(T P Tate) *swvd lft s: hdwy over 2f out: edgd lft 1f out: wknd towards fin* **11/4**[2]

1m 13.28s (-1.92) **Going Correction** -0.475s/f (Firm) **5** Ran SP% **111.0**
Speed ratings (Par 95): **93,90,89,89,86**
CSF £9.34 TOTE £3.00: £1.60, £2.20; EX 11.10.
Owner Kevin Kirkup **Bred** David Barry **Trained** Denton, Co Durham

FOCUS
An open novice stakes run at an even enough gallop.

NOTEBOOK

Kaptain Kirkup(IRE) proved much the best horse in the race, despite fears beforehand that conditions may just be a little quicker than he wants. Phillip Makin always looked happy as he sat a coupleof lengths off the pace up the rail and, switched out to make his challenge over a furlong out, he soon mastered long time leader Ailsa Carmel and drew away a pretty ready winner. He has proved that he handles a sound surface, having won his maiden on good to soft ground, and his trainer reported afterwards that he has improved plenty from his first run. He holds an entry in Redcar´s Two-Year-Old Trophy, which looks a likely target now. (op 5-2)

Ailsa Carmel(IRE) was the most experienced runner in the field butthat meant she was the most exposed and, although she bagged the rail and was allowed to set her own tempo, she was brushed aside by the winner in the closing stages and handicaps looks her best bet later in the season. (op 5-1)

Ingleby Spirit seemed to relish testing ground when off the mark at Haydock on his second start and he didn´t look at home on this faster surface, edging left in the final furlong and not really picking up for pressure. He looks to need easier ground. (op 3-1)

Arabian Pride edged out to the middle of the track, taking Leviathan with him but both looked a little one paced in the closing stages. (tchd 5-1 and 13-2)

Leviathan could only find the one pace under pressure and was disappointing. (op 7-2)

3312 SEATON DELAVAL H'CAP 1m 3y(S)

3:30 (3:31) (Class 2) (0-100,95) 4-Y-O+

£12,462 (£3,732; £1,866; £934; £466; £234) **Stalls** High

Form RPR

-001 **1** **The Osteopath (IRE)**[41] 2045 6-9-1 **89** .... PhillipMakin 10 98
(M Dods) *hld up in midfield on inner: smooth hdwy and nt clr run over 1f out: swtchd between horses and led jst ins fnl f: hld on wl* **10/1**

4600 **2** *1* **Flipando (IRE)**[12] 2933 8-9-4 **95** .... NeilBrown(3) 3 102
(T D Barron) *steadied and swtchd rt s: hld up in rr: hdwy on ins over 2f out: n.m.r ins fnl f: styd on wl to take 2nd nr line* **7/1**[3]

0-30 **3** *nse* **Kay Gee Be (IRE)**[31] 2342 5-9-2 **90** .... JoeFanning 11 97
(W Jarvis) *led tl hdd jst ins fnl f: no ex* **7/1**[3]

0165 **4** *2 ¾* **Wovoka (IRE)**[16] 2787 6-8-8 **82** .... TonyHamilton 1 83
(D W Barker) *hld up in rr on inner: hdwy over 2f out: kpt on same pce fnl f* **28/1**

111- **5** *nk* **Ben Chorley**[371] 3173 5-9-2 **90** .... TPQueally 12 90+
(D R Lanigan) *trckd ldrs: chal over 1f out: sn rdn and one pce* **15/2**

-033 **6** *3 ¼* **Lady Rangali (IRE)**[9] 2999 4-8-4 **83** .... (p) JamieKyne(5) 5 76+
(Mrs A Duffield) *hld up in mid-div: effrt over 2f out: kpt on: nvr nr to chal* **10/1**

0033 **7** *1 ½* **Raptor (GER)**[11] 2939 6-8-11 **85** .... (vt) JimCrowley 7 74
(K R Burke) *mid-div: effrt over 3f out: one pce fnl 2f* **8/1**

5213 **8** *¾* **Ezdeyaad (USA)**[5] 3154 5-8-9 **83** .... DarryllHolland 6 70
(G A Swinbank) *swtchd rt s: sn chsng ldrs: wknd 1f out* **11/2**[2]

2502 **9** *5* **Charlie Tipple**[5] 3154 5-8-8 **82** .... (p) PaulMulrennan 8 58
(T D Easterby) *w ldrs: wknd 2f out* **5/1**[1]

5030 **10** *1 ¾* **Lucky Dance (BRZ)**[8] 3014 7-9-4 **92** .... GregFairley 9 64
(A G Foster) *chsd ldrs: drvn over 2f out: wknd over 1f out* **8/1**

0-40 **11** *11* **Dubai's Touch**[12] 2933 5-9-7 **95** .... RoystonFfrench 2 42
(M Johnston) *mid-div on outer: drvn over 3f out: sn lost pl and bhd* **25/1**

-400 **12** *5* **Sir Xaar (IRE)**[41] 2045 6-8-8 **82** .... (v) TomEaves 4 17
(B Smart) *in rr: lost pl over 2f out: sn bhd* **40/1**

1m 37.8s (-5.60) **Going Correction** -0.475s/f (Firm) **12** Ran SP% **119.0**
Speed ratings (Par 109): **109,108,107,105,104 101,100,99,94,92 81,76**
toteswinger: 1&2 £15.70, 1&3 £11.70, 2&3 £12.80 CSF £77.23 CT £539.30 TOTE £14.50: £3.80, £2.20, £2.70; EX 109.20 TRIFECTA Not won..
Owner Kevin Kirkup **Bred** Joe Rogers **Trained** Denton, Co Durham

FOCUS
It needed a career best from The Osteopath to win off his new mark. The first five all racednear the stands' rail. Sound form amongst the principals.

NOTEBOOK

The Osteopath(IRE), despite facing ground conditions considered to be quicker than ideal, the in-form 6yo got the job done with a decisive turn of foot in the final furlong. Up to a mark of 89 having won a soft ground 7f event here last time off 4lb lower, the gelding bagged a spot along the rail and proved that he doesn´t need to have slow ground to produce his best, bursting on to the scene inside the final furlong. He still looks to be improving and deserves a crack at a big handicap later in the season where he will hopefully get his favoured conditions. (op 9-1)

Flipando(IRE) hasn´t been at his best recently but is nicely treated on his early season efforts and he bounced back with a cracking run in defeat, coming from last up the stands rail and finishing strongly, despite not getting the smoothest of passages. He can win again soon. (op 8-1 tchd 17-2)

Kay Gee Be(IRE) is another who bounced back from a below-par effort and he ran a cracker from the front having bagged the favoured stands rail, suggesting he is capable of ending a lengthy losing run on turf. (op 11-2 tchd 5-1)

Wovoka(IRE), who needs a decent clip over this trip, stayed on from off the pace and is only 2lb higher than when scoring at Doncaster last month, so he remains well enough treated to go in again if things drop right. (op 25-1 tchd 20-1)

Ben Chorley travelled well in the slipstream of the leaders but he didn´t let himself down on ground much quicker than ideal and he is one to be very interested in back on a slower surface. (op 6-1)

3313 ACE TAXIS H'CAP 2m 19y

4:00 (4:00) (Class 4) (0-80,78) 4-Y-O+ **£5,046** (£1,510; £755; £377; £188) **Stalls** Low

Form RPR

0-11 **1** **Markington**[4] 3191 6-8-3 **65** 6ex .... (b) WilliamCarson(5) 3 72+
(P Bowen) *stdd s: hld up in rr: effrt on outside over 2f out: only 5th 1f out: fin strly to ld last 50yds* **5/2**[1]

0/25 **2** *1 ¾* **Sonara (IRE)**[27] 2452 5-8-12 **69** .... PaulMulrennan 9 74
(J Howard Johnson) *led: qcknd over 4f out: hdd towards fin* **25/1**

3003 **3** *¾* **Simonside**[7] 3068 6-8-7 **64** .... TomEaves 4 68
(B Ellison) *chsd ldr: drvn over 2f out: styd on same pce fnl f* **8/1**

0-32 **4** *2 ¼* **Jackday (IRE)**[22] 2614 4-8-2 **59** oh1 .... DuranFentiman 1 60
(T D Easterby) *chsd ldrs: one pce fnl 2f* **5/1**[3]

-566 **5** *1 ¾* **Dzesmin (POL)**[27] 2452 7-9-4 **78** .... FrederikTylicki(3) 12 77
(R A Fahey) *hld up towards rr: hdwy on ins over 3f out: nvr nr ldrs* **6/1**

46-2 **6** *nk* **Tribe**[17] 2760 7-8-7 **64** .... TPQueally 6 63
(P R Webber) *hld up towards rr: hdwy 10f out: trcking ldrs 5f out: one pce fnl 2f* **7/2**[2]

2016 **7** *8* **Danzatrice**[13] 2895 7-9-1 **72** .... JimCrowley 10 61
(C W Thornton) *hld up in rr: drvn over 4f out: hmpd over 3f out: nvr on terms* **11/1**

3-60 **8** *5* **Indonesia**[17] 2766 7-9-2 **73** .... JamieMoriarty 2 56
(T D Walford) *hld up towards rr: effrt 3f out: wknd over 1f out* **12/1**

200/ **9** *3* **Hyper Viper (IRE)**[363] 6379 4-7-12 **60** .... JamieKyne(5) 5 40
(C Grant) *trckd ldrs: lost pl over 3f out* **100/1**

05/0 **10** *¾* **Uptown Lad (IRE)**[10] 2725 10-7-9 **59** oh14 .... BillyCray(7) 7 38
(R Johnson) *hld up in rr: effrt over 4f out: sn bhd* **50/1**

3m 38.15s (-1.25) **Going Correction** +0.075s/f (Good) **10** Ran SP% **115.7**
Speed ratings (Par 105): **106,105,104,103,102 102,98,96,94,94**
toteswingers: 1&2 £11.30, 1&3 £5.10, 2&3 £19.00 CSF £69.03 CT £443.18 TOTE £3.10: £1.40, £4.60, £2.30; EX 64.40 Trifecta £200.40 Pool: £438.79 - 1.62 winning units..
Owner Ron Stepney **Bred** Minster Enterprises Ltd **Trained** Little Newcastle, Pembrokes
■ Stewards' Enquiry : Billy Cray two-day ban:careless riding (Jul 9,11)

FOCUS
The pace wasn´t that strong in this staying handicap. The placed horses were always prominent so Markington did well to win from the rear.
Tribe Official explanation: trainer's rep said gelding was unsuited by the slow early pace.

3314 GOSFORTH DECORATING & BUILDING SERVICES (S) STKS 1m 2f 32y

4:30 (4:30) (Class 5) 3-Y-O+ **£2,849** (£847; £423; £211) **Stalls** Centre

Form RPR

4355 **1** **Keisha Kayleigh (IRE)**[33] 2263 6-8-12 62 .... LanceBetts(5) 6 69
(B Ellison) *hld up in mi-dfield: hdwy to trckd ldrs over 5f out: rdn to ld over 1f out: sn wl clr* **6/4**[1]

1534 **2** *11* **Rose Of Coma (IRE)**[9] 3005 3-8-5 54 .... JamieKyne(5) 5 59+
(Miss Gay Kelleway) *hld up in rr: hdwy on ins over 2f out: nt clr run: swtchd 4 horses wd ins fnl f: styd on strly to snatch 2nd nr line* **7/2**[3]

00 **3** *hd* **Awaken**[10] 2965 8-9-3 48 .... RoystonFfrench 7 47
(Miss Tracy Waggott) *hld up in rr: hdwy on outside to trck ldrs over 4f out: wnt 2nd 1f out: kpt on same pce* **20/1**

6005 **4** *1* **Moonstreaker**[24] 2527 6-9-5 59 .... MichaelJStainton(3) 8 50
(R M Whitaker) *trckd ldrs: t.k.h: wnt modest 2nd 1f out: kpt on same pce* **10/3**[2]

0/55 **5** *2 ½* **Samizdat (FR)**[10] 1738 6-9-8 53 .... (b) DarrenMoffatt 2 45
(James Moffatt) *dwlt: t.k.h: sn trcking ldrs: effrt 3f out: chal over 1f out: sn rdn: wknd fnl 75yds* **9/1**

300- **6** *1 ½* **Roman History (IRE)**[23] 6951 6-9-5 50 .... (p) KellyHarrison(3) 4 42
(Miss Tracy Waggott) *trckd ldrs: led over 6f out: hdd over 1f out: wknd fnl 75yds* **33/1**

0300 **7** *1 ¼* **Run Free**[105] 823 5-9-3 54 .... BMcHugh(5) 1 40
(N Wilson) *t.k.h: led over 1f: trckd ldrs: fdd over 1f out* **12/1**

00-0 **8** *15* **Recoil (IRE)**[19] 2723 4-9-1 44 .... (bt) JohnCavanagh(7) 3 10
(R Johnson) *in rr: drvn whn stmbld 4f out: t.o 3f out* **66/1**

9 *68* **Chantilly Passion (FR)**[403] 8-9-8 0 .... PaulMulrennan 9 —
(B Storey) *w ldrs: led over 8f out: hdd over 6f out: lost pl over 4f out: t.o 3f out: virtually p.u* **66/1**

2m 11.7s (-0.20) **Going Correction** +0.075s/f (Good)
WFA 3 from 4yo+ 12lb **9** Ran SP% **113.7**
Speed ratings (Par 103): **103,94,94,93,91 90,89,77,22**
toteswingers: 1&2 £2.30, 1&3 £7.30, 2&3 £8.50 CSF £6.48 TOTE £2.40: £1.50, £1.40, £2.90; EX 6.80 Trifecta £46.70 Pool: £387.97 - 6.14 winning units..The winner was bought in for 5,800gns.
Owner Koo's Racing Club **Bred** Ronnie Boland **Trained** Norton, N Yorks

FOCUS
An awful race and the pace was very steady so not form to be getting excited about. The winner's best effort since last summer.
Rose Of Coma(IRE) Official explanation: jockey said filly was denied a clear run

3315 EUROPEAN BREEDERS' FUND HOPPINGS STKS (LISTED RACE) (F&M) 1m 2f 32y

5:00 (5:02) (Class 1) 3-Y-O+

£22,708 (£8,608; £4,308; £2,148; £1,076; £540) **Stalls** Centre

Form RPR

1223 **1** **Lady Jane Digby**[10] 2974 4-9-5 98 .... GregFairley 4 103
(M Johnston) *trckd ldrs: effrt 3f out: led wl over 1f out: drvn clr* **2/1**[2]

-400 **2** *5* **Syvilla**[10] 2974 4-9-5 90 .... WilliamCarson 5 93
(Rae Guest) *hld up towards rr: hdwy over 4f out: styd on to take modest 2nd 1f out* **50/1**

3000 **3** *1 ½* **Medici Pearl**[12] 2933 5-9-5 90 .... DavidAllan 8 95+
(T D Easterby) *s.i.s: hdwy on inner 3f out: nt clr run: swtchd outside 1f out: styd on wl towards fin: snatched 3rd on line* **16/1**

1 **4** *nse* **Gripsholm Castle (USA)**[42] 2002 3-8-7 0 .... TPQueally 2 90
(H R A Cecil) *hld up in midfield: n.m.r over 2f out: styd on same pce fnl f* **13/8**[1]

5-30 **5** *2* **Tottie**[20] 2672 3-8-7 92 .... JimCrowley 9 86
(Mrs A J Perrett) *dwlt: effrt on outer over 2f out: kpt on: nvr trbld ldrs* **15/2**[3]

6011 **6** *1* **Queen Martha (USA)**[20] 2662 3-8-7 79 .... PaulMulrennan 6 84
(M A Magnusson) *led: qcknd over 3f out: hdd wl over 1f out: kpt on one pce* **16/1**

/0-5 **7** *¾* **Laughter (IRE)**[19] 2697 4-9-5 89 .... RoystonFfrench 7 82
(Sir Michael Stoute) *trckd ldr: drvn 3f out: hung lft: wknd 1f out* **20/1**

0-40 **8** *2 ¼* **Moon Sister (IRE)**[12] 2933 4-9-5 96 .... DarryllHolland 3 78+
(W Jarvis) *trckd ldrs: nt clr run on ins fr over 2f out: nt rcvr: eased fnl 100yds* **15/2**[3]

2m 11.51s (-0.39) **Going Correction** +0.075s/f (Good)
WFA 3 from 4yo+ 12lb **8** Ran SP% **113.4**
Speed ratings (Par 111): **104,100,98,98,97 96,95,93**
toteswingers: 1&2 £14.30, 1&3 £7.30, 2&3 £20.40 CSF £83.17 TOTE £2.80: £1.10, £10.90, £4.10; EX 100.70 Trifecta £411.90 Part won. Pool: £556.75 - 0.72 winning units..
Owner Miss K Rausing **Bred** Miss K Rausing **Trained** Middleham Moor, N Yorks

FOCUS
A muddling pace to this fillies´ Listed event and that didn´t suit a few of these. Ordinary form for the grade with the winner the best guide.

NOTEBOOK

Lady Jane Digby avoided any trouble on her inside as some of her rivals got in each other's way, and she took the race by the scruff of the neck well over a furlong out before scooting clear to land her first Listed race in impressive style. She loves fast ground, came here in good form having been slightly unlucky not to win a similar race at Warwick last time and had a leading chance at the weights, so plenty was in her favour. A step up to Group company surely awaits. (op 5-2 tchd 11-4)

Syvilla was some way behind Lady Jane Digby at Warick last time and although she emerged best of the rest here, she was once again no match for that rival. Still, connections will be delighted that she has picked up some black type. (op 33-1)

Medici Pearl hasn´t had many goes over this trip but the muddling pace would have helped her on that front and she stayed on well once in the clear on ground that would have been quick enough. This was a good effort. Official explanation: jockey said mare was denied a clear run (op 18-1 tchd 20-1 and 14-1)

Gripsholm Castle(USA) is surely going to be seen in a better light when getting a stronger pace or stepping up in trip. She took a long time to pick up when the pace quickened and is probably best forgiven this. (op 5-4 tchd 11-10 and 7-4 in places)

Tottie kept on at the one pace from well back but was never a factor. (op 8-1 tchd 10-1)
Laughter(IRE) Official explanation: jockey said filly hung left in straight
Moon Sister(IRE) got no run up the inside rail with Darryll Holland sat motionless, and the rider gave up the ghost in the final furlong. She is easily forgiven this. Official explanation: jockey said filly was denied a clear run (op 12-1)

3316 TSG H'CAP 7f
5:30 (5:30) (Class 5) (0-75,74) 3-Y-O **£3,238** (£963; £481; £240) **Stalls** High

Form				RPR
-546	1		**Olympic Dream**[34] 2248 3-8-12 68 FrederikTylicki(3) 13	76
			(R A Fahey) *hld up in mid-div: smooth hdwy over 2f out: led appr fnl f: hld on wl towards fin* 11/4[1]	
130-	2	nk	**Toledo Gold (IRE)**[272] 6247 3-9-5 72 DavidAllan 6	79
			(E J Alston) *led: hung lft thrght: hdd appr fnl f: rallied ins fnl f: no ex* 28/1	
-503	3	3 1/4	**Lost In Paris (IRE)**[6] 3108 3-8-6 59 (b) DuranFentiman 12	58
			(T D Easterby) *chsd ldrs: kpt on same pce appr fnl f* 9/1	
2012	4	hd	**Minturno (USA)**[6] 3108 3-8-10 63 TPQueally 2	61+
			(Mrs A Duffield) *hld up in rr: hdwy on outer effrt over 2f out: chsng ldrs 1f out: kpt on same pce* 10/1	
-504	5	3 1/4	**Lakeman (IRE)**[23] 2578 3-9-1 73 LanceBetts(5) 9	62
			(B Ellison) *chsd ldrs: wknd fnl 150yds* 6/1[3]	
001	6	1 1/4	**Go Alone (IRE)**[31] 2343 3-9-3 70 DarryllHolland 8	56+
			(G A Swinbank) *mid-div: effrt over 3f out: chsng ldrs appr fnl f: sn wknd* 9/2[2]	
3634	7	2	**Dean Iarracht (IRE)**[7] 3062 3-9-0 67 TomEaves 11	47
			(M Dods) *mid-div: effrt over 3f out: lost pl over 1f out* 8/1	
4121	8	3 1/2	**Just Five (IRE)**[34] 2236 3-9-0 72 PatrickDonaghy(5) 3	43
			(M Dods) *in rr: drvn and sme hdwy over 2f out: wknd over 1f out* 9/1	
-000	9	1 3/4	**Cashleen (USA)**[22] 2607 3-8-13 66 (p) JamieMoriarty 5	32
			(K A Ryan) *w ldrs: lost pl over 1f out* 33/1	
0300	10	1 1/4	**Seldom (IRE)**[16] 2786 3-8-9 69 JohnCavanagh(7) 1	32
			(M Brittain) *chsd ldrs on wd outside: lost pl over 3f out: sn bhd* 40/1	
1025	11	nk	**Al Mugtareb (IRE)**[28] 2393 3-9-7 74 TPO'Shea 10	36
			(M Johnston) *a towards rr: nvr a factor* 12/1	
-043	12	hd	**Red China Blues (USA)**[27] 2450 3-8-8 66 JamieKyne(5) 7	28
			(J Howard Johnson) *s.i.s: in rr: bhd fnl 3f* 11/1	

1m 25.51s (-3.19) **Going Correction** -0.475s/f (Firm) **12** Ran SP% **124.2**
Speed ratings (Par 99): **99,98,94,94,91 89,87,83,81,79 79,79**
toteswinger: 1&2 £25.60, 1&3 £10.50, 2&3 £52.30 CSF £96.23 CT £653.82 TOTE £3.20: £1.20, £7.90, £2.70; EX 113.80 TRIFECTA Not won. Place 6: £87.05 Place 5: £47.99.
Owner H Hurst **Bred** H Hurst **Trained** Musley Bank, N Yorks

FOCUS
An open finale but the strong market support for Olympic Dream proved correct. He had the best draw and is rated back to close to his 2yo best.
Dean Iarracht(IRE) Official explanation: jockey said gelding was unsuited by the good to firm (good in places) ground
Just Five(IRE) Official explanation: jockey said gelding was unsuited by the good to firm (good in places) ground
T/Plt: £79.80 to a £1 stake. Pool: £68,139.99. 623.11 winning tickets. T/Qpdt: £14.90 to a £1 stake. Pool: £4,265.35. 211.20 winning tickets. WG

3071 WARWICK (L-H)
Thursday, June 25

OFFICIAL GOING: Good to firm (good in places; 8.4)
Rails from 1m start to 2f moved out 3yards but impact on distances not quantified.
Wind: Moderate half against Weather: Warm with some hazy sunshine

3317 TURFTV.CO.UK MAIDEN AUCTION STKS 5f
2:15 (2:17) (Class 5) 2-Y-O **£3,070** (£906; £453) **Stalls** Low

Form				RPR
	1		**Mdawee (IRE)** 2-8-13 0 RichardKingscote 3	77+
			(Tom Dascombe) *led: narrowly hdd over 1f out: rdn to ld ins fnl f: edgd lft: rdn out* 9/2[2]	
0222	2	1/2	**Reddy To Star (IRE)**[16] 2778 2-8-13 0 PhilipRobinson 6	75
			(C G Cox) *w wnr: slt ld over 1f out: rdn and hdd ins fnl f: kpt on* 4/5[1]	
20	3	1 1/2	**Fenella Rose**[30] 2354 2-8-1 0 AndreaAtzeni(5) 1	63
			(S C Williams) *a.p: swtchd rt and n.m.r wl over 1f out: sn rdn: nt qckn ins fnl f* 5/1[3]	
00	4	3 3/4	**Baby Judge (IRE)**[10] 2978 2-8-11 0 AmirQuinn 4	54
			(M C Chapman) *hld up: pushed along whn nt clr run briefly jst over 2f out: rdn over 1f out: nvr trbld ldrs* 125/1	
	5	1 1/2	**Ballachulish** 2-8-13 0 DaneO'Neill 2	51
			(H Candy) *s.i.s: rdn over 1f out: a bhd* 16/1	
025	6	2	**Tucker's Law**[16] 2792 2-8-9 0 ow1 JamesMillman(3) 5	43
			(B R Millman) *s.i.s: sn in tch: rdn whn stmbld wl over 1f out: sn bhd* 8/1	

61.27 secs (1.67) **Going Correction** +0.225s/f (Good) **6** Ran SP% **108.2**
Speed ratings (Par 93): **95,94,91,85,83 80**
toteswingers: 1&2 £2.00, 1&3 £3.80, 2&3 £1.70 CSF £7.90 TOTE £5.50: £2.50, £1.10; EX 11.30.
Owner Khalifa Al Attiyah **Bred** Miss Elaine Marie Smith **Trained** Lambourn, Berks

FOCUS
An average juvenile maiden.
NOTEBOOK
Mdawee(IRE), a £10,000 breeze-up purchase, made a winning start to his career and in the process made it four wins from four juvenile runners for his stable at the course this term. He showed decent early speed to win the battle for the lead and displayed a very likeable attitude under pressure down the home straight considering this was his first outing. This looks his trip for the short term and there should be more to come, so it will be interesting to see where he turns up next. (op 7-2)
Reddy To Star(IRE) has now been narrowly beaten into second on his last four runs. He was unable to dominate, which he probably prefers, but still ran close to his recent level. It is more likely that he bumped into one here and not his attitude which contributed to another runner-up spot, and he certainly does deserve to go one better. (op 5-6 tchd 10-11)
Fenella Rose came in for good support and returned to the sort of form that saw her finish second to the Albany winner Habaayib on debut in May. She held every chance, but appeared slightly reluctant to go through the gap that appeared when the first pair came under pressure near the furlong pole. She now qualifies for nurseries and could benefit again for this experience. (op 8-1 tchd 9-2)
Baby Judge(IRE), making his debut for new connections after finishing down the field in a claimer last time, posted his best effort thus far on ground probably lively enough for him. He also looks ready for a return to another furlong. (op 150-1)

Ballachulish's yard sent out Amour Propre to win this race last season. The difference here was Amour Propre had the benefit of a previous spin and got very well backed, where as he was a newcomer who proved friendless in the betting ring. He was outpaced from the gates and ran freely, ultimately shaping as though the race was much needed, but better can be expected next time. (op 15-2)
Tucker's Law failed to raise his game for the drop back from 6f and looks to be going the wrong way. Official explanation: jockey said colt stumbled 2f out (op 12-1 tchd 15-2)

3318 RACING UK LIVE IN YOUR LIVING ROOM H'CAP 6f
2:45 (2:45) (Class 3) (0-90,90) 3-Y-O+ **£7,771** (£2,312; £1,155; £577) **Stalls** Low

Form				RPR
0450	1		**Barons Spy (IRE)**[10] 2976 8-9-7 83 JamesDoyle 1	93
			(R J Price) *chsd ldr: rdn to ld over 1f out: edgd lft ins fnl f: r.o* 5/1[3]	
0002	2	nk	**Benllech**[6] 3122 5-9-9 90 MartinLane(5) 2	99
			(D M Simcock) *hld up: pushed along 3f out: rdn 2f out: hdwy over 1f out: swtchd rt ins fnl f: r.o* 7/4[1]	
0050	3	2 1/2	**Phantom Whisper**[26] 2474 6-9-9 88 JamesMillman(3) 6	89
			(B R Millman) *bhd: pushed along 3f out: rdn 2f out: hdwy over 1f out: kpt on one pce fnl f* 13/2	
3160	4	3	**Peter Island (FR)**[26] 2474 6-9-9 85 (v) ChrisCatlin 3	76
			(J Gallagher) *led: rdn and hdd over 1f out: wknd ins fnl f* 9/2[2]	
0-05	5	3 1/2	**Bond City (IRE)**[28] 2405 7-10-0 90 RichardMullen 4	70
			(G R Oldroyd) *prom: rdn over 1f out: wknd fnl f* 8/1	
4020	6	3 1/4	**Pawan (IRE)**[55] 1647 9-9-9 90 (b) AnnStokell(5) 7	60
			(Miss A Stokell) *sn chsng ldrs: rdn over 2f out: wknd over 1f out* 20/1	
-306	7	1 1/4	**Diriculous**[29] 2385 5-9-7 90 DToole(7) 8	56
			(T G Mills) *s.i.s: outpcd* 20/1	
3423	8	2 1/4	**Music Box Express**[2] 3246 5-8-9 71 oh9 DO'Donohoe 5	30
			(George Baker) *s.i.s: hld up and bhd: c wd over 2f out: sn rdn and struggling* 20/1	

1m 12.04s (0.24) **Going Correction** +0.225s/f (Good) **8** Ran SP% **109.9**
Speed ratings (Par 107): **107,106,103,99,94 90,88,85**
toteswingers: 1&2 £3.30, 1&3 £5.50, 2&3 £4.40 CSF £12.96 CT £51.81 TOTE £7.40: £2.10, £1.10, £2.20; EX 13.90.
Owner Barry Veasey **Bred** Tally-Ho Stud **Trained** Ullingswick, H'fords
■ Stewards' Enquiry : Martin Lane four-day ban: used whip with excessive frequency (July 9,11,13,14)

FOCUS
A tight-looking handicap, run at a solid pace. Sound form rated through the runner-up.
NOTEBOOK
Barons Spy(IRE)'s best previous run this season came over 6f and as a former course and distance winner it was unsurprising that the money came for him on this drop back from 7f. He got a lovely passage through the race, showing the required early speed, and kept most gamely to his task inside the final furlong. He is capable of holding his form, but this was his highest winning mark to date and that should be taken into account when he bids to follow up. (op 17-2)
Benllech had finished a narrow second off this mark at Redcar six days earlier. He lost out this time by hitting a flat spot nearing the home turn and, though he was eating into the winner's advantage throughout the last furlong, he was never quite getting there. He is now due to race from a 2lb higher mark and has yet to win away from Polytrack. (tchd 5-2)
Phantom Whisper had been dropped 2lb and ran his race, confirming last-time-out form with the front-running Peter Island. (op 6-1 tchd 9-2)
Peter Island(FR) had his own way out in front, but is still 6lb higher than his last winning mark. (op 4-1 tchd 10-3)
Bond City(IRE) has run creditably in decent sprints the last twice and was not totally disgraced considering the ground was probably quicker than he cares ideally for. Official explanation: jockey said gelding was unsuited by the good to firm (good in places) ground (tchd 7-1)

3319 RACING UK FOCUSED ON RACING MAIDEN STKS 7f 26y
3:20 (3:23) (Class 5) 3-Y-O+ **£2,914** (£867; £433; £216) **Stalls** Low

Form				RPR
36	1		**Turning Top (IRE)**[19] 2710 3-8-12 77 JamieSpencer 8	70+
			(S A Callaghan) *led early: chsd ldr: led wl over 1f out: sn edgd lft: r.o wl* 1/1[1]	
0-0	2	3 1/4	**Orlando's Tale (USA)**[28] 2416 4-9-12 0 DaneO'Neill 4	69
			(J R Fanshawe) *sn led: hung rt bnd over 3f out: hdd wl over 1f out: one pce* 9/1	
5264	3	nk	**Bennelong**[13] 2885 3-9-3 75 (p) MartinDwyer 6	65
			(R M Beckett) *hld up in tch: carried hd high over 1f out: rdn and edgd lft ins fnl f: kpt on same pce* 2/1[2]	
0	4	7	**Double Moon**[36] 2178 3-9-3 0 DO'Donohoe 5	46
			(George Baker) *t.k.h: prom tl rdn and wknd over 1f out* 50/1	
	5	2 1/4	**Scottish Glen** 3-9-3 0 PaulDoe 3	40
			(P R Chamings) *s.i.s: rdn wl over 1f out: a bhd* 8/1[3]	
0	6	3 1/2	**Rock Tech**[78] 1185 4-9-12 0 SimonWhitworth 2	34
			(J R Jenkins) *s.i.s: a in rr* 80/1	
0	7	9	**Ivy The Terrible**[27] 2455 3-8-12 0 SteveDrowne 7	1
			(Dr J D Scargill) *bhd fnl 4f* 66/1	

1m 25.56s (0.96) **Going Correction** -0.20s/f (Firm)
WFA 3 from 4yo 9lb **7** Ran SP% **109.1**
Speed ratings (Par 103): **86,82,81,73,71 67,57**
toteswingers: 1&2 £2.30, 2&3 £1.10 1&3 not won. CSF £10.00 TOTE £1.90: £1.20, £2.90; EX 6.60.Hindford Oak Sioux was withdrawn. Price at time of withdrawal 12/1. Rule 4 applies to all bets - deduction 5p in the pound.
Owner Michael Tabor **Bred** Barouche Stud Ireland Ltd **Trained** Newmarket, Suffolk
■ Hindford Oak Sioux (12/1, unruly at s) was withdrawn. Deduct 5p in the £ under R4.

FOCUS
A moderate maiden, run at a steady pace, and the form is not easy to assess. Easy for the winner, with a doubt over how much ability the third retains.

3320 WARWICK RACECOURSE ETERNAL STKS (LISTED RACE) (FILLIES) 7f 26y
3:50 (3:51) (Class 1) 3-Y-O
£22,708 (£8,608; £4,308; £2,148; £1,076; £540) **Stalls** Low

Form				RPR
5-62	1		**Golden Stream (IRE)**[8] 3016 3-8-12 94 JamieSpencer 7	102+
			(Sir Michael Stoute) *mde all: rdn and edgd rt jst ins fnl f: rdn out* 6/5[1]	
-250	2	1 1/2	**Damaniyat Girl (USA)**[8] 3016 3-8-12 100 (b[1]) LiamJones 5	98
			(W J Haggas) *s.i.s: t.k.h: sn mid-div: nt clr run on ins over 3f out: hdwy over 2f out: sn rdn: swtchd rt and wnt 2nd jst ins fnl f: kpt on one pce* 5/1[2]	
0-10	3	2	**Select (IRE)**[47] 1873 3-8-12 94 RichardMullen 13	93+
			(P W Chapple-Hyam) *hld up towards rr: hdwy and c wd over 2f out: rdn over 1f out: r.o ins fnl f* 40/1	
-035	4	3/4	**Seradim**[17] 2777 3-8-12 99 MartinDwyer 1	91
			(P F I Cole) *a.p: rdn over 1f out: carried rt jst ins fnl f: one pce* 7/1[3]	

6-30 **5** 3 ¼ **Foundation Room (IRE)**[33] 2273 3-8-12 88 SteveDrowne 2 82
(A M Balding) *hld up in tch: rdn and hung bdly lft over 1f out: sn wknd* **8/1**
-101 **6** shd **Aroundthebay**[17] 2761 3-8-12 86 ChrisCatlin 10 82
(H J L Dunlop) *stdd s: hld up in rr: sme prog fnl f: n.d* **28/1**
-063 **7** shd **Favourite Girl (IRE)**[12] 2934 3-8-12 97 GrahamGibbons 11 82
(T D Easterby) *hld up in mid-div: lost pl over 3f out: effrt 2f out: no imp whn carried lft over 1f out* **10/1**
0-25 **7** dht **Ahla Wasahl**[41] 2057 3-8-12 99 AhmedAjtebi 8 82
(D M Simcock) *chsd wnr tl wl over 1f out: wknd fnl f* **33/1**
61 **9** 3 **So Blissful (IRE)**[36] 2179 3-8-12 76 DaneO'Neill 9 74
(T G Mills) *swtchd rt over 1f out: a in rr* **40/1**
16-6 **10** 2 ¾ **Honest Quality (USA)**[57] 1599 3-9-3 98 IanMongan 12 71
(H R A Cecil) *prom: wkng whn hung lft wl over 1f out* **20/1**
4022 **11** nk **Ermine And Velvet**[20] 2673 3-8-12 93 EdwardCreighton 6 65
(C E Brittain) *prom: hung rt bnd over 3f out: sn wknd* **20/1**

1m 22.38s (-2.22) **Going Correction** -0.20s/f (Firm) 11 Ran SP% 115.6
Speed ratings (Par 104): **104,102,100,99,95 95,95,95,91,88 88**
toteswinger: 1&2 £3.20, 1&3 £16.10, 2&3 £29.20 CSF £6.06 TOTE £2.10: £1.10, £1.70, £7.40; EX 8.00.
Owner The Queen **Bred** The Queen **Trained** Newmarket, Suffolk

FOCUS
A competitive Listed prize for 3yo fillies. The form is not the strongest for the class, but still sound enough. The winner ran to a similar level to Ascot.

NOTEBOOK
Golden Stream(IRE) gained some compensation for her second in the Sandringham Handicap at Royal Ascot last week by making all in convincing fashion. The drop back to 7f proved no bother as she was smartly away and handled the tight nature of this track really well. She had her rivals at work turning for home and never really looked like being reeled in. Considering she is by Sadler's Wells, out of a dam that landed the Ribblesdale, it is surprising that she has relished dropping back in trip from 1m2f the last twice, and the best of her has likely still to be seen. A step up to Group company is now firmly on the cards. (op 5-4 tchd 11-8)
Damaniyat Girl(USA) finished well behind the winner at Royal Ascot, but was giving her 6lb and more importantly fared poorly with the draw there. She was equipped with first-time blinkers and awash with sweat, but still got closer to that rival despite not enjoying the same passage through the race. She has a few questions to answer with her temperament now, but there is little doubt she can find a race of this class when things go her way. (tchd 9-2 and 11-2)
Select(IRE) had to come wide around the home bend and took time to hit top gear when straightening up. She motored home inside the final furlong to bag third and this was career-best display. A stiffer track over this distance should suit better and she could build on this. (op 25-1)
Seradim ran her race on this drop back from 1m and return to a sounder surface, confirming her York form with Ahla Wasahl. She helps to set the standard. (op 10-1)
Aroundthebay looks one to take from the race. She had plenty to find on paper, but ran on nicely from well off the pace and is evidently still improving. (op 20-1)
Favourite Girl(IRE) never looked that happy on this step up in distance and return to quicker ground, failing to see it out. (op 17-2 tchd 8-1)

3321 WARWICKRACECOURSE.CO.UK H'CAP 1m 2f 188y
4:20 (4:20) (Class 5) (0-75,75) 3-Y-O £2,914 (£867; £433; £216) Stalls Low

Form RPR
5043 **1** **Parc Des Princes (USA)**[3] 3222 3-8-4 58 ChrisCatlin 2 66
(A M Balding) *hld up in rr: nt clr run briefly over 2f out: hdwy wl over 1f out: edgd rt and led 1f out: r.o* **5/2**[1]
541 **2** 2 ¼ **Dome Rocket**[20] 2681 3-9-7 75 PaulDoe 6 79
(W J Knight) *prom: n.m.r and lost pl after 1f: hdwy over 4f out: led wl over 1f out: sn rdn and hung lft: hdd 1f out: one pce* **7/1**[3]
0-04 **3** 3 **Choral Service**[28] 2415 3-9-4 72 LiamJones 3 71
(W J Haggas) *hld up in tch: pushed along and reminder over 6f out: rdn 2f out: sltly hmpd over 1f out: wknd ins fnl f* **4/1**[2]
-005 **4** 1 ¾ **Shanavaz**[16] 2779 3-8-4 58 DaleGibson 5 54
(Mrs G S Rees) *stmbld s: hld up and bhd: pushed along over 3f out: rdn over 1f out: nvr trbld ldrs* **16/1**
4110 **5** 2 ¾ **Mons Calpe (IRE)**[10] 2982 3-9-6 74 (b) MartinDwyer 1 65
(P F I Cole) *sn led: rdn and hdd wl over 1f out: sn hmpd: wknd fnl f* **5/2**[1]
-405 **6** 1 ½ **King's Masque**[19] 2710 3-9-2 70 DO'Donohoe 4 59
(W R Muir) *led early: t.k.h: chsd ldr tl over 7f out: rdn over 2f out: wknd over 1f out* **15/2**
3256 **7** 5 **Hypnotist (UAE)**[24] 2535 3-9-6 74 EdwardCreighton 7 54
(C E Brittain) *prom: chsd ldr over 7f out: rdn over 2f out: wknd wl over 1f out* **18/1**

2m 17.23s (-3.87) **Going Correction** -0.375s/f (Firm) 7 Ran SP% 112.6
Speed ratings (Par 99): **99,97,95,93,91 90,87**
toteswinger: 1&2 £2.20, 1&3 £2.70, 2&3 £3.50 CSF £20.03 TOTE £2.90: £1.80, £2.80; EX 14.70.
Owner Calzaghe Partnership **Bred** Castletown Stud **Trained** Kingsclere, Hants

FOCUS
A fair handicap for the grade, run at a good pace. A slight personal best from the winner.

3322 BOLLINGER CHAMPAGNE CHALLENGE SERIES H'CAP (FOR GENTLEMAN AMATEUR RIDERS) 1m 22y
4:50 (4:50) (Class 5) (0-70,68) 4-Y-O+ £2,498 (£774; £387; £193) Stalls Low

Form RPR
0260 **1** **Tanforan**[7] 3070 7-11-0 58 MrSWalker 9 65
(B P J Baugh) *a.p: led ent fnl f: drvn out* **13/2**[3]
0401 **2** 1 ½ **Aggbag**[7] 3077 5-10-6 50 MrSDobson 7 54
(J Mackie) *hld up in tch: rdn 2f out: edgd rt wl ins fnl f: kpt on u.p to take 2nd last strides* **3/1**[1]
4020 **3** hd **Justcallmehandsome**[8] 3024 7-10-12 63 (v) MrGOliver(7) 4 67
(D J S Ffrench Davis) *led: edgd rt wl over 1f out: rdn and hdd ent fnl f: no ex and lost 2nd last strides* **9/1**
006 **4** ½ **Dudley Docker (IRE)**[20] 2675 7-11-0 65 (b) MrJPearce(7) 3 67
(T T Clement) *s.s: hld up in rr: rdn and hdwy 1f out: kpt on* **12/1**
0023 **5** ½ **Bavarica**[17] 2764 7-10-12 61 MrRBirkett(5) 10 62
(Miss J Feilden) *hld up: sn mid-div: hdwy 2f out: sn rdn and hung lft: kpt on same pce ins fnl f* **4/1**[2]
0003 **6** nk **Desert Lover (IRE)**[21] 537 7-10-0 49 oh4 MrMPrice(5) 1 50
(R J Price) *hld up in mid-div: pushed along 3f out: rdn over 1f out: kpt on ins fnl f: nvr able to chal* **20/1**
0/00 **7** ¾ **Legal Lover (IRE)**[18] 2746 7-10-11 60 MrStephenHarrison(5) 6 59
(R Hollinshead) *chsd ldr: pushed along over 3f out: edgd lft over 1f out: rdn and fdd ins fnl f* **12/1**
5000 **8** 3 ¾ **Millfield (IRE)**[10] 2977 6-11-5 68 MrNdeBoinville(5) 11 58
(P R Chamings) *s.s: hld up in rr: sme prog 3f out: rdn and btn over 1f out* **20/1**
5520 **9** 4 **Just Oscar (GER)**[12] 2921 5-10-5 52 ow1 (b[1]) MrBenBrisbourne(3) 5 33
(W M Brisbourne) *hld up towards rr: nt clr run briefly 3f out: c wd st: nvr nr ldrs* **8/1**
-050 **10** shd **Naledi**[44] 1974 5-9-12 49 oh4 MrPHardy(7) 2 30
(J R Norton) *a in rr* **33/1**
500/ **11** 16 **Seasons Estates**[1357] 5712 7-11-0 65 MrTGarner(7) 8 9
(F J Brennan) *hld up in mid-div: wknd 3f out* **25/1**

1m 40.77s (-0.23) **Going Correction** -0.20s/f (Firm) 11 Ran SP% 118.9
Speed ratings (Par 103): **93,91,91,90,90 90,89,85,81,81 65**
toteswinger: 1&2 £5.20, 1&3 £10.90, 2&3 £6.50 CSF £25.96 CT £183.90 TOTE £7.70: £2.60, £1.80, £3.60; EX 26.90 Place 6: £8.24 Place 5: £7.04.
Owner F Gillespie **Bred** Bearstone Stud **Trained** Audley, Staffs
■ Stewards' Enquiry : Mr P Hardy jockey saud gelding was unsuited by the good to firm, good in places ground

FOCUS
A weak handicap, confined to gentleman amateur riders. The most accomplished jockeys were on the first two and the winner is rated back to form.
Naledi Official explanation: jockey said gelding was unsuited by the good to firm (good in places) ground
T/Plt: £8.40 to a £1 stake. Pool: £47,944.35. 4,139.94 winning tickets. T/Qpdt: £7.20 to a £1 stake. Pool: £2,653.63. 272.20 winning tickets. KH

3323 - 3330a (Foreign Racing) - See Raceform Interactive

2778 CHESTER (L-H)
Friday, June 26

OFFICIAL GOING: Good to firm (firm in places; 8.5)
Wind: Almost nil Weather: Showers

3331 TRAFFORD CENTRE H'CAP 7f 122y
6:40 (6:40) (Class 5) (0-70,74) 4-Y-O+ £4,209 (£1,252; £625; £312) Stalls Low

Form RPR
0600 **1** **Glenridding**[8] 3076 5-9-4 64 (p) J-PGuillambert 1 74
(J G Given) *mde all: pushed along whn hung rt off bnd wl over 1f out: r.o wl fnl f: wl in command at fin* **5/1**[2]
6000 **2** 2 ½ **H Harrison (IRE)**[18] 2769 9-8-4 57 AndrewHeffernan(7) 5 61
(I W McInnes) *chsd wnr thrght: rdn over 1f out and clsd on wnr briefly: nt qckn ins fnl f: all out to hold on for 2nd at fin* **12/1**
-004 **3** hd **Jilly Why (IRE)**[10] 3002 8-9-0 60 (b) StephenDonohoe 2 63
(Paul Green) *chsd ldrs: pushed along over 2f out: plld out off rail wl over 1f out: styd on u.p ins fnl f* **8/1**
0-06 **4** shd **Mayoman (IRE)**[39] 2145 4-8-12 58 RobertHavlin 3 61
(M Mullineaux) *hld up: nt clr run over 2f out: hdwy over 1f out: r.o ins fnl f: gaining at fin* **14/1**
/5-5 **5** nk **Four Tel**[57] 1634 5-8-11 62 MCGeran(5) 17 64
(N J Vaughan) *hld up: hdwy whn nt clr run over 1f out: running on whn nt clr run and swtchd rt ins fnl f: rapid prog towards fin* **16/1**
-035 **6** 3 ½ **Zabeel Tower**[7] 3097 6-9-10 70 (p) RoystonFfrench 7 64
(R Allan) *midfield: pushed along and hdwy to chse ldrs 2f out: no ex fnl 100yds* **8/1**
-000 **7** 4 ½ **Flashy Max**[16] 2804 4-8-5 51 oh3 (p) SilvestreDeSousa 6 33
(Jedd O'Keeffe) *chsd ldrs: pushed along over 3f out: wknd fnl f* **20/1**
500- **8** ½ **White Ledger (IRE)**[365] 3405 10-7-12 51 oh6 AmyScott(7) 13 32
(R E Peacock) *missed break: bhd: styd on fnl f: nvr rchd ldrs* **100/1**
0110 **9** nk **Sign Of The Cross**[18] 2775 5-9-3 70 BillyCray(7) 9 50
(C R Dore) *towards rr on outside: pushed along and hdwy into midfield 3f out: no imp on ldrs: wknd fnl f* **11/1**
/5-6 **10** 3 **Tobago Reef**[114] 760 5-8-7 60 oh4 ow9 (p) RobbieEgan(7) 4 33
(C W Moore) *in tch: pushed along over 3f out: wknd over 2f out* **25/1**
0-00 **11** 3 **Dashing Daniel**[31] 2366 4-8-6 57 oh1 ow6 (p) DeanHeslop(5) 15 22
(N J Vaughan) *midfield: rdn and wknd over 1f out* **50/1**
3223 **12** 1 **Kildare Sun (IRE)**[21] 2665 7-9-6 66 (p) GregFairley 11 29
(J Mackie) *midfield: pushed along 2f out: wknd over 1f out* **4/1**[1]
0-01 **13** ½ **Bahamian Kid**[8] 3075 4-9-9 74 6ex (p) RichardEvans(5) 12 36
(R Hollinshead) *chsd ldrs tl rdn and wknd 2f out* **7/1**[3]
5200 **14** 1 ¾ **Just Oscar (GER)**[1] 3322 5-8-2 53 ow2 (b) RossAtkinson(5) 14 10
(W M Brisbourne) *a bhd* **33/1**
1335 **U** **Many Welcomes**[31] 2353 4-8-6 52 CatherineGannon 8 —
(B P J Baugh) *got upset in stalls and rrd twice bef s: lft gate wout jockey* **10/1**

1m 32.43s (-1.37) **Going Correction** -0.175s/f (Firm) 15 Ran SP% 123.6
Speed ratings (Par 103): **99,96,96,96,95 92,87,87,87,84 81,80,79,77,—**
toteswingers: 1&2 £15.50, 1&3 £8.60, 2&3 £22.80 CSF £62.10 CT £367.18 TOTE £4.70: £2.40, £3.00, £2.10; EX 46.50.
Owner Tremousser Partnership **Bred** Bolton Grange **Trained** Willoughton, Lincs

FOCUS
Despite the ground being watered and a brief shower before racing, the going was on the firm side of good to firm. A modest handicap where the draw was as usual important and the first four were drawn from the bottom five stalls. The form is not the most solid but alright for the level.
Four Tel ◆ Official explanation: jockey said gelding was denied a clear run
Sign Of The Cross Official explanation: jockey said gelding suffered interference at start

3332 LIVERPOOL JOHN LENNON AIRPORT MAIDEN FILLIES' STKS 7f 2y
7:15 (7:15) (Class 4) 2-Y-O £4,047 (£1,204; £601; £300) Stalls Low

Form RPR
642 **1** **Abandagold (IRE)**[17] 2792 2-9-0 0 StephenDonohoe 2 68+
(P D Evans) *mde all: hung rt off bnd fr 2f out whn pressed: r.o wl and plld out more towards fin* **8/11**[1]
2 2 ¼ **Bideeya (USA)** 2-9-0 0 J-PGuillambert 6 62+
(C E Brittain) *chsd ldrs: outpcd by front pair over 1f out: kpt on to take 2nd towards fin: nt pce of wnr* **7/2**[2]
6U **3** ½ **Sarahthecarer (IRE)**[3] 3249 2-8-7 0 RobbieEgan(7) 5 61
(P M Mooney, Ire) *chsd wnr: pushed along over 3f out: effrt to chal 2f out: no ex 75yds out: sn lost 2nd* **16/1**
4 **4** 7 **Abbi Jicaro**[11] 2978 2-8-9 0 DeanHeslop(5) 4 44
(Mrs L Williamson) *dwlt: plld hrd: hld up: outpcd fnl 2f* **6/1**[3]
0 **5** 14 **Psychopathicsandra (IRE)**[50] 1802 2-8-7 0 BillyCray(7) 1 —
(A Berry) *outpcd in rr after 2f: lost tch over 1f out* **17/2**

1m 27.48s (0.98) **Going Correction** -0.175s/f (Firm) 5 Ran SP% 110.8
Speed ratings (Par 92): **87,84,83,75,59**
CSF £3.59 TOTE £1.60: £1.20, £2.00; EX 2.70.
Owner Bathwick Gold Partnership **Bred** Rocklow Stud **Trained** Pandy, Monmouths

FOCUS
A small field for this modest fillies' maiden and a race best rated through the winner to previous form.

NOTEBOOK
Abandagold(IRE) had the best form on show and, having no problem with the longer trip, made all the running to score on her debut for her new trainer. She did tend to hang to her right coming off the home turn, and reportedly was unsuited by the track, but found for pressure to draw clear. She should be up to winning a nursery at around this trip. (op 5-6 tchd Evens)

Bideeya(USA), the only debutante, chased the first two from the start but was held over a furlong out before staying on for second late on. She is a half-sister to a 1m2f winner and looks likely to be suited by further in time. (op 10-3 tchd 3-1)
Sarahthecarer(IRE) ran her best race so far, challenging the leader turning in before weakening in the final furlong. However, her proximity tends to limit the form. (op 14-1)
Abbi Jicaro, as on her debut, missed the break and was struggling before the home turn. (tchd 11-2 and 13-2)

3333 TRAFFORD CENTRE E B F H'CAP — 1m 2f 75y
7:45 (7:47) (Class 3) (0-95,90) 3-Y-0+ £9,714 (£2,890; £1,444; £721) Stalls High

Form RPR
1 **1** **Alpen Glen**[14] 2877 3-8-11 85 RoystonFfrench 1 97
(M Johnston) *mde all: pushed along and qcknd 2f out: r.o wl and wl in command fnl f* 11/8[1]
1021 **2** 2 ¾ **Eastern Aria (UAE)**[14] 2884 3-8-6 80 GregFairley 4 87
(M Johnston) *chsd wnr thrght: rdn 2f out: lugged in bhd wnr over 1f out: no imp* 7/4[2]
0-23 **3** 3 ¼ **Simplification**[72] 1284 3-8-1 75 FrancisNorton 5 76
(R Hannon) *racd keenly and hld up early: niggled along and nt look happy fr 7f out: styd on to take 3rd wl ins fnl f: n.d to front pair* 15/2[3]
-305 **4** 1 **Amanda Carter**[5] 3189 5-9-2 83 BMcHugh(5) 2 82
(R A Fahey) *racd keenly: trckd ldrs: pushed along over 3f out: nvr able to chal ldrs: wl hld fnl f* 12/1
21-6 **5** ½ **Amanjena**[20] 2697 4-10-0 90 StephenDonohoe 3 88
(A M Balding) *hld up: pushed along 3f out: rdn over 1f out: nvr able to chal: wknd fnl f* 8/1

2m 7.57s (-4.63) **Going Correction** -0.175s/f (Firm) course record
WFA 3 from 4yo+ 12lb 5 Ran SP% 109.0
Speed ratings (Par 107): **111,108,106,105,105**
CSF £3.95 TOTE £2.10: £1.50, £1.40; EX 2.80.
Owner Sheikh Hamdan Bin Mohammed Al Maktoum **Bred** Darley **Trained** Middleham Moor, N Yorks

FOCUS
Another small field for this fillies' handicap but a decent heat and quite interesting with the three-year-olds dominating the market. The race worked out as the betting suggested and the winner could be better than this. The placed horses set the level.

NOTEBOOK
Alpen Glen ◆ had recorded a good time when scoring over 1m4f on her debut and was ridden positively on this drop in trip. She had her rivals in trouble 3f out but had to be kept up to her work in the straight, although she again recorded a decent time on a track that would not have played to her strengths. She looks the sort that will go on again from this. (op 11-10 tchd 6-4)
Eastern Aria(UAE), the winner's stable companion and second-favourite, chased the winner throughout and stuck to her task without ever looking like reeling in her stablemate. She had shown a tendency to hang in the past, but it was less evident this time. (op 3-1)
Simplification was stepping up in trip on her first outing for over two months. She was backed beforehand but was too keen early on and looked ill at ease on the track, having dropped to the rear at halfway. However, she stayed on again and can do better on a more straightforward course and easier ground, or back on Polytrack. Official explanation: jockey said filly was unsuited by the track (op 8-1 tchd 6-1)
Amanda Carter was steadily progressive last season but has struggled after a decent effort on her return. She needs to show something more before she is worth backing again. (op 8-1)
Amanjena has not so far built on the progressive form she showed last autumn. (op 13-2)

3334 LJL AIRPORT H'CAP — 7f 122y
8:15 (8:15) (Class 5) (0-70,70) 3-Y-0 £4,047 (£1,204; £601; £300) Stalls Low

Form RPR
0233 **1** **Rio Cobolo (IRE)**[8] 3053 3-8-12 61 (v) PaulMulrennan 2 66
(Paul Green) *chsd ldrs: pushed along over 3f out: chsd ldr over 2f out: swtchd lft ins fnl f: led 100yds out: kpt up to work* 9/4[1]
3045 **2** ½ **Night Lily (IRE)**[21] 2667 3-9-2 65 StephenDonohoe 5 69
(J Jay) *hld up: rdn and hdwy on outside over 1f out: r.o ins fnl f to take 2nd towards fin* 3/1[3]
-622 **3** 1 ½ **Royal Premium**[9] 3018 3-8-3 52 (v) LiamJones 9 52
(Mrs G S Rees) *led: rdn and qcknd over 2f out: edgd rt fr 1f out: hdd 100yds out: no ex cl home* 5/2[2]
0543 **4** 6 **Piccolo Express**[21] 2652 3-8-10 59 J-PGuillambert 6 44
(B P J Baugh) *chsd ldrs: rdn and outpcd over 1f out: n.d after* 9/1
0-00 **5** ½ **Bounty Reef**[12] 2950 3-8-7 56 (v[1]) CatherineGannon 7 40
(P D Evans) *chsd ldr tl over 2f out: wknd over 1f out* 12/1
5006 **6** 12 **Singapore Girl**[20] 2726 3-8-2 51 oh1 (v[1]) SilvestreDeSousa 1 5
(G R Oldroyd) *hld up: niggled along 4f out: wl bhd fnl f* 11/1

1m 32.41s (-1.39) **Going Correction** -0.175s/f (Firm) 6 Ran SP% 110.4
Speed ratings (Par 99): **99,98,97,91,90 78**
toteswingers: 1&2 £1.90, 1&3 £1.40, 2&3 £2.10 CSF £8.98 CT £15.53 TOTE £2.70: £1.70, £1.90; EX 9.00.
Owner The Keely Gang **Bred** Yvonne & Gerard Kennedy **Trained** Lydiate, Merseyside

FOCUS
A modest contest for three-year-olds, but the time was fractionally faster than the opening race for older horses. The winner isra ted back to his all-weather best with the runner-up a slight improver.

3335 TRAFFORD CENTRE MIDSUMMER H'CAP — 7f 2y
8:50 (8:50) (Class 4) (0-85,85) 4-Y-0+ £5,180 (£1,541; £770; £384) Stalls Low

Form RPR
1254 **1** **Desert Dreamer (IRE)**[11] 2976 8-8-8 75 RichardEvans(5) 7 85
(P D Evans) *s.i.s: hld up: nt clr run 2f out: hdwy whn nt clr run again over 1f out: sn swtchd lft: str run to ld fnl 75yds: wl on top at fin* 14/1
6050 **2** 1 ½ **Gallantry**[17] 2780 7-9-2 83 MCGeran(5) 2 89
(P Howling) *midfield: hdwy over 2f out: rdn to take narrow ld over 1f out: edgd sltly rt ins fnl f: hdd 75yds out: hld by wnr after* 11/1
4255 **3** 1 **Fiefdom (IRE)**[4] 3211 7-8-12 74 PatrickMathers 6 77
(I W McInnes) *midfield: rdn 3f out: effrt and hdwy 2f out: burst through gap to chal strly over 1f out: no ex towards fin* 20/1
-003 **4** ½ **Dingaan (IRE)**[13] 2927 6-9-0 76 (p) WilliamBuick 8 78
(A M Balding) *hld up: hdwy on wd outside wl over 1f out: carried hd awkwardly: r.o ins fnl f: gng on at fin* 8/1[3]
-004 **5** ¾ **Zomerlust**[34] 2266 7-9-1 77 GrahamGibbons 4 77
(J J Quinn) *in tch: rdn over 2f out: chsd ldrs over 1f out: kpt on ins fnl f: nt pce of ldrs* 6/1[2]
0145 **6** 2 **Methaaly (IRE)**[13] 2938 6-9-4 80 (be) FrancisNorton 9 74
(M Mullineaux) *hld up: pushed along over 1f out: kpt on ins fnl f: nvr able to chal* 14/1
1106 **7** 1 ¼ **Billy Dane (IRE)**[17] 2787 5-9-5 85 LiamJones 5 76
(F P Murtagh) *w ldr: led 3f out: rdn and hdd over 1f out: wknd ins fnl f* 10/1
100/ **8** nk **Parisian Dream**[421] 5805 5-9-2 78 RobertHavlin 10 68
(T J Pitt) *hld up: pushed along 3f out: nvr able to get on terms* 28/1
0210 **9** 1 ½ **Gift Horse**[17] 2782 9-9-2 78 (p) CatherineGannon 3 64
(P D Evans) *led: pushed along and hdd 3f out: continued to chal u.p tl wknd over 1f out* 17/2
0351 **10** 14 **Brassini**[13] 2927 4-9-9 85 TGMcLaughlin 1 33
(B R Millman) *trckd ldrs: effrt to chal on outside over 2f out: eased qckly over 1f out: dropped away* 5/4[1]

1m 24.28s (-2.22) **Going Correction** -0.175s/f (Firm) course record 10 Ran SP% 119.3
Speed ratings (Par 105): **105,103,102,101,100 98,97,96,94,78**
toteswingers: 1&2 £28.30, 1&3 £70.30, 2&3 £66.60 CSF £161.53 CT £3135.83 TOTE £14.90: £3.10, £2.90, £5.40; EX 302.80.
Owner R Piff **Bred** Gainsborough Stud Management Ltd **Trained** Pandy, Monmouths
■ Stewards' Enquiry : Patrick Mathers two-day ban: used whip with excessive frequency (Jul 11,13)

FOCUS
Quite a tight handicap with just 11lb covering the entire field. The time was 3.2 seconds faster than the juvenile maiden and the race is best rated through the third to last year's turf form.

3336 JOHN LENNON AIRPORT H'CAP — 1m 2f 75y
9:20 (9:20) (Class 5) (0-70,70) 3-Y-0 £4,047 (£1,204; £601; £300) Stalls High

Form RPR
5-04 **1** **Carter**[9] 3018 3-8-12 59 PaulMulrennan 9 63
(W M Brisbourne) *trckd ldrs: led 3f out: rdn 2f out: strly pressed wl ins fnl f: battled gamely* 13/2[2]
1331 **2** hd **Dark Ranger**[45] 1967 3-8-13 60 RobertHavlin 1 64
(T J Pitt) *trckd ldrs: effrt 2f out: chsd wnr over 1f out: str chal and upsides wl ins fnl f: r.o u.p* 9/4[1]
0-05 **3** 1 **Kristopher James (IRE)**[39] 2131 3-8-4 56 RossAtkinson(5) 15 58
(W M Brisbourne) *racd keenly: in tch: chsd wnr 2f out tl over 1f out: hung lft fr over 1f out: sn chalng: nt qckn towards fin* 12/1
3200 **4** 4 **Duke Of Normandy (IRE)**[32] 2320 3-8-10 57 RoystonFfrench 3 52
(B P J Baugh) *in tch: pushed along 2f out: chsd ldrs over 1f out: kpt on ins fnl f: nt pce to chal ldrs* 14/1
0324 **5** 1 ¾ **Musical Maze**[9] 3019 3-9-4 65 TGMcLaughlin 16 56
(W M Brisbourne) *midfield: rdn and hdwy over 1f out: sn chsd ldrs: one pce fnl 150yds* 9/1
-560 **6** shd **Katie Girl**[9] 3019 3-8-4 51 oh1 (p) LiamJones 4 42
(Mrs G S Rees) *midfield: pushed along 2f out: plugged on at one pce ins fnl f: nvr able to chal* 20/1
000 **7** ½ **Paddy Partridge**[36] 2199 3-8-13 60 LukeMorris 7 50
(N J Vaughan) *missed break: towards rr: pushed along and hdwy into midfield 4f out: one pce fr over 1f out* 7/1[3]
0306 **8** 1 ½ **Jobekani (IRE)**[17] 2779 3-8-6 58 DeanHeslop(5) 10 45
(Mrs L Williamson) *hld up: rdn and hdwy over 1f out: no further prog fnl f* 8/1
0060 **9** 3 ¾ **Hit The Switch**[7] 3099 3-8-10 57 StephenDonohoe 12 37
(Patrick Morris) *bhd: niggled along 7f out: nvr on terms w ldrs* 33/1
00-6 **10** 1 ½ **Zelos Diktator**[67] 1410 3-8-4 51 SilvestreDeSousa 14 28
(J G Given) *hld up: pushed along 2f out: nvr on terms* 22/1
234- **11** 3 ½ **Artesium**[192] 7693 3-8-9 56 GrahamGibbons 5 27
(Patrick Morris) *led: hdd 3f out: wknd over 1f out* 10/1
65-0 **12** 1 **Cherry Belle (IRE)**[12] 2950 3-8-10 57 (v) CatherineGannon 8 26
(P D Evans) *bhd: pushed along 2f out: nvr on terms* 16/1
-230 **13** 4 ½ **Jul's Lad (IRE)**[64] 1470 3-9-3 64 GregFairley 6 24
(M Mullineaux) *racd keenly: prom tl pushed along and wknd 2f out* 20/1

2m 10.84s (-1.36) **Going Correction** -0.175s/f (Firm) 13 Ran SP% 123.9
Speed ratings (Par 99): **98,97,97,93,92 92,91,90,87,86 83,82,79**
toteswinger: 1&2 £3.10, 1&3 £23.40, 2&3 £19.10 CSF £21.05 CT £181.96 TOTE £7.70: £1.80, £1.70, £4.70; EX 19.50 Place 6: £182.25 Place 5: £44.10.
Owner W M Clare **Bred** Dr D G St John And Mrs Sherry Collier **Trained** Great Ness, Shropshire

FOCUS
A decent-sized field for this ordinary handicap despite the withdrawals, and the time was 3.27secs slower than the earlier fillies' handicap. There is little solid form-wise, with the winner and third rated to their juvenile form.
T/Plt: £74.80 to a £1 stake. Pool: £60,927.98. 593.90 winning tickets. T/Qpdt: £19.70 to a £1 stake. Pool: £3,662.13. 136.90 winning tickets. DO

2939 DONCASTER (L-H)
Friday, June 26

OFFICIAL GOING: Good (7.4)
Running rail moved out 4yards increasing distances on round course by 12yards.
Wind: Light half behind Weather: Overcast

3337 E B F SIMPSONMILLAR.CO.UK SOLICITORS MAIDEN FILLIES' STKS — 6f
2:20 (2:21) (Class 5) 2-Y-0 £3,561 (£1,059; £529; £264) Stalls High

Form RPR
03 **1** **Wigan Lane**[17] 2778 2-8-11 0 FrederikTylicki(3) 2 68
(R A Fahey) *mde virtually all: strly pressed fr 2f out: rdn ent fnl f: edgd lft and kpt onwl* 7/2[3]
24 **2** nk **Cherry Bee**[14] 2893 2-9-0 0 JoeFanning 1 67
(M Johnston) *cl up: effrt 2f out: sn rdn and ev ch tl drvn and nt qckn wl ins fnl f* 3/1[2]
3 1 ¼ **Seeking Dubai** 2-9-0 0 TPQueally 7 63
(E F Vaughan) *midfield: pushed along 1/2-way: hdwy wl over 1f out: sn rdn and kpt on ins fnl f: nrst fin* 14/1
4 **4** hd **Proper Littlemadam**[20] 2699 2-8-9 0 Louis-PhilippeBeuzelin(5) 9 64+
(M Botti) *trckd ldrs on inner: effrt 2f out: sn rdn and edgd lft over 1f out: drvn and one pce ins fnl f* 5/2[1]
4 **5** 2 **Perfect Blossom**[27] 2503 2-9-0 0 DanielTudhope 8 57
(I W McInnes) *hld up in rr: hdwy over 2f out and sn swtchd lft: chsd ldrs whn n.m.r over 1f out and sn rdn: wknd ins fnl f* 3/1[2]
05 **6** 2 **The Midshipmaid**[23] 2604 2-9-0 0 TGMcLaughlin 6 51
(Lucinda Featherstone) *trckd ldrs: rdn along over 2f out and grad wknd* 25/1
7 nse **Mooinooi** 2-9-0 0 GrahamGibbons 5 51
(T D Walford) *sn pushed along and a towards rr* 22/1
00 **8** 14 **Antique Diamond (IRE)**[23] 2604 2-9-0 0 NeilChalmers 4 9
(Lucinda Featherstone) *chsd ldrs: rdn along wl over 2f out and sn wknd* 100/1
0 **9** 34 **Woodhouse Mill (IRE)**[13] 2936 2-9-0 0 DO'Donohoe 3 —
(N Tinkler) *s.i.s and a in rr* 100/1

1m 12.69s (-0.91) **Going Correction** -0.375s/f (Firm) 9 Ran SP% 117.6
Speed ratings (Par 90): **91,90,88,88,86 83,83,64,19**
totewingers: 1&2 £2.60, 1&3 £7.10, 2&3 £4.50 CSF £14.41 TOTE £5.10: £1.90, £1.10, £3.10; EX 11.20 Trifecta £88.30 Pool: £533.78 - 4.47 winning units..

Owner David W Armstrong **Bred** D R Botterill **Trained** Musley Bank, N Yorks

FOCUS

An ordinary fillies' maiden dominated by the first two, who tacked over from the lowest stalls to race on the stands' rail. The time compared favourably with that for the older-horse maiden half an hour later and the first two were stepping up on previous form.

NOTEBOOK

Wigan Lane, reverting to 6f after running over the minimum at Chester, just shaded the runner-up throughout and held her off rather cosily with the rider not needing to be hard on her at all. She has a likeable attitude and should progress from this. (op 10-3 tchd 3-1)

Cherry Bee matched strides with the winner for most of the way. Her rider only really went for her in the last half-furlong, but although she kept trying she was always just being held. She is now eligible for nurseries and a step up to 7f should bear fruit. (op 9-4 tchd 10-3)

Seeking Dubai, a half-sister to the smart Presto Vento, looked green and was off the bridle before halfway, but she was staying on at the end. This was a pleasing debut. (op 16-1)

Proper Littlemadam lived up to her name by rearing a couple of times in the paddock. Also fourth on her debut over course and distance, she broke better this time and chased the principals before becoming outpaced a little when the race to the line kicked in. Official explanation: jockey said filly hung left (op 7-2)

Perfect Blossom travelled well at the back and was attempting a forward move when she was slightly short of room a furlong and a half out, although it is doubtful if her finishing position was affected. (op 5-1)

The Midshipmaid showed more than her stablemate Antique Diamond but faded as if not ready for the sixth furlong yet. (tchd 28-1)

Mooinooi's dam won over this trip and was a half-sister to good sprinters Bishops Court, Astonished and Cape Royal. She needed this debut experience and can do considerably better in time. (op 18-1)

3338 SIMPSON MILLAR FAMILY LAW SERVICE MAIDEN STKS 6f

2:50 (2:50) (Class 5) 3-Y-O+ **£3,238** (£963; £481; £240) **Stalls** High

Form — RPR

04 **1** **Medicean Man**[9] 3036 3-9-3 0 .... ClareLindop 2 — 77
(J R Gask) *trckd ldrs: hdwy to chse ldr 2f out: rdn to ld ins fnl f: kpt on* **8/1**

- **2** ½ **Leverage (IRE)** 3-9-3 0 .... RyanMoore 9 — 75+
(L M Cumani) *chsd ldrs: effrt 2f out and sn pushed along: rdn and edgd rt over 1f out: styd on ins fnl f* **4/1**[2]

0302 **3** 2 ¾ **Papillio (IRE)**[18] 2759 4-9-5 67 .... Louis-PhilippeBeuzelin(5) 1 — 68
(J R Fanshawe) *led: rdn clr 2f out: drvn over 1f out: hdd ins fnl f and kpt on same pce* **6/1**

4 1 ¾ **Miss Frangipane (IRE)** 3-8-12 0 .... TPQueally 5 — 56
(J Noseda) *sn pushed along in rr: hdwy 1/2-way: rdn along 2f out: styd on appr fnl f: nrst fin* **11/2**[3]

-624 **5** 9 **Rainy Night**[23] 2602 3-9-3 67 .... NCallan 7 — 32
(R Hollinshead) *trckd ldrs: hdwy 1/2-way: rdn 2f out and sn one pce* **10/3**[1]

-060 **6** shd **Luckette**[16] 2802 3-8-5 40 .... JohnCavanagh(7) 3 — 26
(M Brittain) *chsd ldrs on outer: rdn along 1/2-way and sn wknd* **150/1**

7 ¾ **Running Flush (USA)** 3-9-3 0 .... LukeMorris 13 — 29
(J R Gask) *s.i.s: a towards rr* **16/1**

3 **8** 1 **River Till (IRE)**[15] 2862 3-8-12 0 .... AlanMunro 6 — 21
(W Jarvis) *midfield: rdn along over 2f out and n.d* **4/1**[2]

00 **9** 2 ½ **Whisper Softly (IRE)**[20] 2700 3-8-12 0 .... GrahamGibbons 4 — 13
(T D Walford) *chsd ldr: rdn along 2f out: sn drvn and wknd* **66/1**

0/0- **10** 6 **Pretty Orchid**[296] 5608 4-9-5 0 .... JamieMoriarty 10 — —
(P T Midgley) *a towards rr* **66/1**

11 21 **Into Mac** 3-9-3 0 .... FrancisNorton 12 — —
(N Bycroft) *a in rr: bhd fr 1/2-way* **100/1**

1m 11.01s (-2.59) **Going Correction** -0.375s/f (Firm)
WFA 3 from 4yo 7lb — **11** Ran SP% **114.4**
Speed ratings (Par 103): **102,101,97,95,83 83,82,80,77,69 41**
toteswingers: 1&2 £10.50, 1&3 £10.20, 2&3 £6.20 CSF £38.99 TOTE £8.40: £2.70, £1.50, £2.20; EX 47.70 Trifecta £244.70 Part won. Pool: £330.81 - 0.30 winning units..
Owner Horses First Racing Limited **Bred** Barry Taylor **Trained** Sutton Veny, Wilts

FOCUS

A fairly modest maiden run below the standard time and a second and a half quicker than the earlier maiden for juveniles. The form is not solid and is best rated around the third.

River Till(IRE) Official explanation: trainer said, regarding running, that the filly never travelled

3339 SIMPSON MILLAR SOUND INVESTMENT ADVICE H'CAP 7f

3:25 (3:25) (Class 4) (0-80,79) 4-Y-O+ **£4,857** (£1,445; £722; £360) **Stalls** High

Form — RPR

0-00 **1** **Shotley Mac**[13] 2938 5-9-6 78 .... (b) FrancisNorton 1 — 87
(N Bycroft) *mde virtually all: rdn wl over 1f out: drvn and edgd rt ent fnl f: kpt on gamely* **8/1**

-016 **2** hd **Castles In The Air**[13] 2938 4-9-6 78 .... TonyHamilton 9 — 86
(R A Fahey) *trckd ldrs: hdwy 2f out: rdn to chal and edgd lft ent fnl f: sn drvn and ev ch tl no ex nr fin* **9/2**[2]

0-00 **3** 2 ¼ **Without Prejudice (USA)**[20] 2695 4-9-5 77 .... RyanMoore 2 — 79
(J Noseda) *trckd ldrs on outer: hdwy to chse wnr 2f out: swtchd rt and rdn to chal whn squeezed out ent fnl f: one pce after* **7/1**[3]

2400 **4** 1 **The Galloping Shoe**[11] 2980 4-9-7 79 .... TPQueally 7 — 79
(J Noseda) *dwlt: hld up in rr: swtchd rt and effrt 2f out: sn rdn and styd on ins fnl f: nrst fin* **17/2**

1-00 **5** ½ **Misphire**[13] 2938 6-9-5 77 .... PhillipMakin 5 — 75
(M Dods) *hld up: hdwy 2f out: rdn to chse ldrs over 1f out: drvn and one pce ins fnl f* **18/1**

21-0 **6** hd **Oh So Saucy**[36] 2188 5-9-5 77 .... AlanMunro 6 — 75
(C F Wall) *midfield: hdwy over 2f out: sn rdn and kpt on ins fnl f: nt rch ldrs* **8/1**

0015 **7** 1 ¼ **Xpres Maite**[17] 2791 6-8-8 71 .... (b) AndreaAtzeni(5) 11 — 65
(S R Bowring) *cl up: rdn along over 2f out: grad wknd* **7/1**[3]

540- **8** ½ **Capone (IRE)**[267] 6411 4-8-4 65 .... DominicFox(3) 4 — 58
(Garry Moss) *a towards rr* **66/1**

2252 **9** hd **Tiger Dream**[12] 2939 4-9-2 74 .... NCallan 3 — 67
(K A Ryan) *trkd ldrs: effrt over 2f out: sn rdn along and btn* **3/1**[1]

0000 **10** 6 **He's A Humbug (IRE)**[35] 2235 5-9-0 77 ow10 .... JamesO'Reilly(5) 8 — 53
(J O'Reilly) *in tch: rdn along 3f out: sn wknd* **25/1**

-220 **11** 8 **Oskari**[34] 2261 4-8-2 60 .... DuranFentiman 10 — 15
(P T Midgley) *chsd ldrs: rdn along wl over 2f out and sn wknd* **16/1**

1m 23.86s (-2.44) **Going Correction** -0.375s/f (Firm) — **11** Ran SP% **117.4**
Speed ratings (Par 105): **98,97,95,94,93 93,91,91,91,84 75**
toteswingers: 1&2 £13.20, 1&3 £15.20, 2&3 £6.80 CSF £43.82 CT £273.14 TOTE £9.80: £2.60, £1.90, £3.10; EX 60.70 Trifecta £517.10 Part won. Pool: £698.90 - 0.95 winning units..
Owner J A Swinburne **Bred** N Bycroft **Trained** Brandsby, N Yorks
■ Stewards' Enquiry : Francis Norton two-day ban: used whip with excessive frequency (Jul 11,13)

FOCUS

A fair handicap that looks sound enough rated around the first three. Not many managed to get into it and again a low draw proved beneficial.

3340 SIMPSON MILLAR MAXIMUM COMPENSATION FOR INJURY NOVICE STKS 7f

4:00 (4:00) (Class 3) 2-Y-O **£7,771** (£2,312; £1,155; £577) **Stalls** High

Form — RPR

010 **1** **Avon River**[20] 2702 2-9-5 0 .... RyanMoore 1 — 82+
(R Hannon) *cl up: niggled along 3f out: rdn and qcknd to ld 2f out: drvn and edgd rt over 1f out: kpt on wl* **5/1**

61 **2** 1 ¼ **Victoire De Lyphar (IRE)**[21] 2663 2-9-2 0 .... PaulMulrennan 2 — 76+
(P C Haslam) *set stdy pce: pushed along over 2f out: sn rdn and hdd: drvn and kpt on same pce fnl f* **11/8**[1]

1 **3** shd **Pycian**[48] 1867 2-9-5 0 .... TomEaves 3 — 78+
(Mrs L Stubbs) *trckd ldng pair: effrt whn rdn along and sltly outpcd 2f out: kpt on same pce u.p ent fnl f* **4/1**[3]

351 **4** hd **Reeds Bay (IRE)**[15] 2839 2-9-5 0 .... RichardMullen 4 — 78+
(E S McMahon) *trckd ldrs: rdn along and sltly outpcd 2f out: kpt on same pce u.p ent fnl f* **5/2**[2]

1m 26.84s (0.54) **Going Correction** -0.375s/f (Firm) — **4** Ran SP% **107.3**
Speed ratings (Par 97): **81,79,79,79**
CSF £12.19 TOTE £5.30; EX 10.10.
Owner Jim Horgan **Bred** Poulton Stud **Trained** East Everleigh, Wilts

FOCUS

An interesting little novice event in which all four runners were tackling 7f for the first time, but it proved far from a true test as the pace was pretty steady, only quickening up at around the two pole. The form is muddling and has a dubious look to it.

NOTEBOOK

Avon River, the outsider of the party, went for home first and he showed a commendably professional attitude to put his seal on the race. He had failed to handle the Epsom undulations when unplaced in the Woodcote Stakes last time but might be worth another try in Listed company now. (op 9-2 tchd 4-1)

Victoire De Lyphar(IRE), whose maiden win over 6f came at this venue, set the sedate pace and was the last of the four to come off the bridle, but the winner took first run on him when going for home at the two pole and he could not counter, only just holding on for second in the end as the other pair closed. A galloping type, he will be much more at home off a true pace at this trip but gives the impression that he might be a bit quirky. (tchd 11-10 and 6-4)

Pycian, who came from a seemingly impossible position to win at Haydock first time out, was worst away of the four. He was unsuited by the lack of pace and was running on from the back when it was too late. (op 11-4)

Reeds Bay(IRE), also successful at Haydock, was at the rear throughout in this tactical affair but was running on late and was only beaten about a neck for second. (op 7-2 tchd 9-4)

3341 KEEP THE POST PUBLIC H'CAP 7f

4:35 (4:37) (Class 4) (0-80,80) 3-Y-O **£4,857** (£1,445; £722; £360) **Stalls** High

Form — RPR

-411 **1** **Legal Legacy**[20] 2719 3-8-13 72 .... PhillipMakin 10 — 83
(M Dods) *hld up in midfield: hdwy 2f out: swtchd rifght and rdn over 1f out: qcknd to ld ins fnl f: styd on wl* **5/2**[2]

0-05 **2** 2 ¼ **Diggeratt (USA)**[16] 2821 3-8-13 72 .... PaulMulrennan 9 — 77
(R A Fahey) *in tch: hdwy to chse ldrs 2f out: sn rdn and kpt on ins fnl f: nt rch wnr* **16/1**

212- **3** ¾ **Happy Anniversary (IRE)**[287] 5855 3-9-2 80 .... LeeNewnes(5) 4 — 83
(Mrs D J Sanderson) *trckd ldr: led 2f out and sn rdn: drvn and hdd ins fnl f: kpt on same pce* **14/1**

-001 **4** ½ **Jack Cool (IRE)**[10] 3009 3-9-1 74 6ex .... AdrianMcCarthy 14 — 76
(P W Chapple-Hyam) *midfield whn sltly hmpd after 1f and sn in rr: hdwy 2f out: sn swtchd rt and rdn: kpt on ins fnl f: nrst fin* **9/4**[1]

44-0 **5** 1 **Too Tall**[15] 2845 3-8-12 71 .... WilliamBuick 1 — 70
(L M Cumani) *trckd ldrs: effrt over 2f out: sn rdn and kpt on same pce appr fnl f* **8/1**

2-00 **6** 2 **Kingswinford (IRE)**[13] 2934 3-9-2 80 .... Louis-PhilippeBeuzelin(5) 11 — 73
(P D Evans) *chsd ldrs: rdn along 2f out: sn drvn and one pce* **28/1**

2123 **7** 2 **Head Down**[13] 2926 3-9-6 79 .... RyanMoore 5 — 67
(R Hannon) *in tch: swtchd outside and hdwy to chse ldrs 2f out: sn rdn and no imp* **7/1**[3]

1433 **8** 1 **Riflessione**[5] 3193 3-8-10 72 .... (p) MichaelJStainton(3) 8 — 57
(R A Harris) *chsd ldrs: rdn along over 2f out: sn wknd* **14/1**

1054 **9** nk **Toby Tyler**[33] 2300 3-8-10 69 .... JamieMoriarty 6 — 54
(P T Midgley) *hld up in rr: sme hdwy over 2f out: sn rdn and no imp* **25/1**

0-62 **10** 5 **Moonlight Affair (IRE)**[35] 2227 3-9-1 74 .... DO'Donohoe 15 — 45
(E S McMahon) *a towards rr* **18/1**

0-40 **11** 2 ½ **King's Sabre**[21] 2674 3-9-5 78 .... TolleyDean 2 — 42
(W R Muir) *led: rdn along over 2f out: sn hdd & wknd* **33/1**

15-5 **12** 1 ½ **Doric Echo**[15] 2841 3-9-7 80 .... TomEaves 13 — 40
(B Smart) *a in rr* **28/1**

2-40 **13** ½ **Diddums**[16] 2826 3-9-2 75 .... (b) LiamJones 12 — 34
(J W Hills) *a towards rr* **22/1**

1m 24.06s (-2.24) **Going Correction** -0.375s/f (Firm) — **13** Ran SP% **125.5**
Speed ratings (Par 101): **97,94,93,93,91 89,87,86,85,80 77,75,74**
toteswingers: 1&2 £11.80, 1&3 £11.10, 2&3 £40.70 CSF £41.76 CT £498.92 TOTE £3.90: £1.60, £4.70, £4.40; EX 73.50 TRIFECTA Not won..
Owner D Vic Roper **Bred** D Dowling **Trained** Denton, Co Durham

FOCUS

A fair event run in a time a fifth of a second slower than the earlier older-horse handicap. This looks good form for the grade.

3342 CW RACING CLUB H'CAP 6f

5:05 (5:05) (Class 5) (0-70,70) 3-Y-O **£3,238** (£963; £481; £240) **Stalls** High

Form — RPR

-002 **1** **The Scorching Wind (IRE)**[10] 3010 3-8-10 59 .... RyanMoore 9 — 69
(S C Williams) *trckd ldrs: hdwy to ld 2f out: rdn over 1f out: styd on strly* **6/5**[1]

2000 **2** 2 ¾ **Bobs Dreamflight**[15] 2849 3-9-2 70 .... JamesO'Reilly(5) 3 — 71
(D K Ivory) *trckd ldrs: hdwy 2f out: rdn to chse wnr ins fnl f: kpt on* **17/2**

5152 **3** 2 ½ **Blue Noodles**[11] 2970 3-9-2 65 .... AdrianMcCarthy 5 — 58
(D W Barker) *led: rdn along and hdd 2f out: sn drvn and kpt on same pce* **7/1**[3]

0022 **4** nk **Unbelievable Jeff**[3] 3239 3-7-11 51 oh6 ..... Louis-PhilippeBeuzelin(5) 10 — 43
(S Parr) *chsd ldrs on outer: hdwy 2f out: sn rdn and hung lft: drvn and no imp ins fnl f* **3/1**[2]

6640 **5** 3 **Steel Stockholder**[21] 2662 3-8-7 63 .... JohnCavanagh(7) 8 — 46
(M Brittain) *in rr: rdn along and sme hdwy over 2f out: sn drvn and no imp* **22/1**

202 **6** *6* **She's In The Money**[20] 2700 3-9-5 **68** .... PaulMulrennan 7 31
(J G Given) *prom: rdn along over 2f out and sn wknd* **16/1**

0410 **7** *3* **Volito**[15] 2852 3-9-5 **68** .... JamieMoriarty 4 22
(Jonjo O'Neill) *cl up: rdn along over 2f out: sn wknd* **20/1**

000- **8** *4* **Calley Ho**[192] 7694 3-8-9 **65** .... KristinStubbs(7) 2 6
(Mrs L Stubbs) *sn outpcd and a bhd* **100/1**

1m 11.42s (-2.18) **Going Correction** -0.375s/f (Firm) **8** Ran SP% **109.5**
Speed ratings (Par 99): **99,95,92,91,87 79,75,70**
CSF £11.05 CT £45.01 TOTE £2.20: £1.10, £2.10, £2.00; EX 13.10 Trifecta £153.90 Pool: £301.72 - 1.45 winning units. Place 6: £306.84 Place 5: £148.25.
Owner Chris Watkins And David N Reynolds **Bred** Mark Commins **Trained** Newmarket, Suffolk

FOCUS
A modest sprint handicap but a taking winner and there is a chance this form could be better than rated.
Unbelievable Jeff Official explanation: jockey said gelding hung left

3343 CWU LEGAL SERVICES H'CAP — 1m 4f
5:40 (5:40) (Class 4) (0-85,83) 4-Y-0+ **£4,857** (£1,445; £722; £360) **Stalls** Low

Form RPR

004 **1** **Valmari (IRE)**[46] 1944 6-9-0 **83** .... (b) DebraEngland(7) 2 90
(C E Brittain) *trckd ldr: cl up 4f out: rdn over 2f out: styd on u.p ins fnl f to ld nr fin* **12/1**

14-1 **2** *hd* **Nobelix (IRE)**[164] 142 7-9-3 **79** .... ClareLindop 3 86
(J R Gask) *set stdy pce: jnd 4f out: qcknd 3f out: rdn wl over 1f out: drvn ins fnl f: hdd nr fin: broke leg: dead* **3/1**[2]

1104 **3** *5* **Grand Art (IRE)**[10] 3000 5-8-13 **75** .... JamieMoriarty 5 74
(P T Midgley) *hld up in tch: effrt and rdn along 3f out: drvn 2f out: kpt on ins fnl f: n.d* **4/1**[3]

62-2 **4** *1 ½* **Outlandish**[12] 2945 6-9-1 **77** .... RyanMoore 4 73
(Miss E C Lavelle) *hld up in rr: hdwy over 3f out: rdn along to chse elading pair 2f out: sn drvn and wknd* **5/4**[1]

0-10 **5** *3 ¼* **Paint The Town Red**[42] 2052 4-8-7 **74** .... Louis-PhilippeBeuzelin(5) 1 65
(H J Collingridge) *trckd ldng pair: rdn along over 3f out: sn wknd* **13/2**

2m 35.1s **Going Correction** -0.375s/f (Firm) **5** Ran SP% **110.5**
Speed ratings (Par 105): **85,84,81,80,78**
CSF £46.72 TOTE £13.00: £4.30, £2.20; EX 45.00.
Owner Emmanouil Zografakis **Bred** Airlie Stud **Trained** Newmarket, Suffolk

FOCUS
On a card somewhat short on variety this was the only race run over the round course. It was a steadily run affair and the form is distinctly modest and muddling, with only the first two getting into it.
T/Plt: £304.00 to a £1 stake. Pool: £64,306.32. 154.41 winning tickets. T/Qpdt: £54.70 to a £1 stake. Pool: £3,728.90. 50.40 winning tickets. JR

2758 FOLKESTONE (R-H)
Friday, June 26

OFFICIAL GOING: Good to firm (firm in places; overall 8.8; round 8.5; stands' side 8.6; far side 9.8)
Wind: virtually nil Weather: muggy, warm

3344 BET IRISH DERBY - BETDAQ MEDIAN AUCTION MAIDEN STKS — 7f (S)
2:30 (2:32) (Class 6) 2-Y-0 **£2,729** (£806; £403) **Stalls** Low

Form RPR

5 **1** **Huygens**[21] 2649 2-9-3 0 .... DarryllHolland 14 78+
(D J Coakley) *swtchd rt s and racd far side: t.k.h: chsd ldr tl pushed into overall ld wl over 1f out: clr fnl f: pushed out: 1st of 4 in gp* **25/1**

0 **2** *2 ¾* **Astonishment (IRE)**[18] 2771 2-9-3 0 .... JamesDoyle 9 71
(S Kirk) *swtchd rt s and racd far side: chsd ldrs: rdn to chse wnr over 1f out: edgd rt u.p and no imp ins fnl f: 2nd of 4 in gp* **66/1**

02 **3** *shd* **Al Khimiya (IRE)**[10] 2997 2-8-12 0 .... JamieSpencer 2 70+
(S A Callaghan) *led stands' side: rdn and hung rt fr 2f out: chsd ldng pair and wl clr of stands' side gp over 1f out: kpt on: 1st of 8 in gp* **4/1**[2]

00 **4** *6* **Keen Bidder**[15] 2860 2-9-3 0 .... ChrisCatlin 13 56
(D M Simcock) *swtchd rt s and racd far side and overall ldr tl wl over 1f out: wknd jst over 1f out: 3rd of 4 in gp* **66/1**

0 **5** *7* **Danger Mulally**[32] 2328 2-9-0 0 .... DavidProbert(3) 7 42
(A M Balding) *racd stands' side: bhd: rdn and struggling over 2f out: wl btn fnl 2f: passed btn horses ins fnl f: 2nd of 8 in gp* **14/1**

0 **6** *shd* **Take My Hand**[13] 2919 2-8-12 0 .... EdwardCreighton 3 37
(M R Channon) *racd stands' side: chsd stands' side ldr for 2f out: rdn and wknd 2f out: wl btn after: 3rd of 8 in gp* **20/1**

7 *½* **Spanish Duke (IRE)** 2-9-3 0 .... SebSanders 10 45+
(J L Dunlop) *racd stands' side: s.i.s: sn swtchd lft: bhd: hdwy into midfield 1/2-way: plugged on but nvr on terms: 4th of 8 in gp* **12/1**[3]

030 **8** *3 ¾* **George Baker (IRE)**[10] 2995 2-9-3 0 .... GeorgeBaker 8 32
(George Baker) *racd stands' side: in tch: swtchd rt and rdn over 2f out: drvn and btn 2f out: 5th of 8 in gp* **8/13**[1]

9 *¾* **Another Magic Man (USA)** 2-9-3 0 .... RobertWinston 11 26
(J R Best) *s.i.s: sn swtchd rt and racd far side: a last of gp: lost tch 2f out: 4th of 4 in gp* **16/1**

10 *1 ½* **Valmina** 2-9-3 0 .... (t) RichardSmith 4 26
(Tom Dascombe) *racd stands' side: chsd stands' side ldr after 2f tl over 2f out: sn wknd and wl btn: 6th of 8 in gp* **16/1**

11 *2 ¼* **Little Meadow (IRE)** 2-8-12 0 .... NeilPollard 5 15
(Miss J Feilden) *racd stands' side: a struggling in rr: lost tch over 2f out: 7th of 8 in gp* **100/1**

0 **12** *12* **Rufus Roughcut**[78] 1195 2-9-3 0 .... (t) SaleemGolam 6 —
(S C Williams) *racd stands' side: t.k.h: chsd ldrs tl 1/2-way: sn lost pl: t.o: 8th of 8 in gp* **66/1**

1m 26.57s (-0.73) **Going Correction** -0.125s/f (Firm) **12** Ran SP% **122.1**
Speed ratings (Par 91): **99,95,95,88,80 80,80,75,75,73 70,57**
toteswingers: 1&2 £98.60, 1&3 £12.50, 2&3 £56.30 CSF £1101.77 TOTE £46.40: £7.10, £17.80, £1.20; EX 980.20.
Owner Chris Van Hoorn **Bred** R F And Mrs Knipe **Trained** West Ilsley, Berks

FOCUS
The usual stands' side track bias was eliminated, with the far side penetrometer reading of 9.8 being much quicker than the 8.6 registered stands' side, and it was those who stayed high that came out on top in this opening contest, although the winner had clearly improved. Jamie Spencer, who rode the third, felt the ground was significantly slower stands' side.

NOTEBOOK
Huygens was a well-beaten fifth behind a useful sort on his debut at Bath, and the extra furlong here was always likely to suit. He struck the front inside the two and never looked in any danger once there, running on well for pressure, and looks a nice prospect. However, according to his trainer this race had been the plan, so where he goes next has yet to be decided. (op 18-1)

Astonishment(IRE), always outpaced when well beaten at Windsor on his debut, is bred to appreciate this extra furlong and he improved markedly on that initial effort, sticking on right the way to the line. He should come on again and can find a race at some point. (op 80-1)
Al Khimiya(IRE) ◆, who raced stands' side, left the others in her group a long way behind. Narrowly denied over this trip at Thirsk last time, she ended up down the centre of the track, having hung off the rail, and would surely have gone close to winning had she raced on the other side. (op 6-1)
Keen Bidder took them along far side and, although ultimately well held, he is now qualified for a handicap mark and should fare better in that sphere.
Danger Mulally did best of the remainder stands' side and is another likely sort for nurseries. (op 12-1)
Take My Hand, up 2f in trip, will be qualified for nurseries following one more run. (op 16-1)
Spanish Duke(IRE), a half-brother to Spanish Hidalgo who made some late headway, should improve for the outing. (tchd 10-1)
George Baker(IRE), a creditable seventh in the Windsor Castle Stakes at Royal Ascot and the red-hot favourite on this step up from 5f, was expected to prove suited by the extra quarter mile of this contest. However, he was being niggled at halfway and found little for pressure. He was on the wrong side as things turned out, but this effort was still too bad to be true, the race surely coming too soon. Official explanation: trainer had no explanation for the poor form shown (op 4-6 tchd 4-7, 8-11 in a place)

3345 BET TEST MATCH RUGBY - BETDAQ CLAIMING STKS — 6f
3:05 (3:05) (Class 6) 3-Y-0+ **£2,047** (£604; £302) **Stalls** Low

Form RPR

3605 **1** **Bertie Southstreet**[59] 1587 6-8-12 62 .... (p) SebSanders 5 71
(J R Boyle) *swtchd to r on far rail: mde all: clr after 2f: rdn over 1f out: unchal* **11/2**[2]

3311 **2** *4 ½* **Caribbean Coral**[3] 3242 10-9-1 62 .... GeorgeBaker 2 61
(A B Haynes) *stdd s: hld up towards rr: hdwy and pushed 1/2-way: rdn wl over 1f out: no imp on wnr: wnt 2nd wl ins fnl f* **8/11**[1]

0335 **3** *nk* **Dr Wintringham (IRE)**[8] 3066 3-7-12 60 .... DavidProbert(3) 1 51
(J S Moore) *swtchd to r far side: in tch: hdwy to chse clr wnr jst over 2f out: rdn and no imp over 1f out: lost 2nd wl ins fnl f* **13/2**

5106 **4** *2* **Louphole**[3] 3243 7-9-3 66 .... DarryllHolland 3 56
(J R Jenkins) *swtchd to r far side: hld up in tch in rr: effrt and rdn wl over 1f out: edgd rt and no prog over 1f out* **6/1**[3]

-400 **5** *3 ½* **Noverre To Hide (USA)**[10] 3010 3-8-9 62 ow1 .... RobertWinston 4 41
(J R Best) *swtchd to r far side: chsd wnr tl jst over 2f out: wknd wl over 1f out* **16/1**

0 **6** *12* **Bolshoi King (IRE)**[15] 2856 3-8-5 0 .... TPO'Shea 7 —
(B J Meehan) *awkward leaving stalls: swtchd to r far side: t.k.h early: lost pl and rdn 1/2-way: lost tch 2f out* **28/1**

1m 11.18s (-1.52) **Going Correction** -0.125s/f (Firm)
WFA 3 from 5yo+ 7lb **6** Ran SP% **110.2**
Speed ratings (Par 101): **105,99,98,95,91 75**
CSF £9.63 TOTE £5.40: £2.10, £1.20; EX 10.90.
Owner Horses for Causes **Bred** B Whitehouse **Trained** Epsom, Surrey

FOCUS
All six of the runners raced far side for this claimer. The winner is rated to his winter form but the form is not solid.

3346 BERNIE MILL BIRTHDAY CELEBRATION H'CAP — 2m 93y
3:40 (3:40) (Class 4) (0-80,77) 4-Y-0+ **£6,476** (£1,927; £963; £481) **Stalls** Low

Form RPR

0-00 **1** **Kasban**[27] 2497 5-8-10 **70** .... (tp) MartinLane(5) 1 79
(Ian Williams) *awkward s: hld up in tch: rdn 3f out: drvn and hdwy over 1f out: led wl ins fnl f: styd on wl* **20/1**

40/5 **2** *¾* **Swordsman (GER)**[18] 2760 7-8-10 **65** .... (t) ChrisCatlin 5 73
(C Gordon) *sn led: hrd pressed and rdn 3f out: hdd narrowly 2f out: drvn to ld again ent fnl f: hdd and no ex wl ins fnl f* **16/1**

6-11 **3** *1* **Prairie Hawk (USA)**[135] 502 4-8-10 **65** .... (t) FergusSweeney 7 72
(Tim Vaughan) *trckd ldrs: rdn over 2f out: drvn wl over 1f out: kpt on same pce fnl f* **4/1**[2]

0-11 **4** *1* **Sweetheart**[18] 2760 5-9-4 **73** .... GeorgeBaker 2 79
(Jamie Poulton) *sn chsng ldr: upsides over 3f out: rdn to ld narrowly 2f out: drvn over 1f out: hdd ent fnl f: one pce and lost 2 pls ins fnl f* **11/4**[1]

4511 **5** *¾* **Callisto Moon**[8] 3059 5-9-8 **77** 6ex .... DarryllHolland 3 82
(R Curtis) *in tch: rdn and effrt over 2f out: unable qck and one pce fr over 1f out* **11/4**[1]

0-23 **6** *nk* **Pseudonym (IRE)**[14] 252 7-8-8 **63** .... (t) FrankieMcDonald 6 68
(M F Harris) *prom early: grad stdd and hld up in last pair: pushed along 4f out: edgd rt and hdwy over 1f out: styd on but nt rch ldrs* **8/1**

1232 **7** *15* **Mr Aitch (IRE)**[76] 1215 7-9-7 **76** .... (t) SebSanders 4 63
(R T Phillips) *stdd s: hld up in last pair: effrt over 2f out: rdn and wknd over 1f out: eased ins fnl f* **5/1**[3]

3m 37.93s (0.73) **Going Correction** -0.05s/f (Good) **7** Ran SP% **111.8**
Speed ratings (Par 105): **96,95,95,94,94 94,86**
toteswingers: 1&2 £11.60, 1&3 £16.30, 2&3 £8.30 CSF £264.52 TOTE £28.70: £8.20, £2.80; EX 263.00.
Owner Michael H Watt **Bred** Ardenode Stud **Trained** Portway, Worcs

FOCUS
This had looked a fair staying handicap, with three of the runners bidding for a hat-trick, but all three were unplaced. nevertheless, the form looks sound rated around the four immediately behind the winner.

3347 WEATHERBYS BANK FOLKESTONE HAMMER STKS (H'CAP) — 6f
4:15 (4:16) (Class 4) (0-85,85) 3-Y-0+ **£14,247** (£4,239; £2,118; £1,058) **Stalls** Low

Form RPR

0321 **1** **Zowington**[8] 3057 7-8-11 **77** 6ex .... (v) WilliamCarson(5) 14 87
(S C Williams) *mde all on far side: clr over 1f out: drvn out: 1st of 8 in gp* **9/1**

0610 **2** *1* **Filligree (IRE)**[13] 2911 4-9-5 **83** .... DavidProbert(3) 5 90
(Rae Guest) *racd stands' side: chsd ldrs: rdn to chse stands' side ldr wl over 1f out: chsd wnr ins fnl f: styd on but unable to chal wnr: 1st of 4 in gp* **14/1**

6664 **3** *1* **Spirit Of Sharjah (IRE)**[12] 2941 4-9-10 **85** .... TPO'Shea 10 89
(Miss J Feilden) *racd far side: towards rr: hdwy and swtchd lft jst over 2f out: edgd rt u.p fr over 1f out: kpt on fnl f: nvr gng to rch wnr: 2nd of 8 in gp* **15/2**

0-01 **4** *1 ½* **Luminous Gold**[29] 2418 4-8-12 **73** .... SebSanders 2 72
(C F Wall) *led stands' side gp until ins fnl f: kpt on same pce: 2nd of 4 in gp* **16/1**

0302 **5** *1* **Harlech Castle**[11] 2980 4-9-3 **78** .... (b) GeorgeBaker 13 74
(P F I Cole) *racd on far side: s.i.s: bhd: rdn and hdwy ent fnl 2f out: no imp u.p fnl f: 3rd of 8 in gp* **8/1**

3241 **6** ¾ **Halsion Chancer**[20] 2713 5-8-12 **73** .... RobertWinston 3 66
(J R Best) *racd stands' side: chsd ldrs tl swtchd rt to far side gp and chsd wnr 2f out: drvn and wknd ent fnl f:4th of 8 in gp* **11/2**[2]

13-1 **7** 2¾ **Mabait**[23] 2611 3-9-0 **82** .... ChrisCatlin 7 67
(L M Cumani) *racd far side: bhd: rdn and effrt 2f out: nt clr run and swtchd rt wl over 1f out: nvr trbld ldrs: 5th of 8 in gp* **7/2**[1]

3630 **8** 4 **Merlin's Dancer**[20] 2704 9-9-6 **81** .... ShaneKelly 12 53
(S Dow) *racd far side: chsd ldng pair tl 2f out: sn wknd: 6th of 8 in gp* **16/1**

-510 **9** 1¼ **Earlsmedic**[27] 2474 4-9-9 **84** .... (v) SaleemGolam 4 52
(S C Williams) *racd stands' side: chsd stands' side ldr tl wl over 1f out: sn wknd: 3rd of 4 in gp* **6/1**[3]

0035 **10** nk **Daddy's Gift (IRE)**[14] 2886 3-9-1 **83** .... PatDobbs 9 50
(R Hannon) *racd far side: a in rr: rdn and struggling 1/2-way: 7th of 8 in gp* **12/1**

1024 **11** shd **Rio Royale (IRE)**[14] 2882 3-8-9 **77** .... DarryllHolland 11 44
(Mrs A J Perrett) *racd far side: chsd wnr tl 2f out: sn edgd lft and wknd: 8th of 8 in gp* **12/1**

04-0 **12** ¾ **Flashy Photon**[16] 2828 4-8-11 **72** .... FrankieMcDonald 6 36
(H Candy) *swtchd lft to r stands' side after s: a struggling in rr: 4th of 4 in gp* **25/1**

1m 11.19s (-1.51) **Going Correction** -0.125s/f (Firm)
WFA 3 from 4yo+ 7lb 12 Ran SP% **122.4**
Speed ratings (Par 105): **105,103,102,100,99 98,94,89,87,86 86,85**
toteswingers: 1&2 £26.00, 1&3 £9.90, 2&3 £20.50 CSF £132.66 CT £1020.72 TOTE £9.90: £2.70, £4.20, £2.70; EX 121.80.
Owner O Pointing **Bred** O Pointing **Trained** Newmarket, Suffolk

FOCUS
The far side didn't hold much of an advantage in this 6f sprint, but the winner still came from the highest stall. Those drawn six downwards stayed stands' side, though Halsion Chancer was taken right across to join the far-side group with two to run. The third to his recent best sets the level.
Filligree(IRE) Official explanation: trainer's rep said filly lost a near-fore shoe
Harlech Castle Official explanation: jockey said gelding was slowly away
Rio Royale(IRE) Official explanation: jockey said colt hung both ways

3348 BET IN-RUNNING - BETDAQ H'CAP 1m 4f
4:45 (4:45) (Class 6) (0-60,58) 4-Y-O+ **£2,047** (£604; £302) **Stalls** Low

Form RPR
0343 **1** **Sand Repeal (IRE)**[11] 2971 7-9-4 **58** .... DarryllHolland 1 64
(Miss J Feilden) *sn chsng ldr: rdn to chal over 2f out: led 2f out: kpt on u.p fnl f* **5/2**[1]

0-20 **2** 1¼ **Phoenix Hill (IRE)**[10] 816 7-8-5 **45** .... ChrisCatlin 5 49
(D R Gandolfo) *bhd: detached last 9f out: pushed along 7f out: rdn over 4f out: stl 8th over 1f out: r.o strly fnl f: snatched 2nd on post* **14/1**

0603 **3** nse **Dazzling Begum**[17] 2785 4-8-6 **46** ow1 .... (p) ShaneKelly 7 50
(J Pearce) *in tch in midfield: pushed along over 4f out: n.m.r and swtchd lft over 1f out: chsd wnr 1f out: hung rt and no imp after: lost 2nd on post* **4/1**[2]

3000 **4** ½ **Good Effect (USA)**[44] 1980 5-8-9 **49** .... FrankieMcDonald 9 52
(C P Morlock) *chsd ldrs: pushed along over 3f out: sltly outpcd over 2f out: drvn and hdwy over 1f out: one pce ins fnl f* **12/1**

66-4 **5** 1¾ **Pinnacle Point**[20] 2708 4-8-11 **51** .... (be) FergusSweeney 3 51
(G L Moore) *chsd ldrs: pushed along and chsd ldng pair over 2f out: drvn and hung rt ent fnl f: wknd ins fnl f* **17/2**

5053 **6** ½ **Generous Lad (IRE)**[18] 2762 6-8-5 **45** .... (p) SamHitchcott 8 45
(A B Haynes) *awkward s: sn bustled along: racd in midfield: rdn 5f out: drvn over 2f out: nt qckn over 1f out and one pce fnl f* **5/1**[3]

1440 **7** 4½ **Rough Sketch (USA)**[20] 2725 4-9-1 **55** .... (b[1]) SebSanders 4 47
(Sir Mark Prescott) *racd freely: sn led and clr: rdn over 2f out: hdd 2f out: wknd jst over 1f out* **4/1**[2]

056 **8** 4½ **Karmei**[11] 2975 4-7-12 **45** .... CharlesEddery[(7)] 10 30
(R Curtis) *racd in midfield: pushed along 4f out: rdn over 2f out: one pce and wl hld whn n.m.r 1f out: eased after* **20/1**

100- **9** 21 **Linby (IRE)**[248] 6883 4-8-12 **52** .... RobertWinston 6 4
(Miss Tor Sturgis) *stdd s: t.k.h: hld up in last pair: hdwy over 2f out: rdn and btn wl over 1f out: eased fnl f* **20/1**

2m 39.92s (-0.98) **Going Correction** -0.05s/f (Good) 9 Ran SP% **119.6**
Speed ratings (Par 101): **101,100,100,99,98 98,95,92,78**
toteswingers: 1&2 £7.60, 1&3 £3.90, 2&3 £9.50 CSF £42.11 CT £136.67 TOTE £3.30: £1.20, £3.40, £1.60; EX 52.50.
Owner The Sultans of Speed **Bred** Don Commins **Trained** Exning, Suffolk

FOCUS
They went a fair gallop in what was a low-grade handicap and the form looks sound if limited.
Dazzling Begum Official explanation: jockey said filly hung right

3349 SCREWFIX DIRECT H'CAP 1m 1f 149y
5:15 (5:15) (Class 5) (0-75,74) 3-Y-O+ **£3,885** (£1,156; £577; £288) **Stalls** Centre

Form RPR
-260 **1** **Mick's Dancer**[37] 2183 4-9-6 **66** .... DarryllHolland 2 75
(W R Muir) *t.k.h: chsd ldrs: rn wd bnd 7f out: hdwy to ld 6f out: mde rest: rdn and edgd lft fr over 1f out: styd on wl* **13/8**[1]

6253 **2** 2¾ **Wilbury Star (IRE)**[23] 2600 3-9-2 **74** .... PatDobbs 1 77
(R Hannon) *t.k.h: pressed ldr tl 6f out: chsd wnr 3f out: pressed wnr and edgd lft over 1f out: wknd fnl 100ds* **5/2**[3]

1615 **3** 3 **Vinces**[21] 2678 5-9-6 **66** .... GeorgeBaker 6 63
(T D McCarthy) *s.i.s: t.k.h and sn hld up in tch: carried wd bnd 7f out: wnt 3rd 2f out: rdn and btn jst over 1f out* **2/1**[2]

64-6 **4** 11 **Kattar**[57] 1629 3-8-5 **63** .... (t) ChrisCatlin 4 37
(D M Simcock) *led at stdy gallop tl 6f out: chsd wnr tl 3f out: wknd wl over 1f out: eased whn no ch ins fnl f* **8/1**

2m 4.92s (0.02) **Going Correction** -0.05s/f (Good)
WFA 3 from 4yo+ 12lb 4 Ran SP% **111.1**
Speed ratings (Par 103): **97,94,92,83**
CSF £6.14 TOTE £2.50; EX 7.30 Place 6: £4441.91 Place 5: £807.74.
Owner Perspicacious Punters Racing Club **Bred** Cheveley Park Stud Ltd **Trained** Lambourn, Berks

FOCUS
A moderate handicap with the runner rated 4lb higher than his previous turf form.
T/Plt: £7,492.80 to a £1 stake. Pool: £57,992.97. 5.65 winning tickets. T/Qpdt: £476.20 to a £1 stake. Pool: £5,019.60. 7.80 winning tickets. SP

3310 NEWCASTLE (L-H)
Friday, June 26

OFFICIAL GOING: Good (good to firm in places) changing to good to soft after race 2 (7.25)
Rail realignment from 9f to 4.5f increased advertised distances on the round course by about 35yards.
Wind: Light, half behind Weather: Overcast, raining

3350 KB SHEET METAL & GDBS H'CAP 1m 2f 32y
6:50 (6:51) (Class 5) (0-70,69) 4-Y-O+ **£3,885** (£1,156; £577; £288) **Stalls** Centre

Form RPR
0/00 **1** **High Ambition**[21] 2665 6-9-2 **67** .... FrederikTylicki[(3)] 8 78
(R A Fahey) *dwlt: hld up: hdwy over 4f out: effrt over 2f out: ev ch fnl f: led nr fin* **9/2**[2]

3321 **2** hd **Society Venue**[32] 2314 4-9-7 **69** .... AndrewElliott 10 80
(Jedd O'Keeffe) *chsd ldr: led over 4f out: clr 2f out: jnd fnl f: hdd cl home* **9/2**[2]

3551 **3** 5 **Keisha Kayleigh (IRE)**[1] 3314 6-9-6 **68** 6ex .... NCallan 2 69
(B Ellison) *t.k.h: hld up: hdwy and in tch 3f out: rdn and one pce fnl 2f* **7/2**[1]

0061 **4** shd **Trouble Mountain (USA)**[7] 3121 12-8-11 **59** 6ex .... (t) DaleGibson 12 60
(M W Easterby) *prom: rdn over 4f out: one pce fr 2f out* **25/1**

5415 **5** 2½ **Fell Pack**[24] 2573 5-8-6 **59** .... JamieKyne[(5)] 1 55
(J J Quinn) *midfield: rdn over 3f out: nt pce to chal fnl 2f* **7/2**[1]

5204 **6** ¾ **Grey Command (USA)**[9] 3035 4-9-0 **62** .... AlanMunro 6 56
(M Brittain) *midfield: outpcd 1/2-way: kpt on fnl 2f: nvr rchd ldrs* **20/1**

0060 **7** 3¾ **Monfils Monfils (USA)**[8] 3068 7-9-0 **65** .... NeilBrown[(3)] 3 52
(R E Barr) *hld up: rdn over 3f out: nvr on terms* **12/1**

-062 **8** 2 **Eijaaz (IRE)**[7] 3121 8-9-2 **64** .... MickyFenton 11 47
(G A Harker) *hld up: rdn 3f out: nvr able to chal* **9/1**[3]

030/ **9** 16 **John Forbes**[426] 3446 7-8-10 **65** .... AnthonyBetts[(7)] 7 16
(B Ellison) *chsd ldrs tl wknd fr 3f out: t.o* **25/1**

060- **10** 53 **Miss Ferney**[252] 6786 5-8-7 **55** .... JoeFanning 4 —
(A Kirtley) *cl up tl wknd qckly 3f out: t.o* **66/1**

4-04 **P** **Drumadoon Bay (IRE)**[8] 3061 5-8-2 **50** .... PaulQuinn 5 —
(G A Swinbank) *rdr lost irons leaving stalls: plld hrd: led to over 4f out: brought wd and p.u ent st* **12/1**

2m 14.55s (2.65) **Going Correction** +0.35s/f (Good) 11 Ran SP% **120.1**
Speed ratings (Par 103): **103,102,98,98,96 96,93,91,78,36** —
toteswingers: 1&2 £6.20, 1&3 £4.80, 2&3 £4.70 CSF £24.60 CT £80.54 TOTE £6.20: £2.40, £2.10, £2.20; EX 32.80.
Owner G H Leatham **Bred** A B Phipps **Trained** Musley Bank, N Yorks

FOCUS
The course took the decision to put 5mm of water on the track in the morning and, due to the weather turning, steady rain throughout the afternoon caused the ground to be officially changed to good. The first pair came well clear in this moderate opener with the runner-up posting a personal best.
Drumadoon Bay(IRE) Official explanation: jockey said he lost his irons coming out of stalls

3351 PIRAMAL HEALTHCARE GOSFORTH PARK CUP (H'CAP) 5f
7:25 (7:27) (Class 2) (0-105,102) 3-Y-O+
£12,462 (£3,732; £1,866; £934; £466; £234) **Stalls** High

Form RPR
2001 **1** **Pavershooz**[20] 2716 4-8-7 **84** .... DuranFentiman 10 94
(N Wilson) *led centre: overall ldr ins fnl f: hld on gamely: 1st of 3 in gp* **12/1**

0160 **2** nk **Buachaill Dona (IRE)**[27] 2502 6-9-9 **100** .... AdrianTNicholls 14 109
(D Nicholls) *led and overall ldr stands' side: hung lft and drew clr of that gp wl over 1f out: hdd ins fnl f: kpt on fin: 1st of 6 in gp* **8/1**[3]

4444 **3** ½ **Hamish McGonagall**[20] 2716 4-9-7 **98** .... DavidAllan 9 105
(T D Easterby) *chsd wnr centre: effrt over 2f out: kpt on u.p fnl f: 2nd of 3 in gp* **8/1**[3]

5-10 **4** ¾ **Total Impact**[20] 2716 6-8-8 **85** .... TonyHamilton 11 89
(R A Fahey) *trckd centre ldrs: effrt over 2f out: kpt on ins fnl f: last of 3 in gp* **20/1**

0416 **5** 4 **Indian Trail**[14] 2897 9-8-11 **88** .... (v) PaulQuinn 4 77
(D Nicholls) *in tch far side: smooth hdwy to ld that gp ins fnl f: plld clr of that gp: nt pce of centre: 1st of 7 in gp* **16/1**

40-0 **6** 3¾ **Tabaret**[7] 3122 6-9-0 **91** .... TonyCulhane 15 66
(R M Whitaker) *in tch stands' side: effrt over 2f out: kpt on fnl f: no imp: 2nd of 6 in gp* **50/1**

0000 **7** ¾ **Northern Fling**[27] 2470 5-8-10 **87** .... (p) AndrewMullen 16 59
(D Nicholls) *hld up in tch stands' side: rdn over 2f out: kpt on fnl f: no imp: 3rd of 6 in gp* **14/1**

1060 **8** ¾ **Hitchens (IRE)**[20] 2716 4-9-8 **102** .... NeilBrown[(3)] 17 71
(T D Barron) *dwlt: hld up stands' side: rdn over 2f out: kpt on fnl f: n.d: 4th of 6 in gp* **12/1**

5016 **9** shd **Ishetoo**[20] 2716 5-9-0 **96** .... JamieKyne[(5)] 6 65
(A Dickman) *cl up far side: led that gp over 1f out to ins fnl f: one pce: 2nd of 7 in gp* **14/1**

1523 **10** 2½ **Cheveton**[43] 2012 5-9-5 **96** .... JimCrowley 7 55
(R J Price) *in tch far side: effrt wl over 1f out: one pce fnl f: 3rd of 7 in gp* **7/1**[2]

00-1 **11** ½ **Fathom Five (IRE)**[65] 1457 5-9-5 **96** .... AlanMunro 5 53
(C F Wall) *chsd far side ldr: effrt over 1f out: one pce: 4th of 7 in gp* **8/1**[3]

-100 **12** ½ **Piscean (USA)**[12] 2941 4-9-1 **92** .... DaleGibson 3 47
(T Keddy) *dwlt: bhd far side: sme late hdwy: nvr on terms: 5th of 7 in gp* **33/1**

5532 **13** nk **River Falcon**[20] 2716 9-9-3 **94** .... DanielTudhope 12 48
(J S Goldie) *hld up in tch stands' side: struggling over 2f out: sn btn: 5th of 6 in gp* **10/1**

-022 **14** ¾ **Captain Dunne (IRE)**[20] 2704 4-9-6 **100** .... FrederikTylicki[(3)] 1 51
(T D Easterby) *led far side to over 1f out: sn btn: 6th of 7 in gp* **6/1**[1]

0-05 **15** 1 **Green Manalishi**[51] 1791 8-9-4 **100** .... AmyRyan[(5)] 13 48
(K A Ryan) *prom on outside of stands' side gp: wknd over 2f out: last of 6 in gp* **14/1**

0400 **16** 2¼ **Tournedos (IRE)**[20] 2704 7-9-4 **95** .... JoeFanning 8 34
(D Nicholls) *dwlt: hld up far side: struggling over 2f out: sn btn: last of 7 in gp* **33/1**

60.46 secs (-0.24) **Going Correction** +0.20s/f (Good) 16 Ran SP% **123.1**
Speed ratings (Par 109): **109,108,107,106,100 94,92,91,91,87 86,85,85,84,82 79**
toteswingers: 1&2 £126.00, 1&3 £19.30, 2&3 £16.40 CSF £102.18 CT £833.13 TOTE £15.40: £3.80, £2.60, £2.30, £4.30; EX 181.90.

Owner Mrs Michael John Paver **Bred** Exors Of The Late M J Paver **Trained** Flaxton, N Yorks
■ Stewards' Enquiry : Duran Fentiman one-day ban: used whip with excessive frequency (Jul 11)

FOCUS
This is always ultra-competitive. The field split into three separate groups, with just three runners electing to stay down the middle, and that was the place to be as it developed. The placed horses set the level and the form looks solid.

NOTEBOOK
Pavershooz made his light weight count by making just about all down the centre of the course to follow up his Musselburgh success from a 4lb higher mark. He had questions to answer on the easing surface, but it proved no bother and he has now won both his races since being dropped back to the minimum trip. There was plenty to like about his attitude and he remains unexposed over the distance, so further improvement is certainly not ruled out. The valuable Portland Handicap over an extra half a furlong at Doncaster in September looks an ideal target and connections also fancy a tilt at the Ayr Gold Cup. (op 11-1)
Buachaill Dona(IRE) was 2lb higher than when winning this last season and he only just failed, running a blinder from his unfavourably high draw. The changing surface played into his hands and he deserves to win a decent pot. Perhaps he now really needs another furlong and the Stewards' Cup, in which he finished sixth last term from a 3lb higher mark, will probably figure on his agenda again. (op 14-1)
Hamish McGonagall finished second in this last year from an 8lb higher mark and was not beaten at all far here, but failed to reverse last-time-out form with Pavershooz despite being 4lb better off. He rates a solid benchmark and richly deserves to find another winning turn. (op 9-1)
Total Impact also failed to confirm Musselburgh form with the winner despite a 4lb pull, but he still ran a solid race down the middle of the track. There will be other days for him, but he may enjoy a drop in class.
Indian Trail was one in the race who would not have appreciated the easing ground, so the fact he came clear of those who raced far side dictates this was another commendable effort. He is still weighted to win a nice prize when things go more his way. Official explanation: jockey said gelding was denied a clear run (op 14-1)
Tabaret stepped up massively on the level of his seasonal bow a week earlier and was another not helped by his draw. A return to quicker ground will suit and it would be no surprise to see the cheekpieces back on next time. (tchd 66-1)
Cheveton was back to the mark he scored off at Southwell in the spring but has yet to show the same sparkle on turf that he did last year and is still 9lb above his highest winning turf rating. (op 15-2 tchd 13-2)
Piscean(USA) Official explanation: jockey said colt missed the break
Captain Dunne(IRE) made the running up the far side but the principals raced in the centre and towards the stands' side. He ended up fading out of things and a sharper track plays more to his strengths. Official explanation: vet said gelding injured its mouth in stalls (op 7-1)

3352 PHOENIX SECURITY MAIDEN FILLIES' STKS — 7f
7:55 (7:55) (Class 5) 3-Y-O+ **£4,533** (£1,348; £674; £336) **Stalls** High

Form — RPR
-253 **1** **Kammaan**[17] 2789 3-8-12 70 ... PhilipRobinson 9 — 75+
(M A Jarvis) *prom centre: smooth hdwy to ld 1f out: qcknd clr: eased nr fin* **2/1**[2]
2-33 **2** 4½ **Silk Trail**[12] 2947 3-8-12 0 ... NCallan 4 — 63
(Saeed Bin Suroor) *led centre: overall ldr briefly over 1f out: kpt on same pce fnl f* **10/11**[1]
6-00 **3** 3¾ **Le Reve Royal**[41] 2091 3-8-12 54 ... (p) DavidAllan 5 — 53
(G R Oldroyd) *chsd centre ldrs: rdn over 3f out: one pce fr 2f out* **66/1**
4 ¾ **Pure Heir (USA)** 3-8-12 0 ... PhillipMakin 6 — 51
(T D Barron) *hld up centre: hdwy 2f out: no imp fnl f* **16/1**
55 **5** 3 **Chichen Daawe**[9] 3036 3-8-5 0 ... AnthonyBetts(7) 7 — 43+
(B Ellison) *in tch stands' side tl edgd lft and outpcd over 2f out: n.d after* **50/1**
6 **6** 1½ **Lady Bluesky**[7] 3093 6-9-4 0 ... NeilBrown(3) 3 — 42
(A C Whillans) *hld up centre: pushed along over 3f out: nvr rchd ldrs* **8/1**[3]
0- **7** hd **See That Girl**[237] 7140 3-8-12 0 ... TomEaves 1 — 38
(B Smart) *midfield centre: pushed along over 2f out: sn outpcd* **33/1**
00-0 **8** ¾ **Little Pandora**[64] 1480 5-9-2 40 ... LanceBetts(5) 8 — 39
(L R James) *led and sn clr stands' rail: hdd over 1f out: wknd* **100/1**
00 **9** 3 **Riley Queen Bee (USA)**[7] 3093 3-8-12 0 ... AndrewElliott 10 — 28
(K R Burke) *hld up in tch: rdn and hung lft 3f out: sn btn* **12/1**
0-0 **10** 6 **Arriva La Diva**[9] 3036 3-8-5 0 ... IJBrennan(7) 2 — 12
(J J Quinn) *chsd centre ldrs tl wknd over 2f out* **100/1**

1m 30.1s (1.40) **Going Correction** +0.20s/f (Good)
WFA 3 from 5yo+ 9lb — **10** Ran SP% **118.8**
Speed ratings (Par 100): **100,94,90,89,86 84,84,83,80,73**
toteswingers: 1&2 £1.10, 2&3 £88.00, 1&3 not won. CSF £4.18 TOTE £2.80: £1.30, £1.20, £9.30; EX 4.30.
Owner Sheikh Ahmed Al Maktoum **Bred** Darley **Trained** Newmarket, Suffolk

FOCUS
The ground was predictably changed to good to soft prior to this modest fillies' maiden. This did not take much winning and the form looks weak.
Riley Queen Bee(USA) Official explanation: vet said filly finished distressed

3353 DELOITTE NATIONAL H'CAP — 1m 3y(S)
8:25 (8:29) (Class 4) (0-85,83) 3-Y-O+ **£5,046** (£1,510; £755; £377; £188) **Stalls** High

Form — RPR
5264 **1** **Rosko**[7] 3124 5-8-10 65 ... TomEaves 9 — 71
(B Ellison) *in tch: effrt over 2f out: rdn 2f out: kpt on wl fnl f: led nr fin* **5/1**[3]
2610 **2** ¾ **My Mate Mal**[8] 3070 5-8-4 64 oh2 ... LanceBetts(5) 1 — 68
(B Ellison) *led: rdn over 2f out: kpt on wl fnl f: hdd nr fin* **20/1**
0040 **3** 1½ **Orpen Wide (IRE)**[7] 3116 7-9-11 83 ... (b) LeeVickers(3) 7 — 84
(M C Chapman) *w ldr: rdn 2f out: kpt on same pce wl ins fnl f* **25/1**
-530 **4** nk **Middlemarch (IRE)**[21] 2665 9-8-13 73 ... (v) GaryBartley(5) 8 — 73
(J S Goldie) *bhd: outpcd 1/2-way: hdwy and styng on whn n.m.r briefly ins fnl f: kpt on fin* **12/1**
0-15 **5** 2 **Celtic Lynn (IRE)**[29] 2402 4-9-8 77 ... PhillipMakin 2 — 73
(M Dods) *hld up: hdwy over 2f out: rdn and one pce fnl f* **9/2**[2]
5220 **6** 10 **Handsome Falcon**[14] 2894 5-9-2 74 ... FrederikTylicki(3) 5 — 47
(R A Fahey) *in tch: drvn over 2f out: sn wknd* **9/4**[1]
010 **7** 37 **Byron Bay**[8] 3070 7-8-4 64 oh15 ... JamieKyne(5) 10 — —
(R Johnson) *chsd ldrs tl wknd over 2f out: t.o* **22/1**
0046 **8** 17 **Minority Report**[7] 3124 9-9-5 74 ... (v[1]) AdrianTNicholls 3 — —
(D Nicholls) *dwlt: hld up: rdn over 2f out: sn btn: t.o* **11/1**

1m 45.25s (1.85) **Going Correction** +0.20s/f (Good) — **8** Ran SP% **94.6**
Speed ratings (Par 105): **98,97,95,95,93 83,46,29**
toteswingers: 1&2 £13.10, 1&3 £25.00, 2&3 £28.30 CSF £66.65 CT £1199.66 TOTE £5.50: £1.60, £3.10, £3.90; EX 65.10.
Owner Racing Management & Training Ltd **Bred** Normandie Stud Ltd **Trained** Norton, N Yorks
■ Ellmau was withdrawn (9/2, broke out of stalls). Deduct 15p in the £ under R4.
■ Stewards' Enquiry : Lee Vickers six-day ban: used whip with excessive frequency (Jul 10-11, 13-16)
Tom Eaves two-day ban: one for careless riding; one for using whip with excessive frequency (Jul 11, 13)

FOCUS
This tricky handicap was further complicated when Ellmau burst the stalls open, causing the others to also spring back and there was a false start. The runners got no further than the first furlong pole, but it was unsatisfactory and the form should be treated with caution, with the runner-up the best guide.
Handsome Falcon Official explanation: trainer had no explanation for the poor form shown
Byron Bay Official explanation: jockey said gelding never travelled
Minority Report Official explanation: jockey said gelding hung right throughout

3354 SENDRIG CONSTRUCTION H'CAP — 6f
8:55 (9:02) (Class 5) (0-75,75) 3-Y-O+ **£3,885** (£1,156; £577; £288) **Stalls** High

Form — RPR
-350 **1** **Mark Of Meydan**[18] 2769 4-9-2 67 ... PhillipMakin 16 — 79
(M Dods) *in tch: hdwy to ld over 1f out: pushed out fnl f* **7/1**
6322 **2** 1½ **Soto**[16] 2801 6-8-4 62 ... (b) JamesPSullivan(7) 4 — 69
(M W Easterby) *w ldr: led 2f to over 1f out: kpt on u.p ins fnl f* **9/1**
5260 **3** 1¾ **Ingleby Arch (USA)**[13] 2938 6-9-7 75 ... NeilBrown(3) 13 — 77
(T D Barron) *missed break: bhd tl styd on wl fnl 2f: nrst fin* **9/2**[1]
3101 **4** ½ **Red Cape (FR)**[10] 3001 6-9-9 74 6ex ... AndrewElliott 3 — 74
(Mrs R A Carr) *prom: effrt over 2f out: kpt on same pce fnl f* **12/1**
4533 **5** 4 **Miss Daawe**[6] 3153 5-8-5 61 ... LanceBetts(5) 12 — 48
(B Ellison) *in tch: rdn over 2f out: sn one pce* **9/1**
3131 **6** 1¼ **Swinbrook (USA)**[18] 2769 8-9-6 74 ... (v) FrederikTylicki(3) 9 — 57
(R A Fahey) *hld up: rdn over 2f out: nvr able to chal* **5/1**[2]
4504 **7** nse **Castlebury (IRE)**[20] 2722 4-8-11 62 ... NCallan 7 — 45
(G A Swinbank) *towards rr: drvn and outpcd 1/2-way: sme late hdwy: n.d* **16/1**
0000 **8** hd **Hotham**[13] 2938 6-9-7 72 ... DanielTudhope 1 — 54
(N Wilson) *hld up on outside: rdn 1/2-way: kpt on fnl f: nvr on terms* **25/1**
1-20 **9** 7 **Charles Parnell (IRE)**[18] 2770 6-9-9 74 ... DaleGibson 14 — 34
(M Dods) *hld up in midfield: drvn over 2f out: sn wknd* **11/1**
-060 **10** 4 **Kalhan Sands (IRE)**[20] 2722 4-8-9 65 ... JamieKyne(5) 8 — 12
(J J Quinn) *chsd ldrs: drvn 1/2-way: wknd fnl 2f* **20/1**
16-6 **11** 6 **Another Decree**[74] 1246 4-9-3 68 ... TomEaves 10 — —
(M Dods) *hld up: pushed along over 2f out: nvr on terms* **40/1**
6- **12** 6 **Dream Rainbow**[420] 1790 4-9-0 65 ... (t) MickyFenton 2 — —
(Joss Saville) *hld up: rdn 1/2-way: n.d* **80/1**
-000 **13** 1 **Steel Blue**[8] 3066 9-9-1 66 ... (p) TonyCulhane 11 — —
(R M Whitaker) *sn prom: rdn over 2f out: sn wknd* **33/1**
5000 **14** 6 **Spin Again (IRE)**[34] 2269 4-9-1 66 ... (v[1]) AdrianTNicholls 15 — —
(D Nicholls) *led to over 2f out: sn rdn and wknd* **11/2**[3]

1m 15.8s (0.60) **Going Correction** +0.20s/f (Good) — **14** Ran SP% **119.9**
Speed ratings (Par 103): **104,102,99,99,93 92,91,91,82,77 69,61,59,51**
toteswingers: 1&2 £15.80, 1&3 £18.90, 2&3 £11.30 CSF £64.76 CT £327.34 TOTE £8.90: £2.90, £2.30, £2.90; EX 93.60.
Owner The Bounty Hunters **Bred** The Bounty Hunters **Trained** Denton, Co Durham

FOCUS
A modest sprint in which the runner-up is a solid guide to the form. The visibility was very poor due to heavy fog, but a high draw was clearly an advantage.
Swinbrook(USA) Official explanation: trainer had no explanation for the poor form shown
Dream Rainbow Official explanation: trainer said gelding scoped dirty post-race

3355 KEVIN LEE MEMORIAL H'CAP — 5f
9:30 (9:31) (Class 5) (0-75,72) 3-Y-O **£3,885** (£1,156; £577; £288) **Stalls** High

Form — RPR
0132 **1** **Noodles Blue Boy**[20] 2726 3-9-5 70 ... TonyHamilton 9 — 79
(Ollie Pears) *chsd ldrs: effrt and wnt 2nd over 1f out: kpt on wl fnl f: led nr fin* **9/4**[1]
1215 **2** nk **Taurus Twins**[18] 2774 3-9-4 69 ... (b) JimCrowley 7 — 77
(R J Price) *led: rdn 2f out: kpt on fnl f: hdd nr fin* **9/2**[2]
3465 **3** 7 **York Key Bar**[21] 2683 3-8-4 60 ... (t) LanceBetts(5) 8 — 43
(B Ellison) *s.i.s: bhd and outpcd: kpt on fnl f: nt pce of first two* **6/1**
0434 **4** 2 **Dispol Kylie (IRE)**[6] 3173 3-9-7 72 ... JoeFanning 5 — 48
(P T Midgley) *cl up tl rdn and wknd wl over 1f out* **9/2**[2]
-032 **5** 2 **Rogalt (IRE)**[28] 2439 3-9-3 68 ... TomEaves 3 — 36
(B Smart) *midfield: outpcd 1/2-way: sn btn* **14/1**
-131 **6** 1 **Hysterical Lady**[55] 1686 3-9-7 72 ... AdrianTNicholls 1 — 37
(D Nicholls) *chsd ldrs tl edgd lft and wknd fr 2f out* **11/2**[3]
-002 **7** 2½ **Sleepy Valley (IRE)**[34] 2268 3-8-0 56 ... (p) JamieKyne(5) 4 — 12
(A Dickman) *midfield: rdn 2f out: sn wknd* **20/1**
2546 **8** 12 **Compton Ford**[8] 3063 3-9-0 65 ... (b[1]) PhillipMakin 2 — —
(M Dods) *hld up: rdn 1/2-way: nvr on terms* **16/1**

61.83 secs (1.13) **Going Correction** +0.20s/f (Good) — **8** Ran SP% **114.1**
Speed ratings (Par 99): **98,97,86,83,79 78,74,55**
toteswingers: 1&2 £3.30, 1&3 £6.20, 2&3 £7.40 CSF £12.35 CT £52.18 TOTE £3.40: £1.40, £1.90, £2.00; EX 8.90 Place 6: £78.66 Place 5: £48.83.
Owner Ian Bishop **Bred** Fifehead Farms M C Denning **Trained** Norton, N Yorks

FOCUS
A fairly tight sprint and it is worth taking a positive view of the form. A high draw proved a must.
Hysterical Lady Official explanation: jockey said filly was unsuited by the good to soft ground
Sleepy Valley(IRE) Official explanation: jockey said filly hung badly right final 3f
Compton Ford Official explanation: jockey said gelding was unsuited by the good to soft ground
T/Jkpt: Not won. T/Plt: £132.70 to a £1 stake. Pool: £90,590.80. 498.06 winning tickets. T/Qpdt: £18.00 to a £1 stake. Pool: £5,580.61. 228.90 winning tickets. RY

3163 NEWMARKET (R-H)
Friday, June 26

OFFICIAL GOING: Good to soft
Wind: Almost nil Weather: Overcast

3356 EUROPEAN BREEDERS' FUND MAIDEN FILLIES' STKS — 6f
6:00 (6:00) (Class 4) 2-Y-O **£5,180** (£1,541; £770; £384) **Stalls** Low

Form — RPR
05 **1** **Emma Dora (IRE)**[15] 2860 2-9-0 0 ... DaneO'Neill 6 — 71
(D R C Elsworth) *led: rdn over 2f out: hdd over 1f out: rallied to ld nr fin where rdr dropped whip* **11/1**
2 shd **Water Biscuit** 2-9-0 0 ... JamieSpencer 9 — 71
(B J Meehan) *s.i.s: sn chsng ldrs: led over 1f out: rdn and edgd lft ins fnl f: hdd nr fin* **7/1**
3 shd **L'Enchanteresse (IRE)** 2-9-0 0 ... EddieAhern 8 — 70
(M L W Bell) *hld up: rdn over 1f out: r.o wl ins fnl f* **4/1**[3]
4 hd **Keyta Bonita (IRE)** 2-9-0 0 ... RichardHughes 1 — 70
(M G Quinlan) *hld up: nt clr run and swtchd lft over 1f out: r.o wl ins fnl f* **7/1**

5 ½ **Gundaroo** 2-9-0 0 TedDurcan 2 68
(J L Dunlop) *chsd ldrs: nt clr run over 1f out: rdn ins fnl f: r.o* **2/1**[1]

6 1¼ **Dizziness (USA)** 2-9-0 0 SteveDrowne 5 65
(R Charlton) *dwlt: hld up: hdwy over 1f out: no ex wl ins fnl f* **7/2**[2]

0 7 11 **Anitra's Dance**[16] 2825 2-9-0 0 JimmyQuinn 4 32
(P Howling) *prom: racd keenly: rdn over 2f out: wknd wl over 1f out* **33/1**

0 8 shd **Sisters Warning**[19] 2741 2-9-0 0 MichaelHills 7 31
(J Ryan) *chsd wnr tl rdn over 2f out: wknd over 1f out* **33/1**

1m 15.4s (2.90) **Going Correction** +0.125s/f (Good) **8** Ran SP% **114.8**
Speed ratings (Par 92): **85,84,84,84,83 82,67,67**
toteswingers: 1&2 £3.60, 1&3 £10.50, 2&3 £4.80 CSF £84.99 TOTE £13.90: £2.90, £1.80, £1.60; EX 70.10.
Owner G B Partnership **Bred** Georgestown Stud **Trained** Newmarket, Suffolk

FOCUS
Traditionally, this has been quite a decent maiden, but this year's renewal appeared to lack depth and you could have thrown a blanket over the first five. The form is rated fairly negatively.

NOTEBOOK
Emma Dora(IRE) apparently froze on her debut at Newbury before running with a little promise to finish fifth at Yarmouth. The big positive from this display was her will to win. She was headed over 1f out but knuckled down - despite her rider dropping his whip a few yards from the line - and rallied to score. On the negative side, she looked a little edgy beforehand and had two handlers with her. Her future probably lies in nurseries and much will depend how the assessor rates her. (op 10-1)
Water Biscuit, a January foal, has plenty of stamina in the family on the dam's side, but her sire Bertolini has clearly been an influence for speed. She looked well in herself but left the impression that she'd really tighten up for this. She moved to post sweetly and showed decent early speed before delivering a concerted challenge. Her trainer often introduces above-average types at this track and she may take the beating next time and keep progressing as the season unfolds. (op 4-1)
L'Enchanteresse(IRE) cost 55,000gns as a yearling and hails from the yard that won the race last year. She was another to draw added interest in the preliminaries, appearing a little leggy and leaving the impression that she has some strengthening up to do. She has something of a mixed pedigree. While she is by a Nunthorpe Stakes winner in Kyllachy, a couple of her siblings won over1m2f-plus. She is entitled to have learned plenty from this and can go even closer in a similar race next time. (op 9-2)
Keyta Bonita(IRE)'s jockey booking suggested she had shown a good level of ability at home. She didn't disappoint, shaping well - especially as she had to be switched to the inner rail for a run. (op 9-1)
Gundaroo is a half-sister to a 5f-6f winner at two and the dam was placed on her only start as a two-year-old. She looks a compact filly who will be competitive as a juvenile. She is another who should harden up physically and mentally for the run. (tchd 9-4 tchd 5-2 in places)
Dizziness(USA) is a half-sister to seven winners, including the Group 1 scorer Monzante. On paddock inspection, she appealed as a filly of potential substance, albeit slightly on the leg for her debut, and she moved to post in taking fashion. Drawn wide, she was forced to race on her own, which was not ideal on her debut. An American-bred, the ground may have been a little on the soft side for her. (op 5-1)

3357 DIRECTA UK H'CAP 1m
6:30 (6:31) (Class 5) (0-75,81) 3-Y-O+ **£3,885** (£1,156; £577; £288) **Stalls** Low

Form RPR

5346 1 **King Columbo (IRE)**[7] 3112 4-9-6 **67** TPQueally 11 74
(Miss J Feilden) *racd stands' side: hld up in tch: chsd ldr over 1f out: rdn to ld and edgd lft wl ins fnl f* **6/1**

5005 2 nse **Lord Theo**[7] 3112 5-9-1 **62** RichardHughes 10 69
(N P Littmoden) *racd stands' side: chsd ldr tl led overall over 2f out: rdn over 1f out: hung lft and hdd wl ins fnl f: 2nd of 5 in gp* **14/1**

-203 3 ½ **Hawk's Eye**[7] 3115 3-8-12 **69** (p) JamieSpencer 2 73
(E F Vaughan) *racd stands' side: hld up: swtchd lft and hdwy over 1f out: rdn and ev ch ins fnl f: styd on reluctantly: 3rd of 5 in gp* **11/2**[3]

0035 4 6 **Magnitude**[10] 3008 4-9-8 **69** (p) DaneO'Neill 5 61
(M E Rimmer) *racd far side: chsd ldr tl rdn to ld that gp ins fnl f: no ch w far side: 1st of 4 in gp* **16/1**

65-0 5 nk **Waahej**[7] 3115 3-8-11 **68** RHills 3 57
(J L Dunlop) *racd far side: hld up: hdwy over 2f out: rdn over 1f out: ev ch in that quartet ins fnl f: styd on same pce: 2nd of 4 in gp* **12/1**

6-31 6 1 **Addwaitya**[21] 2675 4-9-11 **72** TedDurcan 9 61
(C F Wall) *racd stands' side: chsd ldrs: rdn over 2f out: wknd over 1f out: 4th of 5 in gp* **5/1**[2]

1511 7 9 **Prince Rossi (IRE)**[31] 2352 5-9-0 **61** (v) EddieAhern 7 29
(A E Price) *overall ldr far side tl over 3f out: sn rdn: wknd fnl f* **7/1**

0531 8 ¾ **Carlitos Spirit (IRE)**[6] 3159 5-10-3 **81** 6ex JamesMillman[(3)] 8 48
(B R Millman) *led stands' side: overall ldr over 3f out: hdd over 2f out: wknd over 1f out: last of 5 in gp* **9/2**[1]

3000 9 3¼ **Guildenstern (IRE)**[7] 3112 7-9-8 **69** JimmyQuinn 4 28
(P Howling) *racd far side: chsd ldrs: rdn and wknd over 2f out: last of 4 in gp* **33/1**

4-61 P **Sonny Parkin**[7] 3112 7-9-1 **69** (v) SimonPearce[(7)] 1 —
(J Pearce) *s.s: wl bhd: swtchd to join stands' side over 6f out: nvr any ch: p.u ins fnl f* **5/1**[2]

1m 40.45s (0.45) **Going Correction** +0.125s/f (Good)
WFA 3 from 4yo+ 10lb **10** Ran SP% **116.9**
Speed ratings (Par 103): **102,101,101,95,95 94,85,84,81,—**
toteswingers: 1&2 £18.30, 1&3 £9.30, 2&3 £19.50 CSF £86.33 CT £500.89 TOTE £6.50: £2.10, £4.60, £1.90; EX 111.60.
Owner Columbian Kings **Bred** Don Commins **Trained** Exning, Suffolk

FOCUS
An unsatisfactory affair as the field split into two groups. Four chose to hug the far-side rail, while eventually five came across towards the stands' side rail. In the end, the first three drifted left to finish in the centre of the track. The form is modest but appears sound with the first three clear.
King Columbo(IRE) Official explanation: trainer's rep said, regarding apparent improvement in form, that the gelding was better suited by being ridden with more restraint.
Addwaitya Official explanation: jockey said gelding was unsuited by the soft ground
Carlitos Spirit(IRE) Official explanation: jockey said gelding had no more to give
Sonny Parkin Official explanation: jockey said gelding lost its action

3358 ADCOCK GROUP CLAIMING STKS 1m
7:00 (7:01) (Class 5) 3-Y-O **£3,885** (£1,156; £577; £288) **Stalls** Low

Form RPR

6022 1 **Fajita**[10] 3009 3-8-9 67 TedDurcan 8 67
(G L Moore) *hld up: pushed along over 2f out: hdwy over 1f out: r.o to ld wl ins fnl f* **9/2**[3]

2205 2 1 **Barbarian**[21] 2685 3-9-0 69 MichaelHills 2 70
(B W Hills) *led: rdn over 1f out: hdd and unable qckn wl ins fnl f* **11/2**

52-3 3 1 **Mootriba**[30] 2375 3-8-8 71 (b) JamieSpencer 9 61
(W J Haggas) *chsd ldrs: rdn and ev ch over 1f out: nt qckn ins fnl f* **2/1**[1]

130 4 1 **Statute Book (IRE)**[23] 2600 3-9-9 76 EddieAhern 3 74
(S Kirk) *chsd ldrs: rdn over 1f out: no ex ins fnl f* **10/1**

-030 5 ¾ **Tidal Force (USA)**[15] 2849 3-9-0 69 TPQueally 5 63
(P F I Cole) *hld up in tch: rdn over 2f out: styd on same pce* **14/1**

-605 6 nk **Brooksby**[9] 3030 3-9-0 70 (b) DaneO'Neill 4 62
(R Hannon) *chsd ldr: rdn over 2f out: hung lft and wknd ins fnl f* **11/1**

-400 7 8 **Granski (IRE)**[15] 2850 3-9-0 63 RichardHughes 10 43
(R Hannon) *hld up: rdn over 1f out: wknd fnl f* **10/3**[2]

0-04 8 4 **Flashgun (USA)**[59] 1595 3-8-4 53 NicolPolli[(5)] 6 28
(M G Quinlan) *hld up: rdn and wknd over 2f out* **25/1**

1m 42.2s (2.20) **Going Correction** +0.125s/f (Good) **8** Ran SP% **117.9**
Speed ratings (Par 99): **94,93,92,91,90 89,81,77**
toteswingers: 1&2 £5.30, 1&3 £1.70, 2&3 £2.70 CSF £30.37 TOTE £4.30: £1.70, £1.70, £1.30; EX 18.30.Fajita was subject to a friendly claim.
Owner W P Flynn **Bred** Mrs Joan Langmead **Trained** Lower Beeding, W Sussex

FOCUS
A modest contest with only one of the field having registered a victory this season. The time reflected the quality of the race with it being five and a half seconds beyond standard and 1.75sec slower than the previous handicap over the same trip. The form is rated around the winner to his maiden form backed up by the fourth.

3359 DIRECTA WINNING SIGNS H'CAP 1m 4f
7:35 (7:36) (Class 4) (0-80,76) 3-Y-O **£5,828** (£1,734; £866; £432) **Stalls** Centre

Form RPR

11-2 1 **Becausewecan (USA)**[87] 1056 3-9-9 **76** RHills 5 84
(M Johnston) *led: hdd over 1f out: edgd and carried lft fnl f: rallied to ld towards fin* **9/2**[3]

6-13 2 ½ **Solar Graphite (IRE)**[36] 2189 3-9-6 **73** EddieAhern 2 80
(J L Dunlop) *s.i.s: rcvrd to chse wnr after 1f tl 7f out: rdn to ld and hung lft fr over 1f out: hdd towards fin* **13/8**[1]

65-5 3 shd **Dazinski**[30] 2371 3-9-2 **69** TedDurcan 1 76
(M H Tompkins) *hld up: hdwy over 6f out: rdn over 1f out: r.o* **7/1**

4-33 4 6 **Royal Trooper (IRE)**[12] 2943 3-8-13 **66** TPQueally 3 63
(J G Given) *plld hrd and prom: trckd wnr 7f out: rdn and wknd over 1f out* **6/1**

4440 5 3½ **Kaolak (USA)**[8] 3050 3-9-7 **74** RichardMullen 6 66
(J Ryan) *prom: pushed along over 3f out: wknd over 1f out* **4/1**[2]

311 6 3¾ **Supernoverre (IRE)**[86] 1063 3-9-9 **76** JimmyQuinn 4 62
(P Howling) *s.i.s: hld up: pushed along over 3f out: wknd over 1f out* **12/1**

2m 33.98s (1.08) **Going Correction** +0.125s/f (Good) **6** Ran SP% **110.8**
Speed ratings (Par 101): **101,100,100,96,94 91**
toteswinger: 1&2 £2.30, 1&3 £2.30, 2&3 £4.00 CSF £11.95 TOTE £3.70: £2.00, £1.50; EX 10.00.

Owner Douglas Livingston **Bred** Tony Holmes & Walter Zent **Trained** Middleham Moor, N Yorks
■ Stewards' Enquiry : Eddie Ahern two-day ban: careless riding (Jul 11, 13)

FOCUS
They went only a steady gallop at the outset and the time was more than six and a half seconds outside standard. The first three were clear and the form is rated fairly positively.
Royal Trooper(IRE) Official explanation: jockey said colt ran too free

3360 EUROPEAN BREEDERS' FUND FILLIES' CONDITIONS STKS 6f
8:05 (8:05) (Class 3) 3-Y-O+ **£10,361** (£3,083; £1,540; £769) **Stalls** Low

Form RPR

20-0 1 **Raggle Taggle (IRE)**[59] 1582 3-8-5 93 EddieAhern 6 92
(R M Beckett) *led to 1/2-way: rdn over 1f out: r.o to ld nr fin* **7/1**

-013 2 hd **Pretty Bonnie**[40] 2102 4-8-12 85 KirstyMilczarek 2 93
(A E Price) *a.p: edgd rt and led over 1f out: sn rdn: hdd nr fin* **9/2**[3]

1-10 3 nk **Mullein**[34] 2271 4-8-12 96 SebSanders 7 92
(R M Beckett) *hld up: hdwy over 1f out: sn rdn: r.o* **15/8**[1]

2260 4 4 **Shaws Diamond (USA)**[21] 2674 3-8-5 77 RichardMullen 3 77
(D Shaw) *s.i.s: sn chsng ldrs: led 1/2-way: rdn: edgd rt and hdd over 1f out: sn hung lft: wknd fnl f* **16/1**

0120 5 3½ **Cake (IRE)**[20] 2704 4-8-12 93 RichardHughes 5 68
(R Hannon) *trckd ldrs: racd keenly: nt clr run and swtchd lft over 1f out: wkng whn hmpd sn after* **11/4**[2]

2210 6 nk **White Shift (IRE)**[6] 3166 3-8-5 78 JimmyQuinn 4 65
(P Howling) *prom: racd keenly: rdn over 1f out: sn wknd* **13/2**

1m 13.05s (0.55) **Going Correction** +0.125s/f (Good)
WFA 3 from 4yo+ 7lb **6** Ran SP% **111.3**
Speed ratings (Par 104): **101,100,100,95,90 89**
toteswingers: 1&2 £6.00, 1&3 £3.10, 2&3 £3.40 CSF £36.89 TOTE £8.70: £3.00, £2.80; EX 60.10.
Owner Lady Marchwood **Bred** Keith Wills **Trained** Whitsbury, Hants

FOCUS
This looked a tight enough race on paper with four of the six runners having winning form this year. The form is muddling and is limited by the fourth.

NOTEBOOK
Raggle Taggle(IRE) had solid claims on her best two-year-old form - she was a narrowly beaten second in a Deauville Listed contest - but you had to look beyond her last, apparently disappointing effort when she was second last in a Listed event at Bath. Her best two runs have now come with give in the ground, but she has won on a fast surface so is versatile and is worth a step back into Listed company in pursuit of some winning black type. (tchd 13-2 and 8-1)
Pretty Bonnie, third on similar ground over this trip on her last start, ran a cracker and just inside the final furlong looked as if she had them all beaten. However, on paper beforehand she did have a bit to find and in the end was just reined in by a rival to whom she was conceding 7lb. She has handled quicker ground in the past, but - by Kyllachy - it would be no surprise if a little underfoot ease suits her down to the ground. She is clearly a filly in form and deserves to be respected if running in similar company in the near future. (op 5-1 tchd 13-2)
Mullein appeared to be travelling with purpose over 2f out. She came there with every chance, but her effort just flattened out. The ground was ideal for her - she has won twice before with cut in the ground - but wasn't good enough on the day. That said, she was only beaten a quarter of a length and is another who can pick up a nice prize in the coming months. (op 2-1 tchd 11-8)
Shaws Diamond(USA) is still a maiden after 11 starts, although she has finished second on no less than four occasions. She showed plenty of dash here, but may be awkward to place off a mark of 77 if returned to handicaps. (op 20-1 tchd 12-1)
Cake(IRE) was short of room approaching the final furlong, but her stamina limitations were exposed. All of her four career wins have come over 5f, and on better ground. (tchd 3-1 tchd 10-3 in places)
White Shift(IRE) has been busy of late and may just welcome a break. (op 6-1 tchd 7-1)

3361 DANWOOD H'CAP 1m 2f
8:40 (8:40) (Class 4) (0-80,80) 3-Y-O+
£5,607 (£1,679; £839; £420; £209; £105) **Stalls** Centre

Form RPR

2410 1 **Summer Winds**[22] 2641 4-9-13 **79** (b) SebSanders 2 88
(T G Mills) *sn chsng ldr: led over 2f out: rdn and edgd lft over 1f out: styd on* **8/1**

1140 **2** *1 ¼* **Manshoor (IRE)**[21] 2671 4-9-10 **76**.................................... EddieAhern 8 83
(Mrs L Wadham) *trckd ldrs: racd keenly: rdn whn nt clr run over 1f out: r.o* **4/1**[3]

1-30 **3** *½* **Wiggy Smith**[29] 2407 10-10-0 **80**.. DaneO'Neill 4 86
(H Candy) *hld up in tch: rdn and edgd lft over 1f out: styd on same pce ins fnl f* **9/4**[1]

3431 **4** *shd* **Buddy Holly**[9] 3024 4-9-3 **76**.................................(v) CharlesEddery(7) 6 81
(Pat Eddery) *led: racd keenly: hdd over 2f out: sn rdn: edgd rt over 1f out: styd on* **5/2**[2]

1334 **5** *2 ¼* **Nassar (IRE)**[32] 2332 6-8-12 **64**...............................(v) KirstyMilczarek 5 65
(G Prodromou) *s.s: hld up: racd keenly: hdwy 2f out: rdn over 1f out: no ex ins fnl f* **13/2**

40-1 **6** *3* **Agapanthus (GER)**[74] 1261 4-9-6 **72**....................................... TPQueally 3 67
(B J Curley) *s.i.s: hld up: hdwy over 2f out: wknd fnl f* **12/1**

2m 11.05s (5.55) **Going Correction** +0.125s/f (Good)
WFA 3 from 4yo+ 12lb **6** Ran SP% **111.5**
Speed ratings (Par 105): **82,81,80,80,78 76**
toteswingers: 1&2 £5.80, 1&3 £3.90, 2&3 £2.50 CSF £38.64 CT £93.58 TOTE £9.70: £3.20, £2.40; EX 48.00.
Owner John Humphreys **Bred** Beechgrove Stud **Trained** Headley, Surrey

FOCUS
This was a far from satisfactory affair with a steady early tempo preceding a desperate sprint from over 2f out. The time backs this up, with it being over eight seconds beyond standard. The form is not the most solid but looks reasonable rated around the placed horses.

3362 DEVIL'S DYKE H'CAP 5f
9:10 (9:10) (Class 4) (0-85,85) 3-Y-O **£5,828** (£1,734; £866; £432) **Stalls** Low

Form RPR

1021 **1** **Mattamia (IRE)**[8] 3053 3-9-7 **85** 6ex........................... JamesMillman(3) 2 94
(B R Millman) *mde all: rdn and r.o wl* **5/2**[2]

2-10 **2** *2* **Dark Lane**[34] 2279 3-9-8 **83**.. JamieSpencer 1 85
(T D Barron) *sn pushed along in rr: hdwy to chse wnr over 1f out: sn rdn and no imp* **11/4**[3]

34-5 **3** *2 ¼* **Fantasy Gladiator**[14] 2888 3-8-8 **69**................................. PatCosgrave 5 63
(R M H Cowell) *chsd wnr tl rdn and hung lft over 1f out: wknd ins fnl f* **9/1**

21 **4** *1 ¼* **Avertor**[20] 2700 3-9-8 **83**.. SteveDrowne 3 72
(R Charlton) *hld up: rdn and hung rt over 1f out: hung lft ins fnl f: n.d* **11/8**[1]

59.89 secs (0.79) **Going Correction** +0.125s/f (Good) **4** Ran SP% **107.3**
Speed ratings (Par 101): **98,94,91,89**
CSF £9.26 TOTE £3.80; EX 8.50 Place 6: £527.44 Place 5: £172.76 .
Owner C Roper **Bred** H G And J R Dutfield **Trained** Kentisbeare, Devon

FOCUS
A one-sided contest and sound enough rated around the first two.
T/Plt: £163.80 to a £1 stake. Pool: £59,603.07. 265.50 winning tickets. T/Qpdt: £132.70 to a £1 stake. Pool: £3,695.60. 20.60 winning tickets. CR

3363 - 3369a (Foreign Racing) - See Raceform Interactive

3331
CHESTER (L-H)
Saturday, June 27

OFFICIAL GOING: Good to firm (good in places; 8.0)
False rail in use adding 5yards per circuit to race distances.
Wind: Almost nil. Weather: Overcast turning bright

3370 THOROUGHBRED REHABILITATION CENTRE NOVICE STKS 5f 16y
2:10 (2:10) (Class 4) 2-Y-O **£5,180** (£1,541; £770; £384) **Stalls** Low

Form RPR

1 **Dancing Red Devil (IRE)** 2-8-3 0........................ SilvestreDeSousa 2 77+
(Paul Green) *chsd ldrs: pushed along 2f out: qcknd to ld over 1f out: r.o wl to draw clr ins fnl f: pushed out* **11/2**

4 **2** *3 ¾* **Bazsharani**[18] 2778 2-8-7 0.................................... CatherineGannon 3 67
(P D Evans) *led: rdn and hdd over 1f out: nt pce of wnr ins fnl f* **10/3**[3]

4102 **3** *2* **Tillys Tale**[22] 2655 2-8-7 0.. PaulPickard(7) 4 67
(P T Midgley) *chsd ldr tl rdn and nt qckn over 1f out: one pce fnl f* **9/4**[2]

4326 **4** *2 ½* **My Mandy (IRE)**[52] 1788 2-8-7 0.............................. StephenDonohoe 5 51+
(Ian Williams) *s.i.s: sn chsd ldrs: rdn over 1f out: wknd fnl f* **15/8**[1]

00 **5** *nk* **Exceed Power**[8] 3101 2-8-7 0.. WilliamBuick 6 50+
(D M Simcock) *racd on wd outside thrght: in tch: effrt over 2f out: wknd fnl f* **12/1**

00 **6** *10* **Another Sold**[33] 2339 2-8-0 0... BillyCray(7) 1 14
(A Berry) *lost pl after 1f: sn bhd and pushed along: wl outpcd appr fnl f* **28/1**

61.59 secs (0.59) **Going Correction** -0.025s/f (Good) **6** Ran SP% **115.2**
Speed ratings (Par 95): **94,88,84,80,80 64**
toteswingers: 1&2 £3.30, 1&3 £2.80, 2&3 £2.00. CSF £24.73 TOTE £6.60: £2.50, £2.30; EX 23.00.
Owner Daniel Britton **Bred** Martin Walsh **Trained** Lydiate, Merseyside

FOCUS
Only fillies took part in this modest novice event which was a weak race for the grade.

NOTEBOOK
Dancing Red Devil(IRE) came home to score comfortably on this racecourse debut and looks a filly with a bright future. She may not have beaten that much, but could have been called the winner off the final turn and showed a professional attitude when straightening for home. Bred to get further in time, the daughter of Desert Style clearly has plenty of speed and her trainer is aiming her at the valuable Tattersalls Ireland Sale Stakes at the Curragh in August, a race he won with Sudden Impact back in 2007. (op 5-1 tchd 9-2)
Bazsharani showed the benefit of her initial experience over course and distance 18 days earlier and led the field until being put in her place by the winner. This was a step in the right direction and she will not mind stepping up a furlong. (op 7-2 tchd 3-1)
Tillys Tale did not lose much in defeat considering she was conceding weight all round, being the only previous winner in the field. She should find her feet when the nurseries begin. (op 5-2 tchd 11-4 in places)
My Mandy(IRE) finished out the back in Lily Agnes over here on her previous outing 53 days earlier, so this clearly represented an easier assignment and she has to rate as disappointing. (op 5-2 tchd 11-4)
Exceed Power was never a serious player on this first outing over the minimum trip and looks to need more time. (op 11-1 tchd 8-1)
Another Sold played up at the start and was always in rear. (op 25-1)

3371 BARCLAYS WEALTH H'CAP 1m 4f 66y
2:40 (2:40) (Class 4) (0-85,81) 3-Y-O **£5,504** (£1,637; £818; £408) **Stalls** Low

Form RPR

222 **1** **Stanstill (IRE)**[19] 2767 3-9-7 **79**.................................... RobertWinston 5 83
(G A Swinbank) *in tch: pushed along 4f out: chal on outside over 2f out: led narrowly over 1f out: all out at fin* **7/2**[2]

51 **2** *nse* **Act Of Kalanisi (IRE)**[22] 2659 3-9-9 **81**......................... J-PGuillambert 1 85+
(M Johnston) *hld up: outpcd 3f out: u.str driving over 1f out: r.o wl and gd prog ins fnl f: fin strly: jst failed* **5/1**[3]

-021 **3** *½* **Cool Strike (UAE)**[14] 2909 3-9-9 **81**.............................(v) WilliamBuick 3 84
(A M Balding) *chsd ldr: pushed along 3f out: str chal fr 2f out: bmpd over 1f out: hung lft and leant on rival ins fnl f: r.o u.p: hld fnl strides* **15/8**[1]

1123 **4** *shd* **Classic Contours (USA)**[22] 2667 3-8-13 **71**................. JamieMoriarty 2 74
(J J Quinn) *chsd ldrs: shkn up 3f out: rdn and nt qckn over 1f out: swtchd rt ins fnl 100yds: r.o and clsd at fin* **11/2**

4651 **5** *nk* **Embsay Crag**[18] 2779 3-8-10 **71**... NeilBrown(3) 6 73
(Mrs K Walton) *led: rdn whn bmpd and hdd over 1f out: continued to chal ins fnl f: hld and one pce fnl strides* **11/2**

3245 **6** *1 ¾* **Musical Maze**[1] 3336 3-7-13 **64**................................... PaulPickard(7) 4 64
(W M Brisbourne) *in rr: pushed along 2f out: kpt on fnl f: nvr able to chal* **12/1**

2m 39.42s (-0.48) **Going Correction** -0.025s/f (Good) **6** Ran SP% **112.1**
Speed ratings (Par 101): **100,99,99,99,99 98**
toteswingers: 1&2 £3.60, 1&3 £2.20, 2&3 £2.30. CSF £20.80 TOTE £4.50: £2.20, £2.60; EX 21.70.
Owner The Twopin Partnership **Bred** E J Daly **Trained** Melsonby, N Yorks

FOCUS
There were three last-time-out winners in this interesting 3yo handicap. The race was run at just an average pace, however, and there was a blanket finish between the first five. There are doubts about the solidity of the form although the majority came into the race in good heart.

3372 HORSERACING ABROAD H'CAP 5f 16y
3:15 (3:17) (Class 3) (0-90,83) 3-Y-O+ **£8,831** (£2,643; £1,321; £660; £329) **Stalls** Low

Form RPR

1312 **1** **Impressible**[7] 3173 3-9-0 **75**... WilliamBuick 5 83
(E J Alston) *broke wl: mde most: drifted rt fr over 1f out: r.o and fnd ex fnl 50yds* **11/4**[2]

0003 **2** *1 ¼* **Bertoliver**[18] 2782 5-9-11 **80**.. CatherineGannon 1 86
(Tom Dascombe) *chsd ldrs: wnt 2nd and chal wnr over 1f out: nt qckn fnl 50yds* **2/1**[1]

0150 **3** *½* **Legal Eagle (IRE)**[11] 3001 4-9-11 **80**........................ StephenDonohoe 3 84
(Paul Green) *bmpd sn after s: chsd ldrs: rdn over 1f out: r.o fnl 100yds: nt quite pce of ldng duo* **11/2**[3]

1640 **4** *¾* **Rasaman (IRE)**[11] 3001 5-9-9 **83**.................................(t) AmyRyan(5) 9 84
(K A Ryan) *in rr: sn niggled along: rdn over 1f out: styd on wl and prog ins fnl f: nt pce to rch ldrs* **22/1**

3003 **5** *½* **Nickel Silver**[7] 3149 4-9-8 **77**.................................(b) SilvestreDeSousa 7 77
(B Smart) *dwlt: racd off the pce: nt clr run fr 2f out tl effrt and sme hdwy on inner to chse ldrs over 1f out: one pce fnl 150yds* **13/2**

6061 **6** *2* **Mr Wolf**[19] 2770 8-9-6 **75**..(p) RobertWinston 6 67
(D W Barker) *upsides and pressed wnr: pushed along 2f out: lost 2nd over 1f out: wknd ins fnl f* **13/2**

0402 **7** *¾* **Foxy Music**[3] 3268 5-9-4 **78**... GaryBartley(5) 8 68
(E J Alston) *hung rt thrght: racd off the pce on outside: outpcd fnl 2f* **8/1**

60.52 secs (-0.48) **Going Correction** -0.025s/f (Good)
WFA 3 from 4yo+ 6lb **7** Ran SP% **117.5**
Speed ratings (Par 107): **102,100,99,98,97 94,92**
toteswingers: 1&2 £2.10, 1&3 £4.10, 2&3 £3.50. CSF £9.12 CT £27.66 TOTE £3.70: £1.90, £1.90; EX 7.80.
Owner Mr & Mrs G Middlebrook **Bred** Mr & Mrs G Middlebrook **Trained** Longton, Lancs
■ Stewards' Enquiry : William Buick four-day ban: careless riding (Jul 11, 13-15)

FOCUS
As expected this good-quality sprint was run at a frantic early pace. The winner is rated close to her Redcar form with the third to his mark.

NOTEBOOK
Impressible gained compensation for a narrow defeat at Redcar a week previously. She helped force the early pace and was there to be shot at when straightening for home, but really put her head down when put under maximum pressure and is clearly a very hardy filly. A likely rise may not be enough to stop her next time. (tchd 5-2 and 3-1 in places)
Bertoliver made a tardy start, but still got a lovely sit through the race just off the early leaders. He looked the most likely winner soon after turning in, but simply found the winner too resolute. (op 11-4 tchd 3-1 in places)
Legal Eagle(IRE) lacked the pace to take advantage of his decent draw and ran a nice race in the circumstances, doing his best work late in the day. (op 8-1)
Rasaman(IRE), two places ahead of the third at Thirsk 11 days earlier, also posted a nice effort from a poor draw and this was much more like it from him. (op 20-1)
Nickel Silver Official explanation: jockey said gelding missed the break
Mr Wolf, 5lb higher, paid for his early exertions and that makes the winner's effort all the more meritorious. (op 9-2 tchd 7-1)
Foxy Music, a stable companion of the winner, finished second when trying to make all at Carlisle three days previously, but got outpaced early on and never seriously figured. He was later reported to have hung right throughout. Official explanation: jockey said gelding hung right

3373 SPORTINGBET.COM MAIDEN STKS 1m 2f 75y
3:50 (3:52) (Class 4) 3-Y-O+ **£5,180** (£1,541; £770; £384) **Stalls** High

Form RPR

3-50 **1** **Norwegian Dancer (UAE)**[32] 2356 3-9-1 75........... StephenDonohoe 4 78+
(E S McMahon) *trckd ldrs: rdn to ld over 1f out: r.o wl fnl f: sn in full control: comf* **7/2**[3]

0-40 **2** *1 ¾* **Spirit Of Dubai (IRE)**[34] 2310 3-8-10 92.......................... WilliamBuick 1 70
(D M Simcock) *sn led: pushed along whn pressed 4f out: drifted rt whn rdn wl over 1f out: sn hdd: styd on same pce and hld fnl 100yds* **7/4**[1]

62-2 **3** *¾* **Tropical Blue**[36] 2230 3-9-1 76....................................... JamieMoriarty 3 73
(Jennie Candlish) *w ldr: stl chalng whn carried rt wl over 1f out: kpt on same pce fnl 100yds* **3/1**[2]

0 **4** *4 ½* **Love In The West (IRE)**[14] 2937 3-8-10 0.................. RobertWinston 2 59
(G A Swinbank) *sn stdd and dropped to rr: outpcd over 2f out: edgd lft u.p over 1f out: no imp on ldrs: wl btn fnl f* **8/1**

5 **5** *2* **Gulf Of Aqaba (USA)**[16] 2843 3-9-1 0.............................. J-PGuillambert 6 60
(M Johnston) *trckd ldrs: pushed along over 3f out: outpcd over 2f out: dropped away ins fnl f* **6/1**

2m 12.11s (-0.09) **Going Correction** -0.025s/f (Good)
WFA 3 from 6yo 12lb **5** Ran SP% **109.0**
Speed ratings (Par 105): **99,97,97,93,91**
toteswingers: 1&2 £6.10. CSF £9.62 TOTE £4.70: £2.00, £1.40; EX 10.60.
Owner Philip Wilkins **Bred** Darley **Trained** Lichfield, Staffs
■ Kayf Commander was withdrawn (14/1, ref to ent stalls). Deduct 5p in the £ under R4.

FOCUS
An ordinary maiden and the form is slightly muddling, although the winner and third ran to form.

Love In The West(IRE) Official explanation: jockey said filly ran green

3374 SPORTINGBET.COM CLAIMING STKS 1m 2f 75y
4:25 (4:26) (Class 5) 3-Y-O+ £4,047 (£1,204; £601; £300) Stalls High

Form RPR
-000 1 **Munsef**[128] 616 7-9-5 95 StephenDonohoe 7 87+
(Ian Williams) *chsd ldrs: wnt 2nd over 3f out: led over 2f out: clr over 1f out: styd on wl and in command fnl f: comf* **13/2**

-134 2 3 3/4 **Gross Prophet**[4] 3245 4-9-3 76 RichardSmith 6 77
(Tom Dascombe) *led: hdd over 2f out: rdn and no ch w wnr fr over 1f out* **9/2**[3]

1003 3 2 1/4 **Samurai Warrior**[3] 3258 4-8-10 67 AndrewHeffernan(7) 4 73
(P D Evans) *in tch: pushed along over 2f out: wnt 3rd over 1f out: plugged on at one pce after* **7/1**

4116 4 4 1/2 **Wind Star**[28] 2468 6-9-8 90 RobertWinston 3 69
(G A Swinbank) *hld up: hdwy into midfield 7f out: clsd on ldrs 3f out: rdn over 2f out: wknd 1f out* **13/8**[1]

0026 5 5 **New England**[18] 2783 7-9-3 57 CatherineGannon 9 55
(W M Brisbourne) *s.i.s: hld up: pushed along over 2f out: nvr able to land a blow* **12/1**

3110 6 7 **Ahlawy (IRE)**[24] 2597 6-9-13 90 (bt) WilliamBuick 2 51
(F Sheridan) *handy: niggled along over 7f out: dropped to rr over 5f out: n.m.r 4f out: nvr able to get on terms after* **4/1**[2]

5 7 6 **Monopole (IRE)**[12] 2981 5-9-8 0 (t) JamieMoriarty 1 35
(P R Webber) *s.i.s: in rr: bmpd 4f out: pushed along over 2f out: nvr on terms* **16/1**

530 8 41 **Scamperdale**[30] 2392 7-9-6 66 J-PGuillambert 8 —
(B P J Baugh) *w ldr: lost pl over 3f out: sn wknd: eased whn wl btn over 1f out: t.o* **25/1**

2m 9.55s (-2.65) **Going Correction** -0.025s/f (Good) 8 Ran SP% **119.5**
Speed ratings (Par 103): **109,106,104,100,96 91,86,53**
toteswingers: 1&2 £7.90, 1&3 £9.30, 2&3 £6.40. CSF £37.48 TOTE £8.40: £2.10, £1.90, £1.80; EX 53.70.
Owner Dr Marwan Koukash **Bred** Shadwell Estate Company Limited **Trained** Portway, Worcs

FOCUS
A good claimer, run at a fair pace but the form is limited by the proximity of the third.

3375 CRUISE NIGHTCLUB H'CAP 7f 2y
4:55 (4:56) (Class 3) (0-90,90) 3-Y-O £8,831 (£2,643; £1,321; £660; £329) Stalls Low

Form RPR
30-0 1 **Brae Hill (IRE)**[43] 2049 3-9-6 **87** StephenDonohoe 2 97
(M L W Bell) *trckd ldrs after 1f: qcknd to ld jst over 1f out: r.o wl and in command fnl f* **9/1**

4-23 2 2 3/4 **Cheviot (USA)**[55] 1705 3-9-5 **86** (p) J-PGuillambert 7 89
(M A Jarvis) *hld up: effrt and hdwy to chse ldrs over 1f out: wnt 2nd 100yds out: nt pce to trble wnr* **6/1**[3]

1214 3 1 **Seek N' Destroy (IRE)**[28] 2504 3-9-3 **84** RobertWinston 3 84
(B W Hills) *led: rdn and hdd jst over 1f out: no ex fnl 100yds* **6/4**[1]

436 4 2 1/4 **Agente Parmigiano (IRE)**[22] 2674 3-9-6 **90** NeilBrown(3) 1 84
(G A Butler) *missed break: hld up in rr: sme hdwy over 1f out: no imp on ldrs and kpt on one pce after* **4/1**[2]

10-6 5 3 1/2 **Advertise**[23] 2638 3-8-4 **71** WilliamBuick 4 56
(A M Balding) *racd keenly: chsd ldr: chal 3f out: rdn over 2f out: wknd over 1f out* **13/2**

0-51 6 shd **Deadly Encounter (IRE)**[16] 2841 3-8-12 **79** JamieMoriarty 6 64
(R A Fahey) *in tch: niggled along and lost pl over 4f out: n.d after* **12/1**

206 7 7 **Lucky Numbers (IRE)**[14] 2934 3-9-4 **85** CatherineGannon 5 51
(Paul Green) *chsd ldrs: pushed along over 2 out: wknd over 1f out* **8/1**

1m 24.89s (-1.61) **Going Correction** -0.025s/f (Good) 7 Ran SP% **116.4**
Speed ratings (Par 103): **108,104,103,101,97 97,89**
toteswingers: 1&2 £8.70, 1&3 £4.60, 2&3 £2.40. CSF £62.59 TOTE £12.40: £4.70, £3.20; EX 83.50 Place 6 £295.86, Place 5 £87.81..
Owner Thurloe Partners **Bred** James Doyle **Trained** Newmarket, Suffolk

FOCUS
There was a solid pace on to this fair three-year-old handicap and the form looks sound enough rated around the placed horses.

NOTEBOOK
Brae Hill(IRE) was well backed and, showing the real benefit of his comeback run 43 days earlier, won most decisively. He got the run of the race just off the leaders and travelled sweetly into the home straight. His response when asked to go clear was immediate and the step up to this trip was much to his liking. No doubt the handicapper will now have his say, but further progression should certainly not be ruled out. (op 11-1 tchd 12-1)

Cheviot(USA) did not enjoy the same sort of passage through the race as the winner, but enjoyed the decent early tempo and looked to get the extra furlong well enough. He rates a sound benchmark and his turn may be nearing once more. (op 5-1 tchd 9-2)

Seek N' Destroy(IRE) did not get an uncontested lead, but still looked to be full of running off the home bend. He found just the same pace when push came to shove and, while he would not have beaten the winner, may have held on for second had he been asked a little sooner for his effort. (op 15-8)

Agente Parmigiano(IRE) again hampered his cause by losing ground with a sluggish start. He is fairly treated at present, but cannot be backed with any confidence until brushing up his act from the gates. (tchd 9-2)

Advertise put it up to the early leader, but he ran keen and paid for those exertions from the home turn. His maiden win last year came on much easier ground and he will probably prefer racing back on a more galloping circuit. Official explanation: jockey said gelding failed to handle the track (op 8-1)

Deadly Encounter(IRE), 2lb higher, was never going to get to the lead here from his moderate draw and his fate was sealed a long way out. It is wise not to judge him too harshly for this. (op 7-1)

Lucky Numbers(IRE) Official explanation: jockey said colt never travelled

T/Plt: £246.70 to a £1 stake. Pool: £65,745.44. 194.52 winning tickets. T/Qpdt: £17.60 to a £1 stake. Pool: £4,122.95. 173.30 winning tickets. DO

3337 DONCASTER (L-H)
Saturday, June 27

OFFICIAL GOING: Good to firm (8.5)
Running rail moved out 4yards increasing distances on round course by 12yards.
Wind: Virtually nil. Weather: Fine and dry

3376 CROWNHOTEL-BAWTRY.COM MAIDEN STKS 7f
6:00 (6:01) (Class 5) 2-Y-O £3,238 (£963; £481; £240) Stalls High

Form RPR
2 1 **Layali Al Andalus**[24] 2588 2-9-3 0 GregFairley 5 92+
(M Johnston) *cl up: led 3f out: rdn and qcknd clr wl over 1f out: easily* **1/1**[1]

32 2 7 **Fonterutoli (IRE)**[22] 2663 2-8-12 0 AndreaAtzeni(5) 7 72
(M Botti) *hld up: swtchd lft to outer 1/2-way: hdwy over 2f out: rdn to chse wnr over 1f out: sn drvn and kpt on: no ch w wnr* **8/1**[3]

5 3 1 1/4 **Cape D'Or (IRE)**[8] 3113 2-9-3 0 RichardHughes 2 68
(R Hannon) *hld up: hdwy to trck ldrs 1/2-way: effrt to chal over 2f out and sn rdn: drvn wl over 1f out and one pce* **6/4**[2]

0 4 1 1/2 **French Seventyfive**[22] 2663 2-9-3 0 GrahamGibbons 4 65
(T D Walford) *hld up in tch: hdwy to chse ldrs wl over 2f out: sn rdn and no imp* **100/1**

4 5 nk **Turf Trivia**[37] 2195 2-9-3 0 FrancisNorton 3 64
(G M Moore) *cl up: led after 2f: rdn along and hdd 3f out: grad wknd* **33/1**

0 6 nk **Green For Luck (IRE)**[29] 2444 2-9-3 0 MickyFenton 6 63
(T P Tate) *led 2f: prom tl rdn along over 3f out and sn wknd* **28/1**

7 34 **Shercon (IRE)** 2-9-3 0 DO'Donohoe 1 —
(N Tinkler) *a in rr: rdn along bef 1/2-way and sn bhd* **100/1**

1m 24.1s (-2.20) **Going Correction** -0.225s/f (Firm) 7 Ran SP% **109.5**
Speed ratings (Par 93): **103,95,93,91,91 91,52**
toteswingers: 1&2 £1.60, 1&3 £1.02, 2&3 £2.40. CSF £8.68 TOTE £2.00: £1.20, £3.40; EX 9.50.
Owner Sheikh Hamdan Bin Mohammed Al Maktoum **Bred** Wood Hall Stud Limited **Trained** Middleham Moor, N Yorks

FOCUS
A decent juvenile maiden and, although it may have lacked strength in depth, it featured a clutch of promising types. They went a solid pace and the form is rated around those in the frame behind the winner.

NOTEBOOK
Layali Al Andalus had shown more than enough on his debut at Ayr 24 days previously to suggest he could collect a prize like this, running on well over 6f to fill second spot behind a rival thought good enough subsequently to contest Royal Ascot's Coventry Stakes. His pedigree indicated he would appreciate this step up in trip, as he is by Halling out of a mare who handled a 1m2f, and he appeared to have ample physical scope for improvement.\n\x\x He looked magnificent beforehand and outshone his rivals in the race, too, taking the lead at halfway, easing over towards the stands' rail, and, when asked to increase the tempo with 2f to run, he strode clear for a comprehensive victory. (tchd 11-10)
Fonterutoli(IRE), the most experienced of these after two earlier outings, had looked no more than a fair prospect when, on the second of those runs, he had taken second in an ordinary 6f auction maiden at Doncaster. He was going the right way, however, if that effort was a guide, though he needed to show marked further progression here to come out on top. He probably did make another step forward, travelling nicely throughout the contest, but he never threatened to finish better than second. (op 7-1 tchd 10-1)
Cape D'Or(IRE) had suffered traffic problems on his first appearance, over 6f at Newmarket just eight days earlier, and, as he represented a yard that continues in fine form with its juveniles, it was no great surprise that he attracted interest in the betting ring. Most youngsters from his stable take a step forward following their initial racecourse experience and, with plenty of stamina in his pedigree, there seemed every chance that he would cope with this longer distance. It would not be fair to state confidently that he did not, based solely on this performance, but he was tiring in the closing stages. (op 13-8 tchd 11-8)
French Seventyfive, almost 14 lengths behind Fonterutoli on his Doncaster debut, fared better this time and seems to be improving, although he will need to make significant further progress to score in this grade.
Turf Trivia, from a successful family both on the Flat and over hurdles, had run better than his finishing position of fourth on his first outing over 6f at Haydock in May might have suggested and looked a potential improver, but he failed to cut much ice against these rivals.
Green For Luck(IRE) had shown a glimmer of ability on his debut, even though he had beaten just two opponents on testing ground at Haydock in May. However, after leading in the early stages here, he dropped away as the pace quickened and posted a tame finishing effort. (op 25-1)

3377 FREEBETS.CO.UK FREE BETS H'CAP 6f
6:35 (6:37) (Class 4) (0-85,85) 4-Y-O+ £4,857 (£1,445; £722; £360) Stalls High

Form RPR
20-0 1 **First In Command (IRE)**[34] 2308 4-8-7 **76** (t) AndreaAtzeni(5) 3 86
(Daniel Mark Loughnane, Ire) *trckd ldrs: hdwy to ld 2f out: sn rdn and hung bdly rt ins fnl f: kpt on* **5/1**[3]

-250 2 1 1/4 **Errigal Lad**[8] 3097 4-9-4 **82** (p) NCallan 5 88
(K A Ryan) *cl up: effrt 2f out and sn rdn: drvn to chse wnr ent fnl f: no imp whn n.m.r towards fin* **7/1**

6030 3 1 1/4 **Haajes**[15] 2897 5-9-4 **82** (t) GregFairley 9 84
(J Balding) *chsd ldrs on stands' rail: rdn along over 2f out: kpt on u.p ins fnl f* **14/1**

0012 4 nk **Grazeon Gold Blend**[11] 3001 6-9-2 **80** (p) GrahamGibbons 7 81
(J J Quinn) *chsd ldrs: rdn along 2f out: drvn over 1f out and sn one pce* **4/1**[2]

0-03 5 1 3/4 **John Keats**[11] 3001 6-8-7 **71** ow1 DanielTudhope 6 66
(J S Goldie) *sltly hmpd s and bhd: rdn along and hdwy 2f out: kpt on u.p ins fnl f: nt rch ldrs* **3/1**[1]

00-0 6 1 **Sundae**[42] 2078 5-9-7 **85** TPQueally 1 77
(C F Wall) *a towards rr* **33/1**

1562 7 1 1/4 **Silver Wind**[14] 2938 4-8-12 **81** (v) RichardEvans(5) 2 69
(P D Evans) *chsd ldrs on outer: rdn along over 2f out: grad wknd* **11/2**

1010 8 1 1/4 **Calmdownmate (IRE)**[19] 2770 4-8-6 **70** SilvestreDeSousa 8 54
(Mrs R A Carr) *led: rdn along and hdd 2f out: sn drvn and wknd* **17/2**

0-26 9 8 **Superduper**[51] 1806 4-9-4 **82** RichardHughes 4 41
(R Hannon) *prom: rdn along wl over 2f out and sn wknd* **9/1**

1m 10.77s (-2.83) **Going Correction** -0.225s/f (Firm) 9 Ran SP% **119.7**
Speed ratings (Par 105): **109,107,105,105,102 101,99,98,87**
toteswingers: 1&2 £7.20, 1&3 £14.50, 2&3 £14.50. CSF £41.37 CT £470.82 TOTE £6.30: £2.10, £2.10, £3.70; EX 68.20.
Owner Raymond Yeung **Bred** Peter & Mrs McCutcheon **Trained** Trim, Co Meath

FOCUS
Just a fair mid-range handicap, but it looked an open affair, with several of the line-up in obviously good form and a couple bidding to re-establish themselves after a relatively poor sequence. They raced in two groups, one near the stands' rail, the other down the middle of the track. The winner was close to last year's form with the placed horses to their marks.

Calmdownmate(IRE) Official explanation: jockey said gelding hung left
Superduper Official explanation: jockey said filly had no more to give

3378 ZESTBARANDGRILL.COM DONCASTER H'CAP 1m (R)
7:05 (7:05) (Class 4) (0-80,80) 4-Y-0+ £4,857 (£1,445; £722; £360) Stalls Low

Form RPR
6213 1 **Bold Cross (IRE)**[12] 2976 6-9-3 76 PaulFitzsimons 6 85
(E G Bevan) *hld up in tch: hdwy to trck ldrs 4f out: effrt 2f out: rdn to ld appr fnl f: styd on* 11/2[3]
-056 2 3/4 **Reel Buddy Star**[9] 3067 4-8-12 71 DanielTudhope 8 78
(G M Moore) *trckd ldrs on outer: hdwy 3f out: rdn to ld 2f out: hdd appr fnl f: sn drvn and kpt on* 6/1
6166 3 1 **Arctic Cape**[15] 2894 4-9-2 75 JoeFanning 5 80
(M Johnston) *prom: effrt over 2f out and ev ch tl drvn ent fnl f and kpt on same pce* 7/1
336- 4 1 1/2 **Jawaab (IRE)**[196] 7670 5-9-2 75 TPQueally 4 76
(Mark Buckley) *chsd ldrs: rdn along 2f out: drvn and kpt on same pce appr fnl f* 17/2
2003 5 1/2 **Ours (IRE)**[25] 2576 6-8-10 69 (p) PatCosgrave 2 69
(John A Harris) *in midfield: hdwy over 2f out: rdn to chse ldrs over 1f out: sn drvn and no imp* 8/1
00 6 6 **Tres Froide (FR)**[21] 2724 4-8-11 70 AndrewElliott 10 55
(N Tinkler) *a in rr* 66/1
040- 7 1 1/2 **Bid For Glory**[266] 6482 5-9-7 80 RichardHughes 3 62
(H J Collingridge) *prom: effrt on inner over 3f out and sn rdn along: wknd over 2f out* 9/2[2]
06 8 1 3/4 **French Art**[13] 2939 4-9-2 75 DO'Donohoe 7 53
(N Tinkler) *a towards rr* 25/1
-251 9 1/2 **Everybody Knows**[51] 1813 4-9-7 80 NCallan 1 56
(Miss Jo Crowley) *led: rdn along 3f out: drvn and hdd 2f out: sn wknd* 5/2[1]

1m 38.59s (-1.11) **Going Correction** -0.225s/f (Firm) 9 Ran SP% **115.9**
Speed ratings (Par 105): **103,102,101,99,99 93,91,90,89**
toteswingers: 1&2 £8.90, 1&3 £6.20, 2&3 Not won. CSF £38.55 CT £234.66 TOTE £5.80: £1.60, £2.30, £2.10; EX 43.50.
Owner E G Bevan **Bred** M Hosokawa **Trained** Ullingswick, H'fords
■ Stewards' Enquiry : Paul Fitzsimons one-day ban: used whip in incorrect place (Jul 11)

FOCUS
Much like the previous event, this looked an open affair, with few in the line-up easy to discount completely. Sound form, with another step forward from the winner.
Bid For Glory Official explanation: jockey said horse had no more to give
Everybody Knows Official explanation: jockey said colt hung right and stumbled approaching furlong mark; vet said colt returned lame

3379 CLUMBER PARK HOTEL AND SPA MAIDEN FILLIES' STKS 1m 2f 60y
7:40 (7:44) (Class 4) 3-Y-0+ £4,857 (£1,445; £722; £360) Stalls Low

Form RPR
22 1 **Interdiamonds**[13] 2943 3-8-12 0 JoeFanning 8 71
(M Johnston) *mde all: rdn clr over 2f out: styd on strly* 5/4[1]
/3 2 3 **Whirlijig (IRE)**[10] 3022 4-9-10 0 RobertWinston 5 65
(G A Swinbank) *trckd wnr: effrt 3f out: rdn over 2f out: sn drvn and kpt on same pce* 12/1[3]
0- 3 4 1/2 **Za Za**[269] 6391 3-8-12 0 TPQueally 9 57
(H R A Cecil) *trckd ldrs: hdwy to chse ldng pair 3f out and sn rdn along: kpt on same pce fnl 2f* 16/1
4 3/4 **Knotgarden (IRE)** 3-8-12 0 WilliamBuick 4 55
(J R Fanshawe) *s.i.s and in rr: hdwy 1/2-way: rdn to chse ldrs over 2f out: kpt on same pce* 12/1[3]
0 5 6 **Flying Phoebe**[30] 2403 3-8-12 0 GregFairley 7 44
(Mrs L Stubbs) *a towards rr* 66/1
44-2 6 1 1/4 **Bessie Lou (IRE)**[29] 2446 3-8-12 74 NCallan 1 42
(K A Ryan) *plld hrd: chsd ldng pair: effrt 4f out: sn rdn and btn 3f out* 11/8[2]
60/0 7 5 **Viola Rosa (IRE)**[21] 2723 4-9-10 40 PatCosgrave 3 32
(J G Given) *in tch: rdn along over 3f out: sn drvn and wknd* 66/1
00-0 8 21 **Ugly Betty**[130] 581 4-9-3 36 BillyCray(7) 2 —
(Bruce Hellier) *a bhd* 66/1

2m 9.29s (-1.91) **Going Correction** -0.225s/f (Firm)
WFA 3 from 4yo 12lb 8 Ran SP% **112.3**
Speed ratings (Par 102): **98,95,92,91,86 85,81,64**
toteswingers: 1&2 £5.80, 1&3 £5.40, 2&3 £11.20. CSF £16.62 TOTE £2.40: £1.10, £2.30, £2.00; EX 14.30.
Owner Syndicate 2007 **Bred** Irish National Stud **Trained** Middleham Moor, N Yorks

FOCUS
Just a run-of-the-mill fillies' maiden, lacking strength in depth, but featuring a small group of likely candidates for a first victory. Very limited form, with the winner only having to run close to her initial efforts.
Knotgarden(IRE) Official explanation: jockey said filly missed the break
Ugly Betty Official explanation: jockey said filly never travelled

3380 FREEBETS.CO.UK FREE BETTING ONLINE H'CAP 1m 6f 132y
8:10 (8:11) (Class 4) (0-85,85) 4-Y-0+ £4,857 (£1,445; £722; £360) Stalls Low

Form RPR
-142 1 **Hawk Mountain (UAE)**[15] 2895 4-8-13 77 GrahamGibbons 1 85
(J J Quinn) *trckd ldng pair: smooth hdwy to take clsr order 4f out: led over 3f out: rdn clr 2f out and styd on strly* 6/4[1]
2123 2 2 1/4 **Saloon (USA)**[8] 3114 5-8-11 75 (p) JamieSpencer 6 80
(Jane Chapple-Hyam) *hld up in rr: hdwy over 3f out: chsd wnr over 2f out: sn rdn: carried hd high and no imp fr wl over 1f out* 5/1[3]
2163 3 4 1/2 **Wild Rhubarb**[14] 2931 4-9-1 79 PhilipRobinson 7 78
(C G Cox) *hld up: effrt and sme hdwy 4f out: rdn along 3f out: drvn to chse ldng pair 2f out and sn no imp* 15/8[2]
0-60 4 14 **Wicked Daze (IRE)**[49] 1863 6-9-7 85 (t) StephenDonohoe 3 66
(Ian Williams) *trckd ldr: hdwy to ld over 4f out: rdn and hdd over 3f out: drvn and wknd over 2f out* 6/1
-402 5 90 **Inspector Clouseau (IRE)**[18] 2783 4-8-6 70 AdrianTNicholls 2 —
(T P Tate) *led: rdn along and hdd over 4f out: sn wknd: wl bhd and eased fnl 2f* 11/1

3m 6.98s (0.28) **Going Correction** -0.225s/f (Firm) 5 Ran SP% **114.1**
Speed ratings (Par 105): **90,88,86,78,30**
toteswingers: 1&2 £2.40. CSF £9.78 TOTE £2.80: £1.30, £1.80; EX 8.00.
Owner P Morrison & N Luck **Bred** Darley **Trained** Settrington, N Yorks

FOCUS
Most of the runners had posted a solid effort on their latest outing and this looked a tricky riddle to solve. They went off at a strong pace, though, and it seemed to find several of them out. The winner produced another step forward.

3381 MOSS PROPERTIES FILLIES' H'CAP 7f
8:45 (8:48) (Class 5) (0-70,70) 3-Y-0+ £3,238 (£963; £481; £240) Stalls High

Form RPR
3321 1 **Mo Mhuirnin (IRE)**[12] 2967 3-9-10 70 PaulHanagan 13 84
(R A Fahey) *hld up towards rr: smooth hdwy over 2f out: rdn to ld 1 1/2f out: clr whn hung lft ins fnl f: styd on wl* 9/4[1]
-632 2 3 1/4 **Ailsa Craig (IRE)**[15] 2879 3-9-3 63 RichardHughes 5 68
(R Hannon) *chsd ldrs: hdwy over 2f out: rdn and ev ch 1 1/2f out: sn drvn: edgd lft and one pce ins fnl f* 13/2
-100 3 nk **Fancy Footsteps (IRE)**[19] 2775 4-10-0 65 PhilipRobinson 8 72
(C G Cox) *prom: effrt over 2f out: sn rdn and ev ch tl drvn and one pce ent fnl f* 6/1[3]
15 4 5 **Laura's Lady (IRE)**[32] 2365 3-8-11 57 RobertWinston 7 48
(G A Swinbank) *towards rr: pushed along and outpcd 1/2-way: rdn and hdwy 2f out: kpt on u.p ins fnl f: nt rch ldrs* 11/2[2]
5000 5 1 3/4 **Milton Of Campsie**[5] 3227 4-9-9 60 (t) AdrianTNicholls 11 49
(S Parr) *led: rdn along and jnd 2f out: sn hdd: drvn and wknd* 40/1
4565 6 1 **City For Conquest (IRE)**[14] 2913 6-8-11 48 (p) PatCosgrave 1 34
(John A Harris) *prom: rdn along over 2f out: sn drvn and grad wknd* 33/1
0043 7 nk **Athboy Auction**[14] 2921 4-8-7 51 (t) RosieJessop(7) 12 36
(H J Collingridge) *s.i.s and in rr tl sme late hdwy* 33/1
-223 8 2 1/2 **Who's Shirl**[12] 2970 3-8-6 55 KellyHarrison(3) 9 31
(C W Fairhurst) *nvr bttr than midfield* 8/1
-234 9 2 3/4 **Lyric Art (USA)**[85] 1098 3-9-2 62 (v[1]) TomEaves 10 30
(B Smart) *t.k.h: chsd ldrs: rdn along 3f out and sn wknd* 12/1
00-0 10 3/4 **Uace Mac**[9] 3066 5-9-9 60 FrancisNorton 4 29
(N Bycroft) *prom: rdn along wl over 2f out: sn wknd* 28/1
0605 11 1 **Slip Star**[10] 3019 6-8-11 48 GregFairley 2 15
(T J Etherington) *chsd ldrs: rdn along over 3f out: sn wknd* 12/1
-006 12 1 **Polemica (IRE)**[22] 2679 3-9-5 65 WilliamBuick 3 26
(E A L Dunlop) *dwlt and towards rr: effrt and sme hdwy on wd outside 3f out: sn rdn and wknd* 7/1

1m 24.67s (-1.63) **Going Correction** -0.225s/f (Firm)
WFA 3 from 4yo+ 9lb 12 Ran SP% **124.5**
Speed ratings (Par 100): **100,96,95,90,88 87,86,83,80,79 78,77**
toteswingers: 1&2 £2.60, 1&3 £14.50, 2&3 £12.60. CSF £17.34 CT £84.20 TOTE £3.40: £1.20, £1.90, £2.70; EX 11.10 Place 6 £68.19, Place 5 £44.78..
Owner Gone West Syndicate **Bred** John McEnery **Trained** Musley Bank, N Yorks

FOCUS
Not a race that could be described as a resounding climax to the evening's entertainment, being a low-grade fillies' handicap featuring a number of runners who are starting to look profoundly disappointing, but a handful might be called consistent in their grade. Modest form with improved performance from the winner.
T/Plt: £50.80 to a £1 stake. Pool: £66,815.79. 959.10 winning tickets. T/Qpdt: £5.80 to a £1 stake. Pool: £6,153.70. 779.70 winning tickets. JR

3210 LINGFIELD (L-H)
Saturday, June 27

OFFICIAL GOING: Turf course - good to firm (firm in places; 8.9); all-weather - standard
Wind: Light, behind race 4; Almost nil races 5 & 6 Weather: Sunny, very warm

3382 BACK OR LAY AT BETDAQ (S) STKS 1m 4f (P)
5:45 (5:45) (Class 6) 3-Y-0+ £2,047 (£604; £302) Stalls Low

Form RPR
2132 1 **Terminate (GER)**[22] 2656 7-9-10 62 (t) JackMitchell(3) 8 57
(Ian Williams) *s.s: hld up in last pair: gd prog on wd outside to ld jst over 2f out: sn drvn and pressed: hld on wl* 7/2[3]
1220 2 1/2 **Sunset Boulevard (IRE)**[16] 2851 6-9-13 59 ChrisCatlin 3 56
(Miss Tor Sturgis) *hld up: trckd ldrs on inner fr 1/2-way: gng wl whn nt clr run over 2f out: prog to chal over 1f out: upsides ins fnl f: nt qckn* 3/1[2]
00-4 3 nk **Champagne Shadow (IRE)**[163] 168 8-9-8 47 (p) JerryO'Dwyer 7 51
(J Pearce) *pushed along in last pair after 4f: drvn and prog on outer over 3f out to press wnr jst over 2f out: nt qckn 1f out* 25/1
-630 4 5 **Tevez**[12] 2975 4-9-5 59 (p) DavidProbert(3) 1 43
(D Donovan) *hld up in 7th: cl enough whn n.m.r 3f out: sn dropped to last and u.p: kpt on again fnl f* 10/1
4-44 5 2 3/4 **Ministerofinterior**[17] 2808 4-9-1 56 (b) JemmaMarshall(7) 4 39
(G L Moore) *trckd ldr 2f: cl up after: gng wl enough whn nt clr run briefly over 2f out: outpcd fr over 1f out* 14/1
6003 6 1 1/2 **Ben Bacchus (IRE)**[33] 2337 7-9-8 47 LukeMorris 9 36
(P W Hiatt) *trckd ldr after 2f to over 3f out: sn lost pl: wknd over 1f out* 16/1
0-30 7 1 **Royal Jet**[49] 1863 7-9-1 82 PNolan(7) 10 35
(Mrs S Leech) *s.i.s: sn prom on outer: rdn to ld narrowly over 3f out: hdd and nt qckn jst over 2f out: wknd over 1f out* 15/8[1]
0 8 2 1/4 **She's A Model**[23] 2633 3-8-3 0 KirstyMilczarek 5 26
(R Ingram) *prom: rdn over 4f out: lost pl over 3f out: wknd rapidly 2f out* 80/1
00-4 9 6 **Timbaa (USA)**[7] 3157 3-8-8 55 RichardKingscote 2 21
(Rae Guest) *mde most to over 3f out: wknd rapidly 2f out* 16/1

2m 35.31s (2.31) **Going Correction** +0.225s/f (Slow)
WFA 3 from 4yo+ 14lb 9 Ran SP% **114.6**
Speed ratings (Par 101): **101,100,100,97,95 94,93,92,88**
toteswingers: 1&2 £1.80, 1&3 £10.00, 2&3 £11.40. CSF £14.31 TOTE £4.70: £1.50, £1.40, £2.90; EX 12.70.The winner was bought in for 3,600gns.
Owner Macable Partnership **Bred** Gestut Hofgut Mappen **Trained** Portway, Worcs

FOCUS
Not much strength in depth to this seller and the form is weak.

3383 MARY DAVIS 80TH BIRTHDAY H'CAP 1m 4f (P)
6:15 (6:15) (Class 6) (0-60,60) 3-Y-0 £2,047 (£604; £302) Stalls Low

Form RPR
-000 1 **Hi Fling**[16] 2865 3-9-3 59 (b[1]) RobertHavlin 16 63
(B J Meehan) *sltly hmpd after 2f: sn cl up on outer: prog 3f out: drvn to ld narrowly over 1f out: asserted last 75yds* 10/1
4200 2 1 **On Cue (IRE)**[29] 2461 3-8-9 51 LukeMorris 15 54
(J M P Eustace) *hld up in midfield: prog over 2f out: rdn to chal over 1f out: pressed wnr tl no ex last 75yds* 14/1

3320 **3** 1 1/4 **Persian Tomcat (IRE)**[16] 2865 3-8-1 50 .... MatthewCosham(7) 7 51
(Miss J Feilden) *s.i.s: hld up in midfield: prog over 2f out: chsd ldng trio over 1f out: kpt on to take 3rd last 75yds* **8/1**[3]

400 **4** 1/2 **Gaselee (USA)**[21] 2710 3-8-13 55 .... ChrisCatlin 5 55
(Rae Guest) *hld up in midfield on inner: gng wl whn trapped bhd wkng rivals fr 3f out: 12th 2f out: gd prog over 1f out: nt rch ldrs* **9/1**

-002 **5** 1/2 **Chic Shanique (USA)**[17] 2802 3-9-2 58 .... RichardKingscote 12 57
(Tom Dascombe) *trckd ldr: led over 4f out: tried to kick on over 2f out: hdd over 1f out: wknd last 75yds* **13/2**[2]

-000 **6** 3/4 **Winterbrook King**[14] 2909 3-8-8 53 .... MarcHalford(3) 11 51
(J R Best) *sltly hmpd after 2f: sn in rr: rdn over 4f out: prog on wd outside over 2f out: kpt on one pce fr over 1f out* **66/1**

050 **7** 1/2 **Twist Again (IRE)**[23] 2640 3-9-3 59 .... JimCrowley 2 56
(P Howling) *hld up wl in rr: gng wl enough 3f out: effrt 2f out: nt qckn over 1f out: one pce after* **9/1**

0563 **8** 2 1/4 **Valkyrie (IRE)**[29] 2461 3-8-10 52 .... (p) KirstyMilczarek 14 45
(N P Littmoden) *rapid prog to go prom after 3f: chsd ldr over 3f out to 2f out: wknd over 1f out* **8/1**[3]

5000 **9** 1/2 **Manolito Montoya (IRE)**[15] 2892 3-8-11 58 ......(v) GabrielHannon(5) 9 51
(J W Hills) *hld up wl in rr: gng wl enough but stl there 3f out: rdn over 2f out: plugged on: no ch* **18/1**

0133 **10** 3 1/2 **First Spirit**[7] 3157 3-9-0 56 .... (p) LPKeniry 3 43
(J S Moore) *settled in rr: struggling over 3f out: no ch fr 2f out* **6/1**[1]

0506 **11** 7 **Dalrymple (IRE)**[20] 2737 3-8-10 55 .... DavidProbert(3) 1 31
(M Madgwick) *cl up on inner: rdn over 3f out: steadily lost pl: wknd over 1f out* **12/1**

5002 **12** 9 **Lilly Blue (IRE)**[22] 2681 3-9-1 60 .... JackMitchell(3) 8 21
(R Brotherton) *cl up bhd ldrs: rdn over 2f out: wknd rapidly wl over 1f out: t.o* **9/1**

0505 **13** 6 **Peak (IRE)**[17] 2809 3-9-4 60 .... (b[1]) TravisBlock 4 12
(H Morrison) *led: drvn and hdd over 4f out: wknd over 3f out: t.o* **11/1**

1030 **14** 60 **Graycliffe (IRE)**[9] 2152 3-9-4 60 .... JerryO'Dwyer 6 —
(Patrick Morris) *s.s: a in last pair: wknd over 4f out: t.o and eased 3f out* **14/1**

2m 34.83s (1.83) **Going Correction** +0.225s/f (Slow) **14** Ran SP% **125.0**
Speed ratings (Par 97): **102,101,100,100,99 99,99,97,97,94 90,84,80,40**
toteswingers: 1&2 £27.00, 1&3 £26.50, 2&3 £27.00. CSF £148.31 CT £1196.45 TOTE £15.10: £4.40, £5.10, £2.50; EX 304.10.
Owner Lady Laidlaw Of Rothiemay **Bred** Redhill Bloodstock & Silfield Bloodstock **Trained** Manton, Wilts

FOCUS
More low-grade stuff and quite a condensed affair with just 10lb covering the 14 runners. No a race to be positive about.
Hi Fling Official explanation: trainer's rep said, regarding apparent improvement in form, that the colt was blinkered for the first time.
Chic Shanique(USA) Official explanation: jockey said filly had no more to give
Lilly Blue(IRE) Official explanation: trainer said filly did not stay the trip
Graycliffe(IRE) Official explanation: jockey said gelding never travelled

3384 BET IN-RUNNING - BETDAQ MEDIAN AUCTION MAIDEN STKS 1m 2f (P)
6:50 (6:50) (Class 6) 3-4-Y-O **£2,729** (£806; £403) **Stalls** Low

Form RPR

4-32 **1** **Andhaar**[39] 2170 3-9-2 77 .... RyanMoore 8 79
(E A L Dunlop) *trckd ldr: led over 2f out and sn dashed 3 l clr: drvn over 1f out: kpt on* **10/11**[1]

3222 **2** 3 **Pyrus Time (IRE)**[14] 2922 3-9-2 76 .... LukeMorris 2 73
(J S Moore) *taken down early: trckd ldng pair: chsd wnr 2f out: threatened to cl over 1f out: sn nt qckn and hld* **15/8**[2]

3-44 **3** 2 3/4 **Nesayem (IRE)**[31] 2375 3-8-11 72 .... ChrisCatlin 3 63
(D M Simcock) *in tch: drvn over 3f out: outpcd over 2f out: styd on u.p to take 3rd jst ins fnl f* **9/1**[3]

4 2 1/2 **Anessia** 3-8-11 0 .... RichardKingscote 4 58
(Tom Dascombe) *prog to go 4th 6f out: pushed along 4f out: outpcd 2f out: no ch after* **16/1**

0- **5** 1/2 **Dovedon Angel**[238] 7140 3-8-11 0 .... JimCrowley 5 57
(Miss Gay Kelleway) *hld up: last pair fr 6f out: cl enough over 2f out: sn outpcd and btn* **33/1**

0 **6** 2 1/2 **Brandy Butter**[30] 2395 3-9-2 0 .... (v[1]) LPKeniry 1 57
(A M Balding) *led: rdn 3f out: hdd over 2f out: wknd tamely over 1f out* **20/1**

7 26 **Nelsons Prospect (IRE)** 4-10-0 0 .... DaneO'Neill 7 5
(R A Teal) *s.s: mostly last: rn green and wknd 3f out: t.o* **33/1**

2m 8.74s (2.14) **Going Correction** +0.225s/f (Slow)
WFA 3 from 4yo 12lb **7** Ran SP% **113.7**
Speed ratings (Par 101): **100,97,95,93,93 91,70**
toteswingers: 1&2 £1.10, 1&3 £1.30, 2&3 £2.40. CSF £2.71 TOTE £2.00: £1.50, £1.70; EX 3.30.
Owner Hamdan Al Maktoum **Bred** Shadwell Estate Company Limited **Trained** Newmarket, Suffolk

FOCUS
Very ordinary maiden form in which the two who dominated the market did so in the race itself, although the contest was effectively over when Ryan Moore made a decisive move to kick clear on the winner at the top of the straight. The form is rated through the winner and makes some sense.

3385 E B F RAY CLARK 75TH BIRTHDAY CELEBRATION MAIDEN STKS 5f
7:20 (7:20) (Class 5) 2-Y-O **£3,885** (£1,156; £577; £288) **Stalls** High

Form RPR

502 **1** **Nepotism**[12] 2979 2-9-3 0 .... DaneO'Neill 5 71
(M S Saunders) *mde all and racd against nr side rail: rdn over 1f out: a holding on: eased last strides* **6/5**[1]

55 **2** 1/2 **Point To Prove**[33] 2335 2-9-3 0 .... JerryO'Dwyer 7 69
(Miss Amy Weaver) *t.k.h early: hld up in tch: effrt and swtchd wd 2f out: swtchd rt jst over 1f out: r.o to take 2nd ins fnl f: clsng fin* **25/1**

03 **3** 1/2 **Val C**[12] 2972 2-8-12 0 .... LukeMorris 1 62
(N P Littmoden) *hanging lft and racd wd: chsd ldrs: wnt 2nd over 1f out: no imp and lost 2nd ins fnl f* **7/2**[3]

05 **4** 1 1/2 **Papageno**[34] 2295 2-9-3 0 .... FergusSweeney 8 62
(J R Jenkins) *hld up bhd ldrs against nr side rail: nt qckn 2f out: reminder 1f out: kpt on one pce* **22/1**

5 1/2 **Where's The Soap (FR)** 2-8-12 0 .... RichardKingscote 3 55
(Tom Dascombe) *pressed wnr: pushed along 1/2-way: lost pl over 1f out: grad fdd* **5/2**[2]

6 19 **Trade Fairle** 2-9-3 0 .... TedDurcan 4 —
(P R Webber) *s.i.s: outpcd and sn t.o* **10/1**

58.22 secs (0.02) **Going Correction** -0.15s/f (Firm) **6** Ran SP% **113.5**
Speed ratings (Par 93): **93,92,91,89,88 57**
toteswingers: 1&2 £6.10, 1&3 £1.20, 2&3 £6.20. CSF £32.34 TOTE £2.20: £1.50, £4.30; EX 48.90.
Owner Chris Scott **Bred** M S Saunders And Chris Scott **Trained** Green Ore, Somerset

FOCUS
Another average maiden and this level could flatter with the runner-up and fourth taking big steps forward.

NOTEBOOK
Nepotism, who was backed as if defeat was out of the question, had the form to win a race like this. He put his experience to good use to bounce out and soon bag the favoured stands' rail and, although he came under pressure over 1f out, he was always holding his rivals. He has plenty of early speed and boasts quite a progressive little profile now so he's capable of better as he moves up into sprint nurseries. (op 9-4)

Point To Prove had been given a little break after a very ordinary effort at Leicester last month, but this was much better as he stayed on strongly once switched out to make his move and he looks to be going the right way now. (op 20-1 tchd 16-1)

Val C didn't get any cover early and was a bit free, but she kept plugging away down the outside and shaped as though she may be worth a try over an extra furlong. Official explanation: jockey said filly hung left throughout (op 11-4 tchd 4-1)

Papageno travelled well in the slipstream of the winner, but he looked a touch one paced when push came to shove. His future looks to lie in low grade handicaps. (op 20-1)

Where's The Soap(FR) shaped with a degree of promise without being able to see her effort through, and ought to be able to build on this next time. (op 2-1 tchd 11-4)

3386 CGG VERITAS H'CAP 5f
7:55 (7:55) (Class 5) (0-75,75) 3-Y-O+ **£3,070** (£906; £453) **Stalls** High

Form RPR

4522 **1** **Matterofact (IRE)**[21] 2712 6-9-4 65 .... DaneO'Neill 5 75
(M S Saunders) *racd on outer: pressed ldrs: led over 1f out: rdn out fnl f and a doing enough* **9/4**[1]

-330 **2** 1 **Rocker**[23] 2637 5-10-0 75 .... RyanMoore 4 81
(G L Moore) *hld up bhd ldrs: rdn and prog over 1f out: wnt 2nd ins fnl f: a hld* **7/2**[2]

0632 **3** 1/2 **Cape Royal**[7] 3162 9-9-10 71 .... (bt) LPKeniry 3 75
(J M Bradley) *hld up bhd ldrs: swtchd to nr side rail over 1f out: kpt on same pce to take 3rd ins fnl f* **11/2**[3]

-100 **4** 1 **Magical Speedfit (IRE)**[36] 2219 4-9-13 74 .... GeorgeBaker 1 75
(G G Margarson) *hld up in detached last: cajoled along to cl fr 2f out: rdn and nt qckn 1f out: one pce* **9/1**

0353 **5** 1/2 **Thoughtsofstardom**[2] 3304 6-8-2 56 oh1 .... CarolineKelly(7) 7 55
(P S McEntee) *racd one off nr side rail: disp ld: led 2f out to over 1f out: fdd ins fnl f* **10/1**

0035 **6** 2 3/4 **Princess Rose Anne (IRE)**[3] 3261 4-10-0 75 .... SteveDrowne 2 64
(J R Best) *racd wdst of all: hld up in tch: shkn up and hanging lft over 1f out: sn btn* **7/1**

3000 **7** 9 **Even Bolder**[14] 2911 6-9-13 74 .... StephenCarson 6 31
(E A Wheeler) *awkward s: pushed up to dispute ld: wknd fr 2f out: eased ins fnl f* **8/1**

060 **8** 2 1/2 **Magic Glade**[88] 1055 10-8-9 56 oh10 .... (b) PatrickMathers 8 4
(Peter Grayson) *racd against nr side rail: disp ld to 1/2-way: sn wknd* **33/1**

58.05 secs (-0.15) **Going Correction** -0.15s/f (Firm) **8** Ran SP% **114.0**
Speed ratings (Par 103): **95,93,92,91,90 85,71,67**
toteswingers: 1&2 £6.50, 1&3 £5.00, 2&3 £1.90. CSF £10.03 CT £37.15 TOTE £3.20: £1.40, £1.80, £1.80; EX 7.70.
Owner Prempro Racing **Bred** Tony Gleeson **Trained** Green Ore, Somerset

FOCUS
A modest sprint handicap with the winner rated back to his best.

3387 BACK OR LAY AT BETDAQ FILLIES' H'CAP 7f
8:25 (8:26) (Class 5) (0-75,74) 3-Y-O **£3,238** (£963; £481; £240) **Stalls** High

Form RPR

5-02 **1** **All For You (IRE)**[16] 2857 3-8-12 65 .... AlanMunro 15 71
(M Botti) *dwlt: hld up in rr and racd against nr side rail: plld out and prog ins fnl 2f: rdn to ld jst over 1f out: styd on wl* **13/2**

1060 **2** 1 1/2 **My Best Bet**[12] 2967 3-9-3 70 .... DarryllHolland 14 72
(M R Channon) *racd against nr side rail: trckd ldrs: plld out jst over 2f out: rdn to chal and upsides over 1f out: outpcd ins fnl f* **6/1**[3]

1-04 **3** 1 1/4 **Young Dottie**[28] 2498 3-9-4 71 .... IanMongan 12 70
(P M Phelan) *pressed ldr: led 2f out: hdd and outpcd jst over 1f out* **9/2**[2]

1223 **4** 3/4 **Perfect Friend**[8] 3102 3-9-7 74 .... RyanMoore 4 71+
(S Kirk) *chsd ldrs towards outer: pushed along over 2f out: effrt u.p over 1f out: one pce after* **5/2**[1]

0-00 **5** 1/2 **Queen Of Thebes (IRE)**[25] 2562 3-9-3 70 .... (t) JimCrowley 10 65
(G L Moore) *dwlt: hld up in rr: effrt over 2f out: nt qckn u.p over 1f out: styd on ins fnl f* **14/1**

3003 **6** 3/4 **Chadwell Spring (IRE)**[11] 3009 3-8-2 62 .... MatthewCosham(7) 2 55+
(Miss J Feilden) *dwlt: racd wd in last: effrt 2f out: plugged on at one pce* **25/1**

0025 **7** 3/4 **Jewelled Reef (IRE)**[14] 2910 3-8-8 61 .... StephenCarson 7 52
(Eve Johnson Houghton) *dwlt: hld up in rr: swtchd to outer over 2f out: sme prog over 1f out: fdd ins fnl f* **16/1**

4160 **8** 3/4 **Lighthearted (FR)**[17] 2827 3-9-2 69 .... LukeMorris 5 58
(C G Cox) *trckd ldrs: rdn 2f out: hanging and sn struggling: plugged on* **12/1**

0-00 **9** 4 1/2 **Sley (FR)**[27] 2515 3-8-3 56 .... (b) NickyMackay 9 33
(B J Meehan) *pressed ldrs: hanging lft whn rdn over 2f out: sn wknd* **20/1**

031- **10** 4 **Speedy Guru**[250] 6858 3-9-4 71 .... DaneO'Neill 13 37
(H Candy) *racd against nr side rail: led to 2f out: wknd rapidly* **9/2**[2]

46-0 **11** 8 **Bella Rowena**[50] 1825 3-9-2 69 .... LPKeniry 6 14
(A M Balding) *t.k.h early: pressed ldrs to 1/2-way: wknd rapily: t.o* **20/1**

1m 22.34s (-0.96) **Going Correction** -0.15s/f (Firm) **11** Ran SP% **126.2**
Speed ratings (Par 96): **99,97,95,95,94 93,92,91,86,82 73**
toteswingers: 1&2 £11.40, 1&3 £20.70, 2&3 £1.10. CSF £47.49 CT £175.21 TOTE £8.00: £2.00, £2.50, £2.20; EX 48.20 Place 6 £60.14, Place 5 £30.77..
Owner Lucky Seven Stable **Bred** Whitewood Stables **Trained** Newmarket, Suffolk

FOCUS
An open fillies' handicap. They finished in a bit of a heap in behind the winner and the form is sound but limited.

T/Plt: £285.50 to a £1 stake. Pool: £57,885.20. 148.00 winning tickets. T/Qpdt: £8.40 to a £1 stake. Pool: £6,011.14. 525.37 winning tickets. JN

3350 NEWCASTLE (L-H)

Saturday, June 27

OFFICIAL GOING: Soft (6.3)

All dolling removed and distances advertised.

Wind: Light, half-behind. Weather: Overcast

3388 FREEBETS.CO.UK CHIPCHASE STKS (GROUP 3) 6f

2:05 (2:05) (Class 1) 3-Y-O+

£37,468 (£14,203; £7,108; £3,544; £1,775; £891) **Stalls** High

Form					RPR
2000	1		**Knot In Wood (IRE)**[7] 3141 7-9-3 100 PaulHanagan 2 (R A Fahey) *pressed ldr: led over 1f out: drvn out fnl f*	7/1	111
316-	2	1 1/4	**Ancien Regime (IRE)**[287] 5891 4-9-3 110 JamieSpencer 10 (Saeed Bin Suroor) *stdd s: t.k.h: hld up: hdwy and rdn over 1f out: hung lft: styd on to go 2nd towards fin: nt rch wnr*	3/1[2]	107
-262	3	1/2	**Pusey Street Lady**[35] 2271 5-9-0 99 TPO'Shea 9 (J Gallagher) *led to over 1f out: kpt on same pce fnl f: lost 2nd towards fin*	9/2[3]	102
0-5	4	1 1/2	**Shallal**[49] 1865 4-9-3 96 TPQueally 1 (P W Chapple-Hyam) *prom: drvn and outpcd over 2f out: rallied fnl f: no imp*	14/1	101
1104	5	3/4	**Arganil (USA)**[35] 2272 4-9-3 104 NCallan 8 (K A Ryan) *prom: rdn over 2f out: no ex ins fnl f*	6/1	98
-405	6	3	**Atlantic Sport (USA)**[28] 2483 4-9-3 107 TonyCulhane 7 (M R Channon) *chsd ldrs: drvn and edgd lft over 2f out: wknd wl over 1f out*	11/4[1]	89
3020	7	nk	**Fullandby (IRE)**[28] 2481 7-9-3 100 GregFairley 4 (T J Etherington) *s.i.s: bhd: shortlived effrt over 2f out: sn btn*	12/1	88

1m 14.03s (-1.17) **Going Correction** +0.10s/f (Good)

WFA 3 from 4yo+ 7lb 7 Ran SP% 111.0

Speed ratings (Par 113): **111,109,108,106,105 101,101**

toteswingers: 1&2 £2.00, 1&3 £3.90, 2&3 £3.20. CSF £26.56 TOTE £6.40: £2.30, £2.10; EX 21.40 Trifecta £15.40 Pool: £384.60 - 15.40 winning units..

Owner Rhodes, Kenyon & Gill **Bred** Rathbarry Stud **Trained** Musley Bank, N Yorks

FOCUS

An ordinary race for the grade with the winner running to his best. They all raced up the middle of the track.

NOTEBOOK

Knot In Wood(IRE) had failed to be placed on his previous five starts in Group company and was comfortably held in the Wokingham last time, but he proved good enough to take this Group 3. He is suited by give underfoot, so conditions were in his favour, and he kept on best having disputed the lead early on, taking full advantage of the runner-up being set plenty to do. His trainer admitted he doesn't believe the seven-year-old is a genuine Group 3 horse and he hopes the handicapper doesn't overreact. Official explanation: trainer said, regarding apparent improvement in form, that the gelding got the run of the race. (tchd 13-2)

Ancien Regime(IRE), a 5f Group 3 winner for Michael Jarvis last season who was making his debut for Godolphin, looked fit enough for this first start in 287 days. However, he appeared to be given an over-confident ride and simply got going too late. He was a little keen under restraint early on, most probably the reason his jockey was eager to get cover, but he still had around four or five lengths to make up on the winner once finally coming under pressure after being switched right 2f out. He ran on, although looked to be hanging left in the closing stages and couldn't make up the ground. (op 11-4)

Pusey Street Lady, trying Group company for the first time after running third in a Listed race on heavy ground at Haydock, had conditions to suit but wasn't quite good enough. She disputed the early running with the winner and there can be no excuses. (op 11-2)

Shallal, well beaten on his return from nearly a year off in a 7f Listed event at Haydock, took too long to pick up on this drop in trip. (op 12-1 tchd 16-1)

Arganil(USA) had returned to form when fourth in the Temple Stakes over 5f on testing ground at Haydock, but he ran below that form this time. He's better suited by the minimum trip and ideally doesn't want extremes of going, hence the reason Polytrack seems to suit him so well. (op 9-2)

Atlantic Sport(USA) was having his first run over 6f since he made a winning debut at Ascot as a juvenile, and the trip promised to suit, but he ran disappointingly. He seemed to be going okay early on, displaying sufficient speed, but he floundered once under pressure. Official explanation: trainer had no explanation for the poor form shown (op 4-1)

Fullandby(IRE) has now yet to be placed in five starts in Group company. (op 8-1)

3389 TOTESCOOP6 H'CAP 6f

2:35 (2:36) (Class 2) (0-100,97) 3-Y-O+

£16,200 (£4,851; £2,425; £1,214; £605; £304) **Stalls** High

Form					RPR
-001	1		**Roker Park (IRE)**[13] 2941 4-9-7 90 (p) NCallan 11 (K A Ryan) *prom: hdwy to ld over 1f out: drvn out*	9/1	103
2-52	2	1 1/2	**Barney McGrew (IRE)**[13] 2941 6-10-0 97 PhillipMakin 7 (M Dods) *taken early to post: dwlt: hld up: hdwy over 2f out: chsd wnr ins fnl f: r.o*	6/1[2]	105
2460	3	1 1/4	**Sunrise Safari (IRE)**[21] 2707 6-8-13 82 (v) PaulHanagan 10 (R A Fahey) *taken early to post: dwlt: towards rr: drvn 1/2-way: hdwy over 1f out: kpt on: wnt 3rd nr fin*	13/2[3]	86
0140	4	shd	**Excusez Moi (USA)**[13] 2941 7-9-12 95 (p) PJMcDonald 9 (Mrs R A Carr) *hld up: hdwy over 1f out: kpt on: no imp clsng stages*	16/1	99
2324	5	1 1/4	**Thebes**[34] 2297 4-9-8 91 GregFairley 8 (M Johnston) *mde most to over 1f out: wknd wl ins fnl f*	6/1[2]	91
3522	6	1/2	**Millfields Dreams**[5] 3206 10-8-4 78 oh8 (p) MarkFlynn(5) 3 (G C Bravery) *in midfield: drvn over 2f out: no imp fnl f*	40/1	76
6614	7	1 3/4	**Ponty Rossa (IRE)**[18] 2780 5-9-3 86 DavidAllan 12 (T D Easterby) *racd alone against stands' rail: rdn over 2f out: no imp*	4/1[1]	78
12-5	8	1/2	**Tajneed (IRE)**[88] 1052 6-9-7 97 NSLawes(7) 13 (D Nicholls) *cl up tl rdn and wknd fr 2f out*	13/2[3]	88
0001	9	2 1/2	**Baldemar**[21] 2707 4-9-4 87 AndrewElliott 4 (K R Burke) *chsd ldrs tl wknd over 1f out*	13/2[3]	70
-000	10	17	**Inter Vision (USA)**[13] 2941 9-9-4 87 DanielTudhope 5 (A Dickman) *hld up: shortlived effrt over 2f out: edgd lft: sn wknd: t.o*	20/1	15
0000	11	4 1/2	**Van Bossed (CAN)**[7] 3141 4-9-7 90 AdrianTNicholls 6 (D Nicholls) *cl up tl rdn and wknd over 1f out: t.o*	14/1	4
0-00	12	11	**Lucky Leigh**[14] 2928 3-8-10 86 TonyCulhane 1 (M R Channon) *in midfield: drvn and wknd over 2f out: eased whn no ch fnl f*	40/1	—

1m 14.32s (-0.88) **Going Correction** +0.10s/f (Good)

WFA 3 from 4yo+ 7lb 12 Ran SP% 120.8

Speed ratings (Par 109): **109,107,105,105,103 102,100,99,96,73 67,53**

toteswingers: 1&2 £4.50, 1&3 £13.90, 2&3 £14.80. CSF £62.30 CT £381.39 TOTE £6.60: £2.30, £2.40, £3.10; EX 45.30 Trifecta £309.70 Part won. Pool: £418.61 - 0.20 winning units..

Owner T Alderson **Bred** Dr Dean Harron **Trained** Hambleton, N Yorks

■ Stewards' Enquiry : Phillip Makin two-day ban: careless riding (Jul 11,13)

FOCUS

A decent, competitive sprint handicap and solid form rated around the first four. The winning time was only 0.29 seconds slower than the earlier Group 3. Most of these raced up the middle of the track.

NOTEBOOK

Roker Park(IRE), back to form in first-time cheekpieces when narrowly defeating Barney McGrew over this trip at Doncaster on quick ground last time, was able to confirm the form on 2lb worse terms under these vastly different conditions. After showing good speed from the outset, he picked up well when asked and was always holding his old rival. He's in the Stewards Cup and that looks an obvious target, particularly considering he's versatile regarding ground conditions. (op 15-2 tchd 7-1)

Barney McGrew(IRE) ran a good race off a career-high mark and is evidently improving. He couldn't reverse recent form with the winner, but emerges with plenty of credit considering he raced further back than the Kevin Ryan-trained horse after a sluggish start. (op 13-2)

Sunrise Safari(IRE) ◆ hasn't won since 2007 and is low on confidence according to his trainer, but there is no doubt he's seriously well handicapped. Things hadn't gone right for him in three starts since running a good second over this course and distance in April and, although this was better, he again didn't get the run of things. He was continually messed about in the pack and had to fight for room, but he finished very well to take a closing third. A strongly run race at this trip, ideally on a non-undulating course, is what he wants, and there are races to be won with him when things finally fall right. (op 15-2 tchd 8-1)

Excusez Moi(USA) bounced back to form after a couple of ordinary efforts. Not for the first time he missed the break, but he finished reasonably well on ground that is probably soft enough for him these days. (op 20-1)

Thebes couldn't sustain his effort after being pressed for the lead and continues to look high enough in the weights, even if the ground was softer than ideal. (op 15-2)

Millfields Dreams ran with credit from 8lb out of the handicap.

Ponty Rossa(IRE) raced alone against the stands' rail almost throughout and was well held. (op 6-1)

Tajneed(IRE) was only 1lb higher than when runner-up in last year's Ayr Gold Cup, but his only outing this year came on Fibresand back in March and his trainer felt he might need the run. (op 6-1)

Baldemar, 5lb higher than when causing a surprise in a similarly competitive race at Epsom on Derby day, had conditions to suit, so this was disappointing. (op 6-1 tchd 7-1)

3390 JOHN SMITH'S NORTHUMBERLAND PLATE (HERITAGE H'CAP) 2m 19y

3:10 (3:12) (Class 2) 3-Y-O+

£110,970 (£33,408; £16,704; £8,334; £4,176; £2,106) **Stalls** Low

Form					RPR
0-05	1		**Som Tala**[11] 2994 6-8-8 92 TonyCulhane 4 (M R Channon) *set mod gallop: mde all: rdn wl over 2f out: hld on gamely fnl f*	16/1	99
11-2	2	3/4	**Wells Lyrical (IRE)**[63] 1519 4-8-7 91 TomEaves 2 (B Smart) *t.k.h: in tch: effrt over 2f out: chsd wnr ins fnl f: r.o fin*	15/2[2]	97
4/12	3	2	**Friston Forest (IRE)**[28] 2501 5-9-10 108 NCallan 3 (Saeed Bin Suroor) *t.k.h: trckd ldrs: smooth hdwy and ev ch over 2f out: sn rdn: edgd lft and lost 2nd ins fnl f: one pce*	14/1	112
2-11	4	3/4	**Hendersyde (USA)**[35] 2283 4-8-6 90 (t) ShaneKelly 5 (W R Swinburn) *hld up ins: hdwy over 2f out: edgd rt and kpt on ins fnl f: nrst fin*	10/1	93
10-4	5	1 3/4	**Electrolyser (IRE)**[43] 2055 4-8-11 95 PaulMulrennan 22 (C G Cox) *towards rr: drvn 4f out: styd on fnl 2f: nvr able to chal*	12/1	96
0033	6	shd	**Tilt**[28] 2486 7-8-7 91 PaulHanagan 12 (B Ellison) *dwlt: sn in midfield: rdn and outpcd wl over 2f out: rallied fnl f: no imp*	14/1	92
00-2	7	1/2	**Ajaan**[52] 1790 5-9-1 99 (b) TPQueally 13 (H R A Cecil) *trckd ldrs: effrt over 2f out: no ex fnl f*	13/2[1]	99
05-1	8	nse	**Hits Only Vic (USA)**[28] 2486 5-9-0 98 DNolan 8 (D Carroll) *in tch: drvn 3f out: one pce fnl 2f*	8/1[3]	98
2335	9	1 1/2	**The Betchworth Kid**[30] 2425 4-8-11 100 JamieKyne(5) 1 (M L W Bell) *hld up: rdn and effrt whn nt clr run and swtchd rt over 2f out: keeping on whn n.m.r briefly ins fnl f: n.d*	17/2	98
0-10	10	6	**Keenes Day (FR)**[11] 2994 4-8-9 93 JoeFanning 7 (M Johnston) *sn w ldr: edgd lft and wknd fr 3f out*	10/1	84
51-3	11	hd	**Meshtri (IRE)**[91] 1007 4-9-0 98 PhilipRobinson 18 (M A Jarvis) *t.k.h: in midfield on outside: effrt 3f out: btn over 1f out*	11/1	89
3335	12	shd	**Buddhist Monk**[28] 2501 4-8-6 90 (t) AdrianTNicholls 14 (Ian Williams) *bhd: rdn over 4f out: nvr able to chal*	50/1	81
6-20	13	1	**Mischief Making (USA)**[37] 2216 4-9-2 100 TGMcLaughlin 19 (E A L Dunlop) *hld up on outside: pushed along over 4f out: nvr on terms*	33/1	89
-630	14	nk	**Carte Diamond (USA)**[52] 1790 8-8-10 94 PhillipMakin 17 (B Ellison) *bhd: rdn 4f out: nvr on terms*	40/1	83
2412	15	8	**Record Breaker (IRE)**[7] 3142 5-8-9 93 5ex (b) RoystonFfrench 20 (M Johnston) *towards rr: rdn 4f out: sn btn*	12/1	72
1-62	16	31	**Meethaaq (USA)**[28] 2471 4-8-6 90 TPO'Shea 16 (Sir Michael Stoute) *t.k.h: in tch tl wknd over 3f out: t.o*	16/1	32
0-00	17	11	**Valentino Rossi (BRZ)**[11] 2994 7-8-10 94 (b[1]) GregFairley 10 (A G Foster) *hld up: hdwy into midfield 1/2-way: wknd 5f out: t.o*	40/1	23

3m 45.1s (5.70) **Going Correction** +0.475s/f (Yiel) 17 Ran SP% 123.5

Speed ratings (Par 109): **104,103,102,102,101 101,101,101,100,97 97,97,96,96,92 77,71**

toteswingers: 1&2 £32.10, 1&3 £61.20, 2&3 £30.10. CSF £129.35 CT £1753.94 TOTE £19.60: £3.60, £2.20, £3.70, £3.40; EX 78.80 Trifecta £1364.10 Pool: £18,065.81 - 9.80 winning units..

Owner Sheikh Ahmed Al Maktoum **Bred** Usk Valley Stud **Trained** West Ilsley, Berks

FOCUS

One of the most prestigious staying handicaps of the season, but this year's race was unsatisfactory for a number of reasons and the form needs treating with caution. For a start, the dolling out of rails was removed and there was fresh ground from the 1m1f point to 4.5f out. That led clerk of the course James Armstrong to predict that "anyone who can get the rail has got an advantage all the way round". The first four emerged from the bottom five stalls and that quartet all raced against the rail for much of the way, suggesting there was indeed a track bias. One final point to note, and just as significant, is they went very steady, even allowing for the conditions, and it proved difficult to make up ground. There are doubts over the form although it should produce future winners. Leading fancies Speed Ticket (lame) and Judgethemoment (ground) were non-runners.

NOTEBOOK

Som Tala produced a game effort, but all things considered, he had an awful lot going for him. He was allowed a soft lead from a favourable draw and was seemingly at an advantage in racing against the rail. His latest effort wasn't too bad when he finished fifth from a poor draw in the Ascot Stakes and the return to front-running tactics suited this dour stayer. It will be a surprise if things fall so kindly again any time soon, however, and he'll be well worth taking on next time, particularly considering this was his first success since 2006. (op 20-1 tchd 22-1)

Wells Lyrical(IRE), off the track for two months after running second at Ripon on his reappearance, ran a cracker in this tougher contest off a 2lb higher mark. This was the softest ground he had encountered, and he was plenty keen enough for much of the way, but he saw his race out well. He's evidently a most progressive stayer and his rider thinks he could be a horse for a race like the Ebor. (op 8-1)
Friston Forest(IRE), beaten just a short head by subsequent Royal Ascot winner Caracciola when conceding 3lb in a 1m6f Listed contest at York on his latest start, was always well placed and had his chance. The ground didn't bother him and he threw down a big challenge to the winner in the straight, but he couldn't sustain his effort. This was his first try at 2m and this trip seemed to stretch him, but this was still a big effort under top weight. (op 16-1)
Hendersyde(USA), 7lb higher than when winning over 1m6f at Newmarket on his previous start, was outpaced when the tempo increased, having raced slightly further back than the front three and, although keeping on, was always held. (op 11-1)
Electrolyser(IRE) ◆, a progressive type at up to 1m4f, fared best of those waited with, despite being drawn out widest, and emerges with credit. This progressive type appeals as one to keep on-side. (tchd 14-1)
Tilt was another to race keenly but he kept on and reversed recent form with Hits Only Vic. (tchd 12-1)
Ajaan, 3lb higher than when runner-up in the Chester Cup (best of those waited with) on his only previous start this year, raced close up for much of the way, although off the inside rail, and was well held in the straight. Like a few of the also-rans, he can be given another chance. (op 8-1 tchd 6-1)
Hits Only Vic(USA) had conditions to suit but couldn't defy a 4lb rise for his recent Haydock win. (op 9-1 tchd 15-2)
The Betchworth Kid, whose trainer teamed up with an inexperienced apprentice to win this two years ago, is a fair bit better than he showed. He was the only runner drawn in the bottom five stalls not to make the frame, but he didn't help his chance by running lazily through the early stages and was soon too far back. Once in the straight, he faced an impossible task, but still would have finished closer with a clearer run. Official explanation: jockey said gelding was denied a clear run (op 9-1)
Keenes Day(FR), a beaten favourite in the Ascot Stakes last time, again ran below expectations and is possibly a bit soft. (op 8-1)
Meshtri(IRE), 3lb higher than when third in the Queen's Prize on his only previous start this year, was unable to dominate from stall 18 and raced far too keenly. Official explanation: jockey said colt had no more to give and was unsuited by the slow early pace (op 12-1)
Meethaaq(USA) Official explanation: jockey said colt was unsuited by the soft ground
Valentino Rossi(BRZ) Official explanation: jockey said horse ran too free

3391 TOTESPORT.COM H'CAP 7f

3:45 (3:47) (Class 2) (0-100,97) 3-Y-O+

£12,462 (£3,732; £1,866; £934; £466; £234) **Stalls** High

Form				RPR
1230	**1**		**Horatio Carter**[8] 3091 4-9-7 **90** (p) NCallan 12 (K A Ryan) *t.k.h: prom: hdwy to ld appr fnl f: hld on wl towards fin* **11/4**[1]	99
0362	**2**	*shd*	**Osteopathic Remedy (IRE)**[7] 3172 5-9-2 **85** PhillipMakin 3 (M Dods) *t.k.h: hld up: hdwy over 1f out: edgd lft and kpt on fnl f: jst hld* **7/2**[2]	93
5340	**3**	¾	**Boy Blue**[18] 2780 4-8-12 **81** DaleGibson 10 (P Salmon) *led to appr fnl f: kpt on u.p ins fnl f* **12/1**	87
0201	**4**	*shd*	**Benandonner (USA)**[24] 2612 6-10-0 **97** PaulHanagan 6 (R A Fahey) *chsd ldrs: drvn fr over 2f out: sltly outpcd over 1f out: kpt on u.p ins fnl f* **7/1**	103
1200	**5**	½	**Opus Maximus (IRE)**[14] 2933 4-9-6 **89** JoeFanning 13 (M Johnston) *w ldr: ev ch appr fnl f: no ex ins fnl f* **9/1**	93
34-6	**6**	*shd*	**Lindoro**[28] 2470 4-9-6 **89** (t) ShaneKelly 5 (W R Swinburn) *hld up: hdwy over 1f out: no imp fnl f* **16/1**	93
0-00	**7**	2 ¾	**Damika (IRE)**[28] 2470 6-9-11 **97** MichaelJStainton(3) 2 (R M Whitaker) *in tch: effrt over 2f out: outpcd appr fnl f* **9/1**	94
0-04	**8**	*shd*	**Game Lad**[43] 2045 7-8-11 **80** (t) DavidAllan 9 (T D Easterby) *dwlt: hld up: hdwy over 2f out: no ex over 1f out* **6/1**[3]	77
6400	**9**	1 ½	**Kings Point (IRE)**[10] 3014 8-9-6 **89** AdrianTNicholls 8 (D Nicholls) *hld up: rdn and edgd lft wl over 2f out: nvr rchd ldrs* **12/1**	82

1m 28.12s (-0.58) **Going Correction** +0.10s/f (Good) **9** Ran SP% **116.9**
Speed ratings (Par 109): **107,106,106,105,105 105,102,101,100**
toteswingers: 1&2 £2.20, 1&3 £7.50, 2&3 £12.30. CSF £12.47 CT £99.02 TOTE £4.00: £1.60, £1.30, £3.30; EX 16.50 Trifecta £439.30 Pool: £653.16 - 1.10 winning units..
Owner T Alderson **Bred** Mrs T Brudenell **Trained** Hambleton, N Yorks

FOCUS
A good, competitive handicap, but they went steady early on, even allowing for the conditions, and the first six finished in a bit of a heap. The form looks solid enough rated around those in the frame behind the winner. They raced up the middle of the track.

NOTEBOOK
Horatio Carter ◆, second of 12 on the far side of the track in the Buckingham Palace at Royal Ascot eight days earlier, coped with the switch to soft ground and just did enough. He didn't help his chance by racing keenly for much of the way and, having looked set to win convincingly when first going for home, he only just held on. He had next to nothing in hand at the line, but gives the impression he can do better again and it would be no surprise to see him remain ahead of the handicapper. (op 4-1)
Osteopathic Remedy(IRE), like the winner, raced keenly early on, but he finished strongly and would have got up in another few strides. He's on a good mark and looks ready to win. (tchd 3-1)
Boy Blue was allowed to set a modest gallop and it was no surprise to see him still bang there at the finish. It remains to be seen whether he can repeat this form next time. (op 14-1)
Benandonner(USA) is versatile regarding ground and trip and he ran well off a mark 3lb higher than when winning over 1m on fast going at Ripon last time. (op 11-2)
Opus Maximus(IRE), racing on the softest ground he has encountered, was close up for a lot of the way but couldn't sustain his challenge. A return to a better surface might suit. (op 8-1)
Lindoro, with the tongue-tie back on, never featured and probably would have preferred a stronger-run race. (op 12-1)

3392 E.B.F./TARMAC MAIDEN STKS 6f

4:20 (4:25) (Class 4) 2-Y-O

£6,231 (£1,866; £933; £467; £233; £117) **Stalls** High

Form				RPR
3	**1**		**The Human League**[8] 3113 2-9-3 0 TonyCulhane 6 (M R Channon) *led to over 4f out: led again over 2f out: sn rdn: kpt on strly fnl f* **9/4**[1]	84+
2	**2**	2	**Chaperno (USA)**[16] 2839 2-9-3 0 JamieSpencer 5 (Saeed Bin Suroor) *dwlt: sn prom: smooth hdwy and ev ch over 1f out: sn rdn: nt qckn ins fnl f* **3/1**[2]	78
3	**3**	8	**My One Weakness (IRE)**[9] 3064 2-8-12 0 LanceBetts(5) 11 (B Ellison) *in tch stands' side: drifted lft fr 1/2-way: outpcd fnl 2f* **5/1**	54
	4	1 ¼	**Lucky Windmill** 2-9-3 0 PJMcDonald 4 (G A Swinbank) *in midfield: pushed along 3f out: no imp fnl 2f* **33/1**	50
	5	3 ¾	**Lowdown (IRE)** 2-9-3 0 RoystonFfrench 10 (M Johnston) *w ldr: led over 4f out to over 2f out: wknd over 1f out* **9/2**[3]	39
	6	6	**Grey Garth (IRE)** 2-9-3 0 PhilipRobinson 3 (J D Bethell) *s.i.s: bhd and outpcd: nvr on terms* **20/1**	21
	7	½	**Elmfield Giant (USA)** 2-9-3 0 PaulHanagan 2 (R A Fahey) *sn prom: rdn and hung lft over 2f out: sn wknd* **8/1**	20
	8	6	**Orpen All Hours (IRE)** 2-8-12 0 PhillipMakin 9 (P C Haslam) *plld hrd: in tch: carried lft over 2f out: sn wknd* **20/1**	—
	9	6	**Dinkys Diamond (IRE)** 2-9-3 0 TomEaves 12 (B Ellison) *unruly bef s: missed break: a struggling stands' side* **20/1**	—

1m 16.53s (1.33) **Going Correction** +0.10s/f (Good) **9** Ran SP% **119.0**
Speed ratings (Par 95): **95,92,81,80,75 67,66,58,50**
toteswingers: 1&2 £2.20, 1&3 £4.20, 2&3 £3.90. CSF £8.85 TOTE £3.70: £1.30, £1.60, £2.00; EX 9.20.
Owner Findlay & Bloom **Bred** C J Murfitt **Trained** West Ilsley, Berks
■ Stewards' Enquiry : Lance Betts three-day ban: careless riding (Jul 11,13, 14)

FOCUS
The first two pulled a long way clear in this maiden and both look above-average colts. Most of these raced up the centre of the track.

NOTEBOOK
The Human League ◆ is a sizeable individual who didn't look totally happy on quick ground when third in a fair maiden on the July course first time up, and he was also hampered at a crucial stage. The money came for him on this switch to a soft surface and he relished the conditions, showing no signs of hanging or carrying his head awkwardly, and there was much to like about this performance. Having shown good speed from the off, he briefly appeared vulnerable when the Godolphin challenger loomed up going well, but the son of Tobougg galloped on relentlessly. He could be Pattern class when there is give underfoot. (op 4-1)
Chaperno(USA), beaten just a short head after running green over this trip on quick ground at Haydock on his debut, again had a sheepskin noseband fitted and this was a decent effort. Made to wait in the stalls much longer than ideal, he unsurprisingly took a few strides to get going when the gates opened and raced off the pace. He looked a big threat to the winner when moving into contention going well around 2f out, but he didn't find enough. Both the way he finished his race and his US pedigree suggests he might do better back on quicker ground, and he should make his mark in the short term, although he lacks size. (op 9-4)
My One Weakness(IRE), third in an ordinary Ripon maiden first time up, was taken towards the stands' rail early on but seemed to resent the move and hung left, ending up in the main group towards the middle. All things considered, this wasn't a bad effort. (op 8-1)
Lucky Windmill, an 8,000gns half-brother to a few winners at around 6f-7f, showed some ability and is entitled to improve.
Lowdown(IRE), a 100,000gns half-brother to a few winners, including Grand Ducal, who was successful in Group 3 company over 1m2f, looked as though the run would bring him on. Despite proving reluctant to load, he showed good early speed in the race before tiring. (op 7-2 tchd 6-1)
Elmfield Giant(USA), a $105,000 half-brother to a winner on an artificial surface in the US, represented the trainer, jockey and owner who won this race with a newcomer last year, but he was on his toes beforehand and didn't run much of a race. (tchd 7-1)

3393 TOTESPORT 0800 221 221 H'CAP 1m 2f 32y

4:50 (4:51) (Class 4) (0-85,84) 3-Y-O+

£4,984 (£1,492; £746; £373; £186; £93) **Stalls** Centre

Form				RPR
0003	**1**		**Kingsdale Orion (IRE)**[3] 3266 5-8-13 **73** LanceBetts(5) 3 (B Ellison) *dwlt: sn chsng ldrs: led over 2f out: hld on wl fnl f* **2/1**[1]	80
1021	**2**	¾	**Dechiper (IRE)**[21] 2724 7-9-1 **70** PaulMulrennan 4 (R Johnson) *hld up in tch: hdwy to chse wnr 2f out: rdn and ev ch ins fnl f: edgd rt: kpt on* **6/1**	75
4000	**3**	2 ¾	**Best Prospect (IRE)**[14] 2933 7-10-0 **83** (t) PhillipMakin 10 (M Dods) *hld up bhd: stdy hdwy on bit over 2f out: chsng ldrs and rdn fnl f: kpt on same pce* **5/1**[3]	83
112	**4**	3 ¾	**Stagecoach Jade (IRE)**[33] 2341 3-8-9 **76** JimmyQuinn 6 (M Johnston) *chsd ldrs: drvn over 2f out: sn outpcd* **3/1**[2]	68
20/6	**5**	1 ¼	**King In Waiting (IRE)**[7] 3154 6-9-4 **78** DeanHeslop(5) 1 (J Hetherton) *t.k.h: led to over 2f out: sn outpcd: n.d after* **40/1**	68
1460	**6**	3	**Destinys Dream (IRE)**[3] 3264 4-8-12 **70** KellyHarrison(3) 11 (Miss Tracy Waggott) *hld up in tch: effrt over 2f out: wknd over 1f out* **14/1**	54
64-6	**7**	2	**Dar Es Salaam**[14] 2932 5-9-10 **79** JamieSpencer 7 (J S Goldie) *sn trcking ldr: rdn and wknd fr 2f out* **5/1**[3]	59

2m 16.56s (4.66) **Going Correction** +0.475s/f (Yiel)
WFA 3 from 4yo+ 12lb **7** Ran SP% **115.1**
Speed ratings (Par 105): **100,99,97,94,93 90,89**
toteswingers: 1&2 £2.90, 1&3 £3.00, 2&3 £4.80. CSF £14.86 CT £52.45 TOTE £3.00: £1.70, £2.30; EX 17.40.
Owner Koo's Racing Club **Bred** Myles And Mrs Joan Doyle **Trained** Norton, N Yorks

FOCUS
Just a fair handicap with the runner-up recording a personal best.
Dar Es Salaam Official explanation: jockey said gelding was unsuited by the soft ground

3394 GRAPHITE RESOURCES H'CAP 1m (R)

5:25 (5:26) (Class 4) (0-85,84) 3-Y-O **£4,984** (£1,492; £746; £373) **Stalls** Centre

Form				RPR
1142	**1**		**Tiger Reigns**[7] 3144 3-9-4 **81** PhillipMakin 1 (M Dods) *trckd ldrs: led over 2f out: hrd pressed fr over 1f out: hld on wl u.p* **11/10**[1]	91
14	**2**	*shd*	**Sunshine Always (IRE)**[16] 2841 3-9-2 **79** TonyCulhane 6 (W J Haggas) *hld up in tch: stdy hdwy over 2f out: ev ch and rdn over 1f out: kpt on fnl f: jst hld* **9/4**[2]	89
01	**3**	16	**Cipher**[18] 2789 3-9-7 **84** RoystonFfrench 2 (M Johnston) *mde most to over 2f out: wknd wl over 1f out* **7/2**[3]	57
-114	**4**	27	**Postman**[47] 1925 3-8-12 **75** TomEaves 5 (B Smart) *w ldr tl wknd fr over 2f out* **8/1**	—

1m 45.33s (1.93) **Going Correction** +0.475s/f (Yiel) **4** Ran SP% **111.7**
Speed ratings (Par 101): **109,108,92,65**
toteswingers: 1&2 £3.10. CSF £4.03 TOTE £2.20; EX 4.20 Place 6 £144.22, Place 5 £47.10..
Owner Joe Buzzeo **Bred** Richard Green And New England Stud **Trained** Denton, Co Durham

FOCUS
Rather surprisingly for such a small field, the lead was contested, with Cipher and Postman taking each other on for much of the way, and that obviously compromised their chances. The winner ran to his Ayr form with the runner-up back to his debut effort.
T/Jkpt: Not won. T/Plt: £53.10 to a £1 stake. Pool: £168,389.64. 2,312.28 winning tickets. T/Qpdt: £7.80 to a £1 stake. Pool: £10,532.10. 989.15 winning tickets. RY

3356 NEWMARKET (R-H)

Saturday, June 27

OFFICIAL GOING: Good (good to soft in places; 6.9)

Wind: Light across Weather: Light rain

3395 DESI DILLINGHAM BIRTHDAY MAIDEN STKS 7f

1:50 (1:51) (Class 4) 2-Y-O **£5,180** (£1,541; £770; £384) **Stalls** High

Form RPR

2 **1** **Missionaire (USA)**[19] 2771 2-9-3 0........................ PaulDoe 5 82+
(W J Knight) *mde all: rdn and hung lft fr over 1f out: r.o* **5/2**[1]

56 **2** *½* **Dubawi Phantom**[15] 2889 2-9-3 0........................ DarryllHolland 8 81
(D M Simcock) *s.i.s: rcvrd to chse wnr over 5f out: rdn over 1f out: sn hung lft and ev ch: unable qckn nr fin* **8/1**

3 *3* **Simenon (IRE)** 2-9-3 0........................ NeilChalmers 4 73+
(A M Balding) *dwlt: hld up: nt clr run 2f out: swtchd rt and hdwy over 1f out: r.o: nt rch ldrs* **20/1**

4 *1 ½* **Nideeb** 2-9-3 0........................ KShea 9 70+
(C E Brittain) *s.i.s: hld up: pushed along 1/2-way: r.o ins fnl f: nrst fin* **12/1**

3 **5** *½* **Irish Jugger (USA)**[17] 2813 2-8-12 0........................ MartinLane(5) 6 68
(K R Burke) *chsd ldrs: rdn over 2f out: wknd fnl f* **4/1**[2]

6 *1* **Baltimore Clipper (USA)** 2-9-3 0........................ TedDurcan 3 66
(P F I Cole) *hld up in tch: racd keenly: rdn over 2f out: wknd over 1f out* **12/1**

0 **7** *1 ½* **Our Boy Barrington (IRE)**[16] 2853 2-9-3 0........................ RichardHughes 10 62
(R Hannon) *chsd ldrs: rdn and edgd lft over 1f out: wknd fnl f* **15/2**[3]

8 *¾* **Suited And Booted (IRE)** 2-9-3 0........................ PatDobbs 2 60
(R Hannon) *dwlt: hld up: nt clr run over 2f out: nvr trbld ldrs* **10/1**

9 *hd* **Timely Jazz (IRE)** 2-9-3 0........................ RobertHavlin 11 60
(B J Meehan) *mid-div: rdn and hung lft over 2f out: wknd over 1f out* **9/1**

10 *3* **Anchorage Boy (USA)** 2-9-3 0........................ JerryO'Dwyer 1 52
(Miss Amy Weaver) *mid-div: rdn over 2f out: wknd over 1f out* **66/1**

6 **11** *2 ½* **Blinka Me**[16] 2860 2-9-3 0........................ MichaelHills 7 46
(M H Tompkins) *stdd s: hld up: plld hrd: rdn over 2f out: wknd over 1f out* **14/1**

1m 27.83s (2.13) **Going Correction** +0.125s/f (Good) **11** Ran SP% **118.8**

Speed ratings (Par 95): **92,91,88,86,85 84,82,82,81,78 75**

toteswingers: 1&2 £6.00, 1&3 £9.10, 2&3 £28.60. CSF £23.32 TOTE £3.10: £1.30, £2.80, £5.20; EX 18.10.

Owner Bluehills Racing Limited **Bred** Mt Joy Stables **Trained** Patching, W Sussex

FOCUS

This maiden has produced the odd smart performer in the past and plenty of subsequent winners, so this should be a race to keep a note of and has been rated positively.

NOTEBOOK

Missionaire(USA) was drawn on the wrong side when making his debut, but still ran with a deal of promise. He proved that he had progressed from that effort with a determined display, and seems sure to get 1m this year. (op 2-1 tchd 11-4 in places)

Dubawi Phantom made the winner work really hard during the final furlong but did not see out the tip as well as that horse did. He should be winning something as a juvenile. (op 11-2)

Simenon(IRE), who cost 60,000gns as a yearling, is bred so have a bit of stamina and showed that he has a future by staying on strongly once getting the hang of things. (op 16-1 tchd 25-1)

Nideeb, a 20,000gns yearling out of an unraced sister to Nell Gwyn winner and Vermeille runner-up Cloud Castle, did not have a clue what was going on early but kept on really well up the incline. A flashy looking chestnut, he has a future. (op 11-1)

Irish Jugger(USA) weakened after sitting close to the leader. It was not a bad run and he will be good enough to find a race in time. (op 5-1)

Baltimore Clipper(USA), who is related to sprinters and hurdlers, looked to have plenty of substance about him and should improve. His head was a little high under pressure, which may have been because he was green.

Our Boy Barrington(IRE) showed pace but did not see out the race. However, he was not given a really hard time in the final furlong when his chance was gone. (op 16-1 tchd 18-1)

Suited And Booted(IRE), a 48,000euros half-brother to three winners, notably to the useful sprinter Cake, held quite a few places during the contest and ran a bit better than his final position suggests, especially as he was hampered a couple of times. (op 12-1)

Timely Jazz(IRE), a 58,000gns half-brother to the useful Iron Fist, who was sixth in this race in 2006, was another to drop out after racing prominently. (op 10-1)

3396 SUNLEY EMPRESS STKS (LISTED RACE) (FILLIES) 6f

2:20 (2:20) (Class 1) 2-Y-O

£17,031 (£6,456; £3,231; £1,611; £807; £405) **Stalls** High

Form RPR

410 **1** **Jira**[8] 3086 2-8-12 0........................ KShea 8 93
(C E Brittain) *s.i.s: sn pushed along in rr: hdwy over 1f out: r.o to ld wl ins fnl f* **15/2**[3]

21 **2** *nk* **Jeanie Johnston (IRE)**[17] 2819 2-8-12 0........................ LiamJones 13 92
(K R Burke) *led: hung lft thrght: rdn over 1f out: hdd wl ins fnl f* **3/1**[2]

16 **3** *½* **Electric Feel**[26] 2557 2-8-12 0........................ AndreaAtzeni 2 91
(M Botti) *hld up: hdwy over 1f out: r.o: nt rch ldrs* **14/1**

3215 **4** *½* **Curtains**[8] 3086 2-8-12 0........................ TedDurcan 4 89
(S Dow) *chsd ldr: rdn and ev ch over 1f out: edgd lft: styd on same pce ins fnl f* **10/1**

41 **5** *½* **Hairspray**[28] 2490 2-8-12 0........................ DarryllHolland 7 88
(M R Channon) *s.i.s: hld up: hdwy over 1f out: styd on* **14/1**

4 **6** *¾* **Vanishing Grey (IRE)**[32] 2354 2-8-12 0........................ RobertHavlin 11 85
(B J Meehan) *prom: rdn over 1f out: styd on same pce ins fnl f* **12/1**

4242 **7** *1 ¾* **Angelena Ballerina (IRE)**[19] 2765 2-8-12 0........................(p) NeilChalmers 3 80
(A Bailey) *chsd ldrs: rdn over 2f out: wknd ins fnl f* **25/1**

1 **8** *1* **Mudaaraah**[25] 2563 2-8-12 0........................ RHills 5 77
(J L Dunlop) *chsd ldrs: rdn over 1f out: wknd fnl f* **2/1**[1]

4610 **9** *1 ¾* **Flyinflyout**[8] 3086 2-8-12 0........................ SamHitchcott 1 72
(M R Channon) *hld up: rdn over 2f out: wknd over 1f out* **40/1**

21U **10** *8* **Kurtanella**[8] 3086 2-8-12 0........................ RichardHughes 10 48
(R Hannon) *sn pushed along and prom: lost pl over 3f out: wknd over 2f out* **12/1**

1m 12.91s (0.41) **Going Correction** +0.125s/f (Good) **10** Ran SP% **114.2**

Speed ratings (Par 98): **102,101,100,100,99 98,96,94,92,81**

toteswingers: 1&2 £5.50, 1&3 £17.30, 2&3 £11.00 CSF £29.58 TOTE £8.90: £1.90, £1.80, £4.60; EX 38.70 TRIFECTA Not won..

Owner Saeed Manana **Bred** W And R Barnett Ltd **Trained** Newmarket, Suffolk

■ Stewards' Enquiry : Liam Jones two-day ban: careless riding (Jul 11,13)

FOCUS

Down the years, the winner of this race has not really gone on to progress into a higher-grade animal, so this could be just ordinary form for the level. The runner-up and fourth set the standard.

NOTEBOOK

Jira, who kept on well from a high draw in the Albany Stakes, looked to have a hopeless task at halfway here, as she was a couple of lengths behind all her rivals. However, her stamina really kicked in when she hit the hill and she ended up winning comfortably. Connections will probably give her an entry in the Lowther Stakes. (op 9-1 tchd 7-1 and 10-1 in places)

Jeanie Johnston(IRE) may well have won had she kept a straight line throughout the race. Noticeably sweating around her neck, she was quite keen in front but kept on powerfully despite going left about 2f out. (op 11-4 tchd 10-3)

Electric Feel beat Angelena Ballerina on her debut and then had a go at beating the Aidan O´Brien-trained filly Lillie Langtry in her own back yard. She travelled strongly here and finished to good effect, but did not get to the leaders quickly enough to cause them any worrying moments. (op 12-1)

Curtains seemed to excel herself in the Albany Stakes last time, when considering her starting price, and was not helped here by the runner-up´s antics, as she got carried across the course with her. (op 11-1 tchd 12-1)

Hairspray, who had been absent since beating Curtains in May, shaped well and ran a similar race to the third. (op 16-1)

Vanishing Grey(IRE) looked a likely winner 2f from home but did not have the pace of those closer to the middle of the course. She is progressing the right way, however. (op 10-1)

Angelena Ballerina(IRE), who finished fourth in the Hilary Needler two starts previously, was always thereabouts and ran her race without posing any problems to the main contenders. The first-time cheekpieces did not have any obvious effect. (op 20-1 tchd 33-1)

Mudaaraah won a Folkestone maiden that has already produced two winners (the second and third), but she was very disappointing in this, considering she had the near-side rail to come up. Official explanation: trainer said filly was found to have a respiratory infection (tchd 15-8 tchd 9-4 and 5-2 in places)

Kurtanella Official explanation: jockey said filly never travelled

3397 TOTESPORT.COM FRED ARCHER STKS (LISTED RACE) 1m 4f

2:50 (2:50) (Class 1) 4-Y-O+ **£22,708** (£8,608; £4,308; £2,148; £1,076) **Stalls** Centre

Form RPR

4-2 **1** **All The Aces (IRE)**[42] 2075 4-9-0 111........................ MichaelHills 4 114+
(M A Jarvis) *a.p: chsd ldr whn wnt centre over 7f out: rdn to ld that gp over 2f out: led overall and hung rt over 1f out: styd on wl* **5/4**[1]

1-01 **2** *6* **Wasan**[30] 2398 4-9-0 110........................ RHills 3 104
(E A L Dunlop) *hld up: wnt centre over 7f out: reminders over 3f out: hdwy and hung rt over 1f out: sn chsng wnr: no ex ins fnl f* **3/1**[2]

0201 **3** *2 ½* **Classic Punch (IRE)**[63] 1523 6-9-0 104........................ DarryllHolland 2 100
(D R C Elsworth) *led: styd stands' side turning for home and racd alone: rdn over 2f out: hdd over 1f out: wknd fnl f* **10/1**[3]

-640 **4** *1 ¾* **Yellowstone (IRE)**[7] 3142 5-9-0 99........................(p) AlanMunro 5 97
(P F I Cole) *trckd ldr: racd keenly: wnt centre over 7f out and led that gp: rdn and hdd over 2f out: hung rt and wknd over 1f out* **14/1**

-312 **5** *20* **Age Of Reason (UAE)**[13] 2955 4-9-0 114........................ TedDurcan 1 65
(Saeed Bin Suroor) *hld up in tch: wnt centre over 7f out: rdn over 3f out: wkng whn hung rt wl over 1f out: eased* **3/1**[2]

2m 30.95s (-1.95) **Going Correction** +0.125s/f (Good) **5** Ran SP% **110.2**

Speed ratings (Par 111): **111,107,105,104,90**

CSF £5.28 TOTE £2.10: £1.30, £1.90; EX 5.10.

Owner A D Spence **Bred** Jack Ronan And Des Ver Hunt Farm Ltd **Trained** Newmarket, Suffolk

FOCUS

On their best form, there was not much to choose between this bunch. Much depended on whether each of them put their best foot forward or had conditions in their favour. The form is muddling.

NOTEBOOK

All The Aces(IRE), who only ran because the ground was suitable, is still lightly raced for his age and won this by a healthy margin once getting to the front. Very talented when conditions are in his favour, he is one to have on your side when raised in grade again. It would not be a surprise to see him take a Group race during the autumn. (tchd 11-8 and 6-4 in places)

Wasan, who was sweating on his neck, has a really good win-to-runs record but disappointed the last time he was tried in this company (it was the only time he was tried in blinkers). He did not always look happy at various stages and failed to make any noticeable impact on the winner. (op 4-1)

Classic Punch(IRE), the winner of this in 2007 and fourth last year, has always gone well fresh and got to the lead easily. The jockey chose to come up the stands´-side rail, a route no-one else took, and the horse looked very tired inside the final furlong. (op 9-1 tchd 13-2)

Yellowstone(IRE), with cheekpieces back on, has become slightly difficult to predict now and did not get home after taking a grip early. (op 16-1 tchd 12-1)

Age Of Reason(UAE), who had an entry in the Northumberland Plate, was the best treated of these on official figures and came into the race on the back of an excellent effort in an Italian Group 1. However, he was soon in trouble up the home straight and his jockey eased right off in the latter stages. Official explanation: jockey said gelding was unsuited by the good (good to soft in places) ground (op 11-4 tchd 7-2)

3398 JOHN BOVINGTON MEMORIAL CRITERION STKS (GROUP 3) 7f

3:25 (3:27) (Class 1) 3-Y-O+

£36,900 (£13,988; £7,000; £3,490; £1,748; £877) **Stalls** High

Form RPR

2446 **1** **Imbongi (SAF)**[62] 1553 5-9-3 114........................ KShea 9 117
(M F De Kock, South Africa) *chsd ldrs: led over 2f out: rdn and edgd lft over 1f out: hung rt ins fnl f: r.o* **8/1**

130- **2** *1 ¼* **Huntdown (USA)**[252] 6815 3-8-8 112........................ TedDurcan 3 111+
(Saeed Bin Suroor) *hld up: hdwy over 1f out: sn rdn: r.o* **9/1**

0310 **3** *shd* **Balthazaar's Gift (IRE)**[91] 1010 6-9-3 111........................ IanMongan 5 113
(C G Cox) *chsd ldrs: rdn and edgd rt over 1f out: r.o* **10/1**

2205 **4** *2 ¾* **Dream Eater (IRE)**[11] 2990 4-9-3 114........................(t) FrancisNorton 4 106+
(A M Balding) *plld hrd: trckd ldrs: rdn over 1f out: styd on same pce* **5/2**[1]

05/3 **5** *½* **Court Masterpiece**[28] 2500 9-9-3 110........................ GrahamGibbons 2 105
(J J Quinn) *hld up in tch: rdn over 1f out: styd on same pce fnl f* **6/1**[3]

233- **6** *1 ¼* **Al Qasi (IRE)**[237] 7157 6-9-3 110........................ RichardMullen 6 101
(P W Chapple-Hyam) *led: rdn and hdd over 2f out: wknd fnl f* **5/1**[2]

5-40 **7** *1 ½* **Winker Watson**[42] 2076 4-9-3 107........................(b[1]) AdrianMcCarthy 7 97
(P W Chapple-Hyam) *s.i.s: hld up: hdwy over 1f out: sn rdn and wknd* **8/1**

2405 **8** *½* **Vitznau (IRE)**[22] 2668 5-9-3 104........................ RichardHughes 1 96+
(R Hannon) *hld up: rdn over 2f out: n.d* **12/1**

15-0 **9** *¾* **Express Wish**[83] 1138 5-9-8 109........................ MichaelHills 8 99
(J Noseda) *chsd ldr: rdn and ev ch over 2f out: wknd fnl f* **12/1**

1m 24.83s (-0.87) **Going Correction** +0.125s/f (Good)

WFA 3 from 4yo+ 9lb **9** Ran SP% **116.2**

Speed ratings (Par 113): **109,107,107,104,103 102,100,100,99**

toteswingers: 1&2 £5.90, 1&3 £7.00, 2&3 £10.40 CSF £77.72 TOTE £4.10: £1.80, £2.40, £2.50; EX 41.30 Trifecta £154.70 Pool: £460.09 - 2.20 winning units..

Owner Sheikh Mohammed Bin Khalifa Al Maktoum **Bred** Summerhill Stud **Trained** South Africa

■ Stewards' Enquiry : Ian Mongan one-day ban: careless riding (Jul 11)

FOCUS

A fair Group 3 in which the winner did not need to run to his best and the third is probably the best guide, in a reasonably sound contest.

The Form Book, Raceform Ltd, Compton, RG20 6NL

NOTEBOOK
Imbongi(SAF), absent since running in the Group 1 Champions' Mile at Sha Tin in April, drifted alarmingly in the betting before the off but that did not stop him at all, and he won comfortably. A dual Guineas winner in his native South Africa, he may not be the easiest to place but was another fine advertisement for the training skills of Mike de Kock. He is to be aimed at the Group 2 Summer Mile, a race the jockey/trainer took last year with Archipenko. (op 4-1)
Huntdown(USA), having his first start for Godolphin, had smart form as a juvenile and was the only three-year-old in the line-up. In rear early, he was a little keen but kept on really well in the latter stages after hitting traffic. He has entries in the Sussex Stakes and the Darley July Cup, so connections clearly think the ability is still there. (op 8-1 tchd 6-1)
Balthazaar's Gift(IRE), making his debut for this stable after leaving Rod Simpson in Dubai, travelled nicely in midfield and kept on in good style. It will be interesting to see in which direction connections go with him next, but he is the sort who could run well in the Stewards Cup again. (tchd 8-1)
Dream Eater(IRE), who would have preferred quicker ground, was really keen after leaving the stalls and may have done a little better with a bit of cover. However, there is no denying that he is finding it difficult to get his head in front. (op 4-1)
Court Masterpiece had been given a nice breather since his return to action and ran very respectably. Connections will surely find him a race this season. (tchd 11-2 and 13-2)
Al Qasi(IRE) had an easy lead on his return to action and ran a satisfactory race. (op 6-1)
Winker Watson, wearing blinkers for the first time, came with an effort a furlong out but lacked the acceleration to get involved. (op 10-1)

3399 TREASURE BEACH HOTEL BARBADOS H'CAP 1m 2f
4:00 (4:00) (Class 2) (0-100,100) 3-Y-0+ **£12,952** (£3,854; £1,926; £962) **Stalls** Centre

Form RPR
3-50 **1** **Alazeyab (USA)**[42] 2077 3-8-12 **96**.................... RHills 6 104
(M A Jarvis) *mde all: rdn over 1f out: edgd lft ins fnl f: styd on gamely* **6/1**
/352 **2** *1* **Wintercast**[15] 2891 4-9-5 **91**.................... TedDurcan 8 97
(W R Swinburn) *chsd ldrs: rdn over 1f out: r.o: wnt 2nd post* **9/4**[1]
-004 **3** *nse* **Proponent (IRE)**[30] 2412 5-9-7 **93**.................... AlanMunro 4 99
(R Charlton) *a.p: rdn to chse wnr 1f out: styng on same pce whn edgd lft towards fin: lost 2nd post* **9/2**[3]
/001 **4** *2 1/2* **Charlie Cool**[127] 644 6-10-0 **100**....................(v) RichardMullen 1 101
(J H M Gosden) *hld up: rdn over 1f out: r.o ins fnl f: nvr nrr* **5/1**
2152 **5** *nse* **Mystery Star (IRE)**[22] 2671 4-9-5 **91**.................... MichaelHills 5 92
(M H Tompkins) *hld up: hdwy over 3f out: rdn over 1f out: no ex fnl f* **3/1**[2]
3124 **6** *12* **Dream Of Fortune (IRE)**[103] 847 5-8-9 **81**.................... PatCosgrave 3 58
(M G Quinlan) *dwlt: bhd: rdn over 2f out: wknd over 1f out* **25/1**
1632 **7** *1 3/4* **Sri Kuantan (IRE)**[31] 2374 5-8-9 **81** oh1....................(t) KShea 7 54
(R C Guest) *plld hrd: trckd wnr tl rdn over 1f out: sn wknd and eased* **14/1**

2m 5.70s (0.20) **Going Correction** +0.125s/f (Good)
WFA 3 from 4yo+ 12lb **7 Ran SP% 115.4**
Speed ratings (Par 109): **104,103,103,101,101 91,90**
toteswingers: 1&2 £4.40, 1&3 £5.80, 2&3 £3.30 CSF £20.33 CT £66.83 TOTE £7.10: £3.50, £1.90; EX 26.80.
Owner Hamdan Al Maktoum **Bred** Shadwell Farm LLC **Trained** Newmarket, Suffolk

FOCUS
A decent handicap and form worth taking at face value.

NOTEBOOK
Alazeyab(USA), the only three-year-old in the race, had been off since proving a little disappointing under a big weight in a Newbury handicap, but dug really deep here to hold off all challengers. There is a suspicion that his rider dictated a modest pace and quickened it at the right time, which would make this unreliable form. (op 7-1 tchd 11-2)
Wintercast, the least exposed runner in the race, ran well when tried over this distance last time and got close to Alazeyab about a furlong out before being outpaced. He did close again in the final stages but was unable to catch the winner. (tchd 5-2 and 11-4 in places)
Proponent(IRE) looked to be returning to form last time (a place in front of Wintercast) and ran well again, but just lacked the toe under his big weight to get to the winner. He is not far off getting his head in front again. (op 5-1)
Charlie Cool, absent since winning for Dhruba Selvaratnam in February, was having his first start for John Gosden and did not have the gears to get on terms as the gallop was steadily increased. However, it was a good effort after a break and he should progress. (op 7-1)
Mystery Star(IRE) is a very consistent sort in handicap company, but his trainer stated before the race that his horse would not like the ground, and he was proved right to some extent, although the gelding was far from disgraced. (op 7-2 after early 4-1 and 9-2 in a place)
Dream Of Fortune(IRE), having his first run on turf since June last year, lost plenty of ground at the start and never played a part in proceedings. (op 16-1)
Sri Kuantan(IRE) was very keen in the early stages here and had nothing left for the fight up the hill. (op 12-1 tchd 11-1)

3400 BETTERBET 08000 898887 EBF FILLIES' H'CAP 1m
4:35 (4:35) (Class 3) (0-90,85) 3-Y-0+ **£9,066** (£2,697; £1,348; £673) **Stalls** High

Form RPR
2212 **1** **Cumana Bay**[5] 3220 3-9-0 **81**.................... PatDobbs 4 89+
(R Hannon) *a.p: chsd ldr over 1f out: rdn to ld ins fnl f: edgd lft: r.o* **7/4**[1]
-211 **2** *1 1/4* **Charlotte Point (USA)**[24] 2607 3-9-3 **84**.................... MichaelHills 5 89
(P F I Cole) *led: rdn over 1f out: hdd and unable qck ins fnl f* **5/2**[2]
30-0 **3** *3/4* **Stan's Cool Cat (IRE)**[26] 2544 3-8-13 **80**.................... TedDurcan 3 83
(P F I Cole) *hld up: rdn over 1f out: r.o ins fnl f: nrst fin* **11/1**
-310 **4** *4* **Spring Adventure**[30] 2399 3-8-12 **79**.................... AlanMunro 1 73
(E A L Dunlop) *chsd ldr tl rdn over 1f out: wknd ins fnl f* **4/1**[3]
1306 **5** *5* **Trumpet Lily**[19] 2768 4-10-0 **85**.................... PatCosgrave 2 69
(J G Portman) *hld up: hdwy over 2f out: rdn and wknd over 1f out* **9/2**

1m 39.4s (-0.60) **Going Correction** +0.125s/f (Good)
WFA 3 from 4yo 10lb **5 Ran SP% 111.5**
Speed ratings (Par 104): **108,106,106,102,97**
CSF £6.50 TOTE £2.90: £1.60, £1.40; EX 4.40.
Owner J R Shannon **Bred** J R Shannon **Trained** East Everleigh, Wilts

FOCUS
Some useful fillies lined up for this, and there was not a great deal to choose between them on official figures. The small field was always going to make it a tactical affair, so the form is a bit muddling.

NOTEBOOK
Cumana Bay has been in excellent heart this season and fully deserved to get her head back in front. A better race and a stronger gallop may see this improving filly do even better. (op 2-1 tchd 9-4 in a place)
Charlotte Point(USA), who has only finished out of the first three once in her career, was a little keen under her jockey, who tried to wind it up from the front, and could not contain Cumana Bay as she challenged. (op 2-1 tchd 11-4 and 3-1 in places)
Stan's Cool Cat(IRE) showed a modicum of promise on her return at Thirsk but probably did not achieve much in this. The trainer reported before the race that she would not like the ground. (op 12-1)
Spring Adventure was not completely disgraced on her handicap debut after showing a good level of ability in maidens, but disappointed in this after holding every chance. (op 9-2)
Trumpet Lily, who ran in a Listed event last time, loomed up going well but weakened quickly once push came to shove. She has won in easy ground so the big weight must have been enough to stop her. (op 5-1 tchd 4-1)

3401 AGORA APPRENTICE H'CAP 7f
5:05 (5:06) (Class 5) (0-70,69) 4-Y-0+ **£3,885** (£1,156; £577; £288) **Stalls** High

Form RPR
-000 **1** **Violent Velocity (IRE)**[49] 1887 6-8-8 **60**.................... IJBrennan(7) 12 74
(J J Quinn) *hld up: hdwy over 2f out: led over 1f out: rdn and edgd lft ins fnl f: styd on* **3/1**[1]
1415 **2** *3/4* **Convince (USA)**[15] 2880 8-8-7 **55**.................... JackDean(3) 9 67
(K M Prendergast) *hld up: hdwy over 2f out: ev ch over 1f out: sn rdn: unable qck towards fin* **7/1**
3536 **3** *3* **King Of The Moors (USA)**[39] 2166 6-9-0 **64**............(p) LeeNewnes(5) 4 68
(R C Guest) *s.i.s: hdwy to join ldr over 5f out: rdn and ev ch over 1f out: no ex ins fnl f* **8/1**
06-6 **4** *nse* **King's Icon (IRE)**[65] 1475 4-8-0 **52** ow2.................... TobyAtkinson(7) 6 56
(M Wigham) *hld up: hdwy over 1f out: rdn and hung lft ins fnl f: nt rch ldrs* **7/1**
0046 **5** *2 1/2* **Compton's Eleven**[12] 2976 8-9-7 **69**.................... MCGeran(3) 5 66
(M R Channon) *hld up: hdwy u.p over 1f out: wknd ins fnl f* **9/2**[2]
0011 **6** *1 1/4* **Another Try (IRE)**[14] 2920 4-8-12 **62**.................... MatthewDavies(5) 2 56
(A P Jarvis) *chsd ldrs: rdn over 2f out: wknd fnl f* **6/1**[3]
665 **7** *1/2* **Majestic Cheer**[26] 2534 5-8-3 **51** ow1....................(p) WilliamCarson(3) 3 43
(John A Harris) *prom: rdn over 2f out: wknd over 1f out* **33/1**
0520 **8** *shd* **Cavalry Guard (USA)**[14] 2921 5-8-4 **52**....................(b) AmyBaker(3) 8 44
(T D McCarthy) *mid-div: rdn over 2f out: wknd over 1f out* **14/1**
4045 **9** *hd* **Rough Rock (IRE)**[9] 3075 4-8-3 **53**.................... RichardRowe(5) 1 44
(C A Dwyer) *racd alone far side: chsd ldrs: rdn over 1f out: hung rt and wknd fnl f* **16/1**
0006 **10** *1* **Ramblin Bob**[3] 3269 4-8-0 **50** oh4.................... CharlesEddery(5) 13 39
(W J Musson) *prom: rdn over 2 out: n.m.r and wknd over 1f out* **33/1**
5644 **11** *1 1/4* **Tri Chara (IRE)**[92] 975 5-8-11 **63**....................(p) DavidKenny(7) 10 48
(R Hollinshead) *led: rdn: hdd & wknd over 1f out* **14/1**

1m 25.69s (-0.01) **Going Correction** +0.125s/f (Good) **11 Ran SP% 118.7**
Speed ratings (Par 103): **105,104,100,100,97 96,95,95,95,94 92**
toteswingers: 1&2 £5.30, 1&3 £8.80, 2&3 £12.80 CSF £24.40 CT £155.34 TOTE £3.90: £1.70, £1.90, £3.10; EX 27.40 Place 6 £110.50, Place 5 £48.40..
Owner Mrs S Quinn **Bred** Miss Jill Finegan **Trained** Settrington, N Yorks

FOCUS
This had looked a wide-open sprint handicap for apprentices, but a nice gamble was landed. The form looks fair for the grade with the third and fourth to recent marks.
Violent Velocity(IRE) Official explanation: trainer said, regarding apparent improvement in form, that horses in his yard had been out of form.
T/Plt: £40.60 to a £1 stake. Pool: £81,068.01. 1,454.70 winning tickets. T/Qpdt: £10.30 to a £1 stake. Pool: £4,116.44. 294.99 winning tickets. CR

3217 WINDSOR (R-H)
Saturday, June 27

OFFICIAL GOING: Good to firm (8.4)
Wind: Moderate ahead Weather: Sunny

3402 TOTEPLACEPOT MAIDEN STKS (DIV I) 6f
2:00 (2:02) (Class 5) 2-Y-0 **£2,388** (£705; £352) **Stalls** High

Form RPR
5 **1** **Lucky General (IRE)**[16] 2844 2-9-3 0.................... RyanMoore 7 93+
(R Hannon) *mde virtually all: c clr over 1f out: easily* **1/1**[1]
2 *6* **Yarra River** 2-9-3 0.................... LPKeniry 11 73+
(A M Balding) *s.i.s: sn rcvrd and in tch: hdwy over 1f out: chsd wnr ins fnl f but nver any ch: jst hld on for 2nd* **20/1**
4 **3** *shd* **Dubai Set**[5] 3218 2-9-3 0.................... DaneO'Neill 4 73+
(R Hannon) *in rr and detached 1st 2f: hdwy fr 2f out: edgd lft over 1f out and qckd fnl f to dispute 2nd cl home but nvr any ch w easy wnr* **7/1**[3]
4 *2 1/4* **Ghost (IRE)** 2-9-0 0.................... PatrickHills(3) 8 66
(B W Hills) *chsd ldrs: rdn over 2f out: styd on same pce fr over 1f out* **14/1**
5 *nk* **Wellington Fair** 2-9-0 0.................... DavidProbert(3) 2 65
(C G Cox) *pressed wnr and stl upsides 2f out: sn drvn: edgd lft and wknd 1f out* **11/1**
3 **6** *8* **Belinsky (IRE)**[12] 2979 2-9-3 0.................... GeorgeBaker 1 41
(S A Callaghan) *chsd ldrs: rdn over 2f out: wknd qckly 1f out* **7/2**[2]
7 *3/4* **Petite Mambo** 2-8-12 0.................... NicolPolli(5) 10 39
(W De Best-Turner) *in rr and green: mod prog fnl f* **100/1**
8 *1/2* **Argyll** 2-9-3 0.................... ChrisCatlin 9 37
(J Pearce) *s.i.s: rr: mod prog fnl f* **66/1**
9 *1 1/4* **Regal Rave (USA)** 2-9-3 0.................... JimCrowley 6 34
(J R Best) *green: a towards rr* **33/1**
0 **10** *1 3/4* **Rebecca Romero**[28] 2494 2-8-12 0.................... EdwardCreighton 5 23
(D J Coakley) *t.k.h: chsd ldrs: hung lft 2f out and sn wknd* **12/1**
11 *61* **Woodface** 2-9-3 0.................... SteveDrowne 3 —
(B J Meehan) *slowly away: green and sn t.o* **28/1**

1m 12.01s (-0.99) **Going Correction** -0.225s/f (Firm) **11 Ran SP% 121.0**
Speed ratings (Par 93): **97,89,88,85,85 74,73,73,71,69** —
toteswingers: 1&2 £8.60, 1&3 £2.50, 2&3 £71.90 CSF £31.09 TOTE £2.30: £1.10, £4.20, £2.50; EX 35.80 Trifecta £324.20 Part won. Pool: £438.23 - 0.85 winning units..
Owner Mrs J Wood **Bred** K Molloy **Trained** East Everleigh, Wilts

FOCUS
Quite an interesting maiden with several major yards represented but the market spoke strongly in favour of the favourite, who was impressive, although the form will take time to settle.

NOTEBOOK
Lucky General(IRE) ◆ was supported in the betting and that proved fully justified, as he ran out an easy winner. He had shown plenty of promise on his debut at Newbury and - typical of horses from this yard - had clearly improved for the outing. He was always in the firing line nearest the rail and, clear entering the final furlong, he won with a good deal in hand. He is quite well thought-of and will now be aimed at the Goffs Million. (op 5-4)
Yarra River, a 20,000gns half-brother to five winners, is bred to be suited by around a mile and was unfancied on this debut. He chased the leaders throughout and stayed on well in the closing stages to do best of the remainder. He should come on a fair amount for the experience. (op 14-1)
Dubai Set, a stable companion of the winner, was another to put up an eyecatching effort. Despite having previous experience he was outpaced in the early stages but then picked up well in the second half of the race despite having to come to the centre of the track. Although a brother to last year's useful two-year-old sprinter Saxford, he gives the impression he will do better over a little further. (op 13-2 tchd 8-1)

Ghost(IRE), a 52,000gns son of Invincible Spirit, showed a fair amount of ability on this debut despite being keen early on. He will need to settle better in future but should improve for the outing. (op 11-1)
Wellington Fair was a springer in the market and showed why he had been supported. Quickly away from the gates, he disputed the running with the more experienced market leaders until tiring in the last furlong or so. He is out of a juvenile debut winner and can be expected to win a race this season on this evidence. (op 25-1 tchd 33-1 and 10-1)
Belinsky(IRE) was the disappointment of the race, having jumped well and raced up with the leaders from the start. However, he was being ridden at around the quarter-mile pole and dropped away in the last furlong. He has some was to go to justify his 160,000gns purchase price. (op 5-1)
Woodface Official explanation: jockey said colt became upset in the stalls

3403 TOTEPLACEPOT MAIDEN STKS (DIV II) — 6f
2:30 (2:31) (Class 5) 2-Y-O — **£2,388** (£705; £352) **Stalls** High

Form — RPR
1 **Dorback** 2-9-3 0 ... DaneO'Neill 5 — 87+
(H Candy) *s.i.s: t.k.h: hdwy over 2f out: drvn to ld jst ins fnl f: styd on strly* **11/2**[3]
2 *1 ½* **Buzzword** 2-9-0 0 ... AhmedAjtebi(3) 11 — 82
(Saeed Bin Suroor) *led: rdn along ins fnl 2f: hung lft u.p and hdd jst ins fnl f: no ch w wnr fnl 100yds but kpt on for clr 2nd* **6/1**
3 *3 ¼* **San Jemeniano (IRE)** 2-9-3 0 ... SteveDrowne 1 — 72
(P W Chapple-Hyam) *trckd ldrs: chal 2f out: wknd fnl f* **8/1**
4 *2 ¼* **Mr David (USA)** 2-9-3 0 ... PaulEddery 2 — 66
(B J Meehan) *chsd ldrs: chal 3f out tl ins fnl 2f: wknd appr fnl f* **5/2**[2]
4 **5** *2 ½* **Bridge Valley**[19] 2771 2-9-3 0 ... RyanMoore 6 — 58
(R Hannon) *broke wl: sn outpcd: sme prog and hung lft over 2f out: nvr in contention* **15/8**[1]
55 **6** *3 ½* **England (IRE)**[15] 2887 2-9-3 0 ... LukeMorris 7 — 48+
(N P Littmoden) *chsd ldrs: rdn over 2f out: sn btn* **25/1**
7 *½* **Panpiper** 2-9-3 0 ... GeorgeBaker 3 — 46+
(G L Moore) *s.i.s: in rr tl mod late prog* **28/1**
8 *13* **Flaming Miracle** 2-9-3 0 ... LPKeniry 8 — 7
(A M Balding) *s.i.s: sn rcvrd and in tch w main gp after 2f: sn pushed along and wknd* **28/1**
0 **9** *5* **Chill Out Charley**[9] 3072 2-9-0 0 ... DavidProbert(3) 4 — —
(J J Bridger) *chsd ldrs over 3f* **66/1**

1m 12.62s (-0.38) **Going Correction** -0.225s/f (Firm) — **9** Ran SP% **116.4**
Speed ratings (Par 93): **93,91,86,83,80 75,75,57,51**
toteswingers: 1&2 £8.20, 1&3 £5.80, 2&3 £8.50 CSF £36.90 TOTE £6.70: £2.10, £1.90, £2.10; EX 30.30 Trifecta £113.60 Pool: £ 338.46 - 2.53 winning units..
Owner Thurloe Thoroughbreds XXIV **Bred** Winterbeck Manor Stud **Trained** Kingston Warren, Oxon

FOCUS
This second division was run 0.61 secs slower than the first leg. With the favourite being unable to get competitive the race was dominated by newcomers. The form is rated positively with the fifth and sixth the best guides.

NOTEBOOK
Dorback ◆, by Kyllachy, who did so well for this colt's syndicate, out of a mare who won over 5f as a juvenile, he missed the break and then was quite keen in the early stages. However, that did not stop him, as he picked up well to challenge over a furlong out and found enough to see off the long-time leader. He looks a speedy sort and can go on to better things and the plan is to have one more run before taking his chance in the DBS St Leger Sales race at the York Ebor meeting. (op 4-1 tchd 7-2)
Buzzword is by Pivotal but has more stamina on the distaff side. He knew his job on this debut though, bouncing out in front and making the running until he drifted left entering the final furlong and let the winner up the rail. He kept going under pressure and can win a similar contest before long. (op 8-1)
San Jemeniano(IRE), a half-brother to five winners, made a decent debut especially considering he was drawn on the outside of the field. He looked like playing a major role inside the final 2f but his effort flattened out and his rider was not unduly hard on him. That kindness should pay dividends in future. (op 9-1 tchd 10-1)
Mr David(USA), who cost $155,000 at the breeze-ups, was a racecourse tip beforehand. He showed up well until fading in the last furlong and a half and is another who should benefit from the run. (op 15-8)
Bridge Valley, a half-brother to the useful Go Nani Go, had shown promise on his debut and was sent off favourite but was outpaced at around halfway and could never get back into contention. He may be better back on an easier surface. (op 7-2)
England(IRE), tracked the leader for much of the way but was gradually left behind from the halfway point. He is the best guide to the level. (op 22-1)

3404 TOTEPOOL MIDSUMMER STKS (LISTED RACE) — 1m 67y
3:00 (3:01) (Class 1) 3-Y-O+ — **£22,708** (£8,608; £4,308; £2,148; £1,076) **Stalls** High

Form — RPR
3254 **1** **Without A Prayer (IRE)**[22] 2668 4-9-7 105 ... RichardKingscote 6 — 114
(R M Beckett) *trckd wnr over 3f: drvn and outpcd 3f out: styd on wl fr over 1f out: qcknd to ld fnl 75yds: won gng away* **6/1**
1121 **2** *1* **Premio Loco (USA)**[28] 2476 5-9-7 110 ... GeorgeBaker 4 — 112
(C F Wall) *t.k.h: trckd ldrs: wnt 2nd 5f out: drvn to chal fr 2f out: led 1f out: hdd and outpcd fnl 75yds* **7/4**[1]
-360 **3** *1* **Laa Rayb (USA)**[28] 2483 5-9-4 107 ... JimCrowley 7 — 106
(M Johnston) *t.k.h: in tch: hdwy over 3f out: rdn to chal fr 2f out and stl upsides 1f out: outpcd ins fnl f* **9/1**
4216 **4** *nk* **Ordnance Row**[33] 2327 6-9-7 111 ... RyanMoore 3 — 109
(R Hannon) *led: rdn over 2f out: hdd 1f out: ouped ins fnl f* **3/1**[2]
0543 **5** *3* **Charlie Farnsbarns (IRE)**[33] 2327 5-9-9 112 ... DaneO'Neill 5 — 104
(B J Meehan) *stdd s: t.k.h in 5th: rdn and effrt fr 3f out: nvr gng pce to chal: wknd fnl f* **10/3**[3]

1m 42.15s (-2.55) **Going Correction** -0.225s/f (Firm) — **5** Ran SP% **108.7**
Speed ratings (Par 111): **103,102,101,100,97**
toteswingers: 1&2 £5.50 CSF £16.55 TOTE £6.90: £2.50, £1.50; EX 19.40.
Owner McDonagh Murphy And Nixon **Bred** Brownstown Stud **Trained** Whitsbury, Hants

FOCUS
A small field but a very tight Listed race judged on official ratings and four of the five were in line entering the last furlong. the form is a bit muddling but is rated something like face value.

NOTEBOOK
Without A Prayer(IRE), whose only previous turf success was on fast ground, stays further than this and was briefly outpaced when the gallop lifted. He found plenty under pressure and, getting a gap entering the final furlong, proved too strong for his rivals. He will be aimed at a Group 3 in Ireland next month. (op 4-1)
Premio Loco(USA), has a good strike rate but he is better known as a Polytrack performer and his recent win at this level was on good ground. He appeared to have every chance and kept going but could not produce his customary turn of foot in the closing stages. (tchd 13-8 and 2-1)
Laa Rayb(USA) has not been able to maintain last season's progression but this was a fair effort and he kept going well under pressure despite having been keen early. (tchd 10-1)
Ordnance Row won the battle for the early lead but then steadied the pace rounding the loop and stacked his rivals up behind. He picked up the pace from the intersection and was still in front entering the final furlong but was run out of it in the closing stages. (op 5-2)
Charlie Farnsbarns(IRE) was settled at the back and did not have the pace to get involved in the last quarter-mile. He has been racing over further recently and would have preferred a stronger gallop at this trip. (op 11-2)

3405 TOTEQUADPOT HERITAGE H'CAP — 6f
3:35 (3:37) (Class 2) (0-105,104) 3-Y-O+
£28,039 (£8,397; £4,198; £2,101; £1,048; £526) **Stalls** High

Form — RPR
1520 **1** **Tamagin (USA)**[7] 3141 6-9-6 100 ... FergusSweeney 11 — 111
(K A Ryan) *led after 1f: drvn along 2f out: in comand ins fnl f: readily* **8/1**
0-50 **2** *1 ½* **Genki (IRE)**[7] 3141 5-9-1 95 ... SteveDrowne 3 — 101+
(R Charlton) *s.i.s: swtchd rt: towards rr: hdwy over 2f out: str run fr over 1f out to chse wnr ins fnl f: but a hld* **12/1**
0000 **3** *2 ¾* **Matsunosuke**[31] 2385 7-9-5 99 ... LukeMorris 16 — 96
(A B Coogan) *in rr: pushed along 1/2-way: hdwy over 1f out: styd on wl fnl f to take 3rd cl home but nvr any ch w ldng duo* **33/1**
0602 **4** *nse* **Mac Gille Eoin**[21] 2707 5-9-0 94 ... JimCrowley 8 — 91
(J Gallagher) *chsd ldrs: rdn and hung bdly lft appr fnl f: no ch w ldng duo ins fnl f and lost 3rd cl home* **7/1**[3]
-210 **5** *½* **Jimmy Styles**[7] 3141 5-9-8 102 ... RyanMoore 10 — 98
(C G Cox) *trckd ldrs: rdn and hdwy 2f out: styng on whn carried bdly lft over 1f out: nt rcvr* **9/4**[1]
400- **6** *2* **Viking Spirit**[266] 6468 7-9-4 98 ... (t) ChrisCatlin 7 — 87
(W R Swinburn) *towards rr: rdn 1/2-way: sme hdwy over 1f out: styd on ins fnl f but nvr any threat* **40/1**
000- **7** *½* **Kostar**[407] 2172 8-9-1 98 ... DavidProbert(3) 14 — 86
(C G Cox) *led 1f: styd chsng wnr: rdn over 2f out: wknd fnl f* **28/1**
2060 **8** *½* **Hogmaneigh (IRE)**[21] 2704 6-9-8 102 ... SaleemGolam 4 — 88
(S C Williams) *s.i.s: in rr: pushed along over 2f out: mod prog fnl f* **18/1**
0230 **9** *½* **Little Pete (IRE)**[21] 2704 4-8-10 90 ... LPKeniry 15 — 74
(A M Balding) *chsd ldrs: rdn: 2f out: wknd and hung bdly lft over 1f out* **20/1**
6-12 **10** *¾* **Eisteddfod**[59] 1608 8-9-9 103 ... GeorgeBaker 6 — 85
(P F I Cole) *chsd ldrs: rdn over 2f out: wknd appr fnl f* **14/1**
-604 **11** *nk* **Oldjoesaid**[21] 2704 5-9-5 99 ... DaneO'Neill 12 — 80
(H Candy) *s.i.s: in rr: sme hdwy on outside over 2f out: nvr in contention* **6/1**[2]
2021 **12** *1 ½* **Fishforcompliments**[17] 2814 5-9-4 98 ... (p) RichardKingscote 5 — 74
(R A Fahey) *chsd ldrs: rdn and wkng whn crossed over 1f out* **7/1**[3]
2341 **13** *2 ¼* **Judd Street**[13] 2948 7-9-10 104 ... (v) StephenCarson 2 — 73
(Eve Johnson Houghton) *sn in tch: rdn on outside over 2f out: wkng whn crossed over 1f out* **16/1**

1m 10.14s (-2.86) **Going Correction** -0.225s/f (Firm) course record **13** Ran SP% **120.3**
Speed ratings (Par 109): **110,108,104,104,103 100,100,99,98,97 97,95,92**
toteswingers: 1&2 £13.70, 1&3 £138.90, 2&3 £101.90 CSF £96.76 CT £3111.56 TOTE £9.90: £3.00, £3.30, £10.30; EX 127.90 TRIFECTA Not won..
Owner Tariq Al Nisf **Bred** Stonehaven Farm LLC **Trained** Hambleton, N Yorks

FOCUS
A high-class sprint handicap in which three of the last five winners scored off marks in the low-100s and the trend continued with a brave win from the front for Tamagin. The runner-up is better than rated and sets the standard just below his Listed form here.

NOTEBOOK
Tamagin(USA), a genuine front-running gelding, soon took the lead and, sticking towards the rail, never looked likely to be reeled in. This was his tenth success on his 50th start, which is a fine strike rate for a sprint handicapper. He may be give a bit of a break now. (op 7-1)
Genki(IRE), who was so disappointing in the Wokingham the previous weekend, put up a much better performance here. Switched in behind the field, he picked up well to chase the winner in the final furlong and this was more like what he was previously capable of. (op 10-1 tchd 14-1)
Matsunosuke has struggled after his terrific spell of form early in the year but this was something of a revival. Helped by a drop in the handicap, he was held up on the rail from his good draw before making late progress to just snatch third. He is capable of winning decent handicaps off this mark and would be interesting if returned to Sandown, where he has a good record on the 5f track. (op 25-1)
Mac Gille Eoin looked to be returning to form at Epsom last time and ran another good race, showing up throughout but ducking left and doing the favourite no favours at about the furlong marker. He is well suited by a sharp, downhill track and is one to keep in mind for races at Goodwood or Epsom in the near future.
Jimmy Styles was favourite for the Wokingham but was drawn on the wrong side. Sent off favourite again, he appeared to have few excuses this time. He tracked the leaders and was pulled out over 2f out. He appeared to be coming to challenge when the third swerved across his path momentarily and from that point he could not pick up. (op 3-1)
Viking Spirit chased the pace throughout and kept on steadily on this first outing since October and on ground faster than suits ideally. (op 33-1)
Kostar broke well but was unable to lead with the winner in the race. This first start since May 2008 should help blow away the cobwebs , and it will be no surprise to see him aimed at the Great St Wilfrid in August, a race he won in 2007. (op 25-1 tchd 33-1)
Eisteddfod chased the leaders early but is not really at his best on ground this fast. (op 16-1)
Oldjoesaid was held up after a tardy start and was at the back at halfway. He was forced to pull to the outside of his field and could make no impression in the last quarter-mile. (op 11-2 tchd 9-2)
Fishforcompliments had returned to form earlier in the month when the cheekpieces were refitted. Off an 8lb higher mark, he showed up early but faded from the intersection. (op 8-1)
Judd Street was held up from his outside draw and never left the rear division. (tchd 14-1)

3406 TOTEEXACTA H'CAP — 1m 3f 135y
4:05 (4:07) (Class 2) (0-100,97) 3-Y-O+ — **£11,656** (£3,468; £1,733; £865) **Stalls** Low

Form — RPR
20-0 **1** **Warringah**[43] 2055 4-9-8 91 ... RyanMoore 8 — 108+
(Sir Michael Stoute) *mde all: pushed along 3f out: sn in command and in n.d fr over 2f out* **5/4**[1]
00-5 **2** *6* **Magicalmysterytour (IRE)**[42] 2075 6-10-0 97 ... ChrisCatlin 2 — 104
(W J Musson) *chsd wnr thrght: rdn over 3f out and nvr any ch but styd on for clr 2nd fnl 2f* **4/1**[2]
2023 **3** *5* **King Supreme (IRE)**[13] 2945 4-9-1 84 ... (b) DaneO'Neill 5 — 82
(R Hannon) *in rr but in tch: hdwy 4f out: rdn over 3f out and nvr nr wnr: styd on same pce in 3rd fr over 2f out* **9/1**
-650 **4** *4 ½* **Resplendent Light**[21] 2706 4-9-6 89 ... MartinDwyer 4 — 79
(W R Muir) *in rr but in tch: hdwy 5f out: drvn to dispute 2nd over 3f out but nver nr wnr: wknd over 2f out* **4/1**[2]
6230 **5** *5* **Encircled**[24] 2597 5-9-4 87 ... FergusSweeney 7 — 69
(J R Jenkins) *in rr but in tch: rdn 4f out: wknd fr 3f out* **25/1**
1-01 **6** *38* **Maadraa (IRE)**[51] 1815 4-8-9 81 oh3 ... DavidProbert(3) 1 — —
(B J Llewellyn) *chsd ldrs 7f: sn wknd: t.o* **7/1**[3]

2m 24.01s (-5.49) **Going Correction** -0.225s/f (Firm) — **6** Ran SP% **110.8**
Speed ratings (Par 109): **109,105,101,98,95 70**
toteswingers: 1&2 £1.60, 1&3 £2.90, 2&3 £3.80 CSF £6.30 CT £27.28 TOTE £2.10: £1.40, £2.50; EX 8.10 Trifecta £61.80 Pool: £432.66 - 5.18 winning units..
Owner Philip Newton **Bred** Philip Newton **Trained** Newmarket, Suffolk

FOCUS
A good handicap but most of the field had something to prove. In the end they finished well strung out. The winner should do better although there are doubts over the form.

NOTEBOOK
Warringah stays really well and Moore negated the possibility of a falsely run race by setting off in front at an even gallop. As expected, the further the horse went the stronger he became and in the end he scored going away. This should help boost his confidence for stiffer tasks in the future, with the Ebor a possible target. (op 6-4)

Magicalmysterytour(IRE) has won on fast but his best form has been on softer going. He ran creditably on his second start of the season and is one to bear in mind, especially if racing on flat track. The Old Newton Cup early next moth could be a feasible target. (op 6-1 tchd 7-1)

King Supreme(IRE) is a fairly decent performer at a lower level but this step up in grade proved too much for him, although he was staying on in the closing stages. (op 6-1 tchd 10-1 place)

Resplendent Light beat the winner in a close finish for last season's Bibury Cup and was only a pound worse off. He came through to challenge over 2f out but paid the penalty for his efforts in the last furlong or so. He is struggling to recapture his form but the Handicapper is gradually easing him down the ratings. (tchd 7-2 and 9-2)

Encircled was always out the back and did not help herself by racing keenly early. (op 20-1)

Maadraa(IRE) came into this in form but was racing from out of the handicap on this big step up in grade and was the first beaten. Official explanation: jockey said gelding lost a front shoe and never travelled (op 6-1)

3407 TOTETRIFECTA H'CAP — 6f
4:40 (4:41) (Class 5) (0-70,70) 3-Y-O+ — **£2,729** (£806; £403) **Stalls** High

Form				RPR
402	**1**		**C'Mon You Irons (IRE)**[14] 2920 4-9-8 **64** .... JimCrowley 16 (M R Hoad) *mde all: hrd drvn fr 2f out: styd on wl thrght fnl f* **9/2**[2]	76
5000	**2**	*1 ½*	**Dvinsky (USA)**[10] 3030 8-9-11 **67** .... (b) PaulDoe 9 (P Howling) *chsd ldrs: wnt 2nd over 3f out: styd on u.p but no imp on wnr fnl 2f: hld on wl for 2nd cl home* **9/1**	74
4200	**3**	*nk*	**Make My Dream**[23] 2637 6-9-7 **68** .... Louis-PhilippeBeuzelin(5) 14 (J Gallagher) *chsd ldrs: rdn 3f out and sn outpcd: styd on again u.p fr over 1f out and clsd on 2nd cl home but no ch w wnr* **14/1**	74
0030	**4**	*3 ¾*	**Gold Express**[7] 3164 6-9-12 **68** .... SaleemGolam 10 (P J O'Gorman) *chsd ldrs: rdn 1/2-way: wknd appr fnl f* **11/2**[3]	62
-000	**5**	*2 ¾*	**Shakespeare's Son**[15] 2880 4-9-6 **62** .... GeorgeBaker 12 (H J Evans) *chsd ldrs: rdn 1/2-way: wknd over 1f out* **9/2**[2]	47
4303	**6**	*1 ¾*	**Gwilym (GER)**[9] 3057 6-9-9 **65** .... DaneO'Neill 7 (D Haydn Jones) *sn chsng ldrs: rdn 1/2-way: wknd ins fnl 2f* **15/2**	45
00-0	**7**	*½*	**Inspainagain (USA)**[53] 1776 5-9-7 **66** .... RussellKennemore(3) 6 (Paul Mason) *in rr: rdn over 3f out: mod prog 2f out: wknd sn after* **50/1**	44
4434	**8**	*2 ¼*	**Sam's Cross (IRE)**[19] 2769 4-9-12 **68** .... PaulEddery 15 (Pat Eddery) *t.k.h: chsd ldrs over 3f* **4/1**[1]	39
-524	**9**	*1 ¾*	**Rhapsilian**[14] 2920 5-8-13 **55** .... (v) StephenCarson 13 (J A Geake) *s.i.s: sn rcvrd to chse ldrs: wknd fr 1/2-way* **8/1**	20
0-00	**10**	*1*	**Boldinor**[32] 2353 6-8-9 **51** oh1 .... FergusSweeney 5 (M R Bosley) *in rr: sme hdwy on outside 3f out: nvr on terms: sn hung rt and wknd* **33/1**	13
220-	**11**	*5*	**Bountiful Bay**[209] 7508 4-8-13 **55** .... (t) LPKeniry 8 (M Salaman) *plld hrd in rr: sn outpcd* **25/1**	—

1m 12.12s (-0.88) **Going Correction** -0.225s/f (Firm)
WFA 3 from 4yo+ 7lb — **11** Ran SP% **120.0**
Speed ratings (Par 103): **96,94,93,88,84 82,81,78,76,75 68**
toteswingers: 1&2 £8.30, 1&3 £11.40, 2&3 £16.70 CSF £45.00 CT £544.82 TOTE £5.40: £1.90, £3.50, £3.80; EX 64.50 Trifecta £489.10 Part won. Pool: £660..96 - 0.85 winning units..
Owner double-r-racing.com **Bred** Airlie Stud **Trained** Lewes, E Sussex

FOCUS
Several absentees, including those drawn in the lowest four stalls, reduced the field for this ordinary handicap. The time was nearly 2 secs slower than the heritage handicap. The winner is rated to his winter form with the runner-up close to his turf mark.
Rhapsilian Official explanation: jockey said mare ran too freely

3408 BET TOTEPOOL AT TOTESPORT.COM FILLIES' H'CAP — 1m 67y
5:10 (5:13) (Class 5) (0-75,75) 3-Y-O+ — **£3,070** (£906; £453) **Stalls** High

Form				RPR
3603	**1**		**Flying Valentino**[14] 2916 5-9-12 **72** .... SteveDrowne 11 (Ian Williams) *trckd ldr after 2f: drvn to ld ins fnl 2f: styd on strly* **14/1**	83
521	**2**	*2 ¾*	**Candy Ride (IRE)**[16] 2856 3-9-5 **75** .... RyanMoore 9 (E A L Dunlop) *chsd ldrs: rdn along 3f out: styd on to chse wnr over 1f out but a readily hld* **15/8**[1]	77
34-3	**3**	*½*	**Sterling Sound (USA)**[51] 1808 3-9-3 **73** .... DaneO'Neill 1 (M P Tregoning) *hld up towards rr: hdwy over 3f out: styd on towards outside and disp 2nd fr 2f out: nvr any ch w wnr: no ex ins fnl f* **4/1**[3]	74
4001	**4**	*1 ¼*	**Very Well Red**[14] 2910 6-9-11 **71** .... TolleyDean 2 (P W Hiatt) *led: rdn 3f out: hdd ins fnl 2f: wknd appr fnl f* **14/1**	71
054	**5**	*nk*	**Kindest**[16] 2856 3-9-2 **72** .... GeorgeBaker 4 (C F Wall) *chsd ldrs: rdn 3f out: hung lft 2f out and sn wknd* **3/1**[2]	69
0033	**6**	*2*	**Hallingdal (UAE)**[12] 2977 4-9-9 **69** .... NeilChalmers 6 (J J Bridger) *rdn over 3f out: a towards rr* **13/2**	64
2016	**7**	*1 ½*	**Tikka Masala (IRE)**[14] 2910 3-8-13 **74** .... (t) RossAtkinson(5) 10 (Tom Dascombe) *awkward out of stalls: t.k.h: a towards rr* **10/1**	63

1m 42.52s (-2.18) **Going Correction** -0.225s/f (Firm)
WFA 3 from 4yo+ 10lb — **7** Ran SP% **115.5**
Speed ratings (Par 100): **101,98,97,96,96 94,92**
toteswingers: 1&2 £5.50, 1&3 £9.50, 2&3 £2.20 CSF £41.62 CT £130.25 TOTE £16.50: £5.40, £1.60; EX 51.20 Trifecta £234.10 Place 6: £288.64, Place 5: £187.60. Pool: £490.52 - 1.55 winning units..
Owner UK Distribution Personnel Ltd **Bred** Helshaw Grange Stud Ltd **Trained** Portway, Worcs

FOCUS
An ordinary fillies' handicap featuring a couple of potentially progressive sorts, but it fell to one of the more established performers. The form looks sound with the race rated around the runner-up and fifth.

T/Plt: £253.70 to a £1 stake. Pool: £69,814.08. 200.85 winning tickets. T/Qpdt: £81.70 to a £1 stake. Pool: £4,785.25. 43.30 winning tickets. ST

3409 - 3411a (Foreign Racing) - See Raceform Interactive

3363 CURRAGH (R-H)
Saturday, June 27

OFFICIAL GOING: Yielding

3412a AUDI PRETTY POLLY STKS (GROUP 1) — 1m 2f
3:40 (3:42) 3-Y-O+
£131,067 (£41,504; £19,660; £6,553; £4,368; £2,184)

			RPR
1		**Dar Re Mi**[44] 2013 4-9-9 .... JimmyFortune 4 (J H M Gosden) *mde all: rdn and chal under 2f out: jnd ins fnl f: drifted sltly rt: kpt on wl and all out* **9/2**[3]	110
2	*shd*	**Beach Bunny (IRE)**[35] 2285 4-9-9 105 .... CDHayes 7 (Kevin Prendergast, Ire) *chsd ldrs in 3rd: rdn to chal under 2f out: jnd ldr ins fnl f: kpt on wl: jst failed* **25/1**	110
3	*1*	**Look Here**[22] 2670 4-9-9 .... SebSanders 6 (R M Beckett) *settled bhd ldrs in 5th: rdn over 2f out: styd on to 3rd ins fnl f: kpt on cl home* **11/8**[1]	108+
4	*1 ¼*	**Lush Lashes**[10] 3012 4-9-9 115 .... KJManning 2 (J S Bolger, Ire) *chsd ldrs in 4th: rdn over 2f out: styd on to 3rd 1f out: no imp on ldrs: kpt on same pce fnl f* **6/1**	106
5	*1 ¼*	**Katiyra (IRE)**[265] 6521 4-9-9 114 .... MJKinane 1 (John M Oxx, Ire) *chsd ldr in 2nd: rdn in 3rd under 2f out: no ex in 4th 1f out: kpt on same pce* **5/2**[2]	103
6	*3*	**Roman Empress (IRE)**[8] 3134 3-8-11 84 .... JMurtagh 3 (A P O'Brien, Ire) *hld up in 6th: rdn and dropped to rr 3f out: no imp* **16/1**	97
7	*1 ¾*	**Jakarta Jazz (IRE)**[13] 2960 3-8-11 96 .... DPMcDonogh 5 (Kevin Prendergast, Ire) *hld up in rr: rdn into 6th 3f out: sn no imp* **50/1**	94

2m 14.0s (4.50) **Going Correction** +0.55s/f (Yiel)
WFA 3 from 4yo 12lb — **7** Ran SP% **114.8**
Speed ratings: **104,103,103,102,101 98,97**
CSF £89.78 TOTE £6.00: £2.70, £5.00; DF 49.50.
Owner Lord Lloyd-Webber **Bred** Watership Down Stud **Trained** Newmarket, Suffolk

FOCUS
There was a lengthy stewards' inquiry. The time was slower than for the maiden. The winner is rated in line with her recent figures.

NOTEBOOK
Dar Re Mi gained a deserved Pattern race success under a fine tactical ride from Fortune. He allowed his mount to dictate things at her own pace. She didn't go mad in front by any means, a tactic chosen to presumably inconvenience the favourite, and it worked to perfection. The rider gradually wound the pace up and brought them towards the centre of the track in the straight. She showed her toughness as she beat off the surprisingly persistent challenge of the runner-up, however, she did continuously lean to her right inside the final furlong, into the runner-up and there was a real question of intimidation. She survived the inevitable stewards' inquiry, but looked somewhat fortunate to do so. (op 7/2)

Beach Bunny(IRE) ran the race of her life, of that there is no doubt. Off the mudding enough pace, she sat very handily and moved up to lay down a challenge to the winner from the two-furlong pole and sustained her challenge all the way to the line. The more imposing winner was leaning into her inside the final furlong and, with a short head in it on the line, it is difficult to accept that the result was not affected.

Look Here ran well enough considering the way the race was run almost certainly failed to play to the strengths of a filly that stays 1m4f very well. She settled behind the leaders, but it took her time to get into her stride once the pace quickened. Predictably, she was doing her best work at the finish but all too late and a return to 12f for the King George or Yorkshire Oaks now looks in the cards. (op 6/4 tchd 5/4)

Lush Lashes did not run as abjectly as she did at Ascot, but in three runs this season she has not shown very many traces of the level of form which saw her win three Group 1s last season and be robbed of a fourth. The ground might have been somewhat softer than she liked but she was unable to quicken when asked two furlongs out and could only keep on at one pace. (op 6/1 tchd 13/2)

Katiyra(IRE) has been found wanting on her forays into Group 1 company in the past and this proved the same, but it was obviously her return to action. She tracked the winner into the straight but once that filly quickened the pace she had no answers. (op 11/4)

3413a AT THE RACES CURRAGH CUP (GROUP 3) — 1m 6f
4:15 (4:16) 3-Y-O+ — **£42,135** (£12,912; £6,116; £2,038; £1,359)

			RPR
1		**Profound Beauty (IRE)**[235] 7188 5-9-8 108 .... PJSmullen 3 (D K Weld, Ire) *settled bhd ldrs in 4th: hdwy in 3rd 3f out: chal 1 1/2f out: rdn to ld 1f out: kpt on wl u.p fnl f* **5/1**	109+
2	*nk*	**Alandi (IRE)**[30] 2425 4-9-11 106 .... MJKinane 4 (John M Oxx, Ire) *chsd ldrs: mainly 3rd: rdn in 4th 3f out: prog whn short of room 1 1/2f out: rdn in 3rd and no imp 1f out: r.o wl cl home to go 2nd* **9/4**[2]	112+
3	*hd*	**Yankee Doodle**[8] 3090 3-8-11 103 ow1 .... JMurtagh 2 (A P O'Brien, Ire) *sn chsd ldr in 2nd: rdn to ld 3f out: chal and drifted lft u.p 1 1/2f out: hdd 1f out: kpt on: no ex cl home* **7/2**[3]	115
4	*4 ½*	**Suailce (IRE)**[30] 2425 4-9-8 98 .... (b) PShanahan 1 (D K Weld, Ire) *hld up in rr: rdn 3f out: no imp over 2f out: kpt on one pce* **18/1**	102
5	*21*	**Mad Rush (USA)**[22] 2677 5-9-11 .... JimmyFortune 5 (L M Cumani) *led: rdn and hdd 3f out: no ex in 2nd 2f out: sn wknd* **7/4**[1]	76

3m 3.35s (-1.35) **Going Correction** +0.25s/f (Good)
WFA 3 from 4yo+ 17lb — **5** Ran SP% **111.3**
Speed ratings: **113,112,112,110,98**
CSF £16.74 TOTE £4.90: £1.90, £1.50; DF 21.40.
Owner Moyglare Stud Farm **Bred** Moyglare Stud Farms **Trained** The Curragh, Co Kildare
■ Stewards' Enquiry : J Murtagh one-day ban: careless riding (Jul 11)

NOTEBOOK
Profound Beauty(IRE) put up close to a career-best performance to win this considering that she was ring-rusty and it did show inside the last. Settled just off the pace and travelling sweetly the whole way, she moved up to challenge a furlong out and ran on well to get the better of the eventual third after a reasonable scrap. She did just get a bit tired close home. The Melbourne Cup is going to be the end of season target once more, although the Irish St Leger looks a natural target for her as well. (op 4/1)

Alandi(IRE) did not get a clear run and was a bit of an unlucky loser. Racing close to the pace, he was tapped for a bit of tactical speed early in the straight, but was running on again when squeezed up between the front two. The interference was caused by the eventual third coming off a straight line. He finished well and would probably have got up in another stride, but he would be hard pressed to get as close to the winner if and when they meet again with race fitness on the side of the winner. (op 9/4 tchd 5/2)

Yankee Doodle, the Queen's Vase second, is an improving colt and might well develop into a Doncaster or Curragh St Leger horse. Tracking the leader and favourite, he moved upsides and attempted to go for his race early in the straight, but the winner had that move covered. Despite his wanderings under pressure, he ran on again late in the day and looks well capable of winning a good contest at this sort of trip. (op 9/2 tchd 5/1)
Mad Rush(USA) has form on this sort of ground, but ran no race. He attempted to make all but dropped away quickly once he was challenged and headed in the straight. He was later reported to be lame. Official explanation: vet said gelding was lame on his right-fore post race (op 7/4 tchd 13/8)

3414 - 3415a (Foreign Racing) - See Raceform Interactive

HAMBURG (R-H)
Saturday, June 27

OFFICIAL GOING: Good

3416a HAMBURGER MEILE FRANZ-GUNTHER VON GAERTNER RENNEN (GROUP 3) 1m
4:20 (4:35) 4-Y-0+ **£31,068** (£9,709; £4,854; £2,913)

RPR
1 **Earl Of Fire (GER)**41 2113 4-9-4 .... DBoeuf 4 113
(W Baltromei, Germany) *mde all: set str pce: hld on gamely whn strly pressed clsng stages* **115/10**
2 *shd* **Sehrezad (IRE)**272 6322 4-9-2 .... JiriPalik 2 111
(Andreas Lowe, Germany) *racd in 3rd: wnt 2nd over 2f out: n.m.r on ins and swtchd lft over 1f out: styd on wl fnl f: jst failed* **166/10**
3 *1 ½* **Liang Kay (GER)**41 2113 4-9-4 .... THellier 6 110
(Uwe Ostmann, Germany) *racd in 8th: hdwy under 2f out: tk 3rd ins fnl f: nt rch front two* **11/10**1
4 *¾* **Forthe Millionkiss (GER)**39 5-9-2 .... WMongil 10 106
(Uwe Ostmann, Germany) *racd in 4th: rdn 1 1/2f out: kpt on* **22/1**
5 *½* **Iolith (GER)**52 4-9-2 .... FilipMinarik 5 105
(J Hirschberger, Germany) *racd in 2nd: rdn and one pce fnl 1 1/2f* **33/1**
6 *nse* **Querari (GER)**69 1395 3-8-10 .... EPedroza 9 109
(A Wohler, Germany) *racd in 6th: kpt on at same pce fnl 2f* **106/10**
7 *1 ¾* **Walzertraum (USA)**267 6461 4-9-2 .... ADeVries 3 101
(J Hirschberger, Germany) *hld up in 9th: nvr able to chal* **71/10**3
8 *4* **Aspectus (IRE)**41 2113 6-9-6 .... AStarke 8 95
(T Mundry, Germany) *hld up in last: nvr nr ldrs* **16/5**2
9 *2* **Konig Concorde (GER)**272 6322 4-9-2 .... ASuborics 12 87
(C Sprengel, Germany) *a in rr* **89/10**
10 *1 ½* **Assahab (GER)**643 6-9-4 .... EFrank 7 85
(U Stech, Germany) *a in rr* **33/1**
11 *4* **Mharadono (GER)**62 6-9-2 .... NRichter 1 74
(P Hirschberger, Germany) *racd in 5th on outside: outpcd fnl 2f* **39/1**
12 *1 ½* **Smart Enough**25 2587 6-9-2 .... RSchistl 11 71
(F Reuterskiold, Sweden) *plld hrd on outside: 7th 1/2-way: wknd under 2f out* **38/1**

1m 34.55s (94.55)
WFA 3 from 4yo+ 10lb **12 Ran SP% 131.5**
(including 10 Euro stake): WIN 125; PL 23, 34, 13; SF 2264.
Owner Frau M Haller **Bred** Frau M Haller **Trained** Germany

NANTES (R-H)
Saturday, June 27

OFFICIAL GOING: Soft

3417a PRIX DES CHEVALIERS BRETVINS (PRIX DE THOUARE) 1m
1:00 (12:59) 3-Y-0 **£12,136** (£4,854; £3,641; £2,427; £1,214)

RPR
1 **Easterland (IRE)**18 3-9-4 .... GMosse 1 91
(A De Royer-Dupre, France)
2 *1* **Chorale D'Anges (FR)**58 3-9-1 .... LHuart 3 86
(M Houdoin, France)
3 *¾* **Emily Blackwell**82 3-9-1 .... JAuge 5 84
(H-A Pantall, France)
4 *1* **Dame Anouska (IRE)**66 1451 3-8-8 .... J-BEyquem 8 75
(E J O'Neill) *racd in 4th on outside: niggled along bef 1/2-way: reminder under 4f out: hrd rdn in 5th over 1 1/2f out: kpt on down outside (10/1)* **10/1**1
5 *hd* **Raise A Mind (IRE)** 3-8-11 .... FVeron 7 78
(H-A Pantall, France)
6 *¾* **Don Salsa (FR)** 3-8-11 .... ARoussel 2 76
(C Diard, France)
7 *2* **Glimmer** 3-8-8 .... IMendizabal 6 68
(H-A Pantall, France)
8 *5* **Crystal Merit (FR)**44 3-9-1 .... NEven 4 64
(R Lecomte, France)

1m 39.78s (99.78) **8 Ran SP% 9.1**
PARI-MUTUEL (including 1 Euro stake): WIN 2.10; PL 1.10, 1.60, 1.30; DF 7.60.
Owner A Fontaine **Bred** Mlle M Bliard **Trained** Chantilly, France

NOTEBOOK
Dame Anouska(IRE), who had been runner-up on fast ground on her debut in April, never looked entirely happy on this soft ground but did stick to her task under pressure.

3419a GRAND PRIX ANJOU BRETAGNE - PRIX CENTENAIRE DU SYNDICAT DES PROPRIETAIRES (LISTED RACE) 1m
3:25 (3:24) 4-Y-0+ **£25,243** (£10,097; £7,573; £5,049; £2,524)

RPR
1 **Prince Fasliyev**39 5-9-4 .... FVeron 6 101
(H-A Pantall, France)
2 *¾* **Slickly Royal (FR)**13 5-8-10 .... IMendizabal 8 91
(P Demercastel, France)
3 *1 ½* **Unquenchable Fire (IRE)**51 4-8-10 .... DBonilla 5 88
(C Ferland, France)
4 *¾* **Barricado (FR)**10 3045 4-8-10 .... J-BEyquem 4 86
(E J O'Neill) *disp 3rd on outside: hrd rdn and sltly outpcd 1 1/2f out: kpt on while edging lft ins fnl f (13/1)*
5 *½* **Rockette (FR)**22 4-8-7 .... CSoumillon 2 82
(Y De Nicolay, France)
6 *snk* **Silky Steps (IRE)**32 4-8-7 .... JAuge 3 81
(H-A Pantall, France)
7 *¾* **Spanish Moss (IRE)**23 8-8-10 .... (b) WWalter 1 83
(A Dupont, France)
8 *1 ½* **Satchmo Bay (FR)**13 8-8-10 .... MickaelForest 7 79
(C Boutin, France)

1m 38.84s (98.84) **8 Ran**
PARI-MUTUEL: WIN 4.30; PL 1.70, 1.70, 1.90; DF 10.60.
Owner P-H Lassen **Bred** Theakston Stud **Trained** France

NOTEBOOK
Barricado(FR) has handled soft ground in the past although his sole win came on fast ground. He was never far away and kept on without having the necessary pace.

3418 - 3419a (Foreign Racing) - See Raceform Interactive

3276 SALISBURY (R-H)
Sunday, June 28

OFFICIAL GOING: Good (good to firm in places; 8.6)
The rails on the far side of the straight course were out 16 feet for the last six and half furlongs.
Wind: Virtually nil Weather: Sunny and very warm

3420 EBF BLAGRAVE MAIDEN STKS (C&G) 6f 212y
2:00 (2:00) (Class 4) 2-Y-0 **£4,695** (£1,397; £698; £348) **Stalls High**

Form RPR
6 1 **Lord Zenith**17 2844 2-9-0 0 .... WilliamBuick 5 89+
(A M Balding) *travelled wl bhd ldrs: led on bit wl over 1f out: rdn clr fnl f* **4/7**1
2 *6* **Cafe Greco** 2-9-0 0 .... FergusSweeney 6 73
(P J Makin) *trckd ldrs: rdn to ld 2f out: sn hdd and lost 2nd: kpt on same pce to regain 2nd nr fin* **40/1**
3 *hd* **Kensei (IRE)** 2-9-0 0 .... SebSanders 1 73
(R M Beckett) *hld up in tch: rdn and stdy prog fr over 2f out: chsd wnr jst over 1f out: no ex whn lost 2nd nr fin* **12/1**3
03 4 *2 ½* **Fire And Stone (IRE)**6 3218 2-9-0 0 .... RichardKingscote 2 66
(Tom Dascombe) *trckd ldr: rdn 3f out: one pce fnl 2f* **12/1**3
5 *shd* **Kajima** 2-9-0 0 .... JimmyFortune 4 66+
(R Hannon) *s.i.s: hld up in tch: rdn over 2f out: sn one pce* **7/2**2
6 *nk* **Sea Dubai** 2-9-0 0 .... JimmyQuinn 7 65
(R Hannon) *s.i.s: swtchd lft 2f out: sn rdn: kpt on same pce* **14/1**
5 7 *7* **Rainsborough**23 2676 2-9-0 0 .... TPO'Shea 9 47
(M R Channon) *led tl 2f out: wkng whn short of room on rails sn after* **50/1**

1m 27.72s (-1.28) **Going Correction** -0.15s/f (Firm) **7 Ran SP% 112.3**
Speed ratings (Par 95): **101,94,93,91,90 90,82**
toteswingers: 1&2 £13.00, 1&3 £3.00, 2&3 £37.10. CSF £29.05 TOTE £1.70: £1.50, £10.70; EX 36.60.
Owner Mrs M E Wates **Bred** Langton Stud And G E M Wates **Trained** Kingsclere, Hants

FOCUS
This is often a decent juvenile maiden and Lord Zenith looks another well above-average winner, although the standard is fluid.

NOTEBOOK
Lord Zenith ◆ looks well above-average. It remains to be seen exactly what he beat but he was most impressive and confirmed the good impression he made in a hot race at Newbury first time up. After travelling best of all, he took a few strides to really get going when first coming under pressure, but ultimately powered clear and looked better the further he went. Understandably he'll now be stepped up in grade, with the Superlative Stakes at the Newmarket July meeting his most likely target, and he must go there with a big chance. Andrew Balding, who reported that the colt wouldn't want extremes of going, intends to keep him to 7f until the Tattersalls Timeform Million sales race in October, but he should stay 1m without a bother. (op 8-11 tchd 4-5 in places)
Cafe Greco, the first foal of 1m-1m2f winner, had no chance with the winner but fared best of the newcomers. He clearly has ability and is open to improvement. (op 33-1)
Kensei(IRE), a 65,000euros purchase who is closely related to, among others, multiple 5f-1m winner Living Symbol, looked the main threat to the winner around two furlongs out, having recovered from going slightly left on leaving the stalls, but he couldn't sustain his effort and weakened late on. He should come on a good deal for the run. (op 10-1 tchd 9-1)
Fire And Stone(IRE) came under pressure a fair way out and failed to make progress. Nurseries will now be an option. (op 13-2)
Kajima ◆, an 82,000gns half-brother to French 7.5f winner Bestofthem, didn't enjoy the clearest of runs through, but was basically just very green. There should be much better to come. (op 9-2)
Sea Dubai, a 23,000gns half-brother to, among others, dual 7f-1m winner Arabian Spirit, was extremely green and raced in a detached last early on, before making some late progress. (tchd 16-1)

3421 BRIAN AMY 60TH BIRTHDAY H'CAP 1m 1f 198y
2:35 (2:37) (Class 5) (0-70,69) 4-Y-0+ **£3,238** (£963; £481; £240) **Stalls High**

Form RPR
00-2 1 **Merrymadcap (IRE)**9 3104 7-9-4 66 .... WilliamBuick 4 74
(M Salaman) *trckd ldr: led 2f out: sn rdn and edgd rt: styd on: hld on wl: drvn out* **9/1**3
4-60 2 *1* **Seventh Cavalry (IRE)**17 2851 4-8-13 61 .... JimmyFortune 1 67
(A King) *hld up: puched along and stdy hdwy fr 3f out: rdn to chse wnr fr wl over 1f out: styd on but a being hld* **14/1**
6001 3 *5* **Surprise Pension (IRE)**34 2332 5-8-5 58 .... JamieKyne(5) 9 54
(J J Quinn) *trckd ldrs: rdn over 2f out: styd on same pce* **5/2**1
1012 4 *¾* **Cossack Prince**34 2331 4-9-7 69 .... IanMongan 11 64
(Mrs L J Mongan) *led: rdn and hdd over 2f out: sn swtchd lft: styd on same pce* **5/2**1
4002 5 *nk* **Artreju (GER)**17 2851 6-8-11 59 .... (p) FergusSweeney 6 53
(G L Moore) *mid-div: rdn and hdwy 2f out: one pce fnl f* **9/1**3
3053 6 *4 ½* **Seventh Hill**16 2878 4-8-10 58 .... JimmyQuinn 5 43
(M Blanshard) *mid-div tl dropped to rr over 5f out: reminders: nvr bk on terms* **8/1**2
0-00 7 *8* **Hey Presto**18 2824 9-7-9 50 oh5 .... (b) RichardRowe(7) 7 19
(R Rowe) *mid-div: nudged along fr over 5f out: btn 3f out* **66/1**
4600 8 *7* **Upstairs**38 2202 5-8-6 54 .... ChrisCatlin 2 9
(P Henderson) *a towards rr* **50/1**
00-0 9 *hd* **Fantastic Morning**13 2983 5-8-12 60 .... (b) SebSanders 10 15
(F Jordan) *trckd ldrs: rdn over 2f out: sn wknd* **33/1**

2m 7.44s (-2.46) **Going Correction** -0.15s/f (Firm) **9 Ran SP% 101.3**
Speed ratings (Par 103): **103,102,98,97,97 93,87,81,81**
toteswingers: 1&2 £7.10, 1&3 £2.40, 2&3 £6.40. CSF £94.51 CT £286.85 TOTE £7.70: £3.40, £3.40, £1.40; EX 62.70.
Owner Mrs N L Young **Bred** Wickfield Farm Partnership **Trained** Upper Lambourn, Berks

FOCUS
A modest handicap run at a strong pace.

3422 K J PIKE & SONS LTD SENIORS' SPRINT H'CAP 5f
3:05 (3:07) (Class 4) (0-80,80) 6-Y-0+ **£6,476** (£1,927; £963; £481) **Stalls** High

Form RPR
436 **1** **Misaro (GER)**15 2911 8-9-0 **76**....(b) DavidProbert(3) 12 88
(R A Harris) *a.p: rdn to ld over 1f out: r.o wl* **6/1**2
2035 **2** *2* **Bahamian Ballet**17 2840 7-8-12 **71**.... StephenDonohoe 3 76
(E S McMahon) *in tch: rdn 3f out: styng on whn swtchd lft over 1f out: wnt 2nd ins fnl f but nvr gng to catch wnr* **9/2**1
4201 **3** *1 1/4* **Brandywell Boy (IRE)**5 3252 6-8-5 **64** 6ex.... RichardThomas 2 65
(D J S Ffrench Davis) *mid-div: hdwy over 2f out: sn rdn: kpt on fnl f* **9/1**
0004 **4** *1/2* **Fantasy Believer**15 2929 11-8-5 **64**.... JimmyQuinn 9 63
(J J Quinn) *mid-div: rdn and hdwy 2f out: kpt on same pce fnl f* **9/2**1
5543 **5** *3/4* **Fromsong (IRE)**31 2397 11-8-4 **68**.... JamieKyne(5) 10 64
(D K Ivory) *trckd ldrs: rdn over 2f out: nt pce to mount chal: short of room ent fnl f: kpt on cl home* **9/1**
-01 **6** *shd* **For Life (IRE)**31 2396 7-8-11 **73**.... NataliaGemelova(3) 4 72+
(J E Long) *taken down early: trckd ldrs: rdn to chal over 2f out: fdd fnl f* **10/1**
0120 **7** *nk* **Desperate Dan**15 2911 8-9-2 **75**....(v) SebSanders 1 70
(A B Haynes) *wnt lft s: towards rr: rdn over 2f out: nvr pce to get on terms* **10/1**
5326 **8** *1* **Forest Dane**26 2564 9-8-9 **68**.... RichardKingscote 7 59
(Mrs N Smith) *s.i.s: bhd: sme late prog: nvr a threat* **15/2**3
-000 **9** *hd* **Blessed Place**19 2799 9-8-3 **62** oh3 ow1....(t) ChrisCatlin 11 52
(D J S Ffrench Davis) *led: rdn whn hdd over 1f out: hld whn short of room ins fnl f* **28/1**
0310 **10** *3/4* **Bold Argument (IRE)**24 2637 6-8-8 **70** ow1.... JackMitchell(3) 5 58
(Mrs P N Dutfield) *a towards rr* **8/1**
0535 **11** *1 1/4* **First Order**6 3212 8-9-2 **80**....(v) AnnStokell(5) 8 63
(Miss A Stokell) *t.k.h in midfield: rdn over 2f out: wknd over 1f out* **12/1**
4-00 **12** *3* **Malapropism**5 3246 9-8-3 **62**....(v) TPO'Shea 6 34
(M R Channon) *sn pushed along: nvr bttr than mid-div* **25/1**
59.90 secs (-1.10) **Going Correction** -0.15s/f (Firm) **12** Ran SP% **126.7**
Speed ratings: **102,98,96,96,94 94,94,92,92,91 89,84**
toteswingers: 1&2 £14.10, 1&3 £12.70, 2&3 £12.40. CSF £35.62 CT £256.66 TOTE £6.00: £2.40, £2.30, £3.60; EX 52.60.
Owner Messrs Criddle Davies Dawson & Villa **Bred** Wilhelm Fasching **Trained** Earlswood, Monmouths

FOCUS
A handicap for six-year-olds and above and, rather surprisingly, the first two finishers from last year's race filled the same positions once again.
Fromsong(IRE) Official explanation: jockey said gelding was denied a clear run
First Order Official explanation: jockey said race came too soon for the gelding

3423 H S LESTER MEMORIAL H'CAP 1m 6f 21y
3:35 (3:36) (Class 4) (0-85,82) 4-Y-0+ **£4,857** (£1,445; £722; £360) **Stalls** Far side

Form RPR
-050 **1** **Sam Lord**15 2931 5-9-3 **78**.... FergusSweeney 6 88
(A King) *hld up: hdwy 3f out: sn rdn: chalng u.str.p whn bmpd over 1f out: led fnl 75yds: drvn clr* **11/4**2
6-15 **2** *2 1/2* **Colonel Flay**15 2931 5-8-8 **72** ow1.... JackMitchell(3) 8 79
(Mrs P N Dutfield) *travelled wl in last: smooth hdwy to join ldrs over 2f out: tk narrow advantage whn bmpd over 1f out: nt qckn whn rdn ent fnl f: hdd fnl 75yds: no ex* **6/4**1
0-30 **3** *3* **Look To This Day**39 2177 4-8-12 **73**.... WilliamBuick 2 75
(R Charlton) *trckd ldr: led over 3f out: sn rdn: hung lft over 1f out: sn hdd: no ex* **7/1**
5463 **4** *2* **Maslak (IRE)**16 2898 5-8-12 **73**.... ChrisCatlin 5 73
(P W Hiatt) *cl up: effrt 3f out: one pce fr over 1f out* **9/2**3
030/ **5** *10* **Cave Of The Giant (IRE)**19 5628 7-7-13 **63** oh3.(b1) DavidProbert(3) 10 49
(T D McCarthy) *led: nudged along over 5f out: rdn and hdd ocver 3f out: sn btn* **16/1**
230- **6** *7* **Bazart**14 3368 7-9-2 **77**....(p) StephenDonohoe 9 53
(B J Llewellyn) *trckd ldr: rdn 3f out: sn wknd* **14/1**
3m 6.90s (-0.50) **Going Correction** -0.15s/f (Firm) **6** Ran SP% **109.9**
Speed ratings (Par 105): **95,93,91,90,85 81**
toteswingers: 1&2 £1.20, 1&3 £3.70, 2&3 £3.00. CSF £6.95 CT £21.11 TOTE £3.70: £2.00, £1.40; EX 7.90.
Owner Winter Madness **Bred** Wickfield Farm Partnership **Trained** Barbury Castle, Wilts

FOCUS
It rained for about ten minutes before this uncompetitive staying handicap.

3424 K J PIKE & SONS LTD AUCTION STKS (CONDITIONS RACE) 6f
4:10 (4:11) (Class 2) 2-Y-0
£8,411 (£2,519; £1,259; £630; £314; £157) **Stalls** High

Form RPR
51 **1** **Orpen Grey (IRE)**10 3072 2-8-8 0.... RichardKingscote 5 101+
(Tom Dascombe) *mde all: shkn up to draw clr over 1f out: eased towards fin: quite impressive* **2/1**1
6310 **2** *8* **Royal Desert**22 2702 2-8-6 0.... TPO'Shea 2 75
(M R Channon) *trckd wnr: rdn over 3f out: styd on to take 2nd over 1f out: no ch w wnr* **9/1**
1 **3** *1/2* **Practitioner**19 2792 2-8-4 0.... ChrisCatlin 6 72
(H J L Dunlop) *hld up: rdn 3f out: little imp tl styd on fr over 1f out: nvr pce to get on terms* **9/2**2
4412 **4** *3/4* **Daniella De Bruijn (IRE)**16 2875 2-8-1 0.... DavidProbert 10 66
(A B Haynes) *chsd ldrs: rdn over 2f out: kpt on same pce* **6/1**
3130 **5** *shd* **King's Approach (IRE)**22 2702 2-8-8 0.... FergusSweeney 8 73
(R Hannon) *in tch: rdn whn swtchd lft 2f out: kpt on same pce* **10/1**
0130 **6** *1/2* **Kirsty's Boy (IRE)**12 2995 2-8-7 0.... JamesDoyle 3 70
(J S Moore) *chsd wnr: rdn wl over 2f out: edgd lft: fdd ins fnl f* **20/1**
034 **7** *1/2* **Timelord (IRE)**34 2328 2-8-4 0.... WilliamBuick 7 66
(S Kirk) *towards rr: struggling 1/2-way: nvr pce to get on terms* **16/1**
2120 **8** *hd* **Shark Man (IRE)**37 2247 2-8-3 0.... NickyMackay 1 64
(P J McBride) *hld up: swtchd lft over 2f out: sn rdn: little imp* **12/1**
0330 **9** *1/2* **French Connexion (IRE)**9 3086 2-7-13 0 ow1.... FrankieMcDonald 9 59
(J S Moore) *in tch tl outpcd over 2f out* **50/1**
21 **10** *3* **Yer Woman (IRE)**41 2135 2-8-2 0.... JimmyQuinn 4 53
(R Hannon) *mid-div: rdn 2f out: wknd ent fnl f* **11/2**3
1m 13.6s (-1.20) **Going Correction** -0.15s/f (Firm) **10** Ran SP% **120.6**
Speed ratings (Par 99): **102,91,90,89,89 88,88,87,87,83**
toteswingers: 1&2 £5.60, 1&3 £2.40, 2&3 £15.40. CSF £22.28 TOTE £2.90: £1.20, £3.40, £1.60; EX 28.00.
Owner The Folly Racers **Bred** John Osborne **Trained** Lambourn, Berks

■ Stewards' Enquiry : James Doyle three-day ban: careless riding (Jul 13-15)

FOCUS
A race with a rich history - previous winners include the likes of Milk It Mick and Sir Percy - and there's every reason to believe this year's race went to a very smart colt. They finished in a bunch in behind, and the beaten horses look ordinary for the level, but Orpen Grey was in a different league.

NOTEBOOK
Orpen Grey(IRE) ◆ soon grabbed the far rail and dominated throughout, gradually winding things up from the front. It's true he was allowed an uncontested lead, but he soon had most of his rivals out of their comfort zone and the further he went, the better he looked. He was nominated for this contest by Tom Dascombe immediately after landing a Warwick maiden in taking fashion and provided his trainer with back-to-back victories in the race following Classic Blade's success 12 months ago. Last year's winner followed up in the July Stakes and that Newmarket Group 2 is now unsurprisingly the aim for Orpen Grey. He'll go there with a sound chance. (tchd 15-8 and 9-4)
Royal Desert was edgy at the start and needed a blindfold for stalls entry, but he still fared best of the rest. This was a fair effort in defeat, but the winner exposed his limitations. (op 8-1 tchd 10-1)
Practitioner, the winner of an ordinary course-and-distance maiden on his debut, ran with credit in third. He'll probably find things easier in nurseries. Official explanation: jockey said gelding suffered interference shortly after start (op 5-1 tchd 11-2)
Daniella De Bruijn(IRE) ran okay and should be a fair type for nurseries. (op 11-1)
King's Approach(IRE) didn't run a bad race but basically wasn't good enough. (op 14-1)
Kirsty's Boy(IRE) Official explanation: jockey said colt hung both ways
Yer Woman(IRE), a recent Windsor maiden winner, proved most disappointing. Official explanation: jockey said filly suffered interference shortly after start (op 5-1 tchd 9-2)

3425 ARMISHAWS REMOVALS AND STORAGE MAIDEN STKS 1m 1f 198y
4:45 (4:47) (Class 5) 3-Y-0+ **£3,885** (£1,156; £577; £288) **Stalls** High

Form RPR
0 **1** **Dangerous Midge (USA)**15 2930 3-9-0 0.... NickyMackay 7 82
(B J Meehan) *trckd ldr: chal 3f out: sn rdn: kpt pressing ldr: led ins fnl f: styd on wl: drvn out* **14/1**
03- **2** *1 3/4* **Alqaffay (IRE)**267 6470 4-9-12 0.... RobertHavlin 13 79
(J H M Gosden) *t.k.h early: trckd ldrs: rdn whn swtchd lft 2f out: styd on ins fnl f: wnt 2nd nr fin* **5/1**3
5-24 **3** *3/4* **Souter Point (USA)**69 1407 3-9-0 85.... JimmyFortune 12 77
(R Charlton) *trckd ldrs: rdn to ld over 2f out: sn hrd pressed: hdd ins fnl f: no ex whn lost 2nd nr fin* **9/4**1
0 **4** *nk* **Vivachi (IRE)**29 2488 3-8-9 0.... RichardKingscote 11 71
(R M Beckett) *led: rdn and hdd over 2f out: kpt pressing ldrs tl no ex ins fnl f* **50/1**
55 **5** *2 1/4* **Jewelled**20 2763 3-8-9 0.... JamesDoyle 1 67
(J W Hills) *hld up bhd: rdn and stdy prog fr over 2f out: swtchd rt over 1f out: styd on* **25/1**
6 *2 3/4* **Sushitan (GER)**412 4-9-12 0.... GeorgeBaker 6 66
(G L Moore) *mid-div: hdwy over 3f out: rdn over 2f out: sn one pce* **20/1**
03 **7** *3 3/4* **Sahaal (USA)**16 2885 3-9-0 0.... TPO'Shea 4 59
(M P Tregoning) *hld up towards rr: rdn and hdwy whn swtchd lft 2f out: one pce fnl f* **6/1**
0-0 **8** *12* **Carbon Print (USA)**13 2981 4-9-12 0.... ChrisCatlin 2 35
(P R Webber) *a towards rr* **66/1**
9 *shd* **Templar Knight** 3-9-0 0.... WilliamBuick 5 35
(Sir Michael Stoute) *mid-div: hdwy 3f out: sn rdn: wknd over 1f out* **10/3**2
5-5 **10** *8* **Pointillist (IRE)**27 2551 3-8-9 0.... SebSanders 10 42
(R M Beckett) *t.k.h in mid-div: rdn over 2f out: wknd over 1f out* **7/1**
11 *25* **Mik** 3-9-0 0.... RichardThomas 8 —
(Dr J R J Naylor) *s.i.s: a towards rr: lost tch fr over 3f out* **80/1**
2m 9.16s (-0.74) **Going Correction** -0.15s/f (Firm)
WFA 3 from 4yo 12lb **11** Ran SP% **117.3**
Speed ratings (Par 103): **96,94,94,93,91 89,86,77,77,70 50**
toteswingers: 1&2 £12.20, 1&3 £8.20, 2&3 £3.00. CSF £79.14 TOTE £17.60: £4.40, £2.10, £1.40; EX 82.70.
Owner Iraj Parvizi **Bred** Tony Holmes & Dr Walter Zent **Trained** Manton, Wilts

FOCUS
A fair maiden.
Pointillist(IRE) Official explanation: jockey said filly ran too free

3426 AXMINSTER CARPETS APPRENTICE H'CAP (WHIPS SHALL BE CARRIED BUT NOT USED) 1m
5:20 (5:20) (Class 6) (0-60,59) 3-Y-O **£3,043** (£905; £452; £226) **Stalls** High

Form RPR
0-00 **1** **Aine's Delight (IRE)**28 2515 3-9-3 **57**.... SimonPearce 4 66
(Andrew Turnell) *rrd leaving stalls: hld up: swtchd lft and hdwy over 2f out: hung rt but chsd ldr over 1f out: kpt on to ld fnl strides* **5/1**3
5066 **2** *hd* **Whotsit (IRE)**14 2950 3-8-7 **52**....(b) LauraPike(5) 2 61
(Miss Amy Weaver) *prom: led over 3f out: clr over 1f out: ct fnl strides* **5/1**3
0000 **3** *9* **Kneesy Earsy Nosey**18 2809 3-8-0 **45**.... SeanPalmer(5) 7 32
(Miss A Stokell) *led tl over 3f out: sltly hmpd over 1f out: fdd* **33/1**
00-4 **4** *hd* **Fire King**20 2763 3-9-1 **55**.... PNolan 3 42
(J A Geake) *chsd ldrs: effrt 3f out: fdd fnl f* **3/1**2
0-60 **5** *1 3/4* **Happy And Glorious (IRE)**123 678 3-8-13 **56**.... AmyScott(3) 1 39
(J W Hills) *racd keenly: cl up tl wknd over 1f out* **12/1**
3436 **6** *3 1/4* **My Best Man**19 2797 3-9-0 **59**....(p) DavidKenny(5) 8 34
(B R Millman) *trckd ldrs: effrt over 2f out: wknd over 1f out* **2/1**1
05 **7** *2* **Kinigi (IRE)**21 2744 3-8-11 **56**.... SPRyan(5) 5 26
(R A Harris) *rrd leaving stalls: towards rr: short lived effrt 2f out* **8/1**
1m 44.3s (0.80) **Going Correction** -0.15s/f (Firm) **7** Ran SP% **113.4**
Speed ratings (Par 97): **90,89,80,80,78 75,73**
toteswingers: 1&2 £7.00, 1&3 £15.80, 2&3 £9.20. CSF £29.33 CT £735.15 TOTE £7.10: £3.90, £3.00; EX 48.30 Place 6 £10.46, Place 5 £7.17..
Owner Dave Murray, Joe Mallon & Peter Ross **Bred** Dr John Hollowood And Aiden Murphy **Trained** Broad Hinton, Wilts

FOCUS
An extremely moderate handicap in which these inexperienced apprentices were not allowed to use their whips. The first two finished clear.
Aine's Delight(IRE) Official explanation: trainer said, regarding apparent improvement in form, that the filly was better suited by the easier ground
T/Plt: £23.50 to a £1 stake. Pool: £59,440.45. 1,845.62 winning tickets. T/Qpdt: £7.50 to a £1 stake. Pool: £3,834.90. 376.50 winning tickets. TM

[3402]WINDSOR (R-H)

Sunday, June 28

OFFICIAL GOING: Good to firm (8.1)

Wind: Almost nil. Weather: Fine, very warm

3427 BET ON TOTEPLACEPOT AT TOTESPORT.COM H'CAP 1m 67y

2:25 (2:26) (Class 5) (0-70,76) 3-Y-O **£2,729** (£806; £403) **Stalls** High

Form RPR

0320 **1** **Hip Hip Hooray**[16] 2884 3-9-2 **65**.............................. JimCrowley 6 72
(L A Dace) *hld up in last trio: prog fr 3f out: rdn over 2f out: swtchd to inner over 1f out: sn led: drvn out* **8/1**

000 **2** *1 ½* **Indian Violet (IRE)**[19] 2795 3-9-6 **69**.............................. TPQueally 5 73
(P F I Cole) *hld up in abt 7th: rdn and prog on outer fr 3f out: wnt 2nd ins fnl f: nvr able to chal* **14/1**

4306 **3** *¾* **Squad**[18] 2809 3-8-9 **58**.............................. TonyCulhane 2 60
(S Dow) *s.i.s: detached in last and rdn 1/2-way: taken to outer over 2f out and gd prog after: styd on to snatch 3rd last stride* **10/1**

0-55 **4** *shd* **Play It Sam**[27] 2548 3-9-2 **65**.............................. AdamKirby 9 67
(W R Swinburn) *hld up in abt 9th: prog 3f out: drvn over 2f out: nvr able to chal: kpt on to press for a pl nr fin* **3/1**[1]

-000 **5** *hd* **Alexander Loyalty (IRE)**[18] 2827 3-8-13 **62**..............(v[1]) NCallan 14 63
(E F Vaughan) *trckd ldng pair: led against rail wl over 2f out: sn edgd lft: hdd and no ex jst over 1f out: lost 2 pls nr fin* **10/1**

1400 **6** *6* **Best In Class**[30] 2432 3-9-7 **70**.............................. CatherineGannon 11 60
(Tom Dascombe) *chsd ldng quartet: rdn 1/2-way: stl chsng but hld whn nt clr run briefly over 1f out: eased last 75yds* **14/1**

-000 **7** *2 ¾* **Temperence Hall (USA)**[12] 3009 3-8-7 **59**..........(v[1]) MarcHalford(3) 13 43
(J R Best) *t.k.h early: led at mostly str pce: hdd wl over 2f out: wandering and wknd: eased ins fnl f* **16/1**

-500 **8** *½* **Count On Guest**[40] 2170 3-9-1 **64**..............(b[1]) AdrianMcCarthy 8 44
(G G Margarson) *t.k.h early: chsd ldr to 3f out: sn lost pl and btn* **25/1**

00-4 **9** *shd* **Precious Secret (IRE)**[68] 1422 3-8-11 **60**.............................. TedDurcan 12 42
(C F Wall) *chsd ldrs: rdn sn after 1/2-way and no prog: wl btn last 2f* **15/2**[3]

05-5 **10** *1 ¾* **Lady Drac (IRE)**[24] 2640 3-9-7 **70**.............................. MichaelHills 7 46
(B W Hills) *chsd ldng trio: rdn over 3f out: lost pl over 2f out: wknd over 1f out* **4/1**[2]

-640 **11** *1 ½* **Novastasia (IRE)**[45] 2001 3-8-12 **61**.............................. ShaneKelly 10 33
(W R Swinburn) *s.s: a in last trio: pushed along and no prog 3f out* **16/1**

-000 **12** *13* **Bermondsey Bob (IRE)**[8] 3159 3-8-7 **56**.............................. SaleemGolam 3 —
(J L Spearing) *chsd ldrs early: u.p and losing pl 1/2-way: last over 2f out: t.o* **40/1**

1m 44.0s (-0.70) **Going Correction** -0.175s/f (Firm) **12** Ran SP% **117.4**
Speed ratings (Par 99): **96,94,93,93,93 87,84,84,84,82 80,67**
toteswingers: 1&2 £19.10, 1&3 £14.20, 2&3 £11.10. CSF £113.65 CT £781.60 TOTE £7.10: £2.90, £4.10, £3.50; EX 91.50 TRIFECTA Not won..
Owner M C S D Racing Partnership **Bred** Mrs R S Evans **Trained** Five Oaks, W Sussex

FOCUS
With a hot day correctly forecast 4mm of water had been put on overnight in a bid to counteract the drying conditions. The time for the opener, which was run at a decent pace, was just over a second outside the standard. The first five finished clear in this modest handicap.
Novastasia(IRE) Official explanation: jockey said filly was slowly away

3428 BET ON TOTESUPER7 AT TOTESPORT.COM H'CAP 5f 10y

2:55 (2:56) (Class 5) (0-70,70) 3-Y-O **£2,729** (£806; £403) **Stalls** High

Form RPR

4424 **1** **Piste**[12] 3003 3-9-4 **67**.............................. EddieAhern 10 72
(B J Meehan) *chsd ldr: rdn wl over 1f out: got through gap against rail fnl f to ld last 75yds* **4/1**[2]

6041 **2** *½* **Dancing Wave**[8] 3176 3-8-2 **58**.............................. AndrewHeffernan(7) 7 61
(M C Chapman) *drvn to ld and sn at least 2 l clr: maintained gallop but edgd off nr side rail fr 2f out: hdd last 75yds* **5/1**[3]

33 **3** *4* **Imaginary Diva**[21] 2740 3-9-2 **65**.............................. AdrianMcCarthy 1 54
(G G Margarson) *chsd ldr: rdn over 2f out: no imp in 3rd over 1f out: one pce* **9/1**

0-06 **4** *¾* **Zelos Girl (IRE)**[21] 2740 3-9-2 **65**..............(e) SaleemGolam 9 51
(Rae Guest) *chsd ldrs: rdn 1/2-way: no imp 2f out: n.d after* **16/1**

0052 **5** *2* **Brynfa Boy**[9] 3118 3-8-8 **57**.............................. TonyCulhane 6 36
(P W D'Arcy) *hld up in tch: hanging lft and nt qckn fr 1/2-way: no prog over 1f out* **7/4**[1]

06 **6** *1 ½* **Cool Art (IRE)**[31] 2393 3-9-7 **70**..............(b) PatrickMathers 8 44
(Peter Grayson) *dwlt: sn outpcd and wl bhd in last: no prog u.p 1/2-way* **16/1**

-050 **7** *1* **Peper Harow (IRE)**[29] 2478 3-8-5 **54**.............................. CatherineGannon 4 24
(M D I Usher) *stdd s and squeezed out sn after: in tch in rr and wdst of all: effrt 1/2-way: sn btn* **13/2**

5-00 **8** *6* **Countrywide City (IRE)**[28] 2520 3-9-7 **70**.............................. LPKeniry 5 18
(Jane Southcombe) *in tch in rr: rdn after 2f: sn struggling: wl bhd over 1f out* **33/1**

60.15 secs (-0.15) **Going Correction** -0.05s/f (Good) **8** Ran SP% **111.1**
Speed ratings (Par 99): **99,98,91,90,87 85,83,73**
toteswingers: 1&2 £3.30, 1&3 £5.70, 2&3 £4.30. CSF £22.80 CT £162.76 TOTE £4.70: £1.70, £2.00, £1.80; EX 18.10 Trifecta £44.20 Pool £249.92 - 4.18 winning units..
Owner Miss Gloria Abbey **Bred** Miss G Abbey **Trained** Manton, Wilts

FOCUS
An ordinary sprint handicap run at a strong pace, and few got into it.
Peper Harow(IRE) Official explanation: jockey said filly was hampered at start

3429 BET IN-PLAY AT TOTESPORT.COM H'CAP 1m 2f 7y

3:25 (3:28) (Class 3) (0-95,90) 3-Y-O **£8,742** (£2,601; £1,300; £649) **Stalls** Low

Form RPR

033 **1** **Midnight Cruiser (IRE)**[17] 2855 3-9-7 **90**.............................. PatDobbs 5 96
(R Hannon) *sn led: jnd and pushed along over 3f out: styd against nr side rail fnl 2f: kpt on wl* **6/1**

-333 **2** *¾* **Something Perfect (USA)**[8] 3165 3-8-11 **80**.............................. TPQueally 4 85
(H R A Cecil) *hld up in last: prog on outer over 2f out: drvn to press wnr over 1f out: edgd rt and flashed tail: nt qckn* **7/1**

-130 **3** *2 ¼* **Legislate**[43] 2077 3-9-3 **86**.............................. MichaelHills 6 86
(B W Hills) *trckd ldng pair to over 3f out: renewed effrt over 2f out but forced to switch to wd outside wl over 1f out: kpt on one pce* **6/4**[1]

4-13 **4** *1* **The Fonz**[38] 2210 3-8-10 **79**.............................. NCallan 1 79+
(Sir Michael Stoute) *trckd wnr: chal and upsides over 3f out to 2f out: hld in 3rd whn crossed and snatched up jst ins fnl f: fdd* **3/1**[2]

1-00 **5** *12* **Dialogue**[22] 2701 3-8-11 **80**.............................. JoeFanning 2 54
(M Johnston) *hld up in 4th: chsd ldng pair over 3f out: nt pce to hold position and squeezed out wl over 2f out: wknd* **9/2**[3]

2m 6.17s (-2.53) **Going Correction** -0.175s/f (Firm) **5** Ran SP% **110.0**
Speed ratings (Par 103): **103,102,100,99,90**
toteswingers: 1&2 £22.70. CSF £42.09 TOTE £6.50: £3.20, £2.40; EX 34.50.
Owner Michael Pescod **Bred** Vincent Hannon **Trained** East Everleigh, Wilts
■ Stewards' Enquiry : N Callan three-day ban: weighed-in 2lb overweight (Jul 13-15)

FOCUS
Another handicap for three-year-olds, and an open race run at a sound pace.

NOTEBOOK
Midnight Cruiser(IRE) made pretty much all of the running and after securing the favoured stands' rail he held on tenaciously. There was a doubt over his stamina for this longer trip but he saw it out well enough. He had proved difficult to place previously this term and it may be that he will struggle to follow up this win. (op 7-1)
Something Perfect(USA), another stepping up in trip, came from the back to keep the winner up to his work but was always just being held. A quirky filly who needed to be walked part of the way to post and was fitted with a rug for stalls entry, she showed her trademark tail-swishing when the pressure was on and looked to keep a bit back for herself. (op 5-1 tchd 9-2 and 15-2)
Legislate was the first of the five to come under pressure and he could merely plug on for third after being obliged to switch to his left. This was a better run than his effort at Newbury in soft ground but he seems best when able to dominate. He might be ready for a try at 1m4f. (tchd 11-8, 13-8 and 7-4 in a place)
The Fonz, who raced a bit freely early on, had his chance, but was held in third when he was hampered by the runner-up over 1f out. He could do with coming down a couple of pounds. (tchd 7-2)
Dialogue has yet to make the frame in any of his six tries on turf and had no chance here after being left short of room over 2f out. (op 15-2 tchd 4-1)

3430 E B F BIGGER ODDS GUARANTEED AT TOTESPORT.COM FILLIES' CONDITIONS STKS 5f 10y

4:00 (4:03) (Class 2) 2-Y-O

£12,462 (£3,732; £1,866; £934; £466; £234) **Stalls** High

Form RPR

3 **1** **Lady Darshaan (IRE)**[9] 3101 2-8-9 0.............................. LPKeniry 3 80+
(J S Moore) *settled in rr: plld out wd over 1f out: drvn and r.o fnl f to ld last strides* **12/1**

5103 **2** *nk* **Kings Of Leo**[15] 2907 2-8-12 0.............................. EddieAhern 2 82
(R Hannon) *led and sn crossed to nr side rail: edgd lft off rail fr 2f out: drvn fnl f: hdd last strides* **6/1**

310 **3** *¾* **Existentialist**[32] 2372 2-8-12 0.............................. TPQueally 7 79
(J G Portman) *wnt lft s and bmpd: hld up in last: looking for run against nr side rail fr 2f out: got through to chse ldr fnl f: hung lft and nt qckn* **3/1**[1]

6212 **4** *2* **Ailsa Carmel (IRE)**[3] 3311 2-8-9 0.............................. EdwardCreighton 9 69
(M R Channon) *prom: rdn to dispute 2nd 2f out: nt qckn over 1f out: hanging lft fnl f* **3/1**[1]

1030 **5** *¾* **Leleyf (IRE)**[9] 3086 2-9-0 0.............................. TonyCulhane 8 71
(M R Channon) *t.k.h early and restrained to rr: stl there whn rn into trble 2f out: shuffled along and nvr on terms after* **4/1**[2]

010 **6** *1 ¼* **Quaker Parrot**[32] 2372 2-8-12 0.............................. RichardSmith 4 65
(Tom Dascombe) *racd wd: cl up: disp 2nd 2f out: fdd fnl f* **16/1**

421 **7** *1 ¼* **White Daffodil (IRE)**[25] 2604 2-8-12 0.............................. PatDobbs 6 60
(R Hannon) *wnt rt s and bmpd: sn chsd ldr: no imp fr 2f out: wknd fnl f* **5/1**[3]

61.05 secs (0.75) **Going Correction** -0.05s/f (Good) **7** Ran SP% **114.5**
Speed ratings (Par 96): **92,91,90,87,85 83,81**
toteswingers: 1&2 £16.00, 1&3 £12.60, 2&3 £3.70. CSF £80.48 TOTE £10.70: £5.90, £2.60; EX 85.80 Trifecta £267.40 Part won. Pool 361.44 - 0.43 winning units..
Owner Coleman Bloodstock Limited **Bred** Michael Woodlock And Seamus Kennedy **Trained** Upper Lambourn, Berks

FOCUS
A decent conditions event but perhaps not a great race for the money. It went to the least experienced filly on show and the one maiden in the field.

NOTEBOOK
Lady Darshaan(IRE) ◆ had been third in a 6f Goodwood maiden on her sole previous start. She needed every yard of this trip to score, running on to collar the leader almost on the post after being switched to the outside, and will benefit from a return to a longer trip. Well regarded, she will be aimed at the Two-Year-Old Trophy at Redcar in October, a race her trainer has won for the past two seasons, with her half-brother Total Gallery last year and with Dubai Dynamo in 2007. (op 10-1 tchd 16-1)
Kings Of Leo got over from her low draw to grab the stands' rail, but she drifted away from the fence under pressure and was caught on the line. This was a creditable run, but she looks exposed now. (op 15-2 tchd 11-2)
Existentialist made all when winning her maiden here and was badly drawn when down the field (behind Leleyf and Quaker Parrot) in the Listed Hilary Needler Stakes at Beverley. After receiving an early bump from White Daffodil she was obliged to race in rear, but when a gap finally opened up for her near the rail she finished quite well, if never quite going to catch the first two. This was a pleasing run in the circumstances. (tchd 11-4 and 4-1)
Ailsa Carmel(IRE), who was making a quick reappearance, has been running over 6f and she just lacked a bit of pace back down at 5f. (op 11-4 tchd 5-2 and 7-2)
Leleyf(IRE), who conceded weight all round, was short of room early on and again at around the halfway stage, and could never really get into the race. (op 6-1 tchd 7-2)
Quaker Parrot, only tenth in the Hilary Needler won by her stablemate Don't Tell Mary, ran respectably, but may not be easy to place in the short term. (tchd 14-1 and 20-1)
White Daffodil(IRE), from the same stable as the runner-up, chased the pace until fading in the final furlong. She really needs 6f. (op 9-2 tchd 6-1)

3431 BET TOTEPOOL AT TOTESPORT.COM H'CAP 1m 67y

4:35 (4:35) (Class 3) (0-90,90) 3-Y-O+ **£7,771** (£2,312; £1,155; £577) **Stalls** High

Form RPR

6351 **1** **The Cayterers**[13] 2977 7-9-1 **80**.............................. MCGeran(5) 2 93+
(A W Carroll) *hld up in last trio and racd on inner: plld out and prog over 2f out: rdn to ld over 1f out: grabbed rail and wl in command fnl f* **15/2**

4631 **2** *2 ¼* **Vainglory (USA)**[10] 3055 5-9-7 **86**.............................. MartinLane(5) 3 94
(D M Simcock) *disp ld tl def advantage 3f out: grabbed nr side rail 2f out: hdd over 1f out: outpcd* **4/1**[1]

13-0 **3** *1 ½* **Film Set (USA)**[36] 2270 3-9-6 **90**..............(t) TedDurcan 7 92
(Saeed Bin Suroor) *disp ld on inner to 3f out: stl nrly on terms 2f out: steadily outpcd* **16/1**

-306 **4** *2 ½* **Guilded Warrior**[19] 2780 6-9-6 **85**.............................. Louis-PhilippeBeuzelin(5) 9 84
(W S Kittow) *hld up bhd ldrs on inner: rdn over 2f out: plugged on but n.d* **9/1**

00-0 **5** *2* **Hurricane Hymnbook (USA)**[24] 2639 4-9-13 **87**.......... MickyFenton 4 81
(Stef Liddiard) *hld up in last: modest prog over 2f out: taken to outer and shuffled along over 1f out: nvr nr ldrs* **16/1**

0034 **6** 1 3/4 **Cape Hawk (IRE)**[29] 2480 5-9-8 85 PatrickHills(3) 6 75
(R Hannon) *cl up bhd ldrs: c wd in home st and struggling u.p fnl 2f* **11/2**[2]

251 **7** 1 1/2 **El Loco Uno (USA)**[22] 2710 3-9-2 86 TPQueally 8 71
(H R A Cecil) *t.k.h early: cl up: racd wd in home st: struggling wl over 1f out* **4/1**[1]

551- **8** 6 **The Which Doctor**[261] 6625 4-10-0 88 ShaneKelly 1 61
(J Noseda) *hld up in last trio: racd wd in home st and no prog: wknd 2f out* **13/2**[3]

0033 **9** 11 **Ballinteni**[24] 2639 7-9-11 85 NCallan 5 32
(M G Quinlan) *in tch: racd wd in home st and sn struggling: wknd rapidly over 2f out: t.o* **7/1**

1m 41.79s (-2.91) **Going Correction** -0.175s/f (Firm)
WFA 3 from 4yo+ 10lb **9** Ran SP% **114.7**
Speed ratings (Par 107): **107,104,103,100,98 97,95,89,78**
toteswingers: 1&2 £7.50, 1&3 £21.30, 2&3 £15.70. CSF £37.33 CT £470.55 TOTE £9.70: £2.70, £1.70, £3.70; EX 34.30 Trifecta £299.20 Part won. Pool £404.45 - 0.43 winning units..
Owner R D Willis and M C Watts **Bred** Acrum Lodge Stud **Trained** Cropthorne, Worcs

FOCUS
A decent handicap run at a good pace. It concerned only a few, with a number of the runners never able to make their presence felt. The rail was again favoured.

NOTEBOOK
The Cayterers won well over C/D earlier this month, but the resultant 6lb rise left him on a career-high mark. He is clearly an improved performer at the age of seven, though, and won this in nice style, quickening up to lead and securing the rail when in command. He seems to like Windsor and it would be no surprise to see him back here before long. (tchd 7-1 and 9-1)
Vainglory(USA), 3lb higher, got the better of a sustained duel with Film Set, the pair of them disputing the lead until the winner swooped, and stuck on in typically tenacious fashion for second. (op 9-2)
Film Set(USA), back on a more suitable surface, came off worse in his tussle with Vainglory, but stuck on for a creditable third. (op 8-1)
Guilded Warrior was beaten only a neck in this event last year when 2lb higher, but has run mainly over shorter since. He plugged on for fourth, but was never really a factor. (op 17-2 tchd 8-1)
El Loco Uno(USA), making his handicap debut on only his second run on turf, sweated up on the way to post. He chased the pace but, in common with the others who raced towards the centre in the straight, was never going to trouble the principals who congregated near the stands' rail. (op 5-1 tchd 7-2)

3432 BET TOTEPOOL ON 0800 221 221 MAIDEN STKS 1m 3f 135y
5:10 (5:10) (Class 5) 3-5-Y-O £2,729 (£806; £403) Stalls Low

Form RPR

0 **1** **Cape Marien (IRE)**[65] 1488 3-8-9 0 TedDurcan 5 68+
(D R Lanigan) *trckd ldr to 5f out: styd cl up: led 4f out and kicked on: rdn and styd on wl fnl 2f* **7/2**[2]

32 **2** 5 **Birdinthehand (FR)**[27] 2538 3-8-9 0 TPQueally 1 57
(H R A Cecil) *cl up: wd bnd over 5f out and lost pl: effrt to go 2nd over 3f out: sn rdn: no imp on wnr fnl 2f* **2/5**[1]

0022 **3** 2 1/2 **Dark Oasis**[51] 1848 3-8-7 58 AndrewHeffernan(7) 3 58
(M C Chapman) *hld up: outpcd over 3f out: plugged on to take 3rd 2f out: n.d* **7/1**[3]

-000 **4** 14 **Jay Gee Wigmo**[18] 2824 4-10-0 48 ShaneKelly 4 41
(A W Carroll) *cl up: wnt 2nd 5f out to 4f out: fdd u.p 3f out: eased fnl f* **33/1**

00 **5** 8 **Iron Master**[16] 2885 3-9-0 0 (t) NeilChalmers 2 21
(J J Bridger) *hld up in last pair: outpcd 4f out: wknd 3f out: sn wl bhd* **33/1**

006- **6** 21 **Brave Knave (IRE)**[297] 5652 4-10-0 48 (t) PatDobbs 6 —
(B De Haan) *plld hrd: led and racd wd of rest early: hanging lft bnd 5f out: hdd & wknd rapidly 4f out: t.o* **33/1**

2m 30.11s (0.61) **Going Correction** -0.175s/f (Firm)
WFA 3 from 4yo 14lb **6** Ran SP% **115.0**
Speed ratings (Par 103): **90,86,85,75,70 56**
toteswingers: 1&2 £1.20, 1&3 £1.40, 2&3 £1.30. CSF £5.46 TOTE £4.20: £1.90, £1.10; EX 9.70 Place 6 £4,704.49, Place 5 £906.00..
Owner Saif Ali **Bred** Darley **Trained** Newmarket, Suffolk
■ Stewards' Enquiry : Pat Dobbs jockey said colt ran too freely

FOCUS
A very weak maiden run at a steady pace.
Brave Knave(IRE) Official explanation: jockey said colt ran too freely
T/Plt: £752.00 to a £1 stake. Pool: £67,325.78. 65.35 winning tickets. T/Qpdt: £94.00 to a £1 stake. Pool: £5,388.40. 42.40 winning tickets. JN

3409 CURRAGH (R-H)
Sunday, June 28

OFFICIAL GOING: Good to yielding

3434a DUBAI DUTY FREE MILLENIUM MILLIONAIRE SAPPHIRE STKS (GROUP 3) 5f
2:10 (2:10) 3-Y-O+

£40,825 (£12,961; £6,165; £2,087; £1,407; £728)

RPR

1 **Benbaun (IRE)**[28] 2523 8-9-5 (b) PJSmullen 8 114
(K A Ryan) *chsd ldrs: 2nd 1/2-way: chal 2f out: impr to ld 1 1/2f out: rdn and kpt on wl fnl f* **5/1**[3]

2 2 1/2 **Snaefell (IRE)**[14] 2959 5-9-8 106 (p) JMurtagh 7 108
(M Halford, Ire) *mid-div: 6th 1/2-way: rdn into 5th 1 1/2f out: 4th 1f out: kpt on fnl f to 2nd cl home* **6/1**

3 hd **Inxile (IRE)**[27] 2555 4-9-5 AdrianTNicholls 6 104
(D Nicholls) *led: rdn and chal 2f out: hdd 1 1/2f out: no ex in 2nd 1f out: kpt on same pce fnl f: lost 2nd cl home* **6/4**[1]

4 nk **Angus Newz**[36] 2271 6-9-2 JAHeffernan 2 100
(M Quinn) *chsd ldrs: 5th 1/2-way: rdn into 4th 1 1/2f out: u.p in 5th 1f out: kpt on same pce fnl f* **33/1**

5 1/2 **Three Rocks (IRE)**[17] 2870 4-9-5 107 KJManning 5 101
(J S Bolger, Ire) *dwlt: in rr: rdn into 7th 1 1/2f out: kpt on fnl f* **10/1**

6 2 1/2 **Judge 'n Jury**[38] 2191 5-9-5 (t) KevinGhunowa 4 92
(R A Harris) *chsd ldrs: 4th 1/2-way: rdn in 3rd 1 1/2f out: no imp 1f out: kpt on one pce* **14/1**

7 shd **Miss Gorica (IRE)**[11] 3039 5-9-2 102 DPMcDonogh 9 89
(Ms Joanna Morgan, Ire) *chsd ldrs: 3rd 1/2-way: rdn and dropped to 6th 1 1/2f out: no ex* **20/1**

8 1 **Captain Gerrard (IRE)**[12] 2991 4-9-5 TomEaves 1 88
(B Smart) *in rr of mid-div thrght: rdn and dropped to rr under 2f out: no imp* **3/1**[2]

60.03 secs (-0.67) **Going Correction** +0.20s/f (Good) **8** Ran SP% **119.4**
Speed ratings: **113,109,108,108,107 103,103,101**
CSF £36.53 TOTE £6.00: £2.00, £1.90, £1.10; DF 47.50.
Owner Ransley, Birks, Hillen **Bred** Dr T A Ryan **Trained** Hambleton, N Yorks

NOTEBOOK
Benbaun(IRE) logged his seventh win at this venue and his second in this race, having won it in 2005. It was also his first win for Kevin Ryan and it was never in doubt in what wasn't the strongest of Group 3s. Always in the front couple, he challenged and went on over a furlong out and powered on up the hill to score decisively. It was a return to his best form and the Prix de l'Abbaye at Longchamp, which he won in 2007, is again his big target. (op 9/2)
Snaefell(IRE) is at his best over a furlong further, but showed a return to his best at Cork a couple of weeks ago and this stiff 5f on easy enough ground would always give him a chance of being involved. He was outpaced when the race took shape after halfway, but he kept on well inside the last without threatening the winner. (op 6/1 tchd 13/2)
Inxile(IRE) ran well enough, but this was more like a 6f race than 5f. He showed his usual early pace but ran out of petrol somewhat inside the last when the winner took over. (op 2/1)
Angus Newz does not portray the form in a particularly flattering light, but this would be close to a career-best effort for her. She was outpaced for much of the way but ran on quite well again inside the last and was probably never nearer.
Judge 'n Jury was beaten over a furlong out and remains below par this term. Official explanation: jockey said gelding hung throughout (op 16/1)
Captain Gerrard(IRE) showed hardly a trace of the form of his Royal Ascot run. After being restrained at the start, he began and finished in pretty much the same position. (op 3/1 tchd 4/1)

3435a DUBAI DUTY FREE FINEST SURPRISE SCURRY (PREMIER H'CAP) 6f 63y
2:40 (2:46) 3-Y-O+ **£44,242** (£12,980; £6,184; £2,106)

RPR

1 **Mountain Coral (IRE)**[16] 2900 5-8-7 84 NGMcCullagh 5 89
(F Oakes, Ire) *mid-div on nr side: hdwy in 8th over 1f out: sn styd on to chal and kpt on wl fnl f to ld cl home* **8/1**[2]

2 1/2 **Dedo (IRE)**[36] 2289 4-9-0 91 DPMcDonogh 2 94
(Kevin Prendergast, Ire) *towards rr on nr side: late hdwy in 10th over 1f out: kpt on wl fnl f to take 2nd cl home* **11/1**

3 3/4 **Irish Heartbeat (IRE)**[63] 1542 4-8-6 83 RMBurke 17 84+
(David P Myerscough, Ire) *chsd ldrs on far side: led under 2f out: rdn and kpt on fnl f: hdd cl home* **25/1**

4 hd **Tornadodancer (IRE)**[16] 2900 6-8-5 87 (b) BACurtis(5) 10 87
(T G McCourt, Ire) *chsd ldrs on nr side: rdn in 5th 1f out: kpt on same pce fnl f* **33/1**

5 shd **Something (IRE)**[9] 3091 7-9-5 96 AdrianTNicholls 1 96
(D Nicholls) *chsd ldrs on nr side: hdwy to 6th 1f out: rdn and kpt on same pce fnl f* **9/2**[1]

6 nk **Joseph Henry**[8] 3141 7-9-6 97 TomEaves 9 96
(D Nicholls) *led on nr side: rdn in 4th 1f out: kpt on same pce fnl f* **12/1**

7 3 **Northburn**[16] 2900 5-8-7 84 KLatham 6 74
(G M Lyons, Ire) *mid-div on nr side: rdn 1 1/2f out: kpt on same pce fnl f* **16/1**

8 1 1/4 **Deal Breaker**[63] 1542 4-8-12 89 KJManning 18 75
(Edward Lynam, Ire) *towards rr on far side: rdn in 9th 1f out: kpt on same pce fnl f* **33/1**

9 1/2 **Kingsdale Ocean (IRE)**[16] 2900 6-8-3 90 (b) LFRoche(10) 14 75
(D K Weld, Ire) *mid-div on far side: rdn in 7th 1f out: no ex fnl f* **16/1**

10 nk **Majestic Times (IRE)**[16] 2900 9-7-13 81 oh1 (b) ShaneFoley(5) 20 65
(Liam McAteer, Ire) *chsd ldr on far side: rdn 2f out: no ex in 3rd over 1f out: no ex fnl f* **33/1**

11 hd **Gist (IRE)**[17] 2870 6-8-13 93 (b) SMGorey(3) 3 76
(W J Martin, Ire) *nvr a factor* **33/1**

12 hd **Nanotech (IRE)**[14] 2959 5-9-9 100 JAHeffernan 11 83
(Jarlath P Fahey, Ire) *chsd ldr on nr side: rdn and wknd 1 1/2f out* **25/1**

13 1/2 **Dahindar (IRE)**[27] 2555 4-9-4 95 (b[1]) MJKinane 7 76
(John M Oxx, Ire) *chsd ldrs on nr side: rdn and wknd 1 1/2f out* **10/1**

14 hd **Georgebernardshaw (IRE)**[17] 2870 4-9-7 105 JPO'Brien(7) 12 86
(A P O'Brien, Ire) *chsd ldrs on nr side: rdn and wknd 1 1/2f out* **9/1**[3]

15 shd **Osterhase (IRE)**[45] 2012 10-9-3 94 (b) FMBerry 22 74
(J E Mulhern, Ire) *overall ldr on far side: hdd under 2f out: wknd fnl f* **14/1**

16 1/2 **Richelieu**[9] 3127 7-8-4 81 oh7 RPCleary 4 60
(J J Lambe, Ire) *a towards rr* **20/1**

17 7 **Funatfuntasia**[17] 2871 5-8-9 86 (p) CDHayes 21 44
(Ms Joanna Morgan, Ire) *chsd ldrs on far side: rdn and wknd 2f out* **20/1**

18 1/2 **Andrea Palladio (IRE)**[25] 2616 3-8-4 88 oh5 WMLordan 13 42
(David Wachman, Ire) *mid-div best: rdn and wknd 2f out* **12/1**

19 5 **Romeo's On Fire (IRE)**[78] 1219 5-8-10 92 EJMcNamara(5) 19 33
(G M Lyons, Ire) *a towards rr* **20/1**

1m 17.59s (-0.41) **Going Correction** +0.20s/f (Good)
WFA 3 from 4yo+ 7lb **19** Ran SP% **124.3**
Speed ratings: **110,109,108,108,107 107,103,101,101,100 100,100,99,99,99 98,89,88,81**
CSF £78.13 TOTE £7.50: £1.90, £2.50, £5.80, £7.50; DF 110.40.
Owner F Oakes **Bred** Frank Oakes **Trained** Dunboyne, Co Meath

NOTEBOOK
Mountain Coral(IRE) is most progressive and this was his fourth win on the bounce.
Something(IRE), back in trip, was produced with every chance from just off the pace a furlong out but could not quite get there. (op 5/1 tchd 6/1)
Joseph Henry showed up strongly until feeling the pinch at the furlong marker and helps to set the level. (op 14/1)

3436a NETJETS RAILWAY STKS (GROUP 2) 6f
3:10 (3:11) 2-Y-O

£69,902 (£22,135; £10,485; £3,495; £2,330; £1,165)

RPR

1 **Alfred Nobel (IRE)**[31] 2422 2-9-1 JMurtagh 3 107
(A P O'Brien, Ire) *chsd ldrs: 4th 1/2-way: hdwy to chal 2f out: led 1 1/2f out: rdn and kpt on wl fnl f* **6/4**[1]

2 1 1/4 **In Some Respect (IRE)**[16] 2899 2-9-1 CDHayes 1 104
(Andrew Oliver, Ire) *chsd ldrs: 3rd 1/2-way: lost pl 2f out: rdn in 5th 1 1/2f out: styd on to 3rd 1f out: kpt on fnl f to go 2nd ins fnl 100yds* **20/1**

3 hd **King Ledley (USA)**[14] 2957 2-9-1 DPMcDonogh 4 103
(Kevin Prendergast, Ire) *settled in rr: gd hdwy on outer to ld 2f out: rdn and hdd 1 1/2f out: no ex in 2nd 1f out: kpt on fnl f: lost 2nd last 100yds* **9/2**

4 1 1/4 **Kitty Kiernan**[27] 2557 2-8-12 KJManning 5 96
(J S Bolger, Ire) *chsd ldr: 2nd 1/2-way: rdn in 4th 2f out: no ex in 5th 1f out: kpt on same pce fnl f* **4/1**[3]

5 3/4 **Rock Jock (IRE)**[70] 1385 2-9-1 PShanahan 2 97
(Tracey Collins, Ire) *hld up towards rr: 5th 1/2-way: in rr and rdn 2f out: styd on to go 4th 1f out: no ex ins fnl f and kpt on same pce* **33/1**

6 2 **Love Lockdown (IRE)**[14] 2957 2-9-1 KLatham 7 91
(G M Lyons, Ire) *led: rdn and hdd 2f out: no ex in 4th 1 1/2f out: wknd over 1f out* **3/1**[2]

1m 15.05s (0.35) **Going Correction** +0.20s/f (Good) **6** Ran SP% **110.9**
Speed ratings: **105,103,103,101,100 97**
CSF £29.14 TOTE £2.40: £1.50, £5.10; DF 48.90.
Owner Derrick Smith **Bred** Lodge Park Stud **Trained** Ballydoyle, Co Tipperary
■ Stewards' Enquiry : K Latham one-day ban: failed to keep straight from stalls (Jul 13)

NOTEBOOK
Alfred Nobel(IRE) ran out as authoritative a winner as his market position deserved. There would not have been much of an indication before now that this horse would have been among the better Ballydoyle juveniles, even at this early stage, but this display marks him down as a quickly improving horse whose progression should continue. Obviously, all the big races open up for him now after this very taking display and he was later quoted as short as 14/1 for next year's 2000 Guineas. (op 7/4)
In Some Respect(IRE) fully justified his trainer's decision to supplement him. He was also just tucked in off the pace, but just got a little bit outpaced when things quickened up. However, he ran on really well once more inside the last but just didn't have the class of the winner. He wants an extra furlong and looks capable of winning a nice race.
King Ledley(USA) probably needs easier ground to be seen at his very best, but he ran a very sound race and rates the best guide to the form. He quickened through on the outside to lead two furlongs out but his run just flattened out somewhat inside the last. (op 4/1)
Kitty Kiernan has not really progressed from her debut victory over Lillie Langtry at Naas last month. She was in a perfect position to challenge past halfway but was onepaced inside the last furlong. (op 7/2)
Rock Jock(IRE) justified the decision to run him and probably ran better than his bare finishing position. Held up just out the back, he came with what looked briefly to be a threatening run a furlong or so out before running out of steam close home. He would have little troubling winning a maiden somewhere on this evidence.
Love Lockdown(IRE) had been supplemented for this, something his trainer had never done before, and maybe he was just feeling the effects of what has been a busy enough few weeks. He led on the rail but produced no real response when he was challenged two furlongs out. (op 7/2)

3438a DUBAI DUTY FREE IRISH DERBY (GROUP 1) (ENTIRE COLTS & FILLIES) 1m 4f
4:20 (4:20) 3-Y-O
£818,446 (£279,611; £133,980; £46,601; £32,038; £17,475)

RPR

1 **Fame And Glory**[22] 2705 3-9-0 120 JMurtagh 12 128
(A P O'Brien, Ire) *settled bhd ldrs: mod 5th 1/2-way: hdwy in 4th ent st: rdn into 2nd 2f out: styd on to ld over 1f out: plld clr fnl f: easily* **8/11**[1]

2 5 **Golden Sword**[22] 2705 3-9-0 118 CO'Donoghue 7 120
(A P O'Brien, Ire) *chsd ldr in mod 2nd: clsr 5f out: impr to ld under 4f out: rdn 3f out: hdd over 1f out: no ex and kpt on same pce* **11/1**

3 1 **Mourayan (IRE)**[49] 1910 3-9-0 108 (b[1]) MJKinane 10 118
(John M Oxx, Ire) *chsd ldrs: mod 3rd 1/2-way: hdwy to 2nd 3f out: rdn in 3rd and no ex 2f out: kpt on same pce* **8/1**[3]

4 10 **Masterofthehorse (IRE)**[22] 2705 3-9-0 119 JAHeffernan 3 102
(A P O'Brien, Ire) *settled mid-div: mod 6th 1/2-way: hdwy in 5th 3f out: rdn in 4th and no imp over 2f out: kpt on same pce* **9/2**[2]

5 8 **Recharge (IRE)**[36] 2288 3-9-0 110 CDHayes 2 90
(Kevin Prendergast, Ire) *in rr of mid-div: mod 7th 4f out: rdn and no imp 3f out: 6th 2f out: styd on to mod 5th over 1f out: kpt on one pce* **20/1**

6 2 1/2 **Gan Amhras (IRE)**[22] 2705 3-9-0 117 KJManning 8 86
(J S Bolger, Ire) *chsd ldrs: mod 4th 1/2-way: rdn in 6th 3f out: no ex in 5th over 2f out: kpt on one pce* **10/1**

7 1/2 **The Bull Hayes (IRE)**[35] 2306 3-9-0 104 (p) FMBerry 6 85
(Mrs John Harrington, Ire) *towards rr for most: rdn in 8th and no imp 3f out: kpt on one pce* **40/1**

8 shd **Loch Long (IRE)**[263] 6589 3-9-0 PShanahan 5 85
(Tracey Collins, Ire) *towards rr for most: nvr a factor* **100/1**

9 3 **Rockhampton (IRE)**[10] 3049 3-9-0 100 SMLevey 13 80
(A P O'Brien, Ire) *led and sn clr: reduced advantage 5f out: rdn and hdd under 4f out: sn no ex and wknd ent st* **200/1**

10 25 **Byzantine**[22] 2729 3-9-0 88 JPO'Brien 9 40
(A P O'Brien, Ire) *chsd ldrs early: sn mid-div: rdn and wknd 4f out: t.o* **200/1**

11 13 **Drumbeat (IRE)**[21] 2756 3-9-0 105 PJSmullen 1 19
(A P O'Brien, Ire) *a towards rr: wknd over 1f out: t.o* **50/1**

2m 30.87s (-6.63) **Going Correction** -0.125s/f (Firm) **11** Ran SP% **115.8**
Speed ratings: **117,113,113,106,101 99,99,98,96,80 71**
CSF £9.63 TOTE £1.70: £1.10, £2.50, £1.80; DF 9.30.
Owner Derrick Smith **Bred** Ptarmigan Bloodstock & Miss K **Trained** Ballydoyle, Co Tipperary
■ The first time since 1957 that there was no overseas runner. A record seventh Irish Derby win for Aidan O'Brien.

FOCUS
No British runner and the absence of Sea The Stars, who was pulled out because of the ground, removed the most fascinating element from the race. However, off a strong gallop Fame And Glory was most impressive and rates a very worthy winner. The runner-up ran a career-best and should continue his improvement.

NOTEBOOK
Fame And Glory ◆ ran out a most commanding winner and would have been very hard to beat even with his Epsom conqueror in attendance given the way the race was run. Well off the pace in fifth at halfway, he started to improve on the approach to the straight and strode clear in terrific style after getting to the front just over a furlong out. The five-length winning margin was the same as that recorded by his sire Montjeu in 1999, and the logical course now would seem to be to train him for the Arc in a further bid to emulate his sire. He could well take in the King George beforehand. (op 4/5 tchd 4/6)
Golden Sword, who had been responsible for the much more modest pace at Epsom, took up second place form the outset and went to the front around three and a half furlongs out once Rockhampton had done his job. At Epsom he was relegated to fifth late on, in a race that clearly favoured the speedier types, but this time he was able to hang on for a fine second. He has maintained the improvement that he showed in winning the Chester Vase and looks a likely St Leger type. (op 10/1 tchd 12/1)
Mourayan(IRE), left to fly the flag for John Oxx, raced in third for much of the way and moved into second when the pacemaker weakened. Though unable to find any extra through the last quarter-mile, this was a good, honest effort by a colt who finished second to Sea The Stars in last year's Beresford Stakes and started the season with a promising effort in third behind Fame And Glory in the Ballysax before a somewhat lack-lustre run in the Derrinstown ruled him out of Epsom. On this evidence he has the makings of a genuine Group 1-standard performer. (op 8/1 tchd 9/1)

Masterofthehorse(IRE) seemed to get the trip well at Epsom, but it looked here as if he was exposed for lack of stamina and he ran well below expectations. (op 7/2)
Gan Amhras(IRE) had no obvious excuses, remembering he is a horse who has a strong middle-distance pedigree and started the season in such fine style with a third behind Sea The Stars at Newmarket. He was well enough placed for most of the way but found nothing when it mattered. (op 9/1)

3437 - 3440a (Foreign Racing) - See Raceform Interactive

3416 HAMBURG (R-H)
Sunday, June 28

OFFICIAL GOING: Good

3441a HANSA-PREIS DER BESITZERVEREINIGUNG (GROUP 2) 1m 4f
4:40 (4:58) 3-Y-O+ **£38,835** (£17,476; £8,738; £4,854; £2,913)

RPR

1 **Flamingo Fantasy (GER)**[38] 2216 4-9-2 ASuborics 3 114
(W Hickst, Germany) *mid-div to st: hdwy to ld over 1f out: hung rt to rails: drvn clr: r.o wl* **48/10**[3]

2 2 **Getaway (GER)**[245] 7008 6-9-4 ADeVries 7 113
(J Hirschberger, Germany) *hld up in rr to st: hdwy fr wl over 1f out: tk 2nd cl home* **6/4**[1]

3 1/2 **Poseidon Adventure (IRE)**[17] 6-9-2 (b) KKerekes 10 110
(W Figge, Germany) *hld up in rr on ins: trckd wnr through fr 2f out: 2nd over 1f out: no ex and lost 2nd cl home* **69/10**

4 hd **Kamsin (GER)**[35] 2309 4-9-6 AStarke 5 114
(P Schiergen, Germany) *4th & pushed along over 3f out: 3rd & taken to middle st: drvn to take narrow ld wl over 1f out: hdd over 1f out: kpt on same pce* **27/10**[2]

5 2 1/2 **Sassoaloro (GER)**[35] 2309 5-9-2 DarryllHolland 4 106
(H Blume, Germany) *a cl up: 5th st: styd on one pce on ins fr over 1f out* **23/1**

6 3/4 **Adelar (GER)**[35] 2309 4-9-2 YLerner 11 104
(W Baltromei, Germany) *mid-div: outpcd 2f out: rallied ins fnl f* **11/1**

7 1 3/4 **Dwilano (GER)**[29] 6-9-2 NRichter 1 102
(P Remmert, Germany) *first to show: trckd ldr in 3rd: 4th st: grad wknd* **44/1**

8 1 3/4 **Ruten (USA)**[38] 2216 4-9-2 JiriPalik 12 99
(Andreas Lowe, Germany) *wnt lft s: sn mid-div on outside: one pce fnl 2f* **21/1**

9 4 **Shawnee Saga (FR)**[38] 2216 4-9-2 WMongil 9 92
(W Baltromei, Germany) *a in rr* **33/1**

10 3 1/2 **Ambassador (GER)**[35] 2309 5-9-4 THellier 6 89
(T Mundry, Germany) *rdn in paddock: racd in mid-div: hdwy and 5th st: wknd over 1f out (reported to have clipped heels)* **11/1**

11 1 **Download (GER)**[7] 3201 4-9-2 LydiaLammers 8 85
(R Gross, Germany) *pressed ldr: 2nd st: sn wknd* **100/1**

12 1 **Soum (GER)**[357] 3773 4-9-2 FilipMinarik 2 84
(J Hirschberger, Germany) *sn led: hdd & wknd wl over 1f out* **35/1**

2m 28.17s (-6.38) **12** Ran SP% **131.2**
TOTE: WIN 58; PL 18, 17, 20; SF 232.
Owner Gestut Park Wiedingen **Bred** Gestut Park Wiedlingen **Trained** Germany

2988 SAINT-CLOUD (L-H)
Sunday, June 28

OFFICIAL GOING: Soft

3442a PRIX DE MALLERET (GROUP 2) (FILLIES) 1m 4f
2:55 (2:55) 3-Y-O **£71,942** (£27,767; £11,044; £11,044; £4,417)

RPR

1 **Ashalanda (FR)**[27] 3-8-9 FDiFede 2 104
(A De Royer-Dupre, France) *s.i.s: sn led: set stdy early pce: qcknd bef 1/2-way: drvn last 100yds: all out* **33/1**

2 shd **Terre Du Vent (FR)**[20] 3-8-9 GMosse 3 104
(Y De Nicolay, France) *disp 4th: 4th st on outside: sn outpcd and rdn: r.o steadily on outside fnl f: jst failed* **20/1**

3 1/2 **Shamakiya (IRE)**[21] 2754 3-8-9 CSoumillon 8 103
(A De Royer-Dupre, France) *hld up disputing 4th: cl 6th st: disp 3rd 2f out: sn drvn: r.o same pce fnl f* **6/4**[1]

3 dht **Kalla**[25] 2622 3-8-9 MGuyon 1 103
(A Fabre, France) *a.p: 3rd st: wnt 2nd briefly ins fnl f: kpt on same pce* **3/1**[2]

5 2 **Villa Molitor (FR)**[42] 2119 3-8-9 SPasquier 4 100
(F Rohaut, France) *hld up: hdwy and 5th st on ins: one pce fnl 2f* **14/1**

6 2 **Liberty Chery**[16] 2989 3-8-9 DBoeuf 5 97
(J E Hammond, France) *hld up towards rr: last st* **20/1**

7 nk **Peinture Rare (IRE)**[27] 3-8-9 ACrastus 6 96
(E Lellouche, France) *hld up: 7th st: rdn wl over 1f out: one pce* **13/2**

8 nk **Enticement**[46] 1988 3-8-9 RyanMoore 7 96
(Sir Michael Stoute) *trckd ldr: pushed along and 2nd st: rdn over 2f out: stl 2nd 1f out: sn wknd: eased clsng stages* **9/2**[3]

2m 30.6s (-9.80) **Going Correction** -0.65s/f (Hard) **8** Ran SP% **115.6**
Speed ratings: **106,105,105,105,104 102,102,102**
PARI-MUTUEL: WIN 2.20 (coupled with Shamakiya); PL 4.00, 2.60, 1.101.10; DF 178.50.
Owner H H Aga Khan **Bred** Haras De Son Altesse L'Aga Khan **Trained** Chantilly, France
■ Stewards' Enquiry : G Mosse eight-day ban: whip abuse (Jul 12-19)
F Di Fede 100euro fine: whip abuse

NOTEBOOK
Ashalanda(FR), in the race as a pacemaker, ended up in the winners' enclosure. Her young jockey set a sensible pace and on several occasions looked over his shoulder to see how his stablemate was going. When he realised a winning chance was on the cards he rode out to the line and the filly gamely held off the runner-up. Now unbeaten in two races, she is unlikely to go through the sales and her exact future has not been decided for the moment. She could stay at Chantilly or might return to her initial base at Pau.
Terre Du Vent(FR) settled down behind the leading group early on and she didn't really engage top gear until one and a half out, then finished best of all, being in front a few metres past the poste. She is very consistent and should at least win a Group 3 race. Something like the Prix de Pomone in Deauville may now be a target.

Shamakiya(IRE) was given every possible chance but couldn't quicken when things warmed up and never looked like catching her pacemaker. Settled in mid-division in the early stages, she was perfectly placed to challenge halfway up the straight and was then one paced inside the final furlong. A highly rated individual, she has yet to show her best form.
Kalla was just a little one paced in the final stages and the firmish ground might not have suited this daughter of Monsun. Always well placed, she did lengthen her stride in the straight but never looked like making it to the head of affairs. This was the first real race of her career and she should make it at a similar level in the future.
Enticement dropped in behind the leader she was going well down the back straight but being niggled along round the final turn. She never quite made it to the front in the straight and then dropped completely out of contention. The jockey felt the ground was on the lively side for the filly.

3443a GRAND PRIX DE SAINT-CLOUD (GROUP 1) 1m 4f
3:30 (3:36) 4-Y-O+ **£221,903** (£88,777; £44,388; £22,175; £11,107)

RPR

1 **Spanish Moon (USA)**[92] 1012 5-9-2 .... RyanMoore 10 119
(Sir Michael Stoute) *racd in 4th to st: 2nd 2f out: drvn to ld 1f out: drvn clr last 150yds: in command fnl 50yds* **8/1**[3]

2 1 ½ **Alpine Rose (FR)**[31] 2428 4-8-13 .... GMosse 2 114
(A De Royer-Dupre, France) *racd in 3rd: 2nd st: led over 2f out to 1f out: r.o same pce* **11/1**

3 1 ½ **Youmzain (IRE)**[23] 2670 6-9-2 .... CSoumillon 6 114
(M R Channon) *hld up: 8th st: hdwy to dispute 4th 2f out: kpt on u.p fnl f* **10/11**[1]

4 snk **Curtain Call (FR)**[42] 2120 4-9-2 .... C-PLemaire 5 114
(L M Cumani) *mid-div: 5th st on ins: 3rd 2f out: one pce fnl f* **11/1**

5 hd **Magadan (IRE)**[28] 2522 4-9-2 .... ACrastus 8 114
(E Lellouche, France) *mid-div: 6th st on outside: rdn to dispute 3rd wl over 1f out: no ex fnl f* **9/2**[2]

6 ¾ **Ideal World (USA)**[28] 2522 4-9-2 .... SPasquier 4 112
(A Fabre, France) *hld up in rr: 9th st: hdwy 1 1/2f out: kpt on fnl f: nrest at fin* **12/1**

7 15 **Scintillo**[28] 2522 4-9-2 .... RichardHughes 7 88
(R Hannon) *hld up: 7th st: hdwy over 2f out: btn wl over 1f out: eased fnl f* **10/1**

8 1 ½ **Full Of Gold (FR)**[17] 4-9-2 .... DBoeuf 9 86
(Mme C Head-Maarek, France) *mid-div: dropped to last bef st: btn 2f out* **20/1**

9 1 ½ **Dream Desert (IRE)**[23] 2671 4-9-2 .... SamHitchcott 1 84
(M R Channon) *s.s: drvn and sn led: hdd over 2f out and sn wknd* **250/1**

10 dist **Petrograd (IRE)**[28] 2522 8-9-2 .... DBonilla 3 —
(E Lellouche, France) *pressed ldr: 3rd and wkng st: sn t.o* **250/1**

2m 27.4s (-13.00) **Going Correction** -0.65s/f (Hard) **10** Ran SP% **120.7**
Speed ratings: **117,116,115,114,114 114,104,103,102,—**
PARI-MUTUEL: WIN 5.90 (coupled with Ideal World): PL 1.80, 1.80, 1.20;DF 35.80.
Owner K Abdulla **Bred** Juddmonte Farms Inc **Trained** Newmarket, Suffolk
■ Stewards' Enquiry : Ryan Moore 100euro fine: whip abuse

NOTEBOOK
Spanish Moon(USA), who is banned from racing in Britain because of a repeated reluctance to enter the stalls, as expected, played up before the start but eventually entered the gates following a slap with the long tom. He did absolutely nothing wrong in the race though and, always well placed, moved up into a challenging position early in the straight and took command running into the final furlong. He ran on really well and looks capable of winning other Group 1 races. His stalls ban in England doesn't end until November so he is will be campaigned in Europe and the USA. The Arc de Triomphe is definitely a target and a trip to Belmont for the Man O'War Stakes in September is not out of the question.
Alpine Rose(FR) put up a fine performance. Settled in second place, she was cruising round the final turn before taking the lead early in the straight. She battled on really well but couldn't hold the winner. The ground was probably a little lively for this Linamix filly and she will now be given a rest until the autumn. Connections are already thinking about the Prix Vermeille, and the Prix de l'Opera has also been mentioned as a target.
Youmzain(IRE), who won this race a year ago, was a rather a disappointing odds-on favourite. He was at the tail of the field and a long way from the leader when the field entered the straight, and although he did make up some late ground he never threatened the first two. Plans will not change and he will almost certainly be in the line-up for the King George VI and Queen Elizabeth Stakes.
Curtain Call(FR) might have found the ground, which dried out considerably during the day, going against him. Nevertheless he put up a sound performance, coming with a run up the far rail and finishing really well, only narrowly failing to take third place. He will now be sent back to Ireland, probably for the Royal Whip in August.
Scintillo played up before the start and was nearly always at the tail of the field. He made an effort to catch the leaders in the straight but it was short-lived. This fast run race was very different from when he won the Grand Prix at Chantilly.
Dream Desert(IRE) set a good pace for the odds-on favourite and was still at the head of affairs until the straight.

3105 MUSSELBURGH (R-H)
Monday, June 29

OFFICIAL GOING: Good to firm (good in places; 7.9)
Wind: Nil Weather: Dry and hazy

3444 BOLLINGER CHAMPAGNE CHALLENGE SERIES H'CAP (FOR GENTLEMAN AMATEUR RIDERS) 2m
6:55 (6:57) (Class 6) (0-65,61) 4-Y-0+ **£2,498** (£774; £387; £193) **Stalls** Low

Form RPR

4123 1 **Monte Pattino (USA)**[18] 2854 5-11-6 **57** ....(vt) MrSDobson 2 64
(C J Teague) *mde virtually all: rdn along 3f out: drvn and hung lft wl over 1f out: kpt on* **11/2**[3]

-122 2 1 ½ **Mystified (IRE)**[9] 3171 6-11-0 **51** ....(tp) MrSWalker 9 56
(R F Fisher) *a.p: cl up 1/2-way: rdn along 3f out: ev ch tl drvn and one pce fnl f* **5/2**[1]

2360 3 hd **Sir Sandicliffe (IRE)**[11] 3073 5-11-7 **61** .... MrBenBrisbourne(3) 7 66
(W M Brisbourne) *hld up and bhd: stdy hdwy 4f out: rdn to chse ldng pair 2f out: drvn and hung lft ins fnl f: kpt on* **5/1**[2]

0-55 4 4 ½ **Kyber**[10] 3095 8-10-11 **53** .... MrPNorton(5) 6 52
(J S Goldie) *hld up towards rr: hdwy on inner 3f out: swtchd lft and rdn wl over 1f out: sn drvn and no imp* **11/2**[3]

32-5 5 hd **Wotchalike (IRE)**[23] 2725 7-10-7 **51** ....(p) MrCWhillans(7) 8 50
(Miss S Johnstone) *in tch: hdwy to chse ldrs 5f out: rdn along 3f out: sn drvn and grad wknd* **6/1**

4003 6 18 **Mayadeen (IRE)**[14] 2969 7-10-9 **51** ....(v) MrBenHamilton(5) 1 29
(R A Fahey) *chsd ldrs whn rn wd bnd after 5f: in tch tl rdn along and outpcd fnl 3f* **11/1**

0-06 7 ¾ **Rocknest Island (IRE)**[14] 2969 6-10-8 **45** ....(v) MrOGreenall 4 22
(P D Niven) *prom: rdn along 6f out and sn wknd* **12/1**

0/0- 8 19 **Named At Dinner**[39] 3718 8-10-1 **45** ....(p) MrGJCockburn(7) 5 —
(Miss Lucinda V Russell) *a in rr: bhd fnl 4f* **100/1**

9 8 **Eimear's Pride (IRE)**[31] 2263 9-10-1 **45** ....(b) MrVPLyons(7) 3 —
(Daniel Mark Loughnane, Ire) *chsd ldrs: rdn along 6f out: sn wknd and bhd fnl 4f* **9/1**

3m 32.25s (-1.25) **Going Correction** -0.275s/f (Firm) **9** Ran SP% **117.3**
Speed ratings (Par 101): **92,91,91,88,88 79,79,69,65**
toteswingers: 1&2 £2.30, 1&3 £6.30, 2&3 £3.30. CSF £19.99 CT £74.14 TOTE £8.00: £2.40, £1.20, £2.00; EX 24.90.
Owner Collins Chauffeur Driven Executive Cars **Bred** Gainsborough Farm Llc **Trained** Station Town, Co Durham

FOCUS
A weak handicap. The first two home slipped the field on the final bend, but while they both had very much the run of things the form still makes sense.

3445 STERLING SPRINT H'CAP 5f
7:25 (7:25) (Class 6) (0-65,64) 4-Y-0+ **£2,590** (£770; £385; £192) **Stalls** Low

Form RPR

1041 1 **Rocketball (IRE)**[10] 3111 4-8-12 **60** .... DeanHeslop(5) 12 69
(Mrs L Williamson) *a.p: rdn to ld over 1f out: kpt on wl fnl f* **6/1**[3]

20-2 2 1 **Wicked Wilma (IRE)**[14] 2966 5-8-11 **59** .... SladeO'Hara(5) 11 64
(A Berry) *cl up: led 1/2-way: rdn and hdd over 1f out: drvn and edgd lft ins fnl f: no ex last 100yds* **6/1**[3]

0100 3 nk **Thunder Bay**[14] 2966 4-9-0 **60** ....(v[1]) FrederikTylicki(3) 4 64
(R A Fahey) *chsd ldrs: rdn along wl over 1f out: drvn and keeping on whn n.m.r ins fnl f* **5/1**[2]

0-00 4 shd **Ingleby Star (IRE)**[13] 3002 4-8-9 **57** ....(p) BMcHugh(5) 1 61
(N Wilson) *midfield: hdwy 2f out: swtchd rt and rdn over 1f out: kpt on ins fnl f* **16/1**

0043 5 1 ¾ **Spirit Of Coniston**[10] 3111 6-8-2 **52** .... PaulPickard(7) 3 50
(P T Midgley) *trckd ldrs: rdn along and outpcd 1/2-way: effrt and nt clr run over 1f out: sn swtchd rt and rdn: kpt on ins fnl f* **13/2**

4201 6 ¾ **Twosheetstothewind**[13] 3002 5-9-6 **63** .... PhillipMakin 13 58
(M Dods) *hld up: hdwy 1/2-way: rdn to chse ldrs over 1f out: wknd ins fnl f* **3/1**[1]

0000 7 2 **Coconut Moon**[13] 3002 7-8-2 **45** .... PaulQuinn 2 33
(A Berry) *towards rr: hdwy 2f out: swtchd rt and rdn over 1f out: nt rch ldrs* **33/1**

0-06 8 ½ **Making Music**[6] 3239 6-8-5 **48** ....(b) DuranFentiman 10 34
(T D Easterby) *led: rdn along and hdd 1/2-way: grad wknd* **14/1**

0540 9 nk **Valiant Romeo**[6] 3239 9-8-5 **48** ....(v) GregFairley 7 33
(R Bastiman) *towards rr: pushed along 1/2-way: rdn wl over 1f out and sme late hdwy* **25/1**

0600 10 1 ½ **King Of Swords (IRE)**[11] 3065 5-9-7 **64** .... PJMcDonald 6 43
(N Tinkler) *a in rr* **12/1**

0-5 11 2 ¼ **Alfie Lee (IRE)**[10] 3109 12-8-3 **51** ow6........................(tp) PatrickDonaghy(5) 5 22
(D A Nolan) *a towards rr* **100/1**

0006 12 1 **Angle Of Attack (IRE)**[22] 2745 4-9-1 **58** .... TomEaves 14 26
(A D Brown) *stmbld s: a towards rr* **22/1**

0-06 13 ½ **Mutayam**[10] 3109 9-8-5 **48** ow3........................(tp) PatrickMathers 9 14
(D A Nolan) *a towards rr* **125/1**

58.88 secs (-1.52) **Going Correction** -0.275s/f (Firm) **13** Ran SP% **116.7**
Speed ratings (Par 101): **101,99,98,98,95 94,91,90,90,87 84,82,81**
toteswingers: 1&2 £4.30, 1&3 £11.40, 2&3 £9.90. CSF £39.16 CT £200.20 TOTE £8.30: £3.10, £1.70, £2.00; EX 36.60.
Owner J Levenson **Bred** John Morris **Trained** Saighton, Cheshire
■ Stewards' Enquiry : Slade O'Hara one-day ban: careless riding (Jul 13)

FOCUS
Eight previous course-and-distance winners lined up here. The race was run at a decent pace and few got seriously involved from off the pace, with the field coming over to the stands' side. Sound form.
Angle Of Attack(IRE) Official explanation: jockey said gelding stumbled coming out of stalls

3446 EUROPEAN BREEDERS' FUND MEDIAN AUCTION MAIDEN STKS 5f
7:55 (7:55) (Class 5) 2-Y-0 **£3,885** (£1,156; £577; £288) **Stalls** Low

Form RPR

6522 1 **Mal And Dave (IRE)**[9] 3152 2-9-3 0........................ AdrianTNicholls 7 69
(D Nicholls) *chsd ldng pair: swtchd rt and rdn wl over 1f out: led briefly ent fnl f: sn hdd and drvn: rallied to ld nr fin* **15/8**[1]

4 2 shd **Mercers Row**[28] 2526 2-9-3 0........................ DanielTudhope 3 69
(A Dickman) *chsd ldrs: swtchd rt and rdn wl over 1f out: styd on to ld ins fnl f: drvn: hdd and no ex nr fin* **18/1**

5242 3 1 ½ **Ignatieff (IRE)**[13] 3006 2-9-3 0........................ TomEaves 1 63
(Mrs L Stubbs) *clsd up: effrt wl over 1f out: sn rdn and kpt on same pce* **2/1**[2]

0000 4 2 ¾ **Camacho Flyer (IRE)**[30] 2467 2-8-10 0........................(p) PaulPickard(7) 2 53
(P T Midgley) *led: rdn along 2f out: drvn and hdd ent fnl f: wknd* **22/1**

60 5 2 ¼ **Charity Fair**[35] 2311 2-8-7 0........................ SladeO'Hara(5) 4 40
(A Berry) *in tch: rdn along 1/2-way: sn no imp* **66/1**

0604 6 1 ½ **Sir Christie**[11] 3058 2-9-3 0........................ PJMcDonald 8 40
(N Tinkler) *chsd ldrs: rdn along 2f out: sn drvn and wknd* **33/1**

7 nk **Licence To Till (USA)** 2-9-3 0........................ GregFairley 6 39
(M Johnston) *s.i.s: rdn along 1/2-way: a towards rr* **11/4**[3]

8 15 **Jigajig** 2-8-12 0........................ BMcHugh(5) 5 —
(N Wilson) *s.i.s: a in rr* **25/1**

59.52 secs (-0.88) **Going Correction** -0.275s/f (Firm) **8** Ran SP% **112.7**
Speed ratings (Par 93): **96,95,93,89,85 83,82,58**
toteswingers: 1&2 £11.40, 1&3 £1.40, 2&3 £8.90. CSF £31.15 TOTE £3.70: £1.50, £4.60, £1.10; EX 33.60.
Owner Dr Marwan Koukash **Bred** Tally-Ho Stud **Trained** Sessay, N Yorks

FOCUS
A poor juvenile maiden rated through the fourth and fifth. The winner is rated to form.

NOTEBOOK
Mal And Dave(IRE), a runner-up the last twice, narrowly got his head in front at the sixth time of asking. He was well away from his modest draw, but hit a flat spot at halfway. He was still close enough when getting second wind and just edged out the more inexperienced runner-up near the line. This was certainly deserved and he ought to find his feet in nurseries. (op 2-1 tchd 9-4 in places)
Mercers Row ◆, fourth on debut at Carlisle, looked the most likely winner when switching wide with his effort. He just ran green when hitting the front, however, and was mugged late on. He looks the part and, with this experience sure to bring him forward again, can soon be placed to gain compensation. (tchd 20-1)
Ignatieff(IRE) had plenty in his favour and held every chance against the stands' rail. He probably paid for forcing the strong early fractions and has a small race in him, but is looking exposed now. (tchd 15-8 and 9-4 in places)

Camacho Flyer(IRE) was dropping back in trip and showed real early dash to lead in first-time cheekpieces. He unsurprisingly paid for his early exertions, but this was his best effort yet. (op 25-1 tchd 28-1)
Licence To Till(USA) has a sprint pedigree and cost $130,000. He was solid enough in the betting for this racecourse bow, without being very popular, and basically proved far too green to do himself justice. That was not surprising considering the early pace and he should leave this behind in due course. (tchd 7-2)

3447 STERLING SOLUTIONS H'CAP — 1m 4f 100y
8:25 (8:25) (Class 5) (0-70,67) 4-Y-O+ — £3,885 (£1,156; £577; £288) Stalls High

Form — RPR
3-02 **1** **Mooted (UAE)**[12] 3035 4-8-9 **60** .... BMcHugh(5) 4 — 66
(Miss J A Camacho) *trckd ldng pair: smooth hdwy 3f out: led over 2f out: rdn wl over 1f out: drvn and wandered ent fnl f: kpt on wl towards fin* **5/2**[2]
4305 **2** 1 ½ **Thorny Mandate**[9] 3169 7-8-8 **54** .... PaulMulrennan 3 — 58
(W M Brisbourne) *hld up in tch: hdwy 4f out: trckd ldng pair over 2f out: sn nt clr run on inner and swtchd lft: rdn to chal over 1f out: sn drvn and ev ch whn rdr dropped whip ins fnl f: one pce towards fin* **5/1**[3]
3046 **3** ¾ **Solas Alainn (IRE)**[19] 2815 4-9-7 **67** ....(b) GregFairley 5 — 70
(M Johnston) *led: rdn along 3f out: hdd over 2f out and sn drvn: wknd ins fnl f* **11/8**[1]
2200 **4** nk **Piper's Song (IRE)**[11] 2783 6-9-2 **62** .... JerryO'Dwyer 2 — 64
(Patrick Morris) *hld up and bhd: hdwy 3f out and sn rdn along: drvn over 1f out: styd on ins fnl f: nrst fin* **11/1**
4666 **5** 6 **Papa's Princess**[10] 3098 5-8-9 **55** .... DanielTudhope 1 — 48
(J S Goldie) *a in rr* **10/1**
\- **6** 2 ¼ **Ptolomeos**[51] 1902 6-8-10 **61** .... PatrickDonaghy(5) 6 — 51
(Thomas McLaughlin, Ire) *chsd ldr: rdn along over 3f out and sn wknd* **25/1**

2m 42.42s (0.42) **Going Correction** -0.275s/f (Firm) — **6** Ran SP% **108.6**
Speed ratings (Par 103): **87,86,85,85,81 79**
toteswingers: 1&2 £2.00, 1&3 £1.10, 2&3 £1.50. CSF £14.11 TOTE £3.70: £1.50, £2.70; EX 12.00.
Owner Axom (XII) **Bred** Darley **Trained** Norton, N Yorks

FOCUS
Previous winning form was thin on the ground in this weak handicap. The time was slow and this is not form to be positive about.

3448 NCB H'CAP — 1m
8:55 (8:55) (Class 6) (0-65,65) 3-Y-O+ — £2,590 (£770; £385; £192) Stalls High

Form — RPR
0210 **1** **San Silvestro (IRE)**[10] 3098 4-9-1 **57** ....(p) BMcHugh(5) 14 — 67
(Mrs A Duffield) *mde all: rdn along over 2f out: drvn over 1f out: kpt on gamely ins fnl f* **11/1**
6102 **2** nk **Forbidden (IRE)**[10] 3094 6-9-12 **63** ....(t) JerryO'Dwyer 8 — 72
(Daniel Mark Loughnane, Ire) *hld up in tch: hdwy 3f out: swtchd lft and rdn to chal wl over 1f out: ev ch tl drvn ins fnl f and no ex towards fin* **11/2**[3]
5056 **3** 1 ¾ **Bold Indian (IRE)**[10] 3110 5-9-1 **52** .... TomEaves 2 — 57
(I Semple) *hld up: hdwy on outer 3f out: rdn wl over 1f out and ev ch tl drvn and one pce ins fnl f* **12/1**
2001 **4** 2 ½ **King Of Legend (IRE)**[10] 3092 5-8-13 **57** ....(t) IJBrennan(7) 3 — 57
(A G Foster) *t.k.h: hld up in midfield: hdwy over 2f out and sn rdn: drvn and kpt on ins fnl f: nrst fin* **12/1**
3365 **5** shd **Mister Jingles**[19] 2804 6-9-5 **56** ....(p) PaulQuinn 4 — 55
(R M Whitaker) *trckd ldrs: hdwy over 2f out: rdn wl over 1f out: wknd ent fnl f* **11/1**
4004 **6** 1 ¾ **Stoic Leader (IRE)**[14] 2968 9-10-0 **65** .... PhillipMakin 7 — 60
(R F Fisher) *midfield: hdwy 3f out: rdn along 2f out: sn drvn and no imp appr fnl f* **14/1**
4023 **7** nk **Carpe Diem**[14] 2968 4-9-1 **55** .... FrederikTylicki(3) 6 — 50
(R A Fahey) *t.k.h early: hld up in rr: hdwy on inner wl over 2f out: n.m.r wl over 1f out and sn swtchd lft: rdn and kpt on appr fnl f: nrst fin* **5/2**[1]
5024 **8** 1 **Grand Diamond (IRE)**[9] 3150 5-9-13 **64** ....(p) DanielTudhope 5 — 56
(J S Goldie) *hld up and bhd tl sme late hdwy* **4/1**[2]
505 **9** ½ **Funky Munky**[51] 1888 4-9-6 **57** .... PJMcDonald 1 — 48
(G A Swinbank) *nvr nr ldrs* **25/1**
6003 **10** 2 ¾ **Wilmington**[10] 3092 5-8-6 **50** .... JakePayne(7) 10 — 35
(Mrs J C McGregor) *hld up: a towards rr* **66/1**
0053 **11** nk **Al Wasef (USA)**[10] 3093 4-9-9 **65** .... GaryBartley(5) 11 — 49
(J S Goldie) *chsd ldrs: rdn along over 3f out and sn wknd* **14/1**
5-00 **12** 1 ½ **Reddy Ronnie (IRE)**[14] 2965 5-8-10 **47** ....(p) GregFairley 12 — 28
(D W Thompson) *chsd ldrs on inner: rdn along wl over 2f out: sn wknd* **33/1**
31-0 **13** 22 **Shunkawakhan (IRE)**[10] 3110 6-9-10 **64** ....(p) NeilBrown(3) 13 — —
(Miss L A Perratt) *chsd ldr: rdn along 3f out: sn drvn and wknd* **28/1**

1m 40.02s (-1.18) **Going Correction** -0.275s/f (Firm)
WFA 3 from 4yo+ 10lb — **13** Ran SP% **121.1**
Speed ratings (Par 101): **94,93,91,89,89 87,87,86,85,83 82,81,59**
toteswingers: 1&2 £25.40, 1&3 £20.70, 2&3 £19.10. CSF £69.33 CT £785.46 TOTE £12.20: £4.00, £2.00, £3.80; EX 129.90.
Owner Middleham Park Racing Xiv **Bred** Canice M Farrell Jnr **Trained** Constable Burton, N Yorks

FOCUS
An open handicap, run at a fair gallop. The race was notable for some hard-luck stories but the form seems pretty sound.
Grand Diamond(IRE) Official explanation: jockey said gelding was denied a clear run

3449 SCOTTISH RACING YOUR BETTER BET H'CAP — 7f 30y
9:25 (9:26) (Class 6) (0-55,55) 3-Y-O — £2,266 (£674; £337; £168) Stalls High

Form — RPR
060- **1** **Dark Moment**[298] 5632 3-8-13 **54** .... DanielTudhope 1 — 58
(A Dickman) *hld up: hdwy over 2f out: rdn over 1f out: drvn ins fnl f: styd on wl to ld last strides* **7/2**[1]
0-00 **2** hd **Native Dame (IRE)**[23] 2709 3-8-3 **49** ....(b) PatrickDonaghy(5) 14 — 52
(Edgar Byrne) *sn led: rdn along over 2f out: drvn over 1f out: hdd and no ex nr line* **14/1**
5040 **3** 1 ½ **Trade Price (GR)**[11] 3063 3-8-7 **51** ....(p) NeilBrown(3) 5 — 50
(I Semple) *hld up: hdwy on outer over 2f out: rdn over 1f out: kpt on u.p ins fnl f* **20/1**
-000 **4** ¾ **Join Up**[16] 2918 3-8-8 **49** .... PaulMulrennan 9 — 46
(W M Brisbourne) *hld up in rr: hdwy on wd outside over 2f out and sn rdn: drvn over 1f out: kpt on ins fnl f* **66/1**
500 **5** 2 ¾ **George Adamson (IRE)**[20] 2789 3-9-0 **55** .... PJMcDonald 11 — 45
(G A Swinbank) *trckd ldrs: hdwy over 3f out: swtchd lft and rdn to chal 2f out: ev ch tl drvn and one pce appr fnl f* **17/2**
-050 **6** ½ **Royal Keva (IRE)**[12] 3018 3-9-0 **55** .... PhillipMakin 6 — 44
(A D Brown) *prom: effrt over 2f out: sn rdn and ev ch tl drvn and one pce appr fnl f* **14/1**
0030 **7** shd **Street Spirit (USA)**[12] 3018 3-8-11 **52** ....(t) DuranFentiman 2 — 40
(T D Easterby) *midfield: hdwy over 2f out: rdn to chse ldrs over 1f out: drvn and wknd ent fnl f* **14/1**
8 nse **Battimoore (IRE)**[12] 3037 3-8-8 **49** .... JerryO'Dwyer 4 — 37
(Daniel Mark Loughnane, Ire) *plld hrd: hld up in rr: effrt over 2f out: sn rdn and sme late hdwy* **7/2**[1]
0-50 **9** ½ **Sardan Dansar (IRE)**[42] 2143 3-8-5 **51** .... BMcHugh(5) 12 — 38
(Mrs A Duffield) *nvr bttr than midfield* **13/2**[3]
606- **10** nk **Igneous**[284] 6059 3-8-8 **49** .... GregFairley 10 — 35
(D W Thompson) *a in rr* **28/1**
-055 **11** 5 **Positivity**[28] 2530 3-8-12 **53** .... TomEaves 8 — 26
(B Smart) *a in rr* **18/1**
0030 **12** nk **Lily Jicaro (IRE)**[12] 3036 3-8-7 **53** .... DeanHeslop(5) 7 — 25
(Mrs L Williamson) *prom: rdn along over 2f out: drvn wl over 1f out and sn wknd* **25/1**
3540 **13** ½ **Jack's House (IRE)**[13] 3010 3-8-10 **54** ....(t) FrederikTylicki(3) 3 — 24
(Miss J A Camacho) *prom: rdn along 3f out and sn wknd* **6/1**[2]
000- **14** 3 **Home Before Dark**[264] 6573 3-8-11 **52** .... PaulQuinn 13 — 14
(R M Whitaker) *midfield: rdn along 3f out and sn wknd* **33/1**

1m 28.73s (-1.57) **Going Correction** -0.275s/f (Firm) — **14** Ran SP% **124.3**
Speed ratings (Par 97): **97,96,95,94,91 90,90,90,89,89 83,83,82,79**
toteswingers: 1&2 £26.10, 1&3 £82.90, 2&3 £82.90. CSF £55.65 CT £908.51 TOTE £5.20: £2.00, £3.70, £10.20; EX 53.70 Place 6 £91.53, Place 5 £59.84.
Owner Construction Crew Racing Partnership **Bred** Wilderbrook Stud **Trained** Sandhutton, N Yorks

FOCUS
A low-grade handicap but the form seems sound enough.
Dark Moment ◆ Official explanation: trainer said, regarding apparent improvement in form, that he believed it had benefited from being gelded last season and appeared better suited by the faster ground.
Battimoore(IRE) Official explanation: jockey said filly hung left throughout
T/Plt: £157.80 to a £1 stake. Pool: £72,873.31. 336.94 winning tickets. T/Qpdt: £70.10 to a £1 stake. Pool: £4,150.00. 43.80 winning tickets. JR

3187 PONTEFRACT (L-H)
Monday, June 29

OFFICIAL GOING: Good to firm (8.7)
The course was dolled out from 6f to winning post but effect on distances not notified.
Wind: Almost nil Weather: Fine and sultry becoming overcast and very humid

3450 PONTEFRACT LADIES' H'CAP (LADY AMATEUR RIDERS) — 1m 2f 6y
2:15 (2:16) (Class 5) (0-70,70) 3-Y-O+ — £3,123 (£968; £484; £242) Stalls Low

Form — RPR
0000 **1** **Gala Sunday (USA)**[37] 2263 9-9-6 **52** ....(bt) MissSBrotherton 4 — 62
(M W Easterby) *chsd ldrs: hdwy on ins to ld 2f out: hld on towards fin* **14/1**
3-36 **2** 1 **Sir Boss (IRE)**[30] 2493 4-10-5 **68** .... MissMSowerby(3) 14 — 76
(D E Cantillon) *hld up towards rr: gd hdwy on outside over 1f out: wnt 2nd last 75yds: nt rch wnr* **9/2**[1]
6202 **3** 2 **Strike Force**[6] 3244 5-9-9 **60** .... MissALHutchinson(5) 13 — 64
(Miss J Feilden) *in rr: swtchd outside over 3f out: chsng ldrs over 1f out: kpt on same pce* **6/1**[2]
-444 **4** 1 **Hurricane Thomas (IRE)**[12] 3023 5-8-12 **51** oh3(v[1]) MissPhillipaTutty(7) 7 — 53
(R A Fahey) *mid-div: hdwy to chse ldrs over 2f out: one pce* **8/1**[3]
-101 **5** 4 **Hi Dancer**[4] 3291 6-10-3 **68** 6ex .... MissEStead(5) 17 — 62
(P C Haslam) *prom: chsng ldrs over 2f out: fdd fnl f* **9/1**
50-4 **6** ½ **Inspirina (IRE)**[20] 2783 5-9-11 **62** .... MissHayleyMoore(5) 6 — 55
(R Ford) *s.v.s: detached in last: hdwy on ins over 2f out: nvr nr ldrs* **9/2**[1]
50-0 **7** 5 **Itsy Bitsy**[146] 377 7-8-12 **51** oh6 .... RosePearson(7) 1 — 34
(W J Musson) *hld up in rr: hdwy over 2f out: nvr nr ldrs* **33/1**
0062 **8** 3 ½ **Ming Vase**[10] 3123 7-9-6 **52** .... MissFayeBramley 3 — 28
(P T Midgley) *chsd ldrs: upsides 2f out: sn wknd* **12/1**
000- **9** 2 **Paparaazi (IRE)**[34] 6189 7-9-5 **56** ow2 ....(p) MissKSharp(5) 11 — 28
(I W McInnes) *s.i.s: hdwy on ins over 2f out: wknd over 1f out* **66/1**
30-4 **10** ½ **Zaplamation (IRE)**[10] 3123 4-9-5 **51** oh5 .... MissADeniel 10 — 22
(D W Barker) *sn chsng ldrs: upsides 2f out: sn wknd* **18/1**
042 **11** 14 **Man Of Gwent (UAE)**[17] 2878 5-10-10 **70** .... MissEFolkes 8 — 13
(P D Evans) *mid-div: lost pl over 2f out: sn bhd* **9/1**
5-60 **12** nse **Jarvo**[157] 275 8-8-12 **51** oh2 .... MissCLWhitehead(7) 2 — —
(I W McInnes) *trckd ldrs: sddle sn slipped: lost pl over 2f out* **50/1**
6030 **13** 2 **King's Ransom**[10] 3112 6-10-5 **65** ....(p) MrsCBartley 5 — 4
(S Gollings) *led: hdd and hunr rt 2f out: sn wknd* **18/1**
0-00 **14** 2 **Swing It Ruby (IRE)**[22] 2742 3-9-4 **69** ow18 .... MissDLenge(7) 9 — 4
(Mrs D J Sanderson) *mid-div: lost pl over 3f out: sn bhd* **80/1**
600- **15** 12 **Right You Are (IRE)**[100] 7373 9-9-0 **53** oh6 ow2 .... MissACraven(7) 12 — —
(Paul Green) *chsd ldrs: lost pl 4f out: bhd fnl 2f: t.o* **66/1**
0344 **16** 14 **Titinius (IRE)**[27] 2569 9-9-6 **52** ....(v[1]) MissEJJones 16 — —
(Micky Hammond) *prom: lost pl over 2f out: sn bhd: t.o* **16/1**

2m 12.36s (-1.34) **Going Correction** -0.05s/f (Good)
WFA 3 from 4yo+ 12lb — **16** Ran SP% **121.6**
Speed ratings (Par 103): **103,102,100,99,96 96,92,89,87,87 76,76,74,72,63 52**
toteswingers: 1&2 £22.30, 1&3 £19.80, 2&3 £7.90. CSF £74.47 CT £433.58 TOTE £14.30: £2.60, £2.00, £1.60, £2.40; EX 146.00.
Owner Steve Hull **Bred** Juddmonte Farms Inc **Trained** Sheriff Hutton, N Yorks
■ Stewards' Enquiry : Miss A Craven one-day ban: used whip when out of contention

FOCUS
This was a typically competitive ladies´ handicap. Ordinary but sound form.
Inspirina(IRE) Official explanation: jockey said gelding missed the break
Jarvo Official explanation: jockey said saddle slipped
King's Ransom Official explanation: jockey said gelding hung right

3451 TED CARTER - A LIFETIME IN RACING FILLIES' H'CAP — 1m 4y
2:45 (2:45) (Class 5) (0-70,69) 3-Y-O+ — £3,238 (£963; £481; £240) Stalls Low

Form — RPR
-160 **1** **Hel's Angel (IRE)**[20] 2786 3-9-9 **69** .... JamieKyne(5) 3 — 76
(Mrs A Duffield) *hld up in rr: gd hdwy on outside 2f out: r.o to ld last 75yds* **11/2**
/00- **2** 1 ¼ **Kassuta**[90] 7535 5-9-2 **47** .... EddieAhern 8 — 53
(R M H Cowell) *trckd ldrs: led over 1f out: hdd and no ex wl ins fnl f* **12/1**

4231 **3** *2* **Singora Lady (IRE)**[8] 3188 4-9-12 **57** 6ex........................ MickyFenton 1 58
(P T Midgley) *s.i.s: hdwy on outer over 3f out: chsng ldrs over 1f out: kpt on same pce* **9/4**[1]

-064 **4** *1 3/4* **Georgie Bee**[42] 2143 3-8-12 **53**.. PaulHanagan 6 48
(T D Walford) *mid-div: effrt over 2f out: kpt on same pce appr fnl f* **5/1**[3]

6524 **5** *1 1/2* **Grethel (IRE)**[11] 3060 5-9-5 **50**.. PaulMulrennan 5 44
(A Berry) *chsd ldrs: n.m.r over 1f out: one pce* **14/1**

0034 **6** *2 3/4* **Premier Krug (IRE)**[6] 3241 3-8-4 **45**.. PaulQuinn 4 31
(P D Evans) *in rr: effrt over 3f out: nvr a threat* **7/1**

0-05 **7** *3 3/4* **Sairaam (IRE)**[34] 2357 3-9-6 **61**.. TPO'Shea 7 38
(J L Dunlop) *led 1f: trckd ldr: led 2f out: sn hdd: wknd 1f out* **9/2**[2]

64-5 **8** *7* **Aquarian Dancer**[16] 748 4-9-0 **45**.. TonyHamilton 2 8
(Jedd O'Keeffe) *hdwy to ld after 1f: hdd 2f out: sn lost pl* **25/1**

1m 45.79s (-0.11) **Going Correction** -0.05s/f (Good)
WFA 3 from 4yo+ 10lb **8** Ran SP% **111.7**
Speed ratings (Par 100): **98,96,94,93,91 88,85,78**
toteswingers: 1&2 £16.80, 1&3 £3.20, 2&3 £8.00 . CSF £64.38 CT £187.41 TOTE £7.50: £2.40, £3.90, £1.30; EX 92.60.
Owner Mrs H Baines & Middleham Park Racing VII **Bred** S White **Trained** Constable Burton, N Yorks
■ Stewards' Enquiry : Jamie Kyne one-day ban: used whip in incorrect place (Jul 13)

FOCUS
Just a modest fillies´ handicap. Sound enough form.

3452 SPINDRIFTER CONDITIONS STKS 6f
3:15 (3:15) (Class 3) 2-Y-O **£7,771** (£2,312; £1,155; £577) **Stalls** Low

Form RPR

3110 **1** **Jack My Boy (IRE)**[23] 2702 2-9-4 0.. PaulHanagan 3 84
(P D Evans) *mde all: styd on wl fnl f: rdn out* **6/1**

1 **2** *1 3/4* **Decree Absolute (USA)**[20] 2793 2-8-13 0........................ PaulFitzsimons 2 74
(Miss J R Tooth) *trckd ldrs: effrt and chsd wnr over 1f out: no imp* **3/1**[2]

3 *5* **Bilash** 2-8-7 0.. TPO'Shea 1 53+
(R Hollinshead) *sn drvn along in last: outpcd over 2f out: kpt on fnl f: nvr on terms* **5/1**[3]

41 **4** *7* **Kylladdie**[43] 2099 2-9-1 0.. MickyFenton 4 40
(T P Tate) *sweating and coltish: sn w wnr: drvn over 2f out: hung rt and wknd over 1f out* **10/11**[1]

1m 17.57s (0.67) **Going Correction** -0.05s/f (Good) **4** Ran SP% **108.3**
Speed ratings (Par 97): **93,90,84,74**
CSF £22.37 TOTE £4.40; EX 13.50.
Owner Terry Earle **Bred** Mrs Sheila Walker **Trained** Pandy, Monmouths

FOCUS
Quite what this form is worth is debatable, with the favourite seriously harming his chance in the preliminaries, but nothing should be taken away from Jack My Boy. Probably not form to be too positive about.

NOTEBOOK
Jack My Boy(IRE) took them along at a decent clip and kept finding to record a third career victory. A drifter in the market, he had finished last of 12 when bidding for a hat-trick in the Woodcote Stakes at Epsom, but the smaller field here helped and he galloped on strongly. He was conceding weight all round, but things will be a lot tougher when he goes back up in grade. Connections will aim him at the Redcar Two-Year-old Trophy. (op 3-1)
Decree Absolute(USA), who caused a 66/1 shock when winning at Salisbury on his debut, moved nicely in behind the speed and stuck on right the way to the line, but never looked like getting to the winner. (op 11-2 tchd 6-1)
Bilash, out of the yard´s useful sprinter Goldeva, was nibbled at beforehand and made an encouraging debut. It was always going to be very tough for him to win this at the first time of asking and he will find easier opportunities. (op 11-1)
Kylladdie, ready winner of a slow-ground Ripon maiden, became very coltish in the paddock and got himself rather warm. He continued to play up down at the start and it clearly affected his performance, being eased off once his chance had gone in the straight. This wasn´t his true form and connections will surely sign him up for a gelding operation following these antics. Official explanation: trainer had no explanation for the poor form shown (op 8-11 tchd 4-6)

3453 EBF PARK SUITE FILLIES' H'CAP 6f
3:45 (3:46) (Class 3) (0-90,83) 3-Y-O+
£9,346 (£2,799; £1,399; £700; £349; £175) **Stalls** Low

Form RPR

0-1 **1** **Sioux Rising (IRE)**[38] 2250 3-9-4 **80**.. PaulHanagan 6 84
(R A Fahey) *chsd ldrs: drvn over 2f out: styd on fnl f: led post* **15/2**

5545 **2** *nse* **Mey Blossom**[13] 2998 4-8-10 **68**........................ MichaelJStainton(3) 4 74
(R M Whitaker) *chsd ldrs: led on ins over 1f out: jst ct* **9/2**[2]

0413 **3** *nk* **Artistic License (IRE)**[9] 3164 4-10-0 **83**........................ DarryllHolland 1 88
(M R Channon) *s.i.s: sn drvn along in last: hdwy and swtchd outside over 1f out: styd on wl: jst hld* **5/1**[3]

2112 **4** *5* **Sweet Gale (IRE)**[12] 3030 5-9-6 **75**........................ FrankieMcDonald 5 64
(Mike Murphy) *in rr: hdwy over 2f out: chsng ldrs whn hmpd appr fnl f: sn wknd* **13/2**

6035 **5** *1/2* **On Offer (IRE)**[12] 3033 3-8-12 **74**.. DavidAllan 9 59
(T D Easterby) *chsd ldrs on outer: upsides over 1f out: wknd jst ins fnl f* **16/1**

1115 **6** *1 1/4* **All The Nines (IRE)**[13] 3001 3-9-7 **83**........................ EdwardCreighton 2 64
(Mrs D J Sanderson) *drvn to ld: edgd rt and hdd over 1f out: sn wknd* **8/1**

6621 **7** *4 1/2* **Mango Music**[9] 3153 6-9-9 **78**.. TPQueally 8 47
(M Quinn) *w ldr fr outside draw: wkng whn hmpd appr fnl f* **4/1**[1]

2214 **8** *1/2* **Bobbie Soxer (IRE)**[26] 2611 3-9-6 **82**.. EddieAhern 7 47
(J L Dunlop) *in rr: effrt over 2f out: chsng ldrs whn hmpd appr fnl f: sn lost pl* **5/1**[3]

1m 16.8s (-0.10) **Going Correction** -0.05s/f (Good)
WFA 3 from 4yo+ 7lb **8** Ran SP% **113.6**
Speed ratings (Par 104): **98,97,97,90,90 88,82,81**
toteswingers: 1&2 £11.30, 1&3 £6.50, 2&3 £6.10. CSF £40.53 CT £186.31 TOTE £8.90: £2.30, £2.40, £2.00; EX 56.10.
Owner Mrs Una Towell **Bred** N And Mrs N Nugent **Trained** Musley Bank, N Yorks
■ Stewards' Enquiry : Darryll Holland one-day ban: used whip down shoulder in forehand position (Jul 13)

FOCUS
This was a wide-open fillies´ sprint handicap and All The Nines and Mango Music ensured they went a strong gallop. Probably fair form for the grade.

NOTEBOOK
Sioux Rising(IRE), who drew clear with the runner-up when winning a C&D maiden last month, looked potentially interesting on thishandicap debut and she showed an excellent attitude for one so inexperienced, battling on gamely and getting up right on the line. Her stable continues in fine form and this daughter of Danetime may well improve again. (op 7-1 tchd 8-1)
Mey Blossom, some 17lb lower than when last winning over a year ago, looked set to end the losing run when coming through a furlong out and kept on right the way to the line, but was just caught on the post. She was out of luck this time, but it is surely not long before she wins again. (op 11-2)
Artistic License(IRE) has been in good form and she ran another fine race, responding to pressure having been last and outpaced to come and hold every chance inside the final furlong. She was unable to pull out that bit extra close home, but this was still a fine effort under a big weight and things may have been different had she not been slow to get going. (op 9-2 tchd 11-2)
Sweet Gale(IRE), 10lb higher than when winning at Leicester two starts back, stayed on late without ever looking likely to be involved, getting slightly impeded in the process. (op 8-1)
On Offer(IRE) continues to fall short and needs some assistance from the handicapper. (op 14-1 tchd 20-1)
All The Nines(IRE) paid the cost for setting such a fast pace and deserve another chance. (op 9-1 tchd 7-1)
Mango Music, winner of this a year ago, helped to set too strong a pace and was already retreating when hampered. (tchd 11-2)
Bobbie Soxer(IRE) moved nicely into contention but couldn´t quicken in the straight and was held when hampered. (op 11-2 tchd 9-2)

3454 WAYNE CONWAY MEMORIAL H'CAP 1m 4f 8y
4:15 (4:16) (Class 5) (0-70,66) 3-Y-O **£3,238** (£963; £481; £240) **Stalls** Low

Form RPR

00-5 **1** **Sparkaway**[89] 1070 3-8-2 **47**.. TPO'Shea 15 56
(W J Musson) *in rr: hdwy on outside over 3f out: led over 1f out: drvn clr* **16/1**

-003 **2** *4 1/2* **Rocky Heights (IRE)**[25] 2635 3-8-10 **55**........................ EddieAhern 4 57+
(J L Dunlop) *chsd ldrs: nt clr run and swtchd ins over 1f out: styd on to take 2nd nr fin* **9/4**[1]

3211 **3** *3/4* **Screaming Brave**[25] 2635 3-9-5 **64**.. TedDurcan 10 65
(M R Channon) *hld up in rr: hdwy on outside over 3f out: wnt 2nd 1f out: styd on same pce* **7/1**[3]

5016 **4** *1 1/2* **Berriedale**[18] 2838 3-8-10 **55**.. TPQueally 5 53
(Mrs A Duffield) *hld up in midfield: effrt and nt clr run 2f out: swtchd outside: styd on wl ins fnl f* **28/1**

-003 **5** *1/2* **Nut Hand (IRE)**[19] 2802 3-8-9 **54**.. DavidAllan 14 51
(T D Easterby) *mid-div: hdwy 4f out: styd on same pce fnl 2f* **16/1**

0-03 **6** *1 3/4* **Pattern Mark**[20] 2790 3-8-9 **54**.. PaulMulrennan 8 49
(Ollie Pears) *hld up in rr: effrt on inner whn nt clr run 2f out: swtchd rt and kpt on wl fnl f* **12/1**

0520 **7** *hd* **Amazing Blue Sky**[12] 3018 3-8-12 **57**.. MickyFenton 2 51
(Mrs R A Carr) *led tl over 1f out: hung rt one pce* **14/1**

-020 **8** *hd* **Deuce**[17] 2881 3-9-3 **62**..(b) StephenCarson 12 56
(Eve Johnson Houghton) *chsd ldrs: one pce appr fnl f* **8/1**

-320 **9** *1 3/4* **Avitus**[33] 2371 3-9-1 **60**.. PaulHanagan 7 51
(Micky Hammond) *trckd ldrs: chal over 2f out: one pce appr fnl f* **12/1**

306 **10** *1/2* **Sadaska**[25] 2633 3-8-7 **52**.. SaleemGolam 3 42
(S C Williams) *mid-div: effrt over 2f out: nvr nr ldrs* **16/1**

-500 **11** *4 1/2* **What A Day**[33] 2370 3-8-10 **60**.. JamieKyne(5) 1 43
(J J Quinn) *chsd ldrs: tk fierce hold: effrt on ins whn hmpd over 1f out: sn wknd* **6/1**[2]

065 **12** *3/4* **The Quiet Genius**[45] 2042 3-9-6 **65**.. TonyHamilton 9 47
(Jedd O'Keeffe) *s.i.s: hld up in rr: nvr on terms* **33/1**

5045 **13** *2 3/4* **Kochanski (IRE)**[18] 2838 3-8-8 **53**.. JoeFanning 6 31
(M Johnston) *chsd ldrs: wkng whn hmpd over 1f out* **14/1**

4504 **14** *49* **Susurrayshaan**[18] 2843 3-8-10 **55**..(p) DaleGibson 11 —
(Mrs G S Rees) *chsd ldrs: drvn 4f out: wkng whn hmpd over 2f out: eased and sn bhd: t.o* **50/1**

2m 37.59s (-3.21) **Going Correction** -0.05s/f (Good) **14** Ran SP% **123.4**
Speed ratings (Par 99): **108,105,104,103,103 102,101,101,100,100 97,96,94,62**
toteswingers: 1&2 £20.70, 1&3 £28.10, 2&3 £3.50. CSF £52.50 CT £295.56 TOTE £31.70: £7.10, £1.70, £2.30; EX 146.10.
Owner KCS Partnership **Bred** Jenny Hall Bloodstock Ltd **Trained** Newmarket, Suffolk
■ Stewards' Enquiry : Eddie Ahern two-day ban: careless riding (Jul 14-15)

FOCUS
This had looked a competitive 3yo handicap, but bottom weight Sparkaway had other ideas and came out well on top. Modest but sound form.
Sparkaway Official explanation: trainer said, regarding apparent improvement in form, that the gelding appreciated the stiff track.
Berriedale Official explanation: jockey said filly was denied a clear run
Pattern Mark Official explanation: jockey said gelding was denied a clear run
Amazing Blue Sky Official explanation: jockey said gelding hung right

3455 MR WOLF SPRINT H'CAP 6f
4:45 (4:47) (Class 4) (0-85,83) 3-Y-O **£5,180** (£1,541; £770; £384) **Stalls** Low

Form RPR

4264 **1** **Big Apple Boy (IRE)**[9] 3144 3-9-6 **82**.. MickyFenton 4 94+
(Jedd O'Keeffe) *sn led: hung lft and wnt clr appr fnl f: eased towards fin* **3/1**[1]

0520 **2** *6* **Indian Art (IRE)**[10] 3116 3-9-6 **82**.. JimmyFortune 7 75
(R Hannon) *hld up in rr: effrt on outside over 2f out: edgd lft and kpt on to take 2nd nr fin* **3/1**[1]

-404 **3** *hd* **Desert Falls**[19] 2821 3-9-4 **83**........................ MichaelJStainton(3) 8 75
(R M Whitaker) *chsd ldrs: drvn over 2f out: kpt on same pce appr fnl f* **10/1**[3]

-316 **4** *hd* **Kersivay**[53] 1803 3-9-0 **76**.. TonyHamilton 3 68
(D W Barker) *chsd ldrs: kpt on same pce appr fnl f* **3/1**[1]

5-40 **5** *2 1/2* **Whatyouwoodwishfor (USA)**[44] 2072 3-9-0 **76**........................ PaulHanagan 6 60
(R A Fahey) *qckly away and led early: chsd ldrs: drvn over 3f out: hung lft and wknd fnl 75yds* **9/2**[2]

211- **6** *3 1/2* **Spiritual Art**[199] 7645 3-8-7 **76**.. HollyHall(7) 2 48
(S A Callaghan) *hld up in rr: effrt on ins whn hmpd over 2f out: sn btn* **11/1**

1m 16.71s (-0.19) **Going Correction** -0.05s/f (Good) **6** Ran SP% **110.6**
Speed ratings (Par 101): **99,91,90,90,87 82**
toteswingers: 1&2 £2.80, 1&3 £7.40, 2&3 £5.30. CSF £11.73 CT £71.87 TOTE £4.30: £2.20, £2.10; EX 14.70.
Owner Highbeck Racing **Bred** Thomas Keane **Trained** Middleham Moor, N Yorks

FOCUS
Nothing got into this as Big Apple Boy made all for an easy success. The form has been rated at face value despite a bit of doubt over what he beat.
Whatyouwoodwishfor(USA) Official explanation: jockey said gelding hung left

3456 WILFRED UNDERWOOD MEMORIAL MAIDEN FILLIES' STKS 1m 2f 6y
5:15 (5:17) (Class 5) 3-4-Y-O **£3,238** (£963; £481; £240) **Stalls** Low

Form RPR

0- **1** **Straits Of Hormuz (USA)**[323] 4897 3-9-0 0........................ JoeFanning 1 75
(M Johnston) *mde all: kpt on wl fnl 2f: hld on towards fin* **15/2**

6-3 **2** *nk* **Brilliana**[18] 2848 3-9-0 0.. TedDurcan 5 74
(D R Lanigan) *hld up in last but wl in tch: effrt over 2f out: tk 2nd last 75yds: jst hld* **4/1**[2]

2-32 **3** *1* **Queen Eleanor**[10] 3100 3-9-0 76 JimmyFortune 2 72
(J H M Gosden) *sn trcking wnr: effrt over 2f out: rdn and hung lft over 1f out: no ex ins fnl f* **8/13**[1]

56-4 **4** *8* **Quiquillo (USA)**[20] 2789 3-9-0 64 TPQueally 4 56
(H R A Cecil) *rn in snatches and hung rt thrght: chsd ldrs: upsides and drvn on outer over 3f out: wl hld whn eased ins fnl f* **7/1**[3]

2m 14.44s (0.74) **Going Correction** -0.05s/f (Good)
WFA 3 from 4yo 12lb **4** Ran SP% **106.2**
Speed ratings (Par 100): **95,94,93,87**
CSF £31.84 TOTE £5.90; EX 29.40.
Owner R S Brookhouse **Bred** Stratford Place Stud **Trained** Middleham Moor, N Yorks

FOCUS
A weakish fillies' maiden which was syeadily run.
Quiquillo(USA) Official explanation: jockey said filly hung right throughout

3457 BEST UK RACECOURSES ON TURFTV H'CAP 1m 4y
5:45 (5:45) (Class 5) (0-75,74) 3-Y-0+ **£3,238** (£963; £481; £240) **Stalls** Low

Form RPR

5310 **1** **Betteras Bertie**[20] 2791 6-9-4 **63** JimmyFortune 4 72
(M Brittain) *s.i.s: in rr: effrt over 3f out: styd on to ld jst ins fnl f: drvn clr* **14/1**

0010 **2** *2 ½* **Desert Hunter (IRE)**[19] 2804 6-8-9 **54** oh1 PaulHanagan 2 57
(Micky Hammond) *hld up in mid-div: hdwy to ld over 2f out: hdd and no ex ins fnl f* **9/1**

064/ **3** *1* **Bold Diktator**[632] 6025 7-9-5 **67** MichaelJStainton(3) 8 68
(R M Whitaker) *hld up in midfield: effrt and nt clr run over 2f out: kpt on fnl f* **25/1**

0313 **4** *1 ½* **Inside Story (IRE)**[28] 2532 7-9-9 **68** (b) EddieAhern 1 66
(C R Dore) *hld up in rr: hdwy and n.m.r over 1f out: styd on ins fnl f: nt rch ldrs* **5/2**[1]

066- **5** *½* **Acclaben (IRE)**[278] 6214 3-8-5 **60** DaleGibson 3 54
(G A Swinbank) *trckd ldrs: drvn over 3f out: outpcd over 2f out: kpt on fnl f* **9/1**

3000 **6** *4* **Pegasus Lad (USA)**[16] 2925 3-9-5 **74** JoeFanning 9 59
(M Johnston) *led early: chsd ldrs: edgd rt and wknd over 1f out* **9/2**[3]

5363 **7** *2 ½* **King Of The Moors (USA)**[2] 3401 6-9-0 **64** (p) LeeNewnes(5) 5 45
(R C Guest) *trckd ldrs: led over 3f out: hdd over 2f out: carried hd awkwardly and lost pl over 1f out* **5/1**

1403 **8** *6* **Kipchak (IRE)**[6] 3243 4-10-0 **73** (p) DarryllHolland 7 41
(C R Dore) *awkward to break: sn led: t.k.h: hdd over 3f out: nt run on and lost pl over 1f out: eased* **7/2**[2]

1m 46.45s (0.55) **Going Correction** -0.05s/f (Good)
WFA 3 from 4yo+ 10lb **8** Ran SP% **116.2**
Speed ratings (Par 103): **95,92,91,90,89 85,83,77**
toteswingers: 1&2 £8.60, 1&3 £16.40 2&3 £12.50. CSF £132.85 CT £3120.10 TOTE £8.50: £3.30, £2.50, £4.60; EX 61.70 Place 6: £215.79, Place 5: £105.60.
Owner Mrs V C Sugden **Bred** Mrs V C Sugden **Trained** Warthill, N Yorks

FOCUS
A moderate, but open handicap. It was run at a sound enough pace and the form looks straightforward enough, if pretty weak.
Inside Story(IRE) Official explanation: jockey said gelding was denied a clear run
Kipchak(IRE) Official explanation: jockey said gelding ran too free
T/Plt: £75.40 to a £1 stake. Pool: £69,110.39. 668.98 winning tickets. T/Qpdt: £27.80 to a £1 stake. Pool: £4,465.80. 118.55 winning tickets. WG

3427 WINDSOR (R-H)
Monday, June 29

OFFICIAL GOING: Good to firm (8.1)
Wind: Virtually nil Weather: Humid

3458 TOTESPORTBINGO.COM FILLIES' MEDIAN AUCTION MAIDEN STKS 5f 10y
6:40 (6:41) (Class 5) 2-Y-O **£2,729** (£806; £403) **Stalls** High

Form RPR

02 **1** **Virginia Hall**[7] 3210 2-9-0 0 SebSanders 9 80+
(Sir Mark Prescott) *mde all: pushed along and c readily clr over 1f out: easily* **9/2**[2]

5 **2** *4 ½* **Excellent Thought**[14] 2972 2-9-0 0 MichaelHills 5 62
(W J Haggas) *chsd wnr thrght: pushed along: hung lft and green fr 2f out but stl hld on wl for 2nd* **2/1**[1]

3 *¾* **Duchess Ravel (IRE)** 2-9-0 0 RyanMoore 7 59
(R Hannon) *s.i.s: sn in tch: rdn along 1/2-way and styd on fr over 1f out to cl on 2nd wl ins fnl f but nvr any ch w wnr* **5/1**[3]

4 *1 ¼* **Yurituni** 2-9-0 0 TonyCulhane 2 55+
(Eve Johnson Houghton) *in rr: outpcd and green: pushed along 2f out: styd on ins fnl f: gng on cl home* **10/1**

04 **5** *nse* **Jessica Hayllar (USA)**[10] 3101 2-8-7 0 MalinHolmberg(7) 3 54
(M L W Bell) *trckd ldrs in 3rd: nudged along 2f out: styd on same pce ins fnl f* **16/1**

6 *½* **So Surreal (IRE)** 2-9-0 0 FergusSweeney 8 53
(G L Moore) *in tch early: outpcd and pushed along 1/2-way: styd on again ins fnl f but nvr anywhere nr ldrs* **16/1**

0060 **7** *nk* **Silvee**[16] 2919 2-9-0 0 LPKeniry 6 52?
(J J Bridger) *chsd ldrs: rdn 1/2-way: one pce fnl 2f* **100/1**

8 *1* **Rosetta Hill** 2-9-0 0 AdrianMcCarthy 4 48
(J R Jenkins) *chsd ldrs: rdn over 2f out: wknd fnl f* **14/1**

9 *nk* **Polish Steps (IRE)** 2-9-0 0 ShaneKelly 1 47
(J A Osborne) *s.i.s: in rr: sme hdwy on outside and green 2f out: nvr rchd ldrs: wknd ins fnl f* **25/1**

10 *23* **Glamour Profession (IRE)** 2-9-0 0 RichardHughes 10 —
(R Hannon) *s.i.s: wl bhd fr 1/2-way* **9/2**[2]

61.07 secs (0.77) **Going Correction** -0.025s/f (Good) **10** Ran SP% **118.7**
Speed ratings (Par 90): **92,84,83,81,81 80,80,78,78,41**
toteswingers: 1&2 £3.00, 1&3 £5.70, 2&3 £5.00. CSF £14.15 TOTE £6.20: £2.10, £1.40, £2.30; EX 18.20.
Owner C G Rowles Nicholson **Bred** Limestone And Tara Studs **Trained** Newmarket, Suffolk

FOCUS
A fair fillies' maiden but nothing could live with Virginia Hall. The winner impressed but the poor seventh will limit the form.

NOTEBOOK
Virginia Hall, a scopey individual, is improving with every run. Well drawn, she was soon in front against the favoured near-side rail and gradually drew clear after finding plenty for pressure, in the process paying a handsome compliment to her Lingfield conqueror, Brambleberry. It's true she had plenty go her way this time, but she's evidently pretty useful and deserves her chance in something better now. (op 10-3 tchd 3-1)
Excellent Thought finished a few places ahead of Virginia Hall when the pair made their debuts in a Warwick maiden earlier in the month, but the Prescott filly has simply made more progress. This still represented some improvement, however, and she gave the impression there might be more to come again next time. (op 11-4 tchd 3-1)
Duchess Ravel(IRE) ◆, a 20,000gns first foal of a 1m2f winner, fared best of the newcomers, keeping on after a slow start, and this was a pleasing performance. She should go close next time and will stay further. (op 13-2)
Yurituni ◆, a 32,000gns half-sister to a number of successful two-year-olds over sprint trips, is out of quite a useful dual 5f winning juvenile. She looked a bit backward in the paddock, and was well behind for most of the way in the race itself, but she ran on in taking fashion under mainly hands-and-heels riding once getting the idea. One to be with next time. (op 16-1 tchd 20-1 and 9-1)
Jessica Hayllar(USA) ran an improved race to be fourth at Goodwood last time, but the booking of a 7lb claimer suggested she might be best watched on this her third run. Nurseries are now an option. (op 14-1)
So Surreal(IRE), a £24,000 purchase, showed ability on her racecourse bow for a trainer who won this last year with a debutante. (op 14-1)
Rosetta Hill was backed at big prices but she showed little after starting slowly. (op 33-1)
Glamour Profession(IRE), a 28,000euros sister to 7f juvenile winner Midnight Cruiser, ran as though something was amiss. Considering she was sent off at a shorter price than her stablemate, who ran third, she should be capable of leaving this effort well behind. (op 4-1)

3459 TOTESPORTGAMES.COM (S) STKS 6f
7:10 (7:10) (Class 6) 3-Y-0+ **£2,047** (£604; £302) **Stalls** High

Form RPR

040/ **1** **Matuza (IRE)**[674] 4827 6-9-3 70 LPKeniry 5 60
(P R Chamings) *sn trcking ldrs: led over 1f out: rdn out fnl f* **9/2**[3]

1022 **2** *¾* **Outer Hebrides**[17] 2876 8-9-3 51 (v) AmyBaker(5) 8 63
(J M Bradley) *s.i.s: in rr tl hdwy on outside 2f out: styd on to chse wnr fnl f but a hld* **16/1**

6051 **3** *nk* **Bertie Southstreet**[3] 3345 6-9-8 62 (p) PatCosgrave 6 62
(J R Boyle) *sn led: rdn over 2f out: hdd over 1f out: styd on u.p ins fnl f but a jst outpcd* **4/1**[2]

2063 **4** *1 ¾* **Duke Of Milan (IRE)**[19] 2806 6-9-3 60 (v[1]) RichardKingscote 1 51
(Tom Dascombe) *in rr: hdwy 2f out: rdn and styd on fr over 1f out and kpt on ins fnl f but nvr gng pce to rch ldrs* **4/1**[2]

350- **5** *½* **Irish Music (IRE)**[398] 2490 4-9-3 67 RyanMoore 13 50
(A P Jarvis) *chsd ldrs: rdn over 2f out: styd on same pce fr over 1f out* **4/1**[2]

0-0 **6** *6* **Richardlionheart (USA)**[52] 1838 3-8-7 0 JackMitchell(3) 11 29
(B Gubby) *s.i.s: in rr: sn rdn along and green: swtchd to outside and mod prog u.p fnl f* **33/1**

0006 **7** *hd* **Fly In Johnny (IRE)**[9] 3162 4-9-0 48 (p) DavidProbert(3) 4 30
(J J Bridger) *w ldr 3f: sn rdn: wknd fr 2f out* **66/1**

0206 **8** *3 ½* **Fyodor (IRE)**[20] 2782 8-8-12 70 (v) RichardEvans(5) 3 19
(P D Evans) *s.i.s: sn rcvrd and hdwy on outside to chse ldrs over 2f out: sn rdn: fnd little and wknd qckly* **3/1**[1]

5006 **9** *4 ½* **Silver Salsa**[19] 2810 3-8-5 47 (v[1]) AdrianMcCarthy 9 —
(J R Jenkins) *chsd ldrs 3f* **66/1**

06 **10** *4* **Bolshoi King (IRE)**[3] 3345 3-8-10 0 (p) MartinDwyer 2 —
(B J Meehan) *in tch: rdn 3f out: hung bdly rt and wknd sn after* **40/1**

1m 14.24s (1.24) **Going Correction** -0.025s/f (Good)
WFA 3 from 4yo+ 7lb **10** Ran SP% **117.4**
Speed ratings (Par 101): **90,89,88,86,85 77,77,72,66,61**
toteswingers: 1&2 £10.90, 1&3 £2.80, 2&3 £10.10. CSF £70.42 TOTE £7.50: £2.20, £2.70, £2.10; EX 87.00.There was no bid for the winner.
Owner P R Chamings **Bred** Round Hill Stud **Trained** Baughurst, Hants

FOCUS
A typical seller run in a time 1.38secs slower than the following maiden for three and four-year-olds. Probably not form to dwell on.

3460 TOTESPORTCASINO.COM MAIDEN STKS 6f
7:40 (7:44) (Class 5) 3-4-Y-O **£2,729** (£806; £403) **Stalls** High

Form RPR

4323 **1** **Maverin (IRE)**[12] 3036 3-9-3 74 RyanMoore 9 77
(J Noseda) *trckd ldr: led ins fnl 2f: drvn clr fnl f* **13/8**[1]

5- **2** *3 ¼* **Russian Spirit**[240] 7141 3-8-12 0 PhilipRobinson 2 62
(M A Jarvis) *chsd ldrs: wnt 2nd over 1f out and kpt on but nvr gng pce to trble wnr* **5/2**[2]

0-53 **3** *1 ½* **Summers Target (USA)**[9] 3161 3-9-3 75 RichardHughes 11 62
(R M H Cowell) *taken down early: trckd ldrs: pushed along fr 2f out: styd on fnl f but nvr gng pce to trble ldng duo* **5/1**[3]

0 **4** *3 ¼* **Akabar**[38] 2250 3-9-3 0 SebSanders 4 51
(R M Beckett) *chsd ldrs: drvn along over 2f out: wknd fnl f* **14/1**

00 **5** *3* **Rosie Two**[11] 3071 3-8-12 0 FergusSweeney 14 37
(W S Kittow) *led tl hdd ins fnl 2f: wknd over 1f out* **66/1**

0 **6** *shd* **A Lot Of Red (IRE)**[9] 3168 3-9-3 0 (t) PatDobbs 10 41
(P J O'Gorman) *in rr: shkn up 2f out: styd on fnl f but nvr in contention* **33/1**

7 *2 ½* **Croeso Ynol** 3-8-12 0 SteveDrowne 6 28
(J L Spearing) *in rr tl mod prog fr over 1f out* **33/1**

0-60 **8** *½* **Guga (IRE)**[77] 1250 3-9-3 55 TonyCulhane 13 32
(George Baker) *broke wl: sn stdd towards rr: pushed along fr 2f out and mod late prog* **50/1**

9 *½* **Sutton Veny (IRE)** 3-8-12 0 ClareLindop 12 25
(J R Gask) *s.i.s: hmpd after 1f: swtchd to outside and sme prog whn hmpd over 2f out and green sn after: nvr nr ldrs* **14/1**

6- **10** *10* **Academy Of War (USA)**[245] 7020 3-9-3 0 LPKeniry 5 —
(J M Bradley) *chsd ldrs: rdn: hmpd and wknd over 2f out* **33/1**

06 **11** *4* **Rock Tech**[4] 3319 4-9-10 0 SimonWhitworth 1 —
(J R Jenkins) *in rr: sme prog on outside 1/2-way: nvr rchd ldrs and wknd over 2f out* **100/1**

000 **12** *13* **Redlynch**[111] 791 4-9-10 20 JimmyQuinn 7 —
(S Parr) *s.i.s sn rcvrd and chsd ldrs tl hmpd and wknd over 2f out* **100/1**

0 **P** **Viva Averti**[57] 1704 4-9-10 0 GeorgeBaker 3 —
(R M Beckett) *chsng ldrs: p.u whn broke leg over 2f out: dead* **25/1**

1m 12.86s (-0.14) **Going Correction** -0.025s/f (Good)
WFA 3 from 4yo 7lb **13** Ran SP% **114.8**
Speed ratings (Par 103): **99,94,92,88,84 84,80,80,79,66 60,43,—**
toteswingers: 1&2 £1.80, 1&3 £1.70, 2&3 £2.20. CSF £4.75 TOTE £2.80: £1.50, £1.50, £1.80; EX 7.50.
Owner Ballygallon Stud Limited **Bred** Ballygallon Stud Limited **Trained** Newmarket, Suffolk

FOCUS
The winning time was 1.38secs quicker than the previous seller. Nothing got into it from the rear and the winner probably only had to match his previous best.

Redlynch Official explanation: jockey said gelding suffered interference in running

3461 £10 FREE PLAY AT TOTESPORTBINGO.COM H'CAP 1m 2f 7y
8:10 (8:12) (Class 4) (0-85,85) 3-Y-0+ **£5,180** (£1,541; £770; £384) **Stalls** Low

Form RPR

0054 **1** **Resurge (IRE)**[11] 3055 4-9-7 **78**.................................. FergusSweeney 4 94
(W S Kittow) *in tch: hdwy 4f out: led ins fnl 2f: drvn clr appr fnl f: easily* **12/1**[3]

0545 **2** *7* **Rio Guru (IRE)**[21] 2768 4-8-10 **72**.............................. MCGeran(5) 1 76
(M R Channon) *in tch: rdn 4f out and one pce: styd on again over 2f out: chsd wnr fnl f: nvr any ch but wl clr of 3rd* **16/1**

1110 **3** *5* **Pelham Crescent (IRE)**[32] 2407 6-9-3 **77**.................. DavidProbert(3) 6 69
(B Palling) *awkward stalls: towards rr: pushed along and sme hdwy fr 3f out: nvr rchd ldrs and styd on for wl hld 3rd fnl f* **12/1**[3]

5520 **4** *1 1/2* **Trans Siberian**[26] 2597 5-9-9 **85**..............(p) Louis-PhilippeBeuzelin(5) 9 74
(P F I Cole) *t.k.h: chsd ldr: slt ld ins fnl 3f: edgd rt and hdd ins fnl 2f: sn wknd* **11/2**[2]

31 **5** *nk* **Racing Hero (IRE)**[15] 2943 3-8-11 **80**........................... RyanMoore 3 68
(J Noseda) *in rr: rdn along 4 out: sme hdwy to cl on ldrs over 2f out but nvr on terms: wknd sn after* **8/13**[1]

4060 **6** *4 1/2* **Roly Boy**[31] 2432 3-8-10 **79** ow1.................................. RichardHughes 5 58
(R Hannon) *in rr: mod prog 3f out: nvr on terms and wknd over 2f out* **14/1**

1630 **7** *3/4* **Quince (IRE)**[41] 2150 6-9-2 **73**..(v) SebSanders 2 51
(J Pearce) *a in rr* **33/1**

326- **8** *18* **Blow Hole (USA)**[269] 6452 4-8-12 **72**.................... RussellKennemore(3) 7 14
(Paul Mason) *chsd ldrs: rdn 4f out: wknd ins fnl 3f* **33/1**

4314 **9** *8* **Buddy Holly**[3] 3361 4-9-7 **85**...................................(v) CharlesEddery(7) 8 11
(Pat Eddery) *t.k.h: led tl hdd ins fnl 3f: wkng whn hmpd: stmbld and eased ins 2f* **12/1**[3]

2m 5.32s (-3.38) **Going Correction** -0.20s/f (Firm)
WFA 3 from 4yo+ 12lb **9** Ran SP% **118.8**
Speed ratings (Par 105): **105,99,95,94,93 90,89,75,68**
toteswingers: 1&2 £24.40, 1&3 £25.00, 2&3 £14.30. CSF £188.47 CT £2341.75 TOTE £17.50: £2.40, £3.20, £2.20; EX 101.50.
Owner Chris & David Stam **Bred** Sweetmans Bloodstock **Trained** Blackborough, Devon
■ Stewards' Enquiry : Louis-Philippe Beuzelin four-day ban: careless riding (Jul 13-16)

FOCUS
This was run at a fast pace and the time was good. A personal best from the winner but the favourite was below form.
Quince(IRE) Official explanation: jockey said gelding suffered interference in running

3462 OVER 50 INSTANT GAMES AT TOTESPORTGAMES.COM FILLIES' H'CAP 1m 3f 135y
8:40 (8:41) (Class 5) (0-70,69) 3-Y-0+ **£2,729** (£806; £403) **Stalls** Low

Form RPR

0016 **1** **Hollow Green (IRE)**[10] 3123 3-8-6 **61**.......................... CatherineGannon 2 69+
(P D Evans) *hld up in rr: hdwy fr 4f out: led over 2f out: drvn 2 l clr appr fnl f: in command whn eased cl home* **16/1**

-003 **2** *1/2* **Persian Memories (IRE)**[28] 2540 3-8-8 **63**................. RichardMullen 8 70
(J L Dunlop) *chsd ldrs: drvn to chal over 2f out: outpcd by wnr appr fnl f: styd on again and clsd as wnr eased cl home* **11/2**

5055 **3** *5* **Uig**[7] 3206 8-9-2 **57**.. KirstyMilczarek 9 55
(H S Howe) *led: hdd over 2f out: and sn hrd drvn styd on same pce to hold 3rd fr over 1f out but nvr any ch w ldng duo* **20/1**

4260 **4** *1 1/2* **Location**[17] 2892 3-7-10 **56**.. AndreaAtzeni(5) 4 51
(Ian Williams) *in tch: hdwy 4f out: rdn to chse ldrs over 2f out: sn no imp: wknd over 1f out* **4/1**[2]

064 **5** *3/4* **Course De Diamante (IRE)**[18] 2847 3-9-0 **69**................... NeilPollard 3 63
(D R Lanigan) *s.i.s: sn rcvrd to chse ldr: rdn over 3f out: wknd 2f out* **5/1**[3]

0-45 **6** *nk* **Silken Promise (USA)**[46] 2006 3-8-11 **66**...................... ShaneKelly 11 60
(W R Swinburn) *in rr: pushed along over 3f out and sme hdwy: nvr rchd ldrs and styd on same pce fnl 2f* **8/1**

3102 **7** *5* **Inis Boffin**[7] 3209 3-9-0 **69**..................................... RichardHughes 6 54
(S Kirk) *hld up in mid-div: rdn and hdwy over 3f out: nvr gng pce to rch ldrs and wknd 2f out* **5/2**[1]

0-56 **8** *3/4* **Chanrossa (IRE)**[18] 2848 3-8-12 **67**.................................. RyanMoore 7 51
(E A L Dunlop) *in rr: detached fr maiden gp 5f out: sn pushed along: only modest rspnse fnl 3f* **9/1**

606- **9** *2 1/4* **Silver Surprise**[194] 7701 5-8-9 **53** oh6.......................... DavidProbert(3) 12 33
(J J Bridger) *chsd ldrs a m* **66/1**

/0-5 **10** *11* **King's Kazeem**[33] 2384 4-10-0 **69**.................................. GeorgeBaker 10 30
(G L Moore) *chsd ldrs a m: sn wknd: eased whn no ch fnl f* **33/1**

2m 28.46s (-1.04) **Going Correction** -0.20s/f (Firm)
WFA 3 from 4yo+ 14lb **10** Ran SP% **116.8**
Speed ratings (Par 100): **95,94,91,90,89 89,86,85,84,76**
toteswingers: 1&2 £17.50, 1&3 £35.40, 2&3 £16.70. CSF £100.08 CT £1787.82 TOTE £17.60: £3.40, £1.50, £3.50; EX 69.80.
Owner Raymond N R Auld **Bred** R N Auld **Trained** Pandy, Monmouths

FOCUS
A modest fillies' handicap dominated by 3yos. A clear personal best from the winner, with the first pair clear.
Inis Boffin Official explanation: jockey said filly had no more to give

3463 100% NEW PLAYER BONUS AT TOTESPORTCASINO.COM H'CAP 1m 67y
9:10 (9:10) (Class 5) (0-70,70) 3-Y-0+ **£2,729** (£806; £403) **Stalls** High

Form RPR

250/ **1** **Expensive Problem**[134] 6-9-9 **65**...................................... IvanLopez 13 76
(R J Smith, Spain) *trckd ldrs: rdn and qcknd on ins to ld appr fnl f: drvn out* **16/1**

0221 **2** *2 1/2* **Dancing Jest (IRE)**[16] 2916 5-9-8 **64**.......................... MartinDwyer 7 69
(Rae Guest) *led: rdn and styd on whn strly chal fr over 2f out: hdd appr fnl f: sn outpcd by wnr but hld on wl for 2nd* **9/2**[2]

0000 **3** *3/4* **Paul's Pet**[14] 2975 4-8-13 **55**.................................... TGMcLaughlin 10 58
(Karen George) *s.i.s: towards rr: hdwy over 2f out: kpt on to take 3rd ins fnl f and gng on cl home but nvr gng pce to trble wnr* **25/1**

3-50 **4** *1 1/2* **Recession Proof (FR)**[18] 2845 3-9-4 **70**........................ PatDobbs 6 68
(S A Callaghan) *in tch: rdn to chse ldrs 3f out: styd on same pce fnl 2f* **13/2**[3]

0333 **5** *1 1/4* **Tignello (IRE)**[16] 2924 4-9-4 **60**...................................... RyanMoore 5 63+
(G L Moore) *chsd ldrs: ev ch and rdn 2f out: hung lft u.p ins fnl f: stl disputing 2nd whn lost action and eased cl home* **15/8**[1]

-540 **6** *1 1/2* **Bahkov (IRE)**[35] 2320 3-8-10 **62**............................ RichardKingscote 3 56+
(Tom Dascombe) *chsd ldrs: rdn 3f out: wknd appr fnl f* **8/1**

2036 **7** *1* **Gazboolou**[11] 3075 5-9-10 **66**.................................... FergusSweeney 2 57
(David Pinder) *in rr: sme hdwy on outside fr 3f out: nvr rchd ldrs* **8/1**

4503 **8** *1* **Nun Today (USA)**[42] 2141 3-7-13 **51** oh1..................(v) JimmyQuinn 8 38
(Karen George) *in tch to 1/2-way* **16/1**

4020 **9** *4* **This Ones For Eddy**[17] 2880 4-10-0 **70**.....................(t) RichardHughes 1 50
(S Parr) *in rr: sme hdwy 3f out: nvr rchd ldrs and wknd 2f out* **15/2**

1m 43.91s (-0.79) **Going Correction** -0.20s/f (Firm)
WFA 3 from 4yo+ 10lb **9** Ran SP% **115.9**
Speed ratings (Par 103): **95,92,91,90,89 87,86,85,81**
toteswingers: 1&2 £33.30, 1&3 £49.60, 2&3 £66.00. CSF £86.84 CT £1813.88 TOTE £11.50: £2.50, £1.80, £6.80; EX 64.70 Place 6 £735.55, Place 5 £513.55.
Owner F Willson **Bred** T J Cooper **Trained** Spain

FOCUS
A modest handicap but it was soundly run. Ordinary form, with the runner-up the best guide.
Tignello(IRE) Official explanation: jockey said saddle slipped
T/Plt: £641.60 to a £1 stake. Pool: £84,886.96. 96.57 winning tickets. T/Qpdt: £95.80 to a £1 stake. Pool: £6,209.53. 47.95 winning tickets. ST

3223 WOLVERHAMPTON (A.W) (L-H)
Monday, June 29

OFFICIAL GOING: Standard
Wind: Almost nil but fresh behind during 5.00 race Weather: Thunderstorm and heavy rain 5.00, light rain 5.30

3464 GREAT OFFERS AT WOLVERHAMPTON-RACECOURSE.CO.UK H'CAP 5f 216y(P)
2:30 (2:31) (Class 6) (0-65,70) 3-Y-O **£2,729** (£806; £403) **Stalls** Low

Form RPR

1321 **1** **Sarasota Sunshine**[14] 2973 3-9-7 **65**...........................(b) LukeMorris 4 69
(N P Littmoden) *hld up in tch: rdn wl over 1f out: r.o to ld wl ins fnl f: drvn out* **2/1**[1]

1140 **2** *1 1/4* **Billy Beetroot (USA)**[8] 3193 3-9-4 **65**..................(t) KevinGhunowa(3) 9 65
(R A Harris) *a.p: rdn wl over 1f out: slt ld ins fnl f: sn hdd: nt qckn* **12/1**

-05 **3** *shd* **Come On Buckers (IRE)**[48] 1958 3-9-1 **62** ow2....... AlanCreighton(3) 6 62
(E J Creighton) *led: rdn 2f out: hdd ins fnl f: kpt on* **40/1**

0061 **4** *2* **Angelo Poliziano**[7] 3229 3-9-12 **70** 6ex................(p) SilvestreDeSousa 2 64
(Mrs A Duffield) *w ldr: rdn over 1f out: ev ch ins fnl f: no ex towards fin* **9/2**[2]

10-0 **5** *2* **Piccolinda**[62] 1588 3-9-4 **62**.. WilliamBuick 5 49
(W R Muir) *in rr: pushed along over 3f out: c wd st: rdn over 1f out: r.o ins fnl f: nrst fin* **17/2**

006 **6** *3* **Two Turtle Doves (IRE)**[16] 2937 3-9-2 **60**...................... SebSanders 12 38
(M Mullineaux) *in tch on outside: lost pl over 3f out: c wd st: rdn wl over 1f out: n.d* **10/1**

5400 **7** *1 1/2* **Dalepak Flyer (IRE)**[69] 1437 3-8-10 **57**........... RussellKennemore(3) 10 30
(Paul Mason) *sn bhd: rdn wl over 1f out: n.d* **40/1**

0304 **8** *1 3/4* **You Avin A Laugh**[7] 3225 3-9-2 **60**........................ CatherineGannon 11 27
(C A Dwyer) *prom: pushed along over 2f out: rdn and wkng whn hung lft wl over 1f out* **20/1**

0-05 **9** *1/2* **Tarruji (IRE)**[33] 2377 3-9-0 **58**.......................................(b[1]) JamieSpencer 7 24
(S A Callaghan) *hld up in rr: short-lived effrt over 2f out* **12/1**

-400 **10** *nk* **Maigh Eo (IRE)**[27] 2562 3-8-13 **57**.......................... StephenDonohoe 3 22
(Patrick Morris) *hld up in tch on ins: rdn over 2f out: wknd wl over 1f out* **80/1**

4015 **11** *1/2* **Deckchair**[10] 3118 3-8-12 **56**......................................(v) FrancisNorton 8 19
(H J Collingridge) *t.k.h in mid-div: lost pl after 2f: sn bhd* **12/1**

2041 **12** *10* **Villaruz (IRE)**[65] 1529 3-9-0 **63**.................................(b) AndreaAtzeni(5) 1 —
(D Flood) *hld up towards rr: sme prog on ins over 3f out: wknd wl over 2f out* **13/2**[3]

1m 15.69s (0.69) **Going Correction** +0.175s/f (Slow) **12** Ran SP% **118.4**
Speed ratings (Par 97): **102,100,100,97,94 90,88,86,85,85 84,71**
toteswingers: 1&2 £8.20, 1&3 £20.30, 2&3 £49.90. CSF £27.42 CT £757.75 TOTE £2.70: £1.20, £4.10, £8.50; EX 36.00 TRIFECTA Not won..
Owner Franconson Partners **Bred** London Thoroughbred S'Vces Ltd & West Bl **Trained** Newmarket, Suffolk

FOCUS
A modest handicap in which the pace did not seem particularly strong. Ordinary form.

3465 CARLSBERG EXPORT (S) STKS 5f 20y(P)
3:00 (3:00) (Class 6) 3-Y-0+ **£2,047** (£604; £302) **Stalls** Low

Form RPR

2005 **1** **Bertbrand**[7] 3227 4-9-0 58..(p) AndreaAtzeni(5) 13 66
(D Flood) *hld up in mid-div: rdn and hung lft over 1f out: running on wl whn carried rt towards fin: led last stride* **10/1**

1522 **2** *hd* **Northern Empire (IRE)**[12] 3020 6-9-10 66...........................(p) NCallan 1 70
(K A Ryan) *sn chsng ldrs: led 1f out: sn edgd rt: rdn whn hung bdly rt wl ins fnl f: hdd last stride* **10/11**[1]

5060 **3** *4* **Diane's Choice**[23] 2712 6-9-0 56............................(e) StephenDonohoe 7 46
(Miss Gay Kelleway) *outpcd in rr: hdwy on ins fnl f: tk 3rd nr fin* **22/1**

2200 **4** *nk* **Spic 'n Span**[7] 3204 4-9-10 65.........................(b) CatherineGannon 3 55
(R A Harris) *led after 1f: rdn and hdd 1f out: sn sltly hmpd: wknd* **4/1**[2]

464 **5** *hd* **Russian Rocket (IRE)**[55] 1776 7-9-5 65......................... TGMcLaughlin 2 49
(Mrs C A Dunnett) *prom: pushed along and sltly outpcd over 2f out: kpt on same pce fnl f* **13/2**[3]

0360 **6** *hd* **Pressed For Time (IRE)**[41] 2162 3-8-8 57.....................(t) JamesDoyle 5 41
(E J Creighton) *led 1f: chsd ldr tl rdn and hung lft wl over 1f out: wknd ins fnl f* **22/1**

4002 **7** *1* **Decider (USA)**[24] 2682 6-9-2 54.............................. KevinGhunowa(3) 11 45
(R A Harris) *chsd ldrs: rdn over 1f out: fdd fnl f* **16/1**

6500 **8** *1 3/4* **Know No Fear**[12] 3031 4-9-5 65............................ GrahamGibbons 4 41
(D Shaw) *hld up in mid-div: lost pl over 2f out: n.d after* **11/1**

-060 **9** *2 1/2* **Woqoodd**[6] 3239 5-9-5 49...(v) FrancisNorton 10 29
(D Shaw) *hld up in mid-div: bhd fnl 2f* **40/1**

3040 **10** *1 1/2* **Tag Team (IRE)**[19] 2812 8-9-0 46..............................(v) MarkCoumbe(5) 8 24
(John A Harris) *a in rr* **66/1**

62.71 secs (0.41) **Going Correction** +0.175s/f (Slow)
WFA 3 from 4yo+ 6lb **10** Ran SP% **121.7**
Speed ratings (Par 101): **103,102,96,95,95 95,93,90,86,84**
toteswingers: 1&2 £3.80, 1&3 £25.70, 2&3 £7.50. CSF £19.88 TOTE £11.30: £2.60, £1.20, £4.40; EX 37.80 Trifecta £336.70 Pool: £477.75 - 1.05 winning units..There was no bid for the winner. Northern Empire was claimed by Mr F Jordan for £6,000.
Owner Barrie Kirby **Bred** R F And S D Knipe **Trained**

FOCUS
An ordinary seller. There was a dramatic finish and some violent swings on the exchanges.

3466 BET WIMBLEDON TENNIS - BETDAQ H'CAP 1m 4f 50y(P)
3:30 (3:30) (Class 4) (0-80,79) 3-Y-O **£5,180** (£1,541; £770; £384) **Stalls** Low

Form RPR
603 **1** **Red Cadeaux**[43] 2104 3-9-0 **72** ..... SebSanders 7 84+
(E A L Dunlop) *hdwy on outside after 2f: reminder 5f out: led wl over 2f out: rdn over 1f out: clr ins fnl f: r.o wl* **9/2**[3]
4-33 **2** *6* **Decorum (USA)**[45] 2038 3-9-5 **77** .....(t) RichardMullen 6 79
(J H M Gosden) *a.p: rdn 5f out: wnt 2nd over 1f out: continually wandered away fr whip: no ch w wnr* **11/4**[2]
0-40 **3** *4* **Guestofthenation (USA)**[39] 2189 3-9-7 **79** ..... RoystonFfrench 9 75
(M Johnston) *prom: led 4f out: rdn and hdd wl over 2f out: wknd 1f out* **11/1**
-033 **4** *5* **Calaloo (IRE)**[19] 2829 3-9-6 **78** ..... SteveDrowne 5 66
(C R Egerton) *bmpd sn after s: hld up: hdwy over 5f out: rdn over 3f out: wknd 2f out* **5/1**
01-0 **5** *33* **Spiritual Treasure (USA)**[12] 3026 3-9-3 **75** ..... JamieSpencer 2 10
(M A Magnusson) *t.k.h: stdd after 1f: hld up: rdn over 3f out: sn struggling* **14/1**
523- **6** *1 3/4* **Naheell**[226] 7343 3-8-13 **71** ..... PhilipRobinson 1 3
(M A Jarvis) *led: hdd 4f out: wknd over 3f out* **5/2**[1]
-020 **7** *1* **Horsley Warrior**[18] 2850 3-9-1 **73** ..... GrahamGibbons 4 3
(E S McMahon) *n.m.r and bmpd sn after s: sn prom: pushed along over 6f out: wknd over 5f out* **12/1**
0-6 **8** *36* **Black Nun**[49] 1937 3-7-12 **61** ..... AndreaAtzeni(5) 3 —
(S Wynne) *hld up and bhd: rdn over 6f out: sn struggling: t.o* **50/1**

2m 41.91s (0.81) **Going Correction** +0.175s/f (Slow) **8** Ran SP% **114.7**
Speed ratings (Par 101): **104,100,97,94,72 70,70,46**
toteswingers: 1&2 £3.30, 1&3 £9.70, 2&3 £4.90. CSF £17.38 CT £126.82 TOTE £6.00: £1.80, £1.20, £3.70; EX 14.60 Trifecta £92.90 Pool: £374.33 - 2.98 winning units..
Owner R J Arculli **Bred** Foursome Thoroughbreds **Trained** Newmarket, Suffolk

FOCUS
A decent handicap for the grade. It was run at a steady pace and they finished well strung out, with the last four virtually walking across the line. The winner can do better and the form is rated through the runner-up.
Black Nun Official explanation: trainer's rep said filly scoped dirty post-race

3467 WOLVERHAMPTON HOLIDAY INN APPRENTICE CLAIMING STKS 7f 32y(P)
4:00 (4:00) (Class 6) 4-Y-O+ **£2,047** (£604; £302) **Stalls** High

Form RPR
1000 **1** **Mocha Java**[17] 2876 6-8-12 58 ..... RossAtkinson 10 64
(M Salaman) *mde virtually all: clr 3f out: rdn over 1f out: narrowly hdd cl home led post* **11/1**
500 **2** *nse* **Sun Catcher (IRE)**[16] 2921 6-8-7 55 .....(p) SimonPearce(3) 6 62
(P G Murphy) *a.p: rdn wl over 1f out: slt ld cl home: hdd post* **22/1**
4001 **3** *1 1/4* **Dabbers Ridge (IRE)**[9] 3174 7-9-7 80 ..... LanceBetts(3) 9 72
(I W McInnes) *hld up in mid-div: hdwy wl over 1f out: rdn and kpt on same pce ins fnl f* **2/1**[1]
4-00 **4** *3/4* **Hanoverian Baron**[10] 3091 4-9-10 85 ..... WilliamCarson 3 70
(D Nicholls) *w wnr tl over 3f out: rdn wl over 1f out: sn wandered: lost 2nd ent fnl f: no ex* **3/1**[2]
45 **5** *2* **Appelouse**[109] 820 4-8-2 0 ..... JamesPSullivan(3) 2 46
(D W Thompson) *in rr: sme hdwy 2f out: nvr trbld ldrs* **33/1**
0046 **6** *3/4* **Ten Pole Tudor**[17] 2876 4-8-8 55 ow1 .....(p) SPRyan(5) 5 52
(R A Harris) *s.s: hdwy on outside 5f out: hung rt bnd over 2f out: wknd ins fnl f* **10/1**
5-0 **7** *3 1/4* **Broughtons Silk**[18] 2856 4-8-8 0 ..... MatthewDavies(3) 7 41
(W J Musson) *dwlt: nvr nr ldrs* **16/1**
0236 **8** *shd* **Haroldini (IRE)**[22] 2746 7-8-5 56 .....(v) AJSmith(7) 1 42
(J Balding) *bhd fnl 3f* **10/1**
0000 **9** *1 1/2* **Strabinios King**[24] 2658 5-9-3 78 ..... BillyCray(3) 11 46
(A Berry) *prom tl rdn and wknd wl over 1f out* **6/1**[3]
6/00 **10** *1 1/4* **Dazzling Colours**[41] 2149 4-8-7 54 ..... JosephineBruning(5) 12 35
(T T Clement) *prom: hung lft over 3f out: wknd over 2f out* **66/1**
0100 **11** *5* **The London Gang**[7] 3224 6-8-7 57 .....(b) JPHamblett(3) 8 19
(S Wynne) *hdwy 5f out: wknd 3f out* **25/1**

1m 30.77s (1.17) **Going Correction** +0.175s/f (Slow) **11** Ran SP% **117.6**
Speed ratings (Par 101): **100,99,98,97,95 94,90,90,88,87 81**
toteswingers: 1&2 £12.70, 1&3 £5.50, 2&3 £6.10. CSF £230.05 TOTE £14.50: £3.00, £4.70, £1.10; EX 173.80 Trifecta £367.80 Part won. Pool: £497.04 - 0.53 winning units..
Owner Oaktree Racing **Bred** A H And C E Robinson Partnership **Trained** Upper Lambourn, Berks

FOCUS
A fair claimer. The pace was fairly steady and the first two held official ratings in the mid-to-upper 50s, so the form is only modest.

3468 EUROPEAN BREEDERS' FUND MAIDEN STKS 7f 32y(P)
4:30 (4:31) (Class 5) 2-Y-O **£3,885** (£1,156; £577; £288) **Stalls** High

Form RPR
22 **1** **Coloursoftheglen (IRE)**[9] 3160 2-9-3 0 ..... RichardKingscote 5 75+
(Tom Dascombe) *mde all: rdn over 1f out: pushed out* **6/4**[1]
2 *2* **Bonfire Knight** 2-9-3 0 .....(t) GrahamGibbons 4 71+
(J J Quinn) *hld up in tch: rdn over 1f out: wnt 2nd ins fnl f: nt trble wnr* **9/1**[3]
30 **3** *1/2* **Motivational (IRE)**[18] 2853 2-9-3 0 ..... ChrisCatlin 10 69
(D R Lanigan) *chsd wnr after 1f: ev ch 2f out: rdn over 1f out: nt qckn and lost 2nd ins fnl f* **10/1**
42 **4** *9* **Bradford (IRE)**[23] 2721 2-9-3 0 ..... AndrewElliott 8 47+
(K R Burke) *sn pushed along and outpcd: rdn over 3f out: sme prog on ins wl over 1f out: nvr nr ldrs* **15/8**[2]
5 *4 1/2* **Bandear (IRE)** 2-8-12 0 ..... JamieSpencer 9 31
(C E Brittain) *s.s: hung lft over 1f out: a bhd* **12/1**
6 *1 3/4* **Port Hill** 2-9-3 0 ..... TGMcLaughlin 6 32
(W M Brisbourne) *s.s: pushed along over 2f out: a bhd* **66/1**
0 **7** *shd* **Reel Love**[43] 2099 2-9-3 0 ..... NCallan 1 31
(J R Holt) *sn prom: rdn and wknd over 1f out* **80/1**
0 **8** *1* **Ellies Image**[16] 2914 2-8-12 0 ..... RoystonFfrench 3 24
(B P J Baugh) *prom: rdn over 3f out: wknd wl over 2f out* **50/1**
00 **9** *1 1/2* **Beach Boy (IRE)**[7] 3226 2-9-3 0 ..... NeilChalmers 7 25
(S Wynne) *prom tl wknd 2f out* **200/1**
0 **10** *3 1/2* **Woodenitbenice**[7] 3226 2-8-12 0 ..... LukeMorris 12 12
(D Shaw) *pushed along: sn mid-div: rdn over 3f out: sn bhd* **200/1**

1m 32.25s (2.65) **Going Correction** +0.175s/f (Slow) **10** Ran SP% **107.2**
Speed ratings (Par 93): **91,88,88,77,72 70,70,69,67,63**
toteswingers: 1&2 £5.20, 1&3 £2.90, 2&3 £8.10. CSF £13.68 TOTE £2.00: £1.10, £2.30, £2.30; EX 16.10 Trifecta £68.80 Pool: £241.90 - 2.60 winning units..
Owner Evan M Sutherland **Bred** Glending Bloodstock **Trained** Lambourn, Berks
■ Execution (12/1) was withdrawn after spreading a plate. Deduct 5p in the £ under R4.

FOCUS
There did not seem to be much strength in depth in this maiden, and the first three pulled a long way clear of the rest. Straightforward form.

NOTEBOOK
Coloursoftheglen(IRE) was not as well drawn as the winner on quick turf upped to this trip at Lingfield last time, but eventually got across to the rail and was only just seen off. He had a decent chance if repeating that form and did the job in determined style under a front-running ride on his AW debut. The third gives this form some substance, and the winner, who is from a good family, should be capable of further progress and should not have much trouble staying an extra furlong this season. (op 13-8 tchd 7-4)
Bonfire Knight ◆ ran a very promising race on his debut. He cost £38,000 as a yearling and is quite well connected, being the first foal of a Listed winner over this trip at three. He should improve for this initial experience and should be able to win a similar race. (op 10-1 tchd 12-1)
Motivational(IRE) sweated up in the preliminaries, but still managed to bounce back from a modest run at Nottingham last time and probably improved a bit on his creditable debut third over 6f at Leicester in May. (op 9-1)
Bradford(IRE) was particularly disappointing. He is closely related to plenty of winners here and abroad and had solid claims on his second in a 6f Newcastle maiden auction last time. However, he was vigorously ridden a long way out, found very little for pressure and may not have handled this surface. (op 2-1 tchd 7-4)
Bandear(IRE) Official explanation: jockey said filly was hampered leaving stalls, rendering it slowly away and ran green

3469 BETDAQ THE BETTING EXCHANGE H'CAP 7f 32y(P)
5:00 (5:01) (Class 4) (0-85,85) 3-Y-O+ **£4,727** (£1,406; £702; £351) **Stalls** High

Form RPR
-500 **1** **Major Phil (IRE)**[25] 2638 3-8-9 **75** ..... WilliamBuick 6 81
(L M Cumani) *chsd ldr after 1f: hdd 2f out: rdn to ld over 1f out: carried lft and hdd ins fnl f: led towards fin: r.o* **9/2**[1]
6536 **2** *1/2* **Capucci**[19] 2822 4-9-7 **78** .....(t) GrahamGibbons 11 86
(J J Quinn) *hdwy after 1f: rdn and hung lft fr over 1f out: led ins fnl f: hdd towards fin* **15/2**
2220 **3** *1 1/4* **Mudhish (IRE)**[31] 2459 4-8-10 **67** .....(b) JamieSpencer 1 72
(C E Brittain) *a.p: swtchd rt wl over 1f out: hung lft fnl f: nt qckn* **8/1**
5064 **4** *hd* **Carleton**[14] 2980 4-9-3 **74** ..... ChrisCatlin 12 78+
(W J Musson) *hld up towards rr: hdwy over 1f out: swtchd rt ins fnl f: fin wl* **11/1**
214 **5** *1* **Imprimis Tagula (IRE)**[10] 3097 5-9-9 **80** .....(v) NeilChalmers 5 81
(A Bailey) *s.i.s: sn mid-div: hdwy wl over 1f out: sn rdn: one pce ins fnl f* **7/1**
0660 **6** *hd* **Stanley Goodspeed**[16] 2927 6-8-13 **70** .....(t) JamesDoyle 2 71
(J W Hills) *led: hdd 4f out: led 2f out: rdn and hdd over 1f out: wknd ins fnl f* **13/2**[3]
01-6 **7** *2 1/2* **Fleeting Star (USA)**[10] 3102 3-8-8 **74** ..... RichardMullen 4 65
(J Noseda) *hld up in tch: wknd wl over 1f out* **6/1**[2]
510/ **8** *2 1/4* **La Voile Rouge**[717] 3504 4-10-0 **85** ..... GeorgeBaker 3 73
(R M Beckett) *prom tl wknd wl over 1f out* **8/1**
4100 **9** *1* **Hustle (IRE)**[10] 3091 4-10-0 **85** ..... SimonWhitworth 7 70
(Miss Gay Kelleway) *s.i.s: a in rr* **14/1**
0006 **10** *1/2* **Joe Caster**[42] 2140 3-9-2 **82** ..... LukeMorris 8 63
(J M P Eustace) *t.k.h in mid-div: rdn and hung rt bnd over 2f out: sn wknd* **16/1**
016- **11** *1 1/2* **Blues Minor (IRE)**[220] 7405 4-8-10 **67** ..... RobertHavlin 9 47
(M Mullineaux) *a towards rr* **50/1**
0-60 **12** *3 1/2* **Binanti**[19] 2828 9-9-4 **75** ..... FrancisNorton 10 45
(P R Chamings) *a in rr* **33/1**

1m 31.49s (1.89) **Going Correction** +0.175s/f (Slow)
WFA 3 from 4yo+ 9lb **12** Ran SP% **118.1**
Speed ratings (Par 105): **96,95,94,93,92 92,89,86,85,85 83,79**
toteswingers: 1&2 £6.00, 1&3 £4.20, 2&3 £7.50. CSF £37.58 CT £269.20 TOTE £6.50: £2.20, £3.40, £1.80; EX 44.00 Trifecta £255.30 Pool: £379.50 - 1.10 winning units..
Owner L Marinopoulos **Bred** Roger Macnair **Trained** Newmarket, Suffolk

FOCUS
A decent handicap run during a heavy shower. It was steadily run and the first three raced near the pace. Sound form among them.

3470 BETDAQ.CO.UK H'CAP 1m 141y(P)
5:30 (5:30) (Class 6) (0-60,66) 3-Y-O+ **£2,729** (£806; £403) **Stalls** Low

Form RPR
46 **1** **Ensnare**[133] 570 4-9-5 **55** ..... StephenDonohoe 7 68
(Ian Williams) *chsd ldr: led over 2f out: sn rdn: edgd lft ins fnl f: drvn out* **17/2**
0351 **2** *3/4* **Ninth House (USA)**[7] 3224 7-10-2 **66** 6ex .....(t) SilvestreDeSousa 12 77
(Mrs R A Carr) *hld up in tch: pushed along over 3f out: rdn wl over 1f out: chsd wnr fnl f: kpt on same pce* **2/1**[1]
5543 **3** *3* **Barodine**[11] 3077 6-8-13 **54** ..... WilliamCarson(5) 1 58
(R J Hodges) *a.p: rdn wl over 1f out: one pce fnl f* **7/2**[2]
0342 **4** *4 1/2* **Time To Regret**[10] 3092 9-8-13 **56** .....(p) AndrewHeffernan(7) 2 50
(I W McInnes) *led: rdn and hdd over 2f out: wknd ins fnl f* **6/1**
0040 **5** *shd* **Djalalabad (FR)**[16] 2924 5-9-5 **55** .....(tp) TGMcLaughlin 6 49
(Mrs C A Dunnett) *hld up towards rr: swtchd rt and hdwy on outside over 2f out: rdn over 1f out: hung lft and wknd ins fnl f* **25/1**
0000 **6** *1/2* **The Grey One (IRE)**[11] 3077 6-9-10 **60** .....(p) JamieSpencer 4 52
(J M Bradley) *hmpd and stdd s: hld up in rr: pushed along over 1f out: nvr nr ldrs* **9/1**
-342 **7** *nk* **Hits Only Cash**[11] 3077 7-9-9 **59** ..... RobertHavlin 9 51
(J Pearce) *hld up in mid-div: pushed along over 3f out: bhd fnl 2f* **5/1**[3]
6000 **8** *3 1/4* **Cross Reef**[22] 2746 4-9-4 **54** .....(p) CatherineGannon 11 38
(R A Harris) *a in rr* **22/1**
5634 **9** *3* **Imperial Djay (IRE)**[16] 2921 4-9-2 **52** ..... NCallan 3 29
(J R Holt) *hld up in mid-div: pushed along and hung lft over 3f out: sn bhd* **9/1**
5160 **10** *3 1/4* **The Graig**[20] 1514 5-9-7 **57** ..... WilliamBuick 8 27
(J R Holt) *hld up in tch: ev ch over 2f out: wknd wl over 1f out* **16/1**

1m 52.27s (1.77) **Going Correction** +0.175s/f (Slow) **10** Ran SP% **131.1**
Speed ratings (Par 101): **99,98,95,91,91 91,90,87,85,82**
toteswingers: 1&2 £10.50, 1&3 £14.40, 2&3 £4.30. CSF £29.25 CT £79.62 TOTE £16.70: £4.10, £1.50, £1.70; EX 69.20 Trifecta £312.20 Part won. Pool: £421.95 - 0.43 winning units. Place 6: £44.08, Place 5: £18.84..
Owner C Owen **Bred** Cheveley Park Stud Ltd **Trained** Portway, Worcs

FOCUS
An ordinary handicap. The pace was steady and not many got into it. The first two pulled clear of the third, who was a long way clear of the rest. The form is rated through the second.
Imperial Djay(IRE) Official explanation: jockey said gelding hung right

T/Jkpt: Not won. T/Plt: £12.20 to a £1 stake. Pool: £63,327.72. 3,761.52 winning tickets. T/Qpdt: £7.00 to a £1 stake. Pool: £4,652.35. 485.80 winning tickets. KH

3240 BRIGHTON (L-H)
Tuesday, June 30

OFFICIAL GOING: Firm (9.4)
Course dolled out 6metres from 6f to 2.5f but effect on distances not notified.
Wind: Moderate, against Weather: Sunny and hot

3471 C & S RUBBISH CLEARANCE H'CAP — 5f 213y
2:30 (2:30) (Class 6) (0-55,55) 3-Y-O+ **£2,331** (£693; £346; £173) **Stalls** Low

Form / RPR
6422 **1** **Itsher**[6] 3281 3-8-8 **55** ....(b) WilliamCarson(5) 6 — 74+
(S C Williams) *chsd ldrs: c alone onto stands' rail ent st: led over 1f out: sn clr: v easily* **5/2**[1]
00 **2** 4 1/2 **Namu**[19] 2852 6-9-5 **54** ....(p) JimCrowley 12 — 57
(Miss T Spearing) *towards rr: hdwy 2f out: rdn and r.o to go 2nd towards fin* **14/1**
-600 **3** 3/4 **Tricky Trev (USA)**[7] 3239 3-8-11 **53** ....(t) JamesDoyle 13 — 52
(S Curran) *mid-div: rdn to chse ldrs 2f out: kpt on fnl f* **50/1**
0460 **4** 1 1/2 **Mandelieu (IRE)**[29] 2529 4-9-1 **50** .... DNolan 7 — 46
(Ollie Pears) *a.p: led after 2f: hdd over 1f out: one pce ins fnl f* **6/1**[3]
000 **5** 1/2 **Scruffy Skip (IRE)**[14] 3007 4-9-3 **52** .... TGMcLaughlin 9 — 47
(Mrs C A Dunnett) *towards rr: rdn over 1f out: mde sme late hdwy* **40/1**
5634 **6** nse **Who's Winning (IRE)**[8] 3208 8-9-2 **51** ....(t) GeorgeBaker 8 — 45
(B G Powell) *in rr: r.o fnl f: nvr nrr* **11/2**[2]
0-00 **7** 1 **Call Me Courageous (IRE)**[30] 2515 3-8-10 **52** ow1 .... SebSanders 2 — 41
(A B Haynes) *led for 2f: rdn and wknd fnl f* **25/1**
3-04 **8** 3/4 **Eleanor Eloise (USA)**[25] 2682 5-9-1 **50** ....(p) ClareLindop 5 — 39
(J R Gask) *mid-div: no hdwy fr over 1f out* **7/1**
404 **9** hd **Ask Jenny (IRE)**[7] 3239 7-9-6 **55** .... RyanMoore 1 — 43
(Patrick Morris) *chsd ldrs tl rdn and wknd fnl f* **13/2**
5002 **10** 2 **Supreme Speedster**[7] 3242 5-8-12 **47** .... SimonWhitworth 3 — 29
(A G Newcombe) *nvr bttr than mid-div* **8/1**
0-45 **11** 3/4 **Ile Royale**[12] 3071 4-8-12 **47** .... ChrisCatlin 14 — 26
(W S Kittow) *wnt rt s: sn mid-div: chsd ldrs 2f out: wknd 1f out* **16/1**
0500 **12** 1/2 **Tightrope (IRE)**[10] 3161 3-8-3 **50** ....(b[1]) AmyBaker(5) 4 — 27
(T D McCarthy) *prom to 1/2-way* **40/1**

69.44 secs (-0.76) **Going Correction** -0.10s/f (Good)
WFA 3 from 4yo+ 7lb — **12** Ran SP% **118.4**
Speed ratings (Par 101): **101,95,94,92,91 91,89,88,88,86 85,84**
toteswingers: 1&2 £9.50, 1&3 £23.60, 2&3 £65.00 CSF £40.35 CT £1445.51 TOTE £2.70: £1.30, £5.10, £11.50; EX 51.80 TRIFECTA Not won..
Owner Itsus **Bred** Old Mill Stud And Partners **Trained** Newmarket, Suffolk

FOCUS
A weak sprint handicap that was all about one horse, Itsher. She had the best place alone on the stands' rail and how literally this form should be taken is open to question.

3472 HARDINGS CATERING MAIDEN STKS — 1m 1f 209y
3:00 (3:02) (Class 5) 3-Y-O+ **£3,406** (£1,019; £509; £254; £126) **Stalls** High

Form / RPR
22 **1** **Rocky's Pride (IRE)**[8] 3221 3-9-0 0 .... RyanMoore 5 — 78+
(J Noseda) *mde all: rdn 2f out: in command and drew clr fnl f* **11/10**[1]
6- **2** 4 **Gordy Bee (USA)**[326] 4826 3-9-0 0 .... PaulEddery 6 — 70
(Pat Eddery) *plld hrd: sn trckd wnr: rdn over 1f out: kpt on but nt pce of wnr* **2/1**[2]
33 **3** 1 3/4 **Bolanderi (USA)**[19] 2857 4-9-12 0 .... ChrisCatlin 1 — 66
(Andrew Turnell) *3rd almost thoughout: rdn wl over 1f out: no imp on first 2 after* **16/1**
0- **4** 3 **Marsool**[410] 2146 3-9-0 0 .... TPO'Shea 2 — 60
(M P Tregoning) *in tch tl rdn and wknd over 1f out* **10/1**
5-35 **5** 4 1/2 **Rockfella**[18] 2892 3-9-0 66 .... JamieSpencer 4 — 59
(D J Coakley) *rrd up s: a same pl: wknd over 1f out: eased ins fnl f* **4/1**[3]
00 **6** 18 **Bedarra Boy**[21] 2795 3-9-0 0 .... SimonWhitworth 3 — 15
(D W P Arbuthnot) *hld up in rr: lost tch 2f out* **80/1**

2m 4.53s (0.93) **Going Correction** -0.10s/f (Good)
WFA 3 from 4yo 12lb — **6** Ran SP% **117.2**
Speed ratings (Par 103): **92,88,87,85,81 67**
toteswingers: 1&2 £1.40, 1&3 £2.90, 2&3 £3.50 CSF £3.82 TOTE £2.00: £1.40, £1.90; EX 5.20.
Owner Cheveley Park Stud **Bred** London Thoroughbred Services Ltd **Trained** Newmarket, Suffolk

FOCUS
A moderate maiden run at an average pace and the jockeys all decided to come over to the stands' rail in the straight. The form seems sound.

3473 BRIGHTON & HOVE STREAMLINE TAXIS (S) STKS — 7f 214y
3:30 (3:33) (Class 6) 3-4-Y-O **£1,942** (£578; £288; £144) **Stalls** Low

Form / RPR
3022 **1** **Lady Florence**[7] 3241 4-8-13 48 .... LPKeniry 6 — 56+
(A B Coogan) *mde all: hung lft ins fnl 2f but wl in command fnl f* **5/2**[1]
4000 **2** 3 **Cognac Boy (USA)**[8] 3225 3-8-13 56 ....(v) ChrisCatlin 8 — 56
(A B Haynes) *in rr: hdwy over 1f out: r.o to go 2nd ins fnl f* **50/1**
/6-0 **3** 3/4 **La Belle Joannie**[8] 3207 4-8-13 48 .... JamesDoyle 4 — 46+
(S Curran) *plld hrd in mid-div: effrt 2f out: kpt on one pce fnl f* **33/1**
006 **4** 3 3/4 **Proud Junior (USA)**[10] 3161 3-8-8 52 .... RyanMoore 2 — 41
(S A Callaghan) *in tch: rdn 2f out: no hdwy tl wnt 4th ins fnl f* **11/4**[2]
-056 **5** 1 1/2 **Bathwick Pursuit**[5] 3303 3-8-8 55 .... JimCrowley 9 — 37
(P D Evans) *trckd wnr tl rdn and wknd wl over 1f out* **5/1**[3]
044 **6** hd **Cash In The Attic**[11] 3108 3-8-3 49 .... CatherineGannon 3 — 32
(M R Channon) *prom tl lost pl 1/2-way: rallied over 2f out: wknd 1f out* **14/1**
3336 **7** 3/4 **Maddy**[20] 2808 4-8-8 48 ....(p) MatthewDavies(5) 7 — 32
(George Baker) *slowly away: a bhd* **6/1**
0030 **8** hd **Lancaster Lad (IRE)**[7] 3241 4-9-4 47 ....(p) SebSanders 1 — 37
(A B Haynes) *slowly away: sme hdwy whn short of room and swtchd lft over 1f out: sn btn* **12/1**
4030 **9** 3 1/2 **Never Sold Out (IRE)**[17] 2912 4-8-13 52 ....(b) MCGeran(5) 5 — 29
(J G M O'Shea) *chsd ldrs tl wknd over 1f out* **8/1**

1m 35.27s (-0.73) **Going Correction** -0.10s/f (Good)
WFA 3 from 4yo 10lb — **9** Ran SP% **116.6**
Speed ratings (Par 101): **99,96,95,91,90 89,89,88,85**
toteswingers: 1&2 £8.30, 1&3 £12.20, 2&3 £33.10 CSF £118.66 TOTE £3.40: £1.30, £6.70, £6.60; EX 79.10 TRIFECTA Not won..The winner was bought in for 4,400gns.
Owner A B Coogan **Bred** The National Stud **Trained** Soham, Cambs

FOCUS
A weak seller but fairly open judged on official ratings. The winner got the favoured stands' rail and probably only had to repeat her C&D latest.

3474 FASTWEBMEDIA H'CAP — 1m 1f 209y
4:00 (4:03) (Class 6) (0-60,60) 3-Y-O **£1,942** (£578; £288; £144) **Stalls** High

Form / RPR
0-00 **1** **Halfway House**[35] 2357 3-9-3 **59** .... JamieSpencer 1 — 67+
(M L W Bell) *in rr tl gd hdwy on stands' rail over 1f out: drvn and responded to ld nr fin* **11/4**[1]
4516 **2** nk **Vita Mia**[19] 2866 3-8-13 **55** .... CatherineGannon 3 — 62
(P D Evans) *mid-div: gd hdwy to ld 5f out: clr over 1f out: ct nr fin* **3/1**[2]
0-40 **3** 6 **Timbaa (USA)**[3] 3382 3-8-8 **55** .... WilliamCarson(5) 9 — 50
(Rae Guest) *chsd ldrs thrght: no ch w first 2 fnl f* **7/1**
600 **4** 2 1/4 **Winrob**[21] 2779 3-8-9 **56** .... Louis-PhilippeBeuzelin(5) 6 — 47
(Patrick Morris) *in rr: hdwy 2f out: hng lft and wknd appr fnl f* **7/1**
0056 **5** 1 1/2 **Dulce Domum**[10] 3157 3-8-4 **46** oh1 ....(v[1]) ChrisCatlin 8 — 34
(A B Haynes) *trckd ldr tl outpcd 2f out: sn btn* **16/1**
5-00 **6** 14 **Cobos**[8] 3217 3-9-4 **60** .... SebSanders 7 — 20
(Ms E L McWilliam) *led tl hdd 5f out: wknd 2f out* **10/1**
-600 **7** 1 1/2 **Gibson Square (USA)**[26] 2635 3-8-8 **50** ....(t) JimCrowley 2 — 7
(S C Williams) *trckd ldrs tl wknd 2f out* **33/1**
3-00 **8** 1 1/4 **Sampower Quin (IRE)**[21] 2779 3-9-3 **59** .... DNolan 4 — 13
(D Carroll) *mid-div: rdn over 3f out: wknd 2f out* **5/1**[3]
60-0 **9** 3 3/4 **Milly Rose**[15] 2973 3-8-6 **53** .... MatthewDavies(5) 5 — —
(George Baker) *mid-div tl lost tch 2f out* **40/1**

2m 1.69s (-1.91) **Going Correction** -0.10s/f (Good) — **9** Ran SP% **113.7**
Speed ratings (Par 97): **103,102,97,96,94 83,82,81,78**
toteswingers: 1&2 £2.70, 1&3 £4.30, 2&3 £5.00 CSF £10.93 CT £50.10 TOTE £3.30: £1.40, £1.50, £2.50; EX 9.40 Trifecta £26.40 Pool: £466.22 - 13.03 winning units..
Owner Ferguson, Le Gassick, Dawson & Mercer **Bred** Usk Valley Stud **Trained** Newmarket, Suffolk
■ Stewards' Enquiry : Chris Catlin one-day ban: careless riding (Jul 14)

FOCUS
Only one of these had won before, and the quality of the race was very modest. The winner was another advantaged by the rail and the first two finished clear.
Halfway House Official explanation: trainer's rep said, regarding apparent improvement in form, that the gelding was better suited by the firm ground, lower grade of race, and wearing a ring bit for the first time.
Timbaa(USA) Official explanation: vet said on return gelding had lost a shoe
Winrob Official explanation: jockey said gelding hung left

3475 VIRTUALAGE.CO.UK H'CAP — 1m 3f 196y
4:30 (4:35) (Class 5) (0-70,65) 3-Y-O+ **£3,406** (£1,019; £509; £254; £126) **Stalls** High

Form / RPR
4400 **1** **Rough Sketch (USA)**[4] 3348 4-9-6 **55** ....(b) SebSanders 1 — 61+
(Sir Mark Prescott) *hld up in rr: short of room on stands' rail over 1f out bef str run u.p to ld towards fin* **7/1**
3501 **2** 1 **Penang Cinta**[7] 3244 6-9-10 **59** 6ex .... CatherineGannon 4 — 63
(P D Evans) *hld up: hdwy to ld 2f out: hung bdly lft fr over 1f out: hdd towards fin* **5/2**[1]
1602 **3** 1 1/2 **Spinning Waters**[17] 2909 3-9-2 **65** ....(p) StephenCarson 5 — 67
(Eve Johnson Houghton) *trckd ldrs: rdn and kpt on one pce fnl f* **9/2**[3]
4053 **4** 3 1/4 **Astrolibra**[12] 3074 5-9-7 **56** .... RyanMoore 2 — 52
(M H Tompkins) *trckd ldr tl wknd over 1f out* **11/4**[2]
0235 **5** hd **Carmela Maria**[8] 3217 4-9-8 **62** .... WilliamCarson(5) 6 — 58
(S C Williams) *led tl lost action and hdd 2f out: sn wknd* **8/1**
00-4 **6** 10 **Majd Aljazeera**[146] 391 3-9-2 **65** .... JimCrowley 3 — 45
(D M Simcock) *w.w in tch: rdn 3f out: wknd over 1f out* **5/1**

2m 33.71s (1.01) **Going Correction** -0.10s/f (Good)
WFA 3 from 4yo+ 14lb — **6** Ran SP% **113.7**
Speed ratings (Par 103): **92,91,90,88,88 81**
toteswingers: 1&2 £3.50, 1&3 £5.00, 2&3 £2.30 CSF £25.31 TOTE £8.20: £3.20, £1.50; EX 28.40.
Owner Edward S A Belcher **Bred** Drama Club Syndicate **Trained** Newmarket, Suffolk

FOCUS
A small field for this ordinary handicap with the top weight 8lb below the race ceiling. Modest form. The early pace was fairly steady.
Rough Sketch(USA) Official explanation: trainer's rep said, regarding apparent improvement in form, that the gelding ran too keen early on last time and was better suited by more patient tactics.
Carmela Maria Official explanation: jockey said filly stumbled 2 1/2f out

3476 KILLER CREATIVE H'CAP — 6f 209y
5:00 (5:00) (Class 5) (0-70,70) 3-Y-O **£3,154** (£944; £472; £236; £117) **Stalls** Low

Form / RPR
-104 **1** **Cavendish Road (IRE)**[21] 2797 3-8-11 **60** .... MartinDwyer 5 — 64
(W R Muir) *a in tch: rdn to ld over 1f out: drvn out* **9/2**[3]
-000 **2** 3/4 **Motor Home**[37] 2300 3-8-9 **58** .... WilliamBuick 8 — 60
(A M Balding) *hld up: hdwy and swtchd lft over 1f out: r.o fnl f* **13/2**
5501 **3** nk **Rocket Rob (IRE)**[14] 3010 3-9-4 **67** .... RyanMoore 4 — 68
(S A Callaghan) *s.i.s: hdwy over 2f out: disp ld appr fnl f: no ex towards fin* **13/8**[1]
5066 **4** nk **Arctic Freedom (USA)**[14] 3009 3-9-1 **64** .... SebSanders 2 — 64
(E A L Dunlop) *hld up: hdwy on stands' side over 1f out: fin strly: nvr nrr* **9/1**
0323 **5** nk **Perfect Class**[17] 2917 3-9-1 **67** ....(b) DavidProbert(3) 6 — 67
(C G Cox) *trckd ldrs: outpcd over 1f out: r.o again ins fnl f* **4/1**[2]
0030 **6** 8 **Yughanni**[10] 3176 3-8-3 **52** .... ChrisCatlin 9 — 30
(C E Brittain) *led tl rdn and hdd over 1f out: wknd qckly* **20/1**
3600 **7** 5 **Auld Arty (FR)**[21] 2786 3-9-7 **70** .... RobertHavlin 3 — 34
(T G Mills) *w ldr tl rdn and wknd over 1f out* **14/1**
-404 **8** 25 **Blackwater Fort (USA)**[20] 2810 3-8-6 **55** .... TPO'Shea 1 — —
(J Gallagher) *a outpcd: t.o ins fnl 2f* **20/1**

1m 22.32s (-0.78) **Going Correction** -0.10s/f (Good) — **8** Ran SP% **115.8**
Speed ratings (Par 99): **100,99,98,98,98 88,83,54**
toteswingers: 1&2 £6.40, 1&3 £2.50, 2&3 £4.00 CSF £34.07 CT £65.17 TOTE £5.70: £1.90, £2.50, £1.10; EX 38.40 Trifecta £201.20 Part won. Pool: £271.92 - 0.73 winning units..
Owner C L A Edginton **Bred** Garry Chong **Trained** Lambourn, Berks

FOCUS
An ordinary handicap and pretty modest form, rated around the winner.

Blackwater Fort(USA) Official explanation: jockey said gelding missed the break and never travelled

3477 JIMMY HEAL MEMORIAL H'CAP 5f 59y
5:30 (5:30) (Class 5) (0-70,70) 3-Y-O+ **£3,280** (£981; £490; £245; £122) **Stalls** Low

Form RPR

5600 **1** **Orpen's Art (IRE)**[7] 3246 4-9-1 **58**.......... RyanMoore 6 65
(S A Callaghan) *a in tch: strly rdn to ld jst ins fnl f: drvn out* **7/1**

3224 **2** ¾ **Louie's Lad**[7] 3252 3-8-0 **52**..........(p) DavidProbert(3) 4 54
(J J Bridger) *trckd ldr: led over 1f out: hdd jst ins fnl f: kpt on but nt pce of wnr* **4/1**[1]

0062 **3** 1 ¾ **Espy**[6] 3261 4-9-13 **70**.......... JamesDoyle 2 68+
(S Kirk) *in rr: hdwy in centre of crse to chal over 1f out: one pce fnl f* **4/1**[1]

0000 **4** 1 **Just Joey**[15] 2966 5-8-8 **51** oh1..........(be) JimCrowley 9 45
(J R Weymes) *led tl rdn and hdd over 1f out: nt qckn fnl f* **28/1**

-613 **5** nk **Pic Up Sticks**[7] 3252 10-9-8 **65**.......... GeorgeBaker 7 58
(B G Powell) *s.i.s: sn in tch: nt clr rn 2f out: nt qckn fr over 1f out* **9/2**[2]

6015 **6** 1 ¼ **Berrymead**[7] 3246 4-8-11 **59** ow2.......... AnnStokell(5) 1 48
(Miss A Stokell) *t.k.h: prom tl wknd over 1f out* **17/2**

3112 **7** nk **Caribbean Coral**[4] 3345 10-9-11 **68** 6ex.......... SebSanders 8 55+
(A B Haynes) *mid-div: effrt on stands' side whn short of room fr over 1f out: nt rcvr* **13/2**[3]

4003 **8** ½ **Lithaam (IRE)**[7] 3239 5-8-9 **52**..........(p) ChrisCatlin 3 38
(J M Bradley) *prom tl rdn and wknd appr fnl f* **9/2**[2]

61.42 secs (-0.88) **Going Correction** -0.10s/f (Good)
WFA 3 from 4yo+ 6lb **8** Ran SP% **116.2**
Speed ratings (Par 103): **103,101,99,97,96 94,94,93**
toteswingers: 1&2 £5.20, 1&3 £5.10, 2&3 £4.90 CSF £35.69 CT £128.50 TOTE £9.80: £3.20, £1.70, £1.20; EX 37.70 TRIFECTA Not won. Place 6: £22.93 Place 5: £8.66.
Owner S A Callaghan & N A Callaghan **Bred** Fin A Co S R L **Trained** Newmarket, Suffolk

FOCUS
A routine sprint handicap and again the stands' rail played a big part in the outcome. Modest form.
Berrymead Official explanation: jockey said filly ran too free
Caribbean Coral Official explanation: jockey said gelding was denied a clear run
T/Plt: £9.40 to a £1 stake. Pool: £70,691.16. 5,487.91 winning tickets. T/Qpdt: £6.00 to a £1 stake. Pool: £4,728.98. 576.90 winning tickets. JS

3291 HAMILTON (R-H)
Tuesday, June 30

OFFICIAL GOING: Good to firm (9.8)
Rail realignment around the loop reduced advertised distances on round course by circa 30yards.
Wind: Light, half behind Weather: Fine, sunny

3478 RACING UK MAIDEN STKS 5f 4y
2:15 (2:15) (Class 5) 2-Y-O **£2,729** (£806; £403) **Stalls** Low

Form RPR

2 **1** **Exgray (IRE)**[32] 2449 2-8-12 0.......... TomEaves 8 73+
(B Smart) *cl up gng wl: led over 1f out: drvn out* **8/15**[1]

6 **2** nk **Melody In The Mist (FR)**[36] 2339 2-8-12 0.......... PhillipMakin 4 72
(T D Barron) *chsd ldrs: effrt 2f out: kpt on wl fnl f: jst hld* **4/1**[2]

3 1 ½ **Yesnabay (USA)** 2-9-3 0.......... PJMcDonald 1 72
(G A Swinbank) *dwlt: hld up: hdwy on outside 1/2-way: rdn and kpt on fnl f: nrst fin* **28/1**

4 1 ½ **Waveband** 2-8-12 0.......... JoeFanning 3 61
(M Johnston) *s.i.s: edgd to outside after 2f: effrt 1/2-way: one pce fnl f* **13/2**[3]

5203 **5** 2 ¼ **Dower Glen**[12] 3058 2-8-12 0.......... PaulMulrennan 6 53
(I Semple) *led to over 1f out: kpt on same pce* **12/1**

0 **6** 2 ½ **Mason Hindmarsh**[24] 2721 2-8-12 0.......... BMcHugh(5) 5 49
(Karen McLintock) *in tch tl rdn and outpcd fr 2f out* **66/1**

500 **7** 5 **Ariel Bender**[21] 2778 2-9-3 0.......... PatrickMathers 2 31
(Peter Grayson) *hld up: rdn 1/2-way: sn wknd* **200/1**

00 **8** 2 ¾ **Ron The Don**[38] 2260 2-8-12 0.......... SladeO'Hara(5) 7 21
(A Berry) *chsd ldrs tl rdn and wknd over 2f out* **200/1**

59.80 secs (-0.20) **Going Correction** -0.20s/f (Firm) **8** Ran SP% **112.2**
Speed ratings (Par 93): **93,92,90,87,84 80,72,67**
toteswingers: 1&2 £2.00, 1&3 £5.00, 2&3 £7.60 CSF £2.79 TOTE £1.60: £1.02, £1.40, £5.50; EX 3.90.
Owner Prime Equestrian **Bred** G H Beeby & Viscount Marchwood **Trained** Hambleton, N Yorks

FOCUS
Due to rail realignment, all races over a 1m or further were approximately 30 yards shorter than the official race distances. Following this opener Tom Eaves described the ground as good to firm, while Joe Fanning said it was nearly good, and that they were kicking the top off a little.

NOTEBOOK
Exgray(IRE) showed plenty of speed to sit handy from the widest stall, but had to see off challengers on both sides in the closing stages. This effort confirmed the promise she showed when a close second behind a useful filly at Musselburgh on her debut, but she's quite a leggy filly who still looks immature, and she might need more time before she fulfils her potential. (op 4-7 tchd 1-2)
Melody In The Mist(FR) stepped up significantly on the form she showed at Redcar on her debut. There might be more to come and she should win a maiden. (op 5-1)
Yesnabay(USA) ◆, a 36,000gns first foal of a useful turf sprinter in the US, has already been gelded. Fitted with a sheepskin noseband for this debut, he started slowest of all but made gradual headway and finished well. He's open to a deal of improvement and should soon be winning. (op 25-1 tchd 33-1)
Waveband ◆, a 75,000gns half-sister to a number of sprint winners, including the smart Classic Encounter, started slowly but recovered to hold a chance around two furlongs out, before weakening. She can be expected to come on a fair bit for this and could be hard to beat next time. (op 11-2)
Dower Glen had her chance against the stands' rail but wasn't good enough. She should find things easier in nurseries. (tchd 14-1)

3479 SCOTTISH RACING CLAIMING STKS 5f 4y
2:45 (2:45) (Class 6) 3-5-Y-O **£2,047** (£604; £302) **Stalls** Centre

Form RPR

0262 **1** **Gap Princess (IRE)**[12] 3066 5-8-10 **69**.......... PaulHanagan 1 64
(R A Fahey) *in tch: outpcd 1/2-way: gd hdwy appr fnl f: led ins fnl f: comf* **2/1**[1]

-051 **2** 1 ½ **Cayman Fox**[13] 3020 4-8-12 **60**..........(e) PJMcDonald 6 61
(James Moffatt) *led and clr: hdd ins fnl f: kpt on* **3/1**[3]

6314 **3** 2 **Silvanus (IRE)**[5] 3295 4-9-3 **66**..........(p) TomEaves 3 58
(I Semple) *prom: effrt over 1f out: one pce fnl f* **4/1**

0600 **4** 1 ¾ **Rightcar Lewis**[11] 3125 4-8-8 **40**..........(b) PatrickMathers 7 43
(Peter Grayson) *dwlt: bhd and outpcd: hdwy over 1f out: kpt on: no imp* **80/1**

2246 **5** ½ **Metroland**[29] 2546 3-8-6 **73**.......... AdrianTNicholls 5 43
(D Nicholls) *unruly bef s: sn chsng clr ldr: rdn and edgd lft over 1f out: wknd ins fnl f* **5/2**[2]

0000 **6** ½ **Rio L'Oren (IRE)**[25] 2686 4-8-7 **48**..........(p) LukeMorris 4 39
(N J Vaughan) *in tch: outpcd 1/2-way: n.d after* **50/1**

000 **7** 3 **Gelert (IRE)**[11] 3125 4-8-8 **40**..........(t) SladeO'Hara(5) 2 34
(A Berry) *sn outpcd and drvn along: no ch fr 1/2-way* **100/1**

59.32 secs (-0.68) **Going Correction** -0.20s/f (Firm)
WFA 3 from 4yo+ 6lb **7** Ran SP% **111.1**
Speed ratings (Par 101): **97,94,91,88,87 87,82**
toteswingers: 1&2 £2.30, 1&3 £1.50, 2&3 £2.70 CSF £7.86 TOTE £2.60: £1.70, £2.40; EX 9.80.Gap Princess was claimed by G. A. Harker for £8000.
Owner Dr W D Ashworth **Bred** D Veitch And Musagd Abo Salim **Trained** Musley Bank, N Yorks
■ Stewards' Enquiry : Slade O'Hara one-day ban: used whip when out of contention (Jul 14)

FOCUS
A weak and uncompetitive claimer. The pace was predictably furious. The winner's form rivals disappointed.
Metroland Official explanation: jockey said filly didn't come down the hill

3480 FREEBETS.CO.UK FREE FOOTBALL BETTING H'CAP 1m 65y
3:15 (3:15) (Class 5) (0-70,70) 3-Y-O **£3,238** (£963; £481; £240) **Stalls** High

Form RPR

0431 **1** **Aldaado (IRE)**[34] 2370 3-9-6 **69**.......... PhillipMakin 5 78+
(M Dods) *in tch: drvn and outpcd over 3f out: rallied to ld over 1f out: kpt on strly to go clr fnl f* **10/11**[1]

-004 **2** 3 ¼ **Petsas Pleasure**[11] 3115 3-9-3 **66**.......... PaulHanagan 1 68
(Ollie Pears) *hld up: rdn and outpcd over 3f out: hdwy and swtchd lft over 1f out: chsd wnr ins fnl f: kpt on: no imp* **15/8**[2]

-202 **3** 1 ½ **Liberty Trail (IRE)**[11] 3093 3-9-7 **70**.......... TomEaves 2 68
(I Semple) *led: rdn 3f out: hung rt and hdd over 1f out: kpt on same pce* **7/1**[3]

4000 **4** ½ **Green Dynasty (IRE)**[21] 2779 3-8-9 **58**..........(b[1]) JoeFanning 7 55
(M Johnston) *t.k.h: cl up: ev ch over 3f out: no ex over 1f out* **16/1**

6-00 **5** 2 ¼ **Fuzzy Cat**[24] 2723 3-8-4 **53**..........(b[1]) FrancisNorton 6 45
(T D Barron) *t.k.h: pressed ldr: rdn and edgd rt over 2f out: outpcd wl over 1f out: n.d after* **16/1**

1m 46.82s (-1.58) **Going Correction** -0.35s/f (Firm) **5** Ran SP% **111.4**
Speed ratings (Par 99): **93,89,88,87,85**
CSF £2.89 TOTE £1.80: £1.10, £1.70; EX 3.50.
Owner A Wynn-Williams, D Graham, D Neale **Bred** Deer Forest Stud **Trained** Denton, Co Durham

FOCUS
A wek handicap but there could be more to come from the winner. The first two finishers were well out the back and looked in trouble at halfway, suggesting the prominent racers went off too fast.

3481 FREEBETS.CO.UK SCOTTISH FOOTBALL FREE BETS H'CAP (QUALIFIER FOR SCOTTISH TROPHY HANDICAP FINAL) 1m 1f 36y
3:45 (3:45) (Class 5) (0-75,75) 3-Y-O+ **£3,885** (£1,156; £577; £288) **Stalls** High

Form RPR

0-21 **1** **Stateside (CAN)**[33] 2390 4-8-9 **56** oh3.......... PaulHanagan 3 66
(R A Fahey) *t.k.h early: trckd ldrs: led over 2f out: drvn fnl f: hld on wl* **3/1**[1]

6665 **2** hd **Talk Of Saafend (IRE)**[6] 3267 4-8-13 **60**.......... RoystonFfrench 9 70
(P Monteith) *hld up towards rr: hdwy 2f out: kpt on wl fnl f: jst hld* **11/1**

200- **3** 2 ¼ **Doon Haymer (IRE)**[259] 6726 4-9-7 **68**.......... PaulMulrennan 1 73
(I Semple) *cl up: ev ch over 2f out: one pce fnl f* **13/2**

35-6 **4** 1 ½ **Regent's Secret (USA)**[13] 3023 9-8-10 **57**..........(p) DanielTudhope 10 59
(J S Goldie) *s.i.s: hld up: hdwy and swtchd lft over 2f out: kpt on fnl f: nrst fin* **4/1**[2]

0-24 **5** 1 **Farne Island**[33] 1556 6-8-4 **56** oh1.......... JamieKyne(5) 5 56
(Micky Hammond) *in tch: effrt over 2f out: edgd rt: one pce appr fnl f* **7/1**

0354 **6** 5 **Masterofceremonies**[20] 2818 6-9-1 **62**.......... DarrenMoffatt 6 52
(James Moffatt) *s.i.s: hld: rdn 3f out: kpt on fnl f: n.d* **9/1**

306- **7** 1 ¼ **Anthemion (IRE)**[347] 4148 12-8-2 **56** oh10.......... JakePayne(7) 7 43
(Mrs J C McGregor) *led tl edgd lft and hdd over 2f out: sn btn* **100/1**

6603 **8** 4 ½ **Theonebox (USA)**[12] 3076 4-10-0 **75**.......... LukeMorris 8 52
(N J Vaughan) *hld up towards rr: drvn 3f out: sn btn* **5/1**[3]

00- **9** 14 **Jim Martin**[262] 6657 4-9-5 **66**.......... PJMcDonald 11 14
(Miss L A Perratt) *dwlt: sn prom: rdn over 3f out: sn wknd* **12/1**

00-0 **10** 3 **Jamieson Gold (IRE)**[10] 3150 6-9-1 **65**.......... NeilBrown(3) 4 7
(Miss L A Perratt) *t.k.h: hld up towards rr: struggling over 3f out: sn wknd* **18/1**

1m 55.73s (-3.97) **Going Correction** -0.35s/f (Firm) **10** Ran SP% **119.8**
Speed ratings (Par 103): **103,102,100,99,98 94,93,89,76,73**
toteswingers: 1&2 £8.20, 1&3 £6.70, 2&3 £15.70 CSF £38.83 CT £205.43 TOTE £2.80: £1.10, £3.30, £2.80; EX 31.70.
Owner P Timmins **Bred** Yvonne Schwabe & Dagmar Schwabe **Trained** Musley Bank, N Yorks
■ Stewards' Enquiry : Daniel Tudhope one-day ban: careless riding (Jul 14)
Paul Hanagan caution: used whip with excessive frequency.

FOCUS
An ordinary handicap but an interesting race for the grade with the unexposed winner beating a potentially well treated trio. The pace was decent.

3482 FREEBETS.CO.UK FREE BETS H'CAP 1m 4f 17y
4:15 (4:16) (Class 6) (0-65,62) 3-Y-O **£1,942** (£578; £288; £144) **Stalls** High

Form RPR

0005 **1** **Suitably Accoutred (IRE)**[27] 2605 3-8-4 **45**.......... SilvestreDeSousa 6 54
(Mrs A Duffield) *cl up: led over 3f out: pushed out fnl f: comf* **16/1**

0-01 **2** 3 ½ **Outland (IRE)**[19] 2865 3-8-12 **53**.......... SaleemGolam 10 57
(M H Tompkins) *prom: effrt and swtchd lft over 2f out: sn chsng wnr: kpt on fnl f: no imp* **10/3**[1]

0-06 **3** 2 ½ **Tillietudlem (FR)**[26] 2627 3-8-8 **49** ow4.......... DanielTudhope 5 49
(J S Goldie) *bhd: rdn over 3f out: styd on wl fnl f: nrst fin* **25/1**

2404 **4** 1 **Addison De Witt**[20] 2802 3-8-12 **53**..........(p) PaulHanagan 7 51
(Micky Hammond) *hld up in tch: effrt over 2f out: hung rt: no imp over 1f out* **6/1**

3-35 **5** 3 ¼ **Peintre D'Argent (IRE)**[35] 2350 3-9-5 **60**.......... LukeMorris 9 53
(N J Vaughan) *midfield: drvn 3f out: no ex over 1f out* **7/2**[2]

-003 **6** 4 **Sydney Cove (IRE)**[26] 2627 3-8-0 **46**.......... JamieKyne(5) 8 32
(R Allan) *t.k.h: hld up: drvn over 3f out: n.d* **18/1**

3324 **7** 1 ¾ **Tae Kwon Do (USA)**[36] 2340 3-9-2 **57**.......... RoystonFfrench 1 41
(Miss J A Camacho) *trckd ldrs tl rdn and wknd over 1f out* **5/1**[3]

6405 **8** 7 **Sharp Sovereign (USA)**[12] 3069 3-9-7 **62**.......... TomEaves 3 34
(I Semple) *rdr slow to remove blindfold and s.v.s: hdwy after 3f: rdn over 3f out: sn wknd* **6/1**

0000 **9** *10* **Best Bidder (USA)**[42] 2152 3-8-9 **50**............................ PaulMulrennan 4 6
(Patrick Morris) *hld up: reminders 1/2-way: struggling fnl 4f* **33/1**
0-04 **10** *14* **Step Fast (USA)**[26] 2627 3-8-6 **47**..................................(b[1]) JoeFanning 2 —
(M Johnston) *led to over 3f out: sn rdn and wknd* **12/1**
2m 34.94s (-3.66) **Going Correction** -0.35s/f (Firm) **10** Ran SP% **116.2**
Speed ratings (Par 97): **98,95,94,93,91 88,87,82,76,66**
toteswingers: 1&2 £10.80, 1&3 £27.60, 2&3 £11.40 CSF £68.69 CT £1357.31 TOTE £20.50: £4.70, £1.60, £5.90; EX 99.10.
Owner Miss Helen Wynne **Bred** Bryan Ryan **Trained** Constable Burton, N Yorks

FOCUS
A moderate handicap but the time was good for the grade. The form is rated around the fourth.
Suitably Accoutred(IRE) Official explanation: trainer's rep said, regarding apparent improvement in form, that the stable had been under a cloud recently and the filly had shown sings of recovery since its previous race.
Sharp Sovereign(USA) Official explanation: jockey said gelding was restless in stalls and he was unable to remove blindfold as gates opened

3483 TURFTV H'CAP 5f 4y
4:45 (4:45) (Class 5) (0-75,74) 3-Y-0+ **£3,238** (£963; £481; £240) **Stalls** Centre

Form RPR
1123 **1** **Argentine (IRE)**[5] 3295 5-9-12 **74**................................(b) PaulMulrennan 5 84
(J A McShane) *t.k.h early: trckd ldrs: effrt 2f out: led ins fnl f: r.o wl* **5/1**[2]
3133 **2** *1 ¾* **Raccoon (IRE)**[11] 3109 9-9-11 **73**.................................... PJMcDonald 6 77
(Mrs R A Carr) *led: pushed along over 1f out: hdd ins fnl f: kpt on* **15/2**
0400 **3** *shd* **Joyeaux**[10] 3164 7-9-0 **62**.. JoeFanning 1 65
(Ollie Pears) *hld up in tch: hdwy over 1f out: r.o fnl f* **10/1**
6001 **4** *¾* **Sir Nod**[6] 3268 7-9-11 **73** 6ex.. PaulHanagan 3 74
(Miss J A Camacho) *in tch: effrt and swtchd over 1f out: kpt on same pce ins fnl f* **7/4**[1]
2054 **5** *1* **Kheylide (IRE)**[5] 3304 3-9-1 **69**................................ EdwardCreighton 8 64
(Mrs D J Sanderson) *prom tl rdn and one pce over 1f out* **14/1**
40-3 **6** *shd* **Ursus**[12] 3065 4-8-7 **55**.. SilvestreDeSousa 7 52
(C R Wilson) *cl up tl rdn and no ex over 1f out* **11/2**[3]
0056 **7** *½* **Mandalay King (IRE)**[15] 2966 4-8-12 **67**.................. JohnCavanagh[(7)] 4 62+
(Mrs Marjorie Fife) *missed break: bhd and rdn along: sme late hdwy: n.d* **17/2**
03-0 **8** *5* **Tadalavil**[10] 3149 4-9-5 **72**... JamieKyne[(5)] 2 49
(Miss L A Perratt) *towards rr: drvn and hung rt fr 1/2-way: sn wknd* **12/1**
59.17 secs (-0.83) **Going Correction** -0.20s/f (Firm)
WFA 3 from 4yo+ 6lb **8** Ran SP% **114.2**
Speed ratings (Par 103): **98,95,95,93,92 92,91,83**
toteswingers: 1&2 £3.20, 1&3 £6.30, 2&3 £8.60 CSF £41.63 CT £361.83 TOTE £5.10: £2.10, £1.80, £2.60; EX 17.20.
Owner D Moriarty **Bred** Tony Hirschfeld & L K Piggott **Trained** Dalkeith, Midlothian

FOCUS
A fair, competitive sprint handicap which was strongly run. Solid form, the winner rated back to his best.
Kheylide(IRE) Official explanation: jockey said gelding hung left throughout
Mandalay King(IRE) Official explanation: jockey said gelding missed the break

3484 FAMILY NIGHT WITH STARS FROM XFACTOR H'CAP 6f 5y
5:15 (5:15) (Class 6) (0-65,64) 3-Y-0+ **£2,047** (£604; £302) **Stalls** Centre

Form RPR
-430 **1** **Optical Illusion (USA)**[15] 2964 5-9-5 **54**...................... PaulHanagan 11 63
(R A Fahey) *trckd ldrs: rdn to ld over 1f out: hdd ins fnl f: rallied gamely to ld cl home* **11/2**[3]
2112 **2** *shd* **Hansomis (IRE)**[10] 3148 5-9-9 **63**................................ JamieKyne[(5)] 6 72
(B Mactaggart) *trckd ldrs: gng wl whn nt clr run over 2f out to over 1f out: squeezed through to ld ins fnl f: hdd cl home* **3/1**[2]
3000 **3** *3 ½* **Elkhorn**[8] 3227 7-9-8 **57**..(b) RoystonFfrench 3 55
(Miss J A Camacho) *dwlt: hld up: hdwy over 1f out: kpt on: nt rch first two* **12/1**
5100 **4** *nk* **Sunley Sovereign**[20] 2812 5-9-0 **49**...................(b) SilvestreDeSousa 10 46
(Mrs R A Carr) *sn drvn in midfield: edgd rt 1/2-way: r.o fnl f: nrst fin* **12/1**
0506 **5** *nk* **Circuit Dancer (IRE)**[19] 2852 9-9-13 **62**........................ FrancisNorton 4 58
(D Nicholls) *cl up tl rdn and no ex fnl f* **7/1**
0403 **6** *hd* **Ingleby Princess**[5] 3296 5-9-2 **54**...............................(p) NeilBrown[(3)] 8 49
(T D Barron) *towards rr: rdn over 2f out: kpt on fnl f: n.d* **11/4**[1]
00 **7** *1 ¼* **Tarus (IRE)**[11] 3125 5-8-3 **45**... BillyCray[(7)] 5 36
(A Berry) *led to over 1f out: sn no ex* **80/1**
0245 **8** *1 ¼* **Howards Tipple**[5] 3296 5-9-5 **54**.............................(p) PaulMulrennan 1 41
(I Semple) *hld up: hdwy over 1f out: n.d* **15/2**
465- **9** *2 ¼* **Blow Your Mind**[322] 4948 3-9-3 **64**............................. BMcHugh[(5)] 9 42
(Karen McLintock) *cl up: ev ch over 1f out: sn wknd* **33/1**
0-50 **10** *2 ¾* **Call Me Rosy (IRE)**[35] 2366 5-8-11 **46**............................ TomEaves 7 17
(B Smart) *s.s: bhd: rdn over 2f out: sn wknd* **25/1**
1m 10.85s (-1.35) **Going Correction** -0.20s/f (Firm)
WFA 3 from 5yo+ 7lb **10** Ran SP% **114.7**
Speed ratings (Par 101): **101,100,96,95,95 95,93,91,88,85**
toteswingers: 1&2 £4.10, 1&3 £10.90, 2&3 £8.90 CSF £21.67 CT £194.27 TOTE £5.90: £2.10, £1.40, £3.40; EX 29.80.
Owner James Gaffney **Bred** Arthur I Appleton **Trained** Musley Bank, N Yorks
■ Stewards' Enquiry : Billy Cray caution: careless riding

FOCUS
A moderate sprint handicap. It was well run and the form is sound.
Sunley Sovereign Official explanation: jockey said gelding hung left
Circuit Dancer(IRE) Official explanation: trainer's rep said gelding bled from the nose
Call Me Rosy(IRE) Official explanation: jockey said mare missed the break

3485 SCOT INDUSTRIAL PRODUCTS MAIDEN STKS 1m 65y
5:45 (5:46) (Class 5) 3-4-Y-0 **£2,590** (£770; £385; £192) **Stalls** High

Form RPR
4-02 **1** **Drum Dragon**[25] 2685 3-8-12 73.................................... SaleemGolam 6 70
(M H Tompkins) *trckd ldrs: led over 2f out: hung lft ins fnl f: styd on* **9/4**[2]
4-5 **2** *¾* **Jeunopse (IRE)**[34] 2375 3-8-12 0................................ TomEaves 2 68+
(B Smart) *in tch: effrt over 2f out: hmpd and swtchd sharply lft over 1f out: kpt on ins fnl f* **12/1**
3 *1 ¾* **Acquavella** 3-8-12 0.. PaulHanagan 5 64+
(R A Fahey) *hld up in tch: outpcd 4f out: styd on fr 2f out: nrst fin* **5/1**[3]
50 **4** *½* **Fernando Torres**[17] 2937 3-8-10 0............................... NSLawes[(7)] 4 68
(D Nicholls) *led to over 2f out: edgd rt wl over 1f out: sn no ex* **16/1**
5 *6* **Oneofapear (IRE)** 3-9-3 0.. PJMcDonald 1 54
(G A Swinbank) *s.i.s: bhd: outpcd 4f out: n.d after* **28/1**
5-60 **6** *10* **More Tea Vicar (IRE)**[91] 1050 3-8-7 60........................ JamieKyne[(5)] 7 26
(Patrick Morris) *trckd ldrs tl rdn and wknd over 2f out* **50/1**

7 *¾* **Curlew (IRE)** 3-9-3 0... JoeFanning 3 30
(M Johnston) *t.k.h: trckd ldrs: effrt and ch over 2f out: sn wknd* **5/4**[1]
1m 46.26s (-2.14) **Going Correction** -0.35s/f (Firm) **7** Ran SP% **110.9**
Speed ratings (Par 103): **96,95,93,93,87 77,76**
toteswingers: 1&2 £2.60, 1&3 £2.20, 2&3 £4.60 CSF £26.60 TOTE £3.10: £1.50, £3.20; EX 17.50 Place 6: £35.95 Place 5: £29.61.
Owner David P Noblett **Bred** Ian Lochhead **Trained** Newmarket, Suffolk

FOCUS
The winning time was 0.56 seconds quicker than the earlier 51-70 handicap for 3yos won by the 69-rated Aldaado. Modest maiden form and is it doubtful what the winner achieved with the favourite disappointing.
T/Plt: £18.10 to a £1 stake. Pool: £60,261.09. 2,427.93 winning tickets. T/Qpdt: £9.10 to a £1 stake. Pool: £3,735.63. 301.10 winning tickets. RY

2996 THIRSK (L-H)
Tuesday, June 30
OFFICIAL GOING: Good (good to firm in places; 9.8)
Wind: Nil

3486 FAIRFAX ARMS GILLING H'CAP 2m
6:30 (6:31) (Class 6) (0-60,58) 4-Y-0+ **£3,139** (£926; £463) **Stalls** Low

Form RPR
60-4 **1** **Spiders Star**[27] 2614 6-8-3 **50**.................................... PaulPickard[(7)] 4 59+
(S G West) *hld up and bhd: swtchd to wd outside and hdwy over 2f out: sn rdn and str run appr fnl f: styd on wl to ld last stride* **12/1**
-324 **2** *hd* **Jackday (IRE)**[5] 3313 4-9-4 **58**.................................... DuranFentiman 8 67
(T D Easterby) *trckd ldrs: hdwy 3f out: swtchd rt and rdn to ld wl over 1f out: drvn ins fnl f: hdd last stride* **7/2**[1]
0-54 **3** *5* **Waterloo Corner**[10] 3171 7-9-0 **54**...................................(p) NCallan 5 57
(R Craggs) *a.p: rdn along wl over 2f out: drvn wl over 1f out: kpt on same pce u.p ent fnl f* **11/2**
30/P **4** *shd* **Patavium (IRE)**[18] 2159 6-8-7 **47**.................................. TonyHamilton 3 50
(E W Tuer) *set stdy pce: qcknd over 4f out: rdn along wl over 2f out: drvn and hdd wl over 1f out: kpt on same pce fnl f* **16/1**
14-0 **5** *1 ¾* **Simple Jim (FR)**[5] 3291 5-8-9 **56**........................ JamesPSullivan[(7)] 9 57
(J Hetherton) *hld up in tch: effrt and hdwy 3f out: rdn 2f out and no imp appr fnl f* **6/1**
0-63 **6** *1 ½* **Terenzium (IRE)**[27] 2614 7-8-10 **50**..............................(p) GregFairley 13 49
(Micky Hammond) *trckd ldr: effrt 4f out and cl up tl rdn along over 2f and grad wknd* **8/1**
20-4 **7** *3 ¾* **Park's Prodigy**[35] 2366 5-8-6 **51**............................(t) PatrickDonaghy[(5)] 10 45
(P C Haslam) *trckd ldrs: effrt 4f out: pushed along over 3f out: sn rdn and wknd wl over 2f out* **5/1**[3]
/00- **8** *1* **Graze On And On**[35] 3126 4-8-5 **45**.......................(p) GrahamGibbons 12 38
(J J Quinn) *chsd ldrs: pushed along over 3f out: rdn wl over 2f out and sn wknd* **4/1**[2]
000 **9** *1 ¾* **Lady Anne Nevill**[11] 3120 5-8-7 **50**........................... KellyHarrison[(3)] 11 41
(C W Fairhurst) *prom: rdn along 3f out: drvn over 2f out and sn wknd* **50/1**
00-0 **10** *1* **Liberty Seeker (FR)**[15] 2971 10-8-6 **51** ow1.............. MarkCoumbe[(5)] 7 41
(John A Harris) *hld up: a bhd* **33/1**
6-00 **11** *½* **Able Dara**[10] 3171 6-8-5 **45**..(p) JimmyQuinn 6 34
(N Bycroft) *hld up: a bhd* **33/1**
0000 **12** *47* **Fan Club**[15] 2965 5-8-5 **45**... AndrewElliott 2 —
(Mrs R A Carr) *hld up towards rr: hdwy on outer to chse ldrs 1/2-way: rdn along over 4f out and sn wknd* **66/1**
3m 30.32s (-2.48) **Going Correction** -0.15s/f (Firm) **12** Ran SP% **122.6**
Speed ratings (Par 101): **100,99,97,97,96 95,93,93,92,91 91,68**
toteswingers: 1&2 £12.80, 1&3 £14.40, 2&3 £3.40 CSF £54.77 CT £269.13 TOTE £12.70: £2.90, £1.40, £2.60; EX 52.70.
Owner Miss Kate Milligan **Bred** Acrum Lodge Stud **Trained** Middleham Moor, N Yorks
■ Simon West's first Flat winner.
■ Stewards' Enquiry : Patrick Donaghy two-day ban: used whip with excessive force (Jul 14-15)

FOCUS
After rain on Sunday night the ground looked on the quick side of good. This was a low-grade 45-58 stayers' handicap and was run at a very steady pace until the final three-quarters of a mile. Modest form at best.
Able Dara Official explanation: jockey said gelding hung right

3487 HELMSLEY CASTLE MAIDEN STKS 6f
7:00 (7:07) (Class 5) 2-Y-0 **£4,274** (£1,271; £635; £317) **Stalls** High

Form RPR
2 **1** **Ballodair (IRE)**[19] 2853 2-9-3 0.................................. TonyHamilton 2 80+
(R A Fahey) *cl up: led 1/2-way: rdn wl over 1f out: drvn and edgd lft ins fnl f: styd on wl* **15/8**[1]
2 *¾* **Call To Arms (IRE)** 2-9-3 0... GregFairley 7 78+
(M Johnston) *trckd ldrs: swtchd lft and hdwy over 2f out: sn chal and ev ch: rdn over 1f out: drvn ins fnl f: no ex last 100yds* **2/1**[2]
00 **3** *5* **Mighty Clarets (IRE)**[25] 2663 2-8-10 0......................... LeeTopliss[(7)] 3 63
(R A Fahey) *chsd ldrs: rdn along 2f out: wandered ins fnl f: kpt on wl towards fin* **25/1**
4 *½* **Layla's Hero (IRE)** 2-9-3 0................................... AdrianTNicholls 8 61+
(D Nicholls) *dwlt and towards rr: hdwy 2f out: sn rdn and kpt on ins fnl f: nrst fin* **16/1**
36 **5** *hd* **Gillburg (USA)**[73] 1358 2-9-3 0.. NCallan 5 61
(K A Ryan) *led: rdn along and hdd 1/2-way: drvn and wknd wl over 1f out* **9/2**[3]
6 *1 ¼* **Mad Millie (IRE)** 2-8-5 0................................... JamesPSullivan[(7)] 10 52
(J Hetherton) *dwlt and towards rr tl styd on fnl 2f: nrst fin* **16/1**
6 **7** *hd* **Lady Lefroy (IRE)**[16] 2940 2-8-5 0........................... TimothyAyres[(7)] 4 51
(R A Fahey) *in tch: pushed along 2f out: sn one pce* **14/1**
60 **8** *1 ¼* **Sweet Baby Jane (IRE)**[42] 2153 2-8-5 0................. FrazerWilliams[(7)] 9 48
(R A Fahey) *a towards rr* **100/1**
6 **9** *nk* **One Cool Deal (IRE)**[15] 2963 2-9-3 0................................ DavidAllan 6 52
(T D Easterby) *rdn 1/2-way and a in rr* **50/1**
10 *45* **Go Win Girl** 2-8-7 0...................................... PatrickDonaghy[(5)] 1 —
(P C Haslam) *dwlt and wnt lft s: a in rr* **50/1**
1m 13.92s (1.22) **Going Correction** +0.025s/f (Good) **10** Ran SP% **113.5**
Speed ratings (Par 93): **92,91,84,83,83 81,80,79,79,19**
toteswingers: 1&2 £1.40, 1&3 £13.70, 2&3 £14.00 CSF £5.50 TOTE £2.80: £1.10, £1.20, £4.70; EX 6.10.
Owner Mrs H Steel **Bred** Mrs Catherine La Mara **Trained** Musley Bank, N Yorks

FOCUS
An interesting six furlong two-year-old maiden race won by the subsequent Gimcrack winner Sir Gerry in 2007. The front pair finished clear and look well above average.

NOTEBOOK

Ballodair(IRE) ◆, runner-up to the subsequent Chesham sixth on his debut at Nottingham, had to dig deep to get the better of the runner-up. He is most unlikely to be given a lenient nursery mark and the novice route may be forced upon him. (op 2-1 tchd 9-4)

Call To Arms(IRE) ◆, a son of Shamardal, came in for good support. He looked a real danger when moving upsides coming to the final furlong but the more experienced winner was a fraction too good. From a good dam-line, he will be even better suited by 7f and should have a bright future. (op 5-2 tchd 15-8)

Mighty Clarets(IRE), although no match for the first two, ran his best race so far. This was his third start and opens up the nursery route. (tchd 20-1)

Layla's Hero(IRE) ◆, a gelded son of One Cool Cat, was cheaply bought. He stayed on in eye-catching style from off the pace and should improve. (op 10-1)

Gillburg(USA), absent for ten weeks and gelded since flopping as an odds-on favourite after a promising debut, gave problems in the paddock. He hung violently left after making the early running and is not straightforward. (op 100-30 tchd 5-1)

Mad Millie(IRE), a springer in the market, was far too keen. Sticking on at the finish after she met trouble over a furlong out, she will hopefully settle better next time. (op 50-1)

Lady Lefroy(IRE) came in for support, but was hopelessly outpaced. With another run under her belt, she looks a likely type for 7f-1m in nursery company. (op 22-1 tchd 9-1)

3488 HARES OF SNAPE H'CAP — 7f

7:30 (7:32) (Class 5) (0-75,75) 3-Y-0+ **£4,274** (£1,271; £635; £317) **Stalls Low**

Form — RPR

6001 **1** **Glenridding**[4] 3331 5-9-7 **68** 6ex....(p) J-PGuillambert 11 — 76
(J G Given) *mde all: rdn over 2f out: drvn appr fnl f and styd on wl* **9/1**

0013 **2** 1 1/4 **Avontuur (FR)**[13] 3021 7-8-9 **61**.... DeanHeslop(5) 2 — 65+
(Mrs R A Carr) *hld up: hdwy on outer over 2f out: rdn wl over 1f out: edgd lft and styd on wl fnl f* **16/1**

0-03 **3** 1/2 **Nufoudh (IRE)**[11] 3105 5-8-6 **56** oh11.... KellyHarrison(3) 6 — 59
(Miss Tracy Waggott) *chsd wnr: rdn along over 2f out: drvn over 1f out: kpt on u.p ins fnl f: n.m.r and lost 2nd nr fin* **66/1**

-400 **4** 2 **Royal Composer (IRE)**[29] 2529 6-8-9 **56** oh2.... GrahamGibbons 5 — 57+
(T D Easterby) *chsd ldrs: rdn along 3f out and styng on whn n.m.r and hmpd wl over 1f out: sn swtchd lft and kpt on ins fnl f* **20/1**

0001 **5** shd **Violent Velocity (IRE)**[3] 3401 6-8-6 **60**.... IJBrennan(7) 7 — 57+
(J J Quinn) *hld up: hdwy 3f out: rdn along 2f out: sn one pce* **5/4**[1]

5040 **6** 1 1/2 **Mozayada (USA)**[14] 2999 5-9-6 **67**.... JimmyQuinn 8 — 60
(M Brittain) *chsd ldrs: rdn along over 3f out: drvn and wknd 2f out* **33/1**

0402 **7** 1 3/4 **Hiccups**[14] 2998 9-9-13 **74**.... DarryllHolland 10 — 63
(M Dods) *hld up: a towards rr* **11/2**[2]

-133 **8** 1 **Pickering**[32] 2438 5-9-11 **72**....(p) AndrewMullen 4 — 58
(E J Alston) *chsd ldng pair: rdn along 3f out: drvn over 2f out and sn wknd* **7/1**[3]

0300 **9** 1 **Dream Express (IRE)**[14] 2998 4-9-10 **71**....(t) PhillipMakin 9 — 54
(M Dods) *a bhd* **16/1**

0-00 **10** 1/2 **Geezers Colours**[17] 2938 4-10-0 **75**.... AndrewElliott 1 — 57
(K R Burke) *a in rr* **40/1**

1m 26.76s (-0.44) **Going Correction** +0.025s/f (Good) **10** Ran SP% **105.7**
Speed ratings (Par 103): **103,101,101,98,98 96,94,93,92,92**
toteswingers: 1&2 £18.50, 1&3 £73.10, 2&3 £33.40. CSF £101.32 CT £5526.17 TOTE £10.50: £2.10, £3.90, £15.50; EX 125.60.
Owner Tremousser Partnership **Bred** Bolton Grange **Trained** Willoughton, Lincs
■ Malcheek was withdrawn (5/1, broke out of stalls). Deduct 15p in the £ under R4.
■ Stewards' Enquiry : Dean Heslop two-day ban: excessive use of the whip (Jul 14-15)

FOCUS

The rain continued to fall in the lead up to this 56-75 handicap. The pace was strong and the field was soon strung out. It was hard to make ground from off the pace. This was not a bad race for the grade but the form is confusing, with the winner confirming his Chester win but the third 12lb out of the weights.

Hiccups Official explanation: jockey said gelding was unsuited by the good (good to firm in places) ground

3489 CARLETON FURNITURE H'CAP — 1m

8:00 (8:03) (Class 4) (0-85,83) 3-Y-0 **£5,569** (£1,657; £828; £413) **Stalls Low**

Form — RPR

3-31 **1** **Yirga**[18] 2890 3-9-4 **80**....(t) LDettori 2 — 87+
(Saeed Bin Suroor) *trckd ldng pair: pushed along wl over 3f out: rdn over 2f out and sn edgd lft: drvn to chal appr fnl f: styd on u.str.p to ld nr line* **4/5**[1]

0100 **2** nk **Johnmanderville**[24] 2696 3-9-0 **76**.... AndrewElliott 4 — 82
(K R Burke) *cl up: effrt over 2f out and sn rdn: drvn over 1f out: led ins fnl f: hdd and no ex nr fin* **9/1**

0401 **3** 3 1/4 **Fesko**[14] 2999 3-9-7 **83**.... GregFairley 1 — 82
(M Johnston) *sn led: rdn along over 2f out: drvn over 1f out: hdd ins fnl f: wknd towards fin* **6/1**[3]

1140 **4** 9 **Cornish Castle (USA)**[28] 2571 3-8-11 **73**....(b[1]) GrahamGibbons 3 — 51
(T D Walford) *a in rr* **14/1**

-221 **5** 5 **Palacefield (IRE)**[36] 2318 3-9-4 **80**.... NCallan 5 — 46
(P W Chapple-Hyam) *hld up: hdwy to chse ldng pair 1/2-way: rdn along wl over 2f out: sn wknd* **3/1**[2]

1m 39.88s (-0.22) **Going Correction** +0.025s/f (Good) **5** Ran SP% **111.5**
Speed ratings (Par 101): **102,101,98,89,84**
CSF £9.00 TOTE £1.70: £1.10, £3.00; EX 7.40.
Owner Godolphin **Bred** Gainsborough Stud Management Ltd **Trained** Newmarket, Suffolk

FOCUS

A fair handicap for three-year-olds. The winner on the bare form of his Sandown win.

Palacefield(IRE) Official explanation: jockey said colt was unsuited by the good (good to firm in places) ground

3490 TURFTV H'CAP — 1m

8:30 (8:31) (Class 6) (0-55,61) 3-Y-0+ **£3,139** (£926; £463) **Stalls Low**

Form — RPR

-536 **1** **Not Now Lewis (IRE)**[15] 2964 5-8-13 **53**.... SladeO'Hara(5) 8 — 61
(F P Murtagh) *in tch: hdwy 3f out: rdn to ld over 1f out: hung lft ent fnl f and sn drvn: jst hld on* **14/1**

0032 **2** hd **Sion Hill (IRE)**[6] 3269 8-9-0 **52**....(p) KellyHarrison(3) 12 — 61+
(John A Harris) *chsd ldng pair: hdwy 3f out: led over 2f out: rdn and hdd over 1f out: hmpd ent fnl f: sn swtchd rt and drvn: styd on wl towards fin: jst failed* **12/1**

3-04 **3** 3/4 **Astroangel**[14] 3007 5-9-2 **51**....(p) NCallan 10 — 57
(M H Tompkins) *chsd ldrs: hdwy over 2f out: sn rdn and ch whn n.m.r ent fnl f: sn drvn and kpt on* **11/1**

0000 **4** 3 1/2 **Fyodorovich (USA)**[15] 2964 4-9-4 **53**.... PAspell 15 — 51
(J S Wainwright) *hld up and bhd: hdwy on inner whn nt clr run and swtchd rt over 2f out: rdn over 1f out: kpt on wl fnl f: nrest at fin* **66/1**

0053 **5** 1/2 **Libre**[14] 3007 9-9-6 **55**.... TolleyDean 3 — 52+
(F Jordan) *hld up in rr: hdwy wl over 2f out: rdn wl over 1f out: styd on wl fnl f: nrest at fin* **10/1**[3]

0265 **6** 2 **Whaston (IRE)**[36] 2314 4-9-3 **52**....(v) JimmyQuinn 16 — 44
(J D Bethell) *midfield: hdwy to chse ldrs 3f out: rdn along 2f out and sn one pce* **11/1**

200- **7** 1 1/4 **Uhuru Peak**[217] 7441 8-8-13 **55**.... JamesPSullivan(7) 5 — 44
(M W Easterby) *dwlt and bhd tl hdwy wl over 2f out: rdn and styd on appr fnl f: nrest at fin* **33/1**

0443 **8** 1 3/4 **Pianoforte (USA)**[6] 3264 7-9-6 **55**....(b) DavidAllan 11 — 40
(E J Alston) *midfield: hdwy on outer to chse ldrs wl over 2f out: sn rdn and no imp fr wl over 1f out* **11/2**[2]

-006 **9** 1 1/4 **Bentley**[24] 2722 5-9-5 **54**....(v) PatCosgrave 4 — 36
(J G Given) *cl up: led over 3f out: rdn along and hdd over 2f out: sn drvn and grad wknd* **25/1**

-000 **10** 1 **Emperor's Well**[49] 1955 10-9-4 **53**....(b) PaulMulrennan 6 — 33+
(M W Easterby) *trckd ldng pair on inner: pushed along 3f out: rdn over 2f out and sn wknd* **11/2**[2]

0403 **11** 5 **Carnival Dream**[12] 3061 4-9-4 **53**....(p) PhillipMakin 13 — 21
(H A McWilliams) *chsd ldrs on outer: rdn along wl over 2f out and sn wknd* **18/1**

0615 **12** shd **All You Need (IRE)**[20] 2812 5-8-13 **55**....(p) DavidKenny(7) 2 — 23
(R Hollinshead) *midfield on inner: sme hdwy over 3f out: rdn wl over 2f out and sn btn* **20/1**

000 **13** 1 1/2 **Strategic Knight (USA)**[33] 2420 4-9-1 **50**.... GrahamGibbons 9 — 15
(R C Guest) *midfield: effrt on outer over 2f out: sn rdn and nvr a factor* **25/1**

05-1 **14** 26 **Hypnotic**[7] 3241 7-9-12 **61** 6ex.... PaulDoe 17 — —
(Jim Best) *in tch on wd outside: rdn along 1/2-way: sn wknd and bhd fnl 2f* **3/1**[1]

60-0 **15** 24 **Miss Ferney**[4] 3350 5-9-6 **55**.... GregFairley 1 — —
(A Kirtley) *led: rdn along and hdd over 3f out: sn wknd and bhd fnl 2f* **66/1**

6633 **P** **Crux**[12] 3070 7-8-9 **51**.... PaulPickard(7) 18 — —
(R E Barr) *a in rr: wl bhd 3f out: sn p.u and dismntd* **10/1**[3]

1m 42.03s (1.93) **Going Correction** +0.20s/f (Good) **16** Ran SP% **128.6**
Speed ratings (Par 101): **98,97,97,93,93 91,89,88,86,85 80,80,79,53,29** —
toteswingers: 1&2 £10.80, 1&3 £36.10, 2&3 £41.90 CSF £170.45 CT £1946.85 TOTE £15.60: £2.70, £2.30, £3.10, £18.60; EX 170.80.
Owner R & J Wharton **Bred** Michael And John Fahy **Trained** Low Braithwaite, Cumbria
■ Stewards' Enquiry : Slade O'Hara two-day ban: careless riding (Jul 15-16)

FOCUS

A low-grade 50-61 handicap and it continued to rain. The first three, who finished clear, were always prominent, and this is modest form.

Carnival Dream Official explanation: jockey said filly was unsuited by the good (good to firm in places) giound

Hypnotic Official explanation: jockey said gelding never travelled

3491 THIRSK CASTLE H'CAP — 5f

9:00 (9:01) (Class 4) (0-85,81) 3-Y-0+ **£5,569** (£1,657; £828; £413) **Stalls High**

Form — RPR

201 **1** **Le Toreador**[10] 3149 4-9-12 **81**....(t) NCallan 5 — 90
(K A Ryan) *cl up: led 1/2-way: rdn wl over 1f out: drvn ins fnl f and hld on gamely* **5/1**

6003 **2** nk **Medici Time**[14] 3002 4-8-7 **62** oh1....(v) GrahamGibbons 8 — 70
(T D Easterby) *in rr: pushed along over 2f out: rdn and hdwy over 1f out: styd on strly ins fnl f* **8/1**

0-30 **3** hd **Sudden Impact (IRE)**[89] 1089 4-9-10 **79**....(e[1]) PaulMulrennan 7 — 86
(Paul Green) *led: hdd and rdn along 1/2-way: rallied wl u.p ent fnl f: kpt on* **28/1**

0422 **4** 1/2 **Artsu**[10] 3149 4-9-5 **74**.... PhillipMakin 1 — 79
(M Dods) *hld up in rr: hdwy 2f out: rdn to chal over 1f out: sn rdn and ev ch tl nt qckn wl ins fnl f* **10/3**[2]

-040 **5** 1 3/4 **Cape Vale (IRE)**[24] 2707 4-9-11 **80**.... AdrianTNicholls 6 — 79
(D Nicholls) *hld up: hdwy to trck ldrs 2f out: effrt and nt clr run over 1f out: sn swtchd lft and rdn: one pce ins fnl f* **4/1**[3]

1 **6** 6 **Crimea (IRE)**[14] 3003 3-9-5 **80**.... GregFairley 2 — 58
(M Johnston) *cl up on outer: effrt 1/2-way and ev ch tl rdn and hung lft wl over 1f out: sn btn* **11/4**[1]

106 **7** 5 **Kyzer Chief**[14] 3002 4-8-10 **65**.... RoystonFfrench 4 — 25
(R E Barr) *cl up: rdn along 1/2-way: sn drvn and outpcd fnl 2f* **12/1**

59.92 secs (0.32) **Going Correction** +0.20s/f (Good)
WFA 3 from 4yo+ 6lb **7** Ran SP% **108.7**
Speed ratings (Par 105): **105,104,104,103,100 91,83**
toteswingers: 1&2 £6.50, 1&3 £17.10, 2&3 £4.50 CSF £37.75 CT £740.54 TOTE £6.00: £2.40, £4.00; EX 51.60 Place 6 £1,252.96, Place 5 £504.31..
Owner Guy Reed **Bred** G Reed **Trained** Hambleton, N Yorks

FOCUS

The rain had stopped but the time suggested that the ground had not been affected. They raced in one group against the stands' side rails and there were traffic problems. The form is best rated around the runner-up.

T/Plt: £530.00 to a £1 stake. Pool: £70,273.06. 96.78 winning tickets. T/Qpdt: £88.00 to a £1 stake. Pool: £4,961.86. 41.70 winning tickets. JR

3441 HAMBURG (R-H)

Tuesday, June 30

OFFICIAL GOING: Good

3493a HAMBURG-DRESDEN-POKAL 141. LANGER HAMBURGER (LISTED RACE) — 2m

6:55 (7:02) 4-Y-0+ **£11,650** (£4,854; £1,942; £971)

RPR

1 **Tarkheena Prince (USA)**[60] 4-8-9.... ASuborics 4 — 103
(C Von Der Recke, Germany) **151/10**

2 5 **Limatus (GER)**[19] 8-8-9.... AStarke 9 — 97
(P Vovcenko, Germany) **58/10**

3 1 **Brisant (GER)**[60] 7-8-9.... MSuerland 2 — 96
(R Suerland, Germany) **31/10**[2]

4 nk **Valdino (GER)**[19] 4-9-4.... RPiechulek 10 — 105
(Uwe Ostmann, Germany) **18/5**[3]

5 1/2 **Miss Naline (FR)** 4-8-6.... FilipMinarik 5 — 92
(Andreas Lowe, Germany) **45/1**

6 1 3/4 **Satier (FR)**[19] 4-8-9 .... AHelfenbein 1 93
(Mario Hofer, Germany) **2/1**[1]
7 1 1/4 **Si Belle (IRE)**[31] 2501 4-8-6 .... ABest 7 89
(Rae Guest) *hld up towards rr: 7th st on outside: rdn 2f out: no hdwy* **63/10**
8 4 1/2 **Sweet Day (GER)** 4-8-6 .... NRichter 8 84
(A Trybuhl, Germany) **22/1**
9 40 **Santero (GER)**[359] 3773 4-8-9 .... HGrewe 6 43
(N Sauer, Germany) **106/10**
10 dist **Longoria (GER)** 5-8-8 ow2 .... APietsch 3 —
(Helga Dewald, Hungary) **37/1**

3m 26.48s (206.48) **10** Ran SP% **131.9**
(including ten euro stakes): WIN 161; PL 34, 21, 20: SF 603.
Owner Bmk Racing **Bred** Whitewood Stable Inc **Trained** Weilerswist, Germany

NOTEBOOK
Si Belle(IRE) picked up black type last year in Germany, but she couldn't land a blow from off the pace this time.

2655 CATTERICK (L-H)
Wednesday, July 1

OFFICIAL GOING: Good to firm (good in places; 9.2)
Wind: Nil Weather: Hot and sunny

3494 RACESPONSORS.CO.UK MEDIAN AUCTION MAIDEN STKS 7f
2:30 (2:32) (Class 5) 2-Y-O **£3,238** (£963; £481; £240) **Stalls** Low

Form RPR
42 1 **Contract Caterer (IRE)**[13] 3052 2-9-3 0 .... MickyFenton 3 77+
(Pat Eddery) *mde all: rdn and qcknd clr over 1f out: kpt on wl* **2/5**[1]
02 2 4 **Desert Forest (IRE)**[22] 2788 2-9-3 0 .... PaulMulrennan 4 66
(J Howard Johnson) *sn chsng wnr: rdn along over 2f out: kpt on u.p appr last: no ch w wnr* **12/1**
3 nk **Aquarian Spirit** 2-9-3 0 .... PaulHanagan 6 65
(R A Fahey) *dwlt: sn in tch: hdwy 1/2-way: rdn to chse ldng pair over 2f out: kpt onfnl f* **10/1**[3]
4 1 1/4 **Jutland** 2-9-3 0 .... GregFairley 5 65+
(M Johnston) *s.i.s and bhd: hdwy 2f out: styd on wl fnl f: nrst fin* **4/1**[2]
00 5 9 **William Arnold**[14] 3032 2-9-0 0 .... KellyHarrison(3) 7 39
(C W Fairhurst) *towards rr: rdn along 1/2-way: nvr a factor* **100/1**
0460 6 nk **Blue Bond**[19] 2896 2-9-3 0 ....(p) JamieMoriarty 1 38
(P T Midgley) *s.i.s: a in rr* **125/1**
3 7 6 **Blue Emirate**[22] 2784 2-9-3 0 .... PhillipMakin 2 22
(P C Haslam) *t.k.h: chsd ldng pair: rdn along 1/2-way and sn wknd* **40/1**

1m 26.35s (-0.65) **Going Correction** -0.30s/f (Firm) **7** Ran SP% **112.4**
Speed ratings (Par 94): **91,86,86,84,74 74,67**
toteswingers: 1&2 £2.40, 1&3 £2.00, 2&3 £3.20 CSF £6.50 TOTE £1.50: £1.10, £3.10; EX 5.70.
Owner ABM Catering Limited **Bred** Tareq Al Mazeedi **Trained** Nether Winchendon, Bucks

FOCUS
The first meeting for almost a month and after three dry days the ground was described as 'quick' but with an excellent covering of grass. A weak maiden.

NOTEBOOK
Contract Caterer(IRE), who did not have luck on his side when narrowly denied at Leicester on his second start, was bustled along to lead. His rider slowed the pace until sending him clear two furlongs out. Heavily eased, he was value double the official margin. It was a weak event and connections will be hoping for a realistic nursery mark. (tchd 8-13 in a place)
Desert Forest(IRE), narrowly beaten in a maiden claimer at Redcar on his second start, is the guide to the overall value of the form. (op 14-1 tchd 16-1)
Aquarian Spirit made a sluggish start but was soon in pursuit of the leaders. He kept on in his own time in the final quarter-mile and will improve both fitness-wise and for the experience. (op 7-1 tchd 13-2)
Jutland, bred for stamina rather than speed, is a well-made newcomer. He gave away many lengths at the start, then hung left in the home straight. Sticking on in his own time, this will have taught him plenty and he will appreciate a more galloping track. He looked second best. (op 9-2)

3495 EUROPEAN BREEDERS' FUND MAIDEN FILLIES' STKS 5f
3:00 (3:01) (Class 5) 2-Y-O **£3,885** (£1,156; £577; £288) **Stalls** Low

Form RPR
04 1 **Totally Invincible (IRE)**[16] 2972 2-9-0 0 .... GrahamGibbons 6 80+
(E S McMahon) *qckly away: sn clr: mde all: rdn over 1f out: kpt on ins fnl f: eased nr fin* **5/4**[1]
0 2 2 **Elusive Sue (USA)**[19] 2893 2-9-0 0 .... PaulHanagan 4 76+
(R A Fahey) *chsd ldrs: hdwy 2f out: rdn to chse wnr over 1f out: kpt on ins fnl f: nt rch wnr* **5/4**[1]
3 10 **Tut (IRE)** 2-9-0 0 .... AndrewElliott 1 44+
(K R Burke) *slowlhy into stride and green in rr: hdwy wl over 1f out: sn rdn and kpt on ins fnl f: bttr for r* **6/1**[2]
5056 4 shd **Mrs Jones And Me (IRE)**[19] 2896 2-9-0 0 .... JamieMoriarty 3 37
(P T Midgley) *chsd ldng pair: rdn along over 2f out: kpt on same pce* **14/1**[3]
060 5 1 1/4 **Coralamber (IRE)**[29] 2575 2-8-9 0 .... MarkCoumbe(5) 2 32
(Garry Moss) *chsd wnr: rdn along 1/2-way: drvn and wknd wl over 1f out* **100/1**
5 6 7 **Bonasera (IRE)**[26] 2655 2-8-9 0 .... SladeO'Hara(5) 5 7
(A Berry) *dwlt: a in rr* **66/1**
0 7 3 **Moonlight Babe (USA)**[28] 2604 2-9-0 0 .... PatrickMathers 7 —
(I W McInnes) *s.i.s: a bhd* **100/1**

58.47 secs (-1.33) **Going Correction** -0.40s/f (Firm) **7** Ran SP% **113.3**
Speed ratings (Par 91): **94,90,74,74,72 61,56**
toteswingers: 1&2 £1.70, 2&3 £1.80, 1&3 not won. CSF £2.86 TOTE £2.40: £1.50, £1.30; EX 3.90.
Owner Premspace Ltd **Bred** Gaetano Drago **Trained** Lichfield, Staffs

FOCUS
The two market leaders were backed to the exclusion of the others.

NOTEBOOK
Totally Invincible(IRE), who made much of the running before fading to finish fourth in a better race at Warwick on her second start, flew the traps and was soon setting a scorching pace. She was never in any danger, despite her trainer's pre-race fears about how she would handle the quick ground as she has a rather choppy action. She is all speed and looks sure to make her mark in nursery company with a trip to Chester next on the agenda. (op 2-1)
Elusive Sue(USA), who did not run up to expectations on her debut at York, went in pursuit of the winner over a furlong out. She kept on to finish a long way clear of the others without ever threatening to trouble the winner. A less sharp track will suit her and she should have no trouble finding a race. (op 11-10 tchd 10-11)
Tut(IRE), a well-made, rangy newcomer, looked to be carrying plenty of condition. After missing a beat at the start, she stayed on nicely to take a distant third on the line. Six or even 7f will suit her much better and she can only improve. (op 11-2 tchd 8-1)
Mrs Jones And Me(IRE), sixth in selling company at York, was on her toes beforehand and, after four previous outings, she is not progressing at all. (op 11-1 tchd 10-1)
Coralamber(IRE), well beaten in three previous starts including in selling company, chased the winner but showed a marked tendency to hang left and she weakened badly in the final furlong.

3496 BIRTHDAY SPONSORSHIP @ RACESPONSORS.CO.UK H'CAP 7f
3:30 (3:30) (Class 4) (0-80,80) 3-Y-O+ **£5,180** (£1,541; £770; £384) **Stalls** Low

Form RPR
4433 1 **Bold Marc (IRE)**[7] 3265 7-9-10 **76** .... AndrewElliott 2 86
(K R Burke) *trckd ldrs on inner: swtchd rt and hdwy to ld wl over 1f out: rdn ent fnl f and styd on gamely* **11/4**[1]
-110 2 1 3/4 **Turn Me On (IRE)**[39] 2266 6-10-0 **80** .... GrahamGibbons 4 85
(T D Walford) *trckd ldrs: hdwy 2f out: rdn to chse wnr and hung lft ent fnl f: kpt on* **5/1**[2]
-666 3 2 **Jonny Lesters Hair (IRE)**[39] 2257 4-9-5 **71** .... PaulMulrennan 10 71
(T D Easterby) *cl up: effrt 2f out and ev ch: rdn and hld whn n.m.r ins fnl f: kpt on same pce* **16/1**
6511 4 1/2 **Summer Dancer (IRE)**[8] 3234 5-9-8 **74** 6ex .... PhillipMakin 5 73+
(P T Midgley) *hld up in rr: hdwy on inner 2f out: effrt and nt clr run ent fnl f: nt rcvr* **11/4**[1]
0530 5 hd **Border Owl (IRE)**[19] 2894 4-9-5 **71** .... DaleGibson 8 69
(P Salmon) *hld up in rr: hdwy 2f out: sn rdn and no imp appr fnl f* **13/2**[3]
2513 6 2 **Kabis Amigos**[12] 3110 7-9-4 **70** ....(b) TonyHamilton 1 66+
(Ollie Pears) *trckd ldrs on inner: effrt over 1f out: rdn and hmpd ent fnl f and nt rcvr* **12/1**
043- 7 1 1/4 **Nuit Sombre (IRE)**[281] 6186 9-9-5 **71** .... SilvestreDeSousa 3 60
(G A Harker) *led: rdn along over 2f out: drvn and hdd wl over 1f out: grad wknd* **9/1**
400- 8 7 **Tina's Best (IRE)**[254] 6864 4-9-6 **72** .... DavidAllan 6 42
(E J Alston) *prom: hdwy on outer to chal over 2f out: sn rdn and ev ch tl wknd appr fnl f* **14/1**
6013 9 13 **Woodsley House (IRE)**[12] 3097 7-9-2 **71** .... NeilBrown(3) 9 6
(A G Foster) *in rr whn slipped bdly home bnd: no ch after* **18/1**

1m 25.3s (-1.70) **Going Correction** -0.30s/f (Firm)
WFA 3 from 4yo+ 8lb **9** Ran SP% **118.8**
Speed ratings (Par 105): **97,95,92,92,91 89,88,80,65**
toteswingers: 1&2 £3.30, 1&3 £9.80, 2&3 £11.60 CSF £17.19 CT £189.67 TOTE £4.50: £1.20, £1.60, £4.10; EX 21.00.
Owner Market Avenue Racing Club Ltd **Bred** Eamon D Delany **Trained** Middleham Moor, N Yorks
■ Stewards' Enquiry : Graham Gibbons three-day ban: careless riding (July 15-17)

FOCUS
A 70-80 handicap and despite their being several confirmed front-runners in the line-up, the pace was not as strong as might have been expected. Straightforward form.
Woodsley House(IRE) Official explanation: jockey said gelding slipped on bend turning for home

3497 SPONSOR A RACE @ RACESPONSORS.CO.UK H'CAP 5f 212y
4:00 (4:06) (Class 4) (0-80,80) 3-Y-O+ **£5,180** (£1,541; £770; £384) **Stalls** Low

Form RPR
1014 1 **Red Cape (FR)**[5] 3354 6-9-7 **74** .... AndrewElliott 4 91
(Mrs R A Carr) *trckd ldr: hdwy to chal 2f out: rdn to ld wl over 1f out and sn clr: r.o strly* **11/4**[1]
0405 2 5 **Cape Vale (IRE)**[1] 3491 4-9-13 **80** .... AdrianTNicholls 8 81
(D Nicholls) *led: rdn over 2f out: drvn and hdd over 1f out: kpt on u.p ins fnl f: no ch w wnr* **4/1**[2]
145 3 1 **Imprimis Tagula (IRE)**[2] 3469 5-9-3 **70** ....(v) NeilChalmers 3 68
(A Bailey) *trckd ldrs: hdwy over 2f out: rdn to chse ldng pair over 1f out: sn drvn and no imp* **5/1**[3]
3341 4 1 1/4 **Maison Dieu**[11] 3148 6-8-8 **61** .... AndrewMullen 6 55
(E J Alston) *hld up towards rr: hdwy 2f out: sn rdn and kpt on ins fnl f: nvr a threat* **5/1**[3]
6030 5 2 3/4 **Rio Sands**[21] 2801 4-8-8 **61** oh1 .... TonyHamilton 2 46
(R M Whitaker) *chsd ldrs on inner: rdn along over 2f out and grad wknd* **14/1**
5000 6 2 1/4 **My Gacho (IRE)**[28] 2589 7-9-10 **77** ....(b) GregFairley 1 55
(M Johnston) *a towards rr* **15/2**
6133 7 shd **Ryedane (IRE)**[16] 2966 7-8-8 **61** oh1 ....(b) DuranFentiman 5 39
(T D Easterby) *a in rr* **9/1**
000- 8 1/2 **Avertuoso**[263] 6651 5-9-8 **75** .... TomEaves 7 51
(B Smart) *chsd ldrs on outer: effrt over 2f out: sn rdn and wknd* **14/1**

1m 10.73s (-2.87) **Going Correction** -0.30s/f (Firm) **8** Ran SP% **115.1**
Speed ratings (Par 105): **107,100,99,97,93 90,90,89**
toteswingers: 1&2 £2.80, 1&3 £3.40, 2&3 £3.90 CSF £13.86 CT £51.84 TOTE £3.20: £1.30, £2.00, £1.80; EX 15.00.
Owner Middleham Park Racing LVI **Bred** Gilles And Mrs Forien **Trained** Huby, N Yorks

FOCUS
What looked a tight-knit 61-80 handicap was turned into a procession by Red Cape who scored in a fast time and is back to something like his old turf form.

3498 ADVERTISE YOUR COMPANY WITH RACESPONSORS.CO.UK MEDIAN AUCTION MAIDEN STKS 5f 212y
4:30 (4:46) (Class 6) 3-4-Y-O **£2,388** (£705; £352) **Stalls** Low

Form RPR
0-00 1 **Neo's Mate (IRE)**[51] 1921 3-8-12 36 .... SilvestreDeSousa 8 54
(Paul Green) *hld up in tch: hdwy over 2f out: rdn to chse ldrs over 1f out: edgd lft ins fnl f and styd on wl to ld last 100yds* **20/1**
6 2 1 1/2 **Roodee King**[25] 2700 3-9-3 0 .... PaulMulrennan 3 54
(Patrick Morris) *chsd ldr: hdwy 2f out: rdn to chal over 1f out: drvn to ld ins fnl f: sn hdd and one pce* **4/1**[1]
4000 3 1 3/4 **Cindy Incidentally**[28] 2603 3-8-12 40 ....(b[1]) MickyFenton 1 43
(Miss Gay Kelleway) *led: rdn along over 2f out and sn jnd: drvn over 1f out: hdd ins fnl f and one pce* **20/1**
4-60 4 2 1/4 **Wrens Hope**[14] 3036 3-8-12 44 .... GrahamGibbons 5 36
(N Bycroft) *chsd ldng pair: effrt 2f out whn n.m.r and swtchd rt wl over 1f out: sn rdn and kpt on same pce* **5/1**[3]
5060 5 2 **Paddy Jack**[15] 3002 4-9-9 49 .... PhillipMakin 11 36
(J R Weymes) *chsd ldrs: rdn along 2f out: sn drvn and no imp appr fnl f* **9/2**[2]
0066 6 1 **Honey Berry (IRE)**[28] 2593 3-8-12 43 ....(v) PaulHanagan 4 26
(Patrick Morris) *dwlt and in rr: sme hdwy over 2f out: sn rdn and nvr a threat* **7/1**
4330 7 2 1/4 **Josphiel (IRE)**[11] 3175 4-8-11 54 ....(b) BillyCray(7) 9 20
(A Berry) *a in rr* **5/1**[3]

0606 **8** *1* **Luckette**[5] 3338 3-8-12 40 ....(v) JoeFanning 10 16
(M Brittain) *t.k.h: chsd ldrs to 1/2-way: sn rdn and wknd* **10/1**

500- **9** *14* **Mister Wilberforce**[240] 7170 3-9-3 35 .... TomEaves 2 —
(M Mullineaux) *dwlt: a outpcd and bhd* **40/1**

1m 13.21s (-0.39) **Going Correction** -0.30s/f (Firm)
WFA 3 from 4yo 6lb **9** Ran SP% **105.1**
Speed ratings (Par 101): **90,88,85,82,80 78,75,74,55**
toteswingers: 1&2 £13.10, 1&3 £33.90, 2&3 £9.00 CSF £79.58 TOTE £27.00: £4.70, £1.50, £3.70; EX 131.50.
Owner Derek A Howard **Bred** Ken Carroll And Miss Marie McCarthy **Trained** Lydiate, Merseyside
■ Neva A Mull Moment was withdrawn (6/1, uns rdr & bolted bef s). R4 applies, deduct 10p in the £.

FOCUS
A dreadful sprint maiden and a candidate for one of the worst races of the year, confirmed by the time two and a half seconds slower than the preceding 61-80 handicap. The runners were at the gate for almost quarter of an hour after the errant behaviour of the eventually withdrawn Neva A Mull Moment. The field was soon well strung out. Seemingly big improvement from the winner.
Josphiel(IRE) Official explanation: jockey said filly hung badly right throughout

3499 GREAT DEALS ON RACESPONSORS.CO.UK H'CAP — 1m 3f 214y
5:00 (5:09) (Class 6) (0-65,65) 4-Y-O+ — **£2,388** (£705; £352) **Stalls** Low

Form — RPR

0105 **1** **Bijou Dan**[16] 2969 8-9-5 **63** .... PJMcDonald 9 71
(G M Moore) *midfield: hdwy to trck ldrs over 4f out: rdn 2f out: drvn over 1f out: edgd lft ins fnl f: styd on strly to ld last 100yds* **9/2**[2]

0-10 **2** *1 ½* **Promise Maker (USA)**[16] 2971 4-8-13 **57** .... GrahamGibbons 8 63
(T D Walford) *led: pushed along and hdd 4f out: cl up: rdn to ld again 1 1/2f out: drvn ins fnl f: hdd and no ex last 100yds* **4/1**[1]

0320 **3** *3* **Andorn (GER)**[19] 2898 5-9-4 **65** .... LeeVickers(3) 7 66
(P A Kirby) *t.k.h: chsd ldrs: rdn along and sltly outpcd 3f out: swtchd rt and drvn over 1f out: styd on ins fnl f* **14/1**

1003 **4** *4* **Mccormack (IRE)**[12] 3121 7-8-3 **47** .... AndrewMullen 4 41
(Miss T Jackson) *trckd ldrs: effrt over 3f out: rdn along to chse ldng pair 2f out: sn drvn and kpt on same pce* **14/1**

6561 **5** *hd* **Dimashq**[13] 3068 7-8-5 **49** .... JoeFanning 6 43
(P T Midgley) *trckd ldrs: hdwy on inner to ld 4f out: rdn along over 2f out: drvn and hdd 1 1/2f out: grad wknd* **7/1**[3]

53-6 **6** *½* **Prince Samos (IRE)**[22] 2791 7-9-2 **65** .... SophieDoyle(5) 5 58
(C A Mulhall) *hld up towards rr: hdwy over 3f out: rdn and kpt on fnl 2f: nt rch ldrs* **33/1**

0000 **7** *3 ¼* **Fan Club**[1] 3486 5-8-2 **46** oh1 .... SilvestreDeSousa 1 34
(Mrs R A Carr) *hld up in rr: effrt and sme hdwy 3f out: sn rdn and n.d* **22/1**

0520 **8** *3 ½* **Fistral**[17] 2944 5-8-7 **51** .... TomEaves 11 33
(P D Niven) *hld up: hdwy and in tch 1/2-way: rdn along over 3f out: slipped on home bnd and grad wknd* **7/1**[3]

-450 **9** *2* **Harcas (IRE)**[16] 2614 7-8-13 **57** .... PaulMulrennan 12 36
(M Todhunter) *prom: rdn along 5f out: sn wknd* **9/1**

5004 **10** *4 ½* **High Profit (IRE)**[9] 3223 5-8-9 **53** .... DarrenMoffatt 2 25
(James Moffatt) *a in rr* **12/1**

/60- **11** *1 ½* **Chip N Pin**[407] 2286 5-8-4 **48** .... DuranFentiman 13 18
(T D Easterby) *chsd ldrs: rdn along 5f out: sn wknd* **17/2**

/5-0 **12** *18* **Princess Of Aeneas (IRE)**[12] 3098 6-8-3 **47** oh1 ow1(p) AndrewElliott 15 —
(A G Foster) *dwlt: a towards rr* **80/1**

40/6 **13** *6* **Green Day Packer (IRE)**[98] 169 5-8-2 **46** oh1 ....(t) PaulHanagan 10 —
(P C Haslam) *cl up: rdn along 4f out and sn wknd* **7/1**[3]

2m 34.97s (-3.93) **Going Correction** -0.30s/f (Firm) **13** Ran SP% **125.8**
Speed ratings (Par 101): **101,100,98,95,95 94,92,90,89,86 85,73,69**
toteswingers: 1&2 £5.30, 1&3 £15.00, 2&3 £14.80 CSF £23.84 CT £245.48 TOTE £4.50: £1.90, £2.10, £4.60; EX 29.40 TRIFECTA Not won.. Place 6: £15.81 Place 5: £11.97.
Owner Bert Markey **Bred** James Thom And Sons **Trained** Middleham Moor, N Yorks

FOCUS
A modest 46-65 handicap and the winner probably only had to run to his May form here. The early gallop was just steady but the pace really picked up starting the final turn.
Fistral Official explanation: jockey said gelding slipped on bend
Green Day Packer(IRE) Official explanation: jockey said he had no explanation for the poor form shown
T/Plt: £11.10 to a £1 stake. Pool: £49,264.30. 3,216.64 winning tickets. T/Qpdt: £11.30 to a £1 stake. Pool: £2,585.70. 168.50 winning tickets. JR

3203 CHEPSTOW (L-H)
Wednesday, July 1

OFFICIAL GOING: Good to firm (8.7)
Wind: Nil Weather: Warm and humid

3500 E.B.F./JOHN SMITH'S MAIDEN STKS — 6f 16y
6:40 (6:41) (Class 5) 2-Y-O — **£3,561** (£1,059; £529; £264) **Stalls** High

Form — RPR

5 **1** **Slice (IRE)**[64] 1577 2-9-3 0 .... NCallan 10 75
(Eve Johnson Houghton) *a.p: rdn 2f out: swtchd lft over 1f out: led ent fnl f: r.o* **4/1**[1]

2 *½* **Red Badge (IRE)** 2-9-3 0 .... EddieAhern 13 74+
(R Hannon) *mid-div: pushed along over 3f out: rdn and hdwy over 1f out: swtchd lft and r.o to take 2nd nr fin* **4/1**[1]

0 **3** *nk* **Miskin Nights**[23] 2771 2-8-9 0 .... DavidProbert(3) 14 68
(B Palling) *w ldr: ev ch wl over 1f out: sn rdn: kpt on towards fin* **100/1**

4 *nse* **Marcus Cicero (IRE)** 2-9-3 0 .... LukeMorris 2 72
(P Winkworth) *a.p: ev ch over 1f out: sn rdn: kpt on ins fnl f* **25/1**

42 **5** *1 ¾* **Bazsharani**[4] 3370 2-8-12 0 .... CatherineGannon 3 62
(P D Evans) *led: rdn 2f out: hdd ent fnl f: no ex towards fin* **9/2**[2]

0 **6** *1* **Glass Of Red (IRE)**[16] 2979 2-8-9 0 .... JackMitchell(3) 8 59
(R M Beckett) *s.i.s: in rr: swtchd rt to stands' rail after 1f: pushed along over 2f out: hdwy fr over 1f out: nrst fin* **16/1**

7 *1 ½* **Flipping** 2-9-3 0 .... LPKeniry 6 60
(W S Kittow) *s.i.s: chsd ldrs after 1f: rdn over 1f out: edgd rt and wknd ins fnl f* **18/1**

8 *½* **Carnaby Street (IRE)** 2-9-3 0 .... PatDobbs 9 58+
(R Hannon) *mid-div: rdn over 2f out: wknd over 1f out* **11/1**

9 *hd* **Avon Grounds** 2-9-3 0 .... PaulFitzsimons 11 58
(J M Bradley) *bhd: rdn over 3f out: sme prog over 1f out: n.d* **100/1**

10 *nk* **Iron Velvet (USA)** 2-9-3 0 .... RoystonFfrench 7 57+
(M Johnston) *sn pushed along and bhd* **11/2**[3]

30 **11** *17* **Trelawny Wells**[32] 2477 2-8-12 0 .... MCGeran(5) 5 6
(M R Channon) *rdn over 3f out: a in rr* **50/1**

12 *16* **The Confessor** 2-9-3 0 .... FergusSweeney 12 —
(H Candy) *outpcd: t.o fnl 2f* **13/2**

13 *9* **Little Buddy** 2-9-3 0 .... JamesDoyle 4 —
(R J Price) *s.s and wnt lft: a in rr: t.o fnl 2f* **33/1**

1m 11.7s (-0.30) **Going Correction** -0.25s/f (Firm) **13** Ran SP% **117.1**
Speed ratings (Par 94): **98,97,96,96,94 93,91,90,90,89 67,45,33**
Tote Swingers: 1&2 £4.60, 2&3 not won, 1&3 not won. CSF £18.68 TOTE £5.20: £1.70, £2.60, £18.40; EX 27.80.
Owner Eden Racing (III) **Bred** John Hutchinson **Trained** Blewbury, Oxon

FOCUS
A sultry evening with the temperature in the high 20s. The going stick recorded 8.7 and the ground rode good to firm as advertised for this modest juvenile maiden in which those drawn high dominated.

NOTEBOOK
Slice(IRE), who ran in a good maiden last time, clearly improved for his first run and showed a professional and willing attitude. He would have found this ground quick enough. Connections are thinking in terms of the valuable Tattersalls Sales race at the Curragh in August. (tchd 9-2)
Red Badge(IRE) looked as though he would come on for his introduction and was the main eye-catcher. Slowly into his stride, once the penny dropped he made significant late headway and only just failed. He will be interesting over this trip next time. (op 5-1 tchd 11-2)
Miskin Nights, with the benefit of one run behind her, broke sharply from a plum draw and was in the firing line all the way. She improved markedly and appeared to appreciate this faster ground. Without getting too carried away, she may be interesting in nursery company in due course. (tchd 80-1)
Marcus Cicero(IRE), a bit playful in the preliminaries, was unfancied in the market and wasn't well drawn. He was bang there with a furlong to run and stayed on well, despite running a little green. He will come on a bundle for this.
Bazsharani had shown ability in two starts over the minimum at Chester and franked the good impression she had previously shown. She is worth trying again over this trip on a less demanding track. (op 5-1)
Avon Grounds, who looked as though the run would bring him on, ran on nicely without his rider getting serious.

3501 JOHN SMITH'S PREMIER CLUB CLAIMING STKS — 1m 14y
7:10 (7:12) (Class 6) 3-Y-O+ — **£2,072** (£616; £308; £153) **Stalls** High

Form — RPR

6600 **1** **Red Current**[18] 2912 5-8-7 45 .... DavidProbert(3) 4 54
(R A Harris) *a.p: led jst over 2f out: rdn over 1f out: drvn out* **6/1**[3]

1100 **2** *¾* **Dichoh**[9] 3211 6-9-5 77 ....(v) EddieAhern 1 61
(M Madgwick) *led: hdd jst over 2f out: sn rdn: kpt on towards fin* **7/2**[2]

0002 **3** *hd* **Captain Jacksparra (IRE)**[16] 2965 5-9-5 75 .... AmyRyan(5) 2 66
(K A Ryan) *t.k.h: a.p: rdn wl over 1f out: kpt on ins fnl f* **1/1**[1]

/050 **4** *shd* **Picture Frame**[11] 3174 5-9-0 52 .... KevinGhunowa(3) 9 59
(J T Stimpson) *hld up and bhd: hdwy on outside over 3f out: rdn 2f out: hrd rdn and no ex towards fin* **25/1**

000- **5** *3 ¼* **Cadeaux Fax**[224] 7379 4-9-5 21 .... TGMcLaughlin 8 53
(B R Millman) *w ldr: rdn 3f out: wknd wl over 1f out* **100/1**

00-0 **6** *6* **Marino Prince (FR)**[13] 3074 4-9-0 47 ....(p) SeanPalmer(7) 10 41
(T Wall) *hld up in tch: rdn 3f out: wknd over 2f out* **40/1**

6026 **7** *1* **Mountain Pass (USA)**[21] 2807 7-9-0 53 ....(p) NCallan 12 32
(B J Llewellyn) *hld up and bhd: swtchd lft and hdwy over 3f out: rdn wl over 1f out: sn wknd* **13/2**

006- **8** *9* **Evianne**[301] 5604 5-8-9 36 .... LukeMorris 5 6
(P W Hiatt) *s.i.s: bhd: rdn over 4f out: no ch fnl 3f* **25/1**

00 **9** *6* **Steamer (IRE)**[36] 2355 3-8-5 0 .... SaleemGolam 6 —
(P Winkworth) *dwlt: in rr: rdn 5f out: no ch fnl 4f* **20/1**

10 *62* **Gunner Be Lucky (IRE)**[17] 6-9-0 0 ....(p) FrankieMcDonald 7 —
(B Palling) *in rr: rdn over 5f out: sn t.o* **66/1**

1m 34.39s (-1.81) **Going Correction** -0.25s/f (Firm)
WFA 3 from 4yo+ 9lb **10** Ran SP% **117.2**
Speed ratings (Par 101): **99,98,98,97,94 88,87,78,72,10**
Tote Swingers: 1&2 £2.10, 2&3 £2.80, 1&3 £1.80. CSF £25.63 TOTE £7.90: £2.10, £1.70, £1.10; EX 59.90.
Owner Ridge House Stables Ltd **Bred** Wretham Stud **Trained** Earlswood, Monmouths

FOCUS
An uncompetitive claimer run at a fair pace. The winner is the best guide to this form, which is less than solid.

3502 JOHN SMITH'S (S) STKS — 7f 16y
7:40 (7:43) (Class 6) 3-Y-O — **£1,942** (£578; £288; £144) **Stalls** High

Form — RPR

2022 **1** **Piazza San Pietro**[6] 3305 3-9-0 72 .... NCallan 6 60
(A B Haynes) *hld up in tch: led over 1f out: sn rdn: r.o* **2/1**[1]

0540 **2** *nk* **Like For Like (IRE)**[7] 3257 3-8-9 54 .... SamHitchcott 8 54
(R J Hodges) *w ldrs on stands' rail: led 3f out: rdn and hdd over 1f out: r.o ins fnl f* **12/1**

-010 **3** *½* **Capo Regime**[9] 3225 3-9-5 70 .... RobertWinston 1 63
(D Nicholls) *in rr: hung rt thrght: hdwy 3f out: rdn 2f out: r.o ins fnl f* **12/1**

-000 **4** *1 ¼* **Spring Secret**[13] 3054 3-9-0 50 .... LukeMorris 2 54
(B Palling) *led: rdn and hdd 3f out: kpt on same pce ins fnl f* **25/1**

-000 **5** *6* **Premier Demon (IRE)**[7] 3257 3-8-9 43 ....(t) PaulDoe 10 33
(P D Evans) *hld up: pushed along 3f out: sn lost pl: n.d after* **66/1**

4004 **6** *hd* **Autumn Morning (IRE)**[7] 3257 3-8-9 50 ....(v[1]) CatherineGannon 3 33
(P D Evans) *hld up: hdwy 4f out: rdn 3f out: sn wknd* **6/1**[3]

4600 **7** *7* **Midnight Bay**[7] 3257 3-9-0 63 .... TonyCulhane 7 19
(M R Channon) *w ldrs tl rdn 2f out: sn wknd* **12/1**

1460 **8** *3 ½* **Trip Switch**[21] 2826 3-9-5 67 .... EddieAhern 9 14
(W R Muir) *in rr: reminders over 5f out: rdn over 3f out: eased whn no ch over 1f out* **9/2**[2]

6-00 **9** *10* **Jhinga Palak (IRE)**[58] 1746 3-8-9 55 ....(t) FrankieMcDonald 4 —
(Mrs K Waldron) *hld up in tch: wknd over 3f out: sn bhd* **50/1**

1m 22.29s (-0.91) **Going Correction** -0.25s/f (Firm) **9** Ran SP% **96.2**
Speed ratings (Par 98): **95,94,94,92,85 85,77,73,62**
Tote Swingers: 1&2 £5.00, 2&3 £1.20, 1&3 £7.20. CSF £18.00 TOTE £2.60: £1.10, £3.00, £2.60; EX 14.70.There was no bid for the winner. Capo Regime was claimed by P Howling for £6000.
Owner K Corke **Bred** T E Pocock **Trained** Limpley Stoke, Bath
■ Gwerthybid was withdrawn (4/1, unruly at start). R4 applies, deduct 20p in the £.

FOCUS
A poor contest for very poor prize-money. The runner-up appears the best guide.
Trip Switch Official explanation: jockey said gelding was unsuited by the track

3503 JOHN SMITH'S EXTRA SMOOTH H'CAP — 1m 4f 23y
8:10 (8:13) (Class 6) (0-60,60) 4-Y-O+ — **£2,266** (£674; £337; £168) **Stalls** Low

Form — RPR

3-00 **1** **Starstruck Peter (IRE)**[97] 528 5-8-10 **52** ....(b) PaulDoe 15 59
(Jim Best) *mde all: rdn clr over 1f out: drvn out* **8/1**

0025 **2** 2¾ **Lady Jinks**[23] 2762 4-8-9 **51** .... EddieAhern 13 54
(R J Hodges) *hdwy after 2f: chsd wnr jst over 3f out: rdn jst over 2f out: styd on same pce* **15/2**

-006 **3** *nk* **Little Sark (IRE)**[12] 3121 4-8-11 **53** .... CatherineGannon 5 55
(P D Evans) *chsd wnr 2f: a.p: rdn over 2f out: styd on one pce fnl f* **20/1**

6404 **4** *1* **Corrib (IRE)**[18] 2912 6-8-4 **49** .... DavidProbert(3) 10 50+
(B Palling) *hld up towards rr: rdn and hdwy on outside over 2f out: edgd lft over 1f out: one pce ins fnl f* **7/1**[3]

0064 **5** *¾* **Le Corvee (IRE)**[13] 3074 7-8-10 **52** .... TolleyDean 6 51+
(A W Carroll) *t.k.h in mid-div: rdn over 2f out: styd on ins fnl f: nvr nr to chal* **7/1**[3]

0 **6** *nse* **Mito**[19] 2877 8-8-6 **48** .... NickyMackay 3 47
(B R Millman) *hld up in mid-div: hdwy 3f out: rdn 2f out: no further prog* **7/1**[3]

00-4 **7** *½* **Personify**[57] 1770 7-8-5 **50** .... KevinGhunowa(3) 4 48
(J L Flint) *plld hrd: prom: rdn over 1f out: wknd wl ins fnl f* **8/1**

0-66 **8** 1½ **Bolton Hall (IRE)**[17] 627 7-8-8 **50** ....(tp) FergusSweeney 16 46
(W K Goldsworthy) *prom: chsd wnr after 2f tl jst over 3f out: rdn and wknd over 2f out* **13/2**[2]

5022 **9** *¾* **Jackie Kiely**[16] 2971 8-8-9 **54** ....(t) JackMitchell(3) 14 49
(R Brotherton) *hld up in tch: lost pl over 5f out: rdn over 2f out: sn wknd* **11/2**[1]

2600 **10** *6* **King Of The Beers (USA)**[18] 2912 5-8-6 **48** ....(p) LukeMorris 7 33
(R A Harris) *hld up towards rr: pushed along over 4f out: sme hdwy over 3f out: wknd over 2f out* **14/1**

006/ **11** *7* **Cat Six (USA)**[20] 6766 5-7-12 **47** .... SeanPalmer(7) 2 21
(T Wall) *a in rr* **66/1**

0/0- **12** 3¾ **Flexible Friend (IRE)**[14] 4366 5-9-1 **57** .... LPKeniry 12 25
(B J Llewellyn) *a in rr* **33/1**

4-00 **13** *44* **Compton Charlie**[27] 2634 5-8-7 **49** .... JamesDoyle 8 —
(J G Portman) *a towards rr: pushed along 4f out: eased whn no ch over 1f out* **25/1**

2m 35.75s (-3.25) **Going Correction** -0.25s/f (Firm) **13** Ran SP% **119.9**
Speed ratings (Par 101): **100,98,97,97,96 96,96,95,94,90 86,83,54**
Tote Swingers: 1&2 not won, 2&3 not won, 1&3 not won. CSF £64.60 CT £1173.18 TOTE £7.80: £3.50, £2.00, £6.20; EX 62.80.
Owner W P K Racing **Bred** Barouche Stud Ireland Ltd **Trained** Lewes, E Sussex
■ Stewards' Enquiry : Sean Palmer one-day ban: used whip when out of contention (Jul 15)

FOCUS
An uncompetitive handicap run at a slow pace. Modest form.
King Of The Beers(USA) Official explanation: jockey said gelding was unsuited by the good to firm ground
Compton Charlie Official explanation: jockey said gelding was unsuited by the track and the good to firm ground

3504 JOHN SMITH'S "NO NONSENSE" RACING H'CAP 1m 14y
8:40 (8:41) (Class 5) (0-75,75) 3-Y-O+ **£3,561** (£1,059; £529; £264) **Stalls** High

Form RPR

4105 **1** **Beautiful Breeze (IRE)**[11] 3144 3-9-7 **75** .... RoystonFfrench 2 81
(M Johnston) *chsd ldrs: n.m.r after 1f: rdn and wnt 2nd 3f out: led 1f out: drvn out* **3/1**[2]

1054 **2** *½* **Bere Davis (FR)**[15] 2998 4-9-9 **73** .... RichardEvans(5) 5 80
(P D Evans) *led: rdn 3f out: hdd 1f out: no ex cl home* **13/8**[1]

/0-0 **3** 4½ **Petomic (IRE)**[42] 2185 4-8-10 **58** .... JackMitchell(3) 1 55
(R M Beckett) *plld hrd: chsd ldr to 3f out: rdn over 2f out: sn swtchd rt: wknd over 1f out* **13/2**

5062 **4** *½* **Tuxedo**[13] 3075 4-9-9 **68** .... LukeMorris 8 64
(P W Hiatt) *hld up and bhd: hdwy 3f out: rdn over 2f out: wknd fnl f* **5/1**[3]

-004 **5** *8* **Lordship (IRE)**[13] 3077 5-8-2 **54** .... JakePayne(7) 3 31
(A W Carroll) *t.k.h: hdwy over 3f out: rdn and wknd over 2f out* **14/1**

00-5 **6** *15* **Silver Blue (IRE)**[14] 2379 6-8-11 **56** ....(v) FergusSweeney 6 —
(W K Goldsworthy) *hld up and bhd: rdn 3f out: sn struggling: eased whn no ch over 1f out* **15/2**

1m 33.54s (-2.66) **Going Correction** -0.25s/f (Firm)
WFA 3 from 4yo+ 9lb **6** Ran SP% **111.5**
Speed ratings (Par 103): **103,102,98,97,89 74**
toteswingers: 1&2 £1.10, 1&3 £6.90, 2&3 £13.90 CSF £8.19 CT £26.20 TOTE £3.90: £2.10, £1.50; EX 9.00.
Owner Crone Stud Farms Ltd **Bred** Patrick M Ryan **Trained** Middleham Moor, N Yorks

FOCUS
A competitive, if modest, small-field handicap run at a fair clip. Sound form.
Bere Davis(FR) Official explanation: jockey said gelding hung left-handed
Silver Blue(IRE) Official explanation: jockey said gelding lost its action

3505 JOHN SMITH'S EXTRA COLD H'CAP 6f 16y
9:10 (9:11) (Class 6) (0-65,64) 3-Y-O+ **£2,266** (£674; £337; £168) **Stalls** High

Form RPR

306- **1** **Onebidkintymill (IRE)**[312] 5261 4-9-8 **59** .... J-PGuillambert 17 71+
(B P J Baugh) *hld up in rr: hdwy 3f out: rdn to ld over 1f out: r.o* **40/1**

1156 **2** *nk* **Mr Skipiton (IRE)**[18] 2920 4-9-5 **56** .... TGMcLaughlin 12 67
(B J McMath) *hld up in rr: rdn and hdwy on stands' rail wl over 1f out: r.o ins fnl f* **11/1**

6000 **3** 1¼ **Stamford Blue**[7] 3283 8-9-10 **61** ....(b) LukeMorris 1 68
(R A Harris) *s.i.s: in rr: pushed along over 3f out: rdn over 2f out: hdwy over 1f out: r.o ins fnl f* **16/1**

2250 **4** *hd* **Plumage**[19] 2879 4-9-9 **60** .... LPKeniry 8 66
(M Salaman) *a.p: ev ch over 1f out: sn rdn: no ex towards fin* **5/1**[2]

3403 **5** *1* **Desert Pride**[19] 2879 4-9-9 **60** ....(v) FergusSweeney 2 63
(W S Kittow) *s.i.s: sn swtchd rt: hld up: hdwy over 1f out: rdn and kpt on towards fin* **10/1**

-026 **6** *½* **Miss Firefly**[23] 2758 4-9-1 **52** .... SamHitchcott 11 54
(R J Hodges) *hld up in mid-div: pushed along over 3f out: hdwy over 1f out: rdn and one pce ins fnl f* **18/1**

01 **7** *nk* **Bohobe (IRE)**[22] 2799 4-9-6 **57** .... NCallan 7 58
(Rae Guest) *mid-div: rdn wl over 1f out: no real prog* **8/1**[3]

0042 **8** *½* **Just Jimmy (IRE)**[9] 3208 4-8-13 **50** .... PaulDoe 16 49
(P D Evans) *hld up and bhd: pushed along over 3f out: rdn over 2f out: nvr trbld ldrs* **3/1**[1]

3553 **9** *2* **Tadlil**[7] 3261 7-8-12 **52** ....(v) DavidProbert(3) 3 45
(J M Bradley) *led: hdd over 1f out: sn rdn: wknd fnl f* **12/1**

40-0 **10** *½* **The Name Is Frank**[9] 3204 4-9-7 **58** .... NickyMackay 13 49
(Mark Gillard) *chsd ldrs: rdn 3f out: wknd over 2f out* **66/1**

-006 **11** *2* **Charlie Delta**[13] 3057 6-9-11 **62** ....(b) CatherineGannon 5 47
(R A Harris) *w ldr tl wknd 2f out* **22/1**

5062 **12** 2¼ **It's A Mans World**[6] 3299 3-8-10 **58** ....(v) JackDean(5) 9 35
(K M Prendergast) *mid-div: rdn 2f out: wknd over 1f out* **10/1**

4040 **13** 2¾ **Hart Of Gold**[6] 3304 5-9-12 **63** ....(p) RobertWinston 6 32
(R A Harris) *mid-div on outside: wknd over 2f out* **16/1**

0162 **14** 2½ **Gioacchino (IRE)**[14] 3031 4-8-13 **53** .... KevinGhunowa(3) 10 14
(R A Harris) *chsd ldrs: rdn over 3f out: wknd wl over 1f out* **14/1**

2536 **15** *12* **Divine Force**[113] 797 3-9-5 **62** .... SimonWhitworth 15 —
(M Wigham) *s.i.s: sn lost tch* **25/1**

1m 10.55s (-1.45) **Going Correction** -0.25s/f (Firm)
WFA 3 from 4yo+ 6lb **15** Ran SP% **122.8**
Speed ratings (Par 101): **105,104,102,102,101 100,100,99,96,96 93,90,86,83,67**
toteswingers: 1&2 £36.90, 1&3 not won, 2&3 £17.50 CSF £430.84 CT £7350.86 TOTE £45.40: £14.30, £4.40, £4.20; EX 485.00 Place 6: £391.87 Place 5: £180.99.
Owner Brian Hatton **Bred** John And Eva Peet **Trained** Audley, Staffs

FOCUS
An ordinary, yet competitive handicap run at a solid pace. They finished in a heap but the form seems sound enough, and the winner could do better.
The Name Is Frank Official explanation: jockey said gelding was unsuited by the good to firm ground
Divine Force Official explanation: jockey said gelding stumbled
T/Plt: £176.90 to a £1 stake. Pool: £76,100.26. 313.90 winning tickets. T/Qpdt: £77.30 to a £1 stake. Pool: £5,374.20. 51.40 winning tickets. KH

3297 KEMPTON (A.W) (R-H)
Wednesday, July 1

OFFICIAL GOING: Standard
Wind: Moderate, across towards stands Weather: Sunny, hot

3506 DAY TIME, NIGHT TIME, GREAT TIME H'CAP 5f (P)
6:20 (6:22) (Class 5) (0-75,75) 3-Y-O **£2,590** (£770; £385; £192) **Stalls** High

Form RPR

-013 **1** **Spring Green**[27] 2632 3-9-7 **75** .... SteveDrowne 2 81
(H Morrison) *mde virtually all: strly pressed fr over 1f out: edgd lft: hld on wl* **4/1**[2]

1-4 **2** *nk* **Night Affair**[27] 2632 3-9-6 **74** .... MartinDwyer 1 79
(D W P Arbuthnot) *t.k.h early and hanging lft bnd after 1f: pressed wnr: sustained chal fr over 1f out: edgd lft and nt qckn last 100yds* **5/1**[3]

343- **3** 2¾ **Clerical (USA)**[209] 7542 3-8-6 **60** ow1 .... RichardMullen 3 55
(R M H Cowell) *racd wd in rr: effrt over 1f out: cajoled into 3rd jst ins fnl f: no imp on ldng pair* **11/1**

2414 **4** 1¼ **Simple Rhythm**[13] 3063 3-8-11 **65** .... TPQueally 8 56
(J G Given) *chsd ldng pair: rdn and no imp over 1f out: lost 3rd jst ins fnl f: fdd* **5/1**[3]

0020 **5** *¾* **Pocket's Pick (IRE)**[19] 2882 3-9-7 **75** .... RyanMoore 9 63+
(G L Moore) *s.s: last tl wnt 4th on inner briefly wl over 1f out: no prog after* **5/1**[3]

1315 **6** *1* **Speak The Truth (IRE)**[48] 2005 3-9-0 **68** ....(p) PatCosgrave 5 52
(J R Boyle) *chsd ldng trio: rdn 2f out: lost pl wl over 1f out: grad fdd* **8/1**

033- **7** 2¾ **Chosen Son (IRE)**[229] 7308 3-9-2 **70** .... TedDurcan 6 44
(P J O'Gorman) *dwlt: a in rr: dropped to last and rdn over 1f out: wknd fnl f* **7/2**[1]

60.92 secs (0.42) **Going Correction** +0.15s/f (Slow) **7** Ran SP% **111.7**
Speed ratings (Par 100): **102,101,97,95,93 92,87**
toteswingers: 1&2 £2.00, 1&3 £10.90, 2&3 £6.70 CSF £22.90 CT £196.59 TOTE £5.10: £2.20, £2.70; EX 18.10.
Owner Nicholas Jones **Bred** Coln Valley Stud **Trained** East Ilsley, Berks

FOCUS
Unusually, the first two came from the two widest stalls to dispute it throughout at a good pace - or as good a pace as is possible around a bend - with the winner always a head or a neck in front. Nothing else got into it.
Chosen Son(IRE) Official explanation: trainer had no explanation for the poor form shown

3507 EUROPEAN BREEDERS' FUND MAIDEN FILLIES' STKS 7f (P)
6:50 (6:51) (Class 5) 2-Y-O **£3,885** (£1,156; £577; £288) **Stalls** High

Form RPR

1 **Blue Angel (IRE)** 2-9-0 0 .... JimmyFortune 5 75+
(R Hannon) *dwlt: last to 3f out: gd prog and rdn over 2f out: clsd to ld last 100yds: styd on wl* **7/1**

02 **2** 1½ **Brunette (IRE)**[14] 3027 2-9-0 0 .... RichardHughes 7 71
(R Hannon) *w ldr to 1/2-way: sn pushed along: clsd again u.p over 1f out: led briefly ins fnl f: no ex last 100yds* **5/2**[2]

52 **3** *1* **Fasilight**[40] 2238 2-9-0 0 .... RyanMoore 2 69
(M Botti) *chsd ldng pair: rdn and hung lft fr over 2f out: drvn to cl on ldrs 1f out: nt qckn* **15/8**[1]

5 **4** *½* **Larkrise Star**[23] 2771 2-9-0 0 .... ChrisCatlin 3 67
(D K Ivory) *settled in last pair: effrt whn hmpd over 2f out and forced lft after: rallied over 1f out: kpt on same pce fnl f* **16/1**

3 **5** 1½ **Lady Valiant**[14] 3027 2-9-0 0 .... SebSanders 10 64
(R M Beckett) *disp ld tl advantage 1/2-way: drvn over 2f out: hdd & wknd ins fnl f* **4/1**[3]

00 **6** *3* **Smicker Smacker**[23] 2765 2-8-9 0 .... MatthewDavies(5) 9 56
(George Baker) *dwlt: sn chsd ldrs: pushed along 1/2-way: fdd 2f out* **66/1**

0 **7** 1½ **Botley Bell**[18] 2914 2-9-0 0 .... DarryllHolland 4 52
(M R Channon) *nvr beyond midfield: rdn and grad wknd fr 2f out* **40/1**

0 **8** 3¾ **It's A Deal (IRE)**[42] 2175 2-9-0 0 .... StephenCarson 1 43
(P Winkworth) *stdd s: in tch on outer: losing pl whn hmpd over 2f out: sn no ch* **33/1**

9 *19* **Aldorable** 2-9-0 0 .... TedDurcan 6 —
(R A Teal) *dwlt: rr green in rr: wknd 3f out: t.o* **16/1**

1m 28.75s (2.75) **Going Correction** +0.15s/f (Slow) **9** Ran SP% **114.5**
Speed ratings (Par 91): **90,88,87,86,84 81,79,75,53**
toteswingers: 1&2 £2.30, 1&3 £3.40, 2&3 £1.90. CSF £24.45 TOTE £8.80: £2.10, £1.30, £1.40; EX 25.60.
Owner Oakley Street Racing **Bred** Whisperview Trading Ltd **Trained** East Everleigh, Wilts
■ Stewards' Enquiry : Ryan Moore two-day ban: careless riding (Jul 15-16)

FOCUS
A decent gallop produced a winner from the rear but, with the runner-up having raced prominently, the result looks a fair one.

NOTEBOOK
Blue Angel(IRE), a 32,000gns Oratorio half-sister to three winners in France, is bred to come into her own from 1m to 1m2f in the long run. Patiently ridden after missing the break, the good gallop eventually enabled her to recover the ground and win going away, with connections expecting her to come on for this first effort. (op 11-1 tchd 5-1)

Brunette(IRE), a stablemate of the winner, did well considering she chased the lively pace, though she is reported to be lazy and Richard Hughes had to give her some strong reminders turning for home. In the circumstances she ran a solid race, having momentarily looked as if she would win. She responded well to pressure and, though hard work, she is capable of winning a similar event. (op 13-8 tchd 3-1)

Fasilight had shown promise in two races on turf and this was a creditable AW debut. She is now qualified for nurseries, but in the meantime she is good enough to have another crack in maiden company on either surface. Official explanation: jockey said filly hung left (op 5-2)

Larkrise Star had shown ability on her debut, which was over 6f on turf, and this confirmed that she can win races. She looks one for the longer term and already stays 7f well. (op 11-1 tchd 10-1)

Lady Valiant, held up after missing the break on her debut, adopted contrasting tactics this time and it is hard to say which suits her the better, though on this occasion she ended up running herself into the ground. However, she has shown enough to give connections something to look forward to when they have sorted that out and she is able to run in nurseries. (op 5-1 tchd 3-1)

Smicker Smacker is not good enough to win a typical maiden but is now qualified for nurseries. (tchd 80-1)

3508 DIGIBET MAIDEN FILLIES' STKS — 1m 3f (P)

7:20 (7:24) (Class 5) 3-Y-0+ — **£2,590** (£770; £385; £192) **Stalls** High

Form				RPR
	1		**Cordoba** 3-8-12 0 ... RyanMoore 8 (Sir Michael Stoute) *s.i.s: settled in rr: 9th 4f out: shkn up and gd prog over 2f out: drvn ahd jst over 1f out: kpt on wl* **5/2[2]**	76+
5-	2	¾	**Blue Nymph**[258] 6759 3-8-12 0 ... JimCrowley 9 (R M Beckett) *s.i.s and pushed along early in rr: rchd 8th 4f out but pushed along again: gd prog on inner over 2f out: chal wl over 1f out: nt qckn* **5/4[1]**	74+
0	3	¾	**Mayolynn (USA)**[34] 2416 3-8-12 0 ... TPQueally 13 (H R A Cecil) *cl up: rdn to ld wl over 2f out: sn clr w 2 rivals: hdd jst over 1f out: kpt on same pce after* **18/1**	73
00-	4	8	**Tuppenny Piece**[208] 7561 3-8-12 0 ... AdamKirby 7 (W R Swinburn) *pressed ldrs: rdn 4f out: wl outpcd over 2f out: plugged on to claim modest 4th fnl f* **66/1**	59
0-6	5	hd	**Crocus Rose**[20] 2847 3-8-12 0 ... ChrisCatlin 2 (H J L Dunlop) *racd wd: wl in tch: outpcd over 2f out: disp modest 4th over 1f out* **20/1**	59
44	6	3	**Best Tune**[24] 2738 3-8-12 0 ... ShaneKelly 11 (J Noseda) *led: hung bdly lft bnd 3f out: sn hdd: continued to hang lft and fdd tamely* **11/1**	54
4	7	hd	**Maid Of Stone (IRE)**[27] 2633 3-8-12 0 ... RobertHavlin 14 (D R C Elsworth) *hld up in midfield: gng wl 4f out: drvn and cl enough over 2f out: sn lft bhd: hung lft whn disputing 4th over 1f out* **12/1**	54+
02-0	8	shd	**Bantu**[19] 2877 4-9-10 75 ... JimmyFortune 3 (J H M Gosden) *hld up in last pair: pushed along over 4f out: effrt on wd outside 3f out: sn wl outpcd: no ch after* **8/1[3]**	53
0-3	9	¾	**Samba Mirander**[14] 3025 3-8-12 0 ... FrancisNorton 10 (C Drew) *reluctant to go to post: mostly pressed ldr: rdn over 3f out: wl outpcd over 2f out: bmpd over 1f out* **33/1**	52
0-0	10	10	**Hallingdal Blue (UAE)**[42] 2181 3-8-12 0 ... IanMongan 5 (H R A Cecil) *racd wd: prom: rdn over 3f out: wknd over 2f out* **50/1**	35
0-0	11	39	**Kaijai (IRE)**[16] 2981 3-8-12 0 ... (t) JerryO'Dwyer 1 (Mrs L C Jewell) *sn last and pushed along: bhd fr 5f out: t.o* **100/1**	—
00	12	7	**Our Last Call (IRE)**[6] 3297 3-8-12 0 ... SebSanders 12 (Sir Mark Prescott) *a in rr: wknd over 4f out: sn t.o* **33/1**	—

2m 23.41s (1.51) **Going Correction** +0.15s/f (Slow)
WFA 3 from 4yo+ 12lb — **12** Ran SP% **120.5**
Speed ratings (Par 100): **100,99,98,93,92 90,90,90,90,82 54,49**
toteswingers: 1&2 £1.30, 1&3 £11.90, 2&3 £10.00 CSF £5.74 TOTE £3.10: £1.40, £1.20, £4.40; EX 6.90.
Owner K Abdulla **Bred** Juddmonte Farms Ltd **Trained** Newmarket, Suffolk
■ Stewards' Enquiry : Ryan Moore two-day ban: careless riding ban (July 15 and 16)

FOCUS
An interesting bunch of lightly raced late developers, which makes it hard to get a solid grip on the form. On the whole it may not be a race to get too excited about, but the first two are worthy of note. The first three were clear.
Kaijai(IRE) Official explanation: jockey said filly never travelled

3509 DIGIBET LONDON MILE H'CAP (LONDON MILE QUALIFIER) — 1m (P)

7:50 (7:54) (Class 4) (0-85,85) 3-Y-0+ — **£4,727** (£1,406; £702; £351) **Stalls** High

Form				RPR
41-	1		**Emirates Sports**[228] 7333 3-9-4 84 ... TedDurcan 14 (Saeed Bin Suroor) *prom: wnt 2nd wl over 2f out: rdn to ld jst over 1f out: jnd fnl f: won on the nod* **5/2[1]**	91+
0-00	2	shd	**Nice To Know (FR)**[12] 3102 5-9-5 76 ... RyanMoore 13 (G L Moore) *dwlt: sn in midfield on inner: prog over 2f out: drvn to chal 1f out: w wnr ins fnl f: pipped on the nod* **17/2**	85
155-	3	½	**Solo Attempt**[298] 5711 3-9-1 81 ... AlanMunro 12 (M Botti) *led over 6f out: kicked on over 2f out: drvn and hdd jst over 1f out: kpt on wl* **20/1**	87
353	4	¾	**Jake The Snake (IRE)**[9] 3211 8-9-2 78 ... AmyBaker(5) 2 (A W Carroll) *dropped in fr wd draw and hld up wl in rr: prog over 2f out: cl up bhd ldng trio 1f out: urged along and nt qckn* **10/1**	84+
0045	5	¾	**Ilie Nastase (FR)**[28] 2612 5-10-0 85 ... FrancisNorton 9 (D Nicholls) *settled midfield: prog to trck ldrs over 2f out: nt qckn over 1f out: shown whip fnl f and kpt on* **13/2[2]**	89
1210	6	1 ¼	**Miss Glitters (IRE)**[27] 2639 4-9-6 77 ... SteveDrowne 3 (H Morrison) *hld up in midfield: outpcd over 2f out and looked to be struggling: shkn up and kpt on over 1f out: nrst fin* **13/2[2]**	78+
6-35	7	nk	**Quirina**[19] 2891 4-9-13 84 ... SebSanders 5 (R M Beckett) *hld up in midfield and racd wd: cl enough over 2f out: sn outpcd: one pce fr over 1f out* **7/1[3]**	85
10-0	8	nk	**Master Fong (IRE)**[27] 2638 3-8-11 77 ... WilliamBuick 7 (B W Hills) *sn gng bdly in rr: last whn reluctant and hung lft bnd 3f out: styd on u.p on outer fr 2f out: nrst fin* **14/1**	75
5064	9	8	**Sparton Duke (IRE)**[7] 3274 4-9-0 71 ... (p) RichardMullen 6 (K A Ryan) *dwlt: wl in rr: rdn on outer 3f out: no real prog and swtchd ins: wknd over 1f out* **8/1**	53
3000	10	1 ½	**Trafalgar Square**[21] 2828 7-9-12 83 ... ShaneKelly 10 (M J Attwater) *dwlt: hld up in rr: shkn up and no prog over 2f out: sn bhd* **25/1**	61
4340	11	1 ¾	**Mister New York (USA)**[23] 2775 4-9-13 84 ... JimmyFortune 11 (Noel T Chance) *chsd ldrs: lost pl rapidly over 2f out: sn bhd* **16/1**	58
-500	12	1 ½	**Sammy The Snake (IRE)**[17] 2941 4-10-0 85 ... AdamKirby 4 (B W Duke) *led for over 1f: chsd ldr to wl over 2f out: wknd rapidly* **100/1**	56
14-0	13	2 ¼	**Portugese Caddy**[18] 2926 3-9-1 81 ... JimCrowley 1 (P Winkworth) *prom tl wknd rapidly wl over 2f out* **50/1**	47

1m 40.72s (0.92) **Going Correction** +0.15s/f (Slow)
WFA 3 from 4yo+ 9lb — **13** Ran SP% **122.6**
Speed ratings (Par 105): **101,100,100,99,98 97,97,97,89,87 85,84,82**
toteswingers: 1&2 £6.20, 1&3 £13.00, 2&3 £65.50 CSF £24.07 CT £307.74 TOTE £3.50: £1.50, £3.90, £6.70; EX 37.80.
Owner Godolphin **Bred** W And R Barnett Ltd **Trained** Newmarket, Suffolk

FOCUS
A competitive race of its type for the money but the pace was only ordinary and the bare form is not that strong. The winner is likely to do better.

3510 DIGIBET.COM H'CAP — 2m (P)

8:20 (8:21) (Class 3) (0-90,90) 4-Y-0+
£7,352 (£2,201; £1,100; £551; £274; £138) **Stalls** High

Form				RPR
4-22	1		**Swingkeel (IRE)**[53] 1863 4-9-0 83 ... JimmyFortune 3 (J L Dunlop) *hld up in 8th: wl off the pce over 4f out: stdy prog gng easily over 3f out: led 1f out: sn clr: decisively* **7/4[1]**	96+
3304	2	3 ¼	**Calculating (IRE)**[14] 3029 5-7-13 71 oh8 ... AndreaAtzeni(3) 5 (M D I Usher) *settled in 7th: outpcd and rdn over 4f out: prog u.p fr 3f out: chal over 1f out: chsd wnr fnl f: kpt on but no ch* **16/1**	76
-056	3	2 ½	**Group Captain**[25] 2706 7-9-7 90 ... RichardHughes 9 (H J Collingridge) *settled in 6th: pushed along and outpcd over 4f out: rallied on inner u.p 2f out: cl enough 1f out: plugged on* **15/2[3]**	92
4-50	4	nk	**Jadalee (IRE)**[41] 2194 6-8-5 74 ... (p) MartinDwyer 2 (G A Butler) *trckd ldr: rdn 4f out: drvn into narrow ld over 2f out: hdd and outpcd 1f out* **8/1**	76
1400	5	1	**Salute (IRE)**[24] 2743 10-8-6 75 ... RobertHavlin 4 (P G Murphy) *trckd ldng trio: wnt 3rd 5f out gng wl: pushed along over 3f out: nt qckn over 2f out: one pce* **28/1**	75
/044	6	1	**Aaim To Prosper (IRE)**[12] 3103 5-8-11 80 ... DarryllHolland 1 (M R Channon) *s.s: rdn up on outer and sn 5th: u.p again 5f out: outpcd over 3f out: rallied briefly over 1f out: sn btn* **17/2**	79
004-	7	4 ½	**Candle**[20] 7108 6-9-5 88 ... JimCrowley 7 (T R George) *led: pressed 4f out: rdn and narrowly hdd over 2f out: wknd rapidly over 1f out* **50/1**	82
2211	8	32	**Kavaloti (IRE)**[81] 1215 5-8-11 80 ... (b) RyanMoore 10 (G L Moore) *hld up in detached last: outpcd fr over 4f out: tried to cl on main gp 3f out: sn no imp: eased: t.o* **5/2[2]**	35
2-22	9	13	**Ursis (FR)**[33] 2445 8-8-3 72 ... ChrisCatlin 6 (S Gollings) *trckd ldng pair to 5f out: wknd rapidly: t.o* **14/1**	12

3m 29.45s (-0.65) **Going Correction** +0.15s/f (Slow) — **9** Ran SP% **116.3**
Speed ratings (Par 107): **107,105,104,103,103 102,100,84,78**
toteswingers: 1&2 £8.90, 1&3 £3.90, 2&3 £11.90 CSF £32.87 CT £173.81 TOTE £3.00: £1.30, £3.50, £2.30; EX 47.90.
Owner Mrs M E Slade **Bred** R J Cornelius **Trained** Arundel, W Sussex

FOCUS
A good-quality handicap for the track, with the modest pace stepping up suddenly over 4f from home, resulting in many of the field suddenly coming off the bridle. The winner impressed but the form is less than solid.

NOTEBOOK
Swingkeel(IRE) ◆ bolted up largely on the bit and looks progressive. He had finished second twice in decent staying handicaps on turf before this and should achieve more success on either surface during the coming months. (op 6-4 tchd 5-4 and 15-8, and 2-1 in places)

Calculating(IRE), a solid performer on Polytrack and Fibresand, did well to chase home the winner from so far out of the handicap. It would be unfortunate if he were to be raised as a result because he has been on a handy mark of late. (op 14-1)

Group Captain was outpaced when the tempo quickened but still came to have his chance. Ideally suited by a strongly-run 1m4f, he does not convince as a natural 2m performer but made a good fist of it until the final 200 yards. (op 7-1)

Jadalee(IRE) has not finished in the first three in the last three seasons but he shows occasional form and this was one of his better efforts. He is handicapped to win a race but would probably be best suited by a stronger gallop and slightly shorter trip. (op 10-1 tchd 12-1)

Salute(IRE) would have been retired had he won this, but he looks set to soldier on following a much better effort than in his previous two races. (op 40-1 tchd 25-1)

Aaim To Prosper(IRE) is running respectably at present but could do with being dropped another couple of pounds. (op 12-1 tchd 14-1)

Kavaloti(IRE), settled at the back, was struggling immediately the pace increased at the end of the back straight, leaving him with a lot to do and that seemed to disappoint him. He is higher in the weights now but can do better if ridden more handily in race run at a more testing gallop. Official explanation: jockey said gelding never travelled (op 7-2 tchd 9-2 and 5-1 in a place)

Ursis(FR) Official explanation: jockey said gelding hung right throughout

3511 KEN DIXON 80TH BIRTHDAY H'CAP — 1m 4f (P)

8:50 (8:51) (Class 6) (0-65,65) 3-Y-0 — **£2,047** (£604; £302) **Stalls** Centre

Form				RPR
600	1		**The Last Don (IRE)**[50] 1963 3-9-6 64 ... TedDurcan 7 (D R Lanigan) *reminders sn after s: in tch in midfield: more reminders 4f out: prog whn hmpd over 2f out: hung rt wl over 1f out: sustained effrt to ld jst over 1f out: fought on wl* **7/1**	74
0-66	2	½	**Incendo**[47] 2048 3-9-5 63 ... WilliamBuick 11 (J R Fanshawe) *hld up in last pair: gd prog over 2f out and swtchd to inner: chal jst over 1f out: pressed wnr hrd fnl f: jst hld* **4/1[1]**	72
00-5	3	4	**Royal Max (IRE)**[12] 3099 3-8-7 51 ... (b[1]) MartinDwyer 2 (C G Cox) *sn led and clr at decent pce: breather 5f out: tried to kick on again wl over 2f out: hdd jst over 1f out: fdd* **10/1**	54
2230	4	9	**Salybia Bay**[9] 3222 3-9-7 65 ... RichardHughes 9 (R Hannon) *chsd ldrs: wnt 3rd briefly over 2f out: wknd rapidly over 1f out* **13/2[3]**	54
0103	5	3	**Primo Dilettante**[21] 2809 3-9-3 61 ... JimCrowley 14 (W J Knight) *hld up bhd ldrs: prog on inner to go 2nd wl over 2f out to over 1f out: wknd* **14/1**	45
0333	6	½	**Good Buy Dubai (USA)**[25] 2709 3-9-2 60 ... ChrisCatlin 8 (J R Best) *s.s: last pair: pushed along sn after 1/2-way: effrt u.p over 2f out: sn n.d* **4/1[1]**	43
0300	7	1 ½	**Alittlemoreflair**[20] 2866 3-8-12 56 ... JerryO'Dwyer 12 (J Pearce) *hld up towards rr on inner: rdn over 3f out: no real prog over 2f out: n.d after* **33/1**	37
2100	8	3 ¾	**Sullenberger (IRE)**[12] 3099 3-9-7 65 ... ShaneKelly 5 (J A Osborne) *hld up towards rr: gng wl enough over 3f out: rdn over 2f out: wknd tamely and rapidly* **16/1**	40
50-3	9	2 ¼	**Windpfeil (IRE)**[20] 2865 3-9-4 62 ... JimmyFortune 13 (J H M Gosden) *trckd ldng pair: wnt 2nd over 4f out to wl over 2f out: wandered and wknd rapidly* **9/2[2]**	33

5106 **10** *5* **Scottish Affair**[43] 2152 3-9-4 62 SebSanders 1 25
(E A L Dunlop) *trckd ldng trio to 3f out: wknd rapidly u.p* **12/1**
3000 **11** *7* **Milemilia (IRE)**[24] 2742 3-8-12 56 TravisBlock 10 8
(H Morrison) *chsd ldr to over 4f out: wknd rapidly 3f out: sn wl bhd* **66/1**

2m 36.26s (1.76) **Going Correction** +0.15s/f (Slow) **11** Ran SP% **117.8**
Speed ratings (Par 98): **100,99,97,91,89 88,87,85,83,80 75**
toteswingers: 1&2 £11.90, 1&3 £19.50, 2&3 £11.50 CSF £35.17 CT £284.47 TOTE £9.50: £3.10, £1.90, £2.00; EX 44.80.
Owner P Brosnan **Bred** Tally-Ho Stud **Trained** Newmarket, Suffolk

FOCUS
On paper, just a routine Polytrack handicap, but the first two were taking a big step up in trip, so they can be rated significantly better than their previous form would suggest. Fair form for the grade, with the first three clear.
The Last Don(IRE) Official explanation: trainer said, regarding apparent improvement in form, that the colt has matured and was suited by the step up in trip.
Windpfeil(IRE) Official explanation: jockey said gelding never travelled

3512 WEATHERBYS BETTRENDS.CO.UK APPRENTICE H'CAP (ROUND 5) 6f (P)
9:20 (9:20) (Class 5) (0-75,74) 3-Y-0+ **£2,590** (£770; £385; £192) **Stalls** High

Form RPR
0030 **1** **Bel Cantor**[18] 2938 6-9-7 70 (p) PaulPickard(3) 6 84
(W J H Ratcliffe) *mde all and nvr less than 2 l clr: styd on wl and in command 1f out: unchal* **8/1**
0650 **2** *3 1/2* **Lethal**[16] 2980 6-8-12 61 RosieJessop(3) 3 64
(Andrew Reid) *chsd wnr thrght: clr of rest but rdn 1/2-way: no imp over 1f out: clung on for 2nd* **12/1**
5-00 **3** *1/2* **Integria**[20] 2849 3-9-0 66 (b1) MartinLane 7 66
(J M P Eustace) *s.i.s: sn disp 4th: prog to chse clr ldng pair wl over 2f out: kpt on fnl f* **12/1**
034 **4** *1 1/4* **Tudor Prince (IRE)**[11] 3164 5-9-9 69 AndreaAtzeni 11 66
(A W Carroll) *s.i.s: hld up off the pce: rdn wl over 2f out: plugged on but no threat at all* **13/8**[1]
0000 **5** *1* **Grand Honour (IRE)**[12] 3115 3-9-3 72 CharlesEddery(3) 5 65
(P Howling) *s.s: outpcd in last: sme prog over 2f out: nvr on terms w ldrs* **33/1**
3405 **6** *1 1/2* **Royal Envoy (IRE)**[21] 2824 6-9-7 67 MCGeran 10 56
(P Howling) *disp 4th and nvr on terms w ldng pair: rdn and no prog wl over 2f out* **7/2**[3]
4-32 **7** *1 3/4* **Billberry**[9] 3211 4-9-6 66 (t) WilliamCarson 4 50
(S C Williams) *chsd clr ldng pair: no imp whn tightened up against rail briefly over 2f out: fdd* **3/1**[2]
0-00 **8** *3/4* **Ejeed (USA)**[18] 2920 4-8-12 58 RossAtkinson 1 39
(Miss Z C Davison) *awkward s: a off the pce in last pair: hanging lft and struggling 1/2-way* **66/1**

1m 12.95s (-0.15) **Going Correction** +0.15s/f (Slow)
WFA 3 from 4yo+ 6lb **8** Ran SP% **116.2**
Speed ratings (Par 103): **107,102,101,100,98 96,94,93**
toteswingers: 1&2 £27.40, 1&3 £3.20, 2&3 £25.60 CSF £98.12 CT £1153.54 TOTE £9.30: £1.80, £4.80, £2.60; EX 87.80 Place 6: £30.63 Place 5: £8.73.
Owner W J H Ratcliffe **Bred** Henry And Mrs Rosemary Moszkowicz **Trained** Newmarket, Suffolk

FOCUS
A strong gallop, but the first and second held those positions throughout. The form has not been rated to positively.
T/Plt: £17.90 to a £1 stake. Pool: £62,175.43. 2,535.21 winning tickets. T/Qpdt: £7.20 to a £1 stake. Pool: £4,990.40. 506.70 winning tickets. JN

3513 - (Foreign Racing) - See Raceform Interactive

3037 FAIRYHOUSE (R-H)
Wednesday, July 1

OFFICIAL GOING: Good

3514a GOLDEN FLEECE STKS (LISTED RACE) 7f
6:30 (6:30) 2-Y-0 **£26,861** (£7,881; £3,754; £1,279)

RPR
1 **Perfect Symmetry (IRE)**[20] 2868 2-9-1 KLatham 5 92
(G M Lyons, Ire) *settled in 3rd on inner: led 2f out: pushed out and kpt on wl fr 1f out* **11/8**[1]
2 *1* **En Un Clin D'Oeil (IRE)**[17] 2956 2-9-1 PJSmullen 1 90
(Ms Joanna Morgan, Ire) *sn led: hdd 2f out: sn drifted sharply lft into centre of crse: 3rd 1f out: sted up and kpt on wl fnl 100yds* **11/4**[2]
3 *2* **Bosphorus Queen (IRE)**[13] 3078 2-8-12 WJSupple 4 82
(P D Deegan, Ire) *t.k.h early and settled in rr: hdwy on inner to go 3rd under 2f out: 2nd 1f out: sn no ex and dropped to 3rd fnl f* **5/1**
4 *1 1/2* **Knight Eagle (IRE)**[29] 2582 2-9-1 DPMcDonogh 3 81
(Kevin Prendergast, Ire) *mainly 4th on outer: stl cl-up 2f out: no imp and kpt on one pce fr 1f out* **9/2**[3]
5 *13* **Light Years Ahead**[12] 3129 2-9-1 KJManning 2 54+
(P D Deegan, Ire) *trckd ldr: 2nd ent st: dropped to 5th under 2f out: no ex over 1f out: eased* **11/1**

1m 28.39s (-2.11) **5** Ran SP% **112.0**
CSF £5.53 TOTE £1.80: £1.40, £1.60; DF 5.90.
Owner Sean Jones **Bred** Forenaghts Stud & Dermot Canti **Trained** Dunsany, Co. Meath

FOCUS
This wasn't a strongly contested event by any means but it turned into an extraordinary contest where the benefit of keeping a straight course proved the winning of the race for Perfect Symmetry.

NOTEBOOK
Perfect Symmetry(IRE) kept tabs on the leaders on the inside and when a gap opened up for him next to the rail in the straight he proved good enough to seize the opportunity. Once getting there he came off the rail himself, but he was good enough to repel the challenge of the filly on his inside and ran on well. It's quite hard to know what level he will operate at best, and what ability he has will be tested in a stronger contest, even at this level. He is an improving horse though. (op 7/4)
En Un Clin D'Oeil(IRE) lost the race at least as much as the winner won. Leading early, he was challenged in the straight and when coming under pressure proceeded to drift quite violently to his left. For all that, he did run on well but it's certain that he gave up quite a bit more ground than the length margin of defeat he suffered. Of course, there's always the possibility that the winner would have found a bit more had he been able to see his main rival. Official explanation: jockey said colt hung badly left in the final 2f (op 9/4 tchd 2/1)
Bosphorus Queen(IRE) ran a fine race and might well be suited by dropping back a furlong in trip. She quickened to try and seize the opportunity presented by the winner just edging off the rail inside the last but she just ran out of steam close home. (op 5/1 tchd 11/2)

3516a IRISH STALLION FARMS EUROPEAN BREEDERS FUND BROWNSTOWN STKS (GROUP 3) (F&M) 7f
7:30 (7:30) 3-Y-0+ **£51,747** (£15,126; £7,165; £2,388)

RPR
1 **Glowing (IRE)**[13] 3082 4-9-6 92 FMBerry 7 104
(Charles O'Brien, Ire) *trckd ldr: 2nd and pushed along ent st: rdr sn lost whip: disp ld fr 1f out: slt advantage fnl 100 yds* **20/1**
2 *shd* **Luminous Eyes (IRE)**[38] 2304 3-9-1 106 (b1) PJSmullen 5 103
(D K Weld, Ire) *trckd ldrs: 3rd 2f out: rdn to dispute ld 1f out: hdd fnl 100 yds: kpt on wl: jst failed* **8/1**
3 *1 1/4* **Kalidaha (IRE)**[27] 2644 4-9-6 99 MJKinane 9 100
(John M Oxx, Ire) *chsd ldrs: 5th 3f out: cl up 6th u.p over 1f out: kpt on one pce into 3rd fnl f* **7/1**[3]
4 *shd* **Miss Gorica (IRE)**[3] 3434 5-9-6 102 CDHayes 2 100
(Ms Joanna Morgan, Ire) *trckd ldrs: 4th appr st: no imp fr over 1f out: kpt on* **14/1**
5 *1/2* **Heart Shaped (USA)**[12] 3088 3-8-12 109 JAHeffernan 4 95
(A P O'Brien, Ire) *mid-div: 7th 3f out: short of room in 5th over 1f out: kpt on* **2/1**[1]
6 *1/2* **Festoso (IRE)**[39] 2271 4-9-6 CO'Donoghue 6 98+
(H J L Dunlop) *mid-div: 6th 3f out: 7th 1 1/2f out: kpt on one pce fnl f* **8/1**
7 *1* **Monivea (IRE)**[14] 3039 3-8-12 94 DJMoran 10 91
(Brian Nolan, Ire) *sn led: 4L clr appr st: sn reduced ld and hdd 1f out: wknd ins fnl f* **20/1**
8 *1 1/4* **Maoineach (USA)**[27] 2644 3-9-3 106 KJManning 12 93
(J S Bolger, Ire) *ponied to s: keen early and settled towards rr on outer: no imp u.p fr under 2f out* **9/2**[2]
9 *1* **Alexander Youth (IRE)**[25] 2728 3-8-12 86 WMLordan 11 85
(David Wachman, Ire) *towards rr on inner: sme hdwy on far rail into 7th 1 1/2f out: no ex fnl f* **20/1**
10 *1 1/2* **Aleagueoftheirown (IRE)**[27] 2644 5-9-6 104 (p) JohnEgan 8 84
(David Wachman, Ire) *a towards rr: kpt on one pce fr 2f out* **20/1**
11 *9* **Chantilly Tiffany**[14] 3012 5-9-9 DPMcDonogh 1 63
(E A L Dunlop) *rr of mid-div on outer: no ex u.p fr under 2f out: eased ins fnl f* **10/1**
12 *4 1/2* **Mooretown Lady (IRE)**[20] 2870 6-9-6 99 (p) PShanahan 3 48
(H Rogers, Ire) *a bhd: eased fnl f* **33/1**

1m 25.9s (-4.60)
WFA 3 from 4yo+ 8lb **12** Ran SP% **124.0**
CSF £173.19 TOTE £21.80: £6.10, £2.80, £2.70; DF 897.50.
Owner Mrs John Magnier **Bred** Millsec Limited **Trained** Straffan, Co Kildare

FOCUS
The form looks pretty strong with the in-form runner-up and third recording small personal bests, and the fourth being rated to the best of her form this summer.

NOTEBOOK
Glowing(IRE) appeared to have plenty on here based on offiicial ratings. A winner over 1m at two, she posted her second success over that same trip at Dundalk in April before finishing fourth at this level over 1m1f at Leopardstown last month. Soon second, she was pushed along turning for home and was disputing the lead over a furlong out after her rider had lost his whip about two furlongs out. She edged ahead about 100 yards from the finish and just held on. Her trainer thinks 7f or a mile on fast ground are her ideal conditions.
Luminous Eyes(IRE), successful at a similar level over this trip at Leopardstown last season, had finished ninth in the Irish 1,000 Guineas on heavy ground on her only previous start this year. Soon close up, she challenged to dispute the lead over a furlong out and, after the winner edged ahead well inside the final furlong, she was coming back at her late on and only just lost out. (op 7/1)
Kalidaha(IRE), lightly raced and a winner on her only start at two and of a 1m handicap from only three attempts last season, had a couple of fair efforts behind her at a similar level this year. She was always in touch and after failing to raise her game under pressure over a furlong out, she kept on in the closing stages. (op 10/1)
Miss Gorica(IRE), back up to a more suitable trip after beating only one home in a 5f Group 3 at the Curragh on Sunday, has done all her winning in handicaps. Soon close up on the outside, she was unable to get to the leaders over a furlong out but kept on in the closing stages. (op 12/1 tchd 16/1)
Heart Shaped(USA), fourth in the 1,000 Guineas and more recently sixth in the Coronation Stakes, was dropping in class and trip here. She race in midfield and had anything but a clear run on the inside approaching the final furlong. That being said, it would be stretching a point to say she was an unlucky loser. She would have finished a bit closer, but while she kept on in the closing stages, she wasn't quickening to any degree. (op 2/1 tchd 7/4)
Festoso(IRE), a Listed winner over 6f on heavy ground at Haydock on her previous start, chased the leaders but found little when asked to raise her effort a furlong and a half out. She kept on towards the finish.
Chantilly Tiffany, fourth in the Group 2 Windsor Forest Stakes at Royal Ascot on her previous start and a winner at this level over this trip on soft ground in Germany last year, never really threatened. After coming under pressure early in the straight it was soon obvious that she was not going to be involved at the finish. (op 8/1)

3517 - 3519a (Foreign Racing) - See Raceform Interactive

3493 HAMBURG (R-H)
Wednesday, July 1

OFFICIAL GOING: Good

3520a PREIS DER SPIELBANK HAMBURG (GROUP 3) (F&M) 1m
7:00 (7:10) 3-Y-0+ **£31,068** (£9,709; £4,854; £2,913)

RPR
1 **Caro Jina (FR)**[59] 3-8-11 THellier 2 99
(A Trybuhl, Germany) *prom: disputing 3rd 1/2-way: disputing 2nd st: pushed along and disputing ld over 2f out: led over 1 1/2f out: styd on u.p* **151/10**
2 *nk* **Whispered Dreams (GER)**[20] 4-9-4 AHelfenbein 9 99
(Mario Hofer, Germany) *cl 2nd: pushed along and disputing 2nd st: disputing ld over 2f out: hdd 1 1/2f out: styd on* **123/10**
3 *nk* **Mambo Light (USA)**[24] 2757 3-8-11 EPedroza 10 98
(A Wohler, Germany) *prom: 4th st: drvn to dispute ld over 2f out: styd on tl no ex cl home* **11/2**
4 *1/2* **Waky Love (GER)**[20] 5-9-6 AStarke 3 99
(P Schiergen, Germany) *hld up: pushed along st: styd on fr over 1f out: nrest at fin* **5/1**[3]
5 *shd* **Manipura (GER)**[66] 4-9-6 HGrewe 8 99
(H Steguweit, Germany) *hld up: last st: nvr in chalng position* **164/10**

6 ½ **Turning For Home (FR)**[55] 1819 4-9-6 FilipMinarik 4 97
(H-A Pantall, France) *hld up: r.o 2f out: in front nk over 1f out: kpt on at one pce* 14/1
7 shd **Silent Sunday (IRE)**[55] 1819 4-9-6 FVeron 7 97
(H-A Pantall, France) *settled towards rr: drvn st: nvr able to chal* 54/10
8 2 **Masquenada (FR)**[20] 4-9-4 WMongil 1 91
(W Baltromei, Germany) *towards rr: drvn ent st: nvr in chalng position* 17/5[2]
9 hd **Rock My Soul (IRE)**[354] 3-8-11 DPorcu 6 90
(Uwe Ostmann, Germany) *hld up: n.d* 134/10
10 ¾ **Addicted (GER)**[24] 2757 3-8-11 ASuborics 5 88
(T Mundry, Germany) *led: pushed along st: hdd over 2f out: wknd over 1f out* 27/10[1]

1m 38.1s (98.10)
WFA 3 from 4yo+ 9lb **10** Ran SP% **130.5**
(Including 10 Euros stake): WIN 161; PL 43, 36, 27; SF 1,362.
Owner Gestut Weiherwiesen **Bred** Mme V Jud-Frei **Trained** Germany

2701 EPSOM (L-H)

Thursday, July 2

OFFICIAL GOING: Good to firm (firm in places; 9.4)
Wind: Light, behind Weather: Fine, hot

3521 OFFICE DEPOT H'CAP 1m 4f 10y

6:20 (6:22) (Class 5) (0-75,75) 4-Y-O+ **£3,238** (£963; £481; £240) **Stalls** Centre

Form RPR
0040 1 **Epsom Salts**[17] 2983 4-8-4 63 JackDean(5) 1 72
(P M Phelan) *dwlt: hld up: 5th and clsng st: wnt 2nd on outer over 2f out: led over 1f out: rdn clr fnl f* 15/2
3334 2 2 ¼ **Watson's Bay**[12] 3169 4-9-0 68 PaulDoe 7 73
(P Howling) *s.s: hld up in last trio: 7th and c wd st: prog 3f out: pressed wnr over 1f out: one pce fnl f* 6/1
-453 3 3 ¾ **Cyborg**[23] 2798 5-9-7 75 RobertHavlin 5 74
(D R C Elsworth) *trckd ldrs: cl 4th st: nt qckn 3f out and sn outpcd: kpt on to take 3rd ins fnl f* 9/2[2]
0015 4 nk **Sinbad The Sailor**[9] 3247 4-8-10 64 ow1 (v) SebSanders 3 63
(J W Hills) *cl up: 3rd st: chsd ldr 3f out to over 2f out: sn outpcd: kpt on to press for 3rd ins fnl f* 11/2[3]
6502 5 3 ¼ **Agente Romano (USA)**[12] 3169 4-9-0 68 (b) DaneO'Neill 4 61
(G A Butler) *mde most: kicked on 3f out: hdd & wknd over 1f out* 9/1
0512 6 4 **Mixing**[9] 3247 7-7-9 56 oh8 KierenFox(7) 6 43
(M J Attwater) *awkward s: last after 4f: detached ent st: plugged on but nvr rchd ldrs* 20/1
4634 7 25 **Maslak (IRE)**[4] 3423 5-9-5 73 LPKeniry 2 20
(P W Hiatt) *chsd ldrs: rdn 1/2-way: 6th and losing pl st: sn bhd: t.o* 6/1
0124 8 3 ½ **Cossack Prince**[4] 3421 4-9-1 69 IanMongan 9 10
(Mrs L J Mongan) *racd wd early: w ldr to over 3f out: wknd rapidly: eased: t.o* 3/1[1]

2m 36.98s (-1.92) **Going Correction** -0.175s/f (Firm) **8** Ran SP% **113.7**
Speed ratings (Par 103): **99,97,95,94,92 89,73,70**
toteswingers: 1&2 £12.30, 1&3 £8.50, 2&3 £6.20 CSF £50.93 CT £225.96 TOTE £9.80: £3.30, £2.40, £1.80; EX 59.50.
Owner The Epsom Racegoers **Bred** Heatherwold Stud **Trained** Epsom, Surrey

FOCUS
A modest handicap, featuring horses with poor wins-to-runs ratios, but it looked competitive enough and few could be dismissed out of hand. The pace, considering the presence of several potential front-runners, was not overly strong and the form is ordinary.
Maslak(IRE) Official explanation: jockey said gelding never travelled
Cossack Prince Official explanation: jockey said gelding ran too free and boiled over

3522 VIKING DIRECT E. B. F. MEDIAN AUCTION MAIDEN STKS 7f

6:50 (6:52) (Class 4) 2-Y-O **£5,180** (£1,541; £770; £384) **Stalls** Low

Form RPR
34 1 **Suffolk Punch (IRE)**[10] 3226 2-9-3 0 LPKeniry 4 80+
(A M Balding) *mde virtually all: shkn up 2f out: in command over 1f out: styd on wl* 9/1
5 2 2 ½ **Interakt**[9] 3249 2-8-12 0 CatherineGannon 2 69
(M R Channon) *pushed up to go prom: 3rd st: chsd wnr 3f out: edgd rt u.p 2f out: no imp after* 5/1[3]
3 2 **Cadley Road (IRE)** 2-9-3 0 DaneO'Neill 3 69
(R Hannon) *hld up in tch: 5th st: rdn over 2f out: kpt on to take 3rd over 1f out: no imp on ldng pair* 15/8[1]
03 4 3 **Dashing Doc (IRE)**[12] 3167 2-9-3 0 RobertHavlin 8 61
(D R C Elsworth) *in tch: 6th st and j. path: effrt on outer over 2f out: wandering and one pce over 1f out* 13/2
0 5 4 **Mountrath**[8] 3270 2-9-3 0 AdamKirby 7 51
(B R Johnson) *pressed wnr to 3f out: grad wknd fnl 2f* 100/1
6 2 **Epic (IRE)** 2-9-3 0 JoeFanning 9 46
(M Johnston) *prom: cl 4th st: rn green and fdd over 2f out* 12/1
7 nk **High Resolution** 2-8-12 0 WilliamCarson(5) 1 46
(S C Williams) *s.i.s: in tch on inner: 7th st: no prog 3f out: grad wknd* 33/1
2 8 7 **Do More Business (IRE)**[38] 2325 2-9-3 0 IanMongan 10 28
(P M Phelan) *a in last pair: struggling 3f out: sn btn* 9/2[2]
5 9 16 **Comedy Act**[14] 3052 2-9-3 0 SebSanders 6 —
(Sir Mark Prescott) *s.s: a in last pair: struggling 3f out: wknd: t.o* 8/1

1m 22.76s (-0.54) **Going Correction** -0.175s/f (Firm) **9** Ran SP% **115.7**
Speed ratings (Par 96): **96,93,90,87,82 80,80,72,53**
toteswingers: 1&2 £5.00, 1&3 £3.40, 2&3 £3.20 CSF £53.60 TOTE £11.20: £2.40, £1.90, £1.40; EX 37.60.
Owner Marcus Evans **Bred** Islanmore Stud **Trained** Kingsclere, Hants

FOCUS
No more than a fair juvenile median auction maiden, although a clutch already had sound placed form. They were taken on by some potential improvers and a couple of newcomers from yards whose two-year-olds are always worth noting. The runner-up is the best guide to the level.

NOTEBOOK
Suffolk Punch(IRE) had shown distinct promise on his debut at Chepstow, filling third over 6f, but he had taken a step backwards when switched to Polytrack at Wolverhampton on his second outing, managing no better than fourth after starting at odds-on. He seemed very much more effective here though, returned to a natural surface and, grabbing the lead early on, he made virtually all the subsequent running and was well on top at the finish. (op 8-1 tchd 7-1)

Interakt had to make some improvement from his initial outing to take this event, but he was representing a stable whose newcomers often progress with experience and could be counted slightly better than his debut fifth of 15 because he had encountered traffic problems. He almost certainly did show improved form here, chasing the winner hard from an early stage and battling on well for his clear second place, but he lacked the gears of his conqueror and may do better when trying 1m. (op 11-2 tchd 9-2)

Cadley Road(IRE), a 110,000euros purchase with plenty to like in his pedigree, represented a stable enjoying an extraordinary year, even by its own high standards, and boasting a powerful team of juveniles. He was well supported in the market and showed promise in the race too, but perhaps unsurprisingly for a newcomer he seemed to find the course cambers a little disconcerting and was not always on an even keel. (op 2-1 tchd 7-4 in places)

Dashing Doc(IRE) looked to set the standard for the rest to aim at, having stepped up markedly on a mildly encouraging all-weather debut when filling third spot behind a well-regarded winner in a Newmarket maiden, but seemed below that level of form here. (op 9-2)

Mountrath Official explanation: jockey said colt hung both ways in straight

Epic(IRE), whose trainer has most of his big two-year-old string in fine shape, is bred to be decent, even though his pedigree suggests he might do better when tackling middle distances next season. He was a significant market drifter, however, and will need to improve on this display if he is to notch a victory before setting out on a three-year-old campaign. (op 13-2)

3523 WHYOFFICEDEPOT.COM H'CAP 7f

7:25 (7:26) (Class 4) (0-85,84) 3-Y-O+ **£4,857** (£1,445; £722; £360) **Stalls** Low

Form RPR
3021 1 **Victoria Sponge (IRE)**[13] 3102 3-9-3 81 DaneO'Neill 3 91+
(R Hannon) *trckd ldng pair: prog against rail to go 2nd 2f out: led over 1f out: sn in command: drvn out* 5/2[1]
2541 2 1 **Desert Dreamer (IRE)**[6] 3335 8-9-5 80 6ex RichardEvans(5) 7 87
(P D Evans) *hld up in 7th: prog 2f out: sn rdn: styd on wl to take 2nd last 150yds: unable to chal* 10/1
5-01 3 1 ¼ **Wellington Square**[20] 2883 4-10-0 84 TravisBlock 2 88+
(H Morrison) *hld up in 5th: effrt over 2f out but sn nt qckn: kpt on fnl f to take 3rd last strides* 4/1[2]
1032 4 nk **Den's Gift (IRE)**[17] 2976 5-10-0 84 (b) AdamKirby 6 87
(C G Cox) *led: pressed 3f out and edgd away fr far rail: hdd over 1f out: one pce and lost 2 pls ins fnl f* 5/1[3]
0333 5 2 ¼ **Ivory Lace**[13] 3104 8-9-0 70 JimCrowley 9 67
(S Woodman) *hld up in 6th on outer: nt qckn over 2f out: no prog after tl kpt on ins fnl f* 8/1
0003 6 nse **Prince Of Thebes (IRE)**[8] 3274 8-9-9 79 PaulDoe 5 76
(M J Attwater) *pressed ldr: upsides 3f out: lost 2nd 2f out: grad fdd* 8/1
4230 7 3 ¼ **Purus (IRE)**[17] 2976 7-9-8 78 SebSanders 8 66
(R A Teal) *hld up in last: nt travel wl downhill: rdn 3f out: no real prog* 14/1
0010 8 2 ¾ **Lodi (IRE)**[20] 2883 4-9-8 78 (t) IanMongan 4 59
(J Akehurst) *chsd ldng trio tl wknd over 2f out: eased fnl f* 8/1

1m 21.23s (-2.07) **Going Correction** -0.175s/f (Firm)
WFA 3 from 4yo+ 8lb **8** Ran SP% **114.3**
Speed ratings (Par 105): **104,102,101,101,98 98,94,91**
toteswingers: 1&2 £5.80, 1&3 £2.50, 2&3 £9.00 CSF £28.59 CT £97.50 TOTE £3.20: £1.50, £2.80, £1.60; EX 20.20.
Owner Simon Leech **Bred** Corrin Stud & Peter McCutcheon **Trained** East Everleigh, Wilts

FOCUS
This was a decent enough handicap and three of the runners lined up having won on their latest outing. Three others had made the first three last time out, so it seems reasonable to describe it as competitive. The form looks sound and worth being positive about.

3524 TOTESPORTCASINO.COM H'CAP 6f

7:55 (7:55) (Class 3) (0-95,94) 3-Y-O+ **£7,771** (£2,312; £1,155; £577) **Stalls** High

Form RPR
6024 1 **Mac Gille Eoin**[5] 3405 5-9-13 94 JimCrowley 5 103
(J Gallagher) *mde all in narrow ld: rdn 2f out: gained def advantage last 100yds* 4/6[1]
2200 2 ¾ **Noble Citizen (USA)**[13] 3116 4-9-9 90 (b) StephenDonohoe 3 97
(D M Simcock) *racd on inner: pressed wnr: persistent chal in st: stl trying whn jockey lost whip 150yds out: no ex* 7/1[3]
2300 3 3 **Abraham Lincoln (IRE)**[26] 2707 5-9-13 94 AdrianTNicholls 4 92
(D Nicholls) *hld up in last: wnt 3rd st: hanging and nt qckn 2f out: no imp after* 11/4[2]
6300 4 14 **Merlin's Dancer**[6] 3347 9-9-0 81 IanMongan 6 37
(S Dow) *hld up in 3rd: last in st: shkn up and no rspnse over 2f out: eased fnl f* 12/1

67.21 secs (-2.19) **Going Correction** -0.175s/f (Firm) course record **4** Ran SP% **106.8**
Speed ratings (Par 107): **107,106,102,83**
toteswingers: 1&2 £4.40. CSF £5.56 TOTE £1.60; EX 3.60.
Owner M C S D Racing Partnership **Bred** M C S D Racing Ltd **Trained** Chastleton, Oxon

FOCUS
A decent handicap, despite the small turn-out, with the lowest-rated runner having an official mark of 81. They went a good pace and the form looks sound.

NOTEBOOK
Mac Gille Eoin had already posted two decent efforts from as many starts on this tricky track, his record on the course standing at one win and one second, and he came back here in good form, having finished fourth over this trip at Windsor five days previously. He was weighted right up to best - 1lb higher than for his latest victory, in fact - but his proven ability to handle this venue's eccentric cambers and undulations marked him out as an obvious contender. He duly won, landing the odds after breaking fast and either holding or disputing the lead throughout, but he needed to pull out all the stops to do so against a runner-up who showed great determination. (op 8-11 tchd 5-6 and 10-11 in a place)

Noble Citizen(USA) has never won at this distance, all three of his victories being registered over 7f, and his last two runs had been disappointing. He ran a blinder here, though, making his challenge right under the inside rail, and might have given the winner even more to do had his rider not dropped his whip when the first two came together - and almost got entangled - in the closing stages. (op 15-2 tchd 11-2)

Abraham Lincoln(IRE) had not had the run of the race on his last visit to this course, being badly hampered when attempting to make ground in an event in which Mac Gille Eoin had taken second, but a 1lb drop in the ratings was at least of minor assistance as he tried to reverse that form.\n\x\x
He certainly got a great deal closer this time, reducing what had been a near 12-length deficit to a total of three and three-quarters, but he never seemed remotely likely to get the upper hand. (op 5-2 tchd 3-1)

Merlin's Dancer was attempting to notch his first success since March 2007 and failed to give his connections any great deal of hope for an imminent improvement in his fortunes. (tchd 10-1)

3525 TOTESPORTBINGO.COM CLAIMING STKS 1m 114y
8:30 (8:31) (Class 5) 3-Y-0+ £3,412 (£1,007; £504) Stalls Low

Form RPR
-403 1 **Ogre (USA)**[9] 3245 4-9-0 74.....(t) PaulDoe 2 71
(P D Evans) *late to post: trckd ldng pair: led on inner wl over 2f out gng wl: in command over 1f out: clr and rdn out fnl f* 5/2[1]
0611 2 2 ½ **Theocritus (USA)**[22] 2808 4-9-3 75..... StephenDonohoe 5 68
(D M Simcock) *hld up in detached last: stl there on wd outside 2f out and rdn: prog jst over 1f out: r.o wl to take 2nd last strides* 8/1
3050 3 hd **Aggravation**[13] 3112 7-9-3 64..... DaneO'Neill 1 70+
(D R C Elsworth) *stdd s: hld up in 7th: hmpd on inner 2f out: plld out wd over 1f out: styd on fnl f to take 3rd last strides* 11/1
0606 4 hd **Roly Boy**[3] 3461 3-8-11 78.....(b) PatDobbs 4 70
(R Hannon) *hld up in 5th: prog to go 2nd over 2f out: no imp on wnr over 1f out: edgd lft fnl f: lost 2 pls last strides* 9/2[3]
0-43 5 2 ½ **Daring Racer (GER)**[10] 3215 6-8-13 53.....(p) IanMongan 8 58
(Mrs L J Mongan) *trckd ldr to 3f out: styd chsng ldrs tl fdd over 1f out* 16/1
2341 6 2 **Fremen (USA)**[22] 2816 9-9-8 83..... AdrianTNicholls 6 73+
(D Nicholls) *s.s: hld up in 6th: swtchd to inner jst over 2f out and prog: keeping on in 3rd whn hmpd ins fnl f: nt rcvr* 10/3[2]
2606 7 2 ½ **Ma Ridge**[10] 3215 5-8-8 45.....(b[1]) AmyBaker[(5)] 7 48
(T D McCarthy) *led to wl over 2f out: sn wknd* 66/1
4055 8 nk **Wasp (AUS)**[19] 2927 7-9-11 80..... JoeFanning 9 59
(W Jarvis) *trckd ldng trio: rdn over 3f out: cl up 2f out: wknd* 5/1

1m 43.28s (-2.82) **Going Correction** -0.175s/f (Firm)
WFA 3 from 4yo+ 10lb 8 Ran SP% **113.3**
Speed ratings (Par 103): **105,102,102,102,100 98,96,95**
toteswingers: 1&2 £5.90, 1&3 £5.50, 2&3 £12.10. CSF £22.87 TOTE £3.50: £1.40, £2.40, £2.10; EX 22.10.
Owner Diamond Racing Ltd **Bred** Gulf Coast Farms LLC **Trained** Pandy, Monmouths

FOCUS
A reasonable race by claiming standards, featuring several runners representing trainers with the nous to put them in on a sensible weight, and only a couple looked out of their depth. The pace was solid, rather than frenetic and the proximity of the fifth and seventh suggests the form horses were not at their best.
Fremen(USA) Official explanation: jockey said gelding suffered interference

3526 LEWIS SILKIN H'CAP 1m 2f 18y
9:00 (9:02) (Class 4) (0-85,85) 3-Y-0+ £4,857 (£1,445; £722; £360) Stalls Low

Form RPR
0212 1 **Eastern Aria (UAE)**[6] 3333 3-9-2 80..... JoeFanning 5 93+
(M Johnston) *mde all: styd alone against far rail in st: pushed wl clr fr over 2f out: eased ins fnl f* 6/5[1]
31-4 2 7 **Barliffey (IRE)**[28] 2641 4-9-6 73.....(v) DaneO'Neill 6 70
(D J Coakley) *dwlt: hld up in last: c wd in st: rdn over 2f out: styd on to take modest 2nd ins fnl f* 4/1[3]
2251 3 3 ¾ **My Shadow**[13] 3104 4-9-3 70..... IanMongan 4 60
(S Dow) *hld up in 3rd: c wd in st: rdn to chse wnr over 1f out: no imp: lost 2nd and wknd ins fnl f* 13/2
-241 4 1 ¾ **Dubai Echo (USA)**[29] 2613 3-9-7 85..... PatDobbs 2 71
(Sir Michael Stoute) *chsd wnr: c wd in st: rdn and btn wl over 2f out: lost 2nd and wknd over 1f out* 5/2[2]

2m 5.97s (-3.73) **Going Correction** -0.175s/f (Firm)
WFA 3 from 4yo+ 11lb 4 Ran SP% **107.4**
Speed ratings (Par 105): **107,101,98,97**
toteswingers: 1&2 £4.20. CSF £6.09 TOTE £2.10; EX 5.60 Place 6: £37.13, Place 5: £10.11..
Owner Sheikh Hamdan Bin Mohammed Al Maktoum **Bred** Darley **Trained** Middleham Moor, N Yorks

FOCUS
Just a run-of-the-mill small-field handicap, with the top weight following the announcement of two non-runners being officially rated 85, but it featured a couple of lightly raced potential improvers. The winner is rated a 6lb improver.
T/Plt: £52.70 to a £1 stake. Pool: £54,745.95. 757.86 winning tickets. T/Qpdt: £5.90 to a £1 stake. Pool: £3,691.50. 460.90 winning tickets. JN

3151 HAYDOCK (L-H)
Thursday, July 2

OFFICIAL GOING: Firm (good to firm in places)
Rail realignment increased advertised distances on the round course by around 10yards
Wind: Light across Weather: Sunny and warm

3527 RITEC CLEAR-SHIELD FILLIES' H'CAP 1m 3f 200y
2:10 (2:10) (Class 5) (0-75,71) 3-Y-0+ £3,238 (£963; £481; £240) Stalls Centre

Form RPR
00-3 1 **Going For Gold**[21] 2847 3-9-1 71..... AlanMunro 4 78
(R Charlton) *trckd ldrs: hdwy 4f out: cl up 3f out: effrt to chal wl over 2f out: rdn to ld over 1f out: kpt on ins fnl f* 11/8[1]
-013 2 3 **Princess Rainbow (FR)**[12] 3151 4-10-0 71..... TPO'Shea 6 73
(Jennie Candlish) *led: jnd and rdn along 3f out: drvn 2f out: hdd over 1f out and kpt on same pce* 11/4[2]
00-5 3 4 ½ **Prelude**[23] 2783 8-9-9 66..... TGMcLaughlin 7 61
(W M Brisbourne) *trckd ldr: effrt 4f out: cl up 3f out and sn rdn: drvn 2f out and ev ch tl grad wknd appr last* 5/1
0-30 4 27 **Babilu**[20] 2898 4-9-9 66..... FergusSweeney 3 18
(A G Newcombe) *trckd ldrs: rdn along over 3f out and sn wknd* 7/2[3]
006/ 5 22 **Lilymay**[671] 4989 9-8-4 54 oh9..... BillyCray[(7)] 5 —
(B P J Baugh) *a in rr: outpcd and bhd fnl 4f* 50/1

2m 33.96s (0.76) **Going Correction** -0.10s/f (Good)
WFA 3 from 4yo+ 13lb 5 Ran SP% **109.6**
Speed ratings (Par 100): **93,91,88,70,55**
toteswingers: 1&2 £2.90, 1&3 not won, 2&3 not won CSF £5.38 TOTE £2.10: £1.40, £1.50; EX 4.40.
Owner The Queen **Bred** The Queen **Trained** Beckhampton, Wilts

FOCUS
A modest fillies' handicap won by the sole three-year-old in the race. The pace was steady and not a race to be too positive about with the runner-up the best guide.

3528 E B F GRETSCH-UNITAS NOVICE FILLIES' STKS 6f
2:40 (2:42) (Class 4) 2-Y-0 £6,476 (£1,927; £963; £481) Stalls Centre

Form RPR
10 1 **Rose Blossom**[15] 3015 2-8-12 0..... PaulHanagan 2 90+
(R A Fahey) *qckly away: mde all: shkn up over 1f out: rdn and edgd lft ins fnl f: kpt on* 8/11[1]
015 2 1 ¾ **Avonrose**[18] 2957 2-9-0 0..... GregFairley 4 87+
(M Johnston) *chsd wnr: rdn along over 2f out: rallied u.p ins fnl f: sn edgd lft and one pce* 9/2[3]
31 3 7 **Lady Springbank (IRE)**[18] 2940 2-9-3 0..... JimCrowley 5 69+
(K R Burke) *trckd ldng pair: effrt and sme hdwy 2f out: sn rdn and btn over 1f out* 9/4[2]
4 16 **Dazakhee** 2-8-6 0..... PJMcDonald 3 10
(P T Midgley) *s.i.s: rn green and a outpcd: bhd whn hung bdly lft fr 1/2-way* 50/1

1m 11.4s (-2.60) **Going Correction** -0.40s/f (Firm) 4 Ran SP% **108.8**
Speed ratings (Par 93): **101,98,89,68**
CSF £4.46 TOTE £1.50; EX 3.30.
Owner Highclere Thoroughbred Racing (Blossom) **Bred** J R Mitchell **Trained** Musley Bank, N Yorks

FOCUS
A good novice event for fillies in which the winner bounced back to her Ascot form with a personal best from the runner-up.

NOTEBOOK
Rose Blossom came unstuck in the Queen Mary last time out, but that was on just her second outing and she had looked a filly of considerable promise when breaking the track record on debut at Hamilton. Stepping up a furlong on this drop back in grade, she made all for a convincing success and could have been called the winner passing the 2f pole. A quick surface clearly suits, but she evidently has some quirks as she took time to load up and drifted markedly left when put under pressure inside the final furlong. She was also getting weight from her two main rivals, but there was still plenty to like about this display and a return to Pattern company is now firmly on the cards. Her trainer indicated the Group 2 Lowther Stakes at York is a likely target and the quick 6f there should be right up her street. (op 4-6 tchd 4-5)
Avonrose ◆, out the back in a good Listed event at Cork 18 days earlier, struggled to go the very early pace yet still rated the chief danger to the winner throughout and posted an improved run in defeat. She was giving 2lb to that rival and looks the type to find another race in the coming weeks. (tchd 4-1 and 5-1)
Lady Springbank(IRE) won readily at Doncaster last time and came into this with a very similar profile to that of her yard's winner of this race in 2006, Precocious Star. She was conceding weight all round, but still met good support to follow up. It was clear from 2f out she was in trouble, however, and this was disappointing. It may well have been this quicker surface that was to blame though, and the suspicion remains the best of her has still to be seen. Official explanation: trainer said filly lost a shoe (op 3-1)
Dazakhee was immediately outpaced and found this way too hot. This was a very stiff initial ask, however, and she should prove sharper for the run. Another furlong should also suit before long. (op 28-1)

3529 TUFFX CONSERVATORY ROOF GLASS H'CAP 6f
3:10 (3:11) (Class 4) (0-80,80) 3-Y-0+ £5,504 (£1,637; £818; £408) Stalls Centre

Form RPR
5000 1 **Sea Rover (IRE)**[16] 2998 5-8-11 63..... GregFairley 12 76
(M Brittain) *mde virtually all: rdn clr wl over 1f out: edgd rt ins fnl f: styd on wl* 7/1
-035 2 4 ½ **John Keats**[5] 3377 6-9-4 70..... DanielTudhope 15 69
(J S Goldie) *hld up in rr: hdwy 2f out: sn rdn and styd on ins fnl f: nt rch wnr* 3/1[1]
1650 3 ¾ **Bahamian Lad**[12] 3164 4-9-9 75..... FergusSweeney 11 71
(R Hollinshead) *in tch: hdwy 1/2-way: rdn to chse wnr over 1f out: kpt on same pce ins fnl f* 8/1
0500 4 1 **Resplendent Alpha**[12] 3164 5-9-3 69..... FrancisNorton 1 62
(P Howling) *rr: hdwy 2f out: sn rdn and kpt on ins fnl f: nrst fin* 10/1
-165 5 1 ¼ **Elijah Pepper (USA)**[12] 3164 4-9-4 70..... ShaneKelly 4 59
(T D Barron) *chsd ldng pair: rdn along 2f out: sn drvn and btn* 13/2[3]
0000 6 ½ **Timber Treasure (USA)**[54] 1885 5-8-13 70.....(b) MartinLane[(5)] 5 57
(Paul Green) *dwlt: a in rr* 10/1
0502 7 6 **No Grouse**[21] 2852 9-8-9 61..... AndrewMullen 13 29
(E J Alston) *in tch: rdn along 1/2-way: wknd 2f out* 8/1
1456 8 6 **Methaaly (IRE)**[6] 3335 6-10-0 80.....(be) AlanMunro 10 29
(M Mullineaux) *cl up: rdn along over 2f out: sn wknd* 7/2[2]

1m 11.63s (-2.37) **Going Correction** -0.40s/f (Firm)
WFA 3 from 4yo+ 6lb 8 Ran SP% **113.5**
Speed ratings (Par 105): **99,93,92,90,89 88,80,72**
toteswingers: 1&2 £6.10, 1&3 £9.90, 2&3 £5.80 CSF £27.86 CT £171.47 TOTE £9.50: £2.50, £1.10, £3.10; EX 32.60.
Owner Mel Brittain **Bred** Darley **Trained** Warthill, N Yorks

FOCUS
Despite the withdrawals this sprint was still an open affair and it was run at a solid pace. The form looks pretty ordinary.
Sea Rover(IRE) Official explanation: trainer's rep said, regarding apparent improvement in form, that the horse had failed to settle in previous races but appeared to benefit from racing prominently over a shorter trip.
Methaaly(IRE) Official explanation: trainer said, regarding running, that the race had come too soon and the gelding would benefit from a break.

3530 VISTA PANELS H'CAP 1m 30y
3:40 (3:40) (Class 3) (0-95,95) 3-Y-0+ £9,066 (£2,697; £1,348; £673) Stalls Low

Form RPR
4123 1 **Pride Of Kings**[20] 2890 3-8-6 82..... GregFairley 4 89
(M Johnston) *trckd ldr: hdwy to ld over 2f out: rdn wl over 1f out: drvn and hung lft ent fnl f: kpt on wl towards fin* 10/11[1]
6002 2 ¾ **Flipando (IRE)**[7] 3312 8-10-0 95..... PhillipMakin 3 102
(T D Barron) *hld up in rr: hdwy over 3f out: trckd ldng pair over 2f out: rdn to chal over 1f out: sn drvn and ev ch: edgd lft ins fnl f and no ex towards fin* 7/4[2]
-500 3 3 ¾ **Mujaadel (USA)**[12] 3172 4-8-13 80..... AndrewMullen 2 78
(D Nicholls) *trckd ldng pair: hdwy on inner 3f out: rdn and ch over 1f out: sn drvn and one pce* 13/2[3]
-403 4 3 ¼ **Summer Gold (IRE)**[21] 2842 5-8-11 78..... ShaneKelly 7 69
(E J Alston) *led: rdn along 3f out: sn hdd & wknd* 10/1

1m 41.41s (-2.39) **Going Correction** -0.10s/f (Good)
WFA 3 from 4yo+ 9lb 4 Ran SP% **111.2**
Speed ratings (Par 107): **107,106,102,99**
CSF £2.89 TOTE £1.80; EX 3.00.

Owner Jaber Abdullah **Bred** Floors Farming And Dominic Burke **Trained** Middleham Moor, N Yorks

FOCUS

Five non-runners meant that what had originally looked a decent handicap essentially boiled down to a match between the two market leaders. The runner-up is rated to his recent best.

NOTEBOOK

Pride Of Kings, taking on his elders for the first time, got his head back in front with a workmanlike display on ground that holds no fears. He was not able to dominate, but that meant he settled better than was the case on his previous run at Sandown, for which he had been upped 3lb. He showed a very honest attitude when sent to the front and, despite edging over to the far rail, was always holding off his main rival at the business end. Another rise is now forthcoming and his light weight was a decisive factor this time, but he should at least continue to pay his way. (op 5-4 tchd 11-8)

Flipando(IRE) ran right up to his best last time out and has form on this sort of ground. He predictably threw down a strong challenge when asked for his effort, but the weight concession proved beyond him. This was a very likeable effort and he really does deserve to go one better again. (op 6-4 tchd 15-8 in places)

Mujaadel(USA), 2lb lower, was first off the bridle down the home straight, but kept to his task well and ran his most encouraging race of the current campaign. He has the ability to defy this mark, but is struggling to find his optimum trip and now may be the time to try him over a little further again. (op 8-1 tchd 12-1)

Summer Gold(IRE), second over course and distance off 2lb higher three weeks earlier, was intent on leading and had her own way out in front. She was easily passed by the winner 3f out, however, and she has become an in-and-out performer. (op 13-2 tchd 11-2)

3531 SAINT-GOBAIN PLANITHERM MAIDEN STKS — 1m 30y

4:10 (4:11) (Class 5) 3-Y-O+ £3,238 (£963; £481; £240) Stalls Low

Form				RPR
20-3	1		**Captain Ellis (USA)**[12] 3155 3-9-0 80 ... AndrewElliott 5	81
			(K R Burke) *t.k.h: trckd ldrs: hdwy 4f out: led wl over 2f out: drvn clr appr fnl f and kpt on wl* **5/4**[1]	
0-3	2	3 ¾	**Flame Of Hestia (IRE)**[40] 2282 3-8-9 0 ... AlanMunro 4	67
			(J R Fanshawe) *t.k.h: trckd ldrs on inner: hdwy 3f out: swtchd rt over 1f out: chsd wnr ins fnl f: sn no imp* **9/2**[3]	
-434	3	2	**Makhaaleb (IRE)**[21] 2845 3-9-0 72 ... TPO'Shea 2	67
			(B W Hills) *trckd ldrs: effrt 3f out and sn rdn along outpcd 2f out: swtchd rt over 1f out: styd on u.p ins fnl f* **3/1**[2]	
0	4	1 ¼	**Lost In The Desert (IRE)**[21] 2856 3-9-0 0 ...(b[1]) J-PGuillambert 6	64
			(M Botti) *prom: led over 5f out: rdn along 3f out: sn hdd and drvn: wknd wl over 1f out* **16/1**	
4	5	5	**Merchant Man**[46] 2104 3-9-0 0 ... PJMcDonald 7	52
			(J D Bethell) *hld up in tch: hdwy to chse ldrs 3f out: sn rdn and wknd fnl 2f* **6/1**	
0	6	10	**Two Tone**[12] 3168 3-9-0 0 ... FergusSweeney 1	28
			(G Woodward) *a in rr* **66/1**	
6	7	61	**Wandering Minstral**[21] 2843 6-9-9 0 ... MickyFenton 8	—
			(H J L Dunlop) *led to over 5f out: rdn along and wknd 4f out* **40/1**	

1m 42.6s (-1.20) **Going Correction** -0.10s/f (Good)
WFA 3 from 6yo 9lb — 7 Ran SP% **111.7**
Speed ratings (Par 103): **102,98,96,95,90 80,19**
toteswingers: 1&2 £2.00, 1&3 £1.80, 2&3 £2.40 CSF £6.94 TOTE £2.20: £1.30, £2.20; EX 7.10.
Owner Mogeely Stud & Mrs Maura Gittins **Bred** Catesby W Clay & Robert P Levy **Trained** Middleham Moor, N Yorks
■ Stewards' Enquiry : T P O'Shea one-day ban: careless riding (Jul 16)

FOCUS

Not a bad maiden, run at a solid pace and the form makes sense rated around the front pair.

3532 RICHARD & DEBBIE SCHWARZ MEMORIAL STAYERS' H'CAP — 1m 6f

4:40 (4:40) (Class 4) (0-85,85) 4-Y-O+ £5,180 (£1,541; £770; £384) Stalls Low

Form				RPR
-665	1		**Hawridge King**[14] 3073 7-8-7 71 ... FergusSweeney 3	81
			(W S Kittow) *trckd ldng pair: hdwy 3f out: rdn to ld over 2f out: qcknd wl over 1f out: kpt on strly ins fnl f* **2/1**[1]	
1651	2	2	**Trip The Light**[16] 3000 4-8-9 73 ... TonyHamilton 6	80
			(R A Fahey) *trckd ldr: cl up 4f out: rdn to chal 3f out: drvn 2f out and ev ch tl sltly outpcd by wnr over 1f out: kpt on ins fnl f* **2/1**[1]	
0-05	3	6	**Mudawin (IRE)**[12] 3146 8-8-8 72 ... DarrenMoffatt 1	72
			(James Moffatt) *set stdy pce: rdn and qcknd 4f out: drvn 3f out: hdd over 2f out and grad wknd* **6/1**[3]	
400-	4	1 ½	**Downing Street (IRE)**[14] 6817 8-8-10 74 ...(p) ShaneKelly 4	71
			(Jennie Candlish) *hld up in tch: effrt over 4f out: sn rdn along and outpcd: kpt on u.p appr last* **8/1**	
10-0	5	3 ¼	**Ragdollianna**[19] 2931 5-8-13 77 ... KirstyMilczarek 2	69
			(Norma Twomey) *dwlt: hld up in rr: hdwy to chse ldrs 4f out: rdn along over 3f out: drvn and wknd over 2f out* **4/1**[2]	

3m 2.62s (-1.68) **Going Correction** -0.10s/f (Good) 5 Ran SP% **112.1**
Speed ratings (Par 105): **100,98,95,94,92**
CSF £6.30 TOTE £2.90: £1.60, £1.60; EX 4.70 Place 6: £7.73 Place 5: £6.24.
Owner Eric Gadsden **Bred** Old Mill Stud **Trained** Blackborough, Devon

FOCUS

A modest staying handicap, run at a fair gallop and the form makes sense, although the winner did not need to match last year's form.

T/Plt: £5.10 to a £1 stake. Pool: £56,093.22. 7,962.03 winning tickets. T/Qpdt: £2.70 to a £1 stake. Pool: £2,567.00. 681.20 winning tickets. JR

3247 NEWBURY (L-H)

Thursday, July 2

OFFICIAL GOING: Good to firm (9.4)

Wind: Virtually nil Weather: Humid

3533 LADBROKES.COM APPRENTICE H'CAP — 1m 3f 5y

6:30 (6:30) (Class 5) (0-70,67) 4-Y-O+ £2,590 (£770; £385; £192) Stalls Centre

Form				RPR
5213	1		**Hatch A Plan (IRE)**[19] 2912 8-8-9 55 ... JPHamblett(3) 6	60
			(Mouse Hamilton-Fairley) *hld up towards rr but in tch: hdwy: nt clr run and swtchd rt 3f out: drvn to ld jst ins fnl f: hung lft u.p fnl 100yds: all out* **5/1**[3]	
0/62	2	nk	**Arab League (IRE)**[17] 2975 4-8-8 51 ... AndreaAtzeni 7	55
			(R J Price) *trckd ldrs 1/2-way: chal 2f out: led briefly 1f out: sn hdd: styd pressing wnr tl carried lft fnl 100yds* **6/4**[1]	
5300	3	½	**Horseshoe Reef (AUS)**[19] 2923 6-9-10 67..(p) Louis-PhilippeBeuzelin 9	70
			(J R Gask) *chsd ldr: t.k.h: led 5f out: rdn 3f out: hdd and rdr dropped whip 1f out: styd chalng tl carried lft fnl 100yds* **15/2**	
-000	4	3 ¾	**Muffett's Dream**[9] 3247 5-8-6 49 oh3 ow1 ... MCGeran 4	46
			(J J Bridger) *led tl hdd 5f out: styd pressing ldr: outpcd fnl 2f: styd on again to take 4th fr eased rival nr fin* **10/1**	
024P	5	1	**Rosy Dawn**[14] 3074 4-8-3 51 ow1 ... DebraEngland(5) 1	49+
			(J J Bridger) *chsd ldrs: drvn to chal fr 2f out: weaking whn hmpd fnl 100yds: eased and lost 4th cl home* **14/1**	
0064	6	9	**Lilleput**[8] 3260 4-8-6 52 ... SophieDoyle(3) 3	32
			(E A Wheeler) *slowly away: in rr: hdwy 3f out: sn rdn: wknd qckly 2f out* **25/1**	
005/	7	3 ½	**Ophistrolie (IRE)**[15] 5739 7-8-0 48 oh3 ... AmyScott(5) 2	22
			(H J Manners) *in tch 7f: sn wknd* **18/1**	
1006	8	½	**Filun**[17] 2983 4-9-2 62 ... SimonPearce(3) 5	35
			(A Middleton) *chsd ldrs 1/2-way: rdn 4f out: wknd qckly over 2f out* **4/1**[2]	

2m 21.19s (-0.01) **Going Correction** -0.125s/f (Firm) 8 Ran SP% **113.3**
Speed ratings (Par 103): **95,94,94,91,90 84,81,81**
toteswingers: 1&2 £2.20, 1&3 £5.60, 2&3 £4.00 CSF £12.66 CT £54.35 TOTE £4.20: £1.50, £1.10, £2.10; EX 9.40.
Owner Hamilton-Fairley Racing **Bred** Camogue Stud Ltd **Trained** Bramshill, Hants
■ Stewards' Enquiry : J P Hamblett four-day ban: careless riding (Jul 16-19)
Debra England three-day ban: failed to ride out for fourth (Jul 16-18)

FOCUS

A hot and muggy night. The track had been watered during the heatwave, the ground was officially described as good to firm with a stick reading of 9.4. Most of the runners were struggling for form in this modest handicap. The pace was very steady, there was a tight finish and the winner had to survive a long stewards' inquiry. The time was over four seconds above standard and the form should be treated with some caution.

Lilleput Official explanation: jockey said filly hung right throughout

3534 JUDDMONTE E B F MAIDEN FILLIES' STKS — 6f 8y

7:05 (7:07) (Class 4) 2-Y-O £5,180 (£1,541; £770; £384) Stalls Centre

Form				RPR
4	1		**Full Mandate (IRE)**[8] 3277 2-9-0 0 ... RichardHughes 6	78+
			(R Hannon) *sn led: drvn along 2f out: qcknd ins fnl f and sn in command: comf* **5/2**[1]	
	2	1 ¼	**Deloria** 2-8-11 0 ... KevinGhunowa(3) 8	74+
			(Eve Johnson Houghton) *in rr but in tch: rdn 3f out and outpcd: gd hdwy appr fnl f and styd on ins fnl f: tk 2nd cl home and gng on but no ch w wnr* **20/1**	
03	3	½	**Zinjbar (USA)**[19] 2914 2-9-0 0 ... PhilipRobinson 10	72
			(C E Brittain) *chsd ldrs: rdn over 2f out: chsd wnr 1f out but nvr any imp: outpcd and lost 2nd cl home* **9/2**[3]	
5	4	3 ¾	**Blushing (IRE)**[8] 3256 2-9-0 0 ... MartinDwyer 4	61
			(B J Meehan) *chsd wnr: rdn 2f out and no imp wknd fnl f* **7/1**	
	5	1 ¾	**Theladyinquestion** 2-9-0 0 ... WilliamBuick 7	56
			(A M Balding) *chsd ldrs: rdn over 2f out: sn outpcd* **12/1**	
4	6	1 ¼	**Knockenduff**[11] 3187 2-9-0 0 ... TonyCulhane 1	52
			(M R Channon) *chsd ldrs: pushed along over 2f out: wknd over 1f out* **11/4**[2]	
	7	2	**Gold Fix (IRE)** 2-8-9 0 ... MCGeran(5) 5	46
			(M R Channon) *outpcd most of way* **16/1**	
0	8	1 ¼	**Candyfloss Girl**[9] 3248 2-9-0 0 ... EddieAhern 3	42
			(H J L Dunlop) *wnt lft s: sn chsng ldrs: wknd 2f out* **28/1**	
	9	24	**Asaba** 2-9-0 0 ... JimmyFortune 2	—
			(S Kirk) *carried lft s: a in rr* **14/1**	

1m 12.98s (-0.02) **Going Correction** -0.125s/f (Firm) 9 Ran SP% **114.4**
Speed ratings (Par 93): **95,93,92,87,85 83,81,79,47**
toteswingers: 1&2 £22.80, 1&3 £2.80, 2&3 £24.70 CSF £52.64 TOTE £3.60: £1.30, £4.50, £1.70; EX 69.50.
Owner Mrs Anna Doyle & Partners **Bred** Con Harrington **Trained** East Everleigh, Wilts

FOCUS

A maiden fillies' race that did not look particularly strong with the placed horses the best guide.

NOTEBOOK

Full Mandate(IRE) made a quick move towards the stands' rail, showed plenty of natural speed and won easing down. This represents a fair step forward from her fourth of six after an awkward start at Salisbury the previous week on her debut. She cost 60,000euros as a yearling, is a half-sister to the pretty useful 6f winner Danidh Dubai and should go on to better things. (tchd 3-1)

Deloria ◆ was the big eyecatcher, as she found a bit of trouble against the near rail but powered home and ran a very promising race on this debut. She is from a good German family, should stay further and will have learned a lot from this initial experience. (op 12-1)

Zinjbar(USA) shaped with promise when third in a 6f Leicester maiden on her second start and her finishing position here gives the form some substance. She may struggle to live up to her six-figure price tag but is bred to come into her own over further next year, so it is encouraging that she is showing promise sprinting this season. (op 6-1 tchd 13-2)

Blushing(IRE) got involved in a damaging battle for the lead with the winner and eventually paid the price for those exertions. She has probably confirmed, but not built on the debut promise of her fourth in a maiden at Bath the previous week. (op 8-1 tchd 6-1)

Knockenduff was the disappointment of the race, having looked a leading contender here after her fourth of 14 in a Pontefract maiden fillies' event on her debut. She had a tough draw to cope with and had to race down the centre of the track, but she did not really pick up for pressure and faded. (op 5-2 tchd 2-1)

Asaba Official explanation: jockey said filly moved poorly throughout

3535 JACKPOT JOY H'CAP — 1m 4f 5y

7:35 (7:36) (Class 4) (0-85,81) 3-Y-O £4,857 (£1,445; £722; £360) Stalls Centre

Form				RPR
-063	1		**Zaaqya**[23] 2796 3-9-3 77 ... RichardHughes 3	86
			(J L Dunlop) *trckd ldr to 4f out: n.m.r and hung rt 2f out: drvn to chal over 1f out: styd pressing ldr tl led last strides* **10/3**[3]	
2104	2	shd	**Ithbaat (USA)**[19] 2925 3-9-7 81 ... JimmyFortune 6	90
			(J H M Gosden) *led: 5l clr 7f out: rdn pushed along whn chal fr 2f out: styd on wl u.p whn jnd thrght fnl f: hdd last strides* **5/1**	
0431	3	6	**Parc Des Princes (USA)**[7] 3321 3-8-4 64 6ex ... WilliamBuick 1	63
			(A M Balding) *hld up in rr: hdwy on outside fr over 3f out: chsd ldng duo 1f out but nvr any ch* **11/4**[1]	
5021	4	¾	**Urban Space**[10] 3222 3-8-9 69 6ex ... EddieAhern 7	67
			(B G Powell) *chsd ldrs: wnt 2nd 4f out: upsides and drvn whn bmpd 2f out: sn one pce and wknd over 1f out* **8/1**	
5001	5	4 ½	**Fong's Alibi**[14] 3054 3-8-8 68 ...(p) SteveDrowne 5	59
			(J S Moore) *hld up in tch: chsd ldrs 4f out: hung lft 3f out and stl hanging and btn whn pushed rt 2f out* **25/1**	
50-6	6	1 ½	**Kayflar (USA)**[13] 3099 3-8-6 66 ... MartinDwyer 4	54
			(P F I Cole) *in rr: rdn 4f out: hung lft u.p and nt run on fr ins fnl 3f* **12/1**	

U1-4 7 75 **Worth A King'S**[20] 2892 3-8-8 **73** Louis-PhilippeBeuzelin(5) 2 —
(Sir Michael Stoute) *chsd ldrs: hrd rdn and wknd 4f out: t.o* **3/1**[2]
2m 33.32s (-2.18) **Going Correction** -0.125s/f (Firm) **7** Ran SP% **114.1**
Speed ratings (Par 102): **102,101,97,97,94 93,43**
toteswingers: 1&2 £3.30, 1&3 £2.00, 2&3 £2.90 CSF £20.13 TOTE £4.20: £2.50, £2.80; EX 14.40.
Owner Hamdan Al Maktoum **Bred** Launceston Stud **Trained** Arundel, W Sussex

FOCUS
A decent handicap. It was an intriguing tactical event and produced a tight finish between Hamdan Al Maktoum's two representatives, who pulled clear of the rest. The form looks pretty solid and could rate higher.

3536 SUNLEY CONDITIONS STKS 7f (S)
8:10 (8:11) (Class 3) 3-Y-0+
£7,477 (£2,239; £1,119; £560; £279; £140) **Stalls** Centre

Form RPR
24-4 1 **Gallagher**[15] 3011 3-8-5 116 MartinDwyer 4 108+
(B J Meehan) *trckd ldr: pushed along and edgd lft fr 2f out: led jst ins fnl f: drvn out* **1/1**[1]
0-12 2 2 **Plum Pudding (IRE)**[27] 2669 6-9-6 105 RichardHughes 2 113
(R Hannon) *led: rdn 2f out: hdd jst ins fnl f and sn outpcd* **5/1**[3]
1-66 3 3½ **Khor Dubai (IRE)**[27] 2673 3-8-8 100 (v) WilliamBuick 3 97
(Saeed Bin Suroor) *in tch: wnt 3rd 3f out: shkn up and kpt on fr over 1f out but nvr nr ldng duo* **12/1**
0020 4 6 **Intrepid Jack**[12] 3140 7-9-2 105 SteveDrowne 1 83
(H Morrison) *chsd ldrs but nvr on terms: rdn over 3f out: wknd over 2f out* **12/1**
6-26 5 2¾ **Patrician's Glory (USA)**[15] 3011 3-8-0 103.. Louis-PhilippeBeuzelin(5) 5 70
(T P Tate) *plld hrd: in tch to 1/2-way: sn rdn and wknd* **4/1**[2]
4050 6 4½ **Vitznau (IRE)**[5] 3398 5-8-13 104 EddieAhern 6 61
(R Hannon) *sn bhd* **17/2**
1m 23.53s (-2.17) **Going Correction** -0.125s/f (Firm)
WFA 3 from 5yo+ 8lb **6** Ran SP% **112.6**
Speed ratings (Par 107): **107,104,100,93,90 85**
toteswingers: 1&2 £2.00, 1&3 £5.20, 2&3 £9.80. CSF £6.46 TOTE £2.20: £1.40, £1.80; EX 5.00.
Owner Brimacombe, McNally, Rickman & Sangster **Bred** Ptarmigan Bloodstock Limited **Trained** Manton, Wilts

FOCUS
A classy event in which the winner did not need to run to his juvenile best. The first two were always prominent and nothing else got into it.

NOTEBOOK
Gallagher was beaten less than a length three times in Group contests as a two-year-old and proved he retains ability when fourth in the Jersey Stakes at Royal Ascot on his belated return last month. He had a clear advantage on official figures, swept alongside the leader a furlong out and forged clear for an authoritative success. His plans are fluid at the moment but he could step up to 1m for his next assignment. (tchd 11-10)
Plum Pudding(IRE) is a specialist on the Rowley track at Newmarket but he has been in great form elsewhere this season, winning at Warwick on his reappearance and finishing a fine second off 105 in an Epsom handicap last time. He had no easy task conceding weight to all his rivals but gave it a good shot from the front and put in another commendable effort. (tchd 9-2 and 6-1)
Khor Dubai(IRE) was the worst in here on BHA figures and was never a factor but he does deserve some credit for doing best of those who came from off the pace. (op 11-1 tchd 10-1)
Intrepid Jack finished tailed off when flying too high in a Group 1 at Royal Ascot last month. He was expected to bounce back to some degree in more realistic company but put in a very laboured effort and, as a former runner-up in a Bunbury Cup, the trip cannot be cited as an excuse. (op 10-1)
Patrician's Glory(USA) was two places and less than two lengths behind Gallagher on these terms when sixth in the Jersey Stakes, but he was beaten out of sight by the winner here. (op 5-1)
Vitznau(IRE) was not at his best in a Group 3 the previous week, was deserted by Richard Hughes here and put in another lacklustre effort. (op 12-1 tchd 14-1)

3537 MATRIX FILLIES' H'CAP 7f (S)
8:40 (8:43) (Class 4) (0-80,80) 3-Y-0+ **£4,857** (£1,083; £1,083; £360) **Stalls** Centre

Form RPR
2234 1 **Perfect Friend**[5] 3387 3-9-1 **74** JimmyFortune 8 83+
(S Kirk) *hld up in rr: gd hdwy over 2f out: drvn to ld jst ins fnl f: hung lft fnl 100yds but a in command* **4/1**[1]
-052 2 ¾ **Ken's Girl**[18] 2949 5-9-2 **67** TonyCulhane 6 75
(W S Kittow) *sn led: narrowly hdd over 3f out: styd pressing ldr and chal 1f out: one pce whn carried lft fnl 100yds* **10/1**
0602 2 dht **My Best Bet**[5] 3387 3-8-6 **70** MCGeran(5) 10 75
(M R Channon) *s.i.s: t.k.h: sn chsng ldrs: rdn and one pce over 2f out: styd on again fr over 1f out: fin wl to dispute 2nd on line but a hld by wnr* **7/1**
0212 4 2¼ **Arabian Pearl (IRE)**[17] 2967 3-8-13 **77** Louis-PhilippeBeuzelin(5) 2 76
(P W Chapple-Hyam) *chsd ldrs: rdn and ev ch fr 2f out: slt ld 1f out: hdd sn after: one pce whn crossed fnl 100yds* **9/2**[2]
2-1 5 ½ **Shangani**[23] 2795 3-8-11 **77** AmyScott(7) 4 75
(H Candy) *chsd ldrs: led over 3f out: rdn over 2f out: hdd 1f out: wknd ins fnl f* **5/1**[3]
2241 6 ½ **Cape Melody**[20] 2879 3-9-2 **75** SteveDrowne 3 71
(H Morrison) *s.i.s: in rr: rdn and sme hdwy fr 2f out but nvr gng pce to trble ldrs* **9/1**
-505 7 4 **Ballyalla**[18] 2948 3-9-7 **80** (t) RichardHughes 1 65
(R Hannon) *chsd ldrs: rdn over 2f out: nvr gng pce to chal: wknd fnl f: eased whn no ch* **13/2**
3213 8 4½ **Cheap Thrills**[27] 2661 3-9-3 **76** EddieAhern 12 49
(J A Osborne) *chsd ldrs over 4f* **8/1**
5-00 9 11 **The Jostler**[13] 3102 4-9-13 **78** WilliamBuick 7 25
(Mrs L Wadham) *a towards rr* **16/1**
1m 24.68s (-1.02) **Going Correction** -0.125s/f (Firm)
WFA 3 from 4yo+ 8lb **9** Ran SP% **116.8**
Speed ratings (Par 102): **100,99,99,96,96 95,90,85,73**PL: Perfect Friend £1.80, Ken's Girl £3.60, My Best Bet £2.10. Exacta: PF-KG £27.20, PF-MBB £16.20. CSF: PF-KG £22.39, PF-MBB £16.28. Tricast: PF-KG-MBB £136.75, PF-MBB-KG £131.44. toteswinger: PF-KG £6.40, PF-MBB £5.60, KG-MBB £25.80. TOTE £5.10.
■ Stewards' Enquiry : Jimmy Fortune two-day ban: careless riding (Jul 16-17)

FOCUS
A fair handicap run at a reasonable pace and the form is best rated around the placed horses.
Arabian Pearl(IRE) Official explanation: jockey said filly was unsuited by the good to firm ground
Ballyalla Official explanation: jockey said saddle slipped
The Jostler Official explanation: jockey said filly was unsuited by the good to firm ground

3538 URBANMAPZ.CO.UK MAIDEN STKS 1m 4f 5y
9:10 (9:11) (Class 5) 3-Y-0+ **£4,209** (£1,252; £625; £312) **Stalls** Centre

Form RPR
0-23 1 **Putra One (IRE)**[66] 1573 3-9-0 83 PhilipRobinson 2 70+
(M A Jarvis) *led 2f: styd trcking clr ldr: qcknd to ld over 2f out: drvn and hung lft ins fnl f: pushed out* **4/9**[1]
-55 2 ¾ **Penolva (IRE)**[14] 3056 3-8-9 0 AndrewElliott 7 64+
(K R Burke) *led after 2f: 8l clr over 5f out: hdd over 2f out: sn rdn: styd 1l down on wnr and rdn and n.m.r on rails and swtchd rt ins fnl f: kpt on same pce* **11/2**[2]
0 3 4 **Miss Doodle**[15] 3025 3-8-9 0 EddieAhern 1 58+
(Eve Johnson Houghton) *rdn in rr 4f out: styd on fr over 2f out to take 3rd ins fnl f but nvr anywhere nr ldng duo* **25/1**
0-40 4 2¼ **Millharbour (IRE)**[21] 2850 3-9-0 70 WilliamBuick 6 59
(B W Hills) *in tch: rdn to chse ldrs and hung lft 3f out: nvr in contention and continued to hang: wknd over 1f out* **11/1**
5 5 **Cecily Parsley** 3-8-9 0 (t) SteveDrowne 4 46+
(H Morrison) *chsd ldrs: rdn and green over 3f out: wknd fr 2f out* **15/2**[3]
04 6 2¾ **Boffin**[19] 2922 4-9-13 0 TonyCulhane 3 47
(Eve Johnson Houghton) *rdn and hung lft over 3f out: a bhd* **40/1**
2m 33.09s (-2.41) **Going Correction** -0.125s/f (Firm)
WFA 3 from 4yo 13lb **6** Ran SP% **111.0**
Speed ratings (Par 103): **103,102,99,98,95 93**
toteswingers: 1&2 £1.10, 1&3 £7.10, 2&3 £12.10. CSF £3.25 TOTE £1.40: £1.10, £2.20; EX 2.90 Place 6: £21.38, Place 5: £14.99..
Owner H R H Sultan Ahmad Shah **Bred** Airlie Stud **Trained** Newmarket, Suffolk

FOCUS
A fair maiden but the winner did not have to run to his previous form to score.
T/Plt: £17.20 to a £1 stake. Pool: £50,805.66. 2,146.26 winning tickets. T/Qpdt: £9.90 to a £1 stake. Pool: £3,427.70. 254.40 winning tickets. ST

3170 REDCAR (L-H)
Thursday, July 2

OFFICIAL GOING: Firm (good to firm in places; 10.5)
Wind: light, half behind Weather: fine and sunny

3539 THE COMMITMENTS ARE PERFORMING HERE ON 29TH AUGUST APPRENTICE CLAIMING STKS 7f
6:10 (6:20) (Class 5) 3-Y-0+ **£2,914** (£867; £433; £216) **Stalls** Centre

Form RPR
0013 1 **Dabbers Ridge (IRE)**[3] 3467 7-9-8 80 GaryBartley(3) 5 71
(I W McInnes) *hld up: outpcd over 2f out: hung lft and chsd ldrs over 1f out: kpt on to ld ins fnl f* **11/8**[1]
0530 2 1¼ **Efidium**[13] 3124 11-9-1 59 JamieKyne(3) 8 60
(N Bycroft) *chsd ldrs: kpt on same pce fnl f* **11/2**[3]
1146 3 1¼ **Seneschal**[20] 2883 8-9-6 75 PNolan(3) 3 62
(A B Haynes) *w ldr: led on bit over 1f out: sn shkn up: fnd nil and hdd ins fnl f: wknd towards fin* **13/8**[2]
0043 4 1½ **Sheik'N'Knotsterd**[12] 3175 4-9-4 53 DeanHeslop(3) 6 56
(J F Coupland) *led tl over 1f out: one pce* **33/1**
0050 5 3½ **Boss Hog**[45] 2133 4-9-1 55 PaulPickard(3) 2 44
(P T Midgley) *in rr: drvn and hdwy 3f out: wknd over 1f out* **12/1**
0-60 6 2 **Borodinsky**[12] 3174 8-9-1 44 AmyRyan(3) 4 38
(R E Barr) *unruly s: chsd ldrs: drvn over 3f out: sn wl outpcd* **66/1**
0/0- 7 18 **Flaming Cat (IRE)**[463] 1025 6-9-1 40 (p) LanceBetts(3) 1 —
(F Watson) *s.v.s: hdwy to chse ldrs over 4f out: sn rdn and lost pl: t.o* **66/1**
1m 24.53s (0.03) **Going Correction** -0.05s/f (Good) **7** Ran SP% **109.2**
Speed ratings (Par 103): **97,95,94,92,88 86,65**
toteswingers: 1&2 £1.40, 1&3 £1.10, 2&3 £2.20 CSF £8.53 TOTE £2.30: £1.60, £2.00; EX 8.30.
Owner M Shirley **Bred** Franco Castelfranci **Trained** Catwick, E Yorks

FOCUS
This was delayed for ten minutes when Yahwudwee broke out of the starting stalls and galloped down the track, while Borodinksy then gave trouble during the re-loading process. The winner did not have to run to his mark and the form is not solid, with the moderate fourth and fifth not beaten far.

3540 GLANBIA NUTRITIONALS NURSERY 5f
6:40 (6:43) (Class 4) 2-Y-0 **£5,180** (£1,541; £770; £384) **Stalls** Centre

Form RPR
21 1 **Singeur (IRE)**[30] 2575 2-9-4 **73** PatCosgrave 6 77
(R Bastiman) *racd alone stands' side: chsd ldrs: edgd lft and styd on wl to ld last 100yds* **4/1**[2]
41 2 1 **Vilnius**[71] 1450 2-8-5 **60** PaulHanagan 1 60
(M R Channon) *swvd lft s: sn chsng ldr: led 1f out: edgd rt: hdd and no ex last 100yds* **9/4**[1]
6313 3 2¾ **Oondiri (IRE)**[27] 2655 2-9-0 **69** (b[1]) DavidAllan 3 59
(T D Easterby) *led: edgd lft: hdd and racd far side over 1f out: wknd* **9/2**[3]
633 4 ¾ **Makbullet**[19] 2936 2-9-7 **76** PaulMulrennan 4 63
(J Howard Johnson) *chsd ldrs: drvn and outpcd over 2f out: kpt on ins fnl f* **4/1**[2]
646 5 3¾ **Prettiest Star (IRE)**[19] 2914 2-8-6 **61** RichardMullen 7 35
(K A Ryan) *swvd rt s: sn outpcd and detached in last: kpt on fnl 2f: nvr on terms* **14/1**
5203 6 1 **Parbold Hill**[20] 2893 2-9-3 **72** (b[1]) PhillipMakin 5 42
(T D Barron) *trckd ldrs: rdn over 2f out: lost pl over 1f out* **5/1**
58.73 secs (0.13) **Going Correction** -0.05s/f (Good) **6** Ran SP% **112.3**
Speed ratings (Par 96): **96,94,90,88,82 81**
toteswingers: 1&2 £2.00, 1&3 £4.00, 2&3 £2.10 CSF £13.44 TOTE £5.80: £2.80, £1.30; EX 16.00.
Owner Ms M Austerfield **Bred** Patrick Cassidy **Trained** Cowthorpe, N Yorks

FOCUS
The first nursery of the current season and a modest affair best rated through the runner-up. The 'official' ratings shown next to each horse are estimated and for information purposes only.

NOTEBOOK
Singeur(IRE) had seemed to be going the right way in his two starts and showed plenty of toughness to knuckle down and take this prize having been pushed along to keep up at the halfway stage. His trainer said he had no particular plans for the Chineur colt, who has an interesting pedigree with plenty of stamina on the dam's side and who holds an entry in the Redcar Two-Year-Old Trophy later in the season. However he will not go up much in the weights for this and could well take another nursery even if he bypasses a possible engagement at Musselburgh on Monday. (op 11-2)

Vilnius was one of the best-backed horses of the day and she ran creditably, albeit in receipt of almost a stone from the winner. She had won what had looked a pretty poor seller on her previous start more than two months earlier, but a couple of subsequent winners had come out of that race and she is probably capable of improving again. (op 3-1)
Oondiri(IRE) who had come unstuck in novice company on her previous start, was quickly away as is her style. With headgear on for the first time, she seemed happy bowling along in front but drifted left as she started to tire and ended up on the far rail as her rivals swept past in the centre of the course. Judged on pedigree, she could do better as she progresses physically. (op 4-1)
Makbullet remains a maiden, which might help connectons find a race for him, but he did not find a great deal when asked to quicken up. (op 3-1)
Parbold Hill took a backward step in the first-time blinkers. (op 6-1 tchd 7-1)

3541 WIN A VIP DAY OUT @ REDCARRACING.CO.UK (S) STKS 1m
7:15 (7:15) (Class 5) 3-4-Y-O £2,729 (£806; £403) Stalls Centre

Form RPR
6050 1 **Arizona John (IRE)**[19] 2938 4-9-2 71 DarryllHolland 10 70+
(N Wilson) *stdd s: hdwy on ins over 2f out: rdn: hung lft and led jst ins fnl f: drvn clr* **11/10**[1]
0033 2 2 ½ **Wiseman's Diamond (USA)**[12] 3174 4-8-4 55 PaulPickard(7) 6 59
(P T Midgley) *chsd ldrs on ins: led over 2f out: hdd jst ins fnl f: no ex* **7/2**[2]
-000 3 5 **Rowaad**[10] 3208 4-9-2 48 (v) GrahamGibbons 5 53
(A E Price) *trckd ldrs: upsides over 2f out: wknd fnl f* **16/1**
0346 4 5 **Premier Krug (IRE)**[3] 3451 3-7-13 45 KellyHarrison(3) 8 34
(P D Evans) *chsd ldrs: wknd over 1f out* **7/1**[3]
446 5 nk **Cash In The Attic**[2] 3473 3-8-2 49 PaulHanagan 9 33
(M R Channon) *in rr-div: hdwy over 3f out: sn chsng ldrs: lost pl over 1f out* **10/1**
60 6 1 ¾ **Flaming Blaze**[26] 2104 3-8-2 0 (t) PatrickDonaghy(5) 1 34
(P C Haslam) *rrd s: in rr: nvr a factor* **100/1**
0042 7 3 ¼ **Nchike**[41] 2234 3-8-7 62 (v) PaulQuinn 3 27
(D Nicholls) *prom: drvn over 3f out: sn lost pl* **11/1**
0-00 8 ½ **Reel Bluff**[13] 3108 3-8-8 50 ow1 TomEaves 7 27
(D W Barker) *led tl over 2f out: lost pl over 1f out* **33/1**
6500 9 1 ½ **Knock Three Times (IRE)**[28] 2627 3-7-11 44 JamieKyne(5) 11 17
(W Storey) *sn drvn along towards rr: bhd fnl 3f* **40/1**
3-00 10 ½ **Karate Queen**[63] 1628 4-8-6 48 AmyRyan(5) 2 18
(R E Barr) *sn outpcd and in rr: bhd fnl 3f* **22/1**
1m 36.66s (-1.34) **Going Correction** -0.05s/f (Good)
WFA 3 from 4yo 9lb 10 Ran SP% **116.4**
Speed ratings (Par 103): **104,101,96,91,91 89,86,85,84,83**
toteswingers: 1&2 £1.80, 1&3 £3.30, 2&3 £14.40 CSF £4.64 TOTE £2.10: £1.02, £2.10, £5.10; EX 6.10.There was no bid for the winner.
Owner B Plows P M Watson J Owen **Bred** Abergwaun Farms **Trained** Flaxton, N Yorks
■ Stewards' Enquiry : Darryll Holland caution: used whip down shoulder in the forehand position.
FOCUS
A very weak heat but the form makes sense.

3542 MARKET CROSS JEWELLERS NURSERY 6f
7:45 (7:45) (Class 6) 2-Y-O £2,388 (£705; £352) Stalls Centre

Form RPR
425 1 **Military Call**[44] 2153 2-8-7 69 RichardMullen 8 74
(E S McMahon) *trckd ldrs: effrt 2f out: sn chsng ldr: styd on to ld last 75yds: all out* **4/1**[2]
2313 2 hd **Transfixed (IRE)**[38] 2319 2-7-13 64 ow3 KellyHarrison(3) 4 68
(P D Evans) *led: wandered appr fnl f: hd wl ins fnl f: kpt on wl towards fin: jst hld* **5/1**[3]
661 3 4 ½ **Saxby (IRE)**[16] 2996 2-8-13 75 SamHitchcott 6 66
(M R Channon) *sn chsng ldrs: effrt over 2f out: n.m.r over 1f out: styd on same pce* **7/2**[1]
6166 4 1 ¾ **Dispol Kabira**[16] 2996 2-8-0 62 DuranFentiman 5 47
(P T Midgley) *hld up: effrt over 2f out: sn rdn: wknd over 1f out* **40/1**
3063 5 ¾ **Gentle Beat (IRE)**[12] 3152 2-8-11 73 DavidAllan 1 56
(T D Easterby) *chsd ldrs: wknd over 1f out* **7/1**
2130 6 ¾ **Dancing Freddy (IRE)**[16] 2995 2-9-7 88 JamieKyne(5) 9 69
(J G Given) *racd stands' side: w ldrs: rdn and edgd rt 2f out: sn wknd* **7/2**[1]
41 7 2 ¾ **Whispered Times (USA)**[28] 2623 2-9-4 80 PaulMulrennan 3 56+
(P C Haslam) *w ldrs: hung lft and lost pl over 1f out* **4/1**[2]
1m 11.28s (-0.52) **Going Correction** -0.05s/f (Good) 7 Ran SP% **116.1**
Speed ratings (Par 92): **101,100,94,92,91 90,86**
toteswingers: 1&2 £3.40, 1&3 £2.20, 2&3 £2.10 CSF £24.82 CT £76.41 TOTE £3.60: £1.40, £4.30; EX 21.30.
Owner J C Fretwell **Bred** Southill Stud **Trained** Lichfield, Staffs
■ Stewards' Enquiry : Kelly Harrison three-day ban: improper riding (Jul 16-18); two-day ban: used whip with excessive frequency (Jul 19-20)
FOCUS
This second nursery of the current season was another ordinary race but the first two finished clear and the form looks sound. The 'official' ratings shown next to each horse are estimated and for information purposes only.
NOTEBOOK
Military Call travelled well behind the early pace and although he did not find a great deal when asked to quicken up, he eventually got the better of the battle. He had been given a six-week break since disappointing when favourite at Musselburgh. At this stage of his career, it is probably wise to give him the benefit of the doubt given that this was just his fourth race, and he may have more to offer now he has got his head in front. Connections were reportedly expecting him to want softer ground. (op 11-2 tchd 6-1)
Transfixed(IRE) was given a strong ride by her apprentice jockey, who was unable to claim her allowance due to overweight. The filly has been a model of consistency, finishing in the first three on all six of her starts, and the way that she was rallying close home suggests she may be as effective stepped up to 7f. (op 8-1 tchd 9-2)
Saxby(IRE) had to drop down to selling company to break his duck on his previous start but should be rated better than this result suggests. He seemed to prop slightly coming out of the stalls and lost ground at the start before also meeting trouble in running when seemingly going quite well 2f out. He is probably worth another chance. (tchd 3-1 and 4-1)
Dispol Kabira was noted staying on at the finish having been scrubbed along from an early stage. (op 33-1)
Dancing Freddy(IRE) looked likely to be involved in the finish with a couple of furlongs to run but seemed to be anchored by his weight and his effort petered out quickly close home. (tchd 5-1)

3543 GO RACING IN YORKSHIRE SUMMER FESTIVAL H'CAP 1m 2f
8:20 (8:20) (Class 4) (0-85,83) 3-Y-O £5,828 (£1,734; £866; £432) Stalls High

Form RPR
0513 1 **Geneva Geyser (GER)**[31] 2545 3-9-5 81 MickyFenton 4 86
(J M P Eustace) *mde all: kpt on wl fnl 2f: hld on wl* **7/2**[3]
1022 2 1 ½ **Sign Of Approval**[15] 3026 3-8-9 76 (p) MartinLane(5) 5 78
(K R Burke) *chsd ldr: chal 4f out: sn rdn: styd on same pce fnl f* **11/4**[2]
1646 3 shd **Hatta Diamond (IRE)**[30] 2571 3-8-10 72 GregFairley 3 74
(M Johnston) *in rr: drvn over 4f out: carried hd high: kpt on wl ins fnl f* **11/4**[2]
2252 4 2 ½ **Gaily Noble (IRE)**[51] 1971 3-9-7 83 PhillipMakin 1 80
(A B Haynes) *hld up in rr: smooth hdwy over 3f out: rdn over 2f out: wknd over 1f out* **85/40**[1]
2m 5.90s (-1.20) **Going Correction** -0.05s/f (Good) 4 Ran SP% **107.6**
Speed ratings (Par 102): **102,100,100,98**
CSF £12.69 TOTE £4.30; EX 7.90.
Owner J C Smith **Bred** Graf And Grafin Von Stauffenberg **Trained** Newmarket, Suffolk
FOCUS
A modest handicap run at a fair pace and best rated around the runner-up.

3544 FAMILY FUN DAY SUNDAY 19TH JULY H'CAP 1m 6f 19y
8:50 (8:50) (Class 5) (0-70,66) 4-Y-O+ £3,885 (£1,156; £577; £288) Stalls High

Form RPR
-241 1 **Master Nimbus**[12] 3171 9-9-4 63 GrahamGibbons 5 69
(J J Quinn) *trckd ldrs: stdy hdwy over 3f out: led 1f out: hld on wl* **10/3**[2]
0511 2 ¾ **Zefooha (FR)**[17] 2969 5-9-4 63 JamieMoriarty 1 68
(T D Walford) *trckd ldrs: drvn 4f out: ev ch 1f out: no ex fnl 75yds* **11/4**[1]
413 3 shd **Dramatic Solo**[26] 2720 4-9-1 65 (b) MartinLane(5) 6 70
(K R Burke) *led: qcknd over 4f out: hdd 1f out: no ex* **8/1**
6543 4 1 ¼ **Cripsey Brook**[12] 3171 11-8-11 56 PaulHanagan 8 59
(K G Reveley) *hld up in rr: effrt 4f out: styd on strly ins fnl f* **10/1**
4012 5 ¾ **Desert Destiny**[14] 3059 9-9-6 65 TonyHamilton 2 67
(C Grant) *trckd ldrs: effrt over 2f out: one pce* **8/1**
5132 6 2 ¼ **Paddy Rielly (IRE)**[23] 2798 4-9-0 66 (p) AndrewHeffernan(7) 4 65
(P D Evans) *t.k.h in midfield: hdwy on ins over 3f out: edgd rt: no imp and edgd lft ins fnl f* **6/1**
0041 7 8 **Lord Oroko**[32] 2519 5-9-2 61 TGMcLaughlin 3 49
(J G M O'Shea) *dwlt: hld up in rr: drvn over 3f out: nvr on terms: wknd fnl f* **11/2**[3]
3m 8.16s (3.46) **Going Correction** -0.05s/f (Good) 7 Ran SP% **110.7**
Speed ratings (Par 103): **88,87,87,86,86 85,80**
toteswingers: 1&2 £2.00, 1&3 £28.50, 2&3 £11.50. CSF £12.07 CT £61.60 TOTE £2.80: £1.80, £1.90; EX 6.60.
Owner J H Hewitt **Bred** A H Bennett **Trained** Settrington, N Yorks
FOCUS
A moderate staying handicap, run at an uneven gallop but the form is straightforward.

3545 REDCARRACING.CO.UK FILLIES' H'CAP 1m 2f
9:20 (9:20) (Class 5) (0-70,70) 3-Y-O+ £3,238 (£963; £481; £240) Stalls High

Form RPR
-440 1 **Tour D'Amour (IRE)**[37] 2362 6-8-11 50 (p) TomEaves 3 55
(R Craggs) *chsd ldrs: effrt and plld wd over 3f out: str run fnl f: led last 50yds* **10/1**
-211 2 1 **Stateside (CAN)**[2] 3481 4-9-6 59 6ex PaulHanagan 5 62
(R A Fahey) *led: qcknd over 4f out: hdd and no ex wl ins fnl f* **5/4**[1]
0-65 3 hd **Charismatic Lady**[44] 2170 3-8-12 62 DarryllHolland 4 65
(M Botti) *chsd ldrs: drvn over 4f out: nt clr run on inner over 2f out: edgd rt over 1f out: kpt on wl ins fnl f* **5/1**[3]
03 4 3 ¼ **Awaken**[7] 3314 8-8-9 48 oh3 GregFairley 1 45
(Miss Tracy Waggott) *early and bolted 4f gng to post: t.k.h towards rr: effrt over 3f out: kpt on: nvr a threat* **20/1**
0545 5 shd **Flora's Pride**[11] 3188 5-9-3 56 PhillipMakin 2 52
(K G Reveley) *hld up in rr: effrt on outside over 2f out: kpt on fnl f* **12/1**
1-04 6 1 ¼ **Chantilly Pearl (USA)**[17] 2967 3-9-6 70 PatCosgrave 8 64
(J G Given) *trckd ldrs: drvn over 4f out: chal over 2f out: hung lft and wknd ins fnl f* **5/2**[2]
004 7 2 ¼ **Waltzalong (IRE)**[27] 2659 3-8-6 56 DuranFentiman 7 45
(T D Easterby) *chsd ldr: chal over 3f out: wknd fnl 2f* **40/1**
0-06 8 5 **Royal Fantasy (IRE)**[12] 3151 6-10-0 67 DavidAllan 6 46
(N Tinkler) *t.k.h in rr: effrt over 3f out: edgd lft and wknd 2f out* **28/1**
2m 8.71s (1.61) **Going Correction** -0.05s/f (Good)
WFA 3 from 4yo+ 11lb 8 Ran SP% **117.1**
Speed ratings (Par 100): **91,90,90,87,87 86,84,80**
toteswingers: 1&2 £2.10, 1&3 £6.40, 2&3 £3.60. CSF £23.29 CT £74.35 TOTE £16.70: £2.80, £1.10, £1.90; EX 34.10 Place 6: £110.87, Place 5: £60.79..
Owner Ray Craggs **Bred** Peter McCutcheon **Trained** Sedgefield, Co Durham
FOCUS
A moderate fillies' handicap and slowly run. The winner and third set the level.
Tour D'Amour(IRE) Official explanation: trainer said, regarding apparent improvement in form, that the mare's penultimate run had come too soon.
T/Plt: £272.50 to a £1 stake. Pool: £41,132.74. 110.18 winning tickets. T/Qpdt: £57.80 to a £1 stake. Pool: £3,143.95. 40.20 winning tickets. WG

3004 YARMOUTH (L-H)
Thursday, July 2

OFFICIAL GOING: Good to firm (9.2)
Wind: nil Weather: sunny and hot

3546 EUROPEAN BREEDERS' FUND MAIDEN STKS 6f 3y
2:30 (2:33) (Class 5) 2-Y-O £3,784 (£1,132; £566; £283; £141) Stalls High

Form RPR
2 1 **Showcasing**[21] 2844 2-9-3 0 JimmyFortune 6 89+
(J H M Gosden) *mde all: pushed along and drew clr ent fnl f: easily* **4/11**[1]
2 3 ½ **Cansili Star** 2-9-3 0 PhilipRobinson 9 76+
(M A Jarvis) *chsd wnr 2f out: outpcd by ldng pair over 1f out: kpt on again ins fnl f to go 2nd towards fin: no ch w wnr* **8/1**[2]
65 3 ½ **Amno Dancer (IRE)**[15] 3017 2-9-3 0 JerryO'Dwyer 4 74
(M H Tompkins) *chsd ldng pair: wnt 2nd 2f out: rdn and tried to chal over 1f out: outpcd by wnr fnl f: lost 2nd towards fin* **100/1**
4 1 ¼ **Azizi** 2-9-3 0 RHills 3 73+
(W J Haggas) *s.i.s: in tch in midfield: pushed along and outpcd ent fnl 2f: kpt on steadily fnl f* **18/1**
0 5 3 **Kahail (USA)**[13] 3113 2-9-3 0 (t) KShea 5 61
(Miss D Mountain) *chsd ldrs: hung lft fr 3f out: rdn and wknd wl over 1f out* **100/1**
6 4 **Professor John (IRE)** 2-9-3 0 ChrisCatlin 8 49
(M L W Bell) *in tch: rdn and struggling wl over 2f out: no ch w ldrs fnl 2f* **50/1**
0 7 ½ **Edward Whymper**[13] 3113 2-9-3 0 SaleemGolam 2 48
(M H Tompkins) *awkward leaving stalls and slowly away: rn v green in rr: n.d* **100/1**

8 ½ **Seamster** 2-9-3 0 .... DO'Donohoe 7 46
(Saeed Bin Suroor) *s.i.s: sn in tch in midfield: rdn jst over 2f out: sn wl btn* **8/1**[2]

9 shd **Demonstrative (USA)** 2-9-3 0 .... RoystonFfrench 11 49+
(M Johnston) *restless in stalls: s.i.s: sn pushed along in rr: sme late hdwy* **10/1**[3]

10 17 **Refuse To Tell** 2-9-3 0 .... NCallan 10 —
(C E Brittain) *s.i.s: sn bustled along: bhd fr 1/2-way: t.o* **33/1**

11 13 **Securitisation (IRE)** 2-9-3 0 .... TPQueally 1 —
(B J Curley) *v.s.a and lost many l s: a t.o* **125/1**

1m 13.66s (-0.74) **Going Correction** -0.20s/f (Firm) 11 Ran SP% **118.6**
Speed ratings (Par 94): **96,91,90,89,85 79,79,78,78,55 38**
toteswingers: 1&2 £2.90, 1&3 £11.00, 2&3 £29.10 CSF £4.04 TOTE £1.50: £1.02, £2.10, £14.30; EX 4.80 Trifecta £296.70 Pool: £557.46 - 1.39 winning units..
Owner K Abdulla **Bred** Juddmonte Farms Ltd **Trained** Newmarket, Suffolk

FOCUS
An ordinary maiden overall but Showcasing is a smart prospect and looks Listed level at least.

NOTEBOOK
Showcasing showed a huge amount of promise when a neck second on his debut in a competitive race at Newbury and did not have to improve on that effort to dispose of these rivals with plenty to spare. He raced enthusiastically in the lead and had matters sewn up in the final furlong. He will not be easily beaten next time. (op 8-15)

Cansili Star ◆ is a smallish, neat colt who is a half-brother to the useful miler Jawaab. He looked as if the race would do him good and this was a pleasing start to his career. He snatched second, but had no chance with the winner. He can certainly score. (op 7-1)

Amno Dancer(IRE) had shown modest form in two 6f maidens but did a little better here, and was comfortably clear of the rest.

Azizi, a small, neat colt, kept on steadily in the closing stages without threatening and showed a degree of promise. (op 16-1)

Kahail(USA) is robust and needed the outing. He tracked the leaders but was never quite on an even keel and might prefer softer ground, although it would have been more encouraging if he had kept straighter. His trainer is 0-40 with two-year-olds in the last five years. (op 66-1)

Professor John(IRE) was a bit backward and eventually well beaten. (op 66-1)

Edward Whymper has a mountain to climb if he is to make a racehorse. (op 150-1)

Seamster cost 90,000gns but is very small and unimpressive and if he proves to be a bargain it will be a big surprise on this evidence. (op 5-1)

Demonstrative(USA) towered over these in the paddock. He was extremely green until the penny dropped late on and can only have benefited from the experience. (op 12-1 tchd 9-1)

Refuse To Tell had two handlers and was sweating and on his toes.

Securitisation(IRE) was on his toes and keen to the post. He completely missed the break and was always tailed off. Official explanation: jockey said colt was slowly away (op 100-1)

3547 AVENUE (S) STKS 6f 3y
3:00 (3:01) (Class 6) 2-Y-0 **£1,942** (£578; £288; £144) **Stalls** High

Form				RPR
0	**1**		**Vested Interest**[45] 2128 2-8-6 0 .... MatthewDavies(5) 7 (George Baker) *mde all: rdn and flashed tail over 1f out: sn clr: in n.d fnl f: pushed out* **11/2**[2]	76+
00	**2**	10	**Steeley Flyer**[16] 2996 2-8-6 0 .... SaleemGolam 9 (P D Evans) *taken down early: hld up towards rr: rdn and effrt over 2f out: drvn over 1f out: wnt modest 2nd ins fnl f: no ch w wnr* **14/1**	41
604	**3**	1 ½	**Ba Jetstream**[10] 3203 2-8-11 0 .... JimmyQuinn 5 (M R Channon) *bhd: rdn and hdwy on outer wl over 2f out: drvn and pressing for modest 2nd over 1f out: plugged on same pce fnl f* **11/1**	41
0060	**4**	nk	**Magneto (IRE)**[19] 2906 2-8-11 0 .... EdwardCreighton 10 (E J Creighton) *chsd ldrs: rdn 2f out: sn wl outpcd by wnr: plugged on same pce fnl f* **22/1**	40
63	**5**	¾	**Acting Elegant**[17] 2978 2-8-3 0 .... DavidProbert(3) 6 (P D Evans) *racd in midfield: rdn over 3f out: drvn and btn 2f out: no ch after* **3/1**[1]	33
540	**6**	shd	**Rakhine (IRE)**[20] 2896 2-8-11 0 ....(b[1]) NCallan 8 (P F I Cole) *chsd wnr tl 1/2-way: sn rdn and reluctant: drvn and wl btn whn hung lft over 1f out* **3/1**[1]	38
034	**7**	1 ¾	**Vaduz**[75] 1364 2-8-6 0 .... ChrisCatlin 1 (M R Channon) *hld up in rr: rdn and effrt 1/2-way: wknd wl over 1f out* **8/1**[3]	27
00	**8**	hd	**Cygnet Committee (IRE)**[13] 3119 2-8-6 0 .... RoystonFfrench 3 (J S Wainwright) *chsd ldrs: wnt 2nd 1/2-way: outpcd by wnr wl over 1f out: lost modest 2nd ins fnl f: fdd* **33/1**	27
0	**9**	½	**Hidden City (IRE)**[20] 2896 2-8-11 0 .... LukeMorris 2 (J S Moore) *sn rdn along on outer: drvn and btn ent fnl 2f: hung lft after* **12/1**	30
	10	hd	**Steel My Heart (IRE)** 2-8-6 0 .... NeilChalmers 4 (Miss D Mountain) *s.i.s: swtchd rt s: a bhd and rn green: no ch whn hung bdly lft over 1f out* **9/1**	25

1m 14.18s (-0.22) **Going Correction** -0.20s/f (Firm) 10 Ran SP% **116.5**
Speed ratings (Par 92): **93,79,77,77,76 76,73,73,72,72**
toteswingers: 1&2 £30.10, 1&3 £10.50, 2&3 £32.50 CSF £79.18 TOTE £7.30: £2.10, £4.50, £2.60; EX 144.60 TRIFECTA Not won..The winner was bought by K. Wainwright for 17,500gns.
Owner Mrs Susan Roy **Bred** Hascombe And Valiant Studs **Trained** Moreton Morrell, Warwicks

FOCUS
Vested Interest was far too good for some very moderate opposition and sets the level.

NOTEBOOK
Vested Interest showed that the ability was there when ninth on his debut on the Southwell all-weather when not knocked about (stayed on without threatening). He was the second consecutive winner to make all and, despite flashing his tail a furlong out, he soon stormed clear. Already gelded, but clearly better than a plater, he attracted a great deal of interest in the ring afterwards and changed hands for 17,500gns. (op 12-1)

Steeley Flyer was taken to post very early. She has tried this company before without success and is obviously limited. (op 22-1)

Ba Jetstream was taken off his feet in the early stages but did pass several rivals from halfway without looking remotely like winning. He is modest. (op 8-1)

Magneto(IRE) looked well, but the drop to a seller did not help. (op 40-1)

Acting Elegant broke better but was below the form she showed in a similar race last time. (op 9-4 tchd 10-3)

Rakhine(IRE) shut up shop soon after halfway despite first-time blinkers, and is going the wrong way with every race. (op 5-2, tchd 10-3 in places)

Hidden City(IRE) looked particularly feeble in the final two furlongs. (op 11-1)

Steel My Heart(IRE) wanted to do everything except go forward and already looks out of love with the game (and this was her debut). (op 14-1)

3548 BET365 BEST ODDS GUARANTEED ON EVERY RACE H'CAP 7f 3y
3:30 (3:31) (Class 5) (0-75,75) 3-Y-0+ **£2,719** (£809; £404; £202) **Stalls** High

Form				RPR
1-04	**1**		**Pressing Matters (IRE)**[12] 3159 3-9-8 **71** ....(p) JimmyQuinn 2 (M Botti) *hld up trcking ldrs: rdn and effrt 2f out: swtchd lft jst ins fnl f: hrd drvn and r.o to ld towards fin* **9/2**[3]	75
-060	**2**	nk	**Registrar**[44] 2166 7-8-11 **52** ....(p) SaleemGolam 1 (Mrs C A Dunnett) *dwlt: in tch on outer: rdn and effrt 2f out: drvn and ev ch wl ins fnl f: no ex nr fin* **12/1**	58
6236	**3**	½	**Mutually Mine (USA)**[13] 3115 3-9-3 **66** ....(p) JerryO'Dwyer 3 (Mrs P Sly) *led: reminder over 2f out: drvn and forged 2 l clr ent fnl f: hdd and no ex towards fin* **11/2**	68
2203	**4**	nk	**Mudhish (IRE)**[3] 3469 4-9-12 **67** ....(b) NCallan 6 (C E Brittain) *swtchd lft after s: hld up in tch: rdn and effrt 2f out: drvn ent fnl f: pressed ldrs fnl 100yds: nt qckn and no imp after* **6/1**	71
3225	**5**	1 ½	**Hobson**[23] 2799 4-9-13 **68** .... StephenCarson 4 (Eve Johnson Houghton) *chsd ldr: rdn and nt qckn wl over 1f out: edging lft and one pce fnl f* **7/2**[1]	68
5201	**6**	2	**Takaamul**[16] 3007 6-9-0 **55** .... NeilChalmers 7 (K A Morgan) *hld up in last pair: rdn and effrt 2f out: no real prog: nvr trbld ldrs* **13/2**	50
1-5	**7**	1	**Iasia (GR)**[56] 1808 3-9-12 **75** .... KShea 9 (Jane Chapple-Hyam) *stdd after s: hld up in last pair: hdwy 3f out: chsd ldrs and rdn over 1f out: hung lft and btn jst ins fnl f* **4/1**[2]	64
00-0	**8**	4 ½	**Sorrel Point**[14] 3077 6-8-5 **49** oh4 ....(t) DavidProbert(3) 8 (H J Collingridge) *chsd ldrs: rdn and wknd wl over 1f out: wl btn fnl f* **66/1**	29
1-00	**9**	21	**Inconspicuous Miss (USA)**[31] 2539 3-8-11 **65**...(t) MatthewDavies(5) 5 (George Baker) *in tch in midfield tl lost pl and rdn 1/2-way: sn lost tch: t.o fnl 2f* **16/1**	—

1m 26.1s (-0.50) **Going Correction** -0.20s/f (Firm)
WFA 3 from 4yo+ 8lb 9 Ran SP% **118.5**
Speed ratings (Par 103): **94,93,93,92,91 88,87,82,58**
toteswingers: 1&2 £15.40, 1&3 £6.40, 2&3 £17.90 CSF £58.33 CT £256.49 TOTE £5.90: £1.90, £4.00, £2.30; EX 58.70 Trifecta £250.40 Part won. Pool: £338.48 - 0.93 winning units..
Owner Giuliano Manfredini **Bred** Lady Legard **Trained** Newmarket, Suffolk

FOCUS
A modest handicap resulting in a bunched finish. The form is muddling and cannot be rated too positively.
Iasia(GR) Official explanation: trainer had no explanation for the poor form shown

3549 NORFOLK NELSON MUSEUM MAIDEN STKS 1m 2f 21y
4:00 (4:01) (Class 5) 3-Y-0+ **£2,775** (£830; £415; £207; £103) **Stalls** Low

Form				RPR
0	**1**		**Laaheb**[13] 3117 3-9-2 0 .... RHills 1 (M A Jarvis) *t.k.h: hld up in midfield: hdwy 4f out: upsides ldr and gng best 3f out: sn led: clr and rdn ent fnl f: comf* **11/4**[1]	91+
034	**2**	2 ½	**Bomber Brown (IRE)**[38] 2338 3-9-2 0 .... NCallan 6 (P W Chapple-Hyam) *t.k.h: led: rdn and hdd over 2f out: chsd wnr and clr of remainder fnl 2f: one pce and hld fnl f* **16/1**	79
424	**3**	6	**Buckie Boy (IRE)**[17] 2981 3-9-2 75 ....(b) TPQueally 4 (H R A Cecil) *s.i.s: bustled along early: racd in last pair: rdn and hdwy over 3f out: edgd lft fr over 1f out: wnt modest 3rd ins fnl f: nvr trbld ldrs* **4/1**[3]	67
0-4	**4**	¾	**Freedom Fire (IRE)**[21] 2857 3-9-2 0 .... LukeMorris 5 (J M P Eustace) *t.k.h: chsd ldr: wnt 2nd briefly 4f out: wknd and racd awkwardly 2f out: lost 3rd ins fnl f* **33/1**	65
5	**5**	3 ½	**Adnams**[12] 3168 3-8-13 0 .... JackMitchell(3) 3 (C F Wall) *t.k.h: hld up towards rr: outpcd and lost tch over 4f out: kpt on to pass btn horses fnl f: nvr trbld ldrs* **7/1**	58+
222	**6**	3 ½	**Luc Jordan**[23] 2789 3-9-2 79 .... KShea 8 (L M Cumani) *hld up in tch: hdwy 4f out: shkn up and hung lft over 2f out: sn wl btn* **3/1**[2]	51
0	**7**	½	**Highway Code (USA)**[19] 2930 3-9-2 0 .... RoystonFfrench 2 (M Johnston) *t.k.h: chsd ldrs: rdn wl over 4f out: drvn 3f out: wknd over 2f out: wl btn after* **4/1**[3]	50
	8	6	**Ann Birkett** 3-8-11 0 .... AmirQuinn 7 (Miss J Feilden) *stdd s: t.k.h: hld up in last pair: lost tch 4f out: sn bhd* **150/1**	33
00	**9**	3	**Cyber Space**[45] 2142 5-9-13 0 .... StephenCarson 9 (B J McMath) *chsd ldr tl 4f out: sn dropped out: wl bhd fnl 2f* **150/1**	32

2m 7.75s (-2.75) **Going Correction** -0.075s/f (Good)
WFA 3 from 5yo 11lb 9 Ran SP% **114.3**
Speed ratings (Par 103): **108,106,101,100,97 95,94,89,87**
toteswingers: 1&2 £10.90, 1&3 £3.60, 2&3 £4.70 CSF £46.28 TOTE £4.10: £1.40, £2.90, £1.70; EX 57.80 Trifecta £407.00 Part won. Pool: £550.10 - 0.63 winning units..
Owner Hamdan Al Maktoum **Bred** Darley **Trained** Newmarket, Suffolk

FOCUS
An ordinary maiden but the winner was impressive and the fourth sets the standard.
Luc Jordan Official explanation: jockey said colt was unsuited by the slow pace.

3550 MR KING & SONS H'CAP 1m 2f 21y
4:30 (4:30) (Class 5) (0-70,70) 3-Y-0+ **£2,719** (£809; £404; £202) **Stalls** Low

Form				RPR
5114	**1**		**Cwm Rhondda (USA)**[13] 3114 4-9-10 **69** .... JackMitchell(3) 2 (P W Chapple-Hyam) *settled in tch: a gng wl: hdwy between horses wl over 1f out: shkn up to ld ins fnl f: sn pushed clr: easily* **11/10**[1]	79+
6026	**2**	1 ½	**Extremely So**[18] 2942 3-8-6 **59** .... ChrisCatlin 4 (P J McBride) *t.k.h: chsd ldr tl 5f out: styd handy: rdn and pressed ldrs 2f out: kpt on u.p to chse wnr fnl 100yds: no imp* **9/1**	63
5021	**3**	hd	**Iceman George**[21] 2851 5-9-1 **57** ....(b) LiamJones 7 (D Morris) *s.i.s and pushed along early: chsd ldrs 6f out: rdn 4f out: chsd ldrs and drvn 2f out: kpt on ins fnl f: no ch w wnr* **8/1**[3]	61
-130	**4**	½	**Locum**[27] 2684 4-9-11 **67** .... JerryO'Dwyer 3 (M H Tompkins) *t.k.h: hld up in tch: effrt and n.m.r over 1f out: sn drvn: swtchd lft ins fnl f: styd on u.p* **4/1**[2]	70
3004	**5**	2	**Sawab**[11] 3188 3-9-3 **70** ....(b) NCallan 5 (C E Brittain) *t.k.h: led: jnd 4f out: rdn over 2f out: hdd ins fnl f: sn btn: eased towards fin* **10/1**	69
0535	**6**	3	**Dragon Slayer (IRE)**[21] 2851 7-8-13 **60** .... GabrielHannon(5) 6 (John A Harris) *stdd s: plld hrd: sn chsng ldrs: wnt 2nd 5f out: upsides ldr 4f out tl over 1f out: wknd fnl f* **12/1**	53

0-60 **7** ½ **Faith And Reason (USA)**[24] 2760 6-9-2 **58** TPQueally 1 50
(B J Curley) *t.k.h: hld up in last pl: hdwy on inner over 2f out: rdn and wknd ent fnl f* **17/2**

2m 9.82s (-0.68) **Going Correction** -0.075s/f (Good)
WFA 3 from 4yo+ 11lb **7** Ran SP% **116.0**
Speed ratings (Par 103): **99,97,97,97,95 93,92**
toteswingers: 1&2 £4.40, 1&3 £2.90, 2&3 £9.10 CSF £12.62 CT £56.10 TOTE £1.80: £1.20, £6.20; EX 14.70 Trifecta £74.70 Pool: £197.88 - 1.96 winning units..
Owner Hintlesham Thoroughbreds **Bred** David Allan **Trained** Newmarket, Suffolk

FOCUS
A modest handicap and the form is limited, although the winner is value for double the winning margin.
Dragon Slayer(IRE) Official explanation: jockey said gelding ran too free

3551 NORFOLK CHAMBER OF COMMERCE H'CAP 1m 1f
5:00 (5:00) (Class 5) (0-75,70) 3-Y-O **£2,719** (£606; £606; £202) **Stalls** Low

Form RPR

4600 **1** **Atacama Sunrise**[21] 2858 3-8-7 **56** DO'Donohoe 3 63
(J Pearce) *stdd s: hld up in last pl: plld to outer and hdwy over 2f out: led ent fnl f: drvn out* **17/2**

1-04 **2** 1 **Mykingdomforahorse**[13] 3099 3-9-4 **67** ChrisCatlin 5 72
(M R Channon) *stdd after s: in tch: rdn and effrt over 2f out: chsd ldrs and unable qck 2f out: styd on fnl 100yds* **3/1**[1]

1-00 **2** dht **Three Ducks**[34] 2432 3-9-6 **69** KShea 8 74
(L M Cumani) *led: edgd rt and jnd over 2f out: hdd ent fnl f: kpt on same pce fnl f* **5/1**

2-03 **4** 2 **Royal Willy (IRE)**[27] 2685 3-9-7 **70** LiamJones 9 71
(W Jarvis) *stdd s: hld up towards rr: rdn and effrt 3f out: no real hdwy: edging lft and one pce fr over 1f out* **13/2**

1-00 **5** 2½ **Moon Lightning (IRE)**[33] 2504 3-9-7 **70** NCallan 6 65
(M H Tompkins) *stdd and dropped in bhd after s: hdwy and stmbld over 2f out: one pce u.p over 1f out: eased whn no ch wl ins fnl f* **9/2**[3]

-404 **6** 1 **Transformer (IRE)**[22] 2809 3-8-12 **61** (v[1]) TPQueally 2 54
(W J Knight) *plld hrd: in tch tl dropped to last pl and rdn 4f out: no ch after: plugged on again ins fnl f* **7/2**[2]

0010 **7** nk **Ocean Countess (IRE)**[45] 2143 3-8-9 **58** (v[1]) JimmyQuinn 7 50
(Miss J Feilden) *in tch: hdwy on inner 4f out: upsides ldr 3f out: rdn 2f out: wknd u.p ent fnl f* **14/1**

000 **8** ½ **Mister Frosty (IRE)**[21] 2863 3-8-9 **58** AdrianMcCarthy 4 49
(G Prodromou) *chsd ldr tl 3f out: sn lost pl: bhd fnl 2f* **18/1**

1m 55.15s (-0.65) **Going Correction** -0.075s/f (Good) **8** Ran SP% **117.9**
Speed ratings (Par 100): **99,98,98,96,94 93,92,92**WIN: 21.30. PL: Atacama Sunrise £2.70, Three Ducks £2.90, Mykingdomforahorse £1.20. EX: AS/TD £24.10, AS/M £27.00. CSF: AS/TD £26.00 AS/M £17.69 TRICAST: AS/TD/M £80.60 AS/M/TD £73.20 toteswingers: AS/TD £13.50, AS/M £9.20, TD/M £4.40 TR27 Owner.

FOCUS
A bunch finish at the end, suggesting that all bar the winner were much of a muchness. The form looks sound enough rated around the third and fourth.
Atacama Sunrise Official explanation: trainer said, regarding apparent improvement in form, that after arriving home after its previous race he found the filly to be in season.

3552 BBC RADIO NORFOLK "HANDS AND HEELS" APPRENTICE SERIES H'CAP 1m 3f 101y
5:30 (5:30) (Class 6) (0-65,65) 4-Y-O+ **£1,942** (£578; £288; £144) **Stalls** Low

Form RPR

3010 **1** **Al Azy (IRE)**[29] 2609 4-8-7 **53** LauraPike(3) 1 61
(D M Simcock) *chsd ldr for 2f: styd chsng ldrs: clsd on ldr 2f out: led 1f out: styd on wl* **9/2**[3]

0-04 **2** 2¼ **Credential**[16] 3004 7-8-1 **47** (p) TobyAtkinson(3) 6 51
(John A Harris) *led: clr 6f out: hung rt fr over 3f out: rdn wl over 1f out: hdd ent fnl f: one pce* **4/1**[2]

0232 **3** 2½ **Clipperdown (IRE)**[19] 2923 8-9-5 **65** (t) DavidKenny(3) 5 65
(E J Creighton) *hld up in midfield: hdwy to chse clr ldr 4f out: rdn and fnd little wl over 1f out: wl hld fnl f* **11/4**[1]

3345 **4** 5 **Nassar (IRE)**[6] 3361 6-9-2 **64** RichardOld(5) 7 55
(G Prodromou) *stdd s: hld up in rr: effrt to chse ldng trio 3f out: no prog and wl btn after* **9/2**[3]

0523 **5** 3½ **Dobravany (IRE)**[69] 969 5-8-3 **49** (v) IJBrennan(3) 2 34
(K A Morgan) *hld up in last pair: shkn up and no rspnse 4f out: n.d* **4/1**[2]

4060 **6** 12 **Cragganmore Creek**[35] 2419 6-8-0 **46** oh1 (v) RyanPowell(3) 8 11
(D Morris) *dwlt: t.k.h: chsd ldr after 2f tl 4f out: sn wknd: wl bhd fnl 2f* **16/1**

0-00 **7** 4½ **Templet (USA)**[16] 3004 9-8-0 **46** oh1 (b) JosephineBruning(3) 3 3
(T T Clement) *chsd ldrs tl lost pl and pushed along 6f out: wl bhd fnl 4f* **33/1**

2m 27.41s (-1.29) **Going Correction** -0.075s/f (Good) **7** Ran SP% **111.9**
Speed ratings (Par 101): **101,99,97,93,91 82,79**
toteswingers: 1&2 £4.40, 1&3 £3.00, 2&3 £2.70 CSF £21.69 CT £56.65 TOTE £5.60: £2.90, £2.70; EX 23.70 Trifecta £61.30 Pool: £313.97 - 3.79 winning units. Place 6: £90.71 Place 5: £73.40.
Owner Dr Marwan Koukash **Bred** Shadwell Estate Company Limited **Trained** Newmarket, Suffolk
■ Laura Pike's first winner since she returned from a three-year sabbatical.

FOCUS
A very moderate event that was soundly run and the form looks reasonable for the grade.
Al Azy(IRE) Official explanation: trainer's rep had no explanation for the apparent improvement in form.
Credential Official explanation: jockey said gelding hung right
T/Plt: £1,001.20 to a £1 stake. Pool: £50,171.78. 36.58 winning tickets. T/Qpdt: £76.70 to a £1 stake. Pool: £4,016.35. 38.70 winning tickets. SP

3553 - 3556a (Foreign Racing) - See Raceform Interactive

[3232]BEVERLEY (R-H)
Friday, July 3

OFFICIAL GOING: Good to firm (9.7)
Wind: Blustery 1/2 against Weather: Fine and sunny

3557 RACING AGAIN TOMORROW H'CAP 1m 1f 207y
6:20 (6:20) (Class 5) (0-75,70) 3-Y-O+ **£3,561** (£1,059; £529; £264) **Stalls** High

Form RPR

3162 **1** **Umverti**[10] 3235 4-9-4 **60** GrahamGibbons 4 70
(N Bycroft) *mde all: drvn and hung lft over 3f out: edgd lft ins fnl f: all out* **5/1**[3]

04-2 **2** hd **Graceful Descent (FR)**[20] 2916 4-9-6 **65** FrederikTylicki(3) 8 75
(R A Fahey) *trckd wnr: effrt over 3f out: upsides over 1f out: kpt on towards fin: jst hld* **5/4**[1]

3312 **3** 3¼ **Dark Ranger**[7] 3336 3-8-7 **60** RobertHavlin 6 64
(T J Pitt) *hld up: hdwy to chse ldrs over 4f out: edgd lft over 1f out: kpt on same pce* **9/4**[2]

4000 **4** 7 **Neon Blue**[18] 2965 8-8-7 **54** AmyRyan(5) 7 44
(R M Whitaker) *s.i.s: hld up in last: drvn over 3f out: nvr on terms* **14/1**

3010 **5** 4½ **General Tufto**[36] 2419 4-9-9 **65** (b) PhillipMakin 5 46
(C Smith) *hld up: hdwy to trck ldrs over 5f out: wknd 2f out: bhd whn eased nr fin* **7/1**

2m 6.35s (-0.65) **Going Correction** -0.125s/f (Firm)
WFA 3 from 4yo+ 11lb **5** Ran SP% **111.0**
Speed ratings (Par 103): **97,96,94,88,85**
toteswingers: 1&2 £4.50. CSF £11.94 TOTE £5.30: £1.90, £1.50; EX 10.50.
Owner Mrs C M Whatley **Bred** N Bycroft **Trained** Brandsby, N Yorks

FOCUS
The rail around the bottom bend had been moved back by one metre to leave the course at its widest configuration. With no confirmed front-runners in this opener, the pace was not strong and it opened the door for the first willing to seize the initiative to dictate the race. Two pulled clear in a prolonged battle from two furlongs out. Modest form.

3558 NATWEST AGRICULTURAL TEAM (S) STKS 7f 100y
6:50 (6:50) (Class 6) 3-Y-O+ **£2,266** (£674; £337; £168) **Stalls** High

Form RPR

3000 **1** **Dream Express (IRE)**[3] 3488 4-9-3 71 PhillipMakin 8 70
(M Dods) *trckd ldrs: t.k.h: hmpd and swtchd lft 2f out: carried hd high and looked reluctant: persuaded to ld last 75yds* **3/1**[2]

0000 **2** 1 **Spin Again (IRE)**[7] 3354 4-9-3 66 FrancisNorton 2 67
(D Nicholls) *led: edgd lft over 1f out: hdd and no ex ins fnl f* **12/1**

0501 **3** ¾ **Arizona John (IRE)**[1] 3541 4-9-3 71 BMcHugh(5) 6 70+
(N Wilson) *hld up towards rr: hdwy over 3f out: styd on fnl f: nt rch 1st 2* **13/8**[1]

3010 **4** 1¼ **Just Sam (IRE)**[23] 2812 4-9-3 57 DuranFentiman 4 62
(R E Barr) *chsd ldrs: upsides jst ins fnl f: kpt on same pce* **14/1**

5302 **5** 2 **Efidium**[1] 3539 11-9-0 59 FrederikTylicki(3) 5 57
(N Bycroft) *in tch: effrt over 2f out: one pce* **6/1**[3]

0-00 **6** 1¼ **Coole Dodger (IRE)**[32] 2527 4-9-3 66 PaulMulrennan 11 54+
(B Ellison) *hld up in rr: hdwy and swtchd rt 2f out: kpt on same pce* **20/1**

0004 **7** 1¼ **Fyodorovich (USA)**[3] 3490 4-9-3 53 PAspell 9 51
(J S Wainwright) *t.k.h in mid-div: kpt on fnl 3f: nvr a threat* **8/1**

4060 **8** 1 **Crocodile Bay (IRE)**[15] 3055 6-8-12 60 (b) MarkCoumbe(5) 3 48
(John A Harris) *trckd ldrs: t.k.h: chal 3f out: wknd over 1f out* **16/1**

00-0 **9** 2½ **Grey Gurkha**[35] 2441 8-9-3 47 PatrickMathers 7 42
(I W McInnes) *s.i.s: nvr on terms* **80/1**

465- **10** 4 **Favouring (IRE)**[349] 528 7-9-0 40 (b) LeeVickers(3) 12 32
(M C Chapman) *chsd ldrs: wknd over 2f out* **66/1**

0-00 **11** 33 **Call Of Ktulu (IRE)**[36] 2404 4-8-12 12 (v[1]) LanceBetts(5) 1 —
(J S Wainwright) *s.s: a bhd: t.o 2f out* **125/1**

1m 32.85s (-0.95) **Going Correction** -0.125s/f (Firm) **11** Ran SP% **117.0**
Speed ratings (Par 101): **100,98,98,96,94 92,91,90,87,82 46**
toteswingers: 1&2 £11.20, 1&3 £2.00, 2&3 £11.40 CSF £37.79 TOTE £4.80: £1.50, £3.70, £1.30; EX 35.60.There was no bid for the winner. Arizona John was claimed by David Penman for £6,000.
Owner J A Wynn-Williams Les Waugh **Bred** Quay Bloodstock **Trained** Denton, Co Durham

FOCUS
A fair seller in which those at the top of the official ratings filled the first three places. Sound form.

3559 EBF WILLIAM JACKSON BAKERY NOVICE STKS 5f
7:25 (7:26) (Class 4) 2-Y-O **£5,180** (£1,541; £770; £384) **Stalls** High

Form RPR

431 **1** **Bould Mover**[15] 3058 2-9-2 0 GrahamGibbons 5 91+
(R Curtis) *mae all: rdn clr over 1f out: v readily* **9/2**[3]

120 **2** 5 **Grand Zafeen**[16] 3015 2-8-11 0 FrancisNorton 4 68
(M R Channon) *bmpd s: drvn to sn chse ldrs: wnt 2nd 1f out: no ch w wnr* **5/4**[1]

1 **3** 1¾ **House Of Frills**[64] 1624 2-8-7 0 PaulMulrennan 1 58
(T D Barron) *sn chsng ldrs: styd on same pce appr fnl f* **22/1**

416 **4** 1 **Sheka**[37] 2372 2-8-11 0 DanielTudhope 6 58
(I W McInnes) *chsd ldrs: outpcd and lost pl over 2f out: kpt on fnl f* **6/1**

1 **5** 1¼ **On The Bounty**[48] 2069 2-9-2 0 TonyHamilton 3 59
(R A Fahey) *wnt rt s: hld up: effrt over 2f out: kpt on: nvr a threat* **4/1**[2]

021 **6** ¾ **Craicattack (IRE)**[10] 3240 2-9-2 0 RobertHavlin 2 56
(J S Moore) *chsd ldrs: rdn and hung bdly lft over 2f out: n.d whn edgd rt fnl f* **7/1**

62.99 secs (-0.51) **Going Correction** -0.125s/f (Firm) **6** Ran SP% **113.8**
Speed ratings (Par 96): **99,91,88,86,84 83**
toteswingers: 1&2 £1.10, 1&3 £10.70, 2&3 £7.20 CSF £10.85 TOTE £6.00: £2.10, £1.50; EX 12.30.
Owner H Downs & D Looney **Bred** K W P Engineering **Trained** Lambourn, Berks

FOCUS
All of the contestants had already registered a win in their short careers, but the winner ran them ragged.

NOTEBOOK
Bould Mover ◆, breaking smartly and showing good early pace, kept up the gallop so that by the final furlong he already had the race won and he carried on to pull well clear of the rest. This was his second decisive win in a row and he looks to be progressing nicely. (op 5-1 tchd 4-1)
Grand Zafeen had been competing in tougher races, including in the Queen Mary at Ascot last time, though admittedly well beaten, and was a warm order for this drop in grade. She was quite keen early tracking the leader, but had no answer from two furlongs out as the winner quickened away. She plugged on well enough to suggest a step up in trip might suit. (op 7-4)
House Of Frills showed early speed and though readily outpaced she stayed on well on the outside of the pack in the straight. Having won a seller on her debut in April this was a solid performance against potentially better rivals. (op 14-1)
Sheka was prominent early but soon dropped to the rear, then made some headway in the straight before getting outpaced. She previously made late headway when well beaten in a Listed race over course and distance in May and looks to need further. (op 13-2 tchd 7-1)
On The Bounty had won on his debut on easy ground at Doncaster in May, but could not pick up on this faster ground. (op 3-1)
Craicattack(IRE) was already under pressure when hanging markedly left as they straightened out for home. Official explanation: jockey said colt hung left-handed (op 17-2)

3560 AUNT BESSIE'S YORKSHIRE PUDDING H'CAP 1m 100y
7:55 (7:55) (Class 4) (0-85,82) 4-Y-O+ **£5,180** (£1,541; £770; £384) **Stalls** High

Form RPR

1053 **1** **Cotswolds**[15] 3055 4-8-12 **73** AndrewMullen 5 82
(M Johnston) *mde all: kpt on wl fnl 2f: unchal* **9/4**[1]

0336 2 2 **Lady Rangali (IRE)**[8] 3312 4-9-2 82 BMcHugh(5) 7 86
(Mrs A Duffield) *drvn to chse ldrs: rdn over 2f out: wnt 2nd over 1f out: no imp* 9/2[2]
6302 3 1 1/4 **Exit Smiling**[15] 3067 7-8-12 80 PaulPickard(7) 4 81
(P T Midgley) *hld up: hdwy 4f out: sn drvn: kpt on same pce fnl 2f* 13/2
2206 4 1/2 **Handsome Falcon**[7] 3353 5-8-10 74 FrederikTylicki(3) 6 74+
(R A Fahey) *hld up: hdwy to trck ldrs 4f out: rdn over 2f out: kpt on ins fnl f* 9/4[1]
0130 5 2 1/4 **Captain Macarry (IRE)**[27] 2695 4-9-7 82 (v) PhillipMakin 2 77
(B Smart) *t.k.h: trckd ldr: effrt over 2f out: wknd fnl f* 5/1[3]
1m 46.2s (-1.40) **Going Correction** -0.125s/f (Firm) 5 Ran SP% 109.7
Speed ratings (Par 105): **102,100,98,98,96**
toteswingers: 1&2 £7.70. CSF £12.43 TOTE £2.70: £1.80, £2.40; EX 13.20.
Owner Sheikh Hamdan Bin Mohammed Al Maktoum **Bred** Gainsborough Stud Management Ltd **Trained** Middleham Moor, N Yorks

FOCUS
There was little pace until the winner picked up the tempo two furlongs from home. Not form to take too positively.

3561 FERGUSON FAWSITT ARMS H'CAP 1m 4f 16y
8:30 (8:33) (Class 6) (0-60,60) 3-Y-0+ **£2,266** (£674; £337; £168) **Stalls** High

Form RPR
-634 1 **Shaylee**[23] 2803 4-9-6 52 GrahamGibbons 2 61
(T D Walford) *unruly s: chsd ldrs: led over 2f out: kpt on wl fnl f* 8/1
0455 2 1 1/2 **Art Value**[13] 3171 4-9-0 46 oh1 (p) FrancisNorton 4 53+
(M Wigham) *mid-div: hdwy over 2f out: sn chsng ldrs: kpt on same pce ins fnl f* 3/1[1]
60-3 3 hd **Astroleo**[26] 2742 3-8-3 48 NickyMackay 3 54
(M H Tompkins) *trckd ldrs: t.k.h: drvn 5f out: outpcd over 2f out: rallied over 1f out: n.m.r ins fnl f: styd on wl towards fin* 9/2[2]
00-0 4 1/2 **Kames Park (IRE)**[180] 40 7-10-0 60 DanielTudhope 9 65+
(R C Guest) *dwlt: hld up in rr: stdy hdwy on wd outsider over 2f out: styd on fnl f* 33/1
3402 5 1 1/2 **Shekan Star**[10] 3233 7-9-6 52 PaulMulrennan 8 55
(K G Reveley) *mid-div: hdwy over 3f out: chsng ldrs over 1f out: one pce* 6/1[3]
6-00 6 5 **Fossgate**[31] 2573 8-9-9 55 PhillipMakin 11 50
(J D Bethell) *hld up in midfield: hdwy on ins 3f out: upsides over 1f out: wknd fnl 150yds* 14/1
60-0 7 6 **Hits Only Time**[38] 2366 4-8-10 49 NeilFarley(7) 6 34
(D Carroll) *led tl over 2f out: lost pl over 1f out* 50/1
00-0 8 4 1/2 **Linby (IRE)**[7] 3348 4-9-3 52 FrederikTylicki(3) 5 30
(Miss Tor Sturgis) *hld up in rr: effrt over 3f out: hung rt and lost pl over 1f out* 28/1
26-0 9 4 1/2 **Markadam**[37] 2370 3-8-12 60 MichaelJStainton(3) 1 31
(Miss S E Hall) *chsd ldrs: drvn to chse ldrs over 3f out: wknd over 1f out* 14/1
0051 10 23 **Suitably Accoutred (IRE)**[3] 3482 3-8-6 51 6ex AndrewMullen 7 —
(Mrs A Duffield) *v unruly s: drvn to sn chse ldrs: jnd ldr 7f out: wknd qckly over 2f out: bhd whn eased* 3/1[1]
0P-0 11 7 **King Of Sparta (USA)**[14] 3098 4-9-0 46 oh1 TonyHamilton 12 —
(T J Fitzgerald) *t.k.h in rr: lost pl 4f out: wl bhd whn eased* 50/1
2m 38.95s (-1.95) **Going Correction** -0.125s/f (Firm)
WFA 3 from 4yo+ 13lb 11 Ran SP% 117.2
Speed ratings (Par 101): **101,100,99,99,98 95,91,88,85,69 65**
toteswingers: 1&2 £4.70, 1&3 £7.30, 2&3 £3.50 CSF £31.39 CT £122.81 TOTE £8.60: £2.30, £1.80, £2.30; EX 43.90.
Owner L C And A E Sigsworth **Bred** L C And Mrs A E Sigsworth **Trained** Sheriff Hutton, N Yorks
■ Stewards' Enquiry : Graham Gibbons two-day ban: careless riding (July 18-19)

FOCUS
Just a moderate handicap but it was run at a sound pace and six runners held some sort of chance a furlong from home. Solid form.
Suitably Accoutred(IRE) Official explanation: jockey said filly never travelled

3562 COCKTAILS AND CALYPSO NIGHT STKS (H'CAP) 5f
9:00 (9:01) (Class 6) (0-65,65) 3-Y-0+ **£2,590** (£770; £385; £192) **Stalls** High

Form RPR
6-01 1 **Solemn**[11] 3204 4-9-3 56 6ex (b) NickyMackay 5 67
(J M Bradley) *chsd ldrs: led over 1f out: hld on towards fin* 14/1
3545 2 3/4 **Dickie Le Davoir**[11] 3224 5-9-6 64 (b[1]) MarkCoumbe(5) 9 72+
(John A Harris) *s.i.s: gd hdwy and nt clr run: swtchd lft appr fnl f: edgd rt ins fnl f: fin wl* 10/1
3-54 3 nk **Select Committee**[15] 3065 4-9-4 57 (p) GrahamGibbons 3 64
(J J Quinn) *chsd ldrs: kpt on wl fnl f* 10/1
0051 4 1 1/2 **Only A Game (IRE)**[23] 2801 4-9-8 61 (p) DanielTudhope 12 63
(I W McInnes) *chsd ldrs: kpt on same pce fnl f* 7/2[1]
001 5 hd **Foreign Rhythm (IRE)**[10] 3239 4-8-1 47 oh1 ow1 JohnCavanagh(7) 6 48
(N Tinkler) *chsd ldrs: drvn over 2f out: kpt on same pce appr fnl f whn sltly hmpd ins fnl f* 18/1
3465 6 nk **Yungaburra (IRE)**[17] 3002 5-9-12 65 (t) PaulMulrennan 15 65+
(J Balding) *mid-div: hdwy over 1f out: n.m.r and hung rt: nvr rchd ldrs* 17/2
1005 7 1/2 **Circle Dance (IRE)**[15] 3057 4-9-4 57 (v) PatrickMathers 8 55
(D Shaw) *in rr: kpt on fnl 2f: nvr nr ldrs* 33/1
0-24 8 nk **Bahamian Ballad**[18] 2966 4-8-11 50 PhillipMakin 16 47
(J D Bethell) *mid-div: effrt on ins 2f out: nvr trbld ldrs* 9/2[2]
6024 9 hd **Strathmore (IRE)**[23] 2812 5-8-12 58 TimothyAyres(7) 7 54
(R A Fahey) *in rr on outer: kpt on fnl 2f: nvr a factor* 12/1
-500 10 1 1/2 **Welcome Approach**[32] 2529 6-8-12 51 TonyHamilton 14 42
(J R Weymes) *prom: fdd ins fnl f* 20/1
4533 11 2 **What A Fella**[14] 3125 3-8-4 48 AndrewMullen 2 32
(Mrs A Duffield) *dwlt: swtchd rt and prom after 1f: wknd appr fnl f* 20/1
1003 12 3 **Thunder Bay**[4] 3445 4-9-4 60 (v) FrederikTylicki(3) 4 33
(R A Fahey) *led tl hdd & wknd over 1f out* 5/1[3]
5000 13 1/2 **Know No Fear**[4] 3465 4-9-9 65 LeeVickers(3) 13 36
(D Shaw) *mid-div: lost pl over 2f out* 33/1
0005 14 1 1/2 **Chipolini (IRE)**[16] 3031 3-7-9 46 oh1 (b[1]) NeilFarley(7) 11 12
(D Carroll) *rrd s: a in rr* 50/1
63.66 secs (0.16) **Going Correction** -0.125s/f (Firm)
WFA 3 from 4yo+ 5lb 14 Ran SP% 122.8
Speed ratings (Par 101): **93,91,91,88,88 88,87,86,86,84 80,76,75,72**
toteswingers: 1&2 £43.40, 1&3 £20.80, 2&3 £42.40 CSF £141.27 CT £1517.97 TOTE £17.70: £4.40, £3.40, £3.70; EX 252.10 Place 6: £41.63, Place 5: £24.75..
Owner E A Hayward **Bred** Cheveley Park Stud Ltd **Trained** Sedbury, Gloucs
■ Stewards' Enquiry : Mark Coumbe two-day ban: careless riding (Jul 17-18); two-day ban: used whip without allowing mount time to respond (Jul 19-20)

FOCUS
This was run at a good pace, although the final time was 0.6 seconds slower than the two-year-old race earlier on the card. Modest form.
Yungaburra(IRE) Official explanation: jockey said gelding was denied a clear run
T/Plt: £158.60 to a £1 stake. Pool: £44,966.90. 206.95 winning tickets. T/Qpdt: £49.00 to a £1 stake. Pool: £3,307.04. 49.90 winning tickets. WG

3376 DONCASTER (L-H)
Friday, July 3

OFFICIAL GOING: Good (good to firm; 8.5) changing to good after race 1 (2.00)
Running rail moved out 4yards increasing distances on round course by 12yards
Wind: Virtually nil Weather: Overcast and heavy rain showers

3563 100TH ANNIVERSARY OF BRITAIN'S FIRST AIRSHOW H'CAP 1m 4f
2:00 (2:00) (Class 5) (0-70,69) 4-Y-0+ **£3,238** (£963; £481; £240) **Stalls** Low

Form RPR
4453 1 **Bollin Greta**[16] 3035 4-9-3 65 DavidAllan 4 76+
(T D Easterby) *trckd ldrs: swtchd rt and smooth hdwy 3f out: led on bit 2f out: sn rdn clr and kpt on* 2/1[1]
00/5 2 2 1/4 **Astronomical (IRE)**[13] 3151 7-8-12 63 RussellKennemore(3) 1 69
(R Hollinshead) *trckd ldrs: effrt wl over 2f out: swtchd rt and rdn wl over 1f out and snchsng wnr: drvn and no imp ins fnl f* 10/1
1650 3 6 **Mustajed**[22] 2851 8-9-3 68 JamesMillman(3) 3 64
(B R Millman) *hld up towards rr: hdwy 3f out: rdn along 2f out: styd on ins fnl f* 7/1[3]
-005 4 3/4 **Royal Flynn**[21] 2898 7-9-0 65 (p) KellyHarrison(3) 2 60
(Mrs K Walton) *dwlt: hld up in rr: hdwy over 2f out and sn rdn: kpt on ins fnl f: nvr nr ldrs* 16/1
6000 5 1 3/4 **Sporting Gesture**[31] 2573 12-8-5 53 DaleGibson 6 45
(M W Easterby) *cl up: effrt over 3f out: sn rdn and grad wknd fnl 2f* 15/2
3212 6 9 **Society Venue**[7] 3350 4-9-7 69 AndrewElliott 7 47
(Jedd O'Keeffe) *led: rdn along 3f out: drvn and hdd 2f out: grad wknd* 11/4[2]
/036 7 22 **Annambo**[32] 2552 9-8-11 59 NCallan 8 2
(Andrew Reid) *chsd ldrs: rdn along over 3f out: sn wknd* 16/1
023 8 41 **Ross Moor**[35] 2442 7-8-12 60 MickyFenton 5 —
(Mike Murphy) *dwlt: a in rr* 8/1
2m 36.35s (1.25) **Going Correction** +0.05s/f (Good) 8 Ran SP% 116.2
Speed ratings (Par 103): **97,95,91,91,89 83,69,41**
toteswingers: 1&2 £11.20, 1&3 £5.80, 2&3 £11.40 CSF £23.66 CT £119.52 TOTE £2.80: £1.20, £4.20, £2.10; EX 26.60 Trifecta £210.00 Part won. Pool: £283.79 - 0.61 winning units..
Owner Sir Neil Westbrook **Bred** Sir Neil & Exors Of Late Lady Westbrook **Trained** Great Habton, N Yorks

FOCUS
The rail was moved out four yards from the bottom of Rose Hill into the straight, increasing race distances on the round course by 12 yards. Rain before racing eased the going from the advertised good to firm, good in places and riders in the first reported that the ground was a bit loose on top. This was just a modest handicap. The pace was fairly steady and only really picked up with half a mile to run. Bollin Greta did it well but there is a bit of doubt over the form.
Ross Moor Official explanation: jockey said gelding slipped on bend and never travelled thereafter

3564 CROWNHOTEL-BAWTRY.COM H'CAP 1m 4f
2:30 (2:30) (Class 4) (0-85,85) 3-Y-0+ **£4,857** (£1,445; £722; £360) **Stalls** Low

Form RPR
04-5 1 **Conquisto**[42] 2249 4-9-13 84 IanMongan 6 93+
(C G Cox) *hld up in rr: hdwy 4f out: nt clr run 3f out: swtchd outside and smooth hdwy to chal 2f out: sn led and qcknd clr appr fnl f: comf* 4/1[2]
1-5 2 3 1/2 **Battle Planner (USA)**[43] 2210 3-9-0 84 GregFairley 9 86+
(M Johnston) *chsd ldr: hdwy 4f out: rdn along 3f out and sn outpcd: rallied wl u.p ins fnl f: kpt on towards fin* 7/2[1]
4-60 3 nk **Dar Es Salaam**[6] 3393 5-9-3 79 GaryBartley(5) 2 81
(J S Goldie) *hld up in tch: effrt on inner and n.m.r 3f out: swtchd rt wl over 1f and sn rdn: kpt on u.p ins fnl f: nrst fin* 15/2
22-0 4 1/2 **Mubrook (USA)**[21] 2891 4-9-12 83 ShaneKelly 7 84
(L M Cumani) *trckd ldrs: hdwy over 3f out: rdn to dispute ld and ev ch over 2f out: drvn whn n.m.r wl over 1f out: sn one pce* 13/2
3150 5 shd **Demolition**[23] 2815 5-10-0 85 (p) DanielTudhope 3 86
(N Wilson) *hld up in rr: hdwy over 4f out: rdn to ld briefly 2f out: sn hdd and drvn: kpt on same pce* 11/2
4024 6 3 3/4 **Spirit Of Adjisa (IRE)**[21] 2898 5-9-6 77 NCallan 5 78+
(Pat Eddery) *trckd ldng pair: effrt 3f out and sn n.m.r: rdn and nt clr run over 2f out: sn btn and eased fnl f* 9/2[3]
5300 7 3 3/4 **Eton Fable (IRE)**[25] 2766 4-8-9 73 (p) PaulPickard(7) 8 62
(W J H Ratcliffe) *led and sn clr: rdn along 4f out: drvn and hdd over 2f out: sn wknd* 7/1
2m 33.91s (-1.19) **Going Correction** +0.05s/f (Good)
WFA 3 from 4yo+ 13lb 7 Ran SP% 113.4
Speed ratings (Par 105): **105,102,102,102,102 99,97**
toteswingers: 1&2 £1.60, 1&3 £10.10, 2&3 £9.20 CSF £18.04 CT £98.83 TOTE £5.60: £2.10, £2.50; EX 27.20 Trifecta £139.70 Pool: £311.52 - 1.65 winning units..
Owner Reid's Racers **Bred** Bricklow Ltd **Trained** Lambourn, Berks

FOCUS
There was an open look beforehand to this handicap, which was run in a time more than two seconds quicker than the 51-70 race half an hour earlier. Soikd form with the winner back to his previous best.
Mubrook(USA) Official explanation: jockey said gelding hung left

3565 FUNKYFASCINATORS.CO.UK FILLIES' H'CAP 5f
3:00 (3:02) (Class 4) (0-80,78) 4-Y-0+ **£4,857** (£1,445; £722; £360) **Stalls** High

Form RPR
-414 1 **Doric Lady**[21] 2886 4-9-6 77 KirstyMilczarek 8 85
(J A R Toller) *chsd ldrs: hdwy 1/2-way: rdn to ld wl over 1f out: drvn and edgd rt ins fnl f: hld on wl* 11/4[1]
-032 2 1/2 **Tartatartufata**[32] 2546 7-8-9 66 (v) PaulMulrennan 3 72
(J G Given) *cl up: effrt to dispute ld over 2f out: sn rdn and ev ch tl drvn and nt qckn ins fnl f* 11/4[1]
00-5 3 nse **Hypnosis**[10] 3236 6-9-7 78 TonyHamilton 6 84
(N Wilson) *broke wl and narrow advantage: rdn along over 2f out: drvn and hdd wl over 1f out: no ex wl ins fnl f* 12/1[3]
2016 4 1/2 **Twosheetstothewind**[4] 3445 5-8-6 63 DaleGibson 5 67
(M Dods) *chsd ldrs: hdwy 2f out: swtchd lft and drvn ins fnl f: kpt on same pce* 4/1[2]
3302 5 5 **Speedy Senorita (IRE)**[8] 3295 4-8-7 69 JamieKyne(5) 4 55
(J J Quinn) *chsd ldrs: rdn along over 2f out: wknd wl over 1f out* 4/1[2]

0100 **6** *hd* **Revue Princess (IRE)**[15] 3065 4-8-9 **66**..........................(b) DavidAllan 1 52
(T D Easterby) *racd wd: cl up: rdn along over 2f out and ev ch tl wknd over 1f out* **12/1**[3]

050 **7** *27* **Wibbadune (IRE)**[13] 3145 5-8-11 **68** ow1.................................. NCallan 2 —
(D Shaw) *s.i.s and a bhd* **16/1**

60.26 secs (-0.24) **Going Correction** +0.125s/f (Good) 7 Ran SP% **114.6**
Speed ratings (Par 102): **106,105,105,104,96 96,52**
toteswingers: 1&2 £2.40, 1&3 £5.50, 2&3 £10.90 CSF £10.44 CT £74.98 TOTE £3.10: £1.80, £1.60; EX 10.90 Trifecta £93.50 Pool: £305.90 - 2.42 winning units..
Owner Buckingham Thoroughbreds I **Bred** Minster Enterprises Ltd **Trained** Newmarket, Suffolk
■ Stewards' Enquiry : Kirsty Milczarek caution: careless riding

FOCUS
A fair fillies' handicap run at a strong pace. The first four were all close to their marks.
Wibbadune(IRE) Official explanation: jockey said mare was slowly away

3566 PATEDDERYRACING.COM PROFESSIONAL RACEHORSE SYNDICATION MAIDEN STKS 7f

3:35 (3:37) (Class 4) 3-Y-O £4,857 (£1,445; £722; £360) **Stalls** High

Form RPR

440 **1** **Dukes Art**[36] 2399 3-9-3 72.. RobertHavlin 3 83
(J A R Toller) *trckd ldrs: hdwy 2f out: rdn over 1f out: styd on to ld last 100yds* **14/1**

2 *nk* **Primaeval** 3-9-3 0.. NCallan 1 82
(J R Fanshawe) *trckd ldrs: hdwy over 2f out: rdn to ld over 1f out: sn drvn: hdd and no ex last 100yds* **10/1**

03- **3** *4 ½* **Navajo Nation (IRE)**[289] 6031 3-9-3 0................................ ShaneKelly 4 70
(B J Meehan) *dwlt: sn trcking ldrs: hdwy over 2f out: rdn wl over 1f out: kpt on same pce* **8/1**[3]

-202 **4** *½* **Arteus**[20] 2917 3-9-3 77.. GregFairley 2 69
(Jane Chapple-Hyam) *cl up in centre: hdwy to ld wl over 2f out and sn rdn: drvn and hdd over 1f out: sn one pce* **13/2**[2]

22 **5** *1* **French Applause (IRE)**[20] 2937 3-9-3 0........................ MickyFenton 7 66
(T P Tate) *racd towards stands rail: cl up: rdn along over 2f out: drvn wl over 1f out and sn btn* **4/9**[1]

50 **6** *½* **Bermondsey Girl**[21] 2885 3-8-12 0.. IanMongan 5 60
(C F Wall) *towards rr: hdwy over 2f out: rdn and hung lft over 1f out: sn no imp* **40/1**

4-U **7** *42* **Sams Lass**[13] 3175 3-8-12 0.. AdrianTNicholls 6 —
(D Nicholls) *led: rdn along 3f out: sn hdd: cl up tl wknd wl over 1f out and eased* **16/1**

0 **8** *1 ¼* **Emerald Hawk (IRE)**[87] 1168 3-9-3 0.............................. PaulMulrennan 8 —
(D H Brown) *s.i.s: racd towards stands rail: a in rr* **50/1**

1m 28.07s (1.77) **Going Correction** +0.125s/f (Good) 8 Ran SP% **119.7**
Speed ratings (Par 102): **94,93,88,87,86 86,38,36**
toteswingers: 1&2 £8.20, 1&3 £5.40, 2&3 £7.70 CSF £148.65 TOTE £22.20: £4.00, £3.10, £2.20; EX 302.00 TRIFECTA Not won..
Owner Matthew Green **Bred** Fern Hill Stud & M Green **Trained** Newmarket, Suffolk
■ Stewards' Enquiry : Robert Havlin one-day ban: used whip with excessive frequency (Jul 17)

FOCUS
An ordinary maiden and not form to take too positively. They split into two groups with half a dozen, including the first four home, racing in the centre, and the beaten favourite leading a pair down the stands' rail. The first two pulled away to fight out the finish.
French Applause(IRE) Official explanation: jockey said gelding hung right
Sams Lass Official explanation: jockey said filly lost her action

3567 WAKEFIELD HOSPICE H'CAP 7f

4:10 (4:10) (Class 3) (0-95,94) 3-Y-O+ £7,771 (£2,312; £1,155; £577) **Stalls** High

Form RPR

0-50 **1** **Musaalem (USA)**[14] 3091 5-9-8 **88**.. RHills 9 105+
(W J Haggas) *dwlt: stdd and swtchd to centre after s: hdwy wl over 2f out: rdn to ld over 1f out and sn clr: comf* **7/2**[1]

120 **2** *3 ½* **Celtic Sultan (IRE)**[14] 3091 5-9-12 **92**.............................. MickyFenton 8 97
(T P Tate) *overall ldr stands rail: rdn along over 2f out: hdd and drvn over 1f out: sn one pce* **5/1**[2]

1200 **3** *3* **Light From Mars**[16] 3014 4-9-8 **91**.............................. JamesMillman[(3)] 5 88
(B R Millman) *trckd ldrs centre: effrt over 2f out: sn rdn and one pce fr over 1f out* **5/1**[2]

-110 **4** *3 ¼* **Soccerjackpot (USA)**[16] 3014 5-10-0 **94**.............................. IanMongan 6 82
(C G Cox) *prom in centre: rdn along over 3f out: drvn and one pce fnl 2f* **11/1**

5320 **5** *1* **Kiwi Bay**[9] 3265 4-9-0 **80**.. PhillipMakin 7 65
(M Dods) *racd stands rail: chsd ldr: rdn along over 2f out and sn btn* **11/2**[3]

033 **6** *½* **Atlantic Story (USA)**[13] 3172 7-9-5 **90**.....(bt) Louis-PhilippeBeuzelin[(5)] 3 74
(M W Easterby) *prom centre: effrt and cl up 2f out: sn rdn and wknd* **5/1**[2]

-055 **7** *5* **Bond City (IRE)**[8] 3318 7-9-10 **90**.............................. PJMcDonald 10 61
(G R Oldroyd) *hld up: bhd fr 1/2-way* **33/1**

321 **8** *2 ¾* **Crime Writer (USA)**[14] 3093 3-8-6 **80**.............................. GregFairley 1 43
(M Johnston) *prom centre: rdn along 1/2-way and sn wknd* **11/2**[3]

1m 25.9s (-0.40) **Going Correction** +0.125s/f (Good)
WFA 3 from 4yo+ 8lb 8 Ran SP% **114.3**
Speed ratings (Par 107): **107,103,99,95,94 94,88,85**
toteswingers: 1&2 £4.40, 1&3 £4.00, 2&3 £6.00 CSF £21.05 CT £86.61 TOTE £3.50: £1.30, £2.10, £1.50; EX 25.50 Trifecta £170.50 Pool: £693.84 - 3.01 winning units..
Owner Hamdan Al Maktoum **Bred** Shadwell Farm LLC **Trained** Newmarket, Suffolk

FOCUS
A decent handicap run more than two seconds quicker than the preceding maiden. As in that race half a dozen took the centre-course route while two runners remained on the stands' side. The winner is back to form and the race has been rated at face value.

NOTEBOOK
Musaalem(USA) had been eased 4lb by the handicapper after finishing down the field in the Buckingham Palace at Royal Ascot, where he raced rather keenly. Held up at the rear of the centre-course group here, he went on with over a furlong left and came clear for a comfortable success, eased down. He is a smart sort when on song and is ideally served by genuine fast ground. (tchd 4-1)
Celtic Sultan(IRE)'s rider decided to race down the rail and the gelding led the field overall before sticking on for second, if no match for the easy winner down the centre. This was a creditable effort in the circumstances and he remains well handicapped on his best form. (op 6-1 tchd 9-2)
Light From Mars ran respectably but the handicapper has him in his pocket now and he looked a little short of pace on this drop in trip. (op 8-1 tchd 9-1)
Soccerjackpot(USA) was last in action at Ascot, where he became upset in the stalls prior to the Hunt Cup. He ran respectably under topweight but is another who will benefit from a return to 1m. (op 8-1)
Kiwi Bay, who went to post early, is a pretty consistent sort and he ran his race again, albeit finishing well held after racing down the stands' rail. (op 5-1 tchd 4-1)
Atlantic Story(USA) pushed the pace down the middle before fading when the pressure was on. He was reported by his jockey to have found the ground too slow. Official explanation: jockey said gelding found the good ground too slow (op 4-1 tchd 11-2)

Crime Writer(USA) disappointed on this handicap debut, dropping away after leading the main bunch down the centre. He probably needs further. (op 13-2 tchd 7-1)

3568 1STSECURITYSOLUTIONS.CO.UK CLAIMING STKS 1m (S)

4:45 (4:47) (Class 5) 4-Y-O+ £2,729 (£806; £403) **Stalls** High

Form RPR

1000 **1** **Flawed Genius**[16] 3014 4-9-6 88.......................................(t) NCallan 4 79
(K A Ryan) *dwlt: sn trcking ldrs: cl up over 2f out: rdn to ld over 1f out: edgd lft and clr ins fnl f* **4/5**[1]

0215 **2** *3* **Aussie Blue (IRE)**[14] 3124 5-8-12 60.............................. MichaelJStainton[(3)] 3 67
(R M Whitaker) *trckd ldrs: hdwy over 2f out: rdn to chse wnr appr last: sn noimp* **10/1**[3]

660 **3** *3 ¼* **Singleb (IRE)**[11] 3211 5-9-1 70.......................................(p) MickyFenton 2 59
(Miss Gay Kelleway) *cl up: effrt 3f out and sn led: rdn along 2f out: hdd over 1f out and kpt on same pce* **11/1**

0-66 **4** *¾* **Superior Duchess**[17] 3007 4-8-8 49 ow2.............................. MichellePayne 1 51
(Jane Chapple-Hyam) *dwlt: a towards rr* **33/1**

1012 **5** *14* **Royal Dignitary (USA)**[13] 3174 9-9-6 85.............................. AdrianTNicholls 6 29
(D Nicholls) *led: rdn along and hdd wl over 2f out: wknd and eased over 1f out* **2/1**[2]

1m 40.1s (0.80) **Going Correction** +0.125s/f (Good) 5 Ran SP% **109.3**
Speed ratings (Par 103): **101,98,94,94,80**
toteswingers: 1&2 £6.80 CSF £9.52 TOTE £1.80: £1.20, £2.90; EX 9.30.
Owner Dubai's Finest **Bred** Darley **Trained** Hambleton, N Yorks

FOCUS
They all raced down the centre in this claimer. It looked a two-horse race on paper, but with Royal Dignitary well below par the path was cleared for the winner. The runner-up is the best guide.
Royal Dignitary(USA) Official explanation: jockey said gelding had no more to give

3569 DONCASTER RACECOURSE SPONSORSHIP CLUB MAIDEN FILLIES' STKS 7f

5:15 (5:18) (Class 4) 3-Y-O+ £4,857 (£1,445; £722; £360) **Stalls** High

Form RPR

2- **1** **Sakhee's Pearl**[267] 6600 3-8-12 0.. MickyFenton 1 75
(Miss Gay Kelleway) *hld up in tch: smooth hdwy 3f out: rdn and qcknd to ld over 1f out: clr ins fnl f* **4/1**[2]

0-0 **2** *7* **Rock Art (IRE)**[19] 2947 3-8-12 0.. NickyMackay 6 56
(B J Meehan) *cl up: effrt 3f out: rdn along over 2f out and ev ch: drvn and hdd over 1f out: kpt on: no ch w wnr* **8/1**[3]

3 *1 ¼* **Cactus Curtsey** 3-8-7 0.............................. Louis-PhilippeBeuzelin[(5)] 4 53
(J R Fanshawe) *hld up: hdwy over 2f out: sn rdn and kpt on ins fnl f* **9/1**

22 **4** *1 ¼* **Global Conquest (IRE)**[9] 3278 3-8-12 0.............................. PaulEddery 7 49
(Pat Eddery) *led: rdn along 3f out: drvn and hdd 2f out: sn btn* **4/7**[1]

0-00 **5** *3 ½* **Kaikoura**[48] 2090 3-8-12 42.. KirstyMilczarek 8 40
(G Woodward) *chsd ldrs: rdn along wl over 2f out: sn one pce* **100/1**

05- **6** *4* **Highland Starlight (USA)**[266] 6622 3-8-12 0.............................. IanMongan 3 29
(C G Cox) *prom: rdn along 1/2-way: wknd over 2f out* **16/1**

0-00 **7** *1 ¼* **Cranworth Blaze**[45] 2157 5-9-3 40.............................. JamesMillman[(3)] 5 26
(T J Etherington) *in tch: rdn along 1/2-way: sn wknd* **100/1**

1m 27.4s (1.10) **Going Correction** +0.125s/f (Good)
WFA 3 from 5yo 8lb 7 Ran SP% **112.6**
Speed ratings (Par 102): **98,90,88,87,83 78,77**
toteswingers: 1&2 £2.10, 1&3 £3.50, 2&3 £3.50 CSF £33.88 TOTE £4.90: £2.00, £3.00; EX 29.60 Trifecta £116.50 Pool: £538.87 - 3.42 winning units. Place 6: £40.05 Place 5: £21.26.
Owner The Peregrina Partnership **Bred** Andrea Wilkinson Gay Kelleway **Trained** Exning, Suffolk

FOCUS
A modest fillies' maiden run in a marginally quicker time than the earlier maiden over the same trip. The whole field raced down the middle of the track. The winner probably only had to match last year's debut form.
T/Plt: £323.40 to a £1 stake. Pool: £51,793.73. 116.90 winning tickets. T/Qpdt: £75.10 to a £1 stake. Pool: £3,867.92. 38.10 winning tickets. JR

3527 HAYDOCK (L-H)

Friday, July 3

OFFICIAL GOING: Good (good to firm in places; 8.4)
Rail realignment increased advertised distances on the round course by around 10yards
Wind: Light, half-against Weather: Fine

3570 BET ONLINE AT CORBETTSPORTS.COM P.J.A. APPRENTICE SERIES H'CAP 5f

6:40 (6:42) (Class 5) (0-75,75) 3-Y-O+ £3,238 (£963; £481; £240) **Stalls** Centre

Form RPR

620 **1** **Top Bid**[25] 2770 5-9-2 **58**.......................................(b) KellyHarrison 8 66
(T D Easterby) *dwlt: hld up: rdn and hdwy over 1f out: r.o to ld ins fnl f: wl on top at fin* **13/2**[3]

3004 **2** *1 ¼* **Distant Vision (IRE)**[14] 3111 6-8-6 **51** oh6..........(b) PatrickDonaghy[(3)] 9 54
(H A McWilliams) *hld up: rdn and hdwy over 1f out: squeezed through gap to chal 100yds out: r.o towards fin: nt rch wnr* **16/1**

1404 **3** *hd* **Peopleton Brook**[13] 3162 7-9-0 **59**.............................. (tp) RossAtkinson[(3)] 1 61
(B G Powell) *a.p: rdn over 1f out: r.o to ld briefly ins fnl f: nt qckn towards fin* **14/1**

0411 **4** *¾* **Rocketball (IRE)**[4] 3445 4-9-7 **66** 6ex.............................. DeanHeslop[(3)] 2 66
(Mrs L Williamson) *led: rdn over 1f out: hdd ins fnl f: no ex cl home* **7/2**[1]

0000 **5** *hd* **Town House**[8] 3304 7-8-2 **51** oh6.. NoraLooby[(7)] 12 50
(B P J Baugh) *racd keenly: showed pce to r promly: rdn to chal over 1f out: styd on same pce fnl 100yds* **50/1**

0043 **6** *1 ¼* **Jilly Why (IRE)**[7] 3331 8-9-3 **62**.......................................(b) MartinLane[(3)] 7 56
(Paul Green) *hld up bhd ldrs: effrt over 1f out: wnt sltly lft ins fnl f: kpt on u.p: nt pce to chal* **5/1**[2]

2300 **7** *½* **Mazzola**[22] 2840 3-9-11 **75**.. MCGeran[(3)] 4 66
(M R Channon) *in rr: rdn over 1f out: kpt on ins fnl f: nvr able to land a blow* **13/2**[3]

0421 **8** *nk* **Red Rosanna**[14] 3118 3-9-13 **74**.............................. RussellKennemore 10 63
(R Hollinshead) *prom: rdn to chal over 1f out: one pce whn n.m.r 100yds out: fdd after* **7/2**[1]

0000 **9** *9* **Miacarla**[61] 1695 6-8-4 **51** oh6.......................................(t) DeclanCannon[(5)] 3 10
(H A McWilliams) *dwlt: hld up: outpcd appr fnl f* **25/1**

006- **10** 4 **Gleaming Spirit (IRE)**[201] 7672 5-8-8 **55**...........(v) AndrewHeffernan(5) 6 —
(Peter Grayson) *prom: pushed along 1/2-way: sn wknd* **25/1**

61.44 secs (0.94) **Going Correction** 0.0s/f (Good)
WFA 3 from 4yo+ 5lb **10** Ran SP% **110.0**
Speed ratings (Par 103): **92,90,89,88,88 86,85,84,70,64**
toteswingers: 1&2 £18.90, 1&3 £11.10, 2&3 £31.90 CSF £95.01 CT £1337.17 TOTE £7.80: £1.90, £6.30, £3.40; EX 82.10.
Owner John & Marilyn Williams **Bred** Southill Stud **Trained** Great Habton, N Yorks

FOCUS
After a dry night 6mm of water was put on during the morning, but this was followed by 8mm of rain in the afternoon. The ground was still officially good, good to firm in places though, and that resulted in quite a few non-runners through the card. Jockeys who rode in the opener were unanimous that the ground was genuinely good all round, and times throughout the evening looked to back that up. Modest and slightly dubious sprint form, although it appears sound enough, and the decent gallop helped to set things up for those coming from off the pace.

3571 SUPPLY UK MAIDEN STKS 6f
7:10 (7:11) (Class 5) 2-Y-O **£3,238** (£963; £481; £240) **Stalls** Centre

Form RPR

2 **1** **Black Snowflake (USA)**[14] 3113 2-9-3 0.......................... AlanMunro 5 85
(Saeed Bin Suroor) *trckd ldrs: rdn and nt qckn over 1f out whn disputing 2nd: r.o ins fnl f to ld fnl 100yds* **8/13**[1]

4 **2** ½ **Gunner Lindley (IRE)**[14] 3113 2-9-3 0.......................... MichaelHills 3 84
(B W Hills) *trckd ldrs: rdn and nt qckn over 1f out whn disputing 2nd: rallied ins fnl f: chal fnl 100yds: kpt on* **9/2**[2]

3 ½ **Our Jonathan** 2-9-3 0.......................... TomEaves 11 82+
(B Smart) *w ldr: led 1/2-way: rdn and abt 2 l clr 1f out: hdd and no ex fnl 100yds* **18/1**

4 **4** 13 **Brasingaman Eric**[13] 3152 2-9-3 0.......................... SilvestreDeSousa 15 43
(Mrs G S Rees) *chsd ldrs: pushed along 2f out: outpcd by front trio over 1f out: no imp after* **9/1**[3]

03 **5** 1½ **Dolphin Rock**[11] 3226 2-9-3 0.......................... DaleGibson 1 39
(Mrs G S Rees) *hld up: rdn 2f out: nvr able to get on terms w ldrs* **33/1**

6 hd **Blue Avon** 2-8-5 0.......................... LeeTopliss(7) 6 33
(R A Fahey) *missed break: bhd: hung lft fr 2f out: kpt on and gained pls ins fnl f: nvr on terms w ldrs* **25/1**

7 hd **Smog (IRE)** 2-9-3 0.......................... RichardMullen 9 37
(B J Meehan) *dwlt: pushed along in rr and green: kpt on and gained pls ins fnl f: nvr on terms w ldrs* **12/1**

8 1½ **Ajara Boy** 2-9-3 0.......................... LukeMorris 17 33
(N J Vaughan) *missed break: in rr: hdwy and in tch after 2f: lost pl and outpcd 1/2-way: hung lft whn n.d over 1f out* **33/1**

9 5 **Lighterman** 2-8-12 0.......................... GaryBartley(5) 14 18
(E J Alston) *racd keenly: led: hdd 1/2-way: wknd 2f out* **25/1**

10 2¾ **Hot Rod Mamma (IRE)** 2-8-7 0.......................... SladeO'Hara(5) 8 —
(A Berry) *s.i.s: hld up: pushed along 2f out: outpcd after* **80/1**

11 2 **Gee Major** 2-9-3 0.......................... GregFairley 4 —
(N J Vaughan) *bmpd s: in rr: pushed along and outpcd 1/2-way* **33/1**

1m 14.79s (0.79) **Going Correction** 0.0s/f (Good) **11** Ran SP% **120.8**
Speed ratings (Par 94): **94,93,92,75,73 73,72,70,64,60 57**
toteswingers: 1&2 £1.20, 1&3 £4.10, 2&3 £7.70 CSF £3.29 TOTE £1.80: £1.10, £1.30, £2.30; EX 2.70.
Owner Godolphin **Bred** Grapestock Llc **Trained** Newmarket, Suffolk

FOCUS
The first three finished a long way clear in this maiden.

NOTEBOOK
Black Snowflake(USA) further strengthened the form of his Newmarket debut by getting up close home. He clearly isn't straightforward given the presence of the noseband, an aid Godolphin rarely seem to use on their horses, but he settled well in midfield here and under a strong ride from Alan Munro (who was riding his first winner for Godolphin), battled on strongly to plunder the prize. His jockey reported afterwards that the colt is still a big baby and he's got a ton of improvement in him, while this ground was plenty quick enough. He has an entry in the big juvenile sales race at Doncaster later in the season. (op 5-4 tchd 11-8)
Gunner Lindley(IRE) ◆, two places behind today's winner at Newmarket on his debut, also stepped forward, staying on strongly to ensure Black Snowflake had to pull out all the stops to score, and this Medicean colt looks a winner waiting to happen. (op 5-2)
Our Jonathan ◆ ran an absolute screamer in third and looks a really nice type for Bryan Smart to go to war with. He bounced out like an old hand to bowl along and set decent fractions, and had most of his rivals under pressure 2f out. Although he was worn down by more experienced rivals close home, he's a sure-fire future winner if building on this and the speed he showed suggests he wouldn't mind dropping back to 5f. (op 16-1 tchd 14-1)
Brasingaman Eric, who was gambled on, was beaten so far into fourth that it's hard to be positive about his performance, but he's bred to want much further in time anyway. (op 28-1)
Ajara Boy was well beaten but shaped with some encouragement. He looked pretty clueless throughout and seemed to want to hang in the final furlong, but he kept going forward and looks capable of improving for the experience. (op 25-1)

3572 GLENCROFT (S) STKS 6f
7:45 (7:47) (Class 4) 2-Y-O **£5,504** (£1,637; £818; £408) **Stalls** Centre

Form RPR

043 **1** **Bluie**[21] 2896 2-8-11 0.......................... AdrianTNicholls 4 68
(D Nicholls) *mde all: rdn over 1f out: r.o wl and in command fnl f* **9/4**[1]

66 **2** 2 **Maoi Chinn Tire (IRE)**[74] 1404 2-8-11 0.......................... LukeMorris 13 62
(J S Moore) *midfield: rdn and hdwy 2f out: wnt 2nd and hung lft fr over 1f out: styd on u.p: no imp on wnr fnl 100yds* **8/1**

3 2¾ **Lord Raglan (IRE)** 2-8-11 0.......................... AndrewElliott 3 54
(K R Burke) *chsd ldrs: rdn and outpcd over 2f out: styd on u.p and hung lft ins fnl f: no threat to front pair* **14/1**

55 **4** shd **Clear Ice (IRE)**[18] 2963 2-8-11 0.......................... TonyCulhane 10 53
(D Nicholls) *a.p: rdn and hung lft fr over 1f out: styd on same pce fnl f* **7/1**

014 **5** 3 **Miami Gator (IRE)**[21] 2896 2-8-11 0.......................... MartinLane(5) 1 49
(K R Burke) *w wnr: rdn and outpcd 2f out: one pce u.p fr over 1f out: no imp* **13/2**[3]

6 shd **Otterton** 2-8-1 0.......................... JamieKyne(5) 2 39
(R Hollinshead) *missed break: bhd: pushed along 2f out: sme prog over 1f out: nvr a threat* **33/1**

4 **7** 5 **Almuntaser (IRE)**[18] 2979 2-8-11 0.......................... StephenDonohoe 9 29
(Ian Williams) *missed break: sn in midfield: effrt to chse ldrs 2f out: wknd ins fnl f* **11/4**[2]

0 **8** 1¾ **That'Lldonowthen (IRE)**[25] 2771 2-8-11 0.......................... NCallan 7 24
(J S Moore) *racd keenly in midfield: rdn over 2f out: wknd over 1f out* **25/1**

0 **9** 1 **Orpen All Hours (IRE)**[6] 3392 2-8-1 0.......................... PatrickDonaghy(5) 6 16
(P C Haslam) *midfield: rdn and sme hdwy over 2f out: wknd over 1f out* **28/1**

504 **10** 7 **Zaskia (IRE)**[32] 2541 2-8-6 0.......................... RichardMullen 14 —
(K A Ryan) *wnt rt s: in tch: rdn over 2f out: wknd over 1f out* **25/1**

0 **11** 15 **Whistling Wind**[57] 1802 2-8-11 0.......................... SilvestreDeSousa 8 —
(Paul Green) *sn bhd and outpcd* **33/1**

000 **12** 34 **Nuts About You (IRE)**[14] 3119 2-7-13 0.......................... BillyCray(7) 5 —
(A Berry) *missed break: bhd: wnt rt after 2f: a bdly outpcd* **100/1**

1m 14.87s (0.87) **Going Correction** 0.0s/f (Good) **12** Ran SP% **119.1**
Speed ratings (Par 96): **94,91,87,87,83 83,76,74,73,63 43,—**
toteswingers: 1&2 £4.70, 1&3 £7.30, 2&3 £7.40 CSF £19.50 TOTE £3.00: £1.60, £2.80, £3.10; EX 23.00.There was no bid for the winner.
Owner The Three K's **Bred** P Baugh **Trained** Sessay, N Yorks

FOCUS
An ordinary seller.

NOTEBOOK
Bluie had run well in an above average seller at York last time and he made the most of what was a much softer contest. Always to the fore, he gradually wound things up from the front and had his rivals on the stretch entering the final furlong. He kept on strongly to get off the mark at the fourth attempt and, although he is running at a very lowly level, does look to be improving with each start and may be able to hold his own in low-grade nurseries. (op 11-4)
Maoi Chinn Tire(IRE) was down in grade which enabled him to show more than in a couple of maidens, and he stayed on well enough to suggest he can win a similar contest granted a bit more improvement. (tchd 7-1)
Lord Raglan(IRE) put in some decent late work to grab third despite edging to his left under pressure, and looks the type to improve plenty for this initial experience, especially when stepped up in trip. (tchd 12-1)
Clear Ice(IRE) kept on at the one speed, having been close enough throughout, and is another who will probably do better over further. (op 11-1 tchd 12-1)

3573 EUROPA SERVICES H'CAP 1m 2f 95y
8:15 (8:15) (Class 4) (0-85,85) 3-Y-0+ **£5,504** (£1,637; £818; £408) **Stalls** Low

Form RPR

-005 **1** **Classic Legend**[17] 2999 4-9-13 **84**.......................... ShaneKelly 9 90
(B J Meehan) *chsd ldr: rdn and chal fr over 3f out: tk narrow ld over 1f out: r.o u.p* **9/4**[1]

0222 **2** nk **Snow Dancer (IRE)**[9] 3267 5-8-7 **67**..........(p) NeilBrown(3) 6 72
(H A McWilliams) *s.i.s: hld up: hdwy to mount str chal fr over 2f out: r.o u.p: hld fnl strides* **7/2**[2]

15 **3** nk **Hallstatt (IRE)**[16] 3026 3-8-10 **78**.......................... GregFairley 3 82
(M Johnston) *hld up: hdwy to ld over 3f out: a strly pressed: hdd narrowly over 1f out: nt qckn fnl strides* **9/4**[1]

200- **4** 7 **Bajan Parkes**[161] 6288 6-9-12 **83**.......................... DavidAllan 10 73
(E J Alston) *led: hdd over 3f out: wknd 2f out* **10/1**

0245 **5** 6 **Shady Gloom (IRE)**[10] 3235 4-9-7 **78**.......................... NCallan 11 56
(K A Ryan) *chsd ldrs: rdn and lost pl over 3f out: n.d after* **5/1**[3]

2m 14.3s (1.30) **Going Correction** +0.05s/f (Good)
WFA 3 from 4yo+ 11lb **5** Ran SP% **109.5**
Speed ratings (Par 105): **105,104,104,98,94**
toteswingers: 1&2 £25.90. CSF £10.21 TOTE £3.60: £1.60, £1.40; EX 13.30.
Owner Mrs Moira McNamara **Bred** B Walters **Trained** Manton, Wilts

FOCUS
A race decimated by non-runners and it turned into a bit of a sprint from 3f out. A bunch finish and the exposed runner-up rather limit the form.

3574 WATERAID FILLIES' H'CAP 1m 30y
8:50 (8:50) (Class 5) (0-75,75) 3-Y-O **£3,238** (£963; £481; £240) **Stalls** Low

Form RPR

1- **1** **Island Sunset (IRE)**[251] 6986 3-9-5 **73**.......................... AlanMunro 7 77
(W R Muir) *stdd s: hld up: pushed along and outpcd 4f out: hdwy to ld over 1f out: r.o wl and in full control fnl f* **5/2**[2]

1-00 **2** 2¾ **Sampower Rose (IRE)**[37] 2370 3-8-8 **62**.......................... DNolan 6 60
(D Carroll) *s.i.s: chsd ldrs: rdn and outpcd over 3f out: clsd to chal and take 2nd over 1f out: nt pce of wnr and no imp fnl f* **17/2**[3]

2515 **3** 10 **Peter's Gift (IRE)**[15] 3062 3-9-4 **72**.......................... NCallan 8 47
(K A Ryan) *led for 1f: remained w ldr: led 2f out: sn rdn: hdd over 1f out: sn wknd* **5/2**[2]

423 **4** 13 **Silent Oasis**[14] 3100 3-9-6 **74**.......................... ShaneKelly 4 19
(B J Meehan) *led after 1f: rdn and hdd 2f out: got unbalanced whn wkng over 1f out: sn hung rt* **6/4**[1]

1m 44.66s (0.86) **Going Correction** +0.05s/f (Good) **4** Ran SP% **107.7**
Speed ratings (Par 97): **97,94,84,71**
toteswingers: 1&2 £25.30. CSF £18.38 TOTE £3.40; EX 18.10.
Owner Mrs J M Muir **Bred** Rathasker Stud **Trained** Lambourn, Berks
■ Stewards' Enquiry : D Nolan two-day ban: used whip with excessive frequency (Jul 17-18)

FOCUS
Another contest depleted by non-runners. The gallop was strong from the outset as Silent Oasis and Peter's Gift traded blows from a long way out, and that only served to set things up for the pair in behind. Weak form, rated around the runner-up.
Silent Oasis Official explanation: trainer had no explanation for the poor form shown

3575 BALFOUR BEATTY H'CAP 1m 6f
9:20 (9:20) (Class 5) (0-70,70) 3-Y-O **£3,238** (£963; £481; £240) **Stalls** Low

Form RPR

-603 **1** **Drop The Hammer**[10] 3233 3-8-7 **56**.......................... SilvestreDeSousa 8 60
(T P Tate) *chsd ldr: pushed along over 3f out: rdn over 2f out: styd on to ld fnl 75yds* **11/1**

-002 **2** nk **Golden Games (IRE)**[30] 2605 3-9-0 **63**.......................... NCallan 9 67+
(J L Dunlop) *midfield: hdwy over 3f out: rdn to ld over 1f out: hdd fnl 75yds* **3/1**[2]

-431 **3** 2¾ **Bollin Judith**[39] 2340 3-8-11 **60**.......................... DavidAllan 5 60+
(T D Easterby) *hld up: pushed along 4f out: rdn over 2f out: hdwy over 1f out: styd on towards fin: nt pce to trble front pair* **11/4**[1]

-304 **4** hd **Ja One (IRE)**[11] 3222 3-9-2 **65**.......................... MichaelHills 6 64
(B W Hills) *chsd ldrs: rdn over 2f out: styd on same pce fnl f* **5/1**[3]

5302 **5** nk **Tropical Bachelor (IRE)**[22] 2838 3-9-5 **68**.......................... TomEaves 11 67
(T J Pitt) *led: rdn over 2f out: hdd over 1f out: one pce fnl f* **11/2**

4460 **6** 2¼ **Mohanad (IRE)**[31] 2567 3-9-3 **66**.......................... TonyCulhane 4 62
(M R Channon) *midfield: pushed along over 3f out: styd on u.p: nt pce to chal: no imp on ldrs* **22/1**

-400 **7** ½ **Blue Tango (IRE)**[74] 1408 3-9-7 **70**.......................... JimCrowley 10 65
(Mrs A J Perrett) *hld up: rdn over 2f out: nvr able to land a blow* **20/1**

0-06 **8** nse **Morning Calm**[21] 2881 3-8-12 **61**..........................(v[1]) GregFairley 3 56
(R Charlton) *racd keenly: chsd ldrs: pushed along 3f out: wknd 2f out* **15/2**

6530 9 3 1/4 **One Scoop Or Two**[24] 2779 3-8-9 58....................(t) StephenDonohoe 7 49
(F Sheridan) *hld up in rr: hung lft u.p fr over 1f out: nvr on terms* **40/1**

3m 13.14s (8.84) **Going Correction** +0.05s/f (Good) **9 Ran SP% 115.4**
Speed ratings (Par 100): **76,75,74,74,73 72,72,72,70**
toteswingers: 1&2 £9.50, 1&3 £6.20, 2&3 £1.90 CSF £43.12 CT £118.71 TOTE £18.90: £3.80, £1.60, £1.80; EX 104.50 Place 6: £161.50, Place 5: £18.65.
Owner A Crowther **Bred** Mrs N J Gidley Wright **Trained** Tadcaster, N Yorks

FOCUS
The pace was just steady and this contest didn't really begin in earnest until the 3f pole. It is hard to rate the form positively.
T/Plt: £113.30 to a £1 stake. Pool: £67,600.25. 435.43 winning tickets. T/Qpdt: £15.20 to a £1 stake. Pool: £4,840.40. 235.05 winning tickets. DO

3420 SALISBURY (R-H)
Friday, July 3

OFFICIAL GOING: Good to firm (9.0)
Wind: Vrtually nil Weather: Hot and humid

3576 "COME SHOPPING AT CASTLEPOINT" BOURNEMOUTH MAIDEN AUCTION FILLIES' STKS 6f 212y
6:30 (6:30) (Class 5) 2-Y-O **£3,885** (£1,156; £577; £288) **Stalls High**

Form RPR

1 **Gobama** 2-8-9 0.................................. SebSanders 2 78+
(J W Hills) *hld up towards rr: stdy prog fr over 3f out: swtchd lft over 2f out: sn rdn and qcknd up wl: edgd rt but led jst over 1f out: r.o wl: readily* **12/1**

35 2 1 1/2 **Just The Tonic**[34] 2494 2-8-7 0.................................. SamHitchcott 6 73
(M R Channon) *trckd ldrs: rdn to ld over 2f out: hdd over 1f out: kpt on but nt pce of wnr* **10/1**

44 3 1 **Bathwick Xaara**[10] 3248 2-8-4 0.................................. SaleemGolam 10 67
(J G Portman) *trckd ldrs: wandered u.p over 1f out: kpt on towards fin* **5/1[2]**

3 4 1/2 **Go Forth North (USA)**[13] 3160 2-8-4 0.................................. LiamJones 12 66+
(M L W Bell) *mid-div: sn pushed along: rdn over 2f out: styng on whn hmpd jst ins fnl f: fin wl* **3/1[1]**

6 5 nk **Giulietta Da Vinci**[10] 3248 2-8-4 0.................................. RichardSmith 13 65+
(R Hannon) *trckd ldrs: rdn over 2f out: swtchd lft over 1f out: kpt on same pce* **11/2[3]**

6 1 1/2 **Sounds Of Thunder** 2-8-7 0.................................. JamesDoyle 9 64+
(H J L Dunlop) *green thrght: s.i.s: sn pushed along in rr: styd on but nvr best of runs fnl f* **25/1**

335 7 nk **Shibhan**[10] 3248 2-8-5 0..................................(p) EdwardCreighton 4 62
(C E Brittain) *trckd ldrs: chal over 3f out: hung rt u.p over 1f out: hung lft jst ins fnl f: fdd* **16/1**

8 1/2 **Expensive Legacy** 2-8-0 0.................................. SophieDoyle(5) 8 60
(H J L Dunlop) *s.i.s: nvr bttr than mid-div* **50/1**

9 nk **Delta Sky (IRE)** 2-8-7 0.................................. JerryO'Dwyer 3 62+
(Miss Amy Weaver) *restrained in rr: stmbld after 2f: sme hdwy u.p whn hmpd ent fnl f: no imp after* **66/1**

10 1 1/4 **Elizabelle (IRE)** 2-8-12 0.................................. PatDobbs 7 63
(R Hannon) *prom: rdn over 3f out: sn btn: wknd over 1f out* **20/1**

0 11 1/2 **Open Glory (FR)**[10] 3249 2-8-12 0.................................. RichardKingscote 1 62
(Tom Dascombe) *led tl u.p over 2f out: wknd fnl f* **13/2**

12 1/2 **Moonraker's Choice (IRE)** 2-8-9 0 ow1.................................. PatrickHills(3) 5 61+
(R Hannon) *t.k.h bhd ldrs: chal over 3f out: wkng whn short of room ent fnl f* **8/1**

13 22 **Nicaldani** 2-8-4 0.................................. JimmyQuinn 14 —
(M Blanshard) *mid-div for 3f: sn bhd* **33/1**

1m 28.3s (-0.70) **Going Correction** -0.25s/f (Firm) **13 Ran SP% 119.2**
Speed ratings (Par 91): **94,92,91,90,90 88,88,87,87,85 85,84,59**
toteswingers: 1&2 £43.30, 1&3 £25.10, 2&3 £8.90 CSF £119.82 TOTE £22.30: £5.30, £4.30, £2.60; EX 188.60.
Owner W Y Chen **Bred** Newsells Park Stud Limited **Trained** Upper Lambourn, Berks

FOCUS
The far rail was dolled out approximately two and a half furlongs from the finish, which allowed horses on the inside to get a run. It also significantly narrowed the course from the three-furlong marker.

NOTEBOOK
Gobama made an impressive debut to provide trainer John Hills with his first two-year-old winner of the season. Ridden with patience, she was kept to the outside to get a clear run and, after getting balanced, showed a good turn of foot. Her immaturity showed, as she drifted right inside the last furlong, but she won with plenty of authority. The ground was probably as fast as she would want and her pedigree, being a daughter of Dr Fong out of an Inchinor mare, would suggest that a mile in her first season wouldn't be a problem. (op 10-1)
Just The Tonic ran another sound race on her third start. She appeared suited by the first attempt at 7f. She was pressing the pace throughout and stayed on really well to the line. She might be interesting in a fillies' nursery over this distance. (tchd 11-1)
Bathwick Xaara failed to confirm May runnning at Newbury with the runner-up, but was another suited by the step up in trip. (tchd 11-2)
Go Forth North(USA) was struggling at halfway and, when she finally did get rolling, was hampered inside the final furlong. It didn't cost her the race, but she may have been placed. (op 11-4 tchd 10-3)
Giulietta Da Vinci, who had finished behind Bathwick Xaara at Newbury, was tapped for pace despite the extra furlong. In her defence, she didn't see much daylight during the last furlong. (op 7-1)
Sounds Of Thunder ran a pleasing debut after looking immature soon after the start. She didn't pick up until late and will need further judged on her stout pedigree. (tchd 28-1)
Shibhan was all over the place going to the last furlong, first going right, then left. This was her fourth run, but hers her third on pretty fast ground, and she may have been feeling it.
Expensive Legacy showed some promise without threatening. (op 66-1)
Delta Sky(IRE) missed the break and got going too late. Official explanation: jockey said filly was slowly away
Open Glory(FR) again raced too freely. (op 8-1)

3577 "COME SHOPPING AT CASTLEPOINT" EMPRISE SERVICES CLAIMING STKS 6f 212y
7:00 (7:00) (Class 5) 3-Y-O+ **£3,238** (£963; £481; £240) **Stalls High**

Form RPR

5202 1 **Indian Art (IRE)**[4] 3455 3-9-5 82.................................. RichardHughes 6 84
(R Hannon) *hld up: hdwy in center fr 3f out: rdn for sustained chal fr 2f out: kpt on to ld wl ins fnl f: asserting nr fin* **13/8[1]**

0514 2 nk **Elna Bright**[13] 3174 4-9-10 88.................................. JamieSpencer 7 83
(P D Evans) *hld up last: smooth prog fr 3f out: shkn up to take narrow advantage wl over 1f out: sn edgd lft: kpt on but no ex whn hdd towards fin* **11/4[2]**

4361 3 6 **Belated Silver (IRE)**[11] 3225 3-8-13 69.................................. RichardKingscote 9 61
(Tom Dascombe) *broke wl: sn settled bhd ldrs: rdn 2f out: sn outpcd by ldng pair* **9/2[3]**

3651 4 1 **Dressed To Dance (IRE)**[58] 1784 5-8-9 79........(b) KevinGhunowa(3) 11 52
(R A Harris) *trckd ldrs: short of room on rails over 3f out: effrt whn gap appeared wl over 2f out: sn outpcd by ldng pair: no ex towards fin* **11/2**

6200 5 4 1/2 **Mr Flannegan**[9] 3257 3-8-5 60.................................. FrankieMcDonald 3 38
(H Candy) *trckd ldrs: led over 3f out: sn rdn: hung lft and hdd wl over 1f out: wknd* **33/1**

-005 6 4 1/2 **Shybutwilling (IRE)**[30] 2603 4-8-10 50.................................. FergusSweeney 4 26
(Mrs P N Dutfield) *short lived effrt over 2f out but nvr on terms* **66/1**

0305 7 1 1/4 **Tidal Force (USA)**[7] 3358 3-8-11 69..................................(b) MartinDwyer 5 29
(P F I Cole) *chsd ldrs: sn pushed along: wknd wl over 1f out* **9/1**

0/5- 8 10 **Carson's Spirit (USA)**[167] 6537 5-9-1 70.................................. JerryO'Dwyer 10 —
(J R Gask) *prom: rdn wl over 2f out: sn wknd* **33/1**

0/0 9 27 **Pitton Justice**[11] 3204 7-8-13 0.................................. RichardThomas 1 —
(Dr J R J Naylor) *led tl over 3f out: sn wknd: t.o* **100/1**

1m 26.65s (-2.35) **Going Correction** -0.25s/f (Firm)
WFA 3 from 4yo+ 8lb **9 Ran SP% 116.7**
Speed ratings (Par 103): **103,102,95,94,89 84,82,71,40**
toteswingers: 1&2 £1.70, 1&3 £2.40, 2&3 £3.70 CSF £6.19 TOTE £2.60: £1.10, £1.60, £1.80; EX 5.40.
Owner Matthew Green **Bred** Michael Woodlock And Seamus Kennedy **Trained** East Everleigh, Wilts

FOCUS
An uncompetitive claimer, but the front pair,who finished clear, are useful on their day. Probably not form to be too positive about.
Dressed To Dance(IRE) Official explanation: jockey said mare ran too free

3578 "COME SHOPPING AT CASTLEPOINT" H'CAP 1m 1f 198y
7:35 (7:36) (Class 4) (0-85,85) 3-Y-O+ **£6,476** (£1,927; £963; £481) **Stalls High**

Form RPR

3-00 1 **St Jean Cap Ferrat**[34] 2468 4-9-12 83..................................(v) PatDobbs 2 92
(P J Hobbs) *wnt bdly lft s: in tch: rdn and gd run to squeeze through on rails over 1f out: chal ent fnl f: slt ld wl ins fnl f: hld on* **22/1**

4331 2 nse **Cill Rialaig**[24] 2796 4-9-6 77.................................. SteveDrowne 6 86
(H Morrison) *in tch: hdwy 3f out: chal 2f out: rdn to ld ent fnl f: narrowly hdd wl ins fnl f: kpt on: jst hld* **2/1[2]**

3-11 3 2 1/4 **Larkham (USA)**[38] 2356 3-9-1 83.................................. SebSanders 10 92+
(R M Beckett) *trckd ldr: swtchd rt over 2f out: nt clr run whn swtchd lft sn after: rdn and abt to mount chal whn squeezed up 1f out: no ch after* **13/8[1]**

0051 4 1 1/4 **Emperor Court (IRE)**[23] 2823 5-9-13 84.................................. FergusSweeney 7 86
(P J Makin) *led: rdn and hrd pressed fr wl over 2f out: drifted lft wl over 1f out: hdd ent fnl f: no ex* **12/1**

2455 5 10 **Basra (IRE)**[29] 2641 6-9-9 80.................................. JamieSpencer 4 62
(Miss Jo Crowley) *hld up in last pair: effrt over 2f out: wknd over 1f out* **9/2[3]**

0000 6 1 1/4 **Goodwood Starlight (IRE)**[14] 3103 4-9-11 82.................................. WilliamBuick 9 62
(G L Moore) *trckd ldr: rdn over 3f out: wknd 2f out* **14/1**

420 7 2 1/4 **Man Of Gwent (UAE)**[4] 3450 5-8-8 70..................................(p) RichardEvans(5) 8 45
(P D Evans) *hld up: hdwy over 3f out: sn rdn: wknd 2f out* **16/1**

2m 6.08s (-3.82) **Going Correction** -0.25s/f (Firm)
WFA 3 from 4yo+ 11lb **7 Ran SP% 114.2**
Speed ratings (Par 105): **105,104,103,102,94 93,91**
toteswingers: 1&2 £12.20, 1&3 £6.90, 2&3 £1.10 CSF £66.18 CT £116.71 TOTE £17.20: £4.70, £1.80; EX 48.40.
Owner R A Green **Bred** J L C Pearce **Trained** Withycombe, Somerset

FOCUS
The cutaway on the far rail over two furlongs out gave an unexpected chance to horses looking to get a run at what is usually a congested part of the course and the winner made the most of it. The form looks solid with the winner back to his best.

3579 "COME SHOPPING AT CASTLEPOINT" DOUGLAND SUPPORT SERVICES NURSERY 6f
8:05 (8:05) (Class 4) 2-Y-O **£4,695** (£1,397; £698; £348) **Stalls High**

Form RPR

503 1 **Michaelmas Daisy**[35] 2457 2-8-2 66 oh5 ow4.................................. MartinDwyer 7 67
(Miss Amy Weaver) *broke wl: mde all: rdn 2f out: r.o wl* **25/1**

432 2 3/4 **Janeiro (IRE)**[30] 2599 2-9-7 85.................................. RichardKingscote 3 84
(Tom Dascombe) *missed break: in last trio but cl enough: hdwy over 2f out: sn rdn r.o to chse wnr over 1f out but a being hld* **7/2[1]**

0340 3 hd **Timelord (IRE)**[5] 3424 2-8-3 67.................................. FrankieMcDonald 5 65
(S Kirk) *in last trio but cl enough: hdwy over 2f out: sn swtchd lft and rdn: edgd rt 1f out: r.o towards fin* **11/2[2]**

51 4 6 **Fleeting Echo**[30] 2595 2-8-4 68.................................. JimmyQuinn 11 48+
(R Hannon) *slowly away: sn pushed along to chse ldrs but tight of room on rails: wknd ent fnl f* **7/2[1]**

0425 5 3/4 **Pullyourfingerout (IRE)**[26] 2735 2-8-7 71.................................. FergusSweeney 10 49
(B G Powell) *s.i.s: sn pushed along in last 3: nvr a threat* **10/1[3]**

045 6 2 **The Shuffler**[29] 2631 2-8-5 69.................................. ChrisCatlin 2 41
(G L Moore) *chsd wnr: rdn over 2f out: wknd over 1f out* **10/1[3]**

5111 7 5 **Anjomarba (IRE)**[21] 2896 2-9-2 85.................................. JackDean(5) 8 42
(W G M Turner) *little slow away: sn trcking ldrs: rdn over 2f out: sn btn* **7/2[1]**

003 8 6 **Lofthouse**[49] 2037 2-8-3 67.................................. CatherineGannon 9 6
(M R Channon) *chsd ldrs: rough passage for over 2f: rdn and wknd over 2f out* **10/1[3]**

1m 14.34s (-0.46) **Going Correction** -0.25s/f (Firm) **8 Ran SP% 113.2**
Speed ratings (Par 96): **93,92,91,83,82 80,73,65**
toteswingers: 1&2 £21.40, 1&3 £22.00, 2&3 £3.50 CSF £108.48 CT £564.28 TOTE £29.70: £5.10, £1.30, £2.00; EX 154.10.
Owner The Michaelmas Daisy Partnership **Bred** M Sharkey **Trained** Newmarket, Suffolk

FOCUS
The 'official' rating shown next to each horse are estimated and for information purposes only. This was a rough race early on.

NOTEBOOK
Michaelmas Daisy was in the right place at the head of affairs. Having finished a close third in a 5f seller last time when she was carried left but stayed on, this extra furlong suited her and she showed plenty of courage on this fourth appearance. However, her intended apprentice partner failed to arrive and instead of carrying 7st 9lb she had 4lb overweight at 8st 2lb which meant she was carrying 9lb more than her long handicap mark of 7st 7lb. It might be hard for her when she is re-evaluated. (tchd 20-1)

Janeiro(IRE) had been progressive in three starts, two on all weather, and once again took a keen hold. When he was brought with his run he still showed a tendency to hang, this time right. He was gaining on the winner although this looks the right trip if he'll settle. (op 3-1)
Timelord(IRE) took a while to get going from the rear, but finished really well and should be able to win off this mark. (op 9-1 tchd 5-1)
Fleeting Echo got a very rough passage when he tried for a run up the inside after a furlong and still had problems after that. It put him at a disadvantage from which he could never really recover his momentum. (op 5-1)
Pullyourfingerout(IRE) was hanging right from halfway and never got into the action. (op 8-1)
Anjomarba(IRE) had done her winning in three sellers, each progressively more valuable, and was allotted joint top-weight. It didn't help when she was squeezed out of a position at halfway but she dropped away tamely soon after. The handicapper seems to have her nailed. (tchd 3-1 and 4-1)
Lofthouse was involved in the bumping with Fleeting Echo, but it didn't seem to have any effect on his chance. (op 7-1)

3580 "COME SHOPPING AT CASTLEPOINT" INDUSTRIAL CLEANING EQUIPMENT H'CAP 6f

8:40 (8:42) (Class 6) (0-65,65) 3-Y-O **£2,914** (£867; £433; £216) **Stalls** High

Form RPR
60-0 **1** **Kuanyao (IRE)**[34] 2496 3-8-10 **54**.............................. FergusSweeney 13 66+
(P J Makin) *racd far side: hld up: hdwy over 2f out: led over 1f out: r.o wl: rdn clr* **6/1**[3]
05-0 **2** *2* **Sister Clement (IRE)**[36] 2417 3-8-13 **57**........................ JamieSpencer 4 63+
(R Hannon) *racd centre: hld up and t.k.h: hdwy over 2f out: sn rdn to ld: hdd over 1f out: kpt on but nt pce of wnr ins fnl f* **3/1**[1]
00 **3** *2 ¼* **Ponting (IRE)**[49] 2048 3-9-2 **60**.. SebSanders 10 58
(R M Beckett) *racd far side: hld up: rdn and hdwy over 2f out: styd on fnl f* **10/3**[2]
2305 **4** *shd* **Vamos (IRE)**[8] 3299 3-9-2 **60**.. WilliamBuick 11 58
(J R Gask) *overall ldr on far side tl over 3f out: sn rdn: kpt chsng ldrs but no ex fnl f* **10/1**
541 **5** *5* **Fyelehk (IRE)**[72] 1465 3-9-4 **62**.................................. TGMcLaughlin 12 44
(B R Millman) *racd far side: chsd ldr: rdn and ev ch briefly 2f out: wknd fnl f* **14/1**
0005 **6** *¾* **Eye For The Girls**[13] 3161 3-8-11 **55**........................ CatherineGannon 2 35
(M R Channon) *chsd ldrs in centre: effrt over 2f out: wknd ent fnl f* **25/1**
1402 **7** *2* **Billy Beetroot (USA)**[4] 3464 3-9-4 **65**....................(t) KevinGhunowa(3) 7 38
(R A Harris) *racd centre: prom rdn over 2f out: wknd 1f out* **8/1**
0-00 **8** *nk* **Suakin Dancer (IRE)**[19] 2950 3-8-13 **57**........................ SteveDrowne 6 29
(H Morrison) *raced centre: a towards rr* **33/1**
6500 **9** *¾* **Marina Walk**[9] 3281 3-8-11 **55**... TravisBlock 3 25
(H Morrison) *racd centre: prom tl wknd over 2f out* **33/1**
4341 **10** *¾* **Pepin (IRE)**[46] 2132 3-8-9 **53**...................................(p) FrankieMcDonald 1 20
(D Haydn Jones) *racd centre: a towards rr* **25/1**
2-32 **11** *6* **Robin The Till**[95] 1032 3-9-7 **65**...................................... RichardHughes 8 13
(R Hannon) *racd centre: prom: overall ldr over 3f out: sn rdn and hdd: qckly wknd* **6/1**[3]
5400 **12** *20* **Azharia**[20] 2913 3-9-3 **61**...(p) MartinDwyer 9 —
(C E Brittain) *towards rr on far side: short lived effrt over 2f out: eased whn btn* **25/1**

1m 13.25s (-1.55) **Going Correction** -0.25s/f (Firm) 12 Ran SP% **120.9**
Speed ratings (Par 98): **100,97,94,94,87 86,83,83,82,81 73,46**
toteswingers: 1&2 £13.10, 1&3 £14.00, 2&3 £5.40 CSF £23.32 CT £71.97 TOTE £9.60: £2.50, £2.20, £1.80; EX 20.80.
Owner D M Ahier **Bred** Newlands House Stud **Trained** Ogbourne Maisey, Wilts

FOCUS
There was a difference of opinion about the best place to race, and with the course very narrow over three furlongs out, the majority of the field ended middle to stands side - unusual when the ground rides on the fast side. Form to be fairly positive about.
Kuanyao(IRE) Official explanation: trainer said, regarding the apparent improvement in form shown, that the gelding had taken time to recover from being gelded and had matured
Robin The Till Official explanation: jockey said gelding lost its action
Azharia Official explanation: jockey said filly was unsuited by the good to firm ground

3581 "COME SHOPPING AT CASTLEPOINT" BOURNEMOUTH FILLIES' H'CAP 1m

9:10 (9:12) (Class 5) (0-70,70) 3-Y-O+ **£4,695** (£1,397; £698; £348) **Stalls** High

Form RPR
3045 **1** **Caster Sugar (USA)**[11] 3209 3-9-1 **63**........................ RichardHughes 14 69
(R Hannon) *mid-div: hdwy on far side rails over 2f out: sn rdn: styd on gamely fnl f: led towards fin: drvn out* **15/2**
562 **2** *shd* **Some Sunny Day**[39] 2338 3-9-7 **69**................................. SteveDrowne 9 75+
(H Morrison) *mid-div: rdn over 3f out: hdwy 2f out: slt ld whn drifted rt jst ins fnl f: hdd nr fin* **6/1**[3]
0324 **3** *nk* **Seasonal Cross**[18] 2977 4-9-4 **57**..................................... SebSanders 6 64
(S Dow) *sn swtchd to far side rails: hld up: hdwy whn nt clr run over 2f out: weaved way through fnl f: r.o and clsng wl at fin* **10/3**[1]
0650 **4** *1 ½* **Dancing Storm**[11] 3217 6-9-4 **57**.................................... ChrisCatlin 11 61
(W S Kittow) *led: rdn and hrd pressed fr 3f out: hdd jst ins fnl f: disputing cl 3rd but hld whn squeezed out towards fin* **8/1**
401 **5** *2* **Miss Mujanna**[19] 2949 4-10-0 **67**.............................. J-PGuillambert 13 66
(J Akehurst) *hld up bhd: rdn over 3f out: styd on fr over 1f out: nvr trbld ldrs* **5/1**[2]
-400 **6** *½* **Fifty (IRE)**[30] 2598 4-9-12 **65**.. PatDobbs 7 63
(R Hannon) *hld up towards rr: rdn over 3f out: styd on fnl f: nrst fin* **16/1**
0504 **7** *1 ¼* **Applesnap (IRE)**[9] 3269 4-9-7 **60**..............................(p) JerryO'Dwyer 2 55
(Miss Amy Weaver) *trckd ldrs: rdn over 3f out: fdd over 1f out* **25/1**
-644 **8** *nk* **Oriental Girl**[20] 2910 4-9-8 **61**....................................(p) JamieSpencer 4 57
(J A Geake) *mid-div: smooth hdwy over 3f out: rdn to chal whn drifted rt over 2f out: hld whn short of room jst ins fnl f* **13/2**
-013 **9** *2 ¾* **Sapphire Rose**[20] 2910 3-9-0 **62**..................................... TravisBlock 12 48
(J G Portman) *trckd ldrs: rdn and ev ch over 2f out: wknd over 1f out* **11/1**
022- **10** *10* **Saharan Royal**[331] 4720 3-9-8 **70**................................... WilliamBuick 5 33
(M Salaman) *wnt lft s: trckd ldr: rdn wl over 2f out: wknd over 1f out* **15/2**

1m 42.32s (-1.18) **Going Correction** -0.25s/f (Firm)
WFA 3 from 4yo+ 9lb 10 Ran SP% **120.1**
Speed ratings (Par 100): **95,94,94,93,91 90,89,89,86,76**
toteswingers: 1&2 £9.50, 1&3 £5.70, 2&3 £5.10 CSF £53.66 CT £185.68 TOTE £8.20: £2.40, £2.10, £1.90; EX 33.30 Place 6: £55.49, Place 5: £12.60.
Owner Mrs James Wigan **Bred** Mrs James Wigan & London TB Services Ltd **Trained** East Everleigh, Wilts
■ Stewards' Enquiry : Steve Drowne caution: careless riding

FOCUS
Once again, the cutaway on the far rail over two furlongs out helped the winner. Just modest form, rated around the third and fourth.
T/Plt: £251.70 to a £1 stake. Pool: £52,856.33. 153.26 winning tickets. T/Qpdt: £49.80 to a £1 stake. Pool: £3,874.62. 57.50 winning tickets. TM

2925 SANDOWN (R-H)

Friday, July 3

OFFICIAL GOING: Good (round course 8.0; sprint course 7.7)
Rail dolled out 3yards from 7f start to 3f marker, creating a'drop in' at that point and increasing distances on round course by 4yards.
Wind: Light, against Weather: Bright, humid

3582 CADOGAN KEELAN WESTALL H'CAP 5f 6y

2:20 (2:20) (Class 3) (0-95,95) 3-Y-O+ **£7,771** (£2,312; £1,155; £577) **Stalls** High

Form RPR
3126 **1** **Canadian Danehill (IRE)**[19] 2946 7-9-2 **85**........................(p) LDettori 12 95
(R M H Cowell) *racd against far rail: chsd ldrs: rdn and effrt 2f out: led ins fnl f: kpt on wl* **8/1**
0541 **2** *¾* **The Jobber (IRE)**[19] 2946 8-9-1 **84**.................................. DaneO'Neill 15 91
(M Blanshard) *hld up in midfield: swtchd to far rail over 1f out and nt clr run briefly: swtchd lft and prog to chse wnr ins fnl f: a hld* **7/1**[3]
-031 **3** *½* **Sharpened Edge**[21] 2888 3-8-6 **80**.................................... LiamJones 10 87+
(B Palling) *lw: racd against far rail: pressed ldr: led over 1f out: hung bdly thrght fnl f and sn hdd: threw it away* **9/2**[1]
-104 **4** *¾* **Northern Dare (IRE)**[27] 2707 5-9-4 **87**............................ SteveDrowne 9 90
(D Nicholls) *s.s: wl in rr and racd off far rail: prog over 1f out: styd on fnl f: nrst fin* **7/1**[3]
0411 **5** *2 ¼* **Equuleus Pictor**[21] 2897 5-9-1 **89**..................................... JackDean(5) 7 83
(J L Spearing) *lw: led but racd off far side rail: hdd over 1f out: wknd ins fnl f* **9/1**
110- **6** *½* **Tony The Tap**[251] 6971 8-9-5 **88**...................................... MartinDwyer 4 81
(W R Muir) *s.v.s: swtchd to r against far rail: last pair tl kpt on fr over 1f out: n.d* **33/1**
1-40 **7** *nk* **Safari Mischief**[27] 2704 6-9-4 **92**.............................. WilliamCarson(5) 8 84
(P Winkworth) *chsd ldrs: rdn 2f out: lost pl over 1f out: no imp fnl f* **9/1**
6003 **8** *1* **Good Gorsoon (USA)**[11] 3212 4-9-1 **84**........................ WilliamBuick 1 72
(B W Hills) *sweating: s.s and swvd lft: mostly in last pair: sme prog fnl f: no ch* **16/1**
4-52 **9** *1 ½* **Kay Two (IRE)**[21] 2897 7-9-4 **87**..(p) TPQueally 3 70
(R J Price) *racd on outer: chsd ldrs: rdn 1/2-way: grad wknd over 1f out* **16/1**
03 **10** *1 ¼* **Jaconet (USA)**[14] 3122 4-9-3 **86**.................................(b) JamieSpencer 2 64
(T D Barron) *swtchd to r alone on nr side: on terms 3f: sn struggling* **11/1**
1205 **11** *1 ¼* **Cake (IRE)**[7] 3360 4-9-10 **93**.. RichardHughes 13 67
(R Hannon) *lw: chsd ldng pair: rdn 2f out: no prog over 1f out: wknd rapidly ins fnl f: eased* **11/2**[2]
1360 **12** *8* **Lesley's Choice**[13] 3166 3-8-10 **84**................................. DarryllHolland 6 27
(R Curtis) *nvr on terms w ldrs: rdn after 2f on outer: wknd 2f out: t.o* **25/1**

61.42 secs (-0.18) **Going Correction** +0.15s/f (Good)
WFA 3 from 4yo+ 5lb 12 Ran SP% **116.6**
Speed ratings (Par 107): **107,105,105,103,100 99,98,97,94,92 90,78**
toteswingers: 1&2 £11.20, 1&3 £10.50, 2&3 £5.60 CSF £61.96 CT £236.54 TOTE £9.30: £2.50, £2.20, £2.30; EX 38.60.
Owner T W Morley **Bred** Skymarc Farm Inc And Dr A J O'Reilly **Trained** Six Mile Bottom, Cambs

FOCUS
A competitive sprint handicap, despite the three non-runners, but as is often the case over this straight 5f the draw played its part with the first four home starting from the five highest stalls. Sound form, the winner back to his best.

NOTEBOOK
Canadian Danehill(IRE), who lost a near-fore shoe when sixth behind The Jobber at Salisbury last month, had never won off a mark this high on turf though he has won off higher on Fibresand. Given a fine ride by Dettori, who had already won three times on him, he was always in a good position behind the leaders against the far rail and once the gap opened up in front of him he made no mistake. Suited by tracks with stiff finishes like this, he is likely to turn out under a 6lb penalty at Newmarket next week. (tchd 17-2)
The Jobber(IRE), winner of this race off 7lb lower four years ago, had been put up 2lb for his narrow Salisbury success last time out though he has won off 11lb higher in his time. After travelling well in the middle of the field, he dived for the inside rail over a furlong from home to follow the winner though and did his best to get to him up the final climb, but could never quite do so. (tchd 15-2)
Sharpened Edge ◆, bumped up 8lb for her all-the-way win on her handicap debut over course and distance last month, basically threw it away. Always up with the pace, she was in front a furlong out when she suddenly hung badly away to her left and by the time she was gathered together and ran on again, it was too late. She would have gone very close to winning had she kept straight and this was most probably just down the inexperience. Compensation surely awaits. Official explanation: jockey said filly hung badly left (op 5-1)
Northern Dare(IRE), successful over this trip on Polytrack in March but without a win on turf in two years, did very well to finish where he did as he lost plenty of ground at the start. He does most of his racing over an extra furlong these days. (op 8-1)
Equuleus Pictor, up another 4lb in his bid for a hat-trick, made much of the running but was already beaten when hampered by the errant Sharpened Edge. He is a much better horse with give and could probably have done with even more rain. (op 6-1)
Tony The Tap, now 8lb higher than for his last win on turf, can be given some credit as he was another to give away plenty of ground at the start. The outing should have brought him on following a nine-month absence. (op 40-1 tchd 25-1)
Good Gorsoon(USA) Official explanation: jockey said colt jumped awkwardly from stalls
Jaconet(USA), winner of six of her last ten starts and still on a career-high mark, was switched to race alone up the stands' rail but the ploy didn't work. (op 10-1 tchd 9-1)
Cake(IRE), back down to her best trip, showed up for a fair way before dropping right out and this was too bad to be true. (op 15-2)

3583 FOUNDATION DEVELOPMENTS DRAGON STKS (LISTED RACE) 5f 6y

2:50 (2:53) (Class 1) 2-Y-O
£17,031 (£6,456; £3,231; £1,611; £807; £405) **Stalls** High

Form RPR
231 **1** **Iver Bridge Lad**[23] 2825 2-9-2 0.. MarcHalford 2 98
(J Ryan) *lw: plld hrd early: hld up: prog 2f out: hrd rdn to ld last 100yds: styd on wl* **14/1**[3]
4413 **2** *½* **Di Stefano**[17] 2995 2-9-2 0.. DarryllHolland 6 96
(M R Channon) *sn lost pl and pushed along in rr: racd against far side rail and prog over 1f out: drvn and squeezed through to press wnr last 100yds: no ex nr fin* **15/8**[1]
10 **3** *½* **Angel's Pursuit (IRE)**[17] 2995 2-9-2 0............................ RichardHughes 3 94
(R Hannon) *lw: hld up in tch: effrt 2f out: nt qckn over 1f out: edgd lft but kpt on ins fnl f* **15/8**[1]

210 **4** *shd* **Absolute Music (USA)**[14] 3086 2-8-11 0 EddieAhern 4 89
(R M H Cowell) *chsd ldrs and racd towards outer: effrt over 1f out: kpt on same pce fnl f* **25/1**

331 **5** *1* **Deal (IRE)**[18] 2972 2-8-11 0 PatDobbs 1 85
(R Hannon) *wnt lft s: last and swtchd to far rail: effrt 1f out: sn no imp on ldrs* **20/1**

3160 **6** *1* **Little Perisher**[17] 2995 2-9-2 0 LDettori 7 87
(A P Jarvis) *racd against far rail: chsd ldr: led overall abt 1f out: hdd and hmpd last 100yds: wknd* **8/1**[2]

1 **7** *shd* **Mdawee (IRE)**[8] 3317 2-9-2 0 RichardKingscote 8 86
(Tom Dascombe) *w'like: led but hung lft thrght and ended against nr side rail 2f out: lost overall ld abt 1f out: fdd* **8/1**[2]

1 **8** *12* **Brambleberry**[11] 3210 2-8-11 0 RichardSmith 5 38
(Tom Dascombe) *w'like: leggy: t.k.h: prom tl wknd rapidly over 1f out: t.o* **25/1**

62.95 secs (1.35) **Going Correction** +0.15s/f (Good) **8 Ran SP% 110.9**
Speed ratings (Par 102): **95,94,93,93,91 90,89,70**
toteswingers: 1&2 £5.30, 1&3 £6.00, 2&3 £1.60 CSF £38.28 TOTE £13.40: £3.20, £1.20, £1.20; EX 52.70.
Owner The Iver Lads **Bred** J C S Wilson Bloodstock **Trained** Newmarket, Suffolk
■ Stewards' Enquiry : Darryll Holland two-day ban: careless riding (Jul 17-18)

FOCUS
A decent juvenile Listed sprint with half the field having run at Royal Ascot.

NOTEBOOK
Iver Bridge Lad was up in class and back down in trip following his five-length romp in a maiden auction event on the Kempton Polytrack, but he had some decent placed form behind some smart performers on turf prior to that. He was inclined to take a strong grip early here, but was still able to deliver a telling challenge which took him to the front inside the last furlong and he kept on finding enough to hold off the runner-up. Obviously held in high regard, he looks a nice prospect. (op 10-1 tchd 9-1)
Di Stefano, a strong-finishing third in the Windsor Castle at Ascot when in front of both Angel's Pursuit and Little Perisher, again found himself rather outpaced after breaking well enough. Gradually creeping into contention as the race progressed, he didn't have a great deal of room to play with on the inside over the last couple of furlongs, but his impetus didn't seem to be interrupted and he had every chance to go past the winner had he been good enough. He has plenty of talent, but doesn't look the easiest of rides. (tchd 7-4 and 2-1 in places)
Angel's Pursuit(IRE) ◆, only eighth when favourite for the Windsor Castle though he missed the break and then met trouble in running, took a while to hit top gear and by the time he did it was too late. He still has scope and an extra furlong should see him winning again. (op 13-8)
Absolute Music(USA), who didn't appear to see out the extra furlong when only tenth in the Albany, was always close to the pace and despite seeing plenty of daylight on the outside of the pack, stayed on pretty well. There should be another day for her. (op 33-1)
Deal(IRE), who upset an odds-on shot on easy ground at Warwick last time, gave away plenty of ground at the start and was then completely taken off her feet, but she stayed on in decent style in the latter stages and, like her stable-companion Angel's Pursuit, looks in need of 6f now. (op 14-1)
Little Perisher, unplaced in Listed company in his last two starts and behind a couple of these in the Windsor Castle, was the most exposed in the line-up but he attracted plenty of market support. He showed plenty of speed on the far side of the track, but he faded up the final climb and was already beaten when hampered by the runner-up. (op 16-1)
Mdawee(IRE), narrow winner of a six-runner Warwick maiden auction contest on debut last month, looked the stable's first string on jockey bookings. He showed decent early speed, but gradually hung right across the track as the race progressed and ended up on the stands' rail. He still wasn't beaten that far and this can probably be put down to inexperience. Official explanation: jockey said colt hung left (op 10-1)
Brambleberry had beaten a subsequent winner when successful on her debut on the Lingfield Polytrack last month, but she was deserted by Richard Kingscote in favour of Mdawee here. After pulling hard in touch early, she eventually dropped right out and has questions to answer now. (op 20-1)

3584 BRITISH LAND EBF MAIDEN STKS 7f 16y
3:25 (3:32) (Class 4) 2-Y-O **£6,476** (£1,927; £963; £481) **Stalls** High

Form RPR

1 **Dreamspeed (IRE)** 2-9-3 0 WilliamBuick 7 79+
(A M Balding) *gd sort: lw: s.s and then hmpd: last tl gd prog on wd outside fr 2f out: sustained effrt to ld last 50yds* **6/1**[2]

2 *1/2* **Poor Prince** 2-9-3 0 PhilipRobinson 6 78
(C G Cox) *w'like: athletic: lw: free to post: trckd ldng pair: prog to ld over 2f out: rdn and kpt on wl fr over 1f out: hdd last 50yds* **20/1**

6 **3** *2 1/4* **Branderburgo (IRE)**[34] 2467 2-9-3 0 MartinDwyer 11 72
(M Botti) *str: pressed ldr: upsides over 2f out: nt qckn wl over 1f out: kpt on same pce fnl f* **11/1**

4 *shd* **Logos Astra (USA)** 2-9-3 0 JamieSpencer 2 72+
(D R Lanigan) *w'like: settled in midfield: pushed along and prog 2f out: tried to cl on ldrs 1f out but hanging: kpt on* **10/1**[3]

6 **5** *3/4* **Number One Guy**[20] 2936 2-9-3 0 TPQueally 1 70
(M H Tompkins) *hld up in 5th: prog over 2f out: chsd ldr wl over 1f out tl wknd ent fnl f* **25/1**

05 **6** *1 1/2* **Bubbly Braveheart (IRE)**[21] 2889 2-9-3 0 NeilChalmers 5 66
(A Bailey) *w'like: leggy: led to over 2f out: outpcd over 1f out: kpt on same pce fnl f* **33/1**

7 *1/2* **Halyard (IRE)** 2-9-3 0 AdamKirby 8 65+
(W R Swinburn) *w'like: athletic: bit bkwd: s.s: mostly in last pair: pushed along over 2f out: sme prog over 1f out: no hdwy fnl f* **20/1**

2 **8** *1 1/2* **Pytheas (USA)**[13] 3170 2-9-3 0 RoystonFfrench 10 61
(M Johnston) *unf: dwlt: keen early and hld up towards rr: rdn and effrt 2f out: modest prog over 1f out: sn no hdwy and btn* **4/6**[1]

9 *1 1/4* **White Devil** 2-9-3 0 LPKeniry 3 58
(A M Balding) *tall: dwlt: tk ferocious hold early: hld up in rr: effrt on outer 1/2-way: flashed tail and no prog 2f out* **50/1**

0 **10** *1/2* **Barastar**[25] 2771 2-9-3 0 EddieAhern 12 57
(J R Boyle) *str: trckd ldng pair on inner tl lost pl and grad wknd fr over 2f out* **50/1**

11 *1 1/2* **Beyond The City (USA)** 2-9-3 0 RichardHughes 4 53
(R Hannon) *w'like: str: scope: lw: dwlt: hld up in last trio: no prog whn pushed along 2f out: no ch after* **11/1**

12 *1/2* **City Of Rome (IRE)** 2-9-3 0 PatDobbs 9 52
(R Hannon) *reluctant to enter stalls: settled in 6th on inner: lost pl 3f out: wl in rr fnl 2f* **40/1**

1m 32.86s (3.36) **Going Correction** -0.075s/f (Good) **12 Ran SP% 122.7**
Speed ratings (Par 96): **77,76,73,73,72 71,70,68,67,66 65,64**
toteswingers: 1&2 £16.90, 1&3 £11.50, 2&3 £30.00 CSF £122.21 TOTE £6.70: £1.90, £4.30, £3.30; EX 148.30.
Owner J C Smith **Bred** Stone Ridge Farm **Trained** Kingsclere, Hants

FOCUS
An interesting maiden that has been won by some smart performers such as No Excuse Needed, Mister Monet and Scintillo within the past ten years. A taking winner despite a very moderate winning time.

NOTEBOOK
Dreamspeed(IRE) ◆, a 62,000gns half-brother to three winners including his smart stable-companion Dream Eater, put up a very taking debut performance. Having taken a broadside from Halyard exiting the stalls, he found himself in last place and still had his 11 rivals in front of him starting up the home straight. He was then forced to circle the entire field in order to make his effort, but maintained it to force his way to the front close to the line. Market support beforehand suggested he was held in high regard and he can be rated even better than the official margin. He looks a very nice prospect. (op 9-1 tchd 5-1)
Poor Prince ◆, out of a half-sister to the top-class sprinter Tamarisk, was ridden much more handily than the winner, but also looked green. Taking it up 2f out, he did little wrong and was only just worn down. With the experience under his belt he shouldn't take long in going one better. (op 16-1 tchd 14-1)
Branderburgo(IRE) ◆, unplaced in a Doncaster maiden on debut in May in which the subsequent Chesham Stakes winner Big Audio was second, was always up there and he had every chance. He may have had the edge in experience on the front pair, but this was still an improvement on his debut effort and he should win races. (op 14-1)
Logos Astra(USA) ◆, a half-brother to a couple of winning milers, was doing some good late work but also looked a little green and he should benefit from the experience. (op 11-1)
Number One Guy, well beaten on his York debut last month, ran much better here and is the type to improve as he goes up in trip. (op 20-1)
Bubbly Braveheart(IRE), who ran much better than on his debut when fifth in a similar contest over course and distance three weeks ago, set the early pace but once joined passing the 3f pole could only stay on at one pace.
Halyard(IRE) ◆, a 58,000gns colt and first foal of the Listed winner Brindisi, was noted staying on late and was by no means knocked about. The stable's youngsters normally improve with racing and he is one to watch. (op 16-1 tchd 25-1)
Pytheas(USA), caught on the line on his Redcar debut, was all the rage to go one better but he was being niggled along soon after reaching the home straight and never threatened to take a hand. Official explanation: jockey said colt was restless in stalls and missed the break (tchd 8-11, 4-5 in places and 5-6 in a place)

3585 HELICAL BAR GALA STKS (LISTED RACE) 1m 2f 7y
4:00 (4:00) (Class 1) 3-Y-O+
£22,708 (£8,608; £4,308; £2,148; £1,076; £540) **Stalls** High

Form RPR

3140 **1** **Kirklees (IRE)**[97] 1012 5-9-5 116 LDettori 1 119+
(Saeed Bin Suroor) *led 1f: trckd ldr: led again over 2f out: shkn up and drew clr over 1f out: readily* **85/40**[1]

1-1 **2** *4* **Covert Ambition**[30] 2597 4-9-5 103 DaneO'Neill 2 110+
(Saeed Bin Suroor) *swtg: hld up: pushed along 4f out: swtchd to outer and rdn over 2f out: prog over 1f out: kpt on to take 2nd last strides* **11/2**

15-1 **3** *3/4* **Tranquil Tiger**[39] 2327 5-9-8 114 (b) TPQueally 5 112
(H R A Cecil) *led after 1f: rdn and hdd over 2f out: no ch w wnr after: lost 2nd last strides* **11/4**[2]

4-12 **4** *1 3/4* **Confront**[28] 2668 4-9-5 110 JamieSpencer 4 105
(Sir Michael Stoute) *lw: t.k.h early: hld up bhd ldrs: rdn and effrt wl over 2f out: no imp wnr over 1f out: one pce* **3/1**[3]

2220 **5** *hd* **Halicarnassus (IRE)**[14] 3089 5-9-5 110 SamHitchcott 7 105
(M R Channon) *lw: chsd ldrs: rdn 4f out: struggling over 2f out: plugged on* **16/1**

6 *6* **Guarino (GER)**[627] 5-9-5 0 RichardHughes 6 93
(G L Moore) *stdd s: hld up in last: detached fr rest and shuffled along 3f out: passed one wkng rival nr fin: nvr nr ldrs* **100/1**

10- **7** *1 1/2* **Democrate**[397] 2654 4-9-5 0 (t) WilliamBuick 3 90
(Saeed Bin Suroor) *trckd ldrs: rdn and cl enough 3f out: btn 2f out: wknd rapidly over 1f out* **20/1**

2m 7.60s (-2.90) **Going Correction** -0.075s/f (Good) **7 Ran SP% 110.7**
Speed ratings (Par 111): **108,104,104,102,102 97,96**
toteswingers: 1&2 £2.90, 1&3 £2.10, 2&3 £3.50 CSF £13.41 TOTE £3.00: £1.50, £3.10; EX 16.70.
Owner Godolphin **Bred** Darley **Trained** Newmarket, Suffolk

FOCUS
A fascinating Listed event which basically looked a straight fight between Godolphin and Prince Khalid Abdulla. The early pace looked decent enough. Decent form for the grade and the winner is up to a Group win again.

NOTEBOOK
Kirklees(IRE), last seen finishing well beaten in the Dubai Sheema Classic in March when events conspired against him, looked very much the best of the Godolphin trio on form and was also the highest rated of these. Content to take a lead from Tranquil Tiger after breaking best, he was back in front passing the 2f pole and soon bolted clear. He looks well worth a try back in something rather better now. (op 3-1 tchd 2-1)
Covert Ambition ◆, winner of a Nottingham maiden and a handicap on the Kempton Polytrack off a mark of 94, was given a more patient ride than the winner. Off the bridle a fair way out, he eventually ran on to finish second at a respectful distance, but he still has some scope and looks up to winning a race like this. (op 7-1 tchd 5-1)
Tranquil Tiger, carrying a 3lb penalty and already a winner five times at this level including when just holding on from Halicarnassus at Goodwood last month, is very effective when allowed to dominate and things looked to be going his way for much of the contest. However, once the winner had got to him he was then merely playing for places. (op 3-1 tchd 10-3 in places)
Confront, who lost a shoe when just beaten in the Diomed at Epsom last month, was trying this trip for the first time. Delivered with his effort soon after turning for home, he found less than expected off the bridle and was beaten before stamina became an issue. He has questions to answer now. (op 15-8 tchd 10-3 in places)
Halicarnassus(IRE), being kept very busy and just beaten by Tranquil Tiger at Goodwood in May, is a very hard horse with whom to get the timing right and more positive tactics didn't work in the Wolferton at Royal Ascot last time. Reverting to waiting tactics here, he never looked like winning. (tchd 14-1)
Guarino(GER), a fair performer in Germany and France, was making his debut for the yard after an absence of 21 months. He never got into the race from off the pace, but this should have blown the cobwebs away.
Democrate, making his debut for Godolphin and not seen since finishing out the back in last year's French Derby when with Andre Fabre, raced in mid-division for much of the way before appearing to blow up. Official explanation: jockey said colt hung right and got tired from 2f out (tchd 18-1 and 25-1)

3586 TAYLOR WESSING H'CAP 1m 2f 7y
4:35 (4:35) (Class 2) (0-100,97) 3-Y-O+
£11,215 (£3,358; £1,679; £840; £419; £210) **Stalls** High

Form RPR

2500 **1** **Fanjura (IRE)**[20] 2933 4-9-7 **90** EddieAhern 9 102
(B W Hills) *hld up towards rr: pushed along over 3f out: rdn and prog 2f out: 3rd ins fnl f: squeezed between rivals to ld last 75yds* **14/1**

4100 **2** *1/2* **Greylami (IRE)**[49] 2055 4-9-4 **87** DarryllHolland 4 98
(T G Mills) *lw: hld up: last 1/2-way: gd prog on outer fr over 2f out: wnt 2nd 1f out: edgd rt but clsd to ld briefly 100yds out: jst outpcd* **6/1**[3]

2-51 **3** 1¼ **Australia Day (IRE)**[21] 2891 6-10-0 **97**........................ MartinDwyer 6 106
(P R Webber) *lw: disp ld at fast pce tl led after 2f: breahter 1/2-way: rdn 2f out: tired over 1f out: battled on but hdd last 100yds* **5/1**[2]

-501 **4** 7 **Mountain Pride (IRE)**[36] 2407 4-9-6 **89**........................ SteveDrowne 2 84
(J L Dunlop) *hld up bhd ldrs gng wl: prog to go 2nd over 2f out: drvn and no imp over 1f out: wknd fnl f* **14/1**

4006 **5** 2¼ **Ramona Chase**[28] 2671 4-9-6 **89**........................ PaulDoe 1 79
(M J Attwater) *s.i.s: rcvrd to chse ldng pair: wnt 2nd over 3f out: drvn over 2f out: sn btn: wknd* **14/1**

11 **6** 2½ **Alpen Glen**[7] 3333 3-8-11 **91** 6ex........................ RoystonFfrench 11 76
(M Johnston) *w ldr at fast pce 2f: chsng after: rdn and dropped to 3rd over 3f out: struggling after* **15/8**[1]

3-01 **7** 4 **Jack Dawkins (USA)**[34] 2468 4-9-13 **96**........................ TPQueally 10 73
(H R A Cecil) *settled in rr: rdn and no prog 3f out: n.d after* **8/1**

-216 **8** 3 **Emerald Wilderness (IRE)**[29] 1301 5-9-11 **94**........ RichardHughes 8 65
(A King) *hld up in rr: in last pair 3f out: shkn up and no prog 2f out: no ch* **20/1**

-000 **9** 32 **Road To Love (IRE)**[13] 3142 6-9-3 **86**........................ LDettori 3 —
(M Johnston) *chsd ldrs: wknd rapidly over 2f out: eased over 1f out: t.o* **8/1**

0-00 **10** ¾ **Alan Devonshire**[16] 3014 4-9-2 **85**........................ DaneO'Neill 7 —
(M H Tompkins) *stdd s: hld up in last tl rapid prog to join ldrs 1/2-way: wknd as rapidly over 3f out: t.o* **50/1**

2m 7.26s (-3.24) **Going Correction** -0.075s/f (Good)
WFA 3 from 4yo+ 11lb **10** Ran SP% **114.7**
Speed ratings (Par 109): **109,108,107,102,100 98,95,92,67,66**
toteswingers: 1&2 £13.80, 1&3 £14.40, 2&3 £5.00 CSF £94.08 CT £484.06 TOTE £17.60: £3.30, £2.20, £1.70; EX 146.80.
Owner Terry Benson **Bred** Patrick F Kelly **Trained** Lambourn, Berks
■ Stewards' Enquiry : Eddie Ahern one-day ban: careless riding (Jul 17)

FOCUS
A decent and competitive handicap with four of the ten runners last-time-out winners. They went a serious early pace and the field were soon well spread out, though the tempo had eased a bit by halfway. The front three pulled well clear in the latter stages and the time was around 0.3 of a second faster than the hand-timed Listed race. The winner is rated back to his early 3yo best.

NOTEBOOK
Fanjura(IRE), disappointing since a fair reappearance effort, was negatively ridden when first tried over this trip two starts ago, but he showed that he gets every yard of it here. Brought with his effort entering the last couple of furlongs, the gap he was aiming for between the second and third was closing as he reached it well inside the last furlong, but he maintained his effort to just prevail. This opens up plenty more options for him. Official explanation: trainer's rep said, regarding apparent improvement in form, that the gelding was better suited by the stronger gallop. (op 16-1 tchd 12-1)
Greylami(IRE), twice well beaten on turf since winning the Rosebery on the Kempton Polytrack off this mark, bounced back to form here. Given plenty to do, he was forced to come widest of all to make his effort up the straight. He did receive a slight nudge from Jack Dawkins around 2f from home though his impetus wasn't affected and he still looked the most likely winner well inside the last furlong, but the winner outbattled him. A strongly run race like this suits him well and he may now head to Glorious Goodwood. (op 15-2 tchd 11-2)
Australia Day(IRE), raised 7lb for his all-the-way victory over course and distance last month, was soon allowed an uncontested lead and it looked for a long way as though he would take some catching, but he couldn't quite hold off the front pair. Unfortunately the margin back to the others is unlikely to persuade the handicapper to drop him. (op 9-2)
Mountain Pride(IRE), unbeaten in two previous outings here, was 8lb higher than when successful over course and distance last time but the easing of the ground would have been a help. Nothing was travelling better than him approaching the last 2f, but he didn't find as much off the bridle as had looked likely and the handicapper looks to have him now. (tchd 12-1 and 16-1)
Ramona Chase, winner of just one of his 23 Flat starts plus one over hurdles, often spoils his chances by pulling hard. He was keen enough again here and although he wasn't entirely disgraced, his record doesn't make him a betting proposition. (op 16-1 tchd 12-1)
Alpen Glen, the only three-year-old and only filly in the field, only made her racecourse debut last month but has been very impressive in winning both of her starts so far. Her defeat of her stable-companion Eastern Aria was boosted when that filly bolted up at Epsom on Thursday evening and although she was carrying a 6lb penalty, she was still 2lb well in compared to her new mark. She broke well, but rather than get involved in a war with Australia Day she was allowed to tuck in behind him. However, once she came off the bridle starting up the home straight the response was bitterly disappointing. It may be that three runs in a little over three weeks proved too much for this inexperienced filly and she is well worth another chance to show her true ability. (op 13-8 tchd 2-1 in places)

3587 PROPERTY RACE DAY H'CAP — 1m 6f
5:05 (5:12) (Class 4) (0-85,80) 3-Y-0+ **£6,476** (£1,927; £963; £481) **Stalls** High

Form RPR

-260 **1** **Alanbrooke**[15] 3069 3-8-13 **80**........................(b[1]) RoystonFfrench 6 94
(M Johnston) *lw: sn prom: led after 2f: mde rest: clr 3f out: galloped on strly* **10/3**[2]

-411 **2** 6 **Strathcal**[22] 2850 3-8-10 **77**........................ SteveDrowne 7 82
(H Morrison) *lw: trckd ldrs: wnt 2nd 3f out: sn rdn and no imp on wnr* **5/2**[1]

03-0 **3** 1½ **All Guns Firing (IRE)**[20] 2930 3-8-8 **75**........................ PhilipRobinson 4 78
(M A Jarvis) *lw: hld up: last and wl off the pce 5f out: prog 3f out and sn rdn: hanging rt but pressed runner-up 1f out: no ex* **4/1**[3]

2-56 **4** 5 **Force Group (IRE)**[21] 2898 5-9-9 **75**........................ TPQueally 3 71
(M H Tompkins) *towards rr: rdn over 4f out: struggling and no real prog 3f out: plugged on* **14/1**

0445 **5** 11 **Profit's Reality (IRE)**[20] 2932 7-9-13 **79**........................ PaulDoe 8 60
(M J Attwater) *hld up in last: t.k.h and prog on outer 1/2-way: wnt 2nd over 4f out to 3f out: wknd* **16/1**

2-21 **6** 2 **It's A Date**[19] 2945 4-10-0 **80**........................ DaneO'Neill 1 58
(A King) *prom: lost pl after 4f: rdn over 3f out: no prog and sn no ch* **7/1**

1310 **7** 37 **Supsonic**[21] 2895 6-8-13 **72**........................ RyanPowell(7) 2 —
(R J Price) *trckd ldrs: wnt 2nd 9f out to over 4f out: wknd rapidly 3f out: t.o* **25/1**

650 **8** 166 **War Party**[20] 2932 5-10-0 **80**........................ DarryllHolland 5 —
(Dr R D P Newland) *led 2f: prom: lost pl 5f out and urged along: wknd and virtually p.u 3f out: eventually fin* **15/2**

3m 2.12s (-4.48) **Going Correction** -0.075s/f (Good)
WFA 3 from 4yo+ 15lb **8** Ran SP% **112.3**
Speed ratings (Par 105): **109,105,104,101,95 94,73,—**
toteswingers: 1&2 £2.60, 1&3 £4.10, 2&3 £3.70 CSF £11.63 CT £32.54 TOTE £4.40: £1.60, £1.60, £2.00; EX 15.40 Place 6: £72.81 Place 5: £37.83.
Owner Sheikh Hamdan Bin Mohammed Al Maktoum **Bred** Miss K Rausing **Trained** Middleham Moor, N Yorks

FOCUS
A fair staying handicap, but several of these were trying this sort of trip for the first time and they finished spread out all over Esher. Improvement from the winner, and form to be fairly positive about.

All Guns Firing(IRE) Official explanation: jockey said gelding hung right
Profit's Reality(IRE) Official explanation: jockey said he was unable to ride out after being struck on the shoulder by a shoe
T/Jkpt: Not won. T/Plt: £366.40 to a £1 stake. Pool: £80,368.32. 160.09 winning tickets. T/Qpdt: £107.90 to a £1 stake. Pool: £5,048.56. 34.60 winning tickets. JN

3317 WARWICK (L-H)
Friday, July 3

OFFICIAL GOING: Sprint course - good; round course - good to firm (good in places; 8.7)
Wind: Moderate behind Weather: Sunny periods

3588 BLUE SQUARE (S) STKS — 1m 2f 188y
2:10 (2:11) (Class 6) 3-Y-O **£2,047** (£604; £302) **Stalls** Low

Form RPR

0-0 **1** **Jeronimo Joe**[39] 2333 3-8-13 0........................ TGMcLaughlin 1 58
(A B Haynes) *hld up in rr: pushed along over 3f out: hdwy on stands' side 2f out: rdn to ld jst over 1f out: drvn out* **22/1**

-406 **2** ¾ **Highland Storm**[11] 3222 3-8-8 70........................(v[1]) MatthewDavies(5) 3 57
(George Baker) *hld up in rr: rdn and hdwy whn swtchd rt over 1f out: r.o u.p on stands' rail ins fnl f: nt rch wnr* **4/6**[1]

1330 **3** 2¾ **First Spirit**[6] 3383 3-8-13 56........................(p) LukeMorris 4 52
(J S Moore) *bhd: pushed along 6f out: rdn and hdwy 3f out: one pce fnl f* **15/2**[2]

00-0 **4** 5 **Just Dan**[30] 2605 3-8-13 52........................ FergusSweeney 5 43
(R Hollinshead) *led 1f: chsd ldr tl over 6f out: rdn wl over 1f out: wknd ins fnl f* **33/1**

0025 **5** hd **Kirkson**[17] 3005 3-8-13 55........................ AdrianMcCarthy 7 43
(P W Chapple-Hyam) *hld up in mid-div: pushed along over 3f out: rdn and edgd lft over 1f out: no hdwy* **11/1**

-005 **6** 1 **Bounty Reef**[7] 3334 3-8-8 55........................(v) StephenDonohoe 2 36
(P D Evans) *t.k.h: sn stdd towards rr: hdwy to chse ldr over 6f out: rdn over 2f out: wknd ins fnl f* **10/1**[3]

00-0 **6** dht **Strongarm**[11] 3222 3-8-10 59........................(b[1]) DavidProbert(3) 6 41
(A Bailey) *led after 1f: rdn and edgd rt whn hdd jst over 1f out: wknd ins fnl f* **25/1**

5-00 **8** 6 **Cherry Belle (IRE)**[7] 3336 3-8-9 55 ow1........................(v) PatCosgrave 9 26
(P D Evans) *hld up in mid-div: pushed along and hdwy over 4f out: rdn wl over 1f out: sn wknd* **28/1**

0-00 **9** 2¼ **Mystic Prince**[19] 2950 3-8-13 57........................ ChrisCatlin 8 26
(Miss Tor Sturgis) *prom: lost pl over 4f out: bhd fnl 3f* **16/1**

40-6 **10** 14 **Blazing Buck**[91] 1105 3-8-13 72........................ TolleyDean 10 1
(A W Carroll) *hld up in tch: rdn and wknd 3f out* **14/1**

2m 21.02s (-0.08) **Going Correction** -0.025s/f (Good) **10** Ran SP% **116.3**
Speed ratings (Par 98): **99,98,96,92,92 91,91,87,85,75**
toteswingers: 1&2 £8.70, 1&3 £21.10, 2&3 £2.50 CSF £36.08 TOTE £32.00: £4.30, £1.10, £2.20; EX 67.70.The winner was bought in for 5,600gns. Highland Storm was claimed by Mrs T Hill for £6,000.
Owner Joe McCarthy **Bred** Bearstone Stud **Trained** Limpley Stoke, Bath
■ Stewards' Enquiry : David Probert one-day ban: careless riding (Jul 17)

FOCUS
A weak heat, run at a decent pace. The favourite was below par.
Bounty Reef Official explanation: jockey said filly ran too freely

3589 BLUE SQUARE CASINO NOVICE AUCTION STKS — 7f 26y
2:40 (2:41) (Class 5) 2-Y-O **£3,238** (£963; £481; £240) **Stalls** Low

Form RPR

1 **1** **Silver Grecian**[13] 3167 2-9-3 0........................ MichaelHills 3 91+
(J Ryan) *chsd ldr after 1f: pushed along to ld over 1f out: shkn up ins fnl f: comf* **4/11**[1]

6421 **2** 4 **Abandagold (IRE)**[7] 3332 2-8-10 0........................ StephenDonohoe 5 72+
(P D Evans) *led: rdn and hdd over 1f out: one pce ins fnl f* **22/1**

2251 **3** 5 **Toga Tiger (IRE)**[13] 3160 2-8-13 0........................ TonyCulhane 4 63+
(M R Channon) *n.m.r s: hld up in last: wnt 3rd jst over 3f out: rdn wl over 1f out: no imp* **11/2**[2]

4 8 **Apostle Of Rome (IRE)** 2-8-9 0........................ CatherineGannon 1 37
(Tom Dascombe) *chsd ldr 1f: bhd fnl 3f* **8/1**[3]

1m 24.31s (-0.29) **Going Correction** -0.025s/f (Good) **4** Ran SP% **104.2**
Speed ratings (Par 94): **100,95,89,80**
CSF £7.99 TOTE £1.20; EX 5.70.
Owner Ocean Trailers Ltd **Bred** Deerfield Farm **Trained** Newmarket, Suffolk

FOCUS
A straightforward task for the progressive Silver Grecian.

NOTEBOOK
Silver Grecian had won so well on his debut at Newmarket. Sent off long odds-on, he won in pretty straightforward fashion and should go on to better things. His trainer thinks a lot of him and there is a possibility he could go to Goodwood or York. (op 1-3)
Abandagold(IRE) is progressing with her racing and set off in front as she did when scoring at Chester. However, she again did not look that comfortable taking the turn into the straight and had no answer when the winner ranged alongside. She was clear of the rest however, and can pick up more races, possibly on a straight track. (op 14-1)
Toga Tiger(IRE) was held up out the back and was close enough making the home turn. However, his rider was hard at work soon afterwards and he could not find another gear. (op 6-1 tchd 13-2)
Apostle Of Rome(IRE), a newcomer from a yard that does well with its juveniles, broke well enough but was left behind by his more experienced rivals from halfway. A half-brother to Book Of Music, better can be expected in time. (tchd 7-1 and 9-1)

3590 BLUE SQUARE SP GUARANTEE MAIDEN STKS — 7f 26y
3:10 (3:12) (Class 5) 3-4-Y-0 **£2,914** (£867; £433; £216) **Stalls** Low

Form RPR

23 **1** **Steel Free (IRE)**[45] 2151 3-8-12 0........................ ChrisCatlin 3 76+
(M L W Bell) *mde all: rdn over 1f out: drvn out* **5/2**[2]

-352 **2** 1½ **Papyrian**[22] 2849 3-9-3 77........................(b[1]) AlanMunro 2 77
(W Jarvis) *hld up in tch: rdn to chse wnr jst over 1f out: nt qckn ins fnl f* **1/1**[1]

0 **3** 2¾ **Prime Circle**[16] 3036 3-9-3 0........................ J-PGuillambert 7 70
(M Johnston) *w wnr: carried hd high and rdn over 1f out: sn lost 2nd: one pce* **9/1**

220 **4** 2¾ **Makaam (USA)**[22] 2862 3-9-3 86........................ TPO'Shea 9 62
(M P Tregoning) *hld up in mid-div: rdn wl over 1f out: kpt on same pce ins fnl f* **9/2**[3]

0 **5** 5 **Lady Lam**[27] 2710 3-8-7 0........................ MatthewDavies(5) 5 44
(George Baker) *w ldrs over 3f: pushed along wl over 1f out: wknd fnl f* **33/1**

000- **6** ½ **Avonlini**[279] 6273 3-8-12 25 .... AdrianMcCarthy 1 42
(B P J Baugh) *t.k.h in mid-div: rdn wl over 1f out: wknd fnl f* **150/1**

04 **7** ½ **Double Moon**[8] 3319 3-9-3 0 .... DO'Donohoe 8 46
(George Baker) *s.i.s: swtchd rt wl over 1f out: a in rr* **40/1**

0-00 **8** 1 **Wivny (USA)**[9] 3269 4-9-6 47 .... FergusSweeney 4 41
(H J Evans) *s.i.s: in rr: rdn and short-lived effrt wl over 1f out* **100/1**

6 **9** 10 **Square Of Gold (FR)**[11] 3207 3-9-3 0 .... TolleyDean 6 16
(A W Carroll) *stdd s: t.k.h: c wd and rdr lost whip ent st over 2f out: sn struggling* **50/1**

1m 23.84s (-0.76) **Going Correction** -0.025s/f (Good)
WFA 3 from 4yo 8lb **9** Ran SP% **115.7**
Speed ratings (Par 103): **103,101,98,95,89 88,88,87,75**
toteswingers: 1&2 £1.20, 1&3 £2.70, 2&3 £4.40 CSF £5.32 TOTE £3.80: £1.10, £1.10, £2.10; EX 5.60.
Owner Recycled Products Limited **Bred** Corduff Stud & B Egan **Trained** Newmarket, Suffolk

FOCUS
Only four mattered in the betting and they duly made the frame. Straightforward form but the winner only had to match her debut effort.

3591 BLUE SQUARE FILLIES' H'CAP — 5f 110y
3:45 (3:45) (Class 5) (0-70,70) 3-Y-0+ **£2,590** (£770; £385; £192) **Stalls** Low

Form RPR

6304 **1** **Keep Dancing (IRE)**[14] 3118 3-8-12 64 .... (p) DavidProbert(3) 9 73
(A M Balding) *hld up and bhd: rdn over 1f out: hdwy on stands' rail fnl f: edgd rt and led cl home* **4/1**[2]

2431 **2** 1 **Feelin Foxy**[27] 2712 5-9-13 70 .... ChrisCatlin 2 77
(J G Given) *led: rdn over 1f out: sn edgd rt: hdd cl home* **7/2**[1]

5415 **3** 1 **Weet A Surprise**[18] 2966 4-9-3 60 .... (v) FergusSweeney 8 64
(J W Unett) *hld up in tch: rdn over 1f out: kpt on ins fnl f* **8/1**[3]

4563 **4** 2½ **Comptonspirit**[20] 2913 5-9-5 62 .... J-PGuillambert 3 57
(B P J Baugh) *a.p: chsd ldr wl over 1f out: rdn fnl f: no ex towards fin* **7/2**[1]

0030 **5** 1¾ **Affirmatively**[20] 2913 4-8-3 51 oh5 .... (bt) AmyBaker(5) 5 40
(A W Carroll) *s.i.s: in rr: rdn and hdwy wl over 1f out: no further prog fnl f* **28/1**

0-40 **6** 3 **Bahamian Bliss**[48] 2088 4-9-1 58 .... (b[1]) JimCrowley 4 37
(J A R Toller) *hld up in mid-div: hdwy 2f out: rdn over 1f out: wknd ins fnl f* **10/1**

5552 **7** 7 **Chantilly Jewel (USA)**[14] 3125 4-8-12 55 .... (v) PatCosgrave 6 10
(R M H Cowell) *chsd ldr tl rdn wl over 1f out: sn wknd* **12/1**

00-2 **8** 1¾ **Jiggalong**[15] 3071 3-8-11 60 .... AlanMunro 7 8
(Jane Chapple-Hyam) *a in rr: eased whn no ch over 1f out* **7/2**[1]

66.11 secs (0.21) **Going Correction** +0.075s/f (Good)
WFA 3 from 4yo+ 5lb **8** Ran SP% **118.0**
Speed ratings (Par 100): **101,99,98,95,92 88,79,77**
toteswingers: 1&2 £4.10, 1&3 £6.20, 2&3 £5.20 CSF £19.11 CT £108.27 TOTE £5.80: £1.50, £1.40, £2.50; EX 20.80.
Owner The C H F Partnership **Bred** Yeomanstown Stud **Trained** Kingsclere, Hants
■ Stewards' Enquiry : David Probert one-day ban: careless riding (Jul 18)

FOCUS
A modest fillies' handicap, but competitive enough. The front pair raced closest to the favoured stands' rail.
Jiggalong Official explanation: jockey said filly lost its action

3592 BLUE SQUARE POKER H'CAP — 6f
4:20 (4:22) (Class 4) (0-80,78) 3-Y-0 **£6,476** (£1,927; £963; £481) **Stalls** Low

Form RPR

5504 **1** **Ben's Dream (IRE)**[21] 2888 3-8-5 65 .... (t) DavidProbert(3) 1 70
(A M Balding) *a.p: rdn to ld over 1f out: rdn out* **11/2**

0311 **2** 1½ **Hand Painted**[23] 2810 3-9-1 72 .... TravisBlock 9 72+
(P J Makin) *hmpd s: hld up in rr: pushed along 3f out: hdwy 2f out: rdn over 1f out: kpt on ins fnl f* **5/1**[3]

4-42 **3** nk **Leftontheshelf (IRE)**[35] 2456 3-9-3 74 .... (p) TolleyDean 4 73
(J L Spearing) *chsd ldr: rdn whn bmpd and carried rt over 2f out: sn lost 2nd: swtchd lft over 1f out: kpt on same pce ins fnl f* **14/1**

6016 **4** nk **Hi Shinko**[14] 3118 3-8-13 70 .... TGMcLaughlin 11 68
(B R Millman) *mid-div: pushed along 3f out: c to stands' rail and rdn 2f out: swtchd lft ins fnl f: r.o towards fin* **22/1**

-061 **5** ½ **Miss Hollybell**[25] 2776 3-9-2 73 .... TPO'Shea 6 70+
(J Gallagher) *half-rrd s: in rr: rdn 2f out: hdwy over 1f out: no ex towards fin* **17/2**

0-00 **6** 1 **Finnegan McCool**[20] 2915 3-9-4 75 .... (p) PatCosgrave 3 68
(R M Beckett) *chsd ldrs: hrd rdn 2f out: fdd wl ins fnl f* **20/1**

2152 **7** hd **Taurus Twins**[7] 3355 3-8-12 69 .... (b) JimCrowley 2 62
(R J Price) *led: c to stands' rail 2f out: rdn and hdd over 1f out: wknd ins fnl f* **10/3**[1]

1-00 **8** 1¼ **Charging Indian (IRE)**[42] 2248 3-9-6 77 .... ChrisCatlin 10 66
(D R Lanigan) *bmpd s: sn outpcd in rr: rdn over 2f out: short-lived effrt over 1f out* **11/1**

601 **9** 6 **New Leyf (IRE)**[16] 3036 3-9-3 74 .... ClareLindop 7 44
(J R Gask) *wnt rt s: hld up in mid-div: wknd 2f out* **9/2**[2]

0-03 **10** 8 **Klynch**[11] 3219 3-9-2 78 .... (b) GabrielHannon(5) 8 22
(B J Meehan) *hmpd s: outpcd* **9/1**

1m 11.86s (0.06) **Going Correction** +0.075s/f (Good) **10** Ran SP% **117.9**
Speed ratings (Par 102): **102,100,99,99,98 97,96,95,87,76**
toteswingers: 1&2 £6.00, 1&3 £11.40, 2&3 £7.40 CSF £33.60 CT £378.75 TOTE £6.50: £2.60, £1.70, £3.10; EX 36.00.
Owner Alan Halsall **Bred** Joe Foley & John Grimes **Trained** Kingsclere, Hants
■ Stewards' Enquiry : Jim Crowley caution: careless riding; two-day ban: careless riding (Jul 17-18)

FOCUS
An ordinary handicap. The form looks pretty sound.
Hand Painted Official explanation: jockey said colt suffered interference at start
Klynch Official explanation: jockey said gelding lost its action

3593 BLUE SQUARE GAMES H'CAP — 1m 6f 213y
4:55 (4:56) (Class 5) (0-70,70) 3-Y-0+ **£3,238** (£963; £481; £240) **Stalls** Low

Form RPR

-236 **1** **Pseudonym (IRE)**[7] 3346 7-9-7 63 .... (t) J-PGuillambert 5 69
(M F Harris) *hld up: hdwy over 4f out: brought to stands' rail 2f out: swtchd lft over 1f out: hrd rdn to ld wl ins fnl f: all out* **4/1**[3]

0130 **2** shd **Zuwaar**[16] 2194 4-10-0 70 .... (tp) StephenDonohoe 7 76
(Ian Williams) *hld up in tch: c to stands' rail wl over 1f out: sn rdn: led 1f out: hdd wl ins fnl f: r.o* **11/2**

4 **3** ¾ **Kristallo (GER)**[18] 2983 4-9-4 60 .... PatCosgrave 2 65
(P R Webber) *chsd ldr: led 2f out: sn rdn: hdd 1f out: nt qckn cl home* **9/4**[1]

24-6 **4** 1¼ **Stoop To Conquer**[81] 751 9-9-8 64 .... VinceSlattery 3 67
(A W Carroll) *hld up and bhd: pushed along over 3f out: hdwy over 2f out: sn rdn: ev ch over 1f out: no ex towards fin* **10/1**

6564 **5** 10 **Lapina (IRE)**[15] 3073 5-9-5 61 .... (p) TravisBlock 6 51
(A Middleton) *hld up and bhd: rdn over 3f out: hdwy 2f out: wknd over 1f out* **8/1**

41-6 **6** 34 **Blue Dynasty (USA)**[32] 2540 3-8-9 68 .... (b[1]) JimCrowley 1 14
(Mrs A J Perrett) *hld up in tch: rdn 6f out: wknd 4f out: bhd fnl 3f: eased over 1f out* **3/1**[2]

7 12 **Vertueux (FR)**[217] 4-9-13 69 .... (t) TolleyDean 9 —
(A W Carroll) *led: pushed clr over 4f out: hdd 2f out: wknd qckly* **33/1**

000 **8** 73 **Brave Beat**[20] 2930 3-8-2 61 oh7 ow4 .... (b[1]) DO'Donohoe 8 —
(H J L Dunlop) *hld up: sn in tch: pushed along after 4f: lost pl 9f out: struggling 7f out: t.o fnl 4f* **28/1**

3m 17.13s (-1.87) **Going Correction** -0.025s/f (Good)
WFA 3 from 4yo+ 17lb **8** Ran SP% **117.7**
Speed ratings (Par 103): **103,102,102,101,96 78,72,33**
toteswingers: 1&2 £4.50, 1&3 £3.10, 2&3 £3.80 CSF £27.10 CT £61.32 TOTE £5.50: £1.70, £2.20, £1.30; EX 29.00.
Owner Mrs D J Brown **Bred** Ballymacoll Stud Farm Ltd **Trained** Paxford, Glos

FOCUS
An ordinary staying handicap featuring several who are better known as hurdlers. It was not strongly run. The runner-up looks the best guide to the form.

3594 BLUE SQUARE APPRENTICE H'CAP — 1m 4f 134y
5:25 (5:25) (Class 6) (0-60,55) 4-Y-0+ **£2,047** (£604; £302) **Stalls** Low

Form RPR

0-04 **1** **Looks The Business (IRE)**[11] 3216 8-8-9 50 .... SPRyan(5) 2 61
(A B Haynes) *mde all: clr over 7f out: pushed along over 3f out: rdn wl over 1f out: edgd rt ins fnl f: styd on* **11/4**[1]

600- **2** 4 **Goldan Jess (IRE)**[18] 3631 5-8-12 48 .... RichardRowe 5 53
(P A Kirby) *hld up and bhd: hdwy over 3f out: rdn over 2f out: wnt 2nd jst ins fnl f: nt trble wnr* **14/1**

0645 **3** 2¾ **Le Corvee (IRE)**[2] 3503 7-8-11 52 .... JakePayne(5) 1 53
(A W Carroll) *hld up in tch: chsd wnr over 5f out: rdn over 1f out: lost 2nd jst ins fnl f: one pce* **10/3**[2]

3633 **4** hd **Barbirolli**[10] 3247 7-9-0 50 .... MatthewLawson 8 50
(W M Brisbourne) *hld up in rr: stdy prog on ins over 5f out: pushed along over 3f out: rdn 2f out: one pce fnl f* **9/2**[3]

10-5 **5** 8 **Jelly Mo**[20] 2912 4-8-10 51 .... AlexEdwards(5) 9 38
(W M Brisbourne) *hld up and bhd: rdn over 2f out: no rspnse* **8/1**

0036 **6** 6 **Ben Bacchus (IRE)**[6] 3382 7-8-9 45 .... JohnCavanagh 6 23
(P W Hiatt) *s.i.s: sn rdn into mid-div: hdwy over 6f out: rdn and wknd wl over 3f out* **10/1**

4066 **7** 6 **Speagle (IRE)**[10] 3244 7-8-2 45 .... MatthewCosham(7) 4 13
(A J Chamberlain) *chsd wnr 2f: prom: rdn over 3f out: sn wknd* **20/1**

5200 **8** 49 **Monaadi (IRE)**[24] 2783 4-8-13 55 .... (v) DavidKenny(6) 7 —
(R Hollinshead) *hdwy to chsd wnr after 2f: lost 2nd over 5f out: sn lost pl: t.o fnl 4f* **9/2**[3]

2m 42.45s (-2.15) **Going Correction** -0.025s/f (Good) **8** Ran SP% **116.6**
Speed ratings (Par 101): **105,102,100,100,95 92,88,58**
toteswingers: 1&2 £10.70, 1&3 £2.80, 2&3 £10.40 CSF £42.97 CT £134.22 TOTE £4.70: £1.80, £4.10, £1.40; EX 52.20 Place 6: £12.79 Place 5: £10.03.
Owner Mould, Harrold, Drewett & Drewett **Bred** Mrs M O'Callaghan **Trained** Limpley Stoke, Bath

FOCUS
A poor handicap. The winner is rated back to something like last year's best, although he might be flattered.
T/Plt: £12.60 to a £1 stake. Pool: £37,852.06. 2,177.36 winning tickets. T/Qpdt: £9.10 to a £1 stake. Pool: £2,706.02. 218.30 winning tickets. KH

3601 - 3603a (Foreign Racing) - See Raceform Interactive

3520 HAMBURG (R-H)
Friday, July 3

OFFICIAL GOING: Good

3604a GROSSER PREIS DER JUNGHEINRICH GABELSTAPLER (GROUP 3) (FILLIES) — 1m 3f
7:05 (7:08) 3-Y-0 **£31,068** (£9,709; £4,854; £2,913)

RPR

1 **Night Magic (GER)**[33] 2524 3-9-2 .... KKerekes 6 108
(W Figge, Germany) *mde all: rdn fnl f: r.o wl* **54/10**[2]

2 ¾ **Miss Europa (GER)**[33] 2524 3-9-2 .... AStarke 3 107
(P Schiergen, Germany) *sn racing in 4th: 4th st: chal on outside fr wl over 1f out: hrd rdn and unable qck fnl f* **3/5**[1]

3 4 **Norderney (GER)**[26] 2757 3-9-2 .... FilipMinarik 4 100
(P Schiergen, Germany) *hld up: 7th st: hdwy to rch 3rd jst over 1f out: nvr nr first two* **112/10**

4 3 **Quillaja (GER)** 3-9-2 .... ASuborics 9 95
(W Hickst, Germany) *s.i.s fr outside draw: hld up in rr: last st: rdn 2f out: styd on one pce* **41/5**[3]

5 ¾ **Sworn Pro (GER)**[33] 2524 3-9-2 .... AHelfenbein 7 94
(Mario Hofer, Germany) *pressed ldr: 2nd st: stl 3rd appr fnl f: sn wknd* **15/1**

6 nse **La Poesie (GER)**[22] 2874 3-9-2 .... DBoeuf 5 94
(W Baltromei, Germany) *hld up: 6th st: effrt on outside fr 2f out: kpt on same pce* **96/10**

7 2 **Near Galante (GER)**[33] 2524 3-9-2 .... EPedroza 2 90
(A Wohler, Germany) *mid-div to 1/2-way: 8th st: sn rdn and btn* **18/1**

8 3½ **Andrea (GER)**[22] 2874 3-9-2 .... THellier 1 84
(H Blume, Germany) *mid-div: 5th st: sn wknd* **96/10**

9 14 **Jambalaya (GER)**[22] 2874 3-9-2 .... ADeVries 8 61
(A Wohler, Germany) *racd in 3rd: rdn 4f out: 3rd st: sn wknd* **17/1**

2m 19.44s (-5.26) **9** Ran SP% **133.1**
(including ten euro stakes): WIN 64; PL 14, 11, 17; SF 161.
Owner Stall Salzburg **Bred** Gestut Etzean **Trained** Germany

3557 BEVERLEY (R-H)

Saturday, July 4

OFFICIAL GOING: Good to firm (9.6)

Wind: Light, half against Weather: Fine and dry

3605 AWARD WINNING COACHMAN CARAVANS CLAIMING STKS 7f 100y

1:45 (1:45) (Class 5) 2-Y-O £2,590 (£770; £385; £192) Stalls High

Form RPR

0 1 **She Knows It All (IRE)**[16] 3058 2-8-2 0 JimmyQuinn 4 57+
(G A Swinbank) *t.k.h: chsd ldrs on inner: hdwy 3f out: swtchd lft and effrt to chal wl over 1f out: rdn to ld appr fnl f: styd on wl* **10/1**

542 2 2 1/4 **Go To Dubai**[15] 3119 2-8-1 0 DaleGibson 7 51
(M W Easterby) *set stdy pce: rdn and qcknd 3f out: jnd and drvn wl over 1f out: hdd appr fnl f and kpt on same pce* **5/4**[1]

3253 3 1/2 **Cassidy K**[18] 2996 2-7-13 0 JamieKyne(5) 6 53+
(J Howard Johnson) *v s.i.s and bhd: hdwy and in tch 1/2-way: rdn wl over 2f out: drvn and kpt on same pce appr fnl f* **10/3**[3]

3255 4 1/2 **Alphacino**[23] 2861 2-8-6 0 SamHitchcott 2 54
(M R Channon) *t.k.h: trckd ldrs: hdwy 3f out: rdn along 2f out: sn drvn and one pce* **10/1**

000 5 hd **Dispol Antonio (IRE)**[18] 2997 2-8-6 0 (v) FrankieMcDonald 3 53
(P T Midgley) *chsd ldr: rdn along 3f out: drvn 2f out and grad wknd* **40/1**

60 6 2 1/4 **Glen Lass**[68] 1569 2-8-4 0 AndrewElliott 1 46
(J S Moore) *chsd ldrs on outer: hung lft home turn: sn rdn and btn 2f out: eased* **11/4**[2]

1m 35.73s (1.93) **Going Correction** -0.125s/f (Firm) 6 Ran SP% **114.8**

Speed ratings (Par 94): **83,80,79,79,79 76**

toteswingers: 1&2 £4.70, 1&3 £23.80, 2&3 £1.10 CSF £23.92 TOTE £10.00: £2.70, £1.40; EX 24.50.She Knows It All was claimed by C. Bjorling for £8000.

Owner John P Jones **Bred** Gerard Callanan **Trained** Melsonby, N Yorks

■ Stewards' Enquiry : Sam Hitchcott caution: used whip down shoulder in forehand position.

Frankie McDonald one-day ban: used whip down shoulder in forehand position (Jul 18)

FOCUS

The rail around the bottom bend had been moved back by one metre, so that the configuration of the track was at its widest. This did not change any of the distances, though. A moderate heat run at a fairly steady pace to kick things off.

NOTEBOOK

She Knows It All(IRE) left her debut form well behind on this drop in class. The step up in trip was the key to her success, as there is a great deal of stamina on her dam's side, and she simply saw it out a lot better than the rest. (op 12-1)

Go To Dubai, second in a seller at Redcar last time, looked to have plenty going for her from the best draw, but although she kept on, the winner was just too good. (op 13-8 tchd 7-4)

Cassidy K ran well considering she lost her race at the start, giving away several lengths when caught with her head over the adjacent stall as the traps opened. She would surely have gone close had she broken on terms. Official explanation: jockey said filly missed the break (op 3-1 tchd 11-4)

Alphacino, the most experienced in the line-up, raced a bit keenly and couldn't pick up in the closing stages. (tchd 9-1)

Dispol Antonio(IRE) has yet to show any worthwhile form. (op 33-1)

Glen Lass found the trip beyond her. (op 3-1)

3606 LEISURE FURNISHINGS MAIDEN STKS 5f

2:15 (2:17) (Class 4) 2-Y-O £4,047 (£1,204; £601; £300) Stalls High

Form RPR

4 1 **Electioneer (USA)**[10] 3256 2-9-3 0 J-PGuillambert 9 79
(M Johnston) *dwlt: sn chsng ldr: cl up 1/2-way: rdn to chal wl over 1f out: led ent fnl f: edgd rt and styd on* **4/1**[3]

26 2 1 1/4 **Trinder**[37] 2388 2-9-3 0 TonyHamilton 13 75
(R A Fahey) *chsd ldrs: hdwy 2f out: rdn to chse ldng pair over 1f out: kpt on u.p ins fnl f: nt rch wnr* **11/4**[1]

6 3 1 1/2 **Mister Hughie (IRE)**[10] 3256 2-9-3 0 SamHitchcott 12 69
(M R Channon) *led: rdn along 2f out: drvn over 1f out: hdd ent fnl f: one pce* **9/2**

5003 4 3 **Bossy Kitty**[17] 3032 2-8-12 0 AndrewElliott 5 53
(N Tinkler) *towards rr: hdwy on outer wl over 1f out: sn rdn and kpt on ins fnl f: nrst fin* **20/1**

4242 5 nse **Trade Secret**[22] 2893 2-9-3 0 JimmyQuinn 3 58
(M Brittain) *in tch on outer: rdn along 2f out: drvn over 1f out: kpt on ins fnl f: nrst fin* **6/1**

42 6 nk **Crushing (IRE)**[16] 3064 2-9-0 0 NeilBrown(3) 8 57
(T D Barron) *chsd ldrs: rdn 2f out: sn drvn and wknd appr fnl f* **7/2**[2]

03 7 2 **Powerful Pierre**[9] 3310 2-9-3 0 PhillipMakin 4 50
(Jedd O'Keeffe) *stdd and swtchd rt s: hld up in rr: hdwy on inner to chse ldrs wl over 1f out: sn rdn and no imp* **25/1**

8 2 1/2 **Summa Cum Laude** 2-8-8 0 PatCosgrave 2 32
(Mrs A Duffield) *towards rr: sme late hdwy on outer: nvr a factor* **50/1**

9 1 1/4 **Countrycraft** 2-8-13 0 AndrewMullen 6 32
(Miss S E Hall) *midfield: rdn along and green 1/2-way: sn wknd* **66/1**

004 10 3 1/2 **Baby Judge (IRE)**[9] 3317 2-9-0 0 LeeVickers(3) 10 24
(M C Chapman) *chsd ldrs to 1/2-way: sn wknd* **80/1**

11 8 **Somewhere Else** 2-8-1 0 BillyCray(7) 7 —
(A Berry) *dwlt: a in rr* **100/1**

0 12 6 **Confessional**[36] 2444 2-9-3 0 JamieMoriarty 11 —
(T D Easterby) *dwlt: plld hrd in midfield whn n.m.r and sltly hmpd after 1f: sn towards rr* **8/1**

63.23 secs (-0.27) **Going Correction** -0.125s/f (Firm) 12 Ran SP% **126.8**

Speed ratings (Par 96): **97,95,92,87,87 87,84,80,78,72 59,50**

toteswingers: 1&2 £4.80, 1&3 £4.30, 2&3 £2.80 CSF £16.02 TOTE £6.10: £1.60, £2.00, £2.70; EX 19.60.

Owner Sheikh Hamdan Bin Mohammed Al Maktoum **Bred** Gainsborough Farm Llc **Trained** Middleham Moor, N Yorks

■ Stewards' Enquiry : J-P Guillambert one-day ban: used whip in incorrect place (Jul 18)

FOCUS

A fair maiden and, as is often the case over this trip here, a high draw proved an advantage.

NOTEBOOK

Electioneer(USA) ran green but showed promise on his debut at Bath, and coming from the stable that he does it was no surprise that he showed improvement for that on this second start. He was able to get over from stall nine to race one off the rail and saw his race out strongly inside the last. He looks the type who could make a mark in nurseries, and should get 6f in time. (op 7-2 tchd 5-1)

Trinder, who is blind in his left eye, got upset in the stalls last time out, and again didn't enjoy the experience. He ran well enough in the race itself, though, albeit from the best draw, staying on once switched. (op 4-1 tchd 9-2)

Mister Hughie(IRE), drawn in stall 12, had finished behind Electioneer at Bath on his debut, but he was well supported to reverse the form, having been as big as 12-1 in the morning. Quickly away, he led on the rail for a long way and had no excuse. (op 7-2 tchd 5-1)

Bossy Kitty came into the race with only moderate form to her name. From an ordinary draw, she ended up racing pretty wide throughout and in the circumstances it wasn't a bad effort. However, she is looking exposed now. (tchd 14-1)

Trade Secret had a low draw to overcome and was another who ended up giving away ground racing wide. He also hung under pressure. Official explanation: jockey said colt moved poorly (op 15-2)

Crushing(IRE) was disappointing but an easier traack should suit this speedy type, and nurseries might provide him with better opportunities. (op 11-2)

3607 COACHMAN CARAVANS QUALITY H'CAP 5f

2:45 (2:45) (Class 4) (0-85,80) 3-Y-O+ £6,476 (£1,927; £963; £481) Stalls High

Form RPR

2552 1 **Baybshambles (IRE)**[9] 3304 5-8-11 68 KellyHarrison(3) 1 77
(R E Barr) *dwlt: hld up towards rr: hdwy on outer wl over 1f out: sn rdn: styd on strly ins fnl f to ld nr fin* **13/2**

1522 2 1 1/4 **Liberty Ship**[16] 3065 4-9-2 70 (bt) JimmyQuinn 4 74
(J D Bethell) *cl up: chal wl over 1f out: rdn to ld and hung rt ins fnl f: drvn: hdd and no ex nr fin* **4/1**[1]

0545 3 shd **Kheylide (IRE)**[4] 3483 3-8-6 68 DominicFox(3) 10 70+
(Mrs D J Sanderson) *in tch on inner: hdwy and n.m.r wl over 1f out: rdn and styng on wl whn hmpd towards fin* **7/1**

1R21 4 1/2 **Sands Crooner (IRE)**[14] 3162 6-9-12 80 (v) PatCosgrave 8 82
(J G Given) *trckd ldrs: smooth hdwy 2f out: rdn to ld over 1f out: drvn and hddnside last: hld whn hmpd nr fin* **11/2**[2]

0100 5 1 1/4 **Pacific Pride**[17] 3021 6-8-12 71 (p) JamieKyne(5) 7 68
(J J Quinn) *led: rdn along 2f out: drvn and hdd over 1f out: grad wknd* **4/1**[1]

205 6 hd **Divine Spirit**[26] 2770 8-9-6 74 PhillipMakin 5 71
(M Dods) *chsd ldrs: rdn along over 2f out: sn drvn and grad wknd* **6/1**[3]

0-30 7 nk **Commander Wish**[14] 3164 6-8-13 67 (p) TGMcLaughlin 3 63
(Lucinda Featherstone) *stmbld s: a in rr* **16/1**

0-60 8 1 **Mullglen**[50] 2058 3-9-3 76 DuranFentiman 9 66
(T D Easterby) *dwlt: hld up in tch: effrt 2f out: sn rdn and wknd* **10/1**

0346 9 3/4 **Green Park (IRE)**[14] 3149 6-9-8 76 (b) DNolan 6 65
(D Carroll) *dwlt: a towards rr* **10/1**

63.38 secs (-0.12) **Going Correction** -0.125s/f (Firm)

WFA 3 from 4yo+ 5lb 9 Ran SP% **119.6**

Speed ratings (Par 105): **95,93,92,92,90 89,89,87,86**

toteswingers: 1&2 £5.10, 1&3 £7.40, 2&3 £5.20 CSF £33.94 CT £193.24 TOTE £8.80: £2.50, £1.50, £2.10; EX 40.00.

Owner Miss S Haykin **Bred** Mrs H F Mahr **Trained** Seamer, N Yorks

■ Stewards' Enquiry : Kelly Harrison two-day ban: careless riding (Jul 21-22)

FOCUS

An ordinary but competitive handicap in which the top weight was rated 5lb below the ceiling for the race. Solid form with a small personal best from the winner.

3608 C.G.I. H'CAP 1m 100y

3:20 (3:21) (Class 4) (0-80,80) 3-Y-O £5,180 (£1,541; £770; £384) Stalls High

Form RPR

01 1 **Desire To Excel (IRE)**[21] 2917 3-9-3 76 JimmyQuinn 5 79
(P F I Cole) *mde all: rdn along over 2f out: drvn over 1f out: edgd rigfht ins fnl f: kpt on gamely* **7/2**[3]

3040 2 1/2 **Kheskianto (IRE)**[13] 3193 3-7-10 62 oh2 ow1 AndrewHeffernan(7) 2 64
(M C Chapman) *wnt lft s: hld up in rr: hdwy on inner 2f out: effrt and nt clr run over 1f out: rdn to chal and ev ch ins fnl f whn n.m.r on inner: kpt on* **9/1**

61 3 nk **Burns Night**[11] 3238 3-9-5 78 J-PGuillambert 6 83+
(M Johnston) *t.k.h: trckd ldng pair: hdwy over 2f out and sn n.m.r: effrt and nt clr run over 1f out and ent fnl f: swtchd lft ins fnl f and fin wl* **6/4**[1]

-120 4 2 1/4 **Russian George (IRE)**[10] 3264 3-9-7 80 DNolan 3 76
(T P Tate) *cl upo: rdn along over 2f out: drvn over 1f out: wknd appr fnl f* **8/1**

4311 5 1 **Aldaado (IRE)**[4] 3480 3-9-2 75 6ex PhillipMakin 4 69
(M Dods) *trckd ldrs on outer: effrt over 2f out and sn rdn: drvn over 1f out and grad wknd* **11/4**[2]

1000 6 1 1/2 **Sanvean (IRE)**[42] 2275 3-9-6 79 SamHitchcott 1 69
(M R Channon) *bmpd s: hld up: a in rr* **16/1**

1m 46.05s (-1.55) **Going Correction** -0.125s/f (Firm) 6 Ran SP% **115.9**

Speed ratings (Par 102): **102,101,101,98,97 96**

toteswingers: 1&2 £10.60, 1&3 £1.40, 2&3 £7.50 CSF £34.01 TOTE £4.70: £1.60, £4.90; EX 44.20.

Owner H R H Sultan Ahmad Shah **Bred** Glending Bloodstock **Trained** Whatcombe, Oxon

■ Stewards' Enquiry : D Nolan caution: used whip down shoulder in forehand position

FOCUS

An interesting little handicap for three-year-olds but the winner was allowed to dictate. The form is not all that solid.

3609 ELTHERINGTON STKS (H'CAP) 2m 35y

3:55 (3:55) (Class 5) (0-70,68) 3-Y-O+ £3,561 (£1,059; £529; £264) Stalls High

Form RPR

0-41 1 **Spiders Star**[4] 3486 6-8-9 56 6ex PaulPickard(7) 4 66+
(S G West) *hld up in rr: hdwy 4f out: rdn and qcknd on outer to ld 2f out: sn clr* **5/4**[1]

-005 2 8 **Lets Roll**[16] 3059 8-10-0 68 DanielTudhope 5 69
(C W Thornton) *trckd ldrs: hdwy on bit whn n.m.r 3f out: swtchd ins and hdwy to chse wnr wl over 1f out: sn no imp* **5/1**

6654 3 3 **Wannarock (IRE)**[16] 3068 4-8-6 49 oh1 KellyHarrison(3) 2 46
(M C Chapman) *trckd ldrs: hdwy 6f out: effrt 3f out: sn rdn and one pce fnl 2f* **7/2**[2]

04-6 4 4 **Feeling Peckish (USA)**[14] 3171 5-8-2 49 oh4 (t) AndrewHeffernan(7) 1 41
(M C Chapman) *led: rdn along over 3f out: drvn and hdd 2f out: sn wknd* **14/1**

10- 5 8 **Quitit (IRE)**[22] 7177 4-9-13 67 (p) TonyHamilton 3 50
(Mrs S A Watt) *trckd ldrs: hdwy after 4f and cl up: rdn along wl over 2f out: sn drvn and wknd wl over 1f out* **4/1**[3]

3m 41.59s (1.79) **Going Correction** -0.125s/f (Firm) 5 Ran SP% **110.0**

Speed ratings (Par 103): **90,86,84,82,78**

toteswingers: 1&2 £5.80, 1&3 not won, 2&3 not won. CSF £7.87 TOTE £1.90: £1.30, £2.20; EX 5.00.

Owner Miss Kate Milligan **Bred** Acrum Lodge Stud **Trained** Middleham Moor, N Yorks

FOCUS
There was little pace on and the race developed into something of a dash up the straight. Weak form.

3610 POWERPART FILLIES' H'CAP 1m 1f 207y
4:25 (4:25) (Class 5) (0-70,64) 3-Y-O £3,238 (£963; £481; £240) Stalls High

Form RPR
660- 1 **Upton Seas**[271] 6524 3-8-8 51 AndrewElliott 4 60
(M W Easterby) *trckd ldr: cl up 1/2-way: led over 2f out and sn rdn: drvn ent fnl f and kpt on wl* **11/1**
5360 2 3 ¾ **Dispol Diva**[29] 2667 3-9-7 64 (v) PhillipMakin 5 65
(P T Midgley) *hld up in rr: hdwy 3f out: rdn and n.m.r 2f out: swtchd lft and drvn ent fnl f: sn chsng wnr and no imp* **5/2**[1]
0-55 3 3 ½ **Astrobrava**[38] 2380 3-8-11 54 JimmyQuinn 2 48
(M H Tompkins) *trckd ldng pair: hdwy 3f out: rdn to chse wnr 2f out: drvn and edgd rt over 1f out: sn one pce* **10/3**[3]
640 4 1 ¾ **Catch Key (IRE)**[38] 2375 3-8-13 56 DuranFentiman 8 47
(T D Easterby) *trckd ldrs: hdwy 3f out: rdn 2f out: sn drvn and swtchd lft over 1f out: sn btn* **8/1**
00-0 5 1 **Desert Fairy**[20] 2942 3-8-8 51 TonyHamilton 7 40
(J W Unett) *led: rdn along and hdd over 2f out: sn wknd* **10/1**
-460 6 hd **Triple Cee (IRE)**[12] 3209 3-9-6 63 SamHitchcott 6 51
(M R Channon) *trckd ldrs: effrt 3f out: sn rdn and wknd over 2f out* **3/1**[2]
62-0 7 18 **Challenging (UAE)**[38] 2370 3-8-11 54 DaleGibson 1 6
(M W Easterby) *a in rr: bhd fr 1/2-way* **8/1**
2m 6.33s (-0.67) **Going Correction** -0.125s/f (Firm) 7 Ran SP% **116.3**
Speed ratings (Par 97): **97,94,91,89,89 88,74**
toteswingers: 1&2 £9.30, 1&3 £11.20, 2&3 £2.20 CSF £39.95 CT £115.30 TOTE £14.80: £6.50, £2.00; EX 49.70.
Owner Stephen J Curtis **Bred** S J Curtis - Park Farm Stud **Trained** Sheriff Hutton, N Yorks
FOCUS
With the top weight rated 6lb below the ceiling, this looked a pretty modest fillies' handicap. Clear improvement from the winner but she probably did not beat much.
Upton Seas ◆ Official explanation: trainer said, regarding apparent improvement in form, that as this was the filly's first run for the yard, he had no explanation.

3611 COACHMAN MAIDEN STKS 5f
5:00 (5:00) (Class 5) 3-Y-O+ £2,914 (£867; £433; £216) Stalls High

Form RPR
0-4 1 **Hitches Dubai (BRZ)**[14] 3175 4-9-8 0 SamHitchcott 13 67
(D Nicholls) *cl up: led after 2f: rdn over 1f out: styd on wl* **5/1**[3]
5-55 2 1 **Majestic Lady (IRE)**[19] 2973 3-8-12 58 JimmyQuinn 7 56
(B W Hills) *chsd ldrs: rdn 2f out: drvn over 1f out and kpt on ins fnl f: nrst fin* **5/1**[3]
665 3 1 ¾ **Aegean King**[46] 2157 3-8-10 0 TobyAtkinson(7) 10 54+
(M Wigham) *in rr: pushed along and swtchd wd to stands rails 1/2-way: rdn over 1f out: styd on strly ins fnl f: nrst fin* **7/1**
60-3 4 1 ½ **Excitable (IRE)**[14] 3176 3-8-9 50 DominicFox(3) 1 43
(Mrs D J Sanderson) *led 2f: cl up: rdn and ev ch over 1f out: sn drvn and wknd ins fnl f* **11/1**
0000 5 1 **Port Ronan (USA)**[14] 3176 3-9-0 48 (p) NeilBrown(3) 6 44
(J S Wainwright) *bhd: swtchd lft and rdn wl over 1f out: kpt on ins fnl f: nrst fin* **25/1**
00- 6 ½ **Residency (IRE)**[282] 6230 3-9-3 0 J-PGuillambert 11 42+
(B Smart) *towards rr: hdwy 1/2-way: effrt and n.m.r wl over 1f out: sn rdn and kpt on ins fnl f: nrst fin* **12/1**
0066 7 3 ½ **Singapore Girl**[8] 3334 3-8-12 47 (v) DuranFentiman 8 24
(G R Oldroyd) *chsd ldrs: rdn along 2f out: grad wknd* **33/1**
500- 8 nse **Gee Gina**[327] 4921 3-8-12 52 JamieMoriarty 4 24
(P T Midgley) *wnt lft s: a towards rr* **33/1**
0 9 nk **Arjemis**[17] 3036 3-8-12 0 PAspell 3 23
(C R Wilson) *s.i.s and a towards rr* **100/1**
6-00 10 hd **Another Luke (IRE)**[46] 2154 3-9-0 53 LeeVickers(3) 2 27
(T J Etherington) *a towards rr* **33/1**
200- 11 ½ **Sea Crest**[257] 6865 3-8-5 63 JohnCavanagh(7) 14 20
(M Brittain) *a in rr* **7/2**[2]
4-03 12 nk **Africa's Star (IRE)**[18] 3003 3-8-12 64 (b¹) TonyHamilton 9 19
(M Dods) *chsd ldrs on inner: rdn along 2f out: sn drvn and wknd* **11/4**[1]
0-0 13 7 **Barley Bree (IRE)**[18] 3003 4-9-3 0 PatCosgrave 12 —
(Mrs A Duffield) *dwlt: a bhd* **14/1**
6 14 2 ½ **Star Addition**[24] 2820 3-9-3 0 AndrewMullen 5 —
(E J Alston) *cl up: rdn along 1/2-way: sn wknd* **25/1**
63.40 secs (-0.10) **Going Correction** -0.125s/f (Firm)
WFA 3 from 4yo 5lb 14 Ran SP% **134.9**
Speed ratings (Par 103): **95,93,90,88,86 85,80,80,79,79 78,78,66,62**
toteswingers: 1&2 £6.80, 1&3 £8.00, 2&3 £11.00 CSF £32.43 TOTE £7.20: £1.80, £2.40, £3.10; EX 39.00 Place 6: £ 103.05 Place 5: £55.23.
Owner Michael Reay **Bred** Haras Valente **Trained** Sessay, N Yorks
FOCUS
A modest maiden. The likes of the second and fifth help with the level.
Residency(IRE) Official explanation: jockey said gelding was denied a clear run
T/Plt: £197.50 to a £1 stake. Pool: £48,134.59. 177.90 winning tickets. T/Qpdt: £44.70 to a £1 stake. Pool: £3,056.95. 50.60 winning tickets. JR

3262 CARLISLE (R-H)
Saturday, July 4

OFFICIAL GOING: Good (good to firm on stands' side in home straight) changing to good after race 2 (7.35)
Wind: Light, half against Weather: Overcast

3612 CLEANEVENT APPRENTICE H'CAP 5f 193y
7:05 (7:05) (Class 5) (0-75,73) 4-Y-O+ £2,729 (£806; £403) Stalls High

Form RPR
0021 1 **Bid For Gold**[17] 3021 5-9-7 70 PatrickDonaghy 1 78
(Jedd O'Keeffe) *prom on outside: hdwy to ld 2f out: sn rdn along: hrd pressed fnl f: hld on wl* **7/1**[3]
0132 2 shd **Avontuur (FR)**[4] 3488 7-8-12 61 DeanHeslop 7 69
(Mrs R A Carr) *hld up: hdwy on ins 2f out: ev ch fnl f: jst hld* **9/1**
-003 3 1 ½ **Eastern Hills**[21] 2938 4-9-10 73 LanceBetts 8 76
(J S Wainwright) *in tch: outpcd after 2f: rallied wl over 1f out: kpt on fnl f* **7/1**[3]
3222 4 2 **Soto**[8] 3354 6-8-12 64 (b) JamesPSullivan(3) 9 60
(M W Easterby) *w ldrs to 2f out: kpt on same pce fnl f* **9/2**[2]
5560 5 ½ **Red River Boy**[11] 3239 4-8-2 54 oh5 PaulPickard(3) 4 49
(C W Fairhurst) *slt ld to 2f out: kpt on same pce fnl f* **28/1**
-010 6 3 **Young Gladiator (IRE)**[12] 3224 4-8-5 57 (b) AmyRyan(3) 3 42
(Miss J A Camacho) *trckd ldrs tl edgd rt and wknd 2f out* **9/1**
1006 7 shd **Imperial Sword**[16] 3065 6-9-0 68 (b) JanWilson(5) 2 53
(T D Barron) *bhd and outpcd: short-lived effrt centre 2f out: sn no imp* **25/1**
1122 8 10 **Hansomis (IRE)**[4] 3484 5-9-0 63 JamieKyne 6 16
(B Mactaggart) *w ldrs tl wknd qckly fr 2f out* **7/4**[1]
2301 U **Buy On The Red**[9] 3304 8-9-3 71 (b) NSLawes(5) 5 —
(D Nicholls) *stmbld and uns rdr leaving stalls* **12/1**
1m 15.15s (1.45) **Going Correction** +0.325s/f (Good) 9 Ran SP% **114.5**
Speed ratings (Par 103): **103,102,100,98,97 93,93,80,—**
toteswingers: 1&2 £14.70, 1&3 £4.40, 2&3 £14.80 CSF £67.30 CT £460.59 TOTE £7.90: £1.80, £2.90, £2.70; EX 55.40.
Owner Paul Chapman And Ba'Tat Investments **Bred** B Minty **Trained** Middleham Moor, N Yorks
■ Stewards' Enquiry : Dean Heslop two-day ban: used whip with excessive frequency (Jul 18-19)
Patrick Donaghy five-day ban: used whip with excessive frequency, down shoulder in the forehand (Jul 18-22)
Jamie Kyne caution: used whip without giving mare time to respond.
FOCUS
A modest apprentices' race in which they raced in one group middle to far side, not one of the riders tried out the stands' side. The form looks straightforward rated around the first three.
Hansomis(IRE) Official explanation: trainer had no explanation for the poor form shown

3613 NORTHERN SECURITY LTD MAIDEN AUCTION STKS 5f 193y
7:35 (7:38) (Class 5) 2-Y-O £2,590 (£770; £385; £192) Stalls High

Form RPR
3 1 **Ask Frank (IRE)**[14] 3147 2-8-11 0 PJMcDonald 4 97+
(G A Swinbank) *in tch: hdwy to ld over 1f out: sn clr* **6/1**[3]
34 2 10 **Lucky Rave**[23] 2839 2-8-11 0 PaulMulrennan 5 70+
(D H Brown) *w ldrs: hung rt and led over 2f out: hdd over 1f out: no ch w wnr* **5/1**[2]
4 3 5 **William Morgan (IRE)**[10] 3262 2-8-11 0 PaulHanagan 3 55+
(R A Fahey) *towards rr: hdwy 2f out: kpt on: nt rch first two* **8/1**
0 4 1 **Firetrap**[35] 2484 2-8-13 0 SilvestreDeSousa 2 51
(Mrs A Duffield) *midfield: effrt u.p over 2f out: sn no imp* **16/1**
0 5 2 **Clever Molly (IRE)**[17] 3032 2-8-4 0 PaulQuinn 7 36
(E J Alston) *led to over 2f out: sn wknd* **25/1**
6 6 1 **Raleigh Quay (IRE)**[9] 3292 2-8-8 0 JamieKyne(5) 9 42
(Micky Hammond) *midfield: outpcd 1/2-way: n.d after* **16/1**
3 7 3 **Hill Of Miller (IRE)**[23] 2860 2-8-13 0 PhillipMakin 1 33
(Rae Guest) *hld up: rdn 1/2-way: nvr on terms* **3/1**[1]
5 8 1 ½ **Fantastic Strike (IRE)**[9] 3292 2-8-9 0 GregFairley 8 25
(M Johnston) *s.i.s: shortlived effrt over 3f out: sn wknd* **3/1**[1]
0 9 10 **Stef And Stelio**[44] 2187 2-9-2 0 TonyCulhane 6 —
(G A Butler) *t.k.h: cl up tl wknd over 2f out* **9/1**
0 10 4 ½ **Kirkby's Gem**[19] 2963 2-8-4 0 DarrenMoffatt 10 —
(A Berry) *in tch to 1/2-way: hung rt and sn wknd* **200/1**
1m 13.21s (-0.49) **Going Correction** -0.225s/f (Firm) 10 Ran SP% **118.2**
Speed ratings (Par 94): **94,80,74,72,70 68,64,62,49,43**
toteswingers: 1&2 £6.50, 1&3 £9.00, 2&3 £5.50 CSF £36.63 TOTE £6.60: £1.50, £2.10, £2.50; EX 36.90.
Owner Frank Hanson **Bred** D Hefin Jones **Trained** Melsonby, N Yorks
FOCUS
The area in front of the stalls was sanded before this race after Buy On Red's misfortune in the opener. The senior riders elected to come wide and race towards the stands' side. Quite an interesting maiden auction race and a winner of real potential.
NOTEBOOK
Ask Frank(IRE), a gelded son of Hawk Wing, had shaped well behind July Stakes-bound Ghostwing on his debut at Ayr. He travelled strongly and came a long way clear in the final furlong. He looks very useful, a step up to novice company will follow and already he looks a very saleable commodity. (tchd 13-2)
Lucky Rave, who had shown a fair level of form in two previous starts both at Haydock, mastered the pacesetter but was almost immediately overwhelmed by the winner. He deserves to find a race. (op 7-2)
William Morgan(IRE) fourth on his debut here ten days earlier, was only sixth a furlong out. He put in some highly pleasing late work and is still learning. (op 15-2 tchd 7-1)
Firetrap, backed at long odds, showed a fair bit more than on his debut five weeks earlier. (op 28-1)
Clever Molly(IRE) showed bags of toe to take them along to past halfway. She needs another outing to qualify for a nursery mark. (tchd 20-1)
Raleigh Quay(IRE) struggled to go the pace and will need a stiffer test in time. (op 28-1)
Hill Of Miller(IRE), third first time at Yarmouth, made a tardy start and was never on terms despite racing hard against the stands'-side rail. (op 11-4 tchd 5-2)
Fantastic Strike(IRE), again well backed, missed a beat at the start. He tended to race towards the centre of the track and could never go the pace. Presumably he shows plenty at home. (op 9-2)

3614 ANDERSONS DENTON HOLME LTD (S) STKS 7f 200y
8:05 (8:07) (Class 6) 3-Y-O £2,047 (£604; £302) Stalls High

Form RPR
0055 1 **Ask Dan (IRE)**[9] 3305 3-8-12 53 (p) PaulHanagan 9 63
(B Smart) *mde all: rdn over 2f out: hld on wl fnl f* **7/2**[3]
3033 2 3 ½ **Paint Splash**[54] 1926 3-8-2 52 DeanHeslop(5) 4 49
(T D Barron) *s.i.s: hld up: hdwy to chse wnr over 1f out: one pce fnl f* **9/4**[1]
154 3 2 ½ **Laura's Lady (IRE)**[7] 3381 3-8-12 55 PJMcDonald 5 48+
(G A Swinbank) *hld up towards rr: drvn and outpcd 3f out: rallied wl over 1f out: no imp fnl f* **3/1**[2]
-606 4 1 ¼ **Haulage Lady (IRE)**[33] 2528 3-8-7 54 (p) GregFairley 2 40
(Karen McLintock) *midfield: outpcd and hung rt 3f out: kpt on fnl f: nrst fin* **10/1**
0000 5 4 **Flynn's Island (IRE)**[15] 3108 3-8-12 48 (v¹) PhillipMakin 7 35
(M Dods) *t.k.h: cl up: rdn over 2f out: btn over 1f out* **14/1**
-000 6 4 ½ **Hettie Hubble**[17] 3031 3-8-10 44 ow3 PaulMulrennan 8 22
(D W Thompson) *midfield: rdn 3f out: wknd fr 2f out* **66/1**
600 7 6 **Indigo Belle (IRE)**[15] 3123 3-8-7 35 (v) SilvestreDeSousa 3 4
(Mrs A Duffield) *hld up: rdn over 3f out: nvr on terms* **25/1**
-005 8 6 **Fifth Amendment**[15] 3093 3-8-7 62 SladeO'Hara(5) 11 —
(A Berry) *chsd ldrs tl wknd over 2f out* **7/1**
-556 9 3 ½ **Smelly Cat**[30] 2624 3-8-0 48 JamesPSullivan(7) 1 —
(D W Thompson) *pressed wnr tl wknd over 2f out* **18/1**
0 10 1 ¼ **Miss Dee Lady (IRE)**[83] 1228 3-8-2 0 LanceBetts(5) 6 —
(Patrick Morris) *s.i.s: a bhd* **40/1**
1m 43.94s (3.94) **Going Correction** +0.45s/f (Yiel) 10 Ran SP% **119.3**
Speed ratings (Par 98): **98,94,92,90,86 82,76,70,66,65**
toteswingers: 1&2 £2.90, 1&3 £2.50, 2&3 £3.20 CSF £11.96 TOTE £4.30: £1.40, £1.40, £1.50; EX 17.50.The winner was sold to A. Tinler for 6,500gns.

Owner EKOS Pinnacle Partnership **Bred** Darley **Trained** Hambleton, N Yorks

FOCUS

Prior to this poor seller the ground was changed to good. Again they raced in one group towards the stands' side in the home straight. The form is not solid with the winner to his juvenile form the best guide.

3615 COORS LIGHT H'CAP 7f 200y

8:35 (8:35) (Class 4) (0-80,85) 3-Y-0+ **£6,476** (£1,927; £963; £481) **Stalls** High

Form RPR

6-26 **1** **Mount Hadley (USA)**[38] 2387 5-9-10 **76** PaulMulrennan 8 89
(G A Butler) *chsd ldrs: effrt over 2f out: styd on ins fnl f to ld nr fin* **13/2**

6131 **2** *hd* **Sunnyside Tom (IRE)**[10] 3264 5-10-0 **80** PaulHanagan 6 92
(R A Fahey) *led: rdn over 2f out: kpt on wl fnl f: hdd nr fin* **7/2**[1]

0615 **3** *3 ¾* **Intersky Charm (USA)**[10] 3264 5-9-0 **66** TonyCulhane 3 69
(R M Whitaker) *cl up: rdn over 2f out: one pce fnl f* **12/1**

3022 **4** *2 ½* **Daaweitza**[10] 3264 6-9-9 **78** NeilBrown(3) 7 75
(B Ellison) *in tch: outpcd over 2f out: rallied fnl f: no imp* **6/1**[3]

0201 **5** *½* **Stevie Gee (IRE)**[10] 3265 5-9-12 **85** PaulPickard(7) 10 81+
(G A Swinbank) *t.k.h: in tch: effrt over 2f out: no ex over 1f out* **9/2**[2]

/000 **6** *1 ¾* **Call Of Duty (IRE)**[16] 3070 4-8-10 **62** DarrenMoffatt 4 53
(Mrs Dianne Sayer) *midfield: drvn 3f out: no imp fr 2f out* **28/1**

04-0 **7** *hd* **Pitbull**[96] 1042 6-8-4 **61** oh1 (p) JamieKyne(5) 1 52
(Mrs G S Rees) *dwlt: hld up: rdn over 2f out: edgd rt and sn outpcd* **20/1**

0640 **8** *½* **Sparton Duke (IRE)**[3] 3509 4-9-0 **71** (p) AmyRyan(5) 9 61+
(K A Ryan) *missed break: bhd: rdn over 3f out: n.d* **8/1**

304 **9** *6* **Middlemarch (IRE)**[8] 3353 9-9-7 **73** (v) DanielTudhope 12 48
(J S Goldie) *bhd: struggling over 3f out: sn btn* **11/1**

0000 **10** *½* **Major Magpie (IRE)**[10] 3265 7-9-10 **76** PhillipMakin 5 49
(M Dods) *t.k.h in midfield: struggling over 2f out: sn wknd* **7/1**

0045 **11** *35* **Forzarzi (IRE)**[19] 2968 5-8-9 **66** oh6 ow5 (p) GaryBartley(5) 11 —
(H A McWilliams) *hld up: rdn 3f out: sn wknd* **33/1**

1m 42.47s (2.47) **Going Correction** +0.45s/f (Yiel)
WFA 3 from 4yo+ 9lb **11 Ran SP% 118.8**
Speed ratings (Par 105): **105,104,101,98,98 96,96,95,89,89 53**
toteswingers: 1&2 £6.60, 1&3 £20.80, 2&3 £12.80 CSF £29.15 CT £278.42 TOTE £8.80: £2.60, £1.60, £4.20; EX 36.70.

Owner Michael Tabor **Bred** Gainsborough Farm Llc **Trained** Newmarket, Suffolk

■ Stewards' Enquiry : Paul Mulrennan caution: used whip without giving gelding time to respond.

FOCUS

Five of these had run in either the Carlisle Bell or the consolation race ten days earlier. Again the whole field came across to the stands' side rail once in line for home. The form is rated at face value with a personal best from the runner-up.

Major Magpie(IRE) Official explanation: jockey said gelding had no more to give

3616 CFM CASH FOR KIDS H'CAP 6f 192y

9:05 (9:06) (Class 5) (0-70,70) 3-Y-0 **£2,590** (£770; £385; £192) **Stalls** High

Form RPR

1245 **1** **Rising Kheleyf (IRE)**[36] 2450 3-9-7 **70** PJMcDonald 1 77
(G A Swinbank) *mde virtually all: rdn and edgd rt over 1f out: hld on gamely fnl f* **11/4**[1]

0133 **2** *hd* **Island Chief**[11] 3234 3-9-1 **64** (p) TonyHamilton 5 70
(K A Ryan) *t.k.h: prom: rdn over 2f out: disp ld ins fnl f: jst hld* **11/4**[1]

2331 **3** *1 ¼* **Rio Cobolo (IRE)**[8] 3334 3-9-1 **64** (v) PaulMulrennan 6 67
(Paul Green) *dwlt: in tch: effrt over 2f out: edgd rt appr fnl f: kpt on same pce ins fnl f* **11/2**[3]

2234 **4** *1* **Diamond Daisy (IRE)**[36] 2450 3-9-0 **63** SilvestreDeSousa 2 63
(Mrs A Duffield) *chsd ldrs: rdn over 2f out: one pce over 1f out* **4/1**[2]

6223 **5** *5* **Royal Premium**[8] 3334 3-8-5 **54** (v) PaulHanagan 4 41
(Mrs G S Rees) *t.k.h: cl up tl wknd wl over 1f out* **4/1**[2]

1m 30.31s (3.21) **Going Correction** +0.45s/f (Yiel) **5 Ran SP% 108.7**
Speed ratings (Par 100): **99,98,97,96,90**
toteswingers: 1&2 £6.70 CSF £10.17 TOTE £3.80: £1.80, £1.80; EX 8.30.

Owner D Bamlet **Bred** J K Thoroughbreds And M Buckley **Trained** Melsonby, N Yorks

■ Stewards' Enquiry : P J McDonald two-day ban: used whip with excessive frequency (Jul 18-19)

FOCUS

A modest contest and again they headed directly for the stands' side rail once in line for home. The form looks straightforward rated around the winner and third.

3617 CFM RADIO ESCALA LIVE HERE TONIGHT MAIDEN H'CAP 2m 1f 52y

9:35 (9:35) (Class 6) (0-65,62) 4-Y-0+ **£2,047** (£604; £302) **Stalls** High

Form RPR

002 **1** **Saxona (IRE)**[12] 3205 5-8-11 **52** StephenDonohoe 8 61+
(Ian Williams) *midfield: effrt over 2f out: edgd lft and chal ins fnl f: led cl home* **3/1**[2]

343- **2** *nse* **Beauchamp Wonder**[278] 6331 4-9-7 **62** PaulHanagan 9 71
(G A Butler) *cl up: led over 2f out: edgd rt and jnd ins fnl f: hdd cl home* **5/1**[3]

5/00 **3** *8* **Uptown Lad (IRE)**[9] 3313 10-8-1 **47** ow2 DeanHeslop(5) 4 46
(R Johnson) *hld up: brought wd over 4f out: sn rdn: rallied over 1f out: kpt on: nt rch wnr and 2nd* **11/1**

23-2 **4** *shd* **Unawatuna**[57] 1851 4-9-2 **60** KellyHarrison(3) 6 59
(Mrs K Walton) *chsd ldrs: outpcd over 3f out: rallied over 1f out: no imp* **2/1**[1]

545/ **5** *3 ¼* **Sea Cove**[21] 240 9-8-4 **45** DarrenMoffatt 5 40
(Mrs Dianne Sayer) *hld up in midfield: rdn over 3f out: kpt on fnl f: nvr rchd ldrs* **50/1**

040 **6** *1 ¾* **Trempari**[16] 3056 6-9-0 **55** TonyCulhane 10 48
(Mike Murphy) *hld up: drvn 4f out: sme late hdwy: nvr on terms* **20/1**

00-0 **7** *¾* **Art Gallery**[20] 302 5-7-13 **45** JamieKyne(5) 12 37
(D W Thompson) *cl up tl outpcd over 3f out: n.d after* **40/1**

3-30 **8** *4* **Amir Pasha (UAE)**[39] 1242 4-8-13 **54** (p) PhillipMakin 3 42
(Micky Hammond) *hld up: struggling over 4f out: sn btn* **7/1**

0-00 **9** *9* **Dance Sauvage**[28] 2725 6-8-7 **48** ow3 PJMcDonald 2 25
(B Storey) *hld up: rdn 4f out: sn btn* **40/1**

20 **10** *1* **Roisin's Prince (IRE)**[6] 2519 7-8-11 **52** (t) GregFairley 7 28
(M Sheppard) *led to over 2f out: sn wknd* **16/1**

6330 **11** *23* **Dawn Wind**[8] 1156 4-8-7 **48** ow1 (bt) TonyHamilton 1 —
(I A Wood) *midfield: struggling over 3f out: sn btn* **16/1**

4m 0.59s (7.59) **Going Correction** +0.45s/f (Yiel) **11 Ran SP% 119.2**
Speed ratings (Par 101): **100,99,96,96,94 93,93,91,87,86 76**
toteswingers: 1&2 £4.60, 1&3 £12.50, 2&3 £9.10 CSF £18.15 CT £147.96 TOTE £4.30: £1.60, £2.20, £3.00; EX 20.20 Place 6: £80.28 Place 5: £22.37.

Owner Mr & Mrs G Middlebrook **Bred** G And Mrs Middlebrook **Trained** Portway, Worcs

■ Stewards' Enquiry : Paul Hanagan caution: used whip down shoulder in the forehand.

FOCUS

A moderate stayers' handicap run at a very steady pace to the halfway mark. The first two are unexposed as stayers and should remain of interest in the short term. Again they all came towards the stands'-side rail once in line for home.

Amir Pasha(UAE) Official explanation: jockey said gelding hung both ways

Roisin's Prince(IRE) Official explanation: jockey said gelding hung left throughout

T/Plt: £66.60 to a £1 stake. Pool: £65,438.37. 716.20 winning tickets. T/Qpdt: £8.90 to a £1 stake. Pool: £5,096.80. 420.42 winning tickets. RY

3570 HAYDOCK (L-H)

Saturday, July 4

OFFICIAL GOING: Good to firm (good in places; 8.4) changing to good after race 5 (4.35)

Rail realignment increased advertised distances on the round course by around 16yards

Wind: Light, across Weather: Showers

3618 BET365 BEST ODDS GUARANTEED H'CAP 1m 3f 200y

2:20 (2:20) (Class 2) (0-100,96) 3-Y-0 **£19,428** (£5,781; £2,889; £1,443) **Stalls** Centre

Form RPR

2010 **1** **Quai D'Orsay**[16] 3051 3-9-4 **93** JoeFanning 7 102
(M Johnston) *mde all: rdn whn pressed over 1f out: jnd by runner-up nr fin: all out to prevail on the nod* **5/1**[3]

-401 **2** *nse* **Thin Red Line (IRE)**[26] 2767 3-8-9 **84** JamieSpencer 3 93
(E A L Dunlop) *trckd leaeders: rdn to chse and chal wnr fr over 1f out: upsides nr fin: jst denied on the nod* **4/1**[2]

-001 **3** *1* **Cosmic Sun**[16] 3051 3-8-13 **88** PaulHanagan 4 96
(R A Fahey) *hld up: pushed along whn nt clr run 3f out: sn outpcd: swtchd rt and hdwy u.p over 1f out: styd on ins fnl f: clsd at fin but nt quite rchd front pair* **11/2**

1510 **4** *1* **Brunston**[16] 3051 3-8-11 **86** SebSanders 1 92
(R Charlton) *hld up: effrt and hdwy on outside over 2f out: chsd ldrs over 1f out: no ex fnl 75yds* **7/2**[1]

1-10 **5** *3 ¼* **Lethal Glaze (IRE)**[15] 3090 3-8-13 **88** EddieAhern 9 89
(R Hannon) *hld up in midfield: lost pl 6f out: pushed along and hdwy to chse ldrs over 3f out: one pce appr fnl f* **14/1**

1-21 **6** *hd* **Becausewecan (USA)**[8] 3359 3-8-4 **79** GregFairley 5 79
(M Johnston) *chsd wnr: rdn 2f out: lost 2nd over 1f out: wknd ins fnl f* **7/1**

3-11 **7** *2* **Rosika**[51] 2008 3-8-9 **84** WilliamBuick 8 81
(Sir Michael Stoute) *hld up: hdwy 7f out: lost pl 3f out: outpcd after* **11/2**

2m 31.49s (-1.71) **Going Correction** +0.025s/f (Good) **7 Ran SP% 108.8**
Speed ratings (Par 106): **106,105,105,104,102 102,101**
toteswingers: 1&2 £5.20, 1&3 £7.30, 2&3 £4.00 CSF £22.67 CT £100.42 TOTE £6.60: £4.10, £2.60; EX 34.00 TRIFECTA Not won..

Owner Sheikh Hamdan Bin Mohammed Al Maktoum **Bred** Miss K Rausing **Trained** Middleham Moor, N Yorks

■ Stewards' Enquiry : Seb Sanders caution: careless riding

FOCUS

The ground had dried out slightly from the previous evening and was officially good to firm, good in places, although some of the jockeys in this contest felt the track was riding loose. This was a decent handicap, although the early pace was nothing special. Solid form, and the race could rate higher.

NOTEBOOK

Quai D'Orsay, 7lb higher than when scoring at Musselburgh last month, was allowed to dictate at his own tempo from the start and that always makes a horse from his stable a dangerous opponent. Gradually winding things up from the front down the long home straight, he kept on finding a bit more under pressure but only held on by the skin of his teeth at the line and it took the judge a long time to separate the first two. (op 13-2 tchd 7-1)

Thin Red Line(IRE) ◆, trying the trip for the first time and put up 6lb for his Pontefract success last month, would probably have been suited by the ordinary gallop. Tracking the pace from the off, he eventually managed to find a gap between the Johnston pair and finished well but failed by a whisker to get up. He can win off this mark. (tchd 7-2 and 9-2)

Cosmic Sun, bumped up 8lb for getting off the mark at the 11th attempt when a 66-1 shot for the King George V Handicap at Royal Ascot, was held up in the early stages. Once pulled out wide for his effort, he finished strongly but could never quite get to the front pair and he could probably have done with a stronger gallop. At least this performance shows he isn't handicapped out of things just yet. (op 5-1 tchd 9-2)

Brunston, who pulled too hard early when around six lengths behind Cosmic Sun at Royal Ascot, enjoyed a 9lb pull here. Keen enough again in last place, he looked dangerous when making his effort down the outside and had every chance over a furlong from home before his effort flattened out. (op 5-1)

Lethal Glaze(IRE), who failed to see out 2m in the Queen's Vase, had won three in a row before that but he was 10lb higher than for the last of those. He could never really get into the race and needs some leniency. (op 10-1)

Becausewecan(USA), a stablemate of the winner and 3lb higher than when winning over this trip at Newmarket eight days earlier, raced a bit too keen in a handy position and he had little left once coming off the bridle. His best form has come on an easier surface. (op 6-1 tchd 15-2)

Rosika, bidding for a hat-trick off a 7lb higher mark and trying the trip for the first time, got shuffled back to last when a couple of her rivals made their efforts down the outside passing the three-furlong pole and there was no way back. (op 7-2)

3619 BET365 LANCASHIRE OAKS (GROUP 2) (F&M) 1m 3f 200y

2:55 (2:56) (Class 1) 3-Y-0+

£56,770 (£21,520; £8,070; £8,070; £2,690; £1,350) **Stalls** Centre

Form RPR

-435 **1** **Barshiba (IRE)**[14] 3139 5-9-5 105 PaulHanagan 8 110
(D R C Elsworth) *racd keenly: chsd ldr: led over 2f out: r.o wl and in command fnl f* **12/1**

1-23 **2** *3 ¾* **Fallen In Love**[23] 2846 3-8-6 98 SteveDrowne 3 104
(J L Dunlop) *in tch: effrt whn nt clr run under 3f out: styd on to chse wnr over 1f out: no imp fnl f* **7/1**

0-24 **3** *1 ½* **Starfala**[35] 2482 4-9-5 100 JamieSpencer 7 102
(P F I Cole) *s.i.s: in rr: pushed along 2f out and struggling to go pce: styd on ins fnl f: fin wl but nvr gng to threaten front 2* **25/1**

-143 **3** *dht* **High Heeled (IRE)**[29] 2672 3-8-6 114 MichaelHills 6 102
(B W Hills) *hld up: rdn and swtchd lft over 2f out: hdwy over 1f out: kpt on but nt pce to chal ldrs* **11/8**[1]

103- **5** *¾* **Saphira's Fire (IRE)**[259] 6819 4-9-5 103 MartinDwyer 2 101
(W R Muir) *hld up: hdwy 3f out: chsd wnr 2f out tl over 1f out: one pce fnl 150yds* **10/1**

1-16 **6** *1 ¾* **Take The Hint**[16] 3047 3-8-6 107 RichardMullen 4 98
(J H M Gosden) *in tch: effrt to chse ldrs over 2f out: no ex ins fnl f* **6/1**[3]

1-25 **7** 4 1/2 **July Jasmine (USA)**[16] 3047 3-8-6 100 WilliamBuick 5 91
(Sir Michael Stoute) *chsd ldrs: rdn over 2f out: sn wknd* **5/1**[2]

043- **8** hd **Miracle Seeker**[338] 4549 4-9-5 102 PhilipRobinson 9 90
(C G Cox) *led: rdn and hdd over 2f out: wknd over 1f out* **16/1**

2m 30.36s (-2.84) **Going Correction** +0.025s/f (Good)
WFA 3 from 4yo+ 13lb **8** Ran SP% **112.1**
Speed ratings (Par 115): **110,107,106,106,106 104,101,101**
Place: Starfala £2.10, High Heeled £0.60 Tote Trifecta: B-FIL-S £169.60 B-FIL-HH £67.80. toteswingers: B&FIL £24.30, B&S £4.30, FIL&S £5.00, B&HH £2.00, FIL&HH £1.00. CSF £88.52 TOTE £12.10: £2.10, £1.80; EX 80.90.
Owner J C Smith **Bred** Littleton Stud **Trained** Newmarket, Suffolk
■ Stewards' Enquiry : Martin Dwyer one-day ban: careless riding (Jul 18)

FOCUS
The early pace was strong and the winning time was 1.13 seconds faster than the opener. Older fillies and mares have held a slight advantage in recent runnings of this contest and the seniors struck again this time. Ordinary form for the grade, Barshiba not needing to improve with the favourite below par.

NOTEBOOK
Barshiba(IRE) hadn't really proved her stamina one way or the other under a positive ride in her first attempt at the trip in the Hardwicke last month, and she took a fierce hold early again here, but she was helped by getting a lead from Miracle Seeker. Once getting the better of that filly coming to the last two furlongs, she found plenty under strong pressure and ran out a deserved winner. The Yorkshire Oaks is now a possibility. (op 10-1)
Fallen In Love, the lowest rated in the field and trying the trip for the first time, was nonetheless well backed. Help up in midfield early, she stayed on well once in the clear entering the last two furlongs but could never get anywhere near the winner. She saw the trip out well enough and looks well up to winning a Listed race at least. (op 10-1 tchd 6-1)
Starfala, a dual winner on Polytrack but yet to win on turf, hasn't been disgraced in a couple of Listed contests this year. She gave away plenty of ground at the start and was last for a long way, but she ran on in decent style towards the end and did well to finish where she did under the circumstances. (tchd 5-4 and 6-4)
High Heeled(IRE), by far the highest rated of these following her fine third to Sariska in the Oaks, was held up before being asked to take closer order starting up the home straight, but she had little room when trying for a gap between Saphira's Fire and Fallen In Love and when she did see daylight it was far too late. She probably wouldn't have been that much closer in any case and this wasn't the ideal advert for the Oaks form. (tchd 5-4 and 6-4)
Saphira's Fire(IRE), not seen since finishing third in a Newmarket Group 2 last October, ran with plenty of credit and should come on for it. She is still lightly raced for a horse of her age. (op 12-1)
Take The Hint, a rather disappointing second favourite when behind July Jasmine in the Ribblesdale, represented a stable that had won this race twice since 2003. She made an effort out wide once into the straight, but it came to little and this was another rather disappointing effort. She slipped up after the line but was none the worse. (tchd 11-2 and 13-2)
July Jasmine(USA) dropped out tamely and this was another modest performance. Shes doesn't seem to be progressing. (op 6-1)

3620 BET365 OLD NEWTON CUP (HERITAGE H'CAP) 1m 3f 200y
3:30 (3:32) (Class 2) 4-Y-0+
£52,963 (£15,861; £7,930; £3,969; £1,980; £994) **Stalls** Centre

Form RPR

3211 **1** **Red Merlin (IRE)**[35] 2475 4-8-10 92 (v) PhilipRobinson 9 107
(C G Cox) *midfield: hdwy over 2f out: chsd ldr over 1f out: r.o to ld ins fnl f: rdn out* **15/2**[1]

0001 **2** 1/2 **Munsef**[7] 3374 7-8-13 95 StephenDonohoe 16 109
(Ian Williams) *in tch: led ent fnl 2f: hdd ins fnl f: styd on u.p but a jst hld after* **25/1**

2-21 **3** 5 **Mezzanisi (IRE)**[47] 2146 4-8-8 90 JamieSpencer 4 96
(M L W Bell) *lost pl early: midfield: swtchd rt and hdwy over 2f out: rdn over 1f out: styd on ins fnl f: nvr able to chal front pair* **9/1**[3]

/161 **4** 1 **Spring Jim**[52] 1990 8-8-8 90 MartinDwyer 14 94
(J R Fanshawe) *hld up: hdwy on outside over 2f out: kpt on u.p ins fnl f: nvr able to chal ldrs* **16/1**

3321 **5** nse **Drill Sergeant**[14] 3142 4-9-10 106 JoeFanning 12 110+
(M Johnston) *chsd ldrs: chal fr 3f out: rdn 2f out: nt qckn over 1f out: styd on same pce ins fnl f* **8/1**[2]

61-2 **6** 3/4 **Hevelius**[35] 2468 4-8-9 91 ShaneKelly 6 94
(W R Swinburn) *s.i.s: racd keenly: hld up: hdwy into midfield over 5f out: pushed along 3f out: carried hd high and looked uncomfortable 2f out: kpt on ins fnl f: nvr landed a blow* **8/1**[2]

4221 **7** 3/4 **Just Lille (IRE)**[9] 3293 6-8-8 90 (p) SilvestreDeSousa 7 92
(Mrs A Duffield) *chsd ldrs: pushed along over 3f out: one pce fr over 1f out* **20/1**

3416 **8** 2 **Dansili Dancer**[14] 3142 7-9-6 102 EddieAhern 3 104+
(C G Cox) *midfield: n.m.r and hmpd under 3f out: sn pushed along: drvn in chsng gp over 1f out: keeping on at one pce and hld whn n.m.r and snatched up ins fnl 100yds* **8/1**[2]

04-0 **9** 1 1/4 **Laterly (IRE)**[50] 2055 4-8-11 93 MickyFenton 5 90
(T P Tate) *sn led: clr fr 9f out to 7f out: hdd ent fnl 2f out: wknd ins fnl f* **16/1**

1-15 **10** hd **Falcativ**[35] 2471 4-8-10 92 DaneO'Neill 8 88
(L M Cumani) *in tch: effrt over 2f out: no imp over 1f out: wknd ins fnl f* **15/2**[1]

1525 **11** 3/4 **Mystery Star (IRE)**[7] 3399 4-8-9 91 SebSanders 10 86+
(M H Tompkins) *towards rr: trying to make hdwy whn nt clr run and swtchd lft over 1f out: sn nt clr run again and continually denied a run: eased ins fnl f* **22/1**

-412 **12** 12 **Yes Mr President (IRE)**[10] 3266 4-8-7 89 MichaelHills 11 65+
(M Johnston) *chsd ldr: upsides 3f out: rdn 2f out: wknd over 1f out: eased whn wl btn ins fnl f* **8/1**[2]

0650 **13** 3 1/4 **Love Galore (IRE)**[28] 2706 4-8-11 93 GregFairley 2 64
(M Johnston) *s.i.s: racd keenly: hld up: struggling 2f out: nvr on terms* **16/1**

065- **14** 8 **Malt Or Mash (USA)**[413] 2192 5-9-7 106 PatrickHills(3) 13 64
(R Hannon) *midfield: rdn over 3f out: wknd over 2f out* **33/1**

111U **15** 1 3/4 **Hatton Flight**[14] 3142 5-9-3 99 (b) WilliamBuick 17 54
(A M Balding) *a bhd: eased whn n.d fnl f* **8/1**[2]

2m 29.75s (-3.45) **Going Correction** +0.025s/f (Good) **15** Ran SP% **122.6**
Speed ratings (Par 109): **112,111,108,107,107 107,106,105,104,104 103,95,93,88,87**
toteswingers: 1&2 £126.70, 1&3 £14.30, 2&3 £113.80 CSF £197.32 CT £1729.01 TOTE £8.80: £2.50, £7.00, £4.20; EX 315.50 Trifecta £2099.00 Part won. Pool: £2,836.50 - 0.20 winning units..
Owner Reid's Allstars **Bred** Keatly Overseas Ltd **Trained** Lambourn, Berks
■ Stewards' Enquiry : Silvestre De Sousa three-day ban: careless riding (Jul 18-20)

FOCUS
A typically red-hot handicap, as would be expected for the money. The pace was strong and the winning time was 0.61 seconds faster than the Lancashire Oaks. The front pair pulled well clear and the winner posted a big personal best.

NOTEBOOK
Red Merlin(IRE), 7lb higher in his bid for a hat-trick, was given a cracking ride. He could be seen travelling extremely well a long way from home and his rider seemed keen not to ask him until the last possible moment. Once pulled out from the slipstream of the runner-up, he found plenty when put under pressure to get up near the line. (op 8-1 tchd 9-1 and 10-1 in places)
Munsef, formerly a Group-class performer for John Dunlop, was favoured by the weights when successful in a Chester claimer last month on his debut for the yard, but he ran a blinder in this much more competitive event. Sent to the front inside the last two furlongs, it looked as though he might score but the winner was right on his tail and found more in the rush to the line. The problem is that considering how far he pulled clear of the others he may well go up a bit for this. (op 20-1)
Mezzanisi(IRE) ◆, very consistent but yet to win on grass, was closely matched with Hatton Flight on their meeting at Epsom in April. He was done few favours just after the start, but he stayed on in pleasing style over the last couple of furlongs to snatch third and was reported to have lost his near-fore shoe. It can only be a matter of time before he breaks his duck on turf. Official explanation: jockey said gelding lost a near-fore shoe (op 12-1)
Spring Jim, 7lb higher than when beating a big field over this trip at York in May, was held up right out the back early but made up plenty of late ground to finish a very creditable fourth.
Drill Sergeant, raised 5lb for his success in the Duke of Edinburgh Stakes at Royal Ascot, was never far away and was one of four disputing the lead two furlongs from home before fading. This was a good effort under his big weight in such a hot race, but he isn't going to be easy to place off this mark. (op 10-1)
Hevelius ◆, 5lb higher than when just beaten at Doncaster in May following a lengthy absence, was trying the trip for the first time. Given plenty to do, he made some eyecatching late headway, having not had a great deal of room. The least exposed in the field, there is probably better to come from him. (op 7-1)
Just Lille(IRE), back off a career-high mark following her victory in a four-runner fillies' conditions event at Hamilton last month, raced handily and kept on well, so it's not impossible she can win off this sort of mark. (op 22-1 tchd 25-1)
Dansili Dancer ◆ got into all sorts of trouble when trying to get closer against the inside rail passing the three-furlong pole. Now 7lb higher than when winning this race two years ago, he can be rated closer than his finishing position. (op 9-1 tchd 10-1)
Laterly(IRE) soon blasted off into a clear lead and was never going to maintain it.
Falcativ, from the stable that had won this three time since 2004, was a disappointing favourite in his bid for a four-timer at Doncaster last time when behind both Dansili Dancer and Drill Sergeant. His trainer was of the opinion that he got too nervous beforehand that day and that he is the sort of horse for whom things need to go right. However, he seemed to have every chance here with no obvious excuses. (op 13-2 tchd 8-1)
Mystery Star(IRE) ran into all sorts of trouble over the last couple of furlongs and was eventually eased right down when his cause became hopeless. Official explanation: jockey said gelding was denied a clear run (op 28-1 tchd 33-1)
Hatton Flight, who lost his rider exiting the stalls in the Duke of Edinburgh, was 5lb higher than when completing a hat-trick before that, but he was very disappointing here. Held up wide off the pace, he never got into the race. William Buick reported that he was never travelling. Official explanation: jockey said gelding never travelled (op 7-1 tchd 13-2)

3621 BET365.COM CONDITIONS STKS 6f
4:05 (4:06) (Class 2) 3-Y-0+
£15,577 (£4,665; £2,332; £1,167; £582; £292) **Stalls** Centre

Form RPR

5-02 **1** **Doncaster Rover (USA)**[35] 2485 3-8-5 103 SteveDrowne 5 107
(D H Brown) *in rr: hdwy over 2f out: led over 1f out: r.o ins fnl f: kpt up to work towards fin* **11/4**[2]

-115 **2** 1/2 **Taqdeyr**[35] 2500 4-8-11 99 PhilipRobinson 4 106
(M A Jarvis) *sn hld up bhd ldrs and racd keenly: rdn and hdwy over 1f out: r.o ins fnl f: tk 2nd and clsd on wnr towards fin* **3/1**[3]

320- **3** 3/4 **Excellerator (IRE)**[275] 6426 3-8-0 98 (t) FrancisNorton 8 98
(George Baker) *racd keenly: led: hung lft and hdd over 1f out: nt qckn ins fnl f: lost 2nd towards fin* **13/2**

2-10 **4** 9 **Instalment**[17] 3011 3-8-5 101 EddieAhern 3 74
(R Hannon) *prom: pushed along 2f out: wknd over 1f out* **7/1**

5030 **5** 2 3/4 **Internationaldebut (IRE)**[14] 3142 4-8-11 92 WilliamBuick 7 66
(S Parr) *showed gd spd w ldr to 2f out: sn wknd* **22/1**

26-4 **6** 3 **Tombi (USA)**[35] 2500 5-8-11 104 PaulMulrennan 1 56
(J Howard Johnson) *prom tl rdn and wknd over 1f out* **9/4**[1]

1m 11.46s (-2.54) **Going Correction** -0.175s/f (Firm)
WFA 3 from 4yo+ 6lb **6** Ran SP% **112.6**
Speed ratings (Par 109): **109,108,107,95,91 87**
toteswingers: 1&2 £2.20, 1&3 £5.10, 2&3 £6.90 CSF £11.49 TOTE £3.70: £1.90, £2.20; EX 14.60.
Owner P Holling I Raeburn S Halsall S Bolland **Bred** Coffeepot Stable **Trained** Maltby, S Yorks

FOCUS
A tight conditions sprint, but they didn't go mad and there was still barely a length covering the six runners inside the last two furlongs. Decent form for the grade, and pretty solid.

NOTEBOOK
Doncaster Rover(USA), who had finished runner-up in a course-and-distance Listed event for three-year-olds in May, was the first of the sextet to be niggled along but the further he went, the better he was going and after being sent to the front on the outside approaching the last furlong, he was always doing just enough. He may head for the Group 3 Shadwell Stakes at Newbury in a couple of weeks' time. (op 7-2)
Taqdeyr, a triple winner on sand before finishing unplaced back on turf at York in May when he reportedly found the ground too quick, was dropping back in trip. His rider attempted to angle him out for an effort coming to the last furlong, but the winner was already there and he lost impetus when colliding with him. He ran on again when finally out in the clear and finished well, but the damage had been done. (tchd 11-4 and 10-3)
Excellerator(IRE), disappointing in her last two starts at two after finishing third in the Princess Margaret, was having her first outing since last October. She took the field along, but was quite keen, so lasted longer than might have been expected. This should have brought her on. (op 9-1)
Instalment, back over probably his best trip after finding the company too hot and the trip too far in the Jersey Stakes, raced close up for a long way before dropping out. He is becoming disappointing. (op 8-1 tchd 6-1)
Internationaldebut(IRE), back to sprinting after his abortive attempt at 1m4f in the Duke of Edinburgh, had plenty on at the weights and was duly put in his place. (op 14-1)
Tombi(USA), marginally best-in at the weights, had finished over two lengths in front of Taqdeyr on his return to action at York in May, so this was far too bad to be true. He was reported to have lost a shoe. Official explanation: jockey said gelding lost a near-fore shoe (tchd 11-4)

3622 POKER AT BET365 H'CAP 6f
4:35 (4:36) (Class 2) (0-100,99) 3-Y-0 **£12,952** (£3,854; £1,444; £1,444) **Stalls** Centre

Form RPR

-426 **1** **Enderby Spirit (GR)**[50] 2035 3-9-6 98 RichardMullen 9 105
(B Smart) *a.p: led wl over 1f out: hung lft ins fnl f: pressed fnl 100yds: r.o u.p and a doing enough* **9/2**[1]

1320 **2** nk **Servoca (CAN)**[36] 2443 3-8-7 85 (t) MichaelHills 10 91
(B W Hills) *hld up: hdwy whn nt clr run and swtchd lft over 1f out: barged through to chse wnr ent fnl f: str chal fnl 100yds: r.o u.p* **7/1**

5244 **3** 1 3/4 **Five Star Junior (USA)**[35] 2469 3-9-1 **93**.......................... ShaneKelly 2 96+
(Mrs L Stubbs) *hld up: rdn whn hdwy and swtchd rt over 1f out: r.o ins fnl f: nt rch front pair* **25/1**

1-40 **3** dht **Noverre To Go (IRE)**[78] 1324 3-8-10 **88**..............(t) RichardKingscote 11 88
(Tom Dascombe) *racd keenly: in tch: rdn to chse ldrs over 1f out: styd on but unable to chal ldrs ins fnl f* **15/2**

-150 **5** 2 1/4 **Dark Mischief**[21] 2934 3-9-0 **92**.. DaneO'Neill 6 85
(H Candy) *midfield: effrt and hdwy to chse ldrs 2f out: kpt on same pce ins fnl f* **11/2**[3]

2060 **6** 1 **Lucky Numbers (IRE)**[7] 3375 3-8-5 **83**.................... SilvestreDeSousa 8 73
(Paul Green) *in tch: pushed along 3f out: sn sltly outpcd: n.m.r and snatched up 1f out: kpt on wout threatening after* **14/1**

200- **7** 1 1/4 **Rosabee (IRE)**[259] 6818 3-9-7 **99**.............................. EdwardCreighton 5 85
(Mrs D J Sanderson) *s.i.s: in rr: sn niggled along: hung rt u.p over 2f out: no imp* **40/1**

1410 **8** nk **Proclaim**[21] 2934 3-9-5 **97**.. JoeFanning 4 82
(M Johnston) *chsd ldrs tl rdn and wknd wl over 1f out* **7/1**

-325 **9** nk **Quanah Parker (IRE)**[21] 2934 3-8-12 **90**........................ SebSanders 1 74
(R M Whitaker) *hld up: effrt 2f out: no imp* **9/2**[1]

10-4 **10** 1 1/4 **Zuzu (IRE)**[42] 2271 3-8-13 **91**.. PhilipRobinson 7 81+
(M A Jarvis) *led: rdn and hdd over 1f out: stl chsng ldrs u.p whn n.m.r and snatched up ins fnl f: sn eased* **5/1**[2]

61-P **11** 2 1/4 **Knavesmire (IRE)**[52] 1987 3-9-2 **94**.............................. PaulMulrennan 3 66
(M Brittain) *in rr: rdn over 3f out: nvr on terms* **50/1**

1m 13.51s (-0.49) **Going Correction** +0.075s/f (Good) **11** Ran SP% **120.1**
Speed ratings (Par 106): **106,105,103,103,100 98,97,96,96,94 91**
Place: FSJ £1.70 NTG £1.60 Tricast: ES,S,FSJ £366.49 ES,S,NTG £98.98. toteswingers: E&S £18.60, ES&FSJ £12.80, ES&NTG £6.60, S&FSJ £8.00, S&NTG £7.90. CSF £36.48 TOTE £5.70: £2.00, £2.70; EX 39.50.
Owner We-Know Partnership **Bred** Stavloi Th Nanou S A **Trained** Hambleton, N Yorks

FOCUS
A competitive sprint handicap and the first three home came from the three highest stalls, but that didn't tell the whole story and this was quite a rough race. The rain appeared to be getting into the ground, as the winning time was over two seconds slower than the preceding conditions event. The second and Noverre To Go set the standard.

NOTEBOOK
Enderby Spirit(GR), whose only previous success came in a Nottingham maiden last October, hasn't been disgraced in Listed company in his last two starts. Making his handicap debut, he attracted good market support and raced close to the pace from the start. Taking it up inside the last two furlongs, he drifted away to his left, causing problems for a few, including the runner-up, but he did just enough to stay in front and was allowed to keep the race in the stewards' room. (op 7-1)

Servoca(CAN), whose only win came on Polytrack, was back up to a more suitable trip after disappointing over the minimum here last time. Held up off the pace, his rider decided to switch left and challenge up the inside of the winner, but in view of the interference he received, had he gone the other way he would probably have won. (op 8-1)

Five Star Junior(USA) ◆, just over three lengths behind Proclaim at Doncaster last time and 5lb better off, never saw any daylight when he needed it and had to be switched right over to the outside to get a run, but he finished in good style. He is yet to win on turf, but it can only be a matter of time. (op 9-1 tchd 10-1)

Noverre To Go(IRE), a dual winner over this trip on Polytrack in December, hadn't been seen since disappointing over an extra furlong at Newbury in April. Never far away, he had every chance and this should have put him spot on. (op 9-1 tchd 10-1)

Dark Mischief, still 6lb higher than when making a successful return to action at Newmarket in May, received a bit of a bump at the end of a chain reaction started by the hanging winner, but it probably made little difference to his finishing position. He needs some help from the handicapper. (op 5-1 tchd 4-1)

Lucky Numbers(IRE), disappointing on his first try over 7f after finishing just behind Quanah Parker in the valuable 6f handicap for three-year-olds at York last month, still had some sort of chance when badly hampered as the runner-up crossed him a furlong from home and there was no way back. (op 12-1)

Rosabee(IRE), a three-time winner as a juvenile for Vicki Haigh and runner-up in the Princess Margaret, was having her first outing since October. She raced apart from the others, closer to the stands' rail, and though she was never a threat, this should have brought her on. (op 33-1)

Quanah Parker(IRE), in front of three of these when a good fifth off this mark in the big 6f handicap for three-year-olds at York last month, raced closest to the far rail and never got into the race at all. (op 11-2 tchd 7-1)

Zuzu(IRE), not disgraced on her return to action in a heavy-ground Listed event over course and distance in May, took them along early but she looked to have run her race when badly hampered inside the last furlong. (op 9-2 tchd 11-2)

3623 CASINO AT BET365.COM H'CAP 5f
5:10 (5:11) (Class 4) (0-80,82) 3-Y-0+ **£6,476** (£1,927; £963; £481) **Stalls** Centre

Form RPR

4210 **1** **Red Rosanna**[1] 3570 3-8-8 **74**.. DavidKenny(7) 12 82
(R Hollinshead) *a.p: led 2f out: flashed tail u.p ins fnl f: kpt up to work towards fin* **6/1**

1211 **2** nk **Tyrannosaurus Rex (IRE)**[25] 2782 5-9-4 **77**................ MartinLane(5) 10 86
(D Shaw) *hld up: rdn and hdwy 2f out: chsd wnr fnl f: r.o* **11/4**[1]

1503 **3** 1 **Legal Eagle (IRE)**[7] 3372 4-9-12 **80**......................... SilvestreDeSousa 5 85
(Paul Green) *a.p: rdn 2f out: edgd lft whn chalng ins fnl f: no ex cl home* **9/2**[2]

3242 **4** 1/2 **The Tatling (IRE)**[12] 3204 12-9-6 **79**................................. JackDean(5) 8 83
(J M Bradley) *in rr: rdn and hdwy 2f out: styd on ins fnl f: nt pce to chal ldrs* **7/1**

361 **5** 2 1/4 **Misaro (GER)**[6] 3422 8-9-7 **82** 6ex.............................(b) SPRyan(7) 2 78
(R A Harris) *chsd ldrs: rdn over 1f out: one pce fnl f* **6/1**

5416 **6** shd **Fivefootnumberone (IRE)**[14] 3173 3-8-13 **79**................ IJBrennan(7) 9 72
(J J Quinn) *got upset in stalls bef r: in rr: rdn 1/2-way to go pce: styd on u.p fnl 100yds: nt rch ldrs* **11/2**[3]

6323 **7** 3/4 **Cape Royal**[7] 3386 9-9-0 **71**....................................(bt) KevinGhunowa(3) 6 63
(J M Bradley) *led: hdd 2f out: wknd ins fnl f* **12/1**

010 **8** 2 1/2 **El Dececy (USA)**[11] 3234 5-9-0 **68**..........................(v[1]) RichardMullen 1 51
(S Parr) *bustled along to chse ldrs: lost pl after 2f: outpcd after* **20/1**

-050 **9** 7 **Lucky Art (USA)**[14] 3173 3-9-4 **77**.................................. PaulMulrennan 4 33
(J Howard Johnson) *hld up bhd ldrs: rdn 2f out: sn btn* **33/1**

60.73 secs (0.23) **Going Correction** +0.175s/f (Good)
WFA 3 from 4yo+ 5lb **9** Ran SP% **116.7**
Speed ratings (Par 105): **105,104,102,102,98 98,97,93,81**
toteswingers: 1&2 £4.40, 1&3 £7.40, 2&3 £3.00 CSF £23.13 CT £82.68 TOTE £7.40: £2.30, £1.50, £1.60; EX 28.90.
Owner Mrs Debbie Hodson **Bred** J R Mitchell **Trained** Upper Longdon, Staffs

FOCUS
The ground was changed to good all round before this race. Just a fair sprint handicap and those who raced widest and came more up the centre of the track held the advantage. The front pair came from the two highest stalls. Solid form for the grade.

3624 FINANCIALS AT BET365.COM H'CAP 1m 30y
5:45 (5:45) (Class 5) (0-75,74) 3-Y-0+ **£4,857** (£1,445; £722; £360) **Stalls** Low

Form RPR

2006 **1** **Celtic Change (IRE)**[10] 3264 5-9-12 **72**..............(bt[1]) StephenDonohoe 5 87
(M Dods) *sn led: rdn 2f out: strly pressed fnl f: all out* **9/2**[2]

53-4 **2** nse **Block Party**[29] 2662 3-9-4 **73**.. RichardMullen 6 86
(R Charlton) *sn chsd wnr: rdn to chal over 1f out: upsides fnl 100yds: r.o u.p* **9/2**[2]

0000 **3** 8 **Goodbye Mr Bond**[10] 3264 9-9-10 **70**............................... ShaneKelly 9 66
(E J Alston) *hld up: rdn over 2f out: hdwy over 1f out: chsd front pair ins fnl f but no imp* **13/2**[3]

-035 **4** 1/2 **River Dee (IRE)**[13] 3193 3-8-2 **62**................................... MartinLane(5) 4 55
(D Donovan) *chsd ldrs: pushed along over 3f out: plugged on at one pce fnl 2f* **7/1**

56-1 **5** hd **Gassin**[23] 2857 3-9-3 **72**.. JamieSpencer 8 65
(M L W Bell) *hld up: sme hdwy over 3f out: rdn over 2f out: wandered over 1f out: no imp after* **9/4**[1]

6304 **6** 2 1/4 **Astrodonna**[14] 3165 4-9-6 **66**.. MichaelHills 10 56
(M H Tompkins) *in rr: pushed along 2f out: sme hdwy over 1f out: nvr able to chal* **12/1**

0200 **7** 13 **This Ones For Eddy**[5] 3463 4-9-3 **70**.......................... ThomasWhite(7) 3 30
(S Parr) *led early: chsd ldrs tl lost pl 5f out: struggling after* **20/1**

2225 **8** 9 **Will He Wish**[21] 2916 13-9-9 **74**..........................(v) MatthewDavies(5) 2 13
(S Gollings) *midfield tl rdn and wknd over 2f out: eased whn wl btn fnl f* **10/1**

1m 44.38s (0.58) **Going Correction** +0.175s/f (Good)
WFA 3 from 4yo+ 9lb **8** Ran SP% **114.5**
Speed ratings (Par 103): **104,103,95,95,95 93,80,71**
toteswingers: 1&2 £3.60, 1&3 £6.10, 2&3 £8.10 CSF £25.07 CT £130.19 TOTE £5.30: £1.70, £1.90, £2.00; EX 25.00 Place 6: £146.11 Place 5: £47.34.
Owner P Taylor **Bred** Wardstown Stud Ltd **Trained** Denton, Co Durham

FOCUS
An ordinary handicap, but there was no hanging about and the front pair eventually pulled right away. Most of the field came up the centre of the track in the home straight, with only one staying against the inside rail. Not many got into it and the winner looks the best guide to this form.
T/Plt: £168.50 to a £1 stake. Pool: £130,259.73. 564.05 winning tickets. T/Qpdt: £41.60 to a £1 stake. Pool: £6,922.15. 122.90 winning tickets. DO

3304 LEICESTER (R-H)
Saturday, July 4

OFFICIAL GOING: Good (good to firm places; 7.9)
Wind: Light behind becoming fresher from race 2 onwards Weather: Cloudy with sunny spells

3625 JOHN SMITH'S FILLIES' H'CAP 5f 218y
2:30 (2:30) (Class 5) (0-70,67) 3-Y-0 **£3,885** (£1,156; £577; £288) **Stalls** Low

Form RPR

4221 **1** **Itsher**[4] 3471 3-8-12 **63** 6ex..(b) WilliamCarson(5) 5 75
(S C Williams) *chsd ldrs: led over 1f out: pushed clr fnl f* **1/1**[1]

0404 **2** 4 **Crystal B Good (USA)**[14] 3161 3-8-13 **59**........................ TonyCulhane 3 58
(J R Best) *chsd ldr tl led 1/2-way: rdn and hdd over 1f out: styd on same pce* **18/1**

6201 **3** 1 **Wotasparkler**[16] 3071 3-9-3 **63**.. RobertHavlin 1 59
(W S Kittow) *hld up: hdwy 1/2-way: rdn over 1f out: one pce* **11/4**[2]

4060 **4** 3 3/4 **Feet Of Fury**[25] 2797 3-9-0 **60**.. JamesDoyle 4 44
(W M Brisbourne) *sn pushed along in rr: swtchd rt and hdwy over 1f out: nt trble ldrs* **8/1**[3]

6-56 **5** 1 3/4 **Lana's Charm**[155] 348 3-8-8 **54**.. TravisBlock 6 32
(P J Makin) *hld up: hung rt thrght: hdwy 1/2-way: sn rdn: wknd fnl f* **18/1**

0006 **6** 1 **Peninsula Girl (IRE)**[19] 2973 3-8-9 **55**................................ TPO'Shea 2 30
(M R Channon) *mid-div: sn pushed along: hdwy 1/2-way: rdn and wknd over 1f out* **12/1**

2020 **7** 3/4 **Song Of Praise**[22] 2888 3-9-7 **67**...................................... JimCrowley 7 40
(M Blanshard) *hld up in tch: racd keenly: rdn over 2f out: wknd over 1f out* **14/1**

-000 **8** 11 **Glorious Dreams (USA)**[19] 2973 3-8-11 **60**..........(p) DavidProbert(3) 8 —
(T J Pitt) *s.i.s: racd keenly and sn led: hdd 1/2-way: wknd over 2f out* **40/1**

1m 11.01s (-1.99) **Going Correction** -0.25s/f (Firm) **8** Ran SP% **115.1**
Speed ratings (Par 97): **103,97,96,91,89 87,86,72**
toteswingers: 1&2 £5.20, 1&3 £1.10, 2&3 £8.50 CSF £23.16 CT £42.49 TOTE £1.80: £1.20, £2.60, £1.40; EX 22.00 Trifecta £64.70 Pool: £542.34 - 6.20 winning units..
Owner Itsus **Bred** Old Mill Stud And Partners **Trained** Newmarket, Suffolk

FOCUS
Good recent efforts were thin on the ground for this, apart from the two last-time-out winners that took their chance, so it did not look a strong contest despite a fair winning time.
Lana's Charm Official explanation: jockey said filly hung right

3626 JOHN SMITH'S EXTRA SMOOTH (S) STKS 5f 218y
3:05 (3:07) (Class 6) 2-Y-0 **£1,942** (£578; £288; £144) **Stalls** Low

Form RPR

50 **1** **Rainsborough**[6] 3420 2-8-11 0.. TonyCulhane 8 58
(M R Channon) *sn bhd: hdwy to chse ldr over 1f out: r.o to ld wl ins fnl f* **14/1**

0 **2** 1 **Audrinna (IRE)**[50] 2047 2-8-1 0..................................(t) NicolPolli(5) 4 50
(M G Quinlan) *s.i.s: sn chsng ldrs: rdn to ld over 1f out: edgd lft and hdd wl ins fnl f* **9/2**[3]

052 **3** 3 1/4 **Hachi**[19] 2978 2-8-6 0.. FergusSweeney 3 40
(J L Spearing) *led: rdn and hdd over 1f out: wknd towards fin* **13/8**[1]

600 **4** 3 1/4 **Polly Macho (IRE)**[48] 2099 2-8-11 0..............................(v[1]) AdamKirby 5 36
(P D Evans) *prom: outpcd 1/2-way: hdwy over 1f out: wknd ins fnl f* **7/4**[2]

50 **5** 2 **Miss Lauz**[31] 2604 2-8-3 0.. DavidProbert(3) 1 25
(R Hannon) *hmpd s: hung rt thrght: sn chsng ldrs: rdn and wknd over 1f out* **16/1**

6505 **6** 4 1/2 **Ytartfawn (IRE)**[25] 2788 2-8-11 0..............................(b[1]) LeeEnstone 6 16
(P T Midgley) *sn pushed along in rr: hdwy 1/2-way: rdn over 2f out: wknd wl over 1f out* **40/1**

066 7 *35* **Carries Lass**[19] 2978 2-8-7 0 ow1....................................(b) JimCrowley 2 —
(J A Osborne) *wnt lft s: sn prom: wknd over 2f out* **16/1**
1m 12.73s (-0.27) **Going Correction** -0.25s/f (Firm) **7** Ran SP% **113.5**
Speed ratings (Par 92): **91,89,85,81,78 72,25**
toteswingers: 1&2 £66.70, 1&3 £7.00, 2&3 £2.00 CSF £73.81 TOTE £13.20: £5.40, £2.50; EX 81.80 Trifecta £371.30 Part won. Pool: £501.85 - 0.86 winning units..The winner was bought in for 6,200gns. Audrinna was claimed by C Bjorling for £7000.
Owner Billy Parish **Bred** Norman Court Stud **Trained** West Ilsley, Berks

FOCUS
A weak contest. The two horses that fought out the finish had not beaten a horse between them in three previous starts.

NOTEBOOK
Rainsborough was dropped in grade for this after finishing last in two maidens. He looked a very unlikely winner at halfway, but he responded well for pressure and got on top in the latter stages. (op 11-1)
Audrinna(IRE), fitted with a tongue-tie for the first time, was another to improve for the ease in grade and did little wrong. (op 5-1 tchd 3-1)
Hachi was not disgraced in a similar contest on her previous outing, but was readily held here after setting the pace. (op 9-4 tchd 5-2 and 11-4 in places)
Polly Macho(IRE), in a first-time visor, possibly had the best form on offer, but offered little once under pressure. (op 15-8 tchd 2-1)
Miss Lauz hung right throughout and played no part in the race. (op 12-1)
Carries Lass Official explanation: jockey said filly lost its action

3627 JOHN SMITH'S EUROPEAN BREEDERS' FUND FILLIES' H'CAP 1m 1f 218y
3:35 (3:36) (Class 4) (0-80,78) 3-Y-0+
£6,854 (£2,052; £1,026; £513; £256; £128) **Stalls** High

Form RPR
0643 1 **La Coveta (IRE)**[18] 3008 4-9-8 **75**.................................... GabrielHannon(5) 1 82
(B J Meehan) *hld up: hdwy over 3f out: rdn ins fnl f: r.o to ld nr fin* **20/1**
4-24 2 *nk* **Visite Royale (USA)**[29] 2679 3-8-9 **73**.......... Louis-PhilippeBeuzelin(5) 8 79
(Sir Michael Stoute) *hld up: hdwy over 1f out: r.o wl towards fin* **6/1**[3]
515 3 *nse* **Stravella (IRE)**[26] 2775 4-9-12 **74**.................................... GeorgeBaker 7 80
(R M Beckett) *led: rdn and edgd lft fnl f: hdd nr fin* **10/1**
1 4 *2 1/4* **Whooshka (USA)**[23] 2848 3-9-5 **78**............................ AdrianMcCarthy 9 80
(P W Chapple-Hyam) *trckd ldrs: rdn over 2f out: nt clr run over 1f out: styd on same pce ins fnl f* **8/1**
0514 5 *hd* **Aphrodisia**[57] 1826 5-9-9 **76**.. WilliamCarson(5) 5 77+
(Ian Williams) *s.s: hld up: r.o ins fnl f: nrst fin* **8/1**
-233 6 *1* **Simplification**[8] 3333 3-9-2 **75**.................................... FergusSweeney 6 74
(R Hannon) *trckd ldr: racd keenly: rdn over 2f out: no ex ins fnl f* **11/1**
4-1 7 *2 3/4* **Mrs Beeton (IRE)**[20] 2947 3-9-4 **77**.................................... AdamKirby 2 71
(W R Swinburn) *chsd ldrs: rdn over 2f out: wknd ins fnl f* **5/1**[2]
-061 8 *1/2* **Mejala (IRE)**[15] 3099 3-8-13 **72**.. TPO'Shea 3 65
(J L Dunlop) *s.i.s: hld up: rdn over 3f out: nt run on* **10/3**[1]
4122 9 *3/4* **Luck Will Come (IRE)**[13] 3188 5-9-9 **71**.................... KirstyMilczarek 10 62
(H J Collingridge) *prom: rdn over 2f out: edgd rt and wknd over 1f out* **9/1**
5452 10 *9* **Rio Guru (IRE)**[5] 3461 4-9-10 **72**.. TonyCulhane 4 45
(M R Channon) *hld up: wknd 3f out* **7/1**
2m 6.57s (-1.33) **Going Correction** -0.075s/f (Good)
WFA 3 from 4yo+ 11lb **10** Ran SP% **120.9**
Speed ratings (Par 102): **102,101,101,99,99 98,96,96,95,88**
toteswingers: 1&2 £37.40, 1&3 £21.20, 2&3 £44.10 CSF £140.37 CT £1300.78 TOTE £22.10: £5.20, £3.00, £3.70; EX 162.10 TRIFECTA Not won..
Owner Mrs Wendy English **Bred** Mrs Noelle Walsh **Trained** Manton, Wilts

FOCUS
This looked the most intriguing race of the day, as plenty of these were far from exposed and looked capable of going on to better things.
Mejala(IRE) Official explanation: jockey said filly never travelled
Rio Guru(IRE) Official explanation: jockey said filly slipped on leaving stalls and was slowly away

3628 JOHN SMITH'S NO NONSENSE H'CAP 7f 9y
4:10 (4:11) (Class 3) (0-95,95) 3-Y-0+
£10,904 (£3,265; £1,632; £817; £407; £204) **Stalls** Low

Form RPR
420- 1 **Big Noise**[280] 6269 5-9-3 **89**........................ Louis-PhilippeBeuzelin(5) 11 99
(Dr J D Scargill) *stdd s: hld up: hdwy over 2f out: rdn to ld and edgd lft 1f out: r.o* **7/1**[3]
0212 2 *1/2* **Woodcote Place**[24] 2828 6-9-5 **86**.. JimCrowley 9 95
(P R Chamings) *chsd ldrs: led over 1f out: sn rdn and hdd: r.o* **12/1**
0050 3 *hd* **Key Signature**[21] 2926 3-8-2 **77**....................................(b[1]) PaulEddery 6 82
(Pat Eddery) *hld up: hdwy over 1f out: sn rdn: r.o* **8/1**
2131 4 *1 3/4* **Bold Cross (IRE)**[7] 3378 6-8-13 **80**.................................. PaulFitzsimons 8 84
(E G Bevan) *hld up in tch: rdn over 2f out: styd on* **15/2**
0130 5 *hd* **Saucy Brown (IRE)**[17] 3011 3-9-4 **93**...................................... PatDobbs 7 93
(R Hannon) *chsd ldr tl led wl over 2f out: rdn: edgd lft and hdd over 1f out: styd on same pce* **8/1**
2604 6 *2* **Masai Moon**[15] 3116 5-9-7 **91**.................................. JamesMillman(3) 5 89
(B R Millman) *prom: hmpd and lost pl over 2f out: styd on ins fnl f* **7/2**[1]
11L4 7 *hd* **Spectait**[77] 1352 7-10-0 **95**.. GeorgeBaker 10 92
(Jonjo O'Neill) *stdd s: bhd: hdwy over 1f out: no ex ins fnl f* **9/1**
1551 8 *nk* **I Confess**[12] 3211 4-8-8 **80**.....................................(b) RichardEvans(5) 2 76
(P D Evans) *led: rdn and hdd wl over 2f out: hung rt over 1f out: styd on same pce* **14/1**
4110 9 *nse* **Oceana Blue**[15] 3102 4-8-13 **83**...................................(t) DavidProbert(3) 1 79
(A M Balding) *hld up: rdn over 2f out: n.d* **9/1**
0-36 10 *1/2* **Golden Desert (IRE)**[15] 3091 5-9-8 **89**.. TPO'Shea 4 84
(T G Mills) *trckd ldrs: plld hrd: rdn and edgd rt over 2f out: wknd over 1f out* **9/2**[2]
00/0 11 *8* **Parisian Dream**[8] 3335 5-8-9 **76**.................................... RobertHavlin 3 49
(T J Pitt) *prom: racd keenly: wknd over 2f out* **40/1**
1m 23.2s (-3.00) **Going Correction** -0.25s/f (Firm)
WFA 3 from 4yo+ 8lb **11** Ran SP% **123.7**
Speed ratings (Par 107): **107,106,106,104,103 101,101,101,101,100 91**
toteswingers: 1&2 £26.90, 1&3 £20.10, 2&3 £11.50 CSF £92.65 CT £714.91 TOTE £8.50: £2.90, £4.40, £3.70; EX 161.50 TRIFECTA Not won..
Owner Theme Tune Partnership **Bred** F B B White **Trained** Newmarket, Suffolk

FOCUS
Quite a few of these came into the race in good heart, so this result should be reliable for the class.

NOTEBOOK
Big Noise, having his first run since last September at Ascot, sat in midfield early before making his bid about two furlongs from home. He battled with the runner-up for a while, but was comfortably on top passing the post. It was a fine training performance and the horse is clearly talented on his day, but this victory is going to push him up the weights again, possibly to a career-high mark. The Abu Dhabi International Stakes on the King George card at Ascot later this month is his target. (op 8-1)
Woodcote Place has been in good heart on both turf and the all-weather, so his good effort helps to give the form a solid look. (op 8-1)
Key Signature, wearing blinkers for the first time, took a while to get organised but kept on well to gain on the first two throughout the final furlong. She has a mainly consistent profile. (op 14-1)
Bold Cross(IRE) has been running regularly since his comeback in May and kept on at the one pace here after settling in midfield. A combination of a drop in trip and a mark of 80 was probably enough to stop him. (op 10-1)
Saucy Brown(IRE), the highest-rated three-year-old in the race, was prominent early before finding little once the tempo increased. (tchd 15-2)
Masai Moon is an infrequent winner but was still fancied to play a part in this race judged on the market support he received. However, he failed to make much impact after losing his place. Official explanation: jockey said gelding was denied a clear run (op 5-1)
Spectait was slowly away and soon under pressure. He never looked that happy for some reason and did well to pass any rivals. (op 13-2 tchd 10-1)
Golden Desert(IRE) pulled very, very hard and unsurprisingly had nothing left for the business end of the race. Official explanation: jockey said gelding ran too free (op 5-1)

3629 JOHN SMITH'S CLAIMING STKS 1m 1f 218y
4:45 (4:46) (Class 5) 3-Y-O
£3,238 (£963; £481; £240) **Stalls** High

Form RPR
-402 1 **Playful Asset (IRE)**[24] 2808 3-8-7 62.......................... JimCrowley 1 59+
(R M Beckett) *hld up: hdwy to chse ldr over 2f out: led over 1f out: rdn clr: eased nr fin* **7/4**[1]
60-0 2 *7* **Moggy (IRE)**[20] 2942 3-8-0 55.................. Louis-PhilippeBeuzelin(5) 4 43
(M L W Bell) *chsd ldrs: hmpd and lost pl 7f out: hdwy over 3f out: outpcd fnl 2f* **7/2**[3]
-004 3 *shd* **Lomica**[33] 2528 3-8-5 49...(p) TPO'Shea 5 43
(Miss J A Camacho) *chsd ldrs: rdn over 3f out: sn hung rt: outpcd fnl 2f* **8/1**
4000 4 *3 1/4* **Granski (IRE)**[8] 3358 3-8-12 62..(b[1]) PatDobbs 2 43
(R Hannon) *hld up: plld hrd: hdwy to ld wl over 6f out: sn clr: wknd and hdd over 1f out* **3/1**[2]
0000 5 *23* **Manolito Montoya (IRE)**[7] 3383 3-9-1 55................ GabrielHannon(5) 7 5
(J W Hills) *chsd ldrs: rdn and wknd over 2f out: eased* **16/1**
0003 6 *16* **Nouailhas**[16] 3054 3-9-2 55.. FergusSweeney 3 —
(R Hollinshead) *dwlt: sn rcvrd to ld: hdd wl over 6f out: wknd 3f out: eased* **9/1**
2m 7.73s (-0.17) **Going Correction** -0.075s/f (Good) **6** Ran SP% **110.6**
Speed ratings (Par 100): **97,91,91,88,70 57**
toteswingers: 1&2 £1.10, 1&3 £2.70, 2&3 £6.70 CSF £7.85 TOTE £2.10: £1.30, £2.50; EX 7.70.Playful Asset was claimed by P. Howling for £6000.
Owner The Macatoo Partnership **Bred** P Murray And Eugene Blaney **Trained** Whitsbury, Hants

FOCUS
A weak-looking claimer, as the two highest-rated runners had official marks of 62.

3630 JOHN SMITH'S EXTRA COLD RATING RELATED MAIDEN STKS 7f 9y
5:20 (5:22) (Class 5) 3-Y-0+
£3,238 (£963; £481; £240) **Stalls** Low

Form RPR
54-3 1 **Diapason (IRE)**[29] 2664 3-8-9 74..................................... RichardSmith 5 72
(Tom Dascombe) *led: rdn over 1f out: edgd lft and hdd ins fnl f: rallied to ld post* **5/4**[1]
-300 2 *shd* **Piccolo Mondo**[14] 3159 3-8-12 67.....................................(t) JimCrowley 7 74
(P Winkworth) *chsd ldrs: rdn over 1f out: edgd lft and hdd ins fnl f: hdd post* **25/1**
62-6 3 *3* **Good For Her**[20] 2947 3-8-9 69.. TPO'Shea 2 64
(J L Dunlop) *prom: rdn over 2f out: hung rt ins fnl f: no ex* **12/1**
0-52 4 *1* **West With The Wind (USA)**[40] 2320 3-8-4 70
Louis-PhilippeBeuzelin(5) 8 61
(P W Chapple-Hyam) *chsd wnr: rdn over 2f out: styd on same pce fnl f* **13/8**[2]
0250 5 *4 1/2* **Bea Menace (USA)**[22] 2879 3-8-9 68.................................. JosedeSouza 6 49
(P F I Cole) *trckd ldrs: racd keenly: rdn over 2f out: wknd fnl f* **15/2**[3]
0630 6 *14* **Mellow Mixture**[22] 2892 3-8-12 70...................................(t) JamesDoyle 4 14
(S Kirk) *chsd ldrs: pushed along 1/2-way: wknd over 2f out* **25/1**
-604 7 *2 1/4* **Just Mustard (USA)**[57] 1831 3-8-12 65.................................. TolleyDean 1 8
(G A Butler) *s.i.s: sn pushed along in rr: wknd over 2f out* **40/1**
3306 8 *3/4* **Fantasy Land (IRE)**[10] 3272 3-8-9 68...............................(bt[1]) RobertHavlin 3 3
(B J Meehan) *s.i.s: hld up: wknd over 2f out* **20/1**
1m 23.84s (-2.36) **Going Correction** -0.25s/f (Firm) **8** Ran SP% **116.9**
Speed ratings (Par 103): **103,102,99,98,93 77,74,73**
toteswingers: 1&2 £8.50, 1&3 £3.60, 2&3 £20.80 CSF £39.91 TOTE £2.30: £1.20, £2.50, £2.00; EX 14.80 Trifecta £95.20 Pool: £467.19 - 3.63 winning units. Place 6: £441.38 Place 5: £346.94.
Owner John Brown **Bred** Miss Alice Fitzgerald **Trained** Lambourn, Berks

FOCUS
Most of these looked to have a chance on their best bits of form but punters only really wanted to be with one.
T/Plt: £814.80 to a £1 stake. Pool: £49,669.33. 44.50 winning tickets. T/Qpdt: £84.20 to a £1 stake. Pool: £3,471.47. 30.50 winning tickets. CR

2852 NOTTINGHAM (L-H)
Saturday, July 4

OFFICIAL GOING: Good (7.7)
Running rail moved out 5yards from increasing distances on round course by about 30yards.
Wind: Light across Weather: Fine

3631 AJA INSURE THEIR MEMBERS FEGENTRI LADY RIDERS' INVITATION H'CAP (FOR LADY AMATEUR RIDERS) 1m 2f 50y
6:20 (6:21) (Class 6) (0-60,58) 4-Y-0+ **£1,977** (£608; £304) **Stalls** Low

Form RPR
4602 1 **Iguacu**[12] 3215 5-9-11 **48**.. MissNGratz 11 58
(George Baker) *mde all: nudged along over 1f out: hld on wl fnl f* **11/2**
004 2 *nk* **Casablanca Minx (IRE)**[12] 3215 6-9-10 **47**......................(b) MissCAllen 7 56
(Miss Gay Kelleway) *hld up in tch: stdd and lost pl after 2f: hdwy on outside over 4f out: rdn over 1f out: sustained chal fnl f: kpt on* **10/1**
5405 3 *7* **Apache Dawn**[10] 3258 5-9-13 **50**...........................(t) MissCJMacmahon 4 45
(A Sadik) *a.p: hrd rdn and edgd lft over 1f out: kpt on same pce to take 3rd towards fin* **16/1**
3/60 4 *1/2* **Captain Oats (IRE)**[19] 2971 6-9-12 **49**.. MissMPlat 5 43
(Mrs P Ford) *t.k.h in tch: stdd and lost pl after 2f: rdn over 2f out: sn edgd lft: kpt on same pce ins fnl f* **16/1**

50-0 **5** *2* **Classic Blue (IRE)**[16] 3077 5-9-13 **50** .... MissLEllison 6 40
(Ian Williams) *hld up and bhd: hdwy on ins over 3f out: ev ch 2f out: sn rdn: wknd fnl f* **4/1**[2]

0306 **6** *1 3/4* **Gamesters Lady**[11] 3247 6-10-1 **52** .... (b) MissADeniel 10 39
(W M Brisbourne) *s.i.s: hld up and bhd: pushed along and sme prog over 3f out: edgd lft over 2f out: wknd fnl f* **9/2**[3]

0030 **7** *2 3/4* **Ba Dreamflight**[19] 2983 4-9-11 **48** .... MissSBrotherton 3 29
(H Morrison) *prom: pushed along over 2f out: wknd wl over 1f out* **5/2**[1]

000- **8** *14* **Tot Hill**[280] 6275 6-9-8 **45** .... MissCEngebretsen 12 —
(C N Kellett) *w wnr tl over 3f out: wknd wl over 2f out* **100/1**

/0-0 **9** *15* **Monmouthshire**[21] 2912 6-9-8 **45** .... (vt) MissCBurri 1 —
(R J Price) *prom tl wknd wl over 3f out* **14/1**

5500 **10** *4 1/2* **Lawyer To World**[37] 2420 5-9-10 **47** .... MrsPWolters-Fierman 2 —
(Mrs C A Dunnett) *prom tl rdn and wknd over 3f out* **28/1**

2m 15.55s (3.85) **Going Correction** +0.225s/f (Good) **10** Ran SP% **114.1**
Speed ratings (Par 101): **93,92,87,86,85 83,81,70,58,54**
toteswingers: 1&2 £6.80, 1&3 £13.60, 2&3 £12.40 CSF £57.92 CT £823.18 TOTE £6.50: £1.80, £2.70, £3.40; EX 39.50.
Owner Derek & Cheryl Holder **Bred** Cheveley Park Stud Ltd **Trained** Moreton Morrell, Warwicks
■ Stewards' Enquiry : Miss C J Macmahon five-day ban: used whip with excessive frequency (Jul 24-28)

FOCUS
A total of 20mm of rain in the preceding 24 hours had turned the going to good, good to soft in places by 8am, but drying conditions subsequently returned it to good ground by race-time. This ordinary opener, part of an established international amateur riders' series, will be of greater significance for the points on offer to the human participants than for the future prospects of most of the horses involved. The first two finished clear having raced up the centre of the home straight but this is not form to take too positively

3632 KONICA MINOLTA EAST (S) STKS 6f 15y
6:50 (6:51) (Class 6) 3-4-Y-O **£2,047** (£604; £302) **Stalls** High

Form RPR

0000 **1** **Pintano**[22] 2879 4-9-2 46 .... (t) CatherineGannon 4 51
(J M Bradley) *a.p: chsd ldr over 3f out: sn pushed along: rdn 2f out: led over 1f out: drvn out* **33/1**

-000 **2** *1/2* **Royal Bloom (IRE)**[12] 3215 4-8-11 46 .... AdamKirby 3 44
(J R Fanshawe) *mid-div: rdn and hdwy 3f out: ev ch 2f out: r.o ins fnl f* **8/1**[3]

063 **3** *hd* **Abhainn (IRE)**[33] 2534 3-8-7 49 .... DavidProbert(3) 11 48
(B Palling) *hld up in mid-div: rdn over 2f out: hdwy on stands' rail fnl f: r.o* **9/2**[2]

000 **4** *2 1/2* **Rambling Rosie (IRE)**[29] 2683 3-8-5 39 .... FrankieMcDonald 8 35
(C Drew) *bmpd s: in rr: hdwy on outside over 2f out: rdn jst over 1f out: one pce ins fnl f* **100/1**

0000 **5** *hd* **Sally's Swansong**[17] 3031 3-8-5 40 .... (p) FrancisNorton 6 34
(M Wellings) *led: crossed to stands' rail after 1f: sn hdd: rdn over 2f out: one pce ins fnl f* **80/1**

600 **6** *4 1/2* **Brazilian Brush (IRE)**[33] 2534 4-9-2 47 .... (t) SteveDrowne 5 26
(J M Bradley) *prom: rdn wl over 1f out: sn wknd* **16/1**

0-03 **7** *nk* **Boundless Applause**[17] 3031 3-8-0 39 .... SophieDoyle(5) 10 19
(I A Wood) *wnt lft s: hld up in mid-div: wknd 2f out* **14/1**

-000 **8** *3/4* **Bilboa**[33] 2534 4-8-11 43 .... (p) MCGeran(5) 2 22
(J M Bradley) *prom: led on outside over 4f out: crossed to stands' rail 2f out: rdn and hdd over 1f out: wknd ins fnl f* **33/1**

5243 **9** *6* **Spinight (IRE)**[9] 3305 3-8-7 61 .... (p) AndreaAtzeni(3) 12 2
(M Botti) *hld up towards rr: rdn over 2f out: no rspnse* **1/1**[1]

0000 **10** *1 3/4* **The Spicer**[21] 2924 4-9-2 52 .... (t) JamesDoyle 7 —
(F Sheridan) *rrd s: sn hld up in mid-div: pushed along over 3f out: wknd over 2f out* **33/1**

0-00 **11** *1* **Bold Hawk**[18] 3010 3-8-10 51 .... (b1) TGMcLaughlin 9 —
(Mrs C A Dunnett) *n.m.r s: rdn 2f out: a in rr* **16/1**

4040 **12** *10* **Cwmni**[27] 2876 3-8-5 48 .... LukeMorris 13 —
(B Palling) *racd on stands' rail: rdn over 2f out: a bhd* **11/1**

1m 16.23s (1.33) **Going Correction** -0.125s/f (Firm) **12** Ran SP% **117.1**
WFA 3 from 4yo 6lb
Speed ratings (Par 101): **86,85,85,81,81 75,75,74,66,63 62,49**
toteswingers: 1&2 £28.70, 1&3 £15.40, 2&3 £5.20 CSF £270.08 TOTE £48.70: £9.30, £2.90, £1.70; EX 361.00.There was no bid for the winner.
Owner J M Bradley **Bred** W L Caley **Trained** Sedbury, Gloucs
■ Stewards' Enquiry : Adam Kirby two-day ban: used whip with excessive frequency (Jul 18-19)
Catherine Gannon one-day ban: used whip in incorrect place (Jul 19)

FOCUS
The defection of the likely favourite, the 74-rated Leftontheshelf, reduced this to a poor-looking seller, and with Spinight running no sort of race, it was left to a trio of sub-50 rated animals to fill the frame. The form looks weak.
Rambling Rosie(IRE) Official explanation: jockey said filly missed the break

3633 GOLDEVA MAIDEN AUCTION FILLIES' STKS 5f 13y
7:20 (7:23) (Class 5) 2-Y-O **£2,590** (£770; £385; £192) **Stalls** High

Form RPR

1 **Skylla** 2-8-8 0 .... JerryO'Dwyer 5 81+
(J R Holt) *hld up and bhd: hdwy on stands' rail over 1f out: rdn to ld ins fnl f: readily* **50/1**

24 **2** *3/4* **Social Grace**[40] 2339 2-8-4 0 .... FrancisNorton 12 73
(D H Brown) *w ldr on stands' rail: led over 2f out: hung lft and rdn over 1f out: hdd ins fnl f: nt qckn* **5/2**[2]

3 **3** *3 1/2* **Poppy N'Penny (IRE)**[18] 3006 2-8-4 0 .... LiamJones 3 60
(W J Haggas) *chsd ldrs: rdn 2f out: one pce fnl f* **2/1**[1]

632 **4** *1 1/4* **Diamond Affair (IRE)**[27] 2741 2-7-13 0 .... NicolPolli(5) 2 56
(M G Quinlan) *hld up in tch: rdn 1f out: one pce* **11/2**[3]

5 *3/4* **Nabrina (IRE)** 2-7-11 0 .... AndrewHeffernan(7) 1 53
(M Brittain) *dwlt: outpcd in rr: hdwy on outside over 2f out: rdn over 1f out: one pce fnl f* **22/1**

6 *1 1/2* **Mrs Mogg** 2-8-8 0 .... LukeMorris 9 52
(N J Vaughan) *prom: swtchd lft over 2f out: rdn over 1f out: wknd ins fnl f* **11/1**

7 *1* **Excelling (IRE)** 2-8-4 0 .... FrankieMcDonald 4 44
(P J Makin) *s.i.s and wnt lft: hld up and bhd: sme prog whn carried lft over 2f out: wknd 1f out* **6/1**

8 *6* **Crystal Bridge** 2-8-1 0 .... DavidProbert(3) 6 23
(Mrs L Williamson) *n.m.r s: sn swtchd rt: outpcd* **50/1**

0 **9** *nk* **Acquaviva**[11] 3248 2-8-4 0 .... CatherineGannon 8 22
(Eve Johnson Houghton) *chsd ldrs: carried lft over 2f out: sn wknd* **16/1**

6 **10** *4* **Cheshire Lady (IRE)**[25] 2778 2-8-12 0 .... TGMcLaughlin 10 15
(W M Brisbourne) *led: hdd over 2f out: sn rdn: wknd wl over 1f out* **25/1**

62.39 secs (1.39) **Going Correction** -0.125s/f (Firm) **10** Ran SP% **117.9**
Speed ratings (Par 91): **83,81,76,74,73 70,69,59,58,52**
toteswingers: 1&2 £20.10, 1&3 £35.00, 2&3 £2.80 CSF £171.38 TOTE £34.30: £8.00, £1.20, £1.20; EX 274.60.
Owner Facts & Figures **Bred** Bearstone Stud **Trained** Peckleton, Leics

FOCUS
The first of two sprint maidens was delayed by repeated, and ultimately futile, attempts to cram Wild Heather into her stall.

NOTEBOOK
Skylla was slowly away, but otherwise knew her job on this debut and stayed on pleasingly with the benefit of the nearside rail to win comfortably. Evidently not unfancied by connections, for whom this was a first-ever juvenile winner, she can count three other sprint winners among her half-siblings. There could be fair nurseries to win with her in time, although probably not from the top of the weights, as she is not the biggest. (op 66-1 tchd 80-1)
Social Grace, who by chasing the pacesetters may have blunted her finishing effort, as she couldn't quicken once the winner sailed past. She fared best of those to race prominently and finished some way clear of the remainder, so an ordinary maiden might be within her grasp. (op 9-4 tchd 3-1)
Poppy N'Penny(IRE) was switched at a vital stage when third on debut at Yarmouth. However, there were no excuses for her here and this run didn't represent a step forward. She will have a little to prove next time. (op 13-8 tchd 6-4)
Diamond Affair(IRE) had been available at up to 14-1 earlier in the evening, but although she raced far less keenly early on than has sometimes been the case, she could still only muster the one speed late on. Low-grade nurseries would seem a better option at this stage. (op 14-1)
Excelling(IRE)'s cause wasn't helped by being pushed left by a rival 2f out and, although it didn't cost her a winning chance, she performed a little better than the bare form suggests. Official explanation: jockey said filly was slowly away and ran green (op 5-1 tchd 9-2)

3634 MATTHEWS & TANNERT MEDIAN AUCTION MAIDEN STKS 5f 13y
7:50 (7:50) (Class 5) 2-Y-O **£2,729** (£806; £403) **Stalls** High

Form RPR

2 **1** **Danny's Choice**[21] 2919 2-8-12 0 .... SebSanders 7 70+
(R M Beckett) *mde all: rdn over 1f out: rdn out* **4/5**[1]

24 **2** *3/4* **Il Forno**[16] 3064 2-9-3 0 .... AdrianTNicholls 1 72
(D Nicholls) *w wnr: rdn over 1f out: nt qckn ins fnl f* **9/4**[2]

0 **3** *1* **Kakapuka**[54] 1920 2-9-3 0 .... KirstyMilczarek 9 69
(Mrs A L M King) *trckd ldrs: swtchd lft wl over 1f out: edgd rt ins fnl f: kpt on one pce* **16/1**

0 **4** *4* **Russian Davis (IRE)**[17] 3032 2-9-3 0 .... EddieAhern 5 54
(R M H Cowell) *hld up: effrt over 2f out: rdn and edgd rt wl over 1f out: swtchd lft and wknd ins fnl f* **8/1**[3]

5 *11* **Bustard Bay (IRE)** 2-9-3 0 .... PatCosgrave 6 15
(J G Given) *s.i.s: hld up: pushed along over 2f out: sn struggling* **16/1**

6 *3/4* **Liberty Power (IRE)** 2-9-0 0 .... DominicFox(3) 4 12
(Garry Moss) *dwlt and bmpd s: pushed along and swtchd rt 2f out: a in rr* **33/1**

0 **7** *1* **Keithshazel (IRE)**[17] 3032 2-8-5 0 .... AndrewHeffernan(7) 8 3
(Garry Moss) *dwlt and bmpd s: a in rr* **33/1**

8 *hd* **Tulip Explosion** 2-8-12 0 .... PaulEddery 3 3
(D Shaw) *hung lft thrght: prom tl wknd over 2f out* **16/1**

61.11 secs (0.11) **Going Correction** -0.125s/f (Firm) **8** Ran SP% **121.0**
Speed ratings (Par 94): **94,92,91,84,67 66,64,64**
toteswingers: 1&2 £1.10, 1&3 £3.30, 2&3 £3.00 CSF £2.98 TOTE £1.60: £1.02, £1.20, £3.50; EX 3.60.
Owner G B Partnership **Bred** R J Cornelius **Trained** Whitsbury, Hants
■ Stewards' Enquiry : Adrian T Nicholls one-day ban: failed to keep straight from stalls (Jul 18)

FOCUS
This race was won in a time 1.28 seconds faster than the preceding contest, and by a runner carrying 4lb more.

NOTEBOOK
Danny's Choice, for whom this looked a gilt-edged opportunity to gain compensation for her Lingfield debut defeat, duly collected under a sympathetic ride. Always travelling well in front, Sanders didn't need the whip to keep the runner-up at bay, and the winning margin could have been greater. There are no firm plans for this Compton Place filly, other than to keep her racing over the minimum trip. (tchd 8-11)
Il Forno had shown decent speed on his previous starts, but never got the opportunity to dictate the pace here. He was clear second best throughout. He did show he handles quick ground, and he qualifies for a mark now. (op 5-2 tchd 11-4)
Kakapuka travelled more kindly than on his debut, and wasn't disgraced over a trip a little shorter than ideal. He had little trouble in keeping hold of third place. (op 20-1)
Russian Davis(IRE)'s effort amounted to less than had seemed likely 2f out. (tchd 9-1)

3635 SHOWTIME PRESENTATIONS H'CAP 1m 2f 50y
8:20 (8:20) (Class 4) (0-80,78) 3-Y-O+ **£5,504** (£1,637; £818; £408) **Stalls** Low

Form RPR

1-64 **1** **Liberally (IRE)**[17] 3034 4-9-11 **75** .... EddieAhern 8 87+
(B J Meehan) *chsd ldr 2f: prom: wnt 2nd again gng wl 3f out: rdn to ld 1f out: drvn out* **4/1**[1]

1045 **2** *1 1/4* **Gilded Age**[12] 3213 3-8-12 **73** .... JoeFanning 5 79
(M Johnston) *led: rdn over 3f out: hdd 1f out: nt qckn* **9/2**[2]

6000 **3** *1* **Danehillsundance (IRE)**[18] 2998 5-9-7 **71** .... (t) SteveDrowne 11 75
(D H Brown) *stdd towards rr sn after s: hdwy wl over 1f out: rdn and kpt on ins fnl f* **12/1**

4304 **4** *2 1/2* **Dear Maurice**[18] 3008 5-9-12 **76** .... SebSanders 4 75
(E A L Dunlop) *hld up towards rr: hdwy on ins over 3f out: swtchd rt over 2f out: sn rdn: wknd fnl f* **7/1**

1103 **5** *nk* **Pelham Crescent (IRE)**[5] 3461 6-9-10 **77** .... DavidProbert(3) 6 75
(B Palling) *hld up in rr: rdn and effrt on outside 2f out: no imp fnl f* **7/1**

5356 **6** *2* **Dragon Slayer (IRE)**[2] 3550 7-8-10 **60** .... PatCosgrave 2 54
(John A Harris) *hld up in mid-div: hdwy over 2f out: rdn wl over 1f out: wknd fnl f* **9/1**

-000 **7** *2 3/4* **Rowan Rio**[10] 3273 4-10-0 **78** .... LiamJones 3 67
(W J Haggas) *hld up in rr: hdwy on ins over 2f out: rdn wl over 1f out: sn wknd* **12/1**

36-4 **8** *1/2* **Hannicean**[17] 3024 5-9-7 **71** .... (t) TGMcLaughlin 1 59
(R W Price) *hld up in tch: pushed along over 3f out: sn wknd* **12/1**

5441 **9** *10* **Supercast (IRE)**[29] 2678 6-9-12 **76** .... LukeMorris 10 44
(N J Vaughan) *prom tl rdn and wknd over 2f out* **5/1**[3]

0-03 **10** ½ **Red Birr (IRE)**[12] 3206 8-9-9 **73**......................................(t) MartinDwyer 9 40
(P R Webber) *hdwy to chse ldr after 2f: pushed along and lost 2nd 3f out: sn wknd* **14/1**

2m 12.51s (0.81) **Going Correction** +0.225s/f (Good)
WFA 3 from 4yo+ 11lb **10** Ran SP% **119.6**
Speed ratings (Par 105): **105,104,103,101,100 99,97,96,88,88**
toteswingers: 1&2 £5.70, 1&3 £14.30, 2&3 £18.20 CSF £22.48 CT £202.51 TOTE £5.10: £2.30, £2.50, £3.50; EX 38.00.

Owner Andrew Rosen **Bred** Waterford Hall Stud **Trained** Manton, Wilts

FOCUS
This was the highest quality race on the card, but the winner could be called some way out. Furlong-for-furlong, this was the fastest time of the night and the form looks solid with the third the best guide.

3636 2008 BEST DRESS LADY "ANITA GOTTS" H'CAP — 1m 2f 50y
8:50 (8:51) (Class 5) (0-75,75) 3-Y-O **£2,590** (£770; £385; £192) **Stalls** Low

Form RPR

5-43 **1** **Kaloni (IRE)**[23] 2858 3-9-5 **73**.. MickyFenton 11 78
(Mrs P Sly) *s.i.s: hld up in rr: hdwy on outside over 2f out: edgd lft and led wl over 1f out: drvn out fnl f* **7/1**

5200 **2** ½ **Amazing Blue Sky**[5] 3454 3-8-3 **57**.................................... LiamJones 9 61
(Mrs R A Carr) *w ldr: led wl over 2f out: sn rdn: hdd over 1f out: kpt on ins fnl f* **8/1**

0-34 **3** *shd* **Bruton Street (USA)**[68] 1573 3-9-7 **75**........................ RichardMullen 1 79+
(J H M Gosden) *s.i.s: hld up in mid-div: pushed along over 3f out: swtchd rt 2f out: rdn and hdwy over 1f out: swtchd rt and styd on wl to take 3rd nr fin* **10/1**

0-23 **4** 1¼ **Demeanour (USA)**[19] 2982 3-9-4 **72**.......................... SebSanders 10 73
(E A L Dunlop) *a.p: rdn jst over 1f out: one pce* **9/2**[1]

-542 **5** *nk* **Cosimo**[9] 3307 3-9-3 **71**..(v) DaneO'Neill 4 72
(Sir Michael Stoute) *a.p: rdn and ev ch 2f out: no ex wl ins fnl f* **9/2**[1]

-214 **6** 5 **Veroon (IRE)**[14] 3156 3-9-4 **72**...................................... J-PGuillambert 6 63
(J G Given) *hld up in tch: rdn and wknd over 2f out* **5/1**[2]

2-00 **7** 9 **Mehendi (IRE)**[39] 2356 3-9-1 **69**..................................(b[1]) MartinDwyer 8 42
(B J Meehan) *led: hdd wl over 2f out: sn rdn: wknd wl over 1f out* **12/1**

-605 **8** *nse* **Abulharith**[35] 2479 3-8-13 **67**...................................... EddieAhern 5 40
(P W Chapple-Hyam) *hld up in rr: rdn over 2f out: sn struggling* **6/1**[3]

01- **9** 5 **Tombov (FR)**[318] 5184 3-9-7 **75**................................. FergusSweeney 7 38
(A King) *a towards rr* **11/1**

2m 13.72s (2.02) **Going Correction** +0.225s/f (Good) **9** Ran SP% **116.0**
Speed ratings (Par 100): **100,99,99,98,98 94,87,87,83**
toteswingers: 1&2 £12.90, 1&3 £11.50, 2&3 £9.90 CSF £61.83 CT £561.58 TOTE £8.20: £2.10, £2.80, £2.40; EX 73.40.

Owner Alan Speechley & John Watt **Bred** Niall Farrell **Trained** Thorney, Cambs

FOCUS
A fair handicap that produced a close finish. The form is ordinary rated around the placed horses.

3637 LIFE&STYLE MAGAZINE H'CAP — 1m 75y
9:20 (9:21) (Class 5) (0-70,69) 3-Y-O+ **£2,590** (£770; £385; £192) **Stalls** Low

Form RPR

2601 **1** **Tanforan**[9] 3322 7-9-0 **62**.. BillyCray(7) 3 70
(B P J Baugh) *hld up towards rr: hdwy on ins over 3f out: led 1f out: drvn out* **16/1**

6-64 **2** ½ **King's Icon (IRE)**[7] 3401 4-8-9 **50**.................................. SteveDrowne 1 57
(M Wigham) *a.p: swtchd rt 2f out: rdn over 1f out: r.o u.p to take 2nd cl home* **7/1**

0005 **3** *nse* **Count Ceprano (IRE)**[11] 3234 5-9-7 **69**...................... SimonPearce(7) 4 75
(C R Dore) *hld up in rr: hdwy on outside over 1f out: str run ins fnl f: rdn and jst failed to take 2nd* **10/1**

-210 **4** 1½ **Focail Eile**[15] 3112 4-9-12 **67**... MickyFenton 8 70
(Miss Gay Kelleway) *led early: hld up in mid-div: hdwy 3f out: ev ch over 1f out: nt qckn wl ins fnl f* **16/1**

3121 **5** *hd* **You've Been Mowed**[12] 3209 3-8-11 **64**..................... AndreaAtzeni(3) 5 65
(R J Price) *t.k.h: hld up in tch: swtchd rt over 2f out: rdn 1f out: kpt on same pce* **4/1**[1]

4001 **6** 1½ **West End Lad**[46] 2166 6-9-13 **68**......................................(b) DaneO'Neill 2 67
(S R Bowring) *t.k.h: sn led: rdn 2f out: hdd 1f out: fdd wl ins fnl f* **5/1**[3]

2464 **7** 2 **Indy Driver**[21] 2916 4-9-11 **66**......................................(p) FrancisNorton 6 60
(J R Fanshawe) *broke wl: sn stdd towards rr: effrt on outside over 2f out: sn rdn: wknd ins fnl f* **9/2**[2]

-010 **8** 1¼ **Night Knight (IRE)**[15] 3115 3-9-4 **68**..............................(v) EddieAhern 9 58
(M L W Bell) *hld up in rr: rdn over 2f out: no rspnse* **14/1**

2655 **9** 1¾ **Kielty's Folly**[37] 2390 5-8-9 **50** oh3........................... GrahamGibbons 10 38
(B P J Baugh) *prom: wnt 2nd jst over 3f out: rdn and ev ch over 1f out: wknd ent fnl f* **10/1**

0-00 **10** 59 **Straboe (USA)**[74] 1423 3-8-0 **50** oh5......................... CatherineGannon 12 —
(S C Williams) *t.k.h: sn w ldr: rdn and lost 2nd jst over 3f out: wknd wl over 2f out: t.o whn eased over 1f out* **50/1**

1064 **11** 2¼ **Blue Charm**[11] 3234 5-10-0 **69**... TomEaves 7 —
(I W McInnes) *rrd and s.s: a in rr: no ch whn lost action and eased over 2f out* **7/1**

1m 47.02s (1.42) **Going Correction** +0.225s/f (Good)
WFA 3 from 4yo+ 9lb **11** Ran SP% **118.4**
Speed ratings (Par 103): **101,100,100,98,98 97,95,94,92,33 31**
toteswingers: 1&2 £20.10, 1&3 £43.10, 2&3 £17.80 CSF £124.70 CT £837.04 TOTE £21.40: £5.10, £2.50, £3.60; EX 251.30 Place 6: £ 266.16 Place 5: £48.91.

Owner F Gillespie **Bred** Bearstone Stud **Trained** Audley, Staffs

FOCUS
This modest handicap was run at a generous pace, and the three runners that helped set it were on the retreat by the furlong pole. The form is rated around the first two.

Blue Charm Official explanation: jockey said gelding was slowly away and lost its action

T/Plt: £251.00 to a £1 stake. Pool: £56,673.15. 164.82 winning tickets. T/Qpdt: £16.90 to a £1 stake. Pool: £4,947.06. 215.80 winning tickets. KH

3582 SANDOWN (R-H)
Saturday, July 4

OFFICIAL GOING: Good (good to firm places)
Wind: Light, against Weather: Becoming bright, very warm

3638 CORAL CHARGE (REGISTERED AS THE SPRINT STKS) (GROUP 3) — 5f 6y
2:05 (2:05) (Class 1) 3-Y-O+

£36,900 (£13,988; £7,000; £3,490; £1,748; £877) **Stalls** High

Form RPR

10 **1** **Ialysos (GR)**[14] 3140 5-9-3 107.. C-PLemaire 9 115
(L M Cumani) *chsd ldrs and racd against far rail: rdn 2f out: prog and squeezed through to chal fnl f: led nr fin* **9/2**[2]

1-21 **2** ½ **Triple Aspect (IRE)**[21] 2928 3-8-12 114.......................... LiamJones 11 111+
(W J Haggas) *lw: nt pce to capitalise on prime draw and 9th after 1f: swtchd to outer after 2f: sn rdn: prog fr 1/2-way: jnd ldr ins fnl f but hung bdly lft last 100yds* **13/8**[1]

0032 **3** *nk* **Masta Plasta (IRE)**[15] 3202 6-9-3 106........................ AdrianTNicholls 5 112
(D Nicholls) *swtg: gd spd to dispute ld and racd against far rail: edgd sltly lft fr 2f out: narrow advantage 1f out: sn jnd: no ex nr fin* **11/1**

0003 **4** ¾ **Matsunosuke**[7] 3405 7-9-3 98.. LukeMorris 1 109
(A B Coogan) *stdd s fr worst draw: hld up in last but sn outpcd and pushed along: stl last whn nt clr run 1f out: r.o wl last 150yds: nrst fin* **66/1**

3410 **5** *hd* **Judd Street**[7] 3405 7-9-3 103..(v) MJKinane 7 109
(Eve Johnson Houghton) *lw: dwlt: off the pce in 10th: taken to outer and pushed along 1/2-way: stl at bk 1f out: gd run fnl f: nrst fin* **28/1**

-123 **6** *nk* **Anglezarke (IRE)**[18] 2991 3-8-9 104................................... DavidAllan 10 103
(T D Easterby) *lw: hld up towards rr against nr side rail: effrt over 1f out: kpt on same pce fnl f: nvr able to chal* **9/2**[2]

1-06 **7** 1¼ **Madame Trop Vite (IRE)**[15] 3202 3-8-9 105........................ NCallan 6 98
(K A Ryan) *chsd ldrs: rdn and stl cl enough 1f out: fdd last 100yds* **20/1**

010 **8** ½ **Duff (IRE)**[14] 3140 6-9-7 109.. KJManning 3 105
(Edward Lynam, Ire) *pressed ldrs: nt qckn and lost pl over 1f out: one pce and no imp fnl f* **11/1**

-150 **9** 1¼ **Total Gallery (IRE)**[17] 3011 3-8-12 103.............................. LPKeniry 8 95
(J S Moore) *hld up in midfield: nt clr run briefly wl over 1f out: sn rdn and lost pl* **10/1**[3]

0040 **10** *nk* **Captain Gerrard (IRE)**[6] 3434 4-9-3 106.......................... TomEaves 2 96
(B Smart) *gd spd fr wd draw to dispute ld: rdn over 1f out: wknd ent fnl f* **20/1**

-005 **11** ½ **Group Therapy**[28] 2704 4-9-3 95.................................. GrahamGibbons 4 94
(N P Littmoden) *chsd ldrs: lost pl and rdn 2f out: sn struggling* **66/1**

60.17 secs (-1.43) **Going Correction** +0.05s/f (Good)
WFA 3 from 4yo+ 5lb **11** Ran SP% **116.2**
Speed ratings (Par 113): **113,112,111,110,110 109,107,106,104,104 103**
toteswingers: 1&2 £2.50, 1&3 £7.30, 2&3 £4.90 CSF £11.33 TOTE £4.70: £1.80, £1.30, £2.30; EX 11.40 Trifecta £60.20 Pool: £1,472.77 - 18.10 winning units..

Owner Mrs M Marinopoulos **Bred** Figaia Stud **Trained** Newmarket, Suffolk

FOCUS
An intriguing Group 3 sprint. It was run at a searching early pace which was highlighted by the proximity of the fourth and fifth, who came from well back. Strong form and sound for the grade, but while Ialysos showed his Golden Jubilee running was all wrong, Triple Aspect did rather throw it away.

NOTEBOOK
Ialysos(GR) failed to show his true colours in the Golden Jubilee a fortnight earlier, but things failed to go his way there as he took a bump and was reported to have been unsuited by the "watered" going. He would certainly not be the first horse to not act on that course and he bounced back to winning ways on this drop in trip/grade with a fairly straightforward success. Well drawn, he showed natural speed to sit just behind the pacesetters and got a dream run against the far rail when Masta Plasta moved off it around the furlong pole. That was no doubt the place to be and everything went his way this time, but he readily confirmed his previous Haydock form with Anglezarke and is obviously a talented sprinter. The Nunthorpe at York in August remains his big target, but he will obviously need to raise his game again back at the top level. (op 4-1 tchd 5-1)

Triple Aspect(IRE) came into this being unbeaten in two runs over course and distance, and looked to have a great chance of maintaining the good record of three-year-olds in this contest. He ran a blinder taking on his elders for the first time, but somewhat predictably got nothing like the same charmed passage as the winner. As was the case when winning here last time, he got taken off his feet early on, but this time the pace was much stronger. He was switched to the outside with his challenge around halfway and looked the most likely winner at the furlong marker. He went off a true line when put under maximum pressure, however, going out to his left, and the ground he lost there, along with that of which he lost in coming to the middle of the track, cost him the verdict. He remains a sprinter on an upward curve and lost very little in defeat, but perhaps now is the time to revert to 6f. (op 15-8 tchd 2-1)

Masta Plasta(IRE) was on his toes in the paddock and awash with sweat through the race. He showed his customary blistering speed to get across from his draw and kept gamely to his task when the challengers mounted. His turn is not looking far off again, but he may need to go abroad again to find that winning opportunity. (op 10-1)

Matsunosuke was faced with a stiff task on this step up from handicap company and was drawn worst of all. He was allowed to find his feet early on and finished strongly, with the early pace playing to his strengths. His proximity should not be used to hold down the form as he does have a very good record over course and distance. (op 50-1)

Judd Street bounced back from a terrible run at Windsor a week previously, when well behind Matsunosuke, and the fact he made a sluggish start actually helped his cause. (op 33-1)

Anglezarke(IRE) posted a career-best when third to Scenic Blast in the King's Stand and confirmed that form with Captain Gerrard. She was also 7lb worse off with the winner for a narrow defeat at Haydock on her penultimate start. (tchd 4-1)

Madame Trop Vite(IRE) showed up well through the early parts and performed very close to her last-time-out form with Masta Plasta. (tchd 25-1 in places)

Duff(IRE) came in for support, but he was edgy beforehand and failed to raise his game for the drop back to the minimum distance. (op 16-1)

3639 CORAL CHALLENGE (HERITAGE H'CAP) — 1m 14y
2:40 (2:41) (Class 2) 3-Y-O+

£62,310 (£18,660; £9,330; £4,670; £2,330; £1,170) **Stalls** High

Form RPR

2-44 **1** **Acrostic**[21] 2933 4-9-0 **94**.. C-PLemaire 3 106
(L M Cumani) *hld up in 10th: prog on outer over 2f out: chsd ldr wl over 1f out: edgd rt but clsd and upsides 100yds out: led last strides* **7/1**[3]

1-10 **2** *hd* **Crackdown (IRE)**[16] 3049 3-8-8 **97**................................... NCallan 12 107
(M Johnston) *lw: t.k.h early: led at decent pce: kicked on 2f out: drvn and jnd 100yds out: battled on wl: hdd last strides* **10/1**

-113 **3** *2* **Mirrored**[16] 3049 3-8-7 **96** ow1 .... RyanMoore 6 101
(Sir Michael Stoute) *hld up in last quartet: rdn on outer over 2f out: prog over 1f out: r.o to take 3rd ins fnl f* **9/2**[1]

02 **4** *1* **Huzzah (IRE)**[17] 3014 4-9-5 **99** .... JimmyFortune 17 104
(B W Hills) *lw: a in ldng quartet: rdn to chse ldr briefly 2f out: outpcd over 1f out: kpt on same pce* **17/2**

06-5 **5** *3/4* **Alfathaa**[17] 3014 4-9-8 **102** .... RHills 7 105+
(W J Haggas) *swtg: stdd s: hld up in last pair: stl there 2f out: taken to outer and prog over 1f out: styd on wl fnl f: nrst fin* **7/1**[3]

1-10 **6** *1 1/4* **Roman Republic (FR)**[16] 3049 3-8-2 **91** .... RoystonFfrench 5 89
(M Johnston) *dwlt: hld up in last pair: taken to outer and rdn over 2f out: styd on fr over 1f out: nrst fin* **6/1**[2]

2310 **7** *1 1/4* **Extraterrestrial**[51] 2015 5-9-2 **99** .... FrederikTylicki(3) 2 96
(R A Fahey) *lw: hld up in abt 12th and racd wd: prog on outer wl over 2f out: disp 3rd over 1f out: wknd fnl f* **16/1**

0-0 **8** *1 1/4* **Smokey Oakey (IRE)**[37] 2410 5-9-10 **104** .... TPQueally 9 98
(M H Tompkins) *dwlt: settled in 9th: rdn over 2f out: no imp on ldrs wl over 1f out: plugged on same pce* **50/1**

01-0 **9** *shd* **Willow Dancer (IRE)**[30] 2639 5-8-10 **90** .... (p) TedDurcan 13 84+
(W R Swinburn) *lw: chsd ldrs in 7th: lost pl fr 3f out and wl in rr 2f out: shkn up and sme prog over 1f out: no hdwy after* **25/1**

4510 **10** *nk* **Ellemujie**[17] 3014 4-8-12 **92** .... RichardHughes 1 87
(D K Ivory) *racd alone on wd outside 1st 2f: chsng ldrs in 8th after 3f: rdn over 2f out: btn over 1f out: eased ins fnl f* **16/1**

-000 **11** *1 1/2* **Opera Prince**[22] 2891 4-8-5 **85** .... ChrisCatlin 14 75
(S Kirk) *a abt same pl on inner: shkn up and no prog over 2f out* **33/1**

5-13 **12** *3 1/2* **Tanto Faz (IRE)**[24] 2822 4-8-7 **87** .... LiamJones 4 69
(W J Haggas) *swtg: t.k.h: chsd ldr: rdn 3f out: wknd 2f out* **20/1**

2201 **13** *nk* **Ace Of Hearts**[49] 2083 10-9-2 **99** .... JackMitchell(3) 10 80
(C F Wall) *reluctant to go to post: prom in abt 5th: u.p 3f out: wknd fr 2f out* **16/1**

2065 **14** *1 1/4* **Blythe Knight (IRE)**[51] 2015 9-9-8 **102** .... GrahamGibbons 15 80
(J J Quinn) *trckd ldrs on inner in abt 6th: rdn over 2f out: sn lost pl: btn over 1f out* **25/1**

4-01 **15** *1* **We'll Come**[10] 3282 5-9-6 **100** .... (b) DarryllHolland 16 76
(M A Jarvis) *swtg: hld up in last trio: pushed along and no rspnse on inner wl over 2f out: nvr a factor* **10/1**

5226 **16** *3/4* **Millfields Dreams**[7] 3389 10-8-0 **80** oh6 ow2 .... (p) LukeMorris 8 54
(G C Bravery) *chsd ldng pair: rdn 3f out: sn lost pl and struggling* **100/1**

1m 40.21s (-3.09) **Going Correction** -0.15s/f (Firm)
WFA 3 from 4yo+ 9lb **16** Ran SP% **122.2**
Speed ratings (Par 109): **109,108,106,105,105 103,102,101,101,100 99,95,95,94,93 92**
toteswingers: 1&2 £21.20, 1&3 £6.20, 2&3 £12.40 CSF £70.07 CT £370.17 TOTE £8.80: £2.50, £2.90, £1.70, £2.90; EX 96.70 Trifecta £756.90 Pool: £22,298 - 21.80 winning units..
Owner L Marinopoulos **Bred** Mrs B A Matthews **Trained** Newmarket, Suffolk

FOCUS
This very valuable handicap is always a cracking heat. There was a sound pace on and, despite some hard luck stories from off the pace, the form still looks solid enough with the fourth the best guide.

NOTEBOOK
Acrostic opened his account for the season at the third time of asking by getting up near the line under a fine ride and gave his stable a quick-fire double. The slight drop back on this stiff track proved ideal and he was produced with perfect timing by Lemaire. This was his first success since winning his maiden last year, but he does not have many miles on the clock and his trainer has excelled with such performers in the past, so there is very likely still more to come. The Totesport Mile at Glorious Goodwood later this month looks a logical next step and, granted a high draw, he would have obvious claims there. He was trimmed from 14-1 to 10-1 with William Hill for that, but others were more impressed and sponsors quoted him at 7-1. (op 15-2 tchd 8-1 in places)
Crackdown(IRE) ◆, visibly sweating through the race, won the battle for the lead and was only mugged in the dying strides. This was certainly his best effort so far and it would be little surprise to see him re-oppose the winner at Goodwood. (tchd 11-1 and 12-1 in places)
Mirrored ◆ ran a massive race when third in the Britannia on his previous outing and was well supported here. He came from well off the pace, but was always getting there too late and never looked like confirming form with the runner-up from his 6lb higher mark. There was still plenty to like about the way he finished his race wide of the pack, however, and there is definitely a decent pot in him this season when things go his way. (op 5-1)
Huzzah(IRE), upped 3lb for coming second in the Royal Hunt Cup, was well positioned turning for home yet had to wait a touch for his challenge around 3f out. He found just the same pace when in the clear, but kept on resolutely and is a very likeable handicapper. He rates the benchmark. (op 9-1 tchd 10-1)
Alfathaa ◆ went into just about every notebook in existence when finishing fifth from a poor draw on his return in the Hunt Cup 17 days earlier. He failed to reverse form with Huzzah, but endured a troubled passage from off the pace and is better than the bare form. (op 13-2 tchd 11-2)
Roman Republic(FR) had to come from behind due to his low draw and showed his run in the Britannia to be wrong, but was another getting there all too late. He needs more use made of him at this distance and one could see him relishing 1m2f. (op 15-2)
Extraterrestrial performed creditably considering he was poorly drawn, but looks held by the Handicapper now.
We'll Come was confidently ridden, but got no sort of run when trying to make up ground on the far rail. Official explanation: jockey said gelding was denied a clear run (op 9-1 tchd 17-2)

3640 CORAL-ECLIPSE (GROUP 1) 1m 2f 7y
3:15 (3:17) (Class 1) 3-Y-O+

£283,850 (£107,600; £53,850; £26,850; £13,450; £6,750) **Stalls** High

Form RPR

1-11 **1** **Sea The Stars (IRE)**[28] 2705 3-8-10 **124** .... MJKinane 5 135+
(John M Oxx, Ire) *lw: hld up in 5th: smooth prog fr 3f out to ld 2f out: rdn and hrd pressed 1f out: dug deep and fended off chalr last 150yds* **4/7**[1]

0-44 **2** *1* **Rip Van Winkle (IRE)**[28] 2705 3-8-10 **119** .... JimmyFortune 6 132
(A P O'Brien, Ire) *hld up towards rr: smooth prog wl over 2f out: wnt 2nd wl over 1f out: potent chal ent fnl f: r.o but hld last 150yds* **11/2**[3]

11-2 **3** *4 1/2* **Conduit (IRE)**[37] 2410 4-9-7 **125** .... RyanMoore 9 123
(Sir Michael Stoute) *settled in last: taken to outer and rdn 3f out: prog to go 3rd over 1f out and cl enough: kpt on but outpcd after* **9/2**[2]

0-61 **4** *5* **Cima De Triomphe (IRE)**[37] 2410 4-9-7 **116** .... C-PLemaire 2 113+
(L M Cumani) *hld up in last trio: effrt whn nt clr run over 2f out: kpt on to take modest 4th jst over 1f out: nvr any ch* **11/1**

4300 **5** *3 3/4* **Steele Tango (USA)**[14] 3139 4-9-7 **110** .... DarryllHolland 1 106
(R A Teal) *chsd clr ldng trio: rdn over 3f out: lost pl over 2f out: no ch after: plugged on* **100/1**

12-0 **6** *1/2* **Jukebox Jury (IRE)**[12] 3230 3-8-10 **110** .... RoystonFfrench 3 105
(M Johnston) *settled in midfield: rdn 4f out: effrt u.p and 4th briefly over 1f out: wknd fnl f* **50/1**

-334 **7** *2 1/2* **Twice Over**[17] 3013 4-9-7 **119** .... TPQueally 8 102
(H R A Cecil) *lw: hld up in rr: last and nt gng wl over 2f out: plugging on to chal for remote 6th whn hmpd 1f out* **14/1**

30 **8** *11* **Malibu Bay (USA)**[27] 2756 3-8-10 **102** .... CO'Donoghue 4 78
(A P O'Brien, Ire) *chsd clr ldng pair tl wknd wl over 2f out* **100/1**

06-0 **9** *6* **Lang Shining (IRE)**[51] 2015 5-9-7 **99** .... RichardHughes 10 80
(Sir Michael Stoute) *led after 1f to 2f out: heavily eased over 1f out* **150/1**

-400 **10** *1 1/2* **Set Sail (IRE)**[18] 2992 3-8-10 **103** .... JAHeffernan 7 63
(A P O'Brien, Ire) *led 1f: pressed other pcemaker to over 2f out: wknd rapidly* **200/1**

2m 3.40s (-7.10) **Going Correction** -0.15s/f (Firm)
WFA 3 from 4yo+ 11lb **10** Ran SP% **117.3**
Speed ratings (Par 117): **122,121,117,113,110 110,108,99,94,93**
toteswingers: 1&2 £1.90, 1&3 £1.40, 2&3 £3.30 CSF £4.37 CT £8.39 TOTE £1.50: £1.02, £2.10, £1.80; EX 4.20 Trifecta £9.90 Pool: £31,619.58 - 2,346.27 winning units..
Owner Christopher Tsui **Bred** Sunderland Holdings **Trained** Currabeg, Co Kildare
■ Sea The Stars became the first horse since Nashwan to achieve the 2000 Guineas, Derby and Eclipse treble.
■ Stewards' Enquiry : Richard Hughes caution: allowed horse to coast home with no assistance.
Royston Ffrench two-day ban: careless riding (Jul 18-19)

FOCUS
Sea The Stars produced a performance right out of the very top drawer, beating another talented three-year-old, with the pair leaving two classic winners trailing the best part of five and ten lengths further adrift at the end of a race run at an end-to-end gallop, thanks to three pacemakers. The winning time of 2min 03.40secs was little more than a second outside Kalaglow's course record, which was set in the 1982 Brigadier Gerard Stakes on an afternoon of outstanding times, and by far the fastest set in the Eclipse in more than 40 years, bettering by almost a second the next best achieved by Mtoto in 1987. Outstanding form, Sea The Stars' RPR of 131 being the best awarded any horse in the world this year, while Rip Van Winkle's 129 is joint second best.

NOTEBOOK
Sea The Stars(IRE), switched here owing to unsuitably soft ground for the Irish Derby the previous weekend, produced a performance right out of the very top drawer. He had already been the first horse since Nashwan to achieve the 2000 Guineas and Derby double, and although his winning margin here was nowhere near so extravagant as Nashwan's 20 years ago, he was beating a better colt. The pair left two classic winners trailing the best part of five and ten lengths further adrift at the end of a race run at an end-to-end gallop, thanks to three pacemakers, and the form looks outstanding. Having broke smartly, he was always best placed of the main protagonists, albeit around ten lengths off the lead still as they turned in. At the 3f marker Kinane glanced over his left shoulder and then eased him out for his challenge. With the leaders tiring, having done their job, he made his ground so easily that he was in front 2f out, and that was plenty soon enough here as Rip Van Winkle had followed him through and Conduit was closing too on the wide outside, having been last into the straight. Around a furlong and a half out they both looked dangers, but by the furlong marker he had only the former to worry about. Rip Van Winkle got to within half a length, but that simply spurred Sea The Stars on. He found plenty and was firmly on top through the last 150 yards or so, winning yet another major prize without enduring that hard a race. It's a shame that running in the King George, as Nashwan did, is now unlikely, for his presence would be just the shot in the arm that race needs. Instead the Juddmonte International at York is now likely to be his next race, and then the Irish Champion Stakes, which is evidently his main target. The Arc, where soft ground tends to be the norm, does not seem high on connections' agenda, and he could make his swansong instead in the Newmarket Champion Stakes. The 5-1 with William Hill to go through the season unbeaten (minimum one more appearance) is not that mean. He is a truly exceptional colt. (op 8-13 tchd 4-6 in places)
Rip Van Winkle(IRE) has now been beaten on all four appearances at this level, but his fourth places in both the 2000 Guineas and Derby showed he was a top-class colt, and reports from Ballydoyle suggested he was held in as high regard as Mastercraftsman and Fame And Glory, if not higher. There is real substance to that claim now, for in running Sea The Stars to a length and pulling four and a half lengths clear of Conduit he did enough to be elevated above his two illustrious stablemates on ratings. The knock he received on Thursday at home cannot have helped, but there was no suggestion it had a significant bearing on his running, as he appeared to be just where Fortune wanted him from the start, with the winner in his sights and ready to pounce, and he followed the winner through to have his chance if good enough. He wasn't quite, but still ran the race of his life. He is obviously a Group 1 winner in waiting, but it is hard to see him beating Sea The Stars. The Sussex Stakes could be his next target. (op 6-1 tchd 13-2 in places)
Conduit(IRE) is a full year older than Sea The Stars, but we still did not know the full extent of his ability going into this race, for he had ended last year on a steep upward curve and had then made a highly encouraging reappearance when failing by the minimum margin to concede 7lb to Cima De Triomphe in a muddling race over this course and distance. Held up at the back of the field, he benefited from the sort of pace that had been such a factor in his Breeders' Cup win and he came from last place to threaten briefly inside the last 2f. Though he couldn't keep tabs on the first two through the final furlong, he finished far enough clear of Cima De Triomphe to suggest he had come on since the Brigadier Gerard. Sir Michael Stoute has not been entirely happy with the way he has looked this year - he was not coltish, however, this time - and he expects him to go on improving, as he did in 2008. The King George is next on the agenda. (op 5-1)
Cima De Triomphe(IRE) was checked momentarily, but it did not make a material difference. He ran a fair race but does not look quite good enough to win one of the major domestic Group 1 races. (op 12-1 tchd 14-1)
Steele Tango(USA) was a bit out of his depth again, but he earned his enterprising connections decent enough money in fifth and will be winning again when his sights are lowered a little.
Jukebox Jury(IRE) turned in a far more encouraging effort after his lacklustre return from injury, for while he was among the first under pressure he got ahead of Cima De Triomphe briefly before fading again in the last furlong. He looks as if he is on his way back.
Twice Over was a disappointment for once. At the back of the field with Conduit straightening up, he was making only laboured headway when checked briefly as he ran up the back of Steele Tango. He was well clear of the three pacemakers, but beaten around 17 lengths. Official explanation: jockey said colt hung right (tchd 16-1 in places)

3641 CORAL DISTAFF (LISTED RACE) (FILLIES) 1m 14y
3:45 (3:47) (Class 1) 3-Y-O

£22,708 (£8,608; £4,308; £2,148; £1,076; £540) **Stalls** High

Form RPR

21 **1** **Strawberrydaiquiri**[47] 2139 3-8-12 **90** .... RyanMoore 5 106+
(Sir Michael Stoute) *trckd ldng pair: pushed along and clsd 2f out: led over 1f out: shkn up and asserted readily* **6/5**[1]

-130 **2** *2* **Say No Now (IRE)**[17] 3016 3-8-12 **90** .... TedDurcan 7 101
(D R Lanigan) *lw: led: rdn and hdd over 1f out: kpt on wl but no match for wnr* **6/1**[3]

1020 **3** *nk* **Wadaat**[29] 2672 3-8-12 **104** .... NCallan 1 100
(C E Brittain) *lw: trckd ldr: rdn to chal 2f out: nrly upsides over 1f out: kpt on same pce fnl f* **11/2**[2]

-160 **4** *3 1/2* **King's Starlet**[17] 3016 3-8-12 **86** .... AlanMunro 2 92
(H Morrison) *hld up in last pair: prog on outer to go 4th 2f out and looked possible danger: sn rdn and btn* **25/1**

4-00 **5** *2 1/2* **Beat Seven**[17] 3016 3-8-12 **102** .... RichardHughes 4 87
(Miss Gay Kelleway) *lw: stdd s: hld up in 7th: effrt over 2f out: sn outpcd: wnt 5th over 1f out: no further prog* **8/1**

0354 **6** *3 1/4* **Seradim**[9] 3320 3-8-12 **97** .... (b1) TPQueally 6 79
(P F I Cole) *plld hrd early: hld up in 4th: rdn and nt qckn over 2f out: fdd* **12/1**

13-0 **7** *4* **Yorksters Girl (IRE)**[77] 1353 3-8-12 97 JimmyFortune 3 70
(M G Quinlan) *swtg: trckd ldrs in 5th: rdn over 2f out: sn wknd* **12/1**

8 *2 ¾* **Young Americans (IRE)**[105] 3-8-12 0 DarrylHolland 9 64
(M Botti) *w'like: lw: mostly in 6th: rdn wl over 2f out: sn struggling* **12/1**

1016 **9** *nse* **Aroundthebay**[9] 3320 3-8-12 86 ChrisCatlin 8 63
(H J L Dunlop) *a in last pair: shkn up and no prog over 2f out: bhd after* **40/1**

1m 42.39s (-0.91) **Going Correction** -0.15s/f (Firm) **9** Ran SP% **115.6**
Speed ratings (Par 105): **98,96,95,92,89 86,82,79,79**
toteswingers: 1&2 £3.10, 1&3 £1.80, 2&3 £3.30 CSF £8.66 TOTE £1.90: £1.30, £2.20, £1.70; EX 10.40 Trifecta £82.10 Pool: £965.66 - 8.70 winning units..

Owner Mrs R J Jacobs **Bred** Newsells Park Stud Limited **Trained** Newmarket, Suffolk

FOCUS
An ordinary fillies' race for the class, but a taking display from the improving winner. The winner runner-up is rated to her previous best.

NOTEBOOK
Strawberrydaiquiri ◆ enhanced her leading stable's decent record in the race. Despite having won her maiden at Windsor by six lengths, she still had plenty to find on this debut in Listed company, but her trainer's last two winners of the race came into it with similar profiles and one of them went on to land the Windsor Forest at Royal Ascot as a four-year-old. She was never far from the pace and it was apparent coming to the 2f pole that she was the one to be on. The course and distance looked perfect for her and a decent test at this trip should prove her optimum. A further step up in class is now on the cards and she appeals as the sort who will really come into her own next year. (op 5-4 tchd 11-10 and 11-8 in places)

Say No Now(IRE) was not disgraced in the Sandringham from a moderate draw last time and that race is working out well. She had her own way out in front and looked to need all of the trip, keeping on gamely once headed by the ready winner. She deserves to find a race of this class. (op 8-1)

Wadaat, well beaten when hampered in the Oaks on her previous outing, would likely have enjoyed a better test on this drop in trip and so was not at all disgraced. Like the first pair, however, she got the run of the race. (op 7-1)

King's Starlet fared best of those to come from behind and ran close to her Royal Ascot form with the runner-up. She can do better in this grade when faced with a stronger pace or perhaps a longer trip. (op 20-1)

Beat Seven had claims at these weights with the runner-up and the fourth, so she has to be considered a little disappointing, but the race was hardly run to suit. (op 15-2 tchd 17-2 and 9-1 in a place)

Seradim was lit up by the application of first-time blinkers and has now run out of excuses. Official explanation: jockey said filly ran too freely (op 11-1 tchd 10-1)

Yorksters Girl(IRE) was having her first run since running down the field in the Fred Darling at Newbury in April and her first outing over this stiffer test. She can be rated a little better than the bare form as she made up her ground nicely down the home straight, but that effort proved costly and she failed to get home. (op 11-1)

3642 CORAL MARATHON (REGISTERED AS THE ESHER STKS) (LISTED RACE) 2m 78y
4:20 (4:21) (Class 1) 4-Y-0+

£22,708 (£8,608; £4,308; £2,148; £1,076; £540) **Stalls** Centre

Form RPR

6-14 **1** **Desert Sea (IRE)**[59] 1790 6-9-0 96 RyanMoore 6 103
(D W P Arbuthnot) *hld up in last: prog on outer to go 2nd over 2f out: drvn to ld over 1f out: gained upper hand last 100yds* **7/2**[2]

5-12 **2** *1* **Victoria Montoya**[21] 2931 4-8-9 85 LPKeniry 1 96
(A M Balding) *lw: w ldr: led 5f out: kicked on over 3f out: hdd over 1f out: fought on wl tl no ex last 100yds* **6/1**

1-22 **3** *1* **Wells Lyrical (IRE)**[7] 3390 4-9-0 93 TomEaves 4 100+
(B Smart) *lw: trckd ldrs: trapped bhd rival 4f out and lost pl: rdn over 3f out: wnt 3rd over 1f out: 3l down fnl f: grad clsng fin* **5/1**[3]

-111 **4** *9* **Judgethemoment (USA)**[18] 2994 4-9-0 97 RichardHughes 3 89
(Jane Chapple-Hyam) *hld up in 5th: taken to r wd 9f out: drvn in 3rd whn rejnd gp 5f out: wnt 2nd u.p over 3f out to over 2f out: wknd over 1f out* **2/1**[1]

14-0 **5** *7* **Gravitation**[35] 2482 4-8-9 108 AlanMunro 2 76
(W Jarvis) *trckd ldrs: effrt 3f out: rdn and hld over 2f out: wknd rapidly* **17/2**

-503 **6** *39* **Amerigo (IRE)**[14] 3143 4-9-0 97 NCallan 5 34
(M A Jarvis) *led to 5f out: wknd rapidly 4f out: t.o* **5/1**[3]

3m 31.9s (-6.80) **Going Correction** -0.15s/f (Firm) **6** Ran SP% **113.7**
Speed ratings (Par 111): **111,110,110,105,102 82**
toteswingers: 1&2 £6.00, 1&3 £3.90, 2&3 £9.60 CSF £24.45 TOTE £5.00: £2.00, £3.30; EX 26.60.

Owner Bonusprint **Bred** Peter McGlynn **Trained** Compton, Berks

FOCUS
A small field, but a competitive line up for this staying prize. the pace was sound and the form looks fairly solid, rated around the first three.

NOTEBOOK
Desert Sea(IRE), last seen finishing fourth in the Chester Cup, swerved the Northumberland Plate a week earlier on account of the soft ground and gained reward with a straightforward display. He was content to bide his time out the back before making his move round the home turn and found plenty for pressure when it mattered. His form figures at the track now read 211 and a crack at the Cesarewitch at Newmarket later in the season looks viable, but that would be ground dependant. It may be the Ebor for him next. (op 5-1)

Victoria Montoya cut out most of the donkey work and showed an honest attitude when pressed throughout the home straight. She was beaten off a mark over 85 at the track on her previous outing so limits the form, but is clearly still improving and stays all day. She too could be an Ebor possible. (op 5-1)

Wells Lyrical(IRE), second in the Northumberland Plate last time, lacked the tactical pace to seriously threaten on this return to quicker ground. He stayed on stoutly towards the finish, however, and remains in good heart. (tchd 9-2 and 11-2 in places)

Judgethemoment(USA) took the Ascot Stakes over an extra 4f at Royal Ascot 18 days earlier and came into this bidding for a four-timer. Having disputed the early lead, he was taken back before being ridden back up to the leaders as the pace slackened going out onto the back straight. He was then taken very wide of runners and began to feel the pinch rounding the turn for home. He was beaten shortly afterwards and this was not his true form, so perhaps his Ascot run had left its mark. (op 5-2 tchd 11-4 in places)

Gravitation showed more than had been the case on her seasonal bow in May, but failed to see out the race like a true stayer. She still has to prove she retains enthusiasm for the game. (op 11-2 tchd 9-1 and 10-1 in places)

Amerigo(IRE) was beaten shortly after turning into the home straight and clearly something went amiss. (op 11-2 tchd 6-1)

3643 10% CASHBACK @ CORAL.CO.UK H'CAP 7f 16y
4:55 (4:56) (Class 3) (0-95,88) 3-Y-0

£7,477 (£2,239; £1,119; £560; £279; £140) **Stalls** High

Form RPR

0411 **1** **Cyflymder (IRE)**[14] 3163 3-9-7 88 RichardHughes 8 95
(R Hannon) *mde all: rdn 2f out: kpet on wl fr over 1f out: a holding on* **5/1**[3]

52-1 **2** *1* **Maswerte (IRE)**[23] 2849 3-9-0 81 NCallan 7 85+
(L M Cumani) *lw: t.k.h: trckd ldrs: looking for gap fr over 2f out: effrt to dispute 2nd over 1f out: kpt on fnl f but a hld* **15/8**[1]

012 **3** *shd* **Santefisio**[14] 3163 3-8-9 76 JimmyFortune 2 80+
(P J Makin) *lw: dwlt: hld up in last: sme prog 2f out: clsng on ldrs whn n.m.r 150yds out: r.o wl nr fin* **8/1**

-516 **4** *nk* **Deadly Encounter (IRE)**[7] 3375 3-8-9 79 FrederikTylicki(3) 6 82
(R A Fahey) *dwlt: sn chsd ldrs: prog on inner 3f out: rdn to dispute 2nd fr over 2f out: kpt on fnl f but a hld* **12/1**

-433 **5** *nk* **Inheritor (IRE)**[16] 3062 3-8-13 80 TomEaves 5 82
(B Smart) *t.k.h early: trckd ldrs and racd on outer: effrt over 2f out: disp 2nd over 1f out: nt qckn ins fnl f* **14/1**

-562 **6** *1 ¾* **Hail Promenader (IRE)**[23] 2841 3-9-0 81 RHills 4 78
(B W Hills) *hld up in 6th: shkn up 2f out: nt qckn over 1f out: kpt on same pce after* **14/1**

-216 **7** *1* **Standpoint**[28] 2696 3-8-12 79 RyanMoore 1 79+
(Sir Michael Stoute) *trckd ldr: rdn 2f out: losing pl whn tightened up last 150yds: eased* **5/1**[3]

1-12 **8** *2 ¼* **Floor Show**[49] 2072 3-9-1 82 TedDurcan 3 71
(E S McMahon) *hld up in last pair: rdn and hanging 2f out: no prog and btn after* **9/2**[2]

1m 29.05s (-0.45) **Going Correction** -0.15s/f (Firm) **8** Ran SP% **118.4**
Speed ratings (Par 104): **96,94,94,94,94 92,90,88**
toteswingers: 1&2 £2.90, 1&3 £5.10, 2&3 £4.20 CSF £15.41 CT £75.68 TOTE £5.30: £1.80, £1.30, £1.90; EX 16.90.

Owner Amblestock Partnership **Bred** Miss Laura G F Ferguson **Trained** East Everleigh, Wilts

FOCUS
A decent handicap. The winner got another uncontested lead, but remains progressive and the form looks good, despite getting somewhat messy in behind.

NOTEBOOK
Cyflymder(IRE), whose stable had won two of the last three runnings of this event, made all to land the hat-trick and is clearly right at the top of his game. Now 4lb higher than when successful at Newmarket a fortnight previously, he was well drawn for one who likes to lead and showed a turn of foot when asked to win the race nearing the final furlong. He has been transformed since joining the stable this season, his success is made more meritorious as he was conceding weight all around and it is hard to gauge just how far he may progress. (tchd 11-2)

Maswerte(IRE) won readily on his seasonal and handicap debut at Newbury 23 days earlier. 6lb higher, he settled just off the winner through the early parts yet failed to settle nearly as well as that rival. He had to wait for his challenge down the home straight, but really got caught out when Cyflymder quickened up. He kept on inside the final furlong and was not beaten far, so with few miles on the clock it is safe to assume the best of him has yet to be seen. (op 5-2)

Santefisio ◆ was 1lb better off with the winner for a short-head defeat at Newmarket last time. He had ground to make up 3f out, but was motoring inside the final furlong and would have gone very close with a better passage. He too is lightly raced and compensation should not be far off, but a more positive ride now looks in order. Official explanation: jockey said gelding was denied a clear run (op 11-2 tchd 5-1)

Deadly Encounter(IRE) had to be ridden from the gates, but emerged with his challenge as a gap opened on the far rail and enjoyed this return to a more galloping track. (op 14-1)

Inheritor(IRE), back down in trip, made his challenge more towards the middle down the home straight and posted a respectable effort. (op 9-1)

Hail Promenader(IRE) was 1lb better off with Deadly Encounter for a neck beating at Haydock, but was ridden more patiently this time and may need more use made of him. (op 12-1 tchd 11-1)

Standpoint was suited by this better ground and got a positive ride, but was held prior to being eased off with something looking to go amiss. (op 6-1 tchd 13-2 and 7-1 in places)

Floor Show, returning from a 49-day break, was 3lb higher and never looked that happy on this return to a quick surface. (op 11-2 tchd 6-1)

3644 CHARLES LEAHY MEMORIAL H'CAP 1m 2f 7y
5:30 (5:30) (Class 4) (0-85,85) 3-Y-0 **£6,476** (£1,927; £963; £481) **Stalls** High

Form RPR

-123 **1** **Sandor**[17] 3026 3-9-7 85 JimmyFortune 6 94
(P J Makin) *trckd ldng pair: rdn 3f out: wnt 2nd 2f out: sustained chal u.p fnl f: led last strides* **9/1**

55-3 **2** *nk* **Nbhan (USA)**[22] 2892 3-8-8 72 C-PLemaire 3 80
(L M Cumani) *led to over 5f out: trckd ldr: led again over 2f out: drvn and hrd pressed fnl f: kpt on but worn down last strides* **11/2**[3]

-035 **3** *1* **Call It On (IRE)**[21] 2935 3-9-4 82 TPQueally 1 88+
(M H Tompkins) *hld up in last trio: effrt on outer over 2f out: hanging and nt qckn wl over 1f out: styd on to take 3rd jst ins fnl f: clsng at fin* **7/1**

621 **4** *2 ½* **Senses (USA)**[30] 2640 3-9-0 78 RyanMoore 7 79
(J Noseda) *lw: trckd ldng trio: shkn up 3f out: hanging and nt qckn 2f out: one pce after* **11/4**[2]

61-3 **5** *2* **Raaeidd (IRE)**[52] 1992 3-9-4 82 NCallan 5 79
(M A Jarvis) *lw: hld up bhd ldrs: effrt on outer to chse ldng pair 2f out: rdn and nt qckn over 1f out: fdd* **2/1**[1]

600 **6** *hd* **Equipe De Nuit**[28] 2701 3-8-10 74 RoystonFfrench 2 71
(S C Williams) *hld up in last: rdn 3f out: struggling and no prog tl styd on ins fnl f* **33/1**

304 **7** *4 ½* **Statute Book (IRE)**[8] 3358 3-8-12 76 RichardHughes 8 64
(S Kirk) *pressed ldr: led over 5f out to over 2f out: sn btn: eased over 1f out* **25/1**

5-33 **8** *3 ½* **Tiger Flash**[70] 1515 3-8-9 73 RHills 4 54
(W J Haggas) *s.i.s and rousted along early: then t.k.h and hld up: wknd tamely fr 3f out* **8/1**

2m 8.92s (-1.58) **Going Correction** -0.15s/f (Firm) **8** Ran SP% **115.8**
Speed ratings (Par 102): **100,99,98,96,95 95,91,88**
toteswingers: 1&2 £8.40, 1&3 £6.90, 2&3 £7.20 CSF £58.20 CT £370.39 TOTE £8.60: £2.30, £2.20, £2.10; EX 30.80 Place 6: £14.53 Place 5: £9.77.

Owner Keith And Brian Brackpool **Bred** Southcourt Stud **Trained** Ogbourne Maisey, Wilts

FOCUS
A very interesting handicap, run at a fair pace but considerably slower than the big race. The form is sound with the first three close to form.

Tiger Flash Official explanation: jockey said colt hung badly right
T/Jkpt: £6,119.00 to a £1 stake. Pool: £25,855.00. 3.00 winning tickets. T/Plt: £22.70 to a £1 stake. Pool: £176,594.00. 5,660.11 winning tickets. T/Qpdt: £10.80 to a £1 stake. Pool: £7,202.00. 489.96 winning tickets. JN

3645 - 3647a (Foreign Racing) - See Raceform Interactive

887 DEAUVILLE (R-H)

Saturday, July 4

OFFICIAL GOING: All-weather - standard; turf course - good to soft

3648a **PRIX YACOWLEF (LISTED RACE) (UNRACED)** **5f**
12:45 (12:47) 2-Y-O **£26,699** (£10,680; £8,010; £5,340; £2,670)

RPR

1 **Sorciere (IRE)** 2-8-13 .... YLerner 1 96
(C Lerner, France) **92/10**[3]

2 1 ½ **Special Duty** 2-8-13 .... SPasquier 3 91
(Mme C Head-Maarek, France) **13/10**[1]

3 1 ½ **Mata Keranjang (USA)** 2-9-2 .... CSoumillon 5 88
(P F I Cole) *prom: pushed along 2f out: drvn and 2nd 1 1/2f out: rdn and kpt on one pce* **19/5**[2]

4 shd **Coriante (FR)** 2-8-13 .... MickaelForest 8 85
(C Boutin, France)

5 hd **Lucky Like (FR)** 2-9-2 .... TThulliez 7 87
(E J O'Neill) *missed break and last: pushed along on outside 2f out: styd on but n.d* **28/1**

6 snk **Constant Lover (IRE)** 2-9-2 .... GBenoist 6 87
(Robert Collet, France)

7 ½ **Around Me (IRE)** 2-8-13 .... OPeslier 4 82
(Robert Collet, France)

8 ¾ **Dangerous Cat (IRE)** 2-8-13 .... MGuyon 9 79
(Mario Hofer, Germany)

9 ¾ **Rosas A Sandra (IRE)** 2-8-13 .... GMosse 2 76?
(C Laffon-Parias, France)

10 1 ½ **La Somome** 2-8-13 .... TJarnet 10 71
(B De Montzey, France)

58.60 secs (1.10) **10** Ran SP% **77.6**
PARI-MUTUEL: WIN 10.20; PL 1.70, 1.10, 1.30; DF 8.70.
Owner Lady O'Reilly **Bred** Petra Bloodstock Agency Ltd **Trained** France

NOTEBOOK
Mata Keranjang(USA), making his debut in this Listed race for newcomers, ran well and is obviously quite well thought-of, having been given an entry in the Gimcrack.
Lucky Like(FR) ran pretty well on this debut, especially considering he missed the break.

3649a **PRIX DE SAINT-PATRICK (LISTED RACE) (C&G) (ROUND)** **1m (R)**
1:15 (1:15) 3-Y-O **£26,699** (£10,680; £8,010; £5,340; £2,670)

RPR

1 **Donativum**[17] 3011 3-8-12 .... LDettori 4 103
(Saeed Bin Suroor) *hld up: 8th and pushed along st: r.o steadily fr over 1 1/2f out to ld cl home: drvn out* **12/5**[1]

2 snk **Polarix**[57] 1858 3-8-12 .... MGuyon 2 103
(H-A Pantall, France)

3 ¾ **Mantoro (GER)**[55] 1915 3-8-12 .... GMosse 1 101
(A De Royer-Dupre, France)

4 hd **Broken In Light (FR)**[27] 2755 3-9-2 ....(b) SPasquier 3 105
(T Larriviere, France)

5 ½ **Glamstar (FR)**[27] 2756 3-8-12 ....(b) IMendizabal 6 99
(J-C Rouget, France)

6 3 **Rock Of Nassau (FR)**[17] 3-8-12 .... DBonilla 8 92
(F Head, France)

7 2 **Partner Shift (IRE)**[51] 3-8-12 .... OPeslier 5 88
(H-A Pantall, France)

8 1 ½ **Silverside (USA)**[27] 2755 3-8-12 .... CSoumillon 7 84
(M Delcher-Sanchez, Spain)

9 1 ½ **Sea Fight (USA)**[35] 3-8-12 .... TThulliez 9 81
(N Clement, France)

1m 41.9s (0.90) **9** Ran SP% **29.4**
PARI-MUTUEL: WIN 3.40; PL 1.70, 3.20, 1.50; DF 30.70.
Owner Godolphin **Bred** Stratford Place Stud **Trained** Newmarket, Suffolk

NOTEBOOK
Donativum, who won the Breeders' Cup Juvenile Turf last season, got in here without a penalty and took full advantage. He only just got there but connections deserve credit for some shrewd placing.

3604 HAMBURG (R-H)

Saturday, July 4

OFFICIAL GOING: Good

3650a **LOTTO HAMBURG TROPHY (GROUP 3)** **6f**
4:45 (5:03) 3-Y-O+ **£38,835** (£17,476; £8,738; £4,854; £2,913)

RPR

1 **Etoile Nocturne (FR)**[33] 5-8-13 .... WMongil 6 104
(W Baltromei, Germany) *sn led: strly chal 1 1/2f out: fnd more fnl stages: kpt on wl* **37/10**

2 ¾ **Lips Arrow (GER)**[21] 4-8-13 .... ASuborics 5 102
(Andreas Lowe, Germany) *in tch: r.o to go 2nd 2f out: strly chal ldr 1 1/2f out: r.o tl no ex fnl 100yds* **87/10**

3 2 **Glad Sky**[21] 3-8-10 .... DPorcu 2 99
(M Rulec, Germany) *a.p: no ex cl home* **32/5**

4 shd **Contat (GER)**[35] 2513 6-9-4 .... RJuracek 7 101
(P Vovcenko, Germany) *sn cl up: effrt 1 1/2f out: kpt on but nt chal ldrs* **23/10**[1]

5 1 ¾ **Key To Pleasure (GER)**[21] 9-9-0 .... AHelfenbein 1 91
(Mario Hofer, Germany) *racd in last to 2f out: styd on at one pce* **94/10**

6 ½ **Shinko's Best (IRE)**[21] 8-9-2 .... HGrewe 2 92
(A Kleinkorres, Germany) *cl up to 1/2-way: wknd fr 2 1/2f out* **18/5**[3]

7 shd **Calrissian (GER)**[32] 5-9-4 .... EPedroza 6 94
(F Reuterskiold, Sweden) *hmpd s: a in rr* **31/10**[2]

1m 10.25s (-2.44) **7** Ran SP% **131.1**
WFA 3 from 4yo+ 6lb
(Including 10 Euros stake): WIN 47; PL 20, 24, 21; SF 376.
Owner Rennstall Gestut Hachtsee **Bred** Scea Haras De St Pair Du Mont **Trained** Germany

3144 AYR (L-H)

Sunday, July 5

OFFICIAL GOING: Good (good to firm in places, 8.3)
Rail realignment increased distances on round course by 15yards.
Wind: Fresh, half against Weather: Cloudy, sunny intervals

3651 **TOTEPLACEPOT H'CAP** **6f**
2:10 (2:13) (Class 6) (0-60,59) 3-Y-O **£2,266** (£674; £337; £168) **Stalls** Low

Form RPR

0-05 1 **Secret City (IRE)**[26] 2786 3-9-1 **56** ....(b) DanielTudhope 11 59
(R Bastiman) *mde all: rdn over 2f out: hld on wl fnl f* **9/2**[1]

2 nk **Blackwell Nation (IRE)**[30] 2687 3-9-1 **56** .... RoystonFfrench 3 58
(Adrian McGuinness, Ire) *prom: effrt over 2f out: kpt on wl fnl f* **9/2**[1]

3460 3 shd **Ba Globetrotter**[10] 3305 3-8-5 **46** .... FrancisNorton 8 48
(M R Channon) *prom: outpcd over 2f out: r.o fnl f: no ex nr fin* **11/2**[2]

0-36 4 3 **Scrapper Smith (IRE)**[16] 3096 3-9-3 **58** .... PJMcDonald 2 50
(A C Whillans) *hld up: hdwy over 1f out: kpt on fnl f: nt rch ldrs* **25/1**

504 5 1 **Moneysupermarket (IRE)**[29] 2700 3-9-1 **59** .... FrederikTylicki[(3)] 4 48
(Patrick Morris) *chsd wnr tl no ex appr fnl f* **20/1**

-530 6 nse **Lucky Buddha**[54] 1969 3-9-2 **57** .... PhillipMakin 9 46
(Jedd O'Keeffe) *dwlt: bhd tl hdwy over 1f out: nvr rchd ldrs* **9/2**[1]

0-35 7 2 ¼ **Lady Zena**[33] 2581 3-8-4 **45** ....(b) DaleGibson 10 27
(M W Easterby) *t.k.h: sn chsng ldrs: hung bdly lft appr fnl f: sn btn* **14/1**

3643 8 3 ½ **Pedregal**[17] 3063 3-8-1 **45** .... KellyHarrison[(3)] 1 15
(J S Goldie) *hld up on ins: rdn 2f out: nvr rchd ldrs* **8/1**[3]

6060 9 1 ¾ **Wee Bizzom**[37] 2450 3-7-11 **45** .... BillyCray[(7)] 7 10
(A Berry) *bhd and sn drvn along: nvr on terms* **100/1**

0000 10 1 ¾ **Bold Bomber**[22] 2918 3-8-9 **50** .... PaulMulrennan 12 9
(Paul Green) *t.k.h: hld up on outside: rdn over 2f out: sn wknd* **9/2**[1]

06-0 11 ¾ **Fifer (IRE)**[54] 1950 3-8-0 **46** .... JamieKyne[(5)] 5 3
(Patrick Morris) *in tch: rdn over 2f out: lost pl wl over 1f out* **50/1**

1m 11.11s (-2.49) **Going Correction** -0.45s/f (Firm) **11** Ran SP% **117.4**
Speed ratings (Par 98): **98,97,97,93,92 92,89,84,82,79 78**
toteswingers: 1&2 £7.30, 1&3 £8.00, 2&3 £6.70 CSF £23.70 CT £116.31 TOTE £5.60: £2.20, £2.60, £2.00; EX 30.90.
Owner Ms M Austerfield **Bred** Miss Karen Theobald **Trained** Cowthorpe, N Yorks

FOCUS
A maiden handicap in all but name.
Lucky Buddha Official explanation: jockey said gelding hung badly left
Pedregal Official explanation: jockey said gelding hung right; trainer said gelding had a breathing problem
Bold Bomber Official explanation: vet said colt finished jarred up

3652 **UNISON CELEBRATING CUBA'S HEALTH SERVICE 50TH MEDIAN AUCTION MAIDEN STKS** **7f 50y**
2:40 (2:41) (Class 5) 2-Y-O **£2,914** (£867; £433; £216) **Stalls** Low

Form RPR

3 1 **Tukitinyasok (IRE)**[15] 3170 2-8-12 0 .... SladeO'Hara[(5)] 1 80
(R F Fisher) *mde all: rdn over 2f out: jnd over 1f out: kpt on gamely* **7/2**[2]

4 2 ½ **Layla's Boy**[18] 3017 2-9-0 0 .... FrederikTylicki[(3)] 2 79
(R A Fahey) *cl up: effrt and ev ch over 1f out: kpt on fnl f: hld nr fin* **11/2**

53 3 8 **Cambuslang (IRE)**[51] 2027 2-9-3 0 .... TomEaves 5 59
(I Semple) *hld up: hdwy over 2f out: no imp fr over 1f out* **25/1**

03 4 2 ½ **Aattash (IRE)**[24] 2839 2-9-3 0 .... TonyCulhane 6 53
(M R Channon) *t.k.h: cl up: rdn over 2f out: sn one pce* **4/1**[3]

26 5 3 **Count Bertoni (IRE)**[30] 2663 2-9-3 0 .... MickyFenton 4 45
(T P Tate) *t.k.h: hld up in tch: effrt and edgd rt over 2f out: sn outpcd* **15/8**[1]

44 6 shd **Abbi Jicaro**[9] 3332 2-8-12 0 .... SilvestreDeSousa 7 40
(Mrs L Williamson) *hld up: rdn over 2f out: sn btn* **66/1**

7 ½ **Ibn Hiyyan (USA)** 2-9-3 0 .... RoystonFfrench 8 44
(M Johnston) *prom on outside: rdn and rn green 3f out: wknd over 2f out* **6/1**

1m 32.79s (-0.61) **Going Correction** -0.25s/f (Firm) **7** Ran SP% **112.0**
Speed ratings (Par 94): **93,92,83,80,77 76,76**
toteswingers: 1&2 £3.60, 1&3 £9.30, 2&3 £7.10 CSF £21.86 TOTE £5.20: £2.50, £2.50; EX 23.40.
Owner Des Johnston **Bred** Newlands House Stud **Trained** Ulverston, Cumbria

FOCUS
A fair juvenile maiden. The first two came well clear.

NOTEBOOK
Tukitinyasok(IRE) made all in dogged fashion to open his account at the second attempt and land some nice bets in the process. He did not have much to find on the level of his pleasing Redcar debut 15 days earlier and that experience had clearly taught him well. He remains open to a bit more improvement and should get another furlong before the year is out. (op 6-1)
Layla's Boy ◆ stepped up nicely on his debut fourth at Hamilton and appreciated the extra furlong, as his pedigree suggested he would. He found the winner too resolute, but finished well clear of the rest and can be placed to find compensation. (op 7-1)
Cambuslang(IRE) looked a possible danger when making up his ground from off the pace, but failed to see out this longer trip like the first pair. A drop back to 6f should see him get closer and he now has the option of nurseries. (op 20-1)
Aattash(IRE) again took time to settle, but failed to raise his game for the step up a furlong and is now looking somewhat exposed. He now qualifies for nurseries. (op 3-1)
Count Bertoni(IRE), up in trip, was unlucky to be hampered at the start at Doncaster last time out, but he got behind of his own accord here and now has something prove with his attitude. (op 9-4)
Abbi Jicaro Official explanation: jockey said filly hung right
Ibn Hiyyan(USA) cost $400,000 as a yearling and boasts a classy US pedigree. He proved very easy to back, however, and despite not being helped by having to race wide from his outside stall, still put in a disappointing debut display. Official explanation: jockey said colt hung right and failed to handle the bend (op 4-1 tchd 13-2)

3653 **TOTESUPER7 H'CAP** **1m 1f 20y**
3:10 (3:12) (Class 6) (0-65,65) 4-Y-O+ **£2,266** (£674; £337; £168) **Stalls** Low

Form RPR

61 1 **Ensnare**[6] 3470 4-9-3 **61** 6ex .... StephenDonohoe 10 71+
(Ian Williams) *trckd ldrs: effrt over 2f out: led and edgd lft ins fnl f: r.o wl* **5/1**[2]

3005 2 ¾ **Diamond Lass (IRE)**[33] 2569 4-8-12 **59** .... FrederikTylicki[(3)] 7 66
(R A Fahey) *prom: rdn over 2f out: styd on wl fnl f: tk 2nd cl home* **5/1**[2]

0004 3 shd **Primo Way**[16] 3098 8-8-11 **55** .... DuranFentiman 6 62+
(D A Nolan) *hld up: hdwy over 1f out: wnt 2nd ins fnl f: kpt on u.p* **20/1**

-212 4 2 ½ **Confide In Me**[24] 2859 5-9-3 **61** ....(t) RoystonFfrench 1 63
(G A Butler) *led after 1f: rdn over 2f out: hdd ins fnl f: one pce* **7/2**[1]

052 **5** ½ **Red Skipper (IRE)**[15] 3150 4-9-0 **58** DavidAllan 14 59
(N Wilson) *led 1f: pressed ldr: rdn over 2f out: no ex ent fnl f* **8/1**[3]
-042 **6** nse **Apache Nation (IRE)**[17] 3070 6-8-13 **57** PhillipMakin 4 58
(M Dods) *midfield: outpcd over 2f out: r.o fnl f* **8/1**[3]
-343 **7** shd **Willyn (IRE)**[16] 3098 4-8-8 **52** (p) DanielTudhope 12 52
(J S Goldie) *in tch: outpcd over 2f out: rallied fnl f: no imp* **17/2**
00-3 **8** ½ **Chin Wag (IRE)**[16] 3094 5-8-7 **56** (p) GaryBartley(5) 2 55
(J S Goldie) *hld up: hdwy over 2f out: no imp over 1f out* **10/1**
0030 **9** 1¾ **Wilmington**[6] 3448 5-8-1 **50** (p) JamieKyne(5) 5 46
(Mrs J C McGregor) *hld up: effrt on outside over 2f out: nvr able to chal* **40/1**
6000 **10** hd **King Of Rhythm (IRE)**[11] 3264 6-8-13 **57** DNolan 8 52
(D Carroll) *midfield: effrt over 2f out: no ex over 1f out* **9/1**
5500 **11** ½ **Bourse (IRE)**[31] 2626 4-9-0 **58** (p) TomEaves 13 52
(A G Foster) *towards rr: drvn 1/2-way: nvr on terms* **20/1**
0-00 **12** 2 **Boy Dancer (IRE)**[25] 2804 6-9-0 **58** GrahamGibbons 11 48
(J J Quinn) *in tch tl rdn and wknd fr 2f out* **16/1**
0-00 **13** dist **Jamieson Gold (IRE)**[5] 3481 6-9-7 **65** PaulMulrennan 3 —
(Miss L A Perratt) *dwlt: a bhd: lost tch fr over 3f out: virtually p.u* **50/1**

1m 56.18s (-2.22) **Going Correction** -0.25s/f (Firm) **13** Ran SP% **127.2**
Speed ratings (Par 101): **99,98,98,96,95 95,95,95,93,93 92,91,—**
toteswingers: 1&2 £8.00, 1&3 £40.40, 2&3 £46.70 CSF £31.12 CT £483.75 TOTE £6.60: £2.30, £2.70, £7.90; EX 46.70.
Owner C Owen **Bred** Cheveley Park Stud Ltd **Trained** Portway, Worcs
FOCUS
A moderate handicap.

3654 TOTESWINGER H'CAP — 1m 5f 13y
3:40 (3:40) (Class 5) (0-70,69) 4-Y-0+ **£3,238** (£963; £481; £240) **Stalls** Low

Form RPR
1301 **1** **Forrest Flyer (IRE)**[16] 3107 5-9-4 **66** PhillipMakin 1 71
(I Semple) *trckd ldrs: effrt over 2f out: led ins fnl f: drvn out* **7/1**
0-14 **2** nk **Ifatfirst (IRE)**[16] 3095 6-9-1 **63** DanielTudhope 4 68
(J S Goldie) *hld up: hdwy over 2f out: kpt on wl fnl f: jst hld* **6/1**[3]
000/ **3** nk **Catskill**[22] 4114 7-8-5 **53** (b) RoystonFfrench 8 58
(Adrian McGuinness, Ire) *prom: outpcd over 2f out: rallied over 1f out: kpt on fin* **4/1**[2]
0203 **4** 1 **Merrion Tiger (IRE)**[17] 3059 4-9-0 **62** TomEaves 3 65
(A G Foster) *set stdy pce: niggled fr 1/2-way: rdn over 2f out: hdd ins fnl f: one pce* **12/1**
-422 **5** 1¼ **Fenners (USA)**[18] 3023 6-8-5 **53** DaleGibson 10 54
(M W Easterby) *midfield: niggled 1/2-way: outpcd over 2f out: kpt on u.p fnl f: nrst fin* **7/1**
0165 **6** 1 **Herrera (IRE)**[23] 2895 4-9-4 **69** FrederikTylicki(3) 6 69
(R A Fahey) *trckd ldr: rdn over 3f out: one pce fnl f* **5/2**[1]
400/ **7** 4 **Eye Candy (IRE)**[27] 2511 8-8-2 **55** (b) JamieKyne(5) 9 49
(Mrs Sandra McCarthy, Ire) *hld up on outside: stdy hdwy to trck ldrs over 3f out: rdn over 2f out: sn outpcd* **14/1**
1601 **8** shd **Ibrox (IRE)**[16] 3098 4-9-5 **67** SilvestreDeSousa 5 61
(A D Brown) *in tch: rdn over 2f out: wknd fnl f* **13/2**
040 **9** 10 **Oh Landino (GER)**[16] 3098 4-8-2 **50** oh5 DuranFentiman 7 29
(P Monteith) *hld up: rdn over 3f out: btn fnl 2f* **80/1**

2m 54.01s (0.01) **Going Correction** -0.25s/f (Firm) **9** Ran SP% **116.8**
Speed ratings (Par 103): **97,96,96,96,95 94,92,92,85**
toteswingers: 1&2 £7.60, 1&3 £8.80, 2&3 £5.90 CSF £49.09 CT £192.55 TOTE £6.70: £2.90, £1.50, £1.80; EX 44.60.
Owner Mrs Camille Macdonald **Bred** Philip Lau **Trained** Carluke, S Lanarks
FOCUS
A competitive staying handicap for the class, run at a routine sort of gallop.

3655 BET TOTEPOOL AT TOTESPORT.COM H'CAP — 7f 50y
4:10 (4:11) (Class 5) (0-70,67) 3-Y-0+ **£2,914** (£867; £433; £216) **Stalls** Low

Form RPR
2344 **1** **Kargan (IRE)**[16] 3105 4-9-5 **58** GrahamGibbons 7 67
(A G Foster) *midfield: effrt over 2f out: led ins fnl f: hld on wl* **3/1**[2]
0465 **2** hd **Compton's Eleven**[8] 3401 8-10-0 **67** TonyCulhane 3 75
(M R Channon) *trckd ldrs: effrt 2f out: ev ch and rdn ins fnl f: nt go past* **3/1**[2]
00-1 **3** 2½ **Tom Tower (IRE)**[16] 3094 5-9-3 **61** JamieKyne(5) 5 63
(A C Whillans) *led: rdn over 2f out: hdd ins fnl f: kpt on same pce* **5/2**[1]
0046 **4** 1¾ **Stoic Leader (IRE)**[6] 3448 9-9-12 **65** SladeO'Hara 8 62
(R F Fisher) *pressed ldr: rdn over 2f out: one pce over 1f out* **12/1**
6-60 **5** 3¼ **Another Decree**[9] 3354 4-9-12 **65** PhillipMakin 2 53
(M Dods) *midfield: rdn and edgd lft 2f out: sn no imp* **9/1**
0120 **6** 2¾ **Botham (USA)**[16] 3092 5-9-2 **55** DanielTudhope 10 36
(J S Goldie) *hld up: rdn over 2f out: nvr able to chal* **8/1**[3]
00-0 **7** 1¾ **Mangano**[16] 3105 5-8-2 **48** oh3 BillyCray(7) 6 24
(A Berry) *hld up: rdn and hung lft over 2f out: sn btn* **66/1**
60-0 **8** 6 **James Street (IRE)**[75] 1438 6-8-2 **48** oh3 (v) AndrewHeffernan(7) 9 8
(Peter Grayson) *towards rr: rdn 3f out: nvr on terms* **80/1**
06-0 **9** ½ **Prospect Court**[15] 3148 7-9-12 **65** PaulMulrennan 1 24
(A C Whillans) *bhd: drvn over 3f out: sn btn* **18/1**
1-00 **10** 17 **Shunkawakhan (IRE)**[6] 3448 6-9-11 **64** (p) TomEaves 4 —
(Miss L A Perratt) *t.k.h: trckd ldrs tl rdn and wknd fr over 2f out* **25/1**

1m 31.06s (-2.34) **Going Correction** -0.25s/f (Firm) **10** Ran SP% **119.2**
Speed ratings (Par 103): **103,102,99,97,94 91,89,82,81,62**
toteswingers: 1&2 £3.00, 1&3 £3.20, 2&3 £3.50 CSF £12.69 CT £25.69 TOTE £4.30: £1.80, £1.50, £1.50; EX 13.20.
Owner M Sawers **Bred** His Highness The Aga Khan's Studs S C **Trained** Haddington, East Lothian
FOCUS
This was run at a fair pace, but nothing got involved from off the pace.
Mangano Official explanation: jockey said gelding hung left

3656 CAMPBELTOWN BAR STEWART SCOTT MEMORIAL H'CAP — 1m
4:40 (4:41) (Class 4) (0-85,85) 3-Y-0+ **£6,476** (£1,927; £963; £481) **Stalls** Low

Form RPR
40-1 **1** **Royal Destination (IRE)**[15] 3155 4-9-11 **82** DaleGibson 8 99+
(J Noseda) *chsd clr ldrs: effrt over 2f out: led ins fnl f: styd on wl u.p* **3/1**[1]
0004 **2** 1 **Cobo Bay**[17] 3067 4-9-9 **85** (b[1]) AmyRyan(5) 4 98
(K A Ryan) *pressed ldr: led over 2f out: hung rt and hdd ins fnl f: kpt on same pce* **11/2**
2401 **3** 4½ **White Deer (USA)**[19] 2998 5-9-9 **80** (v) SilvestreDeSousa 12 83
(G A Harker) *t.k.h: in tch: rdn over 2f out: rallied over 1f out: no imp fnl f* **4/1**[2]
0240 **4** 1¼ **Grand Diamond (IRE)**[6] 3448 5-8-9 **66** oh2 DanielTudhope 7 66+
(J S Goldie) *hld up: rdn and hdwy over 2f out: kpt on fnl f: nrst fin* **5/1**[3]

2130 **5** 1 **Ezdeyaad (USA)**[10] 3312 5-9-12 **83** PJMcDonald 11 80
(G A Swinbank) *led to over 2f out: rdn and one pce over 1f out* **5/1**[3]
6101 **6** 1¼ **Stellite**[16] 3097 9-8-8 **70** GaryBartley(5) 5 65
(J S Goldie) *hld up: effrt over 2f out: no imp over 1f out* **12/1**
0610 **7** 6 **Golden Penny**[11] 3265 4-9-3 **77** NeilBrown(3) 6 58
(A G Foster) *hld up: drvn over 3f out: nvr on terms* **16/1**
0060 **8** 2¾ **Blue Spinnaker (IRE)**[23] 2894 10-9-4 **75** PaulMulrennan 9 49
(M W Easterby) *hld up: rdn over 3f out: n.d* **12/1**
6000 **9** ½ **Defi (IRE)**[16] 3105 7-8-9 **66** oh21 DuranFentiman 2 39
(D A Nolan) *midfield: rdn over 2f out: nvr rchd ldrs* **150/1**
0045 **10** 5 **Cigalas**[16] 3094 4-8-9 **66** oh1 TomEaves 10 28
(Mrs J C McGregor) *in tch tl rdn and wknd over 2f out* **33/1**
552- **11** 10 **Hosanna**[263] 6730 3-8-0 **71** JamieKyne(5) 1 10
(J Barclay) *bhd: struggling over 3f out: sn wknd* **33/1**

1m 39.87s (-3.93) **Going Correction** -0.25s/f (Firm)
WFA 3 from 4yo+ 9lb **11** Ran SP% **121.5**
Speed ratings (Par 105): **109,108,103,102,101 100,94,91,90,85 75**
toteswingers: 1&2 £6.10, 1&3 £3.50, 2&3 £7.40 CSF £20.32 CT £70.31 TOTE £3.60: £1.80, £2.20, £2.20; EX 25.40.
Owner Vimal Khosla **Bred** Miss Deirdre Barry **Trained** Newmarket, Suffolk
FOCUS
This fair handicap was another race run at a sound pace where nothing landed a blow from behind.
Blue Spinnaker(IRE) Official explanation: jockey said gelding never travelled
Cigalas Official explanation: jockey said gelding was unsuited by the good to firm ground
Hosanna Official explanation: jockey said filly never travelled

3657 TOTEEXACTA AMATEUR RIDERS' H'CAP — 5f
5:10 (5:13) (Class 6) (0-60,59) 4-Y-0+ **£2,307** (£709; £354) **Stalls** Low

Form RPR
004 **1** **Ingleby Star (IRE)**[6] 3445 4-11-5 **57** (p) MrsCBartley 3 67
(N Wilson) *chsd ldr: rdn over 2f out: led ins fnl f: kpt on wl* **9/2**
0012 **2** ½ **Toy Top (USA)**[19] 3002 6-11-5 **57** (b) MissSBrotherton 4 65
(M Dods) *led to ins fnl f: kpt on same pce towards fin* **11/4**[1]
360- **3** 1 **Feeling Fresh (IRE)**[215] 7533 4-10-12 **57** MissACraven(7) 6 62+
(Paul Green) *s.i.s and wl bhd: gd hdwy centre over 1f out: fin wl* **10/1**
2560 **4** 1¾ **Conjecture**[30] 2660 7-11-2 **59** MissRBastiman(5) 7 57
(R Bastiman) *chsd ldrs: outpcd 2f out: kpt on u.p fnl f* **3/1**[2]
5550 **5** ½ **Handsinthemist (IRE)**[19] 3002 4-11-1 **53** MrSWalker 9 50
(P T Midgley) *in tch: rdn 2f out: one pce fnl f* **7/2**[3]
-030 **6** 1¼ **Strensall**[30] 2657 12-10-9 **52** MissVBarr(5) 5 44
(R E Barr) *prom tl rdn and no ex over 1f out* **16/1**
0400 **7** shd **Victory Spirit**[16] 3105 5-10-1 **46** ow1 (b) MrJMQuinlan(7) 2 38
(D A Nolan) *hld up in tch: edgd lft and no ex over 1f out* **18/1**
00-0 **8** 10 **Throw The Dice**[16] 3109 7-10-2 **45** MissMMullineaux(5) 8 —
(A Berry) *bhd and sn outpcd: no ch fr 1/2-way* **66/1**
0000 **U** **Coconut Moon**[6] 3445 7-10-0 **45** MissSarahRichardson(7) 1 —
(A Berry) *in tch: outpcd after 1f: sddle slipped 1/2-way: no imp whn uns rdr over 1f out* **25/1**

59.39 secs (-0.71) **Going Correction** -0.45s/f (Firm) **9** Ran SP% **117.6**
Speed ratings (Par 101): **87,86,84,81,81 79,78,62,—**
toteswingers: 1&2 £2.50, 1&3 £6.20, 2&3 £9.10 CSF £17.66 CT £118.65 TOTE £5.70: £1.60, £1.40, £3.40; EX 11.70 Place 6 £58.59, Place 5 £30.01.
Owner Renaissance Racing **Bred** Pat Cosgrove **Trained** Flaxton, N Yorks
FOCUS
A weak sprint, confined to amateur riders.
T/Jkpt: Not won. T/Plt: £264.10 to a £1 stake. Pool: £81,038.91. 224.00 winning tickets. T/Qpdt: £9.10 to a £1 stake. Pool: £5,863.57. 474.10 winning tickets. RY

3471 BRIGHTON (L-H)
Sunday, July 5

OFFICIAL GOING: Firm (good to firm in places; 9.0)
Wind: Moderate, half against Weather: Fine

3658 EUROPEAN BREEDERS FUND MEDIAN AUCTION MAIDEN STKS — 5f 213y
2:30 (2:31) (Class 5) 2-Y-O **£3,784** (£1,132; £566; £283) **Stalls** Low

Form RPR
326 **1** **Velvet Band**[20] 2972 2-8-12 MartinDwyer 2 75+
(P F I Cole) *mde all: rdn clr 1f out: eased nr fin* **11/10**[1]
520 **2** 2½ **Fly Silca Fly (IRE)**[15] 3138 2-8-12 SamHitchcott 4 67
(M R Channon) *chsd wnr: rdn 2f out: nt qckn appr fnl f* **11/10**[1]
0 **3** 1¾ **Panpiper**[8] 3403 2-9-3 GeorgeBaker 5 66
(G L Moore) *hld up in cl 3rd: brought alone middle to stands' side and effrt over 2f out: hrd rdn: one pce* **10/1**[2]
65 **4** 3¼ **Split The Pot (IRE)**[20] 2979 2-9-3 LPKeniry 1 57
(P R Chamings) *cl 4th tl outpcd fnl 2f* **12/1**[3]

1m 10.86s (0.66) **Going Correction** +0.05s/f (Good) **4** Ran SP% **112.0**
Speed ratings (Par 94): **97,93,91,87**
CSF £2.67 TOTE £1.80; EX 2.60.
Owner Denford Stud **Bred** Belgrave Bloodstock Ltd **Trained** Whatcombe, Oxon
FOCUS
A very ordinary juvenile contest, judged on the previous efforts of this quartet.
NOTEBOOK
Velvet Band, stepping back up to 6f, set off in front and never looked in any danger of being caught. It was a comfortable success but she will surely find things much more difficult next time, despite looking like a horse that enjoys getting her head down and battling. (tchd Evens and 5-4 in a place)
Fly Silca Fly(IRE) tracked the winner but could not get past her when push came to shove. (op 13-8 tchd 15-8)
Panpiper was moved towards the stands' side off the home bend but failed to get on terms. He rolled around under pressure, but it was only his second outing and was entitled to be inexperienced. The jockey reported after the race that his mount got a bit lonely away from the rest. (op 13-2)
Split The Pot(IRE) sat third of those that stands towards the far side but was unable to quicken when asked to. (tchd 10-1)

3659 KEW ELECTRICAL H'CAP — 6f 209y
3:00 (3:00) (Class 5) (0-75,74) 3-Y-0+ **£3,406** (£1,019; £509; £254; £126) **Stalls** Low

Form RPR
-402 **1** **My Learned Friend (IRE)**[12] 3243 5-9-13 **73** WilliamBuick 3 80
(A M Balding) *hld up in tch: a gng wl: led wl over 1f out: rdn out* **5/4**[1]
-050 **2** ¾ **Zebrano**[24] 2849 3-9-4 **72** AlanMunro 1 74
(Miss E C Lavelle) *in tch: nt clr run 2f out tl over 1f out: squeezed through to take 2nd 1f out: edgd lft: r.o: a hld* **12/1**

5015 **3** 1 3/4 **Golden Prospect**[11] 3283 5-8-11 **57** .... LiamJones 6 57
(J W Hills) *s.s: in rr: hmpd and rdn 2f out: squeezed through into 3rd whn carried lft 1f out: kpt on same pce* **5/1**[3]

5-10 **4** 8 **Hypnotic**[5] 3490 7-9-3 **63** .... RichardThomas 2 42
(Jim Best) *prom tl wknd over 1f out* **8/1**

-044 **5** nk **Pokfulham (IRE)**[10] 3305 3-8-2 **61** ow2 ....(v) MatthewDavies(5) 4 36
(A P Jarvis) *led tl over 2f out: rdn and rdr dropped rein: wknd over 1f out* **14/1**

0000 **6** 9 **Choreography**[37] 2434 6-10-0 **74** ....(p) PaulDoe 5 41
(Jim Best) *chsd ldrs: wnt 2nd over 4f out: led over 2f out tl wl over 1f out: 5th and wkng whn squeezed appr fnl f: eased down* **9/4**[2]

1m 22.53s (-0.57) **Going Correction** +0.05s/f (Good)
WFA 3 from 5yo+ 8lb **6** Ran SP% **117.4**
Speed ratings (Par 103): **105,104,102,93,92 82**
toteswingers: 1&2 £3.60, 1&3 £1.30, 2&3 £4.80 CSF £18.56 TOTE £2.50: £1.30, £4.60; EX 22.60.
Owner DR E Harris **Bred** B Kennedy **Trained** Kingsclere, Hants
■ Stewards' Enquiry : Alan Munro two-day ban: careless riding (Jul 19-20)

FOCUS
This was a modest handicap, despite a couple of the runners having an official mark in the 70s.
Golden Prospect Official explanation: jockey said gelding was denied a clear run

3660 DOWNS VIEW FARM MAIDEN STKS 7f 214y
3:30 (3:31) (Class 5) 3-Y-O **£3,532** (£1,057; £528; £264; £131) **Stalls** Low

Form RPR

534 **1** nse **Sunceleb (IRE)**[21] 2947 3-8-12 73 .... SteveDrowne 1 69
(H Morrison) *chsd clr ldr: clsd rapidly and led over 1f out: hrd rdn fnl f: hdd and bmpd nr fin: r.o wl* **2/1**[1]

60- **2** **Altimatum (USA)**[253] 6978 3-9-3 0 .... AlanMunro 3 74
(P F I Cole) *hld up off the pce in 3rd: rdn 3f out: drvn to chal 1f out: led and bmpd nr fin: all out* **4/1**

0625 **3** 6 **Cabernet Sauvignon**[12] 3238 3-9-3 70 ....(b[1]) GeorgeBaker 4 60
(J W Hills) *racd freely: led: sn 12 l clr: wandered and hdd over 1f out: no ex* **10/3**[3]

3 **4** 1/2 **Miss Kittyhawk (IRE)**[15] 3168 3-8-12 0 .... JimmyQuinn 2 54
(Rae Guest) *bhd: hdwy to press ldrs over 1f out: wknd fnl f* **9/4**[2]

5 7 **Whiterocks** 3-9-3 0 .... SamHitchcott 5 43
(M R Channon) *dwlt: hld up off the pce in 4th: rdn over 3f out: bhd fnl 2f* **20/1**

1m 37.5s (1.50) **Going Correction** +0.05s/f (Good) **5** Ran SP% **111.9**
Speed ratings (Par 100): **93,94,87,87,80**
CSF £12.64 TOTE £5.80: £2.90, £1.80; EX 18.20.
Owner Stonethorn Stud Farms Limited **Bred** Stonethorn Stud Farms Ltd **Trained** East Ilsley, Berks
■ Stewards' Enquiry : Alan Munro one-day ban: careless riding (Jul 21)

FOCUS
A small field lined up for this maiden, but it was still one of the more interesting races on the card. The stewards took a look into the placings as the first two came close, but let the result stand.
Cabernet Sauvignon Official explanation: jockey said colt ran too free

3661 SOUTHERN RAILWAY H'CAP 1m 1f 209y
4:00 (4:03) (Class 5) (0-70,65) 3-Y-O **£3,154** (£944; £472; £236; £117) **Stalls** High

Form RPR

6-00 **1** **Arcola (IRE)**[13] 3209 3-9-2 **60** .... ChrisCatlin 6 74
(D M Simcock) *dwlt: hld up in rr: rdn 4f out: hdwy to ld 2f out: drew clr and styd on wl: comf* **2/1**[1]

5342 **2** 7 **Rose Of Coma (IRE)**[10] 3314 3-8-10 **54** .... AdrianMcCarthy 1 54
(Miss Gay Kelleway) *t.k.h in 5th: effrt and hrd rdn 2f out: kpt on to take 2nd 1f out: no ch w wnr* **9/2**[2]

0-04 **3** 5 **Jumaana (IRE)**[24] 2865 3-9-3 **61** .... TPO'Shea 5 51
(J L Dunlop) *t.k.h: trckd ldr: led over 6f out tl 2f out: wknd and lost 2nd 1f out* **2/1**[1]

-000 **4** 3/4 **Pursuit Of Purpose**[36] 2489 3-8-5 **49** ....(b[1]) JimmyQuinn 2 38
(G L Moore) *plld hrd in 3rd: rdn over 2f out: sn btn* **14/1**

3-00 **5** 3/4 **Sussex Dancer (IRE)**[25] 2827 3-9-7 **65** .... SteveDrowne 7 52
(J A Osborne) *hld up in 4th: rdn over 2f out: wknd over 1f out* **11/2**[3]

0-06 **6** 11 **Mountain Forest (GER)**[32] 2605 3-8-4 **48** ....(t) WilliamBuick 3 13
(H Morrison) *led over 3f: wknd over 2f out* **11/1**

2m 4.02s (0.42) **Going Correction** +0.05s/f (Good) **6** Ran SP% **115.2**
Speed ratings (Par 103): **100,94,90,89,89 80**
toteswingers: 1&2 £2.20, 1&3 £1.90, 2&3 £1.90 CSF £11.97 TOTE £3.00: £1.90, £1.60; EX 12.50.
Owner Ali Saeed **Bred** Celbridge Estates Ltd **Trained** Newmarket, Suffolk

FOCUS
Virtually none of these came into this contest off the back of a decent effort so, apart from the winner, this is not a race to be following.
Arcola(IRE) Official explanation: trainer's rep said, regarding apparent improvement in form, that the filly was suited by the firm ground and step up in trip.
Mountain Forest(GER) Official explanation: jockey said gelding lost its action

3662 ARGUS H'CAP 7f 214y
4:30 (4:32) (Class 6) (0-65,66) 3-Y-O+ **£2,590** (£770; £385; £192) **Stalls** Low

Form RPR

0221 **1** **Lady Florence**[5] 3473 4-9-3 **54** 6ex .... LPKeniry 4 64
(A B Coogan) *mde all: rdn and hld on gamely fnl 2f: edgd lft: in control nr fin* **3/1**[1]

4503 **2** 3/4 **Daring Dream (GER)**[37] 2458 4-9-1 **57** ....(v) MatthewDavies(5) 5 65
(A P Jarvis) *chsd ldrs: drvn to chal over 1f out: kpt on: jst hld* **8/1**

50-2 **3** nk **Monashee Rock (IRE)**[11] 3258 4-10-1 **66** .... WilliamBuick 8 73
(M Salaman) *hld up in midfield: rdn over 2f out: styd on wl fnl f: clsng at fin* **4/1**[2]

3055 **4** 4 **Fairly Honest**[12] 3241 5-8-6 **48** .... WilliamCarson(5) 1 46
(P W Hiatt) *chsd wnr tl 2f out: sn outpcd* **16/1**

-540 **5** nse **Golden Flight (IRE)**[30] 2685 3-9-5 **65** .... GeorgeBaker 10 63
(J W Hills) *hld up towards rr: rdn over 2f out: styd on fnl f* **15/2**

0056 **6** 2 1/2 **Dynamo Dave (USA)**[11] 3259 4-8-9 **46** oh1 .... SteveDrowne 2 38
(M D I Usher) *towards rr: effrt over 2f out: nt pce to chal* **33/1**

0000 **7** 3 3/4 **Shake On It**[16] 3112 5-9-1 **57** ....(t) MCGeran(5) 9 41
(M R Hoad) *t.k.h towards rr: rdn over 2f out: n.d* **16/1**

211U **8** 3 1/2 **Annes Rocket (IRE)**[25] 2806 4-8-13 **57** .... GemmaElford(7) 6 33
(J C Fox) *s.v.s: plld hrd and anchored in detached last: mod effrt and unbalanced 3f out: n.d* **8/1**

3004 **9** 3/4 **Mystic Touch**[21] 2950 3-8-13 **59** .... AlanMunro 7 33
(Miss E C Lavelle) *hld up in 5th: rdn and wknd 2f out* **13/2**[3]

1200 **10** 4 **Mr Fantozzi (IRE)**[17] 3070 4-9-9 **60** ....(p) ChrisCatlin 3 25
(D Donovan) *prom: rdn over 2f out: sn wknd* **15/2**

1m 36.35s (0.35) **Going Correction** +0.05s/f (Good)
WFA 3 from 4yo+ 9lb **10** Ran SP% **118.8**
Speed ratings (Par 101): **100,99,98,94,94 92,88,85,84,80**
toteswingers: 1&2 £4.40, 1&3 £4.20, 2&3 £7.70 CSF £28.24 CT £98.89 TOTE £3.80: £1.90, £2.70, £1.40; EX 34.00 Trifecta £61.60 Pool: £465.34 - 5.59 winning units.
Owner A B Coogan **Bred** The National Stud **Trained** Soham, Cambs

FOCUS
A modest but open-looking handicap.
Shake On It Official explanation: jockey said gelding ran too free

3663 SUSSEX LIFE H'CAP 5f 59y
5:00 (5:00) (Class 6) (0-65,69) 3-Y-O **£2,590** (£770; £385; £192) **Stalls** Low

Form RPR

2211 **1** **Itsher**[1] 3625 3-9-9 **69** 12ex ....(b) WilliamCarson(5) 7 75
(S C Williams) *sn last: gd hdwy in centre over 1f out: r.o to ld fnl 50yds* **4/7**[1]

4653 **2** 1/2 **Halaak (USA)**[16] 3118 3-9-7 **62** ....(b) ChrisCatlin 4 66
(D M Simcock) *settled in 5th: hdwy 2f out: led over 1f out: hrd rdn fnl f: hdd and nt qckn fnl 50yds* **5/1**[2]

5040 **3** 4 **Bees River (IRE)**[20] 2973 3-8-8 **54** ....(v) MatthewDavies(5) 1 44
(A P Jarvis) *led tl over 1f out: no ex fnl f* **8/1**[3]

5-60 **4** 1 1/4 **Equinity**[10] 3299 3-8-9 **50** .... LiamJones 6 35
(J Pearce) *towards rr: effrt over 2f out: no imp* **18/1**

4050 **5** 2 3/4 **Thumberlina**[47] 2162 3-8-4 **45** ....(p) CatherineGannon 3 20
(Mrs C A Dunnett) *prom tl wknd over 1f out* **16/1**

35-0 **6** 7 **Agnes Love**[15] 3162 3-8-12 **53** .... J-PGuillambert 5 3
(J Akehurst) *in tch in 4th: rdn over 2f out: wknd over 1f out: eased wn btn fnl f* **14/1**

3606 **7** 28 **Pressed For Time (IRE)**[6] 3465 3-9-2 **57** ....(bt[1]) EdwardCreighton 2 —
(E J Creighton) *pressed ldr tl wknd qckly 2f out: bhd and eased fnl f* **20/1**

62.86 secs (0.56) **Going Correction** +0.05s/f (Good) **7** Ran SP% **114.0**
Speed ratings (Par 98): **97,96,89,87,83 72,27**
toteswingers: 1&2 £1.40, 1&3 £2.50, 2&3 £2.70 CSF £3.78 TOTE £1.50: £1.20, £1.80; EX 2.70 Place 6 £14.07, Place 5 £6.36.
Owner Itsus **Bred** Old Mill Stud And Partners **Trained** Newmarket, Suffolk

FOCUS
This race revolved around how Itsher performed under a 12lb penalty after her emphatic success the previous day at Leicester.
Pressed For Time(IRE) Official explanation: jockey said filly lost its action
T/Plt: £20.90 to a £1 stake. Pool: £58,731.97. 2,046.74 winning tickets. T/Qpdt: £5.00 to a £1 stake. Pool: £3,869.60. 568.10 winning tickets. LM

3664 - 3666a (Foreign Racing) - See Raceform Interactive

[3202] CHANTILLY (R-H)
Sunday, July 5

OFFICIAL GOING: Good

3667a PRIX DU BOIS (GROUP 3) 5f
1:15 (1:15) 2-Y-O **£38,835** (£15,534; £11,650; £7,767; £3,883)

RPR

1 **Dolled Up (IRE)**[27] 2-8-10 ow2 .... OPeslier 1 103
(Robert Collet, France) *trckd ldr on rails: led appr fnl f: rdn clr: r.o wl* **12/1**

2 1 **Chantilly Creme (USA)**[18] 3015 2-8-8 .... SPasquier 5 98
(R Gibson, France) *pressed ldr tl gng on at 1/2-way: hdd appr fnl f: rdn and kpt on same pce* **6/1**[3]

3 3/4 **Corporal Maddox**[29] 2702 2-8-11 .... JimCrowley 3 98
(K R Burke) *a in tch in 5th or 6th: beginning to improve whn sltly hmpd over 1f out: drvn and r.o to take 3rd on line* **11/4**[2]

4 nse **Paradise Rain**[22] 2-8-8 .... DBoeuf 2 95
(Mario Hofer, Germany) *disp 3rd: kpt on steadily u.p fnl f: lost 3rd on line* **16/1**

5 3/4 **Kolokol (IRE)**[18] 3044 2-8-11 .... TThulliez 6 95
(D Prod'Homme, France) *drawn on outside: restrained in rr and grad brought to stands' rails: kpt on but nvr able to chal* **20/1**

6 nk **Forum Magnum (USA)**[12] 2-8-11 .... MGuyon 4 94
(A Fabre, France) *trckd ldrs: disputing 3rd on outside 2f out: sn rdn and one pce* **15/8**[1]

7 5 **Ascot Glory (IRE)**[18] 3044 2-8-8 .... DBonilla 7 73
(S Wattel, France) *a in rr: btn wl over 1f out* **14/1**

8 4 **Blue Panis (FR)**[24] 2-8-11 .... THuet 8 62
(F Chappet, France) *led to 1/2-way: wknd qckly 2f out* **6/1**[3]

58.10 secs **Going Correction** +0.10s/f (Good) **8** Ran SP% **115.0**
Speed ratings: **104,102,101,101,99 99,91,85**
PARI-MUTUEL: WIN 16.40; PL 2.70, 2.00, 1.50; DF 116.80.
Owner Mme Anne-Marie Hayes **Bred** Mesnil Investments Ltd **Trained** Chantilly, France

NOTEBOOK
Dolled Up(IRE) put up a fine performance. She was held up on the rail behind the leaders and came with a progressive run to pass the runner-up 100m from the line and won with something in hand. She had previously been second to Siyouni on her first start and it looks like she will re-oppose him in the Prix Robert Papin.
Chantilly Creme(USA), who had previously been fifth in the Queen Mary, put up a good effort. She broke well and led on the rail for much of the race but couldn't go with the winner although she stayed on gamely for second place. (op 5-1)
Corporal Maddox, dropping in trip, produced a slightly disappointing effort, although connections were happy with his run. He slightly missed the break then was held up in mid-division for much of the race and came with a late run. His trainer thinks that 6f will suit him better in the future. The Richmond Stakes at Goodwood is his likely target.
Paradise Rain, well placed behind the leaders, she came with a challenge a furlong out but could reach the leaders and eventually finished fourth. (op 14-1)

3668a PRIX CHLOE (GROUP 3) (FILLIES) 1m 1f
2:25 (2:31) 3-Y-O **£38,835** (£15,534; £11,650; £7,767; £3,883)

RPR

1 **Wilside (IRE)**[31] 3-8-12 .... OPeslier 6 105
(M Delzangles, France) *mid-div: hdwy on outside and 3rd st: edgd rt 1 1/2f out: drvn to ld 50yds out: r.o wl* **12/1**

2 hd **One Clever Cat (IRE)**[38] 3-8-12 .... FPrat 5 105
(T Clout, France) *sweating: 8th st: swtchd lft 2f out: stdy prog on outside: jst failed* **20/1**

3 *nk* **Denomination (USA)**[21] 2952 3-9-1 .... DBoeuf 9 107
(Mme C Head-Maarek, France) *first to show: settled trcking ldr: 2nd st: led 2f out to 50yds out: r.o* **4/1**[1]

4 *3/4* **Providanza (FR)**[27] 2777 3-8-12 .... C-PLemaire 3 102
(M Delzangles, France) *a cl up: 5th st: 3rd whn squeezed up 1 1/2f out: r.o one pce fnl f* **8/1**[3]

5 *3/4* **Black Rose (FR)**[32] 2622 3-8-12 .... IMendizabal 10 101
(F Chappet, France) *last tl hdwy on outside fnl 1 1/2f: nrest at fin* **20/1**

6 *1 1/2* **Mary's Precedent (FR)**[47] 2173 3-8-12 .... YLerner 2 98
(C Lerner, France) *prom: 4th st on ins: wknd wl over 1f out* **14/1**

7 *nse* **Jakonda (USA)**[30] 3-8-12 .... GMosse 1 98
(A De Royer-Dupre, France) *6th st on ins: swtchd lft wl over 1f out: sn rdn and one pce* **8/1**[3]

8 *1 1/2* **Milford Sound**[36] 3-8-12 .... SPasquier 7 94
(A Fabre, France) *hld up: 7th st: brief effrt on outside wl over 1f out: sn one pce* **9/2**[2]

9 *1* **Quiza Quiza Quiza**[42] 2310 3-8-12 .... CSoumillon 4 92
(L Riccardi, Italy) *led after 1f: hdd & wknd 2f out* **10/1**

1m 53.2s (2.10) **Going Correction** +0.475s/f (Yiel) **9 Ran SP% 93.4**
Speed ratings: **109,108,108,107,107 105,105,104,103**
PARI-MUTUEL: WIN 5.50 (coupled with Providanza); PL 4.70, 4.00, 1.90;DF 106.40.
Owner Marquisa De Moratalla **Bred** Kildaragh Stud **Trained** France

NOTEBOOK
Wilside(IRE) battled gamely in the final stages with the second and just held on at the line. Sixth in the early stages, she came with a progressive run in the home straight and ran a brave race. This was something of a surprise and it has not been decided where the filly will go next. (op 11-1)
One Clever Cat(IRE) put up a courageous performance. She was ridden from behind and progressed well to show a fine turn of foot in the last 100m and just failed by a head under her young apprentice jockey.
Denomination(USA), well placed behind the leaders, made her challenge to lead 2f out but could not quite hold onto her advantage. She carried 3lb more than the rest of the field, and her trainer thought that she did not quite get the distance on this track and will be better over a flatter course.
Providanza(FR), always in a good position, tried to join the leaders but could never quite take the advantage although she stayed on for fourth place. (op 9-1)

3669a ETIHAD AIRWAYS PRIX JEAN PRAT (GROUP 1) (C&F) 1m
3:00 (3:04) 3-Y-0 **£221,845** (£88,777; £44,388; £22,175; £11,107)

RPR

1 **Lord Shanakill (USA)**[19] 2992 3-9-2 .... JimCrowley 8 119
(K R Burke) *trckd ldr to st: led 2f out: drvn out* **4/1**[3]

2 *hd* **Oiseau De Feu (USA)**[28] 2755 3-9-2 .... C-PLemaire 1 118
(J-C Rouget, France) *s.i.s: 6th whn began pulling briefly after 2f: 5th st: hdwy wl over 1f out: chsd wnr fnl f: clsd steadily: jst failed* **7/2**[2]

3 *1/2* **Irian (GER)**[56] 1915 3-9-2 .... SPasquier 3 117
(J Hirschberger, Germany) *a in tch: 6th st on ins: edgd towards outside fr 2f out: drvn and r.o wl fnl f: nrest at fin* **5/1**

4 *3* **Calvados Blues (FR)**[28] 2756 3-9-2 .... GMosse 5 110
(P Demercastel, France) *hld up in last two: last st: hdwy over 2f out: kpt on same pce: nvr able to chal* **16/1**

5 *1* **Westphalia (IRE)**[28] 2756 3-9-2 ....(b) JimmyFortune 7 108
(A P O'Brien, Ire) *plld hrd to half-way (worst fr 6f out to 4f out): 4th st: 5th whn ct on ins wl over 1f out: styd on one pce fnl f* **3/1**[1]

6 *1/2* **Handsome Maestro (IRE)**[28] 2755 3-9-2 .... CSoumillon 4 107
(D Smaga, France) *a.p: 4th st: disp 2nd over 1f out: one pce* **10/1**

7 *nk* **Feels All Right (IRE)**[28] 2756 3-9-2 .... OPeslier 6 106
(E Libaud, France) *hld up in last two: 8th st: nvr a factor* **8/1**

8 *1 1/2* **Milanais (FR)**[13] 3230 3-9-2 ....(b) IMendizabal 9 103
(A Chaille-Chaille, France) *led to 2f out: sn wknd* **40/1**

9 *2 1/2* **Indomito (GER)**[22] 3-9-2 .... LLezcano 2 97
(P Vovcenko, Germany) *towards rr early: wnt up to 3rd on outside after 2f: 7th and wkng st* **25/1**

1m 38.9s (0.90) **Going Correction** +0.475s/f (Yiel) **9 Ran SP% 116.3**
Speed ratings: **114,113,113,110,109 108,108,107,104**
PARI-MUTUEL: WIN 7.90; PL 2.80, 2.00, 2.20; DF 18.60.
Owner Mogeely Stud & Mark T Gittins **Bred** Vimal Khosla, Gillian Khosla Et Al **Trained** Middleham Moor, N Yorks
■ The first Group 1 winner for Karl Burke and Jim Crowley.

NOTEBOOK
Lord Shanakill(USA) recorded a well deserved Group 1 victory. After being a little keen in the early stages he was always going well behind the leader Milanais. It was not a strong pace and he took the advantage on the rail a furlong out and battled on courageously with the runner-up to just hold on at the line. He is progressing with every run this season, having had an interrupted preparation before the Guineas, and should be able to win another at this level. His trainer is looking at two possibilities for his next outing, the Sussex Stakes at Goodwood on July 29th and the Prix Jacques le Marois at Deauville on August 16th.
Oiseau De Feu(USA) lost nothing in defeat and never runs a bad race. Mid-division for much of the contest, he came with a challenge to the winner half a furlong out and just failed. He is very consistent and should be capable of running another decent race at this level.
Irian(GER), a German challenger, was outpaced in the early stages of the race but made up lost ground to finish strongly. His jockey said that he needed further to show his best and there is no doubt that he is capable of taking an event of this level over a longer distance.
Calvados Blues(FR), who after being behind for much of the race, finished well without troubling the first three. This was not his ideal trip and he will be better on his return to 1m1f.
Westphalia(IRE), fitted with blinkers for the first time, ran far too freely in the early stages. Held up behind the leaders on the rail, he failed to find a gap and then stayed on one paced.

3650 HAMBURG (R-H)
Sunday, July 5

OFFICIAL GOING: Good

3670a IDEE DEUTSCHES DERBY (GROUP 1) 1m 4f
4:45 (4:50) 3-Y-0 **£291,262** (£97,087; £58,252; £29,126; £9,709)

RPR

1 **Wiener Walzer (GER)**[21] 2954 3-9-2 .... FJohansson 5 111
(J Hirschberger, Germany) *a cl up: 5th st: led over 1 1/2f out: drvn out* **18/5**[2]

2 *1 1/4* **Sordino (GER)**[14] 3-9-2 .... JVictoire 13 109
(W Hickst, Germany) *towards rr to st: hdwy on wd outside 2f out: sn drvn: r.o to take 2nd in last 50yds* **29/1**

3 *nk* **Toughness Danon**[34] 3-9-2 ....(p) EPedroza 10 109
(A Wohler, Germany) *cheek pieces: mid-div: trcking wnr ent st: drvn to rch 2nd ins fnl f: no ex* **17/1**

4 *nk* **Eliot (GER)**[21] 2954 3-9-2 .... THellier 12 108
(T Mundry, Germany) *last after 2f: hdwy on outside and 7th st: disp 2nd ins fnl f: one pce* **127/10**

5 *2* **Quo Dubai (GER)**[34] 2560 3-9-2 .... TedDurcan 16 105
(Mario Hofer, Germany) *carried rt s: hld up in rr: last st: hdwy on outside fnl 2f: nrest at fin* **52/1**

6 *shd* **Ordenstreuer (IRE)**[22] 3-9-2 .... APietsch 2 105
(R Dzubasz, Germany) *trckd ldr: 2nd st: rdn and btn appr fnl f* **29/1**

7 *3/4* **Saphir (GER)**[34] 2560 3-9-2 .... AStarke 7 104
(P Schiergen, Germany) *hld up in rr: styd on fnl 2f: nvr a factor* **61/10**

8 *1 1/4* **Frantic Storm (GER)**[34] 3-9-2 .... DarryllHolland 14 102
(W Hickst, Germany) *hld up: kpt on fnl 2f: nvr a factor* **17/1**

9 *nk* **Egon (IRE)**[21] 2954 3-9-2 .... RichardHughes 11 101
(W Hickst, Germany) *nvr nrr than mid-div* **205/10**

10 *1 1/4* **Hansom (GER)**[34] 2560 3-9-2 .... LDettori 9 99
(Frau E Mader, Germany) *trckd ldrs: 3rd and pushed along st: sn btn* **22/1**

11 *1/2* **Oriental Lion**[21] 2954 3-9-2 .... DPorcu 17 98
(Uwe Ostmann, Germany) *drawn on wd outside: rrd and wnt rt s: sn wl in tch: 6th st: btn 2f out* **122/10**

12 *2 1/2* **Glad Panther**[34] 2560 3-9-2 .... RPiechulek 1 94
(Uwe Ostmann, Germany) *led 2f: 4th st on ins: wknd wl over 1f out* **64/1**

13 *3/4* **Bolivia (GER)**[35] 2524 3-8-13 .... ASuborics 15 90
(W Hickst, Germany) *hmpd s: a in rr* **54/10**[3]

14 *2 1/2* **Suestado (GER)**[34] 3-9-2 .... ADeVries 3 89
(J Hirschberger, Germany) *hld up bhd ldrs: wl in tch tl losing pl appr st: eased* **29/10**[1]

15 *1* **Marlow (GER)**[24] 3-9-2 .... AHelfenbein 6 88
(Mario Hofer, Germany) *mid-div: hdwy on ins 4f out: 7th st: sn btn* **56/1**

16 *1 1/4* **Double Handful (GER)**[24] 3-9-2 .... WMongil 8 86
(M Figge, Germany) *led after 2f to over 1 1/2f out* **86/1**

17 *1 1/2* **Panyu (GER)**[21] 2954 3-9-2 .... FilipMinarik 4 83
(P Schiergen, Germany) *mid-div tl wkng over 3f out: eased* **165/10**

2m 29.56s (-4.99) **17 Ran SP% 130.8**

Owner Gestut Schlenderhan **Bred** Gestut Schlenderhan **Trained** Germany

NOTEBOOK
Wiener Walzer(GER), the stable second string, ran on determinedly to follow up his success in the Union-Rennen the previous month. It was also a poignant success as his owner died recently.

3658 BRIGHTON (L-H)
Monday, July 6

OFFICIAL GOING: Firm (good to firm in places; 9.0)
Wind: Strong, half against Weather: Mainly cloudy

3671 BET365 H'CAP 5f 213y
2:30 (2:31) (Class 6) (0-55,55) 3-Y-0+ **£2,072** (£616; £308; £153) **Stalls Low**

Form RPR

02 1 **Namu**[6] 3471 6-9-5 **54** ....(p) JimCrowley 9 64
(Miss T Spearing) *towards rr: hdwy over 2f out: chsd ldr over 1f out: drvn to ld ins fnl f* **7/1**

005 2 *2* **Scruffy Skip (IRE)**[6] 3471 4-9-3 **52** .... TGMcLaughlin 12 56
(Mrs C A Dunnett) *prom: led 2f out tl ins fnl f: nt qckn* **40/1**

0005 3 *2* **Nawaaff**[13] 3242 4-8-10 **45** .... SamHitchcott 10 42
(M R Channon) *chsd ldrs: drvn along over 2f out: kpt on same pce* **33/1**

0563 4 *nse* **Ishibee (IRE)**[12] 3283 5-8-13 **48** ....(p) NeilChalmers 1 45+
(J J Bridger) *mid-div: hdwy 2f out: hrd rdn over 1f out: one pce fnl f* **13/2**[3]

6346 5 *1/2* **Who's Winning (IRE)**[6] 3471 8-9-1 **50** ....(t) GeorgeBaker 2 45+
(B G Powell) *towards rr: hdwy and in tch whn n.m.r 2f out: styd on same pce* **5/1**[2]

0040 6 *nk* **Davids Mark**[59] 1846 9-9-5 **54** .... SimonWhitworth 3 48+
(J R Jenkins) *bhd: hdwy and nt clr run over 1f out: swtchd lft: rdn and r.o: nrst fin* **18/1**

0266 7 *1 1/4* **Miss Firefly**[5] 3505 4-8-12 **52** ....(b[1]) MCGeran(5) 7 42
(R J Hodges) *led: hung rt and hdd 2f out: wknd over 1f out* **4/1**[1]

6050 8 *hd* **Buail Isteach (IRE)**[41] 2361 4-8-11 **46** ....(b) EdwardCreighton 11 36
(E J Creighton) *sn pushed along towards rr: mod effrt over 2f out: sme late hdwy* **16/1**

0000 9 *3* **Maggie Kate**[40] 2381 4-9-0 **49** ....(p) RobertHavlin 4 29
(R Ingram) *chsd ldrs: effrt over 2f out: wknd over 1f out* **20/1**

0000 10 *hd* **Helping Hand (IRE)**[13] 3239 4-8-11 **53** .... DavidKenny(7) 6 33
(R Hollinshead) *in tch: rdn over 2f out: sn wknd* **13/2**[3]

40-0 11 *nk* **Prince Valentine**[13] 3241 8-9-0 **49** ....(p) FergusSweeney 5 28
(G L Moore) *mid-div: rdn over 2f out: no imp whn sltly hmpd over 1f out* **17/2**

3534 12 *3 1/4* **Elusive Ronnie (IRE)**[97] 1046 3-9-0 **55** ....(p) DarryllHolland 13 23
(R A Teal) *prom over 3f* **16/1**

0002 13 *1 3/4* **Private Passion (IRE)**[23] 2918 3-8-11 **52** .... PaulEddery 8 15
(Pat Eddery) *restless in stalls: s.s: a bhd* **10/1**

1m 11.52s (1.32) **Going Correction** +0.15s/f (Good)
WFA 3 from 4yo+ 6lb **13 Ran SP% 122.6**
Speed ratings (Par 101): **97,94,91,91,90 90,88,88,84,84 83,79,77**
toteswingers: 1&2 £18.20, 1&3 £21.00, 2&3 £134.50 CSF £272.22 CT £5008.07 TOTE £5.50: £2.60, £9.70, £11.20; EX 147.50 TRIFECTA Not won..
Owner Advantage Chemicals Holdings Ltd **Bred** Philip Graham Harvey **Trained** Alcester, Warwicks

FOCUS
A very moderate sprint handicap in which they all raced towards the stands' side rail in the straight. They went a good pace. The winner confirmed last week's placing with the second and fifth.
Miss Firefly Official explanation: jockey said filly hung badly right throughout
Private Passion(IRE) Official explanation: jockey said gelding missed the break

3672 MAGNETIC.UK.COM H'CAP 6f 209y
3:00 (3:02) (Class 6) (0-65,65) 3-Y-0 **£2,331** (£693; £346; £173) **Stalls Low**

Form RPR

000- 1 **Orangeleg**[301] 5754 3-8-2 **46** oh1 .... ChrisCatlin 5 53
(S C Williams) *dwlt: bhd: hdwy on stands' rail 3f out: swtchd lft over 1f out: styd on to ld fnl 30yds* **11/4**[2]

4000 2 *nk* **Sermons Mount (USA)**[49] 2143 3-8-6 **50** .... NeilChalmers 4 56
(Mouse Hamilton-Fairley) *led: edgd over to stands' rail fr 2f out: hrd rdn and kpt on fnl f: hdd fnl 30yds* **20/1**

0660 **3** 2 ³/₄ **Caerus (USA)**[17] 3115 3-9-7 65 JimCrowley 7 64
(W J Knight) *bhd: drvn along over 2f out: styd on to take 3rd ins fnl f* **3/1**[3]

-003 **4** 2 **Kyle Of Bute**[13] 3241 3-8-6 50 RichardMullen 8 43
(J L Dunlop) *t.k.h in tch: effrt over 2f out: hrd rdn over 1f out: one pce* **2/1**[1]

0-60 **5** 2 ¹/₄ **Green Poppy**[38] 2431 3-8-13 57 TPQueally 3 44
(Eve Johnson Houghton) *chsd ldrs: rdn and n.m.r 2f out: wknd jst over 1f out* **15/2**

00-0 **6** 8 **Eager To Bow (IRE)**[63] 1746 3-8-11 55 (b¹) LPKeniry 1 21
(P R Chamings) *chsd ldrs tl hrd rdn and wknd qckly over 1f out* **33/1**

-400 **7** 7 **Handcuff**[55] 1969 3-8-7 51 FergusSweeney 6 —
(J Gallagher) *chsd ldr tl wknd qckly over 1f out: eased whn wl btn ins fnl f* **14/1**

-064 **8** 2 ³/₄ **Give Us A Song (USA)**[129] 705 3-9-7 65 LukeMorris 2 4
(J S Moore) *hld up towards rr: rdn 3f out: bhd fnl 2f* **18/1**

1m 24.55s (1.45) **Going Correction** +0.15s/f (Good) **8** Ran SP% **116.4**
Speed ratings (Par 98): **97,96,93,91,88 79,71,68**
toteswingers: 1&2 £66.90, 1&3 £2.00, 2&3 £10.80 CSF £55.08 CT £177.17 TOTE £4.10: £1.40, £5.00, £2.00; EX 74.10 Trifecta £646.70 Pool: £900.26, 1.03 winning units..
Owner K Harrison, J Allen **Bred** Baroness Bloodstock & Redmyre Bloodstock **Trained** Newmarket, Suffolk

FOCUS
An extremely moderate handicap. It is not a race to be positive about overall, but the winner can do better.
Orangeleg Official explanation: trainer said, regarding apparent improvement in form, that the gelding had matured and strengthened since last season.
Sermons Mount(USA) Official explanation: .

3673 FRIDAY-AD (S) STKS 5f 213y
3:30 (3:31) (Class 6) 3-Y-0+ £1,942 (£578; £288; £144) Stalls Low

Form RPR
4340 **1** **Sam's Cross (IRE)**[9] 3407 4-9-5 68 (bt¹) PaulEddery 3 66+
(Pat Eddery) *hld up in 5th: hdwy and fnd gap over 1f out: qcknd to ld fnl 150yds: pushed clr: comf* **4/5**[1]

-053 **2** 1 ³/₄ **Come On Buckers (IRE)**[7] 3464 3-8-13 60 EdwardCreighton 9 59
(E J Creighton) *led: hrd rdn and hdd fnl 150yds: nt pce of wnr* **11/4**[2]

1064 **3** shd **Louphole**[10] 3345 7-9-10 64 AdrianMcCarthy 8 65
(J R Jenkins) *dwlt: t.k.h towards rr: hdwy on stands' rail 3f out: pressed ldrs gng wl 2f out: rdn and kpt on fnl f* **17/2**[3]

-000 **4** 2 ¹/₂ **Call Me Courageous (IRE)**[6] 3471 3-8-13 51 TPQueally 1 51
(A B Haynes) *t.k.h: pressed ldr: hrd rdn over 1f out: no ex fnl f* **17/2**[3]

0000 **5** 2 ¹/₂ **Mr Loire**[14] 3208 5-9-0 44 (b) MarkCoumbe(5) 5 44
(A J Chamberlain) *dwlt: plld hrd in rr: rdn over 2f out: nt pce to chal* **50/1**

6000 **6** ³/₄ **Briery Lane (IRE)**[28] 2759 8-9-5 41 (p) LPKeniry 6 42
(J M Bradley) *trckd ldrs: shkn up wl over 1f out: sn wknd* **50/1**

/000 **7** nse **Dazzling Colours**[7] 3467 4-9-5 54 (v¹) TGMcLaughlin 4 41
(T T Clement) *chsd ldrs: outpcd and lost pl over 2f out: sn struggling* **28/1**

1m 12.46s (2.26) **Going Correction** +0.15s/f (Good)
WFA 3 from 4yo+ 6lb **7** Ran SP% **110.6**
Speed ratings (Par 101): **90,87,87,84,80 79,79**
toteswingers: 1&2 £1.10, 1&3 £2.30, 2&3 £2.60 CSF £2.86 TOTE £1.90: £1.20, £1.20; EX 3.80 Trifecta £8.50 Pool: £540.86, 46.70 winning units..The winner was sold to John Bridger for 3,500gns.
Owner Pattern Racing UK Ltd **Bred** Gainsborough Stud Management Ltd **Trained** Nether Winchendon, Bucks
■ Stewards' Enquiry : Paul Eddery one-day ban: careless riding (Jul 20)

FOCUS
A weak seller in which they all raced stands' side in the straight. Not form to be in any way positive about.

3674 TERESA PEACE MEMORIAL MAIDEN H'CAP 1m 3f 196y
4:00 (4:02) (Class 5) (0-75,75) 3-Y-O £3,406 (£1,019; £509; £254; £126) Stalls High

Form RPR
-206 **1** **Dice (IRE)**[34] 2567 3-8-13 67 JamieSpencer 5 72
(L M Cumani) *trckd ldrs: led 3f out: jnd and bmpd over 2f out: disp ld after: drvn to get bk up fnl 50yds* **7/2**[2]

0434 **2** hd **My Chestnut Girl (USA)**[14] 3214 3-9-0 68 TPQueally 2 73
(H R A Cecil) *hld up in 5th: hdwy 3f out: hdwy to dispute ld whn bmpd over 2f out: r.o u.p: jst outpcd fnl 50yds* **15/2**

2222 **3** 4 ¹/₂ **Pyrus Time (IRE)**[9] 3384 3-9-7 75 LukeMorris 6 72
(J S Moore) *hld up in rr: hdwy over 2f out: drvn to chse ldng pair 1f out: one pce* **10/1**

005- **4** 3 ¹/₄ **Lava Steps (USA)**[242] 7209 3-8-13 67 JimCrowley 4 59
(P F I Cole) *hld up in 4th: effrt over 2f out: wknd over 1f out* **4/1**[3]

-002 **5** 16 **Sixties Swinger (USA)**[29] 2738 3-8-13 67 PhilipRobinson 1 34
(M A Jarvis) *chsd ldr tl led 4f out: hdd 3f out: wknd 2f out* **7/2**[2]

5525 **6** 16 **Albaasha (IRE)**[11] 3300 3-8-10 64 (v) RHills 3 5
(Sir Michael Stoute) *led tl 4f out: wknd rapidly 3f out: bhd and eased fnl 2f* **3/1**[1]

2m 34.17s (1.47) **Going Correction** +0.15s/f (Good) **6** Ran SP% **110.3**
Speed ratings (Par 100): **101,100,97,95,85 74**
toteswingers: 1&2 £3.70, 1&3 £4.60, 2&3 £8.70 CSF £27.39 TOTE £4.70: £2.50, £3.60; EX 22.00.
Owner DIC Racing Syndicate **Bred** Swordlestown Stud **Trained** Newmarket, Suffolk

FOCUS
A modest handicap for maidens. They again raced stands' side in the straight. The form is rated through the runner-up and doesn't look strong.

3675 QUEEN ALEXANDRA HOSPITAL 90TH BIRTHDAY H'CAP 1m 1f 209y
4:30 (4:32) (Class 6) (0-65,65) 3-Y-0+ £2,590 (£770; £385; £192) Stalls High

Form RPR
0141 **1** **Goose Green (IRE)**[23] 2912 5-9-7 58 DarryllHolland 10 69+
(R J Hodges) *hld up in rr: hdwy 3f out: squeezed through 2f out: led over 1f out: pushed clr* **4/1**[3]

-020 **2** 2 ¹/₂ **Venture Capitalist**[25] 2865 3-9-1 63 JamieSpencer 5 69+
(L M Cumani) *bhd: rdn 4f out: hdwy and nt clr run 2f out: edgd lft over 1f out: styd on to take 2nd fnl 100yds* **3/1**[2]

066- **3** 1 **Recalcitrant**[326] 5020 6-8-9 46 JamesDoyle 9 50
(S Dow) *chsd ldrs: led 3f out tl over 1f out: one pce* **12/1**

-230 **4** 2 ¹/₂ **Shavoulin (USA)**[26] 2830 5-9-0 51 LukeMorris 8 50
(P W Hiatt) *dwlt: towards rr: hdwy 1/2-way: hrd rdn over 1f out: no ex ins fnl f* **11/4**[1]

6-45 **5** 3 **Pinnacle Point**[10] 3348 4-8-12 49 (be) FergusSweeney 3 42
(G L Moore) *chsd ldrs tl wknd over 1f out* **6/1**

00-0 **6** 4 ¹/₂ **Owain James**[36] 2519 4-8-9 46 oh1 (p) NeilChalmers 6 30
(M Salaman) *prom 4f: sn lost pl and struggling towards rr* **33/1**

2323 **7** 2 ¹/₂ **Clipperdown (IRE)**[4] 3552 8-10-0 65 (tp) EdwardCreighton 1 44
(E J Creighton) *bhd: hdwy to chse ldrs over 2f out: wknd over 1f out* **7/1**

/000 **8** 7 **Legal Lover (IRE)**[11] 3322 7-9-5 59 (p) RussellKennemore(3) 7 24
(R Hollinshead) *led after 2f tl 3f out: sn wknd* **25/1**

00-0 **9** 11 **Green Endeavour (CAN)**[11] 3303 3-8-2 50 ow1 (b¹) ChrisCatlin 4 —
(Mrs A J Perrett) *led 2f: wknd 3f out* **28/1**

2m 4.81s (1.21) **Going Correction** +0.15s/f (Good)
WFA 3 from 4yo+ 11lb **9** Ran SP% **116.4**
Speed ratings (Par 101): **101,99,98,96,93 90,88,82,73**
toteswingers: 1&2 £2.60, 1&3 £9.20, 2&3 £10.90. CSF £16.24 CT £132.01 TOTE £3.50: £1.60, £1.50, £4.20; EX 12.70 Trifecta £168.30 Pool: £666.64, 2.93 winning units..
Owner Mrs S G Clapp **Bred** Liam Queally **Trained** Charlton Mackrell, Somerset

FOCUS
A modest handicap in which they raced towards the stands' side in the straight. The winner is rated back to his best.

3676 ST DUNSTANS H'CAP 5f 213y
5:00 (5:00) (Class 5) (0-75,73) 3-Y-O £3,154 (£944; £472; £236; £117) Stalls Low

Form RPR
0555 **1** **Satwa Street (IRE)**[19] 3028 3-9-7 73 RichardMullen 2 84
(D M Simcock) *mde all: rdn clr fnl f* **15/2**

6423 **2** 4 ¹/₂ **Choisharp (IRE)**[20] 3010 3-8-13 65 (b¹) JerryO'Dwyer 4 62
(M Botti) *trckd ldrs: rdn to go 2nd 2f out: nt pce of wnr appr fnl f* **5/2**[1]

6644 **3** ³/₄ **Raimond Ridge (IRE)**[15] 3193 3-9-1 72 MCGeran(5) 3 66+
(M R Channon) *hld up in rr: hdwy and hung lft over 1f out: one pce* **3/1**[3]

2504 **4** 1 ³/₄ **Flamsteed (IRE)**[40] 2377 3-9-1 67 DarryllHolland 6 56
(M Quinn) *chsd ldrs: outpcd 2f out: rallied and hung lft over 1f out: sn wknd* **5/1**

2242 **5** 3 ¹/₂ **Louie's Lad**[6] 3477 3-7-13 54 oh2 (p) DavidProbert(3) 5 31
(J J Bridger) *chsd wnr 4f: sn wknd* **11/4**[2]

1m 10.65s (0.45) **Going Correction** +0.15s/f (Good) **5** Ran SP% **108.7**
Speed ratings (Par 100): **103,97,96,93,89**
toteswingers: 1&2 £7.20. CSF £25.53 TOTE £8.10: £3.20, £1.50; EX 27.90.
Owner Khalifa Dasmal **Bred** Ditta Nardi Raffaele **Trained** Newmarket, Suffolk

FOCUS
An uncompetitive sprint handicap but the clear pick of the C&D times. The form is slightly dubious but the winner has been rated back to somewhere near his winter AW form.

3677 JUICE FM H'CAP 5f 59y
5:30 (5:31) (Class 6) (0-65,65) 3-Y-0+ £2,590 (£770; £385; £192) Stalls Low

Form RPR
0302 **1** **Multahab**[13] 3246 10-9-2 58 (t) MarcHalford(3) 2 69
(M Wigham) *mde all: led field to stands' rail in st: rdn and in control fnl 2f: readily* **7/2**[1]

6001 **2** 2 ¹/₄ **Orpen's Art (IRE)**[6] 3477 4-9-4 64 6ex HollyHall(7) 12 67
(S A Callaghan) *prom: rdn 2f out: kpt on to take 2nd ins fnl f: nt pce of wnr* **9/2**[2]

-000 **3** ³/₄ **Malapropism**[8] 3422 9-9-2 60 MCGeran(5) 4 60+
(M R Channon) *in tch: rdn to chse ldrs ins fnl 2f: edgd lft: one pce* **16/1**

0004 **4** 1 ¹/₄ **Just Joey**[6] 3477 5-8-11 50 (be) DarryllHolland 3 46
(J R Weymes) *in tch: effrt over 2f out: one pce appr fnl f* **8/1**[3]

05-0 **5** 1 **Metal Guru**[185] 15 5-9-5 61 (p) RussellKennemore(3) 10 53
(R Hollinshead) *chsd ldrs: lost pl 2f out: kpt on u.p fnl f* **8/1**[3]

0044 **6** 2 ³/₄ **One Way Ticket**[14] 3204 9-8-7 46 oh1 (tp) NickyMackay 6 28
(J M Bradley) *spd to 1/2-way* **11/1**

6135 **7** nse **Pic Up Sticks**[6] 3477 10-9-9 65 PatrickHills(3) 8 47+
(B G Powell) *hld up towards rr: hdwy to chse ldrs 2f out: no ex 1f out* **9/2**[2]

3535 **8** 1 ¹/₂ **Thoughtsofstardom**[9] 3386 6-8-8 54 CarolineKelly(7) 9 31+
(P S McEntee) *towards rr: rdn and sme hdwy 2f out: wknd over 1f out* **12/1**

5000 **9** ¹/₂ **Gone'N'Dunnett (IRE)**[55] 1957 10-8-7 46 oh1 (v) LukeMorris 7 21
(Mrs C A Dunnett) *rdn along in rr: nvr nr ldrs* **50/1**

-462 **10** 3 **Kalligal**[26] 2811 4-9-1 54 (b) RobertHavlin 1 18
(R Ingram) *mid-div: rdn and btn 2f out* **10/1**

00-0 **11** 6 **Rathmolyon**[61] 1787 4-8-11 50 FrankieMcDonald 5 —
(D Haydn Jones) *prom 2f: sn rdn and lost pl* **28/1**

63.68 secs (1.38) **Going Correction** +0.15s/f (Good)
WFA 3 from 4yo+ 5lb **11** Ran SP% **117.2**
Speed ratings (Par 101): **94,90,89,87,85 81,81,78,77,73 63**
toteswingers: 1&2 £17.60, 1&3 £14.20, 2&3 £4.50. CSF £18.71 CT £226.20 TOTE £3.90: £1.40, £1.90, £5.90; EX 21.60 Trifecta £248.20 Pool: £385.83 - 1.15 winning units. Place 6: £284.00, Place 5: £33.71..
Owner Dave Anderson **Bred** Shadwell Estate Company Limited **Trained** Newmarket, Suffolk

FOCUS
An ordinary sprint handicap. The stands' rail was the place to be again. The winner is rated back to last year's best.
Rathmolyon Official explanation: jockey said filly moved poorly throughout
T/Plt: £595.80 to a £1 stake. Pool: £74,201.53. 90.90 winning tickets. T/Qpdt: £15.60 to a £1 stake. Pool: £6,977.55. 330.20 winning tickets. LM

3444 MUSSELBURGH (R-H)
Monday, July 6

OFFICIAL GOING: Good changing to good to soft (good in places) after race 4 (3.45)
Wind: Light across Weather: Sunny and showers

3678 FREDDIE WILLIAMS (S) STKS 5f
2:15 (2:15) (Class 6) 3-Y-0+ £1,942 (£578; £288; £144) Stalls Low

Form RPR
0000 **1** **Princess Charlmane (IRE)**[20] 3002 6-8-13 47 (p) DNolan 3 60
(C J Teague) *cl up: led after 1f: rdn over 1f out: drvn ins fnl f and hld on gamely* **66/1**

3110 **2** 1 ¹/₄ **Blue Tomato**[26] 2814 8-9-9 77 AdrianTNicholls 2 66
(D Nicholls) *in tch and sn pushed along: hdwy to chse ldng pair over 2f out: swtchd rt and rdn over 1f out: drvn ins fnl f: kpt on same pce* **13/8**[1]

00- **3** 1 **Grudge**[285] 6218 4-9-4 68 TonyHamilton 8 57
(D W Barker) *led 1f: cl up: rdn over 1f out and ev ch tl drvn and one pce ins fnl f* **9/4**[2]

-060 **4** 1 ¹/₂ **Angelofthenorth**[38] 2451 7-8-10 43 KellyHarrison(3) 10 47
(C J Teague) *bhd: hdwy 1/2-way: sn rdn and kpt on appr fnl f: nrst fin* **28/1**

6-2 **5** 3 ¹/₄ **Glenlini**[48] 2157 3-8-8 0 DanielTudhope 1 35
(J S Goldie) *chsd ldrs: rdn along 1/2-way: sn wknd* **4/1**[3]

5000 **6** 2 ¾ **Welcome Approach**[3] 3562 6-9-4 51 PhillipMakin 9 30
(J R Weymes) *sn rdn along and a in rr* **14/1**

56-0 **7** ½ **Westport**[11] 3304 6-9-4 66 PaulMulrennan 7 28
(R Bastiman) *chsd ldrs: rdn along 1/2-way: sn wknd* **7/1**

00-0 **U** **Egyptian Lord**[49] 2130 6-9-4 40 (b) PatrickMathers 4 —
(Peter Grayson) *rrd bdly s: swvd violenty lft into rails and uns rdr sn after s* **100/1**

59.52 secs (-0.88) **Going Correction** -0.10s/f (Good)
WFA 3 from 4yo+ 5lb **8** Ran SP% **114.0**
Speed ratings (Par 101): **103,101,99,97,91 87,86,—**
toteswingers: 1&2 £13.30, 1&3 £16.00, 2&3 £2.30 CSF £172.61 TOTE £69.20: £10.20, £1.20, £1.40; EX 190.10.There was no bid for the winner.
Owner M N Emmerson **Bred** James And Joe Brannigan **Trained** Station Town, Co Durham

FOCUS
A weak seller. The market leaders ran well below par and the winner appeared to find dramatic improvement.
Princess Charlmane(IRE) Official explanation: trainer said, regarding apparent improvement in form, that the mare benefited from the first-time cheek pieces.
Welcome Approach Official explanation: jockey said gelding never travelled

3679 BLUE SQUARE H'CAP 1m 6f
2:45 (2:45) (Class 5) (0-75,75) 4-Y-0+ **£3,885** (£1,156; £577; £288) **Stalls** High

Form RPR
5-23 **1** **Wee Charlie Castle (IRE)**[16] 3150 6-9-7 75 TomEaves 6 81
(I Semple) *hld up: hdwy over 4f out: rdn to chse ldr wl over 1f out: drvn to chal appr fnl f: styd on to ld last 100yds* **10/1**

2004 **2** 2 **Piper's Song (IRE)**[7] 3447 6-8-10 64 ow2 PhillipMakin 4 68
(Patrick Morris) *hld up in rr: hdwy over 3f out: rdn to ld jst over 2f out: drvn and edgd lft ent fnl f: hdd and no ex last 100yds* **15/2**

6323 **3** 6 **Grandad Bill (IRE)**[17] 3107 6-8-1 58 KellyHarrison(3) 5 53
(J S Goldie) *trckd ldng pair: pushed along 5f out: rdn over 3f out and sn cl up: led briefly wl over 2f out: sn hdd: drvn and one pce* **4/1**[3]

3134 **4** ¾ **That'll Do Nicely (IRE)**[18] 3059 6-9-1 69 PaulMulrennan 2 63
(N G Richards) *trckd ldrs: hdwy to chse clr ldr 1/2-way: effrt to dispute ld 3f out and ev ch: sn rdn and btn* **7/2**[2]

0125 **5** 16 **Desert Destiny**[4] 3544 9-8-11 65 TonyHamilton 1 37
(C Grant) *chsd clr ldr: rdn along 7f out and sn wknd* **9/2**

1120 **6** 1 ¼ **Baizically (IRE)**[12] 3266 6-9-2 70 PJMcDonald 7 40
(G A Swinbank) *led and sn clr: rdn along 4f out: drvn 3f out: sn hdd & wknd* **9/4**[1]

3m 3.45s (-1.85) **Going Correction** -0.10s/f (Good) **6** Ran SP% **112.0**
Speed ratings (Par 103): **101,99,96,96,86 86**
toteswingers: 1&2 £5.50, 1&3 £3.40, 2&3 £4.00 CSF £76.95 TOTE £7.00: £2.50, £2.70; EX 52.60.
Owner Mrs Francesca Mitchell **Bred** Bryan Ryan **Trained** Carluke, S Lanarks
■ Stewards' Enquiry : Phillip Makin caution: careless riding

FOCUS
A modest staying handicap run to suit those racing from off the pace. The winner is better than ever this year.

3680 BLUE SQUARE MEDIAN AUCTION MAIDEN STKS 1m 1f
3:15 (3:15) (Class 5) 3-5-Y-0 **£2,590** (£770; £385; £192) **Stalls** High

Form RPR
4004 **1** **Gaselee (USA)**[9] 3383 3-8-12 55 GrahamGibbons 1 69
(Rae Guest) *mde all: pushed clr over 4f out: rdn over 2f out and styd on strly* **13/2**[3]

6 **2** 9 **Moon Money (IRE)**[22] 2943 3-9-3 0 PaulMulrennan 6 55
(K A Ryan) *trckd ldng pair: hdwy to chse wnr over 3f out: rdn along over 2f out: drvn wl over 1f out: sn no imp* **10/3**[2]

-32 **3** 4 **Helieorbea**[13] 3237 3-9-3 0 DavidAllan 7 47
(T D Easterby) *in tch: hdwy to chse ldng pair over 3f out and sn rdn along: drvn wl over 1f out and sn btn* **8/13**[1]

-060 **4** 12 **Ducal Regancy Duke**[16] 3171 5-9-8 28 (p) LanceBetts(5) 5 22
(C J Teague) *chsd wnr: rdn along over 4f out and sn wknd* **100/1**

3060 **5** 2 ¾ **Jobekani (IRE)**[10] 3336 3-9-3 56 TonyHamilton 4 16
(Mrs L Williamson) *a bhd* **20/1**

6 5 **Agricultural** 3-9-3 0 PhillipMakin 2 6
(Mrs L B Normile) *s.i.s and bhd: sme hdwy 1/2-way: sn rdn along and nvr a factor* **20/1**

7 27 **Clanachy** 3-8-12 0 TomEaves 3 —
(A G Foster) *s.i.s: a bhd* **33/1**

1m 54.15s (-0.55) **Going Correction** 0.0s/f (Good)
WFA 3 from 5yo 10lb **7** Ran SP% **111.8**
Speed ratings (Par 103): **96,88,84,73,71 66,42**
toteswingers: 1&2 £1.60, 1&3 £2.30, 2&3 £1.50 CSF £26.22 TOTE £5.80: £2.10, £1.60; EX 28.50.
Owner Mrs Paula Smith **Bred** Flaxman Holdings Ltd **Trained** Newmarket, Suffolk
■ Stewards' Enquiry : Graham Gibbons one-day ban: used his whip when clearly winning (Jul 20)

FOCUS
A very poor maiden. Seemingly much-improved form from the winner but the favourite ran poorly. WWith the rain getting into the ground front-runners were favoured from now on.
Helieorbea Official explanation: trainer had no explanation for the poor form shown

3681 BLUE SQUARE LE GARCON D'OR H'CAP 5f
3:45 (3:46) (Class 4) (0-80,80) 3-Y-0+ **£6,476** (£1,927; £963; £481) **Stalls** Low

Form RPR
-011 **1** **Secret Venue**[18] 3063 3-8-13 66 TonyHamilton 1 73
(Jedd O'Keeffe) *mde most: rdn wl over 1f out: drvn ins fnl f and hld on gamely* **5/1**[3]

2020 **2** nk **Sandwith**[30] 2717 6-9-11 73 GrahamGibbons 8 81
(A G Foster) *cl up: effrt over 1f out and sn ev ch: rdn ent fnl f: drvn and nt qckn towards fin* **7/2**[1]

0000 **3** 2 **Hotham**[10] 3354 6-9-7 69 JamieMoriarty 2 70
(N Wilson) *chsd ldrs: rdn along and sltly outpcd 2f out: kpt on u.p ins fnl f* **10/1**

1332 **4** ¾ **Raccoon (IRE)**[6] 3483 9-9-11 73 PJMcDonald 3 71
(Mrs R A Carr) *cl up: effrt 2f out: sn rdn and ev ch tl n.m.r ent fnl f and sn one pce* **6/1**

-434 **5** 1 ½ **Blown It (USA)**[17] 3096 3-9-9 76 (p) TomEaves 6 67
(I Semple) *towards rr: hdwy 1/2-way: rdn wl over 1f out: kpt on ins fnl f: nt rch ldrs* **12/1**

301U **6** 1 ¼ **Buy On The Red**[2] 3612 8-9-9 71 (b) AdrianTNicholls 4 59
(D Nicholls) *midfield: rdn along over 2f out and sn no hdwy* **4/1**[2]

4005 **7** 1 ½ **Blazing Heights**[17] 3111 6-9-0 62 DanielTudhope 5 45
(J S Goldie) *a in rr* **17/2**

1231 **8** ¾ **Argentine (IRE)**[6] 3483 5-10-4 80 6ex (b) PaulMulrennan 7 60
(J A McShane) *in tch: rdn along on outer 1/2-way: sn wknd* **13/2**

59.70 secs (-0.70) **Going Correction** 0.0s/f (Good)
WFA 3 from 5yo+ 5lb **8** Ran SP% **113.8**
Speed ratings (Par 105): **105,104,101,100,97 95,93,92**
toteswingers: 1&2 £3.70, 1&3 £8.50, 2&3 £7.70 CSF £22.63 CT £168.12 TOTE £7.30: £2.10, £1.40, £2.90; EX 29.10.
Owner Ken And Delia Shaw-KGS Consulting LLP **Bred** Sherwoods Transport Ltd **Trained** Middleham Moor, N Yorks

FOCUS
A competitive sprint. Sound form, the winner taking another step forward.
Argentine(IRE) Official explanation: jockey said gelding hung right

3682 BLUE SQUARE NURSERY 5f
4:15 (4:16) (Class 4) 2-Y-O **£5,180** (£1,541; £770; £384) **Stalls** Low

Form RPR
1000 **1** **Eternal Instinct**[17] 3086 2-9-2 74 GaryBartley(5) 1 79
(J S Goldie) *trckd ldrs: swtchd rt and hdwy 2f out: rdn to chal over 1f out: led ent fnl f and kpt on wl* **9/2**[3]

12 **2** 2 ¼ **Vilnius**[4] 3540 2-8-7 60 CatherineGannon 5 57
(M R Channon) *sn led: rdn along and jnd over 1f out: drvn and hdd ent fnl f: sn one pce* **5/4**[1]

0206 **3** ¾ **Goodbye Earl (IRE)**[16] 3152 2-8-10 68 SladeO'Hara(5) 2 62
(A Berry) *cl up: hanging bdly rt fr 3f out: kpt on same pce fr over 1f out* **10/1**

230 **4** hd **Paradise Dream**[25] 2853 2-8-12 65 TomEaves 4 59
(J Noseda) *cl up: rdn along 2f out: sn drvn and wknd appr fnl f* **3/1**[2]

62.08 secs (1.68) **Going Correction** 0.0s/f (Good) **4** Ran SP% **96.7**
Speed ratings (Par 96): **86,82,81,80**
CSF £8.46 TOTE £5.60; EX 8.80.
Owner J S Goldie, F Connor, G Brown **Bred** Jim Goldie **Trained** Uplawmoor, E Renfrews

FOCUS
The ground was officially changed to good to soft, good in places prior to this moderate nursery. The second and third limit the form and this is not a race to be with. The 'official' ratings shown next to each horse are estimated and for information purposes only.

NOTEBOOK
Eternal Instinct was making her debut in this sphere after contesting the Albany at Royal Ascot on her previous run. She found it all too hot there, but the class drop did the trick and she won tidily under top weight despite having definite questions to answer on the easing surface. She handled it better than her rivals and found the race run to suit, but is clearly a fair filly on her day. (op 4-1 tchd 3-1)
Vilnius finished second in the first nursery of the season at Redcar four days earlier and was a solid favourite. She showed early speed, but was unable to bag the rail, which looked her initial intention. It is likely she ran very close to her recent level, despite the different ground, and she rates the benchmark. (op Evens)
Goodbye Earl(IRE) drifted to the middle of the track from 2f out and proved one paced when push came to shove. She would probably benefit for a drop to plating company. Official explanation: jockey said filly hung right (op 8-1 tchd 11-1)
Paradise Dream made a bright start and got the stands' rail, but his response when asked for maximum effort was most limited. He is bred to be much better than this and his sire has thrown up plenty of soft-ground winners, so he has become very disappointing. Perhaps the application of headgear now would help. (op 7-2)

3683 BLUE SQUARE SP GUARANTEE H'CAP 7f 30y
4:45 (4:46) (Class 6) (0-60,58) 4-Y-0+ **£2,590** (£770; £385; £192) **Stalls** High

Form RPR
-033 **1** **Nufoudh (IRE)**[6] 3488 5-8-2 45 KellyHarrison(3) 8 55
(Miss Tracy Waggott) *mde all: rdn along over 2f out: drvn over 1f out: styd on wl fnl f* **5/2**[1]

-600 **2** 1 ¼ **Only A Splash**[17] 3125 5-8-5 45 SilvestreDeSousa 5 52
(Mrs R A Carr) *a chsng wnr: rdn over 2f out: drvn appr fnl f and kpt on* **33/1**

0-00 **3** 1 ½ **Morocchius (USA)**[20] 3007 4-8-5 50 (p) BMcHugh(5) 6 53
(Miss J A Camacho) *towards rr: hdwy 1/2-way: rdn along to chse ldrs over 2f out: drvn and kpt on fnl f: nrst fin* **14/1**

0005 **4** 1 **Sands Of Barra (IRE)**[17] 3105 6-9-2 56 DanielTudhope 4 56
(I W McInnes) *chsd ldrs: rdn along over 2f out: drvn and hung bdly rt over 1f out: kpt on u.p ins fnl f* **15/2**[3]

4000 **5** nk **Cheery Cat (USA)**[18] 3070 5-8-10 50 (v[1]) TonyHamilton 11 49
(D W Barker) *chsd ldng pair on inner: rdn along over 2f out: drvn over 1f out: sn one pce* **6/1**[2]

-04P **6** 3 ¼ **Drumadoon Bay (IRE)**[10] 3350 5-8-7 50 NeilBrown(3) 2 41
(G A Swinbank) *in rr: sme hdwy on outer wl over 2f out: sn rdn and n.d* **6/1**[2]

0-00 **7** 6 **Warners Bay (IRE)**[26] 2812 4-8-10 50 ow2 PhillipMakin 10 24
(R Bastiman) *a towards rr* **8/1**

0054 **8** 1 ¼ **Fern House (IRE)**[17] 3110 7-7-12 45 (p) BillyCray(7) 3 16
(Bruce Hellier) *a in rr* **14/1**

06-0 **9** 2 ¼ **Anthemion (IRE)**[6] 3481 12-8-1 46 PatrickDonaghy(5) 12 11
(Mrs J C McGregor) *a in rr* **16/1**

0046 **10** 6 **Mr Lu**[16] 3148 4-9-2 56 PaulMulrennan 7 5
(A G Foster) *chsd ldrs: rdn along wl over 2f out: sn wknd and eased over 1f out* **6/1**[2]

1m 30.08s (-0.22) **Going Correction** 0.0s/f (Good) **10** Ran SP% **116.5**
Speed ratings (Par 101): **101,99,97,96,96 92,85,84,81,74**
toteswingers: 1&2 £10.90, 1&3 £8.30, 2&3 £27.80. CSF £100.41 CT £978.82 TOTE £3.20: £1.20, £6.70, £4.00; EX 80.70.
Owner H Conlon **Bred** Swordlestown Stud **Trained** Spennymoor, Co Durham

FOCUS
A very ordinary handicap. The first two home raced in the same order throughout. The winner was well in if last week's Catterick form could be believed, and went some way to confirming that, but the runner-up was 5lb wrong.
Mr Lu Official explanation: trainer said gelding had a breathing problem

3684 ON COURSE BOOKMAKERS SUPPORT MUIRFIELD RDA H'CAP 1m
5:15 (5:15) (Class 6) (0-65,65) 3-Y-O **£2,590** (£770; £385; £192) **Stalls** High

Form RPR
1332 **1** **Island Chief**[2] 3616 3-9-1 64 (p) AmyRyan(5) 2 74
(K A Ryan) *cl up: led after 1f: rdn and 2 l up whn hung violenty lft to stands' rail 1 1/2f out: styd on strly fnl f* **3/1**[2]

-435 **2** 11 **Hawkeyethenoo (IRE)**[19] 3018 3-8-9 53 ow2 (b[1]) PaulMulrennan 1 38
(M W Easterby) *trckd ldng pair: hdwy to chse wnr 3f out: drvn along over 2f out: sn one pce* **7/1**

2002 **3** 1 ¼ **Amazing Blue Sky**[2] 3636 3-8-13 57 SilvestreDeSousa 6 39
(Mrs R A Carr) *led 1f: cl up: rdn along 3f out: drvn over 2f out and sn outpcd* **4/1**[3]

-023 **4** 1 ¾ **Mohawk Ridge**[19] 3018 3-9-2 **60** .... PhillipMakin 7 38
(M Dods) *trckd ldrs: effrt over 3f out and sn pushed along: rdn wl over 2f out and snbtn* **5/4**[1]
66-5 **5** 17 **Acclaben (IRE)**[7] 3457 3-9-2 **60** .... DanielTudhope 3 —
(G A Swinbank) *a in rr* **11/1**
1m 41.41s (0.21) **Going Correction** 0.0s/f (Good) **5** Ran SP% **110.3**
Speed ratings (Par 98): **98,87,85,84,67**
toteswingers: 1&2 £7.00. CSF £22.13 TOTE £3.30: £1.80, £3.50; EX 24.20 Place 6: £2,350.04, Place 5: £1,605.20..
Owner The C H F Partnership **Bred** The C H F Partnership **Trained** Hambleton, N Yorks

FOCUS
A poor 3yo handicap, run at a sound pace. The errant winner could have been rated higher but this is not form to take literally.
T/Plt: £710.90 to a £1 stake. Pool: £63,693.20. 65.40 winning tickets. T/Qpdt: £71.70 to a £1 stake. Pool: £4,848.05. 50.00 winning tickets. JR

3064 **RIPON** (R-H)
Monday, July 6

OFFICIAL GOING: Good (good to firm in places; 8.5)
Wind: Light, half-behind. Weather: overcast

3685 MARKET PLACE (S) STKS — 1m 1f 170y
6:50 (6:51) (Class 6) 3-Y-O **£2,729** (£806; £403) **Stalls** High

Form RPR
04 **1** **Love In The West (IRE)**[9] 3373 3-8-7 .... TPO'Shea 11 54
(G A Swinbank) *trckd ldrs: led over 1f out: kpt on wl* **5/2**[1]
2604 **2** 1 **Location**[7] 3462 3-8-12 56 .... EddieAhern 13 57
(Ian Williams) *trckd ldrs: kpt on to take 2nd jst ins fnl f: no ex* **5/2**[1]
6330 **3** 2 **King's Chorister**[26] 2802 3-8-12 51 ....(t) MickyFenton 8 52
(Miss Gay Kelleway) *hld up in midfield: hdwy over 3f out: hung rt and styd on same pce fnl f* **11/1**[3]
0-03 **4** nk **Bussell Along (IRE)**[56] 1940 3-8-7 54 .... SaleemGolam 6 47
(M L W Bell) *s.i.s: sn chsng ldrs: one pce appr fnl f* **12/1**
-000 **5** 1 ¼ **Mymateeric**[11] 3302 3-8-12 55 ....(b) JimmyQuinn 9 49
(J Pearce) *in midfield: effrt over 3f out: one pce fnl 2f* **16/1**
0405 **6** ½ **Feeling Stylish (IRE)**[27] 2790 3-8-7 45 .... AndrewElliott 14 43
(N Tinkler) *led to over 1f out: fdd* **16/1**
0600 **7** 8 **Terrymene Prince**[13] 3233 3-8-12 40 ....(v) DuranFentiman 12 31
(L A Mullaney) *w ldrs: wknd over 1f out* **100/1**
8 6 **Legnani**[234] 7326 3-8-2 71 ....(p) MatthewDavies(5) 4 14
(George Baker) *mid-div: lost pl over 3f out* **4/1**[2]
-000 **9** 9 **Desdamona (IRE)**[35] 2528 3-8-0 35 ....(t) CharlotteKerton(7) 2 —
(A Berry) *s.s: reminders after s: a bhd* **150/1**
000- **10** 2 **Prom**[339] 4604 3-8-1 45 ow1 .... JohnCavanagh(7) 1 —
(M Brittain) *t.k.h in rr: hdwy on outside over 4f out: sn lost pl* **33/1**
5-00 **11** 1 ¾ **Fat Chance**[17] 3117 3-8-7 44 ....(b[1]) LiamJones 3 —
(Rae Guest) *mid-div: lost pl over 3f out* **16/1**
2m 4.71s (-0.69) **Going Correction** -0.125s/f (Firm) **11** Ran SP% **115.4**
Speed ratings (Par 98): **97,96,94,94,93 92,86,81,74,72 71**
toteswingers: 1&2 £3.90, 1&3 £11.70, 2&3 £5.00. CSF £8.09 TOTE £3.50: £1.80, £1.40, £2.70; EX 11.20.There was no bid for the winner. Location was claimed by Mr R. E. R. Williams for £6,000.
Owner John P Jones **Bred** Noel Brosnan **Trained** Melsonby, N Yorks

FOCUS
The course missed all of the forecast rain but the riders reported it was "good, safe ground". A weak seller run at an ordinary gallop. The form is not solid.
Feeling Stylish(IRE) Official explanation: jockey said filly hung left-handed throughout

3686 PLAY CROQUET AT RIPON SPA HOTEL MAIDEN AUCTION FILLIES' STKS — 6f
7:20 (7:45) (Class 5) 2-Y-O **£2,914** (£867; £433; £216) **Stalls** Low

Form RPR
1 **Shamandar (FR)** 2-8-4 .... KirstyMilczarek 6 78+
(W J Haggas) *w ldr: led after 2f: styd on strly: v readily* **9/2**[3]
4 **2** 3 ¾ **Farmers Wish (IRE)**[27] 2793 2-8-4 .... LiamJones 7 67
(J L Spearing) *chsd ldrs: styd on same pce appr fnl f* **4/1**[2]
3 **3** 2 ½ **City Vaults Girl (IRE)**[15] 3187 2-8-10 .... FrederikTylicki(3) 11 68
(R A Fahey) *mid-div: outpcd over 3f out: styd on fnl 2f* **5/2**[1]
4 6 **Dontbugthebunny (USA)** 2-8-8 .... MatthewDavies(5) 5 50
(George Baker) *s.s: sme hdwy 2f out: nvr nr ldrs* **25/1**
4 **5** ¾ **Zelos Dream (IRE)**[29] 2741 2-8-4 .... SaleemGolam 8 39
(Rae Guest) *chsd ldrs: wknd over 1f out* **14/1**
6 1 **Royal Record** 2-8-7 .... JimmyQuinn 4 39
(M Brittain) *s.i.s: bhd tl sme hdwy fnl 2f* **16/1**
5 **7** 1 ¼ **Daisy Brown**[16] 3152 2-8-4 .... AndrewElliott 10 32
(N Tinkler) *chsd ldrs: lost pl over 1f out* **20/1**
8 ½ **Jozafeen** 2-7-13 .... JamieKyne(5) 3 31
(R Bastiman) *chsd ldrs: wknd over 2f out* **13/2**
042 **9** 2 ¾ **Yawary**[13] 3240 2-8-7 .... EddieAhern 12 37+
(C E Brittain) *swvd bdly rt s: wl bhd: kpt on fnl 2f: nvr on terms* **11/2**
605 **10** 6 **Charity Fair**[7] 3446 2-7-11 .... CharlotteKerton(7) 2 4
(A Berry) *s.i.s: bhd fnl 2f* **66/1**
0400 **11** 1 ¼ **Tagula Pearl (IRE)**[38] 2435 2-8-10 ....(p) PatrickMathers 1 7
(I W McInnes) *led 2f: wknd over 2f out* **33/1**
1m 12.75s (-0.25) **Going Correction** -0.125s/f (Firm) **11** Ran SP% **121.1**
Speed ratings (Par 91): **96,91,87,79,78 77,75,75,71,63 61**
toteswingers: 1&2 £8.40, 1&3 £5.00, 2&3 £1.80. CSF £22.74 TOTE £5.50: £2.40, £1.40, £1.30; EX 30.10.
Owner Mr & Mrs R Scott **Bred** Team Hogdala A B **Trained** Newmarket, Suffolk
■ This race was delayed for 24 minutes after a stalls handler was injured.

FOCUS
Those with previous experience looked fair at best, but there was plenty to like about the winner on her debut. The pace was sound. The form is rated around the winer and second and the winner should be capable of rating a good deal higher.

NOTEBOOK
Shamandar(FR) ♦, out of a dam placed over middle distances, attracted support and created a favourable impression on. She travelled and quickened well and, with improvement likely, should be able to hold her own in stronger company. She should stay 7f. (op 7-1)
Farmers Wish(IRE) jumped off better this time and matched the form of her promising debut effort at Salisbury. While vulnerable to the better sorts in this grade, she should be able to pick up a modest event, either over this trip or 7f. (tchd 7-2 and 9-2)
City Vaults Girl(IRE) had also shown promise on her debut but, while unable to build on that from her double figure draw, she again left the impression that a step up to 7f would be more to her liking. She is in good hands and is likely to be placed to best advantage. (op 11-4 tchd 3-1)
Dontbugthebunny(USA), the first foal of an unraced half-sister to a dual 1m2f winner, was taken off her feet over this trip on her debut. Her future lies in ordinary handicaps over further. (op 18-1)
Zelos Dream(IRE), who hinted at ability on Fibresand on her debut, failed to match that form on this first run on turf. She is likely to remain vulnerable in this type of event. (op 20-1)
Yawary, who had improved with every run, looked to have claims in this company. However, she lost all chance by veering badly right at the start. She will be of more interest in nursery company and is worth another chance. (op 4-1 tchd 7-1)
Charity Fair Official explanation: jockey said filly missed the break

3687 GO RACING IN YORKSHIRE H'CAP — 1m 4f 10y
7:50 (8:04) (Class 4) (0-80,74) 3-Y-O **£5,180** (£1,541; £770; £384) **Stalls** High

Form RPR
41 **1** **Acquisition**[18] 3056 3-9-7 **74** .... EddieAhern 2 77+
(H R A Cecil) *trckd ldrs: effrt over 2f out: led 1f out: kpt on wl towards fin* **6/4**[1]
0505 **2** ¾ **Amethyst Dawn (IRE)**[34] 2571 3-8-8 **61** .... DavidAllan 3 63
(T D Easterby) *w ldr: carried wd: swtchd rt and lft in ld after 2f: hdd 1f out: kpt on wl: no ex towards fin* **10/1**
-334 **3** ¾ **Royal Trooper (IRE)**[10] 3359 3-9-1 **71** .... FrederikTylicki(3) 5 72
(J G Given) *hld up towards rr: effrt on ins over 3f out: n.m.r over 1f out: kpt on wl ins fnl f* **12/1**
-004 **4** 1 **Madamlily (IRE)**[18] 3069 3-9-3 **70** .... GrahamGibbons 4 69
(J J Quinn) *sn chsng ldrs: drvn over 3f out: outpcd and swtchd lft over 1f out: kpt on wl* **11/2**[3]
2663 **5** 2 ¼ **Gosforth Park**[25] 2838 3-8-5 **58** .... JimmyQuinn 6 54
(M Brittain) *dwlt: t.k.h in rr: hdwy on outside over 3f out: sn chsng ldrs: wknd fnl f* **9/2**[2]
0410 **6** 1 ¼ **Highkingofireland**[23] 2925 3-8-12 **70** .... MartinLane(5) 1 64
(K R Burke) *in rr: hdwy over 3f out: sn chsng ldrs: wknd jst ins fnl f* **8/1**
0223 **7** 1 ½ **Dark Oasis**[8] 3432 3-8-0 **58** .... JamieKyne(5) 8 49
(M C Chapman) *chsd ldrs: drvn 4f out: wknd over 1f out* **12/1**
02-0 **P** **Captain Imperial (IRE)**[28] 2767 3-9-7 **74** .... MickyFenton 7 —
(T P Tate) *led: hung violently lft: hdd after 2f: lost pl bnd 6f out: sn heavily eased: p.u over 4f out* **33/1**
2m 34.88s (-1.82) **Going Correction** -0.125s/f (Firm) **8** Ran SP% **112.1**
Speed ratings (Par 102): **101,100,100,99,97 97,96,—**
toteswingers: 1&2 £13.30, 1&3 £7.30, 2&3 £20.30. CSF £17.10 CT £129.19 TOTE £2.20: £1.60, £2.30, £2.60; EX 23.30.
Owner K Abdulla **Bred** Juddmonte Farms Ltd **Trained** Newmarket, Suffolk

FOCUS
A fair handicap that went to the least experienced member of the field. The gallop was only an ordinary one. The form looks sound despite the bunch finish. The winner has more to offer.
Captain Imperial(IRE) Official explanation: jockey said gelding hung violently left throughout

3688 WESTGATE H'CAP — 6f
8:20 (8:27) (Class 3) (0-90,88) 3-Y-O **£8,831** (£2,643; £1,321; £660; £329) **Stalls** Low

Form RPR
-100 **1** **Bajan Tryst (USA)**[44] 2279 3-8-11 **78** .... NCallan 3 85
(K A Ryan) *w ldrs: led over 2f out: edgd rt 1f out: edgd lft wl ins fnl f: hld on* **9/1**
0556 **2** ¾ **Come And Go (UAE)**[16] 3144 3-8-8 **75** .... PJMcDonald 12 80
(G A Swinbank) *w ldrs on outer: no ex wl ins fnl f* **7/1**
0526 **3** 1 ¼ **Kerrys Requiem (IRE)**[23] 2915 3-9-7 **88** .... TonyCulhane 10 96+
(M R Channon) *hld up in rr: hdwy on inner and nt clr run over 2f out: squeezed through on inner ins fnl f: fining wl whn bdly hmpd last 50yds: nt rcvr* **14/1**
1412 **4** 1 ½ **Devil You Know (IRE)**[14] 3219 3-9-2 **83** .... EddieAhern 11 79
(D R C Elsworth) *w ldrs: led over 3f out tl over 2f out: hrd rdn and hung lft: wknd towards fin* **10/3**[1]
4043 **5** nk **Desert Falls**[7] 3455 3-8-13 **83** .... MichaelJStainton(3) 4 78
(R M Whitaker) *chsd ldrs: t.k.h: kpt on same pce fnl f* **16/1**
-302 **6** 1 **The Kyllachy Kid**[19] 3033 3-9-6 **87** .... MickyFenton 9 79
(T P Tate) *hdwy on wd outside over 2f out: sn chsng ldrs: wknd fnl 75yds* **11/2**[3]
-660 **7** nk **Caranbola**[33] 2611 3-8-13 **80** .... DavidAllan 5 71
(M Brittain) *in tch: effrt over 2f out: nvr trbld ldrs* **25/1**
2106 **8** 1 ¼ **White Shift (IRE)**[10] 3360 3-9-1 **82** .... JimmyQuinn 1 69
(P Howling) *hld up on ins: effrt and n.m.r over 2f out: nvr nr ldrs* **11/1**
1551 **9** nk **Midnight Fantasy**[12] 3272 3-8-6 **73** .... SaleemGolam 6 59
(Rae Guest) *in tch: effrt over 2f out: nvr trbld ldrs* **5/1**[2]
5434 **10** shd **Tagula Breeze (IRE)**[18] 3053 3-8-12 **79** .... PatrickMathers 8 65
(I W McInnes) *hld up: effrt on outer 2f out: sn chsng ldrs: fdd fnl f* **12/1**
4301 **11** 12 **Grissom (IRE)**[17] 3096 3-8-8 **75** .... PaulQuinn 2 22
(A Berry) *led 2f: lost pl over 2f out: sn bhd* **10/1**
1m 12.77s (-0.23) **Going Correction** -0.125s/f (Firm) **11** Ran SP% **119.1**
Speed ratings (Par 104): **96,95,93,91,90 89,89,87,87,87 71**
toteswingers: 1&2 £7.10, 1&3 £35.60, 2&3 Not won. CSF £71.66 CT £902.34 TOTE £12.40: £3.00, £2.80, £3.10; EX 114.20.
Owner Mrs Margaret Forsyth & Mrs R G Hillen **Bred** William Patterson & James Glenn **Trained** Hambleton, N Yorks
■ Stewards' Enquiry : N Callan four-day ban: careless riding (Jul 20-23)

FOCUS
A decent handicap run at a good gallop. The third looked an unlucky loser and has been rated back to his best.

NOTEBOOK
Bajan Tryst(USA) had been soundly beaten on his last couple of starts but returned to his best, despite wandering both ways under pressure. He hampered the third-placed finisher, and it is debatable if he would have won had that horse received a trouble-free passage. However, this was still a decent effort on his first run since being gelded and, as he is relatively lightly raced, it will be interesting to see how he progresses. (op 12-1)
Come And Go(UAE), from the in-form Alan Swinbank yard, returned to form dropped to sprinting for the first time this year. He won't be inconvenienced by the return to 7f and should be able to pick up a run of the mill handicap from his current mark. (op 8-1)
Kerrys Requiem(IRE)'s form has been patchy since her last win, but she turned in an eyecatching effort, and would almost certainly have won but for being badly hampered by the winner in the closing stages. She is capable of winning from this mark, but her overall record suggests she would not be one to blindly follow at shorter odds next time.
Devil You Know(IRE), a steadily progressive sprinter, travelled like the best horse in the race, but did not find as much off the bridle as seemed likely. Nevertheless, this was still a solid effort and this unexposed sort is worth another chance. (op 7-2 tchd 4-1)
Desert Falls, a dual Polytrack winner, again ran respectably after racing up with the pace, but he looks to have very little margin for error from his current rating of 83. (op 20-1)

The Kyllachy Kid was not disgraced after racing wide throughout, especially as his best form has been with more give in the ground. He may do better under more suitable conditions. (op 9-2 tchd 4-1 and 6-1 in a place)

3689 BONDGATE H'CAP 1m
8:50 (8:50) (Class 5) (0-70,69) 3-Y-O+ **£3,238** (£963; £481; £240) **Stalls** High

Form RPR

0441 **1** **Montiboli (IRE)**[18] 3070 4-9-9 **64**....(p) NCallan 11 72
(K A Ryan) *trckd ldrs: led over 1f out: wnt 3 l clr: hrd rdn and hld on towards fin* **3/1**[1]

00-0 **2** *nk* **Whipma Whopma Gate (IRE)**[17] 3092 4-8-9 **50** oh2.... DNolan 9 57
(D Carroll) *s.i.s: sn trcking ldrs: n.m.r 1f out: styd on wl towards fin* **33/1**

3655 **3** *3/4* **Mister Jingles**[7] 3448 6-8-12 **56**....(p) MichaelJStainton(3) 4 62
(R M Whitaker) *chsd ldrs: kpt on ins fnl f* **10/1**

4-44 **4** *2* **Veronicas Boy**[55] 1953 3-8-10 **60**.... PJMcDonald 8 59
(G M Moore) *chsd ldrs: kpt on same pce appr fnl f* **12/1**

3400 **5** *1* **Jebel Tara**[30] 2722 4-9-10 **68**....(bt) LeeVickers(3) 13 67
(A D Brown) *led tl over 1f out: sn wknd* **8/1**

0333 **6** *1* **Kalasam**[17] 3124 5-9-9 **64**....(b) DaleGibson 10 60
(M W Easterby) *s.i.s: effrt over 3f out: n.m.r over 1f out: kpt on same pce* **9/2**[3]

-400 **7** *1/2* **Regal Lyric (IRE)**[17] 3124 3-9-3 **67**.... MickyFenton 7 60+
(T P Tate) *in rr: effrt and swtchd wd outside over 3f out: kpt on: nt rch ldrs* **14/1**

3-00 **8** *3 3/4* **Kingsholm**[61] 1014 7-9-2 **62**.... BMcHugh(5) 1 49
(N Wilson) *s.i.s: hdwy on outer over 3f out: wknd over 1f out* **40/1**

-066 **9** *3/4* **Flying Bantam (IRE)**[63] 1741 8-8-11 **55**.... FrederikTylicki(3) 12 40
(J R Norton) *chsd ldrs: drvn over 3f out: wknd over 1f out* **12/1**

-000 **10** *2 1/4* **Natural Rhythm (IRE)**[18] 3070 4-8-10 **51**.... AndrewElliott 6 31
(Mrs R A Carr) *mid-div: hdwy on outside over 5f out: wknd over 1f out* **33/1**

304 **11** *8* **Direct Debit (IRE)**[17] 3112 6-9-9 **64**.... EddieAhern 3 25
(M Wellings) *in rr div: hmpd bnd 5f out: effrt over 3f out: lost pl over 1f out* **4/1**[2]

060- **12** *12* **Ready For Battle (IRE)**[290] 6072 3-8-12 **62**.... JamieMoriarty 2 —
(D W Thompson) *hld up in rr on outside: hdwy over 4f out: hung rt and lost pl over 2f out* **40/1**

1m 39.67s (-1.73) **Going Correction** -0.125s/f (Firm)
WFA 3 from 4yo+ 9lb **12** Ran SP% **116.2**
Speed ratings (Par 103): **103,102,101,99,98 97,97,93,92,90 82,70**
toteswingers: 1&2 £7.70, 1&3 £3.10, 2&3 £30.80. CSF £114.78 CT £887.00 TOTE £3.10: £2.10, £5.00, £2.60; EX 158.50.
Owner Dales Homes Ltd **Bred** A Brudenell, James Boughey & Trickledown Stud **Trained** Hambleton, N Yorks

FOCUS
An ordinary handicap in which the gallop was fair. The principals all raced prominently and this is modest form.
Direct Debit(IRE) Official explanation: jockey said gelding suffered interference in running and never travelled after; trainer said gelding was found to have been struck into and was lame behind

3690 KIRKGATE MAIDEN STKS 1m
9:20 (9:20) (Class 5) 3-Y-O+ **£3,238** (£963; £481; £240) **Stalls** High

Form RPR

-222 **1** **Eastern Warrior**[25] 2856 3-9-3 77.... EddieAhern 6 79
(J W Hills) *mde all: drvn and styd on strly fnl 2f: unchal* **5/4**[1]

40 **2** *3 1/2* **Canyon Ranch**[23] 2937 3-9-3 0.... NCallan 5 71+
(L M Cumani) *trckd wnr: rdn and hung rt over 2f out: no imp: eased towards fin* **10/3**[2]

3 *4 1/2* **Mustakmil (IRE)** 3-9-3 0.... TPO'Shea 4 61
(E A L Dunlop) *chsd ldrs: effrt and hung rt over 3f out: fdd fnl 2f* **9/2**[3]

5203 **4** *hd* **Steel Trade**[13] 3238 3-8-10 71.... JohnCavanagh(7) 11 60
(M Brittain) *mid-div: drvn 4f out: kpt on fnl 2f: nvr a threat* **9/2**[3]

40 **5** *1 3/4* **Brockfield**[23] 2937 3-9-3 0.... DavidAllan 1 56
(M Brittain) *s.i.s: drvn 4f out: kpt on fnl 2f: nvr a factor* **50/1**

6 *4 1/2* **Meml** 3-8-12 0.... JimmyQuinn 7 41
(J D Bethell) *chsd ldrs: effrt over 3f out: lost pl over 2f out* **28/1**

5 **7** *8* **Rose Avelina**[13] 3237 3-8-12 0.... PatrickMathers 10 22
(I W McInnes) *dwlt: in rr: drvn and sme hdwy 4f out: edgd lft and wknd over 2f out* **80/1**

8 *1* **Informal Affair** 3-9-3 0.... AndrewElliott 9 25
(J D Bethell) *s.i.s: sn detached in last* **28/1**

1m 38.97s (-2.43) **Going Correction** -0.125s/f (Firm)
WFA 3 from 4yo 9lb **8** Ran SP% **114.0**
Speed ratings (Par 103): **107,103,99,98,97 92,84,83**
toteswingers: 1&2 £1.60, 1&3 £1.10, 2&3 £3.60. CSF £5.44 TOTE £2.20: £1.10, £1.40, £1.50; EX 7.20 Place 6 £36.31, Place 5 £24.68..
Owner Wai Kuen Chan & Mark Wilson Leung **Bred** Watership Down Stud **Trained** Upper Lambourn, Berks

FOCUS
Not a competitive maiden and the gallop was only fair. It was set by the winner who is the best guide to the form.
T/Plt: £56.90 to a £1 stake. Pool: £74,936.85. 961.01 winning tickets. T/Qpdt: £42.00 to a £1 stake. Pool: £4,980.61. 87.70 winning tickets. WG

3458 WINDSOR (R-H)
Monday, July 6

OFFICIAL GOING: Good to firm (8.9) changing to good after race 2 (6.30)
Rail realignment increased distance of races of a mile and over by 9yards.
Wind: Moderate, across. Weather: Showery

3691 SPORTINGBET APPRENTICE H'CAP 6f
6:00 (6:01) (Class 5) (0-75,73) 4-Y-O+ **£2,729** (£806; £403) **Stalls** High

Form RPR

021 **1** **C'Mon You Irons (IRE)**[9] 3407 4-9-6 **69**.... JackMitchell 3 82
(M R Hoad) *chsd ldrs: wnt sharply lft to r against far rail and led ins fnl 3f: clr over 1f out: easily* **7/2**[1]

0300 **2** *3* **Realt Na Mara (IRE)**[11] 3304 6-8-6 **58**....(p) AmyBaker(3) 11 61
(H Morrison) *in rr: rdn and hdwy in centre of crse fr 2f out: styd on wl fnl f to take 2nd cl home but nvr any ch w easy wnr* **20/1**

0005 **3** *nse* **Shakespeare's Son**[9] 3407 4-8-7 **61**.... SimonPearce(5) 5 64
(H J Evans) *trckd ldrs: wnt to far side ins fnl 3f: sn chsng wnr towards centre but no ch fr ins fnl 2f: lost wl hld 2nd cl home* **12/1**

0031 **4** *2 1/4* **Golden Dixie (USA)**[14] 3208 10-9-2 **72**.... SPRyan(7) 12 68
(R A Harris) *chsd ldrs: styd stands' side and rdn to ld gp of three over 1f out but nvr any ch w centre to far side gp: 1st of 3 in gp* **7/1**

14-5 **5** *shd* **Rondeau (GR)**[14] 3208 4-9-4 **67**.... AndrewMullen 1 63
(P R Chamings) *in tch: racd towards centre of crse fr ins fnl 3f: sn rdn: one pce fnl 2f* **11/2**[3]

2416 **6** *3/4* **Halsion Chancer**[10] 3347 5-9-3 **73**.... KathrynFerguson(7) 13 66
(J R Best) *chsd ldrs: styd stands' side and no ch w centre to far side gp fnl 2f: 2nd of 3 in gp* **15/2**

0116 **7** *1/2* **Super Frank (IRE)**[53] 2011 6-8-12 **68**.... BarryAdams(7) 8 60
(J Akehurst) *led overall tl styd stands' side and hdd ins fnl 3f: no ch w far side gp ins fnl 2f and wknd appr fnl f: last of 3 in gp* **11/1**

1152 **8** *3/4* **Kyllachy Storm**[23] 2911 5-9-7 **73**.... Louis-PhilippeBeuzelin(3) 9 62
(R J Hodges) *s.i.s: sn in tch: racd centre to far side ins fnl 3f: sn rdn: wknd over 1f out* **5/1**[2]

5530 **9** *1/2* **Don Pele (IRE)**[13] 3252 7-9-4 **70**....(p) WilliamCarson(3) 4 58
(R A Harris) *in tch: racd centre to far side fr ins fnl 3f: wknd over 1f out* **12/1**

0355 **10** *4* **Geoffdaw**[123] 762 4-8-11 **63**....(p) RichardEvans(3) 6 38
(P D Evans) *chsd ldrs: racd far side fr ins fnl 3f: wknd* **17/2**

1m 11.84s (-1.16) **Going Correction** -0.10s/f (Good) **10** Ran SP% **117.5**
Speed ratings (Par 103): **103,99,98,95,95 94,94,93,92,87**
toteswingers: 1&2 £13.40, 1&3 £3.20, 2&3 £35.40. CSF £78.01 CT £780.94 TOTE £4.70: £1.60, £7.40, £4.60; EX 126.90.
Owner double-r-racing.com **Bred** Airlie Stud **Trained** Lewes, E Sussex

FOCUS
The field spread across the track in this modest sprint handicap. The winner set the trend for the evening when grabbing the far rail. There is some doubt over the form but he has been rated back to his best at face value.
Rondeau(GR) Official explanation: jockey said gelding hung right throughout
Kyllachy Storm Official explanation: jockey said gelding suffered interference in running

3692 EBF MOIRA HANBURY MEMORIAL MAIDEN STKS 6f
6:30 (6:31) (Class 5) 2-Y-O **£3,885** (£1,156; £577; £288) **Stalls** High

Form RPR

1 **Classic Colori (IRE)** 2-9-3 0.... RichardKingscote 3 88+
(Tom Dascombe) *trckd ldrs: shkn up 2f out: pushed along to ld ins fnl f: comf* **9/4**[1]

43 **2** *1 1/2* **Dubai Set**[9] 3402 2-9-3 0.... GeorgeBaker 7 81
(R Hannon) *disp ld tl over 3f out: styd chalng tl rdn to ld wl over 1f out: hdd and outpcd by wnr ins fnl f but wl clr of 3rd* **9/2**[2]

3 *4* **Al Ghazal (USA)** 2-9-3 0.... DO'Donohoe 2 71+
(Saeed Bin Suroor) *in tch: pushed along and hdwy over 2f out: styd on to take 3rd ins fnl f but nvr any ch w ldng duo* **8/1**

4 **4** *1* **Excellent Guest**[39] 2413 2-8-12 0.... Louis-PhilippeBeuzelin(5) 11 66
(G G Margarson) *rrd stalls and slowly away: rapid hdwy fr 3f out: styng on whn nt clr run ins fnl 2f: kpt on again ins fnl f* **11/2**[3]

5 *1/2* **Luminous Star (USA)** 2-9-3 0.... SebSanders 12 64+
(R M Beckett) *in rr: pushed along 3f out: hdwy fr 2f out: styd on wl fnl f but nvr gng pce to trble ldrs* **16/1**

6 **6** *1 1/4* **Dixi Heights**[33] 2595 2-8-12 0.... PatCosgrave 6 55
(J R Boyle) *disp ld tl slt ld over 3f out: hdd wl over 1f out and wknd qckly* **66/1**

40 **7** *1* **Evergreen Dancer (IRE)**[14] 3218 2-9-3 0.... LPKeniry 16 57
(J R Best) *disp ld tl over 3f out: sn rdn: wknd ins fnl 2f* **33/1**

8 *1 1/2* **Come On Safari (IRE)** 2-9-3 0.... JimCrowley 9 53
(P Winkworth) *chsd ldrs: rdn over 2f out: edgd rt and wknd wl over 1f out* **12/1**

9 *3/4* **Butch And Sundance** 2-9-3 0.... MartinDwyer 8 51+
(B J Meehan) *s.i.s: rcvrd into mid-div but sn rdn and outpcd 1/2-way: kpt on again fnl f* **20/1**

10 *1 1/2* **Start Right** 2-9-3 0.... MichellePayne 5 46
(L M Cumani) *chsd ldrs: shkn up over 2f out: sn wknd* **33/1**

11 *1* **Law Of Attraction (IRE)** 2-9-3 0.... ShaneKelly 1 43
(J R Gask) *in tch: rdn: hung rt and wknd fr 2f out* **33/1**

12 *4* **Royal Box** 2-9-3 0.... PatDobbs 14 31
(R Hannon) *sn rdn and outpcd in rr* **14/1**

13 *1* **Carnival Time (IRE)** 2-9-3 0.... AdamKirby 4 28
(C G Cox) *a outpcd* **16/1**

0 **14** *1 1/4* **Satwa Crown**[14] 3226 2-9-3 0.... StephenDonohoe 10 24
(E A L Dunlop) *outpcd* **50/1**

15 *2 1/2* **Catchanova (IRE)** 2-9-3 0.... PhilipRobinson 15 17+
(Eve Johnson Houghton) *s.i.s: sn rcvrd and in tch: rdn and wkng whn hmpd and stmbld ins fnl 2f* **16/1**

16 *3 1/2* **Kumbeshwar** 2-9-3 0.... TGMcLaughlin 13 —
(P D Evans) *outpcd* **33/1**

1m 12.8s (-0.20) **Going Correction** -0.10s/f (Good) **16** Ran SP% **127.4**
Speed ratings (Par 94): **97,95,89,88,87 86,84,82,81,79 78,73,71,70,66 62**
toteswingers: 1&2 £2.20, 1&3 £13.50, 2&3 £4.60. CSF £11.15 TOTE £3.50: £1.60, £2.20, £3.10; EX 13.90.
Owner The Classic Strollers Partnership **Bred** Frank Dunne **Trained** Lambourn, Berks

FOCUS
A potentially useful maiden, won in great style by the newcomer Classic Colori. This looks good form with the front pair clear.

NOTEBOOK
Classic Colori(IRE) was slowly away but made up the ground without wasting much energy, showed a good cruising speed to sit just behind the leaders, and quickened up well to win with quite a bit of authority. The main form contenders finished in second and fourth, so this looks a solid performance from a decent prospect. He is a half-brother to some useful winners and it is interesting that he is one of just two entries for the Group 2 Gimcrack Stakes from a stable which has had plenty of two-year-old winners. (op 10-3, tchd 7-2 in a place)
Dubai Set had twice caught the eye staying on from well back when in the frame behind better-fancied stablemates in maidens over this course-and-distance. The brother to the very useful Saxford has run another creditable race. He could not cope with the stylish winner but pulled a long way clear of the rest and looks a progressive type. (op 7-2 tchd 11-2 and 6-1 in places)
Al Ghazal(USA) had to weave his way through some traffic problems but stayed on well and has run a very promising race on debut. He is out of a quite useful dual 7f-1m winner who is a sister to the top-class miler/sire Cape Cross. (op 17-2 tchd 10-1)
Excellent Guest reared badly leaving the stalls and got stopped on a couple of occasions in the closing stages but kept grinding away. He made a pleasing debut when fourth of five behind previous winners in a Yarmouth novice event in May and has confirmed that promise. (op 8-1 tchd 5-1)
Luminous Star(USA) did not find a gap until halfway inside the final furlong but quickened up quite nicely. He is well-related, changed hands for 45,000gns at the breeze-ups and has run a very encouraging race on debut, particularly as he is not the most precocious on breeding.

Catchanova(IRE) was reported to have become unbalanced and was eased. Official explanation: jockey said colt became unbalanced and was eased. (op 12-1)

3693 SPORTINGBET.COM H'CAP — 1m 67y

7:00 (7:01) (Class 5) (0-70,70) 3-Y-O — £2,729 (£806; £403) Stalls High

Form — RPR

43-0 **1** Fortunate Bid (IRE)[84] 1252 3-9-4 **67** ... MichaelHills 12 — 74
(B W Hills) *mde all: 5 l clr over 3f out: drvn along 2f out: hld on wl fnl f: unchal* — 7/1[3]

3-00 **2** *1 1/4* **Striding Edge (IRE)**[17] 3115 3-9-5 **68** ... MartinDwyer 1 — 72
(W R Muir) *t.k.h and stdd towards rr whn hmpd after 2f: hdwy over 2f out: styd on to go 2nd 1f out: clsng on wnr ins fnl f but a hld* — 20/1

1-03 **3** *2* **Super Fourteen**[11] 3302 3-8-11 **60** ... PatDobbs 8 — 59
(R Hannon) *chsd wnr: rdn over 3f out: no imp fr 2f out: wknd and lost 2nd 1f out* — 13/2[2]

0221 **4** *hd* **Fajita**[10] 3358 3-9-5 **68** ... GeorgeBaker 4 — 67
(G L Moore) *mid-div: pushed along and hdwy fr 3f out: styd on wl fr over 1f out and kpt on ins fnl f: nt rch ldrs* — 6/1[1]

5-66 **5** *shd* **Mitra Jaan (IRE)**[24] 2892 3-9-4 **67** ... AdamKirby 11 — 66
(W R Swinburn) *chsd ldrs: rdn 3f out: styd on same pce ins fnl 2f* — 10/1

-030 **6** *3* **When Doves Cry**[14] 3209 3-8-12 **61** ... ChrisCatlin 13 — 53
(B W Hills) *s.i.s: in rr: hdwy over 2f out: styd on over 1f out: eased whn no imp on ldrs ins fnl f* — 12/1

5502 **7** *4* **Diamond Twister (USA)**[16] 3159 3-9-7 **70** ... (t) SebSanders 7 — 53
(J R Best) *in tch: rdn over 3f out: nvr gng pce to rch ldrs: wknd over 1f out* — 6/1[1]

00-0 **8** *1/2* **Sircozy (IRE)**[67] 1617 3-8-2 **56** ... WilliamCarson(5) 9 — 37+
(S C Williams) *s.i.s: in rr and styd alone in centre of crse: styd on wl fr over 1f out: fin strly* — 10/1

050 **9** *1 1/2* **Dream On Connie**[17] 3117 3-9-2 **65** ... JimCrowley 3 — 43
(W J Knight) *t.k.h and stdd in rr: styd on fnl 2f: gng on cl home* — 8/1

3640 **10** *nk* **Paymaster In Chief**[12] 3257 3-8-2 **51** oh1 ... (v) DO'Donohoe 6 — 28
(M D I Usher) *chsd ldrs: rdn 3f out: wknd over 2f out* — 66/1

5025 **11** *1 1/2* **Itainteasybeingme**[25] 2863 3-8-9 **58** ... PatCosgrave 10 — 32
(J R Boyle) *chsd ldrs: rdn over 3f out: wknd 2f out* — 20/1

43-0 **12** *shd* **Better In Time (USA)**[77] 1406 3-9-1 **64** ... MichellePayne 2 — 38
(Jane Chapple-Hyam) *a towards rr* — 25/1

0330 **13** *1 3/4* **Love Allowed**[37] 2498 3-8-10 **59** ... RichardKingscote 14 — 36
(Jamie Poulton) *chsd ldrs over 5f* — 33/1

0-35 **14** *29* **Fondant Fancy**[69] 1579 3-9-4 **67** ... PhilipRobinson 5 — —
(H J L Dunlop) *chsd ldrs tl wknd over 3f out* — 7/1[3]

1m 43.26s (-1.44) **Going Correction** -0.05s/f (Good) — **14** Ran SP% **121.7**
Speed ratings (Par 100): **105,103,101,101,101 98,94,93,92,92 90,90,88,59**
toteswingers: 1&2 Not won, 1&3 £10.10, 2&3 £10.00. CSF £147.58 CT £991.00 TOTE £9.50: £3.10, £6.60, £1.70; EX 188.20.
Owner John C Grant **Bred** E O'Leary **Trained** Lambourn, Berks

FOCUS
An ordinary handicap in which the runners had managed just four wins between them in a total of 101 starts. The field all moved towards the far side in the straight. The first five finished clear of the rest and the time was only just outside standard. The form is rated around the runner-up.
Love Allowed Official explanation: jockey said filly hung left
Fondant Fancy Official explanation: jockey said filly stopped quickly

3694 SPORTINGBET H'CAP — 5f 10y

7:30 (7:30) (Class 4) (0-85,84) 3-Y-O+ — £5,180 (£1,541; £770; £384) Stalls High

Form — RPR

0615 **1** **Blue Jack**[22] 2946 4-9-9 **81** ... (b) MartinDwyer 8 — 95+
(W R Muir) *towards rr: hdwy over 2f out: drvn and qcknd to ld 1f out: sn clr: easily* — 5/1[2]

6541 **2** *3 3/4* **Memphis Man**[21] 2980 6-8-11 **74** ... RichardEvans(5) 10 — 74
(P D Evans) *bmpd s and bhd: rapid hdwy over 1f out: str run ins fnl f to take 2nd last strides but no ch w wnr* — 8/1

0-54 **3** *hd* **Olynard (IRE)**[22] 2946 3-9-7 **84** ... SebSanders 11 — 82
(R M Beckett) *in rr: hdwy 2f out: styng on whn n.m.r ins fnl f: kpt on to briefly chse easy wnr cl home: lost 2nd last strides* — 6/1[3]

3302 **4** *hd* **Rocker**[9] 3386 5-9-3 **75** ... GeorgeBaker 12 — 74
(G L Moore) *in tch: chsd ldrs fnl f kpt on cl home but nvr any ch w easy wnr* — 15/2

2114 **5** *nk* **Harry Up**[23] 2911 8-8-8 **66** ... (p) J-PGuillambert 14 — 64
(Andrew Reid) *slt advantage whn strly pressed for ld tl def advantage over 1f out: sn hdd: styd on same pce and lost 2nd wl ins fnl f* — 7/1

6104 **6** *3/4* **Lochstar**[14] 3212 5-9-9 **81** ... LPKeniry 2 — 76
(A M Balding) *chal for ld tl over 1f out: wknd wl ins fnl f* — 9/2[1]

1004 **7** *1/2* **Magical Speedfit (IRE)**[9] 3386 4-9-1 **73** ... TPQueally 6 — 66
(G G Margarson) *in tch: hdwy on rail over 1f out: n.m.r ins fnl f: kpt on cl home* — 22/1

-260 **8** *1 3/4* **Superduper**[9] 3377 4-9-8 **80** ... PatDobbs 7 — 67
(R Hannon) *chsd ldrs: wkng whn hmpd ins fnl f* — 12/1

000 **9** *2 1/2* **Elhamri**[14] 3212 5-9-9 **81** ... JamesDoyle 9 — 59
(S Kirk) *wnt rt s: outpcd most of way* — 14/1

400 **10** *11* **Kelamon**[51] 2088 5-8-11 **69** ... (t) MichellePayne 3 — 8
(S C Williams) *spd to 1/2-way* — 6/1[3]

59.36 secs (-0.94) **Going Correction** -0.05s/f (Good)
WFA 3 from 4yo+ 5lb — **10** Ran SP% **117.5**
Speed ratings (Par 105): **105,99,98,98,97 96,95,93,89,71**
toteswingers: 1&2 £5.50, 1&3 £5.80, 2&3 £15.50. CSF £45.10 CT £247.47 TOTE £6.30: £2.10, £2.50, £2.90; EX 51.50.
Owner Martin P Graham **Bred** Miss S N Ralphs **Trained** Lambourn, Berks
■ Stewards' Enquiry : Seb Sanders one-day ban: careless riding (Jul 20)

FOCUS
A competitive sprint handicap won emphatically by Blue Jack. His improvement has been taken at something like face value.
Magical Speedfit(IRE) Official explanation: jockey said gelding was denied a clear run

3695 WIN@SPORTINGBET.COM H'CAP — 1m 2f 7y

8:00 (8:02) (Class 4) (0-85,86) 3-Y-O+ — £5,180 (£1,541; £770; £384) Stalls Centre

Form — RPR

3511 **1** **The Cayterers**[8] 3431 7-9-11 86 6ex ... MCGeran(5) 3 — 96
(A W Carroll) *hld up in rr: stdy hdwy fr 3f out: drvn to ld 1f out: hld on wl u.p fnl f* — 9/1

0541 **2** *nk* **Resurge (IRE)**[7] 3461 4-10-0 84 6ex ... FergusSweeney 9 — 93
(W S Kittow) *towards rr tl hdwy fr 4f out: slt ld over 2f out: sn rdn: hdd 1f out: styd pressing wnr tl no ex nr fin* — 9/4[2]

1-2 **3** *2* **State Banquet (USA)**[46] 2210 3-9-3 84 ... DarryllHolland 2 — 89
(H Morrison) *trckd ldrs: pushed along over 3f out: chal and rdn 2f out: one pce 1f out: wknd ins fnl f* — 7/4[1]

1062 **4** *5* **Brouhaha**[11] 3301 5-9-9 79 ... RichardKingscote 1 — 74
(Tom Dascombe) *chsd ldrs: drvn to chal fr 3f out: out to 2f out: wknd over 1f out* — 12/1

3201 **5** *1 1/4* **Hip Hip Hooray**[8] 3427 3-8-4 71 6ex ... FrancisNorton 5 — 64
(L A Dace) *t.k.h early in rr: hdwy over 3f out: drvn to chal over 2f out: wknd wl over 1f out* — 16/1

2136 **6** *nse* **Special Reserve (IRE)**[37] 2475 4-9-12 82 ... PatDobbs 8 — 74
(R Hannon) *chsd ldrs: drvn to chal fr 3f out: wknd ins fnl 2f* — 7/1[3]

2-50 **7** *2 3/4* **Threestepstoheaven**[49] 2126 3-8-3 70 ow1 ... ChrisCatlin 7 — 57
(B W Hills) *t.k.h: chsd ldrs: rdn 3f out: wknd 2f out* — 25/1

0621 **8** *9* **Traphalgar (IRE)**[13] 3235 4-10-0 84 ... MartinDwyer 4 — 53
(P F I Cole) *led tl hdd over 2f out: sn wknd: hung lft over 1f out* — 14/1

2m 6.83s (-1.87) **Going Correction** -0.05s/f (Good)
WFA 3 from 4yo+ 11lb — **8** Ran SP% **113.7**
Speed ratings (Par 105): **105,104,103,99,98 98,95,88**
toteswingers: 1&2 £4.80, 1&3 £5.00, 2&3 £3.00. CSF £29.32 CT £52.29 TOTE £10.70: £2.90, £1.60, £1.30; EX 30.10.
Owner R D Willis and M C Watts **Bred** Acrum Lodge Stud **Trained** Cropthorne, Worcs
■ Stewards' Enquiry : Fergus Sweeney three-day ban: used whip with excessive frequency (Jul 20-22)

FOCUS
A decent handicap for the grade involving four last-time-out winners. The first two weere bith well in and the form is rated around the runner-up. The pace was steady and they were tightly grouped turning in, but the first two pulled clear of the third. There was a long gap to the rest.

3696 SPORTINGBET MAIDEN FILLIES' STKS — 1m 67y

8:30 (8:31) (Class 5) 3-4-Y-O — £2,729 (£806; £403) Stalls High

Form — RPR

32- **1** **Applause (IRE)**[269] 6622 3-9-3 0 ... ShaneKelly 2 — 79+
(J Noseda) *t.k.h: trckd ldrs: wnt 2nd ins fnl 3f: shkn up to ld over 1f out: c clr ins fnl f: v easily* — 11/10[1]

2 *3 1/4* **Poppet's Lovein** 3-9-3 0 ... StephenDonohoe 10 — 72
(A B Haynes) *plld hrd: chsd ldr tl led over 5f out: pushed along over 2f out: hdd over 1f out: sn no ch w wnr but styd on wl for clr 2nd* — 50/1

5 **3** *3 3/4* **Insolence (USA)**[22] 2947 3-8-12 0 ... Louis-PhilippeBeuzelin(5) 3 — 63
(Sir Michael Stoute) *slt ld tl over 5f out: styd chsng ldrs: rdn 3f out: styd on same pce fnl 2f* — 7/4[2]

/6 **4** *1 3/4* **Action Girl**[14] 3214 4-9-12 0 ... PatCosgrave 12 — 61
(R M H Cowell) *chsd ldrs: rdn 4f out: outpcd over 2f out: wknd fnl f* — 66/1

P **5** *1 1/2* **Kimberley Rocks (IRE)**[51] 2082 3-9-3 0 ... SebSanders 8 — 55+
(R M Beckett) *s.i.s: in rr tl hdwy over 3f out: kpt on fnl f but nvr in contention* — 33/1

0 **6** *3/4* **Highland Lassie (IRE)**[22] 2947 3-9-3 0 ... TPQueally 9 — 54+
(B J Meehan) *in tch whn hmpd after 3f: drvn and hdwy 3f out: nvr rchd ldrs and wknd 2f out* — 20/1

7 *3/4* **Through The Forest (USA)** 3-9-3 0 ... AdamKirby 14 — 52+
(W R Swinburn) *in tch whn hmpd and dropped to rr after 3f: drvn along over 3f out and no prog* — 14/1

0- **8** *1* **Seeking Faith (USA)**[285] 6205 3-9-3 0 ... IanMongan 5 — 50
(C G Cox) *chsd ldr 5f out tl ins fnl 3f: wknd qckly 2f out* — 25/1

0- **9** *1 1/2* **Salamon**[249] 7093 3-9-3 0 ... MartinDwyer 13 — 46+
(P F I Cole) *mid-div whn hmpd and dropped to rr after 3f: nvr in contention after* — 16/1

10 *1 3/4* **Douchkette (FR)**[58] 3-9-3 0 ... GeorgeBaker 7 — 42
(John Berry) *in tch: rdn and effrt ins fnl 3f: nvr in contention and wknd qckly 2f out* — 33/1

11 *2 1/2* **Countrystyle Lass (IRE)** 3-9-3 0 ... JimCrowley 4 — 36
(P Winkworth) *s.i.s: a towards rr* — 40/1

12 *2 3/4* **Dayanara (USA)** 3-9-3 0 ... PhilipRobinson 1 — 30
(C G Cox) *in tch over 5f* — 12/1[3]

1m 46.77s (2.07) **Going Correction** -0.05s/f (Good)
WFA 3 from 4yo 9lb — **12** Ran SP% **124.6**
Speed ratings (Par 100): **87,83,80,78,76 76,75,74,72,71 68,65**
toteswingers: 1&2 £5.00, 1&3 £1.10, 2&3 Not won. CSF £88.19 TOTE £2.20: £1.10, £8.40, £1.40; EX 158.10.
Owner M Tabor, D Smith & Mrs J Magnier **Bred** John M Weld **Trained** Newmarket, Suffolk

FOCUS
Not much strength in depth in this fillies' maiden, which was slowly run. Guessy form, rated around the winner and third.
Kimberley Rocks(IRE) Official explanation: jockey said, regarding running and riding, that his orders were to drop in, get the filly to relax, work its way through the field and do its best at the end, adding that due to the unsuitable slow early pace, he was unable to get into a rhythm, asked to quicken at the 4f mark and ran on through beaten horses; trainer confirmed, adding that the filly bled on its last run and it was important that it relaxed in the early stages.

3697 EBF MUNNELLY SUPPORT SERVICES H'CAP — 1m 3f 135y

9:00 (9:00) (Class 4) (0-80,78) 3-Y-O+ — £5,375 (£1,599; £799; £399) Stalls Centre

Form — RPR

0-41 **1** **Turjuman (USA)**[21] 2983 4-8-13 **63** ... ChrisCatlin 2 — 67+
(W J Musson) *in rr: hdwy over 3f out: str run fr over 1f out to ld last strides* — 4/1[3]

2143 **2** *nk* **Onemix**[13] 3251 3-8-12 **75** ... MichaelHills 8 — 78
(B W Hills) *led: sn clr: stl 3 l ahd over 1f out but sn rdn: wknd and ct last strides* — 7/2[2]

-411 **3** *hd* **Gloucester**[22] 2818 6-9-13 **77** ... SebSanders 1 — 80
(M J Scudamore) *chsd ldrs: wnt 2nd 4f out: rdn and no imp on wnr 2f out: kpt on wl fnl f and clsng thrght fnl f: chal cl home but nt quite get up* — 9/2

-034 **4** *7* **Wee Sonny (IRE)**[12] 3279 3-8-9 **72** ... RichardKingscote 4 — 63
(Tom Dascombe) *t.k.h early: in tch: pushed along over 3f out: styd on same pce fr over 2f out* — 11/4[1]

3100 **5** *8* **Admirable Duque (IRE)**[46] 2208 3-8-13 **76** ... AdamKirby 7 — 53
(D J S Ffrench Davis) *in rr: rdn and hdwy over 3f out: nvr rchd ldrs: wknd 2f out* — 4/1[3]

-000 **6** *5* **Royal Arthur**[40] 2380 3-8-1 **64** oh16 ow3 ... (b[1]) FrancisNorton 3 — 33
(L A Dace) *chsd ldr to 4f out: sn wknd* — 50/1

134/ **7** *6* **Daryal (IRE)**[103] 5808 8-9-11 **75** ... (b) GeorgeBaker 6 — 33
(G L Moore) *chsd ldrs: rdn 4f out: sn btn* — 14/1

2m 29.21s (-0.29) **Going Correction** -0.05s/f (Good)
WFA 3 from 4yo+ 13lb — **7** Ran SP% **115.7**
Speed ratings (Par 105): **98,97,97,93,87 84,80**
toteswingers: 1&2 £1.70, 1&3 £1.10, 2&3 £1.90. CSF £18.84 CT £64.99 TOTE £5.20: £2.50, £2.20; EX 12.90 Place 6 £56.82, Place 5 £20.15..
Owner I Johnson & John D Jacques **Bred** Shadwell Farm LLC **Trained** Newmarket, Suffolk
■ Stewards' Enquiry : Chris Catlin caution: used whip down shoulder in forehand position.

FOCUS
A fair handicap. It was run at a good pace and the first three finished a long way clear of the rest. Muddling form with the runner-up almost nicking the race. Not form to take too positively.

T/Jkpt: Not won. T/Plt: £47.10 to a £1 stake. Pool: £84,028.04. 1,300.79 winning tickets. T/Qpdt: £11.70 to a £1 stake. Pool: £7,150.46. 449.80 winning tickets. ST

3698 - 3699a (Foreign Racing) - See Raceform Interactive

2747 ROSCOMMON (R-H)

Monday, July 6

OFFICIAL GOING: Heavy

3700a LENEBANE STKS (LISTED RACE) 1m 4f

6:40 (6:41) 3-Y-O+ **£26,861** (£7,881; £3,754; £1,279)

RPR

1 **Alaivan (IRE)**[43] 2306 3-8-10 106 ... MJKinane 4 112+
(John M Oxx, Ire) *sn chsd ldr in 2nd: impr to ld over 2f out: rdn and kpt on strly fr over 1f out: comf* **11/10**[1]

2 3 ½ **Von Jawlensky (IRE)**[10] 3369 3-8-10 ... JAHeffernan 2 106
(A P O'Brien, Ire) *settled in 4th: pushed along in 5th 3f out: styd on to 2nd 2f out: no imp on ldr over 1f out: kpt on same pce* **3/1**[2]

3 7 **Via Galilei (IRE)**[8] 3439 4-9-9 107 ... KJManning 5 96
(J S Bolger, Ire) *chsd ldrs in 3rd: rdn 2f out: no ex over 1f out: kpt on same pce* **5/1**

4 1 **Moiqen (IRE)**[17] 3132 4-9-9 108 ... DPMcDonogh 1 94
(Kevin Prendergast, Ire) *hld up in rr: hdwy to 4th 5f out: rdn 2f out: no imp in 4th over 1f out: kpt on same pce* **14/1**

5 18 **Hindu Kush (IRE)**[18] 3048 4-9-12 ... CDHayes 3 68
(D Nicholls) *sn led: rdn and hdd over 2f out: sn no ex and wknd: eased over 1f out* **9/2**[3]

6 2 **Wanna (IRE)**[43] 2306 3-8-7 89 ... (b) WMLordan 6 58
(T Stack, Ire) *settled in 5th: dropped to rr 5f out: rdn and no imp ent st* **25/1**

2m 49.62s (6.32)
WFA 3 from 4yo 13lb **6 Ran SP% 118.0**
CSF £5.06 TOTE £1.80: £1.80, £2.10; DF 6.40.
Owner H H Aga Khan **Bred** H H The Aga Khan Stud's S C **Trained** Currabeg, Co Kildare

NOTEBOOK
Alaivan(IRE) was a decisive winner. Tracking the leader most of the way, he quickened impressively to the front and won cosily. He looks a progressive horse and could develop into a contender for the Irish St Leger. (op 11/8 tchd 6/4)
Von Jawlensky(IRE) has been employed as a lead horse for Yeats on the Ballydoyle gallops. He was niggled to stay in touch before the straight but kept on strongly inside the final furlong. He's improving and should stay further. (op 7/2)
Via Galilei(IRE) returned to form at the Curragh last weekend but was unable to land a blow here. He tracked the leaders, but once the winner quickened, could make no impression. (op 9/2)
Moiqen(IRE) was held up and travelled well to get within a few lengths of the lead before the turn into the straight. However, he was found wanting when the race developed. (op 10/1)
Hindu Kush(IRE) attempted to make all but faded tamely inside the final quarter-mile. (op 13/2)

3701 - (Foreign Racing) - See Raceform Interactive

3450 PONTEFRACT (L-H)

Tuesday, July 7

OFFICIAL GOING: Good to soft (7.9)

Course dolled out from 6f to winning post but effect on distances not notified.
Wind: Light behind Weather: Sunny periods and heavy showers

3702 DIANNE NURSERY 6f

2:30 (2:31) (Class 4) 2-Y-O **£5,180** (£1,541; £770; £384) **Stalls Low**

Form RPR

0032 1 **Take It To The Max**[23] 2940 2-9-4 77 ... JimmyFortune 8 81
(G M Moore) *hld up towards rr: wd st: gd hdwy wl over 1f out: rdn and str run ins fnl f: hung bdly lft and led nr fin* **5/1**[2]

031 2 nk **Colonel Mak**[12] 3292 2-9-4 77 ... PhillipMakin 1 80
(D H Brown) *trckd ldrs: gd hdwy over 2f out: led over 1f out: rdn ins fnl f: hdd andno ex nr fin* **11/4**[1]

053 3 3 ¾ **Flaneur**[39] 2435 2-8-10 69 ... (b) DavidAllan 6 61
(T D Easterby) *chsd ldrs on outer: hdwy 2f out: rdn over 1f out: kpt on u.p ins fnl f* **14/1**

641 4 3 **Merseyside Star (IRE)**[13] 3262 2-8-10 69 ... NCallan 4 52+
(K R Burke) *led: rdn along 2f out: drvn and hdd over 1f out: wknd ins fnl f* **11/4**[1]

01 5 2 ½ **Bubbelas**[29] 2765 2-9-4 77 ... GrahamGibbons 5 52
(J J Quinn) *hld up in tch: effrt over 2f out: sn rdn and btn* **8/1**[3]

410 6 1 ¼ **Lady Lube Rye (IRE)**[41] 2372 2-8-11 70 ... JamieMoriarty 2 42
(N Wilson) *prom on inner: rdn along 3f out: sn wknd* **14/1**

143 7 2 **King Of Axum (IRE)**[40] 2413 2-9-7 80 ... RoystonFfrench 3 46
(M Johnston) *cl up: rdn along 2f out and sn wknd* **10/1**

664 8 4 ½ **Ice Cool Lady (IRE)**[35] 2563 2-8-11 70 ... TPO'Shea 7 22
(W R Swinburn) *fractious stalls: a in rr* **9/1**

1m 19.18s (2.28) **Going Correction** +0.30s/f (Good) **8 Ran SP% 113.5**
Speed ratings (Par 96): **96,95,90,86,83 81,78,72**
toteswingers: 1&2 £3.70, 1&3 £12.10, 2&3 £13.20 CSF £18.87 CT £179.64 TOTE £5.90: £1.80, £1.80, £3.10; EX 21.40.
Owner Mrs Phillipa Davies **Bred** Whatton Manor Stud **Trained** Middleham Moor, N Yorks

FOCUS
This was just an ordinary nursery but the first pair produced fair efforts to pull clear. The 'official' ratings shown next to each horse are estimated and for information purposes only.

NOTEBOOK
Take It To The Max finished strongly to get up close home. He had shown himself to be effective with cut in the ground when finishing third at Haydock in May and relished the stiffer test this track offered, really coming good from over a furlong out. He hung left close home, but always looked to be getting there and remains capable of better as he goes up to 7f and maybe even 1m. (op 6-1)
Colonel Mak, off the mark in good style at Hamilton last time, travelled well for a long way on this handicap debut and came through to lead over a furlong out, but he couldn´t repel the winner´s late thrust. The speed he showed suggests he will be fine at 5f and he too remains capable of better. (op 7-2)
Flaneur, third behind a useful type at Hamilton last time, didn´t make much appeal on this nursery debut and he ran about as well as could have been expected back in third. (op 20-1 tchd 12-1)
Merseyside Star(IRE), narrow winner of a Carlisle maiden, showed good speed for a long way, but could find no extra from a furlong out and could probably have done without the rain. (op 3-1 tchd 5-2)
Bubbelas, winner of a C&D maiden last month, was one of the first under pressure and proved to be disappointing. (op 5-1)
Lady Lube Rye(IRE), outclassed in the Hilary Needler last time, looked on a relatively stiff mark and struggled. (op 16-1 tchd 9-1)
King Of Axum(IRE) has not really built on his debut victory and was beaten soon after two out. (op 15-2 tchd 14-1)
Ice Cool Lady(IRE), who got upset in the stalls, failed to improve for the move into handicaps and was beaten a long way. She was reported to have hung right in the straight. Official explanation: jockey said filly hung right in straight (op 11-1)

3703 GO RACING IN YORKSHIRE SUMMER FESTIVAL MAIDEN STKS 1m 2f 6y

3:00 (3:00) (Class 5) 3-Y-O+ **£3,885** (£1,156; £577; £288) **Stalls Low**

Form RPR

02/ 1 **Dove (IRE)**[623] 6414 4-9-7 0 ... JimmyFortune 7 75+
(J H M Gosden) *trckd ldrs: hdwy on outer and wd st: led over 1f out: rdn ins fnl f and styd on wl* **5/1**[3]

045 2 3 **Dark Quest**[25] 2877 3-8-10 74 ... EddieAhern 4 69
(J L Dunlop) *a.p: cl up 3f out: rdn to ld wl over 1f out: drvn and hdd appr last: hung rt jst ins fnl f and kpt on same pce* **11/4**[2]

/32 3 ½ **Whirlijig (IRE)**[10] 3379 4-9-7 0 ... PJMcDonald 3 68
(G A Swinbank) *prom: effrt and cl up over 3f out: ev ch 2f out: sn rdn and kpt on same pce fnl f* **12/1**

4 4 6 **Laughing Boy (IRE)**[24] 2930 3-9-1 0 ... JamieSpencer 6 76+
(L M Cumani) *hld up in rr: gd hdwy 3f out: chsd ldrs and swtchd lft over 1f out: swtchd rt: nt clr run and hmpd jst ins fnl f: no ch after* **6/5**[1]

40-3 5 2 ½ **King's Counsel (IRE)**[12] 3294 3-9-1 55 ... SilvestreDeSousa 1 56
(J Hetherton) *led: rdn along 3f out: drvn and hdd wl over 1f out: sn wknd* **50/1**

6 3 ¼ **Prime Classique (USA)** 3-8-10 0 ... TomEaves 2 45
(B Smart) *trckd ldrs: rdn along over 3f out and sn wknd* **33/1**

06 7 nse **Brave Dealer**[24] 2930 3-9-1 0 ... RichardKingscote 8 49
(R Charlton) *hld up: hdwy and in tch 1/2-way: rdn along over 3f out and sn wknd* **12/1**

8 20 **Step At A Time (IRE)** 3-8-10 0 ... RoystonFfrench 5 4
(M Johnston) *dwlt a towards rr: rdn along and outpcd fnl 3f* **20/1**

2m 17.69s (3.99) **Going Correction** +0.30s/f (Good)
WFA 3 from 4yo 11lb **8 Ran SP% 113.8**
Speed ratings (Par 103): **96,93,93,88,86 83,83,67**
toteswingers: 1&2 £2.30, 1&3 £3.80, 2&3 £4.60 CSF £18.73 TOTE £5.90: £1.40, £1.50, £2.00; EX 21.90.
Owner H R H Princess Haya Of Jordan **Bred** Gainsborough Stud Management Ltd **Trained** Newmarket, Suffolk

FOCUS
An interesting maiden. The winner did not need to match her 2yo form, with the fifth rather limiting things.

3704 HARWORTH ESTATES H'CAP 5f

3:30 (3:31) (Class 5) (0-75,72) 3-Y-O **£3,885** (£1,156; £577; £288) **Stalls Low**

Form RPR

0350 1 **Red Kyte**[18] 3096 3-9-7 72 ... (p) NCallan 5 76
(K A Ryan) *cl up: led over 2f out: rdn over 1f out: drvn ins fnl f and kpt on gamely* **7/1**

55 2 nk **Exceed Elegance (IRE)**[15] 3229 3-8-8 59 ... FrancisNorton 8 62
(D Shaw) *trckd ldng pair: hdwy on outer over 2f out: rdn over 1f out: styd on to chal ins fnl f: sn drvn and nt qckn towards fin* **14/1**

-215 3 ½ **Musical Bridge**[18] 3096 3-9-7 72 ... JamieSpencer 1 73
(Mrs L Williamson) *hld up in rr: hdwy 2f out: swtchd lft and hdwy ent fnl f: sn rdn and ev ch tl drvn and nt qckn last 75yds* **5/1**[3]

3121 4 2 ¾ **Dispol Grand (IRE)**[31] 2726 3-9-5 70 ... PhillipMakin 2 61
(P T Midgley) *trckd ldrs: hdwy on inner 2f out: rdn to chal over 1f out: drvn and wknd ins fnl f* **3/1**[2]

1321 5 ½ **Noodles Blue Boy**[11] 3355 3-9-7 72 ... TonyHamilton 7 61
(Ollie Pears) *trckd ldrs: hdwy 2f out: rdn ent fnl f and kpt on same pce* **9/4**[1]

0110 6 2 ¾ **Baby Queen (IRE)**[18] 3118 3-9-1 66 ... GrahamGibbons 6 45
(B P J Baugh) *led: rdn along and hdd over 2f out: drvn over 1f out: wknd appr fnl f* **7/1**

1106 7 10 **Lady Vivien**[25] 2888 3-9-3 68 ... PaulMulrennan 4 11
(D H Brown) *in tch: rdn along 1/2-way: sn wknd* **14/1**

65.24 secs (1.94) **Going Correction** +0.30s/f (Good) **7 Ran SP% 110.8**
Speed ratings (Par 100): **96,95,94,90,89 85,69**
toteswingers: 1&2 £14.90, 1&3 £6.10, 2&3 £12.80 CSF £87.20 CT £510.03 TOTE £7.60: £3.10, £4.20; EX 132.50.
Owner Malih L Al Basti **Bred** Peter Hodgson And Star Pointe Limited **Trained** Hambleton, N Yorks
■ Stewards' Enquiry : N Callan caution: used whip with excessive frequency

FOCUS
This was a modest sprint handicap. The winner produced her best effort of the year.
Red Kyte Official explanation: trainer's rep said, regarding apparent improvement in form, that the filly was better suited by the good to soft ground and fitting of first-time cheek pieces.
Noodles Blue Boy Official explanation: jockey said gelding ran flat
Lady Vivien Official explanation: jockey said filly lost its action

3705 BOOK ONLINE AT PONTEFRACT-RACES.CO.UK H'CAP 1m 2f 6y

4:00 (4:00) (Class 4) (0-85,85) 3-Y-O+ **£5,180** (£1,541; £770; £384) **Stalls Low**

Form RPR

250- 1 **Hollins**[303] 5718 5-8-10 70 ... FrederikTylicki(3) 1 79
(Micky Hammond) *prom on inner: hdwy to ld over 2f out: rdn clr over 1f out: styd on strly* **14/1**

-015 2 3 ½ **Dark Prospect**[34] 2597 4-10-0 85 ... PhilipRobinson 4 88
(M A Jarvis) *a cl up: effrt 2f out: sn rdn and ev ch tl drvn and hung bdly rt ins fnl f: sn edgd lft and one pce* **4/1**[2]

0530 3 nse **Charlie Tokyo (IRE)**[24] 2932 6-9-12 83 ... (v) JamieMoriarty 3 85
(R A Fahey) *hld up towards rr: hdwy 3f out: rdn wl over 1f out: kpt on ins fnl f* **7/1**

200 4 1 ½ **Red Jade**[24] 2933 4-9-13 84 ... NCallan 5 83
(K R Burke) *trckd ldrs: hdwy 3f out: rdn over 2f out and sn one pce* **9/4**[1]

003 5 3 ½ **Applaude**[27] 2817 4-8-10 67 ... JamieSpencer 2 59
(G A Swinbank) *hld up in tch: hdwy 3f out: rdn wl over 1f out and sn no imp* **5/1**[3]

0054 6 2 ½ **Jeer (IRE)**[16] 3189 5-9-1 72 ... DaleGibson 6 59
(M W Easterby) *trckd ldrs: effrt 3f out: rdn over 2f out: drvn and wknd over 1f out* **4/1**[2]

0/65 7 6 **King In Waiting (IRE)**[10] 3393 6-9-1 72 ... SilvestreDeSousa 10 47
(J Hetherton) *a towards rr: rdn along and outpcd fr 3f out* **33/1**

P-00 8 9 **Runswick Bay**[25] 2898 4-8-13 70 ... TomEaves 7 27
(G M Moore) *led: rdn along 3f out: hdd over 2f out and sn wknd* **50/1**

2m 16.31s (2.61) **Going Correction** +0.30s/f (Good)
WFA 3 from 4yo+ 11lb **8 Ran SP% 111.5**
Speed ratings (Par 105): **101,98,98,96,94 92,87,80**
toteswingers: 1&2 £8.50, 1&3 £8.70, 2&3 £5.00 CSF £65.75 CT £422.89 TOTE £15.60: £2.50, £1.80, £2.10; EX 90.00.

Owner R D Bickenson **Bred** Bricklow Ltd And Hyperion Stud Ltd **Trained** Middleham Moor, N Yorks

FOCUS

Just a fair handicap. The winner is rated up 8lb with the runner-up to form.

Jeer(IRE) Official explanation: jockey said gelding ran flat

King In Waiting(IRE) Official explanation: jockey said gelding never travelled

3706 KING RICHARD III H'CAP 6f

4:30 (4:31) (Class 3) (0-90,88) 3-Y-0+

£9,346 (£2,799; £1,399; £700; £349; £175) **Stalls** Low

Form RPR

5452 **1** **Dickie Le Davoir**[4] 3562 5-8-8 **69** oh5 ....(b) JamieSpencer 8 82
(John A Harris) *dwlt and sn swtchd to outer: in rr tl gd hdwy over 2f out: rdn over 1f out: styd on to ld ins fnl f: drvn and wandered: kpt on* **11/1**

0141 **2** *2* **Red Cape (FR)**[6] 3497 6-9-5 **80** 6ex .... AndrewElliott 7 87
(Mrs R A Carr) *trckd ldrs: hdwy and cl up 1/2-way: led 2f out and sn rdn: drvn andhdd ins fnl f: kpt on* **10/1**[3]

1-31 **3** *½* **Eton Rifles (IRE)**[45] 2276 4-9-11 **86** .... PaulMulrennan 12 91
(J Howard Johnson) *in tch: hdwy to chse ldrs over 2f out: rdn wl over 1f out: drvn and kpt on same pce ins fnl f* **15/8**[1]

0112 **4** *nk* **Misplaced Fortune**[19] 3057 4-8-12 **73** .... EddieAhern 4 77
(N Tinkler) *cl up: rdn along to chal and ev ch over 1f out: sn drvn and one pce ins fnl f* **14/1**

2330 **5** *1 ¾* **Solar Spirit (IRE)**[25] 2897 4-9-8 **83** .... GrahamGibbons 9 81
(J J Quinn) *chsd ldrs: rdn along 2f out: drvn over 1f out and kpt on same pce* **11/2**[2]

2502 **6** *2 ¾* **Errigal Lad**[10] 3377 4-9-7 **82** ....(p) NCallan 3 72
(K A Ryan) *cl up on inner: rdn along 2f out abnd ev ch tl drvn and one pce over 1f out* **11/1**

3311 **7** *¾* **Novellen Lad (IRE)**[17] 3172 4-9-11 **86** .... DavidAllan 13 73
(E J Alston) *nvr bttr than midfield* **14/1**

4040 **8** *1 ¼* **Maze (IRE)**[27] 2814 4-9-11 **86** .... TomEaves 10 69
(B Smart) *towards rr: hdwy 2f out: sn rdn and no imp* **20/1**

5-01 **9** *1 ½* **Suzie Quw**[46] 2227 3-8-8 **82** .... DeclanCannon(7) 6 60
(K R Burke) *a towards rr* **20/1**

3501 **10** *¾* **Mark Of Meydan**[11] 3354 4-8-12 **73** .... PhillipMakin 1 49
(M Dods) *a towards rr* **11/1**

2005 **11** *1 ¼* **Opus Maximus (IRE)**[10] 3391 4-9-13 **88** .... RoystonFfrench 5 60
(M Johnston) *sn rdn along and a in rr* **14/1**

0616 **12** *nse* **Mr Wolf**[10] 3372 8-8-13 **74** ....(p) TonyHamilton 11 46
(D W Barker) *led: rdn along and hdd 2f out: sn wknd* **28/1**

0000 **13** *17* **Ajigolo**[31] 2707 6-9-13 **88** .... TPO'Shea 2 5
(N Wilson) *hld up: hdwy and in tch 1/2-way: rdn and wknd 2f out: eased* **33/1**

1m 17.66s (0.76) **Going Correction** +0.30s/f (Good)
WFA 3 from 4yo+ 6lb **13** Ran SP% **120.2**
Speed ratings (Par 107): **106,103,102,102,99 96,95,93,91,90 88,88,66**
toteswingers: 1&2 £11.00, 1&3 £6.30, 2&3 £8.70 CSF £111.32 CT £301.66 TOTE £9.30: £2.50, £3.50, £1.40; EX 56.10.

Owner Stan Wright **Bred** P And Mrs A G Venner **Trained** Eastwell, Leics

FOCUS

This was a fair sprint handicap. The inconsistent winner produced his best effort since winning this last year.

NOTEBOOK

Dickie Le Davoir, having to race from 5lb out of the handicap, came back to form when second in first-time blinkers at Beverley the other day and he came with a well-timed challenge under Spencer to repeat last year´s win in the race. He has largely been in decline over the past year, but is clearly returning to something like his best. (op 10-1)

Red Cape(FR), shouldering a 6lb penalty for winning at Catterick last week, was soon up with the pace and went to the front over a furlong out. He kept on right the way to the line and registered another good effort, but couldn´t match the winner. (op 8-1)

Eton Rifles(IRE), 6lb higher than when winning in heavy ground at Haydock back in May, didn´t find this enough of a test at the distance and never looked like winning. He kept on to just take third and a return to 7f seems in order. (op 9-4)

Misplaced Fortune has been in good form, finishing second off a 2lb lower mark in her bid for a hat-trick at Leicester last time, and she again ran well here on ground that would have been softer than ideal. (op 16-1 tchd 18-1)

Solar Spirit(IRE) is largely consistent, though he again got going too late and remains without a win in handicaps. (op 8-1)

Errigal Lad showed lots of speed but could find no extra in the final furlong. (tchd 12-1)

Mark Of Meydan Official explanation: jockey said gelding never travelled

Ajigolo Official explanation: jockey said horse lost its action

3707 JOHN LOFTHOUSE 50TH BIRTHDAY CELEBRATION MAIDEN STKS 1m 4f 8y

5:00 (5:01) (Class 5) 3-Y-0+ **£3,238** (£963; £481; £240) **Stalls** Low

Form RPR

-233 **1** **Times Up**[18] 3117 3-8-13 79 .... EddieAhern 2 89
(J L Dunlop) *led to 1/2-way: cl up tl led again 2f out: rdn clr over 1f out and styd on strly* **5/2**[2]

6220 **2** *7* **Gibb River (IRE)**[18] 3090 3-8-13 85 .... JimmyFortune 1 78
(P W Chapple-Hyam) *trckd wnr: led 1/2-way: rdn along and hdd over 2f out: sn drvn and plugged on same pce* **6/5**[1]

03-2 **3** *1 ½* **Alqaffay (IRE)**[9] 3425 4-9-12 0 .... RHills 6 76
(J H M Gosden) *trckd ldng pair: smooth hdwy over 3f out: led briefly over 2f out: sn rdn and hdd: wknd fnl f* **5/2**[2]

000- **4** *23* **Transporter (IRE)**[263] 6789 3-8-13 38 .... DavidAllan 4 39
(T D Easterby) *in tch: rdn along over 3f out and sn wl outpcd* **100/1**

0 **5** *1 ¾* **Watchoverme**[22] 2981 3-8-8 0 .... JamieSpencer 3 31
(J R Fanshawe) *in tch: rdn along over 3f out and sn wl outpcd* **20/1**[3]

40-0 **6** *15* **Masking Baldini (IRE)**[18] 3123 5-9-12 40 .... SilvestreDeSousa 5 12
(J Hetherton) *a in rr: bhd fnl 4f* **250/1**

2m 41.92s (1.12) **Going Correction** +0.30s/f (Good)
WFA 3 from 4yo+ 13lb **6** Ran SP% **108.7**
Speed ratings (Par 103): **108,103,102,87,85 75**
toteswingers: 1&2 £1.10, 1&3 £1.50, 2&3 £1.10 CSF £5.51 TOTE £3.10: £1.70, £1.40; EX 5.90.

Owner Mrs I H Stewart-Brown & M J Meacock **Bred** I Stewart-Brown And M Meacock **Trained** Arundel, W Sussex

FOCUS

The front three brought fair form to this maiden. Times Up ran out an easy winner but this is probably not form to take too literally.

3708 RED SHIRT NIGHT ON FRIDAY 17TH JULY H'CAP 1m 4y

5:30 (5:31) (Class 5) (0-70,69) 3-Y-0 **£3,238** (£963; £481; £240) **Stalls** Low

Form RPR

-300 **1** **Cheam Forever (USA)**[35] 2578 3-9-0 **62** .... RichardKingscote 5 67
(R Charlton) *sn led: rdn 2f out: drvn and edgd lft appr last: kpt on u.p ins fnl f* **12/1**

65 **2** *1 ½* **Miss Sophisticat**[23] 2942 3-9-7 **69** ....(v) EddieAhern 7 71
(W J Knight) *cl up: rdn along wl over 1f out: ev ch tl drvn and one pce appr fnl f* **4/1**[2]

-403 **3** *2 ½* **Hilltop Artistry**[15] 3207 3-9-1 **66** .... DavidProbert(3) 4 62
(S W James) *hld up: hdwy 1/2-way: rdn to chse ldrs 2f out: drvn over 1f out and kpt on same pce ins fnl f* **8/1**

5056 **4** *2* **Hey Up Dad**[17] 3156 3-9-1 **63** ....(tp) PhillipMakin 3 54
(M Dods) *trckd ldrs: rdn along over 2f out: sn drvn and no imp appr fnl f* **3/1**[1]

450 **5** *2* **Zouk**[25] 2885 3-9-6 **68** .... AdamKirby 1 55
(W R Swinburn) *hld up towards rr: hdwy over 3f out: rdn over 2f out: drvn wl over 1f out and sn no imp* **4/1**[2]

0-60 **6** *1 ½* **Zelos Diktator**[11] 3336 3-8-2 **50** oh1 .... FrancisNorton 6 33
(J G Given) *in tch: rdn along 3f out: wknd 2f out* **18/1**

0664 **7** *½* **Arctic Freedom (USA)**[7] 3476 3-9-2 **64** .... JimmyFortune 2 46
(E A L Dunlop) *hld up towards rr: effrt over 3f out: sn rdn and nvr a factor* **5/1**[3]

060 **8** *3 ½* **Kentucky Lakes**[31] 2723 3-8-2 **50** .... AndrewMullen 9 24
(Jedd O'Keeffe) *chsd ldrs: rdn along 3f out and sn wknd* **40/1**

0-00 **9** *20* **Jacobite Prince (IRE)**[21] 3009 3-9-0 **62** .... PaulMulrennan 8 —
(M H Tompkins) *v s.i.s and swvd bdly rt s: a wl bhd* **16/1**

1m 46.9s (1.00) **Going Correction** +0.30s/f (Good) **9** Ran SP% **114.1**
Speed ratings (Par 100): **107,105,103,101,99 97,97,93,73**
toteswingers: 1&2 £9.20, 1&3 £7.30, 2&3 £6.30 CSF £58.82 CT £412.45 TOTE £14.30: £3.70, £1.70, £2.70; EX 64.20 Place 6: £250.07 Place 5: £137.56.

Owner H R H Sultan Ahmad Shah **Bred** Robert W McCann Et Al **Trained** Beckhampton, Wilts

■ Stewards' Enquiry : Eddie Ahern caution: used whip with excessive frequency

FOCUS

This was a weak handicap and the form is not strong despite a fair time for the grade.

Zouk Official explanation: trainer's rep said gelding was unsuited by the good to soft ground

Jacobite Prince(IRE) Official explanation: jockey said gelding was slowly away

T/Plt: £803.40 to a £1 stake. Pool: £78,933.66. 71.72 winning tickets. T/Qpdt: £113.70 to a £1 stake. Pool: £6,685.71. 43.50 winning tickets. JR

2741 SOUTHWELL (L-H)

Tuesday, July 7

OFFICIAL GOING: Standard

Wind: Light 1/2 behind Weather: changeable, heavy showers 1st 4 races

3709 BET TOTEPOOL AT TOTESPORT.COM (S) STKS 5f (F)

6:40 (6:41) (Class 6) 2-Y-0 **£2,047** (£604; £302) **Stalls** High

Form RPR

565 **1** **Mahiki**[19] 3072 2-8-1 0 .... JamieKyne(5) 3 63
(S A Callaghan) *fly-jmpd s: sn w ldrs: rdn to ld over 1f out: styd on wl* **9/2**[3]

5542 **2** *2 ¼* **True Red (IRE)**[15] 3203 2-8-6 0 .... AlanMunro 4 55
(B R Millman) *mde most: hdd over 1f out: styd on same pce* **10/3**[1]

0300 **3** *1 ¼* **Southwark Newshawk**[21] 3006 2-8-6 0 .... LiamJones 2 50
(Mrs C A Dunnett) *w ldrs far side: kpt on same pce appr fnl f* **7/2**[2]

4665 **4** *hd* **Drumpellier (IRE)**[25] 2896 2-8-6 0 .... FrankieMcDonald 12 50
(P T Midgley) *sn outpcd in rr: hdwy 2f out: kpt on fnl f* **5/1**

5040 **5** *1* **Zaskia (IRE)**[4] 3572 2-8-6 0 ....(b[1]) RoystonFfrench 11 46
(K A Ryan) *w ldrs stands' side: one pce appr fnl f* **18/1**

00 **6** *hd* **Bookiesindex Girl (IRE)**[26] 2860 2-8-6 0 .... AdrianMcCarthy 1 45
(J R Jenkins) *chsd ldrs far side: one pce fnl 2f* **14/1**

002 **7** *1 ½* **Angie's Nap (USA)**[39] 2457 2-8-1 0 ....(v[1]) Louis-PhilippeBeuzelin(5) 9 40
(P S McEntee) *w ldrs: rdn and wknd fnl f* **13/2**

6060 **8** *¾* **Saachi's Vision (IRE)**[22] 2978 2-8-7 0 ow1 ....(bt) StephenCarson 14 38
(D K Ivory) *chsd ldrs stands' side: wknd appr fnl f* **50/1**

000 **9** *2* **Santas Pal**[35] 2575 2-8-3 0 .... KellyHarrison(3) 5 30
(C J Teague) *w ldrs: wknd over 1f out* **50/1**

05 **10** *2* **Cecil's Gift**[15] 3203 2-8-1 0 .... RossAtkinson(5) 10 23
(W G M Turner) *s.i.s: sn outpcd and bhd: kpt on fnl 2f* **50/1**

00 **11** *hd* **Reel Easy**[85] 1249 2-8-11 0 .... JerryO'Dwyer 8 27
(J R Holt) *sn in rr on stands' side* **66/1**

00 **12** *1 ½* **Keithshazel (IRE)**[3] 3634 2-7-13 0 .... AndrewHeffernan(7) 6 17
(Garry Moss) *mid-div: lost pl over 2f out* **50/1**

00 **13** *8* **Daft Lad**[52] 2069 2-8-11 0 .... TPQueally 13 —
(L A Mullaney) *dwlt: racd stands' side: wl bhd fnl 2f* **20/1**

60.45 secs (0.75) **Going Correction** -0.05s/f (Stan) **13** Ran SP% **119.5**
Speed ratings (Par 92): **92,88,86,86,84 84,81,80,77,74 73,71,58**
toteswingers: 1&2 £4.20, 1&3 £2.50, 2&3 £2.40 CSF £19.00 TOTE £3.40: £1.80, £1.70, £1.40; EX 22.40.The winner was bought in for 9,500gns.

Owner The Mahiki Partnership **Bred** Whatton Manor Stud **Trained** Newmarket, Suffolk

FOCUS

The main action took place up the middle of the track and a low draw proved advantageous in this ordinary juvenile seller. Straightforward low-grade form.

NOTEBOOK

Mahiki had shown just ordinary form in three starts in maiden company, including when well behind the potentially Group-class Orpen Grey at Warwick last time, but this represented a significant drop in grade. She proved a class apart, showing good speed throughout to avoid kickback, and looks better than this level, with her connections going to 9,500gns to buy her back at the subsequent auction. However, a slight note of caution, once in front she wandered slightly and had a good look around. (op 100-30 tchd 3-1)

True Red(IRE), already exposed at this level, showed early speed but simply wasn't good enough. (op 3-1 tchd 7-2)

Southwark Newshawk, one of the few with previous experience of this surface, was well drawn and didn't seem to have an excuse. (op 13-2 tchd 7-1)

Drumpellier(IRE) kept on in the closing stages and fared best of those drawn in a double-figure stall. (op 6-1 tchd 13-2)

Zaskia(IRE), who was trying headgear for the first time, showed early speed but faded late on, possibly racing on a slower part of the track. (op 16-1 tchd 20-1)

3710 TOTESPORT HOME OF POOL BETTING MAIDEN H'CAP 1m (F)
7:10 (7:13) (Class 6) (0-60,60) 3-Y-O+ **£2,047** (£604; £302) **Stalls** Low

Form RPR

-600 **1** **Guga (IRE)**[8] 3460 3-8-12 **55**.............. TonyCulhane 4 63
(George Baker) *chsd ldrs: drvn over 3f out: chsd ldr over 2f out: led 1f out: all out* **11/2**[2]

000 **2** *1 3/4* **Russian Music (USA)**[70] 1592 4-8-13 **47**..............(b) DaleGibson 6 53
(C A Mulhall) *t.k.h: trckd ldrs: led after 3f: hdd 1f out: kpt on same pce* **7/1**[3]

4040 **3** *1* **Jonnie Skull (IRE)**[26] 2863 3-8-12 **55**..............(vt) JerryO'Dwyer 10 57
(P S McEntee) *chsd ldrs: edgd lft over 2f out: kpt on same pce fnl f* **14/1**

0/00 **4** *3 1/2* **Bernix**[34] 2608 7-9-1 **54**.............. Louis-PhilippeBeuzelin(5) 12 50
(N Tinkler) *s.i.s: in rr: kpt on fnl 2f: nt rch ldrs* **40/1**

-000 **5** *shd* **Leelu**[13] 3279 3-9-3 **60**.............. GeorgeBaker 5 53
(D W P Arbuthnot) *s.s: in rr: hdwy over 2f out: kpt on fnl f* **25/1**

0230 **6** *1* **Carpe Diem**[8] 3448 4-9-7 **55**..............(v) TonyHamilton 2 48
(R A Fahey) *chsd ldrs: kpt on one pce appr fnl f* **7/2**[1]

00-0 **7** *1/2* **Cooper Island Kid (USA)**[78] 1408 3-9-1 **58**.............. MickyFenton 7 48
(P W D'Arcy) *s.i.s: racd wd: in rr: hdwy on wd outside over 2f out: styd on: nt rch ldrs* **28/1**

8 *1/2* **Denton (NZ)**[507] 6-9-2 **50**..............(t) LukeMorris 13 41
(J R Gask) *chsd ldrs: wknd appr fnl f* **7/2**[1]

-003 **9** *1 3/4* **Le Reve Royal**[11] 3352 3-9-0 **57**..............(v[1]) DavidAllan 14 42
(G R Oldroyd) *chsd ldrs on outer: outpcd over 4f out: wknd over 2f out* **11/1**

045 **10** *3 3/4* **Final Son**[24] 2922 4-9-7 **55**.............. AlanMunro 9 33
(A P Jarvis) *led 3f: lost pl 3f out* **12/1**

00 **11** *7* **Inchando (FR)**[26] 2851 5-9-11 **59**.............. TolleyDean 3 21
(A W Carroll) *sn in rr and drvn along: bhd fnl 4f* **66/1**

-006 **12** *13* **Rockson (IRE)**[12] 3302 3-8-12 **55**.............. RoystonFfrench 11 —
(B W Hills) *w ldrs: drvn and lost pl over 4f out: wl bhd whn eased 2f out* **11/2**[2]

06-0 **13** *40* **Short Sharp Shock**[46] 2230 3-9-1 **58**.............. TPQueally 1 —
(J Mackie) *s.i.s: sn wl bhd: virtually p.u 3f out* **20/1**

1m 45.09s (1.39) **Going Correction** +0.125s/f (Slow)
WFA 3 from 4yo+ 9lb **13** Ran SP% **126.4**
Speed ratings (Par 101): **98,96,95,91,91 90,90,89,87,84 77,64,24**
toteswingers: 1&2 £11.20, 1&3 not won, 2&3 not won. CSF £44.12 CT £532.62 TOTE £6.40: £3.10, £3.50, £3.70; EX 41.10.
Owner Findlay & Bloom **Bred** Azienda Agricola Loreto Luciani **Trained** Moreton Morrell, Warwicks

FOCUS
A moderate, uncompetitive maiden handicap and few were ever seriously involved. The time was poor; 2.27 seconds slower than the following 3yo claimer.
Guga(IRE) Official explanation: trainer said, regarding apparent improvement in form, that this was the colt's first run on Fibresand, having run promisingly previously and was in lower class.
Short Sharp Shock Official explanation: jockey said colt lost its action

3711 BET TOTEPOOL ON 0800 221 221 CLAIMING STKS 1m (F)
7:40 (7:40) (Class 5) 3-Y-O **£2,729** (£806; £403) **Stalls** Low

Form RPR

0515 **1** **Swiss Art (IRE)**[15] 3225 3-8-9 70.............. SilvestreDeSousa 9 65
(Mrs R A Carr) *chsd ldrs: hung lft and led 1f out: kpt on towards fin* **4/5**[1]

0201 **2** *3/4* **Iron Out (USA)**[12] 3305 3-9-3 65.............. MickyFenton 5 71
(R Hollinshead) *led: edgd rt and hdd 1f out: no ex towards fin* **7/1**[3]

-060 **3** *10* **Aboukir**[13] 3279 3-9-7 67.............. NCallan 3 51
(P F I Cole) *s.i.s: sn chsng ldrs: rdn over 3f out: one pce fnl 2f* **7/1**[3]

0060 **4** *1/2* **Wicklewood**[24] 2918 3-8-13 45.............. TPQueally 10 42
(Mrs C A Dunnett) *w ldrs on outer: one pce fnl 2f* **40/1**

-004 **5** *1/2* **Peace Concluded**[28] 2794 3-8-13 66.............. JamesMillman(3) 8 44
(B R Millman) *hmpd s: sn bhd on outer: reminders after 2f: styd on fnl 2f* **6/1**[2]

006- **6** *1* **Isabella Romee (IRE)**[257] 6931 3-8-10 56 ow2.............. MichellePayne 7 35
(Jane Chapple-Hyam) *in tch: outpcd and lost pl over 4f out: hdwy over 2f out: one pce* **14/1**

0004 **7** *1 3/4* **Off Hand**[46] 2234 3-7-13 48..............(b[1]) KellyHarrison(3) 13 23
(T D Easterby) *s.i.s: hdwy on outside 4f out: one pce fnl 2f* **33/1**

0-04 **8** *4 1/2* **Silent Treatment (IRE)**[12] 3302 3-8-8 58.............. JimmyQuinn 2 18
(Miss Gay Kelleway) *chsd ldrs: rdn over 3f out: wknd over 1f out* **12/1**

6000 **9** *3 1/4* **Terrymene Prince**[1] 3685 3-8-4 40..........(v) Louis-PhilippeBeuzelin(5) 4 11
(L A Mullaney) *chsd ldrs: lost pl 3f out* **66/1**

6-00 **10** *27* **Strevelyn**[11] 2627 3-8-5 44.............. AndrewElliott 6 —
(Mrs A Duffield) *lost pl after 2f: sn bhd: t.o 3f out* **66/1**

1m 42.82s (-0.88) **Going Correction** +0.125s/f (Slow) **10** Ran SP% **117.6**
Speed ratings (Par 100): **109,108,98,97,97 96,94,90,86,59**
toteswingers: 1&2 £1.10, 1&3 £1.70, 2&3 £6.80 CSF £6.92 TOTE £1.50: £1.10, £2.00, £2.60; EX 7.20.Swiss Art was the subject of a friendly claim.
Owner David W Chapman **Bred** John Yarr **Trained** Huby, N Yorks
■ Stewards' Enquiry : Micky Fenton caution: careless riding

FOCUS
The winning time was 2.27 seconds quicker than the 55-rated Guga managed in an earlier handicap.
Peace Concluded Official explanation: jockey said filly suffered interference leaving stalls

3712 £10 FREE PLAY AT TOTESPORTBINGO.COM MAIDEN STKS 6f (F)
8:10 (8:10) (Class 5) 3-4-Y-O **£2,729** (£806; £403) **Stalls** Low

Form RPR

2432 **1** **George Thisby**[17] 3161 3-9-0 72.............. JamesMillman(3) 13 70
(B R Millman) *chsd ldrs on outside: lost pl over 4f out: gd hdwy on outside over 2f out: r.o wl to ld towards fin* **11/10**[1]

-503 **2** *hd* **Defector (IRE)**[29] 2761 3-9-3 72..............(b[1]) GeorgeBaker 11 69
(W R Muir) *sn chsng ldrs: hung lft and led over 1f out: hdd last strides* **4/1**[3]

605- **3** *3 3/4* **Mr Rio (IRE)**[306] 5627 4-9-9 58.............. AlanMunro 5 58
(A P Jarvis) *led tl over 1f out: kpt on same pce* **18/1**

-366 **4** *7* **Abu Derby (IRE)**[43] 2343 3-9-3 70.............. PatCosgrave 3 35
(J G Given) *w ldrs: wknd over 1f out* **10/1**

5 *1 1/2* **Fast Living** 4-9-9 0.............. LiamJones 2 31
(Ms E L McWilliam) *chsd ldrs: upsides 2f out: sn wknd* **33/1**

0 **6** *2* **Crimson Mist**[20] 3036 3-8-10 0.............. IJBrennan(7) 4 23
(J J Quinn) *chsd ldrs: sn drvn along: lost pl over 2f out* **25/1**

7 *3 1/4* **Hohrod** 3-8-12 0.............. MarkCoumbe(5) 6 13
(John A Harris) *s.s: detached in last: sme hdwy 2f out: nvr on terms* **66/1**

8 *1* **Angels And Demons (IRE)** 3-8-5 0.............. AndrewHeffernan(7) 7 5
(Garry Moss) *sn drvn along: lost pl over 4f out: sn in rr* **50/1**

2205 **9** *2 1/4* **Rebel City**[14] 3243 3-9-3 72.............. NCallan 9 3
(S A Callaghan) *w ldrs: lost pl over 1f out: heavily eased ins fnl f* **11/4**[2]

/0-0 **10** *4* **Becky Quick (IRE)**[17] 3155 4-8-11 0.............. CharlotteKerton(7) 12 —
(Bruce Hellier) *sn chsng ldrs: wknd over 2f out* **150/1**

1m 16.7s (0.20) **Going Correction** +0.125s/f (Slow)
WFA 3 from 4yo 6lb **10** Ran SP% **119.5**
Speed ratings (Par 103): **103,102,97,88,86 83,79,78,75,69**
toteswingers: 1&2 £1.50, 1&3 £14.00, 2&3 not won. CSF £5.89 TOTE £2.10: £1.10, £1.10, £4.60; EX 4.80.
Owner Robert Thisby **Bred** Meon Valley Stud **Trained** Kentisbeare, Devon

FOCUS
A modest sprint maiden.
Rebel City Official explanation: jockey said colt had a breathing problem

3713 OVER 50 GAMES AT TOTESPORTGAMES.COM H'CAP 6f (F)
8:40 (8:41) (Class 5) (0-70,70) 3-Y-O+ **£2,729** (£806; £403) **Stalls** Low

Form RPR

0500 **1** **Elusive Fame (USA)**[16] 3193 3-9-4 **67**.............. RoystonFfrench 9 76
(M Johnston) *chsd ldrs: styd on to ld 1f out: kpt on wl* **10/1**

0166 **2** *1 1/4* **Guto**[46] 2225 6-9-4 **64**..............(p) KellyHarrison(3) 6 70
(W J H Ratcliffe) *led: t.k.h: hung rt off bnd 3f out: hdd 1f out: kpt on same pce* **10/1**

-226 **3** *nk* **Elusive Hawk (IRE)**[49] 2168 5-9-13 **70**.............. TPQueally 7 75
(B J Curley) *prom: rdn and outpcd over 3f out: hdwy over 2f out: edgd lft over 1f out: kpt on same pce* **9/2**[2]

2103 **4** *2 1/4* **Dualagi**[13] 3272 5-9-2 **59**.............. GeorgeBaker 2 57
(M R Bosley) *hld up in rr: hdwy and hung rt over 2f out: kpt on fnl f* **12/1**

00-0 **5** *nse* **Yankee Storm**[15] 3211 4-9-13 **70**.............. PatCosgrave 3 68
(M Quinn) *chsd ldrs: kpt on same pce appr fnl f* **22/1**

155 **6** *3/4* **Figaro Flyer (IRE)**[24] 2929 6-9-13 **70**.............. JimmyQuinn 10 65
(P Howling) *prom on outer: kpt on same pce fnl 2f* **15/2**

3505 **7** *3 1/2* **Makshoof (IRE)**[20] 3021 5-9-5 **65**..............(p) NeilBrown(3) 5 49
(I W McInnes) *s.i.s: hdwy over 2f out: nvr a factor* **13/2**[3]

0 **8** *1/2* **Whiteoak Lady (IRE)**[78] 1403 4-9-6 **68**.............. JackDean(5) 14 50
(J L Spearing) *dwlt: sn in rr on outside: hdwy over 2f out: nvr on terms* **10/1**

0305 **9** *2 1/2* **Rio Sands**[6] 3497 4-9-0 **60**.............. MichaelJStainton(3) 4 34
(R M Whitaker) *prom: fdd over 1f out* **16/1**

4050 **10** *1/2* **Back In The Red (IRE)**[13] 3261 5-9-10 **70**..........(b) KevinGhunowa(3) 1 43
(R A Harris) *prominent on inner: outpcd over 3f out: one pce fnl 2f* **16/1**

0050 **11** *1/2* **Circle Dance (IRE)**[4] 3562 4-9-6 **63**..............(v) PatrickMathers 11 34
(D Shaw) *in tch on outer: lost pl over 4f out* **22/1**

3023 **12** *1 3/4* **Papillio (IRE)**[11] 3338 4-9-13 **70**.............. NCallan 8 36
(J R Fanshawe) *w ldr: wknd over 1f out: eased whn wl btn ins fnl f* **7/2**[1]

50-0 **13** *5* **Star Acclaim**[26] 2852 4-9-3 **60**..............(t) AlanMunro 13 10
(E V Stanford) *restless in stalls: in tch on outer: lost pl over 4f out: in rr whn eased* **50/1**

1m 16.98s (0.48) **Going Correction** +0.125s/f (Slow)
WFA 3 from 4yo+ 6lb **13** Ran SP% **122.9**
Speed ratings (Par 103): **101,99,98,95,95 94,90,89,86,85 84,82,75**
toteswingers: 1&2 not won, 1&3 £4.40, 2&3 not won. CSF £107.16 CT £523.90 TOTE £14.40: £5.20, £4.00, £2.50; EX 199.20.
Owner Mark Johnston Racing Ltd **Bred** Summer Wind Farm **Trained** Middleham Moor, N Yorks

FOCUS
A modest sprint handicap.
Guto Official explanation: jockey said gelding hung right throughout
Dualagi Official explanation: jockey said mare hung right throughout
Whiteoak Lady(IRE) Official explanation: jockey said filly was slowly away and resented the kickback
Back In The Red(IRE) Official explanation: jockey said gelding never travelled
Papillio(IRE) Official explanation: jockey said gelding had no more to give

3714 100% NEW PLAYER BONUS AT TOTESPORTCASINO.COM H'CAP 1m 6f (F)
9:10 (9:10) (Class 6) (0-65,63) 4-Y-O+ **£2,047** (£604; £302) **Stalls** Low

Form RPR

6033 **1** **Dazzling Begum**[11] 3348 4-8-4 **46**.............. LiamJones 4 60
(J Pearce) *chsd ldrs: wnt 2nd over 2f out: styd on to ld last 100yds* **12/1**

-400 **2** *1* **Crimson Mitre**[34] 2601 4-9-5 **61**.............. NCallan 5 74
(J Jay) *w ldr: led over 4f out: hdd and no ex ins fnl f* **11/1**

-400 **3** *8* **Swords**[22] 2971 7-8-9 **56**.............. MartinLane(5) 13 57
(R E Peacock) *in rr: hdwy to chse ldrs over 4f out: wnt 3rd over 2f out: one pce* **12/1**

2515 **4** *1 1/4* **Dancing Lyra**[19] 3068 8-9-6 **62**.............. TonyHamilton 9 62
(R A Fahey) *in rr: hdwy over 2f out: styd on fnl f* **7/2**[1]

3054 **5** *2* **Amwell Brave**[33] 2634 8-8-6 **48**.............. AdrianMcCarthy 14 45
(J R Jenkins) *in rr: hdwy 7f out: one pce fnl 3f* **6/1**[3]

-000 **6** *1/2* **Stormy Summer**[17] 3158 4-8-10 **52**..............(t) PatCosgrave 10 48
(R W Price) *in rr: hdwy over 5f out: wnt 2nd 3f out: wknd over 1f out* **20/1**

0-00 **7** *15* **Stagecoach Emerald**[40] 2419 7-8-10 **52** ow4..............(p) MickyFenton 8 27
(R W Price) *prom early: in rr and drvn after 4f: sme hdwy on wd outside over 2f out: nvr on terms* **25/1**

0-00 **8** *5* **Polish Red**[22] 2983 5-9-6 **62**..............(p) JimmyQuinn 7 30
(Jane Chapple-Hyam) *in rr: shkn up and hdwy 6f out: lost pl over 2f out* **8/1**

5-01 **9** *1* **Piverina (IRE)**[20] 3023 4-8-3 **52**.............. AndrewHeffernan(7) 3 19
(Miss J A Camacho) *trckd ldrs: drvn over 4f out: lost pl over 3f out* **13/2**

300- **10** *7* **Leyte Gulf (USA)**[252] 7045 6-9-0 **56**.............. FrankieMcDonald 11 13
(C C Bealby) *dwlt: t.k.h: sn trcking ldrs: lost pl over 3f out* **22/1**

0632 **11** *7* **Blue Jet (USA)**[28] 2785 5-8-5 **47**.............. PaulQuinn 2 —
(R M Whitaker) *led tl over 4f out: wknd 3f out* **5/1**[2]

-300 **12** *4 1/2* **One Tou Many**[17] 3171 4-8-0 **45**.............. KellyHarrison(3) 12 —
(C W Fairhurst) *mid-div: drvn 6f out: sn lost pl: t.o 3f out* **10/1**

3m 9.41s (1.11) **Going Correction** +0.125s/f (Slow) **12** Ran SP% **123.4**
Speed ratings (Par 101): **101,100,95,95,94 93,85,82,81,77 73,71**
toteswingers: 1&2 £24.30, 1&3 £24.30, 2&3 not won. CSF £138.98 CT £1641.05 TOTE £13.40: £5.00, £6.50, £3.00; EX 267.40 Place 6 £202.63, Place 5 £151.12.
Owner Macniler Racing Partnership **Bred** Ian Bryant **Trained** Newmarket, Suffolk

FOCUS
A moderate staying handicap in which the front two pulled well clear.
Blue Jet(USA) Official explanation: jockey said gelding hung right
T/Plt: £225.20 to a £1 stake. Pool: £75,396.37. 244.35 winning tickets. T/Qpdt: £30.50 to a £1 stake. Pool: £5,488.72. 133.10 winning tickets. WG

3464 WOLVERHAMPTON (A.W) (L-H)

Tuesday, July 7

OFFICIAL GOING: Standard

Wind: Moderate across Weather: Showers

3715 CLEANEVENT MAIDEN AUCTION STKS (DIV I) 7f 32y(P)
1:45 (1:47) (Class 5) 2-Y-0 **£3,561** (£1,059; £529; £264) **Stalls** High

Form RPR

2 **1** **Mister Angry (IRE)**[18] 3106 2-8-13 0 J-PGuillambert 7 84+
(M Johnston) *mde all: rdn clr and edgd lft 1f out: r.o wl* **7/4**[2]

2 *7* **Forshour** 2-8-10 0 TedDurcan 6 64
(E S McMahon) *hld up in mid-div: hdwy over 3f out: wnt 2nd 1f out: no ch w wnr* **33/1**

0 **3** *1 ¼* **Llandovery**[17] 3167 2-8-7 0 JackMitchell(3) 11 61
(P J McBride) *hld up: hdwy on outside over 3f out: rdn over 2f out: kpt on same pce to take 3rd wl ins fnl f* **11/1**

5 **4** *1* **Lutine Bell**[18] 3106 2-8-13 0 SebSanders 12 61
(Sir Mark Prescott) *sn w ldrs: ev ch over 2f out: rdn and wknd over 1f out* **6/1**[3]

0 **5** *hd* **Creevy (IRE)**[14] 3249 2-8-6 0 JamesDoyle 1 54
(S Kirk) *s.i.s: outpcd in rr: hdwy over 2f out: rdn over 1f out: one pce* **12/1**

6 *2* **Charlottesometimes (USA)** 2-8-5 0 ow1 RichardMullen 10 48
(D M Simcock) *hld up and bhd: hdwy 2f out: no imp fnl f* **33/1**

0 **7** *2 ¾* **Dimaire**[27] 2825 2-8-4 0 FrankieMcDonald 9 40
(D Haydn Jones) *prom tl rdn and wknd over 2f out* **40/1**

8 *nk* **Execution (IRE)** 2-8-12 0 TGMcLaughlin 3 47
(E A L Dunlop) *hld up in tch on ins: pushed along and wknd over 2f out* **20/1**

3 **9** *½* **Newton Circus**[28] 2793 2-8-12 0 RyanMoore 2 46
(R Hannon) *w wnr: ev ch over 2f out: rdn wl over 1f out: wknd ent fnl f: sn eased* **6/4**[1]

0 **10** *nk* **Dunwhinny**[27] 2825 2-8-10 0 ow1 IanMongan 4 44
(P W D'Arcy) *a bhd* **100/1**

11 *1 ½* **Ivory Jazz** 2-8-9 0 DarryllHolland 8 39
(D K Ivory) *chsd ldrs tl wknd over 3f out* **28/1**

12 *17* **Althabea** 2-8-11 0 ShaneKelly 5 —
(Ian Williams) *s.i.s: outpcd: lost tch fnl 3f* **33/1**

1m 29.19s (-0.41) **Going Correction** -0.10s/f (Stan) 12 Ran SP% **127.1**
Speed ratings (Par 94): **98,90,88,87,87 84,81,81,80,80 78,59**
toteswingers: 1&2 £22.30, 1&3 £6.20, 2&3 £75.80 CSF £71.82 TOTE £2.60: £1.50, £11.80, £3.60; EX 74.50 TRIFECTA Not won..
Owner The Originals **Bred** Darley **Trained** Middleham Moor, N Yorks

FOCUS
The stronger of the two divisions but not a competitive race and, with the market leader disappointing, this did not take as much winning as seemed likely. The winner still impressed and looks useful. The gallop was fair and the winner raced in the centre in the straight.

NOTEBOOK
Mister Angry(IRE) ◆ fully confirmed debut promise on this first run on Polytrack and, while his task was simplified with his main rival disappointing, there was still plenty to like about the way he went about his business. He should prove equally effective over 1m and is the type to win more races. (op 15-8)
Forshour, a gelded first foal of a multiple 6f-7f winner, was easy to back but showed ability on this racecourse debut. He is entitled to improve for this experience and should be able to pick up a minor event in due course.
Llandovery, who hinted at ability at Newmarket on his debut, ran creditably but may be a bit better than the bare facts suggest as he was posted widest from his double-figure draw throughout. Modest nurseries over further will be the way forward with him. (op 10-1 tchd 12-1)
Lutine Bell still looked inexperienced when pressure was applied but, although he got a bit closer to the winner than on their respective debuts at Musselburgh, he left the impression that the best of him would not be seen until he has qualified for a handicap mark. (op 5-1)
Creevy(IRE), who hinted at ability after a tardy start on this all-weather debut and who was not knocked about once clearly held. She ought to do better. (tchd 16-1)
Newton Circus, who had shown promise, despite hanging, over 6f on his recent turf debut, was the disappointment of the race. The vet reported he finished distressed and he looks one to tread carefully with at present. Official explanation: vet said colt returned distressed (op 11-8 tchd 13-8)

3716 CLEANEVENT MAIDEN AUCTION STKS (DIV II) 7f 32y(P)
2:15 (2:17) (Class 5) 2-Y-0 **£3,561** (£1,059; £529; £264) **Stalls** High

Form RPR

04 **1** **Wasmi (IRE)**[21] 3006 2-8-5 0 ChrisCatlin 12 68
(C E Brittain) *t.k.h: w ldr: led 5f out: rdn jst over 1f out: wandered away fr whip ins fnl f: r.o* **20/1**

6 **2** *1 ¼* **Baltimore Clipper (USA)**[10] 3395 2-8-12 0 TedDurcan 9 72+
(P F I Cole) *s.i.s: hld up and bhd: hdwy on outside over 3f out: chsd wnr 2f out: rdn fnl f: kpt on one pce* **4/1**[2]

3 *2 ½* **Abriachan** 2-8-13 0 JerryO'Dwyer 5 67+
(M G Quinlan) *hld up in tch: pushed along 2f out: rdn over 1f out: one pce ins fnl f* **3/1**[1]

4 *3 ¼* **Zaffature** 2-8-6 0 JimmyQuinn 4 52
(M Botti) *hld up: sn in tch: lost pl on ins over 3f out: rallied over 1f out: wknd ins fnl f* **13/2**

5 **5** *1* **Marafong**[27] 2825 2-8-11 0 AmirQuinn 2 54
(Miss J Feilden) *led: hdd 5f out: prom tl rdn and wknd over 1f out* **9/2**[3]

44 **6** *½* **Brasingaman Eric**[4] 3571 2-8-9 0 LiamJones 6 51
(Mrs G S Rees) *hld up in tch: lost pl over 5f out: hung lft and rdn jst over 1f out: no rspnse* **10/1**

0 **7** *4 ½* **Seldom Seen Kid (IRE)**[19] 3064 2-8-10 0 DNolan 11 41
(T D Easterby) *a bhd* **16/1**

53 **8** *5* **Dancing Poppy**[18] 3106 2-8-8 0 ow1 DarryllHolland 8 27
(M R Channon) *w ldrs: ev ch over 2f out: sn rdn: wknd wl over 1f out* **6/1**

9 *2* **Young Firth** 2-8-9 0 ShaneKelly 3 23
(J R Norton) *bmpd s: sn wl in rr* **66/1**

0 **10** *1* **Inittowinit**[17] 3160 2-8-4 0 MartinDwyer 7 16
(W R Muir) *prom: pushed along over 3f out: wknd over 2f out* **25/1**

1m 30.23s (0.63) **Going Correction** -0.10s/f (Stan) 10 Ran SP% **115.9**
Speed ratings (Par 94): **92,90,87,84,82 82,77,71,69,68**
toteswingers: 1&2 £6.00, 1&3 £8.40, 2&3 £4.70 CSF £96.46 TOTE £13.30: £5.80, £1.20, £1.90; EX 61.70 Trifecta £233.30 Part won. Pool: £315.29 - 0.43 winning units..
Owner Saeed Manana **Bred** Airlie Stud **Trained** Newmarket, Suffolk

FOCUS
The lesser of the two divisions strength-wise and a race run over a second slower than the opener. The winner raced centre to far side in the straight. The level is guesyy but the form looks modest.

NOTEBOOK
Wasmi(IRE), stepped up markedly in distance, had the run of the race but turned in a much improved effort on this all-weather debut. She travelled strongly for much of the way and may be able to progress further in ordinary nursery company on this surface.
Baltimore Clipper(USA) looked to have decent claims on his debut form and ran to a similar level after racing on the outside for much of the last half of the contest. While vulnerable to the better sorts in this grade, he should be able to pick up a minor event around this trip. (tchd 7-2)
Abriachan, the first foal of an unraced half-sister to a 7f winner, lacked the experience of the first two but turned in an encouraging debut effort after attracting market support. He should be all the wiser for this run and is sure to improve. (op 7-2)
Zaffature, nibbled at in the market, was far from disgraced without being knocked about on this racecourse debut. She should have no problems staying 1m and is entitled to come on for this experience. (op 8-1)
Marafong, fifth to a subsequent Listed winner at Kempton on his debut, had the run of the race but failed to build on that effort and his rider reported he hung right. He may do better in nurseries. Official explanation: jockey said colt hung right
Brasingaman Eric was not disgraced on this all-weather debut and first run over 7f. He may be suited by a stiffer test of stamina and may do better in ordinary nursery company. (op 16-1)
Young Firth Official explanation: jockey said gelding suffered interference at start

3717 CLEANDOMAIN (S) STKS 1m 141y(P)
2:45 (2:45) (Class 6) 3-Y-0+ **£2,047** (£604; £302) **Stalls** Low

Form RPR

5664 **1** **Beauchamp Viceroy**[12] 3301 5-9-8 84 (tp) RyanMoore 2 88
(G A Butler) *w ldr: led jst over 2f out: clr wl over 1f out: easily* **1/2**[1]

1620 **2** *10* **Northern Desert (IRE)**[21] 3007 10-10-0 70 (p) JamesDoyle 5 71
(S Curran) *hld up towards rr: hdwy on ins over 3f out: wnt 2nd wl over 1f out: sn rdn: no ch w wnr* **14/1**

4600 **3** *3 ¾* **Quick Off The Mark**[26] 2859 4-9-3 62 (t) J-PGuillambert 7 51
(J G Given) *hld up in rr: pushed along and hdwy over 2f out: wnt 3rd wl ins fnl f: n.d* **9/2**[2]

-200 **4** *2 ½* **Sotik Star (IRE)**[101] 841 6-9-8 62 (p) JimmyQuinn 3 51
(K A Morgan) *a.p: wnt 2nd briefly wl over 1f out: sn rdn: wknd ins fnl f* **12/1**[3]

4546 **5** *½* **Everyman**[27] 2830 5-9-8 49 (v) ShaneKelly 8 49
(A W Carroll) *hmpd s: hld up towards rr: short-lived effrt over 2f out* **25/1**

6100 **6** *2 ¼* **Straight Face (IRE)**[24] 2921 5-9-7 52 (e) KylieManser(7) 1 50
(Miss Gay Kelleway) *led: rdn and hdd jst over 2f out: wknd jst over 1f out* **25/1**

0540 **7** *shd* **Obe Royal**[12] 3301 5-9-9 73 (b) RichardEvans(5) 13 55
(P D Evans) *hld up in rr: struggling over 2f out: eased fnl f: sddle slipped* **12/1**[3]

1-00 **8** *2 ¾* **Hi Spec (IRE)**[170] 210 6-9-3 48 (p) ChrisCatlin 9 33
(Miss M E Rowland) *stdd s: hld up in rr: no ch fnl 3f* **50/1**

500 **9** *¾* **Amber Moon**[29] 2768 4-9-4 52 (b) AnnStokell(5) 6 37
(Miss A Stokell) *prom tl wknd over 2f out* **40/1**

0000 **10** *7* **Strategic Knight (USA)**[7] 3490 4-9-8 50 SebSanders 10 20
(R C Guest) *hld up in mid-div: short-lived effrt on outside over 3f out* **40/1**

0/0- **11** *6* **Rosemarkie**[258] 6896 5-9-3 0 LPKeniry 4 1
(J M Bradley) *hld up in tch: wknd over 3f out* **66/1**

1m 49.46s (-1.04) **Going Correction** -0.10s/f (Stan)
WFA 3 from 4yo+ 10lb 11 Ran SP% **122.9**
Speed ratings (Par 101): **100,91,87,85,85 83,83,80,79,73 68**
toteswingers: 1&2 £3.20, 1&3 £2.30, 2&3 £3.80 CSF £9.55 TOTE £1.70: £1.10, £2.70, £1.90; EX 8.10 Trifecta £41.20 Pool: £394.96 - 7.08 winning units..The winner was bought in for 17,500gns.
Owner Erik Penser **Bred** E Penser **Trained** Newmarket, Suffolk

FOCUS
A wide range of ability on show and a race won in clear-cut fashion by the highest rated horse. The winner edged towards the far side in the straight.
Obe Royal Official explanation: jockey said saddle slipped
Amber Moon Official explanation: jockey said filly's nose band broke

3718 CLEAN WASTE SOLUTIONS MEDIAN AUCTION MAIDEN STKS 1m 141y(P)
3:15 (3:18) (Class 6) 3-4-Y-0 **£3,070** (£906; £453) **Stalls** Low

Form RPR

50-3 **1** **Omnium Duke (IRE)**[15] 3228 3-9-3 70 (v) JimmyQuinn 6 73
(J W Hills) *hld up in tch: led 2f out: clr whn rdn jst over 1f out: r.o wl* **9/2**[3]

-602 **2** *4* **Layer Cake**[15] 3228 3-9-3 72 ChrisCatlin 12 64+
(J W Hills) *hld up towards rr: swtchd lft sn after s: hdwy and c v wd st wl over 1f out: wnt 2nd and edgd lft ins fnl f: no ch w wnr* **3/1**[1]

4005 **3** *3* **Gulf President**[22] 2982 3-9-3 62 (v) TonyCulhane 8 57
(M R Channon) *sn pushed along towards rr: rdn and hdwy on outside 3f out: styd on to take 3rd wl ins fnl f* **6/1**

24-0 **4** *2 ¼* **Whisky Jack**[78] 1414 3-9-3 70 MartinDwyer 1 52
(W R Muir) *s.s: hld up in rr: hdwy on ins over 2f out: rdn jst over 1f out: wknd wl ins fnl f* **7/2**[2]

5 *4* **Grand Pere** 3-8-12 0 RichardEvans(5) 4 43
(P D Evans) *hld up in mid-div: lost pl 5f out: n.d after* **20/1**

50P **6** *hd* **Sirjosh**[16] 3192 3-9-3 0 JamesDoyle 3 42
(D Donovan) *led early: chsd ldr: rdn and ev ch over 2f out: sn lost 2nd: wknd wl over 1f out* **9/1**

7 *hd* **Takizada (IRE)**[281] 4-9-8 75 ClareLindop 13 38
(J R Gask) *prom tl wknd 2f out* **12/1**

0-00 **8** *1 ¼* **Chasing Amy**[21] 3010 3-8-12 57 JerryO'Dwyer 11 34
(M G Quinlan) *sn led: rdn and hdd 2f out: sn btn: wknd fnl f* **40/1**

2300 **9** *2 ½* **Jul's Lad (IRE)**[11] 3336 3-9-3 61 (b[1]) SebSanders 2 33
(M Mullineaux) *t.k.h in tch: rdn and hung lft wl over 1f out: wknd fnl f* **14/1**

10 *1* **Annan Rock (IRE)** 3-9-3 0 VinceSlattery 10 31
(W J Musson) *s.s: a in rr* **25/1**

11 *5* **Prince De Fortune** 3-8-10 0 RyanPowell(7) 7 19
(Mrs C A Dunnett) *hld up in tch: wknd over 2f out* **100/1**

P **The Coach** 3-9-3 0 LiamJones 9 —
(T Wall) *dwlt: a in rr: t.o whn p.u 5f out* **66/1**

1m 49.87s (-0.63) **Going Correction** -0.10s/f (Stan)
WFA 3 from 4yo 10lb 12 Ran SP% **117.6**
Speed ratings (Par 101): **98,94,91,89,86 86,85,84,82,81 77,—**
toteswingers: 1&2 £3.90, 1&3 £5.70, 2&3 £4.70 CSF £17.41 TOTE £5.30: £1.60, £1.30, £2.40; EX 10.40 Trifecta £97.10 Pool: £291.54 - 2.22 winning units..
Owner Barnes/ Waterford Hall Stud **Bred** Waterford Hall Stud **Trained** Upper Lambourn, Berks

FOCUS
A moderate maiden in which progressive types were in short supply. The pace was reasonable but this was another race on the card that suited the prominent racers. The winner raced centre to far side in the straight.

Layer Cake Official explanation: jockey said, regarding running and riding, that his orders were to drop in quickly from an unfavourable draw, give the colt a chance early and get it to finish, adding that it was trapped on the final bend behind a runner that was dropping back and hanging preventing him from making his intended run on the inside and compelled to switch having had to wait longer than he wanted.

3719 ENJOY THE LUCKY 7 GROUP OFFER CLAIMING STKS — 5f 216y(P)

3:45 (3:46) (Class 6) 2-Y-O — £2,729 (£806; £403) Stalls Low

Form — RPR

2140 **1** **Diamond Laura**[41] 2372 2-8-12 0 ... CatherineGannon 5 — 76
(P D Evans) *chsd ldrs: outpcd over 4f out: rallied 3f out: led jst over 2f out: rdn wl over 1f out: drifted towards stands' side: r.o wl* **10/11**[1]

130 **2** *3* **Art Jewel (IRE)**[53] 2054 2-8-12 0 ... RyanMoore 4 — 67
(S A Callaghan) *a.p: pushed along and flashed tail over 2f out: rdn and tail wnt like windmill over 1f out: wnt 2nd wl ins fnl f: nt trble wnr* **10/3**[2]

554 **3** *1 1/4* **Gulf Punch**[20] 3027 2-8-5 0 ... ChrisCatlin 6 — 56
(R Hannon) *prom: outpcd after 1f: hdwy over 2f out: chsd wnr wl over 1f out tl rdn and no ex wl ins fnl f* **9/1**

P0 **4** *1 3/4* **Arken Lad**[21] 2997 2-8-12 0 ...(p) JimmyQuinn 7 — 58
(D Donovan) *sn outpcd and bhd: hdwy whn hung rt over 3f out: rdn and one pce ins fnl f* **66/1**

60 **5** *4 1/2* **One Cool Deal (IRE)**[7] 3487 2-9-3 0 ... TedDurcan 8 — 50
(T D Easterby) *sn outpcd: rdn over 3f out: prog on ins wl over 1f out: wknd ins fnl f* **22/1**

0210 **6** *2 1/2* **Kate Skate**[18] 3086 2-8-7 0 ... MartinLane(5) 9 — 37
(Miss Gay Kelleway) *prom: carried rt over 3f out: wkng whn hung lft over 1f out* **9/2**[3]

0 **7** *1* **Rivitivo**[73] 1504 2-8-9 0 ow1 ... TGMcLaughlin 1 — 31
(W M Brisbourne) *s.i.s: outpcd* **66/1**

0340 **8** *3 3/4* **Vaduz**[5] 3547 2-8-4 0 ow2 ... MCGeran(5) 2 — 20
(M R Channon) *sn w ldr: led over 3f out: hdd jst over 2f out: rdn and wknd over 1f out* **20/1**

0 **9** *2* **Three Sons**[27] 2800 2-8-11 0 ...(b) PatrickMathers 3 — 16
(I W McInnes) *led: hdd and hung rt over 3f out: wknd wl over 1f out* **50/1**

1m 15.35s (0.35) **Going Correction** -0.10s/f (Stan) — **9** Ran SP% **117.7**
Speed ratings (Par 92): **93,89,87,85,79 75,74,69,66**
toteswingers: 1&2 £2.20, 1&3 £3.30, 2&3 £3.20 CSF £3.99 TOTE £1.70: £1.10, £1.40, £1.80; EX 5.60 Trifecta £29.70 Pool: £541.45 - 13.47 winning units..Gulf Punch was claimed by M. Harris for £5,000.

Owner Diamond Racing Ltd **Bred** Paul Sweeting **Trained** Pandy, Monmouths

FOCUS

A couple of fair sorts in this strongly run claimer. The winner edged towards the stands' rail in the straight. Straightforward form, rated around the principals.

NOTEBOOK

Diamond Laura had disappointed in Listed company on her previous start but proved well suited by this drop in grade and showed enough, despite edging right late on, to maintain her unbeaten record on sand. This extra furlong seemed to suit but she may not be the easiest to place away from claiming or selling company. (op 5-4 after early 6-4)

Art Jewel(IRE), with the visor left off here, ran creditably in terms of form dropped a fair way in grade but once again did not impress with the way she repeatedly flashed her tail for pressure. She has the ability to win a similar event but does not appeal as one to be taking too short a price about. (tchd 3-1 and 7-2)

Gulf Punch was fairly easy to back and was not disgraced down in both trip and grade. The way she shapes coupled with her pedigree suggests the return to 7f should suit and she may be capable of a little better in ordinary nursery company. (op 6-1)

Arken Lad had previously shown precious little on turf but turned in a much improved effort in the first-time cheekpieces on this all-weather debut. He looks flattered by coming off a strong pace but it will be interesting to see what the handicapper makes of this.

Kate Skate, soundly beaten in a Group 3 at Royal Ascot on her previous start, looked to have fair claims in this company but proved disappointing on this all-weather debut after racing three deep from her draw. (op 11-2)

Vaduz Official explanation: jockey said filly hung right

Three Sons Official explanation: jockey said gelding hung right

3720 CLEAN CONCIERGE H'CAP — 5f 216y(P)

4:15 (4:16) (Class 6) (0-60,65) 3-Y-O+ — £2,388 (£705; £352) Stalls Low

Form — RPR

000- **1** **Sea Land (FR)**[371] 3593 5-8-12 **57** ... LanceBetts(5) 2 — 66
(B Ellison) *bhd: pushed along over 3f out: hdwy jst over 1f out: r.o wl to ld towards fin* **7/1**

30-0 **2** *1 1/2* **Roleplay (IRE)**[21] 3007 4-9-3 **57** ...(b) LukeMorris 6 — 61
(J M P Eustace) *s.i.s: in rr: rdn 3f out: hdwy on ins over 1f out: ev ch wl ins fnl f: nt qckn* **14/1**

0603 **3** *hd* **Diane's Choice**[8] 3465 6-8-11 **56** ...(e) MartinLane(5) 7 — 59
(Miss Gay Kelleway) *hld up: sn in tch: rdn wl over 1f out: led ins fnl f: hdd and no ex towards fin* **10/1**

0051 **4** *1 3/4* **Bertbrand**[8] 3465 4-9-10 **64** 6ex ...(p) SJCraine 3 — 62
(D Flood) *bhd: pushed along and hdwy over 2f out: rdn wl over 1f out: no ex wl ins fnl f* **12/1**

051 **5** *nk* **Great Knight (IRE)**[15] 3227 4-9-4 **58** ... LPKeniry 5 — 55
(S Kirk) *hld up in mid-div: nt clr run on ins over 2f out: hdwy jst over 1f out: sn rdn: one pce ins fnl f* **9/4**[1]

000 **6** *1/2* **Double Carpet (IRE)**[40] 2418 6-9-6 **60** ... FergusSweeney 9 — 55
(G Woodward) *chsd ldr: led 2f out: rdn over 1f out: hdd ins fnl f: fdd* **12/1**

0542 **7** *1 1/2* **Monte Cassino (IRE)**[15] 3227 4-9-0 **59** ... JamesO'Reilly(5) 11 — 49
(J O'Reilly) *bhd: c wd st: rdn and struggling wl over 1f out* **6/1**[3]

0036 **8** *shd* **Best One**[14] 3246 5-9-0 **57** ... KevinGhunowa(3) 1 — 47
(R A Harris) *s.i.s: sn prom on ins: rdn and ev ch over 1f out: wknd wl ins fnl f* **8/1**

0000 **9** *2 1/4* **Blessed Place**[9] 3422 9-9-4 **58** ...(t) ChrisCatlin 12 — 41
(D J S Ffrench Davis) *broke wl: led: hdd 2f out: wknd ins fnl f* **33/1**

0004 **10** *7* **Dhhamaan (IRE)**[15] 3227 4-9-6 **60** ...(b) SebSanders 10 — 20
(Mrs R A Carr) *prom: pushed along over 3f out: rdn and wknd over 2f out: eased fnl f* **11/2**[2]

1m 14.67s (-0.33) **Going Correction** -0.10s/f (Stan) — **10** Ran SP% **118.1**
Speed ratings (Par 101): **98,96,95,93,93 92,90,90,87,77**
toteswingers: 1&2 £28.00, 1&3 £18.40, 2&3 £28.90 CSF £101.10 CT £984.45 TOTE £9.10: £2.70, £4.90, £3.00; EX 145.60 Trifecta £518.90 Part won. Pool: £701.34 - 0.86 winning units..

Owner S Hawe **Bred** Tarworth Bloodstock Ltd **Trained** Norton, N Yorks

FOCUS

A moderate handicap run at a good gallop. The winner raced in the centre while the runner-up made her ground hard against the inside rail.

3721 CE RISK, SAFETY & SECURITY H'CAP — 1m 4f 50y(P)

4:45 (4:45) (Class 5) (0-75,78) 3-Y-O+ — £3,238 (£963; £481; £240) Stalls Low

Form — RPR

6001 **1** **The Last Alzao (IRE)**[28] 2790 3-8-2 **58** ... MartinDwyer 1 — 70+
(R A Fahey) *s.i.s: hld up in mid-div: hdwy over 2f out: rdn wl over 1f out: led jst ins fnl f: r.o wl* **10/1**[3]

6031 **2** *2* **Red Cadeaux**[8] 3466 3-9-8 **78** 6ex ... SebSanders 4 — 87
(E A L Dunlop) *chsd ldr: carried sltly rt 4f out: rdn 2f out: led over 1f out tl jst ins fnl f: nt qckn* **8/11**[1]

2562 **3** *3 1/4* **La Rosa Nostra**[18] 3114 4-10-0 **71** ...(t) ShaneKelly 6 — 75
(W R Swinburn) *led: edgd rt 4f out: rdn and hdd over 1f out: wknd ins fnl f* **11/1**

0054 **4** *1/2* **Shanavaz**[12] 3321 3-7-13 **55** ... CatherineGannon 3 — 58
(Mrs G S Rees) *stdd s: hld up towards rr: pushed along over 2f out: styd on fr over 1f out: nvr nrr* **33/1**

4-05 **5** *nk* **Bushy Dell (IRE)**[43] 2322 4-9-10 **67** ... RyanMoore 7 — 70
(Miss J Feilden) *hld up in tch: pushed along over 3f out: outpcd over 2f out: n.d after* **12/1**

2243 **6** *5* **Baan (USA)**[19] 3073 6-9-5 **62** ... JimmyQuinn 2 — 57
(H J Collingridge) *prom: pushed along over 3f out: wknd wl over 2f out* **5/1**[2]

4046 **7** *4* **Hucking Heat (IRE)**[25] 2878 5-10-0 **71** ...(p) TedDurcan 11 — 59
(R Hollinshead) *stdd s: sn swtchd lft to ins rail: hld up towards rr: sme prog over 3f out: rdn over 2f out: sn struggling* **33/1**

0-05 **8** *nk* **Ameeq (USA)**[44] 591 7-10-0 **71** ... ChrisCatlin 10 — 59
(Dr R D P Newland) *a in rr* **20/1**

/0-4 **9** *6* **Twill (IRE)**[19] 2684 6-9-7 **64** ... VinceSlattery 8 — 42
(D Burchell) *prom: carried sltly rt 4f out: wknd 3f out* **33/1**

00-0 **10** *3 1/4* **Desert Leader (IRE)**[32] 2684 8-8-12 **55** ... TGMcLaughlin 5 — 28
(W M Brisbourne) *hld up in mid-div: pushed along and struggling over 3f out* **80/1**

00- **11** *3* **Tilapia (IRE)**[271] 6607 5-9-6 **70** ... KylieManser(7) 9 — 38
(Miss Gay Kelleway) *dwlt: a in rr: lame* **66/1**

2m 38.44s (-2.66) **Going Correction** -0.10s/f (Stan)
WFA 3 from 4yo+ 13lb — **11** Ran SP% **116.0**
Speed ratings (Par 103): **104,102,100,100,99 96,93,93,89,87 85**
toteswingers: 1&2 £5.00, 1&3 £11.10, 2&3 £4.40 CSF £16.72 CT £88.76 TOTE £8.50: £3.40, £1.02, £3.50; EX 27.00 Trifecta £229.40 Pool: £378.23 - 1.22 winning units..

Owner G Devlin **Bred** G Devlin **Trained** Musley Bank, N Yorks

■ Stewards' Enquiry : Kylie Manser two-day ban: used whip when out of contention (Jul 21-22)

FOCUS

A couple of progressive sorts in an otherwise ordinary handicap. A fair pace picked up leaving the back straight and the winner raced centre to far side in the straight.

Tilapia(IRE) Official explanation: vet said gelding returned lame behind

3722 CE PROPERTY SERVICES GROUP H'CAP — 7f 32y(P)

5:15 (5:16) (Class 6) (0-65,65) 3-Y-O+ — £2,388 (£705; £352) Stalls High

Form — RPR

6-00 **1** **Chief Exec**[48] 2185 7-9-8 **65** ...(b) ClareLindop 1 — 79
(J R Gask) *s.i.s: hld up in rr: swtchd rt and wd ent st: rdn and hdwy whn edgd lft fr over 1f out: rdn and str run to ld wl ins fnl f: r.o wl* **20/1**

0000 **2** *2* **Commando Scott (IRE)**[13] 3265 8-9-4 **64** ... NeilBrown(3) 6 — 72
(I W McInnes) *hld up in mid-div: hdwy wl over 1f out: rdn and kpt on to take 2nd last strides* **12/1**

002 **3** *1/2* **Poppy's Rose**[15] 3224 5-9-2 **59** ... DanielTudhope 3 — 66
(I W McInnes) *led: clr whn rdn over 1f out: hdd and no ex wl ins fnl f: lost 2nd last strides* **5/1**[3]

3512 **4** *1* **Ninth House (USA)**[8] 3470 7-9-8 **65** ...(t) SebSanders 7 — 69
(Mrs R A Carr) *hld up towards rr: swtchd lft over 2f out: hdwy wl over 1f out: sn rdn: kpt on to take 4th last strides* **9/4**[1]

6440 **5** *1/2* **Tri Chara (IRE)**[10] 3401 5-9-6 **63** ...(p) ChrisCatlin 9 — 66
(R Hollinshead) *a.p: chsd ldr over 2f out: rdn over 1f out: one pce and lost 2nd wl ins fnl f* **16/1**

-254 **6** *1 1/2* **Vanadium**[13] 3283 7-9-3 **60** ... RyanMoore 11 — 59
(G L Moore) *s.i.s: hld up in rr: c v wd st: rdn and sme prog over 1f out: edgd lft: nvr trbld ldrs* **9/2**[2]

0100 **7** *1 1/2* **Diego Rivera**[19] 3075 4-9-5 **62** ... FergusSweeney 8 — 57
(P J Makin) *s.i.s: hld up in mid-div: nt clr run briefly over 2f out: rdn jst over 1f out: n.d* **9/2**[2]

34- **8** *2 1/4* **Bonne**[334] 4782 4-9-6 **63** ... PaulFitzsimons 5 — 52
(Miss J R Tooth) *chsd ldrs: pushed along over 2f out: wknd over 1f out* **16/1**

6010 **9** *hd* **Kingsmaite**[30] 2745 8-9-1 **65** ...(b) AndrewYoxall(7) 12 — 53
(S R Bowring) *hld up: sn in tch: rdn over 2f out: c wd st: wknd wl over 1f out* **40/1**

0000 **10** *5* **Guildenstern (IRE)**[11] 3357 7-9-8 **65** ... JimmyQuinn 4 — 40
(P Howling) *hld up in mid-div: pushed along over 3f out: sn bhd* **20/1**

1506 **11** *3 3/4* **Norcroft**[145] 519 7-9-7 **64** ...(p) VinceSlattery 2 — 29
(Mrs C A Dunnett) *chsd ldr tl rdn over 2f out: wknd wl over 1f out* **25/1**

0-00 **12** *23* **Willridge**[25] 2880 4-9-8 **65** ...(tp) LPKeniry 10 — —
(J M Bradley) *chsd ldrs: wknd 3f out: eased whn t.o over 1f out* **66/1**

1m 28.48s (-1.12) **Going Correction** -0.10s/f (Stan) — **12** Ran SP% **120.6**
Speed ratings (Par 101): **102,99,99,98,97 95,94,91,91,85 81,54**
toteswingers: 1&2 £32.30, 1&3 £26.50, 2&3 £27.20 CSF £232.29 CT £1425.72 TOTE £29.50: £6.90, £5.50, £1.70; EX 269.60 Trifecta £326.00 Part won. Pool: £440.66 - 0.10 winning units. Place 6: £59.91 Place 5: £16.82.

Owner For Sale **Bred** C A Cyzer **Trained** Sutton Veny, Wilts

FOCUS

A moderate handicap run at a decent gallop throughout. The winner came down the centre in the straight.

T/Plt: £93.70 to a £1 stake. Pool: £54,948.70. 427.69 winning tickets. T/Qpdt: £19.00 to a £1 stake. Pool: £4,786.63. 186.40 winning tickets. KH

3494 CATTERICK (L-H)

Wednesday, July 8

OFFICIAL GOING: Good (good to soft in places; 8.1)

Wind: Virtually nil Weather: Overcast

3726 GO RACING IN YORKSHIRE SUMMER FESTIVAL (S) STKS 5f

2:20 (2:21) (Class 6) 2-Y-O **£2,047** (£604; £302) **Stalls** Low

Form RPR

315 **1** **On The Piste (IRE)**[28] 2800 2-7-13 0 PaulPickard(7) 9 59
(P T Midgley) *cl up: rdn to ld 1f out: styd on strly* **4/1**[3]

2 *1 3/4* **Izuizorizuain't (IRE)** 2-8-6 0 PJMcDonald 4 53+
(K A Ryan) *green and sn pushed along towards rr: rdn along and hdwy 2f out: styd on ins fnl f: tk 2nd nr line* **5/2**[1]

0604 **3** *nk* **Xaara Star (IRE)**[15] 3240 2-8-6 0 GregFairley 3 52
(Eve Johnson Houghton) *trckd ldrs: hdwy 2f out: rdn to chse wnr ins fnl f: sn drvn and one pce: lost 2nd nr line* **3/1**[2]

00 **4** *4* **Menediva**[17] 3187 2-8-1 0 JamieKyne(5) 5 37
(L A Mullaney) *chsd ldrs: rdn along 2f out: sn one pce* **6/1**

0 **5** *shd* **Chilean Fizz**[17] 3187 2-8-6 0 SilvestreDeSousa 7 37
(Mrs A Duffield) *led: rdn along wl over 1f out: hdd 1f out and sn wknd* **16/1**

500 **6** *6* **Sacred Star (IRE)**[21] 3032 2-8-1 0 ow2 (b[1]) JohnCavanagh(7) 2 17
(M Brittain) *s.i.s and bhd: swtchd rt and rdn 1/2-way: a in rr* **6/1**

00 **7** *6* **Havelock Flyer**[32] 2721 2-8-11 0 TonyHamilton 8 —
(C Grant) *chsd ldrs: rdn along 2f out: sn wknd* **28/1**

62.21 secs (2.41) **Going Correction** +0.30s/f (Good) 7 Ran SP% **111.5**

Speed ratings (Par 92): **92,89,88,82,82 72,62**

toteswingers: 1&2 £2.10, 1&3 £2.20, 2&3 £2.10 CSF £13.67 TOTE £4.90: £1.90, £1.50; EX 14.50.There was no bid for the winner.

Owner Tony Coyle **Bred** C Kelly **Trained** Westow, N Yorks

FOCUS

An ordinary juvenile seller, dominated by fillies. The winner was close to her Yarmouth mark.

NOTEBOOK

On The Piste(IRE) escaped a penalty for her success at this level two starts back and won readily. She went slightly right coming out of the stalls, but soon recovered and showed speed throughout. Once past the line, she jinked slightly and unseated her rider, but it was nothing to worry about. (op 9-2 tchd 5-1)

Izuizorizuain't(IRE), a 10,000gns first foal of a three-time winner on turf in the US, was outpaced for most of the way before making good late headway to get up for second. A stiffer track, or another furlong is likely to suit, and she should improve enough to win at a similarly low level. (op 11-4 tchd 10-3)

Xaara Star(IRE), dropped in trip and grade, ran okay but simply wasn't good enough. (op 9-4 tchd 2-1)

Menediva will probably have to improve to win a similar race. (op 11-1)

Chilean Fizz faded after showing speed and is possibly a short-runner. (op 12-1 tchd 18-1)

3727 BOOK TICKETS ON-LINE AT CATTERICKBRIDGE.CO.UK H'CAP 7f

2:55 (2:55) (Class 5) (0-75,74) 3-Y-O **£3,043** (£905; £452; £226) **Stalls** Low

Form RPR

21-4 **1** **Snow Bay**[37] 2544 3-9-7 74 GregFairley 2 82
(B Smart) *sn led: rdn along and edgd lft over 1f out: hdd ent fnl f: drvn and rallied to ld again nr line* **15/2**

6321 **2** *hd* **Northern Flyer (GER)**[19] 3108 3-8-4 62 JamieKyne(5) 3 69
(J J Quinn) *hld up towards rr: gd hdwy on inner 2f out: rdn to ld ins fnl f: drvn: hdd and nt qckn nr line* **11/4**[1]

0611 **3** *3* **Mister Tinktastic (IRE)**[17] 3193 3-9-4 71 (p) PhillipMakin 1 70
(M Dods) *chsd ldrs: hdwy 2f out: sn rdn and ev ch tl drvn and one pce ins fnl f* **7/2**[2]

6405 **4** *1/2* **Steel Stockholder**[12] 3342 3-8-8 61 DavidAllan 11 59
(M Brittain) *bmpd shortly after s and bhd: swtchd outside and hdwy 2f out: sn rdn and kpt on ins fnl f: nrst fin* **20/1**

1-3 **5** *1/2* **Ursula (IRE)**[48] 2198 3-9-6 73 JamieMoriarty 12 71+
(K R Burke) *in rr: hdwy on inner 2f out: sn rdn and kpt on ins fnl f: nrst fin* **5/1**[3]

00-0 **6** *1* **Mintoe**[33] 2660 3-8-7 60 ow1 (p) TonyHamilton 5 54
(K A Ryan) *cl up: rdn along 2f out: hld whn n.m.r and swtchd rt over 1f out: sn drvn and wknd* **50/1**

53-1 **7** *2 3/4* **Ykikamoocow**[33] 2661 3-9-1 68 SilvestreDeSousa 6 54
(G A Harker) *towards rr: effrt over 2f out: sn rdn and n.d* **15/2**

5033 **8** *1 3/4* **Lost In Paris (IRE)**[13] 3316 3-8-6 59 (b) DuranFentiman 9 40
(T D Easterby) *in tch: effrt on outer 2f out: sn rdn and no imp* **9/1**

4220 **9** *4 1/2* **Top Flight Splash**[23] 2973 3-8-2 55 oh4 (v) DaleGibson 13 24
(Mrs G S Rees) *in tch: rdn along 1/2-way: sn wknd* **33/1**

45-0 **10** *3* **Monaco Mistress (IRE)**[65] 1725 3-8-4 57 AndrewMullen 4 18
(P C Haslam) *chsd ldrs: rdn along over 2f out: sn wknd* **80/1**

4400 **11** *2* **Abbey Steps (IRE)**[23] 2964 3-8-2 55 oh1 (b) DarrenMoffatt 10 11
(T D Easterby) *hmpd sn after s: a in rr* **25/1**

-600 **12** *1/2* **Fitzolini**[23] 2970 3-8-11 64 (v[1]) PaulMulrennan 8 18
(A D Brown) *prom: rdn along 1/2-way: sn wknd* **50/1**

1m 26.23s (-0.77) **Going Correction** 0.0s/f (Good) 12 Ran SP% **115.8**

Speed ratings (Par 100): **104,103,100,99,99 98,94,92,87,84 82,81**

toteswingers: 1&2 £6.00, 1&3 £6.40, 2&3 £3.00 CSF £26.13 CT £86.07 TOTE £9.10: £2.30, £1.70, £1.60; EX 36.60.

Owner Pinnacle Bahamian Bounty Partnership **Bred** West Dereham Abbey Stud **Trained** Hambleton, N Yorks

FOCUS

A modest but competitive handicap and solid form for the grade.

Steel Stockholder Official explanation: jockey said colt suffered interference in running

Fitzolini Official explanation: jockey said gelding had no more to give

3728 5TH REGIMENT ROYAL ARTILLERY "TURMERIC" H'CAP 1m 7f 177y

3:30 (3:31) (Class 4) (0-85,85) 3-Y-O+ **£5,180** (£1,541; £770; £384) **Stalls** Low

Form RPR

5630 **1** **Bergonzi (IRE)**[28] 2815 5-9-1 72 PaulMulrennan 5 77
(J Howard Johnson) *led 3f: trckd ldng pair: hdwy 4f out: led wl over 2f out: rdn clr wl over 1f out: drvn ins fnl f: jst hld on* **20/1**

00-0 **2** *nk* **Always Bold (IRE)**[22] 2994 4-9-11 85 FrederikTylicki(3) 4 92+
(D McCain Jnr) *hld up towards rr: effrt over 2f out: rdn to chse ldng pair over 1f out: styd on strly ins fnl f: jst failed* **9/2**[3]

2000 **3** *3* **Fin Vin De Leu (GER)**[20] 3051 3-8-1 77 AndrewMullen 6 78
(M Johnston) *trckd ldr: hdwy to ld over 4f out: rdn along and hdd wl over 2f out: drvn over 1f out and kpt on same pce* **2/1**[1]

444 **4** *1* **Puy D'Arnac (FR)**[30] 2766 6-9-0 71 PJMcDonald 1 71
(G A Swinbank) *hld up in rr: hdwy 3f out: rdn on outer to chse ldrs 2f out: sn drvn and no imp appr fnl f* **7/2**[2]

1051 **5** *1 3/4* **Bijou Dan**[7] 3499 8-8-7 69 6ex PatrickDonaghy(5) 2 67
(G M Moore) *hld up in tch: hdwy to chse ldrs over 4f out: rdn along 3f out: drvn 2f out and sn one pce* **8/1**

-043 **6** *3* **Luna Landing**[17] 3191 6-9-1 72 TonyHamilton 3 66
(Jedd O'Keeffe) *chsd ldrs: led after 3f: rdn along over 5f out: hdd over 4f out: sn drvn and wknd wl over 2f out* **9/2**[3]

/045 **7** *nk* **My Immortal**[17] 3191 7-8-8 70 JamieKyne(5) 7 64
(J J Quinn) *hld up in rr: hdwy to chse ldrs over 6f out: rdn along over 3f out and sn wknd* **20/1**

3m 29.63s (-2.37) **Going Correction** 0.0s/f (Good)

WFA 3 from 4yo+ 19lb 7 Ran SP% **112.6**

Speed ratings (Par 105): **105,104,103,102,101 100,100**

toteswingers: 1&2 £14.00, 1&3 £12.90, 2&3 £3.00 CSF £102.90 TOTE £33.30: £9.20, £2.50; EX 146.90.

Owner Andrea & Graham Wylie **Bred** Deer Forest Stud **Trained** Billy Row, Co Durham

■ Stewards' Enquiry : Paul Mulrennan two-day ban: used whip in incorrect place (Jul 22-23)

FOCUS

Just a fair staying handicap and muddling form with the runner-up looking a little unlucky.

My Immortal Official explanation: jockey said gelding hung left throughout

3729 CALL 01748 810165 TO BOOK RACEDAY HOSPITALITY H'CAP 5f 212y

4:05 (4:06) (Class 5) (0-75,72) 3-Y-O **£3,043** (£905; £452; £226) **Stalls** Low

Form RPR

31-0 **1** **Real Diamond**[43] 2365 3-8-9 65 JamieKyne(5) 5 72
(A Dickman) *cl up: led over 4f out: rdn wl over 2f out: drvn and wandered ent fnl f: styd on* **7/1**

0016 **2** *2 1/4* **Go Alone (IRE)**[13] 3316 3-9-5 70 PJMcDonald 7 70
(G A Swinbank) *trckd ldrs: hdwy 1/2-way: rdn to chse wnr over 1f out: drvn ins fnl f and sn no imp* **8/1**

0124 **3** *1* **Minturno (USA)**[13] 3316 3-9-1 66 SilvestreDeSousa 6 63
(Mrs A Duffield) *hld up in tch: hdwy over 2f out: rdn wl over 1f out: sn chsng ldrs: kpt on same pce ins fnl f* **2/1**[1]

-026 **4** *nk* **Oriental Rose**[23] 2967 3-9-3 68 PhillipMakin 9 64+
(G M Moore) *hld up and bhd: hdwy on outer 2f out: sn rdn and styd on ins fnl f: nrst fin* **11/1**

-500 **5** *1 1/2* **Sardan Dansar (IRE)**[9] 3449 3-8-2 53 oh2 DuranFentiman 3 44
(Mrs A Duffield) *bhd tl sme late hdwy* **33/1**

1523 **6** *nse* **Blue Noodles**[12] 3342 3-9-2 TonyHamilton 4 58
(Ollie Pears) *trckd ldrs: hdwy 1/2-way: rdn over 2f out: drvn over 1f out and grad wknd* **4/1**[2]

0-46 **7** *1 3/4* **Rossett Rose (IRE)**[18] 3176 3-8-5 56 GregFairley 2 41
(M Brittain) *led: hdd over 4f out: sn rdn along and wknd 2f out* **9/2**[3]

5306 **8** *3/4* **Lucky Buddha**[3] 3651 3-8-1 57 PatrickDonaghy(5) 8 40
(Jedd O'Keeffe) *trckd ldrs: hdwy 1/2-way: rdn to chse wnr over 2f out: drvn over 1f out and grad wknd* **8/1**

1m 13.9s (0.30) **Going Correction** 0.0s/f (Good) 8 Ran SP% **117.5**

Speed ratings (Par 100): **98,95,93,93,91 91,88,87**

toteswingers: 1&2 £9.20, 1&3 £3.30, 2&3 £4.10 CSF £62.65 CT £154.17 TOTE £12.40: £3.20, £3.50, £1.10; EX 65.70.

Owner John H Sissons **Bred** Capt J H Wilson **Trained** Sandhutton, N Yorks

FOCUS

A modest sprint handicap with the favourite rated around his form at this trip, rather than what he has achieved over 7f.

3730 TURFTV.CO.UK H'CAP 7f

4:40 (4:40) (Class 6) (0-65,65) 3-Y-O+ **£2,388** (£705; £352) **Stalls** Low

Form RPR

0000 **1** **He's A Humbug (IRE)**[12] 3339 5-9-9 65 JamesO'Reilly(5) 13 75
(J O'Reilly) *towards rr: hdwy on outer 1/2-way: rdn and edgd lft over 1f out: styd on to ld ins fnl f* **28/1**

0133 **2** *1* **Silly Gilly (IRE)**[17] 3188 5-9-2 58 SladeO'Hara(5) 15 65
(R E Barr) *chsd ldrs: rdn along over 2f out: swtchd rt and styd on ins fnl f* **12/1**

4012 **3** *nk* **Aggbag**[13] 3322 5-8-10 54 DeclanCannon(7) 9 60
(Miss M E Rowland) *in tch: hdwy 2f out: rdn to chse ldrs over 1f out: kpt on ins fnl f* **16/1**

5043 **4** *3/4* **Bertie Vista**[16] 3224 4-9-6 57 (b) DuranFentiman 4 61
(T D Easterby) *led to 1/2-way: rdn over 2f out: sn drvn and one pce appr fnl f* **8/1**

0052 **5** *hd* **Party In The Park**[15] 3234 4-8-13 53 (b) FrederikTylicki(3) 3 57
(Miss J A Camacho) *chsd ldrs: rdn along over 2f out: drvn over 1f out and sn one pce* **6/1**

40-0 **6** *1/2* **Capone (IRE)**[12] 3339 4-9-9 63 DominicFox(3) 12 65
(Garry Moss) *bhd: hdwy on outer 2f out: sn rdn and styd on wl fnl f: nrst fin* **18/1**

1322 **7** *3/4* **Avontuur (FR)**[4] 3612 7-9-5 61 DeanHeslop(5) 5 61
(Mrs R A Carr) *towards rr: rdn along 1/2-way: styd on appr fnl f: nrst fin* **4/1**[1]

1004 **8** *3/4* **Sunley Sovereign**[8] 3484 5-8-9 49 (b) MichaelJStainton(3) 1 47
(Mrs R A Carr) *cl up on inner: led 1/2-way: rdn over 2f out: drvn over 1f out: hdd ins fnl f and wknd qckly* **25/1**

6340 **9** *1/2* **Imperial Djay (IRE)**[9] 3470 4-9-1 52 (p) GregFairley 6 49
(J R Holt) *nvr bttr than midfield* **16/1**

0-03 **10** *nk* **Desert Ben (IRE)**[33] 2660 6-9-7 58 JamieMoriarty 10 54
(C Grant) *chsd ldrs on inner: rdn along 2f out: wknd over 1f out* **28/1**

6-03 **11** *1/2* **Big Slick (IRE)**[32] 2722 4-9-4 55 DavidAllan 2 50
(M Brittain) *hld up: a towards rr* **5/1**[3]

0505 **12** *shd* **Boss Hog**[6] 3539 4-8-11 55 PaulPickard(7) 14 52+
(P T Midgley) *in rr: hdwy on inner over 2f out: sn rdn and wknd* **33/1**

-000 **13** *30* **Reddy Ronnie (IRE)**[9] 3448 5-8-11 48 ow1 IanMongan 11 —
(D W Thompson) *racd wd: a in rr: bhd and eased fnl 2f* **50/1**

60-1 **R** **Dark Moment**[9] 3449 3-8-12 60 6ex NeilBrown(3) 8 —
(A Dickman) *ref to r* **9/2**[2]

1m 27.6s (0.60) **Going Correction** 0.0s/f (Good)

WFA 3 from 4yo+ 8lb 14 Ran SP% **120.6**

Speed ratings (Par 101): **96,94,94,93,93 92,92,91,90,90 89,89,55,—**

toteswingers: 1&2 £38.30, 1&3 £62.20, 2&3 £15.30 CSF £321.50 CT £5627.93 TOTE £31.80: £7.40, £3.20, £4.50; EX 369.80.

Owner J D Walker **Bred** Denis McDonnell **Trained** Doncaster, S Yorks

■ Stewards' Enquiry : Michael J Stainton caution: careless riding.

FOCUS

A moderate handicap run in a time 1.37 seconds slower than earlier 56-75 contest for three-year-olds. The form looks pretty sound rated around the four immediately behind the winner, but not a race to be too positive about.

Boss Hog Official explanation: jockey said gelding was denied a clear run
Reddy Ronnie(IRE) Official explanation: jockey said gelding never travelled

3731 WE RACE AGAIN NEXT WEDNESDAY MEDIAN AUCTION MAIDEN STKS 1m 5f 175y
5:15 (5:16) (Class 5) 3-4-Y-0 **£3,238** (£963; £481; £240) **Stalls** Low

Form RPR
22 **1** **Spiekeroog**[17] 3192 3-8-11 0 IanMongan 1 68+
(H R A Cecil) *trckd ldng pair: pushed along after 5f: hdwy 3f out: brought wd st and rdn to ld wl over 1f out: kpt on strly* **5/4**[2]
-600 **2** 7 **Marillos Proterras**[12] 2236 3-8-6 48 SilvestreDeSousa 6 52
(Mrs A Duffield) *chsd ldrs: rdn along and outpcd 6f out: styd on u.p fnl 2f: tk 2nd wl ins fnl f: no ch w wnr* **80/1**
0463 **3** *nk* **Solas Alainn (IRE)**[9] 3447 4-9-12 67 GregFairley 5 57
(M Johnston) *trckd ldr: cl up 1/2-way: rdn to ld 3f out: drvn 2f out: sn hdd and one pce* **11/2**[3]
00-0 **4** 1 ¾ **Seminal Moment**[27] 2857 3-8-1 42 JamieKyne(5) 3 49
(J G Given) *in rr: hdwy to chse ldrs 1/2-way: rdn along 3f out: sn drvn and plugged on same pce fnl 2f* **50/1**
\- **5** 1 ½ **Roses**[29] 4-9-7 0 PJMcDonald 2 47
(G A Swinbank) *led: rdn along 4f out: hdd 3f out: drvn 2f out and sn wknd* **11/10**[1]
6 30 **Kinetic Art (IRE)**[25] 4-9-9 0 MichaelJStainton(3) 4 7
(R M Whitaker) *s.i.s: a in rr: t.o fnl 3f* **100/1**

3m 3.15s (-0.45) **Going Correction** 0.0s/f (Good)
WFA 3 from 4yo 15lb **6** Ran SP% **111.6**
Speed ratings (Par 103): **101,97,96,95,94 77**
toteswingers: 1&2 £8.90, 1&3 £1.80, 2&3 £10.50 CSF £63.43 TOTE £2.30: £1.40, £8.40; EX 59.20 Place 6 £683.94, Place 5 £352.93.
Owner G Schoeningh **Bred** M J Dawson **Trained** Newmarket, Suffolk

FOCUS
The proximity of two runners rated in the 40s confirms this was a weak maiden.
Kinetic Art(IRE) Official explanation: vet said gelding finished lame
T/Plt: £318.40 to a £1 stake. Pool: £48,876.70. 112.05 winning tickets. T/Qpdt: £63.20 to a £1 stake. Pool: £3,018.02. 35.30 winning tickets. JR

[3506] KEMPTON (A.W) (R-H)
Wednesday, July 8

OFFICIAL GOING: Standard
Wind: Virtually nil Weather: Dull

3732 WEATHERBYS BETTRENDS.CO.UK APPRENTICE H'CAP (ROUND 6) 7f (P)
6:20 (6:20) (Class 5) (0-70,67) 4-Y-0+ **£2,590** (£770; £385; £192) **Stalls** High

Form RPR
6523 **1** **Global Village (IRE)**[16] 3227 4-9-3 60 WilliamCarson 10 71
(Miss D Mountain) *trckd ldrs: drvn to ld appr fnl f: rdn out* **9/4**[1]
0634 **2** 2 ¼ **Duke Of Milan (IRE)**[9] 3459 6-9-5 62 (v) RossAtkinson 9 67
(Tom Dascombe) *towards rr: hdwy over 2f out: rdn and hung lft ins fnl f: tk 2nd cl home but no ch w wnr* **5/1**[2]
0116 **3** *nk* **Another Try (IRE)**[11] 3401 4-9-2 62 MatthewDavies(3) 7 66
(A P Jarvis) *led: rdn 2f out: hdd appr fnl f: sn no ch w wnr: one pce and lost 2nd cl home* **6/1**[3]
050 **4** 1 **Idle Power (IRE)**[26] 2883 11-9-10 67 RichardEvans 8 68
(J R Boyle) *in rr: hdwy over 2f out: styd on appr fnl f: one pce whn carried lft wl ins fnl f: swtchd rt and styd on nr fin* **10/1**
0024 **5** 2 ¾ **Munich (IRE)**[35] 2598 5-9-0 60 PNolan(3) 2 54+
(Mrs S Leech) *s.i.s: in rr and racd on outside into st: sn pushed along: styd on fnl f but nvr in contention* **7/1**
-000 **6** ¾ **Grizedale (IRE)**[25] 2921 10-8-2 50 (tp) KierenFox(5) 6 42
(M J Attwater) *t.k.h: chsd ldrs: rdn over 2f out: wknd fnl f* **33/1**
0314 **7** *nk* **Avoca Dancer (IRE)**[16] 3224 6-9-0 57 (v) JackDean 11 48
(Karen George) *chsd ldrs: rdn over 2f out: wknd fnl f* **8/1**
500 **8** *hd* **Kingsgate Castle**[41] 2418 4-9-1 61 (b) KylieManser(3) 3 52
(Miss Gay Kelleway) *hmpd s and swtchd rt to ins: nvr gng pce to get into contention* **14/1**
5306 **9** 1 **Bigfanofthat (IRE)**[27] 2864 4-9-0 60 JPHamblett(3) 4 48
(M D Squance) *s.i.s: in rr and wd into st: nvr gng pce to get into contention* **16/1**
0404 **10** 2 **Simpsons Gamble (IRE)**[25] 2924 6-8-11 54 (p) MartinLane 5 36
(R A Teal) *t.k.h: chsd ldrs: wknd over 1f out* **10/1**
0060 **11** 1 ¾ **Metropolitan Chief**[15] 3252 5-8-2 48 oh3 SimonPearce(3) 1 26
(P Burgoyne) *rrd s: racd wd into st and bhd: mod prog 2f out: nvr in contention and no ch whn hmpd over 1f out* **25/1**

1m 26.01s (0.01) **Going Correction** +0.025s/f (Slow) **11** Ran SP% **122.9**
Speed ratings (Par 103): **100,97,97,95,92 91,91,91,90,87 85**
toteswingers: 1&2 £2.00, 1&3 £3.00, 2&3 £5.40 CSF £13.68 CT £62.79 TOTE £3.90: £1.50, £1.80, £2.40; EX 15.30.
Owner Mrs Janice Jones **Bred** Kilfrush Stud **Trained** Newmarket, Suffolk

FOCUS
A fairly run race in terms of pace, with the placed horses having occupied a variety of positions mid-contest. The winner was less exposed than most of his rivals and the race has been rated at face value among the principals, with the runner-up close to his winter best and third to his recent form.
Kingsgate Castle Official explanation: jockey said gelding suffered interference at start

3733 EUROPEAN BREEDERS' FUND MAIDEN FILLIES' STKS 6f (P)
6:50 (6:51) (Class 5) 2-Y-0 **£3,885** (£1,156; £577; £288) **Stalls** High

Form RPR
5 **1** **Sand Vixen**[28] 2819 2-9-0 0 TedDurcan 11 83+
(Saeed Bin Suroor) *s.i.s: in rr: hdwy on ins 3f out: swtchd lft and hdwy ins fnl 2f: led appr fnl f: rdn clr ins fnl f: readily* **11/4**[1]
532 **2** 2 ¼ **Miss Lesley**[36] 2575 2-9-0 0 StephenCarson 3 75
(D K Ivory) *chsd ldrs: drvn to ld jst ins fnl 2f: sn edgd lft u.p: hdd appr fnl f: no ch w wnr ins fnl f but styd on wl for clr 2nd* **15/2**
65 **3** 2 ¾ **Astarta (IRE)**[39] 2490 2-9-0 0 JimmyQuinn 9 67
(P F I Cole) *chsd ldrs: rdn and outpcd 2f out: drvn and styd on again fr over 1f out: kpt on but no ch w ldng duo* **8/1**
4 1 **Al Joza** 2-8-11 0 AhmedAjtebi(3) 12 64+
(C E Brittain) *chsd ldrs: rdn 2f out: outpcd fnl f* **9/2**[3]
5 *nse* **A Pocketful Of Rye (IRE)** 2-9-0 0 RobertHavlin 5 64+
(J A Osborne) *in rr: pushed along and green 3f out and again whn styng on over 1f out: kpt on cl home but nvr in contention* **40/1**
30 **6** 2 **Caviar**[17] 3187 2-9-0 0 DaneO'Neill 10 58
(R Hannon) *led over 1f: styd pressing ldr and chal over 2f out tl wl over 1f out: wknd qckly fnl f* **7/2**[2]
00 **7** 3 ¼ **Ellmollell**[25] 2919 2-9-0 0 JamesDoyle 7 48
(S Kirk) *s.i.s: bhd: mod prog fnl 2f* **100/1**
2 **8** 1 **Piccadilly Filly (IRE)**[14] 3271 2-9-0 0 EdwardCreighton 2 45
(E J Creighton) *plld hrd and sn chsng ldrs: on outside into st: drvn to chal and hung lft 2f out: sn btn* **5/1**
560 **9** 2 ½ **Monte Mayor One**[23] 2972 2-9-0 0 AdamKirby 6 38
(D Haydn Jones) *led over 4f out: rdn 3f out: hdd ins fnl 2f: wknd wl over 1f out* **28/1**
10 2 ½ **Maiwand** 2-9-0 0 SebSanders 4 30
(Sir Mark Prescott) *rdn along after 2f: a bhd* **25/1**
0 **11** 7 **Fairywater Grey (IRE)**[16] 3210 2-9-0 0 NeilChalmers 8 9
(J J Bridger) *broke wl: chsd ldrs 2f: bhd fr 1/2-way* **100/1**

1m 13.56s (0.46) **Going Correction** +0.025s/f (Slow) **11** Ran SP% **118.3**
Speed ratings (Par 91): **97,94,90,89,88 86,81,80,77,73 64**
toteswingers: 1&2 £5.50, 1&3 £5.00, 2&3 £10.50 CSF £23.55 TOTE £3.80: £1.20, £2.20, £2.80; EX 14.10.
Owner Godolphin **Bred** Mrs M Campbell-Andenaes **Trained** Newmarket, Suffolk

FOCUS
Probably a reasonable race of its type, with a few future winners in the line-up, but the winner looked a cut above the rest. The pace was good and the runner-up is the guide to the level.

NOTEBOOK
Sand Vixen learnt plenty from her debut and the switch to Polytrack was no problem. Though again missing the break, she was confidently ridden and responded well when asked, with Ted Durcan reporting that he was happy to settle her near the back because the pace was good. She should continue to improve. (op 5-2 tchd 3-1 in a place)
Miss Lesley has done well in 5f maidens and the step up to 6f would have paid dividends had the winner not been in the line-up. She is good enough to win a maiden over either trip, though this extra furlong looks ideal, and nurseries are another option.
Astarta(IRE) has shown enough in maidens to suggest that she can make her mark now she has qualified for a handicap mark. (op 15-2 tchd 9-1)
Al Joza, a half-sister to several winners from 7f to 2m, shaped as if an extra furlong will suit her before long. (op 7-1 tchd 4-1)
A Pocketful Of Rye(IRE) is a sister to the 5f juvenile winner River Rye, but she already needs this trip. Trainer Jamie Osborne thinks she should land a little race, but did not expect her to win on this debut, and so it proved.
Caviar has not built on the promise of her debut, but will be more competitive in nurseries. (op 8-1)
Piccadilly Filly(IRE) had run much better on her debut, when allowed to lead, but her tendency to hang left was again a concern. (op 11-4)

3734 DIGIBET.COM H'CAP 1m 3f (P)
7:20 (7:20) (Class 4) (0-80,80) 3-Y-0+ **£4,727** (£1,406; £702; £351) **Stalls** High

Form RPR
-626 **1** **Action Impact (ARG)**[129] 726 5-9-8 74 RyanMoore 10 87+
(G L Moore) *in tch: pushed along 3f out: str run to chse ldr ins fnl 2f: led fnl 110yds and sn in command: comf* **7/2**[1]
00 **2** 2 **Mafeking (UAE)**[26] 2891 5-9-12 78 JimCrowley 7 85
(M R Hoad) *trckd ldr tl led over 7f out: drvn and qcknd 3 l clr over 2f out: hdd and one pce fnl 110yds* **7/2**[1]
-012 **3** 2 ½ **Inch Lodge**[118] 813 7-8-5 62 (t) WilliamCarson(5) 6 65
(Miss D Mountain) *in tch: rdn over 3f out and styd on fr over 2f out but nvr gng pce to trble ldng duo* **7/1**[2]
-550 **4** 1 ½ **Hambledon Hill**[14] 3279 3-8-0 64 CatherineGannon 2 64
(R Hannon) *in rr: rdn along over 3f out: hdwy over 2f out: styd on fnl f to take 4th cl home* **16/1**
4454 **5** *nk* **Fazbee (IRE)**[15] 3251 3-9-2 80 ShaneKelly 5 80
(P W D'Arcy) *in rr: pushed along and hdwy towards outside fr 4f out: styd on u.p fnl 2f but nvr anywhere nr ldrs* **10/1**
1300 **6** 3 ½ **Avoir Choisi (IRE)**[19] 3115 3-8-10 74 TedDurcan 12 67
(P W Chapple-Hyam) *led tl hdd over 7f out: styd in 2nd but nvr on terms w ldr: reidden over 3f out: lost 2nd ins fnl 2f: wknd fnl f* **8/1**[3]
23/0 **7** ¾ **New World Order (IRE)**[21] 3024 5-8-12 64 RobertHavlin 13 56
(Mrs S Leech) *in rr: sme hdwy on ins over 2f out but anywhere nr ldrs* **25/1**
620/ **8** ¾ **Mister Benedictine**[26] 5001 6-9-1 67 (t) RichardKingscote 4 58
(B W Duke) *chsd ldrs: rdn 4f out: wknd over 2f out* **14/1**
0011 **9** 1 **Maybe I Wont**[20] 3074 4-8-7 64 (p) JPHamblett(5) 8 53
(Lucinda Featherstone) *in tch: rdn 4f out: wknd 3f out* **7/1**[2]
-260 **10** 2 ½ **Aegean Prince**[32] 2706 5-10-0 80 StephenDonohoe 3 64
(P Howling) *s.i.s: a in rr* **12/1**
-100 **11** ¾ **Serious Choice (IRE)**[25] 2931 4-9-10 76 PatCosgrave 11 59
(J R Boyle) *rdn 4f out: a in rr* **11/1**

2m 20.34s (-1.56) **Going Correction** +0.025s/f (Slow)
WFA 3 from 4yo+ 12lb **11** Ran SP% **122.1**
Speed ratings (Par 105): **106,104,102,101,101 98,97,97,96,94 94**
toteswingers: 1&2 £3.50, 1&3 £5.50, 2&3 £6.50 CSF £14.93 CT £84.24 TOTE £3.80: £1.80, £2.00, £1.70; EX 15.90.
Owner T Bowley **Bred** Santa Maria De Araras **Trained** Lower Beeding, W Sussex

FOCUS
Probably the first race ever run to to the accompaniment of a symphony orchestra! The form looks fair for the grade, with the winner progressive last year and the runner-up well treated on his winter form in better races.

3735 DIGIBET CASINO H'CAP 1m (P)
7:50 (7:51) (Class 6) (0-58,60) 3-Y-0+ **£2,047** (£604; £302) **Stalls** High

Form RPR
0501 **1** **Sovereignty (JPN)**[14] 3269 7-9-1 57 SophieDoyle(5) 1 67
(D K Ivory) *in tch: rdn and hung rt 2f out: styd on to ld fnl 110yds: hld on wl* **10/1**
-042 **2** ¾ **Feasible**[25] 2924 4-9-7 58 PatCosgrave 12 66
(J G Portman) *chsd ldrs: rdn and styd on to chal 1f out and stl upsides tl outpcd by wnr fnl 110yds* **4/1**[1]
0003 **3** 1 ½ **Ugenius**[14] 3269 5-8-13 55 WilliamCarson(5) 8 60
(Mrs C A Dunnett) *sn in tch: chsd ldrs 3f out: rdn and styd on to take narrow ld ins fnl 2f: kpt on tl hdd and outpcd fnl 110yds* **11/1**
3424 **4** ¾ **Time To Regret**[9] 3470 9-9-5 56 (p) DanielTudhope 5 59
(I W McInnes) *in rr: hdwy and rdn over 2f out: styd on fnl f but nvr gng pce to rch ldrs* **20/1**
2211 **5** 1 ¼ **Lady Florence**[3] 3662 4-9-9 60 12ex LPKeniry 10 60
(A B Coogan) *sn led: rdn and hdd ins fnl 2f: styd pressing ldrs tl wknd ins fnl f* **5/1**[2]

6455 **6** 1 3/4 **Spoof Master (IRE)**[25] 2924 5-9-4 **55**.............................. JimmyQuinn 14 51
(C R Dore) *sn chsng ldrs: rdn over 2f out: styd on same pce fr over 1f out* **11/1**

2363 **7** hd **Mister Trickster (IRE)**[12] 2830 8-9-7 **58**.............................. GeorgeBaker 2 53
(R Dickin) *s.i.s: in rr: pushed along over 2f out: styd on fnl f but nvr in contention* **15/2**[3]

0003 **8** 3 **Paul's Pet**[9] 3463 4-9-4 **55**.............................. TGMcLaughlin 11 44
(Karen George) *s.i.s: in rr: pushed along ins fnl 3f: mod prog fnl f* **8/1**

025- **9** 3 **Headache**[266] 6735 4-9-2 **53**..............................(t) RichardKingscote 4 35
(B W Duke) *sn chsng ldr: chal over 4f out tl 2f out: wknd over 1f out* **28/1**

4/40 **10** nk **Kickahead (USA)**[38] 2518 7-9-2 **53**..............................(t) StephenDonohoe 9 34
(Ian Williams) *in tch: rdn 3f out: wknd over 2f out* **12/1**

11 2 **Sufficient Warning**[122] 5-9-7 **58**..............................(b[1]) IvanLopez 3 34
(R J Smith) *in rr: no ch whn rdn and hung rt over 2f out* **14/1**

600 **12** 3/4 **Tallulah Sunrise**[41] 2400 4-8-11 **53**.............................. GabrielHannon(5) 7 28
(M D I Usher) *s.i.s: hrd rdn over 2f out: a bhd* **40/1**

0-20 **13** 1 **Chinese Profit**[40] 2458 4-9-3 **54**.............................. SebSanders 13 26
(G C Bravery) *chsd ldrs: rdn 3f out: wknd over 2f out* **14/1**

1m 39.99s (0.19) **Going Correction** +0.025s/f (Slow) **13** Ran SP% **117.0**
Speed ratings (Par 101): **100,99,97,97,95 94,93,90,87,87 85,84,83**
toteswingers: 1&2 £5.90, 1&3 £22.40, 2&3 £8.80 CSF £47.59 CT £470.11 TOTE £6.30: £1.10, £2.20, £4.60; EX 23.00.
Owner Radlett Racing **Bred** Darley Stud Management, L L C **Trained** Radlett, Herts
■ Stewards' Enquiry : Sophie Doyle two-day ban: used whip with excessive frequency (Jul 22-23)

FOCUS
A low-grade but competitive handicap, with several changes of lead in the last two furlongs. The form looks sound rated around the runner-up and fourth.

3736 DIGIBET LONDON MILE H'CAP (LONDON MILE QUALIFIER) 1m (P)
8:20 (8:22) (Class 4) (0-80,80) 3-Y-O+ **£4,727** (£1,406; £702; £351) **Stalls** High

Form RPR

0304 **1** **Gold Express**[11] 3407 6-9-4 **70**.............................. WilliamBuick 4 83+
(P J O'Gorman) *stdd s: hld up in rr: stdy hdwy on outside fr 3f out: qcknd to ld appr fnl f and sn in command: comf* **10/1**

-002 **2** 1 3/4 **Nice To Know (FR)**[7] 3509 5-9-10 **76**.............................. GeorgeBaker 7 85
(G L Moore) *in rr: hdwy over 2f out: styd on to chse wnr fnl f and a hld but styd on wl to hold clr 2nd* **11/2**[2]

1315 **3** 1 3/4 **Highly Regal (IRE)**[70] 1603 4-9-11 **77**..............................(b) LPKeniry 6 82
(R A Teal) *chsd ldrs: rdn to take slt ld ins fnl 2f: hdd appr fnl f and one pce ins fnl f* **8/1**

1665 **4** 1 1/4 **Hawaana (IRE)**[14] 3274 4-9-10 **76**.............................. SebSanders 12 78
(Eve Johnson Houghton) *chsd ldrs: rdn to chal 2f out: outpcd ins fnl f* **11/2**[2]

220- **5** hd **Silver Print (USA)**[257] 6946 3-9-0 **75**.............................. AdamKirby 9 75
(W R Swinburn) *in rr: hdwy on ins over 2f out: kpt on but nvr gng pce to trble ldrs* **7/1**[3]

2532 **6** 3/4 **Wilbury Star (IRE)**[12] 3349 3-8-13 **74**.............................. RyanMoore 1 72
(R Hannon) *stdd towards rr after 1f: hrd drvn over 2f out: styd on u.p ins fnl f and gng on cl home but nvr a threat* **8/1**

10-0 **7** 1/2 **Dustry (IRE)**[35] 2600 3-8-11 **72**.............................. PatDobbs 13 69
(R Hannon) *chsd ldrs: chal over 2f out tl wknd appr fnl f* **33/1**

1100 **8** hd **Sign Of The Cross**[12] 3331 5-9-3 **69**.............................. JimmyQuinn 2 67
(C R Dore) *in rr: hdwy on ins and hung rt over 2f out and over 1f out: styd on cl home* **25/1**

2436 **9** hd **Randama Bay (IRE)**[13] 3301 4-9-6 **72**.............................. TGMcLaughlin 3 70
(I A Wood) *in rr: rdn over 2f out: styd on fnl f: gng on cl home* **20/1**

2166 **10** hd **Paraguay (USA)**[14] 3265 6-9-12 **78**.............................. EdwardCreighton 11 75
(Mrs D J Sanderson) *chsd ldrs: rdn 3f out: wknd over 1f out* **9/1**

2040 **11** nk **Binfield (IRE)**[25] 2910 4-9-3 **69**.............................. JimCrowley 10 66
(B G Powell) *chsd ldrs: rdn and effrt to press ldrs on ins fr 2f out: wknd qckly fnl f* **20/1**

4030 **12** 5 **Salient**[23] 2976 5-9-7 **80**.............................. KierenFox(7) 5 65
(M J Attwater) *chsd ldr: led over 4f out: hdd ins fnl 2f: sn btn* **16/1**

60/0 **13** 7 **Nomoretaxes (BRZ)**[83] 1301 7-9-9 **80**..............................(t) WilliamCarson(5) 8 49
(Miss D Mountain) *chsd ldrs: rdn 4f out: wknd over 2f out* **66/1**

/6-5 **14** 3 3/4 **Quick Release (IRE)**[13] 3301 4-9-12 **78**.............................. NCallan 14 38
(D M Simcock) *sn led: hdd over 4f out: wknd rapidly over 1f out* **5/1**[1]

1m 38.87s (-0.93) **Going Correction** +0.025s/f (Slow)
WFA 3 from 4yo+ 9lb **14** Ran SP% **124.9**
Speed ratings (Par 105): **105,103,101,100,100 99,98,98,98,97 97,92,85,82**
toteswingers: 1&2 £19.10, 1&3 £9.90, 2&3 £6.80 CSF £62.71 CT £478.76 TOTE £14.70: £2.90, £2.20, £2.30; EX 90.20.
Owner N S Yong **Bred** Deerfield Farm **Trained** Newmarket, Suffolk

FOCUS
A good gallop, which was particularly strong for the first three furlongs, played into the hands of the hold-up performers, with the front-runners predictably caving in. The winner, who was unexposed at the trip, improved for it and may do better again granted a well-run race. The runner-up is the guide to the form, with the third, fourth and fifth all running close to their marks, too.

3737 LEONARD CURTIS H'CAP 2m (P)
8:50 (8:50) (Class 5) (0-75,75) 4-Y-O+ **£2,590** (£770; £385; £192) **Stalls** High

Form RPR

1362 **1** **Isabelonabicycle**[24] 2944 4-9-1 **69**.............................. WilliamBuick 7 75+
(A M Balding) *hld up in rr: stdy hdwy 4f out: rdn and qcknd on outside fr 2f out to ld 1f out: edgd rt u.p and styd on wl* **3/1**[1]

-036 **2** 1 **Warrior Conquest**[29] 2798 4-9-0 **68**.............................. JimCrowley 11 73
(W J Knight) *chsd ldrs: rdn 3f out: slt ld over 1f out: sn hdd: kpt on but a readily hld by wnr* **12/1**

3042 **3** hd **Calculating (IRE)**[7] 3510 5-8-6 **63**.............................. AndreaAtzeni(3) 10 68
(M D I Usher) *chsd ldrs: rdn and kpt on fr 2f out: swtchd rt over 1f out: styd on to press for 2nd ins fnl f but no imp on wnr* **9/2**[2]

2440 **4** 3/4 **Alnwick**[20] 3073 5-9-4 **72**.............................. DaneO'Neill 1 76
(P D Cundell) *in tch: rdn and hdwy fr 2f out and sn chsng ldrs: one pce ins fnl f* **8/1**

0304 **5** 1 3/4 **Go Amwell**[14] 3275 6-8-2 **56** oh3.............................. JimmyQuinn 2 58+
(J R Jenkins) *in rr: hrd rdn over 2f out: styd on and hung rt ins fnl f: gng on cl home* **18/1**

4005 **6** nse **Salute (IRE)**[7] 3510 10-9-7 **75**.............................. RobertHavlin 3 77
(P G Murphy) *chsd ldr: led ins fnl 2f: hdd over 1f out: wknd ins fnl f* **25/1**

2405 **7** 3/4 **American Spin**[18] 3143 5-9-7 **75**..............................(e) AdamKirby 8 79+
(L A Dace) *in rr: hdwy over 2f out: prog on ins whn hmpd appr fnl f: nt rcvr* **8/1**

5-01 **8** 1 1/4 **Coda Agency**[21] 3029 6-8-12 **66**.............................. NCallan 6 66
(D W P Arbuthnot) *chsd ldrs: rdn over 3f out: wknd over 1f out* **11/2**[3]

-012 **9** 3/4 **Karky Schultz (GER)**[20] 3074 4-8-5 **59**.............................. LukeMorris 4 58
(J M P Eustace) *in tch: rdn and hung rt over 2f out: mod prog fnl f* **16/1**

4025 **10** 6 **Drum Major (IRE)**[23] 2983 4-9-0 **68**.............................. RyanMoore 5 59
(G L Moore) *t.k.h: led tl hdd ins fnl 2f: wkng whn n.m.r over 1f out* **15/2**

265/ **P** **Jeu D'Esprit (IRE)**[418] 6856 6-8-7 **61**.............................. PaulDoe 9 —
(Mrs L J Mongan) *lost action and p.u after 3f: dead* **50/1**

3m 32.17s (2.07) **Going Correction** +0.025s/f (Slow) **11** Ran SP% **117.2**
Speed ratings (Par 103): **95,94,94,94,93 93,92,92,91,88** —
toteswingers: 1&2 £7.40, 1&3 £2.80, 2&3 £17.80 CSF £40.84 CT £162.14 TOTE £4.00: £1.50, £4.20, £2.30; EX 55.10.
Owner J C & S R Hitchins **Bred** J C , J R And S R Hitchins **Trained** Kingsclere, Hants
■ Stewards' Enquiry : Andrea Atzeni sixteen-day ban: careless riding two days; fourteen days under trotting up procedure; four days deferred (Jul 24-Aug 3)

FOCUS
The pace was a fairly sound one for the trip, allowing the winner's stamina to kick in just in time. The winner is the best guide to the level of the form.
Jeu D'Esprit(IRE) Official explanation: vet said mare pulled up lame

3738 FAREWELL HEAD GROUNDSMAN RICHARD LANGLEY H'CAP 6f (P)
9:20 (9:21) (Class 4) (0-80,80) 3-Y-O+ **£4,727** (£1,406; £702; £351) **Stalls** High

Form RPR

0-21 **1** **Pumpkin**[27] 2862 3-9-3 **77**.............................. RyanMoore 8 88+
(Sir Michael Stoute) *in rr: pushed along over 2f out: hrd rdn over 1f out and str run fnl f to ld cl home: won gng away* **13/8**[1]

6502 **2** 1/2 **Lethal**[7] 3512 6-8-0 **61**.............................. RosieJessop(7) 4 71
(Andrew Reid) *led: rdn over 2f out and kpt narrow advantage whn strly chal fnl f: hdd and outpcd cl home* **12/1**

0451 **3** 1/2 **Mac's Power (IRE)**[21] 3028 3-8-13 **73**..............................(t) WilliamBuick 5 80
(P J O'Gorman) *hld up in rr: stdy hdwy over 2f out: drvn to chal fnl f: fnd no ex and one pce fnl 50yds* **4/1**[2]

4-51 **4** 1 1/4 **Lujeanie**[13] 3299 3-9-1 **75**..............................(p) FergusSweeney 2 78
(D K Ivory) *chsd ldrs: rdn and effrt fr 2f out: wknd fnl 100yds* **7/1**

3500 **5** 1/2 **Kyle (IRE)**[21] 3030 5-9-6 **74**.............................. LPKeniry 3 77
(C R Dore) *in rr: hdwy whn swtchd rt over 1f out: styd on fnl f but nvr gng pce to rch ldrs* **20/1**

0002 **6** nk **Dvinsky (USA)**[11] 3407 8-9-12 **80**..............................(b) JimmyQuinn 7 82
(P Howling) *chsd ldrs: rdn over 2f out: wknd ins fnl f* **12/1**

-056 **7** 3 **Calahonda**[21] 3028 3-9-6 **80**.............................. ShaneKelly 6 71
(P W D'Arcy) *outpcd most of way* **20/1**

1-35 **8** shd **Rare Art**[72] 1567 3-8-13 **73**.............................. PatCosgrave 9 64
(S A Callaghan) *sn outpcd* **16/1**

0301 **9** nk **Bel Cantor**[7] 3512 6-8-13 **70**..............................(p) KellyHarrison(3) 1 61
(W J H Ratcliffe) *chsd ldr: rdn 3f out: wknd over 1f out* **5/1**[3]

1m 12.33s (-0.77) **Going Correction** +0.025s/f (Slow)
WFA 3 from 5yo+ 6lb **9** Ran SP% **118.1**
Speed ratings (Par 105): **106,105,104,103,102 101,97,97,97**
toteswingers: 1&2 £5.10, 1&3 £2.10, 2&3 £9.30 CSF £24.32 CT £67.78 TOTE £2.40: £1.30, £3.00, £1.90; EX 32.70 Place 6 £43.97, Place 5 £31.34.
Owner Cheveley Park Stud **Bred** Cheveley Park Stud Ltd **Trained** Newmarket, Suffolk

FOCUS
A decent gallop set by the runner-up, with the well-backed winner's stamina just coming to her rescue in time. There should be more to come from her as she learns, and this form looks solid rated through the runner-up, third and fourth.
Bel Cantor Official explanation: jockey said horse moved poorly final 2f
T/Plt: £31.80 to a £1 stake. Pool: £65,546.83. 1,501.19 winning tickets. T/Qpdt: £10.80 to a £1 stake. Pool: £5,681.54. 387.44 winning tickets. ST

3382 LINGFIELD (L-H)
Wednesday, July 8

OFFICIAL GOING: Turf course - good to firm (8.7); all-weather - standard
Rail along back straight up to the top of the hill moved in 2metres.
Wind: Light, half against Weather: Cloudy, heavy shower after race 4

3739 POPPY SUPPORT FILLIES' H'CAP 1m 3f 106y
2:10 (2:10) (Class 5) (0-70,66) 3-Y-O+ **£3,070** (£906; £453) **Stalls** High

Form RPR

-142 **1** **Where's Susie**[16] 3216 4-9-10 **62**.............................. GeorgeBaker 3 66
(M Madgwick) *prom: wnt 2nd 3f out: shkn up to cl and led over 1f out: wl in command fnl f* **7/4**[1]

0-05 **2** 1 1/2 **Ubiquitous**[31] 2739 4-8-10 **48** oh3.............................. JamesDoyle 5 48
(S Dow) *hld up in rr: prog fr last trio 4f out to chse ldrs over 2f out: styd on to take 2nd ins fnl f: no real ch w wnr* **10/1**

00 **3** 1 **Sahara Sunshine**[23] 2983 4-9-9 **64**.............................. JackMitchell(3) 4 63
(Mrs L J Mongan) *v s.i.s: last tl prog u.p on wd outside over 2f out: styd on wl to take 3rd nr fin* **16/1**

0004 **4** nk **Muffett's Dream**[6] 3533 5-8-10 **48** oh3.............................. LPKeniry 1 46
(J J Bridger) *led: kicked on over 3f out: hdd over 1f out: one pce and lost 2 pls ins fnl f* **10/1**

5-00 **5** 1 1/4 **The Saucy Snipe**[43] 2357 3-8-10 **60**.............................. JimCrowley 10 56
(P Winkworth) *hld up in rr: outpcd over 3f out: drvn and plugged on same pce fnl 2f: nvr rchd ldrs* **7/1**[3]

0000 **6** hd **Milemilia (IRE)**[7] 3511 3-8-3 **53** ow2..............................(b[1]) AdrianTNicholls 8 49
(H Morrison) *hld up in midfield: effrt on inner to chse ldrs 3f out: hrd rdn and plugged on same pce* **28/1**

3314 **7** nse **Coral Shores**[15] 3244 4-9-9 **66**..............................(v) WilliamCarson(5) 12 62
(P W Hiatt) *pushed up to chse ldr after 1f to 3f out: hrd rdn and nt qckn: fdd over 1f out* **7/2**[2]

6100 **8** 2 1/2 **Soul Singer**[13] 3303 3-8-4 **54**.............................. FrankieMcDonald 11 45
(J G Portman) *hld up in midfield: prog to chse ldrs over 4f out: wd and lost pl sn after gng downhill: effrt again 3f out: sn no hdwy* **40/1**

0620 **9** 2 1/2 **Oronsay**[14] 3259 4-8-11 **49**..............................(t) DaneO'Neill 9 36
(B R Millman) *taken down early: hld up and racd wd: outpcd whn effrt 3f out: no real prog fnl 2f* **14/1**

00-0 **10** 1 1/2 **Extreme Pleasure (IRE)**[24] 2944 4-9-8 **60**.............................. PaulDoe 6 45
(W J Knight) *prom: rdn 4f out: wknd wl over 2f out* **20/1**

5655 **11** 37 **Suhailah**[105] 957 3-8-12 **62**.............................. KirstyMilczarek 7 —
(M J Attwater) *chsd ldrs: lost pl rapidly downhill over 4f out: last and wkng over 2f out: t.o* **25/1**

2m 30.92s (-0.58) **Going Correction** -0.05s/f (Good)
WFA 3 from 4yo+ 12lb **11** Ran SP% **116.3**
Speed ratings (Par 100): **100,98,98,97,97 96,96,95,93,92 65**
toteswingers: 1&2 £5.00, 1&3 £18.30, 2&3 £51.40 CSF £19.18 CT £215.19 TOTE £2.20: £1.40, £3.00, £4.10; EX 17.70 Trifecta £120.90 Part won. Pool: £163.44 - 0.43 winning units..
Owner Recycled Products Limited **Bred** Mrs L R Burrage **Trained** Denmead, Hants

FOCUS
There was 14mm of overnight rain, taking 'firm' out of the going description on the turf course, and a blustery breeze which occasionally veered into the horses in the home straight. The jockeys reported that the ground was loose on top. The pace was only fair for a moderate handicap and the form looks ordianry, with the fourth to her latest mark the best guide.
Suhailah Official explanation: jockey said filly hung right on bend

3740 POPPYSHOP (S) STKS — 1m 2f
2:45 (2:46) (Class 6) 3-Y-O+ — **£2,047** (£604; £302) **Stalls** Low

Form — RPR

5-15 **1** **Slip**[167] 244 4-9-12 82 .... PatCosgrave 3 — 60
(J R Boyle) *trckd ldng pair: smooth prog over 2f out: pushed into ld over 1f out and hanging lft: urged along to hold on nr fin* **1/2**[1]

0505 **2** *nk* **Waterside (IRE)**[16] 3223 10-9-12 60 ....(t) JamesDoyle 5 — 59
(S Curran) *dwlt: settled in last pair: rdn and prog over 2f out: wnt 2nd ins fnl f: clsng on wnr fin* **16/1**

020 **3** *2* **Lytham (IRE)**[50] 2149 8-9-12 60 .... JimCrowley 6 — 55
(A W Carroll) *trckd ldng trio: rdn over 2f out: hanging lft and nt qckn: kpt on fr over 1f out to take 3rd nr fin* **5/1**[2]

4300 **4** *1* **Mrs Slocombe (IRE)**[16] 3209 3-8-4 62 ....(p) KirstyMilczarek 7 — 42
(J Akehurst) *trckd ldr: led over 2f out: rdn and hdd over 1f out: wknd ins fnl f* **10/1**

00/0 **5** *3 ½* **Safari**[16] 3207 6-9-1 37 .... DaneO'Neill 4 — 35
(S Curran) *led to over 2f out: wknd over 1f out* **50/1**

-403 **6** *4* **Timbaa (USA)**[8] 3474 3-8-4 52 .... WilliamCarson(5) 8 — 32
(Rae Guest) *dwlt: a in rr: outpcd fr 3f out: nvr on terms after* **7/1**[3]

7 *18* **Harry Africa (IRE)**[30] 6846 3-8-9 0 ....(v[1]) RichardKingscote 2 — —
(Mrs S Leech) *dwlt: a in rr: lost tch over 2f out: t.o* **50/1**

2m 12.2s (1.70) **Going Correction** -0.05s/f (Good)
WFA 3 from 4yo+ 11lb — 7 Ran SP% **114.7**
Speed ratings (Par 101): **91,90,89,88,85 82,67**
toteswingers: 1&2 £3.50, 1&3 £2.00, 2&3 £6.00 CSF £11.19 TOTE £1.50: £1.10, £3.90; EX 8.60 Trifecta £23.30 Pool: £417.24 - 13.25 winning units..There was no bid for the winner.
Owner M Khan X2 **Bred** Mrs H T Jones **Trained** Epsom, Surrey

FOCUS
An uncompetitive seller on paper run at a less than satisfactory gallop early on. The placed horses have little form on turf and the form looks weak.
Harry Africa(IRE) Official explanation: jockey said gelding hung left

3741 SURREY ROYAL BRITISH LEGION H'CAP — 1m 1f
3:20 (3:21) (Class 6) (0-60,60) 3-Y-O — **£2,047** (£604; £302) **Stalls** Low

Form — RPR

0036 **1** **Chadwell Spring (IRE)**[11] 3387 3-9-4 **60** .... JimCrowley 11 — 67
(Miss J Feilden) *trckd ldr: chal 2f out: hrd rdn over 1f out: narrow ld ins fnl f: asserted nr fin* **7/1**[3]

3060 **2** *½* **Heartsease**[16] 3209 3-9-0 **56** .... PatCosgrave 7 — 62
(J G Portman) *mde most: rdn 2f out: narrowly hdd ins fnl f: kpt on but hld nr fin* **14/1**

6534 **3** *¾* **Evening Sunset (GER)**[16] 3209 3-8-11 **58** .... MCGeran(5) 2 — 62+
(M R Channon) *hld up in rr: prog over 3f out: swtchd rt over 2f out: drvn to take 3rd jst over 1f out: styd on ins fnl f: nrst fin* **5/1**[2]

00-0 **4** *1 ¾* **Caught On Camera**[32] 2709 3-9-1 **57** .... GeorgeBaker 4 — 58
(M L W Bell) *mostly chsd ldng pair: rdn over 2f out and nt qckn: one pce and lost 3rd jst over 1f out* **20/1**

3063 **5** *1* **Squad**[10] 3427 3-9-2 **58** .... DarryllHolland 10 — 57+
(S Dow) *dwlt: hld up in last trio: stl there and plenty to do over 3f out: laboured prog into midfield 2f out: styd on fnl f: nrst fin* **11/4**[1]

0205 **6** *½* **Hector Spectre (IRE)**[14] 3257 3-9-0 **56** .... StephenDonohoe 12 — 54
(K M Prendergast) *hld up in tch: wdst of all bnd over 3f out: no imp on ldrs 2f out: kpt on* **14/1**

3540 **7** *½* **Baby Josr**[27] 2863 3-8-13 **58** ....(vt) JackMitchell(3) 13 — 55
(I A Wood) *s.s: wl in rr: sme prog 6f out: wd and rdn wl over 2f out: styd on fr over 1f out: nrst fin* **10/1**

-053 **8** *1 ¼* **Kristopher James (IRE)**[12] 3336 3-9-2 **58** .... TGMcLaughlin 9 — 52
(W M Brisbourne) *prom: rdn over 2f out: sn outpcd: grad wknd over 1f out* **7/1**[3]

0000 **9** *¾* **The Bully Wee**[36] 2567 3-9-0 **56** .... LukeMorris 8 — 48
(J Jay) *tended to run in snatches: chsd ldrs: u.p and hanging lft whn nt clr run briefly 2f out: fdd* **16/1**

5060 **10** *2 ½* **Dalrymple (IRE)**[11] 3383 3-8-10 **52** ....(v[1]) LPKeniry 14 — 39
(M Madgwick) *mostly in midfield: rdn and no prog over 2f out: fdd* **33/1**

000 **11** *3 ¼* **Tarqua (IRE)**[24] 2947 3-8-10 **52** .... PatDobbs 6 — 32
(R Hannon) *wl plcd on inner: rdn 3f out: no prog: wknd 2f out* **8/1**

0000 **12** *4 ½* **Taste Of Honey (IRE)**[13] 3302 3-8-11 **53** .... KirstyMilczarek 3 — 24
(D W P Arbuthnot) *sn last: looked like tailing off 1/2-way: plugged on* **33/1**

0-60 **13** *3 ¾* **Law And Order**[29] 2797 3-9-1 **57** .... PaulFitzsimons 5 — 20
(Miss J R Tooth) *dwlt: t.k.h and sn trckd ldrs: losing pl whn hmpd over 2f out: sn bhd* **20/1**

-440 **14** *5* **Crown Affair (IRE)**[116] 839 3-8-9 **58** ....(t) AmyScott(7) 1 — 10
(J W Hills) *dwlt: a in last trio: wknd over 2f out: sn bhd* **66/1**

1m 56.46s (-0.14) **Going Correction** -0.05s/f (Good) — 14 Ran SP% **124.6**
Speed ratings (Par 98): **98,97,96,95,94 94,93,92,91,89 86,82,79,74**
toteswingers: 1&2 £28.10, 1&3 £7.80, 2&3 £25.60 CSF £98.39 CT £560.44 TOTE £7.90: £2.50, £3.90, £2.50; EX 166.90 TRIFECTA Not won..
Owner R J Creese **Bred** William P Fogarty **Trained** Exning, Suffolk
■ Stewards' Enquiry : M C Geran two-day ban: careless riding (Jul 22-23)
L P Keniry two-day ban: careless riding (Jul 22-23)

FOCUS
A competitive if modest handicap, run at an even pace, which very few got into. The form looks sound rated mainly around the placed horses.

3742 SURREY BRITISH ARMED FORCES AND VETERANS NURSERY — 5f (P)
3:55 (3:56) (Class 5) 2-Y-O — **£3,238** (£963; £481; £240) **Stalls** High

Form — RPR

6236 **1** **Any Day (IRE)**[22] 3006 2-8-3 **68** .... RichardKingscote 3 — 67
(R M Beckett) *chsd ldng pair: rdn to cl over 1f out: styd nr rail and drvn ahd last strides: hld on* **11/1**[3]

124 **2** *shd* **Soccer (USA)**[41] 2408 2-9-9 **93** ....(t) RossAtkinson(5) 1 — 92
(Tom Dascombe) *sn led: shkn up and narrowly hdd over 1f out: edgd rt but led again ins fnl f: hdd last strides: kpt on wl* **2/1**[1]

3103 **3** *¾* **Six Wives**[35] 2599 2-8-7 **72** .... JamesDoyle 7 — 68
(J A Glover) *pressed ldr: shkn up to ld narrowly over 1f out: edgd rt and hdd ins fnl f: no ex nr fin* **12/1**

666 **4** *2 ½* **Rightcar**[19] 3106 2-7-9 **63** oh6 .... AndreaAtzeni(3) 9 — 50
(Peter Grayson) *racd wd in last trio: off the pce 2f out: styd on to take 4th nr fin* **50/1**

0400 **5** *¾* **Avec Moi**[25] 2919 2-7-12 **63** oh5 .... CatherineGannon 10 — 48
(Mrs C A Dunnett) *t.k.h early: chsd ldng pair: nt qckn fr 2f out: fdd fnl f* **33/1**

51 **6** *¾* **Italian Tom (IRE)**[16] 3203 2-8-7 **72** .... JimCrowley 2 — 54
(S A Callaghan) *dwlt: rcvrd to chse ldrs 1/2-way: outpcd wl over 1f out: n.d after* **3/1**[2]

1032 **7** *2 ½* **Kings Of Leo**[10] 3430 2-8-10 **75** .... PatDobbs 4 — 48
(R Hannon) *settled and sn in last: nvr on terms after: no prog over 1f out* **2/1**[1]

0020 **8** *5* **Angie's Nap (USA)**[1] 3709 2-7-10 **68** oh7 ow5 ....(v) CarolineKelly(7) 5 — 23
(P S McEntee) *restless stalls: in tch tl wknd 2f out* **50/1**

59.53 secs (0.73) **Going Correction** +0.025s/f (Slow) — **8** Ran SP% **114.6**
Speed ratings (Par 94): **95,94,93,89,88 87,83,75**
toteswingers: 1&2 £4.60, 1&3 £4.70, 2&3 £5.30 CSF £33.36 CT £275.54 TOTE £12.90: £2.00, £1.20, £2.60; EX 33.60 Trifecta £128.50 Pool: £740.09 - 4.26 winning units..
Owner R Roberts **Bred** Paul Ennis **Trained** Whitsbury, Hants

FOCUS
An ordinary nursery handicap for poor prize money. The principals were close to their pre-race marks. The 'official' ratings shown next to each horse are estimated and for information purposes only.

NOTEBOOK
Any Day(IRE) broke well, was settled in behind the principals and still looked to have plenty to do inside the final half furlong, but she shot though a gap up the rail and powered home. She seemed to progress with every run in maidens, before taking a backward step on turf last time, but this was a confidence-boosting victory on only her fifth start and she may well progress further. It is worth noting that her jockey reported afterwards that the filly is merely mediocre. (op 10-1 tchd 14-1)
Soccer(USA) ◆ had been highly tried – twice behind the smart Monsieur Chevalier (latterly in Listed company) – and this looked an ideal opportunity to record a second success at the track. Despite looking the winner from a long way out, he either idled in front, but more likely his rider, who never seemed to get too serious, was simply caught napping. He found more when the winner came to him and he was just a bit unlucky. There is plenty more to come. (op 9-4)
Six Wives set a fast pace, but it was far from a cut-throat one. Although she is beginning to look exposed, this was a fair effort and she just weakened in the closing stages. This looks her trip. (op 10-1 tchd 14-1, 16-1 in places)
Rightcar stayed on with some effect. He looks in need of a bit further on this showing. (op 40-1)
Avec Moi didn't have the best of draws, but was left looking a little one-paced nonetheless.
Italian Tom(IRE), who slightly missed the break, found this class hike a bit too much after winning a Chepstow seller but ran his race and there were no real excuses. He was eased once his chance had gone. (op 10-3 tchd 7-2 and 11-4)
Kings Of Leo was bitterly disappointing. She broke well, but then appeared to be reined back and thereafter looked to be run off her feet. There were no obvious excuses. (op 9-4 tchd 5-2 in a place)

3743 ST PETER'S CROSS MEDIAN AUCTION MAIDEN STKS — 6f (P)
4:30 (4:30) (Class 6) 3-4-Y-O — **£2,729** (£806; £403) **Stalls** Low

Form — RPR

6-4 **1** **Regeneration (IRE)**[27] 2862 3-8-10 0 .... HollyHall(7) 8 — 58
(S A Callaghan) *hld up in midfield on outer: outpcd 1/2-way: prog over 1f out: edgd lft but r.o to ld last 100yds: sn clr* **9/2**

000 **2** *1 ½* **Titus Gent**[57] 1958 4-9-9 45 .... KirstyMilczarek 6 — 55
(J Ryan) *chsd ldrs: outpcd 1/2-way: wnt 3rd over 2f out: clsng whn n.m.r and snatched up ins fnl f: kpt on to take 2nd nr fin* **33/1**

0000 **3** *nk* **Temperence Hall (USA)**[10] 3427 3-9-0 59 ....(v) MarcHalford(3) 10 — 52
(J R Best) *t.k.h early: prom on outer: pressed ldr over 3f out and sn clr of rest: hrd rdn wl over 1f out: edgd rt and led briefly ins fnl f: sn outpcd* **20/1**

0042 **4** *1* **Towy Boy (IRE)**[14] 3283 4-9-6 55 ....(v) JackMitchell(3) 5 — 50
(I A Wood) *t.k.h early: pressed ldr: led over 3f out: sn clr w one rival: hrd rdn over 1f out: wknd tamely and hdd ins fnl f* **3/1**[2]

0000 **5** *½* **Wicksy Creek**[14] 3283 4-9-4 40 ....(t) MarkFlynn(5) 7 — 48
(G C Bravery) *chsd ldrs: outpcd fr 1/2-way: rdn and kpt on one pce fr over 1f out* **66/1**

0000 **6** *½* **Jeremiah (IRE)**[22] 3009 3-9-3 67 .... PatCosgrave 4 — 45
(J G Portman) *chsd ldrs: rdn to go 4th over 2f out: tried to cl over 1f out: one pce fnl f* **8/1**

-000 **7** *½* **Bold Hawk**[4] 3632 3-9-3 51 ....(b) TGMcLaughlin 3 — 44
(Mrs C A Dunnett) *settled in rr: wl off the pce 1/2-way: effrt on inner over 1f out: kpt on: nvr rchd ldrs* **50/1**

-226 **8** *2 ¼* **Safari Guide**[42] 2377 3-9-3 75 .... JimCrowley 11 — 37
(P Winkworth) *racd wd in last trio: outpcd 1/2-way: brief effrt 2f out: sn no prog* **11/4**[1]

0- **9** *5* **Django Reinhardt**[264] 6770 3-9-3 0 .... GeorgeBaker 9 — 21
(J R Gask) *settled in rr: outpcd 1/2-way: pushed along and no prog 2f out* **7/2**[3]

00-0 **10** *18* **Pappoose**[43] 2353 4-9-4 49 .... DaneO'Neill 1 — —
(H Candy) *led to over 3f out: sn wknd: t.o* **12/1**

0-00 **11** *4 ½* **May Need A Spell**[25] 2918 3-9-3 52 ....(b[1]) LukeMorris 2 — —
(J G M O'Shea) *sn drvn towards rr: last and wkng 1/2-way: t.o* **50/1**

1m 12.65s (0.75) **Going Correction** +0.025s/f (Slow)
WFA 3 from 4yo 6lb — 11 Ran SP% **124.0**
Speed ratings (Par 101): **96,94,93,92,91 90,90,87,80,56 50**
toteswingers: 1&2 £30.10, 1&3 £16.90, 2&3 £38.00 CSF £153.52 TOTE £6.40: £2.00, £8.00, £5.10; EX 148.30 TRIFECTA Not won..
Owner Tamdown Group Limited **Bred** Tally-Ho Stud **Trained** Newmarket, Suffolk

FOCUS
A weak maiden run at a fair pace and a race of changing fortunes. The form looks shaky and a hard race to rate positively.

3744 PLAYSTOWE MAIDEN AUCTION STKS (DIV I) — 6f (P)
5:05 (5:05) (Class 5) 2-Y-O — **£2,388** (£705; £352) **Stalls** Low

Form — RPR

30 **1** **Florio Vincitore (IRE)**[18] 3138 2-8-9 0 .... JamesDoyle 7 — 75
(E J Creighton) *mde virtually all: drvn over 1f out: hrd pressed fnl f: jst hld on* **5/2**[1]

65 **2** *nse* **Quaestor (IRE)**[33] 2663 2-8-12 0 .... RichardKingscote 8 — 78
(Tom Dascombe) *pressed wnr: drvn and sustained chal fr over 1f out: jst pipped* **5/2**[1]

3 *6* **Kathindi (IRE)** 2-8-9 0 .... LPKeniry 1 — 57
(J S Moore) *chsd ldng pair and sn pushed along: grad outpcd fr 1/2-way* **10/1**

4 *¾* **Phoenix Rose (IRE)** 2-8-4 0 .... AdrianTNicholls 4 — 50
(J R Best) *chsd ldng pair: shkn up 1/2-way: outpcd after: jst hld in battle for 3rd* **10/1**

5 *7* **Captain Bluebird (IRE)** 2-8-12 0 .... JimmyQuinn 2 — 37+
(D Donovan) *s.v.s: a bhd: tk remote 5th nr fin* **9/2**[2]

0 **6** 1/2 **Speedyfix**^{22} 3006 2-8-9 0 .... SaleemGolam 9 32
(Mrs C A Dunnett) *dwlt: t.k.h early: in tch: outpcd fr 1/2-way: wknd over 1f out* **100/1**

7 1 1/2 **Babajaga (IRE)** 2-8-10 0 .... LukeMorris 3 29
(J M P Eustace) *in tch w tail swishing: outpcd fr 1/2-way: wknd over 1f out* **16/1**

8 3 3/4 **Freddie's Girl (USA)** 2-8-4 0 .... JackMitchell$^{(3)}$ 6 14
(Stef Liddiard) *s.v.s: a wl bhd: nvr a factor* **8/1**^{3}

9 38 **Braggadocio** 2-8-12 0 .... JimCrowley 5 —
(P Winkworth) *dwlt: sn last: t.o fr 1/2-way* **8/1**^{3}

1m 13.19s (1.29) **Going Correction** +0.025s/f (Slow) 9 Ran SP% **122.6**
Speed ratings (Par 94): **92,91,83,82,73 72,70,65,15**
toteswingers: 1&2 £2.10, 1&3 £8.50, 2&3 £8.20 CSF £9.09 TOTE £3.50: £1.30, £1.40, £3.00; EX 12.40 Trifecta £140.40 Pool: £296.07 - 1.56 winning units..

Owner Murray & Prosser **Bred** Newsells Park Stud **Trained** Mill Hill, London NW7

FOCUS
An uncompetitive maiden containing plenty of moderate animals and few got into it. The market proved the best guide with the two principals fighting it out. The winner is rated back to his debut form.

NOTEBOOK
Florio Vincitore(IRE), last seen running in the Chesham Stakes at Royal Ascot, got the better of a protracted duel up the straight with his main market rival and just held on. On pedigree he is bred to get further in time and this 6f would have been sharp enough for him. Like his sire, he shows plenty of determination and he will improve for this. (op 11-4 tchd 4-1)
Quaestor(IRE) had the benefit of two moderate runs behind him and left that level of form well behind. He looked better the further they went and, while he was always appearing to be held by the winner, he was in front a couple of strides after the line. He should be very capable of making his mark in nursery company. (tchd 9-4 and 3-1)
Kathindi(IRE) was green going to post and looked as though he would come on a ton for the run. He made a pleasing introduction, however, travelling well and staying on without being posed too many questions, despite going a little wide off the bend. The ability may be limited, but it is there. (op 12-1 tchd 7-1)
Phoenix Rose(IRE) also showed clear signs of ability and will come on a lot for her debut. She was full of running coming off the bend, but was eased once her chance had gone. (op 6-1 tchd 12-1)
Captain Bluebird(IRE), who has a sprinting pedigree, was well backed but looked very green (which was confirmed by his rider), missed the break and was run off his feet. He was given a gentle introduction and his rider accepted the situation. A late foal, he will be better with experience. Official explanation: jockey said colt missed the break and ran green (op 7-1)
Speedyfix Official explanation: jockey said gelding ran green

3745 PLAYSTOWE MAIDEN AUCTION STKS (DIV II) 6f (P)
5:40 (5:42) (Class 5) 2-Y-O £2,388 (£705; £352) Stalls Low

Form RPR

3 **1** **Snow Fairy (IRE)**^{15} 3248 2-8-4 0 .... KirstyMilczarek 4 84+
(E A L Dunlop) *hld up in midfield: prog over 2f out: led wl over 1f out: sn clr: shkn up fnl f* **7/2**^{3}

2 3 1/2 **Baby Dottie** 2-8-4 0 .... CatherineGannon 10 72
(P M Phelan) *trblesme to load in stalls: outpcd and rdn in rr: gd prog on outer over 2f out: chsd wnr over 1f out: rn green and sn no imp* **18/1**

03 **3** 3/4 **Hot Pursuits**^{14} 3271 2-8-4 0 .... NickyMackay 1 69
(H Morrison) *settled in midfield: clsd 2f out: sn outpcd: styd on to take 3rd ins fnl f* **11/4**^{2}

6 **4** 3 **Orsett Lad (USA)**^{18} 3160 2-8-9 0 .... MarcHalford$^{(3)}$ 6 68
(J R Best) *outpcd and rdn in rr: clsd but stl at rr 2f out: sn outpcd again: kpt on fnl f* **25/1**

35 **5** 4 1/2 **Safari Special**^{43} 2348 2-8-9 0 .... JimCrowley 9 52
(P Winkworth) *prom: chsd ldr 1/2-way: clsd to ld 2f out: immediately hdd & wknd* **11/1**

0 **6** 3 3/4 **Flaming Miracle**^{11} 3403 2-8-9 0 .... LPKeniry 7 41
(A M Balding) *dwlt: outpcd and rdn in rr: tried to cl 2f out: sn wknd* **50/1**

0 **7** nk **Private Olley**^{34} 2636 2-8-12 0 .... J-PGuillambert 3 43
(J Akehurst) *chsd ldr to 1/2-way: lost pl rapidly 2f out: eased whn no ch fnl f* **14/1**

4322 **8** 2 3/4 **Janeiro (IRE)**^{5} 3579 2-8-9 0 .... (v^{1}) RichardKingscote 5 31
(Tom Dascombe) *led at str pce: wknd and hdd 2f out* **11/8**^{1}

6 **9** 11 **Trade Fairle**^{11} 3385 2-9-1 0 .... PatCosgrave 8 4
(P R Webber) *dwlt: outpcd and sn t.o* **100/1**

1m 12.03s (0.13) **Going Correction** +0.025s/f (Slow) 9 Ran SP% **118.1**
Speed ratings (Par 94): **100,95,94,90,84 79,78,75,60**
toteswingers: 1&2 £10.60, 1&3 £2.50, 2&3 £15.60 CSF £62.71 TOTE £4.10: £1.50, £5.90, £1.50; EX 90.10 TRIFECTA Not won. Place 6 £172.15, Place 5 £85.45.

Owner Anamoine Ltd **Bred** Windflower Overseas Holdings Inc **Trained** Newmarket, Suffolk

FOCUS
A better division of the maiden and run at a fair pace. The winner improved from her debut and can rate higher.

NOTEBOOK
Snow Fairy(IRE), who showed plenty of ability when third on her Newbury debut, turned this into something of a procession. She travelled sweetly throughout and made her move with 3f to go. She possibly hit the front sooner than her rider would have anticipated but, once clear off the final bend, she put daylight between herself and her rivals. She appears to have plenty of improvement in her. (op 11-4 tchd 5-2)
Baby Dottie showed plenty of promise on her debut. Her outside draw did not help and, though she showed greenness when hanging in towards the rail after turning in, she has ability and will learn a lot form this. This looks her trip for now. (op 25-1)
Hot Pursuits didn't have the best draw on the inside, or a trouble-free passage. She was just getting going when squeezed for room as Baby Dottie hung, and had to be switched. She stayed on well enough to think that she can win a race or two and looks progressive. (op 5-2 tchd 9-4 and 3-1)
Orsett Lad(USA), who had shaped well on his debut on turf here last time, caught the eye staying on in fourth, albeit some way behind the principals. He should come on for the run, according to his trainer. (op 50-1)
Safari Special was up there for a long way, but tired. He probably didn't stay this trip. (tchd 12-1)
Flaming Miracle started tardily and was outpaced, but he showed a glimmer of ability before tiring. (op 66-1)
Private Olley Official explanation: vet said colt returned lame left-fore
Janeiro(IRE), an habitual slow starter, was quickly away this time and led them approaching the straight. However, he quickly and disappointingly folded. He may have not relished the visor. (op 7-4 tchd 2-1 in a place)
T/Plt: £90.00 to a £1 stake. Pool: £41,164.58. 333.80 winning tickets. T/Qpdt: £31.10 to a £1 stake. Pool: £2,874.35. 68.30 winning tickets. JN

3395 NEWMARKET (R-H)
Wednesday, July 8

OFFICIAL GOING: Good (7.7)
All three days of the meeting were staged on the far side track.
Wind: Modest, behind Weather: Overcast

3746 EBF HOTEL CHOCOLAT FILLIES' H'CAP 7f
1:30 (1:32) (Class 2) (0-100,99) 3-Y-O
£24,924 (£5,598; £5,598; £1,868; £932; £468) Stalls Low

Form RPR

-300 **1** **Greenisland (IRE)**^{21} 3016 3-8-13 **89** .... RobertHavlin 11 95
(H Morrison) *racd in centre: led centre gp tl overall ldr 3f out: rdn and pressed over 1f out: styd on gamely to forge ahd fnl f* **66/1**

3211 **2** 3/4 **Mo Mhuirnin (IRE)**^{11} 3381 3-8-4 **80** oh3 .... PaulHanagan 9 84
(R A Fahey) *taken down early: racd in centre gp: in tch in midfield: niggled along 4f out: rdn and unable qck 2f out: rallied u.p and squeezed between horses 1f out: styd on wl u.p: nt rch wnr* **8/1**^{3}

-212 **2** dht **Balaagha (USA)**^{19} 3102 3-8-8 **84** .... RHills 12 88+
(M A Jarvis) *mounted on crse: awkward leaving stalls and v.s.a: racd in centre gp: hld up bhd: swtchd rt and hdwy wl over 1f out: styd on wl ins fnl f: nt rch wnr* **6/1**^{1}

02-3 **4** 1/2 **Pyrrha**^{26} 2882 3-8-6 **82** .... AlanMunro 3 85+
(C F Wall) *lw: racd on far rail: chsd ldrs: rdn and effrt 2f out: chsd wnr briefly ins fnl f: kpt on same pce fnl 100yds* **9/1**

1120 **5** 3/4 **Photographic**^{21} 3016 3-9-4 **94** .... MichaelHills 10 95
(B W Hills) *lw: racd in centre gp: trckd ldrs: rdn and unable qck wl over 1f out: kpt on same pce u.p fnl f* **11/1**

2121 **6** nse **Cumana Bay**^{11} 3400 3-8-9 **85** .... JimmyFortune 14 86
(R Hannon) *lw: racd in centre gp: cl up: rdn to press wnr over 1f out: unable qck ent fnl f: kpt on one pce after* **7/1**^{2}

5-10 **7** 1/2 **Resort**^{62} 1801 3-8-7 **83** .... RyanMoore 15 83
(Sir Michael Stoute) *racd in centre gp: w.w in tch: pushed along 3f out: rdn and unable qck 2f out: edging lft and no imp u.p fnl f* **9/1**

4134 **8** nse **Never Lose**^{25} 2928 3-9-2 **92** .... NCallan 16 91
(C E Brittain) *lw: racd in centre gp: towards rr: rdn and struggling over 2f out: hdwy u.p and swtchd rt over 1f out: styd on fnl 100yds: nt pce to rch ldrs* **9/1**

-305 **9** hd **First City**^{21} 3016 3-9-0 **93** .... AhmedAjtebi$^{(3)}$ 5 92
(D M Simcock) *racd on far side rail: t.k.h: chsd ldrs: effrt to press ldrs and rdn 2f out: wknd u.p ins fnl f* **12/1**

160- **10** 1 **Sea Of Leaves (USA)**^{347} 4403 3-9-0 **90** .... DanielTudhope 13 86
(J S Goldie) *racd in centre gp: t.k.h: wl in tch: rdn jst over 2f out: wknd u.p ent fnl f* **66/1**

106 **11** 1 3/4 **Mastoora (IRE)**^{18} 3163 3-8-2 **83** .... Louis-PhilippeBeuzelin$^{(5)}$ 6 74
(W J Haggas) *racd in centre gp: dwlt: hld up in midfield: rdn and unable qck 2f out: drvn and wknd over 1f out* **12/1**

1-40 **12** 1 3/4 **Arabian Mirage**^{21} 3016 3-9-1 **91** .... MartinDwyer 1 78
(B J Meehan) *racd on far rail: hld up towards rr: pushed along and effrt over 2f out: wknd wl over 1f out* **33/1**

4146 **13** shd **Good Again**^{21} 3016 3-9-3 **93** .... EddieAhern 4 79
(G A Butler) *racd in centre gp: hld up towards rr: rdn and struggling 3f out: nvr trbld ldrs* **7/1**^{2}

00-0 **14** 1/2 **Rosabee (IRE)**^{4} 3622 3-9-9 **99** .... EdwardCreighton 7 84
(Mrs D J Sanderson) *racd in centre gp: stdd s: hld up in rr: nvr a factor* **40/1**

-130 **15** 17 **Lovely Thought**^{21} 3033 3-8-6 **82** .... (p) LiamJones 2 21
(W J Haggas) *racd on far rail: sn bustled along and overall ldr: hdd 3f out: steadily dropped out: t.o and eased ins fnl f* **20/1**

1m 24.09s (-1.61) **Going Correction** -0.15s/f (Firm) 15 Ran SP% **117.2**
Speed ratings (Par 103): **103,102,102,101,100 100,100,100,99,98 96,94,94,93,74**PL: Balaagha £2.60, Mo Mhuirnin £483.30; EX: G-B £343.90; G-MM £483.30; CSF: G-B £195.25, G-MM £243.76; TRICAST: G-B-MM £1,542.42, G-MM-B £1,590.28. toteswingers: 1&2 (B) £67.60, 1&3 (MM) £114.90, 2&3 £7.90 TOTE £85.10: £16.30 TRIF27 Owner.

FOCUS
This had looked a wide-open handicap beforehand, but not that many got into it, the field splitting into two groups, with those in the centre having the upper hand. Sound enough form nevertheless.

NOTEBOOK
Greenisland(IRE) sprang a 66/1 shock. A 1m maiden winner at two who returned with a respectable third in a Listed contest at Dusseldorf in April, she ran better than the bare form suggests at York next time (eased having been hampered), but showed little when an outsider in the Sandringham at Royal Ascot, finishing behind many of these. Dropped 3lb by the handicapper, she led the centre group from an early stage and kept finding when strongly challenged, always looking to be doing enough in the final half furlong. She reportedly liked the good (fast) ground and connections will no doubt go back up in grade with her now. Official explanation: trainer said, regarding apparent improvement in form, that the filly was better suited by being able to dominate. (tchd 100-1 in a place)
Mo Mhuirnin(IRE), racing from 3lb out of the handicap, was effectively 10lb higher than when winning at Doncaster last month and she ran really well in defeat. She began to take closer order passing the three and started to run on well once hitting the rising ground, but never looked like getting to the winner. She has now finished in the first three on each of her last ten starts. (op 9-2)
Balaagha(USA) ran a massive race considering she fell out of the stalls and was the only one to make up appreciable ground. A filly who has her share of temperament, again having to be mounted on the course, she has made a habit of starting slowly and it proved her undoing here. Up 4lb having finished second at Goodwood on her handicap debut, she started to come with a strong run from over a furlong out and was edging closer with every stride as they crossed the line. There is clearly a good deal of ability there, but she is evidently going to remain a tough one to get the best out of. Official explanation: jockey said filly was slowly away (op 9-2)
Pyrrha 'won' the battle of the small group who stayed far side. Third at Goodwood on her reappearance, she was up to 7f for the first time and stuck on well against the rail, but wasn't quite on terms with the front trio. This was a good effort and she saw the trip out well. (op 11-1)
Photographic was progressing well until running a shocker in the Sandringham at Royal Ascot last time, but she showed her true colours here and ran much better, keeping on without being able to quicken on this return to 7f. (op 10-1)
Cumana Bay, a winner over 1m at the course last month, was up 4lb in a stronger heat and ran well without suggesting the return to 7f was in her favour. She is still going the right way. Official explanation: jockey said filly lost its action (tchd 15-2)
Resort, off since reportedly failing to cope with Chester in May, was outpaced when the tempo quickened and could only plug on at the one pace. (op 8-1)
Never Lose, fourth in the 5f Scurry Stakes at Sandown last time, was 10lb higher than when winning at Newbury in May and got going all too late. (op 10-1 tchd 11-1)

First City, who came home well having met trouble when a 66/1 shot in the Sandringham, was 2lb lower here and looked one of the more obvious ones, but stayed towards the far side and faded late on. (op 10-1)

3747 TOTESPORT.COM STKS (HERITAGE H'CAP) 6f

2:00 (2:03) (Class 2) (0-105,104) 3-Y-O

£62,310 (£18,660; £9,330; £4,670; £2,330; £1,170) **Stalls** Low

Form				RPR
1500	**1**		**Total Gallery (IRE)**[4] 3638 3-9-7 **103** ... JMurtagh 11 (J S Moore) *hld up in tch: rdn and hdwy over 1f out: drvn to ld ins fnl f: r.o wl* **11/1**	110
P-06	**2**	*nk*	**Desert Icon (IRE)**[16] 3219 3-7-9 **80** oh5 ... DavidProbert(3) 8 (W J Knight) *prom: chsd ldr 1/2-way: rdn and ev ch over 1f out: led briefly 1f out: sn hdd: kpt on wl but a jst hld by wnr* **40/1**	86
4261	**3**	*3/4*	**Enderby Spirit (GR)**[4] 3622 3-9-3 **104** 6ex ... GaryBartley(5) 14 (B Smart) *hld up towards rr: hdwy 2f out: n.m.r ent fnl f: chsng ldrs and styng on whn swtchd rt wl ins fnl f: nt quite pce to rch ldrs* **14/1**	108
-045	**4**	*hd*	**Rowayton**[18] 3166 3-8-0 **82** ... JimmyQuinn 12 (J D Bethell) *sn led: rdn and hrd pressed over 1f out: hdd 1f out: kpt on same pce fnl f* **20/1**	85
0342	**5**	*nk*	**Parisian Pyramid (IRE)**[25] 2934 3-8-8 **95** ... MartinLane(5) 5 (D Nicholls) *prom: rdn and ev ch 2f out: hrd drvn: edgd rt and one pce fnl f* **9/1**[3]	97
0050	**6**	*3/4*	**Imperial Guest**[25] 2934 3-8-4 **86** ... ChrisCatlin 15 (G G Margarson) *in tch in midfield: rdn and effrt wl over 1f out: kpt on but nvr gng pce to rch ldrs* **40/1**	86
0131	**7**	*3/4*	**Spring Green**[7] 3506 3-7-13 **81** 6ex ... NickyMackay 10 (H Morrison) *towards rr: rdn and hdwy u.p over 1f out: edgd lft and no imp fnl 100yds* **16/1**	78
1-12	**8**	*hd*	**Shamwari Lodge (IRE)**[33] 2674 3-8-12 **94** ... RyanMoore 18 (R Hannon) *lw: hld up bhd: rdn and effrt wl over 1f out: styd on u.p ins fnl f: nt rch ldrs* **11/2**[1]	91+
-200	**9**	*shd*	**Enact**[46] 2270 3-7-13 **86** ... Louis-PhilippeBeuzelin(5) 4 (Sir Michael Stoute) *lw: hld up in midfield: rdn and effrt 2f out: drvn and kpt on same pce fr jst over 1f out* **14/1**	82
4100	**10**	*nk*	**Proclaim**[4] 3622 3-9-1 **97** ... JoeFanning 17 (M Johnston) *lw: chsd ldrs: rdn ent fnl 2f out: wknd u.p ent fnl f* **20/1**	92
21-0	**11**	*1/2*	**Run For The Hills**[54] 2035 3-8-10 **92** ... JimmyFortune 13 (J H M Gosden) *lw: stdd s and dropped in bhd: hld up in rr: swtchd rt and rdn 2f out: hld hd high and no hdwy tl styd on ins fnl f: nvr trbld ldrs* **7/1**[2]	89+
2240	**12**	*hd*	**Akhenaten**[25] 2934 3-8-12 **94** ... TonyCulhane 6 (M R Channon) *bhd: drvn and struggling 1/2-way: sme hdwy u.p fnl f: nvr toubled ldrs* **20/1**	87
110	**13**	*1*	**Sloop Johnb**[25] 2934 3-8-2 **84** ... PaulHanagan 1 (R A Fahey) *stdd after s: hld up in tch: pushed along and hdwy over 2f out: drvn and wknd over 1f out* **25/1**	74
-030	**14**	*3/4*	**Klynch**[5] 3592 3-8-1 **83** ow3 ... (b) RichardThomas 7 (B J Meehan) *s.i.s: a towards rr: nvr trbld ldrs* **66/1**	70
-463	**15**	*1/2*	**Damien (IRE)**[39] 2485 3-9-6 **102** ... MichaelHills 2 (B W Hills) *stdd after s: hld up in midfield: hdwy over 2f out: chsd ldrs and rdn 2f out: wknd over 1f out* **16/1**	88
2000	**16**	*nk*	**Timeteam (IRE)**[16] 3219 3-8-2 **84** ow2 ... (t) MartinDwyer 16 (S Kirk) *t.k.h: hld up towards rr: rdn and no hdwy wl over 1f out: wl hld fnl f* **50/1**	69
-451	**17**	*1*	**Global City (IRE)**[28] 2821 3-9-6 **102** ... (t) LDettori 9 (Saeed Bin Suroor) *in tch in midfield: rdn and struggling over 1f out: eased whn wl btn ins fnl f* **9/1**[3]	84
2641	**18**	*1*	**Big Apple Boy (IRE)**[9] 3455 3-8-6 **88** 6ex ... AndrewElliott 3 (Jedd O'Keeffe) *chsd ldr for 3f out: wknd u.p wl over 1f out* **10/1**	66
-102	**19**	*nse*	**Dark Lane**[12] 3362 3-8-1 **83** ... (p) FrancisNorton 20 (T D Barron) *stdd and dropped in bhd after s: nvr a factor* **18/1**	61

1m 10.67s (-1.83) **Going Correction** -0.15s/f (Firm) **19** Ran SP% **122.1**
Speed ratings (Par 106): **106,105,104,104,103 102,101,101,101,101 100,100,98,97,97 96,95,94,94**
toteswingers: 1&2 £92.30, 1&3 £25.10, 2&3 £111.70 CSF £407.88 CT £6070.69 TOTE £12.30: £2.70, £8.70, £3.40, £5.10; EX 497.40 TRIFECTA Not won..
Owner Coleman Bloodstock Limited **Bred** Michael Woodlock And Seamus Kennedy **Trained** Upper Lambourn, Berks

FOCUS

A competitive field lined up for this heritage handicap and they all raced up the centre of the track. With the aid of a tailwind the pace held up despite the gallop looking strong. Although the runner-up was out of the proper handicap, the form makes sense overall, but it was clearly an advantage to race handily.

NOTEBOOK

Total Gallery(IRE) had been held in Group company recently, but he hadn't raced over his best trip since taking a Listed contest at Ascot on his reappearance, and the return to 6f suited, coupled with a drop in class into handicap company for the first time. Tracking the pace right up the centre of the course, he kept on well to edge ahead on the climb to the line, and he's clearly a bit better than this class. Another Listed race could come his way over this trip on this evidence, and talk of the Abbaye sounds optimistic. (op 14-1)

Desert Icon(IRE) looked to have plenty on his plate from 5lb out of the handicap, but he has had his excuses (broken his pelvis twice) since winning his maiden, and the fact that he ran in the Richmond Stakes at two gives some indication of the regard in which he has been held in the past. Showing good speed up the centre of the track, he posted a career-best effort, although it has to be said that his style of running was suited to the way track was riding. Connections suggested that he's likely to be out again soon to take advantage of his current mark. (op 50-1)

Enderby Spirit(GR), who was 2lb worse in at the weights under his 6lb penalty than he will be when his new mark takes effect, tracked the leaders up the centre of the track but could never quite put down a challenge to the winner, who had given him 3lb and beaten him a neck in a Listed race at Ascot earlier in the season. That form was confirmed and helps set the level. (tchd 16-1 in a place)

Rowayton was given a positive ride and bounced back to her best, having run a bit below form over 5f here last time when the race came a bit quick after a good effort at York on her previous start. She too benefited from racing prominently on a day when those tactics were heavily favoured, though.

Parisian Pyramid(IRE) didn't see it out quite as well as some, but it was another solid effort from this consistent gelding. His losing run is getting longer, but he might be seen at his best on an easier track. (tchd 11-1)

Imperial Guest, who raced more towards the stands' side of the bunch, has slipped to a favourable mark and ran well considering his stable remains largely out of form. He'll be interesting once the winners start going in again.

Spring Green, who was 3lb wrong under her penalty, didn't do badly considering she was held up in a race dominated by the pace horses. She clearly remains at the top of her game and the return to 6f proved no problem. (op 12-1)

Shamwari Lodge(IRE) ◆, who ran well from a tough draw at Epsom last time, stayed on steadily from way back and simply never got involved. With pace holding up he was set an impossible task, and he remains one to be interested in for a similar race. (tchd 6-1 in places)

Enact, who has had her excuses this season, was expected to be suited by the drop back to 6f, but she was drawn low, raced towards the far side of the bunch and never landed a blow. (tchd 16-1)

Proclaim, already due to be dropped 2lb, showed early pace but could not sustain it. He has not progressed since the spring.

Run For The Hills came towards the stands' side as he tried to make up ground from the rear, and ran out of room inside the last. He would have finished a little closer with a clear run, but would still not have troubled the principals. (op 17-2)

Klynch Official explanation: jockey said gelding never travelled

Global City(IRE) Official explanation: jockey said colt had no more to give

Big Apple Boy(IRE) was 3lb well in under his penalty but he raced towards the far side of the bunch and weakened right out of things inside the last. The race might have come too soon for him, or he might be best on a turning track. (op 11-1 tchd 12-1)

3748 IRISH THOROUGHBRED MARKETING CHERRY HINTON STKS (GROUP 2) (FILLIES) 6f

2:35 (2:36) (Class 1) 2-Y-O

£45,416 (£17,216; £8,616; £4,296; £2,152; £1,080) **Stalls** Low

Form				RPR
112	**1**		**Misheer**[21] 3015 2-8-12 0 ... NCallan 10 (C E Brittain) *lw: racd keenly: trckd ldrs and a gng wl: led 2f out: rdn over 1f out: edgd rt but r.o strly to go clr fnl f: readily* **7/2**[3]	108+
311	**2**	*3 1/4*	**Habaayib**[19] 3086 2-8-12 0 ... RHills 6 (E A L Dunlop) *dwlt: hld up in tch: pushed along ent fnl 2f: rdn wl over 1f out: styd on to chse wnr ins fnl f: no imp and wl hld after* **9/4**[1]	98
31	**3**	*nk*	**Lady Darshaan (IRE)**[10] 3430 2-8-12 0 ... JimmyFortune 1 (J S Moore) *dwlt: hld up bhd: pushed along 3f out: hdwy u.p over 1f out: edgd lft u.p fnl f: styd on to press for 2nd nr fin: no ch w wnr* **16/1**	98
114	**4**	*2 1/2*	**Capercaillie (USA)**[21] 3015 2-8-12 0 ... LDettori 9 (M Johnston) *lw: led: rdn and hdd 2f out: outpcd by wnr ent fnl f: edgd lft and lost 2nd ins fnl f: wknd fnl 100yds* **3/1**[2]	90
0110	**5**	*3/4*	**Crown (IRE)**[21] 3015 2-8-12 0 ... RyanMoore 2 (R Hannon) *bhd: niggled along and struggling 4f out: hdwy u.p and swtchd lft over 1f out: plugged on fnl f: no ch w wnr* **33/1**	88
113	**6**	*nk*	**Ceedwell**[21] 3015 2-8-12 0 ... TomEaves 4 (B Smart) *broke wl: racd keenly and prom for 2f: lost pl and pushed along 1/2-way: no ch ldrs fnl 2f: plugged on fnl f* **10/1**	87
01	**7**	*1/2*	**Raddy 'Ell Pauline (IRE)**[14] 3271 2-8-12 0 ... JMurtagh 7 (K A Ryan) *str: scope: racd keenly: pressed ldr after 1f tl over 1f out: sn outpcd by wnr: wknd fnl f* **20/1**	85+
2354	**8**	*1*	**Little Scotland**[22] 2995 2-8-12 0 ... AlanMunro 8 (T D Easterby) *chsd ldrs untl lost pl and rdn over 2f out: wl hld fnl f* **20/1**	82
415	**9**	*nk*	**Hairspray**[11] 3396 2-8-12 0 ... TonyCulhane 5 (M R Channon) *dwlt: a in rr: shkn up 2f out: sn rdn and no prog* **40/1**	81
21	**10**	*2 1/4*	**Swan Wings**[14] 3277 2-8-12 0 ... WilliamBuick 3 (A M Balding) *chsd ldr early: sn niggled along and struggling to go pce: bhd and rdn 2f out: sn wknd* **16/1**	75

1m 10.85s (-1.65) **Going Correction** -0.15s/f (Firm) **10** Ran SP% **113.8**
Speed ratings (Par 103): **105,100,100,96,95 95,94,93,93,90**
toteswingers: 1&2 £2.30, 1&3 £7.70, 2&3 £6.00 CSF £10.84 TOTE £4.00: £1.60, £1.40, £3.00; EX 12.60 Trifecta £226.00 Pool: £733.20 - 2.40 winning units..
Owner Saeed Manana **Bred** New England Stud And Partners **Trained** Newmarket, Suffolk

FOCUS

The Albany Stakes has proved the best guide to finding the winner of this race in recent years, but it was the Queen Mary form that came out on top this time. The winning time was smart, only 0.18sec slower than the three-year-olds recorded in the earlier 0-105 handicap. Solid form and a decent winner in Misheer, but not a vintage running.

NOTEBOOK

Misheer had been well and truly put in her place by the very speedy American filly Jealous Again when runner-up at Ascot, but she'd had a hold-up with a sore back the week before and went there short of work. The step up to 6f here promised to suit her well, and, having travelled strongly behind the pace, she confirmed that expectation by racing away once she hit the rising ground. She shapes as though she'll be suited by 7f, which would bring in the Moyglare as the way to go next, but there has to be some doubt on pedigree about whether she'll be as effective over that distance, especially when one considers that she'll no doubt come up against some more stoutly bred rivals in that Irish Group 1 contest. Sayyedati went to the Moyglare via success in this race, and followed up in the Cheveley Park, so one can expect that to be the route taken by Brittain with this high-class prospect. She is generally a 20-1 chance for the Guineas, but whether she'll get a mile next year must be open to question. (op 3-1 tchd 11-4)

Habaayib, the Albany Stakes winner, was ridden more patiently than the winner, tracking her for much of the way. Unable to make any impression inside the last, she appeared to run below her Ascot form, a view that was supported by her connections, who noted that she was on edge beforehand and that perhaps the race had come too soon for her. There was a suggestion, too, that she may have been coming into season as well, and apparently the plan is to now give her a break and bring her back for the Cheveley Park in the autumn. Official explanation: trainer said filly had come into season (op 5-2 tchd 3-1)

Lady Darshaan(IRE), a half-sister to Total Gallery, who won the previous handicap, is considered to be still quite raw, but this was a highly promising effort from her on this step up in class. A daughter of High Chaparral, she was held up out the back and stayed on strongly to take third. She will get further in time, but is clearly effective over this trip now, and at this stage she looks a leading candidate for the Two-Year-Old Trophy at Redcar later in the year. However, on this evidence she can take a Pattern race before then. (op 25-1)

Capercaillie(USA), who was sent off favourite for the Queen Mary, in which she finished fourth, was fancied by many to reverse Ascot form with Misheer and Ceedwell, but she was a little disappointing, especially as she made the running on a day when pace had been holding up quite well. An easier 6f might suit her, so it wouldn't be a surprise to see her go a bit better if she turns up for the Lowther at York. (tchd 11-4 and 10-3)

Crown(IRE) had plenty of ground to make up on those that finished in front of her in the Queen Mary, although the step up to 6f looked likely to suit. She ran about as well as could be expected.

Ceedwell, third in the Queen Mary, regressed on this step up to 6f and on her first start on ground easier than good to firm. She is by Exceed And Excel and might need it rattling to be at her best. (op 9-1 tchd 11-1)

Raddy 'Ell Pauline(IRE) was taking a big step up in class from a Kempton maiden, and she raced too keenly to get home. There is more to come from her when she settles better. Official explanation: jockey said filly hung right-handed (op 25-1)

Little Scotland has shown solid form in Listed company but is simply not up to this class. (tchd 16-1)

Hairspray, representing last year's winning stable, was another who found the competition too hot.

Swan Wings made all in a Salisbury maiden last time but couldn't lead this field and was struggling to go the pace from before halfway.

3749 ETIHAD AIRWAYS FALMOUTH STKS (GROUP 1) (F&M) 1m

3:10 (3:11) (Class 1) 3-Y-O+

£113,540 (£43,040; £21,540; £10,740; £5,380; £2,700) **Stalls** Low

Form RPR

11-0 **1** **Goldikova (IRE)**^{52} 2120 4-9-5 125 OPeslier 3 116
(F Head, France) *racd keenly: trckd ldr: shkn up to chal over 1f out: rdn to ld ent fnl f: edgd rt u.p: sn stratnd and pushed out fnl 100yds* **7/4**^{1}

5-12 **2** ½ **Heaven Sent**^{21} 3012 6-9-5 111 RyanMoore 7 115
(Sir Michael Stoute) *swtg: stdd after s: hld up in tch: rdn and effrt 2f out: hrd drvn and edgd lft fnl f: wnt 2nd towards fin: nvr quite pce to rch wnr* **8/1**

4-31 **3** ½ **Spacious**^{21} 3012 4-9-5 113 JMurtagh 6 114
(J R Fanshawe) *lw: led at stdy gallop: rdn and qcknd ent fnl 2f: sn hrd pressed: edgd lft and hdd ent fnl f: one pce after* **11/2**^{3}

-543 **4** *nk* **Rainbow View (USA)**^{19} 3088 3-8-10 114 JimmyFortune 4 111
(J H M Gosden) *hld up wl in tch: rdn and effrt jst over 2f out: drvn and hdwy to chse ldrs ent fnl f: r.o but nvr quite pce to chal ldrs* **9/4**^{2}

-361 **5** 6 **Penny's Gift**^{31} 2757 3-8-10 107 JamieSpencer 5 97
(R Hannon) *lw: trckd ldng pair: rdn and wanting to hang rt ent fnl 2f: sn hrd drvn and outpcd: wl btn fnl f* **14/1**

-126 **6** *hd* **San Sicharia (IRE)**^{27} 2870 4-9-5 104 TedDurcan 2 99
(Ms Joanna Morgan, Ire) *hld up in last pair: rdn and outpcd ent fnl 2f: sn drvn and wknd* **80/1**

0113 **7** 1½ **Eva's Request (IRE)**^{21} 3012 4-9-5 109 EdwardCreighton 8 95
(M R Channon) *stdd s: t.k.h: hld up in last pl: rdn jst over 2f out: sn outpcd and wl btn* **20/1**

3-11 **8** 16 **Cosmopolitan**^{18} 3165 4-9-5 88 LDettori 1 59
(J H M Gosden) *racd alone towards far rail: chsd ldrs tl over 2f out: sn wknd: t.o and eased ins fnl f* **28/1**

1m 36.21s (-3.79) **Going Correction** -0.15s/f (Firm)
WFA 3 from 4yo+ 9lb **8** Ran SP% **109.7**
Speed ratings (Par 117): **112,111,111,110,104 104,103,87**
toteswingers: 1&2 £3.80, 1&3 £2.70, 2&3 £4.70 CSF £14.90 TOTE £1.90: £1.10, £2.70, £1.90; EX 14.30 Trifecta £38.10 Pool: £14,186.52 - 275.16 winning units..
Owner Wertheimer Et Frere **Bred** Wertheimer Et Frere **Trained** France

FOCUS
There was little strength-in-depth to this year's renewal, though the form looks solid with Windsor Forest one-two Heaven Sent and Spacious filling the places, albeit in a different order to Ascot, and Rainbow View, who was third to Ghanaati in the Coronation Stakes, finishing a close-up fourth. They again raced down the centre of the track, with the 'big' four drawing clear, and the time was very good, dipping almost half a second under RP standard.

NOTEBOOK
Goldikova(IRE) opened her account for the season without needing to run to her best. A three-time Group 1 winner last term, culminating with a brilliant victory in the Breeders' Cup Mile, she got bogged down by the testing ground on her reappearance in the Prix D'Ispahan, but conditions were much more in her favour here and trainer Freddie Head could not have been more bullish about her chances. Keen through the early stages, sat close to the pace, she eased level with Spacious approaching the two-pole and edged ahead for light pressure over a furlong out. Peslier was reluctant to get too serious with her, giving her just a couple of taps with the whip as she ran around in front, but she was always doing enough and just had to be nudged out hands and heels. A poignant win for her sire Anabaa, who had passed away the day before, this performance was probably still someway below her very best, but she got better as the season went on last year and all roads will lead towards a defence of her Breeders' Cup Mile crown, with races such as the Prix Rothschild and Prix Jacques Le Marois likely to come under consideration along the way. (tchd 6-4, 2-1 and 15-8 in places)
Heaven Sent is a hugely consistent filly, yet amazingly has still to win above Group 3 level. Third in this a year ago, she showed herself to be as good as ever when finishing second to Spacious in the Windsor Forest and, having travelled well in behind the speed, she stayed on well once switched, but never looked like getting to the classy winner. She deserves to find a race at Group 2 level at least and will no doubt contest races such as the Nassau and Sun Chariot once again. (tchd 9-1 in a place)
Spacious didn't live up to expectations at the backend of last season, but she has the size and breeding to make a much better older horse and showed herself to be an improved filly when making all under a fine ride in the Windsor Forest. Considering connections plan on going back up to 1m2f with her at some stage, it was surprising Murtagh didn't go a bit quicker early on her here, as she was always likely to get done for speed by a couple of the others. She kept on right the way to the line and remains capable of better, with the Nassau also likely to come under consideration for her. (op 5-1 tchd 13-2)
Rainbow View(USA), representing the generation responsible for the last three winners of this race, has not lived up to lofty expectations this term, but she met trouble when a running-on third in the Coronation Stakes and looked to hold obvious claims in this. Having chased the early speed, she couldn't quicken immediately when asked, but ran on for pressure and was not beaten far. This was a good effort, for all that it seemed to confirm the 3yo fillies, with the probable exception of Ghanaati and Sariska, are inferior to their elders. She has any number of options now, and will probably go back up in trip at some stage. (tchd 2-1 and 11-4 in places)
Penny's Gift, winner of a Group 2 at Dusseldorf last time, she had earlier finished sixth in the 1000 Guineas and this was about as good a placing as connections could have hoped for. She was trying to hang away to her right passing the two-marker and simply lacked the class to race on with the principals. (op 16-1 tchd 12-1)
San Sicharia(IRE), winner of a 7f Group 3 at Lingfield in May, was trying 1m for the first time since joining current connections and never threatened to get into it, as one would expect for an 80/1 shot. (tchd 100-1)
Eva's Request(IRE), third behind Spacious and Heaven Sent at Ascot, never looked like getting into it and should have fared better. This was not her best form. (op 18-1)
Cosmopolitan, successful off a mark of 84 last time, raced alone on the far side and was quickly beaten from two out. (op 25-1)

3750 MERTOUN PADDOCKS EBF MAIDEN STKS 7f

3:45 (3:46) (Class 2) 2-Y-O **£9,714** (£2,890; £1,444; £721) **Stalls** Low

Form RPR

1 **Elusive Pimpernel (USA)** 2-9-3 0 EddieAhern 4 89+
(J L Dunlop) *w'like: scope: lw: towards rr: pushed along 4f out: swtchd lft and hdwy 2f out: rdn to chse wnr jst ins fnl f: r.o strly to ld fnl 50yds* **12/1**

0 **2** ½ **Timely Jazz (IRE)**^{11} 3395 2-9-3 0 MartinDwyer 10 88+
(B J Meehan) *lw: w ldr tl led over 2f out: rdn wl over 1f out: drvn clr jst ins fnl f: edgd lft u.p: hdd and no ex fnl 50yds* **40/1**

3 2¾ **Poet's Voice** 2-9-3 0 LDettori 9 81+
(Saeed Bin Suroor) *w'like: str: t.k.h: hld up in tch: rdn to chse ldr and edgd rt over 1f out: outpcd by ldr 1f out: plugged on same pce after* **6/1**^{2}

4 ¾ **Emerald Commander (IRE)** 2-9-3 0 RyanMoore 15 79
(R Hannon) *w'like: scope: s.i.s: hld up towards rr: pushed along and hdwy 3f out: rdn to chse ldrs over 1f out: no ex ins fnl f* **6/1**^{2}

5 1¾ **Rasselas (IRE)** 2-9-3 0 MichaelHills 7 75+
(B W Hills) *leggy: s.i.s: rn green in rr: hdwy over 2f out: styng on whn sltly hmpd over 1f out: sn swtchd rt: kpt on steadily fnl f: nvr trbld ldrs* **16/1**

6 *nk* **New Innocence** 2-9-3 0 WilliamBuick 12 74+
(G A Butler) *leggy: hld up in midfield: shuffled bk and in rr whn swtchd rt and rdn 2f out: kpt on steadily fnl f: nvr trbld ldrs* **50/1**

6 **7** 3½ **Gold Diamond (USA)**^{18} 3167 2-9-3 0 RoystonFfrench 11 65
(M Johnston) *led tl rdn and hdd 2f out: edgd rt and wknd u.p over 1f out: wl hld fnl f* **13/2**^{3}

0 **8** *shd* **Erfaan (USA)**^{27} 2844 2-9-3 0 RHills 6 65
(B W Hills) *hld up wl in tch: shkn up 2f out: fnd little and rdn wl over 1f out: sn wknd* **6/1**^{2}

2 **9** *hd* **Liquid Asset (FR)**^{26} 2889 2-9-3 0 DavidProbert 13 64
(A M Balding) *chsd ldrs tl short of room and lost pl over 2f out: sn drvn: keeping on same pce and wl hld whn nt clr run and swtchd lft 1f out* **9/2**^{1}

4 **10** 1¾ **Heading To First**^{18} 3160 2-9-3 0 NCallan 14 60
(C E Brittain) *w'like: trckd ldrs: shkn up to try and chal 2f out: sn rdn and fnd nil: wl btn fnl f* **6/1**^{2}

11 ½ **Ransom Note** 2-9-3 0 PhilipRobinson 3 59+
(B W Hills) *str: bit bkwd: s.i.s: sn pushed along and rn green in rr: edging lft fr wl over 1f out: nvr trbld ldrs* **40/1**

12 4½ **High Holborn (IRE)** 2-9-3 0 JamieSpencer 1 48+
(B J Meehan) *str: bit bkwd: s.i.s: rn green and a in rr: rdn and losing tch whn sltly hmpd over 1f out* **20/1**

0 **13** 4 **Sancho Panza**^{28} 2825 2-9-3 0 TPQueally 5 38
(Miss J Feilden) *unf: prom tl 1/2-way: sn rdn and losing pl: no ch fr wl over 1f out* **100/1**

14 5 **Osorios Trial** 2-9-3 0 JoeFanning 2 25
(M Johnston) *w'like: leggy: in tch: rdn and struggling 3f out: wl bhd fnl 2f* **40/1**

15 27 **Tiger Hawk (USA)** 2-9-3 0 JimmyFortune 8 —
(S A Callaghan) *w'like: s.i.s: rn green and sn detached in last pl: t.o fnl 2f* **25/1**

1m 24.88s (-0.82) **Going Correction** -0.15s/f (Firm) **15** Ran SP% **121.1**
Speed ratings (Par 100): **98,97,94,93,91 91,87,86,86,84 84,79,74,68,37**
toteswingers: 1&2 £61.40, 1&3 £14.70, 2&3 £32.90 CSF £434.73 TOTE £15.10: £4.80, £9.50, £2.40; EX 413.30.
Owner Windflower Overseas Holdings Inc **Bred** Windflower Overseas Holdings Inc **Trained** Arundel, W Sussex

FOCUS
This maiden has a rich history, last year's renewal again working out rather well, and this contest should again produce plenty of winners.

NOTEBOOK
Elusive Pimpernel(USA) ◆ finished strongly, despite drifting left, to get up in the final strides. A half-brother to the yard's smart 3yo Palavicini, it's not often one in these colours makes a winning debut, so the fact he proved good enough first time up suggests he could be smart. Held up through the early stages, he came under quite strong pressure at halfway, but started to stay on really well taken towards the far side and really grabbed at the turf as they hit the rising ground. He is clearly going to stay further than this and looks a horse with a bright future. (tchd 10-1)
Timely Jazz(IRE), who looked very much in need of the experience when ninth over C&D on his recent debut, knew a lot more this time and was soon up on the pace. He struck on over a furlong out and looked all over the winner, but couldn't repel Elusive Pimpernel's late surge. He should find a race on this evidence. (op 50-1)
Poet's Voice ◆, closely related to the stable's useful winner Swan Nebula, he travelled well just in behind the pace and briefly looked like coming with a winning run, but just lacked the speed in the final furlong. This was a pleasing start and he looks an obvious type for a maiden. (op 9-2)
Emerald Commander(IRE) ◆made a very pleasing debut considering he was slowly away. A son of Pivotal who went for £72,000 at the breeze-ups, he stayed on from over two out, but could not race on inside the final furlong. He should know more next time. (op 5-1 tchd 9-2 and 7-1 in a place)
Rasselas(IRE), a son of Danehill Dancer who went for 120,000gns, kept on despite running very green and getting slightly hampered. This initial experience will not be lost on him. (tchd 20-1)
New Innocence, a son of Where Or When from a yard whose juveniles tend to benefit from a run, kept on again having lost his position and will benefit from 1m before long.
Gold Diamond(USA) again showed speed before dropping out and is probably more of a nursery type. (op 8-1 tchd 9-1)
Liquid Asset(FR), runner-up on his debut at Sandown, was just beginning to look in trouble when squeezed for room and he soon lost his position. He was trying to stay on again when denied a clear run and probably deserves another chance to build on that initial promise. (tchd 4-1 and 5-1 in a place)

3751 TURFTV MAIDEN STKS 1m 2f

4:20 (4:22) (Class 3) 3-Y-O **£9,714** (£2,890; £1,444; £721) **Stalls** High

Form RPR

1 **Blizzard Blues (USA)** 3-9-3 0 (b^{1}) JamieSpencer 3 84
(H R A Cecil) *w'like: stdd s: hld up in last pl: gd hdwy over 2f out: chal on bit ent fnl f: sn led and drvn: immediately hung lft and reluctant: stened and rdn out fnl 100yds* **25/1**

2 ¾ **Manifest** 3-9-3 0 TPQueally 9 83+
(H R A Cecil) *athletic: w'like: scope: dwlt: hld up in tch towards rr: effrt and edgd lft jst over 2f out: hdwy and swtchd rt 1f out: kpt on wl to go 2nd towards fin: nvr gng to rch wnr* **11/2**^{3}

042- **3** *nk* **Kansai Spirit (IRE)**^{244} 7204 3-9-3 80 RichardMullen 11 82
(J H M Gosden) *lw: plld hrd: trckd ldng pair: ev ch and rdn 2f out: led briefly ent fnl f: sn hdd and carried lft: stl ev ch tl no ex fnl 75yds: lost 2nd towards fin* **13/2**

0 **4** 1½ **Do The Strand (IRE)**^{81} 1355 3-9-3 0 MichaelHills 2 79
(B W Hills) *w.w in tch: pushed along and hdwy over 3f out: chsd ldrs and drvn over 1f out: one pce and no imp fnl f* **16/1**

2336 **5** *hd* **Simplification**^{4} 3627 3-8-12 75 AlanMunro 1 74
(R Hannon) *chsd ldr: ev ch and rdn jst over 2f out: stl ev ch tl wknd 1f out* **16/1**

6 ¾ **Tinaar (USA)** 3-8-12 0 EddieAhern 4 72+
(G A Butler) *angular: lw: hld up in tch in rr: hdwy towards far side over 2f out: no imp u.p over 1f out* **10/1**

4 **7** 1¾ **Charger**^{19} 3117 3-9-3 0 ShaneKelly 7 74
(J Noseda) *w.w in tch in midfield: rdn and effrt over 2f out: struggling and losing pl whn short of room jst over 1f out: wl hld after* **5/2**^{1}

4420 **8** *shd* **Beauchamp Xerxes**^{19} 3087 3-9-3 101 RyanMoore 12 73+
(G A Butler) *plld hrd: hld up in tch in midfield: n.m.r and lost pl over 2f out sn hmpd and no ch after: plugged on fnl f* **3/1**^{2}

0-60 **9** ½ **Desert Fever**^{19} 3117 3-9-3 59 RHills 6 72?
(B W Hills) *led: rdn wl over 2f out: hdd ent fnl f: wkng whn sltly hmpd jst ins fnl f: sn wl btn and eased* **50/1**

63 **10** *4 1/2* **Reportage (USA)**[44] 2317 3-9-3 0 JimmyFortune 8 63
(J H M Gosden) *lw: t.k.h: hld up wl in tch: rdn and nt qckning whn hmpd jst over 2f out: no ch fnl 2f* **9/1**

00 **11** *1 1/4* **Regal Blush**[24] 2947 3-8-12 0 WilliamBuick 5 56
(A M Balding) *hld up in tch in rr: rdn and effrt over 2f out: sn struggling: wknd wl over 1f out* **50/1**

0 **12** *nk* **Catchmeifyoucan (FR)**[37] 2551 3-9-3 0 PhilipRobinson 13 60
(C G Cox) *w'like: in tch in midfield: hmpd bnd after 2f: pushed along 4f out: struggling and rdn 3f out: sn bhd* **50/1**

55 **13** *6* **Gulf Of Aqaba (USA)**[11] 3373 3-9-3 0 JoeFanning 10 48
(M Johnston) *t.k.h: hld up in midfield: dropped to rr 4f out: lost tch 3f out: eased ins fnl f* **100/1**

2m 8.96s (3.46) **Going Correction** -0.15s/f (Firm) **13** Ran SP% **123.9**
Speed ratings (Par 104): **80,79,79,77,77 77,75,75,75,71 70,70,65**
toteswingers: 1&2 £17.50, 1&3 £21.70, 2&3 £11.20 CSF £160.63 TOTE £21.00: £4.40, £2.20, £2.80; EX 72.30.
Owner Gestut Ammerland **Bred** Ammerland Verwaltung Gmbh & Co Kg **Trained** Newmarket, Suffolk
■ Stewards' Enquiry : Jamie Spencer four-day ban: careless riding (Jul 22-24,26)

FOCUS
Quite a competitive maiden and an eventful finish, but probably ordinary form for the track. It has been rated around the third and the fifith.

NOTEBOOK
Blizzard Blues(USA) managed to win in the first-time blinkers despite hanging badly left across the course and carrying the third with him. A son of Mr Greeley whose dam was a useful middle-distance performer in Germany, the headgear was an obvious concern on this racecourse debut and he was very slowly into stride. Detached in last place, his prospects did not look good, but he made ground with the minimum of fuss under a tentative Jamie Spencer and quickened well when asked for his effort. He found enough to score, surviving a stewards' enquiry (although Spencer picked up a four-day ban) but it was easy to see why he was wearing the blinkers. There is clearly a good deal of ability there and it will be fascinating to see how he progresses. (op 20-1)
Manifest ◆, who is from an excellent family, being a half-brother to Elmaamul and Reams Of Verse, stayed on nicely inside the final furlong to take second behind his stablemate. He showed signs of inexperience and is almost certainly the better long-term prospect of the front pair. He will be suited by further and winning a standard maiden should prove a formality. (op 5-1 tchd 7-1)
Kansai Spirit(IRE), runner-up over 1m at Great Leighs on his final start at two and carrying an official rating of 80, went on inside the two and raced clear with the winner, but he was carried left across to the far rail and could find no extra close home. (op 9-1 tchd 10-1)
Do The Strand(IRE) stayed on late and confirmed the promise shown on debut. He is crying out for 1m4f and remains capable of better, especially once handicapping. (op 14-1 tchd 12-1)
Simplification, fourth off a mark of 75 at Leicester just four days earlier, ran about as well as could have been expected against several less-exposed sorts. (op 12-1)
Tinaar(USA) cost $400,000 as a yearling and, like many from her yard, should come on appreciably for this initial experience. (op 16-1 tchd 8-1)
Charger was another to disappoint, failing to build on a promising effort over C&D last month. He couldn't respond for pressure and has a bit to prove now. (op 10-3 tchd 4-1)
Beauchamp Xerxes, officially rated 101, finished second in a Listed contest at Goodwood two starts back, but was beaten a long way when last in the Group 2 King Edward VII Stakes at Royal Ascot and this effort seemed to confirm he has gone the wrong way. Official explanation: jockey said colt ran too free (op 10-3 tchd 7-2 and 4-1 in a place)

3752 HOME OF RACING H'CAP — 1m
5:30 (5:32) (Class 3) (0-90,88) 3-Y-O+ **£9,714** (£2,890; £1,444; £721) **Stalls** Low

Form RPR

4-22 **1** **Dancourt (IRE)**[25] 2925 3-8-8 **77** RyanMoore 2 87
(Sir Michael Stoute) *lw: trckd ldng pair: rdn to ld over 1f out: a holding runner up fnl f: r.o wl* **3/1**[1]

0034 **2** *1 1/4* **Dingaan (IRE)**[12] 3335 6-9-2 **76** WilliamBuick 5 85
(A M Balding) *hld up in tch in midfield: hdwy over 1f out: rdn hands and heels to chse wnr jst ins fnl f: no imp and wl hld fnl 100yds* **11/1**[3]

2202 **3** *1* **Mujood**[14] 3282 6-9-10 **87** KevinGhunowa[(3)] 7 94
(Eve Johnson Houghton) *led: rdn jst over 2f out: drvn and hdd over 1f out: kpt on same pce fnl f* **25/1**

0464 **4** *nk* **Mastership (IRE)**[18] 3172 5-9-13 **87** (p) GrahamGibbons 1 93
(J J Quinn) *stdd s: t.k.h: hld up in last trio: rdn and hdwy over 1f out: kpt on u.p fnl f: nt pce to rch ldrs* **16/1**

3621 **5** *1* **Marajaa (IRE)**[22] 3008 7-9-10 **84** ChrisCatlin 12 88
(W J Musson) *lw: stdd s: hld up in last trio: pushed along and hdwy jst over 2f out: rdn to chse ldrs ent fnl f: one pce ins fnl f* **14/1**

4013 **6** *nk* **Last Three Minutes (IRE)**[25] 2933 4-9-13 **87** RHills 9 98+
(E A L Dunlop) *stdd s: t.k.h: hld up in last trio: effrt whn n.m.r 2f out tl nt clr run and bdly hmpd ent fnl f: switching rt after tl fnlly in the clr fnl 100yds: r.o: no ch* **3/1**[1]

0162 **7** *3/4* **Castles In The Air**[12] 3339 4-9-8 **82** PaulHanagan 4 84
(R A Fahey) *swtg: wnt rt s: t.k.h: sn chsng ldr: rdn over 2f out: drvn and unable qck 2f out: wknd ent fnl f* **16/1**

4-36 **8** *nse* **Habshan (USA)**[34] 2639 9-9-11 **85** AlanMunro 11 86
(C F Wall) *hld up in midfield: niggled along 3f out: rdn and unable qck ent fnl 2f: plugged on same pce after* **12/1**

6-02 **9** *1 1/4* **Admiral Dundas (IRE)**[26] 2894 4-9-6 **80** JoeFanning 13 79
(W Jarvis) *in tch in midfield: shkn up jst over 2f out: rdn and no prog 2f out: wl hld fnl f* **13/2**[2]

-402 **10** *nk* **Kinsya**[22] 3008 6-9-9 **83** NCallan 3 81
(M H Tompkins) *chsd ldrs: rdn over 2f out: wkng whn edgd sltly rt 1f out: eased whn wl btn towards fin* **11/1**[3]

361 **11** *13* **Turning Top (IRE)**[13] 3319 3-8-9 **78** JamieSpencer 8 44
(S A Callaghan) *in tch: rdn and edgd rt 2f out: sn struggling: btn and eased jst ins fnl f* **12/1**

1m 38.75s (-1.25) **Going Correction** -0.15s/f (Firm)
WFA 3 from 4yo+ 9lb **11** Ran SP% **117.7**
Speed ratings (Par 107): **100,98,97,97,96 96,95,95,94,93 80**
toteswingers: 1&2 £10.70, 1&3 £10.40, 2&3 £23.70 CSF £38.49 CT £702.41 TOTE £3.70: £1.70, £3.40, £5.30; EX 42.40 Place 6 £740.64, Place 5 £209.84.
Owner Ballymacoll Stud **Bred** Ballymacoll Stud Farm Ltd **Trained** Newmarket, Suffolk

FOCUS
This featured a couple of unexposed three-year-olds, and one of them came out on top. Ordinary form for the track and grade.

NOTEBOOK
Dancourt(IRE) ◆ is well bred and had shown plenty of ability in two previous starts in handicaps this term. In contrast to before those two runs, though, he was very strong in the market this time. Tracking the leader up the centre of the track, he was always well placed on a day when early pace had been holding up, and kept on well for pressure when sent on, despite again carrying his head a touch high. He won with a bit more in hand than the winning margin suggests and will be seen to even better effect in a stronger-run race on easier ground. He should be kept on-side and could well develop into a Cambridgeshire horse later in the season. (op 7-2 tchd 11-4)
Dingaan(IRE) came in for each-way support beforehand. A consistent sort, he bumped into an improving three-year-old here, but the fact remains that he is difficult to win with. His losing run now stands at 26, but he is undeniably well handicapped on his best form. (op 20-1)
Mujood set no more than a sensible pace up front and, with conditions favouring those who raced prominently, he was able to hang on for third. He remains on a mark 5lb higher than when last successful. (op 20-1 tchd 16-1)
Mastership(IRE) finished fourth in the Bunbury Cup off 95 at this meeting last year. Off an 8lb lower mark and with cheekpieces fitted for the first time, he stayed on from off the pace to take fourth, but he's become a disappointing sort (losing run of 22) and isn't one to be backing to break that sequence. (op 14-1)
Marajaa(IRE), a winner at Yarmouth last time, was 6lb higher here. He's a confirmed hold-up performer and conditions were not playing to his strengths on this occasion, so in the circumstances he ran a solid race. (tchd 16-1)
Last Three Minutes(IRE) ◆ was unlucky in running at York last time and still looked well handicapped off a 3lb higher mark. However, given the way races were panning out on this day he was always going to struggle trying to make up ground from well off the pace. Denied a clear run and hampered approaching the final furlong, he ran better than his finishing position suggests and, while there's a danger he could be developing into one of those horses that keeps letting punters down, he deserves another chance when a decent pace looks assured. Official explanation: jockey said gelding was denied a clear run (tchd 10-3 in a place)
Castles In The Air was given a good prominent ride but simply failed to get home over this longer trip. He will deserve respect back over 6f or 7f.
Habshan(USA), who won this race last year off a 2lb lower mark, is thoroughly exposed and was comfortably held. (tchd 10-1)
Admiral Dundas(IRE) perhaps could have done with racing more prominently, as he has done when successful in the past, but his stable remains quiet. (op 8-1)
Kinsya would have appreciated softer ground. (op 10-1 tchd 12-1)
Turning Top(IRE), the only other three-year-old in the field apart from the winner, was disappointing on her handicap debut, hanging before being heavily eased. (op 16-1)
T/Jkpt: Not won. T/Plt: £1,965.20 to a £1 stake. Pool: £176,768.80. 65.66 winning tickets. T/Qpdt: £43.80 to a £1 stake. Pool: £11,196.55. 189.10 winning tickets. SP

3753 - 3759a (Foreign Racing) - See Raceform Interactive

3563 DONCASTER (L-H)
Thursday, July 9

OFFICIAL GOING: Soft (6.5)
Rail realignment increased advertised distances on the round course by around 12yards.
Wind: Light across Weather: Overcast and showers

3760 JCT600 MERCEDES-BENZ SOUTH YORKSHIRE APPRENTICE H'CAP — 2m 110y
6:40 (6:40) (Class 6) (0-65,67) 4-Y-O+ **£2,729** (£806; £403) **Stalls** Low

Form RPR

5163 **1** **No Rules**[22] 3029 4-9-2 **55** SimonPearce 10 64
(M H Tompkins) *prom: hdwy to ld over 3f out: rdn clr wl over 1f out: styd on* **7/2**[2]

-636 **2** *7* **Terenzium (IRE)**[9] 3486 7-8-11 **50** (p) AmyRyan 5 51
(Micky Hammond) *hld up in tch: hdwy on inner 4f out: swtchd rt and rdn to chse wnr wl over 1f out: sn drvn: hung lft and no imp* **3/1**[1]

460- **3** *2 1/4* **Spring Breeze**[341] 4652 8-8-11 **55** IJBrennan[(5)] 7 53
(J J Quinn) *hld up in tch: hdwy 4f out: rdn to chse ldrs over 2f out: sn drvn and plugged on one pce* **5/1**[3]

-664 **4** *11* **Royal Premier (IRE)**[26] 2854 6-8-13 **52** (v) SophieDoyle 9 37
(H J Collingridge) *hld up towards rr: hdwy on outer over 3f out: rdn over 2f out: sn wknd* **10/1**

-000 **5** *6* **Flame Creek (IRE)**[40] 2497 13-8-6 **45** MatthewDavies 12 23
(E J Creighton) *hld up in rr: hdwy over 4f out: rdn along 3f out: nvr a factor* **28/1**

06-0 **6** *9* **Muntami (IRE)**[13] 38 8-8-13 **52** DeclanCannon 4 19
(John A Harris) *chsd ldrs: rdn along over 4f out and sn wknd* **10/1**

310 **7** *16* **Agglestone Rock**[48] 2237 4-9-7 **63** DavidKenny[(3)] 11 11
(P A Kirby) *hld up tl sddle slipped and rapid hdwy to ld after 3f: sn wl clr: pushed along and hdd over 3f out: sn wknd* **8/1**

0000 **8** *20* **Fan Club**[8] 3499 5-8-6 **45** JamesPSullivan 6 —
(Mrs R A Carr) *t.k.h: chsd ldrs: rdn along 4f out: sn wknd* **25/1**

6200 **9** *36* **Snowberry Hill (USA)**[31] 2766 6-9-2 **55** JPHamblett 2 —
(Lucinda Featherstone) *a in rr: rdn along and wknd 6f out: t.o fnl 3f* **11/2**

3m 52.99s (12.59) **Going Correction** +0.575s/f (Yiel) **9** Ran SP% **115.9**
Speed ratings (Par 101): **93,89,88,83,80 76,68,59,—**
toteswingers: 1&2 £2.40, 1&3 £6.20, 2&3 £4.10 CSF £14.50 CT £51.70 TOTE £4.10: £1.40, £1.70, £1.80; EX 16.30.
Owner M P Bowring **Bred** R F And S D Knipe **Trained** Newmarket, Suffolk

FOCUS
A modest staying handicap, weakened by the absence of three declared runners who had seemed certain to figure prominently, and the top-rated runner had an official mark of just 63. Rain during the day had changed the ground to soft and the pace was only steady. Weak form, rated around the runner-up.
Agglestone Rock Official explanation: jockey said saddle slipped

3761 EASTSIDE 20TH BIRTHDAY H'CAP — 1m 4f
7:10 (7:10) (Class 4) (0-80,78) 3-Y-O+ **£4,857** (£1,445; £722; £360) **Stalls** Low

Form RPR

0044 **1** **Shaloo Diamond**[15] 3266 4-9-7 **74** MichaelJStainton[(3)] 6 89
(R M Whitaker) *hld up in tch: smooth hdwy 3f out: led on bit 2f out: rdn clr appr fnl f: styd on strly* **6/1**

221 **2** *9* **Interdiamonds**[12] 3379 3-9-0 **77** JoeFanning 7 78
(M Johnston) *led 2f: trckd ldr tl led over 3f out: rdn and hdd 2f out: sn drvn and kpt on: no ch w wnr* **4/1**[2]

0546 **3** *3 3/4* **By Command**[17] 3206 4-9-7 **71** SebSanders 5 66
(J W Hills) *hld up towards rr: hdwy over 3f out: rdn to chse ldng pair over 2f out: sn drvn and one pce* **14/1**

4210 **4** *2 3/4* **Red Wine**[47] 2283 10-9-9 **73** AlanMunro 9 63
(J A Glover) *hld up in rr: hdwy over 3f out: rdn over 2f out: sn drvn and one pce* **10/1**

16-5 **5** *16* **Bavarian Nordic (USA)**[22] 3034 4-10-0 **78** SilvestreDeSousa 1 43
(Mrs A Duffield) *trkd ldrs: hdwy on inner to chse ldng pair 3f out: rdn over 2f out: sn drvn and wknd* **6/1**

21-0 **6** *2* **West With The Wind**[15] 3266 4-9-8 **72** MickyFenton 2 33
(T P Tate) *awkward at s: hdwy to ld after 2f: rdn along over 4f out: hdd over 3f out and sn wknd* **13/2**

5-13 **7** *2 1/2* **Timocracy**[40] 2505 4-10-0 **78** GrahamGibbons 3 35
(T D Walford) *t.k.h: chsd ldng pair: rdn along over 3f out: sn wknd* **7/2**[1]

005 **8** *41* **Spensley (IRE)**[20] 3117 3-8-8 **71** ..... JamieSpencer 8 —
(J R Fanshawe) *hld up: a bhd: eased 3f out: virtually p.u 2f out* **11/2**[3]

2m 40.48s (5.38) **Going Correction** +0.575s/f (Yiel)
WFA 3 from 4yo+ 13lb **8** Ran SP% **115.3**
Speed ratings (Par 105): **105,99,96,94,84 82,81,—**
toteswingers: 1&2 £10.30, 1&3 £11.10, 2&3 £4.20 CSF £30.46 CT £322.74 TOTE £7.20: £2.20, £2.10, £3.50; EX 27.80.
Owner G B Bedford **Bred** Hellwood Stud Farm **Trained** Scarcroft, W Yorks

FOCUS
A fair-to-middling handicap that featured several older horses with sound form and two three-year-olds with the potential to progress. The winner looked improved but this is probably not form to take too positively.
Spensley(IRE) Official explanation: jockey said colt was unsuited by the soft ground

3762 REGIONAL MAGAZINE COMPANY NOVICE FILLIES' STKS 5f
7:45 (7:45) (Class 4) 2-Y-O **£3,885** (£1,156; £577; £288) **Stalls** High

Form RPR

1 **Breathless Kiss (USA)** 2-8-6 0 ..... JamieSpencer 1 71+
(K A Ryan) *dwlt: sn cl up: effrt 2f out and sn rdn: drvn to ld ins fnl f: kpt on* **6/1**[2]

160 **2** *3/4* **High Spice (USA)**[22] 3015 2-9-3 0 ..... EddieAhern 7 79
(R M H Cowell) *led: rdn along wl over 1f out: drvn and hdd ins fnl f: no ex* **8/11**[1]

0106 **3** *1 1/2* **Quaker Parrot**[11] 3430 2-8-12 0 ..... RossAtkinson(5) 2 74
(Tom Dascombe) *chsd ldng pair: rdn along over 2f out: kpt on same pce appr fnl f* **14/1**

4 *2 1/2* **Mosa Mine** 2-8-6 0 ..... PaulHanagan 4 54
(D H Brown) *t.k.h: chsd ldrs: rdn along 2f out: drvn and wknd ent fnl f* **13/2**[3]

0 **5** *1 3/4* **More Lashes (USA)**[55] 2034 2-8-10 0 ..... AlanMunro 6 52
(M G Quinlan) *hld up in tch: swtchd lft and hdwy 2f out: rdn over 1f out and sn btn* **8/1**

5 **6** *1/2* **Nabrina (IRE)**[5] 3633 2-8-3 0 ..... JohnCavanagh(7) 5 50
(M Brittain) *s.i.s: a in rr* **12/1**

62.77 secs (2.27) **Going Correction** +0.475s/f (Yiel) **6** Ran SP% **111.0**
Speed ratings (Par 93): **100,98,96,92,89 88**
toteswingers: 1&2 £1.20, 1&3 £7.90, 2&3 £4.60 CSF £10.64 TOTE £5.50: £1.80, £1.30; EX 9.70.

Owner Mrs Angie Bailey **Bred** Don Mattox & Pam Mattox **Trained** Hambleton, N Yorks
■ Stewards' Enquiry : Eddie Ahern two-day ban: used whip in incorrect place and down shoulder in the forehand (Jul 23-24)

FOCUS
Not the strongest juvenile novices' event ever run, its limitations starting with its being confined to fillies, but the two previous winners had already shown themselves to be above the mundane at their best and at least one of the newcomers had a profile suggesting a close look at the betting would be wise. A nice start from the winner but the third limits things.

NOTEBOOK
Breathless Kiss(USA), a debutante from a yard whose juveniles are always worth a second look, even during a period when, as now, they do not seem to be firing on all cylinders, had fetched $145,000 as a foal. Her breeze-up price had failed to match that, dropping to just $60,000, but she is a half-sister to several sprint winners and her family has proved in the US that they can operate convincingly on turf as well as dirt. She was not the quickest out of stalls, seeming to miss a beat as they opened, but she soon gained a prominent position and, after chasing the runner-up into the final furlong, she found a decent change of gear to collect at her first attempt. (op 4-1)
High Spice(USA) was taking a marked drop in grade for this after tackling a Listed contest at Sandown and the Queen Mary Stakes at Royal Ascot and, while she had clearly been out of her depth in the latter, she had not been disgraced in a race whose form was looking stronger by the day. She had shown with her debut victory at Newmarket in May that she possesses a very professional attitude, not to mention good early pace, and once again she started smartly, soon grabbed the near-side rail, and made a bold bid from the front before being caught in the closing stages. (op 5-6 tchd 10-11and evens in places)
Quaker Parrot had broken her duck on her first appearance at Warwick in May and, although her two subsequent performances had been somewhat disappointing, she had been taking on decent rivals and seemed to have a far easier task against most of these. She ran well, too, posting her best effort since her second-time-out victory, but she could not cope with the front two and will probably need a switch to nursery company if she is to add to her tally in the near future.
Mosa Mine, an inexpensively-purchased daughter of Exceed And Excel, who is racking up winners right, left and centre this season, represented a stable just beginning to find some form after a relatively slow start to the campaign and she showed enough to suggest she can soon be profitably placed. (op 8-1)
More Lashes(USA) had run with a little promise in her only previous race, finishing a six-length seventh at Newbury in May, and, while she needed to up her game markedly to beat the two penalised winners, she did have the advanatge of a 7lb concession from that pair. It was not nearly enough, though, and, on this form, she will struggle to win before she earns a handicap mark. (op 13-2 tchd 9-1)
Nabrina(IRE) had hinted at better to come when fifth on her Nottingham debut five days earlier and, though her stable's two-year-olds have not been pulling up any trees this term, she was nibbled at in the betting. That speculative money was lost, however, as, after starting slowly and perhaps being slightly inhibited by a bandage on her hind leg coming loose and trailing in her wake, she came home a moderate last of six. (op 33-1)

3763 EASTSIDE DOUBLE DECADE FILLIES' H'CAP 1m (S)
8:15 (8:17) (Class 4) (0-80,80) 3-Y-0+ **£5,118** (£1,511; £756) **Stalls** High

Form RPR

00 **1** **Folly Lodge**[41] 2434 5-9-13 **77** ..... SebSanders 5 86
(R M Beckett) *trckd ldng pair: hdwy 2f out and sn led: rdn ins fnl f and styd on wl* **5/1**[3]

4034 **2** *2* **Summer Gold (IRE)**[7] 3530 5-10-0 **78** ..... DavidAllan 3 84+
(E J Alston) *hld up in tch: hdwy 2f out whn nt clr run and sltly hmpd: swtchd lft and rdn over 1f out: kpt on ins fnl f: nrst fin* **8/1**

-441 **3** *1/2* **Honimiere (IRE)**[15] 3267 3-8-13 **72** ..... PJMcDonald 8 73
(G A Swinbank) *chsd ldr: effrt 2f out: sn rdn and kpt on same pce ent fnl f* **5/1**[3]

0-12 **4** *1/2* **Bombina**[28] 2858 3-9-3 **76** ..... AlanMunro 4 76
(P W Chapple-Hyam) *trckd ldrs: hdwy over 2f out: rdn to chse wnr and ev ch over 1f out: drvn and one pce ins fnl f* **11/8**[1]

-362 **5** *2* **Act Green**[23] 2999 3-9-3 **76** ..... (v[1]) JamieSpencer 2 71
(M L W Bell) *wnt lft s: hld up in rr: effrt and sme hdwy over 2f out: sn rdn and btn over 1f out* **9/2**[2]

0100 **6** *9* **Style Award**[41] 2460 4-8-12 **65** ..... KellyHarrison(3) 1 42
(W J H Ratcliffe) *hld up: a in rr* **33/1**

0406 **7** *2 1/2* **Mozayada (USA)**[9] 3488 5-9-3 **67** ..... JoeFanning 7 38
(M Brittain) *led: rdn along 3f out: drvn 2f out: sn hdd & wknd* **20/1**

1m 42.64s (3.34) **Going Correction** +0.475s/f (Yiel)
WFA 3 from 4yo+ 9lb **7** Ran SP% **112.4**
Speed ratings (Par 102): **102,100,99,99,97 88,85**
toteswingers: 1&2 £7.90, 1&3 £3.40, 2&3 £8.00 CSF £41.78 CT £207.64 TOTE £6.60: £2.80, £3.20; EX 26.00.
Owner T D Rootes **Bred** Shutford Stud **Trained** Whitsbury, Hants
■ Stewards' Enquiry : Seb Sanders caution: used whip with excessive frequency

FOCUS
A reasonable fillies' handicap, and, with last year's winner in the line-up racing off top weight again, and from a similar mark, it was obviously well up to scratch based on previous runnings. The form makes sense but is somewhat unconvincing and the winner did not have to improve much on her Southwell reappearance form.

3764 RMC WINNER HELEN WESTWOOD MAIDEN STKS 6f
8:45 (8:53) (Class 5) 3-Y-0+ **£3,412** (£1,007; £504) **Stalls** High

Form RPR

5-2 **1** **Russian Spirit**[10] 3460 3-8-12 0 ..... PhilipRobinson 11 84
(M A Jarvis) *mde all: rdn clr over 1f out: kpt on wl u.p ins fnl f* **3/1**[2]

2 *3/4* **Penitent** 3-9-3 0 ..... SebSanders 5 87
(W J Haggas) *chsd ldrs: rdn along 2f out: styd on strly ins fnl f* **12/1**

32 **3** *7* **Hightime Heroine (IRE)**[34] 2664 3-8-12 0 ..... ShaneKelly 17 60
(J Noseda) *chsd ldrs: hdwy to chse wnr 2f out: sn rdn and one pce appr fnl f* **6/4**[1]

5 **4** *5* **King Of Eden (IRE)**[29] 2820 3-9-3 0 ..... DavidAllan 12 49
(E J Alston) *prom: rdn along 2f out and sn one pce* **66/1**

40 **5** *3/4* **Jill Le Brocq**[22] 3036 3-8-12 0 ..... PJMcDonald 8 41
(M Dods) *unruly s and in stalls: in tch: rdn along over 2f out: drvn and kpt on appr fnl f* **100/1**

4 **6** *1 1/4* **Halcyon Dancer**[20] 3093 3-8-12 0 ..... PhillipMakin 10 37+
(M Dods) *dwlt and rr: hdwy over 2f out: kpt on appr fnl f* **14/1**

5 **7** *2 1/4* **Migliori**[133] 686 3-9-3 0 ..... JoeFanning 15 35+
(Rae Guest) *towards rr tl styd on fnl 2f* **40/1**

8 *3* **Fortezza** 3-8-12 0 ..... AlanMunro 9 20+
(C F Wall) *s.i.s and bhd tl sme late hdwy* **28/1**

0 **9** *1 1/2* **Francis Albert**[33] 2700 3-9-3 0 ..... GeorgeBaker 16 21
(M Mullineaux) *midfield: effrt and sme hdwy on wd outside: 1/2-way: sn rdn and nvr a factor* **28/1**

10 *3/4* **Ex Gracia** 3-8-12 0 ..... PaulMulrennan 13 13
(K A Ryan) *chsd ldrs: rdn along over 2f out and sn wknd* **22/1**

11 *hd* **Spartan Storm (IRE)** 3-8-10 0 ..... JohnCavanagh(7) 7 18
(M Brittain) *dwlt: a in rr* **100/1**

500- **12** *4 1/2* **Billy Cadiz**[308] 5652 4-9-9 38 ..... DanielTudhope 1 —
(N Tinkler) *a towards rr* **200/1**

6-20 **13** *11* **Alpha Tauri (USA)**[62] 1852 3-9-3 77 ..... EddieAhern 14 —
(H R A Cecil) *midfield: rdn along 1/2-way: sn wknd* **9/2**[3]

4 **14** *14* **Shannon Golden**[77] 1476 3-9-3 0 ..... AmirQuinn 3 —
(S R Bowring) *cl up: rdn along over 2f out: sn wknd and eased over 1f out* **100/1**

15 *1/2* **Distant Dreamer (USA)** 3-8-12 0 ..... GrahamGibbons 2 —
(Rae Guest) *a in rr* **33/1**

1m 15.78s (2.18) **Going Correction** +0.475s/f (Yiel)
WFA 3 from 4yo 6lb **15** Ran SP% **119.1**
Speed ratings (Par 103): **104,103,93,87,86 84,81,77,75,74 74,68,53,34,34**
toteswingers: 1&2 £13.90, 1&3 £4.40, 2&3 £12.70 CSF £35.40 TOTE £4.10: £1.70, £3.10, £1.10; EX 39.10.
Owner Cromhall Stud **Bred** Derek R Price **Trained** Newmarket, Suffolk

FOCUS
An ordinary sprint maiden, lacking strength in depth among those with form, but several high-profile stables were represented and a clutch of the newcomers looked interesting on pedigree. More rain fell in the run-up to the off and, with several giving trouble at the start, conditions were dark and miserable for this mainly lightly raced line-up. Not many got into it and the first pair finished clear of the third, who was below par.

3765 EASTSIDE PRIDE OF DONCASTER H'CAP 5f
9:15 (9:20) (Class 5) (0-75,74) 3-Y-0+ **£3,238** (£963; £481; £240) **Stalls** High

Form RPR

4312 **1** **Feelin Foxy**[6] 3591 5-9-8 **70** ..... AlanMunro 5 85
(J G Given) *sn led: rdn wl over 1f out: hdd briefly ent fnl f: sn rallied to ld again and r.o strly* **5/1**[3]

-543 **2** *2* **Select Committee**[6] 3562 4-8-9 **57** ..... (p) GrahamGibbons 3 65
(J J Quinn) *cl up: effrt wl over 1f out: rdn and slt ld ent fnl f: sn drvn: hdd and kpt on same pce* **7/2**[1]

-600 **3** *shd* **First Swallow**[31] 2770 4-8-7 **55** ..... PaulHanagan 9 62
(R A Fahey) *chsd ldrs: rdn along and sltly outpcd 2f out: styd on wl u.p ins fnl f* **9/2**[2]

0-36 **4** *nk* **Ursus**[9] 3483 4-8-7 **55** ..... SilvestreDeSousa 10 61
(C R Wilson) *towards rr: hdwy on outer 2f out: sn rdn and kpt on ins fnl f: nrst fin* **6/1**

1262 **5** *1/2* **La Capriosa**[17] 3229 3-8-11 **64** ..... EddieAhern 4 67
(J A Glover) *dwlt: sn chsng ldrs: effrt on outer and ev ch 2f out: sn rdn and one pce ent fnl f* **16/1**

01 **6** *nk* **Garstang**[36] 2596 6-9-5 **67** ..... (b) GeorgeBaker 1 70
(J Balding) *cl up: rdn and ev ch wl over 1f out: drvn and wknd ent fnl f* **7/1**

056 **7** *nk* **Divine Spirit**[5] 3607 8-9-12 **74** ..... PhillipMakin 8 76
(M Dods) *towards rr: hdwy on outer over 2f out: sn rdn and kpt on same pce* **5/1**[3]

5453 **8** *1/2* **Kheylide (IRE)**[5] 3607 3-9-1 **68** ..... SebSanders 6 67
(Mrs D J Sanderson) *chsd ldrs: rdn along 2f out: sn drvn and wknd* **12/1**

4000 **9** *4* **Ronnie Howe**[14] 3304 5-8-7 **55** oh2 ..... (bt) DaleGibson 7 41
(S R Bowring) *a in rr* **33/1**

62.73 secs (2.23) **Going Correction** +0.475s/f (Yiel)
WFA 3 from 4yo+ 5lb **9** Ran SP% **117.0**
Speed ratings (Par 103): **101,97,97,97,96 95,95,94,88**
toteswingers: 1&2 £5.30, 1&3 £6.70, 2&3 £6.10 CSF £23.22 CT £85.36 TOTE £4.80: £2.00, £1.30, £2.10; EX 30.30 Place 6: £45.93, Place 5: £33.42.
Owner Danethorpe Racing Partnership **Bred** Bearstone Stud **Trained** Willoughton, Lincs

FOCUS
A modest sprint handicap with the top weight rated only 74 and more than one of these had been sorely out of form over recent weeks, but the winner posted a decent effort and is enjoying a fine season. Sound form overall with the best guide.
T/Plt: £53.70 to a £1 stake. Pool: £77,048.20. 1,047.35 winning tickets. T/Qpdt: £13.40 to a £1 stake. Pool: £5,734.80. 314.70 winning tickets. JR

3521 EPSOM (L-H)

Thursday, July 9

OFFICIAL GOING: Good (good to soft in places; 7.6; home straight: stands' side 7.9; far side 7.4)
Rail realignment from the one mile to winning post added 3yards to all races.
Wind: Almost nil Weather: Fine but cloudy

3766 BET TOTEPOOL AT TOTESPORT.COM APPRENTICE H'CAP 1m 2f 18y
6:20 (6:21) (Class 5) (0-75,75) 4-Y-0+ £3,238 (£963; £481; £240) Stalls Low

Form RPR
6-45 1 **Constant Cheers (IRE)**22 3024 6-9-10 75 DavidProbert 7 81
(W R Swinburn) *mde all: set mod pce tl kicked on over 3f out: pressed 2f out: asserted fnl f: rdn out* **7/2**2

0-50 2 1 1/4 **Shesha Bear**17 3217 4-8-12 63 (b1) RussellKennemore 9 66
(W R Muir) *awkward s: sn in tch: chsd ldng pair 1/2-way: rdn 3f out: kpt on fr over 1f out to take 2nd nr fin* **8/1**

0-14 3 nk **Run For Ede's**50 2183 5-9-2 70 JackDean(3) 4 72
(P M Phelan) *t.k.h: trckd ldng pair to 1/2-way: 4th st: rdn 3f out: kpt on fr over 1f out: nvr able to chal* **4/1**3

5012 4 nk **Penang Cinta**9 3475 6-8-1 57 AndrewHeffernan(5) 3 59
(P D Evans) *hld up in 5th: rdn 3f out: kpt on fr over 1f out: nvr able to chal* **9/4**1

1446 5 1/2 **Tecktal (FR)**78 1463 6-8-2 56 oh6 AmyBaker(3) 8 57
(P M Phelan) *trckd wnr: rdn to chal 2f out: stl pressing 1f out: wknd ins fnl f: lost 3 pls nr fin* **16/1**

50/1 6 10 **Expensive Problem**10 3463 6-8-13 71 6ex KierenFox(7) 1 52
(R J Smith) *rrd s and slowly away: hld up in 6th: brought wd in st and sn outpcd: no ch fnl 2f* **11/2**

00-0 7 3 **Dancer's Legacy**70 1633 4-8-10 68 NathanAlison(7) 6 43
(J R Boyle) *t.k.h: hld up and sn wl detached in last: t.o whn pushed along 4f out: no ch* **12/1**

2m 16.98s (7.28) **Going Correction** +0.275s/f (Good) 7 Ran SP% **113.1**
Speed ratings (Par 103): **81,80,79,79,79 71,68**
toteswingers: 1&2 £7.20, 1&3 £4.00, 2&3 £10.60 CSF £30.10 CT £114.69 TOTE £4.30: £2.20, £3.60; EX 25.00.
Owner Mr & Mrs W R Swinburn **Bred** Pendley Farm **Trained** Aldbury, Herts
■ Stewards' Enquiry : Nathan Alison ten-day ban: breach of Rule 158 (Jul 23-Aug 1)

FOCUS
A modest handicap, run at a very steady pace. The form is highly dubious.

Dancer's Legacy Official explanation: jockey said, regarding running and riding, that his orders were to settle the gelding to give it the best chance of staying the longer trip; trainer said gelding had been with him for six weeks and had a wind operation and could be a tricky ride, however he considered that the jockey had lain too far out of his ground in the early stages.

3767 EPSOM TRAINERS OPEN DAY AUGUST 2ND MAIDEN AUCTION STKS 6f
6:50 (6:50) (Class 5) 2-Y-O £3,238 (£963; £481; £240) Stalls High

Form RPR
2 1 **Silver Grey (IRE)**44 2348 2-8-5 0 ow1 RobertHavlin 3 69+
(R Ingram) *cl up: 5th st: grabbed nr side rail and jnd ldrs over 2f out: def advantage over 1f out: drew clr fnl f* **7/2**2

3 2 3 **Cuthbert (IRE)**16 3240 2-8-11 0 KirstyMilczarek 2 66
(W Jarvis) *cl up: 4th whn sltly awkward bnd over 3f out: racd four off rail in st: chal over 2f out: nrly upsides 1f out: kpt on* **7/1**

43 3 hd **Super Duplex**45 2324 2-8-11 0 IanMongan 6 65
(P M Phelan) *disp ld: racd one off rail in st: hanging fr over 2f out: nt qckn over 1f out: kpt on fnl f* **4/1**3

2 4 nk **Cool Valentine**43 2383 2-8-8 0 DavidProbert(3) 7 64
(A M Balding) *hld up in 6th: sltly awkward downhill: wdst of all st: effrt to chal 2f out: nrly upsides 1f out: nt qckn* **9/4**1

00 5 5 **Barastar**6 3584 2-8-9 0 PatCosgrave 5 50+
(J R Boyle) *disp ld: jst unable to hold pl and squeezed out 2f out: no ch after* **33/1**

43 6 10 **Radio City**49 2201 2-8-10 0 JackMitchell(3) 1 21
(R M Beckett) *disp ld: racd three off nr side rail st: wknd rapidly over 1f out: eased and t.o* **9/2**

7 3 **Boogie Waltzer** 2-8-4 0 SaleemGolam 4 3
(S C Williams) *sn outpcd and t.o: lost no further grnd fnl 3f* **20/1**

1m 12.5s (3.10) **Going Correction** +0.275s/f (Good) 7 Ran SP% **111.4**
Speed ratings (Par 94): **90,86,85,85,78 65,61**
toteswingers: 1&2 £3.10, 1&3 £3.80, 2&3 £7.20 CSF £26.17 TOTE £4.20: £2.00, £2.80; EX 31.10.
Owner Z Malik **Bred** Tally-Ho Stud **Trained** Epsom, Surrey

FOCUS
An ordinary juvenile maiden in which the field came stands' side in the home straight. The form has been rated around the third.

NOTEBOOK
Silver Grey(IRE), runner-up over 5f at Chepstow on her debut, raced closest to the stands' rail in the straight, where the best ground undoubtedly was, and she got well on top inside the final furlong, despite her rider putting up 1lb overweight. She was at an advantage, but clearly appreciated the sixth furlong, even though this is as far as she wants to go according to her trainer, and connections will now look to find a conditions race for her. A flat track is expected to suit her even better. (op 5-2)

Cuthbert(IRE), slowly away and green when third on his debut at Brighton, may well have won had he raced as close to the rail as Silver Grey. He was on the slower ground and looks capable of winning a small maiden. (op 10-1 tchd 6-1)

Super Duplex kept on right the way to the line, despite hanging, and has now qualified for nurseries. (op 9-2 tchd 5-1)

Cool Valentine, who shaped with a good deal of promise when second at Lingfield on his debut, struggled to go the early gallop and raced widest of all in the straight. He came with a run and appeared to lead over a furlong out, but that spurt took its toll on what was the slowest ground and he faded late on. He can be rated better than the bare form and deserves another chance. (op 11-4)

Barastar will stand more of a chance in low-grade nurseries. (op 25-1)

Radio City, who was disappointing here, is now also eligible for a provisional handicap rating. (op 11-2)

3768 TOTESPORT HOME OF POOL BETTING H'CAP 1m 4f 10y
7:25 (7:26) (Class 4) (0-80,77) 4-Y-0+ £5,180 (£1,541; £770; £384) Stalls Centre

Form RPR
0-11 1 **Norman The Great**19 3169 5-9-8 76 FergusSweeney 5 82
(A King) *trckd ldr: led narrowly jst over 2f out: hung lft down to far rail over 1f out: hdd ins fnl f: rallied to ld last strides* **6/4**1

202- 2 shd **Yossi (IRE)**31 4955 5-9-9 77 (b) TPQueally 6 83
(Jim Best) *set fair pce: led field down centre of crse in st: shkn up and narrowly hdd jst over 2f out: hung lft 1f out: led again ins fnl f: hdd last strides* **7/2**3

3342 3 4 1/2 **Watson's Bay**7 3521 4-9-0 68 IanMongan 1 67
(P Howling) *trckd ldng pair: shkn up over 2f out: hung lft to far rail over 1f out: no imp* **9/4**2

0050 4 4 1/2 **Waldorf (IRE)**17 3224 4-8-1 58 oh2 DavidProbert(3) 4 50
(W R Muir) *a last: rdn 3f out: edgd lft fr 2f out: no prog* **11/2**

2m 42.86s (3.96) **Going Correction** +0.275s/f (Good) 4 Ran SP% **108.4**
Speed ratings (Par 105): **97,96,93,90**
toteswingers: 1&2 £3.50 CSF £6.86 TOTE £2.50; EX 4.10.
Owner McNeill Racing **Bred** Barton Stud Partnership **Trained** Barbury Castle, Wilts

FOCUS
A modest handicap in which all four runners headed centre-track in the straight before ending up on the far rail having hung left. The front pair set the level of the form.

3769 FLEMING RUSSELL STENT CONDITIONS STKS 1m 2f 18y
7:55 (7:58) (Class 3) 3-Y-0+ £7,477 (£2,239; £1,119; £560) Stalls Low

Form RPR
4425 1 **Fairmile**18 3190 7-9-0 107 (tp) StephenDonohoe 3 92
(Ian Williams) *s.i.s: sn trckd ldr: led against nr side rail wl over 2f out: sn shkn up and tending to hang lft: asserted over 1f out* **1/2**1

060 2 4 **Kaleo**33 2706 5-9-0 76 DarryllHolland 1 84
(S Dow) *t.k.h early: led to wl over 2f out: one pce over 1f out* **7/1**3

5050 3 26 **Play Up Pompey**19 3158 7-8-11 41 DavidProbert(3) 4 32
(J J Bridger) *a in last pair: pushed along after 4f: t.o over 3f out: won duel for distant 3rd* **100/1**

4 4 1/2 **Rugell (ARG)**208 4-9-4 0 TPQueally 2 27
(H R A Cecil) *a in last pair: nt gng wl after 4f: t.o over 3f out* **11/4**2

2m 10.21s (0.51) **Going Correction** +0.275s/f (Good) 4 Ran SP% **106.8**
Speed ratings (Par 107): **108,104,84,80**
CSF £4.45 TOTE £1.60; EX 4.10.
Owner Dr Marwan Koukash **Bred** Pendley Farm **Trained** Portway, Worcs

FOCUS
A straightforward opportunity for Fairmile. The race has been rated around the runner-up.

NOTEBOOK
Fairmile, sporting a first-time cheekpieces/tongue tie combo, did not put the race to bed immediately when asked for his effort, but got well on top over a furlong out and won with plenty in hand, though in fairness he was rated 31lb superior to the runner-up. He is not as good as he used to be, but races similar to this are likely to continue to provide him with chances of winning. That said, connections do have him entered in the Stockholm Cup. (op 4-6)
Kaleo, a one-time smart performer in Germany, has done little since coming to this country and he ran as well as could have been expected against the winner at the weights. (op 12-1 tchd 6-1)
Play Up Pompey kept on back in a distant third, one place better than nearly everybody expected.
Rugell(ARG), a Grade 2 winner back home last November, was conceding 4lb all round and drifted notably in the market beforehand. He was in trouble from an early stage, failing to cope with the unique demands of the track, and was eased having failed to come down the hill. He is better than this, but this effort leaves him with rather a lot to prove. (op 13-8 tchd 3-1)

3770 FLEMING RUSSELL STENT H'CAP 1m 114y
8:30 (8:31) (Class 4) (0-85,82) 3-Y-0+ £5,180 (£1,541; £770; £384) Stalls Low

Form RPR
-500 1 **Northern Spy (USA)**22 3024 5-9-1 66 TPQueally 5 78
(S Dow) *trckd ldrs: cl 4th st: angled across to nr side: led over 2f out and sn grabbed rail: drew rt away over 1f out* **15/2**

-160 2 8 **Twilight Star (IRE)**29 2828 5-9-13 78 DarryllHolland 3 72
(R A Teal) *v awkward s: last but sn in tch: prog in striaght to chse wnr 2f out: sn lft wl bhd* **11/4**2

5240 3 3/4 **Rock Anthem (IRE)**29 2824 5-8-11 62 StephenDonohoe 4 54
(Mike Murphy) *t.k.h early: trckd ldng pair: c towards nr side rail st: outpcd 2f out: edgd rt ins fnl f* **6/1**3

1200 4 1/2 **Tarzan (IRE)**21 3049 3-9-7 82 RoystonFfrench 2 72
(M Johnston) *trckd ldr: c towards nr side in st: lost pl over 2f out and rdn: one pce over 1f out* **13/8**1

3260 5 2 3/4 **Phluke**27 2883 8-9-11 76 StephenCarson 6 65+
(Eve Johnson Houghton) *racd wd: cl up: 5th st: grabbed nr side rail in st but nt pce to ld gp: trying to chal for 3rd whn hmpd ins fnl f: eased* **14/1**

0036 6 1/2 **Prince Of Thebes (IRE)**7 3523 8-10-0 79 PaulDoe 1 62
(M J Attwater) *led: styd alone far side in st: lost overall ld over 2f out: no ch after* **8/1**

1m 47.34s (1.24) **Going Correction** +0.275s/f (Good)
WFA 3 from 5yo+ 10lb 6 Ran SP% **108.6**
Speed ratings (Par 105): **105,97,97,96,94 93**
toteswingers: 1&2 £3.80, 1&3 £5.80, 2&3 £2.70 CSF £26.43 TOTE £10.00: £2.40, £1.90; EX 27.00.
Owner J R May **Bred** Gainsborough Farm Llc **Trained** Epsom, Surrey
■ Stewards' Enquiry : Stephen Donohoe one-day ban: careless riding (Jul 23)

FOCUS
A modest handicap and doubts over the entire field. The favourite has been below his best recently and the winner's best previous efforts had been on the All-Weather, so there are question marks over the form, despite the wide-margin victory.
Twilight Star(IRE) Official explanation: jockey said gelding missed the break
Rock Anthem(IRE) Official explanation: jockey said gelding was unsuited by the slow pace

3771 BET TOTEPOOL ON 0800 221 221 H'CAP 6f
9:00 (9:00) (Class 4) (0-80,79) 3-Y-0+ £5,180 (£1,541; £770; £384) Stalls High

Form RPR
-416 1 **Tyfos**19 3164 4-9-7 73 TGMcLaughlin 6 82
(W M Brisbourne) *pressed ldr: got to nr side rail in st: led 2f out: rdn clr over 1f out: kpt on* **3/1**2

0044 2 1 1/4 **Fantasy Believer**11 3422 11-8-12 64 DarryllHolland 5 69
(J J Quinn) *chsd ldng trio: rdn 2f out: kpt on to take 2nd ins fnl f: unable to chal* **3/1**2

0250 3 nk **We Have A Dream**21 3057 4-9-1 70 DavidProbert(3) 3 74
(W R Muir) *led: failed to get to nr side rail in st: shkn up and hdd 2f out: one pce and lost 2nd ins fnl f* **7/2**3

-440 **4** *1 ¼* **My Kingdom (IRE)**[19] 3163 3-9-6 **78**................................(t) TravisBlock 2 77
(H Morrison) *chsd ldng pair: racd three off rail in st: rdn and nt qckn 2f out: one pce after* **11/4**[1]

5130 **5** *7* **Caprio (IRE)**[42] 2396 4-9-13 **79**.................................... PatCosgrave 9 57
(J R Boyle) *hld up in last: pushed along and outpcd 1/2-way: nvr on terms* **7/1**

1m 10.28s (0.88) **Going Correction** +0.275s/f (Good)
WFA 3 from 4yo+ 6lb **5** Ran SP% **111.4**
Speed ratings (Par 105): **105,103,102,101,91**
toteswingers: 1&2 £3.70. CSF £12.39 TOTE £4.00: £2.00, £1.70; EX 9.20 Place 6: £147.51, Place 5: £45.41..
Owner J Tomlinson/G Williams **Bred** J Tomlinson And G Williams **Trained** Great Ness, Shropshire

FOCUS
The stands' rail again proved decisive in this moderate sprint handicap. The form looks sound but pretty ordinary rated through the runner-up and third.
T/Plt: £259.80 to a £1 stake. Pool: £61,433.05. 172.57 winning tickets. T/Qpdt: £20.90 to a £1 stake. Pool: £5,864.30. 207.06 winning tickets. JN

3344 FOLKESTONE (R-H)
Thursday, July 9

OFFICIAL GOING: Good to firm (firm in places on straight course; straight course: far side 8.9, stands' side 8.4, round course 8.5)
Wind: Fairly Light, Behind Weather: overcast

3772 EUROPEAN BREEDERS' FUND MAIDEN FILLIES' STKS 5f
2:10 (2:11) (Class 5) 2-Y-O **£3,561** (£1,059; £529; £264) **Stalls** Low

Form RPR

22 **1** **Tomintoul Singer (IRE)**[28] 2860 2-9-0 0.............................. IanMongan 10 77+
(H R A Cecil) *trckd ldrs: hdwy to ld 2f out: edgd lft but pushed clr over 1f out: comf* **11/10**[1]

2 *4 ½* **Memory And Magic (USA)** 2-9-0 0.................................... AdamKirby 2 58+
(C G Cox) *in tch: swtchd rt and hdwy wl over 1f out: chsd clr wnr over 1f out: kpt on but no imp on wnr* **20/1**

5 **3** *nse* **Oasis Jade**[15] 3277 2-9-0 0.. PatCosgrave 3 58
(G L Moore) *in tch in rr of main gp: swtchd lft and hdwy wl over 1f out: pressing for 2nd jst ins fnl f: kpt on but no ch w wnr* **40/1**

4 **4** *nk* **Yurituni**[10] 3458 2-9-0 0.. DarryllHolland 9 57
(Eve Johnson Houghton) *in tch in rr of main gp: rdn over 2f out: hdwy 2f out: pressing for 2nd but no ch w wnr fr over 1f out: kpt on same pce fnl f* **3/1**[2]

006 **5** *3 ¼* **Princess Shamal**[17] 3210 2-9-0 0.................................... RobertHavlin 6 45
(J R Jenkins) *sn led: hdd 2f out: sn rdn and edgd rt: wknd over 1f out* **100/1**

5 **6** *4* **Sakile**[18] 3187 2-9-0 0.. AdrianMcCarthy 7 31
(P W Chapple-Hyam) *in tch: rdn and unable qck 2f out: sn swtchd sltly rt and drvn: wknd over 1f out* **10/3**[3]

7 *1 ½* **Titoli Di Coda (IRE)** 2-9-0 0.................................... FergusSweeney 1 25
(L M Cumani) *s.i.s: sn pushed along and outpcd in last pair: nvr on terms* **20/1**

45 **8** *8* **Starburst Excel**[57] 1991 2-9-0 0.................................... JerryO'Dwyer 8 —
(M G Quinlan) *broke wl and led briefly: chsd ldr after tl ent fnl 2f: wknd qckly wl over 1f out: eased whn wl btn fnl f* **16/1**

9 *½* **Graceandgratitude** 2-9-0 0.................................... SaleemGolam 5 —
(S C Williams) *s.i.s: sn outpcd in last* **40/1**

58.44 secs (-1.56) **Going Correction** -0.225s/f (Firm) **9** Ran SP% **117.0**
Speed ratings (Par 91): **103,95,95,95,90 83,81,68,67**
toteswingers: 1&2 £7.20, 1&3 £10.80, 2&3 £11.40 CSF £31.02 TOTE £2.00: £1.20, £4.20, £6.70; EX 16.80 Trifecta £141.60 Pool: £246.99 - 1.29 winning units..
Owner Angus Dundee Distillers plc **Bred** Paul & T J Monaghan **Trained** Newmarket, Suffolk

FOCUS
A moderate juvenile maiden, but the winner was back to her debut form and was quite impressive in putting this race to bed.

NOTEBOOK
Tomintoul Singer(IRE) had the pace to get a prominent slot after a furlong then gradually got over to the preferred stands' rail well over a furlong out and was never in any danger after that. She ought not to be overburdened when switching to nurseries. (op 11-8)
Memory And Magic(USA) ◆ has a pedigree full of winners, most of them over 7f and a mile, so this was a decent debut over a trip too sharp. She also switched right inside the final two furlongs and ended up on what might have been slightly slower ground up the centre, but still managed to get the better of more experienced opposition for second spot. Although she was righly not given a hard time on her debut, she still did enough to learn something and might be very interesting over another furlong next time, given that her stable's juveniles always improve for their first run. (op 16-1)
Oasis Jade ran in the same style as on her debut at Salisbury but came home much better and was only just run out of second. Although she has pace in her pedigree, she does look to need another furlong or a considerably stiffer five than this. (tchd 50-1)
Yurituni caught the eye on her debut at Windsor over this distance and, despite that experience, 5f really is too sharp for her. She was soon off the bridle and then had to come towards the centre of the track but showed a good attitude. Her dam was very quick but did win over 6f and that might suit her daughter, too. (op 10-3 tchd 7-2)
Princess Shamal was better behaved than on her previous appearances but still hung when put under pressure.
Sakile failed to build on a fair debut last time but was towards the centre of the course. (op 11-4 tchd 5-2)
Titoli Di Coda(IRE) is very well connected but was friendless in the market and only got the hang of things very late on.
Starburst Excel hadn't run since May and again showed early pace. She is now eligible for nurseries and her debut run behind Its Alright at Newbury in April, a race that has thrown up six winners, looks a sound effort. (op 14-1)

3773 CECIL TRICE MEMORIAL MAIDEN STKS 7f (S)
2:45 (2:45) (Class 5) 3-Y-O **£2,729** (£806; £403) **Stalls** Low

Form RPR

-332 **1** **Silk Trail**[13] 3352 3-8-12 74.................................... DO'Donohoe 7 66
(Saeed Bin Suroor) *awkward and wnt rt s: mde all: hung rt thrght: pushed along and hung to centre fr 2f out: rdn ins fnl f: a holding runner up* **1/5**[1]

00- **2** *½* **Kessraa (IRE)**[276] 6539 3-9-3 0.................................... DarryllHolland 2 70
(M R Channon) *chsd wnr thrght: rdn and carried rt 2f out: swtchd lft over 1f out: kpt on u.p fnl f* **9/1**[2]

3 *21* **Bobble Rock (IRE)** 3-9-3 0.................................... AdamKirby 4 13
(J R Best) *racd in 4th pl: rdn and lost tch w ldng pair wl over 2f out: wnt poor 3rd over 1f out* **9/1**[2]

4 **4** *10* **Spring Bridge (IRE)** 3-9-3 0.................................... JerryO'Dwyer 1 —
(Mrs L C Jewell) *chsd ldng pair: rdn and struggling wl over 2f out: wl btn after: lost poor 3rd over 1f out: t.o* **33/1**[3]

0-00 **5** *27* **Soldier Soldier**[59] 1941 3-9-3 0....................................(v[1]) RobertHavlin 6 —
(J R Jenkins) *stdd s: hld up in last pl: lost tch qckly over 3f out: t.o fnl 2f* **100/1**

1m 25.4s (-1.90) **Going Correction** -0.225s/f (Firm) **5** Ran SP% **107.3**
Speed ratings (Par 100): **101,100,76,65,34**
CSF £2.45 TOTE £1.10: £1.02, £3.40; EX 2.30.
Owner Godolphin **Bred** Darley **Trained** Newmarket, Suffolk

FOCUS
A poor maiden. The winner made heavy weather of it and is not straightforward.
Bobble Rock(IRE) Official explanation: jockey said colt ran green

3774 LADBROKES.COM H'CAP 2m 93y
3:20 (3:20) (Class 6) (0-60,60) 4-Y-O+ **£2,047** (£604; £302) **Stalls** High

Form RPR

-001 **1** **Starstruck Peter (IRE)**[8] 3503 5-9-2 **58** 6ex............(b) RichardThomas 9 64
(Jim Best) *mde all: 3 l clr and rdn over 2f out: edgd lft over 1f out: styd on wl* **9/2**[3]

3431 **2** *4* **Sand Repeal (IRE)**[13] 3348 7-9-4 **60**.................................... DarryllHolland 8 62
(Miss J Feilden) *chsd wnr after 2f: rdn over 2f out: no imp on wnr and wl hld fnl f* **13/8**[1]

06-0 **3** *4 ½* **Silver Surprise**[10] 3462 5-8-5 **47**.................................... FrankieMcDonald 10 43
(J J Bridger) *chsd wnr for 2f: in tch after: rdn and unable qck whn barging match w rival over 2f out: no ch w ldng pair fnl 2f: plugged on to go 3rd towards fin* **28/1**

-202 **4** *½* **Phoenix Hill (IRE)**[13] 3348 7-8-4 **46** oh1.................................... SaleemGolam 11 41
(D R Gandolfo) *stdd s: hld up in rr: hdwy 5f out: wnt 3rd and barging match w rival over 2f out: drvn and btn wl over 1f out: lost 3rd towards fin* **5/1**

0/0- **5** *4 ½* **Grasp**[47] 2245 7-8-10 **52**.................................... PaulDoe 3 42
(P D Evans) *racd in midfield: hdwy to chse ldng pair 1/2-way tl over 2f out: wknd u.p ent fnl 2f* **9/1**

-030 **6** *shd* **Bob's Your Uncle**[22] 3029 6-8-9 **51**.................................... PatCosgrave 7 40
(J G Portman) *awkward leaving stalls and s.i.s: hld up in last trio: effrt on outer 3f out: no hdwy and wl hld fnl 2f* **4/1**[2]

60-0 **7** *12* **Black Cloud**[15] 3275 6-8-4 **46** oh1.................................... AdrianMcCarthy 2 21
(G P Enright) *t.k.h: hld up in last trio: n.m.r 6f out: rdn and short lived effrt over 3f out: wl bhd fnl 2f* **20/1**

000- **8** *26* **Panadin (IRE)**[188] 4250 7-8-4 **46** oh1....................................(t) LukeMorris 4 —
(Mrs L C Jewell) *racd in midfield: rdn and dropped in rr over 6f out: lost tch u.p 3f out: eased ins fnl f: t.o* **66/1**

3m 39.82s (2.62) **Going Correction** -0.225s/f (Firm) **8** Ran SP% **112.6**
Speed ratings (Par 101): **84,82,79,79,77 77,71,58**
toteswingers: 1&2 £2.70, 1&3 £22.30, 2&3 £11.60 CSF £11.82 CT £175.62 TOTE £6.30: £1.10, £1.10, £7.10; EX 12.10 Trifecta £179.90 Part won. Pool: £243.16 - 0.86 winning units..
Owner W P K Racing **Bred** Barouche Stud Ireland Ltd **Trained** Lewes, E Sussex

FOCUS
A poor staying handicap run at a steady pace, and the first two held those positions throughout.

3775 LADBROKES H'CAP 5f
3:55 (3:55) (Class 5) (0-70,67) 3-Y-O+ **£3,070** (£906; £453) **Stalls** Low

Form RPR

2033 **1** **Green Lagonda (AUS)**[17] 3204 7-8-11 **52**.................................... PaulDoe 7 61
(P D Evans) *chsd ldrs: wnt 2nd over 2f out: led over 1f out: rdn and flashed tail ent fnl f: r.o wl* **3/1**[2]

2001 **2** *1* **Billy Red**[16] 3246 5-9-12 **67**....................................(b) FergusSweeney 1 72
(J R Jenkins) *sn led: hdd and rdn over 1f out: kpt on one pce ins fnl f* **3/1**[2]

2336 **3** *2 ¼* **Step It Up (IRE)**[34] 2680 5-9-7 **62**.................................... PatCosgrave 4 59
(J R Boyle) *chsd ldr tl over 2f out: styd chsng ldrs tl rdn and wknd jst over 1f out* **10/3**[3]

4043 **4** *¾* **Peopleton Brook**[6] 3570 7-9-4 **59**....................................(t) StephenDonohoe 2 54
(B G Powell) *in tch in midfield: edging rt fr over 2f out: no prog u.p fr over 1f out* **11/4**[1]

5000 **5** *1* **Tightrope (IRE)**[9] 3471 3-7-13 **50**....................................(b) AmyBaker(5) 3 39
(T D McCarthy) *in tch tl dropped to in rr and pushed along over 3f out: kpt on fnl f: nvr trbld ldrs* **11/1**

046- **6** *5* **Ava's World (IRE)**[531] 297 5-8-2 **50**.................................... AndrewHeffernan(7) 6 23
(Peter Grayson) *hld up in tch in last pair: rdn 2f out: drvn and wknd qckly over 1f out* **25/1**

58.22 secs (-1.78) **Going Correction** -0.225s/f (Firm) course record
WFA 3 from 5yo+ 5lb **6** Ran SP% **111.9**
Speed ratings (Par 103): **105,103,99,98,97 89**
toteswingers: 1&2 £2.50, 1&3 £2.30, 2&3 £2.40 CSF £12.31 TOTE £4.00: £1.80, £1.50; EX 8.90.
Owner M D Jones **Bred** P Brain **Trained** Pandy, Monmouths

FOCUS
A modest handicap won in a course-record time, and straightforward form to rate through the winner and runner-up.
Peopleton Brook Official explanation: vet said horse lost an off-fore shoe

3776 ODDS ON LADBROKES.COM H'CAP 1m 4f
4:30 (4:30) (Class 5) (0-70,67) 3-Y-O **£3,070** (£906; £453) **Stalls** High

Form RPR

5162 **1** **Vita Mia**[9] 3474 3-8-9 **55**.................................... StephenDonohoe 1 58+
(P D Evans) *chsd ldrs: pushed along over 4f out: rdn and unable qck over 3f out: drvn to chse ldng pair 2f out: edgd out lft over 1f out: styd on dourly fnl 100yds to ld last stride* **5/2**[1]

5013 **2** *shd* **Sumani (FR)**[20] 3099 3-9-3 **63**.................................... DarryllHolland 2 66
(S Dow) *led: rdn over 2f out: edgd lft u.p over 1f out: kpt on tl hdd last stride* **3/1**[2]

1066 **3** *½* **Lake Kalamalka (IRE)**[14] 3300 3-9-7 **67**.................................... IanMongan 3 69
(J L Dunlop) *chsd ldr: rdn and drew clr w ldr over 2f out: drvn and nt qckn over 1f out: plugged on same pce ins fnl f* **7/1**

3203 **4** *3* **Persian Tomcat (IRE)**[12] 3383 3-8-4 **50**.................................... SaleemGolam 5 47
(Miss J Feilden) *dwlt: hld up in last pair: effrt on inner and nt clr run 3f out tl over 2f out: rdn to chse ldrs 2f out: no imp after* **15/2**

6023 **5** *5* **Spinning Waters**[9] 3475 3-9-2 **65**....................................(p) KevinGhunowa(3) 4 54
(Eve Johnson Houghton) *hld up in last pair: pushed along 6f out: rdn and outpcd wl over 2f out: wl hld after* **11/2**[3]

-500 **6** *3* **Luthien (IRE)**[17] 3222 3-9-2 **62**.................................... AdamKirby 6 46
(W R Swinburn) *hld up in rr: rdn and shortlived effrt 3f out: drvn and btn over 2f out* **7/1**

-000 7 18 **Angelica's Art (IRE)**[49] 2192 3-9-2 **62** .... RobertHavlin 7 42
(B J Meehan) *t.k.h: chsd ldrs: rdn and outpcd by ldng pair over 2f out: wknd 2f out: wl btn and eased ent fnl f* **14/1**

2m 38.61s (-2.29) **Going Correction** -0.225s/f (Firm) **7** Ran SP% **112.4**
Speed ratings (Par 100): **98,97,97,95,92 90,78**
toteswingers: 1&2 £1.90, 1&3 £4.00, 2&3 £3.60 CSF £9.79 TOTE £2.90: £1.50, £1.70; EX 9.30.
Owner Countess Of Lonsdale **Bred** Lady Lonsdale **Trained** Pandy, Monmouths

FOCUS
A weak handicap in which the first three came clear. The winner didn't really handle the track and did well to get up, while the runner-up was given a good ride and is the guide to the level of the form.

Spinning Waters Official explanation: jockey said gelding never travelled

3777 LADBROKES.COM FILLIES' H'CAP — 1m 1f 149y
5:05 (5:05) (Class 5) (0-70,64) 3-Y-0+ — **£3,070** (£906; £453) **Stalls** Centre

Form / RPR

4526 1 **Make Amends (IRE)**[21] 3074 4-9-3 **58** .... WilliamCarson(5) 3 65
(R J Hodges) *chsd ldrs: rdn and effrt over 2f out: hdwy between horses wl over 1f out: sn chsng ldr: drvn to ld ins fnl f: styd on wl* **11/1**

24P5 2 1 1/4 **Rosy Dawn**[7] 3533 4-8-7 **50** .... DebraEngland(7) 6 54
(J J Bridger) *led: rdn and fnd ex wl over 1f out: hdd ins fnl f: one pce fnl 100yds* **8/1**

0235 3 2 3/4 **Bavarica**[14] 3322 7-9-3 **60** .... MatthewCosham(7) 8 59
(Miss J Feilden) *dwlt: t.k.h: hld up in last pl: hdwy on outer 2f out: styd on to go 3rd ins fnl f: nvr gng pce to rch ldrs* **7/1**[3]

1032 4 1 3/4 **Lunar River (FR)**[17] 3217 6-9-13 **63** ....(t) FergusSweeney 4 58
(David Pinder) *t.k.h: hld up in last trio: hdwy over 2f out: swtchd lft and effrt 2f out: wknd u.p over 1f out* **7/2**[2]

2212 5 3 **Dancing Jest (IRE)**[10] 3463 5-10-0 **64** .... DarryllHolland 5 53
(Rae Guest) *chsd ldr: pushed along over 3f out: rdn and unable qck jst over 2f out: lost 2nd over 1f out: wknd ent fnl f* **11/8**[1]

4-50 6 3 **Heart Of Tuscany**[49] 2204 3-9-1 **62** .... PaulDoe 7 45
(W J Knight) *dwlt and bustled along leaving stalls: sn t.k.h and hld up in last trio: rdn and effrt on outer over 2f out: sn struggling: wl btn fnl 2f* **17/2**

3606 7 nk **Encore Belle**[39] 2517 4-9-3 **53** .... AdamKirby 1 35
(Mouse Hamilton-Fairley) *s.i.s: hdwy into midfield after 2f: rdn over 2f out: edgd rt and wknd wl over 1f out* **14/1**

2m 2.65s (-2.25) **Going Correction** -0.225s/f (Firm)
WFA 3 from 4yo+ 11lb **7** Ran SP% **113.5**
Speed ratings (Par 100): **100,99,96,95,93 90,90**
toteswingers: 1&2 £8.40, 1&3 £8.00, 2&3 £5.10 CSF £90.86 CT £661.57 TOTE £8.70: £3.90, £2.70; EX 84.00 Trifecta £177.00 Pool: £325.35 - 1.36 winning units. Place 6: £117.45 Place 5: £56.25.
Owner Miss R Dobson **Bred** Moyglare Stud Farm Ltd **Trained** Charlton Mackrell, Somerset

FOCUS
A moderate fillies' handicap rated around the runner-up to her winter best and the third to last month's C&D form.

Dancing Jest(IRE) Official explanation: jockey said mare was unsuited by the track
T/Plt: £112.00 to a £1 stake. Pool: £43,255.60. 281.77 winning tickets. T/Qpdt: £94.60 to a £1 stake. Pool: £2,902.06. 22.70 winning tickets. SP

3746 NEWMARKET (R-H)
Thursday, July 9

OFFICIAL GOING: Good (8.1)
Wind: Fresh behind becoming lighter through the afternoon Weather: Overcast

3778 BAHRAIN TROPHY (GROUP 3) — 1m 5f
1:30 (1:31) (Class 1) 3-Y-0 — **£36,900** (£13,988; £7,000; £3,490; £1,748; £877) **Stalls** High

Form / RPR

1-50 1 **Kite Wood (IRE)**[33] 2705 3-9-0 **108** .... LDettori 7 109+
(Saeed Bin Suroor) *lw: mde all: rdn and edgd rt over 1f out: styd on wl* **2/1**[1]

2144 2 2 1/2 **Tactic**[20] 3090 3-9-0 **95** .... RHills 4 105
(J L Dunlop) *swtg: a.p: chsd wnr over 2f out: rdn and edgd rt 1f out: styd on same pce fnl f* **10/3**[2]

2100 3 4 1/2 **Above Average (IRE)**[21] 3051 3-9-3 **101** .... MichaelHills 5 101
(B W Hills) *hld up in tch: rdn over 2f out: edgd rt over 1f out: no ex fnl f* **16/1**

1-44 4 1 **Free Agent**[20] 3087 3-9-0 **103** .... RyanMoore 6 97
(R Hannon) *chsd wnr tl rdn over 2f out: styd on same pce* **11/2**[3]

-164 5 1/2 **Too Much Trouble**[21] 3050 3-9-0 **99** .... TonyCulhane 3 96
(M R Channon) *hld up: rdn over 3f out: no imp fnl 2f* **15/2**

-164 6 12 **Inhibition**[27] 2989 3-8-11 **93** .... LPKeniry 8 75
(A M Balding) *chsd ldrs: rdn over 2f out: sn wknd* **33/1**

410 7 11 **Dhushan**[20] 3090 3-9-0 **96** .... NCallan 2 61
(M A Jarvis) *hld up: rdn over 2f out: sn wknd: eased fnl f* **7/1**

1345 8 2 1/2 **Popmurphy**[20] 3090 3-9-0 **97** ....(v) JimCrowley 1 58
(K R Burke) *hld up: hdwy 5f out: rdn and wknd over 2f out: hung rt over 1f out* **10/1**

2m 42.01s (-1.99) **Going Correction** -0.025s/f (Good) **8** Ran SP% **114.0**
Speed ratings (Par 110): **104,102,99,99,98 91,84,83**
toteswingers: 1&2 £2.20, 1&3 £5.50, 2&3 £11.40 CSF £8.58 TOTE £3.00: £1.40, £1.70, £3.50; EX 9.70 Trifecta £145.30 Pool: £667.63 - 3.40 winning units..
Owner Godolphin **Bred** Elsdon Farms **Trained** Newmarket, Suffolk

FOCUS
Youmzain in 2006 was probably the best recent winner of this contest, which was promoted to Group 3 level for the first time this season. The winning time took 1/10th of a second off the course record, though this is a rarely used trip. Sound form, although Kite Wood won well without needing to match his best under a good front-running ride.

NOTEBOOK
Kite Wood(IRE) was dropping in class following his runs in the Dante and Derby, his first two outings for Godolphin. Whilst he wasn't disgraced when a close fifth at York, he expended too much energy before the race had even started at Epsom and he got himself warm enough before the start here, but he still proved good enough and his class shone through. Given a front-running masterclass by Dettori, he was bounced straight out in front and set just a fair pace until quickening the tempo inside the last half-mile. He had his rivals stone cold by the time he reached the furlong pole and was well on top by the time they reached the line. He was quoted as low as 10-1 for the St Leger and ought to have a big chance, though he wouldn't want the ground to be any faster than good. He may take in either the Great Voltigeur or the Geoffrey Freer en route. (op 11-4 tchd 3-1 in a place)

Tactic was dropping back in trip after his fourth in the Queen's Vase in which he finished in front of both Popmurphy and Dhushan. He tried to get on terms with the winner entering the last 3f, but although he pulled clear of the others he could make little impression. He may be able to nick a Listed event over this sort of trip. (op 4-1 tchd 9-2 and 5-1 in a place)

Above Average(IRE) had been disappointing since his shock win in the Sandown Classic Trial in April and that race has yet to produce a subsequent winner. Conceding upwards of 3lb to his seven rivals as a result of that victory, he plugged on over the last couple of furlongs but lacked the speed to trouble the front pair. He looks a real grinder and may benefit from an even stiffer test.

Free Agent raced prominently early, but came off the bridle inside the last half-mile and was made to look very one-paced. He didn't improve for the extra furlong and may need to drop back into Listed company in order to win again. (op 9-2 tchd 4-1)

Too Much Trouble, who looked as though he would be suited by the step back up in trip when fourth in the Hampton Court at Royal Ascot, failed to make much impression from off the pace and his best trip is still to be identified. (op 6-1 tchd 8-1 and 10-1 in a place)

Inhibition, the only filly in the field and another stepping up to this trip for the first time, was keen enough in a prominent position early and she didn't get home. A drop in class and trip looks required and she may also need easier ground.

Dhushan, who pulled his chance away in the Queen's Vase, was dropped out last early here but he never got into the race at all and it looks a case of back to the drawing board. (op 11-2)

Popmurphy, fifth in the Queen's Vase, took a hold at the back of the field early but a mid-race move came to nothing and he ended up beaten a long way. (op 12-1)

3779 TNT JULY STKS (GROUP 2) (C&G) — 6f
2:00 (2:02) (Class 1) 2-Y-0 — **£45,416** (£17,216; £8,616; £4,296; £2,152; £1,080) **Stalls** Low

Form / RPR

1 1 **Arcano (IRE)**[28] 2844 2-8-12 0 .... MartinDwyer 10 114+
(B J Meehan) *hld up: swtchd lft and hdwy over 2f out: rdn to chse ldr and edgd rt over 1f out: led ins fnl f: r.o wl* **7/4**[1]

511 2 3/4 **Orpen Grey (IRE)**[11] 3424 2-8-12 0 .... RichardKingscote 3 112
(Tom Dascombe) *led: rdn and edgd rt over 1f out: hdd ins fnl f: r.o* **9/2**[2]

110 3 3 **Red Jazz (USA)**[23] 2993 2-8-12 0 .... MichaelHills 2 103
(B W Hills) *t.k.h to post: hld up: hdwy over 1f out: rdn and hung rt ins fnl f: styd on* **7/1**

5122 4 4 1/2 **Reignier**[21] 3046 2-8-12 0 .... AndrewElliott 7 90
(K R Burke) *chsd ldrs: rdn and edgd rt over 1f out: wknd ins fnl f* **16/1**

31 5 hd **Ghostwing**[19] 3147 2-8-12 0 .... PaulHanagan 1 89+
(R A Fahey) *w'like: hld up: outpcd 1/2-way: r.o ins fnl f: nt trble ldrs* **16/1**

103 6 1 **Angel's Pursuit (IRE)**[6] 3583 2-8-12 0 .... JimmyFortune 8 86
(R Hannon) *lw: chsd ldr tl rdn over 2f out: wknd fnl f* **12/1**

213 7 1/2 **Tawaabb**[21] 3046 2-8-12 0 .... LDettori 5 84
(M R Channon) *lw: prom: rdn over 12f out: wknd fnl f* **8/1**

14 8 hd **Nosedive**[21] 3046 2-8-12 0 .... RyanMoore 4 84
(W J Haggas) *hld up in tch: racd keenly: rdn over 1f out: wknd fnl f* **6/1**[3]

2 9 1 3/4 **Noble Greek (USA)**[29] 2825 2-8-12 0 .... MarcHalford 11 79
(J R Best) *prom: racd keenly: rdn over 2f out: hung rt and wknd over 1f out* **50/1**

26 10 9 **Diamond Johnny G (USA)**[21] 3046 2-8-12 0 .... SteveDrowne 6 52
(J R Best) *plld hrd and prom: rdn: hung lft and wknd over 2f out* **40/1**

11 11 3/4 **Niran (IRE)**[42] 2413 2-8-12 0 .... SebSanders 9 49
(C E Brittain) *hld up: rdn over 2f out: sn wknd* **28/1**

1m 10.53s (-1.97) **Going Correction** -0.025s/f (Good) 2y crse rec **11** Ran SP% **119.7**
Speed ratings (Par 106): **112,111,107,101,100 99,98,98,96,84 83**
Toteswinger: 1&2 £3.70, 1&3 £5.00, 2&3 £7.50 CSF £9.29 TOTE £2.80: £1.50, £2.20, £2.10; EX 12.60 Trifecta £76.00 Pool: £1028.25 -10.00 winning units..
Owner Brimacombe,McNally,Vinciguerra,Sangster **Bred** Yellow Bird Syndicate **Trained** Manton, Wilts

FOCUS
Some really smart 2yos have taken this race in the past but since 2002 only Strategic Prince and Ivan Denisovich have gone on to win another race. However, this looked a strong renewal and the winning time was only fractionally slower than the juvenile record set last year by Elnawin. Very solid form.

NOTEBOOK
Arcano(IRE) was the subject of good reports before he made his racecourse debut and he duly landed his maiden in decent style. That race has already produced three winners and two placed horses from five subsequent runners, so the form looked rock solid. Once again he was very strong in the market and, after taking a few strides to hit top gear, he powered to the front and won comfortably. He looks a bright prospect and at this time there is nothing to suggest that he cannot develop into a top juvenile, but the record of previous winners of this race at three is just enough to put one off backing him at the current odds for next year's Guineas, for which he is top priced 25/1. The Prix Morny is next on the agenda if everything goes to plan, but all options are open. (op 9-4 tchd 5-2 in places)

Orpen Grey(IRE) had a very progressive profile and came from the stable that took this race with Classic Blade last year. In fact, both horses had taken the same prep contest at Salisbury. He went straight to the front and fought off all of his rivals except for the winner, so emerges with plenty of credit. This trip looks about right for him, but he could head for a big sales race in Ireland next and then the Middle Park if everything goes to plan. (op 4-1 tchd 5-1)

Red Jazz(USA) looked a decent prospect early in the season and did not run badly after an absence in the Coventry. On his toes in the paddock here, he stayed on well after getting slightly outpaced and was nicely clear of the rest of the field. The Richmond Stakes at Goodwood could be next for him. (tchd 13-2, 8-1 in places)

Reignier, trying 6f for the first time, ran yet another fantastic race at this level but was ultimately not in the class of at least the first two home. (op 14-1)

Ghostwing ◆, who had progressed from his debut to take a 6f event at Ayr on his next outing by six lengths, was one of the biggest eyecatchers in the race. This was obviously a step up in class and he was at least two lengths behind everything else at one point before flying home inside the two marker. He should provide his owners with something to dream about. (op 25-1)

Angel's Pursuit(IRE), who finished third at Sandown the previous Friday in a Listed event, was never far away and probably ran as well as he should have. (op 14-1 tchd 16-1 in a place)

Tawaabb was behind Reiginer when they met in the Norfolk, and was comfortably held by him again. The step up in trip did not look to suit him. (op 9-1 tchd 10-1)

Nosedive also took part in the Norfolk Stakes after making his racecourse debut only six days before that Group 2 contest, but he got caught up in all the trouble that American raider Yogaroo caused while rolling around. He had no such problems in this and was arguably a little disappointing. (tchd 11-2 and 13-2)

Niran(IRE) was defending an unbeaten record here (neither of the two previous races that he had won looked particularly strong) and represented a trainer with, seemingly, a strong hand of juveniles this season. However, this was a moderate effort and he was beaten before coming to the final furlong. (op 33-1)

3780 BLUE SQUARE STKS (HERITAGE H'CAP) 1m 2f

2:35 (2:36) (Class 2) (0-105,102) 3-Y-O

£49,848 (£14,928; £7,464; £3,736; £1,864; £936) **Stalls** High

Form				RPR
2211	**1**		**Firebet (IRE)**[19] 3144 3-9-5 **100** PaulHanagan 16 (R A Fahey) *lw: hld up: swtchd rt and hdwy over 2f out: rdn to ld ins fnl f: r.o wl* **7/1**[3]	112+
106	**2**	1 ¾	**Roman Republic (FR)**[5] 3639 3-8-10 **91** NCallan 6 (M Johnston) *a.p: rdn and edgd lft over 1f out: sn ev ch: styd on* **7/2**[2]	100
02-1	**3**	nk	**Class Is Class (IRE)**[42] 2416 3-8-8 **89** RyanMoore 4 (Sir Michael Stoute) *str: lw: hld up: hdwy over 1f out: rdn and edgd lft ins fnl f: r.o: nt rch ldrs* **11/4**[1]	97+
-111	**4**	½	**Mister Dee Bee (IRE)**[38] 2535 3-8-8 **89** MichaelHills 12 (B W Hills) *lw: led 1f: chsd ldrs: rdn to ld over 1f out: hdd and unable qck ins fnl f* **14/1**	96
3251	**5**	2	**Changing The Guard**[26] 2935 3-8-7 **88** TonyHamilton 2 (R A Fahey) *hld up: rdn over 2f out: hdwy over 1f out: r.o: nrst fin* **25/1**	91+
-115	**6**	½	**Aqwaal (IRE)**[20] 3087 3-9-7 **102** RHills 10 (E A L Dunlop) *prom: rdn and ev ch over 1f out: no ex ins fnl f* **10/1**	104
3140	**7**	2	**Takaatuf (IRE)**[21] 3051 3-8-6 **87** RoystonFfrench 7 (M Johnston) *led after 1f: rdn and hdd over 1f out: n.m.r and wknd ins fnl f* **20/1**	85
-230	**8**	¾	**Emirates Roadshow (USA)**[21] 3049 3-8-5 **86** TedDurcan 15 (Saeed Bin Suroor) *hld up: hdwy over 3f out: sn rdn: wknd over 1f out* **9/1**	83
2121	**9**	hd	**Eastern Aria (UAE)**[7] 3526 3-8-7 **88** 6ex JoeFanning 1 (M Johnston) *chsd ldrs: rdn: hung lft and wknd over 1f out* **20/1**	84
0315	**10**	¾	**High Severa (IRE)**[28] 2855 3-7-9 **81** oh1 ow2 Louis-PhilippeBeuzelin(5) 11 (K R Burke) *hld up in tch: rdn over 2f out: wknd over 1f out* **33/1**	76
6560	**11**	hd	**Aurorian (IRE)**[21] 3049 3-8-5 **86** MartinDwyer 13 (R Hannon) *dwlt: hld up: rdn over 2f out: sn hung rt: no ch whn hung lft ins fnl f* **40/1**	80
-331	**12**	1 ½	**Clerk's Choice (IRE)**[26] 2925 3-8-2 **83** FrancisNorton 5 (W Jarvis) *hld up in tch: rdn over 2f out: wknd over 1f out* **9/1**	74
2430	**13**	1 ½	**Lasso The Moon**[21] 3051 3-7-12 **79** CatherineGannon 8 (M R Channon) *swtg: mid-div: rdn over 3f out: edgd lft and wknd over 1f out* **20/1**	67
1202	**14**	26	**Union Island (IRE)**[26] 2935 3-8-4 **85** AlanMunro 3 (K A Ryan) *lw: mid-div: rdn 1/2-way: wknd 3f out* **25/1**	21

2m 3.52s (-1.98) **Going Correction** -0.025s/f (Good) **14** Ran SP% **124.5**
Speed ratings (Par 106): **106,104,104,103,102 101,100,99,99,99 98,97,96,75**
toteswingers: 1&2 £8.70, 1&3 £6.20, 2&3 £3.60 CSF £29.67 CT £87.55 TOTE £8.20: £2.50, £2.00, £1.80; EX 40.30 Trifecta £85.20 Pool: £1301.18 - 11.30 winning units..

Owner Mrs H Steel **Bred** Derek Veitch And Saleh Ali Hammadi **Trained** Musley Bank, N Yorks

FOCUS

A red-hot handicap which has produced winners that have gone on to Pattern success in the past, with the likes of Zindabad, Leporello and Formal Decree all successful within the last ten years. They appeared to go a decent pace, but there were still five in a line across the track a furlong from home. The form has been rated around the fourth and fifth, and with plenty of unexposed and progressive types it should work out well.

NOTEBOOK

Firebet(IRE) ◆ was on a hat-trick, having been successful in his first two starts for this yard. Trying this trip for the first time off a 6lb higher mark, he had the highest draw, which would have been a help with the first bend coming up relatively quickly. Settled in the middle of the field early, he was delivered with his effort to hit the front a furlong from home and won going away. He continues on an upward curve and he looks very capable of holding his own in Pattern company. He may now head for the Prix Eugene Adam. (op 6-1 tchd 15-2)

Roman Republic(FR) ◆, making a quick reappearance following his good effort at Sandown five days earlier, like the winner was stepping up to this trip for the first time. Very well backed earlier in the day and again on course, he was never far away and kept on strongly despite edging away to his left slightly up the hill. Already due to drop 1lb, he saw the trip out well enough and he should be winning again before too long. (op 11-2 tchd 6-1 in places)

Class Is Class(IRE) ◆, another to attract good market support, was making his handicap debut over this longer trip and the form of his Yarmouth maiden victory in May has worked out well with the three that finished closest to him all having been successful since. Held up well off the pace, he came off the bridle a fair way out but stayed on strongly up the hill, if hanging away a little to his left. He was the least exposed in this field and there is surely more to come from him. (tchd 3-1)

Mister Dee Bee(IRE), already proven over this sort of trip, was bidding for a four-timer off a 6lb higher mark. Never far away, he was bang there in the firing line a furlong from home before getting run out of the placings. This was another good effort, but the handicapper may have him now. Official explanation: jockey said gelding hung left (op 16-1)

Changing The Guard ◆, a stable companion of the winner, had been raised 4lb for his narrow York success on his first try over this sort of trip. Given plenty to do, having been tucked in from his wide draw, he stayed on strongly over the last couple of furlongs and was still going forward at the line. He is one to keep on the right side.

Aqwaal(IRE), back in trip after his good fifth in the King Edward VII at Royal Ascot, was 17lb higher than when completing a hat-trick at Newbury in May. Never far off the pace, he travelled strongly into a challenging position a furlong out but got tired up the hill. This was a fair effort conceding weight to some progressive and unexposed types and he looks worth a try at Listed level over this sort of trip. (op 9-1)

Takaatuf(IRE) soon adopted his usual position out in front, but was challenged on both sides coming to the last furlong and had no more to offer. (op 25-1)

Emirates Roadshow(USA), normally a front-runner, was ridden more patiently this time. Another trying this trip for the first time and supported in the market beforehand, he made an effort inside the last half-mile but could never get to the leaders and didn't appear to stay. (op 10-1 tchd 11-1)

Eastern Aria(UAE), 8lb higher than when destroying three rivals at Epsom seven days earlier, ended up well beaten but she had to use a lot of energy to take a handy position from the outside stall early, so she can be forgiven this to a degree. (op 16-1)

Clerk's Choice(IRE), raised 6lb for his defeat of a subsequent winner over 1m1f at Sandown last time, was never too far away but he didn't get up the hill and again this extra furlong with a stiff finish looked too much for him. (op 12-1)

Lasso The Moon was reported to have finished lame. Official explanation: vet said colt finished lame

3781 PRINCESS OF WALES'S BLUE SQUARE STKS (GROUP 2) 1m 4f

3:10 (3:11) (Class 1) 3-Y-O+

£56,770 (£21,520; £10,770; £5,370; £2,690; £1,350) **Stalls** High

Form				RPR
0-10	**1**		**Doctor Fremantle**[19] 3139 4-9-2 111 RyanMoore 4 (Sir Michael Stoute) *hld up: hdwy 3f out: chsd ldr over 1f out: sn rdn and hung rt: led ins fnl f: styd on u.p* **8/1**	116
1-41	**2**	nk	**Alwaary (USA)**[50] 2176 3-8-3 107 RHills 8 (J H M Gosden) *hld up: hdwy over 1f out: gng wl and hmpd 1f out: swtchd lft and r.o wl: nvr able to chal: fin 3rd: plcd 2nd* **12/1**	117+
/20-	**3**	½	**Schiaparelli (GER)**[277] 6522 6-9-2 117 TedDurcan 2 (Saeed Bin Suroor) *lengthy: s.i.s: sn rcvrd to ld: rdn and hung rt over 1f out: hdd ins fnl f: carried hd high and edgd lft: styd on: fin 2nd: pl 3rd* **25/1**	115
0506	**4**	nk	**Indian Days**[20] 3089 4-9-2 105 TPQueally 7 (J G Given) *hld up: hdwy 3f out: rdn and hung lft over 1f out: no ex ins fnl f: fin 5th: plcd 4th* **50/1**	108
21	**5**	½	**All The Aces (IRE)**[12] 3397 4-9-2 115 PhilipRobinson 6 (M A Jarvis) *lw: chsd ldrs: rdn over 3f out: lost pl whn hmpd over 1f out: n.d after: fin 6th: plcd 5th* **5/1**[3]	108+
4-14	**6**	4	**Enroller (IRE)**[19] 3139 4-9-2 111 MartinDwyer 1 (W R Muir) *chsd ldr tl rdn and hung rt over 1f out: styd on same pce: fin 4th: plcd 6th* **12/1**	109
-342	**7**	2 ¼	**Drumfire (IRE)**[18] 3190 5-9-2 109 JoeFanning 3 (M Johnston) *hld up: hdwy over 3f out: rdn: edgd rt over 1f out: wknd fnl f* **25/1**	104
2-02	**8**	4 ½	**Campanologist (USA)**[19] 3139 4-9-2 115 LDettori 9 (Saeed Bin Suroor) *prom: rdn whn hmpd over 1f out: sn wknd and eased* **5/2**[2]	96
-114	**9**	3 ½	**Duncan**[34] 2670 4-9-2 120 JimmyFortune 5 (J H M Gosden) *hld up: plld hrd: hdwy over 7f out: wknd and eased fnl f* **2/1**[1]	91

2m 30.7s (-2.20) **Going Correction** -0.025s/f (Good)
WFA 3 from 4yo+ 13lb **9** Ran SP% **114.7**
Speed ratings (Par 115): **106,105,105,102,102 102,100,97,95**
toteswingers: 1&2 £21.10, 1&3 £12.40, 2&3 £17.20 CSF £94.41 TOTE £9.80: £2.10, £2.90, £4.10; EX 122.80 Trifecta £415.80 Part won. Pool: £1460.93 - 0.60 winning units..

Owner K Abdulla **Bred** Juddmonte Farms Ltd **Trained** Newmarket, Suffolk

■ Stewards' Enquiry : Ted Durcan four-day ban: careless riding (Jul 23-24,26-27)

Martin Dwyer three-day ban: careless riding (Jul 23,24,26)

FOCUS

This race has usually been won by a good horse, as the list of previous winners suggests. Virtually all of the nine that lined up were worthy of respect, but there was a messy conclusion to the race, and the form is highly suspect.

NOTEBOOK

Doctor Fremantle did not show his true colours behind Campanologist last time, and he had always fallen just short of this level in the past, but things panned out nicely for him and he won in good style. He clearly has no problem staying 1m4f but his trainer mentioned afterwards that he could go for the Juddmonte International next, which is run over nearly two furlongs shorter. (tchd 9-1)

Alwaary(USA) ◆ was the sole three-year-old in the line-up, an age group that had only proved victorious once in the past 10 years, admittedly from few runners. Off since winning the Listed Cocked Hat Stakes at Goodwood in May, he came with a strong run towards the stands' side before being hampered by Schiaparelli, and was rightly placed second after the stewards had a look. With a clear passage he may well have won, which would have been a tremendous effort. The Gordon Stakes and/or the Great Voltigeur were mentioned for him afterwards and he is currently top priced 14-1 for the St Leger. (op 10-1)

Schiaparelli(GER), who passed the post second, had some very strong form in Group 1 company before joining Godolphin from Peter Schiergen, and he showed some ability on his first outing for Saeed Bin Suroor last year in the Prix Foy after almost a year off. There were plenty of negative vibes for him before the off here and he took up what looked a pacemaking role, but he fought on really well after steadily increasing the pace before wandering inside the latter stages. It was a promising return despite a high head carriage late on, and it will be interesting to see if he can progress this time. (op 20-1)

Indian Days ran a cracker but he has regularly been beaten at this level, so while this was a very commendable effort, his placing is probably not as good as it looks considering the trouble in running of some, and the poor efforts of the market leaders. (tchd 66-1)

All The Aces(IRE) was hampered by Enroller, which made Phillip Robinson snatch his mount up when making some ground. (op 9-2)

Enroller(IRE) passed the post in fourth but was another to be demoted, as he ran across All The Aces, who passed the post in sixth. (op 11-1)

Drumfire(IRE) had not shown enough recently to suggest he could bustle the best of these up and that proved the case. (tchd 28-1)

Campanologist(USA) has proved to be a useful servant to Godolphin since switching to them, but he went from travelling to beaten in a matter of strides, suggesting something was not quite right with him. Official explanation: jockey said colt lost its action (op 7-2 tchd 9-4)

Duncan, who has been improving all year, was disappointing here. His demise looks easy to explain, though, as he was very keen whilst on a long rein, so probably had little left for the fight after his early exertions. Official explanation: jockey said colt ran too free (tchd 15-8 and 9-4)

3782 EUROPEAN BREEDERS' FUND CONDITIONS STKS 6f

3:45 (3:45) (Class 2) 2-Y-O **£12,952** (£3,854; £1,926; £962) **Stalls** Low

Form				RPR
1	**1**		**Awzaan**[22] 3017 2-9-1 0 RHills 4 (M Johnston) *w'like: scope: lw: hld up: swtchd lft and hdwy over 1f out: led 1f out: r.o strly* **9/1**	101+
1	**2**	5	**Amary (IRE)**[42] 2401 2-8-10 0 NCallan 3 (C E Brittain) *leggy: hld up: hdwy over 1f out: sn rdn and hung lft: styd on same pce* **8/1**	81+
1	**3**	2	**Sabii Sands (IRE)**[34] 2676 2-9-1 0 RyanMoore 9 (R Hannon) *lengthy: chsd ldrs: rdn over 3f out: outpcd fr over 1f out* **9/2**[1]	80
01	**4**	½	**Extreme Warrior (IRE)**[20] 3113 2-9-1 0 (b) ChrisCatlin 5 (D R Lanigan) *s.s: hdwy 1/2-way: sn rdn: styd on same pce fr over 1f out* **9/1**	79
1	**5**	nse	**Navajo Chief**[38] 2547 2-9-1 0 AlanMunro 6 (A P Jarvis) *w'like: mid-div: rdn over 2f out: styd on same pce appr fnl f* **16/1**	78
31	**6**	¾	**The Human League**[12] 3392 2-9-1 0 TonyCulhane 2 (M R Channon) *w'like: str: chsd ldrs: rdn over 1f out: no ex* **5/1**[2]	76
6221	**7**	¾	**Footstepsofspring (FR)**[24] 2979 2-9-1 0 JimmyFortune 8 (R Hannon) *hld up: outpcd and hung lft over 2f out: rdn and swtchd rt over 1f out: n.d* **14/1**	74

6231 **8** *1* **Farmer Giles (IRE)**[22] 3032 2-8-13 0.......................... TPQueally 10 69
(M L W Bell) *w'like: str: swtg: sn led: rdn and hdd 1f out: wknd qckly* **6/1**[3]

031 **9** *½* **Lady Pattern (IRE)**[16] 3248 2-8-10 0.......................... LDettori 1 64
(P W D'Arcy) *hld up: hdwy 1/2-way: rdn: hung rt and ev ch over 1f out: wknd ins fnl f* **8/1**

331 **10** *hd* **Swilly Ferry (USA)**[35] 2631 2-8-13 0.......................... MichaelHills 7 67
(B W Hills) *chsd ldr: rdn and ev ch over 1f out: wknd ins fnl f* **6/1**[3]

1m 11.78s (-0.72) **Going Correction** -0.025s/f (Good) **10** Ran SP% **118.2**
Speed ratings (Par 100): **103,96,93,93,92 91,90,89,88,88**
toteswingers: 1&2 £13.00, 1&3 £6.00, 2&3 £9.30 CSF £80.01 TOTE £8.00: £2.60, £3.10, £2.20; EX 49.60.

Owner Hamdan Al Maktoum **Bred** Shadwell Estate Company Limited **Trained** Middleham Moor, N Yorks

FOCUS
A very decent conditions event with all ten runners having been successful in their most recent starts, four of them in their only outings. The early pace was very strong, perhaps too strong, as those that helped set it didn't figure in the finish and the race rather dropped into the laps of those held up. The winning time was 1.25 seconds slower than the July Stakes.

NOTEBOOK
Awzaan ◆ could hardly have won this in more convincing style. Dropped right out early, the only moment of worry for his supporters was when it looked as though he might get stopped in his run 2f from home, but he was switched to his left in plenty of time and, once hitting the front, soon bounded right away. He looks an exciting prospect and will now probably head for the Vintage Stakes over an extra furlong at Glorious Goodwood, a race his stable has won with Lucky Story and Shamardal in recent years. (op 8-1 tchd 10-1)

Amary(IRE), who was relatively weak in the market, travelled well towards the inside of the field and, although she was completely swept aside by the winner's finishing effort, she beat the rest well enough despite still looking as though the experience would do her good. She looks capable of winning a decent race back against her own sex and will no doubt get another chance in Group company at some stage. (op 6-1)

Sabii Sands(IRE), who was sent off a well-backed favourite, came off the bridle at halfway but eventually responded to pressure to just prevail in the separate race for third. He shapes as though he needs an extra furlong. (op 7-1)

Extreme Warrior(IRE), shock 40-1 winner of a course-and-distance maiden the previous month when in front of The Human League, blew the start again here just as he did then, but although he finished well he never had a hope of getting on terms with the winner. He is another who looks as though he will be suited by an extra furlong now. (op 10-1 tchd 11-1)

Navajo Chief, 50-1 winner from Footstepsofspring on his debut over the minimum trip last month, failed to get involved over this extra furlong in this better race but he confirmed the Windsor form with his old rival, so has probably run his race. (op 12-1)

The Human League, successful on soft ground at Newcastle since his defeat by Extreme Warrior on debut, was never far away and would have been a bit closer had he not got into a barging match with Lady Pattern well over a furlong from home. (op 11-2 tchd 9-2)

Farmer Giles(IRE) did far too much too soon and eventually paid for it. (op 5-1 tchd 7-1)

Lady Pattern(IRE) Official explanation: jockey said filly hung right

Swilly Ferry(USA) also did far too much too early. (op 15-2)

3783 PORTLAND PLACE PROPERTIES CONDITIONS STKS — 1m

4:20 (4:20) (Class 2) 3-Y-O
£12,462 (£3,732; £1,866; £934; £466; £234) **Stalls** Low

Form RPR

2330 **1** **Spring Of Fame (USA)**[21] 3050 3-8-12 102.......................... LDettori 4 107
(Saeed Bin Suroor) *lw: stdd after s: hld up: hdwy over 2f out: rdn over 1f out: hung lft and led ins fnl f: r.o* **9/2**

0311 **2** *¾* **Cloudy Start**[14] 3298 3-9-1 108.......................... TPQueally 6 108
(H R A Cecil) *lw: chsd ldrs: led over 2f out: sn rdn and hung lft: hdd ins fnl f: kpt on* **2/1**[1]

10 **3** *½* **Loch Linnhe (USA)**[22] 3011 3-8-12 99.......................... JimmyFortune 2 104
(J H M Gosden) *lw: hld up: hdwy over 2f out: rdn over 1f out: n.m.r ins fnl f: styd on same pce* **5/2**[2]

3-53 **4** *1* **Derbaas (USA)**[47] 2273 3-8-12 104.......................... RHills 7 101
(E A L Dunlop) *hld up: hdwy 3f out: ev ch and hung lft fr 2f out: sn rdn: flashed tail ins fnl f: styd on same pce* **7/2**[3]

2230 **5** *2¼* **Shampagne**[21] 3049 3-9-3 100.......................... MartinDwyer 1 101
(P F I Cole) *chsd ldrs: led 6f out: rdn and hdd over 1f out: styd on same pce: eased towards fin* **11/1**

0403 **6** *9* **Jonnie Skull (IRE)**[2] 3710 3-8-12 51..........................(t) KellyHarrison 5 74?
(P S McEntee) *led 2f: chsd ldrs tl wknd wl over 2f out* **100/1**

6044 **7** *11* **Quick Single (USA)**[14] 3299 3-8-12 63..........................(v) CarolineKelly 3 48
(P S McEntee) *chsd ldrs tl wknd 3f out* **100/1**

1m 38.52s (-1.48) **Going Correction** -0.025s/f (Good) **7** Ran SP% **112.6**
Speed ratings (Par 106): **106,105,104,103,101 92,81**
toteswingers: 1&2 £2.20, 1&3 £2.70, 2&3 £2.00 CSF £13.51 TOTE £5.80: £2.50, £1.70; EX 14.10.

Owner Godolphin **Bred** Brushwood Stable **Trained** Newmarket, Suffolk

■ Stewards' Enquiry : Caroline Kelly two-day ban: used whip when out of contention (Jul 23-24)

FOCUS
Only five of these had any chance of winning, and it produced a really good tussle throughout the final furlong, but the early pace looked sedate and this was effectively a sprint from around the two-furlong pole.

NOTEBOOK
Spring Of Fame(USA) was dropping in trip after looking not to stay on a couple of occasions over 1m2f since joining Godolphin. That decision looked justified as he showed the necessary pace to get on terms before doing enough in front to claim victory. He is probably up to winning a Listed race, but his future lies on synthetics, with Meydan in the winter very much on the agenda. (tchd 4-1 and 5-1)

Cloudy Start was chasing a hat-trick after victories at Epsom and then Kempton and had every chance here after hitting the front. His action is quite pronounced, and one would imagine that he would struggle to handle easy ground if asked to race on it again, despite a good effort on soft on his racecourse debut. (tchd 15-8 tchd 9-4 in a place)

Loch Linnhe(USA) ◆ did the job so well on his racecourse debut this year that connections let him take his chance in the Jersey Stakes on only his second run. He ran a blinder there and finished in front of Total Gallery, who won a hot handicap at this course the previous day (Donativum and Gallagher who were just in front have also landed victories since). However, this contest did not play to his strengths, and he can easily be given another chance. (tchd 9-4 and 3-1)

Derbaas(USA) ran very poorly in the Feilden Stakes on his return to action this year but did much better in the Silver Bowl last time in very heavy ground. He stayed wide of his rivals early in the race before edging left once joining issue, and eventually hung so badly that the jockey could not ride him forward. Ground might be important to him, and an easier surface during the autumn could see him win a fair event, but it is also worth noting that he flashed his tail in the latter stages after getting reminders. Official explanation: jockey said colt hung left-handed (op 9-2)

Shampagne had been very consistent this season until running in the Britannia Stakes at Royal Ascot, where he was well down the field. He set the early fractions in this before being readily swept aside. (op 10-1 tchd 14-1)

3784 RACING UK SKY 432 H'CAP — 5f

4:55 (4:55) (Class 3) (0-95,95) 3-Y-0+ **£9,714** (£2,890; £1,444; £721) **Stalls** Low

Form RPR

1261 **1** **Canadian Danehill (IRE)**[6] 3582 7-9-10 91 6ex..........................(p) LDettori 10 99
(R M H Cowell) *mde all: drifted rt fr 1/2-way: rdn over 1f out: jst hld on* **8/1**

0-06 **2** *hd* **Tabaret**[13] 3351 6-9-9 90.......................... TonyCulhane 7 97+
(R M Whitaker) *a.p: rdn and edgd rt over 1f out: swtchd lft ins fnl f: r.o wl* **25/1**

5412 **3** *1¼* **The Jobber (IRE)**[6] 3582 8-9-3 84.......................... NCallan 1 87
(M Blanshard) *chsd ldrs: rdn over 1f out: styd on same pce towards fin* **13/2**[3]

1552 **4** *nse* **Green Beret (IRE)**[19] 3166 3-9-8 94.......................... JimmyFortune 15 101+
(J H M Gosden) *lw: chsd ldrs: effrt and nt clr run ins fnl f: r.o wl towards fin* **4/1**[1]

2300 **5** *½* **Little Pete (IRE)**[12] 3405 4-9-7 88..........................(v[1]) LPKeniry 3 89
(A M Balding) *prom: sn pushed along: rdn over 1f out: r.o* **12/1**

5 *dht* **Danetime Lily (IRE)**[13] 3368 5-8-12 79..........................(p) TedDurcan 2 80
(Ms Joanna Morgan, Ire) *chsd ldrs: rdn over 1f out: styd on same pce ins fnl f* **20/1**

4165 **7** *¾* **Indian Trail**[13] 3351 9-9-7 88..........................(v) RyanMoore 9 89+
(D Nicholls) *hld up: hmpd over 1f out: r.o ins fnl f: nt rch ldrs* **9/2**[2]

1031 **8** *nk* **Rothesay Dancer**[14] 3295 6-8-12 82.......................... KellyHarrison(3) 17 79+
(J S Goldie) *hld up: r.o ins fnl f: nvr nrr* **16/1**

3504 **9** *½* **Angus Newz**[11] 3434 6-9-9 90.......................... FrancisNorton 13 85
(M Quinn) *chsd ldrs: rdn over 1f out: styng on same pce whn hmpd ins fnl f* **11/1**

R214 **10** *hd* **Sands Crooner (IRE)**[5] 3607 6-8-13 80..........................(v) TPQueally 6 75
(J G Given) *hld up: rdn over 1f out: no imp ins fnl f* **25/1**

3500 **11** *hd* **Ebraam (USA)**[46] 2297 6-8-13 85.......................... MCGeran(5) 4 86+
(P Howling) *hld up: hmpd ins fnl f: nvr trbld ldrs* **11/1**

2046 **12** *¾* **Namir (IRE)**[16] 3236 7-8-9 76 oh2..........................(vt) PatrickMathers 11 67+
(D Shaw) *s.i.s: hld up: hmpd over 1f out: n.d* **28/1**

0040 **13** *2¾* **Magical Speedfit (IRE)**[3] 3694 4-8-9 76 oh3.......................... ChrisCatlin 16 57
(G G Margarson) *hld up: effrt over 1f out: wknd fnl f* **25/1**

4-06 **14** *10* **Flash McGahon (IRE)**[20] 3122 5-9-8 89.......................... AdrianTNicholls 18 34
(D Nicholls) *hld up: wkng whn hung lft over 1f out: b.b.v* **10/1**

58.42 secs (-0.68) **Going Correction** -0.025s/f (Good)
WFA 3 from 4yo+ 5lb **14** Ran SP% **121.7**
Speed ratings (Par 107): **104,103,101,101,100 100,99,99,98,98 97,96,92,76**
toteswingers: 1&2 £39.90, 1&3 £5.80, 2&3 £25.50 CSF £203.34 CT £1425.27 TOTE £7.30: £2.20, £8.20, £2.30; EX 194.40 Place 6: £78.39 Place 5: £49.46.

Owner T W Morley **Bred** Skymarc Farm Inc And Dr A J O'Reilly **Trained** Six Mile Bottom, Cambs

■ Stewards' Enquiry : L Dettori caution: careless riding
Tony Culhane one-day ban: careless riding (Jul 23)

FOCUS
A hot sprint handicap and it was crucial to race up with the pace. The problem was that, although the field came down the centre early, they gradually migrated towards the stands' rail and several that had been held up for a late run met traffic problems.

NOTEBOOK
Canadian Danehill(IRE), carrying a 6lb penalty for his Sandown victory six days earlier, has won off this mark on Fibresand. Sent straight into the lead, he was in the ideal position as things turned out and, although he gradually edged over to the stands' rail as the race progressed, he kept on finding a bit more and hung on to win with nothing to spare. He is in cracking form at the moment, but he may be given a break now.

Tabaret, without a win in over a year but still 3lb higher, was never too far away but, although he put in a strong late run up the hill, he just failed to get there. This was much better and he would be interesting if able to reproduce it, but he isn't the most consistent.

The Jobber(IRE), beaten less than a length by Canadian Danehill at Sandown, had a 6lb pull here. Always close to the pace, he had every chance and did his best and appeared to have few excuses. He is already due to go up 2lb which won't make life any easier. (op 15-2 tchd 6-1)

Green Beret(IRE) ◆, less exposed than most in this line-up, raced close to the pace towards the nearside of the field, but just as he tried to put in an effort against the stands' rail the winner had got there before him and he ran out of room. He may not have won otherwise, but he would have finished closer and there are more sprints to be won with him. (op 9-2)

Little Pete(IRE), visored for the first time, finished strongly but he is putting together a lengthy losing run. (op 14-1 tchd 10-1)

Danetime Lily(IRE) saw plenty of daylight on the outside of the field, but she had every chance and ran her race. (op 14-1 tchd 10-1)

Indian Trail got the strong pace he needs, but he found a troubled passage on the near side and his finishing effort was too late. He would also have preferred the ground to have been quicker. Official explanation: jockey said gelding was denied a clear run (op 4-1)

Rothesay Dancer, back on a career-high mark, was weak in the market beforehand but was another to finish well and wasn't disgraced. (op 10-1)

Angus Newz was probably in the right place in a handy position early as things turned out, but she looked to have run her race well when getting badly hampered inside the last furlong. She is already due to go up 5lb. (op 10-1)

Ebraam(USA) found every bit of trouble going and a line can be put through this performance. Official explanation: jockey said gelding was denied a clear run (op 14-1 tchd 10-1)

Namir(IRE) was another to get into all sorts of trouble and this performance can be ignored. Official explanation: jockey said gelding was denied a clear run (op 25-1)

Flash McGahon(IRE), the subject of quite a plunge, was slightly hampered against the stands' rail passing the 2f pole and was knocked back to last. He seemed virtually unrideable after that and it transpired that he had broken a blood-vessel. Official explanation: trainer said gelding bled from the nose (op 20-1)

T/Jkpt: Not won. T/Plt: £152.50 to a £1 stake. Pool: £181,066.64. 866.40 winning tickets. T/Qpdt: £47.70 to a £1 stake. Pool: £7,533.36. 116.65 winning tickets. CR

3588 WARWICK (L-H)

Thursday, July 9

OFFICIAL GOING: Good to firm (good in places; 8.4)
Wind: Moderate across Weather: Fine

3785 EUROPEAN BREEDERS' FUND MEDIAN AUCTION MAIDEN STKS (DIV I) — 7f 26y

1:45 (1:46) (Class 5) 2-Y-O **£3,399** (£1,011; £505; £252) **Stalls** Low

Form RPR

05 **1** **Danger Mulally**[13] 3344 2-9-3 0.......................... NeilChalmers 3 68
(A M Balding) *w ldr: led over 3f out: c towards stands' side: rdn and edgd lft over 1f out: narrowly hdd jst ins fnl f: led last strides* **9/1**

0 **2** *hd* **Sir Bruno (FR)**[21] 3052 2-9-0 0 .... DavidProbert(3) 9 67
(B Palling) *led: hdd over 3f out: c to stands' side: rdn wl over 1f out: slt ld jst ins fnl f: hdd last strides* **80/1**

45 **3** *shd* **Bridge Valley**[12] 3403 2-9-3 0 .... PatDobbs 5 67
(R Hannon) *hld up in mid-div: hdwy 2f out: rdn over 1f out: ev ch ins fnl f: r.o* **9/1**

02 **4** *1* **Many A Slip**[17] 3218 2-9-3 0 .... JamieSpencer 8 65
(J L Dunlop) *hld up in mid-div: hdwy 2f out: ev ch 1f out: sn rdn: nt qckn towards fin* **3/1**[2]

6 **5** *1 1/4* **Agony And Ecstasy**[50] 2175 2-8-9 0 .... JackMitchell(3) 10 56
(R M Beckett) *a.p: rdn over 1f out: one pce* **3/1**[2]

06 **6** *3/4* **Wing Of Faith**[24] 2979 2-9-3 0 .... EddieAhern 1 60
(S Kirk) *hld up in tch: rdn and ev ch wl over 1f out: wknd ins fnl f* **15/2**[3]

7 *1/2* **Caracal** 2-9-3 0 .... J-PGuillambert 7 58+
(M Johnston) *s.i.s: in rr: rdn 2f out: nvr trbld ldrs* **9/4**[1]

0 **8** *2 1/2* **Petite Mambo**[12] 3402 2-8-12 0 .... NicolPolli(5) 6 52
(W De Best-Turner) *prom: ev ch 2f out: rdn and wknd 1f out* **100/1**

9 *3 1/2* **Downtoobusiness** 2-9-3 0 .... TGMcLaughlin 4 43
(Karen George) *s.i.s: rdn jst over 1f out: a in rr* **50/1**

1m 25.84s (1.24) **Going Correction** -0.125s/f (Firm) 9 Ran SP% **116.7**
Speed ratings (Par 94): **87,86,86,85,84 83,82,79,75**
toteswingers: 1&2 £23.90, 1&3 £6.80, 2&3 £16.60 CSF £492.38 TOTE £14.00: £2.50, £13.10, £1.70; EX 611.80.
Owner John Dwyer **Bred** D Robb **Trained** Kingsclere, Hants

FOCUS
The first two filled the front two positions throughout and the time was 1.11 seconds slower than the second division won by Mingun Bell, suggesting the bare form is modest. They raced middle to stands' side in the straight. It has been rated around the principals.

NOTEBOOK
Danger Mulally raced on the wrong side of the track at Folkestone on his second start and he showed himself much better than that effort implied. After displaying good speed throughout, he was joined on both sides in the straight but showed a good attitude to prevail. He should be competitive in ordinary nurseries. (op 11-1)
Sir Bruno(FR) stepped up massively on the form he showed when failing to beat a rival at Leicester on his debut. Racing closest to the stands'-side rail in the straight, he kept on but was just held. (op 66-1 tchd 100-1)
Bridge Valley fared best of those who raced off the pace, keeping on for pressure up the middle of the track. He can now switch to nurseries. (op 5-1)
Many A Slip, stepped up a furlong in trip, looked a danger early in the straight but didn't see his race out as well as the front three. Official explanation: jockey said colt had a breathing problem (tchd 5-2 and 7-2)
Agony And Ecstasy, one of only two fillies, didn't appear to improve much on the form she showed on her debut over 6f at Goodwood. (op 11-4)
Wing Of Faith travelled quite well but didn't pick up. He now has the option of nurseries and can be expected to do better, possibly back over shorter. (op 8-1 tchd 7-1)
Caracal, a 32,000gns half-brother to five winners, including smart 5f-7f performer Nufoos, was a well-backed favourite but he was too green to do himself justice. Having played up beforehand, unshipping his rider in the paddock, he struggled to lay up in the race itself after starting very slowly. He should have learnt plenty. (op 9-2)

3786 EUROPEAN BREEDERS' FUND MEDIAN AUCTION MAIDEN STKS (DIV II) 7f 26y
2:20 (2:21) (Class 5) 2-Y-O **£3,399** (£1,011; £505; £252) **Stalls Low**

Form RPR

33 **1** **Mingun Bell (USA)**[21] 3052 2-9-3 0 .... EddieAhern 3 79+
(H R A Cecil) *hld up in mid-div: swtchd rt and hdwy wl over 1f out: sn rdn: r.o wl u.p to ld nr fin* **2/1**[1]

4 **2** *1/2* **Duplicity**[15] 3270 2-9-3 0 .... DaneO'Neill 7 78
(R Hannon) *chsd ldr: led wl over 1f out: sn rdn: edgd rt ent fnl f: hdd nr fin* **8/1**

3 *1 1/4* **Wriggle (IRE)** 2-9-3 0 .... LiamJones 8 75
(W J Haggas) *hld up in tch: ev ch ins fnl f: rdn and nt qckn* **15/2**[3]

02 **4** *1/2* **Astonishment (IRE)**[13] 3344 2-9-0 0 .... DavidProbert(3) 11 73
(S Kirk) *a.p: rdn wl over 1f out: edgd rt jst ins fnl f: nt qckn* **14/1**

4 **5** *1 3/4* **Dream Spinner**[27] 2889 2-9-3 0 .... RichardMullen 12 69
(J L Dunlop) *swtchd lft sn after s: hld up in rr: hdwy 2f out: no imp fnl f* **12/1**

023 **6** *hd* **Al Khimiya (IRE)**[13] 3344 2-8-12 0 .... JamieSpencer 1 64+
(S A Callaghan) *hld up towards rr: hdwy on ins over 2f out: rdn over 1f out: no further prog* **5/2**[2]

0 **7** *6* **Truly Magic**[29] 2825 2-8-12 0 .... MickyFenton 5 49
(H J L Dunlop) *led: hdd wl over 1f out: sn wknd* **50/1**

8 *nk* **Constant Contact** 2-9-3 0 .... NeilChalmers 4 53
(A M Balding) *s.i.s: a in rr* **14/1**

6 **9** *2 3/4* **Meer Und Wind (GER)**[20] 3101 2-8-12 0 .... PatDobbs 2 42
(P R Webber) *hld up: pushed along and bhd fnl 2f* **22/1**

0 **10** *20* **Little Buddy**[8] 3500 2-9-0 0 .... RussellKennemore(3) 6 —
(R J Price) *s.i.s: a in rr: t.o fnl 2f* **100/1**

11 *7* **Kit Kat** 2-8-12 0 .... MatthewDavies(5) 9 —
(George Baker) *mid-div: pushed along over 5f out: sn bhd: t.o fnl 2f* **50/1**

1m 24.73s (0.13) **Going Correction** -0.125s/f (Firm) 11 Ran SP% **115.1**
Speed ratings (Par 94): **94,93,92,91,89 89,82,82,78,56 48**
toteswingers: 1&2 £3.10, 1&3 £7.10, 2&3 £10.70 CSF £17.92 TOTE £2.70: £1.10, £2.20, £2.60; EX 19.60.
Owner Niarchos Family **Bred** Paula W Cline **Trained** Newmarket, Suffolk

FOCUS
The winning time was 1.11 seconds quicker than the first division won by Danger Mulally. They raced all over the place in the straight, with the main action taking place up the middle of the track. The fourth and fifth set the level for now.

NOTEBOOK
Mingun Bell(USA) raced too keenly when ridden from the front at Leicester on his previous start (beaten at odds on), and the switch to more patient tactics suited. He travelled kindly in about mid-division, but was still set plenty to do and took a while to get going once switched right into the clear in the straight, before eventually getting on top near the line to win a shade cosily. He gave the impression he was still learning his job and can be expected to show improved form next time. (op 3-1)
Duplicity stepped up on the form he showed when fourth in a Polytrack maiden on his debut, but was simply beaten by a better one on the day. He might find a similar race, but will also have the option of nurseries after one more run. (tchd 7-1)
Wriggle(IRE), a 55,000euros already gelded half-brother to 6f winner Guertino, fared best of the newcomers, looking a big threat about a furlong out, before fading near the line. He might improve enough to find a similar contest. (op 12-1)
Astonishment(IRE) looked flattered by the bare result of his recent second placing at Folkestone, but this was a solid effort. He should find his level in nurseries. (op 11-1 tchd 9-1)
Dream Spinner could make no impression and didn't seem to improve on the form he showed at Sandown first time up. (op 16-1)
Al Khimiya(IRE) raced more towards the inside than most of these in the straight and might have been on the slowest part of the track. She can be given another chance, especially in handicap company. Official explanation: jockey said filly was hampered at start (op 6-4)
Constant Contact Official explanation: jockey said gelding ran green

3787 RACING UK LIVE IN YOUR LIVING ROOM H'CAP 6f
2:55 (2:55) (Class 4) (0-85,87) 3-Y-O+
£6,231 (£1,866; £933; £467; £233; £117) **Stalls Low**

Form RPR

40-2 **1** **Baunagain (IRE)**[19] 3164 4-9-12 **80** .... JamieSpencer 10 92
(P W Chapple-Hyam) *a.p: led 4f out: c to stands' side wl over 1f out: rdn ins fnl f: r.o wl* **11/2**[3]

0-01 **2** *2 1/2* **First In Command (IRE)**[12] 3377 4-9-10 **81** .... (t) FrederikTylicki(3) 5 86
(Daniel Mark Loughnane, Ire) *a.p: rdn and ev ch over 1f out: nt qckn wl ins fnl f* **7/2**[2]

30-0 **3** *2* **Golden Destiny (IRE)**[54] 2079 3-9-4 **78** .... EddieAhern 2 76
(P J Makin) *led 2f: a.p: rdn over 1f out: no ex ins fnl f* **8/1**

0211 **4** *nk* **Victoria Sponge (IRE)**[7] 3523 3-9-13 **87** 6ex .... DaneO'Neill 1 84
(R Hannon) *hld up and bhd: hdwy wl over 1f out: sn rdn: one pce fnl f* **5/2**[1]

5412 **5** *1* **Memphis Man**[3] 3694 6-9-1 **74** .... RichardEvans(5) 6 69
(P D Evans) *hld up in tch: pushed along over 2f out: wknd over 1f out* **8/1**

0404 **6** *1 3/4* **Koraleva Tectona (IRE)**[27] 2883 4-9-6 **74** .... PaulEddery 4 64
(Pat Eddery) *hld up and bhd: pushed along and effrt over 1f out: eased whn btn wl ins fnl f* **11/2**[3]

0044 **7** *1 3/4* **Dig Deep (IRE)**[15] 3268 7-9-1 **69** .... (t) LiamJones 9 54
(J J Quinn) *hld up in tch: pushed along and wknd over 1f out* **14/1**

1m 10.14s (-1.66) **Going Correction** -0.125s/f (Firm) course record
WFA 3 from 4yo+ 6lb 7 Ran SP% **110.5**
Speed ratings (Par 105): **106,102,100,99,98 95,93**
toteswingers: 1&2 £3.90, 1&3 £5.70, 2&3 £5.60 CSF £23.23 CT £143.26 TOTE £4.30: £1.90, £2.30; EX 19.70.
Owner P Ransley **Bred** Patrick Doyle **Trained** Newmarket, Suffolk

FOCUS
A fair sprint handicap in which it paid to race handily. They raced towards the stands' side in the straight. The form looks sound rated around the runner-up to the best of his form in this country.

3788 TURFTV.CO.UK H'CAP 1m 6f 213y
3:30 (3:32) (Class 5) (0-75,73) 3-Y-O+ **£3,885** (£1,156; £577; £288) **Stalls Low**

Form RPR

0-21 **1** **Rare Ruby (IRE)**[28] 2854 5-9-5 **64** .... ShaneKelly 3 70
(Jennie Candlish) *hld up in tch: rdn to chal wl over 1f out: led jst ins fnl f: drvn out* **4/1**[1]

0335 **2** *nk* **Longboat Key**[18] 3192 3-8-8 **70** .... (b[1]) J-PGuillambert 1 75
(M Johnston) *hld up and bhd: rdn 2f out: hdwy over 1f out: styd on to take 2nd cl home* **11/2**[2]

6 **3** *1 3/4* **Dantari (IRE)**[21] 631 4-9-3 **62** .... JamieSpencer 7 65
(Evan Williams) *a.p: chsd ldr after 3f: rdn over 3f out: led over 2f out: c to stands' side st: hdd jst ins fnl f: no ex towards fin* **11/2**[2]

5033 **4** *1 1/4* **Kiho**[17] 3216 4-8-9 **54** oh1 .... (b) EddieAhern 9 55
(Eve Johnson Houghton) *swtchd lft sn after s: hld up and bhd: c to stands' rail st: nt clr run and swtchd lft jst over 1f out: styd on ins fnl f: nt rch ldrs* **12/1**[3]

540- **5** *1/2* **Converti**[22] 5148 5-8-9 **54** oh6 .... (b) PaulEddery 5 55
(H J Manners) *hld up and bhd: pushed along over 3f out: rdn 2f out: hdwy over 1f out: one pce ins fnl f* **40/1**

-022 **6** *1 1/2* **My Mate Max**[21] 3073 4-10-0 **73** .... (p) MickyFenton 4 72
(R Hollinshead) *led early: prom: rdn over 1f out: wknd ins fnl f* **11/2**[2]

43 **7** *3/4* **Kristallo (GER)**[6] 3593 4-9-1 **60** .... DaneO'Neill 6 58
(P R Webber) *hld up in tch: ev ch over 2f out: c to stands' side st: rdn wl over 1f out: wknd fnl f* **4/1**[1]

130/ **8** *4* **Secret Ploy**[628] 6335 9-10-0 **73** .... TravisBlock 8 66
(H Morrison) *pushed along to sn ld: rdn over 3f out: hdd over 2f out: wknd jst over 1f out* **11/2**[2]

604- **9** *2 1/2* **Corum (IRE)**[277] 3891 6-9-7 **69** .... LeeVickers(3) 2 58
(Mrs K Waldron) *hld up in tch: settled into mid-div after 3f: rdn and effrt over 1f out: wknd fnl f* **40/1**

3m 16.87s (-2.13) **Going Correction** -0.125s/f (Firm)
WFA 3 from 4yo+ 17lb 9 Ran SP% **114.1**
Speed ratings (Par 103): **100,99,98,98,97 97,96,94,93**
toteswingers: 1&2 £3.60, 1&3 £3.60, 2&3 £6.10 CSF £25.73 CT £118.66 TOTE £4.10: £1.50, £2.00, £2.30; EX 23.60.
Owner Mrs Judith Ratcliff **Bred** Robert And Michelle Dore **Trained** Basford Green, Staffs
■ Stewards' Enquiry : Dane O'Neill caution: careless riding

FOCUS
A modest staying handicap in which they raced middle to stands' side in the straight. The fifth, who was 6lb wrong, casts some doubt on the level of the form.

3789 EUROPEAN BREEDERS' FUND FILLIES' H'CAP 7f 26y
4:05 (4:05) (Class 4) (0-80,80) 3-Y-O+ **£6,799** (£2,023; £1,011; £505) **Stalls Low**

Form RPR

1-33 **1** **Perfect Silence**[27] 2886 4-9-7 **73** .... EddieAhern 1 83
(C G Cox) *chsd ldr: led over 2f out: c to stands' rail st: rdn and hdd wl over 1f out: led ins fnl f: drvn out* **9/4**[2]

0344 **2** *1/2* **Support Fund (IRE)**[25] 2949 5-9-4 **70** .... DaneO'Neill 7 79
(Eve Johnson Houghton) *hld up and bhd: hdwy 2f out: rdn over 1f out: r.o u.p to take 2nd nr fin* **13/2**[3]

-021 **3** *hd* **All For You (IRE)**[12] 3387 3-8-7 **70** .... FrederikTylicki(3) 4 75
(M Botti) *a.p: led wl over 1f out: sn rdn: hdd ins fnl f: no ex and lost 2nd nr fin* **6/4**[1]

-255 **4** *4* **Valatrix (IRE)**[24] 2980 4-9-9 **78** .... JackMitchell(3) 3 76
(C F Wall) *prom: styd alone far side st: rdn over 1f out: btn whn edgd rt ins fnl f* **8/1**

4-40 **5** *1 1/2* **Mamlakati (IRE)**[17] 3219 3-9-4 **78** .... PatDobbs 9 69
(R Hannon) *swtchd lft sn after s: t.k.h in rr: rdn over 1f out: no rspnse* **40/1**

-400 **6** *5* **Aunt Nicola**[27] 2886 3-9-5 **79** .... JamieSpencer 2 56
(M L W Bell) *hld up in tch: lost pl over 2f out: sn struggling* **17/2**

6-00 **7** *1 1/2* **Stand In Flames**[40] 2491 4-9-2 **68** .... ShaneKelly 8 44
(Pat Eddery) *led over 1f: w ldr: c to stands' side and sltly hmpd jst over 2f out: wknd wl over 1f out* **33/1**

1m 23.25s (-1.35) **Going Correction** -0.125s/f (Firm)
WFA 3 from 4yo+ 8lb 7 Ran SP% **111.1**
Speed ratings (Par 102): **102,101,101,96,94 89,87**
toteswingers: 1&2 £2.90, 1&3 £1.70, 2&3 £2.00 CSF £16.15 CT £25.95 TOTE £4.00: £1.70, £2.40; EX 15.60.
Owner Wild Beef Racing (Mr & Mrs R J Vines) **Bred** R J Vines **Trained** Lambourn, Berks

FOCUS
A fair fillies' handicap, well-run and sound form. They all raced towards the stands' side, with the exception of Valatrix.
Aunt Nicola Official explanation: jockey said filly hung right throughout

3790 WARWICKRACECOURSE.CO.UK H'CAP 7f 26y
4:40 (4:40) (Class 5) (0-75,75) 3-Y-O **£2,914** (£867; £433; £216) **Stalls** Low

Form RPR
1-50 **1** **Iasia (GR)**[7] 3548 3-9-7 **75** MichellePayne 5 83
(Jane Chapple-Hyam) *a.p: led wl over 1f out: rdn out* **9/1**
0-65 **2** 3 **Advertise**[12] 3375 3-9-1 **69** NeilChalmers 10 69
(A M Balding) *chsd ldr tl c to stands' side wl over 1f out: sn rdn and edgd rt: kpt on ins fnl f: nt trble wnr* **4/1**[3]
003 **3** 1 1/2 **Ymir**[41] 2431 3-8-3 **57** (p) LiamJones 2 53
(M J Attwater) *led: c to stands' side st: hdd wl over 1f out: sn rdn: no ex and lost 2nd wl ins fnl f* **10/1**
0015 **4** 1 1/2 **Jimwil (IRE)**[24] 2970 3-9-7 **75** (b) PhillipMakin 7 67+
(M Dods) *s.v.s: hld up and bhd: rdn over 1f out: nvr trbld ldrs* **3/1**[2]
0061 **5** shd **Secret Hero**[30] 2797 3-8-11 **65** DaneO'Neill 8 57
(R Hannon) *chsd ldrs: pushed along over 3f out: wknd over 2f out* **13/8**[1]
10 **6** 32 **Special Cuvee**[72] 1595 3-8-13 **67** JamieSpencer 9 —
(A B Haynes) *hld up and bhd: pushed along over 2f out: eased whn no ch over 1f out* **9/1**

1m 24.01s (-0.59) **Going Correction** -0.125s/f (Firm) **6** Ran SP% **112.2**
Speed ratings (Par 100): **98,94,92,91,91 54**
toteswingers: 1&2 £6.60, 1&3 £6.00, 2&3 £6.50 CSF £43.88 CT £366.52 TOTE £11.00: £4.20, £2.80; EX 57.00.
Owner Mrs M Marinopoulos **Bred** Figaia Stud **Trained** Newmarket, Suffolk

FOCUS
Most of these raced stands' side in the straight, but the winner raced up the middle. The form looks weak as the runner-up hasn't been at his best this year, the third's form isn't solid and the fourth blew the start again.
Jimwil(IRE) Official explanation: jockey said gelding missed the break
Secret Hero Official explanation: jockey said colt never travelled
Special Cuvee Official explanation: trainer said gelding was unsuited by the good to firm (good in places) ground

3791 RACING UK MAIDEN STKS 1m 4f 134y
5:15 (5:15) (Class 5) 3-Y-0+ **£2,914** (£867; £433; £216) **Stalls** Low

Form RPR
2 **1** **Doggerbank (IRE)**[17] 3214 3-8-9 0 EddieAhern 2 73+
(H R A Cecil) *chsd ldr tl 9f out: prom: c to stands' rail wl over 1f out: sn rdn: led jst ins fnl f: r.o* **8/11**[1]
-243 **2** nse **Souter Point (USA)**[11] 3425 3-9-0 85 SteveDrowne 7 77+
(R Charlton) *hld up: c to stands' side st: hdwy whn nt clr run over 1f out: rdn and r.o towards fin: jst failed to take 2nd: fin 3rd: plcd 2nd* **11/4**[2]
6 **3** 1 1/4 **Sally Forth**[16] 3250 3-8-9 0 PatDobbs 4 71
(R Charlton) *a.p: wnt 2nd 9f out: c to stands' side st: rdn and ev ch whn edgd rt over 1f out: nt qckn wl ins fnl f: jst hld on for 2nd: plcd 3rd* **25/1**
4 4 **De Soto**[22] 8-10-0 0 (t) DaneO'Neill 5 70
(P R Webber) *s.s: hld up: prog over 7f out: c to stands' side st: btn whn swtchd lft over 1f out* **14/1**
34 **5** 1/2 **Little Prudence**[27] 2877 3-8-9 0 J-PGuillambert 8 64
(R M Beckett) *led: hung rt fr wl over 1f out: rdn and hdd jst ins fnl f: wknd* **6/1**[3]
05 **6** 7 **Warrants Attention (IRE)**[17] 3205 3-9-0 0 NeilChalmers 6 58
(A M Balding) *hld up in rr: pushed along over 2f out: rdn and hung rt over 1f out: sn struggling* **66/1**
7 39 **Thunderonthemount**[110] 4-10-0 0 LiamJones 1 —
(M J Attwater) *t.k.h towards rr: pushed along over 7f out: prog 6f out: wknd over 3f out: eased over 2f out* **100/1**

2m 47.96s (3.36) **Going Correction** -0.125s/f (Firm)
WFA 3 from 4yo+ 14lb **7** Ran SP% **111.9**
Speed ratings: **84,83,83,80,80 76,55**
toteswingers: 1&2 £7.80, 1&3 £1.10, 2&3 £8.60 CSF £2.74 TOTE £1.90: £1.10, £2.40; EX 2.90 Place 6: £647.70 Place 5: £88.44.
Owner G Schoeningh **Bred** Airlie Stud **Trained** Newmarket, Suffolk

FOCUS
An ordinary, steadily run maiden in which they raced stands' side in the straight. The runner-up is becoming disappointing and the winner only had to match his debut form to get off the mark.
Little Prudence Official explanation: jockey said filly hung right
T/Plt: £1,851.30 to a £1 stake. Pool: £41,084.38. 16.20 winning tickets. T/Qpdt: £72.90 to a £1 stake. Pool: £4,289.26. 43.50 winning tickets. KH

3138 ASCOT (R-H)
Friday, July 10

OFFICIAL GOING: Good (good to firm in places; overall 10.0, straight 10.2, round 9.9)
Rail realignment increased distance of 4.45 race by 8yards and 3.00 and 5.20 races by 16yards.
Wind: fairly modest against Weather: overcast

3792 ICAP EBF MAIDEN STKS 6f
2:25 (2:27) (Class 3) 2-Y-0 **£7,771** (£2,312; £1,155; £577) **Stalls** Low

Form RPR
62 **1** **Trailblazing**[16] 3262 2-9-3 0 JoeFanning 9 82+
(M Johnston) *w ldr tl led over 2f out: edgd lft but rdn clr over 1f out: styd on strly fnl f* **5/1**[1]
2 1 1/2 **Taajub (IRE)** 2-9-3 0 LiamJones 3 78+
(W J Haggas) *in tch: lost pl over 3f out: switching rt looking for run over 2f out: chsd wnr and edging rt fr over 1f out: kpt on but no imp* **5/1**[1]
0 **3** 3 1/2 **Sheer Force (IRE)**[29] 2844 2-9-3 0 ShaneKelly 1 67
(W J Knight) *trckd ldrs: hdwy and upsides ldrs gng wl over 2f out: shkn up and nt qckn 2f out: drvn and wandered u.p over 1f out: one pce fnl f* **13/2**[2]
4 shd **Frozen Power (IRE)** 2-9-3 0 NCallan 8 67
(Saeed Bin Suroor) *chsd ldrs: rdn and unable qck jst over 2f out: kpt on same pce fnl f* **5/1**[1]
60 **5** 2 1/2 **He's Invincible**[29] 2853 2-9-3 0 PaulEddery 7 59
(B J Meehan) *s.i.s: hld up in tch towards rr: rdn 3f out: carried rt over 2f out: plugged on same pce fr over 1f out: nvr pce to threaten ldrs* **33/1**
6 3 1/4 **Fireback** 2-9-0 0 DavidProbert(3) 4 52+
(A M Balding) *v.s.a: bhd: rdn 3f out: plugged on past btn horses fnl f: n.d* **10/1**
36 **7** shd **Pintura**[73] 1590 2-9-3 0 TonyCulhane 11 49
(M R Channon) *in tch: rdn over 2f out: drvn and wknd wl over 1f out* **20/1**
8 6 **Satwa Son (IRE)** 2-9-3 0 DO'Donohoe 12 31+
(E A L Dunlop) *wnt rt s: hld up in tch towards rr: rdn over 2f out: sn struggling: wl hld and edging lft whn veered bdly rt over 1f out: eased ins fnl f* **20/1**
023 **9** 1 **Fantastic Prince**[37] 2588 2-9-3 0 SebSanders 2 28+
(P F I Cole) *led narrowly tl rdn and hdd over 2f out: wknd qckly wl over 1f out: eased whn no ch fnl f* **7/1**[3]
10 1 **Tatawor (IRE)** 2-9-3 0 SteveDrowne 10 25
(M P Tregoning) *s.i.s: hld up towards rr: rdn 3f out: struggling and wanting to hang rt ent fnl 2f: sn outpcd and wl btn* **12/1**
05 **11** 12 **House Red (IRE)**[29] 2839 2-8-10 0 HeatherCork(7) 5 —
(B W Hills) *in tch tl dropped to rr over 3f out: t.o* **50/1**

1m 16.42s (2.02) **Going Correction** +0.15s/f (Good) **11** Ran SP% **107.0**
Speed ratings (Par 98): **92,90,85,85,81 77,77,69,68,66 50**
toteswingers: 1&2 £5.20, 1&3 £5.80, 2&3 £11.60 CSF £22.83 TOTE £4.10: £1.60, £2.00, £2.50; EX 24.80 Trifecta £188.30 Pool: £290.14 - 1.14 winning units.
Owner Sheikh Hamdan Bin Mohammed Al Maktoum **Bred** Darley **Trained** Middleham Moor, N Yorks

FOCUS
A dry night led to a change in the going description to good, good to firm in places, with the GoingStick reading 10.2 on the straight course and 9.9 on the round course. There were one or two interesting newcomers in this line-up, but in the end previous experience told.

NOTEBOOK
Trailblazing, having his third start, put his previous experience to good use to come out on top. His rider didn't have to get too serious but the colt still won quite comfortably in the end, and presumably he will go down the nursery route now. (op 6-1 tchd 9-2)
Taajub(IRE) ◆, a half-brother to dual 5f-6f winner Polish Pride, holds an entry in the Gimcrack. He got outpaced at halfway but, once switched, really began to get the hang of things inside the final two furlongs. He showed his inexperience by hanging right, though, and the more professional winner had his measure in the closing stages. He should have learnt plenty from this and should take some beating next time. (op 11-2 tchd 13-2)
Sheer Force(IRE), who finished in midfield behind subsequent July Stakes winner Arcano on his debut in a hot maiden at Newbury, had the stands'-rail draw in one, and tried to make the most of it, but he still looked green when put under pressure and can be expected to step up again from this. (op 5-1 tchd 7-1)
Frozen Power(IRE), who cost 500,000gns, is a half-brother to the dual 1,000 Guineas winner Finsceal Beo. He ran a perfectly satisfactory race on his debut, only being narrowly beaten for third, and should come on for the run. (tchd 9-2 and 11-2)
He's Invincible had been comfortably held in his first two starts but this was more promising and it wouldn't be a surprise to see him do better in nurseries in time.
Fireback missed the break and was soon struggling out the back, but he passed a few late on and looks capable of better with this run under his belt. (tchd 8-1)
Fantastic Prince was disappointing, struggling from two furlongs out and failing to run to the level of his previous two starts.

3793 SPARGONET H'CAP 2m
3:00 (3:00) (Class 3) (0-95,90) 3-Y-0+
£7,477 (£2,239; £1,119; £560; £279; £140) **Stalls** High

Form RPR
2601 **1** **Alanbrooke**[7] 3587 3-8-5 **86** 6ex (b) JoeFanning 2 100+
(M Johnston) *mde all: rdn and qcknd wl clr jst over 2f out: in n.d after: unchal* **4/5**[1]
-114 **2** 5 **Sweetheart**[14] 3346 5-8-10 **72** NCallan 5 79
(Jamie Poulton) *chsd ldng pair: wnt 2nd 4f out: rdn and nt pce of wnr jst over 2f out: plugged on* **9/1**[3]
-533 **3** 2 3/4 **Bernie The Bolt (IRE)**[28] 2881 3-7-9 **79** oh5 DavidProbert(3) 4 83+
(A M Balding) *hld up in last trio: hdwy on outer 3f out: modest 4th and no prog ent fnl 2f: wnt 3rd fnl 100yds: nvr nr wnr* **8/1**[2]
-001 **4** 3/4 **Kasban**[14] 3346 5-8-6 **73** (tp) MartinLane(5) 9 76
(Ian Williams) *in tch in midfield: rdn and chsd ldng pair over 3f out: hrd drvn and no prog over 2f out: lost 3rd fnl 100yds* **12/1**
-060 **5** 13 **Inchnadamph**[28] 2895 9-9-10 **86** (t) TonyCulhane 6 73
(T J Fitzgerald) *hld up in last trio: hdwy on inner over 3f out: rdn and no hdwy over 2f out: wl btn after* **16/1**
00-0 **6** 10 **Whenever**[27] 2931 5-9-0 **76** SteveDrowne 8 51
(R T Phillips) *s.i.s: bustled along early: racd in last trio: pushed along 1/2-way: rdn over 4f out: no ch fnl 2f* **18/1**
-122 **7** 5 **Mr Crystal (FR)**[19] 3191 5-9-1 **80** NeilBrown(3) 3 49
(Micky Hammond) *in tch in midfield: rdn and losing pl over 5f out: drvn and struggling 4f out: t.o over 1f out* **11/1**
13 **8** 65 **Eighteenfifty**[125] 787 5-8-9 **71** ShaneKelly 1 —
(N J Henderson) *chsd wnr tl 4f out: wknd qckly 3f out: virtually p.u fnl 2f: t.o* **9/1**[3]

3m 27.42s (-1.58) **Going Correction** +0.15s/f (Good)
WFA 3 from 4yo+ 19lb **8** Ran SP% **113.8**
Speed ratings (Par 107): **109,106,105,104,98 93,90,58**
toteswingers: 1&2 £2.20, 1&3 £4.90, 2&3 £5.50 CSF £8.73 CT £35.18 TOTE £1.80: £1.10, £1.90, £2.40; EX 8.40 Trifecta £21.90 Pool: £802.63 - 27.04 winning units..
Owner Sheikh Hamdan Bin Mohammed Al Maktoum **Bred** Miss K Rausing **Trained** Middleham Moor, N Yorks

FOCUS
The winner was again impressive in defying a penalty, being value for further than the winning margin, and he looks a smart stayer in the making. The runner-up and fourth ran close to their previous Folkestone form and the level looks solid.

NOTEBOOK
Alanbrooke, who was 4lb well in at the weights under his penalty, enjoyed the run of the race out in front and found plenty when kicked on at the top of the straight. Apparently a lazy sort, the step up to staying distances, coupled with the application of blinkers and adoption of positive tactics has seen him make giant strides, and there is plenty more to come from him in this sphere. Following two quick runs, though, he will now be given a bit of a break. (op 6-5 tchd 5-4 in places)
Sweetheart, who ran one of her best races over hurdles at this venue, tracked the winner throughout and ran a solid race in second, but she had no chance with the improving three-year-old, and the handicapper might just be in charge now. (op 7-1)
Bernie The Bolt(IRE), who was racing from 5lb out of the handicap, was held up in rear and came widest round the bend into the straight. He certainly got the longer trip well. (op 9-1 tchd 7-1)
Kasban, who had Sweetheart back in fourth when successful at Folkestone last time out, couldn't confirm that form on 4lb worse terms. Perhaps the headgear didn't work as well on this occasion. (tchd 16-1)
Inchnadamph threatened to run on for a place turning into the straight but his effort proved short-lived. A stronger all-round pace and quicker ground would have suited him. (op 12-1 tchd 20-1)

The Form Book, Raceform Ltd, Compton, RG20 6NL

Whenever never got into a challenging position. (op 16-1 tchd 20-1)

3794 IRON STAND WINKFIELD NOVICE STKS 7f

3:35 (3:36) (Class 4) 2-Y-O £6,476 (£1,927; £963; £481) Stalls Low

Form				RPR
	1		**Black Spirit (USA)** 2-8-5 0 ....(t) DavidProbert(3) 5	86+
			(C G Cox) *trckd ldng pair: hdwy to ld wl over 1f out: edgd lft u.p over 1f out: r.o wl and a jst holding runner up fnl f* **15/2**	
	2	hd	**Prompter** 2-8-8 0 .... HayleyTurner 7	86+
			(M L W Bell) *hld up in last pair: hdwy on outer 1/2-way: ev ch 2f out: clr w wnr and drvn ent fnl f: r.o but a jst hld* **5/2**1	
	3	5	**Cockney Class (USA)** 2-8-8 0 .... JoeFanning 2	73+
			(B J Meehan) *s.i.s: t.k.h: hld up in tch in rr: shkn up and rn green 2f out: hung rt and pushed along hands and heels fr over 1f out: wnt 3rd ins fnl f: no ch w ldng pair* **12/1**	
0	4	2 1/4	**Suited And Booted (IRE)**13 3395 2-8-12 0 .... SebSanders 1	71
			(R Hannon) *led: pressed ent fnl 2f: rdn and hdd wl over 1f out: wknd u.p over 1f out* **3/1**2	
010	5	1 1/2	**Queen's Hawk**20 3138 2-9-2 0 .... NCallan 4	72
			(D J Coakley) *chsd ldr: ev ch and rdn jst over 2f out: edgd lft u.p wl over 1f out: drvn and wknd over 1f out* **4/1**3	
	6	2 1/4	**Red Courtier** 2-8-8 0 .... SteveDrowne 6	58+
			(P F I Cole) *dwlt: rn green in rr: swtchd lft and hdwy after 2f: chsd ldrs over 4f out: rdn and rn green jst over 2f out: sn btn and bhd* **4/1**3	

1m 28.98s (0.98) **Going Correction** +0.15s/f (Good) **6 Ran SP% 113.0**
Speed ratings (Par 96): **100,99,94,91,89 87**
toteswingers: 1&2 £7.70, 1&3 £6.60, 2&3 £2.10 CSF £26.90 TOTE £10.00: £4.10, £1.90; EX 40.00.
Owner A D Spence **Bred** Arundel Farm Llc **Trained** Lambourn, Berks

FOCUS
Six of the last eight winners had had a previous outing but the majority of this field were making their racecourse debuts, and it was two of the newcomers who fought out the finish. The first two came nicely clear and look good recruits.

NOTEBOOK
Black Spirit(USA) is a half-brother to six winners including Sun Chariot winner Majestic Roi, and, although apparently not fully wound up for his debut, showed plenty of ability to cosily hold off the persistent challenge of Prompter inside the final furlong. He is well regarded and is likely to take his chance in Pattern company next. (op 7-1 tchd 8-1)
Prompter ◆, a son of Motivator out of a half-sister to high-class miler Prior´s Lodge, travelled noticeably well on the outside of the bunch but just came up short in the battle to the line. The winner had the benefit of the rail, though, and with the pair finishing well clear, the form looks sound, and he shouldn't be long in going one better. He was Hayley Turner's first ride back since winning her appeal against a one-year ban from riding on medical grounds (op 7-4 tchd 11-4)
Cockney Class(USA), whose dam was quite a useful triple winner in the US, was far too keen for his own good through the early stages. He can do better for this experience, but his pedigree suggests he might turn out to be at his best over sprint distances. (op 11-1 tchd 14-1)
Suited And Booted(IRE) had shaped with a bit of promise on his debut at Newmarket but, after making the early running, was soon put in his place. He's another bred to be more effective over a sprint trip. (op 11-2)
Queen's Hawk, who finished in midfield in the Chesham on his previous start, was disappointing and might not like this track. (op 7-1 tchd 7-2)
Red Courtier was too green to do himself justice on his debut, but he's out of a Group 2 winning mare and should be capable of better in time. (op 10-3 tchd 3-1)

3795 ALDERMORE H'CAP 6f

4:10 (4:21) (Class 3) (0-90,89) 3-Y-O+ £7,771 (£2,312; £1,155; £577) Stalls Low

Form				RPR
2341	1		**Street Power (USA)**23 3030 4-8-12 74 .... SteveDrowne 4	84
			(J R Gask) *s.i.s: hld up in rr: hdwy on outer 3f out: rdn and edgd lft over 1f out: drvn to ld jst ins fnl f: all out* **7/2**2	
23-1	2	hd	**Cape Rock**28 2880 4-8-13 75 .... PaulDoe 3	84+
			(W J Knight) *t.k.h: trckd ldrs on stands' rail: rdn and effrt 2f out: hanging rt after: r.o fnl 100yds: pressing wnr nr fin: jst hld* **10/1**	
-400	3	1	**Spitfire**41 2470 4-9-13 89 .... TonyCulhane 1	95+
			(J R Jenkins) *wnt rt s: t.k.h: hld up in midfield tl shuffled bk to rr over 3f out: nt clr run and swtchd lft over 1f out: gd hdwy and edging rt 1f out: fin wl: snatched 3rd last stride* **28/1**	
1311	4	hd	**Lemon N Sugar (USA)**28 2886 4-9-6 82 .... ShaneKelly 12	88
			(J Noseda) *w ldr: gng wl over 2f out: pushed into ld over 1f out: rdn ent fnl f: hdd and flashed tail u.p jst ins fnl f: one pce and hld whn short of room nr fin: lost 3rd last stride* **5/2**1	
40-0	5	2 3/4	**Hurricane Spirit (IRE)**21 3091 5-9-9 88 .... MarcHalford(3) 2	85
			(J R Best) *s.i.s: hld up in rr: switching rt looking for run 2f out: nt clr run wl over 1f out tl over 1f out: no hdwy u.p ent fnl f* **20/1**	
1-10	6	4 1/2	**Al Gillani (IRE)**84 1321 4-9-3 79 .... SebSanders 9	61
			(J R Boyle) *t.k.h: hld up wl in tch: shkn up and edging lft wl over 1f out: sn wknd* **20/1**	
0-00	7	nse	**Gentle Guru**48 2271 5-9-7 83 .... LiamJones 10	65
			(R T Phillips) *t.k.h: hld up in midfield: hdwy to chse ldrs 3f out: ev ch and rdn 2f out: edgd lft and wkng whn sltly hmpd jst ins fnl f* **33/1**	
3263	8	4 1/2	**Orpenindeed (IRE)**47 2297 6-9-10 89 ....(p) AndreaAtzeni(3) 8	57
			(M Botti) *led: rdn and hung rt wl over 1f out: wknd over 1f out* **6/1**3	
321-	9	17	**Fabreze**366 3838 4-9-13 89 .... NCallan 6	2+
			(P J Makin) *plld hrd: hld up in tch: shkn up whn nt clr run and bdly hmpd over 1f out: bhd and eased after* **8/1**	

1m 15.84s (1.44) **Going Correction** +0.15s/f (Good) **9 Ran SP% 101.2**
Speed ratings (Par 107): **96,95,94,94,90 84,84,78,55**
toteswingers: 1&2 £3.00, 1&3 £18.90, 2&3 £32.30 CSF £25.90 CT £505.19 TOTE £5.00: £1.90, £3.20, £5.80; EX 31.50 Trifecta £387.00 Part won. Pool: £523.05 - 0.50 winning units..
Owner Horses First Racing Limited **Bred** John Hawkins **Trained** Sutton Veny, Wilts

FOCUS
This looked a decent little sprint handicap on paper, but a false start was called after stalls one and two failed to open, and only Street Power and Cape Rock were successfully restrained by their riders and prevented from going much further than a furlong. It was probably no coincidence that the pair finished first and second in the re-run, with Spitfire, who was one of the two whose stall failed to open first time round, finishing third. Three of the field were declared non-runners after crossing the finishing line, and with the others having taken various amounts out of themselves, the overall form is questionable. The race itself was run at a fairly ordinary early pace. The winner has been rated at face value to his All-Weather mark.

NOTEBOOK
Street Power(USA) had only previously won on Polytrack, but specialists on that surface often go well at this track and, having travelled well towards the outside of the bunch, he quickened up well to take the favourite's measure and held on narrowly from the fast-finishing runner-up. He got in here off a 6lb lower mark than his all-weather rating, so was entitled to run well, and Steve Drowne is now unbeaten in three starts on him, but his success has to be seen in the context of the false start beforehand. (op 6-1)
Cape Rock, who finally got his head in front over 7f at Chepstow last time out, stayed on well along the stands' rail inside the final furlong but just came up short. He is just as effective over this trip as 7f and should continue to run his race. (op 8-1 tchd 12-1)
Spitfire, whose stall didn't open first time round, didn't settle towards the stands' rail, but he still had more energy left than some of his rivals who had run half the track following the false start, and he finished well to take third. This might flatter him. (op 25-1 tchd 33-1)
Lemon N Sugar(USA) ◆ impressed in winning at Goodwood last time and the form had been given a couple of boosts by the third and fourth going in next time so a 7lb higher mark looked very fair. However, she was drawn on the wide outside and she'd gone half a furlong before her rider realised that there was a false start and she went further than the eventual winner and second before her rider was able to dismount and walk her back to the start. In the re-run she showed up well throughout and simply lacked that little bit extra at the finish, which was perfectly understandable in the circumstances, and she looks very much the one to take from the race. (op 11-4 tchd 9-4 and 3-1 in places)
Hurricane Spirit(IRE) was the other one fortunate enough to have his stall fail to open and his energy preserved for the race proper. He still looks too high in the handicap. (op 25-1 tchd 33-1)
Al Gillani(IRE) raced keenly having taken a while to pull up after the false start. (op 14-1)
Gentle Guru was another keen in the race itself.
Orpenindeed(IRE) went further than most after the false start and ran below market expectations. His effort in the re-run can be ignored. (op 9-1)
Fabreze was another who took a long time to pull up after the false start, and he also pulled hard in the race itself. (op 15-2)

3796 GOUDHURST GAME H'CAP 1m (R)

4:45 (4:50) (Class 3) (0-95,90) 3-Y-O+ £7,771 (£2,312; £1,155; £577) Stalls High

Form				RPR
-400	1		**Dubai's Touch**15 3312 5-10-0 90 ....(b1) JoeFanning 9	103
			(M Johnston) *s.i.s: bhd: hdwy over 3f out: chsd ldr over 2f out: rdn to ld 2f out: sn clr: styd on wl* **12/1**	
01	2	3	**One Way Or Another (AUS)**20 3154 6-9-13 89 .... ClareLindop 5	95
			(J R Gask) *t.k.h: hld up in tch in rr: hmpd jst over 3f out: nt clr run 3f out tl swtchd lft and hdwy over 2f out: chsd wnr over 1f out: edgd rt and no imp fnl f* **10/3**1	
-013	3	2 1/4	**Sarah Park (IRE)**15 3301 4-9-0 76 .... ShaneKelly 10	77
			(B J Meehan) *led: rdn and kicked on 3f out: hdd 2f out: sn outpcd by wnr: wl hld fnl f: plugged on* **9/1**	
5-35	4	2 1/2	**Stevie Thunder**54 2101 4-9-7 88 ....(t) MartinLane(5) 6	88+
			(Ian Williams) *chsd ldrs tl bdly hmpd and shuffled bk over 3f out: switching lft and n.m.r wl over 2f out: no ch fnl 2f* **11/2**	
-600	5	nk	**Isphahan**41 2480 6-9-6 85 ....(v) DavidProbert(3) 1	79
			(A M Balding) *prom on outer: chsd ldr 3f out: shkn up and fnd nil over 2f out: sn edging rt and wl btn* **9/1**	
106	6	7	**Spring Goddess (IRE)**24 3008 8-9-5 81 .... TonyCulhane 11	59
			(A P Jarvis) *stdd s: hld up in rr: c wd and hdwy over 2f out: sn no prog and wl btn* **40/1**	
0346	7	nk	**Cape Hawk (IRE)**12 3431 5-9-9 85 .... PatDobbs 4	63+
			(R Hannon) *hld up wl in tch: hmpd over 3f out: nt clr run and hmpd again wl over 2f out: trying to make hdwy on inner whn hit in face by rivals whip 2f out: no ch* **5/1**3	
40-2	8	nk	**Motafarred (IRE)**16 3265 7-8-13 78 .... NeilBrown(3) 3	55
			(Micky Hammond) *w ldrs: pushed along and edgd rt over 3f out: losing pl whn edgd rt again wl over 2f out: no ch after* **9/2**2	
5000	9	16	**Bomber Command (USA)**62 1861 6-8-10 75 ....(bt) PatrickHills(3) 2	15
			(J W Hills) *w ldrs: wnt 2nd over 3f out tl 3f out: wkng u.p whn edgd rt jst over 2f out: t.o fnl f* **12/1**	

1m 41.56s (0.86) **Going Correction** +0.15s/f (Good) **9 Ran SP% 111.1**
Speed ratings (Par 107): **101,98,95,93,92 85,85,85,69**
toteswingers: 1&2 £31.70, 1&3 £20.80, 2&3 £4.30 CSF £49.11 CT £369.96 TOTE £9.80: £2.10, £1.50, £2.20; EX 46.50 Trifecta £494.90 Part won. Pool: £668.81 - 0.43 winning units..
Owner Salem Suhail **Bred** Miss S N Ralphs **Trained** Middleham Moor, N Yorks
■ Stewards' Enquiry : Neil Brown five-day ban: careless riding (Jul 24 - 28)

FOCUS
Not a bad handicap class-wise, but in-form horses were thin on the ground. They went a good gallop and the first two came from off the pace. The runner-up is the guide to the level of the form.

NOTEBOOK
Dubai's Touch had been well held in his previous three starts this term but as a result he'd been dropped 12lb to a career-low mark. Down in grade, blinkered for the first time and representing a stable very much in form, he travelled up sweetly in the straight, got first run on the favourite and held him off comfortably. This was a dramatic return to form and presumably he will now go for the totesport Mile at Goodwood, a race in which he was third last year off 100, and for which he picks up a 3lb penalty. He was cut by a few firms but 40-1 was still available post-race. (op 16-1)
One Way Or Another(AUS) got the good pace he needs but he was still fairly keen. Hampered on the turn into the straight, he tended to hang right when going in pursuit of the winner, and could make no impression. (tchd 3-1 and 7-2)
Sarah Park(IRE) took them along but was not left alone in front. As a result she simply helped set it up for the closers. Third was a good effort in the circumstances and she remains one to be interested in when looking likely to get her own way. (op 13-2 tchd 10-1)
Stevie Thunder, who was badly hampered on the turn into the straight, shaped a bit better than the bare form. His best efforts have come on softer ground. (op 4-1)
Isphahan was done no favours by being brought widest around the home bend having disputed the pace up front. He predictably found little in the closing stages. (op 10-1)
Cape Hawk(IRE), whose last win came in this race last year off a 4lb higher mark, endured a rough passage and not too many conclusions should be drawn from this effort. He is already due to be dropped 2lb in future handicaps. (op 6-1 tchd 13-2)

3797 STONELL APPRENTICE H'CAP 1m 4f

5:20 (5:20) (Class 4) (0-85,85) 4-Y-O+ £7,123 (£2,119; £1,059; £529) Stalls High

Form				RPR
-143	1		**Run For Ede's**1 3766 5-8-6 70 .... JackDean(3) 5	79
			(P M Phelan) *stdd s: t.k.h: hld up wl bhd: hdwy 6f out: rdn to chse clr ldr over 2f out: clsd u.p over 1f out: swtchd lft ins fnl f: sn led: styd on* **10/1**	
-033	2	1/2	**Relative Strength (IRE)**21 3103 4-9-1 76 ....(v) DavidProbert 7	84
			(A M Balding) *chsd ldr: allowed ldr to go wl clr over 8f out: lost 2nd over 5f out: drvn to chse ldr 3f out tl over 2f out: clsd ent fnl f: wnt 2nd fnl 75yds: kpt on* **4/1**3	
-401	3	1	**Dakiyah (IRE)**16 3273 5-9-3 81 ....(p) RossAtkinson(3) 8	87
			(Mrs L J Mongan) *racd wl off the pce in midfield: stl plenty to do and swtchd to outer and rdn over 2f out: swtchd rt over 1f out: edgd rt after: styd on wl to go 3rd wl ins fnl f: kpt on* **10/1**	
4006	4	2	**Capable Guest (IRE)**19 3189 7-9-2 80 ....(v) MCGeran(3) 6	83
			(M R Channon) *t.k.h early: hld up wl off the pce in midfield: dropped to rr over 3f out: rdn over 2f out: styd on to go 4th wl ins fnl f: nvr trbld ldrs* **20/1**	
0300	5	3/4	**Robby Bobby**20 3180 4-9-3 83 .... MatthewLawson(5) 2	85
			(M Johnston) *racd freely: led: drew wl clr over 8f out: 10 l clr 3f out: rdn 2f out: hung lft over 1f out: hdd fnl 100yds: fdd* **16/1**	

4455 **6** *3* **Profit's Reality (IRE)**[7] 3587 7-9-1 **79**...................... WilliamCarson(3) 3 76
(M J Attwater) *racd off the pce in midfield: pushed along 3f out: no hdwy u.p over 2f out* **20/1**

0-03 **7** *3 3/4* **Overturn (IRE)**[18] 3213 5-9-10 **85**...................................... AndreaAtzeni 1 76
(W R Swinburn) *rrd s and v.s.a: wl bhd: sme hdwy 5f out: rdn and no prog over 2f out* **11/4**[2]

5012 **8** *6* **Gifted Leader (USA)**[27] 2932 4-9-5 **83**.............................. MartinLane(3) 4 65
(Ian Williams) *t.k.h: chsd ldrs: chsd clr ldr over 5f out tl 3f out: sn wknd* **5/2**[1]

-600 **9** *33* **Paktolos (FR)**[37] 2597 6-9-3 **83**..................................(b) SimonPearce(5) 9 12
(A King) *s.i.s: hld up wl in rr: lost tch over 3f out: t.o* **12/1**

2m 34.3s (1.80) **Going Correction** +0.15s/f (Good) **9** Ran SP% **116.5**
Speed ratings (Par 105): **100,99,99,97,97 95,92,88,66**
toteswingers: 1&2 £6.50, 1&3 £14.30, 2&3 £4.40 CSF £50.28 CT £410.88 TOTE £14.30: £3.40, £1.80, £3.50; EX 64.50 Trifecta £453.00 Pool: £801.98 - 1.31 winning units. Place 6: £100.36 Place 5: £56.39..
Owner Ede's (uk) Ltd **Bred** Mrs James Wigan & London TB Services Ltd **Trained** Epsom, Surrey

FOCUS
No more than a fair handicap, and they went only steady early, but Robby Bobby raced freely in front, keen to go faster, and in the end Matthew Lawson relented and let his mount stride on. The form is messy but has been rated around the third to her recent All-Weather win.
Robby Bobby Official explanation: jockey said gelding ran too free
Overturn(IRE) Official explanation: jockey said the gelding reared leaving the stalls
Paktolos(FR) Official explanation: jockey said gelding never travelled
T/Plt: £72.60 to a £1 stake. Pool: £71,207.76. 715.96 winning tickets. T/Qpdt: £22.20 to a £1 stake. Pool: £4,080.81. 135.80 winning tickets. SP

3500 CHEPSTOW (L-H)
Friday, July 10

OFFICIAL GOING: Good to firm (good in places)
Wind: mild breeze Weather: overcast with light showers

3798 CROWN AT WHITEBROOK APPRENTICE H'CAP — 1m 4f 23y
6:30 (6:30) (Class 5) (0-70,68) 4-Y-0+ **£2,590** (£770; £385; £192) **Stalls** Low

Form RPR

-362 **1** **Sir Boss (IRE)**[11] 3450 4-9-10 **68**...................................... RosieJessop 2 78+
(D E Cantillon) *t.k.h in rr: smooth hdwy to ld on bit over 3f out: sn pushed clr: comf* **10/11**[1]

306- **2** *2 1/2* **Bert's Memory**[209] 7658 5-8-4 **51** oh1 ow2.................. DebraEngland(3) 6 55
(Jennie Candlish) *mid-div: hdwy over 3f out: rdn to chse wnr wl over 2f out: sn hung rt: styd on but nvr any ch* **20/1**

000/ **3** *4 1/2* **Picot De Say**[63] 5886 7-8-2 **49** oh1.............................. RichardRowe(3) 9 46
(C Roberts) *hld up towards rr: hdwy 3f out: sn rdn: styd on same pce* **9/2**[3]

0-50 **4** *6* **Great View (IRE)**[47] 2294 10-8-9 **58**..................................(p) LauraPike(5) 8 45
(Mrs A L M King) *slowly away: bhd: styd on past btn horses fr 2f out: nvr a threat* **4/1**[2]

600/ **5** *1/2* **Waziri (IRE)**[460] 5587 8-8-0 **49** oh4..................... JosephineBruning(5) 10 35
(M Hill) *t.k.h: trckd ldrs: rdn 3f out: wknd over 1f out* **66/1**

4000 **6** *2 1/2* **Bespoke Boy**[18] 3206 4-8-5 **52**.. DavidKenny(3) 4 34
(Mrs N S Evans) *led tl over 3f out: sn rdn: wknd over 1f out* **33/1**

00 **7** *1 1/2* **Tara's Garden**[29] 2859 4-8-7 **51**.. PNolan 5 31
(M Blanshard) *w ldr: rdn 4f out: sn hld: wknd 2f out* **25/1**

0-60 **8** *7* **Sweet Request**[95] 1156 5-7-12 **49** oh3..............(b[1]) MatthewCosham(7) 3 18
(Dr J R J Naylor) *trckd ldrs: effrt 4f out: wknd over 2f out* **40/1**

06 **P** **Mito**[9] 3503 8-8-5 **49** oh1.. JemmaMarshall 1 —
(B R Millman) *t.k.h: trckd ldrs: sddle slipped and jnd ldr over 5f out tl 4f out: bhd whn p.u 2f out: nt rcvr* **15/2**

2m 35.13s (-3.87) **Going Correction** -0.225s/f (Firm) **9** Ran SP% **117.8**
Speed ratings (Par 103): **103,101,98,94,94 92,91,86,—**
toteswingers: 1&2 £0.00, 1&3 £1.10, 2&3 £6.90 CSF £27.14 CT £63.05 TOTE £2.10: £1.10, £3.30, £1.40; EX 18.50.
Owner Don Cantillon Racing **Bred** Mrs E R Cantillon **Trained** Newmarket, Suffolk

FOCUS
A weak apprentice riders' race in which Sir Boss ran out a convincing winner on his first try at the trip.
Mito Official explanation: jockey said that her saddle slipped

3799 E.B.F./LINDLEY CATERING NOVICE STKS — 5f 16y
7:00 (7:01) (Class 4) 2-Y-0 **£5,180** (£1,541; £770; £384) **Stalls** High

Form RPR

2 **1** **Roodle**[16] 3277 2-8-7 0.. AlanMunro 2 77
(Eve Johnson Houghton) *little slowly away and bmpd: chsd ldrs: rdn whn swtchd lft 2f out: r.o wl to ld ins fnl f: drvn out* **13/2**

021 **2** *nk* **Virginia Hall**[11] 3458 2-8-11 0.. SebSanders 6 80
(Sir Mark Prescott) *led: rdn 2f out: drifted lft and hdd ins fnl f: kpt on* **2/1**[1]

4 **3** *2* **Waveband**[10] 3478 2-8-7 0.. AndrewMullen 4 69+
(M Johnston) *little slowly away and bmpd: chsd ldrs: rdn over 2f out: styd on to go 3rd nr fin: nt pce to mount chal* **15/2**

1230 **4** *3/4* **Red Avalanche (IRE)**[24] 2995 2-9-5 0............................... JimmyQuinn 1 78
(P F I Cole) *prom: rdn and ev ch fr 2f out tl 1f out: kpt on same pce* **4/1**[3]

621 **5** *7* **Palisades Park**[18] 3218 2-9-2 0... SteveDrowne 5 50
(R Hannon) *prom: rdn over 2f out: wknd jst over 1f out* **9/4**[2]

58.86 secs (-0.44) **Going Correction** -0.325s/f (Firm) **5** Ran SP% **109.2**
Speed ratings (Par 96): **90,89,86,85,73**
CSF £19.53 TOTE £7.80: £2.40, £1.30; EX 15.90.
Owner Mrs R F Johnson Houghton **Bred** Mrs H Johnson Houghton & Mrs R F Johnson Hought **Trained** Blewbury, Oxon

FOCUS
This had the feel of a decent novice stakes with the runner-up setting the level of the form.

NOTEBOOK
Roodle ◆ justified her tall home reputation by seeing off three previous winners. Still very green, the homebred filly was slowly away from the starting stalls, but settled well behind the leaders. Once switched out to make her challenge, she responded well to a couple of smacks of the whip. She looked inexperienced once in front, but had enough in the locker to hold on from the more experienced runner-up. She looks a nice filly and it was significant that she was allowed to take on previous winners rather than win her maiden. Connections intimated that they'll be looking for some black type for her now, so a Listed race for fillies looks on the cards. (op 6-1 tchd 11-2 and 7-1)
Virginia Hall boxed on gamely, having always been front rank. Although she lacks the scope of the winner, she was conceding 4lb to that rival. This was no mean effort and there are more races to be won with her. (op 15-8 tchd 13-8)
Waveband could never get into it, but kept on well up the stands' rail to suggest she has come on for her debut. (op 10-1 tchd 12-1)
Red Avalanche(IRE) was the most experienced horse in the field. He bounced back from a disappointing effort in the Windsor Castle Stakes, but is pretty exposed. Although he ran well, giving weight all round proved beyond him. Nurseries are likely to be his bag now. (tchd 9-2)
Palisades Park dropped right away and this was not his true running. (op 5-2 tchd 2-1)

3800 "WAITROSE CALDICOT IS NOW OPEN" H'CAP — 1m 14y
7:35 (7:43) (Class 5) (0-70,70) 3-Y-0+ **£3,238** (£963; £481; £240) **Stalls** High

Form RPR

6253 **1** **Sir Ike (IRE)**[133] 706 4-9-8 **61**...(t) ShaneKelly 8 71
(W S Kittow) *trckd ldrs: led over 2f out: sn rdn: hrd pressed thrght fnl f: hld on gamely: all out* **10/1**

30-0 **2** *hd* **Chatanoogachoochoo**[41] 2493 4-9-7 **60**......................... JimmyQuinn 3 69
(M Hill) *bmpd s: mid-div: hdwy 3f out: rdn 2f out: str chal thrght fnl f: jst hld* **11/1**

3-40 **3** *4 1/2* **Russian Angel**[22] 3074 5-8-9 **48** oh2............................ FergusSweeney 6 47
(Jean-Rene Auvray) *hld up towards rr: hdwy 3f out: rdn to chse ldrs 2f out: cl enough 3rd whn little short of room and swtchd lft 1f out: nt pce of ldrs ins fnl f* **20/1**

2264 **4** *1* **Red Suede Shoes**[15] 3309 3-9-5 **70**............................ JamesMillman(3) 4 65
(B R Millman) *squeezed out s: towards rr: hdwy in centre over 2f out: sn rdn: styd on same pce fnl f* **8/1**

1-60 **5** *nk* **Addiena**[35] 2684 5-9-10 **63**... AlanMunro 12 59
(B Palling) *led for 2f: prom: rdn 3f out: one pce fnl 2f* **14/1**

3335 **6** *1* **Tignello (IRE)**[11] 3463 4-9-7 **60**.. GeorgeBaker 2 57
(G L Moore) *bmpd s: prom: rdn over 2f out: sn one pce: hmpd ins fnl f* **3/1**[1]

0535 **7** *hd* **Libre**[10] 3490 9-9-2 **55**.. SebSanders 5 48
(F Jordan) *wnt sltly lft s: towards rr: struggling and hanging lft 4f out: sme prog 3f out but nvr trbld ldrs* **15/2**

3022 **8** *1/2* **Amber Ridge**[21] 3112 4-9-0 **53**.. JamesDoyle 9 45
(B P J Baugh) *prom: rdn over 3f out: wknd over 1f out* **9/2**[2]

0063 **9** *4 1/2* **Charles Darwin (IRE)**[20] 3159 6-10-0 **67**.......................... SteveDrowne 1 49
(M Blanshard) *hld up: a in rr* **12/1**

/00- **10** *1 1/4* **Heavenly Saint**[327] 5119 4-9-0 **58**......................... ByronMoorcroft(5) 10 37
(C Roberts) *mid-div: hdwy 3f out: sn rdn: wknd over 1f out* **50/1**

5110 **11** *3/4* **Prince Rossi (IRE)**[14] 3357 5-9-8 **61**.................................(v) EddieAhern 7 38
(A E Price) *s.i.s: sn swtchd to standside rails: hdwy to ld after 2f: rdn whn hdd over 2f out: sn wknd* **11/2**[3]

0004 **12** *2 1/4* **Jay Gee Wigmo**[12] 3432 4-8-9 **48**.. TolleyDean 11 20
(A W Carroll) *chsd ldrs for over 3f* **33/1**

1m 34.48s (-1.72) **Going Correction** -0.325s/f (Firm)
WFA 3 from 4yo+ 9lb **12** Ran SP% **122.9**
Speed ratings (Par 103): **95,94,90,89,89 88,87,87,82,81 80,78**
toteswingers: 1&2 not won, 2&3 not won 1&3 not won CSF £117.24 CT £2207.37 TOTE £14.10: £3.70, £4.60, £6.10; EX 232.60.
Owner Mrs Susan Arnesen **Bred** Martin Francis **Trained** Blackborough, Devon

FOCUS
An ordinary contest, but it produced a stirring finish with a protracted duel throughout the final furlong, and the pair, who have run personal bests, pulled well clear of the rest.
Tignello(IRE) Official explanation: jockey said the gelding was denied a clear run
Prince Rossi(IRE) Official explanation: jockey said that the gelding became upset prior to the start

3801 THE CROWN AT CELTIC MANOR H'CAP — 7f 16y
8:05 (8:11) (Class 4) (0-85,80) 3-Y-0+ **£5,180** (£1,541; £770; £384) **Stalls** High

Form RPR

0-00 **1** **Arthur's Edge**[25] 2977 5-9-2 **69**... SteveDrowne 8 78
(B Palling) *mde all: kpt on wl to assert ent fnl f: rdn out* **16/1**

501 **2** *1 1/4* **Ocean Transit (IRE)**[25] 2976 4-9-13 **80**........................... JamesDoyle 9 86
(R J Price) *prom: rdn over 2f out: kpt on but hld ent fnl f* **10/1**

1230 **3** *1/2* **Head Down**[14] 3341 3-9-0 **78**.. PatrickHills(3) 10 80
(R Hannon) *in tch: nt clr run on rails 3f out tl 2f out: rdn whn swtchd lft for effrt over 1f out: drifted lft and no ex ins fnl f* **9/1**

3-62 **4** *nse* **Greensward**[27] 2926 3-9-5 **80**.. EddieAhern 4 82
(B J Meehan) *s.i.s: bhd: hdwy over 3f out: rdn to chal for 2nd over 1f out: kpt on same pce ins fnl f* **2/1**[1]

5310 **5** *2 3/4* **Carlitos Spirit (IRE)**[14] 3357 5-9-10 **80**..................... JamesMillman(3) 7 77
(B R Millman) *chsd ldrs tl rdn over 3f out: styd on same pce fnl 2f* **9/1**

0542 **6** *3/4* **Bere Davis (FR)**[9] 3504 4-9-6 **73**... AlanMunro 1 68
(P D Evans) *rrd leaving stalls: in last trio but racd alone in centre: hdwy over 3f: sn rdn: fdd fnl f* **11/4**[2]

5412 **7** *hd* **Desert Dreamer (IRE)**[8] 3523 8-9-8 **80**........................ RichardEvans(5) 3 75
(P D Evans) *s.i.s: in last pair: hdwy over 3f out: effrt over 2f out: wknd over 1f out* **11/2**[3]

32/0 **8** *3 3/4* **Apex**[16] 3274 8-9-2 **74**... AmyBaker(5) 5 58
(M Hill) *chsd ldrs: effrt over 2f out: wknd over 1f out* **12/1**

1m 22.04s (-1.16) **Going Correction** -0.325s/f (Firm)
WFA 3 from 4yo+ 8lb **8** Ran SP% **118.1**
Speed ratings (Par 105): **93,91,91,90,87 86,86,82**
toteswingers: 1&2 £6.40, 2&3 not won 1&3 not won CSF £166.73 CT £1076.34 TOTE £19.70: £5.10, £3.50, £3.20; EX 269.30.
Owner Mrs Annabelle Mason **Bred** Christopher J Mason **Trained** Tredodridge, Vale Of Glamorgan

FOCUS
A turn-up as Arthur's Edge saw off all challengers from the front to bounce back to form.

3802 CROWN HOTELS & RESTAURANTS SPRINT (HANDICAP STKS) — 6f 16y
8:40 (8:40) (Class 2) (0-100,98) 3-Y-£12,616 (£3,776; £1,888; £944; £470) **Stalls** High

Form RPR

3245 **1** **Thebes**[13] 3389 4-9-6 **90**.. JimmyQuinn 8 101
(M Johnston) *led for 1f: prom: led 3f out: shkn up to qcknd clr over 1f out: readily* **9/4**[1]

4501 **2** *6* **Barons Spy (IRE)**[15] 3318 8-9-3 **87**.................................. JamesDoyle 3 78
(R J Price) *trckd ldrs: rdn over 2f out: kpt on to go 2nd ent fnl f but no ch w wnr* **7/1**

00-6 **3** *3/4* **Viking Spirit**[13] 3405 7-9-13 **97**..(t) ShaneKelly 9 86
(W R Swinburn) *hld up: hdwy over 3f out: rdn over 2f out: kpt on but nt pce to mount chal* **15/2**

2260 **4** *nk* **Millfields Dreams**[6] 3639 10-8-5 **80** oh6 ow2............ MarkCoumbe(5) 10 68
(G C Bravery) *s.i.s: towards rr: struggling 1/2-way: hdwy whn nt clr run and swtchd off rails over 1f out: r.o* **12/1**

230- **5** *2* **Ginobili (IRE)**[272] 6644 3-9-8 **98**...................................(b[1]) SebSanders 7 80
(Stef Liddiard) *plld hrd: led after 1f: hdd 3f out: sn rdn: remained chsng wnr tl fdd fnl f* **8/1**

0503 **6** *nk* **Phantom Whisper**[15] 3318 6-9-3 **87**.................................. AlanMunro 4 68
(B R Millman) *struggling fr over 3f out: nvr bttr than mid-div* **13/2**[3]

06-0 **7** *1* **Pearly Wey**[20] 3141 6-9-12 **96**.. EddieAhern 2 73
(C G Cox) *awkward leaving stalls: hld up: rdn over 3f out: little imp* **7/1**

000- **8** ¾ **Galeota (IRE)**[244] 7243 7-9-6 **97** CharlesEddery(7) 6 72
(R Hannon) *s.i.s: sn mid-div: rdn 3f out: wknd over 1f out* **22/1**

1-40 **9** 3 ¼ **Osiris Way**[20] 3141 7-9-10 **94** GeorgeBaker 1 59
(P R Chamings) *chsd ldrs: rdn 3f out: wknd over 1f out* **11/2**[2]

69.55 secs (-2.45) **Going Correction** -0.325s/f (Firm)
WFA 3 from 4yo+ 6lb **9** Ran SP% **119.4**
Speed ratings (Par 109): **109,101,100,99,96 96,95,94,89**
toteswingers: 1&2 £4.80, 1&3 not won, 2&3 not won CSF £19.23 CT £104.98 TOTE £3.40: £1.30, £2.30, £2.60; EX 17.10.
Owner Sheikh Hamdan Bin Mohammed Al Maktoum **Bred** Whitsbury Manor Stud And Mrs M E Slade **Trained** Middleham Moor, N Yorks

FOCUS
This looked a competitive sprint handicap on paper, but in a race where several were not at their best it was turned into a rout.

NOTEBOOK
Thebes quickened clear about a furlong and a half out and was out on his own passing the furlong marker. He maintained his advantage, thrashing his rivals and continuing the cracking form of his stable. He relished the return to quicker ground, having not run to his capabilities on soft at Newcastle last time. This performance underlines what a force he is when on song and given his favoured conditions. (op 4-1)
Barons Spy(IRE) was no match for the winner, but saw the hill out well enough to hold off the rest. Given he was racing off a 4lb higher mark than when scoring at Warwick last time, this was another good run. (op 6-1)
Viking Spirit stayed on from off the pace and appears to be working his way back to form. His stable have been fairly quiet recently, but they have had a couple of winners in the last day or two and this was another decent performance. (op 13-2 tchd 8-1)
Millfields Dreams was last early, but did plenty of late running to grab fourth. Although he was never a threat, this was encouraging given he was effectively racing from 8lb out of the handicap including the 2lb overweight. (op 16-1 tchd 18-1)
Ginobili(IRE) was less exposed than most and, although he faded away having been front rank early, he showed good speed and is sure to come on for this first start in 272 days. (op 11-1)
Osiris Way Official explanation: jockey said the gelding lost its action

3803 JOIN CHEPSTOW RACECOURSE WINE CLUB @ WINEAUX.CO.UK FILLIES' H'CAP — 1m 14y
9:10 (9:12) (Class 5) (0-70,69) 3-Y-O **£3,238** (£963; £481; £240) **Stalls** High

Form RPR

-620 **1** **Ethics Girl (IRE)**[31] 2790 3-9-0 62 AlanMunro 10 75
(John Berry) *mid-div: rdn over 2f out: hdwy over 1f out: swtchd lft ent fnl f: r.o strly: led nr fin* **5/1**[3]

0-41 **2** *hd* **Royal Superlative**[18] 3207 3-9-5 67 SebSanders 9 79
(R M Beckett) *prom: led over 2f out: sn rdn: ct nr fin* **3/1**[1]

0250 **3** *7* **Jewelled Reef (IRE)**[13] 3387 3-8-12 60 ShaneKelly 3 56
(Eve Johnson Houghton) *mid-div: hdwy 2f out: effrt over 1f out: fdd ins fnl f: jst hld on for 3rd* **8/1**

5622 **4** *nse* **Some Sunny Day**[7] 3581 3-9-7 69 SteveDrowne 1 65
(H Morrison) *wnt lft s: sn struggling and detached: hdwy over 1f out: styd wl ins fnl f: jst failed to snatch 3rd: nvr nrr* **4/1**[2]

-130 **5** ½ **Second To Nun (IRE)**[26] 2950 3-8-12 60 FergusSweeney 2 55
(Jean-Rene Auvray) *prom for 3f: sn rdn: wknd over 1f out* **12/1**

-005 **6** 2 ½ **Queen Of Thebes (IRE)**[13] 3387 3-9-6 68 (t) GeorgeBaker 6 57
(G L Moore) *led tl over 2f out: sn rdn: wknd over 1f out* **8/1**

604 **7** *hd* **Rockabout (IRE)**[18] 3221 3-8-12 60 EddieAhern 4 49
(B J Meehan) *chsd ldrs: rdn over 2f out: wknd wl over 1f out* **8/1**

05-5 **8** *9* **Peal Park**[35] 2652 3-8-7 55 JimmyQuinn 8 23
(Karen George) *rrd bdly leaving stalls: a in rr* **25/1**

600- **9** *21* **Jarrah Bay**[256] 7015 3-8-4 52 AndrewMullen 7 —
(J G M O'Shea) *plld hrd: hld up towards rr: wknd wl over 1f out* **33/1**

1m 34.15s (-2.05) **Going Correction** -0.325s/f (Firm) **9** Ran SP% **109.5**
Speed ratings (Par 97): **97,96,89,89,89 86,86,77,56**
toteswingers: 1&2 £1.60, 1&3 £16.50, 2&3 £7.60 CSF £17.03 CT £77.03 TOTE £5.90: £2.10, £1.60, £2.80; EX 21.10 Place 6: £511.77 Place 5: £368.63.
Owner The 1997 Partnership **Bred** Newsells Park Stud **Trained** Newmarket, Suffolk
■ Stewards' Enquiry : Alan Munro one-day ban: used whip without giving filly time to respond (Jul 24)

FOCUS
A fair race for the grade with the much improved front pair fighting out a cracking finish.
Peal Park Official explanation: jockey said that the filly reared leaving the stalls
Jarrah Bay Official explanation: jockey said that the filly failed to handle the track
T/Plt: £403.20 to a £1 stake. Pool: £51,120.51. 92.54 winning tickets. T/Qpdt: £141.60 to a £1 stake. Pool: £4,308.06. 22.50 winning tickets. TM

3370 CHESTER (L-H)
Friday, July 10

OFFICIAL GOING: Good to firm
Rail realignment increased distances by around 10yards per circuit and the false rail was in place.
Wind: Almost nil Weather: Fine

3804 RIPPLEFFECT.COM H'CAP — 7f 122y
6:40 (6:41) (Class 4) (0-80,78) 3-Y-O **£5,828** (£1,734; £866; £432) **Stalls** Low

Form RPR

6036 **1** **Athania (IRE)**[16] 3281 3-8-8 65 (v1) RichardMullen 8 69
(A P Jarvis) *wnt lft s: stdd and sn swtchd lft: hld up towards rr: hdwy on outside wl over 1f out: sn rdn: r.o to ld wl ins fnl f* **28/1**

3313 **2** 1 ¼ **Rio Cobolo (IRE)**[6] 3616 3-8-7 64 (v) SilvestreDeSousa 3 65
(Paul Green) *a.p on ins: rdn to ld over 1f out: hdd and no ex wl ins fnl f* **5/2**[1]

30-2 **3** *nk* **Toledo Gold (IRE)**[15] 3316 3-9-7 78 GrahamGibbons 9 78
(E J Alston) *led: rdn and hdd over 1f out: no ex wl ins fnl f* **6/1**[2]

4210 **4** ¾ **Doc Jones (IRE)**[23] 3028 3-9-3 74 StephenDonohoe 6 72+
(P D Evans) *wnt rt s: hld up in tch: rdn and ev ch over 1f out: nt qckn ins fnl f* **11/1**

0250 **5** ½ **Al Mugtareb (IRE)**[15] 3316 3-9-1 72 AdrianTNicholls 2 69
(M Johnston) *s.i.s: sn pushed along in rr: reminder over 4f out: rdn and hdwy on outside over 1f out: nvr able to chal* **17/2**

2531 **6** 1 ½ **Kammaan**[14] 3352 3-9-7 78 PhilipRobinson 1 71
(M A Jarvis) *hld up: hdwy on ins wl over 1f out: no imp fnl f* **5/2**[1]

650 **7** *1* **Lucky Dan (IRE)**[15] 3304 3-8-3 60 FrancisNorton 4 56+
(Paul Green) *t.k.h: sn in tch: hmpd and lost pl wl over 1f out: n.d after* **20/1**

2030 **8** ½ **Richo**[20] 3163 3-9-6 77 (b) PaulMulrennan 7 67
(D H Brown) *hmpd s: sn swtchd lft: hld up towards rr: nt clr run on ins wl over 1f out: n.d after* **15/2**[3]

140- **9** *6* **Amber Sunset**[244] 7241 3-9-4 78 KevinGhunowa(3) 5 53
(J Jay) *chsd ldr: ev ch 2f out: sn rdn and wknd* **16/1**

1m 33.92s (0.12) **Going Correction** -0.025s/f (Good) **9** Ran SP% **116.1**
Speed ratings (Par 102): **98,96,96,95,95 93,92,92,86**
toteswingers: 1&2 £20.50, 1&3 £23.30, 2&3 £1.90 CSF £98.27 CT £500.54 TOTE £37.70: £7.90, £1.50, £1.80; EX 156.30.
Owner A L R Morton **Bred** Mrs Anne Marie Burns **Trained** Middleham Moor, N Yorks
■ Stewards' Enquiry : Silvestre De Sousa caution: used whip with excessive frequency

FOCUS
After 4mm rain over the past five days and 4mm watering the previous day, the ground was described as "just about perfect". The rail was out five yards from the 6f marker and the false rail was in place turning in. A modest 60-78 three-year-old handicap and, as is the rule here, the pace was sound. The second and fourth set the level.
Kammaan Official explanation: jockey said filly was unsuited by the good to firm ground
Lucky Dan(IRE) Official explanation: jockey said gelding was denied a clear run

3805 THORNEYCROFT SOLICITORS CONDITIONS STKS — 5f 16y
7:10 (7:12) (Class 2) 2-Y-O **£9,777** (£2,926; £1,463; £731; £364) **Stalls** Low

Form RPR

041 **1** **Totally Invincible (IRE)**[9] 3495 2-8-9 0 RichardMullen 6 84
(E S McMahon) *chsd ldrs: wnt 2nd wl over 1f out: sn swtchd rt: r.o u.p to ld last stride* **7/2**[2]

10 **2** *shd* **Mdawee (IRE)**[7] 3583 2-8-11 0 PhilipRobinson 1 86
(Tom Dascombe) *led after 1f: rdn ins fnl f: hdd last stride* **7/4**[1]

2215 **3** 1 ¾ **Archers Road (IRE)**[34] 2714 2-9-7 0 CatherineGannon 7 90
(M R Channon) *sn chsng ldrs: rdn over 1f out: kpt on same pce to take 3rd towards fin* **7/1**

2063 **4** ½ **Goodbye Earl (IRE)**[4] 3682 2-8-6 0 FrancisNorton 2 73?
(A Berry) *wnt rt s: led 1f: chsd ldr tl wl over 1f out: rdn and one pce fnl f: lost 3rd towards fin* **20/1**

1 **5** *1* **Dancing Red Devil (IRE)**[13] 3370 2-8-9 0 SilvestreDeSousa 4 72
(Paul Green) *played up in stalls: hmpd on ins after 1f: sn wl in rr: rdn and hdwy over 1f out: nvr trbld ldrs* **7/2**[2]

1606 **6** *9* **Little Perisher**[7] 3583 2-9-0 0 StephenDonohoe 5 45
(A P Jarvis) *sn pushed along and outpcd* **6/1**[3]

05 **7** ½ **Psychopathicsandra (IRE)**[14] 3332 2-8-6 0 CharlotteKerton 3 35
(A Berry) *s.i.s: outpcd* **100/1**

61.32 secs (0.32) **Going Correction** -0.025s/f (Good) **7** Ran SP% **113.3**
Speed ratings (Par 100): **96,95,93,92,90 76,75**
toteswingers: 1&2 £1.90, 1&3 £4.70, 2&3 £2.40 CSF £9.87 TOTE £4.90: £2.40, £1.60; EX 12.20.
Owner Premspace Ltd **Bred** Gaetano Drago **Trained** Lichfield, Staffs
■ Stewards' Enquiry : Catherine Gannon two-day ban: careless riding (Jul 24- 26)

FOCUS
Five of the seven runners in this Class 2 event were previous winners and the pace was fast and furious. The proximity of the fourth tends to limit ithe form.

NOTEBOOK
Totally Invincible(IRE), who made all when a clear cut maiden winner at Catterick, had to accept a lead this time. She had to switch from the inner, once in line for home, but she put her head down and made up two lengths inside the final 75 yards to get up on the line. She could now take another step up in class, the Molecomb at Goodwood is on her agenda. (op 3-1 tchd 9-2)
Mdawee(IRE), seventh in Listed company at Sandown seven days earlier, soon had them strung out from his plum draw. After looking likely to hang on, he just missed out and is clearly all speed. (op 13-8)
Archers Road(IRE), given a five-week break after already running eight times this season, had to give weight away and had the worst of the draw. He ran up to his best and is very tough. (op 6-1)
Goodbye Earl(IRE), having her eighth start and only third off a provisional nursery mark of 68 at Musselburgh four days earlier, gave problems in the paddock and went to post late after being mounted in the saddling boxes. She matched strides with the leader but weakened noticeably near the line. This seemed to mark a big improvement, but it may be best to take it with a pinch of salt. (op 22-1)
Dancing Red Devil(IRE), who took a Class 4 event here on her debut here two weeks earlier, became very upset in the stalls. Soon run off her feet, she stuck on in good style in the straight and this will have taught her plenty. She would be interesting in a nursery. (op 9-2 tchd 3-1)
Little Perisher, just ahead of Mdawee when sixth in that Sandown Listed race, was edgy in the stalls and could never go the pace. This sharp, turning track did not seem to suit. (op 15-2)

3806 11TH RUNNING OF KATHLEEN B. CORBETT MEMORIAL H'CAP — 5f 16y
7:45 (7:46) (Class 3) (0-95,94) 3-Y-O **£9,777** (£2,926; £1,463; £731; £364) **Stalls** Low

Form RPR

5150 **1** **Glamorous Spirit (IRE)**[20] 3173 3-8-6 82 KevinGhunowa(3) 4 91
(R A Harris) *mde all: rdn jst over 1f out: drvn out* **20/1**

2215 **2** ¾ **Noble Storm (USA)**[27] 2928 3-9-7 94 GrahamGibbons 8 100
(E S McMahon) *chsd ldrs: rdn and edgd lft over 1f out: chsd wnr fnl f: nt qckn* **10/3**[1]

2226 **3** *nk* **Lenny Bee**[20] 3166 3-8-6 79 PaulMulrennan 2 84
(D H Brown) *s.i.s: sn mid-div: hdwy on ins whn nt clr run bnd wl over 1f out: sn rdn: kpt on same pce ins fnl f* **7/2**[2]

1064 **4** ½ **Brenin Taran**[20] 3166 3-9-0 87 StephenDonohoe 5 90+
(D M Simcock) *hld up in rr: pushed along and hung lft fr over 1f out: r.o ins fnl f: nrst fin* **8/1**

2101 **5** 1 ½ **Red Rosanna**[6] 3623 3-8-7 80 6ex RichardKingscote 1 78
(R Hollinshead) *prom: wnt 2nd briefly wl over 1f out: one pce ins fnl f* **7/2**[2]

-006 **6** *1* **Kingswinford (IRE)**[14] 3341 3-8-5 78 CatherineGannon 6 72
(P D Evans) *towards rr: pushed along 2f out: c wd st: n.d* **25/1**

3121 **7** ½ **Impressible**[13] 3372 3-8-7 80 FrancisNorton 9 73
(E J Alston) *chsd wnr tl wl over 1f out: sn n.m.r: wknd ins fnl f* **7/1**

5223 **8** *3* **Titus Andronicus (IRE)**[20] 3173 3-8-12 85 RichardMullen 7 67
(K A Ryan) *hmpd sn after s: towards rr: rdn over 1f out: eased whn no ch wl ins fnl f* **6/1**[3]

59.89 secs (-1.11) **Going Correction** -0.025s/f (Good) **8** Ran SP% **114.0**
Speed ratings (Par 104): **107,105,105,104,102 100,99,94**
toteswingers: 1&2 £10.50, 1&3 £15.00, 2&3 £2.40 CSF £85.31 CT £297.65 TOTE £19.10: £3.40, £1.30, £1.70; EX 111.60.
Owner Robert Bailey **Bred** Carlo Soria **Trained** Earlswood, Monmouths

FOCUS
A 78-94, three-year-olds' only sprint handicap. The pace was furious and the form looks sound.

NOTEBOOK
Glamorous Spirit(IRE), well beaten twice on turf since winning from the same mark on the all-weather at Kempton in May, had a favourable draw and took them along at a breakneck pace. She knuckled down when hotly challenged in the home straight and would not be denied. Official explanation: trainer said, regarding the apparent improvement of form that the filly is better suited to racing around a bend (op 14-1)

Noble Storm(USA), reckoned to be not at his best when fifth in a Listed race at Sandown a month earlier, was drawn towards the outside. He kept tabs on the winner, but after drawing almost upsides at the line, came off second best. (op 4-1 tchd 9-2)
Lenny Bee had an inside draw but missed the break slightly. He was closing on the leaders when left short of room coming off the final turn and was just found lacking. A more orthodox track would have suited him better. Official explanation: jockey said colt missed the break (tchd 4-1 in places)
Brenin Taran, squeezed out at the start, was detached in last. Despite a tendency to hang, he made up a good deal of ground once in line for home. With better luck, he would have gone very close. (tchd 9-1)
Red Rosanna had the plum draw but lacked the raw pace to dominate. (tchd 4-1)
Kingswinford(IRE), down 6lb after three below-par efforts this year, stayed on after getting outpaced and needs a stiffer test. (op 22-1)
Impressible, 5lb higher than when accounting for older horses here last time, had the worst of the draw and her chance had already gone when she was left short of room. (op 6-1)
Titus Andronicus(IRE), drawn wide, was another to meet trouble soon after the start and this normally speedy sort was never on terms. This run is best overlooked. Official explanation: jockey said gelding suffered interference at the start (op 7-1)

3807 ASTBURY WREN NURSERY — 6f 18y
8:15 (8:16) (Class 4) 2-Y-O — **£5,828** (£1,734; £866; £432) **Stalls** Low

Form				RPR
3132	**1**		**Transfixed (IRE)**[8] 3542 2-8-0 **61** ... CatherineGannon 9 *(P D Evans) hld up in tch: wnt 2nd wl over 1f out: sn rdn: led ins fnl f: r.o* **11/2**[3]	68+
5031	**2**	1 ½	**Michaelmas Daisy**[7] 3579 2-8-2 **63** 6ex ... AdrianTNicholls 1 *(Miss Amy Weaver) pushed along early to ld: rdn wl over 1f out: hdd ins fnl f: nt qckn* **3/1**[2]	66
140	**3**	½	**Antonius Moris (IRE)**[24] 2995 2-9-7 **82** ... RichardKingscote 2 *(Tom Dascombe) hld up in rr: pushed along 3f out: hdwy over 1f out: kpt on towards fin* **13/2**	83
033	**4**	1	**Regardless**[33] 2741 2-8-4 **65** ... SilvestreDeSousa 4 *(Mrs G S Rees) prom: hung rt bnd after 2f: pushed along 3f out: sn sltly outpcd: rdn wl over 1f out: one pce ins fnl f* **7/1**	63
0305	**5**	8	**Leleyf (IRE)**[12] 3430 2-9-4 **79** ... DarryllHolland 7 *(M R Channon) prom: pushed wd bnd after 2f: ev ch over 2f out: rdn and wknd over 1f out* **13/2**	53
5000	**6**	17	**Ariel Bender**[10] 3478 2-7-11 **65** oh7 ow6 ... AndrewHeffernan(7) 5 *(Peter Grayson) s.i.s: in rr: rdn over 3f out: lost tch wl over 1f out* **33/1**	—
21	**7**	3	**Gwynedd (IRE)**[27] 2919 2-9-2 **77** ... RichardMullen 3 *(E S McMahon) t.k.h: sn w ldr: wknd wl over 1f out: eased fnl f* **9/4**[1]	—

1m 15.0s (1.20) **Going Correction** -0.025s/f (Good) 7 Ran SP% **113.3**
Speed ratings (Par 96): **91,89,88,87,76 53,49**
toteswingers: 1&2 £2.80, 1&3 £6.90, 2&3 £4.70 CSF £21.90 CT £108.39 TOTE £6.10: £2.80, £2.10; EX 22.80.
Owner Mrs I M Folkes **Bred** Rathasker Stud **Trained** Pandy, Monmouths

FOCUS
An ordinary nursery rated around the first two. The 'official' ratings shown next to each horse are estimated and for information purposes only.

NOTEBOOK
Transfixed(IRE), twice a winner in selling company and placed on her other four starts, must be as tough as old boots. Despite having the worst of the draw she was soon in pursuit of the leaders towards the inner. She readily mastered the pacesetter and was firmly in command at the line. (op 7-1)
Michaelmas Daisy, who carried overweight and was racing from out of the handicap when showing much-improved form to take a nursery at Salisbury on her fourth start, was in effect 3lb better in. Drawn one, she was determined to lead but in the end was very much second best. She will have a lot more to do when her new mark kicks in. (tchd 11-4)
Antonius Moris(IRE), out of his depth at Royal Ascot, made up a lot of ground from the rear and was putting in some solid work at the finish on his fourth start. He had looked awkward on his first two starts but seems to be getting the hang of things. (op 5-1 tchd 7-1)
Regardless, below form on her third start on the all-weather, ducked right at the first bend. Tapped for toe soon after halfway, she stuck on all the way to the line and is still learning. A more orthodox track will see her in a better light. (op 13-2)
Leleyf(IRE), having her seventh start, was pushed wide on the first bend. She dropped away once in line for home and is already looking fully exposed. (op 7-1 tchd 15-2)
Gwynedd(IRE), a Lingfield maiden winner when dropped back to 5f on her second start, looked potentially leniently treated. She raced far too keenly upsides the leader and dropped out going into the final turn. Her rider eased her right up as if something had gone amiss. Official explanation: jockey said, regarding the running and riding of the filly, that the filly ran too free and had no more to give (op 5-2)

3808 HOLLYOAKS H'CAP — 1m 2f 75y
8:50 (8:50) (Class 4) (0-85,83) 3-Y-O — **£5,828** (£1,734; £866; £432) **Stalls** High

Form				RPR
-501	**1**		**Norwegian Dancer (UAE)**[13] 3373 3-9-7 **83** ... StephenDonohoe 1 *(E S McMahon) hld up in last: pushed along and hdwy over 1f out: sn rdn and hung lft: r.o to ld cl home* **9/4**[3]	89+
153	**2**	½	**Hallstatt (IRE)**[7] 3573 3-9-2 **78** ... AdrianTNicholls 4 *(M Johnston) chsd ldr tl over 5f out: rdn to ld ent fnl f: hdd cl home* **2/1**[2]	83+
-450	**3**	3	**Digger Derek (IRE)**[65] 1792 3-8-6 **68** ... TonyHamilton 6 *(R A Fahey) led early: hld up in 3rd: wnt 2nd over 5f out: led wl over 1f out: sn rdn: edgd lft and hdd ent fnl f: one pce* **8/1**	67
26-1	**4**	2 ¼	**Chapter And Verse (IRE)**[94] 1168 3-9-5 **81** ... PhilipRobinson 2 *(B W Hills) t.k.h: sn led: hdd wl over 1f out: sn rdn: wknd ins fnl f* **15/8**[1]	76

2m 12.4s (0.20) **Going Correction** -0.025s/f (Good) 4 Ran SP% **110.0**
Speed ratings (Par 102): **98,97,95,93**
CSF £7.17 TOTE £3.00; EX 8.00.
Owner Philip Wilkins **Bred** Darley **Trained** Lichfield, Staffs

FOCUS
Just four runners for this three-year-old handicap with the runner-up the best guide to the level.
Chapter And Verse(IRE) Official explanation: jockey said gelding was unsuited by the good to firm ground

3809 MORSON AND XCHANGING PATNERSHIP H'CAP — 1m 4f 66y
9:20 (9:20) (Class 5) (0-75,74) 3-Y-O+ — **£4,047** (£1,204; £601; £300) **Stalls** Low

Form				RPR
0-46	**1**		**Inspirina (IRE)**[11] 3450 5-9-2 **62** ... TonyHamilton 3 *(R Ford) s.i.s: hld up in mid-div: hdwy on outside 2f out: led jst over 1f out: pushed out* **9/2**[3]	72
1645	**2**	2	**Valdan (IRE)**[24] 3000 5-10-0 **74** ... StephenDonohoe 7 *(P D Evans) hld up towards rr: hdwy on outside 2f out: rdn 1f out: styd on to take 2nd cl home: nt trble wnr* **4/1**[2]	81
4606	**3**	½	**Destinys Dream (IRE)**[13] 3393 4-9-5 **68** ... KellyHarrison(3) 12 *(Miss Tracy Waggott) hld up in rr: nt clr run wl over 1f out: sn swtchd lft and hdwy on ins: kpt on ins fnl f* **20/1**	74
2401	**4**	½	**Drawn Gold**[25] 2971 5-9-0 **60** ... GrahamGibbons 5 *(R Hollinshead) chsd ldr: rdn to ld briefly over 1f out: no ex and lost two pls cl home* **10/1**	65
3203	**5**	¾	**Andorn (GER)**[9] 3499 5-9-2 **65** ... RussellKennemore(3) 4 *(P A Kirby) t.k.h: a.p: rdn jst over 1f out: one pce* **16/1**	69
3052	**6**	1 ½	**Thorny Mandate**[11] 3447 7-8-11 **57** oh3 ... PaulMulrennan 9 *(W M Brisbourne) hld up in rr: pushed along whn sltly hmpd wl over 1f out: n.d* **9/1**	59
-201	**7**	nk	**New Tricks**[36] 2627 3-8-9 **68** ... (b) JamieMoriarty 6 *(I Semple) t.k.h: prom: rdn wl over 1f out: sn wknd* **8/1**	69
4025	**8**	½	**Inspector Clouseau (IRE)**[13] 3380 4-9-8 **68** ... FrancisNorton 2 *(T P Tate) racd keenly: led: rdn and hdd over 1f out: wknd ins fnl f* **6/1**	68
0-53	**9**	2	**Prelude**[8] 3527 8-9-6 **66** ... DarryllHolland 1 *(W M Brisbourne) hld up in mid-div: pushed along and wknd wl over 1f out* **3/1**[1]	63

2m 38.6s (-1.30) **Going Correction** -0.025s/f (Good)
WFA 3 from 4yo+ 13lb 9 Ran SP% **118.3**
Speed ratings (Par 103): **103,101,101,101,100 99,99,98,97**
toteswingers: 1&2 £3.30, 1&3 £28.60, 2&3 £33.90 CSF £23.52 CT £330.61 TOTE £5.60: £2.00, £1.70, £4.40; EX 24.40 Place 6: £103.28 Place 5: £48.71.
Owner Miss Gill Quincey **Bred** Mohammad Al-Qatami **Trained** Cotebrook, Cheshire

FOCUS
A 68-74 handicap run at a very sound pace and the form looks solid rated around the placed horses.
T/Plt: £305.70 to a £1 stake. Pool: £63,501.08. 151.60 winning tickets. T/Qpdt: £155.30 to a £1 stake. Pool: £3,947.08. 18.80 winning tickets. KH

3533 NEWBURY (L-H)
Friday, July 10

OFFICIAL GOING: Good to firm (9.1)
Rail on bends between 7f and 5f moved out increasing distances on round course by about 14yards.
Wind: Moderate ahead Weather: Overcast

3810 PETER BAKER FOUNDATION E B F MAIDEN FILLIES' STKS (IN AID OF SWINGS & SMILES) — 7f (S)
6:20 (6:25) (Class 4) 2-Y-O — **£5,180** (£1,541; £770; £384) **Stalls** Centre

Form				RPR
3	**1**		**Middle Club**[17] 3249 2-9-0 0 ... RyanMoore 3 *(R Hannon) chsd ldrs: wnt 2nd 2f out: drvn and 2 l down 1f out: styd on wl ins fnl f to ld cl home then j. winning line* **7/2**[3]	83+
32	**2**	½	**Secret Queen**[17] 3249 2-9-0 0 ... MartinDwyer 11 *(B J Meehan) led and t.k.h: pushed along and clr 1f out: pushed along ins fnl f: hdd cl home* **7/4**[1]	82+
	3	4	**Chelsea Morning (USA)** 2-9-0 0 ... MichaelHills 13 *(B W Hills) in rr: pushed along and hdwy over 2f out: styd on to take 3rd ins fnl f but nvr any ch w ldng duo* **10/3**[2]	72
0	**4**	1	**Universal Circus**[17] 3249 2-8-9 0 ... MatthewDavies(5) 4 *(M R Channon) chsd ldrs: rdn over 2f out: styd on tl outpcd by ldng duo fnl f and sn lost 3rd* **100/1**	70
	5	¾	**Calatrava Cape (IRE)** 2-9-0 0 ... IanMongan 5 *(J L Dunlop) s.i.s: in rr: hdwy over 2f out: styd on fr over 1f out but nvr in contention* **12/1**	68+
0	**6**	5	**Glamour Profession (IRE)**[11] 3458 2-9-0 0 ... SimonWhitworth 2 *(R Hannon) sn in tch: pushed along and hung lft and one pce 2f out: styd on again cl home* **80/1**	55
	7	½	**Rose Alba (IRE)** 2-9-0 0 ... DaneO'Neill 12 *(J L Dunlop) sn outpcd in rr: shkn up over 2f out: kpt on fnl f but nvr in contention* **33/1**	54
4	**8**	2 ¼	**Love Action (IRE)**[17] 3249 2-9-0 0 ... PatDobbs 9 *(R Hannon) s.i.s: in rr: pushed along 2f out: stl in rr whn n.m.r and edgd rt ins fnl f: mod prog nr fin* **8/1**	48+
0	**9**	shd	**Gold Fix (IRE)**[8] 3534 2-9-0 0 ... PaulDoe 1 *(M R Channon) in tch: hdwy on outside to chse ldrs 3f out: sn pushed along: wknd over 1f out* **80/1**	48
	10	4 ½	**Mahjong Girl** 2-8-11 0 ... JackMitchell(3) 8 *(R M Beckett) s.i.s: sn in tch: sme prog 3f out: pushed along 2f out and sn wknd* **25/1**	37
0	**11**	nk	**Madj's Baby**[31] 2792 2-9-0 0 ... KirstyMilczarek 14 *(H S Howe) in tch early: towards rr fr 1/2-way* **66/1**	36
	12	2	**Hulcote Rose (IRE)** 2-9-0 0 ... JimmyFortune 15 *(S Kirk) chsd ldrs: rdn and effort 2f out: wknd over 1f out: no ch whn hmpd on ins fnl f* **28/1**	31+
2	**13**	3	**Bideeya (USA)**[14] 3332 2-8-11 0 ... AhmedAjtebi(3) 10 *(C E Brittain) chsd ldrs tl wknd over 2f out: no ch whn hmpd on ins fnl f* **14/1**	24+
64	**14**	17	**Three's A Crowd**[18] 3210 2-9-0 0 ... RobertHavlin 6 *(D R C Elsworth) chsd ldrs tl wknd qckly over 2f out* **40/1**	—

1m 26.9s (1.20) **Going Correction** +0.05s/f (Good) 14 Ran SP% **124.8**
Speed ratings (Par 93): **95,94,89,88,87 82,81,79,78,73 73,71,67,48**
toteswingers: 1&2 £2.50, 1&3 £3.80, 2&3 £2.80 CSF £9.92 TOTE £4.40: £1.80, £1.40, £1.80; EX 13.80.
Owner R J McCreery **Bred** Stowell Hill Ltd **Trained** East Everleigh, Wilts

FOCUS
A fair fillies' maiden and the form looks decent with the first two clear.

NOTEBOOK
Middle Club ◆ looked the stable first string on jockey bookings and attracted plenty of support. She raced near the pace, but it looked like she would have to settle for second until she found a surging run to steal the race close home and reverse course-and-distance debut form with the runner-up. She is a half-sister to Anna Mona, a quite useful 1m3f winner in France, so it is encouraging that she is showing winning form over 7f at this early stage of her career. She looks a determined type and should go on to better things. (op 4-1 tchd 9-2)
Secret Queen ◆ set the target on the form of her debut second. She dictated the pace and looked in control, but after kicking clear approaching the 2f pole she showed a slight tendency to hang into the stands' rail and was just caught. This was still a creditable effort and she pulled a long way clear of the rest. She should not have much trouble gaining compensation for this defeat in a similar race. (op 2-1 tchd 11-8)
Chelsea Morning(USA) was always fighting a losing battle after starting slowly, but she kept on steadily and showed a bit of promise and ability on her debut. She cost $200,000 as a yearling and is out of a useful 7f-1m winner at three in France, who was later a 1m3f Grade 3 winner in US. (op 13-2 tchd 3-1)
Universal Circus was tailed off at 66-1 behind the first two on her debut but she left that form well behind. She has an interesting mixture of speed and stamina in her pedigree, but shaped here like an extra furlong would suit.

Calatrava Cape(IRE) looked inexperienced and never got into the race, but she stayed on steadily to pull a long way clear of the rest on her debut. She is from a middle-distance family and should progress with time. (op 9-1)
Love Action(IRE) finished less than a length behind the winner on her debut, so this has to rate as a disappointing effort. However, she did not really get the breaks when she needed them and could be worth another chance to confirm her debut promise. (op 13-2)

3811 AXMINSTER CARPETS H'CAP 1m 2f 6y
6:50 (6:54) (Class 5) (0-70,72) 4-Y-O+ **£3,238** (£963; £481; £240) **Stalls** Low

Form RPR
122 **1** **Jo'Burg (USA)**[32] 2764 5-9-7 **70** .... RyanMoore 6 81
(Lady Herries) *slowly away: hld up: hdwy 3f out: grad moved rt to outside and str run fr 2f out to ld fnl 110yds: readily* **3/1**[1]
0-06 **2** *1* **Mount Hermon (IRE)**[22] 3055 5-9-7 **70** .... (b) JimmyFortune 2 79
(H Morrison) *trckd ldrs: led over 2f out: hrd drvn over 1f out: hdd and nt qckn fnl 110yds* **5/1**[2]
0021 **3** *1 1/2* **Love In The Park**[18] 3215 4-8-7 **59** .... JackMitchell(3) 15 65+
(R Brotherton) *stdd in rr: stl l last over 3f out: swtchd rt to outside and gd hdwy fr 2f out: styd on wl to take 3rd ins fnl f but nt rch ldng duo* **6/1**[3]
6153 **4** *shd* **Vinces**[14] 3349 5-9-1 **64** .... KirstyMilczarek 12 70
(T D McCarthy) *mid-div: rdn and hdwy over 2f out: chsd ldrs over 1f out: no imp and styd on same pce ins fnl f* **12/1**
0052 **5** *1 1/4* **Lord Theo**[14] 3357 5-9-2 **65** .... RobertHavlin 9 68
(N P Littmoden) *in tch: shkn up and n.m.r ins fnl 3f: styd on u.p fr over 1f out but nvr a threat* **12/1**
6002 **6** *1 3/4* **Clovis**[16] 3259 4-9-2 **65** .... (p) DaneO'Neill 11 65
(N P Mulholland) *in rr: pushed along and hdwy fr 2f out: styd on thrght fnl f but nvr gng pce to be competitive* **16/1**
624/ **7** *1/2* **Mexican Bob**[457] 5273 6-8-13 **62** .... IanMongan 16 61
(C E Longsdon) *towards rr: hdwy fr 4f out: chsd ldrs fr over 2f out and wl there over 1f out: one pce ins fnl f* **14/1**
1310 **8** *3* **Megalala (IRE)**[35] 2678 8-8-11 **60** .... NeilChalmers 4 53
(J J Bridger) *led: rdn over 3f out: hdd over 2f out: styd front rnk tl wknd fnl f* **16/1**
0-21 **9** *3/4* **Merrymadcap (IRE)**[12] 3421 7-9-9 **72** 6ex .... JerryO'Dwyer 7 63
(M Salaman) *trckd ldrs: wnt 2nd over 4f out: rdn over 2f out: wknd qckly appr fnl f* **9/1**
3-00 **10** *1 1/2* **Alfie Tupper (IRE)**[23] 3024 6-9-7 **70** .... MartinDwyer 3 58
(J R Boyle) *t.k.h in rr: hdwy on ins to trck ldrs over 3f out: rdn and edgd rt over 2f out: wknd sn after* **14/1**
005- **11** *1 3/4* **Lady Maya**[322] 5215 4-8-2 **51** oh6 .... FrankieMcDonald 5 36
(P Henderson) *in rr: hrd drvn fr over 2f out: mod prog ins fnl f* **100/1**
-550 **12** *nse* **Colour Trooper (IRE)**[39] 2552 4-9-2 **65** .... (p) JoeFanning 13 50
(P Winkworth) *in tch: chsd ldrs and rdn over 3f out: wknd fr 2f out* **20/1**
0100 **13** *14* **Hilbre Court (USA)**[21] 3124 4-8-13 **67** .... (p) JackDean(5) 10 24
(B P J Baugh) *in rr: brief effrt ins fnl 3f: nvr rchd ldrs and sn wknd* **18/1**
000 **14** *7* **Tallulah Sunrise**[2] 3735 4-8-1 **53** .... DavidProbert(3) 14 —
(M D I Usher) *chsd ldr tl over 4f out: wknd fr 3f out* **25/1**
0000 **15** *34* **Royal Island (IRE)**[102] 1042 7-8-11 **60** .... VinceSlattery 8 —
(M G Quinlan) *chsd ldrs: rdn 4f out: wknd qckly 3f out: t.o* **40/1**

2m 6.31s (-2.49) **Going Correction** -0.15s/f (Firm) 15 Ran SP% **123.7**
Speed ratings (Par 103): **103,102,101,100,99 98,98,95,95,93 92,92,81,75,48**
toteswingers: 1&2 £5.30, 1&3 £2.90, 2&3 £9.60 CSF £16.38 CT £88.89 TOTE £3.60: £1.50, £2.60, £2.10; EX 24.40.
Owner Seymour Bloodstock (uk) Ltd **Bred** Tim Cooper **Trained** Patching, W Sussex
■ Stewards' Enquiry : Martin Dwyer caution: careless riding

FOCUS
A modest though well-run handicap and sound form for the grade.
Merrymadcap(IRE) Official explanation: jockey said gelding hung right-handed

3812 GARDNER MECHANICAL SERVICES H'CAP 1m (S)
7:25 (7:26) (Class 4) (0-80,79) 3-Y-O+ **£5,828** (£1,734; £866; £432) **Stalls** Centre

Form RPR
4205 **1** **Credit Swap**[21] 3116 4-9-2 **76** .... TobyAtkinson(7) 7 87
(M Wigham) *hld up towards rr but in tch: gd hdwy fr 2f out: drvn to ld towards stands' side jst ins fnl f: pushed out* **16/1**
613 **2** *1 1/2* **Burns Night**[6] 3608 3-9-2 **78** .... JoeFanning 6 83
(M Johnston) *trckd ldrs: rdn: swtchd rt to stands rail and qcknd to take slt ld over 1f out: hdd jst ins fnl f: sn outpcd by wnr but kpt on for 2nd* **2/1**[1]
0232 **3** *1/2* **Effigy**[22] 3055 5-9-11 **78** .... DaneO'Neill 2 84
(H Candy) *trckd ldrs: narrow ld 3f out: sn rdn: styd towards centre of crse and hdd appr fnl f: styd on same pce ins fnl f* **9/4**[2]
22-3 **4** *3* **Burma Rock (IRE)**[31] 2795 3-9-1 **77** .... RyanMoore 3 74
(L M Cumani) *t.k.h: trckd ldrs: rdn over 2f out: sn hung lft to centre of crse: wknd fnl f* **5/2**[3]
0336 **5** *2 1/4* **Hallingdal (UAE)**[13] 3408 4-9-2 **69** .... NeilChalmers 4 63
(J J Bridger) *s.i.s: rr: hdwy over 2f out: chsd ldrs over 1f out but nvr on terms: sn wknd* **33/1**
5101 **6** *17* **April Fool**[16] 3258 5-9-8 **75** .... (v) RichardThomas 5 30
(J A Geake) *w ldr: led after 2f: hdd and rdn 3f out: wknd qckly 2f out* **18/1**
3634 **7** *12* **Grey Boy (GER)**[20] 3154 8-9-3 **70** .... JimmyFortune 1 —
(A W Carroll) *t.k.h: slt ld 2f: styd front rnk tl wknd qckly over 2f out* **14/1**

1m 39.07s (-0.63) **Going Correction** +0.05s/f (Good) 7 Ran SP% **113.4**
WFA 3 from 4yo+ 9lb
Speed ratings (Par 105): **105,103,103,100,97 80,68**
toteswingers: 1&2 £8.30, 1&3 £9.80, 2&3 £1.02 CSF £47.65 CT £102.80 TOTE £18.30: £5.20, £1.60; EX 58.50.
Owner Your Golf Travel Ltd **Bred** Jeremy Green And Sons **Trained** Newmarket, Suffolk

FOCUS
There was a fair pace on in this fair handicap, despite the smallish field, and the form looks sound enough.
Burns Night Official explanation: jockey said colt hung right-handed
April Fool Official explanation: jockey said gelding ran flat
Grey Boy(GER) Official explanation: jockey said gelding ran too free

3813 GT EXHIBITIONS MAIDEN STKS 6f 8y
7:55 (7:56) (Class 4) 3-Y-O **£5,828** (£1,734; £866; £432) **Stalls** Centre

Form RPR
-2 **1** **Leverage (IRE)**[14] 3338 3-9-3 0 .... RyanMoore 8 79+
(L M Cumani) *t.k.h early: trckd ldrs: qcknd to ld 1f out: drvn and asserted ins fnl f kpt on strly cl home* **4/7**[1]
2 *3/4* **Major Lawrence (IRE)** 3-9-3 0 .... JimmyFortune 1 77+
(J Noseda) *s.i.s: sn wl there: pushed along 2f out: green and one pce: drvn and styd on again ins fnl f and tk 2nd nr fin but a hld by wnr* **9/4**[2]
6 **3** *1 1/4* **Milldown Story**[50] 2205 3-8-12 0 .... DaneO'Neill 9 68
(B R Millman) *t.k.h: led: rdn 2f out: hdd 1f out: sn no ch w wnr: kpt on same pce and lost 2nd nr fin* **12/1**[3]
0 **4** *1/2* **Fiftyfourth Street**[41] 2496 3-9-3 0 .... (t) TravisBlock 2 71
(P J Makin) *s.i.s: pushed along and hdwy over 2f out: styd on wl fnl f but nvr quite gng pce to rch ldrs* **50/1**
0 **5** *5* **Weekend Away (IRE)**[46] 2317 3-9-3 0 .... PatDobbs 12 55
(S Kirk) *s.i.s: rr: pushed along 2f out: styd on fnl f but nvr a threat* **25/1**
6 **6** *nse* **Yashkur**[43] 2403 3-8-12 0 .... MartinDwyer 11 50
(C E Brittain) *s.i.s: rr: pushed along 2f out: styd on fnl f: nvr a threat* **28/1**
0 **7** *3/4* **Cardenio (USA)**[20] 3161 3-8-12 0 .... ClareLindop 6 48
(J R Gask) *in rr: pushed along and hung lft 2f out: sme prog fnl f* **40/1**
0 **8** *1* **Running Flush (USA)**[14] 3338 3-9-3 0 .... JerryO'Dwyer 3 50
(J R Gask) *chsd ldr: rdn fr 3f out: wknd wl over 1f out* **33/1**
6-0 **9** *7* **Academy Of War (USA)**[11] 3460 3-8-12 0 .... JackDean(5) 10 27
(J M Bradley) *chsd ldrs: rdn 1/2-way: sn btn* **66/1**
10 *18* **Orpen Lady** 3-8-12 0 .... PaulFitzsimons 7 —
(J M Bradley) *slowly away: green on outside: sn rdn: hung rt ins fnl 3f: sn wknd* **66/1**

1m 13.61s (0.61) **Going Correction** +0.05s/f (Good) 10 Ran SP% **119.7**
Speed ratings (Par 102): **97,96,94,93,87 86,85,84,75,51**
toteswingers: 1&2 £1.02, 1&3 £2.90, 2&3 £4.10 CSF £1.93 TOTE £1.60: £1.02, £1.20, £2.40; EX 2.30.
Owner Ron Levi & Stuart Roden **Bred** Azienda Agricola Santucci Silvano **Trained** Newmarket, Suffolk

FOCUS
There did not seem much strength in depth here and the first four pulled a long way clear of the rest.

3814 BERRY BROS MAGNUM H'CAP 1m 5f 61y
8:30 (8:30) (Class 5) (0-75,75) 4-Y-O+ **£3,238** (£963; £481; £240) **Stalls** Low

Form RPR
4533 **1** **Cyborg**[8] 3521 5-9-7 **75** .... RyanMoore 2 84
(D R C Elsworth) *trckd ldrs: chal fr over 2f out: slt advantage appr fnl f: sn rdn: kpt on and a readily holding runner up* **2/1**[1]
4221 **2** *nk* **Summer Lodge**[23] 3035 6-8-8 **65** .... DavidProbert(3) 10 74
(J A Glover) *trckd ldr: chal fr 4f out: narrow ld fr 3f out: rdn over 2f out: hdd appr fnl f: styd on but a hld by wnr* **13/2**
3-30 **3** *5* **Act Three**[41] 2497 5-8-6 **60** .... NeilChalmers 4 64
(Mouse Hamilton-Fairley) *hld up in rr: hdwy on ins whn nt clr run ins fnl 3f: swtchd rt 2f out: styd on wl appr fnl f: tk 3rd ins fnl f but no ch w ldng duo* **16/1**
3104 **4** *1/2* **Party Palace**[19] 2798 5-8-2 **56** oh5 .... KirstyMilczarek 3 57
(H S Howe) *led tl narrowly hdd 3f out: styd pressing ldrs to 2f out: wknd fnl f* **16/1**
0401 **5** *5* **Epsom Salts**[8] 3521 4-8-10 **69** 6ex .... JackDean(5) 6 62
(P M Phelan) *chsd ldrs: rdn along 3f out: wknd 2f out* **11/2**[3]
0-51 **6** *1 1/2* **Venir Rouge**[17] 3247 5-8-10 **69** .... MCGeran(5) 7 60
(M Salaman) *in rr: rdn over 3f out: nvr gng pce to get into contention* **4/1**[2]
1320 **7** *2* **Augustus John (IRE)**[80] 1435 6-9-0 **71** .... JackMitchell(3) 9 59
(R Brotherton) *chsd ldrs: rdn over 3f out: wknd qckly 2f out* **12/1**
0-03 **8** *1 3/4* **Trachonitis (IRE)**[20] 3169 5-9-4 **72** .... JimmyFortune 1 57
(J R Jenkins) *s.i.s: hld up in rr: hdwy and nt clr run 3f out: qcknd to trck ldrs in 3rd over 2f out: sn rdn: little respnse and wknd qckly* **6/1**

2m 52.42s (0.42) **Going Correction** -0.15s/f (Firm) 8 Ran SP% **115.8**
Speed ratings (Par 103): **92,91,88,88,85 84,83,82**
toteswingers: 1&2 £2.90, 1&3 £11.60, 2&3 £12.40 CSF £15.82 CT £162.53 TOTE £3.10: £1.60, £1.90, £4.20; EX 11.70.
Owner J C Smith **Bred** G And Mrs Middlebrook **Trained** Newmarket, Suffolk

FOCUS
A moderate handicap and the field finished well spread out.
Trachonitis(IRE) Official explanation: jockey said gelding ran too free

3815 SWINGS AND SMILES FILLIES' H'CAP 7f (S)
9:00 (9:03) (Class 5) (0-75,73) 3-Y-O **£3,238** (£963; £481; £240) **Stalls** Centre

Form RPR
0500 **1** **Peper Harow (IRE)**[12] 3428 3-7-13 **54** .... DavidProbert(3) 4 55
(M D I Usher) *stdd s: sn trcking ldrs: drvn to ld 1f out: hld on under pressue fnl f: all out* **12/1**
00-4 **2** *1/2* **Lucy Brown**[16] 3278 3-9-2 **68** .... RyanMoore 12 71+
(R Hannon) *plld hrd and stdd rr after 1f: rdn 2f out: hdwy whn nt clr run and swtchd rt to stands rail 1f out: str run ins fnl f: fin wl but nt rch wnr* **7/2**[2]
-403 **3** *hd* **Sweet Possession (USA)**[42] 2455 3-8-13 **65** .... JimmyFortune 2 64
(A P Jarvis) *trckd ldrs: rdn over 1f out: styd on u.p fnl f and gng on cl home but nt pce of wnr* **9/2**[3]
4-00 **4** *nk* **Dicey Affair**[15] 3299 3-8-8 **60** .... PatDobbs 6 58
(G L Moore) *hld up in rr but in tch: gd hdwy over 1f out: styng on whn rdr dropped reins and edgd lft ins fnl f: sn rcvrd: fin strly but nt quite rch ldrs* **20/1**
6022 **5** *1 1/4* **My Best Bet**[8] 3537 3-9-1 **72** .... MCGeran(5) 1 67
(M R Channon) *chsd ldrs: led 2f out: hdd 1f out: wknd fnl 50yds* **5/4**[1]
306- **6** *4* **Champagne Fizz (IRE)**[294] 6087 3-9-2 **68** .... DaneO'Neill 9 52
(Miss Jo Crowley) *led tl hdd 2f out: wknd fnl f* **8/1**
00-0 **7** *shd* **Allexes (IRE)**[35] 2679 3-9-0 **69** .... JackMitchell(3) 11 53
(J R Boyle) *chsd ldrs: rdn over 2f out: wknd over 1f out* **12/1**
-000 **8** *7* **Thefillyfromepsom**[63] 1839 3-8-2 **54** .... (v[1]) FrankieMcDonald 5 19
(P M Phelan) *chsd ldrs over 4f* **20/1**

1m 26.81s (1.11) **Going Correction** +0.05s/f (Good) 8 Ran SP% **120.9**
Speed ratings (Par 97): **95,94,94,93,92 87,87,79**
toteswingers: 1&2 £8.60, 1&3 £7.70, 2&3 £3.00 CSF £56.91 CT £223.77 TOTE £19.00: £3.60, £1.40, £1.60; EX 115.80 Place 6: £12.44 Place 5: £10.66.
Owner Mr & Mrs Richard Hames & Friends 1 **Bred** R And Mrs Hames **Trained** Upper Lambourn, Berks

FOCUS
This was weakened by the non-runners. There was just a steady pace on and the form is muddling.
Dicey Affair Official explanation: jockey said that he dropped his reins on the run to the line
T/Plt: £51.60 to a £1 stake. Pool: £63,863.93. 902.97 winning tickets. T/Qpdt: £27.90 to a £1 stake. Pool: £3,341.40. 88.50 winning tickets. ST

3778 NEWMARKET (R-H)

Friday, July 10

OFFICIAL GOING: Good to firm (good in places; 8.5)

Wind: Fresh behind Weather: Overcast

3816 PREMIER TRAVEL H'CAP — 1m

1:30 (1:30) (Class 2) (0-100,97) 3-Y-O

£24,924 (£7,464; £3,732; £1,868; £932; £468) **Stalls** Low

Form				RPR
-610	1		**Brief Encounter (IRE)**[22] 3049 3-9-2 **90** .... LPKeniry 4 (A M Balding) *hld up: hdwy over 3f out: rdn to ld ins fnl f: styd on* **5/1**	100+
-102	2	3/4	**Crackdown (IRE)**[6] 3639 3-9-9 **97** .... RoystonFfrench 6 (M Johnston) *swtg: led: rdn and hung lft over 1f out: hdd and edgd rt ins fnl f: styd on* **11/4**[1]	105
-216	3	1	**Sovereign Remedy (USA)**[27] 2935 3-9-0 **88** .... LDettori 9 (Saeed Bin Suroor) *lw: hld up: hdwy over 3f out: rdn and edgd lft over 1f out: styd on* **7/2**[2]	94+
6600	4	hd	**Canwinn (IRE)**[22] 3049 3-8-11 **85** .... (v) SamHitchcott 8 (M R Channon) *hld up: rdn over 2f out: r.o ins fnl f: nt rch ldrs* **25/1**	90
15	5	3/4	**Thousand Miles (IRE)**[55] 2096 3-8-10 **84** .... RichardMullen 2 (P W Chapple-Hyam) *lw: a.p: chsd ldr over 2f out: rdn over 1f out: styd on same pce ins fnl f* **16/1**	88
4011	6	1/2	**Kyllachy Star**[27] 2926 3-9-2 **90** .... TonyHamilton 3 (R A Fahey) *prom: racd keenly: lost pl 5f out: hdwy u.p and edgd lft over 1f out: no imp ins fnl f* **8/1**	92
1310	7	2 3/4	**Spinners End (IRE)**[20] 3144 3-8-7 **81** .... JimCrowley 10 (K R Burke) *hld up in tch: racd keenly: rdn over 2f out: wknd ins fnl f* **20/1**	77
0220	8	3/4	**Ermine And Velvet**[15] 3320 3-9-3 **91** .... MartinDwyer 7 (C E Brittain) *chsd ldr tl rdn over 2f out: wknd ins fnl f* **50/1**	85
331	9	1 3/4	**Mohtashem (IRE)**[28] 2885 3-9-2 **90** .... RHills 5 (Sir Michael Stoute) *lw: prom: rdn over 2f out: wknd over 1f out* **9/2**[3]	80
6-00	10	7	**Archie Rice (USA)**[35] 2674 3-9-2 **90** .... AlanMunro 1 (W Jarvis) *hld up: rdn over 3f out: wknd wl over 1f out* **14/1**	71

1m 38.45s (-1.55) **Going Correction** -0.075s/f (Good) **10** Ran SP% **118.0**

Speed ratings (Par 106): **104,103,102,102,101 100,98,97,95,88**

toteswingers: 1&2 £3.60, 1&3 £6.80, 2&3 £3.30 CSF £18.99 CT £56.61 TOTE £6.70: £2.10, £1.40, £1.90; EX 24.30 Trifecta £274.80 Pool: £631.46 1.70 - winning units.

Owner Thurloe Thoroughbreds XXII **Bred** Ballyhane Stud **Trained** Kingsclere, Hants

FOCUS

A smaller field than in previous years, and not as competitive as it might have been, but this was still a decent 3yo handicap. They raced up the middle of the track early on, but the winner went left in the closing stages and ended up tight against the far rail. Sound form, with the runner-up a fair guide.

NOTEBOOK

Brief Encounter(IRE) did well to reel in the Johnston runner considering that one set just an ordinary gallop. He ran below expectations when fancied to go well in the Britannia Stakes at Royal Ascot, but showed his true worth this time. He edged slightly left late on, possibly intimidated by the runner-up, but still won readily enough and looks potentially Listed class. (op 11-2 tchd 6-1)

Crackdown(IRE), who was 5lb ahead of the Handicapper following his recent second at Sandown, was allowed a soft lead and set no more than an ordinary gallop. Not sweating like he did at Sandown, there can be no excuses, although he did edge slightly left under pressure. He's in the totesport Mile at Goodwood, but would have to run off his new mark of 102, and it's possible he'll want 1m2f before long. (op 10-3 tchd 7-2)

Sovereign Remedy(USA), dropped back in trip after failing to prove his stamina for 1m2f, raced wide without cover for most of the way. He couldn't muster the pace to pose a serious threat, yet only just held on for third and doesn't look particularly well handicapped. (op 5-1, tchd 11-2 in a place)

Canwinn(IRE) ◆, held up early, stayed on well but all too late after getting outpaced about two furlongs out. He seems to be running into form and, having dropped to a very favourable mark, there could be a nice handicap in him this season, possibly at Glorious Goodwood. (op 20-1)

Thousand Miles(IRE) probably found this ground quicker than ideal. (tchd 14-1)

Kyllachy Star had shown improved form to win back-to-back handicaps over 7f, but a modestly run 1m didn't suit and he could not effect a 6lb rise. He can be given another chance. (op 6-1)

Spinners End(IRE) was too keen. (op 25-1, tchd 28-1 in a place)

Ermine And Velvet, the only filly, now looks poorly handicapped.

Mohtashem(IRE) looked a good prospect when winning his maiden at Goodwood, but this was very disappointing. (op 4-1)

3817 MEYDAN SUPERLATIVE STKS (GROUP 2) — 7f

2:00 (2:00) (Class 1) 2-Y-O

£45,416 (£17,216; £8,616; £4,296; £2,152; £1,080) **Stalls** Low

Form				RPR
11	1		**Silver Grecian**[7] 3589 2-9-0 0 .... MichaelHills 7 (J Ryan) *hld up: pushed along 2 out: plenty to do over 1f out: str run to ld wl ins fnl f: rdn out* **5/1**[3]	104+
0113	2	1	**Roi De Vitesse (IRE)**[26] 2957 2-9-0 0 .... JamesMillman 5 (B R Millman) *chsd ldrs: rdn over 2f out: led 1f out: edgd lft and hdd wl ins fnl f* **25/1**	102
15	3	3/4	**Shakespearean (IRE)**[20] 3138 2-9-0 0 .... RoystonFfrench 9 (M Johnston) *lw: hld up: hdwy over 1f out: r.o* **16/1**	100
51	4	nk	**Lucky General (IRE)**[13] 3402 2-9-0 0 .... RyanMoore 8 (R Hannon) *prom: stdd and lost pl over 5f out: rdn and nt clr run wl over 1f out: hung lft and r.o ins fnl f* **8/1**	99+
61	5	1/2	**Lord Zenith**[12] 3420 2-9-0 0 .... LPKeniry 6 (A M Balding) *sn trcking ldrs: outpcd over 1f out: hmpd ins fnl f: styd on* **9/2**[2]	98+
2	6	nse	**Emperor Claudius (USA)**[20] 3138 2-9-0 0 .... JMurtagh 3 (A P O'Brien, Ire) *lw: sn pushed along and prom: led over 5f out: rdn over 2f out: hdd 1f out: sn hung lft and no ex* **13/8**[1]	98
421	7	1 1/4	**Big Audio (IRE)**[20] 3138 2-9-0 0 .... JimmyFortune 2 (R Hannon) *lw: prom: rdn over 2f out: looked hld whn hmpd and eased ins fnl f* **5/1**[3]	94+
61	8	1/2	**Silenceofthewind (USA)**[15] 3310 2-9-0 0 .... JimCrowley 1 (K R Burke) *str: lw: led: racd keenly: hdd over 5f out but remained w ldr: rdn and ev ch over 1f out: looked hld whn hmpd and eased ins fnl f* **20/1**	95+

1m 24.37s (-1.33) **Going Correction** -0.075s/f (Good) **8** Ran SP% **115.2**

Speed ratings (Par 106): **104,102,102,101,101 101,99,99**

toteswingers: 1&2 £14.70, 1&3 £11.90, 2&3 £29.80 CSF £112.83 TOTE £5.30: £1.60, £6.90, £4.20; EX 130.40 TRIFECTA Not won..

Owner Ocean Trailers Ltd **Bred** Deerfield Farm **Trained** Newmarket, Suffolk

■ A first Group-race winner for trainer John Ryan.

■ Stewards' Enquiry : J Murtagh four-day ban: careless riding (Jul 24-28)

FOCUS

Subsequent Group 1 winners Dubawi and Horatio Nelson appear on the recent roll of honour, but this is a race with something of a mixed pedigree. This year's edition looked strong on paper, but it was a very messy race with several of the field finding trouble in the latter stages. The Chesham Stakes at Royal Ascot had looked a key piece of form, with the winner, second and fifth meeting here, but the principals from that race failed to fire. The field finished in a heap, covered by not much more than four lengths, and this form does not look too solid.

NOTEBOOK

Silver Grecian was the sole unbeaten candidate and he stretched his record to three from three. Held up in rear this time, having raced prominently on his debut over C&D and when following up at Warwick, he was looking for a run from over two out and was still nearer last entering the final furlong, but he burst through in the final 50 yards to win well. There are no immediate plans for him but a race like the Champagne Stakes at Doncaster might be suitable later in the season. He has a nice mix of speed and stamina and his trainer hopes he will make a Guineas candiate, although quotes of 33/1 look about right at this stage. (op 6-1)

Roi De Vitesse(IRE), the most experienced member of the line-up with four runs behind him, was tackling 7f for the first time, and his regular rider was unable to claim his usual 3lb allowance. After chasing the pace, he stayed on for pressure to lead briefly entering the last but could not prevent the winner from surging past. This was a decent effort but he avoided all the trouble and perhaps lacks the scope of some of his rivals.

Shakespearean(IRE), still green on his second start when fifth in the Chesham, was niggled along at halfway but avoided the trouble down the outside and stayed on for third. He turned around Ascot form with the pair who finished in front of him and remains a nice long-term prospect. (tchd 20-1)

Lucky General(IRE), the longer priced of the Hannon pair, had finished sixth on his debut behind July Stakes winner Arcano before taking a 6f Windsor maiden. After briefly having to wait for a run, he dived left under pressure, colliding with Lord Zenith, before staying on for fourth. He is worth persevering with at this trip. (op 10-1)

Lord Zenith was outpaced by the leaders at the business end and was already under pressure when getting bumped by Lucky General. This was a little disappointing but it could be that a flatter track suits him. Official explanation: jockey said colt was denied a clear run (tchd 4-1)

Emperor Claudius(USA), who had been obliged to come from behind at Ascot after meeting trouble leaving the stalls, was up with the pace all the way here but came under pressure with 2f to run. He edged to his left under Murtagh's right-handed drive inside the last, tightening up both Silenceofthewind and Big Audio, and faded out of the frame in the last half-furlong. He had previously looked progressive and this was a backward step. (op 6-4 tchd 15-8 and 2-1 in places)

Big Audio(IRE) finished a short-head in front of Emperor Claudius when winning the Chesham but was unable to confirm that form on the same terms. He was being niggled at by halfway but had been switched to the rail and was in the process of running on when his path was blocked inside the last. That ended what chance he had, and he should be not be written off. (op 6-1)

Silenceofthewind(USA) travelled strongly against the rail, disputing the running with Emperor Claudius. He could not quicken when let down and appeared held when the O'Brien colt edged into him inside the last final furlong, relegating him quickly to last place. He holds an entry in the National Stakes over this trip but this free-running sort gave the impression he would not mind reverting to 6f.

3818 LADBROKES BUNBURY CUP (HERITAGE H'CAP) — 7f

2:35 (2:37) (Class 2) 3-Y-O+

£62,310 (£18,660; £9,330; £4,670; £2,330; £1,170) **Stalls** Low

Form				RPR
-122	1		**Plum Pudding (IRE)**[8] 3536 6-9-10 **105** .... RyanMoore 5 (R Hannon) *lw: mde all: rdn over 1f out: edgd rt ins fnl f: styd on gamely* **12/1**	113
21/1	2	nk	**Captain Brilliance (USA)**[21] 3116 4-9-3 **98** .... JMurtagh 1 (J Noseda) *str: chsd ldrs: rdn over 2f out: swtchd rt ins fnl f: r.o* **3/1**[1]	105
-134	3	3/4	**Mutheeb (USA)**[21] 3091 4-9-8 **103** .... LDettori 7 (Saeed Bin Suroor) *lw: prom: chsd ldr 5f out: rdn over 2f out: styd on* **7/1**[2]	108
0006	4	shd	**Joseph Henry**[12] 3435 7-9-0 **95** .... RHills 13 (D Nicholls) *alwqays prom: rdn over 1f out: edgd lft ins fnl f: r.o* **33/1**	100
0-55	5	2 1/4	**Racer Forever (USA)**[21] 3091 6-9-9 **104** .... (b) JimmyFortune 14 (J H M Gosden) *hld up: swtchd rt and hdwy over 1f out: r.o wl ins fnl f: nt rch ldrs* **12/1**	103+
4-43	6	1/2	**Redford (IRE)**[21] 3091 4-9-5 **100** .... JamieSpencer 12 (M L W Bell) *swtg: hld up: swtchd rt and hdwy over 2f out: rdn over 1f out: styd on same pce ins fnl f* **10/1**	97+
2-41	7	1	**Signor Peltro**[41] 2470 6-9-1 **96** .... DaneO'Neill 3 (H Candy) *mid-div: hdwy 1/2-way: rdn over 1f out: styd on same pce fnl f* **8/1**[3]	91
3340	8	nk	**Nota Bene**[20] 3141 7-9-3 **98** .... RobertHavlin 4 (D R C Elsworth) *racd keenly: trckd ldr 2f: remained handy: nt clr run and lost pl over 1f out: styd on ins fnl f* **40/1**	92
4540	9	1 1/2	**Orpsie Boy (IRE)**[20] 3141 6-8-10 **96** .... Louis-PhilippeBeuzelin(5) 16 (N P Littmoden) *hld up: rdn over 2f out: r.o ins fnl f: nvr nrr* **33/1**	86
0-30	10	3/4	**Dhaular Dhar (IRE)**[21] 3091 7-9-3 **98** .... DanielTudhope 11 (J S Goldie) *lw: hld up: rdn over 2f out: n.d* **28/1**	86
2014	11	hd	**Benandonner (USA)**[13] 3391 6-9-2 **97** .... TonyHamilton 9 (R A Fahey) *prom: rdn and lost pl over 2f out: n.d after* **25/1**	84
-000	12	hd	**Shifting Star (IRE)**[21] 3091 4-9-0 **95** .... (t) AdamKirby 17 (W R Swinburn) *hld up: hdwy 1/2-way: rdn: edgd lft and wknd over 1f out* **20/1**	82
0/6-	13	1 1/4	**Headford View (IRE)**[13] 3411 5-9-0 **95** .... (p) SPasquier 2 (James Halpin, Ire) *hld up in tch: nt clr run and lost pl over 2f out: rallied over 1f out: sn wknd* **22/1**	78
3603	14	nk	**Laa Rayb (USA)**[13] 3404 5-9-10 **105** .... RoystonFfrench 20 (M Johnston) *hld up: rdn over 2f out: a in rr* **14/1**	88
6063	15	1 1/4	**Spanish Bounty**[26] 2948 4-9-0 **95** .... TPQueally 6 (J G Portman) *swtg: mid-div: hdwy 1/2-way: rdn and wknd over 1f out* **33/1**	74
0400	16	3/4	**Beaver Patrol (IRE)**[20] 3141 7-9-5 **100** .... RichardMullen 10 (Eve Johnson Houghton) *mid-div: rdn and lost pl 1/2-way: in rr whn hmpd wl over 1f out: n.d* **50/1**	77
1110	17	3/4	**Mister Hardy**[21] 3091 4-8-13 **97** .... FrederikTylicki(3) 15 (R A Fahey) *hld up: hdwy 1/2-way: rdn and wknd over 1f out* **16/1**	72
0552	18	3/4	**Al Muheer (IRE)**[21] 3091 4-9-4 **99** .... MartinDwyer 18 (C E Brittain) *hld up: rdn over 2f out: a in rr* **20/1**	72
0041	19	2 3/4	**Giganticus (USA)**[21] 3091 6-9-3 **98** .... MichaelHills 8 (B W Hills) *mid-div: dropped in rr over 4f out* **9/1**	64

1m 23.39s (-2.31) **Going Correction** -0.075s/f (Good) **19** Ran SP% **130.0**

Speed ratings (Par 109): **110,109,108,108,106 105,104,104,102,101 101,101,99,99,97 96,96,95,92**

toteswingers: 1&2 £5.10, 1&3 £12.10, 2&3 £4.20 CSF £44.21 CT £292.62 TOTE £11.10: £2.00, £1.70, £2.30, £6.20; EX 44.60 Trifecta £180.20 Pool: £2,362.60 - 9.70 winning units..

Owner Hyde Sporting Promotions Limited **Bred** Tom Deane **Trained** East Everleigh, Wilts

FOCUS

They all raced far side, meaning low drawn runners were at an advantage and, with the winner making all, it also paid to race handy. All things considered, those in high stalls had next to no chance and would surely have been better off trying their luck against the stands' rail. A slight personal best from the winner.

NOTEBOOK

Plum Pudding(IRE) was allowed an uncontested lead from a favourable draw and produced a very smart performance under joint-top weight. He only just held off the fast-finishing runner-up, and Ryan Moore, who deserves credit for a fine ride, felt the gelding was all out. He's in the totesport Mile but, while a 3lb penalty on top of his new mark of 107 will make things much tougher, he won't be top weight if Bankable takes his chance, and it's not out of the question he could repeat this type of performance granted one of the top boxes. He's a best-price 16/1 shot for the Goodwood race, but whatever, he'll surely be contesting Listed and Group 3 contests before long. (op 11-1)

Captain Brilliance(USA) ◆, raised 8lb for an impressive success over this course and distance on his return from nearly two years off last month, just got going too late. Drawn in stall one, he was always well positioned but didn't respond when first asked to pick up over two furlongs out, with the winner catching him flat footed after quickening from the front, before then running on well once switched off the rail inside the final furlong, only just failing to get up. He would probably have won had the early pace been stronger and he'll surely bid for compensation in the valuable Abu Dhabi International Stakes at Ascot at the end of the month. Considering he'll be able to race off the same mark, his chance will be obvious and quotes of around 6/1 seem about right, but anyone backing him ante-post will hope for a favourable draw. (op 7-2, tchd 4-1 in a place)

Mutheeb(USA), fourth when favourite for the Buckingham Palace at Royal Ascot, ran a solid race in defeat. Like the front pair, he was always well positioned from a good draw and had his chance. This was only his fifth start and he looks progressive. (op 15-2)

Joseph Henry ◆ deserves plenty of credit for faring best of those from a double-figure stall, keeping on well having managed to get a handy position out wide. He's in the totesport Mile and the Stewards' Cup.

Racer Forever(USA), dropped in from his high stall, finished best of those held up and ran about as well as could have been expected. He's another in the Abu Dhabi International Stakes at Ascot and is around about a 16/1 shot. (tchd 16-1 in a place)

Redford(IRE) ◆ was soon out the back after a sluggish start and was switched towards the inside. He travelled well and made more headway than most, but he had no chance with the leaders considering how the race developed. Like a few of these, he's in the big 7f handicap at Ascot at the end of the month and is entitled to go well. (op 15-2)

Signor Peltro, 4lb higher than when winning at Doncaster on his previous start, didn't travel well enough to make full use of his favourable draw. (op 10-1)

Nota Bene sat handy from his good draw but was keen early and didn't see his race out. He's better over shorter. (op 33-1, tchd 50-1 in a place)

Orpsie Boy(IRE) was left with far too much to do after being given a waiting ride from his outside stall.

Dhaular Dhar(IRE) was another not helped by a wide draw. (op 25-1 tchd 33-1)

Shifting Star(IRE) was caught wide throughout from his unfavourable draw. (op 25-1 tchd 28-1)

Headford View(IRE), 5lb higher than when winning at the Curragh on her previous start, didn't make use of stall two and lacked the pace to pose a threat. (tchd 20-1 and 25-1)

Laa Rayb(USA) had no chance from stall 20. (tchd 16-1 in a place)

Giganticus(USA), who landed this race off a mark 94 in 2007, was 7lb higher than when winning the Buckingham Palace from a few of today's rivals on his previous start, but he forfeited a reasonable draw with a rather negative ride and never featured. Whatever, though, he should still have finished closer and something might have been amiss. Official explanation: jockey said gelding ran flat (tchd 10-1 in a place)

3819 DARLEY JULY CUP (BRITISH LEG OF THE GLOBAL SPRINT CHALLENGE) (GROUP 1) 6f

3:10 (3:11) (Class 1) 3-Y-O+

£227,080 (£86,080; £43,080; £21,480; £10,760; £5,400) **Stalls** Low

Form	Pos	Dist	Horse	Jockey	RPR
54-2	**1**		**Fleeting Spirit (IRE)**[24] 2991 4-9-2 114 (J Noseda) *lw: trckd keenly: racd keenly: led over 1f out: sn rdn and hung lft: swvd rt ins fnl f: r.o: hung lft nr fin* **12/1**	TPQueally 9	123
-114	**2**	*1¼*	**Main Aim**[24] 2990 4-9-5 116 (Sir Michael Stoute) *lw: led 5f out: pushed along and hdd 2f out: hrd rdn fr over 1f out: hung lft and hmpd ins fnl f: r.o* **14/1**	RyanMoore 10	123+
6114	**3**	*½*	**J J The Jet Plane (SAF)**[20] 3140 5-9-5 119 (M F De Kock, South Africa) *b: lw: hld up in tch: jnd ldrs 2f out: sn rdn styd on* **13/2**[3]	KShea 5	120
0141	**4**	*1*	**Paco Boy (IRE)**[24] 2990 4-9-5 124 (R Hannon) *lw: hld up: pushed along over 2f out: sn outpcd: r.o wl ins fnl f: nt rch ldrs* **9/2**[2]	JimmyFortune 1	117+
-020	**5**	*nk*	**King's Apostle (IRE)**[20] 3140 5-9-5 114 (W J Haggas) *chsd ldrs: rdn over 2f out: running on whn hung lft and hmpd ins fnl f: nt rcvr* **20/1**	JMurtagh 13	119+
10-4	**6**	*hd*	**African Rose**[40] 2523 4-9-2 115 (Mme C Head-Maarek, France) *hld up: rdn over 1f out: r.o ins fnl f: nt trble ldrs* **25/1**	SPasquier 11	112
24-0	**7**	*1¼*	**Takeover Target (AUS)**[54] 2116 10-9-5 119 (Joe Janiak, Australia) *led 1f: chsd ldr tl led 2f out: sn rdn and hdd: no ex ins fnl f* **16/1**	JayFord 8	111
2000	**8**	*1¼*	**Equiano (FR)**[24] 2991 4-9-5 109 (B W Hills) *chsd ldrs: rdn over 1f out: wknd ins fnl f* **66/1**	(b) MichaelHills 7	107
6-10	**9**	*shd*	**Prime Defender**[54] 2116 5-9-5 109 (B W Hills) *hld up: rdn over 1f out: n.d* **66/1**	RHills 3	107
1	**10**	*1*	**Scenic Blast (AUS)**[24] 2991 5-9-5 120 (Daniel Morton, Australia) *lw: hld up: racd keenly: hdwy over 1f out: rdn and edgd lft ins fnl f: fnd nil* **11/8**[1]	StevenArnold 2	104
0204	**11**	*1*	**Intrepid Jack**[8] 3536 7-9-5 105 (H Morrison) *s.i.s: sn pushed along in rr: sme hdwy over 4f out: wknd over 1f out* **125/1**	JimCrowley 6	100
0-01	**12**	*12*	**Art Connoisseur (IRE)**[20] 3140 3-8-13 119 (M L W Bell) *hld up: rdn over 1f out: a in rr: eased ins fnl f* **12/1**	JamieSpencer 4	62
16-2	**13**	*6*	**Ancien Regime (IRE)**[13] 3388 4-9-5 109 (Saeed Bin Suroor) *hld up: rdn over 2f out: sn wknd* **25/1**	LDettori 12	43

69.58 secs (-2.92) **Going Correction** -0.075s/f (Good)

WFA 3 from 4yo+ 6lb **13** Ran SP% **117.8**

Speed ratings (Par 117): **116,114,113,112,111 111,110,108,108,106 105,89,81**

toteswingers: 1&2 £30.10, 1&3 £8.60, 2&3 £10.00 CSF £154.74 TOTE £15.50: £3.50, £5.00, £2.90; EX 127.50 Trifecta £1816.60 Pool: £13,993.26 - 5.70 winning units..

Owner The Searchers **Bred** Mrs Bernadette Hayden **Trained** Newmarket, Suffolk

FOCUS

A terrific July Cup on paper, well up to scratch, with Australian and South African challengers taking on the best European sprinters. Royal Ascot form was richly represented, by the King's Stand first and second and the winners of the Golden Jubilee and Queen Anne Stakes. Racing down the centre, they did not appear to go off particularly quickly, but the time was just .07 of a second outside Stravinsky's track record, set in this race ten years ago. The race was slightly unsatisfactory in some ways though, with those held up, including the three Ascot winners, failing to get into it, and the winner having to survive an enquiry after causing interference to both the runner-up and the fifth inside the final furlong.

NOTEBOOK

Fleeting Spirit(IRE) had been due to head straight for the Nunthorpe in August following her second to Scenic Blast in the King's Stand, but she had been working so well recently that she was allowed to take her chance. She broke quickly, thanks to a new stalls routine first used on her at Ascot, travelled well in touch and burst clear over a furlong out. Inside the last, with the race in the bag, she hung badly to her left before swerving back to the right when her jockey took corrective action, interfering with Main Aim who in turn rolled on to King's Apostle. The filly was clearly the best horse on the day and her wayward action, which connections could not account for, did not improve her final position. She will head to York and the Nunthorpe now and will be hard to beat on this evidence, with the return to 5f not a problem for her. (op 16-1)

Main Aim had looked set to go for the Golden Jubilee at Ascot following his Group 3 win over 7f at Haydock, but he stepped up to 1m instead, finishing fourth to Paco Boy in the Queen Anne. Dropped back to sprinting now, the colt ran a cracker, with the fast ground no inconvenience to him. Soon in front, he came off the bridle with 2f to run and the winner quickly swept past. He stuck to his guns but was held in second when she veered sharply across him inside the last.

J J The Jet Plane(SAF), unsuited by the lack of an even gallop when fourth in the Golden Jubilee, ran his race here, sticking on after showing prominently towards the far side. He has winning form over 7f and could step up to an intermediate trip in the Prix Maurice de Gheest at Deauville. (op 8-1 tchd 6-1)

Paco Boy(IRE), the Queen Anne winner, had not run over sprint distances since he was a 2yo and had since proved himself at the top level over 7f and 1m. His participation here had been in doubt in the lead up to the race due to fears over fast ground. With Richard Hughes suspended Jimmy Fortune took over and the colt was held up, although further from the pace than usual, and he found himself outpaced going into the dip before finishing with a real flourish to snatch fourth. He loses nothing in defeat and may revert to a mile in the Sussex Stakes. (tchd 5-1 in a place)

King's Apostle(IRE) was ridden by Johnny Murtagh, who was preferred to Liam Jones. Without the visor this time, the Duke of York runner-up raced in touch and was running on, nearest to the stands' rail, when he had to be snatched up to avoid Main Aim who himself had been hampered by the winner. The incident probably cost King's Apostle third place. (op 16-1)

African Rose, who went to post early, ran a sound race with no obvious excuses. The rearranged Haydock Sprint Cup she won at Doncaster last September was not a strong Group 1. (op 20-1)

Takeover Target(AUS), who missed Ascot with a temperature, showed plenty of pace but faded late on. He was also seventh on his only previous appearance in this race, behind Les Arcs three years ago. Sadly he was found to have cracked his near-hind cannonbone and has been retired. He won 21 races, including seven at Group 1 level, and earned more than £2.5m. (op 12-1)

Equiano(FR) was not discredited but remains below form and is more effective over 5f.

Prime Defender ran okay but wasn't good enough. (op 50-1)

Scenic Blast(AUS), so impressive when beating Fleeting Spirit in the King's Stand, was bitterly disappointing in his bid to become the first winner of that race to follow up here since Never So Bold 24 years ago. Held up towards the rear, he was asked to pick up at about the two pole, his rider apparently confident he had plenty of horse underneath him, but the response was very short-lived. The return to 6f should not have posed a problem and this was his first defeat on a straight track. This was not his running. (op 13-8 tchd 7-4 in places)

Art Connoisseur(IRE), winner of the Golden Jubilee, didn't do himself justice, although there were doubts about his Ascot form, with the market leaders below par and speculation that the ground had been overwatered. Reunited with Jamie Spencer, he was another held up out the back and failed to respond when asked to pick up before being eased. (op 10-1)

Ancien Regime(IRE) Official explanation: jockey said colt lost its action

3820 NGK SPARK PLUGS E B F MAIDEN FILLIES' STKS 6f

3:45 (3:47) (Class 2) 2-Y-O **£9,714** (£2,890; £1,444; £721) **Stalls** Low

Form	Pos	Dist	Horse	Jockey	RPR
32	**1**		**Bella Swan**[27] 2914 2-9-0 0 (W R Swinburn) *w'like: scope: lw: trckd ldrs: rdn to ld and hung rt ins fnl f: r.o* **3/1**[1]	AdamKirby 5	85+
2	**2**	*¾*	**Water Biscuit**[14] 3356 2-9-0 0 (B J Meehan) *unf: scope: led: rdn over 1f out: hdd and edgd rt ins fnl f: styd on* **7/1**[3]	JamieSpencer 4	83+
	3	*4*	**Outshine** 2-9-0 0 (J H M Gosden) *w'like: athletic: hld up: hdwy and hung rt over 1f out: r.o: nt trble ldrs* **9/1**	JimmyFortune 8	71+
	4	*½*	**Ghazwah** 2-9-0 0 (J H M Gosden) *w'like: scope: lw: w ldr: tl rdn 2f out: sn edgd rt: wknd fnl f* **6/1**[2]	RHills 3	69+
32	**5**	*nk*	**Babylonian**[34] 2699 2-9-0 0 (M Johnston) *leggy: chsd ldrs: rdn over 1f out: wknd fnl f* **10/1**	RoystonFfrench 6	68
5	**6**	*¾*	**Areeda (IRE)**[34] 2711 2-9-0 0 (C E Brittain) *w'like: scope: prom: rdn over 2f out: hung rt and wknd fnl f* **20/1**	MartinDwyer 14	66+
	7	*1¼*	**Dubawi Heights** 2-9-0 0 (S A Callaghan) *str: lw: s.i.s: sn pushed along and prom: rdn and wknd over 1f out* **15/2**	LDettori 2	62
	8	*1½*	**Star Twilight** 2-9-0 0 (D R Lanigan) *leggy: mid-div: pushed along 1/2-way: wknd over 1f out* **14/1**	ChrisCatlin 1	58
	9	*1*	**Excellent Day (IRE)** 2-9-0 0 (M R Channon) *unf: hld up: rdn over 2f out: hung rt over 1f out: n.d* **22/1**	SamHitchcott 11	55+
	10	*nk*	**Larehaan (USA)** 2-9-0 0 (B W Hills) *w'like: s.i.s: hld up: rdn and edgd lft over 2f out: sn wknd* **11/1**	MichaelHills 7	54
	11	*1*	**Silent Secret (IRE)** 2-9-0 0 (R Hannon) *unf: s.i.s: a in rr* **7/1**[3]	RyanMoore 12	51
	12	*4*	**Faithful Duchess (IRE)** 2-9-0 0 (E A L Dunlop) *str: bit bkwd: hld up: a in rr: rdn over 2f out: sn wknd* **33/1**	JimCrowley 9	39
	13	*½*	**Golden Pippin** 2-9-0 0 (R Hannon) *str: bit bkwd: dwlt: a in rr* **50/1**	RichardMullen 13	37
	14	*¾*	**Precious Coral (IRE)** 2-9-0 0 (S A Callaghan) *w'like: scope: bit bkwd: hld up: a in rr: wknd over 2f out* **16/1**	LPKeniry 10	35

1m 12.13s (-0.37) **Going Correction** -0.075s/f (Good) **14** Ran SP% **130.0**

Speed ratings (Par 97): **99,98,92,92,91 90,88,86,85,85 83,78,77,76**

toteswingers: 1&2 £3.70, 1&3 £9.50, 2&3 £6.40 CSF £24.54 TOTE £4.30: £1.70, £2.10, £3.50; EX 22.80.

Owner Pendley Farm **Bred** Pendley Farm **Trained** Aldbury, Herts

FOCUS

Often a very decent fillies' maiden - recent winners include Fantasia and Gossamer - and this should produce plenty of nice types. They started off racing towards the far side, but were spread out across the track at the line. Improved form from the first two, who both look decent.

NOTEBOOK

Bella Swan is held in high regard - she might have gone for the Cherry Hinton had she won last time - and she got off the mark at the third attempt in decent enough style, despite hanging right about a furlong out, possibly shying away from the runner-up's jockey's whip. She may now be aimed at the Group 3 Princess Margaret Stakes at Ascot. (op 4-1, tchd 9-2 in places)

Water Biscuit, given a positive ride against the far rail, flashed her tail when first hit with the whip but still ran on and pulled a long way clear of the remainder. This confirmed the promise she showed when runner-up in a muddling contest over this course and distanced on her debut and she should win a similar race. (tchd 13-2 and 15-2)

Outshine, a £32,000 half-sister to eight winners, including smart 6f-1m winner Warming Trends, has been given a Lowther entry. She continually went right under pressure and ended up towards the stands' rail, but she still showed ability. She should have learnt plenty and it's hoped she'll be less wayward next time. (op 8-1 tchd 10-1)

Ghazwah ◆ didn't see her race out after showing speed, but she wasn't given a hard time by Richard Hills inside the final furlong and should be capable of better. (op 13-2 tchd 8-1)

Babylonian didn't seem to have any excuses, but she's bred to want further and now has the option of nurseries. (op 9-1)

Areeda(IRE), who's entered in the Moyglare Stakes, was another to hang right but still stepped up on her debut showing. Official explanation: jockey said filly was unsuited by the good to firm, good in places ground (op 16-1)

Dubawi Heights ◆, a 72,000gns half-sister to triple 6f-1m winner Generous Thought, out of 6f juvenile scorer, is another with a Lowther entry. She ran green but showed ability and can do better. (op 8-1 tchd 7-1)

Star Twilight is bred to want further. (op 12-1 tchd 11-1)

Larehaan(USA) started slowly and gave the impression she'll come on for the experience. (op 16-1 tchd 20-1)

Silent Secret(IRE) was solid in the market but was another to start slowly and never featured. (op 9-1 tchd 10-1 and 11-1 i n a place)

3821 WEATHERBYS NURSERY — 7f

4:20 (4:20) (Class 2) 2-Y-O £12,952 (£3,854; £1,926; £962) Stalls Low

Form				RPR
41	1		**Lamh Albasser (USA)**[20] 3170 2-9-0 **86** ... LDettori 2	94+
			(Saeed Bin Suroor) *lengthy: hld up: hdwy over 2f out: shkn up to ld over 1f out: r.o: eased nr fin* **3/1**[1]	
312	2	1 1/4	**Tres Coronas (IRE)**[56] 2041 2-8-2 **74** ow1 ... ChrisCatlin 6	77
			(T D Barron) *led: rdn and hung rt fr over 2f out: hdd over 1f out: styd on* **5/1**[2]	
011	3	2	**Sir Parky (IRE)**[28] 2875 2-9-7 **93** ... JimmyFortune 7	91
			(R Hannon) *lw: chsd ldr: edgd rt over 2f out: sn rdn: styd on* **6/1**[3]	
4231	4	hd	**Rock Of Love (IRE)**[17] 3232 2-9-6 **92** ... RoystonFfrench 8	89
			(M Johnston) *prom: rdn and carried rt over 2f out: nt clr run wl over 1f out: swtchd lft: styd on* **15/2**	
6431	5	1/2	**Master Of Dance (IRE)**[16] 3256 2-8-7 **79** ow1 ... RyanMoore 9	75
			(R Hannon) *lw: hld up: hdwy u.p over 1f out: nt trble ldrs* **5/1**[2]	
2510	6	2 3/4	**Bell's Ocean (USA)**[21] 3086 2-7-12 **75** ... Louis-PhilippeBeuzelin(5) 5	64
			(J Ryan) *hld up in tch: rdn over 1f out: edgd lft and wknd ins fnl f* **6/1**[3]	
524	7	2 3/4	**Ginger Grey (IRE)**[33] 2735 2-8-2 **74** ow1 ... MartinDwyer 3	56
			(S A Callaghan) *hld up: rdn over 2f out: hdwy over 1f out: wknd fnl f* **25/1**	
644	8	6	**Ant Music (IRE)**[24] 2997 2-7-13 **71** ... AdrianMcCarthy 4	38
			(J S Moore) *prom: rdn over 2f out: wknd over 1f out* **16/1**	
521	9	2 3/4	**Jehu**[24] 2997 2-8-8 **80** ... SamHitchcott 1	41
			(M R Channon) *chsd ldrs tl rdn and wknd over 1f out* **14/1**	

1m 24.97s (-0.73) **Going Correction** -0.075s/f (Good) **9** Ran SP% **115.1**

Speed ratings (Par 100): **101,99,97,97,96 93,90,83,80**

toteswingers: 1&2 £2.90, 1&3 £3.50, 2&3 £4.70 CSF £17.77 CT £84.33 TOTE £3.80: £1.70, £2.00, £2.20; EX 20.80.

Owner Godolphin **Bred** Stonestreet Thoroughbred Holdings Llc **Trained** Newmarket, Suffolk

■ Stewards' Enquiry : Jimmy Fortune caution: careless riding

FOCUS

A decent nursery and the winning time was only 0.60 seconds slower than Silver Grecian recorded in the Group 2 Superlative Stakes earlier on the card. They all started off up the middle of the track and that's where the winner stayed, but a few of these drifted towards the stands' side late on, including the runner-up. The form should work out well.

NOTEBOOK

Lamh Albasser(USA) was gelded after being extremely wayward on his racecourse debut and has quickly developed into a very useful juvenile. He was forced to work hard to win a maiden at Redcar last time, but improved on that form with a decisive success on this switch to nursery company. Having travelled strongly, he ran straight and true under pressure and ultimately won a shade cosily. There should be more to come. (op 7-2 tchd 4-1 in places)

Tres Coronas(IRE) looked well treated for his nursery bow, even allowing for 1lb overweight, and promised to be suited by this step up in trip. He edged right under pressure, but had his chance and was simply beaten by a better one on the day. He might step up to 1m now. Official explanation: jockey said gelding hung right-handed (op 9-2 tchd 11-2)

Sir Parky(IRE), bidding for a hat-trick after wins in minor company over sprint trips, ended up against the stands' rail after drifting right but didn't run badly. (op 11-2)

Rock Of Love(IRE) is a little better than he showed as Sir Parky carried him right towards the stands' rail inside the final three furlongs and then took his ground. Official explanation: jockey said colt was carried across (op 8-1)

Master Of Dance(IRE), the winner of as 5.5f maiden on his previous start, didn't convince over this longer trip, struggling to land a telling blow having been held up. (tchd 9-2 and 11-2)

Bell's Ocean(USA), the only filly, hails from a stable in great form with their two-year-olds but she didn't offer much. (op 8-1 tchd 11-2)

3822 EGERTON HOUSE STABLES H'CAP — 1m 4f

4:55 (4:57) (Class 3) (0-90,90) 3-Y-O+ £9,714 (£2,890; £1,444; £721) Stalls High

Form				RPR
0213	1		**Cool Strike (UAE)**[13] 3371 3-8-6 **81** ...(v) LPKeniry 16	93
			(A M Balding) *mde all: rdn and hung lft fr over 1f out: styd on* **9/1**	
0-30	2	1 3/4	**Manyriverstocross (IRE)**[27] 2932 4-9-11 **87** ... JamieSpencer 17	96
			(A King) *a.p: rdn to chse wnr and hung lft over 1f out: kpt on* **13/2**	
-601	3	1 1/2	**Classic Vintage (USA)**[16] 3280 3-9-0 **89** ... JimCrowley 13	96+
			(Mrs A J Perrett) *lw: s.i.s: hld up: hdwy over 2f out: rdn and edgd lft over 1f out: styd on* **6/1**[3]	
1051	4	2 1/2	**Gordonsville**[20] 3146 6-9-10 **86** ... DanielTudhope 14	89
			(J S Goldie) *hld up: hdwy over 2f out: rdn and edgd lft over 1f out: no ex ins fnl f* **14/1**	
-226	5	3 1/4	**Sahrati**[16] 3273 5-9-13 **89** ...(p) MartinDwyer 8	87
			(D R C Elsworth) *prom: rdn over 2f out: wknd fnl f* **12/1**	
0-43	6	3/4	**William Blake**[19] 3189 4-9-9 **85** ... RoystonFfrench 9	82
			(M Johnston) *lw: chsd wnr: rdn over 2f out: wknd fnl f* **9/1**	
-662	7	5	**Nice Time (IRE)**[26] 2942 3-7-12 **73** oh1 ... NickyMackay 5	62
			(M H Tompkins) *mid-div: hdwy over 3f out: rdn and wknd 2f out* **16/1**	
0563	8	1 1/4	**Group Captain**[9] 3510 7-9-9 **90** ... Louis-PhilippeBeuzelin(5) 3	77
			(H J Collingridge) *hld up: rdn over 3f out: wknd over 2f out* **20/1**	
5310	9	nk	**Clear Reef**[41] 2486 5-9-7 **83** ... MichellePayne 10	69
			(Jane Chapple-Hyam) *plld hrd and prom: stdd and lost pl over 8f out: hdwy over 3f out: wknd over 2f out* **33/1**	
-532	10	1	**Jabal Tariq**[16] 3273 4-9-9 **85** ... RHills 6	70
			(B W Hills) *hld up: hdwy over 4f out: wknd over 2f out* **14/1**	
-000	11	1 3/4	**Sereth (IRE)**[55] 2085 6-10-0 **90** ... TPQueally 11	72
			(B J Curley) *s.i.s: hld up: a in rr* **40/1**	
3000	12	1 1/4	**Grand Passion (IRE)**[37] 2597 9-9-12 **88** ... ChrisCatlin 12	68
			(C F Wall) *hld up: a in rr: rdn and wknd over 2f out* **50/1**	
-564	13	3 1/2	**Force Group (IRE)**[7] 3587 5-8-13 **75** ... SaleemGolam 4	49
			(M H Tompkins) *prom: rdn over 3f out: wknd over 2f out* **28/1**	
61	14	11	**Pictorial (USA)**[39] 2551 3-8-7 **82** ... RyanMoore 15	39
			(Sir Michael Stoute) *lw: mid-div: lost pl 8f out: rdn over 3f out: wknd over 2f out: eased fnl f* **5/1**[2]	
6612	15	10	**Bullet Man (USA)**[19] 3189 4-9-10 **86** ... JimmyFortune 2	27
			(L M Cumani) *sn prom: rdn over 3f out: wknd over 2f out: eased fnl f* **4/1**[1]	

2m 28.31s (-4.59) **Going Correction** -0.075s/f (Good)

WFA 3 from 4yo+ 13lb **15** Ran SP% **126.7**

Speed ratings (Par 107): **112,110,109,108,106 105,102,101,101,100 99,98,96,88,82**

toteswingers: 1&2 £15.90, 1&3 £8.60, 2&3 £13.80 CSF £66.26 CT £393.86 TOTE £10.10: £3.00, £3.20, £2.50; EX 111.00 Place 6: £217.74 Place 5: £143.92..

Owner Mrs P Hastings **Bred** Darley **Trained** Kingsclere, Hants

FOCUS

They came down the centre of the track in the straight. Not many got into the race, the winner making all, and those drawn high dominated. The form may not prove that solid.

NOTEBOOK

Cool Strike(UAE) is an improved performer this year since being fitted with a visor. Put up a stone after winning at Bath, he was just held from this mark at Chester, but did not handle the bends and was unable to reach the front there, whereas he could dictate things this time. He looked in trouble when coming under pressure and edged to his left, but stayed on well in the end. He is a galloper who will stay further and could win a nice race on the Flat, but he also has obvious potential as a jumper. (op 10-1 tchd 8-1)

Manyriverstocross(IRE) racded close to the pace and chased the winner hard through the last two furlongs. Third under Spencer to subsequent Old Newton Cup winner Red Merlin first time out before running too keen from a bad draw in an amateurs' race, he could be ready for a try over further. (op 9-1 tchd 10-1)

Classic Vintage(USA), in contrast to the front two, improved from the back of the field. He briefly posed a threat but could make no further impression inside the last. This was a solid effort in the circumstances off a 4lb higher mark than when winning at Salisbury. (op 7-1 tchd 15-2)

Gordonsville, 4lb higher than when winning over 1m5f at Ayr, came from a little way off the pace to go after the leaders but was unable to quicken late on. This was another creditable effort. (op 18-1 tchd 20-1)

Sahrati looks rated up to his best on turf and is a stone higher than he is on sand. Another who was always up with the pace, he could not race on with the principals in the last quarter-mile. (op 11-1 tchd 10-1)

William Blake ran creditably and finished clear of the remainder, but after chasing the winner his stamina over this longer trip was just waning late on. (op 12-1)

Group Captain Official explanation: jockey said gelding hung right

Pictorial(USA) was making his handicap debut after just two starts in maidens. This trip was expected to suit and he was well drawn, but he missed the break and could never get into the race. He is probably worth another chance. (op 4-1 tchd 6-1)

Bullet Man(USA) got over from his low draw to race prominently but weakened tamely and before his stamina for this longer trip could be fully tested. Official explanation: jockey said colt stopped quickly (op 5-1)

T/Jkpt: Not won. T/Plt: £258.00 to a £1 stake. Pool: £178,367.31. 504.53 winning tickets. T/Qpdt: £27.90 to a £1 stake. Pool: £11,458.16. 303.50 winning tickets. CR

2932 YORK (L-H)

Friday, July 10

OFFICIAL GOING: Good (8.3)

Course at innermost configuration and all distances as advertised.

Wind: Light across Weather: Overcast - sunny periods

3823 CAKEMARK E B F MAIDEN STKS — 7f

2:15 (2:16) (Class 3) 2-Y-O £7,641 (£2,273; £1,136; £567) Stalls Low

Form				RPR
	1		**Emirates Dream (USA)** 2-9-3 0 ... TedDurcan 8	81+
			(Saeed Bin Suroor) *midfield: hdwy 3f out: rdn to chse ldng pair wl over 1f out: styd on ins fnl f to ld nr fin* **2/1**[1]	
	2	nk	**Laureldean Spirit (IRE)** 2-8-12 0 ... PaulHanagan 11	73+
			(R A Fahey) *cl up: rdn to ld over 1f out: edgd lft ins fnl f: hdd and no ex nrfin* **5/1**[3]	
3	3	3/4	**Marie De Medici (USA)**[30] 2819 2-8-12 0 ... J-PGuillambert 3	71+
			(M Johnston) *cl up: led over 2f out: sn rdn and hdd over 1f out: drvn and kpt on ins fnl f* **11/4**[2]	
	4	6	**Hoss Cartwright (IRE)** 2-9-3 0 ... PaulMulrennan 10	64+
			(J Howard Johnson) *chsd ldrs: rdn along over 2f out: grad wknd* **33/1**	
06	5	1/2	**The Caped Crusader (IRE)**[22] 3052 2-9-3 0 ... MickyFenton 2	60
			(T P Tate) *led: rdn along and hdd over 2f out: sn drvn and grad wknd* **50/1**	
	6	1 3/4	**Jimmy The Poacher (IRE)** 2-9-3 0 ... DavidAllan 5	55
			(T D Easterby) *sn pushed along in rr: hdwy on inner wl over 2f out: kpt on appr fnl f: nrst fin* **16/1**	
2	7	1	**We'll Deal Again**[54] 2099 2-9-3 0 ... DaleGibson 6	53
			(M W Easterby) *chsd ldrs: rdn along over 2f out: grad wknd* **13/2**	
	8	4	**Bun Oir (USA)** 2-9-3 0 ... PatCosgrave 12	43
			(R Hannon) *midfield: pushed along and green 1/2-way: n.d* **10/1**	
	9	1 1/4	**Escape Artist** 2-9-3 0 ... DNolan 9	40
			(T D Easterby) *a towards rr* **50/1**	
0	10	7	**Moonlight Blaze**[15] 3310 2-9-3 0 ... AndrewElliott 1	22
			(C W Fairhurst) *midfield: rdn along 1/2-way: sn wknd* **100/1**	
	11	1 3/4	**Newtons Cradle (IRE)** 2-9-3 0 ... PhillipMakin 4	18
			(J Howard Johnson) *in rr fr 1/2-way* **20/1**	

1m 26.27s (0.97) **Going Correction** 0.0s/f (Good) **11** Ran SP% **117.6**

Speed ratings (Par 98): **94,93,92,85,85 83,82,77,76,68 66**

toteswingers: 1&2 £4.10, 1&3 £1.80, 2&3 £3.50 CSF £11.85 TOTE £3.00: £1.30, £2.20, £1.50; EX 14.00.

Owner Godolphin **Bred** Kilroy Thoroughbred Partnership **Trained** Newmarket, Suffolk

FOCUS

A decent maiden featuring a couple that had already shown some ability and some interesting newcomers. It is hard to be sure of the level of the form, but the first three pulled a very long way clear of the rest and the race looks worth rating at least this high.

NOTEBOOK

Emirates Dream(USA) ◆, an $850,000 yearling out of a high-class performer at up to 1m1f on dirt in the US, did well to win this as he was slow to break and then appeared to have little chance of catching the leader inside the last furlong, but he never stopped trying and got up in the very dying strides. He should get further and has a future. (tchd 9-4)

Laureldean Spirit(IRE) ◆, a 150,000euros half-sister to a couple of winners including the high-class Nahoodh, attracted market support on this debut. Having been prominent from the off, she appeared to have done everything right and looked the certain winner inside the last furlong, but she got tired in the very latter stages and was mugged on the line. Her winning turn is merely delayed. (op 8-1)

Marie De Medici(USA), who finished in front of a subsequent winner when third on her Haydock debut last month, is bred to have been suited by this extra furlong. Always up there, she had every chance but was inclined to hang inside the last furlong and couldn't get back at the front pair. Perhaps she still needed the experience and she should break her duck before too long. (tchd 3-1 in a place)

Hoss Cartwright(IRE), a 25,000euros yearling and already gelded, made some late progress without being knocked about and, although well adrift of the leading trio at the line, this was a pleasing enough introduction. (op 40-1)

The Caped Crusader(IRE) made much of the running and, although he was swamped over the last couple of furlongs, this was still probably an improvement on his first two efforts. Nurseries are likely to be his thing. (op 40-1)

Jimmy The Poacher(IRE) ◆, a 29,000euros half-brother to his smart stable-companion Ponty Rossa, showed enough on this debut without being given a hard time, and the experience will not be lost on him. (op 14-1)

We'll Deal Again, who 'won' the race on his side when runner-up on his debut at Ripon in May, was up there early but was left behind over the last couple of furlongs. A recent entry in a seller suggests he isn't considered a world-beater, but he probably needs more time and, given his breeding, he would be of real interest if tried on sand. (op 5-1)

Newtons Cradle(IRE), a 32,000gns half-brother to the winning juvenile sprinter El Soprano, was backed at big prices but he proved far too green on this debut and looks to need more time and experience. (op 33-1)

3824 CUISINE DE FRANCE SUMMER STKS (GROUP 3) (F&M) 6f

2:45 (2:45) (Class 1) 3-Y-O+ **£38,519** (£14,566; £7,280; £3,640) **Stalls** High

Form RPR

11-0 **1** **Serious Attitude (IRE)**[68] 1698 3-8-10 111 EddieAhern 1 113
(Rae Guest) *trckd ldrs on outer: hdwy 2f out: rdn to chal over 1f out: r.o ins fnl f to ld nr fin* **7/2**[2]

-113 **2** *hd* **Lesson In Humility (IRE)**[20] 3140 4-9-4 109 AndrewElliott 2 115
(K R Burke) *cl up: led over 2f out: rdn over 1f out: drvn ins fnl f: hdd and nt qckn nr fin* **5/2**[1]

-131 **3** *3 ¾* **Look Busy (IRE)**[48] 2272 4-9-6 103 SladeO'Hara 11 105
(A Berry) *hld up in rr: hdwy 1/2-way: n.m.r 2f out: effrt whn nt clr run and hmpd 1f out: squeezed through and rdn to chse ldng pair: kpt on same pce* **14/1**

3131 **4** *½* **Swiss Diva**[27] 2934 3-8-10 101 DarryllHolland 9 105+
(D R C Elsworth) *hld up in tch: hdwy whn nt clr run and swtchd lft 1f out: sn rdn and kpt on wl fnl f: nrst fin* **15/2**

2623 **5** *shd* **Pusey Street Lady**[13] 3388 5-9-2 99 FrancisNorton 4 99
(J Gallagher) *led: rdn along 1/2-way and sn hdd: drvn over 1f out: hung rt 1f out and sn wknd* **18/1**

0-31 **6** *¾* **Danehill Destiny**[41] 2485 3-8-10 102 (t) PaulHanagan 6 96
(W J Haggas) *prom: rdn along 2f out and ev ch: drvn and n.m.r ent fnl f: sn wknd* **9/2**[3]

1144 **7** *½* **Diana's Choice (SAF)**[26] 2948 5-9-2 110 PatCosgrave 5 95
(M F De Kock, South Africa) *chsd ldrs: rdn and ev ch 2f out: sn drvn and hld whn hmpd 1f out: wknd after* **9/1**

0466 **8** *1 ½* **Infamous Angel**[34] 2703 3-8-10 100 TedDurcan 10 89
(R Hannon) *a in rr* **33/1**

0630 **9** *7* **Favourite Girl (IRE)**[15] 3320 3-8-10 96 DavidAllan 3 67
(T D Easterby) *chsd ldrs: rdn along over 2f out: sn wknd* **10/1**

69.82 secs (-2.08) **Going Correction** 0.0s/f (Good)
WFA 3 from 4yo+ 6lb **9** Ran SP% **114.7**
Speed ratings (Par 113): **113,112,107,107,106 105,105,103,93**
toteswingers: 1&2 £120.70, 1&3 £63.00, 2&3 £16.10 CSF £12.57 TOTE £3.90: £1.70, £1.40, £2.90; EX 6.70 Trifecta £36.50 Pool: £375.04 - 7.60 winning units..

Owner Derek J Willis & Rae Guest **Bred** Paddy Twomey **Trained** Newmarket, Suffolk

FOCUS

A fascinating Group 3 sprint for the girls run at a strong pace and, although a couple met trouble in running, class told and the two market leaders pulled clear. The winner has been rated as improving a length on her two-year-old form.

NOTEBOOK

Serious Attitude(IRE), winner of last season's Cheveley Park for which she escaped a penalty here, was back to sprinting after appearing not to stay in the 1000 Guineas. Not best away, she nonetheless travelled powerfully down the wide outside and maintained her effort to get up near the line. This looks to be her game and she is now likely to go for the Prix Maurice du Gheest at Deauville over an extra half furlong. (op 10-3 tchd 3-1)

Lesson In Humility(IRE), back down in class following her cracking effort to finish third in the Golden Jubilee, was one of those to help force the pace and she looked likely to score when shaking off the other two pacesetters over a furlong out, but despite a couple of trademark swishes of the tail she gave her all and was mugged close to the line. (op 11-4 tchd 2-1 in a place)

Look Busy(IRE), fourth in this race last year, just keeps on improving and beat the boys in the Group 2 Temple Stakes at Haydock last time, but that victory saddled her with a 4lb penalty here. Held up early, she endured a troubled passage when trying to get closer, especially when trying for a gap between Diana's Choice and Pusey Street Lady, and once through she never had a hope of getting near the front pair. She seems to stay this trip, but all ten of her wins have come over the minimum. (op 12-1 tchd 10-1)

Swiss Diva ◆, upped in class after winning the big three-year-old handicap over course and distance last month off a mark of 91, also met plenty of trouble. She travelled well off the pace but when trying for a run between Diana's Choice and Danehill Destiny, the gap quickly closed and she was forced to switch out to her left. She ran on well when out in the clear and looks well worth another try at this level. Official explanation: jockey said filly was denied a clear run (op 8-1)

Pusey Street Lady has been running well in Group and Listed company this season, but she is without a win since March of last year. She ran fast for a long way, but was held from over a furlong out and may have preferred softer ground. (tchd 16-1)

Danehill Destiny, who beat a subsequent winner in a Haydock Listed event last time, raced up with the leaders closest to the stands' rail but didn't get home. (op 5-1 tchd 11-2)

Diana's Choice(SAF), an ordinary fourth of six on her British debut in a Salisbury Listed event last month, was reported to have come on from that but she never looked like winning and now has plenty to prove. (op 8-1)

3825 CARAVAN CHAIRMAN'S CHARITY STKS (H'CAP) 7f

3:20 (3:20) (Class 4) (0-85,84) 3-Y-O+ **£6,476** (£1,927; £963; £481) **Stalls** Low

Form RPR

1650 **1** **Smarty Socks (IRE)**[20] 3172 5-9-2 79 PaulPickard(7) 16 90
(P T Midgley) *towards rr on outer: hdwy over 2f out: swtchd rt to stands' rail and rdn wl over 1f out: styd on to ld ins fnl f: r.o strly* **33/1**

12-3 **2** *1 ½* **Happy Anniversary (IRE)**[14] 3341 3-9-2 80 EdwardCreighton 11 84
(Mrs D J Sanderson) *hld up towards rr: hdwy and pushed along over 2f out: rdn wl over 1f out: snswtchd rt and drvn: styd on ins fnl f* **10/1**

1412 **3** *½* **Red Cape (FR)**[3] 3706 6-9-10 80 6ex AndrewElliott 9 86
(Mrs R A Carr) *cl up: effrt 2f out: sn rdn and ev ch tl drvn and nt qckn ins fnl f* **13/2**[2]

-001 **4** *hd* **Shotley Mac**[14] 3339 5-9-13 83 (b) FrancisNorton 4 88
(N Bycroft) *led: rdn along over 2f out: drvn over 1f out: hdd ins fnl f: kpt on same pce* **12/1**

4603 **5** *1* **Sunrise Safari (IRE)**[13] 3389 6-9-7 82 (v) BMcHugh(5) 8 84
(R A Fahey) *chsd ldrs: rdn along 2f out: drvn over 1f out: one pce ins fnl f* **16/1**

6643 **6** *½* **Spirit Of Sharjah (IRE)**[14] 3347 4-10-0 84 DarryllHolland 5 85
(Miss J Feilden) *in tch: hdwy to chse ldrs over 2f out: sn rdn and kpt on same pce appr fnl f* **12/1**

2520 **7** *½* **Tiger Dream**[14] 3339 4-8-13 74 (p) AmyRyan(5) 6 74
(K A Ryan) *cl up: effrt 2f out: sn rdn and ev ch tl drvn and wknd ins fnl f* **14/1**

-121 **8** *hd* **Johannes (IRE)**[21] 3122 6-9-12 82 PaulHanagan 14 81
(R A Fahey) *t.k.h: hld up towards rr: hdwy over 2f out and sn rdn: kpt on appr fnl f: nt rch ldrs* **9/2**[1]

-003 **9** *2* **Without Prejudice (USA)**[14] 3339 4-9-7 77 EddieAhern 12 71
(J Noseda) *dwlt and rr: swtchd lft and hdwy over 2f out: sn rdn and n.d* **8/1**[3]

1102 **10** *nk* **Turn Me On (IRE)**[9] 3496 6-9-10 80 JamieMoriarty 1 73
(T D Walford) *a towards rr* **20/1**

3205 **11** *1 ¼* **Kiwi Bay**[7] 3567 4-9-10 80 PhillipMakin 7 69
(M Dods) *t.k.h: hld up in rr: hdwy over 2f out: sn rdn and n.d* **20/1**

5452 **12** *1* **Mey Blossom**[11] 3453 4-8-9 68 MichaelJStainton(3) 13 55
(R M Whitaker) *in tch on outer: rdn along 2f out: and grad wknd* **14/1**

2206 **13** *¾* **Bravely (IRE)**[20] 3172 5-9-4 74 TedDurcan 3 59
(T D Easterby) *rrd s and s.i.s: a in rr* **14/1**

0033 **14** *½* **Eastern Hills**[6] 3612 4-8-12 73 LanceBetts(5) 10 56
(J S Wainwright) *promient: rdn along over 2f out: sn drvn and wknd* **12/1**

4013 **15** *3 ¼* **White Deer (USA)**[5] 3656 5-9-10 80 (b) MickyFenton 2 55
(G A Harker) *chsd ldrs: rdn along over 2f out: sn wknd* **17/2**

1m 24.3s (-1.00) **Going Correction** 0.0s/f (Good)
WFA 3 from 4yo+ 8lb **15** Ran SP% **123.7**
Speed ratings (Par 105): **105,103,102,102,101 100,100,99,97,97 95,94,93,93,89**
toteswingers: 1&2 £10.40, 1&3 £8.60, 2&3 £41.40 CSF £335.78 CT £2490.90 TOTE £55.00: £12.70, £4.20, £2.10; EX 1436.80.

Owner R G Fell **Bred** Mick McGinn **Trained** Westow, N Yorks

FOCUS

A competitive handicap in which the field came centre-to-stands' side in the home straight. Several were well backed which suggests that a few were well fancied, but there was a shock result and there is a chance that this race was influenced by a track bias. The third and fourth are the guide to the form.

Without Prejudice(USA) Official explanation: jockey said gelding missed the break
Bravely(IRE) Official explanation: jockey said gelding reared at the start
White Deer(USA) Official explanation: jockey said gelding hung badly right in the straight

3826 CADBURY CUP (HANDICAP STKS) 1m 4f

3:55 (3:57) (Class 2) (0-100,92) 3-Y-O+ **£11,527** (£3,430; £1,714; £856) **Stalls** Centre

Form RPR

0013 **1** **Cosmic Sun**[6] 3618 3-8-11 88 PaulHanagan 10 94
(R A Fahey) *chsd ldng pair: rdn and cl up over 2f out: led wl over 1f out: drvn ent fnl f and styd on gamely towards fin* **7/2**[2]

453 **2** *¾* **Lochiel**[30] 2815 5-9-8 86 PJMcDonald 4 91
(G A Swinbank) *trckd ldrs: hdwy 3f out: rdn to chal 2f out: drvn to dispute ld over 1f out and ev ch tl no ex last 75yds* **10/1**

6504 **3** *nk* **Resplendent Light**[13] 3406 4-9-8 86 EddieAhern 8 91
(W R Muir) *midfield: hdwy 3f out: rdn wl over 1f out: swtchd lft and drvn ins fnl f: styd on towards fin* **22/1**

1 **4** *½* **Whispering Gallery**[23] 3022 3-9-1 92 J-PGuillambert 3 96
(M Johnston) *trckd ldr: cl up 3f out: rdn to ld over 2f out: hdd wl over 1f out and sn drvn: wknd ins fnl f* **2/1**[1]

-330 **5** *1 ¼* **Rajeh (IRE)**[24] 2994 6-9-11 89 JamieMoriarty 9 91+
(J L Spearing) *hld up towards rr: hdwy over 3f out: rdn and n.m.r over 1f out: swtchd lft and kpt on ins fnl f: nrst fin* **16/1**

1-00 **6** *½* **Red Kestrel (USA)**[34] 2706 4-9-5 88 AmyRyan(5) 7 89
(K A Ryan) *hld up towards rr: hdwy over 2f out: rdn wl over 1f out: drvn and no imp appr fnl f* **20/1**

123 **7** *shd* **Hillview Boy (IRE)**[27] 2932 5-9-3 81 MickyFenton 6 82
(J S Goldie) *hld up in rr: hdwy over 2f out: rdn wl over 1f out: sn no imp* **10/1**

-420 **8** *shd* **King Fingal (IRE)**[16] 3266 4-8-11 80 JamieKyne(5) 5 81
(J J Quinn) *a in midfield* **7/1**

6300 **9** *6* **Carte Diamond (USA)**[13] 3390 8-10-0 92 PhillipMakin 11 83
(B Ellison) *prom on outer: rdn along over 3f out and sn wknd* **20/1**

0342 **10** *½* **Rosbay (IRE)**[23] 3034 5-9-4 82 DavidAllan 1 72
(T D Easterby) *chsd ldrs: hdwy and cl up 3f out: rdn over 2f out and grad wknd* **25/1**

1133 **11** *4 ½* **Martyr**[20] 3142 4-9-13 91 DarryllHolland 2 74
(R Hannon) *led: rdn along 3f out: hdd over 2f out: sn drvn and wknd* **6/1**[3]

2m 32.09s (-1.11) **Going Correction** 0.0s/f (Good)
WFA 3 from 4yo+ 13lb **11** Ran SP% **124.1**
Speed ratings (Par 109): **103,102,102,101,101 100,100,100,96,96 93**
toteswingers: 1&2 £5.10, 1&3 £9.50, 2&3 £9.70 CSF £38.27 CT £696.72 TOTE £5.00: £1.60, £3.30, £7.00; EX 32.70.

Owner The Cosmic Cases **Bred** M Wassall **Trained** Musley Bank, N Yorks

■ Stewards' Enquiry : Eddie Ahern caution: careless riding
Paul Hanagan caution: careless riding

FOCUS

A decent handicap run at just a fair pace and this time the whole field came right up the stands' rail in the home straight. The form has been taken at face value for now but is unlikely to prove solid given the bunched finish.

NOTEBOOK

Cosmic Sun, 1lb well in compared to his new mark, needs a strong pace as his King George V Handicap victory showed, and he didn't have the race run to suit at Haydock six days earlier. Although this wasn't exactly run at a scorching pace, it was solid enough for him and, having been handy from the start, he battled on to gain a very game victory. He is likely to step up in trip now and may return here next month for the Melrose. (op 9-2 tchd 5-1 in a place)

Lochiel was a good third off 1lb higher in the Lanark Silver Bell at Hamilton last time and that race has already produced three subsequent winners. He put in a strong effort from the middle of the field entering the last 2f and just lost out following a protracted duel. (op 8-1 tchd 15-2)

Resplendent Light, who continues to slide down the weights after some modest efforts so far this season, put in a very strong finish and this was his best effort for some time. He is still 4lb above his last winning mark, but on this evidence he can win off it. (op 25-1 tchd 18-1)

Whispering Gallery, who slammed a 78-rated rival by ten lengths on his debut in a Hamilton maiden auction last month, was sent off a well-backed favourite. Always close to the pace, he bagged the stands' rail in the straight, which appeared such an advantage in the previous contest, but already looked beaten when becoming short of room inside the last furlong. Given his lack of experience, it's probably best to forgive him this, and he is probably capable of much more. (op 7-2)

Rajeh(IRE), dropping back a mile after finishing in midfield in the Ascot Stakes, was making a rare appearance over a trip this short, so it was no great surprise to see him come off the bridle a long way out before finishing well. A return to further is needed. (op 14-1)

Red Kestrel(USA), who didn't sparkle in his first two starts for the yard, was down another 4lb and performed better this time, making a little headway over the last couple of furlongs. He still has a bit of scope and better can probably be expected. (op 25-1)

Hillview Boy(IRE), a good third from a bad draw in the Queen Mother's Cup over course and distance last month, didn't have a lot of room to play with when trying to get closer over the last couple of furlongs and he remains unexposed on the Flat. Official explanation: jockey said gelding was denied a clear run (op 8-1)

Martyr, running well in recent months and off the same mark as when third in the Duke Of Edinburgh, was allowed his own way out of front but he put up limited resistence when challenged and dropped away very disappointingly. Official explanation: jockey said gelding ran too free (op 5-1 tchd 13-2)

3827 MR KIPLING EXCEEDINGLY GOOD STKS (H'CAP) 1m 6f

4:30 (4:36) (Class 3) (0-95,90) 3-Y-O **£7,641** (£2,273; £1,136; £567) **Stalls** Low

Form				RPR
3112	1		**Akmal**[16] 3280 3-9-7 **88** ... EddieAhern 1	98+

(J L Dunlop) *trckd ldrs: hdwy 3f out: led 2f out: sn jnd and rdn: drvn ins fnl f and kpt on gamely towards fin* **9/2**[2]

210 **2** *nse* **Sabotage (UAE)**[21] 3090 3-9-9 **90** ... J-PGuillambert 2 — 100+
(M Johnston) *hld up in rr: hdwy on inner 3f out: rdn to chal wl over 1f out: sn drvn and ev ch tl no ex nr fin* **5/1**[3]

-222 **3** *6* **Astrodiva**[23] 3022 3-8-8 **75** ... TedDurcan 4 — 77
(M H Tompkins) *hld up in tch: hdwy 3f out: rdn 2f out: drvn over 1f out: styd on u.p ins fnl f* **10/1**

0313 **4** *3 ½* **Deauville Flyer**[22] 3069 3-7-13 **71** oh1 ... JamieKyne(5) 5 — 68
(T D Easterby) *hld up towards rr: hdwy on outer over 3f out: rdn to chse ldrs 2f out: sndrvn and wknd: hung lft ins fnl f* **13/2**

3111 **5** *9* **Antigua Sunrise (IRE)**[22] 3069 3-8-13 **80** ... PaulHanagan 3 — 65
(R A Fahey) *hld up in rr: hdwy 5f out: rdn to chse ldrs 3f out: drvn 2f out and sn btn* **4/1**[1]

2410 **6** *31* **Talimos (IRE)**[21] 3090 3-9-1 **82** ... PatCosgrave 7 — 23
(R M Beckett) *chsd ldrs on outer: rdn along 5f out: drvn and wknd 3f out* **9/1**

5-31 **7** *24* **Kris Kin Line (IRE)**[27] 2922 3-8-10 **77** ... DarryllHolland 8 — —
(Sir Michael Stoute) *cl up: rdn along 3f out and sn wknd* **4/1**[1]

0-46 **8** *23* **Kudu Country (IRE)**[22] 3069 3-8-8 **75** ... MickyFenton 6 — —
(T P Tate) *led: rdn along over 3f out: drvn and hddc 2f out: sn wknd and virtually p.u appr fnl f* **14/1**

2m 58.77s (-1.43) **Going Correction** 0.0s/f (Good) **8** Ran SP% **113.9**
Speed ratings (Par 104): **104,103,100,98,93 75,61,48**
toteswingers: 1&2 £5.10, 1&3 £9.50, 2&3 £9.70 CSF £26.98 CT £211.61 TOTE £5.40: £1.90, £2.00, £2.80; EX 29.10.
Owner Hamdan Al Maktoum **Bred** Shadwell Estate Company Limited **Trained** Arundel, W Sussex
■ Stewards' Enquiry : Eddie Ahern caution: used whip with excessive frequency

FOCUS

A decent handicap with several of these attempting this sort of trip for the first time, but despite what looked a very ordinary pace it proved far too much for a few and they finished spread all over the Knavesmire. The first two, who raced furthest from the stands' rail in the home straight, pulled well clear of the others and produced a cracking finish. The third and fourth are the best guide.

NOTEBOOK

Akmal, who has been running consistently well this season, was up another 2lb despite getting beaten last time and was one of those trying beyond 1m4f for the first time. It proved no problem for him though, especially as he had to get every yard in order to get the better of the runner-up, and he remains a progressive sort. (op 6-1)

Sabotage(UAE) ◆, making his handicap debut after finishing a rather disappointing ninth in the Queen's Vase, returned to form here. Given a patient ride, he came to win his race and lost nothing in defeat. Unraced before last month, he still has plenty of scope and shouldn't take long in regaining the winning thread. (op 9-2 tchd 11-2)

Astrodiva, making her handicap debut after three consecutive seconds, including when thrashed by Whispering Gallery (fourth in the previous contest) at Hamilton last time, was racing over half a mile further than she had attempted before. Despite hanging away to her right over the last furlong or so, she plugged on to finish third at a respectable distance but the jury is still out over her stamina. (op 11-1)

Deauville Flyer, nearly four lengths behind Antigua Sunrise at Ripon last time and 7lb better off, put in an effort towards the nearside of the group coming to the last quarter-mile and managed to turn the form around with the Fahey filly, but he too failed to convince that he stayed this trip. (op 11-2 tchd 7-1)

Antigua Sunrise(IRE), up another 8lb in her bid for a four-timer and trying this trip for the first time, was inclined to race in snatches and, although still in with a chance of a place coming to the last 2f, her stamina then seemed to ebb away. (op 7-2 tchd 9-2 in a place)

Talimos(IRE) Official explanation: jockey said gelding hung right throughout

Kris Kin Line(IRE) was well in with Sabotage on their meeting at Goodwood in May, albeit over half a mile shorter, but he came off the bridle fully 3f out and folded very quickly. He had struggled to beat an habitual loser in a Polytrack maiden last time, so may be harshly handicapped at present. Official explanation: jockey said colt lost its action (op 5-1)

Kudu Country(IRE) Official explanation: jockey said gelding lost its action

3828 WARBURTONS, BAKERS BORN & BRED APPRENTICE STKS (H'CAP) 5f

5:05 (5:07) (Class 4) (0-80,80) 3-Y-O+ **£5,180** (£1,541; £770; £384) **Stalls** High

Form — RPR

0000 **1** **Highland Warrior**[22] 3065 10-8-9 **63** ... PaulPickard(2) 6 — 75
(P T Midgley) *towards rr and sn pushed along: hdwy whn nt clr run 2f out: sn swtchd lft and rdn over 1f out: styd on wl to ld last 100yds* **16/1**

060 **2** *¾* **Kyzer Chief**[10] 3491 4-8-13 **65** ... DeanHeslop 4 — 74
(R E Barr) *chsd ldrs: hdwy to ld wl over 1f out: drvn ins fnl f: hdd and no ex last 100yds* **9/1**

0-22 **3** *1 ¼* **Wicked Wilma (IRE)**[11] 3445 5-8-9 **61** oh2 ... SladeO'Hara 1 — 66
(A Berry) *trckd ldrs: hdwy 2f out: rdn to chal and ev ch whn hung lft ent fnl f: kpt on same pce* **11/1**

201 **4** *¾* **Top Bid**[7] 3570 5-8-12 **64** 6ex ... (b) JamieKyne 3 — 66
(T D Easterby) *in tch: rdn along to chse ldrs 2f out: kpt on u.p ins fnl f* **7/1**

0614 **5** *nk* **Angelo Poliziano**[11] 3464 3-8-13 **70** ... (p) LanceBetts 12 — 69
(Mrs A Duffield) *chsd ldrs: rdn 2f out: drvn and hung lft ent fnl f: one pce* **17/2**

1005 **6** *½* **Mister Laurel**[27] 2915 3-9-3 **78** ... (b[1]) LeeTopliss(4) 2 — 75
(R A Fahey) *in tch on outer: rdn along 2f out: kpt on same pce appr fnl f* **20/1**

0001 **7** *2 ¼* **Sea Rover (IRE)**[8] 3529 5-8-13 **69** 6ex ... JohnCavanagh(4) 5 — 60
(M Brittain) *cl up: rdn along 2f out: sn drvn and wknd over 1f out* **9/2**[1]

5521 **8** *1 ¼* **Baybshambles (IRE)**[6] 3607 5-9-6 **74** 6ex ... DeclanCannon(2) 9 — 60
(R E Barr) *slowly intio stride: hdwy and in tch 1/2-way: sn rdn and btn* **6/1**[3]

2050 **9** *nk* **High Curragh**[24] 3001 6-9-12 **80** ... (p) AmyRyan(2) 10 — 65
(K A Ryan) *cl up: rdn wl over 1f out: drvn and wknd ent fnl f* **11/2**[2]

30-0 **10** *¾* **Northern Bolt**[105] 985 4-9-10 **80** ... NSLawes(4) 7 — 63
(D Nicholls) *led: rdn along over 2f out: drvn and hdd wl over 1f out: wkng whn hmpd ent fnl f* **12/1**

1005 **11** *2 ¾* **Pacific Pride**[6] 3607 6-9-1 **71** ... (v) IJBrennan(4) 11 — 44
(J J Quinn) *prom: rdn along 2f out: sn wknd* **10/1**

0060 **12** *hd* **Lord Of The Reins (IRE)**[24] 3001 5-9-6 **72** ... PatrickDonaghy 8 — 44
(J G Given) *s.i.s and a bhd* **14/1**

59.24 secs (-0.06) **Going Correction** 0.0s/f (Good)
WFA 3 from 4yo+ 5lb **12** Ran SP% **123.3**
Speed ratings (Par 105): **100,98,96,95,95 94,90,88,88,87 82,82**
toteswingers: 1&2 £45.30, 1&3 £51.60, 2&3 £21.50 CSF £158.96 CT £1699.54 TOTE £28.20: £6.00, £3.60, £3.00; EX 241.60 Place 6: £478.24 Place 5: £394.91..
Owner R Wardlaw **Bred** Rowcliffe Stud **Trained** Westow, N Yorks

FOCUS

A competitive sprint handicap run at a strong early pace and another dramatic finish. The third and fourth have been rated close to their marks.

Wicked Wilma(IRE) Official explanation: jockey said gelding hung left

Top Bid Official explanation: jockey said gelding was denied a clear run

Lord Of The Reins(IRE) Official explanation: jockey said gelding missed the break

T/Plt: £700.40 to a £1 stake. Pool: £77,427.18. 80.69 winning tickets. T/Qpdt: £198.90 to a £1 stake. Pool: £3,522.28. 13.10 winning tickets. JR

3829 - 3838a (Foreign Racing) - See Raceform Interactive

3792 ASCOT (R-H)

Saturday, July 11

OFFICIAL GOING: Good to firm (good in places on round course; overall 10.3, straight 10.4 round 10.3)

Rail realignment increased distance of 2.20 race by 16yards and 2.50 race by 8yards.

Wind: fairly modest, half against Weather: light rain

3839 TOTESCOOP6 STKS (HERITAGE H'CAP) 7f

1:50 (1:52) (Class 2) 3-Y-O

£31,155 (£9,330; £4,665; £2,335; £1,165; £585) **Stalls** Low

Form — RPR

1412 **1** **Secret Society**[23] 3049 3-9-5 **96** ... JamieSpencer 4 — 109+
(M L W Bell) *stdd and hmpd s: hld up in rr: switching rt fr 3f out: gng wl on outer wl over 1f out: chsd ldr jst ins fnl f: drvn to chal ins fnl f: r.o wl to ld last strides* **10/3**[2]

2110 **2** *hd* **Suruor (IRE)**[23] 3049 3-8-11 **88** ... JimCrowley 2 — 100
(D M Simcock) *hld up in rr: hdwy on outer wl over 2f out: rdn to ld over 1f out: r.o wl tl hdd and no ex last strides* **9/1**

-663 **3** *2 ½* **Khor Dubai (IRE)**[9] 3536 3-9-7 **98** ... (v) TedDurcan 3 — 103
(Saeed Bin Suroor) *wnt rt s: trckd ldrs: nt clr run ent fnl 2f: squeezed between horses and ev ch wl over 1f out: sn hung rt: edgd lft and one pce fnl f* **12/1**

4410 **4** *2 ½* **Invisible Man**[23] 3049 3-8-8 **85** ... RichardMullen 1 — 84
(J H M Gosden) *wnt rt s: led: rdn and edgd rt ent fnl 2f: hdd over 1f out: wknd ent fnl f* **5/1**[3]

364 **5** *2 ½* **Agente Parmigiano (IRE)**[14] 3375 3-8-12 **89** ... (p) RichardHughes 5 — 81
(G A Butler) *t.k.h early: hld up towards rr: nt clr run 2f out: sn swtchd lft: drvn and no hdwy over 1f out* **16/1**

0-11 **6** *½* **Sioux Rising (IRE)**[12] 3453 3-8-7 **84** ... AlanMunro 9 — 74
(R A Fahey) *t.k.h: in tch: pushed along over 3f out: wknd u.p wl over 1f out* **11/1**

4403 **7** *1* **Feeling Fab (FR)**[16] 3293 3-8-9 **86** ... RoystonFfrench 8 — 74
(M Johnston) *stdd s: t.k.h: hld up in midfield: hdwy on outer over 3f out: ev ch and rdn 2f out: wknd and hung lft fr over 1f out* **33/1**

-400 **8** *6* **Satwa Laird**[23] 3049 3-8-8 **85** ... SteveDrowne 7 — 57
(E A L Dunlop) *chsd ldng pair: rdn over 2f out: wknd qckly wl over 1f out* **6/1**

0-31 **9** *½* **Captain Ellis (USA)**[9] 3531 3-8-6 **83** ... (p) AndrewElliott 10 — 53
(K R Burke) *pressed ldr: rdn and ev ch jst over 2f out: wkng and btn whn n.m.r over 1f out* **16/1**

5214 **10** *4 ½* **Espiritu (FR)**[23] 3049 3-9-6 **97** ... (v) JimmyFortune 6 — 55
(J Noseda) *hld up in last trio: rdn and no rspnse over 2f out: nvr a factor* **3/1**[1]

1m 26.45s (-1.55) **Going Correction** +0.075s/f (Good) **10** Ran SP% **119.8**
Speed ratings (Par 106): **111,110,107,105,102 101,100,93,93,87**
toteswingers: 1&2 £8.80, 1&3 £7.00, 2&3 £16.20. CSF £34.66 CT £271.85 TOTE £3.80: £1.80, £3.60, £4.20; EX 31.40 Trifecta £352.40 Pool: £1090.59 - 2.29 winning units..
Owner Sheikh Marwan Al Maktoum **Bred** Darley **Trained** Newmarket, Suffolk

FOCUS

A decent three-year-old handicap run at a fair gallop, and the front two pulled nicely clear. They all raced towards the stands' side, but the first two raced away from the rail in the closing stages.

NOTEBOOK

Secret Society ◆ apparently surprised Jamie Spencer by how well he picked up when second in the Britannia Stakes - his jockey felt if anything he got there too soon - so he was given an exaggerated waiting ride this time. However, after making good headway on the bridle, having been last early, he was asked to sit in behind the running-on Suruor until just over a furlong out, and didn't respond immediately when finally asked to win his race. He edged slightly left under hands-and-heels pressure, before his rider went for the whip in the final few yards and forced him in front in the last strides. He had spread both hind plates beforehand and apparently also lost a front shoe during the race, which Spencer felt was pricking him, suggesting that's why he didn't pick up as well as last time. Whatever the case, this was a decent effort off a 6lb higher mark and there's good reason to believe he is even better than the bare result. A colt with a terrific cruising speed, he's equally effective over this trip and 1m and is entered in both the Abu Dhabi International back over this course and distance on July 25, and the Totesport Mile at Goodwood on 31 July. He should go well in whatever race connections choose, granted a good draw. (tchd 7-2)

Suruor(IRE) was below form under too prominent a ride in the Britannia, but left that effort behind with a career-best effort under more patient tactics. Having travelled well, he went readily to the front and stayed on strongly for pressure, but was just picked off. (op 14-1)

Khor Dubai(IRE), racing in a handicap for the first time this year, had his chance after briefly being short of room about two furlongs out, but didn't run straight and proved no match for the front two, who simply look more progressive. (tchd 10-1)

Invisible Man was given a positive ride, but he couldn't confirm Britannia placings with Suruor. (op 8-1 tchd 9-1)

Agente Parmigiano(IRE) didn't get the clearest of runs and had to be switched inside, but he wasn't unlucky. (tchd 11-1)

Sioux Rising(IRE), the winner of her last two starts, both gained over 6f at Pontefract, raced keenly early on over this longer trip and never looked like defying a 4lb rise. (op 6-1)

Satwa Laird ran nowhere near the form he showed in the Britannia. (op 15-2 tchd 8-1)

Espiritu(FR), fourth at the Royal meeting, was covered up towards the inside for most of the way, but found nothing when asked to pick up. Official explanation: jockey said colt was never travelling (op 10-3 tchd 7-2 in places)

3840 EURO EARTHWORKS H'CAP — 1m 2f

2:20 (2:20) (Class 3) (0-90,93) 3-Y-O+ **£7,771** (£2,312; £1,155; £577) **Stalls High**

Form | | | | RPR

1-03 **1** **Shamali**[29] 2891 4-9-8 **84** ... RHills 3 102+
(W J Haggas) *hld up wl bhd: stl plenty to do over 2f out: gd hdwy 2f out: chsd ldr over 1f out: rdn to ld ins fnl f: sn clr: readily* **7/2**[2]

2231 **2** 2 ¾ **Mabuya (UAE)**[17] 3279 3-8-8 **81** ... FergusSweeney 11 91+
(P J Makin) *chsd ldr tl over 8f out: wnt 2nd again 3f out: shkn up to ld 2f out: sn rdn clr: hdd ins fnl f: no ch w wnr* **3/1**[1]

36-4 **3** 2 **Jawaab (IRE)**[14] 3378 5-8-13 **75** ... RichardMullen 12 81
(Mark Buckley) *stdd s: t.k.h: hld up in rr: hdwy towards inner over 2f out: chsd ldng pair jst ins fnl f: no imp* **25/1**

0-11 **4** 1 ½ **Shavansky**[19] 3213 5-9-8 **87** ... JamesMillman(3) 6 90
(B R Millman) *hld up in rr: hdwy and n.m.r ent fnl 2f: rdn over 1f out: plugged on to go 4th wl ins fnl f: nvr trbld ldrs* **8/1**

5-42 **5** ½ **Spell Caster**[32] 2796 4-9-8 **87** ... JackMitchell(3) 2 89
(R M Beckett) *t.k.h: chsd ldng trio: rdn to chse ldng pair over 2f out: drvn and no imp wl over 1f out* **15/2**

0-40 **6** 5 **Snoqualmie Boy**[47] 2342 6-9-11 **87** ... JimmyFortune 10 79
(T P Tate) *hld up off the pce in midfield: effrt wl over 2f out: rdn and no imp over 1f out* **14/1**

12-0 **7** 1 ¼ **Black Rain**[84] 1357 4-9-0 **76** ... AlanMunro 7 65
(M Wigham) *stdd to rr after s: t.k.h: hld up wl bhd: swtchd lft and effrt jst over 2f out: no prog* **20/1**

331 **8** 1 ¾ **Midnight Cruiser (IRE)**[13] 3429 3-9-6 **93** ... RichardHughes 4 79
(R Hannon) *t.k.h: hld up off the pce in midfield: rdn and effrt 3f out: drvn and no prog over 2f out: wknd* **5/1**[3]

0000 **9** ¾ **Road To Love (IRE)**[8] 3586 6-9-5 **81** ... RoystonFfrench 9 65
(M Johnston) *led: qcknd 8f out: rdn and hdd 2f out: wknd qckly over 1f out* **14/1**

0065 **10** 10 **Ramona Chase**[8] 3586 4-9-10 **86** ... PaulDoe 8 50
(M J Attwater) *stdd s: plld hrd and hdwy on outer to chse ldr over 8f out tl 3f out: wknd u.p over 2f out* **16/1**

0000 **11** 11 **Rowan Rio**[7] 3635 4-8-10 **72** ... MichaelHills 1 14
(W J Haggas) *stdd and swtchd rt s: hld up wl bhd: rdn and lost tch wl over 2f out: t.o* **25/1**

2m 7.15s (0.15) **Going Correction** +0.075s/f (Good)
WFA 3 from 4yo+ 11lb **11** Ran SP% **118.4**
Speed ratings (Par 107): **102,99,98,97,96 92,91,90,89,81 72**
toteswinger: 1&2 £2.80, 1&3 £18.00, 2&3 £14.50. CSF £14.11 CT £221.62 TOTE £5.00: £2.10, £1.50, £7.80; EX 17.50 TRIFECTA Not won..
Owner Abdulla Al Khalifa **Bred** Sheikh Abdulla Bin Isa Al-Khalifa **Trained** Newmarket, Suffolk

FOCUS

A decent handicap. The early pace looked steady, resulting in a few of these racing keenly, before noticeably increasing after about three furlongs or so.

NOTEBOOK

Shamali ◆ did well to win so readily considering he still had plenty to do turning into the straight, and the runner-up had got first run on the field when kicked into a clear lead around two furlongs out. He has taken a couple of runs to come to himself this year, just like last season, but his trainer, who sounds quite sweet on him, is not ruling out the Ebor. Although he is by Selkirk, his dam won over 1m6f and both Bet365 and Totesport cut him to 20-1 from 33s. (tchd 10-3, 4-1 in places)

Mabuya(UAE) made a bold bid early in the straight, but he had been a little keen early and couldn't resist the winner's late challenge. A good effort off a 6lb higher mark than when winning at Salisbury on his previous start. (op 7-2 tchd 4-1 in places)

Jawaab(IRE) has yet to win beyond 1m. He seemed to get the trip okay, but still couldn't land a telling blow. (op 28-1 tchd 33-1)

Shavansky ◆, bidding for a hat-trick off a 5lb higher mark than when winning at Lingfield on his latest outing, was under pressure in an unpromising position turning into the straight before running on. He should prove suited by a return to more positive tactics.

Spell Caster, the only filly, was a bit keen early and finished up well held. A 4lb rise for her recent second at Salisbury looks harsh. (op 7-1 tchd 8-1)

Black Rain was reported to have hung right. Official explanation: jockey said gelding hung right (op 22-1)

Midnight Cruiser(IRE) was only 3lb higher than when winning at Windsor on his previous start, but he was a little keen early and never featured. (op 6-1)

Road To Love(IRE) continues to finish his races tamely. (op 12-1)

Rowan Rio Official explanation: jockey said gelding lost its action

3841 TOTESPORT.COM SUMMER MILE STKS (GROUP 2) — 1m (R)

2:50 (2:52) (Class 1) 4-Y-O+ **£56,770** (£21,520; £10,770; £5,370; £2,690; £1,350) **Stalls High**

Form | | | | RPR

1-03 **1** **Aqlaam**[25] 2990 4-9-1 117 ... RHills 6 120
(W J Haggas) *stdd s: sn t.k.h and hdwy to trck ldrs: chsd ldr wl over 1f out: rdn to ld 1f out: kpt on wl* **15/8**[1]

-124 **2** ½ **Confront**[8] 3585 4-9-1 109 ... JimmyFortune 9 119
(Sir Michael Stoute) *sn pressing ldr: led 3f out: rdn jst over 2f out: drvn and hdd 1f out: kpt on same pce fnl f* **12/1**

4461 **3** ½ **Imbongi (SAF)**[14] 3398 5-9-1 114 ... KShea 1 118
(M F De Kock, South Africa) *hld up in tch: hdwy on outer jst over 2f out: chsd ldng pair ent fnl f: kpt on wl but nvr quite getting to ldrs* **4/1**[3]

2054 **4** 5 **Dream Eater (IRE)**[14] 3398 4-9-1 112 ... (t) LPKeniry 7 107
(A M Balding) *led narrowly tl 3f out: drvn over 2f out: wknd ent fnl f* **12/1**

43-2 **5** 2 ¼ **Cesare**[25] 2990 8-9-1 118 ... JamieSpencer 2 101
(J R Fanshawe) *niggled along early: bhd: rdn and effrt over 2f out: no rspnse and wl hld after* **9/4**[2]

2541 **6** 5 **Without A Prayer (IRE)**[14] 3404 4-9-1 112 ... RichardKingscote 4 90
(R M Beckett) *in tch in midfield: lost pl 1/2-way: rdn 3f out: sn struggling and wl btn fnl 2f* **12/1**

2164 **7** 5 **Ordnance Row**[14] 3404 6-9-1 110 ... RichardHughes 8 78
(R Hannon) *w.w in tch towards rr: rdn and effrt on inner over 2f out: no hdwy: eased whn wl btn fnl f* **25/1**

1m 39.92s (-0.78) **Going Correction** +0.075s/f (Good) **7** Ran SP% **112.5**
Speed ratings (Par 115): **106,105,105,100,97 92,87**
toteswinger: 1&2 £4.50, 1&3 £2.20, 2&3 £5.10. CSF £24.18 TOTE £2.70: £1.60, £4.40; EX 23.10 Trifecta £91.50 Pool: £1585.80 - 12.82 winning units..
Owner Hamdan Al Maktoum **Bred** Granham Farm **Trained** Newmarket, Suffolk

FOCUS

This looked like a decent Group 2. A modest early gallop wasn't satisfactory, but it's hard to argue too much with the result.

NOTEBOOK

Aqlaam suffered a fractured pelvis (although it wasn't displaced) after winning last year's Jersey Stakes and has taken a while to rediscover his best form but, having been well beaten in the Lockinge on his return, his latest third in the Queen Anne offered more hope. Eased slightly in grade, he had to work hard to justify favouritism and was only workmanlike, but the muddling early gallop was hardly conducive to a big performance, and this more than confirmed his recovery. He was a little keen early, but was sensibly ridden by Richard Hills, ensuring he was close up throughout, and although taking a while to get on top in the straight, he battled on well. It's not unreasonable to expect him to step forward again, this being only his third start after serious injury, and a stronger-run race should suit better. He could be aimed at the Prix Jacques le Marois, before a possible tilt at the Queen Elizabeth II Stakes back over this course and distance, and William Haggas even mentioned the Breeders' Cup. However, it's likely he'll be kept apart from the same owner's Ghanaati. (op 9-4 tchd 5-2 in places)

Confront, dropped in trip, recovered from a sluggish start to help force the pace, and even though he got the run of things to an extent, this was still a fine effort. There was much to like about the way he stuck on for pressure and, having taken time to fulfil his potential, there could be more to come. (tchd 11-1)

Imbongi(SAF), whose trainer won this race last year with Archipenko, is another who probably would have preferred a better gallop but he ran on well to pull a long way clear of the remainder. He won a 7f Group 3 at Newmarket on his previous start and is evidently in top form. (op 7-2)

Dream Eater(IRE), too keen when behind Imbongi over 7f at the July course last time, didn't improve for the step back up in distance and simply does not stay 1m in high-class company. (op 16-1)

Cesare's hold-up style was totally unsuited to the way the race unfolded and he could not confirm Queen Anne form with Aqlaam. But even so, he did seem to run a little flat and was reported to have never been travelling. Official explanation: jockey said gelding was never travelling (tchd 5-2)

Without A Prayer(IRE) confirmed recent Windsor placings with Ordnance Row, but in truth was still not good enough. (op 11-1 tchd 10-1)

3842 RUDDY NURSERY — 6f

3:25 (3:26) (Class 4) 2-Y-O **£6,476** (£1,927; £963; £481) **Stalls Low**

Form | | | | RPR

41 **1** **Soul Heaven**[45] 2383 2-8-8 **75** ... JamieSpencer 8 77
(M L W Bell) *s.i.s: hld up bhd: swtchd rt and hdwy on outer over 2f out: drvn and hung lft ent fnl f: r.o to ld towards fin* **4/1**[1]

210 **2** nk **Step In Time (IRE)**[21] 3138 2-9-1 **82** ... RoystonFfrench 1 83
(M Johnston) *w ldr: rdn to ld 2f out: hdd jst ins fnl f: rallied to ld again fnl 100yds tl hdd and no ex towards fin* **4/1**[1]

6414 **3** nk **Merseyside Star (IRE)**[4] 3702 2-8-2 **69** ... AndrewElliott 5 69
(K R Burke) *t.k.h: hld up wl in tch: swtchd lft and hdwy over 1f out: rdn and qcknd to ld jst ins fnl f: hld hd high u.p and hdd fnl 100yds: no ex* **5/1**[2]

1100 **4** ½ **Desert Auction (IRE)**[25] 2995 2-9-7 **88** ... RichardHughes 6 87
(R Hannon) *s.i.s: bhd: pushed along over 2f out: hdwy on stands' rail over 1f out: drvn and ev ch ent fnl f: unable qck fnl 100yds* **13/2**

01 **5** ½ **Cultured Pride (IRE)**[22] 3101 2-8-12 **79** ... SteveDrowne 9 76
(R Hannon) *hld up in rr: hdwy on outer over 2f out: drvn and ev ch but edging rt over 1f out: unable qck fnl f* **14/1**

6613 **6** 3 **Saxby (IRE)**[9] 3542 2-8-4 **76** ow1 ... MCGeran(5) 7 64
(M R Channon) *w.w in tch: rdn and effrt to press ldrs 2f out: wknd u.p ent fnl f* **11/1**

031 **7** 3 ¼ **Wigan Lane**[15] 3337 2-8-4 **71** ... AlanMunro 2 49
(R A Fahey) *prom: ev ch and rdn 2f out: drvn and wknd over 1f out* **6/1**[3]

455 **8** nk **Master Mylo (IRE)**[51] 2187 2-7-7 **67** oh4 ow2 ... RyanPowell(7) 4 44
(Mrs L C Jewell) *bmpd s: sn rcvrd and led: hdd 2f out: wknd over 1f out* **33/1**

3403 **9** 3 ½ **Timelord (IRE)**[8] 3579 2-8-2 **69** ... CatherineGannon 3 36
(S Kirk) *wnt rt s: chsd ldrs: rdn 3f out: struggling 2f out and sn bhd* **7/1**

1m 15.12s (0.72) **Going Correction** +0.075s/f (Good) **9** Ran SP% **114.7**
Speed ratings (Par 96): **98,97,97,96,95 91,87,87,82**
toteswinger: 1&2 £1.20, 1&3 £3.60, 2&3 £4.70. CSF £19.61 CT £81.07 TOTE £3.60: £1.70, £1.70, £1.90; EX 12.10 Trifecta £39.20 Pool: £856.59 - 16.17 winning units..
Owner Lady Bamford **Bred** Lady Bamford **Trained** Newmarket, Suffolk

FOCUS

A very competitive nursery. They started off towards the stands' side, but were spread out all the way across to the middle of the track at the line.

NOTEBOOK

Soul Heaven ◆ started slowly and seemed to run in snatches. His chance still looked very much in the balance a furlong out, with it not clear whether he would run on, but he found just enough for strong pressure, despite edging left. He had been off for over six weeks since winning his maiden and ran like a horse who had forgotten some of that earlier experience. He should improve from this, especially when stepped up in trip - by Oratorio; dam placed over 1m6f - and could stay ahead of the handicapper. (op 3-1)

Step In Time(IRE), who fared best of the high-drawn runners in the Chesham, ran well on this drop in trip. Given a positive ride, he kept on gamely for pressure and probably won't mind a return to 7f.
Merseyside Star(IRE), a little keen early, ran on when switched left towards the inside in the closing stages and had his chance, but was worried out of it near the line. He looks as though he might be suited by a drop back to 5f. (op 8-1)
Desert Auction(IRE), well held in Listed company on his last two starts, found this easier but didn't help his chance with a slow start. He kept on against the near-side rail but was always just held. (op 6-1 tchd 5-1)
Cultured Pride(IRE) edged right over to the middle of the track in the closing stages and didn't perform badly in the circumstances. She should have more to offer. (op 16-1)
Saxby(IRE) hasn't progressed as expected from his impressive win in an above-average seller. (op 9-1)
Wigan Lane ran nowhere near the form she showed when winning a weak Doncaster maiden. (tchd 15-2)
Timelord(IRE) was below his best. (op 11-1 tchd 13-2)

3843 NORMAN COURT STUD FILLIES' H'CAP — 1m (S)
4:00 (4:02) (Class 3) (0-90,87) 3-Y-O+ **£7,771** (£2,312; £1,155; £577) **Stalls** Low

Form — RPR
-401 **1** **Desert Kiss**[31] 2824 4-9-2 **74** ... JimmyFortune 5 — 82
(W R Swinburn) *mde all: set stdy gallop tl rdn and qcknd ent fnl 2f out: drvn and a finding enough fnl f* **4/1**[3]
6-11 **2** 1 ¼ **Alsace Lorraine (IRE)**[36] 2665 4-9-12 **84** ... JamieSpencer 4 — 89+
(J R Fanshawe) *stdd s: hld up in last pair: hdwy 1/2-way trckd ldrs over 2f out: swtchd rt and rdn 2f out: wanting to hang lft after: bmpd ent fnl f: kpt on same pce* **2/1**[1]
3142 **3** nk **Silver Games (IRE)**[16] 3293 3-9-1 **87** ... MCGeran(5) 2 — 89+
(M R Channon) *t.k.h: hld up in tch: swtchd rt looking for run over 1f out: barged between horses and effrt jst over 1f out: continually leaned on and n.m.r fnl f: kpt on same pce* **3/1**[2]
0512 **4** ¾ **Miss Mojito (IRE)**[16] 3302 3-7-9 **69** ow4 ... (t) KierenFox(7) 7 — 69
(J W Hills) *stdd s and sn swtchd lft: hld up bhd: hdwy on outer ent fnl 2f: kpt on same pce fr over 1f out* **7/1**
5205 **5** ¾ **Al Sabaheya**[22] 3102 3-9-2 **83** ... TedDurcan 1 — 82
(C E Brittain) *trckd ldr tl 1/2-way: styd handy: shkn up 2f out: nt clr run after tl ent fnl f: one pce* **11/1**
-052 **6** 1 ¼ **Diggeratt (USA)**[15] 3341 3-8-7 **74** ... RoystonFfrench 6 — 70
(R A Fahey) *t.k.h: cl up: trckd wnr 1/2-way: rdn over 2f out: wknd ent fnl f: btn whn hmpd ins fnl f* **5/1**

1m 44.68s (4.08) **Going Correction** +0.075s/f (Good)
WFA 3 from 4yo 9lb — 6 Ran SP% **115.8**
Speed ratings (Par 104): **82,80,80,79,78 77**
toteswinger: 1&2 £1.80, 1&3 £2.70, 2&3 £1.80. CSF £13.00 CT £26.78 TOTE £6.20: £2.20, £1.80; EX 13.60 Trifecta £24.70 Pool: £924.03 - 27.64 winning units..
Owner The Capers **Bred** C R Mason **Trained** Aldbury, Herts
■ Stewards' Enquiry : Jamie Spencer three-day ban: careless riding (July 27,28,30)
M C Geran three-day ban: careless riding (July 26-28)

FOCUS
Quite a good fillies' handicap on paper, but the pace was steady and the bare result needs treating with caution as there was plenty of scrimmaging in behind the winner.

NOTEBOOK
Desert Kiss, 7lb higher than when winning on the Polytrack at Kempton, very much allowed the run of the race in front. She travelled well and found plenty for pressure, but the bare result needs treating with caution. (op 9-2 tchd 5-1)
Alsace Lorraine(IRE) bumped into Silver Games on several occasions in the closing stages and couldn't defy a 7lb rise for her Doncaster success. The steady pace was against her and she shouldn't be judged too harshly. (op 7-4 tchd 9-4 in a place)
Silver Games(IRE) tried to squeeze through a narrow gap between horses over a furlong out and probably would have got up for second with a clear run, but Jamie Spencer aboard the runner-up seemed determined to keep her blocked in. She is a little better than she showed here. (op 7-2)
Miss Mojito(IRE)'s 7lb claimer put up 4lb overweight. Like most of these, she probably would have preferred a stronger-run race. (op 8-1 tchd 9-1)
Al Sabaheya didn't really improve for the removal of blinkers and switch to more patient tactics. (op 10-1 tchd 9-1)
Diggeratt(USA) had never raced over a trip this far and was keen off the steady pace. (op 7-1)

3844 KELTBRAY CUP H'CAP — 5f
4:35 (4:37) (Class 2) (0-105,104) 3-Y-O+
£11,215 (£3,358; £1,679; £840; £419; £210) **Stalls** Low

Form — RPR
0-40 **1** **Sonny Red (IRE)**[58] 2012 5-9-4 **96** ... RichardHughes 8 — 106
(D Nicholls) *chsd ldrs: rdn and hdwy over 1f out: drvn to chse ldr ins fnl f: r.o wl to ld last strides* **5/1**[3]
0050 **2** hd **Group Therapy**[7] 3638 4-9-3 **95** ... SteveDrowne 1 — 104
(N P Littmoden) *chsd ldrs: ev ch 2f out: rdn to ld ent fnl f: r.o wl tl hdd and no ex last strides* **10/1**
5230 **3** 2 ½ **Cheveton**[15] 3351 5-9-4 **96** ... JimCrowley 7 — 96
(R J Price) *hmpd s: towards rr: switching rt and hdwy over 1f out: r.o fnl f to snatch 3rd last stride: nvr pce to rch ldrs* **4/1**[1]
006 **4** shd **Judge 'n Jury**[13] 3434 5-9-4 **99** ... (t) KevinGhunowa(3) 13 — 99
(R A Harris) *chsd ldr: ev ch and rdn 2f out: led over 1f out tl ent fnl f: wknd fnl 100yds and lost 3rd on post* **15/2**
10-6 **5** ½ **Tony The Tap**[8] 3582 8-8-9 **87** ... TedDurcan 9 — 85
(W R Muir) *stdd s: bhd: rdn over 1f out: edging rt but r.o wl ins fnl f: nvr trbld ldrs* **9/1**
0-10 **6** 1 ¼ **Fathom Five (IRE)**[15] 3351 5-9-4 **96** ... AlanMunro 4 — 90
(C F Wall) *wnt rt s and rdr lost iron: sn rcvrd and led: rdn and edgd rt 2f out: hdd over 1f out: wknd fnl f* **9/2**[2]
0034 **7** 3 ½ **Matsunosuke**[7] 3638 7-9-12 **104** ... RoystonFfrench 3 — 85
(A B Coogan) *a bhd: shkn up 2f out: no hdwy and nvr on terms* **8/1**
1046 **8** 2 ¼ **Lochstar**[5] 3694 5-8-7 **85** oh4 ... LPKeniry 10 — 58
(A M Balding) *restless in stalls: chsd ldrs: rdn 2f out: wknd u.p jst over 1f out: eased ins fnl f* **6/1**
100- **9** 1 ¾ **Hadaf (IRE)**[288] 6239 4-8-9 **87** ... RHills 11 — 54
(M P Tregoning) *dwlt: a towards rr: brief effrt wl over 1f out: eased whn no ch ins fnl f* **9/1**

59.94 secs (-0.56) **Going Correction** +0.075s/f (Good)
WFA 3 from 4yo+ 5lb — 9 Ran SP% **121.1**
Speed ratings (Par 109): **107,106,102,102,101 99,94,90,87**
toteswinger: 1&2 £7.80, 1&3 £4.50, 2&3 £11.20. CSF £56.52 CT £225.25 TOTE £4.50: £1.90, £3.40, £1.70; EX 47.10 Trifecta £278.30 Pool: £725.86 - 1.93 winning units..
Owner Alex Nicholls E Maher & J E Greaves **Bred** Denis Bergin **Trained** Sessay, N Yorks

FOCUS
A decent, competitive sprint handicap in which those that raced prominently seemed to hold an advantage.

NOTEBOOK
Sonny Red(IRE) had offered encouragement on both his starts for this yard, but he had been off for two months and this good looked plenty quick enough. As it turned out, he handled conditions just fine on Ascot's rather unique surface and responded well to pressure to get up in the final strides. His connections paid only 5,000gns for him last October, but it's clear he retains plenty of ability and he's in the Stewards' Cup, for which he is now a best-price 25-1 chance. (op 4-1 tchd 11-2)
Group Therapy travelled well and pulled clear of the remainder, but he was nabbed near the line. He looks up to winning a similar race.
Cheveton was slightly squeezed out at the start and never really recovered, finishing well for a place but never looking a winning threat. (op 9-2 tchd 5-1 in a place)
Judge 'n Jury showed plenty of speed but didn't see his race out. He's struggling to recapture his best form, but this wasn't a bad effort and he's one to keep in mind when the ground is soft. (op 8-1)
Tony The Tap finished well but had far too much ground to make up. (op 11-1 tchd 12-1)
Fathom Five(IRE)'s rider seemed to lose an iron coming out of the stalls, but the partnership quickly recovered. The gelding showed speed but is another who probably wants easier ground. (op 15-2)
Matsunosuke was given his usual hold-up ride but never featured. (op 13-2 tchd 6-1)
Lochstar, 4lb out of the handicap, didn't want to go into the stalls and was restless when eventually stepping forward. (op 7-1 tchd 8-1)
Hadaf(IRE) offered nothing after 288 days off for a yard that has been very quiet. (op 10-1 tchd 12-1)

3845 THAMES HOSPICE CARE H'CAP — 5f
5:10 (5:10) (Class 4) (0-85,82) 3-Y-O+ **£6,476** (£1,927; £963; £481) **Stalls** Low

Form — RPR
001 **1** **Mandurah (IRE)**[30] 2840 5-9-12 **82** ... RichardHughes 8 — 94
(D Nicholls) *led: racd in centre and sn wl clr: rdn over 1f out: kpt on: unchal* **15/2**[3]
5040 **2** 3 ¼ **Esteem Machine (USA)**[27] 2946 5-9-11 **81** ... JamieSpencer 4 — 81+
(R A Teal) *v.s.a: bhd: swtchd into centre after 1f: stl last over 1f out: r.o u.p to go 2nd nr fin: nvr nr wnr* **16/1**
0000 **3** nk **Even Bolder**[14] 3386 6-9-2 **72** ... StephenCarson 9 — 71
(E A Wheeler) *stdd after s: hld up wl in rr: rdn and hdwy over 1f out: chsd clr wnr ins fnl f: no real imp: hung lft and lost 2nd nr fin* **33/1**
-643 **4** ½ **All Spin (IRE)**[16] 3299 3-8-6 **67** ... AndrewElliott 10 — 62
(A P Jarvis) *dwlt: outpcd in midfield: rdn 1/2-way: kpt on u.p fnl f: nvr nr wnr* **14/1**
4012 **5** ¾ **Efistorm**[28] 2929 8-9-12 **82** ... JimmyFortune 1 — 76
(C R Dore) *bhd: swtchd into centre after 1f: pushed along over 2f out: styd on ins fnl f: nvr nr wnr* **9/1**
0313 **6** nse **Sharpened Edge**[8] 3582 3-9-6 **81** ... CatherineGannon 6 — 73
(B Palling) *awkward leaving stalls: sn chsng ldrs: rdn 1/2-way: chsd clr wnr 1f out: no imp and wknd fnl 100yds* **11/4**[1]
-231 **7** ¾ **Our Piccadilly (IRE)**[64] 1836 4-9-8 **78** ... FergusSweeney 2 — 70
(W S Kittow) *chsd ldrs: rdn to chse clr wnr 2f out: no imp and wknd 1f out* **8/1**
3211 **8** 1 **Zowington**[15] 3347 7-9-7 **82** ... (v) WilliamCarson(5) 11 — 70
(S C Williams) *a outpcd towards rr: rdn over 2f out: n.d* **7/1**[2]
1350 **9** hd **Pic Up Sticks**[5] 3677 10-8-9 **65** ... RHills 5 — 52
(B G Powell) *stdd s: wl bhd: n.d* **18/1**
1-22 **10** 2 ¼ **Ivory Silk**[27] 2946 4-9-6 **76** ... (b) SteveDrowne 3 — 55
(J R Gask) *chsd clr wnr tl rdn and hung rt 2f out: wknd over 1f out: eased whn no ch fnl f* **11/4**[1]

60.25 secs (-0.25) **Going Correction** +0.075s/f (Good)
WFA 3 from 4yo+ 5lb — 10 Ran SP% **119.5**
Speed ratings (Par 105): **105,99,99,98,97 97,96,94,94,90**
toteswinger: 1&2 £22.30, 1&3 £40.30, 2&3 £45.80. CSF £122.37 CT £3705.73 TOTE £9.40: £2.90, £4.20, £6.80; EX 147.50 TRIFECTA Not won. Place 6: £34.30, Place 5: £8.92..
Owner Martin Hignett **Bred** Michael Lyons **Trained** Sessay, N Yorks

FOCUS
This looked quite a competitive sprint handicap, but it was a strange race to watch. Several of these missed the break, but the winner was quickly into stride and, leading the field up the middle of the track, there was soon a good 12 or so lengths from first to last, with the backmarker the eventual runner-up.
Sharpened Edge Official explanation: jockey said filly missed the break
T/Plt: £31.40 to a £1 stake. Pool: £120,135.76. 2,785.74 winning tickets. T/Qpdt: £8.10 to a £1 stake. Pool: £6,539.05. 596.45 winning tickets. SP

3804 CHESTER (L-H)
Saturday, July 11

OFFICIAL GOING: Good to firm (8.3)
Running rail moved out 7yards from 6f to top of home straight increasing distances by 14yards per circuit and the false rail was in place.
Wind: Almost nil Weather: Fine

3846 TOTEPOOL CITY PLATE (LISTED RACE) — 7f 2y
2:25 (2:26) (Class 1) 3-Y-O+
£22,708 (£8,608; £4,308; £2,148; £1,076; £540) **Stalls** Low

Form — RPR
6210 **1** **Regal Parade**[21] 3140 5-9-2 107 ... AdrianTNicholls 4 — 110
(D Nicholls) *chsd ldrs: dropped to midfield after 2f: swtchd rt and hdwy over 1f out: led ent fnl f: sn edgd lft: r.o u.p whn pressed: a doing enough towards fin* **11/4**[2]
3103 **2** ½ **Balthazaar's Gift (IRE)**[14] 3398 6-9-2 111 ... DarryllHolland 1 — 109
(C G Cox) *hld up: swtchd lft and hdwy over 1f out: chal wnr ins fnl 150yds: r.o u.p: hld cl home* **13/8**[1]
10-2 **3** 2 ¾ **Hartley**[59] 1987 3-8-8 97 ... GrahamGibbons 6 — 98
(J D Bethell) *chsd ldr: rdn and chal over 1f out: edgd rt and nt qckn ins fnl f* **17/2**
1010 **4** ¾ **Ocean's Minstrel**[24] 3011 3-8-11 104 ... JerryO'Dwyer 10 — 99
(J Ryan) *missed break and wnt rt s: hld up: effrt over 1f out: styd on ins fnl f: nvr able to rch ldrs* **14/1**
1010 **5** ¾ **Nashmiah (IRE)**[22] 3088 3-8-6 103 ... AhmedAjtebi 5 — 92
(C E Brittain) *chsd ldrs: effrt over 1f out: nt qckn: kpt on same pce ins fnl f* **15/2**[3]
44-0 **6** nk **Red Dune (IRE)**[35] 2703 4-8-11 99 ... J-PGuillambert 3 — 91
(M A Jarvis) *hld up: rdn over 1f out: kpt on ins fnl f: nvr able to chal* **10/1**
0455 **7** 1 ¼ **Ilie Nastase (FR)**[10] 3509 5-9-2 84 ... AndrewMullen 2 — 93
(D Nicholls) *hld up: niggled along 4f out: effrt into midfield 2f out: no imp on ldrs: outpcd appr fnl f* **20/1**

The Form Book, Raceform Ltd, Compton, RG20 6NL

1202 **8** ¾ **Celtic Sultan (IRE)**[8] 3567 5-9-2 92........................ StephenDonohoe 8 91
(T P Tate) *led: rdn over 1f out: hdd ent fnl f: fdd* **9/1**

4160 **9** *11* **Carcinetto (IRE)**[21] 3141 7-8-11 98........................ RichardEvans 9 56
(P D Evans) *racd on outside: chsd ldrs: pushed along 4f out: wknd wl over 1f out* **50/1**

1m 24.97s (-1.53) **Going Correction** +0.075s/f (Good)
WFA 3 from 4yo+ 8lb **9** Ran SP% **119.5**
Speed ratings (Par 111): **111,110,107,106,105 105,103,102,90**
toteswinger: 1&2 £1.30, 1&3 £5.50, 2&3 £4.20. CSF £7.92 TOTE £3.80: £1.70, £1.30, £2.30; EX 6.70 Trifecta £39.90 Pool: £420.92 - 7.80 winning units..
Owner Dab Hand Racing **Bred** Highclere Stud And Harry Herbert **Trained** Sessay, N Yorks

FOCUS
Two came away in this Listed contest and it was Regal Parade who stayed on just the stronger. It looks ordinary form for the grade.

NOTEBOOK
Regal Parade stayed on just the stronger. Winner of a conditions event at York two starts back, he performed creditably to be beaten just over six lengths when a 66-1 shot for the Golden Jubilee Stakes at Royal Ascot and capitalised on this marked drop in grade. He picked up well once switched at the top of the straight and always looked to be holding the runner-up on the run to the line. He continues to get better and may well be up to winning a Group contest. (op 7-2)
Balthazaar's Gift(IRE), third in a Group 3 at Newmarket on his recent debut for the yard, readily made ground towards the inside and challenged the winner strongly inside the final furlong, but was always getting the worst of the argument. He has never been the easiest to win with, but can surely find a race at this sort of level. (op 2-1)
Hartley, who dead-heated for second in a good handicap at York on his reappearance, travelled like a decent horse and kept on back in third. This was a good effort against proven performers and he looks a horse with a bright future. (tchd 10-1)
Ocean's Minstrel ideally likes to lead, but that was always going to be tricky from stall ten and he had to be held up following a sluggish start. He stayed on late for fourth, bouncing back from a poor effort in the Jersey Stakes, and remains capable of winning again at this level when things drop right. (op 12-1)
Nashmiah(IRE), a well-beaten eighth in the Coronation Stakes last time, already has two Listed wins to her name this season but she lacked the basic speed to make an impact. (op 7-1)
Red Dune(IRE) burst a blood vessel at Epsom last time and was ridden with greater restraint on this occasion. She kept on late, having been held up, and we should learn more about what she is capable of next time. (op 9-1)
Celtic Sultan(IRE) was driven to lead, but always looked set to struggle to fend off some of these and was quickly beaten. (op 17-2 tchd 8-1)

3847 BET TOTEPOOL AT TOTESPORT.COM H'CAP 1m 2f 75y
2:55 (2:56) (Class 4) (0-80,80) 4-Y-0+ **£5,828** (£1,734; £866; £432) **Stalls** High

Form RPR

2601 **1** **Mick's Dancer**[15] 3349 4-8-12 71........................ DarryllHolland 8 86
(W R Muir) *chsd ldr: led after 2f: mde rest: rdn over 1f out: r.o ins fnl f: kpt up to work towards fin* **5/1**[2]

6001 **2** *1* **Wing Play (IRE)**[28] 2923 4-8-10 69........................(p) TravisBlock 10 82
(H Morrison) *hld up early: chsd along 6f out: n.m.r over 5f out: hdwy on outside 4f out: chsd ldrs 3f out: wnt 2nd jst over 1f out: styd on wl towards fin to cl but nt quite get to wnr* **8/1**

200 **3** 2¾ **Royal Amnesty**[31] 2815 6-9-5 78........................(b) TomEaves 6 86
(I Semple) *missed break: hld up: hdwy 2f out: styd on ins fnl f: no imp on front pair fnl 100yds* **9/1**

6112 **4** 2¾ **Theocritus (USA)**[9] 3525 4-8-13 72........................ StephenDonohoe 3 75
(D M Simcock) *off the bridle thrght: bhd: hdwy on outside 2f out: styd on ins fnl f: nvr gng pce to get to ldrs* **11/2**[3]

-461 **5** *nk* **Inspirina (IRE)**[1] 3809 5-8-8 67 6ex........................ DaleGibson 7 69
(R Ford) *racd keenly: midfield: hdwy 6f out: chal and wnt 2nd 3f out: rdn and lost 2nd over 1f out: one pce ins fnl f* **9/2**[1]

3443 **6** 1¼ **Johnston's Baby (IRE)**[17] 3267 7-8-3 62........................ AndrewMullen 9 62
(E J Alston) *chsd ldrs: rdn over 2f out: btn over 1f out* **10/1**

5003 **7** ½ **Mujaadel (USA)**[9] 3530 4-9-2 78........................ AhmedAjtebi(3) 2 77
(D Nicholls) *led for 2f: hit rail wl over 7f out: chsd ldrs after: pushed along over 1f out: wknd fnl f* **7/1**

6124 **8** 2¾ **I'm In The Pink (FR)**[19] 3206 5-8-8 72........................ RichardEvans(5) 4 65
(P D Evans) *hld up: rdn 2f out: nvr on terms w ldrs* **11/2**[3]

4140 **9** *24* **Templetuohy Max (IRE)**[20] 3189 4-9-1 74........................(v) GrahamGibbons 5 22
(J D Bethell) *chsd ldrs: hmpd wl over 7f out: lost pl over 4f out: stl in tch whn n.m.r and hmpd wl over 2f out: bhd after and eased* **10/1**

4200 **10** *5* **Man Of Gwent (UAE)**[8] 3578 5-8-9 68........................ JerryO'Dwyer 11 —
(P D Evans) *rdn along after s: hdwy to go prom after 2f: pushed along 3f out: wknd over 2f out: eased whn wl btn over 1f out* **28/1**

2m 9.81s (-2.39) **Going Correction** +0.075s/f (Good) **10** Ran SP% **120.9**
Speed ratings (Par 105): **112,111,109,106,106 105,105,102,83,79**
toteswinger: 1&2 £3.40, 1&3 £13.40, 2&3 £113.50. CSF £46.52 CT £358.00 TOTE £5.10: £2.00, £3.30, £3.10; EX 31.90.
Owner Perspicacious Punters Racing Club **Bred** Cheveley Park Stud Ltd **Trained** Lambourn, Berks

FOCUS
This was a modest handicap and Darryll Holland was seen to excellent effect on Mick's Dancer. The runner-up is the guide to the level of the form.
Theocritus(USA) Official explanation: vet said gelding bled from the nose
I'm In The Pink(FR) Official explanation: jockey said gelding was unsuited by the good to firm ground
Templetuohy Max(IRE) Official explanation: jockey said gelding suffered interference in running
Man Of Gwent(UAE) Official explanation: jockey said gelding was struck into behind

3848 TOTESWINGER CITY WALL STKS (LISTED RACE) 5f 16y
3:30 (3:30) (Class 1) 3-Y-0+
£22,708 (£8,608; £4,308; £2,148; £1,076; £540) **Stalls** Low

Form RPR

-325 **1** **Borderlescott**[25] 2991 7-9-0 112........................ PatCosgrave 2 109
(R Bastiman) *broke wl: sn lost pl: nt clr run whn in midfield 3f out: qcknd to make prog on ins over 1f out: led 100yds out: r.o gamely* **6/5**[1]

0400 **2** *1* **Captain Gerrard (IRE)**[7] 3638 4-9-0 105........................ TomEaves 4 105
(B Smart) *hld up: trckd ldrs after 1f: nt clr run over 1f out: sn rdn: r.o ins fnl f but hld* **9/1**

1230 **3** *nk* **Hoh Hoh Hoh**[25] 2991 7-9-0 104........................ StephenDonohoe 3 104
(R J Price) *prom: effrt to chal 1f out: led ins fnl f: hdd 100yds out: nt qckn cl home* **7/1**[3]

2140 **4** *nk* **Sohraab**[21] 3141 5-9-0 100........................ DarryllHolland 10 103+
(H Morrison) *sn n.m.r and hmpd: towards rr: str run on wd outside fnl f: clsd rapidly on ldrs at fin* **14/1**

5040 **5** ½ **Angus Newz**[2] 3784 6-8-9 95........................(v) J-PGuillambert 8 96
(M Quinn) *towards rr: nt clr run wl over 1f out: sn swtchd lft and nt clr run: styd on ins fnl f: nt pce of ldrs* **20/1**

6520 **6** ½ **Rievaulx World**[25] 2991 3-8-9 100........................ AdrianMcCarthy 1 97
(K A Ryan) *led: rdn over 1f out: hdd and edgd rt ins fnl f: no ex fnl 50yds* **11/1**

4000 **7** ½ **Tournedos (IRE)**[15] 3351 7-9-0 93........................ PaulQuinn 6 97+
(D Nicholls) *fly-jmpd s: bhd: prog and r.o ins fnl f: nt pce to quite get to ldrs* **33/1**

0323 **8** *hd* **Masta Plasta (IRE)**[7] 3638 6-9-0 106........................ AdrianTNicholls 5 97
(D Nicholls) *prom: rdn over 1f out: no ex fnl 75yds* **7/2**[2]

4263 **9** 1¾ **Strike Up The Band**[35] 2704 6-9-0 100........................ AndrewMullen 7 90
(D Nicholls) *chsd ldrs: pushed along over 1f out: outpcd fnl f* **16/1**

-050 **10** *hd* **Green Manalishi**[15] 3351 8-9-0 98........................ JohnEgan 11 90
(K A Ryan) *towards rr: wnt into midfield 3f out: rdn over 1f out: no real imp whn n.m.r briefly ins fnl 75yds: dropped away* **16/1**

60.33 secs (-0.67) **Going Correction** +0.075s/f (Good)
WFA 3 from 4yo+ 5lb **10** Ran SP% **124.6**
Speed ratings (Par 111): **108,106,105,105,104 103,103,102,99,99**
toteswinger: 1&2 £3.90, 1&3 £2.00, 2&3 £6.50. CSF £14.74 TOTE £2.20: £1.20, £2.30, £2.10; EX 15.30 Trifecta £55.40 Pool: £1177.45 - 15.70 winning units..
Owner James Edgar & William Donaldson **Bred** James Clark **Trained** Cowthorpe, N Yorks

FOCUS
This looked an excellent opportunity for last year's Nunthorpe winner Borderlescott to open his account for the season and his class got him through. He did not need to be at his best to win, and the form is muddling.

NOTEBOOK
Borderlescott, last year's Nunthorpe winner, had been found an excellent opportunity to open his account for the season and, despite not getting the best of trips around the inside, his class saw him through. Fifth in the King's Stand at Royal Ascot last time, he escaped a penalty and was rightly made a short-price favourite. He was squeezed for room on more than one occasion, but stayed on strongly against the inside rail, and this hugely consistent 7yo continues to perform up to a high level. (op 7-4 tchd 11-10)
Captain Gerrard(IRE), one place ahead of the winner at Royal Ascot, has been disappointing in two starts since and this good showing in second seemed to further emphasise his inconsistency. He finished well for second, having been denied a clear run, and can surely find a race at this level. (op 8-1 tchd 15-2)
Hoh Hoh Hoh, behind the front pair at Ascot, had earlier been in good form, and he came back to something like his best here. He has yet to win at pattern level, but certainly deserves to. (tchd 6-1)
Sohraab ◆, a C&D winner in May, was hampered early and soon came under pressure, but finished very strongly down the outside and would have been second in a few more strides. He may well have been unlucky. (tchd 16-1)
Angus Newz, unplaced in a handicap at Newmarket just two days earlier, is a very tough mare and she ran with credit in the visor, keeping on having been short of room. (op 16-1 tchd 25-1)
Rievaulx World is all about speed but he probably went a bit too quick off the front. (op 9-1 tchd 12-1)
Tournedos(IRE) blew any chance he had at the start. Official explanation: jockey said gelding missed the break
Masta Plasta(IRE) faded disappointingly and didn't appear to be at his best. (op 4-1)
Strike Up The Band Official explanation: trainer said gelding was unsuited by the good to firm ground

3849 BET TOTEPOOL ON 0800 221 221 MAIDEN AUCTION STKS 5f 16y
4:05 (4:05) (Class 5) 2-Y-O **£4,047** (£1,204; £601; £300) **Stalls** Low

Form RPR

242 **1** **Social Grace**[7] 3633 2-8-4 0........................ AdrianTNicholls 4 73
(D H Brown) *mde all: rdn to qckn over 1f out: kpt up to work and hld on wl at fin* **11/8**[1]

62 **2** *nk* **She's Ok (IRE)**[22] 3101 2-8-1 0........................ AhmedAjtebi(3) 8 72
(C E Brittain) *racd keenly: w wnr: rdn and nt qckn over 1f out: r.o cl home* **11/4**[2]

3 2½ **Just Mandy (IRE)** 2-8-7 0 ow1........................ StephenDonohoe 2 66+
(R A Fahey) *in rr: rdn and hdwy over 1f out: styd on ins fnl f: nt pce to chal front pair* **10/3**[3]

4 *nk* **Art Summer** 2-8-6 0........................ AdrianMcCarthy 3 64
(D M Simcock) *trckd ldrs: rdn over 1f out: one pce ins fnl f* **8/1**

0 **5** *1* **Hot Rod Mamma (IRE)**[8] 3571 2-8-4 0........................ AndrewMullen 1 58
(A Berry) *dwlt: racd keenly: hld up: effrt over 1f out: nvr able to chal ldrs: no ex ins fnl f* **12/1**

0 **6** *16* **Crystal Bridge**[7] 3633 2-8-4 0........................ PaulQuinn 7 —
(Mrs L Williamson) *trckd ldrs: wknd 2f out: sn bhd* **33/1**

62.38 secs (1.38) **Going Correction** +0.075s/f (Good) **6** Ran SP% **113.6**
Speed ratings (Par 94): **91,90,86,86,84 58**
toteswinger: 1&2 £1.10, 1&3 £1.90, 2&3 £2.60. CSF £5.53 TOTE £2.30: £1.60, £1.80; EX 3.30.
Owner Norton Common Farm Racing **Bred** R G Percival **Trained** Maltby, S Yorks

FOCUS
A modest and uncompetitive maiden that was dominated by the front two in the market.

NOTEBOOK
Social Grace, second in two of her three previous starts, was soon in front and won the race when kicking off the final bend, just finding enough to hold the persistent runner-up. She deserved this win and is likely to take her chance in next weekend's Super Sprint if getting in. (op 7-4)
She's Ok(IRE), claimed in the final strides at Goodwood over 6f last time, held every chance and stuck on right the way to the line, but the winner always just looked to be holding on. She is now eligible for nurseries. (op 5-2)
Just Mandy(IRE), whose dam was a juvenile winner over 6f, kept on without threatening to win on this racecourse debut and should learn from the experience. (op 7-2)
Art Summer, out of a prolific winning sprint handicapper, comes from a yard that have yet to get going with their juveniles and she should be wiser with this run under her belt. (op 7-1 tchd 13-2)
Hot Rod Mamma(IRE) improved on her debut effort. (op 10-1 tchd 9-1)

3850 TOTESPORT HOME OF POOL BETTING H'CAP 1m 7f 195y
4:40 (4:40) (Class 4) (0-85,83) 3-Y-0+ **£5,828** (£1,734; £866; £432) **Stalls** Low

Form RPR

512 **1** **Act Of Kalanisi (IRE)**[14] 3371 3-8-9 83........................ J-PGuillambert 5 88+
(M Johnston) *led: hdd 9f out: continued to chse ldr tl lost pl 4f out: sn stuck in pocket on rail: rdn over 1f out: str run ins fnl 75yds to ld fnl stride* **2/1**[1]

1302 **2** *hd* **Zuwaar**[8] 3593 4-9-2 71........................(tp) StephenDonohoe 2 76
(Ian Williams) *hld up bhd ldrs: wnt 2nd 4f out: rdn to ld jst over 1f out: hrd pressed ins fnl f: hdd fnl stride* **7/2**[3]

2214 **3** *hd* **Aleatricis**[21] 3146 4-10-0 83........................ GrahamGibbons 1 88+
(J J Quinn) *prom: lost pl over 4f out: outpcd over 3f out: rallied ins fnl f: r.o and clsd strly at fin* **6/1**

5022 **4** *nk* **Dolly Penrose**[21] 3146 4-9-13 82........................ DarryllHolland 4 86
(M R Channon) *prom: led 9f out: rdn and hdd jst over 1f out: r.o u.p and continued to chal ins fnl f: nt qckn fnl strides* **9/4**[2]

3603 **5** *1* **Sir Sandicliffe (IRE)**[12] 3444 5-8-4 **64** oh1.................. DeanHeslop(5) 3 67
(W M Brisbourne) *missed break: in rr: pushed along 4f out and outpcd: effrt whn hung lft over 1f out: kpt on but nvr able to chal* **6/1**

3m 33.66s (5.66) **Going Correction** +0.075s/f (Good)
WFA 3 from 4yo+ 19lb **5** Ran SP% **114.9**
Speed ratings (Par 105): **93,92,92,92,92**
toteswinger: 1&2 £6.30. CSF £9.79 TOTE £2.30: £1.50, £2.10; EX 5.40.
Owner Mrs Joan Keaney **Bred** Mrs Joan Keaney **Trained** Middleham Moor, N Yorks

FOCUS
This was a messy race and all five runners finished in a bunch as they crossed the line, but the winner can rate higher in future.

3851 TOTEEXACTA APPRENTICE H'CAP 7f 122y
5:15 (5:16) (Class 5) (0-70,72) 4-Y-O+ **£4,047** (£1,204; £601; £300) **Stalls** Low

Form RPR

335U **1** **Many Welcomes**[15] 3331 4-8-3 **52**........................ JemmaMarshall(3) 9 61+
(B P J Baugh) *bmpd s: in tch: rdn over 1f out: gd run ins fnl f to ld nr fin* **25/1**

0011 **2** *½* **Glenridding**[11] 3488 5-9-7 **72**................................(p) RosieJessop(5) 11 79
(J G Given) *led: qcknd abt 5 l clr over 2f out: rdn over 1f out: all out fnl 100yds: ct nr fin* **4/1**[2]

0015 **3** *½* **Violent Velocity (IRE)**[11] 3488 6-9-6 **66**...................... JamesO'Reilly 5 72
(J J Quinn) *midfield: hdwy over 1f out: edgd lft ins fnl 100yds: r.o and clsd nr fin* **3/1**[1]

3414 **4** *1* **Maison Dieu**[10] 3497 6-9-1 **61**.............................. AndrewMullen 15 65
(E J Alston) *hld up: hdwy on ins rail over 1f out: styd on ins fnl f: nt quite pce to get to ldrs* **12/1**

00-0 **5** *nk* **Danzig Fox**[183] 108 4-8-1 **54** oh1 ow3........................ AlexEdwards(7) 1 57
(M Mullineaux) *racd keenly: in tch: rdn over 1f out: edgd rt ins fnl 100yds: nt qckn* **14/1**

5020 **6** *¾* **No Grouse**[9] 3529 9-8-9 **60**.. DTDaSilva(5) 3 61
(E J Alston) *midfield: hdwy on wd outside over 1f out: kpt on ins fnl f: nt pce to chal ldrs* **14/1**

0002 **7** *nk* **H Harrison (IRE)**[15] 3331 9-8-9 **58**............................ DeanHeslop(3) 12 58
(I W McInnes) *w ldr tl outpcd by that rival over 2f out: no ex ins fnl f* **8/1**

5400 **8** *1 ½* **Obe Royal**[4] 3717 5-9-8 **68**.......................................(b) RichardEvans 6 65
(P D Evans) *midfield: rdn over 1f out: nvr able to chal* **11/1**

5-60 **9** *½* **Tobago Reef**[15] 3331 5-7-12 **51** oh4...............(v[1]) JosephineBruning(7) 8 46
(C W Moore) *racd keenly: chsd ldrs: rdn over 2f out: wknd ins fnl f* **50/1**

2000 **10** *1 ½* **Just Oscar (GER)**[15] 3331 5-8-2 **51** oh3................... RossAtkinson(3) 4 43
(W M Brisbourne) *s.i.s: hld up: rdn 2f out: nvr on terms w ldrs* **25/1**

0054 **11** *nk* **Sands Of Barra (IRE)**[5] 3683 6-8-10 **56**.................... PatrickDonaghy 2 47
(I W McInnes) *wnt rt s: racd keenly: chsd ldrs: rdn over 2f out: wknd ins fnl f* **5/1**[3]

341- **12** *nk* **Zennerman (IRE)**[324] 5198 6-8-13 **64**......................(b) PaulPickard(5) 13 54
(W M Brisbourne) *a bhd* **12/1**

0036 **13** *1 ¼* **Desert Lover (IRE)**[16] 3322 7-7-12 **51** oh4..................... JakePayne(7) 7 38
(R J Price) *n.m.r s: a bhd* **18/1**

-060 **14** *3* **Avoncreek**[31] 2812 5-7-12 **51** oh6.................................. NoraLooby(7) 14 31
(B P J Baugh) *racd keenly: niggled along over 4f out: a bhd* **66/1**

1m 34.12s (0.32) **Going Correction** +0.075s/f (Good) **14** Ran SP% **126.2**
Speed ratings (Par 103): **101,100,100,99,98 97,97,96,95,94 93,93,92,89**
toteswinger: 1&2 £34.80, 1&3 £30.80, 2&3 £1.90. CSF £125.96 CT £408.28 TOTE £36.40: £7.30, £1.90, £1.90; EX 276.10 Place 6: £19.52, Place 5: £14.62..
Owner Gang Of Four **Bred** Mrs F Wilson **Trained** Audley, Staffs

FOCUS
A low-grade handicap run at a sound pace. The third, fourth and fifth have been rated close to their marks.
Avoncreek Official explanation: jockey said gelding hung right throughout
T/Plt: £8.90 to a £1 stake. Pool: £89,361.32. 7,286.51 winning tickets. T/Qpdt: £3.90 to a £1 stake. Pool: £4,522.05. 846.80 winning tickets. DO

3478 HAMILTON (R-H)
Saturday, July 11

OFFICIAL GOING: Good to firm (10.3)
Rail realignment around the loop reduced distances on round course by 30yards.
Wind: Almost nil Weather: Fine, sunny

3852 FREEBETS.CO.UK FREE FOOTBALL BETTING APPRENTICE RIDERS' H'CAP (ROUND 2) 6f 5y
6:05 (6:07) (Class 6) (0-60,60) 3-Y-O+ **£2,388** (£705; £352) **Stalls** Low

Form RPR

60-3 **1** **Feeling Fresh (IRE)**[6] 3657 4-9-5 **57**.................... MatthewLawson(3) 4 64
(Paul Green) *s.i.s: swtchd rt and hdwy to go prom after 2f: ev ch over 1f out: led wl ins fnl f: kpt on* **3/1**[2]

0642 **2** *shd* **Magical Song**[16] 3296 4-9-2 **51**.......................................(b) JamieKyne 9 58
(J Balding) *led: rdn 2f out: edgd rt and hdd wl ins fnl f: r.o* **7/4**[1]

0006 **3** *1 ¾* **Hettie Hubble**[7] 3614 3-8-3 **49** oh1 ow3........................ AdamCarter(5) 5 48
(D W Thompson) *hld up: rdn 1/2-way: hdwy over 1f out: r.o fnl f* **33/1**

0003 **4** *¾* **Elkhorn**[11] 3484 7-9-6 **55**....................................(b) DeclanCannon 1 54
(Miss J A Camacho) *dwlt: bhd tl hdwy over 1f out: kpt on fnl f: nrst fin* **4/1**[3]

0003 **5** *2 ¾* **Kneesy Earsy Nosey**[13] 3426 3-8-0 **46** oh1................. SeanPalmer(5) 2 34
(Miss A Stokell) *hld up: rdn over 2f out: kpt on but no imp fnl f* **25/1**

0000 **6** *nk* **Steel Blue**[15] 3354 9-9-11 **60**.......................................(p) AmyRyan 6 49
(R M Whitaker) *chsd ldrs tl rdn and no ex over 1f out* **8/1**

0005 **7** *4 ½* **Obe One**[21] 3148 9-8-13 **48** oh1 ow2........................ ByronMoorcroft 11 23
(A Berry) *in tch tl wknd over 2f out* **16/1**

000- **8** *1 ¼* **Second Reef**[341] 4679 7-8-13 **51** oh1 ow5.................. GarryWhillans(3) 8 22
(T A K Cuthbert) *chsd ldrs tl wknd over 1f out* **50/1**

0-00 **9** *3* **Quicks The Word**[40] 2529 9-8-13 **51**.......................... DavidKenny(3) 7 12
(T A K Cuthbert) *chsd ldrs tl rdn and wknd fr 2f out* **18/1**

5560 **10** *6* **Smelly Cat**[7] 3614 3-8-2 **46**.. SoniaEaton(3) 10 —
(D W Thompson) *sn outpcd: no ch fnl 2f* **28/1**

1m 11.27s (-0.93) **Going Correction** -0.225s/f (Firm)
WFA 3 from 4yo+ 6lb **10** Ran SP% **115.8**
Speed ratings (Par 101): **97,96,94,93,89 89,83,81,77,69**
toteswinger: 1&2 £1.10, 1&3 £53.60, 2&3 £14.80. CSF £8.24 CT £140.65 TOTE £3.80: £1.80, £1.10, £12.00; EX 11.30.
Owner Paul Green (Oaklea) **Bred** J Mahon **Trained** Lydiate, Merseyside

FOCUS
A low-grade sprint in which half the runners were out of the handicap proper. As a result the form has not been rated positively. They set off at fair clip.

Obe One Official explanation: jockey said saddle slipped.

3853 FREEBETS.CO.UK SCOTTISH FOOTBALL FREE BETS MAIDEN (S) STKS 5f 4y
6:35 (6:36) (Class 6) 3-Y-O+ **£2,388** (£705; £352) **Stalls** Low

Form RPR

5330 **1** **What A Fella**[8] 3562 3-8-9 **46**..................................(p) AmyRyan(5) 2 51
(Mrs A Duffield) *in tch: effrt over 2f out: led wl ins fnl f: r.o* **11/4**[2]

0-00 **2** *nk* **Arriva La Diva**[15] 3352 3-8-4 **35**.. JamieKyne(5) 4 45
(J J Quinn) *w ldr: led 2f out: sn rdn: hdd wl ins fnl f: r.o* **11/2**[3]

0605 **3** *¾* **Paddy Jack**[10] 3498 4-9-0 **46**.................................(be) MarkCoumbe(5) 10 48
(J R Weymes) *led to 2f out: kpt on u.p fnl f* **14/1**

-030 **4** *½* **Africa's Star (IRE)**[7] 3611 3-8-9 **60**............................. TonyHamilton 7 41
(M Dods) *blkd s: sn pushed along in rr: hdwy and edgd rt 2f out: r.o fnl f* **11/8**[1]

000 **5** *½* **Whisper Softly (IRE)**[15] 3338 3-8-9 **50**............................ PJMcDonald 3 39
(T D Walford) *in tch stands' side: drvn 1/2-way: kpt on fnl f: no imp* **12/1**

045 **6** *¾* **Badtanman**[23] 3063 3-8-7 **41**...............................(b) AndrewHeffernan(7) 1 41
(Peter Grayson) *sn outpcd stands' side: hdwy over 1f out: nrst fin* **20/1**

6004 **7** *1 ¼* **Rightcar Lewis**[11] 3479 4-9-0 **45**............................(b) PaulMulrennan 8 33
(Peter Grayson) *wnt rt s: chsd ldrs tl wknd over 1f out* **20/1**

000 **8** *6* **Tarus (IRE)**[11] 3484 5-8-13 **41** ow4......................... ByronMoorcroft(3) 11 15
(A Berry) *cl up tl rdn and wknd over 1f out* **20/1**

0000 **9** *3 ¼* **Gelert (IRE)**[11] 3479 4-9-0 **40**.............................(bt) SladeO'Hara(5) 6 4
(A Berry) *bmpd s: a outpcd* **33/1**

00-0 **10** *10* **Sokoke**[43] 2451 8-9-0 **27**... GaryBartley(5) 12 —
(D A Nolan) *chsd ldrs tl wknd fr 2f out* **150/1**

59.71 secs (-0.29) **Going Correction** -0.225s/f (Firm)
WFA 3 from 4yo+ 5lb **10** Ran SP% **116.4**
Speed ratings (Par 101): **93,92,91,90,89 88,86,76,71,55**
toteswinger: 1&2 £5.40, 1&3 £8.30, 2&3 £6.00. CSF £16.80 TOTE £3.80: £1.20, £2.10, £2.60; EX 20.10.There was no bid for the winner.
Owner Trevor Wilson **Bred** C J Murfitt **Trained** Constable Burton, N Yorks
■ Stewards' Enquiry : Amy Ryan one-day ban: excessive use of the whip (Jul 26)

FOCUS
Poor fare by any standards and very few of these had ever threatened to win. The winner has been rated in line with this year's form.

3854 FREEBETS.CO.UK FREE BETS CLAIMING STKS 1m 3f 16y
7:05 (7:05) (Class 6) 4-Y-O+ **£2,388** (£705; £352) **Stalls** High

Form RPR

-253 **1** **Tufton**[22] 3123 6-8-13 **75**.. TonyHamilton 4 67
(R A Fahey) *t.k.h early: trckd ldrs: rdn over 3f out: effrt and edgd rt over 1f out: led wl ins fnl f: styd on* **5/4**[1]

0106 **2** *½* **Birkside**[17] 3266 6-9-7 **75**.. PaulMulrennan 3 74
(Miss L A Perratt) *led: rdn 3f out: hdd wl ins fnl f: kpt on* **2/1**[2]

1241 **3** *3* **Lucayan Dancer**[22] 3123 9-8-8 **66**.................................... AmyRyan(5) 6 61
(D Nicholls) *t.k.h early: in tch: effrt over 2f out: sn no imp* **3/1**[3]

5-64 **4** *nk* **Regent's Secret (USA)**[11] 3481 9-8-4 **55**...............(p) JamieKyne(5) 1 56
(J S Goldie) *trckd ldr: rdn over 3f out: one pce fr 2f out* **12/1**

2m 24.62s (-0.98) **Going Correction** -0.225s/f (Firm) **4** Ran SP% **110.5**
Speed ratings (Par 101): **94,93,91,91**
toteswinger: 1&2 £2.70. CSF £4.16 TOTE £2.40; EX 4.30.
Owner G Brogan **Bred** Gainsborough Stud Management Ltd **Trained** Musley Bank, N Yorks

FOCUS
A modest contest and the early pace was not strong. The proximity of the fourth limits the form.

3855 MCNAIR BUILDERS MERCHANTS H'CAP 5f 4y
7:40 (7:40) (Class 4) (0-80,80) 3-Y-O+ **£6,476** (£1,927; £963; £481) **Stalls** Low

Form RPR

16 **1** **Crimea (IRE)**[11] 3491 3-9-5 **78**.. JoeFanning 10 90
(M Johnston) *pressed ldr: led over 1f out: rdn out* **5/1**[3]

-303 **2** *1 ½* **Sudden Impact (IRE)**[11] 3491 4-9-11 **79**...............(e) SilvestreDeSousa 3 87
(Paul Green) *led to over 1f out: kpt on same pce fnl f* **13/2**

0-06 **3** *1 ¼* **The Nifty Fox**[17] 3268 5-9-6 **74**.. TomEaves 6 78
(T D Easterby) *trckd ldrs gng wl: effrt over 1f out: r.o fnl f* **11/1**

2310 **4** *1 ¼* **Argentine (IRE)**[5] 3681 5-9-12 **80**.........................(b) PaulMulrennan 9 79
(J A McShane) *in tch: rdn over 1f out: kpt on same pce fnl f* **9/1**

4003 **5** *1 ¼* **Joyeaux**[11] 3483 7-8-3 **62**.. JamieKyne(5) 5 57
(Ollie Pears) *s.i.s: bhd: hdwy whn nt clr run and swtchd rt over 1f out: r.o* **10/1**

4324 **6** *1 ¼* **Atlantic Beach**[25] 3001 4-9-2 **70**.............................(b[1]) TonyHamilton 4 60
(R A Fahey) *cl up tl rdn and wknd ent fnl f* **2/1**[1]

5350 **7** *2 ¼* **First Order**[13] 3422 8-9-5 **78**.......................................(v) AnnStokell(5) 1 60
(Miss A Stokell) *prom tl wknd appr fnl f* **25/1**

4521 **8** *2 ¼* **Dickie Le Davoir**[4] 3706 5-8-13 **72** 6ex.................(b) MarkCoumbe(5) 7 46
(John A Harris) *sn outpcd and bhd: nvr on terms* **4/1**[2]

3-00 **9** *6* **Tadalavil**[11] 3483 4-8-10 **69**.. AmyRyan(5) 8 21
(Miss L A Perratt) *in tch tl rdn and wknd fr 1/2-way* **40/1**

58.08 secs (-1.92) **Going Correction** -0.225s/f (Firm)
WFA 3 from 4yo+ 5lb **9** Ran SP% **117.0**
Speed ratings (Par 105): **106,103,101,99,97 95,92,88,78**
toteswinger: 1&2 £7.30, 1&3 £5.80, 2&3 £17.90. CSF £37.97 CT £345.82 TOTE £5.40: £2.10, £2.30, £3.10; EX 47.90.
Owner Sheikh Hamdan Bin Mohammed Al Maktoum **Bred** Lodge Park Stud **Trained** Middleham Moor, N Yorks

FOCUS
A fair sprint handicap run at a good pace, and rated around the first two.
Crimea(IRE) Official explanation: the trainer was unable to offer an explanation for the apparent improvement of form
Argentine(IRE) Official explanation: jockey said regarding the running and riding, that he had ridden the horse exactly the same as when he had won on the gelding two runs ago and this was to get cover and produce the gelding late in the race. However, when the gaps came it failed to quicken; vet said gelding was lame on its left fore
First Order Official explanation: jockey said gelding ran too free early on

3856 FAIR FRIDAY NEXT WEEK H'CAP 6f 5y
8:10 (8:12) (Class 5) (0-75,75) 3-Y-O **£3,885** (£1,156; £577; £288) **Stalls** Low

Form RPR

500 **1** **Lucky Dan (IRE)**[1] 3804 3-8-6 **60**........................ SilvestreDeSousa 1 69
(Paul Green) *hld up in tch: hdwy to ld appr fnl f: r.o strly* **12/1**

-550 **2** *2 ½* **Fathey (IRE)**[26] 2970 3-8-11 **65**.................................... TonyHamilton 6 66
(R A Fahey) *w ldr: led briefly over 1f out: kpt on same pce ins fnl f* **5/2**[1]

4442 **3** *2* **Cheyenne Red (IRE)**[25] 3003 3-8-13 **67**............................ PJMcDonald 3 62
(M Dods) *t.k.h: cl up: effrt and ev ch over 1f out: one pce fnl f* **3/1**[2]

3343 **4** 1 1/4 **Captain Scooby**[24] 3033 3-9-4 72 (p) PaulMulrennan 2 63
(R M Whitaker) *prom: effrt over 2f out: one pce appr fnl f* **10/3**[3]
0325 **5** 4 1/2 **Rogalt (IRE)**[15] 3355 3-8-11 65 TomEaves 7 41
(B Smart) *led tl hung rt and hdd over 1f out: sn wknd* **5/1**
36-0 **6** 8 **Granny McPhee**[78] 1491 3-9-4 72 JoeFanning 4 23
(A Bailey) *dwlt: sn in tch: rdn and wknd fr 2f out* **8/1**
1m 10.71s (-1.49) **Going Correction** -0.225s/f (Firm) **6** Ran SP% **112.1**
Speed ratings (Par 100): **100,96,94,92,86 75**
toteswinger: 1&2 £6.40, 1&3 £4.90, 2&3 £3.40. CSF £41.94 TOTE £11.00: £3.20, £1.90; EX 47.40.
Owner B & B Hygiene Limited **Bred** Mountarmstrong Stud **Trained** Lydiate, Merseyside

FOCUS
Just a run-of-the-mill event, with the top weight officially rated 75, but a clutch of the runners were lightly raced. It has been rated around the runner-up to his recent best.

3857 JLS DEBUT "BEAT AGAIN" OUT MONDAY H'CAP (QUALIFIER FOR SCOTTISH TROPHY HANDICAP SERIES FINAL) 1m 65y
8:45 (8:46) (Class 5) (0-75,70) 3-Y-0+ **£3,238** (£963; £481; £240) **Stalls** High

Form RPR
0042 **1** **Petsas Pleasure**[11] 3480 3-9-3 66 TomEaves 3 70
(Ollie Pears) *pressed ldr: led 2f out: hrd pressed fnl f: hld on wl* **6/1**[3]
2320 **2** *shd* **Shadowtime**[17] 3264 4-9-4 65 AndrewHeffernan(7) 2 71
(Miss Tracy Waggott) *t.k.h: in tch: effrt and chsd wnr over 1f out: ev ch ins fnl f: r.o* **9/2**[2]
0221 **3** 2 **King Pin**[22] 3124 4-9-8 62 PaulMulrennan 8 63
(Miss Tracy Waggott) *hld up in tch: outpcd 3f out: rallied fnl f: nt rch first two* **4/5**[1]
0356 **4** *nk* **Zabeel Tower**[15] 3331 6-10-0 68 (p) TonyHamilton 5 69
(R Allan) *trckd ldrs: effrt over 1f out: one pce fnl f* **14/1**
0306 **5** 1 **Island Music (IRE)**[21] 3150 4-9-3 62 JamieKyne(5) 7 60
(J J Quinn) *hld up: effrt over 2f out: no imp fnl f* **11/1**
0530 **6** 5 **Al Wasef (USA)**[12] 3448 4-9-4 63 GaryBartley(5) 6 50
(J S Goldie) *led to 2f out: wknd fnl f* **12/1**
1m 46.5s (-1.90) **Going Correction** -0.225s/f (Firm)
WFA 3 from 4yo+ 9lb **6** Ran SP% **110.7**
Speed ratings (Par 103): **100,99,97,97,96 91**
toteswinger: 1&2 £2.80, 1&3 £1.50, 2&3 £1.10. CSF £31.41 CT £41.20 TOTE £6.80: £2.90, £2.90; EX 23.40 Place 6: £193.08, Place 5: £126.35..
Owner PSB Holdings Ltd **Bred** Psb Holdings Ltd **Trained** Norton, N Yorks

FOCUS
A trappy handicap and muddling form rated around the runner-up.
T/Plt: £712.70 to a £1 stake. Pool: £51,841.71. 53.10 winning tickets. T/Qpdt: £104.00 to a £1 stake. Pool: £4,877.56. 34.70 winning tickets. RY

3631 NOTTINGHAM (L-H)
Saturday, July 11

OFFICIAL GOING: Good to firm
Running rail moved out 5yards from increasing distances on round course by about 30yards.
Wind: Light across Weather: Overcast

3858 EUROPEAN BREEDERS' FUND MAIDEN FILLIES' STKS 6f 15y
2:15 (2:15) (Class 5) 2-Y-0 **£3,885** (£1,156; £577; £288) **Stalls** High

Form RPR
4 **1** **Miss Smilla**[99] 1097 2-9-0 0 TonyCulhane 8 77+
(K A Ryan) *chsd ldrs: rdn over 1f out: led ins fnl f: r.o wl* **10/1**
5 **2** 2 1/4 **Gundaroo**[15] 3356 2-9-0 0 ShaneKelly 5 70
(J L Dunlop) *sn led: rdn and edgd lft over 1f out: hdd and unable qck ins fnl f* **7/4**[1]
23 **3** 1 1/4 **Nina Rose**[33] 2771 2-9-0 0 DaneO'Neill 11 66
(C G Cox) *mid-div: hdwy over 2f out: sn rdn: styd on* **5/2**[2]
4 3/4 **Diamond Duchess (IRE)** 2-9-0 0 NeilPollard 1 64+
(D R Lanigan) *hld up: hdwy over 2f out: styd on same pce ins fnl f* **66/1**
5 *nk* **Admirable Duchess** 2-9-0 0 FrankieMcDonald 13 63+
(D J S Ffrench Davis) *prom: hmpd and lost pl over 2f out: hdwy over 1f out: rdn and swtchd lft ins fnl f: r.o* **50/1**
00 **6** 1 1/4 **Botley Bell**[10] 3507 2-9-0 0 NickyMackay 14 59+
(M R Channon) *dwlt: in rr whn hmpd over 2f out: hdwy over 1f out: hmpd ins fnl f: nt trble ldrs* **40/1**
7 1 **Admire The View (IRE)** 2-9-0 0 SaleemGolam 7 56+
(D R Lanigan) *mid-div: hdwy over 2f out: styng on same pce whn hmpd ins fnl f* **25/1**
0 **8** 1 **Thewinnatakesitall**[19] 3226 2-8-11 0 KellyHarrison(3) 4 53
(H J Evans) *chsd ldrs: hung lft: rdn over 1f out: wknd ins fnl f* **125/1**
9 3 **Whirly Dancer** 2-9-0 0 TPQueally 9 44+
(H R A Cecil) *s.i.s: outpcd: sme hdwy over 1f out: wknd fnl f* **9/2**[3]
10 *hd* **Fairy Promises (USA)** 2-9-0 0 PaulEddery 3 44
(Pat Eddery) *s.i.s: sn pushed along and prom: rdn over 2f out: wknd over 1f out* **9/1**
11 20 **Green Shoots** 2-8-11 0 MichaelJStainton(3) 10 —
(M E Sowersby) *chsd ldrs: edgd rt over 2f out: sn wknd* **100/1**
3 **12** 17 **Gypsy Jazz (IRE)**[17] 3262 2-9-0 0 DO'Donohoe 12 —
(Jennie Candlish) *s.i.s: eased fr over 4f out* **16/1**
1m 15.31s (0.41) **Going Correction** -0.05s/f (Good) **12** Ran SP% **119.6**
Speed ratings (Par 91): **95,92,90,89,88 87,85,84,80,80 53,31**
toteswingers: 1&2 £11.20, 1&3 £3.40, 2&3 £1.10 CSF £27.67 TOTE £11.90: £3.60, £1.20, £1.20; EX 38.50.
Owner Findlay & Bloom **Bred** Lady Bland **Trained** Hambleton, N Yorks
■ Stewards' Enquiry : Frankie McDonald six-day ban: careless riding (July 25- 30) two-day ban: careless riding (July 31- 2 Aug)

FOCUS
A fair maiden in which previous experience proved crucial with the first three home all having run at least once. This field wasn't really big enough to split, so they call came up the stands' rail. The second, third and sixth help set the level.

NOTEBOOK
Miss Smilla had been a warm favourite when only fourth of six on her Musselburgh debut in April, though it transpired that she had thrown a splint, but the absence since then had obviously done her good and she was a different filly here. She was relatively weak in the market beforehand, which might have been a worry given her connections, but it made no difference and, having tracked the leader throughout, she saw her race out well once sent to the front inside the last furlong. She should continue to improve and looks the type to make her mark in nurseries. (op 15-2)
Gundaroo, fifth of eight on her Newmarket debut last month when not getting the clearest of runs, started favourite for that race and was sent off a well-backed market leader again here. She had no excuses this time as she took the field along for a long way and just came up against a rival with a superior turn of foot. Official explanation: jockey said filly was unsuited by the good to firm/good in places ground; this was confirmed by the trainer's representative (op 5-2)
Nina Rose, placed on varying ground in her first two starts, stayed on up the stands' rail to snatch third but never looked likely to catch the front pair. Nurseries now become an option for her. (tchd 3-1)
Diamond Duchess(IRE) ◆, an 80,000euros foal but a 34,000gns yearling, is a half sister to five winners. Tucked in from the outside stall, she was brought to hold every chance over a furlong from home before lack of a previous outing took its toll, but she still fared best of the newcomers. The stable's youngsters usually come on for a run and a couple of her siblings stayed very well, so she should improve with experience and a longer trip.
Admirable Duchess ◆, a 20,000gns half-sister to the winning sprinter Lenny Bee, lost her place when she became outpaced in the middle of the contest but she stayed on again late, though she did cause some interference to a few when switched left inside the last furlong. This was an encouraging enough start. (tchd 66-1)
Botley Bell, well beaten in her first two starts, ran better this time and was one of those hampered inside the last furlong. She may do better in nurseries now that she has qualified. (op 50-1)
Admire The View(IRE) ◆, a 55,000gns half-sister to a winning juvenile over 6f, was another to meet some trouble when staying on inside the last furlong. She is likely to come on a fair bit for this. (op 40-1)
Gypsy Jazz(IRE) Official explanation: jockey said filly hung left throughout

3859 PG MAN MEMORIAL H'CAP 6f 15y
2:45 (2:47) (Class 6) (0-65,65) 3-Y-0 **£1,942** (£578; £288; £144) **Stalls** High

Form RPR
1460 **1** **Bold Ring**[33] 2776 3-8-7 56 SophieDoyle(5) 12 62
(E J Creighton) *racd stands' side: hld up: hdwy over 2f out: rdn to ld and edgd lft ins fnl f: r.o* **12/1**
-360 **2** 1 1/4 **First Blade**[74] 1595 3-8-9 53 (b[1]) FrankieMcDonald 3 55
(S R Bowring) *racd far side: chsd ldr: led that gp over 2f out: rdn and ev ch w stands' side fr over 1f out: unable qck towards fin: 1st of 4 in gp* **20/1**
415 **3** *nse* **Fyelehk (IRE)**[8] 3580 3-9-1 59 TGMcLaughlin 13 61
(B R Millman) *racd stands' side: chsd ldrs: swtchd rt over 2f out: led over 1f out: sn rdn and hung lft: hdd and unable qck ins fnl f: 2nd of 10 in gp* **6/1**[2]
-320 **4** 1 1/2 **Robin The Till**[8] 3580 3-9-7 65 DaneO'Neill 1 62
(R Hannon) *racd far side: prom: chsd ldr of that gp 2f out: sn rdn and ev ch: no ex ins fnl f: 2nd of 4 in gp* **7/1**[3]
0000 **5** 1 **Cashleen (USA)**[16] 3316 3-9-5 63 (b[1]) DO'Donohoe 6 57
(K A Ryan) *chsd ldr stands' side: rdn 1/2-way: led over 2f out: sn hung lft: hdd over 1f out: styd on same pce: 3rd of 10 in gp* **10/1**
0-20 **6** *hd* **Jiggalong**[8] 3591 3-9-2 60 MichellePayne 14 53+
(Jane Chapple-Hyam) *racd stands' side: hld up: r.o ins fnl f: nvr nrr: 4th of 10 in gp* **10/1**
00-2 **7** 1 **Exopuntia**[21] 3175 3-8-9 56 MichaelJStainton(3) 9 46
(R M Whitaker) *racd stands' side: sn outpcd: r.o ins fnl f: nvr nrr: 5th of 10 in gp* **8/1**
-430 **8** 3/4 **Theta Wave (USA)**[106] 986 3-9-5 63 ShaneKelly 10 51
(J R Gask) *edgd rt s: sn led stands's side: rdn and hdd over 2f out: wknd fnl f: 6th of 10 in gp* **12/1**
400- **9** 1/2 **Black Salix (USA)**[362] 4020 3-8-10 54 PaulEddery 15 40
(Mrs P Sly) *racd stands' side: sn outpcd: styd on ins fnl f: nvr nrr: 7th of 10 in gp* **16/1**
00-6 **10** *shd* **Avonlini**[8] 3590 3-8-6 50 NeilChalmers 17 36
(B P J Baugh) *racd stands' side: outpcd: nvr nrr: 8th of 10 in gp* **28/1**
0532 **11** 3/4 **Come On Buckers (IRE)**[5] 3673 3-9-1 62 AlanCreighton(3) 2 45
(E J Creighton) *led far side: rdn: hung rt and hdd over 2f out: wknd over 1f out: 3rd of 4 in gp* **8/1**
05-0 **12** *hd* **Lady Dinsdale (IRE)**[30] 2862 3-8-8 52 NickyMackay 11 35
(T Keddy) *s.i.s and hmpd s: racd stands' side: hdwy 4f out: rdn and wknd over 1f out: 9th of 10 in gp* **20/1**
6130 **13** 1 1/2 **West Leake (IRE)**[30] 2852 3-9-5 63 TPQueally 16 41
(B W Hills) *racd stands' side: prom: rdn 1/2-way: wknd over 1f out: last of 10 in gp* **5/1**[1]
0066 **14** 2 1/2 **Peninsula Girl (IRE)**[7] 3625 3-8-7 51 (v[1]) TonyCulhane 4 21
(M R Channon) *racd far side: chsd ldr tl rdn 1/2-way: hung rt and wknd wl over 1f out: last of 4 in gp* **12/1**
1m 14.79s (-0.11) **Going Correction** -0.05s/f (Good) **14** Ran SP% **125.8**
Speed ratings (Par 98): **98,96,96,94,92 92,91,90,89,89 88,88,86,82**
toteswingers: 1&2 £63.80, 1&3 £9.10, 2&3 £53.10 CSF £242.78 CT £1641.33 TOTE £15.20: £5.30, £6.80, £1.60; EX 390.50.
Owner Daniel Creighton **Bred** J A Pickering & T Pears **Trained** Mill Hill, London NW7

FOCUS
The ground was officially changed to good to firm before this race. A competitive sprint handicap, but a moderate one all the same. The field split into two with a smaller group of four going far side while the larger group came up the stands' rail. The result would suggest there was no great advantage with two from each side filling the first four places, but the pair that raced stands' side both hung away to their left late on and ended up in the centre. The runner-up and fourth are the guide to the form.
Come On Buckers(IRE) Official explanation: jockey said gelding lost its action

3860 NOTTINGHAM EVENING POST H'CAP 5f 13y
3:20 (3:20) (Class 5) (0-70,70) 3-Y-0+ **£2,729** (£806; £403) **Stalls** High

Form RPR
645 **1** **Russian Rocket (IRE)**[12] 3465 7-9-1 59 TGMcLaughlin 11 70
(Mrs C A Dunnett) *racd far side: hld up: hdwy over 1f out: rdn to ld ins fnl f: r.o* **11/1**
0601 **2** 1 1/4 **Flying Applause**[30] 2852 4-9-8 69 (bt) RussellKennemore(3) 3 76
(S R Bowring) *racd far side: chsd ldr: rdn and ev ch 1f out: sn hung rt: styd on same pce: 2nd of 11 in gp* **6/1**[3]
4000 **3** 3/4 **Digital**[26] 2980 12-9-6 64 (v) TonyCulhane 8 68
(M R Channon) *racd far side: hld up: pushed along 1/2-way: r.o u.p ins fnl f: nrst fin: 3rd of 11 in gp* **20/1**
0331 **4** 1 **Green Lagonda (AUS)**[2] 3775 7-9-0 58 6ex SaleemGolam 13 58
(P D Evans) *led stands' side duo: rdn over 1f out: styd on: 1st of that pair* **4/1**[2]
0322 **5** 1/2 **Tartatartufata**[8] 3565 7-9-8 66 (v) TPQueally 2 65
(J G Given) *racd far side: sn led: rdn over 1f out: edgd rt: hdd and no ex ins fnl f: 4th of 11 in gp* **9/4**[1]
2013 **6** 3/4 **Brandywell Boy (IRE)**[13] 3422 6-9-4 62 RichardThomas 6 58
(D J S Ffrench Davis) *racd far side: sn prom: rdn 1/2-way: edgd rt over 1f out: styd on same pce fnl f: 5th of 11 in gp* **8/1**

500 **7** *hd* **Wibbadune (IRE)**[8] 3565 5-9-4 **65**.............................. KellyHarrison(3) 1 60
(D Shaw) *racd far side: s.i.s: hld up: r.o ins fnl f: nvr trbld ldrs: 6th of 11 in gp* **33/1**
0050 **8** *½* **Monsieur Reynard**[31] 2801 4-8-13 **57**....................(b) KirstyMilczarek 15 50
(J M Bradley) *chsd ldr stands' side: effrt over 1f out: styd on same pce: eased nr fin: last of 2 that side* **20/1**
5530 **9** *1 ¼* **Tadlil**[10] 3505 7-8-9 **53**..(v) NickyMackay 7 42
(J M Bradley) *racd far side: s.i.s: hld up: rdn over 1f out: n.d: 7th of 11 in gp* **12/1**
2500 **10** *¾* **Hereford Boy**[28] 2929 5-9-4 **67**...................................(p) SophieDoyle(5) 5 53
(D K Ivory) *racd far side: mid-div: rdn 1/2-way: wknd ins fnl f: 8th of 11 in gp* **10/1**
100- **11** *nse* **Wreningham**[213] 7621 4-9-4 **62**... ShaneKelly 4 48
(M D Squance) *racd far side: plld hrd and prom: rdn over 1f out: sn wknd: 9th of 11 in gp* **20/1**
6000 **12** *3 ½* **King Of Swords (IRE)**[12] 3445 5-9-4 **62**....................... DO'Donohoe 12 35
(N Tinkler) *racd far side: a in rr: 10th of 11 in gp* **25/1**
600 **13** *7* **Bookiesindex Boy**[33] 2758 5-8-11 **55**..................(v) SimonWhitworth 10 3
(J R Jenkins) *racd far side: sn chsng ldrs: rdn: hung rt and wknd over 1f out: last of 11 in gp* **33/1**

60.30 secs (-0.70) **Going Correction** -0.05s/f (Good) **13** Ran SP% **125.3**
Speed ratings (Par 103): **103,101,99,98,97 96,95,95,93,91 91,86,75**
toteswingers: 1&2 £9.40, 1&3 £25.20, 2&3 £30.90 CSF £71.85 CT £1369.95 TOTE £10.80: £3.30, £1.90, £5.90; EX 96.30.
Owner Mrs Christine Dunnett **Bred** Tally-Ho Stud **Trained** Hingham, Norfolk

FOCUS
A modest sprint with around half the field sporting some kind of headgear. The jockeys must have decided that the far side of the track was favoured as all bar two went straight over to race centre-to-far side, but the fourth horse was one of the pair to come up the stands' rail and he wasn't beaten far. He has been rated close to his recent best, with the runner-up rated as running his best race since this time last year.
Wibbadune(IRE) Official explanation: jockey said mare missed the break
Monsieur Reynard Official explanation: jockey said gelding ran too free

3861 DG TAXIS GET YOU HOME SAFELY H'CAP 1m 6f 15y
3:55 (3:56) (Class 4) (0-80,80) 3-Y-O **£6,476** (£1,927; £963; £481) **Stalls** Low

Form RPR
5654 **1** **Lombok**[38] 2605 3-8-6 **65**.. HayleyTurner 3 77
(M L W Bell) *hld up: hdwy over 2f out: rdn to ld over 1f out: hung lft ins fnl f: styd on wl* **6/1**
-021 **2** *2 ½* **Perfect Shot (IRE)**[19] 3205 3-9-6 **79**................................. ShaneKelly 7 87
(J L Dunlop) *a.p: chsd ldr 5f out: rdn to ld over 2f out: hdd over 1f out: hmpd ins fnl f: sn swtchd rt: styd on same pce* **7/2**[2]
1234 **3** *1 ¼* **Classic Contours (USA)**[14] 3371 3-8-5 **71**.................... IJBrennan(7) 2 77
(J J Quinn) *chsd ldrs: rdn over 3f out: styd on same pce fnl f over 1f out* **9/2**[3]
2231 **4** *5* **Shemoli**[20] 3192 3-9-7 **80**.. TonyCulhane 5 79
(M A Jarvis) *chsd ldr tl led over 6f out: rdn and hdd over 2f out: wknd over 1f out* **11/4**[1]
0110 **5** *nk* **Taste The Wine (IRE)**[30] 2866 3-8-11 **70**......................... DaneO'Neill 4 69
(J S Moore) *hld up: hdwy u.p over 2f out: wknd over 1f out* **7/2**[2]
2-23 **6** *4 ½* **Tropical Blue**[14] 3373 3-9-3 **76**... TPQueally 8 69
(Jennie Candlish) *plld hrd and prom: pushed along over 6f out: rdn over 3f out: n.m.r and wknd over 2f out* **10/1**
0-01 **7** *11* **Captain Flack**[21] 3157 3-8-3 **62**...................................(b) KirstyMilczarek 6 39
(J A R Toller) *sn led: hdd over 6f out: rdn and wknd over 3f out* **25/1**

3m 6.26s (1.26) **Going Correction** +0.075s/f (Good) **7** Ran SP% **116.5**
Speed ratings (Par 102): **99,97,96,94,93 91,84**
toteswingers: 1&2 £5.30, 1&3 £4.80, 2&3 £3.90 CSF £28.10 CT £104.35 TOTE £8.80: £3.50, £1.80; EX 37.10.
Owner J L C Pearce **Bred** J L C Pearce **Trained** Newmarket, Suffolk
■ Stewards' Enquiry : Hayley Turner two-day ban: careless riding (July 26-27)
I J Brennan three-day ban: careless riding (July 26-28)

FOCUS
A reasonable three-year-old handicap in which only two of these had raced over this extended trip before. Although two horses disputed the lead from the start, the pace looked a sensible one. The race has been rated around the runner-up progressing in line with his Windsor run in May and the third recording a personal best.

3862 NOTTINGHAM RACECOURSE MORE THAN JUST RACING (S) STKS 1m 75y
4:30 (4:30) (Class 6) 3-4-Y-O **£2,047** (£604; £302) **Stalls** Low

Form RPR
32 **1** **Shared Moment (IRE)**[25] 3005 3-8-4 0...................(p) KellyHarrison(3) 9 64
(Ollie Pears) *hld up: hdwy over 3f out: led over 1f out: shkn up and r.o wl ins fnl f* **4/1**[3]
0332 **2** *4 ½* **Wiseman's Diamond (USA)**[9] 3541 4-8-13 55.. RussellKennemore(3) 3 56
(P T Midgley) *hld up in tch: led over 1f out: sn rdn and hdd: outpcd ins fnl f* **11/4**[1]
6-03 **3** *2 ¼* **La Belle Joannie**[11] 3473 4-9-2 44.................................. DaneO'Neill 14 51
(S Curran) *hld up: racd keenly: hdwy over 2f out: rdn over 1f out: styd on same pce* **18/1**
6003 **4** *2* **Quick Off The Mark**[4] 3717 4-9-2 52.................................(t) TPQueally 2 46
(J G Given) *prom: rdn and ev ch over 1f out: wknd ins fnl f* **7/2**[2]
5 **5** *shd* **Jenny's Pride (IRE)**[19] 3228 3-8-7 0............................ NickyMackay 12 44
(John A Harris) *hld up: hdwy 1/2-way: led over 2f out: rdn edgd lft and hdd over 1f out: wknd ins fnl f* **8/1**
0060 **6** *3* **Buckle Up**[25] 3005 3-8-7 40..(p) SophieDoyle(5) 13 42
(D K Ivory) *chsd ldrs: led over 3f out: hdd over 2f out: wknd fnl f* **66/1**
6000 **7** *2 ¼* **Midnight Bay**[10] 3502 3-8-12 56......................................(v) TonyCulhane 15 37
(M R Channon) *hld up: sme hdwy over 2f out: n.d* **16/1**
00R- **8** *½* **Dry Speedfit (IRE)**[214] 7373 4-9-7 52.................................... PaulEddery 1 38
(Micky Hammond) *chsd ldrs: rdn over 2f out: wknd over 1f out* **16/1**
9 *6* **Sybil's Surprise**[73] 4-9-2 0.. SaleemGolam 16 19
(J Mackie) *s.i.s: outpcd* **66/1**
4-06 **10** *1 ½* **Monte Mayor Eagle**[106] 986 3-8-7 52................(b) FrankieMcDonald 10 14
(D Haydn Jones) *prom: rdn 1/2-way: sn wknd* **20/1**
0000 **11** *3 ½* **Autumn Charm**[26] 2975 4-8-11 41.............................. JPHamblett(5) 7 8
(Lucinda Featherstone) *hld up: a in rr* **33/1**
0-04 **12** *1 ¾* **Welcome Applause (IRE)**[23] 3054 3-8-2 49..........(b[1]) NicolPolli(5) 6 —
(M G Quinlan) *led: rdn and hdd over 3f out: wknd over 2f out* **28/1**
13 *14* **Bar Blu (IRE)**[79] 4-9-2 0..(t) ShaneKelly 5 —
(G A Swinbank) *s.s: outpcd* **12/1**
00-0 **14** *2 ¾* **Calley Ho**[15] 3342 3-8-5 60.............................. KristinStubbs(7) 8 —
(Mrs L Stubbs) *prom: jnd ldrs 1/2-way: hung lft and wknd over 2f out* **20/1**
15 *58* **Dave Diamond** 3-8-12 0.. TGMcLaughlin 11 —
(P D Evans) *s.s: outpcd* **25/1**

1m 46.15s (0.55) **Going Correction** +0.075s/f (Good)
WFA 3 from 4yo 9lb **15** Ran SP% **127.5**
Speed ratings (Par 101): **100,95,93,91,91 88,85,85,79,78 74,72,58,56,—**
toteswingers: 1&2 £3.70, 1&3 £8.30, 2&3 £5.80 CSF £15.00 TOTE £4.90: £1.80, £1.50, £3.70; EX 18.50.The winner was bought in for 6,600gns.
Owner We-Know Partnership **Bred** Mrs E R Cantillon **Trained** Norton, N Yorks

FOCUS
A very poor seller and not form to dwell on, though the right horses fought out the finish. The winner has been rated as recording a personal best, with the runner-up close to her recent form in this grade.

3863 CIRCUS DAY 30TH JULY H'CAP 1m 75y
5:05 (5:05) (Class 5) (0-70,70) 3-Y-O+ **£2,590** (£770; £385; £192) **Stalls** Low

Form RPR
0016 **1** **West End Lad**[7] 3637 6-9-9 **68**.........................(b) RussellKennemore(3) 3 79
(S R Bowring) *trckd ldrs: racd keenly: led over 2f out: rdn clr fnl f* **9/1**
0322 **2** *3 ¼* **Sion Hill (IRE)**[11] 3490 8-8-10 **55**..........................(p) KellyHarrison(3) 15 58
(John A Harris) *chsd ldr: led over 3f out: hdd over 2f out: styd on same pce fnl f* **10/1**
0003 **3** *1 ½* **Rowaad**[9] 3541 4-8-9 **51** oh3...................................(v) KirstyMilczarek 13 51
(A E Price) *a.p: rdn over 2f out: hung lft over 1f out: styd on same pce* **25/1**
0203 **4** *shd* **Justcallmehandsome**[16] 3322 7-9-3 **64**..................(v) SophieDoyle(5) 9 64
(D J S Ffrench Davis) *chsd ldrs: rdn over 2f out: styd on same pce fnl f* **11/1**
6011 **5** *hd* **Tanforan**[7] 3637 7-9-2 **65**... BillyCray(7) 4 64
(B P J Baugh) *prom: rdn over 2f out: nt clr run over 1f out: swtchd rt: styd on same pce* **13/2**[2]
0105 **6** *½* **General Tufto**[8] 3557 4-9-3 **64**................................(b) MatthewDavies(5) 7 62+
(C Smith) *s.i.s: hld up: rdn over 1f out: r.o ins fnl f: nvr nrr* **16/1**
0053 **7** *¾* **Count Ceprano (IRE)**[7] 3637 5-9-7 **70**........................ SimonPearce(7) 5 66+
(C R Dore) *hld up: rdn over 2f out: r.o ins fnl f: nvr nrr* **5/1**[1]
-065 **8** *nse* **Bivouac (UAE)**[22] 3098 5-9-5 **61**...................................... ShaneKelly 17 57
(G A Swinbank) *broke wl: stdd into midfield after 1f: hdwy over 3f out: sn rdn: hung lft and wknd over 1f out* **15/2**[3]
3630 **9** *2 ½* **King Of The Moors (USA)**[12] 3457 6-9-1 **62**............(p) LeeNewnes(5) 2 53
(R C Guest) *s.i.s: hld up: hdwy over 3f out: sn rdn: wknd over 1f out* **9/1**
00-0 **10** *1 ½* **Uhuru Peak**[11] 3490 8-8-5 **54**...............................(t) JamesPSullivan(7) 10 41
(M W Easterby) *mid-div: rdn over 3f out: wknd over 1f out: eased ins fnl f* **25/1**
5200 **11** *10* **Cavalry Guard (USA)**[14] 3401 5-8-4 **51** oh1................(b) AmyBaker(5) 1 15
(T D McCarthy) *mid-div: rdn over 3f out: sn wknd* **18/1**
/0-5 **12** *3 ½* **Perez Prado (USA)**[21] 3155 4-9-6 **62**............................ TGMcLaughlin 6 18
(W Jarvis) *hld up: rdn and wknd over 3f out* **12/1**
30-0 **13** *1 ¾* **Dannios**[47] 2320 3-8-11 **62**... DaneO'Neill 12 14
(L M Cumani) *s.i.s: a in rr: rdn and wknd over 3f out* **12/1**
64/3 **14** *10* **Bold Diktator**[12] 3457 7-9-11 **67**...................................... TonyCulhane 16 —
(R M Whitaker) *hld up: a in rr: wknd 3f out* **12/1**
300- **15** *3 ½* **Hardanger (IRE)**[379] 3438 4-9-4 **60**.................................... TPQueally 8 —
(T J Fitzgerald) *led: hdd over 3f out: wknd over 2f out* **16/1**

1m 45.4s (-0.20) **Going Correction** +0.075s/f (Good)
WFA 3 from 4yo+ 9lb **15** Ran SP% **127.0**
Speed ratings (Par 103): **104,100,99,99,98 98,97,97,95,93 83,80,78,68,64**
toteswingers: 1&2 £21.00, 1&3 £47.60, 2&3 £55.60 CSF £100.77 CT £2235.89 TOTE £8.80: £3.30, £2.30, £8.70; EX 76.40.
Owner K Nicholls **Bred** Keith Nicholls **Trained** Edwinstowe, Notts

FOCUS
A modest handicap with recent winning form thin on the ground and another race where half the field were fitted with some sort of headgear. With a few of these happiest when forcing the pace, a solid gallop was always likely and the winning time was 0.75 seconds faster than the seller. The winner has been rated as recording a 5lb personal best, with the runner-up and third close to their recent marks.
Cavalry Guard(USA) Official explanation: jockey said that the gelding was unsuited by the good to firm ground
Bold Diktator Official explanation: jockey said the gelding stumbled leaving the stalls

3864 BETFAIR APPRENTICE TRAINING SERIES H'CAP 1m 2f 50y
5:40 (5:40) (Class 5) (0-75,72) 4-Y-O+ **£2,590** (£770; £385; £192) **Stalls** Low

Form RPR
4406 **1** **Can Can Star**[24] 3024 6-9-7 **72**.................................. DebraEngland(3) 8 83
(A W Carroll) *a.p: led over 2f out: rdn clr fnl f* **7/1**
002 **2** *4 ½* **Princelywallywogan**[40] 2537 7-9-0 **62**................................. BillyCray 12 64
(John A Harris) *plld hrd and prom: led over 8f out: hdd over 7f out: chsd ldr tl led again over 4f out: rdn and hdd over 2f out: sn hung rt: styd on same pce fr over 1f out* **9/1**
3-06 **3** *¾* **Proficiency**[30] 2859 4-8-7 **55**....................................(b[1]) MatthewDavies 6 56
(T D Walford) *hld up: rdn over 2f out: hdwy over 1f out: nt rch ldrs* **5/1**[2]
1 **4** *2* **Hippolytus**[21] 3151 4-9-5 **72**... IJBrennan(5) 1 69
(J J Quinn) *prom: pushed along 1/2-way: rdn over 2f out: wknd ins fnl f* **3/1**[1]
-123 **5** *hd* **Granary Girl**[30] 2859 7-8-12 **60**.. SimonPearce 4 56
(J Pearce) *hld up: hdwy over 1f out: wknd wl ins fnl f* **17/2**
6262 **6** *¾* **Cry Alot Boy**[30] 2843 6-9-10 **72**.. PNolan 9 67
(K A Morgan) *s.s: plld hrd: hdwy to ld over 7f out: hdd over 4f out: rdn over 2f out: wknd over 1f out* **14/1**
00-4 **7** *2 ¼* **Jenny Soba**[26] 2971 6-8-12 **60**... JPHamblett 2 50
(Lucinda Featherstone) *prom: lost pl over 6f out: rdn 1/2-way: wknd over 2f out* **20/1**
0614 **8** *1 ½* **Trouble Mountain (USA)**[15] 3350 12-8-10 **58**.........(t) JamesPSullivan 7 45
(M W Easterby) *hld up: rdn over 3f out: a in rr* **16/1**
0033 **9** *shd* **Samurai Warrior**[14] 3374 4-9-6 **68**...................................... LeeNewnes 3 55
(P D Evans) *sn led: hdd over 8f out: chsd ldrs: rdn over 2f out: wknd over 1f out* **13/2**[3]
3060 **10** *2 ¼* **Portrush Storm**[17] 3264 4-8-6 **61**..................................... NeilFarley(7) 11 43
(D Carroll) *s.i.s: hld up: plld hrd: hdwy 1/2-way: wknd 2f out* **33/1**
240 **11** *2 ¼* **Old Romney**[57] 2052 5-9-5 **72**... LauraPike(5) 10 50
(P Howling) *chsd ldrs tl wknd over 2f out* **8/1**

2m 11.57s (-0.13) **Going Correction** +0.075s/f (Good) **11** Ran SP% **119.4**
Speed ratings (Par 103): **103,99,98,97,97 96,94,93,93,91 89**
toteswingers: 1&2 £15.40, 1&3 £9.70, 2&3 £16.20 CSF £69.68 CT £348.27 TOTE £10.20: £2.50, £5.00, £2.00; EX 96.60 Place 6: £912.41, Place 5: £657.05..
Owner K F Coleman **Bred** A W And I Robinson **Trained** Cropthorne, Worcs
■ Stewards' Enquiry : P Nolan jockey said gelding ran too free

FOCUS
A moderate apprentice handicap run at a very uneven pace, but an emphatic winner. He has been rated close to his winter all-weather form, with the sixth rated 3lb off the best of his maiden form despite racing keenly.
Cry Alot Boy Official explanation: jockey said that the gelding ran too free
T/Plt: £887.20 to a £1 stake. Pool: £44,542.32. 36.65 winning tickets. T/Qpdt: £104.10 to a £1 stake. Pool: £3,252.45. 23.10 winning tickets. CR

3576 SALISBURY (R-H)

Saturday, July 11

OFFICIAL GOING: Good changing to good to soft after race 1 (6.20) and to soft after race 2 (6.50)
Rail dolled out 8 feet on far side between 6f and 4f marker but impact on distances not notified.
Wind: Brisk across Weather: Rain

3865 BATHWICK TYRES NOVICE AUCTION STKS 6f
6:20 (6:21) (Class 5) 2-Y-O £3,885 (£1,156; £577; £288) Stalls High

Form					RPR
1	1		**Dick Turpin (IRE)**[33] 2771 2-9-4 0 ... PatDobbs 2 (R Hannon) *sn disputing cl 2nd: trckd ldr 3f out: qcknd to ld gng wl jst ins fnl 2f: pushed clr ins last: readily* **8/11**[1]	99+
051	2	6	**Perfect Ch'I (IRE)**[30] 2860 2-8-8 0 ... RichardMullen 8 (I A Wood) *drvn fr stalls and wnt sharply lft to get narrow ld on stands' rail: kpt slt advantage: rdn 3f out: hdd ins fnl 2f: no ch w wnr fnl f but hld on wl for 2nd* **7/1**[3]	71
	3	½	**Chocolate Cookie (IRE)** 2-8-4 0 ... RichardSmith 10 (R Hannon) *in rr: pushed along and hdwy fr 3f out: drvn and styd on wl fnl 2f: pressed for 2nd ins fnl f but nvr any ch w easy wnr* **33/1**	68+
130	4	1 ½	**Raine's Cross**[25] 2993 2-9-1 0 ... JimCrowley 9 (P Winkworth) *pressed ldrs and stl upsides over 3f out tl over 2f out: wknd u.p over 1f out* **3/1**[2]	72
1	5	4 ½	**Drift And Dream**[25] 3006 2-8-10 0 ... AlanMunro 6 (C F Wall) *chsd ldrs: rdn 3f out: wknd 2f out* **8/1**	54
051	6	4 ½	**Emma Dora (IRE)**[15] 3356 2-9-1 0 ... RobertHavlin 1 (D R C Elsworth) *in rr: mod prog fnl f* **18/1**	45
60	7	1 ¼	**Fantastic Pick**[25] 2997 2-8-12 0 ... MichaelHills 7 (B J Meehan) *rdn after 2f: a towards rr* **25/1**	38
	8	nk	**Weliketobouggie** 2-8-11 0 ... JamesDoyle 3 (J S Moore) *slowly away: a in rr* **50/1**	36
20	9	11	**Pherousa**[18] 3248 2-8-5 0 ow1 ... EdwardCreighton 5 (M Blanshard) *plld hrd early: in tch 2f: sn in rr* **66/1**	—
0	10	5	**Bush Master**[82] 1404 2-8-9 0 ... PatrickHills(3) 11 (R Hannon) *early spd: sn bhd* **25/1**	—

1m 14.82s (0.02) **Going Correction** -0.125s/f (Firm) 10 Ran SP% **125.9**
Speed ratings (Par 94): **94,86,85,83,77 71,69,69,54,47**
toteswinger: 1&2 £3.50, 1&3 £3.40, 2&3 £40.80. CSF £7.33 TOTE £1.80: £1.10, £3.00, £7.60; EX 10.20.
Owner John Manley **Bred** John McEnery **Trained** East Everleigh, Wilts

FOCUS
The going was changed to good (from good, good to firm in places) shortly before racing after 4.5mm of rain since Friday night, but jockeys returning after the opener asserted that it was good to soft, and that only a little more rain would turn it to genuinely soft going. This fair-looking novice stakes was run in steady rain and saw all competitors make a beeline to the stands' rail at the earliest opportunity. The form has been rated around the runner-up.

NOTEBOOK
Dick Turpin(IRE), who looked superb on the way to post, had made all when recording a most taking debut victory at Windsor last month, but let Perfect Ch'i give him a tow until inside the two on this occasion. The response when asked to go on was decisive and impressive. Already a very mature-looking juvenile and the best of Arakan's first crop so far, connections will find him a conditions race next en route to a possible tilt at the Group 2 Richmond Stakes at Goodwood. (tchd 10-11)
Perfect Ch'I(IRE), who was well supported, was rigorously ridden by Richard Mullen after a slow start to claim both the lead and the stands' rail, and she stuck to the task determinedly once headed. A decent fillies' novice or handicap contest should be attainable at least. (op 14-1)
Chocolate Cookie(IRE), stablemate of the winner and a Weatherbys Super Sprint entry, made eyecatching progress in the final furlong, having struggled to lay up with the pace early on. There is certainly a decent maiden to be won with her if improving from her debut as so many from her yard do. (op 40-1)
Raine's Cross hasn't gone on from his Bath win in April and he was unable to sustain his effort to the line this time. (tchd 11-4 and 7-2)
Drift And Dream ran too wastefully early on to give herself a chance of staying the extra furlong. (op 17-2 tchd 9-1)

3866 HORSESFIRSTRACING.COM H'CAP 6f
6:50 (6:50) (Class 5) (0-75,75) 3-Y-O+ £3,238 (£963; £481; £240) Stalls High

Form					RPR
6430	1		**Hillside Lad**[16] 3299 3-8-11 64 ... (p) JimCrowley 1 (R M Beckett) *grabbed stands' rail and sn slt ld: rdn over 2f out: hld on u.p thrght fnl f* **16/1**	66
2331	2	1	**Bateleur**[17] 3261 5-9-1 67 ... MCGeran(5) 9 (M R Channon) *hld up in rr but in tch: hdwy and rdn over 2f out: styd on u.p and tk 2nd cl home but nt rch wnr* **13/2**	67
-543	3	nk	**Cativo Cavallino**[38] 2598 6-8-12 62 ... NataliaGemelova(3) 2 (J E Long) *w wnr: rdn over 2f out and stl ev ch 1f out: styd on ins fnl f tl no ex fnl 50yds: lost 2nd cl home* **12/1**	61
0003	4	hd	**Stamford Blue**[10] 3505 8-8-12 59 ... (b) CatherineGannon 3 (R A Harris) *sn pressing ldrs: rdn over 2f out: stl ev ch 1f out: no ex fnl 50yds* **11/2**[3]	57
0314	5	2	**Golden Dixie (USA)**[5] 3691 10-9-11 72 ... TedDurcan 7 (R A Harris) *towards rr: hdwy on outside and hung rt 1/2-way: nvr gng pce to rch ldrs and styd on same pce fr over 1f out* **7/1**	64
1034	6	1 ½	**Dualagi**[4] 3713 5-8-12 59 ... RichardKingscote 5 (M R Bosley) *plld hrd: stdd in tch: rdn over 2f out: styd on same pce fr over 1f out* **4/1**[2]	46
0306	7	½	**Ghost Dancer**[16] 3304 5-9-0 64 ... (p) KevinGhunowa(3) 6 (J M Bradley) *plld hrd: chsd ldrs: hung rt over 2f out: wknd wl over 1f out* **20/1**	50
42	8	¾	**Catalan Bay (AUS)**[21] 3153 5-10-0 75 ... (v[1]) ClareLindop 4 (J R Gask) *plld hrd: pressed ldrs: rdn: hung rt and wknd over 2f out* **3/1**[1]	58
0515	9	2 ¼	**Great Knight (IRE)**[4] 3720 4-8-11 58 ... JamesDoyle 8 (S Kirk) *hit stall gates and s.i.s: styd rr but in tch: wknd 2f out* **8/1**	34

1m 16.35s (1.55) **Going Correction** +0.15s/f (Good)
WFA 3 from 4yo+ 6lb 9 Ran SP% **115.7**
Speed ratings (Par 103): **95,93,93,93,90 88,87,86,83**
toteswinger: 1&2 £30.20, 1&3 £78.80, 2&3 £4.00. CSF £115.95 CT £1313.80 TOTE £22.30: £4.90, £2.10, £4.30; EX 110.60.
Owner P Hickey **Bred** B Whitehouse **Trained** Whitsbury, Hants

FOCUS
The going was officially changed to good to soft ahead of this contest, another run in the rain. Few got involved behind the all-the-way winner in a race run in a time 1.5 seconds slower than the opener. The race has been rated around the runner-up to his Bath effort, but the form looks dubious.

3867 EBF BATHWICK TYRES MAIDEN STKS 6f 212y
7:25 (7:25) (Class 4) 2-Y-O £4,695 (£1,397; £698; £348) Stalls High

Form					RPR
	1		**Blakey's Boy** 2-9-3 0 ... TedDurcan 8 (J L Dunlop) *s.i.s: rr: moved over to stands' rail and v green: stl last ins fnl 3f: hdwy over 2f out: shkn up and green over 1f out but styd on wl to go 2nd sn after: rdn ins fnl f: led fnl 50yds: won gng away* **12/1**	80+
2	2	1 ¼	**Lean Machine**[21] 3167 2-9-3 0 ... JimmyFortune 9 (R Hannon) *c on to stands' rail and led: 2 l clr and pushed along ins fnl 2f: rdn fnl f: hdd and outpcd fnl 50yds* **1/1**[1]	77
	3	¾	**Royal Etiquette (IRE)** 2-9-3 0 ... RichardMullen 1 (H J L Dunlop) *broke wl: stdd towards rr after 3f: hdwy and nt clr run and switche rt 2f out: kpt on fnl f but nt rch ldng duo* **25/1**	75+
2	4	1 ¼	**Cafe Greco**[13] 3420 2-9-3 0 ... FergusSweeney 5 (P J Makin) *trckd ldrs: wnt 2nd and j. path 3f out: sn rdn and no imp on wnr: lost 2nd 1f out: wknd ins fnl f* **9/2**[2]	72
	5	4 ½	**Themanforacrisis (IRE)** 2-9-3 0 ... GeorgeBaker 3 (R M Beckett) *broke wl stdd after 2f but in tch: hdwy over 2f out: nvr rchd ldrs: wknd fnl f* **10/1**	61
	6	shd	**Pebblesonthebeach** 2-9-3 0 ... AlanMunro 4 (J W Hills) *in rr: pushed along over 2f out: sme prog fr over 1f out and kpt on cl home but nvr in contention* **20/1**	61
	7	2 ¼	**White Dart** 2-9-3 0 ... EdwardCreighton 12 (M R Channon) *s.i.s: hdwy 1/2-way: chsd ldrs u.p over 2f out: no imp and wknd over 1f out* **6/1**[3]	55
	8	3	**Caucus** 2-9-3 0 ... SteveDrowne 2 (J L Dunlop) *slowly away: in rr: sme prog towards centre of crse 1/2-way: nvr anywhere nr ldrs and sn wknd* **20/1**	47+
	9	7	**Brave Ghurka** 2-9-3 0 ... JamesDoyle 11 (S Kirk) *chsd ldr tl 3f out: wknd qckly over 2f out* **25/1**	30
	10	8	**Bury St Edmunds** 2-9-3 0 ... RobertHavlin 7 (A G Newcombe) *chsd ldrs: rdn 1/2-way: wknd ins fnl 3f* **50/1**	10

1m 30.51s (1.51) **Going Correction** +0.15s/f (Good) 10 Ran SP% **118.4**
Speed ratings (Par 96): **97,95,94,93,88 88,85,82,74,64**
toteswinger: 1&2 £4.70, 1&3 £42.90, 2&3 £14.50. CSF £23.49 TOTE £13.30: £3.30, £1.10, £6.60; EX 31.90.
Owner The Blue Bar Partnership **Bred** T E Pocock And Westbury Bloodstock **Trained** Arundel, W Sussex

FOCUS
Officially soft going by the time of this maiden, in which only two had previously seen a racecourse. A smart piece of jockeyship helped win the day here. The runner-up and fourth help set the level.

NOTEBOOK
Blakey's Boy, who was steadily brought over to the stands' rail with only one other horse behind him, was given time to settle by his rider before setting him alight two furlongs out. The gaps came in time, but he couldn't really be classed as a lucky winner, and there may be more to come as a few signs of greenness were still evident. (op 9-1)
Lean Machine, whose connections were worried that he might not be suited by the going, was additionally undone by the effort expended to secure the early lead, and then by drifting off the stands' rail with work still to be done over a furlong out. He remains of interest despite this reversal granted more conducive conditions. Official explanation: jockey said colt hung right-handed throughout (op 10-11 tchd 4-5)
Royal Etiquette(IRE) needed time to recover from a bump after a couple of furlongs, but he subsequently benefited from electing to follow the winner through the emerging gap on the rail late on. A reasonable debut. Official explanation: jockey said colt was denied a clear run
Cafe Greco, second over course and distance on debut last month, didn't see out the race as well this time despite the adoption of similar racing tactics and is worth another chance to claim a routine maiden back on a sounder surface. (op 5-1 tchd 4-1)
Themanforacrisis(IRE)'s effort faltered as quickly as it began, but connections can take heart that of his six half-siblings to have won races (including three juveniles), only one did so on debut. (op 14-1)
White Dart, a 60,000gns yearling who came in for late support, got mired in the worse ground nearer the centre of the course, and is probably better than the bare form suggests. (op 10-1 tchd 12-1)

3868 GRANT GLOVER MEMORIAL H'CAP 1m
7:55 (7:58) (Class 4) (0-85,85) 3-Y-O £4,857 (£1,445; £722; £360) Stalls High

Form					RPR
3-10	1		**Elliptical (USA)**[35] 2701 3-9-2 80 ... JimCrowley 5 (G A Butler) *led 1f: trckd ldr: led again on stands' rail appr fnl 2f: drvn and hld on wl whn strly chal thrght fnl f* **12/1**	93
14-3	2	½	**Rafiqa (IRE)**[21] 3163 3-9-4 85 ... JackMitchell(3) 2 (C F Wall) *stdd mid-div on ins: swtchd rt over 2f out: waited for a run sn after then qcknd to chse wnr 1f out: styd on to chal ins fnl f but a jst hld* **11/4**[2]	96+
-423	3	4	**Star Links (USA)**[24] 3030 3-9-4 82 ... JimmyFortune 10 (R Hannon) *chsd wnr: wnt 2nd over 1f out but nvr on terms: wknd into 3rd sn after and one pce* **11/1**	84
1-61	4	1 ¼	**Glowing Praise**[16] 3309 3-9-2 80 ... RichardMullen 1 (E S McMahon) *plld hrd: broke wl and stdd in bhd ldrs: rdn 2f out: chsd ldrs ins fnl f but one pce and no imp* **5/2**[1]	79
4-15	5	¾	**Imaam**[29] 2890 3-9-1 79 ... TedDurcan 9 (J L Dunlop) *dropped out s and c to r in rr on stands' rail: bmpd over 5f out: hdwy on ins over 2f out: kpt on over 1f out but nvr gng pce to get competitve* **12/1**	76
0456	6	1 ¼	**Quinsman**[16] 3309 3-8-5 69 ... RichardKingscote 3 (J S Moore) *chsd ldrs: rdn and outpcd over 3f out: nvr in contention after* **20/1**	64
5134	7	nk	**Roar Of Applause**[29] 2890 3-9-2 80 ... MichaelHills 12 (B J Meehan) *mid-div: sme hdwy on outside over 2f out: nvr gng pce to get into contention and wknd appr fnl f* **10/1**[3]	74+

10-0 **8** 3 ¾ **Swift Chap**[105] 1001 3-9-2 **80**.................... AlanMunro 8 65
(B R Millman) *in tch: rdn and bhd fr 3f out* **16/1**
060 **9** 1 ¾ **Efficiency**[38] 2600 3-8-11 **75**.................... SteveDrowne 11 56
(M Blanshard) *rdn over 4f out: a towards rr* **33/1**
61- **10** nk **Sky High Kid (IRE)**[194] 7810 3-8-2 **66**.................... CatherineGannon 7 46
(M R Channon) *led after 1f: hdd appr fnl 2f: sn wknd* **33/1**
1105 **11** nse **Global**[17] 3282 3-9-4 **85**.................... PatrickHills(3) 6 65
(R Hannon) *chsd ldrs on outside: rdn over 2f out: wknd qckly over 1f out* **14/1**
-005 **12** 7 **Sapphire Prince (USA)**[22] 3115 3-8-7 **74**.................... MarcHalford(3) 4 38
(J R Best) *plld hrd: bmpd over 5f out: a in rr* **16/1**

1m 43.74s (0.24) **Going Correction** +0.15s/f (Good) **12** Ran SP% **117.1**
Speed ratings (Par 102): **104,103,99,98,97 96,95,92,90,90 90,83**
toteswinger: 1&2 £14.40, 1&3 £24.00, 2&3 £7.40. CSF £43.53 CT £385.14 TOTE £17.10: £4.20, £1.60, £2.70; EX 58.20.
Owner Keen As Mustard **Bred** Lavin Bloodstock **Trained** Newmarket, Suffolk

FOCUS
Another race in which the winner raced prominently on the rail. The form has been rated at face value around the third, fourth and fifth for now.
Glowing Praise Official explanation: jockey said gelding was unsuited by the soft ground

3869 PICADOR CHEVROLET H'CAP 1m 4f
8:30 (8:30) (Class 5) (0-75,73) 3-Y-0+ **£3,238** (£963; £481; £240) **Stalls** Low

Form RPR
-235 **1** **Curacao**[51] 2189 3-9-5 **70**.................... JimCrowley 1 75
(Mrs A J Perrett) *disp 2nd: c over to stands' side and chal over 2f out: led wl over 1f out: drvn out ins fnl f* **11/2**
6503 **2** 1 ½ **Mustajed**[8] 3563 8-9-11 **66**....................(b) JamesMillman(3) 4 69+
(B R Millman) *dispured 2nd: rdn and styd towards centre of crse fr 3f out but stl upsides and rdn 2f out: pressed wnr 1f out: no ex fnl 75yds* **4/1**[2]
-602 **3** 1 ¼ **Seventh Cavalry (IRE)**[13] 3421 4-9-13 **65**.................... JimmyFortune 2 66
(A King) *hld up in rr: stdy hdwy 3f out: pressed ldrs and rdn ins fnl 2f: fnd no ex u.p and one pce ins fnl f* **9/2**[3]
3422 **4** 1 **Bagber**[29] 2892 3-9-8 **73**.................... SteveDrowne 7 72
(H J L Dunlop) *sn led: rdn and c towards stands' side 3f out: kpt narrow advantage tl hdd & wknd wl over 1f out* **11/4**[1]
113 **5** 1 ½ **Screaming Brave**[12] 3454 3-8-13 **64**.................... TedDurcan 3 61
(M R Channon) *hld up in rr: swtchd sharply to get stands' rail over 3f out: qcknd to chal 2f out: wknd fnl f* **9/2**[3]
10 **6** nk **Majehar**[46] 2351 7-9-9 **61**.................... RobertHavlin 6 57
(A G Newcombe) *chsd ldrs: rdn 3f out: wknd fnl f* **16/1**
63-6 **7** 17 **Yvonne Evelyn (USA)**[19] 3217 4-9-10 **62**.................... ClareLindop 5 31
(J R Gask) *plld hrd: towards rr: wknd qckly 3f out* **10/1**

2m 41.36s (3.36) **Going Correction** +0.15s/f (Good)
WFA 3 from 4yo+ 13lb **7** Ran SP% **113.4**
Speed ratings (Par 103): **94,93,92,91,90 90,78**
toteswinger: 1&2 £4.70, 1&3 £6.30, 2&3 £5.00. CSF £27.11 TOTE £6.40: £3.00, £2.40; EX 24.00.
Owner Mrs S Conway, Coombelands Racing Stables **Bred** Granham Farm **Trained** Pulborough, W Sussex

FOCUS
This was the only race run around the loop this evening, and having taken the inner rail around it, the field only started to drift towards the stands from around three furlongs out. Muddling form rated around the runner-up and third to their recent best.

3870 EUROPEAN BREEDERS' FUND LADIES EVENING FILLIES' H'CAP 1m
9:00 (9:00) (Class 3) (0-95,89) 3-Y-0
£9,969 (£2,985; £1,492; £747; £372; £187) **Stalls** High

Form RPR
10-3 **1** **Ave**[70] 1679 3-9-7 **89**.................... JimmyFortune 1 100+
(Sir Michael Stoute) *racd stands' side in gp of 3 tl field merged 4f out: qcknd to ld on bit over 2f out: shkn up and clr fnl f: easily* **9/4**[1]
2341 **2** 4 **Perfect Friend**[9] 3537 3-8-11 **79**.................... JamesDoyle 4 81
(S Kirk) *in rr: pushed along 3f out: hdwy over 2f out: styd on wl appr fnl f and chsd wnr ins fnl f but nvr any ch* **4/1**[2]
2-1 **3** ¾ **Farleigh**[68] 1752 3-8-3 **74**.................... DavidProbert(3) 10 74+
(A M Balding) *chsd ldrs in centre of crse: rdn and effrt over 2f out: edgd lft over 1f out and ins fnl f: kpt on same pce* **4/1**[2]
-246 **4** shd **Fanditha (IRE)**[21] 3165 3-9-2 **84**.................... PatDobbs 3 84
(R Hannon) *in tch: chsd ldrs in centre of crse: hdwy over 2f out: squeezed through to chsd ldrs over 1f out: one pce* **12/1**
-321 **5** ½ **Sparkling Crystal (IRE)**[19] 3220 3-8-7 **75**.................... MichaelHills 9 74+
(B W Hills) *led in centre of crse tl hdd over 3f out: edgd rt over 1f out: one pce ins fnl f* **5/1**[3]
3050 **6** 4 ½ **Miss Beat (IRE)**[30] 2846 3-9-3 **85**.................... SteveDrowne 7 73
(B J Meehan) *s.i.s: c to stands' side in gp of 3 tl field merged 4f out: wknd fr 2f out* **17/2**
0006 **7** 5 **Sanvean (IRE)**[7] 3608 3-8-7 **75**.................... CatherineGannon 2 52
(M R Channon) *racd in centre of crse tl field merged 4f out and led 3f out: hdd over 2f out: wknd over 1f out* **20/1**
120- **8** 2 ¼ **Such Optimism**[259] 6982 3-9-5 **87**.................... GeorgeBaker 5 59
(R M Beckett) *led gp of 3 on stands' side but bhd maiden gp tl field merged 4f out: wknd 2f out* **10/1**

1m 44.44s (0.94) **Going Correction** +0.15s/f (Good) **8** Ran SP% **119.5**
Speed ratings (Par 101): **101,97,96,96,95 91,86,83**
toteswinger: 1&2 £1.90, 1&3 £3.50, 2&3 £5.20. CSF £11.99 CT £34.92 TOTE £3.30: £1.10, £2.10, £2.20; EX 17.80 Place 6: £169.26, Place 5: £112.32..
Owner Plantation Stud **Bred** Plantation Stud **Trained** Newmarket, Suffolk

FOCUS
The feature race of the evening was won in a time 0.7 seconds slower than the three-year-old handicap over the same distance, albeit with the going having endured another hour's worth of deterioration. It was still a reasonable contest despite the defection of likely favourite Suba. The form is a bit messy with the winner getting the favoured rail, but it has been rated at face value for now, with the runner-up rated within a length of her 7f form and the third up 3lb on her maiden win.

NOTEBOOK
Ave was one of only three runners to opt for the stands' side throughout, with the remainder staying centre field until halfway. Despite conceding weight all round, the daughter of Danehill Dancer travelled supremely well throughout, and nothing looked likely to catch her once given the office two furlongs out. Jimmy Fortune noted after the race that the winner enjoyed this first try of soft going and that she will stay further still, which ought to enhance her chances of being found the right follow-up race. (op 2-1 tchd 5-2)
Perfect Friend fared best of those who raced in the centre, having declined the pace Sparkling Crystal cut out in that group. Although ultimately a well-beaten second best, she still served notice that she can stay 1m on turf at this first attempt. Already a winner on extremes of going, she should be able to land a slightly easier fillies' mile than this. (op 9-2 tchd 5-1)
Farleigh had the worst draw and was compelled to stay wide with Sparkling Crystal on her left for nearly the whole contest, so she did well in the circumstances. Only three races and one handicap into her career, she should be given the opportunity to prove there is more to come. (op 11-2)
Fanditha(IRE), a 7f maiden winner here last September, has not looked quite up to defying her mark in handicaps yet and this performance didn't constitute a great leap forward. (op 11-1 tchd 10-1)
Miss Beat(IRE) never recovered from a slow start. She was being beaten in handicaps off 12lb lower before unsuccessful tilts at Listed company the last twice, and she's going to prove hard to place for now. (op 12-1 tchd 14-1)
T/Plt: £53.70 to a £1 stake. Pool: £54,391.89. 739.31 winning tickets. T/Qpdt: £9.60 to a £1 stake. Pool: £4,854.03. 371.10 winning tickets. ST

3823 YORK (L-H)
Saturday, July 11

OFFICIAL GOING: Good to firm (good in places; 8.7) changing to good to firm after race 4 (3.45)
Course at innermost configuration and all distances as advertised.
Wind: light, half behind Weather: fine and sunny

3871 JOHN SMITH'S AND R.A.F. LINTON-ON-OUSE STKS (NURSERY H'CAP) 5f
2:05 (2:08) (Class 3) 2-Y-0 **£7,123** (£2,119; £1,059; £529) **Stalls** High

Form RPR
4140 **1** **Gertmegalush (IRE)**[29] 2896 2-8-4 **70**.................... PaulHanagan 2 74
(J D Bethell) *uns rdr leaving paddock and rn loose: mde all: styd on wl ins fnl f* **25/1**
210 **2** 1 ½ **Kingdom Of Light**[23] 3046 2-9-7 **87**....................(t) RyanMoore 8 86
(J Howard Johnson) *lw: w ldr: chall over 1f out: no ex ins fnl f* **10/3**[1]
122 **3** 1 ½ **Vilnius**[5] 3682 2-7-9 **64** oh1.................... DavidProbert(3) 4 57
(M R Channon) *lw: chsd ldrs: kpt on wl fnl f* **7/2**[2]
10 **4** hd **Mon Brav**[35] 2702 2-9-2 **82**.................... DNolan 7 74+
(D Carroll) *prom: outpcd over 2f out: styd on fnl f* **4/1**[3]
3 **5** 3 ¼ **Tom Folan**[66] 1788 2-8-9 **75**.................... MartinDwyer 6 56
(H J Collingridge) *rrd and uns rdr bef s: in rr: hdwy of 2f out: sn chsng ldrs: wknd ins fnl f* **10/1**
1033 **6** 1 ½ **Six Wives**[3] 3742 2-8-4 **70**.................... DuranFentiman 10 45
(J A Glover) *chsd ldrs: wknd over 1f out* **12/1**
1023 **7** 1 ¼ **Tillys Tale**[14] 3370 2-8-0 **73**.................... PaulPickard(7) 3 44
(P T Midgley) *hld up: hdwy over 2f out: wknd over 1f out* **7/1**
420 **8** 1 ¼ **Final Ovation (IRE)**[29] 2896 2-8-11 **80**.................... FrederikTylicki(3) 5 46
(J J Quinn) *chsd ldrs: wknd over 1f out* **8/1**
0320 **9** 11 **Mr Smithson (IRE)**[35] 2714 2-8-1 **72**........(v[1]) Louis-PhilippeBeuzelin(5) 9 —
(B Ellison) *s.v.s: hung lft and a detached in last* **11/1**

58.29 secs (-1.01) **Going Correction** -0.15s/f (Firm) **9** Ran SP% **117.9**
Speed ratings (Par 98): **102,99,97,96,91 89,87,85,67**
toteswingers: 1&2 £14.80, 1&3 £16.30, 2&3 £2.00 CSF £109.23 CT £380.11 TOTE £38.50: £7.10, £1.60, £1.70; EX 176.60 Trifecta £448.20 Part won. Pool: £605.80 - 0.30 winning units..
Owner Business Development Consultants Limited **Bred** Kildare Racing Syndicate **Trained** Middleham Moor, N Yorks

FOCUS
This looked a modest nursery for the class, but the form is straightforward, with the third the marker. The winning time suggested the ground was riding quick.

NOTEBOOK
Gertmegalush(IRE) made all to score, despite getting loose and unseating his rider on the way to post. He was well beaten in a seller at this venue on his previous outing, but aggressive tactics back over this sharper test did the trick and a return to quicker ground suited. This was undoubtedly a career-best effort. Official explanation: trainer's representative said, regarding the apparent improvement of form, that the gelding appeared suited by the quicker ground (op 22-1 tchd 20-1)
Kingdom Of Light finished out the back in the Norfolk Stakes at Royal Ascot last month, but was reported to have lost his action and had obvious claims if returning to his previous level. He was never far away and looked like the winner at the furlong marker, but the winner was not for catching. It rates a solid effort under top weight, but he had the benefit of the rail. This looks about as good as he is. (op 11-4)
Vilnius, 1lb out of the weights, was supported on this return to a quicker surface but lacked the speed to land a telling blow. She was not helped by having to make her effort down the middle of the track, however, and her turn is not looking far away. (op 11-2)
Mon Brav also lacked the natural pace to get seriously involved on this drop in grade, but finished his race in the style of a horse who will appreciate stepping back up a furlong. (op 7-2)
Mr Smithson(IRE) Official explanation: jockey said gelding was slow away

3872 JOHN SMITH'S "NO NONSENSE RACING" STKS (H'CAP) 1m
2:35 (2:36) (Class 2) (0-100,99) 3-Y-0+ **£11,656** (£3,468; £1,733; £865) **Stalls** Low

Form RPR
0-21 **1** **City Of The Kings (IRE)**[23] 3067 4-9-5 **90**.................... SilvestreDeSousa 2 101
(G A Harker) *chsd ldrs: led appr fnl f: jst hld on* **7/1**[1]
-240 **2** nse **Webbow (IRE)**[22] 3091 7-9-0 **90**.................... Louis-PhilippeBeuzelin(5) 12 101
(N Tinkler) *mid-div: effrt over 3f out: ev ch fnl f: jst hld* **9/1**
0001 **3** 1 ½ **Flawed Genius**[8] 3568 4-9-3 **88**....................(t) NCallan 14 95
(K A Ryan) *swtchd lft after s: bhd: hdwy over 2f out: hung lft and styd and styng on ins fnl f* **16/1**
6-00 **4** 1 ¼ **Lang Shining (IRE)**[7] 3640 5-10-0 **99**.................... RyanMoore 13 104
(Sir Michael Stoute) *lw: hld up in midfield: effrt on outside 3f out: styd on same pce approachinmg fnl f* **10/1**
-303 **5** nk **Kay Gee Be (IRE)**[16] 3312 5-9-7 **92**.................... ChrisCatlin 10 96
(W Jarvis) *chsd ldrs: led over 2f out: hdd appr fnl f: one pce* **12/1**
4523 **6** nk **Gala Casino Star (IRE)**[23] 3067 4-8-13 **84**....................(b[1]) PaulHanagan 6 87
(R A Fahey) *chsd ldrs: one pce fnl 2f* **15/2**[2]
1060 **7** 2 ¼ **Billy Dane (IRE)**[15] 3335 5-8-10 **84**.................... FrederikTylicki(3) 15 82
(F P Murtagh) *lw: chsd ldrs: ev ch tl wknd jst ins fnl f* **22/1**
-615 **8** ¾ **Spinning**[21] 3172 6-8-7 **83**....................(b) DeanHeslop(5) 7 79
(T D Barron) *s.i.s: bhd: hdwy on outside over 2f out: nvr rchd ldrs* **20/1**
2010 **9** hd **Tartan Gigha (IRE)**[22] 3091 4-9-9 **94**.................... JoeFanning 5 90
(M Johnston) *mid-div: effrt and n.m.r over 3f out: one pce fnl 2f* **8/1**[3]
3622 **10** hd **Osteopathic Remedy (IRE)**[14] 3391 5-9-3 **88**.................... TonyHamilton 3 83
(M Dods) *lw: trckd ldrs: t.k.h: wknd fnl f* **7/1**[1]
1654 **11** 1 ¼ **Wovoka (IRE)**[16] 3312 6-8-6 **82**.................... BMcHugh(5) 19 74
(D W Barker) *in rr: effrt over 2f out: nvr on terms* **25/1**
4013 **12** 2 ¼ **Fesko**[11] 3489 3-8-3 **83**.................... MartinDwyer 8 70
(M Johnston) *led tl hdd over 2f out: lost pl over 1f out* **14/1**
115 **13** nk **Esoterica (IRE)**[32] 2780 6-9-3 **88**.................... DanielTudhope 11 75
(J S Goldie) *mid-div: sme hdwy whn hmpd over 2f out: nvr on terms* **16/1**

5020 **14** ¾ **Charlie Tipple**[16] 3312 5-8-13 **84**................................(p) PaulMulrennan 16 69
(T D Easterby) *mid-div: effrt over 3f out: wknd 2f out* **25/1**
0300 **15** 2½ **Lucky Dance (BRZ)**[16] 3312 7-9-2 **90**................................ NeilBrown(3) 9 69
(A G Foster) *mid-div: effrt on outside 3f out: wknd over 1f out* **22/1**
20 **16** *hd* **Final Verse**[24] 3014 6-9-7 **92**................................ SebSanders 4 71
(M Salaman) *mid-div: effrt over 3f out: wknd over 1f out* **9/1**
1234 **17** 3 **Moheebb (IRE)**[17] 3265 5-8-9 **80** oh1................................(b) MickyFenton 1 52
(Mrs R A Carr) *in rr: bhd fnl 3f* **14/1**

1m 37.33s (-1.47) **Going Correction** -0.15s/f (Firm)
WFA 3 from 4yo+ 9lb **17** Ran SP% **130.9**
Speed ratings (Par 109): **101,100,99,98,97 97,95,94,94,94 92,90,90,89,87 86,83**
toteswingers: 1&2 £23.90, 1&3 £35.30, 2&3 £77.40 CSF £67.18 CT £1033.27 TOTE £8.10: £2.20, £3.20, £3.80, £2.70; EX 87.30 TRIFECTA Not won..
Owner John J Maguire **Bred** Tom McDonald **Trained** Thirkleby, N Yorks
■ Stewards' Enquiry : Silvestre De Sousa two-day ban: used whip in the incorrect place.(July 26-27)

FOCUS
A very competitive handicap, run at an average pace. Another personal best from the winner, who enjoyed a nice run through the race, and a personal best too from the second, with the third to form.

NOTEBOOK
City Of The Kings(IRE) proved game at the business end and has now got the best of a tight finish on his last two outings. He was just 1lb higher than when scoring at Ripon 23 days earlier and this return to quicker ground was in his favour. His low draw was an advantage and he got a lovely sit through the race. There could well be more to come while he remains in such form. (op 8-1)
Webbow(IRE) ◆ just lost out in the bobbing finish and also showed a game attitude. He did not enjoy a trouble-free run and did not fare well with his draw, so he emerges with plenty of credit. This is his optimum trip and he deserves another winning turn. (op 10-1)
Flawed Genius landed a claimer last time, but that obviously did his confidence a power of good and he posted a solid effort from off the pace, despite failing to confirm previous Thirsk form with the runner-up. His trainer has done well with him this term and intends to take him to the Galway Festival later this month.
Lang Shining(IRE) was deployed as Conduit's pacemaker in last week's Eclipse, but got a much more patient ride over this shorter trip. He kept on for pressure and was not disgraced under his big weight, but looks held by the handicapper. (op 9-1)
Kay Gee Be(IRE) raced handily and had his chance against the far rail down the home straight. He remains in good heart, but is on a losing run.
Gala Casino Star(IRE) was equipped with first-time blinkers, but it made little difference and he was beaten further by the winner than when losing out on 1lb worse terms at Ripon last time. He helps to set the level. (tchd 8-1)
Osteopathic Remedy(IRE) spoilt his cause by refusing to settle and did not look happy on the fast ground. Official explanation: jockey said gelding ran too free (tchd 6-1)

3873 50TH JOHN SMITH'S CUP (HERITAGE H'CAP) 1m 2f 88y
3:10 (3:11) (Class 2) 3-Y-O+ **£97,140** (£28,905; £14,445; £7,215) **Stalls** Low

Form RPR
1111 **1** **Sirvino**[44] 2392 4-8-8 **92**................................ NeilBrown(3) 16 105
(T D Barron) *hld up in rr: hdwy on ins over 2f out: wnt 2nd over 1f out: r.o wl to ld last 100yds* **16/1**
3-21 **2** 2¾ **Kingdom Of Fife**[47] 2342 4-9-6 **101**................................(v) RyanMoore 13 109
(Sir Michael Stoute) *lw: led: qcknd over 3f out: hdd and no ex ins fnl f* **11/2**[1]
5342 **3** 2½ **Albaqaa**[28] 2933 4-9-0 **95**................................ PaulHanagan 18 98+
(R A Fahey) *swtchd lft after s: hld up in rr: hdwy and nt clr run over 2f out: styd on wl fnl f: tk 3rd nr fin* **15/2**[2]
/112 **4** *nk* **Seeking The Buck (USA)**[19] 3213 5-8-8 **89**................................ SebSanders 4 92
(R M Beckett) *prom: effrt over 2f out: styd on same pce fnl 2f* **8/1**[3]
-144 **5** 3 **Ladies Best**[57] 2031 5-9-0 **95**................................ JamieMoriarty 1 92
(B Ellison) *lw: hld up in rr: hdwy 3f out: kpt on fnl f* **20/1**
6-26 **6** 2¼ **Sweet Lightning**[80] 1460 4-8-6 **87**................................ MartinDwyer 20 80
(W R Muir) *swtg: chsd ldrs: wknd over 1f out* **10/1**
-156 **7** 2 **Unbreak My Heart (IRE)**[47] 2342 4-8-9 **93**................................ FrederikTylicki(3) 8 82
(R A Fahey) *lw: mid-div: effrt over 2f out: kpt on same pce fnl 2f* **16/1**
0003 **8** 2 **Medici Pearl**[16] 3315 5-8-9 **90**................................ DavidAllan 3 75
(T D Easterby) *in rr div: hdwy over 3f out: kpt on: nvr nr ldrs* **25/1**
6434 **9** 5 **Re Barolo (IRE)**[22] 3089 6-9-2 **102**................................ Louis-PhilippeBeuzelin(5) 11 78
(M Botti) *mid-div: drvn over 6f out: nvr a threat* **16/1**
-501 **10** 1¼ **Alazeyab (USA)**[14] 3399 3-8-9 **101** 5ex................................ PhilipRobinson 17 74
(M A Jarvis) *trckd ldrs: lost pl over 1f out* **20/1**
-230 **11** ¾ **Deep Winter**[70] 1673 4-8-6 **87**................................ TonyHamilton 7 59
(R A Fahey) *in rr: hdwy on ins 3f out: nvr on terms* **25/1**
6500 **12** 1¾ **Love Galore (IRE)**[7] 3620 4-8-12 **93**................................ JoeFanning 21 61
(M Johnston) *s.i.s: hdwy 6f out: wknd over 2f out* **40/1**
-024 **13** *shd* **Nanton (USA)**[24] 3014 7-8-13 **94**................................ DanielTudhope 15 62
(J S Goldie) *in rr: effrt over 4f out: nvr on terms* **16/1**
4-00 **14** 2 **Laterly (IRE)**[7] 3620 4-8-12 **93**................................ MickyFenton 5 57
(T P Tate) *in rr: nvr on terms* **33/1**
2612 **15** *hd* **Moonquake (USA)**[22] 3089 4-9-8 **103**................................ LDettori 22 67
(Saeed Bin Suroor) *lw: trckd ldrs: wknd over 1f out* **15/2**[2]
1-01 **16** 2 **Riggins (IRE)**[42] 2480 5-9-1 **96**................................ NCallan 2 56
(L M Cumani) *swtg: mid-div: effrt 3f out: sn wknd* **11/2**[1]
12-0 **17** 6 **Ra Junior (USA)**[105] 1009 3-8-3 **98**................................ DavidProbert(3) 10 47
(B J Meehan) *prom: drvn along 6f out: lost pl over 3f out* **18/1**
11-5 **18** 7 **Ben Chorley**[16] 3312 5-8-9 **90**................................ ChrisCatlin 9 26
(D R Lanigan) *s.i.s: t.k.h: sn trcking ldrs: wknd over 3f out* **16/1**

2m 7.18s (-5.32) **Going Correction** -0.15s/f (Firm)
WFA 3 from 4yo+ 11lb **18** Ran SP% **131.8**
Speed ratings (Par 109): **115,112,110,110,108 106,104,103,99,98 97,96,96,94,94 92,87,82**
toteswingers: 1&2 £33.90, 1&3 £44.20, 2&3 £12.10 CSF £99.45 CT £749.72 TOTE £22.20: £4.80, £2.00, £2.60, £2.20; EX 167.50 Trifecta £2608.10 Pool: £34539.84 - 9.80 winning units..
Owner Theo Williams and Charles Mocatta **Bred** A W J Perry **Trained** Maunby, N Yorks

FOCUS
A cracking running of this valuable handicap and the form looks rock-solid. Another clear personal best from the winner, and a personal best from the second too. A race that looks sure to work out.

NOTEBOOK
Sirvino ◆ maintained his unbeaten record this season with a most impressive display, under an outstanding ride by the up-and-coming Neil Brown. He came into this 27lb higher than when winning on his seasonal return and had been hiked up 8lb for an easy win at Ayr on his previous outing in May. Settled way off the pace, he caught the eye rounding the final bend and stuck to the far rail in the home straight. He took a little time to master the runner-up, but found another gear when put under maximum pressure.
Kingdom Of Fife ◆ made most in the Zetland Gold Cup off a 9lb lower mark last time out and set out to repeat the feat here. He won the battle for the lead, but proved somewhat free, and that would not have helped his cause in the last furlong. Time will likely tell the concession of 9lb to the winner was an impossible task, however, and he still ran a blinder in defeat to finish a clear second-best. There is still another big pot in him before the season's end and he could be hard to peg back in a race like the Cambridgeshire. (op 13-2 tchd 5-1)
Albaqaa had been laid out for this and was backed to give his stable a third consecutive success in the race, despite not having a good draw. He was sweating through the race, but that is a common trait of his, and he turned in a career-best effort to stay on for third. He will defy this sort of mark when things go his way. (op 12-1)
Seeking The Buck(USA) has excelled since joining his current stable and ran another improved race in defeat. However, the handicapper looks to have his measure now. He could still gain further reward for his consistency this term. (op 9-1)
Ladies Best ◆ stayed on stoutly from off the pace, but this trip is probably an inadequate test these days. There is a race to be won with him off this mark and he could be an Ebor possible. (op 25-1)
Sweet Lightning ran well from his outside draw and should go forward from this first outing for 80 days. (op 11-1 tchd 12-1)
Unbreak My Heart(IRE) was never a serious player from off the pace. This surface was quicker than he cares for, however, and he is one to keep on side in the latter stages of the season.
Moonquake(USA) was not helped by being housed widest of all and dropped out down the home straight. He was later reported to have run flat. Official explanation: jockey said colt ran flat (op 17-2 tchd 7-1)
Riggins(IRE), 7lb higher, proved disappointing on this step up in trip. He got warm beforehand which cannot have helped. Official explanation: trainer's representative had no explanation for the poor form shown (op 9-2)
Ben Chorley Official explanation: jockey said gelding was unsuited by the good to firm, good in places going

3874 JOHN SMITH'S EXTRA SMOOTH SILVER CUP (H'CAP) (LISTED RACE) 1m 6f
3:45 (3:46) (Class 1) (0-110,110) 3-Y-O+**£23,704** (£8,964; £4,480; £2,240) **Stalls** Low

Form RPR
5-10 **1** **Hits Only Vic (USA)**[14] 3390 5-9-0 **97**................................ DNolan 10 107
(D Carroll) *hld up: hdwy 3f out: styd on wl to ld post* **16/1**
0-01 **2** *shd* **Warringah**[14] 3406 4-9-4 **101**................................ RyanMoore 2 111
(Sir Michael Stoute) *lw: led: qcknd over 3f out: jst ct* **9/2**[3]
0-52 **3** *nse* **Magicalmysterytour (IRE)**[14] 3406 6-8-13 **96**................................ ChrisCatlin 3 106
(W J Musson) *hld up: hdwy over 2f out: styd on wl fnl f: jst hld* **8/1**
-534 **4** 6 **Sugar Ray (IRE)**[20] 3190 5-9-7 **104**................................(vt) MartinDwyer 8 105
(Saeed Bin Suroor) *lw: hld up: effrt over 3f out: kpt on one pce fnl 2f* **14/1**
0101 **5** *nk* **Quai D'Orsay**[7] 3618 3-7-13 **97**................................ SilvestreDeSousa 5 98
(M Johnston) *lw: chsd ldrs: wnt cl 2nd over 3f out: fdd appr fnl f* **10/3**[2]
3215 **6** 3 **Drill Sergeant**[7] 3620 4-9-8 **105**................................ JoeFanning 6 102
(M Johnston) *chsd ldrs: effrt over 3f out: fdd fnl f* **9/1**
0-66 **7** 3¼ **Bulwark (IRE)**[21] 3143 7-9-0 **97**................................(v) MickyFenton 4 89
(Ian Williams) *dwlt: detached last and drvn along: nvr on terms* **22/1**
/123 **8** *nk* **Friston Forest (IRE)**[14] 3390 5-9-11 **108**................................ LDettori 1 100
(Saeed Bin Suroor) *chsd ldrs: rdn and n.m.r on inner 2f out: sn wknd* **3/1**[1]
-311 **9** 30 **Furmigadelagiusta**[20] 3190 5-9-13 **110**................................ NCallan 12 60
(K R Burke) *hld up in midfield: effrt over 4f out: lost pl over 2f out: bhd whn eased* **11/2**
0-25 **10** 10 **Hobby**[26] 2974 4-8-13 **96**................................ SebSanders 7 32
(R M Beckett) *chsd ldrs: lost pl over 3f out: bhd whn eased* **33/1**

2m 56.37s (-3.83) **Going Correction** -0.15s/f (Firm)
WFA 3 from 4yo+ 15lb **10** Ran SP% **122.6**
Speed ratings (Par 111): **104,103,103,100,100 98,96,96,79,73**
toteswingers: 1&2 £17.90, 1&3 £24.10, 2&3 £10.60 CSF £91.11 CT £642.06 TOTE £23.00: £4.10, £2.20, £2.80; EX 100.70 Trifecta £297.40 Pool: £1245.99 - 3.10 winning units..
Owner Kell-Stone & Watson **Bred** Peter E Blum **Trained** Sledmere, E Yorks
■ Stewards' Enquiry : D Nolan five-day ban: used whip with excessive frequency (July 25-29)

FOCUS
There was a thrilling three-way finish to this Listed staying handicap. Solid form, with another personal best from the winner and the placed horses improving on recent form to come clear of the fourth, who was close to form.

NOTEBOOK
Hits Only Vic(USA) was not seen to best effect in the Northumberland Plate a fortnight earlier and showed his true colours here on ground quicker than ideal. He has been well handled by connections and this was his best effort so far. It was also just his third outing of the year, so further improvement remains possible, and he will be entered in all the big staying handicaps. The Ebor could be next, but that would likely be ground-dependent. (op 12-1)
Warringah made all at Windsor last time out and was again allowed an easy time out in front. He nearly pulled off the same tactics again and this relentless galloper lost nothing in defeat. (op 7-2 tchd 5-1)
Magicalmysterytour(IRE) travelled sweetly through the race and only lost out by the smallest of margins. He is now clearly back in top form and is another who would have found the ground plenty fast enough. He would be interesting, if heading to the Ebor. (op 9-1 tchd 11-1)
Sugar Ray(IRE) had the visor back on. He ran on when the race was effectively over. He is one to avoid for win-only betting. (op 12-1 tchd 10-1)
Quai D'Orsay ◆ was the sole three-year-old in the race and was getting lumps of weight. He looked a possible winner when hitting top gear 2f out, but ultimately failed to see out the longer distance. He can go in again when reverting to 1m4f. (op 9-2)
Friston Forest(IRE) failed to run to his Northumberland Plate form on the contrasting surface. Official explanation: jockey said horse ran flat (op 7-2)
Furmigadelagiusta came here on the back of a career-best display at Pontefract and has shown a liking for this track before. He was never in the hunt on this step up in trip under top weight and now has a little to prove. Official explanation: jockey said horse was never travelling (op 6-1 tchd 13-2)

3875 JOHN SMITH'S 50 YEARS OF RACING SPONSORSHIP MEDIAN AUCTION MAIDEN STKS 6f
4:20 (4:21) (Class 4) 2-Y-O **£6,670** (£1,984; £991; £495) **Stalls** High

Form RPR
22 **1** **Chaperno (USA)**[14] 3392 2-9-3................................ LDettori 8 88+
(Saeed Bin Suroor) *athletic: lw: trckd ldrs: smooth hdwy over 2f out: shkn up to ld appr fnl f: sn clr: v readily* **13/8**[1]
0 **2** 4 **Iron Velvet (USA)**[10] 3500 2-9-3................................ MartinDwyer 4 76+
(M Johnston) *w'like: lw: chsd ldrs: outpcd over 2f out: styd on fnl f: tk 2nd towards fin* **16/1**
2 **3** ¾ **George Benjamin**[24] 3032 2-8-10................................ NSLawes(7) 11 72
(D Nicholls) *str: lw: mde most: hdd appr fnl f: kpt on same pce* **14/1**
4 **4** 1½ **Seven Of Diamonds (IRE)**[44] 2401 2-8-12................................(t) DavidAllan 10 62
(T D Easterby) *mid-div: hdwy and n.m.r over 2f out: kpt on wl fnl f* **20/1**
03 **5** *shd* **Tislaam (IRE)**[24] 3017 2-9-3................................ SamHitchcott 14 67
(M R Channon) *chsd ldrs: one pce fnl 2f* **17/2**
43 **6** 1¼ **William Morgan (IRE)**[7] 3613 2-9-0................................ FrederikTylicki(3) 15 63
(R A Fahey) *in rr: effrt and nt clr run over 2f out: styds on fnl f* **16/1**
5 **7** ½ **Uddy Mac**[24] 3032 2-8-12................................ ChrisCatlin 7 57+
(N Bycroft) *mid-div: drvn over 2f out: one pce* **50/1**
8 ½ **Gold Rules** 2-9-3................................ SebSanders 9 61+
(L M Cumani) *w'like: str: scope: bit bkwd: in rr div: effrt and n.m.r over 2f out: nvr a factor* **16/1**

9 ½ **Beat Baby (IRE)** 2-9-0 .... NeilBrown(3) 12 59
(J Howard Johnson) *leggy: bit bkwd: b.hind: s.s: sme hdwy over 2f out: sn wknd* **25/1**

05 **10** 1 ½ **More Lashes (USA)**[2] 3762 2-8-12 .... MickyFenton 1 49
(M G Quinlan) *chsd ldrs: wknd over 1f out* **25/1**

42 **11** ½ **Paradise Spectre**[24] 3017 2-9-3 ....(v[1]) JamieMoriarty 3 53
(K R Burke) *unf: w ldrs: hung rt and wknd over 1f out* **4/1**[2]

03 **12** ½ **Olympic Ceremony**[47] 2311 2-9-3 .... PaulHanagan 6 51
(R A Fahey) *w'like: lw: a towards rr* **11/2**[3]

13 1 ½ **Tribal Myth (IRE)** 2-9-3 .... NCallan 5 47
(K A Ryan) *str: bit bkwd: s.s: hdwy to chse ldrs 3f out: wknd over 1f out* **14/1**

1m 11.15s (-0.75) **Going Correction** -0.15s/f (Firm) **13** Ran SP% **129.4**
Speed ratings (Par 96): **99,93,92,90,90 88,88,87,86,84 84,83,81**
toteswingers: 1&2 £9.70, 1&3 £9.40, 2&3 £49.00 CSF £34.59 TOTE £2.70: £1.40, £6.00, £3.20; EX 33.50.
Owner Godolphin **Bred** Bruce Berenson & Laurie Berenson **Trained** Newmarket, Suffolk

FOCUS
A fair juvenile maiden. The winner improved again and is the type to rate higher in a better race. The runner-up caught the eye again too.

NOTEBOOK
Chaperno(USA) got off the mark at the third try and completed the task in great style. He moved beautifully through the race and could have been called the winner some way out. This quicker ground proved much more to his liking, and the manner in which he did the business here, would suggest he can hold his own in better company. (op 7-4 tchd 6-4)
Iron Velvet(USA) ◆ showed his debut run to be wrong and turned in a promising effort. He ought to prove hard to beat next time, especially if tackling a stiffer test. (tchd 20-1)
George Benjamin, second at Ripon on debut 24 days previously, showed decent early pace and got the extra furlong well enough, but was outstayed by the first pair. A drop back to the minimum looks on the cards and he should win races this year. (op 12-1)
Seven Of Diamonds(IRE), equipped with a first-time tongue tie, fared best of those to come from off the pace and would have been a little closer with a better run around 2f out. (op 10-1)
Tislaam(IRE) showed up well for a long way against the rail, but lacked the tactical pace when it mattered. He now has the option of nurseries and looks sure to benefit for a step up to 7f. (op 14-1)
William Morgan(IRE) ◆ was his stable's second string on jockey bookings, but he ran very well in defeat. He would have been closer with a clearer passage and looks one to take from the race. He can now go the nursery route (tchd 14-1 and 22-1)
Gold Rules ran better than his finishing position suggests and will leave this behind in time. (op 12-1 tchd 11-1)
More Lashes(USA) Official explanation: jockey said filly ran flat
Paradise Spectre was disappointing in the first-time visor. He was later reported to have hung left. Official explanation: jockey said colt hung right handed throughout (op 9-2)
Olympic Ceremony, up in trip, was disappointing on this first outing since being gelded and now has it to prove. (op 15-2)

3876 JOHN SMITH'S YORKSHIRE'S FINEST STKS (MAIDEN FILLIES) 7f
4:55 (4:56) (Class 4) 3-4-Y-O **£6,540** (£1,946; £972; £485) **Stalls** Low

Form RPR

2604 **1** **Shaws Diamond (USA)**[15] 3360 3-9-0 77 .... NCallan 8 78
(D Shaw) *b: mde all: kpt on gamely fnl f: hld on wl towards fin* **7/2**[2]

33 **2** ¾ **Barynya**[64] 1844 3-9-0 0 .... RyanMoore 6 76
(Sir Michael Stoute) *lw: trckd ldrs: effrt 3f out: chal over 1f out: no ex wl ins fnl f* **10/11**[1]

0-0 **3** 4 **In Secret**[65] 1804 3-9-0 0 .... SebSanders 7 65
(J L Dunlop) *s.i.s: hld up in rr: hdwy over 2f out: hung lft: kpt on to take modest 3rd ins fnl f* **11/1**

0 **4** 2 ¼ **Fine Silk (USA)**[22] 3093 3-9-0 0 .... MickyFenton 5 59
(B Smart) *leggy: dwlt: sn chsng wnr: drvn to chal over 3f out: wknd over 1f out* **25/1**

-60 **5** 14 **Langland Bay**[32] 2795 3-9-0 0 .... MartinDwyer 3 21
(W R Muir) *trckd ldrs: lost pl over 2f out* **12/1**

00-3 **6** 2 ¼ **Alacity (IRE)**[61] 1922 3-9-0 40 .... ChrisCatlin 1 15
(N Bycroft) *in rr: drvn over 3f out: sn bhd* **40/1**

7 5 **Pete's Passion** 3-9-0 0 .... PaulHanagan 4 2
(R A Fahey) *w'like: lw: in rr: rdn over 3f out: sn bhd* **9/2**[3]

1m 24.27s (-1.03) **Going Correction** -0.15s/f (Firm) **7** Ran SP% **115.1**
Speed ratings (Par 105): **99,98,93,91,75 72,66**
toteswingers: 1&2 £1.80, 1&3 £6.30, 2&3 £3.90 CSF £7.15 TOTE £4.30: £2.10, £1.50; EX 7.80.
Owner Mrs Lyndsey Shaw **Bred** John J Greely Iv & Richard Sturgill **Trained** Danethorpe, Notts

FOCUS
A modest fillies' maiden, run at an ordinary pace. Not much of a race for the track.
Langland Bay Official explanation: jockey said filly was unsuited by the good to firm, good in places going

3877 JOHN SMITH'S CASK STKS (H'CAP) 6f
5:30 (5:32) (Class 3) (0-95,95) 3-Y-O+ **£7,771** (£2,312; £1,155; £577) **Stalls** High

Form RPR

1000 **1** **Striking Spirit**[21] 3141 4-9-11 **93** .... MickyFenton 11 106
(D Nicholls) *mde virtually all: styd on wl fnl f* **15/2**

0011 **2** 1 ¾ **Pavershooz**[15] 3351 4-9-4 **86** .... DuranFentiman 7 93
(N Wilson) *lw: racd wd: w wnr: styd on same pce ins fnl f* **9/2**[2]

-062 **3** 2 **Tabaret**[2] 3784 6-9-5 **90** ....(p) MichaelJStainton(3) 9 91
(R M Whitaker) *chsd ldrs: hung lft and kpt on same pce appr fnl f* **9/1**

336 **4** shd **Atlantic Story (USA)**[8] 3567 7-9-8 **90** ....(bt) SebSanders 14 90
(M W Easterby) *chsd ldrs: kpt on same pce appr fnl f* **12/1**

5620 **5** ½ **Silver Wind**[14] 3377 4-8-13 **81** ....(v) MartinDwyer 10 80
(P D Evans) *chsd ldrs: one pce fnl 2f* **20/1**

0000 **6** nk **Inter Vision (USA)**[14] 3389 9-9-0 **82** .... DanielTudhope 2 80+
(A Dickman) *in rr: hdwy and n.m.r over 1f out: kpt on ins fnl f* **18/1**

4-00 **7** 1 **Kaldoun Kingdom (IRE)**[42] 2502 4-9-7 **92** .... FrederikTylicki(3) 16 87
(R A Fahey) *in rr: hdwy over 1f out: nt rch ldrs* **5/1**[3]

6255 **8** ¾ **Wyatt Earp (IRE)**[22] 3122 8-9-1 **83** .... DaleGibson 3 75
(P Salmon) *chsd ldrs: one pce fnl 2f* **14/1**

-420 **9** nk **Harrison George (IRE)**[22] 3091 4-9-8 **90** .... PaulHanagan 1 81+
(R A Fahey) *stmbld s: in rr: swtchd lft over 1f out: r.o* **4/1**[1]

0160 **10** 1 ½ **Ishetoo**[15] 3351 5-9-8 **95** .... BMcHugh(5) 17 81
(A Dickman) *in rr: hdwy 2f out: styd on ins fnl f: nvr on terms* **12/1**

6404 **11** nse **Rasaman (IRE)**[14] 3372 5-9-0 **82** ....(tp) NCallan 5 68
(K A Ryan) *rrd s: in rr: nvr on terms* **20/1**

0000 **12** hd **Ajigolo**[4] 3706 6-9-6 **88** .... JamieMoriarty 4 74
(N Wilson) *dwlt: nvr on terms* **40/1**

0124 **13** 1 ½ **Grazeon Gold Blend**[14] 3377 6-8-7 **80** ......(p) Louis-PhilippeBeuzelin(5) 8 61
(J J Quinn) *chsd ldrs: wknd over 1f out* **14/1**

1-P0 **14** 1 **Knavesmire (IRE)**[7] 3622 3-9-3 **91** .... DavidAllan 15 69
(M Brittain) *sn in rr* **25/1**

0010 **15** 3 **Sea Rover (IRE)**[1] 3828 5-8-1 **76** oh4 .... JohnCavanagh(7) 6 44
(M Brittain) *mid-div: lost pl over 2f out* **20/1**

4-00 **16** 1 ¾ **Silver Guest**[22] 3091 4-9-5 **87** .... SamHitchcott 13 49
(M R Channon) *sn in rr* **40/1**

3460 **17** 4 **Green Park (IRE)**[7] 3607 6-8-8 **76** oh2 ....(b) DNolan 12 26
(D Carroll) *mid-div: lost pl over 2f out* **33/1**

69.83 secs (-2.07) **Going Correction** -0.15s/f (Firm)
WFA 3 from 4yo+ 6lb **17** Ran SP% **136.5**
Speed ratings (Par 107): **107,104,102,101,101 100,99,98,98,96 96,95,93,92,88 86,80**
toteswingers: 1&2 £5.10, 1&3 £20.60, 2&3 £11.80 CSF £42.26 CT £330.74 TOTE £9.60: £2.20, £1.90, £2.80, £3.50; EX 48.40 Place 6: £73.75, Place 5: £43.55..
Owner N & Z Aboobaker & Bon Accord Racing **Bred** Juddmonte Farms Ltd **Trained** Sessay, N Yorks

FOCUS
A typically wide-open sprint. The field shunned the far side, and nothing got into the race from off the pace.

NOTEBOOK
Striking Spirit ran well in the Wokingham last time out and, 2lb lower here, made all in determined fashion. His natural early pace was well suited to this sharp track and it was a very good weight-carrying performance. (op 9-1 tchd 10-1)
Pavershooz was 2lb higher in this quest for the hat-trick and ran a solid race in defeat back on quicker ground. This easy 6f was fine for him and he was another whose style was suited to this track, but perhaps 5f is now his ideal trip. He remains in great heart and looks an ideal candidate for the Portland over the intermediate trip at Doncaster in September. (op 5-1 tchd 11-2 in places)
Tabaret only just missed out at Newmarket two days earlier and ran another fine race in defeat. He is now back to near his previous best, but will be due a rise in the handicap. (op 8-1)
Atlantic Story(USA) showed up nicely over a test sharper than ideal. He also got himself warm, so deserves credit and his turn is probably not too far off again. (op 16-1)
Silver Wind displayed good early pace and bounced back to form for the return to this venue. He has a mediocre win record, though. (tchd 22-1)
Inter Vision(USA) bounced back to form and ran a touch better than the bare form as he met some trouble. (op 20-1 tchd 25-1)
Kaldoun Kingdom(IRE) was expected to relish the extra furlong, but this track doesn't play to his strengths and he is another with a poor strike-rate. (op 6-1 tchd 8-1)
Harrison George(IRE) blew his chance at the start and so did well to finish so close. He is worth another chance. Official explanation: jockey said colt stumbled at the start (op 9-2 tchd 7-2)
T/Jkpt: Not won. T/Plt: £40.60 to a £1 stake. Pool: £195,078.44. 3,501.12 winning tickets.
T/Qpdt: £13.10 to a £1 stake. Pool: £8,135.98. 457.23 winning tickets. WG

3878 - 3880a (Foreign Racing) - See Raceform Interactive

[3433] CURRAGH (R-H)
Saturday, July 11

OFFICIAL GOING: Straight course - yielding; round course - good to yielding changing to soft on both courses after race 3 (3.30)

3881a KEENELAND MINSTREL STKS (GROUP 3) 7f
4:00 (4:01) 3-Y-O+ **£41,966** (£12,266; £5,810; £1,936)

RPR

1 **Three Rocks (IRE)**[13] 3434 4-9-7 107 .... KJManning 6 111
(J S Bolger, Ire) *hld up in rr: hdwy in 3rd over 2f out: led 1 1/2f out: rdn and kpt on wl fnl f* **8/1**

2 1 ¼ **Georgebernardshaw (IRE)**[13] 3435 4-9-7 105 .... JAHeffernan 3 108
(A P O'Brien, Ire) *settled bhd ldrs: 5th 1/2-way: rdn into 4th 2f out: u.p over 1f out: kpt on fnl f to 2nd cl home* **16/1**

3 ¾ **Mad About You (IRE)**[62] 1913 4-9-7 112 ....(b) PJSmullen 8 106
(D K Weld, Ire) *chsd ldrs: 2nd 1/2-way: impr to chal 2f out: rdn in 2nd over 1f out: no ex and kpt on same pce fnl f: lost 2nd cl home* **7/2**[3]

4 2 ½ **Al Qasi (IRE)**[14] 3398 6-9-7 .... MJKinane 5 99
(P W Chapple-Hyam) *chsd ldrs: 4th 1/2-way: rdn in 5th 2f out: no imp over 1f out: kpt on same pce fnl f* **3/1**[2]

5 1 ¾ **Jumbajukiba**[13] 3437 6-9-12 112 ....(b) FMBerry 9 100
(Mrs John Harrington, Ire) *led: rdn and hdd 1 1/2f out: no ex and wknd fr over 1f out* **2/1**[1]

6 1 ½ **Rock Of Rochelle (USA)**[21] 3141 4-9-10 108 .... ShaneFoley 4 93
(A Kinsella, Ire) *chsd ldrs early: towards rr bef 1/2-way: rdn in mod 6th and no ex 2f out: kpt on one pce* **7/1**

7 8 **Snaefell (IRE)**[13] 3434 5-9-10 106 ....(p) RPCleary 7 72
(M Halford, Ire) *chsd ldr: 3rd 1/2-way: rdn and wknd 3f out* **9/1**

1m 28.61s (1.51) **Going Correction** +0.55s/f (Yiel) **7** Ran SP% **120.0**
Speed ratings: **113,111,110,107,105 104,95**
CSF £123.13 TOTE £9.60: £4.40, £4.30; DF 108.50.
Owner Mrs J S Bolger **Bred** Michael Poland & Aerial Bloods **Trained** Coolcullen, Co Carlow

NOTEBOOK
Three Rocks(IRE) has shown himself to be versatile in terms of distance and ground. Held up at the back of the field, he travelled well into third place over 2f out before going to the front one and a half furlongs out. He kept on well and was always in command inside the final furlong. He found 5f too short for him on his previous start, but he has wins over 6f and 7f to his credit and has also been placed over 1m. There should be more to come from him. (op 7/1)
Georgebernardshaw(IRE), both of whose wins were on heavy ground, disappointed in a handicap here on his previous start having shown signs of a return to form when third in a 7f Group 3 on good ground at Leopardstown. He made steady headway from 2f out and, while he never looked likely to trouble the winner, he stayed on to go second close home. (op 14/1)
Mad About You(IRE), a winner at this level over the same course and trip in April, had finished in the frame on both her subsequent starts. Returning from a two-month break, she was soon tracking the leaders and was second at halfway. She failed to find much over 1f out and just kept on, losing second spot near the finish. (op 3/1 tchd 4/1)
Al Qasi(IRE) has done all his winning over 6f and won a Group 3 here last season. Well suited by soft ground, he tracked the leaders but never posed much of a threat after being pushed along at halfway. Fifth 2f out, he kept on inside the final furlong. (op 3/1 tchd 100/30)
Jumbajukiba, something of a Curragh specialist and well suited by soft ground, was attempting to win this race for the second consecutive year. As usual, he set off in front but he was never able to get away from his rivals and was done with once headed by the winner one and a half furlongs out. (op 9/4 tchd 15/8)

3882a KEENELAND INTERNATIONAL STKS (GROUP 3) 1m 1f
4:30 (4:30) 3-Y-O+ **£44,174** (£12,912; £6,116; £2,038)

RPR

1 **Famous Name**[13] 3437 4-9-7 117 .... PJSmullen 7 114+
(D K Weld, Ire) *chsd ldrs: 3rd 1/2-way: impr to 2nd over 2f out: led 1 1/2f out: rdn and kpt on wl fnl f* **2/5**[1]

2 2 **Staying On (IRE)**[44] 2410 4-9-7 ....(t) AdamKirby 1 110
(W R Swinburn) *led: rdn and hdd 1 1/2f out: no ex and kpt on same pce fnl f* **4/1**[2]

3 3 ½ **Red Rock Canyon (IRE)**[4] 3725 5-9-7 103 CO'Donoghue 6 103
(A P O'Brien, Ire) *chsd ldr in 2nd: rdn in 3rd 2f out: no imp 1 1/2f out: kpt on same pce* 14/1[3]

4 1 ¾ **Rockhampton (IRE)**[13] 3438 3-8-11 100 JAHeffernan 2 98
(A P O'Brien, Ire) *hld up in rr: rdn into 4th 2f out: no imp 1 1/2f out: kpt on one pce* 20/1

5 2 ½ **Deauville Vision (IRE)**[23] 3082 6-9-4 106 (p) RPCleary 3 91
(M Halford, Ire) *racd mainly 4th: rdn and no ex over 2f out: sn rr and no imp: kpt on one pce* 14/1[3]

6 1 ¾ **Chintz (IRE)**[22] 3088 3-8-11 103 WMLordan 8 89
(David Wachman, Ire) *settled in 5th: rr and rdn over 2f out: no imp in mod 5th 1 1/2f out: kpt on one pce* 16/1

R **Estrela Brage (USA)**[83] 1387 6-9-7 102 DPMcDonogh 4 —
(Edward Lynam, Ire) *ref to r* 25/1

1m 57.43s (2.53) **Going Correction** +0.625s/f (Yiel)
WFA 3 from 4yo+ 10lb 7 Ran SP% **119.3**
Speed ratings: **113,111,108,106,104 102,—**
CSF £2.65 TOTE £1.40: £1.10, £2.70; DF 2.70.
Owner K Abdulla **Bred** Juddmonte Farms Ltd **Trained** The Curragh, Co Kildare

NOTEBOOK
Famous Name was the clear form pick as his price indicated and he won quite easily after tracking the leaders and going to the front one and a half furlongs out. He was never in any danger and afterwards trainer Dermot Weld said it will be either Prix Jacques Le Marois at Deauville or the Arlington Million next, with the French race more likely.
Staying On(IRE) had performed well since achieving his fourth win in a 1m Listed race at Doncaster in April. Touched off by Doctor Fremantle at this level over 1m2f at Chester, he performed creditably when a close up, and hampered, sixth in another 1m2f Group 3 at Sandown, won by Cima de Triomphe. All his wins and those two Group 3 efforts were on quick ground and conditions here were very different, but he set off in front and, although always playing second fiddle to the winner from one and a half furlongs out, he did keep on to the line. (op 9/2)
Red Rock Canyon(IRE), who has a couple of Group 1 first three placings to his credit, has been a pacemaker and a lead horse for Ballydoyle for much of his career. He belatedly got off the mark in a maiden over this trip at Roscommon on Tuesday and ran a solid race here without looking a likely winner. He raced in second place until over 2f out from where he kept on at the same pace. (op 16/1)
Rockhampton(IRE) acted as pacemaker for Fame And Glory in the Irish Derby in which he was beaten 30 lengths. Held up back in trip here, he kept on from 2f out and closed steadily without ever posing a real threat.
Deauville Vision(IRE), whose five wins include two at Listed level, is well suited by soft ground and after a disappointing run on good ground on her previous start she put in a better effort here, although unable to make much impression from one and a half furlongs out. She is in-foal and retirement is not far away. (op 12/1)
Estrela Brage(USA) Official explanation: jockey said gelding refused to race after a fair start was effected

3883 - 3891a (Foreign Racing) - See Raceform Interactive

[3648]DEAUVILLE (R-H)
Saturday, July 11

OFFICIAL GOING: Turf course - good; all-weather - fast

3892a PRIX AMANDINE (LISTED RACE) (FILLIES) (STRAIGHT) 7f
1:15 (1:19) 3-Y-O **£26,699** (£10,680; £8,010; £5,340; £2,670)

RPR

1 **Emergency**[32] 3-8-12 SPasquier 5 101
(D Smaga, France)

2 nk **Soneva (USA)**[62] 1918 3-9-2 CSoumillon 6 104
(Y De Nicolay, France) 33/10[1]

3 snk **Rosey De Megeve**[16] 3330 3-8-12 OPeslier 1 100
(F Rohaut, France)

4 ¾ **Select (IRE)**[16] 3320 3-8-12 TThulliez 3 98
(P W Chapple-Hyam) *trckd ldrs on rails in 4th: looking for gap fr 1 1/2f out: 6th whn got through 110yds out: fin wl* 31/1[2]

5 1 **Ciel Rouge (FR)**[41] 2521 3-8-12 C-PLemaire 9 95
(J-C Rouget, France)

6 nse **Peace Camp (USA)**[85] 3-8-12 JVictoire 4 95
(A Fabre, France)

7 1 ½ **Chausson Dore (IRE)**[30] 3-8-12 TJarnet 7 91
(A De Royer-Dupre, France)

8 2 **Maggi Fong**[58] 2026 3-8-12 MGuyon 11 85
(H-A Pantall, France)

9 1 **Novita (FR)**[33] 2777 3-9-2 DBoeuf 10 87
(P Schiergen, Germany)

1m 24.2s (-4.10) 9 Ran SP% **26.4**
PARI-MUTUEL: WIN 10.70; PL 2.00, 1.40, 1.80; DF 11.90.
Owner K Abdulla **Bred** Juddmonte Farms Ltd **Trained** Lamorlaye, France

NOTEBOOK
Select(IRE), placed in a Listed contest on her previous start, did not get the clearest of runs and finished strongly. She could be up to winning a similar contest on fast ground.

3893 - (Foreign Racing) - See Raceform Interactive

[3878]CURRAGH (R-H)
Sunday, July 12

OFFICIAL GOING: Round course - soft; straight course - soft to heavy changing to heavy on both courses after race 3 (3.05)

3894a KILBOY ESTATE STKS (LISTED RACE) (FILLIES) 1m 1f
2:35 (2:36) 3-Y-O+ **£30,021** (£8,808; £4,196; £1,429)

RPR

1 **She's Our Mark**[25] 3012 5-9-10 106 DMGrant 8 104+
(Patrick J Flynn, Ire) *mid-div: mod 7th 1/2-way: rdn in mod 4th 3f out: clsr in 3rd 2f out: styd on wl to ld ins fnl f* 9/4[1]

2 2 **Latin Love (IRE)**[14] 3437 3-8-12 93 ow1 JMurtagh 2 97
(David Wachman, Ire) *led and sn clr: rdn clr 2 1/2f out: reduced advantage 2f out: hdd ins fnl f: no ex cl home* 8/1

3 1 ¼ **Timabiyra (IRE)**[28] 2960 3-8-11 96 FMBerry 4 93+
(John M Oxx, Ire) *in rr: rdn fr 3f out: kpt on wout threatening to go 3rd fnl f* 14/1

4 nk **Miss Keller (IRE)**[21] 3195 3-8-11 100 MJKinane 11 92
(John M Oxx, Ire) *trckd ldrs in mod 3rd: rdn and wnt mod 2nd under 3f out: no imp fr 1 1/2f out* 3/1[2]

5 2 **Always Be True (IRE)**[49] 2304 3-8-11 WMLordan 7 88
(David Wachman, Ire) *trckd ldrs: mod 6th 1/2-way: rdn and kpt on same pce fr 3f out* 14/1

6 10 **Lady Deauville (FR)**[27] 2974 4-9-12 HayleyTurner 6 73
(R Curtis) *trckd ldr in mod 2nd: rdn fr 2 1/2f out: wknd fr 2f out* 8/1

7 3 ½ **Luminous Eyes (IRE)**[11] 3516 3-9-2 105 (b) PJSmullen 1 65
(D K Weld, Ire) *towards rr: no imp fr 3f out* 4/1[3]

8 1 ¾ **Tactful (IRE)**[36] 2697 4-9-7 DPMcDonogh 10 57
(R M Beckett) *trckd ldrs: mod 4th 1/2-way: rdn and no imp fr 3f out* 14/1

2m 0.06s (5.16) **Going Correction** +0.775s/f (Yiel)
WFA 3 from 4yo+ 10lb 8 Ran SP% **118.0**
Speed ratings: **108,106,105,104,103 94,91,89**
CSF £21.98 TOTE £2.30: £1.20, £1.90, £3.80; DF 15.80.
Owner B & M Syndicate **Bred** M Barrett & Redmyre Bloodstock **Trained** Carrick-On-Suir, Co Waterford

NOTEBOOK
She's Our Mark was sent off a well-backed favourite and while she won, she did give her supporters a few anxious moments. She stayed on strongly from what looked an unpromising position and in the end ran on well close home to score for a third time at stakes level. She has been a great money-spinner for connections and has held her form well over the last couple of seasons. She is well served by testing ground and she should continue to prosper at this level. (op 5/2)
Latin Love(IRE) ran a brave race in defeat and, while she was given an easy lead, this represented an improved effort on the part of the three-year-old. She picked up some more valuable black type here and on this evidence, she should get her turn at this level.
Timabiyra(IRE) finished well to snatch third. (op 10/1)
Miss Keller(IRE) ran well but couldn't hold on for third. (op 7/2)
Lady Deauville(FR) was back on a soft surface and at the right level but was well beaten. She has yet to win a race earlier in the year than August. (op 6/1)
Luminous Eyes(IRE) was disappointing but one can put a line through this run as she is better than this form and she probably found the ground far too testing. (op 9/2)

3895a JEBEL ALI STABLES & RACECOURSE ANGLESEY STKS (GROUP 3) 6f 63y
3:05 (3:05) 2-Y-O **£42,346** (£12,424; £5,919; £2,016)

RPR

1 **Walk On Bye (IRE)**[15] 3410 2-8-12 WMLordan 1 106
(T Stack, Ire) *chsd ldrs on outer: cl 5th 1/2-way: rdn 1 1/2f out: led 1f out: styd on wl: comf* 7/4[1]

2 1 ¾ **King Ledley (USA)**[14] 3436 2-9-1 103 (b[1]) DPMcDonogh 6 104
(Kevin Prendergast, Ire) *chsd ldrs: cl 3rd 1/2-way: rdn fr 2f out: wnt 2nd ins fnl f: kpt on* 9/2[3]

3 ¾ **Beethoven (IRE)**[22] 3138 2-9-1 JMurtagh 4 102
(A P O'Brien, Ire) *chsd ldrs: cl 4th 1/2-way: rdn fr 2f out: kpt on same pce in 3rd fnl f* 4/1[2]

4 ¾ **En Un Clin D'Oeil (IRE)**[11] 3514 2-9-1 PJSmullen 3 100
(Ms Joanna Morgan, Ire) *led and disp: rdn fr 2f out: hdd 1f out: no ex* 9/1

5 3 ½ **Capulet Monteque (IRE)**[17] 3323 2-8-12 JamieSpencer 8 87
(T Stack, Ire) *in rr: sme prog fr under 2f out: mod 5th 1f out: no ex* 25/1

6 2 ½ **Air Chief Marshal (IRE)**[26] 2993 2-9-1 96 JAHeffernan 2 82
(A P O'Brien, Ire) *led and disp: rdn and hdd 2f out: sn no imp* 5/1

7 5 ½ **Eireannach (IRE)**[98] 1135 2-9-1 KJManning 5 67
(J S Bolger, Ire) *chsd ldrs: rdn and no imp fr 2f out* 8/1

8 3 **Diamondgeezer Luke (IRE)**[32] 2832 2-9-1 FMBerry 7 58
(F Costello, Ire) *in rr: no imp fr 1/2-way* 66/1

1m 20.82s (2.82) **Going Correction** +0.575s/f (Yiel) 8 Ran SP% **117.7**
Speed ratings: **104,101,100,99,95 91,84,80**
CSF £10.27 TOTE £2.80: £1.40, £1.80, £1.60; DF 12.90.
Owner M V Magnier **Bred** Tower Bloodstock **Trained** Golden, Co Tipperary

NOTEBOOK
Walk On Bye(IRE) looked a decent type in supplementing the course maiden win gained on her debut. The market got it right, with the Danehill Dancer filly attracting good support in a race in which the two Aidan O´Brien-trained colts were easy enough to back. Produced on the outside in a race run at a fair pace in the conditions, Walk On Bye quickened up well when asked for her effort a furlong out. Her major target is a Goffs-backed confined event, but races such as the Lowther and the Prix Morny could also be on her agenda. In the longer term she could turn out to be a 1000 Guineas prospect if she can build on this solidly professional performance. (op 9/4 tchd 6/4)
King Ledley(USA) won the first two-year-old race of the season and is proving a reliable sort. His run here provides a link to a couple of the more promising Irish-trained juvenile colts, since he was beaten only a little farther here than when third behind Alfred Nobel in the Railway Stakes. (op 5/1)
Beethoven(IRE) could not quicken after coming under pressure around 2f and probably needs further.
En Un Clin D'Oeil(IRE) probably ran to a similar level of form as when second in a weak Listed race at Fairyhouse. He is quite capable, though he may not be an easy horse to place at this stage. (op 10/1 tchd 12/1)
Capulet Monteque(IRE), a stablemate of the winner, picked up useful experience here and should be capable of a maiden success in due course. (op 33/1)
Air Chief Marshal(IRE) helped set the pace, but had been headed two out and failed to bounce back from his modest effort in the Coventry. (op 11/2)
Eireannach(IRE) was disappointing in view of the fact that he had won on softish ground at the venue in April.

3896a DARLEY IRISH OAKS (GROUP 1) (FILLIES) 1m 4f
3:40 (3:40) 3-Y-O
£272,330 (£92,718; £44,174; £14,563; £10,194; £5,339)

RPR

1 **Sariska**[37] 2672 3-9-0 JamieSpencer 3 123+
(M L W Bell) *mid-div: 7th 5f out: 4th travelling strly 3f out: led on bridle ins fnl f: nt extended* 1/1[1]

2 3 **Roses For The Lady (IRE)**[28] 2960 3-9-0 100 FMBerry 9 112
(John M Oxx, Ire) *led: rdn along 5f out: hdd ins fnl f: kpt on same pce wout troubling easy wnr* 25/1

3 4 ½ **Midday**[37] 2672 3-9-0 TPQueally 1 105
(H R A Cecil) *trckd ldrs: 3rd 5f out: rdn in 2nd 3f out: dropped to 3rd over 1f out: no ex* 9/2[3]

4 4 **Grace O'Malley (IRE)**[28] 2960 3-9-0 101 PJSmullen 6 98
(D K Weld, Ire) *trckd ldrs: 5th 5f out: rdn in 4th fr 2 1/2f out: kpt on one pce* 12/1

5 4 ½ **Oh Goodness Me**[37] 2672 3-9-0 106 KJManning 4 91
(J S Bolger, Ire) *trckd ldrs: rdn in 3rd 3f out: sn no ex* 10/1

6 3 ½ **Roman Empress (IRE)**[15] 3412 3-9-0 94 JMurtagh 2 86
(A P O'Brien, Ire) *mid-div: 6th 5f out: rdn and no imp fr 3f out* 16/1

7 15 **Rory Anna (IRE)**[28] 2960 3-9-0 79 RPCleary 11 62
(John J Walsh, Ire) *in rr: no imp fr 5f out* 150/1

8 *10* **Chirkova (USA)**[49] 2306 3-9-0 93 JAHeffernan 10 46
(A P O'Brien, Ire) *trckd ldr in 2nd: rdn fr 4f out: sn wknd* **50/1**
9 *25* **Belle Chose (IRE)**[9] 3602 3-9-0 66 DMGrant 8 6
(John Joseph Murphy, Ire) *a bhd* **66/1**
10 *22* **Beauty O' Gwaun (IRE)**[60] 1996 3-9-0 (b[1]) MJKinane 7 —
(John M Oxx, Ire) *trckd ldrs in 3rd: rdn and wknd fr 4f out* **4/1**[2]

2m 45.84s (8.34) **Going Correction** +1.075s/f (Soft) **10** Ran SP% **118.8**
Speed ratings: **115,113,110,107,104 102,92,85,68,54**
CSF £36.58 TOTE £2.20: £1.10, £6.90, £2.00; DF 51.80.
Owner Lady Bamford **Bred** Lady Bamford **Trained** Newmarket, Suffolk

FOCUS
A deeply impressive performance by Sariska, who was completing the Epsom/Irish Oaks double.

NOTEBOOK
Sariska became the third filly during the current decade to complete the Epsom/Irish Oaks double, and did so with astonishing ease under an ultra-confident ride. One rarely sees such overwhelming superiority at this level, and though much can be explained by the fact that she simply handled the ground much better than her main market rival, it would be unfair not to salute this as a deeply impressive performance from a filly having only the fifth run in her career. She heads now for the Yorkshire Oaks with outstanding credentials, with the Arc as the logical target thereafter. (op 11/10)
Roses For The Lady(IRE) made the running and kept on to finish a clear second-best. She had disappointed on her two starts since winning a decent early-season maiden at Leopardstown, and this was a revelation in the circumstances. The Park Hill Stakes could be next for her. (op 33/1)
Midday would not have been suited by the ground, but there is also a strong possibility that Sariska has simply improved more since Epsom, and that was clearly on Henry Cecil´s mind afterwards when expressing the view that he would not want to take on the winner again. (op 4/1)
Grace O'Malley(IRE), winner of a Group 3 at Cork last time, travelled well and stayed on back in fourth, but couldn't quicken in the ground. This was an improved effort and she remains capable of better. (op 14/1)
Oh Goodness Me, a remote seventh behind Sariska at Epsom, was just a little closer this time. However, it looks as if she does not stay 1m4f effectively, with the compensation that there is possibly a decent prize to be won with her over a shorter trip, judged on her third to Again in the Irish 1000 Guineas.
Roman Empress(IRE) has not progressed in the manner that Aidan O´Brien anticipated early in the season, and the others were hopelessly outclassed.

3898a LADBROKES ROCKINGHAM H'CAP (PREMIER HANDICAP) 5f
4:45 (4:45) 3-Y-0+
£52,514 (£16,689; £7,951; £2,708; £1,834; £961)

RPR
1 **Just For Mary**[16] 3368 5-8-4 80 oh7 RPCleary 3 84
(Daniel Mark Loughnane, Ire) *in rr: hdwy on far side 2f out: edgd sltly lft over 1f out: led ins fnl f: kpt on wl* **9/1**
2 *1* **Senor Benny (USA)**[28] 2959 10-9-5 95 (b) FMBerry 12 95
(M McDonagh, Ire) *chsd ldrs: rdn to dispute ld 1 1/2f out: hdd under 1f out: kpt on same pce* **14/1**
3 *nk* **Majestic Times (IRE)**[14] 3435 9-7-13 80 oh1 (b) DEMullins(5) 6 79
(Liam McAteer, Ire) *chsd ldrs: rdn 2f out: kpt on wout threatening in 3rd ins fnl f* **25/1**
4 *2* **Douze Points (IRE)**[17] 3325 3-8-7 88 (b) WMLordan 9 78
(Joseph G Murphy, Ire) *towards rr: hdwy on far side 2f out: sltly checked 1 1/2f out: kpt on wout threatening fnl f* **12/1**
5 *hd* **Santo Padre (IRE)**[16] 3368 5-8-8 84 DPMcDonogh 14 75
(David Marnane, Ire) *chsd ldrs: rdn to dispute ld 1 1/2f out: hdd 1f out: sn no ex* **12/1**
6 *½* **Brave Falcon (IRE)**[56] 2108 5-8-9 92 (p) JPO'Brien(7) 1 81
(Leo J Temple, Ire) *towards rr: kpt on wout threatening fr 2f out* **14/1**
7 *shd* **Fol Hollow (IRE)**[19] 3236 4-9-9 99 AdrianTNicholls 8 88
(D Nicholls) *broke wl and led: rdn and hdd 2f out: sn no ex* **9/2**[1]
8 *½* **Danetime Lily (IRE)**[3] 3784 5-7-11 80 oh1 (p) KTO'Neill(7) 15 67
(Ms Joanna Morgan, Ire) *towards rr: hdwy into 2nd and rdn 2f out: sn no ex* **8/1**[3]
9 *½* **Tornadodancer (IRE)**[14] 3435 6-8-6 87 (b) BACurtis(5) 10 72
(T G McCourt, Ire) *chsd ldrs: no ex fr 2f out* **10/1**
10 *1 ¾* **Croisultan (IRE)**[17] 3325 3-9-2 104 (b[1]) GFCarroll(7) 2 81
(Liam McAteer, Ire) *prom: rdn and no imp fr 2f out* **14/1**
11 *½* **Fly By Magic (IRE)**[16] 3368 5-8-1 80 oh5 SMGorey(3) 17 57
(Patrick Carey, Ire) *chsd ldrs: led 2f out: rdn and hdd 1 1/2f out: sn wknd* **20/1**
12 *1* **Mountain Coral (IRE)**[14] 3435 5-9-3 93 NGMcCullagh 4 67
(F Oakes, Ire) *mid-div: no imp fr 2f out* **13/2**[2]
13 *3* **Cihangir (IRE)**[16] 3368 4-8-8 84 PJSmullen 7 47
(D K Weld, Ire) *chsd ldrs: no imp fr 2f out* **8/1**[3]
14 *1 ¾* **Nanotech (IRE)**[14] 3435 5-9-2 99 CPHarrison(7) 18 55
(Jarlath P Fahey, Ire) *a towards rr* **16/1**
15 *8* **Impossible Dream (IRE)**[3] 3836 5-9-12 102 KJManning 16 30
(A Kinsella, Ire) *a bhd* **12/1**

63.36 secs (2.66) **Going Correction** +0.775s/f (Yiel)
WFA 3 from 4yo+ 5lb **15** Ran SP% **130.4**
Speed ratings: **109,107,106,103,103 102,102,101,100,98 97,95,90,88,75**
CSF £139.04 CT £3153.07 TOTE £9.40: £2.60, £4.60, £6.90; DF 128.20.
Owner Andrew Doyle **Bred** Cheveley Park Stud **Trained** Trim, Co Meath

NOTEBOOK
Fol Hollow(IRE), who came into this off the back of a win on fast ground, has won on easy going but this was more testing and he could not respond when taken on for the lead. (op 4/1)
Impossible Dream(IRE) Official explanation: jockey said horse never travelled on the ground

3899 - 3907a (Foreign Racing) - See Raceform Interactive

4368 MAISONS-LAFFITTE (R-H)
Sunday, July 12

OFFICIAL GOING: Good

3908a PRIX DE RIS-ORANGIS (GROUP 3) 6f (S)
3:30 (3:48) 3-Y-0+ **£38,835** (£15,534; £11,650; £7,767; £3,883)

RPR
1 **Tiza (SAF)**[80] 1576 7-9-4 (p) DBoeuf 3 115
(A De Royer-Dupre, France) *last to over 2f out: hdwy on stands' side but stl only 7th appr fnl f: r.o wl to ld cl home* **7/1**
2 *nk* **Delvita (FR)**[23] 3202 5-8-10 OPeslier 4 106
(J-V Toux, France) *pressed ldr: hrd rdn 2f out: responded gamely to ld narrowly 100yds out: hdd cl home* **14/1**
3 *nse* **Aiboa (IRE)**[75] 1596 3-8-5 CSoumillon 9 106
(L A Urbano-Grajales, France) *trckd ldrs in 5th: rdn over 1f out: squeezed through narrow gap to hold ev ch 100yds out: no ex cl home* **9/2**[2]
4 *1* **Mariol (FR)**[20] 3231 6-9-0 GBenoist 7 107
(Robert Collet, France) *hld up: swtchd outside and hdwy over 1f out: tk 4th cl home* **20/1**
5 *snk* **Strike The Deal (USA)**[22] 3140 4-9-0 (b) PhilipRobinson 11 106
(J Noseda) *led: rdn under 2f out: hdd 100yds out: one pce* **6/1**[3]
6 *1 ½* **Blue Cayenne (FR)**[33] 4-8-10 TJarnet 2 97
(Mlle S-V Tarrou, France) *disp 3rd on stands' side: rdn and one pce fr over 1f out* **20/1**
7 *nk* **Contest (IRE)**[23] 3202 5-9-0 (b) SPasquier 8 100
(C Theodorakis, Greece) *disp 3rd towards centre: hrd rdn to dispute 2nd over 1f out: one pce: btn whn sltly hmpd cl home* **14/1**
8 *hd* **Planet Five (USA)**[54] 3-8-8 C-PLemaire 6 99
(P Bary, France) *a midfield on outside* **7/2**[1]
9 *10* **As De Trebol (USA)**[43] 2513 3-8-8 IMendizabal 5 67
(G Arizkorreta Elosegui, Spain) *a in rr: brief effrt under 2f out: sn btn* **6/1**[3]
10 *1* **Mood Music**[42] 2523 5-9-4 (b) MGuyon 1 69
(Mario Hofer, Germany) *a in rr: rdn and btn over 2f out* **16/1**
11 **Only Green (IRE)**[20] 3231 3-8-5 DBonilla 10 61
(F Head, France) *cl up early: pushed along and lost pl bef 1/2-way* **9/1**

1m 11.2s (-2.20)
WFA 3 from 4yo+ 6lb **11** Ran SP% **120.2**
PARI-MUTUEL: WIN 10.90; PL 2.80, 3.60, 1.80; DF 44.30.
Owner J-C Seroul **Bred** Daytona Stud (pty) Ltd **Trained** Chantilly, France
■ Stewards' Enquiry : Philip Robinson 100euro fine: whip abuse

NOTEBOOK
Tiza(SAF) put up a very game performance to repeat his success in the race in 2007. He was given a perfect ride by his first-time jockey who waited patiently at the tail of the field until steadily progressing on the rail to hit the front near the line. He had not run since April and connections are thinking about going for the Prix Maurice de Gheest, although it is more likely he will go for the Prix de Meautry at the end of August, a race he won last year.
Delvita(FR), ridden quickly to the head of affairs, she took control with Strike The Deal for much of the race and was just headed in the final few yards. This was a good performance.
Aiboa(IRE), winner of her two previous starts this season, was settled behind the leaders and finished with a good run but could never quite catch the first two.
Mariol(FR), winner of this race last year, was slightly outpaced during the middle stages of the race but put up a finishing run on the outside.
Strike The Deal(USA), well up for most of the race on the outside, he had nothing extra to offer in the last 100m. This was a slightly disappointing effort, although he got no peace up front, and it has not been decided where he will go next.

3651 AYR (L-H)
Monday, July 13

OFFICIAL GOING: Good to firm (8.1) (meeting abandoned after race 3 (3.00) due to unsafe ground)
Wind: Fresh, half against Weather: Cloudy

3909 VICTOR CHANDLER H'CAP 5f
2:00 (2:04) (Class 6) (0-65,63) 3-Y-0+ **£2,388** (£705; £352) **Stalls** High

Form RPR
0164 1 **Twosheetstothewind**[10] 3565 5-9-9 62 (p) FrederikTylicki(3) 8 76
(M Dods) *trckd ldrs: rdn to ld 1f out: hld on wl fnl f* **9/2**[2]
041 2 *¾* **Ingleby Star (IRE)**[8] 3657 4-9-8 63 6ex (p) BMcHugh(5) 6 74
(N Wilson) *prom: effrt over 1f out: chsd wnr ins fnl f: r.o* **5/1**[3]
0604 3 *1 ½* **Angelofthenorth**[7] 3678 7-8-9 45 PaulHanagan 11 51
(C J Teague) *midfield: drvn 1/2-way: hdwy over 1f out: kpt on fnl f* **12/1**
0042 4 *1 ¾* **Dubai To Barnsley**[24] 3109 4-9-0 55 GaryBartley(5) 5 55
(D A Nolan) *towards rr: hdwy over 1f out: kpt on fnl f* **5/1**[3]
-223 5 *hd* **Wicked Wilma (IRE)**[3] 3828 5-9-10 60 PaulMulrennan 10 59
(A Berry) *led to 1f out: sn outpcd* **10/3**[1]
0050 6 *5* **Blazing Heights**[7] 3681 6-9-9 62 KellyHarrison(3) 1 43
(J S Goldie) *s.i.s: hld up on outside: rdn 2f out: nvr able to chal* **14/1**
060- 7 *1 ½* **Town And Gown**[303] 5911 4-9-1 51 DanielTudhope 2 27
(J S Goldie) *hld up: rdn 1/2-way: nvr on terms* **22/1**
0001 8 *nk* **Princess Charlmane (IRE)**[7] 3678 6-9-3 53 6ex (p) DNolan 9 28
(C J Teague) *w ldr: rdn 2f out: wknd appr fnl f: eased ins fnl f* **10/1**
0000 9 *2* **Miacarla**[10] 3570 6-8-2 45 (t) DeclanCannon(7) 4 12
(H A McWilliams) *s.i.s: towards rr: struggling 1/2-way: sn btn* **25/1**

59.31 secs (-0.79) **Going Correction** -0.275s/f (Firm) **9** Ran SP% **106.2**
Speed ratings (Par 101): **95,93,91,88,88 80,77,77,74**
CSF £23.36 CT £205.28 TOTE £5.40: £1.60, £2.10, £2.50; EX 23.70.
Owner P Taylor **Bred** Mrs R D Peacock **Trained** Denton, Co Durham

FOCUS
Despite a couple of sharp showers late in the morning, the ground remained Good to Firm, with a going stick reading of 8.1. The time advertised the fast ground. The stalls were set on the stands' rail for a competitive handicap, run at a strong pace, and the form looks straightforward, rated around the placed horses.
Princess Charlmane(IRE) Official explanation: jockey said saddle slipped

3910 VICTORCHANDLER.COM MEDIAN AUCTION MAIDEN STKS 6f
2:30 (2:32) (Class 5) 2-Y-0 **£2,914** (£867; £433; £216) **Stalls** High

Form RPR
5 1 **Lord Aeryn (IRE)**[18] 3310 2-9-3 0 PaulHanagan 8 69+
(R A Fahey) *trckd ldrs: drvn and outpcd 2f out: rallied to ld ins fnl f: kpt on wl* **7/4**[2]
2 *¾* **Always Dazzling** 2-8-12 0 AndrewElliott 4 62
(M Johnston) *trckd ldrs: ev ch and edgd lft over 1f out: led briefly ins fnl f: kpt on* **12/1**
3 *½* **So Bazaar (IRE)** 2-9-3 0 PJMcDonald 7 65
(G A Swinbank) *hld up in tch: rdn 2f out: no imp tl styd on wl fnl f: nrst fin* **10/1**
4 *1 ½* **Bahraj (USA)** 2-8-12 0 JoeFanning 2 56
(M Johnston) *led to ins fnl f: kpt on same pce* **6/1**[3]
5 *4 ½* **Ballycommon (USA)** 2-9-3 0 PaulMulrennan 3 47+
(K A Ryan) *dwlt: t.k.h: sn trcking ldrs: effrt over 1f out: wknd ins fnl f* **11/8**[1]
0 6 *10* **Jigajig**[14] 3446 2-9-3 0 JamieMoriarty 6 17
(N Wilson) *cl up tl hung lft and wknd 2f out: slipped and fell jst after line* **100/1**

7 7 **Daphne Du Maurier (IRE)** 2-8-12 0............................ TonyHamilton 5 —
(I Semple) *green in paddock: s.s: bhd and outpcd whn hung bdly lft over 2f out: nvr on terms* **33/1**

1m 12.6s (-1.00) **Going Correction** -0.275s/f (Firm) **7** Ran SP% **113.5**
Speed ratings (Par 94): **95,94,93,91,85 72,62**
CSF £22.30 TOTE £2.10: £1.40, £4.50; EX 21.60.

Owner Mrs H Steel **Bred** Woodhouse Syndicate **Trained** Musley Bank, N Yorks

FOCUS

Probably a modest, but eventful maiden run at a fairly decent pace, particularly in the middle stages of the race. The winner looks capable of better.

NOTEBOOK

Lord Aeryn(IRE), who holds an entry in the Two-Year-Old Trophy, appeared to benefit from his debut at Newcastle. He broke smartly enough but then seemed to be run off his feet a little bit when the pace intensified. Fortunately, the gap opened in plenty of time and he justified market support, though the penny took a while to drop. In the end he won a shade cosily and will get a bit further than this. (op 5-2)

Always Dazzling, whose half-sister was a 7f winner in France, does not hold any fancy entries, but made a promising debut. She wasn't quickly away but took a keen hold and probably could have done with a bit of cover. Though she showed her inexperience, hanging a little left, she stuck on gamely to the line and will come on for this. (tchd 11-1)

So Bazaar(IRE) also made an eyecatching debut. He ran green and looked a little headstrong, but followed the winner through to some effect. Though he was passing beaten horses at the time, he looked as though he would come on a great deal for the experience. (op 11-1 tchd 9-1)

Bahraj(USA), who also has no fancy entries but an interesting pedigree (unraced dam was a sister to 1000 Guineas winner Shadayid and a half-sister to Fath) showed plenty of ability on her debut. She showed up well for a long way before being eased inside the final furlong. She was blowing hard afterwards and will be better for it. (op 4-1)

Ballycommon(USA), who holds a Gimcrack entry, was well backed but ran very green. Fitted with a noseband, as his trainer often does with his horses, he still carried his head high. (op 6-4 tchd 13-8 tchd 7-4 in a place)

Jigajig seemed to improve a little after a disappointing debut at Musselburgh, but still looked extremely green and tried to jump the line, slipping in the process and unshipping his rider. He is best avoided until he learns a bit more. Official explanation: jockey said colt hung left-handed throughout (op 66-1)

Daphne Du Maurier(IRE) was all over the shop on her debut and darted left, right across the track approaching 2f out. (op 25-1)

3911 UP TO £125 FREET BET AT VICTORCHANDLER.COM H'CAP 1m 2f

3:00 (3:00) (Class 5) (0-70,69) 3-Y-O+ **£2,914** (£867; £433; £216) **Stalls** Low

Form RPR

2656 1 **Whaston (IRE)**[13] 3490 4-8-10 **51**............................(v) GrahamGibbons 10 58
(J D Bethell) *mde all: rdn clr over 2f out: styd on wl fnl f* **12/1**

3430 2 1 1/4 **Willyn (IRE)**[8] 3653 4-8-7 **53** ow1............................ GaryBartley(5) 1 57
(J S Goldie) *chsd ldrs: effrt over 2f out: kpt on fnl f: nt rch wnr* **10/1**

0-24 3 6 **Tamasou (IRE)**[24] 3104 4-9-7 **67**............................ MarkCoumbe(5) 5 59
(Garry Moss) *t.k.h: cl up: rdn over 2f out: wknd fnl f* **17/2**[3]

6665 4 4 1/2 **Papa's Princess**[14] 3447 5-8-9 **53**............................ KellyHarrison(3) 8 36
(J S Goldie) *midfield: avoided trble over 3f out: sn rdn and outpcd* **14/1**

6-24 5 17 **Darfour**[24] 3094 5-9-4 **59**............................ DanielTudhope 2 8
(J S Goldie) *in tch: rdn whn slipped bdly and rdr lost irons over 3f out: nt rcvr* **10/1**

403/ S **Balwearie (IRE)**[821] 1042 8-8-8 **52**............................ FrederikTylicki(3) 13 —
(Miss L A Perratt) *chsd ldrs: 4th and rdn whn slipped and fell over 3f out* **20/1**

0004 S **Neon Blue**[10] 3557 8-8-5 **51**............................(p) AmyRyan(5) 3 —
(R M Whitaker) *missed break: bhd: slipped up over 3f out* **20/1**

002 B **Hawkit (USA)**[24] 3098 8-9-1 **56**............................ PaulMulrennan 6 —
(P Monteith) *hld up: b.d over 3f out* **12/1**

6652 B **Talk Of Saafend (IRE)**[13] 3481 4-9-9 **64**............................ TonyHamilton 11 —
(P Monteith) *hld up in midfield: b.d over 3f out* **6/1**[2]

2030 B **All In The Red (IRE)**[19] 3266 4-10-0 **69**............................(p) JoeFanning 12 —
(A Crook) *hld up: b.d over 3f out* **16/1**

0-02 B **Whipma Whopma Gate (IRE)**[7] 3689 4-8-10 **51** oh2 ow1..... DNolan 7 —
(D Carroll) *hld up: b.d over 3f out* **6/1**[2]

344 B **Northside Prince (IRE)**[38] 2667 3-8-13 **65**............................ PJMcDonald 9 —
(G A Swinbank) *in tch whn b.d over 3f out* **11/4**[1]

2m 8.27s (-3.73) **Going Correction** -0.275s/f (Firm)
WFA 3 from 4yo+ 11lb **12** Ran SP% **121.4**
Speed ratings (Par 103): **103,102,97,93,80 —,—,—,—,— —,—**
CSF £129.71 CT £1081.08 TOTE £18.60: £4.90, £3.90, £3.10; EX 110.90 Trifecta £180.10 Part won. Pool: £243.50 - 0.50 winning units. Place 6: 26.78 Place 5: £11.99..

Owner Clarendon Thoroughbred Racing **Bred** Herbertstown Stud Ltd **Trained** Middleham Moor, N Yorks

FOCUS

An inconclusive handicap as far as form analysis goes, for there was carnage entering the home turn on the round course as two horses slipped independently of each other on the slick surface - not helped by sharp showers on fast ground prior to racing - and brought down all but five runners. The field was well-bunched at the time and the first two offer the best guide to the level.

3912 NEW WEBSITE AT VICTORCHANDLER.COM H'CAP 6f

() (Class 5) (0-70,) 3-Y-O+ £

3913 BEST ODDS GUARANTEED VICTOR CHANDLER FILLIES' H'CAP 6f

() (Class 4) (0-85,) 3-Y-O+ £

3914 VICTORCHANDLER.COM H'CAP 1m

() (Class 4) (0-85,) 3-Y-O £

3915 JOB MAN H'CAP 7f 50y

() (Class 6) (0-65,) 3-Y-O+ £

3916 CALL VICTOR CHANDLER 08000 78 78 78 APPRENTICE H'CAP 1m 2f

() (Class 6) (0-65,) 3-Y-O £

3691 WINDSOR (R-H)

Monday, July 13

OFFICIAL GOING: Good (good to firm in places; 7.8)

Rail realignment increased distances of races of a mile and over by 22yards.

Wind: Light, behind Weather: Sunny, warm

3917 SPORTINGBET.COM APPRENTICE H'CAP 5f 10y

6:30 (6:31) (Class 5) (0-75,74) 3-Y-O+ **£2,729** (£806; £403) **Stalls** High

Form RPR

1025 1 **Colorus (IRE)**[69] 1776 6-9-0 **65**............................(p) JosephineBruning(5) 5 73
(W J H Ratcliffe) *trckd ldng pair: styd in centre fr 1/2-way: clsd to ld over 1f out: hrd pressed after: urged along and edgd ahd nr fin* **9/1**

5221 2 hd **Matterofact (IRE)**[16] 3386 6-9-3 **68**............................ JakePayne(5) 2 75
(M S Saunders) *trckd ldng trio: styd centre fr 1/2-way: prog to join wnr over 1f out: upsides after: nt qckn nr fin* **5/1**[2]

4125 3 1 1/4 **Memphis Man**[4] 3787 6-10-0 **74**............................ SimonPearce 8 77
(P D Evans) *taken down early: outpcd in 10th and sn wl off the pce: styd against nr side rail fr 1/2-way: hrd rdn and r.o fr over 1f out: tk 3rd last strides* **5/1**[2]

3036 4 nk **Gwilym (GER)**[16] 3407 6-9-4 **64**............................ JPHamblett 7 65
(D Haydn Jones) *off the pce in midfield: styd centre fr 1/2-way: prog u.p over 1f out: chsd ldng pair fnl f: one pce* **9/1**

0000 5 1 1/4 **Blessed Place**[6] 3720 9-8-11 **57**............................(p) BillyCray 3 54
(D J S Ffrench Davis) *led: hdd and no ex over 1f out* **16/1**

5435 6 3/4 **Fromsong (IRE)**[15] 3422 11-9-8 **68**............................ SophieDoyle 9 62
(D K Ivory) *taken down early: off the pce in midfield: rdn 1/2-way: kpt on fnl f: nvr on terms* **9/2**[1]

0412 7 hd **Dancing Wave**[15] 3428 3-8-8 **59**............................ AndrewHeffernan 11 51
(M C Chapman) *drvn to join ldr: u.p thrght: upsides over 1f out: sn wknd* **5/1**[2]

0-00 8 1 **Danzadil (IRE)**[19] 3272 3-8-1 **55**............................ CharlesEddery(3) 4 43
(R A Teal) *dwlt: outpcd in 9th and wl off the pce: drvn and kpt on fr over 1f out: n.d* **28/1**

0513 9 2 1/2 **Bertie Southstreet**[14] 3459 6-9-5 **65**............................(p) PNolan 1 46
(J R Boyle) *s.s: off the pce in midfield: taken to far side of crse wl over 1f out: nvr on terms* **7/1**[3]

1006 10 3 3/4 **Bold Rose**[35] 2776 3-8-11 **62**............................(p) LeeNewnes 6 27
(M D I Usher) *dwlt: bdly outpcd and sn t.o: kpt on fnl f* **14/1**

00-0 11 34 **Calabaza**[83] 1421 7-8-4 **55** oh3............................(p) KierenFox(5) 10 —
(M J Attwater) *nt on terms in midfield: wknd wl over 1f out: eased: t.o: b.b.v* **33/1**

59.62 secs (-0.68) **Going Correction** -0.05s/f (Good)
WFA 3 from 6yo+ 5lb **11** Ran SP% **119.6**
Speed ratings (Par 103): **103,102,100,100,98 97,96,95,91,85 30**
toteswinger: 1&2 £42.50, 1&3 £42.50, 2&3 £2.10. CSF £54.56 CT £260.09 TOTE £12.50: £3.60, £2.10, £2.20; EX 81.00.

Owner J Sheard & W J S Ratcliffe **Bred** M Ervine **Trained** Newmarket, Suffolk

FOCUS

A modest apprentice handicap and straightforward form. The field ended up racing over most of the track with those racing down the centre coming out on top.

Calabaza Official explanation: trainer said gelding bled from the nose

3918 E B F SPORTINGBET.COM MAIDEN STKS 5f 10y

7:00 (7:05) (Class 4) 2-Y-O **£4,695** (£1,397; £698; £348) **Stalls** High

Form RPR

1 **Tropical Treat** 2-8-12 0............................ SebSanders 4 80+
(R M Beckett) *trckd ldrs: prog 2f out: rdn to ld over 1f out: r.o wl* **4/1**[2]

2 1 1/2 **Bush Tucker (IRE)** 2-9-3 0............................ JimCrowley 6 80+
(P Winkworth) *green in preliminaries: off the pce in 7th: prog over 1f out: reminder ent fnl f: styd on to take 2nd last 100yds: gng on wl fin* **9/1**

63 3 2 1/4 **Mister Hughie (IRE)**[9] 3606 2-9-3 0............................ TonyCulhane 11 71
(M R Channon) *reluctant to enter stalls: mde most: styd against nr side rail fr 1/2-way: hdd over 1f out: edgd lft and outpcd* **7/2**[1]

33 4 1 3/4 **Look Whos Next**[25] 3072 2-9-3 0............................ RichardMullen 8 64
(E S McMahon) *t.k.h: pressed ldrs: disp 2nd over 1f out: sn fdd* **13/2**[3]

0040 5 1 3/4 **Baby Judge (IRE)**[9] 3606 2-8-10 0............................ AndrewHeffernan(7) 7 58
(M C Chapman) *chsd ldrs: rdn 2f out: grad fdd* **200/1**

5 6 1 **Softly Spoken**[18] 3306 2-8-12 0............................ ShaneKelly 1 49
(A W Carroll) *trckd ldrs: pushed along to dispute 2nd whn jockey dropped whip over 1f out: wknd* **100/1**

7 2 **Pose (IRE)** 2-8-12 0............................ RichardHughes 10 42
(R Hannon) *w ldr to 1/2-way: wknd and nt pushed over 1f out* **15/2**

3033 8 shd **Mrs Boss**[21] 3210 2-8-11 0 ow2............................(v[1]) JamesMillman(3) 2 44
(B R Millman) *rel to r: early reminders and wl bhd in last pair: sme prog 1/2-way: nvr a threat* **13/2**[3]

9 8 **Cockney Colonel (USA)** 2-9-0 0............................ AlanCreighton(3) 5 18
(E J Creighton) *reluctant to enter stalls: sn u.p: a bhd* **25/1**

10 shd **Coolree Star (IRE)** 2-9-3 0............................ MartinDwyer 3 18
(W R Muir) *s.s: a wl bhd in last pair* **28/1**

59.83 secs (-0.47) **Going Correction** -0.05s/f (Good) **10** Ran SP% **99.4**
Speed ratings (Par 96): **101,98,95,92,89 87,84,84,71,71**
toteswinger: 1&2 £13.10, 1&3 £9.60, 2&3 £18.80. CSF £26.48 TOTE £5.60: £2.00, £2.60, £1.70; EX 48.10.

Owner J C Smith **Bred** R J Cornelius **Trained** Whitsbury, Hants

FOCUS

Time might show that there was little strength in depth here. The third and fifth set the level although the first two can do better.

NOTEBOOK

Tropical Treat overcame immaturity to win her first race with some authority. Her dam was quick, won on her debut, then graduated to Pattern grade and the entry that had been made for the Lowther gave an indication that she had shown connections some ability. She gave the impression she might get a little further. Her trainer revealed that the winner would have been out earlier but for a slight injury but has always shown plenty of pace. (tchd 6-1)

Bush Tucker(IRE) was very immature in the preliminaries and took a long time to get going but nothing came home better apart from the winner. This will have taught him a lot. (op 16-1 tchd 8-1)

Mister Hughie(IRE) was truculent before stalls entry - he might have been set off by the antics of withdrawn Wellington Fair - and made the most of his experience but was beaten by two newcomers with more potential. He looks the type for a nursery. (op 9-2)

Look Whos Next has now run the same style of race in each of his three appearances and didn't get home again. He could be another candidate for a nursery. (op 8-1 tchd 6-1)

Softly Spoken showed more this time than on debut. (op 80-1 tchd 66-1)

Pose(IRE) showed pace on her debut then got tired. Her stable's runners always improve and she might be alright over another furlong. (op 6-1 tchd 8-1)

Mrs Boss didn't appear to stay 6f but doesn't seem to have the pace for a sharp 5f. Official explanation: jockey said filly missed the break and was never travelling (op 6-1)
Cockney Colonel(USA) was another who was a handful at the stalls having been taken to post early. (op 66-1)

3919 SPORTINGBET.COM (S) STKS — 1m 3f 135y
7:30 (7:32) (Class 6) 3-4-Y-O — **£2,047** (£604; £302) **Stalls** Centre

Form — RPR

-002 **1** **Diktalina**[23] [3157] 3-8-4 53 ... MartinDwyer 16 — 56
(W R Muir) *led after 3f: kicked at least 3 l clr over 3f out: drvn and hung across trck to far side fnl 2f: unchal* **11/2**[1]

4400 **2** *3 ¾* **Dhania (IRE)**[49] [2320] 3-8-9 67 ... (b[1]) LPKeniry 5 — 55
(R A Teal) *hld up in midfield: prog over 3f out: drvn to chse wnr 1f out: nt look keen and no imp* **8/1**[3]

0-00 **3** *4* **Pagan Flight (IRE)**[31] [2881] 3-8-9 56 ... JimCrowley 1 — 48
(Mrs A J Perrett) *s.i.s: hld up in midfield: prog 5f out and sn prom: chsd wnr over 2f out to 1f out: wknd* **14/1**

6400 **4** *1 ¼* **Paymaster In Chief**[7] [3693] 3-8-6 50 ... (v) DavidProbert[(3)] 9 — 46
(M D I Usher) *hld up in midfield: rdn over 3f out: plugged on in centre fnl 2f: n.d* **8/1**[3]

4600 **5** *2* **Musashi (IRE)**[23] [3158] 4-9-8 53 ... (p) IanMongan 2 — 42
(Mrs L J Mongan) *dwlt: rcvrd and sn prom: chsd wnr 1/2-way to over 2f out: fdd* **7/1**[2]

0000 **6** *1* **Primera Rossa**[19] [3257] 3-8-4 40 ... CatherineGannon 15 — 35
(J S Moore) *dwlt: hld up in last trio: rdn over 4f out: sme prog in centre fr over 2f out: nvr rchd ldrs* **50/1**

45-0 **7** *shd* **Sponge**[23] [3158] 4-9-8 57 ... RichardKingscote 11 — 40
(P R Chamings) *hld up in last trio: shkn up 4f out: sme prog into midfield 2f out: rdn and kpt on: nvr nr ldrs* **20/1**

0-03 **8** *1 ½* **April's Daughter**[21] [3217] 4-9-0 54 ... JamesMillman[(3)] 13 — 33
(B R Millman) *cl up: rdn 4f out: outpcd over 3f out: no prog fnl 2f* **11/2**[1]

0400 **9** *nk* **Bestowed**[13] [2859] 4-9-1 52 ... AndrewHeffernan[(7)] 4 — 37
(M C Chapman) *hld up: last after 4f: stl there 4f out: hrd rdn and sme prog over 2f out: nvr on terms w ldrs* **66/1**

-060 **10** *9* **Chalk Hill Blue**[21] [3209] 3-7-13 52 ... SophieDoyle[(5)] 3 — 17
(Eve Johnson Houghton) *chsd ldrs: racd wdst of all st: outpcd over 3f out: wknd over 1f out* **16/1**

460 **11** *2 ¼* **Classical Rhythm (IRE)**[41] [2580] 4-9-8 57 ... SebSanders 12 — 18
(J R Boyle) *t.k.h: cl up tl wknd wl over 3f out: sn bhd* **7/1**[2]

0300 **12** *1 ¼* **It's My Day (IRE)**[20] [3244] 4-9-8 58 ... MickyFenton 10 — 16
(C Gordon) *hld up in rr: u.p and no prog over 3f out: bhd after* **20/1**

50-0 **13** *2 ½* **Echo Forest**[21] [3215] 3-8-9 44 ... SteveDrowne 8 — 12
(J R Best) *sn restrained into midfield: rdn 4f out: wknd 3f out: bhd after* **33/1**

0565 **14** *16* **Bathwick Pursuit**[13] [3473] 3-8-10 50 ow1 ... RichardHughes 14 — —
(P D Evans) *t.k.h: led 3f: trckd wnr to 1/2-way: wknd rapidly over 4f out: t.o* **7/1**[2]

0-00 **15** *39* **Kaijai (IRE)**[12] [3508] 3-8-4 42 ... (t) SaleemGolam 6 — —
(Mrs L C Jewell) *a in rr: wknd 5f out: wl t.o* **66/1**

2m 30.09s (0.59) **Going Correction** -0.05s/f (Good)
WFA 3 from 4yo 13lb — **15** Ran SP% **120.5**
Speed ratings (Par 101): **96,93,90,90,88 88,87,86,86,80 79,78,76,66,40**
toteswinger: 1&2 £4.20, 1&3 £5.70, 2&3 £29.70. CSF £45.27 TOTE £6.50: £1.80, £3.50, £6.00; EX 28.80.The winner was bought in for 5,000gns.
Owner Foursome Thoroughbreds **Bred** Foursome Thoroughbreds **Trained** Lambourn, Berks

FOCUS
A moderate seller and not a race to be positive about.
It's My Day(IRE) Official explanation: jockey said gelding hung badly left
Bathwick Pursuit Official explanation: jockey said colt lost its action

3920 SPORTINGBET.COM MAIDEN STKS — 6f
8:00 (8:07) (Class 5) 2-Y-O — **£2,729** (£806; £403) **Stalls** High

Form — RPR

2 **1** **Buzzword**[16] [3403] 2-9-3 0 ... LDettori 15 — 89+
(Saeed Bin Suroor) *disp ld tl led 2f out: hung lft fr over 1f out but sn clr: ended against far rail: eased nr fin* **8/11**[1]

5 **2** *3* **Joe Packet**[49] [2324] 2-9-3 0 ... SaleemGolam 13 — 76+
(J G Portman) *trckd ldrs: pushed along 2f out: prog over 1f out: kpt on wl to take 2nd ins fnl f: no ch w wnr* **50/1**

2 **3** *½* **Red Badge (IRE)**[12] [3500] 2-9-3 0 ... RichardHughes 12 — 74
(R Hannon) *w wnr to 2f out: sn outpcd: kpt on but lost 2nd ins fnl f* **7/2**[2]

4 *2* **Yaa Wayl (IRE)** 2-9-3 0 ... PhilipRobinson 4 — 68
(M A Jarvis) *w wnr to 2f out: grad fdd jst over 1f out* **20/1**

0 **5** *2 ½* **Rockabilly Rebel**[21] [3218] 2-9-3 0 ... MichaelHills 10 — 61
(B W Hills) *chsd ldrs: rdn 2f out: outpcd over 1f out: fdd ins fnl f* **16/1**

6 **6** *2* **Breeze Of The Air**[38] [2649] 2-9-3 0 ... SamHitchcott 8 — 55
(M R Channon) *chsd ldrs: rdn over 2f out: outpcd and hanging over 1f out: fdd* **25/1**

63 **7** *¾* **Imperial Warrior**[34] [2792] 2-9-3 0 ... SteveDrowne 14 — 52
(H Morrison) *dwlt: sn rchd midfield: reminder 2f out: sn outpcd: kpt on steadily* **8/1**[3]

8 *1* **Flying Destination** 2-9-3 0 ... PaulDoe 6 — 49+
(W J Knight) *in tch on outer: lost pl 2f out: pushed along and grad wknd* **66/1**

0 **9** *4* **Woodface**[16] [3402] 2-9-3 0 ... JimmyFortune 11 — 37
(B J Meehan) *dwlt: nvr bttr than midfield: rdn and btn 2f out* **100/1**

10 *4* **Edgewater (IRE)** 2-9-3 0 ... MartinDwyer 5 — 25
(B J Meehan) *dwlt: a towards rr: pushed along and struggling 1/2-way: wknd* **25/1**

11 *nk* **South African Gold (USA)** 2-9-3 0 ... MickyFenton 7 — 24
(J M P Eustace) *reluctant to enter stalls: dwlt: a wl in rr: lft bhd fr over 2f out* **25/1**

12 *½* **R Woody** 2-9-3 0 ... TravisBlock 3 — 23
(Mrs L C Jewell) *s.s: a in rr and sn pushed along* **100/1**

13 *2* **Just A Monkey** 2-9-3 0 ... TonyCulhane 2 — 17
(R Curtis) *s.s: detached in last and sn rdn: a bhd* **50/1**

14 *7* **Flash For Freedom (USA)** 2-9-3 0 ... JimCrowley 16 — —
(J R Best) *dwlt: sn in tch against nr side rail: wknd rapidly 2f out: t.o* **50/1**

1m 12.44s (-0.56) **Going Correction** -0.05s/f (Good) — **14** Ran SP% **122.8**
Speed ratings (Par 94): **101,97,96,93,90 87,86,85,80,74 74,73,70,61**
toteswinger: 1&2 £10.60, 1&3 £1.10, 2&3 £65.30. CSF £72.17 TOTE £1.80: £1.10, £9.50, £1.50; EX 69.20.
Owner Godolphin **Bred** Darley **Trained** Newmarket, Suffolk

FOCUS
An uncompetitive maiden though the time was good.

NOTEBOOK
Buzzword confirmed the promise shown here on his debut late last month but again showed a worrying tendency to hang to his left. He had the race well won when he decided to deviate and only went straight once he got to the far rail. He gives the impression he will get a bit further. (op 5-6 tchd 10-11 and 11-10 in a place and 1-1 in places)
Joe Packet is not fashionably bred and was a £500 buyback but has a good attitude. He was tapped for pace at halfway but battled back well to get second. His sire wanted a mile to win at two and this one is worth a try over another furlong. (tchd 40-1)
Red Badge(IRE) ran a sound second race and was more on the pace this time than on his debut when second. (op 10-3 tchd 4-1)
Yaa Wayl(IRE) ran a most encouraging debut but looked very green and only wanted to lug left from over two out. He's from a good family and should be alright when he straightens out. (op 16-1)
Rockabilly Rebel ran the same style of race as on his debut, doing a lot from the front, he might be better just off the pace. (op 14-1 tchd 12-1 and 20-1)
Imperial Warrior took a long time to get motivated as he did on his previous outing and needs to sharpen up. (op 10-1)
Flying Destination showed enough to make a better showing next time. (op 80-1)

3921 SPORTINGBET.COM FILLIES' H'CAP — 1m 67y
8:30 (8:31) (Class 4) (0-80,83) 3-Y-O+ — **£4,857** (£1,445; £722; £360) **Stalls** High

Form — RPR

3050 **1** **Romany Princess (IRE)**[18] [3301] 4-10-0 77 ... RichardHughes 4 — 85+
(R Hannon) *hld up in last pair: ready prog fr 2f out: rdn to ld last 100yds: sn in command: decisively* **6/1**[3]

0120 **2** *1 ¼* **Tinshu (IRE)**[34] [2796] 3-9-4 76 ... MartinDwyer 5 — 79
(D Haydn Jones) *hld up towards rr: prog over 2f out: rdn to ld jst over 1f out: hdd and outpcd last 100yds* **9/1**

3104 **3** *1* **Spring Adventure**[16] [3400] 3-9-5 77 ... (v[1]) JimmyFortune 10 — 78
(E A L Dunlop) *led to over 4f out: led again over 3f out and styd against nr side rail: hdd and one pce jst over 1f out* **10/1**

-402 **4** *3* **Penzena**[23] [3165] 3-8-9 67 ... JimCrowley 11 — 61
(W J Knight) *chsd ldrs: rdn over 2f out: disp 2nd over 1f out: sn fdd* **6/1**[3]

32-5 **5** *½* **Lyceana**[23] [3165] 4-9-12 75 ... PhilipRobinson 1 — 68
(M A Jarvis) *racd wd: wl in tch: rdn over 2f out: cl enough over 1f out: fdd* **10/1**

06-6 **6** *½* **Chateauneuf (IRE)**[31] [2885] 3-8-1 62 ... DavidProbert[(3)] 9 — 54
(B W Hills) *sn chsd ldrs: rdn over 2f out: nt qckn over 1f out: fdd* **16/1**

2-15 **7** *10* **Respite**[58] [2072] 3-9-0 72 ... MichaelHills 7 — 41
(W J Haggas) *dwlt: last and nvr gng wl: no real prog 2f out: eased fnl f* **9/4**[1]

4-31 **8** *4* **Diapason (IRE)**[9] [3630] 3-9-0 72 ... RichardKingscote 2 — 31
(Tom Dascombe) *racd wd: w ldr: led over 4f out to over 3f out: wknd rapidly 2f out: eased fnl f* **10/3**[2]

1m 43.88s (-0.82) **Going Correction** -0.05s/f (Good)
WFA 3 from 4yo+ 9lb — **8** Ran SP% **116.5**
Speed ratings (Par 102): **102,100,99,96,96 95,85,81**
toteswinger: 1&2 £22.00, 1&3 £23.00, 2&3 £16.70. CSF £58.98 CT £538.61 TOTE £6.20: £1.80, £2.90, £3.10; EX 52.30.
Owner Con Harrington **Bred** St Simon Foundation **Trained** East Everleigh, Wilts

FOCUS
No early pace which saw several of these doing too much too soon. The form looks sound rated around the placed horses.
Respite Official explanation: jockey said filly was never travelling
Diapason(IRE) Official explanation: jockey said filly ran too free and was not suited by the track

3922 SPORTINGBET.COM H'CAP — 1m 3f 135y
9:00 (9:00) (Class 4) (0-85,83) 3-Y-O — **£5,180** (£1,541; £770; £384) **Stalls** Centre

Form — RPR

-144 **1** **History Lesson**[19] [3280] 3-9-7 83 ... RichardHughes 1 — 88
(R Hannon) *mde virtually all: set stdy pce tl kicked on over 2f out: sn jnd: drvn and gained upper hand fnl f* **3/1**[2]

0161 **2** *¾* **Hollow Green (IRE)**[14] [3462] 3-8-5 67 ... CatherineGannon 4 — 71
(P D Evans) *hld up in last: pushed along over 3f out: wnt 2nd over 2f out: sn jnd wnr: drvn and upsides over 1f out: nt qckn ins fnl f* **7/1**[3]

1 **3** *1 ¼* **Plymouth Rock (IRE)**[28] [2981] 3-9-6 82 ... ShaneKelly 3 — 84
(J Noseda) *sn trckd wnr: stmbld after 1f: nt qckn and dropped to 3rd over 2f out: hrd rdn over 1f out: kpt on but nvr able to chal* **4/7**[1]

2200 **4** *26* **Divinatore**[31] [2892] 3-8-3 65 ... (p) MartinDwyer 5 — 23
(D Haydn Jones) *cl up: rdn and wknd 4f out: sn bhd: t.o* **14/1**

2m 30.66s (1.16) **Going Correction** -0.05s/f (Good) — **4** Ran SP% **107.8**
Speed ratings (Par 102): **94,93,92,75**
toteswinger: 1&2 £5.70 CSF £19.29 TOTE £4.50; EX 15.00 Place 6: £255.75 Place 5: £109.11.
Owner The Queen **Bred** The Queen **Trained** East Everleigh, Wilts

FOCUS
Only four runners, but a tactical race and the form is a bit muddling.
T/Jkpt: Not won. T/Plt: £380.80 to a £1 stake. Pool: £86,746.92. 166.29 winning tickets. T/Qpdt: £143.30 to a £1 stake. Pool: £7,206.78. 37.20 winning tickets. JN

[3715] WOLVERHAMPTON (A.W) (L-H)
Monday, July 13

OFFICIAL GOING: Standard changing to standard to fast after race 1 (6.20)
Wind: Light half behind Weather: Light showers

3923 BET AFTER THE OFF AT LADBROKES.COM CLASSIFIED CLAIMING STKS — 1m 4f 50y(P)
6:20 (6:20) (Class 6) 3-Y-O+ — **£2,729** (£806; £403) **Stalls** Low

Form — RPR

0046 **1** **Resplendent Ace (IRE)**[30] [2923] 5-9-9 59 ... JimmyQuinn 8 — 66
(P Howling) *hld up towards rr: hdwy over 3f out: rdn to ld jst ins fnl f: drvn out* **9/2**[1]

0200 **2** *½* **Deuce**[14] [3454] 3-8-9 59 ... (b) RobertWinston 6 — 64
(Eve Johnson Houghton) *hld up in mid-div: nt clr run over 2f out: hdwy on ins wl over 1f out: sn rdn: wnt 2nd ins fnl f: styd on* **5/1**[2]

0265 **3** *3 ¾* **New England**[16] [3374] 7-9-7 59 ... GeorgeBaker 7 — 57
(W M Brisbourne) *hld up in mid-div: hdwy over 4f out: wnt 2nd 3f out: rdn over 1f out: one pce ins fnl f* **5/1**[2]

0360 **4** *¾* **Annambo**[10] [3563] 9-9-6 56 ... (p) J-PGuillambert 9 — 55
(Andrew Reid) *a.p: led over 3f out: rdn jst over 2f out: hdd jst ins fnl f: wknd towards fin* **22/1**

203 **5** *¾* **Lytham (IRE)**[5] [3740] 8-9-7 60 ... HayleyTurner 1 — 55
(A W Carroll) *hld up towards rr: pushed along and hdwy over 2f out: rdn wl over 1f out: one pce* **6/1**[3]

3546 **6** *1 ½* **Masterofceremonies**[13] 3481 6-9-6 60...................... RoystonFfrench 2 51
(James Moffatt) *dwlt: hld up in rr: nt clr run and swtchd rt over 3f out: hdwy on wd outside over 2f out: rdn and hung lft over 1f out: no further prog* **9/1**

-01 **7** *5* **Jeronimo Joe**[10] 3588 3-8-12 60...................... TGMcLaughlin 4 48
(A B Haynes) *hld up in mid-div: rdn and lost pl 4f out: n.d after* **14/1**

5115 **8** *6* **World Of Choice (USA)**[41] 2580 4-9-9 59..................(b) DaleGibson 10 37
(M W Easterby) *hld up in rr: pushed along and hdwy 3f out: nt clr run and lost pl over 2f out: n.d after* **11/1**

0000 **9** *1 ½* **Mister Frosty (IRE)**[11] 3551 3-8-8 55...................... AdrianMcCarthy 12 32
(G Prodromou) *hld up in mid-div: hdwy on outside over 4f out: pushed along and wknd 2f out* **40/1**

-60 **10** *8* **Black Nun**[14] 3466 3-8-5 60......................................(b[1]) KirstyMilczarek 5 16
(S Wynne) *chsd ldr: led over 5f out tl over 3f out: wkng whn n.m.r on ins wl over 2f out* **40/1**

2202 **11** *2* **Sunset Boulevard (IRE)**[16] 3382 6-9-6 59...................... ChrisCatlin 11 15
(Miss Tor Sturgis) *chsd ldrs: pushed along and wknd 2f out* **9/2**[1]

0-06 **12** *26* **Strongarm**[10] 3588 3-8-3 52..(b) NeilChalmers 3 —
(A Bailey) *led: hdd over 5f out: wknd wl over 3f out: eased whn no ch fnl 2f* **66/1**

2m 38.73s (-2.37) **Going Correction** -0.10s/f (Stan)
WFA 3 from 4yo+ 13lb **12** Ran SP% **119.7**
Speed ratings (Par 101): **103,102,100,99,99 98,94,90,89,84 83,65**
toteswinger: 1&2 not won, 1&3 £5.30, 2&3 £22.20. CSF £26.34 TOTE £7.70: £1.40, £3.00, £1.80; EX 33.90.No claims for this race.
Owner Paul Howling **Bred** Newlands House Stud **Trained** Newmarket, Suffolk

FOCUS
A moderate but reasonably competitive claimer. They seemed to go a good pace throughout and the form looks pretty sound for the grade.
Sunset Boulevard(IRE) Official explanation: jockey said gelding had no more to give

3924 BET WITH LADBROKES ON 0800 777 888 H'CAP 7f 32y(P)
6:50 (6:51) (Class 5) (0-75,75) 3-Y-0+ **£3,885** (£1,156; £577; £288) **Stalls** High

Form RPR
6105 **1** **Volochkova (USA)**[29] 2949 3-9-4 73..................................(t) AdamKirby 6 79
(J R Fanshawe) *bmpd sn after s: hld up towards rr: rdn and hdwy jst over 1f out: edgd lft jst ins fnl f: r.o to ld cl home* **9/2**[2]

5124 **2** *hd* **Ninth House (USA)**[6] 3722 7-9-9 70......................(t) SilvestreDeSousa 8 78
(Mrs R A Carr) *hld up in rr: pushed along over 2f out: rdn and hdwy on outside fnl f: r.o to take 2nd last stride* **5/1**[3]

4000 **3** *hd* **Autumn Blades (IRE)**[19] 3265 4-10-0 75................... RobertWinston 12 82
(A Bailey) *hld up in mid-div: hdwy on outside over 2f out: hung lft over 1f out: led briefly towards fin: kpt on* **8/1**

0100 **4** *½* **Kingsmaite**[6] 3722 8-8-11 65.............................(b) AndrewYoxall[(7)] 7 71+
(S R Bowring) *hld up in mid-div: pushed along whn n.m.r over 2f out: c wd st: rdn jst over 1f out: kpt on ins fnl f* **28/1**

0002 **5** *1* **Spin Again (IRE)**[10] 3558 4-9-1 62...................... AdrianTNicholls 10 65
(D Nicholls) *sn chsng ldr: led 2f out: sn rdn: hdd towards fin: no ex* **6/1**

4056 **6** *½* **Royal Envoy (IRE)**[12] 3512 6-9-4 65...................... TolleyDean 11 67
(P Howling) *hld up in rr: swtchd rt jst over 1f out: rdn and r.o ins fnl f: nrst fin* **14/1**

2600 **7** *2 ¾* **A Big Sky Brewing (USA)**[20] 3234 5-9-6 72............... DeanHeslop[(5)] 9 67
(T D Barron) *chsd ldrs: pushed along over 2f out: wknd 1f out* **18/1**

2135 **8** *nk* **Jord (IRE)**[44] 2473 5-9-6 67...................................... StephenDonohoe 1 61
(J A Glover) *led: rdn and hdd 2f out: wknd ins fnl f* **8/1**

4300 **9** *nk* **Trade Centre**[28] 2976 4-9-12 73.. DaneO'Neill 4 66
(W R Muir) *hld up in mid-div: pushed along over 2f out: wknd over 1f out* **4/1**[1]

-400 **10** *1 ¾* **Diddums**[17] 3341 3-9-3 72... ChrisCatlin 3 57
(J W Hills) *hld up towards rr: short-lived effrt on ins over 1f out* **12/1**

16-0 **11** *3* **Blues Minor (IRE)**[14] 3469 4-9-4 65.........................(be) GeorgeBaker 2 45
(M Mullineaux) *prom tl rdn and wknd over 1f out* **20/1**

1m 28.58s (-1.02) **Going Correction** -0.10s/f (Stan)
WFA 3 from 4yo+ 8lb **11** Ran SP% **119.2**
Speed ratings (Par 103): **101,100,100,99,98 98,95,94,94,92 89**
toteswinger: 1&2 £3.40, 1&3 £30.60, 2&3 £8.90. CSF £27.74 CT £181.25 TOTE £5.30: £1.50, £1.80, £3.70; EX 32.30.
Owner Mrs C C Regalado-Gonzalez **Bred** Robert N Clay & Fair Way Equine Llc **Trained** Newmarket, Suffolk

FOCUS
Quite a competitive handicap, but a decent gallop helped set this up for those held up. The form looks sound.

3925 CARLSBERG EXPORT MAIDEN AUCTION STKS 5f 216y(P)
7:20 (7:21) (Class 5) 2-Y-O **£3,070** (£906; £453) **Stalls** Low

Form RPR
342 **1** **Lucky Rave**[9] 3613 2-8-9 0...................................... JamieSpencer 8 76
(D H Brown) *hld up in mid-div: hdwy over 2f out: rdn to ld ins fnl f: r.o wl* **9/4**[2]

642 **2** *3 ¼* **Listillo (USA)**[21] 3226 2-9-1 0...................................... DaneO'Neill 6 72
(H J L Dunlop) *chsd ldr: led over 1f out: rdn and hdd ins fnl f: no ex* **5/1**[3]

056 **3** *3* **Agent Boo**[56] 2128 2-8-11 0...................................... StephenDonohoe 9 59
(E S McMahon) *a.p: pushed along over 2f out: rdn wl over 1f out: one pce* **16/1**

4 *hd* **Pan American** 2-8-9 0.. FergusSweeney 11 57+
(P J Makin) *hld up in rr: pushed along over 2f out: rdn and hdwy over 1f out: kpt on ins fnl f: nvr nrr* **16/1**

242 **5** *½* **Il Forno**[9] 3634 2-8-13 0...................................... AdrianTNicholls 5 59
(D Nicholls) *led: rdn and hdd over 1f out: wknd ins fnl f* **6/4**[1]

00 **6** *1 ½* **Rebecca Romero**[16] 3402 2-8-4 0...................................... NickyMackay 1 46
(D J Coakley) *s.i.s: hld up in rr: sme prog over 1f out: sn rdn: n.d* **33/1**

444 **7** *2 ¾* **Marosh (FR)**[40] 2599 2-8-13 0...................................... PatCosgrave 4 46
(R M H Cowell) *chsd ldrs: lost pl after 2f: pushed along over 2f out: n.d after* **33/1**

00 **8** *5* **Anitra's Dance**[17] 3356 2-8-4 0...................................... JimmyQuinn 10 22
(P Howling) *a in rr* **66/1**

00 **9** *2* **Orpen All Hours (IRE)**[10] 3572 2-8-6 0...................... RoystonFfrench 12 18
(P C Haslam) *hld up and bhd: short-lived effrt on outside 3f out* **100/1**

10 *¾* **Valkov** 2-8-4 0.. RichardSmith 3 14
(Tom Dascombe) *prom: lost pl over 3f out: rdn over 2f out: eased whn no ch jst over 1f out* **12/1**

4330 **11** *4 ½* **Midnight Uno**[23] 3160 2-8-4 0..(v[1]) JackDean[(5)] 2 6
(W G M Turner) *towards rr: pushed along over 3f out: rdn and struggling over 2f out* **50/1**

1m 14.74s (-0.26) **Going Correction** -0.10s/f (Stan) **11** Ran SP% **117.2**
Speed ratings (Par 94): **97,92,88,88,87 85,82,75,72,71 65**
toteswinger: 1&2 £6.50, 1&3 £6.00, 2&3 £7.80. CSF £13.59 TOTE £3.70: £1.10, £1.20, £6.00; EX 12.20.
Owner Ron Hull **Bred** Cothi Bloodstock **Trained** Maltby, S Yorks

FOCUS
No more than a fair juvenile maiden. The pace was strong.

NOTEBOOK
Lucky Rave paid a big compliment to Ask Frank, the ten-length Carlisle maiden winner he chased home last time. This Lucky Story colt seemed to appreciate the decent gallop and responded well to pressure to get up and ultimately win quite readily. He was getting weight from the next two home, so it would probably be unwise to get carried away, but he looks a nursery type. (op 2-1 tchd 5-2)
Listillo(USA) went off quickly in order to keep tabs on early leader Il Forno, who ended up dropping away, and didn't do much once in front in the straight. He was obviously getting tired, and still looked a little green, but whatever, this was not bad effort under top weight. (op 7-2)
Agent Boo was never too far away but simply wasn't good enough. He might find things slightly easier in nurseries.
Pan American, an 8,000gns half-brother to French 1m 3yo winners Battlestar, Burnished Steel and Chinese Cookie, fared best of the newcomers. He should have learnt plenty and is likely to be suited by further. (op 20-1)
Il Forno weakened tamely in the straight, even allowing for having set a very quick pace. On this evidence he'll be suited by a return to 5f. (op 15-8 tchd 2-1)
Rebecca Romero showed some ability after starting slowly and is one to keep in mind for nurseries later in the season. Official explanation: jockey said filly did not face the kick-back
Orpen All Hours(IRE) Official explanation: jockey said filly was keen early and hung badly right-handed in the latter stages

3926 BETTER PRICES, BIGGER WINS AT LADBROKES.COM (S) STKS 5f 20y(P)
7:50 (7:50) (Class 6) 3-4-Y-0 **£2,047** (£604; £302) **Stalls** Low

Form RPR
2004 **1** **Spic 'n Span**[14] 3465 4-9-10 64..................................(b) RobertWinston 1 69
(R A Harris) *mde all: clr wl over 1f out: pushed along fnl f: r.o* **4/1**[2]

2660 **2** *½* **Miss Firefly**[7] 3671 4-8-9 50...................................... WilliamCarson[(5)] 4 60+
(R J Hodges) *hld up in mid-div: hdwy whn nt clr run wl over 1f out: nt clr run ent fnl f: swtchd rt ins fnl f: rdn and fin wl: nt rch wnr: unlucky* **8/1**

4602 **3** *1 ¾* **Dancing Welcome**[21] 3225 3-8-9 50..............................(b) NickyMackay 6 49
(J M Bradley) *mid-div: pushed along and lost pl over 3f out: c wd st: str run to take 3rd last strides* **12/1**

5460 **4** *½* **Compton Ford**[17] 3355 3-9-5 65...................................... StephenDonohoe 8 57
(M Dods) *a.p: rdn over 1f out: one pce fnl f* **16/1**

-660 **5** *nse* **Rebecca De Winter**[31] 2888 3-8-9 69...................... FergusSweeney 5 47
(David Pinder) *chsd ldrs: pushed along over 1f out: rdn and one pce fnl f* **4/1**[2]

6 *hd* **Mata Hari Blue** 3-8-9 0.. JerryO'Dwyer 2 46
(J R Holt) *mid-div: sn pushed along: hdwy on ins wl over 1f out: sn rdn: one pce fnl f* **28/1**

3335 **7** *½* **Bahamian Ceilidh**[18] 3304 3-8-9 68...................... RichardSmith 10 45
(Tom Dascombe) *chsd wnr tl rdn over 1f out: one pce* **3/1**[1]

0514 **8** *3* **Bertbrand**[6] 3720 4-9-10 60..(p) SJCraine 3 46
(D Flood) *in rr: rdn wl over 1f out: nvr nr ldrs* **11/2**[3]

-600 **9** *3 ¼* **Sonhador**[38] 2683 3-9-0 60...................................... AdrianMcCarthy 9 27
(G Prodromou) *chsd ldrs tl rdn and wknd over 2f out* **33/1**

0440 **10** *2* **Transcentral**[21] 3225 3-8-9 52...................................... TGMcLaughlin 7 15
(W M Brisbourne) *s.i.s and hmpd s: a wl in rr* **22/1**

4005 **11** *6* **Piccaso's Sky**[38] 2651 3-9-0 50..(v[1]) DaneO'Neill 12 —
(A B Haynes) *s.i.s: a in rr* **40/1**

61.56 secs (-0.74) **Going Correction** -0.10s/f (Stan)
WFA 3 from 4yo 5lb **11** Ran SP% **118.2**
Speed ratings (Par 101): **101,100,97,96,96 96,95,90,85,82 72**
toteswinger: 1&2 £6.70, 1&3 £7.70, 2&3 £15.60. CSF £34.68 TOTE £5.10: £2.10, £2.10, £2.10; EX 45.20.There was no bid for the winner.
Owner Mrs Ruth M Serrell **Bred** C A Cyzer **Trained** Earlswood, Monmouths

FOCUS
A standard seller with the winner the best guide to the form backed up by the third.
Transcentral Official explanation: jockey said filly jumped awkwardly leaving the stalls

3927 BET ON THE ASHES AT LADBROKES.COM H'CAP 1m 5f 194y(P)
8:20 (8:21) (Class 6) (0-65,65) 4-Y-0+ **£2,388** (£705; £352) **Stalls** Low

Form RPR
34-0 **1** **Dot's Delight**[23] 3158 5-8-2 46 oh1...................... SilvestreDeSousa 13 51
(M G Rimell) *hld up in mid-div: hdwy on ins over 2f out: led wl over 1f out: sn rdn: edgd rt ins fnl f: drvn out* **10/1**

5433 **2** *1 ¼* **Barodine**[14] 3470 6-8-5 54...................................... WilliamCarson[(5)] 5 57
(R J Hodges) *hld up in rr: hdwy on ins 2f out: swtchd lft wl ins fnl f: sn tk 2nd: styd on* **12/1**

4015 **3** *½* **Zalkani (IRE)**[40] 2601 9-9-3 61...................................... JerryO'Dwyer 9 64
(J Pearce) *hld up in rr: stdy hdwy on outside over 3f out: c wd st: rdn wl over 1f out: styd on to take 3rd post* **17/2**

0-30 **4** *shd* **Smooth As Silk (IRE)**[20] 3247 4-9-7 65...................... HayleyTurner 7 67
(C R Egerton) *hld up in tch: chal gng wl 2f out: rdn jst over 1f out: no ex towards fin* **14/1**

4003 **5** *nk* **Swords**[6] 3714 7-8-12 56...................................... ChrisCatlin 11 58
(R E Peacock) *hld up in mid-div: hdwy over 2f out: rdn and styd on towards fin* **5/1**[2]

6005 **6** *½* **Follow The Dream**[18] 3303 6-8-8 52...................... TGMcLaughlin 12 53
(Karen George) *hld up towards rr: rdn and hdwy on outside whn hung lft over 1f out: nvr able to chal* **25/1**

4603 **7** *2 ¼* **Adage**[19] 3275 6-8-2 46..(tp) FrankieMcDonald 10 44
(David Pinder) *hld up in rr: pushed along on outside over 2f out: c v wd st: rdn and no imp fnl f* **6/1**[3]

-024 **8** *2 ¾* **Ready To Crown (USA)**[85] 494 5-8-8 52...................... RobertWinston 3 46
(J Mackie) *hld up in tch: nt clr run ent st wl over 1f out: sn wknd* **9/1**

300- **9** *7* **King's Fable (USA)**[353] 4391 6-8-13 57...................... StephenDonohoe 4 41
(Karen George) *s.i.s: hld up towards rr: sltly hmpd briefly over 1f out: eased whn no ch ins fnl f* **14/1**

0011 **10** *½* **Starstruck Peter (IRE)**[4] 3774 5-9-5 63 6ex............(b) RichardThomas 6 50
(Jim Best) *led: pushed along over 2f out: hdd wl over 1f out: sn wknd: eased whn no ch wl ins fnl f* **2/1**[1]

2-00 **11** *5* **Munching Mike (IRE)**[19] 3275 6-8-2 46 oh1..............(v[1]) JimmyQuinn 1 30
(K M Prendergast) *prom: chsd ldr over 8f out: rdn over 2f out: wknd wl over 1f out: eased whn no ch ins fnl f* **25/1**

-030 **12** *2 ¼* **Cecina Marina**[23] 3171 6-8-2 **46** oh1........................ KirstyMilczarek 8 20
(Mrs K Walton) *chsd ldr tl over 8f out: rdn and wknd 8f out* **50/1**
066/ **13** *26* **Great Quest (IRE)**[496] 5283 7-8-13 **57**........................ RoystonFfrench 2 —
(James Moffatt) *a towards rr: lost tch fnl 3f: t.o* **25/1**
3m 4.00s (-2.00) **Going Correction** -0.10s/f (Stan) **13** Ran SP% **128.4**
Speed ratings (Par 101): **101,100,100,99,99 99,98,96,92,92 89,88,73**
toteswinger: 1&2 not won, 1&3 not won, 2&3 £15.20. CSF £128.69 CT £1091.32 TOTE £12.30: £3.80, £5.10, £3.20; EX 226.30.
Owner Mrs S E Lindley **Bred** M W And Mrs B A Littlewort **Trained** Leafield, Oxon

FOCUS
The pace seemed muddling - most of these were still well bunched at the top of the straight - and the form needs treating with caution. The placed horses are rated close to their recent marks but the form is muddling.

3928 SSG CLEANING CONTRACTORS LTD H'CAP 7f 32y(P)
8:50 (8:50) (Class 3) (0-95,94) 3-Y-O **£7,443** (£2,227; £1,113; £556; £277) **Stalls** High

Form RPR
016 **1** **More Time Tim (IRE)**[38] 2669 4-9-3 **84**........................ PatCosgrave 4 93
(J R Boyle) *w ldr: led over 3f out: rdn over 1f out: drvn out* **7/1**[3]
550 **2** *1* **Bond City (IRE)**[10] 3567 7-9-7 **88**........................ SilvestreDeSousa 10 94
(G R Oldroyd) *hld up towards rr: hdwy wl over 1f out: sn rdn: r.o u.p to take 2nd ins fnl f: kpt on* **25/1**
0644 **3** *½* **Carleton**[14] 3469 4-8-8 **75** oh1........................ ChrisCatlin 8 80
(W J Musson) *t.k.h in mid-div: rdn and hdwy 1f out: tk 3rd wl ins fnl f: kpt on* **3/1**[1]
4-66 **4** *2* **Lindoro**[16] 3391 4-9-7 **88**........................(t) AdamKirby 5 87
(W R Swinburn) *hld up in tch on ins: pushed along 2f out: rdn jst over 1f out: no ex ins fnl f* **3/1**[1]
0150 **5** *shd* **Xpres Maite**[17] 3339 6-9-6 **87**........................(b) DaneO'Neill 7 86
(S R Bowring) *s.i.s: sn hld up in mid-div: hdwy 2f out: c wd st: rdn over 1f out: one pce* **14/1**
1050 **6** *nse* **Lastroarofdtiger (USA)**[23] 3156 3-8-3 **78** ow1........ RoystonFfrench 2 74
(K R Burke) *t.k.h: prom: ev ch over 2f out: sn rdn: one pce whn edgd lft ins fnl f* **14/1**
-504 **7** *1 ½* **Dixey**[30] 2927 4-9-11 **92**........................ TedDurcan 1 87
(M A Jarvis) *led: hdd over 3f out: rdn over 1f out: wknd ins fnl f* **11/2**[2]
0060 **8** *hd* **Jack Junior (USA)**[26] 3014 5-9-13 **94**........................ AdrianTNicholls 9 90
(D Nicholls) *prom: rdn 2f out: btn whn hmpd ins fnl f* **8/1**
-004 **9** *nk* **Aflaam (IRE)**[38] 2665 4-8-12 **79**........................ TolleyDean 6 72
(P Howling) *s.i.s: pushed along over 2f out: a in rr* **10/1**
5266 **10** *10* **Silver Hotspur**[115] 893 5-8-12 **79**........................ FergusSweeney 3 45
(C R Dore) *s.i.s: hld up towards rr: rdn wl over 1f out: sn struggling: eased whn no ch ins fnl f* **16/1**
1m 28.32s (-1.28) **Going Correction** -0.10s/f (Stan)
WFA 3 from 4yo+ 8lb **10** Ran SP% **121.1**
Speed ratings (Par 107): **103,101,101,99,98 98,97,96,96,85**
toteswinger: 1&2 £49.20, 1&3 £3.90, 2&3 not won. CSF £169.34 CT £659.67 TOTE £8.70: £3.30, £6.60, £1.70; EX 203.40.
Owner M Khan X2 **Bred** Glending Bloodstock **Trained** Epsom, Surrey

FOCUS
The winning time wasn't great for the grade, only 0.26 seconds quicker than the 73-rated Volochkova managed earlier on the card, but they didn't seem to go as quick in this race. The winner took another step forward.

NOTEBOOK
More Time Tim(IRE), well beaten on the turf at Epsom last time, appreciated the return to an artificial surface and won readily, taking his record on both Polytrack and Fibresand to 5-8. Although the time could have been better, his record on sand is impressive and he could turn out to be very useful. (op 13-2)
Bond City(IRE), dropped in from the widest stall, was very keen early but still produced a good finishing effort when getting a run towards the inside in the straight. This was a good effort all things considered.
Carleton, 1lb out of the handicap, travelled quite well in about mid-division and kept on in the straight, but he was never getting to the winner. (op 7-2)
Lindoro failed to pick up for pressure and is becoming frustrating. (op 7-2)
Xpres Maite has yet to win off a mark this high. (op 16-1)
Lastroarofdtiger(USA), carrying 1lb overweight, was a little keen early and didn't see his race out. He's not progressed since winning a maiden over an extended 1m here in March. Official explanation: jockey said colt ran too free (op 12-1)
Dixey raced with the winner for much of the way but was beaten before the straight. (tchd 6-1)
Jack Junior(USA) Official explanation: jockey said gelding suffered interference in running

3929 WATCH LIVE SPORT AT LADBROKES.COM H'CAP 1m 141y(P)
9:20 (9:20) (Class 6) (0-60,60) 3-Y-O+ **£2,388** (£705; £352) **Stalls** Low

Form RPR
2056 **1** **Hector Spectre (IRE)**[5] 3741 3-9-2 **60**................(v[1]) StephenDonohoe 6 72
(K M Prendergast) *hld up in mid-div: pushed along and hdwy over 2f out: led ins fnl f: drvn clr: r.o wl* **8/1**
0006 **2** *3 ¾* **The Grey One (IRE)**[14] 3470 6-9-7 **58**................(p) KevinGhunowa(3) 4 62
(J M Bradley) *t.k.h in mid-div: hdwy on outside 3f out: hung rt over 2f out: rdn over 1f out: kpt on same pce to take 2nd wl ins fnl f* **8/1**
0040 **3** *1 ¼* **Dhhamaan (IRE)**[6] 3720 4-9-12 **60**................(b) SilvestreDeSousa 8 61
(Mrs R A Carr) *led: rdn over 1f out: hdd ins fnl f: one pce* **14/1**
6001 **4** *½* **Red Current**[12] 3501 5-9-4 **52**........................ FrankieMcDonald 3 52
(R A Harris) *hld up towards rr: nt clr run over 2f out: hdwy wl over 1f out: rdn and styd on to take 4th nr fin* **9/1**
455 **5** *¾* **Appelouse**[14] 3467 4-9-7 **55**........................ RoystonFfrench 10 53
(D W Thompson) *s.i.s: sn rcvrd to chse ldr: rdn over 2f out: lost 2nd 1f out: fdd wl ins fnl f* **25/1**
3002 **6** *½* **Mayfair's Future**[18] 3303 4-9-7 **55**........................ AdrianMcCarthy 9 52
(J R Jenkins) *hld up in tch: rdn 2f out: wknd ins fnl f* **12/1**
3420 **7** *shd* **Hits Only Cash**[14] 3470 7-9-11 **59**................(p) RobertHavlin 13 56
(J Pearce) *swtchd lft sn after s: hld up in rr: pushed along over 3f out: rdn and sme prog 1f out: nvr nrr* **12/1**
0000 **8** *1* **Our Kes (IRE)**[32] 2859 7-9-8 **56**........................ JimmyQuinn 2 51
(P Howling) *s.i.s: sn hld up in mid-div: n.m.r on ins bnd 7f out: pushed along over 3f out: rdn wl over 1f out: no hdwy* **15/2**[3]
000 **9** *1* **King Of The Beers (USA)**[12] 3503 5-9-5 **60**................(p) SPRyan(7) 5 52
(R A Harris) *hld up towards rr: pushed along over 4f out: rdn wl over 1f out: no rspnse* **28/1**
10 *½* **Precious Citizen (USA)**[281] 6513 4-9-2 **50**........................ ClareLindop 7 41
(J R Gask) *hld up in mid-div: pushed along over 3f out: struggling whn c v wd st* **14/1**
5-00 **11** *½* **Broughtons Silk**[14] 3467 4-9-3 **51**........................ ChrisCatlin 11 41
(W J Musson) *hld up in rr: pushed along wl over 1f out: no rspnse* **5/1**[2]
2360 **12** *6* **Haroldini (IRE)**[14] 3467 7-9-6 **54**................(v) RobertWinston 1 30
(J Balding) *hld up in tch: rdn over 3f out: wknd over 2f out* **10/1**
6021 **13** *5* **Iguacu**[9] 3631 5-9-1 **54**........................ MatthewDavies(5) 12 19
(George Baker) *prom: rdn over 2f out: sn wknd: c wd st* **9/2**[1]
1m 49.61s (-0.89) **Going Correction** -0.10s/f (Stan)
WFA 3 from 4yo+ 10lb **13** Ran SP% **123.9**
Speed ratings (Par 101): **99,95,94,94,93 93,92,92,91,90 90,84,80**
toteswinger: 1&2 not won, 1&3 not won, 2&3 £48.90. CSF £73.44 CT £903.86 TOTE £11.10: £4.30, £3.70, £5.10; EX 92.70 Place 6: £242.17 Place 5: £149.09.
Owner Alchemy Bloodstock **Bred** D & R Burns **Trained** Sellack, H'fords

FOCUS
A moderate handicap run at an honest pace and the form looks reasonable for the grade.
Haroldini(IRE) Official explanation: jockey said gelding lost its action
Iguacu Official explanation: jockey said gelding was never travelling
T/Plt: £676.40 to a £1 stake. Pool: £61,619.92. 66.50 winning tickets. T/Qpdt: £50.00 to a £1 stake. Pool: £5,725.98. 84.70 winning tickets. KH

3930 - 3933a (Foreign Racing) - See Raceform Interactive

LE TOUQUET (L-H)
Sunday, July 12

OFFICIAL GOING: Good

3934a PRIX SAINT POL SUR TERNOISE (MAIDEN) 7f
6:00 (12:00) 2-Y-O **£5,825** (£2,330; £1,748; £1,165; £583)

RPR
1 **Tall Chief (IRE)**[19] 2-9-2........................ RonanThomas 80
(R Pritchard-Gordon, France)
2 *3* **Zomorroda (IRE)**[35] 2-8-12........................(b) WVion 69
(R Gibson, France)
3 *½* **Tussian Bere (FR)**[14] 2-9-2........................ JAuge 71
(E J O'Neill) *always prominent, went clear with 2 others over 2f out, outpaced by winner final f, lost 2nd close home*
4 *5* **La Joie (FR)** 2-8-12........................ JBensimon 55
(J P J Dubois, France)
5 *8* **Kaldougold (BEL)** 2-8-8........................ EBureller 31
(Andre Hermans, Belgium)
6 *snk* **Bellona (FR)** 2-8-8........................ JCabre 30
(D Allard, France)
7 *10* **Doun Pearl (FR)** 2-8-8........................ AHamelin 5
(F Vermeulen, France)
8 *1 ½* **Offert (FR)** 2-8-8........................ FLefebvre —
(J Van Handenhove, France)
9 *15* **Zifron (IRE)** 2-8-11........................ BDeKoninck —
(F Caenepeel, France)
9 Ran
PARI-MUTUEL (including 1 Euro stake): WIN 2.20; PL 1.70, 1.90, 1.70;DF 4.60.
Owner Khalifa Dasmal **Bred** Jean Van Gysel **Trained** France

DIEPPE (R-H)
Monday, July 13

OFFICIAL GOING: Soft

3935a PRIX DE BELIMONT (MAIDEN) (C&G) 7f
1:05 (1:06) 2-Y-O **£6,796** (£2,718; £2,039; £1,359; £680)

RPR
1 **Maroon Machine (IRE)** 2-8-12........................ TThulliez 77
(E J O'Neill) *racd in 2nd tl led 2f out: r.o wl: comf* **31/10**[1]
2 *1* **Sir Des Brousses (FR)** 2-8-12........................ ACrastus 75
(F Chappet, France)
3 *1* **Signal (FR)**[15] 2-8-11........................ ALemaitre(5) 76
(F Head, France)
4 *¾* **Porzapone (FR)** 2-8-12........................ J-MBreux 70
(N Clement, France)
5 *snk* **Lazarus (FR)** 2-9-2........................ EWehrel 74
(J Parize, France)
6 *2* **Darwind (FR)** 2-8-7........................(b) EBureller(5) 65
(J-L Pelletan, France)
7 *¾* **Spectacle Du Mars (FR)** 2-8-12........................ MSautjeau 63
(C Martens, France)
8 *3* **Leiloken (FR)** 2-8-9........................ BRaballand(3) 56
(F-X De Chevigny, France)
9 *1* **Tinder Ball (FR)** 2-8-9........................ MBarzalona(3) 53
(J Van Handenhove, France)
10 *hd* **Mana Kourou (FR)** 2-9-2........................ AlexisBadel 57
(D Windrif, France)
0 **Calvero (FR)**[20] 2-9-2........................ GBenoist —
(Robert Collet, France)
0 **Don Fanucci (FR)** 2-8-12........................ JCrocquevieille —
(M Boutin, France)
0 **Money For Nothing (FR)** 2-8-12........................ TJarnet —
(R Pritchard-Gordon, France)
0 **Be My Gallery (FR)** 2-8-12........................ SRuis —
(J-P Gallorini, France)
1m 25.84s (85.84) **14** Ran SP% **24.4**
PARI-MUTUEL (including 1 Euro stake): WIN 4.10; PL 1.80, 3.90, 2.60;DF 34.00.
Owner G A Lucas & A E Hunt **Bred** G Brochard **Trained** Southwell, Notts

NOTEBOOK
Maroon Machine(IRE) is Eoghan O'Neill's first winner in France since he set up a satellite yard near Argentan this year.

3605 BEVERLEY (R-H)

Tuesday, July 14

OFFICIAL GOING: Good to firm (good in places; 9.7)

Wind: Light across Weather: Fine and dry

3936 BOOK ONLINE AT BEVERLEY-RACECOURSE.CO.UK CLAIMING STKS — 7f 100y

2:15 (2:16) (Class 5) 3-Y-O **£2,590** (£770; £385; £192) **Stalls** High

Form RPR

1210 **1** **Just Five (IRE)**[19] 3316 3-9-1 72 ... PhillipMakin 8 75
(M Dods) *mde all: pushed clr 2f out: unchal* **8/11**[1]

041 **2** 7 **Love In The West (IRE)**[8] 3685 3-8-8 0 ... RobertWinston 7 51
(G A Swinbank) *chsd wnr: rdn over 2f out: drvn wl over 1f out and kpt on same pce* **15/8**[2]

0040 **3** ¾ **Off Hand**[7] 3711 3-8-1 48 ... (b) PaulHanagan 1 42
(T D Easterby) *wnt lft s: sn chsng ldrs: rdn along over 2f out: drvn wl over 1f out: sn one pce* **18/1**[3]

00-0 **4** *hd* **Supera (IRE)**[59] 2082 3-8-2 49 ... NickyMackay 3 43
(M H Tompkins) *trckd ldrs: effrt 3f out and sn rdn: drvn 2f out and kpt on same pce* **18/1**[3]

050 **5** 13 **Pollish**[26] 3063 3-7-9 38 ow1 ... BillyCray(7) 5 10
(A Berry) *a towards rr* **150/1**

0 **6** ½ **Simply Sensational (IRE)**[43] 2543 3-8-0 0 ... JamieKyne(5) 2 12
(Patrick Morris) *v.s.a: a bhd* **100/1**

4455 **7** 6 **Herecomesbella**[14] 2737 3-8-2 50 ... FrankieMcDonald 4 —
(P G Murphy) *in tch: rdn along 1/2-way: sn wknd* **25/1**

1m 32.77s (-1.03) **Going Correction** -0.175s/f (Firm) **7** Ran SP% **108.7**

Speed ratings (Par 100): **98,90,89,88,74 73,66**

toteswingers: 1&2 £1.30, 1&3 £2.70, 2&3 £3.10 CSF £1.96 TOTE £1.80: £1.10, £1.40; EX 2.50.

Owner Just Five Racing Partners **Bred** Rathbarry Stud **Trained** Denton, Co Durham

■ Stewards' Enquiry : Jamie Kyne one-day ban: used whip when out of contention (July 28)

FOCUS

A dry night and warm day ensured the ground remained on the quick side. An uncompetitive race in which the second favourite proved disappointing. The gallop was only moderate at best but the form makes sense.

3937 RACING UK ON SKY 432 MAIDEN AUCTION STKS — 5f

2:45 (2:46) (Class 5) 2-Y-O **£3,238** (£963; £481; £240) **Stalls** High

Form RPR

32 **1** **Emerald Girl (IRE)**[20] 3263 2-8-4 0 ... PaulHanagan 7 69
(R A Fahey) *wnt rt s: sn trcking ldrs: hdwy 2f out: rdn to ld ins fnl f: styd on* **4/1**[2]

3264 **2** 2 **My Mandy (IRE)**[17] 3370 2-8-9 0 ow1 ... StephenDonohoe 10 67
(Ian Williams) *cl up: rdn to ld wl over 1f out: drvn ent fnl f: sn hdd and kpt on same pce* **6/1**[3]

4 **3** 1 ¼ **Flow Chart (IRE)**[75] 1623 2-8-9 0 ... PhillipMakin 5 62
(T D Barron) *chsd ldrs: hdwy 2f out: sn rdn and kpt on same pce ent fnl f* **4/1**[2]

0 **4** *shd* **Cian Rooney (IRE)**[50] 2311 2-9-2 0 ... SilvestreDeSousa 12 72+
(Mrs A Duffield) *midfield: sltly outpcd and swtchd lft 1/2-way: sn rdn and styng on whn swtchd rt to inner ent fnl f: chsd ldrs and nt clr run ins fnl f: sn swtchd lft and kpt on* **28/1**

5 1 ¼ **Wijikura (IRE)** 2-8-9 0 ... MickyFenton 13 61+
(J J Quinn) *sn outpcd in rr: hdwy 1/2-way: swtchd outside and rdn wl over 1f out: styd on wl ins fnl f: nrst fin* **16/1**

42 **6** 1 **Saint Sebastian (IRE)**[19] 3306 2-8-9 0 ... GrahamGibbons 9 54
(E S McMahon) *led: rdn along and hdd wl over 1f out: sn drvn and wknd appr fnl f* **10/3**[1]

33 **7** 1 ½ **My One Weakness (IRE)**[17] 3392 2-8-11 0 ... TomEaves 11 50
(B Ellison) *chsd ldrs on inner: rdn along 2f out: grad wknd* **6/1**[3]

554 **8** 1 ¾ **Clear Ice (IRE)**[11] 3572 2-8-9 0 ... AdrianTNicholls 4 42
(D Nicholls) *a towards rr* **16/1**

9 4 ½ **Selina Rio** 2-8-4 0 ... AndrewMullen 1 21
(L A Mullaney) *dwlt and a towards rr* **125/1**

10 6 **Wedding Dream** 2-8-8 0 ... PaulMulrennan 8 —
(K A Ryan) *midfield: rdn along 1/2-way: sn wknd* **14/1**

000 **11** 2 ½ **Daft Lad**[7] 3709 2-8-9 0 ... (v[1]) DuranFentiman 6 —
(L A Mullaney) *chsd ldrs: rdn along 1/2-way and sn wknd* **150/1**

12 10 **Calders** 2-7-11 0 ... BillyCray(7) 3 —
(A Berry) *s.i.s: a bhd* **150/1**

63.06 secs (-0.44) **Going Correction** -0.175s/f (Firm) **12** Ran SP% **115.6**

Speed ratings (Par 94): **96,92,90,90,88 87,84,81,74,65 61,45**

toteswingers: 1&2 £5.30, 1&3 £4.60, 2&3 £4.40 CSF £27.40 TOTE £4.30: £1.60, £2.10, £1.60; EX 32.00.

Owner M Wynne **Bred** Tally-Ho Stud **Trained** Musley Bank, N Yorks

FOCUS

An ordinary maiden but a decent gallop and this race should throw up its share of winners. The form looks modest rated around the principals, but the fifth home caught the eye.

NOTEBOOK

Emerald Girl(IRE) is a steadily progressive individual who showed a good attitude to get off the mark at the third attempt. She should prove equally effective back over 6f and may be able to win in ordinary nursery company. (op 10-3 tchd 9-2)

My Mandy(IRE) has had a few chances but she returned to something like her best from a favourable draw and she looks a good guide to the worth of this form. While vulnerable to the more progressive types in this grade, she should be able to pick up a minor event. (op 5-1)

Flow Chart(IRE), as on his debut in April, attracted support and showed more than enough to suggest a small race can be found. He will be better suited by the step up to 6f and is one to keep an eye on. (op 6-1 tchd 3-1)

Cian Rooney(IRE) ◆ bettered his debut effort by some way, despite his relative inexperience and a tendency to edge to his right under pressure. He is open to further improvement and will be one to note in ordinary nursery company in due course. (op 20-1)

Wijikura(IRE) ◆, the third foal of a half-sister to one placed in the Prix De Diane, was the eyecatcher of the race. Despite being taken off his feet, he picked up most encouragingly without being knocked about and should improve with this experience behind him. He will be suited by the step up to 6f and is sure to win a race. (op 12-1 tchd 10-1)

Saint Sebastian(IRE), from a yard among the winners, attracted support but failed to build on his improved Leicester effort back over this shorter trip. However, he would not be one to write off just yet. (op 7-2 tchd 4-1)

Clear Ice(IRE) Official explanation: jockey said, regarding the poor form shown, that he had ridden the gelding before and instructions were to ride him as he found him on the day, adding that he had a poor draw and he wished to get across to the rail, but was intimidated by another runner

3938 GO RACING IN YORKSHIRE SUMMER FESTIVAL H'CAP — 5f

3:15 (3:15) (Class 6) (0-60,60) 3-Y-O+ **£2,266** (£674; £337; £168) **Stalls** High

Form RPR

-600 **1** **Greek Secret**[66] 1889 6-8-11 55 ow5 ... (b) JamesO'Reilly(5) 16 63
(J O'Reilly) *n.m.r and stmbld after 1f: midfield: hdwy 2f out: rdn over 1f out: str run ent fnl f: styd on wl to ld nr fin* **16/1**

-011 **2** ¾ **Solemn**[11] 3562 4-9-7 60 ... (b) SteveDrowne 11 65+
(J M Bradley) *led: rdn clr ent fnl f: sn drvn: hdd and no ex nr fin* **5/2**[1]

400 **3** ½ **Darcy's Pride (IRE)**[29] 2966 5-9-2 55 ... (t) TonyHamilton 5 59
(P T Midgley) *midfield: hdwy on outer wl over 1f out: sn rdn and chsd ldrs ent fnl f: drvn and kpt on towards fin* **20/1**

0240 **4** ½ **Strathmore (IRE)**[11] 3562 5-9-3 56 ... PaulHanagan 4 58+
(R A Fahey) *stdd and swtchd rt s: hld up in rr: hdwy on inner and n.m.r over 1f out: sn rdn and kpt on ins fnl f: nrst fin* **10/1**

5335 **5** *nk* **Miss Daawe**[18] 3354 5-9-6 59 ... TomEaves 2 60+
(B Ellison) *in tch on outer: hdwy to chse ldrs wl over 1f out: rdn ent fnl f: kpt on same pce* **14/1**

0000 **6** ½ **Half A Crown (IRE)**[28] 3002 4-8-8 47 ... (p) PaulMulrennan 17 46
(D W Barker) *trckd ldrs on inner: effrt 2f out: sn rdn: drvn and edgd lft ent fnl f: kpt on same pce* **8/1**[3]

0005 **7** ½ **Port Ronan (USA)**[10] 3611 3-8-1 50 ... (p) JamieKyne(5) 6 45
(J S Wainwright) *rr: hdwy on outer wl over 1f out: sn rdn and kpt on ins fnl f: nrst fin* **28/1**

0-34 **8** ¾ **Excitable (IRE)**[10] 3611 3-8-3 50 ... DominicFox(3) 9 42
(Mrs D J Sanderson) *chsd ldrs: rdn along wl over 1f out: n.m.r appr fnl f: sn one pce* **10/1**

5656 **9** 1 ¾ **City For Conquest (IRE)**[17] 3381 6-8-7 46 ... (b) FrankieMcDonald 13 34
(John A Harris) *hld up towards rr: effrt and sme hdwy 2f out: nvr a factor* **12/1**

1000 **10** *shd* **Almaty Express**[22] 3212 7-9-7 60 ... (b) PhillipMakin 8 48
(J R Weymes) *cl up: rdn wl over 1f out and grad wknd appr fnl f* **16/1**

000U **11** *hd* **Coconut Moon**[9] 3657 7-8-7 46 oh1 ... PaulQuinn 12 33
(A Berry) *in rr: rdn along 1/2-way: nvr a factor* **40/1**

0514 **12** ½ **Only A Game (IRE)**[11] 3562 4-9-7 60 ... (p) SilvestreDeSousa 7 45
(I W McInnes) *midfield: effrt and sme hdwy wl over 1f out: sn rdn and n.d* **11/2**[2]

015 **13** ¾ **Foreign Rhythm (IRE)**[11] 3562 4-8-3 49 ... JohnCavanagh(7) 14 31
(N Tinkler) *midfield: pushed along 1/2-way: rdn wl over 1f out: no imp whn n.m.r appr fnl f* **10/1**

0005 **14** 2 **Whisper Softly (IRE)**[3] 3853 3-8-6 50 ... PJMcDonald 10 23
(T D Walford) *cl up: rdn along 2f out: sn drvn and wknd over 1f out* **25/1**

62.46 secs (-1.04) **Going Correction** -0.175s/f (Firm)

WFA 3 from 4yo+ 5lb **14** Ran SP% **123.0**

Speed ratings (Par 101): **101,99,99,98,97 96,96,94,92,91 91,90,89,86**

toteswingers: 1&2 £12.10, 1&3 £44.20, 2&3 £15.20 CSF £54.78 CT £876.95 TOTE £21.90: £6.10, £1.30, £7.80; EX 72.50.

Owner The Boot & Shoe Ackworth Partnership **Bred** James Clark **Trained** Doncaster, S Yorks

■ Stewards' Enquiry : James O'Reilly caution: used whip above shoulder height

FOCUS

A run-of-the mill-sprint and one run at a decent gallop throughout. The winner carried 5lb overweight and probably limits the form.

Strathmore(IRE) Official explanation: jockey said gelding was denied a clear run

3939 BUSINESS EXPO HERE ON 1 OCTOBER H'CAP — 7f 100y

3:45 (3:46) (Class 6) (0-65,64) 3-Y-O **£2,428** (£722; £361; £180) **Stalls** High

Form RPR

2344 **1** **Diamond Daisy (IRE)**[10] 3616 3-9-5 62 ... SilvestreDeSousa 3 67
(Mrs A Duffield) *trckd ldrs: effrt over 2f out and sn rdn: hdwy on outer over 1f out: led ent fnl f: edgd rt: flashed tail and drvn out* **5/1**[2]

3212 **2** ¾ **Northern Flyer (GER)**[6] 3727 3-9-0 62 ... JamieKyne(5) 7 71+
(J J Quinn) *trckd ldrs: effrt on inner and nt clr run over 1f out: swtchd rt and rdn to chse wnr ins fnl f: styd on strly towards fin* **8/11**[1]

0354 **3** 1 ½ **River Dee (IRE)**[10] 3624 3-8-10 60 ... HollyHall(7) 4 59
(D Donovan) *trckd ldng pair: hdwy over 2f out: rdn to chal and edgd rt over 1f out: led briefly appr last: sn hdd and one pce* **13/2**[3]

5406 **4** ½ **Bahkov (IRE)**[15] 3463 3-8-11 59 ... RossAtkinson(5) 6 57
(Tom Dascombe) *led: rdn along 2f out: drvn and edgd lft over 1f out: edgd rt and hdd appr last: one pce* **10/1**

060- **5** 1 ½ **Liteup My World (USA)**[241] 7333 3-9-7 64 ... TomEaves 2 58+
(B Ellison) *s.i.s and wnt lft s: in rr tl hdwy over 2f out: sn rdn and no imp fr over 1f out* **10/1**

0066 **6** 1 ¼ **Two Turtle Doves (IRE)**[15] 3464 3-9-2 59 ... MickyFenton 1 50
(M Mullineaux) *wnt lft s: in rr tl hdwy to chse ldrs on outer 2f out: sn rdn and wknd* **33/1**

000- **7** 5 **Melkatant**[252] 7172 3-8-3 46 ... DuranFentiman 5 25
(N Bycroft) *cl up: rdn along over 2f out: sn drvn and wknd* **40/1**

1m 33.06s (-0.74) **Going Correction** -0.175s/f (Firm) **7** Ran SP% **111.5**

Speed ratings (Par 98): **97,96,94,93,92 90,85**

toteswingers: 1&2 £1.50, 1&3 £2.30, 2&3 £2.00 CSF £8.56 TOTE £5.10: £2.50, £1.10; EX 10.20.

Owner John and Elaine Culf and John Gatenby **Bred** Thomas F Brennan & Holborn Trust Co Ltd **Trained** Constable Burton, N Yorks

FOCUS

A moderate handicap run at only a fair pace and one in which the runner-up looked an unlucky loser. The winner sets the standard.

3940 MARY ELIZABETH WESTWOOD CELEBRATION H'CAP (124TH YEAR OF THE WATT MEMORIAL STKS) — 2m 35y

4:15 (4:15) (Class 4) (0-85,74) 3-Y-O+ **£12,952** (£3,854; £1,926; £962) **Stalls** High

Form RPR

61 **1** **Pseudonym (IRE)**[11] 3593 7-9-1 65 ... (t) J-PGuillambert 4 72
(M F Harris) *hld up: hdwy 3f out: rdn to chse ldrs wl over 1f out: led ins fnl f: sn drvn and hld on wl nr fin* **6/1**[3]

3352 **2** *nse* **Longboat Key**[5] 3788 3-8-1 70 ... (b) JimmyQuinn 5 77+
(M Johnston) *hld up in tch: n.m.r on inner and lost pl whn outpcd 3f out: rr and swtchd wd over 2f out: sn rdn and styd on strly to chal ins fnl f: drvn and edgd rt nr fin: jst hld* **2/1**[1]

6014 **3** 3 ½ **Miss Keck**[23] 3191 5-9-1 65 ... PJMcDonald 2 68
(G A Swinbank) *trckd ldng pair: hdwy 3f out: rdn to chse ldr over 2f out: drvn over 1f out and kpt on same pce* **7/1**

1043 **4** *hd* **Grand Art (IRE)**18 3343 5-9-10 74 PaulMulrennan 3 77
(P T Midgley) *hld up in rr: hdwy over 2f out: rdn to chse ldrs over 1f out: kpt on same pce* **17/2**

0052 **5** *nk* **Lets Roll**10 3609 8-8-8 65 PaulPickard(7) 8 67
(C W Thornton) *hld up in tch: hdwy 1/2-way: led 3f out and sn rdn clr: drvn over 1f out: hdd ins fnl f and wknd* **10/1**

0160 **6** *1 1/2* **Danzatrice**19 3313 7-9-3 70 FrederikTylicki(3) 6 70
(C W Thornton) *hld up in rr: hdwy on outer 3f out: rdn to chse ldrs wl over 1f out: sn drvn and wknd over 1f out* **9/1**

3011 **7** *3 1/2* **Yonder**22 3216 5-9-3 67 (b1) SteveDrowne 9 63
(H Morrison) *hld up towards rr: hdwy on inner: pushed along over 3f out: sn rdn and wknd over 2f out* **5/1**2

30/0 **8** *8* **John Forbes**18 3350 7-8-13 63 TomEaves 1 50
(B Ellison) *trckd ldrs: led after 3f: rdn along and hdd 3f out: sn wknd* **40/1**

231 **9** *nk* **Monte Pattino (USA)**15 3444 5-8-12 62 (vt) PaulHanagan 7 48
(C J Teague) *led 3f: cl up tl hld again over 4f out: rdn and hdd 3f out: sn drvn and wknd* **10/1**

3m 34.84s (-4.96) **Going Correction** -0.175s/f (Firm)
WFA 3 from 5yo+ 19lb **9** Ran SP% **117.9**
Speed ratings (Par 105): **105,104,103,103,102 102,100,96,96**
toteswingers: 1&2 £3.20, 1&3 £6.20, 2&3 £4.80 CSF £18.82 CT £88.01 TOTE £7.00: £1.80, £1.50, £2.40; EX 20.90.

Owner Mrs D J Brown **Bred** Ballymacoll Stud Farm Ltd **Trained** Paxford, Glos

■ Stewards' Enquiry : Jimmy Quinn three-day ban: used whip with excessive frequency without giving mount time to respond and down the horse's shoulder in the forehand position (Jul 28, 30, 31)

FOCUS
A few in-form types in an ordinary handicap. The pace was moderate until lifting around 3f out and the third and fourth help set the level with the winner back to his best.

3941 LEVY BOARD H'CAP 1m 100y
4:45 (4:46) (Class 4) (0-80,80) 3-Y-O+ £4,727 (£1,406; £702; £351) Stalls High

Form RPR

0003 **1** **Danehillsundance (IRE)**10 3635 5-9-5 71 (t) SteveDrowne 9 80
(D H Brown) *trckd ldrs on inner: swtchd lft and hdwy over 2f out: sn chal: rdn to ld ent fnl f: drvn and kpt on wl towards fin* **9/4**1

3023 **2** *1* **Exit Smiling**11 3560 7-9-6 79 PaulPickard(7) 7 86
(P T Midgley) *hld up in tch: swtchd outside and effrt 2f out: sn rdn and styd on u.p ins fnl f: nrst fin* **13/2**

-560 **3** *nse* **Atabaas Allure (FR)**33 2874 3-9-5 80 J-PGuillambert 2 85
(M Johnston) *led: rdn along 2f out: drvn and hdd ent fnl f: kpt on u.p* **4/1**2

0-4 **4** *1 1/2* **Addikt (IRE)**32 2894 4-9-8 77 FrederikTylicki(3) 8 82+
(G A Harker) *trckd ldrs on inner: hdwy 2f out: styng on whn nt clr run ins fnl f: kpt on* **4/1**2

2000 **5** *shd* **Collateral Damage (IRE)**20 3265 6-9-9 75 (t) DavidAllan 3 78
(T D Easterby) *hld up in rr: hdwy over 2f out: rdn to chse ldrs over 1f out: sn drvn and kpt on same pce* **10/1**

1601 **6** *3* **Hel's Angel (IRE)**15 3451 3-8-12 73 SilvestreDeSousa 4 67
(Mrs A Duffield) *t.k.h: prom: rdn along over 2f out: grad wknd* **9/2**3

-000 **7** *2* **Rising Shadow (IRE)**30 2941 8-10-0 80 JimmyQuinn 6 71
(C W Thornton) *dwlt: hld up in rr: effrt and sme hdwy on inner 3f out: sn rdn and nvr nr ldrs* **40/1**

21-0 **8** *3 1/2* **Tenjack King**32 2894 4-9-12 78 MickyFenton 1 61
(Joss Saville) *chsd ldrs on outer: rdn along wl over 2f out and sn wknd* **50/1**

1m 45.81s (-1.79) **Going Correction** -0.175s/f (Firm)
WFA 3 from 4yo+ 9lb **8** Ran SP% **115.8**
Speed ratings (Par 105): **101,100,99,98,98 95,93,89**
toteswingers: 1&2 £4.10, 1&3 £3.60, 2&3 £4.80 CSF £17.99 CT £55.73 TOTE £3.60: £1.30, £1.90, £1.40; EX 18.50.

Owner J P Hardiman **Bred** J P Hardiman **Trained** Maltby, S Yorks

FOCUS
Not the strongest of handicaps for the money and the ordinary gallop suited those up with the pace. Nevertheless, the form looks sound.
Hel's Angel(IRE) Official explanation: jockey said filly ran too freely

3942 TURFTV APPRENTICE H'CAP 1m 100y
5:15 (5:15) (Class 6) (0-65,65) 3-Y-O £1,942 (£578; £288; £144) Stalls High

Form RPR

4352 **1** **Hawkeyethenoo (IRE)**8 3684 3-8-7 51 (b) JamesPSullivan(3) 3 57
(M W Easterby) *t.k.h early: chsd ldrs: hdwy 1/2-way: led wl over 2f out and sn clr: rdn and hung rt over 1f out: kpt on* **5/1**2

0041 **2** *1 1/4* **Gaselee (USA)**8 3680 3-9-6 61 6ex WilliamCarson 9 64
(Rae Guest) *led: rdn along and hdd wl over 2f out: drvn and rallied appr fnl f: kpt on u.p: nt rch wnr* **8/15**1

555 **3** *3 3/4* **Chichen Daawe**18 3352 3-8-5 51 IJBrennan(5) 5 46
(B Ellison) *trckd ldrs on inner: effrt over 2f out: sn rdn and kpt on same pce* **9/1**3

0-00 **4** *2 3/4* **Lambourn Genie (UAE)**31 2909 3-8-8 49 RossAtkinson 6 37
(Tom Dascombe) *hld up towards rr: hdwy 3f out: rdn along to chse ldrs 2f out: sn no imp* **16/1**

020- **5** *3 3/4* **Aven Mac (IRE)**281 6524 3-8-3 51 (p) TerenceFury(7) 4 31
(N Bycroft) *rrd s: a towards rr* **33/1**

4-56 **6** *2 1/2* **Hector's House**53 2230 3-9-7 65 AmyRyan(3) 2 39
(M Dods) *t.k.h: chsd ldrs: rdn and hung lft over 2f out: sn wknd* **10/1**

0400 **7** *1/2* **Benozzo Gozzoli**57 2143 3-8-6 50 PNolan(3) 1 23
(H Morrison) *towards rr: hung lft bnd after 3f: nvr a factor* **33/1**

56-6 **8** *hd* **Lady Norlela**183 135 3-8-2 46 oh1 PaulPickard(3) 8 18
(T J Fitzgerald) *cl up: rdn along 1/2-way: sn wknd* **33/1**

1m 45.86s (-1.74) **Going Correction** -0.175s/f (Firm) **8** Ran SP% **115.7**
Speed ratings (Par 98): **101,99,96,93,89 87,86,86**
toteswingers: 1&2 £1.40, 1&3 £4.50, 2&3 £2.60 CSF £8.04 CT £21.20 TOTE £6.10: £1.50, £1.02, £2.60; EX 9.80.

Owner Forbes Connor **Bred** S Leigh & R Leigh & Islandmore Stud **Trained** Sheriff Hutton, N Yorks

FOCUS
A moderate handicap. The pace was only fair and the first two pulled clear, with the winner the best guide to the form.

Benozzo Gozzoli Official explanation: jockey said gelding hung left on the bend turning into the straight

3943 LADY JANE BETHELL MEMORIAL LADY RIDERS' H'CAP (FOR LADY AMATEUR RIDERS) 1m 1f 207y
5:45 (5:46) (Class 6) (0-65,64) 3-Y-O+ £1,873 (£581; £290; £145) Stalls High

Form RPR

0011 **1** **The Last Alzao (IRE)**7 3721 3-9-8 64 6ex MrsVFahey(5) 13 76+
(R A Fahey) *in tch: hdwy to chse ldrs over 2f out: styd on ent fnl f to ld last 100yds* **11/4**1

0001 **2** *1 1/4* **Gala Sunday (USA)**15 3450 9-10-2 56 (bt) MissSBrotherton 14 63
(M W Easterby) *trckd ldrs on inner: hdwy over 3f out: led wl over 2f out: rdn clr over 1f out: drvn ins fnl f: hdd and no ex last 100yds* **9/2**2

3336 **3** *1 1/4* **Kalasam**8 3689 5-10-5 64 MissJoannaMason(5) 4 69
(M W Easterby) *in tch: rdn along and sltly outpcd over 2f out: styd on appr fnl f: nrst fin* **9/1**

4025 **4** *3/4* **Shekan Star**11 3561 7-9-11 51 MrsCBartley 16 54
(K G Reveley) *chsd ldrs: hdwy over 3f out: rdn to chse ldr 2f out: drvn and one pce appr fnl f* **6/1**3

0300 **5** *3/4* **Ba Dreamflight**10 3631 4-9-2 47 MissVCartmel(5) 5 49
(H Morrison) *towards rr: hdwy 3f out: sn rdn and kpt on appr fnl f: nrst fin* **14/1**

-064 **6** *shd* **Mayoman (IRE)**18 3331 4-9-13 58 MissMMullineaux(5) 6 59
(M Mullineaux) *towards rr: hdwy over 2f out: sn rdn and kpt on appr fnl f: nrst fin* **11/1**

0006 **7** *1 1/4* **Call Of Duty (IRE)**10 3615 4-10-0 59 MissECSayer(5) 1 62+
(Mrs Dianne Sayer) *towards rr: hdwy on inner: 2f out: rdn and styng on whn nt clr run over 1f out: swtchd lft and kpt on ins fnl f: nrst fin* **20/1**

00-0 **8** *6* **Paparaazi (IRE)**15 3450 7-9-8 53 (p) MissKSharp(5) 2 40
(I W McInnes) *towards rr: sme hdwy 3f out: sn rdn and nvr nr ldrs* **33/1**

4053 **9** *3/4* **Apache Dawn**10 3631 5-9-5 48 (t) MissCJMacmahon(3) 3 33
(A Sadik) *a in midfield* **28/1**

5245 **10** *1 1/4* **Grethel (IRE)**15 3451 5-9-1 48 MissSarahRichardson(7) 17 31
(A Berry) *towards rr: hdwy 1/2-way: rdn and in tch 2f out: wknd over 1f out* **22/1**

6304 **11** *1 3/4* **Tevez**17 3382 4-10-3 57 (v) MissLEllison 11 36
(D Donovan) *dwlt: sn chsng ldr: rdn along 3f out: wknd 2f out* **9/1**

000 **12** *1/2* **Kingsholm**8 3689 7-10-3 62 MissKellyBurke(5) 8 40
(N Wilson) *a in rr* **33/1**

3000 **13** *nk* **Run Free**19 3314 5-9-11 51 MissADeniel 12 29
(N Wilson) *chsd ldrs: rdn along over 3f out: wknd over 2f out* **33/1**

0-00 **14** *3/4* **Hits Only Time**11 3561 4-9-3 48 MissKECooper(5) 10 24
(D Carroll) *led: rdn along over 3f out: hdd wl over 2f out: sn drvn and wknd* **22/1**

-600 **P** **Jarvo**15 3450 8-9-2 49 (v) MissCLWhitehead(7) 15 —
(I W McInnes) *a in rr: sddle slipped and lost tch over 3f out: p.u wl over 1f out* **66/1**

2m 4.35s (-2.65) **Going Correction** -0.175s/f (Firm)
WFA 3 from 4yo+ 11lb **15** Ran SP% **121.4**
Speed ratings (Par 101): **103,102,101,100,99 99,98,93,93,92 90,90,89,89,—**
toteswingers: 1&2 £3.40, 1&3 £8.10, 2&3 £10.00 CSF £12.48 CT £101.42 TOTE £3.50: £1.80, £1.70, £3.30; EX 13.20 Place 6: £8.89 Place 5: £8.41.
Owner G Devlin **Bred** G Devlin **Trained** Musley Bank, N Yorks
■ Stewards' Enquiry : Miss K Sharp one-day ban: used whip when out of contention (Jul 28)
Miss C J Macmahon one-day ban: used whip when out of contention (Jul 30)
Miss A Deniel one-day ban: used whip when out of contention (Jul 28)
FOCUS
An ordinary handicap in which a fair gallop picked up turning for home. The placed horses set the level.
Tevez Official explanation: jockey said gelding had a breathing problem
Jarvo Official explanation: jockey said saddle slipped
T/Jkpt: Not won. T/Plt: £8.20 to a £1 stake. Pool: £72,772.00. 6,471.70 winning tickets. T/Qpdt: £3.80 to a £1 stake. Pool: £3,509.68. 680.20 winning tickets. JR

3671 BRIGHTON (L-H)
Tuesday, July 14

OFFICIAL GOING: Good to firm (good in places; 8.2)
Rail dolled out 5m from 6f pole to 2.5f but impact on distances not quantified.
Wind: Fresh, against Weather: Fine

3944 3663 FIRST FOR FOODSERVICE MEDIAN AUCTION MAIDEN STKS 5f 213y
2:30 (2:31) (Class 6) 2-Y-O £2,775 (£830; £415; £207; £103) Stalls Low

Form RPR

6 **1** **Professor John (IRE)**12 3546 2-9-3 0 HayleyTurner 4 81+
(M L W Bell) *hld up in 4th: rdn 3f out: hdwy over 1f out: drvn to ld fnl 100yds* **9/2**2

2 **2** *3/4* **Faith Jicaro (IRE)**34 2819 2-8-12 0 JamieSpencer 7 74
(Mrs L Williamson) *trckd ldng pair: led jst over 1f out: hung lft and hdd fnl 100yds: nt qckn* **8/15**1

065 **3** *6* **Volatilis (IRE)**35 2793 2-9-3 0 DarryllHolland 3 61
(J W Hills) *pushed along thrght: led tl jst over 1f out: wknd fnl f* **11/2**3

6 **4** *2 3/4* **Charlottesometimes (USA)**7 3715 2-8-12 0 RichardMullen 1 48
(D M Simcock) *chsd ldr tl hrd rdn and wknd over 1f out* **33/1**

5 *29* **Holkham** 2-9-3 0 IanMongan 2 —
(N P Littmoden) *dwlt: a last: rdn 3f out: nt handle trck and sn lost tch: eased whn no ch fnl 2f* **16/1**

1m 11.6s (1.40) **Going Correction** +0.05s/f (Good) **5** Ran SP% **107.6**
Speed ratings (Par 92): **92,91,83,79,40**
CSF £7.08 TOTE £4.40: £1.70, £1.30; EX 7.40.
Owner Paddy Barrett **Bred** Manfred Wurtenberger **Trained** Newmarket, Suffolk
■ Stewards' Enquiry : Jamie SpencerM one-day ban: careless riding (Aug 2)
FOCUS
An ordinary juvenile maiden but the second improved on her debut and third and fourth help set the level. They all raced towards the stands' side in the straight, continuing the theme of recent meetings, but the front two were not tight against the rail.
NOTEBOOK
Professor John(IRE) improved a good deal on the form he showed when sixth behind the potentially smart colt, Showcasing, on his debut at Yarmouth. Having raced towards the rear, he was slightly short of room when looking to make ground against the stands' rail early in the straight and was forced to switch. However, once in the clear he stayed on strongly for pressure and readily mastered the favourite. He looks the type to keep improving and should do okay in nurseries.

Faith Jicaro(IRE), reeled in the early leader Volatilis without any fuss in the straight and had her chance, but the winner was too good. She again displayed a bit of knee action and the drying ground might not have suited. Her trainer is just 1-113 with her two-year-olds since 2002. Jamie Spencer reported the filly was unsuited by the track. Official explanation: trainer said filly was unsuited by the track (op 4-7)
Volatilis(IRE) led the field over to the stands' side in the straight, but he didn't look totally comfortable in front, having to be niggled to hold his position, and was soon beaten. A return to more patient tactics might suit. (op 13-2)
Charlottesometimes(USA), well beaten on her debut over 7f at Wolverhampton, was again well held and doesn't look up to winning a maiden like this one.
Holkham, a half-brother to, among others, very smart sprinter Torosay Spring, was very green throughout and didn't look comfortable on the track, but an entry in a seller next week suggests connections believe he has his limitations. He was reported to have hung left throughout. Official explanation: jockey said colt hung left throughout (op 11-1)

3945 CATERING SERVICES INTERNATIONAL H'CAP — 5f 213y
3:00 (3:00) (Class 5) (0-75,79) 3-Y-0+ **£3,280** (£981; £490; £245; £122) **Stalls** Low

Form | | | | RPR
0000 **1** **Highland Harvest**[22] 3211 5-9-9 **69** .... RobertHavlin 3 77
(Jamie Poulton) *cl 3rd tl jnd ldr over 2f out: disp ld fnl f: drvn to get on top nr fin* **15/2**
5551 **2** *hd* **Satwa Street (IRE)**[8] 3676 3-9-13 **79** 6ex .... RichardMullen 2 86
(D M Simcock) *led: claimed stands' rail and jnd by runner-up over 2f out: disp ld and hrd rdn fnl f: no ex fnl strides* **5/4**[1]
0400 **3** *3* **Magical Speedfit (IRE)**[5] 3784 4-9-13 **73** .... DaneO'Neill 5 71
(G G Margarson) *hld up in 4th: rdn over 2f out: one pce fnl f* **9/2**[2]
0156 **4** *2* **Berrymead**[14] 3477 4-8-10 **61** ow5 .... AnnStokell(5) 7 53
(Miss A Stokell) *pushed along in last: struggling over 2f out: kpt on fnl f: n.d* **14/1**
423 **5** *3* **Leftonthesheif (IRE)**[11] 3592 3-9-8 **74** .... (p) TolleyDean 8 55
(J L Spearing) *chsd ldr 3f: n.m.r and dropped to 4th sn after: wknd over 1f out* **5/1**[3]
5222 **6** *3 1/4* **Northern Empire (IRE)**[15] 3465 6-9-6 **66** .... (p) DarryllHolland 4 38
(F Jordan) *stdd s: hld up in 5th: rdn to dispute 3rd in centre 2f out: hung lft over 1f out: sn wknd* **11/2**

1m 10.38s (0.18) **Going Correction** +0.05s/f (Good)
WFA 3 from 4yo+ 6lb — **6** Ran SP% **113.1**
Speed ratings (Par 103): **100,99,95,93,89 84**
toteswingers: 1&2 £5.50, 1&3 £5.10, 2&3 £1.80 CSF £17.75 CT £47.41 TOTE £9.70: £3.70, £1.50; EX 23.40 Trifecta £81.40 Pool: £256.59 - 2.33 winning units..
Owner J Wotherspoon **Bred** John Wotherspoon **Trained** Lewes, E Sussex

FOCUS
An ordinary sprint handicap with the winner appreciating the drop in trip and grade. They were all taken towards the stands' side in the straight but, just as in the opener, the winner raced off the rail.
Northern Empire(IRE) Official explanation: jockey said gelding was unsuited by the track

3946 RIDGEVIEW SPARKLING WINE H'CAP — 7f 214y
3:30 (3:30) (Class 6) (0-60,62) 3-Y-0+ **£2,590** (£770; £385; £192) **Stalls** Low

Form | | | | RPR
223 **1** **Mick Is Back**[34] 2807 5-9-11 **58** .... (v) DaneO'Neill 14 65
(G G Margarson) *rn wout declared tongue-strap: chsd ldrs: led over 1f out: hld on wl* **5/1**[2]
-043 **2** *1/2* **Astroangel**[14] 3490 5-9-5 **52** .... (p) GeorgeBaker 7 58
(M H Tompkins) *s.s: hld up in rr: smooth hdwy 2f out: rdn to chal ins fnl f: nt qckn* **11/2**[3]
0004 **3** *shd* **Spring Secret**[13] 3502 3-8-13 **55** .... TonyCulhane 10 59
(B Palling) *led after 1f tl 6f out: styd prom: briefly disp ld 2f out: kpt on gamely* **18/1**
0002 **4** *1* **Cognac Boy (USA)**[14] 3473 3-9-0 **56** .... (v) FergusSweeney 1 57
(A B Haynes) *hld up in midfield: smooth hdwy to chal over 1f out: one pce fnl f* **16/1**
0423 **5** *1 3/4* **Gracechurch (IRE)**[20] 3259 6-9-8 **55** .... DarryllHolland 5 54
(R J Hodges) *hld up towards rr: hdwy on stands' rail 2f out: styd on u.p fnl f* **13/2**
0002 **6** *1/2* **Motor Home**[14] 3476 3-9-0 **59** .... DavidProbert(3) 8 55
(A M Balding) *mid-div: rdn and hdwy in centre over 2f out: no ex over 1f out* **3/1**[1]
0500 **7** *5* **Buail Isteach (IRE)**[8] 3671 4-8-13 **46** .... (b) EdwardCreighton 2 33
(E J Creighton) *towards rr: effrt 3f out: nt pce to trble ldrs fnl 2f* **33/1**
3300 **8** *2 1/4* **Love Allowed**[8] 3693 3-9-3 **59** .... PaulDoe 9 38
(Jamie Poulton) *led 1f: styd prom: briefly disp ld 2f out: sn wknd* **20/1**
-504 **9** *2 1/4* **Billy Smart (IRE)**[42] 2577 3-8-10 **52** .... TravisBlock 6 26
(D J S Ffrench Davis) *s.s: bhd: rdn 3f out: sme hdwy in centre 2f out: wknd over 1f out* **10/1**
4005 **10** *hd* **Noverre To Hide (USA)**[18] 3345 3-8-13 **55** .... (v[1]) RichardThomas 4 29
(J R Best) *prom: led 6f out tl wknd qckly 2f out* **25/1**
35-0 **11** *hd* **Percys Corismatic**[20] 3257 3-8-10 **52** .... HayleyTurner 12 25
(J Gallagher) *rdn over 4f out: a bhd* **40/1**
2-55 **12** *5* **Dark Camellia**[31] 2921 4-9-6 **53** .... RichardMullen 3 17
(H J L Dunlop) *chsd ldrs: rdn over 2f out: hung lft and wknd wl over 1f out: eased whn wl btn fnl f* **17/2**
0230 **13** *hd* **Sularno**[20] 3269 5-9-10 **57** .... RobertHavlin 15 20
(J Pearce) *chsd ldrs over 5f: eased whn no ch over 1f out* **16/1**

1m 36.29s (0.29) **Going Correction** +0.05s/f (Good)
WFA 3 from 4yo+ 9lb — **13** Ran SP% **121.0**
Speed ratings (Par 101): **100,99,99,98,96 96,91,88,86,86 86,81,81**
toteswingers: 1&2 £7.60, 1&3 £17.40, 2&3 £18.50 CSF £31.70 CT £468.80 TOTE £5.70: £1.40, £2.70, £6.10; EX 38.80 Trifecta £127.20 Part won. Pool: £171.96 - 0.10 winning units..
Owner M Jenner & G Margarson **Bred** J E Abbey **Trained** Newmarket, Suffolk

FOCUS
A very moderate but competitive handicap and the form looks reasonable rated around those in the frame behind the winner. They raced middle to stands' side, but the near rail was no advantage.
Love Allowed Official explanation: jockey said filly hung left throughout
Noverre To Hide(USA) Official explanation: jockey said gelding ran too free
Dark Camellia Official explanation: jockey said filly had no more to give

3947 MATTHEW CLARK DRINKS H'CAP — 5f 59y
4:00 (4:00) (Class 6) (0-55,54) 3-Y-0+ **£2,072** (£616; £231; £231) **Stalls** Low

Form | | | | RPR
4503 **1** **Joss Stick**[21] 3242 4-9-0 **53** .... DavidProbert(3) 7 60
(J J Bridger) *towards rr: sltly hmpd after 100yds: rdn over 2f out: hdwy over 1f out: r.o to ld fnl 50yds* **6/1**
0300 **2** *hd* **Lily Jicaro (IRE)**[15] 3449 3-8-9 **50** .... NeilChalmers 5 55
(Mrs L Williamson) *s.i.s: bhd: drvn along over 2f out: rapid hdwy fnl f: tk 2nd fnl strides* **20/1**
0030 **3** *3/4* **Lithaam (IRE)**[14] 3477 5-8-12 **53** .... (p) JackDean(5) 9 57
(J M Bradley) *prom: led over 1f out: hrd rdn fnl f: hdd and nt qckn fnl 50yds* **11/2**[3]
6003 **3** *dht* **Tricky Trev (USA)**[14] 3471 3-8-9 **50** .... (t) LPKeniry 2 52
(S Curran) *prom: styd alone far side st: kpt on fnl f* **9/2**[2]
0000 **5** *1/2* **Maggie Kate**[8] 3671 4-8-13 **49** .... (b[1]) FergusSweeney 4 51
(R Ingram) *chsd ldrs: effrt 2f out: hld whn n.m.r fnl 100yds* **10/1**
0044 **6** *1/2* **Just Joey**[8] 3677 5-8-13 **49** .... (be) DarryllHolland 12 49
(J R Weymes) *dwlt: sn in midfield: rdn and styd on same pce fnl 2f: no imp* **6/1**
6033 **7** *nse* **Diane's Choice**[7] 3720 6-9-4 **54** .... (v) DaneO'Neill 8 54
(Miss Gay Kelleway) *dwlt and n.m.r s: sn in tch: drvn to chal over 1f out: wknd fnl f* **11/4**[1]
640 **8** *2 3/4* **Sandy Par**[36] 2758 4-9-4 **54** .... (b) HayleyTurner 1 44
(J M Bradley) *led tl wknd over 1f out: hung lft: 6th and btn whn squeezed 100yds out* **11/1**
0005 **9** *2* **Mr Loire**[8] 3673 5-8-6 **47** ow2 .... (b) MarkCoumbe(5) 3 30
(A J Chamberlain) *s.s: outpcd: a bhd* **33/1**
-000 **10** *1/2* **Walragnek**[32] 2879 5-9-0 **50** .... (b[1]) RobertHavlin 6 31
(J G M O'Shea) *dwlt: towards rr: sltly hmpd after 100yds: hrd rdn and n.d fnl 2f* **16/1**

63.38 secs (1.08) **Going Correction** +0.05s/f (Good)
WFA 3 from 4yo+ 5lb — **10** Ran SP% **119.8**
Speed ratings (Par 101): **93,92,91,91,90 89,89,85,82,81**PL: Lithaam £1/00 Tricky Trev £1.20TRI:Joss Stick/Lily Jicaro/Lithaam £352.83 Joss Stick/Lily Jicaro/Tricky Trev £303.83toteswingers: 1&2 £7.60, Joss Stick&Lithaam £3.80Lily Jicaro&Lithaam £11.30,Joss Stick&Tricky Trev £2.20, Lily Jicaro&Tricky Trev £9.4027 CSF £Owner CT £Gayler William Chambers TOTE £Bred: £K W Green, £Trained, £Liphook, Hants.
■ Stewards' Enquiry : David Probert one-day ban: careless riding (Jul 28)

FOCUS
A moderate sprint handicap and the form looks dubious with little solid.
Diane's Choice Official explanation: jockey said mare suffered interference at the start

3948 MATTHEW CLARK WINES (S) STKS — 6f 209y
4:30 (4:31) (Class 6) 3-Y-0+ **£1,942** (£578; £288; £144) **Stalls** Low

Form | | | | RPR
-000 **1** **Goodbye Cash (IRE)**[34] 2812 5-9-4 47 .... PaulDoe 9 58
(P D Evans) *prom: led over 2f out: hrd rdn: hld on wl* **16/1**
6342 **2** *1 3/4* **Duke Of Milan (IRE)**[6] 3732 6-9-4 60 .... (v) RichardSmith 6 53
(Tom Dascombe) *hld up in rr: hdwy 2f out: chsd wnr over 1f out: nt qckn fnl f* **13/8**[1]
5414 **3** *2 1/4* **Landucci**[21] 3242 8-9-9 62 .... (p) DaneO'Neill 1 52
(S Curran) *trckd ldrs: hrd rdn rdn over 1f out: one pce* **5/2**[2]
540 **4** *1 1/2* **Fun In The Sun**[35] 2794 5-9-9 54 .... FergusSweeney 2 48
(A B Haynes) *bhd: rdn over 2f out: styd on to take modest 4th 1f out* **16/1**
3550 **5** *1 3/4* **Geoffdaw**[8] 3691 4-8-13 63 .... (v) RichardEvans(5) 5 38
(P D Evans) *t.k.h: prom: outpcd and losing pl whn hmpd 2f out: kpt on again fnl f* **4/1**[3]
0000 **6** *3 3/4* **The Jailer**[32] 2876 6-8-8 45 .... (v) MCGeran(5) 8 23
(J G M O'Shea) *led tl over 2f out: wknd wl over 1f out* **25/1**
1006 **7** *shd* **Straight Face (IRE)**[7] 3717 5-9-9 52 .... (b) DarryllHolland 7 33
(Miss Gay Kelleway) *hld up in 6th: swtchd alone to centre over 2f out: sn rdn and btn: wkng whn hung lft over 1f out* **11/1**
0160 **8** *nk* **Straitjacket**[19] 3302 3-8-10 53 .... (p) PaulFitzsimons 3 27
(Miss J R Tooth) *hld up in 5th: rdn 3f out: wknd 2f out* **16/1**

1m 23.26s (0.16) **Going Correction** +0.05s/f (Good)
WFA 3 from 4yo+ 8lb — **8** Ran SP% **116.5**
Speed ratings (Par 101): **101,99,96,94,92 88,88,87**
toteswingers: 1&2 £6.80, 1&3 £7.80, 2&3 £1.80 CSF £43.42 TOTE £19.70: £3.70, £1.20, £1.20; EX 60.20 Trifecta £148.30 Pool: £332.71 - 1.66 winning units..The winner was bought in for 2,900gns.
Owner Mrs I M Folkes **Bred** Mrs A C Peters **Trained** Pandy, Monmouths
■ Stewards' Enquiry : M C Geran one-day ban: failed to keep straight from stalls (July 30)

FOCUS
An ordinary seller and little solid or reliable form to go on. The main action took place towards the far side of the track.

3949 IT FIRST H'CAP — 1m 1f 209y
5:00 (5:02) (Class 6) (0-60,66) 3-Y-0+ **£2,590** (£770; £385; £192) **Stalls** High

Form | | | | RPR
3100 **1** **Megalala (IRE)**[4] 3811 8-9-13 **60** .... NeilChalmers 2 68
(J J Bridger) *mde all: drvn along and hld on gamely fnl 2f* **14/1**
-001 **2** *nk* **Arcola (IRE)**[9] 3661 3-9-8 **66** 6ex .... JamieSpencer 5 74+
(D M Simcock) *hld up in rr of midfield: nt clr run over 2f out: gd hdwy over 1f out: drvn to chal fnl f: nt qckn fnl 75yds* **7/4**[1]
4044 **3** *2* **Corrib (IRE)**[13] 3503 6-9-0 **47** .... TonyCulhane 13 51
(B Palling) *chsd ldrs: rdn to chal 2f out: one pce fnl f* **12/1**
1035 **4** *1 3/4* **Primo Dilettante**[13] 3511 3-8-11 **58** .... DavidProbert(3) 8 58
(W J Knight) *prom: rdn to chal 2f out: no ex fnl f* **10/1**
1411 **5** *hd* **Goose Green (IRE)**[8] 3675 5-10-3 **64** 6ex .... DarryllHolland 6 64+
(R J Hodges) *hld up in rr: rdn and styd on fnl 2f: nvr nrr* **4/1**[2]
-435 **6** *3 1/2* **Daring Racer (GER)**[12] 3525 6-9-6 **53** .... (p) IanMongan 1 46
(Mrs L J Mongan) *prom: drvn along 2f out: wknd over 1f out* **12/1**
0-05 **7** *3/4* **Classic Blue (IRE)**[10] 3631 5-9-0 **47** .... (t) PaulEddery 7 38
(Ian Williams) *hld up in midfield: hdwy to chal 2f out: wknd fnl f: eased whn wl btn* **16/1**
0534 **8** *hd* **Astrolibra**[14] 3475 5-9-7 **54** .... GeorgeBaker 12 45
(M H Tompkins) *bhd: drvn along and sme hdwy over 2f out: no further prog* **5/1**[3]
0000 **9** *3 1/2* **Space Pirate**[24] 3158 4-8-13 **46** oh1 .... (v) RobertHavlin 14 30
(J Pearce) *s.s: bhd: sme hdwy into midfield 4f out: rdn 3f out: sn outpcd* **33/1**
06-0 **10** *1/2* **Evianne**[13] 3501 5-8-13 **46** oh1 .... HayleyTurner 4 29
(P W Hiatt) *chsd ldrs tl wknd 3f out* **66/1**
0-40 **11** *2 1/2* **Personify**[13] 3503 7-8-11 **47** .... (p) KevinGhunowa(3) 9 25
(J L Flint) *hld up in 6th: promising effrt and pressed ldrs 3f out: hrd rdn and wknd 2f out* **20/1**
0-05 **12** *18* **Bermacha**[37] 2746 4-9-6 **56** .... NataliaGemelova(3) 3 —
(J E Long) *plld hrd in last: n.d fnl 3f: eased whn no ch fnl 2f* **33/1**

2m 3.79s (0.19) **Going Correction** +0.05s/f (Good)
WFA 3 from 4yo+ 11lb — **12** Ran SP% **122.2**
Speed ratings (Par 101): **101,100,99,97,97 94,94,94,91,90 88,74**
toteswingers: 1&2 £9.30, 1&3 £26.20, 2&3 £7.50 CSF £38.87 CT £328.07 TOTE £17.20: £4.20, £1.60, £4.60; EX 67.10 TRIFECTA Not won..
Owner Tommy Ware **Bred** Joseph Gallagher **Trained** Liphook, Hants

FOCUS
A moderate handicap run at a steady pace but the form looks sound rated around the three immediately behind the winner. The main action took place towards the far side in the straight.
Bermacha Official explanation: trainer said filly was unsuited by the good to firm ground

3950 ABI ISMAIL CCI RETIREMENT APPRENTICE H'CAP 1m 3f 196y
5:30 (5:30) (Class 6) (0-65,64) 4-Y-O+ £2,590 (£770; £385; £192) Stalls High

Form RPR
0124 1 **Penang Cinta**[5] 3766 6-9-4 61 RichardEvans(3) 5 71
(P D Evans) *prom: pressed ldr fr 1/2-way: drvn to ld ins fnl f* 11/4[1]
-011 2 ½ **Sagunt (GER)**[36] 2762 6-9-9 63 JackMitchell 6 72
(S Curran) *led and restrained in front: set steady pce: qcknd over 3f out: hrd rdn and hdd ins fnl f: kpt on* 4/1[2]
1223 3 1 ¼ **Jafaru**[21] 3244 5-8-11 56 (b) JemmaMarshall(5) 1 63
(G L Moore) *dwlt: t.k.h: sn in tch: pressed ldrs 1/2-way: outpcd over 1f out: styd on nr fin* 4/1[2]
2006 4 1 **Turner's Touch**[22] 3223 7-8-2 49 (b) HarryBentley(7) 3 54
(G L Moore) *s.s: hld up in rr: hmpd 5f out: hdwy to chse ldrs on rail over 2f out and nvr much room after: kidded along: hld whn hmpd fnl 100yds* 25/1
2023 5 4 ½ **Strike Force**[15] 3450 5-8-12 59 SPRyan(7) 2 57
(Miss J Feilden) *hld up in 5th: effrt 3f out: outpcd fnl 2f* 4/1[2]
4P-0 6 ¾ **Bundle Up**[40] 6-8-4 47 JackDean(3) 7 44
(J L Flint) *hld up in rr: drvn along 4f out: btn over 2f out* 13/2[3]
5204 7 ¾ **Star Choice**[29] 2975 4-9-5 64 (v) SimonPearce(5) 4 60
(J Pearce) *chsd ldrs: rdn and outpcd over 3f out: sn struggling in rr* 8/1
2m 36.34s (3.64) **Going Correction** +0.05s/f (Good) 7 Ran SP% **115.0**
Speed ratings (Par 101): **89,88,87,87,84 83,83**
toteswingers: 1&2 £2.80, 1&3 £3.10, 2&3 £2.90 CSF £14.13 TOTE £3.90: £1.90, £2.10; EX 15.80 Place 6: £ 27.75 Place 5: £23.34.
Owner Trevor Gallienne **Bred** Mrs A K H Ooi **Trained** Pandy, Monmouths
■ Stewards' Enquiry : Richard Evans one-day ban: excessive use of the whip (Jul 28)
FOCUS
A modest handicap for apprentice riders who had not ridden more than 50 winners. The pace was steady, the main action took place far side in the straight and the form looks muddling.
T/Plt: £27.90 to a £1 stake. Pool: £69,248.59. 1,809.03 winning tickets. T/Qpdt: £13.90 to a £1 stake. Pool: £4,514.92. 239.65 winning tickets. LM

3709 SOUTHWELL (L-H)
Tuesday, July 14

OFFICIAL GOING: Standard
Wind: Light across Weather: Showers

3951 VICTOR CHANDLER & NOTTINGHAM FOREST FC MAIDEN FILLIES' STKS 1m 4f (F)
6:40 (6:40) (Class 5) 3-Y-O+ £3,885 (£1,156; £577; £288) Stalls Low

Form RPR
022- 1 **Choral Festival**[315] 5590 3-8-12 73 SebSanders 6 73+
(Sir Mark Prescott) *hld up in tch: led over 3f out: hung lft wl over 1f out: sn rdn: hung rt wl ins fnl f: styd on* 7/4[2]
5-2 2 1 **Blue Nymph**[13] 3508 3-8-12 0 PaulHanagan 5 71+
(R M Beckett) *chsd ldrs: led over 3f out: sn rdn and hdd: hmpd wl over 1f out: styd on* 11/10[1]
45 3 2 ¾ **Jabroot (IRE)**[30] 2943 3-8-12 0 PhilipRobinson 7 67
(M A Jarvis) *s.s: hld up: hdwy over 3f out: sn rdn: no imp fnl f* 4/1[3]
05 4 6 **Strategic Princess (IRE)**[21] 3250 3-8-12 0 JosedeSouza 1 57
(P F I Cole) *s.i.s: sn chsng ldrs: led over 9f out: rdn and hdd over 3f out: wknd over 2f out* 20/1
-00 5 1 **Lady Oaksey**[50] 2323 3-8-12 0 FrankieMcDonald 3 55?
(W S Kittow) *led: hdd over 9f out: chsd ldr tl rdn 4f out: wknd 3f out* 100/1
6 43 **Bandeau Charmer**[404] 6-9-6 0 ByronMoorcroft(5) 2 —
(C N Kellett) *sn outpcd: bhd fr 1/2-way: t.o* 100/1
0 7 1 ¼ **Yanbu (USA)**[47] 2416 4-9-11 0 JamieMackay 4 —
(R W Price) *prom: racd keenly: rdn over 4f out: wknd over 3f out* 100/1
2m 41.32s (0.32) **Going Correction** 0.0s/f (Stan)
WFA 3 from 4yo+ 13lb 7 Ran SP% **111.7**
Speed ratings (Par 100): **98,97,95,91,90 62,61**
toteswingers: 1&2 £1.02, 1&3 £1.10, 2&3 £2.00 CSF £3.82 TOTE £3.20: £1.50, £1.20; EX 4.40.
Owner Cheveley Park Stud **Bred** Cheveley Park Stud Ltd **Trained** Newmarket, Suffolk
FOCUS
The going was standard and the opening event was quite a decent fillies' maiden for the track. The first three in the market pulled a long way clear of the rest, the first two set a good standard and the form could work out.

3952 BEST ODDS GUARANTEED @ VICTOR CHANDLER NURSERY 5f (F)
7:10 (7:10) (Class 6) 2-Y-O £2,729 (£806; £403) Stalls High

Form RPR
5651 1 **Mahiki**[7] 3709 2-8-12 69 6ex JamieKyne(5) 7 71
(S A Callaghan) *chsd ldrs: led over 1f out: sn rdn: edgd lft ins fnl f: all out* 3/1[1]
0145 2 shd **Lucky Mellor**[41] 2599 2-9-4 69 SebSanders 5 72
(D K Ivory) *led: rdn and hdd over 1f out: rallied and carried lft ins fnl f: r.o* 3/1[1]
3200 3 2 ¾ **Mr Smithson (IRE)**[3] 3871 2-9-7 72 TomEaves 3 65
(B Ellison) *sn pushed along in rr: hdwy u.p over 1f out: no imp ins fnl f* 9/2[2]
6664 4 hd **Rightcar**[6] 3742 2-8-6 57 PatrickMathers 4 49
(Peter Grayson) *chsd ldrs: rdn 3f out: styd on same pce appr fnl f* 12/1
0004 5 8 **Camacho Flyer (IRE)**[15] 3446 2-8-5 63 (p) PaulPickard(7) 1 27
(P T Midgley) *chsd ldrs: rdn 1/2-way: wknd over 1f out* 9/2[2]
4405 6 2 ¾ **Mind The Monarch**[22] 3210 2-9-1 66 JimmyQuinn 6 20
(R A Teal) *prom: rdn over 3f out: wknd 2f out* 14/1
000 7 1 **Countrywide Ice (IRE)**[50] 2339 2-8-1 52 (b[1]) PaulHanagan 2 —
(K A Ryan) *hung lft sn after s: rel to r: a wl bhd* 13/2[3]
60.59 secs (0.89) **Going Correction** 0.0s/f (Stan) 7 Ran SP% **114.1**
Speed ratings (Par 92): **92,91,87,87,74 69,68**
toteswingers: 1&2 £2.10, 1&3 £4.40, 2&3 £1.80 CSF £11.93 TOTE £3.10: £1.10, £2.30; EX 8.40.
Owner The Mahiki Partnership **Bred** Whatton Manor Stud **Trained** Newmarket, Suffolk
■ Stewards' Enquiry : Jamie Kyne one-day ban: careless riding (Jul 30)
FOCUS
A modest nursery, involving several fairly exposed types. The first two had a sustained duel and nothing got into it from behind, so they set the level. The 'official' ratings shown next to each horse are estimated and for information purposes only.

NOTEBOOK
Mahiki was bought in for 9,500gns after comfortably cashing in on the drop to selling company over course and distance seven days earlier. She had more to do on her nursery debut under a penalty, but travelled smoothly and showed some fighting spirit to repel the persistent runner-up. She seems to have a good cruising speed for this grade and has struck up an excellent partnership with Jamie Kyne. She will go up for this success, but should be able to win more races and looks highly effective on this surface. (op 100-30 tchd 7-2)
Lucky Mellor could not quite land a gamble, but deserves plenty of credit for a feisty display. He ruined his chance by hanging and pulling hard when faced with tough tasks in novice stakes events on his last two runs, but bounced back to form at the scene of his auction maiden win in May. (op 6-1 tchd 13-2 and 11-4)
Mr Smithson(IRE) got detached and looked reluctant with a visor tried at York on Saturday. He put in a much better effort with the headgear discarded on his all-weather debut, but carried his head awkwardly in the closing stages and could continue to be vulnerable off a prohibitive looking mark. (op 4-1 tchd 7-2)
Rightcar did well to finish fourth when 6lb out of the weights and forced to race wide in a 5f nursery on Polytrack last week. He was never really a factor here back off his correct rating switched to Fibresand. (op 7-1)
Countrywide Ice(IRE) put in a particularly quirky display in first-time blinkers, veering sharply to the left exiting the stalls and showing little enthusiasm to try and claw back the deficit. Official explanation: jockey said gelding hung left badly at the start (op 6-1 tchd 5-1 and 7-1)

3953 NEW WEBSITE @ VICTORCHANDLER.COM CLAIMING STKS 6f (F)
7:40 (7:40) (Class 6) 3-Y-O £2,266 (£674; £337; £168) Stalls Low

Form RPR
50 1 **Kinigi (IRE)**[16] 3426 3-7-10 55 ow3 AndrewHeffernan(7) 6 59
(R A Harris) *s.i.s: sn prom: led 2f out: rdn and edgd lft ins fnl f: hung rt nr fin: jst hld on* 33/1
5151 2 hd **Swiss Art (IRE)**[7] 3711 3-8-7 70 SilvestreDeSousa 7 62
(Mrs R A Carr) *prom: pushed along over 4f out: rdn to chse wnr over 1f out: styd on u.p* 5/6[1]
3410 3 3 ¼ **Pepin (IRE)**[11] 3580 3-8-6 56 FrankieMcDonald 4 51
(D Haydn Jones) *w ldr: plld hrd: ev ch 2f out: sn rdn: styd on same pce fnl f* 15/2[3]
600- 4 hd **Coconut Shy**[256] 7107 3-8-9 85 (t) AdrianMcCarthy 3 53
(G Prodromou) *dwlt: hld up: hdwy over 2f out: rdn over 1f out: styd on same pce fnl f* 4/1[2]
0604 5 1 **Wicklewood**[7] 3711 3-8-8 45 (v[1]) TGMcLaughlin 2 49?
(Mrs C A Dunnett) *sn pushed along in rr: bhd 1/2-way: r.o ins fnl f: nrst fin* 20/1
-000 6 3 ½ **Daisy Moses (IRE)**[22] 3225 3-8-5 65 AdrianTNicholls 1 35
(D Nicholls) *led: plld hrd: hdd 2f out: sn rdn and wknd* 15/2[3]
066 7 13 **Cool Art (IRE)**[16] 3428 3-8-8 70 (b) PatrickMathers 5 —
(Peter Grayson) *chsd ldrs: rdn 1/2-way: wknd over 2f out* 14/1
1m 16.69s (0.19) **Going Correction** 0.0s/f (Stan) 7 Ran SP% **112.5**
Speed ratings (Par 98): **98,97,93,93,91 87,69**
toteswingers: 1&2 £3.90, 1&3 not won, 2&3 £5.80 CSF £59.99 TOTE £61.60: £6.70, £1.90; EX 71.10.Swiss Art was the subject of a friendly claim.
Owner Brian Hicks **Bred** Corduff Stud **Trained** Earlswood, Monmouths
FOCUS
A decent claimer, but there was a surprise winner which suggests the form is pretty weak.
Kinigi(IRE) Official explanation: trainer said, regarding the apparent improvement in form shown, that the filly appeared suited by her return to racing on fibresand
Coconut Shy Official explanation: jockey said filly was affected by the kickback
Cool Art(IRE) Official explanation: jockey said gelding lost its action

3954 BEST ODDS GUARANTEED @ VICTORCHANDLER.COM H'CAP 1m 6f (F)
8:10 (8:10) (Class 5) (0-70,68) 3-Y-O
£2,492 (£746; £373; £186; £93; £46) Stalls Low

Form RPR
0-33 1 **Astroleo**[11] 3561 3-8-2 49 oh1 NickyMackay 6 54
(M H Tompkins) *prom: rdn over 4f out: chsd clr ldr 3f out: led over 1f out: hung rt ins fnl f: styd on* 5/4[1]
-035 2 1 ¼ **Oke Bay**[32] 2881 3-8-8 55 ow1 (v) SebSanders 1 58
(R M Beckett) *sn pushed along and prom: led over 10f out: clr 3f out: rdn and hdd over 1f out: carried rt ins fnl f: styng on same pce whn hmpd towards fin* 4/1[2]
4000 3 2 ¾ **Blue Tango (IRE)**[11] 3575 3-9-7 68 PaulHanagan 4 67
(Mrs A J Perrett) *hld up: hdwy 8f out: drvn to chse ldr briefly over 3f out: cl enough over 1f out: no ex ins fnl f* 4/1[2]
0-04 4 20 **Just Dan**[11] 3588 3-8-5 52 ow2 GrahamGibbons 8 23
(R Hollinshead) *prom: rdn 6f out: wknd over 3f out: t.o* 12/1
0035 5 5 **Nut Hand (IRE)**[15] 3454 3-8-5 52 DaleGibson 3 16
(T D Easterby) *led: hdd over 10f out: chsd ldr: rdn over 4f out: wknd over 3f out* 9/2[3]
3-00 6 57 **Fire Me Gun**[148] 570 3-8-2 49 oh2 DuranFentiman 5 —
(M Mullineaux) *sn outpcd: t.o fnl 8f* 40/1
5600 7 3 **Diktaram**[24] 3157 3-7-12 50 oh4 ow1 (v[1]) JamieKyne(5) 2 —
(J R Weymes) *in tch: pushed along 10f out: sn lost tch: t.o fnl 8f* 33/1
3m 9.68s (1.38) **Going Correction** 0.0s/f (Stan) 7 Ran SP% **115.7**
Speed ratings (Par 100): **96,95,93,82,79 46,45**
toteswingers: 1&2 £1.10, 1&3 £5.30, 2&3 £1.80 CSF £6.79 CT £15.35 TOTE £2.00: £1.10, £4.30; EX 7.50.
Owner Mystic Meg Limited **Bred** Mystic Meg Limited **Trained** Newmarket, Suffolk
FOCUS
A modest handicap run during a heavy downpour. There was a slow-motion finish and the first three were miles clear of the rest. the placed horses are to their dubious recent form.

3955 VICTORCHANDLER.COM/FOREST H'CAP 1m (F)
8:40 (8:42) (Class 5) (0-70,66) 3-Y-O £3,432 (£1,021; £510; £254) Stalls Low

Form RPR
0004 1 **Uncle Brit**[74] 1656 3-9-2 61 SebSanders 6 71+
(Sir Mark Prescott) *chsd ldrs: reminders 6f out: rdn over 3f out: led over 1f out: idled ins fnl f: edgd lft nr fin* 9/4[2]
1006 2 ¾ **Echo Dancer**[27] 3026 3-9-7 66 RobertWinston 1 74
(S A Callaghan) *sn pushed along and prom: jnd ldr over 4f out: led 3f out: rdn and hdd over 1f out: styd on* 4/1[3]
2012 3 nse **Iron Out (USA)**[7] 3711 3-9-6 65 MickyFenton 2 73
(R Hollinshead) *led 5f: led again over 1f out: sn hdd: styd on same pce ins fnl f* 13/8[1]
6005 4 11 **Highly Acclaimed**[42] 2579 3-8-9 54 SilvestreDeSousa 4 37
(Mrs A Duffield) *prom: rdn over 3f out: wknd 2f out* 8/1
0420 5 ¾ **Nchike**[12] 3541 3-9-3 62 (v) AdrianTNicholls 7 43
(D Nicholls) *prom: rdn over 4f out: wknd over 3f out* 14/1
04-0 6 7 **Miss Perfectionist**[19] 3299 3-9-6 65 JimmyQuinn 8 30
(P Howling) *hld up: sme hdwy over 2f out: sn wknd* 33/1

6-00 **7** *5* **Inside Knowledge (USA)**[66] 1882 3-8-8 **53**...............(p) PaulHanagan 5 6
(G Woodward) *chsd ldrs tl rdn and wknd over 3f out* **22/1**
460 **8** *hd* **Nimmy's Special**[49] 2357 3-8-9 **54**.................. DuranFentiman 3 7
(M Mullineaux) *s.i.s: outpcd* **50/1**
1m 42.82s (-0.88) **Going Correction** 0.0s/f (Stan) **8** Ran SP% **115.9**
Speed ratings (Par 100): **104,103,103,92,91 84,79,79**
toteswingers: 1&2 £1.50, 1&3 £3.30, 2&3 £1.50 CSF £11.72 CT £17.68 TOTE £3.00: £1.40, £1.10, £1.40; EX 11.80.
Owner P J D Pottinger **Bred** Heather Raw **Trained** Newmarket, Suffolk

FOCUS
They went a fair pace in this modest handicap and the first three in the market powered a long way clear of the rest. The form looks solid and the winner could be a progressive type.

3956 VICTOR CHANDLER SPONSORS OF NOTTINGHAM FOREST FC H'CAP 6f (F)
9:10 (9:11) (Class 4) (0-85,85) 3-Y-0+ **£5,180** (£1,541; £770; £384) **Stalls** Low

Form RPR
020 **1** **Luscivious**[36] 2770 5-9-6 **78**..........................(p) GrahamGibbons 7 91+
(J A Glover) *sn chsng ldrs: led over 4f out: rdn clr fnl f: eased towards fin* **25/1**
0-20 **2** *2 1/4* **Hits Only Jude (IRE)**[31] 2938 6-9-0 **72**.................... DNolan 6 78
(D Carroll) *chsd ldrs: rdn over 2f out: styd on same pce fnl f* **12/1**
0100 **3** *2 1/2* **Calmdownmate (IRE)**[17] 3377 4-9-1 **73**............... PaulMulrennan 13 71+
(Mrs R A Carr) *chsd ldrs: rdn over 2f out: edgd lft and no ex fnl f* **10/1**
/21- **4** *shd* **Choiseau (IRE)**[397] 2981 4-9-10 **82**..................... PaulHanagan 1 80+
(Pat Eddery) *prom: outpcd over 3f out: r.o ins fnl f* **8/1**
-200 **5** *1 1/4* **Charles Parnell (IRE)**[18] 3354 6-9-10 **82**................ DaleGibson 3 76
(M Dods) *mid-div: drvn along 1/2-way: no imp fnl f* **16/1**
0-00 **6** *hd* **Northern Bolt**[4] 3828 4-9-3 **75**........................ AdrianTNicholls 11 68
(D Nicholls) *led: hdd over 4f out: rdn over 2f out: wknd ins fnl f* **18/1**
2603 **7** *1* **Ingleby Arch (USA)**[18] 3354 6-9-10 **85**.................. NeilBrown(3) 2 75
(T D Barron) *hld up: hdwy and nt clr run over 1f out: nvr nrr* **11/2**[3]
1453 **8** *1/2* **Imprimis Tagula (IRE)**[13] 3497 5-9-3 **80**..............(v) LeeNewnes(5) 8 68
(A Bailey) *chsd ldrs: rdn over 2f out: edgd rt and wknd over 1f out* **9/2**[1]
300 **9** *3 1/4* **Don Pele (IRE)**[8] 3691 7-8-12 **70**.....................(p) RobertWinston 9 48
(R A Harris) *prom: rdn 1/2-way: wknd over 1f out* **20/1**
5015 **10** *3/4* **Silent Hero**[22] 3220 3-9-4 **82**........................ PhilipRobinson 12 56+
(M A Jarvis) *dwlt: outpcd: rdn and swtchd lft 2f out: n.d* **5/1**[2]
-004 **11** *3/4* **Hanoverian Baron**[15] 3467 4-9-6 **78**....................(b[1]) FrancisNorton 5 51
(D Nicholls) *sn drvn along: a in rr* **25/1**
3025 **12** *7* **Harlech Castle**[18] 3347 4-9-5 **84**..................... DTDaSilva(7) 10 35
(P F I Cole) *unruly in stalls: sn outpcd* **16/1**
-050 **13** *2 1/2* **Cool Sands (IRE)**[29] 2964 7-8-10 **68**....................(v) J-PGuillambert 4 11
(J G Given) *sn outpcd* **12/1**
1156 **14** *1 3/4* **All The Nines (IRE)**[15] 3453 3-9-4 **82**.................. SebSanders 14 19
(Mrs D J Sanderson) *prom: rdn 1/2-way: wknd 2f out* **9/1**
1m 14.78s (-1.72) **Going Correction** 0.0s/f (Stan)
WFA 3 from 4yo+ 6lb **14** Ran SP% **125.3**
Speed ratings (Par 105): **111,108,104,104,102 102,101,100,96,95 94,84,81,79**
toteswingers: 1&2 not won, 1&3 not won, 2&3 £37.20 CSF £305.22 CT £3283.53 TOTE £26.10: £4.80, £5.60, £4.70; EX 262.30 Place 6 £29.48, Place 5 £25.92.
Owner Paul J Dixon **Bred** R J Turner **Trained** Babworth, Notts
■ Stewards' Enquiry : D T Da Silva two-day ban: careless riding (Jul 28, 30)

FOCUS
A decent handicap run at a furious pace with the runner-up setting the level. The field avoided the far rail and raced towards the centre to stands' side.
Silent Hero Official explanation: jockey said gelding was outpaced throughout
Hanoverian Baron Official explanation: jockey said gelding suffered interference at the start
T/Plt: £50.20 to a £1 stake. Pool: £55,059.33. 799.89 winning tickets. T/Qpdt: £45.30 to a £1 stake. Pool: £4,683.96. 76.40 winning tickets. CR

[3546]YARMOUTH (L-H)
Tuesday, July 14

OFFICIAL GOING: Soft
Wind: Almost nil Weather: hot and sunny after torrential downpours before racing

3957 EBF TOTEPLACEPOT MAIDEN STKS 7f 3y
6:20 (6:22) (Class 5) 2-Y-0 **£3,784** (£1,132; £566; £283; £141) **Stalls** High

Form RPR
4 **1** **Nideeb**[17] 3395 2-9-3 0.. KShea 2 88+
(C E Brittain) *sn trcking ldr: led wl over 1f out: pushed clr fnl f: easily* **4/1**[2]
5 **2** *5* **Lowdown (IRE)**[17] 3392 2-9-3 0.......................... RoystonFfrench 1 73
(M Johnston) *led and abt 2 l clr: hdd wl over 1f out w rest floundering: rdn and one pce after* **11/2**
3 *2 1/2* **Akula (IRE)** 2-9-3 0.. LiamJones 6 66+
(M H Tompkins) *midfield: outpcd over 2f out: tk poor 3rd wl ins fnl f* **66/1**
4 *1 3/4* **Dr Finley (IRE)** 2-9-3 0.................................. PatCosgrave 3 62
(M L W Bell) *drvn along 1/2-way: chsd ldrs: outpcd in mod 3rd 2f out: lost 3rd wl ins fnl f* **20/1**
0 **5** *7* **Rezwaan**[20] 3270 2-9-3 0.................................. TPO'Shea 7 44
(E A L Dunlop) *rdn fr 1/2-way: struggling over 2f out* **33/1**
4 **6** *2 1/2* **Kavak**[24] 3167 2-9-3 0.................................. JerryO'Dwyer 9 38
(M Botti) *pressed ldng pair tl fdd over 2f out* **5/1**
0 **7** *3 1/2* **Seamster**[12] 3546 2-9-3 0.................................. TedDurcan 10 29
(Saeed Bin Suroor) *labouring in rr after 3f: eased fnl f* **9/2**[3]
8 *3 1/2* **Notice Given** 2-9-3 0.................................. TPQueally 5 21
(H R A Cecil) *rn green and sn pushed along: nvr gng wl: struggling wl over 2f out* **9/4**[1]
00 **9** *9* **Dunwhinny**[7] 3715 2-9-3 0.................................. ShaneKelly 8 —
(P W D'Arcy) *last away: nvr gng pce: eased fnl f: t.o* **100/1**
00 **10** *2* **Rufus Roughcut**[18] 3344 2-9-3 0.......................... SaleemGolam 4 —
(S C Williams) *cl up tl 1/2-way: sn dropped out: eased fnl f: t.o* **100/1**
(-86.60) 2y crse rec **10** Ran SP% **112.2**
toteswingers: 1&2 £5.40, 1&3 not won, 2&3 not won. CSF £24.13 TOTE £5.40: £1.60, £1.60, £10.60; EX 29.10.
Owner Saeed Manana **Bred** Rabbah Bloodstock Limited **Trained** Newmarket, Suffolk

FOCUS
The course elected to water the final 7f in the home straight, so after enduring 20mm of rain in an unexpected mid-afternoon downpour it was unsurprisingly changed to soft before the opener. This looked an interesting juvenile maiden, but the exaggerated beaten distances strongly suggests few managed to handle the ground and that the form is suspect, despite the winner having progressed from his debut.

NOTEBOOK
Nideeb ran distinctly green in a fair maiden at Newmarket on his debut 17 days earlier on easy ground. He handled the surface better than the rest here, but has come on since his initial run and looks a horse of potential. His trainer is enjoying a great season with his juveniles and this close relation to Warrsan looks one to follow. (tchd 7-2)
Lowdown(IRE), fifth on his debut at Newcastle, had market support and was again given a positive ride. He was a sitting duck for the winner from the 2f pole and did not look particularly happy on the ground, so this rates an improved effort. He would not mind a drop back to 6f in the short term and can find a race when racing on a sounder surface. (op 8-1 tchd 5-1)
Akula(IRE), whose dam is a half-sister to Eva's Request among others, came home nicely after taking time to get the hang of things and looks sure to come on a bundle for the experience. (tchd 80-1)
Dr Finley(IRE) is a half-brother to two winners at up to 1m1f and was not obviously fancied for this debut. He ran a similar race to the third and it would be little surprise to see him get closer with the run under his belt. (op 33-1)
Rezwaan had not shown a lot on his debut at Kempton last month, but this offered a little more hope. He is another who wants better ground and should come into his own when faced with a longer trip.
Kavak was the pick of those with previous experience after his debut fourth at Newmarket and was a possible improver for the different ground here. He fell in a hole when the race got serious, however. (op 9-2 tchd 11-2)
Seamster looked all at sea on the taxing surface. (op 7-1 tchd 15-2)
Notice Given arrived at the track with a good reputation and holds a Gimcrack entry. As a half-brother to two winning sprinters it was somewhat surprising to see him start off at 7f though and, after running green early on, his supporters knew their fate before halfway. He is no doubt better than this, but needs quicker ground and most probably dropping back a furlong. Official explanation: trainer's rep said, regarding the poor form shown, that the colt was unsuited by the soft ground (op 6-4)

3958 TOTESWINGER (S) NURSERY 7f 3y
6:50 (6:51) (Class 6) 2-Y-0 **£1,942** (£578; £288; £144) **Stalls** High

Form RPR
5333 **1** **Highcliffe Bridge (IRE)**[25] 3119 2-9-0 **52**.............. CatherineGannon 7 53
(P D Evans) *bhd early and pushed along and edging lft: clsd 1/2-way: led wl over 1f out: 2 l clr ins fnl f: racd idly but a holding rival* **3/1**[1]
424 **2** *1/2* **Scilly Breeze**[21] 3232 2-9-6 **58**.............................. LiamJones 3 58
(A M Hales) *cl up: wnt 2nd wl over 1f out: rdn and sustained effrt fnl 100yds: a hld* **4/1**[2]
606 **3** *2 3/4* **Glen Lass**[10] 3605 2-9-5 **57**.................................. TPQueally 6 50
(J S Moore) *chsd ldrs 4f: bdly outpcd and rdn over 2f out: plugged on again to go modest 3rd wl ins fnl f* **9/2**[3]
004 **4** *1 1/4* **Treasury Bond**[25] 3119 2-8-10 **48**...................... RoystonFfrench 2 38
(P T Midgley) *late to paddock and mounted on crse: last and drvn after 2f: clsd 3f out: wl hld fnl f* **13/2**
002 **5** *1 1/4* **Steeley Flyer**[12] 3547 2-9-3 **55**.......................... SaleemGolam 5 42
(P D Evans) *last away after dwling: effrt 1/2-way: wknd over 1f out* **6/1**
433 **6** *1 1/4* **Lairy (IRE)**[48] 2376 2-9-2 **59**.......................... MatthewDavies(5) 4 43
(M F Harris) *t.k.h and sn led: rdn and hdd wl over 1f out: sn btn* **11/2**
4606 **7** *14* **Blue Bond**[13] 3494 2-8-5 **46**.......................(b[1]) KellyHarrison(3) 1 —
(P T Midgley) *late to paddock: t.k.h and racing v awkwardly: w ldrs over 4f: eased and t.o fnl f* **16/1**
ms (-86.60) **7** Ran SP% **112.1**
toteswingers: 1&2 £2.80, 1&3 £3.20, 2&3 £4.30 CSF £14.46 TOTE £4.50: £2.70, £2.90; EX 13.40.The winner was sold to Nick Littmoden for 5,600gns.
Owner Graham George Evans **Bred** R N Auld **Trained** Pandy, Monmouths

FOCUS
A very weak nursery and not a race to be positive about. The 'official' ratings shown next to each horse are estimated and for information purposes only.

NOTEBOOK
Highcliffe Bridge(IRE) shed her maiden tag at the sixth attempt, despite still showing signs of inexperience. She made her move more towards the stands' rail nearing 2f out and was not in any real danger after hitting the front. Her best previous run came on deteriorating ground over course and distance two runs back so soft clearly suits her, and she is value for a little further, but this is obviously her level. (op 5-1)
Scilly Breeze is a touch flattered by his proximity, but best of the rest easily enough. (op 100-30 tchd 3-1 and 9-2)
Glen Lass again went out to her left under pressure, but was doing her best work towards the finish and has one of these in her when becoming more streetwise. (op 5-1 tchd 4-1)
Treasury Bond got behind early on and made some late headway, but never looked like reversing his last-time-out form with the winner on this much softer ground, despite being weighted to do so. (op 7-1 tchd 8-1)
Blue Bond Official explanation: jockey said gelding hung right

3959 TOTEQUADPOT H'CAP 5f 43y
7:20 (7:23) (Class 5) (0-70,62) 3-Y-0+ **£2,719** (£809; £404; £202) **Stalls** High

Form RPR
5502 **1** **Silver Prelude**[41] 2596 8-9-5 **55**..............................(t) KShea 9 66
(S C Williams) *broke fast and mde all: travelled strly and drew clr over 1f out: edgd lft: pushed out: unchal* **4/1**[3]
1662 **2** *1 3/4* **Guto**[7] 3713 6-9-5 **58**..............................(p) KellyHarrison(3) 3 62
(W J H Ratcliffe) *chsd wnr after 2f: rdn and nvr got in a blow fnl 2f* **9/4**[1]
2436 **3** *3/4* **Taboor (IRE)**[134] 727 11-8-12 **48**...................... RoystonFfrench 4 49
(R M H Cowell) *bhd: drvn w no rspnse wl over 2f out: kpt on ins fnl f to snatch 3rd* **10/1**
5520 **4** *shd* **Chantilly Jewel (USA)**[11] 3591 4-9-4 **54**..................(v) PatCosgrave 2 55
(R M H Cowell) *uns rdr gng down: sn urged along: chsd ldrs: drvn 1/2-way: btn wl over 1f out: lost 3rd nr fin* **8/1**
052 **5** *1* **Triple Dream**[21] 3252 4-9-10 **60**..............................(p) TPQueally 5 57
(J M Bradley) *chsd ldrs: rdn 1/2-way: racd awkwardly: btn 2f out* **11/4**[2]
0000 **6** *2* **Gone'N'Dunnett (IRE)**[8] 3677 10-8-9 **45**..................(v) LiamJones 6 35
(Mrs C A Dunnett) *chsd wnr for 2f: rdn and sn struggling* **18/1**
0505 **7** *1/2* **Thumberlina**[9] 3663 3-8-4 **45**..............................(p) CatherineGannon 7 31
(Mrs C A Dunnett) *drvn and struggling fr 1/2-way: plugged on* **8/1**
65.50 secs (3.30) **Going Correction** +0.75s/f (Yiel)
WFA 3 from 4yo+ 5lb **7** Ran SP% **114.0**
Speed ratings (Par 103): **103,100,99,98,97 94,93**
toteswingers: 1&2 £2.00, 1&3 £10.70, 2&3 £3.40 CSF £13.37 CT £81.74 TOTE £3.60: £1.10, £2.20; EX 16.60.
Owner Mrs A Shone **Bred** Bearstone Stud **Trained** Newmarket, Suffolk

FOCUS
This ordinary sprint saw the field congregate down the middle of the track. The winner is rated to his last winning turf mark but there is little solid in behind.

Triple Dream Official explanation: jockey said gelding was unsuited by the soft ground

3960 TOTEEXACTA H'CAP — 1m 1f
7:50 (7:52) (Class 5) (0-70,70) 3-Y-0+ £2,719 (£809; £404; £202) Stalls Low

Form RPR
1300 1 **Becuille (IRE)**[26] 3070 4-9-8 64 ...(b[1]) JimmyFortune 11 73
(B J Meehan) *plld hrd: sn chsng ldr: edging rt whn led up centre of crse 2f out: hdd over 1f out: cajoled to ld again fnl 100yds: all out* **8/1**
3566 2 1 ¼ **Dragon Slayer (IRE)**[10] 3635 7-9-2 58 ... PatCosgrave 9 64
(John A Harris) *bhd: prog over 3f out: led over 1f out: drvn and hdd 100yds out: nt qckn* **9/2**[3]
036 3 3 ¼ **Young Star Gazer**[25] 3120 3-9-2 68 ... TPQueally 10 66
(H R A Cecil) *settled in midfield: effrt 3f out: rdn 2f out: one pce fnl f* **6/1**
33-6 4 ½ **Intikama (IRE)**[33] 2857 3-9-4 70 ... TedDurcan 3 67
(M H Tompkins) *settled in midfield: rdn 2f out: plugged on but n.d fnl f* **8/1**
4400 5 ½ **Bromhead (USA)**[20] 3274 3-8-12 64 ...(t) LiamJones 4 60
(Mrs C A Dunnett) *plld hrd: stdd in midfield after 4f: rdn and outpcd over 2f out: kpt on ins fnl f: no ch* **16/1**
0525 6 1 ¾ **Lord Theo**[4] 3811 5-9-9 65 ... ShaneKelly 8 58
(N P Littmoden) *trckd ldrs: led wl over 2f out: rdn and hdd 2f out: btn over 1f out* **7/2**[1]
0560 7 3 ¼ **Moon Mix (FR)**[79] 1537 6-8-9 51 oh4 ...(v) DO'Donohoe 7 37
(J R Jenkins) *plld hrd in last: n.m.r on ins home turn: clsd gng wl on far rails 2f out: rdn and fnd nil 1f out: fdd tamely* **33/1**
0354 8 hd **Magnitude**[18] 3357 4-9-11 67 ...(p) RoystonFfrench 5 52
(M E Rimmer) *prom: drvn 3f out: sn lost pl* **4/1**[2]
/03- 9 10 **Fly With The Stars (USA)**[62] 7446 4-10-0 70 ... StephenDonohoe 6 33
(A B Haynes) *sn drvn along: in rr and nvr gng wl: struggling in last 4f out: t.o* **33/1**
020- 10 nk **Maximus Aurelius (IRE)**[227] 7494 4-10-0 70 ... LPKeniry 1 33
(J Jay) *led: drvn 3f out: hdd wl over 2f out: wknd qckly: eased and t.o* **16/1**

1m 59.23s (3.43) **Going Correction** +0.275s/f (Good)
WFA 3 from 4yo+ 10lb — 10 Ran SP% **114.6**
Speed ratings (Par 103): **95,93,91,90,90 88,85,85,76,76**
toteswingers: 1&2 £16.80, 1&3 £8.60, 2&3 £3.20 CSF £43.10 CT £196.27 TOTE £10.50: £2.20, £1.70, £2.70; EX 48.70.
Owner Ms Susan McKeon **Bred** Tally-Ho Stud **Trained** Manton, Wilts

FOCUS
A moderate handicap, run at a routine pace and modest form rated around the placed horses..
Lord Theo Official explanation: trainer said gelding was unsuited by the soft ground
Fly With The Stars(USA) Official explanation: trainer said gelding was unsuited by the soft ground

3961 BET TOTEPOOL AT TOTESPORT.COM CLAIMING STKS — 1m 2f 21y
8:20 (8:20) (Class 6) 3-Y-0+ £1,942 (£578; £288; £144) Stalls Low

Form RPR
-100 1 **Invasian (IRE)**[41] 2597 8-9-8 81 ... ShaneKelly 5 87+
(P W D'Arcy) *taken down early: mde all: qcknd clr over 2f out: in n.d after: eased ins fnl f* **9/4**[1]
0330 2 8 **Samurai Warrior**[3] 3864 4-9-6 68 ...(p) StephenDonohoe 6 66
(P D Evans) *a chsng ldr: drvn and completely outpcd 2f out: jst hung on to poor 2nd* **7/2**[3]
5200 3 hd **Khun John (IRE)**[20] 3273 6-9-6 73 ... TPO'Shea 7 66
(W J Musson) *detached in last trio: drvn and effrt up centre 3f out: sn hung lft: wnt 3rd 2f out: grad catching 2nd but nvr anywhere nr wnr* **7/1**
3360 4 5 **Maddy**[14] 3473 4-8-4 46 ...(p) MatthewDavies(5) 4 46
(George Baker) *detached in last trio: drvn 3f out: no ch and hanging lft fnl 2f* **12/1**
1510 5 6 **Polish Power (GER)**[57] 2129 9-9-6 80 ... LPKeniry 8 45
(J S Moore) *settled 3rd and clr of other trio: rdn over 3f out: fdd bdly 2f out: t.o* **11/4**[2]
-000 6 17 **Jacobite Prince (IRE)**[7] 3708 3-8-7 62 ... TedDurcan 1 11
(M H Tompkins) *detached in last trio: t.o over 2f out: eased sn after* **9/1**

2m 11.87s (1.37) **Going Correction** +0.275s/f (Good)
WFA 3 from 4yo+ 11lb — 6 Ran SP% **109.9**
Speed ratings (Par 101): **105,98,98,94,89 76**
toteswingers: 1&2 £2.60, 1&3 £4.00, 2&3 £2.00. CSF £9.91 TOTE £2.80: £2.00, £2.60; EX 11.00.
Owner Paul D'Arcy **Bred** Dr Karen Monica Sanderson **Trained** Newmarket, Suffolk

FOCUS
This was a case of game over after a furlong as confirmed front-runner Invasion got an easy lead and it was apparent 3f out he had his rivals in trouble. The form is rated around the first two.
Polish Power(GER) Official explanation: jockey said horse was never travelling

3962 BET TOTEPOOL ON 0800 221 221 H'CAP — 1m 6f 17y
8:50 (8:50) (Class 5) (0-70,69) 3-Y-0+ £2,719 (£809; £404; £202) Stalls High

Form RPR
0-51 1 **Sparkaway**[15] 3454 3-8-10 54 ... TPO'Shea 6 65+
(W J Musson) *hld up: shkn up and outpcd 4f out tl rallied wl over 1f out: led 1f out: one reminder then hld on wl wout recrse to whip* **7/4**[2]
5-53 2 nk **Dazinski**[18] 3359 3-9-11 69 ... TedDurcan 5 79+
(M H Tompkins) *pressed ldr: urged along 4f out: led wl over 1f out: rdn and hdd 1f out: kpt on for driving but a jst hld* **1/1**[1]
3060 3 8 **Sadaska**[15] 3454 3-8-4 48 ... SaleemGolam 1 47
(S C Williams) *led at dawdle: rdn and hdd wl over 1f out: wknd qckly fnl f* **13/2**[3]
0005 4 1 ½ **Mid Valley**[40] 2634 6-9-2 45 ... DO'Donohoe 3 42
(J R Jenkins) *t.k.h in last: rdn and outpcd over 2f out* **16/1**
0005 5 1 ½ **Flame Creek (IRE)**[5] 3760 13-8-13 45 ... AlanCreighton(3) 7 40
(E J Creighton) *racd enthusiastically in 3rd tl wnt 2nd home turn: chal 3f out: effrt sn petered out: plodded fnl 2f* **28/1**

3m 19.8s (12.20) **Going Correction** +0.275s/f (Good)
WFA 3 from 5yo+ 15lb — 5 Ran SP% **109.0**
Speed ratings (Par 103): **76,75,71,70,69**
toteswingers: 1&2 £3.30 CSF £3.76 TOTE £2.60: £1.50, £1.20; EX 3.90 Place 6 £40.05, Place 5 £9.00..
Owner KCS Partnership **Bred** Jenny Hall Bloodstock Ltd **Trained** Newmarket, Suffolk

FOCUS
This moderate staying handicap was run at a steady gallop until the runners headed into the home turn. The first pair came well clear but the form is limited.
T/Plt: £56.90 to a £1 stake. Pool: £63,278.91. 810.43 winning tickets. T/Qpdt: £9.00 to a £1 stake. Pool: £5,880.90. 480.96 winning tickets. IM

3963 - 3966a (Foreign Racing) - See Raceform Interactive

3230 LONGCHAMP (R-H)
Tuesday, July 14

OFFICIAL GOING: Good to soft

3967a PRIX ROLAND DE CHAMBURE (LISTED RACE) — 7f
5:40 (5:41) 2-Y-O £26,699 (£10,680; £8,010; £5,340; £2,670)

RPR
1 **Colonial (IRE)**[37] 2-8-11 ... MGuyon 4 106+
(A Fabre, France)
2 2 ½ **American Nizzy (FR)**[41] 2-8-8 ... CSoumillon 1 94
(Y De Nicolay, France) **4/1**[1]
3 3 **Foresta (FR)**[9] 2-8-8 ... TJarnet 3 86
(B De Montzey, France)
4 snk **Yushka (FR)**[33] 2-8-8 ... C-PLemaire 5 86
(P Bary, France)
5 ¾ **Ladoga**[27] 3044 2-8-8 ... SPasquier 6 84
(R Gibson, France)
6 1 **Quintalina (FR)**[4] 2-8-8 ...(p) ACrastus 7 82
(C Boutin, France)
7 3 **Barzan (IRE)**[38] 2702 2-8-11 ... RichardKingscote 8 77
(Tom Dascombe) *s.i.s: sn racing in 5th: 6th and pushed along 1/2-way: 6th st: sn rdn and btn (18/1)*

1m 19.8s (-0.90) **Going Correction** -0.10s/f (Good) — 7 Ran SP% **20.0**
Speed ratings: **102,99,95,95,94 93,90**
PARI-MUTUEL: WIN 1.50; PL 1.10, 1.30, 2.50; DF 3.30.
Owner Sheikh Mohammed **Bred** Darley **Trained** Chantilly, France

NOTEBOOK
Barzan(IRE), a winner over 6f on fast ground, had run well enough in the Woodcote but did not get home over the longer trip on the soft ground.

3968a PRIX DE THIBERVILLE (LISTED RACE) (FILLIES) — 1m 4f
6:10 (6:11) 3-Y-O £26,699 (£10,680; £8,010; £5,340; £2,670)

RPR
1 **Shamakiya (IRE)**[16] 3442 3-9-2 ... CSoumillon 7 102
(A De Royer-Dupre, France)
2 snk **Jakonda (USA)**[9] 3668 3-8-12 ... C-PLemaire 10 98
(A De Royer-Dupre, France)
3 3 **Lasting Applause (IRE)**[29] 3-8-12 ... TThulliez 6 93
(F Doumen, France)
4 snk **Irish Queen (FR)**[32] 2989 3-8-12 ... MGuyon 4 93
(H-A Pantall, France)
5 3 **Dubai Rose**[23] 3-8-12 ...(b) DBoeuf 8 88
(H-A Pantall, France)
6 1 ½ **Landskia (FR)**[37] 2754 3-8-12 ... OPeslier 9 86
(A Fabre, France)
7 ½ **Faldal**[54] 2190 3-8-12 ... RichardKingscote 5 85
(Tom Dascombe) *sn cl up: settled in 4th on rail: cl 6th st: nt clr run over 2f out: sn rdn: kpt on one pce (38/1)*
8 ¾ **Palme Royale (IRE)**[41] 2622 3-8-12 ...(p) ACrastus 1 84
(E Lellouche, France)
9 10 **Gainful (USA)**[41] 2622 3-8-12 ... SPasquier 3 68
(D Smaga, France)

2m 30.7s (0.30) **Going Correction** +0.10s/f (Good) — 9 Ran
Speed ratings: **105,104,102,102,100 99,99,98,92**
PARI-MUTUEL: WIN 1.50; PL 1.10, 2.80, 3.50; DF 9.00.
Owner H H Aga Khan **Bred** His Highness The Aga Khan's Studs S C **Trained** Chantilly, France

NOTEBOOK
Faldal, a winner at 1m2f was stepping up in trip and encountering a soft surface for the first time. In mid-division for much of the race, she was outpaced in the straight and never looked like taking a hand in the finish.

3969a PRIX MAURICE DE NIEUIL (GROUP 2) — 1m 6f
6:45 (6:44) 4-Y-O+ £71,942 (£27,767; £13,252; £8,835; £4,417)

RPR
1 **Voila Ici (IRE)**[30] 2955 4-9-2 ... MDemuro 6 114
(V Caruso, Italy) *racd in 3rd: wnt 2nd after 4f: 2nd st: rdn wl over 1f out: led 100yds out: all out* **5/1**[3]
2 shd **Winkle (IRE)**[30] 2955 4-8-8 ... C-PLemaire 5 106
(M Delzangles, France) *2nd for 4f: a wl in tch: 4th st on outside: drvn to chal 150yds out: ev ch: unable qck last strides* **8/1**
3 nk **Shemima**[47] 2428 4-8-12 ... CSoumillon 3 110
(A De Royer-Dupre, France) *hld up in 5th to st: pushed along 2f out: outpcd tl r.o u.str driving in fnl f: tk 3rd in last 50yds* **7/2**[2]
4 1 **Pointilliste (USA)**[58] 2118 6-8-11 ... ACrastus 1 107
(E Lellouche, France) *led: rdn wl over 1f out: hdd 100yds out: no ex and lost 3rd in last 50yds* **2/1**[1]
5 1 ½ **La Boum (GER)**[47] 2428 6-8-8 ... TJarnet 2 102
(Robert Collet, France) *wnt 3rd after 5f: 3rd st on ins: cl 4th 1f out: one pce* **10/1**
6 3 **Bannaby (FR)**[58] 2118 6-9-4 ... JGrosjean 4 108
(M Delcher-Sanchez, Spain) *hld up in rr: last st: kpt on one pce* **7/2**[2]

2m 59.0s (179.00) — 6 Ran SP% **114.6**
PARI-MUTUEL: WIN 7.00; PL 3.30, 4.80; SF 43.70.
Owner Scuderia Incolinx **Bred** Soc Finanza Locale Consulting Srl **Trained** Italy
■ Stewards' Enquiry : M Demuro 200euro fine: whip abuse

NOTEBOOK
Voila Ici(IRE), an Italian-trained colt, put up very brave effort although his jockey was fined for his use of the whip. Always well up and raced in second place for much of the race. He kept on gamely from one and a half out and just managed to repel the challenges in the final few strides. Well suited by the true pace, he may well be aimed at the Prix du Cadran at the end of the year and is not entered in the Arc de Triomphe. Connections may take a look at the Grand Prix de Deauville or the Grand Prix at Baden-Baden.
Winkle(IRE) was again beaten by the Italian winner but she put in a very brave effort and also survived a Steward's enquiry into possible interference in the straight. Settled in fourth position, she quickened from one and a half out battled gamely to the line. She was staying on well at the finish and may well head for the Prix de Pomone at Deauville.
Shemima, given a lot to do, was still one but last in the straight. Her effort began 2f out and she ran on really well throughout the final furlong. Ridden closer to the pace she may well have gone closer, and the most likely plan is for her to come back to this track for the Prix de Lutece in September.

Pointilliste(USA) as usual tried to make every yard of the running and this brave six-year-old stuck to his guns and only began to weaken inside the final furlong. He is a brave individual and connections are now looking at a tilt at the Grosser Preis von Baden.

3970a JUDDMONTE GRAND PRIX DE PARIS (GROUP 1) (C&F) 1m 4f
7:20 (7:20) 3-Y-O £332,854 (£133,165; £66,582; £33,262; £16,660)

RPR

1 **Cavalryman**[43] 2561 3-9-2 .... MGuyon 6 121+
(A Fabre, France) *mid-div: 5th st on outside: drvn to ld 1f out: r.o wl* **4/1**[2]

2 1 ½ **Age Of Aquarius (IRE)**[38] 2705 3-9-2 .... JMurtagh 1 118
(A P O'Brien, Ire) *trckd ldr: led 3f out to 1f out: r.o one pce* **9/2**[3]

3 2 **Mastery**[25] 3090 3-9-2 .... LDettori 7 115
(Saeed Bin Suroor) *mid-div: clsd up over 3f out: 2nd st: drvn and ev ch 1 1/2f out: one pce fr dist* **14/1**

4 snk **Freemantle**[26] 3050 3-9-2 .... JAHeffernan 5 115
(A P O'Brien, Ire) *racd in 3rd: 3rd st on rail: stl disputing 3rd ins fnl f: no ex last 100yds* **10/1**

5 nk **Wajir (FR)**[37] 2756 3-9-2 .... ACrastus 8 114
(E Lellouche, France) *hld up in rr: last st: kpt on one pce to take 5th cl home* **14/1**

6 1 ½ **Beheshtam (FR)**[37] 2756 3-9-2 .... CSoumillon 4 112
(A De Royer-Dupre, France) *hld up in 7th: 7th and nt clr run ent st: cl 5th and hrd rdn wl over 1f out: one pce* **6/4**[1]

7 3 **Black Bear Island (IRE)**[25] 3087 3-9-2 .... CO'Donoghue 3 107
(A P O'Brien, Ire) *racd in 6th to st: btn 2f out* **8/1**

8 dist **Hail Caesar (IRE)**[4] 3888 3-9-2 ....(b) SMLevey 2 —
(A P O'Brien, Ire) *led tl wknd qckly 3f out: 5th st: sn t.o* **100/1**

2m 27.6s (-2.80) **Going Correction** +0.10s/f (Good) **8 Ran SP% 112.7**
Speed ratings: **116,115,113,113,113 112,110,—**
PARI-MUTUEL: WIN 4.40; PL 2.30, 4.40, 2.50; DF 22.70.
Owner Sheikh Mohammed **Bred** Darley **Trained** Chantilly, France

NOTEBOOK
Cavalryman looked the part in the paddock and finally won his first Group event with something in hand. in mid-division for much of the early stages, he was beautifully positioned in the straight to make his final surge to the line. He took the advantage just over one out and then stayed on well. A very progressive indivdual, he has now won three of his six races and can only go on to better things. There were no immediate plans after the race but he may well be supplemented for the Arc de Triomphe with a run before in the Prix Niel.
Age Of Aquarius(IRE) lost nothing in defeat and put up a courageous performance. His pacemaker set a blazing early gallop but he ran out of steam just before the straight. Taking the lead at this point, he stayed on throughout the final two and a half furlongs but had nothing in hand when the winner caught him in the final stages. He certainly stays well and his trainer feels he is still improving. There are no plans for the moment.
Mastery put up a fine effort from this colt at this level. In fourth position coming into the straight, he was challenging for the lead a furlong and a half out. He failed to quicken late on and then held on bravely to keep third place. Beaten by better rivals on the day, he can make his mark at Group level again.
Freemantle settled in third position for much of this race, but just stayed on throughout the two and a half furlong straight. He only missed third place by a narrow margin.

3726 CATTERICK (L-H)
Wednesday, July 15

OFFICIAL GOING: Good to soft (7.8)
Wind: Virtually nil Weather: Sunny periods and heavy showers

3971 ST TERESA'S HOSPICE NOVICE AUCTION STKS 7f
2:30 (2:30) (Class 5) 2-Y-O £3,238 (£963; £481; £240) Stalls Low

Form RPR

21 1 **Mister Angry (IRE)**[8] 3715 2-9-5 0................ GregFairley 3 79+
(M Johnston) *led: rdn and hdd 2f out: drvn and rallied to ld ins fnl f: kpt on* **8/15**[1]

022 2 nk **Desert Forest (IRE)**[14] 3494 2-8-10 0................ FrederikTylicki(3) 5 70
(J Howard Johnson) *cl up: rdn to ld 2f out: drvn over 1f out: hdd ins fnl f and no ex towards fin* **16/1**

3 3 1 **Aquarian Spirit**[14] 3494 2-8-13 0................ PaulHanagan 1 68+
(R A Fahey) *chsd ldrs on inner: hdwy 2f out: sn rdn and kpt on ins fnl f* **11/2**[3]

352 4 nk **Just The Tonic**[12] 3576 2-8-6 0................ SamHitchcott 2 60
(M R Channon) *trckd ldrs: hdwy 2f out and sn rdn: drvn ins fnl f and kpt on* **9/2**[2]

56 5 3 ¾ **Durham Reflection (IRE)**[41] 2623 2-9-1 0................ TonyHamilton 7 60
(J Howard Johnson) *a towards rr* **100/1**

015 6 7 **Bubbelas**[8] 3702 2-8-10 0................ PaulMulrennan 6 37
(J J Quinn) *chsd ldng pair: rdn along on outer over 2f out and sn wknd* **20/1**

1m 29.26s (2.26) **Going Correction** +0.30s/f (Good) **6 Ran SP% 110.4**
Speed ratings (Par 94): **99,98,97,97,92 84**
toteswingers: 1&2 £2.10, 1&3 £1.40, 2&3 £2.80 CSF £10.70 TOTE £1.60: £1.20, £3.40; EX 7.70.
Owner The Originals **Bred** Darley **Trained** Middleham Moor, N Yorks

FOCUS
After 4mm rain over the previous 24 hours the ground was reckoned ´on the soft side of good´. A fair juvenile contest with the winner running to his maiden form.

NOTEBOOK
Mister Angry(IRE), conceding upwards of 4lb all round, followed up his runaway Wolverhampton success but he had to battle hard. After being headed he traded at 4/1 on the exchanges but, really putting his head down and battling, he regained the advantage near the line. He looks essentially a stayer and a mile on a more galloping track will suit him a lot better. (op 4-6)
Desert Forest(IRE), runner-up in a weak maidenhere, had previously occupied the same placing in a claimer at Redcar. He took on the winner and traded at 1/5 when showing ahead but in the end he just missed out. On paper this was a much-improved effort. (op 14-1 tchd 12-1)
Aquarian Spirit, a neck behind Desert Forest when they were second and third over this course and distance two weeks earlier, had no excuse and this may be as good as she is at present. (op 15-2 tchd 8-1)
Just The Tonic, in receipt of weight all round, was encountering easy ground for the first time on her fourth career start. She is already looking fully exposed. (op 7-2)

Bubbelas, well beaten from a provisional nursery mark of 77 at Pontefract, again disappointed and her maiden success was on fast ground. (op 18-1 tchd 16-1)

3972 GO RACING IN YORKSHIRE SUMMER FESTIVAL (S) STKS 5f 212y
3:00 (3:02) (Class 6) 3-Y-O+ £2,047 (£604; £302) Stalls Low

Form RPR

1060 1 **Paddy Bear**[27] 3065 3-9-0 67................ PaulHanagan 8 71
(R A Fahey) *chsd ldr: effrt 2f out: rdn to ld wl over 1f out: sn hung lft: kpt on* **4/1**[2]

4036 2 4 **Ingleby Princess**[15] 3484 5-8-9 54................ PhillipMakin 7 48
(T D Barron) *trckd ldrs: hdwy over 2f out and sn rdn: drvn and one pce appr fnl f* **11/4**[1]

00-0 3 nk **Sea Salt**[65] 1924 6-8-11 61................ KellyHarrison(3) 12 52
(R E Barr) *chsd ldng pair: rdn along and hdwy 2f out: sn drvn and kpt on same pce* **10/1**

4604 4 1 ½ **Mandelieu (IRE)**[15] 3471 4-9-0 49................ TonyHamilton 2 47
(Ollie Pears) *dwlt: sn hld: rdn along over 2f out: drvn and hdd wl over 1f out: grad wknd* **9/2**[3]

0000 5 1 **Rainbow Bay**[41] 2628 6-8-11 45................(p) FrederikTylicki(3) 9 44
(Miss Tracy Waggott) *towards rr: hdwy over 2f out: sn rdn and no imp* **16/1**

5005 6 ¾ **Sardan Dansar (IRE)**[7] 3729 3-8-3 49................ SilvestreDeSousa 10 36
(Mrs A Duffield) *chsd ldrs: rdn along and outpcd 1/2-way: n.d after* **13/2**

0060 7 3 ¾ **Bentley**[15] 3490 5-9-0 52................(v) PaulMulrennan 5 30
(J G Given) *chsd ldrs on inner: rdn along 1/2-way: sn wknd* **8/1**

0-00 8 ¾ **Little Pandora**[19] 3352 5-8-2 44................ JamesPSullivan(7) 4 22
(L R James) *a in rr* **25/1**

0-20 9 4 **Bonnet O'Bonnie**[71] 1781 5-8-4 48................ JamieKyne(5) 11 10
(J Mackie) *a bhd* **16/1**

1m 15.17s (1.57) **Going Correction** +0.30s/f (Good)
WFA 3 from 4yo+ 6lb **9 Ran SP% 114.0**
Speed ratings (Par 101): **101,95,95,93,91 90,85,84,79**
toteswingers: 1&2 £2.30, 1&3 £9.80, 2&3 £8.90 CSF £15.19 TOTE £4.70: £1.50, £1.40, £3.40; EX 14.20.The winner was bought in 5,500 gns.
Owner J A & Kay Campbell **Bred** The Racing Guild **Trained** Musley Bank, N Yorks
■ Stewards' Enquiry : James P Sullivan one-day ban: used whip when out of contention (Jul 30)

FOCUS
There was a heavy shower between the first two races. A very moderate contest but a clear winner.

3973 FULL MONTY H'CAP 5f
3:30 (3:30) (Class 4) (0-85,85) 3-Y-O £5,180 (£1,541; £770; £384) Stalls Low

Form RPR

-600 1 **Mullglen**[11] 3607 3-8-9 **73**................ DavidAllan 3 81
(T D Easterby) *prom: effrt 2f out: rdn over 1f out: styd on to ld ins fnl f: drvn and kpt on wl towards fin* **9/1**

2230 2 hd **Titus Andronicus (IRE)**[5] 3806 3-9-2 **85**................ AmyRyan(5) 5 92
(K A Ryan) *led: rdn: edgd rt and hdd jst ins fnl f: drvn and rallied wl towards fin* **7/2**[3]

1641 3 1 ½ **Ingleby Lady**[25] 3173 3-9-0 **81**................ NeilBrown(3) 4 83
(T D Barron) *trckd ldrs: hdwy 2f out: rdn and ev ch ent fnl f: sn drvn and one pce* **3/1**[2]

100 4 ½ **Sloop Johnb**[7] 3747 3-9-6 **84**................ PaulHanagan 2 84
(R A Fahey) *trckd ldrs: hdwy 2f out and sn rdn: led briefly jst ins fnl f: sn drvn: hdd and one pce* **5/2**[1]

1-01 5 2 ¼ **Real Diamond**[7] 3729 3-8-2 **71** 6ex................ JamieKyne(5) 1 63
(A Dickman) *trckd ldrs on inner: pushed along and lost pl after 2f: sn rdn and nvr a factor* **7/1**

3600 6 5 **Lesley's Choice**[12] 3582 3-9-2 **80**................(p) GregFairley 7 54
(R Curtis) *wnt rt s: sn chsng ldrs: cl up 1/2-way: rdn 2f out and sn wknd* **16/1**

4344 7 3 ½ **Dispol Kylie (IRE)**[19] 3355 3-8-6 **70**................(p) PJMcDonald 8 31
(P T Midgley) *wnt rt s: in tch on outer: rdn along over 2f out and sn btn* **12/1**

61.82 secs (2.02) **Going Correction** +0.475s/f (Yiel) **7 Ran SP% 111.9**
Speed ratings (Par 102): **102,101,99,98,94 86,81**
toteswingers: 1&2 £5.60, 1&3 £5.10, 2&3 £3.40 CSF £38.60 CT £116.25 TOTE £11.40: £5.00, £2.10; EX 39.40.
Owner Richard Taylor & Philip Hebdon **Bred** Rosyground Stud **Trained** Great Habton, N Yorks
■ Stewards' Enquiry : David Allan one-day ban: used whip with excessive frequency (Jul 30)

FOCUS
A tight 70-85 three-year-olds only sprint handicap and in the conditions the pace was fast and furious.

3974 SUBSCRIBE TO RACING UK CLAIMING STKS 1m 3f 214y
4:00 (4:00) (Class 6) 3-Y-O+ £2,388 (£705; £352) Stalls Low

Form RPR

5615 1 **Dimashq**[14] 3499 7-9-5 47................ MickyFenton 3 54
(P T Midgley) *trckd ldrs: hdwy to ld 4f out: rdn clr wl over 1f out: drvn ins fnl f and hld on gamely* **12/1**

0424 2 1 **Den Maschine**[20] 3303 4-9-8 52................ DNolan 11 55
(Ollie Pears) *a.p: hdwy to chse wnr over 3f out: rdn over 2f out: drvn over 1f out: kpt on towards fin* **6/1**[2]

0315 3 ½ **Rosewin (IRE)**[22] 3233 3-8-1 56................ JamieKyne(5) 1 52+
(O Brennan) *hld up in tch on inner: hdwy 4f out: swtchd rt and rdn over 2f out: drvn to chse ldrs and edgd lft ins fnl f: kpt on wl towards fin* **7/1**[3]

5154 4 nse **Dancing Lyra**[8] 3714 8-9-10 62................ PaulHanagan 7 57
(R A Fahey) *trckd ldrs: hdwy 3f out: rdn along over 2f out: drvn over 1f out: kpt on u.p ins fnl f* **15/8**[1]

6334 5 ¾ **Barbirolli**[12] 3594 7-8-13 48................ PaulPickard(7) 8 51
(W M Brisbourne) *hld up towards rr: hdwy 1/2-way: chsd ldrs over 3f out: rdn along over 2f out: drvn and n.m.r ins fnl f: nrst fin* **8/1**

4544 6 7 **Wulimaster (USA)**[20] 3291 6-9-2 46................ PaulMulrennan 2 36
(D W Barker) *hld up in rr: hdwy on inner 3f out: rdn to chse ldrs wl over 1f out: sn drvn and btn* **16/1**

3400 7 1 **Desert Hawk**[27] 3074 8-9-6 45................ LiamJones 5 39
(W M Brisbourne) *hld up towards rr: hdwy 1/2-way: rdn along over 3f out: no imp fnl 2f* **40/1**

3300 8 1 **Karmest**[28] 3019 5-9-9 65................(b) SilvestreDeSousa 13 40
(A D Brown) *chsd ldrs: rdn along over 4f out and sn wknd* **10/1**

30-4 9 8 **Rawaabet (IRE)**[17] 3233 7-9-3 46................(t) RussellKennemore(3) 9 24
(R Hollinshead) *s.i.s: a in rr* **20/1**

640 10 17 **Son Of Monsieur**[26] 3120 3-8-3 0................ DuranFentiman 4 —
(G R Oldroyd) *chsd ldrs: rdn along 4f out: sn wknd* **22/1**

3-66 11 2 ½ **Prince Samos (IRE)**[14] 3499 7-9-10 62................ TomEaves 6 —
(C A Mulhall) *a in rr: rdn along 1/2-way: bhd fnl 3f* **12/1**

000 **12** *4 ½* **Runswick Bay**[8] 3705 4-9-6 70 PJMcDonald 10 —
(G M Moore) *led: rdn along and hdd 4f out: sn wknd* **18/1**

06 **13** *40* **Italiano**[22] 3233 10-9-11 0 (b) FrederikTylicki(3) 14 —
(Mrs Marjorie Fife) *chsd ldr: rdn along afder 5f: sn lost pl and bhd fnl 4f* **80/1**

2m 42.93s (4.03) **Going Correction** +0.30s/f (Good)
WFA 3 from 4yo+ 13lb **13** Ran SP% **121.1**
Speed ratings (Par 101): **98,97,97,96,96 91,91,90,85,73 72,69,42**
.Dancing Lyra was claimed by A. Leyshon for £6000. Den Maschine was claimed by P. Morgan for £5000. Rosewin was claimed by A Dickman for £6000. Wulimaster was claimed by P Hearn for £2000.\n\x\x

Owner A Bell **Bred** Darley **Trained** Westow, N Yorks

FOCUS
A low-grade claimer run at a sound pace but those in the frame behind the winner were all claimed.

3975 TURFTV MEDIAN AUCTION MAIDEN STKS 7f
4:30 (4:30) (Class 6) 3-Y-O £2,388 (£705; £352) Stalls Low

Form RPR
40-4 **1** **Whispering Spirit (IRE)**[54] 2236 3-8-12 65 SilvestreDeSousa 5 59+
(Mrs A Duffield) *chsd ldng pair: tk clsr order 3f out: rdn 2f out and sn led: clr over 1f out: kpt on* **5/4**[1]

0003 **2** *4 ½* **Cindy Incidentally**[14] 3498 3-8-12 43 (b) MickyFenton 4 43
(Miss Gay Kelleway) *led and sn clr: rdn along over 2f out: sn hdd and kpt on same pce* **14/1**

00 **3** *2* **Elusive Style (IRE)**[36] 2789 3-8-9 0 MichaelJStainton(3) 12 38
(S P Griffiths) *in tch: rdn along 2f out: styd on appr last: nrst fin* **100/1**

0- **4** *¾* **Unconsoled**[285] 6453 3-8-5 60 PaulPickard(7) 10 36
(J Hetherton) *chsd clr ldr: rdn along over 2f out: drvn over 1f out and sn wknd* **11/1**

5 *3 ½* **Camomile** 3-8-12 0 TonyHamilton 9 26+
(K A Ryan) *trckd ldrs: hdwy on outer 3f out: sn rdn and ev ch tl wknd wl over 1f out* **7/1**

6 *1 ¼* **There We Go (IRE)** 3-9-3 0 PJMcDonald 1 28
(G A Swinbank) *s.i.s: a towards rr* **13/2**[3]

04 **7** *3 ¼* **Hopeful Lady**[22] 3237 3-8-12 0 TomEaves 7 14
(I W McInnes) *a towards rr* **66/1**

8 *¾* **Targs (IRE)** 3-9-3 0 PatrickMathers 2 17
(Peter Grayson) *s.i.s: a bhd* **28/1**

9 *1 ½* **Skybob** 3-9-3 0 GregFairley 8 13
(D W Thompson) *s.i.s: a bhd* **20/1**

10 *1 ¼* **Prince Maggio** 3-9-3 0 PaulHanagan 11 10
(Pat Eddery) *s.i.s: a bhd* **11/2**[2]

11 *33* **Mareva** 3-8-12 0 PaulMulrennan 3 —
(Ollie Pears) *midfield: rdn along 2f out: sn hung lft: wknd and eased* **25/1**

1m 30.58s (3.58) **Going Correction** +0.30s/f (Good) **11** Ran SP% **115.2**
Speed ratings (Par 98): **91,85,83,82,78 77,73,72,71,69 31**
toteswingers: 1&2 £5.40, 1&3 £24.80, 2&3 £26.80 CSF £19.39 TOTE £1.80: £1.10, £2.90, £19.80; EX 18.50.

Owner Middleham Park Racing XLII **Bred** David Barry **Trained** Constable Burton, N Yorks

FOCUS
A weak median auction maiden race run at a break-neck gallop and they were soon very well strung out.

3976 CATTERICKBRIDGE.CO.UK H'CAP 1m 3f 214y
5:00 (5:01) (Class 5) (0-70,70) 3-Y-O £3,238 (£963; £481; £240) Stalls Low

Form RPR
0-32 **1** **Omokoroa (IRE)**[27] 3069 3-9-7 70 LiamJones 14 80
(M H Tompkins) *trckd ldrs: hdwy 3f out: rdn to ld 2f out: drvn ins fnl f and kpt on wl* **7/4**[1]

4044 **2** *1 ½* **Addison De Witt**[15] 3482 3-8-2 51 (v[1]) FrancisNorton 4 58
(Micky Hammond) *hld up towards rr: gd hdwy on inner over 3f out: rdn to chse wnr wl over 1f out: sn hung rt: drvn and hung lft ins fnl f: no imp towards fin* **9/1**

3602 **3** *5* **Dispol Diva**[11] 3610 3-9-1 64 (v) PhillipMakin 2 63
(P T Midgley) *hld up in midfield: hdwy over 3f out: rdn to chse ldrs on wd outside wl over 1f out: sn drvn and no imp* **6/1**[3]

00-3 **4** *2 ¼* **Sergeant Pink (IRE)**[54] 2230 3-9-0 66 FrederikTylicki(3) 10 62
(S Gollings) *chsd ldrs: rdn along over 3f out: drvn 2f out: plugged on same pce* **8/1**

0544 **5** *1 ½* **Shanavaz**[8] 3721 3-8-6 55 PaulHanagan 5 48
(Mrs G S Rees) *trckd ldrs: hdwy 1/2-way: led 3f out: rdn and hdd 2f out: sn drvn and wknd* **12/1**

2146 **6** *4 ½* **Veroon (IRE)**[11] 3636 3-9-7 70 (b) PaulMulrennan 6 56
(J G Given) *led: rdn along over 3f out: sn hdd: drvn and grad wknd fnl 2f* **10/1**

0600 **7** *3 ¼* **Hit The Switch**[19] 3336 3-7-11 53 JamesPSullivan(7) 1 34
(Patrick Morris) *a in rr* **33/1**

6002 **8** *18* **Marillos Proterras**[7] 3731 3-8-2 51 oh3 SilvestreDeSousa 7 3
(Mrs A Duffield) *a towards rr* **14/1**

5606 **9** *2* **Katie Girl**[19] 3336 3-7-11 51 oh3 (p) JamieKyne(5) 13 —
(Mrs G S Rees) *cl up: rdn along over 4f out and sn wknd* **33/1**

00-0 **10** *10* **Full Blue**[41] 2633 3-8-2 51 oh1 AndrewElliott 8 —
(S C Williams) *chsd ldrs on inner: rdn along over 4f out and sn wknd* **4/1**[2]

0400 **11** *dist* **Cooperman**[40] 2667 3-7-12 54 oh4 ow3 PaulPickard(7) 11 —
(P T Midgley) *chsd ldrs: hung rt and rn wd paddock bnd: sn bhd: t.o fr 1/2-way* **33/1**

2m 42.0s (3.10) **Going Correction** +0.30s/f (Good) **11** Ran SP% **124.0**
Speed ratings (Par 100): **101,100,96,95,94 91,89,77,75,69** —
toteswingers: 1&2 £5.80, 1&3 £2.70, 2&3 £6.80 CSF £19.84 CT £80.95 TOTE £2.70: £1.60, £3.10, £1.70; EX 25.50 Place 6: £67.47 Place 5: £48.48.

Owner Brendan Richardson **Bred** Peter McCutcheon **Trained** Newmarket, Suffolk

FOCUS
A modest 51-70 handicap run at a sensible pace.

Full Blue Official explanation: trainer said filly lost her near fore shoe

T/Plt: £81.50 to a £1 stake. Pool: £45,623.68. 408.60 winning tickets. T/Qpdt: £29.30 to a £1 stake. Pool: £2,925.64. 73.70 winning tickets. JR

3732 KEMPTON (A.W) (R-H)
Wednesday, July 15

OFFICIAL GOING: Standard
Wind: Moderate, across (away from stands) Weather: Changeble with showers

3977 WEATHERBYS PRINTING APPRENTICE H'CAP (ROUND 7) 1m 3f (P)
6:20 (6:20) (Class 4) (0-80,80) 4-Y-O+ £4,727 (£1,406; £702; £351) Stalls High

Form RPR
300 **1** **Scamperdale**[18] 3374 7-9-5 78 KierenFox(5) 4 93+
(B P J Baugh) *hld up in abt 7th: smooth prog over 2f out: pushed into ld over 1f out: sn clr: eased last 50yds* **28/1**

-100 **2** *4* **Balnagore**[32] 2923 5-9-1 69 MartinLane 5 74
(J L Dunlop) *led 2f: styd prom: shkn up to ld again 3f out: drvn and hdd over 1f out: no ch w wnr but kpt on* **12/1**

0031 **3** *1 ¾* **Kingsdale Orion (IRE)**[18] 3393 5-9-8 76 LanceBetts 11 78
(B Ellison) *chsd ldrs: pushed along 4f out: nvr pce to mount a chal after: kpt on to take 3rd last stride* **5/1**[3]

40-1 **4** *shd* **Latin Scholar (IRE)**[23] 3206 4-9-5 76 ByronMoorcroft(3) 2 78
(A King) *racd on outer: trckd ldrs: smooth prog to go 2nd over 2f out: poised to chal sn after: shkn up and fnd nil: wknd fnl f* **8/1**

1342 **5** *¾* **Gross Prophet**[18] 3374 4-9-7 75 RossAtkinson 1 75
(Tom Dascombe) *restrained s: hld up in last: outpcd and pushed along 3f out: swtchd to inner 2f out: r.o fnl f: nvr nr ldrs* **6/1**

-504 **6** *¾* **Jadalee (IRE)**[14] 3510 6-9-0 71 (p) SimonPearce(3) 9 70
(G A Butler) *t.k.h: hld up in abt 8th: pushed along over 3f out: plugged on fnl 2f: n.d* **4/1**[2]

2240 **7** *2* **Wind Flow**[21] 3273 5-9-3 74 (v) AndrewHeffernan(3) 3 69
(C A Dwyer) *led after 2f to over 4f out: cl up to 2f out: wknd* **10/1**

1002 **8** *4* **Dichoh**[14] 3501 6-9-7 75 (v) JackDean 10 63
(M Madgwick) *chsd ldrs: pushed along and stl wl in tch whn squeezed out over 2f out: nt rcvr and wknd* **16/1**

0123 **9** *1* **Inch Lodge**[7] 3734 7-8-8 62 WilliamCarson 8 48
(Miss D Mountain) *prom on outer: wnt 2nd 6f out: led over 4f out to 3f out: wknd 2f out* **7/2**[1]

2460 **10** *2* **My Mentor (IRE)**[118] 886 5-8-11 68 RosieJessop(3) 7 51
(Sir Mark Prescott) *a in last pair: struggling fnl 3f* **10/1**

2m 21.43s (-0.47) **Going Correction** +0.01s/f (Slow) **10** Ran SP% **119.5**
Speed ratings (Par 105): **101,98,96,96,96 95,94,91,90,89**
toteswingers: 1&2 £23.30, 1&3 £25.70, 2&3 £13.40 CSF £335.14 CT £1973.89 TOTE £23.80: £7.50, £4.30, £2.20; EX 336.30.

Owner Saddle Up Racing **Bred** Mrs J A Prescott **Trained** Audley, Staffs

FOCUS
There was a modest pace which increased half a mile from home, but the winner was always travelling strongly and won with remarkable ease.

Scamperdale Official explanation: trainer said, regarding the improved form shown, that the gelding is much better on the all weather, was unsuited by the track at Chester and was badly off at the weights in what was a valuable claimer

3978 BOOK KEMPTON TICKETS ON 0844 579 3008 NURSERY 7f (P)
6:50 (6:51) (Class 5) 2-Y-O £2,590 (£770; £385; £192) Stalls High

Form RPR
2513 **1** **Toga Tiger (IRE)**[12] 3589 2-9-7 82 DarryllHolland 6 87
(M R Channon) *chsd ldr: rdn and edgd lft over 2f out: no imp tl styd on wl fnl f to ld last strides* **15/2**

0004 **2** *nk* **Whippers Love (IRE)**[25] 3147 2-8-2 63 RoystonFfrench 2 67
(M Johnston) *led: at least 2 l clr fr over 2f out: hrd rdn over 1f out: wknd and hdd last strides* **11/2**[3]

000 **3** *3 ½* **Sixpenny Moon (USA)**[22] 3249 2-8-3 64 JimmyQuinn 3 60
(R Hannon) *hld up in last pair and racd wd: outpcd over 2f out: styd on fr over 1f out to take 3rd jst ins fnl f: nrst fin* **14/1**

033 **4** *3 ¼* **Zinjbar (USA)**[13] 3534 2-8-11 72 SebSanders 1 59
(C E Brittain) *dwlt: racd wd: in tch: rdn and nt qckn over 2f out: plugged on to take 3rd briefly 1f out* **5/2**[1]

1200 **5** *¾* **Shark Man (IRE)**[17] 3424 2-9-0 78 JackMitchell(3) 5 64
(P J McBride) *a in midfield: rdn and no imp on ldrs over 2f out: sn n.d* **15/2**

5640 **6** *3 ¾* **Cane Cat (IRE)**[32] 2919 2-7-10 60 DavidProbert(3) 7 36
(A W Carroll) *awkward s but sn chsd wnr to over 2f out: wknd rapidly fnl f* **20/1**

241 **7** *1 ¼* **Ragsta (IRE)**[30] 2978 2-8-6 67 RichardSmith 8 40
(R Hannon) *dwlt: sn chsd ldrs: rdn over 2f out: no prog: wknd over 1f out* **4/1**[2]

01 **8** *4* **Ananda Kanda (USA)**[54] 2226 2-8-8 74 LanceBetts(5) 4 37
(B Ellison) *fractious preliminaries: dwlt: a in rr: rdn over 3f out: sn struggling* **11/2**[3]

1m 26.51s (0.51) **Going Correction** +0.01s/f (Slow) **8** Ran SP% **114.3**
Speed ratings (Par 94): **97,96,92,88,88 83,82,77**
toteswingers: 1&2 £3.90, 1&3 £19.30, 2&3 £16.50 CSF £48.05 CT £569.56 TOTE £8.50: £2.20, £2.50, £3.20; EX 50.50.

Owner Ridgeway Downs Racing **Bred** Daniel Spaight **Trained** West Ilsley, Berks

■ Stewards' Enquiry : Darryll Holland one-day ban: used whip with excessive frequency (Jul 30)

FOCUS
A good performance by the winner off top weight and with the first two clear the form could be better than rated. The 'official' ratings shown next to each horse are estimated and for information purposes only.

NOTEBOOK
Toga Tiger(IRE) looked held by the runner-up for much of the final 2f but he had shown before that he enjoys a scrap, and just got on top near the finish. This was an excellent start to his nursery career and, while he will be off an even higher mark in future, this tough sort takes his racing well and should continue to give supporters a run for their money. (op 7-1 tchd 13-2)

Whippers Love(IRE) improved for switch to handicap company, the step up in trip, change of surface and better form of his stable. Which of those factors were particularly responsible will become clearer as the season progresses, but he put up a spirited show in defeat and should be placed to go one better. (op 9-2 tchd 13-2)

Sixpenny Moon(USA) had shown minor promise in three maidens but nurseries should be the making of her. On this evidence she already gets 7f really well, and an even stiffer test should suit. (op 12-1)

Zinjbar(USA), well-backed, had shown promise in her last two races, both on turf, so this nursery debut was rather disappointing. She can do better, but it remains to be seen whether she acts as well on sand as she has done on grass. (op 5-1)

Shark Man(IRE)'s form has begun to tail off after a promising start, and the step up to 7f did not fix the problem. He looked a fair sprinter earlier in the year and can do much better when on song. (op 10-1 tchd 7-1)

Cane Cat(IRE), stepping up from 5f, failed to stay but showed plenty of speed and is worth a try at 6f. (op 25-1)

Ragsta(IRE), running in her first handicap, looked more effective at 5f and 6f in her maidens. (tchd 7-2)

Ananda Kanda(USA) put in by far her best performance on heavy ground, but she got into a state beforehand this time and may not have run her race. Official explanation: jockey said filly was unsuited by the surface (op 7-2 tchd 7-1)

3979 EBF EPSOM TRAINERS OPEN DAY AUGUST 2ND MAIDEN FILLIES' STKS — 7f (P)

7:20 (7:21) (Class 4) 2-Y-O — **£5,018** (£1,493; £746; £372) **Stalls** High

Form — RPR

1 **Sent From Heaven (IRE)** 2-9-0 0 ... MichaelHills 13 — 80+
(B W Hills) *s.s: sn rcvrd to midfield on inner: waiting for room 3f out tl eased out and prog 2f out: led 1f out: pushed out firmly: decisively* **9/4**[1]

0 2 1 ¾ **Magic Lantern**[46] 2494 2-9-0 0 ... PatDobbs 5 — 76
(R Hannon) *wl plcd prog to trck ldr 2f out: clsd to chal jst over 1f out: pressed wnr briefly fnl f: sn hld but styd on wl* **5/1**[3]

0 3 6 **Amtaar**[22] 3249 2-9-0 0 ... SebSanders 2 — 61
(C E Brittain) *dwlt: forced to r v wd at rr of main gp: effrt on outer over 2f out: sn outpcd: styd on fnl f to take 3rd last strides* **16/1**

54 4 hd **Larkrise Star**[14] 3507 2-9-0 0 ... ChrisCatlin 10 — 60
(D K Ivory) *mde most: kicked on 3f out: hdd & wknd 1f out: lost 3rd last strides* **3/1**[2]

4 5 ½ **Zaffature**[8] 3716 2-9-0 0 ... JimmyQuinn 4 — 59
(M Botti) *in tch in midfield: shkn up and outpcd over 2f out: edgd rt but styd on fr over 1f out* **8/1**

6 ¾ **Chicha Morada (USA)** 2-9-0 0 ... RichardMullen 12 — 57+
(D M Simcock) *in rr of main gp: shkn up over 2f out: sn outpcd: n.d after but styd on fnl f to press for a pl nr fin* **20/1**

7 4 ½ **In The Slips (USA)** 2-9-0 0 ... MartinDwyer 6 — 46+
(P F I Cole) *sn pushed along: detached in last trio after 3f: nvr on terms: pushed along and plugged on fnl 2f* **10/1**

00 8 1 ¼ **It's A Deal (IRE)**[14] 3507 2-9-0 0 ... JimCrowley 7 — 43
(P Winkworth) *chsd ldrs: rdn over 2f out: wknd rapidly over 1f out* **33/1**

00 9 nk **Dragonessa (IRE)**[23] 3226 2-8-11 0 ... DavidProbert(3) 9 — 42
(B Palling) *w ldr to 3f out: wknd rapidly over 1f out* **50/1**

0 10 1 ¼ **Expensive Legacy**[12] 3576 2-8-9 0 ... SophieDoyle(5) 11 — 39
(H J L Dunlop) *detached in last trio after 3f: nvr a factor after* **11/1**

11 13 **Sunshine Buddy** 2-9-0 0 ... JerryO'Dwyer 3 — 6
(J R Holt) *dwlt: detached in last trio after 3f: t.o* **40/1**

5 12 4 **Chinoise (IRE)**[30] 2978 2-9-0 0 ... IanMongan 14 — —
(P M Phelan) *w ldng pair 2f: wknd rapidly 2f out: t.o* **16/1**

1m 26.62s (0.62) **Going Correction** +0.01s/f (Slow) — **12** Ran SP% **124.8**
Speed ratings (Par 93): **96,94,87,86,86 85,80,78,78,77 62,57**
toteswingers: 1&2 £3.30, 1&3 £13.80, 2&3 £21.20 CSF £14.07 TOTE £3.30: £1.50, £2.20, £5.90; EX 16.20.

Owner Triermore Stud **Bred** C O P Hanbury **Trained** Lambourn, Berks

FOCUS

The time was almost the same as the previous race, and strictly speaking Toga Tiger's performance rates slightly the better, but that may be deceptive in the long run. The first two here pulled clear and the winner in particular looks useful.

NOTEBOOK

Sent From Heaven(IRE) ◆, well backed to make a winning debut, scored in the style of a filly to be followed. A Footstepsinthesand half-sister to the current middle-distance three-year-old Above Average, she will stay further than this as she matures, and looks a decent prospect. Connections expect to be able to step her up to Listed company at least, and the Sweet Solera at Newmarket is a possible target. (tchd 3-1)

Magic Lantern, a Halling half-sister to the 1m2f winner Papality, predictably improved for the step up to 7f and deserves full credit for being the only runner to finish anywhere near the impressive winner. She is easily capable of winning a similar race, and looks a nice sort for the rest of season. (op 4-1)

Amtaar had done nothing on her debut, but this 65,000gns Nayef filly acted well on the Polytrack and went much better this time despite the unhelpful draw. She appears to take after her sire more than her sprinter dam Emerald Fire, and can continue to progress. (tchd 14-1)

Larkrise Star was ridden more positively this time but the result was still the same insofar as she was just run out of the first three. She is capable of winning races, with 7f nurseries an obvious option. (op 9-2)

Zaffature, who will be ready for nurseries after one more run, has shown enough to give connections something to look forward to. (op 7-1 tchd 6-1)

Chicha Morada(USA), by the US dirt perfomer Tale Of The Cat, is bred to race at trips up to just beyond 1m. She made a satisfactory debut and is worth watching for signs of improvement.

In The Slips(USA), a half-sister to two winners up to 7f, is by the sprinter-7f winner More Than Ready but out of a 1m4f winner. On this evidence, she has inherited her dam's stamina, and longer trips should suit this debutante. (op 12-1)

It's A Deal(IRE), an Indian Haven half-sister to seven winners, has yet to establish her likely trip but she will be much more comfortable in handicaps now she is qualified. (op 66-1)

Dragonessa(IRE), a Red Ransom filly out of a dam placed at distances up to 1m4f, is worth trying at longer trips now she is handicapped. (op 66-1 tchd 100-1)

3980 DIGIBET.COM LONDON MILE H'CAP (LONDON MILE QUALIFIER) — 1m (P)

7:50 (7:51) (Class 5) (0-70,70) 3-Y-O+ — **£2,590** (£770; £385; £192) **Stalls** High

Form — RPR

2-30 1 **Assail**[30] 2981 3-9-3 68 ... TravisBlock 1 — 83+
(H Morrison) *t.k.h early: racd wd: sn prom: prog to go 2nd 3f out: edgd lft but led wl over 1f out: kpt edging lft but styd on strly* **25/1**

0033 2 2 ¾ **Ugenius**[7] 3735 5-8-8 55 ... WilliamCarson(5) 3 — 65
(Mrs C A Dunnett) *racd wd towards rr: drvn and gd prog on outer 2f out: wnt 2nd ins fnl f: no threat to wnr* **11/1**

1003 3 1 **Fancy Footsteps (IRE)**[18] 3381 4-9-13 69 ... AdamKirby 7 — 77
(C G Cox) *hld up in midfield: prog through rivals wl over 2f out to chal over 1f out: edgd rt and one pce fnl f* **9/2**[1]

0-41 4 1 ¾ **Chief Red Cloud (USA)**[20] 3302 3-9-1 66 ... ShaneKelly 12 — 67
(K R Burke) *hld up towards rr: prog gng wl fr over 2f out: drvn to press ldrs jst over 1f out: effrt petered out* **9/2**[1]

2124 5 ¾ **Confide In Me**[10] 3653 5-9-5 61 ... (t) HayleyTurner 14 — 63
(G A Butler) *settled in last trio: plenty to do whn rdn wl over 2f out: prog over 1f out: kpt on fnl f: nrst fin* **11/2**[2]

6102 6 1 ¼ **My Mate Mal**[19] 3353 5-9-4 65 ... LanceBetts(5) 13 — 64
(B Ellison) *mde most at decent pce to wl over 1f out: wknd fnl f* **10/1**

005- 7 1 ¼ **Causeway King (USA)**[286] 6423 3-9-3 68 ... DaneO'Neill 10 — 62
(A King) *in tch in midfield on inner: lost pl and rr wl over 2f out: kpt on again fnl f: n.d* **16/1**

300- 8 hd **Leptis Magna**[245] 6544 5-9-4 60 ... JimCrowley 8 — 55
(T E Powell) *t.k.h: hld up in tch: swtchd to inner and effrt 2f out: wknd fnl f* **25/1**

4506 9 ¾ **Ocean Legend (IRE)**[21] 3274 4-9-13 69 ... TPO'Shea 5 — 62
(Miss J Feilden) *racd wd: trckd ldrs: u.p but cl enough over 2f out: nt qckn: wknd fnl f* **8/1**[3]

4040 10 2 ¾ **Simpsons Gamble (IRE)**[7] 3732 6-8-12 54 ... (p) LPKeniry 11 — 41
(R A Teal) *in tch: rdn towards rr wl over 2f out: no prog and sn btn* **20/1**

-000 11 8 **Shanzu**[36] 2796 4-10-0 70 ... (b) GeorgeBaker 9 — 38
(G L Moore) *pressed ldng pair: cl up wl over 2f out: sn wknd rapidly* **14/1**

5041 12 ¾ **Copper King**[32] 2924 5-8-9 51 oh1 ... ChrisCatlin 4 — 17
(Miss Tor Sturgis) *settled in last trio: rdn and no prog 3f out: bhd after* **12/1**

603 13 hd **Singleb (IRE)**[12] 3568 5-9-12 68 ... (p) DarryllHolland 6 — 33
(Miss Gay Kelleway) *sn last and pushed along: struggling sn after 1/2-way* **10/1**

-006 14 3 ¾ **Cobos**[15] 3474 3-8-12 63 ... (p) SaleemGolam 2 — 17
(Ms E L McWilliam) *mostly chsd ldr to 3f out: wknd rapidly* **50/1**

1m 39.49s (-0.31) **Going Correction** +0.01s/f (Slow)
WFA 3 from 4yo+ 9lb — **14** Ran SP% **124.0**
Speed ratings (Par 103): **101,98,97,95,94 93,92,92,91,88 80,79,79,75**
toteswingers: 1&2 £33.80, 1&3 £28.80, 2&3 £11.80 CSF £277.60 CT £1526.78 TOTE £37.80: £9.10, £3.10, £2.00; EX 208.20.

Owner M J Watson **Bred** M J Watson **Trained** East Ilsley, Berks

FOCUS

The good gallop should have helped the hold-up performers, so this was a fine effort from the always-handy winner, who also had to overcome the disadvantage of racing three wide all the way.

3981 DIGIBET.COM FILLIES' H'CAP — 1m (P)

8:20 (8:21) (Class 4) (0-85,85) 3-Y-O — **£4,727** (£1,406; £702; £351) **Stalls** High

Form — RPR

320 1 **Mosqueras Romance**[102] 1128 3-8-9 73 ... DarryllHolland 6 — 86+
(M Botti) *led after 2f: 2 l clr and gng strly over 2f out: pushed further clr over 1f out: unchal* **4/1**[3]

3235 2 2 ¼ **Perfect Class**[15] 3476 3-7-13 66 ... DavidProbert(3) 7 — 71
(C G Cox) *sn restrained to last: plenty to do whn effrt over 2f out: styd on to take 2nd last 100yds: no ch to chal* **6/1**

2112 3 ¾ **Charlotte Point (USA)**[18] 3400 3-9-7 85 ... MartinDwyer 3 — 88
(P F I Cole) *rrd s: pressed wnr after 2f: rdn and no imp over 2f out: lost 2nd last 100yds* **85/40**[1]

3561 4 ¾ **Russian Rave**[35] 2827 3-8-8 72 ... RichardKingscote 1 — 73
(J G Portman) *hld up and racd wd: prog to chse ldng pair over 3f out: rdn over 2f out: one pce* **7/2**[2]

-360 5 4 ½ **Welsh Anthem**[34] 2845 3-8-6 70 ... ChrisCatlin 4 — 61
(W R Muir) *led 2f: lost pl and rdn in rr 1/2-way: struggling fr 3f out* **14/1**

6-00 6 11 **Miss Eze**[53] 2270 3-9-4 82 ... HayleyTurner 8 — 46
(M L W Bell) *t.k.h early: hld up: rdn over 3f out: wknd rapidly over 2f out: t.o* **4/1**[3]

1m 39.0s (-0.80) **Going Correction** +0.01s/f (Slow) — **6** Ran SP% **115.2**
Speed ratings (Par 99): **104,101,101,100,95 84**
toteswingers: 1&2 £4.10, 1&3 £1.90, 2&3 £2.20 CSF £28.12 CT £63.47 TOTE £5.10: £2.40, £3.50; EX 25.10.

Owner Mrs R J Jacobs **Bred** Newsells Park Stud Limited **Trained** Newmarket, Suffolk

FOCUS

There was no early gallop, despite three of them vying for the lead, and the winner was in the ideal position to kick for home off the turn, a winning move which never looked like failing. However the early dawdle did not suit many of the others.

3982 DIGIBET CASINO H'CAP — 7f (P)

8:50 (8:50) (Class 5) (0-75,75) 3-Y-O — **£2,590** (£770; £385; £192) **Stalls** High

Form — RPR

1320 1 **Arachnophobia (IRE)**[28] 3028 3-9-5 73 ... PaulEddery 8 — 79
(Pat Eddery) *mostly chsd ldr: wound up fr over 2f out: produced to ld last 150yds: sn wl in command* **8/1**

-400 2 1 ¾ **King's Sabre**[19] 3341 3-8-11 65 ... MartinDwyer 3 — 66
(W R Muir) *led and crossed fr wd draw: drvn over 1f out: hdd and outpcd last 150yds* **12/1**

2100 3 ½ **Kiss A Prince**[43] 2578 3-9-0 68 ... HayleyTurner 1 — 68+
(D K Ivory) *dropped in fr wd draw and hld up last: prog 2f out: rdn and styd on wl fnl f to take 3rd last strides* **28/1**

0005 4 ½ **Grand Honour (IRE)**[14] 3512 3-9-2 70 ... IanMongan 9 — 68
(P Howling) *racd wd towards rr: rdn over 2f out: prog over 1f out: styd on fnl f: nrst fin* **11/1**

5153 5 ½ **Peter's Gift (IRE)**[12] 3574 3-9-4 72 ... DarryllHolland 10 — 69
(K A Ryan) *t.k.h: hld up bhd ldrs on inner: effrt over 2f out: chsd ldng pair over 1f out: no imp fnl f: lost 2 pls nr fin* **7/1**

1600 6 ¾ **Woolston Ferry (IRE)**[25] 3159 3-9-4 72 ... FergusSweeney 5 — 67
(David Pinder) *prom: shkn up to dispute 3rd 2f out: nt qckn sn after: fdd fnl f* **16/1**

3-02 7 ½ **Foxtrot Alpha (IRE)**[35] 2827 3-9-2 70 ... JimCrowley 14 — 64+
(P Winkworth) *plld hrd: hld up towards rr: prog on inner 2f out: no imp 1f out: fdd* **13/2**

-400 8 2 **The Desert Saint**[34] 2849 3-8-12 69 ... (v[1]) DavidProbert(3) 12 — 57
(A M Balding) *nvr beyond midfield: rdn over 2f out: one pce over 1f out: wknd fnl f* **8/1**

-041 9 2 ½ **Pressing Matters (IRE)**[13] 3548 3-9-6 74 ... (b[1]) JimmyQuinn 6 — 55
(M Botti) *awkward s: racd wd in midfield: nt qckn over 2f out: drvn and no imp on ldrs after: wknd fnl f* **6/1**[3]

425- 10 ½ **Florentia**[314] 5628 3-9-0 68 ... SebSanders 7 — 48
(Sir Mark Prescott) *t.k.h early: hld up in midfield: lost pl and struggling in rr over 2f out: sn n.d* **9/2**[1]

61-0 11 1 ¾ **Zim Ho**[52] 2300 3-8-13 67 ... DaneO'Neill 2 — 42
(J Akehurst) *t.k.h: racd wd: pressed ldng pair to wl over 2f out: lost pl qckly* **20/1**

-431 12 1 ½ **Intolerable (IRE)**[25] 3161 3-9-0 75 ... RichardFelton(7) 13 — 46
(R M Beckett) *a in rr and sn struggling: no ch fr over 2f out* **11/2**[2]

1m 26.21s (0.21) **Going Correction** +0.01s/f (Slow) — **12** Ran SP% **126.0**
Speed ratings (Par 100): **98,96,95,94,94 93,92,90,87,87 85,83**
toteswingers: 1&2 £31.20, 1&3 £13.20, 2&3 £76.90 CSF £106.79 CT £2634.21 TOTE £11.30: £2.70, £4.60, £8.30; EX 159.50.

Owner Pat Eddery Racing (Sharpo) **Bred** Michael Staunton **Trained** Nether Winchendon, Bucks

FOCUS
A modest pace until early in the straight suited those who raced handily.

3983 PANORAMIC BAR & RESTAURANT H'CAP 7f (P)
9:20 (9:20) (Class 6) (0-65,71) 3-Y-0+ £2,047 (£604; £302) Stalls High

Form RPR

5231 1 **Global Village (IRE)**[7] 3732 4-8-13 **60** .... WilliamCarson(5) 5 69+
(Miss D Mountain) *sn trckd ldng pair: effrt on outer to ld over 1f out: over a l clr wl ins fnl f: jst lasted* **11/8**[1]

-001 2 ½ **Chief Exec**[8] 3722 7-10-1 **71** 6ex........ (b) ClareLindop 1 78
(J R Gask) *hld up in last: sme prog 2f out: stl only 9th 1f out: threaded through and str run to take 2nd nr fin* **14/1**

-024 3 ½ **Resentful Angel**[57] 2166 4-9-0 **63**........ (b[1]) TobyAtkinson(7) 3 69
(Pat Eddery) *hld up towards rr on outer: hanging and nt qckn over 2f out: rapid prog jst over 1f out: r.o wl to snatch 3rd nr fin* **14/1**

360 4 nse **Castano**[21] 3283 5-8-13 **58**........ JamesMillman(3) 6 64
(B R Millman) *wl in rr on inner: prog fr 2f out: styd on to take 2nd last 50yds: lost 2 pls fnl strides* **20/1**

5022 5 ¾ **Lethal**[7] 3738 6-8-12 **61**........ RosieJessop(7) 2 65
(Andrew Reid) *disp ld at str pce tl def advantage after 3f: drvn and hdd over 1f out: fdd and lost 4 pls last 50yds* **8/1**[2]

000 6 nse **Kingsgate Castle**[7] 3732 4-9-5 **61**........ (b) IanMongan 14 65
(Miss Gay Kelleway) *pressed ldrs: rdn to chal 2f out: nt qckn over 1f out: 3rd ins fnl f: lost 3 pls nr fin* **20/1**

0245 7 2½ **Munich (IRE)**[7] 3732 5-9-4 **60**........ JimCrowley 10 57
(Mrs S Leech) *towards rr: sme prog on inner over 2f out: shkn up over 1f out: no hdwy after* **9/1**[3]

00-1 8 ½ **Sea Land (FR)**[8] 3720 5-9-2 **63** 6ex........ LanceBetts(5) 7 59
(B Ellison) *chsd ldrs: rdn over 2f out: nt qckn and no imp over 1f out: wknd fnl f* **8/1**[2]

0001 9 ½ **Mocha Java**[16] 3467 6-9-1 **62**........ RossAtkinson(5) 8 56
(M Salaman) *disp ld at str pce for 3f: drvn 3f out: wknd over 1f out* **14/1**

5060 10 3½ **Norcroft**[8] 3722 7-9-8 **64**........ (p) VinceSlattery 9 49
(Mrs C A Dunnett) *a towards rr: shkn up and no prog wl over 2f out: no ch after* **33/1**

450 11 nk **Convallaria (FR)**[23] 3224 6-9-2 **58**........ (b) GeorgeBaker 12 42
(C F Wall) *hld up on inner: prog 3f out: chsd ldrs u.p wl over 1f out: sn wknd* **10/1**

-006 12 ½ **Coole Dodger (IRE)**[12] 3558 4-9-5 **61**........ RoystonFfrench 4 44
(B Ellison) *prom on outer: lost pl 1/2-way: struggling in rr over 2f out* **33/1**

002 13 hd **Sun Catcher (IRE)**[16] 3467 6-8-10 **59**........ (p) SimonPearce(7) 13 41
(P G Murphy) *pushed along in midfield 1/2-way: struggling over 2f out* **16/1**

3556 14 1½ **Sew'N'So Character (IRE)**[48] 2400 8-9-7 **63**........ (b) DaneO'Neill 11 41
(M Blanshard) *a in last pair: rdn on outer 3f out: sn btn* **12/1**

1m 25.69s (-0.31) **Going Correction** +0.01s/f (Slow) **14** Ran SP% **132.4**
Speed ratings (Par 101): **101,100,99,99,98 98,96,95,94,90 90,89,89,88**
toteswingers: 1&2 £5.40, 1&3 £11.00, 2&3 £14.20 CSF £7.00 CT £214.51 TOTE £2.20: £1.60, £3.70, £4.20; EX 23.00 Place 6: £4628.36 Place 5: £1021.69.
Owner Mrs Janice Jones **Bred** Kilfrush Stud **Trained** Newmarket, Suffolk
■ Stewards' Enquiry : Clare Lindop three-day ban: careless riding (Jul 30-31, Aug 2)

FOCUS
They went a decent gallop, but the strong finishers got going just too late.
Lethal Official explanation: jockey said gelding hung right
T/Plt: £6,446.80 to a £1 stake. Pool: £57,403.57. 6.50 winning tickets. T/Qpdt: £528.50 to a £1 stake. Pool: £7,070.94. 9.90 winning tickets. JN

3739 LINGFIELD (L-H)
Wednesday, July 15

OFFICIAL GOING: Turf course - good to firm (9.2) all-weather - standard
Wind: Breezy, behind Weather: overcast, blustery

3984 WEATHERBYS BANK MAIDEN STKS 1m 1f
2:20 (2:21) (Class 5) 3-4-Y-0 £2,729 (£806; £403) Stalls Low

Form RPR

-542 1 **Almuktahem**[22] 3238 3-9-2 **75**........ (v[1]) RHills 8 83
(Sir Michael Stoute) *mde all: pressed and rdn 3f out: forged ahd ent fnl f: styd on wl* **2/1**[2]

2 2 2½ **Shakalaka (IRE)**[44] 2551 3-9-2 **79**........ GeorgeBaker 3 78
(G L Moore) *trckd ldng trio: chsd wnr over 2f out: shkn up ent 2f out: drvn and fnd nil over 1f out: one pce* **11/8**[1]

6 3 3¼ **Ebony Eyes**[26] 3100 3-8-11 0........ JimCrowley 1 66
(W J Knight) *chsd wnr: rdn and effrt over 3f out: wknd u.p wl over 1f out* **12/1**

03 4 9 **Mayolynn (USA)**[14] 3508 3-8-11 0........ TPQueally 5 46
(H R A Cecil) *chsd ldng pair: rdn and racd awkwardly over 3f out: sn btn* **8/1**

5-50 5 6 **Peal Park**[5] 3803 3-8-11 **55**........ TGMcLaughlin 7 33
(Karen George) *stdd s: t.k.h: hld up in rr: lost tch 4f out: nvr a factor* **80/1**

500 6 4½ **Calling Birds (IRE)**[54] 2220 3-8-11 **48**........ (p) JimmyQuinn 4 23
(Karen George) *in tch in midfield tl over 4f out: sn struggling and no ch fnl 3f* **100/1**

5 7 1 **Grand Pere**[8] 3718 3-9-2 0........ StephenDonohoe 6 26
(P D Evans) *taken down early: t.k.h: hld up in tch: struggling 4f out: sn wl btn* **50/1**

8 3½ **Emiratesdotcom** 3-9-2 0........ RoystonFfrench 2 18
(M Johnston) *s.i.s: a wl bhd: lost tch 4f out* **5/1**[3]

9 19 **Barnes Bridge** 4-9-5 0........ KierenFox(7) 9 —
(M J Attwater) *v s.i.s: sn rdn along: a last: t.o fnl 4f* **66/1**

1m 55.21s (-1.39) **Going Correction** +0.01s/f (Good)
WFA 3 from 4yo 10lb **9** Ran SP% **116.6**
Speed ratings (Par 103): **106,103,100,92,87 83,82,79,62**
toteswingers: 1&2 £1.70, 1&3 £4.90, 2&3 £3.90 CSF £5.17 TOTE £2.80: £1.40, £1.10, £2.30; EX 4.60 Trifecta £20.30 Pool: £297.37 - 10.83 winning units..
Owner Hamdan Al Maktoum **Bred** Shadwell Estate Company Limited **Trained** Newmarket, Suffolk

FOCUS
Not a particularly strong maiden.
Emiratesdotcom Official explanation: jockey said gelding was never travelling

3985 CELEBRATING THE LIFE OF JASON STOCKTON H'CAP 1m 2f
2:50 (2:50) (Class 6) (0-65,66) 3-Y-O £2,047 (£604; £302) Stalls Low

Form RPR

0-44 1 **Fire King**[17] 3426 3-8-8 **52**........ RobertHavlin 11 65+
(J A Geake) *hld up in tch: hdwy to trck ldng pair 4f out: led gng wl 3f out: pushed clr over 2f out: in n.d after: eased towards fin* **8/1**

0015 2 5 **Fong's Alibi**[13] 3535 3-9-7 **65**........ (p) LPKeniry 5 66
(J S Moore) *hld up towards rr: rdn and hdwy 3f out: drvn to chse clr wnr over 1f out: no imp: plugged on for clr 2nd* **5/1**[3]

006 3 2¼ **Bedarra Boy**[15] 3472 3-8-11 **55**........ MartinDwyer 4 52
(D W P Arbuthnot) *s.i.s: pushed along in last: reminder 7f out: hdwy and edging lft 2f out: kpt on to go modest 3rd ins fnl f: nvr nr ldrs* **20/1**

100 4 2¾ **Clippity Clop (IRE)**[42] 2605 3-9-4 **62**........ ShaneKelly 12 53
(J A Osborne) *hld up towards rr: hdwy 5f out: drvn and pressing for 2nd whn edgd lft 2f out: no prog and wl btn over 1f out* **10/1**

0040 5 nk **Wahan (USA)**[29] 3005 3-8-5 **49**........ (t) HayleyTurner 1 39
(C E Brittain) *hld up towards rr: effrt towards inner 3f out: drvn and no prog wl over 1f out* **17/2**

-044 6 1¾ **Wellesley**[34] 2863 3-9-3 **61**........ AdamKirby 7 48
(W R Swinburn) *chsd ldrs: rdn to chse wnr wl over 2f out: sn outpcd and wl hld fnl 2f: lost 2nd over 1f out: wknd* **10/3**[1]

0-66 7 7 **Kayfiar (USA)**[13] 3535 3-9-6 **64**........ JimmyQuinn 8 37
(P F I Cole) *hld up in tch in midfield: lost pl and dropped to rr on downhill run 4f out: wl bhd fnl 3f* **9/2**[2]

-000 8 14 **Do Be Brave (IRE)**[20] 3302 3-8-11 **55**........ DaneO'Neill 10 —
(Paul Mason) *dwlt: sn bustled along and hdwy to chse leaedr 8f out: drvn and ev ch briefly 3f out: sn struggling: wl bhd and eased fnl f: t.o* **16/1**

0064 9 1½ **Proud Junior (USA)**[15] 3473 3-8-6 **50**........ ChrisCatlin 9 —
(S A Callaghan) *chsd ldr tl 8f out: styd chsng ldrs tl lost pl 4f out: wl bhd fnl 3f: t.o* **8/1**

-605 10 2¾ **Happy And Glorious (IRE)**[17] 3426 3-8-8 **52**........ RHills 6 —
(J W Hills) *sn led: rdn and hdd 3f out: sn wknd: bhd and eased fr over 1f out: t.o* **12/1**

2m 10.87s (0.37) **Going Correction** +0.01s/f (Good) **10** Ran SP% **118.1**
Speed ratings (Par 98): **94,92,90,89 88,82,71,70,68**
toteswingers: 1&2 £7.00, 1&3 £37.80, 2&3 £22.90 CSF £48.42 CT £783.05 TOTE £11.00: £3.60, £1.80, £5.60; EX 28.70 TRIFECTA Not won..
Owner Dr J M Leigh **Bred** Dr J M Leigh **Trained** Kimpton, Hants

FOCUS
A weak handicap bordering on selling class.
Proud Junior(USA) Official explanation: jockey said colt failed to come down the hill

3986 WEATHERBYS BLOODSTOCK INSURANCE H'CAP 2m
3:20 (3:20) (Class 5) (0-75,73) 3-Y-0+ £2,729 (£806; £403) Stalls Low

Form RPR

0/52 1 **Swordsman (GER)**[19] 3346 7-9-7 **66**........ ChrisCatlin 3 76
(C Gordon) *chsd ldr tl led 5f out: mde rest: drvn clr over 1f out: styd on wl* **7/2**[2]

4-06 2 5 **Mohawk Star (IRE)**[22] 1435 8-9-6 **65**........ (v) GeorgeBaker 2 69
(I A Wood) *stdd s: hld up in last pair: pushed along over 5f out: hdwy on outer 4f out: chsd ldrs and drvn over 2f out: no ch w wnr fnl f: plugged on to go 2nd fnl 100yds* **9/1**

6-26 3 ¾ **Tribe**[20] 3313 7-9-4 **63**........ DaneO'Neill 6 66
(P R Webber) *stdd s: hld up in last pair: hdwy 8f out: chsd wnr over 4f out: rdn over 3f out: drvn and btn over 1f out* **7/2**[2]

643 4 2¼ **Whitcombe Spirit**[39] 2725 4-8-10 **55**........ RobertHavlin 4 55
(Jamie Poulton) *hld up in tch: hung lft over 3f out: rdn 3f out: wknd wl over 1f out* **4/1**[3]

45/0 5 9 **Fixation**[30] 2983 5-8-10 **55**........ LPKeniry 5 45
(Mrs L C Jewell) *hld up in tch: rdn and brief effrt 3f out: sn btn* **33/1**

11-0 6 9 **Casual Garcia**[67] 1863 4-10-0 **73**........ SebSanders 1 52
(Sir Mark Prescott) *led: reminders 9f out: rdn 7f out: hdd 5f out: steadily lost pl: bhd fr 3f out* **3/1**[1]

0063 7 14 **Little Sark (IRE)**[14] 3503 4-8-9 **54** oh1........ StephenDonohoe 7 26
(P D Evans) *chsd ldrs: lost pl and rdn over 4f out: wl btn 3f out: eased fnl f* **6/1**

3m 34.94s (0.14) **Going Correction** +0.01s/f (Good) **7** Ran SP% **116.7**
Speed ratings (Par 103): **99,96,96,95,90 86,79**
toteswingers: 1&2 £7.00, 1&3 £3.00, 2&3 £8.20 CSF £35.14 TOTE £4.50: £2.60, £3.60; EX 46.60 TRIFECTA Not won..
Owner Mrs Kate Digweed **Bred** M Beining **Trained** Morestead, Hants

FOCUS
This didn't look a strong race even before the desperate effort by favourite Casual Garcia, so it isn't form to get excited about.
Whitcombe Spirit Official explanation: trainer said gelding was unsuited by the good to firm going

3987 EUROPEAN BREEDERS' FUND MAIDEN FILLIES' STKS 6f (P)
3:50 (3:51) (Class 5) 2-Y-O £3,561 (£1,059; £529; £264) Stalls Low

Form RPR

1 **Puff (IRE)** 2-9-0 0........ SebSanders 9 80+
(R M Beckett) *stdd s: in rr: wd bnd 2f out and stl modest 9th wl over 1f out: str run ent fnl f: wnt 2nd ins fnl f: led towards fin* **10/3**[1]

20 2 1 **Piccadilly Filly (IRE)**[7] 3733 2-9-0 0........ EdwardCreighton 4 77
(E J Creighton) *led: clr 1/2-way: wl clr over 1f out: wknd ins fnl f and hdd towards fin* **13/2**

6 3 1¼ **So Surreal (IRE)**[16] 3458 2-9-0 0........ FergusSweeney 2 73
(G L Moore) *hmpd s: sn in tch: rdn to chse clr ldr wl over 1f out: no prog tl styd on u.p fnl 100yds* **10/1**

4 4 2 **Mellifera**[21] 3271 2-9-0 0........ AdamKirby 8 67
(W R Swinburn) *chsd ldrs tl lost pl over 3f out: hdwy and rdn over 1f out: kpt on fnl f* **7/2**[2]

45 5 nk **Pastel Blue (IRE)**[21] 3271 2-9-0 0........ HayleyTurner 10 66
(M L W Bell) *t.k.h: hld up towards rr: hdwy and rdn jst over 2f out: kpt on same pce fr over 1f out* **7/1**

6 2¾ **Luluti (IRE)** 2-9-0 0........ JamieSpencer 11 58+
(S A Callaghan) *s.i.s: bhd: rn green and wd bnd 2f out: kpt on fnl f: nvr on terms* **6/1**[3]

7 ½ **Suzi's A Smartlady (IRE)** 2-9-0 0........ RoystonFfrench 5 57
(M Johnston) *s.i.s: sn in tch: rdn and struggling ent fnl 2f: edgd lft wl over 1f out: wl hld after* **7/1**

8 ½ **Exearti** 2-9-0 0........ DaneO'Neill 7 55
(Paul Mason) *s.i.s: a in rr: rdn 3f out: kpt on same pce fnl 2f: nvr nr ldrs* **50/1**

0 **9** 2¾ **Slasl**[21] 3271 2-9-0 0 J-PGuillambert 1 47
(C E Brittain) *chsd ldr: outpcd 1/2-way: lost modest 2nd wl over 1f out: sn wknd* **33/1**

10 5 **Hope'N'Reason (USA)** 2-9-0 0 RichardMullen 6 32
(D M Simcock) *wnt rt at s: hld up in midfield: effrt on inner 2f out: wknd qckly over 1f out* **20/1**

050 **11** 12 **Dolly Will Do**[55] 2201 2-9-0 0 JimCrowley 3 —
(N P Mulholland) *wnt lft s: sn rcvrd and chsd ldrs: wknd qckly over 2f out: t.o over 1f out* **100/1**

1m 12.33s (0.43) **Going Correction** -0.05s/f (Stan) **11** Ran SP% **117.7**
Speed ratings (Par 91): **95,93,92,89,88 85,84,83,80,73 57**
toteswingers: 1&2 £7.10, 1&3 £9.80, 2&3 £14.60 CSF £24.63 TOTE £4.30: £1.80, £1.20, £3.70; EX 32.30.
Owner Mrs David Aykroyd **Bred** Yeomanstown Stud **Trained** Whitsbury, Hants

FOCUS
The form of this fillies' maiden is straightforward. There was in-running carnage on the exchanges here as £9k got matched at 1.01 on Piccadilly Filly, who looked home and hosed when around six lengths clear entering the final furlong.

NOTEBOOK
Puff(IRE) came from the clouds to win going away. Her cause looked fairly hopeless as she was towards the back of the field and sat quite wide leaving the back, but she began to make steady headway around the home bend and, once straightened up for home, she took off down the middle of the track and stormed home to score in pretty exhilarating style. Bred to fairly speedy, connections have given her a Lowther entry suggesting she's been showing plenty at home. (tchd 3-1 and 4-1)
Piccadilly Filly(IRE) had proved very difficult to settle at Kempton last time so connections opted to let her stride out in front this time. Despite again racing a little freely early, the tactics looked to have paid off in the straight where she was clear, but she ran out of steam close home and was cut down. If connections can get her to settle a little better she is sure to win a similar race. (op 5-1)
So Surreal(IRE) had shaped with only minor promise at Windsor on her debut but this was a good step forward and she kept on well without having the turn of foot of the winner. She is going the right way and shapes as though she may already appreciate another furlong. (op 12-1 tchd 14-1)
Mellifera ◆, who was three lengths behind Piccadilly Filly at Kempton on her debut, stayed on from off the pace and saw her race out much better than first time up, so she's going forward and looks to have a maiden in her. (op 4-1)
Pastel Blue(IRE) ◆ isn't having much luck with draws at the moment. Having again been stuck out wide here, she stayed on well enough to suggest she's got the ability to do better. (op 6-1 tchd 15-2)
Suzi's A Smartlady(IRE) reportedly failed to handle the bend. Official explanation: jockey said filly failed to handle the bend (op 9-1 tchd 11-1)

3988 EBF PAUL KELLEWAY MEMORIAL CLASSIFIED STKS 1m (P)
4:20 (4:22) (Class 3) 3-Y-0+ £8,742 (£2,601; £1,300; £649) Stalls High

Form RPR

-550 **1** **Tudor Key (IRE)**[27] 3049 3-8-9 87 JimCrowley 7 94
(Mrs A J Perrett) *led tl over 5f out: chsd ldr after tl rdn to chal 2f out: styd on gamely to ld last stride* **5/1**[2]

3-03 **2** *shd* **Film Set (USA)**[17] 3431 3-8-9 90 (t) TedDurcan 9 94
(Saeed Bin Suroor) *t.k.h: trckd ldr tl led over 5f out: hrd pressed and rdn 2f out: hld on to narrow ld tl hdd last stride* **7/2**[1]

2610 **3** ½ **Dalradian (IRE)**[33] 2890 3-8-9 88 ShaneKelly 3 92+
(W J Knight) *stdd after s: hld up in rr: hdwy gng wl 2f out: swtchd lft and effrt 1f out: chsd ldng pair and drvn ins fnl f: kpt on same pce fnl 100yds* **7/2**[1]

51-0 **4** 2¼ **The Which Doctor**[17] 3431 4-9-4 88 TPQueally 5 89
(J Noseda) *stdd s: hld up in rr: pushed along 3f out: hdwy wl over 1f out: drvn ent fnl f: kpt on but nt pce to rch ldrs* **6/1**[3]

4200 **5** 1 **Arabian Spirit**[48] 2412 4-9-4 90 JamieSpencer 6 87
(E A L Dunlop) *hld up in tch: rdn and effrt 2f out: drvn and unable qck ent fnl f: wknd ins fnl f* **7/2**[1]

0000 **6** ½ **Bomber Command (USA)**[5] 3796 6-9-1 89 PatrickHills(3) 4 85
(J W Hills) *in tch: rdn 3f out: drvn and no imp over 1f out* **25/1**

0502 **7** 2¾ **Gallantry**[19] 3335 7-8-13 90 MCGeran(5) 2 79
(P Howling) *chsd ldrs: rdn 3f out: wknd u.p ent fnl f* **9/1**

-000 **8** 16 **Grand Vista**[117] 5-9-4 85 (t) GeorgeBaker 8 59
(G L Moore) *stdd s: t.k.h: hld up in rr: effrt on outer and hanging rt 3f out: wknd 2f out: eased fr over 1f out: t.o* **20/1**

1m 37.98s (-0.22) **Going Correction** -0.05s/f (Stan)
WFA 3 from 4yo+ 9lb **8** Ran SP% **116.2**
Speed ratings (Par 107): **99,98,98,96,95 94,91,75**
toteswingers: 1&2 £7.00, 1&3 £3.00, 2&3 £8.20 CSF £23.29 TOTE £6.20: £1.80, £1.70, £1.80; EX 29.70 Trifecta £255.50 Pool: £573.35 - 1.66 winning units..
Owner Coombelands Racing Syndicate **Bred** Gainsborough Stud Management Ltd **Trained** Pulborough, W Sussex

FOCUS
A decent contest on paper but the early gallop wasn't strong and that played into the hands of the front two, who upped the tempo around the home turn and settled down to fight out a sustained dual through the final furlong with nothing from behind getting in a significant blow.

NOTEBOOK
Tudor Key(IRE), who wasn't totally disgraced in the Britannia Stakes at Royal Ascot, stuck on gamely to edge out Film Set in the final strides and bag his first win of the year. Although this was his first taste of Polytrack, he's bred to thrive on it and this was his best effort of the season so far, but both he and the runner-up are probably a bit flattered by the bare result given the way things panned out. (op 13-2)
Film Set(USA) was a bit keen early as he sat close to Tudor Key and he actually held a neck advantage turning into the straight, but he was unable to fend off the persistent challenge from that rival in the final furlong. This was a solid enough effort but he doesn't appear to be improving at the moment. (op 3-1)
Dalradian(IRE) has done well in the circumstances for he ideally wants a much stronger pace to chase and, having made a big move from off the pace to get within striking distance of the front two over a furlong out, his effort petered out a touch. He looks on good terms with himself and remains of distinct interest in a more strongly run contest. (op 3-1, tchd 4-1 in places)
The Which Doctor is another to shape with promise having been held up last early and this was a step forward on his disappointing Windsor reappearance. (op 11-2 tchd 13-2)
Arabian Spirit was a touch disappointing given he wasn't far off the pace early. He dropped away in the straight and is not seeing out his races at the moment. (op 11-2)
Gallantry Official explanation: jockey said gelding was never travelling
Grand Vista Official explanation: jockey said horse hung right

3989 FOREST ROW H'CAP 6f (P)
4:50 (4:50) (Class 5) (0-75,75) 3-Y-0 £2,729 (£806; £403) Stalls Low

Form RPR

4065 **1** **Comadoir (IRE)**[25] 3159 3-9-5 73 FergusSweeney 11 81
(Miss Jo Crowley) *mde all: sn crossed to inner: rdn clr wl over 1f out: in n.d fnl f: unchal* **12/1**

0003 **2** 4½ **Temperence Hall (USA)**[7] 3743 3-8-2 56 oh2 (v) RichardThomas 9 50
(J R Best) *bmpd s: chsd wnr: sltly hmpd over 5f out: rdn and nt pce of wnr wl over 1f out: no ch w wnr after: hld on for 2nd* **16/1**

4330 **3** 1¾ **Riflessione**[19] 3341 3-9-7 75 (b) ChrisCatlin 6 63
(R A Harris) *chsd ldrs: rdn and unable qck 2f out: drvn and plugged on same pce fnl f* **10/1**[3]

6443 **4** 1¼ **Raimond Ridge (IRE)**[9] 3676 3-8-13 72 MCGeran(5) 1 56
(M R Channon) *racd in midfield: rdn and hdwy wl over 1f out: one pce and no imp fnl f* **5/1**[2]

2-40 **5** ¾ **Good Humoured**[72] 1730 3-8-8 62 SebSanders 7 44+
(Sir Mark Prescott) *hmpd s: bhd: hdwy on outer 3f out: wd bnd 2f out: sn rdn and no prog after* **2/1**[1]

0200 **6** ½ **Song Of Praise**[11] 3625 3-9-7 75 JimmyQuinn 3 55
(M Blanshard) *t.k.h: hld up in tch: rdn and unable qck 2f out: drvn and one pce fr over 1f out* **10/1**[3]

1002 **7** 1¾ **Beautiful Filly**[21] 3272 3-9-2 70 (b) RichardMullen 10 44
(D M Simcock) *s.i.s: dropped in towards rr: drvn and effrt ent fnl 2f: n.d* **5/1**[2]

33-0 **8** ½ **Chosen Son (IRE)**[14] 3506 3-9-1 69 TedDurcan 2 42
(P J O'Gorman) *chsd ldrs: rdn and unable qck 2f out: wknd qckly over 1f out* **10/1**[3]

5360 **9** 3¼ **Divine Force**[14] 3505 3-8-8 62 SimonWhitworth 4 24
(M Wigham) *awkward leaving stalls and slowly away: a in rr* **50/1**

0440 **10** ½ **Quick Single (USA)**[6] 3783 3-8-12 66 (v) AdamKirby 8 27
(P S McEntee) *wnt rt and bmpd s: a bhd: nvr a factor* **20/1**

0205 **11** 1 **Pocket's Pick (IRE)**[14] 3506 3-9-6 74 (t) GeorgeBaker 5 32
(G L Moore) *dwlt: towards rr: reminders and no rspnse wl over 2f out: wknd 2f out* **14/1**

1m 11.58s (-0.32) **Going Correction** -0.05s/f (Stan) **11** Ran SP% **120.9**
Speed ratings (Par 100): **100,94,91,90,89 88,86,85,81,80 79**
toteswingers: 1&2 £7.10, 1&3 £9.80, 2&3 £14.60 CSF £193.53 CT £2041.82 TOTE £14.50: £4.30, £4.20, £3.90; EX 297.90 TRIFECTA Not won. Place 6: £511.26 Place 5: £392.09..
Owner Mrs Liz Nelson **Bred** J S Bolger **Trained** Whitcombe, Dorset
■ Stewards' Enquiry : Fergus Sweeney two-day ban: careless riding (Jul 30-31)

FOCUS
Hard to know what to make of this as the winner blasted out from his wide stall and never saw another rival, with very few getting into a challenging position.
T/Plt: £320.60 to a £1 stake. Pool: £53,484.43. 121.76 winning tickets. T/Qpdt: £95.10 to a £1 stake. Pool: £3,316.24. 25.80 winning tickets. SP

3990 - 3992a (Foreign Racing) - See Raceform Interactive

3256 BATH (L-H)
Thursday, July 16

OFFICIAL GOING: Good to firm (10.3) changing to good after race 4 (7.55)
Wind: Nil Weather: Raining

3993 NESTLE PROFESSIONAL NURSERY 5f 11y
6:20 (6:23) (Class 5) 2-Y-0 £4,209 (£1,252; £625; £312) Stalls Centre

Form RPR

1063 **1** **Quaker Parrot**[7] 3762 2-8-8 72 RichardKingscote 3 74
(Tom Dascombe) *led early: chsd ldr: rdn to ld 1f out: r.o* **10/3**[2]

0320 **2** 1¼ **Kings Of Leo**[8] 3742 2-9-7 85 EddieAhern 1 83
(R Hannon) *sn led: rdn wl over 1f out: hdd 1f out: nt qckn* **9/2**

2361 **3** *nk* **Any Day (IRE)**[8] 3742 2-8-10 74 6ex SebSanders 5 70
(R M Beckett) *hld up: hdwy wl over 1f out: kpt on ins fnl f* **9/2**

333 **4** ¾ **La Fortunata**[33] 2919 2-8-9 73 AdrianMcCarthy 4 67
(J R Jenkins) *chsd ldrs: kpt on same pce fnl f* **7/2**[3]

6100 **5** 1¼ **Flyinflyout**[19] 3396 2-8-7 76 MCGeran(5) 2 65
(M R Channon) *s.i.s: hld up: hdwy on ins over 2f out: btn over 1f out* **5/2**[1]

61.94 secs (-0.56) **Going Correction** -0.175s/f (Firm) **5** Ran SP% **110.2**
Speed ratings (Par 94): **97,95,94,93,91**
CSF £17.86 TOTE £4.10: £2.50, £2.10; EX 20.30.
Owner Timeform Betfair Racing Club Partnership **Bred** Mrs D Du Feu And Trickledown Stud **Trained** Lambourn, Berks

FOCUS
Only five runners, all fillies, but a tight handicap on paper. The 'official' ratings shown next to each horse are estimated and for information purposes only.

NOTEBOOK
Quaker Parrot, making her nursery debut, ultimately won with some authority. She had finished nearly five lengths behind Kings Of Leo when when second and sixth at Windsor over this trip last month, but this race was run much more to the liking of Quaker Parrot. This time she had her adversary to aim at plus a 13lb pull. She gives the impression she wouldn't have trouble with the extra half furlong. (op 3-1 tchd 7-2)
Kings Of Leo had plenty on with top weight and although she played to the winner's strengths by giving her a target, she has to be ridden this way to perform to her optimum. However, a mark of 85 is going to make things pretty tough. (op 5-1 tchd 4-1)
Any Day(IRE) ran with credit under a 6lb penalty for winning a nursery at Lingfield last time, when Kings Of Leo didn't fire when held up. She was tried over 6f earlier in the season and while she might not quite have got it then, she gave the impression she would now be suited by a bit further. (tchd 5-1)
La Fortunata, in a nursery for the first time, has done all her racing at this distance but again didn't have required pace throughout the last furlong. Her pedigree suggests she might be worth a try over another furlong. (tchd 3-1 and 4-1)
Flyinflyout had been racing in much better class over 6f without success since winning over an extended 5f here in May. On this evidence she does need a stiffer test than the minimum. (op 11-4 tchd 3-1)

3994 COCA COLA CLASSIC CLAIMING STKS 5f 161y
6:50 (6:50) (Class 5) 3-Y-0+ £3,561 (£1,059; £529; £264) Stalls Centre

Form RPR

0221 **1** **Piazza San Pietro**[15] 3502 3-9-1 68 (p) SebSanders 5 72
(A B Haynes) *mde all: drvn out wl ins fnl f* **3/1**[2]

0-00 **2** ¾ **The Name Is Frank**[15] 3505 4-8-8 52 EddieAhern 8 59
(Mark Gillard) *w wnr: rdn fnl f: kpt on* **10/1**

6602 **3** 2½ **Miss Firefly**[3] 3926 4-8-2 50 WilliamCarson(5) 2 50
(R J Hodges) *a.p: rdn over 1f out: one pce* **11/4**[1]

1404 **4** 3½ **One More Round (USA)**[57] 2184 11-8-7 65 ow2 (b) RichardEvans(5) 6 43
(P D Evans) *hld up in rr: sme hdwy on outside over 1f out: rdn and kpt on to take 4th wl ins fnl f* **6/1**

-300 **5** 1½ **Mr Forthright**[24] 3204 5-8-11 46 (p) JackDean(5) 9 42
(J M Bradley) *prom: rdn over 1f out: wknd ins fnl f* **16/1**

2060 **6** 1 **Fyodor (IRE)**[17] 3459 8-8-10 65 (v) StephenDonohoe 1 33
(P D Evans) *prom: rdn over 1f out: sn wknd* **7/2**[3]

0056 **7** 11 **Shybutwilling (IRE)**[13] 3577 4-8-7 48 FergusSweeney 4 —
(Mrs P N Dutfield) *hld up and bhd: rdn over 1f out: sn struggling* **16/1**

4006 **8** *2* **Talamahana**[24] 3204 4-8-4 43.....................(v) DavidProbert(3) 7 —
(A B Haynes) *prom tl wknd over 2f out* **22/1**

500- **9** *8* **Professor Malone**[226] 7521 4-8-12 45..................... TravisBlock 3 —
(M S Tuck) *in rr: pushed along over 3f out: rdn and struggling over 1f out: eased fnl f* **50/1**

1m 10.07s (-1.13) **Going Correction** -0.175s/f (Firm)
WFA 3 from 4yo+ 5lb **9** Ran SP% **115.3**
Speed ratings (Par 103): **100,99,95,91,89 87,73,70,59**
toteswingers: 1&2 £4.20, 1&3 £2.00, 2&3 £4.50. CSF £33.02 TOTE £3.40: £1.10, £2.90, £1.50; EX 35.80.
Owner K Corke **Bred** T E Pocock **Trained** Limpley Stoke, Bath

FOCUS
A weak claimer run at only a moderate pace for the first furlong and a half. The form is best rated around the runner-up.
Shybutwilling(IRE) Official explanation: jockey said filly lost its action

3995 SHIRES FAMOUS PIES H'CAP 5f 161y
7:25 (7:25) (Class 4) (0-80,78) 3-Y-O+ **£6,308** (£1,888; £944; £472; £235) **Stalls** Centre

Form RPR

5660 **1** **Whiskey Junction**[24] 3212 5-9-9 **75**..................... SebSanders 4 84
(M Quinn) *mde all: rdn wl over 1f out: drvn out* **6/1**[3]

3260 **2** *1* **Forest Dane**[18] 3422 9-8-9 **66**..................... SophieDoyle(5) 6 72
(Mrs N Smith) *hld up: hdwy over 2f out: rdn 1f out: kpt on u.p ins fnl f* **13/2**

2424 **3** *1* **The Tatling (IRE)**[12] 3623 12-9-7 **78**..................... JackDean(5) 1 80
(J M Bradley) *hld up in tch: rdn over 1f out: kpt on same pce ins fnl f* **7/1**

3312 **4** *shd* **Bateleur**[5] 3866 5-8-10 **67**..................... MCGeran(5) 2 69
(M R Channon) *a.p: n.m.r and swtchd lft jst over 1f out: rdn and nt qckn ins fnl f* **2/1**[1]

1520 **5** *2* **Kyllachy Storm**[10] 3691 5-9-7 **73**..................... DarryllHolland 5 68
(R J Hodges) *w wnr tl rdn wl over 1f out: fdd towards fin* **3/1**[2]

4666 **6** *3* **Blushing Maid**[33] 2913 3-8-5 **62**..................... KirstyMilczarek 3 47
(H S Howe) *s.i.s: hld up in rr: hdwy over 2f out: rdn wl over 1f out: wknd ins fnl f* **12/1**

2100 **7** *½* **Gift Horse**[20] 3335 9-9-5 **76**.....................(p) RichardEvans(5) 7 59
(P D Evans) *hld up: pushed along over 3f out: struggling whn rdn 2f out* **15/2**

1m 10.47s (-0.73) **Going Correction** -0.025s/f (Good)
WFA 3 from 5yo+ 5lb **7** Ran SP% **117.9**
Speed ratings (Par 105): **103,101,100,100,97 93,92**
toteswingers: 1&2 £8.30, 1&3 £10.40, 2&3 £11.50. CSF £45.67 CT £282.34 TOTE £8.50: £2.20, £3.90; EX 35.80.
Owner Steven Astaire **Bred** Mrs I A Balding **Trained** Newmarket, Suffolk

FOCUS
Persistent rain meant that riders decided to take the prescribed deviation to the stands' side up the straight and once again the right tactics off a steady pace were to be in front from the start. The form is not that convincing but does make some sense at face value.
Blushing Maid Official explanation: jockey said filly was unsuited by the good to firm ground

3996 CARLSBERG H'CAP 1m 5y
7:55 (7:56) (Class 4) (0-80,78) 3-Y-O+ **£6,308** (£1,888; £944; £472; £235) **Stalls** Low

Form RPR

0342 **1** **Dingaan (IRE)**[8] 3752 6-9-11 **76**..................... DavidProbert(3) 9 86
(A M Balding) *hld up in mid-div: swtchd lft and hdwy wl over 1f out: sn rdn: led ins fnl f: drvn out* **7/2**[1]

6266 **2** *1 ½* **Magroom**[22] 3283 5-8-9 **62**..................... WilliamCarson(5) 1 69
(R J Hodges) *hld up towards rr: hdwy over 3f out: chsd ldr over 2f out: led over 1f out tl ins fnl f: nt qckn: jst hld on for 2nd* **7/1**

0-23 **3** *nse* **Monashee Rock (IRE)**[11] 3662 4-9-4 **66**..................... ChrisCatlin 8 73
(M Salaman) *hld up in rr: pushed along and hdwy over 3f out: ev ch 1f out: rdn and nt qckn ins fnl f: jst hld for 2nd* **13/2**[3]

2403 **4** *2 ¼* **Rock Anthem (IRE)**[7] 3770 5-9-0 **62**..................... StephenDonohoe 6 64
(Mike Murphy) *hld up in rr: hdwy over 1f out: rdn and one pce fnl f* **9/1**

5001 **5** *1 ¼* **Major Phil (IRE)**[17] 3469 3-9-8 **78**..................... EddieAhern 2 77
(L M Cumani) *hld up in tch: pushed along over 2f out: rdn over 1f out: wknd ins fnl f* **7/2**[1]

0014 **6** *1 ½* **Very Well Red**[19] 3408 6-9-9 **71**..................... DarryllHolland 7 66
(P W Hiatt) *led: rdn and hdd over 1f out: wknd ins fnl f* **9/1**

1016 **7** *shd* **April Fool**[6] 3812 5-9-13 **75**.....................(v) RichardThomas 4 70
(J A Geake) *chsd ldr tl over 2f out: sn pushed along: wknd fnl f* **11/1**

5426 **8** *2 ½* **Bere Davis (FR)**[6] 3801 4-9-8 **75**..................... RichardEvans(5) 3 64+
(P D Evans) *prom: pushed along over 3f out: nt clr run over 2f out: wknd over 1f out* **6/1**[2]

0-02 **9** *nse* **Sunny Future (IRE)**[24] 3207 3-8-8 **71**..................... JakePayne(7) 5 60
(M S Saunders) *played up in stalls: s.s: a in rr* **16/1**

1m 40.92s (0.12) **Going Correction** -0.025s/f (Good)
WFA 3 from 4yo+ 8lb **9** Ran SP% **118.8**
Speed ratings (Par 105): **98,96,96,94,92 91,91,88,88**
toteswingers: 1&2 £33.10, 1&3 £4.20, 2&3 £33.10. CSF £29.38 CT £155.77 TOTE £4.90: £2.10, £2.40, £2.50; EX 28.30.
Owner Lady C S Cadbury **Bred** Mrs Gill Wilson **Trained** Kingsclere, Hants

FOCUS
A fair handicap. It was well run and the form is sound.
Bere Davis(FR) Official explanation: jockey said gelding hung left-handed

3997 ECHO FALLS CHASE H'CAP 2m 1f 34y
8:25 (8:27) (Class 6) (0-65,65) 4-Y-O+ **£2,914** (£867; £433; £216) **Stalls** Centre

Form RPR

-526 **1** **Brave Bugsy (IRE)**[29] 3029 6-8-5 **52**.....................(v) DavidProbert(3) 6 61
(A M Balding) *s.i.s: hld up: hdwy over 7f out: rdn over 2f out: led ins fnl f: styd on* **11/4**[1]

3-01 **2** *nk* **Star Of Pompey**[22] 3275 5-8-10 **54**..................... SebSanders 1 63
(A B Haynes) *chsd ldr: led over 8f out tl over 4f out: led over 2f out: hrd rdn and hdd ins fnl f: styd on* **3/1**[2]

1044 **3** *¾* **Party Palace**[6] 3814 5-8-7 **51**..................... KirstyMilczarek 7 59
(H S Howe) *led: hdd over 8f out: led over 4f out tl over 2f out: sn rdn: styd on same pce ins fnl f* **11/2**

-660 **4** *15* **Bolton Hall (IRE)**[15] 3503 7-8-4 **48**.....................(tp) FrankieMcDonald 3 38
(W K Goldsworthy) *stdd s: hld up in rr: hdwy over 4f out: sn struggling: pushed along over 3f out: tk modest 4th jst ins fnl f* **16/1**

0252 **5** *4 ½* **Lady Jinks**[15] 3503 4-8-7 **51**..................... EddieAhern 9 36
(R J Hodges) *hld up: pushed along over 3f out: n.d after* **6/1**

2220 **6** *¾* **Dream In Blue**[25] 3191 4-9-7 **65**..................... ChrisCatlin 8 49
(J A Osborne) *hld up in tch: pushed along over 6f out: wknd over 4f out* **16/1**

0410 **7** *1 ½* **Lord Oroko**[14] 3544 5-9-1 **59**..................... DarryllHolland 2 41
(J G M O'Shea) *t.k.h in rr: rdn and short-lived effrt over 2f out* **9/2**[3]

0660 **8** *2 ¾* **Speagle (IRE)**[13] 3594 7-7-9 **46** oh1..................... RichardRowe(7) 10 25
(A J Chamberlain) *prom tl wknd over 3f out* **40/1**

3m 52.65s (0.75) **Going Correction** -0.025s/f (Good) **8** Ran SP% **113.7**
Speed ratings (Par 101): **97,96,96,89,87 86,86,84**
toteswingers: 1&2 £3.30, 1&3 £3.80, 2&3 £6.80. CSF £11.09 CT £40.72 TOTE £3.50: £1.30, £1.30, £2.30; EX 10.90.
Owner West Mercia Fork Trucks Ltd **Bred** James F Hanly **Trained** Kingsclere, Hants
■ Stewards' Enquiry : Kirsty Milczarek one-day ban: used whip with excessive frequency (Jul 30)

FOCUS
A weak staying handicap which was not strongly run and that had only four of the field in with a serious chance of the home turn. The form makes sense.

3998 LINDLEY CATERING H'CAP 5f 11y
8:55 (8:55) (Class 5) (0-75,75) 3-Y-O+ **£4,209** (£1,252; £625; £312) **Stalls** Centre

Form RPR

1200 **1** **Desperate Dan**[18] 3422 8-9-2 **73**.....................(v) PNolan(7) 10 83
(A B Haynes) *s.i.s whn rdr sltly late removing blindfold: sn wl in rr: pushed along 3f out: hdwy 1f out: str run to ld towards fin* **10/1**

2212 **2** *1 ¾* **Matterofact (IRE)**[3] 3917 6-9-4 **68**..................... SebSanders 7 72
(M S Saunders) *hld up and bhd: hdwy whn swtchd lft wl over 1f out: sn rdn: ev ch wl ins fnl f: kpt on* **2/1**[1]

3230 **3** *hd* **Cape Royal**[12] 3623 9-9-3 **70**.....................(bt) KevinGhunowa(3) 8 73
(J M Bradley) *w ldr: led over 3f out: rdn ins fnl f: hdd towards fin* **18/1**

0136 **4** *½* **Brandywell Boy (IRE)**[5] 3860 6-8-12 **62**..................... RichardThomas 2 63
(D J S Ffrench Davis) *chsd ldrs: rdn over 1f out: kpt on same pce ins fnl f* **14/1**

3000 **5** *nk* **Mazzola**[13] 3570 3-8-13 **72**..................... MCGeran(5) 1 71
(M R Channon) *w ldrs: rdn jst over 1f out: edgd rt and nt qckn ins fnl f* **16/1**

3363 **6** *¾* **Step It Up (IRE)**[7] 3775 5-8-12 **62**..................... StephenDonohoe 4 60
(J R Boyle) *hld up and bhd: pushed along over 1f out: kpt on ins fnl f: nvr able to chal* **11/1**

0-04 **7** *hd* **Heaven**[22] 3261 4-9-8 **72**..................... DarryllHolland 6 69
(P J Makin) *bhd: pushed along over 2f out: rdn and sme prog 1f out: nvr trbld ldrs* **6/1**[3]

0623 **8** *½* **Espy**[16] 3477 4-9-6 **70**..................... EddieAhern 5 68+
(S Kirk) *chsd ldrs: rdn 2f out: no hdwy fnl f* **8/1**

3314 **9** *½* **Green Lagonda (AUS)**[5] 3860 7-8-8 **58** 6ex..................... PaulDoe 9 54+
(P D Evans) *chsd ldrs: outpcd and rdn over 2f out: nt clr run and swtchd lft ins fnl f: n.d* **9/2**[2]

-625 **10** *1 ½* **Ocean Blaze**[47] 2472 5-9-11 **75**..................... ChrisCatlin 11 63
(B R Millman) *led: hdd over 3f out: rdn jst over 1f out: wkng whn n.m.r ins fnl f* **9/1**

61.83 secs (-0.67) **Going Correction** -0.025s/f (Good)
WFA 3 from 4yo+ 4lb **10** Ran SP% **122.1**
Speed ratings (Par 103): **104,101,100,100,99 98,98,97,96,94**
toteswingers: 1&2 £2.70, 1&3 £30.00, 2&3 £25.60. CSF £31.82 CT £378.24 TOTE £8.60: £2.80, £1.40, £4.90; EX 53.70 Place 6: £117.51, Place 5: £34.01..
Owner Joe McCarthy **Bred** Sheikh Amin Dahlawi **Trained** Limpley Stoke, Bath
■ Stewards' Enquiry : M C Geran two-day ban: careless riding (Jul 31, Aug 2)

FOCUS
A modest handicap which was strongly run. The form reads sound enough.
Ocean Blaze Official explanation: trainer said mare was cut on its near fore
T/Plt: £201.10 to a £1 stake. Pool: £40,355.15. 146.47 winning tickets. T/Qpdt: £43.20 to a £1 stake. Pool: £3,712.82. 63.50 winning tickets. KH

3760 DONCASTER (L-H)
Thursday, July 16

OFFICIAL GOING: Good to soft (good in places; 7.6)
With the running rail moved out by four yards to the entrance of the straight, the distances of the final two races were increased by 12 yards.
Wind: Virtually nil Weather: Overcast

3999 ROBINSONS DESIGNER FASHION AT BAWTRY AMATEUR RIDERS' H'CAP 5f
6:35 (6:38) (Class 6) (0-65,63) 3-Y-O+ **£2,637** (£811; £405) **Stalls** High

Form RPR

001 **1** **Highland Warrior**[6] 3828 10-11-7 **63**..................... MrSWalker 12 77
(P T Midgley) *dwlt and towards rr: gd hdwy 2f out: str run to ld jst ins fnl f and sn clr* **5/2**[1]

420 **2** *3* **Rocket Ruby**[44] 2581 3-10-8 **54**..................... MrsMMorris 8 56
(D Shaw) *sn led: rdn wl over 1f out: drvn and hdd jst ins fnl f: kpt on same pce* **16/1**

-040 **3** *hd* **Lake Chini (IRE)**[28] 3065 7-10-11 **58**.....................(b) MissJoannaMason(5) 3 60
(M W Easterby) *prom: effrt 2f out: sn rdn and ev ch tl drvn ent fnl f and one pce* **7/1**[3]

0436 **4** *¾* **Jilly Why (IRE)**[13] 3570 8-10-12 **61**.....................(b) MissACraven(7) 14 60+
(Paul Green) *in rr: hdwy wl over 1f out: sn rdn and styd on ins fnl f: nrst fin* **9/1**

5605 **5** *nk* **Red River Boy**[12] 3612 4-10-7 **49**..................... MrSDobson 4 47
(C W Fairhurst) *bhd: hdwy wl over 1f out: sn rdn and styd on to chse ldrs ins fnl f: no imp towards fin* **12/1**

0005 **6** *1* **Town House**[13] 3570 7-9-12 **45**..................... MissAWallace(5) 16 40
(B P J Baugh) *in tch: hdwy 2f out: sn rdn and kpt on same pce ins fnl f* **14/1**

3300 **7** *½* **The History Man (IRE)**[21] 3304 6-10-8 **55**.....................(b) MissMMullineaux(5) 13 48
(M Mullineaux) *midfield: rdn along 1/2-way: kpt on u.p ins fnl f: nt rch ldrs* **9/1**

5140 **8** *¾* **Only A Game (IRE)**[2] 3938 4-10-11 **60**.....................(p) MissHBethell(7) 6 50
(I W McInnes) *prom: rdn along 2f out: grad wknd* **11/1**

0000 **9** *½* **Helping Hand (IRE)**[10] 3671 4-10-6 **53**..................... MrStephenHarrison(5) 17 41
(R Hollinshead) *in tch: rdn along 1/2-way: n.d* **5/1**[2]

-000 **10** *1* **Mission Impossible**[106] 1060 4-11-2 **63**..................... MissEStead(5) 1 48
(P C Haslam) *nvr bttr than midfield* **22/1**

0000 **11** *1* **Ronnie Howe**[7] 3765 5-10-6 **53**.....................(bt) MrKApark(5) 15 34
(S R Bowring) *midfield: rdn along over 2f out and sn wknd* **25/1**

4653 **12** *nk* **York Key Bar**[20] 3355 3-10-9 **60**..................... MrDaleSwift(5) 5 39
(B Ellison) *s.i.s: racd alone far side: a in rr* **20/1**

6005 **13** *1 ¼* **Sofinella (IRE)**[24] 3204 6-9-10 **45**..................... MissSPPearce(7) 9 21
(A W Carroll) *sn cl up: disp ld 1/2-way: rdn 2f out and sn wknd* **25/1**

03-0 **14** ½ **Windjammer**[41] 2657 5-10-7 **56**.......... MissRWilson(7) 10 30
(L A Mullaney) *cl up: rdn along 1/2-way and sn wknd* **25/1**

0005 **15** 1¼ **Wicksy Creek**[8] 3743 4-9-10 **45**.......... MrMMarris(7) 7 14
(G C Bravery) *a towards rr* **50/1**

61.42 secs (0.92) **Going Correction** +0.175s/f (Good)
WFA 3 from 4yo+ 4lb **15** Ran SP% **128.9**
Speed ratings (Par 101): **99,94,93,92,92 90,89,88,87,86 84,84,82,81,79**
toteswingers: 1&2 £12.00, 1&3 £4.10, 2&3 £20.30. CSF £45.60 CT £276.62 TOTE £3.60: £1.10, £5.60, £3.60; EX 44.30.
Owner R Wardlaw **Bred** Rowcliffe Stud **Trained** Westow, N Yorks

FOCUS
A modest amateur riders' handicap. Straightforward form with the winner close to his York mark.

4000 CAMPANILE HOTEL DONCASTER NOVICE STKS 6f
7:05 (7:15) (Class 4) 2-Y-O **£3,885** (£1,156; £577; £288) **Stalls** High

Form RPR

2 **1** **Summerinthecity (IRE)**[33] 2936 2-8-11 0.......... LDettori 6 85+
(J Noseda) *trckd ldr: swtchd lft and hdwy 2f out: rdn to chal 1f out: sn drvn and styd on u.p to ld nr fin* **5/6**[1]

1 **2** nk **Skylla**[12] 3633 2-8-10 0.......... JerryO'Dwyer 5 83
(J R Holt) *led: rdn along wl over 1f out: drvn ent fnl f: hdd and no ex towards fin* **5/1**

1 **3** 3¾ **Jairzihno**[21] 3306 2-9-1 0.......... RobertWinston 4 78+
(J R Best) *dwlt: hld up in rr: hdwy over 2f out: rdn wl over 1f out and ch tl drvn and one pce ent fnl f* **4/1**[2]

01 **4** 6 **Haltela (IRE)**[33] 2936 2-9-4 0.......... NCallan 2 62
(K A Ryan) *chsd ldng pair: rdn along 2f out: and wknd over 1f out* **9/2**[3]

01 **5** 9 **Dixie Bright (USA)**[24] 3226 2-9-4 0.......... PaulMulrennan 1 35
(J G Given) *cl up on outer: rdn along over 2f out and sn wknd* **20/1**

1m 13.81s (0.21) **Going Correction** +0.175s/f (Good) **5** Ran SP% **114.2**
Speed ratings (Par 96): **105,104,99,91,79**
toteswingers: 1&2 £4.00. CSF £5.84 TOTE £1.60: £1.20, £2.00; EX 5.80.
Owner Mrs Susan Roy **Bred** J Costello **Trained** Newmarket, Suffolk

FOCUS
Probably not a race about which to get too carried away, although the first two home are both worth keeping on the right side of, albeit for different reasons.

NOTEBOOK
Summerinthecity(IRE) enjoyed the perfect trip on the stands' rail, but when pulled out to throw down his challenge to the pacesetting Skylla, he seemed to take an age to get on top. Judged by the run of fourth-home Haltela, the winner had almost certainly come on plenty for his debut, as he reversed York placings in no uncertain terms and there could well be further to come now that he has got his head in front. Winning trainer Jeremy Noseda reported that the colt had suffered from sore shins since his debut and that he had only been able to get only two half-speed pieces of work into him since that race, making his performance here all the more laudable. Nurseries will now be his game and he shouldn't be overburdened in that sphere. (op Evens tchd 4-5 and 11-10 in places)
Skylla, who was not entirely unbacked when scoring at 50-1 on her debut, got loose at the start and cantered riderless down the home straight before being caught and allowed to take her chance. She showed an abundance of natural speed in front and looked for a long time as she was going to hold off her rivals. There are races to be won with her and she has the pace to go back to 5f. (op 11-2 tchd 6-1 and 4-1)
Jairzihno had broken his duck in what seemed only an average maiden on his debut. He kept on at one pace close home but could prove hard to place now. (op 11-2)
Haltela(IRE) may not have run to his best, but even so it's hard to see him beating the winner again despite the fact that he was giving him 7lb here. (op 4-1 tchd 11-2)
Dixie Bright(USA) Official explanation: jockey said colt lost off hind plate and hung left-handed throughout

4001 E B F SOCIETY LIFESTYLE & LEISURE MAGAZINE MAIDEN FILLIES' STKS 7f
7:35 (7:41) (Class 4) 2-Y-O **£5,459** (£1,612; £806) **Stalls** High

Form RPR

0 **1** **Clarietta**[23] 3249 2-9-0 0.......... TedDurcan 3 78+
(J L Dunlop) *trckd ldr: hdwy 2f out: rdn to ld 1f out: styd on strly* **7/2**[2]

6 **2** 2½ **Jeannie Galloway (IRE)**[26] 3147 2-9-0 0.......... RichardMullen 1 72
(A G Foster) *sn led: rdn along 2f out: drvn and hdd 1f out: kpt on gamely u.p ins fnl f* **33/1**

30 **3** nk **Crystal Gale (IRE)**[37] 2793 2-9-0 0.......... JamieSpencer 13 71
(W J Knight) *wnt lft s: a.p: effrt and cl up over 2f out: rdn wl over 1f out and ev ch tl drvn and edgd lft ent fnl f: kpt on same pce* **6/1**[3]

4 nse **Carioca (IRE)** 2-9-0 0.......... LDettori 10 71
(M Botti) *hld up towards rr: hdwy 3f out: swtchd rt and effrt to chse ldrs wl over 1f out: sn rdn and kpt on same pce ins fnl f* **14/1**

5 2½ **Saafia (USA)** 2-9-0 0.......... NCallan 5 65+
(M Johnston) *in tch: hdwy 3f out and sn chsng ldrs: rdn wl over 1f out and no imp appr fnl f* **15/2**

6 1¼ **Touch Tone** 2-9-0 0.......... MichaelHills 6 62
(B W Hills) *t.k.h and sn in midfield: hdwy on outer and edgd lft 3f out: rdn to chse ldrs 2f out: sn edgd lft and wknd* **6/4**[1]

0 **7** 4 **Jelly Bean**[25] 3187 2-9-0 0.......... JimmyQuinn 9 52
(K A Ryan) *chsd ldrs: rdn along and lost pl 1/2-way: swtchd lft and drvn over 2f out: n.d* **50/1**

8 hd **Keenes Royale** 2-9-0 0.......... PaulMulrennan 7 51
(P C Haslam) *green: a towards rr* **33/1**

05 **9** 11 **Billy's Bid**[23] 3232 2-8-11 0.......... FrederikTylicki(3) 12 24
(I W McInnes) *hmpd s: a in rr* **100/1**

0 **10** 28 **Howdoyalikemenow (IRE)**[51] 2360 2-9-0 0.......... RobertWinston 11 —
(K A Ryan) *sltly hmpd s: sn cl up: rdn along 3f out and sn wknd* **50/1**

04 **11** 2¼ **Lady Bucket**[58] 2161 2-9-0 0.......... SilvestreDeSousa 4 —
(Paul Green) *rrd s and slowly away: a wl bhd* **100/1**

1m 28.23s (1.93) **Going Correction** +0.175s/f (Good) **11** Ran SP% **106.7**
Speed ratings (Par 93): **95,92,91,91,88 87,82,82,70,38 35**
toteswingers: 1&2 £20.10, 1&3 £6.70, 2&3 £32.10. CSF £104.60 TOTE £4.10: £1.60, £7.20, £2.10; EX 162.20.
Owner Bluehills Racing Limited **Bred** Hesmonds Stud Ltd **Trained** Arundel, W Sussex

FOCUS
By now, light rain had arrived and conditions were starting to become damp.

NOTEBOOK
Clarietta took a while to reach top gear, but once she hit the front she didn't look like stopping and she was well on top at the finish. She hails from a fine family, who tend to improve with age and experience and there ought to be plenty more to come in the future, particularly over 1m and beyond next season. (op 3-1 tchd 11-4)
Jeannie Galloway(IRE), sent to the front having broken well from her outside draw, proved an entirely different prospect with the experience of her debut under her belt. She travelled nicely in front and kept on gutsily when challenged on all sides in the closing stages. (op 25-1)
Crystal Gale(IRE) had failed to run her race when bumped soon after the start on her previous outing, but did better here and the way she kept on again in the final strides suggested that she might even be worth stepping up to 1m.
Carioca(IRE) kept on well once switched to the stands' rail. (op 9-1)
Saafia(USA) didn't get the clearest of runs and looked as if she would come on plenty for this. (op 14-1)
Touch Tone failed to live up to market expectations. She was a bit keen in the early stages when not getting much cover on the outside, but even so this was disappointing. (op 7-4)
Keenes Royale shaped with some promise on her racecourse bow. If she has half of the ability of her dam, Prix de l'Opera winner Kinnaird, then she will be all right.
Howdoyalikemenow(IRE) Official explanation: jockey said filly had no more to give
Lady Bucket Official explanation: jockey said filly reared on leaving the stalls

4002 CLUMBER PARK HOTEL & SPA CONDITIONS STKS 1m (S)
8:10 (8:10) (Class 3) 4-Y-O+ **£7,771** (£2,312; £1,155; £577) **Stalls** High

Form RPR

0010 **1** **Dream Lodge (IRE)**[27] 3089 5-8-9 102.......... FrederikTylicki(3) 2 106
(R A Fahey) *trckd ldng pair in centre: swtchd lft and hdwy over 2f out: rdn over 1f out: drvn and edgd rt ins fnl f: styd on to ld nr line* **10/1**

00 **2** nse **Perks (IRE)**[27] 3089 4-8-12 104.......... JimmyQuinn 1 106
(J L Dunlop) *hld up in rr centre: swtchd rt and hdwy over 2f out: rdn over 1f out: led jst ins fnl f: snd drvn and edgd lft: hdd nr line* **11/2**[2]

20-6 **3** ¾ **Moyenne Corniche**[32] 2953 4-8-9 105.......... JamieSpencer 4 101
(M L W Bell) *overall ldr in centre: rdn along over 2f out: drvn and hdd jst ins fnl f: hld whn n.m.r and hmpd nr line* **11/1**

/111 **4** 1 **Forgotten Voice (IRE)**[29] 3014 4-8-9 112.......... LDettori 3 99
(J Noseda) *trckd ldr centre: effrt over 2f out: sn rdn and wknd wl over 1f out* **8/15**[1]

60 **5** 1¾ **Bushman**[47] 2476 5-8-9 103.......... RichardMullen 5 95
(D M Simcock) *racd alone on stands' rail: prom: rdn wl over 1f out: outpcd appr fnl f* **15/2**[3]

1m 39.24s (-0.06) **Going Correction** +0.175s/f (Good) **5** Ran SP% **109.8**
Speed ratings (Par 107): **107,106,106,105,103**
CSF £58.09 TOTE £9.00: £2.30, £2.00; EX 40.80.
Owner The G-Guck Group **Bred** C H Wacker Iii **Trained** Musley Bank, N Yorks

FOCUS
The race of the night, although it left questions unanswered afterwards with Forgotten Voice clearly underperforming and the winner probably not having to improve. The first four raced in Indian file up the middle.

NOTEBOOK
Dream Lodge(IRE) had broken the course record when winning this contest 12 months ago (for a different stable) and again clocked a very respectable time in the conditions. He had never got into the race over 1m2f at Royal Ascot on his previous start but seemed to be staying on well enough at the finish and he needed every yard of this trip to get on top, hinting that a move back up in distance could yet produce further reward. A bit of give in the ground clearly didn't do his chances any harm and although he was pulled up and dismounted after the finish, that was purely because the bridle had slipped through his mouth. (op 12-1 tchd 16-1)
Perks(IRE) finished just in front of the winner at Royal Ascot when probably ridden handily enough with hindsight. He again ran a cracker in what was his most realistic assignment of the campaign. He may continue to find handicaps a struggle off his current rating, but given his liking for soft ground, connections may just be able to find a weak Group race in Europe for him later this season. (op 6-1 tchd 5-1)
Moyenne Corniche tried to make all in the middle of the course and made a good fist of it for a long way. He was beaten when short of room close home and probably ran to near enough his mark. Like the others, he doesn't look obviously well treated in handicaps. (op 16-1)
Forgotten Voice(IRE) failed to pick up when asked to quicken and did not run up to same level of form he showed in taking the Hunt Cup. He may have had the best of the draw there, but even so he took one of the most competitive handicaps of the season with contemptuous ease off a mark of 101 and he must be better than he showed here. Maybe the ground wasn't to the colt's satisfaction. Trainer Jeremy Noseda was keeping his own counsel after the race. (tchd 1-2 and 4-7 in places)
Bushman was the only one of the quintet to race on the stands' rail. He looked to be fairly close to the pace at halfway but didn't pick up. He made a good impression last season and could be worth another chance, despite being quite expensive to follow this year. (op 13-2 tchd 8-1)

4003 MOSS PROPERTIES H'CAP 1m 2f 60y
8:40 (8:40) (Class 4) (0-85,85) 4-Y-O+ **£4,857** (£1,445; £722; £360) **Stalls** Low

Form RPR

3512 **1** **Plaisterer**[31] 2977 4-9-2 **83**.......... JackMitchell(3) 8 100+
(C F Wall) *hld up in rr: hdwy wl over 2f out: swtchd lft over 1f out and str run appr fnl f: led last 100yds* **4/1**[2]

0441 **2** 1¾ **Shaloo Diamond**[7] 3761 4-8-13 **80** 6ex.......... MichaelJStainton(3) 1 89
(R M Whitaker) *trckd ldng pair: hdwy over 2f out: swtchd lft and rdn to ld wl over 1f out: drvn ins fnl f: hdd and no ex last 100yds* **3/1**[1]

30 **3** 5 **Rangefinder**[55] 2242 5-9-4 **82**.......... DaneO'Neill 12 82
(L M Cumani) *trckd ldrs: hdwy 3f out: rdn to chse ldng pair wl over 1f out: sn drvn and kpt on same pce ins fnl f* **7/1**[3]

002 **4** 1½ **Magic Echo**[61] 2073 5-9-7 **85**.......... PhillipMakin 11 82
(M Dods) *sn trcking ldr: hdwy to ld 2 1/2f out: rdn and hdd over 1f out: sn drvn and kpt on same pce ins fnl f* **8/1**

0-20 **5** 2 **Harry The Hawk**[34] 2898 5-8-6 **70**.......... PJMcDonald 9 63
(T D Walford) *t.k.h: in tch: hdwy on outer 3f out: sn rdn and kpt on same pce fnl 2f* **16/1**

6-55 **6** 1¼ **Bavarian Nordic (USA)**[7] 3761 4-9-0 **78**.......... SilvestreDeSousa 7 68
(Mrs A Duffield) *midfield: stdy hdwy 4f out: swtchd lft and effrt to chse ldrs over 2f out: sn rdn and ch tl drvn and wknd appr fnl f* **20/1**

4620 **7** 3½ **Hurlingham**[22] 3266 5-9-0 **78**.......... PaulMulrennan 6 62
(M W Easterby) *midfield: hdwy on inner to chse ldrs 3f out: rdn over 2f out and sn btn* **14/1**

03-6 **8** nk **Coeur De Lionne (IRE)**[29] 3034 5-9-0 **78**.......... TedDurcan 3 61
(E A L Dunlop) *a towards rr* **33/1**

12-6 **9** 8 **Red Fama**[177] 226 5-8-12 **76**.......... JimmyQuinn 10 44
(N Bycroft) *chsd ldrs: rdn along over 4f out and sn wknd* **16/1**

0003 **10** 1½ **Best Prospect (IRE)**[19] 3393 7-9-4 **82**.......... (t) JamieSpencer 14 47
(M Dods) *hld up: a bhd* **7/1**[3]

4346 **11** 1¼ **Black Dahlia**[22] 3267 4-8-6 **70**.......... RichardMullen 4 33
(J A Glover) *led: rdn along 3f out: hdd 2 1/2f out and sn wknd* **18/1**

1-30 **12** 1½ **Moves Goodenough**[49] 2407 6-9-1 **82**.......... NeilBrown(3) 2 42
(A G Foster) *t.k.h: chsd ldrs on inner: rdn along over 3f out and sn wknd* **16/1**

2m 13.47s (2.27) **Going Correction** +0.375s/f (Good) **12** Ran SP% **118.4**
Speed ratings (Par 105): **105,103,99,98,96 95,93,92,86,85 84,82**
toteswingers: 1&2 £1.30, 1&3 £9.00, 2&3 £5.30. CSF £16.33 CT £82.41 TOTE £5.30: £2.10, £1.80, £3.00; EX 14.50.
Owner David Andrews Plastering **Bred** Vogue Development Company (kent) Ltd **Trained** Newmarket, Suffolk

FOCUS
A fair handicap which was quite steadily run. Plaisterer impressed, looking better than the bare form, and the first two came clear.

4004 CROWNHOTEL-BAWTRY.COM H'CAP — 1m 2f 60y
9:10 (9:11) (Class 5) (0-70,70) 3-Y-O — £3,412 (£1,007; £504) Stalls Low

Form — RPR

0023 **1** **Amazing Blue Sky**[10] 3684 3-8-10 **59** ...... SilvestreDeSousa 2 — 71
(Mrs R A Carr) *mde all: rdn 2f out: drvn ent fnl f and styd on gamely* **12/1**

0304 **2** *2 1/2* **Punch Drunk**[32] 2942 3-9-5 **68** ...... LDettori 14 — 75
(J G Given) *sn trcking wnr: effrt to chal 2f out and sn ev ch: rdn appr fnl f and kpt on same pce* **5/1**[3]

530 **3** *1 1/2* **Tapis Wizard**[28] 3069 3-9-5 **68** ...... PaulMulrennan 13 — 72
(M W Easterby) *chsd ldrs: rdn along and sltly outpcd 3f out: styd on u.p appr fnl f: nrst fin* **8/1**

-042 **4** *3/4* **Mykingdomforahorse**[14] 3551 3-9-5 **68** ...... SamHitchcott 6 — 71+
(M R Channon) *hld up: hdwy on inner 3f out: rdn to chse ldng pair and ch 2f out: sn drvn and kpt on same pce* **7/2**[1]

6-44 **5** *5* **Quiquillo (USA)**[17] 3456 3-9-1 **64** ...... TPQueally 9 — 57+
(H R A Cecil) *hld up: hdwy 3f out: rdn over 2f out: styd on appr fnl f: nt rch ldrs* **20/1**

-600 **6** *2* **Desert Fever**[8] 3751 3-8-10 **59** ...... MichaelHills 4 — 48
(B W Hills) *chsd ldrs: rdn along over 2f out and grad wknd* **4/1**[2]

034 **7** *5* **Countenance**[40] 2710 3-9-7 **70** ...... NCallan 15 — 49
(W J Haggas) *in tch: hdwy over 3f out: rdn along over 2f out: sn drvn and wknd wl over 1f out* **12/1**

-000 **8** *nk* **Flannel (IRE)**[47] 2479 3-9-4 **67** ...... TedDurcan 11 — 45
(J R Fanshawe) *midfield: rdn along 3f out: nvr a factor* **33/1**

-440 **9** *2* **Brad's Luck (IRE)**[22] 3279 3-8-10 **59** ...... FrancisNorton 8 — 33
(M Blanshard) *bhd tl sme late hdwy* **18/1**

5020 **10** *1 1/4* **Diamond Twister (USA)**[10] 3693 3-9-7 **70** ......(t) RobertWinston 1 — 41
(J R Best) *chsd ldrs: rdn along 3f out: drvn over 2f out and grad wknd* **16/1**

5000 **11** *1* **What A Day**[17] 3454 3-8-9 **58** ...... JamieMoriarty 16 — 27
(J J Quinn) *a towards rr* **25/1**

5055 **12** *3 1/2* **Dark Echoes**[35] 2865 3-8-4 **53** ...... DaleGibson 12 — 15
(Jedd O'Keeffe) *in tch: rdn along 4f out: sn wknd* **25/1**

00 **13** *3/4* **Arabian Silk (IRE)**[152] 548 3-7-11 **53** ...... JosephineBruning(7) 10 — 14
(D M Simcock) *in rr fr 1/2-way* **33/1**

0564 **14** *3 1/4* **Hey Up Dad**[9] 3708 3-9-0 **63** ...... PhillipMakin 3 — 17
(M Dods) *nvr bttr than midfield* **12/1**

0030 **15** *43* **Le Reve Royal**[9] 3710 3-8-8 **57** ......(p) PJMcDonald 5 — —
(G R Oldroyd) *a towards rr* **40/1**

-300 **16** *40* **Eddie Boy**[27] 3099 3-8-12 **61** ...... JamieSpencer 18 — —
(M L W Bell) *stdd s: hld up: a last* **8/1**

2m 13.79s (2.59) **Going Correction** +0.375s/f (Good) — **16** Ran SP% **136.1**
Speed ratings (Par 100): **104,102,100,100,96 94,90,90,88,87 86,84,83,80,46 14**
toteswingers: 1&2 £28.50, 1&3 £21.70, 2&3 £16.00. CSF £73.94 CT £542.31 TOTE £14.50: £2.90, £1.50, £2.30, £1.80; EX 108.20 Place 6: £88.02, Place 5: £49.38..
Owner David W Chapman **Bred** Hong Kong Breeders Club **Trained** Huby, N Yorks

FOCUS
A big field but, in all probability, not a great race and those outside the first six failed to show any conspicuous promise for the future. An improved effort from the seemingly exposed winner.
Eddie Boy Official explanation: jockey said gelding lost a front shoe
T/Jkpt: £35,091.60 to a £1 stake. Pool: £49,424.84. 1.00 winning ticket. T/Plt: £98.20 to a £1 stake. Pool: £73,654.28. 547.26 winning tickets. T/Qpdt: £57.60 to a £1 stake. Pool: £3,724.78. 47.80 winning tickets. JR

3766 EPSOM (L-H)
Thursday, July 16

OFFICIAL GOING: Good (overall 8.0, straight: stands' side 8.5; far side 8.1)
Rail realignment from the one mile to winning post added 3yards to all races.
Wind: breezy, across Weather: bright, partly cloudy, raining heavily last race

4005 TOTEPLACEPOT CLAIMING STKS — 7f
6:10 (6:10) (Class 5) 3-Y-O+ — £3,238 (£963; £481; £240) Stalls Low

Form — RPR

4031 **1** **Ogre (USA)**[14] 3525 4-9-1 73 ......(t) PaulDoe 3 — 76
(P D Evans) *awkward leaving stalls and s.i.s: hld up in rr: hdwy over 3f out: rdn to ld narrowly 2f out: r.o wl and asserted fnl 75yds:* **6/4**[1]

305 **2** *1* **Caprio (IRE)**[7] 3771 4-9-7 79 ...... HayleyTurner 4 — 79
(J R Boyle) *chsd ldr: carried into centre over 3f out: rdn and ev ch ent fnl 2f: no ex fnl 75yds* **7/1**[3]

6056 **3** *3/4* **Brooksby**[20] 3358 3-7-8 67 ......(b) CharlesEddery(7) 6 — 64+
(R Hannon) *hld up in tch: hanging lft fr over 3f out: n.m.r over 2f out: chsng ldrs but stl hanging bdly ent fnl f: kpt on but unable to chal* **12/1**

6064 **4** *shd* **Roly Boy**[14] 3525 3-8-8 72 ...... PatDobbs 1 — 68
(R Hannon) *chsd ldrs: rdn to ld 3f out: hdd 2f out: wknd jst ins fnl f: keeping on same pce whn bmpd fnl 100yds* **4/1**[2]

-644 **5** *1* **Carmenero (GER)**[24] 3211 6-9-3 70 ...... MartinDwyer 8 — 70
(W R Muir) *hld up towards rr: hdwy over 3f out: rdn to chse ldrs 2f out: keeping on same pce and hld whn hmpd ins fnl f: swtchd rt and one pce fnl 100yds* **4/1**[2]

02-0 **6** *6* **Mystic Roll**[49] 2418 6-8-11 51 ......(e[1]) MichellePayne 5 — 48
(Jane Chapple-Hyam) *hld up in rr: brief effrt towards inner over 3f out: struggling over 2f out and wl hld after* **40/1**

-315 **7** *13* **Resplendent Nova**[176] 232 7-9-1 72 ...... IanMongan 2 — 17
(P Howling) *led: c centre st: hdd 3f out: wknd ent fnl 2f: wl btn and eased ins fnl f* **9/1**

1m 23.11s (-0.19) **Going Correction** +0.05s/f (Good)
WFA 3 from 4yo+ 7lb — **7** Ran SP% **112.6**
Speed ratings (Par 103): **103,101,101,100,99 92,78**
toteswingers: 1&2 £2.70, 1&3 £4.30, 2&3 £16.70. CSF £12.42 TOTE £2.10: £1.50, £2.00; EX 9.70.Ogre was subject of a friendly claim.
Owner Diamond Racing Ltd **Bred** Gulf Coast Farms LLC **Trained** Pandy, Monmouths

FOCUS
The ground was described as good, but the going stick suggested that in the straight the ground was quicker up the stands' side (8.5) than on the far side (8.1). There was also a sounder strip four or five horse widths off the inside rail, which had been moved out a couple of yards from the tight inside line. It was estimated that this has added 3yds to race distances. There was a strong southerly wind blowing across the track into the stands. All but Mystic Roll could be given a chance at the ratings in this reasonable claimer. The form is rated around the fourth.
Brooksby Official explanation: jockey said filly hung left all the way up the straight

4006 EUROPEAN BREEDERS' FUND MAIDEN STKS — 7f
6:40 (6:43) (Class 4) 2-Y-O — £5,180 (£1,541; £770; £384) Stalls Low

Form — RPR

562 **1** **Dubawi Phantom**[19] 3395 2-9-3 0 ...... JimCrowley 5 — 83
(D M Simcock) *in tch: hdwy to ld and edgd lft over 2f out: styd on wl to forge ahd ins fnl f: rdn out* **11/4**[1]

2 *1 1/4* **Sea Lord (IRE)** 2-9-3 0 ...... RoystonFfrench 2 — 80
(M Johnston) *sn chsng ldr: ev ch and edgd lft u.p ent fnl 2f: outpcd by ldng pair over 1f out: rallied ins fnl f to go 2nd nr fin* **9/2**

2 **3** *nk* **Yarra River**[19] 3402 2-9-3 0 ...... LPKeniry 4 — 79
(A M Balding) *chsd ldng pair: ev ch and rdn ent fnl 2f: no ex and btn whn edgd lft wl ins fnl f: lost 2nd nr fin* **7/2**[3]

0 **4** *1 1/2* **Deauville Post (FR)**[34] 2889 2-9-3 0 ...... PatDobbs 1 — 75+
(R Hannon) *s.i.s: sn in tch in midfield: outpcd and rdn over 2f out: swtchd rt over 1f out: rallied and edgd lft ins fnl f: styng on fin: nt pce to rch ldrs* **10/3**[2]

63 **5** *3/4* **Branderburgo (IRE)**[13] 3584 2-9-3 0 ...... MartinDwyer 6 — 74+
(M Botti) *taken down early: led: hdd over 2f out: outpcd and hmpd ent fnl 2f: swtchd rt over 1f out: kpt on fnl f* **11/2**

5 **6** *3 1/2* **Whiepa Snappa (IRE)**[26] 3160 2-9-3 0 ...... IanMongan 7 — 65
(P M Phelan) *wnt rt s: bhd: effrt on outer 3f out: edging lft but kpt on steadily fr over 1f out: nvr nr ldrs* **25/1**

50 **7** *3 1/4* **My Red Kite**[34] 2889 2-8-12 0 ...... GabrielHannon(5) 8 — 57
(G D Blake) *carried rt s: a in rr: outpcd and lost tch over 3f out: n.d* **40/1**

0 **8** *2 3/4* **Killusty Fancy (IRE)**[38] 2771 2-9-3 0 ...... SteveDrowne 3 — 50
(D J S Ffrench Davis) *in tch tl lost pl 4f out: rdn and lost tch over 3f out: no ch after* **100/1**

0 **9** *3/4* **Rodrigo De Freitas (IRE)**[42] 2631 2-9-3 0 ...... PatCosgrave 9 — 48
(J R Boyle) *restless in stalls: carried rt s: rn green and pushed along in rr: lost tch over 3f out: wl btn whn hung lft 2f out* **100/1**

1m 24.03s (0.73) **Going Correction** +0.05s/f (Good) — **9** Ran SP% **113.8**
Speed ratings (Par 96): **97,95,95,93,92 88,84,81,80**
toteswingers: 1&2 £3.50, 1&3 £2.10, 2&3 £3.90. CSF £15.01 TOTE £3.20: £1.50, £2.30, £1.70; EX 12.40.
Owner Sultan Ali **Bred** Plantation Stud **Trained** Newmarket, Suffolk

FOCUS
This looked a fair maiden beforehand and they went a decent gallop.

NOTEBOOK
Dubawi Phantom's second at Newmarket last time has been advertised by a number of those who finished behind him that day, and a reproduction of that form (RPR of 82) looked likely to make him difficult to beat here. It wasn't a walk in the park, though, as he had to dig deep to see off Yarra River, but he was nicely on top inside the last. It's unlikely he improved on his Newmarket effort, and his connections will now look for a little novice race for him. (tchd 9-4 and 3-1)
Sea Lord(IRE) made a promising racecourse debut for a stable with a good record with its 2yos at this track. He holds a Gimcrack entry, but he's by Cape Cross out of a French 1m2f Listed winner, and he rallied well over this 7f having been outpaced a furlong and a half out. A big, scopey sort, a maiden shouldn't be too long in coming his way on this evidence. (op 5-1 tchd 13-2)
Yarra River showed promise on his debut when second to a smart rival at Windsor, and this extra furlong promised to suit him on pedigree. He didn't look to be beaten for stamina, but his best chance of success might come once he gets to race in nurseries. (op 11-4)
Deauville Post(FR), who showed some ability on his debut despite being green, again finished his race well. He too looks like he will be more of a nursery type in due course. (op 3-1 tchd 4-1)
Branderburgo(IRE) set a decent clip out in front and looked to pay for those efforts in the latter stages. He's now had the three runs required to allow him to compete in nurseries and will have better opportunities in that sphere. (op 8-1 tchd 5-1)
Whiepa Snappa(IRE) struggled to go the early pace but stayed on past some beaten horses late on. He needs a bit more time. (tchd 28-1)

4007 TOTEPOOL H'CAP — 1m 4f 10y
7:15 (7:18) (Class 4) (0-80,77) 4-Y-O+ — £5,180 (£1,541; £770; £384) Stalls Centre

Form — RPR

1431 **1** **Run For Ede's**[6] 3797 5-8-11 **70** ...... RossAtkinson(5) 7 — 77
(P M Phelan) *stdd s: hld up in last pair: swtchd rt and hdwy on outer over 3f out: rdn and chal over 1f out: led and hung lft ins fnl f: r.o wl* **3/1**[1]

5615 **2** *3/4* **Graylyn Ruby (FR)**[27] 3114 4-9-0 **68** ...... MartinDwyer 5 — 74
(J Jay) *in tch: rdn and lost pl over 3f out: bhd and drvn 2f out: r.o strly fnl f: wnt 2nd fnl 75yds: nt rch wnr* **11/1**

3423 **3** *3/4* **Watson's Bay**[7] 3768 4-9-0 **68** ...... IanMongan 2 — 74+
(P Howling) *t.k.h: hld up in tch in last trio: swtchd rt and rdn jst over 2f out: hdwy to press ldrs 1f out: keeping on same pce whn hmpd and eased wl ins fnl f* **5/1**

-600 **4** *1/2* **Risque Heights**[29] 3024 5-9-2 **70** ...... PatCosgrave 8 — 74
(J R Boyle) *hld up in last pair: hdwy to trck ldrs over 2f out: rdn to ld wl over 1f out: sn edgd lft: hdd ins fnl f: no ex fnl 100yds* **20/1**

3305 **5** *1 3/4* **Soundbyte**[35] 2854 4-8-13 **67** ...... JimCrowley 1 — 68+
(J Gallagher) *trckd ldrs: nt clr run and outpcd jst over 2f out: kpt on u.p fnl f: nt pce to rch ldrs* **7/1**

4113 **6** *5* **Gloucester**[10] 3697 6-9-9 **77** ...... GeorgeBaker 6 — 70
(M J Scudamore) *trckd ldrs on outer: rdn and effrt 3f out: nt qckn u.p 2f out: sn wl btn* **4/1**[3]

600 **7** *shd* **Classical Rhythm (IRE)**[3] 3919 4-8-4 **58** oh1 ...... HayleyTurner 4 — 51
(J R Boyle) *chsd ldr tl rdn to ld 3f out: drvn and hdd wl over 1f out: sn wknd* **20/1**

02-2 **8** *32* **Yossi (IRE)**[7] 3768 5-9-9 **77** ......(b) SteveDrowne 3 — 19
(Jim Best) *dwlt: sn pushed up to ld: hdd 3f out: sn dropped out: wl btn and eased fnl f: t.o* **7/2**[2]

2m 38.54s (-0.36) **Going Correction** +0.05s/f (Good) — **8** Ran SP% **114.2**
Speed ratings (Par 105): **103,102,102,101,100 97,97,75**
toteswingers: 1&2 £7.60, 1&3 £3.80, 2&3 £10.70. CSF £36.47 CT £157.06 TOTE £3.00: £1.30, £3.80, £2.10; EX 37.20.
Owner Ede's (uk) Ltd **Bred** Mrs James Wigan & London TB Services Ltd **Trained** Epsom, Surrey
■ Stewards' Enquiry : Ross Atkinson three-day ban: careless riding (Jul 30-31, Aug 2)

FOCUS
Three of these came into the race officially ahead of the handicapper, and it was one of those who came out on top. It was not a bad race for the grade and the form has been rated at something like face value.

4008 NOBBY CLARKE'S 70TH BIRTHDAY CELEBRATION H'CAP — 1m 2f 18y
7:45 (7:49) (Class 4) (0-80,80) 3-Y-O — £5,180 (£1,541; £770; £384) Stalls Low

Form — RPR

412 **1** **Dome Rocket**[21] 3321 3-9-5 **76** ......(p) JimCrowley 9 — 83
(W J Knight) *chsd ldr: rdn to ld 2f out: drvn clr over 1f out: edgd lft but r.o strly fnl f* **9/2**[2]

1532 **2** 1 ½ **Hallstatt (IRE)**[6] 3808 3-9-7 **78** RoystonFfrench 8 82+
(M Johnston) *dwlt: sn in tch: pushed along and unable qck over 3f out: drvn and hdwy over 1f out: duelling for 2nd 1f out: r.o but nvr gng to rch wnr* **9/2**[2]

31 **3** nse **Funday**[24] 3214 3-9-6 **77** GeorgeBaker 3 81+
(G L Moore) *s.i.s: t.k.h: hld up in last pair: swtchd rt and rdn jst over 2f out: duelling for 2nd 1f out: r.o but nvr gng to rch wnr* **11/4**[1]

5164 **4** 2 ¾ **Advisor (FR)**[34] 2884 3-9-6 **77** HayleyTurner 6 75
(M L W Bell) *hld up in tch: rdn and effrt over 2f out: hdwy between horses over 1f out: chsd wnr briefly ent fnl f: sn no imp: wknd fnl 100yds* **5/1**[3]

116 **5** 2 ¾ **Supernoverre (IRE)**[20] 3359 3-9-4 **75** IanMongan 4 68
(P Howling) *t.k.h: hld up in last trio: rdn and effrt on outer 3f out: no prog and nvr trbld ldrs* **16/1**

6003 **6** shd **Cruikadyke**[21] 3307 3-9-6 **77** MartinDwyer 1 70
(P F I Cole) *led: pushed along over 3f out: drvn and hdd 2f out: wknd ent fnl f* **9/1**

-321 **7** ¾ **Andhaar**[19] 3384 3-9-9 **80** DO'Donohoe 5 72
(E A L Dunlop) *t.k.h: trckd ldrs: rdn and ev ch 3f out: wknd u.p over 1f out: eased towards fin* **12/1**

-134 **8** 30 **Ballet Dancer (IRE)**[29] 3026 3-9-2 **73** PhilipRobinson 2 4
(M A Jarvis) *nvr gng wl: a last trio: lost tch qckly jst over 2f out: eased fnl f: t.o* **8/1**

2m 9.60s (-0.10) **Going Correction** +0.05s/f (Good) **8** Ran SP% **114.4**
Speed ratings (Par 102): **102,100,100,98,96 96,95,71**
toteswingers: 1&2 £5.50, 1&3 £4.00, 2&3 £2.40. CSF £25.04 CT £65.06 TOTE £5.40: £2.20, £2.00, £1.30; EX 30.40.
Owner Bluehills Racing Limited **Bred** Hesmonds Stud Ltd **Trained** Patching, W Sussex

FOCUS
The early pace here was only steady and as a result those that raced prominently were at an advantage. The winner is rated up 4lb with the next two shaping better than the bare form.
Hallstatt(IRE) Official explanation: jockey said colt hung both ways throughout
Funday Official explanation: jockey said filly missed the break
Advisor(FR) Official explanation: vet said colt finished lame
Ballet Dancer(IRE) Official explanation: trainer said filly had a breathing problem

4009 EPSOM TRAINERS OPEN DAY 2ND AUGUST H'CAP 7f
8:20 (8:20) (Class 4) (0-80,78) 3-Y-O+ **£5,180** (£1,541; £770; £384) **Stalls** Low

Form RPR

3442 **1** **Support Fund (IRE)**[7] 3789 5-9-7 **70** ShaneKelly 5 79
(Eve Johnson Houghton) *hld up bhd: hdwy on outer over 2f out: gd hdwy over 1f out: led ins fnl f: r.o wl* **4/1**[1]

4500 **2** 1 ¼ **Napoletano (GER)**[23] 3243 8-9-0 **63** (p) HayleyTurner 4 69
(S Dow) *plld hrd: hdwy to ld over 4f out: rdn over 2f out: hdd wl over 1f out: stl ev ch tl hdd and nt pce of wnr ins fnl f: kpt on* **12/1**

3210 **3** ½ **Crime Writer (USA)**[13] 3567 3-9-8 **78** RoystonFfrench 3 80
(M Johnston) *led tl over 4f out: drvn to ld narrowly again wl over 1f out: hdd and nt pce of wnr ins fnl f: lost 2nd nr fin* **9/2**[2]

6606 **4** 1 **Stanley Goodspeed**[17] 3469 6-9-5 **68** (vt[1]) JamesDoyle 6 70
(J W Hills) *dwlt and short of room sn after s: bhd: pushed along over 3f out: drvn and effrt on outer 2f out: r.o ins fnl f: nt rch ldrs* **5/1**[3]

4652 **5** hd **Compton's Eleven**[11] 3655 8-9-4 **67** TonyCulhane 2 68
(M R Channon) *hld up in tch towards rr: pushed along: rdn and hdwy 2f out: chsng ldrs whn nt clr run jst ins fnl f: nvr able to chal* **4/1**[1]

061- **6** 1 **Shamrock Lady (IRE)**[279] 6627 4-10-0 **77** JimCrowley 7 76
(J Gallagher) *chsd ldr for over 1f: styd chsng ldrs: drvn 3f out: wkng whn short of room and sltly hmpd 1f out* **14/1**

000 **7** ½ **Buxton**[31] 2980 5-9-12 **75** (t) PatDobbs 8 72
(R Ingram) *in tch in midfield: rdn and unable qck over 2f out: plugged on same pce fnl f* **14/1**

0504 **8** ½ **Idle Power (IRE)**[8] 3732 11-9-9 **72** MartinDwyer 1 68
(J R Boyle) *plld hrd: chsd ldrs: swtchd rt and rdn 2f out: unable qck and btn 1f out* **11/1**

1463 **9** 1 ¼ **Seneschal**[14] 3539 8-9-12 **75** GeorgeBaker 9 79+
(A B Haynes) *hld up in last trio: hdwy jst over 2f out: pressed ldrs and edgd lft 1f out: lost action and eased ins fnl f* **8/1**

1m 23.38s (0.08) **Going Correction** +0.05s/f (Good)
WFA 3 from 4yo+ 7lb **9** Ran SP% **115.3**
Speed ratings (Par 105): **101,99,99,97,97 96,95,95,93**
toteswingers: 1&2 £14.10, 1&3 £3.50, 2&3 £17.70. CSF £52.14 CT £224.36 TOTE £5.50: £1.80, £3.90, £1.90; EX 70.00.
Owner R F Johnson Houghton **Bred** W Maxwell Ervine **Trained** Blewbury, Oxon

FOCUS
Most of these looked pretty exposed beforehand, but the race was run at a good pace. Straightforward form.
Seneschal Official explanation: jockey said gelding lost its action

4010 TOTESWINGER H'CAP 1m 114y
8:50 (8:51) (Class 5) (0-75,73) 3-Y-O **£3,238** (£963; £481; £240) **Stalls** Low

Form RPR

0451 **1** **Caster Sugar (USA)**[13] 3581 3-9-1 **65** PatDobbs 3 70
(R Hannon) *chsd ldrs: chsd clr ldr and rdn over 2f out: styd on wl ins fnl f to ld last strides* **5/1**[3]

3-44 **2** hd **Aurora Sky (IRE)**[35] 2849 3-9-7 **71** J-PGuillambert 8 75
(J Akehurst) *led: pushed clr 3f out: 3 l clr whn j. shadow and wnt lft ins fnl f: ct last strides* **7/2**[1]

0635 **3** 1 **Squad**[8] 3741 3-8-8 **58** TonyCulhane 7 60
(S Dow) *s.i.s: bhd and pushed along: hdwy over 1f out: r.o wl to snatch 3rd last strides* **6/1**

4405 **4** hd **Kaolak (USA)**[20] 3359 3-9-9 **73** (v) PatCosgrave 10 75
(J Ryan) *chsd ldrs: rdn and outpcd over 2f out: rallied u.p 1f out: one pce towards fin* **6/1**

3011 **5** 1 ¾ **Edgeworth (IRE)**[27] 3115 3-9-8 **72** GeorgeBaker 1 70
(B G Powell) *hld up towards rr: hdwy to chse ldng pair over 2f out: drvn and one pce fr over 1f out* **4/1**[2]

0500 **6** ¾ **Dream On Connie**[10] 3693 3-9-1 **65** ShaneKelly 9 61
(W J Knight) *towards rr: rdn and hdwy in center 2f out: one pce and no imp fnl f* **12/1**

5040 **7** 12 **Billy Smart (IRE)**[2] 3946 3-8-4 **54** oh2 NickyMackay 4 24
(D J S Ffrench Davis) *racd in midfield: rdn and struggling over 3f out: wl bhd fnl 2f* **20/1**

6-0 **8** 2 ¼ **D'Artagnans Dream**[38] 2763 3-8-7 **62** (p) GabrielHannon[(5)] 5 27
(G D Blake) *s.i.s: a in rr: lost tch 3f out* **28/1**

-620 **9** 4 **Saturn Way (GR)**[45] 2548 3-9-6 **70** LPKeniry 2 26
(P R Chamings) *a bhd: lost tch 3f out* **10/1**

60-0 **10** 3 ½ **Sultans Way (IRE)**[27] 3115 3-8-13 **63** MartinDwyer 6 11
(P F I Cole) *chsd ldr tl over 2f out: sn dropped out: eased fnl f* **10/1**

1m 46.4s (0.30) **Going Correction** +0.05s/f (Good) **10** Ran SP% **121.5**
Speed ratings (Par 100): **100,99,98,98,97 96,85,83,80,77**
toteswingers: 1&2 £4.20, 1&3 £5.80, 2&3 £5.80. CSF £23.96 CT £112.77 TOTE £4.40: £1.50, £2.00, £2.40; EX 15.80 Place 6: £14.87, Place 5: £7.76..
Owner Mrs James Wigan **Bred** Mrs James Wigan & London TB Services Ltd **Trained** East Everleigh, Wilts

FOCUS
This ordinary handicap was run in driving rain and poor light, with thunder and lightning all about. Dramatic weather, and a dramatic finish. The form makes sense.
T/Plt: £11.00 to a £1 stake. Pool: £58,482.48. 3,880.10 winning tickets. T/Qpdt: £6.20 to a £1 stake. Pool: £3,808.16. 453.90 winning tickets. SP

3852 HAMILTON (R-H)
Thursday, July 16

OFFICIAL GOING: Good to firm (good in places) changing to good (good to firm in places) after race 4 (4.00)
Rail realignment around the loop decreased advertised distances on the Round course by around 30yards.
Wind: Almost nil Weather: Overcast, showers

4011 SCOTTISH RACING MAIDEN AUCTION STKS 5f 4y
2:20 (2:22) (Class 5) 2-Y-O **£2,729** (£806; £403) **Stalls** Low

Form RPR

4 **1** **Layla's Hero (IRE)**[16] 3487 2-8-11 0 AdrianTNicholls 1 72
(D Nicholls) *prom: led over 1f out: drifted rt and styd on strly fnl f* **5/1**[2]

05 **2** 2 ½ **Clever Molly (IRE)**[12] 3613 2-8-4 0 PaulQuinn 7 56
(E J Alston) *t.k.h: led to over 1f out: kpt on same pce fnl f* **66/1**

62 **3** ¾ **Melody In The Mist (FR)**[16] 3478 2-8-6 0 PJMcDonald 4 55
(T D Barron) *dwlt: sn in tch: effrt 2f out: edgd lft and styd on fnl f: nrst fin* **4/9**[1]

04 **4** shd **Firetrap**[12] 3613 2-8-11 0 SilvestreDeSousa 5 60
(Mrs A Duffield) *sn outpcd: hdwy on outside 1/2-way: rdn and one pce fnl f* **9/1**[3]

00 **5** 1 ½ **Kirkby's Gem**[12] 3613 2-7-11 0 BillyCray[(7)] 3 48
(A Berry) *cl up: drvn and outpcd 2f out: no imp fnl f* **200/1**

65 **6** ½ **Aintwogrand (IRE)**[27] 3101 2-8-4 0 GregFairley 6 46
(M R Channon) *trckd ldrs: rdn and ev ch over 1f out: sn no ex* **11/1**

7 9 **Ochilview Warrior (IRE)** 2-8-10 0 DanielTudhope 8 19
(R Bastiman) *bhd and outpcd: no ch fr 1/2-way* **40/1**

60.10 secs (0.10) **Going Correction** -0.10s/f (Good) **7** Ran SP% **108.7**
Speed ratings (Par 94): **95,91,89,89,87 86,72**
toteswingers: 1&2 £7.10, 1&3 £2.00, 2&3 £6.20 CSF £180.45 TOTE £4.30: £1.50, £7.60; EX 89.20.
Owner Dr Marwan Koukash **Bred** Epona Bloodstock Ltd **Trained** Sessay, N Yorks

FOCUS
There was a downpour before this contest which would have taken any sting out of the ground and the winning rider described the going as 'lovely'. This looked only a modest maiden auction event.

NOTEBOOK
Layla's Hero(IRE) had caught the eye when a running-on fourth over an extra furlong on his Thirsk debut, so at first glance it seemed a surprise to see him dropping in trip for this second start, but this performance justified the move. Not best away, he nonetheless had no trouble laying up towards the nearside of the field. Sent to the front coming to the last furlong, he quickened up smartly and despite hanging away a little to his right he always had matters under control. The stiffer track seemed to help him as the further they went, the better he travelled and there should be more to come from him in nurseries. (op 9-2 tchd 11-2)
Clever Molly(IRE), a couple of lengths behind Firetrap at Carlisle earlier this month, showed good speed out in front and stayed on well to hold off the rest of the field and reverse the Carlisle form. She also now qualifies for nurseries. (op 40-1)
Melody In The Mist(FR), beaten just a neck over C&D last month, was sent off a red-hot favourite. Slow to break, she admittedly didn't have much room to play with entering the last 2f and had to be switched towards the stands' rail, but although staying on she never looked like catching the front pair and this was disappointing. She is bred to get further, so hopefully she will improve as she goes up in trip. (op 1-2)
Firetrap, who had hinted at ability in his first two starts, was being niggled from some way out and, though, he was close enough 2f from home, he was soon left behind. (op 8-1 tchd 15-2)
Kirkby's Gem, who failed to beat a rival in her first two starts, improved here in that she didn't finish last. (op 100-1)
Aintwogrand(IRE), who didn't seem to get home when stepped up to 6f at Goodwood last time, was weak in the market. She ran fast for a long way before fading and she doesn't seem to be progressing. (op 7-1)
Ochilview Warrior(IRE), a £7,000 half-brother to three winners, proved far too green from the off. (op 25-1)

4012 HAMILTON-PARK.CO.UK CLAIMING STKS 5f 4y
2:50 (2:51) (Class 6) 3-Y-O+ **£2,266** (£674; £337; £168) **Stalls** Low

Form RPR

3063 **1** **Obe Gold**[22] 3268 7-9-8 83 (v) AdrianTNicholls 4 87
(D Nicholls) *prom: sn niggled along: drvn 1/2-way: hdwy and edgd rt over 1f out: led ins fnl f: r.o* **6/4**[1]

3324 **2** ¾ **Raccoon (IRE)**[10] 3681 9-8-13 73 PJMcDonald 1 75
(Mrs R A Carr) *led: rdn 2f out: hdd ins fnl f: kpt on u.p* **2/1**[2]

0500 **3** 1 ¾ **High Curragh**[6] 3828 6-9-3 80 (p) AmyRyan[(5)] 6 78
(K A Ryan) *trckd ldr: rdn over 2f out: kpt on same pce fnl f* **85/40**[3]

46-6 **4** 8 **Ava's World (IRE)**[7] 3775 5-7-13 50 AndrewHeffernan[(7)] 8 33
(Peter Grayson) *in tch on outside: drvn 2f out: sn wknd* **50/1**

0000 **5** ½ **Gelert (IRE)**[5] 3853 4-8-11 40 DanielTudhope 7 36
(A Berry) *chsd ldrs to 1/2-way: sn rdn and wknd* **100/1**

60.11 secs (0.11) **Going Correction** 0.0s/f (Good) **5** Ran SP% **108.3**
Speed ratings (Par 101): **99,97,95,82,81**
toteswingers: 1&2 £2.80 CSF £4.66 TOTE £2.60: £1.30, £1.50; EX 4.60.
Owner D Nicholls **Bred** Mrs M Mason **Trained** Sessay, N Yorks

FOCUS
Only three of these had a realistic chance at the weights in this modest claimer and they finished almost exactly as adjusted official ratings suggested they should. The pace was ordinary, however, and the winning time was a fraction slower than the opening 2yo maiden.

4013 BILL AND DAVID MCHARG MEMORIAL H'CAP 1m 65y
3:25 (3:25) (Class 6) (0-65,65) 3-Y-O **£2,266** (£674; £337; £168) **Stalls** High

Form RPR

5343 **1** **Evening Sunset (GER)**[8] 3741 3-9-0 **58** PaulHanagan 4 69
(M R Channon) *set stdy pce: rdn and drew clr fr 2f out: unchal* **9/4**[1]

004 **2** *7* **Winrob**[16] 3474 3-8-5 **54**........................ JamieKyne(5) 1 48
(Patrick Morris) *prom: outpcd over 2f out: styd on fnl f to take 2nd cl home: no ch w wnr* **25/1**

0332 **3** *shd* **Paint Splash**[12] 3614 3-8-3 **52**........................ DeanHeslop(5) 6 46
(T D Barron) *hld up in tch: hdwy to chse wnr over 2f out: sn no imp: no ex and lost 2nd cl home* **8/1**[3]

0-1R **4** *nk* **Dark Moment**[8] 3730 3-9-1 **59**........................ DanielTudhope 7 52
(A Dickman) *s.v.s: hdwy off slow pce to join gp after 2f: outpcd over 3f out: rallied wl over 1f out: no imp fnl f* **9/4**[1]

06-0 **5** *1½* **Tahfeez (IRE)**[82] 1508 3-9-2 **60**........................(p) TomEaves 2 50
(I Semple) *cl up: outpcd wl over 1f out: n.d after* **8/1**[3]

0551 **6** *2* **Ask Dan (IRE)**[12] 3614 3-9-2 **60**........................(p) PhillipMakin 3 45
(M Dods) *rrd s: t.k.h early: hld up in tch: effrt on outside over 2f out: no imp over 1f out* **9/2**[2]

25-0 **7** *11* **Izzy Lou (IRE)**[24] 3228 3-9-4 **65**........................(b[1]) NeilBrown(3) 5 23
(K A Ryan) *sn cl up: wandered u.p and wknd fr 3f out* **16/1**

1m 49.5s (1.10) **Going Correction** 0.0s/f (Good) **7** Ran SP% **111.7**
Speed ratings (Par 98): **94,87,86,86,85 83,72**
toteswingers: 1&2 £14.30, 1&3 £2.60, 2&3 £19.60 CSF £56.82 TOTE £3.10: £1.70, £10.60; EX 39.90.
Owner Liam Mulryan **Bred** Newsells Park Stud Ltd **Trained** West Ilsley, Berks
■ Stewards' Enquiry : Neil Brown caution: used whip when out of contention

FOCUS
This was a weak handicap and also a very steadily run affair in the early stages, which played right into the hands of the winner. The form is not rated too positively.
Ask Dan(IRE) Official explanation: jockey said gelding reared on leaving the stalls

4014 ALWAYS TRYING OPEN MAIDEN STKS — 1m 3f 16y
4:00 (4:00) (Class 5) 3-Y-O+ **£2,590** (£770; £385; £192) **Stalls High**

Form — RPR

1 **Urban Poet (USA)** 3-9-2 0........................ GregFairley 10 97+
(M Johnston) *trckd ldrs: led over 2f out: sn pushed clr: eased ins fnl f: readily* **3/1**[2]

-226 **2** *9* **Proud Times (USA)**[37] 2789 3-9-2 77........................ PJMcDonald 9 73
(G A Swinbank) *hld up in tch: outpcd over 3f out: rallied over 1f out: chsd wnr ins fnl f: no imp* **7/2**[3]

3 **3** *1* **Acquavella**[16] 3485 3-8-11 0........................ PaulHanagan 4 66
(R A Fahey) *prom: drvn and outpcd over 3f out: rallied over 1f out: kpt on fnl f* **11/4**[1]

4 *nk* **Clientele (USA)** 3-9-2 0........................ AndrewElliott 1 71+
(M Johnston) *t.k.h: led to over 2f out: sn one pce: no ex and lost 2nd ins fnl f* **9/1**

4-52 **5** *12* **Jeunopse (IRE)**[16] 3485 3-8-11 70........................ TomEaves 2 44
(B Smart) *t.k.h: in tch: effrt over 3f out: edgd rt and wknd fr 2f out* **5/1**

62 **6** *3½* **Moon Money (IRE)**[10] 3680 3-8-13 0........................ NeilBrown(3) 5 43
(K A Ryan) *t.k.h: cl up tl rdn and wknd over 2f out* **13/2**

6 **7** *7* **Agricultural**[10] 3680 3-8-11 0........................ JamieKyne(5) 8 30
(Mrs L B Normile) *bhd: struggling 1/2-way: sn btn* **100/1**

8 *34* **Go Man Go (IRE)**[18] 7-9-8 0........................ BMcHugh(5) 6 —
(B Storey) *dwlt: bhd: lost tch 1/2-way: t.o* **200/1**

2m 23.71s (-1.89) **Going Correction** 0.0s/f (Good)
WFA 3 from 5yo+ 11lb **8** Ran SP% **115.4**
Speed ratings (Par 103): **106,99,98,98,89 87,82,57**
toteswingers: 1&2 4.40, 1&3 £2.70, 2&3 £4.20 CSF £14.14 TOTE £3.20: £1.50, £1.60, £1.50; EX 15.90.
Owner Sheikh Hamdan Bin Mohammed Al Maktoum **Bred** Claiborne Farm **Trained** Middleham Moor, N Yorks

FOCUS
A more interesting older-horse maiden than you often get at this time of year, with a few having shown promise and a couple of fascinating newcomers from the Johnston yard. Urban Poet impressed but there are doubts over what he beat. The early pace threatened to be slow, but it quickened up after a couple of furlongs and it was soon reasonable enough.

4015 RACING UK STKS (H'CAP) — 6f 5y
4:35 (4:35) (Class 5) (0-75,74) 3-Y-O+ **£4,533** (£1,348; £674; £336) **Stalls Low**

Form — RPR

3211 **1** **Tangerine Trees**[21] 3296 4-9-5 **67**........................ TomEaves 3 79+
(B Smart) *mde all: hrd pressed fr over 1f out: kpt on gamely fnl f* **11/4**[1]

0560 **2** *nk* **Mandalay King (IRE)**[16] 3483 4-9-2 **64**........................ PJMcDonald 1 75
(Mrs Marjorie Fife) *rrd s: sn cl up: ev ch and rdn over 1f out: kpt on fnl f: hld towards fin* **7/1**

0030 **3** *2½* **Leonid Glow**[33] 2938 4-9-12 **74**........................ DanielTudhope 2 77
(M Dods) *in tch: effrt 2f out: kpt on fnl f: nt rch first two* **11/2**[3]

3220 **4** *½* **Avontuur (FR)**[8] 3730 7-8-11 **64**........................ DeanHeslop(5) 6 65
(Mrs R A Carr) *cl up: outpcd over 2f out: kpt on ins fnl f: no imp* **6/1**

0034 **5** *½* **Elkhorn**[5] 3852 7-8-2 **55**........................(b) JamieKyne(5) 7 55
(Miss J A Camacho) *dwlt: hld up: effrt over 1f out: nvr able to chal* **13/2**

0060 **6** *¾* **Imperial Sword**[12] 3612 6-8-11 **66**........................(b) JanWilson(7) 5 63
(T D Barron) *in tch on outside: shkn up over 2f out: no imp over 1f out* **20/1**

4301 **7** *shd* **Optical Illusion (USA)**[16] 3484 5-8-9 **57**........................ PaulHanagan 4 54
(R A Fahey) *chsd ldrs tl rdn and no ex over 1f out* **3/1**[2]

1m 12.35s (0.15) **Going Correction** +0.10s/f (Good) **7** Ran SP% **111.9**
Speed ratings (Par 103): **103,102,99,98,97 96,96**
toteswingers: 1&2 £4.60, 1&3 £3.90, 2&3 £9.10 CSF £21.23 TOTE £2.90: £1.80, £4.70; EX 26.90.
Owner Tangerine Trees Partnership **Bred** Mrs B A Matthews **Trained** Hambleton, N Yorks

FOCUS
A fair sprint handicap in which the front pair pulled nicely clear. Another small step forward from Tangerine Trees.

4016 HAMILTON PARK LADIES NIGHT H'CAP — 6f 5y
5:10 (5:11) (Class 6) (0-60,60) 3-Y-O+ **£2,266** (£674; £337; £168) **Stalls Low**

Form — RPR

1206 **1** **Botham (USA)**[11] 3655 5-9-2 **55**........................ DanielTudhope 8 66
(J S Goldie) *hld up: gd hdwy over 1f out: led ins fnl f: kpt on strly* **13/2**[3]

150 **2** *2* **Future Gem**[23] 3239 3-8-2 **51**........................(p) JamieKyne(5) 2 55
(A Dickman) *prom: outpcd over 2f out: kpt on to go 2nd wl ins fnl f: r.o* **10/1**

0000 **3** *¾* **Meydan Groove**[27] 3108 3-7-9 **46** oh1........................ MatthewLawson(7) 7 48
(R Johnson) *led to over 1f out: r.o ins fnl f* **22/1**

0064 **4** *½* **Andrasta**[26] 3153 4-8-7 **53**........................ CharlotteKerton(7) 1 54
(A Berry) *chsd ldrs: led over 1f out to ins fnl f: no ex* **33/1**

0063 **5** *½* **Dalarossie**[28] 3066 4-8-11 **55**........................ GaryBartley(5) 10 54
(E J Alston) *trckd ldrs: effrt over 2f out: one pce fnl f* **5/1**[2]

0040 **6** *½* **Sunley Sovereign**[8] 3730 5-8-8 **47**........................(b) AndrewElliott 6 45
(Mrs R A Carr) *midfield: drvn over 2f out: no imp over 1f out* **5/1**[2]

300- **7** *3* **Just Spike**[258] 7118 6-9-1 **54**........................ PaulHanagan 3 42
(B P J Baugh) *hld up: pushed along over 3f out: no imp fr 2f out* **9/2**[1]

2450 **8** *3¾* **Howards Tipple**[16] 3484 5-8-13 **52**........................(p) TomEaves 11 28
(I Semple) *hld up: rdn over 2f out: btn fnl f* **7/1**

0030 **9** *½* **Owed**[39] 2745 7-8-7 **46** oh1........................(tp) GregFairley 4 21
(R Bastiman) *cl up tl rdn and wknd over 1f out* **20/1**

-046 **10** *3¾* **Actabou**[21] 3296 4-8-8 **52**........................ BMcHugh(5) 9 15
(F P Murtagh) *bhd: drvn over 3f out: nvr on terms* **25/1**

0000 **11** *¾* **Piccolo Pete**[29] 3031 4-8-4 **48** oh1 ow2........................(b[1]) LanceBetts(5) 12 8
(R Johnson) *midfield on outside: struggling 1/2-way: btn over 1f out* **33/1**

1m 12.45s (0.25) **Going Correction** +0.10s/f (Good)
WFA 3 from 4yo+ 5lb **11** Ran SP% **105.3**
Speed ratings (Par 101): **102,99,98,97,97 96,92,87,86,81 80**
toteswingers: 1&2 £12.90, 1&3 £18.20, 2&3 £34.60 CSF £50.72 CT £981.65 TOTE £7.30: £2.00, £2.30, £5.90; EX 64.90 Place 6: £257.46 , Place 5: £37.10.
Owner J S Morrison **Bred** France Weiner & Neal Hayias **Trained** Uplawmoor, E Renfrews

FOCUS
A competitive sprint handicap, but a poor one and weakened further by the withdrawal of Circuit Dancer who got upset in the stalls. The field came down the centre of the track and the leaders may have gone off a shade too quick as the front pair came from well off the pace. The winning time was 1/10th of a second slower than the preceding 56-75 handicap. The form is straightforward. Circuit Dancer was withdrawn (6/1, unruly in stalls). R4 applies, deduct 10p in the £.
T/Plt: £213.50 to a £1 stake. Pool: £45,876.97. 156.80 winning tickets. T/Qpdt: £24.40 to a £1 stake. Pool: £3,925.60. 118.90 winning tickets. RY

3625 LEICESTER (R-H)
Thursday, July 16
OFFICIAL GOING: Good to firm (good in places)
Wind: Light behind Weather: Cloudy with sunny spells

4017 LADBROKES.COM NURSERY — 5f 218y
2:10 (2:10) (Class 4) 2-Y-O **£3,885** (£1,156; £577; £288) **Stalls Low**

Form — RPR

2456 **1** **Angel Of Fashion (IRE)**[22] 3271 2-8-5 **67**........................ FrancisNorton 3 74
(B W Hills) *chsd ldr: edgd rt fr over 3f out: rdn to ld ins fnl f: r.o wl* **6/1**

365 **2** *3¼* **Gillburg (USA)**[16] 3487 2-8-10 **72**........................(p) NCallan 4 69
(K A Ryan) *led: rdn and hdd over 1f out: ev ch ins fnl f: styd on same pce* **7/1**

1321 **3** *¾* **Transfixed (IRE)**[6] 3807 2-8-11 **73** 6ex........................ StephenDonohoe 7 68
(P D Evans) *chsd ldrs: rdn over 2f out: styd on same pce fnl f* **15/8**[1]

2261 **4** *nk* **Danzoe (IRE)**[28] 3064 2-9-7 **83**........................ LDettori 6 77
(D Donovan) *hld up: hdwy over 2f out: rdn to ld over 1f out: sn edgd lft: hdd and no ex ins fnl f* **5/2**[2]

4124 **5** *hd* **Daniella De Bruijn (IRE)**[18] 3424 2-9-2 **78**........................ JamesDoyle 2 72
(A B Haynes) *hld up in tch: rdn over 2f out: edgd rt and no imp fnl f* **4/1**[3]

1m 10.89s (-2.11) **Going Correction** -0.275s/f (Firm) **5** Ran SP% **110.1**
Speed ratings (Par 96): **103,98,97,97,97**
toteswingers: 1&2 £16.60. CSF £42.22 TOTE £8.60: £3.90, £3.10; EX 22.30.
Owner John Sillett **Bred** Grangemore Stud **Trained** Lambourn, Berks

FOCUS
This looked a fair nursery, considering the form of the top three in the weights. The 'official' ratings shown next to each horse are estimated and for information purposes only.

NOTEBOOK
Angel Of Fashion(IRE), who was ridden by Francis Norton for the first time, showed early promise but her form had levelled out a bit. However, she reproduced her best form to win in decisive fashion under the stands'-side rail. If she repeats this sort of effort, she can win in handicap company again. (tchd 15-2)
Gillburg(USA) was given time after his second run - he was gelded as well - but proved a little disappointing last time when not looking completely straightforward. It was no surprise to see cheekpieces applied for his handicap debut and there didn't look a lot wrong with his attitude here, simply being beaten by a better horse on the day after leading early. (op 8-1 tchd 13-2)
Transfixed(IRE) sat just behind the leaders but couldn't pick up for pressure when the tempo increased. She did stay on again about 50 yards from the winning post but was comfortably held. (op 5-2)
Danzoe(IRE), the easy winner of a Ripon maiden last time, loomed up looking a big danger just over a furlong out, but that move soon came to nothing, and the jockey was not hard on him thereafter. (op 2-1 tchd 3-1)
Daniella De Bruijn(IRE) never featured at any stage with a winning chance. (tchd 7-2 and 9-2)

4018 LADBROKES.COM (S) STKS — 5f 2y
2:40 (2:41) (Class 6) 2-Y-O **£1,942** (£578; £288; £144) **Stalls Low**

Form — RPR

1 **Annia Galeria (IRE)** 2-8-6 0 ow3........................ KevinGhunowa(3) 8 58
(A B Haynes) *chsd ldrs: led 4f out: rdn and hdd over 1f out: rallied u.p to ld nr fin* **7/1**[3]

2 *nk* **Ishe A Lord** 2-8-6 0........................ JackDean(5) 9 58
(W G M Turner) *chsd ldrs: led over 1f out: sn rdn and edgd lft: hdd nr fin* **10/1**

2 **3** *1½* **Izuizorizuain't (IRE)**[8] 3726 2-8-6 0........................ RichardMullen 3 54+
(K A Ryan) *sn outpcd: hdwy and nt clr run fr over 1f out tl r.o wl and grabbed 3rd nr fin: nvr able to chal* **1/1**[1]

6320 **4** *nk* **Musiara**[60] 2100 2-8-6 0........................ SamHitchcott 7 47
(M R Channon) *a.p: rdn 1/2-way: no ex wl ins fnl f: lost 3rd nr fin* **10/3**[2]

00 **5** *nse* **That'Lldonowthen (IRE)**[13] 3572 2-8-11 0........................ LPKeniry 1 52
(J S Moore) *chsd ldrs: outpcd over 1f out: styd on wl towards fin* **25/1**

0 **6** *1½* **Althabea**[9] 3715 2-8-11 0........................ StephenDonohoe 6 46
(Ian Williams) *prom: outpcd 1/2-way: n.d after* **50/1**

05 **7** *1¼* **Grace Jicaro**[94] 1249 2-8-6 0........................ NeilChalmers 4 37
(Mrs L Williamson) *s.i.s: hld up: hdwy 2f out: wknd ins fnl f* **12/1**

000 **8** *3¼* **Beach Boy (IRE)**[17] 3468 2-8-11 0........................ LiamJones 5 30
(S Wynne) *sn pushed along in rr: rdn: edgd rt and wknd over 1f out* **66/1**

0600 **P** **Saachi's Vision (IRE)**[9] 3709 2-8-7 0 ow1........................(bt) StephenCarson 2 —
(D K Ivory) *led 1f: chsd ldrs tl eased wl over 2f out: n.m.r sn after: p.u over 1f out* **20/1**

60.66 secs (0.66) **Going Correction** -0.275s/f (Firm) **9** Ran SP% **114.4**
Speed ratings (Par 92): **83,82,80,79,79 77,75,69,—**
toteswingers: 1&2 £16.70, 1&3 £2.70, 2&3 £6.00 CSF £68.75 TOTE £9.40: £2.00, £4.10, £1.10; EX 55.50 Trifecta £183.60 Part won. Pool: £248.20 - 0.50 winning units..There was no bid for the winner. Izuizorizuain't was the subject of a friendly claim.
Owner WCR V - The Conkwell Connection **Bred** Jay Gee Partnership **Trained** Limpley Stoke, Bath

FOCUS
An ordinary-looking seller in which the favourite was very unlucky.

NOTEBOOK
Annia Galeria(IRE), a half-sister to winners, including the once very useful Collateral Damage, does not look the biggest but she knew her job (she had been given a couple of racecourse gallops recently) and came home strongly once getting to the stands'-side rail. This was a fair effort considering her jockey was putting up 3lb overweight and it will be interesting to see whether she progresses much from this success. (op 15-2 tchd 8-1)
Ishe A Lord, a bigger, lengthier type than the winner, also looked to know what was required and shaped well after racing handily. She was green under pressure and will improve. (op 11-1 tchd 14-1)
Izuizorizuain't(IRE) got outpaced soon after leaving the stalls, but could be seen staying on really well when meeting a wall of horses. Once in the clear, she flew home and would have been in front in another 50 yards. Official explanation: jockey said filly was denied a clear run (tchd 5-6 and 11-10)
Musiara, beaten over 15 lengths last time, had every chance but failed to pick up for pressure. (op 7-2 tchd 11-4)
That'Lldonowthen(IRE) had not shown much in two previous races but posted a better effort here. (op 20-1)
Althabea finished last on his debut and was swiftly dropped in grade. He showed more promise at this level and could be found an opening before the end of the season. Official explanation: jockey said colt lost its action (op 28-1)
Grace Jicaro, absent since the middle of April, carries her tail high and flashes it under pressure. (tchd 14-1)
Saachi's Vision(IRE) Official explanation: vet said filly was lame behind

4019 LADBROKESCASINO.COM H'CAP — 7f 9y
3:15 (3:15) (Class 4) (0-80,77) 3-Y-O+ — £4,857 (£1,445; £722; £360) Stalls Low

Form				RPR
0006	1		**My Gacho (IRE)**[15] 3497 7-9-8 **73** ....(v) J-PGuillambert 2	80
			(M Johnston) *chsd ldr tl c stands' side and led that gp over 4f out: rdn and hdd over 1f out: sn carried rt: rallied u.p to ld post* **7/1**	
0-02	2	*nse*	**Orlando's Tale (USA)**[21] 3319 4-9-11 **76** .... DaneO'Neill 10	83
			(J R Fanshawe) *trckd ldr in centre: rdn over 1f out: r.o u.p to ld last strides: hdd post* **10/1**	
0-00	3	*hd*	**Cook's Endeavour (USA)**[61] 2072 3-9-2 **74** .... NCallan 6	78
			(K A Ryan) *overall ldr in centre: rdn over 1f out: hdd last strides* **5/1**[2]	
3026	4	*hd*	**Balata**[24] 3211 4-9-4 **69** .... TGMcLaughlin 1	75
			(B R Millman) *hld up: swtchd stands' side over 4f out: hdwy over 2f out: rdn to ld that gp and hung rt fr over 1f out: r.o* **8/1**	
1124	5	4 ½	**Sweet Gale (IRE)**[17] 3453 5-9-10 **75** .... AlanMunro 4	69
			(Mike Murphy) *s.i.s: hld up: swtchd to stands' side over 4f out: hdwy over 2f out: rdn and carried rt fr over 1f out: no ex ins fnl f* **9/2**[1]	
-010	6	*1*	**Bahamian Kid**[20] 3331 4-9-7 **72** ....(p) GeorgeBaker 9	63
			(R Hollinshead) *stdd s: hld up: swtchd stands' side over 4f out: r.o ins fnl f: nvr trbld ldrs* **8/1**	
0100	7	*6*	**Lodi (IRE)**[14] 3523 4-9-12 **77** ....(t) AdamKirby 7	52
			(J Akehurst) *hld up: swtchd stands' side over 4f out: effrt over 2f out: wknd wl over 1f out* **7/1**	
2100	8	¾	**Champain Sands (IRE)**[22] 3264 10-8-11 **62** .... AndrewMullen 3	35
			(E J Alston) *chsd ldrs: swtchd stands' side over 4f out: rdn over 2f out: sn wknd* **11/1**	
553	9	*4*	**Fiefdom (IRE)**[20] 3335 7-9-9 **74** .... PatrickMathers 8	36
			(I W McInnes) *chsd ldrs: swtchd stands' side over 4f out: rdn and wknd wl over 1f out* **13/2**[3]	

1m 23.3s (-2.90) **Going Correction** -0.275s/f (Firm)
WFA 3 from 4yo+ 7lb — **9** Ran SP% **112.8**
Speed ratings (Par 105): **105,104,104,104,99 98,91,90,85**
toteswingers: 1&2 £8.10, 1&3 £26.90, 2&3 £13.70 CSF £72.31 CT £381.92 TOTE £7.30: £2.20, £3.40, £2.00; EX 44.50 Trifecta £48.70 Pool: £224.02 -3.40 winning units..
Owner Grant Mercer **Bred** Mount Coote Stud **Trained** Middleham Moor, N Yorks
■ Stewards' Enquiry : T G McLaughlin three-day ban: careless riding (Jul 30-Aug 1)

FOCUS
Not many of these came into this race in good heart, so this result may not be completely reliable, especially as two horses raced well away from their rivals. However , the form looks straightforward with the solid fourth the best guide.
My Gacho(IRE) Official explanation: trainer had no explanation for the improved form shown
Cook's Endeavour(USA) Official explanation: jockey said gelding stumbled and lost his iron
Balata Official explanation: jockey said gelding hung right

4020 LADBROKES.COM MELTON MOWBRAY CONDITIONS STKS — 1m 1f 218y
3:50 (3:50) (Class 3) 3-Y-O — £7,569 (£2,265; £1,132; £566; £282) Stalls High

Form				RPR
2530	1		**Big Bound (USA)**[28] 3050 3-9-3 100 .... RichardMullen 2	103
			(J H M Gosden) *chsd ldr: rdn over 2f out: led wl over 1f out: r.o gamely* **4/1**[2]	
4-16	2	*hd*	**Libel Law**[69] 1822 3-9-3 97 .... PhilipRobinson 3	103
			(M A Jarvis) *trckd ldrs: plld hrd: wnt 2nd over 1f out: rdn and ev ch ins fnl f: r.o* **5/2**[1]	
0-00	3	3 ¾	**Misdaqeya**[29] 3016 3-8-12 97 .... RHills 1	90
			(B W Hills) *plld hrd and prom: lost pl over 6f out: rdn over 3f out: hdwy over 1f out: no imp fnl f* **5/1**[3]	
	4	*7*	**Rendezvous (IRE)**[263] 3-9-3 0 .... NCallan 6	81
			(Sir Michael Stoute) *hld up: rdn over 2f out: wknd over 1f out* **5/1**[3]	
1	5	*9*	**In Footlights (USA)**[26] 3168 3-9-3 0 .... LDettori 5	71
			(Saeed Bin Suroor) *led: rdn and hdd wl over 1f out: sn wknd* **5/2**[1]	

2m 4.26s (-3.64) **Going Correction** -0.275s/f (Firm) — **5** Ran SP% **110.5**
Speed ratings (Par 104): **103,102,99,94,87**
toteswingers: 1&2 £7.30 CSF £14.32 TOTE £5.10: £1.30, £1.90; EX 16.00.
Owner Lady Rothschild **Bred** Carwell Equities Ltd **Trained** Newmarket, Suffolk
■ Stewards' Enquiry : Philip Robinson one-day ban: used whip without giving colt time to respond (Jul 30)

FOCUS
This race has gone to some smart horses recently, so the winner is probably a decent sort and the form looks straightforward rated around the first two.

NOTEBOOK
Big Bound(USA), representing last year's winning trainer, was well beaten in the Listed Hampton Court Stakes last time, but was shaping like a progressive horse before that reverse. He already held a verdict over the runner-up in the Dee Stakes earlier in the year, so it was surprising that he was sent off at much bigger odds than that rival. Always close up, he found plenty for pressure and can win more of this type of event. (op 7-2 tchd 9-2 in a place)
Libel Law, absent since finishing down the field in the Group 3 Dee Stakes, pulled his jockey's arms out in the early stages, but still looked a likely winner a furlong out. Hard though the pair tried, they could not get past the winner, but one would imagine he will be sharper next time. (tchd 2-1)
Misdaqeya, who had some good form at two, was slightly detached turning in before running on inside the final furlong. She never posed a serious threat. (op 7-1)
Rendezvous(IRE), having his first outing for Sir Michael Stoute, was beaten at 1/5 on his final start for Andre Fabre and did not show a great deal on this British debut. (op 4-1)
In Footlights(USA) made an instant impact on his debut last month, winning by a couple of lengths at Newmarket. He was handed an easy lead, so it was slightly worrying that he dropped out at a rapid rate when joined and passed. (op 11-4 tchd 3-1, 4-1 in a place)

4021 LADBROKES.COM CLAIMING STKS — 1m 3f 183y
4:25 (4:25) (Class 5) 4-Y-O+ — £3,238 (£963; £481; £240) Stalls High

Form				RPR
1001	1		**Invasian (IRE)**[2] 3961 8-8-10 81 .... PaulPickard(7) 12	82
			(P W D'Arcy) *racd keenly: trckd ldr tl led over 7f out: shkn up and clr 2f out: comf* **9/4**[1]	
5025	2	1 ¾	**Agente Romano (USA)**[14] 3521 4-8-7 67 ....(b) AlanMunro 7	69
			(G A Butler) *mid-div: hdwy over 3f out: rdn to chse wnr 2f out: edgd rt and styd on ins fnl f: nvr able to chal* **7/2**[2]	
4105	3	*1*	**Nawamees (IRE)**[4] 2743 11-8-7 65 ....(p) JamesDoyle 1	67
			(P D Evans) *sn pushed along and prom: rdn over 2f out: styd on* **4/1**[3]	
-020	4	*7*	**Lady Valentino**[43] 2608 5-8-2 50 .... DaleGibson 11	51
			(B D Leavy) *s.i.s: hld up: rdn over 3f out: hdwy over 1f out: n.d* **16/1**	
6450	5	4 ½	**Special Chapter (IRE)**[52] 2333 4-8-0 35 .... JimmyQuinn 9	42
			(A B Haynes) *mid-div: hdwy over 3f out: rdn and wknd over 1f out* **80/1**	
-452	6	*8*	**Into The Light**[21] 3308 4-9-3 70 ....(v[1]) RichardMullen 5	46
			(E S McMahon) *trckd ldrs: wnt 2nd 3f out: sn rdn: wknd wl over 1f out* **4/1**[3]	
0-40	7	2 ¾	**Rawaabet (IRE)**[1] 3974 7-8-9 46 ow7 ....(t) RussellKennemore(3) 8	37
			(R Hollinshead) *hld up: rdn over 3f out: wknd over 2f out* **33/1**	
-043	8	*13*	**Channel Crossing**[21] 3308 7-8-13 59 .... LiamJones 4	17
			(S Wynne) *led: hdd over 7f out: chsd wnr tl rdn over 3f out: sn wknd* **25/1**	
5/5-	9	*9*	**No Supper (IRE)**[114] 758 5-9-3 0 .... DaneO'Neill 6	7
			(Tim Vaughan) *hld up: rdn and wknd 3f out* **12/1**	

2m 29.2s (-4.70) **Going Correction** -0.275s/f (Firm) — **9** Ran SP% **114.6**
Speed ratings (Par 103): **104,102,102,97,94 89,87,78,72**
toteswingers: 1&2 £2.80, 1&3 £5.40, 2&3 £4.40 CSF £9.95 TOTE £3.20: £1.20, £1.60, £1.60; EX 11.70 Trifecta £24.80 Pool: £345.48 - 10.29 winning units..Agente Romano was claimed by R E R Williams for £5,000.
Owner Paul D'Arcy **Bred** Dr Karen Monica Sanderson **Trained** Newmarket, Suffolk

FOCUS
A couple of these were rated as being at least fair, but the majority of them were modest performers, so this probably did not take a great deal of winning. The winner did not have to run to recent form and the runner-up is the best guide.

4022 LADBROKES.COM MOUNTSORREL MAIDEN STKS — 1m 1f 218y
5:00 (5:01) (Class 5) 3-4-Y-O — £3,238 (£963; £481; £240) Stalls High

Form				RPR
2-23	1		**Seaway**[33] 2937 3-9-0 80 ....(t) LDettori 11	66+
			(Saeed Bin Suroor) *led: hdd over 2f out: rallied to ld over 1f out: eased nr fin* **8/11**[1]	
66	2	1 ¼	**Arashi**[48] 2446 3-9-0 0 ....(p) TGMcLaughlin 1	63
			(Lucinda Featherstone) *hld up: rdn over 2f out: hdwy over 1f out: styd on to go 2nd nr fin:* **28/1**	
54	3	*hd*	**Bow To No One (IRE)**[21] 3297 3-8-9 0 .... AlanMunro 8	58
			(A P Jarvis) *trckd wnr: racd keenly: led over 2f out: rdn and hdd over 1f out: styd on same pce ins fnl f: lost 2nd nr fin* **7/2**[2]	
00	4	¾	**Stormy Morning**[80] 1573 3-9-0 0 .... AdamKirby 5	62
			(W R Swinburn) *hld up: hdwy over 2f out: sn rdn: styd on* **10/1**	
00-	5	*shd*	**Flodden Field**[243] 7336 3-9-0 0 .... RichardMullen 3	61
			(P W Chapple-Hyam) *chsd ldrs: rdn over 2f out: styd on* **7/1**[3]	
	6	2 ¼	**Reset City** 3-8-9 0 .... RobertHavlin 2	52
			(A B Haynes) *plld hrd: trckd ldrs: rdn over 2f out: no ex ins fnl f* **20/1**	
	7	*38*	**Billy The Gas**[222] 4-9-10 0 .... J-PGuillambert 6	—
			(N Tinkler) *s.s: hld up: lost tch over 3f out: t.o* **150/1**	

2m 8.76s (0.86) **Going Correction** -0.275s/f (Firm)
WFA 3 from 4yo 10lb — **7** Ran SP% **110.6**
Speed ratings (Par 103): **85,84,83,83,83 81,50**
toteswingers: 1&2 £3.70, 1&3 £1.70, 2&3 £5.90 CSF £26.52 TOTE £1.60: £1.30, £5.30; EX 22.30 Trifecta £83.70 Pool: £312.30 - 2.76 winning units..
Owner Godolphin **Bred** Newsells Park Stud Limited **Trained** Newmarket, Suffolk

FOCUS
Several key non-runners left this looking a weak maiden. The pace was very steady and the form looks messy, with the winner not having to match his best to score.

4023 LADBROKES.COM APPRENTICE H'CAP — 5f 218y
5:30 (5:32) (Class 5) (0-70,65) 3-Y-O+ — £3,885 (£1,156; £577; £288) Stalls Low

Form				RPR
2504	1		**Plumage**[15] 3505 4-9-6 **58** .... LeeNewnes 9	67
			(M Salaman) *a.p: chsd ldr over 1f out: rdn to ld ins fnl f: r.o* **3/1**[1]	
0053	2	*1*	**Shakespeare's Son**[10] 3691 4-9-9 **61** ....(b[1]) SimonPearce 8	67
			(H J Evans) *led: rdn over 1f out: hdd and unable qckn ins fnl f* **4/1**[2]	
651/	3	¾	**Moral Duty (USA)**[403] 4-9-10 **65** .... LauraPike(3) 6	69+
			(J S Moore) *sn pushed along in rr: rdn 1/2-way: hung rt over 1f out: r.o ins fnl f: eased nr fin* **7/1**[3]	
4035	4	1 ½	**Desert Pride**[15] 3505 4-9-9 **60** ....(v) JemmaMarshall 2	59
			(W S Kittow) *plld hrd: sn trcking ldr: rdn over 1f out: no ex ins fnl f* **7/1**[3]	
-000	5	½	**Boldinor**[19] 3407 6-8-10 **48** .... KylieManser 11	45
			(M R Bosley) *prom: rdn 1/2-way: no ex ins fnl f* **10/1**	
0600	6	1 ¾	**Metropolitan Chief**[8] 3732 5-8-5 **46** oh1 ....(p) RyanPowell(3) 4	38
			(P Burgoyne) *s.i.s: hdwy over 2f out: rdn over 1f out: wknd ins fnl f* **33/1**	
5050	7	2 ½	**Makshoof (IRE)**[9] 3713 5-9-10 **65** ....(p) IJBrennan(3) 10	49
			(I W McInnes) *hld up: outpcd 1/2-way: n.d after* **9/1**	
0-00	8	*shd*	**Union Jack Jackson (IRE)**[21] 3304 7-8-5 **46** oh1.(b) TobyAtkinson(3) 7	29
			(John A Harris) *chsd ldrs: rdn 1/2-way: wknd 2f out* **66/1**	
0305	9	*1*	**Affirmatively**[13] 3591 4-8-8 **46** oh1 ....(bt) PaulPickard 3	26
			(A W Carroll) *s.i.s: hmpd sn after s: a in rr* **16/1**	
4230	10	*nse*	**Music Box Express**[21] 3318 5-9-10 **62** .... MatthewDavies 5	42
			(George Baker) *s.i.s: edgd lft sn after s: hdwy over 4f out: rdn 1/2-way: wknd 2f out* **8/1**	
0006	11	*9*	**Captain Peachey**[43] 2603 3-8-0 **46** oh1 .... KierenFox(3) 1	—
			(B R Millman) *chsd ldrs tl wknd over 2f out* **20/1**	

1m 12.16s (-0.84) **Going Correction** -0.275s/f (Firm)
WFA 3 from 4yo+ 5lb — **11** Ran SP% **115.3**
Speed ratings (Par 103): **94,92,91,89,89 86,83,83,81,81 69**
toteswingers: 1&2 £3.60, 1&3 £6.80, 2&3 £8.50 CSF £13.95 CT £76.37 TOTE £2.90: £1.80, £1.80, £2.30; EX 16.30 Trifecta £315.40 Part won. Pool: £426.24 - 0.71 winning units. Place 6: £151.77, Place 5: £10.18.
Owner Mrs N L Young **Bred** The Duke Of Devonshire & Floors Farming **Trained** Upper Lambourn, Berks

FOCUS
A moderate handicap that produced a good finish and it was a slight personal best from the winner.

T/Plt: £60.50 to a £1 stake. Pool: £47,319.51. 570.28 winning tickets. T/Qpdt: £10.20 to a £1 stake. Pool: £3,520.50. 255.30 winning tickets. CR

4024 - 4027a (Foreign Racing) - See Raceform Interactive

3832 LEOPARDSTOWN (L-H)

Thursday, July 16

OFFICIAL GOING: Yielding

4028a SILVER FLASH STKS (GROUP 3) (FILLIES) 7f
6:30 (6:32) 2-Y-O **£39,186** (£11,497; £5,477; £1,866)

RPR

1 **Cabaret (IRE)**20 3364 2-8-12 ... JMurtagh 5 106+
(A P O'Brien, Ire) *mde all: rdn clr 1 1/2f out: kpt on wl fnl f: comf* **2/1**1

2 4 1/2 **Alshahbaa (IRE)**53 2302 2-8-12 ... DPMcDonogh 1 94
(Kevin Prendergast, Ire) *chsd ldrs in 3rd: rdn 2f out: kpt on same pce fr over 1f out: wnt 2nd cl home* **2/1**1

3 shd **Kitty Kiernan**18 3436 2-8-12 97 ...(t) KJManning 6 94
(J S Bolger, Ire) *chsd ldr in 2nd: rdn 2f out: no imp on ldr over 1f out: kpt on same pce fnl f: lost 2nd cl home* **2/1**1

4 1/2 **Velvet Flicker (IRE)**20 3366 2-8-12 89 ... CDHayes 4 92
(Kevin Prendergast, Ire) *racd mainly 4th: rdn 2f out: kpt on same pce fr over 1f out* **9/1**2

5 11 **Strandhill (IRE)**7 3832 2-8-12 ...(t) DJMoran 3 65
(Brian Nolan, Ire) *dwlt: a in rr: rdn and no imp ent st* **66/1**3

1m 28.32s (-0.38) **Going Correction** +0.15s/f (Good) **5** Ran SP% **111.5**
Speed ratings: **108,102,102,102,89**
CSF £6.37 TOTE £2.20: £1.70, £1.40; DF 6.60.
Owner Mrs John Magnier **Bred** Epona Bloodstock Ltd **Trained** Ballydoyle, Co Tipperary

NOTEBOOK
Cabaret(IRE), originally due to be ridden by Heffernan prior to Famous being withdrawn, made all the running to supplement a maiden win gained at The Curragh on her second start. The market was unable to split the front three in the betting in the five-runner field, but the result could hardly have been more emphatic, with the Galileo filly never in any danger after extending her advantage from under two furlongs down. She comes from a family in which there is plenty of stamina and can be rated a smart long-term prospect. (op 2/1 tchd 7/4)
Alshahbaa(IRE), who made a favourable impression in winning first time out in the heavy over 6f at The Curragh in May, was no match for the winner but kept on well enough to edge out Kitty Kiernan for second place.
Kitty Kiernan, who was fitted with a tongue-tie for the first time, has failed to go forward since beating the Albany Stakes runner-up Lillie Langtry first time out at Naas. However, Jim Bolger's fine record with fillies means that it would be premature to write her off, and she is worth persevering with in Pattern company. (op 2/1 tchd 5/2)
Velvet Flicker(IRE) did not ran badly in terms of how close she finished to the placed horses, but never posed any sort of threat. (op 8/1)

4033a CHALLENGE STKS (LISTED RACE) 1m 6f
9:00 (9:00) 3-Y-O+ **£26,861** (£7,881; £3,754; £1,279)

RPR

1 **Profound Beauty (IRE)**19 3413 5-9-9 108 ... PJSmullen 5 108+
(D K Weld, Ire) *settled in 5th: hdwy in 3rd 2f out: rdn into 2nd over 1f out: styd on to ld ins fnl 150yds: kpt on wl* **6/4**1

2 3/4 **Yankee Doodle**19 3413 3-8-10 109 ... JMurtagh 1 108+
(A P O'Brien, Ire) *settled bhd ldrs in 4th: rdn 2f out: styd on to go 3rd over 1f out: kpt on to take 2nd ins fnl f: nt rch wnr* **4/1**3

3 3/4 **Aliyfa (IRE)**18 3439 3-8-7 96 ... NGMcCullagh 2 104
(John M Oxx, Ire) *led: rdn 2f out: kpt on: hdd fnl 150yds and no ex: kpt on same pce* **25/1**

4 1 **Fergus McIver (IRE)**54 2288 3-8-10 105 ...(b) KJManning 3 106
(J S Bolger, Ire) *hld up in rr: rdn into 5th over 1f out: kpt on same pce fnl f* **12/1**

5 2 1/2 **Alandi (IRE)**19 3413 4-9-12 107 ... MJKinane 4 104
(John M Oxx, Ire) *chsd ldrs in 3rd: rdn 3f out: no ex in 5th under 2f out: kpt on one pce fr 1 1/2f out* **7/4**2

6 shd **Von Jawlensky (IRE)**10 3700 3-8-10 103 ... JAHeffernan 6 102
(A P O'Brien, Ire) *chsd ldr in 2nd: pushed along 4f out: kpt on u.p: no ex over 1f out: wknd* **12/1**

2m 59.3s (-1.70) **Going Correction** +0.15s/f (Good)
WFA 3 from 4yo+ 14lb **6** Ran SP% **115.6**
Speed ratings: **110,109,109,108,107 107**
CSF £8.40 TOTE £2.40: £1.50, £2.00; DF 7.10.
Owner Moyglare Stud Farm **Bred** Moyglare Stud Farms **Trained** The Curragh, Co Kildare

FOCUS
This Listed event amounted to a re-run of the Group 3 Curragh Cup. The form looks sound.

NOTEBOOK
Profound Beauty(IRE) accomplished the task in style, held up before improving her position around a quarter of a mile out and staying on well to assert inside the last furlong. Fifth in last year's Melbourne Cup, she has the race as her main target again this year. With a year of added maturity, which may help in the crucial stamina department, she has the look of a major contender, especially when her trainer's proven track-record is factored into the equation. Dermot Weld indicated that he is considering the options of the Yorkshire Oaks and the Irish St Leger en route to Australia. (op 7/4)
Yankee Doodle ◆, third to the winner in the Curragh Cup last time, went one place better, running a sound race without being quite good enough to match the winner in the closing stages. He has only a Wexford maiden win to his name, but is enjoying a good season. His second in the Queen's Vase proves that he stays further than this, and it may be realistic to hope that he could mature into a Cup horse over the next season or two. (op 7/2)
Aliyfa(IRE) made the running, and it was only late in the day that she gave best, a career-best display by the 96-rated filly who outperformed her stablemate Alandi.
Fergus McIver(IRE), trying the trip for the first time, was easy to back and failed to make a significant impression. (op 10/1)
Alandi(IRE) was unlucky in the Curragh Cup, but he had no excuses here and was disappointing. (op 7/4 tchd 6/4)
T/Jkpt: @468.60. Pool of @10,000.00 - 16 winning units. T/Plt: @12.40. Pool of @10,756.80 - 646 winning units. II

4029 - 4033a (Foreign Racing) - See Raceform Interactive

4011 HAMILTON (R-H)

Friday, July 17

OFFICIAL GOING: Good (9.3)
Rail realignment reduced advertised distances on round course by about 30yards.
Wind: Light, half-against Weather: Overcast

4034 JOHN RAMSAY CHASER APPRENTICE SERIES H'CAP (ROUND 3) 1m 1f 36y
6:20 (6:20) (Class 6) (0-60,58) 4-Y-O+ **£2,388** (£705; £352) **Stalls** High

Form RPR

06-6 1 **Phantom Serenade (IRE)**28 3092 4-8-9 **48** ... LanceBetts 3 58
(M Dods) *set stdy pce: rdn and hung lft 2f out: kpt on wl fnl f* **7/1**

4600 2 1 3/4 **Rossini's Dancer**29 3070 4-8-12 **56** ...(p) LeeTopliss(5) 10 63
(R A Fahey) *hld up: hdwy to chse wnr over 1f out: r.o fnl f* **4/1**3

2-00 3 6 **Tender Moments**40 2746 5-8-6 **52** ... RichardOliver(7) 9 48
(B Smart) *hld up: rdn over 3f out: kpt on fnl f: n.d* **15/2**

4 1/2 **Louisa (GER)**698 5-9-5 **58** ... DeclanCannon 2 53
(P Monteith) *s.i.s: bhd tl hdwy over 1f out: no imp fnl f* **16/1**

0563 5 2 3/4 **Bold Indian (IRE)**18 3448 5-8-8 **52** ... RossSmith(5) 8 41
(I Semple) *plld hrd in tch: hdwy and cl up over 2f out: rdn and wknd over 1f out* **11/4**1

0014 6 3 1/4 **King Of Legend (IRE)**18 3448 5-8-12 **56** ...(t) IJBrennan(5) 1 39
(A G Foster) *prom: effrt over 3f out: wknd over 1f out* **10/3**2

4-50 7 1 **Aquarian Dancer**18 3451 4-7-13 **45** ... EleanorMcGowan(7) 5 26
(Jedd O'Keeffe) *in midfield on outside: outpcd over 3f out: n.d after* **28/1**

0000 8 19 **Fan Club**8 3760 5-8-6 **45** ... JamesPSullivan 6 —
(Mrs R A Carr) *t.k.h: chsd ldrs tl wknd over 2f out: t.o* **28/1**

0-06 9 nse **Mystical Ayr (IRE)**28 3094 7-8-8 **50** ... MatthewLawson(3) 7 —
(Miss L A Perratt) *t.k.h: cl up tl wknd over 2f out: t.o* **14/1**

2m 1.20s (1.50) **Going Correction** +0.15s/f (Good) **9** Ran SP% **113.5**
Speed ratings (Par 101): **99,97,92,91,89 86,85,68,68**
toteswingers: 1&2 £5.60, 1&3 £14.40, 2&3 £6.20. CSF £34.47 CT £214.25 TOTE £7.60: £2.00, £2.10, £3.10; EX 49.20.
Owner North Briton Racing **Bred** Redpender Stud Ltd **Trained** Denton, Co Durham
■ Stewards' Enquiry : Lee Topliss three-day ban: careless riding (Jul 31, Aug 2-3); two-day ban: used whip with excessive frequency (Aug 4-5)

FOCUS
An ordinary handicap. It was run at a very steady pace and the first two finished a long way clear of the rest.
Bold Indian(IRE) Official explanation: vet said gelding suffered diaphragmatic flutter

4035 JOHN SMITH'S EXTRA SMOOTH NURSERY 6f 5y
6:55 (6:55) (Class 4) 2-Y-O **£5,180** (£1,541; £770; £384) **Stalls** Low

Form RPR

0312 1 **Colonel Mak**10 3702 2-9-2 **77** ... PhillipMakin 1 91+
(D H Brown) *hld up in tch: smooth hdwy to ld 1f out: qcknd clr: readily* **6/4**1

21 2 6 **Ballodair (IRE)**17 3487 2-9-6 **81** ... TonyHamilton 2 77
(R A Fahey) *cl up: led and overall ldr over 2f out: hdd 1f out: no ch w wnr* **15/8**2

31 3 8 **Maison Brillet (IRE)**50 2388 2-9-7 **82** ... PaulMulrennan 3 54
(J Howard Johnson) *led stands' side gp to over 2f out: sn outpcd* **5/1**3

220 4 4 1/2 **Baileys Vision**28 3086 2-9-0 **75** ... GregFairley 5 34
(M Johnston) *racd alone centre: overall ldr to over 2f out: sn wknd* **11/2**

000 5 3 1/2 **Weetentherty**50 2388 2-7-13 **60** ...(v) DuranFentiman 4 8
(J S Goldie) *chsd ldrs: rdn 1/2-way: sn wknd* **25/1**

1m 13.66s (1.46) **Going Correction** +0.15s/f (Good) **5** Ran SP% **110.7**
Speed ratings (Par 96): **96,88,77,71,66**
CSF £4.64 TOTE £2.40: £1.40, £1.80; EX 5.00.
Owner Norton Common Farm Racing **Bred** Peter Baldwin **Trained** Maltby, S Yorks

FOCUS
It was raining heavily during this interesting nursery, a race which involved three previous winners, and the pace was furious. The 'official' ratings shown next to each horse are estimated and for information purposes only.

NOTEBOOK
Colonel Mak quickened clear in a course-and-distance maiden auction on good to firm before going close off this mark on his nursery debut on slow ground last week. He sat off the blistering pace here, moved smoothly into contention and forged clear in impressive style. He looks a really nice type, who has a high cruising speed and good turn of foot. He could go on to much better things and looks one to follow. (op 2-1)
Ballodair(IRE) was runner-up to the subsequent Chesham Stakes sixth on debut before justifying strong support at Thirsk last month. He looked on a realistic mark for his first skirmish in nursery company and ran a fair race but could not cope with the potentially useful winner. He will face more feasible opportunities in the weeks ahead. (op 2-1)
Maison Brillet(IRE) beat Baileys Vision in an Ayr maiden last time on his second start, but was under pressure and flailing against the near rail a long way out in this race. (op 4-1)
Baileys Vision blasted into the lead up the centre of the track but was in trouble at the 2f pole. She seemed to be kicking up more turf than the others, so may have been on a slower part of the track, but this still has to rate as a disappointing effort. (op 6-1 tchd 5-1)

4036 GUINNESS (S) STKS 5f 4y
7:25 (7:25) (Class 6) 3-Y-O+ **£2,266** (£674; £337; £168) **Stalls** Centre

Form RPR

1102 1 **Blue Tomato**11 3678 8-9-6 77 ...(p) AdrianTNicholls 6 82+
(D Nicholls) *hld up in tch: hdwy to ld over 1f out: drvn clr* **11/4**2

3242 2 4 1/2 **Raccoon (IRE)**1 4012 9-9-6 73 ... PJMcDonald 8 66
(Mrs R A Carr) *chsd ldrs: effrt 2f out: kpt on same pce fnl f* **5/2**1

0000 3 2 **The Bear**50 2389 6-9-0 60 ... AndrewElliott 7 52
(Miss L A Perratt) *led to over 1f out: sn no ex* **10/1**

0424 4 1 3/4 **Dubai To Barnsley**4 3909 4-9-0 55 ... PaulMulrennan 2 46
(D A Nolan) *chsd ldrs: ev ch and rdn over 1f out: sn no ex* **7/2**

3143 5 1 1/2 **Silvanus (IRE)**17 3479 4-9-1 67 ...(p) PatrickDonaghy(5) 4 47
(I Semple) *t.k.h: hld up: hdwy 1/2-way: wknd over 1f out* **3/1**3

0000 6 13 **Howards Prince**30 3020 6-9-0 41 ... DuranFentiman 1 —
(D A Nolan) *cl up tl rdn and wknd wl over 1f out* **100/1**

61.29 secs (1.29) **Going Correction** +0.35s/f (Good)
WFA 3 from 4yo+ 4lb **6** Ran SP% **112.5**
Speed ratings (Par 101): **103,95,92,89,87 66**
toteswingers: 1&2 £1.90, 1&3 £3.80, 2&3 £3.90. CSF £10.12 TOTE £2.70: £1.60, £2.20; EX 4.90.The winner was sold to Mr Ken McGarrity for £3,500.
Owner Dab Hand Racing **Bred** Bearstone Stud **Trained** Sessay, N Yorks

FOCUS
A reasonable seller. The two market leaders held the highest official ratings in the field and filled the first two positions. The form is rated through the winner and fourth.

4037 JOHN SMITH'S SCOTTISH STEWARDS' CUP (H'CAP) 6f 5y
7:55 (7:57) (Class 2) (0-105,105) 3-Y-0+

£21,808 (£6,531; £3,265; £1,634; £815; £409) **Stalls** Centre

Form RPR
1002 **1** **Quest For Success (IRE)**[34] 2927 4-8-11 **90**............ TonyHamilton 13 100
(R A Fahey) *prom: effrt over 2f out: led ins fnl f: r.o wl* **14/1**
5201 **2** ½ **Tamagin (USA)**[20] 3405 6-9-12 **105**............(p) SebSanders 11 114
(J Pearce) *led tl hung lft and hdd ins fnl f: kpt on at fin* **11/1**
0011 **3** *nk* **Roker Park (IRE)**[20] 3389 4-9-1 **94**............(p) NCallan 1 102
(K A Ryan) *bhd: gd hdwy over 1f out: r.o strly fnl f* **6/1**[3]
0001 **4** *nk* **Knot In Wood (IRE)**[20] 3388 7-9-5 **103**............ BMcHugh(5) 8 110
(R A Fahey) *trckd ldrs: effrt over 2f out: kpt on u.p fnl f* **4/1**[1]
1404 **5** *1* **Excusez Moi (USA)**[20] 3389 7-9-2 **95**............(p) PJMcDonald 14 99
(Mrs R A Carr) *dwlt: hld up: hdwy over 1f out: no imp fnl f* **25/1**
6-46 **6** *1* **Tombi (USA)**[13] 3621 5-9-11 **104**............ PaulMulrennan 6 105
(J Howard Johnson) *in midfield: drvn over 3f out: rallied over 1f out: r.o fnl f* **20/1**
2-50 **7** *hd* **Tajneed (IRE)**[20] 3389 6-9-3 **96**............ AdrianTNicholls 7 96
(D Nicholls) *chsd ldrs: drvn 1/2-way: one pce whn n.m.r ins fnl f* **8/1**
2451 **8** *shd* **Thebes**[7] 3802 4-9-3 **96** 6ex............ GregFairley 10 96
(M Johnston) *cl up: effrt and ev ch over 1f out: no ex ins fnl f* **9/2**[2]
040- **9** 1½ **Protector (SAF)**[251] 7245 8-9-2 **95**............(t) AndrewMullen 5 90
(A G Foster) *bhd and drvn along: hdwy over 1f out: nrst at fin* **50/1**
0160 **10** ½ **Baby Strange**[27] 3141 5-8-8 **92**............(v[1]) MartinLane(5) 2 86
(D Shaw) *in tch: effrt over 2f out: wknd fnl f* **12/1**
-522 **11** *shd* **Barney McGrew (IRE)**[20] 3389 6-9-5 **98**............ PhillipMakin 9 92
(M Dods) *reluctant to enter stalls: sn in midfield: effrt over 1f out: no ex ins fnl f* **8/1**
0050 **12** 1½ **Opus Maximus (IRE)**[10] 3706 4-8-9 **88**............ AndrewElliott 4 77
(M Johnston) *bhd and sn pushed along: nvr on terms* **22/1**
0210 **13** *6* **Fishforcompliments**[20] 3405 5-8-12 **98**............ LeeTopliss(7) 16 69
(R A Fahey) *in tch on outside: rdn over 2f out: sn wknd* **16/1**
0305 **14** *2* **Internationaldebut (IRE)**[13] 3621 4-8-12 **91**............ LeeEnstone 15 56
(J Balding) *in midfield: struggling 1/2-way: btn wl over 1f out* **33/1**
3-00 **15** ½ **Santiago Atitlan**[161] 434 7-8-6 **92**............ DeclanCannon(7) 12 56
(P Monteith) *bhd and sn drvn along: nvr on terms* **100/1**

1m 13.09s (0.89) **Going Correction** +0.35s/f (Good) **15 Ran SP% 122.1**
Speed ratings (Par 109): **108,107,106,106,105 103,103,103,101,100 100,98,90,88,87**
toteswingers: 1&2 £21.90, 1&3 £15.70, 2&3 £6.10. CSF £149.89 CT £1066.36 TOTE £19.50: £5.40, £2.90, £2.20; EX 188.70.
Owner Morebrooke Ltd **Bred** Desmond Monaghan **Trained** Musley Bank, N Yorks

FOCUS
A classy sprint handicap. The field gradually shifted towards the centre to stands' side. The first two were always near the pace and there was an exciting finish. The first two produced personal bests with the third to his mark.

NOTEBOOK
Quest For Success(IRE) had come up a bit short in 6f handicaps since finding his feet over 7f last autumn. However, he produced a tremendously gutsy display off a career-high mark to take this highly competitive race and beat a more strongly fancied stablemate Knot In Wood. He should not go up much for this win, has won on ground ranging from firm to heavy and should be able to win more races. (op 10-1)

Tamagin(USA) set a furious pace and did really well to keep grinding away off his highest ever mark on his first run since joining his current yard for 70,000gns. He is a quality trailblazer who should continue to give it a good shot in these high-class handicaps. (op 9-1)

Roker Park(IRE) got outpaced but finished best of all against the near rail. He took his form to a new level with cheekpieces applied when landing back-to-back handicaps on fast and testing ground last month and took another step forward here. (op 5-1)

Knot In Wood(IRE) was caught a bit flat-footed at a vital stage but showed his usual determination to rally and get involved at the finish. He added a Group 3 to his long list of sprint wins at Newcastle last month and put in a creditable effort in his attempt to win this race for a third successive year. (op 5-1)

Excusez Moi(USA) travelled smoothly into contention but was not quite able to land a telling blow in his bid to register his fourth win of the year. Life can get to him at times but the seven-year-old is still a very dangerous opponent in top handicaps when in the mood. (op 20-1)

Tombi(USA) did not get the best of runs and rates a bit better than his finishing position suggests. He managed to put a flop in a Haydock conditions event behind him. (op 25-1 tchd 28-1)

Tajneed(IRE) had every chance but is struggling to hit the heights of his Great St Wilfrid win and Ayr Gold Cup second last season. (tchd 9-1)

Thebes showed up well for a long way but he could not sustain his effort and the arrival of rain may have blunted his weapons. He could bounce back next time and gave the impression that he could take some catching switched back to 5f. (op 11-2 tchd 6-1 in a place)

Baby Strange provided stiff resistance but couldn't quite hold Knot In Wood's late surge in this race last year. He had obvious claims on 6lb better terms with that rival but ran a bit flat in a first-time visor. (op 14-1)

4038 JOHN SMITH'S STAYERS H'CAP 1m 5f 9y
8:30 (8:32) (Class 4) (0-85,83) 3-Y-0+ **£5,828** (£1,734; £866; £432) **Stalls** High

Form RPR
0330 **1** **Toujours Souriante**[41] 2715 3-7-12 **66** oh1............ AndrewMullen 6 76+
(M Johnston) *prom: drvn and outpcd 4f out: rallied 2f out: swtchd and led ins fnl f: styd on wl* **13/2**
111 **2** 3¾ **Chookie Hamilton**[28] 3095 5-9-1 **75**............ PatrickDonaghy(5) 1 79
(I Semple) *cl up: led over 1f out to ins fnl f: kpt on same pce* **9/2**[3]
2124 **3** *5* **Phoenix Flight (IRE)**[87] 1435 4-10-0 **83**............ SebSanders 7 80
(Sir Mark Prescott) *t.k.h: hld up: hdwy over 3f out: rdn and edgd rt over 2f out: one pce fr wl over 1f out* **5/4**[1]
1062 **4** *nse* **Birkside**[6] 3854 6-9-6 **75**............ PaulMulrennan 5 71
(Miss L A Perratt) *led: rdn over 2f out: hdd over 1f out: sn no ex* **15/2**
531- **5** *5* **Prince Rhyddarch**[276] 6727 4-8-13 **68**............ TonyHamilton 2 57
(I Semple) *cl up tl rdn and wknd over 2f out* **7/2**[2]

2m 55.55s (1.65) **Going Correction** +0.35s/f (Good)
WFA 3 from 4yo+ 13lb **5 Ran SP% 109.9**
Speed ratings (Par 105): **108,105,102,102,99**
toteswingers: 1&2 £22.10. CSF £33.57 TOTE £9.00: £3.00, £1.80; EX 49.60.
Owner J S Morrison **Bred** Baldernock Bloodstock Ltd **Trained** Middleham Moor, N Yorks

FOCUS
Not many runners, but a competitive event and a race of wildly changing fortunes. The early pace was brisk but it slackened during the middle part of the race.

4039 ARTHUR GUINNESS 250TH H'CAP 1m 3f 16y
9:00 (9:00) (Class 6) (0-65,70) 3-Y-0 **£2,266** (£674; £337; £168) **Stalls** High

Form RPR
60-5 **1** **Alicante**[78] 1626 3-9-5 **60**............ SebSanders 10 71+
(Sir Mark Prescott) *cl up: led over 2f out: edgd rt: drvn and styd on strly* **11/4**[2]
60-0 **2** 2¼ **Ballade De La Mer**[38] 2790 3-8-4 **45**............ GregFairley 4 51+
(A G Foster) *chsd ldrs: outpcd 4f out: rallied to chse wnr over 1f out: r.o fnl f* **66/1**
-063 **3** *6* **Tillietudlem (FR)**[17] 3482 3-8-4 **45**............ DuranFentiman 1 41
(J S Goldie) *hld up: outpcd over 4f out: rallied 2f out: no imp fnl f* **8/1**
-552 **4** ½ **Penolva (IRE)**[15] 3538 3-9-2 **57**............ AndrewElliott 2 52
(K R Burke) *led to 3f out: rdn and kpt on same pce fnl 2f* **2/1**[1]
6-45 **5** 4½ **Petella**[59] 2164 3-9-2 **57**............ PJMcDonald 11 44
(C W Thornton) *hld up: outpcd over 4f out: rallied 2f out: sn n.d* **16/1**
0036 **6** *5* **Sydney Cove (IRE)**[17] 3482 3-7-11 **45**............ JamesPSullivan(7) 3 24
(R Allan) *plld hrd: cl up: led briefly 3f out: wknd over 1f out* **25/1**
0053 **7** *7* **Gulf President**[10] 3718 3-9-7 **62**............(v) NCallan 9 29
(M R Channon) *prom: effrt over 2f out: sn wknd* **4/1**[3]
002 **8** *59* **Real Desire**[22] 3294 3-9-5 **60**............(p) PhillipMakin 8 —
(I Semple) *hld up in tch: struggling over 4f out: t.o* **5/1**

2m 27.39s (1.79) **Going Correction** +0.35s/f (Good) **8 Ran SP% 119.0**
Speed ratings (Par 98): **107,105,101,100,97 93,88,45**
toteswingers: 1&2 £51.50, 1&3 £7.00, 2&3 £38.60. CSF £139.08 CT £1332.23 TOTE £3.90: £1.30, £11.30, £1.70; EX 171.40.
Owner Miss K Rausing **Bred** Miss K Rausing **Trained** Newmarket, Suffolk

FOCUS
A low-grade handicap but it did involve some unexposed types, they finished well strung out and the winner could be a progressive middle-distance performer.
Alicante Official explanation: trainer's rep said, regarding apparent improvement in form, that the filly had been suited by the step up in trip.
Penolva(IRE) Official explanation: trainer said filly was found to be heavily in season
Real Desire Official explanation: trainer said gelding was found to be distressed

4040 SMIRNOFF H'CAP (A QUALIFIER FOR THE SCOTTISH TROPHY HANDICAP SERIES FINAL) 1m 1f 36y
9:30 (9:30) (Class 5) (0-70,70) 3-Y-0+ **£3,238** (£963; £481; £240) **Stalls** High

Form RPR
00-3 **1** **Doon Haymer (IRE)**[17] 3481 4-9-13 **68**............ PhillipMakin 8 79
(I Semple) *hld up in tch: hdwy to ld over 1f out: edgd lft ins fnl f: hld on wl* **9/4**[1]
4034 **2** *nk* **Casino Night**[22] 3293 4-9-11 **66**............ PaulMulrennan 2 76
(F P Murtagh) *prom: effrt and ev ch over 1f out: kpt on fnl f: hld towards fin* **7/1**
-644 **3** 3½ **Regent's Secret (USA)**[6] 3854 9-9-0 **55**............(v) DanielTudhope 9 59
(J S Goldie) *s.i.s: hld up: hdwy over 2f out: kpt on fnl f: nt rch first two* **9/2**[3]
0043 **4** 1¾ **Primo Way**[12] 3653 8-9-0 **55**............ DuranFentiman 6 55
(D A Nolan) *hld up: effrt over 2f out: no imp fr over 1f out* **14/1**
100 **5** 4½ **El Dececy (USA)**[13] 3623 5-9-11 **66**............ NCallan 4 58
(J Balding) *led to over 1f out: edgd rt u.p: sn btn* **7/1**
0000 **6** *shd* **Natural Rhythm (IRE)**[11] 3689 4-8-10 **51**............ PJMcDonald 1 43
(Mrs R A Carr) *cl up tl rdn and wknd fr 2f out* **28/1**
2000 **7** *3* **This Ones For Eddy**[13] 3624 4-9-11 **66**............ LeeEnstone 5 52
(J Balding) *trckd ldrs tl rdn and no ex wl over 1f out* **14/1**
0006 **8** 2½ **Pegasus Lad (USA)**[18] 3457 3-9-6 **70**............(b[1]) GregFairley 7 50
(M Johnston) *hld up in tch: effrt over 3f out: wknd over 2f out* **3/1**[2]

2m 1.97s (2.27) **Going Correction** +0.35s/f (Good)
WFA 3 from 4yo+ 9lb **8 Ran SP% 115.7**
Speed ratings (Par 103): **103,102,99,98,94 93,91,89**
toteswingers: 1&2 £2.80, 1&3 £3.30, 2&3 £5.70. CSF £19.01 CT £65.72 TOTE £3.40: £1.10, £2.00, £2.10; EX 15.10 Place 6 £245.08, Place 5 £106.07..
Owner Gordon McDowall **Bred** Roland Lerner **Trained** Carluke, S Lanarks

FOCUS
A fair handicap, run at a solid pace.
El Dececy(USA) Official explanation: jockey said gelding had no more to give
T/Plt: £204.00 to a £1 stake. Pool: £51,032.11. 182.60 winning tickets. T/Qpdt: £62.80 to a £1 stake. Pool: £4,443.05. 52.30 winning tickets. RY

3618 HAYDOCK (L-H)
Friday, July 17

OFFICIAL GOING: Good to soft changing to soft after race 1 (2.20)
Rail realignment increased distances on round course by about 21yards.
Wind: overcast, persistent rain Weather: light 1/2 against

4041 STAINLESS WIRE LTD MAIDEN STKS 7f 30y
2:20 (2:21) (Class 5) 2-Y-0 **£3,238** (£963; £481; £240) **Stalls** Low

Form RPR
42 **1** **Gunner Lindley (IRE)**[14] 3571 2-9-3 0............ SebSanders 9 79
(B W Hills) *trckd ldr: chal 3f out: led over 1f out: hld on wl* **11/4**[2]
6 **2** ¾ **Fine Sight**[64] 2017 2-9-3 0............ PatDobbs 1 77
(R Hannon) *led tl 3f out: kpt on wl: no ex ins fnl f* **7/1**
3 *nk* **Realisation (USA)** 2-9-3 0............ GregFairley 10 76
(M Johnston) *swvd rt s: hdwy on outside to join ldrsover 3f out: styd on same pce ins fnl f* **7/2**[3]
2 **4** 3½ **Cansili Star**[15] 3546 2-9-3 0............ PhilipRobinson 6 68
(M A Jarvis) *w ldrs: led 3f out: hdd over 1f out: wknd jst ins fnl f* **6/4**[1]
5 2¾ **Tominator** 2-9-3 0............ HayleyTurner 2 61
(R Hollinshead) *sn chsng ldrs: wknd appr fnl f* **16/1**
6 2½ **Verona Lad** 2-9-3 0............ ShaneKelly 7 55+
(Jennie Candlish) *s.v.s: kpt on fnl 2f: nvr a factor* **40/1**
6 **7** 1½ **Port Hill**[18] 3468 2-9-3 0............ PaulMulrennan 8 51
(W M Brisbourne) *trckd ldrs: effrt over 3f out: wknd 2f out* **100/1**
8 *1* **Lord Wheathill** 2-8-12 0............ DeanHeslop(5) 3 49
(Mrs L Williamson) *in rr: effrt over 4f out: wknd 3f out* **80/1**

1m 35.75s (5.55) **Going Correction** +0.50s/f (Yiel) **8 Ran SP% 111.9**
Speed ratings (Par 94): **88,87,86,82,79 76,75,73**
toteswingers: 1&2 £4.20, 1&3 £3.60, 2&3 £4.40. CSF £21.01 TOTE £3.20: £1.10, £2.10, £1.20; EX 16.00.
Owner P McNamara, N Browne, S Richards **Bred** Marston Stud **Trained** Lambourn, Berks

FOCUS
Following 13mm of rain overnight and more before this opener the ground had eased to Good to Soft, except from the winning post around to the 1m start, where is was described as Good to Firm. The runners came right over to the stands' rail once into the home straight and this looked hard work for these two-year-olds. The winning time was 7.45 seconds slower than standard, suggesting that the ground was indeed testing. The form is rated around the winner ans slightly negatively.

NOTEBOOK
Gunner Lindley(IRE), a good second here earlier in the month in a race where the front three pulled miles clear of the rest, had been shaping as though this extra furlong would suit, which was backed up by his breeding. Always up with the pace, his rider seized the position closest to the stands' rail when the field came across and that might have been crucial. He showed a good attitude to keep battling away once in front entering the last 2f and still seems to be improving. His ability to handle this ground suggests he could be in for a good autumn. (op 13-8)
Fine Sight, not seen since just a fair debut effort at York in May, set the early pace and to his credit he rallied very gamely when seeming likely to drop away passing the 3f pole. Another bred to have been suited by this longer trip, there should be a maiden waiting for him granted a similar test. (op 8-1)
Realisation(USA), a half-brother to a winning juvenile sprinter, swerved right exiting the stalls but he was soon travelling well enough in the middle of the field. He had every chance coming to the last 2f and as things turned out he may not have been helped by racing furthest from the stands' rail. He looked as though he will benefit from the experience and should win races. (op 13-2 tchd 7-1)
Cansili Star, a Derby entry, had finished a clear second behind a Gosden hotpot on his Yarmouth debut earlier in the month with a subsequent winner back in sixth, so he appeared to have strong credentials. Always up with the pace, he had every chance but dropped away rather tamely inside the last furlong. He is better than this and is worth another chance back on a quicker surface. (op 7-4 tchd 15-8)
Tominator, a 7,500gns half-brother to a multiple winner at up to 1m, ran well until blowing up coming to the last furlong. He is highly regarded by connections, who expect him to improve with racing, and he looks one for the future. (tchd 18-1)

4042 HAYDOCK PARK ANNUAL BADGEHOLDERS CLUB CLAIMING STKS — 1m 2f 95y
2:55 (2:55) (Class 5) 3-4-Y-O — **£3,238** (£963; £481; £240) **Stalls** Low

Form — RPR
0233 **1** **King Supreme (IRE)**[20] 3406 4-9-10 82 ....(b) PatDobbs 5 — 75+
(R Hannon) *stmbld s: trckd ldrs: wnt 2nd 3f out: styd on to ld ins fnl f: drvn out* **5/4**[1]
5-52 **2** 1 1/4 **Visions Of Johanna (USA)**[49] 2437 4-9-9 82 ....(p) PaulHanagan 1 — 71+
(R A Fahey) *led: rdn and hung lft over 1f out: hdd and no ex ins fnl f* **5/4**[1]
000- **3** *hd* **Game Roseanna**[263] 7016 3-8-2 55 .... JimmyQuinn 4 — 60
(W M Brisbourne) *trckd ldrs: effrt over 4f out: kpt on fnl 2f: styd on ins fnl f* **20/1**[3]
-016 **4** *24* **Maadraa (IRE)**[20] 3406 4-9-9 78 ....(p) StephenDonohoe 2 — 28+
(B J Llewellyn) *swvd rt: sn chsng ldrs: sn drvn along: reminders after 1f: lost pl over 2f out: bhd whn eased fnl f* **6/1**[2]
2m 19.53s (6.53) **Going Correction** +0.50s/f (Yiel)
WFA 3 from 4yo 10lb — **4** Ran SP% **107.9**
Speed ratings (Par 103): **102,101,100,81**
toteswingers: 1&2 £2.90 CSF £3.02 TOTE £2.30; EX 2.90.
Owner Brian C Oakley **Bred** Miss Joan Murphy **Trained** East Everleigh, Wilts

FOCUS
The going was changed to Soft all round before this contest. A modest claimer and they went a very sensible pace in the conditions. Again the runners all came over to the stands' rail in the home straight. The third is the key to the form.

4043 FREE £25 BET AT CORBETTSPORTS.COM H'CAP — 5f
3:30 (3:30) (Class 4) (0-80,80) 3-Y-0+ — **£5,504** (£1,637; £818; £408) **Stalls** Centre

Form — RPR
3032 **1** **Sudden Impact (IRE)**[6] 3855 4-9-10 79 ....(e) SilvestreDeSousa 8 — 91
(Paul Green) *w ldrs stands' side: styd on to ld ins fnl f: rdn out* **9/4**[1]
5033 **2** 1 3/4 **Legal Eagle (IRE)**[13] 3623 4-9-4 80 .... PaulPickard(7) 6 — 86
(Paul Green) *led tl hdd and no ex ins fnl f* **11/2**[3]
16 **3** 2 3/4 **Garstang**[8] 3765 6-8-12 67 ....(b) PJMcDonald 7 — 63
(J Balding) *trckd ldrs: effrt over 2f out: hung rt and looked reluctant* **17/2**
0540 **4** 1 1/4 **Steelcut**[23] 3268 5-9-9 78 .... PaulHanagan 4 — 69
(R A Fahey) *hld up: effrt over 2f out: kpt on same pce* **9/1**
1015 **5** 3 1/4 **Red Rosanna**[7] 3806 3-8-12 78 .... DavidKenny(7) 5 — 58
(R Hollinshead) *hld up: effrt on outside over 2f out: wknd over 1f out* **6/1**
4166 **6** 1/2 **Fivefootnumberone (IRE)**[13] 3623 3-9-5 78 ....(p) StephenDonohoe 10 — 58+
(J J Quinn) *chsd ldrs: drvn over 2f out: hung lft and lost pl over 1f out* **9/2**[2]
020 **7** 1 1/2 **Foxy Music**[20] 3372 5-9-9 78 .... ShaneKelly 1 — 50
(E J Alston) *swvd lft s: sn w ldrs: wknd over 1f out* **12/1**
6-00 **8** *9* **Prospect Court**[12] 3655 7-8-10 65 .... FrancisNorton 9 — 5
(A C Whillans) *sn drvn along in rr: bhd fnl 2f* **11/1**
61.98 secs (1.48) **Going Correction** +0.50s/f (Yiel)
WFA 3 from 4yo+ 4lb — **8** Ran SP% **115.2**
Speed ratings (Par 105): **108,105,100,98,93 92,90,76**
toteswingers: 1&2 £1.70, 1&3 £5.40, 2&3 £8.30. CSF £14.93 CT £88.11 TOTE £2.60: £1.30, £1.50, £3.00; EX 13.80.
Owner Terry Cummins **Bred** Owen Bourke **Trained** Lydiate, Merseyside

FOCUS
A fair sprint handicap, in which they once again came over to race on the stands' side, and for the third contest in a row the winner raced closest to the rail. It also provided a one-two for trainer Paul Green. Straightforward form.
Fivefootnumberone(IRE) Official explanation: jockey said gelding hung left

4044 BJORN AGAIN HERE TOMORROW EVENING H'CAP — 6f
4:05 (4:06) (Class 4) (0-85,82) 3-Y-0 — **£5,504** (£1,637; £818; £408) **Stalls** Centre

Form — RPR
0300 **1** **Klynch**[9] 3747 3-9-4 79 ....(b) SebSanders 5 — 87
(B J Meehan) *w ldrs: led 2f out: hld on wl towards fin* **33/1**
0606 **2** *nk* **Lucky Numbers (IRE)**[13] 3622 3-9-6 81 .... SilvestreDeSousa 2 — 88
(Paul Green) *w ldrs on outer: chal over 1f out: no ex towards fin* **9/2**[3]
041 **3** 1 1/2 **Medicean Man**[21] 3338 3-8-13 74 .... StephenDonohoe 3 — 77
(J R Gask) *s.i.s: hdwy over 2f out: styd on same pce fnl f* **6/1**
-212 **4** 1 1/2 **Lochan Mor**[37] 2826 3-9-2 77 .... HayleyTurner 10 — 75
(M L W Bell) *mid-div: effrt over 2f out: kpt on same pce* **4/1**[2]
3010 **5** *nse* **Grissom (IRE)**[11] 3688 3-8-9 75 .... SladeO'Hara(5) 7 — 75+
(A Berry) *mid-div: lost pl over 3f out: hdwy on ins and nt clr run 2f out: repeatedly denied clr run and swtchd lft: plld wdst of all ins fnl f: edgd lft and kpt on wl* **33/1**
-112 **6** 1/2 **Dametime (IRE)**[28] 3096 3-9-0 78 ....(t) AndreaAtzeni(3) 11 — 74
(Daniel Mark Loughnane, Ire) *sn trcking ldrs stands' side: effrt over 2f out: wknd over 1f out* **11/1**
5562 **7** *3* **Come And Go (UAE)**[11] 3688 3-9-0 75 .... PJMcDonald 1 — 62
(G A Swinbank) *sn chsng ldrs on outside: wknd over 1f out* **8/1**
0435 **8** 1 1/2 **Desert Falls**[11] 3688 3-9-3 81 .... MichaelJStainton(3) 6 — 64
(R M Whitaker) *w ldrs: wknd over 1f out* **25/1**
5 **9** 1 1/4 **Soul Sista (IRE)**[56] 2227 3-8-6 72 .... JackDean(5) 4 — 51
(J L Spearing) *chsd ldrs on outer: lost pl over 2f out* **14/1**
-062 **10** *8* **Desert Icon (IRE)**[9] 3747 3-9-0 75 .... ShaneKelly 9 — 30
(W J Knight) *led: hdd 2f out: sn lost pl: bhd whn eased: hung lft and sn lost pl* **5/2**[1]
1m 16.57s (2.57) **Going Correction** +0.50s/f (Yiel) — **10** Ran SP% **116.9**
Speed ratings (Par 102): **102,101,99,97,97 96,92,90,89,78**
toteswingers: 1&2 £17.00, 1&3 £22.40, 2&3 £6.90. CSF £174.25 CT £1034.58 TOTE £26.10: £5.80, £2.00, £2.40; EX 208.10.
Owner L P R Partnership **Bred** J C S Wilson Bloodstock **Trained** Manton, Wilts

FOCUS
A decent handicap featuring a couple of progressive and unexposed types, plus a couple that were well in compared to their new marks. Again the field came up the stands' side, but the race produced a surprise winner who didn't race tight against the rail. He produced a personal best on turf.
Desert Icon(IRE) Official explanation: jockey said gelding hung left

4045 TURFTV.CO.UK H'CAP — 1m 6f
4:40 (4:40) (Class 4) (0-85,85) 3-Y-O — **£5,504** (£1,637; £818; £408) **Stalls** Centre

Form — RPR
-105 **1** **Lethal Glaze (IRE)**[13] 3618 3-9-7 85 .... PatDobbs 3 — 94+
(R Hannon) *trckd ldr: reminders 6f out: chal over 2f out: led over 1f out: edgd rt and drew clr ins fnl f* **9/4**[1]
60-0 **2** *6* **Royal Diamond (IRE)**[70] 1829 3-8-3 67 .... JimmyQuinn 1 — 68
(Sir Mark Prescott) *led: t.k.h: hdd over 1f out: edgd lft: kpt on same pce* **4/1**[3]
01-0 **3** *2* **Dulcie**[57] 2190 3-8-10 77 .... JackMitchell(3) 5 — 76
(M H Tompkins) *hld up: pushed along 5f out: kpt on fnl 3f: edgd lft and one pce fnl f* **9/2**
514 **4** *5* **Citizenship**[41] 2715 3-8-9 73 .... ShaneKelly 2 — 65
(Ian Williams) *trckd ldrs: effrt over 3f out: chal over 2f out: wknd fnl f* **5/2**[2]
-625 **5** *10* **Monetary Fund (USA)**[53] 2317 3-8-9 73 .... StephenDonohoe 4 — 52
(G A Butler) *hld up: effrt over 4f out: lost pl 3f out: bhd whn eased ins fnl f* **7/1**
3m 10.5s (6.20) **Going Correction** +0.50s/f (Yiel) — **5** Ran SP% **110.0**
Speed ratings (Par 102): **102,98,97,94,88**
toteswingers: 1&2 £6.50. CSF £11.37 TOTE £3.10: £1.90, £1.70; EX 11.20.
Owner Nigel Morris **Bred** B Kennedy **Trained** East Everleigh, Wilts

FOCUS
The majority of these had question marks against them with regards to the trip and they went a fair pace in the conditions, which made it a decent test. Again the runners came stands' side in the straight. The winner ran to his Royal Ascot mark.

4046 BEST HORSE RACING ON SKY CHANNEL 432 H'CAP — 1m 30y
5:15 (5:15) (Class 5) (0-75,71) 3-Y-0+ — **£3,238** (£963; £481; £240) **Stalls** Low

Form — RPR
0-13 **1** **Tom Tower (IRE)**[12] 3655 5-9-4 61 .... PatDobbs 13 — 73
(A C Whillans) *mde all: c stands' side: styd on wl to forge clr fnl f* **12/1**
0115 **2** 3 1/4 **Tanforan**[6] 3863 7-9-1 65 .... BillyCray(7) 4 — 70
(B P J Baugh) *t.k.h in midfield: nt clr run stands' side over 2f out: chsd wnr appr fnl f: edgd lft and no imp* **10/1**
4-00 **3** 3 3/4 **Pitbull**[13] 3615 6-8-10 58 ....(p) JackDean(5) 5 — 55
(Mrs G S Rees) *s.i.s: hld up in rr: effrt 3f out: hung lft and one pce fnl f* **8/1**
002 **4** *2* **Nisaal (IRE)**[36] 2842 4-10-0 71 ....(t) StephenDonohoe 3 — 63
(J J Quinn) *in tch: drvn 3f out: hung lft: one pce* **6/1**[3]
4350 **5** *hd* **Silk Gallery (USA)**[95] 1241 4-8-4 52 ....(t) SophieDoyle(5) 10 — 44
(E J Alston) *trckd ldrs: t.k.h: chsd wnr and edgd lft over 1f out: wknd jst ins fnl f* **33/1**
3134 **6** 4 1/2 **Inside Story (IRE)**[18] 3457 7-9-11 68 ....(b) ShaneKelly 2 — 50
(C R Dore) *in rr: drvn 4f out: lost pl over 2f out* **6/1**[3]
2154 **7** 1 1/2 **Ergo (FR)**[41] 2724 5-9-8 70 ....(b) SladeO'Hara(5) 9 — 49
(James Moffatt) *dwlt: in rr: effrt on stands' side over 3f out: sn wknd* **7/1**
60 **8** 2 1/2 **French Art**[20] 3378 4-9-13 70 .... PhilipRobinson 14 — 43
(N Tinkler) *racd keenly: styd wd 1st 2f: chsd wnr: drvn 3f out: lost pl 2f out* **3/1**[1]
2152 **9** *4* **Aussie Blue (IRE)**[14] 3568 5-9-0 60 .... MichaelJStainton(3) 6 — 24
(R M Whitaker) *chsd ldrs: lost pl over 1f out* **9/2**[2]
1m 49.04s (5.24) **Going Correction** +0.50s/f (Yiel) — **9** Ran SP% **115.1**
Speed ratings (Par 103): **93,89,86,84,83 79,77,75,71**
toteswingers: 1&2 £7.50, 1&3 £12.30, 2&3 £13.50. CSF £124.23 CT £1027.73 TOTE £12.60: £3.40, £3.50, £2.60; EX 67.30 Place 6: £328.43 Place 5: £170.56.
Owner Play Fair Partnership **Bred** C J Foy **Trained** Newmill-On-Slitrig, Borders

FOCUS
An ordinary handicap weakened further by five non-runners, but they went a fair pace in the conditions and again came up the stands' rail in the straight. The winner is rated back to his best.
T/Plt: £226.30 to a £1 stake. Pool: £60,194.39. 194.13 winning tickets. T/Qpdt: £43.80 to a £1 stake. Pool: £4,133.70. 69.80 winning tickets. WG

3810 NEWBURY (L-H)
Friday, July 17

OFFICIAL GOING: Soft
Wind: Virtually nil early, brisk ahead after race 4 Weather: Dull, overecast

4047 HIGHCLERE THOROUGHBRED RACING EBF MAIDEN FILLIES' STKS — 6f 8y
2:00 (2:02) (Class 4) 2-Y-O — **£6,476** (£1,927; £963; £481) **Stalls** High

Form — RPR
1 **Conniption (IRE)** 2-9-0 0 .... MartinDwyer 10 — 88+
(B J Meehan) *s.i.s: sn in tch: improed to go 2nd 1f out: sn drvn and qcknd ins fnl f to ld fnl 110yds: sn clr: easily* **12/1**
2 4 1/2 **Zubova** 2-9-0 0 .... RichardHughes 5 — 75+
(R Hannon) *s.i.s: swtchd rt to stands rail: hdwy 2f out: rdn and styd on wl fnl f to take 2nd cl home but nvr any ch w easy wnr* **7/1**
3 *hd* **Cash Queen Anna (IRE)** 2-9-0 0 .... MichaelHills 4 — 74+
(B W Hills) *broke wl but sn outpcd: hdwy on outside but green fr ins fnl 2f: styd on wl fnl f to press for 2nd nr fin but nvr any ch w easy wnr* **10/1**
4 3/4 **Poppy Seed** 2-9-0 0 .... RyanMoore 12 — 72
(R Hannon) *trckd ldrs: led jst ins fnl 2f: rdn over 1f out: hdd fnl 110yds: wknd into 4th nr fin* **5/1**[3]

5 **5** *2 ½* **Love Match**[41] 2699 2-9-0 0........ SteveDrowne 2 64
(R Charlton) *chsd ldrs: rdn 2f out: wknd ins fnl f* **4/1[2]**

6 *1* **Transvaal Sky** 2-9-0 0........ RichardKingscote 11 61+
(Tom Dascombe) *rr: pushed along 2f out: styd on wl fnl f but nvr in contention* **11/1**

00 **7** *½* **Gold Fix (IRE)**[7] 3810 2-9-0 0........ TonyCulhane 8 60
(M R Channon) *chsd ldrs: rdn over 2f out: wknd appr fnl f* **25/1**

8 *1* **Paleo (IRE)** 2-9-0 0........ FergusSweeney 6 57
(R Hannon) *pressed ldrs 4f: wknd approachinf fnl f* **16/1**

9 *¾* **Ridgeway Sapphire** 2-8-9 0........ LeeNewnes(5) 7 54
(M D I Usher) *chsd ldrs: rdn over 2f out: sn wknd* **66/1**

00 **10** *4* **Open Glory (FR)**[14] 3576 2-8-9 0........ RossAtkinson(5) 1 42
(Tom Dascombe) *stdd s: a in rr* **10/1**

6 **11** *2 ¾* **Asaab (IRE)**[26] 3187 2-9-0 0........ KShea 16 34+
(C E Brittain) *led tl hdd jst ins fnl 2f: wknd over 1f out: no ch whn n.m.r ins fnl f* **7/2[1]**

12 *1 ½* **Joan's Legacy** 2-8-9 0........ GabrielHannon(5) 13 30
(J C Fox) *s.i.s: sn in tch: rdn 1/2-way: wknd over 2f out* **66/1**

1m 16.66s (3.66) **Going Correction** +0.625s/f (Yiel) **12** Ran SP% **118.3**
Speed ratings (Par 93): **100,94,93,92,89 88,87,86,85,79 76,74**
toteswingers: 1&2 £24.90, 1&3 £19.90, 2&3 £7.00. CSF £92.57 TOTE £14.60: £4.20, £2.30, £2.90; EX 145.80.
Owner Exors of the Late F C T Wilson **Bred** Barronstown Stud **Trained** Manton, Wilts

FOCUS
The going had changed dramatically following 9.5mm of overnight rain and a further 12.5mm since midday, and was officially described as Soft. The ground was viewed as being quite fresh, though, and the runners were getting through it, which is perhaps why the time of the opener wasn't too bad. The newcomers dominated in what was probably a decent fillies' maiden.

NOTEBOOK
Conniption(IRE), who cost 225,000gns, is bred to appreciate further than this in time and she got well on top inside the final furlong, coming away to win in quite impressive fashion. She wasn't the quickest out the stalls, but was soon tracking the speed and clearly had no problem with the testing conditions. She is highly regarded by her trainer and a rise in grade surely beckons now. (tchd 14-1)
Zubova, whose dam was a middle-distance winner, is by a sire who appreciated some cut in the ground and she stayed on late for second. She lacked the speed of the winner, but is going to appreciate 7f before long and should improve for the experience. (op 11-2)
Cash Queen Anna(IRE), who cost 50,000euros, will want further than this in time and she too stayed on well inside the final furlong. Runners from this yard often benefit from a run and she looks capable of winning a standard maiden. (tchd 11-1)
Poppy Seed, a sister to quite useful sprint winners, went on inside the two and looked the likely winner at one stage, but Conniption quickly mastered her inside the final furlong and she was run out of the places close home. She showed plenty of ability and may well benefit from a sounder surface. (op 7-2 tchd 11-2)
Love Match travelled well for a long way on her debut at Doncaster and was expected to have improved for that experience. She again showed plenty of speed, but could find no extra inside the final furlong and was a tad disappointing. She has yet to race on a sound surface, though, so probably deserves another chance. (op 3-1 tchd 9-2)
Transvaal Sky, whose sales price increased to £50,000 as a yearling, comes from a yard that do exceptionally well with their juveniles and she made a little late headway under an educational ride. Improvement should be forthcoming and better ground may also help. (op 10-1)
Gold Fix(IRE) is now qualified for nurseries. (op 33-1 tchd 50-1)
Paleo(IRE), a late-foaled daughter of Indian Ridge, showed up well to a point towards the outer.
Asaab(IRE), who got going late when sixth on her debut at Pontefract, had clearly learnt from that and was soon in front on the rail. She came under pressure two out, though, and was quickly beaten. (op 13-2 tchd 3-1)

4048 HIGHCLERE THOROUGHBRED RACING EBF MAIDEN STKS 7f (S)
2:35 (2:38) (Class 4) 2-Y-O **£6,476** (£1,927; £963; £481) **Stalls** High

Form RPR
4 **1** **Emerald Commander (IRE)**[9] 3750 2-9-3 0........ RyanMoore 8 88+
(R Hannon) *trckd ldrs: slt advantage appr fnl 2f: pushed along to assert ins fnl f: easily* **4/5[1]**

2 *2 ½* **Texan Star (IRE)** 2-9-3 0........ NickyMackay 14 80+
(J H M Gosden) *w ldrs: upsides fr 3f out tl 2f out: sn chsng wnr and kpt on wl but no ch thrght fnl f* **10/1[3]**

3 *2 ¾* **Chain Of Events** 2-9-3 0........ MichaelHills 12 73
(B W Hills) *in tch: hdwy to trck ldrs 3f out: styd on fnl 2f but nvr gng pce of ldng duo* **16/1**

4 *½* **Gene Autry (USA)** 2-9-3 0........ KShea 7 72+
(R Hannon) *s.i.s: hld up towards rr: stdy hdwy over 3f out: trckd ldrs ins fnl 2f: styd on fnl f but nvr quite gng pce to get into contention* **20/1**

5 *1 ½* **Ultravox (USA)** 2-9-3 0........ JamieSpencer 16 68+
(B J Meehan) *rr: pushed along and stl bhd 3f out: hdwy fr 2f out: styd on wl fnl f and gng on cl home* **14/1**

6 *1 ¼* **Walcot Square (IRE)** 2-9-3 0........ SteveDrowne 6 65
(R Charlton) *chsd ldrs: rdn 3f out: wknd appr fnl f* **25/1**

7 *1 ½* **Banana Republic (IRE)** 2-9-3 0........ LDettori 4 61
(P F I Cole) *in tch: pushed along 3f out: outpcd fnl 2f* **16/1**

8 *½* **Poltergeist (IRE)** 2-9-3 0........ RichardHughes 5 60
(R Hannon) *slt advantage: hdd approachung fnl 2f: wknd over 1f out* **8/1[2]**

9 *2 ¼* **Haatheq (USA)** 2-9-3 0........ AlanMunro 10 54
(J L Dunlop) *rr: sme prog over 2f out: nvr rchd ldrs and sn bhd* **16/1**

10 *1 ¼* **Mandarin Express** 2-9-3 0........ MartinDwyer 15 51
(B J Meehan) *rr: rdn over 3f out: sme prog fr 2f out* **33/1**

11 *1 ¾* **Il Portico** 2-9-3 0........ TonyCulhane 9 47
(M R Channon) *chsd ldrs over 4f* **50/1**

12 *shd* **Claimant (IRE)** 2-9-3 0........ PaulFitzsimons 18 46
(Miss J R Tooth) *pressed ldrs to 3f out: wknd qckly over 2f out* **66/1**

13 *nk* **Fancy Star** 2-9-3 0........ RobertWinston 17 46
(B W Hills) *s.i.s: a towards rr* **33/1**

4 **14** *¾* **Apostle Of Rome (IRE)**[14] 3589 2-9-3 0........ RichardKingscote 1 44
(Tom Dascombe) *pressed ldrs over 4f* **25/1**

1m 31.06s (5.36) **Going Correction** +0.625s/f (Yiel) **14** Ran SP% **121.9**
Speed ratings (Par 96): **94,91,88,87,85 84,82,82,79,78 76,75,75,74**
toteswingers: 1&2 £6.10, 1&3 £6.80, 2&3 £31.30. CSF £8.39 TOTE £1.90: £1.20, £3.00, £4.10; EX 14.30.
Owner W P Drew **Bred** Grangecon Stud **Trained** East Everleigh, Wilts

FOCUS
The rain had started to come down even harder and these were atrocious conditions for juveniles. They raced down the centre of the course in this contest. Only two of these had the benefit of previous experience.

NOTEBOOK
Emerald Commander(IRE), a well-backed favourite, ran out a cosy winner. A promising fourth in what looked to be a good maiden at Newmarket's July meeting last week, these ground conditions were not expected to present a problem for the son of Pivotal and he came right away from a furlong out. The fact he had a run under his belt was a big help, but he is clearly a horse of some potential and it will be interesting to see where he pitches up next. (op 11-10)
Texan Star(IRE), an 85,000gns son of Galileo, also has speed in his pedigree and was the only one backed against the favourite. He was soon prominent and held every chance from two out, but in the end the winner possessed a bit too much pace. This was a really promising start and he should have no trouble winning a maiden. (op 14-1 tchd 16-1)
Chain Of Events, a brother to smart middle-distance performer Top Lock, holds a Derby entry and this was a very pleasing debut. Slowly away, he couldn't quicken for pressure, but stayed on nicely inside the final furlong and is going to benefit from the combination of a step up in trip on faster ground. (op 14-1)
Gene Autry(USA), a half-brother to turf and dirt winners in the US, travelled well and stuck on nicely enough having ended up on the far side. He wasn't given a hard time, being viewed as more of a long-term prospect by his trainer, but there are definitely races to be won with him this year. (tchd 16-1)
Ultravox(USA), a 65,000gns first foal of a half-sister to the smart Lord Admiral, never really got into it but did keep on late widest of all and he was another not given the hardest of times. This was a pleasing start.
Walcot Square(IRE), a half-brother to useful performer Furnace, holds a Derby engagement and didn't run too badly considering the ground looked against him. (op 22-1)
Banana Republic(IRE), related to winners abroad, never got into it, just keeping on at the one pace. (op 11-1)
Poltergeist(IRE), a half-brother to 2,000 Guineas runner-up Vital Equine, was soon up on the pace and travelled powerfully. He came under pressure two out, though, and slowly faded, looking far from happy on the going. There is probably better to come from him on faster ground. (op 6-1)
Apostle Of Rome(IRE) Official explanation: jockey said colt was unsuited by the soft ground

4049 ROSE BOWL STKS - SPONSORED BY COMPTON BEAUCHAMP ESTATES LTD (LISTED RACE) 6f 8y
3:10 (3:10) (Class 1) 2-Y-O
£17,031 (£6,456; £3,231; £1,611; £807; £405) **Stalls** High

Form RPR
42 **1** **Duplicity**[8] 3786 2-9-0 0........ RichardHughes 4 95
(R Hannon) *hld up and trckd ldrs: shkn up and qcknd to ld wl over 1f out: in command whn edgd rt cl home* **15/2**

1425 **2** *1* **Hearts Of Fire**[31] 2995 2-9-0 0........ PaulEddery 7 92
(Pat Eddery) *stdd s: hld up to trck ldrs: swtchd lft and qckknd ins fnl 2f: rdn to press wnr over 1f out: no imp u.p ins fnl f and hld whn carried rt cl home* **11/2[2]**

315 **3** *½* **Deal (IRE)**[14] 3583 2-8-9 0........ SteveDrowne 3 86
(R Hannon) *in tch: rdn along over 2f out: styd on to go 3rd fnl f and kpt on to press for 2nd cl home but no imp on wnr* **10/1**

1522 **4** *6* **Walkingonthemoon**[41] 2702 2-9-0 0........ RichardKingscote 5 73
(Tom Dascombe) *disp ld and t.k.h tl slt advantage over 2f out: hdd wl over 1f out and sn wknd* **8/11[1]**

3102 **5** *11* **Royal Desert**[19] 3424 2-9-0 0........ TonyCulhane 6 40
(M R Channon) *disp ld tl over 2f out: sn rdn: hung lft u.p and wknd 2f out* **22/1**

0152 **6** *6* **Avonrose**[15] 3528 2-8-9 0........ RobertWinston 1 17+
(M Johnston) *chsd ldrs: rdn 1/2-way: sn bhd* **13/2[3]**

1m 17.49s (4.49) **Going Correction** +0.625s/f (Yiel) **6** Ran SP% **111.8**
Speed ratings (Par 102): **95,93,93,85,70 62**
toteswingers: 1&2 £4.80, 1&3 £2.90, 2&3 £9.70. CSF £46.13 TOTE £7.10: £2.70, £2.80; EX 42.60.
Owner The Early Bath P'ship & Bloomsbury Stud **Bred** Bloomsbury Stud **Trained** East Everleigh, Wilts

FOCUS
This wasn't the strongest of Listed contests and the defection of morning favourite Showcasing weakened it further. The form isn't worth a great deal.

NOTEBOOK
Duplicity, who improved on his debut effort when finishing second in a 7f maiden at Warwick last time, is by a soft-ground sire and he showed markedly improved form, running on strongly for pressure and winning with a bit to spare. He was suited by the drop in trip, though connections mentioned the Horris Hill, back here over 7f, may be his target. (op 8-1 tchd 7-1)
Hearts Of Fire, winner of the Brocklesby earlier in the season, ran arguably his best race yet when fifth in the Windsor Castle at Royal Ascot last time and he looked the likely winner here when switched to challenge inside the two. The winner, who edged across him close home, stayed on too strongly in the end, but he did see out the sixth furlong and can probably pick up a conditions race somewhere. (op 8-1)
Deal(IRE), a stablemate of the winner who was fifth in this grade at Sandown last time, isn't the biggest but she continues to get better with each run and kept on well inside the final furlong to press for second. (op 7-1 tchd 13-2)
Walkingonthemoon set the standard, having finished second in the Woodcote Stakes last time, but he didn't look overly happy on ground that may have been too soft, for all that his trainer believes he doesn't want it quick. He was a bit keen early and faded inside the final furlong. (op 5-6)
Royal Desert, blown away by a very useful sort at Salisbury last time, stopped quickly. (op 20-1 tchd 25-1)
Avonrose was having her first experience of soft ground and finished well beaten. Official explanation: jockey said filly was unsuited by the soft ground (op 5-1 tchd 7-1)

4050 EP 50 YEARS AT NEWBURY FILLIES' H'CAP 1m 2f 6y
3:45 (3:49) (Class 4) (0-80,80) 3-Y-O **£4,857** (£1,445; £722; £360) **Stalls** Low

Form RPR
0-03 **1** **Stan's Cool Cat (IRE)**[20] 3400 3-9-7 **80**........ LDettori 9 87
(P F I Cole) *stdd s: hld up in rr tl stdy hdwy ins fnl 3f: drvn and qcknd over 1f out: str chal fnl 110yds: led last strides* **9/1**

0002 **2** *hd* **Accede**[24] 3251 3-9-5 **78**........ RyanMoore 1 85
(J G Portman) *hld up in rr: stdy hdwy on ins fr over 2f out: squeezed through to chal 1f out and led fnl 110yds: ct last strides* **8/1[3]**

0-1 **3** *shd* **Straits Of Hormuz (USA)**[18] 3456 3-9-4 **77**........ RobertWinston 14 84
(M Johnston) *led: rdn and kpt slender ld whn strly chal fr over 3f out: hdd fnl 110yds: styd on gamely* **12/1**

-431 **4** *2 ¾* **Kaloni (IRE)**[13] 3636 3-9-3 **76**........ MickyFenton 4 77
(Mrs P Sly) *mid-div: hdwy 3f out chsd ldrs and rdn 2f out: styd on fnl f but nt pce of ldng trio* **8/1[3]**

5031 **5** *1 ½* **Burza**[24] 3251 3-8-10 **72**........ KevinGhunowa(3) 3 70
(J Mackie) *trckd ldrs: rdn 3f out and chal fr over 2f out and stl upsides over 1f out: wknd fnl f* **12/1**

-144 **6** *1 ¾* **At A Great Rate (USA)**[44] 2607 3-9-4 **77**........ TPQueally 10 72
(H R A Cecil) *trckd ldrs: n.m.r and briefly lost position over 2f out: rdn and rallied to press ldrs again over 1f out: wknd ins fnl f* **9/2[1]**

14-0 **7** *¾* **Lady Rusty (IRE)**[58] 2174 3-8-11 **70**........ SaleemGolam 11 63
(P Winkworth) *t.k.h: chsd ldrs: rdn over 2f out: wknd over 1f out* **13/2[2]**

3-16 **8** 1/2 **Featherweight (IRE)**52 2356 3-9-2 **75**.............................. AlanMunro 12 67
(B W Hills) *t.k.h: trckd ldrs: chal fr over 3f out tl ins fnl 2f: wknd qckly appr fnl 2f* **10/1**

0010 **9** 14 **Saa'Ida (IRE)**41 2701 3-9-4 **77**.............................. KShea 5 41
(C E Brittain) *rr: sme hdwy on outside 3f out: nvr rchd ldrs and wknd over 2f out* **12/1**

0-62 **10** 4 **Levitation (IRE)**33 2947 3-9-1 **74**.............................. FergusSweeney 6 30
(W S Kittow) *rr: hdwy on outside over 3f out: nvr quite gng pce to get into contention and wknd sn after* **12/1**

1020 **11** 2 3/4 **Inis Boffin**18 3462 3-8-12 **71**.............................. JamieSpencer 8 22
(S Kirk) *chsd ldr after 3f: upsides 4f out tl ins fnl 3f: wkng whn n.m.r over 2f out: eased whn no ch* **16/1**

2m 12.68s (3.88) **Going Correction** +0.375s/f (Good) **11** Ran SP% **109.5**
Speed ratings (Par 99): **99,98,98,96,95 93,93,92,81,78 76**
toteswingers: 1&2 £9.30, 1&3 £10.60, 2&3 £13.70. CSF £66.84 CT £643.82 TOTE £8.00: £2.50, £2.80, £3.60; EX 49.00 Trifecta £113.70 Part won. Pool: £153.68 - 0.50 winning units..
Owner Stan James Syndicate 1 **Bred** Barronstown Stud **Trained** Whatcombe, Oxon
■ Leceile was withdrawn (6/1, ref to ent stalls). R4 applies, deduct 10p in the £.

FOCUS
This was a wide-open fillies' handicap and the fact they didn't go much of a gallop meant there were any number in with a chance until over a furlong out.

4051 TKP SURFACING H'CAP 5f 34y
4:20 (4:21) (Class 5) (0-70,70) 3-Y-O+ **£2,590** (£770; £385; £192) **Stalls** High

Form RPR

5-02 **1** **Sister Clement (IRE)**14 3580 3-8-10 **59**.............................. JamieSpencer 5 73+
(R Hannon) *trckd ldrs: wnt 2nd 2f out: led over 1f out and drvn to assert ins fnl f: sn clr: eased cl home* **11/4**1

0005 **2** 3 1/4 **Blessed Place**4 3917 9-8-12 **57**.............................. FergusSweeney 11 57
(D J S Ffrench Davis) *led: clr after 2f: rdn 2f out: hdd over 1f out: no ch w wnr ins fnl f but hld on wl to hold 2nd* **9/1**

00 **3** 1/2 **Reigning Monarch (USA)**41 2713 6-8-1 **51** oh6.(b1) RossAtkinson(5) 3 50
(Miss Z C Davison) *towards rr and pushed along 3f out: hdwy 2f out: styd on to go 3rd fnl f and clsng on 2nd nr fin: no ch w wnr* **25/1**

6230 **4** 2 3/4 **Espy**1 3998 4-9-11 **70**.............................. RyanMoore 12 59
(S Kirk) *hld up in rr: stl bhd whn nt clr run over 1f out and ins fnl f: swtchd lft and qcknd sn after: fin wl* **9/2**3

5041 **5** nk **Plumage**1 4023 4-8-13 **58**.............................. AlanMunro 1 46
(M Salaman) *chsd ldrs towards outside: nvr quite on terms: wknd fnl f* **7/2**2

0420 **6** 1 1/4 **Avrilo**23 3281 3-8-2 **51** oh1.............................. RichardKingscote 2 33
(M S Saunders) *chsd ldrs: rdn 1/2-way: wknd appr fnl f* **12/1**

0060 **7** hd **Fly In Johnny (IRE)**18 3459 4-8-6 **51** oh3.............(p) FrankieMcDonald 6 33
(J J Bridger) *chsd ldrs early: outpcd 1/2-way: sme hdwy whn nt clr run ins fnl f: kpt on cl home* **40/1**

0065 **8** 3 1/4 **Trivia (IRE)**24 3252 5-8-6 **51** oh3.............................. NeilChalmers 13 22
(J J Bridger) *chsd ldrs 3f* **18/1**

4626 **9** shd **Green Onions**39 2774 3-9-3 **66**.............................. SteveDrowne 9 35
(D J S Ffrench Davis) *chsd ldr 3f: sn wknd* **9/1**

1556 **10** nk **Figaro Flyer (IRE)**10 3713 6-9-8 **67**.............................. TPQueally 10 36
(P Howling) *t.k.h: hld up in tch: rdn and outpcd fr 1/2-way: no ch whn hmpd jst insde fnl f* **16/1**

1041 **11** 1/2 **Welsh Opera**109 1041 4-9-6 **65**.............................. SaleemGolam 7 32
(S C Williams) *nt clr run over 1f out and jst ins fnl f: so a towards rr* **16/1**

0003 **12** 3/4 **Malapropism**11 3677 9-8-12 **57**.............................. TonyCulhane 14 22
(M R Channon) *chsd ldrs to 1/2-way* **11/1**

65.27 secs (3.87) **Going Correction** +0.625s/f (Yiel)
WFA 3 from 4yo+ 4lb **12** Ran SP% **126.4**
Speed ratings (Par 103): **94,88,88,83,83 81,80,75,75,74 74,72**
toteswingers: 1&2 £9.60, 1&3 £22.60, 2&3 £61.30. CSF £30.77 CT £550.18 TOTE £3.70: £1.90, £3.80, £7.30; EX 41.10.
Owner P Byrne **Bred** J Egan, J Corcoran And J Judd **Trained** East Everleigh, Wilts

FOCUS
A low-grade sprint handicap.
Espy Official explanation: jockey said gelding was denied a clear run
Figaro Flyer(IRE) Official explanation: jockey said gelding hung right-handed
Welsh Opera Official explanation: jockey said filly was denied a clear run

4052 SHADWELL "NUNNERY STUD" CONDITIONS STKS 7f (S)
4:55 (4:57) (Class 3) 3-Y-O
£7,477 (£2,239; £1,119; £560; £279; £140) **Stalls** High

Form RPR

12- **1** **The Cheka (IRE)**321 5507 3-8-9 104.............................. AlanMunro 1 106
(Eve Johnson Houghton) *stdd s and awkward: rr but in tch: hdwy over 1f out: rdn and styd on strly ins fnl f: led cl home* **9/2**3

-023 **2** nk **Ashram (IRE)**30 3011 3-8-12 110..............................(v) LDettori 3 108
(Saeed Bin Suroor) *led: pushed along to keep advantage fr over 1f out: rdn ins fnl f: ct cl home* **7/4**1

41-0 **3** shd **Summer Fete (IRE)**93 1293 3-8-7 100.............................. RobertWinston 2 103
(B Smart) *stdd s and awkward: t.k.h and disp 2nd tl chsd ldr fr 2f out: drvn to chal ins fnl f: kpt on wl tl nt qckn cl home* **7/1**

161- **4** 6 **Tropical Paradise (IRE)**261 7075 3-8-4 92.............................. SaleemGolam 4 85
(P Winkworth) *t.k.h: chsd ldrs: rdn over 2f out: wknd over 1f out* **20/1**

1030 **5** 12 **Kaabari (USA)**58 2174 3-8-5 83 ow1.............................. EdwardCreighton 6 56
(C E Brittain) *chsd ldrs: rdn over 3f out: sn no ch* **40/1**

32-5 **6** 3 1/4 **Bonnie Charlie**22 3298 3-8-12 104.............................. RichardHughes 5 55+
(R Hannon) *disp 2nd tl over 2f out: sn wknd: eased whn no ch fnl f* **15/8**2

1m 29.93s (4.23) **Going Correction** +0.625s/f (Yiel) **6** Ran SP% **109.0**
Speed ratings (Par 104): **100,99,99,92,78 75**
toteswingers: 1&2 £1.90, 1&3 £3.20, 2&3 £2.60. CSF £12.08 TOTE £5.70: £2.40, £1.20; EX 14.10.
Owner Anthony Pye-Jeary And Mel Smith **Bred** James Robert Mitchell **Trained** Blewbury, Oxon

FOCUS
An interesting conditions event.

NOTEBOOK
The Cheka(IRE) did well to make a winning comeback. A smart juvenile who has had his return delayed with minor problems such as sore shins and muscle pulls, not being seen since finishing second in the Group 3 Solario Stakes at Sandown last August, he was held up just in what was a steadily run race and looked in a bit of trouble over a furlong out. However, he eventually hit top stride and just managed to do enough. This was a really encouraging effort, especially as his trainer expected him to come on quite a bit for it as he is hard to get fit, and he is now expected to go back up in grade, with the QEII at Ascot in September being an ambitious target. (tchd 4-1 and 5-1)

Ashram(IRE) has posted useful efforts the last twice, finishing third in a first-time visor in the Jersey Stakes latest, and he looked to have been given a soft time of things on the front. He didn't look overly keen when coming under pressure, but did keep on right the way to the line and will no doubt pick up a similar contest at some stage. That said, he wouldn't be one to ever take too short a price about. (op 11-8 tchd 15-8)
Summer Fete(IRE), C&D winner of a Listed contest in soft ground last October, had been off since finishing well held in the Nell Gwyn in April and she seemed to appreciate the return to slower ground. She did well considering she was very keen through the early stages and should come on for this. (op 8-1 tchd 11-2)
Tropical Paradise(IRE), twice a winner at two, was allowed to take her chance and didn't run too badly against classier types. She isn't going to be the easiest to place, but should find easier opportunities. (op 25-1 tchd 18-1)
Kaabari(USA) had no previous experience of ground such as this and she was outclassed. (tchd 50-1)
Bonnie Charlie, a smart juvenile who ran as though in need of the outing when fifth over 1m at Kempton on his reappearance, he should have been fine in the ground, but came under strong pressure over two out and stopped quickly. This was clearly not his form, leaving connections baffled, and he has still to show he has trained on. Richard Hughes reported he moved poorly throughout. Official explanation: jockey said colt moved poorly throughout (op 9-4 tchd 7-4)

4053 AXA WINTERTHUR WEALTH MANAGEMENT APPRENTICE H'CAP 1m 3f 5y
5:30 (5:32) (Class 5) (0-75,70) 4-Y-O+ **£2,590** (£770; £385; £192) **Stalls** Low

Form RPR

1000 **1** **Sky Quest (IRE)**44 2601 11-8-10 **61**.............................. NathanAlison(5) 7 71
(J R Boyle) *hld up in rr tl hdwy over 4f out: chsd ldr ins fnl 3f: drvn to ld over 1f out: pushed clr ins fnl f* **10/1**

2324 **2** 3 1/4 **Bramalea**42 2650 4-9-3 **66**.............................. JPO'Brien(3) 5 71
(B W Duke) *led at str pce: c towards centre of crse and rdn ins fnl 3f: hdd over 1f out and sn no ch w wnr and looked tired ins fnl f but kpt on for clr 2nd* **11/4**2

43-2 **3** 4 1/2 **Beauchamp Wonder**13 3617 4-9-10 **70**.............................. CharlesEddery 1 68
(G A Butler) *disp 2nd tl chsd ldr 6f out: rdn and no imp over 3f out and sn dropped bk to 3rd: no prog fnl 2f* **5/2**1

000- **4** 8 **Robert The Brave**256 5512 5-9-3 **68**.............................. KierenFox(5) 4 53
(P R Webber) *hld up in rr: rdn and mod prog over 3f out: nvr in contention and sn wknd* **14/1**

2355 **5** 2 1/4 **Carmela Maria**17 3475 4-9-0 **60**.............................. TobyAtkinson 6 41
(S C Williams) *disp 2nd tl dropped bk to 3rd 6f out: wknd fr 4f out* **11/4**2

6 4 1/2 **Ocean Of Peace (FR)**232 6-8-4 **55**.............................. AlexEdwards(5) 2 29
(M R Bosley) *awkward leaving stalls: a in rr* **6/1**3

000/ **7** 19 **John Charles (IRE)**26 3798 7-8-5 **56**.............................. RyanPowell(5) 3 —
(B De Haan) *s.i.s: a wl bhd* **25/1**

2m 27.02s (5.82) **Going Correction** +0.375s/f (Good) **7** Ran SP% **115.8**
Speed ratings (Par 103): **93,90,87,81,79 76,62**
toteswingers: 1&2 £4.80, 1&3 £5.90, 2&3 £1.80. CSF £38.64 CT £91.94 TOTE £12.80: £4.50, £1.60; EX 38.50 Place 6: £441.34 Place 5: £84.70.
Owner M C Cook **Bred** Pendley Farm **Trained** Epsom, Surrey

FOCUS
They went a decent gallop in this apprentices' handicap. The runner-up helps with the level.
John Charles(IRE) Official explanation: jockey said gelding never travelled
T/Jkpt: Not won. T/Plt: £1,872.00 to a £1 stake. Pool: £73,982.85. 28.85 winning tickets. T/Qpdt: £115.80 to a £1 stake. Pool: £5,165.75. 33.00 winning tickets. ST

3816 NEWMARKET (R-H)
Friday, July 17

OFFICIAL GOING: Soft
A pre-racing deluge changed the ground from "good to firm" to "soft". While there was plenty of cut, the times suggested the ground was not desperate.
Wind: Light, behind. Weather: Heavy rain clearing

4054 HEATH H'CAP 1m 2f
5:40 (5:43) (Class 5) (0-70,69) 3-Y-O+ **£3,885** (£1,156; £577; £288) **Stalls** Centre

Form RPR

0213 **1** **Iceman George**15 3550 5-9-2 **57**..............................(b) TPQueally 16 66
(D Morris) *chsd ldrs: led over 1f out: edgd rt ins fnl f: rdn out* **8/1**

-430 **2** 1 1/2 **Streets Apart (USA)**29 3068 4-9-7 **62**..............................(p) AdamKirby 17 68
(W R Swinburn) *led: hdd over 6f out: chsd ldr tl led again 3f out: rdn and hdd over 1f out: styd on same pce* **12/1**

1405 **3** hd **Peter Grimes (IRE)**34 2909 3-9-0 **65**.............................. DaneO'Neill 2 71
(H J L Dunlop) *prom: lost pl over 4f out: hdwy 3f out: rdn over 1f out: styd on same pce ins fnl f* **14/1**

0-00 **4** 3/4 **Carbon Print (USA)**19 3425 4-9-1 **56**.............................. TedDurcan 13 61
(P R Webber) *hld up: swtchd lft over 4f out: hdwy over 2f out: rdn over 1f out: styd on* **12/1**

1056 **5** 1/2 **General Tufto**6 3863 4-9-4 **64**..............................(b) MatthewDavies(5) 18 68
(C Smith) *hld up: hdwy over 3f out: rdn over 1f out: styd on same pce fnl f* **16/1**

0-00 **6** 3 **Sitwell**46 2551 3-8-12 **66**.............................. PatrickHills(3) 7 64
(J R Fanshawe) *hld up: hdwy over 3f out: rdn over 1f out: wknd ins fnl f* **16/1**

5/0- **7** 1 1/2 **Bobby Charles**254 7202 8-9-12 **67**.............................. JamesDoyle 5 63
(Dr J D Scargill) *hld up: effrt over 3f out: rdn and wknd over 1f out* **11/2**2

035 **8** 1/2 **M'Lady Rousseur (IRE)**30 3025 3-8-8 **64**.............................. AmyBaker(5) 11 59
(D R C Elsworth) *hld up: rdn over 3f out: nt clr run and swtchd lft over 2f out: nt trble ldrs* **16/1**

1340 **9** hd **King Of Connacht**24 3247 6-9-0 **55**..............................(p) SteveDrowne 4 49
(M Wellings) *hld up: swtchd rt over 2f out: sn rdn: n.d* **12/1**

2230 **10** shd **Dark Oasis**11 3687 3-7-12 **56**.............................. AndrewHeffernan(7) 15 50
(M C Chapman) *s.i.s: sn chsng ldrs: rdn and wknd over 1f out* **14/1**

0452 **11** 9 **Night Lily (IRE)**21 3334 3-9-2 **67**..............................(p) LPKeniry 14 45
(J Jay) *hld up: nt clr run over 2f out: sn rdn: wknd over 1f out* **13/2**3

0104 **12** 35 **Director's Chair**36 2851 4-9-10 **65**..............................(p) JerryO'Dwyer 10 —
(Miss J Feilden) *prom: rdn over 2f out: sn wknd and eased* **16/1**

0 **13** 4 1/2 **Martin's Friend (USA)**30 3024 4-9-10 **65**..............................(b1) MartinDwyer 1 —
(Mrs L Wadham) *chsd ldr tl led over 6f out: hdd & wknd 3f out* **33/1**

022 **P** **Princelywallywogan**6 3864 7-9-7 **62**.............................. PatCosgrave 12 —
(John A Harris) *prom tl wknd over 2f out: eased: p.u fnl f* **4/1**1

2m 9.76s (4.26) **Going Correction** +0.125s/f (Good)
WFA 3 from 4yo+ 10lb **14** Ran SP% **122.7**
Speed ratings (Par 103): **87,85,85,85,84 82,81,80,80,80 73,45,41,—**
toteswingers: 1&2 £26.20, 1&3 £27.00, 2&3 £59.80. CSF £102.64 CT £1342.69 TOTE £7.50: £2.30, £4.20, £5.90; EX 80.00.
Owner D & L Racing **Bred** T J And J Wells **Trained** Newmarket, Suffolk

FOCUS
The first two home were both prominent throughout, and both raced close to the stands' rail, holding off several attempted challenges in mid-track.
King Of Connacht Official explanation: jockey said gelding did not handle the soft ground

4055 ENCON INSULATION MAIDEN FILLIES' STKS 7f
6:10 (6:14) (Class 4) 2-Y-O **£5,180** (£1,541; £770; £384) **Stalls** Low

Form RPR
1 **Champagnelifestyle** 2-9-0 0 .... MichaelHills 3 85+
(B W Hills) *a.p: led 3f out: rdn out* **9/1**
2 1 1/4 **Qaraaba** 2-9-0 0 .... RHills 13 82+
(J L Dunlop) *a.p: chsd wnr over 2f out: rdn over 1f out: styd on same pce ins fnl f* **9/2[2]**
3 3 3/4 **Dyna Waltz** 2-9-0 0 .... NickyMackay 17 73+
(J H M Gosden) *chsd ldrs: rdn over 1f out: styd on same pce* **9/2[2]**
4 4 **Duty And Destiny (IRE)** 2-9-0 0 .... MartinDwyer 14 63
(B J Meehan) *ponied to s: led: rdn and hdd 3f out: wknd over 1f out* **8/1[3]**
5 3/4 **Black Sapphire** 2-9-0 0 .... JerryO'Dwyer 16 61
(Miss Amy Weaver) *chsd ldrs: rdn over 2f out: edgd lft and wknd over 1f out* **50/1**
6 hd **Magnificence** 2-9-0 0 .... RyanMoore 8 60
(Sir Michael Stoute) *racd keenly: w ldr 3f out: rdn and wknd over 1f out* **11/4[1]**
7 nse **Puteri (IRE)** 2-9-0 0 .... TedDurcan 10 60
(M A Jarvis) *prom: rdn over 2f out: sn hung lft and wknd* **16/1**
8 2 **Pastello** 2-9-0 0 .... ChrisCatlin 11 55
(R Hannon) *s.s: sn mid-div: wknd 2f out* **25/1**
9 1/2 **Red Amy** 2-9-0 0 .... TPQueally 4 54
(M L W Bell) *mid-div: rdn over 2f out: sn wknd* **18/1**
10 1 **Romancea (USA)** 2-9-0 0 .... JamieSpencer 7 51
(E F Vaughan) *s.i.s: a in rr* **10/1**
11 shd **Astronomer's Dream** 2-9-0 0 .... LPKeniry 15 51
(E F Vaughan) *hld up: shkn up over 1f out: n.d* **33/1**
12 3/4 **Gift Of Love (IRE)** 2-9-0 0 .... DaneO'Neill 12 49
(D R C Elsworth) *s.s: hdwy 1/2-way: rdn and wknd 2f out* **20/1**
13 1/2 **Winged (IRE)** 2-8-11 0 .... PatrickHills(3) 5 48
(B W Hills) *s.i.s: in rr: wknd over 2f out* **22/1**

1m 29.35s (3.65) **Going Correction** +0.225s/f (Good) **13** Ran SP% **122.2**
Speed ratings (Par 93): **88,86,82,77,76 76,76,74,73,72 72,71,71**
toteswingers: 1&2 £8.90, 1&3 £6.70, 2&3 £8.10. CSF £47.34 TOTE £7.10: £2.10, £2.60, £2.20; EX 66.10.
Owner Betfair Club ROA **Bred** Sunny Days Ltd **Trained** Lambourn, Berks

FOCUS
In a contest for unraced fillies, the first two were clearly going best from halfway and looked a cut above the others in these conditions, though some of the others should do better on faster ground. In contrast to the first race, which took place around a bend, the first and second occupied the middle of the track, a trend which continued for the rest of the meeting.

NOTEBOOK
Champagnelifestyle, a 140,000gns foal but unsold as a yearling, is a daughter of Montjeu and was probably happier on the soft ground than many of her rivals. A half-sister to a 1m2f winner in France, she should stay at least that far next season. (op 10-1 tchd 8-1)
Qaraaba ◆, whose dam won at 1m4f, is also bred to come into her own over middle distances and this was a good start to her career. Like the winner, she travelled particularly well, and this daughter of the top-class Shamardal should go one better. (op 7-2 tchd 5-1)
Dyna Waltz, out of the French 1,000 Guineas winner Valentine Waltz, also has prospects. By the high-class US 1m2f performer Dynaformer, she should progress and win races. (tchd 11-2)
Duty And Destiny(IRE), who was ponied early to the start, looked very green when asked for her effort. A 180,000euros sister to the 1m2f winner Mississippian, this daughter of Montjeu can step up on this as she gains experience. (op 9-1 tchd 12-1)
Black Sapphire, a Motivator half-sister to three winners up from 6f to 1m3f, exceeded market expectations. Purchased for 15,000gns earlier this year, she can win races in the long term if keeping up the good work. (op 66-1)
Magnificence, not the biggest but fit and well, is a half-sister to six winners up to 1m2f and, being by Sadler's Wells, will need at least that distance as she matures. Though not justifying favouritism, she showed enough to suggest that there should be better to come. (op 7-2 tchd 5-2)
Puteri(IRE), a One Cool Cat half-sister to three winners from 7f to 1m3f, made a satisfactory debut and deserves a chance to show what she can do on faster ground. (op 9-1)
Pastello, by the Australian speedster Exceed and Excel out of a juvenile 5f winner, is bred to sprint, but the fact that she started her career over 7f suggests she has not been setting the gallops alight. However, in light of her performance a drop back to 6f is worth considering. (op 20-1)
Red Amy, a 48,000gns Hawk Wing filly out of a well-related 1m2f winner, will have to improve to win a maiden but did show some ability. Her family background suggests she should improve with racing. (op 16-1 tchd 20-1)

4056 TURFTV H'CAP 7f
6:45 (6:46) (Class 4) (0-85,85) 3-Y-O **£5,828** (£1,734; £866; £432) **Stalls** Low

Form RPR
3-21 1 **Shabib (USA)**[87] 1422 3-9-7 **83** .... RHills 8 94+
(B W Hills) *s.i.s: sn chsng ldrs: rdn over 1f out: r.o u.p to ld ins fnl f: edgd rt towards fin* **10/3[1]**
261 2 2 1/4 **Invincible Isle (IRE)**[42] 2664 3-9-2 **78** .... TPQueally 13 83
(H R A Cecil) *a.p: led over 2f out: rdn over 1f out: edgd rt and hdd ins fnl f: styd on same pce* **6/1[3]**
6010 3 3/4 **New Leyf (IRE)**[14] 3592 3-8-12 **74** .... SteveDrowne 1 77
(J R Gask) *racd keenly: led: rdn and hdd over 2f out: ev ch ins fnl f: styd on same pce* **16/1**
-264 4 hd **Wannabe King**[55] 2270 3-9-9 **85** .... TedDurcan 6 88
(D R Lanigan) *dwlt: hld up: hdwy u.p over 1f out: edgd lft ins fnl f: nt rch ldrs* **7/2[2]**
0402 5 1 3/4 **Kheskianto (IRE)**[13] 3608 3-7-11 **66** oh2 .... AndrewHeffernan(7) 5 64
(M C Chapman) *hld up: plld hrd: hdwy over 1f out: nt rch ldrs* **20/1**
0021 6 1 1/4 **The Scorching Wind (IRE)**[21] 3342 3-8-5 **67** .... ChrisCatlin 7 62
(S C Williams) *hld up in tch: rdn over 1f out: styd on same pce* **7/2[2]**
0103 7 shd **Capo Regime**[16] 3502 3-8-7 **69** .... MichaelHills 2 63
(P Howling) *stdd s: hld up: plld hrd: rdn over 2f out: n.d* **33/1**
21-0 8 1 **Baariq**[76] 1679 3-9-6 **82** .... MartinDwyer 11 74
(P W Chapple-Hyam) *w ldr tl rdn over 2f out: edgd lft and wknd over 1f out* **16/1**
9 5 **The Happy Hammer (IRE)**[44] 2600 3-8-4 **66** oh3 .... JamieMackay 3 44
(E V Stanford) *mid-div: rdn 1/2-way: wknd over 2f out: in rr whn hung rt fnl f* **10/1**

1m 27.93s (2.23) **Going Correction** +0.225s/f (Good) **9** Ran SP% **110.4**
Speed ratings (Par 102): **96,93,92,92,90 88,88,87,81**
toteswingers: 1&2 £3.30, 1&3 £9.60, 2&3 £17.70. CSF £20.67 CT £208.21 TOTE £3.10: £1.40, £2.00, £3.90; EX 12.40.
Owner Hamdan Al Maktoum **Bred** Shadwell Farm LLC **Trained** Lambourn, Berks
■ Dukes Art was withdrawn (8/1, spread plate at s). R4 applies, deduct 10p in the £.

FOCUS
The early pace was slack, and the first three were always in the leading quartet.
New Leyf(IRE) Official explanation: jockey said colt hung right throughout
Summers Target(USA) Official explanation: jockey said gelding was unsuited by the soft ground

4057 JULY COURSE MAIDEN STKS 1m
7:15 (7:17) (Class 4) 3-Y-O **£5,180** (£1,541; £770; £384) **Stalls** Low

Form RPR
05-2 1 **Splendorinthegrass (IRE)**[46] 2543 3-9-3 94 .... RyanMoore 6 93+
(R Charlton) *hld up in tch: racd keenly: led over 2f out: rdn clr fnl f* **7/4[1]**
-223 2 9 **Park Lane**[53] 2318 3-9-3 77 .... MichaelHills 13 73
(B W Hills) *chsd ldrs: rdn over 3f out: edgd lft and wknd over 1f out: wnt 2nd nr fin* **4/1[2]**
5-53 3 1/2 **Sabi Star**[36] 2856 3-9-3 77 .... NickyMackay 10 72
(J H M Gosden) *led: rdn: edgd lft and hdd over 2f out: wknd fnl f: lost 2nd nr fin* **11/2[3]**
0- 4 1 3/4 **Netta (IRE)**[300] 6117 3-8-12 0 .... TPQueally 2 63
(P J Makin) *bmpd s: hld up: racd keenly: hdwy u.p and hung lft over 1f out: wknd fnl f* **16/1**
5 nk **Landofthefourones (USA)** 3-9-3 0 .... TedDurcan 1 68+
(D R Lanigan) *hld up: hdwy u.p over 2f out: hung lft: wknd over 1f out* **25/1**
0 6 3/4 **Primera Vista**[27] 3168 3-9-3 0 .... MichellePayne 17 66
(L M Cumani) *hld up in tch: rdn over 2f out: wknd over 1f out* **25/1**
0-0 7 3/4 **Matilda Poliport**[89] 1380 3-8-12 0 .... AdamKirby 7 59+
(W R Swinburn) *hld up: pushed along over 2f out: styd on ins fnl f: nvr trbld ldrs* **33/1**
6-2 8 2 1/4 **Gordy Bee (USA)**[17] 3472 3-9-3 0 .... PaulEddery 4 59
(Pat Eddery) *hld up: hdwy u.p over 2f out: wknd over 1f out* **6/1**
0 9 shd **Beat Companion**[50] 2395 3-9-3 0 .... PatCosgrave 9 59
(P Howling) *s.s: sn mid-div: rdn and hung lft over 2f out: sn wknd* **66/1**
3 10 1 1/4 **Cactus Curtsey**[14] 3569 3-8-12 0 .... JamieSpencer 15 51
(J R Fanshawe) *chsd ldrs: rdn over 2f out: wknd over 1f out* **14/1**
11 1/2 **Fulfilment (IRE)** 3-8-12 0 .... ChrisCatlin 5 50
(W J Musson) *sn pushed along in rr: n.d* **50/1**
40 12 nse **Maid Of Stone (IRE)**[16] 3508 3-8-12 0 .... DaneO'Neill 11 50
(D R C Elsworth) *plld hrd and prom: wknd 2f out* **33/1**
206- 13 1/2 **Indian Tonic (IRE)**[208] 7754 3-8-12 78 .... MartinDwyer 8 49
(W Jarvis) *mid-div: rdn over 3f out: wknd over 2f out* **28/1**
0 14 6 **Fiancee (IRE)**[91] 1327 3-8-12 0 .... SteveDrowne 3 36
(R Charlton) *hld up: pushed along over 3f out: sn lost tch* **20/1**
0 15 3/4 **Douchkette (FR)**[11] 3696 3-8-12 0 .... TGMcLaughlin 12 34
(John Berry) *mid-div: rdn and wknd over 2f out* **50/1**
16 10 **Head First** 3-8-12 0 .... LPKeniry 14 12
(W Jarvis) *s.i.s: sn mid-div: wknd 3f out* **66/1**

1m 40.59s (0.59) **Going Correction** +0.225s/f (Good) **16** Ran SP% **127.3**
Speed ratings (Par 102): **106,97,96,94,94 93,92,90,90,89 88,88,88,82,81 71**
toteswingers: 1&2 £1.70, 1&3 £3.30, 2&3 £5.10. CSF £7.68 TOTE £2.50: £1.10, £1.90, £2.20; EX 10.20.
Owner B E Nielsen **Bred** Ballylinch Stud **Trained** Beckhampton, Wilts

FOCUS
An above-average maiden, and a decent pace in the soft ground created a good test, which makes the winner's performance all the more taking.

4058 NEWMARKET NIGHTS H'CAP 1m 2f
7:45 (7:48) (Class 3) (0-95,95) 3-Y-O
£9,346 (£2,799; £1,399; £700; £349; £175) **Stalls** Centre

Form RPR
01 1 **Laaheb**[15] 3549 3-8-10 **82** .... RHills 4 91
(M A Jarvis) *mde all: rdn over 1f out: styd on gamely* **7/2[1]**
-10 2 3/4 **Sopranist**[76] 1678 3-9-6 **95** .... PatrickHills(3) 8 103
(J H M Gosden) *chsd wnr: rdn and ev ch over 1f out: styd on same pce ins fnl f* **16/1**
1230 3 2 1/4 **Mutamaashi**[29] 3049 3-9-2 **88** .... MichaelHills 5 92
(W J Haggas) *dwlt: hld up: hdwy over 2f out: rdn over 1f out: no ex ins fnl f* **5/1[3]**
0-00 4 1 1/2 **Master Fong (IRE)**[16] 3509 3-8-4 **76** oh1 .... ChrisCatlin 2 77
(B W Hills) *chsd ldrs: rdn and hung lft over 2f out: styd on same pce appr fnl f* **33/1**
5422 5 9 **Just Like Silk (USA)**[35] 2884 3-8-6 **78** .... NickyMackay 10 63
(G A Butler) *prom: rdn over 3f out: edgd lft and wknd over 1f out* **4/1[2]**
-210 6 nk **Sam Sharp (USA)**[41] 2701 3-8-10 **82** .... TPQueally 7 66
(H R A Cecil) *prom: rdn over 2f out: wknd over 1f out* **6/1**
20-1 7 4 **Yorgunnabelucky (USA)**[28] 3120 3-9-6 **92** .... RyanMoore 3 69
(M Johnston) *hld up: rdn and hung lft over 2f out: sn wknd* **7/2[1]**
-300 8 3/4 **Classically (IRE)**[34] 2930 3-8-6 **78** .... SteveDrowne 6 54
(R Charlton) *stdd s: hld up: rdn over 3f out: wknd over 2f out* **7/1**

2m 5.64s (0.14) **Going Correction** +0.125s/f (Good) **8** Ran SP% **116.7**
Speed ratings (Par 104): **104,103,101,100,93 92,89,89**
toteswingers: 1&2 £9.50, 1&3 £3.70, 2&3 £12.30. CSF £60.13 CT £281.85 TOTE £5.40: £1.80, £3.20, £2.20; EX 39.10.
Owner Hamdan Al Maktoum **Bred** Darley **Trained** Newmarket, Suffolk

FOCUS
Just an ordinary gallop, and it paid to be handy, with the winner making all and the runner-up always second. The race was notable for the Hills family of jockeys filling the first three places.

NOTEBOOK
Laaheb left his debut performance a long way behind last time, and this confirmed that he is on the upgrade. Though he had the run of the race, he kept galloping away much better than most and, though connections have no major plans at present, he looks capable of tackling better company. (op 3-1 tchd 9-2)
Sopranist, disappointing in a Listed race last time, showed that he can win more races at the right level. Though safely held by the winner, they dominated throughout and it was a fine effort conceding so much weight. (op 9-1)
Mutamaashi can be rated a little higher than his position suggests because, unlike the first two, he was held up in the rear off a modest tempo. He had been highly tried in his two previous races and is not far off finding the right opportunity. (op 11-2 tchd 7-1)
Master Fong(IRE) has looked an awkward ride in recent races and, though he ran much better here, his tendency to hang does not make him the most attractive of investments. (op 25-1)
Just Like Silk(USA), withdrawn once on heavy ground, was having his first race on soft and it produced an unusually poor performance from this otherwise reliable sort. (op 9-2 tchd 5-1)
Sam Sharp(USA), a comfortable winner on soft ground in May, has been disappointing since in his last two races. (op 15-2 tchd 5-1 and 8-1 in a place)

Yorgunnabelucky(USA) was impressive when winning on fast ground in his previous race but he flopped on heavy before that, so the late rain probably ruined his chance. (tchd 4-1)

4059 HUGHES CONDITIONS STKS — 5f

8:20 (8:21) (Class 3) 3-Y-O+

£9,346 (£2,799; £1,399; £700; £349; £175) **Stalls** Low

Form — RPR

3400 **1** **Nota Bene**[7] 3818 7-8-9 98 ... RyanMoore 9 106
(D R C Elsworth) *chsd ldrs: rdn to ld ins fnl f: r.o* **4/1**[3]

436 **2** *1* **Icelandic**[46] 2550 7-9-0 105 ... (t) JamieSpencer 1 107
(F Sheridan) *hld up: hdwy over 1f out: rdn ins fnl f: r.o* **10/3**[2]

-305 **3** *1/2* **Peace Offering (IRE)**[48] 2481 9-9-0 104 ... TedDurcan 11 105
(D Nicholls) *chsd ldrs: led over 3f out: rdn and edgd lft over 1f out: hdd and unable qck ins fnl f* **9/4**[1]

0405 **4** *2 3/4* **Angus Newz**[6] 3848 6-8-9 95 ... (v) PatCosgrave 10 91
(M Quinn) *chsd ldr: rdn and ev ch over 1f out: no ex ins fnl f* **8/1**

123- **5** *shd* **Befortyfour**[339] 4957 4-8-9 107 ... RHills 6 90
(M A Jarvis) *prom: rdn over 1f out: styd on same pce* **6/1**

00-0 **6** *1 1/4* **Galeota (IRE)**[7] 3802 7-8-11 97 ... PatrickHills(3) 2 91
(R Hannon) *sn pushed along in rr: hdwy 2f out: rdn and wknd ins fnl f* **25/1**

0-40 **7** *3 1/4* **Zuzu (IRE)**[13] 3622 3-8-0 91 ... Louis-PhilippeBeuzelin(5) 3 74
(M A Jarvis) *led: hdd over 3f out: pushed along 1/2-way: wknd fnl f* **9/1**

5350 **8** *5* **Thoughtsofstardom**[11] 3677 6-8-2 54 ... CarolineKelly(7) 12 56
(P S McEntee) *plld hrd and prom: wknd over 1f out* **100/1**

4400 **9** *2 1/4* **Quick Single (USA)**[2] 3989 3-8-9 63 ... (v) JerryO'Dwyer 8 52
(P S McEntee) *sn outpcd* **100/1**

59.25 secs (0.15) **Going Correction** +0.225s/f (Good)
WFA 3 from 4yo+ 4lb — **9** Ran SP% **115.1**
Speed ratings (Par 107): **107,105,104,100,100 98,92,84,81**
toteswingers: 1&2 £4.00, 1&3 £2.90, 2&3 £2.30. CSF £17.58 TOTE £5.60: £1.80, £1.60, £1.40; EX 20.10.
Owner The Malzee Partnership **Bred** Usk Valley Stud **Trained** Newmarket, Suffolk

FOCUS

A good sprint gallop set things up for two come-from-behind performers in a race featuring a number of horses who are high in the handicap, making it a decent contest of its type.

NOTEBOOK

Nota Bene has been largely in the wilderness in recent seasons but the testing tempo set the race up nicely for him on this return to 5f. All his previous wins had been at 6f, but he was well backed to win this so the return to form was not unexpected. (op 6-1)

Icelandic was outpaced early on but he emerged as a danger as the tempo took its toll on others. Previously a winner at trips from 6f to an extended 1m, he did well considering the drop to 5f, but he has a good record on soft ground so the late afternoon rain probably helped him. (op 3-1 tchd 7-2 and 4-1 in places)

Peace Offering(IRE), winner of this last year, deserves credit for hanging on to third place after setting the lively tempo. Nine times a winner at this trip in the past, he is still in cracking shape and is capable of making it ten. (op 7-2)

Angus Newz, who acts well on softish ground, is on a tough handicap mark at present so it makes sense to target races like this. She had a bit to do at the weights in this company but showed plenty of speed until the effort of pressing the pace had the final say. (op 7-1)

Befortyfour had a fine season last year but, like several in this line-up, he is now handicapped out of most races. He ran satisfactorily considering it was his first outing since last August and is one to keep in mind if connections can find a similar opportunity. (op 7-2)

Galeota(IRE) has won three times on softish ground, but he was not favourably weighted against these opponents. (tchd 20-1)

Zuzu(IRE), a winner on good to soft, had a tough task at the weights but this lightly-raced filly can be given another chance in the right company. (op 17-2 tchd 8-1)

4060 MICHAEL WRIGHT RACING H'CAP — 1m

8:50 (8:54) (Class 5) (0-75,75) 4-Y-O+ — **£3,885** (£1,156; £577; £288) **Stalls** Low

Form — RPR

66-6 **1** **Northern Jem**[63] 2052 5-9-6 72 ... JamieSpencer 16 82
(Jane Chapple-Hyam) *hld up: hdwy over 2f out: led 1f out: rdn clr* **6/1**[2]

1105 **2** *2* **Bookiebasher Babe (IRE)**[29] 3060 4-8-11 63 ... JerryO'Dwyer 17 69
(M Quinn) *racd alone and led overall in centre: rdn and hdd over 1f out: styd on same pce fnl f* **16/1**

2-53 **3** *nk* **Manere Bay**[35] 2880 4-8-13 65 ... TPQueally 2 70
(J L Dunlop) *s.i.s: hld up: hdwy over 3f out: rdn and ev ch over 1f out: styd on same pce ins fnl f* **4/1**[1]

3461 **4** *5* **King Columbo (IRE)**[21] 3357 4-9-0 71 ... Louis-PhilippeBeuzelin(5) 4 65
(Miss J Feilden) *chsd ldrs: led overall over 1f out: sn rdn and hdd: wknd ins fnl f* **4/1**[1]

015 **5** *1 1/4* **Miss Mujanna**[14] 3581 4-9-1 67 ... J-PGuillambert 10 59
(J Akehurst) *led far side gp tl rdn and hdd over 1f out: wknd fnl f* **14/1**

0503 **6** *6* **Aggravation**[15] 3525 7-8-12 64 ... RyanMoore 5 42
(D R C Elsworth) *hld up: rdn over 1f out: n.d* **9/1**

0000 **7** *4* **Eastern Gift**[52] 2351 4-9-6 72 ... MickyFenton 6 42
(Miss Gay Kelleway) *awkward leaving stalls: hld up: hdwy over 3f out: rdn over 1f out: wknd qckly ins fnl f* **10/1**

0-26 **8** *3/4* **Al Rayanah**[29] 3077 6-8-4 56 oh1 ... (p) SaleemGolam 11 24
(G Prodromou) *s.i.s: hld up: rdn over 2f out: hung lft over 1f out: n.d* **33/1**

0-01 **9** *1/2* **Grand Vizier (IRE)**[22] 3301 5-9-6 72 ... TedDurcan 12 39
(C F Wall) *hld up: rdn over 3f out: wknd 2f out* **8/1**[3]

1126 **10** *1 3/4* **Elisiario (IRE)**[37] 2828 4-9-9 75 ... PatCosgrave 13 38
(J R Boyle) *s.i.s: hdwy over 6f out: rdn and wknd over 1f out* **9/1**

2000 **11** *5* **Mr Fantozzi (IRE)**[12] 3662 4-8-8 60 ... (p) ChrisCatlin 7 12
(D Donovan) *chsd ldrs: rdn 1/2-way: wknd 3f out* **25/1**

3400 **12** *8* **Mister New York (USA)**[16] 3509 4-9-1 67 ... (b) GeorgeBaker 3 1
(Noel T Chance) *hld up: rdn and hung lft over 3f out: sn wknd: eased over 1f out* **16/1**

1m 41.56s (1.56) **Going Correction** +0.225s/f (Good) — **12** Ran SP% **119.7**
Speed ratings (Par 103): **101,99,98,93,92 86,82,81,81,79 74,66**
toteswingers: 1&2 £29.60, 1&3 £9.80, 2&3 £23.60. CSF £99.06 CT £439.54 TOTE £7.90: £2.80, £3.00, £2.00; EX 221.80 Place 6 £92.61, Place 5 £12.63..
Owner Norcroft Park Stud **Bred** Norcroft Park Stud **Trained** Newmarket, Suffolk

FOCUS

The first two both came up the centre of the course, with Bookiebasher Babe having raced alone in mid-track throughout and the winner arriving from behind on the stands' side of the main group, who had congregated more towards the far rail.

Grand Vizier(IRE) Official explanation: jockey said gelding was unsuited by the soft ground

T/Plt: £49.10 to a £1 stake. Pool: £59,321.29. 880.55 winning tickets. T/Qpdt: £5.70 to a £1 stake. Pool: £4,536.76. 587.40 winning tickets. CR

3858 NOTTINGHAM (L-H)

Friday, July 17

OFFICIAL GOING: Soft (heavy in places) changing to heavy after race 1 (2.10)

Wind: Light across Weather: Heavy rain before racing, raining after 4.30

4061 SUBSCRIBE TO RACING UK H'CAP — 6f 15y

2:10 (2:11) (Class 5) (0-70,70) 3-Y-O — **£2,590** (£770; £385; £192) **Stalls** High

Form — RPR

0-01 **1** **Rafta (IRE)**[23] 3281 3-8-2 58 ... JosephineBruning(7) 8 78+
(T T Clement) *s.i.s: hld up: hdwy on outside over 3f out: led over 2f out: sn hung lft: clr over 1f out: reminder and edgd rt ins fnl f: unchal* **15/2**

3054 **2** *10* **Vamos (IRE)**[14] 3580 3-8-9 58 ... (b[1]) ChrisCatlin 9 48
(J R Gask) *a.p: rdn and edgd rt 2f out: kpt on to take 2nd cl home: no ch w wnr* **9/2**[3]

3211 **3** *nk* **Sarasota Sunshine**[18] 3464 3-9-6 69 ... (b) AdamKirby 7 58
(N P Littmoden) *hld up and bhd: pushed along and hdwy 2f out: rdn and edgd rt over 1f out: chsd wnr wl ins fnl f: lost 2nd cl home* **7/2**[2]

5243 **4** *1 3/4* **Where's Reiley (USA)**[28] 3096 3-9-1 67 ... NeilBrown(3) 13 51
(T D Barron) *racd sltly detached on stands' rail: prom: hung lft wl over 1f out: sn rdn and btn* **5/1**

31-0 **5** *3 1/4* **Speedy Guru**[20] 3387 3-9-2 70 ... Louis-PhilippeBeuzelin(5) 11 44
(H Candy) *w ldrs: led 3f out tl over 2f out: sn rdn: hung lft over 1f out: wknd ins fnl f* **5/2**[1]

0-00 **6** *hd* **Clear Hand**[24] 3241 3-8-2 51 oh2 ... (b[1]) AdrianMcCarthy 4 25
(B R Millman) *led 3f: rdn and wknd 2f out* **40/1**

0060 **7** *1* **Bold Rose**[4] 3917 3-8-13 62 ... IanMongan 3 33
(M D I Usher) *w ldrs: rdn 2f out: wknd ins fnl f* **14/1**

1300 **8** *17* **West Leake (IRE)**[6] 3859 3-9-0 63 ... (b[1]) RHills 12 —
(B W Hills) *s.i.s: in rr: rdn over 2f out: eased whn no ch wl over 1f out* **9/1**

1m 16.96s (2.06) **Going Correction** +0.35s/f (Good) — **8** Ran SP% **116.5**
Speed ratings (Par 100): **100,86,86,83,79 79,78,55**
toteswingers: 1&2 £6.80, 1&3 £1.90, 2&3 £3.30. CSF £41.91 CT £140.46 TOTE £12.30: £3.50, £2.00, £1.10; EX 45.20.
Owner R L Gray **Bred** Thomas And Linda Heffernan **Trained** Newmarket, Suffolk

FOCUS

With 18mm of rain overnight rain and with further heavy showers during the morning the going had changed to soft, heavy in places. A depleted field for this handicap with not a lot of soft ground form on offer, making this a tricky little heat.

Speedy Guru Official explanation: vet said on examination that the filly had set fast

4062 EUROPEAN BREEDERS' FUND MAIDEN STKS — 6f 15y

2:45 (2:46) (Class 5) 2-Y-O — **£3,885** (£1,156; £577; £288) **Stalls** High

Form — RPR

440 **1** **Running Mate (IRE)**[29] 3046 2-9-3 0 ... RichardMullen 9 75+
(J H M Gosden) *a.p: led wl over 1f out: clr whn rdn ins fnl f: eased towards fin* **9/4**[1]

2 *2 3/4* **Jamarjo (IRE)** 2-9-3 0 ... IanMongan 1 62+
(S Gollings) *hld up: rdn and hdwy over 1f out: wnt 2nd ins fnl f: no ch w wnr* **6/1**[3]

0 **3** *5* **Law Of Attraction (IRE)**[11] 3692 2-9-3 0 ... AdamKirby 8 47
(J R Gask) *w ldr: rdn over 1f out: wknd ins fnl f* **9/1**

30 **4** *4* **Hill Of Miller (IRE)**[13] 3613 2-9-3 0 ... ChrisCatlin 3 35
(Rae Guest) *led: pushed along and hdd wl over 1f out: sn wknd* **3/1**[2]

5 *11* **Tasmeem (IRE)** 2-9-3 0 ... RHills 7 2
(B W Hills) *hld up: rdn and swvd bdly lft wl over 1f out: sn no ch and eased* **9/4**[1]

R **Field Elect** 2-9-3 0 ... SJCraine 5 —
(Garry Moss) *s.s: wnt bdly lft: ref to r* **25/1**

1m 18.95s (4.05) **Going Correction** +0.50s/f (Yiel) — **6** Ran SP% **114.7**
Speed ratings (Par 94): **93,89,82,77,62** —
toteswingers: 1&2 £15.50, 1&3 £1.30, 2&3 £8.30. CSF £16.73 TOTE £3.50: £1.60, £3.00; EX 16.60.
Owner H R H Princess Haya Of Jordan **Bred** Paul Ennis **Trained** Newmarket, Suffolk

FOCUS

The going had changed to heavy for this maiden which had a couple of interesting debutants. The field decided to race down the centre after Rafta's runaway success in the opener.

NOTEBOOK

Running Mate(IRE) had been highly tried last time when never threatening in the Norfolk Stakes at Royal Ascot, but appreciated this drop in class and step back up to 6f to run out a decisive winner. Tracking the leaders, he came through to take the lead over a furlong out and soon put the race to bed, being heavily eased towards the finish. A good-looking individual who seemed to relish the conditions, he should have plenty of opportunities in the near future. (tchd 2-1 and 5-2)

Jamarjo(IRE) was no match for his race-hardened counter part but he made a pleasing debut. Not unfancied beforehand and related to plenty of winners, he was doing his best work at the end but was ultimately flattered by his proximity to the winner. If he can build on this a little opportunity should fall his way. (op 10-1 tchd 11-1)

Law Of Attraction(IRE) took them along at a fair pace for much of the way but was a spent force over a furlong out. Nonetheless it was a step in the right direction. (op 10-1 tchd 11-1)

Hill Of Miller(IRE) raced prominently until fading tamely over a furlong out. This was a slightly disappointing effort. (op 7-2)

Tasmeem(IRE), a 135,000gns purchase, was another who is related to plenty of winners but ran extremely green and after an untidy start was struggling when veering 2f out before being eased. In good hands, he should improve on this. Official explanation: jockey said colt jinked left under pressure (op 2-1 tchd 15-8 and 11-4 in places)

4063 BEST RACECOURSES ON RACING UK NURSERY — 6f 15y

3:20 (3:21) (Class 5) 2-Y-O — **£3,070** (£906; £453) **Stalls** High

Form — RPR

450 **1** **Ginger Ted (IRE)**[60] 2128 2-7-13 65 ... JamieKyne(5) 3 67
(R C Guest) *hld up: hdwy over 2f out: led jst over 1f out: edgd rt jst ins fnl f: sn rdn: edgd rt towards fin: r.o* **5/2**[2]

1403 **2** *nk* **Antonius Moris (IRE)**[7] 3807 2-9-7 82 ... RichardSmith 2 83
(Tom Dascombe) *w ldr: led over 2f out: rdn and hdd jst over 1f out: bmpd sltly jst ins fnl f: carried sltly rt towards fin: kpt on* **11/4**[3]

4336 **3** *7* **Lairy (IRE)**[3] 3958 2-7-12 59 ... JamieMackay 5 39
(M F Harris) *w ldrs: rdn and wknd over 1f out* **12/1**

455 **4** *4* **Masked Dance (IRE)**[62] 2069 2-8-12 73 ... RichardMullen 1 41
(K A Ryan) *led: hdd over 2f out: rdn and wkng whn swvd rt over 1f out* **2/1**[1]

0256 **5** *12* **Tucker's Law**[22] 3317 2-8-12 73 ... TGMcLaughlin 4 5
(B R Millman) *hld up: pushed along 2f out: sn rdn and struggling* **7/1**

1m 18.7s (3.80) **Going Correction** +0.50s/f (Yiel) — **5** Ran SP% **108.8**
Speed ratings (Par 94): **94,93,84,78,62**
toteswingers: 1&2 £12.30. CSF £9.45 TOTE £4.60: £2.00, £1.20; EX 12.30.

Owner Shaun Taylor **Bred** T Counihan **Trained** Stainforth, S Yorks
■ Stewards' Enquiry : Jamie Kyne one-day ban: careless riding (Jul 31)

FOCUS
Only a small field for this nursery but all five could have a case made for them. The 'official' ratings shown next to each horse are estimated and for information purposes only.

NOTEBOOK
Ginger Ted(IRE) made full use of his handy mark and his more than capable rider's useful allowance to grind out success. Patiently ridden on the heels of the leaders before taking it up over a furlong out, he was soon hanging in the conditions, although was always just doing enough to repel the rallying runner up. He had put in some encouraging efforts before disappointing on the Fibresand last time, and with the removal of the blinkers that he had worn the last twice, it would be no surprise to see him follow up, although connections might wait for an autumn campaign as he loves to get his toe in. (op 5-1)
Antonius Moris(IRE), the only winner in the field, was beaten off same mark at Chester last time after struggling to get competitive in the Windsor Castle Stakes but he set a fair standard here. He took them along before the winner headed him before the furlong marker and he stuck to his task well inside the final furlong. He has a likeable attitude and can go one better again before long. (op 13-8, tchd 3-1 in places)
Lairy(IRE) had bits and pieces of form to give him a shout here but he failed to see out the trip in the conditions. (op 8-1)
Masked Dance(IRE), gelded since his last run, raced up with the pace but wandered under pressure from 2f out before fading. Official explanation: jockey said gelding ran round under pressure (op 9-4 tchd 15-8)
Tucker's Law, although a shade disappointing since being runner up at Salisbury, can be forgiven this run on his nursery debut for he did not get home in the conditions. (op 8-1 tchd 17-2)

4064 RACING UK ON CHANNEL 432 H'CAP — 1m 75y
3:55 (3:56) (Class 4) (0-85,85) 3-Y-0+
£6,231 (£1,866; £933; £467; £233; £117) **Stalls Low**

Form — RPR
0042 **1** **Cobo Bay**[12] 3656 4-9-8 **85**..........(b) AmyRyan(5) 8 — 99
(K A Ryan) *led over 1f out: w ldr: led over 3f out tl over 2f out: led wl over 1f out: sn edgd rt and rdn: r.o* — **5/4**[1]
0014 **2** 1 1/2 **Jack Cool (IRE)**[21] 3341 3-9-0 **80**.......... AdrianMcCarthy 2 — 89
(P W Chapple-Hyam) *a.p: squeezed through between horses and wnt 2nd over 3f out: led over 2f out: rdn and hdd wl over 1f out: ev ch ins fnl f: nt qckn* — **5/1**[2]
4 **3** 5 **Full Victory (IRE)**[29] 3076 7-8-11 **69**.......... IanMongan 9 — 68
(R A Farrant) *broke wl: sn stdd: hld up in tch: rdn wl over 1f out: tk 3rd ins fnl f: no imp on ldng pair* — **8/1**[3]
/04- **4** 5 **Prime Exhibit**[440] 1806 4-9-12 **84**.......... GeorgeBaker 6 — 72
(R Charlton) *hld up towards rr: hdwy over 2f out: hung lft over 1f out: wknd ins fnl f* — **5/1**[2]
20 **5** 14 **Toto Skyllachy**[34] 2933 4-9-11 **83**.......... J-PGuillambert 4 — 38
(T P Tate) *prom: led over 6f out tl over 3f out: pushed along and wknd over 2f out* — **5/1**[2]
1000 **6** 3 1/2 **Hustle (IRE)**[18] 3469 4-9-11 **83**.......... SimonWhitworth 3 — 30
(Miss Gay Kelleway) *in rr: pushed along and struggling over 4f out* — **33/1**
0624 **7** 3 1/2 **Brouhaha**[11] 3695 5-9-7 **79**.......... RichardSmith 7 — 18
(Tom Dascombe) *hld up: struggling whn rdn and hung lft to r alone on ins rail wl over 1f out: eased fnl f* — **10/1**

1m 50.92s (5.32) **Going Correction** +0.80s/f (Soft)
WFA 3 from 4yo+ 8lb — **7** Ran SP% **117.6**
Speed ratings (Par 105): **105,103,98,93,79 76,72**
toteswingers: 1&2 £1.30, 1&3 £2.50, 2&3 £23.10. CSF £8.38 CT £36.30 TOTE £2.00: £1.30, £2.50; EX 11.00.
Owner The C H F Partnership **Bred** The C H F Partnership **Trained** Hambleton, N Yorks

4065 RACINGUK.TV (S) STKS — 1m 2f 50y
4:30 (4:30) (Class 6) 3-Y-0 — **£2,047** (£604; £302) **Stalls Low**

Form — RPR
0-04 **1** **Phoenix Enforcer**[25] 3217 3-8-4 68..........(p) DO'Donohoe 4 — 59
(George Baker) *chsd ldr: led over 5f out: c towards stands' rail and rdn wl over 1f out: styd on* — **8/13**[1]
0-02 **2** 3 **Moggy (IRE)**[13] 3629 3-7-13 52.......... Louis-PhilippeBeuzelin(5) 3 — 54
(M L W Bell) *hld up: hdwy to chse wnr over 4f out: rdn over 2f out: no ex ins fnl f* — **7/2**[2]
4004 **3** 7 **Paymaster In Chief**[4] 3919 3-8-9 50..........(p) RichardMullen 1 — 46
(M D I Usher) *hld up in tch: rdn over 3f out: sn btn* — **6/1**[3]
0360 **4** 25 **Fleur De'Lion (IRE)**[23] 3257 3-8-4 47..........(b) RichardSmith 7 — —
(S Kirk) *hld up: rdn and wknd over 3f out* — **25/1**
5000 **5** 51 **Independent James (IRE)**[53] 2340 3-8-4 49.......(v[1]) WilliamCarson(5) 8 — —
(S C Williams) *led: hdd over 5f out: wknd qckly over 4f out: t.o* — **9/1**
600 **6** 2 1/2 **Black Nun**[4] 3923 3-8-4 60..........(v[1]) AdrianMcCarthy 5 — —
(S Wynne) *prom: sn pushed along: lost pl over 5f out: sn lost tch: t.o* — **20/1**

2m 23.22s (11.52) **Going Correction** +1.125s/f (Soft) — **6** Ran SP% **117.0**
Speed ratings (Par 98): **98,95,90,70,29 27**
toteswingers: 1&2 £1.10, 1&3 £1.20, 2&3 £1.80. CSF £3.37 TOTE £1.90: £1.70, £1.30; EX 4.30.There was no bid for the winner. Moggy was claimed by G.A. Harker for £6,000.
Owner Codrington, Crabtree, Jacovou **Bred** The Hill Stud **Trained** Moreton Morrell, Warwicks
■ King's Chorister (8/1) was withdrawn due to unsuitable ground. R4 applies, deduct 10p in the £. New market formed.

FOCUS
A weak seller and they finished well strung out.

4066 VISITNOTTINGHAM.COM MAIDEN FILLIES' STKS — 1m 2f 50y
5:05 (5:07) (Class 5) 3-Y-0 — **£2,914** (£867; £433; £216) **Stalls Low**

Form — RPR
-526 **1** **Phillipina**[42] 2672 3-8-9 103.......... Louis-PhilippeBeuzelin(5) 2 — 88+
(Sir Michael Stoute) *a gng wl: led over 2f out: clr wl over 1f out: v easily* — **2/5**[1]
2 8 **Samaaha** 3-8-11 0.......... AhmedAjtebi(3) 3 — 68+
(Saeed Bin Suroor) *s.i.s: sn hld up in tch: pushed along over 3f out: rdn 2f out: wnt 2nd ins fnl f: no ch w wnr* — **5/1**[2]
0 **3** 5 **Noble Attitude**[27] 3175 3-8-9 0.......... WilliamCarson(5) 1 — 59
(N Tinkler) *w ldr: led briefly wl over 2f out: sn rdn and no ch w wnr: lost 2nd ins fnl f* — **66/1**
0-0 **4** 1 3/4 **Salamon**[11] 3696 3-9-0 0.......... JosedeSouza 5 — 56
(P F I Cole) *hld up in tch: rdn and wknd over 1f out* — **25/1**
4 **5** nk **Anessia**[20] 3384 3-9-0 0.......... RichardSmith 10 — 55
(Tom Dascombe) *led: hdd wl over 2f out: rdn and wknd wl over 1f out* — **16/1**
3-0 **6** 3 1/2 **Nawojka (IRE)**[36] 2856 3-9-0 0.......... J-PGuillambert 4 — 49
(J G Given) *a in rr: rdn wl over 1f out: no rspnse* — **10/1**[3]

05- **7** 24 **Hindford Oak Sioux**[293] 6273 3-9-0 0.......... AdrianMcCarthy 8 — —
(Mrs L Williamson) *prom: pushed along over 3f out: rdn and wknd over 2f out: eased whn no ch over 1f out* — **50/1**

2m 25.1s (13.40) **Going Correction** +1.125s/f (Soft) — **7** Ran SP% **110.4**
Speed ratings (Par 97): **91,84,80,79,78 76,56**
toteswingers: 1&2 £1.02, 1&3 £12.40, 2&3 £23.20. CSF £2.48 TOTE £1.20: £1.02, £2.60; EX 2.60 Place 6: £14.82 Place 5: £5.19.
Owner Cheveley Park Stud **Bred** Cheveley Park Stud Ltd **Trained** Newmarket, Suffolk
■ Silk And Satin was withdrawn (7/1, ref to ent stalls). R4 applies, deduct 10p in the £.

FOCUS
A fillies' maiden which centred around the participation of the useful winner.
T/Plt: £8.90 to a £1 stake. Pool: £43,721.94. 3,552.98 winning tickets. T/Qpdt: £2.50 to a £1 stake. Pool: £2,848.39. 814.11 winning tickets. KH

3702 PONTEFRACT (L-H)
Friday, July 17

OFFICIAL GOING: Soft (heavy in places)
Wind: Light, half-behind. Weather: Heavy rain

4067 COUNTRYWIDE FREIGHT MAIDEN AUCTION STKS — 6f
6:35 (6:35) (Class 4) 2-Y-O — **£4,533** (£1,348; £674; £336) **Stalls Low**

Form — RPR
30 **1** **Tamanaco (IRE)**[33] 2940 2-8-9 0.......... JamieMoriarty 13 — 74
(T D Walford) *cl up: led 2f out: rdn and hdd jst over 1f out: led again ins fnl f and kpt on wl* — **4/1**[2]
2 3/4 **Miss Taken (IRE)** 2-8-4 0.......... PaulQuinn 7 — 67
(D Carroll) *in tch: hdwy over 2f out: rdn to ld briefly jst over 1f out: drvn and hdd ins fnl f: kpt on same pce* — **12/1**
2 **3** nk **Bonfire Knight**[18] 3468 2-9-2 0..........(t) TomEaves 8 — 78
(J J Quinn) *trckd ldrs: effrt 2f out: sn rdn and sltly outpcd: kpt on u.p ins fnl f* — **9/4**[1]
65 **4** 2 **Sejanus**[27] 3147 2-8-11 0.......... TPO'Shea 11 — 67
(K A Ryan) *chsd ldrs: hdwy and cl up 2f out: sn rdn and one pce appr fnl f* — **10/1**
5 1 3/4 **Sir Louis** 2-8-11 0.......... PaulHanagan 6 — 62+
(R A Fahey) *t.k.h: towards rr: hdwy over 2f out: sn rdn and no imp appr fnl f* — **8/1**
0 **6** 2 1/4 **Meetings Man (IRE)**[44] 2610 2-8-11 0.......... DaleGibson 3 — 55
(Micky Hammond) *towards rr and rdn along 1/2-way: sme hdwy over 2f out: n.d* — **25/1**
7 3/4 **Coolella (IRE)** 2-7-13 0.......... JamieKyne(5) 2 — 46
(J R Weymes) *dwlt and towards rr: swtchd wd and sme hdwy 2f out: nvr a factor* — **16/1**
00 **8** 2 **Seldom Seen Kid (IRE)**[10] 3716 2-8-9 0.......... DavidAllan 9 — 45
(T D Easterby) *led: rdn along and hdd 2f out: sn drvn and wknd over 1f out* — **11/1**
03 **9** 1 **Nave (USA)**[44] 2610 2-9-2 0.......... FrancisNorton 12 — 49
(M Johnston) *chsd ldrs: rdn along over 2f out and sn wknd* — **9/2**[3]
10 21 **Micky's Knock Off (IRE)** 2-8-8 0 ow2.......... NeilBrown(3) 10 — —
(R C Guest) *s.i.s: a in rr* — **25/1**

1m 21.92s (5.02) **Going Correction** +0.475s/f (Yiel) — **10** Ran SP% **118.8**
Speed ratings (Par 96): **85,84,83,80,78 75,74,71,70,42**
toteswingers: 1&2 £16.20, 1&3 £1.20, 2&3 £28.40. CSF £52.30 TOTE £5.40: £1.80, £4.50, £1.50; EX 64.80.
Owner Pedro Rosas **Bred** Tom Kelly **Trained** Sheriff Hutton, N Yorks
■ Stewards' Enquiry : Tom Eaves one-day ban: used whip with excessive force (Jul 31)
Paul Hanagan one-day ban: careless riding (Jul 31)
Jamie Moriarty caution: used whip with excessive frequency.

FOCUS
Racing went ahead only after two official inspections of the course after incessant heavy rain had made the going testing, conditions having being just on the fast side of good at the start of the day. However, at least the effects of the ground were offset by a tailwind in the home straight and despite the rain continuing to pour during the first race, these two-year-olds did seem to handle the mud fairly well in the circumstances. That impression was confirmed by the winning time for the first race, which although some seven seconds above standard, suggested that the ground was probably the official 'soft, heavy in places' rather than anything more severe. Jockeys described conditions as testing but safe. Rather than taking the usual soft-ground route and cutting the bend in order to tack across to the stands' side in the home straight, the runners remained fairly wide from the start.

NOTEBOOK
Tamanaco(IRE) had shaped with plenty of promise when third on his first start and winner Shakespearean had franked that form subsequently in pattern company with fourth-home Abandagold also scoring since. Consequently, he was quite well-fancied next time out at Doncaster but connections were reportedly worried about the quicker ground there and those fears were apparently realised when he weakened quickly out of contention. Back on a surface that suited better, he knuckled down well here to regain the lead at the furlong-pole and on this evidence (backed up by his pedigree) 7f and further ought to hold no fears. (tchd 7-2)
Miss Taken(IRE) was the subject of some late support in the betting and ran a good race in defeat, only being worried out of it by the winner in the last 100 yards. A relatively cheap purchase, she was getting weight from these rivals but a similar auction maiden ought to come her way on this showing and her pedigree offers an interesting mix of stamina and speed. (op 20-1)
Bonfire Knight, giving 7lb to the winner, travelled powerfully on his debut over 7f and again looked to be going best of all until losing his place with a couple of furlongs to run as the field jostled for position. Gathered together, he picked up again and was going on nicely at the finish. This experience, added to that of his debut, will not be lost on him and it would be no surprise to see him go and prove to be quite decent. (op 3-1 tchd 15-8)
Sejanus ran his best race and is qualified for nurseries now. (op 11-1 tchd 9-1)
Sir Louis caught the eye when making some ground from off the pace with a furlong to run. His effort peetered out close home, but he showed some promise and is well worth another chance. (op 11-2)

4068 TOTESWINGER FILLIES' H'CAP — 1m 4f 8y
7:05 (7:07) (Class 5) (0-75,72) 3-Y-0+ — **£3,238** (£963; £481; £240) **Stalls Low**

Form — RPR
1621 **1** **Umverti**[14] 3557 4-10-0 **65**.......... FrancisNorton 7 — 77
(N Bycroft) *set stdy pce: qcknd over 3f out: rdn and qcknd clr wl over 1f out: kpt on strly* — **8/1**
2124 **2** 5 **Kings Maiden (IRE)**[32] 2969 6-9-11 **62**.......... PAspell 3 — 66
(James Moffatt) *hld up towards rr: hdwy on outer to trck ldrs 5f out: effrt and cl up 2f out: rdn to chse wnr whn hung lft over 1f out: drvn and kpt on same pce ins fnl f* — **6/1**[3]
50-1 **3** 3 1/4 **Mooteeah (IRE)**[48] 2488 3-9-9 **72**.......... TPO'Shea 9 — 71
(M A Jarvis) *trckd ldrs: smooth hdwy and cl up 4f out: chal 2f out: sn rdn and wknd over 1f out* — **5/2**[1]

The Form Book, Raceform Ltd, Compton, RG20 6NL

2353 **4** 2 1/2 **Cheers For Thea (IRE)**[37] 2803 4-9-6 **57**.......................... DavidAllan 2 52
(T D Easterby) *hld up: hdwy 3f out: sn rdn to chse ldrs 2f out: sn drvn and plugged on same pce* **6/1**[3]

2112 **5** *nk* **Stateside (CAN)**[15] 3545 4-9-10 **61**............................ PaulHanagan 1 56+
(R A Fahey) *t.k.h: trckd ldrs: effrt 3f out: sn rdn and outpcd 2f out* **6/1**[3]

0-00 **6** *14* **Miss Ferney**[17] 3490 5-8-6 **50**............................ PaulPickard(7) 8 24
(A Kirtley) *a in rr* **80/1**

0044 **7** *5* **Madamlily (IRE)**[11] 3687 3-9-7 **70**............................ TomEaves 5 36
(J J Quinn) *trckd ldng pair: rdn along 4f out: sn wknd* **10/3**[2]

-653 **8** *12* **Charismatic Lady**[15] 3545 3-8-12 **64**............................ AndreaAtzeni(3) 4 12
(M Botti) *chsd wnr: rdn along over 4f out: sn wknd* **12/1**

2m 51.76s (10.96) **Going Correction** +0.925s/f (Soft)
WFA 3 from 4yo+ 12lb **8** Ran SP% **114.5**
Speed ratings (Par 100): **100,96,94,92,92 83,79,71**
toteswingers: 1&2 £13.20, 1&3 £7.50, 2&3 £3.30. CSF £55.01 CT £154.89 TOTE £11.20: £2.60, £1.90, £1.20; EX 68.60.
Owner Mrs C M Whatley **Bred** N Bycroft **Trained** Brandsby, N Yorks

FOCUS
The winner set just a steady pace but the field still finished well spread out, with several of the line-up evidently totally failing to act in the conditions.

4069 GARY, MICK AND MALTRAVERS H'CAP 5f
7:35 (7:35) (Class 3) (0-90,87) 3-Y-0+
£9,346 (£2,799; £1,399; £700; £349; £175) **Stalls** Low

Form RPR

1044 **1** **Northern Dare (IRE)**[14] 3582 5-9-11 **87**............................ FrancisNorton 1 96
(D Nicholls) *trckd ldrs on inner: hdwy 2f out: led wl over 1f out: rdn clr ent fnl f: styd on strly* **11/2**[2]

0303 **2** 1 3/4 **Haajes**[20] 3377 5-9-4 **80**............................(t) DavidAllan 14 83+
(J Balding) *in midfield: hdwy on wd outside wl over 1f out: rdn and styd on wl fnl f* **8/1**

3305 **3** 1/2 **Solar Spirit (IRE)**[10] 3706 4-9-2 **83**............................(p) JamieKyne(5) 2 84
(J J Quinn) *cl up: effrt to chal 2f out: sn rdn and ev ch tl drvn appr fnl f and kpt on same pce* **13/2**

520 **4** *2* **Kay Two (IRE)**[14] 3582 7-9-10 **86**............................(p) StephenDonohoe 8 80
(R J Price) *led: rdn along 2f out: sn hdd and drvn: one pce appr fnl f* **6/1**[3]

-061 **5** 3/4 **Turnkey**[29] 3066 7-9-2 **85**............................ NSLawes(7) 11 76
(D Nicholls) *in rr: hdwy 2f out: sn rdn and styd on wl fnl f: nrst fin* **7/1**

0125 **6** 1/2 **Efistorm**[6] 3845 8-9-6 **82**............................ ShaneKelly 10 71
(C R Dore) *chsd ldrs: rdn along 2f out: drvn and wknd appr fnl f* **8/1**

0460 **7** *1* **Namir (IRE)**[8] 3784 7-8-12 **74**............................(vt) PatrickMathers 3 60
(D Shaw) *in midfield: gd hdwy 2f out: rdn to chse ldrs over 1f out: wknd ins fnl f* **20/1**

4224 **8** 3 1/4 **Artsu**[17] 3491 4-8-12 **74**............................(p) TomEaves 9 48
(M Dods) *t.k.h: chsd ldrs: rdn 2f out and sn btn* **9/2**[1]

-104 **9** *4* **Total Impact**[21] 3351 6-9-8 **84**............................ PaulHanagan 7 44
(R A Fahey) *towards rr: rdn along 1/2-way: nvr a factor* **7/1**

1146 **10** 1 1/4 **Chjimes (IRE)**[25] 3212 5-9-11 **87**............................ IanMongan 5 42
(C R Dore) *a in rr* **20/1**

31-0 **11** *6* **Albertine Rose**[34] 2928 3-9-7 **87**............................ LiamJones 13 20
(W R Muir) *in tch on outer: rdn along 1/2-way and sn wknd* **18/1**

64.66 secs (1.36) **Going Correction** +0.475s/f (Yiel)
WFA 3 from 4yo+ 4lb **11** Ran SP% **123.2**
Speed ratings (Par 107): **108,105,104,101,100 99,97,92,86,84 74**
toteswingers: 1&2 £13.30, 1&3 £8.20, 2&3 £11.30. CSF £51.68 CT £301.62 TOTE £7.50: £2.50, £2.20, £3.20; EX 66.40.
Owner Dr Marwan Koukash **Bred** Frank Moynihan **Trained** Sessay, N Yorks

NOTEBOOK
Northern Dare(IRE) had thrown his chance away with a slow start on his latest start at Sandown, but jumped out well here and was able to get his favoured prominent early pitch. Ridden with confidence, he was booted into a clear advantage off the home turn and maintained the lead to the line on ground which he appreciates. The worry for connections now is that the handicapper will take a severe view of a fairly authoritative victory, when it fact he probably only had to run up to his mark to win rather than improve upon it. After all, the overall strength of the race in which he finished fourth at Epsom on Derby day looks some way better than this. He's in the Stewards' Cup but that might not be his track. Besides, he's more likely to get these sort of conditions later in the season - at Ayr, perhaps. (op 5-1 tchd 9-2)
Haajes may be best on the all-weather, but his best turf form has come with cut in the ground and he confirmed recent signs that suggested he was coming back to form. He was rattling home in the final 100 yards and is down to a handicap mark from which he can win in the weeks ahead. (op 10-1)
Solar Spirit(IRE) is becoming expensive to follow, but ran another sound race having been towards the fore throughout. The handicapper is showing him no mercy and the first-time application of cheekpieces didn't seem to bring about any dramatic improvement in form. (op 15-2 tchd 8-1)
Kay Two(IRE) probably wasn't quite at his best and may have found the ground too testing, for all that he has good form in good to soft conditions. (op 15-2 tchd 8-1)
Turnkey was hard ridden to make his challenge but kept on well enough towards the finish. He wants to go back over 6f. (op 8-1 tchd 13-2)
Artsu is another perennial heart-breaker. He looked to have plenty in his favour here but cheekpieces didn't help him. (op 11-2 tchd 4-1)
Total Impact looked all at sea on the surface. (op 8-1)

4070 COLSTROPE CUP H'CAP 1m 4y
8:05 (8:06) (Class 5) (0-70,70) 3-Y-0+ **£3,238** (£963; £481; £240) **Stalls** Low

Form RPR

-554 **1** **Play It Sam**[19] 3427 3-9-0 **64**............................(t) ShaneKelly 9 74
(W R Swinburn) *led: rdn over 1f out: drvn and edgd rt ins fnl f: hdd last 100yds: drvn and rallied to ld nr line* **6/1**

0035 **2** 1/2 **Ours (IRE)**[20] 3378 6-9-11 **67**............................(p) StephenDonohoe 7 78
(John A Harris) *hld up towards rr: gd hdwy wl over 1f out: rdn ent fnl f: led last 100yds: hdd nr fin* **7/2**[1]

3445 **3** 4 1/2 **Hypnotic Gaze (IRE)**[27] 3156 3-8-13 **63**............................ PaulHanagan 3 62
(J Mackie) *chsd ldrs: rdn 2f out: drvn over 1f out and sn one pce* **9/2**[3]

-444 **4** 1 1/4 **Veronicas Boy**[11] 3689 3-8-10 **60**............................ DavidAllan 10 56
(G M Moore) *prom: rdn along 2f out: drvn over 1f out and wknd appr fnl f* **9/2**[3]

0102 **5** 1 3/4 **Desert Hunter (IRE)**[18] 3457 6-8-7 **54**............................ JamieKyne(5) 13 48
(Micky Hammond) *prom: rdn along 2f out: sn wknd* **5/1**

0005 **6** 1 3/4 **Poca A Poca (IRE)**[25] 3207 5-8-8 **53** oh3 ow2(p) RussellKennemore(3) 1 43
(G C Bravery) *hld up: a towards rr* **22/1**

2-60 **7** *nk* **Distant Pleasure**[29] 3077 5-9-0 **56**............................ TomEaves 11 45
(M Dods) *hld up in tch: hdwy 3f out: sn rdn along and btn over 2f out* **4/1**[2]

-565 **8** *24* **Scotch And Soda (IRE)**[67] 1922 3-8-5 **55**............................ DaleGibson 4 —
(Jedd O'Keeffe) *a towards rr* **16/1**

1m 51.31s (5.41) **Going Correction** +0.475s/f (Yiel)
WFA 3 from 4yo+ 8lb **8** Ran SP% **119.8**
Speed ratings (Par 103): **91,90,86,84,83 81,80,56**
toteswingers: 1&2 £7.30, 1&3 £7.90, 2&3 £6.80. CSF £28.71 CT £106.04 TOTE £5.80: £2.00, £1.60, £1.70; EX 23.80.
Owner P W Harris **Bred** Shortgrove Manor Stud **Trained** Aldbury, Herts

FOCUS
Another slow pace in the early stages, with the jockeys understandably keen to keep things sensible in the conditions.

4071 RED SHIRT NIGHT MAIDEN H'CAP 1m 2f 6y
8:40 (8:41) (Class 5) (0-70,68) 3-Y-0+ **£3,238** (£963; £481; £240) **Stalls** Low

Form RPR

-063 **1** **Proficiency**[6] 3864 4-9-9 **55**............................(b) JamieMoriarty 1 64
(T D Walford) *hld up in tch: hdwy to chse ldrs 3f out: rdn wl over 1f out: styd on to ld ent fnl f: sn drvn and hld on wl* **3/1**[1]

-02B **2** 1/2 **Whipma Whopma Gate (IRE)**[4] 3911 4-9-2 **48**............................ IanMongan 10 56
(D Carroll) *hld up in rr: hdwy 3f out: rdn to chse ldrs wl over 1f out: swtchd rt ent fnl f: sn drvn and styd on strly: jst hld* **11/2**[3]

3240 **3** 1 3/4 **Saborido (USA)**[35] 2881 3-9-7 **63**............................(b[1]) PaulHanagan 7 68
(Mrs A J Perrett) *prom: effrt 3f out: rdn over 2f out and ev ch tl drvn and one pce ins fnl f* **11/2**[3]

555 **4** *6* **Jewelled**[19] 3425 3-9-12 **68**............................ TPO'Shea 4 62
(J W Hills) *trckd ldrs: hdwy 1/2-way: led wl over 3f out: rdn 2f out: drvn and hdd ent fnl f: wknd* **5/1**[2]

2304 **5** *9* **Shavoulin (USA)**[11] 3675 5-9-5 **51**............................(p) ShaneKelly 6 29
(P W Hiatt) *prom: rdn along over 2f out: drvn wl over 1f out and sn wknd* **7/1**

42-4 **6** *14* **Wing Diva (IRE)**[190] 90 4-9-13 **59**............................ TomEaves 8 12
(B Smart) *hld up: plld hrd: hdwy to chse ldrs 1/2-way: wknd 3f out* **5/1**[2]

0-00 **7** *58* **Tump Mac**[27] 3174 5-8-13 **45**............................ FrancisNorton 13 —
(N Bycroft) *led: rdn along and hdd over 3f out: sn wknd* **33/1**

00/ **8** *3* **Tar (IRE)**[84] 6553 5-10-0 **60**............................(b) StephenDonohoe 14 —
(John A Harris) *a bhd: t.o fnl 3f* **9/1**

2m 24.77s (11.07) **Going Correction** +0.925s/f (Soft)
WFA 3 from 4yo+ 10lb **8** Ran SP% **114.5**
Speed ratings (Par 103): **92,91,90,85,78 67,20,18**
toteswingers: 1&2 £4.10, 1&3 £3.00, 2&3 £12.00. CSF £19.74 CT £85.51 TOTE £4.30: £1.80, £1.40, £1.90; EX 21.30.
Owner G Mett Racing **Bred** Gainsborough Stud Management Ltd **Trained** Sheriff Hutton, N Yorks
■ Stewards' Enquiry : Jamie Moriarty one-day ban: used whip with excessive frequency (Jul 31)

FOCUS
A painfully slow-motion finish.

4072 "BETTER LATE THAN NEVER" H'CAP 6f
9:10 (9:10) (Class 5) (0-75,74) 3-Y-0+ **£3,238** (£963; £481; £240) **Stalls** Low

Form RPR

0211 **1** **C'Mon You Irons (IRE)**[11] 3691 4-9-7 **69**............................ IanMongan 3 85
(M R Hoad) *styd nr ins rail and cl up: led 2f out: sn clr and swtchd wd to stands' rail wl over 1f out: r.o strly* **7/2**[1]

4520 **2** *6* **Mey Blossom**[7] 3825 4-9-6 **71**............................ MichaelJStainton(3) 10 68
(R M Whitaker) *in tch on outer: hdwy 2f out: rdn to chse wnr ent fnl f: sn drvn and no imp* **12/1**

023 **3** 2 1/2 **Poppy's Rose**[10] 3722 5-8-11 **59**............................ TomEaves 8 48
(I W McInnes) *in tch: hdwy 2f out: rdn to chse ldrs over 1f out: drvn and kpt on ins fnl f: nrst fin* **6/1**[3]

0211 **4** 1/2 **Bid For Gold**[13] 3612 5-9-7 **74**............................ JamieKyne(5) 12 61
(Jedd O'Keeffe) *chsd ldrs on outer: cl up 2f out and sn rdn: drvn and one pce fr over 1f out* **7/1**

0002 **5** *hd* **Commando Scott (IRE)**[10] 3722 8-9-9 **74**............................ NeilBrown(3) 6 61
(I W McInnes) *led to 1/2-way: cl up whn n.m.r and lost pl 2f out: styd on ins fnl f* **8/1**

0006 **6** 1/2 **Redwater River**[45] 2579 5-8-2 **55** oh3............................(b) DeanHeslop(5) 2 40
(Mrs R A Carr) *chsd ldrs: effrt 2f out: sn rdn and kpt on same pce appr fnl f* **28/1**

2214 **7** 2 1/2 **Labisa (IRE)**[28] 3102 3-9-5 **72**............................ TravisBlock 1 49
(H Morrison) *hld up: hdwy to chse ldrs wl over 1f out: sn rdn and wknd* **7/1**

5210 **8** *5* **Dickie Le Davoir**[6] 3855 5-9-10 **72** 6ex............................ StephenDonohoe 9 33
(John A Harris) *dwlt: a towards rr* **9/2**[2]

6000 **9** *4* **Royal Challenge**[39] 2769 8-8-13 **61**............................ PatrickMathers 4 9
(I W McInnes) *a towards rr* **33/1**

30-0 **10** *1* **Prince Namid**[55] 2276 7-9-5 **67**............................ FrancisNorton 11 12
(D Nicholls) *cl up: led 1/2-way: rdn and hdd 2f out: sn drvn and wknd* **9/1**

5005 **11** *nk* **Kyle (IRE)**[9] 3738 5-9-12 **74**............................ ShaneKelly 5 18
(C R Dore) *cl up: rdn along over 2f out: sn wknd and eased* **11/1**

1m 19.2s (2.30) **Going Correction** +0.475s/f (Yiel)
WFA 3 from 4yo+ 5lb **11** Ran SP% **123.2**
Speed ratings (Par 103): **103,95,91,91,90 90,86,80,74,73 73**
toteswingers: 1&2 £6.80, 1&3 32.50£, 2&3 £21.20. CSF £49.75 CT £258.05 TOTE £4.30: £1.80, £3.90, £2.70; EX 62.00 Place 6 £50.69, Place 5 £30.66. .
Owner double-r-racing.com **Bred** Airlie Stud **Trained** Lewes, E Sussex

FOCUS
The progressive C'Mon You Irons completed a hat-trick in fine style.
T/Plt: £36.10 to a £1 stake. Pool: £64,183.42. 1,297.55 winning tickets. T/Qpdt: £10.80 to a £1 stake. Pool: £3,838.73. 261.45 winning tickets. JR

3667 CHANTILLY (R-H)
Friday, July 17

OFFICIAL GOING: Soft

4073a PRIX DE SAINT-FIRMIN (MAIDEN) (C&G) 6f
1:05 (1:05) 2-Y-0 **£11,650** (£4,660; £3,495; £2,330; £1,165)

RPR

1 **Melodyman (FR)**[28] 2-9-2............................ SPasquier 84
(N Clement, France)

2 *snk* **Lucky Like (FR)**[13] 3648 2-9-2............................ TThulliez 84
(E J O'Neill) *prom: led over 1f out: hdd nr fin* **58/10**[1]

1.13.6 (2.20) **9** Ran
Owner Mlle E De Waldner **Bred** Pierre Lepeudry **Trained** Chantilly, France

4041 **HAYDOCK** (L-H)

Saturday, July 18

OFFICIAL GOING: Soft (good to soft in places; 7.7)

Rail realignment increased distances on round course by about 21yards.

Wind: Fresh, against Weather: Sunny periods

4074 BET ONLINE AT CORBETTSPORTS.COM P.J.A. APPRENTICE SERIES H'CAP — 1m 2f 95y

6:40 (6:41) (Class 5) (0-75,75) 3-Y-O — **£3,238** (£963; £481; £240) **Stalls** Low

Form — RPR

41 **1** **Lady Luachmhar (IRE)**[62] 2104 3-9-10 **75**.................... FrederikTylicki 3 87+
(R A Fahey) *hld up: hdwy to trck ldrs 1/2-way: rdn to chal 2f out: led ent fnl f: sn edgd lft u.p: kpt on wl* **10/11**[1]

6515 **2** 3/4 **Embsay Crag**[21] 3371 3-9-0 **72**.................................. IJBrennan(7) 1 81
(Mrs K Walton) *led: wd st to stands' rail: rdn and jnd 2f out: drvn and hdd ent fnl f: kpt on gamely u.p* **11/2**[2]

2456 **3** 7 **Musical Maze**[21] 3371 3-8-6 **62**.................................. PaulPickard(5) 7 59
(W M Brisbourne) *t.k.h: cl up: wd st: n.m.r and swtchd lft 3f out: rdn to chse ldng pair 2f out: sn drvn and kpt on same pce* **7/1**[3]

4106 **4** 8 **Highkingofireland**[12] 3687 3-9-0 **68**.......................... MartinLane(3) 6 51
(K R Burke) *t.k.h early: hld up: hdwy and wd st: sn chsng ldrs: rdn over 2f out: drvn and one pce fr wl over 1f out* **8/1**

0530 **5** 1 1/4 **Kristopher James (IRE)**[10] 3741 3-8-3 **57**................ RossAtkinson(3) 2 38
(W M Brisbourne) *t.k.h: hld up: hdwy to chse ldrs 3f out: sn rdn and wknd over 2f out* **9/1**

43-5 **6** 2 **Heading East (IRE)**[110] 1040 3-9-4 **72**........................ AmyRyan(3) 5 49
(K A Ryan) *in tch: effrt 3f out: rdn over 2f out and sn wknd* **18/1**

2004 **7** 21 **Duke Of Normandy (IRE)**[22] 3336 3-7-12 **56** oh1.......... KierenFox(7) 4 —
(B P J Baugh) *t.k.h: chsd ldrs and sddle slipped after 2f: wknd 3f out* **16/1**

2m 18.43s (5.43) **Going Correction** +0.50s/f (Yiel) — **7 Ran SP% 112.5**

Speed ratings (Par 100): **107,106,100,94,93 91,75**

toteswingers: 1&2 £2.10, 1&3 £2.00, 2&3 £2.70. CSF £6.03 CT £21.10 TOTE £1.90: £1.30, £2.40; EX 5.40.

Owner Mrs H Steel **Bred** Stone Ridge Farm **Trained** Musley Bank, N Yorks

■ Stewards' Enquiry : I J Brennan three-day ban: careless riding (Aug 2-4)

FOCUS

A weak apprentices' handicap, but still a fair effort from Lady Luachmhar, who was conceding weight all round. There is more to come from her. A few of these raced keenly off a predictably steady early pace and they all raced towards the stands' side in the straight.

Duke Of Normandy(IRE) Official explanation: jockey said saddle slipped

4075 E. B. F. S KELLY'S HAWTHORN ESTATES MAIDEN STKS — 6f

7:10 (7:11) (Class 5) 2-Y-O — **£3,885** (£1,156; £577; £288) **Stalls** Centre

Form — RPR

0 **1** **Flipping**[17] 3500 2-9-3 0.. FergusSweeney 7 79+
(W S Kittow) *trckd ldr: smooth hdwy to ld over 2f out: rdn clr wl over 1f out: styd on strly* **3/1**[3]

45 **2** 3 1/2 **Capacity (IRE)**[35] 2936 2-9-3 0.. GregFairley 3 69
(M Johnston) *trckd ldrs: hdwy over 2f out: rdn to chse wnr over 1f out: sn drvn and no imp* **9/4**[1]

40 **3** 2 3/4 **Bitter Honey**[39] 2778 2-8-12 0.. MickyFenton 5 55
(Mrs G S Rees) *led: rdn along and hdd over 2f out: sn drvn and kpt on same pce* **6/1**

4 hd **Romeos Girl** 2-8-12 0.. TPO'Shea 8 55
(Jennie Candlish) *s.i.s and bhd: hdwy 1/2-way: rdn 2f out: edgd lft over 1f out and kpt on ins fnl f: nrst fin* **22/1**

40 **5** 4 1/2 **Almuntaser (IRE)**[15] 3572 2-9-3 0.. TomEaves 4 46
(Ian Williams) *chsd ldrs: rdn 2f out: sn hung lft and wknd* **12/1**

00 **6** 8 **Alfalasteeni**[49] 2484 2-8-12 0.. MartinLane(5) 6 22
(Ian Williams) *chsd ldrs: rdn along 1/2-way: sn edgd rt to stands' rail and outpcd* **66/1**

00 **7** 1 3/4 **Public Service (IRE)**[29] 3113 2-9-3 0.................................. SebSanders 1 17
(B J Meehan) *chsd ldrs on outer: rdn along over 2f out and sn wknd* **5/2**[2]

8 2 3/4 **Anna's Boy** 2-8-12 0.. SladeO'Hara(5) 2 9
(A Berry) *s.i.s and bhd: rdn and hung bdly lft 1/2-way* **16/1**

1m 17.87s (3.87) **Going Correction** +0.50s/f (Yiel) — **8 Ran SP% 118.0**

Speed ratings (Par 94): **94,89,85,85,79 68,66,62**

toteswingers: 1&2 £2.60, 1&3 £3.40, 2&3 £2.80. CSF £10.60 TOTE £3.90: £1.10, £1.30, £1.60; EX 12.90.

Owner Reg Gifford **Bred** D R Tucker **Trained** Blackborough, Devon

FOCUS

Probably a pretty ordinary juvenile maiden, and just fair form. The main action took place up the middle of the track.

NOTEBOOK

Flipping readily justified market support, improving a good deal on the form he showed on quick ground first time at Chepstow. Always travelling well up the middle of the track, he had appeared to commit plenty soon enough, but ran on powerfully for pressure. He looks potentially useful under these sorts of conditions, but his ability to handle quicker going is still to be proved. (op 11-2)

Capacity(IRE), who failed to build on his debut promise when a beaten favourite in a fair York maiden last time, was always close up and had his chance, but the winner was much too good. He looks only modest on what we've seen so far, but he's still learning his job, and it would be no surprise to see a better performance before long. (op 15-8 tchd 11-4)

Bitter Honey didn't see her race out after showing good speed and looks worth another try over 5f. (op 7-1 tchd 11-2)

Romeos Girl, a £4,800 half-sister to winners over 6f, 7f, and 1m2f, has a nasty scar on her off-hind. She started very slowly, but gradually got the idea and nearly grabbed third. She should have learnt plenty. (op 16-1)

Almuntaser(IRE) was never seen with a chance but he has the option of nurseries and might do better back on quicker ground. (op 10-1 tchd 8-1)

Alfalasteeni ended up alone against the stands' rail and was beaten a fair way. (tchd 50-1)

Public Service(IRE) was under pressure by halfway and offered nothing, seemingly not handling the bad ground, even though his breeding offered hope. (op 3-1 tchd 10-3 in places)

Anna's Boy, already gelded, started slowly and hung over towards the far rail late on, never getting competitive at any stage. (op 20-1)

4076 LESLEY WHITTAKER RETIREMENT AT LAST NURSERY — 5f

7:40 (7:40) (Class 5) 2-Y-O — **£2,100** (£2,100; £481; £240) **Stalls** Centre

Form — RPR

003 **1** **Duke Of Rainford**[45] 2595 2-7-12 **53** oh6.................(bt[1]) PaulHanagan 7 51
(Ian Williams) *trckd ldrs: trckd lft: rdn and hdwy ent fnl f: sn drvn and styd on strly to join ldr on line* **15/2**[3]

35 **1** dht **Tom Folan**[7] 3871 2-9-3 **72**.......................................(p) SebSanders 2 70
(H J Collingridge) *trckd ldrs: hdwy 1/2-way: rdn to ld over 1f out: drvn ins fnl f and hld on gamely* **4/1**[2]

106 **3** nse **Lady Lube Rye (IRE)**[11] 3702 2-8-12 **67**..................... JamieMoriarty 1 65
(N Wilson) *cl up: effrt to chal 2f out: sn rdn: drvn and ev ch ins fnl f: nt qckn nr line* **12/1**

0000 **4** hd **Countrywide Ice (IRE)**[4] 3952 2-7-12 **53** oh1..................(b) PaulQuinn 5 50+
(K A Ryan) *dwlt and in rr: hdwy on outer whn bumper 2f out: rdn over 1f out: styd on strly ins fnl f: edgd rt and no ex towards fin* **11/1**

223 **5** 2 **Vilnius**[7] 3871 2-8-7 **62**.. FrancisNorton 10 52
(M R Channon) *led: rdn along 2f out: drvn over 1f out: hdd ent fnl f and wknd* **13/8**[1]

0006 **6** 2 3/4 **Ariel Bender**[8] 3807 2-7-11 **55** oh5 ow2........................ AndreaAtzeni(3) 3 35
(Peter Grayson) *in rr: hdwy 1/2-way: swtchd sharply lft 2f out: sn rdn to chse ldrs: drvn and wknd over 1f out* **12/1**

043 **7** 1 **Tarrants Way**[24] 3263 2-8-4 **59**.. TPO'Shea 6 35
(Jennie Candlish) *trckd ldrs: n.m.r 2f out: sn rdn and wknd appr fnl f* **4/1**[2]

64.30 secs (3.80) **Going Correction** +0.50s/f (Yiel) — **7 Ran SP% 113.6**

Speed ratings (Par 94): **89,89,88,88,85 81,79**WIN: Tom Folan £2.50, Duke Of Rainford £5.00; PL: TF £2.00, DOR £3.60; EX: TF-DOR £24.40, DOR-TF £18.00; CSF: TF-DOR £16.37, DOR-TF £18.38; TRICAST: TF-DOR-LLR £163.75, DOR-TF-LLR £178.14. toteswingers: TF&DOR £6.20, 1&3 (TF) £7.10, 1&3 (DOR) £14.80. CSF £0.0027 CT £Owner TOTE £Dr Marwan Koukash: £Bred, £Worksop Manor Stud, £Trained, £Portway, Worcs .

Owner Tapas Partnership **Bred** Chippenham Lodge Stud Ltd **Trained** Exning, Suffolk

■ Stewards' Enquiry : Andrea Atzeni caution: careless riding.

FOCUS

The first four finished almost in a line and this looks limited form, although the principals all showed improvement to some degree. They raced towards the stands' side, but the rail seemed no real advantage. The 'official' ratings shown next to each horse are estimated and for information purposes only.

NOTEBOOK

Duke Of Rainford, who had the tongue-tie on again and was also equipped with first-time blinkers, looked held for much of the closing stages but Paul Hanagan conjured a strong, late run out of him once switching off the rail and he forced a dead-heat. He's at the right end of the handicap, but already looks hard work and doesn't appeal as one to be following. (op 3-1 tchd 9-2)

Tom Folan looked to be in danger of regressing prior to this - she was keen two starts back and then unshipped her rider before the start last time - but she was clearly suited by both the fitting of cheekpieces and the switch to soft ground. Given a typically strong Sanders ride, she proved a willing partner and crucially had her head down on crossing the line. This daughter of Namid looks ideally suited by an easy surface. (op 3-1 tchd 9-2)

Lady Lube Rye(IRE) showed good speed on this drop back in trip and kept on, but she was just held. (op 10-1 tchd 9-1)

Countrywide Ice(IRE) was given reminders with the whip soon after the start and never travelled at any stage. However, once slightly bumped and pushed wide by Ariel Bender around two furlongs out, he decided to run on and looked a big threat, but his effort possibly flattened out near the line. He has ability but doesn't look one to trust. (op 14-1 tchd 20-1)

Vilnius had finished in front of today's winner at York last time but, after showing good speed towards the stands' rail, she didn't see her race out, presumably not going through the ground late on. (op 7-4 tchd 2-1)

Tarrants Way ◆ was very free and found nothing for pressure. He did show ability, though, and could be a different proposition on a quick surface over an easy 5f. (op 5-1 tchd 10-3)

4077 GEORGE & FLO 50TH ANNIVERSARY CONDITIONS STKS — 7f 30y

8:10 (8:10) (Class 3) 3-Y-O+ — **£9,714** (£2,890; £1,444; £721) **Stalls** Low

Form — RPR

5-60 **1** **Welsh Emperor (IRE)**[49] 2483 10-9-9 **106**...................... MickyFenton 1 106
(T P Tate) *led: qcknd 3f out: rdn and qcknd 2f out: drvn and hdd briefly ins fnl f: rallied gamely u.p to ld again nr line* **10/11**[1]

120- **2** hd **Prime Spirit (IRE)**[372] 3920 3-8-8 **95**.................................. TomEaves 2 95
(B Smart) *trckd ldng pair: cl up 1/2-way: rdn to chal 2f out: drvn and slt ld ins fnl f: hdd and no ex nr line* **9/2**[3]

40-0 **3** 7 **Appalachian Trail (IRE)**[70] 1865 8-9-1 **103**...................(b) PhillipMakin 5 81
(I Semple) *cl up: effrt 3f out: rdn wl over 1f out and ev ch tl drvn and wknd ent fnl f* **5/2**[2]

240 **4** 5 **Balcarce Nov (ARG)**[112] 1009 4-9-4 **98**........................ PaulMulrennan 3 72
(T P Tate) *in rr: hdwy 3f out: rdn to chse ldrs over 2f out: sn wknd* **10/1**

1m 33.73s (3.53) **Going Correction** +0.50s/f (Yiel)

WFA 3 from 4yo+ 7lb — **4 Ran SP% 108.2**

Speed ratings (Par 107): **99,98,90,85**

CSF £5.28 TOTE £1.80; EX 3.70.

Owner Mrs Sylvia Clegg **Bred** Times Of Wigan Ltd **Trained** Tadcaster, N Yorks

FOCUS

A decent contest, despite the small field. They raced up the middle of the track in the straight. The form is rated through the first two.

NOTEBOOK

Welsh Emperor(IRE), without the blinkers this time, had the ground to suit and was allowed to dominate, as he likes to, although both the runner-up and third-placed finisher ensured he was kept honest. He really had to work for this victory when joined in the straight, but he showed he retains plenty of enthusiasm with a gutsy effort. This was his first success since he won this race last year and he'll probably be vulnerable back up in grade. (tchd Evens in places)

Prime Spirit(IRE) ◆ did well to produce such a big effort considering he had been off for over a year and was a little keen early. A smart effort after so long away from the track, he could prove pattern class if building on this. (op 6-1 tchd 4-1)

Appalachian Trail(IRE) was best off at the weights but was readily left behind by the front two and has yet to strike form this year. (op 10-3)

Balcarce Nov(ARG), an ex-Argentinean-trained colt who showed very useful form on quick turf in Dubai for these owners earlier in the year, was never out of last place on his British debut after 112 days off. He carried his head at an angle under pressure and looked totally unsuited by the soft ground. It won't be difficult to give him another chance. (op 13-2)

4078 ANNE ROWLANDS MEMORIAL C.R.U.K. H'CAP — 1m 6f

8:40 (8:40) (Class 4) (0-85,82) 4-Y-O+ — **£5,504** (£1,637; £818; £408) **Stalls** Low

Form — RPR

0224 **1** **Dolly Penrose**[7] 3850 4-9-7 **82**.. FrancisNorton 10 87
(M R Channon) *trckd ldng pair: smooth hdwy over 2f out: chal on bit over 1f out: shkn up ent fnl f: sn rdn and styd on to ld nr fin* **6/4**[1]

-053 **2** hd **Mudawin (IRE)**[16] 3532 8-8-11 **72** ow2.............................. PhillipMakin 3 77
(James Moffatt) *led: rdn along wl over 2f out: drvn over 1f out: kpt on gamely u.p ins fnl f: hdd and no ex nr fin* **15/2**

0132 **3** 3 **Princess Rainbow (FR)**[16] 3527 4-8-11 **72**........................ TPO'Shea 7 73
(Jennie Candlish) *trckd ldr: rdn along over 2f out: drvn wl over 1f out: kpt on same pce ins fnl f* **9/2**[3]

-231 **4** 12 **Wee Charlie Castle (IRE)**[12] 3679 6-9-2 **77**........................ TomEaves 4 62
(I Semple) *hld up in rr: hdwy 3f out: rdn along 2f out: sn drvn and wknd wl over 1f out* **5/1**

4444 **5** *5* **Puy D'Arnac (FR)**[10] 3728 6-8-8 **69**........................ PaulMulrennan 2 48
(G A Swinbank) *t.k.h: hld up: effrt and hdwy over 3f out: sn rdn along and wknd 2f out* **3/1**[2]

3m 10.54s (6.24) **Going Correction** +0.50s/f (Yiel) **5** Ran SP% **111.6**
Speed ratings (Par 105): **102,101,100,93,90**
toteswingers: 1&2 £14.50. CSF £13.16 TOTE £2.70: £1.50, £3.40; EX 14.20.
Owner M Channon **Bred** Jethro Bloodstock **Trained** West Ilsley, Berks

FOCUS
Not many runners but still a fair staying handicap. The first two set the level. The pace seemed ordinary and they raced up the centre of the track in the straight.

4079 JOAN HEWISON MEMORIAL C.R.U.K. H'CAP — 1m 30y
9:10 (9:12) (Class 5) (0-70,73) 3-Y-O **£3,238** (£963; £481; £240) **Stalls** Low

Form RPR

545 **1** **Kindest**[21] 3408 3-9-9 **70**........................ GeorgeBaker 4 77+
(C F Wall) *midfield on inner: hdwy over 3f out: chal 2f out: rdn to ld over 1f out: drvn ins fnl f and hld on wl: jinked lft nr line* **9/2**[2]

00-3 **2** *1* **Speed Dating**[75] 1740 3-8-12 **59**........................ SebSanders 11 64+
(Sir Mark Prescott) *hld up in tch: hdwy 3f out: chal 2f out and sn rdn: drvn ent fnl f and ev ch tl no ex towards fin: hld whn hmpd and wnt lft nr line* **11/8**[1]

6-40 **3** *½* **Flying Silks (IRE)**[39] 2797 3-9-1 **62**........................ TPO'Shea 6 66
(J R Gask) *hld up in rr: hdwy wl over 2f out: rdn over 1f out: kpt on ins fnl f* **8/1**

6340 **4** *hd* **Dean Iarracht (IRE)**[23] 3316 3-9-4 **65**........................ PhillipMakin 14 68
(M Dods) *wnt rt s: hld up in rr: hdwy 3f out: rdn to chse ldrs over 1f out: styng on 3rd whn hmpd nr line* **11/1**

3-01 **5** *6* **Fortunate Bid (IRE)**[12] 3693 3-9-12 **73**........................ GregFairley 13 63
(Mrs L Stubbs) *t.k.h: led: rdn along over 2f out: hdd over 1f out and wknd* **11/2**[3]

-001 **6** *¾* **Neo's Mate (IRE)**[17] 3498 3-7-12 **52**........................ PaulPickard(7) 5 40
(Paul Green) *t.k.h: chsd ldr: rdn along 3f out: drvn over 2f out and grad wknd* **28/1**

-000 **7** *7* **Iron Man Of Mersey (FR)**[33] 2982 3-8-8 **55**........................ PaulQuinn 9 28
(A W Carroll) *towards rr: hdwy 1/2-way: chsd ldrs 3f out: sn rdn and wknd 2f out* **8/1**

5434 **8** *6* **Piccolo Express**[22] 3334 3-8-10 **57**........................ PaulMulrennan 1 17
(B P J Baugh) *chsd ldrs on inner: rdn along 3f out: sn wknd* **33/1**

-300 **9** *1 ¾* **Rose Cheval (USA)**[74] 1774 3-9-6 **67**........................ FrancisNorton 8 23
(M R Channon) *chsd ldrs: rdn along wl over 2f out and sn wknd* **28/1**

404 **10** *4 ½* **Black River Falls (USA)**[23] 3294 3-8-8 **55**........................ TomEaves 12 —
(I Semple) *chsd ldrs on outer: rdn along 3f out and sn wknd* **14/1**

1m 47.89s (4.09) **Going Correction** +0.50s/f (Yiel) **10** Ran SP% **122.7**
Speed ratings (Par 100): **99,98,97,97,91 90,83,77,75,71**
toteswingers: 1&2 £3.60, 1&3 £11.30, 2&3 £5.60. CSF £11.50 CT £51.90 TOTE £5.20: £1.80, £1.30, £2.50; EX 14.70 Place 6 £19.45, Place 5 £16.41.
Owner Peter Botham **Bred** Gainsborough Stud Management Ltd **Trained** Newmarket, Suffolk

FOCUS
Not a bad handicap for the grade. The first four finished clear and the form has been rated on the positive side. The main action took place up the middle of the track in the straight.
T/Plt: £40.10 to a £1 stake. Pool: £69,054.64. 1,255.95 winning tickets. T/Qpdt: £30.50 to a £1 stake. Pool: £4,670.96. 113.20 winning tickets. JR

3984 LINGFIELD (L-H)
Saturday, July 18

OFFICIAL GOING: Turf course - good; all-weather - standard
Wind: Fresh, half behind Weather: overcast

4080 EUROPEAN BREEDERS' FUND MAIDEN STKS — 7f
5:55 (5:56) (Class 5) 2-Y-O **£3,561** (£1,059; £529; £264) **Stalls** High

Form RPR

1 **Cumulus Nimbus** 2-9-3 0........................ PatDobbs 9 82+
(R Hannon) *hld up in midfield: swtchd lft and smooth hdwy over 2f out: pushed into ld over 1f out: pushed clr fnl f: readily* **7/1**

05 **2** *3 ½* **Chairman Pat (USA)**[24] 3270 2-9-3 0........................ RichardKingscote 10 70
(Tom Dascombe) *led narrowly on stands' rail: rdn 2f out: hdd over 1f out: no ch w wnr fnl f: kpt on to hold 2nd* **5/1**[3]

00 **3** *nk* **Avow (USA)**[28] 3138 2-9-3 0........................(b[1]) JamesDoyle 7 70
(J S Moore) *pressed ldr: ev ch and drvn wl over 1f out: nt pce of wnr fnl f: kpt on* **20/1**

32 **4** *1 ½* **Cuthbert (IRE)**[9] 3767 2-9-3 0........................ RobertHavlin 8 66
(W Jarvis) *trckd ldrs: rdn and swtchd lft whn nt clr run briefly over 1f out: sn drvn and kpt on same pce fnl f* **9/4**[1]

0 **5** *2 ½* **Spanish Duke (IRE)**[22] 3344 2-9-3 0........................ RichardMullen 12 60+
(J L Dunlop) *t.k.h early: hld up in midfield: rdn and rn green ent fnl 2f: sn outpcd and wl hld after* **5/2**[2]

6 *6* **Drews Lane** 2-8-7 0........................(t) MCGeran(5) 4 40
(W G M Turner) *wnt bdly lft s: in tch in midfield on outer: rdn and rn green 3f out: sn outpcd: nvr trbld ldrs* **80/1**

7 *2* **Azlak (USA)** 2-9-3 0........................ ChrisCatlin 3 40
(C E Brittain) *hmpd s and s.i.s: away in rr gp: nvr a factor* **12/1**

20 **8** *shd* **Do More Business (IRE)**[16] 3522 2-9-3 0........................ IanMongan 1 39
(P M Phelan) *hmpd s and s.i.s: swtchd rt and in rr on stands' rail: rdn and struggling wl over 2f out: no ch whn nt clr run and swtchd lft 1f out* **12/1**

50 **9** *¾* **Dear Mr Fantasy (IRE)**[34] 2940 2-9-0 0........................ PatrickHills(3) 6 37
(J W Hills) *chsd ldrs: rdn jst over 2f out: sn struggling: wl bhd fnl f* **33/1**

00 **10** *nse* **Fairywater Grey (IRE)**[10] 3733 2-8-12 0........................ JerryO'Dwyer 13 32
(J J Bridger) *in tch in midfield tl 1/2-way: sn struggling and rdn: no ch fnl 2f* **66/1**

11 *2 ½* **Press To Reset** 2-9-3 0........................ SaleemGolam 11 31
(W G M Turner) *awkward leaving stalls and v.s.a: sn pushed along: a bhd* **66/1**

1m 23.18s (-0.12) **Going Correction** -0.30s/f (Firm) **11** Ran SP% **115.8**
Speed ratings (Par 94): **88,84,83,81,79 72,69,69,68,68 66**
toteswingers: 1&2 £7.50, 1&3 £37.80, 2&3 £18.40. CSF £39.80 TOTE £8.30: £2.30, £2.30, £5.30; EX 32.30.
Owner Mrs John Lee **Bred** Chantilly Bloodstock Agency **Trained** East Everleigh, Wilts

FOCUS
A fair juvenile turf maiden, those having already run looking no better than moderate, but it was made more interesting by the presence of a clutch of debutants from stables doing well with their two-year-olds this term.

NOTEBOOK
Cumulus Nimbus does not boast the pedigree to suggest he is likely to become one of his yard's leading lights, but was not a cheap buy. He was easy to back, drifting markedly on the exchanges, but was always travelling well and, after making progress from mid-division just after halfway, he quickened stylishly to take the lead at the furlong pole and register a smooth debut victory. (op 8-1 tchd 13-2)
Chairman Pat(USA) had posted two solid previous performances, one on turf, one on Polytrack, and had been backed on both occasions. This race appeared to represent a slightly easier assignment than either of those earlier outings and, as his young trainer has quickly earned a reputation for shrewd placement, it was no surprise that he attracted punters' cash and figured toward the head of the market. He broke quickly from the gates, grabbing the lead after making a beeline for the generally favoured stands'-side rail, and, although he could not match the finishing pace of the winner, he stayed on gamely to beat the remainder. (op 7-1)
Avow(USA) had shown little on his two previous outings, the second of which was admittedly in a Listed event at Royal Ascot, but his stable has been in better form in recent weeks and, wearing first-time blinkers, he stepped up markedly on those two efforts. He is now qualified for nurseries and, provided the headgear continues to make a difference, he can be placed successfully in the near future. (op 16-1)
Cuthbert(IRE) lined up with two placed efforts to his name, the latter an encouraging second over 6f at Epsom, and, as his dam stayed 1m2f, there seemed an excellent chance that he would improve for this longer distance. Whether he did is a moot point, as he never threatened to collect, but he ran another solid race and should be able to notch a first success, perhaps in nurseries, for which this third run qualifies him. (op 5-2)
Spanish Duke(IRE) had attracted market attention on his Folkestone debut three weeks previously, but, after a slow start, he failed to cut much ice. Runners from his stable often improve significantly for their first experience of racing, though, and, despite a late drift in the betting, he was still a short price to make up for his debut defeat. He is proving expensive to follow and, after pulling quite hard in the early stages here, he failed to produce much of a challenge at the business end of the race. (op 2-1 tchd 11-4)
Drews Lane Official explanation: jockey said filly hung badly left throughout
Azlak(USA) Official explanation: jockey said colt was hampered at start
Do More Business(IRE) had made a promising debut over 5f at Goodwood in May, albeit in selling company, but he had disappointed when the subject of a gamble over 7f at Epsom on his only subsequent start. He again ran below market expectations in this event, hardly improving his chances by breaking slowly from the stalls. Official explanation: jockey said gelding was hampered at start (tchd 9-1)

4081 BOB KIERNAN MEMORIAL NURSERY — 6f
6:25 (6:25) (Class 5) 2-Y-O **£3,238** (£963; £481; £240) **Stalls** High

Form RPR

514 **1** **Fleeting Echo**[15] 3579 2-8-0 **65**........................ RichardThomas 4 76+
(R Hannon) *w ldrs: rdn to ld ent fnl f: r.o strly and drew wl clr ins fnl f: easily* **9/2**[3]

3213 **2** *3* **Transfixed (IRE)**[2] 4017 2-7-11 **69**........................ AndrewHeffernan(7) 7 68
(P D Evans) *rrd s and s.i.s: sn bustled along to chse ldrs: led over 4f out: rdn: edgd lft and hdd ent fnl f: nt pce of wnr fnl f* **9/4**[1]

3310 **3** *1 ½* **Swilly Ferry (USA)**[9] 3782 2-9-7 **86**........................ EddieAhern 6 81
(B W Hills) *chsd ldr tl short of room and eased bk after 1f: chsd ldrs: effrt on outer to chse ldng pair wl over 1f out: rdn and unable qck over 1f out: one pce after* **3/1**[2]

041 **4** *5* **Wasmi (IRE)**[11] 3716 2-8-3 **68**........................ ChrisCatlin 5 48
(C E Brittain) *led tl over 4f out: chsd ldr after tl 2f out: sn rdn: wknd over 1f out* **5/1**

645 **5** *nk* **Bubbly Bellini (IRE)**[28] 3167 2-8-11 **76**........................ NeilChalmers 1 55
(A Bailey) *a struggling to go pce in last pair and pushed along: nvr nr ldrs* **8/1**

433 **6** *3 ¼* **Super Duplex**[9] 3767 2-8-10 **75**........................ IanMongan 2 44
(P M Phelan) *stdd and dropped in bhd after s: rdn and edgd lft over 2f out: sn lost tch* **8/1**

1m 10.3s (-0.90) **Going Correction** -0.30s/f (Firm) **6** Ran SP% **112.8**
Speed ratings (Par 94): **94,90,88,81,80 76**
toteswingers: 1&2 £2.30, 1&3 £2.20, 2&3 £2.50. CSF £15.22 TOTE £5.70: £3.00, £1.50; EX 14.60.
Owner P J & Mrs J P Haycock **Bred** P J Haycock **Trained** East Everleigh, Wilts

FOCUS
Not the greatest nursery and more than one of the contenders looked to have a harsh rating on what they had achieved to date. The 'official' ratings shown next to each horse are estimated and for information purposes only.

NOTEBOOK
Fleeting Echo, who had appeared to make considerable progress from her debut when scoring over 5f on her second start at Kempton, then seemed to take a step backwards on her latest outing, leaving her with a bit to prove. Whatever had caused her to flop when sent off co-favourite at Salisbury, 15 days earlier, was firmly put behind her here, as she soon established a handy position and, once asked to quicken approaching the final furlong, she strode clear for a decisive win. (op 4-1 tchd 11-2)
Transfixed(IRE) boasted solid form in this type of event, having already contested three juvenile handicaps, and, while she is no superstar, her previous efforts indicated that she was not badly treated on her estimated mark of 69. She again ran well, probably close to her best, but despite breaking fast enough to take advantage of racing against the stands' rail, she simply could not cope with the winner's finishing burst. (op 4-1)
Swilly Ferry(USA) has been on the go since the start of the turf season, having made a pleasing debut when third in the Brocklesby at Doncaster. However, his form has not been entirely consistent and his latest effort, admittedly in a good-class event at Newmarket, had been slightly disappointing. He ran a fair race here, figuring prominently from the outset, but, with an estimated mark of 86, he does not look favourably treated. (op 5-2 tchd 10-3)
Wasmi(IRE) had produced progressive form in her three previous starts, the latest of which had resulted in a victory over 7f at Wolverhampton. She had shown enough speed in the past to suggest a drop in trip was not a major drawback. She ran a curious race for one with her profile, chasing the pace early on but fading tamely in the closing stages. (op 7-2)
Bubbly Bellini(IRE) had managed no better than fourth in his three previous starts and, on the basis of those performances, he seemed to have at least his share of weight for this first sortie into a nursery. He ran that way too, not showing enough to suggest he can win, unless dropped a few pounds. Official explanation: jockey said gelding never travelled (tchd 17-2, 9-1 in a place)
Super Duplex had done little wrong on his three previous starts, making the first four each time, but the races he had been contesting were all auction events. He seemed out of his depth from this mark against these rivals. (op 12-1 tchd 15-2)

4082 JOHN SCHOLES 80TH BIRTHDAY H'CAP — 6f
6:55 (6:57) (Class 6) (0-65,65) 3-Y-O+ **£2,047** (£604; £302) **Stalls** High

Form RPR

0034 **1** **Stamford Blue**[7] 3866 8-9-0 **59**........................(b) SPRyan(7) 2 69
(R A Harris) *towards rr: hdwy on outer jst over 2f out: drvn and edgd lft ent fnl f: led ins fnl f: pushed out towards fin* **14/1**

5433 **2** *1 ¼* **Cativo Cavallino**[7] 3866 6-9-7 **62**........................ NataliaGemelova(3) 6 68
(J E Long) *towards rr in centre: rdn over 2f out: hdwy wl over 1f out: edgd rt but styd on wl to chse wnr fnl 100yds: kpt on* **10/1**

3353 **3** 1 1/2 **Dr Wintringham (IRE)**[22] 3345 3-8-12 **55**.......................... TedDurcan 9 56+
(Karen George) *s.i.s: bhd: stl last over 2f out: hdwy on outer over 1f out: styd on steadily fnl f: wnt 3rd nr fin: nvr gng to rch ldng pair* **16/1**

-140 **4** 1/2 **Efisio Princess**[37] 2864 6-9-5 **57**.......................... RichardThomas 12 57
(J E Long) *w ldr on stands' rail: led over 4f out: rdn over 1f out: hdd ins fnl f: wknd fnl 75yds* **10/1**

0002 **5** 1/2 **Sermons Mount (USA)**[12] 3672 3-8-10 **53**.................... NeilChalmers 4 51
(Mouse Hamilton-Fairley) *w ldrs: wnt 2nd 4f out: ev ch and rdn 2f out: wknd u.p jst ins fnl f* **16/1**

2546 **6** *nse* **Vanadium**[11] 3722 7-9-7 **59**.......................... RyanMoore 16 58
(G L Moore) *hld up in tch: rdn and nt qckn 2f out: edging lft u.p over 1f out: plugged on ins fnl f: nt pce to rch ldrs* **11/2**[1]

3140 **7** 1/2 **Avoca Dancer (IRE)**[10] 3732 6-9-4 **56**...................(v) TGMcLaughlin 17 53
(Karen George) *in tch in midfield on stands' rail: rdn and no real prog wl over 1f out tl kpt on fnl 100yds: nvr pce to threaten ldrs* **13/2**[2]

6050 **8** 1 3/4 **Bollin Franny**[41] 2745 5-8-10 **48**.......................... KirstyMilczarek 18 40+
(J E Long) *led on stands' rail: hdd over: chsd ldng pair after: rallied u.p over 1f out: wknd jst ins fnl f: eased whn wl btn towards fin* **16/1**

0600 **9** 2 1/4 **Fly In Johnny (IRE)**[1] 4051 4-8-10 **48**..................(p) RichardKingscote 8 33
(J J Bridger) *s.i.s: a in rr gp: rdn over 2f out: sme modest late hdwy: nvr nr ldrs* **33/1**

4620 **10** *nse* **Kalligal**[12] 3677 4-9-1 **53**..........................(b) RobertHavlin 14 38
(R Ingram) *taken down early: s.i.s: bhd: rdn and effrt jst over 2f out: n.d* **25/1**

0000 **11** 1/2 **Kaystar Ridge**[26] 3227 4-8-11 **49**..........................(bp) JerryO'Dwyer 15 32
(D K Ivory) *in tch: sn rdn along: wkng whn edgd rt 2f out: no ch fr over 1f out* **16/1**

0052 **12** 3/4 **Scruffy Skip (IRE)**[12] 3671 4-9-0 **52**..................(v) SaleemGolam 1 33
(Mrs C A Dunnett) *in tch: rdn and nt qckn ent fnl 2f out: sn wknd* **16/1**

0032 **13** 7 **Temperence Hall (USA)**[3] 3989 3-8-6 **52**..............(v) MarcHalford(3) 13 12
(J R Best) *chsd ldrs: drvn jst over 2f out: wknd wl over 1f out: eased whn no ch ins fnl f* **13/2**[2]

0-0 **14** 1/2 **Cheap Street**[185] 155 5-9-12 **64**.......................... NickyMackay 7 23
(J G Portman) *hld up in rr: rdn and effrt but stl plenty to do whn nt clr run and hmpd 2f out: n.d* **12/1**

4020 **15** 3 1/2 **Billy Beetroot (USA)**[15] 3580 3-9-8 **65**..................(b) ChrisCatlin 3 13
(R A Harris) *chsd ldrs: rdn and struggling jst over 2f out: wl bhd fr over 1f out* **16/1**

05-3 **16** 13 **Mr Rio (IRE)**[11] 3712 4-9-8 **60**.......................... RichardMullen 11 —
(A P Jarvis) *chsd ldrs tl 1/2-way: sn lost pl: t.o and eased fnl f* **9/1**[3]

1m 10.67s (-0.53) **Going Correction** -0.05s/f (Good)
WFA 3 from 4yo+ 5lb **16** Ran SP% **126.7**
Speed ratings (Par 101): **101,99,97,96,96 95,95,92,89,89 89,88,78,78,73 56**
toteswingers: 1&2 £25.10, 1&3 £29.10, 2&3 £48.10. CSF £152.85 CT £2298.72 TOTE £18.90: £3.40, £2.80, £5.10, £3.20; EX 143.70.
Owner Brian Hicks **Bred** Mrs Wendy Miller **Trained** Earlswood, Monmouths

FOCUS
A modest handicap, featuring a large field of seemingly closely-matched sprinters, so the draw, which usually favours high numbers and had appeared to do so in the first event on the card, looked likely to play a part in deciding the result. Heavy rain greeted the runners as they arrived at the start.
Dr Wintringham(IRE) Official explanation: jockey said filly missed the break
Mr Rio(IRE) Official explanation: trainer said gelding was unsuited by the good going

4083 BURRIDGE RACING AND GOLF TROPHIES CLAIMING STKS 1m (P)
7:25 (7:25) (Class 6) 3-5-Y-O **£2,047** (£604; £302) **Stalls** High

Form RPR

0023 **1** **Captain Jacksparra (IRE)**[17] 3501 5-9-8 72.................... RyanMoore 9 82
(K A Ryan) *w ldr tl led over 5f out: mde rest: rdn clr over 1f out: kpt on wl u.p fnl f* **7/4**[1]

5142 **2** 1 3/4 **Elna Bright**[15] 3577 4-9-4 83.......................... RichardEvans(5) 11 79+
(P D Evans) *stdd after s: hld up in last pair: pushed along and hdwy wl over 1f out: rdn to go modest 4th jst over 1f out: r.o strly to go 2nd wl ins fnl f: clsng but nvr gng to rch wnr: too much to do* **7/4**[1]

040 **3** 1 1/4 **Statute Book (IRE)**[14] 3644 3-9-1 75.......................... PatDobbs 12 74
(S Kirk) *hld up towards rr: hdwy on outer over 3f out: chsd wnr 2f out: sn rdn and unable qck wl over 1f out: one pce after: lost 2nd wl ins fnl f* **5/1**[2]

0000 **4** 3 3/4 **Shake On It**[13] 3662 5-8-13 54..........................(t) IanMongan 5 58
(M R Hoad) *trckd ldrs: chsd wnr over 3f out tl 2f out: wknd u.p over 1f out* **33/1**

5030 **5** 3 3/4 **Nun Today (USA)**[19] 3463 3-8-0 55..........................(p) JimmyQuinn 10 43
(Karen George) *stdd s: hld up in rr: rdn and outpcd over 2f out: no ch after* **22/1**

0 **6** 5 **Annan Rock (IRE)**[11] 3718 3-8-9 0.......................... VinceSlattery 2 41
(W J Musson) *hld up towards rr: nt clr run and shuffled bk to last over 2f out: rdn over 1f out: no hdwy* **66/1**

26-0 **7** 1 1/2 **Blow Hole (USA)**[19] 3461 4-8-10 72.................... RussellKennemore(3) 8 36
(Paul Mason) *dwlt: sn chsng ldrs: rdn over 2f out: sn outpcd and wl btn over 1f out* **12/1**[3]

40-0 **8** 3 **Musigny (USA)**[37] 2863 3-8-9 62.......................... ChrisCatlin 6 31
(W Jarvis) *hld up in tch in midfield: rdn over 3f out: wknd over 2f out and sn wl bhd* **33/1**

0050 **9** 1 1/2 **Noverre To Hide (USA)**[4] 3946 3-8-6 55..............(v) MarcHalford(3) 7 28
(J R Best) *a towards rr: rdn and struggling wl over 2f out: bhd whn rn wd bnd 2f out* **12/1**[3]

00 **10** 1 1/4 **Rony Dony (IRE)**[51] 2415 5-9-3 0..........................(t) EdwardCreighton 3 27
(M E Rimmer) *led narrowly tl over 5f out: drvn over 3f out: wknd wl over 2f out: wl bhd fnl 2f* **100/1**

1m 38.11s (-0.09) **Going Correction** +0.075s/f (Slow)
WFA 3 from 4yo+ 8lb **10** Ran SP% **117.5**
Speed ratings (Par 101): **103,101,100,96,92 87,86,83,81,80**
toteswingers: 1&2 £1.10, 1&3 £1.80, 2&3 £2.70. CSF £4.44 TOTE £2.70: £1.10, £1.30, £1.70; EX 5.50.
Owner J Duddy,B McDonald,A Heeney,M McMenamin **Bred** Quay Bloodstock **Trained** Hambleton, N Yorks

FOCUS
There was very little strength in depth in this Polytrack claimer, particularly after the defection of likely favourite Agente Parmigiano. Just three runners appeared to have a serious chance at the weights, with most of the others looking out of their depth.

4084 HAPPY BIRTHDAY GEOFF BOWRY (S) STKS 1m 2f (P)
7:55 (7:55) (Class 6) 3-Y-O+ **£2,047** (£604; £302) **Stalls** Low

Form RPR

410/ **1** **Guiseppe Verdi (USA)**[714] 4147 5-9-5 83.......................... ChrisCatlin 11 53+
(Miss Tor Sturgis) *t.k.h: chsd ldr 8f out: upsides ldr gng wl over 2f out: rdn to ld jst over 1f out: r.o wl and holding runner-up towards fin* **2/1**[1]

5105 **2** 1/2 **Polish Power (GER)**[4] 3961 9-9-11 80.......................... LPKeniry 9 58+
(J S Moore) *v.s.a: hld up bhd: hdwy on outer over 2f out: gd hdwy u.p over 1f out: chsd wnr ins fnl f: kpt on but hld towards fin* **2/1**[1]

-000 **3** 3 1/4 **Platoche (IRE)**[38] 2830 4-9-5 49..........................(t) EddieAhern 3 46
(G A Butler) *chsd ldrs: rdn and unable qck ent fnl 2f out: kpt on same pce u.p fnl f: wnt 3rd last strides* **7/1**[3]

4-00 **4** *hd* **Felicia**[57] 2221 4-8-11 45.......................... NataliaGemelova(3) 6 41
(J E Long) *led: rdn over 2f out: hdd jst over 1f out: wknd and lost 2 pls fnl 100yds* **20/1**

0006 **5** 1 **Primera Rossa**[5] 3919 3-7-13 40.......................... SophieDoyle(5) 8 39
(J S Moore) *hld up wl in tch in midfield: rdn ent fnl 2f out: nt clr run briefly jst over 1f out: plugged on same pce fnl f: nvr pce to trble ldrs* **33/1**

0 **6** *nk* **Dramatic Jewel (USA)**[26] 3207 3-8-9 0.......................... SteveDrowne 4 43
(J W Hills) *hld up in tch in midfield: effrt u.p on inner 2f out: no prog fr over 1f out* **25/1**

-033 **7** 3 1/4 **La Belle Joannie**[7] 3862 4-9-0 46.......................... PaulDoe 13 33
(S Curran) *s.i.s: t.k.h: hld up in rr: rdn and effrt ent fnl 2f: no prog wl btn over 1f out* **9/2**[2]

000- **8** 1 3/4 **Infinite Patience**[360] 4298 4-9-0 48.......................... KirstyMilczarek 7 29
(T D McCarthy) *t.k.h: chsd ldr tl 8f out: chsd ldrs after tl wknd u.p wl over 1f out* **33/1**

0000 **9** *nk* **Romantic Interlude (IRE)**[50] 2461 3-8-4 50.............(v) RichardMullen 1 29
(A P Jarvis) *t.k.h: hld up in last trio: rdn and btn jst over 2f out: no ch and racd awkwardly fnl f* **25/1**

00- **10** 1/2 **Spin Sister**[225] 7561 3-8-4 0.......................... JamieMackay 5 28
(J Gallagher) *hld up in last trio: rdn and struggling over 2f out: wl bhd and hung rt over 1f out* **66/1**

006 **11** 1 1/4 **Calling Birds (IRE)**[3] 3984 3-8-4 48..........................(p) JimmyQuinn 12 26
(Karen George) *s.i.s: t.k.h: hld up in midfield: rdn and losing pl whn n.m.r wl over 1f out: wl bhd and eased ins fnl f* **28/1**

2m 8.54s (1.94) **Going Correction** +0.075s/f (Slow)
WFA 3 from 4yo+ 10lb **11** Ran SP% **120.6**
Speed ratings (Par 101): **95,94,92,91,91 90,88,86,86,86 85**
toteswingers: 1&2 £1.30, 1&3 £4.00, 2&3 £3.60. CSF £5.39 TOTE £3.20: £1.50, £1.50, £2.10; EX 6.90.There was no bid for the winner.
Owner Miss Tor Sturgis **Bred** Runnymede Farm Inc And Catesby W Clay **Trained** Lambourn, Berks

FOCUS
Much of the form for this contest made grim reading and a number of the runners look set to become perennial strugglers. However, the front two in the market stood out, and both had successes on this surface to their name.
Polish Power(GER) Official explanation: jockey said horse was slowly away
Infinite Patience Official explanation: trainer said filly scoped dirty post race

4085 SEAFORD RUGBY FC FILLIES' H'CAP 1m 2f (P)
8:25 (8:26) (Class 5) (0-75,75) 3-Y-O+ **£2,729** (£806; £403) **Stalls** Low

Form RPR

-323 **1** **Queen Eleanor**[19] 3456 3-9-5 **75**.......................... RichardMullen 3 81
(J H M Gosden) *t.k.h: trckd ldrs: rdn ent fnl 2f out: swtchd rt and drvn jst over 1f out: r.o wl to ld on post* **7/1**

1220 **2** *nse* **Luck Will Come (IRE)**[14] 3627 5-9-11 **71**.................... JimmyQuinn 11 77
(H J Collingridge) *stdd after s: hld up in tch in last pair: hdwy on inner over 2f out: rdn to chal 1f out: drvn to ld ins fnl f: r.o: hdd on post* **9/2**[2]

-335 **3** 1 1/4 **Entreat**[41] 2738 3-9-2 **72**.......................... RyanMoore 12 76
(Sir Michael Stoute) *dwlt: sn pushed up to trck ldr: led 2f out: sn rdn: drvn and hrd pressed 1f out: hdd ins fnl f: no ex fnl 75yds* **11/4**[1]

5-34 **4** 1 1/4 **Kapsiliat (IRE)**[29] 3100 3-9-2 **72**.......................... TPQueally 2 73
(J Noseda) *t.k.h: hld up wl in tch in midfield: rdn and edging lft over 1f out: kpt on u.p fnl 100yds* **10/1**

6-32 **5** 3/4 **Brilliana**[19] 3456 3-9-5 **75**.......................... TedDurcan 5 75
(D R Lanigan) *in tch: rdn and effrt to dispute 3rd 2f out: unable qck and drvn over 1f out: kpt on again fnl 100yds* **14/1**

-160 **6** 1/2 **Supaverdi (USA)**[49] 2495 4-10-0 **74**.......................... SteveDrowne 8 73+
(H Morrison) *dwlt: short of room and eased bk after 1f: hld up wl in tch in rr: pushed along 4f out: rdn and no hdwy over 2f out: kpt on fnl 100yds: nvr pce to rch ldrs* **5/1**[3]

0005 **7** 1 **Leelu**[11] 3710 3-8-2 **58**.......................... KirstyMilczarek 7 55
(D W P Arbuthnot) *led at stdy gallop: rdn and hdd 2f out: wknd fnl f* **33/1**

-320 **8** 3/4 **Lady Brora**[58] 2212 4-9-13 **73**.......................... LPKeniry 10 68
(A M Balding) *dwlt: sn in tch on outer: rdn and unable qck bnd jst over 2f out: one pce and wl hld after* **8/1**

00-4 **9** 7 **Full Of Nature**[65] 2008 3-9-5 **75**.......................... EddieAhern 4 56
(S Kirk) *s.i.s: hld up in wl in tch in rr: drvn and dropped to last 3f out: lost tch wl over 1f out: eased wl ins fnl f* **8/1**

0-52 **10** 3 3/4 **Zeyadah (IRE)**[31] 3025 3-9-0 **70**.......................... ChrisCatlin 6 44
(M A Jarvis) *t.k.h: in tch tl lost pl and pushed along over 4f out: rdn and wl btn over 2f out: no ch whn hung rt and eased ins fnl f* **9/1**

2m 6.48s (-0.12) **Going Correction** +0.075s/f (Slow)
WFA 3 from 4yo+ 10lb **10** Ran SP% **124.9**
Speed ratings (Par 100): **103,102,101,100,100 99,99,98,92,89**
toteswingers: 1&2 £2.10, 1&3 £7.80, 2&3 £3.70. CSF £41.51 CT £111.98 TOTE £8.20: £2.60, £1.30, £1.80; EX 51.80 Place 6 £55.35, Place 5 £10.51.
Owner Cheveley Park Stud **Bred** Cheveley Park Stud Ltd **Trained** Newmarket, Suffolk

FOCUS
Punters were set a complex riddle to solve, as this looked an open event featuring a number of solid older handicappers alongside a smaller group of potential three-year-old improvers.
T/Plt: £60.50 to a £1 stake. Pool: £61,116.80. 736.75 winning tickets. T/Qpdt: £8.00 to a £1 stake. Pool: £6,804.78. 626.56 winning tickets. SP

4047 NEWBURY (L-H)
Saturday, July 18

OFFICIAL GOING: Soft (good to soft in places) changing to good to soft after race 2 (2.20)
Running rail moved out increasing distances by about 7yards on round course.
Wind: Moderate, ahead Weather: Overcast

4086 RACING UK CONDITIONS STKS 7f (S)
1:50 (1:50) (Class 3) 2-Y-O
£7,477 (£2,239; £1,119; £560; £279; £140) **Stalls** Centre

Form RPR

0113 **1** **Sir Parky (IRE)**[8] 3821 2-9-2 0.......................... RichardHughes 8 91
(R Hannon) *trckd ldrs: rdn and styd on fr over 1f out to take slt ld fnl 110yds: hld on wl* **11/4**[2]

13 **2** *nk* **Practitioner**[20] 3424 2-8-10 0 .... EddieAhern 6 84
(H J L Dunlop) *towards rr but in tch: rdn over 2f out: gd prog over 1f out: styd on and str chal fnl 110yds: no ex cl home* **5/1**[3]

31 **3** *1 ½* **Tukitinyasok (IRE)**[13] 3652 2-8-8 0 ow3 .... SladeO'Hara(5) 9 84
(R F Fisher) *sn led: shkn up 2f out: kpt on tl hdd fnl 110yds: edgd lft and wknd sn after* **11/2**

13 **4** *1 ½* **Sabii Sands (IRE)**[9] 3782 2-8-13 0 .... RyanMoore 3 80
(R Hannon) *lw: trckd ldr: drvn over 2f out: styd pressing ldrs tl wknd ins fnl f: wl hld whn carried lft cl home* **5/2**[1]

014 **5** *2* **Extreme Warrior (IRE)**[9] 3782 2-8-13 0 ....(b) ChrisCatlin 5 75
(D R Lanigan) *chsd ldrs: rdn over 2f out: wknd fnl f* **15/2**

00 **6** *3 ¾* **Petite Mambo**[9] 3785 2-8-10 0 .... PaulEddery 10 62?
(W De Best-Turner) *s.i.s: a outpcd* **100/1**

13 **7** *12* **Pycian**[22] 3340 2-8-13 0 .... TPQueally 7 35
(Mrs L Stubbs) *t.k.h: in tch: rdn 3f out: wknd over 2f out* **7/1**

1m 29.7s (4.00) **Going Correction** +0.45s/f (Yiel) **7** Ran SP% **112.5**
Speed ratings (Par 98): **95,94,92,91,88 84,70**
toteswingers: 1&2 £3.10, 1&3 £3.40, 2&3 £5.10. CSF £16.29 TOTE £3.10: £1.80, £2.60; EX 15.90.
Owner Sir David Seale **Bred** Swordlestown Stud **Trained** East Everleigh, Wilts
■ Stewards' Enquiry : Eddie Ahern four-day ban: used whip with excessive frequency (Aug 2-5)

FOCUS
The running rail was moved out increasing distances by about seven yards on the round course. 17.5mm of rain the previous day had turned the going soft. However, a warm, dry, breezy morning had improved conditions to Soft, Good to Soft in places. This could have resulted in making the going sticky and the winning rider reported the ground to be dead. Conditions were not helped by a headwind in the straight. The ground change after declaration time meant there were a large number of non-runners throughout the card. Sir Parky ran to form and the runner-up produced a marked step up.

NOTEBOOK
Sir Parky(IRE) lost out on favouritism to his stable companion, despite having the yard's number one rider on board, and battled on gamely to record his third success in five starts. A dual winner on fast going who had appeared to stay 7f on his previous run, the question was how he would handle the soft ground. He was giving weight all round and won well, despite not looking totally suited by the going. He is clearly a genuine sort who should win more races. (op 5-2 tchd 3-1 in a place)
Practitioner, a winner over 6f on fast ground, also had questions to answer regarding the ground and trip, although he is bred to get it. He picked up for pressure and came with a run between horses to challenge inside the final furlong, only to find the winner too strong near the line. (op 11-2 tchd 9-2)
Tukitinyasok(IRE), the only runner to have won over the trip, albeit on fast ground, made the running but started to hang as the race got serious and could find no extra when challenged. A return to faster ground will be in his favour. (op 15-2 tchd 8-1)
Sabii Sands(IRE) had proved effective at 6f on good and fast ground but was one of the first under pressure. He was probably beaten by the going rather than the extra furlong. (tchd 11-4)
Extreme Warrior(IRE), another 6f fast-ground winner, looked outclassed at this level and may do better in handicaps. (tchd 7-1 and 8-1)
Petite Mambo, who looked dull in his coat beforehand, had little chance on previous form and did not help his chance by missing the break.
Pycian was too keen early then drifted under pressure and dropped away over 1f out as if something was amiss. His rider reported that he was unsuited by the ground. Official explanation: jockey said gelding was unsuited by the soft (good to soft places) ground (op 15-2 tchd 13-2)

4087 SHADWELL STKS (REGISTERED AS THE HACKWOOD STAKES) (GROUP 3) 6f 8y
2:20 (2:21) (Class 1) 3-Y-O+

£36,900 (£13,988; £7,000; £3,490; £1,748; £877) **Stalls** Centre

Form RPR

-111 **1** **High Standing (USA)**[28] 3141 4-9-3 105 .... RyanMoore 11 118+
(W J Haggas) *lw: hld up towards rr but in tch: gd hdwy fr over 2f out: led 1f out: pushed along ins fnl f and sn in command: edgd rt cl home* **5/2**[1]

-100 **2** *1 ¼* **Prime Defender**[8] 3819 5-9-3 109 .... RobertWinston 7 114
(B W Hills) *chsd ldrs: drvn along fr 3f out: styd on u.p to take 2nd fnl 50yds but no ch w wnr* **5/1**[3]

-021 **3** *1 ¼* **Doncaster Rover (USA)**[14] 3621 3-8-12 103 .... SteveDrowne 14 109
(D H Brown) *in tch: rdn and one pce over 2f out: styd on fr over 1f out and tk 3rd fnl 50yds but nvr a threat to ldng duo* **6/1**

223- **4** *nk* **War Artist (AUS)**[372] 3922 6-9-3 115 .... TPQueally 8 109+
(J M P Eustace) *bit bkwd: sn led: rdn ins fnl 2f: hdd 1f out: wknd into 4th fnl 50yds* **3/1**[2]

-616 **5** *7* **Festoso (IRE)**[17] 3516 4-9-0 102 .... RichardMullen 1 84
(H J L Dunlop) *s.i.s: sn in tch: rdn over 2f out and sn btn* **10/1**

-003 **6** *7* **Edge Closer**[47] 2550 5-9-3 108 .... RichardHughes 3 64
(R Hannon) *lw: racd isolated towards far side but pressed ldr: ev ch over 2f out tl wknd qckly over 1f out: eased whn no ch* **12/1**

-060 **7** *2* **Madame Trop Vite (IRE)**[14] 3638 3-8-9 104 .... AlanMunro 13 54+
(K A Ryan) *chsd ldrs tl wknd qckly over 2f out* **14/1**

54 **8** *3 ¾* **Shallal**[21] 3388 4-9-3 96 .... LDettori 6 46
(P W Chapple-Hyam) *chsd ldrs tl wknd qckly over 2f out* **14/1**

1m 13.62s (0.62) **Going Correction** +0.45s/f (Yiel)
WFA 3 from 4yo+ 5lb **8** Ran SP% **114.6**
Speed ratings (Par 113): **113,111,109,109,99 90,87,82**
toteswingers: 1&2 £4.80, 1&3 £8.30, 2&3 £6.50. CSF £15.41 TOTE £3.10: £1.50, £1.70, £2.20; EX 15.70 Trifecta £79.40 Pool: £568.81- 5.30 winning units..
Owner Findlay & Bloom **Bred** Dr Melinda Blue **Trained** Newmarket, Suffolk

FOCUS
This competitive Group 3 sprint has either been won by a battle-hardened sprinter or an improver, with three-year-olds having a good record. This year's renewal fell to an improver, with High Standing taking another step forward. The placed horses set a solid standard.

NOTEBOOK
High Standing(USA) ◆, although his previous wins were on a sound surface or Polytrack, had no problem at all with the conditions and scored in what looked a decent time, having been settled off the pace. This was an emphatic success against a couple of good yardsticks and he will now go for a Group 3 at the Curragh. However, he looks the sort who could have a decent chance in something like the Betfred Sprint Cup at Haydock early in September. (tchd 9-4 and 11-4)
Prime Defender is a fair yardstick at Listed and Group 3 level and appeared to run his race, although proving no match for the winner. A slight note of caution is that, like the winner and fourth, his best form has been on fast going. (op 11-2 tchd 9-2)
Doncaster Rover(USA) is another who is best on a sound surface, although he does have some form on easier ground. He ran pretty well stepping up in grade against his elders and seems to be progressing with racing. (op 8-1)
War Artist(AUS) was having his first start since finishing third in the 2008 July Cup, having had several problems, not least of them colic. He showed plenty of dash on this return to action until getting tired in the ground in the last furlong, and looks more than capable of winning at this level back on a fast surface. He will go for a conditions race at Doncaster next. (tchd 4-1)
Festoso(IRE) goes well on this sort of ground but compromised her chance with a slow start and never got competitive. (op 9-1)
Edge Closer disputed the running with the fourth but could not respond to pressure and was eased down inside the last furlong. He tends to come to himself around August time and a return to faster ground may produce some improvement on his efforts so far this season. Richard Hughes reported that his mount had a breathing problem. Official explanation: jockey said horse had a breathing problem (op 10-1)
Madame Trop Vite(IRE), who was on her toes beforehand, chased the leaders early but was struggling a fair way from home (op 12-1)
Shallal, who had form on soft ground, showed up early but was under pressure at halfway and dropped away. His rider reported that he moved poorly throughout. Official explanation: jockey said colt moved poorly throughout (op 16-1 tchd 12-1)

4088 BATHWICK TYRES EBF FILLIES' STKS (H'CAP) 1m (S)
2:50 (2:52) (Class 2) (0-100,92) 3-Y-O+

£12,462 (£3,732; £1,866; £934; £466; £234) **Stalls** Centre

Form RPR

-110 **1** **Cosmopolitan**[10] 3749 4-9-10 **88** .... RichardMullen 11 96
(J H M Gosden) *trckd ldr: rdn to take narrow ld appr fnl f: hld on u.p thrght fnl f* **5/1**[3]

012 **2** *nk* **Ocean Transit (IRE)**[8] 3801 4-9-2 **80** .... JamesDoyle 12 87
(R J Price) *led: drvn 2f out: narrowly hdd appr fnl f: styd on to press wnr thrght fnl f: no ex cl home* **14/1**

-112 **3** *nk* **Full Of Love (IRE)**[57] 2248 3-8-9 **81** .... RobertWinston 3 86
(B W Hills) *stdd in rr and t.k.h early: drvn and hdwy fr over 2f out: styd on between horses ins fnl f and kpt on but nvr quite gng pce to rch ldng duo* **10/3**[1]

10-0 **4** *hd* **Club Tahiti**[37] 2846 3-8-13 **85** .... EddieAhern 2 89
(R Charlton) *t.k.h early and hld up in rr: rdn over 2f out: styd on wl thrght fnl f but nvr quite gng pce to chal nr fin* **11/1**

1423 **5** *½* **Silver Games (IRE)**[7] 3843 3-8-10 **87** .... MCGeran(5) 7 90
(M R Channon) *chsd ldrs: rdn over 2f out: styd on wl thrght fnl f: no ex cl home* **15/2**

2-21 **6** *shd* **Ainia**[30] 3060 4-8-7 **76** .... MartinLane(5) 13 81
(D M Simcock) *lw: chsd ldrs tl rdn and one pce over 2f out: styd on again u.p ins fnl f and kpt on cl home* **8/1**

1340 **7** *1 ¼* **Never Lose**[10] 3746 3-9-6 **92** .... RyanMoore 10 92
(C E Brittain) *s.i.s: hld up in tch: rdn and hdwy to chse ldrs 2f out but nvr quite on terms: one pce ins fnl f* **11/2**

01 **8** *4 ½* **Folly Lodge**[9] 3763 5-9-5 **83** .... GeorgeBaker 5 75
(R M Beckett) *lw: chsd ldrs: rdn 3f out: wknd over 1f out* **9/2**[2]

40-0 **9** *15* **Izzibizzi**[70] 1860 4-9-3 **81** .... TPQueally 9 40
(E A L Dunlop) *chsd ldrs: rdn 3f out: wknd sn after* **16/1**

1m 42.63s (2.93) **Going Correction** +0.45s/f (Yiel)
WFA 3 from 4yo+ 8lb **9** Ran SP% **117.1**
Speed ratings (Par 96): **103,102,102,102,101 101,100,95,80**
toteswingers: 1&2 £16.20, 1&3 £2.90, 2&3 £10.80. CSF £72.54 CT £268.86 TOTE £5.20: £2.00, £3.90, £1.40; EX 84.70 Trifecta £324.60 Pool: £658.16 - 1.50 winning units.
Owner H R H Princess Haya Of Jordan **Bred** G S Shropshire **Trained** Newmarket, Suffolk

FOCUS
The ground was officially changed to good to soft before this race. A decent, competitive fillies' handicap that produced a close finish, with the first six separated by only a length and a half. The runner-up helps with the level.

NOTEBOOK
Cosmopolitan was out of her depth in a Group 1 last time, but previously had a good record at a lower level and put up a game display to hold on, having been up with the pace throughout. She is steadily progressive and may be able to score at Listed level before too long. (op 4-1 tchd 11-2)
Ocean Transit(IRE) is another on the upgrade and ran another fine race over this longer trip, battling on bravely having been upsides the winner throughout. Her optimum trip had looked to be 7f, but this performance opens up more options. (op 12-1)
Full Of Love(IRE) is yet another improver but had been well beaten on her only previous try on soft ground. She came from the back and ran on well enough, but a return to a sounder surface will be in her favour. (op 9-2 tchd 3-1)
Club Tahiti ◆ was the eyecatcher of the race. Dropping back in trip having made her reappearance over 1m2f. She was held up off the pace and had to make her challenge on the outside of her field, slightly away from the main action. She finished strongly though, and this daughter of Hernando, named after the owners' resort in Lanzarote, should soon have her day in the sun. (tchd 14-1)
Silver Games(IRE) is a genuine and fairly consistent type and probably a fair guide to the level of this form. She had every chance before fading and a return to faster ground will be in her favour. (op 8-1 tchd 7-1)
Ainia, another consistent filly, had her chance but seemed to find the step up in grade too much in the closing stages. She can win more races at a lower level. (op 15-2 tchd 9-1)
Never Lose acts on easy ground but was stepping up in trip. Held up off the pace, she made some headway over a furlong out but could not sustain the effort. (op 13-2)
Folly Lodge was the disappointment of the race, having come into this with form on soft ground. She appeared to have every chance but weakened under pressure and appeared to find the step up in class beyond her. (op 5-1 tchd 11-2)
Izzibizzi had today's winner behind when scoring on soft ground here last October, but was well below that level of form here. (op 14-1)

4089 WEATHERBYS SUPER SPRINT 5f 34y
3:25 (3:26) (Class 2) 2-Y-O

£98,480 (£41,860; £19,700; £11,820; £7,860; £5,900) **Stalls** Centre

Form RPR

1115 **1** **Monsieur Chevalier (IRE)**[30] 3046 2-8-12 0 .... RichardHughes 2 105+
(R Hannon) *lw: towards rr and stl plenty to do 2f out: smooth hdwy wl over 1f out: qcknd smartly ins fnl f to ld fnl 30yds: cosily* **2/1**[1]

1 **2** *½* **Shamandar (FR)**[12] 3686 2-7-12 0 .... KirstyMilczarek 10 89+
(W J Haggas) *str: rrd stalls: bhd: swtchd rt to stands' side and hdwy fr 2f out: str run to ld fnl 110yds: hdd and outpcd fnl 30yds* **5/1**[2]

2153 **3** *1 ½* **Archers Road (IRE)**[8] 3805 2-8-7 0 .... SamHitchcott 23 93
(M R Channon) *chsd ldrs: rdn over 2f out: led appr fnl f: hdd and one pce fnl 110yds* **16/1**

2304 **4** *1 ½* **Red Avalanche (IRE)**[8] 3799 2-8-13 0 ....(t) LDettori 20 93
(P F I Cole) *rr: pushed along after 2f: hdwy over 1f out: styd on wl thrght fnl f: gng on cl home* **16/1**

2110 **5** *hd* **Here Now And Why (IRE)**[30] 3046 2-8-2 0 .... RichardMullen 24 82
(K A Ryan) *lw: in tch: chsd ldrs and one pce 2f out: styd on again fnl f: kpt on cl home* **14/1**

3260 **6** *1* **Star Rover (IRE)**[30] 3046 2-8-9 0 .... StephenDonohoe 13 85
(P D Evans) *led: hrd drvn fr 1/2-way: hdd appr fnl f: wknd fnl 110yds* **20/1**

1306 **7** *¾* **Kirsty's Boy (IRE)**[20] 3424 2-8-5 0 .... DO'Donohoe 11 78
(J S Moore) *towards rr: rdn along 1/2-way: hdwy appr fnl f: kpt on ins fnl f but nvr gng pce to rch ldrs* **66/1**

3 **8** *nk* **Chocolate Cookie (IRE)**[7] 3865 2-7-13 0 .... FrancisNorton 5 72+
(R Hannon) *s.i.s: in rr: hmpd 1/2-way: hdwy over 1f out: styd on ins fnl f but nvr in contention* **16/1**

316 **9** 1/2 **Above Limits (IRE)**[29] 3086 2-8-0 0........................ RichardKingscote 12 71
(Tom Dascombe) *lw: chsd ldr: drvn to chal fr 2f out: wknd ins fnl f* **7/1**[3]
3055 **10** 1 1/2 **Leleyf (IRE)**[8] 3807 2-8-5 0.. EdwardCreighton 17 70+
(M R Channon) *s.i.s: sn in tch: rdn and one pce whn hmpd over 1f out: no ex ins fnl f* **100/1**
0001 **11** *hd* **Eternal Instinct**[12] 3682 2-8-4 0.. AlanMunro 25 68
(J S Goldie) *chsd ldrs: rdn 1/2-way: wknd 1f out* **33/1**
1004 **12** *nse* **Desert Auction (IRE)**[7] 3842 2-8-10 0........................ SteveDrowne 18 74
(R Hannon) *lw: rr: sn pushed along: sme prog fnl f* **33/1**
6215 **13** *shd* **Palisades Park**[8] 3799 2-8-10 0.. RyanMoore 21 74
(R Hannon) *lw: trckd ldrs: rdn 2f out: no imp and wknd fnl f* **16/1**
2222 **14** 3/4 **Reddy To Star (IRE)**[23] 3317 2-8-5 0..........................(b[1]) EddieAhern 19 66
(C G Cox) *pressed ldrs: ev ch 2f out tl wknd 1f out* **25/1**
210 **15** *nk* **Itsthursdayalready**[32] 2995 2-8-7 0.. ChrisCatlin 8 67
(J G Given) *chsd ldrs: drvn to chal wl over 1f out: wknd fnl f* **40/1**
3103 **16** 1/2 **Existentialist**[20] 3430 2-8-3 0.. SaleemGolam 9 64+
(J G Portman) *s.i.s: in rr: hdwy 2f out: styng on whn hmpd ins fnl f and nt rcvr* **33/1**
1 **17** 3/4 **Reach For The Sky (IRE)**[54] 2328 2-7-12 0............. AdrianMcCarthy 3 54
(R Hannon) *chsd ldrs: rdn 1/2-way: wknd fnl f* **12/1**
2421 **18** *nse* **Social Grace**[7] 3849 2-7-12 0.. JamieKyne 7 53
(D H Brown) *sn rdn: outpcd* **33/1**
615 **19** 1/2 **Strike Shot**[36] 2875 2-8-12 0.. TPQueally 14 66
(W R Muir) *chsd ldrs: rdn 1/2-way: wknd over 1f out* **33/1**
3300 **20** 1 1/2 **French Connexion (IRE)**[20] 3424 2-7-12 0.................... SophieDoyle 1 46
(J S Moore) *a in rr* **100/1**

62.86 secs (1.46) **Going Correction** +0.45s/f (Yiel) **20** Ran SP% **129.6**
Speed ratings (Par 100): **106,105,102,100,100 98,97,96,96,93 93,93,93,91,91 90,89,89,88,86**
toteswingers: 1&2 £4.70, 1&3 £46.60, 2&3 £40.40. CSF £9.72 TOTE £3.20: £2.10, £2.30, £6.00; EX 17.60 Trifecta £508.00 Pool: £17,300.09 - 25.20 winning units.
Owner Mrs Valerie Hubbard & Ian Higginson **Bred** Tally-Ho Stud **Trained** East Everleigh, Wilts

FOCUS

This sales race always attracts a big field and is usually won by a really speedy juvenile, the best having been being Lyric Fantasy and Superstar Leo. The majority of winners had come from high numbered stalls, although two recent winners were drawn in box one. Richard Hannon had been responsible for six previous winners and eight placed horses and was represented by four this time, including the winner. The pace was strong and this is solid form with the third a good yardstick.

NOTEBOOK

Monsieur Chevalier(IRE) had the best form in the race, having won the Listed National Stakes at Sandown and finished fifth, after being hampered, in the Norfolk Stakes. He bounced back to winning ways here with an ultimately cosy success. He appeared to have a poor draw but Richard Hughes was at his coolest, switching inside and holding him up before producing him late on to collar the second well inside the last furlong. He looks worth another try at Group level and gives the impression another furlong will suit, so a race like the Richmond Stakes at Goodwood could be on the agenda. (op 11-4)

Shamandar(FR) ◆, whose trainer had won this twice in the last nine years, ran a terrific race on only her second start, especially considering she reared as the gates opened and lost a length or so. Given a good ride by Milczarek, she got across towards the stands' rail and looked the most likely winner when striking the front, only for the favourite to appear on her outside finishing more strongly. She was clear of the rest and looks up to winning a Listed race, possibly against her own sex, with the Firth Of Clyde at Ayr a suitable target. (op 9-2 tchd 11-2 in a place)

Archers Road(IRE), a useful multiple winner at 5f on a sound surface, had a good draw and ran another terrific race, striking the front over a furlong out and keeping on well when headed. He ran pretty close to Windsor May form with the winner, which suggests the form is solid. (op 20-1)

Red Avalanche(IRE), winner over 5f on easy ground (the only previous occasion he had encountered a soft surface) had a tongue tie on for the first time and a decent draw. He ran pretty well without quite having the pace of the principals.

Here Now And Why(IRE), a useful dual winner over 5f on fast ground and closely matched with the third on debut form, could not quite run to that level. He had a very good draw and performed quite well on his first encounter with a soft surface. (op 16-1)

Star Rover(IRE), a tough, consistent juvenile, didn't look great beforehand but raced up with the pace from the start and only faded out of it in the last furlong. This was a decent effort after a short break.

Kirsty's Boy(IRE), a 5f winner on good ground, had a lot to find with Star Rover on Ascot form but got much closer on this easier surface.

Chocolate Cookie(IRE) ◆ is one to take from the race. She came into this having made a promising debut at Salisbury but was dropping in trip, had a relatively poor draw and her lack of experience caused her to miss the break. She was then hampered by both the runner-up and fourth when trying to get a clear passage, before staying on towards the stands' side in the final furlong. She should be soon winning, probably back at 6f. (op 20-1 tchd 22-1)

Above Limits(IRE), a 5f winner on fast ground when her action and bandages suggested easier going might suit, had since finished ahead of a couple of her rivals in the Albany Stakes. On her toes beforehand, she showed plenty of pace on the front end, but was keen and always doing a little too much. She tired in the closing stages but could be useful if settling better in future. (op 6-1 tchd 8-1 in a place)

Reddy To Star(IRE) was on his toes in the paddock.

Existentialist was also on her toes in the preliminaries and the rider reported that she was denied a clear run. Official explanation: jockey said filly was denied a clear run

4090 SHADWELL BEECH HOUSE STUD STKS (REGISTERED AS THE STEVENTON STAKES) (LISTED RACE) 1m 2f 6y

3:55 (3:59) (Class 1) 3-Y-0+

£22,708 (£8,608; £4,308; £2,148; £1,076; £540) **Stalls** Low

Form RPR
1026 **1** **Crime Scene (IRE)**[43] 2677 6-9-3 113............................ AhmedAjtebi 5 112
(Saeed Bin Suroor) *led at mod pce: drvn over 2f out and styd on wl whn strly chal fr sn after: kpt on ins fnl f: edgd rt cl home* **25/1**
1-12 **2** 1 **Covert Ambition**[15] 3585 4-9-3 109.. LDettori 11 110
(Saeed Bin Suroor) *lw: trckd ldrs: shkn up and qcknd to chal travelling ok 2f out: sn rdn: no imp on wnr ins fnl f and readily hld whn swtchd lft cl home* **11/8**[1]
-666 **3** *hd* **Traffic Guard (USA)**[142] 698 5-9-3 114........................... EddieAhern 8 109
(P F I Cole) *t.k.h: in tch: hdwy over 2f out: drvn fr over 1f out: kpt on wl cl home to press for 2nd but nvr gng pce to rch wnr* **15/2**
012- **4** *nk* **Blue Monday**[266] 6980 8-9-3 115.................................... SteveDrowne 3 109+
(R Charlton) *bit bkwd: hld up in tch: hdwy over 2f out and sn rdn: styd on wl fr over 1f out and kpt on cl home but nvr gng pce to rch wnr* **9/2**[2]
0-00 **5** 2 1/4 **Smokey Oakey (IRE)**[14] 3639 5-9-3 102.......................... LiamJones 12 104
(M H Tompkins) *hld up in rr but in tch: pushed along and sme prog 2f out: nvr quite gng pce to rch ldrs but styd on fnl f* **7/1**
-365 **6** 1 1/2 **Heliodor (USA)**[56] 2277 3-8-9 102 ow2.......................... RichardHughes 10 103
(R Hannon) *hld up in rr but in tch: swtchd rt and sme hdwy over 2f out: sn rdn and nvr really on terms: wknd fnl f* **20/1**
020- **7** 2 3/4 **Mutajarred**[259] 7145 5-9-3 105.. RyanMoore 2 96
(W J Haggas) *b: trckd ldrs: rdn rdn over 2f out: no imp and wknd over 1f out* **5/1**[3]
-0 **8** 4 1/2 **Rock Ascot (URU)**[177] 261 5-9-3 95.................................... LPKeniry 7 87
(G L Moore) *trckd wnr tl rdn over 2f out: sn wknd* **50/1**

2m 12.06s (3.26) **Going Correction** +0.30s/f (Good)
WFA 3 from 4yo+ 10lb **8** Ran SP% **111.8**
Speed ratings (Par 111): **98,97,97,96,95 93,91,88**
toteswingers: 1&2 £6.60, 1&3 £14.50, 2&3 £2.80. CSF £55.52 TOTE £22.40: £3.60, £1.20, £2.20; EX 45.40.
Owner Godolphin **Bred** Gainsborough Stud Management Ltd **Trained** Newmarket, Suffolk
■ Prince Siegfried (10/1, bolted bef s) was withdrawn. R4 applies, deduct 5p in the £.

FOCUS

A good Listed race that usually falls to one of the major yards, and a tight-looking affair judged on official ratings. A number of these had questions to answer. It was dominated by the Godolphin pair, but not in the order the market anticipated. The pace was slow and this is not form to be too positive about.

NOTEBOOK

Crime Scene(IRE) won the St Simon Stakes here back in 2007 and had scored on easy going at Nad al Sheba in January this year. Well suited by the return to this ground, he made all on this drop in trip and found plenty when asked, despite wandering across his stable companion entering the last furlong. His trainer intends to keep him at this trip in the future. (op 14-1)

Covert Ambition won his maiden on easy ground and made a decent return in this trip and grade behind Kirklees at Sandown. However, he again lost out to a stable companion despite appearing to have every chance, and looks worth trying over 1m4f now. (op 7-4 tchd 15-8 and 2-1 in places)

Traffic Guard(USA) was having his first run since returning from Dubai in February and put up a decent performance, especially considering he was keen early on. He is capable of even better on this ground, witness his close second to New Approach in the Irish Champion Stakes, and this run should have put him right. (tchd 7-1 and 8-1)

Blue Monday likes this track and came into this with a record of two wins and two seconds in four runs here. He performed well on this first start since last October and presumably connections will be targeting the Arc Trial (which he has won twice in the past) back here in September, and the St Simon Stakes. (op 4-1 tchd 7-2)

Smokey Oakey(IRE) has been struggling since winning the 2008 Brigadier Gerard Stakes but the return to easier ground seemed to produce a better effort. (op 10-1 tchd 12-1)

Heliodor(USA), the only three-year-old remaining in therace, travelled well for some way but couldn't pick up. (op 18-1 tchd 16-1)

Mutajarred looked pretty fit beforehand despite having been off the track for 259 days but was disappointing. (op 6-1)

Rock Ascot(URU), having his first run in this country and his initial start for the trainer, was the first beaten. (op 66-1 tchd 40-1)

4091 SHADWELL "STANDING FOR SUCCESS" H'CAP 1m 2f 6y

4:30 (4:31) (Class 3) (0-95,95) 3-Y-0+

£7,477 (£2,239; £1,119; £560; £279; £140) **Stalls** Low

Form RPR
6604 **1** **King Charles**[36] 2891 5-9-9 **90**.. RichardHughes 8 101
(E A L Dunlop) *hld up in tch: pushed along over 2f out: hdwy over 1f out: rdn and styd on strly ins fnl f to ld fnl 75yds: sn in command* **11/2**[2]
-100 **2** 3/4 **Cheshire Prince**[35] 2932 5-9-7 **88**.. LiamJones 6 97
(W M Brisbourne) *led: rdn and styd on gamely whn strly chal fr over 2f out: hdd and nt pce of wnr fnl 75yds* **33/1**
1-02 **3** 1 3/4 **Safari Sunup (IRE)**[78] 1642 4-9-12 **93**........................ RobertWinston 10 99
(P Winkworth) *chsd ldr: drvn chal fr over 2f out tl ins fnl f whn outpcd into 3rd* **11/2**[2]
-000 **4** 3/4 **Heron Bay**[28] 3142 5-10-0 **95**... GeorgeBaker 4 99
(C F Wall) *lw: hld up in rr: hdwy over 2f out: styd on fr over 1f out and kpt on cl home but nvr gng pce to rch ldrs* **14/1**
0064 **5** 1/2 **Capable Guest (IRE)**[8] 3797 7-8-11 **78**......................(v) SamHitchcott 1 81
(M R Channon) *sn chsng ldrs: rdn along 3f out: styd on same pce fnl 2f* **16/1**
3-0 **6** *nk* **Jaser**[91] 1352 4-9-9 **90**... TPQueally 7 92
(P W Chapple-Hyam) *lw: chsd ldrs: rdn over 2f out: styd on same pce fr over 1f out* **15/2**[3]
000- **7** 2 1/4 **Monreale (GER)**[292] 6346 5-8-9 **76** oh1............................ VinceSlattery 9 74
(D E Pipe) *in rr: pushed along over 2f out: mod prog fnl f* **33/1**
-603 **8** *shd* **Dar Es Salaam**[15] 3564 5-8-11 **78**.. AlanMunro 3 76
(J S Goldie) *t.k.h early: chsd ldrs: rdn 3f out: wknd ins fnl 2f* **12/1**
0/13 **9** 3 **Bugaku**[45] 2597 4-9-10 **91**.. RyanMoore 11 83
(Sir Michael Stoute) *lw: chsd ldrs: rdn over 3f out: btn over 2f out* **11/8**[1]
/0-0 **10** 1 3/4 **Kevkat (IRE)**[45] 2597 8-9-6 **87**.................................... StephenDonohoe 5 75
(D E Pipe) *a towards rr* **33/1**
00 **11** *shd* **Final Verse**[7] 3872 6-9-9 **90**.. LPKeniry 2 78
(M Salaman) *t.k.h early: hld up in rr tl hdwy 3f out: drvn to chse ldrs sn after: wknd qckly ins fnl 2f* **16/1**

2m 10.31s (1.51) **Going Correction** +0.30s/f (Good)
WFA 3 from 4yo+ 10lb **11** Ran SP% **119.6**
Speed ratings (Par 107): **105,104,103,102,102 101,99,99,97,96 96**
toteswingers: 1&2 £29.80, 1&3 £4.30, 2&3 £28.80. CSF £177.81 CT £1037.62 TOTE £7.20: £2.00, £9.70, £2.00; EX 234.40.
Owner Khalifa Sultan **Bred** Hunscote House Farm Stud **Trained** Newmarket, Suffolk

FOCUS

Another good handicap that in previous runnings had tended to fall to an improving performer rated in the 80s. The pace was fairly sound and the time was 1.75secs faster than the preceding Listed race. The third and fourth help set the level.

NOTEBOOK

King Charles, who had not scored since September 2007, but had been contesting some hot handicaps, and had form on easy ground. Appreciating this less competitive contest, he travelled well off the pace and picked up once he got an opening to give Richard Hughes a treble on the day. (tchd 6-1)

Cheshire Prince is a Chester specialist, but has won elsewhere. He is suited by a faster surface, but was given an easy lead and kept finding for pressure, only to be run down late by the winner. He will probably go up for this, so may appear at Newmarket next Friday before his revised mark takes effect.

Safari Sunup(IRE) can be a little inconsistent, but he has won on this surface and he seemed to run his race, challenging the runner-up from fairly early in the straight and sticking on. He looks as if the Handicapper has his measure at present. (op 15-2)

Heron Bay has not won since taking the King George V Handicap at Royal Ascot over two years ago, but he was down to his lowest mark since winning that race. He has shown in the past that he handles cut in the ground and gave the impression he retains some ability with his effort here. (op 12-1 tchd 16-1)

Capable Guest(IRE), another on a long losing run, was under pressure a fair way out but stuck to his task and is well handicapped on his best form. (op 14-1)

Jaser likes this ground and travelled as if he would play a bigger part in the finish than he did. Perhaps the longer trip found him out. (op 8-1)

Bugaku, a big horse, had finished third to Covert Ambition, the runner-up in the preceding contest, on his latest start. However, that market confidence proved misplaced as he was under pressure soon after turning for home and finished well beaten. Ryan Moore could offer no explanation for the poor performance. Official explanation: jockey said he had no explanation for the poor form shown (op 2-1 tchd 5-4 and 9-4 in a place)

4092 SHADWELL "DUBAI SUMMER FESTIVAL" H'CAP — 2m

5:05 (5:05) (Class 4) (0-80,82) 4-Y-0+ £4,857 (£1,445; £722; £360) Stalls Low

Form				RPR
0446	1		**Aaim To Prosper (IRE)**[17] 3510 5-9-3 **76**......(v[1]) SamHitchcott 2	86
			(M R Channon) *in tch: hdwy 4f out: drvn to take slt ld over 2f out and kpt it whn persistently chal to the line: all out* **16/1**	
4404	2	*shd*	**Alnwick**[10] 3737 5-8-12 **71**...... AlanMunro 11	81
			(P D Cundell) *trckd ldr: drvn to chal fr over 2f out: and styd upsides wnr u.p tl no ex last stride* **17/2**	
/521	3	4 ½	**Swordsman (GER)**[3] 3986 7-8-13 **72** 6ex...... RichardHughes 6	76
			(C Gordon) *chsd ldrs: rdn over 3f out: styd on same pce fr over 1f out* **9/2**[3]	
52-0	4	4	**Absolut Power (GER)**[70] 1863 8-9-4 **77**...... TravisBlock 5	77
			(J A Geake) *drvn to ld and sn 6l clr: c wd to r alone in centre of crse over 4f out: kpt ld tl hdd over 2f out and edgd lft: wknd over 1f out* **20/1**	
5331	5	*shd*	**Cyborg**[8] 3814 5-9-9 **82**...... RyanMoore 3	82
			(D R C Elsworth) *lw: rr: hdwy 4f out: drvn to chse ldrs over 2f out: wknd over 1f out* **4/1**[2]	
-323	6	6	**Cleaver**[36] 2895 8-9-7 **80**...... GeorgeBaker 10	72
			(Lady Herries) *hld up in rr: pushed along fr 3f out: hd high: wandered lft and rt: nt keen and nvr in contention* **7/2**[1]	
0423	7	9	**Calculating (IRE)**[10] 3737 5-7-9 **61** oh8...... BillyCray[(7)] 4	43
			(M D I Usher) *c to centre of crse over 4f out: a towards rr:* **10/1**	
3621	8	3 ¼	**Isabelonabicycle**[10] 3737 4-8-12 **71**...... LPKeniry 7	49
			(A M Balding) *rr: sme prog 3f out: nvr in contention and sn wknd* **4/1**[2]	
0-40	9	6	**Winged D'Argent (IRE)**[65] 2018 8-9-2 **75**......(b) SteveDrowne 9	45
			(B J Llewellyn) *disp 2nd 6f out to 4f out: sn wknd* **16/1**	
40-5	10	1	**Converti**[9] 3788 5-7-11 **61** oh10......(b) SophieDoyle[(5)] 8	30
			(H J Manners) *in tch tl c towards centre of crse and wknd 4f out* **50/1**	

3m 33.85s (1.85) **Going Correction** +0.30s/f (Good) **10** Ran SP% **118.5**
Speed ratings (Par 105): **107,106,104,102,102 99,95,93,90,90**
toteswingers: 1&2 £20.70, 1&3 £13.00, 2&3 £8.40. CSF £147.26 CT £725.07 TOTE £16.50: £4.30, £2.10, £1.90; EX 125.90 Place 6 £60.63, Place 5 £19.08.
Owner CGA Racing Partnership 2 **Bred** Stephanie Hanly **Trained** West Ilsley, Berks

FOCUS
An ordinary staying handicap. The form is rated around the first two, who finished clear.
Isabelonabicycle Official explanation: jockey said filly was unsuited by the good to soft ground
T/Jkpt: Not won. T/Plt: £45.30 to a £1 stake. Pool: £133,920.48. 2,157.79 winning tickets. T/Qpdt: £15.70 to a £1 stake. Pool: £6,519.78. 307.30 winning tickets. ST

4054 NEWMARKET (R-H)

Saturday, July 18

OFFICIAL GOING: Good (good to soft in places; 7.5)
Wind: Fresh, across Weather: Cloudy with sunny spells

4093 LETTERGOLD MAIDEN STKS — 6f

2:00 (2:01) (Class 4) 2-Y-0 £5,180 (£1,541; £770; £384) Stalls High

Form				RPR
4	1		**Mr David (USA)**[21] 3403 2-9-3 0...... JamieSpencer 7	83
			(B J Meehan) *trckd ldrs: rdn to ld and hung lft ins fnl f: r.o* **7/4**[1]	
4	2	1 ¼	**Ghost (IRE)**[21] 3402 2-9-3 0...... MichaelHills 6	79
			(B W Hills) *led: rdn over 1f out: hung lft and hdd ins fnl f: styd on same pce* **7/1**[3]	
4	3	3	**Marine Spirit (GER)**[49] 2477 2-9-3 0...... TedDurcan 1	70
			(Saeed Bin Suroor) *chsd ldr: rdn over 1f out: no ex ins fnl f* **5/2**[2]	
	4	½	**Centigrade (IRE)** 2-9-3 0...... HayleyTurner 11	69+
			(W J Haggas) *hld up: hdwy over 1f out: r.o: nrst fin* **14/1**	
	5	3 ¼	**Comedy Hall (USA)** 2-9-3 0...... GregFairley 12	59+
			(M Johnston) *s.i.s: rn green in rr: rdn over 2f out: hdwy and hung lft over 1f out: wknd fnl f* **8/1**	
	6	½	**Waabel** 2-9-3 0...... RHills 2	58
			(M A Jarvis) *mid-div: hdwy over 2f out: hung lft and wknd over 1f out* **9/1**	
	7	¾	**Ongoodform (IRE)** 2-9-3 0...... ShaneKelly 3	55
			(P W D'Arcy) *s.s: hld up: sme hdwy over 1f out: n.d* **33/1**	
0	8	2 ¼	**Argyll**[21] 3402 2-9-3 0...... DaneO'Neill 9	49
			(J Pearce) *mid-div: rdn over 2f out: sn wknd* **100/1**	
	9	*nk*	**Lethal Combination (USA)** 2-9-3 0...... TonyCulhane 4	48
			(W J Haggas) *s.i.s: rn green in rr: hung lft over 2f out: n.d* **20/1**	
5	10	¾	**Captain Bluebird (IRE)**[10] 3744 2-9-3 0...... JimmyQuinn 8	45
			(D Donovan) *chsd ldrs: rdn over 2f out: wknd over 1f out* **66/1**	
0	11	½	**Precious Coral (IRE)**[8] 3820 2-8-12 0...... SimonWhitworth 14	39
			(S A Callaghan) *hld up: rdn: hung lft and wknd over 1f out* **100/1**	

1m 13.4s (0.90) **Going Correction** +0.075s/f (Good) **11** Ran SP% **116.4**
Speed ratings (Par 96): **97,95,91,90,86 85,84,81,81,80 79**
toteswingers: 1&2 £3.20, 1&3 £1.30, 2&3 £2.70. CSF £14.13 TOTE £2.70: £1.30, £1.90, £1.50; EX 12.80.
Owner Gold Group International Ltd **Bred** Mr & Mrs R David Randal **Trained** Manton, Wilts

FOCUS
A bright and breezy morning led to the ground drying out from soft overnight to good to soft, soft in places. Jockeys returning from the opener said that it was dead, tacky ground and the time was more than three seconds outside standard. The holding surface was always likely to test the juveniles in the opening race and very few got into it. It was no coincidence that the first three home all had the benefit of a previous run with their experience put to good use as they raced to the fore throughout. Not easy form to rate.

NOTEBOOK
Mr David(USA), a $155,000 breeze-up buy who was fourth of nine on his debut at Windsor, was entitled to be sharper both mentally and physically for this and paddock inspection revealed that he was ready for this, albeit slightly warm. He tracked the modest pace cut out early on by Ghost and did the job in professional fashion. He proved he handled easy ground, although connections said he won despite disliking the underfoot conditions. He will now be trained for a shot at the Gimcrack Stakes, and with his yard having such a strong hand of two-year-old colts this season, he would have to be respected in such company. (tchd 15-8 and 2-1 in places)
Ghost(IRE) made a relatively promising debut at Windsor where he was fourth to subsequent Superlative Stakes fourth Lucky General. That outing wasn't wasted and he lost nothing in defeat, made a valiant effort to make all and didn't go down without a fight, displaying a good attitude to suggest a similar race should come his way. (op 6-1)
Marine Spirit(GER) didn't enjoy the most straightforward of introductions at Goodwood in late May where he took a keen hold before being hit on the nose by a rival's whip. There were no such problems here as he raced prominently before not being able to go on with the first two home. (op 9-4 tchd 2-1)
Centigrade(IRE) ◆, who caught the eye in the paddock, while leaving the impression that he would physically benefit for a race, made a satisfactory debut in fourth. He was given a considerate introduction by his rider and there should be significant improvement to come. (op 16-1 tchd 12-1)
Comedy Hall(USA) is another from whom there should be good, solid progression from this first start. He was slowly away and had to make up a fair amount of ground, although he was helped by the modest early tempo. Understandably green for his racecourse bow, he should markedly step up on this effort next time. (op 16-1)
Waabel looked as if the race would tighten him up and displayed a fluent action to hint that a better surface would see him in a better light. (op 8-1 tchd 10-1)
Precious Coral(IRE)hung left under pressure and the vet reported that he had a breathing problem. Official explanation: vet said filly had a breathing problem

4094 PLANTATION STUD STKS (REGISTERED AS THE APHRODITE STAKES) (LISTED RACE) (F&M) — 1m 4f

2:35 (2:35) (Class 1) 3-Y-0+
£22,708 (£8,608; £4,308; £2,148; £1,076; £540) Stalls Centre

Form				RPR
4351	1		**Barshiba (IRE)**[14] 3619 5-9-9 108...... JamieSpencer 3	114
			(D R C Elsworth) *hung lft thrght: mde virtually all: rdn over 1f out: styd on wl* **9/2**[3]	
2352	2	3	**Princess Taylor**[33] 2974 5-9-2 97...... TedDurcan 5	103
			(M Botti) *a.p: rdn to chse wnr over 1f out: styd on same pce fnl f* **14/1**	
-433	3	3 ¾	**Uvinza**[30] 3047 3-8-4 101...... GregFairley 8	97
			(W J Knight) *trckd wnr racd keenly: rdn over 1f out: wknd ins fnl f* **17/2**	
212	4	4	**Flame Of Gibraltar (IRE)**[30] 3047 3-8-4 103...... JimmyQuinn 7	91
			(H R A Cecil) *hld up: rdn over 2f out: hdwy over 1f out: wknd fnl f* **15/8**[1]	
3-41	5	*shd*	**Splashdown**[37] 2846 3-8-8 102 ow1...... DaneO'Neill 9	95
			(L M Cumani) *prom: rdn over 2f out: hung lft and wknd over 1f out* **5/2**[2]	
4002	6	¾	**Syvilla**[23] 3315 4-9-2 90...... WilliamCarson 4	90
			(Rae Guest) *dwlt: hld up: rdn over 2f out: wknd over 1f out* **33/1**	
0203	7	3 ½	**Wadaat**[14] 3641 3-8-4 104...... HayleyTurner 1	84
			(C E Brittain) *prom: rdn over 3f out: wknd over 2f out* **14/1**	
1-40	8	1 ¾	**Mooakada (IRE)**[30] 3047 3-8-4 94...... RHills 2	82
			(J H M Gosden) *s.i.s: hld up: rdn over 2f out: wknd over 1f out* **11/1**	

2m 28.05s (-4.85) **Going Correction** -0.10s/f (Good)
WFA 3 from 4yo+ 12lb **8** Ran SP% **116.7**
Speed ratings (Par 111): **112,110,107,104,104 104,101,100**
toteswingers: 1&2 £7.80, 1&3 £7.80, 2&3 £15.90. CSF £64.80 TOTE £5.30: £1.70, £3.40, £2.40; EX 50.70 Trifecta £236.00 Pool: £382.72 - 1.20 winning units.
Owner J C Smith **Bred** Littleton Stud **Trained** Newmarket, Suffolk

FOCUS
An ordinary contest for the grade and once again it paid to race handily as the first three home were always the leading trio. The time was less than a second beyond standard, which was a good effort in the testing ground. A personal best from Barshiba.

NOTEBOOK
Barshiba(IRE) set the fractions throughout. She goes from strength to strength and this win was every bit as convincing as her success in the Lancashire Oaks two weeks earlier. What makes it all the more notable is the weight - both for age and the 7lb penalty for her Group 2 win - that she was giving to her rivals. Once again the forcing tactics worked a treat and, if anything, she travelled even better here than at Haydock where she was somewhat keen. She is a stakes winner over both 1m2f and 1m4f and will now come under consideration for the Nassau Stakes and the Yorkshire Oaks, where she will have to take on an altogether different class of filly.
Princess Taylor three career wins have come on a sounder surface but she is proving versatile as to ground, backing up a second-place effort in similar conditions in the same grade at Warwick with another solid effort. Despite running consistently, she may just be the sort who always finds one better each time. (op 11-1)
Uvinza, who always runs with credit and this was the third race on the trot that she has made the frame in stakes company. She turned the tables on Ribblesdale Stakes second Flame Of Gibraltar, having been a length and quarter behind her at Royal Ascot. She deserves success in Listed company at least, but probably needs to find a little more improvement, which she is open to, as a three-year-old. (op 12-1)
Flame Of Gibraltar(IRE) was one of the first off the bridle and didn't travel nearly as well as she did in the Ribblesdale. Perhaps it was the ground as she was clearly weary through the final strides. However, with this being only the fourth race of her life, she is certainly shouldn't be written off. (op 2-1, tchd 9-4 in places)
Splashdown who while never competitive on the day, probably found the ground against her. She impressed with the tenacious style of her victory in Listed company at Newbury and should fare better back on a sounder surface. (op 11-4 tchd 7-2)
Syvilla was never a factor stepped up in trip.
Mooakada(IRE) is becoming something of a disappointment after her Newmarket debut success last autumn but Richard Hills reported that she had a breathing problem. Official explanation: jockey said filly had a breathing problem (op 14-1)

4095 ADNAMS H'CAP — 1m

3:05 (3:06) (Class 2) (0-100,89) 3-Y-0 £12,462 (£3,732; £1,866; £934) Stalls High

Form				RPR
-035	1		**Bravo Echo**[28] 3163 3-9-3 **83**...... RobertHavlin 5	89
			(J H M Gosden) *trckd ldr: rdn to ld over 1f out: styd on* **6/1**[3]	
142	2	½	**Sunshine Always (IRE)**[21] 3394 3-9-1 **81**...... TonyCulhane 8	86
			(W J Haggas) *hld up: hdwy over 2f out: rdn and ev ch over 1f out: styd on* **6/5**[1]	
0-41	3	*hd*	**Aim To Achieve (IRE)**[23] 3297 3-8-7 **74**...... MichaelHills 3	78
			(B W Hills) *led: rdn over 2f out: edgd rt and hdd over 1f out: styd on* **6/1**[3]	
2-12	4	4 ½	**Maswerte (IRE)**[14] 3643 3-9-2 **82**...... DaneO'Neill 7	77
			(L M Cumani) *trckd ldrs: rdn over 2f out: styd on same pce appr fnl f* **15/8**[2]	

1m 40.58s (0.58) **Going Correction** +0.075s/f (Good) **4** Ran SP% **108.8**
Speed ratings (Par 106): **100,99,99,94**
toteswingers: 1&2 £7.50. CSF £13.81 TOTE £7.70; EX 15.50.
Owner K Abdulla **Bred** Juddmonte Farms Ltd **Trained** Newmarket, Suffolk

FOCUS
The steady early gallop contributed to a time that was approaching four seconds beyond standard. The winner is rated back to his better juvenile form.

NOTEBOOK
Bravo Echo, a striking-looking colt, he was in danger of becoming expensive to follow this season after impressing with the style of his maiden success at Leicester last backend. The step up to a mile and the ease in the ground were probably both in his favour as he wore down the third and then repelled Sunshine Always. He responded gamely to his rider's urgings - albeit with a slight flick of the tail - and maybe, having got his head back in front, will build on this further. (tchd 5-1)

Sunshine Always(IRE) did nothing wrong in suffering this reverse, although his followers have seen him turned over as favourite in two of his last three starts. He is likely to edge up the handicap again after another narrow defeat, but is still open to improvement and should add to his sole career victory. (op 6-4 tchd 13-8 and 15-8 in a place)
Aim To Achieve(IRE) is another lightly raced type who should build on her Kempton maiden win, secured on her previous start. Handed a mark of 74 for her first crack at handicaps, she tried to make all and went down by only a length. The Handicapper is unlikely to alter her rating and she should keep on progressing to make her of interest in future races. (op 9-2)
Maswerte(IRE) was involved in quite a battle when finishing second at Sandown a couple of weeks ago and that may have left a mark on him. The ground may also have been a little on the soft side for him, given that his sole career win came on a fast surface at Newbury. This was his first crack at 1m, which may also stretch his stamina. (tchd 7-4)

4096 EUROPEAN BREEDERS' FUND FILLIES' H'CAP 6f
3:35 (3:36) (Class 3) (0-95,93) 3-Y-0+
£9,346 (£2,799; £1,399; £700; £349; £175) **Stalls** High

Form RPR
41-3 **1** **Bounty Box**[40] 2774 3-8-11 **78** ... TedDurcan 1 89+
(C F Wall) *trckd ldrs: led over 1f out: sn rdn: edgd lft and r.o wl* **9/2**[2]
-200 **2** *2 1/2* **Crystal Moments**[28] 3145 3-9-4 **85** ... JamieSpencer 5 88
(E A L Dunlop) *hld up: hdwy over 1f out: hrd rdn ins fnl f: no imp* **14/1**
000 **3** *1/2* **Quiet Elegance**[34] 2941 4-9-3 **79** ... JimmyQuinn 13 81
(E J Alston) *hld up: rdn over 1f out: r.o wl ins fnl f: nt rch ldrs* **12/1**
-026 **4** *1/2* **Brierty (IRE)**[32] 2999 3-8-12 **79** ... GregFairley 3 78
(D Carroll) *chsd ldrs: rdn 1/2-way: styd on u.p* **12/1**
0132 **5** *shd* **Pretty Bonnie**[22] 3360 4-9-8 **87** ... NataliaGemelova(3) 4 87
(A E Price) *chsd ldrs: rdn over 1f out: styd on* **13/2**[3]
-000 **6** *1 1/4* **Gentle Guru**[8] 3795 5-9-3 **79** ... DaneO'Neill 6 75
(R T Phillips) *hld up: hdwy u.p and hung lft over 1f out: nt trble ldrs* **10/1**
3625 **7** *1 1/4* **Act Green**[9] 3763 3-8-8 **75** ...(v) HayleyTurner 7 66
(M L W Bell) *hld up: hdwy 1/2-way: sn rdn: wknd over 1f out* **9/1**
6210 **8** *nk* **Mango Music**[19] 3453 6-9-1 **77** ... PatCosgrave 2 68
(M Quinn) *led: hdd over 2f out: rdn and ev ch over 1f out: wknd ins fnl f* **10/1**
4141 **9** *nk* **Doric Lady**[15] 3565 4-9-4 **80** ... RobertHavlin 8 70
(J A R Toller) *prom: rdn and ev ch over 1f out: wknd ins fnl f* **4/1**[1]
0-01 **10** *hd* **Raggle Taggle (IRE)**[22] 3360 3-9-12 **93** ... RHills 12 82
(R M Beckett) *chsd ldr tl led over 2f out: rdn: edgd lft and hdd over 1f out: wknd ins fnl f* **13/2**[3]

1m 12.1s (-0.40) **Going Correction** +0.075s/f (Good)
WFA 3 from 4yo+ 5lb **10** Ran SP% **115.1**
Speed ratings (Par 104): **105,101,101,100,100 98,96,96,96,95**
toteswingers: 1&2 £11.70, 1&3 £18.30, 2&3 £39.60. CSF £64.58 CT £720.46 TOTE £5.40: £1.80, £3.40, £5.10; EX 66.80.
Owner John E Sims **Bred** Farmers Hill Stud **Trained** Newmarket, Suffolk

FOCUS
A soundly run race for this decent handicap. A nice effort from the winner and the form looks solid in behind.

NOTEBOOK
Bounty Box returned over 5f last month to finish a respectable third of six at Windsor. She was entitled to strip fitter for her second race of the year and underfoot conditions were similar to her maiden win, with the step back up to 6f also likely to suit, judged on her two-year-old form. She broke smartly to track the speed cut out by Mango Music and quickened decisively over 1f out. She ran on in the final strides, and is an improving filly who it is likely to pay to stay on the right side of. Ease in the ground would appear to be a significant plus for this daughter of Bahamian Bounty and there is likely to be more to come. (op 10-3)
Crystal Moments, for whom this marked something of a return to form, had lost her way somewhat after a reappearance second to Swiss Diva at Lingfield back in early May. However, down 5lb since finishing last of ten at Ayr, she produced a much-improved effort. She is now just 1lb higher than her best winning mark and has to be of interest next time, particularly if returned to the all-weather. on which she has enjoyed a fair degree of success. (op 16-1 tchd 12-1)
Quiet Elegance benefited from the true tempo as she came from way out the back to finish her race strongly. She had previously done nothing to write home about this season, but this was encouraging for her connections. (op 14-1)
Brierty(IRE) fared respectably on this drop back to 6f, having raced over 7f and 1m earlier this year. (tchd 14-1)
Pretty Bonnie moved well to post, but may now be in the grip of the Handicapper. (op 5-1)
Act Green has apparently regressed since breaking her maiden at Great Leighs last autumn with this drop to 6f bringing about no improvement. In mitigation, her last two runs have been with cut in the ground and it may well be that she is better suited by a faster surface. (op 12-1)
Doric Lady gave way late on as she was unable to build on her win at Doncaster earlier in the month. Maybe a return to the minimum trip will suit, although she has gone up 7lb this season. (op 9-2, tchd 5-1 in places)
Raggle Taggle(IRE) was successful in a conditions race over course and distance last month but weakened away under top weight. (op 8-1)

4097 NATIONAL STUD MAIDEN STKS 7f
4:10 (4:11) (Class 4) 3-Y-0 **£5,180** (£1,541; £770; £384) **Stalls** High

Form RPR
2 **1** **Penitent**[9] 3764 3-9-3 0 ... ShaneKelly 9 87+
(W J Haggas) *dwlt: hld up: hdwy 3f out: led over 1f out: rdn and r.o wl* **11/8**[1]
43 **2** *2 3/4* **Truly Asia (IRE)**[26] 3221 3-9-3 0 ... HayleyTurner 3 80+
(R Charlton) *hld up: hdwy over 1f out: r.o: nt trble wnr* **12/1**
3 *nk* **El Ameen** 3-9-3 0 ... GregFairley 8 79+
(M Johnston) *sn prom: rdn over 2f out: hung lft over 1f out: r.o* **12/1**
2- **4** *1/2* **Great Art (IRE)**[428] 2146 3-9-3 0 ... JamieSpencer 4 78
(P W Chapple-Hyam) *hld up: hdwy over 2f out: hrd rdn and edgd rt over 1f out: no ex ins fnl f* **5/1**[3]
5 *3/4* **Paisley** 3-8-12 0 ... DaneO'Neill 7 71+
(L M Cumani) *s.i.s: bhd: hdwy over 1f out: r.o: nt rch ldrs* **25/1**
030 **6** *nk* **Sahaal (USA)**[20] 3425 3-9-3 75 ... RHills 10 75
(M P Tregoning) *chsd ldr: led 3f out: rdn: edgd lft and hdd wl over 1f out: no ex ins fnl f*
26-3 **7** *1* **Equinine (IRE)**[37] 2849 3-8-12 68 ... MichaelHills 12 67
(B W Hills) *prom: led wl over 1f out: sn rdn and hdd: wknd ins fnl f* **7/2**[2]
06-6 **8** *6* **Isabella Romee (IRE)**[11] 3711 3-8-12 52 ... MichellePayne 11 51
(Jane Chapple-Hyam) *chsd ldrs: rdn over 2f out: wknd over 1f out* **80/1**
34 **9** *1 1/4* **Miss Kittyhawk (IRE)**[13] 3660 3-8-7 0 ... WilliamCarson(5) 5 48
(Rae Guest) *prom: rdn over 2f out: sn wknd* **25/1**
0-0 **10** *5* **Cativo**[75] 1745 3-8-11 0 ow2 ...(t) JamesMillman(3) 6 36
(B R Millman) *led: hdd 3f out: rdn and wkng whn hung lft over 1f out* **100/1**
11 *6* **Dancing Ghost (IRE)** 3-8-12 0 ... TGMcLaughlin 1 18
(Jane Chapple-Hyam) *s.s: outpcd* **40/1**
12 *18* **Lhashan** 3-8-12 0 ... TonyCulhane 2 —
(M A Jarvis) *chsd ldrs tl wknd over 2f out* **33/1**

1m 25.7s **Going Correction** +0.075s/f (Good) **12** Ran SP% **118.3**
Speed ratings (Par 102): **103,99,99,98,98 97,96,89,88,82 75,55**
toteswingers: 1&2 £5.60, 1&3 £4.50, 2&3 £12.10. CSF £19.16 TOTE £2.40: £1.30, £2.90, £2.90; EX 20.40.
Owner Cheveley Park Stud **Bred** Cheveley Park Stud Ltd **Trained** Newmarket, Suffolk

FOCUS
They went a proper pace throughout with the time reflecting the going description. This was an above-average three-year-old maiden for the time of year with the winner building on his good debut effort.
Great Art(IRE) Official explanation: jockey said colt hung right closing stages

4098 NEWMARKETRACECOURSES.CO.UK H'CAP 1m 6f 175y
4:45 (4:46) (Class 4) (0-85,83) 4-Y-0+ **£5,828** (£1,734; £866; £432) **Stalls** Centre

Form RPR
5046 **1** **Jadalee (IRE)**[3] 3977 6-8-11 **71** ...(p) ShaneKelly 3 80
(G A Butler) *mde all: rdn over 1f out: styd on wl* **7/1**
3100 **2** *3* **Clear Reef**[8] 3822 5-9-7 **81** ...(p) MichellePayne 6 86
(Jane Chapple-Hyam) *chsd wnr: rdn over 1f out: styng on same pce whn hung rt wl ins fnl f* **11/2**[3]
4633 **3** *1* **Solas Alainn (IRE)**[10] 3731 4-8-5 **65** ...(b) GregFairley 1 69
(M Johnston) *chsd ldrs: rdn over 2f out: styd on same pce fnl f* **11/2**[3]
1232 **4** *6* **Saloon (USA)**[21] 3380 5-9-1 **75** ...(p) JamieSpencer 5 71
(Jane Chapple-Hyam) *hld up and bhd: hdwy over 2f out: sn rdn: wknd fnl f* **10/3**[2]
0501 **5** *1 1/4* **Sam Lord**[20] 3423 5-9-9 **83** ... DaneO'Neill 7 77
(A King) *prom: racd keenly: rdn over 2f out: wknd over 1f out* **5/2**[1]
-303 **6** *2 1/2* **Look To This Day**[20] 3423 4-8-11 **71** ...(p) HayleyTurner 4 62
(R Charlton) *hld up: rdn over 3f out: wknd over 1f out* **7/1**
2600 **7** *dist* **Aegean Prince**[10] 3734 5-9-3 **77** ... JimmyQuinn 2 —
(P Howling) *hld up and bhd: lost tch fnl 6f: eased fnl 2f* **20/1**

3m 7.59s (-3.71) **Going Correction** -0.10s/f (Good) **7** Ran SP% **112.2**
Speed ratings (Par 105): **105,103,102,99,99 97,—**
toteswingers: 1&2 £9.40, 1&3 £6.60, 2&3 £6.70. CSF £42.77 TOTE £8.40: £3.90, £3.70; EX 53.80.
Owner Brian Shrubsall & Stef Stefanou **Bred** Hawthorn Villa Stud **Trained** Newmarket, Suffolk

FOCUS
This staying handicap was a steadily run race in which the time was more than four seconds beyond standard. The winner only had to reproduce this year's AW form.
Aegean Prince Official explanation: jockey said gelding returned lame

4099 TURFTV H'CAP 5f
5:20 (5:20) (Class 3) (0-95,95) 3-Y-0+ **£9,714** (£2,890; £1,444; £721) **Stalls** High

Form RPR
1 **Biniou (IRE)**[63] 2094 6-9-13 **95** ... JamieSpencer 3 111
(R M H Cowell) *dwlt: hld up: hdwy over 1f out: rdn to ld and hung rt ins fnl f: r.o wl* **4/1**[3]
0211 **2** *2 1/4* **Mattamia (IRE)**[22] 3362 3-9-1 **90** ... JamesMillman(3) 2 97
(B R Millman) *led: rdn over 1f out: hdd and unable qck ins fnl f* **9/2**
-016 **3** *3* **Dragon Flame (IRE)**[35] 2929 6-8-3 **76** oh3 ... WilliamCarson(5) 10 73
(M Quinn) *prom: pushed along 1/2-way: hrd rdn over 1f out: hung lft ins fnl f: styd on* **9/1**
5010 **4** *nk* **Bahamian Babe**[28] 3166 3-9-2 **88** ... HayleyTurner 1 83
(M L W Bell) *chsd ldr: rdn 2f out: no ex fnl f* **8/1**
2315 **5** *3/4* **Affluent**[28] 3145 3-9-1 **87** ... DaneO'Neill 8 79
(R Charlton) *trckd ldrs: rdn over 1f out: no ex* **5/2**[1]
115 **6** *nk* **Equuleus Pictor**[15] 3582 5-9-2 **89** ... JackDean(5) 9 81
(J L Spearing) *chsd ldrs: rdn over 1f out: no ex ins fnl f* **11/4**[2]

58.59 secs (-0.51) **Going Correction** +0.075s/f (Good)
WFA 3 from 4yo+ 4lb **6** Ran SP% **114.5**
Speed ratings (Par 107): **107,103,98,98,96 96**
toteswingers: 1&2 £2.20, 1&3 £5.00, 2&3 £6.90. CSF £22.53 CT £151.23 TOTE £4.20: £2.20, £2.50; EX 12.70 Place 6 £1,026.59, Place 5 £843.14.
Owner Stennett, Dasmal, Rix, Barr, Mrs Penney **Bred** Kilfrush And Knocktoran Studs **Trained** Six Mile Bottom, Cambs

FOCUS
The pace was strong despite the small field. Biniou returned towards his better form.

NOTEBOOK
Biniou(IRE)put up a smart performance and defied a 5lb rise in the weights for his Thirsk win to land this in a time less than a second beyond standard. Twice a Listed winner in soft conditions in France, he relished getting his toe in here to come from last to first after missing the break. He overcame top weight with the minimum of fuss to lead inside the final furlong and all the evidence suggests that he may just remain ahead of the Hhandicapper for the time being, granted his favoured underfoot conditions. Connections will now target the Stewards' Cup, in which he'd have to carry a penalty for his latest win. (op 7-2 tchd 3-1)
Mattamia(IRE) had previously recorded successive wins and ran another cracking race, easily beating all bar Biniou. He remains very much of interest and shouldn't be too long in adding to his tally of three career wins, especially given that he is versatile as to ground. Official explanation: jockey said gelding hung right (op 4-1 tchd 7-2)
Dragon Flame(IRE) ran a respectable race and is probably now in the grip of the Handicapper. (op 8-1 tchd 13-2)
Bahamian Babe, another who is held by the assessor, has also shown best form on a fast surface. (op 15-2 tchd 7-1)
Affluent gained a commanding handicap success at Windsor in May but found the surface too quick – according to her jockey – when failing to land a blow last month at Ayr. Dropped 3lb in the handicap, there were no such excuses here on that account and she was well supported. However, she could never get competitive and it looks as if the Handicapper also has her measure. (op 3-1 tchd 4-1)
Equuleus Pictor, who is suited by cut in the ground, is 4lb higher than for his last success and faded out of it late on. (op 10-3 tchd 4-1)
T/Plt: £1,811.50 to a £1 stake. Pool: £84,992.12. 34.25 winning tickets. T/Qpdt: £219.70 to a £1 stake. Pool: £4,899.49. 16.50 winning tickets. CR

3685 RIPON (R-H)
Saturday, July 18

OFFICIAL GOING: Soft (heavy in places)
Wind: Fresh, half behind Weather: Overcast

4100 EUROPEAN BREEDERS' FUND MAIDEN FILLIES' STKS 5f
2:30 (2:32) (Class 4) 2-Y-0 **£5,180** (£1,541; £770; £384) **Stalls** Low

Form RPR
5202 **1** **Fly Silca Fly (IRE)**[13] 3658 2-9-0 0 ... TPO'Shea 10 73
(M R Channon) *mde all: rdn 2f out: styd on strly fnl f* **7/4**[1]

The Form Book, Raceform Ltd, Compton, RG20 6NL

2 2 1/4 **Tell Me A Story** 2-8-7 0 .... JohnCavanagh(7) 1 65
(M Brittain) *pressed wnr: effrt over 2f out: kpt on same pce ins fnl f* **16/1**

60 3 1 1/2 **Lady Lefroy (IRE)**[18] 3487 2-9-0 0 .... TonyHamilton 12 60
(R A Fahey) *prom: effrt over 2f out: kpt on same pce fnl f* **7/2**[2]

4 1 **Cross Key (IRE)** 2-9-0 0 .... PaulHanagan 6 56+
(R A Fahey) *in tch: rn green and outpcd over 2f out: kpt on steadily fnl f: no imp* **5/1**[3]

0 5 2 1/4 **Summa Cum Laude**[14] 3606 2-9-0 0 .... SebSanders 13 48
(Mrs A Duffield) *chsd ldrs tl rdn and wknd over 1f out* **11/2**

0 6 3 1/2 **Miss Roma (IRE)**[83] 1534 2-8-11 0 .... AndreaAtzeni(3) 5 35
(R A Harris) *unruly bef s: rrd s: bhd: hdwy and in tch over 2f out: wandered and wknd over 1f out* **25/1**

7 9 **Kookie** 2-9-0 0 .... TomEaves 3 3
(R E Barr) *s.v.s: nvr on terms* **12/1**

8 15 **Superior Service** 2-8-11 0 ow2 .... JamesO'Reilly(5) 7 —
(C C Bealby) *uns rdr and loose leaving paddock: s.i.s: sn wl bhd* **12/1**

62.27 secs (1.57) **Going Correction** +0.15s/f (Good) **8** Ran SP% **115.8**
Speed ratings (Par 93): **93,89,87,85,81 76,61,37**
toteswingers: 1&2 £6.10, 1&3 £1.50, 2&3 £8.60. CSF £33.41 TOTE £2.50: £1.10, £2.50, £1.60; EX 36.50 Trifecta £38.40 Pool: £166.31 - 3.20 winning units.
Owner Aldridge Racing Partnership **Bred** Glenlogan Park Stud **Trained** West Ilsley, Berks

FOCUS

The meeting did well to survive considering the course had taken 62.5mm of rain over the previous 36 hours. The rail on the bend out of the back straight had been moved out five yards. Testing conditions for these juvenile fillies, described as slow and tacky by the riders.

NOTEBOOK

Fly Silca Fly(IRE) put her experience to good use and made just about all the running. Her efforts in maidens either side of being outclassed at Royal Ascot gave her a sound chance in this company, and she coped with the ground well enough to get off the mark. Her trainer has now sent out three winners of this race in the last six years. (op 15-8 tchd 9-4)

Tell Me A Story, out of that prolific racemare Cantina and is a half-sister to Miss Lovat, who won over this trip at two, shaped with plenty of promise on this debut. She looks to have inherited plenty of speed and should be able to find a little race. (tchd 12-1)

Lady Lefroy(IRE), who was well supported, ran a fair race back in third, but she will have better opportunities in nurseries. (op 6-1)

Cross Key(IRE), a half-sister to a sprint winner in Italy, looked the stable's first string on paper, but she was weak in the market and ran green. There should be better to come from her with this outing under her belt. (op 10-3)

Summa Cum Laude, in contrast to her debut, showed up prominently for a long way but didn't see her race out. She probably needs a bit more time. Official explanation: jockey said filly hung left (op 13-2)

Miss Roma(IRE) reared up as the stalls opened and almost unseated her rider. (op 33-1)

Kookie was very slowly away and gave them all a huge head start. (op 16-1)

4101 GO RACING IN YORKSHIRE (S) STKS 6f

3:00 (3:00) (Class 6) 2-Y-O **£1,680** (£1,680; £385; £192) **Stalls** Low

Form RPR

6654 1 **Drumpellier (IRE)**[11] 3709 2-7-13 0 .... PaulPickard(7) 5 60
(P T Midgley) *mde all: rdn 2f out: kpt on fnl f: jnd post* **3/1**[1]

520 1 *dht* **Pure Nostalgia (IRE)**[27] 3187 2-8-7 0 ow1 .... PaulMulrennan 3 61
(J Howard Johnson) *prom: effrt over 2f out: kpt on wl fnl f to dead-heat on post* **3/1**[1]

065 3 5 **Flashy Lover (IRE)**[25] 3240 2-8-6 0 .... TPO'Shea 7 45
(M R Channon) *t.k.h: cl up tl rdn and nt qckn fr 2f out* **9/2**[2]

4 1/2 **Patachou** 2-8-3 0 .... AndreaAtzeni(3) 1 44
(Rae Guest) *dwlt: bhd and outpcd: hdwy fr 2f out: nvr able to chal* **11/2**

5 *nk* **Drinking Buddy** 2-8-11 0 .... (t) NCallan 6 48
(K A Ryan) *dwlt: bhd and drvn along: hdwy 1/2-way: no imp fr 2f out* **5/1**[3]

0 6 20 **Nicosia**[33] 2978 2-8-6 0 .... PaulHanagan 9 —
(M R Channon) *s.i.s: a outpcd and bhd: eased whn no ch fnl f* **14/1**

00 7 2 1/2 **Three Sons**[11] 3719 2-8-11 0 .... (b) DanielTudhope 8 —+
(I W McInnes) *t.k.h early: chsd ldrs: wkng whn hmpd over 2f out: eased whn no ch fnl f* **25/1**

000 8 6 **Ron The Don**[18] 3478 2-8-11 0 .... PhillipMakin 2 —
(A Berry) *in tch tl rdn and wknd fr 1/2-way: eased whn no ch fnl f* **33/1**

1m 15.65s (2.65) **Going Correction** +0.25s/f (Good) **8** Ran SP% **113.7**
Speed ratings (Par 92): **92,92,85,84,84 57,54,46**WIN: Drumpellier £1.90, Pure Nostalgia £2.20; PL: D £1.20, PN £1.60, FL £1.60; EX: D-PN £5.70, PN-D £6.00; CSF: D-PN £5.87, PN-D £5.87; toteswingers: D&PN £2.10, 1&3 (D) £1.80, 1&3 (PN) £2.60. TRIFECTA D-PN-FL £2027 Owner.There was no bid for the winner.
Owner Transcend Bloodstock LLP **Bred** Chesters Stud Ltd **Trained** Billy Row, Co Durham
■ Stewards' Enquiry : Paul Mulrennan four-day ban: used whip with excessive frequency (Aug 2-5)

FOCUS

A bit of a guessing game with these two-year-olds on the ground, but two of the runners with most experience ended up fighting it out, and the judge couldn't split them. The dead-heaters finished clear.

NOTEBOOK

Drumpellier(IRE) appreciated the return to 6f, raced a touch keenly at the head of affairs, but kept responding to pressure. She clearly appreciates some give in the ground, having previously run her best race on good to soft at York. (tchd 7-2)

Pure Nostalgia(IRE) had run on good to firm ground in her previous three starts and, being by Choisir out of a mare who did her winning on good ground or quicker, this testing surface was far from certain to suit. She saw her race out strongly, though, joining Drumpellier on the line, and some will argue that the 1lb overweight put up by her rider was the difference between dead-heating and winning outright. (tchd 7-2)

Flashy Lover(IRE), who was weak in the betting, took too much out of herself in racing keenly and didn't see her race out. (op 3-1)

Patachou, a sister to a winner over 1m and a half-sister to multiple 7f-1m winner Trafalgar Square, ran green but showed some ability on her debut. (op 8-1)

Drinking Buddy, who is out of a mare who won seven times over 6f and 7f, also showed signs of inexperience on his debut. (op 4-1)

4102 SKY BET SUPPORTING THE YORKSHIRE RACING FESTIVAL H'CAP 1m 1f 170y

3:30 (3:30) (Class 4) (0-85,85) 3-Y-O **£6,938** (£2,076; £1,038; £519; £258) **Stalls** High

Form RPR

1-20 1 **Distant Memories (IRE)**[35] 2935 3-9-2 83 .... MickyFenton 1 96
(T P Tate) *t.k.h early: cl up: led over 3f out: drvn and kpt on strly fnl 2f* **4/1**[2]

6213 2 3 3/4 **Mr Freddy (IRE)**[28] 3156 3-8-4 71 .... PaulHanagan 10 76
(R A Fahey) *cl up: effrt and ev ch 3f out: kpt on same pce appr fnl f* **3/1**[1]

2340 3 2 1/2 **Moheebb (IRE)**[7] 3872 5-9-8 79 .... (b) PaulMulrennan 2 79
(Mrs R A Carr) *prom: rdn over 2f out: sn no imp: styd on to take 3rd cl home* **9/1**

1-35 4 1/2 **Raaeidd (IRE)**[14] 3644 3-9-1 82 .... PhilipRobinson 12 81
(M A Jarvis) *hld up: hdwy to chse ldrs over 2f out: sn rdn and one pce: lost 3rd cl home* **4/1**[2]

0313 5 1/2 **Kingsdale Orion (IRE)**[3] 3977 5-9-0 76 .... LanceBetts(5) 8 74
(B Ellison) *in tch: drvn and outpcd 3f out: no imp fr 2f out* **4/1**[2]

3362 6 15 **Lady Rangali (IRE)**[15] 3560 4-9-10 81 .... SebSanders 5 47
(Mrs A Duffield) *hld up in tch on outside: rdn over 3f out: wknd over 2f out* **8/1**[3]

3320 7 2 1/4 **Wind Shuffle (GER)**[24] 3265 6-9-8 79 .... DanielTudhope 6 40
(J S Goldie) *led to 3f out: wkng whn n.m.r over 2f out* **12/1**

2m 6.59s (1.19) **Going Correction** +0.25s/f (Good)
WFA 3 from 4yo+ 10lb **7** Ran SP% **113.8**
Speed ratings (Par 105): **105,102,100,99,99 87,85**
toteswingers: 1&2 £1.80, 1&3 £11.60, 2&3 £6.90. CSF £16.25 CT £99.64 TOTE £4.20: £2.30, £2.40; EX 14.90 Trifecta £173.30 Part won. Pool: 234.25 - 0.86 winning units..
Owner Mrs Fitri Hay **Bred** Kildaragh Stud **Trained** Tadcaster, N Yorks
■ Stewards' Enquiry : Paul Hanagan caution: careless riding.

FOCUS

The three-year-olds dominated the betting and it was one of that trio that came out on top.

4103 RIPON BELL-RINGER H'CAP 1m 4f 10y

4:00 (4:01) (Class 2) (0-100,93) 3-Y-O **£15,577** (£4,665; £2,332; £1,167) **Stalls** High

Form RPR

-142 1 **Kings Destiny**[42] 2715 3-9-4 90 .... PhilipRobinson 6 102+
(M A Jarvis) *mde all: shkn up and qcknd clr 2f out: eased towards fin* **11/4**[2]

0221 2 2 1/4 **Lady Artemisia (IRE)**[25] 3250 3-8-10 82 .... PaulMulrennan 2 89
(M L W Bell) *t.k.h early: chsd ldrs: effrt and chsd wnr over 3f out: rdn and one pce fr over 1f out* **9/1**

0631 3 2 3/4 **Zaaqya**[16] 3535 3-8-13 85 .... TPO'Shea 5 88
(J L Dunlop) *t.k.h early: prom: rdn and outpcd 3f out: no imp fr 2f out* **13/2**[3]

21-1 4 25 **Fortuni (IRE)**[78] 1643 3-9-6 92 .... SebSanders 3 57+
(Sir Mark Prescott) *trckd wnr: rdn 4f out: wknd 2f out: lost tch and eased fnl f* **4/6**[1]

2m 39.95s (3.25) **Going Correction** +0.35s/f (Good) **4** Ran SP% **110.0**
Speed ratings (Par 106): **103,101,99,83**
toteswingers: 1&2 £8.80. CSF £20.96 TOTE £3.30; EX 12.80.
Owner Dennis Yardy **Bred** D A Yardy **Trained** Newmarket, Suffolk

FOCUS

An interesting handicap despite the small field. It's never wise to let Philip Robinson have his own way out in front, but that's what happened here and he was able to dictate from start to finish.

NOTEBOOK

Kings Destiny was allowed the run of thing out in front but he quickened away in the closing stages, only having to be pushed out to score, and on this steadily progressive gelding will soon be rated in the 100s. Effective on quick ground as well as soft, he looks the type to bag a big handicap before the season is out. (op 2-1 tchd 3-1)

Lady Artemisia(IRE) briefly threatened to throw down a challenge to the winner two furlongs out, but she was soon left behind. It wasn't a bad effort on her handicap debut, but perhaps better ground suits her ideally. (op 7-1 tchd 13-2)

Zaaqya, who had been put up 8lb for winning narrowly at Newbury last time, didn't look at home in these much softer conditions, as she looked to be making heavy weather of it from some way out. (op 4-1)

Fortuni(IRE) was the big disappointment of the race. A St Leger entry suggested connections have a high opinion of him, and in that light a 14lb rise in the weights for his Lingfield success, taking him to a mark of 92, looked perfectly fair. However, despite being well supported, he never looked likely to land the odds, struggling from some way out on his turf debut. Perhaps he just didn't handle the conditions, as he is surely better than this. Official explanation: trainer had no explanation for the poor form shown (op 5-4 tchd 11-8)

4104 GO RACING IN YORKSHIRE SUMMER FESTIVAL H'CAP 1m

4:35 (4:35) (Class 4) (0-85,86) 3-Y-O **£6,938** (£2,076; £1,038; £519; £258) **Stalls** High

Form RPR

2-50 1 **Keys Of Cyprus**[24] 3265 7-9-5 76 .... PaulQuinn 8 85+
(D Nicholls) *t.k.h: hld up: hdwy 2f out: squeezed through appr fnl f: led wl ins fnl f: comf* **13/2**

4550 2 1/2 **Ilie Nastase (FR)**[7] 3846 5-10-1 86 .... (b) AndrewMullen 7 93
(D Nicholls) *t.k.h: led: rdn over 2f out: hdd ins fnl f: r.o* **5/1**[2]

02-0 3 *hd* **Celtic Step**[36] 2894 5-9-4 75 .... DavidAllan 13 81
(P D Niven) *w ldr: rdn over 2f out: led briefly ins fnl f: kpt on* **8/1**

5236 4 1 1/4 **Gala Casino Star (IRE)**[7] 3872 4-9-13 84 .... (v[1]) PaulHanagan 10 88
(R A Fahey) *t.k.h early: prom: drvn over 2f out: kpt on same pce fnl f* **5/2**[1]

6150 5 *nk* **Spinning**[7] 3872 6-9-11 82 .... (b) PhillipMakin 11 85
(T D Barron) *missed break: bhd: rdn and outpcd 3f out: rallied over 1f out: no imp ins fnl f* **6/1**[3]

-000 6 2 1/4 **Nevada Desert (IRE)**[30] 3067 9-8-12 72 .... MichaelJStainton(3) 14 70
(R M Whitaker) *t.k.h early: trckd ldrs: drvn over 2f out: no imp fr over 1f out* **12/1**

413 7 4 1/2 **Salerosa (IRE)**[31] 3019 4-8-9 66 .... PaulMulrennan 1 54
(Mrs A Duffield) *t.k.h early: hld up in tch: effrt over 2f out: wknd over 1f out* **7/1**

0130 8 *nk* **Fesko**[7] 3872 3-9-3 82 .... TPO'Shea 12 70
(M Johnston) *trckd ldrs tl rdn and wknd wl over 1f out* **17/2**

1m 43.83s (2.43) **Going Correction** +0.45s/f (Yiel)
WFA 3 from 4yo+ 8lb **8** Ran SP% **114.7**
Speed ratings (Par 105): **105,104,104,103,102 100,96,95**
toteswingers: 1&2 £7.00, 1&3 £10.10, 2&3 £8.90. CSF £38.95 CT £266.77 TOTE £9.20: £2.60, £2.20, £2.90; EX 34.30 Trifecta £128.60 Pool: £285.04 - 1.64 winning units.
Owner The Beasley Gees **Bred** Juddmonte Farms **Trained** Sessay, N Yorks
■ Stewards' Enquiry : David Allan one-day ban: careless riding (Aug 2)
Andrew Mullen two-day ban: used whip with excessive frequency without giving gelding time to respond (Aug 2-3)

FOCUS

There was no great gallop on and the place to be was at the front. In the circumstances the winner did well to catch the front pair.

Keys Of Cyprus Official explanation: jockey said gelding hung right

Spinning Official explanation: jockey said gelding never travelled

4105 MIKE RIDGWAY WINS WITH THE YORKSHIRE POST MAIDEN H'CAP 6f

5:10 (5:10) (Class 5) (0-70,65) 3-Y-O+ **£3,885** (£1,156; £577; £288) **Stalls** Low

Form RPR

6002 1 **Only A Splash**[12] 3683 5-8-9 48 .... PaulMulrennan 15 56
(Mrs R A Carr) *mde all: rdn over 2f out: edgd lft ins fnl f: hld on wl* **5/1**[2]

005 2 *nk* **Cardinal**[28] 3175 4-8-13 55 .... AndreaAtzeni(3) 2 62
(R A Harris) *hld up: gd hdwy over 1f out: kpt on wl fnl f* **6/1**[3]

3 1 1/4 **Minnola**107 1077 4-9-2 **55** MickyFenton 4 58
(Rae Guest) *in tch: effrt over 2f out: hdwy and edgd rt over 1f out: r.o fnl f* **13/2**

6-06 4 1/2 **Nino Zachetti (IRE)**31 3018 3-8-4 **48** PatrickMathers 8 49
(E J Alston) *prom: rdn over 2f out: effrt over 1f out: kpt on same pce ins fnl f* **18/1**

0330 5 2 1/4 **Lost In Paris (IRE)**10 3727 3-9-1 **59** (b) DavidAllan 13 53
(T D Easterby) *pressed wnr: rdn over 2f out: no ex fnl f* **9/2**1

3400 6 hd **Imperial Djay (IRE)**10 3730 4-8-10 **49** (p) DanielTudhope 6 44
(J R Holt) *in tch: rdn and edgd rt over 1f out: one pce fnl f* **7/1**

0400 7 1 1/4 **La Gifted**31 3018 3-8-9 **53** TPO'Shea 10 43
(M R Channon) *midfield: effrt over 2f out: no imp over 1f out* **8/1**

0-00 8 2 1/4 **Our Apolonia (IRE)**29 3108 3-7-11 **48** CharlotteKerton(7) 17 31
(A Berry) *bhd and early reminders: sme late hdwy: nvr on terms* **20/1**

/0-0 9 1/2 **Pretty Orchid**22 3338 4-8-11 **50** TonyHamilton 12 33
(P T Midgley) *chsd ldrs tl rdn and wknd fr 2f out* **28/1**

-460 10 5 **Rossett Rose (IRE)**10 3729 3-8-2 **53** JohnCavanagh(7) 1 20+
(M Brittain) *racd centre to stands' side: hung rt to join main gp 1/2-way: nvr on terms* **14/1**

-050 11 1/2 **Venetian Lady**53 2365 3-8-6 **50** PaulHanagan 18 15
(Mrs A Duffield) *trckd ldrs: rdn over 2f out: wknd over 1f out* **16/1**

00-0 12 nk **Home Before Dark**19 3449 3-8-4 **48** PaulQuinn 20 12
(R M Whitaker) *trckd ldrs tl rdn and wknd fr 2f out* **20/1**

000- 13 3/4 **Monsieur Jourdain (IRE)**297 6214 3-8-10 **54** DuranFentiman 7 16
(T D Easterby) *dwlt: bhd and sn rdn along: nvr on terms* **25/1**

6-00 14 2 **Dark Velvet (IRE)**39 2786 3-8-11 **60** (b1) GaryBartley(5) 5 16+
(E J Alston) *dwlt and swtchd to r alone stands' side sn after s: nvr on terms* **20/1**

60-0 15 2 3/4 **Ready For Battle (IRE)**12 3689 3-9-1 **59** JamieMoriarty 11 7
(D W Thompson) *bhd: drvn over 3f out: nvr on terms* **40/1**

1m 14.91s (1.91) **Going Correction** +0.35s/f (Good)
WFA 3 from 4yo+ 5lb **15** Ran SP% **127.9**
Speed ratings (Par 103): **101,100,98,98,95 95,93,90,89,83 82,81,80,78,74**
toteswingers: 1&2 £8.90, 1&3 £9.10, 2&3 £5.40. CSF £33.46 CT £211.03 TOTE £4.90: £1.90, £2.60, £2.90; EX 41.00 Trifecta £47.10 Pool: £149.18 - 2.34 winning units. Place 6 £89.41, Place 5 £56.42.
Owner David W Chapman **Bred** Mrs M J Hills **Trained** Huby, N Yorks

FOCUS
With the top three in the weights non-runners, this was effectively a 0-60 maiden handicap. The majority of the field raced up the far-side rail, with only Dark Velvet racing up the stands' side. Rossett Rose started racing half-heartedly towards the stands' side before edging over to race with the far-side group at around halfway. Both finished well held.
Venetian Lady Official explanation: jockey said filly hung left in straight
T/Plt: £108.10 to a £1 stake. Pool: £67,839.54. 457.70 winning tickets. T/Qpdt: £92.10 to a £1 stake. Pool: £3,075.10. 24.70 winning tickets. RY

4106 - 4112a (Foreign Racing) - See Raceform Interactive

3908MAISONS-LAFFITTE (R-H)
Saturday, July 18

OFFICIAL GOING: Good to soft

4113a PRIX MESSIDOR (GROUP 3) (STRAIGHT) 1m (S)
2:35 (2:37) 3-Y-0+ **£38,835** (£15,534; £11,650; £7,767; £3,883)

RPR

1 **Alnadana (IRE)**42 2703 4-8-12 CSoumillon 4 112
(A De Royer-Dupre, France) *mde all: qckng clr fnl f: pushed out* **4/5**1

2 3 **Mr Brock (SAF)**30 3085 6-9-1 DBoeuf 1 108
(Mme C Head-Maarek, France) *disputing 2nd: 3rd 1/2-way: drvn 1 1/2f out and dropped bk: rallied fnl f to take 2nd on line* **9/1**

3 hd **Putney Bridge (USA)**78 1658 4-9-1 SPasquier 5 108
(Mme C Head-Maarek, France) *cl up disputing 2nd: 2nd 1/2-way: pushed along over 2f out: rdn and nt pce of wnr fr over 1f out: lost 2nd on line* **32/5**

4 1/2 **Chopastair (FR)**56 2292 8-9-1 JVictoire 6 106
(T Lemer, France) *in tch in 4th on outside: effrt 1 1/2f out: styd on at one pce* **49/10**2

5 1 1/2 **Dovil Boy (IRE)**26 3230 3-8-7 C-PLemaire 7 101
(S Wattel, France) *racd in 5th: last 1/2-way: pushed along 2f out: rdn over 1f out: nt pce of ldrs* **59/10**3

6 shd **Rainbow Dancing**51 2428 4-8-12 TJarnet 3 100
(Mlle H Van Zuylen, France) *hld up in last: 5th 1/2-way: pushed along 1 1/2f out: nvr in chalng position* **15/1**

1m 38.7s (-3.60)
WFA 3 from 4yo+ 8lb **6** Ran SP% **116.8**
PARI-MUTUEL: WIN 1.80; PL 1.40, 2.60; SF 12.20.
Owner H H Aga Khan **Bred** Haras De Son Altesse L'Aga Khan Scea **Trained** Chantilly, France

NOTEBOOK
Alnadana(IRE) never gave connections a moment of anxiety in landing her first Group event. Slowish into her stride, she was soon up with the pace and then dominated the race from 2f out. The others never got a look in, she was in a class of her own and looks capable of making it at an even higher level. Connections are not sure of her next race but she has been entered in the Beverly D Stakes at Arlington Park.
Mr Brock(SAF) ran a little free early on and begun a progressive run from two out. He stayed on bravely to beat his stablemate by a narrow margin for second place and looks to be settling down well in France. A similar race may well come his way in the future.
Putney Bridge(USA) enjoys running over the straight mile at this track. Third in the early stages in a slowly run race, he was given every chance and only lost second place late on.
Chopastair(FR) was probably unsuited by a poor early gallop. He was one paced in the final stages and never looked like filling a better pace.

3539REDCAR (L-H)
Sunday, July 19
4114 Meeting Abandoned - Waterlogged

4121 - 4127a (Foreign Racing) - See Raceform Interactive

2757DUSSELDORF (R-H)
Sunday, July 19

OFFICIAL GOING: Soft

4128a DEUTSCHLAND-PREIS (GROUP 1) 1m 4f
3:35 (3:51) 3-Y-0+ **£87,379** (£33,981; £16,505; £8,252; £4,369)

RPR

1 **Getaway (GER)**21 3441 6-9-6 SHellyn 1 119+
(J Hirschberger, Germany) *first to show: settled a cl 3rd on ins to st: qcknd between ldrs to ld appr fnl f: r.o wl* **23/10**3

2 3/4 **Flamingo Fantasy (GER)**21 3441 4-9-6 ASuborics 5 117
(W Hickst, Germany) *hld up in 6th but a wl in tch: hdwy and 4th st: r.o steadily on outside fr over 1f out to take 2nd on line* **19/10**1

3 nse **Appel Au Maitre (FR)**17 5-9-6 FJohansson 4 117
(Wido Neuroth, Norway) *pressed ldr on outside: 2nd st: tk narrow ld 1 1/2f out: hdd appr fnl f: lost 2nd on line* **74/10**

4 2 1/2 **Kamsin (GER)**21 3441 4-9-6 AStarke 3 113
(P Schiergen, Germany) *led after 1f tl hdd 1 1/2f out: styd on same pce* **11/5**2

5 1 3/4 **Ambassador (GER)**21 3441 5-9-6 THellier 7 110
(T Mundry, Germany) *cl 4th to st: one pce fr over 1f out* **14/1**

6 4 1/2 **Tres Rapide (IRE)**56 2309 4-9-3 DBoeuf 6 100
(H-A Pantall, France) *hld up in last pl but a wl in tch: 6th st: nvr a factor* **57/10**

7 26 **Download (GER)**21 3441 4-9-6 HGrewe 2 61
(R Gross, Germany) *racd in 5th tl wkng over 3f out: last st: sn wl bhd* **26/1**

2m 28.51s (-1.03) **7** Ran SP% **133.2**
(including ten euro stakes): WIN 33; PL 15, 14, 14; SF 131.
Owner Baron G Von Ullmann **Bred** Baron G Von Ullmann **Trained** Germany

NOTEBOOK
Getaway(GER), having his second run since joining Jens Hirschberger from Andre Fabre, came back to something like his best with a stylish win. The Arc will be his target again.

1718FRANKFURT (L-H)
Sunday, July 19

OFFICIAL GOING: Soft

4129a FRAPORT AG-POKAL (GROUP 3) 1m
4:00 (4:48) 3-Y-0+ **£31,068** (£9,709; £4,854; £2,913)

RPR

1 **Sehrezad (IRE)**22 3416 4-9-0 JiriPalik 6 114
(Andreas Lowe, Germany) *disp 4th: hdwy on outside on fnl turn to ld 3f out: brought wd ent st: easily* **7/5**1

2 9 **Querari (GER)**22 3416 3-8-8 ow2 EPedroza 1 94
(A Wohler, Germany) *hld up: hdwy on ins and 3rd st: no ch w wnr fr over 1f out* **37/10**3

3 3 **Konig Concorde (GER)**22 3416 4-9-2 LennartHammer-Hansen 7 88
(C Sprengel, Germany) *6th st on ins: kpt on one pce* **12/1**

4 1 3/4 **Iolith (GER)**22 3416 4-9-2 AGoritz 2 84
(J Hirschberger, Germany) *rdn to take early ld: sn hdd and settled in 4th: 4th st: sn btn* **31/10**2

5 2 **Waky Love (GER)**18 3520 5-8-13 FilipMinarik 5 76
(P Schiergen, Germany) *hld up in rr to st: no hdwy* **43/5**

6 12 **Abbashiva (GER)**27 3231 4-9-4 NRichter 4 54
(T Mundry, Germany) *led after 1f: hdd 3f out: 2nd st: trckd wnr over towards stands' side: sn btn* **124/10**

7 1 1/2 **Setareh (GER)**14 4-9-2 PConvertino 8 48
(P Olsanik, Germany) *trckd ldrs tl wkng over 3f out* **17/1**

8 nk **Forthe Millionkiss (GER)**22 3416 5-9-6 DPorcu 3 52
(Uwe Ostmann, Germany) *pressed ldr to 1/2-way: 5th st: sn btn: eased fnl f* **68/10**

1m 39.02s (99.02)
WFA 3 from 4yo+ 8lb **8** Ran SP% **131.3**
(including ten euro stakes): WIN 24; PL 13, 26, 23; SF 89.
Owner Stall Phillip **Bred** Acorn Stud **Trained** Germany

VICHY
Sunday, July 19

OFFICIAL GOING: Very soft

4130a PRIX EQUIDIA 10ANS - PRIX DE NERIS LES BAINS (MAIDEN) (FILLIES) 1m
1:30 (1:30) 3-Y-0 **£10,194** (£4,077; £3,058; £2,039; £1,019)

RPR

1 **Madonna Incognito (USA)** 3-8-10 FPrat(6) 73
(F Rohaut, France)

2 1/2 **Fait Accompli (GER)**48 3-9-2 FBlondel 72
(J E Hammond, France)

3 snk **Libia (IRE)**27 3-8-10 GMasure(6) 72
(C Laffon-Parias, France)

4 2 1/2 **Beguiler** 3-8-12 MGuyon 62
(H-A Pantall, France)

5 hd **Dame Anouska (IRE)**22 3417 3-9-2 TThulliez 65
(E J O'Neill) *sn pressing ldrs: wnt 2nd after 3f: tk narrow ld 1 1/2f out: rdn and hdd ent fnl f: one pce* **51/10**1

6 2 **Freeze Style (FR)**30 3-9-2 MNobili 61
(B Dutruel, France)

7 1 1/2 **Olga D'Or (USA)**227 7549 3-9-2 (p) SPasquier 57
(R Gibson, France)

8 1/2 **Rosa Rosa (FR)** 3-8-12 LProietti 52
(X Betron, France)

9 6 **La Fee Merchante (FR)** 3-9-2 (p) NRomeo 42
(P Khozian, France)

10 4 **Alrescha (IRE)** 3-9-2 ....(p) TPiccone 33
(B Dutruel, France)
11 **Maille Tartare (FR)** 3-8-12 .... J-MSanchez 29
(Mme A Charbonnier, France)
1m 42.94s (102.94) 11 Ran SP% **16.4**
PARI-MUTUEL (including one euro stakes): WIN 4.80; PL 1.90, 2.40,2.20; DF 22.00.
Owner BS Racing Sarl **Bred** Mrs B & L Mabee **Trained** Sauvagnon, France

3909 AYR (L-H)

Monday, July 20

OFFICIAL GOING: Good (7.0)
A sprint-only card following the problems on the bend at the previous meeting.
Wind: Fresh, half against Weather: Overcast, showers

4131 BUD AND JOE PIERONI MEMORIAL H'CAP 6f

2:30 (2:33) (Class 5) (0-70,70) 3-Y-O **£3,070** (£906; £453) **Stalls** Low

Form RPR
1243 1 **Minturno (USA)**[12] [3729] 3-9-2 **65** ....(p) PaulMulrennan 6 68+
(Mrs A Duffield) *t.k.h: trckd ldrs: effrt over 1f out: led ins fnl f: r.o* **11/4**[1]
0 2 ¾ **Battimoore (IRE)**[21] [3449] 3-8-2 **51** oh2 .... WMLordan 5 52
(Daniel Mark Loughnane, Ire) *led to ent fnl f: kpt on u.p* **7/1**
552 3 shd **Exceed Elegance (IRE)**[13] [3704] 3-8-11 **60** .... FrancisNorton 7 61
(D Shaw) *t.k.h: w ldr: led briefly ent fnl f: kpt on fin* **4/1**[3]
0162 4 2¾ **Go Alone (IRE)**[12] [3729] 3-9-7 **70** .... PJMcDonald 2 62
(G A Swinbank) *trckd ldrs: effrt 2f out: one pce fnl f* **3/1**[2]
602- 5 2¼ **Pacific Bay (IRE)**[306] [6017] 3-9-2 **65** .... TonyHamilton 8 50
(R A Fahey) *trckd ldrs tl rdn and no ex over 1f out* **3/1**[2]
0050 6 4½ **Fifth Amendment**[16] [3614] 3-8-7 **61** ow1 .... SladeO'Hara(5) 4 31
(A Berry) *cl up: lost pl 1/2-way: sn rdn and wknd* **33/1**
1m 13.17s (-0.43) **Going Correction** -0.075s/f (Good) **6** Ran SP% **112.1**
Speed ratings (Par 100): **99,98,97,94,91 85**
toteswingers: 1&2 £3.20, 1&3 £1.90, 2&3 £3.60. CSF £21.76 CT £74.37 TOTE £3.80: £1.70, £2.80; EX 23.80.
Owner Trevor Wilson **Bred** Robert C Francis **Trained** Constable Burton, N Yorks

FOCUS
This was a modest 3yo sprint. The winner basically ran to from although the runner-up is a slight worry from 2lb wrong.

4132 EUROPEAN BREEDERS FUND HOMECOMING MAIDEN 6f

3:00 (3:00) (Class 4) 2-Y-O **£5,018** (£1,493; £746; £372) **Stalls** Low

Form RPR
3 1 **Yesnabay (USA)**[20] [3478] 2-9-3 0 .... PJMcDonald 6 86+
(G A Swinbank) *dwlt: t.k.h and sn trckd ldrs: effrt and led 1f out: qcknd clr* **5/2**[3]
2 2 7 **Benrish (IRE)**[30] [3147] 2-9-3 0 .... TomEaves 3 65
(B Smart) *t.k.h: cl up: lft in ld over 4f out: rdn and hdd 1f out: kpt on same pce* **2/1**[2]
3 3 1 **Lord Raglan (IRE)**[17] [3572] 2-9-3 0 .... AndrewElliott 4 62
(K R Burke) *cl up: carried rt after 2f: swtchd lft to join main gp far side over 2f out: sn rdn: one pce fnl f* **8/1**
262 4 hd **Trinder**[16] [3606] 2-9-3 0 .... TonyHamilton 5 61
(R A Fahey) *t.k.h: cl up: effrt and ev ch over 1f out: sn one pce* **15/8**[1]
6 5 13 **Sydney Bridge**[26] [3263] 2-9-3 0 .... JamieMoriarty 1 22
(I Semple) *led tl drifted bdly rt and hdd over 4f out: struggling 1/2-way: no imp whn drifted lft over 1f out* **33/1**
1m 13.5s (-0.10) **Going Correction** -0.075s/f (Good) **5** Ran SP% **110.7**
Speed ratings (Par 96): **97,87,86,86,68**
toteswingers: 1&2 £7.40. CSF £7.97 TOTE £3.30: £1.40, £1.90; EX 8.00.
Owner Mrs I Gibson **Bred** Denis O'Flynn **Trained** Melsonby, N Yorks

FOCUS
A bit of a messy race but there was no denying Yesnabay's superiority over his rivals. He looks a useful prospect and the form is solid.

NOTEBOOK
Yesnabay(USA), a promising third behind a useful sort over 5f on his debut at Hamilton, was always going to be suited by this extra furlong and really came strong late on, despite being slowly away and pulling hard early. He came right away, having shown a bright change of pace, and looks a horse of considerable promise. (op 3-1 tchd 9-4)
Benrish(IRE) shaped with a good deal of promise when second having run very green on his debut over C&D and he seemed to run his race, but was no match for the winner. He will benefit from a seventh furlong before long. (tchd 9-4 in places)
Lord Raglan(IRE) ran well considering he was carried into the centre of the track by Sydney Bridge and then had to go back across to the far side. He kept on to just take third and looks to have a small race in him. (op 10-1 tchd 11-1)
Trinder, who is blind in his left eye, was soon close on the pace and held every chance but couldn't quicken. He is starting to look exposed now. (tchd 7-4 and 9-4)
Sydney Bridge drifted badly right and was the first one beaten. Official explanation: jockey said colt hung right (op 28-1)

4133 WISECALL CLAIMING STKS 6f

3:30 (3:30) (Class 6) 3-Y-O+ **£2,047** (£604; £302) **Stalls** Low

Form RPR
0001 1 **Dream Express (IRE)**[17] [3558] 4-9-5 69 .... PhillipMakin 7 68
(M Dods) *t.k.h: hld up in tch: nt clr run over 2f out: carried hd high and hdwy to ld ins fnl f: rdn out* **3/1**[2]
1016 2 nk **Stellite**[15] [3656] 9-8-13 70 .... GaryBartley(5) 3 69+
(J S Goldie) *prom: nt clr run on ins over 2f out tl swtchd rt and hdwy appr fnl f: styd on to take 2nd towards fin* **7/2**[3]
-555 3 shd **Ice Planet**[53] [2389] 8-8-9 60 .... DeanHeslop(5) 10 62
(Mrs R A Carr) *prom on outside: effrt over 2f out: kpt on u.p fnl f* **8/1**
4/0- 4 hd **Teachers Choice (IRE)**[9] [3880] 6-9-11 0 .... WMLordan 6 72
(Adrian McGuinness, Ire) *cl up: led over 1f out to ins fnl f: kpt on* **10/1**
0-30 5 4 **Chin Wag (IRE)**[15] [3653] 5-9-1 55 ....(v[1]) DanielTudhope 4 49
(J S Goldie) *cl up tl rdn and wknd over 1f out* **18/1**
0000 6 5 **Strabinios King**[21] [3467] 5-9-5 60 .... FrancisNorton 9 37
(A Berry) *hld up: shkn up 2f out: sn wknd* **16/1**
601 7 nse **Paddy Bear**[5] [3972] 3-9-0 67 .... TonyHamilton 1 37
(R A Fahey) *led to over 1f out: sn wknd* **2/1**[1]
000 8 3¾ **Another Luke (IRE)**[16] [3611] 3-9-2 49 .... AndrewElliott 5 27
(T J Etherington) *bhd: struggling over 2f out: nvr on terms* **100/1**
1m 12.96s (-0.64) **Going Correction** -0.075s/f (Good)
WFA 3 from 4yo+ 5lb **8** Ran SP% **112.9**
Speed ratings (Par 101): **101,100,100,100,94 88,88,83**
toteswingers: 1&2 £2.80, 1&3 £5.70, 2&3 £3.60. CSF £13.58 TOTE £3.90: £1.20, £1.70, £2.30; EX 15.90.
Owner J A Wynn-Williams Les Waugh **Bred** Quay Bloodstock **Trained** Denton, Co Durham

FOCUS
This was a fairly competitive claimer, but there were doubts over most of these coming into the race and the form is muddling. The runer-up has been rated a half-length winner.

4134 INTECHNOLOGY SERVICES H'CAP 6f

4:00 (4:00) (Class 4) (0-80,80) 3-Y-O+ **£6,476** (£1,927; £963; £481) **Stalls** Low

Form RPR
2503 1 **We Have A Dream**[11] [3771] 4-9-1 **69** .... PhillipMakin 13 78
(W R Muir) *mde all on stands' rail: rdn over 2f out: hld on wl fnl f: 1st of 7 in gp* **8/1**[3]
0003 2 hd **Hotham**[14] [3681] 6-9-0 **68** .... JamieMoriarty 15 76
(N Wilson) *trckd stands' side ldrs: drvn 2f out: kpt on wl fnl f: jst hld: 2nd of 7 in gp* **8/1**[3]
4161 3 ¾ **Tyfos**[11] [3771] 4-9-9 **77** .... TGMcLaughlin 10 83
(W M Brisbourne) *pressed wnr stands' side: rdn over 2f out: kpt on u.p ins fnl f: 3rd of 7 in gp* **11/2**[1]
2204 4 nk **Avontuur (FR)**[4] [4015] 7-8-5 **64** .... DeanHeslop(5) 4 69
(Mrs R A Carr) *led far side gp: rdn over 2f out: kpt on fnl f: nt rch stands' side ldrs: 1st of 8 in gp* **8/1**[3]
5- 5 nk **Dash Back (USA)**[23] [3411] 4-9-8 **76** .... WMLordan 3 80
(Adrian McGuinness, Ire) *chsd far side ldrs: effrt over 1f out: kpt on fnl f: 2nd of 8 in gp* **14/1**
5-23 6 ¾ **Finsbury**[40] [2812] 6-8-2 **61** .... JamieKyne(5) 1 63
(J S Goldie) *missed break: bhd far side: hdwy over 1f out: r.o fnl f: 3rd of 8 in gp* **9/1**
0130 7 ¾ **Woodsley House (IRE)**[19] [3496] 7-8-13 **70** .... NeilBrown(3) 8 69
(A G Foster) *hld up far side: hdwy over 1f out: r.o fnl f: no imp: 4th of 8 in gp* **12/1**
004- 8 4½ **Distant Sun (USA)**[395] [3203] 5-9-8 **76** .... TonyHamilton 14 61
(Miss L A Perratt) *hld up stands' side: hdwy over 1f out: r.o fnl f: nvr rchd ldrs: 4th of 7 in gp* **14/1**
0352 9 1¾ **John Keats**[18] [3529] 6-9-1 **69** .... DanielTudhope 9 48
(J S Goldie) *hld up stands' side: rdn over 2f out: sme late hdwy: n.d: 5th of 7 in gp* **6/1**[2]
3104 10 ½ **Argentine (IRE)**[9] [3855] 5-9-12 **80** ....(b) PaulMulrennan 11 58
(J A McShane) *prom stands' side: rdn over 2f out: no ex over 1f out: 6th of 7 in gp* **14/1**
-000 11 2½ **Tadalavil**[9] [3855] 4-8-11 **65** .... AndrewElliott 6 35
(Miss L A Perratt) *cl up far side tl edgd lft and wknd wl over 1f out: 5th of 8 in gp* **50/1**
4345 12 1¾ **Blown It (USA)**[14] [3681] 3-9-1 **74** ....(p) TomEaves 12 38
(I Semple) *prom stands' side tl rdn and wknd wl over 1f out: 7th of 7 in gp* **18/1**
3300 13 shd **Regal Royale**[51] [2472] 6-8-7 **61** oh1 ....(v) JamieMackay 7 25
(Peter Grayson) *dwlt: bhd far side: rdn 1/2-way: btn over 1f out: 6th of 8 in gp* **33/1**
52-0 14 8 **Hosanna**[15] [3656] 3-8-6 **65** .... PJMcDonald 5 3
(J Barclay) *prom far side tl wknd over 2f out: 7th of 8 in gp* **66/1**
0623 15 15 **Dazzling Bay**[40] [2814] 9-9-7 **75** ....(b) DavidAllan 2 —
(T D Easterby) *prom far side tl wknd over 2f out: eased whn no ch fnl f: last of 8 in gp* **10/1**
1m 12.05s (-1.55) **Going Correction** -0.075s/f (Good)
WFA 3 from 4yo+ 5lb **15** Ran SP% **121.4**
Speed ratings (Par 105): **107,106,105,105,104 103,102,96,94,93 90,88,88,77,57**
toteswingers: 1&2 £18.80, 1&3 £6.10, 2&3 £13.90. CSF £70.19 CT £390.16 TOTE £7.80: £2.40, £4.00, £2.60; EX 72.60.
Owner The Dreaming Squires **Bred** Whitsbury Manor Stud **Trained** Lambourn, Berks

FOCUS
Not that many got into this ordinary handicap and the near-side group came out on top. The front runners either side 'won' their races. The winner turned around Epsom form with the third.

4135 GILES INSURANCE STKS (HERITAGE H'CAP) 5f

4:30 (4:31) (Class 2) 3-Y-O+ **£25,904** (£7,708; £3,852; £1,924) **Stalls** Low

Form RPR
0112 1 **Pavershooz**[9] [3877] 4-8-9 **88** .... DuranFentiman 4 101
(N Wilson) *cl up far side: led that gp 1/2-way: drvn and kpt on strly fnl f: 1st of 9 in gp* **13/2**[2]
0-41 2 1½ **Just For Mary**[8] [3898] 5-8-0 **79** 6ex .... WMLordan 1 86+
(Daniel Mark Loughnane, Ire) *slowly away: bhd far side: gd hdwy over 1f out: chsd wnr ins fnl f: r.o: 2nd of 9 in gp* **8/1**[3]
5320 3 hd **River Falcon**[24] [3351] 9-9-1 **94** .... DanielTudhope 14 101
(J S Goldie) *hld up stands' side: gd hdwy over 1f out: led that gp nr fin: 1st of 7 in gp* **16/1**
204 4 hd **Reverence**[51] [2481] 8-9-9 **102** .... TGMcLaughlin 11 108
(E J Alston) *cl up stands' side: led that gp over 1f out tl nr fin: 2nd of 7 in gp* **20/1**
60-0 5 shd **Sea Of Leaves (USA)**[12] [3746] 3-8-5 **88** .... PJMcDonald 5 93
(J S Goldie) *hld up towards rr far side: effrt over 1f out: r.o fnl f: 3rd of 9 in gp* **33/1**
1313 6 hd **Look Busy (IRE)**[10] [3824] 4-9-5 **103** .... SladeO'Hara(5) 10 108+
(A Berry) *missed break: bhd on outside of far side gp: hdwy 2f out: r.o fnl f: 4th of 9 in gp* **3/1**[1]
00-2 7 ½ **Aegean Dancer**[96] [1278] 7-8-7 **86** ow1 .... TomEaves 8 89
(B Smart) *cl up far side: effrt over 2f out: one pce fnl f: 5th of 9 in gp* **16/1**
6151 8 ½ **Blue Jack**[14] [3694] 4-8-10 **89** ....(b) PaulMulrennan 12 90
(W R Muir) *chsd stands' side ldrs: effrt 2f out: one pce fnl f: 3rd of 7 in gp* **8/1**[3]
0310 9 hd **Rothesay Dancer**[11] [3784] 6-7-12 **82** .... JamieKyne(5) 16 83
(J S Goldie) *hld up stands' side: effrt and swtchd lft over 1f out: no imp: 4th of 7 in gp* **20/1**
/0-0 10 1¼ **Copper Dock (IRE)**[24] [3368] 5-8-8 **90** ....(p) NeilBrown(3) 17 86
(T G McCourt, Ire) *led stands' to over 1f out: one pce whn n.m.r ins fnl f: 5th of 7 in gp* **33/1**
2112 11 shd **Tyrannosaurus Rex (IRE)**[16] [3623] 5-8-1 **80** .... FrancisNorton 15 76
(D Shaw) *trckd stands' side ldrs: effrt over 2f out: one pce fnl f: 6th of 7 in gp* **14/1**
0200 12 hd **Fullandby (IRE)**[23] [3388] 7-9-5 **98** .... TonyHamilton 13 93
(T J Etherington) *bhd stands' side: drvn over 2f out: nvr able to chal: last of 7 in gp* **16/1**
2611 13 1¼ **Canadian Danehill (IRE)**[11] [3784] 7-9-1 **94** ....(p) PhillipMakin 2 85
(R M H Cowell) *chsd far side ldrs: rdn and edgd rt 2f out: sn outpcd: 6th of 9 in gp* **16/1**
040 14 nk **Stoneacre Lad (IRE)**[28] [3212] 6-8-0 **79** ....(b) JamieMackay 6 68
(Peter Grayson) *towards rr far side: drvn 1/2-way: nvr on terms: 7th of 9 in gp* **33/1**

3221 **15** 3/4 **Peak District (IRE)**[28] 3212 5-8-10 **94**.............................. AmyRyan(5) 9 81
(K A Ryan) *t.k.h: in tch far side tl wknd over 1f out: 8th of 9 in gp* **10/1**

0220 **16** 7 **Captain Dunne (IRE)**[24] 3351 4-9-7 **100**.............................. DavidAllan 3 62
(T D Easterby) *led far side to 1/2-way: wknd over 1f out: last of 9 in gp* **14/1**

58.59 secs (-1.51) **Going Correction** -0.075s/f (Good)
WFA 3 from 4yo+ 4lb **16** Ran SP% **124.9**
Speed ratings (Par 109): **109,106,106,105,105 105,104,103,103,101 101,101,99,98,97 86**
toteswingers: 1&2 £8.90, 1&3 £35.40, 2&3 £40.30. CSF £55.18 CT £840.39 TOTE £7.50: £2.10, £2.30, £3.60, £3.40; EX 64.00.
Owner Mrs Michael John Paver **Bred** Exors Of The Late M J Paver **Trained** Flaxton, N Yorks

FOCUS
An open and valuable handicap and it was no surprise to see the far-side group come out on top this time as there was more pace on that side of the track. Pretty solid form with a personal best from the winner.

NOTEBOOK
Pavershooz, 2lb higher than when finishing second over 6f at York in his bid for a hat-trick earlier in the month, had recorded his two prior victories over this trip and this win showed that he is still on the up. Soon tracking the speed, he got to the front just past halfway and stayed on well for pressure. There may well be more to come from this progressive sprinter. He may well take in the Portland and Ayr Gold Cup later in the season. (op 8-1)
Just For Mary, another progressive type who came into this on a hat-trick following back-to-back wins at the Curragh, ran really well under the 6lb penalty, especially as he got a bit too far back following a slow start. He too continues to improve. (op 9-1)
River Falcon ran his usual race, staying on well late having been outpaced. He nosed through to 'win' the race on the stands' side and the hardy veteran will no doubt continue to pay his way. (tchd 14-1)
Reverence is not the performer he once was, but he had run well on two of his three starts this year and he recorded another solid effort in defeat. His rating remains very high, though, and conditions races are likely to represent his best chance of winning these days. (tchd 22-1)
Sea Of Leaves(USA), who ran well to a point over 7f on his recent debut for the yard, appreciated the return to sprinting and looks capable of landing a decent handicap at some stage.
Look Busy(IRE), who won the race last year, ran a big race considering she lost ground at the start. Though 3lb higher than when scoring last term, she has got even better this season, winning the Group 2 Temple Stakes in May, and this run shows she is still capable of posting big runs in handicaps. (op 10-3 tchd 7-2)
Aegean Dancer, off since finishing second at Beverley in April, was putting up 1lb overweight and he ran well for a long way. (tchd 20-1)
Copper Dock(IRE) showed speed stands' side before fading. (tchd 40-1)
Canadian Danehill(IRE) Official explanation: jockey said gelding hung right-handed from halfway

4136 HOMECOMING H'CAP 5f
5:00 (5:02) (Class 5) (0-70,68) 3-Y-0+ **£2,914** (£867; £433; £216) **Stalls** Low

Form RPR
0412 **1** **Ingleby Star (IRE)**[7] 3909 4-9-2 60..............................(p) GaryBartley(5) 3 72
(N Wilson) *trckd ldrs: led over 1f out: drvn out fnl f* **7/4**[1]

1641 **2** 1 3/4 **Twosheetstothewind**[7] 3909 5-10-1 68 6ex..................(p) PhillipMakin 1 74
(M Dods) *hld up: hdwy to chse wnr over 1f out: edgd lft: r.o fnl f* **7/2**[2]

0600 **3** 1 **Kalhan Sands (IRE)**[24] 3354 4-9-4 62.............................. JamieKyne(5) 5 64
(J J Quinn) *hld up: hdwy on outside over 1f out: kpt on fnl f: no imp* **20/1**

6145 **4** 1 1/4 **Angelo Poliziano**[10] 3828 3-9-11 68..............................(p) PaulMulrennan 6 65
(Mrs A Duffield) *cl up: effrt over 2f out: one pce fnl f* **9/2**[3]

0644 **5** 1 3/4 **Andrasta**[4] 4016 4-8-7 53.............................. CharlotteKerton(7) 4 44
(A Berry) *towards rr: effrt 1/2-way: no imp over 1f out* **16/1**

0003 **6** 3/4 **The Bear**[3] 4036 6-9-7 60.............................. AndrewElliott 8 49
(Miss L A Perratt) *led to over 1f out: wknd ent fnl f* **13/2**

0030 **7** 1/2 **Thunder Bay**[17] 3562 4-9-7 60..............................(v) TonyHamilton 2 47
(R A Fahey) *hld up in tch: drvn over 2f out: no imp over 1f out* **13/2**

60-0 **8** 1 1/2 **Town And Gown**[7] 3909 4-8-12 51.............................. DanielTudhope 7 32
(J S Goldie) *cl up tl rdn and wknd over 1f out* **33/1**

59.38 secs (-0.72) **Going Correction** -0.075s/f (Good)
WFA 3 from 4yo+ 4lb **8** Ran SP% **117.0**
Speed ratings (Par 103): **102,99,97,95,92 91,90,88**
toteswingers: 1&2 £1.90, 1&3 £8.50, 2&3 £13.30. CSF £8.18 CT £89.91 TOTE £2.60: £1.20, £1.60, £4.70; EX 5.40.
Owner Renaissance Racing **Bred** Pat Cosgrove **Trained** Flaxton, N Yorks

FOCUS
A moderate handicap run in a creditable time compared with the previous race. Straightforward form.

4137 GILES INSURANCE CORPORATE H'CAP 5f
5:30 (5:30) (Class 6) (0-60,58) 3-Y-O **£2,047** (£604; £302) **Stalls** Low

Form RPR
-002 **1** **Arriva La Diva**[9] 3853 3-8-0 45.............................. JamieKyne(5) 7 54
(J J Quinn) *mde all: rdn 2f out: kpt on wl fnl f* **8/1**

202 **2** 2 **Rocket Ruby**[4] 3999 3-9-0 54.............................. FrancisNorton 4 56
(D Shaw) *t.k.h: w ldr: rdn over 1f out: one pce fnl f* **11/4**[1]

3301 **3** 2 1/2 **What A Fella**[9] 3853 3-8-8 48..............................(p) PaulMulrennan 1 41
(Mrs A Duffield) *t.k.h: in tch: effrt over 1f out: no imp fnl f* **11/2**

2 **4** 1 1/4 **Blackwell Nation (IRE)**[15] 3651 3-9-4 58.............................. WMLordan 6 47
(Adrian McGuinness, Ire) *prom: effrt 2f out: outpcd fnl f* **10/3**[2]

30-0 **5** 1 1/4 **Makaykla**[37] 2918 3-9-3 57.............................. DavidAllan 3 41
(E J Alston) *chsd ldrs: drvn and outpcd 1/2-way: n.d after* **7/2**[3]

456 **6** 3 1/4 **Badtanman**[9] 3853 3-8-5 45..............................(b) JamieMackay 2 17
(Peter Grayson) *s.i.s: sn drvn in rr: nvr on terms* **20/1**

6430 **7** 1/2 **Pedregal**[15] 3651 3-8-5 45.............................. DuranFentiman 8 16
(J S Goldie) *sn bhd and outpcd: edgd lft 1/2-way: nvr on terms* **12/1**

40-0 **8** 6 **Mary West (IRE)**[105] 1157 3-8-3 50.............................. JamesPSullivan(7) 5 —
(Patrick Morris) *prom tl edgd rt and wknd fr 2f out* **50/1**

59.69 secs (-0.41) **Going Correction** -0.075s/f (Good) **8** Ran SP% **112.9**
Speed ratings (Par 98): **100,96,92,90,88 83,82,73**
toteswingers: 1&2 £4.70, 1&3 £4.50, 2&3 £2.50. CSF £29.53 CT £132.55 TOTE £12.60: £2.50, £1.30, £1.70; EX 28.10 Place 6: £89.94, Place 5: £33.74..
Owner Allan Stennett **Bred** Mickley Stud, Stennett, Hillside Racing **Trained** Settrington, N Yorks

FOCUS
This was a low-grade contest but the time was reasonable. The winner was 3lb wrong at the weights but there was no fluke, with the runner-up a fair guide to the form.
Pedregal Official explanation: jockey said gelding never travelled
T/Plt: £109.00 to a £1 stake. Pool: £69,416.96. 464.68 winning tickets. T/Qpdt: £20.70 to a £1 stake. Pool: £5,104.70. 182.20 winning tickets. RY

[3936]BEVERLEY (R-H)
Monday, July 20

OFFICIAL GOING: Good (good to soft in places; 8.4)
Wind: Fresh, against Weather: Sunny periods

4138 GO RACING IN YORKSHIRE SUMMER FESTIVAL CLAIMING STKS 5f
6:00 (6:00) (Class 5) 2-Y-O **£2,729** (£806; £403) **Stalls** High

Form RPR
1401 **1** **Diamond Laura**[13] 3719 2-8-12 0.............................. CatherineGannon 6 71+
(P D Evans) *mde all: rdn appr fnl f and sn clr: styd on* **2/7**[1]

50 **2** 5 **Daisy Brown**[14] 3686 2-8-7 0.............................. JimmyQuinn 9 47
(N Tinkler) *hld up in rr: hdwy 1/2-way: rdn wl over 1f out: styd on ent fnl f: nrst fin* **11/1**[3]

06 **3** nk **High Rolling**[27] 3232 2-9-2 0.............................. DNolan 7 55
(T D Easterby) *chsd ldrs on inner: rdn along wl over 1f out: kpt on same pce* **28/1**

004 **4** 2 1/4 **Menediva**[12] 3726 2-7-12 0.............................. PaulPickard(7) 2 36
(L A Mullaney) *trckd ldrs: hdwy to chse wnr wl over 1f out: sn rdn and wknd appr fnl f* **25/1**

000 **5** 7 **Cygnet Committee (IRE)**[18] 3547 2-8-6 0..............(p) RoystonFfrench 1 12
(J S Wainwright) *chsd ldrs: rdn along 1/2-way: sn wknd* **100/1**

00 **6** 1 **Foricherforpoorer**[55] 2360 2-8-7 0.............................. PaulQuinn 4 9
(N Tinkler) *hmpd s: a bhd: rdn 1/2-way: sn hung bdly lft* **100/1**

000 **7** 2 **Three Sons**[2] 4101 2-8-4 0..............................(b) LanceBetts(5) 3 4
(I W McInnes) *wnt rt s: midfield: rdn along 1/2-way and sn wknd* **66/1**

0564 **8** nk **Mrs Jones And Me (IRE)**[19] 3495 2-8-4 0.............................. PaulHanagan 5 —
(P T Midgley) *cl up: rdn along over 2f out: sn drvn and wknd wl over 1f out: eased* **7/1**[2]

64.36 secs (0.86) **Going Correction** +0.10s/f (Good) **8** Ran SP% **109.4**
Speed ratings (Par 94): **97,89,88,84,73 72,68,68**
toteswingers: 1&2 £1.30, 1&3 £4.80, 2&3 £15.10. CSF £3.41 TOTE £1.20: £1.02, £2.10, £4.30; EX 4.20.Diamond Laura was claimed by Mrs Ruth Carr for £13,000.
Owner Diamond Racing Ltd **Bred** Paul Sweeting **Trained** Pandy, Monmouths

FOCUS
After 22mm of rain three days earlier, the ground had dried out and was reckoned to be just on the slow side. Easy for the winner who was the clear pre-race form choice.

NOTEBOOK
Diamond Laura, already a winner of a maiden and claimer on the all-weather at Wolverhampton, had finished fourth in a Listed race at York. She was sent off at prohibitive odds and, pushed along, came well clear. (op 2-5)
Daisy Brown, who unseated her rider on the way to post, was taking a drop in grade on her third start. She stayed on from off the pace to take a modest second. This, at least, opens up the nursery route for her., (op 12-1 tchd 14-1)
High Rolling, who hung badly on the home turn in a maiden over an extended 7f here, behaved himself on his third start, dropped back to the minimum trip. A seller ought to be within his compass. (op 16-1 tchd 33-1)
Menediva, fourth in selling company at Catterick, finished clear of the remainder. (tchd 22-1 and 28-1)
Foricherforpoorer Official explanation: jockey said filly hung left throughout
Mrs Jones And Me(IRE), having her sixth career start, had 11lb to find with the winner on RPRs. She seemed to pay a heavy price for trying to match strides with the favourite. Official explanation: jockey said filly hung left throughout (op 11-2 tchd 15-2)

4139 BEVERLEY BNI MEETS AT THE RACECOURSE H'CAP 1m 1f 207y
6:30 (6:31) (Class 5) (0-75,72) 3-Y-O+ **£3,238** (£963; £481; £240) **Stalls** High

Form RPR
4413 **1** **Honimiere (IRE)**[11] 3763 3-9-7 72.............................. RobertWinston 1 87
(G A Swinbank) *trckd ldrs: hdwy on outer over 3f out: led over 2f out and sn edgd rt: rdn and hung rt wl over 1f out: clr ent fnl f: kpt on* **3/1**[2]

4-22 **2** 5 **Graceful Descent (FR)**[17] 3557 4-10-0 69.............................. PaulHanagan 6 74
(R A Fahey) *trckd ldng pair: pushed along whn lost pl over 5f out and sn rdn: hdwy on inner whn n.m.r 2f out: sn rdn to chse wnr: drvn over 1f out and one pce* **13/8**[1]

0110 **3** 1/2 **Maybe I Wont**[12] 3734 4-9-4 64..............................(p) JPHamblett(5) 2 68
(Lucinda Featherstone) *hld up towards rr: hdwy over 3f out: rdn to chse ldng pair over 1f out: snd drvn and one pce* **7/1**

550 **4** 3 **Gulf Of Aqaba (USA)**[12] 3751 3-8-11 62.............................. GregFairley 5 60
(M Johnston) *dwlt: sn trcking ldrs on inner: rdn along 3f out and sn one pce* **11/1**

3140 **5** 3/4 **Coral Shores**[12] 3739 4-9-7 65..............................(v) AndreaAtzeni(3) 3 62
(P W Hiatt) *clsd up: led briefly 3f out: sn rdn and hdd: n.m.r 2f out and sn wknd* **6/1**[3]

000 **6** 2 3/4 **Kingsholm**[6] 3943 7-9-2 60.............................. FrederikTylicki(3) 7 51
(N Wilson) *dwlt: hld up in rr: hdwy over 3f out: rdn to chse ldrs 2f out: sn btn* **9/1**

-000 **7** 6 **Able Dara**[20] 3486 6-8-9 50 oh5..............................(b) JimmyQuinn 4 29
(N Bycroft) *a in rr* **40/1**

500- **8** 52 **Orchestrion**[203] 7039 4-8-11 52.............................. RoystonFfrench 8 —
(Miss T Jackson) *led: rdn along and hdd 3f out: sn wknd* **66/1**

2m 6.50s (-0.50) **Going Correction** +0.025s/f (Good)
WFA 3 from 4yo+ 10lb **8** Ran SP% **112.1**
Speed ratings (Par 103): **103,99,98,96,95 93,88,47**
toteswingers: 1&2 £1.10, 1&3 £3.10, 2&3 £2.80. CSF £7.91 CT £28.55 TOTE £4.00: £1.30, £1.10, £2.10; EX 8.20.
Owner Mrs J Porter & Mrs David Parkinson **Bred** Peter Collier **Trained** Melsonby, N Yorks

FOCUS
A modest 50-69 handicap run at a sensible pace. The form has been rated at face value.
Kingsholm Official explanation: trainer's rep said gelding lost a near-fore shoe

4140 SKY BET SUPPORTING THE YORKSHIRE RACING FESTIVAL H'CAP 7f 100y
7:00 (7:01) (Class 5) (0-75,74) 3-Y-O+ **£4,533** (£1,348; £674; £336) **Stalls** High

Form RPR
0060 **1** **Moonage Daydream (IRE)**[31] 3124 4-9-1 57..............................(b) DNolan 11 66
(T D Easterby) *hld up: stdy hdwy on inner whn nt clr run and swtchd lft wl over 1f out: squeezed through and rdn to chse ldr ins fnl f: styd on wl to ld nr line* **12/1**

2115 **2** nk **Lady Florence**[12] 3735 4-9-2 58.............................. LPKeniry 7 66
(A B Coogan) *led: rdn clr wl over 1f out: drvn ins fnl f: hdd and no ex nr fin* **10/1**

0153 **3** 1 1/2 **Violent Velocity (IRE)**[9] 3851 6-9-4 67.............................. IJBrennan(7) 10 71
(J J Quinn) *hld up: hdwy 3f out: rdn over 1f out: kpt on same pce ins fnl f* **6/1**

2451 **4** *nse* **Rising Kheleyf (IRE)**[16] 3616 3-9-10 **73** .... RobertWinston 6 74
(G A Swinbank) *midfield: hdwy on outer over 3f out: rdn to chse ldrs 2f out: drvn and one pce ent fnl f* **11/2**[3]
5050 **5** *hd* **Boss Hog**[12] 3730 4-8-9 **51** oh1 .... LeeEnstone 4 55+
(P T Midgley) *midfield: hdwy on outer over 2f out: rdn to chse ldrs over 1f out: kpt on u.p ins fnl f* **50/1**
0526 **6** *½* **Diggeratt (USA)**[9] 3843 3-9-8 **74** .... FrederikTylicki(3) 1 73
(R A Fahey) *cl up: chsd ldr 1/2-way: rdn along 2f out: drvn over 1f out: kpt on same pce* **5/1**[2]
1332 **7** *nk* **Silly Gilly (IRE)**[12] 3730 5-8-10 **59** .... PaulPickard(7) 9 61
(R E Barr) *chsd ldrs: rdn along wl over 2f out: drvn and n.m.r over 1f out: kpt on* **6/1**
-330 **8** *hd* **Business Class (BRZ)**[59] 2235 4-9-6 **62** .... AdrianTNicholls 12 63
(D Nicholls) *chsd ldr: rdn along wl over 2f out and grad wknd* **18/1**
045 **9** *½* **Lordship (IRE)**[19] 3504 5-8-3 **52** .... JakePayne(7) 5 52+
(A W Carroll) *stdd s: hld up in rr: hdwy on inner whn nt clr run wl over 1f: keeping on whn hmpd ins fnl f and nt rcvr* **20/1**
4004 **10** *hd* **Royal Composer (IRE)**[20] 3488 6-8-12 **54** .... PaulHanagan 3 53
(T D Easterby) *a in rr* **11/1**
6553 **11** *1½* **Mister Jingles**[14] 3689 6-8-12 **57** .... (p) MichaelJStainton(3) 8 53
(R M Whitaker) *chsd ldrs: rdn along over 2f out: sn drvn and wknd* **9/2**[1]
43-0 **12** *8* **Nuit Sombre (IRE)**[19] 3496 9-10-0 **70** .... RoystonFfrench 2 46
(G A Harker) *a towards rr* **25/1**

1m 34.36s (0.56) **Going Correction** +0.025s/f (Good)
WFA 3 from 4yo+ 7lb **12** Ran SP% **119.8**
Speed ratings (Par 103): **97,96,94,94,94 94,93,93,92,92 91,81**
toteswingers: 1&2 £41.40, 1&3 £22.80, 2&3 £7.10. CSF £125.19 CT £802.56 TOTE £17.40: £4.40, £3.90, £1.60; EX 231.80.
Owner Rio Grande Partnership **Bred** Miss Nicola Kent **Trained** Great Habton, N Yorks

FOCUS
A modest 51-70 handicap. It was strongly run, but they stuck to the inside rail in the home straight, resulting in traffic problems. The form looks pretty sound.
Lordship(IRE) Official explanation: jockey said gelding was denied a clear run

4141 CARL SKELTON HAPPY BIRTHDAY H'CAP 5f
7:30 (7:31) (Class 5) (0-75,75) 3-Y-0+ **£3,238** (£963; £481; £240) **Stalls** High

Form RPR
0-00 **1** **Prince Namid**[3] 4072 7-9-3 **67** .... AdrianTNicholls 6 78+
(D Nicholls) *towards rr and rdn along 1/2-way: swtchd wd and hdwy wl over 1f out: str run ent fnl f: styd on to ld nr fin* **20/1**
432 **2** *nk* **Select Committee**[11] 3765 4-8-8 **58** .... (v) JimmyQuinn 12 68
(J J Quinn) *trckd ldrs on inner: hdwy wl over 1f out and sn rdn: drvn to ld ins fnl f: hdd and no ex nr fin* **4/1**[2]
4600 **3** *1¾* **Green Park (IRE)**[9] 3877 6-9-8 **72** .... (b) DNolan 4 76
(D Carroll) *midfield: hdwy and in tch 1/2-way: rdn to chse ldrs over 1f out: drvn and kpt on ins fnl f* **20/1**
0014 **4** *½* **Sir Nod**[20] 3483 7-9-11 **75** .... RobertWinston 8 77
(Miss J A Camacho) *chsd ldrs on inner: hdwy 2f out: sn rdn and kpt on ins fnl f* **15/2**
0352 **5** *hd* **Bahamian Ballet**[22] 3422 7-9-5 **72** .... AndreaAtzeni(3) 13 73
(E S McMahon) *cl up: led 1/2-way: rdn wl over 1f out: drvn and hdd ins fnl f: wknd* **10/3**[1]
0403 **6** *1* **Lake Chini (IRE)**[4] 3999 7-8-8 **58** .... (b) DaleGibson 9 56
(M W Easterby) *dwlt: sn rdn along in midfield: drvn over 1f out and kpt on same pce* **9/1**
2404 **7** *¾* **Strathmore (IRE)**[6] 3938 5-8-6 **56** .... PaulHanagan 1 51
(R A Fahey) *stdd s and swtchd rt: hdwy on inner 2f out: sn rdn and no imp appr fnl f* **11/1**
00-0 **8** *nse* **Avertuoso**[19] 3497 5-9-8 **72** .... RoystonFfrench 11 67
(B Smart) *chsd ldrs: rdn along 2f out: drvn and wknd appr fnl f* **14/1**
560 **9** *1½* **Divine Spirit**[11] 3765 8-9-5 **72** .... FrederikTylicki(3) 7 61
(M Dods) *chsd ldrs: rdn along over 2f out: sn wknd* **10/1**
-300 **10** *3¼* **Commander Wish**[16] 3607 6-8-10 **65** .... (p) JPHamblett(5) 5 43
(Lucinda Featherstone) *stdd s: hld up: a in rr* **28/1**
011 **11** *½* **Highland Warrior**[4] 3999 10-9-3 **74** 6ex .... PaulPickard(7) 3 50
(P T Midgley) *dwlt: a in rr* **7/1**[3]
1006 **12** *¾* **Revue Princess (IRE)**[17] 3565 4-8-11 **64** .... (b) MichaelJStainton(3) 10 37
(T D Easterby) *led to 1/2-way: cl up tl rdn along and wknd wl over 1f out* **22/1**

63.58 secs (0.80) **Going Correction** +0.10s/f (Good) **12** Ran SP% **118.8**
Speed ratings (Par 103): **103,102,99,98,98 97,95,95,93,88 87,86**
toteswingers: 1&2 £20.20, 1&3 £62.40, 2&3 £16.80. CSF £94.41 CT £1684.26 TOTE £28.50: £7.10, £1.80, £5.10; EX 192.30.
Owner T Gould **Bred** Mrs R D Peacock **Trained** Sessay, N Yorks

FOCUS
A 56-75 sprint handicap and again the idea that horses cannot win over 5f at Beverley if they come wide was proved wide of the mark. The winner is rated to last year's best.
Prince Namid Official explanation: trainer's rep said, regarding apparent improvement in form, that the gelding was possibly suited by being held up.
Lake Chini(IRE) Official explanation: jockey said gelding never travelled

4142 SPS GROUP MAIDEN H'CAP 2m 35y
8:00 (8:00) (Class 6) (0-65,59) 3-Y-0 **£2,590** (£770; £385; £192) **Stalls** High

Form RPR
2043 **1** **Strikemaster (IRE)**[24] 2350 3-8-13 **56** .... LanceBetts(5) 1 69
(B Ellison) *stdd s: hld up and bhd: gd hdwy on outer over 3f out: cl up 2f out: led over 1f out and sn clr* **3/1**[1]
0-02 **2** *8* **Kidson (USA)**[39] 2866 3-8-10 **51** .... FrederikTylicki(3) 3 54
(George Baker) *trckd ldng pair: effrt over 3f out: rdn and bmpd over 2f out: drvn to dispute ld and ev ch over 1f out: kpt on: no ch w wnr* **3/1**[1]
2300 **3** *1¼* **Dark Oasis**[3] 4054 3-8-10 **55** .... AndrewHeffernan(7) 4 56
(M C Chapman) *hld up towards rr: hdwy 3f out: rdn to chse ldrs wl over 1f out: kpt on ins fnl f* **9/1**[3]
6033 **4** *2¾* **Saffron's Son (IRE)**[24] 2605 3-8-12 **50** .... (v) LeeEnstone 10 48
(P T Midgley) *hld up in rr: hdwy on inner 3f out: rdn 2f out: drvn over 1f out and sn one pce* **16/1**
0020 **5** *1¼* **Marillos Proterras**[5] 3976 3-9-1 **53** .... (p) RoystonFfrench 11 49
(Mrs A Duffield) *trckd ldrs: hdwy 4f out: cl up and ev ch whn bmpd over 2f out: sn rdn and grad wknd* **20/1**
0565 **6** *1¼* **Dulce Domum**[20] 3474 3-8-7 **45** .... KirstyMilczarek 6 40
(A B Haynes) *cl up: led after 7f: rdn along 3f out: drvn and hung lft over 2f out: hdd & wknd over 1f out* **16/1**
-000 **7** *24* **Miss Gibboa (IRE)**[35] 2790 3-8-12 **50** .... RobertWinston 8 16
(P C Haslam) *chsd ldrs: rdn along over 3f out and sn wknd* **9/1**[3]
0006 **8** *4* **Milemilia (IRE)**[12] 3739 3-8-12 **50** .... (b) AdrianTNicholls 9 11
(H Morrison) *chsd ldrs on inner: rdn along over 4f out and sn wknd* **16/1**
0600 **9** *6* **Red Margarita (IRE)**[25] 3303 3-8-12 **50** .... RobertHavlin 13 4
(D R C Elsworth) *in tch: rdn along 1/2-way: sn wknd* **6/1**[2]
00-4 **10** *2¼* **Transporter (IRE)**[13] 3707 3-8-7 **45** .... PaulHanagan 7 —
(T D Easterby) *led 7f: cl up tl rdn along 3f out and sn wknd* **12/1**
0040 **11** *½* **Waltzalong (IRE)**[18] 3545 3-9-1 **53** .... DNolan 5 4
(T D Easterby) *trckd ldrs on outer: pushed along over 4f out: sn rdn and wknd* **33/1**
-050 **12** *8* **Sairaam (IRE)**[21] 3451 3-9-4 **59** .... MichaelJStainton(3) 2 —
(C Smith) *a in rr* **33/1**

3m 40.06s (0.26) **Going Correction** +0.025s/f (Good) **12** Ran SP% **120.3**
Speed ratings (Par 98): **100,96,95,94,93 92,80,78,75,74 74,70**
toteswingers: 1&2 £2.60, 1&3 £5.50, 2&3 £3.20. CSF £10.60 CT £72.24 TOTE £4.10: £1.60, £1.40, £2.90; EX 10.90.
Owner Dan Gilbert **Bred** Dr Peter Harms **Trained** Norton, N Yorks
■ Stewards' Enquiry : Lee Enstone two-day ban: careless riding (Aug 3-4)

FOCUS
The only 2m maiden handicap for three-year-olds in the calendar provided a clear-cut winner of some potential in Strikemaster, who was much improved for this longer trip. Sound form. The pace was steady until the last 5f.

4143 LEVY BOARD H'CAP 1m 100y
8:30 (8:31) (Class 4) (0-85,80) 3-Y-0 **£4,727** (£1,406; £702; £351) **Stalls** High

Form RPR
053 **1** **Splinter Cell (USA)**[42] 2767 3-9-4 **80** .... AndreaAtzeni(3) 2 87
(M Botti) *wnt lft s: hld up in rr: swtchd lft and hdwy 2f out: rdn to chse ldrs over 1f out: drvn ins fnl f and styd on to ld last stride* **9/4**[2]
-020 **2** *nse* **Peaceful Rule (USA)**[44] 2715 3-8-9 **68** .... AdrianTNicholls 6 75
(D Nicholls) *led: rdn over 2f out: drvn over 1f out: edgd lft u.p ins fnl f: hdd online* **20/1**
1144 **3** *3* **Postman**[23] 3394 3-9-0 **73** .... RoystonFfrench 1 73
(B Smart) *hld up in rr: hdwy 2f out and sn rdn: drvn and kpt on ins fnl f: no imp towards fin* **20/1**
6132 **4** *1¼* **Burns Night**[10] 3812 3-9-7 **80** .... GregFairley 5 77
(M Johnston) *dwlt: sn chsng ldr and t.k.h: cl up 1/2-way: rdn to chal 2f out and ev ch tl drvn and hld whn n.m.r ent fnl f: wknd* **5/4**[1]
1-00 **5** *4½* **Trumpstoo (USA)**[68] 1992 3-9-2 **75** .... PaulHanagan 4 62
(R A Fahey) *plld hrd: chsd ldrs: effrt on outer whn sltly hmpd 2f out: sn rdn and btn* **13/2**[3]
021 **6** *nk* **Drum Dragon**[20] 3485 3-9-0 **73** .... SaleemGolam 7 59
(M H Tompkins) *trckd ldng pair on inner: rdn along wl over 2f out: drvn over 1f out: wknd appr fnl f* **7/1**

1m 47.4s (-0.20) **Going Correction** +0.025s/f (Good) **6** Ran SP% **110.6**
Speed ratings (Par 102): **102,101,98,97,93 92**
toteswingers: 1&2 £6.90, 1&3 £14.70, 2&3 £14.00. CSF £38.69 TOTE £2.90: £1.30, £5.90; EX 26.90.
Owner Op - Center **Bred** Old Carhue Stud **Trained** Newmarket, Suffolk
■ Stewards' Enquiry : Adrian T Nicholls two-day ban: used whip with excessive frequency (Aug 3-4)
Andrea Atzeni caution: used whip with excessive frequency.

FOCUS
A fair three-year-olds' handicap run at a sound pace. The winner is back close to his early-season form.

4144 HAPPY BIRTHDAY KATIE IGGULDEN H'CAP 1m 100y
9:00 (9:00) (Class 5) (0-75,71) 3-Y-0+ **£2,914** (£867; £433; £216) **Stalls** High

Form RPR
0006 **1** **Natural Rhythm (IRE)**[3] 4040 4-8-9 **51** oh3 .... (b) JimmyQuinn 7 58
(Mrs R A Carr) *t.k.h: mde all: stdd over 3f out: qcknd over 2f out: rdn clr wl over 1f out: kpt on wl u.p ins fnl f* **10/1**
3065 **2** *½* **Island Music (IRE)**[9] 3857 4-9-4 **60** .... (p) PaulHanagan 5 66+
(J J Quinn) *hld up in rr: hdwy on inner 2f out: swtchd lft and rdn over 1f out: drvn ent fnl f: styd on: nt rch wnr* **6/1**[3]
640 **3** *1¼* **Blue Charm**[16] 3637 5-9-8 **69** .... LanceBetts(5) 6 72
(I W McInnes) *dwlt: sn in tch on inner: hdwy 3f out: rdn wl over 1f out: drvn over 1f out: kpt on ins fnl f* **13/2**
2101 **4** *1½* **San Silvestro (IRE)**[21] 3448 4-9-1 **62** .... (p) BMcHugh(5) 1 62
(Mrs A Duffield) *t.k.h: chsd wnr: rdn along over 2f out: drvn over 1f out: one pce* **15/8**[1]
1000 **5** *½* **Sign Of The Cross**[12] 3736 5-9-11 **67** .... LPKeniry 8 65
(C R Dore) *trckd ldng pair on inner: effrt over 2f out and sn rdn: drvn over 1f out kpt on same pce* **10/3**[2]
2250 **6** *1¾* **Will He Wish**[16] 3624 13-10-0 **70** .... (v) KirstyMilczarek 4 64
(S Gollings) *chsd ldrs: rdn along over 2f out: drvn over 1f out and no imp* **8/1**
4-00 **7** *1* **Wednesdays Boy (IRE)**[32] 3070 6-8-8 **53** .... (p) FrederikTylicki(3) 3 45
(P D Niven) *a in rr* **11/1**

1m 49.29s (1.69) **Going Correction** +0.025s/f (Good)
WFA 3 from 4yo+ 8lb **7** Ran SP% **114.0**
Speed ratings (Par 103): **92,91,90,88,88 86,85**
toteswingers: 1&2 £2.20, 1&3 £6.40, 2&3 £3.10. CSF £66.83 CT £421.80 TOTE £10.30: £5.40, £2.00; EX 33.60 Place 6 £107.30, Place 5 £93.14.
Owner Michael Hill **Bred** Mark Commins **Trained** Huby, N Yorks

FOCUS
A modest 51-70 handicap and a tactical affair. Muddling form.
T/Plt: £137.30 to a £1 stake. Pool: £57,625.25. 306.24 winning tickets. T/Qpdt: £132.40 to a £1 stake. Pool: £4,269.20. 23.85 winning tickets. JR

3917 WINDSOR (R-H)
Monday, July 20

OFFICIAL GOING: Good to firm
Wind: Light, behind Weather: Fine but cloudy

4145 COOLMORE EXCELLENT ART MAIDEN STKS 1m 2f 7y
6:20 (6:22) (Class 5) 3-4-Y-0 **£2,729** (£806; £403) **Stalls** Centre

Form RPR
1 **Mary Goodnight** 3-8-12 0 .... EddieAhern 1 78
(J Noseda) *dwlt: green early but trckd ldr after 3f: shkn up to ld wl over 1f out: styd on wl fnl f* **11/1**
04 **2** *3½* **Vivachi (IRE)**[22] 3425 3-8-12 0 .... RichardKingscote 10 71
(R M Beckett) *led: gng strly over 3f out: rdn and hdd wl over 1f out: kpt on but no ch w wnr* **3/1**[2]
06 **3** *hd* **Phantom Ridge (IRE)**[25] 3297 3-8-12 0 .... RichardHughes 13 71
(R Hannon) *trckd ldr 3f: styd prom: rdn and nt qckn over 2f out: kpt one pce after* **9/1**

0 **4** 3 **Templar Knight**[22] 3425 3-9-3 0 RyanMoore 2 70
(Sir Michael Stoute) *dwlt: sn pressed ldrs: pushed along over 3f out: nt qckn u.p 2f out: fdd fnl f* **11/4**[1]

6 **5** hd **Westlin' Winds (IRE)**[129] 828 3-9-3 0 SteveDrowne 5 69
(C R Egerton) *s.s: sn in midfield: rdn and outpcd fr 3f out: kpt on fr over 1f out* **33/1**

43 **6** 2½ **Lacrosse**[166] 391 3-9-3 0 PhilipRobinson 11 64
(M A Jarvis) *dwlt: wl in rr: rdn over 4f out: taken to wd outside and effrt over 2f out: kpt on: n.d* **4/1**[3]

55 **7** ½ **Adnams**[18] 3549 3-9-0 0 JackMitchell(3) 16 63
(C F Wall) *restless stalls: dwlt: wl in rr: nudged along and prog fr over 2f out: reminder 1f out: styd on: nvr nr ldrs* **17/2**

8 3 **Ten Day Wonder**[82] 4-9-8 0 J-PGuillambert 9 52
(R W Price) *dwlt: wl in rr: pushed along over 4f out: sme prog fr 2f out: nvr on terms* **100/1**

00- **9** 2 **Molly The Witch (IRE)**[301] 6166 3-8-12 0 PatDobbs 6 48
(M P Tregoning) *in tch: outpcd fr 3f out: hanging lft after and wknd* **20/1**

00 **10** 2¾ **Whispered Lands (IRE)**[35] 2981 3-8-12 0 PatCosgrave 12 43
(J R Boyle) *rdn in midfield 1/2-way: sn struggling* **100/1**

5 **11** 1 **Whiterocks**[15] 3660 3-9-3 0 SamHitchcott 4 46
(M R Channon) *s.s: a in rr: rdn over 4f out: brief effrt on outer 3f out: sn btn* **66/1**

6 **12** ¾ **Celtic Lass**[33] 3025 3-8-12 0 TedDurcan 15 39
(M A Jarvis) *chsd ldrs tl wknd fr wl over 2f out* **25/1**

13 ½ **Ingenue** 3-8-5 0 RosieJessop(7) 3 38
(Sir Mark Prescott) *s.s: last and struggling over 4f out: no ch* **50/1**

0-0 **14** 2½ **Seeking Faith (USA)**[14] 3696 3-8-12 0 AdamKirby 8 33
(C G Cox) *wl plcd tl wknd rapidly fr 3f out* **40/1**

2m 8.39s (-0.31) **Going Correction** -0.075s/f (Good)
WFA 3 from 4yo 10lb 14 Ran SP% **119.9**
Speed ratings (Par 103): **98,95,95,92,92 90,90,87,86,83 83,82,82,80**
toteswingers: 1&2 £14.30, 1&3 £13.60, 2&3 £6.30. CSF £41.64 TOTE £12.70: £3.70, £2.20, £2.70; EX 50.10.
Owner Capt J Macdonald-Buchanan **Bred** Hascombe And Valiant Studs **Trained** Newmarket, Suffolk

FOCUS
The bare form looks just fair.
Lacrosse ◆ Official explanation: jockey said colt ran green
Adnams ◆ Official explanation: jockey said gelding was unsuited by the good to firm ground

4146 CADOGAN CHARITY (S) STKS 1m 3f 135y
6:50 (6:51) (Class 6) 3-Y-0+ **£1,978** (£584; £292) **Stalls** Centre

Form RPR
-005 **1** **The Saucy Snipe**[12] 3739 3-8-1 57 DavidProbert(3) 2 56
(P Winkworth) *prom: wnt 2nd 3f out and sn pressed ldr: rdn to ld narrowly over 1f out: pushed out last 150yds and a holding on* **3/1**[2]

1053 **2** nk **Nawamees (IRE)**[4] 4021 11-9-12 65 (p) RyanMoore 3 65
(P D Evans) *led: rdn and pressed 3f out: narrowly hdd over 1f out: kpt on wl u.p but a hld* **5/6**[1]

1000 **3** 5 **Soul Singer**[12] 3739 3-8-9 51 RichardKingscote 7 52
(J G Portman) *settled bhd ldrs: effrt 3f out: cl enough to ldng pair over 1f out: wknd fnl f* **16/1**

5454 **4** 2½ **Tabulate**[138] 760 6-9-2 45 IanMongan 6 43
(P Howling) *hld up in last: stdy prog on outer fr over 2f out: in tch w ldrs over 1f out: shkn up and sn wknd* **25/1**

2525 **5** 2¼ **Lady Jinks**[4] 3997 4-9-2 51 RichardHughes 1 39
(R J Hodges) *reluctant to go nr stalls: keen early: mostly chsd ldr to 3f out: sn wknd* **4/1**[3]

0/05 **6** 6 **Safari**[12] 3740 6-9-2 39 DaneO'Neill 4 29
(S Curran) *hld up in 6th: cl enough 3f out: rdn and fnd nil over 2f out: wknd* **66/1**

0646 **7** 16 **Lilleput**[18] 3533 4-9-2 49 StephenCarson 8 2
(E A Wheeler) *s.s: sn prom: wknd rapidly 3f out: t.o* **40/1**

2m 30.25s (0.75) **Going Correction** -0.075s/f (Good)
WFA 3 from 4yo+ 12lb 7 Ran SP% **113.2**
Speed ratings (Par 101): **94,93,90,88,87 83,72**
toteswingers: 1&2 £1.40, 1&3 £6.70, 2&3 £12.60. CSF £5.74 TOTE £4.60: £2.00, £1.30; EX 7.30.There was no bid for the winner.
Owner Mrs F A Veasey **Bred** Mrs F A Veasey **Trained** Chiddingfold, Surrey

FOCUS
An ordinary seller.

4147 WINDSOR PARTNERS LTD EBF MAIDEN FILLIES' STKS 6f
7:20 (7:25) (Class 4) 2-Y-0 **£5,569** (£1,657; £828; £413) **Stalls** High

Form RPR
5322 **1** **Miss Lesley**[12] 3733 2-8-9 0 JamesO'Reilly(5) 3 78
(D K Ivory) *dwlt: sn prom on outer: rdn to go 2nd 2f out: styd on to ld narrowly ins fnl f: hld on wl* **9/1**

520 **2** nk **Itwasonlyakiss (IRE)**[33] 3015 2-9-0 0 MichaelHills 14 77
(J W Hills) *led and r against nr side rail: rdn 2f out: narrowly hdd ins fnl f: nt qckn and jst hld nr fin* **4/1**[2]

3 **3** 2½ **Outshine**[10] 3820 2-9-0 0 JimmyFortune 4 70
(J H M Gosden) *chsd ldr after 2f to 2f out: nt qckn u.p: one pce fr over 1f out* **6/4**[1]

4 hd **Candleshoe (IRE)** 2-9-0 0 RichardHughes 16 69
(R Hannon) *in tch in midfield: swtchd lft jst over 2f out: effrt over 1f out: styd on: nvr able to chal* **5/1**[3]

53 **5** nk **Oasis Jade**[11] 3772 2-9-0 0 RyanMoore 15 68
(G L Moore) *cl up against nr side rail: shkn up 2f out: one pce after* **8/1**

6 1 **Fair Nella** 2-9-0 0 TPO'Shea 7 65+
(J G Portman) *nervous ent stalls: s.s: taken steadily and wl in rr: pushed along fr 2f out: kpt on fr over 1f out: nrst fin* **80/1**

7 shd **Whipperway (IRE)** 2-9-0 0 SamHitchcott 10 65
(M R Channon) *wl in rr: pushed along bef 1/2-way: kpt on fnl 2f: nvr rchd ldrs* **40/1**

0 **8** 2 **Freddie's Girl (USA)**[12] 3744 2-9-0 0 AdamKirby 13 59
(Stef Liddiard) *chsd ldrs: shkn up briefly 2f out: grad fdd* **66/1**

46 **9** 2 **Pepi Royal (IRE)**[51] 2494 2-9-0 0 J-PGuillambert 2 53
(Pat Eddery) *in tch in rr: carried lft 2f out: grad wknd* **16/1**

0600 **10** 1½ **Silvee**[21] 3458 2-8-11 0 DavidProbert(3) 12 48
(J J Bridger) *awkward s: spd to chse ldr 2f: sn lost pl: fdd fnl 2f* **200/1**

11 9 **Avon Krystal** 2-9-0 0 PatDobbs 6 21
(R Hannon) *s.v.s: immediately t.o: no prog fr 1/2-way* **25/1**

0 **12** ½ **Restyle**[84] 1569 2-8-9 0 SophieDoyle(5) 5 20
(D K Ivory) *a in rr on wd outside: wknd 2f out: t.o* **100/1**

1m 12.54s (-0.46) **Going Correction** -0.25s/f (Firm) 12 Ran SP% **114.2**
Speed ratings (Par 93): **93,92,89,89,88 87,87,84,81,79 67,67**
toteswingers: 1&2 £4.30, 1&3 £8.50, 2&3 £2.50. CSF £42.37 TOTE £10.60: £2.30, £1.70, £1.30; EX 54.70.
Owner Mrs L A Ivory **Bred** Richard Kent **Trained** Radlett, Herts

FOCUS
There were four non-runners, including two fillies who were withdrawn after getting upset at the start, and the bare form looks no better than fair with the winner's profile tempering enthusiasm for the form.

NOTEBOOK
Miss Lesley had shown ability on her last three starts and found this a suitable opportunity to get off the mark. She looks a pretty straightforward filly and stayed on well to get the better of a protracted dual with the runner-up, having been handily placed throughout from her low draw. A fair sort for nurseries, she should stay 7f. (op 8-1 tchd 10-1)
Itwasonlyakiss(IRE), dropped in grade after being outclassed in the Queen Mary, and upped in trip, showed good speed throughout from her handy draw, appearing suited by being allowed to bowl along. She got the sixth furlong okay, but has the speed for 5f. (op 7-2)
Outshine didn't seem to improve on the form she showed in what had looked quite a good maiden at the July course ten days earlier. She was inclined to race a little keenly early and was soon held by the front pair. A drop back to 5f might help, but it remains to be seen whether she'll progress. (op 15-8)
Candleshoe(IRE) ◆, a 50,000gns half-sister to 1m2f winner Keepers Knight, out of a 6f scorer, has plenty of size about her and kept on nicely from off the pace once switched. She's open to a deal of improvement, particularly on easier ground considering she's by Danehill Dancer, and her dam's win was gained on good to soft. (op 6-1)
Oasis Jade has ability and should find her level in nurseries. (op 17-2 tchd 9-1)
Fair Nella, a £10,000 purchase who is related to a number of winners over varying trips, stayed on after a slow start and should improve. (op 66-1)
Pepi Royal(IRE) ◆, ridden with just hands-and-heels and stuck out very wide, might be one to look out for in a weak nursery. Official explanation: vet said filly sustained superficial cuts to its hock (op 14-1 tchd 9-1)

4148 ANIMAL HEALTH TRUST H'CAP 6f
7:50 (7:53) (Class 4) (0-85,85) 3-Y-O **£5,180** (£1,541; £770; £384) **Stalls** High

Form RPR
-543 **1** **Olynard (IRE)**[14] 3694 3-9-4 82 RichardKingscote 3 93
(R M Beckett) *trckd ldrs on outer: rdn 2f out: prog to ld jst ins fnl f: sn wl in command* **9/1**

3112 **2** 1¾ **Hand Painted**[17] 3592 3-8-9 73 TravisBlock 4 79
(P J Makin) *settled in midfield: effrt 2f out: styd on to dispute 2nd ins fnl f: no imp on wnr* **8/1**[3]

0506 **3** hd **Imperial Guest**[12] 3747 3-9-7 85 DaneO'Neill 7 90
(G G Margarson) *settled in midfield: prog 2f out: rdn to chal jst over 1f out: one pce fnl f* **13/2**[2]

5041 **4** ¾ **Ben's Dream (IRE)**[17] 3592 3-8-3 70 (t) DavidProbert(3) 2 73
(A M Balding) *wl in rr: rdn on outer 2f out: styd on fr over 1f out: nrst fin but no threat* **8/1**[3]

2104 **5** ½ **Doc Jones (IRE)**[10] 3804 3-8-10 74 ow1 RichardHughes 1 75
(P D Evans) *settled in rr on outer: prog fr 2f out: rdn to chse ldrs 1f out: nt qckn: eased last 50yds* **14/1**

-103 **6** ½ **Ray Of Joy**[33] 3028 3-9-5 83 EddieAhern 9 82
(J R Jenkins) *w ldr: led wl over 1f out: hdd & wknd jst ins fnl f* **16/1**

1300 **7** 1¼ **Lovely Thought**[12] 3746 3-9-2 80 (b) RyanMoore 5 75
(W J Haggas) *w ldng pair to wl over 1f out: wandering and lost pl sn after* **13/2**[2]

4033 **8** nk **Evelyn May (IRE)**[48] 2562 3-8-11 75 MichaelHills 8 69
(B W Hills) *hld up in last: taken towards outer over 1f out and shkn up: kpt on but nvr nr ldrs* **16/1**

-626 **9** 1¾ **Cut The Cackle (IRE)**[38] 2882 3-9-4 82 IanMongan 12 71
(P Winkworth) *mde most against nr side rail to wl over 1f out: sn wknd* **20/1**

10-1 **10** 1½ **Perfect Pride (USA)**[38] 2882 3-9-7 85 AdamKirby 10 69
(C G Cox) *hmpd s: in tch: first one pushed along bef 1/2-way: no imp fr 2f out: fdd* **7/2**[1]

-210 **11** hd **Anacreon (IRE)**[96] 1291 3-8-8 72 RichardMullen 6 55
(J H M Gosden) *a wl in rr: shkn up wl over 1f out: no prog* **8/1**[3]

0615 **12** ½ **Miss Hollybell**[17] 3592 3-8-9 73 TPO'Shea 11 55
(J Gallagher) *wnt lft s: a in rr: nt clr run on inner over 2f out: no ch after: eased fnl 50yds* **16/1**

1m 11.15s (-1.85) **Going Correction** -0.25s/f (Firm) 12 Ran SP% **121.3**
Speed ratings (Par 102): **102,99,99,98,97 97,95,95,92,90 90,89**
toteswingers: 1&2 £5.40, 1&3 £31.00, 2&3 £16.80. CSF £81.11 CT £510.42 TOTE £11.90: £3.30, £3.00, £2.70; EX 69.90.
Owner R Roberts **Bred** Redmyre Bloodstock & John Cullinan **Trained** Whitsbury, Hants

FOCUS
A fair sprint handicap.
Perfect Pride(USA) Official explanation: trainer had no explanation for the poor form shown
Miss Hollybell Official explanation: jockey said filly was denied a clear run

4149 SPORTINGBET.COM H'CAP 1m 67y
8:20 (8:22) (Class 5) (0-75,75) 3-Y-O+ **£2,729** (£806; £403) **Stalls** High

Form RPR
3041 **1** **Gold Express**[12] 3736 6-9-9 70 TedDurcan 6 88
(P J O'Gorman) *reluctant to enter stalls: stdd s: hld up in rr: prog fr 3f out to go 2nd jst over 2f out: rdn to ld over 1f out: drew clr* **13/2**

3044 **2** 4½ **Dear Maurice**[16] 3635 5-10-0 75 (v[1]) JimmyFortune 9 82
(E A L Dunlop) *led: at least 2 l clr over 2f out: hdd over 1f out: styd on but no match for wnr* **4/1**[1]

-002 **3** 3¼ **Striding Edge (IRE)**[14] 3693 3-9-2 71 EddieAhern 7 69
(W R Muir) *trckd ldrs: wnt 2nd 3f out to jst over 2f out: wl outpcd after* **9/2**[2]

6654 **4** nk **Hawaana (IRE)**[12] 3736 4-9-12 73 PaulDoe 12 72
(Eve Johnson Houghton) *hld up in abt 7th: rdn wl over 2f out and no real prog: edgd rt fr over 1f out: plugged on* **5/1**[3]

0-00 **5** 3¼ **Dustry (IRE)**[12] 3736 3-9-1 70 RyanMoore 5 60
(R Hannon) *sn last: urged along 5f out: plugged on fr over 2f out: no ch* **14/1**

0-05 **6** shd **Cool Ebony**[32] 3076 6-9-11 72 TravisBlock 3 64
(P J Makin) *chsd ldr to 3f out: grad wknd* **14/1**

4-02 **7** ¾ **Foxtrot Charlie**[35] 2982 3-8-11 66 (b) IanMongan 13 54
(P Winkworth) *s.i.s: keen early and sn trckd ldrs: rdn over 3f out: wknd 2f out* **12/1**

0302 **8** 2¾ **Binnion Bay (IRE)**[30] 3158 8-8-11 58 (b) NeilChalmers 8 42
(J J Bridger) *stdd s: hld up in last trio: shkn up 2f out: nvr a factor* **25/1**

5326 **9** 1/2 **Wilbury Star (IRE)**[12] 3736 3-9-4 73 RichardHughes 11 53
(R Hannon) hld up in abt 8th: rdn in midfield over 2f out: no imp over 1f out: eased fnl 150yds 6/1
00 **10** 1 1/4 **Tara's Garden**[10] 3798 4-8-6 56 oh9 (b[1]) JackMitchell(3) 4 36
(M Blanshard) wl in tch on outer: rdn wl over 2f out: wknd 66/1
1260 **11** 7 **Wunder Strike (USA)**[49] 2548 3-8-4 62 DavidProbert(3) 2 23
(J R Boyle) a wl in rr: struggling sn after 1/2-way: sn bhd 20/1
015- **12** 14 **It's Josr**[293] 6353 4-8-11 58 (b) RichardMullen 1 —
(I A Wood) chsd ldrs: rdn over 3f out: hanging and wknd over 2f out: eased over 1f out: t.o 33/1

1m 42.32s (-2.38) **Going Correction** -0.075s/f (Good)
WFA 3 from 4yo+ 8lb **12** Ran SP% **116.5**
Speed ratings (Par 103): **108,103,100,99,96 96,95,93,92,91 84,70**
toteswingers: 1&2 £5.20, 1&3 £3.40, 2&3 £3.80. CSF £30.81 CT £130.35 TOTE £7.90: £2.70, £2.30, £2.10; EX 32.30.
Owner N S Yong **Bred** Deerfield Farm **Trained** Newmarket, Suffolk

FOCUS
A fair handicap for the grade won impressively by Gold Express, who was the only winner on the card to record a time under standard.
Striding Edge(IRE) Official explanation: jockey said gelding was unsuited by the good to firm ground
It's Josr Official explanation: jockey said gelding hung right throughout

4150 PATEDDERYRACING.COM PROFESSIONAL RACEHORSE SYNDICATION H'CAP 1m 2f 7y

8:50 (8:51) (Class 5) (0-70,70) 3-Y-O+ £2,729 (£806; £403) **Stalls** Centre

Form RPR
-355 **1** **Rockfella**[20] 3472 3-8-12 64 EddieAhern 5 70
(D J Coakley) led: rdn and narrowly hdd over 2f out: kpt pressing ldr: rallied to ld again wl ins fnl f 8/1
0-P0 **2** nk **Fine Tolerance**[33] 3025 3-7-11 52 DavidProbert(3) 14 57
(J R Boyle) trckd ldr: clsd to chal over 3f out: narrow ld over 2f out: kpt on but hdd wl ins fnl f 80/1
333 **3** 1 1/4 **Bolanderi (USA)**[20] 3472 4-9-13 69 RichardHughes 15 72+
(Andrew Turnell) hld up wl in rr: stl in last trio 3f out: swtchd out wd and prog 2f out: rdn and styd on to take 3rd ins fnl f: unable to chal 7/1[3]
4-6 **4** 3/4 **Eurotanz (IRE)**[65] 2091 3-8-11 63 SteveDrowne 10 64
(H Morrison) trckd ldng pair: rdn and nt qckn over 2f out: one pce after 4/1[2]
1612 **5** 1 **Hollow Green (IRE)**[7] 3922 3-8-10 67 RichardEvans(5) 4 66+
(P D Evans) hld up towards rr: rapid prog to join ldng pair 3f out: nt qckn jst over 2f out: hld whn jockey dropped whip wl over 1f out: fdd 11/4[1]
1304 **6** 1 1/4 **Locum**[18] 3550 4-9-10 66 TedDurcan 1 63
(M H Tompkins) hld up in last trio: pushed along and no real prog 3f out: rdn and styd on fr over 1f out: nrst fin 8/1
4235 **7** 1 1/2 **Gracechurch (IRE)**[6] 3946 6-8-8 55 MCGeran(5) 12 49
(R J Hodges) hld up in midfield: rdn on inner wl over 2f out: no prog: fdd fnl f 9/1
3365 **8** 3/4 **Hallingdal (UAE)**[10] 3812 4-9-11 67 TPO'Shea 11 59
(J J Bridger) t.k.h: hld up: last 4f out: shuffled along and nvr nr ldrs 14/1
2131 **9** 1/2 **Hatch A Plan (IRE)**[18] 3533 8-9-2 58 NeilChalmers 2 49
(Mouse Hamilton-Fairley) hld up in midfield: effrt on outer over 2f out: no imp on ldrs jst over 1f out: fdd fnl f 12/1
0-00 **10** 1/2 **Dancer's Legacy**[11] 3766 4-9-10 66 PatCosgrave 3 56
(J R Boyle) trckd ldng pair: rdn wl over 2f out: wknd over 1f out 33/1
400 **11** hd **Old Romney**[9] 3864 5-9-7 70 LauraPike(7) 9 60
(P Howling) s.s: plld hrd and hld up in last: taken to wd outside over 3f out: shuffled along and nvr nr ldrs 25/1
34-0 **12** 2 1/2 **Rehabilitation**[42] 2773 4-9-7 63 (tp) AdamKirby 7 48
(W R Swinburn) settled in midfield: rdn and no prog wl over 2f out: sn wknd 14/1

2m 8.61s (-0.09) **Going Correction** -0.075s/f (Good)
WFA 3 from 4yo+ 10lb **12** Ran SP% **120.4**
Speed ratings (Par 103): **97,96,95,95,94 93,92,91,91,90 90,88**
toteswingers: 1&2 £51.70, 1&3 £14.80, 2&3 £103.40. CSF £544.94 CT £4645.78 TOTE £9.20: £3.00, £9.10, £2.70; EX 440.10 Place 6 £93.74, Place 5 £36.24.
Owner L M A Hurley **Bred** Ascagnano S P A **Trained** West Ilsley, Berks

FOCUS
A modest handicap in which it paid to race handy.
Hallingdal(UAE) Official explanation: jockey said filly was denied a clear run
Old Romney Official explanation: jockey said gelding ran too free
T/Plt: £126.60 to a £1 stake. Pool: £80,143.97. 461.87 winning tickets. T/Qpdt: £36.50 to a £1 stake. Pool: £6,684.43. 135.35 winning tickets. JN

3957 YARMOUTH (L-H)

Monday, July 20

OFFICIAL GOING: Good to soft changing to good (good to soft in places) after race 1 (2.15)
Wind: almost nil Weather: warm but overcast

4151 NORFOLK BROADS MEDIAN AUCTION MAIDEN STKS 1m 1f

2:15 (2:16) (Class 6) 3-5-Y-O £2,590 (£770; £385; £192) **Stalls** Low

Form RPR
0342 **1** **Bomber Brown (IRE)**[18] 3549 3-9-0 75 JackMitchell(3) 3 75
(P W Chapple-Hyam) mde all: rdn 1f out: styd on wl: cosily 11/4[1]
0 **2** 1 **Starkat**[44] 2710 3-8-12 0 KirstyMilczarek 7 68
(J A R Toller) t.k.h in midfield: effrt and rdn 4f out: outpcd 2f out: kpt on wl fnl 100yds: snatched 2nd: nt rch wnr 50/1
2240 **3** nse **Mt Kintyre (IRE)**[39] 2855 3-9-3 75 TPQueally 5 73
(M H Tompkins) t.k.h: prom: rdn and no imp 2f out: kpt on to go 2nd 100yds out tl fnl stride 9/1
00-0 **4** 1 1/4 **Ela Gorrie Mou**[73] 1844 3-8-7 47 MCGeran(5) 10 65
(T T Clement) stdd in rr: a lot to do 3f out: prog 2f out: gng on wl ins fnl f 100/1
652 **5** 1/2 **Miss Sophisticat**[13] 3708 3-8-12 72 (v) PaulDoe 6 64
(W J Knight) pressed wnr: rdn 2f out: no ex ins fnl f: lost 2nd fnl 100yds 9/2[3]
2 **6** 3/4 **Espero (IRE)**[30] 3155 3-9-3 82 DarryllHolland 14 67
(R A Farrant) chsd ldrs: effrt 3f out: chal 2f out: styng on at one pce whn hung lft 1f out 4/1[2]
/64 **7** 1 1/4 **Action Girl**[14] 3696 4-9-7 0 JimCrowley 12 60
(R M H Cowell) towards rr: effrt and rdn 3f out: nvr able to chal: btn 2f out 50/1
5 **8** 2 1/4 **Valfurva (IRE)**[25] 3297 3-8-12 0 MartinDwyer 3 55
(L M Cumani) bhd early: rdn 6f out: sme prog to chse ldrs on far rails 3f out: no imp after 8/1
020- **9** 4 **Tamarah**[275] 6818 3-8-12 76 PhilipRobinson 11 46
(Miss D Mountain) cl up: rdn 4f out: fdd 3f out 7/1
10 7 **Sula Dream** 3-9-3 0 DO'Donohoe 8 35
(J Pearce) bhd: last and pushed along 5f out: struggling bdly after 100/1
11 1 1/4 **Red Oriental**[18] 3-8-12 87 ShaneKelly 1 28
(N P Littmoden) ponied to s early: midfield: rdn 4f out: btn 3f out 8/1
66 **12** 4 **Yashkur**[10] 3813 3-8-12 0 KShea 13 19
(C E Brittain) towards rr: rdn and struggling 3f out 20/1
0 **13** 17 **Hilltop Alchemy**[30] 3168 3-9-3 0 AdrianMcCarthy 9 —
(J R Jenkins) last away and sn drvn: nvr gng wl in last pair: t.o 3f out: eased fnl 2f 100/1

1m 55.4s (-0.40) **Going Correction** 0.0s/f (Good)
WFA 3 from 4yo 9lb **13** Ran SP% **121.2**
Speed ratings (Par 101): **101,100,100,98,98 97,96,94,91,84 83,80,65**
toteswingers: 1&2 £39.90, 1&3 £6.00, 2&3 £113.80. CSF £172.15 TOTE £3.00: £1.10, £14.00, £4.20; EX 157.10 TRIFECTA Not won..
Owner Baggies Racing **Bred** Camogue Stud Ltd **Trained** Newmarket, Suffolk

FOCUS
An ordinary maiden. The form makes some sense and has been rated at face value, although the fourth is a worry.
Espero(IRE) Official explanation: jockey said colt hung left
Valfurva(IRE) Official explanation: trainer's rep said filly coughed excessively after the race
Red Oriental Official explanation: trainer said filly was unsuited by the good to soft ground

4152 FIRSTBET.COM 0800 230 0800 #50 MATCHED BET MEDIAN AUCTION MAIDEN STKS 7f 3y

2:45 (2:48) (Class 6) 2-Y-O £2,590 (£770; £385; £192) **Stalls** High

Form RPR
1 **Syrian** 2-9-3 0 HayleyTurner 7 83+
(M L W Bell) hld up in tch: led 1f out: readily 6/4[1]
024 **2** 1 1/2 **Astonishment (IRE)**[11] 3786 2-9-3 0 JamesDoyle 2 76
(S Kirk) a.p: led 2f out: rdn and hdd 1f out: nt qckn: hld on for 2nd 7/1[3]
04 **3** hd **Universal Circus**[10] 3810 2-8-12 0 DarryllHolland 5 71
(M R Channon) led: hdd 2f out: rdn over 1f out: kpt on towards fin 9/2[2]
4 5 **Iron Condor** 2-8-12 0 WilliamCarson(5) 12 63
(J M P Eustace) s.i.s: hld up and bhd: hdwy and hung lft fr over 2f out: pushed along over 1f out: no imp on ldng trio fnl f 25/1
5 3 3/4 **Cornish Beau (IRE)** 2-9-3 0 TPQueally 10 54
(M H Tompkins) hld up in tch: pushed along and hung lft fr over 2f out: wknd over 1f out 16/1
424 **6** 1 1/2 **Bradford (IRE)**[21] 3468 2-8-12 0 (v[1]) MartinLane(5) 6 50
(K R Burke) prom: pushed along over 2f out: wknd wl over 1f out 9/2[2]
7 1 1/4 **Chandrayaan** 2-9-3 0 StephenDonohoe 1 47
(E A L Dunlop) dwlt: in rr: pushed along and sme prog over 2f out: rdn and wknd over 1f out 25/1
6 **8** 6 **The Frying Pan (IRE)**[33] 3027 2-8-12 0 (b[1]) ShaneKelly 8 27
(Dr J D Scargill) prom tl rdn and wknd over 2f out 100/1
9 1 **Carlcol Girl** 2-8-12 0 (v[1]) LiamJones 3 25
(Mrs C A Dunnett) s.i.s: a bhd 100/1
0 **10** 3 **Walnut Rise**[29] 3187 2-8-5 0 AshleyMorgan(7) 11 17
(M H Tompkins) bhd fnl 4f 100/1
06 **11** 9 **Thaliwarru**[28] 3218 2-9-3 0 TonyCulhane 15 —
(G G Margarson) hung lft thrght: sn bhd 33/1
0 **12** 1 **Kit Kat**[11] 3786 2-8-12 0 MatthewDavies(5) 16 —
(George Baker) chsd ldrs: push along over 3f out: rdn and struggling wl over 2f out 100/1
0 **13** 1 3/4 **Anchorage Boy (USA)**[23] 3395 2-9-3 0 JerryO'Dwyer 9 —
(Miss Amy Weaver) sn rdn along and bhd 66/1
60 **14** nk **Polebrook**[36] 2940 2-9-3 0 AdrianMcCarthy 4 —
(J R Jenkins) mid-div: pushed along and lost pl over 3f out: eased whn no ch over 1f out 150/1
00 **15** 1 **Lochbroom Sunset**[39] 2853 2-9-3 0 (t) JimCrowley 14 —
(S C Williams) s.i.s: sn hld up in mid-div: rdn over 2f out: sn wknd 100/1
16 6 **Flag Of Glory** 2-9-3 0 GeorgeBaker 13 —
(C F Wall) sn wl in rr: eased whn no ch over 1f out 12/1

1m 28.54s (1.94) **Going Correction** +0.15s/f (Good) **16** Ran SP% **120.2**
Speed ratings (Par 92): **94,92,92,86,82 80,78,72,70,67 57,56,54,53,52 45**
toteswingers: 1&2 £3.90, 1&3 £3.40, 2&3 £5.10. CSF £11.74 TOTE £2.40: £1.40, £2.30, £1.80; EX 13.10 Trifecta £40.90 Pool: £260.92 - 4.72 winning units.
Owner Highclere Thoroughbred Racing (Donoghue) **Bred** B Walters **Trained** Newmarket, Suffolk

FOCUS
A modest juvenile maiden. The form should work out.

NOTEBOOK
Syrian ◆ justified confidence with a comfortable debut success. He raced in midfield and took time to settle, but was full of running when asked to close on the leaders passing the 2f marker. He showed signs of inexperience coming to the final furlong, but stamped his authority on the race soon afterwards and cruised home under hands-and-heels riding. As a son of Hawk Wing, an easy surface should prove ideal for him and he is bred to come into his own as a 3yo, but looks well up to making his mark at a higher level this season. The step up to 1m should also be well within his reach this term and he should improve for the run, so rates one to follow. Connections will reportedly look for a novice race next. (op 7-4 tchd 2-1 in a place)
Astonishment(IRE) proved game in defeat and provides a decent benchmark for the race. A small maiden could come his way, but nurseries look his best option. (op 6-1 tchd 5-1)
Universal Circus was bidding to enhance her yard's excellent record in the race and was given every chance under a positive ride. She now qualifies for nurseries and should not be that long in winning. (op 5-1)
Iron Condor is a half-brother to his stable's stout stayer At The Money. He posted a pleasing display, probably wants 1m already and should improve nicely for this initial experience. (tchd 20-1 and 33-1)
Cornish Beau(IRE) was representing the stable that took this last year. However, the representative on that occasion had the benefit of a previous outing and their juvenile always improve for a run. With that in mind he put in a fair debut effort and should get closer next time. (op 25-1 tchd 33-1)
Bradford(IRE) raced in a first-time visor and downed tools around 2f out, before the extra furlong came into play. He now becomes one to swerve. (op 4-1 tchd 5-1)
Flag Of Glory Official explanation: jockey said colt ran very green

4153 COMPASS TAXIS 01493 445544 (S) STKS 6f 3y

3:15 (3:18) (Class 6) 2-Y-O £1,942 (£578; £288; £144) **Stalls** High

Form RPR
0 **1** **Coolree Star (IRE)**[7] 3918 2-8-12 0 MartinDwyer 3 67
(W R Muir) wnt rt s: prom: led over 1f out: rdn and hld on after prolonged tussle fnl f 33/1

045 **2** *nse* **Jessica Hayllar (USA)**[21] 3458 2-8-7 0 JamieSpencer 6 62
(M L W Bell) *stdd s: midfield and rdn 1/2-way: clsd to press wnr fr 1f out: drvn and ev ch tl btn on nod* **11/8**[1]

1 **3** *7* **Annia Galeria (IRE)**[4] 4018 2-8-13 0 StephenDonohoe 9 47
(A B Haynes) *led: rdn and hdd over 1f out: sn wknd* **7/2**[2]

0 **4** *nk* **Steel My Heart (IRE)**[18] 3547 2-8-3 0 ow1 WilliamCarson(5) 1 41
(Miss D Mountain) *cl up on outside: rdn and swishing tail and wavering fnl 2f: v reluctant: btn 1f out* **33/1**

0230 **5** *½* **Bond Together**[38] 2896 2-8-12 0 PaulDoe 5 44+
(P D Evans) *hmpd s: rdn in rr: styd on ins fnl f: wnt lft: unable to chal* **6/1**

0200 **6** *1 ¾* **Angie's Nap (USA)**[12] 3742 2-8-2 0 Louis-PhilippeBeuzelin(5) 8 33
(P S McEntee) *racd freely: prom: rdn and fdd over 1f out: fin v weakly* **12/1**

006 **7** *5* **Botley Bell**[9] 3858 2-8-7 0 TonyCulhane 7 18
(M R Channon) *s.i.s: pushed along in rr: struggling over 2f out* **5/1**[3]

50 **8** *10* **Last Orders (IRE)**[70] 1939 2-8-12 0 ChrisCatlin 2 —
(M G Quinlan) *sn pushed along in rr: struggling over 2f out: t.o* **28/1**

0 **9** *4 ½* **Cockney Colonel (USA)**[7] 3918 2-8-12 0 EdwardCreighton 12 —
(E J Creighton) *taken down early: dwlt: rn green and drvn in rr: struggling over 2f out: t.o* **66/1**

1m 15.45s (1.05) **Going Correction** +0.15s/f (Good) **9** Ran SP% **113.8**
Speed ratings (Par 92): **99,98,89,89,88 86,79,66,60**
toteswingers: 1&2 £9.90, 1&3 £19.10, 2&3 £2.00. CSF £76.93 TOTE £44.70: £7.20, £1.10, £1.60; EX 118.70 Trifecta £389.80 Part won. Pool: £526.87 - 0.63 winning units..The winner was bought by Paul Dixon for 10,000gns. Annia Galeria was claimed by C A Dwyer for £5,000. Jessica Hayllar was claimed by G Blum for £5,000.
Owner Mrs J M Muir **Bred** D Johnson **Trained** Lambourn, Berks

FOCUS
A typically poor juvenile seller in which the first pair dominated.

NOTEBOOK
Coolree Star(IRE) ran distinctly green on his debut at Windsor a week previously, but that experience had obviously had the desired effect as he travelled best of all through the race on under a positive ride. He looked in trouble when the runner-up headed him at the furlong pole, but he proved game against the stands' rail and rallied to get back on top where it mattered. The extra furlong helped his cause and he is entitled to further improvement, but looks to have found his level. (op 25-1)
Jessica Hayllar(USA), back up in trip, was well supported for this drop in class and only just missed out. She initially came under pressure around halfway, before coming back onto the bridle, but her jockey again had to get serious with her to get her head in front. With 100yards to run it appeared as if she would go in, but she lacked the resolution of the winner and that rival did have the benefit of a rail to run against. She is clearly well up to winning in this class, but is not one to be taking a short price about. (op 7-4 tchd 15-8)
Annia Galeria(IRE) was the sole winner in attendance having scored on her debut over 5f four days earlier. She had her chance and looked to get the extra furlong, but shaped as though the run probably came a little too soon. (op 6-1)
Steel My Heart(IRE) appeared uninterested when finishing last in this class over C&D on her debut 18 days earlier. This was obviously a big step up on that display, but she got herself warm beforehand and looks to have issues.
Bond Together tended to run in snatches and would likely benefit for the application of headgear. (tchd 11-2)

4154 GEORGE SMITH "LIFETIME IN RACING" H'CAP 6f 3y
3:45 (3:49) (Class 5) (0-75,74) 3-Y-0+ **£1,764** (£1,764; £404; £202) **Stalls** High

Form RPR

0050 **1** **Kyle (IRE)**[3] 4072 5-9-10 **72** ShaneKelly 2 80
(C R Dore) *towards rr: rdn and swtchd rt wl over 1f out: str run ins fnl f to dispute ld and force dead-heat on line* **8/1**

010 **1** *dht* **Bohobe (IRE)**[19] 3505 4-8-4 **57** WilliamCarson(5) 6 65
(Rae Guest) *t.k.h towards rr: rdn 2f out: outpcd over 1f out: kpt on wl ins fnl f to dispute ld and force dead-heat on line* **6/1**[3]

3-40 **3** *hd* **Rosie Says No**[48] 2579 4-8-11 **59** (p) JimCrowley 5 66
(R M H Cowell) *racd freely and prom: drvn ahd ins fnl f: jst ct* **9/1**

-014 **4** *1 ¾* **Luminous Gold**[24] 3347 4-9-11 **73** GeorgeBaker 3 75
(C F Wall) *reluctant to enter stall: led: rdn 1f out: fnd little: hdd and nt qckn ins fnl f* **2/1**[1]

1253 **5** *½* **Memphis Man**[7] 3917 6-9-7 **74** RichardEvans(5) 4 74
(P D Evans) *taken down early: last away: t.k.h: sn pressing ldrs: rdn over 1f out: no ex ins fnl f* **7/2**[2]

-000 **6** *nk* **Geezers Colours**[20] 3488 4-9-5 **72** MartinLane(5) 7 71
(K R Burke) *last early: swtchd lft to outside 3f out: effrt 2f out: unable to chal fnl f but kpt on steadily: fin lame* **22/1**

34-0 **7** *6* **Bonne**[13] 3722 4-9-1 **63** PaulFitzsimons 1 43
(Miss J R Tooth) *cl up: rdn over 2f out: fdd over 1f out* **12/1**

5032 **8** *8* **Defector (IRE)**[13] 3712 3-9-5 **72** (b) MartinDwyer 8 26
(W R Muir) *t.k.h in rr: drvn over 2f out: little rspnse: wl btn over 1f out* **8/1**

1m 15.25s (0.85) **Going Correction** +0.15s/f (Good)
WFA 3 from 4yo+ 5lb **8** Ran SP% **114.1**
Speed ratings (Par 103): **100,100,99,97,96 96,88,77**WIN: Kyle £4.70, Bohobe £3.90. PL: K £2.60, B £1.90, Rosie Says No £2.70. EX: K-B £23.20, B-K £29.70. CSF: K-B £27.33, B-K £26.13. TRICAST: K-B-RSN £222.47, B-K-RSN £215.62. toteswingers: K&B £5.40, K&RSN £10.70, B&RSN £10.10. TRIFECTA Pool: £5227 Owner.
Owner Tremousser Partnership **Bred** Bryan Ryan **Trained** Newmarket, Suffolk

FOCUS
A fair sprint handicap run a fifth of a second faster than the preceding seller, and like that contest it produced a really close finish.
Geezers Colours Official explanation: vet said gelding returned lame

4155 RACING WELFARE HBLB H'CAP 6f 3y
4:15 (4:23) (Class 6) (0-55,53) 3-Y-0 **£1,942** (£578; £288; £144) **Stalls** High

Form RPR

0056 **1** **Eye For The Girls**[17] 3580 3-9-0 **52** DarryllHolland 3 58
(M R Channon) *chsd ldrs: rdn over 2f out: sn edgd lft: gd prog 1f out: edgd rt: led fnl 100yds: kpt on wl* **5/1**[1]

0004 **2** *½* **Call Me Courageous (IRE)**[14] 3673 3-8-12 **50** TPQueally 5 54
(A B Haynes) *t.k.h early: cl up: rdn over 2f out: outpcd over 1f out: styd on to go 2nd wl ins fnl f: a hld* **8/1**

0040 **3** *½* **Rapanui Belle**[27] 3246 3-8-2 **45** MartinLane(5) 4 47
(G L Moore) *prom: rdn to ld 1f out: hdd fnl 100yds: nt qckn: lost 2nd nr fin* **20/1**

-0U5 **4** *nk* **Always The Sun**[27] 3245 3-8-7 **45** DO'Donohoe 10 46
(P Leech) *bdly outpcd: stl virtually t.o over 2f out: prodigious prog fnl f: too much to do* **66/1**

6023 **5** *shd* **Dancing Welcome**[7] 3926 3-8-12 **50** (b) NickyMackay 12 51
(J M Bradley) *sn drvn along: towards rr tl tried to cl over 1f out: swtchd lft and kpt on: unable to chal* **11/2**[2]

-002 **6** *2* **Native Dame (IRE)**[21] 3449 3-9-0 **52** (b) PaulFitzsimons 8 47
(Edgar Byrne) *drvn 1/2-way: nvr bttr than midfield: btn over 1f out* **8/1**

5050 **7** *½* **Thumberlina**[6] 3959 3-8-7 **45** (v) AdrianMcCarthy 9 38
(Mrs C A Dunnett) *led: rdn and hdd 1f out: sn lost pl but plugged on* **20/1**

6045 **8** *1* **Wicklewood**[6] 3953 3-8-3 **46** ow1 (v) WilliamCarson(5) 15 36
(Mrs C A Dunnett) *chsd ldrs tl rdn and no ex over 1f out* **7/1**[3]

440 **9** *1 ¼* **Kings On The Roof**[48] 2577 3-9-0 **52** JimCrowley 7 38
(G C Bravery) *chsd ldrs: drvn 2f out: wknd ins fnl f* **14/1**

5-00 **10** *½* **Lady Dinsdale (IRE)**[9] 3859 3-8-11 **49** ShaneKelly 11 33
(T Keddy) *s.s: plld hrd in rr: btn wl over 1f out* **16/1**

5606 **11** *1 ½* **Songful (IRE)**[90] 1420 3-8-4 **49** TobyAtkinson(7) 13 29
(Pat Eddery) *v awkward to load: sn rdn: prom tl rdn and fdd over 1f out* **7/1**[3]

0150 **12** *4* **Deckchair**[21] 3464 3-9-0 **52** (v) LiamJones 14 19
(H J Collingridge) *cl up tl 1/2-way: fdd qckly over 1f out: eased whn btn ins fnl f* **11/1**

60 **R** **Dedante**[48] 2581 3-9-0 **52** ChrisCatlin 1 —
(D K Ivory) *mounted on crse and reluctant to go to s: ref to r* **16/1**

1m 15.93s (1.53) **Going Correction** +0.15s/f (Good) **13** Ran SP% **117.1**
Speed ratings (Par 98): **95,94,93,93,93 90,89,88,86,86 84,78,—**
toteswingers: 1&2 £8.60, 1&3 £30.90, 2&3 £51.10. CSF £42.39 CT £544.50 TOTE £4.90: £2.00, £2.70, £8.70; EX 37.30 Trifecta £326.00 Part won. Pool: £440.64 - 0.43 winning units..
Owner Heart Of The South Racing **Bred** John And Caroline Penny **Trained** West Ilsley, Berks

FOCUS
A decidedly weak 3yo handicap and it is hard to be positive about the form.
Eye For The Girls Official explanation: trainer's rep said, regarding apparent improvement in form, that the gelding had appreciated the good (good to soft places) ground.

4156 J & H SIMPSON CHARTERED ACCOUNTANTS H'CAP 1m 3f 101y
4:45 (4:48) (Class 6) (0-60,58) 3-Y-0+ **£2,072** (£616; £308; £153) **Stalls** Low

Form RPR

1-06 **1** **Amazing King (IRE)**[48] 2573 5-9-9 **58** LeeVickers(3) 12 68
(P A Kirby) *led after 2f: clr whn rdn 2f out: drvn out ins fnl f* **6/1**[3]

606 **2** *1 ½* **Galiotto (IRE)**[32] 3056 3-8-4 **47** ChrisCatlin 3 54
(C F Wall) *hld up in mid-div: hdwy over 3f out: wnt 2nd 2f out: rdn over 1f out: styd on towards fin: nt rch wnr* **18/1**

0120 **3** *½* **Karky Schultz (GER)**[12] 3737 4-9-7 **58** WilliamCarson(5) 11 64
(J M P Eustace) *s.i.s: hld up towards rr: nt clr run over 4f out: hdwy whn nt clr run and swtchd lft over 2f out: swtchd rt wl over 1f out: sn rdn: styd on towards fin* **9/1**

042 **4** *4 ½* **Casablanca Minx (IRE)**[16] 3631 6-9-5 **51** (b) MickyFenton 9 50
(Miss Gay Kelleway) *hld up towards rr: rdn and edgd lft 3f out: hdwy over 2f out: no imp fnl f* **22/1**

-012 **5** *1 ¼* **Outland (IRE)**[20] 3482 3-8-10 **53** TPQueally 16 49
(M H Tompkins) *hld up in mid-div: hdwy over 4f out: rdn over 2f out: wknd over 1f out* **4/1**[1]

0-04 **6** *2* **Acclaim To Fame (IRE)**[41] 2790 3-8-1 **49** MartinLane(5) 13 42
(K R Burke) *hld up in mid-div: effrt over 4f out: sn rdn: wknd over 2f out* **14/1**

5600 **7** *nk* **Moon Mix (FR)**[6] 3960 6-9-1 **47** AdrianMcCarthy 5 39
(J R Jenkins) *s.i.s: hld up in rr: rdn jst over 1f out: nvr nr ldrs* **33/1**

0240 **8** *½* **Ready To Crown (USA)**[7] 3927 5-9-6 **52** GeorgeBaker 2 44
(J Mackie) *hld up in tch on ins: sltly outpcd 4f out: rdn 2f out: sn btn* **18/1**

0025 **9** *¾* **Chic Shanique (USA)**[23] 3383 3-9-0 **57** RichardSmith 7 47
(Tom Dascombe) *led 2f: chsd ldr tl over 5f out: rdn over 2f out: wknd over 1f out* **16/1**

4552 **10** *¾* **Art Value**[17] 3561 4-9-0 **46** (p) DarryllHolland 10 35
(M Wigham) *stdd sn after s: hld up towards rr: pushed along over 3f out: rdn over 2f out: n.d* **13/2**

4000 **11** *½* **Nicky Nutjob (GER)**[41] 2790 3-8-5 **48** (b[1]) DO'Donohoe 1 36
(J Pearce) *s.i.s: rdn 3f out: a in rr* **50/1**

0005 **12** *11* **Captain Mainwaring**[34] 3004 4-8-8 **45** (p) Louis-PhilippeBeuzelin(5) 15 15
(N P Littmoden) *s.i.s: hld up in rr: pushed along over 3f out: rdn and struggling over 2f out: eased whn no ch fnl f* **25/1**

-000 **13** *17* **Polish Red**[13] 3714 5-9-11 **57** (p) JamieSpencer 14 —
(Jane Chapple-Hyam) *prom: chsd wnr over 5f out: rdn over 3f out: lost 2nd and wknd over 2f out: eased whn no ch over 1f out* **8/1**

0-52 **14** *6* **Silent Act (USA)**[72] 1893 3-9-1 **58** JimCrowley 8 —
(Mrs A J Perrett) *prom: rdn and hung lft 3f out: wknd qckly: eased whn no ch over 1f out* **5/1**[2]

2m 28.36s (-0.34) **Going Correction** 0.0s/f (Good)
WFA 3 from 4yo+ 11lb **14** Ran SP% **121.6**
Speed ratings (Par 101): **101,99,99,96,95 93,93,93,92,92 91,83,71,67**
toteswingers: 1&2 £32.90, 1&3 £16.00, 2&3 £32.70. CSF £105.82 CT £980.53 TOTE £7.90: £3.40, £6.20, £3.00; EX 173.50 TRIFECTA Not won..
Owner The New Venture Partnership **Bred** Kraemer Partnership **Trained** Castleton, N Yorks

FOCUS
A moderate handicap, run at an ordinary pace. Straightforward form.
Silent Act(USA) Official explanation: trainer had no explanation for the poor form shown

4157 CRH TRANSPORT TRAINING H'CAP 1m 2f 21y
5:15 (5:17) (Class 6) (0-65,64) 3-Y-0 **£2,072** (£616; £308; £153) **Stalls** Low

Form RPR

0-05 **1** **My Girl Jode**[39] 2858 3-8-12 **55** TPQueally 6 68
(M H Tompkins) *racd keenly on heels of ldrs: effrt to ld over 2f out: rdn clr over 1f out: nvr looked in danger after* **7/2**[1]

0-20 **2** *2 ¼* **Jachol (IRE)**[31] 3099 3-8-10 **53** TonyCulhane 7 62
(W J Haggas) *prom: rdn over 4f out: swtchd rt and outpcd wl over 1f out: wnt 2nd over 1f out: edgd lft: nvr any ch w wnr* **9/2**[2]

2426 **3** *3 ¾* **Beaubrav**[35] 2982 3-9-5 **62** ShaneKelly 9 63
(P W D'Arcy) *chsd ldr after 3f: rdn 3f out: lost 2nd over 1f out: plodded on* **9/2**[2]

3040 **4** *3 ¼* **Bubses Boy**[35] 2982 3-8-13 **56** JamieSpencer 8 51
(M L W Bell) *sn tacked lft fr outside to ld on rails: rdn and hdd over 2f out: fdd over 1f out* **9/2**[2]

0-40 **5** *¾* **Precious Secret (IRE)**[22] 3427 3-8-12 **55** MartinDwyer 11 48
(C F Wall) *pushed along in rr early: nvr bttr than midfield: effrt 3f out: one pce and btn over 2f out* **7/1**[3]

-004 **6** *2* **Lambourn Genie (UAE)**[6] 3942 3-8-6 **49** RichardSmith 2 38
(Tom Dascombe) *slowly away: bhd: effrt to trck ldrs 3f out: rdn and wknd over 2f out* **14/1**

0-00 **7** *3 ¾* **Vin De Rose**[28] 3228 3-8-3 **46** ow1 DO'Donohoe 1 28
(John A Harris) *v late to paddock: plld hrd and prom early: sn dropped to rr: no ch fnl 4f* **50/1**

4005 **8** *4 ½* **Bromhead (USA)**[6] 3960 3-9-7 **64**....................(t) LiamJones 3 37
(Mrs C A Dunnett) *taken down early: plld hrd in rr: rdn 4f out: lost tch 3f out: t.o* **10/1**
000 **9** *5* **Dolores Ortiz (IRE)**[46] 2640 3-9-3 **60**.................... JimCrowley 5 23
(S C Williams) *midfield: rdn over 4f out: sn labouring: t.o* **14/1**
-050 **10** *9* **Penperth**[26] 3274 3-8-12 **60**....................(b¹) WilliamCarson(5) 4 5
(J M P Eustace) *taken down early: bhd: brought wd after home turn: rdn and sn struggling: t.o* **25/1**

2m 9.84s (-0.66) **Going Correction** 0.0s/f (Good) **10** Ran SP% **117.5**
Speed ratings (Par 98): **102,100,97,94,94 92,89,85,81,74**
toteswingers: 1&2 £5.40, 1&3 £3.70, 2&3 £5.70. CSF £19.27 CT £72.41 TOTE £3.80: £1.60, £1.50, £2.00; EX 24.40 Trifecta £88.10 Pool: £316.93 - 2.66 winning units.
Owner Jackie & George Smith **Bred** G A E And J Smith Bloodstock **Trained** Newmarket, Suffolk

FOCUS
A moderate 3yo handicap but the time was respectable and the form has been rated fairly positively.

4158 GREAT YARMOUTH TOURIST AUTHORITY APPRENTICE H'CAP 1m 2f 21y
5:45 (5:45) (Class 6) (0-60,60) 4-Y-0+ **£1,942** (£578; £288; £144) **Stalls** Low

Form RPR
5662 **1** **Dragon Slayer (IRE)**[6] 3960 7-9-0 **58**.................... TobyAtkinson(3) 3 68
(John A Harris) *plld hrd in midfield: effrt 2f out: unleashed to ld 120yds out: dashed clr* **2/1**[1]
5062 **2** *2 ¾* **Fantasy Ride**[34] 3004 7-8-8 **49**.................... SimonPearce 5 54
(J Pearce) *hld up in rr: gd prog on far rails over 3f out: led over 1f out: 2 l clr ent fnl f: hdd 120yds out and immediately outpcd* **11/4**[2]
6300 **3** *2 ¼* **Jiminor Mack**[34] 3004 6-8-5 **46** oh1.................... DeclanCannon 11 46
(W J H Ratcliffe) *last away: effrt towards centre 3f out: no imp over 1f out* **25/1**
000- **4** *1 ¾* **Domesday (UAE)**[327] 5389 8-8-2 **46** oh1.................... JosephineBruning(3) 8 43
(T T Clement) *prom: pushed along over 1f out: one pce and sn btn* **33/1**
4000 **5** *¾* **Desert Hawk**[5] 3974 8-8-0 **46** oh1.................... KierenFox(5) 7 41
(W M Brisbourne) *hdwy 4f out: hung lft fnl f: kpt on wout threatening* **11/1**
0-55 **6** *¾* **Jelly Mo**[17] 3594 4-8-2 **48**.................... AlexEdwards(5) 6 42
(W M Brisbourne) *cl up: led 3f out tl over 1f out: sn btn* **14/1**
-350 **7** *3 ¾* **Dusk**[24] 2975 4-9-2 **60**....................(b) DavidKenny(3) 2 46
(Mrs S J Humphrey) *midfield: effrt 3f out: shkn up over 2f out: sn no rspnse* **33/1**
0 **8** *nk* **Vanilla Bally (ISR)**[179] 256 4-9-0 **55**.................... MatthewDavies 9 40
(George Baker) *chsd ldrs: wknd over 2f out* **22/1**
0000 **9** *1 ¼* **Dazzling Colours**[14] 3673 4-8-2 **46** oh1....................(v) SoniaEaton(3) 1 29
(T T Clement) *led tl hdd over 4f out: steadily lost pl* **33/1**
0-00 **10** *½* **Itsy Bitsy**[21] 3450 7-8-5 **46** oh1.................... JemmaMarshall 13 28
(W J Musson) *t.k.h on outside: dropped to rr bef st: sn struggling* **13/2**[3]
-306 **11** *5* **Magic Amigo**[64] 775 8-8-2 **46** oh1.................... CharlesEddery(3) 12 18
(J R Jenkins) *t.k.h: prom tl wknd over 3f out* **25/1**
0-05 **12** *9* **Gifted Heir (IRE)**[31] 3092 5-8-0 **46** oh1.................... NatashaEaton(5) 10 —
(A Bailey) *sddle sn slipped: chsd ldrs: drvn ahd over 4f out: sn hanging rt: hdd 3f out: t.o* **12/1**

2m 10.31s (-0.19) **Going Correction** 0.0s/f (Good) **12** Ran SP% **116.9**
Speed ratings (Par 101): **100,97,96,94,94 93,90,90,89,88 84,77**
toteswingers: 1&2 £2.30, 1&3 £15.50, 2&3 £16.10. CSF £6.39 CT £95.36 TOTE £2.30: £1.40, £1.50, £7.20; EX 7.20 Trifecta £149.70 Part won. Pool: £202.43 - 0.43 winning units. Place 6: £216.50, Place 5: £70.78..
Owner Carl Would **Bred** Arandora Star Syndicate **Trained** Eastwell, Leics

FOCUS
A weak handicap, and the winner probably only had to match his previous effort here.
Gifted Heir(IRE) Official explanation: jockey said saddle slipped
T/Jkpt: Not won. T/Plt: £576.40 to a £1 stake. Pool: £71,778.15. 90.90 winning tickets. T/Qpdt: £139.60 to a £1 stake. Pool: £5,530.70. 29.30 winning tickets. IM

4159 - 4162a (Foreign Racing) - See Raceform Interactive

FFOS LAS (L-H)
Tuesday, July 21

OFFICIAL GOING: Good
The first Flat meeting at Ffos Las, not counting a recent Arab fixture. With this being a new track there is as yet unsufficient data to calculate speed figures.
Wind: Moderate across Weather: Showers

4163 E.B.F./JAMIE YEATES MEMORIAL MAIDEN STKS 6f
2:30 (2:33) (Class 4) 2-Y-0 **£4,857** (£1,445; £722; £360) **Stalls** High

Form RPR
35 **1** **Our Dream Queen**[73] 1866 2-8-12 0.................... MichaelHills 8 70+
(B W Hills) *hld up: nt clr run briefly and hdwy over 1f out: led jst ins fnl f: r.o wl* **10/11**[1]
2332 **2** *1 ¼* **Going French (IRE)**[28] 3232 2-9-3 0.................... TonyCulhane 6 69
(R Curtis) *t.k.h: prom: wnt 2nd over 4f out: led over 1f out: rdn and hdd jst ins fnl f: nt qckn* **10/1**
6 **3** *½* **Could It Be Magic**[115] 994 2-8-12 0.................... JackDean(5) 7 68
(W G M Turner) *chsd ldr over 1f: prom: pushed along over 2f out: kpt on fnl f* **3/1**[2]
46 **4** *4 ½* **Yeah**[34] 3017 2-9-3 0.................... SJCraine 1 54
(Patrick Morris) *hld up in tch: rdn over 1f out: wknd fnl f* **66/1**
03 **5** *hd* **Miskin Nights**[20] 3500 2-8-9 0.................... DavidProbert(3) 4 49
(B Palling) *led: rdn and hdd over 1f out: wknd fnl f* **4/1**[3]
6 *22* **Tanto Quanto (IRE)** 2-9-3 0.................... SteveDrowne 2 —
(W R Muir) *s.i.s: outpcd* **16/1**

1m 11.14s (71.14) **6** Ran SP% **113.8**
toteswingers: 1&2 £2.70, 1&3 £1.10, 2&3 £5.10 CSF £11.85 TOTE £1.90: £1.30, £1.90; EX 7.20.
Owner Lady Richard Wellesley **Bred** Marston Stud And Fleming Thoroughbreds **Trained** Lambourn, Berks
■ Wee Bobbie (50/1) was withdrawn (ref to ent stalls).

FOCUS
A weak juvenile maiden won in ready fashion by Our Dream Queen. She and the runner-up set the level.

NOTEBOOK
Our Dream Queen had disappointed in a good maiden at Haydock last time, but shaped with a good deal of promise when third on debut and she capitalised on this easier target. Always travelling well, she quickened nicely once in the clear and is the sort to progress further in nurseries. (op 5-4 tchd 11-8)
Going French(IRE) has now finished either second or third on all five starts. He struck the front over a furlong out, but was quickly claimed by the winner. A race will no doubt fall his way eventually. (op 5-1)
Could It Be Magic, a keeping-on sixth in the Brocklesby on debut, had not been seen since and ran a reasonable race on this return. (op 9-2)
Yeah is now eligible for nurseries and should fare better in that sphere. (tchd 50-1)
Miskin Nights showed speed and is the type to fare better in nurseries. (op 7-2 tchd 10-3)
Tanto Quanto(IRE), whose dam's two previous foals have achieved little, was always outpaced and looks to need further. (op 14-1)

4164 SHUFFLEBOTTOM STEEL FRAMED BUILDINGS MAIDEN FILLIES' STKS 6f
3:00 (3:01) (Class 5) 3-Y-0+ **£3,238** (£963; £481; £240) **Stalls** High

Form RPR
4-U0 **1** **Sams Lass**[18] 3566 3-8-9 0.................... AhmedAjtebi(3) 2 79
(D Nicholls) *mde all: rdn and edgd rt ins fnl f: r.o wl* **14/1**
05- **2** *1 ½* **Kyleene**[281] 6696 3-8-12 0.................... ShaneKelly 1 74
(J Noseda) *hld up in tch: rdn over 1f out: chsd wnr ins fnl f: no imp whn swtchd lft towards fin* **10/3**[2]
63 **3** *1* **Milldown Story**[11] 3813 3-8-12 0.................... DaneO'Neill 4 71
(B R Millman) *chsd ldr: rdn over 1f out: nt qckn* **7/4**[1]
0 **4** *3 ¼* **Sutton Veny (IRE)**[22] 3460 3-8-12 0.................... ClareLindop 7 61
(J R Gask) *t.k.h: prom: pushed along over 2f out: btn over 1f out* **40/1**
-525 **5** *1 ¼* **Morning Queen (IRE)**[27] 3281 3-8-12 **60**....................(p) IanMongan 8 57
(C G Cox) *t.k.h in tch: btn 2f out* **9/2**
-552 **6** *½* **Majestic Lady (IRE)**[17] 3611 3-8-12 **58**.................... MichaelHills 9 55
(B W Hills) *bhd: rdn over 1f out: nvr trbld ldrs* **4/1**[3]
0 **7** *1* **Rebel Woman**[118] 951 3-8-12 0.................... TonyCulhane 6 52
(J A Osborne) *hld up in mid-div: effrt over 2f out: wknd over 1f out* **16/1**
0056 **8** *7* **Poca A Poca (IRE)**[4] 4070 5-8-12 **48**....................(p) MarkCoumbe(5) 5 29
(G C Bravery) *s.s: outpcd* **66/1**
0 **9** *9* **Croeso Ynol**[22] 3460 3-8-12 0.................... SteveDrowne 3 —
(J L Spearing) *dwlt: in rr: rdn over 2f out: sn struggling* **25/1**

69.31 secs (69.31)
WFA 3 from 5yo 5lb **9** Ran SP% **118.0**
toteswingers: 1&2 £17.60, 1&3 £11.60, 2&3 £1.70 CSF £61.11 TOTE £20.00: £4.30, £1.90, £1.10; EX 62.90.
Owner Robert Reid **Bred** Lordship Stud Limited **Trained** Sessay, N Yorks

FOCUS
This was a fairly weak fillies' sprint maiden. The winner showed big improvement and the form has been taken at face value.
Croeso Ynol Official explanation: jockey said filly was never travelling

4165 DURALOCK PERFORMANCE FENCING NURSERY 5f
3:30 (3:30) (Class 4) 2-Y-0 **£4,857** (£1,445; £722; £360) **Stalls** High

Form RPR
5220 **1** **Mijas Playa**[54] 2408 2-8-13 **77**.................... DavidProbert(3) 6 78
(C A Dwyer) *a.p: led on bit wl over 1f out: rdn ins fnl f: edgd lft last strides: r.o* **4/1**[3]
6422 **2** *nk* **Listillo (USA)**[8] 3925 2-8-11 **72**.................... DaneO'Neill 3 72
(H J L Dunlop) *a.p: rdn over 1f out: ev ch ins fnl f: nt qckn* **3/1**[2]
2132 **3** *1 ¾* **Transfixed (IRE)**[3] 4081 2-8-8 **69**.................... PaulDoe 9 63
(P D Evans) *chsd ldrs: rdn over 1f out: kpt on to take 3rd wl ins fnl f: nt trble ldng pair* **5/2**[1]
1110 **4** *nk* **Anjomarba (IRE)**[18] 3579 2-9-2 **82**.................... JackDean(5) 7 75
(W G M Turner) *led: narrowly hdd over 2f out: rdn and edgd lft wl over 1f out: one pce* **6/1**
5422 **5** *½* **True Red (IRE)**[14] 3709 2-7-7 **61** oh3 ow2.................... CharlesEddery(7) 1 52+
(B R Millman) *outpcd in rr: late prog: nvr nrr* **10/1**
2235 **6** *½* **Vilnius**[3] 4076 2-8-1 **62**.................... CatherineGannon 10 51
(M R Channon) *w ldr: slt ld over 2f out: hdd and rdn over 1f out: one pce* **9/2**

58.75 secs (58.75) **6** Ran SP% **115.1**
toteswingers: 1&2 £3.90, 1&3 £4.00, 2&3 £1.20 CSF £16.91 CT £35.23 TOTE £5.20: £2.60, £2.00; EX 13.70.
Owner R S G Jones **Bred** T E Pocock **Trained** Burrough Green, Cambs

FOCUS
A competitive looking nursery despite the small field and the form looks sound, if only fair. The 'official' ratings shown next to each horse are estimated and for information purposes only.

NOTEBOOK
Mijas Playa had been off the track since finishing down the field in the National Stakes, but her previous maiden form suggested she would be a player in this company, and she came in for a bit of support. Travelling well throughout, she only won narrowly, but the margin does not do her justice as she looked comfortably on top at the finish. She could find further success in nurseries on this evidence. (op 5-1 tchd 7-2)
Listillo(USA) put up a solid effort. He appreciated the drop back to 5f and was the only one to give the winner a race. (op 9-2)
Transfixed(IRE), one of the more experienced runners in the line-up, looked to find the drop back to the minimum against her and will be suited by going back up to 6f. The handicapper might have her measure for the time being, though. (op 9-4 tchd 3-1)
Anjomarba(IRE) showed early speed but was struggling with two furlongs to run, and perhaps her busy campaign is beginning to take its toll. (op 5-1 tchd 13-2)
True Red(IRE) never got competitive. (op 7-1)
Vilnius raced keenly on the rail and didn't get home. (op 4-1)

4166 1ST SIGNS & GRAPHICS FILLIES' H'CAP 1m 2f (R)
4:00 (4:01) (Class 3) (0-95,93) 3-Y-0+ **£7,771** (£2,312; £1,155; £577) **Stalls** Low

Form RPR
6125 **1** **Hollow Green (IRE)**[1] 4150 3-7-10 **69** ow2.. Louis-PhilippeBeuzelin(5) 5 82
(P D Evans) *hld up and bhd: stdy prog 3f out: rdn over 1f out: led ins fnl f: r.o* **12/1**
14 **2** *1* **Charity Belle (USA)**[40] 2846 3-9-11 **93**.................... JimmyFortune 2 104
(J H M Gosden) *hld up: hdwy over 3f out: led over 1f out: rdn and hdd ins fnl f: nt qckn* **3/1**[2]
210 **3** *3 ¼* **Polly's Mark (IRE)**[33] 3051 3-9-6 **88**.................... IanMongan 3 93
(C G Cox) *hld up and bhd: n.m.r on ins over 5f out: pushed along over 3f out: hdwy over 2f out: rdn and edgd lft over 1f out: one pce* **9/4**[1]
2054 **4** *3* **Light Dubai (IRE)**[34] 3022 3-8-0 **68**.................... CatherineGannon 4 67
(M R Channon) *a.p: led 3f out: rdn and hdd over 1f out: wknd fnl f* **11/1**
1432 **5** *8* **Onemix**[15] 3697 3-8-10 **78**.................... MichaelHills 1 61
(B W Hills) *sn chsng ldr: ev ch over 2f out: wknd wl over 1f out* **4/1**[3]
0051 **6** *6* **Classic Legend**[18] 3573 4-10-0 **86**.................... ShaneKelly 6 57
(B J Meehan) *led: rdn and hdd 3f out: wknd wl over 1f out* **3/1**[2]

2m 7.28s (127.28)
WFA 3 from 4yo 10lb **6** Ran SP% **116.8**
toteswingers: 1&2 £8.10, 1&3 £5.60, 2&3 £3.40 CSF £49.75 TOTE £10.70: £3.00, £1.80; EX 31.80.
Owner Raymond N R Auld **Bred** R N Auld **Trained** Pandy, Monmouths

FOCUS
A fair fillies' handicap. Another personal best from the winner.

NOTEBOOK
Hollow Green(IRE), a beaten-favourite when fifth at Windsor the previous evening, had earlier been in good form and she came right back to her best, staying on strongly to get well on top late on, despite her rider putting up 2lb overweight. A tough sort, she is taking her racing well and should continue to progress. (op 10-1)
Charity Belle(USA), an easy maiden winner who ran with credit when fourth in a Listed contest at Newbury last time, travelled well on this handicap debut and went on over a furlong out, but the massive weight concession to the winner eventually told. (op 5-2)
Polly's Mark(IRE), outclassed at Royal Ascot last time, stayed on again having lost her position after she became short of room. (op 5-2 tchd 11-4)
Light Dubai(IRE) ran well without suggesting she is up to winning at present. (op 12-1 tchd 10-1)
Onemix faded late on having been in with every chance two out. (op 9-2 tchd 5-1)
Classic Legend, a winner at Haydock last time, was readily brushed aside and dropped right out in the end. (op 7-2 tchd 11-4)

4167 TOPPERS WALES H'CAP 6f
4:30 (4:33) (Class 4) (0-80,80) 3-Y-O+ **£4,857** (£1,445; £722; £360) **Stalls** High

Form RPR
4052 **1** **Cape Vale (IRE)**[20] 3497 4-9-9 **79** AhmedAjtebi(3) 3 89
(D Nicholls) *mde all: rdn ins fnl f: r.o wl* **9/4**[1]
2416 **2** 1 1/2 **Cape Melody**[19] 3537 3-9-3 **75** SteveDrowne 6 79
(H Morrison) *hld up: hdwy over 3f out: rdn over 1f out: wnt 2nd ins fnl f: nt trble wnr* **13/2**[3]
6514 **3** 1 1/4 **Dressed To Dance (IRE)**[18] 3577 5-9-7 **77** (b) KevinGhunowa(3) 5 78
(R A Harris) *s.i.s: bhd: rdn and hdwy wl over 1f out: kpt on ins fnl f* **16/1**
000 **4** shd **Don Pele (IRE)**[7] 3956 7-9-2 **69** (p) CatherineGannon 4 70
(R A Harris) *hld up in tch: rdn over 2f out: chsd wnr over 1f out tl ins fnl f: no ex* **20/1**
2013 **5** 3 3/4 **Wotasparkler**[17] 3625 3-7-13 **62** Louis-PhilippeBeuzelin(5) 7 50
(W S Kittow) *chsd wnr: rdn over 2f out: lost 2nd and wknd over 1f out* **9/2**[2]
2604 **6** shd **Millfields Dreams**[11] 3802 10-9-0 **72** (p) MarkCoumbe(5) 10 60
(G C Bravery) *in rr: rdn over 2f out: late prog: nvr nrr* **16/1**
3100 **7** 1 3/4 **Bold Argument (IRE)**[23] 3422 6-9-1 **68** RobertHavlin 9 51
(Mrs P N Dutfield) *hld up and bhd: rdn over 2f out: kpt on ins fnl f: n.d* **16/1**
-600 **8** 1/2 **Polar Annie**[36] 2980 4-9-3 **70** DaneO'Neill 8 51
(M S Saunders) *hld up in tch: pushed along over 3f out: rdn and wknd over 2f out* **7/1**
3001 **9** 2 3/4 **Miss Chamanda (IRE)**[29] 3219 3-9-8 **80** JimmyFortune 1 51
(P D Evans) *hld up in tch: rdn over 2f out: wknd fnl f* **13/2**[3]
3145 **10** 3/4 **Golden Dixie (USA)**[10] 3866 10-9-1 **71** DavidProbert(3) 2 41
(R A Harris) *prom tl rdn and wknd over 2f out* **8/1**

69.78 secs (69.78)
WFA 3 from 4yo+ 5lb **10 Ran SP% 121.6**
toteswingers: 1&2 £5.20, 1&3 £8.90, 2&3 £20.20 CSF £18.06 CT £197.18 TOTE £3.20: £1.50, £2.10, £3.70; EX 13.70.
Owner Lady O'Reilly **Bred** Derek Veitch **Trained** Sessay, N Yorks

FOCUS
A modest sprint that saw Cape Vale finally end his losing run, taking advantage of a good mark. The runner-up produced a slight personal best.

4168 NATURAL UK H'CAP 2m (R)
5:00 (5:01) (Class 5) (0-70,65) 3-Y-O+ **£2,590** (£770; £385; £192) **Stalls** Low

Form RPR
2-02 **1** **Black Or Red (IRE)**[64] 2127 4-9-7 **56** (b) CatherineGannon 4 71
(I A Wood) *hld up in rr: hdwy on ins over 3f out: led over 2f out: rdn clr over 1f out: styd on wl* **5/1**[3]
533- **2** 9 **Ambrose Princess (IRE)**[54] 7260 4-9-5 **54** JimmyFortune 6 58
(M J Scudamore) *a.p: wnt 2nd over 3f out: ev ch over 2f out: one pce* **3/1**[1]
3600 **3** 2 3/4 **Double Spectre (IRE)**[42] 2798 7-9-11 **60** DaneO'Neill 7 61
(Jean-Rene Auvray) *hld up towards rr: hdwy 4f out: rdn and outpcd over 2f out: styd on to take 3rd wl ins fnl f* **16/1**
4-00 **4** 2 1/4 **The Composer**[62] 2182 7-8-13 **48** SteveDrowne 10 46
(M Blanshard) *hld up in mid-div: hdwy 5f out: wknd over 1f out* **28/1**
3044 **5** 2 3/4 **Ja One (IRE)**[18] 3575 3-8-13 **65** MichaelHills 5 60
(B W Hills) *hld up towards rr: hdwy over 4f out: wknd over 1f out* **7/2**[2]
63 **6** 6 **Dantari (IRE)**[12] 3788 4-9-13 **62** ShaneKelly 1 50
(Evan Williams) *led early: a.p: led over 5f out: rdn over 3f out: hdd over 2f out: sn wknd* **3/1**[1]
6604 **7** 13 **Bolton Hall (IRE)**[5] 3997 7-8-10 **48** (tp) DavidProbert(3) 9 20
(W K Goldsworthy) *stdd s: hdwy into mid-div after 3f: jnd ldrs 8f out: wknd over 5f out* **16/1**
1402 **8** 25 **Colourful Move**[27] 3275 4-9-8 **57** RobertHavlin 3 —
(P G Murphy) *sn led: hdd over 5f out: wknd over 3f out* **5/1**[3]
/0-5 **9** 2 **Grasp**[12] 3774 7-9-1 **50** (v) PaulDoe 2 —
(P D Evans) *s.i.s: sn hld up in tch: pushed along over 5f out: wknd over 4f out* **20/1**
200/ **10** 8 **Amazing Valour (IRE)**[211] 3814 7-9-7 **63** (b) AshleyMorgan(7) 8 —
(P Bowen) *prom tl rdn and wknd over 7f out* **20/1**

3m 29.86s (209.86)
WFA 3 from 4yo+ 17lb **10 Ran SP% 130.3**
toteswingers: 1&2 £6.10, 1&3 £17.00, 2&3 £15.30 CSF £22.52 CT £241.78 TOTE £5.50: £1.60, £1.70, £7.70; EX 37.40.
Owner Cherries Racing **Bred** Dr John Hollowood And Aiden Murphy **Trained** Upper Lambourn, Berks
■ Stewards' Enquiry : Michael Hills one-day ban: careless riding (Aug 4)

FOCUS
This moderate staying handicap was turned into a rout by Black Or Red, who is rated back to something like his best.
Bolton Hall(IRE) Official explanation: jockey said gelding hung right throughout
Colourful Move Official explanation: jockey said colt hung right in the home straight

4169 EPS H'CAP 1m 4f (R)
5:30 (5:32) (Class 5) (0-75,74) 4-Y-O+ **£2,590** (£770; £385; £192) **Stalls** Low

Form RPR
3621 **1** **Sir Boss (IRE)**[11] 3798 4-9-7 **74** DaneO'Neill 6 86+
(D E Cantillon) *hld up towards rr: smooth prog on outside 3f out: led wl over 1f out: sn clr and edgd lft: easily* **7/4**[1]
45-0 **2** 5 **Mae Cigan (FR)**[34] 3029 6-8-8 **61** SteveDrowne 4 60
(M Blanshard) *hld up in mid-div: hdwy over 3f out: styd on one pce fnl f: tk 2nd post* **13/2**
5032 **3** shd **Mustajed**[10] 3869 8-8-12 **68** (b) JamesMillman(3) 7 67
(B R Millman) *hld up in tch: led over 2f out: rdn and hdd wl over 1f out: sn no ch w wnr: lost 2nd post* **6/1**[3]
504- **4** 3 1/4 **Dark Energy**[8] 4592 5-8-12 **65** (t) JimmyFortune 1 59
(M J Scudamore) *dwlt: hld up in rr: rdn over 2f out: styd on ins fnl f: tk 4th nr fin* **18/1**
0042 **5** nk **Piper's Song (IRE)**[15] 3679 6-8-4 **62** Louis-PhilippeBeuzelin(5) 8 55
(Patrick Morris) *hld up towards rr: hdwy over 3f out: rdn over 2f out: wknd over 1f out* **15/2**
1326 **6** 2 3/4 **Paddy Rielly (IRE)**[19] 3544 4-8-12 **65** (p) PaulDoe 2 54
(P D Evans) *a.p: led over 3f out: rdn and hdd over 2f out: wknd wl over 1f out* **13/2**
3003 **7** hd **Horseshoe Reef (AUS)**[19] 3533 6-9-1 **68** (p) ClareLindop 3 57
(J R Gask) *led: hdd over 3f out: wknd over 2f out* **14/1**
1 **8** 7 **Enlightenment (IRE)**[87] 501 9-9-1 **71** DavidProbert(3) 5 48
(Evan Williams) *s.i.s: sn hld up in mid-div: wknd over 2f out* **5/1**[2]
1030 **9** 8 **Imperial Harry**[101] 952 6-9-4 **71** RobertHavlin 10 36
(Jean-Rene Auvray) *hld up and bhd: rdn over 3f out: sn struggling* **33/1**
0553 **10** 13 **Uig**[22] 3462 8-8-2 **55** oh1 CatherineGannon 9 —
(H S Howe) *chsd ldr tl rdn over 4f out: wknd over 3f out* **18/1**

2m 36.76s (156.76) **10 Ran SP% 125.9**
toteswingers: 1&2 £4.70, 1&3 £4.50, 2&3 £9.80 CSF £15.01 CT £62.12 TOTE £2.60: £1.40, £1.90, £1.90; EX 19.90 Place 6: £75.68 Place 5: £46.13.
Owner Don Cantillon Racing **Bred** Mrs E R Cantillon **Trained** Newmarket, Suffolk

FOCUS
This was a low-grade middle-distance handicap which was quite steadily run. The winner is rated value for 8l.
Piper's Song(IRE) Official explanation: jockey said gelding stumbled twice
Uig Official explanation: jockey said mare stopped quickly
T/Plt: £58.10 to a £1 stake. Pool: £65,234.06. 818.79 winning tickets. T/Qpdt: £48.00 to a £1 stake. Pool: £3,840.00. 59.10 winning tickets. KH

3951 SOUTHWELL (L-H)
Tuesday, July 21

OFFICIAL GOING: Standard
Wind: Fresh, half against Weather: Overcast turning showery

4170 VICTORCHANDLER.COM/FOREST APPRENTICE H'CAP 1m 3f (F)
6:20 (6:20) (Class 6) (0-65,61) 4-Y-O+ **£1,942** (£578; £288; £144) **Stalls** Low

Form RPR
-042 **1** **Credential**[19] 3552 7-8-8 **48** PaulPickard(3) 1 58
(John A Harris) *mde all: rdn and hung rt fnl 2f: jst hld on* **5/1**[3]
0005 **2** nk **Altos Reales**[60] 2233 5-8-9 **46** JamieKyne 8 55
(J G Given) *a.p: chsd wnr over 2f out: rdn and carried rt ins fnl f: styd on* **4/1**[2]
0000 **3** 1 3/4 **King Of The Beers (USA)**[8] 3929 5-9-4 **60** (p) SPRyan(5) 2 67
(R A Harris) *hld up: rdn over 4f out: hdwy over 2f out: r.o* **8/1**
004- **4** 2 3/4 **Gulnaz**[223] 7632 4-8-5 **45** BillyCray(3) 10 47
(Mrs G S Rees) *prom: rdn and hung lft 2f out: styd on same pce* **25/1**
2233 **5** 6 **Jafaru**[7] 3950 5-9-7 **61** (b) JemmaMarshall(3) 7 53
(G L Moore) *s.i.s: hld up: hdwy over 4f out: rdn over 3f out: wknd wl over 1f out* **3/1**[1]
000- **6** 6 **Mean Machine (IRE)**[206] 7782 7-8-3 **45** AlexEdwards(5) 11 26
(J W Unett) *prom: rdn over 3f out: wknd over 2f out* **50/1**
0000 **7** hd **Autumn Charm**[10] 3862 4-8-6 **46** ow1 JPHamblett(3) 9 27
(Lucinda Featherstone) *chsd wnr: rdn over 3f out: wknd over 2f out* **50/1**
4-01 **8** 1 1/4 **Dot's Delight**[8] 3927 5-9-0 **51** 6ex LanceBetts 6 30
(M G Rimell) *chsd ldrs: rdn over 3f out: wknd over 2f out* **6/1**
0606 **9** 2 1/2 **Cragganmore Creek**[19] 3552 6-8-8 **45** (v) RossAtkinson 3 20
(D Morris) *sn pushed along: a in rr: wknd wl over 3f out* **8/1**
0530 **10** 21 **Apache Dawn**[7] 3943 5-8-6 **48** TobyAtkinson(5) 5 —
(A Sadik) *prom: lost pl 1/2-way: wknd wl over 3f out* **16/1**
/004 **11** 10 **Bernix**[14] 3710 7-9-2 **53** MCGeran 4 —
(N Tinkler) *sn pushed along: a in rr: wknd wl over 3f out* **14/1**

2m 26.23s (-1.77) **Going Correction** -0.15s/f (Stan) **11 Ran SP% 118.5**
Speed ratings (Par 101): **100,99,98,96,92 87,87,86,84,69 62**
toteswingers: 1&2 £5.40, 1&3 £13.00, 2&3 £6.70. CSF £25.22 CT £158.49 TOTE £4.90: £1.20, £2.30, £2.50; EX 25.80.
Owner Mrs A E Harris **Bred** Rockwell Bloodstock **Trained** Eastwell, Leics

FOCUS
4mm of rain fell during the day and the ground was as the official. A modest handicap in which the pace was fair. The winner and runner-up ended up towards the stands' side in the closing stages. Sound form.
Dot's Delight Official explanation: jockey said mare was unsuited by the fibresand surface
Bernix Official explanation: jockey said gelding had no more to give

4171 VICTOR CHANDLER SPONSORS OF NOTTINGHAM FOREST F.C. H'CAP 1m (F)
6:50 (6:51) (Class 5) (0-70,70) 3-Y-O+ **£3,238** (£963; £481; £240) **Stalls** Low

Form RPR
1512 **1** **Swiss Art (IRE)**[7] 3953 3-9-11 **70** SilvestreDeSousa 4 79
(Mrs R A Carr) *mid-div: sn pushed along: hdwy over 3f out: rdn to ld over 1f out: r.o* **11/2**[3]
100 **2** 1 **Byron Bay**[5] 3353 7-9-5 **56** (p) GrahamGibbons 9 65
(R Johnson) *led: rdn and hdd over 1f out: styd on same pce towards fin* **12/1**
2200 **3** 1 **Oskari**[25] 3339 4-10-0 **65** PaulMulrennan 3 71
(P T Midgley) *a.p: rdn over 3f out: outpcd over 1f out: styd on ins fnl f* **14/1**
0041 **4** 1/2 **Uncle Brit**[7] 3955 3-9-8 **67** 6ex SebSanders 11 70
(Sir Mark Prescott) *dwlt: hdwy over 6f out: rdn over 3f out: edgd lft and no ex ins fnl f* **9/4**[1]
-300 **5** 3 1/4 **Allformary**[42] 2786 3-9-10 **69** TomEaves 13 65
(B Smart) *chsd ldrs: rdn over 2f out: wknd fnl f* **16/1**
0565 **6** 1/2 **General Tufto**[4] 4054 4-9-7 **63** (b) MatthewDavies(5) 2 60
(C Smith) *sn pushed along in rr: rdn over 3f out: r.o ins fnl f: nvr nrr* **6/1**
0-00 **7** 1 1/4 **Star Acclaim**[14] 3713 4-8-11 **55** (t) TobyAtkinson(7) 6 49
(E V Stanford) *prom: rdn over 2f out: sn hung lft: wknd over 1f out* **80/1**
3521 **8** 2 **Hawkeyethenoo (IRE)**[7] 3942 3-7-13 **51** (b) JamesPSullivan(7) 1 38
(M W Easterby) *s.i.s: sn prom: rdn over 2f out: wknd over 1f out* **9/2**[2]
0-00 **9** 17 **Saute**[78] 1729 3-9-1 **60** AdamKirby 12 8
(W R Swinburn) *mid-div: rdn over 5f out: wknd over 3f out* **14/1**
60-0 **10** 2 3/4 **Chosen Forever**[57] 2312 4-9-10 **61** PJMcDonald 10 5
(G R Oldroyd) *mid-div: rdn 1/2-way: sn lost tch* **16/1**
2000 **11** 2 1/2 **Kingaroo (IRE)**[56] 2357 3-8-8 **60** AndrewHeffernan(7) 8 —
(Garry Moss) *chsd ldrs tl rdn and wknd over 3f out* **12/1**

0-00 12 2 ½ **Grey Gurkha**[18] 3558 8-8-9 46........................ PatrickMathers 7 —
(I W McInnes) *s.i.s: sn pushed along: bhd fr 1/2-way* **66/1**

1m 42.84s (-0.86) **Going Correction** -0.15s/f (Stan)
WFA 3 from 4yo+ 8lb **12** Ran SP% **121.8**
Speed ratings (Par 103): **98,97,96,95,92 91,90,88,71,68 66,63**
toteswingers: 1&2 £14.90, 1&3 £12.50, 2&3 £8.60. CSF £72.11 CT £902.42 TOTE £5.60: £2.40, £3.80, £4.50; EX 71.60.
Owner Brian Morton **Bred** John Yarr **Trained** Huby, N Yorks

FOCUS
A run-of-the-mill handicap in which the pace was fair. The winner ended up against the inside rail and the form looks fair for the grade.
Grey Gurkha Official explanation: jockey said horse did not face the kickback

4172 VICTOR CHANDLER & NOTTINGHAM FOREST F.C. H'CAP 6f (F)
7:20 (7:21) (Class 6) (0-60,61) 3-Y-O **£2,590** (£770; £385; £192) **Stalls** Low

Form RPR
3602 1 **First Blade**[10] 3859 3-8-9 **53**........................(b) RussellKennemore[(3)] 5 61
(S R Bowring) *w ldr tl led over 2f out: sn rdn: jst hld on* **9/2**[2]
-005 2 hd **Fuzzy Cat**[21] 3480 3-8-2 **48**........................(b) DeanHeslop[(5)] 9 55+
(T D Barron) *sn pushed along in rr: rdn 1/2-way: hdwy over 1f out: r.o: jst failed* **14/1**
0550 3 1 ½ **Positivity**[22] 3449 3-8-9 **50**........................ TomEaves 10 52
(B Smart) *prom: outpcd over 2f out: swtchd lft over 1f out: styd on ins fnl f* **33/1**
003 4 1 ¼ **Ponting (IRE)**[18] 3580 3-9-3 **58**........................ SebSanders 7 56
(R M Beckett) *a.p: rdn to chs wnr over 1f out: no ex ins fnl f* **13/8**[1]
4550 5 1 ½ **Freepressionist**[36] 2973 3-8-13 **59**........................ JamieKyne[(5)] 1 52
(R A Teal) *chsd ldrs: rdn over 2f out: styd on same pce appr fnl f* **7/1**[3]
4103 6 1 ¼ **Pepin (IRE)**[7] 3953 3-9-1 **56**........................ FrankieMcDonald 6 45
(D Haydn Jones) *prom: rdn over 3f out: styd on same pce fnl 2f* **17/2**
-060 7 1 ¼ **Monte Mayor Eagle**[10] 3862 3-8-8 **49**........................(b) SimonWhitworth 11 34
(D Haydn Jones) *in rr: sme hdwy over 3f out: n.d* **14/1**
4120 8 1 ¾ **Dancing Wave**[8] 3917 3-9-1 **59**........................ LeeVickers[(3)] 4 39
(M C Chapman) *led: rdn and hdd over 2f out: wknd fnl f* **8/1**
5030 9 2 **Bold Account (IRE)**[34] 3031 3-8-0 **48**........................ PaulPickard[(7)] 3 21
(Garry Moss) *hld up: sme hdwy 2f out: sn wknd* **28/1**
501 10 nse **Kinigi (IRE)**[7] 3953 3-8-13 **61** 6ex........................ AndrewHeffernan[(7)] 8 34
(R A Harris) *rrd leaving stalls: a bhd* **10/1**
000- 11 19 **Merry May**[235] 7468 3-8-4 **45**........................ SilvestreDeSousa 2 —
(S Kirk) *sn outpcd: bhd fr 1/2-way* **40/1**

1m 15.43s (-1.07) **Going Correction** -0.15s/f (Stan) **11** Ran SP% **121.7**
Speed ratings (Par 98): **101,100,98,97,95 93,91,89,86,86 61**
toteswingers: 1&2 £17.00, 1&3 £31.70, 2&3 £31.70. CSF £66.94 CT £1927.68 TOTE £5.60: £2.10, £4.70, £4.80; EX 71.60.
Owner S R Bowring **Bred** S R Bowring **Trained** Edwinstowe, Notts

FOCUS
Another modest handicap and one in which the pace was sound. The winner raced towards the centre in the straight and the form is sound for the grade.

4173 BEST ODDS GUARANTEED @ VICTOR CHANDLER NOVICE STKS 6f (F)
7:50 (7:50) (Class 5) 2-Y-O **£4,094** (£1,209; £604) **Stalls** Low

Form RPR
0212 1 **Virginia Hall**[11] 3799 2-8-11 0........................ SebSanders 4 75
(Sir Mark Prescott) *mde all: rdn and edgd rt fr over 1f out: r.o* **2/5**[1]
301 2 ¾ **Florio Vincitore (IRE)**[13] 3744 2-9-2 0........................ EdwardCreighton 6 78
(E J Creighton) *a.p: rdn to chse wnr over 1f out: r.o* **9/2**[2]
4 3 3 ½ **Gold Crusher (USA)**[66] 2087 2-8-12 0........................ PatCosgrave 2 63
(R M H Cowell) *s.i.s: sn chsng ldrs: rdn and hung lft over 1f out: no ex fnl f* **11/2**[3]
3003 4 7 **Southwark Newshawk**[14] 3709 2-8-0 0........................ RyanPowell[(7)] 5 37
(Mrs C A Dunnett) *trckd ldrs: racd keenly: rdn and wknd 2f out* **28/1**
0405 5 1 ¾ **Baby Judge (IRE)**[8] 3918 2-8-5 0........................ AndrewHeffernan[(7)] 3 37
(M C Chapman) *s.i.s: sn hung rt and outpcd* **50/1**
6060 6 1 ¼ **Blue Bond**[7] 3958 2-8-5 0........................ PaulPickard[(7)] 7 33
(P T Midgley) *sn outpcd* **100/1**

1m 15.8s (-0.70) **Going Correction** -0.15s/f (Stan) **6** Ran SP% **111.4**
Speed ratings (Par 94): **98,97,92,83,80 79**
toteswingers: 1&2 £1.02, 1&3 £1.20, 2&3 £4.30. CSF £2.55 TOTE £1.30: £1.02, £2.30; EX 2.50.
Owner C G Rowles Nicholson **Bred** Limestone And Tara Studs **Trained** Newmarket, Suffolk

FOCUS
An uncompetitive event run at a decent gallop. The first three pulled clear and the winner raced centre to stands side in the straight. The form is rated around the first two.

NOTEBOOK
Virginia Hall, who attracted plenty of support, had the best form and got the run of the race. She did not have to improve to win in workmanlike fashion on her Fibresand debut on her first start over this trip. She is a consistent sort who should continue to give a good account and connections, who feel she will stay 7f, are now reportedly eyeing some black type for her. (op 4-9 tchd 4-11)
Florio Vincitore(IRE) had more on his plate than when successful on his Polytrack debut, but ran creditably against a useful rival on this first start on Fibresand. He should prove equally effective over 7f and he appeals as the sort to win again. (op 4-1 tchd 5-1)
Gold Crusher(USA), who showed ability on his debut, travelled strongly for a long way and turned in an improved effort on this all-weather debut, and on only his second start. He should progress further once qualified for a handicap mark. (op 9-2 tchd 13-2)
Southwark Newshawk had her limitations firmly exposed in this grade and her future lies in low-grade handicap company. (op 20-1)

4174 NEW WEBSITE @ VICTORCHANDLER.COM MAIDEN STKS 5f (F)
8:20 (8:20) (Class 5) 3-Y-O+ **£4,776** (£1,410; £705) **Stalls** High

Form RPR
00 1 **Evna (USA)**[38] 2937 3-8-5 0........................ FrazerWilliams[(7)] 12 72
(R A Fahey) *mid-div: hdwy 1/2-way: led over 1f out: shkn up and r.o wl* **33/1**
00-6 2 2 ½ **Residency (IRE)**[17] 3611 3-9-3 0........................ TomEaves 9 68
(B Smart) *chsd ldrs: rdn and ev ch over 1f out: outpcd ins fnl f* **10/1**
25-0 3 2 **Florentia**[6] 3982 3-8-12 68........................ SebSanders 8 56
(Sir Mark Prescott) *sn pushed along and prom: outpcd 1/2-way: styd on to go 3rd wl ins fnl f* **7/2**[1]
04 4 1 **Fiftyfourth Street**[11] 3813 3-9-3 0........................(t) TravisBlock 4 57
(P J Makin) *dwlt: hdwy over 3f out: rdn over 1f out: no ex ins fnl f* **9/2**[3]
40 5 1 **Shannon Golden**[12] 3764 3-9-0 0........................ RussellKennemore[(3)] 7 54
(S R Bowring) *led: racd keenly: rdn and hdd over 1f out: wknd ins fnl f* **33/1**
23 6 2 ½ **Air Lion (USA)**[145] 686 3-9-3 0........................ PatCosgrave 11 45
(R M H Cowell) *s.s: hdwy 1/2-way: sn rdn: hung lft and wknd over 1f out* **4/1**[2]
3664 7 1 ¼ **Abu Derby (IRE)**[14] 3712 3-9-3 68........................ PaulMulrennan 6 40
(J G Given) *w ldr tl rdn 1/2-way: wknd over 1f out* **13/2**
50 8 5 **Qualitas**[34] 3036 3-9-3 0........................ DaleGibson 5 22
(M W Easterby) *mid-div: rdn and lost pl over 3f out: n.d after* **20/1**
0000 9 ¾ **Chenin (IRE)**[29] 3229 3-8-12 40........................ LPKeniry 2 15
(Peter Grayson) *chsd ldrs: rdn 1/2-way: wknd wl over 1f out* **100/1**
0660 10 ½ **Singapore Girl**[17] 3611 3-8-12 45........................(v) SilvestreDeSousa 3 13
(G R Oldroyd) *dwlt: outpcd* **33/1**
4-20 11 4 **Little Calla (IRE)**[43] 2776 3-8-12 60........................ DO'Donohoe 1 —
(E A L Dunlop) *s.i.s: sn outpcd* **6/1**
12 ½ **Foxholes Lodge** 4-9-2 0........................ GrahamGibbons 10 —
(J D Bethell) *s.i.s: outpcd* **20/1**

59.03 secs (-0.67) **Going Correction** -0.15s/f (Stan)
WFA 3 from 4yo 4lb **12** Ran SP% **116.5**
Speed ratings (Par 103): **99,95,91,90,88 84,82,74,73,72 66,65**
toteswingers: 1&2 £27.20, 1&3 £33.70, 2&3 £11.30. CSF £308.31 TOTE £39.90: £7.40, £2.30, £1.60; EX 549.30.
Owner Dr Marwan Koukash **Bred** George Brunacini & Bona Terra Farms **Trained** Musley Bank, N Yorks

FOCUS
Not a strong maiden and one in which several market leaders disappointed. Tricky form to pin down. The pace was sound and the winner raced centre to stands side.
Air Lion(USA) Official explanation: jockey said colt was slowly away
Singapore Girl Official explanation: jockey said filly was slow away

4175 BEST ODDS GUARANTEED @ VICTORCHANDLER.COM H'CAP 1m 6f (F)
8:50 (8:50) (Class 5) (0-70,70) 3-Y-O **£3,238** (£963; £481; £240) **Stalls** Low

Form RPR
0-04 1 **Seminal Moment**[13] 3731 3-7-11 **51** oh1........................ JamieKyne[(5)] 3 60
(J G Given) *chsd ldr tl led over 5f out: rdn over 1f out: styd on wl* **12/1**
6001 2 2 **The Last Don (IRE)**[20] 3511 3-9-7 **70**........................ TedDurcan 7 76+
(D R Lanigan) *hld up: hdwy over 4f out: rdn over 2f out: styd on wl: wnt 2nd cl home* **5/4**[1]
000- 3 nk **Veiled**[272] 6901 3-9-1 **64**........................ SebSanders 6 70
(Sir Mark Prescott) *a.p: chsd wnr over 4f out: rdn over 1f out: styd on same pce ins fnl f: lost 2nd cl home* **6/1**
20 4 23 **Eightdaysaweek**[52] 2479 3-8-8 **57**........................ LPKeniry 5 31
(S Kirk) *hld up in tch: plld hrd: rdn and wknd over 2f out* **11/4**[2]
6031 5 9 **Drop The Hammer**[18] 3575 3-8-12 **61**........................ SilvestreDeSousa 2 22
(T P Tate) *prom: rdn over 4f out: wknd 3f out* **5/1**[3]
0-00 6 ½ **Wolverton (IRE)**[32] 3117 3-8-2 **51** oh1........................ DaleGibson 1 11
(N P Littmoden) *led: hdd over 5f out: rdn and wknd over 3f out* **25/1**

3m 5.74s (-2.56) **Going Correction** -0.15s/f (Stan) **6** Ran SP% **113.6**
Speed ratings (Par 100): **101,99,99,86,81 81**
toteswingers: 1&2 £1.80, 1&3 £9.60, 2&3 £2.80. CSF £28.32 TOTE £9.10: £4.10, £1.20; EX 37.60 Place 6: £204.45, Place 5: £92.26..
Owner Moonfleet Racing **Bred** Whitsbury Manor Stud **Trained** Willoughton, Lincs

FOCUS
A couple of previous winners in an ordinary handicap. The gallop was only a modest one and the first three pulled clear, posting fair form for the grade. The winner raced in the centre in the straight.
Drop The Hammer Official explanation: jockey said filly was unsuited by the fibresand surface
T/Plt: £417.30 to a £1 stake. Pool: £63,504.14. 111.08 winning tickets. T/Qpdt: £42.30 to a £1 stake. Pool: £6,381.76. 111.40 winning tickets. CR

4151 YARMOUTH (L-H)
Tuesday, July 21

OFFICIAL GOING: Good (7.2) changing to good to soft after race 1 (2.15)
Wind: fairly light, half against Weather: overcast, light rain

4176 JOHN SMITH'S MAIDEN AUCTION STKS 6f 3y
2:15 (2:16) (Class 5) 2-Y-O **£2,978** (£886; £442; £221) **Stalls** High

Form RPR
0 1 **Butch And Sundance**[15] 3692 2-9-2 0........................ MartinDwyer 11 77
(B J Meehan) *s.i.s: towards rr: hdwy over 2f out: shkn up and hung lft over 1f out: led 1f out: hung lft thrght ins fnl f: hld on wl* **6/1**[3]
2 shd **Kings Bayonet** 2-8-12 0........................ TPQueally 10 73+
(H R A Cecil) *s.i.s and hmpd s: bhd: stdy hdwy 3f out: led over 1f out: sn rdn and edging lft: hdd narrowly 1f out: carried lft fnl f: r.o but a jst hld* **13/2**
0 3 1 ¼ **Ivory Jazz**[14] 3715 2-8-10 0 ow1........................ KShea 6 67
(D K Ivory) *dwlt: sn in tch in midfield: hdwy over 2f out: drvn to press ldrs over 1f out: carried lft and kpt on same pce fnl f* **100/1**
33 4 1 **Poppy N'Penny (IRE)**[17] 3633 2-8-4 0........................ TPO'Shea 7 60+
(W J Haggas) *hld up wl in tch: n.m.r and swtchd rt 2f out: sn rdn and unable qck: rallied u.p ins fnl f: r.o wl to go 4th nr fin* **4/1**[2]
5 ½ **Wanchai Whisper** 2-8-4 0........................ JimmyQuinn 4 57
(W J Haggas) *s.i.s: bhd: hdwy and edging rt looking for run over 1f out: hung lft ent fnl f: r.o wl fnl f: gng on fin* **12/1**
652 6 hd **Quaestor (IRE)**[13] 3744 2-8-12 0........................ RichardKingscote 8 64
(Tom Dascombe) *prom: ev ch and rdn wl over 1f out: nt pce of ldng trio 1f out: lost 2 pls nr fin* **3/1**[1]
00 7 1 ¼ **Edward Whymper**[19] 3546 2-8-9 0........................ SaleemGolam 12 57
(M H Tompkins) *s.i.s: bhd: hdwy over 2f out: styng on but hld whn racd awkwardly ins fnl f: nvr nr ldrs* **16/1**
8 4 **Red Barcelona (IRE)** 2-8-12 0........................ TedDurcan 15 48
(M H Tompkins) *v s.i.s: bhd and sn pushed along: sme hdwy fnl f: n.d* **16/1**
0 9 ¾ **Email Exit (IRE)**[33] 3072 2-8-12 0........................ SebSanders 1 46
(C F Wall) *towards rr: hdwy into midfield over 2f out: rdn and wknd over 1f out* **16/1**
4005 10 3 ½ **Avec Moi**[13] 3742 2-8-4 0........................ FrancisNorton 9 27
(Mrs C A Dunnett) *stdd and wnt rt s: racd keenly: sn pressing ldr: wknd quickly wl over 1f out: wl btn whn sltly hmpd ins fnl f* **50/1**
11 2 ½ **Strike A Deal (IRE)** 2-8-8 0........................ JackMitchell[(3)] 14 27
(C F Wall) *s.i.s: a in rr and sn pushed along: nvr a factor* **15/2**
06 12 8 **Speedyfix**[13] 3744 2-8-9 0........................ HayleyTurner 13 1
(Mrs C A Dunnett) *led tl over 1f out: wknd qckly and sn bhd* **100/1**
0 13 5 **Babajaga (IRE)**[13] 3744 2-8-6 0........................ WilliamCarson[(5)] 5 —
(J M P Eustace) *stdd s: a towards rr: lost tch and flashing tail wl over 1f out* **40/1**

1m 16.45s (2.05) **Going Correction** +0.175s/f (Good) **13** Ran SP% **116.1**
Speed ratings (Par 94): **93,92,91,89,89 88,87,81,80,76 72,62,55**
toteswingers: 1&2 £11.30, 1&3 £68.70, 2&3 £58.40 CSF £43.08 TOTE £7.80: £2.30, £2.60, £9.90; EX 43.40 TRIFECTA Not won..
Owner Abbott Racing Limited **Bred** Hellwood Stud Farm **Trained** Manton, Wilts

■ Stewards' Enquiry : Martin Dwyer 16-day ban (takes into account previous offences; three days deferred): careless riding (Aug 7-19)

FOCUS

A few of the jockeys felt the ground was riding on the soft side and the official description was duly changed from good, to good to soft after this opener. This was just a modest juvenile maiden, in which the winner improved.

NOTEBOOK

Butch And Sundance improved on the form he showed when down the field on his debut in a decent Windsor maiden and won despite hanging badly left in the closing stages, in the process carrying the runner-up across the track. He had to survive a Stewards' enquiry and might have been a slightly fortunate winner. Whatever, though, things are likely to be tougher next time and it's hoped he will be less wayward in future. (tchd 13-2)

Kings Bayonet, an £11,000 half-brother to 6f juvenile winners Retaliate and Melody King, recovered well from a sluggish start and was produced with a chance inside the final two furlongs, only to have his prospects compromised by being continually intimidated and taken left all the way across the track by the winner late on. He showed plenty of ability and should find a similar race. (op 5-1 tchd 8-1)

Ivory Jazz stepped up massively on the form he showed over 7f on Polytrack first time up. He still showed signs of inexperience, being niggled along a fair way out, and there ought to be more to come. Official explanation: jockey said colt ran greenly (op 66-1)

Poppy N'Penny(IRE), upped in trip, kept on but was never a threat. She might find her level in weak nurseries. (op 9-2 tchd 7-2)

Wanchai Whisper stayed on from a long way back once in the clear, despite running green. She displayed quite a fluent action and might appreciate better ground.

Quaestor(IRE) didn't see his race out after showing speed and was disappointing. He might be better suited by better ground, or a drop back to 5f. (op 7-2 tchd 11-4)

Speedyfix Official explanation: trainer said gelding was struck into

4177 JOHN SMITH'S (S) STKS — 1m 2f 21y

2:45 (2:45) (Class 6) 3-Y-O — £1,942 (£578; £288; £144) Stalls Low

Form — RPR

3303 **1** **King's Chorister**[15] 3685 3-8-12 51 ....(t) MickyFenton 5 — 55+
(Miss Gay Kelleway) *hld up towards rr: nt clr run over 2f out tl wl over 1f out: sn swtchd rt: str run 1f out to ld fnl 100yds: drvn out* **11/1**

40-0 **2** *½* **Myttons Maid**[71] 1940 3-8-7 42 ....(p) NeilChalmers 3 — 49
(A Bailey) *led: rdn over 2f out: drvn and kpt on wl over 1f out: hdd fnl 100yds: kpt on trying but a hld after* **100/1**

-034 **3** *1* **Bussell Along (IRE)**[15] 3685 3-8-7 52 .... HayleyTurner 1 — 47
(M L W Bell) *s.i.s: towards rr: rdn 3f out: swtchd rt to outer and drvn over 2f out: styd on to chse ldng pair ins fnl f: styng on steadily fin* **7/1**[3]

4056 **4** *2 ¼* **King's Masque**[26] 3321 3-8-12 66 .... MartinDwyer 2 — 48
(W R Muir) *broke wl: grad stdd bk and hld up towards rr: hdwy on inner 3f out: chsd ldr ent fnl 2f out: drvn and pressed ldr over 1f out tl wknd fnl 100yds* **6/4**[1]

010 **5** *nk* **Jeronimo Joe**[8] 3923 3-9-4 60 .... SebSanders 7 — 53
(A B Haynes) *restless in stalls: stdd s: plld hrd early: hld up towards rr: hdwy over 4f out: rdn to chse ldng pair 1f out: no imp after and lost 2 pls fnl 100yds* **14/1**

545 **6** *5* **Extracurricular (USA)**[54] 2395 3-8-8 60 ow1 .... RyanMoore 8 — 33
(M Botti) *chsd ldrs: rdn 4f out: wknd u.p over 1f out* **4/1**[2]

00-2 **7** *nk* **Art Discovery (IRE)**[196] 64 3-8-12 52 ....(b[1]) TedDurcan 10 — 36
(M H Tompkins) *s.i.s: hld up in rr: rdn and effrt over 2f out: no prog and n.d* **20/1**

-003 **8** *1* **Pagan Flight (IRE)**[8] 3919 3-8-12 56 ....(t) JimCrowley 9 — 34
(Mrs A J Perrett) *s.i.s: sn pushed along and hdwy: chsd ldr after 1f tl ent fnl 2f: sn looked reluctant and wknd* **8/1**

0-04 **9** *shd* **Supera (IRE)**[7] 3936 3-8-7 49 .... SaleemGolam 6 — 29
(M H Tompkins) *chsd ldr for 1f: styd chsng ldrs tl wknd u.p 2f out* **20/1**

0-06 **10** *7* **Cool Libby (IRE)**[27] 3257 3-8-7 47 .... TPO'Shea 4 — 15
(A B Haynes) *broke wl: t.k.h and grad stdd bk to rr: bhd and rdn over 3f out: no hdwy and sn lost tch* **22/1**

2m 12.93s (2.43) **Going Correction** +0.025s/f (Good) — **10** Ran SP% **113.5**
Speed ratings (Par 98): **91,90,89,88,87 83,83,82,82,77**
toteswingers: 1&2 £48.90, 1&3 £6.30, 2&3 £39.90 CSF £808.90 TOTE £15.20: £2.70, £8.20, £2.10; EX 962.30 TRIFECTA Not won..There was no bid for the winner.
Owner K J Holdings Ltd Kingsclub Syndicate **Bred** Cheveley Park Stud Ltd **Trained** Exning, Suffolk

FOCUS

A weak seller in which the form horses were disappointing. Not a race to be positive about.

4178 JOHN SMITH'S EXTRA COLD H'CAP — 1m 3f 101y

3:15 (3:16) (Class 6) (0-65,66) 3-Y-O — £2,072 (£616; £308; £153) Stalls Low

Form — RPR

0-51 **1** **Alicante**[4] 4039 3-9-8 66 6ex .... SebSanders 8 — 78+
(Sir Mark Prescott) *chsd ldr: led wl over 2f out: sn clr and in n.d: rdn out ins fnl f* **7/4**[1]

0005 **2** *3 ¼* **Mymateeric**[15] 3685 3-8-8 52 ....(b) LiamJones 10 — 56
(J Pearce) *sn niggled along towards rr: hdwy on wd outside 3f out: wnt modest 3rd over 2f out: edging lft but chsd clr wnr over 1f out: no imp* **80/1**

0500 **3** *¾* **Twist Again (IRE)**[24] 3383 3-8-12 56 .... JimmyQuinn 7 — 60+
(P Howling) *s.i.s: sn in tch in midfield: nt clr run and shuffled bk to rr 4f out: swtchd to outer and hdwy 3f out: hung lft and wnt 3rd over 1f out: kpt on but nvr nr wnr* **22/1**

0-44 **4** *8* **Freedom Fire (IRE)**[19] 3549 3-9-7 65 .... MickyFenton 5 — 54
(J M P Eustace) *led: rdn and clr w wnr wl over 2f out sn hdd: no ch w wnr fnl 2f: lost 2 pls over 1f out and wl btn fnl f* **9/1**[3]

0-30 **5** *2 ¼* **Windpfeil (IRE)**[20] 3511 3-9-2 60 ....(p) NickyMackay 11 — 46
(J H M Gosden) *hld up in tch: rdn and effrt 4f out wnt modest 3rd 3f out: no prog and wl btn fnl 2f* **12/1**

135 **6** *1 ¼* **Screaming Brave**[10] 3869 3-9-4 62 .... DarryllHolland 9 — 45
(M R Channon) *s.i.s and sn pushed along in rr: hdwy u.p 4f out: wnt modest 3rd 2f out tl over 1f out: no prog and wl btn after* **12/1**

0-04 **7** *shd* **Riptide**[30] 3192 3-9-6 64 .... GeorgeBaker 12 — 47
(C F Wall) *stdd after s: hld up in rr: n.m.r over 3f out: sn rdn and sme modest hdwy but nvr on terms* **12/1**

0202 **8** *1 ½* **Venture Capitalist**[15] 3675 3-9-5 63 .... RyanMoore 15 — 44
(L M Cumani) *s.i.s: sn in midfield on outer: lost pl bnd 5f out: rallied briefly u.p 4f out: sn wl btn and no ch fnl 3f* **11/1**

0-00 **9** *½* **Cooper Island Kid (USA)**[14] 3710 3-8-11 55 .... EddieAhern 4 — 35
(P W D'Arcy) *dwlt: sn pushed up to chse ldrs: rdn and unable qck 4f out: sn btn and no ch fnl 3f* **50/1**

0000 **10** *9* **Very Distinguished**[32] 3099 3-8-7 51 .... EdwardCreighton 2 — 16
(M G Quinlan) *s.i.s: a bhd: rdn and no rspnse over 3f out* **66/1**

0-64 **11** *3 ¾* **Khayar (IRE)**[37] 2943 3-9-5 63 ....(t) TPQueally 13 — 21
(M H Tompkins) *hld up in rr: rdn and effrt on outer 4f out: sn toiling and bhd* **12/1**

0001 **12** *33* **Hi Fling**[24] 3383 3-9-7 65 ....(b) MartinDwyer 16 — —
(B J Meehan) *chsd ldng pair tl 3f out: sn wandering u.p and lost pl: t.o and eased fr over 1f out* **20/1**

01 **13** *3 ¾* **Cape Marien (IRE)**[23] 3432 3-9-3 61 .... TedDurcan 3 — —
(D R Lanigan) *s.i.s: sn in tch: rdn and wknd qckly 4f out: t.o and eased fr wl over 1f out* **9/2**[2]

2m 29.3s (0.60) **Going Correction** +0.025s/f (Good) — **13** Ran SP% **117.4**
Speed ratings (Par 98): **98,95,95,89,87 86,86,85,85,78 75,51,49**
toteswingers: 1&2 £26.20, 1&3 £13.30, 2&3 £46.90 CSF £233.12 CT £2383.05 TOTE £2.70: £1.40, £18.50, £8.20; EX 215.10 TRIFECTA Not won..
Owner Miss K Rausing **Bred** Miss K Rausing **Trained** Newmarket, Suffolk

FOCUS

A modest contest, but a well-handicapped winner who was value for extra. A positive view has been taken of the form, which is decent for the grade.

Screaming Brave Official explanation: trainer said gelding was unsuited by the good to soft ground

Hi Fling Official explanation: trainer said colt was unsuited by the good to soft ground

Cape Marien(IRE) Official explanation: trainer said filly was unsuited by the good to soft ground

4179 STANLEY THREADWELL MEMORIAL FILLIES' H'CAP — 1m 3y

3:45 (3:48) (Class 5) (0-70,70) 3-Y-O+ — £2,849 (£847; £423; £211) Stalls High

Form — RPR

-552 **1** **Surprise Party**[40] 2863 3-9-5 63 .... GeorgeBaker 2 — 72
(C F Wall) *hld up towards rr: hdwy over 2f out: chsng ldrs wl over 1f out: swtchd rt and rdn to ld over 1f out: sn hrd pressed: styd on gamely to forge ahd fnl 75yds* **3/1**[1]

3046 **2** *2* **Astrodonna**[17] 3624 4-10-0 64 .... RyanMoore 12 — 70
(M H Tompkins) *hld up in rr: hdwy 2f out: rdn to chal and edgd rt over 1f out: ev ch and drvn ent fnl f: btn fnl 75yds and wknd towards fin* **7/1**

00-2 **3** *2* **Kassuta**[22] 3451 5-8-12 48 .... EddieAhern 4 — 49
(R M H Cowell) *in tch effrt to ld wl over 1f out: sn hdd: nt pce of ldng pair fnl f* **9/2**[2]

0060 **4** *hd* **Polemica (IRE)**[24] 3381 3-9-4 62 .... JamieSpencer 11 — 61
(E A L Dunlop) *v.s.a: hld up in last pl: hdwy 2f out: drvn and hung lft fr over 1f out: kpt on same pce u.p fnl f* **20/1**

-003 **5** *3 ½* **Turkish Lokum**[33] 3075 3-8-13 62 .... WilliamCarson(5) 5 — 53
(J M P Eustace) *hld up towards rr: hdwy on far side jst over 2f out: chsd ldrs and rdn over 1f out: wknd fnl f* **10/1**

0-02 **6** *4 ½* **Rock Art (IRE)**[18] 3569 3-9-12 70 .... MartinDwyer 7 — 51
(B J Meehan) *led tl rdn and hdd wl over 1f out: struggling whn hmpd and swtchd rt over 1f out: wl btn fnl f* **9/1**

00-0 **7** *1* **Black Salix (USA)**[10] 3859 3-8-8 52 .... MickyFenton 9 — 30
(Mrs P Sly) *t.k.h: hld up in rr: nt clr run and hmpd ent fnl 2f: swtchd rt over 1f out: nvr nr ldrs* **33/1**

066- **8** *1 ½* **Dance Club (IRE)**[266] 7052 3-9-5 63 .... LiamJones 3 — 38
(W Jarvis) *s.i.s: t.k.h: sn in tch: pressed ldrs and drvn 2f out: sn edgd lft and wknd* **28/1**

-000 **9** *¾* **Broughtons Silk**[8] 3929 4-9-1 51 .... TPQueally 14 — 26
(W J Musson) *hld up towards rr: hdwy jst over 2f out: shkn up and hung lft 2f out: sn wl btn* **28/1**

-456 **10** *1 ¾* **One Cool Kitty**[41] 2827 3-9-2 63 .... JackMitchell(3) 6 — 32
(M G Quinlan) *stdd after s: hld up in tch in midfield: rdn over 2f out: drvn and wknd 2f out* **12/1**

1052 **11** *2* **Bookiebasher Babe (IRE)**[4] 4060 4-9-13 63 .... FrancisNorton 13 — 29
(M Quinn) *w ldr: rdn over 2f out: wknd qckly wl over 1f out* **13/2**[3]

160/ **12** *8* **Memphis Marie**[619] 6762 5-9-0 50 .... EdwardCreighton 1 — —
(P J McBride) *chsd ldrs on outer: wknd qckly over 2f out: wl bhd after* **66/1**

6400 **13** *13* **Novastasia (IRE)**[23] 3427 3-8-9 56 ....(p) AndreaAtzeni(3) 10 — —
(W R Swinburn) *in tch in midfield: rdn and struggling over 3f out: wl btn whn sltly hmpd over 2f out: t.o fnl f* **20/1**

4-00 **14** *10* **Cocktail Party (IRE)**[43] 2776 3-9-0 58 .... ChrisCatlin 8 — —
(J W Hills) *stdd after s: plld hrd and hld up in midfield: rdn over 3f out: sn struggling: t.o fr wl over 1f out* **33/1**

1m 42.0s (1.40) **Going Correction** +0.175s/f (Good)
WFA 3 from 4yo+ 8lb — **14** Ran SP% **119.6**
Speed ratings (Par 100): **100,98,96,95,92 87,86,85,84,82 80,72,59,49**
toteswingers: 1&2 £6.40, 1&3 £4.50, 2&3 £7.40 CSF £21.43 CT £97.74 TOTE £3.90: £1.80, £2.10, £1.80; EX 29.10 Trifecta £54.40 Pool: £301.75 - 4.10 winning units..
Owner The Leap Year Partnership **Bred** Farmers Hill Stud **Trained** Newmarket, Suffolk

FOCUS

A modest fillies' handicap run at a fair pace. The form is solid.

Black Salix(USA) Official explanation: jockey said filly was denied a clear run

4180 FREEBETS.CO.UK OFFICIAL ROCHDALE FC KIT SPONSORS MAIDEN STKS — 7f 3y

4:15 (4:19) (Class 5) 3-4-Y-O — £2,849 (£847; £423; £211) Stalls High

Form — RPR

1 **Laafet**[40] 4-9-10 0 .... JimmyQuinn 11 — 76
(K A Morgan) *a.p: ev ch and rdn over 1f out: led ins fnl f: drvn out* **50/1**

0 **2** *½* **Betony (USA)**[64] 2142 3-8-12 0 .... HayleyTurner 3 — 67
(M L W Bell) *trckd ldrs: n.m.r briefly wl over 1f out: rdn to chse ldng pair over 1f out: pressed ldrs ins fnl f: kpt on u.p to go 2nd last strides* **12/1**

2226 **3** *hd* **Luc Jordan**[19] 3549 3-9-3 79 .... MichellePayne 4 — 71
(L M Cumani) *in tch: hdwy to ld over 2f out: rdn over 1f out: hdd ins fnl f: unable qck u.p fnl 100yds: lost 2nd last strides* **15/8**[1]

00-2 **4** *5* **Kessraa (IRE)**[12] 3773 3-9-3 73 .... DarryllHolland 5 — 58
(M R Channon) *sn pushed up to ld: hdd and rdn over 2f out: sn hung lft u.p: outpcd over 1f out: wl hld fnl f* **5/1**

0-5 **5** *nk* **Eyes Like A Hawk (IRE)**[52] 2496 3-8-12 0 ....(t) RichardKingscote 6 — 52
(Tom Dascombe) *in tch in midfield: pushed along over 2f out: outpcd and rdn wl over 1f out: kpt on fnl f: nvr pce to trble ldrs* **9/2**[3]

3 **6** *1 ¼* **Bobble Rock (IRE)**[12] 3773 3-9-3 0 .... RobertWinston 8 — 53
(J R Best) *s.i.s: bhd on outer: hdwy 3f out: nudged along and outpcd wl over 1f out: one pce ins fnl f* **33/1**

0/ **7** *½* **So Glamorous**[659] 5868 4-9-5 0 .... GeorgeBaker 7 — 50
(C F Wall) *t.k.h: hld up in midfield: rdn and struggling over 2f out: no prog fnl 2f* **25/1**

00 **8** *shd* **Haling Park (UAE)**[42] 2795 3-8-12 0 .... RichardMullen 12 — 47
(G L Moore) *hld up towards rr: rdn and no prog jst over 2f out: no ch fr wl over 1f out* **40/1**

0 **9** *nk* **Prince De Fortune**[14] 3718 3-9-3 0 .... TGMcLaughlin 2 — 51
(Mrs C A Dunnett) *chsd ldr: ev ch and rdn jst over 2f out: btn over 1f out: fdd ins fnl f* **50/1**

10 3 ½ **Squander** 3-8-12 0 .... RyanMoore 9 36
(Sir Michael Stoute) *a bhd and sn pushed along: edgd lft over 1f out: nvr a factor* **7/2[2]**
11 2 ¾ **Mumtaz Begum** 4-9-2 0 .... NataliaGemelova[(3)] 10 32
(J E Long) *s.i.s: a in rr: wl bhd whn edgd lft over 1f out* **100/1**
1m 30.21s (3.61) **Going Correction** +0.175s/f (Good)
WFA 3 from 4yo 7lb 11 Ran SP% **113.7**
Speed ratings (Par 103): **86,85,85,79,79 77,77,77,76,72 69**
toteswingers: 1&2 £57.80, 1&3 £19.80, 2&3 £5.00 CSF £518.90 TOTE £59.40: £9.50, £3.00, £1.20; EX 665.80 TRIFECTA Not won..
Owner J D M Stables **Bred** Gainsborough Stud Ltd **Trained** Newmarket, Suffolk

FOCUS
Just an ordinary maiden and the time was 1.08 seconds slower than the following handicap. Shaky form.

4181 JOHN SMITH'S H'CAP 7f 3y
4:45 (4:46) (Class 5) (0-75,75) 3-Y-O+ **£2,719** (£809; £404; £202) **Stalls** High

Form RPR
0624 1 **Tuxedo**[20] 3504 4-9-6 **67** .... DarryllHolland 2 75
(P W Hiatt) *chsd clr ldr tl over 2f out: rdn and sltly outpcd wl over 1f out: hdwy u.p ent fnl f: led fnl 100yds: r.o wl* **17/2**
4630 2 1 ½ **Seneschal**[5] 4009 8-10-0 **75** .... RyanMoore 9 79
(A B Haynes) *chsd ldrs: wnt 2nd over 2f out: ev ch 2f out: drvn to ld ent fnl f: edgd lft u.p: hdd and nt pce of wnr fnl 100yds* **11/2[2]**
0003 3 ½ **Autumn Blades (IRE)**[8] 3924 4-10-0 **75** .... RobertWinston 8 78
(A Bailey) *t.k.h: hld up towards rr: hdwy 3f out: led gng wl over 1f out: rdn and wanting to hang lft and hdd ent fnl f: nt qckn after* **15/2**
-320 4 ½ **Billberry**[20] 3512 4-8-13 **60** .... (t) JamieSpencer 7 61
(S C Williams) *stdd after s: hld up in last pl: shkn up and hdwy 2f out: drvn to chse ldrs 1f out: kpt on same pce fnl 100yds* **11/2[2]**
-003 5 ½ **Integria**[20] 3512 3-8-7 **66** .... (b) WilliamCarson[(5)] 4 63
(J M P Eustace) *chsd ldrs: rdn and unable qck wl over 1f out: edgd rt u.p and kpt on fnl f: nt pce to chal ldrs* **5/1[1]**
450 6 1 **Lordship (IRE)**[1] 4140 5-8-2 **56** oh4 .... JakePayne[(7)] 6 53
(A W Carroll) *taken down early: stdd s: t.k.h: hld up in midfield: effrt to chse ldrs 2f out: sn rdn: wknd 1f out* **14/1**
0530 7 3 ¼ **Count Ceprano (IRE)**[10] 3863 5-9-8 **69** .... HayleyTurner 1 57
(C R Dore) *hld up in tch in midfield: rdn and unable qck 2f out: sn struggling* **13/2[3]**
4030 8 1 ¼ **Kipchak (IRE)**[22] 3457 4-10-0 **75** .... (p) EddieAhern 3 60
(C R Dore) *led and clr tl 3f out: hdd wl over 1f out: sn wknd* **8/1**
0050 9 ¾ **Sapphire Prince (USA)**[10] 3868 3-9-1 **72** .... MarcHalford[(3)] 5 55
(J R Best) *stdd s: hld up bhd: rdn and no rspnse ent fnl 2f* **12/1**
3150 10 hd **Resplendent Nova**[5] 4005 7-9-11 **72** .... JimmyQuinn 10 55
(P Howling) *hld up in tch in midfield: shuffled bk and dropped to rr: shkn up and no hdwy over 1f out* **12/1**
1m 29.13s (2.53) **Going Correction** +0.175s/f (Good)
WFA 3 from 4yo+ 7lb 10 Ran SP% **116.2**
Speed ratings (Par 103): **92,90,89,89,88 87,83,82,81,81**
toteswingers: 1&2 £8.50, 1&3 £10.90, 2&3 £5.90 CSF £54.55 CT £377.65 TOTE £10.10: £3.20, £2.10, £3.00; EX 63.60 Trifecta £179.80 Pool: £340.25 - 1.40 winning units..
Owner Phil Kelly **Bred** Gainsborough Stud Management Ltd **Trained** Hook Norton, Oxon

FOCUS
A modest handicap run at a strong pace. Straightforward form.

4182 JOHN SMITH'S NO NONSENSE H'CAP 5f 43y
5:15 (5:16) (Class 6) (0-60,61) 4-Y-O+ **£2,183** (£644; £322) **Stalls** High

Form RPR
0450 1 **Rough Rock (IRE)**[24] 3401 4-8-9 **51** .... JerryO'Dwyer 6 57
(C A Dwyer) *chsd ldrs: rdn over 2f out: swtchd lft over 1f out: styd on u.p to ld wl ins fnl f: all out* **11/1**
0006 2 ½ **Gone'N'Dunnett (IRE)**[7] 3959 10-8-4 **46** oh1 .... (v) FrancisNorton 7 50
(Mrs C A Dunnett) *awkward leaving stalls: sn pushed along and wl outpcd in rr: hdwy on stands' rail over 1f out: r.o strly fnl f to go 2nd nr fin: nt quite rch wnr* **50/1**
0056 3 ½ **Town House**[5] 3999 7-8-4 **46** oh1 .... LiamJones 9 48
(B P J Baugh) *in tch: rdn and effrt over 1f out: ev ch and drvn 1f out: nt qckn fnl 100yds* **12/1**
600 4 nse **Mansii**[38] 2921 4-8-11 **53** .... (t) ChrisCatlin 5 55
(P J McBride) *s.i.s: sn outpcd in rr: hdwy over 1f out: str run fnl f: nt rch ldrs* **22/1**
00-0 5 hd **Wreningham**[10] 3860 4-9-4 **60** .... TGMcLaughlin 8 61
(M D Squance) *pressed ldr: rdn over 2f out: ev ch u.p 1f out: no ex fnl 100yds* **20/1**
0303 6 ½ **Lithaam (IRE)**[7] 3947 5-8-11 **53** .... (p) RyanMoore 1 53
(J M Bradley) *chsd ldrs: rdn over 2f out: led 1f out: hdd wl ins fnl f: no ex and lost 4 pls towards fin* **3/1[2]**
5204 7 1 ½ **Chantilly Jewel (USA)**[7] 3959 4-8-12 **54** .... (v) EddieAhern 4 48
(R M H Cowell) *stdd s: hld up off pce towards rr: swtchd rt and rdn wl over 1f out: kpt on but nvr pce to rch ldrs* **10/1**
5021 8 ¾ **Silver Prelude**[7] 3959 8-9-5 **61** 6ex .... (t) KShea 10 52
(S C Williams) *sn led: rdn over 1f out: edgd lft and hdd 1f out: sn btn: eased wl ins fnl f* **11/8[1]**
4363 9 12 **Taboor (IRE)**[7] 3959 11-8-6 **48** .... RichardMullen 2 —
(R M H Cowell) *racd off the pce towards rr: rdn and no hdwy 2f out eased ins fnl f* **7/1[3]**
-000 10 8 **Wivny (USA)**[18] 3590 4-8-5 **47** .... TPO'Shea 3 —
(H J Evans) *s.i.s: a wl outpcd: t.o and eased fnl f* **50/1**
64.80 secs (2.60) **Going Correction** +0.175s/f (Good) 10 Ran SP% **117.8**
Speed ratings (Par 101): **86,85,84,84,84 83,80,79,60,47**
toteswingers: 1&2 £41.10, 1&3 £14.90, 2&3 £22.20 CSF £464.03 CT £6512.77 TOTE £13.30: £3.10, £4.50, £3.30; EX 330.90 TRIFECTA Not won..
Owner M M Foulger **Bred** Mrs B Stroomer **Trained** Burrough Green, Cambs
■ Stewards' Enquiry : Jerry O'Dwyer two-day ban: used whip in the incorrect place (Aug 4-5)

FOCUS
A moderate sprint handicap. The pace was predictably strong with Silver Prelude going off in front as usual. The winner is rtaed to his recent handicap best.
Taboor(IRE) Official explanation: vet said gelding was lame
Wivny(USA) Official explanation: jockey said filly lost her action

4183 FREEBETS.CO.UK FOR FOOTBALL & RACING FREEBETS H'CAP 6f 3y
5:45 (5:47) (Class 6) (0-60,60) 3-Y-O+ **£2,072** (£616; £308; £153) **Stalls** High

Form RPR
1562 1 **Mr Skipiton (IRE)**[20] 3505 4-9-6 **57** .... TGMcLaughlin 3 73
(B J McMath) *in tch in midfield: rdn and hdwy over 2f out: led over 1f out: clr fnl f: styd on wl* **7/1**
0-52 2 1 ¾ **Big Boom**[40] 2864 4-9-1 **52** .... FrancisNorton 15 62+
(M Quinn) *chsd ldrs: rdn and chsd ldr over 2f out: chsd wnr fr over 1f out: kpt on same pce u.p fnl f* **4/1[1]**
0500 3 2 ¼ **Circle Dance (IRE)**[14] 3713 4-9-1 **52** .... (v) RobertWinston 4 55
(D Shaw) *towards rr: pushed along 4f out: hdwy over 2f out: drvn to chse ldng pair ent fnl f: no imp* **12/1**
6622 4 nk **Guto**[7] 3959 6-9-7 **58** .... RyanMoore 8 60
(W J H Ratcliffe) *chsd ldrs: drvn 2f out: kpt on same pce fr over 1f out* **9/2[2]**
0222 5 nk **Outer Hebrides**[22] 3459 8-8-13 **55** .... (v) AmyBaker[(5)] 5 56
(J M Bradley) *bhd: edging lft to far side and hdwy over 2f out: chsd ldrs and rdn over 1f out: no imp fnl f* **12/1**
0520 6 ½ **Scruffy Skip (IRE)**[3] 4082 4-9-1 **52** .... LiamJones 2 51
(Mrs C A Dunnett) *chsd ldrs: rdn ent fnl 2f: wknd u.p jst over 1f out* **20/1**
0532 7 2 **Shakespeare's Son**[5] 4023 4-9-2 **60** .... (b) SimonPearce[(7)] 10 53
(H J Evans) *stdd s: racd keenly and sn chsng ldrs: pushed along and wknd over 1f out* **13/2[3]**
4400 8 3 ¾ **Mafaheem**[29] 3227 7-9-6 **57** .... StephenDonohoe 7 38
(A B Haynes) *s.i.s: bhd and reminder sn after s: sme late hdwy: nvr nr ldrs* **20/1**
0046 9 2 ½ **Secret Dubai (IRE)**[29] 3227 4-9-0 **58** .... KristinStubbs[(7)] 11 31
(Mrs L Stubbs) *wnt rt s and slowly away: hdwy into midfield 1/2-way: edging lft and no hdwy after* **20/1**
-004 10 nk **Hilltop Legacy**[33] 3071 6-9-4 **55** .... AdrianMcCarthy 6 27
(J R Jenkins) *s.i.s: a bhd and sn rdn: nvr trbld ldrs* **50/1**
0602 11 ¾ **Registrar**[19] 3548 7-9-3 **54** .... (p) SaleemGolam 13 24
(Mrs C A Dunnett) *stdd s racd in midfield: rdn over 2f out: sn btn* **10/1**
400- 12 2 ¼ **Bahama Baileys**[385] 3581 4-9-2 **53** .... (b) ChrisCatlin 1 15
(C A Dwyer) *led: rdn and hdd over 1f out: sn dropped out* **33/1**
053- 13 shd **Proud Killer**[333] 5233 6-9-5 **56** .... EddieAhern 9 18
(J R Jenkins) *a towards rr: n.d* **20/1**
5300 14 3 ¾ **Tadlil**[10] 3860 7-8-13 **50** .... (v) NickyMackay 14 —
(J M Bradley) *chsd ldrs: rdn and hung lft over 2f out: sn wknd* **25/1**
3-00 15 4 ½ **Yeoman Of England (IRE)**[33] 3075 3-9-4 **60** .... (b[1]) GeorgeBaker 16 —
(C F Wall) *stdd s: hld up in rr: effrt and looked reluctant jst over 2f out: sn wl btn* **20/1**
54-2 16 8 **Mandhooma**[197] 45 3-9-2 **58** .... DarryllHolland 12 —
(P W Hiatt) *chsd ldr tl over 2f out: sn wknd: wl bhd and eased ins fnl f* **16/1**
1m 15.18s (0.78) **Going Correction** +0.175s/f (Good)
WFA 3 from 4yo+ 5lb 16 Ran SP% **126.9**
Speed ratings (Par 101): **101,98,95,95,94 94,91,86,83,82 81,78,78,73,67 57**
toteswingers: 1&2 £10.50, 1&3 £28.60, 2&3 £19.00 CSF £31.83 CT £362.27 TOTE £8.60: £2.40, £1.10, £3.30, £2.30; EX 59.50 TRIFECTA Not won. Place 6: £ 382.72 Place 5: £99.95..
Owner Steve & Ros Chaplin-Brown **Bred** Darragh O'Reilly **Trained** Newmarket, Suffolk

FOCUS
A weak sprint handicap but not a bad race for the grade. They raced all over the place in the closing stages and the front two were split by the width of the track at the line, with the winner towards the far side.
Mandhooma Official explanation: trainer said filly was unsuited by the good to soft ground
T/Jkpt: Not won. T/Plt: £571.40 to a £1 stake. Pool: £90,744.91. 115.92 winning tickets. T/Qpdt: £19.40 to a £1 stake. Pool: £7,333.35. 279.10 winning tickets. SP

4184 - 4186a (Foreign Racing) - See Raceform Interactive

3971 CATTERICK (L-H)
Wednesday, July 22

OFFICIAL GOING: Soft (good to soft in places; 7.4)
Wind: fresh, half behind Weather: overcast with showers, becoming fine and sunny after race 2

4187 EUROPEAN BREEDERS' FUND MAIDEN STKS 5f 212y
2:20 (2:20) (Class 5) 2-Y-O **£3,691** (£1,098; £548; £274) **Stalls** Low

Form RPR
4 1 **Ejaab**[80] 1700 2-9-3 0 .... TPO'Shea 6 76
(W J Haggas) *chsd ldng pair: hdwy to go 2nd 1f out: hung lft: styd on to ld nr fin* **11/4[2]**
6334 2 1 ¼ **Makbullet**[20] 3540 2-9-0 0 .... FrederikTylicki[(3)] 2 72
(J Howard Johnson) *led after 1f: rdn over 1f out: hdd towards fin* **13/8[1]**
0 3 3 **Licence To Till (USA)**[23] 3446 2-9-3 0 .... GregFairley 7 63
(M Johnston) *led 1f: chsd ldr: hung lft over 1f out: sn wknd* **16/1**
3 4 4 ½ **Newbury Street**[85] 1590 2-9-3 0 .... PaulHanagan 5 50
(R A Fahey) *mid-div: outpcd and lost pl over 4f out: kpt on fnl 2f: nvr on terms* **4/1[3]**
5 3 **Destiny's Dancer** 2-8-12 0 .... PhillipMakin 3 36
(P C Haslam) *s.i.s: hdwy over 4f out: wknd over 1f out* **20/1**
46 6 12 **Leopard Hills (IRE)**[32] 3170 2-9-3 0 .... TomEaves 8 —
(J Howard Johnson) *sn outpcd and in rr: t.o 3f out* **11/1**
0 7 1 ¼ **Calders**[8] 3937 2-8-5 0 .... BillyCray[(7)] 4 —
(A Berry) *mid-div: lost pl over 4f out: sn bhd* **200/1**
8 20 **Smirfys Copper (IRE)** 2-8-12 0 .... AdrianTNicholls 1 —
(D Nicholls) *s.v.s: a detached in last: t.o 4f out* **8/1**
1m 15.93s (2.33) **Going Correction** +0.275s/f (Good) 8 Ran SP% **115.3**
Speed ratings (Par 94): **95,93,89,83,79 63,61,35**
toteswingers: 1&2 £1.80, 1&3 £7.50, 2&3 £5.60 CSF £7.69 TOTE £3.80: £1.70, £1.20, £3.20; EX 9.60.
Owner Hamdan Al Maktoum **Bred** Manor Farm Stud (rutland) & Miss S Hoare **Trained** Newmarket, Suffolk

FOCUS
Very few got into this modest juvenile maiden. The runner-up helps with the level.

NOTEBOOK
Ejaab, fourth of six on his debut at Newmarket back in May, had been given time to strengthen and coped just fine with the slower ground. Soon chasing the early pacesetters, who looked to go a bit too fast, he gradually reeled them in down the straight and got on top close home. He should go on from this again and remains capable of better in nurseries. (tchd 10-3 in places)
Makbullet, fourth at Redcar on his recent handicap debut, was soon right up with the pace and went to the front turning in. He had too many guns for the third, but was unable to hold on from the winner inside the final furlong. He shows plenty of speed and should find a race eventually. (op 5-2)
Licence To Till(USA) was quickly into stride and soon duelling for the lead with the runner-up. He couldn't quicken at the end, but this still represented a big improvement on his debut effort. He has a bit of scope and will come on again for this. (op 14-1)

Newbury Street never got into it and may be more of a nursery type. (op 10-3 tchd 11-4)

4188 RACING UK (S) STKS 7f
2:50 (2:50) (Class 6) 2-Y-O £2,047 (£604; £302) Stalls Low

Form RPR

4 **1** **Sultan's Choice**[41] 2861 2-8-6 0 PaulHanagan 7 60
(P D Evans) *chsd ldrs: led over 1f out: briefly hdd ins fnl f: kpt on wl* **3/1**[2]

2554 **2** *nk* **Alphacino**[18] 3605 2-8-11 0 TPO'Shea 2 64
(M R Channon) *hld up in rr: hdwy over 3f out: chal over 1f out: led briefly ins fnl f: no ex* **10/1**

6043 **3** *5* **Ba Jetstream**[20] 3547 2-8-11 0 TonyCulhane 9 52
(M R Channon) *chsd ldrs: chal over 2f out: one pce over 1f out* **14/1**

0 **4** *¾* **Sassanian (IRE)**[55] 2388 2-8-8 0 FrederikTylicki(3) 6 50+
(J Howard Johnson) *in rr: styd on wl fnl 2f: nt rch ldrs* **11/4**[1]

5 *1 ¾* **Kwami Biscuit** 2-8-11 0 SilvestreDeSousa 4 46
(G A Harker) *s.i.s: drvn over 3f out: kpt on fnl 2f: nvr rchd ldrs* **20/1**

0431 **6** *hd* **Mary Helen**[41] 2861 2-8-12 0 DuranFentiman 12 46
(W M Brisbourne) *s.i.s: hdwy over 4f out: sn chsng ldrs: wknd over 1f out* **8/1**

1664 **7** *1* **Dispol Kabira**[20] 3542 2-8-12 0 PhillipMakin 5 44
(P T Midgley) *mid-div: effrt 3f out: nvr nr ldrs* **8/1**

0 **8** *¾* **Maiwand**[14] 3733 2-8-8 0 ow2 StephenDonohoe 3 38
(Sir Mark Prescott) *chsd ldrs: wknd over 1f out* **15/2**[3]

605 **9** *hd* **One Cool Deal (IRE)**[15] 3719 2-8-11 0 (b[1]) DavidAllan 11 40
(T D Easterby) *led tl over 1f out: sn wknd* **16/1**

00 **10** *20* **Rivitivo**[15] 3719 2-8-6 0 PaulQuinn 1 —
(W M Brisbourne) *s.i.s: drvn to sn chse ldrs: lost pl over 2f out: bhd fnl 2f: t.o* **50/1**

0 **11** *6* **Moondarra Blade**[33] 3119 2-8-11 0 (v[1]) GrahamGibbons 8 —
(J R Weymes) *dwlt: sme hdwy 4f out: sn lost pl: bhd fnl 2f: t.o* **100/1**

1m 30.31s (3.31) **Going Correction** +0.275s/f (Good) 11 Ran SP% **115.0**
Speed ratings (Par 92): **92,91,85,85,83 82,81,80,80,57 50**
The winner was bought in for 11,000gns. Alphacino was claimed by P C Haslam for £6,000. Ba Jetstream was claimed by F Jordan for £6,000. Sassanian was claimed by Jane Chapple-Hyam for £6,000.
Owner Jim Ennis **Bred** Littleton Stud **Trained** Pandy, Monmouths

FOCUS
Not the greatest of sellers and obviously limited form. The runer-up is probably the key.

NOTEBOOK
Sultan's Choice, who shaped with promise when fourth behind Mary Helen on her debut at Yarmouth last month and has since changed stables, was faced with similar conditions here and she found more when challenged and briefly headed by the runner-up. She is going to stay further on breeding and may be worth her place in a low-grade nursery. (tchd 4-1 in places)
Alphacino had finished quite a bit behind the winner at Yarmouth and was again comfortably held at Beverley last time. He made ground wide and came through to narrowly take it up, but the winner pulled out a bit more and he was forced to settle for second. (op 12-1)
Ba Jetstream kept on at the one pace back in third and didn't seem inconvenienced by the rise in trip, though he certainly didn't improve for it. (op 16-1)
Sassanian(IRE) was soon outpaced on this drop in grade and didn't find his stride until the race was all over. He still looked green and should find a race at this level before long. (op 3-1 tchd 7-2)
Kwami Biscuit, related to several minor winners, made a little late headway and should improve for the experience. (op 16-1)
Dispol Kabira Official explanation: jockey said filly was unsuited by the track
Maiwand showed early speed before fading and looks a horse of very limited ability. (op 7-1 tchd 8-1)

4189 SKY BET SUPPORTING THE YORKSHIRE RACING FESTIVAL H'CAP 5f
3:20 (3:20) (Class 4) (0-85,83) 3-Y-O+ £5,180 (£1,541; £770; £384) Stalls Low

Form RPR

-063 **1** **The Nifty Fox**[11] 3855 5-9-1 73 DavidAllan 5 88
(T D Easterby) *trckd ldrs: shkn up over 2f out: led over 1f out: edgd lft ins fnl f: styd on wl* **11/4**[2]

3121 **2** *1 ¾* **Feelin Foxy**[13] 3765 5-9-3 75 AlanMunro 4 83
(J G Given) *chsd ldrs: chal 1f out: hld whn sltly hmpd nr fin* **5/2**[1]

0512 **3** *4 ½* **Cayman Fox**[22] 3479 4-8-6 64 oh4 (e) PJMcDonald 7 56
(James Moffatt) *led: hdd over 1f out: hung rt and sn fdd* **6/1**[3]

14-0 **4** *2 ¼* **Go Go Green (IRE)**[60] 2259 3-9-7 83 PhillipMakin 2 67
(D H Brown) *sn chsng ldrs: outpcd after 2f: wknd over 1f out* **5/2**[1]

0602 **5** *2* **Kyzer Chief**[12] 3828 4-8-9 67 TomEaves 6 44
(R E Barr) *trckd ldrs: wknd over 1f out* **8/1**

60.37 secs (0.57) **Going Correction** +0.275s/f (Good)
WFA 3 from 4yo+ 4lb 5 Ran SP% **109.2**
Speed ratings (Par 105): **106,103,96,92,89**
CSF £9.80 TOTE £3.40: £1.80, £1.50; EX 7.30.
Owner Roy Peebles **Bred** Mrs Norma Peebles **Trained** Great Habton, N Yorks

FOCUS
This was a modest sprint handicap, dominated by 'foxes'. Sound form.

4190 HAPPY BIRTHDAY TRACY-ANN COOPER NURSERY 7f
3:50 (3:50) (Class 5) 2-Y-O £3,238 (£963; £481; £240) Stalls Low

Form RPR

5210 **1** **Jehu**[12] 3821 2-9-7 76 TonyCulhane 1 81
(M R Channon) *in rr: drvn 4f out: sn wl detached in last: gd hdwy on wd outside 2f out: str run to ld post* **15/2**

553 **2** *shd* **Storm Hawk (IRE)**[27] 3306 2-8-10 65 PaulEddery 9 70
(Pat Eddery) *w ldrs: drvn 4f out: lost pl over 2f out: rallied over 1f out: styd on wl to ld last 50yds: hdd last stride* **5/1**[3]

0042 **3** *1 ¾* **Whippers Love (IRE)**[7] 3978 2-8-11 66 GregFairley 6 66
(M Johnston) *led: rdn 3 l clr 1f out: hdd and no ex wl ins fnl f* **5/2**[1]

5422 **4** *1* **Go To Dubai**[18] 3605 2-8-2 57 DaleGibson 7 55
(M W Easterby) *sn chsng ldrs: wnt 2nd 1f out: kpt on same pce* **6/1**

0005 **5** *1* **Dispol Antonio (IRE)**[18] 3605 2-8-4 59 (v) DuranFentiman 2 54
(P T Midgley) *hld up in rr: hdwy over 3f out: kpt on same pce fnl 2f* **66/1**

654 **6** *¾* **Urban Clubber**[37] 2963 2-9-0 72 FrederikTylicki(3) 5 66
(J Howard Johnson) *in rr div: lost pl 4f out: hdwy over 2f out: kpt on fnl f* **7/2**[2]

0635 **7** *1 ¼* **Gentle Beat (IRE)**[20] 3542 2-9-4 73 DavidAllan 4 63
(T D Easterby) *sn chsng ldrs: one pce fnl 2f* **10/1**

516 **8** *1 ¼* **Underworld Dandy**[40] 2875 2-8-13 68 TomEaves 8 55
(P D Evans) *chsd ldrs: lost pl 4f out* **20/1**

6465 **9** *6* **Prettiest Star (IRE)**[20] 3540 2-7-11 57 JamieKyne(5) 3 29
(K A Ryan) *dwlt: in rr: sme hdwy 3f out: sn lost pl and bhd* **9/1**

1m 29.66s (2.66) **Going Correction** +0.275s/f (Good) 9 Ran SP% **118.9**
Speed ratings (Par 94): **95,94,92,91,90 89,88,86,80**
toteswingers: 1&2 £8.30, 1&3 £5.50, 2&3 £3.20 CSF £46.16 CT £123.32 TOTE £9.20: £2.60, £3.00, £1.20; EX 43.90.
Owner Box 41 **Bred** W P Churchward And Mrs C Hue-Williams **Trained** West Ilsley, Berks

FOCUS
A competitive-looking if ordinary nursery. The winner did well to get involved from the rear. The 'official' ratings shown next to each horse are estimated and for information purposes only.

NOTEBOOK
Jehu, detached and ridden along at halfway, was still stone last straightening for home, but began to run on strongly widest of all and just got up to deny Storm Hawk. He ran a shocker on his recent handicap debut at Newmarket, but had been dropped 4lb and seemed to appreciate the softer ground. His dam was placed over middle distances and he is going to benefit from a step up to 1m on this evidence. (op 8-1 tchd 13-2)
Storm Hawk(IRE), who had run in three sprint maidens, was always likely to benefit from the step up to 7f, and he stayed on again having lost his position, but was unable to quite fend off the winner. There is a small race in him. (op 7-1 tchd 9-1)
Whippers Love(IRE) only found one too good when attempting to make all at Kempton last time and he looked the likely winner here when kicking off the final bend, but was ultimately reeled in and had to settle for third. (tchd 11-4 in places)
Go To Dubai, who had twice finished runner-up at selling/claiming level, held every chance but couldn't race on from a furlong out. (op 12-1)
Dispol Antonio(IRE) never really featured.
Urban Clubber was under strong pressure turning in and failed to pick up. (op 5-1)

4191 YORKSHIRE RADIO H'CAP 5f 212y
4:20 (4:20) (Class 6) (0-60,58) 3-Y-O+ £2,460 (£732; £365; £182) Stalls Low

Form RPR

0016 **1** **Neo's Mate (IRE)**[4] 4079 3-8-10 52 SilvestreDeSousa 11 60
(Paul Green) *dwlt: in rr: hdwy 2f out: str run to ld nr fin* **16/1**

1502 **2** *nk* **Future Gem**[6] 4016 3-8-4 51 (p) JamieKyne(5) 10 58
(A Dickman) *swvd rt s: hdwy 4f out: sn chsng ldrs: hung lft 1f out: kpt on wl to go 2nd nr fin* **9/1**

0066 **3** *¾* **Redwater River**[5] 4072 5-8-10 52 (b) DeanHeslop(5) 7 58+
(Mrs R A Carr) *led: hrd drvn 2f out: hdd last 50yds* **6/1**[3]

1350 **4** *½* **Jord (IRE)**[9] 3924 5-8-11 48 (p) StephenDonohoe 3 52
(J A Glover) *in rr: hdwy on wd outside 2f out: styd on wl ins fnl f* **5/1**[2]

0005 **5** *nk* **Rainbow Bay**[7] 3972 6-8-3 45 (p) PaulPickard(5) 9 48
(Miss Tracy Waggott) *prom: effrt over 2f out: styd on same pce fnl f* **22/1**

5604 **6** *½* **Conjecture**[17] 3657 7-9-7 58 GregFairley 12 59
(R Bastiman) *trckd ldrs: chal over 2f out: one pce fnl f* **25/1**

0000 **7** *2 ¼* **King Of Swords (IRE)**[11] 3860 5-9-7 58 DavidAllan 5 52
(N Tinkler) *s.i.s: hdwy 2f out: nvr nr ldrs* **12/1**

0104 **8** *¾* **Just Sam (IRE)**[19] 3558 4-9-7 58 PhillipMakin 6 50
(R E Barr) *chsd ldrs: fdd 1f out* **7/1**

-030 **9** *nk* **Desert Ben (IRE)**[14] 3730 6-9-4 55 JamieMoriarty 8 46
(C Grant) *in rr: nvr a factor* **28/1**

6003 **10** *hd* **First Swallow**[13] 3765 4-9-4 55 (p) TonyHamilton 2 45
(R A Fahey) *chsd ldrs: hmpd on ins and lost pl over 4f out: hdwy and edgd rt 2f out: swtchd lft 1f out: nvr a factor* **4/1**[1]

1620 **11** *½* **Gioacchino (IRE)**[21] 3505 4-8-9 53 SPRyan(7) 4 42
(R A Harris) *chsd ldrs: drvn 3f out: wknd jst ins fnl f* **7/1**

6004 **12** *½* **Nacho Libre**[34] 3066 4-9-6 57 DaleGibson 1 44
(M W Easterby) *hld up on ins: hmpd and lost pl after 150yds: in rr and drvn 3f out* **12/1**

1m 16.23s (2.63) **Going Correction** +0.275s/f (Good)
WFA 3 from 4yo+ 5lb 12 Ran SP% **118.9**
Speed ratings (Par 101): **93,92,91,90,90 89,86,85,85,85 84,83**
toteswingers: 1&2 £11.60, 1&3 £24.20, 2&3 £14.90 CSF £149.72 CT £975.73 TOTE £23.70: £5.50, £3.50, £1.80; EX 128.90.
Owner Derek A Howard **Bred** Ken Carroll And Miss Marie McCarthy **Trained** Lydiate, Merseyside

FOCUS
A moderate handicap. The first two both showed a bit of improvement.

4192 TURFTV CLAIMING STKS 5f
4:50 (4:51) (Class 6) 3-Y-O+ £2,388 (£705; £352) Stalls Low

Form RPR

0631 **1** **Obe Gold**[6] 4012 7-9-7 83 (v) AdrianTNicholls 3 75
(D Nicholls) *hood removed v late: swvd rt s: reminders: sn drvn along: hdwy over 2f out: hrd rdn over 1f out: edgd lft and kpt on to ld wl ins fnl f* **5/6**[1]

0500 **2** *¾* **Lucky Art (USA)**[18] 3623 3-8-11 72 (p) FrederikTylicki(3) 6 69
(J Howard Johnson) *led: hdd and no ex last 50yds* **11/1**[3]

4040 **3** *1 ¾* **Rasaman (IRE)**[11] 3877 5-9-2 81 (p) AmyRyan(5) 10 66
(K A Ryan) *bmpd s: trckd ldrs on outside: effrt 2f out: styd on ins fnl f* **2/1**[2]

0010 **4** *1* **Princess Charlmane (IRE)**[9] 3909 6-8-9 53 ow1 (p) DNolan 8 50
(C J Teague) *swvd rt s: chsd ldrs: kpt on same pce appr fnl f* **28/1**

6043 **5** *nk* **Angelofthenorth**[9] 3909 7-8-8 43 AndrewElliott 5 48
(C J Teague) *chsd ldrs: kpt on same pce appr fnl f* **20/1**

5505 **6** *1 ¼* **Handsinthemist (IRE)**[17] 3657 4-8-1 52 (v[1]) PaulPickard(5) 7 42
(P T Midgley) *chsd ldrs on outside: one pce fnl 2f* **20/1**

6044 **7** *2 ¼* **Mandelieu (IRE)**[7] 3972 4-8-4 49 JamieKyne(5) 9 37
(Ollie Pears) *bmpd s: towards rr: kpt on fnl 2f: nvr nr ldrs* **25/1**

-600 **8** *9* **Yahwudhee (FR)**[55] 2389 4-8-9 60 JamesPSullivan(7) 1 11
(N Wilson) *chsd ldrs: edgd rt and lost pl over 1f out* **100/1**

033/ **9** *¾* **Glencairn Star**[843] 873 8-9-7 65 TonyHamilton 11 14
(F Watson) *hld up on outer: lost pl over 2f out* **66/1**

0 **10** *½* **Fire Up The Band**[35] 3020 10-8-4 46 BillyCray(7) 4 2
(A Berry) *in rr: bhd fnl 3f* **100/1**

61.02 secs (1.22) **Going Correction** +0.275s/f (Good)
WFA 3 from 4yo+ 4lb 10 Ran SP% **116.5**
Speed ratings (Par 101): **101,99,97,95,94 92,89,74,73,72**
toteswingers: 1&2 £3.20, 1&3 £2.20, 2&3 £3.80 CSF £10.80 TOTE £2.10: £1.10, £2.50, £1.30; EX 13.30.Lucky Art was claimed by R Carr for £12,000. Obe Gold was claimed by D Mountain for £15,000.
Owner D Nicholls **Bred** Mrs M Mason **Trained** Sessay, N Yorks

FOCUS
A fair claimer. The winner did not need to be at his best with the likes of the fourth and fifth limiting the form.

4193 BETFAIR APPRENTICE TRAINING SERIES H'CAP 1m 3f 214y
5:20 (5:20) (Class 6) (0-65,64) 4-Y-0+ £2,729 (£806; £403) Stalls Low

Form RPR

0/P4 **1** **Patavium (IRE)**[22] 3486 6-8-6 45........................ JamesPSullivan 14 53+
(E W Tuer) *t.k.h on outer in rr: hdwy to trck ldrs 7f out: outpcd over 3f out: hdwy over 2f out: styd on to ld jst ins fnl f* **8/1**

-102 **2** *1* **Promise Maker (USA)**[21] 3499 4-9-7 60........................ AmyRyan 9 66
(T D Walford) *led: drvn over 2f out: hdd and no ex jst ins fnl f* **4/1**[1]

0222 **3** *2 1/4* **Border Tale**[21] 3291 9-8-11 50........................ LanceBetts 2 53
(James Moffatt) *w ldrs: chal over 2f out: kpt on same pce fnl f* **7/1**

06-2 **4** *hd* **Bert's Memory**[12] 3798 5-8-9 51........................ DebraEngland(3) 5 53
(Jennie Candlish) *hld up in rr: hdwy over 6f out: sn chsng ldrs: hung bdly rt over 1f out and ended up stands' side: kpt on same pce ins fnl f: eased and lost 3rd nr line* **6/1**[3]

0550 **5** *1/2* **Golden Future**[41] 2859 6-8-11 50........................ JamieKyne 4 52
(P D Niven) *in rr div: drvn over 5f out: gd hdwy on ins over 2f out: sn chsng ldrs: kpt on same pce* **10/1**

0-40 **6** *hd* **Jenny Soba**[11] 3864 6-9-5 58........................ JPHamblett 12 59
(Lucinda Featherstone) *chsd ldrs: drvn over 3f out: one pce fnl 2f* **20/1**

1235 **7** *nk* **Granary Girl**[11] 3864 7-9-6 59........................ SimonPearce 11 60+
(J Pearce) *hld up in rr: stmbld bnd over 7f out: hdwy 2f out: kpt on: nt rch ldrs* **14/1**

4155 **8** *1 1/4* **Fell Pack**[26] 3350 5-9-0 58........................ IJBrennan(5) 10 57
(J J Quinn) *hld up towards rr: hdwy on ins over 2f out: nvr nr ldrs* **6/1**[3]

3345 **9** *1/2* **Barbirolli**[7] 3974 7-8-8 47........................ PaulPickard 7 45
(W M Brisbourne) *chsd ldrs: effrt over 2f out: one pce* **9/2**[2]

-000 **10** *5* **Punta Galera (IRE)**[24] 1000 6-8-8 50........................ JohnCavanagh(3) 6 40
(Paul Green) *hld up in rr: stmbld bnd over 7f out: bhd fnl 2f* **33/1**

4-00 **11** *8* **Hunting Haze**[58] 2344 6-8-6 45........................ DeclanCannon 1 22
(A Crook) *sn trcking ldrs: edgd rt and lost pl 2f out* **66/1**

5-00 **12** *1 1/4* **Fleetwood Flame**[33] 3100 4-8-3 45........................ MatthewLawson(3) 8 20
(W M Brisbourne) *t.k.h: trckd ldrs: lost pl 5f out: sn bhd* **66/1**

2m 43.73s (4.83) **Going Correction** +0.275s/f (Good) **12 Ran SP% 116.8**
Speed ratings (Par 101): **94,93,91,91,91 91,91,90,89,86 81,80**
toteswingers: 1&2 £9.80, 1&3 £16.80, 2&3 £3.70 CSF £38.35 CT £237.35 TOTE £12.90: £3.40, £1.60, £1.90; EX 54.60 Place 6: £45.92 Place 5: £30.91.
Owner J A Nixon **Bred** M Channon **Trained** Great Smeaton, N Yorks
■ Stewards' Enquiry : John Cavanagh caution: used whip when out of contention
Jamie Kyne seven-day ban: used whip in the forehand in apprentice training race (tbn)
Debra England ten-day ban: failure to ride out for 3rd place (tbn)
Matthew Lawson seven-day ban: used whip in the forehand in apprentice training race (tbn)

FOCUS
They went just a steady pace in what was a low-grade handicap and the form is a bit muddling.
T/Plt: £47.40 to a £1 stake. Pool: £49,995.12. 768.81 winning tickets. T/Qpdt: £15.90 to a £1 stake. Pool: £3,658.56. 169.80 winning tickets. WG

4017 LEICESTER (R-H)
Wednesday, July 22

OFFICIAL GOING: Good to soft changing to soft after race 4 (7.55)
Wind: Fresh behind Weather: Showers

4194 FOSTON MAIDEN AUCTION STKS 7f 9y
6:10 (6:11) (Class 5) 2-Y-0 £2,914 (£867; £433; £216) Stalls Low

Form RPR

65 **1** **Giulietta Da Vinci**[19] 3576 2-8-4 0........................ FrancisNorton 4 71
(R Hannon) *led: hdd over 5f out: chsd ldr tl led again over 2f out: rdn over 1f out: r.o* **2/1**[2]

42 **2** *2 1/2* **Layla's Boy**[17] 3652 2-8-12 0........................ PaulHanagan 7 73
(R A Fahey) *s.i.s: hdwy over 5f out: rdn to chse wnr 2f out: edgd lft ins fnl f: styd on same pce* **11/10**[1]

0 **3** *2* **Elizabelle (IRE)**[19] 3576 2-8-9 0........................ PatDobbs 10 65
(R Hannon) *prom: rdn over 2f out: styd on same pce fnl f* **11/1**

6 **4** *4* **Revoltinthedesert**[42] 2819 2-8-7 0........................ RichardMullen 12 53
(E S McMahon) *sn outpcd: r.o ins fnl f: nrst fin* **6/1**[3]

66 **5** *hd* **Breeze Of The Air**[9] 3920 2-8-10 0........................ SamHitchcott 3 55
(M R Channon) *chsd ldrs: rdn over 2f out: wknd over 1f out* **33/1**

0 **6** *nk* **Tribal Myth (IRE)**[11] 3875 2-8-12 0........................ GrahamGibbons 1 57
(K A Ryan) *chsd ldr tl led over 5f out: hdd over 2f out: wknd over 1f out* **33/1**

5 **7** *1/2* **Bustard Bay (IRE)**[18] 3634 2-8-13 0........................ HayleyTurner 2 56
(J G Given) *mid-div: hdwy over 4f out: rdn over 2f out: sn wknd* **80/1**

00 **8** *2 3/4* **Zachary Boy (IRE)**[51] 2533 2-8-10 0........................ DaneO'Neill 9 46
(B G Powell) *sn pushed along in rr: sme hdwy 1/2-way: rdn and wknd over 2f out* **100/1**

9 *9* **Hellenio** 2-8-11 0........................ DO'Donohoe 11 25
(S C Williams) *s.i.s: rn green and outpcd* **50/1**

10 *10* **Double Rollover** 2-8-9 0........................ ChrisCatlin 8 —
(W R Muir) *sn outpcd* **33/1**

1m 26.41s (0.21) **Going Correction** -0.10s/f (Good) **10 Ran SP% 116.6**
Speed ratings (Par 94): **94,91,88,84,84 83,83,80,69,58**
toteswingers: 1&2 £1.02, 1&3 £5.90, 2&3 £20.10. CSF £4.37 TOTE £2.70: £1.30, £1.10, £2.90; EX 5.90.
Owner Mrs J K Powell **Bred** Mrs J K Powell **Trained** East Everleigh, Wilts

FOCUS
Jockeys involved in the first reckoned the ground was riding as per the official description. There was very little depth to this modest maiden, in which the field raced down the centre of the track. The winner showed improved form.

NOTEBOOK
Giulietta Da Vinci was one of only a couple that appeared to hold a serious chance, having shown fair form in two maidens confined to her own sex, and her cheap auction price meant she got in here off a low weight. Always close up and racing quite keenly, she fought off the favourite and was nicely on top in the last half furlong. She should be competitive in nurseries. (op 11-4 tchd 3-1)
Layla's Boy's second at Ayr to Tukitinyasok was the best form on offer but he was a little disappointing, not the best away from the stalls and coming under pressure on the outside with 2f to run before lacking the pace to really trouble the filly. It may be that he prefers a sounder surface. (op 5-6)
Elizabelle(IRE), the Hannon second string, stayed on well enough for third and was not far off her debut form with stablemate Giulietta Da Vinci. There is a lot of speed on the dam's side of her pedigree and she is a half-sister to high-class sprinter Orizaba, but her sire is Gold Cup winner Westerner and she seems to have inherited her share of stamina from him. (op 12-1 tchd 14-1)
Revoltinthedesert was the subject of support, evidently expected to leave her debut running behind on this easier surface and over an extra furlong. The increased yardage certainly seemed to suit her, as after coming off the bridle before halfway she stayed on late to shade a bunch finish for fourth. (op 7-1 tchd 9-2)
Breeze Of The Air raced a little freely and did not entirely convince that he wanted this extra furlong and was denied fourth late on. He is now eligible for nurseries.
Tribal Myth(IRE) showed more prominently than he had on his York debut but he faded as if not ready yet for 7f. (op 40-1)
Bustard Bay(IRE), who became warm beforehand, improved on what he showed first time but probably needs more time. (op 66-1)
Hellenio was always in rear after missing the break but was not knocked about. This half-brother to the smart Sans Frontiere and Kootenay should not be written off and should improve considerably in time. (op 33-1)

4195 ABTECHPOWER.CO.UK NURSERY 5f 218y
6:45 (6:46) (Class 4) 2-Y-0 £3,885 (£1,156; £577; £288) Stalls Low

Form RPR

054 **1** **Rosedale**[56] 2383 2-7-12 56........................ AdrianMcCarthy 10 57
(J A R Toller) *s.i.s: sn prom: rdn to ld over 1f out: r.o* **25/1**

440 **2** *3/4* **Folletta (IRE)**[33] 3101 2-8-12 70........................ PatDobbs 2 69
(R Hannon) *chsd ldrs: rdn over 2f out: r.o* **20/1**

15 **3** *1 1/2* **On The Bounty**[19] 3559 2-9-4 76........................ PaulHanagan 4 70
(R A Fahey) *led: rdn and hdd over 1f out: edgd rt and styd on same pce ins fnl f* **6/1**[3]

066 **4** *1* **Wing Of Faith**[13] 3785 2-8-6 64........................ JamesDoyle 1 55
(S Kirk) *mid-div: hdwy over 3f out: sn rdn: styd on* **16/1**

4251 **5** *nse* **Military Call**[20] 3542 2-9-1 73........................ RichardMullen 9 64
(E S McMahon) *hld up: plld hrd: rdn over 2f out: hdwy over 1f out: nt rch ldrs* **15/8**[1]

6136 **6** *1 1/4* **Saxby (IRE)**[11] 3842 2-9-0 72........................ SamHitchcott 8 59
(M R Channon) *prom: lost pl over 2f out: rallied over 1f out: no ex ins fnl f* **9/1**

0105 **7** *1 1/4* **Queen's Hawk**[12] 3794 2-9-7 79........................ TPO'Shea 7 63
(D J Coakley) *hld up: rdn over 2f out: n.d* **10/1**

031 **8** *1 1/2* **Duke Of Rainford**[4] 4076 2-7-13 54 6ex ow1.............(bt) FrancisNorton 5 36
(Ian Williams) *plld hrd: trckd ldrs: rdn over 1f out: wknd fnl f* **9/2**[2]

501 **9** *5* **Ginger Ted (IRE)**[5] 4063 2-8-10 71 6ex.............(p) NeilBrown(3) 3 35
(R C Guest) *hld up: pushed along over 2f out: sn wknd* **7/1**

1m 13.99s (0.99) **Going Correction** 0.0s/f (Good) **9 Ran SP% 113.3**
Speed ratings (Par 96): **93,92,90,88,88 86,85,83,76**
toteswingers: 1&2 not won, 1&3 £37.60, 2&3 £5.50. CSF £426.46 CT £3381.94 TOTE £26.30: £5.90, £4.00, £2.40; EX 274.00.
Owner Alan Gibson **Bred** Alan Gibson **Trained** Newmarket, Suffolk

FOCUS
A modest nursery in which the winner improved a length on her previous form. The 'official' ratings shown next to each horse are estimated and for information purposes only.

NOTEBOOK
Rosedale's Polytrack fourth last time had been well advertised and she got in off bottom weight on her nursery debut. Always in touch down the outer, she went on to win a shade readily despite edging to her left once in front. Her trainer thinks she should get 7f a bit further down the line. (op 14-1 tchd 33-1)
Folletta(IRE), without the cheekpieces this time, was always up with the pace and she stuck on willingly for second, despite showing the tail-flashing trait that was in evidence on each of her first three starts. Described as a lazy filly, this was a definite step forward. (op 16-1 tchd 22-1)
On The Bounty made the running but could not counter when tackled by the winner. He seems well at home in easy ground but shaped as if perhaps 5f is his trip. (tchd 7-1)
Wing Of Faith, on his nursery debut, was always in a similar position without being able to quicken and did not conclusively convince that the drop back to 6f was what he wanted. (op 10-1)
Military Call, 4lb higher than when winning at Redcar, improved under pressure from the furlong pole before coming to the end of his tether in the final 50 yards. (op 9-4 tchd 7-4)
Saxby(IRE) could not turn around Redcar form with Military Call despite an 8lb pull and is not really progressing. (op 12-1 tchd 14-1)
Queen's Hawk could never get into the race on this drop in class, and may not have handled the easier ground. (op 13-2)
Duke Of Rainford was out of the handicap despite his penalty for dead-heating at Haydock recently. He took quite a tug and looked hard work for his rider before fading. Official explanation: jockey said gelding ran too free (op 11-2 tchd 4-1)
Ginger Ted(IRE), tried in cheekpieces (has worn blinkers) and penalised for his Nottingham win, was always in rear and a slight stumble after 2f made no difference to this disappointing display. (tchd 5-1)

4196 OSBASTON (S) STKS 1m 60y
7:20 (7:20) (Class 6) 3-Y-0 £1,942 (£578; £288; £144) Stalls High

Form RPR

-041 **1** **Phoenix Enforcer**[5] 4065 3-8-12 68.............(p) DO'Donohoe 2 60
(George Baker) *hld up: hdwy over 3f out: r.o u.p to ld nr fin* **11/10**[1]

0060 **2** *1/2* **Rockson (IRE)**[15] 3710 3-8-6 52........................ FrancisNorton 10 53
(B W Hills) *a.p: racd keenly: rdn to ld over 1f out: edgd rt ins fnl f: hdd nr fin* **15/2**[3]

0-06 **3** *5* **Davana**[30] 3221 3-8-6 40........................ RichardKingscote 11 42
(W J H Ratcliffe) *hld up: hdwy over 3f out: rdn and swtchd lft over 1f out: styd on same pce: wnt 3rd wl ins fnl f* **40/1**

0606 **4** *2* **Buckle Up**[11] 3862 3-8-11 41........................ SaleemGolam 7 42
(D K Ivory) *sn chsng ldr: rdn and ev ch wl over 1f out: wknd ins fnl f* **33/1**

4000 **5** *1 1/2* **Handcuff**[16] 3672 3-8-11 49........................ TPO'Shea 9 38
(J Gallagher) *led: rdn over 2f out: hdd over 1f out: wknd ins fnl f* **80/1**

0000 **6** *1/2* **August Days (IRE)**[28] 3257 3-8-6 50........................ AdrianMcCarthy 5 32
(J Pearce) *prom: rdn over 3f out: wknd over 1f out* **33/1**

0-60 **7** *1/2* **Blazing Buck**[19] 3588 3-8-11 69........................ TolleyDean 14 36
(A W Carroll) *sn outpcd and bhd: styd on ins fnl f: nvr nrr* **20/1**

0 **8** *2 1/2* **Angels And Demons (IRE)**[15] 3712 3-8-9 0 ow3..... GrahamGibbons 8 28
(Garry Moss) *s.i.s: hld up: rdn over 3f out: n.d* **66/1**

0603 **9** *3 1/2* **Aboukir**[15] 3711 3-8-11 62.............(t) HayleyTurner 4 22
(P F I Cole) *s.i.s: swtchd rt sn after s: rdn over 2f out: n.d* **9/2**[2]

6-00 **10** *3 1/2* **New Beginning (FR)**[47] 2685 3-8-6 60.............(b[1]) RichardMullen 6 9
(H J L Dunlop) *chsd ldrs: rdn over 3f out: wknd 2f out: eased over 1f out* **10/1**

0-03 **11** *16* **Digit**[48] 2624 3-8-7 57 ow1........................ TomEaves 1 —
(B Smart) *hld up: plld hrd: hdwy over 3f out: rdn and wknd over 2f out: t.o* **11/1**

-006 **12** *8* **Terracotta Warrior**[22] 3005 3-8-11 48........................ ChrisCatlin 13 —
(J Jay) *awkward leaving stalls: a in rr: bhd fr 1/2-way: t.o* **33/1**

4550 **13** *5* **Herecomesbella**[8] 3936 3-8-6 50..........................(b) FrankieMcDonald 12 —
(P G Murphy) *s.i.s: a in rr: wknd over 3f out: t.o* **50/1**

1m 46.81s (1.71) **Going Correction** +0.10s/f (Good) **13** Ran SP% **115.7**
Speed ratings (Par 98): **95,94,89,87,86 85,85,82,79,75 59,51,46**
toteswingers: 1&2 £3.20, 1&3 £14.90, 2&3 not won. CSF £8.35 TOTE £1.90: £1.10, £3.00, £7.10; EX 12.10.The winner was bought in for 6,500gns. Rockson was claimed by Ian Williams for £6,000.
Owner Codrington, Crabtree, Jacovou **Bred** The Hill Stud **Trained** Moreton Morrell, Warwicks

FOCUS
A pretty moderate race but the first winner, who ran close to her Nottingham form, is above average for the grade.

4197 IBSTOCK H'CAP 1m 3f 183y
7:55 (7:56) (Class 4) (0-80,80) 4-Y-0+ **£4,857** (£1,445; £722; £360) **Stalls** High

Form RPR
-216 **1** **It's A Date**[19] 3587 4-9-6 79.. TPQueally 5 89
(A King) *mde all: qcknd over 3f out: rdn over 1f out: styd on wl* **10/3**[3]

4-10 **2** *2½* **Rotative**[28] 3273 4-9-5 78..(p) AdamKirby 3 84
(W R Swinburn) *chsd wnr: rdn over 3f out: hung rt over 1f out: no imp fnl f* **5/2**[2]

42-1 **3** *2¼* **Hada Men (USA)**[50] 2566 4-9-3 76.................................. DaneO'Neill 2 78
(L M Cumani) *s.i.s: sn chsng ldrs: rdn over 2f out: edgd rt over 1f out: styd on same pce* **11/8**[1]

2204 **4** *11* **Distinctive Image (USA)**[65] 2146 4-9-7 80.................... ChrisCatlin 8 65
(R Hollinshead) *hld up: racd keenly: hdwy over 4f out: rdn and wknd over 2f out* **6/1**

5 *29* **Sotelo**[814] 7-8-13 72.. TomEaves 4 10
(S Gollings) *prom: lost pl over 4f out: sn bhd* **33/1**

2m 37.19s (3.29) **Going Correction** +0.20s/f (Good) **5** Ran SP% **111.0**
Speed ratings (Par 105): **97,95,93,86,67**
toteswingers: 1&2 £8.20. CSF £12.09 TOTE £3.90: £2.20, £1.70; EX 11.00.
Owner Horace 5 **Bred** Mrs F M Gordon **Trained** Barbury Castle, Wilts

FOCUS
A fair handicap which was always in danger of turning into a tactical affair and that is how it proved, as the winner made all. Other than the last pair swapping places the order never changed. The form is rtaed around the front pair.

4198 EUROPEAN BREEDERS' FUND FILLIES' H'CAP 7f 9y
8:25 (8:26) (Class 4) (0-80,80) 3-Y-0 **£6,308** (£1,888; £944; £472; £235) **Stalls** Low

Form RPR
-011 **1** **Rafta (IRE)**[5] 4061 3-7-12 64 6ex.......................... JosephineBruning(7) 1 74+
(T T Clement) *s.i.s: hld up: hdwy 3f out: led over 1f out: readily* **15/8**[1]

0-42 **2** *1¼* **Belle Des Airs (IRE)**[40] 2886 3-9-7 80..................... RichardKingscote 5 87
(R M Beckett) *led: rdn and hdd over 1f out: styd on same pce ins fnl f* **7/2**[2]

-124 **3** *2¾* **Bombina**[13] 3763 3-9-3 76.. AdrianMcCarthy 7 76
(P W Chapple-Hyam) *plld hrd and prom: rdn over 1f out: styd on same pce fnl f* **11/2**[3]

-620 **4** *1* **Moonlight Affair (IRE)**[26] 3341 3-9-0 73.................. GrahamGibbons 10 70
(E S McMahon) *s.i.s: hdwy over 4f out: rdn over 1f out: no ex ins fnl f* **16/1**

0060 **5** *¾* **Sanvean (IRE)**[11] 3870 3-8-11 70.............................. SamHitchcott 2 65
(M R Channon) *hld up: rdn over 4f out: hdwy over 1f out: nt trble ldrs* **33/1**

452- **6** *¾* **Solitary**[338] 5147 3-9-3 76.. DaneO'Neill 3 69
(H Candy) *chsd ldrs: effrt over 2f out: styd on same pce appr fnl f* **8/1**

0445 **7** *2¾* **Maggie Lou (IRE)**[39] 2926 3-9-3 76............................. TomEaves 12 61
(K A Ryan) *prom: rdn over 2f out: edgd rt over 1f out: wknd ins fnl f* **16/1**

4006 **8** *1¾* **Aunt Nicola**[13] 3789 3-9-2 75.................................... HayleyTurner 6 56
(M L W Bell) *trckd ldrs: plld hrd: wknd over 1f out* **25/1**

5-53 **9** *8* **Darcey**[37] 2967 3-9-0 73.. PaulHanagan 8 32
(R A Fahey) *w ldr tl rdn over 2f out: wknd over 1f out* **6/1**

1m 27.43s (1.23) **Going Correction** +0.30s/f (Good) **9** Ran SP% **116.3**
Speed ratings (Par 99): **104,102,99,98,97 96,93,91,82**
toteswingers: 1&2 £1.60, 1&3 £5.20, 2&3 £4.40. CSF £8.39 CT £30.25 TOTE £2.10: £1.20, £1.50, £2.00; EX 8.30.
Owner R L Gray **Bred** Thomas And Linda Heffernan **Trained** Newmarket, Suffolk

FOCUS
Following rain through the evening the going description was amended to soft before this race. Fair handicap form.

4199 DINGLEY MAIDEN STKS 5f 218y
8:55 (9:02) (Class 5) 3-Y-0+ **£2,914** (£867; £433; £216) **Stalls** Low

Form RPR
1 **Aegean Shadow** 3-8-5 0.. TobyAtkinson(7) 6 65+
(M Wigham) *s.i.s: hdwy over 2f out: rdn to ld ins fnl f: r.o* **33/1**

6 **2** *1* **Mata Hari Blue**[9] 3926 3-8-12 0.................................. JerryO'Dwyer 8 62
(J R Holt) *chsd ldrs: rdn to ld and hung rt 1f out: hdd and unable qck ins fnl f* **14/1**

626- **3** *3¼* **Verinco**[242] 7426 3-9-3 77.. TomEaves 13 57
(B Smart) *trckd ldrs: rdn over 1f out: styd on same pce* **7/2**[1]

50 **4** *½* **Migliori**[13] 3764 3-9-3 0... RichardMullen 7 55+
(Rae Guest) *hld up: hdwy 1/2-way: rdn over 1f out: nt rch ldrs* **8/1**

-000 **5** *nse* **Flute Magic**[34] 3075 3-9-3 60....................................(t[1]) ChrisCatlin 4 55
(W S Kittow) *prom: rdn over 2f out: styd on same pce appr fnl f* **25/1**

54 **6** *½* **Dilli Dancer**[42] 2820 4-8-12 0.................................... GabrielHannon(5) 16 48
(G D Blake) *led: rdn and hdd 1f out: wknd ins fnl f* **6/1**

55 **7** *¾* **Satwa Star (IRE)**[41] 2857 3-9-3 0.............................. DaneO'Neill 9 51
(E A L Dunlop) *prom: rdn over 2f out: no ex fnl f* **4/1**[2]

0 **8** *nk* **Fortezza**[13] 3764 3-8-12 0.. AlanMunro 5 45+
(C F Wall) *s.s: hdwy over 1f out: nt trble ldrs* **8/1**

9 *2¾* **Clever Omneya (USA)** 3-8-12 0.................................. DO'Donohoe 17 36
(J R Jenkins) *s.s: hdwy over 2f out: sn rdn: wknd fnl f* **50/1**

60 **10** *1¼* **Square Of Gold (FR)**[19] 3590 3-9-3 0......................... TolleyDean 10 37
(A W Carroll) *mid-div: hdwy over 1f out: wknd and eased ins fnl f* **66/1**

000- **11** *½* **Hayley's Girl**[265] 7097 3-8-12 46................................ NeilChalmers 14 31
(S W James) *chsd ldrs: rdn over 2f out: wknd over 1f out* **100/1**

0 **12** *8* **Hohrod**[15] 3712 3-8-12 0.. MarkCoumbe(5) 18 10
(John A Harris) *s.i.s: sn chsng ldrs: rdn 1/2-way: wknd over 2f out* **66/1**

06 **13** *¾* **A Lot Of Red (IRE)**[23] 3460 3-9-3 0...........................(t) PatDobbs 2 8
(P J O'Gorman) *hld up: wknd over 2f out* **28/1**

14 *5* **Luisa Tetrazzini (IRE)** 3-8-12 0.................................. PaulHanagan 3 —
(K A Ryan) *s.s: a in rr* **5/1**[3]

0-0 **15** *10* **Django Reinhardt**[14] 3743 3-9-3 0................................ TPO'Shea 1 —
(J R Gask) *mid-div: rdn over 2f out: sn wknd and eased* **20/1**

1m 15.3s (2.30) **Going Correction** +0.40s/f (Good)
WFA 3 from 4yo+ 5lb **15** Ran SP% **123.0**
Speed ratings (Par 103): **100,98,94,93,93 92,91,91,87,86 85,74,73,67,53**
toteswingers: 1&2 £24.80, 1&3 £28.60, 2&3 £15.30. CSF £426.20 TOTE £42.90: £6.70, £4.70, £2.00; EX 689.60 Place 6: £68.12, Place 5: £58.20..
Owner Theobalds Stud 2 **Bred** Theobalds Stud **Trained** Newmarket, Suffolk

FOCUS
Most of the field were in the stalls for around seven minutes prior to this race as a couple of runners played up. This was a pretty weak maiden and it is not form to rate too positively.
Flute Magic Official explanation: jockey said gelding hung left
Django Reinhardt Official explanation: jockey said gelding lost its action
T/Plt: £69.00 to a £1 stake. Pool: £67,562.54. 714.66 winning tickets. T/Qpdt: £19.60 to a £1 stake. Pool: £5,794.06. 217.70 winning tickets. CR

4080 LINGFIELD (L-H)
Wednesday, July 22

OFFICIAL GOING: Standard
Wind: fresh, behind Weather: overcast, quite breezy

4200 ASHURST WOOD MEDIAN AUCTION MAIDEN STKS (DIV I) 7f (P)
2:00 (2:00) (Class 5) 2-Y-0 **£2,388** (£705; £352) **Stalls** Low

Form RPR
43 **1** **Dubai Miracle (USA)**[28] 3270 2-9-3 0............................ JimCrowley 4 79+
(D M Simcock) *chsd ldrs: effrt and lft in ld bnd 2f out: sn clr: drvn and r.o wl fnl f* **13/8**[1]

2 *2¼* **Duster** 2-9-3 0.. SteveDrowne 1 73+
(H Morrison) *t.k.h: w ldr tl led over 4f out: hung rt and hdd bnd 2f out: r.o fnl f but no imp* **16/1**

3 **3** *2¼* **Kathindi (IRE)**[14] 3744 2-9-3 0.................................. TedDurcan 2 68
(J S Moore) *t.k.h: led narrowly tl over 4f out: w ldr tl carried wd bnd 2f out: no ch w wnr after: kpt on* **33/1**

64 **4** *1¼* **Orsett Lad (USA)**[14] 3745 2-9-3 0............................ RobertWinston 5 65
(J R Best) *chsd ldrs: cl up whn carried wd bnd 2f out: kpt on same pce after* **16/1**

54 **5** *1½* **Lutine Bell**[15] 3715 2-9-3 0.. SebSanders 6 61
(Sir Mark Prescott) *dwlt: sn in tch in midfield: rdn over 2f out: no prog and wl hld after* **7/1**[2]

3 **6** *2* **Wriggle (IRE)**[13] 3786 2-9-3 0.................................... LiamJones 7 56
(W J Haggas) *t.k.h: hld up in tch in midfield: rdn and effrt ent fnl 2f: wknd over 1f out* **13/8**[1]

7 *shd* **Dromore (IRE)** 2-9-3 0.. MartinDwyer 3 58+
(A M Balding) *v.s.a: bhd: stl last wl over 2f out: hdwy ent fnl 2f: kpt on steadily: nvr nr ldrs* **14/1**[3]

8 *1½* **Electric City (IRE)** 2-8-12 0..................................... EdwardCreighton 10 47
(M G Quinlan) *a towards rr: nvr trbld ldrs* **100/1**

00 **9** *15* **Satwa Crown**[16] 3692 2-9-3 0..................................... DO'Donohoe 11 14
(E A L Dunlop) *a in rr: lost tch over 2f out* **100/1**

0 **10** *½* **Seeker Rainbow**[32] 3160 2-8-12 0.............................. FrankieMcDonald 9 8
(Mrs L C Jewell) *t.k.h: in tch in midfield: rdn and struggling 3f out: wl bhd fnl 2f* **100/1**

11 *2* **Rock Of Behistun (IRE)** 2-9-0 0................................ DominicFox(3) 8 8
(P L Gilligan) *t.k.h: hld up in tch in rr: lost tch over 2f out* **100/1**

1m 26.29s (1.49) **Going Correction** +0.025s/f (Slow) **11** Ran SP% **114.0**
Speed ratings (Par 94): **92,89,86,85,83 81,81,79,62,61 59**
toteswingers: 1&2 £11.40, 1&3 £10.00, 2&3 £20.20 CSF £33.22 TOTE £2.60: £1.10, £3.70, £3.60; EX 28.30 TRIFECTA Not won..
Owner Ahmad Al Shaikh **Bred** Brylynn Farm, Inc **Trained** Newmarket, Suffolk

FOCUS
A modest maiden and a two-horse contest according to the market. This was a race dominated by those that raced handily and the winner is rated to form.

NOTEBOOK
Dubai Miracle(USA), who had already shown ability in a couple of starts on Polytrack, raced handily and was presented with a large inviting gap on the inside off the final bend when the leaders ran wide. Soon in front, he made no mistake and looks the type to make his mark in nurseries. Connections believe he will stay much further than this. (op 7-4 tchd 6-4)
Duster ◆, not sold for £800 as a yearling after fetching 9,000gns as a foal, ran a blinder on this debut especially as he raced keenly in front early and lost ground when very awkward rounding the home bend. The fact that he still stayed on to finish a clear second does him credit, and as the stable's youngsters usually improve a good deal with experience the future does look bright for him.
Kathindi(IRE), a fair third here on debut, is bred to have been suited by this extra furlong and he ran well for a long way before being done for finishing speed. He may do better once qualifying for a mark.
Orsett Lad(USA), back up in trip, took a keen grip just behind the leaders early and wasn't done many favours when the leader carried him wide off the final bend, but his winning chance wasn't affected. He is another that may do better in nurseries now that he qualifies. (tchd 18-1 and 20-1 in places)
Lutine Bell attracted good market support, but although he plugged on late he was never getting there quickly enough. He looks one for handicaps over further in due course. (op 12-1)
Wriggle(IRE), just behind a subsequent Listed winner when third on his Warwick debut earlier in the month, was well placed for a long way but he found very little off the bridle rounding the home bend and was apparently disappointing. However, it transpired that he had lost a hind shoe so he is probably worth another chance. Official explanation: vet said gelding lost a hind shoe (op 11-8 and 7-4 in places)
Dromore(IRE) ◆, a 14,000gns half-brother to four winners including the top-class Storming Home, completely fluffed the start but he was noted doing some fair late work without being by any means knocked about. Better can be expected in due course. (tchd 18-1)

4201 ASHURST WOOD MEDIAN AUCTION MAIDEN STKS (DIV II) 7f (P)
2:30 (2:32) (Class 5) 2-Y-0 **£2,388** (£705; £352) **Stalls** Low

Form RPR
4 **1** **Azizi**[20] 3546 2-9-3 0... RHills 3 73+
(W J Haggas) *chsd ldr: chal and shied at rivals whip wl over 1f out: rdn to ld ent fnl f: rn green but sn pushed clr: easily* **2/7**[1]

00 **2** *3½* **Bush Master**[11] 3865 2-9-3 0...................................... PatDobbs 2 64
(R Hannon) *led: hrd pressed and edgd rt wl over 1f out: hdd ent fnl f: no ch w wnr after* **40/1**

3 *2* **Christopher Wren (USA)** 2-9-3 0............................... RobertWinston 8 59+
(J R Best) *stdd towards rr after 1f: pushed along and hdwy ent fnl 2f: edgd lft but kpt on steadily fr over 1f out: wnt 3rd ins fnl f* **14/1**

0 **4** 1 1/2 **Execution (IRE)**[15] 3715 2-9-3 0 .... DO'Donohoe 1 56
(E A L Dunlop) *chsd ldrs: rdn and unable qck ent fnl 2f: plugged on same pce fnl f* **33/1**

U00 **5** shd **New York Lights (IRE)**[77] 1783 2-8-7 0 .... LeeNewnes(5) 6 50
(M D I Usher) *taken down early: chsd ldrs: rdn and outpcd by ldng pair 2f out: one pce after: no ch whn edgd rt nr fin* **100/1**

0 **6** 1/2 **Weliketobouggie**[11] 3865 2-9-3 0 .... TedDurcan 9 54
(J S Moore) *stdd after s: hdwy on inner 2f out: keeping on but wl hld whn nt clr run and swtchd rt ins fnl f: nvr nr ldrs* **20/1**

0 **7** 1 1/2 **Downtoobusiness**[13] 3785 2-9-3 0 .... TGMcLaughlin 7 50
(Karen George) *dwlt: in tch in midfield: rdn and struggling over 2f out: no ch fnl 2f* **100/1**

8 6 **Naseby (USA)** 2-9-3 0 .... SteveDrowne 10 35
(R Charlton) *in tch on outer: rdn over 3f out: wknd u.p jst over 2f out* **8/1**[2]

06 **9** 3/4 **Glass Of Red (IRE)**[21] 3500 2-8-12 0 .... SebSanders 5 28
(R M Beckett) *chsd ldrs tl wknd u.p over 2f out: wl bhd over 1f out* **11/1**[3]

10 14 **Man In The Mirror (IRE)** 2-9-0 0 .... DominicFox(3) 4 —
(P L Gilligan) *in tch in rr: rdn 4f out: sn lost tch: t.o over 2f out* **50/1**

1m 26.04s (1.24) **Going Correction** +0.025s/f (Slow) **10** Ran SP% **118.0**
Speed ratings (Par 94): **93,89,86,85,84 84,82,75,74,58**
toteswingers: 1&2 £7.50, 1&3 £3.50, 2&3 £59.90 CSF £30.35 TOTE £1.40: £1.02, £10.60, £3.40; EX 15.90 Trifecta £151.90 Pool: £457.97 - 2.23 winning units..
Owner Hamdan Al Maktoum **Bred** Shadwell Estate Company Limited **Trained** Newmarket, Suffolk

FOCUS
The winning time was 0.25 seconds quicker than the first division. Modest form.

NOTEBOOK
Azizi, by a Guineas winner out of a Guineas winner, was given a nice introduction at Yarmouth in a hot-looking maiden, a race that had already produced a winner. The betting suggested he was going to win easily, but it was far from a straightforward task for him, as he took an age to get on top whilst still looking green. Not overly big, he will need to improve considerably to win next time, using the runner-up as a form marker. (op 4-11 tchd 2-5 in places)
Bush Master, who finished last on his previous outing, was allowed an easy lead, one he only relinquished late on. Of course, he may have improved for a switch to Polytrack, but it is probably easier to believe at this stage that he is only modest. (op 33-1)
Christopher Wren(USA), whose dam was a winner in America, was on his toes before the off and showed plenty of signs of greenness during the race. A big sort, he got the idea towards the end and stayed on well. (op 16-1)
Execution(IRE) looked to have improved from his first run and shaped nicely.
New York Lights(IRE) shaped better having shown virtually nothing in three previous starts. (op 150-1)
Weliketobouggie ◆, who still looked a bit inexperienced, was forced to switch off the inside rail inside the furlong maker and hinted at better to come. (op 28-1 tchd 33-1)
Naseby(USA), an $82,000 yearling, showed very little after starting from a wide draw. (op 10-1 tchd 11-1)
Glass Of Red(IRE), who had a blanket for stalls entry, was prominent early but dropped away alarmingly over two furlongs from home. (op 8-1)

4202 HARTFIELD H'CAP 7f (P)
3:00 (3:01) (Class 5) (0-70,70) 3-Y-0+ **£2,729** (£806; £403) **Stalls** Low

Form RPR

4006 **1** **Best In Class**[24] 3427 3-9-4 67 .... TedDurcan 1 74
(Tom Dascombe) *chsd ldrs: wnt 2nd 5f out: rdn over 2f out: drvn over 1f out: led ins fnl f: r.o wl* **7/1**[3]

2360 **2** 1 1/4 **Ever Cheerful**[49] 2598 8-9-5 61 .... (p) SteveDrowne 2 68
(A B Haynes) *led: rdn ent fnl 2f: drvn over 1f out: hdd ins fnl f: no ex* **11/1**

0006 **3** nk **Loyal Royal (IRE)**[30] 3224 6-8-9 56 .... (b) JackDean(5) 8 62
(J M Bradley) *stdd s: hld up in rr: hdwy jst over 2f out: swtchd rt wl over 1f out: chsd ldrs 1f out: kpt on same pce fnl 100yds: wnt 3rd nr fin* **10/1**

0200 **4** nk **Admiral Sandhoe (USA)**[41] 2849 3-9-5 68 .... JimCrowley 3 70
(Mrs A J Perrett) *chsd ldrs: disp 2nd pl 3f out: rdn over 2f out: drvn and one pce fr over 1f out: lost 3rd nr fin* **7/1**[3]

0006 **5** 2 **Grizedale (IRE)**[14] 3732 10-8-2 51 oh3 .... (tp) KierenFox(7) 4 51
(M J Attwater) *pushed along early: chsd ldrs 5f out: cajoled along 2f out: pushed along and hld hd high over 1f out: no prog* **40/1**

4000 **6** 1 3/4 **Obe Royal**[11] 3851 5-9-9 70 .... (v) RichardEvans(5) 7 65+
(P D Evans) *stdd after s: hld up in rr: rdn and hdwy over 1f out: kpt on fnl f: nvr nr ldrs* **4/1**[1]

0305 **7** 1/2 **Nun Today (USA)**[4] 4083 3-8-6 55 .... (p) JimmyQuinn 14 46
(Karen George) *hld up wl bhd: rdn and gd hdwy jst over 1f out: kpt on but nvr nr ldrs* **28/1**

1640 **8** 1 1/4 **Divertimenti (IRE)**[54] 2459 5-9-10 66 .... (b) EddieAhern 10 57
(C R Dore) *in tch in midfield: rdn and effrt ent fnl 2f: drvn and no hdwy over 1f out: wknd ins fnl f* **7/1**[3]

3050 **9** 1/2 **Fools Gold**[71] 1964 4-9-4 68 .... RussellKennemore(3) 12 57
(Paul Mason) *in tch in midfield on outer: rdn and unable qck over 2f out: no prog and wl hld after* **20/1**

0600 **10** nk **Norcroft**[7] 3983 7-9-4 63 .... (p) AndreaAtzeni(3) 11 51
(Mrs C A Dunnett) *towards rr: rdn and effrt jst over 2f out: no hdwy and n.d* **9/1**

50P6 **11** nk **Sirjosh**[15] 3718 3-8-4 60 .... (t) HollyHall(7) 9 45
(D Donovan) *chsd ldr tl rdn and wknd jst over 2f out* **20/1**

0-02 **12** 2 **Roleplay (IRE)**[15] 3720 4-8-10 57 .... (b) WilliamCarson(5) 6 39
(J M P Eustace) *racd in midfield on inner: rdn and nt qckn over 2f out: drvn and wknd wl over 1f out* **11/2**[2]

0-05 **13** 3/4 **Piccolinda**[23] 3464 3-8-12 61 .... MartinDwyer 5 38
(W R Muir) *hld up bhd: rdn and nt clr run wl over 1f out: nvr on terms* **12/1**

1600 **14** 1 1/4 **Straitjacket**[8] 3948 3-8-8 57 .... (p) PaulFitzsimons 13 31
(Miss J R Tooth) *s.i.s: bhd: rdn and wd bnd 2f out: n.d* **33/1**

1m 24.54s (-0.26) **Going Correction** +0.025s/f (Slow)
WFA 3 from 4yo+ 7lb **14** Ran SP% **126.4**
Speed ratings (Par 103): **102,100,100,99,97 95,95,93,93,92 92,90,89,87**
toteswingers: 1&2 £19.70, 1&3 £31.10, 2&3 £34.00 CSF £80.36 CT £813.27 TOTE £8.90: £2.80, £4.50, £3.30; EX 75.80 TRIFECTA Not won..
Owner Mrs A Shone **Bred** Michael Clarke **Trained** Lambourn, Berks

FOCUS
A modest, if competitive handicap, and another race where it paid to be handy with few making any real impression from off the pace. Straightforward form.
Roleplay(IRE) Official explanation: jockey said filly lost a near-fore shoe

4203 BROADSTONE AMBLE H'CAP 6f (P)
3:30 (3:33) (Class 5) (0-70,74) 3-Y-0+ **£2,729** (£806; £403) **Stalls** Low

Form RPR

4-55 **1** **Rondeau (GR)**[16] 3691 4-9-8 66 .... JimCrowley 2 82+
(P R Chamings) *chsd ldr tl led jst over 3f out: rdn wl over 1f out: styd on strly fnl f* **7/2**[2]

0643 **2** 2 1/2 **Louphole**[16] 3673 7-9-6 64 .... EddieAhern 12 72
(J R Jenkins) *stdd and swtchd lft s: hld up bhd: hdwy over 2f out: rdn to chse wnr 1f out: no imp after* **7/1**[3]

5000 **3** 2 1/4 **Hereford Boy**[11] 3860 5-9-6 64 .... (b) RobertHavlin 10 65
(D K Ivory) *bhd: niggled along after 1f: hdwy towards inner over 1f out: r.o to go 3rd wl ins fnl f: nvr nr ldrs* **8/1**

3000 **4** 1/2 **Regal Royale**[2] 4134 6-9-2 60 .... (v) AdamKirby 8 60
(Peter Grayson) *s.i.s: sn rdn along: hdwy to press wnr 3f out: drvn and outpcd over 1f out: wknd ins fnl f* **16/1**

5130 **5** 1/2 **Bertie Southstreet**[9] 3917 6-9-7 65 .... (p) TGMcLaughlin 9 63
(Karen George) *chsd ldrs: drvn and unable qck 2f out: wknd ent fnl f* **14/1**

-060 **6** 3/4 **Lieutenant Pigeon**[65] 2145 4-8-11 58 .... RussellKennemore(3) 1 54
(Paul Mason) *led tl jst over 3f out: chsd wnr tl 1f out: wknd u.p ins fnl f* **25/1**

6006 **7** nk **Metropolitan Chief**[6] 4023 5-8-3 52 oh6 ow1 ...... (p) WilliamCarson(5) 11 47
(P Burgoyne) *stdd and swtchd rt s: tk kn hold: hld up towards rr: rdn and effrt on inner wl over 1f out: nvr trbld ldrs* **20/1**

-406 **8** 1/2 **Bahamian Bliss**[19] 3591 4-9-4 62 .... KirstyMilczarek 3 55
(J A R Toller) *in tch in midfield: rdn and unable qck 2f out: wknd jst over 1f out* **7/1**[3]

2211 **9** 3 1/2 **Piazza San Pietro**[6] 3994 3-9-11 74 6ex .... (p) SebSanders 6 56
(A B Haynes) *stdd s: t.k.h: hld up in midfield: rdn and unable qck jst over 2f out: btn over 1f out: eased ins fnl f* **11/4**[1]

6000 **10** 1 **Fly In Johnny (IRE)**[4] 4082 4-8-7 51 oh3 .... (v[1]) FrankieMcDonald 5 30
(J J Bridger) *awkward leaving stalls: short of room after 1f: bhd and hanging rt bnd 4f out: nvr on terms after* **40/1**

11 14 **Compton Classic**[91] 1468 7-9-12 70 .... (p) PatCosgrave 7 4
(J R Boyle) *t.k.h: in tch whn hmpd and lost pl over 4f out: bhd fr 4f out: lost tch and eased wl over 1f out: t.o* **10/1**

1m 11.59s (-0.31) **Going Correction** +0.025s/f (Slow)
WFA 3 from 4yo+ 5lb **11** Ran SP% **117.7**
Speed ratings (Par 103): **103,99,96,96,95 94,93,93,88,87 68**
toteswingers: 1&2 £4.00, 1&3 £8.20, 2&3 £7.10 CSF £27.67 CT £188.76 TOTE £4.90: £1.80, £1.80, £2.80; EX 25.80 Trifecta £253.00 Part won. Pool: £341.92 - 0.97 winning units..
Owner The Foxford House Partnership **Bred** Ippotour Stud **Trained** Baughurst, Hants

FOCUS
Not many of these had shown a great deal last time, so this is probably only very modest form overall despite the winning time being reasonable. The form is sound and the winner produced a useful performance.
Piazza San Pietro Official explanation: trainer's rep said gelding was unsuited by the kickback
Compton Classic Official explanation: jockey said gelding ran too free

4204 HINDLEAP WALK H'CAP 5f (P)
4:00 (4:01) (Class 6) (0-65,64) 3-Y-0+ **£2,047** (£604; £302) **Stalls** High

Form RPR

3560 **1** **Bluebok**[27] 3304 8-9-2 60 .... (bt) JackDean(5) 10 69
(J M Bradley) *chsd ldrs: ev ch and drvn over 1f out: led jst ins fnl f: r.o wl* **12/1**

5-06 **2** 3/4 **Agnes Love**[17] 3663 3-9-0 57 .... J-PGuillambert 4 62
(J Akehurst) *w ldr: ev ch 2f out: drvn to ld ent fnl f: sn hdd and kpt on one pce after* **11/1**

451 **3** shd **Russian Rocket (IRE)**[11] 3860 7-9-11 64 .... TGMcLaughlin 6 70
(Mrs C A Dunnett) *trckd ldrs: nt clr run on inner and switched rt over 1f out: drvn and r.o fnl f: nt rch wnr* **4/1**[1]

-340 **4** 3/4 **Excitable (IRE)**[8] 3938 3-8-4 50 .... DominicFox(3) 8 52
(Mrs D J Sanderson) *s.i.s: in rr: pushed along jst over 2f out: gd hdwy on outer jst ins fnl f: fin wl: nt rch ldrs* **9/1**[3]

251- **5** nk **Summer Rose**[203] 7835 4-8-13 52 .... (v[1]) EddieAhern 1 54
(R M H Cowell) *sn led: hrd pressed and rdn wl over 1f out: hdd ent fnl f: wknd fnl 75yds* **4/1**[1]

0360 **6** nk **Best One**[15] 3720 5-8-13 55 .... (b) KevinGhunowa(3) 5 56
(R A Harris) *towards rr: effrt over 1f out: drvn and hung lft ins fnl f: kpt on but nvr pce to rch ldrs* **4/1**[1]

-300 **7** 1 1/2 **Fantasy Fighter (IRE)**[159] 540 4-9-0 53 .... JimmyQuinn 2 49
(J J Quinn) *dwlt: towards rr: n.m.r over 1f out: sn swtchd rt and flashed tail u.p: sme late hdwy: nvr trbld ldrs* **7/1**[2]

60-0 **8** shd **Jane's Payoff (IRE)**[195] 83 4-9-11 64 .... (t) RichardThomas 9 59
(Mrs L C Jewell) *in tch in midfield: rdn and unable qck wl over 1f out: no prog fnl f* **25/1**

3050 **9** 1 **Affirmatively**[6] 4023 4-8-3 45 .... (tp) AndreaAtzeni(3) 3 37
(A W Carroll) *dwlt: in tch in midfield: pushed along and effrt on inner 2f out: drvn over 1f out: no real prog* **12/1**

6400 **10** 11 **Woodcote (IRE)**[54] 2460 7-9-9 62 .... (vt) AdamKirby 7 14
(Peter Grayson) *s.i.s: a bhd: lost tch 2f out: eased ins fnl f* **12/1**

58.86 secs (0.06) **Going Correction** +0.025s/f (Slow)
WFA 3 from 4yo+ 4lb **10** Ran SP% **117.8**
Speed ratings (Par 101): **100,98,98,97,96 96,94,93,92,74**
toteswingers: 1&2 £15.40, 1&3 £10.20, 2&3 £8.60 CSF £137.55 CT £645.65 TOTE £15.80: £3.00, £2.00, £2.10; EX 131.90 TRIFECTA Not won..
Owner E A Hayward **Bred** E Duggan And D Churchman **Trained** Sedbury, Gloucs

FOCUS
A typically tight Lingfield Polytrack sprint, albeit a modest one. Straightforward form.

4205 ASHDOWN FOREST MAIDEN STKS 1m 4f (P)
4:30 (4:33) (Class 5) 3-Y-0+ **£2,729** (£806; £403) **Stalls** Low

Form RPR

2433 **1** **Souter Point (USA)**[13] 3791 3-9-1 80 .... SteveDrowne 10 72
(R Charlton) *trckd ldrs: wnt 2nd gng wl over 2f out: rdn to ld 1f out: drvn out* **2/1**[1]

00 **2** 1 **Danse On Wood**[38] 2943 3-9-1 0 .... ShaneKelly 6 70
(J Noseda) *trckd ldrs: wnt 2nd 5f out: led over 3f out: rdn and hdd 1f out: unable qck fnl f* **12/1**

6 **3** 1 1/4 **Sushitan (GER)**[24] 3425 4-9-13 67 .... GeorgeBaker 13 68
(G L Moore) *t.k.h: hld up in tch: hdwy 5f out: chsd ldng trio and clr of remainder over 2f out: rdn and edgd lft over 1f out: kpt on same pce fnl f* **11/1**

00 **4** hd **Madison Park (IRE)**[33] 3117 3-9-1 0 .... (bt) TPQueally 7 68
(H R A Cecil) *s.i.s: hld up towards rr: hdwy 5f out: chsd ldng pair and clr of remainder over 2f out: rdn and nt qckn 2f out: one pce u.p fr over 1f out* **13/2**

5 13 **Eloise** 3-8-10 0 .... SebSanders 1 42
(Sir Mark Prescott) *sn pushed along: in tch in midfield: rdn 6f out: drvn and struggling 4f out: no ch w ldrs fnl 3f out: plugged on* **6/1**[3]

0-2 **6** 3 3/4 **Canton Road**[34] 3056 3-9-1 0 .... MartinDwyer 4 41
(P F I Cole) *t.k.h: chsd ldr tl led over 8f out: hdd over 3f out: rdn and wknd qckly over 2f out: wl btn after* **9/4**[2]

06 **7** *2 ½* **Brandy Butter**[25] 3384 3-8-12 0 .... DavidProbert(3) 3 37
(A M Balding) *led tl over 8f out: chsd ldr tl 5f out: sn lost pl u.p: no ch fnl 3f* **25/1**

05 **8** *1 ¼* **Watchoverme**[15] 3707 3-8-10 0 .... JimCrowley 11 30
(J R Fanshawe) *s.i.s: sn pushed along in rr: rdn and struggling 5f out: wl bhd fnl 3f* **33/1**

0 **9** *hd* **Megavista (USA)**[41] 2848 3-8-7 0 .... RussellKennemore(3) 2 30
(Paul Mason) *s.i.s: a towards rr: rdn and toiling bdly over 4f out: sn wl bhd* **66/1**

10 *29* **First Maid** 3-8-3 0 .... AndrewHeffernan(7) 5 —
(A B Haynes) *s.i.s: sn pushed along and in tch: rdn and struggling bdly over 4f out: wl t.o fnl 2f* **100/1**

0 **11** *4 ½* **Barnes Bridge**[7] 3984 4-9-6 0 .... KierenFox(7) 12 —
(M J Attwater) *s.i.s: a wl bhd and rdn along: lost tch over 4f out: wl t.o fnl 2f* **150/1**

12 *38* **Williamtown Lad (IRE)**[459] 8-9-13 0 .... PatCosgrave 8 —
(J R Boyle) *awkward leaving stalls and v.s.a: hdwy to join ldrs after 2f: rdn and lost pl qckly over 5f out: hopelessly t.o fnl 2f* **100/1**

2m 32.34s (-0.66) **Going Correction** +0.025s/f (Slow)
WFA 3 from 4yo+ 12lb **12** Ran SP% **118.7**
Speed ratings (Par 103): **103,102,101,101,92 90,88,87,87,68 65,39**
toteswingers: 1&2 £6.50, 1&3 £4.80, 2&3 £16.90 CSF £26.65 TOTE £3.00: £1.20, £3.60, £3.20; EX 28.30 Trifecta £156.20 Part won. Pool: £211.16 - 0.30 winning units..
Owner Michael Pescod **Bred** Earl Silver & Michael Eiserman **Trained** Beckhampton, Wilts
■ Stewards' Enquiry : Russell Kennemore caution: used whip when out of contention
Kieren Fox caution: used whip when out of contention

FOCUS
A modest maiden in which the favourite did not have to match his best form. The first four finshed clear.
Megavista(USA) Official explanation: jockey said filly hung right throughout

4206 FOREST ROW H'CAP 1m 4f (P)
5:00 (5:02) (Class 5) (0-75,72) 3-Y-O **£2,729** (£806; £403) **Stalls** Low

Form RPR

4313 **1** **Parc Des Princes (USA)**[20] 3535 3-8-10 **64** .... DavidProbert(3) 7 76+
(A M Balding) *awkward leaving stalls: hld up in rr: hdwy but stl only 5th wl over 1f out: sn swtchd rt: edgd lft and chsd clr ldr ent fnl f: qcknd to ld fnl 100yds: sn clr: easily* **9/4**[2]

0132 **2** *3 ½* **Sumani (FR)**[13] 3776 3-9-2 **67** .... IanMongan 8 71
(S Dow) *led after 1f and set stdy gallop: rdn and kicked clr over 2f out: stl clr ins fnl f: hdd fnl 100yds: no ch w wnr after* **8/1**

-234 **3** *1 ½* **Demeanour (USA)**[18] 3636 3-9-7 **72** .... JimmyFortune 5 74
(E A L Dunlop) *hld up in tch: hdwy to chse ldrs 3f out: rdn and unable qck wl over 1f out: kpt on same pce after* **5/1**[3]

0021 **4** *2 ½* **Diktalina**[9] 3919 3-8-6 **57** 6ex .... MartinDwyer 3 55
(W R Muir) *led for 1f: chsd ldr after: rdn and nt pce of ldr over 2f out: lost 2nd 1f out: wknd fnl f* **10/1**

002- **5** *3 ½* **Rock Relief (IRE)**[272] 6923 3-9-2 **67** .... SebSanders 1 59
(Sir Mark Prescott) *t.k.h: trckd ldrs: rdn and unable qck over 2f out: drvn and btn over 1f out: eased wl ins fnl f* **15/8**[1]

-506 **6** *2 ½* **Heart Of Tuscany**[13] 3777 3-8-8 **59** ....(p) JimCrowley 2 47
(W J Knight) *t.k.h: hld up in tch: pushed along and unable qck over 2f out: wl btn fnl 2f* **22/1**

500- **7** *13* **Mr Deal**[301] 6199 3-8-3 **54** .... JimmyQuinn 6 21
(Eve Johnson Houghton) *stdd s: t.k.h: hld up in last trio: hdwy to chse ldrs on outer 8f out: rdn and btn 3f out* **16/1**

0-46 **8** *7* **Majd Aljazeera**[22] 3475 3-8-8 **62** ....(t) AhmedAjtebi(3) 4 18
(D M Simcock) *t.k.h: hld up in tch in last trio: rdn and struggling bdly over 3f out sn lost tch* **20/1**

2m 32.47s (-0.53) **Going Correction** +0.025s/f (Slow) **8** Ran SP% **117.4**
Speed ratings (Par 100): **102,99,98,97,94 93,84,79**
toteswingers: 1&2 £4.10, 1&3 £2.30, 2&3 £5.10 CSF £21.41 CT £83.29 TOTE £2.80: £1.10, £2.00, £2.10; EX 20.10 Trifecta £51.10 Pool: £406.47 - 5.88 winning units. Place 6: £172.30 Place 5: £71.45.
Owner The James Gang **Bred** Castletown Stud **Trained** Kingsclere, Hants

FOCUS
A reasonable three-year-old handicap, though the early pace wasn't strong and it developed into something of a sprint over the last half-mile. The winning time was 0.13 seconds slower than the preceding maiden and the form is sound.
T/Jkpt: £6,333.10 to a £1 stake. Pool: £111,499.57. 12.50 winning tickets. T/Plt: £74.60 to a £1 stake. Pool: £61,243.84. 598.64 winning tickets. T/Qpdt: £33.00 to a £1 stake. Pool: £4,243.30. 95.00 winning tickets. SP

3638 SANDOWN (R-H)
Wednesday, July 22

OFFICIAL GOING: Good to firm (good in places on sprint course; round 9.1, sprint 8.8)
Wind: Fresh, against Weather: Fine but cloudy

4207 "ALFIE RAN THE MARATHON" APPRENTICE H'CAP 1m 2f 7y
6:00 (6:00) (Class 5) (0-75,75) 4-Y-O+ **£3,238** (£963; £481; £240) **Stalls** High

Form RPR

0230 **1** **Ross Moor**[19] 3563 7-8-7 **58** .... AndreaAtzeni 1 68
(Mike Murphy) *dwlt: t.k.h: hld up in last pair: rdn 3f out: gd prog on outer fr 2f out to chse ldr ent fnl f: styd on wl to ld last strides* **12/1**

221 **2** *hd* **Jo'Burg (USA)**[12] 3811 5-9-7 **75** .... MartinLane(3) 4 85
(Lady Herries) *hld up in 7th: rdn 3f out: prog on outer over 2f out: led over 1f out and sn 2 l clr: kpt on fnl f: collared last strides* **11/4**[1]

-502 **3** *6* **Shesha Bear**[13] 3766 4-8-7 **63** ....(b) MatthewDavies(5) 3 61
(W R Muir) *hld up bhd ldrs: rdn wl over 2f out: sme prog over 1f out: plugged on to take 3rd ins fnl f* **11/1**

5463 **4** *1 ¼* **By Command**[13] 3761 4-9-4 **69** .... PatrickHills 2 64
(J W Hills) *hld up tl plld way through to ld after 3f: injected pce and sn clr: hdd & wknd over 1f out* **10/1**

-330 **5** *nse* **Mega Watt (IRE)**[28] 3273 4-9-6 **74** ....(p) Louis-PhilippeBeuzelin(3) 9 69
(W Jarvis) *t.k.h: led at slow pce for 3f: chsd ldr: rdn and no imp 3f out: fdd over 1f out* **7/1**[3]

-600 **6** *½* **Faith And Reason (USA)**[20] 3550 6-8-2 **56** ....(v) WilliamCarson(3) 7 50
(B J Curley) *dwlt: hld up in midfield: shkn up over 2f out: no real prog* **8/1**

-105 **7** *11* **Paint The Town Red**[26] 3343 4-9-8 **73** .... JackMitchell 5 45
(H J Collingridge) *a in last pair: rdn and lost tch 3f out: sn wl bhd* **16/1**

11 **8** *5* **Ensnare**[17] 3653 4-8-12 **66** .... JackDean(3) 6 28
(Ian Williams) *t.k.h: trckd ldr 3f: styd prom: rdn wl over 2f out: lost pl over 1f out: wknd v rapidly fnl f* **10/3**[2]

003 **9** *7* **Sahara Sunshine**[14] 3739 4-8-9 **63** .... RossAtkinson(3) 8 11
(Mrs L J Mongan) *dwlt: t.k.h and sn prom: rdn and wknd 3f out: t.o* **8/1**

2m 12.13s (1.63) **Going Correction** -0.025s/f (Good) **9** Ran SP% **115.5**
Speed ratings (Par 103): **92,91,87,86,86 85,76,72,67**
toteswingers: 1&2 £9.70, 1&3 £39.40, 2&3 £8.10. CSF £45.16 CT £383.01 TOTE £16.70: £3.90, £1.70, £2.60; EX 64.80.
Owner M Murphy **Bred** R T And Mrs Watson **Trained** Westoning, Beds
■ Stewards' Enquiry : Patrick Hills two-day ban: careless riding (Aug 5-6)

FOCUS
Following an early crawl, By Command injected some much-needed pace after three furlongs. Even though he went clear, there was a knock-on effect on the rest of the field, and the overall consequence was to bring two hold-up performers to the fore at the finish. The winner was back to something like his best form. The first two finished clear.

4208 BGC NURSERY 5f 6y
6:30 (6:32) (Class 5) 2-Y-O **£3,238** (£963; £481; £240) **Stalls** High

Form RPR

210 **1** **Yer Woman (IRE)**[24] 3424 2-9-7 **75** .... RichardHughes 5 81+
(R Hannon) *racd against rail in midfield: prog to chse ldr jst over 1f out: r.o to ld last 75yds: cosily* **9/2**[2]

15 **2** *1* **Drift And Dream**[11] 3865 2-8-9 **66** .... JackMitchell(3) 9 68
(C F Wall) *racd against rail: disp ld tl def advantage wl over 1f out: clr ent fnl f: hdd and outpcd last 75yds* **9/4**[1]

436 **3** *1* **Radio City**[13] 3767 2-9-2 **70** .... TedDurcan 4 69
(R M Beckett) *racd against rail: hld up in last pair: prog 2f out: r.o to take 3rd ins fnl f: unable to chal* **16/1**

033 **4** *1 ½* **Val C**[25] 3385 2-9-2 **70** .... ShaneKelly 2 63
(N P Littmoden) *restless stalls and propped s: hld up in last pair: plenty to do whn swtchd to inner and effrt jst over 1f out: r.o to take 4th last 100yds: no ch* **11/1**

456 **5** *2 ½* **The Shuffler**[19] 3579 2-9-1 **69** .... GeorgeBaker 3 53
(G L Moore) *hld up towards rr: shkn up 2f out: no prog jst over 1f out: outpcd* **25/1**

552 **6** *1 ¼* **Point To Prove**[25] 3385 2-9-1 **74** .... MartinLane(5) 1 54
(Miss Amy Weaver) *mostly racd wd: chsd ldrs: lost pl sn after 1/2-way: n.d fr over 1f out* **8/1**

5240 **7** *hd* **Ginger Grey (IRE)**[12] 3821 2-9-2 **70** ....(b[1]) LDettori 10 49
(S A Callaghan) *chsd ldng pair: nt qckn wl over 1f out: losing pl whn n.m.r jst ins fnl f* **5/1**[3]

005 **8** *½* **Exceed Power**[25] 3370 2-8-8 **62** .... EddieAhern 8 39
(D M Simcock) *w ldr: edging lft and fnd nil wl over 1f out: wknd* **7/1**

054 **9** *½* **Papageno**[25] 3385 2-9-0 **68** .... SteveDrowne 7 44
(J R Jenkins) *trckd ldng pair: nt qckn 2f out: ended up wd and wkng fnl f* **12/1**

63.49 secs (1.89) **Going Correction** +0.25s/f (Good) **9** Ran SP% **115.0**
Speed ratings (Par 94): **94,92,90,88,84 82,82,81,80**
toteswingers: 1&2 £2.80, 1&3 £10.80, 2&3 £12.60. CSF £14.95 CT £147.58 TOTE £4.80: £1.80, £1.60, £4.40; EX 16.50.
Owner Mrs R McArdle **Bred** Mrs Clodagh McStay **Trained** East Everleigh, Wilts

FOCUS
The 'official' ratings shown next to each horse are estimated and for information purposes only. The first three raced closest to the far rail throughout, and the fourth switched to the rail for her final run, so there appeared to be a significant bias. The pace was ordinary until halfway, but three of the first four came from behind so no damage was done. Improved form from the winner.

NOTEBOOK
Yer Woman(IRE) had produced a similar performance when winning at Windsor, and her running style suggests that a stiff 5f like this suits her well. Her attempt at 6f last time was unsuccessful, but she looks likely to be able to handle that trip before long. A 5f or 6f nursery at Goodwood is the plan. (op 4-1 tchd 10-3)
Drift And Dream flopped over 6f in her previous race, but in her case 5f looks to be the ideal trip for the time being. She has plenty of pace and should find other suitable opportunities. (op 11-4 tchd 3-1)
Radio City gives the impression that longer trips are within his scope even though his best form to date is at 5f. He ran badly over the extra furlong at Epsom, but that was probably down to factors other than stamina and it would no surprise to see him winning a 6f nursery on a more conventional track.
Val C has shown promise in all her races to date and on this evidence she would also be interesting over an extra furlong. Although she had to switch to find a run, she was compensated to some extent by ending up on the faster strip. (op 17-2 tchd 8-1)
The Shuffler was first home of those who raced on the apparently slower ground. His handicap rating has seemed to be on the high side in two races so far. (op 16-1)
Point To Prove, who raced on the apparently slower ground, is good enough to find a nursery off a lower mark than on this first attempt. (op 12-1)

4209 DEVINE HOMES E B F MAIDEN STKS 7f 16y
7:05 (7:05) (Class 4) 2-Y-O **£5,180** (£1,541; £770; £384) **Stalls** High

Form RPR

3 **1** **Cadley Road (IRE)**[20] 3522 2-9-3 0 .... RichardHughes 10 89+
(R Hannon) *mde all: stretched away fr 2f out: maintained gallop fnl f: unchal* **13/8**[1]

2 *2 ½* **High Twelve (IRE)** 2-9-3 0 .... JimmyFortune 11 83
(J H M Gosden) *wl plcd bhd ldrs: effrt over 2f out: wnt 2nd over 1f out: styd on wl but no imp on wnr* **10/3**[2]

4 **3** *5* **Logos Astra (USA)**[19] 3584 2-9-3 0 .... TedDurcan 7 70
(D R Lanigan) *chsd wnr: outpcd fr 2f out: lost 2nd over 1f out: no ch after but hld on for 3rd* **7/1**

4 *1* **Spa's Dancer (IRE)** 2-9-3 0 .... MichaelHills 4 68
(J W Hills) *dwlt: sn prom on outer: outpcd fr 2f out: plugged on* **15/2**

5 *¾* **Stags Leap (IRE)** 2-9-3 0 .... SteveDrowne 5 66
(R Hannon) *prom: outpcd fr 2f out: shuffled along and plugged on* **40/1**

4 **6** *nk* **Jutland**[21] 3494 2-9-3 0 .... RoystonFfrench 6 65
(M Johnston) *a midfield: pushed along over 2f out: outpcd whn n.m.r wl over 1f out: kpt on* **5/1**[3]

7 *nse* **Mecox Bay (IRE)** 2-9-3 0 .... MartinDwyer 1 65
(A M Balding) *dwlt and dropped in fr outside draw: mostly in last trio: shkn up 3f out: sme prog fnl f: nvr on terms* **20/1**

8 *3 ¼* **Book Of Truth (USA)** 2-9-3 0 .... GeorgeBaker 8 57
(D M Simcock) *in tch in midfield: pushed along over 2f out: no real prog: sn outpcd: fdd fnl f* **50/1**

9 *4* **Phonic (IRE)** 2-9-3 0 .... EddieAhern 9 47
(J L Dunlop) *settled in last pair: pushed along and no prog over 2f out* **33/1**

0 **10** *2* **High Resolution**[20] 3522 2-8-12 0 .... WilliamCarson(5) 3 42
(S C Williams) *towards rr but in tch on outer: shkn up and wknd 2f out* **50/1**

11 4 **Cuckoo Rock (IRE)** 2-9-3 0 PatCosgrave 2 32
(J G Portman) *s.s: rn green and a wl bhd in last* **40/1**

1m 28.97s (-0.53) **Going Correction** -0.025s/f (Good) **11** Ran SP% **118.6**
Speed ratings (Par 96): **102,99,93,92,91 91,91,87,82,80 75**
toteswingers: 1&2 £2.40, 1&3 £2.40, 2&3 £7.00. CSF £6.56 TOTE £2.90: £1.30, £1.80, £2.10; EX 7.60.
Owner J R May **Bred** A Panetta **Trained** East Everleigh, Wilts

FOCUS
This was a decent-looking maiden, and the winner put in an exciting performance from the front. Solid maiden form.

NOTEBOOK
Cadley Road(IRE) ◆ had come on a bundle for his promising debut and he quickly put the race to bed two furlongs out after setting a respectable if unspectacular tempo. He looks progressive and is one to follow with interest, but connections will takes things gradually with him, with the Goffs Million over 1m at The Curragh his first big target. (op 5-4 tchd 7-4)
High Twelve(IRE) ◆, a 380,000gns Montjeu half-brother to a juvenile 5f winner and out of the high-class French sprinter Much Faster, clearly has much more stamina than that thanks to his sire. He shaped with great promise against the once-raced winner and should have no problem winning his maiden before going on to better things. (op 3-1 tchd 9-4)
Logos Astra(USA) learnt plenty from his course-and-distance debut and, though well held, was up against two useful-looking juveniles. He is capable of winning a typical maiden. (tchd 8-1)
Spa's Dancer(IRE), a Danehill Dancer half-brother to two winners up to 1m2f , is entered for the National Stakes and the Derby. While he has to improve to land either of those, he made a satisfactory debut in this above-average maiden and should win races. (op 8-1 tchd 14-1)
Stags Leap(IRE), a 110,000euros Refuse To Bend out of the well-related French miler Swingsky, is bred to be smart and is one to keep an eye on. A Derby entry and stablemate of the winner, he was keen to post and should come on plenty. (op 50-1 tchd 33-1)
Jutland was one of those with the benefit of a previous outing and, while others showed more promise, he should find a suitable opportunity against lesser opponents. (op 10-1)
Mecox Bay(IRE), by Noverre out of the 6f winner Birdsong, comes from a fine family, many of whom stayed middle distances. He should come on for the experience, and looks likely to appreciate 1m later in the season. (op 33-1)

4210 BGC & THE CHILDREN'S TRUST ANNIVERSARY H'CAP 7f 16y
7:40 (7:40) (Class 3) (0-90,90) 3-Y-O **£7,771** (£2,312; £1,155; £577) **Stalls** High

Form RPR
-310 **1** **Broad Cairn**[39] 2926 3-8-11 **80** SteveDrowne 6 86+
(R Charlton) *t.k.h early: hld up in last: prog on outer fr 2f out: rdn and styd on wl to ld last 100yds: readily* **11/1**
4233 **2** ½ **Star Links (USA)**[11] 3868 3-8-13 **82** RichardHughes 2 87
(R Hannon) *stdd s: hld up and sn in 4th: shkn up and prog on outer over 2f out: rdn to ld jst ins fnl f: hdd and hld last 100yds* **4/1**[2]
155 **3** 1¾ **Thousand Miles (IRE)**[12] 3816 3-9-1 **84** JimmyFortune 1 84
(P W Chapple-Hyam) *trckd ldr: pushed firmly into ld over 1f out: hdd and rdn jst ins fnl f: fnd nil* **9/2**[3]
3055 **4** 1¼ **Sohcahtoa (IRE)**[69] 2004 3-9-4 **90** PatrickHills(3) 7 87
(R Hannon) *hld up in 5th: shkn up over 2f out: no prog tl kpt on ins fnl f: nvr nr ldrs* **8/1**
41-1 **5** *shd* **Emirates Sports**[21] 3509 3-9-4 **87** LDettori 5 83
(Saeed Bin Suroor) *trckd ldng pair to 2f out: effrt over 1f out and cl enough: nt qckn and btn ent fnl f* **13/8**[1]
2103 **6** 1¼ **Crime Writer (USA)**[6] 4009 3-8-9 **78** RoystonFfrench 3 71
(M Johnston) *led: kicked on over 2f out: hdd over 1f out: wknd fnl f* **5/1**

1m 29.63s (0.13) **Going Correction** -0.025s/f (Good) **6** Ran SP% **112.4**
Speed ratings (Par 104): **98,97,95,94,93 92**
toteswingers: 1&2 £9.10, 1&3 £14.30, 2&3 £3.20. CSF £53.55 CT £228.33 TOTE £14.10: £5.10, £2.40; EX 64.30.
Owner The Queen **Bred** The Queen **Trained** Beckhampton, Wilts

FOCUS
The pace was ordinary and there was something of a sprint to the line in the last two furlongs. Messy form, but the winner did it well and can rate higher.

NOTEBOOK
Broad Cairn had flopped on his handicap debut here last month, when connections felt he was too keen, but he had been off for 40 days since then and this was a return to his previous progressive profile. He did well to come from last place considering the lack of testing pace, and 1m should be within his range later in the year, though Roger Charlton - who rates him a very genuine sort - will keep him to 7f for the time being. Official explanation: trainer said, regarding apparent improvement in form, that more patient tractics were used. (op 17-2 tchd 8-1)
Star Links(USA) continues to run consistently without winning, suggesting that this mark is not beyond him if he continues to improve. He is equally at home over at 7f and 1m. (op 9-2 tchd 5-1)
Thousand Miles(IRE) has run some good races over 1m and this showed he is also effective at 7f, but he did not finish the job off after taking the lead. He will probably have to drop a couple of pounds to win again, with a step back up in trip likely to suit. Official explanation: jockey said colt hung right-handed (tchd 4-1 and 5-1)
Sohcahtoa(IRE), off the track for 69 days and gelded since his last run, has been given a chance by the handicapper and ran a solid race. He will be a tricky horse to place since he is still likely to be relatively high in the weights against less exposed rivals, but an extra furlong would be in his favour. (op 11-1)
Emirates Sports has looked handy on Polytrack in his last two starts, and this showed that he is able enough on turf too. However, he took a while to pick up on the dash to the line and should be suited by a return to 1m. (op 6-4 tchd 11-8)
Crime Writer(USA) looks effective at 7f but his handicap mark has been a couple of pounds too high and, even though he was able to dictate the tempo, that was crucial in a competitive finish. (op 6-1 tchd 13-2)

4211 CHILDREN'S TRUST "CHANGING LIVES" H'CAP 1m 14y
8:15 (8:15) (Class 4) (0-80,83) 3-Y-O+ **£4,857** (£1,445; £722; £360) **Stalls** High

Form RPR
0501 **1** **Romany Princess (IRE)**[9] 3921 4-10-2 **83** 6ex RichardHughes 3 93+
(R Hannon) *hld up in 7th: prog fr 2f out: weaved through to go 2nd jst ins fnl f: sustained effrt to ld last 50yds* **5/1**[2]
10- **2** 1 **Burgundy Ice (USA)**[263] 7144 3-9-5 **80** LDettori 8 85+
(Saeed Bin Suroor) *fast away: led: grad upped tempo fr 3f out: looked in command over 1f out: drvn fnl f: mugged last 50yds* **4/1**[1]
5010 **3** 1¼ **Thunder Gorge (USA)**[40] 2894 4-9-7 **74** JimCrowley 2 78
(Mouse Hamilton-Fairley) *hld up in 6th: effrt on outer over 2f out: drvn and styd on fr over 1f out: tk 3rd ins fnl f: nvr able to chal* **11/1**
0611 **4** 1½ **Marvo**[38] 2939 5-9-10 **77** TedDurcan 1 78
(M H Tompkins) *hld up in 10th: effrt on outer 3f out: drvn and styd on fnl 2f: nvr pce to threaten ldrs* **6/1**[3]
2221 **5** 1 **Eastern Warrior**[16] 3690 3-9-2 **77** EddieAhern 6 74
(J W Hills) *t.k.h early in 4th: chsd ldng pair over 2f out: hrd rdn wl over 1f out: fdd ins fnl f* **4/1**[1]
0300 **6** *hd* **Salient**[14] 3736 5-9-11 **78** PaulDoe 5 76
(M J Attwater) *chsd ldr after 2f: drvn and wandering 2f out: lost 2nd and wknd jst ins fnl f* **16/1**
420- **7** 5 **Daniel Thomas (IRE)**[268] 7014 7-9-8 **75** KirstyMilczarek 11 62
(Mrs A L M King) *dwlt: settled in 9th: pushed along on inner over 2f out: no prog: wl off the pce over 1f out* **33/1**
2513 **8** ½ **My Shadow**[20] 3526 4-9-3 **70** IanMongan 4 56
(S Dow) *hld up in 8th: effrt towards outer over 2f out: sn no prog u.p and btn* **12/1**
3153 **9** 4 **Highly Regal (IRE)**[14] 3736 4-9-10 **77** (b) DarryllHolland 10 53
(R A Teal) *trckd ldng quartet: rdn over 2f out: sn lost pl: wknd over 1f out* **15/2**
2605 **10** 2 **Phluke**[13] 3770 8-9-4 **74** KevinGhunowa(3) 9 46
(Eve Johnson Houghton) *chsd ldr 2f: drvn over 3f out: wknd over 2f out* **18/1**
-300 **11** 8 **Bustan (IRE)**[48] 2641 10-9-11 **78** GeorgeBaker 7 31
(G C Bravery) *dwlt: a last: rdn and struggling 3f out: t.o* **16/1**

1m 41.93s (-1.37) **Going Correction** -0.025s/f (Good)
WFA 3 from 4yo+ 8lb **11** Ran SP% **118.7**
Speed ratings (Par 105): **105,104,102,101,100 100,95,94,90,88 80**
toteswingers: 1&2 £3.50, 1&3 £11.90, 2&3 £10.50. CSF £25.58 CT £217.33 TOTE £7.00: £2.20, £1.90, £3.50; EX 25.60.
Owner Con Harrington **Bred** St Simon Foundation **Trained** East Everleigh, Wilts

FOCUS
Trebles for jockey Richard Hughes and trainer Richard Hannon. The pace set by the runner-up was solid enough and this is solid form, with the third the best guide.
Bustan(IRE) Official explanation: jockey said gelding was slowly away

4212 CHILDREN'S TRUST 25TH ANNIVERSARY H'CAP 1m 6f
8:45 (8:45) (Class 4) (0-85,85) 4-Y-O+ **£4,857** (£1,445; £722; £360) **Stalls** High

Form RPR
5115 **1** **Callisto Moon**[26] 3346 5-9-1 **77** (p) DarryllHolland 4 87
(R Curtis) *mde all at decent pce: drvn and styd on stoutly fr 2f out* **11/4**[1]
0-10 **2** 2¼ **Haarth Sovereign (IRE)**[42] 2815 5-9-3 **79** (t) ShaneKelly 2 86
(W R Swinburn) *hld up in last trio: prog on outer over 2f out: chsd wnr wl over 1f out: hrd rdn and edgd rt after: no imp* **8/1**
660- **3** 2 **Black Jacari (IRE)**[26] 5098 4-9-6 **82** JimmyFortune 6 88+
(A King) *settled in last trio: nt qckn 3f out: dropped to last jst over 2f out: plld out and kpt on again over 1f out: tk 3rd nr fin* **7/2**[3]
6651 **4** ¾ **Hawridge King**[20] 3532 7-8-12 **77** JamesMillman(3) 3 80
(W S Kittow) *chsd wnr after 4f: rdn 3f out: no imp 2f out: sn lost 2nd: fdd ins fnl f* **4/1**
325/ **5** 1½ **Alessano**[858] 698 7-9-9 **85** GeorgeBaker 1 86
(G L Moore) *hld up in detached last: effrt to join chsng gp 2f out: pushed along and wknd over 1f out* **14/1**
4013 **6** 1 **Dakiyah (IRE)**[12] 3797 5-9-5 **81** (p) IanMongan 5 81
(Mrs L J Mongan) *dwlt: rcvrd to chse wnr for 4f: styd prom: drvn 3f out: wkng on inner whn n.m.r wl over 1f out* **10/3**[2]

3m 3.51s (-3.09) **Going Correction** -0.025s/f (Good) **6** Ran SP% **109.7**
Speed ratings (Par 105): **107,105,104,104,103 102**
toteswingers: 1&2 £5.30, 1&3 £2.70, 2&3 £15.10. CSF £23.26 TOTE £3.10: £2.00, £3.00; EX 22.10 Place 6: £93.10, Place 5: £49.70..
Owner B Bedford & Mrs Gill White **Bred** Barton Stud **Trained** Lambourn, Berks

FOCUS
Generally a sound pace for the trip, though the winner eased it a fraction at halfway, saving more than enough for the final dash. The form is rated at face value.
Haarth Sovereign(IRE) Official explanation: jockey said gelding hung right in home straight
T/Plt: £93.10 to a £1 stake. Pool: £78,026.30. 611.30 winning tickets. T/Qpdt: £49.70 to a £1 stake. Pool: £6,296.54. 93.75 winning tickets. JN

4213 - 4218a (Foreign Racing) - See Raceform Interactive

3993 BATH (L-H)
Thursday, July 23

OFFICIAL GOING: Good (7.8)
Wind: Light against Weather: Showers

4219 ASSET PROPERTY BROKERS MEDIAN AUCTION MAIDEN STKS 5f 161y
2:20 (2:20) (Class 6) 2-Y-O **£2,072** (£616; £308; £153) **Stalls** Centre

Form RPR
1 **Dark Eyes (IRE)** 2-8-12 0 CatherineGannon 16 78+
(D J Coakley) *s.i.s: hld up towards rr: pushed along over 2f out: hdwy on outside wl over 1f out: sn edgd lft: rdn to ld towards fin* **40/1**
432 **2** ¾ **Dubai Set**[17] 3692 2-9-3 0 PatDobbs 15 81
(R Hannon) *hld up: sn in tch: pushed along over 2f out: edgd lft and led jst over 1f out: rdn and hdd towards fin* **10/11**[1]
3 1¾ **Chips O'Toole (IRE)** 2-9-3 0 NickyMackay 9 75
(B J Meehan) *s.i.s: hld up and bhd: hdwy on outside over 2f out: rdn and ev ch 1f out: nt qckn wl ins fnl f* **9/1**[3]
0 **4** 1¾ **Come On Safari (IRE)**[17] 3692 2-9-3 0 LukeMorris 10 69
(P Winkworth) *a.p: ev ch wl over 1f out: sn n.m.r and rdn: one pce ins fnl f* **10/1**
03 **5** 1¾ **Kakapuka**[19] 3634 2-9-3 0 KirstyMilczarek 7 63
(Mrs A L M King) *led: hdd and n.m.r on ins jst over 1f out: wknd ins fnl f* **15/2**[2]
00 **6** ¾ **Candyfloss Girl**[21] 3534 2-8-9 0 DavidProbert(3) 14 56+
(H J L Dunlop) *hld up in mid-div: hdwy 2f out: rdn over 1f out: wknd fnl f* **50/1**
0 **7** 2 **Avongate**[52] 2533 2-9-3 0 FrancisNorton 6 54+
(R Hannon) *prom: pushed along over 2f out: rdn and wknd over 1f out* **16/1**
8 *nk* **Feeling Fragile (IRE)** 2-9-3 0 PaulEddery 4 53
(Pat Eddery) *dwlt: in rr: pushed along and sme hdwy over 2f out: swtchd rt over 1f out: no further prog* **40/1**
0 **9** ¾ **West Leake Star (IRE)**[42] 2853 2-9-3 0 RobertWinston 5 60+
(B W Hills) *hld up in mid-div on ins: pushed along over 2f out: nt clr run and swtchd rt over 1f out: no hdwy* **14/1**
10 1 **Kapelad Junior (IRE)** 2-9-3 0 JamieMackay 12 47
(Pat Eddery) *dwlt: hld up in rr on ins: nvr nr ldrs* **40/1**
11 1¾ **Knockback (IRE)** 2-9-3 0 DO'Donohoe 2 42
(P R Chamings) *s.i.s: outpcd in rr: n.d* **100/1**
12 2½ **Primo De Vida (IRE)** 2-9-3 0 SebSanders 8 33
(R M Beckett) *s.i.s: sn mid-div: pushed along over 2f out: no imp whn carried rt over 1f out* **9/1**[3]
0 **13** 6 **Greenore Gordon**[108] 1147 2-9-3 0 TGMcLaughlin 13 14
(M S Saunders) *w ldr: pushed along over 2f out: wknd wl over 1f out* **16/1**
14 7 **Set In Ice** 2-8-12 0 JackDean(5) 11 —
(Mark Gillard) *s.s: outpcd* **100/1**

60 **15** *8* **Trade Fairle**[15] 3745 2-9-3 0........................(v[1]) FergusSweeney 17 —
(P R Webber) *s.i.s: in rr: rdn wl over 2f out: sn struggling* **150/1**

1m 11.58s (0.38) **Going Correction** -0.025s/f (Good) **15** Ran SP% **123.6**
Speed ratings (Par 92): **96,95,92,90,88 87,84,83,82,81 79,75,67,58,47**
toteswingers: 1&2 £18.60, 1&3 £59.30, 2&3 £5.30. CSF £78.47 TOTE £51.40: £9.80, £1.10, £3.80; EX 137.70 Trifecta £175.70 Part won. Pool: £237.52 - 0.30 winning units..
Owner Barliffey Racing **Bred** Amanda Brundenell & Roger Simmons **Trained** West Ilsley, Berks
■ Stewards' Enquiry : Pat Dobbs two-day ban: careless riding (Aug 6-7)

FOCUS
A modest maiden with a couple already having shown experience, plus some interesting newcomers. The early gallop was strong, but perhaps they went too quick as the front pair both came from off the pace. Several shaped well down the field.

NOTEBOOK
Dark Eyes(IRE) ◆, an 800euros half-sister to two winners at up to 2m and representing last year's winning stable, missed the break from her wide stall and took a keen hold early, but she got stronger as the race progressed and came with a withering run down the wide outside to hit the front in the final 50 yards. Despite her price there was no fluke about this and she should have a future. (op 66-1)
Dubai Set, who boasted the best form coming into this having progressed in each of three starts on fast ground at Windsor, was sent off a hot favourite. He was produced from the middle of the field to hold every chance a furlong from home, but despite coming under strong pressure he couldn't quite hold off the filly. He should find a maiden before long, though he doesn't have the scope of a few of these. (op 11-10 tchd 6-5 and 5-4 in places)
Chips O'Toole(IRE), a 30,000gns colt, came through to hold every chance on the outside a furlong out before being done for finishing speed. Out of a dual winner at up to 1m3f, he is stoutly bred on the dam's side and should progress with experience as he goes up in trip. (op 14-1)
Come On Safari(IRE), almost ten lengths behind Dubai Set when in midfield on his Windsor debut, attracted market support and was still in with a shout when slightly buffeted about coming to the last furlong, but it probably made little difference to his finishing position. This was still an improvement, though. (op 12-1 tchd 8-1)
Kakapuka, who stepped up from his debut effort when third at Nottingham earlier in the month, showed good speed to take them along early but he looked to have run his race when getting hampered against the inside rail by the runner-up over a furlong from home. He now qualifies for nurseries. (op 6-1 tchd 8-1)
Candyfloss Girl, well beaten in a couple of Newbury maidens, showed a bit more here and wasn't knocked about late on. She may also do better in nurseries in due course. (op 40-1)
Greenore Gordon Official explanation: jockey said gelding had been struck into behind

4220 OPTIMUMRACING.CO.UK (S) STKS 1m 2f 46y
2:55 (2:57) (Class 6) 4-Y-0+ **£1,942** (£578; £288; £144) **Stalls** Low

Form RPR
6245 **1** **Don Pietro**[80] 6-8-12 67........................ GabrielHannon(5) 2 61
(R Curtis) *t.k.h: a.p: chsd ldr over 7f out: led over 2f out: rdn over 1f out: r.o* **7/1**
3302 **2** *nk* **Samurai Warrior**[9] 3961 4-9-8 68........................(p) CatherineGannon 10 65
(P D Evans) *t.k.h: prom: led over 8f out: pushed along and hdd over 2f out: sn rdn: ev ch ins fnl f: kpt on* **15/8**[1]
465 **3** *2 ½* **Everyman**[16] 3717 5-9-3 49........................(p) MattieBatchelor 8 55
(A W Carroll) *hld up: hdwy over 6f out: rdn 2f out: kpt on same pce fnl f* **14/1**
-030 **4** *½* **April's Daughter**[10] 3919 4-8-12 54........................ PaulEddery 7 49
(B R Millman) *hld up towards rr: hdwy on ins 3f out: swtchd rt over 2f out: rdn wl over 1f out: kpt on u.p ins fnl f* **10/1**
1321 **5** *¾* **Terminate (GER)**[26] 3382 7-9-8 62........................(tp) PaulDoe 5 58
(Ian Williams) *s.v.s: in rr: rdn over 3f out: hdwy over 2f out: styd on towards fin: nvr nrr* **5/1**[3]
6060 **6** *7* **Encore Belle**[14] 3777 4-8-12 50........................(v[1]) FrankieMcDonald 11 34
(Mouse Hamilton-Fairley) *rel to r: in rr: hdwy 3f out: rdn wl over 1f out: sn wknd* **12/1**
0-00 **7** *8* **Almowj**[59] 2317 6-9-3 37........................ JosedeSouza 12 23
(G H Jones) *plld hrd in rr: pushed along 3f out: rdn 2f out: swtchd rt over 1f out: nvr nr ldrs* **100/1**
/00- **8** *2 ¼* **Alannah (IRE)**[357] 4564 4-8-12 40........................ SimonWhitworth 3 13
(Mrs P N Dutfield) *led: hdd over 8f out: rdn and wknd over 2f out: eased over 1f out* **100/1**
550- **9** *1 ¾* **Charlie Be (IRE)**[352] 4707 4-9-3 46........................ AmirQuinn 1 15
(Mrs P N Dutfield) *hld up in mid-div: rdn over 2f out: sn wknd* **66/1**
00-0 **10** *3 ¼* **Trireme (IRE)**[72] 1967 5-9-3 48........................(t) NickyMackay 4 8
(K A Morgan) *hld up towards rr: pushed along over 4f out: rdn wl over 2f out: sn struggling* **33/1**
/0-0 **11** *3 ½* **Rosemarkie**[16] 3717 5-8-12 40........................(p) SaleemGolam 9 —
(J M Bradley) *t.k.h: prom: rdn over 3f out: wknd wl over 2f out* **66/1**
4206 **12** *42* **Ghufa (IRE)**[15] 2851 5-9-3 65........................(p) DO'Donohoe 6 —
(George Baker) *s.i.s: hdwy 9f out: lost pl 7f out: t.o fnl 3f* **10/3**[2]

2m 10.7s (-0.30) **Going Correction** -0.025s/f (Good) **12** Ran SP% **118.4**
Speed ratings (Par 101): **100,99,97,97,96 91,84,82,81,78 76,42**
toteswingers: 1&2 £4.90, 1&3 £16.70, 2&3 £8.10. CSF £20.37 TOTE £6.90: £2.60, £1.10, £3.70; EX 26.00 Trifecta £291.50 Pool: £405.79 - 1.03 winning units..The winner was bought in for 4,000gns. Samurai Warrior was claimed by J. E. Snowden for £6,000.
Owner Mrs Joanna Hughes **Bred** B N And Mrs Toye **Trained** Lambourn, Berks

FOCUS
Only a few held a realistic chance in this moderate seller. The pace was ordinary, but even so very few ever got into it and the front pair were always up there. The front pair are better than this grade on their best form, but not necessarily here.
Terminate(GER) Official explanation: jockey said gelding missed the break

4221 EUROPEAN BREEDERS' FUND NOVICE STKS 5f 11y
3:30 (3:30) (Class 4) 2-Y-0 **£4,857** (£1,445; £722; £360) **Stalls** Centre

Form RPR
041 **1** **Stargaze (IRE)**[76] 1835 2-9-2 0........................ DavidProbert(3) 4 93
(A M Balding) *w ldr: hrd rdn fnl f: led last stride* **5/2**[2]
1036 **2** *hd* **Angel's Pursuit (IRE)**[14] 3779 2-9-5 0........................ PatDobbs 1 92
(R Hannon) *wnt rt s: led: rdn ins fnl f: hdd last stride* **8/13**[1]
2210 **3** *4* **Avonvalley**[37] 2995 2-8-11 0........................ TGMcLaughlin 2 70
(M S Saunders) *sltly hmpd s: t.k.h: trckd ldrs: rdn over 1f out: wknd ins fnl f* **7/1**[3]
26 **4** *2* **Emma Jean Lass (IRE)**[81] 1706 2-8-7 0........................ LukeMorris 3 59
(J S Moore) *hld up: jnd ldrs on outside over 2f out: rdn and wknd over 1f out* **28/1**

62.71 secs (0.21) **Going Correction** -0.025s/f (Good) **4** Ran SP% **106.4**
Speed ratings (Par 96): **97,96,90,87**
CSF £4.37 TOTE £3.20; EX 5.20.
Owner David Brownlow **Bred** Dermot Brennan And Associates Ltd **Trained** Kingsclere, Hants

FOCUS
A race that always attracts only a small field, won last year by the high-class sprinter Amour Propre. Whether this year's renewal will produce anything of his quality is debatable, but the two market leaders dominated the contest and produced a thrilling finish. Stargaze confirmed his good Lingfield impression and the form makes sense.

NOTEBOOK
Stargaze(IRE) ◆, easy winner of a modest Lingfield maiden on his third outing, needs a fast surface and he wouldn't have run here had the ground got any softer, so the drying conditions were very much in his favour. Settled on the shoulder of the favourite from the start, he looked to be getting the worst of the argument entering the last furlong, but then conjured up another effort which took him to the front right on the line. On this evidence another furlong wouldn't bother him and he looks a nice young sprinting prospect. (tchd 11-4)
Angel's Pursuit(IRE), down in class and in trip after failing to see out the extra furlong in the July Stakes, tried to it from the front and looked to be in control half a furlong from home, but the winner's rally proved just too much for him. He may need the ground quicker than this, but may not be the easiest to place from now on. (op 4-6 tchd 4-7 and 8-11 in places)
Avonvalley, well beaten in the Windsor Castle last month, had finished ahead of Stargaze here in April but her rival has progressed the more of the pair since then. After having been done few favours by Angel's Pursuit exiting the stalls, she took a strong hold in behind the leaders and didn't find much once off the bridle. She was the most exposed in the field and may also not be easiest to place. (op 6-1)
Emma Jean Lass(IRE), beaten much further by Leleyf on fast ground at Salisbury last time having finished only a short head behind her on the Lingfield Polytrack before that, saw plenty of daylight on the wide outside and, although she had every chance, she just didn't look good enough against the three previous winners. (op 22-1)

4222 NONSTOP IT SECURITY SPECIALISTS CLAIMING STKS 5f 11y
4:05 (4:05) (Class 6) 3-Y-0+ **£2,072** (£616; £308; £153) **Stalls** Centre

Form RPR
4243 **1** **The Tatling (IRE)**[7] 3995 12-9-6 78........................ JackDean(5) 2 76
(J M Bradley) *hld up: stdy prog over 2f out: nt clr run over 1f out: rdn to ld ins fnl f: readily* **5/4**[1]
0330 **2** *2* **Diane's Choice**[9] 3947 6-8-9 56........................(e) DavidProbert(3) 9 56
(Miss Gay Kelleway) *hld up and bhd: hdwy wl over 1f out: led 1f out: rdn and hdd ins fnl f: nt qckn* **7/2**[2]
0060 **3** *2 ¼* **Talamahana**[7] 3994 4-8-10 43........................(v) TGMcLaughlin 3 46
(A B Haynes) *in rr: pushed along 3f out: rdn and hdwy whn swtchd lft to ins rail 1f out: swtchd rt wl ins fnl f: kpt on to take 3rd cl home* **33/1**
265 **4** *½* **Godfrey Street**[111] 1104 6-9-7 72........................(p) FergusSweeney 7 55
(A G Newcombe) *w ldr: led over 2f out: hdd 1f out: sn rdn: fdd towards fin* **8/1**
060 **5** *1* **Meikle Barfil**[30] 3239 7-8-13 43........................(tp) LukeMorris 1 44
(J M Bradley) *t.k.h: prom: rdn 1f out: wknd wl ins fnl f* **50/1**
5402 **6** *shd* **Like For Like (IRE)**[22] 3502 3-8-8 55........................ KirstyMilczarek 5 42
(R J Hodges) *prom: rdn jst over 1f out: wknd fnl f* **7/1**
4005 **7** *2 ½* **Nordic Light (USA)**[43] 2811 5-8-12 40........................(bt) KevinGhunowa(3) 8 36
(J M Bradley) *led: hdd over 2f out: rdn wl over 1f out: wknd ins fnl f* **33/1**
-002 **8** *3 ¾* **The Name Is Frank**[7] 3994 4-8-13 52........................ SebSanders 6 21
(Mark Gillard) *n.m.r and squeezed out sn after s: sn chsng ldrs: rdn and wknd over 2f out* **9/2**[3]

62.70 secs (0.20) **Going Correction** -0.025s/f (Good)
WFA 3 from 4yo+ 4lb **8** Ran SP% **116.3**
Speed ratings (Par 101): **97,93,90,89,87 87,83,77**
toteswingers: 1&2 £2.30, 1&3 £11.20, 2&3 £20.60. CSF £5.81 TOTE £2.00: £1.10, £1.60, £7.20; EX 8.20 Trifecta £307.40 Pool: £440.38 - 1.06 winning units..The Name Is Frank was claimed by P. D. Evans for £4,000.
Owner J M Bradley **Bred** Patrick J Power **Trained** Sedbury, Gloucs

FOCUS
A fair claimer, despite a wide variety of abilities, and they seemed to go a decent pace from the off. The Tatling did not need to match his recent best, with the third rather limiting the form.

4223 JOIN ONLINE AT OPTIMUMRACING.CO.UK H'CAP 5f 11y
4:40 (4:41) (Class 5) (0-70,70) 3-Y-0 **£2,719** (£809; £404; £202) **Stalls** Centre

Form RPR
2113 **1** **Mythical Blue (IRE)**[31] 3229 3-8-13 **65**........................ DavidProbert(3) 5 83
(J M Bradley) *mde all: rdn clr jst ins fnl f: r.o wl* **7/2**[1]
4206 **2** *4* **Avrilo**[6] 4051 3-8-2 **51** oh1........................ NickyMackay 1 55
(M S Saunders) *a.p: rdn over 2f out: chsd wnr jst over 1f out: no imp* **8/1**
0164 **3** *1 ¾* **Hi Shinko**[20] 3592 3-9-7 **70**........................ TGMcLaughlin 4 67
(B R Millman) *chsd ldrs: rdn and edgd rt over 1f out: one pce* **11/2**[3]
4301 **4** *¾* **Hillside Lad**[12] 3866 3-9-4 **67**........................(p) SebSanders 8 62
(R M Beckett) *prom: rdn on outside over 1f out: wknd ins fnl f* **9/2**[2]
5-16 **5** *6* **Silky Way (GR)**[31] 3229 3-9-3 **66**........................ RobertWinston 6 39
(P R Chamings) *chsd wnr: rdn 2f out: lost 2nd jst over 1f out: wknd fnl f* **9/2**[2]
005 **6** *hd* **Rosie Two**[24] 3460 3-8-3 **52**........................ FrancisNorton 9 24
(W S Kittow) *hld up: swtchd lft wl over 2f out: sn bhd* **12/1**
1460 **7** *1 ¼* **Jolly Ranch**[31] 3229 3-8-6 **55**........................ SimonWhitworth 7 23
(A G Newcombe) *hld up in tch: wknd over 1f out* **25/1**
0000 **8** *1* **Tarqua (IRE)**[15] 3741 3-7-9 **51** oh3........................ CharlesEddery(7) 10 15
(R Hannon) *racd wd: bhd fnl 3f* **20/1**
61-0 **9** *½* **Sky High Kid (IRE)**[12] 3868 3-9-0 **63**........................ CatherineGannon 2 25
(M R Channon) *sn outpcd* **6/1**

61.97 secs (-0.53) **Going Correction** -0.025s/f (Good) **9** Ran SP% **115.7**
Speed ratings (Par 100): **103,96,93,92,83 82,80,79,78**
toteswingers: 1&2 £6.60, 1&3 £4.20, 2&3 £9.50 CSF £32.15 CT £151.31 TOTE £3.80: £1.50, £2.90, £2.20; EX 32.00 Trifecta £217.00 Pool: £419.42 - 1.43 winning units..Miss Leona was withdrawn. Price at time of withdrawal was 80/1. Rule 4 does not apply.
Owner Clifton Hunt **Bred** John O'Dowd **Trained** Sedbury, Gloucs

FOCUS
An ordinary sprint handicap, but an open betting heat which was run in driving rain. With so many that like to go from the front in opposition, a decent pace was always very likely and the winning time was 0.73 seconds faster than the claimer. The winner looks back to his 2yo best.

4224 BET365 FILLIES' H'CAP 1m 2f 46y
5:10 (5:11) (Class 5) (0-70,70) 3-Y-0 **£2,719** (£809; £404; £202) **Stalls** Low

Form RPR
221 **1** **Air Maze**[148] 678 3-9-6 **69**........................ SebSanders 6 70
(Sir Mark Prescott) *hld up: hdwy on outside over 2f out: led jst over 1f out: hrd rdn fnl f: all out* **7/4**[1]
3605 **2** *hd* **Welsh Anthem**[8] 3981 3-9-7 **70**........................(b) RobertWinston 9 71
(W R Muir) *sn led: rdn and hdd jst over 1f out: ev ch ins fnl f: r.o* **9/1**
4606 **3** *¾* **Triple Cee (IRE)**[19] 3610 3-8-11 **60**........................ EdwardCreighton 2 59
(M R Channon) *hdwy on ins after 2f: rdn 2f out: styd on towards fin* **10/1**

3604 **4** ½ **Fleur De'Lion (IRE)**[6] 4065 3-7-13 **51** oh4 .... DavidProbert(3) 1 49
(S Kirk) *hld up in rr: swtchd rt over 2f out: rdn and hdwy on outside over 1f out: fin wl* **40/1**

0152 **5** 1 **Fong's Alibi**[8] 3985 3-9-2 **65** ....(p) LukeMorris 3 61
(J S Moore) *hld up: pushed along and hdwy 2f out: swtchd rt over 1f out: sn rdn: kpt on same pce ins fnl f* **9/2**[2]

1-04 **6** 4 **Red Reef**[40] 2909 3-8-13 **62** .... PatDobbs 4 50
(D J Coakley) *s.i.s: hld up in rr: pushed along over 2f out: rdn and hdwy on outside wl over 1f out: wknd ins fnl f* **12/1**

0056 **7** 7 **Bounty Reef**[20] 3588 3-8-2 **51** oh1 .... CatherineGannon 7 25
(P D Evans) *t.k.h: hld up towards rr: pushed along 3f out: rdn wl over 1f out: no rspnse* **20/1**

0602 **8** 2 **Heartsease**[15] 3741 3-8-9 **58** .... SaleemGolam 12 28
(J G Portman) *led early: chsd ldr tl over 2f out: sn rdn: wknd over 1f out* **6/1**[3]

04 **9** 2¾ **Eightdaysaweek**[2] 4175 3-8-8 **57** .... JamesDoyle 11 22
(S Kirk) *s.i.s: pushed along 3f out: rdn over 1f out: a in rr* **12/1**

0130 **10** 2¼ **Sapphire Rose**[20] 3581 3-8-11 **60** .... TravisBlock 5 20
(J G Portman) *hld up in mid-div: pushed along over 2f out: wkng whn nt clr run briefly over 1f out* **12/1**

0600 **11** 2 **Chalk Hill Blue**[10] 3919 3-8-3 **52** .... FrancisNorton 10 8
(Eve Johnson Houghton) *prom tl rdn and wknd over 2f out* **25/1**

00 **12** 2 **Annes Sound (IRE)**[49] 2627 3-8-4 **53** .... KirstyMilczarek 8 5
(Patrick Morris) *prom: pushed along and hung lft into rail over 2f out: sn wknd: eased whn no ch over 1f out* **40/1**

2m 11.3s (0.30) **Going Correction** -0.025s/f (Good) **12** Ran SP% **124.5**
Speed ratings (Par 97): **97,96,96,95,95 91,86,84,82,80 79,77**
toteswingers: 1&2 £6.80, 1&3 £7.40, 2&3 £19.60. CSF £18.93 CT £131.64 TOTE £3.10: £1.40, £3.50, £3.40; EX 24.80 Trifecta £69.60 Pool: 423.82 - 4.50 winning units..
Owner Plantation Stud **Bred** Pontchartrain Stud And Revilo Park Stud **Trained** Newmarket, Suffolk

FOCUS
A modest fillies' handicap with seven of these maidens coming into it. The winner made hard work of it and there are doubts over the solidity of this form.
Annes Sound(IRE) Official explanation: jockey said filly hung left-handed
T/Plt: £30.30 to a £1 stake. Pool: £45,747.37. 1,099.45 winning tickets. T/Qpdt: £12.30 to a £1 stake. Pool: £2,976.34. 178.60 winning tickets. KH

3999 DONCASTER (L-H)
Thursday, July 23

OFFICIAL GOING: Good (good to soft in places; 7.6)
Wind: Moderate, against Weather: Sunny periods

4225 DONCASTER MINSTER H'CAP 6f
6:15 (6:15) (Class 5) (0-70,70) 4-Y-0+ **£3,412** (£1,007; £504) **Stalls** High

Form RPR

0-06 **1** **Capone (IRE)**[15] 3730 4-8-13 **62** .... HayleyTurner 7 72
(Garry Moss) *dwlt: hld up towards rr: hdwy over 2f out: led over 1f out: rdn ins fnl f and kpt on wl* **8/1**[2]

2014 **2** ½ **Top Bid**[13] 3828 5-8-9 **61** ....(b) KellyHarrison(3) 13 69
(T D Easterby) *midfield: hdwy 2f out: rdn to chse wnr ent fnl f and sn ev ch tl drvn and nt qckn last 75yds* **9/1**[3]

5003 **3** 1 **Circle Dance (IRE)**[2] 4183 4-8-0 **54** ow2 ....(v) MartinLane(5) 4 59
(D Shaw) *hld up towards rr: hdwy over 2f out: swtchd lft and rdn over 1f out: kpt on u.p ins fnl f: nrst fin* **12/1**

0406 **4** nk **Sunley Sovereign**[7] 4016 5-8-2 **51** oh4 ....(p) SilvestreDeSousa 10 55
(Mrs R A Carr) *in tch: pushed along 1/2-way: rdn to chse ldrs 2f out: drvn over 1f out and kpt on same pce* **11/1**

0000 **5** 3 **Captain Royale (IRE)**[51] 2579 4-7-11 **53** oh6 ow2 AndrewHeffernan(7) 1 48
(Miss Tracy Waggott) *cl up: rdn to ld over 2f out: drvn and hdd over 1f out: grad wknd* **50/1**

6012 **6** ½ **Flying Applause**[12] 3860 4-9-4 **70** ....(bt) RussellKennemore(3) 9 63
(S R Bowring) *chsd ldrs: rdn along 2f out: sn drvn and kpt on same pce* **8/1**[2]

-000 **7** 1½ **Fulford**[87] 1558 4-8-4 **53** ow1 .... AdrianTNicholls 15 41
(M Brittain) *racd towards stands' rail: towards rr: hdwy wl over 1f out: sn rdn and kpt on ins fnl f: nrst fin* **40/1**

2003 **8** nk **Make My Dream**[26] 3407 6-9-5 **68** .... AlanMunro 18 55
(J Gallagher) *red towards stands' rail and towards rr: effrt and sme hdwy wl over 1f out: nvr a factor* **12/1**

0-00 **9** ½ **Chosen One (IRE)**[42] 2852 4-9-0 **63** .... TomEaves 12 49
(B Smart) *chsd ldrs: rdn along over 2f out: sn drvn and wknd wl over 1f out* **14/1**

63 **10** nse **Glasshoughton**[33] 3148 6-9-7 **70** .... PhillipMakin 5 56
(M Dods) *hld up towards rr: hdwy 2f out: n.m.r and rdn wl over 1f out: sn no imp* **8/1**[2]

0/0- **11** 1¾ **Danum Dancer**[460] 1485 5-9-3 **69** .... LeeVickers(3) 6 49
(N Bycroft) *chsd ldrs to 1/2-way: sn wknd* **33/1**

0500 **12** nk **Makshoof (IRE)**[7] 4023 5-9-0 **63** ....(b[1]) PatrickMathers 14 42
(I W McInnes) *sn rdn along and bhd tl sme late hdwy* **25/1**

4152 **13** 2½ **Convince (USA)**[26] 3401 8-8-7 **59** .... AndreaAtzeni(3) 20 30
(K M Prendergast) *racd towards stands' rail: a in rr* **11/2**[1]

0600 **14** 2½ **Avoncreek**[12] 3851 5-8-4 **53** oh6 ow2 .... AndrewElliott 17 16
(B P J Baugh) *racd towards stands' rail: a in rr* **33/1**

4405 **15** 4½ **Tri Chara (IRE)**[16] 3722 5-8-11 **60** ....(p) GrahamGibbons 11 9
(R Hollinshead) *prom: rdn along 1/2-way: sn wknd* **16/1**

6560 **16** ¾ **City For Conquest (IRE)**[9] 3938 6-7-12 **52** oh5 ow1(b) PaulPickard(5) 19 —
(John A Harris) *racd nr stands' rail: a towards rr* **33/1**

00-0 **17** 1½ **Billy Cadiz**[14] 3764 4-8-2 **51** oh6 .... JimmyQuinn 16 —
(N Tinkler) *racd towards stands' rail: in tch: rdn along 1/2-way: sn wknd* **66/1**

0001 **18** ½ **He's A Humbug (IRE)**[15] 3730 5-9-2 **70** ....(v) JamesO'Reilly(5) 3 10
(J O'Reilly) *chsd ldrs on outer: effrt over 2f out: sn rdn and wknd* **12/1**

006 **19** 7 **Double Carpet (IRE)**[16] 3720 6-8-4 **53** .... PaulHanagan 2 —
(G Woodward) *led: rdn along and hdd over 2f out: sn wknd* **20/1**

1m 14.49s (0.89) **Going Correction** +0.20s/f (Good) **19** Ran SP% **126.0**
Speed ratings (Par 103): **102,101,100,99,95 94,92,92,91,91 89,89,85,82,76 75,73,72,71**
toteswingers: 1&2 £18.50, 1&3 £58.90, 2&3 £44.40. CSF £72.96 CT £905.52 TOTE £10.00: £2.50, £3.00, £3.70, £3.20; EX 110.20.
Owner Brooklands Racing **Bred** S J Macdonald **Trained**

FOCUS
A breezy day saw the ground dry out to good, good to soft in places. The jockeys reported it to be good. Mainly exposed performers in an ordinary handicap. The pace was sound but the four that raced towards the stands' rail could never land a blow with the larger centre group. The form reads fairly sound.
Convince(USA) Official explanation: trainer said, regarding running, that the gelding was unsuited by the good ground

4226 HENDERSON GARAGE DOORS MAIDEN AUCTION FILLIES' STKS 7f
6:45 (6:47) (Class 4) 2-Y-O **£3,885** (£1,156; £577; £288) **Stalls** High

Form RPR

0 **1** **Celestial Tryst**[29] 3263 2-8-8 0 .... PJMcDonald 12 72
(G M Moore) *in rr and sn pushed along: hdwy 3f out: swtchd outside and rdn to chse ldr over 1f out: chal and hung lft ent fnl f: sn led and kpt on wl towards fin* **12/1**

2 nk **Court Gown (IRE)** 2-8-8 0 .... RichardMullen 13 73+
(E S McMahon) *t.k.h: hld up in rr: hdwy 3f out: n.m.r over 2f out: swtchd lft and n.m.r wl over 1f out: rdn and qcknd to chse wnr ins fnl f: edgd lft and kpt on wl towards fin* **14/1**

4 **3** 2¼ **Diamond Duchess (IRE)**[12] 3858 2-8-10 0 .... PhilipRobinson 1 68
(D R Lanigan) *in tch: pushed along and hdwy to chse ldrs over 2f out: rdn wl over 1f out: kpt on ins fnl f* **7/1**[2]

4 shd **Enjoyment** 2-8-6 0 .... HayleyTurner 3 63
(M L W Bell) *midfield: gd hdwy on outer over 2f out: led wl over 1f out: rdn over 1f out: hdd ent fnl f: wknd* **11/1**

33 **5** nk **City Vaults Girl (IRE)**[17] 3686 2-8-7 0 .... PaulHanagan 5 64
(R A Fahey) *chsd ldrs: rdn along and outpcd 1/2-way: swtchd rt and hdwy u.p wl over 1f out: kpt on ins fnl f* **4/1**[1]

6 **6** 2¾ **Royal Record**[17] 3686 2-8-5 0 .... AlanMunro 2 55
(M Brittain) *trckd ldrs: hdwy 1/2-way: rdn to ld briefly over 2f out: hdd wl over 1f out and wknd appr fnl f* **25/1**

0 **7** nk **Ashkalara**[64] 2175 2-8-6 0 .... AndrewElliott 6 55
(H S Howe) *dwlt and towards rr: hdwy into midfield 1/2-way: rdn along over 2f out: drvn wl over 1f out: kpt on same pce* **33/1**

8 1 **Magic Millie (IRE)** 2-8-5 0 ow1 .... GrahamGibbons 8 52+
(J Hetherton) *towards rr: pushed along and hdwy over 3f out: sn rdn and no imp fnl 2f* **50/1**

50 **9** 2 **Uddy Mac**[12] 3875 2-8-4 0 .... SilvestreDeSousa 14 46
(N Bycroft) *towards rr: hdwy 3f out: rdn and in tch over 2f out: sn drvn and wknd* **8/1**[3]

10 3 **Liebelei (USA)** 2-8-12 0 .... ShaneKelly 11 46
(H J L Dunlop) *a towards rr* **11/1**

0 **11** ½ **Delta Sky (IRE)**[20] 3576 2-8-6 0 ow1 .... JerryO'Dwyer 4 39
(Miss Amy Weaver) *dwlt: sn led: rdn along and hdd 1/2-way: wknd wl over 2f out* **20/1**

3524 **12** 1¼ **Just The Tonic**[8] 3971 2-8-0 0 .... JamieKyne(5) 7 35
(M R Channon) *cl up: led 1/2-way: rdn along and hdd over 2f out: sn wknd* **4/1**[1]

44 **13** 9 **Proper Littlemadam**[27] 3337 2-8-5 0 .... JimmyQuinn 9 12
(M Botti) *prom: rdn along over 2f out and sn wknd* **9/1**

00 **14** 31 **Lady Navara (IRE)**[48] 2663 2-8-4 0 .... AdrianTNicholls 10 —
(M Brittain) *in tch: rdn along 3f out and sn wknd* **150/1**

1m 28.49s (2.19) **Going Correction** +0.20s/f (Good) **14** Ran SP% **118.8**
Speed ratings (Par 93): **95,94,92,91,91 88,88,87,84,81 80,79,69,33**
toteswingers: 1&2 £47.80, 1&3 £26.00, 2&3 £20.80. CSF £159.37 TOTE £14.40: £4.30, £4.90, £2.80; EX 246.30.
Owner Celestial Tryst Partnership **Bred** The Welcome Alliance **Trained** Middleham Moor, N Yorks

FOCUS
In all probability no more than a modest maiden but a race that should throw up its share of winners. The pace was reasonable and the majority raced in the centre.

NOTEBOOK
Celestial Tryst, taken off her feet over 5f on quick ground on her debut, proved much better suited by this trip on decent ground and showed much-improved form to justify the support that had seen her backed from 80-1 downwards. She'll have no problems with 1m, has a good attitude and may be capable of better. (op 80-1 tchd 9-1)
Court Gown(IRE) ◆, a half-sister to a couple of winners over middle distances, shaped with plenty of promise after being denied room at a crucial stage on this racecourse debut. She should prove equally effective over 1m and is sure to pick up a similar event. (op 11-1 tchd 10-1)
Diamond Duchess(IRE) fully confirmed the promise shown on her debut over this longer trip. She is open to further improvement and she should be able to pick up a minor event in due course.
Enjoyment ◆, who has winners in her pedigree, shaped with plenty of promise until tiring in the closing stages on this debut and looks a bit better than this bare form. She should be all the wiser for this experience and is one to keep a close eye on in similar company next time. (op 9-1 tchd 12-1)
City Vaults Girl(IRE) was one of the first off the bridle but kept plugging away over a trip that was expected to be in her favour. She may do better over further, granted a suitable test of stamina in nursery company. (op 10-3 tchd 3-1)
Royal Record, upped in distance, bettered the form shown at Ripon on her debut. While she is likely to remain vulnerable in this type of event, she may do better in run-of-the-mill nurseries. (op 50-1)

4227 SKY BET SUPPORTING YORKSHIRE RACING FESTIVAL H'CAP 6f
7:20 (7:23) (Class 4) (0-80,85) 3-Y-O **£4,857** (£1,445; £722; £360) **Stalls** High

Form RPR

35 **1** **Ursula (IRE)**[15] 3727 3-9-1 **73** .... AndrewElliott 8 85+
(K R Burke) *hld up in rr: hdwy and n.m.r wl over 1f out: rdn and gd hdwy appr fnl f: styd on strly to ld last 100yds* **7/1**[2]

5-21 **2** 1¾ **Russian Spirit**[14] 3764 3-9-5 **77** .... PhilipRobinson 2 83
(M A Jarvis) *led: rdn clr wl over 1f out: hdd and no ex last 100yds* **6/4**[1]

-002 **3** 2 **Merry Diva**[32] 3193 3-9-1 **73** .... AlanMunro 1 73
(C F Wall) *prom: effrt to chse ldr 2f out and sn rdn: drvn appr fnl f and kpt on same pce* **11/1**

0066 **4** ¾ **Kingswinford (IRE)**[13] 3806 3-9-3 **75** .... RichardMullen 7 72
(P D Evans) *in tch: pushed along 1/2-way: sn rdn and kpt on u.p appr fnl f* **15/2**[3]

3434 **5** 2 **Captain Scooby**[12] 3856 3-8-12 **70** ....(v[1]) HayleyTurner 6 61
(R M Whitaker) *chsd ldrs: hdwy 2f out and sn rdn: drvn and wknd appr fnl f* **9/1**

4340 **6** ½ **Tagula Breeze (IRE)**[17] 3688 3-9-5 **77** ....(p) TomEaves 3 66
(I W McInnes) *midfield: hdwy 2f out: sn rdn and no imp* **33/1**

4300 **7** hd **Spiritofthewest (IRE)**[33] 3173 3-9-6 **78** .... PhillipMakin 10 67
(D H Brown) *in rr tl sme late hdwy* **8/1**

3001 **8** hd **Klynch**[6] 4044 3-9-8 **85** 6ex ....(b) GabrielHannon(5) 5 73
(B J Meehan) *a towards rr* **20/1**

6600 **9** ½ **Caranbola**[17] 3688 3-9-4 **76** .... DavidAllan 4 63
(M Brittain) *chsd ldr: rdn along over 2f out: sn drvn and wknd* **33/1**

-405 **10** *15* **Whatyouwoodwishfor (USA)**[24] 3455 3-9-2 **74**........... PaulHanagan 9 13
(R A Fahey) *midfield: rdn along 1/2-way: sn wknd* **12/1**
0-23 **11** *8* **Toledo Gold (IRE)**[13] 3804 3-9-6 **78**.................... ShaneKelly 11 —
(E J Alston) *racd wd: chsd ldr: rdn along 1/2-way: sn wknd* **17/2**
1m 13.96s (0.36) **Going Correction** +0.20s/f (Good) **11** Ran SP% **122.6**
Speed ratings (Par 102): **105,102,100,99,96 95,95,95,94,74 63**
toteswingers: 1&2 £5.00, 1&3 £10.80, 2&3 £3.30. CSF £18.27 CT £122.35 TOTE £8.60: £2.90, £1.20, £2.30; EX 30.20.
Owner Tweenhills Racing XIV **Bred** Rathbarry Stud **Trained** Middleham Moor, N Yorks

FOCUS
A fair sprint in which the two least exposed runners were the only ones to figure in the last half of the race. The pace was sound and the form looks sound.
Toledo Gold(IRE) Official explanation: jockey said colt hung left

4228 KEEPMOAT "DELIVERING COMMUNITY REGENERATION" FILLIES' H'CAP 7f
7:50 (7:52) (Class 3) (0-90,86) 3-Y-0+
£7,477 (£2,239; £1,119; £560; £279; £140) **Stalls** High

Form RPR
60-6 **1** **Jeninsky (USA)**[40] 2927 4-9-6 **81**.................... AndreaAtzeni(3) 4 91
(Rae Guest) *trckd ldrs: hdwy over 2f out: rdn to ld wl over 1f out: drvn ins fnl f and styd on gamely* **8/1**[3]
2-32 **2** *1 1/4* **Happy Anniversary (IRE)**[13] 3825 3-8-12 **82**........... LeeNewnes(5) 10 86
(Mrs D J Sanderson) *trckd ldrs: smooth hdwy over 2f out: chal over 1f out and sn rdn: drvn and ev ch whn edgd lft ins fnl f: no ex towards fin* **4/1**[1]
-155 **3** *1* **Celtic Lynn (IRE)**[27] 3353 4-9-4 **76**.................... TomEaves 7 80
(M Dods) *hld up: hdwy over 2f out: swtchd rt and rdn to chse ldng pair 1f out: kpt on same pce u.p ins fnl f* **12/1**
2-1 **4** *nse* **Sakhee's Pearl**[20] 3569 3-9-6 **85**.................... MickyFenton 8 86
(Miss Gay Kelleway) *hld up towards rr: hdwy 2f out: rdn to chse ldrs over 1f out: kpt on ins fnl f* **13/2**[2]
-005 **5** *2 1/2* **Misphire**[27] 3339 6-9-4 **76**.................... PhillipMakin 6 73
(M Dods) *hld up: hdwy over 2f out: sn rdn: kpt on ins fnl f: nt rch ldrs* **12/1**
113- **6** *1/2* **Prescription**[301] 6225 4-10-0 **86**.................... SebSanders 9 82+
(Sir Mark Prescott) *stdd s and swtchd lft: gd hdwy on outer 1/2-way: chsd ldrs 2f out: sn rdn and wknd over 1f out* **4/1**[1]
231 **7** *4 1/2* **Steel Free (IRE)**[20] 3590 3-9-1 **80**.................... HayleyTurner 1 61
(M L W Bell) *prom: hdwy on outer to ld 3f out: rdn and hdd wl over 1f out: sn drvn and wknd appr fnl f* **10/1**
-P00 **8** *2* **Knavesmire (IRE)**[12] 3877 3-9-6 **85**.................... DavidAllan 5 61
(M Brittain) *led: rdn along and hdd 3f out: sn drvn and wknd* **50/1**
0560 **9** *2 3/4* **Calahonda**[15] 3738 3-8-5 **75**.................... PaulPickard(5) 2 43
(P W D'Arcy) *prom: rdn along 3f out and sn wknd* **8/1**[3]
-010 **10** *4* **Suzie Quw**[16] 3706 3-8-11 **81**.................... MartinLane(5) 3 38
(K R Burke) *prom: rdn along over 3f out: wknd over 2f out* **20/1**
0503 **11** *4* **Key Signature**[19] 3628 3-9-1 **80**....................(b) ShaneKelly 11 26
(Pat Eddery) *a in rr* **8/1**[3]
1m 28.36s (2.06) **Going Correction** +0.20s/f (Good)
WFA 3 from 4yo+ 7lb **11** Ran SP% **117.9**
Speed ratings (Par 104): **96,94,93,93,90 89,84,82,79,74 70**
toteswingers: 1&2 £4.60, 1&3 £14.80, 2&3 £14.10. CSF £40.10 CT £394.77 TOTE £11.10: £3.40, £1.80, £4.30; EX 55.50.
Owner J M Beever **Bred** Dr R And Mrs Smiser West & Mr And Mrs M **Trained** Newmarket, Suffolk

FOCUS
Another fair handicap and one run at a fair gallop throughout. Personal bests from the first two.

NOTEBOOK
Jeninsky(USA) had looked exposed but clearly benefited from her reappearance run and showed she retains all her ability. She showed a decent attitude under pressure but life is going to be tougher from a mark in the mid 80s against the more progressive sorts after reassessment. (op 9-1 tchd 10-1)
Happy Anniversary(IRE) is a model of consistency and turned in another solid effort in defeat. She looks a good guide to the level of this form and should continue to give a good account in this type of event. (op 5-1tchd 11-2 in a place)
Celtic Lynn(IRE) has little in hand of her current mark but ran creditably after travelling strongly for a long way. She may be worth another try over 1m. (tchd 11-1 and 14-1)
Sakhee's Pearl looked on a fairly stiff mark for this handicap debut after an easy course and distance maiden win and was far from disgraced. She should stay 1m and may do better as she gains experience. (op 15-2)
Misphire, on the same mark as when last successful, was not disgraced under suitable conditions but is going to have to show a bit more before she is a solid betting proposition. (op 8-1)
Prescription ◆, a progressive sort on turf and Polytrack last year, raced with the choke out in the early stages but shaped as though retaining plenty of ability on this first run since September and on this first start over this trip. She will be all the better for this outing and is one to keep an eye on over this trip or back over 6f. (op 7-2 tchd 3-1)

4229 MOSS PROPERTIES H'CAP 1m 4f
8:25 (8:25) (Class 5) (0-75,75) 3-Y-0+ **£3,238** (£963; £481; £240) **Stalls** Low

Form RPR
-205 **1** **Harry The Hawk**[7] 4003 5-9-9 **70**.................... GrahamGibbons 7 79
(T D Walford) *trckd ldrs: hdwy over 3f out: led 2f out: drvn ent fnl f and hld on wl* **10/1**
-321 **2** *3/4* **Omokoroa (IRE)**[8] 3976 3-8-10 **74** 6ex.................... MartinLane(5) 8 82
(M H Tompkins) *hld up towards rr: hdwy 1/2-way: trckd ldrs 4f out: effrt to chse wnr 2f out: sn rdn and ev ch tl drvn and no ex wl ins fnl f* **3/1**[1]
0-65 **3** *2* **Crocus Rose**[22] 3508 3-8-3 **62**.................... JimmyQuinn 1 70+
(H J L Dunlop) *towards rr: hdwy on inner 3f out: sn n.m.r and swtchd rt over 2f out: sn rdn and styd on strly ins fnl f: nrst fin* **16/1**
0246 **4** *hd* **Spirit Of Adjisa (IRE)**[20] 3564 5-10-0 **75**....................(b) ShaneKelly 4 79
(Pat Eddery) *hld up: hdwy over 3f out: swtchd lft to inner 2f out: sn rdn and kpt on same pce fnl f* **7/1**
556 **5** *1/2* **Bavarian Nordic (USA)**[7] 4003 4-10-0 **75**.................... SilvestreDeSousa 5 79
(Mrs A Duffield) *t.k.h: hld up in rr: hdwy on outer over 3f out: chsd ldrs 2f out: rdn and no imp appr fnl f* **14/1**
01-5 **6** *1* **Scene Two**[83] 1643 3-9-1 **74**.................... SebSanders 3 76
(L M Cumani) *trckd ldrs: hdwy on outer over 3f out: rdn along 2f out: sn edgd lft: drvn appr fnl f and wknd* **5/1**[3]
22 **7** *9* **Sweet Hollow**[41] 2877 3-8-12 **71**.................... PhilipRobinson 9 59
(C G Cox) *chsd ldrs: rdn along 4f out: drvn 3f out and sn wknd* **10/3**[2]
323 **8** *1* **Whirlijig (IRE)**[16] 3703 4-9-12 **73**.................... PJMcDonald 2 59
(G A Swinbank) *prom: rdn along to dispute ld 3f out: drvn over 2f out and sn wknd* **9/1**
0/52 **9** *2 1/4* **Astronomical (IRE)**[20] 3563 7-9-1 **65**.................... RussellKennemore(3) 10 47
(R Hollinshead) *prom: chsd ldr after 3f: rdn to ld 3f out: drvn and hdd over 2f out and sn wknd* **16/1**

050- **10** *22* **Wild Fell Hall (IRE)**[364] 4343 6-9-1 **67**.................... PaulPickard(5) 6 14
(J Hetherton) *towards rr: rapid hdwy on outer to chse ldrs after 5f: prom 5f out: rdn along over 3f out and sn wknd* **40/1**
2-0P **P** **Captain Imperial (IRE)**[17] 3687 3-9-1 **74**.................... MickyFenton 11 —
(T P Tate) *led: rdn along 4f out: hdd 3f out: lost action and sn p.u* **50/1**
2m 35.73s (0.63) **Going Correction** +0.20s/f (Good)
WFA 3 from 4yo+ 12lb **11** Ran SP% **119.2**
Speed ratings (Par 103): **105,104,103,103,102 102,96,95,93,79 —**
toteswingers: 1&2 £7.30, 1&3 £47.00, 2&3 £13.90. CSF £40.62 CT £492.31 TOTE £7.40: £2.30, £1.60, £4.20; EX 34.60.
Owner David Dickson **Bred** Robe Farm Stud **Trained** Sheriff Hutton, N Yorks

FOCUS
A couple of unexposed performers in an ordinary handicap and the form is fair for the grade. The gallop was reasonable.
Captain Imperial(IRE) Official explanation: jockey said gelding returned distressed

4230 CROWNHOTEL-BAWTRY.COM H'CAP 1m 2f 60y
8:55 (8:57) (Class 5) (0-70,70) 3-Y-0 **£3,238** (£963; £481; £240) **Stalls** Low

Form RPR
0231 **1** **Amazing Blue Sky**[7] 4004 3-9-2 **65** 6ex.................... SilvestreDeSousa 1 73
(Mrs R A Carr) *mde all: rdn over 2f out: drvn over 1f out: kpt on gamely ins fnl f* **5/2**[2]
-051 **2** *1 3/4* **My Girl Jode**[3] 4157 3-8-7 **61** 6ex.................... MartinLane(5) 4 65
(M H Tompkins) *hld up towards rr: hdwy on outer 1/2-way: trckd ldrs 3f out: rdn to chse wnr 2f out: sn drvn and ch tl edgd rt jst ins fnl f and sn no ex* **10/11**[1]
-000 **3** *1 1/4* **Inside Knowledge (USA)**[9] 3955 3-8-1 **53**.................... AndreaAtzeni(3) 3 55
(G Woodward) *hld up on inner: hdwy 3f out: rdn and n.m.r over 2f out: drvn to chse ldng pair over 1f out: kpt on ins fnl f* **50/1**
0-35 **4** *4 1/2* **King's Counsel (IRE)**[16] 3703 3-8-11 **60**.................... PaulHanagan 6 53
(J Hetherton) *chsd wnr to 1/2-way: prom tl rdn along wl over 2f out and sn one pce* **20/1**
0650 **5** *3/4* **The Quiet Genius**[24] 3454 3-8-13 **62**.................... TonyHamilton 2 53
(Jedd O'Keeffe) *dwlt: a in rr* **28/1**
-406 **6** *3 1/4* **Sham Sheer**[48] 2667 3-9-2 **65**....................(v[1]) SebSanders 5 50
(L M Cumani) *trckd ldng pair: hdwy to chse wnr 1/2-way: rdn along 3f out: drvn over 2f out and sn wknd* **15/2**[3]
2034 **7** *1/2* **Steel Trade**[17] 3690 3-9-7 **70**.................... DavidAllan 7 54
(M Brittain) *chsd ldrs on outer: rdn along 3f out: drvn over 2f out and sn wknd* **10/1**
2m 12.96s (1.76) **Going Correction** +0.20s/f (Good) **7** Ran SP% **112.0**
Speed ratings (Par 100): **100,98,97,94,93 90,90**
toteswingers: 1&2 £1.10, 1&3 £16.10, 2&3 £12.50. CSF £4.87 CT £70.28 TOTE £3.70: £1.90, £1.50; EX 6.10 Place 6 £149.86, Place 5 £37.74.
Owner David W Chapman **Bred** Hong Kong Breeders Club **Trained** Huby, N Yorks

FOCUS
A run-of-the-mill handicap in which the pace was just fair. The two previous winners dominated in the closing stages and the first three pulled clear. The winner seems better than ever but the form is a little shaky.
T/Jkpt: Not won. T/Plt: £341.10 to a £1 stake. Pool: £68,258.85. 146.05 winning tickets. T/Qpdt: £16.60 to a £1 stake. Pool: £8,004.20. 354.70 winning tickets. JR

4005 EPSOM (L-H)
Thursday, July 23

OFFICIAL GOING: Good to firm
Wind: Strong, half against Weather: Sunny

4231 TOTESPORTCASINO.COM H'CAP 5f
6:05 (6:05) (Class 4) (0-80,73) 3-Y-0 **£4,857** (£1,445; £722; £360) **Stalls** High

Form RPR
5013 **1** **Rocket Rob (IRE)**[23] 3476 3-9-1 **67**.................... RyanMoore 5 75
(S A Callaghan) *off the pce in 5th: clsd fr 1/2-way: squeezed through to ld over 1f out: sn wl in command: pushed out* **11/4**[1]
0005 **2** *1 1/4* **Mazzola**[7] 3998 3-9-6 **72**.................... SamHitchcott 2 76
(M R Channon) *rrd bdly s: last tl prog over 1f out: styd on to take 2nd fnl 100yds: no imp wnr* **3/1**[2]
2153 **3** *3/4* **Musical Bridge**[16] 3704 3-9-6 **72**.................... JimmyFortune 3 73
(Mrs L Williamson) *racd towards outer: pressed ldrs: rdn 2f out: nt qckn 1f out: one pce after* **11/2**[3]
-503 **4** *nk* **Leadenhall Lass (IRE)**[29] 3281 3-9-1 **67**.................... IanMongan 6 67
(P M Phelan) *pressed ldr: upsides over 1f out: hanging and nt qckn: sn btn* **11/4**[1]
0130 **5** *3 3/4* **Amosite**[34] 3118 3-9-7 **73**....................(b) RichardHughes 4 59
(J R Jenkins) *led against nr side rail to over 1f out: wknd rapidly* **7/1**
2425 **6** *1 1/4* **Louie's Lad**[17] 3676 3-8-2 **54** oh2....................(p) FrankieMcDonald 1 36
(J J Bridger) *racd on wd outside: w ldrs 3f: hanging and wknd rapidly* **16/1**
55.72 secs (0.02) **Going Correction** +0.075s/f (Good) **6** Ran SP% **112.1**
Speed ratings (Par 102): **102,100,98,98,92 90**
toteswingers: 1&2 £3.50, 1&3 £4.50, 2&3 £6.30. CSF £11.27 TOTE £3.90: £2.00, £2.50; EX 16.00.
Owner Bill Hinge, J Searchfield & N Callaghan **Bred** Mrs Marita Rogers **Trained** Newmarket, Suffolk

FOCUS
A modest sprint, run at a strong pace. The time was respectable and the form has been rated slightly on the positive side.

4232 TOTESPORTGAMES.COM H'CAP 5f
6:35 (6:35) (Class 4) (0-85,84) 4-Y-0+ **£5,180** (£1,541; £770; £384) **Stalls** High

Form RPR
3024 **1** **Rocker**[17] 3694 5-8-13 **74**.................... RyanMoore 6 84
(G L Moore) *settled in last trio: prog wl over 1f out to press ldr ent fnl f: drvn ahd last 100yds* **4/1**[1]
0032 **2** *1* **Bertoliver**[26] 3372 5-9-5 **80**.................... DaneO'Neill 5 86
(Tom Dascombe) *cl up towards nr side rail: wnt 2nd 2f out: rdn to ld over 1f out: hdd and outpcd last 100yds* **4/1**[1]
2310 **3** *3/4* **Our Piccadilly (IRE)**[12] 3845 4-8-12 **78**........ Louis-PhilippeBeuzelin(5) 7 84+
(W S Kittow) *settled in last trio and racd against nr side rail: clsd over 1f out: rdn and nowhere to go ent fnl f: snatched up 75yds out but hld on for 3rd* **5/1**[2]
530- **4** *nse* **Handsome Cross (IRE)**[335] 5250 8-8-11 **72**.................... RichardHughes 4 75
(W J Musson) *stdd s: hld up in last: prog jst over 1f out: nt qckn towards outer fnl 100yds: pushed out* **7/1**

615 **5** *nse* **Misaro (GER)**[19] 3623 8-9-8 **83**..........(b) GregFairley 3 86
(R A Harris) *racd towards outer: wl on terms: shkn up and nt qckn over 1f out: one pce after* **12/1**

1604 **6** *1 ¾* **Peter Island (FR)**[28] 3318 6-9-9 **84**..........(v) TPO'Shea 9 81
(J Gallagher) *racd against nr side rail: led after 1f to over 1f out: sn btn* **5/1**[2]

225 **7** *6* **Drifting Gold**[29] 3272 5-9-1 **76**..........(b) AdamKirby 2 51
(C G Cox) *racd wdst of all: on terms w ldrs to 2f out: hanging and wknd* **11/2**[3]

3004 **8** *11* **Merlin's Dancer**[21] 3524 9-9-2 **77**..........(b) IanMongan 1 12
(S Dow) *led 1f: chsd ldr to 2f out: wknd rapidly: burst blood vessel* **25/1**

55.33 secs (-0.37) **Going Correction** +0.075s/f (Good) **8** Ran SP% **112.8**
Speed ratings (Par 105): **105,103,102,102,102 99,89,72**
toteswingers: 1&2 £1.80, 1&3 £3.50, 2&3 £4.80. CSF £19.32 CT £79.60 TOTE £3.40: £1.30, £1.10, £2.30; EX 8.60.
Owner Sir Eric Parker **Bred** Sir Eric Parker **Trained** Lower Beeding, W Sussex

FOCUS
This fair sprint was run to suit the closers and there was a blanket finish for the places. The form is straightforward.
Merlin's Dancer Official explanation: jockey said gelding bled from the nose

4233 EBF "SHOP LOCAL" AT ASHLEY CENTRE MAIDEN STKS 6f
7:10 (7:10) (Class 4) 2-Y-O **£5,180** (£1,541; £770; £384) **Stalls** High

Form RPR
4 **1** **Frozen Power (IRE)**[13] 3792 2-9-3 0..........DO'Donohoe 5 78+
(Saeed Bin Suroor) *sn pushed along to chse clr ldng pair: prog to go 2nd 2f out: clsd grad fnl f: led last strides* **10/3**[3]

43 **2** *nk* **Waveband**[13] 3799 2-8-12 0..........GregFairley 2 72
(M Johnston) *led: 2 l clr 2f out: rdn over 1f out: kpt on: hdd last strides* **3/1**[2]

34 **3** *½* **King Of Reason**[28] 3310 2-9-3 0..........RyanMoore 1 76
(D M Simcock) *off the pce in 5th: shkn up over 2f out: styd on fr over 1f out: wnt 3rd fnl f and clsng at fin* **15/2**

5 **4** *2 ½* **Where's The Soap (FR)**[26] 3385 2-8-12 0..........RichardKingscote 3 63+
(Tom Dascombe) *settled in last and off the pce: pushed along over 2f out: styd on encouragingly fnl f* **12/1**

5 **5** *4* **Key Breeze**[54] 2467 2-9-3 0..........JimmyFortune 6 56
(J H M Gosden) *pressed ldr and sn clr of rest: lost 2nd 2f out and sn wknd* **9/4**[1]

6 *¾* **Al Adham** 2-9-0 0..........AhmedAjtebi(3) 4 54
(Saeed Bin Suroor) *sn off the pce: 4th st: wknd 2f out: nt handle crse* **13/2**

69.54 secs (0.14) **Going Correction** -0.05s/f (Good) **6** Ran SP% **111.6**
Speed ratings (Par 96): **97,96,95,92,87 86**
toteswingers: 1&2 £4.60, 1&3 £4.60, 2&3 £3.20. CSF £13.54 TOTE £3.50: £1.70, £2.30; EX 10.50.
Owner Godolphin **Bred** Rathbarry Stud **Trained** Newmarket, Suffolk

FOCUS
A fair juvenile maiden, run at a solid pace.

NOTEBOOK
Frozen Power(IRE), fourth on debut at Ascot 13 days earlier, did just enough to open his account at the second time of asking. He took time to hit full stride, but was always going to reel in the runner-up at the business end and looks a useful prospect. As a half-brother Finsceal Beo, he is certainly bred to handle better company and another furlong should suit before long. (op 11-4)
Waveband got mugged late on, having cut out a lot of the donkey work, and deserves credit. This was her best run yet and she now becomes eligible for nurseries. (tchd 11-4 and 7-2)
King Of Reason came in for support and was doing his best work towards the finish, suggesting another furlong may now suit ideally. He is another who now has the option of nurseries. (op 8-1 tchd 6-1)
Where's The Soap(FR) was taken off her feet through the early parts as the leaders set a strong pace but was keeping on steadily late in the day on this step up from 5f. Her rider later reported she failed to act on the track. Official explanation: jockey said filly was unsuited by the track
Key Breeze, returning from a 54-day break, put it up to the runner-up through the first half of the race and eventually paid the price. Official explanation: jockey said colt ran too freely (op 11-4 tchd 3-1)
Al Adham did not go unbacked for his racecourse bow and showed some ability but may benefit for a drop to 5f in the short term. He will also prove happier on a more conventional course. (op 8-1 tchd 5-1)

4234 PADDOCKS MAIDEN FILLIES' STKS 1m 2f 18y
7:40 (7:45) (Class 5) 3-Y-O+ **£3,238** (£963; £481; £240) **Stalls** Low

Form RPR
43 **1** **Critical Path (IRE)**[55] 2433 3-8-13 0..........DaneO'Neill 4 79+
(A M Balding) *trckd ldng pair: shkn up 3f out: clsd u.p over 1f out: led ent fnl f: styd on wl* **2/1**[1]

22 **2** *1 ½* **Kinetix**[42] 2848 3-8-13 0..........JimmyFortune 2 74
(J H M Gosden) *trckd ldr: shkn up to try to cl over 2f out: hanging and nt qckn over 1f out: sn dropped to 3rd: kpt on to take 2nd again nr fin* **5/2**[2]

-32 **3** *1 ¼* **Toolentidhaar (USA)**[28] 3297 5-9-9 0..........GeorgeBaker 7 72
(Andrew Turnell) *led: gng bttr than rivals over 2f out: rdn over 1f out: hdd ent fnl f: wknd and lost 2nd nr fin* **8/1**

53 **4** *nk* **Insolence (USA)**[17] 3696 3-8-13 0..........RyanMoore 5 71
(Sir Michael Stoute) *hld up in 4th: shkn up on outer 3f out: no imp on ldrs: kpt on same pce fnl f* **7/2**[3]

63 **5** *6* **Ebony Eyes**[8] 3984 3-8-13 0..........RichardHughes 6 59
(W J Knight) *hld up in 5th: shkn up 3f out: no prog after: pushed along and wl btn over 1f out* **9/2**

6550 **6** *73* **Suhailah**[15] 3739 3-8-13 60..........PaulDoe 1 —
(M J Attwater) *dropped to last over 6f out: hung bdly rt ent st: t.o after* **100/1**

2m 9.82s (0.12) **Going Correction** -0.05s/f (Good)
WFA 3 from 5yo 10lb **6** Ran SP% **114.4**
Speed ratings (Par 100): **97,95,94,94,89 31**
toteswingers: 1&2 £2.30, 1&3 £4.20, 2&3 £5.30. CSF £7.55 TOTE £3.20: £1.50, £1.70; EX 6.30.
Owner Trebles Holford Thoroughbreds **Bred** Trebles Holford Farm Thoroughbreds **Trained** Kingsclere, Hants

FOCUS
A modest fillies' maiden, run at a steady pace. The first two progressed.
Suhailah Official explanation: jockey said filly hung right

4235 TOTESPORTBINGO.COM H'CAP 1m 4f 10y
8:15 (8:18) (Class 5) (0-70,70) 3-Y-O+ **£3,238** (£963; £481; £240) **Stalls** Centre

Form RPR
4615 **1** **Inspirina (IRE)**[12] 3847 5-9-11 **67**..........RichardHughes 5 75+
(R Ford) *dwlt: t.k.h and hld up in tch: swift prog to trck ldr over 7f out: led gng easily jst over 2f out: wl in command after: eased nr fin* **7/4**[1]

4465 **2** *¾* **Tecktal (FR)**[14] 3766 6-8-5 **52**..........JackDean(5) 2 57
(P M Phelan) *t.k.h: trckd ldr to over 7f out: 3rd st: rdn over 2f out: chsd wnr over 1f out: kpt on but nvr any ch* **12/1**

4233 **3** *hd* **Watson's Bay**[7] 4007 4-9-10 **66**..........IanMongan 8 71+
(P Howling) *dwlt: hld up in 7th: effrt whn nt clr run 2f out: nt clr run again over 1f out: swtchd ins ent fnl f: r.o: nrst fin* **3/1**[2]

3200 **4** *1 ¼* **Augustus John (IRE)**[13] 3814 6-9-11 **70**..........JackMitchell(3) 6 73
(R Brotherton) *wl in tch: 6th st: gng wl on outer 3f out: shkn up and nt qckn 2f out: disp 2nd over 1f out: one pce* **20/1**

/010 **5** *¾* **Mossmann Gorge**[35] 3074 7-8-6 **51**..........(p) KevinGhunowa(3) 1 52
(A Middleton) *t.k.h: trckd ldrs: 5th and pushed along st: effrt to dispute 2nd over 1f out: nt qckn* **20/1**

-030 **6** *shd* **Trachonitis (IRE)**[13] 3814 5-10-0 **70**..........RyanMoore 7 71
(J R Jenkins) *dwlt: hld up in 8th: effrt over 2f out: plld out wd and rdn wl over 1f out: kpt on: n.d* **7/1**[3]

4P52 **7** *2 ½* **Rosy Dawn**[14] 3777 4-8-4 **53** ow1..........DebraEngland(7) 4 50
(J J Bridger) *led at modest pce: hdd jst over 2f out: wknd over 1f out* **16/1**

6004 **8** *hd* **Risque Heights**[7] 4007 5-10-0 **70**..........PatCosgrave 9 67
(J R Boyle) *dwlt: hld up in 9th: hanging lft and shuffled along fr over 2f out: nvr on terms* **10/1**

3660 **9** *3 ¾* **City Stable (IRE)**[34] 3114 4-8-6 **55**..........TobyAtkinson(7) 3 46
(M Wigham) *dwlt: hld up in last: shkn up and no prog 3f out* **20/1**

5126 **10** *nk* **Mixing**[21] 3521 7-8-2 **51** oh2..........KierenFox(7) 10 42
(M J Attwater) *trckd ldrs: 4th st: lost pl over 2f out: sn wknd* **25/1**

2m 42.59s (3.69) **Going Correction** -0.05s/f (Good) **10** Ran SP% **114.7**
Speed ratings (Par 103): **85,84,84,83,83 82,81,81,78,78**
toteswingers: 1&2 £7.20, 1&3 £1.60, 2&3 £8.10. CSF £22.09 CT £60.12 TOTE £2.40: £1.40, £3.70, £1.40; EX 29.30.
Owner Miss Gill Quincey **Bred** Mohammad Al-Qatami **Trained** Cotebrook, Cheshire

FOCUS
This moderate handicap was another race run at a steady pace. The form is messy, with the winner value for 2l and back to something like last year's best.
Watson's Bay Official explanation: jockey said colt was denied a clear run
City Stable(IRE) Official explanation: jockey said gelding ran too freely

4236 EDE'S COMMERCIAL MOVER OF THE YEAR H'CAP 7f
8:45 (8:48) (Class 4) (0-85,84) 3-Y-O+ **£5,180** (£1,541; £770; £384) **Stalls** Low

Form RPR
6436 **1** **Spirit Of Sharjah (IRE)**[13] 3825 4-10-0 **84**..........TPO'Shea 6 92+
(Miss J Feilden) *hld up: 6th st: plenty to do 3f out: prog over 2f out: chsd ldng pair over 1f out: hanging lft but styd on wl to ld last 50yds* **8/1**

3064 **2** *½* **Guilded Warrior**[25] 3431 6-9-9 **84**..........Louis-PhilippeBeuzelin(5) 3 91
(W S Kittow) *trckd ldr: clr w him st: rdn to ld narrowly wl over 1f out: kpt on u.p: hdd last 50yds* **6/1**[3]

1602 **3** *1 ¾* **Twilight Star (IRE)**[14] 3770 5-9-7 **77**..........RichardHughes 2 79
(R A Teal) *led: clr w one rival st: narrowly hdd wl over 1f out: kpt on wl and nrly upsides ins fnl f: eased whn hld last 75yds* **11/2**[2]

6440 **4** *1 ½* **Pippbrook Gold**[45] 2775 4-8-10 **69**..........JackMitchell(3) 4 67
(J R Boyle) *in tch: 4th st: chsd clr ldng pair 3f out: no real imp: lost 3rd over 1f out: kpt on* **8/1**

6064 **5** *1 ¾* **Stanley Goodspeed**[7] 4009 6-8-12 **68**..........(vt) RyanMoore 1 62
(J W Hills) *chsd ldng pair to 3f out: hanging and nt qckn after: no imp fnl 2f* **10/3**[1]

-043 **6** *1* **Young Dottie**[26] 3387 3-8-2 **70**..........RossAtkinson(5) 7 61
(P M Phelan) *hld up in 7th: rdn and hanging bdly lft over 2f out: no ch after: plugged on* **10/3**[1]

6525 **7** *3* **Compton's Eleven**[7] 4009 8-8-13 **69**..........SamHitchcott 5 52
(M R Channon) *dwlt: hld up in 5th: nt qckn over 2f out: n.d after* **8/1**

3401 **8** *1 ¾* **Sam's Cross (IRE)**[17] 3673 4-8-12 **68**..........(bt) DaneO'Neill 9 46
(J J Bridger) *hld up in last: shkn up and no prog 3f out* **16/1**

1m 23.15s (-0.15) **Going Correction** -0.05s/f (Good)
WFA 3 from 4yo+ 7lb **8** Ran SP% **115.0**
Speed ratings (Par 105): **98,97,95,93,91 90,87,85**
toteswingers: 1&2 £8.30, 1&3 £3.90, 2&3 £8.40. CSF £55.26 CT £289.65 TOTE £9.90: £2.20, £2.20, £1.90; EX 39.20 Place 6 £28.30, Place 5 £15.91.
Owner A Dee **Bred** Mrs Kathleen Reynolds **Trained** Exning, Suffolk

FOCUS
Few got involved from off the pace in this modest handicap. The winner is rated up a length on this year's best form.
T/Plt: £14.70 to a £1 stake. Pool: £52,712.86. 2,606.25 winning tickets. T/Qpdt: £5.90 to a £1 stake. Pool: £4,576.80. 570.30 winning tickets. JN

3772 FOLKESTONE (R-H)
Thursday, July 23

OFFICIAL GOING: Round course - good to firm (firm in places; 8.0); straight course - firm (good to firm in places; far side 8.5, stands' side 9.1)
Wind: fresh, across Weather: bright, quite breezy

4237 CHRISTINE AND CHERYL - THE BROADSTAIRS BABES APPRENTICE H'CAP 6f
5:55 (5:55) (Class 5) (0-70,70) 3-Y-O **£2,729** (£806; £403) **Stalls** Low

Form RPR
153 **1** **Fyelehk (IRE)**[12] 3859 3-9-6 **59**..........JamesMillman 4 67
(B R Millman) *taken down early: mde all: clr fr 4f out: pushed along over 1f out: kpt on wl: unchal* **2/1**[1]

6532 **2** *2 ¼* **Halaak (USA)**[18] 3663 3-9-3 **63**..........(b) LauraPike(7) 1 64
(D M Simcock) *s.i.s: bhd: clsd and in tch over 3f out: rdn over 1f out: styd on to chse wnr wl ins fnl f: nvr a threat* **5/2**[2]

4601 **3** *1 ¼* **Bold Ring**[12] 3859 3-9-7 **60**..........AlanCreighton 2 57
(E J Creighton) *t.k.h: hld up in tch: rdn and effrt to chse clr wnr over 1f out: kpt on but no imp: lost 2nd wl ins fnl f* **5/1**[3]

4000 **4** *1* **Quick Single (USA)**[6] 4059 3-9-10 **63**..........(vt) MarcHalford 6 57
(P S McEntee) *chsd ldng pair: shkn up over 2f out: drvn and unable qck over 1f out: plugged on same pce* **16/1**

005 **5** *2* **Josiah Bartlett (IRE)**[43] 2810 3-8-6 **48**..........(vt[1]) AmyBaker(3) 3 36
(P S McEntee) *v.s.a: a bhd: rdn and no hdwy 2f out: kpt on ins fnl f: n.d* **20/1**

0060 **6** *1* **Imperial Skylight**[37] 3010 3-9-1 **59**..........MatthewDavies(5) 5 43
(M R Channon) *hld up in tch: effrt and swtchd rt wl over 1f out: sn rdn and no hdwy* **8/1**

505 7 shd **Calypso Girl (IRE)**[40] 2920 3-9-4 **60** RichardEvans(3) 8 44
(P D Evans) *chsd wnr tl over 1f out: wknd u.p ent fnl f* **15/2**
1m 11.1s (-1.60) **Going Correction** -0.325s/f (Firm) 7 Ran SP% **112.1**
Speed ratings (Par 100): **97,94,92,91,88 87,86**
toteswingers: 1&2 £1.70, 1&3 £1.70, 2&3 £2.10. CSF £6.87 CT £19.82 TOTE £2.60: £2.00, £2.70; EX 8.60.
Owner The Links Partnership **Bred** Camogue Stud Ltd **Trained** Kentisbeare, Devon

FOCUS
All seven runners elected to stay stands' side but this weak apprentice riders' handicap was over as a contest some way out as the well supported Fyelehk dominated proceedings from the outset. He was one of four winners on the straight course. Not a race to be too positive about.
Calypso Girl(IRE) Official explanation: jockey said filly was unsuited by the firm ground

4238 TOTESWINGER (S) STKS 6f
6:25 (6:26) (Class 6) 3-Y-0+ **£2,047** (£604; £302) **Stalls** Low

Form RPR
0566 1 **Dynamo Dave (USA)**[18] 3662 4-9-0 41 (b) RobertHavlin 9 53
(M D I Usher) *chsd ldr: wnt clr w ldr over 2f out: led gng wl 2f out: rdn clr over 1f out: drvn ins fnl f: kpt on* **16/1**
4044 2 1 **One More Round (USA)**[7] 3994 11-9-1 65 (b) RichardEvans(5) 6 56
(P D Evans) *stdd s: hld up in rr: hdwy to chse clr ldng pair over 1f out: rdn to chse wnr and edging rt ins fnl f: kpt on but nvr gng to rch wnr* **3/1**[2]
0005 3 2 3/4 **Boldinor**[7] 4023 6-8-9 48 KylieManser(5) 12 41
(M R Bosley) *hld up in last pair: effrt and n.m.r wl over 1f out: sn swtchd rt and rdn: kpt on to go 3rd wl ins fnl f: nvr trbld ldrs* **9/1**
0001 4 1 **Pintano**[19] 3632 4-9-1 51 (t) AmyBaker(5) 1 44
(J M Bradley) *led on stands' rail: pushed clr w wnr over 2f out: rdn and hdd 2f out: sn outpcd by wnr: wl hld whn edgd rt and lost 2 pls ins fnl f* **9/2**
300- 5 4 1/2 **Bluebird Chariot**[327] 5491 6-9-0 45 SteveDrowne 7 23
(J M Bradley) *chsd ldrs: pushed along and outpcd 1/2-way: no ch w ldrs after* **20/1**
0002 6 1 1/4 **Royal Bloom (IRE)**[19] 3632 4-8-9 46 (p) J-PGuillambert 11 14
(J R Fanshawe) *nvr gng wl: in tch but sn pushed along: rdn and outpcd 3f out: wl btn fnl 2f* **7/2**[3]
4040 7 13 **Ridgeway Silver**[48] 2683 3-8-4 58 ChrisCatlin 4 —
(M D I Usher) *chsd ldrs: rdn and outpcd 3f out: wknd wl over 1f out: wl bhd and eased ins fnl f* **11/4**[1]
1m 12.14s (-0.56) **Going Correction** -0.325s/f (Firm)
WFA 3 from 4yo+ 5lb 7 Ran SP% **112.7**
Speed ratings (Par 101): **90,88,85,83,77 76,58**
toteswingers: 1&2 £14.70, 1&3 £13.40, 2&3 £6.70. CSF £61.75 TOTE £13.30: £5.20, £2.70; EX 87.90.There was no bid for the winner.
Owner Donaghey Usher **Bred** Barry Weisbord And Margaret Santulli **Trained** Upper Lambourn, Berks

FOCUS
The five non-runners rendered this a very weak contest even for this grade. Another winner to make most, Dynamo Dave has been rated to his old form.
One More Round(USA) Official explanation: jockey said gelding was not suited by the track
Boldinor Official explanation: jockey said gelding was denied a clear run
Ridgeway Silver Official explanation: jockey said filly hung right throughout

4239 EBF TOTEQUADPOT MAIDEN FILLIES' STKS 7f (S)
7:00 (7:05) (Class 5) 2-Y-0 **£4,209** (£1,252; £625; £312) **Stalls** Low

Form RPR
522 1 **Hasty (IRE)**[29] 3270 2-9-0 0 MichaelHills 8 86
(B W Hills) *mde all and sn crossed to stands' rail: pushed clr w rival over 2f out: kpt on wl fr over 1f out* **4/1**[2]
6 2 1 **Pollenator (IRE)**[30] 3249 2-9-0 0 SteveDrowne 2 85+
(R Hannon) *t.k.h: chsd ldrs: chsd wnr and swtchd rt over 1f out: kpt on but nvr quite pce to chal wnr* **9/4**[1]
5 3 11 **Bandear (IRE)**[24] 3468 2-9-0 0 J-PGuillambert 1 58+
(C E Brittain) *v.s.a: rn green in last pl: hdwy and wnt poor 4th wl over 1f out: plugged on to snatch 3rd nr fin* **50/1**
0 4 nk **Star Twilight**[13] 3820 2-9-0 0 ChrisCatlin 7 55
(D R Lanigan) *t.k.h: chsd wnr: clr w wnr over 2f out: rdn and lost 2nd over 1f out: sn wknd: tired fnl f and lost 3rd nr fin* **25/1**
6 5 10 **Sounds Of Thunder**[20] 3576 2-9-0 0 RobertHavlin 9 30
(H J L Dunlop) *wnt rt s: t.k.h: chsd ldrs tl pushed along and struggling 1/2-way: sn bhd* **33/1**
0 6 8 **Boogie Waltzer**[14] 3767 2-8-9 0 WilliamCarson(5) 3 —
(S C Williams) *in tch towards rr: pushed along and struggling over 3f out: sn wl bhd: t.o* **66/1**
0 7 2 **Goodwood Diva**[34] 3101 2-9-0 0 JimCrowley 6 —
(J L Dunlop) *a towards rr: rdn and lost tch over 3f out: wl bhd after: t.o* **12/1**
8 8 **Montelissima (IRE)** 2-9-0 0 LDettori 4 —
(E A L Dunlop) *wnt rt s and s.i.s: in tch on outer tl 1/2-way: sn bhd: t.o and eased fnl f* **8/1**[3]
1m 25.47s (-1.83) **Going Correction** -0.325s/f (Firm) 8 Ran SP% **79.8**
Speed ratings (Par 91): **97,95,83,82,71 62,60,50**
toteswingers: 1&2 £1.70, 1&3 £9.00, 2&3 Not won. CSF £6.21 TOTE £2.50: £1.20, £1.10, £10.10; EX 6.20.
Owner Richard Morecombe & James Netherthorpe **Bred** Mrs C S Acham **Trained** Lambourn, Berks
■ Interakt was withdrawn (7/4, unruly in stalls). R4 applies, deduct 35p in the £.

FOCUS
The withdrawal of Interakt at the start weakened this fillies' maiden significantly and the front two ended up coming a long way clear suggesting those in behind aren't very good at this stage and the form isn't strong. The first two were well placed near the rail throughout.

NOTEBOOK
Hasty(IRE) isn't anything out of the ordinary but had the best form in the book and was able to make it fourth time lucky having stayed on well up the stands' rail to hold off Pollenator. She saw this trip out well, handled the quick ground well and looks booked for a mark somewhere in the low 70s for nurseries now. (op 2-1)
Pollenator(IRE) attracted plenty of market support so was clearly expected to step up on her Newbury maiden form. She did so, chasing the winner all the way home, drawing miles clear of the rest and there is clearly a similar race in her granted just normal progress. (op 6-1)
Bandear(IRE) stayed on to snatch third from Star Twilight and, given she is bred to want a much stiffer test of stamina than this, she didn't shape at all badly. She looks one to keep an eye on for handicaps.
Star Twilight was front rank early but she dropped away tamely and hasn't really improved on her ordinary debut. (op 28-1)
Boogie Waltzer Official explanation: jockey said filly was unsuited by the firm ground

Montelissima(IRE) Official explanation: jockey said filly lost its action

4240 TOTETRIFECTA H'CAP 7f (S)
7:35 (7:36) (Class 6) (0-65,65) 3-Y-0 **£2,047** (£604; £302) **Stalls** Low

Form RPR
2505 1 **Bea Menace (USA)**[19] 3630 3-9-7 65 (b[1]) JimCrowley 1 73
(P F I Cole) *mde all: gng best over 2f out: drvn and styd on wl fnl f* **9/2**[3]
0025 2 2 **Sermons Mount (USA)**[5] 4082 3-8-9 53 RobertHavlin 4 56
(Mouse Hamilton-Fairley) *stdd s and slowly away: hld up in rr: hdwy on stands' rail 3f out: chsd wnr wl over 1f out: drvn and no imp fnl f* **9/2**[3]
1041 3 7 **Cavendish Road (IRE)**[23] 3476 3-9-5 63 DarryllHolland 7 47
(W R Muir) *chsd ldr tl wl over 2f out: sn rdn: chsd ldng pair and drvn over 1f out: wl btn1f out: wknd fnl f: jst hld 3rd pl* **9/4**[1]
0034 4 shd **Kyle Of Bute**[17] 3672 3-8-4 48 AdrianMcCarthy 9 32
(J L Dunlop) *bmpd s: a towards rr: rdn and struggling 1/2-way: wnt poor 4th over 1f out: plugged on and pressing for 3rd on post: nvr nr ldrs* **7/1**
0026 5 2 1/4 **Native Dame (IRE)**[3] 4155 3-8-3 52 (b) WilliamCarson(5) 13 30
(Edgar Byrne) *chsd ldrs tl 3f out: sn struggling and wl btn* **14/1**
-000 6 3 3/4 **Suakin Dancer (IRE)**[20] 3580 3-8-9 53 SteveDrowne 12 21
(H Morrison) *stdd s: a in rr: rdn and toiling 1/2-way: nvr a factor* **16/1**
-004 7 7 **Dicey Affair**[13] 3815 3-9-3 61 LDettori 2 10
(G L Moore) *in tch: hdwy to chse clr wnr wl over 2f out tl wl over 1f out: wknd qckly* **4/1**[2]
05-6 8 6 **Highland Starlight (USA)**[20] 3569 3-9-7 65 ChrisCatlin 8 —
(C G Cox) *wnt rt and bmpd rival s: sn chsng ldrs: lost pl qckly 1/2-way: sn wl bhd: t.o* **25/1**
500- P **Daily Planet (IRE)**[227] 7607 3-7-11 46 oh1 (p) AmyBaker(5) 5 —
(B W Duke) *in tch tl burst blood vessel and lost tch rapidly wl over 3f out: eventually p.u and dismntd wl ins fnl f* **66/1**
1m 25.32s (-1.98) **Going Correction** -0.325s/f (Firm) 9 Ran SP% **117.5**
Speed ratings (Par 98): **98,95,87,87,85 80,72,65,—**
toteswingers: 1&2 £4.00, 1&3 £1.90, 2&3 £1.80. CSF £25.59 CT £57.68 TOTE £6.70: £2.20, £1.90, £1.20; EX 24.70.
Owner The Comic Strip Heroes **Bred** Stuart McPhee **Trained** Whatcombe, Oxon

FOCUS
Another poor contest in which few made any serious impact. Another front-running winner, with the first pair clear.
Dicey Affair Official explanation: jockey said filly ran flat
Daily Planet(IRE) Official explanation: jockey said gelding bled from the nose

4241 TOTEEXACTA H'CAP 1m 4f
8:05 (8:06) (Class 6) (0-65,65) 3-Y-0 **£2,047** (£604; £302) **Stalls** Low

Form RPR
-001 1 **Halfway House**[23] 3474 3-9-7 65 ChrisCatlin 4 79+
(M L W Bell) *stdd s: hld up wl off the pce in last pl: hdwy over 3f out: chsd ldr 2f out: rdn to ld over 1f out: styd on wl and clr fnl f* **4/1**[2]
0032 2 5 **Persian Memories (IRE)**[24] 3462 3-9-7 65 LDettori 1 70
(J L Dunlop) *awkward leaving stalls: racd wl off the pce in last trio: rdn and hdwy to chse ldr over 2f out: led over 2f out: drvn and hdd over 1f out: no ch w wnr fnl f* **6/4**[1]
0530 3 4 1/2 **Gulf President**[6] 4039 3-9-4 62 DarryllHolland 7 59
(M R Channon) *reminders sn after s: racd wl off the pce in last pair: hdwy over 2f out: c wd and rdn 2f out: wnt modest 3rd ins fnl f: nvr trbld ldrs* **8/1**
2403 4 nk **Saborido (USA)**[6] 4071 3-9-5 63 JimCrowley 2 59
(Mrs A J Perrett) *nvr gng wl and sn niggled along: racd off the pce in midfield: rdn and dropped to last 3f out: no prog and wl hld 2f out: sme hdwy u.p fnl f: nvr nr ldrs* **13/2**
-060 5 3 1/4 **Morning Calm**[20] 3575 3-9-1 59 (v) SteveDrowne 8 50
(R Charlton) *chsd ldr: j. path 9f out: lost 2nd and rdn over 2f out: sn nt clr run and swtchd lft: struggling whn hmpd 2f out: sn wl btn* **5/1**[3]
2034 6 nk **Persian Tomcat (IRE)**[14] 3776 3-7-12 49 MatthewCosham(7) 5 40
(Miss J Feilden) *dwlt: sn in midfield: n.m.r on inner over 3f out tl 2f out: sn rdn and btn* **11/2**
5000 7 9 **Count On Guest**[25] 3427 3-9-1 59 AdrianMcCarthy 3 35
(G G Margarson) *prom in main gp: rdn and clsd 3f out: wknd u.p 2f out and wl btn after* **25/1**
0006 8 2 1/4 **Royal Arthur**[17] 3697 3-7-11 46 oh1 (b) AmyBaker(5) 6 19
(L A Dace) *led and sn wl clr: stl 10 l ld 3f out: wknd qckly and hdd over 2f out: sn dropped out and bhd* **66/1**
2m 37.69s (-3.21) **Going Correction** -0.15s/f (Firm) 8 Ran SP% **121.8**
Speed ratings (Par 98): **104,100,97,97,95 95,89,87**
toteswingers: 1&2 £1.50, 1&3 £10.80, 2&3 £5.70. CSF £11.20 CT £47.72 TOTE £4.10: £1.90, £1.10, £3.70; EX 7.90.
Owner Ferguson, Le Gassick, Dawson & Mercer **Bred** Usk Valley Stud **Trained** Newmarket, Suffolk

FOCUS
This was run at a strong pace and the form looks fair for the grade and sound overall. The winner is unexposed and a big improver.
Royal Arthur Official explanation: jockey said gelding ran too free

4242 TOTEPOOL H'CAP 1m 1f 149y
8:35 (8:35) (Class 4) (0-85,85) 3-Y-0 **£4,727** (£1,406; £702) **Stalls** Centre

Form RPR
-041 1 **Sequillo**[38] 2982 3-8-12 76 JimCrowley 3 79
(R Hannon) *hld up in 3rd pl: rdn 2f out: hdwy between horses and drvn to ld ins fnl f: idled and edgd lft towards fin* **3/1**[2]
-311 2 1 **Yirga**[23] 3489 3-9-7 85 (t) LDettori 1 86
(Saeed Bin Suroor) *trckd ldr: rdn and pressed ldr over 2f out: drvn 2f out: led narrowly ent fnl f: hdd and no ex ins fnl f* **2/5**[1]
6006 3 nk **Equipe De Nuit**[19] 3644 3-8-2 71 WilliamCarson(5) 4 71
(S C Williams) *led: shkn up and hung lft bnd jst over 2f out: rdn wl over 1f out: hdd ent fnl f: kpt on same pce after* **8/1**[3]
2m 4.27s (-0.63) **Going Correction** -0.15s/f (Firm) 3 Ran SP% **107.5**
Speed ratings (Par 102): **96,95,94**
CSF £4.84 TOTE £2.70; EX 5.80 Place 6 £51.61, Place 5 £37.53.
Owner White Beech Farm **Bred** Redmyre Bloodstock And S Hillen **Trained** East Everleigh, Wilts

FOCUS
A three-runner race, and the fact the trio finished on top of each other suggests the gallop was not strong. Messy form.
T/Plt: £40.80 to a £1 stake. Pool: £46,198.67. 826.47 winning tickets. T/Qpdt: £6.90 to a £1 stake. Pool: £4,329.84. 459.70 winning tickets. SP

4207 SANDOWN (R-H)

Thursday, July 23

OFFICIAL GOING: Good to firm (round 9.1; sprint 8.8)

Wind: Moderate across Weather: Bright intervals

4243 EUROPEAN BREEDERS' FUND MAIDEN STKS 5f 6y

2:10 (2:12) (Class 4) 2-Y-O **£5,180** (£1,541; £770; £384) **Stalls** High

Form RPR

1 **Final Answer** 2-9-3 0 .... RichardMullen 9 80+
(E S McMahon) *mde all at mod pce first f: qckrd fr over 1f out: in command thrght fnl f: comf* **7/2**[2]

0 2 1 ¼ **Excellent Day (IRE)**[13] 3820 2-8-12 0 .... DarryllHolland 10 71
(M R Channon) *trckd ldrs: rdn to chse wnr over 1f out: styd on thrght fnl f but a comf hld* **6/1**

05 3 3 ½ **Rockabilly Rebel**[10] 3920 2-9-3 0 .... MichaelHills 12 63
(B W Hills) *hld up in tch: pushed along and hdwy over 1f out: styd on fnl f but nvr gng pce to trble ldng duo* **9/1**

4 4 ½ **Tarita (IRE)**[62] 2238 2-8-12 0 .... RichardHughes 4 56
(R Hannon) *chsd wnr tl over 1f out: styd on same pce fnl f* **11/2**[3]

303 5 ¾ **Thomas Baines (USA)**[84] 1630 2-9-3 0 .... JimmyFortune 5 58
(M L W Bell) *t.k.h: in tch: pushed along and sme prog over 2f out: rdn and no imp ins fnl f and hung lft nr fin* **7/1**

5 6 ¾ **Ballachulish**[28] 3317 2-9-3 0 .... DaneO'Neill 6 56
(H Candy) *chsd ldrs: rdn 2f out: outpcd appr fnl f* **16/1**

7 nk **Autocracy** 2-9-3 0 .... RyanMoore 2 55
(W J Haggas) *chsd ldrs: drvn and outpcd 1/2-way: n.d after* **11/4**[1]

8 2 **The Strig** 2-9-3 0 .... SteveDrowne 3 47
(S C Williams) *s.i.s: in rr tl sme prog fnl f* **100/1**

9 2 ¼ **Recette** 2-8-12 0 .... RobertHavlin 7 34
(R Ingram) *s.i.s: a towards rr* **33/1**

0 10 4 ½ **Securitisation (IRE)**[21] 3546 2-9-3 0 .... TPQueally 1 23
(B J Curley) *s.i.s: a in rr* **100/1**

11 nk **Old Devil Moon (IRE)** 2-9-3 0 .... JamesDoyle 8 22
(T G Mills) *sn outpcd* **12/1**

62.00 secs (0.40) **Going Correction** -0.025s/f (Good) 11 Ran SP% **119.6**

Speed ratings (Par 96): **95,93,87,86,85 84,83,80,76,69 69**

toteswingers: 1&2 £7.10, 1&3 £9.40, 2&3 £10.60. CSF £25.32 TOTE £3.90: £1.70, £2.40, £3.10; EX 27.10.

Owner J C Fretwell **Bred** Wood Hall Stud Limited **Trained** Lichfield, Staffs

FOCUS

The ground had dried out overnight so that there was no 'Good in places' in the official description. An interesting sprint maiden with several newcomers having decent pedigrees. The winner is the type to do better although he was favoured by racing towards the stands' rail.

NOTEBOOK

Final Answer ◆ knew his job first time and, breaking quickly from the stalls, made all the running. He soon got to the favoured far rail and was always in command from that point. A half-brother to several sprinters, he looks to have a bright future and, although he has no major entries at present, should be stepping up in grade before long, with the Roses Stakes at York offering a feasible opportunity, and the Flying Childers a possible along with the Mill Reef. (op 9-2 tchd 3-1)

Excellent Day(IRE) is bred to stay further and improved considerably on her debut, chasing the winner throughout the last furlong without making much impression but coming clear of the rest. She was wearing small bandages around her front legs, which came loose in the closing stages but it did not appear to hamper her. She is entered in the Lowther Stakes, so is obviously well regarded and, although that might be a little ambitious at this stage, she should have no difficulty getting off the mark. (op 7-1)

Rockabilly Rebel put up his best effort so far on this drop in trip. He had the best draw and was never far away, but had no chance with the first two and may be better off in nurseries, for which he now qualifies. (op 15-2)

Tarita(IRE) had not run since making her debut over 6f in May. She showed plenty of early speed from her low draw before tiring in the last furlong. (op 7-2 tchd 10-3)

Thomas Baines(USA) was the most experienced runner in the line-up but was another reappearing after a break. Despite being gelded in the interim, he was quite keen early on and could only stay on at the one pace in the closing stages. (op 13-2)

Ballachulish improved on his debut effort and should do better once handicapped. (op 25-1 tchd 33-1)

Autocracy, a half-brother to several good winners, most notably Group 1 winner Reverence. The stable had won this last season with Triple Aspect, who was also making his debut and went on to win at Group 3 level but Autocracy was drawn on the outside of the field and never reached the front rank. He looked as if the experience will not be lost on him and better can be expected in time. (op 4-1)

The Strig was coltish in the paddock before this debut and then missed the break and had to race wide early. In the circumstances this was not a bad effort. (op 80-1 tchd 200-1 in a place)

4244 THE LUBRICATORS H'CAP 5f 6y

2:45 (2:47) (Class 4) (0-80,80) 3-Y-O **£4,857** (£1,445; £722; £360) **Stalls** High

Form RPR

0-03 1 **Golden Destiny (IRE)**[14] 3787 3-9-3 76 .... (p) JimmyFortune 3 83
(P J Makin) *broke wl: stdd: hung lft and reminder after 2f: drvn over 1f out and qcknd to ld jst ins fnl f: rdn out* **7/1**[3]

-213 2 1 **Strictly**[33] 3166 3-9-7 **80** .... RyanMoore 1 84+
(Sir Michael Stoute) *in rr: sn hanging rt: nt clr run through hanging rt 2f out: swtchd lft and hdwy over 1f out: chsd wnr ins fnl f and stl edging rt: fnd no ex* **11/8**[1]

3136 3 1 ¼ **Sharpened Edge**[12] 3845 3-9-7 **80** .... SteveDrowne 5 79
(B Palling) *sn disputing ld: rdn 1/2-way: hdd jst ins fnl f: sn one pce* **13/8**[2]

2414 4 3 **Cecily**[80] 1727 3-9-3 **76** .... PatCosgrave 2 64
(Sir Mark Prescott) *sn disputing ld: styd chalng and rdn 1/2-way: stl upsides wl over 1f out: wknd ins fnl f* **11/1**

021 5 2 ¼ **Chris's Jem**[84] 1617 3-8-9 **68** .... RichardHughes 4 48+
(J R Jenkins) *trckd ldrs: hdwy and nt clr run over 1f out: n.m.r jst ins fnl f: eased whn hld* **12/1**

61.13 secs (-0.47) **Going Correction** -0.025s/f (Good) 5 Ran SP% **108.7**

Speed ratings (Par 102): **102,100,98,93,90**

CSF £16.82 TOTE £8.10: £2.60, £1.10; EX 17.50.

Owner H J W Davies P Spencer-Jones M H Holland **Bred** Yeomanstown Stud **Trained** Ogbourne Maisey, Wilts

FOCUS

A small field consisting of fillies for this three-year-old handicap but the time was 0.87 secs faster than the opening juvenile contest. The winner is rated close to her best.

Chris's Jem Official explanation: jockey said filly was denied a clear run

4245 WEATHERBYS BLOODSTOCK INSURANCE STAR STKS (LISTED RACE) 7f 16y

3:20 (3:20) (Class 1) 2-Y-O

£17,031 (£6,456; £3,231; £1,611; £807; £405) **Stalls** High

Form RPR

10 1 **Mudaaraah**[26] 3396 2-8-12 0 .... RHills 1 101+
(J L Dunlop) *s.i.s: hld up in rr: str run on outside fr over 1f out: led fnl 110yds: r.o strly* **7/1**[3]

31 2 ½ **Middle Club**[13] 3810 2-8-12 0 .... RyanMoore 3 99
(R Hannon) *in rr but in tch: hdwy on outside over 2f out: slt ld appr fnl f: rdn and hdd fnl 110yds: kpt on* **9/2**[2]

010 3 ½ **Bikini Babe (IRE)**[33] 3138 2-8-12 0 .... GregFairley 6 98
(M Johnston) *trckd ldrs: t.k.h early: rdn and outpcd over 2f out: rallied to chal appr fnl f: sn edgd rt: nt qckn fnl 110yds* **12/1**

01 4 1 ¼ **Gallic Star (IRE)**[40] 2914 2-8-12 0 .... DarryllHolland 7 98+
(M R Channon) *in tch: nt clr run fr ins fnl 2f tl appr fnl f whn swtchd rt and styd on strly ins fnl f: fin wl: nt rcvr* **7/4**[1]

1105 5 3 ¼ **Crown (IRE)**[15] 3748 2-8-12 0 .... RichardHughes 8 87
(R Hannon) *in rr: hdwy whn briefly n.m.r appr fnl 2f: shkn up and kpt on fnl f but nvr in contention* **8/1**

313 6 hd **Lady Springbank (IRE)**[21] 3528 2-8-12 0 .... JimCrowley 5 86
(K R Burke) *t.k.h: trckd ldr after 1f: drvn to take slt ld ins fnl 2f: hdd appr fnl f: wknd ins fnl f* **18/1**

1 7 3 ¼ **Bahati (IRE)**[54] 2494 2-8-12 0 .... TPQueally 4 78
(J G Portman) *t.k.h: chsd ldrs: rdn and stl green 2f out: sn wknd* **15/2**

41 8 2 ¼ **Mistic Magic (IRE)**[30] 3249 2-8-12 0 .... JimmyFortune 2 73
(P F I Cole) *sn led: rdn 3f out: hdd ins fnl 2f: btn whn hmpd on rail jst ins fnl f* **10/1**

1m 28.86s (-0.64) **Going Correction** -0.075s/f (Good) 8 Ran SP% **112.0**

Speed ratings (Par 102): **100,99,98,97,93 93,89,87**

toteswingers: 1&2 £6.30, 1&3 £14.30, 2&3 £7.80. CSF £36.77 TOTE £8.00: £2.20, £1.70, £2.80; EX 43.00.

Owner Hamdan Al Maktoum **Bred** Shadwell Estate Company Limited **Trained** Arundel, W Sussex

■ Stewards' Enquiry : Greg Fairley one-day ban: careless riding (Aug 6)

FOCUS

Not a great renewal of this Listed contest but all the runners were previous winners. A race that normally falls to one of the major yards; John Dunlop had been responsible for three previous winners this century and increased his tally. The form could be rated around 4lb higher.

NOTEBOOK

Mudaaraah ◆, a winner on her debut from two subsequent winners at Folkestone, she had reportedly been suffering from a respiratory infection when beaten in a Listed race last time. Up in trip this time, she was held up from her outside draw and got a clear run down the outside in what was a somewhat rough race. There are no definite plans for her but her trainer mentioned the May Hill so might have that in his mind. (op 11-2 tchd 15-2)

Middle Club, who built on her debut third behind Mistic Magic when scoring at Newbury over this trip, was another held up and her rider was the first of those at the back to make a forward move. She got to the front but drifted right in doing so, doing no favours to Bahati, who was beginning to struggle at the time, and reducing the space for those nearer the rail. She kept on under pressure but was comfortably held by the winner. (op 5-1 tchd 6-1)

Bikini Babe(IRE) appeared to be a little unlucky as she failed to get the early lead - which she had done when scoring here last month - and then had to wait for an opening before staying on well under pressure. She has some good entries but looks a real galloper and the step up to a mile will be in her favour. (op 16-1)

Gallic Star(IRE) ◆ was probably the most unlucky. She was settled off the pace but moved onto the heels of the leaders going well over 2f out, only to be denied any sort of run until it was too late. Once in the open she did run on and would not have been far away with a clear passage. She can be given another chance. Official explanation: jockey said filly was denied a clear run (tchd 13-8 and 15-8 and 2-1 in places)

Crown(IRE) was held up in the rear but was beginning her challenge when caught up in the backwash of the interference. She stayed on again at the end but was not close enough to say she would have played a major role. She had now been held in three starts at Group and Listed level and does not look up to this class. She would be an ideal type for a sales race but does not appear to have any suitable entries. (op 6-1 tchd 11-2)

Lady Springbank(IRE) showed up early but was quite keen and not surprisingly paid the penalty in the closing stages. (op 16-1 tchd 20-1)

Bahati(IRE) had won on her debut in May but had been absent since. She was another to race prominently, and quite keenly, and was one of the first beaten. (op 10-1 tchd 7-1)

Mistic Magic(IRE) made the early running but could not sustain the pace and was on the retreat when hampered by the third over a furlong out. (op 11-1 tchd 14-1)

4246 LEATHERHEAD MAIDEN STKS 1m 14y

3:55 (3:57) (Class 5) 3-4-Y-O **£3,238** (£963; £481; £240) **Stalls** High

Form RPR

04-0 1 **Directorship**[68] 2074 3-9-2 0 .... RichardKingscote 6 83+
(P R Chamings) *hld up in rr: stdy hdwy on outside over 2f out: drvn to ld fnl 110yds: styd on strly* **14/1**

2-43 2 ½ **Poyle Meg**[29] 3278 3-8-11 75 .... (p) JimCrowley 5 77
(R M Beckett) *chsd ldrs: rdn 2f out: styd on to take slt ld jst ins fnl f: hdd and nt qckn fnl 110yds* **17/2**

-523 3 3 ½ **Ithinkbest**[34] 3120 3-9-2 80 .... RyanMoore 11 74
(Sir Michael Stoute) *sn led: rdn along 3f out: narrowly hdd 2f out: styd chalng and stl ev ch 1f out: outpcd ins fnl f* **15/8**[1]

4 nk **El Libertador (USA)**[327] 5523 3-9-2 0 .... StephenCarson 3 73
(E A Wheeler) *trckd ldrs: led gng wl 2f out: shkn up and hdd jst ins fnl f: wknd cl home* **50/1**

40 5 4 **Count Lucien**[40] 2930 3-9-2 0 .... JimmyFortune 12 64
(J H M Gosden) *chsd ldrs: rdn along over 2f out: wknd fnl f* **11/2**[3]

0 6 1 ½ **Bengal Tiger**[68] 2082 3-9-2 0 .... NeilChalmers 8 61+
(A M Balding) *in rr: pushed along 3f out: styd on fr over 1f out: gng on cl home* **8/1**

60-1 7 1 ¼ **Altimatum (USA)**[18] 3660 3-9-2 76 .... RichardHughes 10 58
(P F I Cole) *chsd ldrs: rdn 3f out: wknd appr fnl f* **7/2**[2]

8 hd **Ultimate Respect (USA)** 3-9-2 0 .... GregFairley 1 57
(M Johnston) *in tch: rdn along over 3f out: no ch fnl 2f* **11/2**[3]

0 9 1 **Through The Forest (USA)**[17] 3696 3-8-11 0 .... AdamKirby 2 50+
(W R Swinburn) *in rr: pushed along 3f out: mod prog fnl f* **25/1**

0-5 10 5 **Major Value**[31] 3221 3-9-2 0 .... IanMongan 9 43
(C G Cox) *chsd ldr over 5f: hung rt and sn wknd* **50/1**

05 11 10 **Lady Lam**[20] 3590 3-8-6 0 .... MatthewDavies(5) 4 15
(George Baker) *a in rr* **100/1**

12 3 1/2 **Lilly Royal (IRE)** 3-8-11 0 .... SteveDrowne 7 7
(B Palling) *uns rdr bef s: a in rr* **50/1**
1m 43.14s (-0.16) **Going Correction** -0.075s/f (Good) 12 Ran SP% **126.8**
Speed ratings (Par 103): **97,96,93,92,88 87,85,85,84,79 69,66**
toteswingers: 1&2 £12.90, 1&3 £10.40, 2&3 £4.40. CSF £132.79 TOTE £19.70: £3.90, £2.30, £1.30; EX 91.10.
Owner Mrs Lyon, Mrs Hayton & Exors Mrs Jenkins **Bred** Mrs D O Joly **Trained** Baughurst, Hants

FOCUS
A fair maiden and a number of runners attracted market support, but it fell to an outsider. There are mixed messages from the form, which has been rated at face value.

4247 WISECALL CLAIMS ASSISTANCE H'CAP 1m 2f 7y
4:30 (4:33) (Class 3) (0-90,89) 3-Y-O+ **£7,771** (£2,312; £1,155; £577) **Stalls High**

Form RPR
-221 1 **Dancourt (IRE)**[15] 3752 3-8-12 **83** .... RyanMoore 3 97
(Sir Michael Stoute) *hld up in tch: pushed along and hdwy on outside over 2f out: led wl over 1f out: drvn out ins fnl f* **8/11**[1]
1050 2 4 **Press The Button (GER)**[47] 2706 6-10-0 **89** .... PatCosgrave 7 95
(J R Boyle) *led: 3 l clr 4f out: pushed along and kpt advantage fr over 2f out tl hdd wl over 1f out: sn no ch w wnr but kpt on wl for 2nd* **16/1**
4101 3 1 1/4 **Summer Winds**[27] 3361 4-9-8 **83** ....(b) JimmyFortune 6 87
(T G Mills) *racd in 2nd 2f: styd chsng ldrs: rdn fr 3f out: styd on same pce fr over 1f out* **22/1**
-303 4 1 3/4 **Wiggy Smith**[27] 3361 10-9-5 **80** .... DaneO'Neill 4 80
(H Candy) *in tch: drvn along fr 3f out: styd on fr over 1f out but nvr gng pce to get into contention* **16/1**
1-42 5 2 **Barliffey (IRE)**[21] 3526 4-8-12 **73** ....(v) DarryllHolland 8 69
(D J Coakley) *hld up in rr: sme hdwy and pushed along 2f out: edgd rt and lft over 1f out: kpt on cl home* **8/1**[3]
5322 6 1 1/4 **Hallstatt (IRE)**[7] 4008 3-8-9 **80** .... RHills 5 74
(M Johnston) *chsd ldr after 2f: rdn and no imp 3f out: wknd qckly over 1f out* **10/3**[2]
400- 7 8 **Rayhani (USA)**[283] 6698 6-9-12 **87** .... AndrewMullen 2 65
(D Nicholls) *stdd s: a in rr* **16/1**
2m 7.87s (-2.63) **Going Correction** -0.075s/f (Good)
WFA 3 from 4yo+ 10lb 7 Ran SP% **114.1**
Speed ratings (Par 107): **107,103,102,101,99 98,92**
toteswingers: 1&2 £4.80, 1&3 £3.00, 2&3 £13.50. CSF £15.01 CT £146.61 TOTE £1.80: £1.20, £4.40; EX 17.90.
Owner Ballymacoll Stud **Bred** Ballymacoll Stud Farm Ltd **Trained** Newmarket, Suffolk

FOCUS
A decent handicap that is usually won by a horse rated in the high-70s to low-80s which included the majority of this year's runners. The punters only wanted to know about the first three in the betting and the favourite scored in decisive fashion, showing big improvement. Solid form.

NOTEBOOK
Dancourt(IRE) ◆ had won in good style on his previous start and followed up in similar fashion on his first try over this far. He sat off the pace before making his effort down the outside and, once he got to the front, the result was never in doubt. He ran on strongly and looks more than capable of picking up a high-class handicap if he keeps progressing, with the Cambridgeshire looking the obvious target. (op 5-6 tchd 4-6 and 10-11 in places and evens in a place)
Press The Button(GER) made the running and did his best to expose any stamina flaws in the favourite. He held off a couple of challengers before the winner arrived on the scene and kept galloping, despite having no chance with that rival. (op 12-1 tchd 20-1)
Summer Winds has improved for the fitting of blinkers and put behind him a poor effort when last running over course and distance. He was up in grade here and the impression is that his improvement has not plateaued yet. (op 16-1 tchd 25-1)
Wiggy Smith was 4lb better off with today's third on previous running but is a veteran now and a drop in grade may offer his best chance of winning again. (op 12-1)
Barliffey(IRE) was always out the back and never got involved, although he did stay on late. (op 9-1 tchd 13-2)
Hallstatt(IRE) chased the leaders for much of the way and had his chance but faded rather tamely. This was disappointing but he was also well beaten on his only other try on a right-handed track, so he may prove better suited to going the other way around. (op 9-2 tchd 5-1)

4248 TEDDINGTON H'CAP 1m 6f
5:00 (5:01) (Class 3) (0-95,91) 3-Y-O **£7,771** (£2,312; £1,155; £577) **Stalls High**

Form RPR
-121 1 **King Of Wands**[29] 3276 3-9-3 **86** .... RyanMoore 5 103+
(J L Dunlop) *hld up in tch: hdwy whn nt clr run ins fnl 3f: swtchd lft over 2f out: sn drvn and qcknd to ld wl over 1f out: clr whn edgd lft cl home: easily* **6/4**[1]
3113 2 8 **Final Victory**[29] 3280 3-9-2 **85** .... DarryllHolland 1 90
(A M Balding) *in tch: hdwy 3f out: drvn to ld over 2f out: hdd wl over 1f out and sn no ch w wnr but kpt on for clr 2nd* **10/3**[3]
3130 3 5 **Clowance House**[34] 3090 3-9-7 **90** .... DaneO'Neill 3 88
(R Charlton) *led: rdn and hdd 3f out: wknd fr 2f out* **9/4**[2]
-133 4 3/4 **Cry For The Moon (USA)**[29] 3276 3-8-12 **81** .... JimCrowley 6 78
(Mrs A J Perrett) *trckd ldr: chal over 5f out: led 3f out: hdd over 2f out: wknd qckly fnl f* **13/2**
3m 3.32s (-3.28) **Going Correction** -0.075s/f (Good) 4 Ran SP% **107.2**
Speed ratings (Par 104): **106,101,98,98**
toteswingers: 1&2 £3.10. CSF £6.54 TOTE £2.30; EX 5.80 Place 6: £89.80 Place 5: £26.31..
Owner Normandie Stud Ltd **Bred** Normandie Stud Ltd **Trained** Arundel, W Sussex

FOCUS
A decent and quite a tight staying handicap for three-year-olds, although the field was cut by a third due to withdrawals. It was a bit tactical, but the form has been taken at face value.

NOTEBOOK
King Of Wands ◆, whose trainer had been responsible for two recent winners, was well backed to make it three. He duly did so in runaway fashion, overcoming being kept in a pocket by the runner-up halfway up the straight to race clear once switched outside. He looks a really progressive sort and the Melrose Handicap at York seems an obvious target next. (op 5-4 tchd 13-8)
Final Victory is another who has progressed well but had a bit to find with the winner on early season form, and was trying this trip for the first time. He was the only one to pose any sort of threat to the winner, but in the end was well held and he might be best dropping back to 1m4f. (tchd 11-4)
Clowance House had previously looked short of pace at 1m4f and appeared not to stay 2m last time, so this intermediate trip looked a reasonable option. He made the running but could not pick up when the others quickened, before galloping on again. He gives the impression that he lacks a change of gear and may have been better going faster. A similar type to useful juvenile hurdler Franchoek, it would not be surprising if he went jumping this winter. (op 11-4 tchd 2-1)
Cry For The Moon(USA) had twice been beaten over this trip by today's winner but was ridden positively, taking on the third early in the straight but then fading. A big, long-striding colt, he may be worth trying from the front back over 1m4f, but is the sort the jumping fraternity will be coveting. (op 15-2)
T/Plt: £94.40 to a £1 stake. Pool: £64,915.14. 501.87 winning tickets. T/Qpdt: £9.20 to a £1 stake. Pool: £4,951.00. 394.46 winning tickets. ST

4249 - (Foreign Racing) - See Raceform Interactive

4027 LEOPARDSTOWN (L-H)
Thursday, July 23
OFFICIAL GOING: Yielding to soft (soft in places)

4250a KOREAN RACING AUTHORITY TYROS STKS (GROUP 3) 7f
6:30 (6:31) 2-Y-O **£39,186** (£11,497; £5,477; £1,866)

RPR
1 **Cape Blanco (IRE)**[43] 2832 2-9-1 .... JMurtagh 1 106+
(A P O'Brien, Ire) *sn led: rdn clr over 1f out: eased ins fnl 50yds: impressive* **1/2**[1]
2 3 1/2 **Marfach (USA)**[17] 3698 2-9-1 ....(p) KJManning 3 95
(J S Bolger, Ire) *dwlt: sn 4th: rdn into 3rd 2f out: kpt on same pce fr over 1f out: styd on to 2nd on line* **12/1**
3 shd **Perfect Symmetry (IRE)**[22] 3514 2-9-1 97 .... KLatham 5 95
(G M Lyons, Ire) *towards rr early: hdwy to 3rd 1/2-way: 2nd 3f out: rdn 2f out: no imp on ldr over 1f out: kpt on same pce: lost 2nd on line* **6/1**[3]
4 2 1/2 **Kingdom Of Munster (IRE)**[58] 2367 2-9-1 .... JAHeffernan 2 89
(A P O'Brien, Ire) *chsd ldr in 2nd: pushed along in 3rd 3f out: rdn in 4th 2f out: no imp and kpt on same pce* **9/1**
5 nk **Miracle Match (IRE)**[29] 3285 2-9-1 .... FMBerry 4 88
(Mrs John Harrington, Ire) *chsd ldrs in 3rd early: towards rr 1/2-way: rdn and no imp 2f out: kpt on one pce* **5/1**[2]
1m 32.73s (4.03) **Going Correction** +0.425s/f (Yiel) 5 Ran SP% **115.3**
Speed ratings: **93,89,88,86,85**
CSF £8.44 TOTE £1.40: £1.10, £5.80; DF 8.70.
Owner D Smith, Mrs J Magnier, M Tabor **Bred** Jack Ronan & Des Vere Hunt Far **Trained** Ballydoyle, Co Tipperary

FOCUS
The winner was impressive in the end but did enjoy the run of the race.

NOTEBOOK
Cape Blanco(IRE), all the rage in the betting, kept his unbeaten record intact by making virtually all the running. He had opened his account narrowly in a Fairyhouse maiden over this trip when he looked green and the benefit of that initial effort was clear to see here. He soon established a lead and the outcome was never in doubt despite some concerns beforehand about the ground for the son of Galileo. Quoted at 25-1 with Boylesports for next year's 2,000 Guineas, his trainer Aidan O'Brien described him as a lovely moving horse who is in all those races, with the Futurity mentioned as a possible target. (op 8/13)
Marfach(USA)'s win in testing ground at Roscommon had worked out well afterwards and he plugged on in the straight to snatch second in the dying strides. Although he handled this ground, he'll probably be more effective on a sounder surface. (op 12/1 tchd 14/1)
Perfect Symmetry(IRE) could not raise his game after chasing the leader into the straight. He had won a Listed event last time at Fairyhouse on good ground and he'll be better judged when he gets that ground next time. (op 5/1 tchd 13/2)

4253a MELD STKS (GROUP 3) 1m 2f
8:00 (8:00) 3-Y-O+ **£39,126** (£11,436; £5,417; £1,805)

RPR
1 **She's Our Mark**[11] 3894 5-9-4 106 .... DMGrant 8 109
(Patrick J Flynn, Ire) *prom early: sn in mid-div: 6th 1/2-way: rdn into 2nd over 1f out: sn chal: styd on to ld last 100yds: kpt on wl: pressed cl home and all out* **10/1**[3]
2 shd **Lord Admiral (USA)**[42] 2870 8-9-7 108 ....(b) MJKinane 7 112
(Charles O'Brien, Ire) *hld up towards rr: hdwy to 5th over 1f out: kpt on wl fnl f to chal ins fnl 50yds: jst hld* **28/1**
3 1 1/4 **Casual Conquest (IRE)**[60] 2303 4-10-0 122 ....(t) PJSmullen 5 116
(D K Weld, Ire) *chsd ldrs: 4th 1/2-way: hdwy in 2nd 2f out: impr to ld 1 1/2f out: rdn and chal 1f out: hdd last 100yds and no ex: kpt on same pce* **8/13**[1]
4 2 **Beach Bunny (IRE)**[26] 3412 4-9-4 113 .... CDHayes 3 102
(Kevin Prendergast, Ire) *mid-div: 5th 1/2-way: rdn 2f out: styd on to 3rd over 1f out: kpt on same pce fnl f* **10/3**[2]
5 4 **Red Rock Canyon (IRE)**[9] 3964 5-9-7 103 .... CO'Donoghue 2 97
(A P O'Brien, Ire) *sn led: rdn and hdd 1 1/2f out: no ex and kpt on one pce* **20/1**
6 1 1/4 **Chief Lone Eagle (USA)**[60] 2306 3-8-11 101 .... JMurtagh 4 95
(A P O'Brien, Ire) *chsd ldr in 2nd: pushed along 3f out: no ex in 3rd 2f out: wknd* **12/1**
7 hd **Malibu Bay (USA)**[19] 3640 3-8-11 102 .... JAHeffernan 6 94
(A P O'Brien, Ire) *hld up towards rr: rdn in 7th and no ex 1 1/2f out: kpt on one pce* **16/1**
8 18 **Crossing**[118] 993 8-9-4 98 .... KJManning 1 55
(William J Fitzpatrick, Ire) *chsd ldrs: 3rd 1/2-way: rdn in 4th 2f out: sn no ex and wknd* **66/1**
2m 8.74s (0.54) **Going Correction** +0.425s/f (Yiel)
WFA 3 from 4yo+ 10lb 8 Ran SP% **117.4**
Speed ratings: **114,113,112,111,108 107,106,92**
CSF £235.74 TOTE £7.10: £2.40, £8.20, £1.10; DF 456.60.
Owner B & M Syndicate **Bred** M Barrett & Redmyre Bloodstock **Trained** Carrick-On-Suir, Co Waterford

FOCUS
The runner-up and fourth have been rated to their solid form from the backend of 2008.

NOTEBOOK
She's Our Mark was hard ridden to mount a challenge early in the straight and ran on strongly, even when the favourite took a length or two out of her. It was admirable the way she found more when the runner-up came to challenge and she is a very tough mare. She deserves a crack at a higher level than Group 3. (op 10/1 tchd 12/1)
Lord Admiral(USA) ran his best race for some time on ground which was on the soft side and over a trip he's never won over. Held up off the pace as usual, he came with a sustained run from the rear in the straight but just found the winner too much of a tough nut to crack. Given everything, it was probably as good a performance as he has managed to date. (op 25/1)
Casual Conquest(IRE) was bitterly disappointing. He had shown himself to be a bona fide Group 1 class horse after his impressive win in the Tattersalls Gold Cup but this was a major step backwards. He had a perfect position throughout and seemed to be responding well when asked to go and win his race early in the straight, but for a horse of his class he capitulated quite tamely when challenged. He was obviously a long way below his best. (op 4/7)
Beach Bunny(IRE) also ran well below the form of her unlucky second in the Pretty Polly Stakes. Chasing the leaders, she was not able to make much of an impression when asked for her effort inside the final quarter mile. (op 7/2)

4254 - 4256a (Foreign Racing) - See Raceform Interactive

3839 ASCOT (R-H)

Friday, July 24

OFFICIAL GOING: Good

Wind: Virtually nil Weather: Showery

4257 JOHN GUEST MAIDEN FILLIES' STKS 6f

2:40 (2:42) (Class 3) 2-Y-O £7,123 (£2,119; £1,059; £529) Stalls Centre

Form	Pos	Dist	Horse	Jockey	RPR
	1		**Walk On Water** 2-9-0 0 (H R A Cecil) *w'like: scope: lw: mde virtually all: pushed along 2f out: styd on strly thrght fnl f* **6/1**	TPQueally 1	83
3	2	1 1/4	**Seeking Dubai**[28] 3337 2-9-0 0 (E F Vaughan) *lw: chsd ldrs: disp 2nd over 2f out: sn drvn to chse wnr and kpt on wl but a hld* **8/1**	RyanMoore 4	79
	3	1	**Bab At The Bowster (IRE)** 2-9-0 0 (W J Haggas) *str: broke wl: stdd to trck ldrs: pushed along and sltly outpcd over 2f out: drvn and styd on wl fnl f: gng on cl home* **5/1**[3]	LiamJones 5	76+
2	4	1 1/4	**Zubova**[7] 4047 2-9-0 0 (R Hannon) *s.i.s: in rr: gd hdwy ins fnl 3f: disp 2nd over 2f out: sn pushed along: one pce ins fnl f* **11/10**[1]	RichardHughes 8	73
	5	3/4	**Emirates Hills** 2-9-0 0 (E F Vaughan) *w'like: bit bkwd: s.i.s: in rr: hdwy over 2f out: nvr gng pce to trble ldrs and one pce fnl f* **33/1**	JimCrowley 6	70
	6	1/2	**Battlemaiden (IRE)** 2-9-0 0 (Saeed Bin Suroor) *w'like: athletic: s.i.s and wnt lft s: pushed along and hdwy over 2f out: kpt on fnl f but nvr gng pce to be competitive* **7/2**[2]	LDettori 3	69+
	7	hd	**Galachiya** 2-9-0 0 (C E Brittain) *w'like: neat: in rr: pushed along 3f out: hdwy: edgd rt and green over 2f out: nvr rchd ldrs and one pce fr over 1f out* **33/1**	HayleyTurner 9	68
	8	3	**Carnaval Court (IRE)** 2-8-11 0 (A M Balding) *w'like: tall: towards rr: pushed along and hdwy to get in bhd ldrs over 3f out: drvn over 2f out: wknd appr fnl f* **20/1**	DavidProbert(3) 7	59
	9	14	**Tai Hang (IRE)** 2-9-0 0 (A P Jarvis) *unf: chsd wnr tl over 2f out: wknd qckly* **66/1**	ChrisCatlin 2	17

1m 18.31s (3.91) **Going Correction** +0.50s/f (Yiel) **9** Ran SP% **124.0**

Speed ratings (Par 95): **93,91,90,88,87 86,86,82,63**

toteswingers: 1&2 £5.10, 1&3 £6.10, 2&3 £4.20 CSF £54.04 TOTE £7.00: £1.70, £2.00, £2.00; EX 46.80 Trifecta £632.10 Pool: £1101.97 - 1.29 winning units..

Owner Bloomsbury Stud **Bred** Bloomsbury Stud **Trained** Newmarket, Suffolk

FOCUS

Following 3.5mm of rain overnight and a further 4mm since the morning, the ground had eased from that advertised and was officially changed to Good all round. Fillies with previous experience had won three of the past four runnings of this race, but this time it went to a newcomer. The level of the form is guessy.

NOTEBOOK

Walk On Water, from a family that has been very successful in Australia and New Zealand, certainly knew her job at the first time of asking. Soon in the lead, she was able to dominate throughout and found plenty when asked to quicken from the front around a furlong from home. She doesn't hold any big-race entries this season, but she looks a nice prospect nonetheless and was given quotes of 25-1 for the 1,000 Guineas with Stan James and Cashmans. (op 15-2 tchd 5-1 and 8-1 in places)

Seeking Dubai, a fair third in an ordinary Doncaster maiden on debut last month, stepped up on that effort here and she ran on again to finish a clear second after getting outpaced. On this evidence another furlong will suit her. (op 9-1 tchd 10-1)

Bab At The Bowster(IRE), a 24,000gns half-sister to the dual winner at up to 1m1f Full Of Love, was keen just behind the leaders early and, like the runner-up, she also ran on late after coming off the bridle a fair way out. She is bred to need further and this performance backed that up. (op 7-1 tchd 9-2)

Zubova, runner-up to a decent prospect on softer ground at Newbury seven days earlier, went off a short-priced favourite even though her rider had warned beforehand that she may not have come on much from that debut effort. The signs were even more ominous when she got upset in the stalls, and although she moved into the contest smoothly enough following a tardy start, the writing was on the wall when she came under strong pressure over a furlong from home. She is bred to appreciate further and holds an entry in the Fillies' Mile, but she now has a bit to prove. (op 10-11 tchd 5-6, 11-8 in places and 5-4 in places)

Emirates Hills, a 55,000gns filly out of an unraced half-sister to Pastoral Pursuits and Goodricke, showed enough on this debut to suggest that races can be won with her. (op 66-1)

Battlemaiden(IRE), a 125,000gns 2yo and half-sister to the smart 1m2f-winner Natalie Jane, missed the break and an effort towards the nearside of the track over a furlong from home amounted to little. She is another bred to need further and is probably capable of much better. (op 9-2 tchd 6-1)

Galachiya, a 34,000gns filly out of a winner on turf in the US, showed a little bit on this debut. (op 50-1)

Carnaval Court(IRE), a sister to her useful stable-companion Foundation Room, proved far too green to do herself justice on this debut. (op 33-1 tchd 16-1)

4258 JOHN GUEST E B F MAIDEN STKS 7f

3:15 (3:15) (Class 3) 2-Y-O £7,771 (£2,312; £1,155; £577) Stalls Centre

Form	Pos	Dist	Horse	Jockey	RPR
2	1		**Sea Lord (IRE)**[8] 4006 2-9-3 0 (M Johnston) *w'like: scope: mde all: pushed along over 2f out: hrd drvn whn strly chal thrght fnl f: asserted cl home* **9/4**[2]	GregFairley 1	84
	2	nk	**Pounced (USA)** 2-9-3 0 (J H M Gosden) *w'like: scop: str: s.i.s: hld up towards rr: stdy hdwy fr 2f out: qcknd to trck wnr 1f out: pushed along and str chal thrght fnl f tl no ex cl home* **14/1**	JimmyFortune 10	83+
44	3	1 1/4	**Excellent Guest**[18] 3692 2-9-3 0 (G G Margarson) *in tch: hdwy 3f out: trckd wnr gng ok 2f out: pushed along over 1f out: outpcd by ldng duo ins fnl f but kpt on* **9/1**	TPQueally 9	80
4	4	2 1/4	**Gene Autry (USA)**[7] 4048 2-9-3 0 (R Hannon) *lw: str: scope: trckd ldrs: travelling smoothly over 2f out: drvn along sn after and no imp: one pce fr over 1f out* **6/4**[1]	RichardHughes 4	75
0	5	7	**High Holborn (IRE)**[16] 3750 2-9-3 0 (B J Meehan) *chsd ldrs: rdn over 2f out: wknd over 1f out* **20/1**	LDettori 6	57
	6	1/2	**Big Wave Bay (IRE)** 2-9-3 0 (A P Jarvis) *w'like: broke wl: chsd ldrs tl drvn along and outpcd over 4f out: styd on again fr over 1f out but nvr a threat* **66/1**	JimCrowley 2	56
	7	1/2	**Valiant Knight (FR)** 2-9-3 0 (R Hannon) *str: in tch: rdn 3f out: wknd fr ins fnl 2f* **25/1**	RyanMoore 3	55
6	8	4 1/2	**Fireback**[14] 3792 2-9-0 0 (A M Balding) *leggy: fly j. s and s.i.s: sn rcvrd to chse ldrs: wl there and rdn 3f out: wknd ins fnl 2f* **20/1**	DavidProbert(3) 8	43
	9	1/2	**Almutaham (USA)** 2-9-3 0 (J L Dunlop) *w'like: scope: bit bkwd: s.i.s: immature in rr but pushed along and sme prog 3f out: nvr nr ldrs and sn fdd* **7/1**[3]	RHills 5	42
0	10	3 3/4	**White Dart**[13] 3867 2-9-3 0 (M R Channon) *w'like: sn chsng wnr: rdn 3f out: wknd 2f out* **25/1**	DarryllHolland 7	33

1m 31.58s (3.58) **Going Correction** +0.50s/f (Yiel) **10** Ran SP% **118.6**

Speed ratings (Par 98): **99,98,97,94,86 86,85,80,79,75**

toteswingers: 1&2 £5.30, 1&3 £3.50, 2&3 £6.70 CSF £30.49 TOTE £3.50: £1.40, £3.00, £2.40; EX 22.60 Trifecta £144.40 Pool: £1108.70 - 5.68 winning units..

Owner Sheikh Hamdan Bin Mohammed Al Maktoum **Bred** Darley **Trained** Middleham Moor, N Yorks

FOCUS

An interesting maiden in which previous experience probably made all the difference. The first four finished clear of the rest and the key to the race is whether the third and fourth can back this up.

NOTEBOOK

Sea Lord(IRE), who had finished runner-up in an Epsom maiden over this trip eight days earlier, was keen to post and keen out in front during the race itself, but every time he was asked to pull out a bit more he kept on finding and saw his race out in typically game fashion. He is entered for the Gimcrack, Champagne and Royal Lodge, and the way he won this the last two of those look the more viable options. (op 5-2 tchd 11-4 in a place)

Pounced(USA) ◆, a half-brother to four winners at up to 1m2f including the smart Big Bound, ran green at the back of the field early and took a while to realise what was required. The penny eventually dropped, however, and he made relentless progress to get into a challenging position, but the last thing he probably needed was get involved in a battle with a Johnston inmate with previous racecourse experience and he just fell short. Nonetheless, this was a very encouraging debut and the Champagne Stakes entrant looks a nice colt in the making. (op 10-1 tchd 9-1)

Excellent Guest, owned by the race sponsor, had lost ground at the start in both of his previous starts over 6f, but also showed plenty of ability. He broke well enough this time, had every chance and stayed on pretty well. He is entered in both the Gimcrack and Middle Park and whilst those are probably beyond him, he should still be up to winning a race or two. (op 10-1 tchd 8-1)

Gene Autry(USA), from a yard that has won this race three times during the decade, had finished a promising fourth behind an odds-on stable companion on soft ground at Newbury the previous week. Very well backed throughout the day, he seemed to be in a good position behind the leaders the whole way, but found disappointingly little off the bridle. This may have come a bit too soon and, clearly held in high regard, he shouldn't be written off yet. (op 13-8 tchd 7-4 in places)

High Holborn(IRE) probably ran better than when very green on his Newmarket debut, but he probably still needs more time. (op 28-1 tchd 18-1)

Big Wave Bay(IRE), out of a triple winner over 7f, was being ridden along in a detached last from a long way out and merely ran on past beaten horses. (tchd 80-1)

Valiant Knight(FR), a 115,000euros yearling having fetched just 40,000euros as a foal, is out of a 1m4f Listed winner in France. He didn't show much on this debut, but is probably capable of better as he gains experience and he will appreciate further.

Almutaham(USA), a $260,000 half-brother to the 1m2f winner Natural Flair, was very well backed beforehand but he never got into the race after a slow start. He holds entries in the Champagne Stakes and the Royal Lodge and is likely to leave this effort well behind in due course. Official explanation: jockey said colt was slowly away (op 14-1)

4259 EBF TRANSFORMERS AND RECTIFIERS VALIANT STKS (LISTED RACE) (F&M) 1m (R)

3:50 (3:51) (Class 1) 3-Y-O+

£25,546 (£9,684; £4,846; £2,416; £1,210; £607) Stalls High

Form	Pos	Dist	Horse	Jockey	RPR
211	1		**Strawberrydaiquiri**[20] 3641 3-8-11 105 (Sir Michael Stoute) *lw: sn trcking ldr: drvn and qcknd to ld appr fnl f: hld on wl cl home* **4/6**[1]	RyanMoore 2	106+
2122	2	1	**Balaagha (USA)**[16] 3746 3-8-7 87 (M A Jarvis) *s.i.s: t.k.h towards rr: gd hdwy ins fnl 2f: drvn and qcknd to chse wnr ins fnl f: styd on wl but a hld* **10/1**	RHills 10	100
3001	3	2	**Greenisland (IRE)**[16] 3746 3-8-7 94 (H Morrison) *lw: sn led: rdn and styd on fr over 2f out: hdd appr fnl f and lost 2nd ins fnl f but hld on wl for 3rd* **20/1**	RobertHavlin 3	95
-256	4	nk	**Perfect Star**[62] 2285 5-9-1 99 (C G Cox) *chsd ldrs: rdn over 2f out: styd on same pce u.p fnl f* **7/1**[3]	AdamKirby 5	97
0-10	5	3/4	**Rosaleen (IRE)**[37] 3012 4-9-5 98 (B J Meehan) *lw: chsd ldrs: rdn over 2f out: styd on same pce frn over 1f out* **11/1**	LDettori 6	99
0-22	6	nse	**Lady Francesca**[83] 1667 3-8-7 101 (W R Muir) *in tch: pushed along 3f out: one pce over 2f out: swtchd lft wl over 1f out: kpt on again ins fnl f but nvr a threat* **13/2**[2]	DarryllHolland 8	93
3050	7	1 1/2	**First City**[16] 3746 3-8-7 92 (D M Simcock) *towards rr: rdn over 3f out: sme prog on ins over 2f out: nvr gng pce to get into contention and one pce* **28/1**	ChrisCatlin 7	89
10	8	1 1/2	**Folly Lodge**[6] 4088 5-9-1 83 (R M Beckett) *pushed along and hung rt over 2f out: a towards rr* **40/1**	JimmyFortune 4	88
0022	9	7	**Nice To Know (FR)**[16] 3736 5-9-1 74 (G L Moore) *lw: s.i.s: pushed along 3f out: little rspnse and a bhd* **66/1**	RichardHughes 11	72

1m 42.57s (1.87) **Going Correction** +0.50s/f (Yiel)

WFA 3 from 4yo+ 8lb **9** Ran SP% **115.4**

Speed ratings (Par 111): **110,109,107,106,105 105,104,102,95**

toteswingers: 1&2 £7.00, 2&3 £14.30, 1&3 not won CSF £7.93 TOTE £1.70: £1.10, £2.50, £4.30; EX 10.00 Trifecta £92.90 Pool: £1657.45 - 13.20 winning units..

Owner Mrs R J Jacobs **Bred** Newsells Park Stud Limited **Trained** Newmarket, Suffolk

FOCUS

Three-year-olds had won the first six runnings of this contest until the four-year-old Baharah broke the trend last year, but normality was restored with the classic generation filling the first three places this time around. Ordinary fillies' Listed form but Strawberrydaiquiri continues on the upgrade and the form is pretty sound.

NOTEBOOK

Strawberrydaiquiri, representing the yard that took this race three years in a row between 2004 and 2006, had improved markedly in each of her three outings so far and was a convincing winner of a similar event confined to three-year-olds at Sandown earlier in the month. Carrying a 4lb penalty as a result, she was always in a great position just behind the leader and once sent to the front over a furlong out the race was soon in the bag. There is almost certainly even more to come from her. (tchd 8-11)

Balaagha(USA), who is talented but also a bit of a character, had finished less than a length behind Greenisland after a slow start at Newmarket last time, but she was 5lb worse off with that filly here. She showed her dark side by proving very reluctant to go out onto the track and although she didn't fluff the start as badly as she can, she then took a strong hold on the outside of the field. Given all of that, she obviously has a ton of ability as she managed to put in a decent late effort and wasn't beaten far by the favourite at the line. The extra furlong wasn't a problem and if she were to apply herself properly then she could win a race like this, but that's a big 'if'. (op 9-1 tchd 17-2 and 8-1 in places)

Greenisland(IRE), up in class following her 66/1 surprise victory at Newmarket, had the run of the race out in front and though unable to hold off the front pair from over a furlong out, still ran with plenty of credit and showed that her win was no fluke.

Perfect Star, winner of a soft-ground Listed fillies' handicap over C&D in September 2007, has been running with credit at a similar level this year and she also ran well to fare best of the older generation, especially as she didn't have a lot of room to play with after turning in. (op 9-1 tchd 13-2)

Rosaleen(IRE), proven at this level and back in the right sort of company after finishing seventh in the Windsor Forest, was always in about the same place and she had every chance, but she was up against some more progressive fillies under a 4lb penalty here and found the task beyond her. (op 10-1)

Lady Francesca, runner-up in a similar event at Goodwood when last seen in May, was joint best in with the favourite at the weights and she was running on well at the death after having to be switched out wide for her effort. She is yet to win a race, but she has the ability and connections are keen to step her up in trip. (op 8-1)

4260 JOHN GUEST BROWN JACK STKS (H'CAP) 2m

4:25 (4:25) (Class 2) (0-100,96) 3-Y-O+ **£12,952** (£3,854; £1,926; £962) **Stalls** High

Form RPR

1412 **1** **Darley Sun (IRE)**[30] 3276 3-8-2 **83** ow1 ChrisCatlin 3 102+
(D M Simcock) *swtg: t.k.h: trckd ldr after 4f: drvn 3f out led 2f out: forged clr wl over 1f out: readily* **3/1**[2]

6011 **2** *10* **Alanbrooke**[14] 3793 3-9-1 **96** (b) GregFairley 4 100
(M Johnston) *led: pushed along over 3f out: hdd 2f out: one pce and no ch w wnr wl over 1f out but hld on for hrd-pressed 2nd* **13/8**[1]

0514 **3** *¾* **Gordonsville**[14] 3822 6-9-7 **85** RyanMoore 5 88
(J S Goldie) *in rr but in tch: drvn along over 3f out: styd on fnl 2f and kpt on to press for 2nd cl home but nvr anywhere nr wnr* **7/1**

500- **4** *shd* **Highland Legacy**[349] 4843 5-10-0 **92** HayleyTurner 1 95
(M L W Bell) *b: lw: in rr but in tch: rdn 4f out: styd on fnl 2f and disp wl hld 3rd cl home but nvr anywhere nr wnr* **20/1**

-114 **5** *6* **Hendersyde (USA)**[27] 3390 4-9-12 **90** (t) AdamKirby 2 85
(W R Swinburn) *chsd ldrs: wnt 3rd 4f out: sn rdn and no imp on ldng duo: hung rt u.p fr 3f out: wknd 2f out* **4/1**[3]

5/30 **6** *22* **Ermine Sea**[38] 2994 6-9-8 **86** RichardHughes 6 55
(Miss H C Knight) *lw: chsd ldr 4f: rdn 5f out: wknd into 4th 4f out: wknd 3f out: eased whn no ch fnl 2f* **8/1**

3m 32.7s (3.70) **Going Correction** +0.50s/f (Yiel)
WFA 3 from 4yo+ 17lb **6** Ran SP% **111.5**
Speed ratings (Par 109): **110,105,104,104,101 90**
toteswingers: 1&2 £1.60, 1&3 £4.00, 2&3 £2.50 CSF £8.18 TOTE £4.00: £2.30, £1.40; EX 9.20.
Owner Abdullah Saeed Belhab **Bred** Manfred Hoffer & Ballygrelihan Farm **Trained** Newmarket, Suffolk

FOCUS
An interesting staying handicap even though the pace looked nothing out of the ordinary, but ultimately it was a one-horse race. Big improvement from the winner for this longer trip, with the third the best guide.

NOTEBOOK
Darley Sun(IRE) had been beaten in a tactical four-runner event at Salisbury last month, but even that form was made to look better when the winner bolted up by eight lengths at Sandown the previous evening. Trying this trip for the first time, he was keen enough just behind the leaders in the first half of the contest, but it made no difference because as soon as he swept past the favourite 2f out, he then just went further and further clear. Quite what the form amounts to is hard to say and he is obviously a well-handicapped colt, but connections believe that the extra quarter mile suited him well. He may now go for either the Melrose and/or the Doncaster Cup, and in the longer term he may be a Cesarewitch type. (op 10-3 tchd 7-2 and 4-1 in a place)

Alanbrooke, transformed by blinkers and easy winner of his last two starts including over C&D last time, was 10lb higher in his bid for a hat-trick. He was again allowed his own way out in front and gradually wound up the pace over the last half-mile, but he was completely blown away by the winner passing the 2f pole and it was all he could do to hang on to second. The handicapper may have him now, but he was also taking on better company than he has been beating. (op 6-4 tchd 11-8, 7-4 and 15-8 in places)

Gordonsville, in good form so far this year and back up to a more suitable trip, made some late progress without offering a threat and he remains 3lb above his highest winning mark. (op 9-1 tchd 10-1)

Highland Legacy, once a promising young stayer but not seen for almost a year following a couple of disappointing efforts, would have appreciated the easing of the ground beforehand and he stayed on from the home bend to finish a creditable third. Hopefully he will remain sound and he is entitled to benefit a good deal from this. (op 25-1)

Hendersyde(USA), who did best of those held up when fourth in the Northumberland Plate last time, was inclined to run in snatches and found very little under strong pressure rounding the home turn when he started to hang. This was disappointing. (tchd 9-2)

Ermine Sea, who ran much better than his finishing position would suggest having met plenty of trouble on the home bend in the Ascot Stakes at the Royal meeting, had the same thing happen to him at the same spot here when he was hampered by Hendersyde, but he had already been under pressure for some time so was in no way unlucky. (op 7-1)

4261 OCTOBER CLUB H'CAP (SUPPORTED BY THE ANDY STEWART CHARITABLE FOUNDATION) 1m 2f

5:00 (5:00) (Class 2) (0-105,102) 3-Y-O+
£11,215 (£3,358; £1,260; £1,260; £419; £210) **Stalls** High

Form RPR

5001 **1** **Fanjura (IRE)**[21] 3586 4-9-7 **95** LDettori 4 105
(B W Hills) *lw: led: rdn and hdd appr fnl 2f: rallied over 1f out and styd on gamely to ld again fnl 110yds: pushed out and wl on top cl home* **6/1**[3]

-436 **2** *½* **William Blake**[14] 3822 4-8-9 **83** GregFairley 9 92
(M Johnston) *trckd ldr: drvn to ld appr fnl 2f: sn one pce: hdd and no ex fnl 110yds* **5/1**[2]

6312 **3** *1 ¼* **Vainglory (USA)**[26] 3431 5-8-13 **87** HayleyTurner 10 94
(D M Simcock) *chsd ldrs: rdn 3f out: styd on fnl 2f but nvr gng pce to rch ldng duo* **7/1**

5014 **3** *dht* **Mountain Pride (IRE)**[21] 3586 4-9-0 **88** SteveDrowne 3 95
(J L Dunlop) *lw: mid-div: hdwy on outside fr over 2f out: styd on wl thrght fnl f but nvr gng pce of ldng duo* **16/1**

5412 **5** *1* **Resurge (IRE)**[18] 3695 4-9-0 **88** FergusSweeney 2 93
(W S Kittow) *in tch: rdn over 2f out: styd on fr over 1f out but nvr gng pce to get into contention* **6/1**[3]

0136 **6** *1* **Last Three Minutes (IRE)**[16] 3752 4-8-13 **87** RichardHughes 5 90+
(E A L Dunlop) *hld up in rr: pushed along and stl plenty to do over 2f out: kpt on fnl 2f: styng on cl home but nvr gng pce to get into contention* **15/8**[1]

026- **7** *3 ¼* **Pinch Of Salt (IRE)**[322] 5677 6-8-13 **90** DavidProbert(3) 6 86
(A M Balding) *in rr: rdn along over 3f out: mod prog fnl f* **14/1**

4-10 **8** *1 ¾* **Full Speed (GER)**[33] 3189 4-8-11 **85** RobertWinston 1 78
(G A Swinbank) *t.k.h early: chsd ldrs: rdn over 2f out: sn btn* **28/1**

65-0 **9** *6* **Malt Or Mash (USA)**[20] 3620 5-9-11 **102** PatrickHills(3) 8 83
(R Hannon) *in tch: rdn 3f out and sn wknd* **33/1**

5540 **10** *21* **Wise Dennis**[148] 697 7-9-12 **100** JimCrowley 7 39
(A P Jarvis) *rr: rdn over 4f out: sn lost tch* **20/1**

2m 9.75s (2.75) **Going Correction** +0.50s/f (Yiel) **10** Ran SP% **116.2**
Speed ratings (Par 109): **109,108,107,107,106 106,103,102,97,80**PL: Mountain Pride £2.10, Vainglory £1.30 TRI: Fanjura/William Blake/Mountain Pride £229.31, Fanjura/William Blake/Vainglory £108.02 toteswingers: 1&2 £5.00, 1& Mountain Pride £3.50, 1&Vainglory £3.10, MP&William Blake £6.20, Vainglory&WB £4.30 CSF £35.10 CT £229.27 TOTE £Owner: £Terry Benson, £Bred, £Patrick F Kelly, £TrainedLambourn, Berks.

FOCUS
A decent handicap, but a race dominated by those that raced handily and the first three home basically held those positions throughout. The form makes sense.

NOTEBOOK
Fanjura(IRE) had been raised 5lb for his Sandown victory at the start of the month when he was held up, but he was ridden very differently this time. Soon able to get across from his low draw in front, he set just a fair gallop and looked in trouble when headed for a few strides by the runner-up passing the 2f pole, but he then rallied in very game style to force his head back in front where it mattered. This was a decent effort to outbattle a Johnston horse and he remains at the top of his game. (op 9-2)

William Blake, from a yard that has won this race three times since 2000, was back over a more suitable trip after failing to see out 1m4f at Newmarket last time. Inclined to race keenly in a handy position, he nonetheless looked the most likely winner when looming alongside the leader passing the 2f pole, but his rival kept pulling out a bit more. He tries hard, but is without a win since April of last year yet remains 3lb higher. (op 6-1 tchd 7-1 and 15-2 in places)

Vainglory(USA), up another 1lb having been running consistently well at around 1m recently, was always in about the same place and was staying on well at the line, but he could never quite get there. He has now been placed a few times over this trip and stamina wasn't an issue. (tchd 20-1 in a place)

Mountain Pride(IRE), around nine lengths behind Fanjura at Sandown last time and 6lb better off, would have appreciated the rain and was staying on well down the outside over the last couple of furlongs without quite managing to get there. He still fared best of those that tried to come from off the pace. (tchd 20-1 in a place)

Resurge(IRE), 4lb higher than when just beaten under a penalty at Windsor last time having bolted up off 10lb lower at the same track before that, ran okay but never looked like winning and the handicapper now looks to be in charge. (tchd 11-2)

Last Three Minutes(IRE), unplaced in his only previous try over this far, needs delivering late and things hadn't gone right for him in either start since winning off 7lb lower on the Lingfield Polytrack in May. He was given an impossible task in trying to come from last place here given the way the race panned out, however, and although he stayed on he was never going to get anywhere near. He shouldn't be judged too harshly on this. (op 9-4)

Pinch Of Salt(IRE), reappearing after a ten-month absence and yet to win on turf after 12 attempts, never got involved but connections had warned beforehand that he was likely to need it, so better can be expected. (tchd 16-1)

4262 NATIONWIDE ACCIDENT REPAIR SERVICES H'CAP 1m (S)

5:35 (5:36) (Class 4) (0-85,85) 3-Y-O+ **£6,476** (£1,927; £963; £481) **Stalls** Centre

Form RPR

2051 **1** **Credit Swap**[14] 3812 4-9-2 **80** TobyAtkinson(7) 5 98
(M Wigham) *hld up in rr: stdy hdwy over 2f out: drvn to ld ins fnl f: edgd lft: pushed out* **6/1**[2]

0P0 **2** *1 ½* **Foolin Myself**[41] 2933 4-9-12 **83** HayleyTurner 12 98
(M L W Bell) *lw: trckd ldr: led 2f out: rdn and hung lft u.p and hdd ins fnl f: styd on same pce* **14/1**

2323 **3** *4 ½* **Effigy**[14] 3812 5-9-7 **78** FergusSweeney 10 83
(H Candy) *swtg: in tch: hdwy over 3f out: pressed ldrs and rdn 2f out: outpcd fnl f* **9/2**[1]

6005 **4** *6* **Isphahan**[14] 3796 6-9-8 **82** (v) DavidProbert(3) 15 73
(A M Balding) *towards rr: rdn 3f out: styd on fr 2f out and kpt on fnl f but nvr anywhere nr ldng trio* **9/1**

0324 **5** *½* **Den's Gift (IRE)**[22] 3523 5-10-0 **85** (b) AdamKirby 8 75
(C G Cox) *led tl hdd 2f out: wknd over 1f out* **8/1**

0133 **6** *nse* **Sarah Park (IRE)**[14] 3796 4-9-5 **76** LDettori 14 66
(B J Meehan) *in tch: rdn and hdwy to chse ldrs over 2f out: nvr quite on terms and sn wknd* **8/1**

-210 **7** *3 ¼* **Merrymadcap (IRE)**[14] 3811 7-9-1 **72** RobertWinston 9 54
(M Salaman) *lw: in tch: rdn and sme prog over 2f out: nvr rchd ldrs and sn wknd* **25/1**

-360 **8** *hd* **Habshan (USA)**[16] 3752 9-9-13 **84** JimCrowley 11 66
(C F Wall) *in tch: rdn to chse ldrs 3f out: wknd ins fnl 2f* **12/1**

5300 **9** *7* **Marning Star**[63] 2243 4-8-11 **71** ow3 PatrickHills(3) 7 37
(Ian Williams) *prssed ldrs: rdn 3f out: wknd qckly ins fnl 2f* **33/1**

4430 **10** *3 ¼* **Green Agenda**[34] 3144 3-8-12 **77** GregFairley 2 35
(M Johnston) *pressed ldrs over 5f* **12/1**

361 **11** *13* **Athania (IRE)**[14] 3804 3-8-4 **69** ChrisCatlin 4 —
(A P Jarvis) *lw: wl bhd fr 1/2-way* **12/1**

0000 **12** *¾* **Trafalgar Square**[23] 3509 7-9-5 **76** RobertHavlin 3 —
(M J Attwater) *wl bhd fr 1/2-way* **25/1**

231 **13** *8* **Mick Is Back**[10] 3946 5-8-9 **64** 6ex (v) KirstyMilczarek 1 —
(G G Margarson) *fly j. leaving stalls: wl bhd fr 1/2-way* **16/1**

0000 **14** *18* **Opera Prince**[20] 3639 4-9-11 **82** JamesDoyle 6 —
(S Kirk) *in tch to 1/2-way: sn bhd* **7/1**[3]

0000 **15** *1 ¼* **Shanzu**[9] 3980 4-8-13 **70** (b) SteveDrowne 16 —
(G L Moore) *bhd fr 1/2-way* **66/1**

1m 44.97s (4.37) **Going Correction** +0.50s/f (Yiel)
WFA 3 from 4yo+ 8lb **15** Ran SP% **124.9**
Speed ratings (Par 105): **98,96,92,86,85 85,82,82,75,71 58,58,50,32,30**
toteswingers: 1&2 £29.10, 1&3 £4.60, 2&3 £26.80 CSF £87.30 CT £434.06 TOTE £6.40: £2.30, £5.80, £2.50; EX 138.20 Trifecta £399.50 Pool: £1079.82 - 2.00 winning units. Place 6: £60.82 Place 5: £19.55.
Owner Your Golf Travel Ltd **Bred** Jeremy Green And Sons **Trained** Newmarket, Suffolk

FOCUS
A competitive handicap, but in the end they finished spread out all over Berkshire. The runners raced as a group down the centre of the track early, but gradually edged over towards the far rail as the contest progressed. The last seven winners of this event have been rated at least 80. The first two came clear and it is hard to know how literally to take this form.

Opera Prince Official explanation: jockey said gelding lost its action

T/Jkpt: £4,735.20 to a £1 stake. Pool: £13,338.80. 2.00 winning tickets. T/Plt: £68.40 to a £1 stake. Pool: £113,485.67. 1,209.66 winning tickets. T/Qpdt: £7.00 to a £1 stake. Pool: £8,099.62. 849.49 winning tickets. ST

3798 CHEPSTOW (L-H)

Friday, July 24

OFFICIAL GOING: Soft (heavy in places; 6.4)

Wind: Almost nil Weather: Fine

4263 BETINTERNET.COM AMATEUR RIDERS' H'CAP 1m 4f 23y

6:20 (6:22) (Class 6) (0-65,65) 3-Y-0+ **£2,186** (£677; £338; £169) **Stalls** Low

Form RPR

0112 **1** **Sagunt (GER)**[10] 3950 6-11-5 **63**.................. MissFayeBramley 6 72
(S Curran) *a.p: led on bit 3f out: rdn jst over 1f out: edgd lft ins fnl f: r.o* **15/2**

/622 **2** *3* **Arab League (IRE)**[22] 3533 4-10-4 **53**.................. MrMPrice(5) 2 57
(R J Price) *hld up in mid-div: rdn over 3f out: hdwy wl over 1f out: swtchd rt ins fnl f: styd on u.p to take 2nd towards fin: nt trble wnr* **4/1**[1]

30- **3** *nk* **Allez Frank (GER)**[11] 6136 8-10-6 **55**.................. MrPJTolman(5) 16 59
(A E Jones) *hld up in rr: swtchd rt to outside over 4f out: rdn over 2f out: gd hdwy fnl f: edgd lft cl home: fin wl* **25/1**

0532 **4** *1 ½* **Nawamees (IRE)**[4] 4146 11-11-7 **65**..................(p) MissEFolkes 7 66
(P D Evans) *chsd ldr: ev ch 3f out: rdn and edgd lft wl over 1f out: one pce: lost 2 pls towards fin* **8/1**

000 **5** *1 ¾* **Inchando (FR)**[17] 3710 5-10-7 **54** ow1.................. MrMJJSmith(3) 8 53
(A W Carroll) *t.k.h towards rr: pushed along over 2f out: hdwy whn edgd lft wl over 1f out: sn rdn: no further prog fnl f* **20/1**

666/ **6** *1 ¾* **Intersky Music (USA)**[19] 4334 6-10-8 **52** ow2.................. MrAJBerry 1 48
(Jonjo O'Neill) *dwlt: hld up in rr: rdn over 4f out: styd on fnl f: n.d* **9/1**

4332 **7** *¾* **Barodine**[11] 3927 6-10-3 **54**.................. MissKClark(7) 12 49
(R J Hodges) *hld up in mid-div: no hdwy fnl 2f* **11/1**

106/ **8** *1 ¾* **Lady Romanov (IRE)**[43] 7175 6-11-2 **65**..................(p) MissMBryant(5) 4 57
(P Butler) *hld up in mid-div: no hdwy fnl 2f* **66/1**

0006 **9** *1 ¼* **Bespoke Boy**[14] 3798 4-10-4 **51** ow1.................. MrBenBrisbourne(3) 13 41
(Mrs N S Evans) *led: rdn and hdd 3f out: carried lft and wknd over 1f out* **25/1**

000- **10** *½* **Queen Excalibur**[9] 4366 10-10-1 **48**..................(p) MissIsabelTompsett(3) 5 37
(B J Llewellyn) *hld up in mid-div: stdy prog 3f out: rdn and wknd jst over 1f out* **16/1**

11 *3* **Sonate De La Tour (FR)**[254] 4-10-4 **55**.................. MrTJFlint(7) 10 39
(J L Flint) *prom: pushed along over 5f out: rdn 3f out: sn edgd lft: wknd 2f out* **33/1**

25-5 **12** *nse* **Parnassian**[196] 103 9-10-8 **52**..................(v) MissSBrotherton 15 36
(J A Geake) *hld up in mid-div: rdn over 2f out: stdy hdwy 3f out: rdn and wknd jst over 1f out* **5/1**[2]

0060 **13** *5* **Filun**[22] 3533 4-10-11 **60**..................(p) MissJodieHughes(5) 11 36
(A Middleton) *prom: ev ch 3f out: sn rdn: wkng whn hung lft over 1f out* **25/1**

-556 **14** *2 ¾* **Inn For The Dancer**[43] 734 7-9-13 **48**..... MissSarah-JaneDurman(5) 14 20
(J C Fox) *s.i.s: a in rr* **33/1**

2 **15** *¾* **Rudry World (IRE)**[36] 3068 6-10-9 **58**.................. MissMMullineaux(5) 17 28
(M Mullineaux) *a in rr* **7/1**[3]

5-00 **16** *10* **Sponge**[11] 3919 4-10-8 **57**.................. MrNdeBoinville(5) 3 11
(P R Chamings) *hld up in mid-div: wknd over 4f out* **28/1**

2m 49.33s (10.33) **Going Correction** +0.60s/f (Yiel) **16** Ran SP% **123.4**
Speed ratings (Par 101): **89,87,86,85,84 83,82,81,80,80 78,78,75,73,72 66**
CSF £34.08 CT £739.87 TOTE £8.60: £1.90, £1.90, £4.30, £1.40; EX 46.80.
Owner L M Power **Bred** Gestut Schlenderhan **Trained** Hatford, Oxon

FOCUS
The pace was reasonable, if not as fast as they often go in amateur riders' races, and the strong finishers arrived too late to trouble the winner. Modest form.

4264 WATTS TRUCK AND VAN CLAIMING STKS 2m 49y

6:50 (6:50) (Class 6) 3-Y-0+ **£2,072** (£616; £308; £153) **Stalls** High

Form RPR

-304 **1** **Babilu**[22] 3527 4-9-4 63.................. JackDean(5) 7 54
(A G Newcombe) *hld up towards rr: smooth prog over 3f out: rdn to ld over 1f out: styd on* **9/4**[1]

0-00 **2** *1* **Hill Of Clare (IRE)**[60] 2318 7-9-2 37.................. AmyBaker(5) 10 51
(G H Jones) *s.s: hld up in rr: hdwy and rdn over 3f out: styd on u.p to take 2nd last stride* **33/1**

0406 **3** *hd* **York Cliff**[158] 566 11-9-7 48.................. LukeMorris 9 51
(W M Brisbourne) *t.k.h: a.p: rdn to ld briefly over 1f out: styd on u.p: lost 2nd last stride* **8/1**

600/ **4** *3 ¾* **Menelaus**[12] 5948 8-9-10 50..................(p) NeilChalmers 4 50
(K A Morgan) *sn led: hdd over 11f out: chsd clr ldr: led briefly 4f out: sn rdn: wknd 2f out* **13/2**

410- **5** *¾* **Sonnengold (GER)**[324] 5613 8-8-13 52.................. ByronMoorcroft(5) 6 43
(B J Llewellyn) *led early: a.p: led over 3f out: rdn whn hung lft and hdd over 1f out: wknd fnl f* **10/3**[2]

6 *1 ½* **Lansdowne Princess**[38] 7-9-5 0.................. FrankieMcDonald 5 42
(G A Ham) *dwlt: hld up towards rr: sme hdwy on ins over 3f out: rdn and wknd over 2f out* **33/1**

0220 **7** *24* **Jackie Kiely**[23] 3503 8-9-12 53..................(t) PatCosgrave 1 20
(R Brotherton) *prom: rdn and wknd over 3f out* **4/1**[3]

/0-0 **8** *8* **Flexible Friend (IRE)**[9] 3503 5-9-0 52..................(bt) RichardRowe(7) 2 5
(B J Llewellyn) *hld up: rdn and struggling over 3f out* **20/1**

00-0 **9** *98* **Flying Goose (IRE)**[189] 187 5-9-7 60.................. KevinGhunowa(3) 8 —
(R A Harris) *s.s: plld hrd in rr: gd hdwy to ld over 11f out: hdd over 4f out: wknd rapidly: t.o* **12/1**

3m 58.97s (20.07) **Going Correction** +0.60s/f (Yiel) **9** Ran SP% **116.6**
Speed ratings (Par 101): **73,72,72,70,70 69,57,53,4**
CSF £87.92 TOTE £3.40: £1.60, £5.10, £2.50; EX 56.40.Babilu was claimed by Dai Burchell for £10,000.
Owner Paul Moulton **Bred** Paul Wyatt Ranby Hall **Trained** Yarnscombe, Devon

FOCUS
A weak claimer which has been rated at face value even though the second appears to have run her best race for three years.
Flying Goose(IRE) Official explanation: jockey said gelding ran too free and then bolted

4265 PLAY LIVE CASINO AT BETINTERNET.COM MAIDEN AUCTION STKS 6f 16y

7:20 (7:22) (Class 5) 2-Y-0 **£2,719** (£809; £404; £202) **Stalls** Centre

Form RPR

42 **1** **Farmers Wish (IRE)**[18] 3686 2-8-4 0.................. FrankieMcDonald 1 69+
(J L Spearing) *w ldr: led over 3f out: rdn and edgd lft briefly ins fnl f: rdn out* **6/4**[1]

453 **2** *2 ¼* **Bridge Valley**[15] 3785 2-8-13 0.................. RichardHughes 8 69+
(R Hannon) *hld up: hdwy over 2f out: chsd wnr over 1f out: rdn fnl f: nt qckn* **15/8**[2]

3 *3 ½* **Weekend Millionair (IRE)** 2-8-9 0.................. SamHitchcott 2 55
(P D Evans) *hld up: pushed along and hdwy over 3f out: rdn over 2f out: one pce* **14/1**

0 **4** *6* **Smog (IRE)**[21] 3571 2-8-13 0.................. PatCosgrave 3 41
(B J Meehan) *led: hdd over 3f out: rdn over 2f out: wknd over 1f out* **11/2**[3]

0 **5** *2 ¼* **City Of Rome (IRE)**[21] 3584 2-9-2 0.................. PatDobbs 5 37
(R Hannon) *hld up: rdn over 2f out: sn struggling* **25/1**

6 *4* **Quinner (IRE)** 2-8-9 0.................. PaulDoe 7 18
(P D Evans) *hld up: sn in tch: pushed along 3f out: hung lft and wknd over 2f out* **10/1**

7 *1 ¾* **Dancealot Lady (USA)** 2-8-4 0.................. LukeMorris 6 8
(P Winkworth) *prom: rdn and wknd 3f out* **14/1**

8 *5* **Madam Isshe** 2-7-12 0 ow1.................. JakePayne(7) 4 —
(M S Saunders) *s.i.s: hdwy over 4f out: wknd over 2f out* **50/1**

1m 15.41s (3.41) **Going Correction** +0.60s/f (Yiel) **8** Ran SP% **118.4**
Speed ratings (Par 94): **101,98,93,85,82 77,74,68**
toteswingers: 1&2 £1.10, 1&3 £5.00, 2&3 £18.80 CSF £4.71 TOTE £2.60: £1.20, £1.30, £2.10; EX 4.40.
Owner D J Oseman **Bred** Frank Moynihan **Trained** Kinnersley, Worcs

FOCUS
Not a maiden to get excited about, but the first two - who were the most experienced runners - pulled clear and set a fair standard based on previous form. They can both rate higher.

NOTEBOOK
Farmers Wish(IRE) has shown more speed as she has gained experience, and these tactics suited her. Though she had to work to see off the runner-up, she did it in workmanlike style and her early pace will be useful in nursery company. (op 7-4 tchd 2-1)
Bridge Valley, dropping back in trip, continues to show ability without being quite good enough to win his maiden. Not knocked about when held by the winner, he may well get there if he keeps trying, but he looks a likely sort for a 7f nursery. (op 2-1 tchd 5-2)
Weekend Millionair(IRE) proved hard to get into the stalls but put that behind him with a respectable debut. An Arakan half-brother to two winners at 1m2f and 1m3f, and out of a dam who raced over 1m as a juvenile, he will be suited by longer trips as the season progresses. (op 18-1 tchd 9-1)
Smog(IRE), a 30,000gns yearling, is out of a miler and a half-brother to winners up to 1m2f, so even though he showed his fair share of early toe, he is likely to appreciate 7f. (op 4-1)
City Of Rome(IRE) cost 55,000euros as a yearling but has not lived up to the price-tag in two races to date. He is bred to sprint, but both outings have been over 7f and he has shown little in either. (op 22-1 tchd 20-1)
Quinner(IRE) is related to several speedy types up to 7f, but it is hard to assess his prospects on the basis of a soft-ground debut. (op 12-1 tchd 8-1)

4266 E.B.F./SIGN UP BONUS AT BETINTERNET.COM FILLIES' H'CAP 7f 16y

7:50 (7:51) (Class 5) (0-70,70) 3-Y-0+ **£4,533** (£1,348; £674; £336) **Stalls** Centre

Form RPR

50-6 **1** **Miss Bootylishes**[102] 1256 4-9-6 **65**.................. KevinGhunowa(3) 5 74
(A B Haynes) *chsd ldr: rdn 2f out: led over 1f out: hung lft ins fnl f: rdn out* **14/1**

0522 **2** *1 ¼* **Ken's Girl**[22] 3537 5-10-0 **70**.................. PatCosgrave 4 76
(W S Kittow) *led: rdn and hdd over 1f out: kpt on* **7/2**[3]

300- **3** *5* **Queen Sally (IRE)**[291] 6535 3-9-0 **68**.................. RossAtkinson(5) 3 58
(Tom Dascombe) *hld up in tch: rdn 2f out: wknd over 1f out* **14/1**

2063 **4** *1 ½* **Foreign Investment (IRE)**[32] 3209 3-9-4 **67**.................. PaulDoe 1 52
(P D Evans) *hld up in tch: rdn over 2f out: wknd over 1f out* **10/3**[2]

6322 **5** *2 ¼* **Ailsa Craig (IRE)**[27] 3381 3-9-0 **63**..................(p) RichardHughes 10 42
(R Hannon) *prom: rdn over 2f out: wknd wl over 1f out* **9/4**[1]

0-02 **6** *7* **Chatanoogachoochoo**[14] 3800 4-9-9 **65**.................. TravisBlock 6 28
(M Hill) *hld up towards rr: rdn over 3f out: sn struggling* **6/1**

-000 **7** *2* **Palais Polaire**[128] 874 7-8-9 **51** oh2..................(p) RichardThomas 9 9
(J A Geake) *hld up in mid-div: pushed along over 3f out: sn struggling* **16/1**

0- **8** *½* **Neat 'n Tidy**[128] 3559 5-8-4 **51** oh6.................. AmyBaker(5) 7 8
(A E Jones) *hld up towards rr: pushed along over 3f out: sn toiling* **66/1**

0000 **9** *hd* **Cross Reef**[25] 3470 4-8-9 **51** oh1..................(p) LukeMorris 8 7
(R A Harris) *in rr: pushed along over 3f out: sn toiling* **18/1**

606 **10** *2 ½* **Missrepresentation**[30] 3278 3-9-1 **64**.................. RichardSmith 11 10
(J C Fox) *a in rr: pushed along and toiling 3f out* **40/1**

1m 27.15s (3.95) **Going Correction** +0.60s/f (Yiel)
WFA 3 from 4yo+ 7lb **10** Ran SP% **118.8**
Speed ratings (Par 100): **101,99,93,92,89 81,79,78,78,75**
toteswingers: 1&2 £19.90, 1&3 £23.10, 2&3 £21.00 CSF £63.86 CT £562.41 TOTE £15.40: £3.80, £1.60, £4.20; EX 52.40.
Owner Mrs H Adams & Miss C Berry **Bred** T P Young And D Hanson **Trained** Limpley Stoke, Bath

FOCUS
They went a decent gallop, but it proved hard to make ground in the soft going and nothing came from behind to have a chance. Modest form, rated around the first two.
Ailsa Craig(IRE) Official explanation: jockey said filly was unsuited by the soft (heavy in places) ground

4267 BEST ODDS GUARANTEED AT BETINTERNET.COM H'CAP 7f 16y

8:20 (8:20) (Class 5) (0-75,74) 3-Y-O **£3,238** (£963; £481; £240) **Stalls** Centre

Form RPR

0502 **1** **Zebrano**[19] 3659 3-9-6 **73**.................. ChrisCatlin 3 83
(Miss E C Lavelle) *t.k.h early: sn stdd towards rr: stdy prog over 3f out: led over 2f out: drvn ins fnl f: r.o* **3/1**[2]

0615 **2** *1* **Secret Hero**[15] 3790 3-8-11 **64**.................. RichardHughes 5 71
(R Hannon) *a.p: rdn to chse wnr over 1f out: kpt on* **7/4**[1]

0225 **3** *8* **My Best Bet**[14] 3815 3-9-5 **72**.................. SamHitchcott 2 58
(M R Channon) *fly j. s: hld up and bhd: pushed along over 2f out: rdn and hdwy wl over 1f out: wknd fnl f* **5/1**[3]

-020 **4** *1 ¼* **Sunny Future (IRE)**[8] 3996 3-9-4 **71**.................. TGMcLaughlin 1 53
(M S Saunders) *s.i.s: sn prom: led 5f out: rdn and hdd over 2f out: wknd over 1f out* **9/1**

2123 **5** *5* **Hellbender (IRE)**[182] 276 3-9-7 **74**.................. JamesDoyle 7 43
(S Kirk) *led 2f: prom tl rdn and wknd wl over 1f out* **8/1**

50-3 **6** *1* **One Cool Mission (IRE)**[184] 236 3-8-5 **58**..................(t) RichardSmith 6 24
(Tom Dascombe) *hld up in rr: pushed along over 3f out: struggling whn rdn over 2f out* **9/1**

0-60 **7** *nk* **Cruise Control**[66] 2165 3-7-13 **55**.................. DavidProbert(3) 4 20
(R J Price) *prom: ev ch 3f out: rdn and wkng whn hung lft jst over 1f out* **20/1**

1m 27.85s (4.65) **Going Correction** +0.60s/f (Yiel) **7** Ran SP% **113.9**
Speed ratings (Par 100): **97,95,86,85,79 78,78**
toteswingers: 1&2 £1.50, 1&3 £2.60, 2&3 £3.20 CSF £8.60 CT £23.76 TOTE £3.60: £2.10, £1.70; EX 9.40.

Owner Caloona Racing **Bred** P R Attwater **Trained** Wildhern, Hants

FOCUS

The first two pulled well clear but several of the others were probably unsuited by the soft ground. Modest form overall, the winner rated to the best view of her 2yo form.

4268 BET ON GLORIOUS GOODWOOD AT BETINTERNET.COM H'CAP 5f 16y
8:55 (8:55) (Class 5) (0-70,70) 3-Y-O+ £2,914 (£867; £433; £216) Stalls Centre

Form RPR

0112 **1** **Solemn**[10] 3938 4-8-12 **60**...(b) DavidProbert(3) 1 69
(J M Bradley) *a.p: rdn over 1f out: led ins fnl f: edgd rt: r.o* **2/1**[1]

2303 **2** *hd* **Cape Royal**[8] 3998 9-9-8 **70**....................................(bt) KevinGhunowa(3) 7 78
(J M Bradley) *led: drifted rt to stands' rail 2f out: rdn and hdd ins fnl f: r.o* **8/1**

0341 **3** *1* **Stamford Blue**[6] 4082 8-8-13 **65** 6ex.................................(b) SPRyan(7) 6 69
(R A Harris) *hld up: hdwy 3f out: rdn over 2f out: kpt on ins fnl f* **7/2**[2]

6666 **4** *1* **Rockfield Lodge (IRE)**[31] 3242 4-8-12 **57**......................... LukeMorris 2 58
(R A Harris) *a.p: rdn and ev ch over 1f out: no ex wl ins fnl f* **15/2**

4366 **5** *1 1/2* **My Best Man**[26] 3426 3-8-8 **57**..................................(t) ChrisCatlin 3 51
(B R Millman) *hld up: pushed along and hdwy over 2f out: rdn over 1f out: wknd wl ins fnl f* **10/1**

0003 **6** *1 1/4* **Digital**[13] 3860 12-9-4 **63**...(v) SamHitchcott 5 54
(M R Channon) *sn bdly outpcd: late hdwy: nrst fin* **8/1**

2122 **7** *3 1/4* **Matterofact (IRE)**[8] 3998 6-9-9 **68**............................... TGMcLaughlin 8 47
(M S Saunders) *hld up: hdwy 3f out: rdn and wknd jst over 1f out* **5/1**[3]

61.87 secs (2.57) **Going Correction** +0.60s/f (Yiel)
WFA 3 from 4yo+ 4lb **7** Ran SP% **115.3**
Speed ratings (Par 103): **103,102,101,99,97 95,89**
toteswingers: 1&2 £7.40, 1&3 £4.20, 2&3 £2.40 CSF £19.17 CT £53.07 TOTE £2.90: £1.70, £3.50; EX 17.30 Place 6: 33.96 Place 5: £16.91.
Owner E A Hayward **Bred** Cheveley Park Stud Ltd **Trained** Sedbury, Gloucs

FOCUS

Another race which favoured those who raced close to the pace. The two stablemates who battled the finish were wide apart, with the winner in the middle of the track and the runner-up drifting to the stands' rail, but there was probably no advantage to be had anywhere on the course. Straightforward form.

T/Plt: £71.70 to a £1 stake. Pool: £57,337.17. 583.38 winning tickets. T/Qpdt: £20.60 to a £1 stake. Pool: £5,374.82. 192.30 winning tickets. KH

4093 NEWMARKET (R-H)
Friday, July 24

OFFICIAL GOING: Good (8.2) changing to good to soft after race 2 (6.10)

The ground was described as "on the slow side of good" by the clerk of the course after 3.5mm of rain earlier in the day.

Wind: fairly modest, across Weather: showery

4269 BOLLINGER CHAMPAGNE CHALLENGE SERIES H'CAP (FOR GENTLEMAN AMATEUR RIDERS) 1m 2f
5:40 (5:41) (Class 5) (0-70,70) 3-Y-O+ £3,123 (£968; £484; £242) Stalls Centre

Form RPR

2353 **1** **Bavarica**[15] 3777 7-10-9 **60**... MrRBirkett(5) 14 71+
(Miss J Feilden) *trckd ldng trio: wl clr of remainder: cruised up to ld wl over 1f out: sn rdn clr: in n.d fnl f: eased nr fin* **12/1**

-504 **2** *2 1/2* **Recession Proof (FR)**[25] 3463 3-10-7 **68**.................. MrJohnEnnis(5) 1 73+
(S A Callaghan) *hld up wl off the pce towards rr: hdwy 3f out: drvn to chse clr wnr over 1f out: kpt on but no imp* **6/1**[2]

/3-0 **3** *9* **Sagarich (FR)**[5] 1261 5-10-3 **56**................................ MrJMQuinlan(7) 13 43
(M G Quinlan) *chsd ldr tl over 4f out: rdn and unable qck over 2f out: wl btn over 1f out: plugged on to go modest 3rd ins fnl f* **11/2**[1]

0001 **4** *2* **Sky Quest (IRE)**[7] 4053 11-11-1 **61**.............................. MrSDobson 11 44
(J R Boyle) *hld up wl off the pce towards rr: hdwy 3f out: rdn over 1f out: no prog but plugged on to go modest 4th nr fin* **13/2**[3]

0050 **5** *1/2* **Wicksy Creek**[8] 3999 4-9-12 **51** oh5...............................(t) MrMMarris(7) 3 33
(G C Bravery) *racd keenly: chsd ldng pair tl wnt 2nd over 4f out: upsides ldr over 2f out tl wl over 1f out: wknd over 1f out: lost 2 pls ins fnl f* **100/1**

1123 **6** *1* **Blockley (USA)**[81] 1732 5-10-13 **66**.............................. MrJHodson(7) 7 46
(Ian Williams) *stdd s: wl bhd: niggled along 7f out: rdn over 2f out: sme hdwy fnl f: nvr on terms* **10/1**

0000 **7** *3 1/4* **Rowan Rio**[13] 3840 4-11-3 **70**...................................... MrDJEustace(7) 4 44
(W J Haggas) *stdd s: hld up wl bhd: rdn and effrt 2f out: swtchd lft over 1f out: nvr on terms* **14/1**

3242 **8** *2 1/4* **Bramalea**[7] 4053 4-11-6 **66**...(p) MrRO'Sullivan 9 35
(B W Duke) *racd keenly: led: jnd and rdn over 2f out: hdd wl over 1f out: sn wknd* **10/1**

0262 **9** *2 1/2* **Extremely So**[22] 3550 3-10-0 **59**................................ MrPCollington(3) 8 23
(P J McBride) *stdd after s: hld up off the pce in midfield: rdn and struggling over 3f out: wl bhd fnl 2f* **9/1**

0025 **10** *1/2* **Artreju (GER)**[26] 3421 6-10-8 **59**...........................(p) MrJoshuaMoore(5) 5 22
(G L Moore) *stdd s: t.k.h: hld up wl off the pce towards rr: hdwy 3f out: rdn and wknd over 1f out: wl btn fnl f* **10/1**

0000 **11** *3/4* **Our Kes (IRE)**[11] 3929 7-10-3 **56**................................ MrJBanks(7) 12 18
(P Howling) *racd wl off the pce in midfield: rdn and struggling over 3f out: wl bhd fnl 2f* **33/1**

1201 **12** *22* **High Five Society**[56] 2458 5-10-8 **59**........................(bt) MrKApark(5) 10 —
(S R Bowring) *racd wd: a towards rr: lost tch 3f out: t.o and eased ins fnl f* **14/1**

2m 10.09s (4.59) **Going Correction** +0.225s/f (Good)
WFA 3 from 4yo+ 10lb **12** Ran SP% **105.2**
Speed ratings (Par 103): **90,88,80,79,78 78,75,73,71,71 70,53**
toteswingers: 1&2 £18.50, 1&3 £16.40, 2&3 £5.50 CSF £66.38 CT £329.15 TOTE £11.20: £3.50, £2.20, £2.30; EX 80.10.
Owner Miss J Feilden **Bred** Juddmonte Farms **Trained** Exning, Suffolk
■ Iceman George was withdrawn (6/1, spread a plate). Deduct 10p in the 3 under R4.

FOCUS

A run-of-the-mill amateur riders' handicap featured a strong early gallop that saw the field strung out like washing through the first half mile. The time was fair, but with rain through the card this race had the best of the ground. The winner is the best guide to the form.

4270 PORTLAND PLACE PROPERTIES MAIDEN STKS 1m 4f
6:10 (6:12) (Class 4) 3-Y-O £5,180 (£1,541; £770; £384) Stalls Centre

Form RPR

63 **1** **Galilean Moon**[42] 2877 3-8-12 0... RyanMoore 3 77+
(Sir Michael Stoute) *chsd ldrs: rdn over 2f out: drvn and chsd ldng pair jst over 1f out: styd on u.str.p to ld fnl 50yds* **5/1**[3]

26 **2** *1/2* **Cotillion**[35] 3117 3-9-3 0.. KShea 5 81
(W J Haggas) *s.i.s and short of room s: t.k.h: hld up in rr: hdwy on stands' side 3f out: chal and hung lft wl over 1f out: sn led but stl hanging lft: hdd and no ex fnl 50yds* **4/1**[2]

2242 **3** *1 3/4* **Decision**[35] 3117 3-9-3 86.. DarryllHolland 7 78
(C G Cox) *led: hrd pressed and rdn ent fnl 2f: hdd over 1f out: carried lft 1f out: one pce and btn fnl 100yds* **11/4**[1]

4 *1 3/4* **Rougham** 3-9-3 0... LPKeniry 1 75+
(A M Balding) *s.i.s: hld up bhd: stdy hdwy 4f out: chsng ldrs and pushed along whn hmpd wl over 1f out: kpt on same pce fnl f* **16/1**

-343 **5** *3 3/4* **Bruton Street (USA)**[20] 3636 3-9-3 77......................... JimmyFortune 11 69
(J H M Gosden) *chsd ldrs: shkn up to chse ldr over 3f out: ev ch and rdn ent fnl 2f: keeping on same pce whn hmpd wl over 1f out: wknd ent fnl f* **11/4**[1]

03 **6** *1 1/2* **Miss Doodle**[22] 3538 3-8-12 0...................................... MickyFenton 2 62
(Eve Johnson Houghton) *in tch on outer: hdwy to chse ldrs over 3f out: shkn up 3f out: rdn and btn wl over 1f out* **28/1**

436 **7** *1/2* **Lacrosse**[4] 4145 3-9-3 0..(p) TPO'Shea 8 66
(M A Jarvis) *s.i.s: t.k.h and sn in tch in midfield: rdn 3f out: unable qck over 2f out: wl hld over 1f out* **14/1**

0-3 **8** *20* **Za Za**[27] 3379 3-8-12 0.. TPQueally 4 29
(H R A Cecil) *stdd s: hld up towards rr: rdn and btn 3f out: sn wl bhd* **16/1**

9 *3/4* **Velvet Nayef** 3-8-12 0... DO'Donohoe 10 28
(J Pearce) *s.i.s and pushed along early: a in rr: rdn and lost tch 3f out: t.o* **80/1**

05 **10** *shd* **Flying Phoebe**[27] 3379 3-8-12 0.................................... DaneO'Neill 6 28
(Mrs L Stubbs) *chsd ldr tl over 3f out: sn wknd: wl bhd fnl 2f: t.o* **66/1**

50- **11** *18* **Watch The Master**[218] 7720 3-9-3 0............................... JerryO'Dwyer 9 4
(B I Case) *stdd s: t.k.h: hld up towards rr: rdn and lost tch 3f out: t.o* **80/1**

2m 34.93s (2.03) **Going Correction** +0.225s/f (Good) **11** Ran SP% **115.8**
Speed ratings (Par 102): **102,101,100,99,96 95,95,82,81,81 69**
toteswingers: 1&2 £6.30, 1&3 £2.60, 2&3 £6.20 CSF £24.61 TOTE £6.30: £2.40, £1.70, £1.60; EX 29.30.
Owner D Smith, Mrs J Magnier, M Tabor **Bred** Meon Valley Stud **Trained** Newmarket, Suffolk
■ Stewards' Enquiry : K Shea caution: careless riding

FOCUS

The going was changed to good to soft after this race. An ordinary maiden dominated by those with the best form in the book already. The form is rated around the third.

4271 SPORTINGBET.COM NURSERY 7f
6:40 (6:42) (Class 4) 2-Y-O £5,180 (£1,541; £770; £384) Stalls High

Form RPR

004 **1** **Keen Bidder**[28] 3344 2-7-12 **60**...................................... NickyMackay 5 64
(D M Simcock) *t.k.h: hld up in tch towards rr: rdn and effrt over 2f out: drvn and hdwy but edging lft over 1f out: flashed tail u.p: led fnl 100yds: r.o strly* **11/1**

221 **2** *2* **Coloursoftheglen (IRE)**[25] 3468 2-9-7 **83**............. RichardKingscote 1 82
(Tom Dascombe) *chsd ldrs: wnt 2nd 3f out: ev ch over 1f out: rdn to ld 1f out: hdd fnl 100yds: nt pce of wnr after* **5/2**[1]

15 **3** *3/4* **Leviathan**[29] 3311 2-9-7 **83**.. MickyFenton 10 80
(T P Tate) *hld up in tch in last pair: hdwy over 2f out: ev ch and rdn over 1f out: kpt on same pce ins fnl f* **13/2**

034 **4** *hd* **Dashing Doc (IRE)**[22] 3522 2-9-2 **78**............................... DaneO'Neill 4 75
(D R C Elsworth) *t.k.h: hld up in tch towards rr: effrt and rdn over 2f out: chsd ldrs over 1f out: drvn 1f out: kpt on same pce fnl f* **9/2**[3]

0420 **5** *3/4* **Yawary**[18] 3686 2-8-3 **65**.. LiamJones 9 60
(C E Brittain) *in tch: effrt jst over 2f out: ev ch and rdn over 1f out: unable qck ent fnl f: one pce after* **12/1**

4255 **6** *3/4* **Pullyourfingerout (IRE)**[21] 3579 2-8-2 **69**... Louis-PhilippeBeuzelin(5) 7 62+
(B G Powell) *in tch: rdn and edgd lft jst over 2f out: keeping on same pce whn sltly hmpd and swtchd rt over 1f out: kpt on but nvr pce to trble ldrs* **16/1**

523 **7** *2 1/4* **Fasilight**[23] 3507 2-8-12 **74**... JimmyQuinn 8 61
(M Botti) *led: rdn over 1f out: hdd 1f out: sn drvn and wknd fnl f* **12/1**

4315 **8** *nk* **Master Of Dance (IRE)**[14] 3821 2-9-3 **79**........................ RyanMoore 6 66+
(R Hannon) *stdd after s: hld up in tch towards rr: shkn up and nt clr run jst over 2f out: drvn and no prog over 1f out* **10/3**[2]

501 **9** *2 1/4* **Rainsborough**[20] 3626 2-8-8 **70**....................................... TPO'Shea 3 51
(M R Channon) *stdd s: hld up in tch in last pair: rdn and no prog wl over 1f out* **20/1**

3331 **10** *21* **Highcliffe Bridge (IRE)**[10] 3958 2-7-7 **60** 6ex ow2... CharlesEddery(7) 2 —
(N P Littmoden) *chsd ldr tl 3f out: wknd qckly jst over 2f out: eased ins fnl f: t.o* **20/1**

1m 27.83s (2.13) **Going Correction** +0.35s/f (Good) **10** Ran SP% **122.3**
Speed ratings (Par 96): **101,98,97,97,96 95,93,93,90,66**
CSF £40.68 CT £205.31 TOTE £14.30: £3.90, £1.70, £2.50; EX 78.60.
Owner J M Cook **Bred** Llety Stud **Trained** Newmarket, Suffolk
■ Stewards' Enquiry : Nicky Mackay nine-day ban: used whip with excessive frequency without giving colt time to respond (August 7-15)

FOCUS

The 'official' ratings shown next to each horse are estimated and for information purposes only. Quite a competitive nursery on paper with plenty of these still to show their true worth. The form should prove sound.

NOTEBOOK

Keen Bidder, who had been quietly progressive in maidens, continued that improvement by staying on strongly to assert in the final furlong and win going away. He clearly has no trouble handling ground on the soft side, and the way he shaped here suggests another furlong will suit him well. He comes from a yard in cracking form and he has more to offer. (op 8-1)

Coloursoftheglen(IRE) was always close up and travelling strongly, but he was outstayed in the final furlong. This is another solid run and he's proving most consistent, so it would be no surprise were he to bag a similar event some time soon. (op 7-2 tchd 4-1 in places)

Leviathan posted an improved effort on this step up in trip, having struggled a bit in novice company at Newcastle last time. He saw the 7f out well and looks to be going the right way. (op 8-1)

Dashing Doc(IRE), a half-brother to the stable's Barshiba and making his handicap debut, is another who shaped with promise, charting his course towards the far side of the group. His trainer reported him to be something of a slow learner at home, so there ought to be a deal more to come. (op 4-1)

Pullyourfingerout(IRE) is more exposed and, although he kept plugging away, he seems to lack a bit of tactical speed.

Fasilight travelled very strongly at the head of affairs before dropping away and there is enough speed on the dam's side of her pedigree to suggest a drop back to 6f might help. (op 11-1)

4272 SPORTINGBET.COM E B F CONDITIONS STKS 6f

7:10 (7:10) (Class 3) 2-Y-O **£9,066** (£2,697; £1,348; £673) **Stalls** High

Form				RPR
4150	**1**		**Hairspray**[16] 3748 2-9-0 0 ... DarryllHolland 1 (M R Channon) *stdd and dropped in bhd after s: plld out and hdwy jst over 1f out: edgd rt ins fnl f: qcknd to ld fnl 100yds: r.o wl* **11/2**[2]	88
1	**2**	*nk*	**Blue Angel (IRE)**[23] 3507 2-9-0 0 ... JimmyFortune 2 (R Hannon) *chsd ldng pair: pushed along over 2f out: wnt 2nd 2f out: rdn to ld over 1f out: hdd fnl 100yds: kpt on but hld by wnr after* **8/1**[3]	87
3121	**3**	*1 ¼*	**Colonel Mak**[7] 4035 2-8-13 0 ... PhillipMakin 8 (D H Brown) *hld up in tch: nt clr run on rail over 1f out: swtchd lft and hdwy ent fnl f: chsng ldrs whn nt clr run and swtchd lft again ins fnl f: kpt on same pce fnl 100yds* **4/7**[1]	85+
2210	**4**	*1 ¼*	**Footstepsofspring (FR)**[15] 3782 2-9-5 0 ... RyanMoore 5 (R Hannon) *led at stdy gallop: rdn 2f out: hdd over 1f out: wknd ins fnl f* **8/1**[3]	85
0	**5**	*3 ¾*	**Dubawi Heights**[14] 3820 2-8-8 0 ... SimonWhitworth 6 (S A Callaghan) *hld up wl in tch: nt clr run and shuffled bk over 1f out: swtchd lft ent fnl f: no ch w ldrs after* **16/1**	64+
	6	*6*	**Maldon Prom (IRE)** 2-8-10 0 ... TPQueally 4 (C A Dwyer) *s.i.s: sn rcvrd and chsd ldr tl 2f out: wknd jst over 1f out* **16/1**	46
0	**7**	*2*	**Gessabelle**[59] 2354 2-8-8 0 ... (t) JimmyQuinn 7 (P S McEntee) *s.i.s: a detached in last pl: struggling over 2f out* **200/1**	38

1m 14.5s (2.00) **Going Correction** +0.35s/f (Good) **7 Ran SP% 113.5**
Speed ratings (Par 98): **100,99,97,96,91 83,80**
toteswingers: 1&2 £7.50, 1&3 £1.10, 2&3 £1.40 CSF £46.66 TOTE £7.30: £2.50, £2.10; EX 35.50.

Owner John Breslin **Bred** J Breslin **Trained** West Ilsley, Berks

FOCUS

Only seven runners but a messy little contest as, unlike the previous race, the field congregated up the stands' rail. Straightforward form, with the winner rated to her mark.

NOTEBOOK

Hairspray was out of harm's way wide of the field and, having made good headway to challenge, she kept on well to repel Blue Angel and add to her fast-ground Lingfield maiden win earlier in the year. She had been flying too high in recent starts but this was a much more suitable task on paper and she proved herself fully effective on ground with cut, as so many by her sire do. The handicapper is likely to ensure nurseries are going to be out of the question now so connections are probably going to be forced into stepping her back up in class, and a fillies' Listed contest would seem a suitable target. (op 6-1 tchd 15-2)

Blue Angel(IRE) is clearly held in some regard given her entry in the Fillies' Mile but having won her maiden over 7f, this drop back to 6f appeared to be a potential issue. She was being niggled along some way out but stayed on well and was closing in on the winner again close home. She looks booked for a step back up in trip now and there are more races to be won with her. (op 7-1 tchd 6-1)

Colonel Mak brought the best form into the race courtesy of his recent Hamilton nursery win and he is proven on soft ground, but he got stuck behind horses along the rail and was forced to switch twice to get clear. In the end he wasn't closing on the winner so it's hard to be dogmatic that he'd have won with a clear route, but he'd probably have finished closer. He remains one to keep onside. Official explanation: jockey said colt was denied a clear run (op 8-11)

Footstepsofspring(FR) dropped away after making the running and the combination of the penalty and the slow ground put paid to his chance. (op 15-2)

Dubawi Heights travelled quite well towards the back and, although left behind, her rider never got vigorous at any stage and she came home quite nicely. She has some big-race entries and although they look fanciful on the bare form of this, it is clear we have yet to see the best of her and she's one to keep an eye on. (op 11-1 tchd 20-1 in places)

4273 SPORTINGBET.COM H'CAP 6f

7:40 (7:41) (Class 3) (0-90,90) 3-Y-O+ **£9,066** (£2,697; £1,348; £673) **Stalls** High

Form				RPR
3126	**1**		**Aye Aye Digby (IRE)**[48] 2707 4-9-10 **88** ... DaneO'Neill 10 (H Candy) *trckd ldrs: rdn to ld over 1f out: styd on gamely u.p fnl f* **2/1**[1]	98
-211	**2**	*½*	**Pumpkin**[16] 3738 3-9-0 **83** ... RyanMoore 11 (Sir Michael Stoute) *led for 1f: pressed ldr tl led again 2f out: hdd and rdn over 1f out: unable qck u.p fnl f* **9/4**[2]	90
1001	**3**	*¾*	**River Kirov (IRE)**[34] 3164 6-9-0 **78** ... NickyMackay 12 (M Wigham) *stdd s: hld up in tch: swtchd rt and effrt wl over 1f out: drvn and chsd ldrs ent fnl f: kpt on same pce fnl 100yds* **16/1**	84
0030	**4**	*¾*	**Good Gorsoon (USA)**[21] 3582 4-9-4 **82** ... FrancisNorton 4 (B W Hills) *racd freely: led after 1f tl 2f out: stl ev ch and rdn over 1f out: no ex ins fnl f* **10/1**	86
00/0	**5**	*¾*	**Hamoody (USA)**[76] 1868 5-9-12 **90** ... JimmyFortune 8 (P W Chapple-Hyam) *hld up in tch: effrt wl over 1f out: chsd ldrs and drvn ent fnl f: no imp fnl 100yds* **20/1**	91
2110	**6**	*1 ½*	**Zowington**[13] 3845 7-9-1 **82** ... (v) WilliamCarson(3) 6 (S C Williams) *hld up in tch in midfield: rdn and unable qck wl over 1f out: plugged on same pce fnl f* **16/1**	78
4133	**7**	*hd*	**Artistic License (IRE)**[25] 3453 4-9-7 **85** ... DarryllHolland 1 (M R Channon) *nvr travelling: sn niggled along towards rr: rdn and btn 2f out* **10/1**	81
350-	**8**	*hd*	**Muftarres (IRE)**[291] 6532 4-8-7 **76** ... Louis-PhilippeBeuzelin(5) 5 (G A Butler) *w.w wl in tch: rdn and unable qck ent fnl 2f out: sn struggling* **16/1**	71
0-00	**9**	*4 ½*	**Burnwynd Boy**[34] 3172 4-9-7 **85** ... PhillipMakin 3 (D Nicholls) *rrd at s and v.s.a: a in last pair: rdn and lost tch 2f out* **20/1**	66
4004	**10**	*1*	**The Galloping Shoe**[28] 3339 4-9-0 **78** ... TPQueally 2 (J Noseda) *rrd s and slowly away: a in rr: rdn and lost tch ent fnl 2f* **8/1**[3]	56

1m 13.52s (1.02) **Going Correction** +0.35s/f (Good)
WFA 3 from 4yo+ 5lb **10 Ran SP% 120.6**
Speed ratings (Par 107): **107,106,105,104,103 101,101,100,94,93**
toteswingers: 1&2 £2.50, 1&3 £14.50, 2&3 £4.30 CSF £6.88 CT £52.69 TOTE £3.40: £1.40, £1.50, £2.80; EX 8.60.

Owner Trolley Action **Bred** G J King **Trained** Kingston Warren, Oxon

■ Stewards' Enquiry : Dane O'Neill He is a game and tough and his work at home has been strong. He is a bit more consistent this year. - Dane O'Neill, jockey

FOCUS

A decent handicap for the grade. It was not strongly run and it paid to be close to the pace, and none of the hold-up horses featured. Sound form among the principals.

NOTEBOOK

Aye Aye Digby(IRE) was well backed to return to winning ways, having been most unlucky in his run at Epsom last time, and off the same mark, he duly obliged. He was never far off the pace and, having moved up to challenge well over a furlong out, he kept pulling out more to keep Pumpkin at bay in the closing stages. He was well suited by the return to this more conventional track and he's a talented sprint handicapper on his day, providing he gets the strong pace that seems to suit. (op 3-1 tchd 10-3)

Pumpkin probably posted a career-best effort in defeat. This was a stronger race than Kempton last time and she was up 6lb, so she's clearly taken another step forward and she stayed on well, having been front rank throughout. (tchd 11-4 and 3-1 in places)

River Kirov(IRE) had questions to answer on easy ground but he also ran a cracker, keeping on strongly despite ideally wanting quicker conditions. He is 3lb above his highest winning mark but is clearly still competitive. (op 10-1)

Good Gorsoon(USA) was very free through the early stages but he soon settled down to bowl along at the head of affairs. His early antics probably took their toll in the closing stages but this was an encouraging effort. Official explanation: jockey said colt ran too free (tchd 8-1)

Hamoody(USA) also took a step forward by keeping on well up the far side despite conditions not really being suitable. (op 16-1)

Zowington fared best of the hold-up horses but was never a factor. (op 22-1)

4274 WIN AT SPORTINGBET.COM H'CAP 1m 4f

8:10 (8:11) (Class 3) (0-90,89) 3-Y-O+ **£9,066** (£2,697; £1,010; £1,010) **Stalls** Centre

Form				RPR
14	**1**		**Remember Ramon (USA)**[107] 1184 6-9-6 **81** ... GeorgeBaker 1 (J R Gask) *mde all: rdn wl over 1f out: pressed ins fnl f: styd on gamely and holding runner up fnl 50yds* **12/1**	88
-406	**2**	*¾*	**Snoqualmie Boy**[13] 3840 6-9-9 **84** ... MickyFenton 7 (T P Tate) *stdd s: hld up in last pl: hdwy over 1f out: chsd wnr ent fnl f: rdn to press wnr ins fnl f: unable qck and hld fnl 50yds* **16/1**	90
00-3	**3**	*2 ¼*	**Kensington Oval**[57] 2407 4-9-11 **86** ... RyanMoore 4 (Sir Michael Stoute) *t.k.h: hld up in tch in last pair: hdwy over 3f out: rdn to chse ldrs ent fnl 2f: drvn and wknd ent fnl f* **7/4**[1]	88
0-13	**3**	*dht*	**Straits Of Hormuz (USA)**[7] 4050 3-8-4 **77** ... GregFairley 5 (M Johnston) *t.k.h: chsd wnr tl wl over 2f out: drvn and outpcd wl over 1f out: kpt on again ins fnl f* **10/3**[3]	79+
0000	**5**	*shd*	**Sereth (IRE)**[14] 3822 6-9-12 **87** ... TPQueally 8 (B J Curley) *t.k.h: hld up in tch: rdn and hung lft over 2f out: drvn over 1f out: kpt on ins fnl f* **16/1**	89
3440	**6**	*7*	**Humble Opinion**[38] 2994 7-10-0 **89** ... JimmyFortune 2 (A King) *chsd ldrs: wnt 2nd wl over 2f out: pressed wnr and drvn over 1f out: wknd ent fnl f: eased whn btn ins fnl f* **9/1**	80
532	**U**		**Lochiel**[14] 3826 5-9-12 **87** ... LPKeniry 3 (G A Swinbank) *rrd and stmbld bdly as stalls opened and uns rdr* **3/1**[2]	—

2m 37.09s (4.19) **Going Correction** +0.525s/f (Yiel)
WFA 3 from 4yo+ 12lb **7 Ran SP% 113.9**
Speed ratings (Par 107): **107,106,105,105,104 100,—**
toteswingers: 1&2 £27.60, 1&KO £2.10, 2&KO £4.30 2&SOH £5.30, 1&SOH £4.10 CSF £169.39 TOTE £13.00: £3.80, £4.90; EX 173.70.

Owner Mrs M Findlay **Bred** Bruce T Hundley **Trained** Sutton Veny, Wilts

FOCUS

Dramatic stuff at the start as Lochiel got himself in a right pickle as the stalls opened and he tumbled out of contention, rendering this much less competitive. It was steadily run and the winner made all. Rather muddling form, rated around the winner.

NOTEBOOK

Remember Ramon(USA) hasn't raced on turf since 2007 but he had been in good form on the all-weather earlier this year and he bounced back from a 107-day break to make all and see this out gutsily up the hill. He was allowed to dictate at just an ordinary pace but to his credit he dug deep when push came to shove and remains fairly unexposed on turf, so there is no reason why he can't add to this. (tchd 11-1 and 14-1)

Snoqualmie Boy was tackling this trip for the first time and he saw it out really well to post his best effort of the campaign. He is clearly not the horse he was two to three years ago but he's not badly treated now if able to build on this. (op 12-1)

Kensington Oval was a bit disappointing and looks very one-paced. There were no excuses for him and he's just not progressing. (op 3-1)

Straits Of Hormuz(USA) rallied in the closing stages but didn't have the tactical speed to stick with the front two. (op 3-1)

Sereth(IRE) kept on well in the closing stages and he's clearly going to be interesting when the money's down.

4275 SPORTINGBET H'CAP 1m

8:45 (8:47) (Class 5) (0-75,75) 3-Y-O **£3,885** (£1,156; £577; £288) **Stalls** High

Form				RPR
30-1	**1**		**Paquerettza (FR)**[85] 1626 3-9-8 **74** ... PhillipMakin 12 (D H Brown) *trckd ldrs: led 2f out: sn rdn: drvn ent fnl f: styd on gamely* **7/2**[1]	80+
0220	**2**	*1*	**Implication**[43] 2845 3-9-7 **73** ... TPQueally 5 (E A L Dunlop) *hld up wl in tch: hdwy to chse ldrs over 1f out: rdn and swtchd rt ins fnl f: kpt on u.p to go 2nd nr fin: nt pce to rch wnr* **12/1**	77+
2214	**3**	*nk*	**Fajita**[18] 3693 3-9-2 **68** ... RyanMoore 2 (G L Moore) *chsd ldrs: pushed along jst over 2f out: rdn to chse wnr over 1f out: drvn and unable qck fnl f: lost 2nd nr fin* **5/1**[2]	71
0002	**4**	*1 ¼*	**Indian Violet (IRE)**[26] 3427 3-9-3 **69** ... JimmyFortune 11 (P F I Cole) *stdd s: hld up in last pl: hdwy on stands' side 2f out: chsd ldrs and rdn over 1f out: kpt on fnl f but nvr pce to rch ldrs* **13/2**[3]	69+
1030	**5**	*½*	**Capo Regime**[7] 4056 3-9-3 **69** ... MickyFenton 1 (P Howling) *stdd s: t.k.h: hld up in tch in rr: hdwy on far side 2f out: rdn over 1f out: one pce and no imp fnl f* **33/1**	68
0115	**6**	*1 ½*	**Edgeworth (IRE)**[8] 4010 3-9-1 **72** ... Louis-PhilippeBeuzelin(5) 13 (B G Powell) *in tch: rdn ent fnl 2f: drvn and kpt on same pce fr over 1f out* **8/1**	68
0062	**7**	*shd*	**Echo Dancer**[10] 3955 3-9-0 **66** ... HayleyTurner 4 (S A Callaghan) *chsd ldr tl over 1f out: sn drvn and unable qck: btn 1f out* **11/1**	62
33	**8**	*2*	**Ymir**[15] 3790 3-8-4 **56** ... (p) LiamJones 7 (M J Attwater) *led tl 2f out: sn rdn: wknd over 1f out* **33/1**	47
-00	**9**	*hd*	**D'Artagnans Dream**[8] 4010 3-8-6 **63** ow1 ... (p) GabrielHannon(5) 10 (G D Blake) *hld up in tch towards rr: rdn and effrt wl over 1f out: unable qck and no imp after* **50/1**	54
6-03	**10**	*hd*	**Markhesa**[85] 1632 3-9-2 **68** ... GeorgeBaker 3 (C F Wall) *hld up towards rr: hdwy on far side over 2f out: chsd ldrs and rdn over 1f out: racd awkwardly and wknd ent fnl f* **10/1**	58
20-5	**11**	*shd*	**Silver Print (USA)**[16] 3736 3-9-9 **75** ... DaneO'Neill 6 (W R Swinburn) *s.i.s: hld up in tch in rr: rdn and effrt jst over 2f out: sn edgd lft and no hdwy* **5/1**[2]	65

1000 **12** *3* **Dontuwishitwereso**[67] 2137 3-8-7 **59**.................................... LPKeniry 8 42
(P W D'Arcy) *t.k.h: hld up wl in tch: n.m.r and shuffled bk over 2f out: rdn 2f out: no hdwy* **28/1**

0-31 **13** *2* **Omnium Duke (IRE)**[17] 3718 3-9-9 **75**...........................(v) JimmyQuinn 9 53
(J W Hills) *t.k.h: hld up wl in tch: rdn wl over 1f out: sn btn* **16/1**

1m 41.64s (1.64) **Going Correction** +0.35s/f (Good) **13** Ran SP% **122.3**
Speed ratings (Par 100): **105,104,103,102,101 100,100,98,98,97 97,94,92**
toteswingers: 1&2 £8.40, 1&3 £5.60, 2&3 £3.80 CSF £47.36 CT £223.20 TOTE £5.30: £1.90, £3.00, £1.90; EX 47.50 Place 6: £1156.38 Place 5: 495.07.
Owner J B Smith & J M Smith **Bred** Newsells Park Stud **Trained** Maltby, S Yorks

FOCUS
A wide-open handicap in which a steady early pace meant a few raced a bit keenly and it paid to be close to the pace. The form is a bit muddling and the winner did not need to improve on her Redcar effort, although she is capable of doing so.
Indian Violet(IRE) Official explanation: jockey said gelding hung left
Capo Regime Official explanation: jockey said gelding hung right
T/Plt: £709.30 to a £1 stake. Pool: £54,791.85. 56.39 winning tickets. T/Qpdt: £189.10 to a £1 stake. Pool: £4,139.82. 16.20 winning tickets. SP

3486 THIRSK (L-H)

Friday, July 24

OFFICIAL GOING: Good (good to soft in places; 8.8)
Wind: moderate 1/2 behind Weather: changeable, showers

4276 SKY BET SUPPORTING YORKSHIRE RACING FESTIVAL MAIDEN STKS (DIV I) 7f

1:30 (1:41) (Class 5) 3-Y-O+ **£3,950** (£1,175; £587; £293) **Stalls** Low

Form RPR

0 **1** **Ms Sophie Eleanor (USA)**[34] 3175 3-8-12 0................ PhillipMakin 10 66
(T D Barron) *trckd ldr: chal over 2f out: rdn to ld over 1f out: drvn out* **10/1**

2 *2* **Ordoney (IRE)** 4-9-10 0.. SebSanders 1 65+
(L M Cumani) *s.i.s: in rr: hdwy on outside over 2f out: styd on strly fnl f: will improve* **4/1**[3]

0-3 **3** *shd* **Neva A Mull Moment (IRE)**[53] 2543 3-9-3 0............ AdrianTNicholls 6 65
(D Nicholls) *taken to post early and walked down: led: hdd over 2f out: kpt on same pce* **9/1**

00 **4** *shd* **Arjemis**[20] 3611 3-8-12 0.. PAspell 11 60
(C R Wilson) *chsd ldrs: one pce fnl 2f* **150/1**

6 **5** *7* **Simola**[38] 3003 3-8-12 0..................................... TonyHamilton 12 41
(R A Fahey) *swvd rt at s: chsd ldrs: one pce fnl 2f* **9/1**

6 *1 3/4* **Beat The Shower** 3-8-12 0.................................... BMcHugh(5) 5 41
(P D Niven) *s.i.s: sn midfield: pushed along over 3f out: nvr a factor* **50/1**

7 *nk* **Morning Dress (USA)** 3-9-3 0............................ RoystonFfrench 4 40
(M Johnston) *in tch: drvn over 3f out: wknd over 1f out* **10/3**[1]

8 *1 3/4* **Needy McCredie** 3-8-12 0.............................. PaulMulrennan 13 31
(J R Turner) *s.s: in rr: sme hdwy 2f out: nvr on terms* **100/1**

9 *shd* **Fabled Dancer (IRE)** 3-9-3 0................................... DavidAllan 2 35
(E J Alston) *in rr: bhd fnl 2f* **25/1**

10 *4* **Clash City Rocker** 3-9-3 0.................................. PJMcDonald 9 25
(G A Swinbank) *unruly in stalls: mid-div: bhd fnl 2f* **16/1**

11 *5* **Mutajaaser (USA)** 4-9-10 0...................................... JimmyQuinn 7 11
(K A Morgan) *gave problems in stalls: chsd ldrs: drvn over 3f out: sn btn* **7/2**[2]

12 *38* **Doctor Of Music (IRE)** 3-9-3 0................................. TomEaves 14 —
(B Smart) *s.v.s: reminders after s: sn t.o* **20/1**

1m 29.82s (2.62) **Going Correction** +0.275s/f (Good)
WFA 3 from 4yo 7lb **12** Ran SP% **112.5**
Speed ratings (Par 103): **96,93,93,93,85 83,83,81,81,76 70,27**
toteswingers: 1&2 £6.30, 1&3 £8.20, 2&3 £6.60 CSF £41.46 TOTE £10.70: £2.50, £1.60, £2.10; EX 46.80.
Owner J Browne **Bred** Whose Your Daddy? Breeding Llc **Trained** Maunby, N Yorks
■ Blastie (8/1) withdrawn; unseated rider and bolted on way to start. Rule 4 applies, deduct 10p in the £.

FOCUS
Rain started just before this opening race and the jockeys reported the going was good to soft. A moderate-looking older-horse maiden in which only four had previous experience and the betting was open, although there was early money for the newcomer Mutajaaser and also for Blastie. However, the latter decanted his rider on the way to the start and ran loose, which resulted in his withdrawal. It was the slowest of the three C&D times, on probably the quickest ground. The form looks modest.

4277 SKY BET SUPPORTING YORKSHIRE RACING FESTIVAL MAIDEN STKS (DIV II) 7f

2:00 (2:08) (Class 5) 3-Y-O+ **£3,950** (£1,175; £587; £293) **Stalls** Low

Form RPR

1 **Wood Fairy** 3-8-12 0.. PaulHanagan 4 69+
(R A Fahey) *chsd ldrs: led over 1f out: hld on wl towards fin* **5/1**[3]

00- **2** *3/4* **Safari Song (IRE)**[273] 6944 3-9-0 0...................... FrederikTylicki(3) 14 72
(B Smart) *mid-div: hdwy over 2f out: chsd wnr fnl f: no ex wl ins fnl f* **10/1**

46 **3** *6* **Halcyon Dancer**[15] 3764 3-8-12 0............................ PhillipMakin 5 51
(M Dods) *led tl hdd over 1f out: wknd fnl f* **11/2**

45- **4** *hd* **Battle Royal (IRE)**[293] 6480 3-9-3 0.......................... TomEaves 9 55
(B Smart) *chsd ldrs: drvn 3f out: kpt on same pce appr fnl f* **7/2**[2]

5 *nk* **Tobrata** 3-8-10 0.. JohnCavanagh(7) 3 54+
(M Brittain) *s.i.s: bhd: hdwy on outside 2f out: kpt on wl ins fnl f* **50/1**

0-6 **6** *1* **Elements (IRE)**[63] 2229 3-8-12 0................................ DavidAllan 10 47
(E J Alston) *chsd ldrs: drvn 3f out: one pce* **10/1**

7 *1/2* **Severio (IRE)** 3-8-12 0.. AndrewElliott 12 45
(K R Burke) *t.k.h: lost pl over 4f out: wandered and kpt on fnl 2f* **14/1**

8 *3* **Forward Planning (USA)** 3-8-12 0........................ RoystonFfrench 13 37
(M Johnston) *chsd ldrs: drvn over 3f out: fdd over 1f out* **3/1**[1]

00- **9** *3* **Occasion**[291] 6530 4-9-5 0...................................... PJMcDonald 7 32
(G M Moore) *trckd ldrs: wknd over 1f out* **40/1**

06 **10** *4* **Crimson Mist**[17] 3712 3-8-12 0................................ JamieKyne(5) 2 23
(J J Quinn) *mid-div: hdwy on ins over 2f out: wknd 1f out* **16/1**

40- **11** *shd* **Consequence**[213] 7773 3-9-3 0............................... DanielTudhope 1 23
(A Dickman) *a towards rr* **150/1**

12 *10* **Romantic Bond** 3-8-12 0...................................... DuranFentiman 8 —
(T D Easterby) *in rr and sn drvn along: wl bhd fnl 2f* **25/1**

13 *14* **Mister Biscuit (USA)** 3-9-3 0.............................. PaulMulrennan 6 —
(Miss L A Perratt) *s.i.s: wl bhd fnl 2f* **20/1**

1m 28.68s (1.48) **Going Correction** +0.275s/f (Good)
WFA 3 from 4yo 7lb **13** Ran SP% **123.7**
Speed ratings (Par 103): **102,101,94,94,93 92,92,88,85,80 80,69,53**
toteswingers: 1&2 £12.00, 1&3 £5.70, 2&3 £12.10 CSF £53.87 TOTE £5.30: £2.20, £3.40, £2.10; EX 53.60.
Owner B H Farr **Bred** Worksop Manor Stud **Trained** Musley Bank, N Yorks

FOCUS
This looked the stronger of the two divisions, although it was somewhat weakened by the withdrawal of the forecast favourite, and the time was 1.14secs quicker. Little form to go on, and it has been rated around the third and fourth.
Forward Planning(USA) Official explanation: jockey said filly hung right throughout

4278 EUROPEAN BREEDERS' FUND MAIDEN FILLIES' STKS 7f

2:30 (2:35) (Class 4) 2-Y-O **£5,666** (£1,686; £842; £420) **Stalls** Low

Form RPR

0 **1** **Admire The View (IRE)**[13] 3858 2-9-0 0.................................. NCallan 4 90+
(D R Lanigan) *chsd ldr: led on bit 2f out: shkn up and wnt clr 1f out: eased towards fin* **15/2**[2]

6 **2** *7* **Mad Millie (IRE)**[24] 3487 2-9-0 0........................ GrahamGibbons 2 69+
(J Hetherton) *led: qcknd over 4f out: hdd 2f out: eased wl ins fnl f whn no ch w wnr* **28/1**

46 **3** *7* **Knockenduff**[22] 3534 2-9-0 0................................. TonyCulhane 3 59+
(M R Channon) *s.i.s: hdwy on ins whn hmpd and lost pl after 2f: hdwy 2f out: styd on wl to snatch modest 3rd post* **7/1**[1]

44 **4** *nk* **Seven Of Diamonds (IRE)**[13] 3875 2-9-0 0....................(t) DavidAllan 12 50
(T D Easterby) *chsd ldrs: drvn over 3f out: one pce* **9/1**[3]

5 *2 1/4* **Hedgerow (IRE)** 2-9-0 0... DanielTudhope 5 45+
(A Dickman) *s.i.s: sme hdwy on wd outside over 2f out: nvr nr ldrs* **66/1**

60 **6** *1/2* **Emeralds Spirit (IRE)**[57] 2388 2-9-0 0........................ TonyHamilton 8 43
(J R Weymes) *t.k.h: mid-div: kpt on fnl 2f: nvr nr ldrs* **40/1**

0 **7** *1/2* **Captain's Paradise (IRE)**[32] 3226 2-9-0 0.................. SebSanders 10 42
(Sir Mark Prescott) *chsd ldrs: hung lft and wknd 2f out* **22/1**

8 *2* **Buzz Bird** 2-9-0 0.. PhillipMakin 11 37
(T D Barron) *in rr: nvr a factor* **50/1**

4 **9** *2 3/4* **Dazakhee**[22] 3528 2-9-0 0.. PJMcDonald 7 30
(P T Midgley) *s.i.s: in rr div: hung lft 2f out: nvr on terms* **50/1**

10 *10* **Timeless Elegance (IRE)** 2-9-0 0........................... PaulMulrennan 6 5
(J Howard Johnson) *t.k.h in mid-div: hmpd and lost pl after 2f: bhd fnl 2f* **28/1**

6 **11** *3* **Blue Avon**[21] 3571 2-9-0 0....................................... PaulHanagan 9 —
(R A Fahey) *chsd ldrs: drvn over 4f out: sn lost pl: bhd fnl 2f* **20/1**

1m 28.25s (1.05) **Going Correction** +0.275s/f (Good) **11** Ran SP% **58.1**
Speed ratings (Par 93): **105,97,89,88,86 85,84,82,79,68 64**
toteswingers: 1&2 £10.40, 1&3 £4.40, 2&3 £12.40 CSF £43.58 TOTE £4.40: £1.60, £4.30, £1.40; EX 58.70.
Owner Saif Ali & Saeed H Altayer **Bred** Mountgrange Stud Ltd, T Stewart & A Stroud **Trained** Newmarket, Suffolk
■ Marie De Medici (4/6) withdrawn (got upset and sat down in the stalls); Rule 4 applies, deduction 55p in the £.
■ Stewards' Enquiry : Paul Hanagan caution: used whip when out of contention

FOCUS
A fair juvenile fillies' contest run 0.43 secs faster than the quickest of the two divisions of the preceding older-horse maiden. Marie De Medici was the clear choice on previous form. However, she played up and went down in the stalls which resulted in her being withdrawn. The winner impressed with the second the key to the level.

NOTEBOOK
Admire The View(IRE) ◆, a 55,000gns half-sister to a winning juvenile over 6f, had shown promise on her debut over 6f and was well backed to build on that. Always travelling well up with the pace, she cruised to the front 2f out and came right away before being eased down. The time was decent and she looks to have a future. (op 16-1)
Mad Millie(IRE) had shown promise on her debut over 6f here at the end of the previous month and was given a positive ride that stretched the field out and meant nothing got into it from off the pace. She can win a small race but her future will ultimately lie in handicaps at around this trip. (op 25-1)
Knockenduff was the unlucky horse of the race, as she was hampered in some scrimmaging at the end of the back straight which left her with a lot to do. She ran on once in line for home and may have finished second with a clear run, but wouldn't have beaten the winner. The handicap route is open to her now. (op 11-2 tchd 15-2)
Seven Of Diamonds(IRE) had shown promise in 6f maidens on fast ground and ran well again, although tiring late on. She is another who is now qualified for nurseries.
Hedgerow(IRE) has plenty of winners in her family and showed a measure of promise on this debut, running on late in the wake of the third. (op 28-1)

4279 HABTON (S) H'CAP 1m

3:05 (3:06) (Class 6) (0-65,65) 3-Y-O **£2,978** (£886; £442; £221) **Stalls** Low

Form RPR

042 **1** **Winrob**[8] 4013 3-8-10 **54**... KLatham 14 57
(Patrick Morris) *chsd ldrs: styd on fnl 2f: led nr fin* **14/1**

3031 **2** *hd* **King's Chorister**[3] 4177 3-8-8 **57** 6ex......................(t) KylieManser(5) 6 60
(Miss Gay Kelleway) *mid-div: hdwy over 2f out: styd on wl fnl f: jst failed* **15/2**[3]

-206 **3** *nk* **Jiggalong**[13] 3859 3-9-0 **58**.................................. MichellePayne 7 60
(Jane Chapple-Hyam) *chsd ldrs: led over 1f out: hdd towards fin* **9/1**

3323 **4** *1 3/4* **Paint Splash**[8] 4013 3-8-3 **52**............................. DeanHeslop(5) 17 50
(T D Barron) *chsd ldrs on outer: wknd towards fin* **14/1**

321 **5** *hd* **Shared Moment (IRE)**[13] 3862 3-9-1 **62**...............(p) KellyHarrison(3) 18 60
(Ollie Pears) *mid-div on outer: hdwy over 2f out: styd on wl ins fnl f* **4/1**[1]

0004 **6** *nk* **Join Up**[25] 3449 3-8-5 **49**..................................... DuranFentiman 4 46
(W M Brisbourne) *in tch: effrt over 2f out: kpt on wl ins fnl f* **28/1**

0-06 **7** *1 3/4* **Mintoe**[16] 3727 3-8-13 **57**...(p) NCallan 8 50
(K A Ryan) *t.k.h: led: hdd over 1f out: edgd rt and sn fdd* **7/1**[2]

-003 **8** *1* **Castle Myth (USA)**[39] 2681 3-8-6 **55**...................... LanceBetts(5) 16 46
(B Ellison) *in rr: kpt on fnl 2f: nvr a factor* **25/1**

1000 **9** *2 1/2* **Why Nee Amy**[38] 3005 3-8-1 **50**........................(p) PaulPickard(5) 11 35
(T Keddy) *in rr div: effrt over 2f out: nvr on terms* **20/1**

0054 **10** *hd* **Highly Acclaimed**[10] 3955 3-8-10 **54**..........(p) SilvestreDeSousa 2 38
(Mrs A Duffield) *prom: effrt over 2f out: one pce* **11/1**

5516 **11** *1 1/2* **Ask Dan (IRE)**[8] 4013 3-9-2 **60**.........................(p) PhillipMakin 12 41
(M Dods) *mid-div: effrt over 2f out: nvr a factor* **12/1**

0540 **12** *3* **Weet In Nerja**[91] 1492 3-8-7 **51**........................... GrahamGibbons 10 25
(J W Unett) *in tch: hdwy on ins over 3f out: wknd over 1f out* **50/1**

040 **13** *2* **Silent Treatment (IRE)**[17] 3711 3-8-12 **56**...............(t) PaulHanagan 15 25
(Miss Gay Kelleway) *a towards rr* **16/1**

4600 **14** *5* **Rossett Rose (IRE)**[6] 4105 3-8-2 **53**........................ JohnCavanagh(7) 3 11
(M Brittain) *chsd ldrs: lost pl over 2f out* **25/1**

0000 **15** *1 ½* **Midnight Bay**[13] 3862 3-8-8 **52**.. TonyCulhane 9 6
(M R Channon) *a towards rr* **18/1**

06 **16** *2 ¾* **Special Cuvee**[15] 3790 3-9-7 **65**...................................... SebSanders 13 13
(A B Haynes) *s.i.s: swtchd lft after s: bhd: hdwy on ins over 2f out: wknd over 1f out* **12/1**

400- **17** *28* **Blue Dagger (IRE)**[280] 6787 3-9-2 **60**.......................... PaulMulrennan 5 —
(P C Haslam) *in rr: t.o 2 f out* **40/1**

1m 42.91s (2.81) **Going Correction** +0.275s/f (Good) **17** Ran SP% **122.8**
Speed ratings (Par 98): **96,95,95,93,93 93,91,90,88,87 86,83,81,76,74 72,44**
toteswingers: 1&2 £28.50, 1&3 £31.10, 2&3 £16.30 CSF £106.51 CT £1051.82 TOTE £16.00: £4.00, £2.30, £3.10, £4.50; EX 109.60.The winner was bought in for 10,000gns. Shared Moment was claimed by J. Gallagher for £10,000.

Owner Cruise Nightspot **Bred** Mrs J A Chapman **Trained** Tarporley, Cheshire

■ A winner for Irish-based South African jockey Keagan Latham.

FOCUS
A big field for this seller and it produced a close finish. The form is sound.

4280 STANLAND LAUNDRY H'CAP 1m 4f
3:40 (3:40) (Class 4) (0-80,80) 3-Y-O **£5,569** (£1,657; £828; £413) **Stalls** Low

Form RPR

3343 **1** **Royal Trooper (IRE)**[18] 3687 3-8-8 **70**...................... FrederikTylicki(3) 9 78
(J G Given) *hld up in last: gd hdwy on outside 3f out: led over 1f out: styd on strly* **6/1**[2]

303 **2** *1 ¾* **Tapis Wizard**[8] 4004 3-8-9 **68**...................................... PaulMulrennan 1 73+
(M W Easterby) *trckd ldrs: effrt 3f out: swtchd rt over 1f out: styd on same pce* **9/1**

5052 **3** *4* **Amethyst Dawn (IRE)**[18] 3687 3-8-2 **61**...................... DuranFentiman 6 60
(T D Easterby) *led tl over 1f out: one pce* **13/2**[3]

221- **4** *1 ¼* **Kind Heart**[241] 7445 3-9-7 **80**.. SebSanders 2 77
(Sir Mark Prescott) *racd freely: trckd ldr: rdn over 2f out: edgd lft and wknd fnl f* **6/1**[2]

2262 **5** *hd* **Proud Times (USA)**[8] 4014 3-9-4 **77**........................... PJMcDonald 8 73
(G A Swinbank) *hld up in rr: drvn and hdwy on ins over 2f out: edgd rt over 1f out: swtchd lft ins fnl f: nvr nr ldrs* **11/1**

3-03 **6** *10* **All Guns Firing (IRE)**[21] 3587 3-9-1 **74**.....................(t) PhilipRobinson 3 54
(M A Jarvis) *chsd ldrs: drvn 4f out: lost pl over 2f out* **6/4**[1]

-403 **7** *4 ½* **Guestofthenation (USA)**[25] 3466 3-9-3 **76**............... RoystonFfrench 7 49
(M Johnston) *in rr: reminders over 5f out: sme hdwy over 3f out: lost pl over 2f out* **7/1**

-566 **8** *3 ¾* **Hector's House**[10] 3942 3-8-7 **66** ow1................................ TomEaves 5 33
(M Dods) *mid-div: drvn over 5f out: hung bdly lft and lost pl over 2f out* **50/1**

2m 38.86s (2.66) **Going Correction** +0.275s/f (Good) **8** Ran SP% **114.7**
Speed ratings (Par 102): **102,100,98,97,97 90,87,85**
toteswingers: 1&2 £6.70, 1&3 £5.10, 2&3 £12.40 CSF £58.05 CT £361.79 TOTE £6.90: £1.80, £3.00, £1.90; EX 44.00.

Owner J Barson **Bred** Western Bloodstock **Trained** Willoughton, Lincs

FOCUS
This was no more than a modest handicap. The form is fair for the grade with the runner-up the best guide.

Proud Times(USA) Official explanation: jockey said gelding was denied a clear run approaching line

All Guns Firing(IRE) Official explanation: jockey said gelding had a breathing problem

4281 MALLION SPOUT FILLIES' H'CAP 6f
4:15 (4:15) (Class 5) (0-70,70) 3-Y-O+ **£4,274** (£1,271; £635; £158; £158) **Stalls** High

Form RPR

0111 **1** **Rafta (IRE)**[2] 4198 3-9-3 **70** 12ex........................... JosephineBruning(7) 8 79+
(T T Clement) *mid-div: hdwy on outer over 1f out: r.o to ld jst ins fnl f: kpt on wl* **5/4**[1]

4364 **2** *1 ¼* **Jilly Why (IRE)**[8] 3999 8-9-6 **61**.................................(b) PaulMulrennan 11 67
(Paul Green) *chsd ldrs: led over 1f out: hdd and no ex jst ins fnl f* **15/2**[3]

0056 **3** *¾* **Sardan Dansar (IRE)**[9] 3972 3-8-3 **49**........................ RoystonFfrench 15 52
(Mrs A Duffield) *in rr: hdwy on ins 2f out: swtchd lft: styd on strly ins fnl f* **22/1**

00U0 **4** *hd* **Coconut Moon**[10] 3938 7-8-7 **48** oh3................................ PaulQuinn 14 51
(A Berry) *chsd ldrs: kpt on same pce appr fnl f: eased nr fin* **50/1**

0233 **4** *dht* **Poppy's Rose**[7] 4072 5-9-4 **59**....................................... DanielTudhope 7 62
(I W McInnes) *in rr: hdwy over 2f out: no clr run: hung lft and swtchd lft jst ins fnl f: kpt on* **4/1**[2]

0000 **6** *¾* **Dorn Dancer (IRE)**[51] 2590 7-9-10 **65**.......................... TonyHamilton 9 57
(W M Brisbourne) *s.i.s: swtchd rt after s: hdwy 2f out: styd on same pce fnl f* **14/1**

0-00 **7** *3* **Uace Mac**[27] 3381 5-8-11 **57**... JamieKyne(5) 1 22
(N Bycroft) *racd v wd: overall ldr: hdd over 1f out: sn wknd* **50/1**

0035 **8** *½* **Joyeaux**[13] 3855 7-9-7 **62**... DuranFentiman 10 53
(Ollie Pears) *chsd ldrs: hung lft and fdd over 1f out* **12/1**

-240 **9** *½* **Bahamian Ballad**[21] 3562 4-8-8 **49**...........................(v) PaulHanagan 12 12
(J D Bethell) *chsd ldrs: wknd over 1f out* **9/1**

6050 **10** *nk* **Slip Star**[27] 3381 6-8-7 **48** oh2.................................... GrahamGibbons 16 10
(T J Etherington) *w ldrs: wknd 2f out* **20/1**

0500 **11** *6* **Venetian Lady**[6] 4105 3-8-4 **50**................................(b[1]) SilvestreDeSousa 4 —
(Mrs A Duffield) *swvd lft s: chsd ldrs on outer: hung lft and lost pl over 1f out* **40/1**

-000 **12** *nk* **Little Pandora**[9] 3972 5-8-0 **48** oh3........................... JamesPSullivan(7) 2 —
(L R James) *mid-div on outer: lost pl 2f out* **100/1**

1006 **13** *2 ½* **Style Award**[15] 3763 4-9-5 **63**.................................(p) KellyHarrison(3) 6 —
(W J H Ratcliffe) *mid-div: lost pl over 3f out: sn bhd* **33/1**

005 **14** *15* **Sally's Swansong**[20] 3632 3-8-3 **49** oh3 ow1..............(p) AndrewElliott 3 —
(M Wellings) *s.i.s: sn in rr on outer: bhd fnl 2f* **150/1**

1m 12.78s (0.08) **Going Correction** +0.075s/f (Good)
WFA 3 from 4yo+ 5lb **14** Ran SP% **120.6**
Speed ratings (Par 100): **102,100,99,99,99 94,83,93,82,82 74,73,64,53**
toteswingers: 1&2 £4.70, 1&3 £10.00, 2&3 £22.20 CSF £10.24 CT £153.52 TOTE £2.50: £1.20, £2.10, £4.80; EX 11.80.

Owner R L Gray **Bred** Thomas And Linda Heffernan **Trained** Newmarket, Suffolk

■ Stewards' Enquiry : Paul Quinn three-day ban: failed to ride out for 4th place (Aug 7-9)

FOCUS
Another big field for this sprint but a moderate contest with the top weight 5lb below the race ceiling. The winner still looked well treated despite her double penalty and ran close to her recent level, with the placed form ordinary.

Sally's Swansong Official explanation: trainer said filly lost an off-fore shoe

4282 MICHAEL GRANT MEMORIAL MEDIAN AUCTION MAIDEN STKS 5f
4:50 (5:00) (Class 5) 2-Y-O **£4,274** (£1,271; £635; £317) **Stalls** High

Form RPR

4 **1** **Yaa Wayl (IRE)**[11] 3920 2-9-3 0.................................. PhilipRobinson 11 81
(M A Jarvis) *chsd ldrs: hung lft and led 1f out: styd on strly towards fin* **9/4**[2]

634 **2** *1 ¾* **Goodbye Earl (IRE)**[14] 3805 2-8-7 0............................ SladeO'Hara(5) 2 70
(A Berry) *w ldrs: kpt on same pce ins fnl f* **16/1**

2 **3** *2 ¼* **Secret Millionaire (IRE)**[97] 1358 2-9-3 0............................ KLatham 7 67
(Patrick Morris) *unruly s: mid-div: hdwy over 2f out: swtchd ins over 1f out: styd on ins fnl f* **6/4**[1]

63 **4** *hd* **Silver In The Sand**[53] 2526 2-8-12 0......................... GrahamGibbons 10 61
(J D Bethell) *led tl hdd and no ex 1f out* **25/1**

633 **5** *nk* **Mister Hughie (IRE)**[11] 3918 2-9-3 0............................... TonyCulhane 6 65
(M R Channon) *unruly s: mid-div: hdwy to chse ldrs 2f out: kpt on same pce fnl f* **4/1**[3]

6 *¾* **Shi Shan** 2-9-3 0.. TomEaves 5 62+
(T D Barron) *s.i.s: sn outpcd and bhd: hdwy 2f out: styd on wl ins fnl f* **40/1**

42 **7** *hd* **Mercers Row**[25] 3446 2-9-3 0...................................... DanielTudhope 8 61
(A Dickman) *gave problems s: mid-div: hdwy to chse ldrs 2f out: kpt on same pce* **9/1**

8 *9* **Lieu Day Louie (IRE)** 2-9-3 0..................................... DuranFentiman 3 29
(N Wilson) *s.s: a bhd* **100/1**

6005 **9** *½* **Miccolo**[42] 2893 2-9-3 0.. PJMcDonald 1 27
(P T Midgley) *chsd ldrs on outer: lost pl over 1f out* **150/1**

0 **10** *1 ¾* **Micky's Knock Off (IRE)**[7] 4067 2-8-10 0.......................... JRoberts(7) 4 21
(R C Guest) *gave problems s: chsd ldrs: wknd rapidly over 1f out* **150/1**

59.81 secs (0.21) **Going Correction** +0.075s/f (Good) **10** Ran SP% **115.3**
Speed ratings (Par 94): **101,98,94,94,93 92,92,77,77,74**
toteswingers: 1&2 £4.00, 1&3 £4.50, 2&3 £9.50 CSF £35.08 TOTE £3.40: £1.30, £2.70, £1.20; EX 34.90.

Owner Sheikh Ahmed Al Maktoum **Bred** Ballylinch Stud **Trained** Newmarket, Suffolk

FOCUS
In past years this juvenile maiden has fallen to something with experience and that has appeared more significant than having a high draw. They were waiting in the stalls a long time after Reel Credit Crunch (33/1, withdrawn) broke out. The level was set around the time and the runner-up.

NOTEBOOK

Yaa Wayl(IRE), a promising fourth on his debut over 6f on fast ground, his sire and dam both had form on soft ground so the ease in the going may have been to his advantage. He looked in trouble over a furlong out but picked up well to settle matters and can be expected to build on this. (op 2-1 tchd 4-1)

Goodbye Earl(IRE) is an exposed, modest performer who ran her race and probably sets the standard here. She has yet to score but seems to be running well again after a couple of below-par efforts. (op 12-1)

Secret Millionaire(IRE) is well bred and made an encouraging debut from the front in a race that is working out. He may have lost his race at the start, as he played up before eventually going into the stalls and then missed the break slightly. He may have also been unsuited by the cut in the ground but looked better than this on his previous start. (op 2-1 tchd 5-4)

Silver In The Sand had finished ahead of Mercers Row previously and the pair ran pretty close to that form this time. He made much of the running and was unlucky not to make the frame, being caught for third close home. (op 22-1 tchd 28-1)

Mister Hughie(IRE) was another who was reluctant to load but ran reasonably considering he raced more towards the middle of the track. (op 5-1)

Shi Shan ◆ was possibly the one to take out of the race. Making his debut, this speedily-bred sort was last at halfway but responded to a couple of hefty reminders to finish well and reach the heels of the placed horses. He will be better for the experience. (tchd 33-1)

4283 SUTTON BANK "HANDS AND HEELS" APPRENTICE SERIES H'CAP 5f
5:20 (5:27) (Class 5) (0-75,72) 3-Y-O+ **£4,274** (£1,271; £635; £317) **Stalls** High

Form RPR

0052 **1** **Blessed Place**[7] 4051 9-8-10 **55**.................................... DebraEngland 10 62
(D J S Ffrench Davis) *gave problems gng to s: chsd ldrs stands' side: styd on wl fnl f: led last strides* **9/2**[2]

4121 **2** *shd* **Ingleby Star (IRE)**[4] 4136 4-9-7 **66** 6ex..........................(p) PaulPickard 9 73
(N Wilson) *w ldr towards stands' side: kpt on wl fnl f* **9/4**[1]

4153 **3** *shd* **Weet A Surprise**[21] 3591 4-8-12 **60**............................(v) AlexEdwards(3) 7 67
(J W Unett) *in tch: hdwy over 1f out: styd on wl towards fin* **9/1**

0-3 **4** *hd* **Grudge**[18] 3678 4-9-6 **65**.. MatthewLawson 4 71
(Ollie Pears) *racd towards centre: led: hdd nr fin* **20/1**

2235 **5** *shd* **Wicked Wilma (IRE)**[11] 3909 5-8-12 **60**......................... SeanPalmer(3) 1 66
(A Berry) *chsd ldrs on outside: kpt on wl ins fnl f* **10/1**

0122 **6** *shd* **Toy Top (USA)**[19] 3657 6-8-13 **58**...................................(b) JamieKyne 2 63
(M Dods) *missed break: in rr: hdwy over 1f out: styd on wl ins fnl f* **15/2**

3355 **7** *1 ½* **Miss Daawe**[10] 3938 5-8-11 **59**......................................(t) AnthonyBetts(3) 5 59
(B Ellison) *sn outpcd and in rr: hdwy over 1f out: nvr rchd ldrs* **7/1**[3]

5210 **8** *1 ¾* **Baybshambles (IRE)**[14] 3828 5-9-13 **72**.............................. DavidKenny 6 66
(R E Barr) *outpcd and in rr after 2f: kpt on fnl f: nvr on terms* **14/1**

0251 **9** *¾* **Colorus (IRE)**[11] 3917 6-9-12 **71** 6ex.....................(p) JosephineBruning 8 62
(W J H Ratcliffe) *w ldrs on outside: hung lft and wknd appr fnl f* **17/2**

06-0 **10** *6* **Gleaming Spirit (IRE)**[21] 3570 5-8-8 **53**...........(v) AndrewHeffernan 11 22
(Peter Grayson) *in rr: swtchd centre after 1f: bhd fnl 2f* **40/1**

59.53 secs (-0.07) **Going Correction** +0.075s/f (Good) **10** Ran SP% **116.7**
Speed ratings (Par 103): **103,102,102,102,102 102,99,96,95,86**
toteswingers: 1&2 £2.90, 1&3 £10.60, 2&3 £7.00 CSF £15.01 CT £87.58 TOTE £6.20: £2.10, £1.50, £3.10; EX 15.60 TRIFECTA Place 6: £197.06 Place 5: £69.29.

Owner S J Edwards **Bred** Mrs W H Gibson Fleming **Trained** Lambourn, Berks

FOCUS
A high draw has been important in previous runnings of this apprentice sprint and was so again, although the field were spread across the track at the line. The time was 0.28secs faster than the preceding juvenile maiden but it produced a desperate finish with less than half a length separating the first six. Straightforward form.

Toy Top(USA) Official explanation: jockey said mare missed the break

T/Plt: £184.00 to a £1 stake. Pool: £53,072.96. 210.47 winning tickets. T/Qpdt: £13.40 to a £1 stake. Pool: £3,899.60. 214.80 winning tickets. WG

[3871]YORK (L-H)

Friday, July 24

OFFICIAL GOING: Good (7.3)
Wind: Light across Weather: Sunny periods

4284 J. & S. SEDDON PAINTING APPRENTICE STKS (H'CAP) 1m
6:00 (6:01) (Class 5) (0-70,70) 3-Y-O **£5,051** (£1,503; £751; £375) **Stalls** Low

Form RPR

-440 **1** **Flapper (IRE)**[40] 2942 3-8-8 **59**.. AmyScott(5) 5 67
(J W Hills) *sn led: rdn along 3f out: drvn over 1f out: kpt on ins fnl f* **13/2[3]**

0356 **2** *¾* **Harriet's Girl**[33] 3193 3-9-7 **70**.. MartinLane(3) 9 76
(K R Burke) *t.k.h: hld up in rr: hdwy on inner over 3f out: swtchd rt and rdn to chse ldrs wl over 1f out: swtchd lft and drvn ent fnl f: kpt on* **20/1**

-005 **3** *hd* **Moon Lightning (IRE)**[22] 3551 3-9-2 **67**.................. AshleyMorgan(5) 6 73
(M H Tompkins) *trckd ldrs: hdwy over 3f out: rdn 2f out: drvn ent fnl f: kpt on wl towards fin* **10/1**

4054 **4** *½* **Steel Stockholder**[16] 3727 3-8-9 **60**.......................... JohnCavanagh(5) 4 64
(M Brittain) *hld up in rr: hdwy 3f out: swtchd wd and rdn wl over 1f out: kpt on ins fnl f: nrst fin* **12/1**

2026 **5** *nk* **She's In The Money**[28] 3342 3-9-5 **65**........................ FrederikTylicki 1 69
(R A Fahey) *t.k.h: midfield: hdwy 3f out: rdn to chse ldrs 2f out: sn drvn and kpt on same pce* **7/1**

0123 **6** *1* **Iron Out (USA)**[10] 3955 3-9-3 **68**............................ SimonPearce(5) 2 69
(R Hollinshead) *chsd ldrs on inner: rdn along and outpcd 3f out: styd on u.p appr fnl f* **11/2[2]**

055 **7** *1* **Fantino**[29] 3309 3-9-5 **65**.. MichaelJStainton 11 64
(J Mackie) *chsd ldrs: rdn along 3f out: grad wknd* **16/1**

3123 **8** *1* **Dark Ranger**[21] 3557 3-9-0 **63**.................................... LanceBetts(3) 12 60
(T J Pitt) *t.k.h: chsd ldng pair: effrt 3f out: sn rdn along and wknd 2f out* **13/2[3]**

1535 **9** *4* **Peter's Gift (IRE)**[9] 3982 3-9-5 **68**.............................. AmyRyan(3) 10 56
(K A Ryan) *a towards rr* **8/1**

5121 **10** *2* **Swiss Art (IRE)**[3] 4171 3-9-3 **66** 6ex................................ DeanHeslop(3) 8 49
(Mrs R A Carr) *t.k.h: hld up: effrt on inner 3f out: sn rdn and nvr a factor* **5/1[1]**

20-5 **11** *7* **Aven Mac (IRE)**[10] 3942 3-7-12 **51**............................ TerenceFury(7) 7 18
(N Bycroft) *a in rr* **40/1**

04 **12** *14* **Lost In The Desert (IRE)**[22] 3531 3-9-8 **68**..................(b) JackMitchell 3 —
(M Botti) *chsd ldr: rdn along over 3f out: sn wknd* **12/1**

1m 42.9s (4.10) **Going Correction** +0.225s/f (Good) **12 Ran SP% 119.9**
Speed ratings (Par 100): **88,87,87,86,86 85,84,83,79,77 70,56**
toteswingers: 1&2 £35.80, 1&3 £24.20, 2&3 £41.30 CSF £130.23 CT £1299.53 TOTE £8.60: £2.80, £5.60, £4.60; EX 179.80.
Owner Abbott Racing Partners **Bred** Celbridge Estates Ltd **Trained** Upper Lambourn, Berks

FOCUS
A modest handicap restricted to apprentices who had not ridden more than 50 winners. The raced middle to far side in the straight. Ordinary form, with a slight personal best from the winner.

4285 SYMPHONY GROUP STKS (H'CAP) 6f
6:30 (6:30) (Class 4) (0-80,80) 4-Y-0+ **£5,180** (£1,541; £770; £384) **Stalls** High

Form RPR

5602 **1** **Mandalay King (IRE)**[8] 4015 4-8-5 **64**............................ PJMcDonald 11 76
(Mrs Marjorie Fife) *hld up in rr: hdwy 1/2-way: swtchd rt to stands' rail 2f out: rdn over 1f out: led ins fnl f: styd on strly* **11/1**

3032 **2** *1 ¼* **Haajes**[7] 4069 5-9-7 **80**..(t) DavidAllan 6 88+
(J Balding) *trckd ldrs towards centre: hdwy 1/2-way: led 2f out and sn hdd: drvn ent fnl f: sn hdd and kpt on same pce* **8/1[3]**

1124 **3** *1* **Misplaced Fortune**[17] 3706 4-9-0 **73**............................ SebSanders 16 78
(N Tinkler) *racd towards stands rail: hdwy over 2f out: sn rdn to chse ldrs and hung lft wl over 1f out: drvn and kpt on same pce fnl f* **8/1[3]**

0032 **4** *1 ¾* **Hotham**[4] 4134 6-8-9 **68**.. DanielTudhope 12 67
(N Wilson) *s.i.s and in rr: hdwy 2f out: sn rdn and styd on ins fnl f: nrst fin* **9/2[1]**

6003 **5** *hd* **Green Park (IRE)**[4] 4141 6-8-13 **72**..(b) DNolan 3 71
(D Carroll) *chsd ldrs: rdn along and hdwy 2f out: drvn over 1f out: wknd ins fnl f* **12/1**

2044 **6** *1 ½* **Avontuur (FR)**[4] 4134 7-8-0 **64**.................................. DeanHeslop(5) 2 58
(Mrs R A Carr) *dwlt: hdwy on outer to ld after 2f: rdn along and hdd 2f out: grad wknd* **9/1**

0006 **7** *1 ¼* **Steel Blue**[13] 3852 9-8-3 **62** oh4 ow1........................(p) RoystonFfrench 5 52
(R M Whitaker) *midfield: hdwy wl over 2f out: rdn to chse ldrs wl over 1f out: wknd appr fnl f* **50/1**

4-00 **8** *½* **Bonne**[4] 4154 4-8-5 **64** ow1..(b[1]) PaulFitzsimons 9 52
(Miss J R Tooth) *in rr tl hdwy 2f out: sn rdn: edgd lft and no imp* **40/1**

6030 **9** *2* **Ingleby Arch (USA)**[10] 3956 6-9-2 **75**.......................... PaulMulrennan 4 57
(T D Barron) *cl up: rdn along over 2f out and ev ch tl drvn and wknd over 1f out* **20/1**

-654 **10** *1 ¼* **Istiqdaam**[37] 3021 4-8-6 **65**.. DaleGibson 7 43
(M W Easterby) *s.i.s and bhd tl sme late hdwy* **14/1**

5010 **11** *1* **Mark Of Meydan**[17] 3706 4-9-0 **73**.............................. TomEaves 13 48
(M Dods) *nvr bttr than midfield* **16/1**

000 **12** *nk* **Great Charm (IRE)**[57] 2405 4-9-7 **80**.......................... PaulHanagan 8 54
(M L W Bell) *chsd ldrs: rdn along over 2f out: sn wknd* **7/1[2]**

0224 **13** *2* **Daaweitza**[20] 3615 6-9-5 **78**.................................. J-PGuillambert 14 45
(B Ellison) *a towards rr* **18/1**

000- **14** *3* **Loch Jipp (USA)**[356] 4617 4-9-7 **80**................................ PAspell 10 38
(J S Wainwright) *wnt rt s: a towards rr* **80/1**

-240 **15** *¾* **Bonnie Prince Blue**[41] 2938 6-9-1 **74**........................ AdrianTNicholls 15 29
(D Nicholls) *a towards rr* **11/1**

0100 **16** *1 ¾* **Sea Rover (IRE)**[13] 3877 5-8-13 **72**................................ NCallan 1 22
(M Brittain) *led 2f: rdn along 1/2-way and sn wknd* **25/1**

1m 12.45s (0.55) **Going Correction** +0.225s/f (Good) **16 Ran SP% 119.3**
Speed ratings (Par 105): **105,103,102,99,99 97,95,95,92,90 89,89,86,82,81 79**
toteswingers: 1&2 £14.60, 1&3 £7.90, 2&3 £15.90 CSF £89.86 CT £782.55 TOTE £13.10: £3.20, £2.40, £1.90, £1.80; EX 108.20.
Owner R W Fife **Bred** Forenaghts Stud And Dermot Cantillon **Trained** Stillington, N Yorks

FOCUS
A good sprint handicap for the grade. All the pace looked to be towards the middle of the track early on, but as the race unfolded it became clear those stands' side were not disadvantaged and there was no apparent draw/track bias.

Bonnie Prince Blue Official explanation: jockey said gelding never travelled

4286 RACINGUK.COM MEDIAN AUCTION MAIDEN STKS 7f
7:00 (7:01) (Class 4) 2-Y-O **£5,180** (£1,541; £770; £384) **Stalls** Low

Form RPR

1 **Vale Of York (IRE)** 2-9-0 0.. AhmedAjtebi(3) 10 91+
(Saeed Bin Suroor) *trckd ldrs: smooth hdwy 3f out: led 2f out: rdn over 1f out: styd on wl* **4/1[3]**

2 *2 ¼* **Hot Prospect** 2-9-3 0.. PhilipRobinson 11 83+
(M A Jarvis) *prom: effrt to dispute ld 3f out: sn rdn and ev ch tl drvn: edgd lft and one pce appr fnl f* **3/1[2]**

3 *1 ¾* **Our Joe Mac (IRE)** 2-9-3 0.. PaulHanagan 1 79+
(R A Fahey) *trckd ldrs: hdwy wl over 2f out: rdn to chse ldng pair wl over 1f out: kpt on same pce* **10/1**

4 **4** *9* **Hoof It**[49] 2663 2-9-3 0.. PaulMulrennan 12 57
(M W Easterby) *in rr: hdwy over 2f out: sn rdn and kpt on same pce: nvr nr ldrs* **8/1**

5 *1 ¾* **Mark Anthony (IRE)** 2-9-3 0.. NCallan 3 52
(K A Ryan) *cl up: rdn along 3f out: drvn: hung lft and wknd 2f out* **16/1**

0 **6** *nk* **Start Right**[18] 3692 2-9-3 0.. SebSanders 9 51+
(L M Cumani) *towards rr: hdwy 1/2-way: in tch over 2f out: sn rdn and wknd wl over 1f out* **18/1**

7 *nk* **Palio Square (USA)** 2-9-3 0.. AndrewElliott 4 51
(K R Burke) *bhd and rdn along 1/2-way: sme late hdwy* **33/1**

0 **8** *3 ½* **Claimant (IRE)**[7] 4048 2-9-3 0.................................... PaulFitzsimons 6 42
(Miss J R Tooth) *towards rr: effrt and sme hdwy 1/2-way: sn rdn and nvr a factor* **66/1**

0 **9** *1* **Dead Womans Pass (IRE)**[29] 3310 2-8-12 0............. DanielTudhope 7 34
(N Wilson) *a in rr* **66/1**

02 **10** *1* **Iron Velvet (USA)**[13] 3875 2-9-3 0.............................. RoystonFfrench 2 37
(M Johnston) *cl up on inner: rdn along 3f out: wknd qckly* **2/1[1]**

000 **11** *2 ¾* **Kerolad (IRE)**[29] 3310 2-8-12 0.. BMcHugh(5) 13 30
(N Wilson) *a towards rr* **150/1**

12 *34* **Sovereign Secure (IRE)** 2-8-12 0.................................... TomEaves 8 —
(Lee Smyth, Ire) *led: rdn along 1/2-way: sn hdd & wknd* **50/1**

1m 26.04s (0.74) **Going Correction** +0.225s/f (Good) **12 Ran SP% 118.2**
Speed ratings (Par 96): **104,101,99,89,87 86,86,82,81,80 77,38**
toteswingers: 1&2 £3.60, 1&3 £11.40, 2&3 £2.90 CSF £16.13 TOTE £5.20: £1.90, £1.50, £2.30; EX 18.50.
Owner Godolphin **Bred** Stock Vale Ltd **Trained** Newmarket, Suffolk

FOCUS
This looked a decent maiden; three potentially above-average newcomers pulled well clear, but there were also some interesting performances further down the field. Strong form which could have been rated higher. The main action took place towards of the centre of the course in the straight, although the winner gradually edged across towards the stands' rail late on.

NOTEBOOK
Vale Of York(IRE) ◆, a 23,000gns purchase before going through the sales ring again at two for 65,000gns, has quite a big stride and this galloping track suited, although his knee action suggests he might not want the ground too quick. Although he was stuck wide early on, his high draw was by no means a disadvantage and, after racing close up, he travelled strongly into the straight. Once asked to stretch, he settled this quite readily under gentle persuasion, but did run noticeably green in the closing stages. He has a Gimcrack entry, but whilst he has plenty of natural speed, it remains to be seen if he's a sprinter. Whatever, though, he looks a smart prospect and deserves his chance in a decent race. (op 7-2 tchd 5-1)
Hot Prospect ◆, a 230,000gns colt, who is closely related to middle-distance winner Mount Helicon, and a half-brother to Ayr Gold Cup winner Regal Parade, has some notable entries, including the Champagne Stakes and the Royal Lodge. He showed up well throughout, travelling enthusiastically under a positive ride, but the winner simply had a bit too much speed for him in the straight. To his credit, he kept on right the way to the line, without being given a hard time, and this was a very satisfactory introduction. (op 7-2 tchd 11-4)
Our Joe Mac(IRE) ◆, a 25,000euros purchase, out of a 7f winner, ran with real credit in third, coming up against a couple of useful types but pulling a long way clear of the remainder. (op 12-1 tchd 9-1)
Hoof It shaped well on his debut over 6f at Doncaster in a race that has worked out well, but he had been off for nearly two months since then and still looked green. He has plenty of ability and will be of particular interest when sent handicapping. (op 13-2)
Mark Anthony(IRE), a 7,000gns purchase, out of a 1m winner, was a little keen early and hung left when first placed under pressure. He might have been green but still might be best watched next time. (tchd 20-1)
Start Right ◆, out of a 1m4f winner, will surely continue to do better with time and distance and is one to look out for in nurseries later in the season is. (op 25-1)
Palio Square(USA) ◆, not sold at $150,000, is out of quite a useful multiple dirt sprint winner at two and three in the US, and is entered in both the Gimcrack and Champagne Stakes. He looked as though the run would bring him on fitness wise and was very green early, but he caught the eye in the closing stages, gradually getting the idea. From a stable whose juveniles often improve significantly for a run, he'll be of serious interest next time, particularly if Jim Crowley is booked considering he is 4-7 on two-year-olds for these owners in the last five years. (op 40-1)
Iron Velvet(USA), a staying-on second over 6f here last time, was one of a few who showed speed but he was in trouble early in the straight and was beaten before stamina became an issue. This was a very disappointing performance. Official explanation: trainer had no explanation for the poor form shown (op 9-4 tchd 15-8)

4287 EUROPEAN BREEDERS' FUND LYRIC STKS (LISTED RACE) (F&M) 1m 2f 88y
7:30 (7:30) (Class 1) 3-Y-O+
£22,708 (£8,608; £4,308; £2,148; £1,076; £540) **Stalls** Low

Form RPR

1433 **1** **High Heeled (IRE)**[20] 3619 3-8-8 **114**.............................. MichaelHills 1 114
(B W Hills) *in tch: hdwy 3f out: rdn to chal wl over 1f out: drvn to ld ins fnl f: kpt on* **1/1[1]**

0-31 **2** *2 ¼* **Ave**[13] 3870 3-8-8 **98**.. RichardMullen 6 109
(Sir Michael Stoute) *sn led: rdn along over 2f out: drvn wl over 1f out: hdd ins fnl f and no ex* **3/1[2]**

050- **3** *3 ¾* **Sweet Lilly**[280] 6781 5-9-4 **106**................................ EdwardCreighton 4 102
(M R Channon) *plld hrd in rr: hdwy 3f out: rdn to chse ldng pair over 1f out: sn drvn and one pce ent fnl f* **9/1**

-400 **4** *2 ¼* **Moon Sister (IRE)**[29] 3315 4-9-4 **96**................................ SebSanders 3 98
(W Jarvis) *prom: rdn along 3f out: drvn and hld whn n.m.r wl over 1f out and sn wknd* **14/1**

00-1 **5** *4 ½* **Short Affair**[48] 2697 4-9-4 **95**.. NCallan 5 89
(L M Cumani) *hld up in rr: hdwy 3f out: rdn over 2f out: sn drvn and no imp* **5/1[3]**

0030 **6** *2* **Medici Pearl**[13] 3873 5-9-4 **88**.. DavidAllan 7 86
(T D Easterby) *trckd ldrs: hdwy on outer 1/2-way: rdn to chse ldr 3f out: wknd over2f out* **20/1**

0 **7** *13* **Young Americans (IRE)**[20] 3641 3-8-8 0 .... J-PGuillambert 8 61
(M Botti) *prom: rdn along 4f out and sn wknd* **66/1**

8 *½* **Clare Glen (IRE)**[30] 3289 3-8-8 0 .... TomEaves 2 60
(Lee Smyth, Ire) *chsd ldrs to 1/2-way: sn wknd* **66/1**

2m 12.83s (0.33) **Going Correction** +0.225s/f (Good)
WFA 3 from 4yo+ 10lb **8** Ran SP% **116.1**
Speed ratings (Par 111): **107,105,102,100,96 95,84,84**
toteswingers: 1&2 £1.30, 1&3 £2.70, 2&3 £4.80 CSF £4.14 TOTE £2.00: £1.10, £1.10, £1.80; EX 5.30.
Owner Mr And Mrs Steven Jenkins **Bred** Ballylinch Stud **Trained** Lambourn, Berks

FOCUS
A decent fillies' Listed contest in which the winner set a good standard. The form has been rated at face value with High Heeled close to her Oaks level. The pace seemed just ordinary for much of the way and they raced towards the stands' side in the straight.

NOTEBOOK
High Heeled(IRE) found the ground too firm when disappointing in the Lancashire Oaks on her previous start, but conditions were more suitable this time and she returned to something like the form she showed when third in the Epsom Oaks. For a while it looked as though she had been set plenty to do, with one of her main dangers, Ave, allowed a soft time up front, and that one also grabbed the stands' rail in the straight. However, this daughter of High Chaparral displayed a determined attitude in the straight and was nicely on top in good time. She is now likely to be aimed at the Yorkshire Oaks, provided there is some give underfoot, and on this evidence the return to 1m4f will not be a problem. (tchd 6-5 and 5-4 in a place)
Ave ◆, the impressive winner of a 1m handicap off a mark of 89 on soft ground at Salisbury last time, ran well on this step up in grade. While the drying ground meant she didn't get her favoured easy going, it put less emphasis on stamina for this first try at 1m2f and she was allowed the run of the race in front. She had her chance after grabbing the near rail in the straight and posted a career-best performance, but was simply outstayed by a classy rival late on. Clearly improving into a smart filly, she could do even better back at around 1m on soft ground. (op 7-2)
Sweet Lilly was unable to repeat last year's success in this race, but she still ran well. Quite a big filly, she was expected to need the run after 280 days off, and not for the first time she pulled hard for much of the way, so she did well to get so close. (tchd 15-2 and 10-1)
Moon Sister(IRE) was always handily placed and ran respectably, but she simply wasn't good enough. (op 16-1 tchd 12-1)
Short Affair, an ex-Italian-trained filly who defeated a subsequent Listed winner when landing a handicap off a mark of 89 on her British debut, struggled on this step up in class. She was set plenty to do considering how the race was run, but in truth she simply couldn't muster the speed to get involved and probably would have preferred easier ground. (op 6-1)

4288 SKY BET SUPPORTING YORKSHIRE RACING FESTIVAL CLAIMING STKS — 1m 4f
8:00 (8:00) (Class 4) 3-Y-O+ **£5,180** (£1,541; £770; £384) **Stalls** Centre

Form RPR

505 **1** **Demolition**[21] 3564 5-9-8 84 .... (p) DanielTudhope 7 84
(N Wilson) *fly leapt s: hld up in rr: smooth hdwy 4f out: chal 2f out: rdn to ld over 1f out: clr ins fnl f: styd on* **9/1**

0/00 **2** *3 ½* **John Forbes**[10] 3940 7-8-11 63 .... LanceBetts(5) 1 72
(B Ellison) *led 2f: chsd ldr tl rdn along and outpcd over 2f out: drvn and rallied ent fnl f: kpt on wl towards fin* **66/1**

0011 **3** *¾* **Invasian (IRE)**[8] 4021 8-8-12 81 .... PaulPickard(5) 4 72
(P W D'Arcy) *cl up: led after 2f: rdn along 3f out: drvn 2f out: hdd over 1f out and one pce* **9/4**[2]

4-00 **4** *hd* **Lost Soldier Three (IRE)**[96] 1383 8-9-12 92 .... AdrianTNicholls 8 81
(D Nicholls) *hld up in tch: hdwy 4f out: chsd ldng pair 3f out: sn rdn and ch tl drvn wl over 1f out and one pce* **8/1**[3]

4251 **5** *2 ¼* **Fairmile**[15] 3769 7-9-12 105 .... (bt[1]) NCallan 2 77
(Ian Williams) *chsd ldng pair: smooth hdwy 4f out: chal wl over 2f out and ev ch tl rdn 2f out and sn wknd* **5/4**[1]

2010 **6** *11* **Realism (FR)**[42] 2898 9-8-9 70 .... JamesPSullivan(7) 6 49
(M W Easterby) *hld up in rr: hdwy and in tch over 3f out: sn rdn and wknd* **12/1**

0624 **7** *11* **Birkside**[7] 4038 6-9-7 75 .... PaulMulrennan 5 37
(Miss L A Perratt) *hld up in tch: hdwy to trck ldrs 4f out: effrt 3f out: sn rdn and btn* **16/1**

2110 **8** *19* **Eseej (USA)**[121] 952 4-9-12 75 .... DavidAllan 3 11
(P W Hiatt) *chsd ldrs: rdn along over 3f out: wknd wl over 2f out* **33/1**

505- **P** **Longspur**[398] 3258 5-9-7 70 .... DaleGibson 9 —
(M W Easterby) *a bhd: t.o 1/2-way: p.u 4f out: dismntd* **66/1**

2m 34.75s (1.55) **Going Correction** +0.225s/f (Good) **9** Ran SP% **115.8**
Speed ratings (Par 105): **103,100,100,100,98 91,83,71,—**
toteswingers: 1&2 £113.10, 1&3 £4.30, 2&3 £28.20 CSF £446.47 TOTE £10.00: £2.10, £9.20, £1.20; EX 295.30.
Owner M Wormald **Bred** P D And Mrs Player **Trained** Flaxton, N Yorks

FOCUS
This looked a good claimer, and it was strongly run. The form is rated around the winner with the runner-up a slight doubt.
Fairmile Official explanation: trainer had no explanation for the poor form shown
Eseej(USA) Official explanation: trainer said gelding lost a front shoe
Longspur Official explanation: jockey said gelding returned distressed

4289 TANITH BUTTERS CELEBRATION FOR BREAKTHROUGH BREAST CANCER STKS (H'CAP) — 5f 89y
8:30 (8:30) (Class 4) (0-80,79) 3-Y-O **£5,180** (£1,541; £770; £384) **Stalls** High

Form RPR

0264 **1** **Brierty (IRE)**[6] 4096 3-9-7 79 .... DNolan 2 83
(D Carroll) *dwlt and bmpd sltly s: in tch: hdwy wl over 1f out: swtchd lft and rdn to chal ins fnl f: drvn and kpt on to ld post* **7/1**

0111 **2** *shd* **Secret Venue**[18] 3681 3-8-11 69 .... TonyHamilton 1 73+
(Jedd O'Keeffe) *wnt rt s: cl up: led 2f out and sn rdn: drvn and jnd ins fnl f: edgdlft: hdd and nt qckn on line* **11/4**[2]

0056 **3** *1 ¼* **Mister Laurel**[14] 3828 3-9-4 76 .... (b) PaulHanagan 4 76
(R A Fahey) *chsd ldrs: rdn along and outpcd bef 1/2-way: hdwy over 1f out: kpt on u.p ins fnl f: nrst fin* **5/1**

2263 **4** *¾* **Lenny Bee**[14] 3806 3-9-7 79 .... PaulMulrennan 7 76
(D H Brown) *slt ld: rdn along and hdd 2f out: drvn and ev ch over 1f out tl drvn: edgd lft and wknd ins fnl f* **5/2**[1]

1214 **5** *1 ¼* **Dispol Grand (IRE)**[17] 3704 3-8-12 70 .... NCallan 6 62
(P T Midgley) *cl up: rdn along over 2f out: sn drvn and wknd over 1f out* **4/1**[3]

4241 **6** *1 ¼* **Piste**[26] 3428 3-8-13 71 .... AndrewMullen 5 59
(Miss T Jackson) *trckd ldrs on inner: effrt and hdwy wl over 1f out: rdn and nt clr run ins fnl f: eased nr fin* **12/1**

65.42 secs (1.12) **Going Correction** +0.225s/f (Good) **6** Ran SP% **112.1**
Speed ratings (Par 102): **100,99,97,96,94 92**
toteswingers: 1&2 £3.50, 1&3 £3.50, 2&3 £2.80 CSF £26.36 TOTE £8.10: £3.70, £2.20; EX 32.10 Place 6: £142.45 Place 5: 36.30.
Owner G P Clarke **Bred** Fortbarrington Stud **Trained** Sledmere, E Yorks

■ Stewards' Enquiry : D Nolan five-day ban: used whip with excessive frequency down the shoulder in forehand position (Aug 7-11)

FOCUS
A fair 3yo sprint. Half of this six-strong field contested a fast pace for much of the way and paid for that late on.
T/Plt: £197.90 to a £1 stake. Pool: £71,492.58. 263.68 winning tickets. T/Qpdt: £22.30 to a £1 stake. Pool: £4,809.12. 158.96 winning tickets. JR

4290 - 4292a (Foreign Racing) - See Raceform Interactive

4257 ASCOT (R-H)
Saturday, July 25

OFFICIAL GOING: Good (good to firm in places on straight course; straight: stands' side 9.3, centre 9.7, far side 9.4, round 8.5)
An important Arab race was run between the King George and the 5.35, won by Nayef Al Khalidiah and Christophe Lemaire.
Wind: virtualy nil Weather: bright, partly cloudy

4293 LONGINES H'CAP (LADIES RACE) — 7f
1:25 (1:29) (Class 3) (0-90,90) 3-Y-O+ **£7,495** (£2,324; £1,161; £580) **Stalls** Centre

Form RPR

1620 **1** **Castles In The Air**[17] 3752 4-9-12 82 .... MrsVFahey(5) 6 97
(R A Fahey) *in tch: pushed along and hdwy over 2f out: led over 1f out: r.o strly and drew wl clr fnl f* **9/1**

-360 **2** *4 ½* **Golden Desert (IRE)**[21] 3628 5-10-9 88 .... MsKWalsh 8 91
(T G Mills) *lw: t.k.h: hld up in rr: hdwy 3f out: rdn and edgd rt u.p over 1f out: chsd wnr ent fnl f: sn outpcd by wnr: kpt on* **5/1**[1]

-001 **3** *1 ½* **Arthur's Edge**[15] 3801 5-9-7 72 .... MissFayeBramley 10 71
(B Palling) *swtg: led: jnd and rdn 2f out: hdd over 1f out: wknd and lost 2nd ent fnl f* **12/1**

-364 **4** *6* **King's Colour**[146] 726 4-9-5 70 oh4 .... MissLHorner 18 53
(B R Johnson) *b: s.i.s: bhd: gd hdwy over 3f out: jnd ldr and rdn over 2f out: wknd over 1f out* **28/1**

1323 **5** *1 ¾* **Secret Night**[46] 2780 6-10-3 82 .... (v) MissEJJones 4 60
(C G Cox) *t.k.h: hld up in midfield: rdn and effrt whn edgd rt over 2f out: edgd lft u.p 1f out: plugged on but nvr nr ldrs* **15/2**[2]

6-00 **6** *1 ¾* **South Cape**[36] 3091 6-10-1 85 .... (p) MissHayleyMoore(5) 2 58
(G L Moore) *hld up in rr: rdn and effrt over 2f out: kpt on fnl f but nvr gng pce to rch ldrs* **14/1**

3040 **7** *½* **Middlemarch (IRE)**[21] 3615 9-9-6 71 .... (v) MrsCBartley 9 43
(J S Goldie) *sn bhd: rdn after 2f: hdwy u.p and edging rt 2f out: styd on but nvr nr ldrs* **25/1**

8 *shd* **Achak (IRE)**[13] 3904 3-10-4 90 .... (b[1]) MissNCarberry 1 62
(G M Lyons, Ire) *stdd s: hld up in rr: hdwy wl over 2f out: rdn and no prog over 1f out* **9/1**

4021 **9** *½* **My Learned Friend (IRE)**[20] 3659 5-9-8 76 .... MissMSowerby(3) 3 46
(A M Balding) *hld up towards rr: rdn and effrt over 2f out: no imp fr wl over 1f out* **9/1**

1422 **10** *¾* **Elna Bright**[7] 4083 4-10-1 80 .... MissEFolkes 12 48
(P D Evans) *s.i.s: hdwy and in tch in midfield 1/2-way: rdn ent fnl 2f: sn struggling* **16/1**

4103 **11** *1 ½* **Pravda Street**[36] 3116 4-10-10 89 .... (b) MissSBrotherton 11 53
(P F I Cole) *lw: chsd ldr tl over 2f out: wknd wl over 1f out: wl bhd fnl f: sddle slipped* **8/1**[3]

0006 **12** *5* **Bomber Command (USA)**[10] 3988 6-9-5 70 oh2 .... (b) MissLEllison 16 21
(J W Hills) *chsd ldrs tl rdn and wknd ent fnl 2f: wl bhd fnl f* **20/1**

4115 **13** *½* **Shaded Edge**[70] 2086 5-9-5 70 .... MrsSMoore 13 19
(D W P Arbuthnot) *racd in midfield: pushed along and lost pl 1/2-way: rdn and no prog over 2f out: wl btn after* **16/1**

0366 **14** *½* **Prince Of Thebes (IRE)**[16] 3770 8-9-10 75 .... MissADeniel 19 23
(M J Attwater) *lw: chsd ldrs tl rdn and wknd over 2f out* **33/1**

4120 **15** *2 ¼* **Desert Dreamer (IRE)**[15] 3801 8-10-0 82 .... MissIsabelTompsett(3) 14 24
(P D Evans) *s.i.s: a in rr* **28/1**

4000 **16** *2* **Kings Point (IRE)**[28] 3391 8-10-3 87 .... MissERamstrom(5) 17 24
(D Nicholls) *lw: chsd ldrs untl 1/2-way: wknd 3f out: wl bhd fnl f* **16/1**

1m 28.89s (0.89) **Going Correction** +0.15s/f (Good)
WFA 3 from 4yo+ 7lb **16** Ran SP% **120.0**
Speed ratings (Par 107): **100,94,93,86,84 82,81,81,81,80 78,72,72,71,69 66**
toteswingers: 1&2 £10.80, 1&3 £30.50, 2&3 £25.20 CSF £48.84 CT £554.78 TOTE £12.00: £2.50, £2.00, £4.00, £9.30; EX 69.00 Trifecta £693.50 Pool: £937.28 - 1.00 winning units..
Owner Jim McGrath **Bred** Newgate Stud Company **Trained** Musley Bank, N Yorks
■ Stewards' Enquiry : Ms K Walsh two-day ban: used whip with excessive frequency (tbn)
Miss E Folkes caution: used whip with excessive frequency

FOCUS
One of the best ladies' races of the season, featuring several regulars in the contest, including the previous two winners. The last three runnings have suggested that a middle draw is best and that proved the case again, as the field came up the centre of the track and those drawn on the flanks struggled. The form is rated around the runner-up, with improvement from the winner.

NOTEBOOK
Castles In The Air was a late springer in the market and ran out a clear-cut winner. Tracking the pace early, he took the lead at the 2f pole and came right away under hands-and-heels riding. This was his first win beyond 6f, but he had proved his stamina for this trip over 1m last time. He could well be competing in heritage handicaps, if maintaining this level of form. (op 14-1)
Golden Desert(IRE) won this last year and made a bold bid to follow-up, but was no match for the winner. Held up off the pace not far behind the winner, he made good headway to chase the winner over a furlong out, but that rival was just hitting top gear and drew away from him.
Arthur's Edge came into this in good heart, had an experienced rider aboard and made much of the running. He kept going, once headed, to claim the minor placing. (op 16-1)
King's Colour, 4lb out of the handicap, ran well from his high draw on only his third start on turf. On this evidence, he can pick up an ordinary handicap. (op 50-1)
Secret Night finished runner-up in this last year, but was 7lb higher, and never reached the front rank this time. (tchd 7-1 and 8-1)
South Cape is a capable sort at this trip, having finished fifth in the heritage handicap on this card a year ago. He was 2lb below his last winning mark and had cheekpieces fitted, but had a low draw and raced on the nearside of the field. He was staying on at the finish, giving the impression that he is worth another try at 1m. (op 16-1 tchd 12-1)
Middlemarch(IRE) won this two years ago and had dropped back to the same mark. He stayed on without ever threatening. (op 20-1)
Achak(IRE) was the only three-year-old in the race, but had the highest official rating and was equipped with blinkers for the first time. On his toes beforehand, he was held up off the pace from his low draw, under pressure some way from home and never looked like mounting a serious challenge. (op 6-1)
My Learned Friend(IRE) was another who was unable to get competitive from his low draw. (op 12-1)

Pravda Street likes to lead but could not do so with the third in the race and, although he showed up for a long way, was on retreat at the quarter-mile pole, although his rider later reported that the saddle slipped. Official explanation: jockey said saddle slipped (op 10-1)

Bomber Command(USA) was on his toes beforehand. (op 22-1)

4294 HUGGIES WINKFIELD STKS (LISTED RACE) 7f

2:00 (2:02) (Class 1) 2-Y-O

£17,031 (£6,456; £3,231; £1,611; £807; £405) **Stalls** Centre

Form RPR

41 **1** **Nideeb**[11] 3957 2-9-2 0 .... RyanMoore 6 104
(C E Brittain) *lw: dwlt: hld up in tch in last pair: hdwy over 2f out: rdn to chal over 1f out: drew clr w runner up fnl f: drvn and r.o wl to ld on post* **11/2**[3]

233 **2** *nse* **Party Doctor**[35] 3138 2-9-2 0 .... RichardKingscote 5 104
(Tom Dascombe) *wanting to hang rt thrght: trckd ldrs: jnd ldr jst over 2f out: led wl over 1f out: sn hrd pressed and rdn: drew clr w wnr fnl f: drvn and stl lugging rt ins fnl f: r.o but hdd on post* **9/4**[2]

15 **3** *9* **Navajo Chief**[16] 3782 2-9-2 0 .... AlanMunro 7 82
(A P Jarvis) *t.k.h: led narrowly: rdn 2f out: sn hdd: wknd over 1f out: no ch w ldng pair fnl f* **33/1**

411 **4** *1* **Lamh Albasser (USA)**[15] 3821 2-9-2 0 .... TedDurcan 3 79
(Saeed Bin Suroor) *lw: stdd s: hld up in tch in last pair: hdwy and edgd lft 2f out: chsd ldng trio wl over 1f out: sn rdn and struggling: wl btn whn edgd rt 1f out* **15/8**[1]

21 **5** *4 ½* **Missionaire (USA)**[28] 3395 2-9-2 0 .... JimCrowley 1 68
(W J Knight) *hld up wl in tch: rdn and effrt 2f out: unable qck and edgd rt wl over 1f out: sn btn* **13/2**

1101 **6** *10* **Jack My Boy (IRE)**[26] 3452 2-9-2 0 .... JimmyFortune 4 43
(P D Evans) *w ldr tl ent fnl 2f out: sn drvn and wknd: btn whn edgd lft wl over 1f out* **20/1**

1 **7** *7* **Invincible Prince (IRE)**[31] 3270 2-9-2 0 .... SebSanders 2 25
(R M Beckett) *w'like: in tch: pushed along 1/2-way: rdn 3f out: wkng whn squeezed and hmpd wl over 1f out: wl bhd after* **11/1**

1m 29.28s (1.28) **Going Correction** +0.15s/f (Good) **7 Ran SP% 110.3**
Speed ratings (Par 102): **98,97,87,86,81 69,61**
toteswingers: 1&2 £2.60, 1&3 £17.50, 2&3 £13.10 CSF £16.98 TOTE £6.10: £2.90, £1.90; EX 17.30.
Owner Saeed Manana **Bred** Rabbah Bloodstock Limited **Trained** Newmarket, Suffolk

FOCUS
A decent Listed race in which Raven's Pass was by far the best of the three previous winners. It developed into a real battle in the last 2f with the principals drawing well clear of the rest, in a time just 0.38secs slower than the opening ladies' race.

NOTEBOOK
Nideeb ◆, from the family of Cloud Castle and Warrsan, had finished 5l behind Missionaire on his debut. He had won a 7f maiden on soft next time, but looked to have a bit to find. He was held up early, but followed the runner-up, and battled well under pressure to get up on the line. He looks progressive, but will now be given a break before being brought back for the Royal Lodge, here in September. (op 6-1 tchd 13-2)

Party Doctor the only non-winner in the line-up, had arguably the best form, having finished third in the Chesham and been beaten by two subsequent winners (including July Stakes winner Arcano) before that, but he was on his toes beforehand. He travelled well before coming through to lead inside the last quarter-mile and battled on well under pressure, only to have victory snatched away on the post. He deserves to pick up a good race and will go for the Acomb Stakes at York next. (tchd 2-1 and 5-2)

Navajo Chief, a debut winner over 5f on fast ground and fifth in a conditions race subsequently, was up in trip and made the running. He could not respond to the challenges of the first two but kept going for third. (tchd 28-1)

Lamh Albasser(USA) was gelded after his first run, but then won his next two over 7f on fast ground. He travelled well off the pace, but did not appear to be striding out when let down. He could only keep on at the one pace. (op 7-4 tchd 2-1)

Missionaire(USA), warm beforehand, had beaten the winner decisively on his previous start and, although that colt had clearly improved in the interim, he ran nowhere near that form. With the third from that race winning at Newmarket earlier in the afternoon, the form is beginning to look decent, so it may have been that this colt was unsuited by the faster going here. (op 8-1)

Jack My Boy(IRE), a three-time winner at 6f on fast and easy ground at a lower level, was up in trip and grade and, after racing close to the lead until halfway, dropped out under pressure and does not look up to this level. (op 14-1 tchd 12-1)

Invincible Prince(IRE), whose dam is a half-sister to the top-class sprinter Somnus, had made a promising winning debut over 7f on Polytrack from an outside draw. The next three home had won since, but his rider was niggling along from an early stage here, and he could be another who found the fast ground against him. (op 10-1 tchd 12-1)

4295 PRINCESS MARGARET ABU DHABI STKS (GROUP 3) (FILLIES) 6f

2:40 (2:40) (Class 1) 2-Y-O

£31,223 (£11,836; £5,923; £2,953; £1,479; £742) **Stalls** Centre

Form RPR

16 **1** **Lady Of The Desert (USA)**[38] 3015 2-8-12 0 .... MartinDwyer 5 103+
(B J Meehan) *stdd s: hld up in tch: hdwy to trck ldrs 1/2-way: led gng wl 2f out: rdn and qcknd over 1f out: r.o wl fnl f* **5/2**[1]

41 **2** *1 ½* **Full Mandate (IRE)**[23] 3534 2-8-12 0 .... RichardHughes 6 98+
(R Hannon) *chsd clr ldr: clsd and ev ch 2f out: sn rdn: unable qckn w wnr over 1f out: edgd rt but kpt on gamely to hold 2nd pl* **7/1**

51 **3** *1* **Sand Vixen**[17] 3733 2-8-12 0 .... TedDurcan 3 95
(Saeed Bin Suroor) *stdd s: t.k.h: hld up in rr: hdwy 2f out: pressing for 2nd ent fnl f: kpt on but no imp on wnr* **7/1**

4101 **4** *nk* **Jira**[28] 3396 2-8-12 0 .... KShea 8 94
(C E Brittain) *lw: w.w in midfield: hdwy over 2f out: pressed ldrs 2f out: rdn and nt pce of wnr over 1f out: kpt on same pce fnl f* **9/2**[3]

212 **5** *1 ¾* **Jeanie Johnston (IRE)**[28] 3396 2-8-12 0 .... JimCrowley 4 89
(K R Burke) *swtg: racd in midfield: rdn and unable qck over 2f out: one pce and no imp fnl 2f* **4/1**[2]

21 **6** *½* **Roodle**[15] 3799 2-8-12 0 .... AlanMunro 7 87
(Eve Johnson Houghton) *stdd s: hld up in last pl: swtchd rt and effrt wl over 1f out: no prog fnl f* **14/1**

210 **7** *1 ¼* **Swan Wings**[17] 3748 2-8-12 0 .... JimmyFortune 2 84
(A M Balding) *in tch: rdn and unable qck over 2f out: kpt on same pce fnl 2f* **20/1**

153 **8** *3 ½* **Deal (IRE)**[8] 4049 2-8-12 0 .... RyanMoore 9 73
(R Hannon) *prom early: sn stdd and dropped in bhd: rdn 3f out: no hdwy and wl btn fnl 2f* **11/1**

1602 **9** *5* **High Spice (USA)**[16] 3762 2-8-12 0 .... EddieAhern 1 58
(R M H Cowell) *racd freely: led and sn clr: hdd and rdn 2f out: sn wknd and bhd fnl f* **25/1**

1m 14.95s (0.55) **Going Correction** +0.15s/f (Good) **9 Ran SP% 115.4**
Speed ratings (Par 101): **102,100,98,98,95 95,93,88,82**
toteswingers: 1&2 £3.60, 1&3 £7.10, 2&3 £9.40 CSF £20.55 TOTE £3.50: £1.50, £1.90, £2.70; EX 21.40 Trifecta £445.30 Pool: £1685.05 - 2.80 winning units..
Owner Jaber Abdullah **Bred** Rabbah Bloodstock Llc **Trained** Manton, Wilts

FOCUS
A well-established Group 3 that has produced some useful fillies, the best this century being Russian Rhythm. None of the trainers responsible for the last ten winners were represented in this year's renewal. A lowish draw had been important in the two previous runnings, but this was the smallest field since 2004 and they raced up the centre of the track. There was not much depth to this renewal but the winner is sure to rate higher.

NOTEBOOK
Lady Of The Desert(USA) ◆, a daughter of champion juvenile filly Queen's Logic, was a clear winner on her debut from four subsequent scorers. She had tried to stay with Jealous Again in the Queen Mary which had cost her in the end, and was ridden with more restraint this time. She came through to lead inside the last 2f and scored decisively. She looks the sort that will make her mark in races such as the Lowther and Cheveley Park, both of which her dam won, and is quoted at between 20/1-33/1 for next year's 1000 Guineas. (op 3-1, tchd 10-3 in places)

Full Mandate(IRE), on her toes beforehand, ran a fine race, especially considering she was quite keen early. A half-sister to the pretty useful 6f winner Danidh Dubai, she reversed debut running with both Swan Wings and Roodle and is clearly on the upgrade. (op 10-1 tchd 5-1 and 11-1 in places)

Sand Vixen, a half-sister to, among others, the very useful sprinter So Will I, had improved on her debut to beat a subsequent winner on Polytrack on her second start. She ran pretty well on this step up in grade, but drifted and had nothing more to offer in the closing stages. (op 8-1 tchd 9-1)

Jira, who beat Party Doctor (narrowly beaten in the previous race) on her second start, had narrowly beaten Jeanie Johnston at Newmarket. She appeared to have every chance but could not quicken late on, although she improved on that earlier form. (op 4-1)

Jeanie Johnston(IRE), who made the running on her two most recent starts, and had been narrowly beaten by Jira in a Listed race last time, was not ridden as positively on this occasion and never got to the front rank, despite staying on in the closing stages. (tchd 9-2 and 5-1 in places)

Roodle had finished ahead of today's runner-up on her debut and had beaten three previous scorers and a subsequent winner in a Chepstow novice event next time. She was stepping up in trip and grade and it proved too much for her, although she was keeping on at the end. (op 12-1)

Swan Wings had beaten both the runner-up and fifth when winning her maiden, but she tried to race up with the early pace here and weakened under pressure in the last 2f. (op 16-1)

Deal(IRE) made a good start but was soon struggling to go the pace. (op 12-1 tchd 10-1)

High Spice(USA) blasted off in front and paid the penalty in the second half of the race. (op 20-1)

4296 EMIRATES NBD CUP (HERITAGE H'CAP) 1m (S)

3:15 (3:17) (Class 2) 3-Y-O

£28,039 (£8,397; £4,198; £2,101; £1,048; £526) **Stalls** Centre

Form RPR

0-45 **1** **Sri Putra**[76] 1915 3-9-7 **105** .... PhilipRobinson 5 113
(M A Jarvis) *hld up towards rr: swtchd rt and hdwy over 2f out: led over 1f out: hrd pressed and edgd lft u.p ent fnl f: styd on wl to assert fnl 100yds* **12/1**

4513 **2** *½* **Peking Prince**[35] 3144 3-7-9 **82** oh3 .... (v[1]) DavidProbert[(3)] 2 89
(A M Balding) *lw: travelled wl: hld up in tch: hdwy to chal on bit and edgd rt ent fnl f: stl ev ch whn bmpd ins fnl f: rdn: edgd lft and nt qckn fnl 150yds* **4/1**[2]

2140 **3** *nk* **Espiritu (FR)**[14] 3839 3-8-13 **97** .... (v) JMurtagh 1 103
(J Noseda) *stdd s: hld up towards rr: rdn and gd hdwy over 1f out: chal and edgd rt ent fnl f: drvn and no ex fnl 100yds* **7/1**

0002 **4** *3 ¼* **Fullback (IRE)**[85] 1641 3-8-6 **90** .... LukeMorris 4 89
(J S Moore) *in tch: pushed along over 3f out: rdn over 2f out: chsng ldrs and n.m.r over 1f out: nt pce of ldng trio fnl f* **28/1**

-110 **5** *6* **Desert Creek (IRE)**[37] 3049 3-8-13 **97** .... RyanMoore 11 82
(Sir Michael Stoute) *t.k.h: hld up in rr: swtchd rt and hdwy over 2f out: rdn to chse wnr briefly over 1f out: wknd qckly fnl f* **3/1**[1]

1340 **6** *hd* **Roar Of Applause**[14] 3868 3-7-12 **82** oh3 .... (b[1]) NickyMackay 3 67
(B J Meehan) *t.k.h: chsd ldr: ev ch 2f out: sn rdn: jst beginning to weaken whn sltly hmpd over 1f out: fdd fnl f* **20/1**

1002 **7** *1 ¾* **Johnmanderville**[25] 3489 3-7-12 **82** oh2 .... AdrianMcCarthy 6 63
(K R Burke) *led: rdn and hrd pressed 2f out: hdd over 1f out: wknd qckly jst over 1f out* **28/1**

1231 **8** *3* **Pride Of Kings**[23] 3530 3-8-2 **86** .... RoystonFfrench 7 60
(M Johnston) *chsd ldrs: rdn wl over 2f out: wknd qckly wl over 1f out* **6/1**[3]

103 **9** *10* **Loch Linnhe (USA)**[16] 3783 3-9-4 **102** .... JimmyFortune 8 53
(J H M Gosden) *restless in stalls: t.k.h: hld up wl in tch in midfield: edgd rt and rdn over 2f out: sn hung rt and btn: eased ins fnl f* **13/2**

5501 **10** *13* **Tudor Key (IRE)**[10] 3988 3-8-7 **91** .... JimCrowley 10 12
(Mrs A J Perrett) *t.k.h: hld up in tch in midfield: pushed along 1/2-way: rdn and wknd qckly over 2f out: t.o* **14/1**

-500 **11** *½* **Weald Park (USA)**[70] 2077 3-8-11 **95** .... RichardHughes 9 15
(R Hannon) *hld up in rr: niggled along 1/2-way: rdn and btn wl over 2f out: t.o* **16/1**

1m 40.59s (-0.01) **Going Correction** +0.15s/f (Good) **11 Ran SP% 117.0**
Speed ratings (Par 106): **106,105,105,101,95 95,94,91,81,68 67**
toteswingers: 1&2 £10.80, 1&3 £11.50, 2&3 £8.60 CSF £57.93 CT £366.08 TOTE £15.30: £3.70, £1.90, £2.50; EX 82.40 Trifecta £871.50 Pool: £2508.77 - 2.13 winning units..
Owner H R H Sultan Ahmad Shah **Bred** Glebe Stud And Partners **Trained** Newmarket, Suffolk

FOCUS
A good heritage handicap and a smart effort from the winner, showing big improvement.

NOTEBOOK
Sri Putra had raced in Group company on his last three starts, but had come back from his last outing in the German 2000 Guineas with health problems, so had been given a break since. Dropped into handicap company for the first time, he hit the front 2f out, going well, but appeared to idle entering the final furlong and was briefly headed. However, when his rider got serious, he picked up well and was going away near the line. He won this off a mark of 105 and looks well up to winning at Listed level. (tchd 11-1)

Peking Prince was at the other end of the handicap and was 3lb 'wrong' at the weights. Despite being keen early in the first-time visor, he came through to join the leaders going extremely well, but when the winner rallied, he could not pick up again. This was still a creditable effort. (op 5-1)

Espiritu(FR), who had been a narrowly beaten fourth in the Britannia over course and distance in June, was another who was quite keen early. He had every chance a furlong out before being unable to find any extra under pressure. (op 8-1)

Fullback(IRE), a useful all-weather performer, was having his first start since the beginning of May. Making his turf debut, he was the first to be pushed along, but kept responding to his rider and stayed on. Although well beaten by the first three, he finished clear of the rest. (op 20-1 tchd 16-1)

Desert Creek(IRE), representing last year's winning owner/trainer/jockey combination, appeared to have every chance 2f out, when he was upsides the winner, but could not pick up from that point. (tchd 11-4 and 10-3)

Roar Of Applause, another racing from out of the handicap on this step up in grade, was keen in the first-time blinkers and, as a result, faded in the last 2f. (op 16-1)
Johnmanderville made the early running, before tiring, but has been held on three runs at this grade and is below this level. (op 33-1 tchd 25-1)
Pride Of Kings likes really fast ground, but was another stepping up in grade and weakened at the business end. (op 15-2)
Loch Linnhe(USA), making his handicap debut on his fourth start, got warm beforehand and rather upset in the stalls, and never got seriously involved. (op 5-1)
Tudor Key(IRE), on his toes beforehand, had been raised 4lb for a narrow success on Polytrack last time. He was never far away but dropped out from over 2f out. (op 16-1)
Weald Park(USA), dropping back in trip, was held up in the rear but was struggling soon after halfway. (tchd 14-1)

4297 ABU DHABI INTERNATIONAL STKS (HERITAGE H'CAP) 7f

3:50 (3:57) (Class 2) 3-Y-O+

£93,465 (£27,990; £13,995; £7,005; £3,495; £1,755) **Stalls** Centre

Form RPR

5520 **1** **Al Muheer (IRE)**[15] 3818 4-8-10 **99**....(b) SebSanders 20 110
(C E Brittain) *hld up wl bhd: n.m.r wl over 1f out: rdn and gd hdwy over 1f out: led jst ins fnl f: edgd rt u.p but hld on wl fnl f* **40/1**

4121 **2** ½ **Secret Society**[14] 3839 3-8-3 **99** 3ex.... HayleyTurner 16 106
(M L W Bell) *swtg: hld up towards rr: hdwy 2f out: chsd ldr gng wl over 1f out: rdn to ld 1f out: immediately hdd: battled on wl but a jst hld* **5/1**[2]

-436 **3** 1 ½ **Redford (IRE)**[15] 3818 4-8-11 **100**.... RichardHughes 11 106
(M L W Bell) *lw: stdd s: hld up wl bhd: stl last 3f out: n.m.r briefly 2f out: hdwy over 1f out: r.o to chse ldng pair ins fnl f: no imp fnl 100yds* **10/1**

-502 **4** 1 ¼ **Genki (IRE)**[28] 3405 5-8-7 **96**.... SteveDrowne 22 98
(R Charlton) *v awkward leaving stalls and v.s.a: hld up bhd: hdwy on far side over 2f out: chsd ldrs and rdn over 1f out: kpt on same pce fnl f* **20/1**

-410 **5** 1 ½ **Signor Peltro**[15] 3818 6-8-7 **96**.... DaneO'Neill 5 94
(H Candy) *hld up in midfield: hdwy gng wl 3f out: rdn to ld over 1f out: drvn and hdd 1f out: outpcd fnl f* **20/1**

1152 **6** ¾ **Taqdeyr**[21] 3621 4-8-10 **99**.... PhilipRobinson 8 95+
(M A Jarvis) *lw: racd keenly: chsd ldr tl led 5f out tl wl over 2f out: stl ev ch and rdn 2f out: outpcd over 1f out: plugged on same pce fnl f* **12/1**

0410 **7** 2 **Giganticus (USA)**[15] 3818 6-8-9 **98**.... EddieAhern 12 89
(B W Hills) *bmpd s: hld up in rr: n.m.r whn looking for run 2f out: styd on fr over 1f out: nvr gng to rch ldrs* **25/1**

-555 **8** ½ **Racer Forever (USA)**[15] 3818 6-9-1 **104**....(b) JimmyFortune 2 93
(J H M Gosden) *hld up in midfield: shkn up wl over 1f out: rdn and fnd little over 1f out: wl hld fnl f* **14/1**

0240 **9** nk **Nanton (USA)**[14] 3873 7-8-5 **94**.... MartinDwyer 13 83
(J S Goldie) *bhd and rdn over 5f out: styd on past btn horses fr over 1f out: nvr nr ldrs* **33/1**

5400 **10** ¾ **Orpsie Boy (IRE)**[15] 3818 6-8-7 **96**.... KirstyMilczarek 4 83
(N P Littmoden) *in tch: hdwy to chse ldrs ent fnl 2f: rdn and unable qck wl over 1f out: sn btn* **50/1**

21-1 **11** 2 **Roaring Forte (IRE)**[64] 2241 4-8-10 **99**.... RyanMoore 17 80
(W J Haggas) *chsd ldrs: disputing 2nd pl and rdn 2f out: wknd u.p over 1f out* **9/2**[1]

1022 **12** 2 **Crackdown (IRE)**[15] 3816 3-8-1 **97**.... RoystonFfrench 6 69
(M Johnston) *led for 2f: chsd ldrs after tl wknd u.p wl over 1f out* **9/1**[3]

4510 **13** shd **Thebes**[8] 4037 4-8-4 **93** 3ex.... GregFairley 10 68
(M Johnston) *chsd ldr tl wnt 2nd over 4f out: led wl over 2f out tl drvn and hdd over 1f out: sn wknd* **33/1**

1440 **14** 3 ½ **Diana's Choice (SAF)**[15] 3824 5-9-7 **110**....(t) PatCosgrave 7 76
(M F De Kock, South Africa) *awkward leaving stalls and v.s.a: hld up bhd: short-lived effrt u.p and hung rt ent fnl 2f: sn wl btn* **66/1**

1/12 **15** 2 ½ **Captain Brilliance (USA)**[15] 3818 4-8-9 **98**.... JMurtagh 15 57
(J Noseda) *lw: in tch in midfield: rdn over 2f out: wknd u.p wl over 1f out* **9/2**[1]

0-30 **16** ½ **Stubbs Art (IRE)**[142] 771 4-9-2 **105**....(bt) KShea 3 63
(M F De Kock, South Africa) *awkward leaving stalls and s.i.s: a towards rr: swtchd lft and brief effrt 2f out: nvr nr ldrs* **20/1**

3202 **17** hd **Dohasa (IRE)**[44] 2870 4-9-6 **109**.... KLatham 14 66
(G M Lyons, Ire) *in tch tl rdn and btn over 2f out: wl bhd fnl f* **18/1**

-300 **18** nse **Dhaular Dhar (IRE)**[15] 3818 7-8-9 **98**.... DanielTudhope 18 55
(J S Goldie) *t.k.h: hld up in midfield: effrt and edgd rt ent fnl 2f: sn wknd* **40/1**

150 **19** 2 ¾ **Esoterica (IRE)**[14] 3872 6-7-13 **88**....(v) NickyMackay 21 38
(J S Goldie) *lw: s.i.s: a in rr: effrt and edgd lft over 2f out: sn bhd* **100/1**

400 **20** 4 **Leandros (FR)**[16] 3836 4-8-11 **105**....(p) EJMcNamara(5) 1 44
(G M Lyons, Ire) *in tch tl rdn and wknd over 2f out: wl bhd fr over 1f out* **40/1**

2301 **21** 2 ¼ **Horatio Carter**[28] 3391 4-8-4 **93**.... AlanMunro 19 26
(K A Ryan) *chsd ldrs: rdn over 2f out: wknd 2f out: wl bhd and eased ins fnl f* **25/1**

1m 26.86s (-1.14) **Going Correction** +0.15s/f (Good)
WFA 3 from 4yo+ 7lb **21** Ran SP% **131.4**
Speed ratings (Par 109): **112,111,109,108,106 105,103,102,102,101 99,97,96,92,90 89,89,89,86,81 78**
toteswingers: 1&2 £175.20, 1&3 £100.90, 2&3 £12.40 CSF £217.54 CT £2281.98 TOTE £53.30: £9.60, £1.70, £2.40, £4.50; EX 597.40 Trifecta £2726.50 Pool: £18164.96 - 4.93 winning units..
Owner Saeed Manana **Bred** Foursome Thoroughbreds **Trained** Newmarket, Suffolk

FOCUS
Traditionally a high-class and fiercely competitive handicap. The pace was strong and the winning time was 2.03secs faster than the opening ladies' handicap, with the first three coming from well off the pace. The Bunbury Cup looked the key form race for this with the runner-up, fifth, sixth, seventh and four further behind renewing rivalry. A clear personal best from Al Muheer.

NOTEBOOK
Al Muheer(IRE) finished last but one in the Bunbury Cup, but raced without his usual blinkers there. He has a good record on this track which includes a good second in the Buckingham Palace Handicap over Course and distance at the royal meeting. He spread a plate beforehand, but that was fixed before the start, and was held up in the race. He followed the runner-up through and was galvanised by Seb Sanders, who was at his strongest and responded willingly to strike the front inside the last furlong and resist the second's renewed challenge. Official explanation: trainer said, regarding apparent improvement in form, that the colt benefitted by having blinkers re-fitted and appeared better suited by the track.
Secret Society ◆ has developed into a really high-class handicapper, being touched off in the Britannia before winning a valuable handicap over course and distance last month. He was raised 3lb for that success and looked the winner when moving smoothly into contention inside the final 2f. His rider was keen not to hit the front too soon, waiting tactics having suited him so well last time, but unfortunately the winner arrived on the scene with plenty of momentum and swept by before he was able to respond. He ran on but was unable to reel in his rival, although he lost nothing in defeat. He looks sure to play a major part in similar races for the rest of the season. (op 13-2)
Redford(IRE) was beaten just over a length by today's winner in the Buckingham Palace and was 3lb better off. He followed the winner through and finished well, but arrived on the scene a little too late. He has a big handicap in him and will be of major interest with cut in the ground. (op 11-1 tchd 9-1)
Genki(IRE) had gained all his wins at 6f and had not run over this trip since his racecourse debut. He came from off the pace to look a big threat 2f out, but appeared not to get home. He won the Shergar Sprint Cup two years ago and that race might give him a chance for compensation. (op 16-1)
Signor Peltro has always looked the type to win a race like this and, when he cruised to the front 2f out, it appeared his time had come. However, he was unable to respond to the strong late finishers and it may be he will appreciate the return to a sharper or flatter track. (tchd 22-1)
Taqdeyr ◆ had gained all three of his wins on sand, but had shown a high level of form at 6f-7f on turf. However, he was very keen on this occasion (his rider later reported that he ran too free) and pulled his way to the front after 2f. Fortunately, he settled once there and in the circumstances ran a really good race, considering that the first three came from well off the pace. Official explanation: jockey said gelding ran too free (op 14-1)
Giganticus(USA) had finished last in the Bunbury Cup last time, but before that had beaten today's winner in the Buckingham Palace. He was 3lb worse off this time, but was held up out the back before staying on when the race was over.
Racer Forever(USA) is a regular in this type of contest and is a good guide to the level, as he is never far away. On this occasion, he travelled well before his effort petered out. He has not won for over a year now, but is only 1lb lower than for that last success. (op 16-1)
Nanton(USA), on his toes beforehand, usually runs over further than this and it was no surprise he was being pushed along before halfway. He kept finding, though, and stayed on steadily in the closing stages. (tchd 40-1)
Orpsie Boy(IRE) finished ninth in the Bunbury Cup and put up a similar performance under a more positive ride. He has not won on turf since scoring here over two years ago and remains 8lb higher.
Roaring Forte(IRE) is a really progressive type, but his front-running style made him vulnerable in a race with so much pace. He raced with the leaders, but was in trouble as soon as the principals arrived on the scene. (tchd 11-2 in places)
Crackdown(IRE) has been running well over a furlong further and was, unsurprisingly, given a positive ride. However, he raced more towards the stands' side, away from the main action, and could not sustain his effort. (op 12-1, tchd 14-1 in places)
Captain Brilliance(USA) had done best of these in the Bunbury Cup and he came to have every chance over 2f out before fading markedly in the closing stages. He rider allowed him to come home in his own time and later reported that the colt hung left from halfway. He is clearly better than this. Official explanation: jockey said colt hung left from halfway (tchd 5-1 and 11-2 in place)

4298 KING GEORGE VI AND QUEEN ELIZABETH STKS (SPONSORED BY BETFAIR) (GROUP 1) 1m 4f

4:25 (4:31) (Class 1) 3-Y-O+

£567,700 (£215,200; £107,700; £53,700; £26,900; £13,500) **Stalls** High

Form RPR

1-23 **1** **Conduit (IRE)**[21] 3640 4-9-7 125.... RyanMoore 2 127
(Sir Michael Stoute) *broke wl but stdd bk and racd in last trio: hdwy over 3f out: plld out and rdn ent fnl 2f: led over 1f out: edgd rt ins fnl f: r.o wl* **13/8**[1]

4-12 **2** 1 ¾ **Tartan Bearer (IRE)**[38] 3013 4-9-7 122.... MJKinane 4 125
(Sir Michael Stoute) *stdd after s: hld up in midfield: hdwy over 3f out: rdn to ld wl over 1f out: sn chal and drvn: hdd over 1f out: keeping on same pce and hld whn hmpd and swtchd lft fnl 100yds* **7/2**[2]

0-11 **3** hd **Ask**[50] 2670 6-9-7 120.... OPeslier 7 124
(Sir Michael Stoute) *lw: chsd ldrs: hdwy over 3f out: rdn and chal between horses ent fnl 2f out: kpt on same pce fnl f* **9/1**

-413 **4** 2 ¼ **Alwaary (USA)**[16] 3781 3-8-9 113.... RHills 3 120
(J H M Gosden) *stdd after s: t.k.h: hld up in last pair: clsd over 3f out: plld out and rdn 2f out: chsd ldng trio ins fnl f: kpt on but no imp* **12/1**

4152 **5** 4 **Golden Sword**[27] 3438 3-8-9 119.... JMurtagh 1 114
(A P O'Brien, Ire) *chsd ldng pair tl wnt 2nd over 5f out: pushed along and clsd over 3f out: rdn to ld over 2f out: hdd wl over 1f out: wknd over 1f out* **9/2**[3]

3-33 **6** 2 ½ **Look Here**[28] 3412 4-9-4 118.... SebSanders 8 107
(R M Beckett) *lw: a towards rr and niggled along: rdn and effrt whn n.m.r over 2f out: sn struggling and wl hld fnl 2f* **7/1**

0-35 **7** 2 **Frozen Fire (GER)**[50] 2670 4-9-7 117.... JAHeffernan 6 107
(A P O'Brien, Ire) *chsd ldr tl over 5f out: rdn 4f out: drvn and struggling 3f out: sn bhd* **20/1**

3004 **8** 8 **Rockhampton (IRE)**[14] 3882 3-8-9 100.... CO'Donoghue 5 94
(A P O'Brien, Ire) *led: clr over 8f out: rdn and hdd wl over 2f out: sn dropped out* **125/1**

0210 **9** 87 **Scintillo**[27] 3443 4-9-7 114.... RichardHughes 9 —
(R Hannon) *stdd after s: hld up in last pl: rdn and lost tch over 3f out: virtually p.u fnl 2f: t.o* **66/1**

2m 28.73s (-3.77) **Going Correction** +0.15s/f (Good)
WFA 3 from 4yo+ 12lb **9** Ran SP% **115.7**
Speed ratings (Par 117): **118,116,116,115,112 110,109,104,46**
toteswingers: 1&2 £1.90, 1&3 £4.30, 2&3 £5.60 CSF £7.24 CT £37.94 TOTE £2.50: £1.10, £1.60, £2.20; EX 5.60 Trifecta £22.70 Pool: £26866.85 - 872.38 winning units..
Owner Ballymacoll Stud **Bred** Ballymacoll Stud Farm Ltd **Trained** Newmarket, Suffolk
■ A result that virtually guarantees the trainers' championship for Sir Michael Stoute.
■ Stewards' Enquiry : Ryan Moore three-day ban: careless riding (Aug 8-10)
M J Kinane caution: used whip down shoulder in forehand position

FOCUS
The top mid-season middle-distance Group 1 race in Europe with the list of previous winners a roll-call of champions - Duke Of Marmalade, Dylan Thomas, Galileo, Montjeu and Daylami having all won this in the previous ten years. Not a vintage renewal, with top middle-distance three-year-olds Sea The Stars and Fame And Glory both missing, but it still looked up to standard, with the Irish Derby second, the Coronation Cup winner, and the previous year's Irish Derby, Oaks, St Leger and Breeders' Cup Turf winners all taking their chances. It proved a triumph for Sir Michael Stoute, who trained the first three home, and Ballymacoll Stud who own the first two. Straightforward form to rate, with Ask probably the best guide and Conduit back to his Breeders' Cup best.

NOTEBOOK
Conduit(IRE) had the highest official rating in the race and got the better of a real battle with his stable companions in the straight. Always travelling well, he hit the front going into the last furlong and battled on well despite edging into his rivals, particularly the runner-up, late on, which cost his rider a three-day ban. He had run creditably in both his previous starts this season at 1m2f, but the return to this distance showed him at his best and, clearly one of the top performers in the world at this trip, he will now be campaigned with a second Breeders' Cup Turf as the main objective. The Arc could well come into consideration too. (tchd 15-8 in places)
Tartan Bearer(IRE) is an admirably consistent type and had followed a similar path to his stable companion, having both his runs this season over 1m2f. He ran his race and was done no favours by the winner inside the furlong, although it did not affect the result. If he is to avoid his stable companion, the Arc looks the logical target, although as he has yet to win beyond 1m2f the Irish Champion Stakes and the Breeders' Cup Classic could come into the equation. (tchd 9-2)

Ask has peaked this year, at the age of six, and followed up his Coronation Cup success with another fine effort, if not quite having the pace to hold off his stablemates. Another try at both the Arc and the Canadian International could fit into his schedule. (op 11-1)

Alwaary(USA) did best of the three-year-olds, staying on from off the pace without ever looking like troubling the principals. He is progressing with racing and will go for the Great Voltigeur next, in an attempt to win his first Group race. He should make up into a fine four-year-old. (op 14-1)

Golden Sword was the Ballydoyle number one, following creditable efforts in both the Epsom and Irish Derby. He had yet to score above Group 3 level though and, although showing in front early in the straight, was brushed aside by the older horses. The St Leger seems to offer his best chance of success at this level. (tchd 5-1 in places)

Look Here finished third to Conduit in the St Leger last season and had been touched off by Ask and Youmzain in a desperate finish to the Coronation Cup on her return. She appeared close enough turning in, but found little and was somewhat disappointing, although the surface may have been too quick, as she is ideally suited by good ground. The Yorkshire Oaks looks an obvious next port of call, although it might come a little too soon. (op 8-1)

Frozen Fire(GER) has struggled since winning last year's Irish Derby (when Tartan Bearer was back in fourth) and, although he was ridden positively, he could not pick up once in line for home. (tchd 25-1 in places)

Rockhampton(IRE) made sure it was a decent gallop before dropping away. (op 200-1 tchd 100-1)

Scintillo, who was restrained early, never got out of last position and finished tailed off. Something must have been amiss.

4299 CANISBAY BLOODSTOCK H'CAP — 1m 4f
5:35 (5:35) (Class 4) (0-85,85) 3-Y-O — **£6,476** (£1,927; £963; £481) **Stalls** High

Form — RPR

2221 **1** **Stanstill (IRE)**[28] 3371 3-9-5 **83** ... RobertWinston 6 — 89
(G A Swinbank) *t.k.h: led for 2f: chsd ldr tl led again over 5f out: rdn and kicked on over 2f out: hrd pressed over 1f out: hld on gamely fnl f* **9/2**[2]

-134 **2** ¾ **The Fonz**[27] 3429 3-9-0 **78** ... RyanMoore 2 — 83
(Sir Michael Stoute) *lw: t.k.h: trckd ldrs: rdn to chse wnr 2f out: pressed wnr over 1f out: unable qck and hld fnl f* **7/1**

1234 **3** ¾ **Non Dom (IRE)**[31] 3276 3-8-11 **75** ... SteveDrowne 9 — 81+
(H Morrison) *lw: t.k.h: in tch tl shuffled bk towards rr after 1f: effrt on inner over 2f out: nt clr run and switching lft over 1f out tl swtchd rt bk to rail 1f out: r.o wl but unable to rch ldng pair* **15/2**

-132 **4** 1 ¾ **Solar Graphite (IRE)**[29] 3359 3-8-9 **73** ... EddieAhern 4 — 74+
(J L Dunlop) *t.k.h: hld up in tch: rdn and unable qck over 2f out: kpt on u.p fnl f but nvr pce to chal ldrs* **2/1**[1]

6214 **5** 1 **Senses (USA)**[21] 3644 3-9-0 **78** ...(v[1]) MJKinane 5 — 77
(J Noseda) *stdd after s: hld up in tch in rr: plld out and hdwy jst over 2f out: racd v awkwardly u.p: no prog fnl f* **6/1**[3]

-005 **6** hd **Dialogue**[27] 3429 3-8-12 **76** ... RoystonFfrench 8 — 75
(M Johnston) *t.k.h: trckd ldrs: switching lft over 2f out: chsd ldng pair and drvn over 1f out: no imp: lost 3 pls ins fnl f* **20/1**

2212 **7** 3 ¼ **Interdiamonds**[16] 3761 3-8-12 **76** ... GregFairley 1 — 70
(M Johnston) *t.k.h: hld up in tch towards rr: rdn and unable qck over 2f out: no prog after* **8/1**

1441 **8** 5 **History Lesson**[12] 3922 3-9-7 **85** ... JimmyFortune 3 — 71
(R Hannon) *lw: chsd ldr tl led after 2f: slowed pce and hdd over 5f out: ev ch 3f out: sn rdn and unable qck: wknd wl over 1f out* **8/1**

2m 34.77s (2.27) **Going Correction** +0.15s/f (Good) — **8** Ran SP% **117.0**
Speed ratings (Par 102): **98,97,97,95,95 95,92,89**
toteswingers: 1&2 £4.50, 1&3 £8.00, 2&3 £11.10 CSF £36.63 CT £232.90 TOTE £6.20: £2.00, £1.70, £2.30; EX 41.80 Trifecta £245.80 Pool: £2269.54 - 6.83 winning units. Place 6: £144.49 Place 5: £46.72.
Owner The Twopin Partnership **Bred** E J Daly **Trained** Melsonby, N Yorks

FOCUS
A fair three-year-old handicap in which the early pace was steady. It paid to race close to the pace. The winner is rated up 5lb and the form could be rated higher.
T/Jkpt: Not won. T/Plt: £162.50 to a £1 stake. Pool: £189,194.69. 849.43 winning tickets. T/Qpdt: £28.50 to a £1 stake. Pool: £11,460.58. 297.20 winning tickets. SP

4200 LINGFIELD (L-H)
Saturday, July 25

OFFICIAL GOING: Good (good to firm in places)
Wind: Fresh, half behind Weather: Becoming fine

4300 WALK BEYOND THE PALE H'CAP — 1m 2f
5:45 (5:45) (Class 6) (0-65,65) 3-Y-O+ — **£2,047** (£604; £302) **Stalls** Low

Form — RPR

0213 **1** **Love In The Park**[15] 3811 4-9-10 **60** ... PatCosgrave 5 — 69+
(R Brotherton) *settled in 6th: rdn 4f out: hdwy fr 2f out: wnt 3rd and swtchd to rail 1f out: r.o to ld nr fin* **5/2**[1]

051 **2** ½ **Sceilin (IRE)**[31] 3259 5-9-1 **51** ...(t) SaleemGolam 10 — 59
(J Mackie) *v free to post: prom: wnt 2nd after 3f: hrd rdn over 2f out: led 1f out: kpt on u.p: hdd nr fin* **11/1**

0 **3** 1 ¾ **Precious Citizen (USA)**[12] 3929 4-9-0 **50** ... LukeMorris 14 — 55
(J R Gask) *chsd ldrs: outpcd and struggling to hold pl over 4f out: looked wl btn tl styd on again fnl 2f: hung lft* **20/1**

P520 **4** ½ **Rosy Dawn**[2] 4235 4-9-2 **52** ... JerryO'Dwyer 4 — 56
(J J Bridger) *led and set gd gallop: rdn over 3f out: hdd 1f out: kpt on same pce* **16/1**

1534 **5** ½ **Vinces**[15] 3811 5-9-9 **64** ... AmyBaker[(5)] 13 — 67
(T D McCarthy) *dwlt: towards rr: effrt and hrd rdn over 2f out: styd on wl fr over 1f out: gng on at fin* **8/1**

0324 **6** hd **Lunar River (FR)**[16] 3777 6-9-12 **62** ...(t) FergusSweeney 3 — 64
(David Pinder) *t.k.h towards rr: rdn and hdwy 2f out: n.m.r and no imp fnl f* **8/1**

4115 **7** hd **Goose Green (IRE)**[11] 3949 5-9-10 **63** ... WilliamCarson[(3)] 2 — 65
(R J Hodges) *chsd ldrs: 3rd into st: hrd rdn 3f out: no ex fnl f* **11/2**[2]

1245 **8** 1 ¼ **Confide In Me**[10] 3980 5-9-10 **60** ...(t) HayleyTurner 11 — 59
(G A Butler) *2nd for 3f: chsd ldrs after: hrd rdn over 2f out: wknd over 1f out* **6/1**[3]

6000 **9** hd **Classical Rhythm (IRE)**[9] 4007 4-9-5 **55** ... TGMcLaughlin 12 — 54
(J R Boyle) *mid-div: rdn 4f out: nt pce to chal* **20/1**

0026 **10** 1 ¼ **Clovis**[15] 3811 4-10-0 **64** ...(p) DaneO'Neill 6 — 60
(N P Mulholland) *dwlt: last tl drvn along and passed a few btn rivals over 3f out: nvr nr ldrs* **14/1**

4040 **11** 3 ¼ **Millway Beach (IRE)**[33] 3222 3-9-3 **63** ... StephenCarson 7 — 53
(Pat Eddery) *mid-div: outpcd 4f out: sn struggling in rr* **12/1**

3135 **12** 4 **Mix N Match**[45] 2830 5-9-3 **53** ... EdwardCreighton 9 — 35
(R M Stronge) *dwlt: a in last pair: hrd rdn and no ch fnl 3f* **16/1**

2m 11.6s (1.10) **Going Correction** +0.10s/f (Good)
WFA 3 from 4yo+ 10lb — **12** Ran SP% **124.4**
Speed ratings (Par 101): **99,98,97,96,96 96,96,95,94,93 91,88**
toteswingers: 1&2 £24.70, 1&3 £23.00, 2&3 not won CSF £33.63 CT £463.56 TOTE £3.10: £1.80, £3.90, £5.90; EX 41.90.
Owner Arthur Clayton **Bred** New England Stud And Partners **Trained** Elmley Castle, Worcs
■ Stewards' Enquiry : Luke Morris one-day ban: careless riding (Aug 8)

FOCUS
A low-grade handicap but a few came here in decent nick. Straightforward form. The pace was strong thanks to Rosy Dawn, who had them strung out entering the straight.

4301 SWEET JOHNNIE HAYES H'CAP — 2m
6:15 (6:15) (Class 5) (0-70,69) 3-Y-O+ — **£2,729** (£806; £403) **Stalls** Low

Form — RPR

33-2 **1** **Ambrose Princess (IRE)**[4] 4168 4-8-13 **54** ... PatCosgrave 1 — 62
(M J Scudamore) *in tch: pressed ldrs 5f out: rdn 4f out: drvn to ld 1f out: styd on* **10/3**[2]

51/3 **2** 1 ¼ **Doubly Guest**[47] 2760 5-10-0 **69** ... DaneO'Neill 12 — 76
(B W Hills) *sn prom: led after 6f: hrd rdn over 2f out: hld on gamely tl hdd 1f out: nt qckn* **5/2**[1]

0056 **3** 2 ¼ **Follow The Dream**[12] 3927 6-8-10 **51** ... TGMcLaughlin 8 — 55
(Karen George) *hld up towards rr: rdn and hdwy 3f out: wnt 3rd over 2f out: hung lft over 1f out: one pce* **20/1**

-062 **4** 3 ½ **Mohawk Star (IRE)**[10] 3986 8-9-10 **65** ...(v) GeorgeBaker 9 — 65
(I A Wood) *mid-div: rdn over 4f out: kpt on u.p wout threatening fnl 2f* **8/1**

012 **5** 4 **Star Of Pompey**[9] 3997 5-9-4 **59** ... SebSanders 7 — 54
(A B Haynes) *mid-div: hdwy 5f out: drvn to go 3rd 3f out: sn outpcd* **9/2**[3]

6-03 **6** 15 **Silver Surprise**[16] 3774 5-8-9 **50** oh5 ... LukeMorris 10 — 27
(J J Bridger) *in rr of midfield: rdn 6f out: n.d whn rn wd into st* **40/1**

406 **7** 1 **Trempari**[21] 3617 6-8-11 **52** ... HayleyTurner 13 — 28
(Mike Murphy) *bhd: rdn 4f out: nvr nr ldrs* **33/1**

0362 **8** 1 ¾ **Warrior Conquest**[17] 3737 4-9-13 **68** ... PaulDoe 5 — 42
(W J Knight) *chsd ldrs: wnt 2nd 6f out: drvn along 4f out: wknd 3f out* **11/2**

3-20 **9** 27 **Shy**[44] 2854 4-9-13 **68** ... StephenCarson 4 — 9
(P Winkworth) *led 4f: cl up tl wknd qckly over 4f out: sn bhd* **10/1**

006/ **10** 43 **Letham Island (IRE)**[31] 7178 5-9-0 **55** ...(p) FergusSweeney 3 — —
(R M Stronge) *prom: led after 4f tl after 6f: hrd rdn and wknd rapidly over 5f out: t.o fnl 4f* **33/1**

3m 34.99s (0.19) **Going Correction** +0.10s/f (Good) — **10** Ran SP% **118.5**
Speed ratings (Par 103): **103,102,101,99,97 90,89,88,75,53**
toteswingers: 1&2 £2.20, 1&3 £8.80, 2&3 £33.20 CSF £11.85 CT £144.62 TOTE £4.70: £2.00, £1.20, £2.30; EX 12.60.
Owner The Yes No Wait Sorries **Bred** Tally-Ho Stud **Trained** Bromsash, Herefordshire

FOCUS
Not a strong staying handicap. Straightforward form, the winner rated to last year's best.

4302 CLAIRE LARBY 21ST BIRTHDAY MAIDEN AUCTION STKS — 5f
6:45 (6:46) (Class 6) 2-Y-O — **£2,388** (£705; £352) **Stalls** High

Form — RPR

0 **1** **Excelling (IRE)**[21] 3633 2-8-5 ... ChrisCatlin 7 — 85+
(P J Makin) *dwlt: towards rr of main gp but sn in tch and gng wl: smooth hdwy to ld wl over 1f out: pushed clr: comf* **3/1**[1]

0 **2** 5 **Morgans Choice**[33] 3218 2-8-11 ... PaulDoe 10 — 73
(J L Spearing) *slt ld nr stands' rail tl wl over 1f out: nt pce of wnr* **17/2**

4 **3** 2 ¼ **Art Summer**[14] 3849 2-8-6 ... AdrianMcCarthy 6 — 60
(D M Simcock) *t.k.h: chsd ldrs towards centre: rdn over 2f out: one pce* **7/2**[2]

200 **4** ½ **Pherousa**[14] 3865 2-8-4 ... LukeMorris 3 — 56
(M Blanshard) *towards rr: sme hdwy and in tch 2f out: hrd rdn over 1f out: no imp* **20/1**

6436 **5** 1 ¾ **Flapjack**[61] 2328 2-8-6 ... HayleyTurner 5 — 52
(R Hannon) *sn outpcd and drvn along in rr: n.m.r 2f out: sme late hdwy* **4/1**[3]

6 ½ **Miss Kitty Grey (IRE)** 2-8-6 ... StephenCarson 11 — 50
(J R Boyle) *w ldr on stands' rail tl outpcd and btn 2f out* **12/1**

0 **7** ¾ **Satin Princess (IRE)**[40] 2972 2-8-4 ow1 ... WilliamCarson[(3)] 2 — 48
(Paul Mason) *hld up towards rr in centre: hdwy 2f out: hung lft and hrd rdn: wknd 1f out* **25/1**

0 **8** 1 ¾ **Titoli Di Coda (IRE)**[16] 3772 2-8-8 ... DaneO'Neill 9 — 43
(L M Cumani) *prom over 2f: sn rdn and lost pl* **12/1**

24 **9** ½ **Diamond Affair (IRE)**[21] 3633 2-8-5 ow1 ... EdwardCreighton 1 — 38
(M G Quinlan) *in tch and sn pushed along towards centre: drvn along over 2f out: sn wknd* **15/2**

56 **10** 3 ½ **Softly Spoken**[12] 3918 2-7-13 ... AmyBaker[(5)] 8 — 25
(A W Carroll) *prom: hrd rdn 2f out: wknd qckly over 1f out* **20/1**

11 11 **Fast Elaine (IRE)** 2-8-5 ... SaleemGolam 4 — —
(Mrs L C Jewell) *missed break and lost 12 l: a t.o* **33/1**

58.01 secs (-0.19) **Going Correction** -0.10s/f (Good) — **11** Ran SP% **121.2**
Speed ratings (Par 92): **97,89,85,84,81 81,79,77,76,70 53**
toteswingers: 1&2 £4.20, 1&3 £3.50, 2&3 £7.80 CSF £28.58 TOTE £3.90: £1.50, £2.50, £1.90; EX 39.40.
Owner R P Marchant,D A Poole,G Moss **Bred** J Joyce **Trained** Ogbourne Maisey, Wilts

FOCUS
A weak maiden auction, but the winner impressed and looks potentially useful. The form is rated around the third and fourth.

NOTEBOOK

Excelling(IRE), well backed, won in impressive style and is clearly held in some regard. Sent off at short odds on debut at Nottingham, she was slowly away and looked badly in need of the experience. The daughter of Exceed And Excel was again a bit tardy from the gates, but soon got a decent position behind the pace. She travelled with real purpose before being asked to make her move entering the final couple of furlongs. In front well over a furlong out, she scooted away to justify market support and mark herself down as a potentially useful filly, although it remains to be seen if she beat anything of note. (op 4-1 tchd 9-2)

Morgans Choice was also strong in the market, and although he raced a little too freely at the head of affairs, he showed good speed. He kept on well to hold on for second and this was clearly a big step forward from his debut. (op 16-1)

Art Summer shaped well on debut, so it was a bit disappointing she couldn't make a better fist of this with experience under her belt. She kept on well down the middle, but she lacked a change of gear and looks ordinary. (op 3-1)

Pherousa bounced back from a couple of very poor efforts to keep on for fifth, but she looks more of a low grade nursery type.

Flapjack made a bit of late headway, but lacked tactical speed in the early stages of the race. She's becoming quite exposed now. (op 11-4)

4303 BILL & SHIRLEY BORRIE GOLDEN WEDDING CELEBRATION MEDIAN AUCTION MAIDEN STKS 7f

7:20 (7:22) (Class 6) 3-5-Y-O **£2,388** (£705; £352) **Stalls** High

Form RPR

5-65 **1** **Learo Dochais (USA)**[61] 2336 3-9-3 72 PhilipRobinson 2 76
(M A Jarvis) *mde all: c across to stands' rail over 5f out: rdn over 1f out: hld on wl fnl f: eased fnl strides* **9/2**[2]

2 *2* **Golden Button (IRE)** 4-9-5 SebSanders 1 69+
(Sir Mark Prescott) *stdd s and swtchd to stands' rail: hld up towards rr: shkn up over 2f out: gd hdwy over 1f out: r.o to take 2nd on line: should improve* **15/2**

2260 **3** *shd* **Safari Guide**[17] 3743 3-9-3 72 LukeMorris 9 70
(P Winkworth) *prom: pressed wnr 3f out: hrd rdn over 1f out: nt qckn fnl f* **5/1**[3]

-023 **4** *3 ½* **Formula (USA)**[75] 1931 3-9-3 77 PatDobbs 8 61
(R Hannon) *hld up in tch in 5th: effrt and swtchd lft 2f out: one pce appr fnl f* **10/11**[1]

040- **5** *1 ¼* **Fitz**[229] 7600 3-9-3 43 PatCosgrave 4 58
(M Salaman) *awkward leaving stalls: t.k.h in tch in 6th: effrt and wnt 3rd ins fnl 2f: wknd jst over 1f out* **33/1**

0 **6** *5* **Tiger Breeze (USA)**[46] 2795 3-9-3 IanMongan 5 44
(Miss Jo Crowley) *hmpd s: hld up in midfield: rdn over 2f out: sn btn* **16/1**

-350 **7** *3 ½* **Fondant Fancy**[19] 3693 3-8-12 65 DaneO'Neill 6 30
(H J L Dunlop) *t.k.h: w ldrs: hrd rdn and hung lft over 2f out: wknd wl over 1f out* **16/1**

60 **8** *6* **Stylish Mover**[129] 869 4-9-10 RobertHavlin 10 21
(R Ingram) *mid-div: rdn and struggling fnl 3f* **33/1**

00 **9** *1* **Any Secrets**[33] 3228 3-9-3 TGMcLaughlin 11 16
(Karen George) *outpcd and bhd: rdn 3f out: nvr nr ldrs* **66/1**

0 **10** *4 ½* **Prince Maggio**[10] 3975 3-9-3 (b[1]) HayleyTurner 7 —
(Pat Eddery) *s.s and wnt bdly lft s: outpcd: a wl bhd* **50/1**

4 **11** *15* **Spring Bridge (IRE)**[16] 3773 3-9-3 LPKeniry 3 —
(Mrs L C Jewell) *t.k.h: prom on outer: hrd rdn over 2f out: sn wknd* **66/1**

1m 23.6s (0.30) **Going Correction** -0.10s/f (Good)
WFA 3 from 4yo 7lb **11** Ran SP% **121.6**
Speed ratings (Par 101): **94,91,91,87,86 80,76,69,68,63 46**
toteswingers: 1&2 £7.20, 1&3 £3.40, 2&3 £3.00 CSF £38.28 TOTE £5.60: £1.60, £2.20, £1.40; EX 36.30.
Owner Mrs Lynn Mernagh **Bred** D J Stable **Trained** Newmarket, Suffolk

FOCUS
A modest maiden in which the winner made all up the rail. He is rated back to his best.

4304 PACEY MACEY'S BIRTHDAY SURPRISE H'CAP 7f

7:55 (7:56) (Class 5) (0-70,70) 3-Y-O **£2,729** (£806; £403) **Stalls** High

Form RPR

506 **1** **Bermondsey Girl**[22] 3566 3-8-11 60 SebSanders 11 73+
(C F Wall) *hld up in 6th on stands' rail: swtchd lft and drvn into ld over 1f out: jst holding runner-up at fin* **11/1**

0216 **2** *½* **The Scorching Wind (IRE)**[8] 4056 3-9-4 67 (t) ChrisCatlin 5 78
(S C Williams) *towards rr: rdn 4f out: gd hdwy over 1f out: swtchd to stands' rail and wnt 2nd ins fnl f: clsng at fin: jst hld* **6/1**[3]

0-01 **3** *3 ¾* **Kuanyao (IRE)**[22] 3580 3-8-12 61 FergusSweeney 10 62+
(P J Makin) *t.k.h: trckd ldrs: rdn over 2f out: swtchd lft towards centre over 1f out: one pce* **4/6**[1]

0000 **4** *nk* **Bermondsey Bob (IRE)**[27] 3427 3-8-2 51 oh3 LiamJones 7 51
(J L Spearing) *t.k.h: prom: led briefly wl over 1f out: one pce* **50/1**

0020 **5** *1 ½* **Lilly Blue (IRE)**[28] 3383 3-8-10 59 PatCosgrave 9 55
(R Brotherton) *mid-div: rdn 3f out: sme late hdwy* **40/1**

0054 **6** *1* **Grand Honour (IRE)**[10] 3982 3-9-4 67 IanMongan 1 60
(P Howling) *towards rr: rdn over 2f out: sme hdwy over 1f out: nt pce to chal* **33/1**

-440 **7** *½* **Megasecret**[44] 2849 3-9-7 70 PatDobbs 12 62
(R Hannon) *sluggish s: sn rdn to join ldrs on stands' rail: wknd over 1f out* **11/2**[2]

-600 **8** *nse* **Day In Dubai**[56] 2478 3-8-3 52 CatherineGannon 3 44
(J J Bridger) *prom on outer tl hrd rdn and wknd over 1f out* **66/1**

3100 **9** *¾* **Royal Crest**[46] 2797 3-8-13 62 LPKeniry 2 52
(J A Osborne) *towards rr: rdn over 2f out: nvr trbld ldrs* **25/1**

4-04 **10** *hd* **Whisky Jack**[18] 3718 3-9-2 65 (b) GeorgeBaker 4 54
(W R Muir) *s.s: sn swtchd to stands' rail: bhd: rdn over 2f out: n.d* **16/1**

-020 **11** *2 ¼* **Foxtrot Alpha (IRE)**[10] 3982 3-9-7 70 LukeMorris 8 53
(P Winkworth) *slt ld tl wknd wl over 1f out* **12/1**

1-00 **12** *25* **Zim Ho**[10] 3982 3-9-1 64 DaneO'Neill 6 —
(J Akehurst) *t.k.h in midfield: hrd rdn and wknd 3f out: bhd whn eased over 1f out* **33/1**

1m 23.08s (-0.22) **Going Correction** -0.10s/f (Good) **12** Ran SP% **127.2**
Speed ratings (Par 100): **97,96,92,91,90 88,88,88,87,87 84,56**
toteswingers: 1&2 £6.10, 1&3 £2.70, 2&3 £2.60 CSF £77.21 CT £108.93 TOTE £13.80: £3.50, £2.50, £1.10; EX 96.80.
Owner Whatton Manor Stud & Ne'er Do Wells II **Bred** Whatton Manor Stud **Trained** Newmarket, Suffolk

FOCUS
A modest handicap won by the least-exposed runner, and fair form for the grade. The front pair raced on the favoured stands' rail.
Bermondsey Girl Official explanation: trainer said, regarding apparent improvement in form, that the filly was suited by its first run in a handicap
Whisky Jack Official explanation: jockey said gelding missed the break

4305 WYCH CROSS H'CAP 7f 140y

8:25 (8:30) (Class 6) (0-65,65) 3-Y-O+ **£2,047** (£604; £302) **Stalls** Centre

Form RPR

4640 **1** **Indy Driver**[21] 3637 4-9-13 64 (p) HayleyTurner 12 79
(J R Fanshawe) *mid-div on stands' rail: rdn over 3f out: gd hdwy to ld over 1f out: sn clr: easily* **6/1**[3]

5466 **2** *4 ½* **Vanadium**[7] 4082 7-9-6 57 GeorgeBaker 17 61
(G L Moore) *hld up in tch: nt clr run 2f out: effrt and squeezed over 1f out: r.o to chse easy wnr ins fnl f* **9/2**[2]

4006 **3** *1 ¼* **Fifty (IRE)**[22] 3581 4-9-11 62 PatDobbs 10 63
(R Hannon) *mid-div: swtchd lft and hdwy over 1f out: drvn to go 3rd ent fnl f: kpt on same pce* **11/1**

-001 **4** *1* **Aine's Delight (IRE)**[27] 3426 3-8-8 60 SimonPearce(7) 1 57+
(Andrew Turnell) *mid-div in centre: hdwy to chse ldrs 2f out: no ex over 1f out* **14/1**

-230 **5** *½* **Gun For Sale (USA)**[75] 1940 4-9-0 51 FergusSweeney 18 49
(P J Makin) *s.s: hld up in rr: nt clr run 2f out: weaved through and r.o fr over 1f out: nrst fin* **8/1**

0012 **6** *hd* **Chief Exec**[10] 3983 7-9-6 57 (b) ChrisCatlin 14 54
(J R Gask) *sn last: rdn 3f out: styd on wl fr over 1f out: nvr nrr* **4/1**[1]

-000 **7** *1 ¾* **Onenightinlisbon (IRE)**[52] 2598 5-9-8 59 PatCosgrave 9 52
(J R Boyle) *pressed ldr: led 2f out: edgd rt and hdd over 1f out: sn wknd* **16/1**

06-6 **8** *¾* **Champagne Fizz (IRE)**[15] 3815 3-9-6 65 DaneO'Neill 2 54+
(Miss Jo Crowley) *prom in centre: hrd rdn and hung lft 2f out: wknd over 1f out* **25/1**

045 **9** *hd* **Star Strider**[39] 3007 5-9-2 58 KylieManser(5) 4 49
(Miss Gay Kelleway) *s.s: hdwy into midfield after 2f: chsd ldrs 3f out: rdn and wknd 2f out* **20/1**

2320 **10** *¾* **Fly By Nelly**[41] 2949 3-9-4 63 TravisBlock 6 50
(H Morrison) *t.k.h: prom tl wknd over 1f out* **15/2**

0405 **11** *2* **Batchworth Blaise**[61] 2330 6-9-0 51 CatherineGannon 11 35
(E A Wheeler) *dwlt: t.k.h in rr: swtchd lft and wd to centre 4f out: hdwy and in tch 2f out: wknd over 1f out* **16/1**

0153 **12** *nk* **Golden Prospect**[20] 3659 5-9-6 57 LiamJones 5 40
(J W Hills) *dwlt: towards rr: mod effrt 3f out: n.d* **10/1**

10-0 **13** *½* **Station Place**[75] 1940 4-9-4 55 StephenDonohoe 13 37
(A B Haynes) *led on stands' rail tl wknd 2f out* **33/1**

0004 **14** *¾* **Shake On It**[7] 4083 5-9-6 57 (tp) IanMongan 3 37
(M R Hoad) *prom tl wknd ins fnl 2f: btn whn squeezed over 1f out* **33/1**

0000 **15** *¾* **Royal Island (IRE)**[15] 3811 7-9-6 57 VinceSlattery 15 36
(M G Quinlan) *towards rr: rdn over 2f out: nvr trbld ldrs* **33/1**

030- **16** *9* **Coup De Torchon (FR)**[327] 5574 4-9-4 55 LPKeniry 7 12
(J A Osborne) *mid-div tl rdn and wknd 2f out* **66/1**

1m 31.27s (-1.03) **Going Correction** -0.10s/f (Good)
WFA 3 from 4yo+ 8lb **16** Ran SP% **130.1**
Speed ratings (Par 101): **101,96,95,94,93 93,91,91,90,90 88,87,87,86,85 76**
toteswingers: 1&2 £4.80, 1&3 £19.10, 2&3 £14.10 CSF £31.71 CT £270.28 TOTE £7.20: £2.10, £2.00, £2.80, £4.40; EX 35.10 Place 6: £48.91, Place 5: £19.20.
Owner Mrs C C Regalado-Gonzalez **Bred** Miss K Rausing **Trained** Newmarket, Suffolk

FOCUS
A weak 0-65 handicap and another race in which the rail was favoured. The winner is rated back to his best with the next two close to recent marks.
Gun For Sale(USA) Official explanation: jockey said gelding ran too free and hung both ways closing stages
Batchworth Blaise Official explanation: jockey said gelding was denied a clear run
Station Place Official explanation: jockey said filly hung left throughout
T/Plt: £73.80 to a £1 stake. Pool: £49,651.66. 490.51 winning tickets. T/Qpdt: £13.70 to a £1 stake. Pool: £6,373.25. 342.20 winning tickets. LM

3388 NEWCASTLE (L-H)

Saturday, July 25

OFFICIAL GOING: Good to soft (soft in places; 6.5)
Wind: Fresh, half against Weather: Cloudy, bright

4306 HILTON NEWCASTLE GATESHEAD NURSERY 6f

2:30 (2:30) (Class 5) 2-Y-O **£3,238** (£963; £481; £240) **Stalls** High

Form RPR

0533 **1** **Flaneur**[18] 3702 2-8-5 67 (b) PJMcDonald 6 72
(T D Easterby) *mde all stands' rail: rdn 2f out: kpt on strly fnl f* **9/2**[3]

420 **2** *2* **Paradise Spectre**[14] 3875 2-8-13 80 MartinLane(5) 4 79
(K R Burke) *in tch: smooth hdwy over 2f out: effrt over 1f out: ev ch ins fnl f: kpt on same pce last 75yds* **11/1**

030 **3** *1* **Olympic Ceremony**[14] 3875 2-8-8 70 TonyHamilton 9 66
(R A Fahey) *prom: effrt and rdn 2f out: kpt on same pce ins fnl f* **7/1**

010 **4** *1 ½* **Ananda Kanda (USA)**[10] 3978 2-9-2 83 LanceBetts(5) 8 75
(B Ellison) *hld up ins: rdn and hdwy over 1f out: no further imp fnl f* **18/1**

41 **5** *4 ½* **Miss Smilla**[14] 3858 2-9-4 80 PaulMulrennan 5 58
(K A Ryan) *hld up: drvn and outpcd over 2f out: rallied appr fnl f: nvr rchd ldrs* **10/3**[2]

2021 **6** *¾* **Fly Silca Fly (IRE)**[7] 4100 2-8-12 74 TonyCulhane 3 50
(M R Channon) *chsd ldrs: outpcd over 2f out: n.d after* **3/1**[1]

6050 **7** *9* **Charity Fair**[19] 3686 2-7-5 60 oh9 CharlotteKerton(7) 7 9
(A Berry) *dwlt and wnt lft s: reminders after 2f: hdwy on outside and hung lft 1/2-way: wknd over 2f out* **40/1**

533 **8** *2 ¾* **Cambuslang (IRE)**[20] 3652 2-7-10 63 JamieKyne(5) 2 —
(I Semple) *in tch tl wknd qckly over 2f out* **6/1**

030 **9** *1* **Powerful Pierre**[21] 3606 2-8-4 66 DaleGibson 1 —
(Jedd O'Keeffe) *t.k.h: chsd ldrs tl wknd over 2f out* **14/1**

1m 16.27s (1.07) **Going Correction** +0.025s/f (Good) **9** Ran SP% **115.7**
Speed ratings (Par 94): **93,90,89,87,81 80,68,64,63**
toteswingers: 1&2 £10.30, 1&3 £14.50, 2&3 £37.30 CSF £52.80 CT £345.15 TOTE £5.60: £1.80, £3.00, £2.60; EX 56.40.
Owner Jeremy Gompertz **Bred** C R Mason **Trained** Great Habton, N Yorks
■ Stewards' Enquiry : Charlotte Kerton one-day ban: used whip when out of contention (Aug 8)

FOCUS
This looked nothing more than a fair, at best, nursery when considering all of the runner's form. A couple of jockeys that rode in the race described the going as dead. It appeared an advantage to be close to the rail. The 'official' ratings shown next to each horse are estimated and for information purposes only.

NOTEBOOK
Flaneur has improved since blinkers were fitted, and his most recent effort had been franked by the subsequent wide-margin win of the horse just in front of him. Quickly away and moved to the stands'-side rail here, he kept on really well and fought on bravely to repel all challengers. (op 13-2)
Paradise Spectre, without a visor this time, was held up off the pace, travelling strongly, before being produced to have every chance a furlong out. A big, robust sort, he tried hard but could not get to the front. (op 10-1 tchd 12-1)
Olympic Ceremony, one place behind Paradise Spectre last time, got locked away in a pocket behind the leader during the earl stages, but did have enough time to make an impact when in the clear. (op 6-1 tchd 11-2)
Ananda Kanda(USA) looked dangerous for a few strides after coming from off the gallop, before her effort flattened out. (op 12-1)
Miss Smilla, said to be edgy in the paddock, became outpaced when the tempo lifted and never got into the race with a serious chance. (op 3-1 tchd 7-2)
Fly Silca Fly(IRE), who was free to post, took an uncompetitive maiden at Ripon recently on easy ground but was soon in trouble here. The jockey was hard at work but halfway and she posed no threat. (tchd 9-4)

Powerful Pierre Official explanation: vet said gelding finished lame

4307 PHOENIX SECURITY MAIDEN AUCTION STKS (DIV I) 7f

3:00 (3:01) (Class 4) 2-Y-O **£4,209** (£1,252; £625; £312) **Stalls** Centre

Form RPR

3 **1** **Bahamian Music (IRE)**[39] 2997 2-8-6 0 ow1 .... TonyHamilton 4 74+
(R A Fahey) *t.k.h: hld up: hdwy wl over 1f out: led ins fnl f: drvn out* **3/1**[2]

4 **2** 1 ½ **Hoss Cartwright (IRE)**[15] 3823 2-8-9 0 .... PaulMulrennan 8 73+
(J Howard Johnson) *w ldr: led 1/2-way to ins fnl f: kpt on same pce* **9/2**

3 5 **Sunnandaeg** 2-8-10 0 .... JamieMoriarty 1 62
(I Semple) *in tch on outside: effrt over 2f out: plugged on fnl f: nt rch first two* **10/1**

0 **4** nk **Caracal**[16] 3785 2-8-10 0 .... AndrewMullen 2 61
(M Johnston) *cl up tl rdn and nt qckn over 1f out* **4/1**[3]

3 **5** nk **So Bazaar (IRE)**[12] 3910 2-8-9 0 .... PJMcDonald 3 59
(G A Swinbank) *t.k.h: led to 1/2-way: rdn and no ex fr over 1f out* **2/1**[1]

0 **6** 2 **Young Firth**[18] 3716 2-8-2 0 .... PaulPickard(5) 10 52
(J R Norton) *in tch: outpcd and hung lft over 2f out: sn no imp* **50/1**

7 3 **Kai Broon (IRE)** 2-8-3 0 .... JamieKyne(5) 6 46
(Miss Lucinda V Russell) *dwlt: bhd: rdn and green 3f out: nvr able to chal* **18/1**

0 **8** 8 **Lighterman**[22] 3571 2-8-7 0 .... DaleGibson 7 25
(E J Alston) *chsd ldrs to 1/2-way: sn lost pl* **40/1**

0 **9** 7 **Eeny Mac (IRE)**[63] 2260 2-8-2 0 .... MartinLane(5) 5 —
(N Bycroft) *in tch: drvn and outpcd after 3f: sn no ch* **33/1**

0 **10** 14 **No Quarter (IRE)**[39] 2997 2-8-9 0 ow1 .... PhillipMakin 9 —
(A Dickman) *in tch: hung lft and outpcd 1/2-way: sn btn* **14/1**

1m 30.91s (2.21) **Going Correction** +0.025s/f (Good) **10 Ran SP% 124.9**
Speed ratings (Par 96): **88,86,80,80,79 77,74,65,57,41**
toteswingers: 1&2 £3.60, 1&3 £11.50, 2&3 £19.70 CSF £18.29 TOTE £4.10: £1.40, £2.10, £2.60; EX 18.40.
Owner R A Fahey **Bred** Genesis Green Stud Ltd **Trained** Musley Bank, N Yorks

FOCUS
The first of two divisions of this maiden looked marginally stronger than the following event but although the first two came clear it was still only ordinary form. They can probably rate higher.

NOTEBOOK
Bahamian Music(IRE) was really well supported on her debut and put up an encouraging performance, which she duly built on here despite pulling hard. One would imagine that she should get a mile. (op 7-2)
Hoss Cartwright(IRE) is a lengthy type who did very little wrong. Still a bit green under pressure, he kept on well and has the scope to be better with time. (op 11-2 tchd 6-1)
Sunnandaeg, who cost £31,000 as a yearling, seemed to be edging left early but got the idea late on, and slipped into third inside the final furlong. (op 8-1 tchd 7-1)
Caracal helped to set the pace for a short while, but got outpaced before keeping on again. He looked to improve on his first effort. (op 5-1)
So Bazaar(IRE), an eyecathcer on his debut, was a big disappointment in this, as he was travelling well with the runner-up at the head of affairs before dropping away tamely a furlong out, losing a couple of places in the latter stages. (op 9-4 tchd 11-4 tchd 3-1 in places)
Young Firth got behind but stayed on nicely to be best of the rest. (op 80-1)
No Quarter(IRE) Official explanation: jockey said gelding hung left-handed

4308 PHOENIX SECURITY MAIDEN AUCTION STKS (DIV II) 7f

3:35 (3:35) (Class 4) 2-Y-O **£4,209** (£1,252; £625; £312) **Stalls** Centre

Form RPR

33 **1** **Aquarian Spirit**[10] 3971 2-8-9 0 .... TonyHamilton 10 75
(R A Fahey) *chsd ldrs: led over 1f out: drvn clr fnl f* **11/10**[1]

2 4 ½ **Beat The Rush** 2-8-9 0 ow1 .... PhillipMakin 2 64+
(Miss J A Camacho) *dwlt: bhd: gd hdwy over 1f out: chsd wnr ins fnl f: kpt on: no imp* **16/1**

45 **3** 1 ¼ **Turf Trivia**[28] 3376 2-8-7 0 .... FrederikTylicki(3) 7 62
(G M Moore) *w ldrs: rdn over 2f out: one pce fnl f* **6/1**[2]

40 **4** ¾ **Rigid**[35] 3138 2-8-2 0 .... JamieKyne(5) 1 57
(J G Given) *led to over 1f out: kpt on same pce* **6/1**[2]

5 **5** 2 **Cosmic Orbit**[35] 3170 2-8-11 0 .... TonyCulhane 4 56
(K R Burke) *t.k.h early: in tch: outpcd over 2f out: n.d after* **10/1**[3]

0 **6** 5 **Dinkys Diamond (IRE)**[28] 3392 2-8-2 0 .... LanceBetts(5) 8 39
(B Ellison) *chsd ldrs: drvn over 2f out: sn outpcd* **20/1**

7 6 **Master Leon** 2-8-7 0 .... PaulMulrennan 9 24
(B Smart) *dwlt: bhd: outpcd 1/2-way: n.d* **10/1**[3]

0 **8** 4 ½ **Somewhere Else**[21] 3606 2-7-13 0 .... KellyHarrison(3) 5 8
(A Berry) *towards rr: effrt 3f out: sn rdn and wknd* **80/1**

9 ½ **Thescottishsoldier** 2-8-8 0 .... PJMcDonald 6 13
(A G Foster) *dwlt: hld up: shkn up over 2f out: wknd over 1f out* **14/1**

10 5 **Irish Eyes** 2-8-3 0 .... PatrickDonaghy(5) 3 —
(Jedd O'Keeffe) *bhd: struggling over 3f out: sn btn* **20/1**

1m 30.02s (1.32) **Going Correction** +0.025s/f (Good) **10 Ran SP% 117.7**
Speed ratings (Par 96): **93,87,86,85,83 77,70,65,65,59**
toteswingers: 1&2 £11.20, 1&3 £2.50, 2&3 £36.50 CSF £21.62 TOTE £2.20: £1.10, £4.50, £2.30; EX 22.30.
Owner P S Cresswell & Mrs P A Morrison **Bred** Whitwell Bloodstock **Trained** Musley Bank, N Yorks
■ Stewards' Enquiry : Lance Betts one-day ban: careless riding (Aug 8)

FOCUS
Only half of those with previous racecourse experience showed a bit of promise in any of their starts, so it is unlikely that many winners will probably emerge from this contest in the near future. Aquarian Spirit found the expected improvement.

NOTEBOOK
Aquarian Spirit had run well in two previous starts and set a decent standard to aim at, and although he took a while to pick up, he won comfortably after going clear. One would imagine he will head to handicaps now. (op 6-4 tchd 13-8 and Evens)
Beat The Rush, who had already been gelded, created a good impression on this his first start. He took a while to get the hang of things but flew home once the penny had dropped. (op 12-1)
Turf Trivia shared the early pace and kept on for pressure. (op 15-2)
Rigid, taking a drop in class, was visibly warm and tended to wander around a bit at the end of the race. (op 5-1)
Cosmic Orbit showed promise in a maiden that had already produced winners on debut, and he travelled well here off the pace until about two out. He is probably better than this result suggests. (tchd 9-1)
Dinkys Diamond(IRE) was pushed along throughout. (tchd 16-1)

Thescottishsoldier, a half-brother to a very useful 2yo last season, travelled nicely for a lot of the race and shaped better than his final position suggested. (tchd 12-1)

4309 MAMMA MIA AT ARENA THIS CHRISTMAS H'CAP 6f

4:10 (4:10) (Class 3) (0-90,90) 3-Y-O

£7,477 (£2,239; £1,119; £560; £279; £140) **Stalls** High

Form RPR

0563 **1** **Mister Laurel**[1] 4289 3-8-7 76 .... TonyHamilton 8 88
(R A Fahey) *mde virtually all stands' rail: rdn 2f out: kpt on strly to go clr fnl f* **11/2**[3]

5263 **2** 4 **Kerrys Requiem (IRE)**[19] 3688 3-9-7 90 .... TonyCulhane 6 89
(M R Channon) *t.k.h early: stdd bhd ldrs: effrt and chsd wnr over 1f out: one pce fnl f* **5/1**[2]

0105 **3** 3 ¼ **Grissom (IRE)**[8] 4044 3-7-13 75 .... BillyCray(7) 7 64
(A Berry) *disp ld tl rdn and outpcd wl over 1f out* **20/1**

51 **4** 2 ¾ **Ursula (IRE)**[2] 4227 3-8-5 79 6ex .... MartinLane(5) 2 59
(K R Burke) *hld up in tch: effrt over 2f out: sn no imp: btn fnl f* **5/4**[1]

045 **5** 2 ½ **Lakeman (IRE)**[30] 3316 3-7-10 72 .... JamesPSullivan(7) 4 44
(B Ellison) *in tch: drvn and outpcd 3f out: n.d after* **17/2**

6001 **6** 1 ½ **Mullglen**[10] 3973 3-8-7 76 .... PaulMulrennan 3 43
(T D Easterby) *prom on outside tl hung lft and wknd over 2f out* **7/1**

0355 **7** 1 ¼ **On Offer (IRE)**[26] 3453 3-8-0 72 .... (b[1]) KellyHarrison(3) 1 35
(T D Easterby) *w ldrs tl wknd qckly over 1f out* **8/1**

1m 14.49s (-0.71) **Going Correction** +0.025s/f (Good) **7 Ran SP% 115.4**
Speed ratings (Par 104): **105,99,95,91,88 86,84**
toteswingers: 1&2 £3.50, 1&3 £7.80, 2&3 £11.40 CSF £33.33 CT £511.63 TOTE £7.30: £2.90, £2.40; EX 33.30.
Owner The Cosmic Cases **Bred** Mrs M Bryce **Trained** Musley Bank, N Yorks

FOCUS
Most of these had either won a race this season or shown at least one piece of decent from, but it is hard to know how literally to take this. The winner was in the best place up front on the rail.

NOTEBOOK
Mister Laurel, running in no headgear this time, finished third the previous night at York over about five and a half furlongs, but did the job nicely less than 24 hours later after bagging the stands'-side rail. (op 8-1 tchd 9-2)
Kerrys Requiem(IRE), who looked unlucky at Ripon last time, was tracked the winner and had every chance, but could not close the gap. It was probably a good effort giving away a stone to the winner, although it has to be said she has only one success to her name so far. (op 11-4)
Grissom(IRE) looked very high in the handicap and kept on well without being a threat. (op 11-1)
Ursula(IRE) came right back to her best when winning in good style at Doncaster two days previously, and shouldered a penalty here for that win. However, she was very disappointing this time and was beaten before the two-furlong pole. (op 15-8 tchd 5-2)
Lakeman(IRE) kept on but was never a danger at any stage. (op 10-1 tchd 12-1)
Mullglen, up in trip, was eased considerably late on after seeming to want to hang left for much of the race. Official explanation: jockey said gelding hung badly left-handed (op 13-2 tchd 5-1 tchd 8-1 in places)
On Offer(IRE), wearing blinkers for the first time, was unbeaten in two starts over this course and distance when soft appeared in the going, but was much too keen and failed to get home. (op 15-2 tchd 7-1)

4310 PIMMS BEESWING H'CAP 7f

4:45 (4:45) (Class 3) (0-95,93) 3-Y-O+

£9,346 (£2,799; £1,399; £700; £349; £175) **Stalls** Centre

Form RPR

4644 **1** **Mastership (IRE)**[17] 3752 5-9-0 87 .... (p) JamieKyne(5) 2 98
(J J Quinn) *hld up and bhd: smooth hdwy over 2f out: rdn to ld ins fnl f: kpt on wl* **14/1**

313 **2** ½ **Eton Rifles (IRE)**[18] 3706 4-9-4 86 .... PaulMulrennan 5 96
(J Howard Johnson) *trckd ldrs gng wl: led over 1f out to ins fnl f: r.o* **3/1**[1]

0421 **3** ¾ **Cobo Bay**[8] 4064 4-9-4 91 .... (b) AmyRyan(5) 7 99
(K A Ryan) *t.k.h early: cl up: led briefly 2f out: one pce fnl f* **11/2**[3]

6501 **4** 2 **Smarty Socks (IRE)**[15] 3825 5-8-11 84 .... PaulPickard(5) 8 87
(P T Midgley) *dwlt: hld up: hdwy over 1f out: nvr rchd ldrs* **8/1**

6220 **5** ½ **Osteopathic Remedy (IRE)**[14] 3872 5-9-5 87 .... PhillipMakin 3 88
(M Dods) *in tch: effrt over 2f out: one pce over 1f out* **9/2**[2]

3000 **6** 1 ½ **Lucky Dance (BRZ)**[14] 3872 7-9-5 87 .... (b[1]) TonyCulhane 6 84
(A G Foster) *in tch: drvn and outpcd over 2f out: no imp over 1f out* **16/1**

2015 **7** 1 **Stevie Gee (IRE)**[21] 3615 5-9-3 85 .... PJMcDonald 1 79
(G A Swinbank) *hld up and bhd: rdn and effrt over 2f out: nvr able to chal* **10/1**

40-0 **8** nk **Protector (SAF)**[8] 4037 8-9-11 93 .... (t) TonyHamilton 12 87
(A G Foster) *midfield: drvn and outpcd over 2f out: n.d after* **20/1**

0014 **9** 1 **Shotley Mac**[15] 3825 5-8-11 84 .... (b) MartinLane(5) 9 75
(N Bycroft) *led to 2f out: sn rdn and btn* **8/1**

-000 **10** 1 **Santiago Atitlan**[8] 4037 7-9-3 85 .... JamieMoriarty 4 73
(P Monteith) *towards rr: struggling 1/2-way: nvr on terms* **66/1**

2005 **11** 4 ½ **Arabian Spirit**[10] 3988 4-9-6 88 .... DaleGibson 11 64
(E A L Dunlop) *trckd ldrs: drvn 3f out: wknd qckly over 1f out* **9/1**

1m 27.59s (-1.11) **Going Correction** +0.025s/f (Good) **11 Ran SP% 118.7**
Speed ratings (Par 107): **107,106,105,103,102 101,99,99,98,97 92**
toteswingers: 1&2 £12.40, 1&3 £13.00, 2&3 £3.80 CSF £56.37 CT £275.10 TOTE £19.10: £4.30, £1.80, £2.00; EX 68.60.
Owner Dark Horse Racing Partnership Two **Bred** Darley **Trained** Settrington, N Yorks

FOCUS
A wide-open handicap in which they raced down the centre. Sound form.

NOTEBOOK
Mastership(IRE) had gone a long time without winning, but under a fine waiting ride by his talented jockey, he was forced to go past once challenging the second, and did just enough to win. His previous record is enough to put one off backing him to do this next time. (op 10-1 tchd 16-1)
Eton Rifles(IRE) ◆ is a progressive performer, who had shaped as though a return to 7f would suit at Pontefract last time. Always up with the pace, he got the rest of his rivals nicely beaten before being mugged close home by a seasoned handicapper. He is one to keep the faith with. (op 10-3 tchd 11-4)
Cobo Bay is ideally suited by give in the ground and won over a mile on heavy last time. Raised 6lb and very keen here in the early stages, he had the run of the race but wandered from one side to another under pressure, which ended his chance of collecting again. (tchd 7-1 tchd 8-1 in places)
Smarty Socks(IRE), who was slowly away, came home strongly for fourth but never figured with a hope of winning. (tchd 9-1)
Osteopathic Remedy(IRE) was produced to get to the leaders but he failed to bridge the gap. He has won off this mark before but, considering his other victories, needs an ease in the weights judged on this run. (tchd 4-1 and 5-1)
Lucky Dance(BRZ), wearing blinkers for the first time, kept on quite well inside the final furlong and ran better than he had done for a while. Official explanation: jockey said horse stumbled leaving stalls (op 20-1)

Arabian Spirit has shown his best form when there has been give in the ground, so this effort has to go down as a disappointing one. Official explanation: jockey said colt ran flat (op 11-1)

4311 EMIRATES AIRLINES H'CAP 5f

5:20 (5:20) (Class 4) (0-85,85) 3-Y-0+ **£5,046** (£1,510; £755; £377; £188) **Stalls** High

Form RPR

2060 **1** **Bravely (IRE)**[15] 3825 5-8-12 **72** PaulMulrennan 7 81
(T D Easterby) *trckd ldrs gng wl: rdn to ld ins fnl f: jst hld on* **5/1**[3]

0201 **2** *hd* **Luscivious**[11] 3956 5-8-12 **75** (p) FrederikTylicki(3) 8 83
(J A Glover) *led stands' rail to ins fnl f: kpt on wl u.p nr fin: jst hld* **13/8**[1]

0000 **3** *1 3/4* **Tadalavil**[5] 4134 4-8-1 **66** oh1 JamieKyne(5) 6 68
(Miss L A Perratt) *bhd: edgd to stands rail and hdwy over 1f out: kpt on wl fnl f* **16/1**

6025 **4** *3/4* **Kyzer Chief**[3] 4189 4-8-4 **67** (p) KellyHarrison(3) 4 66
(R E Barr) *cl up tl rdn and one pce fnl f* **5/1**[3]

0110 **5** *1 1/4* **Highland Warrior**[5] 4141 10-8-11 **71** TonyCulhane 3 66
(P T Midgley) *in tch: effrt 2f out: no imp fnl f* **8/1**

-060 **6** *nk* **Flash McGahon (IRE)**[16] 3784 5-9-4 **85** NSLawes(7) 2 79
(D Nicholls) *hld up in tch: shkn up 2f out: no imp fnl f* **16/1**

0202 **7** *6* **Sandwith**[19] 3681 6-9-0 **74** PJMcDonald 1 46
(A G Foster) *chsd ldrs tl rdn and wknd fr 2f out* **9/2**[2]

61.36 secs (0.66) **Going Correction** +0.025s/f (Good) **7** Ran SP% **112.5**

Speed ratings (Par 105): **95,94,91,90,88 88,78**

toteswingers: 1&2 £2.50, 1&3 £10.00, 2&3 £7.20 CSF £13.12 CT £117.01 TOTE £5.50: £3.00, £1.70; EX 15.60.

Owner Habton Farms **Bred** James F Hanly **Trained** Great Habton, N Yorks

FOCUS

There were reasons for thinking virtually all of these could not win judged on recent efforts, so this race is unlikely to produce too many winners in the coming months, unless they make dramatic improvement. The first two raced on the favoured rail.

Sandwith Official explanation: jockey said gelding hung left final 3f

4312 COLAS AND A-ONE CLAIMING STKS 7f

5:50 (5:50) (Class 6) 3-Y-0+ **£2,072** (£616; £308; £153) **Stalls** Centre

Form RPR

0106 **1** **Young Gladiator (IRE)**[21] 3612 4-8-9 56 (b) FrederikTylicki(3) 10 65
(Miss J A Camacho) *mde all stands' rail: rdn over 2f out: kpt on wl fnl f* **9/1**

-240 **2** *1 1/4* **Moody Tunes**[31] 3264 6-9-0 69 MartinLane(5) 11 69
(K R Burke) *trckd ldrs: effrt over 2f out: kpt on u.p fnl f* **8/1**

0060 **3** *2 1/2* **Straight Face (IRE)**[11] 3948 5-8-7 51 (b) JamieKyne(5) 7 55
(Miss Gay Kelleway) *in tch: effrt over 2f out: kpt on fnl f: tk 3rd cl home* **20/1**

0011 **4** *nk* **Dream Express (IRE)**[5] 4133 4-9-1 69 PhillipMakin 6 57+
(M Dods) *hld up: hdwy over 1f out: kpt on fnl f: nrst fin* **7/2**[2]

0-03 **5** *nse* **Sea Salt**[10] 3972 6-8-10 58 KellyHarrison(3) 9 55
(R E Barr) *chsd ldrs: effrt over 2f out: wknd and lost two pls cl home* **14/1**

-300 **6** *1 3/4* **Ozone Trustee (NZ)**[36] 3123 5-8-13 70 PJMcDonald 13 50
(G A Swinbank) *midfield: rdn 2f out: no imp fnl 2f* **9/1**

6540 **7** *7* **Wovoka (IRE)**[14] 3872 6-9-9 81 TonyHamilton 1 41
(K A Ryan) *hld up and bhd: shkn up over 1f out: nvr nr ldrs* **11/4**[1]

0300 **8** *2* **Richo**[15] 3804 3-8-10 77 (b) PaulMulrennan 3 27
(D H Brown) *dwlt: swtchd rt s: hld up: rdn over 2f out: sn wknd* **6/1**[3]

0206 **9** *3 1/2* **No Grouse**[14] 3851 9-8-12 59 AndrewMullen 2 15
(E J Alston) *midfield: struggling over 2f out: sn btn* **20/1**

1026 **10** *9* **My Mate Mal**[10] 3980 5-8-12 65 LanceBetts(5) 8 —
(B Ellison) *chsd ldrs tl wknd qckly over 2f out* **7/1**

0460 **11** *2 1/2* **Mr Lu**[19] 3683 4-9-1 55 (t) TonyCulhane 12 —
(A G Foster) *towards rr: outpcd over 2f out: sn btn* **20/1**

006- **12** *8* **Resolute Defender (IRE)**[228] 4683 4-8-12 50 JamieMoriarty 4 —
(R Johnson) *bhd: drvn over 3f out: nvr on terms* **66/1**

1m 27.59s (-1.11) **Going Correction** +0.025s/f (Good)

WFA 3 from 4yo+ 7lb **12** Ran SP% **129.2**

Speed ratings (Par 101): **107,105,102,102,102 100,92,90,86,75 72,63**

toteswingers: 1&2 £16.70, 1&3 £39.60, 2&3 £45.10 CSF £82.52 TOTE £12.90: £3.70, £3.30, £6.30; EX 118.20.Young Gladiator was subject to a friendly claim.

Owner Barrett,Hope,Postill,Adamson,Wainwright **Bred** Edmond And Richard Kent **Trained** Norton, N Yorks

FOCUS

Not many of the runners could be fancied on form or at the weights. It was very much a case of who wanted it most on the day. The form has been rated around Young Gladiator, another winner to race on the rail.

Wovoka(IRE) Official explanation: jockey said gelding was denied a clear run

Richo Official explanation: jockey said gelding missed the break

4313 PIMMS APPRENTICE H'CAP 1m 3y(S)

6:25 (6:26) (Class 6) (0-60,60) 3-Y-0+ **£2,072** (£616; £308; £153) **Stalls** Centre

Form RPR

0-40 **1** **Zaplamation (IRE)**[26] 3450 4-8-10 **46** oh1 IJBrennan(2) 13 57
(J J Quinn) *hld up: hdwy 1/2-way: led over 1f out: rdn clr fnl f* **9/2**[1]

06 **2** *7* **Josephine Malines**[9] 3070 5-9-4 **52** (p) DebraEngland 2 47+
(Mrs A Duffield) *prom: effrt and chsd wnr over 1f out: one pce fnl f* **9/1**

1002 **3** *4 1/2* **Byron Bay**[4] 4171 7-9-1 **49** (p) GarryWhillans 1 34
(R Johnson) *led: clr 1/2-way: hdd over 1f out: sn outpcd* **8/1**[3]

5000 **4** *5* **Bourse (IRE)**[20] 3653 4-9-3 **55** (b[1]) LeeTopliss(4) 4 29
(A G Foster) *bhd: effrt 3f out: no imp fnl 2f* **8/1**[3]

000 **5** *shd* **Plenilune (IRE)**[43] 2894 4-9-12 **60** JohnCavanagh 12 33
(M Brittain) *prom: outpcd 1/2-way: rallied over 1f out: no imp* **10/1**

5361 **6** *3* **Not Now Lewis (IRE)**[25] 3490 5-9-9 **57** NSLawes 5 23
(F P Murtagh) *hld up in tch: outpcd 3f out: n.d after* **6/1**[2]

-000 **7** *3/4* **Grey Gurkha**[4] 4171 8-8-12 **46** AmyScott 8 11
(I W McInnes) *bhd: effrt on outside 3f out: btn over 1f out* **28/1**

6-61 **8** *5* **Phantom Serenade (IRE)**[8] 4034 4-9-7 **55** DavidKenny 9 8
(M Dods) *in tch tl wknd over 2f out* **6/1**[2]

4244 **9** *11* **Time To Regret**[17] 3735 9-9-7 **55** (p) MatthewLawson 7 —
(I W McInnes) *prom to 1/2-way: sn lost pl* **8/1**[3]

1m 44.37s (0.97) **Going Correction** +0.025s/f (Good)

WFA 3 from 4yo+ 8lb **9** Ran SP% **102.6**

Speed ratings (Par 101): **96,89,84,79,79 76,75,70,59**

toteswingers: 1&2 £5.40, 1&3 £6.30, 2&3 £9.90 CSF £32.70 CT £168.06 TOTE £4.80: £1.80, £2.50, £2.00; EX 28.20 Place 6: £88.19, Place 5: £29.68.

Owner Andrew Turton & David Barker **Bred** Mesnil Investments Ltd And Deerpark Stud **Trained** Settrington, N Yorks

■ Red Skipper was withdrawn (4/1, deduc t 20p in the £.)

■ Stewards' Enquiry : Garry Whillans one-day ban: used whip with excessive frequency (Aug 8)

I J Brennan one-day ban: used whip when clearly winning (Aug 8)

FOCUS

A lot of very ordinary performers took their chance in this. The form is probably on a par with selling-grade company. Only the winner and third made for the favoured stands' rail.

T/Plt: £140.70 to a £1 stake. Pool: £58,265.95. 302.26 winning tickets. T/Qpdt: £12.60 to a £1 stake. Pool: £4,190.76. 245.72 winning tickets. RY

4269 NEWMARKET (R-H)

Saturday, July 25

OFFICIAL GOING: Good (7.9)

Wind: Light across Weather: Cloudy with sunny spells

4314 NSPCC E B F MAIDEN STKS 7f

1:50 (1:50) (Class 4) 2-Y-0 **£5,180** (£1,541; £770; £384) **Stalls** Low

Form RPR

3 **1** **Simenon (IRE)**[28] 3395 2-9-3 0 LPKeniry 13 88
(A M Balding) *chsd ldrs: rdn ins fnl f: styd on to ld nr fin* **6/1**[3]

02 **2** *nk* **Timely Jazz (IRE)**[17] 3750 2-9-3 0 RobertWinston 6 87
(B J Meehan) *chsd ldr tl led over 2f out: rdn ins fnl f: hdd nr fin* **13/8**[1]

3 *2 3/4* **Waseet** 2-9-3 0 ShaneKelly 3 80+
(J L Dunlop) *s.s: hld up: hdwy over 1f out: nt rch ldrs* **28/1**

5 **4** *4* **Rasselas (IRE)**[17] 3750 2-9-3 0 MichaelHills 14 70
(B W Hills) *led: hdd over 2f out: sn rdn: wknd ins fnl f* **11/4**[2]

5 *2 1/2* **Society Rock (IRE)** 2-9-3 0 GeorgeBaker 15 64+
(J R Fanshawe) *hld up in tch: rdn and hung lft over 1f out: sn wknd* **20/1**

6 *nk* **Super Collider** 2-9-3 0 DarryllHolland 9 63+
(M A Jarvis) *hld up: effrt over 2f out: nt trble ldrs* **20/1**

7 *3/4* **Ted Spread** 2-9-3 0 LiamJones 17 62
(M H Tompkins) *mid-div: rdn over 2f out: sn edgd lft: n.d* **100/1**

8 *1* **Lost Cause** 2-9-3 0 FergusSweeney 4 59+
(R Charlton) *mid-div: rdn over 2f out: sn hung lft and wknd* **33/1**

9 *1/2* **Harlestone Times (IRE)** 2-9-3 0 IanMongan 11 58+
(J L Dunlop) *s.s: bhd tl styd on ins fnl f: nvr nrr* **100/1**

0 **10** *nk* **Bun Oir (USA)**[15] 3823 2-9-3 0 PatDobbs 18 57
(R Hannon) *prom: rdn 1/2-way: wknd over 2f out* **33/1**

11 *hd* **Navy List (FR)** 2-9-0 0 AhmedAjtebi(3) 10 57
(Saeed Bin Suroor) *dwlt: pushed along 1/2-way: a in rr* **14/1**

12 *1* **Pleasant Day (IRE)** 2-9-3 0 RobertHavlin 5 54
(B J Meehan) *mid-div: sn pushed along: n.d* **66/1**

0 **13** *1 1/2* **Azlak (USA)**[7] 4080 2-9-3 0 ChrisCatlin 16 50
(C E Brittain) *chsd ldrs tl rdn and wknd over 2f out* **80/1**

14 *hd* **Plus Ultra (IRE)** 2-9-3 0 (b[1]) TPQueally 12 50
(H R A Cecil) *s.s: sme hdwy over 2f out: sn hung lft and wknd* **16/1**

15 *5* **Chat De Soie (IRE)** 2-8-12 0 CatherineGannon 7 32
(J S Moore) *sn pushed along: a in rr* **100/1**

0 **16** *3 1/4* **Boycott (IRE)**[35] 3167 2-9-3 0 RichardMullen 8 29
(J H M Gosden) *prom: rdn over 2f out: wknd wl over 1f out* **20/1**

17 *3/4* **Bojangles Andrews** 2-9-0 0 PatrickHills(3) 2 27
(B G Powell) *mid-div: sn pushed along: wknd wl over 2f out* **100/1**

1m 25.37s (-0.33) **Going Correction** -0.125s/f (Firm) **17** Ran SP% **121.9**

Speed ratings (Par 96): **96,95,92,87,85 84,83,82,82,81 81,80,78,78,72 69,68**

toteswingers: 1&2 £3.10, 1&3 £50.10, 2&3 £16.60 CSF £14.24 TOTE £8.00: £2.00, £1.60, £7.50; EX 19.30.

Owner Mr Greenwood, Ms James & Mr Cockburn **Bred** Max Morris **Trained** Kingsclere, Hants

FOCUS

There were several interesting newcomers on show for looked a pretty strong maiden, but it was two with previous experience that dominated. They both progressed.

NOTEBOOK

Simenon(IRE) just got the better of Timely Jazz close home. A most promising third over C&D on debut (running on well having met trouble), he knew a bit more this time and came to challenge the favourite over a furlong out. He took a while to master him, being helped by Winston having difficulties with his reins close home, but is a horse with plenty of physical scope and he is expected to stay 1m. (op 7-1 tchd 9-2)

Timely Jazz(IRE), who had finished behind the winner on debut before going close in a good maiden at the July meeting, travelled like a decent horse and went to the front over 2f out. He was strongly challenged and possibly in the process of being passed when his rider got in a muddle with the reins, which sealed his fate. He clearly has plenty of ability and should find a standard maiden at some stage. (op 15-8 tchd 2-1)

Waseet ◆ made a really promising debut. Slowly away, he got behind before staying on really well inside the final quarter mile, being the only one to make headway from the pack. A son of Selkirk whose dam was an unraced half-sister to Sakhee, he is going to benefit from an extra furlong before long (holds a Derby entry) and looks a horse of considerable potential. (op 40-1)

Rasselas(IRE), just over five lengths behind Timely Jazz here on debut, was soon in front but couldn't quicken on with the principals and was ultimately a shade disappointing.

Society Rock(IRE) ◆, related to a 2yo winner in Germany, travelled well in behind the speed until over 2f out and was then unable to race on, looking green under pressure. He should learn from this and can be expected to improve next time. (op 28-1 tchd 33-1)

Super Collider ◆, a 230,000gns purchase related to several smart performers, holds numerous big-race entries, namely in Champagne and Royal Lodge, and he was noted going on close home. He wasn't given a particularly hard time and should learn a good deal from the experience. (op 14-1)

Ted Spread, whose dam was a dual-purpose performer, comes from a yard whose juveniles often benefit markedly for a run and, as a result, this has to go down as a nice introduction.

Lost Cause, a son of Dubawi whose dam won over 1m2f, hung under pressure and didn't get home, but should improve. (op 66-1)

Harlestone Times(IRE), from a slow-maturing family, got going late and clearly has a future.

Navy List(FR), who has a blend of speed and stamina in his pedigree, never left the rear and is clearly on of his stable's lesser lights. (op 8-1)

4315 SPORTINGBET.COM H'CAP 1m 2f

2:20 (2:21) (Class 3) (0-95,95) 3-Y-0+

£8,723 (£2,612; £1,306; £653; £326; £163) **Stalls** Centre

Form RPR

2160 **1** **Emerald Wilderness (IRE)**[22] 3586 5-9-9 **90** (b) FergusSweeney 2 97
(A King) *s.i.s: hld up: plld hrd: hdwy 6f out: rdn over 1f out: r.o to ld wl ins fnl f* **14/1**

1002 **2** *3/4* **Cheshire Prince**[7] 4091 5-9-10 **91** LiamJones 3 97
(W M Brisbourne) *led: rdn over 2f out: edgd lft and hdd wl ins fnl f* **16/1**

1 **3** *3/4* **Persian Peril**[81] 1779 5-9-1 **82** RobertWinston 8 86
(G A Swinbank) *trckd ldr: plld hrd: rdn and ev ch over 1f out: hung lft ins fnl f: styd on same pce* **4/1**[2]

1366 **4** *1/2* **Special Reserve (IRE)**[19] 3695 4-8-13 **80** PatDobbs 1 83
(R Hannon) *prom: rdn over 1f out: swtchd lft ins fnl f: styd on same pce* **10/1**

6041 **5** ½ **King Charles**[7] 4091 5-10-0 95 TPQueally 6 97
(E A L Dunlop) *hld up: hdwy fnl f: sn hung lft and nt run on* **3/1**[1]
6-14 **6** 2 **Chapter And Verse (IRE)**[15] 3808 3-8-3 80 ChrisCatlin 4 78
(B W Hills) *hld up: hdwy over 2f out: sn rdn: wknd ins fnl f* **15/2**
-020 **7** nk **Admiral Dundas (IRE)**[17] 3752 4-8-13 80 RobertHavlin 7 77
(W Jarvis) *hld up in tch: rdn over 2f out: wknd fnl f* **4/1**[2]
0/ **8** 7 **Canongate**[288] 5-9-7 88 LPKeniry 5 71
(Miss E C Lavelle) *hld up: plld hrd: rdn over 2f out: wknd over 1f out* **11/2**[3]

2m 7.96s (2.46) **Going Correction** +0.05s/f (Good)
WFA 3 from 4yo+ 10lb 8 Ran SP% **113.8**
Speed ratings (Par 107): **92,91,90,90,90 88,88,82**
toteswingers: 1&2 £23.10, 1&3 £19.70, 2&3 £5.30 CSF £204.98 CT £1063.31 TOTE £18.50: £4.90, £2.80, £1.70; EX 125.80 TRIFECTA Not won..
Owner Terry Warner & David Sewell **Bred** Mrs Joan Murphy **Trained** Barbury Castle, Wilts

FOCUS
They went just a steady gallop in this and the form is a bit messy, although it makes sense among the principals.

NOTEBOOK
Emerald Wilderness(IRE), well beaten at Sandown on his recent return to the Flat, is currently rated quite a bit lower on turf compared to the AW and he stuck on really well having got the front a furlong out. The return of the the blinkers clearly helped and this versatile sort may well go novice chasing as some stage. (op 10-1)
Cheshire Prince, back to form when second to King Charles at Newbury last week, very much had the run of things out in front and kept on right the way to the line having been headed, but was never getting back up. (op 8-1)
Persian Peril ◆, off since winning on the Fibresand at Southwell in May, was 6lb higher for this return to turf and didn't help his chances by pulling through the early stages. He eventually settled into the race and held every chance, but those earlier exertions ultimately took their toll. Official explanation: jockey said gelding ran too free (op 9-2)
Special Reserve(IRE) had been dropped 2lb and he didn't run too badly considering the race wouldn't have been run to suit. (op 7-1)
King Charles, 5lb higher than when winning at Newbury last weekend, was unable to get into this, being unsuited by the way the race was run, and hung under pressure. (op 10-3 tchd 11-4 and 7-2 in places)
Chapter And Verse(IRE), the only 3yo in the field, failed to meet with expectation on his recent handicap debut at Chester and again disappointed. (op 7-1 tchd 13-2)
Admiral Dundas(IRE), backed beforehand, never got into it. (op 7-1 tchd 15-2)
Canongate, an ex-French performer, pulled early and never threatened. Official explanation: jockey said horse ran too free (op 8-1 tchd 5-1)

4316 SPORTINGBET H'CAP 1m
2:50 (2:51) (Class 3) (0-90,89) 3-Y-O
£8,723 (£2,612; £1,306; £653; £326; £163) **Stalls** Low

Form RPR
4104 **1** **Invisible Man**[14] 3839 3-9-3 83 RobertHavlin 6 92+
(J H M Gosden) *hld up: hdwy over 1f out: rdn to ld ins fnl f: r.o* **10/3**[1]
2163 **2** 2 **Sovereign Remedy (USA)**[15] 3816 3-9-9 89 ChrisCatlin 9 94
(Saeed Bin Suroor) *trckd ldrs: led over 2f out: rdn over 1f out: hdd and unable qck ins fnl f* **10/3**[1]
-100 **3** nk **Resort**[17] 3746 3-8-12 83 Louis-PhilippeBeuzelin(5) 5 87
(Sir Michael Stoute) *led: hdd over 2f out: rdn and ev ch ins fnl f: styd on same pce* **7/1**
164- **4** 1 **Watergate (IRE)**[261] 7214 3-9-7 87 StephenDonohoe 2 89
(Sir Mark Prescott) *hld up: hdwy over 1f out: r.o: nt rch ldrs* **25/1**
126 **5** nk **Militarist (USA)**[63] 2281 3-9-8 88 RichardMullen 1 89
(J H M Gosden) *s.i.s: sn prom: rdn and edgd rt over 1f out: styd on same pce* **10/1**
-146 **6** 2 ¾ **Hunterview**[79] 1801 3-9-8 88 DarryllHolland 8 83
(M A Jarvis) *dwlt: hld up: rdn over 2f out: hung lft over 1f out: no ex* **4/1**[2]
2505 **7** 8 **Al Mugtareb (IRE)**[15] 3804 3-8-5 71 LiamJones 7 47
(M Johnston) *chsd ldrs: rdn over 2f out: wknd over 1f out* **16/1**
1-41 **8** 2 ¼ **Snow Bay**[17] 3727 3-8-13 79 TPQueally 3 50
(B Smart) *trckd ldrs: racd keenly: rdn over 2f out: sn hung lft and wknd* **5/1**[3]

1m 37.96s (-2.04) **Going Correction** -0.125s/f (Firm) 8 Ran SP% **114.1**
Speed ratings (Par 104): **105,103,102,101,101 98,90,88**
toteswingers: 1&2 £3.50, 1&3 £6.70, 2&3 £6.50 CSF £14.44 CT £72.01 TOTE £3.90: £1.40, £1.60, £2.70; EX 13.30 Trifecta £112.60 Pool: £334.85 - 2.20 winning units..
Owner H R H Princess Haya Of Jordan **Bred** Darley **Trained** Newmarket, Suffolk

FOCUS
This was a decent 3yo handicap which was well run. Solid form.

NOTEBOOK
Invisible Man got the job done in style. Fourth off a 2lb higher mark over 7f at Ascot last time, this often front-runner wasn't made as much use of on this occasion and the change of tactics seemed to suit. He quickly asserted inside the final furlong and remains capable of better. (op 11-2)
Sovereign Remedy(USA), third in a good handicap over C&D at the July meeting, was ridden more prominently on this occasion and ultimately got the better of a prolonged battle with Resort, but he could do nothing as the winner swept past. (op 7-2 tchd 4-1)
Resort looked worth another go at 1m, having lacked the speed to make an impact in a 7f handicap at the course last time, and she was happy to bowl along in front. However, as with the runner-up, there was no change of pace and she just lost out on second. (tchd 9-1)
Watergate(IRE), making his belated 3yo debut, has a stiff enough mark for what he actually achieved at two, but he was going on nicely close home and is entitled to come on considerably for the outing. (op 16-1 tchd 28-1)
Militarist(USA), also representing connections of the winner, hasn't really gone on as expected, but this wasn't so bad from a mark of 88. (op 11-2)
Hunterview is beginning to come back down the weights, but remains 10lb higher than when winning at Southwell in March and he never looked like making an impact here. Official explanation: jockey said gelding hung both ways
Al Mugtareb(IRE) dropped right out having been up there early. (op 20-1)
Snow Bay, raised 5lb for winning over 7f at Catterick last time, hung under pressure and didn't look a happy horse. (tchd 9-2 and 11-2)

4317 SPORTINGBET.COM E B F FILLIES' STKS (H'CAP) 7f
3:25 (3:26) (Class 2) (0-100,98) 3-Y-O+ **£16,190** (£4,817; £2,407; £1,202) **Stalls** Low

Form RPR
2-34 **1** **Pyrrha**[17] 3746 3-8-7 84 ChrisCatlin 6 93
(C F Wall) *mde all: rdn and hung lft ins fnl f: r.o* **3/1**[2]
2-00 **2** 2 ¼ **Vitoria (IRE)**[87] 1599 3-8-10 87 RichardMullen 8 90
(B Smart) *trckd ldrs: rdn and hung lft ins fnl f: no imp* **20/1**
10-5 **3** ¾ **Lassarina (IRE)**[98] 1353 3-9-6 97 MichaelHills 2 98
(B W Hills) *hld up: hdwy over 2f out: rdn over 1f out: styd on same pce ins fnl f* **11/4**[1]
1051 **4** shd **Volochkova (USA)**[12] 3924 3-7-11 79 oh4.(t) Louis-PhilippeBeuzelin(5) 4 80+
(J R Fanshawe) *hld up: rdn over 2f out: r.o ins fnl f: nt rch ldrs* **16/1**

1 **5** hd **Adoring (IRE)**[62] 2298 3-8-5 82 LiamJones 9 82
(W J Haggas) *hld up in tch: rdn over 1f out: styd on same pce ins fnl f* **3/1**[2]
2114 **6** 1 ¾ **Victoria Sponge (IRE)**[16] 3787 3-8-8 85 PatDobbs 3 80
(R Hannon) *prom: rdn over 1f out: wknd ins fnl f* **5/1**[3]
1100 **7** 2 ¾ **Oceana Blue**[21] 3628 4-8-11 81 (t) LPKeniry 7 72
(A M Balding) *chsd wnr tl rdn and wknd over 1f out* **10/1**
6041 **8** 1 ¼ **Shaws Diamond (USA)**[14] 3876 3-8-2 79 PatrickMathers 5 64
(D Shaw) *hmpd s: sn prom: rdn over 2f out: sn wknd* **25/1**

1m 25.35s (-0.35) **Going Correction** -0.125s/f (Firm)
WFA 3 from 4yo+ 7lb 8 Ran SP% **116.9**
Speed ratings (Par 96): **97,94,93,93,93 91,88,86**
toteswingers: 1&2 £11.10, 1&3 £3.00, 2&3 £11.90 CSF £59.90 CT £185.77 TOTE £4.30: £1.60, £4.50, £1.50; EX 60.40 TRIFECTA Not won..
Owner Lady Juliet Tadgell **Bred** Hong Kong Breeders Club **Trained** Newmarket, Suffolk

FOCUS
The winner set a steady pace and made all, but the form is worth taking at face value with the next few close to their marks.

NOTEBOOK
Pyrrha quickened off the front to record her first win of the season. Fourth in a decent contest over C&D at the July meeting, she was 2lb higher here, but comes from a yard going very well and, despite ending up on the far rail, she was always in control inside the final furlong. This progressive filly has definitely improved for the step up to 7f and may even go up to 1m at some stage. Another handicap is on the agenda next, but connections will no doubt be keen to gain some black type with her later on in the season. (op 5-2 tchd 10-3)
Vitoria(IRE) had run dreadfully on both previous starts this season, but she had been given a break, was down 3lb and also expected to be suited by the return to 7f. She got warm beforehand and hung under pressure, but did stay on for second and this effort suggests that she had trained on. Official explanation: jockey said filly hung badly left (tchd 18-1)
Lassarina(IRE) had twice run well in Group contests behind Lahaleeb since winning on debut, including when fifth in the Fred Darling on her seasonal return (dual Oaks heroine Sariska fourth), but missed an engagement at Royal Ascot. Well backed at the head of the market, she recovered from a sluggish start to race prominently, but couldn't quicken when asked for her effort and was beaten from over a furlong out. She should be sharper next time, though, and looks likely to improve for the step up to 1m. (op 7-2 tchd 5-2)
Volochkova(USA), who was having to race from 4lb out of the handicap, ran on late having been held up and would certainly have been helped by stronger gallop. All things considering, this was a good effort and she is clearly progressing. (op 14-1 tchd 20-1)
Adoring(IRE), another to get warm beforehand, beat subsequent two-time winner Pumpkin on her debut and she looked potentially interesting ahead of this handicap debut. She ran well, despite looking as though a faster pace would have suited, and may be up to winning off this mark. (op 4-1 tchd 9-2)
Victoria Sponge(IRE) is beginning to lose her form and may be a shade high in the weights. (tchd 11-2)
Shaws Diamond(USA) Official explanation: jockey said filly hung left throughout

4318 BALLYGALLON STUD, IRELAND NSPCC MEDIAN AUCTION MAIDEN STKS 6f
4:00 (4:03) (Class 4) 2-Y-O **£4,533** (£1,348; £674; £336) **Stalls** Low

Form RPR
2 **1** **Blue Maiden**[32] 3248 2-8-12 0 CatherineGannon 3 80
(P J McBride) *chsd ldrs tl led over 2f out: rdn ins fnl f: r.o* **9/4**[2]
2 ½ **Mon Cadeaux** 2-9-3 0 LPKeniry 4 85+
(A M Balding) *s.i.s: hdwy and hmpd over 2f out: swtchd lft over 1f out: rdn and ev ch ins fnl f: unable qck nr fin* **10/3**[3]
3 **3** 1 ¼ **San Jemeniano (IRE)**[28] 3403 2-9-3 0 TPQueally 6 80
(P W Chapple-Hyam) *trckd ldrs: plld hrd: rdn and edgd lft ins fnl f: styd on* **1/1**[1]
4 9 **Zenarinda** 2-8-12 0 LiamJones 7 48
(M H Tompkins) *hld up: rdn over 2f out: wknd over 1f out* **33/1**
0 **5** 1 ¼ **Golden Pippin**[15] 3820 2-8-12 0 PatDobbs 1 44
(R Hannon) *led: rdn and hdd over 2f out: wknd over 1f out* **20/1**
56 **6** 4 ½ **Watch Chain (IRE)**[37] 3064 2-8-10 0 AshleyMorgan(7) 2 36
(M H Tompkins) *racd keenly: w ldr tl rdn 2f out: wknd over 1f out* **33/1**
7 23 **Tumbled Again** 2-9-3 0 DarryllHolland 5 —
(M E Rimmer) *s.s: outpcd* **14/1**

1m 13.8s (1.30) **Going Correction** -0.125s/f (Firm) 7 Ran SP% **121.2**
Speed ratings (Par 96): **86,85,83,71,70 64,33**
toteswingers: 1&2 £2.10, 1&3 £1.50, 2&3 £1.60 CSF £10.89 TOTE £3.80: £1.90, £2.40; EX 10.60.
Owner Peter Charter **Bred** Kirtlington Stud Ltd **Trained** Newmarket, Suffolk

FOCUS
No more than a modest maiden by the courses standards, rated around the winner and third.

NOTEBOOK
Blue Maiden, second on her debut at Newbury, knew more this time and went on inside the two. She had to fight hard when the runner-up came up her inside, but she had an experience edge and if anything was just beginning to edge away again close home. She is no star, but should improve for further and can make her mark in nurseries. (op 5-2 tchd 7-2)
Mon Cadeaux, whose pedigree is a blend of speed and stamina, wasn't the quickest away and he engaged in a brief barging match with the favourite when trying to switch out for a run. He ended going up the rail and held every chance, but could find no extra close home. This was a promising start and he should be able to win an ordinary maiden. (op 5-1 tchd 11-2)
San Jemeniano(IRE), third on his debut at Windsor, managed to hold the runner-up in, but he failed to quicken sufficiently when asked for his effort and was always being held inside the final furlong. (tchd 10-11 and 6-5 after early 5-4)
Zenarinda, a daughter of Zamindar, looked as though this run would do her good. (op 40-1 tchd 28-1)
Golden Pippin was readily brushed aside and is more of a nursery prospect. (op 16-1)

4319 NSPCC H'CAP 1m 5f
4:35 (4:36) (Class 4) (0-80,80) 3-Y-O **£5,180** (£1,541; £770; £384) **Stalls** Centre

Form RPR
2312 **1** **Sherman McCoy**[33] 3222 3-9-1 75 JamesMillman(3) 1 85
(B R Millman) *a.p: rdn to ld 2f out: styd on wl* **7/2**[1]
21 **2** 2 **Doggerbank (IRE)**[16] 3791 3-9-7 78 TPQueally 12 85
(H R A Cecil) *hld up: hdwy over 3f out: jnd wnr and hung lft fr 2f out: sn rdn: nt run on and hung rt nr fin* **4/1**[2]
6-56 **3** 2 ¼ **Moresco**[95] 1431 3-9-2 73 AdamKirby 9 76
(W R Swinburn) *chsd ldrs: rdn over 3f out: outpcd wl over 1f out: hung lft and styd on ins fnl f* **16/1**
3014 **4** nk **Excelsior Academy**[30] 3300 3-8-12 74 Louis-PhilippeBeuzelin(5) 3 77
(B J Meehan) *hld up in tch: rdn over 1f out: styd on same pce* **20/1**
-332 **5** 3 ¼ **Decorum (USA)**[26] 3466 3-9-6 77 (t) RobertHavlin 4 75
(J H M Gosden) *led 7f: chsd ldr: rdn and ev ch 2f out: sn edgd lft: wknd ins fnl f* **17/2**

5-06 **6** *hd* **Perception (IRE)**[44] 2850 3-8-9 **66**..............................(v[1]) PatDobbs 10 64
(R Charlton) *chsd ldrs: rdn over 2f out: wknd fnl f* **8/1**

04 **7** *½* **Headline Act**[70] 2084 3-9-9 **80**.............................. RichardMullen 6 77
(J H M Gosden) *s.i.s: hld up: rdn over 3f out: styd on ins fnl f: n.d* **11/2**[3]

5504 **8** *1 ¼* **Hambledon Hill**[17] 3734 3-8-5 **62**.............................. CatherineGannon 2 57
(R Hannon) *trckd ldr: racd keenly: led 6f out: rdn and hdd 2f out: wknd fnl f* **20/1**

0-33 **9** *1 ¼* **Daredevil Dan**[67] 2170 3-8-13 **70**.............................. LiamJones 7 63
(M H Tompkins) *dwlt: hld up: rdn over 3f out: wknd over 1f out* **9/1**

0214 **10** *9* **Urban Space**[23] 3535 3-8-11 **68**.............................. StephenDonohoe 5 48
(B G Powell) *hld up: rdn over 2f out: sn wknd* **16/1**

1050 **11** *7* **Haljaferia (UAE)**[36] 3090 3-9-3 **74**.............................. MichaelHills 11 43
(D R C Elsworth) *hld up: plld hrd: rdn over 3f out: wknd wl over 1f out: eased fnl f* **8/1**

2m 47.89s (3.89) **Going Correction** +0.05s/f (Good) **11** Ran SP% **121.6**
Speed ratings (Par 102): **90,88,87,87,85 85,84,84,83,77 73**
toteswingers: 1&2 £3.70, 1&3 £17.10, 2&3 £13.70 CSF £17.94 CT £197.74 TOTE £5.10: £2.00, £1.90, £3.90; EX 20.90.
Owner Mustajed Partnership **Bred** Horizon Bloodstock Limited **Trained** Kentisbeare, Devon

FOCUS
This was an ordinary handicap and the field massed far side in the straight. Pretty ordinary form for the grade.
Haljaferia(UAE) Official explanation: jockey said gelding moved poorly throughout

4320 NSPCC APPRENTICE H'CAP 1m 2f
5:10 (5:10) (Class 5) (0-75,73) 3-Y-O **£3,885** (£1,156; £577; £288) **Stalls** Centre

Form RPR

030- **1** **Point Of Light**[285] 6701 3-8-6 **60**.............................. RosieJessop(5) 5 71+
(Sir Mark Prescott) *led 1f: chsd ldrs: rdn to ld and edgd lft ins fnl f: styd on* **11/4**[1]

4054 **2** *¾* **Kaolak (USA)**[9] 4010 3-9-3 **73**..............................(v) RyanPowell(7) 6 82
(J Ryan) *s.i.s: rcvrd to ld after 1f: rdn over 1f out: rdr nrly dropped whip sn after: edgd lft and hdd ins fnl f: styd on same pce* **11/4**[1]

4046 **3** *5* **Transformer (IRE)**[23] 3551 3-8-6 **58**.............. Louis-PhilippeBeuzelin(3) 4 57
(W J Knight) *hld up in tch: rdn over 2f out: edgd rt and no ex fnl f* **6/1**[3]

2-33 **4** *9* **Mile High Lad (USA)**[171] 389 3-9-4 **72**.............. MatthewDavies(5) 7 53
(George Baker) *chsd ldr 8f out: rdn over 3f out: hung lft over 1f out: sn wknd* **4/1**[2]

3-64 **5** *2 ¾* **Intikama (IRE)**[11] 3960 3-9-0 **68**.............................. AshleyMorgan(5) 3 44
(M H Tompkins) *prom: rdn over 2f out: wknd over 1f out* **4/1**[2]

040 **6** *4* **Mac Wolf**[75] 1941 3-8-8 **60**.............................. NicolPolli(3) 8 28
(M G Quinlan) *s.s: a in rr: rdn and wknd over 2f out* **20/1**

2m 7.35s (1.85) **Going Correction** +0.05s/f (Good) **6** Ran SP% **112.4**
Speed ratings (Par 100): **94,93,89,82,80 76**
toteswingers: 1&2 £2.00, 1&3 £3.80, 2&3 £3.50 CSF £10.50 CT £39.45 TOTE £3.20: £1.90, £2.10; EX 9.80 Place 6: £63.31 Place 5: £41.44.
Owner Syndicate 2007 **Bred** Watership Down Stud **Trained** Newmarket, Suffolk
■ Stewards' Enquiry : Rosie Jessop three-day ban: used whip with excessive frequency (Aug 8-10)

FOCUS
This was a moderate apprentices' handicap. It was steadily run and the second, who set the pace, is the best guide.
T/Plt: £80.20 to a £1 stake. Pool: £77,908.88. 708.37 winning tickets. T/Qpdt: £14.50 to a £1 stake. Pool: £4,895.80. 248.70 winning tickets. CR

3865 SALISBURY (R-H)
Saturday, July 25

OFFICIAL GOING: Good to firm (good in places; 8.7)
Wind: Virtually nil Weather: Sunny

4321 CHIPMUNK EQUINE DUST EXTRACTED HORSE BEDDING CARNARVON H'CAP (FOR GENTLEMEN AMATEUR RIDERS) 1m
6:00 (6:00) (Class 5) (0-75,70) 3-Y-O+ **£3,123** (£968; £484; £242) **Stalls** High

Form RPR

5001 **1** **Gallego**[31] 3283 7-10-8 **62**.............................. MrMPrice(5) 10 70
(R J Price) *s.i.s: hld up: carried lft 3f out: shkn up and hdwy fr 2f out: r.o wl to ld fnl 50yds: pushed out* **4/1**[1]

3-30 **2** *1* **Mr Udagawa**[61] 2320 3-10-7 **69**.............................. MrJSherwood(5) 8 72
(R M Beckett) *led for over 1f: prom: led 4f out: rdn 2f out: no ex whn hdd fnl 50yds* **5/1**[2]

-403 **3** *1* **Russian Angel**[15] 3800 5-9-11 **56** oh10.............................. MrTRDavid(5) 6 54
(Jean-Rene Auvray) *chsd ldrs tl lost pl over 4f out: hdwy over 2f out: styd on same pce fnl f* **16/1**

2531 **4** *1* **Sir Ike (IRE)**[15] 3800 4-11-1 **67**..............................(t) MrBenBrisbourne(3) 4 68
(W S Kittow) *mid-div: hdwy 4f out: effrt 3f out: kpt on same pce fnl 2f* **6/1**

0064 **5** *1 ½* **Dudley Docker (IRE)**[30] 3322 7-10-9 **65**..............................(p) MrJPearce(7) 12 62
(T T Clement) *mid-div: hdwy over 4f out: shkn up over 1f out: sn one pce* **14/1**

2034 **6** *4* **Justcallmehandsome**[14] 3863 7-10-8 **64**..............................(v) MrGOliver(7) 2 52
(D J S Ffrench Davis) *chsd ldrs: rdn over 3f out: sn one pce: wknd ins fnl f* **10/1**

3020 **7** *nse* **Binnion Bay (IRE)**[5] 4149 8-10-4 **58**..............................(b) MrAshleyBird(5) 9 46
(J J Bridger) *v.s.a: bhd: rdn over 3f out: little imp* **22/1**

4360 **8** *hd* **Randama Bay (IRE)**[17] 3736 4-11-2 **70**.............................. MrCMartin(5) 1 57
(I A Wood) *stmbld leaving stalls: a towards rr* **11/2**[3]

00/- **9** *1 ½* **Akram (IRE)**[17] 4731 7-11-0 **63**.............................. MrAJBerry 7 47
(Jonjo O'Neill) *trckd ldrs: effrt over 2f out: sn btn* **5/1**[2]

11U0 **10** *nk* **Annes Rocket (IRE)**[20] 3662 4-10-1 **57**.............................. MrTGarner(7) 11 40
(J C Fox) *t.k.h: hld up: swtchd lft 3f out: sn rdn: no imp* **16/1**

100- **11** *16* **A One (IRE)**[272] 5912 10-9-13 **60** oh11 ow4.............................. MrJBanks(7) 3 —
(H J Manners) *led after 1f tl 4f out: sn rdn: wknd 3f out* **66/1**

1m 44.52s (1.02) **Going Correction** -0.15s/f (Firm)
WFA 3 from 4yo+ 8lb **11** Ran SP% **116.4**
Speed ratings (Par 103): **88,87,86,85,83 79,79,79,77,77 61**
toteswingers: 1&2 £5.50, 1&3 £13.90, 2&3 £25.30 CSF £23.27 CT £288.96 TOTE £4.10: £1.80, £2.40, £5.40; EX 34.90.
Owner My Left Foot Racing Syndicate **Bred** Mrs C C Regalado-Gonzalez **Trained** Ullingswick, H'fords

FOCUS
The going was reported as good to firm in the last two furlongs, but goodish further out. A moderate race with no obvious pace, but within its context the form looks solid enough despite the third being 10lb wrong.

Binnion Bay(IRE) Official explanation: jockey said gelding missed the break

4322 DEREK BURRIDGE LTD CLAIMING STKS 1m
6:30 (6:31) (Class 5) 3-4-Y-O **£3,238** (£963; £481; £240) **Stalls** High

Form RPR

0036 **1** **Cruikadyke**[9] 4008 3-9-3 76.............................. MartinDwyer 4 87
(P F I Cole) *j. and wnt rt leaving stalls: sn niggled along in rr: hdwy over 2f out: led over 1f out: r.o: rdn out* **7/1**[3]

0563 **2** *2 ¼* **Brooksby**[9] 4005 3-8-2 67..............................(b) RichardThomas 9 67
(R Hannon) *led: rdn whn veered lft 2f out: sn hdd: continued to drift further lft but kpt on: nt pce of wnr* **14/1**

0403 **3** *2 ½* **Statute Book (IRE)**[7] 4083 3-8-10 75.............................. ShaneKelly 8 69
(S Kirk) *bmpd leaving stalls: towards rr: hdwy 2f out: sn rdn to chse ldrs: kpt on fnl f* **12/1**

2303 **4** *1 ¾* **Head Down**[15] 3801 3-8-11 78.............................. RichardHughes 10 65
(R Hannon) *hld up towards rr: prog whn swtchd lft over 3f out: sn rdn: styd on same pce* **1/1**[1]

-220 **5** *1 ½* **Indian Skipper (IRE)**[43] 2894 4-9-4 75.............................. NickyMackay 7 63
(M H Tompkins) *chsd ldrs: rdn over 2f out: sn hung lft: one pce fnl f* **5/2**[2]

0 **6** *shd* **Flying Gazebo (IRE)**[33] 3207 3-8-5 0.............................. MarcHalford(3) 3 59
(J S Moore) *s.i.s: towards rr: sme late prog: nvr a factor* **50/1**

00-5 **7** *¾* **Cadeaux Fax**[24] 3501 4-9-0 52.............................. TolleyDean 6 57
(B R Millman) *in tch tl outpcd over 2f out* **66/1**

0045 **8** *1 ½* **Peace Concluded**[18] 3711 3-8-4 63..............................(p) KirstyMilczarek 2 49
(B R Millman) *mid-div: rdn over 3f out: wknd ent fnl f* **25/1**

4100 **9** *1 ¾* **Solent Ridge (IRE)**[66] 2186 4-8-13 73..............................(p) SophieDoyle(5) 1 53
(J S Moore) *chsd ldr: rdn over 2f out: wknd over 1f out* **16/1**

3600 **10** *8* **Tender Charm (USA)**[30] 3302 3-8-6 55.............................. RichardKingscote 5 28
(R M Beckett) *in tch: rdn over 4f out: wknd 2f out* **33/1**

1m 41.41s (-2.09) **Going Correction** -0.15s/f (Firm)
WFA 3 from 4yo 8lb **10** Ran SP% **121.6**
Speed ratings (Par 103): **104,101,99,97,96 95,95,93,91,83**
toteswingers: 1&2 £8.70, 1&3 £9.40, 2&3 £11.90 CSF £98.54 TOTE £10.30: £2.30, £3.30, £3.40; EX 142.10.
Owner Mrs Fitri Hay **Bred** Alan Gibson **Trained** Whatcombe, Oxon

FOCUS
There was more early pace in this claimer than in the amateurs' race and the final time was over three seconds quicker. The form is rated around the placed horses with the winner close to his 2yo form.
Brooksby Official explanation: jockey said filly hung left-handed
Indian Skipper(IRE) Official explanation: jockey said gelding hung left-handed

4323 BLACK GROUSE MAIDEN STKS 6f
7:05 (7:06) (Class 4) 2-Y-O **£3,885** (£1,156; £577; £288) **Stalls** High

Form RPR

2 **1** **Deloria**[23] 3534 2-8-12 0.............................. AlanMunro 7 72+
(Eve Johnson Houghton) *prom: rdn and edgd sltly lft over 1f out: led briefly jst ins fnl f: rallied to regain ld on nod line* **6/4**[1]

035 **2** *nse* **Tislaam (IRE)**[14] 3875 2-9-3 0.............................. TedDurcan 4 77+
(M R Channon) *hld up bhd: swtchd lft over 1f out: r.o strly but edgd rt to ld ins fnl f: lost on nod* **7/1**

5 **3** *1* **Admirable Duchess**[14] 3858 2-8-12 0.............................. KirstyMilczarek 9 69
(D J S Ffrench Davis) *led: rdn 2f out: kpt on gamely but no ex whn hdd jst ins fnl f* **9/1**

0 **4** *1* **Edgewater (IRE)**[12] 3920 2-9-3 0.............................. NickyMackay 10 71
(B J Meehan) *trckd ldrs: rdn over 2f out: kpt on but nt pce to chal* **20/1**

06 **5** *½* **Flaming Miracle**[17] 3745 2-9-3 0.............................. NeilChalmers 2 69
(A M Balding) *mid-div: swtchd lft 2f out: sn rdn: r.o fnl f* **50/1**

5 **6** *2 ½* **Luminous Star (USA)**[19] 3692 2-9-3 0.............................. JimCrowley 1 62
(R M Beckett) *prom: rdn 2f out: sn one pce* **9/2**[2]

0 **7** *2 ¼* **Joan's Legacy**[8] 4047 2-8-12 0.............................. RichardSmith 11 50
(J C Fox) *nvr bttr than mid-div* **80/1**

0 **8** *1* **Regal Rave (USA)**[28] 3402 2-9-0 0.............................. MarcHalford(3) 8 52
(J R Best) *mid-div: rdn 3f out: wknd ent fnl f* **33/1**

9 *5* **Mawaddah (IRE)** 2-9-3 0.............................. RichardHughes 3 37
(R Hannon) *racd green: s.i.s: a towards rr* **11/2**[3]

10 *1* **Whitechapel** 2-9-3 0.............................. MartinDwyer 6 34
(W R Muir) *s.i.s: a towards rr* **7/1**

1m 15.41s (0.61) **Going Correction** -0.15s/f (Firm) **10** Ran SP% **119.5**
Speed ratings (Par 96): **89,88,87,86,85 82,79,77,71,69**
toteswingers: 1&2 £8.70, 1&3 £9.40, 2&3 £11.90 CSF £12.77 TOTE £2.70: £1.10, £2.60, £3.00; EX 18.20.
Owner Skeltools Ltd **Bred** A B Phipps **Trained** Blewbury, Oxon

FOCUS
Two determined juveniles set up an exciting finish as they battled to the line together. The form is held down by the time but the first two can do better.

NOTEBOOK
Deloria just got up in the drive to the line. Racing prominently throughout, she veered left when under pressure in the final furlong, but responded in gritty fashion when headed. Having shown promise when second on her debut at Newbury, she was a warm order to go one better here, and although it may have been closer than expected, the tenacity she demonstrated should stand her in good stead. (op 13-8 tchd 2-1)
Tislaam(IRE) travelled well before making a strong forward move wide of the field, looking likely to swoop past. However, he began making his run as the winner began to veer left and that may have just put him off for a stride. He has improved with each race and the ground he made up here suggests he should be up to winning soon. (tchd 13-2)
Admirable Duchess tried to make all but was just outpaced in the final furlong. This was another solid effort from a filly who was the youngest in the field by around eight weeks. (tchd 11-1)
Edgewater(IRE) stayed on without having the pace of the protagonists. This was an improvement on his debut run and the gelding is slowly progressing. (op 14-1)
Flaming Miracle, who was fractious before the start, was keen in the race and could not go the early pace, although he did stay on a bit. He might be of more interest when tackling handicaps. (op 40-1 tchd 33-1)
Luminous Star(USA), weak in the market, faded after showing early speed and did not build on his debut run at Windsor. (op 10-3)

4324 COLD SERVICE LTD MAIDEN STKS 6f
7:35 (7:36) (Class 5) 3-Y-O+ **£3,885** (£1,156; £577; £288) **Stalls** High

Form RPR

1 **High Achieved** 3-8-12 0.............................. AlanMunro 3 72
(P W Chapple-Hyam) *slowly away: sn mid-div: rdn and hdwy over 2f out: chal over 1f out: led fnl 100yds: r.o wl* **7/2**[3]

65 **2** *¾* **Present Alchemy**[64] 2229 3-9-3 0.............................. SteveDrowne 1 75
(H Morrison) *mid-div: hdwy to trck ldr 3f out: led 2f out: sn rdn: hdd fnl 100yds: kpt on but no ex* **3/1**[2]

4 **3** 2½ **Miss Frangipane (IRE)**29 3338 3-8-12 0 RichardHughes 5 62
(J Noseda) *wnt sltly lft s: chsd ldrs: rdn over 2f out: kpt on same pce fnl f* **6/4**1

4 1 **The Wee Chief (IRE)** 3-9-3 0 RichardSmith 6 64
(J C Fox) *hld up towards rr: rdn and hdwy wl over 1f out: r.o: nrst fin* **40/1**

06 **5** 1½ **Chandika**56 2496 3-8-12 0 TedDurcan 16 54
(C G Cox) *t.k.h trcking ldrs: rdn wl over 1f out: fdd ins fnl f* **7/1**

04 **6** 2½ **Akabar**26 3460 3-9-3 0 JimCrowley 7 51
(R M Beckett) *a mid-div* **10/1**

7 1¼ **Turbo Shandy**3 6-9-8 0 RichardThomas 12 47
(D Burchell) *s.i.s: towards rr: sme late prog: nvr a danger* **25/1**

-006 **8** ½ **Clear Hand**8 4061 3-9-3 47 (b) TolleyDean 15 45
(B R Millman) *led: rdn and hdd 2f out: fdd fnl f* **100/1**

00 **9** 1¼ **Cardenio (USA)**15 3813 3-8-12 0 NickyMackay 11 36
(J R Gask) *in tch tl squeezed up and lost pl after 1f: sn bhd: nvr bk on terms* **40/1**

05- **10** ½ **Sparkling Suzie**381 3837 3-8-7 0 SophieDoyle(5) 13 35
(J S Moore) *in tch: rdn over 2f out: wknd over 1f out* **28/1**

11 1 **Red Willow** 3-8-9 0 NataliaGemelova(3) 9 32
(J E Long) *s.i.s: outpcd early: a towards rr* **66/1**

U **Louise Sauvage** 3-8-12 0 NeilChalmers 18 —
(M D I Usher) *s.i.s: towards rr of mid-div whn: short of whn uns rdr and crashed through rails 3f out* **50/1**

1m 14.22s (-0.58) **Going Correction** -0.15s/f (Firm)
WFA 3 from 4yo+ 5lb **12 Ran SP% 125.4**
Speed ratings (Par 103): **97,96,92,91,89 86,84,83,82,81 80,—**
toteswingers: 1&2 £4.20, 1&3 £2.50, 2&3 £2.20 CSF £14.81 TOTE £5.60: £1.80, £1.50, £1.10; EX 17.80.
Owner Lady Bamford **Bred** Millsec Limited **Trained** Newmarket, Suffolk
■ Stewards' Enquiry : Sophie Doyle six-day ban: careless riding (Aug 8-13)

FOCUS
Just a modest maiden, held down by the likes of the eighth, but a nice start from the winner.

4325 OLIVER GRUBB 15TH BIRTHDAY H'CAP 1m 6f 21y
8:10 (8:10) (Class 5) (0-75,75) 3-Y-O+ £3,238 (£963; £481; £240)

Form RPR

2351 **1** **Curacao**14 3869 3-9-10 75 JimCrowley 9 83
(Mrs A J Perrett) *mid-div: rdn and hdwy 3f out: str chal fr 2f out: led ins fnl f: styd on wl: rdn out* **4/1**3

-012 **2** ½ **Devil To Pay**44 2850 3-9-8 73 TedDurcan 8 81
(J L Dunlop) *hld up in last trio: hdwy 3f out: rdn to take v narrow advantage 2f out: hdd ins fnl f: kpt on but no ex* **7/4**1

532 **3** ½ **Dazinski**11 3962 3-9-8 73 AlanMunro 4 80+
(M H Tompkins) *mid-div: struggling 4f out: swtchd lft and hdwy 2f out: styd on ins fnl f: clsng at fin* **5/2**2

0154 **4** 9 **Sinbad The Sailor**23 3521 4-9-10 61 (v) RichardHughes 7 55
(J W Hills) *led: rdn over 3f out: hdd 2f out: wknd fnl f* **12/1**

33 **5** 2½ **Dramatic Solo**23 3544 4-10-0 65 (b) RichardMullen 1 56
(K R Burke) *trckd ldr: rdn and ev ch 2f out: wknd ent fnl f* **11/1**

-303 **6** 5 **Act Three**15 3814 5-9-8 59 ShaneKelly 5 43
(Mouse Hamilton-Fairley) *kpt away fr the others: hld up last: rdn over 3f out: edgd lft and no imp* **12/1**

0361 **7** 1 **Haafhd Time (IRE)**30 3303 3-8-9 60 RichardKingscote 2 43
(Tom Dascombe) *trckd ldr: rdn 4f out: wknd over 1f out* **14/1**

1005 **8** 131 **Admirable Duque (IRE)**19 3697 3-9-9 74 (b) JimmyFortune 3 —
(D J S Ffrench Davis) *hld up in last trio: lost action and eased fr 3f out* **18/1**

3m 4.21s (-3.19) **Going Correction** -0.15s/f (Firm)
WFA 3 from 4yo+ 14lb **8 Ran SP% 120.6**
Speed ratings (Par 103): **103,102,102,97,95 93,92,—**
toteswingers: 1&2 £2.10, 1&3 £2.40, 2&3 £1.90 CSF £12.15 CT £21.38 TOTE £5.90: £1.60, £1.40, £1.40; EX 13.90.
Owner Mrs S Conway, Coombelands Racing Stables **Bred** Granham Farm **Trained** Pulborough, W Sussex

FOCUS
With no obvious pace, the race was run at a steady tempo, but it picked up half-a-mile from home and set up a close finish with the first three pulling clear of the field. They all look progressive.
Act Three Official explanation: jockey said mare was unsuited by the good to firm (good in places) ground
Admirable Duque(IRE) Official explanation: jockey said gelding felt lame during race, but returned sound

4326 FAMOUS GROUSE H'CAP 6f 212y
8:40 (8:41) (Class 4) (0-85,85) 3-Y-O £4,857 (£1,445; £722; £360) Stalls Centre

Form RPR

3100 **1** **Spinners End (IRE)**15 3816 3-9-2 80 JimCrowley 3 88
(K R Burke) *a.p: led 2f out: kpt on wl: drvn out* **16/1**

5626 **2** ½ **Hail Promenader (IRE)**21 3643 3-9-2 80 AlanMunro 1 87
(B W Hills) *in tch: rdn over 2f out: styd on ins fnl f: wnt 2nd nr fin* **25/1**

0123 **3** nk **Santefisio**21 3643 3-9-0 78 SteveDrowne 5 84
(P J Makin) *hmpd leaving stalls: sn in tch: rdn and ev ch 2f out: kpt on but no ex fnl f: lost 2nd nr fin* **9/4**1

4000 **4** 1½ **Satwa Laird**14 3839 3-9-4 82 MartinDwyer 8 84+
(E A L Dunlop) *hld up towards rr: hdwy 2f out: sn rdn: styd on same pce fnl f* **7/1**3

1216 **5** nk **Cumana Bay**17 3746 3-9-7 85 RichardHughes 13 86
(R Hannon) *trckd ldrs: rdn over 2f out: kpt on same pce* **9/2**2

-006 **6** 1 **Finnegan McCool**22 3592 3-8-8 72 (p) RichardKingscote 10 70
(R M Beckett) *led tl 2f out: fdd fnl f* **25/1**

1234 **7** ¾ **Time Medicean**38 3033 3-9-4 82 TedDurcan 9 78
(M R Channon) *nvr bttr than mid-div* **9/2**2

3412 **8** 2½ **Perfect Friend**14 3870 3-9-1 79 JimmyFortune 7 69
(S Kirk) *a towards rr* **7/1**3

05-0 **9** ¾ **Bougie Daize**44 2845 3-8-2 71 SophieDoyle(5) 12 59
(C G Cox) *prom: rdn over 2f out: wknd ent fnl f* **20/1**

501 **10** 1¾ **Iasia (GR)**16 3790 3-9-2 80 MichellePayne 4 63
(Jane Chapple-Hyam) *a towards rr* **12/1**

-120 **11** ¾ **Floor Show**21 3643 3-9-4 82 RichardMullen 6 63
(E S McMahon) *t.k.h: restrained in mid-div: rdn over 2f out: wknd over 1f out* **20/1**

1m 27.6s (-1.40) **Going Correction** -0.15s/f (Firm) **11 Ran SP% 122.9**
Speed ratings (Par 102): **102,101,101,99,99 97,97,94,93,91 90**
toteswingers: 1&2 £23.70, 1&3 £6.80, 2&3 £12.70 CSF £372.33 CT £1023.94 TOTE £24.40: £5.40, £4.40, £1.60; EX 251.20 Place 6: £38.61, Place 5: £19.01..
Owner Mogeely Stud & Mrs Maura Gittins **Bred** P D Savill **Trained** Middleham Moor, N Yorks

FOCUS
A muddling early pace allowed the winner to quicken from the front two furlongs out. The enterprising tactic paid off. The form might not prove as strong as the race looked beforehand but the first two produced personal bests.
Floor Show Official explanation: jockey said colt was unsuited by the good to firm (good in places) ground
T/Plt: £46.50 to a £1 stake. Pool: £48,480.35. 760.98 winning tickets. T/Qpdt: £3.10 to a £1 stake. Pool: £5,820.16. 1,387.70 winning tickets. TM

4284 YORK (L-H)
Saturday, July 25

OFFICIAL GOING: Good (7.6) changing to good to firm after race 6 (4.50)
Wind: moderate 1/2 against Weather: fine

4327 SKYPOKER.COM STKS (NURSERY) 5f
2:05 (2:05) (Class 3) 2-Y-O £6,799 (£2,023; £1,011; £505) Stalls High

Form RPR

211 **1** **Singeur (IRE)**23 3540 2-9-1 79 NCallan 7 86
(R Bastiman) *trckd ldrs: chal over 1f out: r.o to ld nr fin* **9/2**1

0034 **2** nk **Bossy Kitty**21 3606 2-7-12 62 SilvestreDeSousa 5 68
(N Tinkler) *mid-div: hdwy over 2f out: led over 1f out: hdd nr fin* **12/1**

321 **3** 2¾ **Emerald Girl (IRE)**11 3937 2-8-6 70 PaulHanagan 13 66+
(R A Fahey) *sn outpcd and in rr: hdwy on ins over 1f out: styd on wl towards fin* **5/1**2

063 **4** ½ **Lady Lube Rye (IRE)**7 4076 2-8-3 67 DuranFentiman 3 61
(N Wilson) *chsd ldrs: kpt on same pce appr fnl f* **12/1**

3133 **5** 2¼ **Oondiri (IRE)**23 3540 2-8-4 68 JohnEgan 9 54
(T D Easterby) *chsd ldrs stands' side: one pce fnl 2f* **10/1**

4143 **6** hd **Merseyside Star (IRE)**14 3842 2-8-5 69 AndrewElliott 11 54
(K R Burke) *sn outpcd and in rr: kpt on fnl 2f: nvr nr ldrs* **5/1**2

1306 **7** ¾ **Dancing Freddy (IRE)**23 3542 2-9-7 85 LDettori 6 68
(J G Given) *mid-div: effrt 2f out: nvr nr ldrs* **8/1**

2423 **8** 1 **Ignatieff (IRE)**26 3446 2-8-8 72 TomEaves 2 51
(Mrs L Stubbs) *led tl hdd over 1f out: sn fdd* **12/1**

1401 **9** 1 **Gertmegalush (IRE)**14 3871 2-8-12 76 JimmyQuinn 12 52
(J D Bethell) *s.v.s: sme hdwy and edgd lft over 1f out: nvr on terms* **7/1**3

0336 **10** 1 **Six Wives**14 3871 2-8-4 68 FrancisNorton 10 40
(J A Glover) *mid-div: effrt over 2f out: nvr a factor* **20/1**

2614 **11** ¾ **Danzoe (IRE)**9 4017 2-9-1 79 MickyFenton 1 48
(D Donovan) *chsd ldrs on outside: wknd appr fnl f* **12/1**

0066 **12** 29 **Ariel Bender**7 4076 2-7-12 62 oh16 (b1) JamieMackay 4 —
(Peter Grayson) *s.s: bhd and drvn along: t.o* **80/1**

59.71 secs (0.41) **Going Correction** +0.075s/f (Good) **12 Ran SP% 121.0**
Speed ratings (Par 98): **99,98,94,93,89 89,88,86,85,83 82,35**
toteswingers: 1&2 £16.70, 1&3 £2.90, 2&3 £16.00 CSF £60.42 CT £290.33 TOTE £5.70: £2.20, £3.10, £2.00; EX 74.20 Trifecta £235.80 Part won. Pool: £318.66 - 0.50 winning units..
Owner Ms M Austerfield **Bred** Patrick Cassidy **Trained** Cowthorpe, N Yorks

FOCUS
The rail had been moved out by three yards from 1m1f out to the entrance to the home straight, adding seven yards to race distances of 1m and over. A drying night and breezy conditions left the ground riding just on the fast side of good in the opinion of riders involved in the opener, a fair nursery in which they went a good clip, and the time was only 1.91sec ouside the standard. The runner-up appeared to show big improvement on the face of things and the winner is progressive.

NOTEBOOK
Singeur(IRE) tracked the pace close to the stands' rail, soon travelling strongly. He showed a likeable attitude to get the better of the runner-up and complete a hat-trick. Raised 6lb following his Redcar nursery win, he will return to that track in the autumn for the Listed totescoop6 Two-Year-Old Trophy and is set to have just one more run in the interim. Official explanation: four-day ban: used whip with excessive frequency (Aug 8-11) (op 5-1 tchd 6-1)
Bossy Kitty was under pressure by halfway but she responded and had every chance, just finding the colt too strong late on. This was a thoroughly creditable handicap debut, albeit from a fairly lowly mark. (op 14-1)
Emerald Girl(IRE) was another appearing in a handicap for the first time. She was somewhat outpaced for most of the contest and although she ran on nicely against the rail inside the last furlong, it was all too late and she was never going to trouble the pair who fought out the finish. Stiffer tracks probably suit her. (op 9-2 tchd 4-1)
Lady Lube Rye(IRE) went early to post. Unable to race with the front pair inside the last furlong and run out of third close home, she probably performed close to the form she showed when third in a race of this nature at Haydock a week earlier. (tchd 11-1)
Oondiri(IRE) represented the yard successful in two of the three previous runnings of this race, including with the smart Anglezarke last year. A disappointment tried in blinkers behind today's winner at Redcar, she showed pace up the stands' side before fading. (op 9-1)
Merseyside Star(IRE) made late progress from the rear once switched but probably found the drop to 5f on this flat track a bit sharp. (op 6-1)
Ignatieff(IRE) possessed the pace to lead overall down the centre but he faded once headed and has an exposed look now. (op 20-1)
Gertmegalush(IRE) made all over course and distance last time but a repeat performance was never on the cards after he fluffed the start. He was making a little headway from the rear late on when he ran into traffic problems and his rider had to ease him. He is a bit of a character and not one for maximum faith. Official explanation: jockey said gelding was slowly away
Danzoe(IRE), able to race off 4lb lower, was running over 5f for the first time since his debut. He was caught out wide from his low draw and found things happening a little too quickly. (op 9-1)

4328 SKYBET.COM E B F FILLIES' STKS (H'CAP) 1m 2f 88y
2:35 (2:35) (Class 3) (0-90,90) 3-Y-O+ £9,714 (£2,890; £1,444; £721) Stalls Low

Form RPR

0342 **1** **Summer Gold (IRE)**16 3763 5-9-3 79 DavidAllan 11 87
(E J Alston) *t.k.h in rr: hdwy over 3f out: led over 1f out: hld on towards fin* **12/1**

021- **2** hd **Spouk**239 7474 4-9-1 77 MichellePayne 10 85
(L M Cumani) *trckd ldrs: led over 2f out: hdd over 1f out: kpt on wl towards fin* **8/1**

1115 **3** 2 **Antigua Sunrise (IRE)**15 3827 3-8-6 78 PaulHanagan 3 82
(R A Fahey) *s.i.s: sn chsng ldrs: styd on same pce fnl 2f* **9/2**2

4520 **4** 1½ **Rio Guru (IRE)**21 3627 4-8-10 72 SamHitchcott 1 73
(M R Channon) *dwlt: hld up in rr: hdwy over 7f out: sn chsng ldrs: kpt on same pce fnl 2f* **25/1**

-305 **5** 2½ **Tottie**30 3315 3-9-2 88 (p) NCallan 5 84
(Mrs A J Perrett) *restless in stalls: mid-div: effrt over 3f out: one pce fnl 2f* **6/1**3

1014 **6** 3½ **Off Chance**31 3267 3-8-2 74 DuranFentiman 7 64+
(T D Easterby) *hld up in rr: hdwy over 3f out: sn chsng ldrs: wknd over 1f out* **14/1**

6431 **7** *2* **La Coveta (IRE)**[21] 3627 4-8-13 **80** GabrielHannon(5) 6 66
(B J Meehan) *hld up in last: hdwy on stands' side over 3f out: wknd over 1f out* **12/1**
2300 **8** *3* **Deep Winter**[14] 3873 4-9-3 **84** BMcHugh(5) 12 64
(R A Fahey) *trckd ldrs: drvn over 3f out: wknd 2f out* **14/1**
-115 **9** *1 ¼* **Aromatic**[46] 2796 3-8-11 **83** LDettori 2 61
(J H M Gosden) *trckd ldrs: effrt over 3f out: wknd over 1f out* **9/4**[1]
1-53 **10** *nk* **Suzi Spends (IRE)**[49] 2697 4-9-7 **83** JimmyQuinn 9 60
(H J Collingridge) *mid-div: effrt on outside over 2f out: sn wknd* **10/1**
024 **11** *2 ½* **Magic Echo**[9] 4003 5-9-9 **85** TomEaves 4 58
(M Dods) *led tl hdd over 2f out: sn wknd* **12/1**

2m 10.93s (-1.57) **Going Correction** +0.075s/f (Good)
WFA 3 from 4yo+ 10lb **11** Ran SP% **123.7**
Speed ratings (Par 104): **109,108,107,106,104 101,99,97,96,96 94**
toteswingers: 1&2 £2.60, 1&3 £17.50, 2&3 £13.10 CSF £110.04 CT £510.61 TOTE £16.30: £4.10, £2.50, £1.90; EX 107.50 TRIFECTA Not won..
Owner J Stephenson **Bred** Rathbarry Stud **Trained** Longton, Lancs
■ Stewards' Enquiry : David Allan four-day ban: used whip with excessive frequency (Aug 8-11)

FOCUS
A fair fillies' handicap and solid form for the grade. The field came over to race centre-to-stands' side in the home straight. The winner produced a clear personal best with the runner-up an improver.

NOTEBOOK
Summer Gold(IRE), held up again, improved from the rear travelling strongly but briefly looked like encountering trouble as the pacemaker edged across her approaching the two-furlong pole. Soon in front, she had a battle on to quell a persistent runner-up but emerged on top and her rider reported that she was idling a little in front. She used to be quite keen but is settling better and seems an improved mare as a result.
Spouk had not raced since landing a maiden on the Lingfield Polytrack in late November. Never far from the pace, she was unable to quicken up but responded very gamely to pressure and went down narrowly. She is from a fine family and there is improvement in her, but she may need time to get over this. (op 7-1)
Antigua Sunrise(IRE) was found out by the step up to 1m6f last time following a hat-trick of wins over lm4f. This shorter trip was not entirely in her favour but she stuck on well near the stands' rail and remains in good heart. (op 6-1)
Rio Guru(IRE) recovered from a tardy start to run her race and is a pretty consistent performer if forgiven a poor run at Leicester on her previous outing. (op 20-1)
Tottie was fitted with cheekpieces for this initial handicap experience. She was a little short of room over two furlongs out and became a bit unbalanced before plugging on at the same pace. She did not stay the 1m4f of the Oaks but may be worth another try at that trip. (op 9-1)
Off Chance was suited by the drying ground, but although she made some headway from the back, she could never get involved. (op 12-1)
La Coveta(IRE), who was put up 5lb following her win at Leicester, was never a factor. (op 11-1)
Aromatic was well placed up the straight but she weakened rather tamely in the last furlong and a half and has now run back-to-back lacklustre races. Official explanation: jockey said filly ran flat (op 3-1)
Magic Echo made the running but could not hold on in the straight and dropped away to finish last. She could have done with some rain. (op 10-1)

4329 SKY BET YORK STKS (GROUP 2) 1m 2f 88y
3:10 (3:11) (Class 1) 3-Y-0+
£56,770 (£21,520; £10,770; £5,370; £2,690; £1,350) **Stalls** Low

Form RPR
1401 **1** **Kirklees (IRE)**[22] 3585 5-9-2 117 LDettori 1 116+
(Saeed Bin Suroor) *trckd ldr: led over 2f out: drvn rt out* **1/1**[1]
-010 **2** *1 ¼* **Allied Powers (IRE)**[58] 2410 4-9-2 106 PaulHanagan 9 113+
(M L W Bell) *hld up: hdwy over 5f out: styd on to take 2nd ins fnl f* **16/1**
5450 **3** *½* **Kings Gambit (SAF)**[119] 1012 5-9-2 110 MickyFenton 8 112
(T P Tate) *hld up in mid-div: stdy hdwy over 3f out: styd on same pce fnl f* **25/1**
-164 **4** *¾* **Curtain Call (FR)**[27] 3443 4-9-2 114 NCallan 4 111
(L M Cumani) *trckd ldrs: chal 3f out: styd on same pce fnl f* **9/2**[2]
2043 **5** *1* **Monitor Closely (IRE)**[37] 3050 3-8-6 108 AdrianTNicholls 2 109
(P W Chapple-Hyam) *trckd ldrs: effrt 3f out: kpt on same pce* **5/1**[3]
-105 **6** *3 ¾* **Tazeez (USA)**[38] 3013 5-9-2 113 TPO'Shea 7 102
(J H M Gosden) *led: qcknd over 4f out: hdd over 2f out: wknd over 1f out* **7/1**
-005 **7** *2 ¾* **Smokey Oakey (IRE)**[7] 4090 5-9-2 105 JimmyQuinn 5 97
(M H Tompkins) *hld up in rr: hdwy on wd outside over 3f out: nvr a factor* **20/1**
2205 **8** *21* **Halicarnassus (IRE)**[22] 3585 5-9-2 110 SamHitchcott 6 57
(M R Channon) *in rr: rdn over 3f out: sn lost pl and bhd* **25/1**
9 *2 ¾* **Macorville (USA)**[644] 6335 6-9-2 105 TomEaves 3 52
(G M Moore) *mid-div: rdn over 3f out: sn lost pl and bhd* **50/1**

2m 10.27s (-2.23) **Going Correction** +0.075s/f (Good)
WFA 3 from 4yo+ 10lb **9** Ran SP% **117.6**
Speed ratings (Par 115): **111,110,109,109,108 105,103,86,84**
toteswingers: 1&2 £5.20, 1&3 £10.60, 2&3 £59.30 CSF £19.38 TOTE £2.00: £1.10, £3.30, £5.70; EX 22.10 Trifecta £449.60 Pool: £789.98 - 1.30 winning units..
Owner Godolphin **Bred** Darley **Trained** Newmarket, Suffolk

FOCUS
The form looks sound but is pretty ordinary for the grade, but Kirklees won well despite not having to be at his best. Again the runners made for the centre of the track in the straight. The pace was fairly steady and nothing got into the race from the rear until it was as good as over.

NOTEBOOK
Kirklees(IRE) impressed in a Listed race at Sandown earlier in the month and he followed up in dominant style. Tracking the pace travelling strongly, he was in front with two furlongs to run and although he edged over to the stands' rail as the pursuers closed, he was well in command through the last furlong. A winner in Group 1 company as a juvenile, he is in fine form and deserves another crack at the top grade, which may come over C&D in the Juddmonte International next month. He would have plenty to find with Sea The Stars for one there. (op 11-8 tchd 10-11)
Allied Powers(IRE) did best of those who raced in the rear and was finishing quite well against the stands' rail, but too late to trouble the favourite unduly. Winner of a Listed handicap over 1m4f at Hamilton two runs back, he will not mind a return to that trip. (op 14-1 tchd 20-1)
Kings Gambit(SAF) ◆ was without the tongue tie on this debut for Tom Tate and first start since finishing last in the Sheema Classic (five places behind Kirklees) in March. He made a very promising British debut, staying on for third after travelling well in midfield, and will be suited by a true gallop at this trip. (op 28-1 tchd 33-1)
Curtain Call(FR) is suited by give in the ground and the drying conditions were not in his favour. He ran well, always up with the pace, but could not quicken with the winner and was caught for second spot well inside the last furlong. Easier conditions and a return to 1m4f will be to his benefit. (tchd 5-1)
Monitor Closely(IRE), the only three-year-old taking part, lacked a change of gear off this fairly steady pace but kept trying to the line. This consistent colt may remain a little difficult to place successfully but looks worth a try over 1m4f on this evidence. (op 6-1 tchd 7-1)
Tazeez(USA) bit off more than he could chew in Group 1 company at Royal Ascot last time. After making the running he could not prevent the winner from moving past and he weakened out of the frame in the final furlong. Official explanation: jockey said gelding ran flat (op 11-2 tchd 5-1)
Macorville(USA), who had not run since the autumn of 2007 and whose best form has come over 1m6f-plus, dropped right away in the straight. (op 66-1)

4330 SKY BET DASH (HERITAGE H'CAP) 6f
3:45 (3:46) (Class 2) (0-105,104) 3-Y-0+
£31,155 (£9,330; £4,665; £2,335; £1,165; £585) **Stalls** High

Form RPR
0014 **1** **Knot In Wood (IRE)**[8] 4037 7-9-4 **103** BMcHugh(5) 9 114
(R A Fahey) *chsd ldrs: styd on gamely to ld nr fin* **9/1**[2]
5220 **2** *hd* **Barney McGrew (IRE)**[8] 4037 6-9-3 **97** TomEaves 6 107
(M Dods) *chsd ldrs: led over 1f out: hdd nr fin* **28/1**
4045 **3** *1 ¾* **Excusez Moi (USA)**[8] 4037 7-9-0 **94** (p) SilvestreDeSousa 8 99
(Mrs R A Carr) *dwlt: in rr: hdwy over 2f out: kpt on wl fnl f* **14/1**
-000 **4** *¾* **Kaldoun Kingdom (IRE)**[14] 3877 4-8-10 **90** PaulHanagan 13 92
(R A Fahey) *in rr: hdwy over 2f out: swtchd lft and styd on fnl f* **9/1**[2]
-500 **5** *nse* **Tajneed (IRE)**[8] 4037 6-9-1 **95** AdrianTNicholls 3 97
(D Nicholls) *chsd ldr: led over 2f out: hdd over 1f out: kpt on same pce* **14/1**
2040 **6** *nk* **Intrepid Jack**[15] 3819 7-9-9 **103** (b[1]) TravisBlock 14 104
(H Morrison) *chsd ldrs: kpt on wl fnl f* **20/1**
103 **7** *hd* **Mullein**[29] 3360 4-8-9 **92** JackMitchell(3) 16 92
(R M Beckett) *mid-div: hdwy towards stands' side 2f out: kpt on wl fnl f* **16/1**
/12- **8** *1 ¼* **Al Khaleej (IRE)**[441] 1982 5-9-8 **102** JimmyQuinn 19 98+
(E A L Dunlop) *s.i.s: swtchd towards centre after 1f: r.o wl appr fnl f: nt rch ldrs* **10/1**[3]
6235 **9** *1* **Pusey Street Lady**[15] 3824 5-9-4 **98** TPO'Shea 12 91
(J Gallagher) *chsd ldrs: fdd appr fnl f* **14/1**
0113 **10** *hd* **Roker Park (IRE)**[8] 4037 4-9-1 **95** (p) NCallan 15 88
(K A Ryan) *mid-div: effrt over 2f out: nvr a threat* **11/2**[1]
3203 **11** *nse* **River Falcon**[5] 4135 9-8-9 **94** GaryBartley(5) 5 86
(J S Goldie) *in rr: kpt on fnl 2f: nvr a factor* **16/1**
2303 **12** *1 ½* **Cheveton**[14] 3844 5-9-1 **95** JamesDoyle 7 83+
(R J Price) *s.v.s: detached in rr tl kpt on fnl 2f* **18/1**
000 **13** *½* **Damika (IRE)**[28] 3391 6-8-12 **95** MichaelJStainton(3) 18 81
(R M Whitaker) *led one other stands' side: nvr nr ldrs* **16/1**
-400 **14** *2 ¼* **Aldermoor (USA)**[63] 2279 3-8-10 **95** DavidAllan 17 74
(S C Williams) *in rr: nvr on terms* **25/1**
0001 **15** *¾* **Striking Spirit**[14] 3877 4-9-6 **100** MickyFenton 4 76
(D Nicholls) *led tl over 2f out: sn wknd* **10/1**[3]
0415 **16** *½* **Valery Borzov (IRE)**[59] 2385 5-9-10 **104** FrancisNorton 11 79
(D Nicholls) *chsd ldrs: lost pl over 1f out* **14/1**
502 **17** *4* **Bond City (IRE)**[12] 3928 7-8-9 **89** J-PGuillambert 1 51
(G R Oldroyd) *mid-div: effrt over 2f out: wknd and eased 1f out* **50/1**
0-63 **18** *2 ½* **Viking Spirit**[15] 3802 7-9-1 **95** (t) LDettori 20 49
(W R Swinburn) *racd w one others stands' side: sn outpcd and in rr* **14/1**
1305 **19** *8* **Something (IRE)**[27] 3435 7-9-1 **95** PaulQuinn 2 23
(D Nicholls) *mid-div: lost pl 2f out: bhd whn eased* **14/1**

1m 10.78s (-1.12) **Going Correction** +0.075s/f (Good)
WFA 3 from 4yo+ 5lb **19** Ran SP% **130.5**
Speed ratings (Par 109): **110,109,107,106,106 105,105,104,102,102 102,100,99,96,95 95,89,86,75**
toteswingers: 1&2 £26.60, 1&3 £39.80, 2&3 £55.10 CSF £259.20 CT £3532.47 TOTE £10.70: £2.40, £6.60, £4.40, £2.80; EX 414.20 Trifecta £2055.20 Part won. Pool: £2777.32 - 0.10 winning units..
Owner Rhodes, Kenyon & Gill **Bred** Rathbarry Stud **Trained** Musley Bank, N Yorks
■ Stewards' Enquiry : B McHugh one-day ban: used whip with excessive frequency (Aug 8)

FOCUS
A valuable and highly competitive sprint. The pace was down the centre and the pair who remained on the stands' side had no chance. Good form, with personal bests from the first two and most of these rated close to their best.

NOTEBOOK
Knot In Wood(IRE) was always close up and he battled on willingly as always to just shade the runner-up. He has developed into a smart performer and this win off a BHA mark off 103 followed his success in the Group 3 Chipchase Stakes at Newcastle two runs back. Next weekend's Stewards' Cup, in which he has been third and sixth in the last two years, looks a logical target for him. (op 11-1)
Barney McGrew(IRE) did nothing wrong and lost out on the nod. He was 7lb higher than when gaining his most recent win and this excellent effort is not going to earn him any leniency from the handicapper. (tchd 33-1)
Excusez Moi(USA), from a yard in form, missed the kick again but came through late for third. Like the runner-up, he is a good way above his latest winning mark, but he is performing with credit. (op 16-1)
Kaldoun Kingdom(IRE) has edged down the weights this year and he ran a solid race in fourth with no apparent excuses. (op 12-1)
Tajneed(IRE) ◆ did best of the four David Nicholls runners. He would ideally like some cut in the ground and this good run augurs well for a successful late summer and autumn. (op 16-1 tchd 12-1)
Intrepid Jack, tried in blinkers for the first time, ran well in this more suitable company - he was out of his depth in the July Cup - but he just faded out of the frame in the last half-furlong. (op 25-1 tchd 18-1)
Mullein was dropped 4lb after finishing fourth in a fillies' conditions event at Newmarket last time. She ran a decent race here but lacked a change of pace against the stands' rail in the final furlong. (op 14-1)
Al Khaleej(IRE) ◆ had not been out since finishing second in the Victoria Cup at Ascot in May 2008 and this was an encouraging reappearance. After missing the break from his high stall, he was switched to chase the main body of the field down the centre and he was making some eyecatching headway when it was all over. The return to 7f will suit him. (op 9-1)
Pusey Street Lady ran creditably on her return to handicap company but could not race on with the leaders inside the last furlong. (op 22-1)
Roker Park(IRE) arrived in fine heart and was a neck in front of Knot In Wood when they were third and fourth at Hamilton recently. He was close enough a furlong and a half out but could not sustain his effort inside the last furlong. (op 6-1)
Cheveton Official explanation: jockey said gelding missed the break
Striking Spirit, a recent course-and-distance winner, blazed the trail but was beaten with two furlongs to run. (op 9-1)
Viking Spirit was one of the pair who raced alone on the stands' side and he can be forgiven this. (op 16-1)

Something(IRE) Official explanation: jockey said gelding never travelled

4331 SKYVEGAS.COM MEDIAN AUCTION MAIDEN STKS 6f
4:15 (4:16) (Class 4) 2-Y-O £6,670 (£1,984; £991; £495) Stalls High

Form RPR

1 **Rodrigo De Torres** 2-9-3 0 .... NCallan 6 89+
(K R Burke) *sn trcking ldrs: n.m.r 2f out: squeezed through and led over 1f out: sn drew clr* **8/1**

3 2 3 ½ **L'Enchanteresse (IRE)**[29] 3356 2-8-12 0 .... MickyFenton 9 72
(M L W Bell) *led: qcknd over 2f out: hdd over 1f out: kpt on same pce* **3/1**[2]

3 *shd* **Distinctive** 2-8-12 0 .... TomEaves 5 72+
(B Smart) *rrd s: sn chsng ldrs: outpcd over 2f out: edgd rt over 1f out: styd on wl towards fin* **20/1**

2 4 2 **Loveinthesand (IRE)**[45] 2813 2-9-3 0 .... TPO'Shea 2 71
(M Johnston) *chsd ldrs: rdn 2f out: kpt on same pce* **2/1**[1]

42 5 3 **Key Art (IRE)**[67] 2161 2-9-3 0 .... LDettori 1 62
(J Noseda) *trckd ldrs: effrt over 1f out: sn wknd* **4/1**[3]

6 2 **Emerald Glade (IRE)** 2-8-12 0 .... DavidAllan 7 51
(T D Easterby) *t.k.h in mid-div: effrt 2f out: kpt on: nvr nr ldrs* **8/1**

00 7 13 **Woodface**[12] 3920 2-8-12 0 .... GabrielHannon(5) 8 17
(B J Meehan) *dwlt: sn outpcd and drvn along: wl bhd fnl 2f* **25/1**

8 21 **Coronaria** 2-8-12 0 .... PaulHanagan 3 —
(W J Haggas) *t.k.h: trckd ldrs: lost pl after 2f: bhd and eased fnl f* **13/2**

1m 13.29s (1.39) **Going Correction** +0.075s/f (Good) **8 Ran SP% 122.5**
Speed ratings (Par 96): **93,88,88,85,81 78,61,33**
toteswingers: 1&2 £7.30, 1&3 £12.80, 2&3 £12.90 CSF £34.72 TOTE £9.20: £2.40, £1.60, £4.40; EX 54.80.
Owner Mogeely Stud & Mrs Maura Gittins **Bred** Worksop Manor Stud **Trained** Middleham Moor, N Yorks

FOCUS
An interesting maiden in which the first two in the market set a fair standard, but it was one of the newcomers, Rodrigo De Torres, who prevailed in fine style. He looks sure to rate as least as good as this.

NOTEBOOK
Rodrigo De Torres ◆, after tracking the pace, burst between horses approaching the final furlong and quickened right away, looking a colt with a bright future. A scopey individual whose dam was placed over this trip at two before winning over 1m the following season, he holds entries in most of the top backend races, including the Champagne (over 7f) and Middle Park Stakes. He will need to improve on the bare form he showed here but should be kept on the right side. (op 15-2 tchd 7-1)
L'Enchanteresse(IRE), third at Newmarket on her debut, travelled well enough in front nearest the stands' rail but gave the impression she was still green. She could not respond when tackled by the winner and would have lost second in another stride. Her turn will come but her Cheveley Park entry looks fanciful, for all that she came up against a potentially smart colt. (tchd 5-2)
Distinctive ◆ missed the break but was soon in touch. She picked up well late on and needed another stride to grab second. The first foal of a maiden sprinter in the US, she should have no problem landing a little race before long. (op 25-1 tchd 16-1)
Loveinthesand(IRE) was green when a beaten favourite at Hamilton first time and does not look the finished article yet. After tracking his market rival, he came under pressure with two furlongs to run and could not race on with the leaders. Easier ground may help. (tchd 5-2)
Key Art(IRE) made the frame on his first two starts but had been off the track since May. He was put in his place here and may not have seen out the sixth furlong, but is now eligible for nursery duty. (tchd 9-2)
Emerald Glade(IRE), who was supported on-course, is a 16,000gns buy whose dam is a half-sister to the smart Baron's Pit. After racing keenly through the early parts, she was never a factor, but she could be capable of better. (op 25-1)
Coronaria was reported to have been badly struck into. She may be worth another chance when she recovers. Official explanation: trainer said filly returned in jured (op 8-1 tchd 9-1)

4332 SKY BET SUPPORTING THE YORKSHIRE RACING FESTIVAL (H'CAP) 2m 88y
4:50 (4:50) (Class 3) (0-90,90) 4-Y-O+ £9,066 (£2,697; £1,348; £673) Stalls Low

Form RPR

0532 1 **Mudawin (IRE)**[7] 4078 8-8-6 75 .... JohnEgan 11 84
(James Moffatt) *mid-div: hdwy 7f out: effrt over 3f out: styd on to ld ins fnl f* **12/1**

1421 2 1 ½ **Hawk Mountain (UAE)**[28] 3380 4-9-0 83 .... GrahamGibbons 10 90
(J J Quinn) *trckd ldr: led over 2f out: hdd and no ex ins fnl f* **11/4**[1]

0605 3 ½ **Inchnadamph**[15] 3793 9-8-13 82 ....(t) DavidAllan 3 88
(T J Fitzgerald) *trckd ldrs: effrt over 3f out: hung bdly rt and kpt on fnl f* **14/1**

-606 4 ½ **Kiribati King (IRE)**[47] 2766 4-8-2 71 oh1 ....(v[1]) TPO'Shea 6 77
(M R Channon) *t.k.h in midfield: hdwy on outside over 4f out: styd on same pce appr fnl f* **10/1**[3]

3022 5 ½ **Zuwaar**[14] 3850 4-8-2 71 ....(vt[1]) AdrianTNicholls 9 76
(Ian Williams) *s.i.s: in rr: hdwy over 3f out: hrd rdn and chsng ldrs over 1f out: styd on same pce* **9/1**[2]

0436 6 2 **Luna Landing**[17] 3728 6-8-2 71 oh2 .... FrancisNorton 7 74
(Jedd O'Keeffe) *dwlt: in rr: drvn over 4f out: one pce fnl 2f* **12/1**

-401 7 5 **Nemo Spirit (IRE)**[43] 2895 4-9-7 90 .... NCallan 4 87
(W R Muir) *led tl over 3f out: wknd over 1f out* **11/4**[1]

0434 8 2 ½ **Grand Art (IRE)**[11] 3940 5-8-5 74 .... DuranFentiman 1 68
(P T Midgley) *in rr: hdwy to chse ldrs over 3f out: wknd over 1f out* **12/1**

2-60 9 6 **Red Fama**[9] 4003 5-8-6 75 .... JimmyQuinn 5 61
(N Bycroft) *trckd ldrs: effrt over 3f out: wknd 2f out* **9/1**[2]

1656 10 5 **Herrera (IRE)**[20] 3654 4-8-2 71 oh3 .... PaulHanagan 2 51
(R A Fahey) *trckd ldrs: quite free: wknd over 2f out* **9/1**[2]

0-30 11 23 **Dreams Jewel**[34] 604 9-7-9 71 oh20 .... RichardRowe(7) 8 24
(C Roberts) *s.i.s: sme hdwy over 4f out: sn lost pl and bhd: t.o 2f out* **40/1**

3m 35.28s (0.78) **Going Correction** +0.075s/f (Good) **11 Ran SP% 124.6**
Speed ratings (Par 107): **106,105,105,104,104 103,101,99,96,94 82**
toteswingers: 1&2 £37.70, 1&3 £22.40, 2&3 £8.30 CSF £47.80 CT £495.89 TOTE £16.10: £3.80, £1.60, £4.70; EX 51.80.
Owner John Macgregor **Bred** Shadwell Estate Company Limited **Trained** Cartmel, Cumbria
■ Stewards' Enquiry : T P O'Shea one-day ban: careless riding (Aug 8)

FOCUS
An ordinary staying handicap for York, run at a reasonable pace. The fourth looks a sound guide to the level.

NOTEBOOK
Mudawin(IRE) had gone 21 races and the best part of three years since last tasting success, in the 2006 Ebor here, but he had dropped a long way in the weights in that period and came here following a couple of solid efforts in small fields at Haydock. Not making the running this time, he sat a little off the pace before coming with his challenge down the outer and wearing down the leader inside the last furlong. He is not in the Ebor but could go for the Mallard Handicap at Doncaster.
Hawk Mountain(UAE) shadowed the pacesetting Nemo Spirit, with whom he was 5lb worse off on their meeting here last month, before striking for home with more than three furlongs to run. That was plenty early enough and he was eventually worn down inside the last furlong, but he did keep on well enough to hold second. He remains generally progressive and should continue to give a good account. (op 7-2 tchd 4-1)
Inchnadamph has been dropped 7lb since the start of the season and he stayed on well enough for third despite hanging to his right. He has become well handicapped but is not particularly consistent. (op 11-1)
Kiribati King(IRE) has been dropped 7lb since the start of the season and he stayed on well enough for third despite hanging to his right. He has become well handicapped but is not particularly consistent. (tchd 11-1)
Zuwaar, tried with a visor in place of cheekpieces, made some progress from the rear without quite landing a blow. (tchd 8-1)
Nemo Spirit(IRE) made all over course and distance last month and attempted to replicate that victory off this 3lb higher mark, but he was never left alone up front and he faded once headed in the straight. This ground was faster than ideal for him. (op 3-1 tchd 10-3)
Red Fama, who has yet to find his form in a light campaign, was close enough early in the home straight but he patently failed to see out this longer trip. (op 11-1)

4333 SKYBINGO.COM STKS (H'CAP) 7f
5:25 (5:27) (Class 4) (0-80,80) 3-Y-O+ £6,476 (£1,927; £963; £481) Stalls Low

Form RPR

0045 1 **Zomerlust**[29] 3335 7-9-10 76 ....(v) GrahamGibbons 11 89
(J J Quinn) *chsd ldrs: led over 1f out: sn clr: pushed out* **8/1**

3040 2 2 ½ **Tevez**[11] 3943 4-8-4 61 oh6 ....(t) DeanHeslop(5) 6 67
(D Donovan) *sn last: hdwy on wd outside over 2f out: styd on wl to take 2nd nr fin* **25/1**

130 3 1 **Salerosa (IRE)**[7] 4104 4-8-13 65 .... SilvestreDeSousa 14 68
(Mrs A Duffield) *rr-div: drvn over 3f out: hdwy on outside over 2f out: wnt 2nd over 1f out: kpt on same pce* **9/1**

5114 4 ¾ **Summer Dancer (IRE)**[24] 3496 5-9-9 75 .... NCallan 9 76
(P T Midgley) *hld up in midfield: n.m.r over 2f out: sn chsng ldrs: kpt on same pce appr fnl f* **13/2**[2]

1520 5 4 **Convince (USA)**[2] 4225 8-8-8 65 oh2 ow4 .... BMcHugh(5) 17 55+
(K M Prendergast) *chsd ldrs on outer: wknd over 1f out* **20/1**

3202 6 1 **Shadowtime**[14] 3857 4-9-1 67 .... JohnEgan 5 55
(Miss Tracy Waggott) *mid-div: drvn over 3f out: kpt on: nvr a threat* **12/1**

1346 7 *nk* **Inside Story (IRE)**[8] 4046 7-8-13 68 ....(b) MichaelJStainton(3) 4 55
(C R Dore) *s.i.s: hdwy over 2f out: nvr nr ldrs* **25/1**

6205 8 1 ¼ **Silver Wind**[14] 3877 4-9-7 80 ....(v) AndrewHeffernan(7) 18 64
(P D Evans) *chsd ldrs on outer: wknd over 1f out* **16/1**

4331 9 6 **Bold Marc (IRE)**[24] 3496 7-10-0 80 .... AndrewElliott 12 47
(K R Burke) *prom: lost pl over 1f out* **8/1**

4000 10 3 ½ **Malcheek (IRE)**[39] 3001 7-9-9 75 .... DavidAllan 16 33
(T D Easterby) *chsd ldrs on outer: lost pl over 1f out* **20/1**

0112 11 1 ¼ **Glenridding**[14] 3851 5-9-8 74 ....(p) J-PGuillambert 10 29
(J G Given) *led tl hdd & wknd over 1f out* **8/1**

5-10 12 1 ½ **Maxwell Hawke (IRE)**[70] 2072 3-9-3 79 .... JackMitchell(3) 3 27
(P W Chapple-Hyam) *chsd ldrs: lost pl over 1f out: fin lame* **6/1**[1]

5-50 13 3 **Doric Echo**[29] 3341 3-9-4 77 .... TomEaves 2 16
(B Smart) *chsd ldrs on inner: lost pl over 1f out* **40/1**

2-03 14 1 **Celtic Step**[7] 4104 5-9-9 75 .... LDettori 1 15
(P D Niven) *hld up: sme hdwy on ins over 2f out: wknd and eased over 1f out* **7/1**[3]

0-00 15 1 ½ **Mesbaah (IRE)**[63] 2257 5-9-4 70 .... PaulHanagan 15 6
(R A Fahey) *mid-div on outer: lost pl over 2f out* **9/1**

2660 16 7 **Silver Hotspur**[12] 3928 5-9-6 72 .... JimmyQuinn 8 —
(C R Dore) *mid-div: lost pl 3f out: sn bhd* **33/1**

1m 24.25s (-1.05) **Going Correction** -0.025s/f (Good) **16 Ran SP% 129.6**
WFA 3 from 4yo+ 7lb
Speed ratings (Par 105): **105,102,101,100,95 94,94,92,85,81 80,78,75,74,72 64**
toteswingers: 1&2 £67.60, 1&3 £21.30, 2&3 £68.20 CSF £210.69 CT £1873.99 TOTE £9.10: £2.00, £6.40, £3.20, £1.70; EX 335.60 Place 6: £404.90 Place 5: 176.80.
Owner Dawson And Quinn **Bred** The Lavington Stud **Trained** Settrington, N Yorks

FOCUS
The going was officially amended to good to firm before this race. This was a competitive handicap run at a scorching pace and they finished strung out. The form should hold up, although the proximity of the second casts doubts. They raced down the centre once more.
Shadowtime Official explanation: trainer said gelding was unsuited by the good to firm ground
Maxwell Hawke(IRE) Official explanation: vet said gelding spread a near-fore plate and finished lame
Celtic Step Official explanation: trainer said gelding was unsuited by the good to firm ground
T/Plt: £353.80 to a £1 stake. Pool: £144,934.67. 299.04 winning tickets. T/Qpdt: £67.10 to a £1 stake. Pool: £7,210.18. 79.48 winning tickets. WG

4130 VICHY
Saturday, July 25

OFFICIAL GOING: Soft

4334a PRIX MADAME JEAN COUTURIE (LISTED RACE) (FILLIES) 1m 2f
12:15 (12:18) 3-Y-O £26,699 (£10,680; £8,010; £5,340; £2,670)

RPR

1 **Danehill's Pearl (IRE)**[44] 2846 3-8-11 .... DBonilla 2 103
(Tom Dascombe) *racd keenly on ins in 7th: brought to outside rail w field ent st: led under 2f out: sn rdn: edgd lft: drvn out* **46/1**[2]

2 1 **Flash Dance (IRE)**[51] 3-8-11 .... MGuyon 13 101
(H-A Pantall, France)

3 *nse* **Black Rose (FR)**[20] 3668 3-8-11 .... THuet 7 101
(F Chappet, France)

4 1 **Eclair De Lune (GER)**[41] 2952 3-8-11 .... SPasquier 12 99
(Y De Nicolay, France) **9/5**[1]

5 *nk* **Superstition (FR)**[44] 3-8-11 .... DBoeuf 3 98
(W Hefter, Germany)

6 ½ **Conti Di Luna (FR)**[40] 3-8-11 .... BrigitteRenk 8 97
(Mlle B Renk, France)

7 1 **Satwa Ruby (FR)**[37] 3050 3-8-11 .... TThulliez 11 95
(J De Roualle, France)

8 1 ½ **Street Romance (USA)**[30] 3330 3-8-11 .... GBenoist 1 92
(D Smaga, France)

9 1 **Symba's Dream (USA)**[36] 3137 3-8-11 .... IMendizabal 10 90
(J-C Rouget, France)

10 *nk* **Parcelle Perdue (FR)**[30] 3330 3-8-11 .... ACrastus 4 90
(Mme C Dufreche, France)

0 **Vadiya (FR)**^{40} 3-8-11 .... CSoumillon 6 —
(A De Royer-Dupre, France)
0 **Magdala (FR)** 3-8-11 .... FBlondel 9 —
(F Rohaut, France)
2m 11.36s (2.76) **12** Ran SP% **37.8**
PARI-MUTUEL (including 1 Euro stake): WIN 46.40; PL 10.70, 2.90, 3.70;DF 141.80.
Owner Paul Murphy **Bred** Azienda Agricola Mediterranea **Trained** Lambourn, Berks

NOTEBOOK
Danehill's Pearl(IRE) appreciates plenty of dig in the ground and earned herself valuable black type with this success. Racing in mid-division early on, she quickened early in the straight and took control of this Listed event with a full two furlongs left to run. She dominated the final stages and has now probably earned at tilt at the Group 3 Prix de la Nonette at Deauville next month.

4335a PRIX YVES PARENTI 1m
1:50 (1:55) 4-Y-O+ **£10,680** (£4,272; £3,204; £2,136; £1,068)

RPR
1 **Marek (GER)**^{38} [3045] 6-9-4 .... HanaMouchova 4 100
(W Sonntag Jr, Germany)
2 *1* **Lord Silvano (GER)**^{446} [1885] 5-9-2 .... RKoplik 3 96
(M Lisek, Czech Republic)
3 *3* **Val d'Espoir (IRE)**^{38} [3045] 5-8-11 .... MGuyon 8 84
(H-A Pantall, France)
4 *3/4* **Nolhac (FR)**^{443} 5-9-4 .... MBarzalona 1 89
(P Khozian, France)
5 *1/2* **Air Bag (FR)**^{133} 5-8-8 .... AlexisBadel 9 78
(Mme C Barande-Barbe, France)
6 *nk* **Avanguardia (GER)**^{76} 4-8-12 .... ACardine 2 81
(D Prod'Homme, France)
7 *3/4* **Call Me Kitty (FR)**^{20} 4-8-10 .... IMendizabal 10 77
(U Suter, France)
8 *nk* **Barricado (FR)**^{28} [3419] 4-9-6 ....(p) TThulliez 11 87
(E J O'Neill) *disp 4th on outside: c to outside rail ent st: rdn 1 1/2f out: sn one pce* **6/1**^{1}
9 *4* **Le Ribot (GER)**^{167} [465] 5-9-4 .... GBocskai 12 76
(Carmen Bocskai, Switzerland)
10 *10* **Poquelino (IRE)**^{2249} 11-8-11 .... FForesi 7 46
(Gabriel Mosse, France)
11 **Butterfly Flip (FR)** 5-8-8 .... BRaballand 5 43
(J-P Perruchot, France)
1m 44.15s (104.15) **11** Ran SP% **14.3**
PARI-MUTUEL: WIN 3.60; PL 1.70, 2.70, 3.80; DF 12.50.
Owner Stall Europa **Bred** Gestut Rottgen **Trained** Germany

NOTEBOOK
Barricado(FR) has only achieved fair handicap form in Britain.

4293 ASCOT (R-H)
Sunday, July 26

OFFICIAL GOING: Round course - good (good to firm in places; 9.1) straight course - good to firm (stands' side 10.2; centre 10.8; far side 10.4)
Wind: Moderate, against Weather: Overcast

4336 E B F GL EVENTS OWEN BROWN CROCKER BULTEEL MAIDEN STKS (C&G) 6f
2:15 (2:15) (Class 4) 2-Y-O **£6,476** (£1,927; £963; £481) **Stalls** Centre

Form RPR
1 **Quarrel (USA)** 2-9-0 0 .... MichaelHills 8 87+
(W J Haggas) *stdd s: hld up in tch in last pair: hdwy 2f out: pushed along over 1f out: chsd ldr ins fnl f: pushed out hands and heels to ld fnl 75yds: r.o wl* **9/2**^{3}
2 *3/4* **Atlaal (USA)** 2-9-0 0 .... RHills 5 83+
(M A Jarvis) *restless stalls: wnt rt s: in tch: hdwy to press ldrs 3f out: led wl over 1f out: rdn over 1f out: hdd and no ex fnl 75yds* **7/4**^{1}
3 *1/2* **Right Step** 2-9-0 0 .... AlanMunro 1 81
(A P Jarvis) *racd keenly: led after 1f: hdd wl over 1f out: sn rdn: rn green and hung both ways over 1f out: kpt on u.p fnl f* **20/1**
4 *hd* **Advertisement (USA)** 2-9-0 0 .... ShaneKelly 3 81
(J Noseda) *w ldrs: chsd ldr over 4f out: ev ch 2f out: rdn wl over 1f out: kpt on same pce fnl f* **4/1**^{2}
5 *7* **Hierarch (IRE)** 2-9-0 0 .... RichardHughes 6 60
(R Hannon) *bmpd s: stdd and dropped in bhd: rdn and effrt ent fnl 2f: wknd over 1f out* **9/2**^{3}
6 *2* **Kilt Rock (IRE)** 2-9-0 0 .... StephenDonohoe 4 54
(T G Mills) *led for 1f: chsd ldrs after tl lost pl over 2f out: towards rr and wkng whn hung lft 2f out: wl btn after* **8/1**
7 *1 1/4* **Starwatch** 2-9-0 0 .... LPKeniry 7 50
(J J Bridger) *restless stalls: in tch in last pair: pushed along 3f out: rdn and struggling over 2f out: wl btn after* **66/1**
8 *1/2* **Gordon Flash** 2-9-0 0 .... PatDobbs 2 48
(R Hannon) *in tch: rdn and struggling jst over 2f out: sn wknd* **16/1**
1m 16.27s (1.87) **Going Correction** +0.175s/f (Good) **8** Ran SP% **116.0**
Speed ratings (Par 96): **94,93,92,92,82 80,78,77**
toteswingers: 1&2 £3.30, 1&3 £16.00, 2&3 £7.20 CSF £13.01 TOTE £5.60: £1.70, £1.30, £3.90; EX 11.40 Trifecta £376.80 Part won. Pool £509.21 - 0.80 winning units..
Owner St Albans Bloodstock LLP **Bred** Rosemont Farm Llc **Trained** Newmarket, Suffolk

FOCUS
The ground was riding much as the previous day according to the jockeys in the first. Richard Hughes felt it was a little more chewed up, but did not think that could be used as an excuse. There was no previous form to go on in this race confined to debutants and the first four finished in a heap, clear of the others. Atlantic Sport had Aqlaam back in third in a good renewal two years ago but otherwise this event has thrown up little of note in the past decade. This year's running has been rated around the averages but Quarrel looks a potentially smart colt.

NOTEBOOK
Quarrel(USA) won it well and looks a colt with a future. An £80,000 buy at the breeze-ups, he has an American dirt pedigree and is out of a winner at 6f-1m in the US. He had reportedly been working well, but his trainer felt that he would not be quite ready and he was weak in the market. Held up, he came under pressure with 2f to run but picked up well down the outside to wear down the favourite in the last 75 yards, with his rider not needing to get serious with him. He holds Group-race entries, including the Gimcrack next month, but would need to improve considerably on the bare form of this win, promising though his performance was. (op 11-2)
Atlaal(USA) did not get the best of breaks but was soon in the front rank. He showed narrowly in front going to the final furlong but could not hold off the winner and his stride was shortening near the line. He is another with Pattern-race entries, including the Middle Park over this trip, but while he should win a maiden he does not look up to that class. (op 5-2 tchd 11-4 in places)
Right Step edged left when upsides than came back in the opposite direction when given a smack to correct him, before straightening up to secure third. This was a pleasing debut from this modestly bred colt, on whom the experience will not be lost. (op 16-1)
Advertisement(USA) fetched $400,000 as a foal but was unsold at $300,000 as a yearling. He was always in the front rank and had every chance, but betrayed his inexperience when the pressure was on and could not quicken up. This was a promising debut. (op 11-4)
Hierarch(IRE) is a half-brother to Dazzling Dancer and Defi out of a winning half-sister to the high-class Petrushka. After taking a bump at the start, he could not prevent the four principals pulling away from him once the race became serious. (tchd 11-2)
Kilt Rock(IRE), a £50,000 buy whose dam won the Breeders' Cup Juvenile Fillies', showed pace but back-pedalled quickly when things hotted up. He should build on this. (op 7-1)

4337 LIVERPOOL UNIVERSITY EQUINE VETS MAIDEN FILLIES' STKS 1m (S)
2:50 (2:51) (Class 4) 3-Y-O **£7,123** (£2,119; £1,059; £529) **Stalls** Centre

Form RPR
4-33 1 **Sterling Sound (USA)**^{29} [3408] 3-9-0 72 .... PatDobbs 8 87
(M P Tregoning) *hld up in main gp: hdwy 3f out: chsd ldr over 2f out: ev ch and carried rt fr 2f out: led fnl 100yds: styd on wl* **7/1**^{3}
232- 2 *nk* **Mezenah**^{267} [7141] 3-9-0 79 .... RHills 2 86
(Saeed Bin Suroor) *chsd clr ldr: clsd qckly over 2f out and sn led: drew clr w wnr but hung bdly rt u.p 2f out: hdd and no ex fnl 100yds* **8/11**^{1}
0-03 3 *6* **In Secret**^{15} [3876] 3-9-0 0 .... RichardHughes 3 72+
(J L Dunlop) *stdd s: hld up in rr: pushed along over 2f out: rdn to go modest 4th wl over 1f out: no ch w ldng pair: wnt 3rd wl ins fnl f* **20/1**
6 4 *1/2* **Tinaar (USA)**^{18} [3751] 3-9-0 0 .... EddieAhern 7 70
(G A Butler) *prom in main gp: rdn wl over 3f out: chsd clr ldng pair 2f out: no imp and wl hld after: lost 3rd wl ins fnl f* **11/4**^{2}
30 5 *19* **Cactus Curtsey**^{9} [4057] 3-9-0 0 .... JimCrowley 6 25
(J R Fanshawe) *t.k.h: hld up in rr of main gp: rdn over 3f out: wknd over 2f out: wl btn fnl 2f: t.o* **33/1**
6 *2 1/2* **Love Call (IRE)** 3-9-0 0 .... DarryllHolland 1 19
(W R Muir) *s.i.s: pushed along 1/2-way: rdn 3f out: wknd qckly over 2f out and sn wl bhd: t.o* **22/1**
2 7 *1* **Poppet's Lovein**^{20} [3696] 3-9-0 0 .... StephenDonohoe 4 16
(A B Haynes) *mounted on crse: restless stalls: led and sn wl clr: edgd lft and wknd over 2f out: sn hdd and dropped out: t.o* **14/1**
1m 40.79s (0.19) **Going Correction** +0.175s/f (Good) **7** Ran SP% **115.8**
Speed ratings (Par 99): **106,105,99,99,80 77,76**
toteswingers: 1&2 £2.40, 1&3 £5.70, 2&3 £3.50 CSF £12.73 TOTE £8.70: £3.10, £1.20; EX 13.80 Trifecta £129.90 Pool £850.04 - 4.84 winning units..
Owner Miss K Rausing **Bred** Liberation Farm And Brandywine Farm Llc **Trained** Lambourn, Berks

FOCUS
Just a fair maiden, lacking strength in depth. They raced down the centre of the course, with the filly who finished last holding a long lead at halfway, but the two principals drifted across the track from the two pole and ended up on the inside rail. They finished clear.
Poppet's Lovein Official explanation: jockey said filly ran too freely

4338 ASCOT TV RED BUTTON H'CAP 6f
3:25 (3:26) (Class 4) (0-85,84) 3-Y-O **£7,123** (£2,119; £1,059; £529) **Stalls** Centre

Form RPR
-155 1 **Rapid Water**^{34} [3219] 3-8-9 72 .... LPKeniry 11 86+
(A M Balding) *trckd ldrs: led gng wl jst over 2f out: rdn over 1f out: r.o wl fnl f* **7/2**^{1}
1-60 2 *3/4* **Fleeting Star (USA)**^{27} [3469] 3-8-9 72 ....(v^{1}) TPQueally 12 83+
(J Noseda) *hld up in tch: rdn and effrt to chse wnr over 1f out: r.o but a hld fnl f* **14/1**
5512 3 *3 1/4* **Satwa Street (IRE)**^{12} [3945] 3-9-5 82 .... StephenDonohoe 9 83
(D M Simcock) *hld up in tch: shkn up wl over 1f out: drvn and hdwy over 1f out: chsd ldng pair ins fnl f: no imp* **10/1**
1060 4 *2* **White Shift (IRE)**^{20} [3688] 3-8-11 81 .... KierenFox$^{(7)}$ 10 76
(P Howling) *hld up towards rr: hdwy and rdn 2f out: chsd ldrs over 1f out: wknd 1f out* **25/1**
0103 5 *1/2* **New Leyf (IRE)**^{9} [4056] 3-8-11 74 .... SteveDrowne 4 67
(J R Gask) *prom: chsd wnr 2f out tl over 1f out: wknd u.p ent fnl f* **9/1**
4033 6 *hd* **Sweet Possession (USA)**^{16} [3815] 3-8-3 66 .... ChrisCatlin 2 58
(A P Jarvis) *in tch: rdn 2f out: plugged on u.p ins fnl f: nvr pce to threaten ldrs* **20/1**
6062 7 *2 1/4* **Lucky Numbers (IRE)**^{9} [4044] 3-9-7 84 .... FrancisNorton 5 69
(Paul Green) *t.k.h: in tch: rdn and hdwy over 2f out: wknd u.p over 1f out* **13/2**^{3}
6214 8 *shd* **Reject**^{43} [2917] 3-8-12 75 .... LiamJones 1 60
(W J Haggas) *in tch: rdn to chse ldrs and hung rt wl over 1f out: wknd ent fnl f* **9/2**^{2}
2140 9 *1 1/2* **Bobbie Soxer (IRE)**^{27} [3453] 3-9-4 81 .... EddieAhern 8 61
(J L Dunlop) *hld up towards rr: hdwy to chse ldrs ent fnl 2f: rdn 2f out: sn btn* **8/1**
33 10 *1/2* **Summers Target (USA)**^{27} [3460] 3-8-9 72 .... JimCrowley 6 50
(R M H Cowell) *stdd s: hld up in rr: hdwy and rdn over 2f out: chsd ldrs 2f out: sn drvn and wknd* **12/1**
1001 11 *82* **Bajan Tryst (USA)**^{20} [3688] 3-9-6 83 .... RichardHughes 3 —
(K A Ryan) *sn led: hdd jst over 2f out: wknd rapidly: virtually p.u fr over 1f out* **15/2**
1m 14.83s (0.43) **Going Correction** +0.175s/f (Good) **11** Ran SP% **118.7**
Speed ratings (Par 102): **104,103,98,96,95 95,92,91,89,89** —
toteswingers: 1&2 £12.80, 1&3 £6.90, 2&3 £16.20 CSF £54.97 CT £363.39 TOTE £4.10: £1.40, £3.70, £3.70; EX 55.40 Trifecta £602.20 Pool £976.65 - 1.20 winning units..
Owner J C Smith **Bred** Littleton Stud **Trained** Kingsclere, Hants
■ Stewards' Enquiry : Kieren Fox caution: used whip with excessive frequency

FOCUS
A decent handicap for the grade. The field soon split into two groups before merging going to the furlong pole, and it was those who raced in the six-strong group down the centre who came out on top, with the first four home coming out of the four highest stalls. The form may not prove that solid, but the first two pulled clear and gave the impression that they have more to offer.
Bajan Tryst(USA) Official explanation: trainer had no explanation for the poor form shown

4339 SODEXO PRESTIGE CLASSIFIED STKS 1m 2f
4:00 (4:00) (Class 2) 3-Y-O+ **£11,215** (£3,358; £1,679; £840) **Stalls** High

Form RPR
-031 1 **Shamali**^{15} [3840] 4-9-6 92 .... RHills 2 107+
(W J Haggas) *chsd ldr: led gng best jst over 2f out: rdn and clr over 1f out: comf* **1/2**^{1}
0043 2 *3 3/4* **Proponent (IRE)**^{29} [3399] 5-9-6 95 .... AlanMunro 1 100
(R Charlton) *t.k.h: hld up in 3rd pl: rdn and effrt over 2f out: chsd wnr over 1f out: no imp and wl hld fnl f* **5/1**^{2}

2210 **3** *3 ¼* **Just Lille (IRE)**[22] 3620 6-9-3 89..(p) TPQueally 4 90
(Mrs A Duffield) *led: rdn 3f out: hdd jst over 2f out: wknd u.p over 1f out* **11/2**[3]

5111 **4** *12* **The Cayterers**[20] 3695 7-9-6 91.................................. RichardHughes 5 69
(A W Carroll) *stdd s: hld up in last pl: rdn and effrt on inner over 2f out: no prog: wl btn wl over 1f out* **8/1**

2m 6.49s (-0.51) **Going Correction** +0.175s/f (Good)
WFA 3 from 4yo+ 10lb **4** Ran SP% **109.8**
Speed ratings (Par 109): **109,106,103,93**
CSF £3.49 TOTE £1.50; EX 3.20.
Owner Abdulla Al Khalifa **Bred** Sheikh Abdulla Bin Isa Al-Khalifa **Trained** Newmarket, Suffolk

FOCUS
Quite a valuable race of its type, and the pace was decent considering the small field. Shamali impressed and this form can be taken at face value.

NOTEBOOK
Shamali ◆ proved much too good for his opponents. An impressive winner of a handicap over course and distance last time, for which he was raised 8lb, he settled well in second here and quickly sealed victory once striking the front with 2f to run, showing his powerful stride as he pulled clear. He is very much one to keep on the right side but may not go for the Ebor, for which he has picked up a 4lb penalty, as his rider thinks he won't stay the 1m6f. (op 8-11 tchd 4-5 in places)
Proponent(IRE) was rather keen in the first part of the race. He stayed on well enough for second and continues to perform creditably, but the winner was much too strong on these terms. (op 10-3 tchd 11-2 in places)
Just Lille(IRE) set a decent pace but could do nothing to counter when the winner eased past and soon lost second spot too. (op 13-2)
The Cayterers arrived on a four-timer, having taken three Windsor handicaps, but he could never get out of last place and was eased when well beaten inside the final furlong. Official explanation: jockey said gelding lost its action (op 7-1)

4340 CASINO AT THE EMPIRE STKS (HERITAGE H'CAP) 1m 4f
4:35 (4:36) (Class 2) (0-105,104) 3-Y-0+

£24,924 (£7,464; £3,732; £1,868; £932; £468) **Stalls** High

Form RPR

0012 **1** **Munsef**[22] 3620 7-9-7 101 .... EddieAhern 11 110
(Ian Williams) *hld up wl in tch: rdn and n.m.r briefly over 2f out: sn swtchd lft and hdwy: chsd ldr over 1f out: ev ch ins fnl f: r.o wl u.p to ld nr fin* **9/1**

5250 **2** *shd* **Mystery Star (IRE)**[22] 3620 4-8-11 91.............................. TPQueally 3 100
(M H Tompkins) *hld up in tch in midfield: rdn and hdwy over 2f out: chsd ldrs and edgd rt u.p over 1f out: led jst over 1f out: r.o wl tl hdd nr fin* **20/1**

2102 **3** *1 ¼* **Sabotage (UAE)**[16] 3827 3-8-3 95.............................. AdrianTNicholls 7 102+
(M Johnston) *in tch: rdn over 2f out: swtchd lft and drvn over 1f out: styd on wl u.p fnl f: nt rch ldng pair* **9/2**[1]

4311 **4** *½* **Run For Ede's**[10] 4007 5-7-9 78 oh4.......................... DavidProbert(3) 15 84+
(P M Phelan) *stdd s: hld up in rr: hdwy on inner jst over 2f out: swtchd lft ent fnl f: styd on wl fnl f: nt rch ldrs* **16/1**

4120 **5** *1* **Record Breaker (IRE)**[29] 3390 5-9-5 99..................(b) RoystonFfrench 4 104
(M Johnston) *chsd ldr tl led 3f out: rdn over 2f out: 2 l clr wl over 1f out: hdd jst over 1f out: wknd fnl 75yds* **7/1**[3]

-045 **6** *hd* **Storyland (USA)**[37] 3103 4-8-9 89.............................. KirstyMilczarek 12 93+
(W J Haggas) *stdd s: t.k.h hld up wl in rr: stl last 2f out: sn swtchd lft and hdwy: styd on wl fnl f: nt rch ldrs* **8/1**

1614 **7** *1* **Spring Jim**[22] 3620 8-8-9 89.................................... MichaelHills 8 92
(J R Fanshawe) *hld up towards rr: swtchd lft and hdwy 2f out: kpt on fnl f but nvr pce to rch ldrs* **12/1**

1-26 **8** *nse* **Hevelius**[22] 3620 4-8-10 90.................................... ShaneKelly 2 93+
(W R Swinburn) *stdd s: t.k.h: hld up in midfield: rdn 3f out: swtchd lft jst over 2f out: kpt on but nvr pce to rch ldrs* **6/1**[2]

1002 **9** *nk* **Greylami (IRE)**[23] 3586 4-8-10 90................................ ChrisCatlin 13 92
(T G Mills) *stdd after s: t.k.h: hld up in rr: effrt on outer bnd over 2f out: kpt on: nvr trbld ldrs* **11/1**

6-43 **10** *1 ¼* **Jawaab (IRE)**[15] 3840 5-7-13 79 oh4 ow1...................... FrancisNorton 14 82+
(Mark Buckley) *t.k.h: hld up towards rr: rdn 2f out: keeping on same pce whn hmpd and snatched up over 1f out: kpt on fnl f* **33/1**

-500 **11** *hd* **Night Crescendo (USA)**[36] 3142 6-8-10 90..................(p) JimCrowley 1 90
(Mrs A J Perrett) *t.k.h: chsd ldrs: rdn and unable qck over 2f out: keeping on same pce whn edgd lft over 1f out: one pce fnl f* **12/1**

3005 **12** *1 ¾* **Robby Bobby**[16] 3797 4-8-1 81.................................. AndrewMullen 6 78
(M Johnston) *plld hrd: hld up towards rr: rdn 3f out: no prog whn hmpd swtchd rt over 1f out: nvr nr ldrs* **16/1**

2013 **13** *1 ¾* **Classic Punch (IRE)**[29] 3397 6-9-5 104...... Louis-PhilippeBeuzelin(5) 10 98
(D R C Elsworth) *led tl rdn and hdd 3f out: wknd u.p over 1f out* **20/1**

4031 **14** *nk* **Overrule (USA)**[32] 3266 5-8-10 90.............................. DaneO'Neill 9 84
(B Ellison) *hld up in midfield: shuffled bk towards rr 3f out: rdn and no prog over 2f out* **9/1**

30-0 **15** *13* **Strategic Mount**[36] 3142 6-9-8 102.............................. AlanMunro 5 75
(P F I Cole) *s.i.s: t.k.h: chsd ldrs after 1f: rdn and wknd over 2f out: wl bhd and eased ins fnl f* **20/1**

2m 32.18s (-0.32) **Going Correction** +0.175s/f (Good)
WFA 3 from 4yo+ 12lb **15** Ran SP% **128.8**
Speed ratings (Par 109): **108,107,107,106,106 105,105,105,105,104 104,102,101,101,92**
toteswingers: 1&2 £38.80, 1&3 £10.40, 2&3 £27.20 CSF £189.78 CT £938.96 TOTE £11.10: £3.50, £7.00, £2.00; EX 207.20 Trifecta £1626.60 Part won. Pool £2,198.24 - 0.30 winning units..
Owner Dr Marwan Koukash **Bred** Shadwell Estate Company Limited **Trained** Portway, Worcs

FOCUS
A competitive heritage handicap, but the pace did not look all that strong and they finished in something of a heap. Muddling form, but likely to be of some relevance to the 1m4f handicaps run here at the Shergar Cup and September festival meetings. Munsef is rated to last year's best.

NOTEBOOK
Munsef was never far from the lead and he gave chase as Record Breaker attempted to get clear in the stright. The runner-up soon shaded him, but he battled on well to force his head in front close home. He shrugged off a 6lb rise for his second to Red Merlin in the Old Newton Cup at Haydock and is at top form at present. He will go for the Ebor, for which he collects a 4lb penalty. (tchd 8-1)
Mystery Star(IRE) was 6lb better off with the winner from their meeting at Haydock, where he encountered trouble in running. Obliged to race wide, he took a slender lead inside the last but Munsef proved just the stronger after a good duel. This solid effort proves his effectiveness at 1m4f.
Sabotage(UAE), the only 3yo in the field and dropping back in trip, stayed on well to secure third after enjoying a clearer passage than most. This was a likeable effort but in all probablility he would be flying too high if taking up his Great Voltigeur entry. He may benefit from a return to 1m6f. (op 5-1 tchd 11-2 and 6-1 in places)
Run For Ede's ◆ ran a cracker on her hat-trick bid, racing from 4lb out of the weights so effectively off an 8lb higher mark, although she had a leading apprentice taking off 3lb. Held up at the back as usual, she improved down the rail in the straight before edging off the fence under pressure late on.
Record Breaker(IRE) found the combination of 2m and soft ground too much for him in the Northumberland Plate but was just 1lb higher here than when second to a stablemate in the Duke Of Edinburgh at the Royal meeting. He kicked for home off the turn and went two lengths up, but was worn down inside the last. (op 8-1 tchd 17-2)
Storyland(USA) was last of all turning in before making good progress. Things have not gone her way this season but she is capable of winning a nice prize if everything falls right for her, although given her running style that is a fairly big 'if'. (tchd 15-2)
Spring Jim ran his race again and was another closing at the line. (tchd 14-1)
Hevelius, who was having only his fifth run, was involved in some buffeting in midfield going to the furlong pole but was keeping on again afterwards. (op 13-2 tchd 11-2)
Greylami(IRE)'s Sandown second looked better in the light of winner Fanjura following up here. He improved from the back down the outer in the straight without getting into contention and seemed to see out the longer trip. (tchd 10-1 and 12-1 in places)
Jawaab(IRE), who was 4lb out of the weights, would have finished closer than he did on this first try beyond 1m2f had he not been hampered at the furlong pole. Official explanation: jockey said gelding suffered interference in running
Night Crescendo(USA) straightened for home in third place but was unable to quicken up.
Robby Bobby again took a tug and remains out of form. (op 20-1)
Classic Punch(IRE) got to the front but was given no peace by Record Breaker and seems best suited by smaller fields. (op 25-1)
Overrule(USA), the Cumberland Plate winner, never got into it off his 11lb higher mark. (op 11-1)
Strategic Mount showed prominently but failed to settle, and he dropped right away in the straight. He is not himself at present. (op 22-1)

4341 GL EVENTS OWEN BROWN HONG KONG SPRINT STKS (HERITAGE H'CAP) 5f
5:10 (5:11) (Class 2) 3-Y-0+

£31,155 (£9,330; £4,665; £2,335; £1,165; £585) **Stalls** Centre

Form RPR

64 **1** **Judge 'n Jury**[15] 3844 5-9-1 98..............................(t) KevinGhunowa(3) 9 108
(R A Harris) *chsd ldrs: rdn over 2f out: hrd drvn over 1f out: styd on wl to ld fnl 100yds: drvn out* **14/1**

4443 **2** *½* **Hamish McGonagall**[30] 3351 4-9-4 98............................ DavidAllan 18 106
(T D Easterby) *racd in midfield: hdwy 1/2-way: chsd ldrs and rdn 2f out: r.o u.p fnl f: wnt 2nd nr fin* **9/2**[1]

1600 **3** *hd* **Ishetoo**[15] 3877 5-9-1 95.. TPQueally 25 102
(A Dickman) *towards rr: rdn and hdwy jst over 2f out: kpt on wl u.p fnl f: wnt 3rd last strides* **10/1**[3]

0410 **4** *hd* **Fol Hollow (IRE)**[14] 3898 4-8-9 96.............................. NSLawes(7) 6 103
(D Nicholls) *chsd clr ldr: rdn 2f out: clsd and edgd rt over 1f out: pressed wnr ins fnl f: no ex and lost 2 pls nr fin* **16/1**

1650 **5** *nk* **Indian Trail**[17] 3784 9-8-8 88...................................(v) PaulQuinn 26 93
(D Nicholls) *wl bhd: hdwy 2f out: rdn ent fnl f: r.o wl ins fnl f: nt rch ldrs* **10/1**[3]

-616 **6** *nk* **Rowe Park**[85] 1676 6-9-10 104.................................. SteveDrowne 8 108
(Mrs L C Jewell) *bhd: rdn jst over 2f out: hdwy u.p over 1f out: kpt on fnl f: unable to rch ldrs* **25/1**

0-65 **7** *nk* **Tony The Tap**[15] 3844 8-8-2 85.............................. DavidProbert(3) 24 88
(W R Muir) *v.s.a: wl bhd: hdwy jst over 1f out: styd on strly fnl f: nt rch ldrs* **10/1**[3]

0502 **8** *¾* **Group Therapy**[15] 3844 4-9-4 98................................ ShaneKelly 17 99
(N P Littmoden) *stdd s: hld up in midfield: hdwy over 2f out: chsd ldrs and rdn over 1f out: kpt on same pce ins fnl f* **11/1**

0011 **9** *½* **Mandurah (IRE)**[15] 3845 5-8-9 89............................ AdrianTNicholls 3 88
(D Nicholls) *chsd ldrs: rdn over 2f out: drvn and swtchd lft over 1f out: kpt on but nvr pce to rch ldrs* **7/1**[2]

2210 **10** *½* **Peak District (IRE)**[6] 4135 5-9-0 94............................ DarryllHolland 1 91
(K A Ryan) *led and sn clr: rdn and edgd rt over 1f out: hdd fnl 100yds: wknd towards fin* **14/1**

4123 **11** *¾* **The Jobber (IRE)**[17] 3784 8-8-0 85...................... Louis-PhilippeBeuzelin(5) 4 79
(M Blanshard) *wnt rt s: bhd: hdwy u.p over 1f out: no imp ins fnl f* **16/1**

0000 **12** *hd* **Tournedos (IRE)**[15] 3848 7-8-13 93.............................. DaneO'Neill 2 87
(D Nicholls) *v.s.a: wl bhd: hdwy over 1f out: kpt on u.p fnl f: nvr trbld ldrs* **20/1**

-106 **13** *1* **Fathom Five (IRE)**[15] 3844 5-9-1 95.............................. AlanMunro 10 85
(C F Wall) *hld up in midfield: hdwy jst over 2f out: rdn over 1f out: wknd jst ins fnl f* **16/1**

0000 **14** *½* **Van Bossed (CAN)**[29] 3389 4-8-6 86............................ DO'Donohoe 19 74
(D Nicholls) *chsd ldrs: rdn over 2f out: wknd ent fnl f* **25/1**

155 **15** *hd* **Misaro (GER)**[3] 4232 8-8-3 83...................................(b) LukeMorris 22 70
(R A Harris) *chsd ldrs: rdn and struggling over 2f out: drvn and wknd wl over 1f out* **25/1**

-400 **16** *1* **Safari Mischief**[23] 3582 6-8-11 91.............................. JimCrowley 20 75
(P Winkworth) *s.i.s: a in rr: rdn 2f out: no prog and nvr trbld ldrs* **20/1**

0332 **17** *1* **Legal Eagle (IRE)**[9] 4043 4-8-3 83 ow3.......................... ChrisCatlin 12 63
(Paul Green) *chsd ldrs but sn niggled along: struggling ent fnl 2f: bhd over 1f out* **12/1**

1000 **18** *5* **Piscean (USA)**[30] 3351 4-8-10 90................................ LiamJones 15 52
(T Keddy) *v.s.a and lost all ch s: nvr on terms* **18/1**

0500 **19** *1* **Green Manalishi**[15] 3848 8-9-1 95.............................. EddieAhern 14 54
(K A Ryan) *racd in midfield: rdn over 2f out: wknd over 1f out: eased whn no ch ins fnl f* **33/1**

60.15 secs (-0.35) **Going Correction** +0.175s/f (Good)
WFA 3 from 4yo+ 4lb **19** Ran SP% **134.2**
Speed ratings (Par 109): **109,108,107,107,107 106,106,104,104,103 102,101,100,99,99 97,95,87,86**
toteswingers: 1&2 £6.40, 1&3 £69.50, 2&3 £28.00 CSF £74.41 CT £716.13 TOTE £18.80: £3.50, £2.10, £3.40, £5.40; EX 98.80 TRIFECTA Not won. Place 6 £46.26, Place 5 £25.16..
Owner Mrs Ruth M Serrell **Bred** C A Cyzer **Trained** Earlswood, Monmouths

FOCUS
The big race of the day, saved until last. This was a very open sprint although there were seven non-runners including the leading fancies Befortyfour, Crimea and Sonny Red. Those drawn lowest seemed at a disadvantage. There was a bunch finish and the form makes sense.

NOTEBOOK
Judge 'n Jury enjoyed a superb second half to last season, winning five times between August and October and seeing his handicap mark rise 37lb in the process. Things had not gone his way this term, but he bounced back to form with a fairly decisive victory, giving his yard back to-back winners of this race. A smart performer when things go his way, he was able to race off 7lb lower than when last successful. He is not in the Stewards' Cup.
Hamish McGonagall has been running creditably this term without reward and he ran well again, staying on to grab second late on. The handicapper will have noted this, though. (op 6-1)
Ishetoo stayed on for third to post his best performance since pipping Peak District at York in May. (op 16-1 tchd 9-1)
Fol Hollow(IRE) did best of the four David Nicholls runners who took part (another three were taken out) and this was a good effort from the number 6 stall. He had run well at the Curragh last time considering he was unsuited by the heavy ground. (tchd 18-1)

Indian Trail has not had things go his way since winning the Vodafone Dash on Derby day but he ran a sound race here and was putting in decent late work.
Rowe Park, who threw a splint in the Palace House Stakes in May, ran well off topweight on this return.
Tony The Tap, who was fourth in this two years ago, did very well to finish where he did after missing the break badly. He is well suited by having a strong pace to chase. Official explanation: jockey said gelding was slowly away (op 11-1)
Group Therapy went up 3lb after finishing second over course-and-distance last time and that anchored him here. (op 10-1)
Mandurah(IRE), raised 7lb for this hat-trick bid, made late progress from his unfavourably low draw and remains in fine form. (op 11-2)
Peak District(IRE) showed blistering pace to lead the field nearest the stands' rail and was only headed with half a furlong to run. This is the way to ride him. (op 18-1 tchd 20-1)
Tournedos(IRE) was another to miss the break, but he was running on when it was all over and has become attractively weighted these days.
Piscean(USA) Official explanation: jockey said colt was very slowly away
T/Jkpt: Not won. T/Plt: £37.40 to a £1 stake. Pool: £144,019.59. 2,808.62 winning tickets. T/Qpdt: £21.50 to a £1 stake. Pool: £8,611.20. 296.38 winning tickets. SP

3612 CARLISLE (R-H)

Sunday, July 26

OFFICIAL GOING: Good (good to soft in places; 7.6)
Wind: Fresh, half-against. Weather: Overcast, showers

4342 STOBARTGROUP.COM MAIDEN AUCTION STKS — 5f
1:50 (1:50) (Class 5) 2-Y-O — £2,590 (£770; £385; £192) Stalls High

Form — RPR
2 **1** **Patch Patch**[38] 3058 2-8-9 0 ... PhillipMakin 3 — 71+
(M Dods) *mde all: rdn over 1f out: edgd lft and kpt on wl fnl f: comf* **6/5**[1]
044 **2** 2 1/4 **Firetrap**[10] 4011 2-8-9 0 ... PaulMulrennan 2 — 61
(Mrs A Duffield) *chsd ldrs: drvn 1/2-way: rallied and edgd rt over 1f out: kpt on same pce fnl f* **11/4**[2]
6406 **3** 3 **Lord's Seat**[38] 3058 2-8-9 0 ... TomEaves 4 — 50
(A Berry) *prom: outpcd 1/2-way: kpt on fnl f: n.d* **33/1**
4 hd **Kristen Jane (USA)** 2-8-2 0 ... JamieKyne(5) 1 — 47
(Miss L A Perratt) *wnt lft and fly j. s: bhd: effrt and rn green over 1f out: nvr able to chal* **9/1**
5 1 1/4 **Boss's Destination** 2-8-12 0 ... PJMcDonald 6 — 48+
(G A Swinbank) *green in paddock: dwlt: bhd: rdn 1/2-way: nvr rchd ldrs* **9/2**[3]
5 **6** 1 1/4 **Prince Fortune**[68] 2167 2-8-9 0 ... TonyHamilton 7 — 40
(Mrs L Stubbs) *t.k.h: w ldr tl rdn and wknd ent fnl f* **16/1**
64.52 secs (3.72) **Going Correction** +0.425s/f (Yiel) — 6 Ran SP% **109.1**
Speed ratings (Par 94): **87,83,78,78,76 74**
toteswingers: 1&2 £1.80, 1&3 £2.90, 2&3 £8.10. CSF £4.35 TOTE £2.20: £1.50, £1.80; EX 3.90.

Owner J M & Mrs E E Ranson **Bred** Mrs A M Young **Trained** Denton, Co Durham
FOCUS
This was a weak and uncompetitive maiden, but there should be more to come from the winner.
NOTEBOOK
Patch Patch, second on his debut at Musselburgh, knew more this time and was soon disputing the lead. Driven ahead over a furlong out, he stayed on well for pressure and looks likely to get an extra furlong before long. (op 5-4 tchd Evens and 11-8 in places)
Firetrap is getting a little better with each run and he stayed on to take a clear second, but was always being held by the winner. He may be the type to fare better in low-grade nurseries. (op 5-2 tchd 3-1)
Lord's Seat kept plugging away for pressure and may find an opening at a lower level. (op 28-1 tchd 40-1)
Kristen Jane(USA), who cost £19,000 at the breeze-ups, fly-jumped leaving the stalls and was soon outpaced. She ran on late, though, and should benefit from an extra furlong. (op 8-1 tchd 10-1)
Boss's Destination, a half-brother to winners at up to 1m2f, looked green beforehand and was soon outpaced following a slow start. He will benefit from more time. (op 6-1)
Prince Fortune faded having shown early speed.

4343 CFM CASH FOR KIDS H'CAP — 5f
2:25 (2:25) (Class 5) (0-70,68) 3-Y-O — £2,590 (£770; £385; £192) Stalls High

Form — RPR
-364 **1** **Scrapper Smith (IRE)**[21] 3651 3-8-10 57 ... PJMcDonald 4 — 65
(A C Whillans) *bhd tl hdwy over 1f out: led ins fnl f: styd on wl* **9/1**
4423 **2** 3/4 **Cheyenne Red (IRE)**[15] 3856 3-9-4 65 ... PhillipMakin 7 — 70
(M Dods) *hld up: hdwy 2f out: ev ch ins fnl f: r.o u.p* **11/4**[1]
0350 **3** 2 **Iachimo**[36] 3176 3-8-0 52 ... MartinLane(5) 5 — 50
(K R Burke) *t.k.h early: cl up: effrt 2f out: kpt on same pce fnl f* **16/1**
1454 **4** 1 3/4 **Angelo Poliziano**[6] 4136 3-9-7 68 ... (b[1]) SebSanders 8 — 60
(Mrs A Duffield) *cl up: led after 2f to ins fnl f: no ex* **11/4**[1]
523 **5** shd **Exceed Elegance (IRE)**[6] 4131 3-8-13 60 ... TomEaves 2 — 51
(D Shaw) *trckd ldrs: effrt 2f out: one pce fnl f* **7/2**[2]
5045 **6** 1 1/2 **Moneysupermarket (IRE)**[21] 3651 3-8-11 58 ... TonyHamilton 1 — 44
(Patrick Morris) *prom tl hung rt and no ex fr over 1f out* **18/1**
40-0 **7** 4 1/2 **Adozen Dreams**[94] 1469 3-8-3 55 ... JamieKyne(5) 6 — 25
(N Bycroft) *led 2f: cl up tl hung rt and wknd over 1f out* **40/1**
5001 **8** 2 **Lucky Dan (IRE)**[15] 3856 3-9-6 67 ... PaulMulrennan 3 — 29
(Paul Green) *in tch: outpcd 1/2-way: btn over 1f out* **5/1**[3]
62.85 secs (2.05) **Going Correction** +0.425s/f (Yiel) — 8 Ran SP% **115.8**
Speed ratings (Par 100): **100,98,95,92,92 90,83,79**
toteswingers: 1&2 £4.20, 1&3 £20.00, 2&3 £12.60. CSF £34.52 CT £397.46 TOTE £10.10: £2.20, £1.40, £3.90; EX 42.50.
Owner A C Whillans **Bred** John Costello **Trained** Newmill-On-Slitrig, Borders
FOCUS
A modest sprint handicap which was strongly run. The winner was back to his 2yo best.
Lucky Dan(IRE) Official explanation: jockey said gelding ran flat

4344 PES CLAIMING STKS — 7f 200y
3:00 (3:00) (Class 6) 3-Y-O+ — £2,047 (£604; £302) Stalls High

Form — RPR
2402 **1** **Moody Tunes**[1] 4312 6-9-4 69 ... MartinLane(5) 9 — 76
(K R Burke) *trckd ldrs: led over 1f out: styd on strly* **9/2**[3]
0430 **2** 2 1/2 **Red China Blues (USA)**[8] 3316 3-8-9 64 ... PaulMulrennan 3 — 62
(J Howard Johnson) *chsd clr ldng trio: effrt over 2f out: kpt on fnl f: nt rch wnr* **10/1**
2115 **3** nk **Rowan Lodge (IRE)**[37] 3123 7-9-9 65 ... (b) JamieMoriarty 2 — 69
(Ollie Pears) *hld up on outside: effrt over 2f out: edgd rt u.p over 1f out: r.o* **2/1**[1]
4020 **4** 2 1/4 **Hiccups**[26] 3488 9-9-5 74 ... PhillipMakin 6 — 59
(M Dods) *t.k.h: hld up: effrt over 2f out: no imp fnl f* **3/1**[2]
0600 **5** 1/2 **Portrush Storm**[15] 3864 4-8-12 58 ... (b) SebSanders 11 — 51
(D Carroll) *led tl edgd rt and hdd over 1f out: sn no ex* **9/1**
3006 **6** 2 **Ozone Trustee (NZ)**[1] 4312 5-9-3 70 ... PJMcDonald 7 — 51
(G A Swinbank) *hld up in tch: rdn 3f out: no imp fnl 2f* **8/1**
4430 **7** 3 1/2 **Pianoforte (USA)**[26] 3490 7-9-3 54 ... (b) TGMcLaughlin 4 — 42
(E J Alston) *hld up: pushed along over 2f out: nvr able to chal* **16/1**
0/ **8** 4 **Divine Design (IRE)**[18] 3754 5-8-5 0 ... (t) PatrickDonaghy(5) 10 — 25
(Seamus G O'Donnell, Ire) *dwlt: hld up: rdn and effrt over 2f out: sn wknd* **40/1**
0-00 **9** 5 **Recoil (IRE)**[31] 3314 4-9-1 42 ... (bt) TomEaves 8 — 18
(R Johnson) *chsd ldr tl hung rt and wknd over 2f out* **100/1**
0/00 **10** 3 3/4 **Beauchamp Unique**[31] 3291 6-8-11 45 ... (b[1]) TonyHamilton 1 — —
(E J Cooper) *s.i.s: bhd: struggling over 3f out: sn btn* **50/1**
1m 42.13s (2.13) **Going Correction** +0.375s/f (Good)
WFA 3 from 4yo+ 8lb — 10 Ran SP% **118.0**
Speed ratings (Par 101): **104,101,101,98,98 96,92,88,83,80**
toteswingers: 1&2 £9.80, 1&3 £3.90, 2&3 £8.00. CSF £48.99 TOTE £5.80: £1.90, £2.70, £1.40; EX 46.20.Red China Blues was claimed by Mr Brian Morton for £6,000.
Owner Geoffrey Hamilton **Bred** Llety Stud **Trained** Middleham Moor, N Yorks
FOCUS
This was quite a competitive claimer. It was strongly run and the form is sound.

4345 STOBART GROUP LADY AMATEUR RIDERS' CUMBRIAN TROPHY H'CAP — 1m 3f 107y
3:35 (3:35) (Class 4) (0-80,78) 4-Y-O+ — £6,246 (£1,937; £968; £484) Stalls Low

Form — RPR
0033 **1** **Simonside**[31] 3313 6-9-8 65 ... MissLEllison 1 — 75
(B Ellison) *enterprisingly rdn: mde all: sn clr: given breather 1/2-way: kicked clr over 2f out: styd on wl: unchal* **13/2**[3]
1 **2** 1 1/4 **Saga De Tercey (FR)**[105] 1231 4-10-7 78 ... MissSBrotherton 8 — 85
(G A Swinbank) *chsd wnr: effrt over 1f out: kpt on fnl f* **5/4**[1]
0342 **3** 2 **Casino Night**[9] 4040 4-9-13 70 ... MissADeniel 6 — 74
(F P Murtagh) *hld up: hdwy 2f out: rdn and one pce fnl f* **14/1**
2433 **4** 3 1/4 **Edas**[31] 3291 7-9-3 65 ... MissHCuthbert(5) 7 — 63
(T A K Cuthbert) *t.k.h: prom: effrt 2f out: outpcd fnl f* **8/1**
-142 **5** 1 1/4 **Ifatfirst (IRE)**[21] 3654 6-9-8 65 ... MrsCBartley 4 — 61
(J S Goldie) *hld up: rdn 3f out: no imp fnl 2f* **13/2**[3]
4 **6** 2 3/4 **Louisa (GER)**[9] 4034 5-8-11 59 oh1 ... RachelKing(5) 5 — 51
(P Monteith) *prom tl rdn and no ex fr over 2f out* **16/1**
0212 **7** 6 **Dechiper (IRE)**[29] 3393 7-10-0 71 ... MissLHorner 3 — 52
(R Johnson) *hld up: effrt over 2f out: sn btn* **5/1**[2]
0600 **8** 1 3/4 **Monfils Monfils (USA)**[30] 3350 7-9-0 62 ... MissMMullineaux(5) 2 — 41
(R E Barr) *plld hrd: in tch on outside tl wknd fr 3f out* **28/1**
2m 29.77s (6.67) **Going Correction** +0.375s/f (Good) — 8 Ran SP% **114.9**
Speed ratings (Par 105): **90,89,87,85,84 82,78,76**
toteswingers: 1&2 £5.40, 1&3 £16.40, 2&3 £4.70. CSF £15.14 CT £111.19 TOTE £8.80: £2.00, £1.20, £2.20; EX 28.00.
Owner Racing Management & Training Ltd **Bred** Keith Richardson **Trained** Norton, N Yorks
FOCUS
A typically low-grade amateur riders' handicap in which the winner made all. The form is ratest around the third.
Dechiper(IRE) Official explanation: trainer had no explanation for the poor form shown

4346 PENRITH BUILDING SUPPLIES H'CAP — 6f 192y
4:10 (4:10) (Class 5) (0-75,73) 3-Y-O+ — £3,238 (£963; £481; £240) Stalls High

Form — RPR
0006 **1** **Timber Treasure (USA)**[24] 3529 5-9-3 67 ... MartinLane(5) 12 — 76
(Paul Green) *dwlt: sn prom: rdn and led ins fnl f: r.o wl* **10/1**
5502 **2** 3/4 **Fathey (IRE)**[15] 3856 3-8-13 65 ... TonyHamilton 8 — 69
(R A Fahey) *cl up: rdn and ev ch over 1f out: kpt on fin* **4/1**[2]
3025 **3** 3/4 **Efidium**[23] 3558 11-8-10 60 ... JamieKyne(5) 11 — 65
(N Bycroft) *hld up in midfield: outpcd 3f out: rallied over 1f out: r.o* **16/1**
4411 **4** shd **Montiboli (IRE)**[20] 3689 4-9-2 68 ... (p) JamesPSullivan(7) 10 — 73
(K A Ryan) *led to ins fnl f: kpt on same pce* **5/2**[1]
3564 **5** nk **Zabeel Tower**[15] 3857 6-9-7 66 ... (p) PJMcDonald 9 — 70
(R Allan) *hld up in midfield: hdwy over 1f out: kpt on ins fnl f* **9/2**[3]
500- **6** 3 3/4 **Hartshead**[295] 6482 10-9-11 70 ... JamieMoriarty 6 — 64
(W Storey) *hld up: nt clr run over 2f out: kpt on fnl f: nvr rchd ldrs* **16/1**
244/ **7** 2 **Prime Aspiration (USA)**[636] 6544 4-9-13 72 ... TomEaves 7 — 60
(B Smart) *trckd ldrs tl edgd lft and wknd over 1f out* **10/1**
0540 **8** 1 1/2 **Fern House (IRE)**[20] 3683 7-8-2 54 oh9 ... (p) CharlotteKerton(7) 4 — 38
(Bruce Hellier) *hld up: rdn and edgd rt 2f out: sn no imp* **80/1**
-000 **9** 2 3/4 **Prospect Court**[9] 4043 7-9-1 60 ... PaulMulrennan 3 — 37
(A C Whillans) *prom tl rdn and wknd over 2f out* **28/1**
000- **10** 1 3/4 **Frill A Minute**[264] 7178 5-8-4 54 oh9 ... PatrickDonaghy(5) 5 — 26
(Miss L C Siddall) *trckd ldrs tl wknd over 2f out* **150/1**
0000 **11** nk **Major Magpie (IRE)**[22] 3615 7-10-0 73 ... PhillipMakin 1 — 44
(M Dods) *hld up: hdwy on outside 3f out: sn wknd* **6/1**
00-0 **12** 8 **Hardanger (IRE)**[15] 3863 4-8-11 56 ... TGMcLaughlin 8 — 6
(T J Fitzgerald) *plld hrd: hld up: struggling over 3f out: sn btn* **28/1**
1m 30.77s (3.67) **Going Correction** +0.375s/f (Good)
WFA 3 from 4yo+ 7lb — 12 Ran SP% **119.8**
Speed ratings (Par 103): **94,93,92,92,91 87,85,83,80,78 78,68**
toteswingers: 1&2 £8.50, 1&3 £`4.00, 2&3 £11.20. CSF £49.56 CT £498.90 TOTE £11.00: £2.40, £1.40, £4.20; EX 64.70.
Owner Gary Williams **Bred** London Thoroughbred Services & Derry Mee **Trained** Lydiate, Merseyside
FOCUS
This was an open handicap, though not that many actually got into it. The form is rated around the fourth and fifth.
Timber Treasure(USA) Official explanation: trainer's rep said, regarding apparent improvement in form, that the gelding may have benefited from no headgear.
Hardanger(IRE) Official explanation: jockey said colt slipped on bend approximately 4 1/2f out.

4347 LANSON CHAMPAGNE MAIDEN STKS — 1m 1f 61y
4:45 (4:46) (Class 5) 3-Y-O+ — £2,590 (£770; £385; £192) Stalls High

Form — RPR
-242 **1** **Visite Royale (USA)**[22] 3627 3-8-12 77 ... TomEaves 4 — 73
(Sir Michael Stoute) *in tch: hdwy to ld over 1f out: hrd pressed and edgd rt ins fnl f: hld on wl* **1/2**[1]
-324 **2** nk **Starla Dancer (GER)**[33] 3238 3-8-12 70 ... TonyHamilton 10 — 72
(R A Fahey) *trckd ldrs: effrt and ev ch fr over 1f out: kpt on fnl f: hld cl home* **10/3**[2]

3 1 **First Bay (IRE)** 3-9-3 0 .... PhillipMakin 2 76+
(J Howard Johnson) *bhd: hdwy u.p over 3f out: kpt on wl fnl f: nrst fin* **33/1**

6- 4 7 **Nakoma (IRE)**[327] 5042 7-9-0 0 .... AnthonyBetts[(7)] 7 56
(B Ellison) *missed break: bhd: effrt over 3f out: no imp fnl 2f* **33/1**

05 5 3 **Born To Perform**[31] 3294 4-9-12 0 .... PJMcDonald 13 55
(G A Swinbank) *in tch: outpcd 3f out: rallied over 1f out: no imp fnl f* **14/1**

66 6 1 3/4 **Lady Bluesky**[30] 3352 6-9-7 0 .... PaulMulrennan 5 46
(A C Whillans) *hld up: rdn over 3f out: kpt on: n.d* **20/1**

00 7 nk **Highway Code (USA)**[24] 3549 3-9-3 0 .... SebSanders 12 49
(M Johnston) *trckd ldrs: led over 3f out to over 1f out: sn btn* **8/1**[3]

6 8 7 **There We Go (IRE)**[11] 3975 3-8-12 0 .... MartinLane[(5)] 1 34
(G A Swinbank) *hld up: struggling over 3f out: nvr on terms* **40/1**

0604 9 1 3/4 **Ducal Regancy Duke**[20] 3680 5-9-9 32 .... (v[1]) LeeVickers[(3)] 6 31
(C J Teague) *led to over 3f out: sn drvn: wknd over 2f out* **100/1**

45 10 7 **Merchant Man**[24] 3531 3-9-3 0 .... JamieMoriarty 3 14
(J D Bethell) *hld up: struggling 3f out: nvr on terms* **25/1**

00-0 11 9 **Diamond Jo (IRE)**[79] 1825 3-8-5 0 .... JamesPSullivan[(7)] 8 —
(Patrick Morris) *in midfield: struggling over 3f out: sn wknd* **150/1**

0 12 1/2 **Anacot Steel (IRE)**[65] 2229 4-9-12 0 .... SJCraine 11 —
(Patrick Morris) *missed break: a bhd* **200/1**

0 13 66 **Sally O'Riley**[37] 3120 3-8-7 0 .... (p) JamieKyne[(5)] 14 —
(F Watson) *trckd ldrs tl wknd over 3f out* **150/1**

1m 59.33s (1.73) **Going Correction** +0.375s/f (Good)
WFA 3 from 4yo+ 9lb 13 Ran SP% **127.3**
Speed ratings (Par 103): **100,99,98,92,89 88,88,81,80,74 66,65,7**
toteswingers: 1&2 £2.20, 1&3 £10.10, 2&3 £12.40. CSF £2.41 TOTE £1.60: £1.02, £1.60, £7.10; EX 2.70.
Owner Mrs Elizabeth Moran **Bred** Brushwood Stable **Trained** Newmarket, Suffolk

FOCUS
This was an uncompetitive maiden and red-hot favourite Visite Royale made incredibly hard work of winning. She did not need to match her best and is rated 6lb off.

4348 "CARLISLE LIVE '09" AFTER RACING TODAY H'CAP — 1m 1f 61y
5:20 (5:20) (Class 5) (0-70,66) 3-Y-O — **£3,238** (£963; £481; £240) **Stalls High**

Form RPR

0-32 1 **Speed Dating**[8] 4079 3-9-1 60 .... SebSanders 3 72
(Sir Mark Prescott) *in tch: effrt over 2f out: drvn to ld ins fnl f: r.o wl* **11/10**[1]

4453 2 3/4 **Hypnotic Gaze (IRE)**[9] 4070 3-8-12 62 .... MartinLane[(5)] 6 72
(J Mackie) *cl up: led over 2f out to ins fnl f: kpt on u.p* **8/1**[3]

3404 3 6 **Dean Iarracht (IRE)**[8] 4079 3-9-6 65 .... TonyHamilton 1 62
(M Dods) *in midfield: drvn over 3f out: kpt on fnl f: nrst fin* **8/1**[3]

4444 4 1/2 **Veronicas Boy**[9] 4070 3-8-13 58 .... (p) PaulMulrennan 2 54
(G M Moore) *cl up: rdn over 2f out: sn one pce* **10/1**

5160 5 1 3/4 **Ask Dan (IRE)**[2] 4279 3-9-1 60 .... (p) PhillipMakin 10 53
(M Dods) *led to over 2f out: one pce over 1f out* **12/1**

4503 6 6 **Digger Derek (IRE)**[16] 3808 3-9-7 66 .... JamieMoriarty 13 46
(R A Fahey) *in tch: rdn over 3f out: outpcd fnl 2f* **5/1**[2]

4050 7 11 **Sharp Sovereign (USA)**[26] 3482 3-9-0 59 .... TomEaves 14 16
(I Semple) *in midfield: drvn over 3f out: btn fnl 2f* **12/1**

0506 8 3 **Royal Keva (IRE)**[27] 3449 3-8-3 53 .... JamieKyne[(5)] 11 4
(A D Brown) *towards rr: drvn over 3f out: nvr on terms* **25/1**

4000 9 3 1/4 **Tropical Duke (IRE)**[79] 1842 3-8-11 56 .... LeeEnstone 4 —
(R E Barr) *bhd: struggling over 3f out: nvr on terms* **33/1**

0366 10 1 1/4 **Sydney Cove (IRE)**[9] 4039 3-7-11 49 oh2 ow2 .... JamesPSullivan[(7)] 8 —
(R Allan) *hld up on outside: drvn over 3f out: sn btn* **33/1**

0-00 11 6 **Ready For Battle (IRE)**[8] 4105 3-8-4 54 .... (p) PaulPickard[(5)] 7 —
(D W Thompson) *prom tl rdn and wknd over 3f out* **100/1**

06-0 12 3 1/2 **Igneous**[27] 3449 3-7-12 50 ow3 .... DeclanCannon[(7)] 12 —
(D W Thompson) *bhd: struggling over 3f out: sn btn* **50/1**

6064 13 13 **Haulage Lady (IRE)**[22] 3614 3-8-2 52 .... (p) PatrickDonaghy[(5)] 15 —
(Karen McLintock) *hld up: rdn 4f out: nvr on terms* **25/1**

1m 58.73s (1.13) **Going Correction** +0.375s/f (Good) 13 Ran SP% **123.2**
Speed ratings (Par 100): **102,101,96,95,94 88,78,76,73,72 66,63,52**
toteswingers: 1&2 £4.00, 1&3 £4.10, 2&3 £12.50. CSF £9.95 CT £54.59 TOTE £2.00: £1.30, £2.30, £2.50; EX 11.40 Place 6 £20.55, Place 5 £17.32.
Owner Cheveley Park Stud **Bred** Cheveley Park Stud Ltd **Trained** Newmarket, Suffolk
■ Stewards' Enquiry : Seb Sanders two-day ban: used whip with excessive frequency (Aug 9-10)

FOCUS
This was only a moderate handicap but the form looks fair for the grade.
Tropical Duke(IRE) Official explanation: jockey said gelding was unsuited by the track
T/Plt: £36.00 to a £1 stake. Pool: £50,848.55. 1,029.16 winning tickets. T/Qpdt: £11.80 to a £1 stake. Pool: £3,819.26. 238.70 winning tickets. RY

4067 PONTEFRACT (L-H)
Sunday, July 26

OFFICIAL GOING: Good (good to firm in places) changing to good after race 3 (3.15)
Wind: Moderate, half-against. Weather: overcast, showers, heavy rain race 7

4349 JOHN RANSOME ACCOUNTANCY SERVICES LTD MAIDEN STKS — 5f
2:05 (2:06) (Class 4) 2-Y-O — **£4,533** (£1,348; £674; £336) **Stalls Low**

Form RPR

04 1 **Cian Rooney (IRE)**[12] 3937 2-9-3 0 .... TonyCulhane 4 74
(Mrs A Duffield) *mde all: rdn and hld on wl* **11/4**[1]

2 3/4 **Saddlers Lodge** 2-9-3 0 .... RobertWinston 9 71+
(G A Swinbank) *swvd rt s: hdwy on outside over 2f out: styd on fnl f: nt rch wnr* **11/4**[1]

050 3 1 1/4 **More Lashes (USA)**[15] 3875 2-8-12 0 .... PaulHanagan 6 62
(M G Quinlan) *chsd ldrs: kpt on same pce fnl f* **10/1**

4 1 1/4 **Little Rufus** 2-9-3 0 .... JimmyQuinn 1 62
(K A Morgan) *in rr: hdwy on ins and n.m.r over 1f out: kpt on* **20/1**

5 5 hd **Wijikura (IRE)**[12] 3937 2-9-3 0 .... GrahamGibbons 3 62
(J J Quinn) *chsd ldrs: kpt on same pce appr fnl f* **3/1**[2]

05 6 3 3/4 **Hot Rod Mamma (IRE)**[15] 3849 2-8-12 0 .... AndrewElliott 2 43+
(A Berry) *hdwy over 2f out: sn chsng ldrs: hung lft and wknd appr fnl f* **28/1**

43 7 6 **Flow Chart (IRE)**[12] 3937 2-9-3 0 .... TPO'Shea 7 26
(T D Barron) *chsd ldrs: lost pl over 1f out* **5/1**[3]

8 3 3/4 **Azzez Life** 2-8-10 0 .... JRoberts[(7)] 5 13
(R C Guest) *s.i.s: sn chsng ldrs: lost pl over 1f out: sn bhd* **100/1**

64.80 secs (1.50) **Going Correction** -0.025s/f (Good) 8 Ran SP% **113.3**
Speed ratings (Par 96): **87,85,83,81,81 75,65,59**
toteswingers: 1&2 £2.20, 1&3 £3.60, 2&3 £8.90. CSF £10.29 TOTE £3.80: £1.50, £1.40, £2.40; EX 10.90.
Owner Findlay & Bloom **Bred** Rossenarra Stud **Trained** Constable Burton, N Yorks
■ Stewards' Enquiry : Andrew Elliott caution: careless riding

FOCUS
A modest maiden. The winner, third and fifth set the level.

NOTEBOOK
Cian Rooney(IRE), who attracted market support, was given a positive ride and kept on really well to get off the mark. One would presume that he will head for nurseries now. (op 7-2 tchd 9-2)
Saddlers Lodge, who was slowly away, ran a bit green for a while but made a pleasing debut, especially as he finished to the outside of his rivals. He is bred to want further. (op 3-1 tchd 7-2)
More Lashes(USA) took a grip in the early stages, so did well to keep on to collect third. (op 9-1 tchd 8-1)
Little Rufus, who is bred to be quick, was not given a really hard time on his first start, and shaped with a degree of promise. He should progress mentally for the run. (op 16-1 tchd 12-1)
Wijikura(IRE) was a place behind the winner last time at Beverley on his debut, but failed to build on that effort significantly. (op 10-3 tchd 11-4)
Flow Chart(IRE) was well below the form he showed at Beverley last time and was disappointing. Official explanation: jockey said gelding had no more to give (op 4-1 tchd 11-2)

4350 YORKSHIRE SOCIETY H'CAP — 1m 4f 8y
2:40 (2:40) (Class 5) (0-70,70) 3-Y-O+ — **£3,885** (£1,156; £577; £288) **Stalls Low**

Form RPR

0005 1 **Sporting Gesture**[23] 3563 12-8-7 54 oh4 ow2 .... BMcHugh[(5)] 12 64
(M W Easterby) *hld up towards rr: hdwy on ins and nt clr run over 2f out: 3rd and hung lft over 1f out: styd on to ld wl ins fnl f* **20/1**

6340 2 nk **Maslak (IRE)**[24] 3521 5-10-0 70 .... TonyCulhane 11 80
(P W Hiatt) *chsd ldrs: chal over 2f out: led over 2f out: hdd and no ex last 75yds* **12/1**

2411 3 5 **Master Nimbus**[14] 3544 9-9-9 65 .... GrahamGibbons 15 67
(J J Quinn) *in tch: wnt 2nd over 2f out: fdd fnl 150yds* **9/2**[1]

0054 4 7 **Royal Flynn**[23] 3563 7-9-4 60 .... (b[1]) DanielTudhope 4 51
(Mrs K Walton) *s.i.s: hmpd bnd after 2f: hdwy over 3f out: nvr nr ldrs* **11/1**

4225 5 3/4 **Fenners (USA)**[21] 3654 6-8-10 52 oh1 .... DaleGibson 8 42
(M W Easterby) *in rr: hmpd bnd after 2f: hdwy over 4f out: nvr nr ldrs* **7/1**[3]

3011 6 nk **Forrest Flyer (IRE)**[21] 3654 5-9-10 69 .... FrederikTylicki[(3)] 14 58
(I Semple) *mid-div: drvn 3f out: nvr nr ldrs* **5/1**[2]

0035 7 5 **Applaude**[19] 3705 4-9-11 67 .... RobertWinston 5 48
(G A Swinbank) *chsd ldrs: outpcd over 2f out: sn fdd* **9/1**

6151 8 10 **Dimashq**[11] 3974 7-8-10 52 oh1 .... MickyFenton 1 17
(P T Midgley) *trckd ldrs: led 4f out: hdd over 2f out: wknd over 1f out* **8/1**

9 2 1/2 **Lady Rose Anne (IRE)**[31] 3328 4-9-12 68 .... TPO'Shea 9 29
(T D Barron) *hld up in rr: hmpd bnd after 2f: sme hdwy 4f out: sn wknd* **12/1**

/650 10 6 **King In Waiting (IRE)**[19] 3705 6-9-10 66 .... JimmyQuinn 2 18
(J Hetherton) *chsd ldrs: drvn over 4f out: sn wknd* **33/1**

5434 11 7 **Cripsey Brook**[24] 3544 11-8-9 54 .... MichaelJStainton[(3)] 3 —
(K G Reveley) *s.i.s: in rr whn hmpd bnd after 2f: sn drvn along: nvr on terms* **8/1**

2034 12 62 **Merrion Tiger (IRE)**[21] 3654 4-9-6 62 .... (b[1]) PatCosgrave 7 —
(A G Foster) *t.k.h: led tl 4f out: wknd qckly: sn wl t.o: virtually p.u* **14/1**

0/0- 13 58 **Northerner (IRE)**[309] 6115 6-8-11 58 oh7 ow6 .... JamesO'Reilly[(5)] 10 —
(J O'Reilly) *chsd ldrs: drvn over 5f out: lost pl over 4f out: sn t.o: virtually p.u* **66/1**

2m 37.38s (-3.42) **Going Correction** -0.025s/f (Good) 13 Ran SP% **119.2**
Speed ratings (Par 103): **110,109,106,101,101 101,97,91,89,85 80,39,—**
toteswingers: 1&2 £12.90, 1&3 £13.30, 2&3 £9.80. CSF £238.72 CT £1283.49 TOTE £23.90: £5.10, £4.20, £2.50; EX 167.90.
Owner Steve Hull **Bred** C C Bromley And Son **Trained** Sheriff Hutton, N Yorks

FOCUS
A really wide range of abilities were on show for this handicap, so the form is difficult to assess accurately. The winner was wrong in the weights but the form has been rated at face value.
King In Waiting(IRE) Official explanation: jockey said gelding had no more to give
Merrion Tiger(IRE) Official explanation: jockey said gelding ran too free

4351 GRAHAM ROCK MEMORIAL H'CAP — 1m 2f 6y
3:15 (3:16) (Class 5) (0-70,69) 3-Y-O+ — **£3,885** (£1,156; £577; £288) **Stalls Low**

Form RPR

5040 1 **Castlebury (IRE)**[30] 3354 4-9-5 60 .... RobertWinston 4 67
(G A Swinbank) *trckd ldrs: led over 1f out: hdd 1f out: kpt on to ld last 50yds: all out* **5/1**[2]

-003 2 nk **Pitbull**[9] 4046 6-9-1 56 .... (p) JimmyQuinn 8 62
(Mrs G S Rees) *dwlt: t.k.h in rr: hdwy 5f out: plld wd over 2f out: slt ld 1f out: hung lft: hdd wl ins fnl f* **11/2**[3]

-233 3 1 1/4 **Dontpaytheferryman (USA)**[134] 377 4-8-10 51 .... PaulHanagan 2 55
(R A Fahey) *led tl over 2f out: kpt on same pce fnl f* **11/8**[1]

-060 4 shd **Royal Fantasy (IRE)**[24] 3545 6-9-4 62 .... (p) KellyHarrison[(3)] 9 66
(N Tinkler) *hld up in rr: hdwy on ins and nt clr run over 1f out: styd on fnl f* **40/1**

0620 5 3/4 **Ming Vase**[27] 3450 7-8-9 50 .... MickyFenton 6 52
(P T Midgley) *hld up in rr: effrt 2f out: styd on fnl f* **17/2**

60-5 6 4 1/2 **Noche De Reyes**[47] 2789 4-8-13 54 .... PatCosgrave 1 47
(E J Alston) *t.k.h: sn chsng ldrs: effrt over 3f out: wknd over 1f out* **12/1**

030B 7 7 **All In The Red (IRE)**[13] 3911 4-9-11 69 .... (p) FrederikTylicki[(3)] 7 48
(A Crook) *in rr: hdwy on outside over 5f out: sn chsng ldrs: wknd over 1f out* **10/1**

0-00 8 2 3/4 **Kaiser Willie (IRE)**[48] 1416 3-7-13 50 .... NickyMackay 5 24
(B W Duke) *chsd ldrs: lost pl over 1f out* **20/1**

0-00 9 63 **Rainbow Zest**[100] 1332 6-9-3 58 .... GrahamGibbons 3 —
(W Storey) *prom: lost pl 3f out: bhd whn eased over 1f out: sn t.o: virtually p.u* **14/1**

2m 14.02s (0.32) **Going Correction** -0.025s/f (Good)
WFA 3 from 4yo+ 10lb 9 Ran SP% **115.3**
Speed ratings (Par 103): **97,96,95,95,95 91,85,83,33**
toteswingers: 1&2 £4.80, 1&3 £2.50, 2&3 £1.10. CSF £32.57 CT £57.21 TOTE £6.20: £2.20, £1.80, £1.10; EX 32.10.
Owner Mrs V McGee & A Butler **Bred** Miss Nicola Ann Adams **Trained** Melsonby, N Yorks

FOCUS
None of those that had run recently looked to be in any sort of form, so this was a very modest event, but it produced a thrilling finish. The winner was close to his best.

4352 SKY BET SUPPORTING THE YORKSHIRE RACING FESTIVAL POMFRET STKS (LISTED RACE) 1m 4y
3:50 (3:50) (Class 1) 3-Y-0+
£25,546 (£9,684; £4,846; £2,416; £1,210; £607) **Stalls** Low

Form RPR
-410 **1** **Khateeb (IRE)**[37] 3089 4-9-1 108 (t) TPO'Shea 7 112
(M A Jarvis) *trckd ldrs: wnt 2nd over 2f out: drvn to ld appr fnl f: ducked lft ins fnl f: styd on wl* **13/2**
4-30 **2** *1 ¾* **Orizaba (IRE)**[40] 2992 3-8-7 108 AhmedAjtebi 3 106
(Saeed Bin Suroor) *led: qcknd over 2f out: hdd appr fnl f: styd on same pce* **15/8**[1]
002 **3** *¾* **Perks (IRE)**[10] 4002 4-9-1 104 JimmyQuinn 5 106
(J L Dunlop) *dwlt: sn trckd ldrs: styd on same pce fnl f* **4/1**[3]
0101 **4** *hd* **Dream Lodge (IRE)**[10] 4002 5-9-1 105 PaulHanagan 2 106
(R A Fahey) *chsd ldrs: effrt over 2f out: kpt on same pce* **11/4**[2]
0-03 **5** *2 ¾* **Appalachian Trail (IRE)**[8] 4077 8-9-1 102 FrederikTylicki 1 99
(I Semple) *hld up in rr: effrt over 2f out: nvr nr ldrs* **25/1**
0014 **6** *4* **Charlie Cool**[29] 3399 6-9-1 99 AndrewElliott 6 90
(Mrs R A Carr) *hld up in rr: effrt over 2f out: nvr a factor* **20/1**
00-0 **7** *9* **Supaseus**[171] 417 6-9-1 108 RobertWinston 8 68
(H Morrison) *chsd ldr: drvn over 2f out: lost pl over 1f out* **11/1**
0-00 **8** *3 ½* **Rosabee (IRE)**[18] 3746 3-8-6 99 ow4 EdwardCreighton 10 57
(Mrs D J Sanderson) *in rr: drvn 5f out: lost pl over 2f out* **66/1**
-030 **9** *7* **Courageous (IRE)**[57] 2500 3-8-7 100 RichardMullen 9 41
(B Smart) *t.k.h in rr: hdwy 3f out: hung lft and lost pl 2f out* **22/1**

1m 43.43s (-2.47) **Going Correction** -0.025s/f (Good)
WFA 3 from 4yo+ 8lb **9** Ran SP% **117.6**
Speed ratings (Par 111): **111,109,108,108,105 101,92,89,82**
toteswingers: 1&2 £2.30, 1&3 £1.90, 2&3 £1.50. CSF £18.75 TOTE £8.10: £2.20, £1.60, £1.10; EX 23.50.
Owner Hamdan Al Maktoum **Bred** Kilfrush Stud **Trained** Newmarket, Suffolk

FOCUS
This looked by far the most competitive renewal of this Listed race, being run for the third time. Hardly any of them could be ruled out with any degree of confidence, and the lowest rated of the nine runners was rated 95. That said, the form is fairly ordinary for the grade.

NOTEBOOK
Khateeb(IRE) was disappointing over further last time, but he bounced right back to his best over 1m here. Given a good ride by his jockey, he was produced to get to the front 1f out and, despite wandering a little, won by a comfortable margin. (tchd 6-1)
Orizaba(IRE) was taking a significant drop in class for this and had the run of the race. His rider steadily increased the tempo and got the rest of the field beaten except for Khateeb. This is probably his level now. (op 9-4 tchd 5-2)
Perks(IRE) looked a big danger when making a bid over 1f out, but he seemed to hang towards the inside rail under pressure. (op 10-3)
Dream Lodge(IRE) kept on but was never quite getting on terms and couldn't confirm recent Doncaster placings with Perks. (op 9-2)
Courageous(IRE) Official explanation: jockey said colt ran too free

4353 TOLENT CONSTRUCTION H'CAP (SPONSORED BY AMBITEMP) 6f
4:25 (4:25) (Class 3) (0-90,91) 3-Y-0+
£9,346 (£2,799; £1,399; £700; £349; £175) **Stalls** Low

Form RPR
6035 **1** **Sunrise Safari (IRE)**[16] 3825 6-9-1 82 (v) FrederikTylicki(3) 13 94
(R A Fahey) *in rr: plld wdst of all 2f out: str run to ld last 50yds: won gng away* **13/2**[2]
4200 **2** *1 ¼* **Harrison George (IRE)**[15] 3877 4-9-10 88 PaulHanagan 2 96
(R A Fahey) *in rr: drvn and hdwy over 2f out: chal ins fnl f: no ex* **7/2**[1]
5012 **3** *¾* **Barons Spy (IRE)**[16] 3802 8-9-9 87 JamesDoyle 12 93
(R J Price) *chsd ldrs: led over 1f out: hdd wl ins fnl f: kpt on same pce* **20/1**
1041 **4** *3 ¼* **Dancing Maite**[43] 2938 4-9-3 84 RussellKennemore(3) 6 80+
(S R Bowring) *w ldrs: led over 2f out: hdd over 1f out: fdd ins fnl f* **12/1**
2240 **5** *shd* **Daaweitza**[2] 4285 6-9-0 78 J-PGuillambert 1 76+
(B Ellison) *sn last and drvn along: hdwy 2f out: nt clr run 1f out: styd on wl towards fin* **18/1**
4003 **6** *1* **Spitfire**[16] 3795 4-9-11 89 RobertWinston 9 81
(J R Jenkins) *s.i.s: effrt and swtchd lft 2f out: kpt on: nvr nr ldrs* **8/1**[3]
2111 **7** *1 ¼* **C'Mon You Irons (IRE)**[9] 4072 4-9-1 79 IanMongan 4 67
(M R Hoad) *chsd ldrs: wknd appr fnl f* **7/2**[1]
2550 **8** *2* **Wyatt Earp (IRE)**[15] 3877 8-9-3 81 DaleGibson 3 63
(P Salmon) *mid-div: effrt over 2f out: lost pl over 1f out* **20/1**
4123 **9** *½* **Red Cape (FR)**[16] 3825 6-9-3 81 AndrewElliott 11 61
(Mrs R A Carr) *chsd ldrs: wknd over 1f out* **10/1**
0003 **10** *1 ½* **Quiet Elegance**[8] 4096 4-9-1 79 JimmyQuinn 14 54
(E J Alston) *hld up in rr: effrt 2f out: sn rdn and wknd* **16/1**
3010 **11** *1* **Bel Cantor**[18] 3738 6-8-12 79 (p) KellyHarrison(3) 5 51
(W J H Ratcliffe) *led tl over 2f out: lost pl over 1f out* **12/1**
0000 **12** *7* **Northern Fling**[30] 3351 5-9-7 85 TonyCulhane 15 35
(D Nicholls) *chsd ldrs: lost pl over 2f out* **20/1**

1m 16.36s (-0.54) **Going Correction** -0.025s/f (Good) **12** Ran SP% **118.8**
Speed ratings (Par 107): **102,100,99,95,94 93,91,89,88,86 85,75**
toteswingers: 1&2 £7.60, 1&3 £29.90, 2&3 £18.40. CSF £28.53 CT £431.00 TOTE £7.10: £2.40, £1.90, £4.20; EX 33.30.
Owner Timeform Betfair Racing Club Ltd **Bred** Mervyn Stewkesbury **Trained** Musley Bank, N Yorks
■ Stewards' Enquiry : Frederik Tylicki caution: used whip with excessive frequency

FOCUS
A decent handicap, and solid form. The early pace was frenetic, which really helped the winner.

NOTEBOOK
Sunrise Safari(IRE) had gone a long time without success and you would have wanted very long odds at halfway that he was going to collect here, but as the pace faltered up front, he came with a strong finish down the middle of the course to win nicely. (op 9-1)
Harrison George(IRE), a stablemate of the winner, did everything right to get past the third, but never saw the winner coming. (op 3-1 tchd 5-2)
Barons Spy(IRE) gradually worked his way into the race and appeared to run up to form. (tchd 25-1)
Dancing Maite, one of the early pacesetters, held an advantage over 1f out, but could not sustain his momentum. (op 11-1 tchd 14-1)
Daaweitza, much like the winner, struggled in the early stages but got going up the hill, and went past plenty of tired rivals. Official explanation: jockey said gelding was denied a clear run (op 20-1)
Spitfire did not look the easiest ride when his jockey manoeuvred him through rivals. (op 9-1 tchd 10-1)
C'Mon You Irons(IRE), chasing a four-timer, was settled in behind the three leaders and ran like a horse high enough in the handicap now. (op 4-1)

4354 RALPH ROBINSON MEMORIAL MAIDEN STKS 1m 4y
5:00 (5:01) (Class 5) 3-4-Y-0 **£3,238** (£963; £481; £240) **Stalls** Low

Form RPR
4 **1** **Clientele (USA)**[10] 4014 3-9-3 0 GregFairley 13 82+
(M Johnston) *mde all: rdn and styd on strly fnl 2f: readily* **5/2**[2]
630 **2** *2 ½* **Reportage (USA)**[18] 3751 3-9-3 74 NickyMackay 1 73
(J H M Gosden) *hdwy 5f out: sn chsng ldrs: wnt 2nd ins fnl f: no imp* **9/2**[3]
3 *½* **Laureldeans Best (IRE)** 3-8-12 0 PaulHanagan 12 67+
(R A Fahey) *in rr: hdwy over 2f out: styd on wl ins fnl f: improve* **7/1**
0- **4** *2 ½* **Dance Card**[282] 6791 4-9-6 0 (t) PatCosgrave 7 63
(A G Foster) *chsd wnr: kpt on same pce appr fnl f* **33/1**
5 *1* **Tripbiyah (USA)** 3-9-3 0 RobertWinston 6 64
(G A Swinbank) *chsd ldrs: rdn: hung lft and carried hd awkwardly over 2f out: one pce* **20/1**
-323 **6** *nk* **Merdaam**[53] 2613 3-9-3 80 TPO'Shea 2 63
(J L Dunlop) *swvd rt s: chsd ldrs: rdn over 2f out: kpt on one pce* **7/4**[1]
5-36 **7** *13* **Rascal In The Mix (USA)**[36] 3175 3-8-12 0 J-PGuillambert 3 28
(R M Whitaker) *in rr: sn drvn along: hdwy 3f out: nvr on terms* **20/1**
00 **8** *1* **Angels And Demons (IRE)**[4] 4196 3-8-5 0 AndrewHeffernan(7) 9 26
(Garry Moss) *mid-div: sme hdwy over 2f out: nvr a factor* **66/1**
06- **9** *3 ¼* **K'Gari (USA)**[347] 4968 3-8-12 0 LanceBetts(5) 5 24
(B Ellison) *bhd and drvn along: sme hdwy 2f out: nvr on terms* **40/1**
50 **10** *12* **Rose Avelina**[20] 3690 3-8-12 0 PatrickMathers 4 —
(I W McInnes) *in rr: nvr on terms* **100/1**
00- **11** *5* **High Tensile**[282] 6789 3-8-12 0 MickyFenton 10 —
(J G Given) *in rr: rn wd bnd after 2f: bhd fnl 3f* **80/1**
06 **12** *2* **Two Tone**[24] 3531 3-9-3 0 JamesDoyle 8 —
(G Woodward) *mid-div: lost pl 3f out* **100/1**
0 **13** *20* **Skybob**[11] 3975 3-9-3 0 IanMongan 15 —
(D W Thompson) *in tch: lost pl over 3f out: t.o 2f out* **80/1**
14 *3* **Slumdog (IRE)** 4-9-6 0 MarkCoumbe(5) 14 —
(Garry Moss) *t.k.h in midfield: lost pl 4f out: t.o 2f out* **66/1**

1m 45.57s (-0.33) **Going Correction** -0.025s/f (Good)
WFA 3 from 4yo 8lb **14** Ran SP% **118.0**
Speed ratings (Par 103): **100,97,97,94,93 93,80,79,75,63 58,56,36,33**
toteswingers: 1&2 £3.40, 1&3 £4.20, 2&3 £5.80. CSF £12.85 TOTE £3.30: £1.60, £1.70, £2.60; EX 14.50.
Owner Sheikh Hamdan Bin Mohammed Al Maktoum **Bred** Liberation Farm, Oratis & Cho Llc **Trained** Middleham Moor, N Yorks

FOCUS
A fair maiden for the track and time of year and the winner looks above average.
Tripbiyah(USA) Official explanation: jockey said gelding ran green
Merdaam Official explanation: jockey said colt never travelled

4355 BARNEY AND MICHAEL BRENNAN MEMORIAL H'CAP 5f
5:30 (5:31) (Class 5) (0-70,70) 3-Y-0+ **£3,238** (£963; £481; £240) **Stalls** Low

Form RPR
0324 **1** **Hotham**[2] 4285 6-9-4 68 BMcHugh(5) 6 75+
(N Wilson) *dwlt: gd hdwy on wd outside over 1f out: fin fast to ld last stride* **3/1**[1]
2625 **2** *shd* **La Capriosa**[17] 3765 3-9-0 63 RobertWinston 4 69+
(J A Glover) *led: kpt on gamely fnl f: hdd post* **13/2**[3]
5420 **3** *1* **Monte Cassino (IRE)**[19] 3720 4-8-11 61 oh5 ow10.. JamesO'Reilly(5) 8 64
(J O'Reilly) *s.i.s: gd hdwy on ins 2f out: upsides ins fnl f: no ex* **25/1**
0600 **4** *2 ½* **Lord Of The Reins (IRE)**[16] 3828 5-9-11 70 PatCosgrave 7 64+
(J G Given) *mid-div: hdwy over 1f out: kpt on ins fnl f: nt rch ldrs* **20/1**
3050 **5** *¾* **Rio Sands**[19] 3713 4-8-10 58 MichaelJStainton(3) 1 49
(R M Whitaker) *chsd ldrs on ins: one pce fnl 2f* **25/1**
3550 **6** *hd* **Miss Daawe**[2] 4283 5-8-9 59 (t) LanceBetts(5) 10 50
(B Ellison) *chsd ldrs: fdd appr fnl f* **6/1**[2]
0150 **7** *nk* **Foreign Rhythm (IRE)**[12] 3938 4-8-3 51 oh3 KellyHarrison(3) 2 41
(N Tinkler) *chsd ldrs: one pce fnl 2f* **40/1**
5634 **8** *¾* **Comptonspirit**[23] 3591 5-9-2 61 J-PGuillambert 13 48
(B P J Baugh) *w ldrs on outer: wknd over 1f out* **9/1**
003 **9** *nk* **Darcy's Pride (IRE)**[12] 3938 5-8-10 55 (t) MickyFenton 9 41
(P T Midgley) *in rr: hdwy on ins over 1f out: nvr on terms* **9/1**
0435 **10** *3* **Spirit Of Coniston**[27] 3445 6-8-7 52 DuranFentiman 11 27
(P T Midgley) *chsd ldrs: wknd over 1f out* **20/1**
1400 **11** *nk* **Only A Game (IRE)**[10] 3999 4-8-13 58 (p) DanielTudhope 14 32
(I W McInnes) *w ldrs on outer: lost pl over 1f out* **33/1**
4322 **12** *1* **Select Committee**[6] 4141 4-8-13 58 (v) GrahamGibbons 12 28
(J J Quinn) *mid-div: effrt on outer over 2f out: hung lft over 1f out: wknd and eased ins fnl f* **3/1**[1]
4656 **13** *1 ¼* **Yungaburra (IRE)**[23] 3562 5-9-6 65 (p) PaulHanagan 15 31
(J Balding) *stmbld s: a bhd* **20/1**

63.82 secs (0.52) **Going Correction** -0.025s/f (Good)
WFA 3 from 4yo+ 4lb **13** Ran SP% **125.0**
Speed ratings (Par 103): **94,93,92,88,87 86,86,85,84,79 79,77,75**
toteswingers: 1&2 £2.90, 1&3 £19.70, 2&3 £22.30. CSF £21.58 CT £431.81 TOTE £3.80: £1.40, £2.60, £6.50; EX 20.70 Place 6 £25.70, Place 5 £15.63..
Owner Far 2 Many Sues **Bred** Capt J H Wilson **Trained** Flaxton, N Yorks
■ Stewards' Enquiry : Robert Winston one-day ban: used whip with excessive frequency (Aug 9)

FOCUS
This was run in driving rain, but that did not stop the leaders going off at a good clip. Trciky form to rate, with the third not helping things.
Yungaburra(IRE) Official explanation: jockey said gelding stumbled at start
T/Plt: £45.90 to a £1 stake. Pool: £67,026.63. 1,064.14 winning tickets. T/Qpdt: £7.40 to a £1 stake. Pool: £4,955.88. 491.00 winning tickets. WG

4356 - (Foreign Racing) - See Raceform Interactive

3893 CURRAGH (R-H)
Sunday, July 26

OFFICIAL GOING: Heavy

4357a GRANGECON STUD STKS (LISTED RACE) 5f
2:40 (2:40) 2-Y-0 **£28,441** (£8,344; £3,975; £1,354)

RPR
1 **Arctic (IRE)**[24] 3553 2-9-1 PShanahan 1 108+
(Tracey Collins, Ire) *mde all: qcknd clr fr over 1f out: r.o strly: impressive* **11/4**[2]

2 5 **Sole Power**[29] 3410 2-9-1 .... PJSmullen 3 90
(Edward Lynam, Ire) *sn cl up in 2nd: rdn and outpcd fr over 1f out: same pce ins fnl f* **7/4**[1]
3 1 1/2 **Velvet Flicker (IRE)**[10] 4028 2-8-12 98.................... DPMcDonogh 4 82
(Kevin Prendergast, Ire) *hld up in 5th: rdn over 1 1/2f out: mod 4th 1f out: kpt on same pce* **8/1**
4 nk **Dream Deer**[14] 3902 2-9-1 95.................................. WJSupple 2 84
(P D Deegan, Ire) *settled 4th: rdn 1 1/2f out: mod 3rd under 1f out: one pce* **7/2**[3]
5 2 1/2 **Dancing Red Devil (IRE)**[16] 3805 2-8-12 .... FMBerry 6 72
(Paul Green) *in rr: rdn bef 1/2-way: no ex fr 2f out* **6/1**
6 1 3/4 **Rigid Rock (IRE)**[15] 3884 2-9-1 78..................................... KJManning 5 69
(J T Gorman, Ire) *chsd ldrs in 3rd: rdn 1/2-way: no ex fr under 2f out* **25/1**

65.09 secs (4.39) **Going Correction** +0.95s/f (Soft) **6** Ran SP% **114.5**
Speed ratings: **102,94,91,91,87 84**
CSF £8.25 TOTE £3.30: £1.90, £1.80; DF 8.60.
Owner R A Pegum **Bred** Darley **Trained** The Curragh, Co Kildare

NOTEBOOK
Dancing Red Devil(IRE) found this all too hot and likely failed to act on the ground. (op 7/1)

4359a CAMAS PARK & ASHTOWN HOUSE PHOENIX STKS (GROUP 1) (ENTIRE COLTS & FILLIES) 6f

3:40 (3:41) 2-Y-O
£126,747 (£41,553; £19,708; £6,601; £4,417; £2,233)

RPR
1 **Alfred Nobel (IRE)**[28] 3436 2-9-1 110.................................. JMurtagh 3 113+
(A P O'Brien, Ire) *hld up in rr: 6th and hdwy on outer over 1f out: 2nd wl ins fnl f: sn rdn to chal: r.o strly to ld cl home* **5/4**[1]
2 1/2 **Air Chief Marshal (IRE)**[14] 3895 2-9-1 94........................... JPO'Brien 4 110
(A P O'Brien, Ire) *cl up: led 1/2-way: rdn and edgd clr 2f out: strly pressed wl ins fnl f: hdd cl home* **33/1**
3 2 1/2 **Walk On Bye (IRE)**[14] 3895 2-8-12 .... WMLordan 6 99
(T Stack, Ire) *hld up towards rr: 7th 1/2-way: prog into 4th under 1 1/2f out: kpt on u.p* **11/8**[2]
4 1/2 **In Some Respect (IRE)**[28] 3436 2-9-1 .... PJSmullen 8 101
(Andrew Oliver, Ire) *cl 4th: 3rd and chal 2f out: 2nd under 1 1/2f out: no imp u.p ins fnl f: kpt on* **16/1**
5 1/2 **Beethoven (IRE)**[14] 3895 2-9-1 .... CO'Donoghue 5 99
(A P O'Brien, Ire) *trckd ldrs in 5th: prog into 3rd over 1f out: no imp ins fnl f* **12/1**[3]
6 2 1/2 **King Ledley (USA)**[14] 3895 2-9-1 107...........................(b) DPMcDonogh 2 92
(Kevin Prendergast, Ire) *chsd ldrs in 6th: rdn and no imp fr 2f out* **12/1**[3]
7 6 **Rock Jock (IRE)**[28] 3436 2-9-1 .... PShanahan 7 74
(Tracey Collins, Ire) *prom in 3rd: 2nd 2f out: sn wknd u.p* **20/1**
8 28 **Reggae Dancer (IRE)**[4] 4213 2-9-1 77.................................. SMLevey 1 —
(A P O'Brien, Ire) *led to 1/2-way: wknd qckly and eased: t.o* **100/1**

1m 20.32s (5.62) **Going Correction** +0.95s/f (Soft) **8** Ran SP% **116.5**
Speed ratings: **100,99,96,95,94 91,83,46**
CSF £48.83 TOTE £2.30: £1.10, £7.10, £1.20; DF 37.80.
Owner Derrick Smith **Bred** Lodge Park Stud **Trained** Ballydoyle, Co Tipperary
■ Aidan O'Brien's tenth win in the last 11 runnings of this race.

FOCUS
It's tricky to know how good the winner is as the time was poor and the runner-up has shown surprising improvement after looking exposed as well below this level. The fourth and fifth offer hope that the form will be okay, though.

NOTEBOOK
Alfred Nobel(IRE) was ridden like a good horse and passed the test in what wasn't the strongest renewal of this contest. Tracking his main market rival, Murtagh had to get really serious when it became obvious that one was starting to struggle, and pulled towards the outside. He quickened and sustained his run all the way to the line to get up close home. Whereas the bare form doesn't add up to a huge amount, the way the victory was achieved shouldn't be underestimated and he is undoubtedly an improving colt. However, stiffer tests await. (op 11/10 tchd 11/8)
Air Chief Marshal(IRE) responded positively around halfway to take a few lengths out of the remainder of the field and was only worn down close home. He had looked reasonably well exposed prior to this, so his proximity to the winner on face value doesn't lend the form a strong look, but this does look to be a much-improved effort.
Walk On Bye(IRE) had her limitations exposed to an extent, but there are still good races to be won with her. Held up off the pace, she did make some progress once asked for her effort inside the two furlong pole but was rather one-paced in doing so and she just kept on through beaten horses. (op 5/4 tchd 6/4)
In Some Respect(IRE) is still a maiden but won't remain so for very much longer. He raced prominently towards the outside of the field and was still travelling two furlongs out but could not find what was required. It was still a decent performance.

4360a SYCAMORE LODGE EQUINE HOSPITAL H'CAP 6f

4:10 (4:10) 3-Y-O+ £9,727 (£2,266; £999; £577)

RPR
1 **Invincible Force (IRE)**[79] 1821 5-9-2 82...........................(b) FMBerry 15 99+
(Paul Green) *mde all: clr to over 1f out: kpt on wl whn pressed ins fnl f* **13/2**[3]
2 1 3/4 **Daring Man (IRE)**[7] 4122 4-8-13 79............................(t) CO'Donoghue 14 88
(M J P O'Brien, Ire) *mid-div: hdwy into 5th after 1/2-way: mod 2nd under 1 1/2f out: chal ins fnl f: kpt on u.p* **12/1**
3 3 1/2 **Luisant**[8] 4108 6-9-10 90.. MJKinane 5 88
(J A Nash, Ire) *hld up: 11th and hdwy 2f out: 6th over 1f out: kpt on* **14/1**
4 nk **Irish Heartbeat (IRE)**[16] 3829 4-9-4 84................................ JMurtagh 9 81
(David P Myerscough, Ire) *prom: 2nd 1/2-way: rdn and no imp fr 2f out: kpt on same pce* **9/2**[1]
5 5 **Majestic Times (IRE)**[14] 3898 9-8-9 80...........................(b) DEMullins(5) 4 61
(Liam McAteer, Ire) *hld up: rdn over 2f out: mod 8th 1 1/2f out: kpt on* **10/1**
6 1 1/2 **Pax Soprana (IRE)**[15] 3880 3-8-9 80............................... NGMcCullagh 13 55
(Edward P Harty, Ire) *trckd ldrs: 4th 1/2-way: rdn over 2f out: one pce* **8/1**
7 1 3/4 **Hazelwood Ridge (IRE)**[15] 3880 6-7-13 70 oh13.................. BACurtis(5) 7 41
(James Bernard McCabe, Ire) *chsd ldrs: rdn over 2f out: mod 7th and no ex fr over 1f out* **25/1**
8 5 **First In Command (IRE)**[17] 3787 4-8-10 81....................(t) GFCarroll(5) 12 36
(Daniel Mark Loughnane, Ire) *trckd ldrs: 3rd 1/2-way: sn rdn: no ex fr under 2f out* **6/1**[2]
9 2 1/2 **Whiteball Wonder (IRE)**[15] 3880 3-8-6 77.......................(p) RPCleary 3 23
(M Halford, Ire) *4th early: 6th after 1/2-way: no ex fr 2f out* **8/1**
10 1 **Fit The Cove (IRE)**[8] 4108 9-9-1 81..............................(t) WJSupple 6 25
(H Rogers, Ire) *prom early: 3rd bef 1/2-way: no ex fr 2 1/2f out* **9/1**
11 4 1/2 **Cihangir (IRE)**[14] 3898 4-9-3 83... PJSmullen 11 12
(D K Weld, Ire) *in rr of mid-div: no imp fr over 2f out* **12/1**
12 1 **Scalded Cat (IRE)**[51] 2688 6-8-4 70 oh23.............................. WMLordan 8 —
(Sean P Hennessy, Ire) *a bhd* **50/1**
13 3/4 **Kingsdale Ocean (IRE)**[16] 3829 6-9-5 88.....................(b) SMGorey(3) 10 12
(D K Weld, Ire) *chsd ldrs on far side to 1/2-way: wknd over 2f out* **16/1**
14 1 1/2 **Toasted Special (USA)**[63] 2308 4-8-12 78................................ KLatham 2 —
(W McCreery, Ire) *towards rr on stand's side: rdn 1/2-way: no ex fr 2f out* **20/1**
15 9 **Gunga Din (IRE)**[8] 4108 5-9-7 92...................................(b) ShaneFoley(5) 1 —
(A Kinsella, Ire) *sn trailing in rr: eased fr over 1f out* **16/1**

1m 17.17s (2.47) **Going Correction** +0.95s/f (Soft)
WFA 3 from 4yo+ 5lb **15** Ran SP% **131.5**
Speed ratings: **121,118,114,113,106 104,102,95,92,91 85,83,82,80,68**
CSF £88.10 CT £1118.48 TOTE £8.30: £1.90, £4.90, £3.80; DF 130.30.
Owner Terry Cummins **Bred** Robert Wilson **Trained** Lydiate, Merseyside

FOCUS
The winner is a very useful sort on soft ground and has been rated close to his 2008 best.

NOTEBOOK
Invincible Force(IRE) was well backed and made all for a determined success. He relishes soft ground and his form figures over this course and distance now read 1211. He could well return here before the season's end. Official explanation: trainer's assistant said, regarding the apparent improvement of form, that there had been a bug in the stable, during that time their horses had been running badly; the horses now appeared healthier and had returned to form (op 7/1)

4361 - 4362a (Foreign Racing) - See Raceform Interactive

2954 COLOGNE (R-H)

Sunday, July 26

OFFICIAL GOING: Good

4363a SILBERNE PEITSCHE (GROUP 3) 6f 110y

4:20 (4:37) 3-Y-O+ £31,068 (£9,709; £4,854; £2,913)

RPR
1 **Contat (GER)**[22] 3650 6-9-5 .... RJuracek 10 103
(P Vovcenko, Germany) *prom: 2nd 1/2-way: led over 2f out: rdn and r.o fr over 1f out: drvn out* **19/5**[2]
2 3/4 **Zaya (GER)**[36] 4-9-2 .... SHellyn 2 98
(A Wohler, Germany) *towards rr of mid-div: effrt and r.o fr over 1 1/2f out: fin strly and sn 2nd ins fnl fur;ong: nrest at fin* **71/1**
3 shd **Muriel (IRE)**[49] 2757 3-8-9 .... JiriPalik 1 96
(Andreas Lowe, Germany) *towards rr: r.o wl fr over 1f out: jst missed 2nd* **197/10**
4 1 **Lips Arrow (GER)**[22] 3650 4-9-2 .... AGoritz 6 95
(Andreas Lowe, Germany) *prom: 3rd st: drvn 2f out: kpt on steadily* **58/10**
5 1 1/4 **Sarabia (GER)**[43] 3-8-9 .... EPedroza 5 89
(A Wohler, Germany) *hld up: pushed along on ins 2f out: styd on at one pce fr 1 1/2f out: n.d* **124/10**
6 1 3/4 **Tertio Bloom (SWE)**[34] 3231 4-9-5 .... FJohansson 8 89
(F Reuterskiold, Sweden) *hld up: pushed along st: n.d* **112/10**
7 3/4 **Key To Pleasure (GER)**[22] 3650 9-9-5 .... WMongil 3 87
(Mario Hofer, Germany) *prom: 4th st: sn drvn and one pce* **106/10**
8 hd **Lukrecia (IRE)**[49] 2757 3-8-9 .... AStarke 7 82
(P Schiergen, Germany) *mid-div: n.d* **39/10**[3]
9 2 1/2 **Trajano (USA)**[57] 2513 4-9-5 ....(b) JLermyte 9 79
(T Callejo-Solana, Spain) *led 1 1/2f: 5th st: one pce* **8/5**[1]
10 1 1/2 **Florentiner (GER)**[16] 6-9-5 .... ADeVries 4 75
(A Trybuhl, Germany) *cl up: led after 1 1/2f: pushed along st: hdd over 2f out: wknd fr over 1 1/2f out* **145/10**

1m 17.91s (77.91)
WFA 3 from 4yo+ 5lb **10** Ran SP% **131.4**
TOTE: WIN 48; PL 26, 60, 55; SF 1,734.
Owner Stall Sunny **Bred** Klaus Laakman **Trained** Germany

2560 MUNICH (L-H)

Sunday, July 26

OFFICIAL GOING: Good

4364a GROSSER DALLMAYR-PREIS BAYERISCHES ZUCHTRENNEN (GROUP 1) 1m 2f

4:00 (4:14) 3-Y-O+ £88,350 (£34,951; £17,476; £9,709)

RPR
1 **Pressing (IRE)**[56] 2525 6-9-6 .... NCallan 7 118
(M A Jarvis) *4th early: disputing cl 2nd st: led 2f out: hung lft 150yds out: 2 l clr 100yds out: pushed out* **2/1**[1]
2 3/4 **Precious Boy (GER)**[42] 2953 4-9-6 .... ASuborics 3 116
(W Hickst, Germany) *hld up: 7th st: r.o wl fr 1 1/2f out fin strly fnl f: nrest at fin* **10/3**[3]
3 1 1/2 **Trincot (FR)**[39] 3013 4-9-6 .... LDettori 1 113
(Saeed Bin Suroor) *cl 2nd early: disputing 2nd st: rdn to chse wnr over 1 1/2f out: lost momentum whn crossed by wnr 150yds out: no ex* **9/4**[2]
4 5 **Integral (GER)**[56] 2525 5-9-6 .... DPorcu 4 103
(R Rohne, Germany) *led after 3f: drvn and hdd 2f out: styd on at one pce u.p* **33/1**
5 hd **Lady Alida**[36] 3186 3-8-7 .... FilipMinarik 8 100
(W Figge, Germany) *hld up in last: styd on fr over 1 1/2f out to take 5th 1f out: n.d* **14/1**
6 3 **Northern Glory**[252] 6-9-6 .... KKerekes 2 97
(W Figge, Germany) *in tch: 4th st: styd on tl no ex fr over 1f out* **22/1**
7 1/2 **Assahab (GER)**[29] 3416 6-9-6 .... APietsch 5 96
(U Stech, Germany) *led and set slow pce first 3f: dropped bk to 5th 1/2-way: 6th and n.d st* **50/1**
8 1 1/2 **Liang Kay (GER)**[29] 3416 4-9-6 .... THellier 6 93
(Uwe Ostmann, Germany) *mid-div: nvr a threat* **6/1**

2m 11.27s (2.30)
WFA 3 from 4yo+ 10lb **8** Ran SP% **117.4**
TOTE: WIN 27; PL 13, 15, 15; SF 86.
Owner Gary A Tanaka **Bred** Agricola Del Parco **Trained** Newmarket, Suffolk

NOTEBOOK
Pressing(IRE) notched his second career win at the top level. He hung left having hit the front, hampering Trincot in the process, but the result was left unchanged by the Stewards.
Trincot(FR) was hampered by the winner inside the final furlong but he was held at the time.

4113 MAISONS-LAFFITTE (R-H)
Sunday, July 26

OFFICIAL GOING: Good to soft

4365a PRIX DE LA PEPINIERE (LISTED RACE) (F&M) (LEFT-HANDED) 1m 2f 110y
2:20 (2:23) 4-Y-0+ £25,243 (£10,097; £2,773; £5,049; £2,524)

RPR

1 **Synergy (FR)**[30] 4-8-11 ..... OPeslier 13 110
(Y Durepaire, Spain)
2 ¾ **Burn The Breeze (IRE)**[24] 4-8-11 ..... TJarnet 2 108
(Mlle H Van Zuylen, France) 20/1[1]
3 6 **Peachmelba (USA)**[49] 4-8-11 ..... C-PLemaire 15 97
(J-C Rouget, France)
4 2 **Stella Di Quattro**[22] 5-8-11 ..... RPiechulek 4 93
(Uwe Ostmann, Germany)
5 snk **Midnight Dreamer**[23] 4-8-11 ..... CSoumillon 14 93
(J E Hammond, France)
6 1½ **La Tournesol (GER)**[104] 4-8-11 ..... DBoeuf 1 90
(P Schiergen, Germany)
7 ¾ **Lunduv (IRE)**[22] 4-8-11 ..... MDemuro 11 88
(C Von Der Recke, Germany)
8 snk **Audaz**[24] 4-8-11 ..... DBonilla 10 88
(C Laffon-Parias, France)
9 hd **Sakza (IRE)**[36] 3184 4-8-11 ..... GMasure 5 88
(M Delzangles, France)
10 ¾ **Starmaria (FR)**[82] 5-8-11 ..... (p) BHubert 12 86
(N Leenders, France)
0 **Calissee (FR)**[36] 3184 5-8-11 ..... SPasquier 3 —
(J De Roualle, France)
0 **Liberally (IRE)**[22] 3635 4-8-11 ..... JimmyFortune 9 —
(B J Meehan) *in rr: 12th st: nvr a factor* 23/1[2]
0 **Albisola (IRE)**[59] 2428 4-9-2 ..... JVictoire 6 —
(Robert Collet, France)
0 **Lumiere Astrale (FR)**[38] 4-8-11 ..... GMosse 7 —
(A De Royer-Dupre, France)
0 **Tubular Bells (USA)**[22] 4-8-11 ..... MGuyon 8 —
(H-A Pantall, France)

2m 8.50s (128.50) **15 Ran SP% 8.9**
PARI-MUTUEL: WIN 7.20; PL 2.40, 4.60, 2.10; DF 63.00.
Owner De La Fuente Stud **Bred** J Stulen **Trained** Spain

4366a PRIX ROBERT PAPIN (GROUP 2) (C&F) 5f 110y
2:50 (2:55) 2-Y-0 £71,942 (£27,767; £13,252; £8,835; £4,417)

RPR

1 **Special Duty**[22] 3648 2-8-13 ..... SPasquier 5 113
(Mme C Head-Maarek, France) *racd freely and rn green on the outside: pressed ldr: led over 1f out: rdn out* 8/1
2 1½ **Siyouni (FR)**[39] 3044 2-9-2 ..... CSoumillon 1 111+
(A De Royer-Dupre, France) *hld up in 5th early: hdwy between horses to hold ev ch 1f out: sn hrd rdn and nt pce of wnr* 1/2[1]
3 hd **Dolled Up (IRE)**[21] 3667 2-8-13 ..... OPeslier 4 107
(Robert Collet, France) *racd in 4th on outside: rdn 1 1/2f out: sn pressing ldrs: kpt on* 7/1[3]
4 ½ **Orpen Shadow (IRE)**[36] 3185 2-9-2 ..... DVargiu 2 109
(B Grizzetti, Italy) *led to over 1f out: one pce* 4/1[2]
5 2½ **Wonderfilly (FR)**[45] 2-8-13 ..... GBenoist 6 97
(P Demercastel, France) *a in rr* 14/1
6 dist **Golden Ramon (IRE)**[19] 2-8-13 ..... MDemuro 3 —
(B Grizzetti, Italy) *cl up tl lost pl qckly bef 1/2-way: eased* 22/1

64.40 secs (-2.90) **6 Ran SP% 121.3**
PARI-MUTUEL: WIN 8.50; PL 2.00, 1.20; SF 16.20.
Owner K Abdulla **Bred** Juddmonte Farms Ltd **Trained** Chantilly, France
■ Stewards' Enquiry : D Vargiu two-day ban: whip abuse (Aug 9-10)

NOTEBOOK
Special Duty, unlucky in her first outing at Deauville, made amends on this occasion. Always well up on the outside, she went into the lead at the furlong marker and then stayed on really well. She was a maiden before this Group 2 event and she looks to have a very bright future. She has already been marked down for the Group 1 Prix Morny at Deauville on August 23rd and she has considerable scope for improvement. The extra half furlong should also be an advantage.
Siyouni(FR) was asked a question for the first time in his life having previously hacked up in three other races. He was settled behind the leaders and moved into a challenging position at the distance but couldn't quicken inside the final furlong. It was a disappointing performance by the odds-on favourite but he shouldn't be written off. His trainer felt that he needs a longer trip and his next outing may come in the 7f Prix la Rochette in September. (op 4-6)
Dolled Up(IRE), always on the outside of the field, was well placed at the halfway stage and was putting in her best work in the dying stages. She only failed by a head to take second place and the stamina in her pedigree suggests she may well appreciate a longer trip. It would be no surprise to see her in the line-up for the Prix du Calvados at Deauville next month.
Orpen Shadow(IRE) tried to lead from pillar to post and was going well during much of the race. Under pressure at the furlong marker, though, he was unable to accelerate and eventually stayed on one-paced for fourth place. He will now be rested after a strenuous start to the season and will return for the Gran Criterium at San Siro in October.

4367a PRIX EUGENE ADAM (GROUP 2) (STRAIGHT COURSE) 1m 2f (S)
3:20 (3:23) 3-Y-0 £221,359 (£85,437; £40,777; £27,184; £13,592)

RPR

1 **Debussy (IRE)**[37] 3087 3-9-2 ..... JimmyFortune 9 115
(J H M Gosden) *cl up: led after 2 1/2f: rdn and r.o over 2f out: styd on wl ins fnl f* 10/1
2 ½ **World Heritage**[42] 2951 3-9-2 ..... SPasquier 8 114
(P Bary, France) *in tch on outside: pushed along and hdwy 2 1/2f out: rdn and 2nd over 1 1/2f out: nt rch wnr ins fnl f* 6/1[3]
3 2 **Prince Siegfried (FR)**[31] 3298 3-9-2 ..... C-PLemaire 2 110
(Saeed Bin Suroor) *in tch: 4th 1/2-way: pushed along to chse ldrs 2 1/2f out: rdn and no ex fr over 1f out* 9/1
4 1½ **Cashelgar (IRE)**[38] 3050 3-9-2 ..... GMosse 3 107
(A De Royer-Dupre, France) *led 2 1/2f: cl 3rd 1/2-way: pushed along 3f out: drvn over 2f out: styd on same pce* 9/4[1]
5 nk **Ideology**[28] 3-9-2 ..... MGuyon 6 106
(A Fabre, France) *prom: 2nd 1/2-way: drvn over 2f out: unable qck* 10/1
6 ½ **Allybar (IRE)**[34] 3230 3-9-2 ..... OPeslier 5 105
(C Laffon-Parias, France) *towards rr: effrt over 2f out: no imp* 13/2
7 nk **Vesuve (IRE)**[49] 2756 3-9-2 ..... ACrastus 1 105
(E Lellouche, France) *mid-div: effrt and sme hdwy over 2f out: rdn and no ex fr over 1f out* 4/1[2]
8 8 **Night Of Magic (IRE)**[63] 2310 3-8-13 ..... MDemuro 7 86
(H Steinmetz, Germany) *towards rr: nvr a factor* 14/1
9 15 **Mr Kintyre (ITY)**[56] 3-9-2 ..... PConvertino 4 59
(S Cannavo, Italy) *last 1/2-way: n.d* 20/1

2m 2.80s (0.40) **9 Ran SP% 118.0**
PARI-MUTUEL: WIN 22.80; PL 6.10, 3.30, 3.30; DF 68.10.
Owner H R H Princess Haya Of Jordan **Bred** Darley **Trained** Newmarket, Suffolk

NOTEBOOK
Debussy(IRE), back in trip, put up a really impressive performance and was given a fine ride by his jockey. At the head of affairs soon after the start, he was asked to set a sensible gallop before pace was injected a furlong and a half out. He then stayed on really well throughout the final furlong. He was without blinkers on this occasion and that was certainly another advantage. His options are now a tilt at the Prix Guillaume d'Ornano over a similar distance at Deauville or a possible supplement into the Juddmonte International at York.
World Heritage was given quite a lot to do in the early stages when settled back in sixth place. He made a forward move from the two-furlong marker but could never peg back the winner. He will now be aimed at the Guillaume d'Ornano at Deauville.
Prince Siegfried(FR) was given every possible chance. In mid-division early on, he was asked to quicken from a furlong and a half out but could only stay on one-paced, and his jockey felt that the ground was a little lively for the colt.
Cashelgar(IRE) was certainly not suited by the firmish ground but he still ran a fair race. Given every chance, he was tucked in behind the leader but couldn't quicken when things warmed up in front of the stands. He still stayed on bravely to the line, though, and he could well be raced over a longer distance next time out.

MOSCOW (R-H)
Saturday, July 18

OFFICIAL GOING: Standard

4369a PRESIDENT OF THE RUSSIAN FEDERATION STKS (DIRT) 1m 4f
10:20 (12:00) 4-Y-0+ £135,049

RPR

1 **Monomakh (USA)**[336] 4-9-4 ..... VMelekhov —
(A Chuguevets, Russia)
2 nk **Sunshine Lemon (USA)** 5-9-4 ..... ALiakhov —
(A H Derov, Russia)
3 3½ **Galiego (RUS)** 5-9-4 ..... SKruglykhin —
(A Chuguevets, Russia)
4 4 **Bronze Cannon (USA)**[28] 3139 4-9-4 ..... JimmyFortune —
(J H M Gosden) *prominent, quickened to press leader approaching straight, driven and dropped to 4th entering straight, kept on same pace*

2m 40.0s (160.00) **11 Ran**
.
Owner Donskoi Stud **Bred** **Trained** Russia

4170 SOUTHWELL (L-H)
Monday, July 27

OFFICIAL GOING: Standard
Wind: moderate 1/2 behind Weather: mainly fine

4370 EUROPEAN BREEDERS' FUND MAIDEN STKS 5f (F)
2:15 (2:16) (Class 5) 2-Y-0 £3,885 (£1,156; £577; £288) Stalls High

Form RPR

0 1 **Star Promise**[40] 3032 2-8-7 0 ..... DeanHeslop(5) 9 76
(T D Barron) *s.i.s: hdwy over 3f out: led over 1f out: r.o strly: readily* 20/1
32 2 2¾ **Yeadon**[56] 2526 2-9-3 0 ..... PaulHanagan 4 71
(R A Fahey) *chsd ldrs: hrd drvn over 2f out: styd on fnl f: no imp* 4/9[1]
36 3 shd **Belinsky (IRE)**[30] 3402 2-9-3 0 ..... TPQueally 1 71
(S A Callaghan) *trckd ldrs: kpt on same pce fnl f* 4/1[2]
5640 4 2¾ **Mrs Jones And Me (IRE)**[7] 4138 2-8-12 0 ..... (v[1]) PaulMulrennan 3 56
(P T Midgley) *led tl hdd over 1f out: sn fdd* 66/1
4450 5 1¾ **Hairs Vital (IRE)**[25] 4368 2-8-10 0 ..... DeclanCannon(7) 2 55
(E J O'Neill) *chsd ldrs: sn drvn along: wknd fnl f* 9/1[3]
04 6 4 **Russian Davis (IRE)**[23] 3634 2-9-3 0 ..... GrahamGibbons 7 40
(R M H Cowell) *hmpd sn after s: racd towards stands' side fr 2f out: nvr a factor* 16/1
06 7 ½ **Miss Roma (IRE)**[9] 4100 2-8-12 0 ..... ChrisCatlin 6 34
(R A Harris) *swtchd lft after s to r towards far side: mid-div: hrd rdn and hung rt over 1f out: nvr a factor* 66/1
4055 8 1¾ **Baby Judge (IRE)**[6] 4173 2-9-0 0 ..... (b[1]) LeeVickers(3) 8 32
(M C Chapman) *chsd ldrs: hung lft and lost pl over 1f out* 100/1
0 9 5 **Tulip Explosion**[23] 3634 2-8-12 0 ..... PaulEddery 5 9+
(D Shaw) *chsd ldrs: outpcd 2f out: sn wknd: eased ins fnl f* 100/1
0 10 4 **Wedding Dream**[13] 3937 2-8-12 0 ..... NCallan 10 —
(K A Ryan) *prom: rdn and outpcd over 2f out: sn lost pl* 33/1

59.47 secs (-0.23) **Going Correction** -0.175s/f (Stan) **10 Ran SP% 117.8**
Speed ratings (Par 94): **94,89,89,85,82 75,75,72,64,57**
toteswingers: 1&2 £5.30, 1&3 £11.80, 2&3 £12.10. CSF £29.79 TOTE £32.30: £5.30, £1.02, £1.40; EX 62.20.
Owner Coney Farms **Bred** Coney Farms **Trained** Maunby, N Yorks

FOCUS
A modest juvenile maiden.

NOTEBOOK
Star Promise overcame a couple of negatives. For a start, stall nine seemed far from ideal judging by both the result in behind, and recent races over this straight 5f, and she was also always squeezed out at the start. She did well to recover before ultimately winning in a decisive fashion and could be one to keep on side in ordinary nursery company.
Yeadon was the clear form pick following two reasonable runs on turf, but he had been off for a couple of months and has apparently had a wind operation since lest seen. Trying Fibresand for the first time, he proved disappointing, not travelling all that well and only getting up for a laboured second near the line. However, he was entitled to need this and should do better in nurseries, with a step back up to 6f and a return to turf likely to suit. (op 8-15 tchd 4-7)
Belinsky(IRE) showed good speed throughout and had his chance. He might be capable of a little better over this trip on quick turf now he's eligible for nurseries. (op 7-2)

Mrs Jones And Me(IRE) is already exposed as very moderate and her proximity does little for the form, even if she did improve slightly for the first-time visor and switch to Fibresand. (op 100-1)
Hairs Vital(IRE), well held in a couple of runs in France lately, including in blinkers, got warm beforehand and had to be ridden along pretty much throughout to try and hold his position. (tchd 10-1)
Russian Davis(IRE) was outpaced throughout but will be one to look out for in a nursery over 7f-plus. Official explanation: jockey said colt suffered interference shortly after start

4371 BET AFTER THE OFF AT LADBROKES.COM NURSERY 7f (F)

2:45 (2:46) (Class 5) 2-Y-O £2,729 (£806; £403) **Stalls Low**

Form RPR

330 **1** **My One Weakness (IRE)**[13] 3937 2-8-7 **63**........................ TomEaves 4 69
(B Ellison) *sn led: hdd 3f out: kpt on wl: led last stride* **4/1**[3]

654 **2** *shd* **Sejanus**[10] 4067 2-8-11 **67**........................ NCallan 7 73
(K A Ryan) *w ldrs: led over 2f out: edgd lft fnl f: hdd post* **7/2**[2]

303 **3** *7* **Motivational (IRE)**[28] 3468 2-9-7 **77**........................ ChrisCatlin 8 66
(D R Lanigan) *chsd ldrs on outer: drvn 3f out: carried hd high: wknd fnl f* **9/4**[1]

035 **4** *½* **Dolphin Rock**[24] 3571 2-8-12 **68**........................ DaleGibson 3 55
(Mrs G S Rees) *chsd ldrs: drvn over 3f out: outpcd over 2f out: kpt on fnl f* **7/1**

000 **5** *nk* **Welsh Legacy (IRE)**[35] 3218 2-7-9 **56** oh2 ow2.............. AmyBaker(5) 1 43
(B W Duke) *s.i.s: in rr and sn drvn along: kpt on wl fnl f* **50/1**

5543 **6** *2¾* **Gulf Punch**[20] 3719 2-8-8 **64**........................ JamieMackay 5 44
(M F Harris) *s.i.s: sn drvn along: nvr on terms* **25/1**

601 **7** *2½* **Belle Eponine**[38] 3119 2-8-4 **60**........................ FrancisNorton 2 33
(E J O'Neill) *led early: w ldrs: hung rt bnd 4f out: lost pl over 1f out* **6/1**

0563 **8** *3* **Agent Boo**[14] 3925 2-8-6 **62** ow1........................ GrahamGibbons 6 28
(E S McMahon) *w ldrs: led 3f out: sn hdd: wknd over 1f out* **8/1**

1m 30.19s (-0.11) **Going Correction** -0.075s/f (Stan) **8** Ran SP% **116.7**
Speed ratings (Par 94): **97,96,88,88,87 84,81,78**
toteswingers: 1&2 £4.40, 1&3 £2.30, 2&3 £2.60. CSF £18.87 CT £38.93 TOTE £5.80: £1.80, £1.50, £1.30; EX 31.30.
Owner Koo's Racing Club **Bred** Epona Bloodstock Ltd **Trained** Norton, N Yorks

FOCUS
An ordinary nursery.

NOTEBOOK
My One Weakness(IRE) improved for this step up in trip on his nursery debut and also coped well with Fibresand at the first attempt. Handily placed from the off, he was under pressure before the runner-up but kept responding to pressure and displayed a willing attitude. He should remain competitive in similar events. (op 9-2 tchd 5-1)
Sejanus, like the winner, benefited from the step up in trip on this first try in handicap company. A long way clear of the remainder, he should find a similar race. (tchd 4-1)
Motivational(IRE) did not look totally keen to run on in the straight, carrying his head a touch high and seeming to resent kickback, and finished well adrift of the front pair. (op 9-2)
Dolphin Rock did not improve for this step up in trip and doesn't look particularly well handicapped. (op 13-2 tchd 15-2)
Welsh Legacy(IRE) was outpaced and didn't go a yard early, before finally running on when the race was as good as over. He is likely to benefit from even further. (op 66-1)

4372 BET WITH LADBROKES ON 0800 777 888 CLAIMING STKS 6f (F)

3:15 (3:15) (Class 6) 3-Y-O+ £2,047 (£604; £302) **Stalls Low**

Form RPR

1316 **1** **Swinbrook (USA)**[31] 3354 8-9-0 74........................(v) PaulHanagan 8 71
(R A Fahey) *hmpd sn after s: hdwy over 3f out: styd on to ld 1f out: drvn out* **13/8**[1]

262 **2** *1* **Wiltshire (IRE)**[42] 2964 7-8-9 55........................(v) TonyCulhane 10 63
(P T Midgley) *mid-div on outer: sn drvn along: hdwy and edgd lft over 1f out: hung lft and styd on to take 2nd ins fnl f* **8/1**

00-4 **3** *½* **Coconut Shy**[13] 3953 3-8-13 79........................(t) FrederikTylicki(3) 9 72
(G Prodromou) *trckd ldrs: chal over 2f out: kpt on same pce fnl f* **9/1**

0020 **4** *1½* **Decider (USA)**[28] 3465 6-8-11 54........................(p) KevinGhunowa(3) 11 61
(R A Harris) *t.k.h: w ldr: led over 2f out: hdd 1f out: kpt on same pce* **25/1**

5003 **5** *3* **High Curragh**[11] 4012 6-9-12 76........................(p) NCallan 5 64
(K A Ryan) *wnt rt s: led tl over 2f out: wknd over 1f out* **13/2**[3]

5320 **6** *hd* **Come On Buckers (IRE)**[16] 3859 3-8-4 62.............. SophieDoyle(5) 2 51
(E J Creighton) *chsd ldrs: outpcd 3f out: no threat after* **20/1**

2005 **7** *1* **Charles Parnell (IRE)**[13] 3956 6-9-8 80........................ DaleGibson 4 56
(M Dods) *chsd ldrs: sn drvn along: lost pl 2f out* **5/2**[2]

0300 **8** *2½* **Owed**[11] 4016 7-9-2 48........................(tp) DanielTudhope 1 42
(R Bastiman) *sn in rr: sme hdwy on ins over 2f out: wknd over 1f out* **33/1**

65-0 **9** *6* **Favouring (IRE)**[24] 3558 7-8-1 40........................(v) AndrewHeffernan(7) 7 15
(M C Chapman) *hmpd sn after s: lost pl over 4f out: sn detached in rr and drvn along* **200/1**

00/0 **10** *7* **Days Of Thunder (IRE)**[83] 1773 4-8-9 41.............. MarkCoumbe(5) 3 —
(B R Summers) *t.k.h in rr: lost pl over 4f out: sn detached in rr* **150/1**

1m 15.94s (-0.56) **Going Correction** -0.075s/f (Stan)
WFA 3 from 4yo+ 5lb **10** Ran SP% **113.8**
Speed ratings (Par 101): **100,98,98,96,92 91,90,87,79,69**
toteswingers: 1&2 £3.70, 1&3 £4.70, 2&3 £7.30. CSF £14.43 TOTE £2.40: £1.20, £2.40, £2.10; EX 12.80.Swinbrook was claimed by C R Dore for £6,000.
Owner Mark A Leatham **Bred** Bill Bronstad **Trained** Musley Bank, N Yorks

FOCUS
A reasonable claimer run at a decent pace. The winner probably did not have to run to form.

4373 WATCH LIVE SPORT AT LADBROKES.COM H'CAP 1m 4f (F)

3:45 (3:45) (Class 6) (0-65,65) 3-Y-O+ £2,047 (£604; £302) **Stalls Low**

Form RPR

4002 **1** **Crimson Mitre**[20] 3714 4-10-0 **65**........................ NCallan 10 79+
(J Jay) *sn trcking ldrs: led 3f out: sn drvn clr: hung lft: styd on strly: readily* **3/1**[1]

6001 **2** *2½* **Guga (IRE)**[20] 3710 3-8-12 **61**........................ TonyCulhane 9 69
(George Baker) *trckd ldrs: t.k.h: led over 3f out: sn hdd: styd on same pce* **9/1**

0-61 **3** *½* **Three Strings (USA)**[91] 1568 6-9-9 **63**..............(p) FrederikTylicki(3) 12 70
(P D Niven) *hld up in rr: hdwy on outside over 4f out: styd on fnl 2f* **5/1**[2]

1402 **4** *1* **Almahaza (IRE)**[50] 2746 5-9-10 **61**........................ NeilChalmers 11 66
(A J Chamberlain) *hld up in rr: hdwy over 4f out: chsng ldrs over 2f out: one pce* **15/2**

0003 **5** *2¾* **King Of The Beers (USA)**[6] 4170 5-9-1 **59**..............(p) SPRyan(7) 3 60
(R A Harris) *sn in rr and drvn along: hdwy over 4f out: nvr rchd ldrs* **12/1**

00 **6** *nse* **Giant Sequoia (USA)**[68] 2181 5-9-9 **60**..............(t) VinceSlattery 13 61
(A J Chamberlain) *in rr: hdwy 5f out: kpt on: nvr trbld ldrs* **6/1**[3]

0035 **7** *7* **Swords**[14] 3927 7-9-5 **56**........................ ChrisCatlin 6 46
(R E Peacock) *in rr: sn drvn along: hdwy 4f out: wknd over 1f out* **13/2**

-304 **8** *3¾* **Smooth As Silk (IRE)**[14] 3927 4-10-0 **65**........................ PaulHanagan 14 49
(C R Egerton) *hld up on outer: sme hdwy over 4f out: sn lost pl: eased ins fnl f* **12/1**

4600 **9** *2¼* **My Mentor (IRE)**[12] 3977 5-10-0 **65**........................(b) SebSanders 1 45
(Sir Mark Prescott) *drvn early to ld: hdd over 3f out: lost pl over 1f out: eased* **14/1**

06/0 **10** *1* **Cat Six (USA)**[26] 3503 5-8-10 **47** oh2........................(p) GrahamGibbons 7 26
(T Wall) *chsd ldrs: reminders over 5f out: sn lost pl* **100/1**

3000 **11** *¾* **Karmest**[12] 3974 5-10-0 **65**........................ TomEaves 4 42
(A D Brown) *chsd ldrs: reminders 5f out: sn lost pl* **33/1**

0050 **12** *10* **Sommersturm (GER)**[95] 1478 5-9-10 **61**........................ TPQueally 2 22
(B J Curley) *t.k.h: w ldr: drvn over 4f out: sn lost pl: bhd whn eased fnl f* **25/1**

0000 **13** *1½* **Flannel (IRE)**[11] 4004 3-9-0 **63**........................ RoystonFfrench 8 22
(J R Fanshawe) *mid-div: drvn and lost pl over 4f out: sn bhd* **20/1**

2m 39.69s (-1.31) **Going Correction** -0.075s/f (Stan)
WFA 3 from 4yo+ 12lb **13** Ran SP% **125.6**
Speed ratings (Par 101): **101,99,99,98,96 96,91,89,87,87 86,79,78**
toteswingers: 1&2 £7.90, 1&3 £4.30, 2&3 £10.70. CSF £31.58 CT £138.62 TOTE £3.60: £1.50, £4.40, £1.60; EX 46.40.
Owner D Clarke **Bred** R Withers **Trained** Newmarket, Suffolk

FOCUS
A fair handicap for the grade. Improved form from the first two with the next pair close to their marks.

4374 GET THE VIP TREATMENT AT LADBROKESCASINO.COM H'CAP 6f (F)

4:15 (4:17) (Class 5) (0-75,73) 3-Y-O+ £2,729 (£806; £403) **Stalls Low**

Form RPR

2263 **1** **Elusive Hawk (IRE)**[20] 3713 5-9-9 **70**........................ TPQueally 6 83
(B J Curley) *trckd ldrs: hrd drvn over 1f out: styd on to ld last 100yds* **7/2**[1]

-202 **2** *1¼* **Hits Only Jude (IRE)**[13] 3956 6-9-11 **72**........................ DanielTudhope 1 81
(D Carroll) *trckd ldrs on inner: led over 3f out: hdd and no ex fnl 100yds* **7/2**[1]

0-05 **3** *1* **Yankee Storm**[20] 3713 4-9-7 **68**........................ FrancisNorton 9 74
(M Quinn) *trckd ldrs: styd on same pce fnl f* **16/1**

0320 **4** *1¼* **Defector (IRE)**[7] 4154 3-9-6 **72**........................(p) NCallan 5 73
(W R Muir) *chsd ldrs: kpt on same pce fnl 2f* **12/1**[3]

1003 **5** *1* **Calmdownmate (IRE)**[13] 3956 4-9-12 **73**........................ PaulMulrennan 10 72+
(Mrs R A Carr) *chsd ldrs: hung lft over 1f out: kpt on same pce* **5/1**[2]

5001 **6** *3½* **Elusive Fame (USA)**[20] 3713 3-9-6 **72**........................(b[1]) RoystonFfrench 4 58
(M Johnston) *dwlt: detached in last and sn drvn along: hdwy over 2f out: nt rch ldrs* **5/1**[2]

5-03 **7** *3* **Florentia**[6] 4174 3-9-0 **66**........................ SebSanders 3 43
(Sir Mark Prescott) *led tl over 3f out: wknd over 1f out* **12/1**[3]

6000 **8** *½* **A Big Sky Brewing (USA)**[14] 3924 5-9-5 **71**..............(b) DeanHeslop(5) 7 47
(T D Barron) *mid-div: effrt 3f out: nvr nr ldrs* **20/1**

0500 **9** *2¼* **Cool Sands (IRE)**[13] 3956 7-9-5 **66**........................(v) TomEaves 8 35
(J G Given) *sn outpcd and in rr: swtchd wd after 1f: nvr on terms* **50/1**

3255 **10** *6* **Captain Kallis (IRE)**[58] 2478 3-8-11 **63**........................(t) PaulHanagan 13 12
(D J S Ffrench Davis) *chsd ldrs on outer: lost pl 3f out: bhd whn eased ins fnl f* **16/1**

6260 **11** *5* **Green Onions**[10] 4051 3-8-11 **68**........................(b[1]) GabrielHannon(5) 12 —
(D J S Ffrench Davis) *chsd ldrs on outer: hung rt and lost pl over 2f out* **33/1**

0201 **12** *11* **Romantic Verse**[126] 937 4-9-3 **67**........................ MichaelJStainton(3) 2 —
(S Curran) *hrd drvn to chse ldrs: lost pl over 4f out: sn bhd: eased* **33/1**

1m 15.36s (-1.14) **Going Correction** -0.075s/f (Stan)
WFA 3 from 4yo+ 5lb **12** Ran SP% **117.5**
Speed ratings (Par 103): **104,102,101,99,98 93,89,88,85,77 71,56**
toteswingers: 1&2 £3.50, 1&3 £10.00, 2&3 £15.20. CSF £14.25 CT £175.80 TOTE £4.20: £1.50, £2.00, £3.60; EX 19.90.
Owner Curley Leisure **Bred** J Fike **Trained** Newmarket, Suffolk

FOCUS
A fair handicap for the grade, run in a time 0.58 seconds quicker than the earlier claimer won by then 74-rated Swinbrook. Several of these are proven over C&D and this is solid form.
Calmdownmate(IRE) Official explanation: jockey said gelding hung left
Elusive Fame(USA) Official explanation: jockey said gelding failed to handle the bend

4375 SOUTHWELL LADIES DAY 16TH AUGUST H'CAP 7f (F)

4:45 (4:46) (Class 6) (0-65,65) 3-Y-O+ £2,047 (£604; £302) **Stalls Low**

Form RPR

0332 **1** **Ugenius**[12] 3980 5-9-5 **56**........................ TonyCulhane 5 69
(Mrs C A Dunnett) *chsd ldrs: led appr fnl f: drvn out* **9/2**[2]

6-41 **2** *3* **Regeneration (IRE)**[19] 3743 3-9-6 **64**........................ TPQueally 4 66
(S A Callaghan) *sn chsng ldrs: led over 4f out: hdd appr fnl f: no ex* **11/4**[1]

6000 **3** *½* **Norcroft**[5] 4202 7-9-11 **62**........................(v) VinceSlattery 2 66
(Mrs C A Dunnett) *trckd ldrs on ins: reminder 3f out: upsides over 1f out: styd on same pce* **33/1**

0600 **4** *1¾* **Crocodile Bay (IRE)**[24] 3558 6-9-1 **57**..............(b) MarkCoumbe(5) 10 56+
(John A Harris) *s.i.s: hdwy on wd outside over 2f out: styd on fnl f* **12/1**

0362 **5** *1* **Ingleby Princess**[12] 3972 5-8-11 **53**........................ DeanHeslop(5) 8 49
(T D Barron) *prom: lost pl over 4f out: styd on down outside fnl 2f* **14/1**

0000 **6** *1¼* **Run Free**[13] 3943 5-9-2 **53**........................(p) DanielTudhope 6 46
(N Wilson) *led tl over 4f out: hung lft over 2f out: fdd appr fnl f* **10/1**

0010 **7** *1* **Mocha Java**[12] 3983 6-9-4 **60**........................ RossAtkinson(5) 1 50
(M Salaman) *rr-div: reminders 4f out: kpt on fnl 2f: nvr nr ldrs* **15/2**[3]

0000 **8** *4½* **Kingaroo (IRE)**[6] 4171 3-8-9 **60**........................(p) AndrewHeffernan(7) 14 35
(Garry Moss) *sn bhd and drvn along: sme hdwy on ins over 2f out: nvr a factor* **33/1**

-605 **9** *4½* **Langland Bay**[16] 3876 3-9-7 **65**........................ SebSanders 7 28
(W R Muir) *chsd ldrs: lost pl over 1f out* **14/1**

0-41 **10** *hd* **Whispering Spirit (IRE)**[12] 3975 3-9-2 **65**........................ BMcHugh(5) 13 27
(Mrs A Duffield) *mid-div: effrt on outer over 3f out: hung lft over 2f out: nvr a factor* **9/1**

1004 **11** *9* **Kingsmaite**[14] 3924 8-9-7 **65**........................(b) AndrewYoxall(7) 11 6+
(S R Bowring) *swtchd lft after s: sn detached and bhd* **10/1**

2-60 **12** *½* **Thurston (IRE)**[55] 2578 3-9-2 **65**........................(b) GabrielHannon(5) 12 2
(D J S Ffrench Davis) *chsd ldrs on outer: hung lft and wknd 2f out* **33/1**

4-06 **13** *11* **Miss Perfectionist**[13] 3955 3-9-2 **60**........................ FrancisNorton 9 —
(P Howling) *chsd ldrs: lost pl over 3f out* **50/1**

666- **14** *4* **Ros Cuire (IRE)**[329] 5561 4-9-9 **60** NCallan 3 —
(W A Murphy, Ire) *s.i.s: sme hdwy on ins over 2f out: sn wknd: eased over 1f out* **40/1**

1m 29.85s (-0.45) **Going Correction** -0.075s/f (Stan)
WFA 3 from 4yo+ 7lb **14** Ran SP% **119.0**
Speed ratings (Par 101): **99,95,95,93,91 90,89,84,79,78 68,67,55,50**
toteswingers: 1&2 £3.70, 1&3 £25.70, 2&3 £23.50. CSF £16.23 CT £325.57 TOTE £5.70: £2.20, £1.80, £9.10; EX 20.90.
Owner Mrs Christine Dunnett **Bred** Three Acres Stud **Trained** Hingham, Norfolk

FOCUS
A moderate handicap. The winner is rated back to his best with the second doing best of the 3yos.
Langland Bay Official explanation: jockey said filly had a breathing problem
Ros Cuire(IRE) Official explanation: jockey said colt never travelled

4376 BOOK TICKETS @ SOUTHWELL-RACECOURSE.CO.UK APPRENTICE H'CAP 1m (F)
5:15 (5:18) (Class 6) (0-55,55) 3-Y-0+ **£2,047** (£604; £302) Stalls Low

Form RPR

4555 **1** **Appelouse**[14] 3929 4-9-6 **53** DTDaSilva 10 64+
(D W Thompson) *in rr: gd hdwy on outside over 2f out: led over 1f out: drvn out* **8/1**

/6-0 **2** *3/4* **Benitez Bond**[48] 2789 4-8-11 **49** AnthonyBetts(5) 8 58
(G R Oldroyd) *t.k.h: w ldrs: kpt on same pce ins fnl f* **25/1**

0123 **3** *1 1/2* **Aggbag**[19] 3730 5-9-7 **54** GarryWhillans 6 60
(Miss M E Rowland) *mid-div: hdwy on outer over 2f out: styd on same pce appr fnl f* **9/2**[2]

25-0 **4** *3* **Headache**[19] 3735 4-9-5 **52** (t) HollyHall 7 51
(B W Duke) *t.k.h: led tl hdd appr fnl f: fdd* **7/1**

-260 **5** *1/2* **Al Rayanah**[10] 4060 6-9-7 **54** (p) DebraEngland 4 52
(G Prodromou) *reluctant to go on to crse: s.i.s: hdwy 3f out: sn chsng ldrs: kpt on: nvr a threat* **6/1**[3]

005/ **6** *1 1/4* **Thistle**[12] 1893 8-9-2 **54** ChrisHough(5) 14 49
(George Baker) *chsd ldrs on outer: drvn over 4f out: outpcd over 2f out: kpt on one pce* **11/1**

000 **7** *nk* **Tara's Garden**[7] 4149 4-9-0 **47** (b) RichardRowe 9 41
(M Blanshard) *in rr: hdwy on ins and nt clr run over 2f out: swtchd rt: nvr nr ldrs* **12/1**

-000 **8** *2* **Hi Spec (IRE)**[20] 3717 6-8-10 **48** (p) AlexEdwards(5) 2 38
(Miss M E Rowland) *in rr: hdwy on ins over 2f out: wknd over 1f out* **33/1**

000 **9** *nk* **Star Acclaim**[6] 4171 4-9-8 **55** (t) CharlesEddery 3 44
(E V Stanford) *chsd ldrs: lost pl over 1f out* **40/1**

0014 **10** *2 1/4* **Red Current**[14] 3929 5-9-2 **52** SPRyan(3) 12 36
(R A Harris) *reluctant to load: chsd ldrs: wknd 2f out* **7/2**[1]

0660 **11** *3* **Flying Bantam (IRE)**[21] 3689 8-9-5 **52** JohnCavanagh 5 29
(J R Norton) *chsd ldrs: drvn 3f out: sn lost pl* **16/1**

0000 **12** *1* **Legal Lover (IRE)**[21] 3675 7-9-1 **48** DavidKenny 11 23
(R Hollinshead) *chsd ldrs: lost pl over 2f out* **10/1**

6/6- **13** *13* **Toberogan (IRE)**[267] 7160 8-9-2 **52** KierenFox(3) 1 —
(W A Murphy, Ire) *s.i.s: in rr and drvn along: hung lft over 2f out: sn bhd: eased* **20/1**

1m 44.56s (0.86) **Going Correction** -0.075s/f (Stan) **13** Ran SP% **123.3**
Speed ratings (Par 101): **92,91,89,86,86 85,84,82,82,80 77,76,63**
toteswingers: 1&2 £50.40, 1&3 £6.90, 2&3 £22.70. CSF £203.31 CT £1024.19 TOTE £10.90: £3.50, £7.10, £1.60; EX 276.50 Place 6: £8.03 Place 5: £7.01.
Owner J A Moore **Bred** Bolton Grange **Trained** Bolam, Co Durham

FOCUS
A weak handicap restricted to apprentices who had not ridden more than ten winners. The pace seemed only steady early on. The third is a sound guide to the form.
T/Plt: £9.60 to a £1 stake. Pool: £63,304.57. 4,765.17 winning tickets. T/Qpdt: £7.70 to a £1 stake. Pool: £3,629.37. 346.50 winning tickets. WG

4145 WINDSOR (R-H)
Monday, July 27

OFFICIAL GOING: Good (good to soft in places)
Rail realignment increased distances of races of a mile and over by 15yards.
Wind: Fresh, behind. Weather: Sunny

4377 EBF SEVENTH HEAVEN EVENTS MAIDEN STKS 6f
6:10 (6:10) (Class 4) 2-Y-0 **£4,857** (£1,445; £722; £360) Stalls High

Form RPR

2 **1** **Planet Red (IRE)**[101] 1323 2-9-3 0 RichardHughes 8 83+
(R Hannon) *chsd ldrs: shkn up over 2f out: clsd on ldng pair jst over 1f out: led last 150yds: kpt on wl* **2/1**[2]

0 **2** *nk* **Carnaby Street (IRE)**[26] 3500 2-9-3 0 PatDobbs 3 82+
(R Hannon) *pressed ldr: rdn to ld narrowly over 1f out: edgd lft sn after: hdd fnl 150yds: kpt on wl* **28/1**

42 **3** *3 1/4* **Ghost (IRE)**[9] 4093 2-9-3 0 MichaelHills 7 72
(B W Hills) *led: racd against nr side rail fr 1/2-way: rdn and hdd over 1f out: hd quite high and nt qckn* **10/11**[1]

4 *3 1/4* **Burgau Royal** 2-9-3 0 EdwardCreighton 4 63
(M R Channon) *unruly preliminaries: chsd ldrs: shkn up over 2f out: sn outpcd: kpt on fnl f* **25/1**

5 *1 1/2* **Onyx Of Arabia (IRE)** 2-9-3 0 JimmyFortune 11 58
(B J Meehan) *dwlt: rcvrd and prom: shkn up and outpcd fr 2f out: hanging lft over 1f out: one pce* **16/1**[3]

040 **6** *1 1/4* **Durham Town (IRE)**[33] 3270 2-9-0 0 JackMitchell(3) 10 54
(D K Ivory) *a in midfield: rdn and outpcd fr over 2f out: no ch after* **50/1**

0 **7** *1/2* **Mandarin Express**[10] 4048 2-9-3 0 MartinDwyer 5 53
(B J Meehan) *chsd ldrs: rdn on wd outside over 2f out: sn fdd* **50/1**

8 *1 1/2* **Confucius Fortune (IRE)** 2-9-3 0 PatCosgrave 1 48
(J R Boyle) *dwlt and wnt lft s: outpcd in last trio: nvr on terms* **66/1**

9 *4 1/2* **Drubinca** 2-9-3 0 AdamKirby 2 35
(S C Williams) *outpcd in last trio: nvr a factor: wl bhd last 2f* **66/1**

10 *2 1/4* **Humidor (IRE)** 2-9-3 0 SteveDrowne 6 28
(R Charlton) *dwlt: outpcd in last trio: nvr a factor* **16/1**[3]

11 *19* **Dauntsey Park (IRE)** 2-9-3 0 FergusSweeney 9 —
(Miss Tor Sturgis) *dwlt: in tch in midfield to 1/2-way: wknd rapidly: t.o* **16/1**[3]

1m 12.37s (-0.63) **Going Correction** -0.05s/f (Good) **11** Ran SP% **117.6**
Speed ratings (Par 96): **102,101,97,92,90 89,88,86,80,77 52**
toteswingers: 1&2 £8.90, 1&3 £1.02, 2&3 £6.40. CSF £65.70 TOTE £3.20: £1.20, £4.20, £1.10; EX 45.00.
Owner Jamie Perryman & Richard Morecombe **Bred** J Breslin **Trained** East Everleigh, Wilts

FOCUS
The stands' rail was dolled out five yards at six furlongs down to one yard at the winning post. The top bend was dolled out nine yards from the innermost line adding fifteen and a half yards to race distances of a mile or more. Two horses cornered the market.

NOTEBOOK
Planet Red(IRE), having his first run since making a favourable impression on debut when second to Walkingonthemoon at Newbury back in April, who landed the spoils. Connections reported a lung infection was the reason for the delayed reappearance. This extra furlong certainly helped as he didn't really find his stride until going to the last, but won with something in hand. However, there is plenty of pace in his pedigree and this may be as far as he wants at present. (tchd 9-4)
Carnaby Street(IRE), the winner's stablemate, was friendless in the market despite showing signs of ability on debut at Chepstow and like the majority of his stable's juvenile runners had matured mentally for the experience and was on the pace throughout. With Planet Red out of the way he'd have been a good winner and he will be hard to beat in this grade next time. (op 33-1)
Ghost(IRE) was a well-backed favourite on the strength of two good placed efforts so far, the latest being the best when second to Mr David at Newmarket. However, he has to go down as disappointing. Once again he showed pace to lead and had the rail to help him - it was possible the better ground was up the middle - but he didn't find much when put under pressure. There's plenty of stamina on the dam's side and maybe he is worth a try over further. Official explanation: jockey said colt ran flat (op 11-10)
Burgau Royal produced a decent debut effort without ever looking like troubling the first three but was getting to grips with things throughout the last furlong and, after perhaps another run over this trip, could be worth a step up. His stable's juveniles usually improve considerably for the first run.
Onyx Of Arabia(IRE) looked very immature when put under pressure on debut but showed enough to warrant a second look next time. He'll be sharper and comes from a speedy family. (op 14-1)
Durham Town(IRE) looked awkward on the fence when ridden at halfway. (tchd 66-1)
Mandarin Express was a little isolated towards the outside and looks as though he'll need a stiffer test than this.
Confucius Fortune(IRE) Official explanation: jockey said gelding was slowly away

4378 THAMES FIAT 500C H'CAP 1m 2f 7y
6:40 (6:40) (Class 5) (0-75,75) 3-Y-0+ **£2,729** (£806; £403) Stalls Low

Form RPR

322 **1** **Falcon Rock (IRE)**[40] 3024 4-9-13 **74** RichardHughes 7 91
(S A Callaghan) *dwlt: hld up in 11th: prog fr 4f out: swtchd to inner wl over 1f out: sustained effrt to ld last 150yds: r.o wl* **11/4**[1]

0012 **2** *1* **Wing Play (IRE)**[16] 3847 4-9-11 **72** (p) ShaneKelly 6 87
(H Morrison) *w.w in midfield: prog on outer fr 3f out: led wl over 1f out: hdd last 150yds: r.o but hld after* **13/2**

1420 **3** *6* **Apotheosis**[44] 2923 4-9-5 **66** AdamKirby 4 69
(W R Swinburn) *trckd ldng pair: rdn to ld briefly 2f out: wl outpcd fr jst over 1f out* **6/1**[3]

00-5 **4** *3 3/4* **Dove Cottage (IRE)**[110] 1179 7-9-11 **72** FergusSweeney 12 68
(W S Kittow) *taken down early and free to post: w ldr: led 4f out to 2f out: cl up over 1f out: wknd* **20/1**

-441 **5** *7* **Fire King**[12] 3985 3-8-13 **60** RichardThomas 11 42
(J A Geake) *in tch: chsd ldrs over 3f out: rdn and steadily wknd fr over 2f out* **5/1**[2]

3130 **6** *1* **Pha Mai Blue**[61] 2387 4-9-5 **66** JimmyFortune 9 46
(J R Boyle) *hld up in 12th: rdn and sme prog on inner 3f out: nvr on terms: lft bhd by ldrs fnl 2f* **20/1**

2003 **7** *nk* **Khun John (IRE)**[13] 3961 6-9-9 **70** ChrisCatlin 1 49
(W J Musson) *hld up in detached last: pushed along and passed sme stragglers fr 3f out: nvr on terms: lft wl bhd by ldrs fnl 2f* **25/1**

44 **8** *2 1/2* **Rose Row**[56] 2552 5-9-7 **68** MartinDwyer 14 42
(Mrs Mary Hambro) *awkward s: sn prom: pushed along 4f out: wknd fr 3f out* **5/1**[2]

4-00 **9** *5* **Portugese Caddy**[26] 3509 3-9-4 **75** IanMongan 10 39
(P Winkworth) *a towards rr: shkn up and no prog over 3f out* **50/1**

015- **10** *1 3/4* **Awatuki (IRE)**[240] 7493 6-9-8 **69** PatCosgrave 5 29
(J R Boyle) *in tch in midfield: hrd rdn 3f out: wknd sn after* **16/1**

0300 **11** *shd* **Imperial Harry**[6] 4169 6-9-10 **71** (v) JerryO'Dwyer 8 31
(Jean-Rene Auvray) *chsd ldrs to 1/2-way: losing pl 4f out: struggling and wl in rr 2f out* **40/1**

12 *1 1/4* **Illicit**[301] 4-9-11 **75** RussellKennemore(3) 2 33
(Paul Mason) *in tch: pushed along to chse ldrs 4f out: wknd rapidly 3f out* **66/1**

13 *2 1/4* **Mississippian (IRE)**[27] 5-10-0 **75** (t) MichaelHills 3 28
(C J Mann) *mde most to 4f out: wknd rapidly* **20/1**

2m 7.38s (-1.32) **Going Correction** -0.05s/f (Good)
WFA 3 from 4yo+ 10lb **13** Ran SP% **117.5**
Speed ratings (Par 103): **103,102,97,94,88 88,87,85,81,80 80,79,77**
toteswingers: 1&2 £3.40, 1&3 £7.60, 2&3 £11.50. CSF £18.26 CT £100.37 TOTE £3.40: £1.60, £2.80, £2.60; EX 16.50.
Owner Michael Tabor **Bred** Barronstown Stud **Trained** Newmarket, Suffolk

FOCUS
A modest handicap won by Falcon Rock under a good ride. He had shaped better than the bare form the last twice.

4379 SPORTINGBET.COM MAIDEN AUCTION STKS 5f 10y
7:10 (7:10) (Class 4) 2-Y-0 **£3,885** (£1,156; £577; £288) Stalls High

Form RPR

06 **1** **Royal Blade (IRE)**[53] 2636 2-8-4 0 MatthewDavies(5) 4 71
(A P Jarvis) *mde all: rdn and edgd lft to centre of crse over 1f out: kpt on wl* **33/1**

4222 **2** *3/4* **Listillo (USA)**[6] 4165 2-8-13 0 DaneO'Neill 3 72
(H J L Dunlop) *pressed wnr and sn clr of rest: rdn and nt qckn wl over 1f out: edgd rt and kept on fnl f* **15/8**[2]

30 **3** *3/4* **Chocolate Cookie (IRE)**[9] 4089 2-8-7 0 ow2 RichardHughes 5 63
(R Hannon) *chsd ldng pair: pushed along after 2f and nt on terms: clsd grad u.p fnl f: nvr able to chal* **8/15**[1]

00 **4** *3 3/4* **Looks Like Slim**[48] 2792 2-8-11 0 JosedeSouza 1 54
(P F I Cole) *dwlt: off the pce in last trio: pushed along 1/2-way: plugged on fnl f: nvr on terms* **33/1**

000 **5** *2* **Ellmolell**[19] 3733 2-8-6 0 JamesDoyle 2 42+
(S Kirk) *sn off the pce in last trio: shkn up 2f out: nvr on terms* **40/1**

64 **6** *2 1/4* **Charlottesometimes (USA)**[13] 3944 2-8-4 0 ChrisCatlin 6 32
(D M Simcock) *pushed along in last trio after 2f: nvr on terms* **16/1**[3]

60.42 secs (0.12) **Going Correction** -0.05s/f (Good) **6** Ran SP% **114.2**
Speed ratings (Par 96): **97,95,94,88,85 81**
toteswingers: 1&2 £30.00, 1&3 £5.50, 2&3 £1.02. CSF £96.22 TOTE £29.70: £10.60, £1.20; EX 207.80.
Owner Christopher Shankland **Bred** Miss Sarah Sands **Trained** Middleham Moor, N Yorks

FOCUS
A turn-up in this weak race but no fluke as Royal Blade made all.

NOTEBOOK

Royal Blade(IRE) left his previous two runs well behind him. He had shown pace on both occasions, once over 6f, but it had been nearly two months since the last of them and this time he had the benefit of experience and extra strength to last home. He did wander a little under pressure but was entitled to as he hadn't seen another horse from the stalls. (op 25-1)

Listillo(USA) finished second for the fourth time and it has to be said that he does not look compeletely straightforward, giving the impression that at times his mind is elsewhere - he actually appeared to jump a shadow near the finish. He was staying on and on this evidence might be better over 6f. (op 11-4)

Chocolate Cookie(IRE) was cutting through the field when finishing eighth in the Super Sprint over this trip at Newbury last time. On her debut over 6f at Salisbury she was staying on and she was struggling over the minimum here and needs at least another furlong, possibly a seventh on pedigree. (op 40-85 tchd 4-7)

Looks Like Slim was tardy at the start once again but that had no effect on his placing over a distance that seems too short - his first two runs had been over 6f. (tchd 25-1)

Ellmollell needs further than this. (op 50-1)

4380 SOUTHERN COUNTIES FUELS FILLIES' H'CAP 6f

7:45 (7:46) (Class 4) (0-80,80) 3-Y-0+ **£4,857** (£1,445; £722; £360) **Stalls** High

Form RPR

2-15 **1** **Shangani**[25] 3537 3-9-2 **77** AmyScott(7) 11 85
(H Candy) *t.k.h: trckd ldng pair: wnt 2nd 2f out: edgd lft over 1f out: pushed into ld jst ins fnl f: eased nr fin* **13/2**[3]

-021 **2** *hd* **Sister Clement (IRE)**[10] 4051 3-9-0 **68** RichardHughes 10 75+
(R Hannon) *stdd s: hld up in midfield: shkn up 2f out: clsng on ldng pair whn no room jst ins fnl f: swtchd rt: hrd rdn and r.o: nrly ct wnr napping* **6/4**[1]

0010 **3** *1* **Miss Chamanda (IRE)**[6] 4167 3-9-12 **80** StephenDonohoe 9 84
(P D Evans) *led: rdn over 1f out: edgd lft and hdd jst ins fnl f: nt qckn* **20/1**

0044 **4** *3* **Top Town Girl**[33] 3272 3-9-6 **77** JackMitchell(3) 8 71
(R M Beckett) *pressed ldr to 2f out: edgd lft and fdd fnl f* **25/1**

3041 **5** *¾* **Keep Dancing (IRE)**[24] 3591 3-8-12 **69** (p) DavidProbert(3) 2 61
(A M Balding) *t.k.h on outer: cl up: outpcd fr over 1f out* **5/1**[2]

1310 **6** *½* **Spring Green**[19] 3747 3-9-10 **78** SteveDrowne 7 68+
(H Morrison) *dwlt: settled towards rr: rdn and effrt against nr side rail 2f out: no real imp* **5/1**[2]

0006 **7** *½* **Gentle Guru**[9] 4096 5-10-0 **77** JamesDoyle 3 66
(R T Phillips) *taken down early: mostly in last trio: in tch to over 2f out: sn outpcd u.p* **16/1**

0-42 **8** *1 ¼* **Lucy Brown**[17] 3815 3-9-2 **70** PatDobbs 6 55
(R Hannon) *dwlt: rcvrd to trck ldrs: rdn 2f out: sn btn* **10/1**

0410 **9** *¾* **Welsh Opera**[10] 4051 4-8-11 **60** (t) MichellePayne 5 42
(S C Williams) *settled in last trio: effrt on outer wl over 1f out: no prog: wknd fnl f* **33/1**

000 **10** *2 ¾* **Bonne**[3] 4285 4-9-0 **63** (b) PaulFitzsimons 4 37
(Miss J R Tooth) *dwlt: a in last trio: pushed along and struggling fr 1/2-way* **40/1**

1m 12.07s (-0.93) **Going Correction** -0.05s/f (Good)
WFA 3 from 4yo+ 5lb **10** Ran SP% **115.6**
Speed ratings (Par 102): **104,103,102,98,97 96,96,94,93,89**
toteswingers: 1&2 £5.60, 1&3 £24.10, 2&3 £12.10. CSF £15.84 CT £184.35 TOTE £6.00: £2.60, £1.40, £4.30; EX 22.40.
Owner Henry Candy **Bred** R S A Urquhart **Trained** Kingston Warren, Oxon
■ Stewards' Enquiry : Stephen Donohoe two-day ban: careless riding (Aug 10-11)

FOCUS

A competitive fillies' sprint but they didn't go a great pace. A high draw seemed significant and the form is rated around the third.

4381 NIRVANASPA.CO.UK MAIDEN STKS 1m 67y

8:15 (8:16) (Class 5) 3-4-Y-0 **£2,729** (£806; £403) **Stalls** High

Form RPR

3-42 **1** **Block Party**[23] 3624 3-9-3 78 RichardHughes 7 81+
(R Charlton) *led: stdd and hdd over 4f out: led again over 3f out: shkn up over 1f out: readily drew clr fnl f* **8/13**[1]

06 **2** *3 ½* **Highland Lassie (IRE)**[21] 3696 3-8-12 0 MartinDwyer 5 64+
(B J Meehan) *settled in midfield: rdn and prog against nr side rail over 2f out: wnt 2nd over 1f out: kpt on but no ch w wnr* **20/1**

P5 **3** *1 ½* **Kimberley Rocks (IRE)**[21] 3696 3-8-12 0 PatCosgrave 1 58
(R M Beckett) *settled towards rr: prog over 3f out: shkn up to dispute 2nd jst over 1f out: kpt on at one pce* **20/1**

0 **4** *7* **Countrystyle Lass (IRE)**[21] 3696 3-8-12 0 IanMongan 12 41
(P Winkworth) *trckd ldng quartet: effrt 3f out: rdn to chse ldrs and cl enough over 1f out: wknd* **66/1**

5 *nk* **Rinky Dink Lady (IRE)** 3-8-12 0 AdamKirby 4 40
(W R Swinburn) *dwlt: hld up in last pair: wl off the pce over 3f out: pushed along and nvr on terms after* **11/1**[3]

-533 **6** *½* **Sabi Star**[10] 4057 3-9-3 77 JimmyFortune 2 44
(J H M Gosden) *trckd wnr: hung lft bnd 5f out: led over 4f out to over 3f out: hanging bdly lft and wknd rapidly over 1f out* **3/1**[2]

50 **7** *½* **Grand Pere**[12] 3984 3-8-12 0 RichardEvans(5) 8 43
(P D Evans) *prom: pushed along over 3f out: stl cl enough u.p wl over 1f out: wknd rapidly* **50/1**

8 *shd* **Secret Desert** 3-9-3 0 StephenDonohoe 3 43
(D M Simcock) *s.s: a in rr: struggling over 3f out* **16/1**

04- **9** *2* **Miskin Flyer**[240] 7498 3-8-9 0 DavidProbert(3) 6 33
(B Palling) *prom: rdn on outer 3f out: wknd rapidly wl over 1f out* **25/1**

06 **10** *nk* **Annan Rock (IRE)**[9] 4083 3-9-3 0 VinceSlattery 10 37
(W J Musson) *a in rr: wl bhd 3f out: no ch after* **50/1**

1m 44.15s (-0.55) **Going Correction** -0.05s/f (Good) **10** Ran SP% **119.9**
Speed ratings (Par 103): **100,96,95,88,87 87,86,86,84,84**
toteswingers: 1&2 £4.80, 1&3 £8.00, 2&3 £20.80. CSF £22.55 TOTE £1.60: £1.02, £5.20, £4.10; EX 18.60.
Owner B E Nielsen **Bred** John Ellis **Trained** Beckhampton, Wilts

FOCUS

A weakish maiden and Block Party had nothing to beat with his main rival disappointing. The winner is value for extra.

4382 SPORTINGBET.COM H'CAP 1m 3f 135y

8:45 (8:45) (Class 5) (0-70,74) 3-Y-0+ **£2,729** (£806; £403) **Stalls** Low

Form RPR

1251 **1** **Hollow Green (IRE)**[6] 4166 3-9-7 **74** 6ex Louis-PhilippeBeuzelin(5) 6 78
(P D Evans) *hld up in 6th: prog on outer over 2f out: rdn to take narrow ld ent fnl f: hld on wl* **5/2**[1]

-052 **2** *hd* **Ubiquitous**[19] 3739 4-8-12 **48** JamesDoyle 2 51
(S Dow) *trckd ldng trio: effrt over 2f out: chal and upsides 1f out: kpt on wl but jst hld nr fin* **15/2**

-P02 **3** *1* **Fine Tolerance**[7] 4150 3-8-1 **52** DavidProbert(3) 1 54
(J R Boyle) *t.k.h early: trckd ldr: rdn to ld narrowly over 1f out: hdd ent fnl f: nt qckn last 100yds* **11/4**[2]

600- **4** *½* **Amical Risks (FR)**[225] 7676 5-8-13 **49** ChrisCatlin 5 50
(W J Musson) *hld up in last prog on wd outside over 2f out: rdn to chal 1f out: nt qckn last 150yds* **9/1**

1001 **5** *1 ½* **Megalala (IRE)**[13] 3949 8-10-0 **64** NeilChalmers 7 62
(J J Bridger) *led: edgd lft and hdd over 1f out: nt qckn and sn btn* **7/1**

653 **6** *1 ¼* **Everyman**[4] 4220 5-8-13 **49** (p) ShaneKelly 8 45
(A W Carroll) *trckd ldng pair tl nt qckn and lost pl over 2f out: n.d fr over 1f out* **9/2**[3]

05-0 **7** *¾* **Lady Maya**[17] 3811 4-8-10 **46** oh1 MartinDwyer 3 41?
(P Henderson) *hld up in 5th: shuffled along over 3f out: no prog whn shkn up 2f out* **20/1**

2m 30.95s (1.45) **Going Correction** -0.05s/f (Good)
WFA 3 from 4yo+ 12lb **7** Ran SP% **112.4**
Speed ratings (Par 103): **93,92,92,91,90 90,89**
toteswingers: 1&2 £20.30, 1&3 £1.10, 2&3 £2.50. CSF £20.80 CT £53.36 TOTE £3.30: £2.00, £4.00; EX 23.30 Place 6 £26.81, Place 5 £22.20..
Owner Raymond N R Auld **Bred** R N Auld **Trained** Pandy, Monmouths

FOCUS

A steadily run maiden and the form is a bit muddling. The winner confirmed her previous improvement.

Everyman Official explanation: jockey said gelding hung right

T/Plt: £18.30 to a £1 stake. Pool: £78,310.58. 3,112.45 winning tickets. T/Qpdt: £15.60 to a £1 stake. Pool: £4,758.54. 224.80 winning tickets. JN

4176 YARMOUTH (L-H)

Monday, July 27

OFFICIAL GOING: Good (good to soft in places)

All dolling out removed and distances as advertised.

Wind: virtually nil Weather: showery

4383 EAST COAST TRUCKERS FILLIES' MAIDEN AUCTION STKS 5f 43y

2:30 (2:33) (Class 6) 2-Y-0 **£2,590** (£770; £385; £192) **Stalls** High

Form RPR

0 **1** **Right Rave (IRE)**[38] 3113 2-8-5 0 CatherineGannon 12 66+
(P J McBride) *hld up in rr: hdwy over 1f out: rdn and qcknd to ld ins fnl f: sn in command: pushed out* **4/1**[2]

45 **2** *2 ½* **Zelos Dream (IRE)**[21] 3686 2-8-4 0 SaleemGolam 1 55
(Rae Guest) *dwlt: sn rcvrd and chsng ldrs: rdn over 1f out: kpt on same pce u.p fnl f: wnt 2nd fnl 75yds* **16/1**

0034 **3** *½* **Southwark Newshawk**[6] 4173 2-8-3 0 ow2 WilliamCarson(3) 7 55
(Mrs C A Dunnett) *led: rdn over 2f out: hdd over 1f out: stl ev ch and edgd lft 1f out: nt pce of wnr ins fnl f: kpt on* **28/1**

4 *½* **Peter's Follie** 2-8-7 0 RichardKingscote 8 54+
(Tom Dascombe) *in tch in midfield: outpcd and lost pl wl over 1f out: rallied fnl f: gng on at fin* **9/2**[3]

065 **5** *shd* **Princess Shamal**[18] 3772 2-8-8 0 AdrianMcCarthy 10 55
(J R Jenkins) *t.k.h: hld up wl in tch: hdwy over 2f out: rdn to ld over 1f out: hdd ins fnl f: no ex and lost 3 pls fnl 75yds* **50/1**

6 *1 ¼* **Labretella (IRE)** 2-8-6 0 NickyMackay 3 48
(M H Tompkins) *rrd s and v.s.a: detached in last pl tl hdwy over 1f out: styd on wl fnl f: gng on at fin* **28/1**

3350 **7** *½* **Shibhan**[24] 3576 2-8-5 0 (p) JimmyQuinn 4 49+
(C E Brittain) *in tch: rdn and unable qck over 1f out: keeping on same pce whn short of room and hmpd jst ins fnl f: no ch after* **5/2**[1]

0050 **8** *2* **Avec Moi**[6] 4176 2-8-4 0 DO'Donohoe 6 37
(Mrs C A Dunnett) *hld up towards rr: rdn ent fnl 2f: no prog* **50/1**

240 **9** *1* **Diamond Affair (IRE)**[2] 4302 2-8-4 0 WilliamBuick 2 34
(M G Quinlan) *racd keenly: chsd ldr tl over 1f out: sn rdn: wkng whn n.m.r jst ins fnl f* **7/1**

10 *10* **Casewick Star** 2-8-4 0 LiamJones 9 —
(P W D'Arcy) *sn pushed along towards rr: rdn 1/2-way: sn struggling and bhd* **25/1**

65.51 secs (3.31) **Going Correction** +0.30s/f (Good) **10** Ran SP% **99.8**
Speed ratings (Par 89): **85,81,80,79,79 77,76,73,71,55**
toteswingers: 1&2 £8.40, 1&3 £15.20, 2&3 £12.10. CSF £42.09 TOTE £4.60: £1.90, £3.20, £4.20; EX 56.40 TRIFECTA Not won..
Owner Jason Anderson **Bred** Garry Chong **Trained** Newmarket, Suffolk

FOCUS

The going was changed to Good, Good to Soft in places following 3mm of overnight rain and a further 5mm in the morning. This was a weak fillies' maiden.

NOTEBOOK

Right Rave(IRE), soon in trouble over 6f on her debut at Newmarket, had clearly learnt a good deal from that and coped just fine with the drop to 5f. The slower ground was clearly a help and she stayed on strongly against the rail to get well on top inside the final half furlong. (tchd 9-2)

Zelos Dream(IRE) failed to build on a promising debut effort when a well-beaten fifth at Ripon last time, but this was much more like it and she is the type to win a small race once contesting low-grade nurseries. (op 12-1)

Southwark Newshawk, whose rider was putting up 2lb overweight, is exposed as a moderate sort, finishing third in a seller two starts back, and she ran about as well as could have been expected. Her trainer does well at this course and it wouldn't surprise to see her win a seller here at some stage. (op 22-1)

Peter's Follie, bred to stay further than this, comes from a yard that does really well with its juveniles and she made some late headway to just snatch fourth. She should come on a good deal for this and will appreciate the step up to 6f. (tchd 11-2)

Princess Shamal made good headway to come through to lead over a furlong out, but the move took its toll and she could find no extra inside the final furlong, losing out on the places. (tchd 66-1)

Labretella(IRE) made quite a pleasing debut considering she reared at the start and was very slow to get going. She stayed on nicely inside the final furlong and should come on markedly for run. Official explanation: jockey said filly missed the break (op 25-1)

Shibhan had only modest form but was sent off favourite for a stable going well. She was already held when hampered late on. Official explanation: jockey said filly was denied a clear run (tchd 2-1)

Diamond Affair(IRE) Official explanation: jockey said filly ran too keen

4384 HIPS AT ECEA.CO.UK (S) STKS 6f 3y

3:00 (3:04) (Class 6) 2-Y-O **£1,942** (£578; £288; £144) **Stalls** High

Form RPR

P04 **1** **Arken Lad**[20] 3719 2-8-11 0 (p) JimmyQuinn 14 60
(D Donovan) *t.k.h: pressed ldr: led narrowly 2f out: pushed along and hld hd high ent fnl f: asserted fnl 75yds: a jst doing enough* **16/1**

2 *hd* **Rescent** 2-8-6 0 SaleemGolam 5 55+
(Rae Guest) *s.i.s: rn green and sn pushed along in rr: swtchd lft over 1f out: r.o wl fnl f: wnt 2nd towards fin: nt quite rch wnr* **50/1**

60 **3** *hd* **Ibmab**[48] 2788 2-8-11 0 TGMcLaughlin 11 59+
(Mrs L Stubbs) *bhd: pushed along 1/2-way: hdwy u.p and edging lft ent fnl f: r.o wl fnl f: wnt 3rd towards fin: nt rch wnr* **66/1**

635 **4** *¾* **Acting Elegant**[25] 3547 2-8-6 0 CatherineGannon 7 52
(P D Evans) *racd in midfield: rdn 2f out: drvn over 1f out: kpt on fnl f but nvr quite pce to rch ldrs* **12/1**

656 **5** *½* **Aintwogrand (IRE)**[11] 4011 2-8-6 0 SamHitchcott 9 51
(M R Channon) *stdd after s: hld up towards rr: hdwy over 2f out: rdn and unable qck 2f out: kpt on steadily u.p fnl f* **6/1**[3]

005 **6** *½* **That'Lldonowthen (IRE)**[11] 4018 2-8-11 0 LPKeniry 3 54
(J S Moore) *led: rdn and narrowly hdd 2f out: stl ev ch tl wknd fnl 75yds* **20/1**

000 **7** *hd* **Lochbroom Sunset**[7] 4152 2-8-8 0 (t) WilliamCarson(3) 6 53+
(S C Williams) *restless in stalls: in tch in midfield tl outpcd and dropped to rr 4f out: swtchd rt to stands' rail 2f out: styd on fnl f: nt rch ldrs* **14/1**

6043 **8** *¾* **Xaara Star (IRE)**[19] 3726 2-8-6 0 (b[1]) RichardMullen 2 46
(Eve Johnson Houghton) *taken down early: w ldrs: ev ch and rdn 2f out: stl ev ch tl wknd ins fnl f* **13/2**

0523 **9** *shd* **Hachi**[23] 3626 2-8-6 0 LiamJones 10 46
(J L Spearing) *chsd ldrs: rdn and unable qckn over 2f out: kpt on same pce u.p fr over 1f out* **10/3**[1]

0060 **10** *3 ½* **Botley Bell**[7] 4153 2-8-6 0 (v[1]) NickyMackay 15 35
(M R Channon) *dropped in bhd after s: hld up towards rr: rdn and effrt over 2f out: sn hanging lft u.p over 1f out: no real prog* **10/1**

6004 **11** *¾* **Polly Macho (IRE)**[23] 3626 2-8-11 0 PaulDoe 8 38
(P D Evans) *chsd ldrs: rdn over 3f out: struggling over 2f out: no ch ent fnl f* **8/1**

00 **12** *8* **Hidden City (IRE)**[25] 3547 2-8-11 0 (p) LukeMorris 12 14
(J S Moore) *racd in midfield: rdn and struggling 1/2-way: wl bhd fr over 1f out* **40/1**

00 **13** *9* **Howdoyalikemenow (IRE)**[11] 4001 2-8-6 0 (b[1]) DO'Donohoe 4 —
(K A Ryan) *wnt rt s: sn struggling and rdn along: lost tch 1/2-way* **25/1**

14 *1 ½* **Angela Jones** 2-8-6 0 EddieAhern 1 —
(D K Ivory) *rn green: in tch in midfield tl wknd qckly over 2f out: wl bhd over 1f out* **25/1**

15 *3 ¾* **Now Look Who'Shere** 2-8-11 0 StephenDonohoe 13 —
(E S McMahon) *s.i.s: sn detached in last pl: t.o* **5/1**[2]

1m 17.61s (3.21) **Going Correction** +0.30s/f (Good) **15** Ran SP% **126.2**
Speed ratings (Par 92): **90,89,89,88,87 87,86,85,85,81 80,69,57,55,50**
toteswingers: 1&2 £9.60, 1&3 £55.40, 2&3 £284.50. CSF £688.47 TOTE £18.00: £4.20, £10.50, £17.20; EX 1207.40 TRIFECTA Not won..The winner was bought in for 3,000gns. Rescent was the subject of a friendly claim.
Owner Philip Mclaughlin **Bred** Heather Raw **Trained** Newmarket, Suffolk
■ Stewards' Enquiry : William Carson one-day ban: excessive use of the whip (Aug 10)

FOCUS
A really competitive seller and it was a clean-sweep for outsiders.

NOTEBOOK
Arken Lad ran his best race yet when fourth in first-time cheekpieces at Wolverhampton last time and improved again to take this. Soon up with the pace, he kept finding for strong pressure, despite carrying his head a shade high, and stayed on well to just do enough. He is clearly going the right way and was bought in for £3,000. (tchd 18-1 and 20-1 in a place)
Rescent, a daughter of Reset, got a bump at the start and was soon outpaced. Strongly ridden with only two behind her at halfway, she finally started to pick up from over a furlong out and in the end only just failed to get there. This was a promising start and she should learn from the experience, suggesting a similar race can come her way.
Ibmab may well have been unlucky. As with the runner-up, he was in rear and under strongly pressure, but began to stay on when hampered and only lost out by a neck in the end.
Acting Elegant, fifth in a course and distance seller last time, kept on right the way to the line and looks seemed to appreciate the ease in the going. (op 10-1)
Aintwogrand(IRE) travelled well but couldn't quicken from over a furlong out. (tchd 15-2)
Lochbroom Sunset kept on against the stands' rail, finishing just ahead of the favourite. (op 16-1 tchd 25-1)
Xaara Star(IRE), in first-time blinkers, was swamped inside the final furlong having been up there on the pace from an early stage. (op 7-1 tchd 15-2)
Hachi, who should have been bang there on form, was disappointing and her rider reported she was never travelling. Official explanation: jockey said filly never travelled (op 4-1 tchd 3-1)
Polly Macho(IRE) Official explanation: jockey said gelding hung right
Now Look Who'Shere, for whom there was a ton of money beforehand, was soon detached in last and ran too bad to be true. (op 12-1)

4385 TIME & TIDE MUSEUM MAIDEN AUCTION STKS 7f 3y

3:30 (3:34) (Class 6) 2-Y-O **£2,590** (£770; £385; £192) **Stalls** High

Form RPR

3220 **1** **Janeiro (IRE)**[19] 3745 2-8-12 0 RichardKingscote 1 87+
(Tom Dascombe) *t.k.h: chsd ldrs: rdn and ev ch 2f out: drvn to ld ent fnl f: styd on strly to draw clr fnl f* **11/2**

622 **2** *2 ¼* **She's Ok (IRE)**[16] 3849 2-8-7 0 JimmyQuinn 15 76
(C E Brittain) *pressed ldr tl led 2f out: rdn and hdd ent fnl f: nt pce of wnr ins fnl f* **4/1**[3]

3 *1 ½* **Venutius** 2-8-9 0 StephenDonohoe 2 74
(E S McMahon) *in tch in midfield: rdn over 2f out: hdwy u.p over 1f out: wnt 3rd ins fnl f: kpt on* **14/1**

34 **4** *1 ¾* **Go Forth North (USA)**[24] 3576 2-8-4 0 WilliamBuick 5 65
(M L W Bell) *hld up wl in tch: swtchd rt and rdn wl over 1f out: drvn and no imp over 1f out: no ch w ldrs fnl f* **11/4**[2]

55 **5** *3* **Marafong**[20] 3716 2-8-12 0 AmirQuinn 12 65
(Miss J Feilden) *led tl hdd 2f out: wknd u.p over 1f out* **28/1**

04 **6** *1 ¾* **Execution (IRE)**[5] 4201 2-9-1 0 DO'Donohoe 4 64
(E A L Dunlop) *racd keenly: hld up in rr: hdwy over 3f out: rdn ent fnl 2f: sn btn* **25/1**

4 **7** *¾* **Keyta Bonita (IRE)**[31] 3356 2-8-4 0 RichardMullen 14 51+
(M G Quinlan) *stdd and dropped in towards rr after s: hdwy over 3f out: rdn ent fnl 2f: no prog and wl btn over 1f out* **5/2**[1]

8 *¾* **Sparkling Crown** 2-7-11 0 RyanPowell(7) 8 49
(J Ryan) *hld up in rr: shkn up ent fnl 2f: sn struggling and wl hld over 1f out* **50/1**

60 **9** *4 ½* **Blinka Me**[30] 3395 2-8-12 0 SaleemGolam 6 46
(M H Tompkins) *in tch in midfield: rdn 3f out: struggling ent fnl 2f: sn wl btn* **25/1**

10 *3 ¾* **Forgotten Army (IRE)** 2-8-5 0 AshleyMorgan(7) 9 37
(M H Tompkins) *s.i.s: a bhd: rdn over 3f out: n.d* **50/1**

11 *nk* **Noverre Over There (IRE)** 2-8-9 0 MickyFenton 3 33
(M E Rimmer) *v.s.a and wnt rt s: in rr: sme hdwy 3f out: rdn ent fnl 2f: sn wl btn* **100/1**

0 **12** *½* **Carlcol Girl**[7] 4152 2-8-7 0 (v) LiamJones 7 30
(Mrs C A Dunnett) *in tch in midfield tl struggling 1/2-way: wl bhd fnl 2f* **100/1**

13 *8* **Lauberhorn** 2-8-9 0 EddieAhern 11 12
(Eve Johnson Houghton) *in tch tl rdn and wknd qckly over 2f out: wl bhd fnl f* **14/1**

1m 29.19s (2.59) **Going Correction** +0.30s/f (Good) **13** Ran SP% **121.0**
Speed ratings (Par 92): **97,94,92,90,87 85,84,83,78,74 73,73,64**
toteswingers: 1&2 £5.80, 1&3 £15.00, 2&3 £14.10. CSF £26.89 TOTE £6.60: £2.10, £1.70, £4.80; EX 22.60 Trifecta £240.90 Part won. Pool: 325.57 - 0.43 winning units..
Owner Basing Bellman Newton Stroud **Bred** J Hutchinson **Trained** Lambourn, Berks

FOCUS
This was a moderate maiden auction.

NOTEBOOK
Janeiro(IRE) had been running consistently well until disappointing in a first-time visor at Lingfield last time, but the headgear was dispensed with here and he stayed on too strongly for the runner-up inside the final furlong. The step up to 7f was clearly in his favour and there could be more to come from him at this distance in nurseries. Official explanation: trainer said, regarding apparent improvement in form, on its previous run the gelding was visored first time and ran too free (op 5-1 tchd 6-1)
She's Ok(IRE), up to 7f for the first time, travelled well and went on two out, but she couldn't stay on as strongly as the winner. She should see it out better on a faster surface and can win a race at some stage. (op 9-2 tchd 7-2)
Venutius, who has a blend of speed and stamina in his pedigree, chased the early pace and stayed on well inside the final furlong to take third. He is entitled to improve and should stay 1m. (op 22-1 tchd 25-1)
Go Forth North(USA) has not really gone on from a promising debut and was made to look paceless. This run sees her qualified for nurseries now, though, and she will benefit from an extra furlong before long. (op 9-4)
Marafong has now finished fifth on all three starts and is another likely to find opportunities in handicaps. (op 25-1)
Keyta Bonita(IRE), who may well have been unlucky when beaten just half a length in fourth on her debut at Newmarket, was entitled to go close here with that run under her belt, but she found little for strong pressure and was beaten well over a furlong out. Official explanation: trainer's rep said filly was unsuited by the good (good to soft places) ground (op 11-4 tchd 3-1)

4386 MARTIN FOULGER MEMORIAL H'CAP 7f 3y

4:00 (4:01) (Class 4) (0-80,80) 3-Y-O+ **£4,667** (£1,397; £698; £349; £173) **Stalls** High

Form RPR

1 **1** **Dukes Art**[24] 3566 3-9-3 **75** RobertHavlin 4 80
(J A R Toller) *trckd ldrs: swtchd lft and effrt over 1f out: drvn to chal ent fnl f: led ins fnl f: drvn out* **4/1**[1]

052 **2** *nk* **Caprio (IRE)**[11] 4005 4-9-13 **78** EddieAhern 3 85
(J R Boyle) *led at stdy pce tl 4f out: rdn to ld again over 1f out: hdd and unable qck ins fnl f* **8/1**

5060 **3** *½* **Ocean Legend (IRE)**[12] 3980 4-9-2 **67** (v[1]) JimmyQuinn 5 73
(Miss J Feilden) *t.k.h: hld up in tch: pushed along over 2f out: swtchd lft and rdn over 1f out: pressed ldrs ent fnl f: kpt on same pce fnl 100yds* **7/1**[3]

0033 **4** *nk* **Autumn Blades (IRE)**[6] 4181 4-9-11 **76** (p) RobertWinston 8 81+
(A Bailey) *stdd after s: hld up in last pair: shkn up and effrt over 1f out: edging lft ins fnl f: no hdwy tl kpt on fnl 100yds:* **4/1**[1]

420 **5** *¾* **Catalan Bay (AUS)**[16] 3866 5-9-9 **74** LukeMorris 2 77
(J R Gask) *plld hrd: w ldr tl led 4f out tl rdn and hdd over 1f out: no ex u.p ins fnl f* **9/2**[2]

1-06 **6** *½* **Oh So Saucy**[31] 3339 5-9-11 **76** GeorgeBaker 6 77+
(C F Wall) *stdd s: hld up in last pair: n.m.r wl over 1f out: sn shkn up and unable qck: no prog whn short of room 100yds out and swtchd rt nr fin* **4/1**[1]

1-00 **7** *23* **Baariq**[10] 4056 3-9-8 **80** WilliamBuick 1 16
(P W Chapple-Hyam) *plld hrd: hld up wl in tch: rdn over 2f out: sn wknd: eased fnl f* **7/1**[3]

1m 29.05s (2.45) **Going Correction** +0.30s/f (Good)
WFA 3 from 4yo+ 7lb **7** Ran SP% **114.3**
Speed ratings (Par 105): **98,97,97,96,95 95,69**
toteswingers: 1&2 £5.50, 1&3 £7.30, 2&3 £9.30. CSF £35.53 CT £215.99 TOTE £5.10: £2.30, £2.80; EX 33.30 Trifecta £151.10 Pool: £794.59 - 3.89 winning units..
Owner Matthew Green **Bred** Fern Hill Stud & M Green **Trained** Newmarket, Suffolk

FOCUS
Nothing seemed obviously fancied in this fair handicap. It was run at an ordinary pace, with the field coming more to the stands' side from halfway, and each of the runners held a chance of sorts. The form looks a bit muddling with the runner-up the best guide.
Baariq Official explanation: trainer's rep said gelding was unsuited by the good (good to soft places) ground

4387 SHIRLEY GILL MEMORIAL H'CAP 6f 3y

4:30 (4:30) (Class 4) (0-85,85) 3-Y-O+ **£4,792** (£1,425; £712; £355) **Stalls** High

Form RPR

0-06 **1** **Sundae**[30] 3377 5-9-9 **82** GeorgeBaker 9 94
(C F Wall) *mde all: pushed along and qcknd over 1f out: in command fnl 100yds: eased towards fin* **13/2**

0013 **2** *1 ¼* **River Kirov (IRE)**[3] 4273 6-8-12 **78** TobyAtkinson(7) 7 85
(M Wigham) *t.k.h: hld up in tch: hdwy to chse wnr 1f out: sn swtchd lft and rdn: kpt on same pce fnl 100yds* **11/4**[2]

2535 **3** *¾* **Memphis Man**[7] 4154 6-9-1 **74** PaulDoe 1 79
(P D Evans) *taken down early: stdd and dropped in bhd after s: rdn and effrt jst over 2f out: drvn to chse ldng pair 1f out: no imp fnl f* **15/2**

1613 **4** *2* **Tyfos**[7] 4134 4-9-4 **77** TGMcLaughlin 6 75
(W M Brisbourne) *t.k.h: hld up towards rr tl hdwy to chse wnr 4f out: rdn ent fnl 2f: lost 2nd 1f out: wknd ins fnl f* **9/4**[1]

5026 **5** *shd* **Errigal Lad**[20] 3706 4-9-9 **82** (p) EddieAhern 5 80
(K A Ryan) *chsd ldr tl 4f out: lost pl and bhd over 2f out: rdn 2f out: sme hdwy ins fnl f: no ch w ldrs* **11/2**[3]

1460 **6** *2 ¾* **Chjimes (IRE)**[10] 4069 5-9-11 **84** LPKeniry 3 73
(C R Dore) *hld up in rr: shkn up ent fnl 2f: rdn and no prog over 1f out: wl btn fnl f* **25/1**

44 7 1/2 **Tudor Prince (IRE)**26 3512 5-8-10 **69** TolleyDean 2 56
(A W Carroll) *chsd ldrs: rdn jst over 2f out: drvn and wknd over 1f out: wl btn fnl f* **8/1**

1m 14.68s (0.28) **Going Correction** +0.30s/f (Good) 7 Ran SP% **112.9**
Speed ratings (Par 105): **110,108,107,104,104 100,100**
toteswingers: 1&2 £5.20, 1&3 £8.30, 2&3 £4.80. CSF £24.06 CT £136.06 TOTE £10.10: £4.30, £2.00; EX 28.60 Trifecta £322.50 Pool: £496.89 - 1.14 winning units..
Owner Peter Gregory **Bred** Jeremy Green And Sons **Trained** Newmarket, Suffolk

FOCUS
A fair sprint handicap but sound enough rated around the placed horses.

4388 FIRSTBET.COM 0800 230 0800 £50 MATCHED BET H'CAP 2m
5:00 (5:00) (Class 6) (0-65,65) 4-Y-0+ **£1,942** (£578; £288; £144) **Stalls** High

Form RPR
2436 **1** **Baan (USA)**20 3721 6-9-2 **60** JimmyQuinn 16 69
(H J Collingridge) *in tch: hdwy and rdn over 3f out: drvn to ld ent fnl 2f: kpt on u.p fnl f* **11/1**
1631 **2** *nk* **No Rules**18 3760 4-8-10 **61** SimonPearce(7) 9 70
(M H Tompkins) *t.k.h: chsd ldr 4f out: styd chsng ldrs: ev ch 2f out: clr w wnr ent fnl f: kpt on but a jst hld* **7/2**1
6025 **3** *5* **Rose Bien**43 2944 7-8-12 **56** (p) RichardKingscote 12 59
(P J McBride) *sltly hmpd s: sn rcvrd and led: hdd 10f out: rdn to ld again over 3f out: hdd over 2f out: outpcd by ldng pair jst over 1f out: plugged on* **6/1**2
0331 **4** *3 3/4* **Dazzling Begum**20 3714 4-8-8 **52** LiamJones 13 50
(J Pearce) *t.k.h: hld up in midfield: rdn and effrt 4f out: wnt modest 4th ent fnl f: no imp* **8/1**
00-0 **5** *3 1/4* **Leyte Gulf (USA)**20 3714 6-8-8 **52** LPKeniry 4 46
(C C Bealby) *t.k.h: hld up in midfield tl hdwy to ld 10f out: rdn and hdd over 3f out: wknd jst over 2f out* **33/1**
6044 **6** *3/4* **Lady Sorcerer**47 2830 4-8-10 **54** ow1 (v) TGMcLaughlin 15 47
(A P Jarvis) *v.s.a and swtchd lft s: hld up wl in rr: effrt on outer over 3f out: styd on past btn horses: nvr nr ldrs* **14/1**
643- **7** *1/2* **Alvee (IRE)**308 6168 4-9-7 **65** EddieAhern 7 58
(J R Fanshawe) *t.k.h: hld up wl in tch: rdn 4f out: sn struggling: no ch fnl 3f* **7/2**1
-551 **8** *1/2* **Squirtle (IRE)**39 3073 6-9-1 **59** LukeMorris 14 51
(W M Brisbourne) *chsd ldrs: wnt 2nd after 4f tl 10f out: styd chsng ldrs: rdn 4f out: wknd u.p over 2f out* **7/1**3
0054 **9** *1 1/2* **Mid Valley**13 3962 6-8-2 **46** oh1 AdrianMcCarthy 8 36
(J R Jenkins) *stdd s: plld hrd: hld up towards rr: hdwy into midfield 6f out: rdn and btn 3f out* **33/1**
-300 **10** *2 1/2* **Chiff Chaff**5 1154 5-8-6 **50** SamHitchcott 6 37
(C R Dore) *hld up in midfield: rdn and effrt on inner over 3f out: wknd over 2f out* **16/1**
6000 **11** *3/4* **Moon Mix (FR)**7 4156 6-8-2 **46** (v) NickyMackay 5 32
(J R Jenkins) *stdd s: t.k.h: hld up in rr: lost tch over 3f out* **25/1**
644 **12** *11* **Royal Premier (IRE)**18 3760 6-8-6 **50** (v) DO'Donohoe 11 23
(H J Collingridge) *in tch tl 1/2-way: lost pl and bhd 6f out: lost tch over 3f out: t.o* **16/1**
000 **13** *46* **Sugar State**27 970 4-8-2 **46** oh1 CatherineGannon 10 —
(J L Spearing) *t.k.h: hld up in last pair: rdn 6f out: t.o fnl 3f* **100/1**

3m 38.49s (3.89) **Going Correction** +0.30s/f (Good) 13 Ran SP% **119.8**
Speed ratings (Par 101): **102,101,99,97,95 95,95,94,94,92 92,87,64**
toteswingers: 1&2 £8.90, 1&3 £10.70, 2&3 £5.00. CSF £48.25 CT £261.77 TOTE £11.50: £3.10, £1.60, £2.10; EX 62.70 Trifecta £285.30 Part won. Pool: £385.56 - 0.53 winning units..
Owner Greenstead Hall Racing Ltd **Bred** Shadwell Farm Inc **Trained** Exning, Suffolk

FOCUS
They went a steady gallop through the early stages of this contest, so it was surprising to see two horses pull clear. The form is not solid and is best rated through the winner.
Sugar State Official explanation: jockey said gelding never travelled

4389 NORFOLK AND SUFFOLK ANIMAL TRUST LADY RIDERS' H'CAP 1m 3y
5:30 (5:31) (Class 6) (0-65,65) 3-Y-0+ **£1,873** (£581; £290; £145) **Stalls** High

Form RPR
6200 **1** **Barataria**33 3264 7-10-5 **65** MissRBastiman(5) 6 76
(R Bastiman) *stdd s: hld up in rr: hdwy 1/2-way: chsd ldr 2f out: sn ev ch: pushed along over 1f out: led fnl 100yds: kpt on* **10/1**
0662 **2** *3/4* **Whotsit (IRE)**29 3426 3-9-0 **54** (b) MissVCartmel(5) 1 61
(Miss Amy Weaver) *led: rdn wl over 1f out: hdd and no ex fnl 100yds* **11/1**
3222 **3** *1/2* **Sion Hill (IRE)**16 3863 8-9-10 **56** ow1 (p) MissABevan(5) 9 64
(John A Harris) *chsd ldrs: wnt 2nd over 3f out tl 2f out: edgd lft and kpt on same pce fnl f* **7/1**3
2450 **4** *7* **Munich (IRE)**12 3983 5-10-3 **58** MissSBrotherton 3 49
(Mrs S Leech) *in tch: hdwy to chse ldrs 1/2-way: rdn over 2f out: sn struggling: no ch fr over 1f out* **4/1**1
4034 **5** *1 3/4* **Rock Anthem (IRE)**11 3996 5-9-12 **60** MissSLWatson(7) 10 47
(Mike Murphy) *racd in midfield: hdwy 1/2-way: rdn and btn wl over 1f out* **9/1**
-004 **6** *1/2* **Winterfell**41 3010 3-9-3 **55** MissGAndrews(3) 14 40
(C F Wall) *stdd s: hld up towards rr: hdwy 1/2-way: chsd ldrs and rdn 2f out: sn drvn and btn* **7/1**3
150- **7** *1 1/2* **A Dream Come True**332 5472 4-9-13 **61** MissECrossman(7) 8 43
(D K Ivory) *chsd ldrs: rdn and struggling 3f out: no ch fnl 2f* **25/1**
5350 **8** *3/4* **Libre**17 3800 9-9-12 **53** MissEJJones 5 33
(F Jordan) *in tch: rdn and racd v awkwardly over 2f out: wknd 2f out and wl btn after* **10/1**
0220 **9** *9* **Amber Ridge**17 3800 4-9-7 **53** MissAWallace(5) 16 12
(B P J Baugh) *a towards rr: struggling bdly fr 1/2-way* **11/1**
310 **10** *4* **Mick Is Back**3 4262 5-9-13 **61** (v) MissKMargarson(7) 15 10
(G G Margarson) *stdd s: a bhd: lost tch 3f out: no ch whn hung bdly lft over 2f out* **5/1**2
-050 **11** *7* **Gifted Heir (IRE)**7 4158 5-9-5 **46** oh1 MissLHorner 12 —
(A Bailey) *s.i.s: a in rr: toiling bdly fr 1/2-way: t.o* **25/1**
00-6 **12** *1 3/4* **Highway Magic (IRE)**72 2084 3-9-9 **63** MissKellyBurke(5) 2 —
(A P Jarvis) *chsd ldr tl over 3f out: sn dropped out: wl bhd fnl 2f: t.o* **25/1**
3300 **13** *3* **Dawn Wind**23 3617 4-9-5 **46** oh1 (v) MissFayeBramley 7 —
(I A Wood) *s.i.s: a in rr: lost tch 1/2-way: t.o fnl f* **33/1**

1m 42.99s (2.39) **Going Correction** +0.30s/f (Good)
WFA 3 from 4yo+ 8lb 13 Ran SP% **121.0**
Speed ratings (Par 101): **100,99,98,91,90 89,88,87,78,74 67,65,62**
toteswingers: 1&2 £24.00, 1&3 £10.10, 2&3 £7.70. CSF £111.66 CT £856.90 TOTE £14.10: £4.70, £3.80, £2.00; EX 114.30 TRIFECTA Not won. Place 6: £4,399.97 Place 5: £1,292.79.
Owner Coal Trade Partnership **Bred** Hesmonds Stud Ltd **Trained** Cowthorpe, N Yorks

FOCUS
This was a typically low-grade lady riders' handicap. The winner ran close to hos all-weather best backed up by the third to his turf best.
Gifted Heir(IRE) Official explanation: jockey said horse never travelled
T/Jkpt: Not won. T/Plt: £18,675.30 to a £1 stake. Pool: £74,445.47. 2.91 winning tickets. T/Qpdt: £33.80 to a £1 stake. Pool: £7,625.87. 166.55 winning tickets. SP

4390 - 4391a (Foreign Racing) - See Raceform Interactive

GALWAY (R-H)
Monday, July 27

OFFICIAL GOING: Soft

4392a CLAREGALWAYHOTEL.IE H'CAP 7f
7:35 (7:35) (50-70,70) 3-Y-O **£7,044** (£1,641; £723; £417)

RPR
1 **Tellelle (IRE)**43 2958 3-9-7 70 DEMullins(5) 13 77
(Liam McAteer, Ire) *a.p: in front 2f out: styd on wl u.p fnl f* **9/1**
2 *1 1/2* **Out Of Honour (IRE)**40 3038 3-9-7 68 PBBeggy(3) 15 71
(John Geoghegan, Ire) *trckd ldrs: 3rd u.p 2f out: sn 2nd and kpt on wout matching wnr ins fnl f* **7/1**3
3 *3* **Spavento (IRE)**21 3699 3-9-2 70 (p) CPHoban(10) 8 65
(William Durkan, Ire) *mid-div: rdn in 8th bef st: sn chsd ldrs and no imp: kpt on same pce ins fnl f* **5/1**2
4 *2 1/2* **Carygali (IRE)**19 3754 3-9-1 64 MACleere(5) 11 52
(John Joseph Murphy, Ire) *towards rr: gd hdwy on inner into 4th bef st: sn no imp u.p and kpt on same pce* **20/1**
5 *1 3/4* **Tradewinds**8 4126 3-9-7 65 DPMcDonogh 12 48
(Mrs Prunella Dobbs, Ire) *chsd ldrs: 5th bef st: sn no imp u.p and kpt on same pce* **16/1**
6 *2* **No Trimmings (IRE)**32 3327 3-9-5 63 PJSmullen 2 41
(Gerard Keane, Ire) *towards rr: kpt on wout threatening u.p fr bef st* **9/1**
7 *nk* **Ain Jalout (IRE)**22 3664 3-9-8 66 CDHayes 4 43
(M Phelan, Ire) *towards rr: hdwy into 7th bef st: sn no imp and kpt on same pce u.p* **14/1**
8 *1 3/4* **Ucanchoose (IRE)**9 4110 3-9-8 66 WJLee 5 38
(Andrew Slattery, Ire) *mid-div: 8th early: no imp fr bef st* **9/1**
9 *nk* **Rio Cobolo (IRE)**17 3804 3-9-6 64 (b1) FMBerry 9 36
(Paul Green) *trckd ldrs: dropped to 6th bef st: sn no ex u.p* **10/3**1
10 *1 3/4* **Red Humour (IRE)**16 3880 3-9-9 70 (b) CPGeoghegan(3) 14 37
(M McDonagh, Ire) *led: hdd 2f out: no ex u.p st* **33/1**
11 *1 1/4* **Lift The Gloom**22 3664 3-9-4 67 (b) GFCarroll(5) 1 31
(Andrew Oliver, Ire) *chsd ldrs: 7th early: no ex fr bef st* **12/1**
12 *3/4* **Alyazwa**76 1976 3-9-12 70 DBDias 6 32
(Joseph Quinn, Ire) *a towards rr* **40/1**
13 *5* **Bridal Dance (IRE)**15 3903 3-9-7 65 WMLordan 7 13
(T Stack, Ire) *mid-div best: no ex fr bef st* **14/1**
14 *hd* **Elusive Moon (IRE)**43 2958 3-9-8 66 KJManning 10 14
(J T Gorman, Ire) *prom: 4th under 3f out: sn lost pl and wknd u.p* **12/1**
15 *3 1/2* **Bahamian Reward (IRE)**14 3932 3-9-7 68 PTownend(3) 3 6
(W J Burke, Ire) *in rr of mid-div: no ex appr st* **33/1**

1m 36.09s (4.49) 15 Ran SP% **129.9**
CSF £73.46 CT £373.78 TOTE £10.80: £3.20, £3.30, £1.90; DF 113.50.
Owner Ms Ashley O'Leary **Bred** Ms Ashley O'Leary **Trained** Navan, Co Meath

NOTEBOOK
Ain Jalout(IRE) Official explanation: jockey gelding received a check in the straight due to general bunching and lost ground
Rio Cobolo(IRE) came into this in good form but had blinkers replacing the usual visor. However, that good run has been on first ground and, although he has won on heavy going, the soft ground appeared to find him out this time. (op 7/2)

4393 - (Foreign Racing) - See Raceform Interactive

4073
CHANTILLY (R-H)
Monday, July 27

OFFICIAL GOING: Good

4394a PRIX DE BAGATELLE (FILLIES) (LISTED RACE) 1m
2:00 (2:03) 3-Y-0 **£26,699** (£10,680; £8,010; £5,340; £2,670)

RPR
1 **Mary's Precedent (FR)**22 3668 3-8-11 YLerner 3 100
(C Lerner, France)
2 *3/4* **Picture Hat (USA)**16 3-8-11 MGuyon 8 98
(H-A Pantall, France)
3 *shd* **Sweet Hearth (USA)**26 3-8-11 GMosse 2 98
(A De Royer-Dupre, France) **2/1**1
4 *1/2* **Golden Clou (FR)**32 3330 3-8-11 SPasquier 5 97
(P Demercastel, France)
5 *1* **Alice De La Vis (FR)**27 3-8-11 JVictoire 7 95
(J De Roualle, France)
6 *3/4* **Coronata (ITY)**64 3-8-11 PConvertino 6 93
(M Innocenti, Italy)
7 *snk* **Prise De Risque (FR)**49 2777 3-8-11 FPrat 9 92
(T Clout, France)
8 *2 1/2* **Enchanting Muse (USA)**358 4673 3-8-11 GBenoist 1 87
(Robert Collet, France)
9 *1 1/2* **Causa Proxima (FR)**32 3330 3-8-11 C-PLemaire 10 83
(A De Royer-Dupre, France)
10 *5* **Riotista (IRE)**310 6102 3-8-11 TThulliez 4 72
(E J O'Neill) *a in rr*

1m 40.0s (2.00) 10 Ran SP% **33.3**
PARI-MUTUEL: WIN 4.70; PL 1.50, 2.00, 1.40; DF 22.30.
Owner J Romel **Bred** Mme A Tamgni & Cocheese Bloodstock Anstalt **Trained** France

NOTEBOOK
Riotista(IRE), Listed placed a sa juvenile, was having her first run since September and was at the back throughout.

4138 BEVERLEY (R-H)

Tuesday, July 28

OFFICIAL GOING: Good to firm (good in places; 9.2)

Wind: Fresh half against Weather: Blustery and cloudy

4396 E B F HOLDERNESS PONY CLUB MAIDEN STKS 7f 100y

2:00 (2:05) (Class 5) 2-Y-O £3,885 (£1,156; £577; £288) Stalls High

Form RPR

1 **Spying** 2-9-3 0 SilvestreDeSousa 16 82+
(Mrs A Duffield) *t.k.h: cl up: effrt 2f out: swtchd lft and rdn to chal ent fnl f: sn led and kpt on strly* **13/2**[3]

2 2 **Aquarius Star (IRE)** 2-8-12 0 PaulEddery 11 72+
(Pat Eddery) *in tch: rn green and sltly outpcd over 2f out: rdn and hdwy over 1f out: styd on wl fnl f* **3/1**[2]

20 3 nk **Pytheas (USA)**[25] 3584 2-9-3 0 RoystonFfrench 3 76
(M Johnston) *sn led: rdn 2f out: drvn and hdd jst ins fnl f sn one pce* **11/4**[1]

6 4 1 1/2 **New Innocence**[20] 3750 2-9-3 0 ShaneKelly 10 73
(G A Butler) *trckd ldrs: hdwy 3f out: rdn to chse ldr 2f out: sn drvn and one pce appr fnl f* **3/1**[2]

63 5 2 **Could It Be Magic**[7] 4163 2-9-0 0 JackDean(3) 9 68
(W G M Turner) *in tch: hdwy to chse ldrs 3f out: rdn over 2f out and kpt on same pce* **7/1**

0 6 1 1/4 **Elmfield Giant (USA)**[31] 3392 2-9-3 0 TonyHamilton 13 65
(R A Fahey) *towards rr: hdwy 1/2-way: rdn to chse ldrs over 2f out: sn no imp* **20/1**

7 8 **Towneley Arms (IRE)** 2-9-0 0 FrederikTylicki(3) 8 46
(G A Harker) *in rr tl styd on fnl 2f: nvr nr ldrs* **80/1**

065 8 3/4 **The Caped Crusader (IRE)**[18] 3823 2-9-3 0 MickyFenton 15 45
(T P Tate) *towards rr: hdwy 1/2-way: rdn rdn to chse ldrs wl over 2f out: sn drvn and wknd* **25/1**

0 9 1/2 **Escape Artist**[18] 3823 2-9-3 0 DavidAllan 1 43
(T D Easterby) *towards rr: hdwy on outer over 3f out: sn in tch and rdn along wl over 2f out: sn wknd* **100/1**

00 10 9 **Brave Ambition (IRE)**[42] 2996 2-8-10 0 AndrewHeffernan(7) 12 22
(Garry Moss) *chsd ldrs on inner: rdn along 1/2-way: sn wknd* **200/1**

0 11 hd **Sarmad (USA)**[74] 2047 2-8-12 0 SebSanders 4 17
(C E Brittain) *dwlt: a in rr* **20/1**

12 1 1/2 **Ainthegorgeous** 2-9-3 0 PaulMulrennan 14 18
(P T Midgley) *s.i.s: a in rr* **66/1**

13 5 **Storm Command (IRE)** 2-9-3 0 TomEaves 7 6
(B Smart) *s.i.s: a bhd* **40/1**

14 12 **Moi Mel** 2-8-12 0 DuranFentiman 5 —
(L A Mullaney) *a in rr* **150/1**

1m 33.33s (-0.47) **Going Correction** -0.20s/f (Firm) **14** Ran SP% **123.2**

Speed ratings (Par 94): **94,91,91,89,87 85,76,75,75,65 64,63,57,43**

toteswingers: 1&2 £7.20, 1&3 £8.60, 2&3 £4.60. CSF £25.46 TOTE £9.00: £2.90, £2.00, £1.60; EX 34.60.

Owner Evelyn Duchess Of Sutherland **Bred** Evelyn Duchess Of Sutherland **Trained** Constable Burton, N Yorks

FOCUS

After a dry night the ground was described as good to firm, good in places. A maiden with mixed abilities on show, but it was run at a sound pace and it should throw up plenty of winners. Two of the newcomers filled first and second place.

NOTEBOOK

Spying was well backed beforehand and came home well from his good draw despite being keen in the early stages and should continue to progress. (op 20-1 tchd 6-1)

Aquarius Star(IRE), who cost 230,000gns as a yearling, was another to attract support in the betting ring and stayed on well in the final couple of furlongs after running very green early in the race. The daughter of Danehill Dancer should have no problem going one better in the near future. (op 4-1)

Pytheas(USA) had disappointed last time out after showing definite ability on his debut at Redcar. He cut out much of the early running and, although his Royal Lodge entry looks highly unlikely, he should be placed to good effect, especially when stepped up in trip. (op 3-1 tchd 4-1)

New Innocence had also shown ability on his debut at Newmarket but still looked green here and didn't really handle the bends that well. He might be more of a nursery type. Official explanation: jockey said colt was unsuited by the good to firm (good in places) ground (op 5-2)

Elmfield Giant(USA) is very well bred and in the right hands. There should be more to come from him. (op 14-1)

The Caped Crusader(IRE) Official explanation: jockey said colt hung right

4397 NATIONAL FESTIVAL CIRCUS (S) H'CAP 1m 4f 16y

2:35 (2:35) (Class 6) (0-65,57) 3-Y-O £2,266 (£674; £337; £168) Stalls High

Form RPR

0450 1 **Kochanski (IRE)**[29] 3454 3-9-6 50 RoystonFfrench 5 57
(M Johnston) *chsd ldng pair: effrt over 2f out and sn rdn along: drvn and styd on to ld ins fnl f: edgd rt and kpt on* **7/2**[2]

0006 2 1 1/4 **Winterbrook King**[31] 3383 3-9-2 46 RobertWinston 2 51
(J R Best) *hld up in rr: hdwy on outer 3f out: rdn wl over 1f out: styd on u.p ins fnl f: nrst fin* **13/2**

0334 3 1 **Saffron's Son (IRE)**[8] 4142 3-9-6 50 (b[1]) LeeEnstone 1 53
(P T Midgley) *dwlt: hld up and t.k.h: gd hdwy on inner 3f out: rdn to ld over 1f out and sn drvn: hdd ins fnl f and one pce* **8/1**

0043 4 3 **Lomica**[24] 3629 3-9-0 49 (p) BMcHugh(5) 9 48
(Miss J A Camacho) *trckd ldr: hdwy to ld over 3f out: rdn over 2f out: drvn and hdd over 1f out: wknd ent fnl f* **4/1**[3]

0065 5 2 **Primera Rossa**[10] 4084 3-9-1 45 LukeMorris 3 40
(J S Moore) *chsd ldrs: rdn along 4f out: wknd wl over 2f out* **11/1**

0312 6 1 3/4 **King's Chorister**[4] 4279 3-9-13 57 6ex (t) MickyFenton 6 50
(Miss Gay Kelleway) *hld up in rr: hdwy on outer over 4f out: rdn to chse ldrs over 2f out: sn drvn and btn over 1f out* **10/3**[1]

-044 7 8 **Just Dan**[14] 3954 3-9-4 48 TonyHamilton 8 28
(R Hollinshead) *led: rdn along and hdd over 3f out: sn wknd* **9/1**

0035 8 14 **Kneesy Earsy Nosey**[17] 3852 3-8-11 46 ow1 AnnStokell(5) 4 3
(Miss A Stokell) *a in rr* **33/1**

0000 9 6 **Desdamona (IRE)**[22] 3685 3-8-8 45 BillyCray(7) 7 —
(A Berry) *chsd ldrs to 1/2-way: sn wknd and bhd fnl 3f* **125/1**

2m 40.03s (-0.87) **Going Correction** -0.20s/f (Firm) **9** Ran SP% **111.8**

Speed ratings (Par 98): **94,93,92,90,89 88,82,73,69**

toteswingers: 1&2 £5.30, 1&3 £7.10, 2&3 £7.70. CSF £25.31 CT £165.06 TOTE £4.50: £1.50, £2.10, £2.10; EX 27.20.There was no bid for the winner.

Owner J R Gough **Bred** Gainsborough Stud Management Ltd **Trained** Middleham Moor, N Yorks

FOCUS

This form didn't look as strong as one would expect from a seller for three-year-olds, but it was run at an even pace thanks to Just Dan, who cut out much of the early running before fading in the final two furlongs. The winner was close to her early 2yo form.

King's Chorister Official explanation: jockey said gelding was unsuited by the good to firm (good in places) ground

4398 LYNNE HOPE COMMUNICATIONS CELEBRATION MAIDEN AUCTION FILLIES' STKS 5f

3:10 (3:11) (Class 5) 2-Y-O £2,914 (£867; £433; £216) Stalls High

Form RPR

2 1 **Tell Me A Story**[10] 4100 2-8-4 0 SilvestreDeSousa 3 69+
(M Brittain) *trckd ldrs: hdwy 2f out: rdn to ld over 1f out: drvn ins fnl f and kpt on gamely* **7/2**[3]

32 2 3/4 **Dance For Julie (IRE)**[37] 3187 2-8-11 0 PaulMulrennan 4 73+
(P C Haslam) *trckd ldrs: effrt and nt clr run wl over 1f out: sn swtchd lft and rdn: chal ent fnl f and ev ch tl drvn and no ex towards fin* **2/1**[2]

2 3 4 **Miss Taken (IRE)**[11] 4067 2-8-4 0 PaulQuinn 8 52
(D Carroll) *cl up: stdd after 1f: sn lost pl and towards rr: hdwy over 1f out: sn rdn and kpt on ins fnl f* **15/8**[1]

502 4 1 **Daisy Brown**[8] 4138 2-8-1 0 KellyHarrison(3) 5 48
(N Tinkler) *hld up: hdwy whn bmpd wl over 1f out: sn rdn and edgd lft: kpt on ins fnl f* **14/1**

5 2 1/2 **Luv U Noo** 2-8-4 0 RoystonFfrench 2 39
(K R Burke) *led: rdn along 1/2-way and sn hdd: drvn wl over 1f out: sn edgd rt and wknd* **12/1**

0 6 6 **Selina Rio**[14] 3937 2-8-4 0 DuranFentiman 6 18
(L A Mullaney) *cl up: led 2f out: sn rdn: hdd over 1f out and sn wknd* **66/1**

06 7 3 1/2 **Crystal Bridge**[17] 3849 2-8-1 0 ow2 DeanHeslop(5) 7 7
(Mrs L Williamson) *chsd ldrs on inner: rdn along over 2f out and sn wknd* **100/1**

8 8 **Remember Dougie (IRE)** 2-7-11 0 BillyCray(7) 9 —
(A Berry) *dwlt and bhd: rdn and hung bdly rt 1/2-way* **16/1**

63.77 secs (0.27) **Going Correction** -0.075s/f (Good) **8** Ran SP% **113.1**

Speed ratings (Par 91): **94,92,86,84,80 71,65,52**

toteswingers: 1&2 £2.10, 1&3 £2.00, 2&3 £2.00. CSF £10.65 TOTE £5.00: £1.60, £1.10, £1.20; EX 9.80.

Owner Northgate Grey **Bred** R Kinsey **Trained** Warthill, N Yorks

■ Stewards' Enquiry : Paul Mulrennan 16-day ban (takes into account previous offences; four days deferred): excessive use of the whip (Aug 14-25)

Billy Cray two-day ban: excessive use of the whip (Aug 11-12)

FOCUS

A maiden lacking strength in depth, but it produced a cracking finish with the first three in the market coming home in front.

NOTEBOOK

Tell Me A Story had finished runner-up in a similar contest at Ripon recently on soft ground and proved that was no fluke on quicker ground here. She seems to have a likeable attitude and can win again, although she will be harder to place from now on. (tchd 10-3)

Dance For Julie(IRE) had the best form coming into the race, albeit over 6f, and should have no problems getting her head in front in a similar contest when stepped back up to that trip. She can also go down the nursery route. (op 5-2 tchd 7-4)

Miss Taken(IRE) was also down in trip a furlong after making a pleasing debut at Pontefract 11 days ago. In rear at halfway, she came home well enough to suggest she could take a hand at this level when upped in trip. Official explanation: jockey said filly slipped leaving stalls (op 5-2)

Daisy Brown, despite being the most experienced in the line-up, still looked green and unbalanced and can improve on this. (op 10-1 tchd 16-1)

Luv U Noo showed plenty of early speed and might be worth a crack over the minimum distance. (op 9-1 tchd 14-1)

4399 "I DO" WEDDING FAIR 9TH AUGUST H'CAP 5f

3:45 (3:46) (Class 5) (0-75,72) 3-Y-O+ £3,238 (£963; £481; £240) Stalls High

Form RPR

3220 1 **Select Committee**[2] 4355 4-8-11 58 (v) TomEaves 6 68
(J J Quinn) *trckd ldrs: effrt over 1f out: sn rdn and styd on ins fnl f to ld nr fin* **7/1**

4546 2 nk **Peninsular War**[60] 2443 3-9-7 72 SebSanders 9 80
(K R Burke) *led: rdn clr appr last: drvn ins fnl f: hdd and nt qckn nr fin* **13/2**[3]

0035 3 1 **Green Park (IRE)**[4] 4285 6-9-11 72 (b) DanielTudhope 5 78
(D Carroll) *swtchd rt after s and hld up: hdwy on inner wl over 1f out: swtchd lft and rdn ins fnl f: kpt on: nrst fin* **12/1**

2100 4 1/2 **Baybshambles (IRE)**[4] 4283 5-9-11 72 PhillipMakin 12 76
(R E Barr) *chsd ldrs: hdwy wl over 1f out and sn rdn: drvn ins fnl f: hld whn n.m.r towards fin* **9/2**[1]

0310 5 2 1/2 **Requisite**[35] 3252 4-9-11 72 (v) TonyHamilton 10 67
(I A Wood) *stmbld s and bhd: hdwy on inner wl over 1f out: sn rdn and kpt on ins fnl f: nrst fin* **9/1**

4600 6 nse **Namir (IRE)**[11] 4069 7-9-10 71 (vt) TedDurcan 8 66
(D Shaw) *trckd ldrs gng wl: effrt over 1f out: sn rdn and n.m.r: one pce* **7/1**

0060 7 1 1/4 **Steel Blue**[4] 4285 9-8-10 57 (p) J-PGuillambert 1 47
(R M Whitaker) *in tch on outer: rdn along 2f out and sn no imp* **28/1**

-001 8 2 **Prince Namid**[8] 4141 7-9-1 69 6ex NSLawes(7) 7 52
(D Nicholls) *prom: rdn wl over 1f out and wknd appr fnl f* **5/1**[2]

4530 9 1 3/4 **Kheylide (IRE)**[19] 3765 3-9-2 67 EdwardCreighton 13 43
(Mrs D J Sanderson) *dwlt: sn rdn along and a in rr* **17/2**

54U 10 3/4 **Nomoreblondes**[33] 3304 5-9-7 68 (p) PaulMulrennan 2 42
(P T Midgley) *prom: rdn along 2f out and sn wknd* **25/1**

610- 11 shd **Azygous**[220] 7743 6-8-5 59 JamesPSullivan(7) 3 33
(M W Easterby) *stdd s and a in rr* **50/1**

1-00 11 dht **Braille**[50] 2770 4-9-5 66 JamieMoriarty 4 40
(T D Walford) *dwlt: a towards rr* **25/1**

62.64 secs (-0.86) **Going Correction** -0.075s/f (Good)

WFA 3 from 4yo+ 4lb **12** Ran SP% **114.5**

Speed ratings (Par 103): **103,102,100,100,96 96,94,90,88,86 86,86**

toteswingers: 1&2 £4.80, 1&3 £12.10, 2&3 £10.80. CSF £48.07 CT £536.91 TOTE £5.90: £2.20, £2.50, £3.80; EX 42.60.

Owner Which Bits Mine Syndicate **Bred** Llety Stud **Trained** Settrington, N Yorks

■ Stewards' Enquiry : N S Lawes caution: careless riding

FOCUS

A 56-75 sprint handicap and as expected it was run at a good gallop. A modest race but solid form.

Kheylide(IRE) Official explanation: jockey said gelding missed the break

4400 WILFORD WATTS MEMORIAL H'CAP 1m 100y
4:20 (4:21) (Class 4) (0-85,84) 3-Y-O+ £5,180 (£1,541; £770; £384) **Stalls** High

Form RPR
0061 **1** **Celtic Change (IRE)**[24] 3624 5-9-8 **78**..............(bt) PhillipMakin 13 87
(M Dods) *mde all: rdn clr over 2f out: styd on wl u.p fnl f* **7/1**
2064 **2** *1* **Handsome Falcon**[25] 3560 5-8-13 **72**........................ FrederikTylicki(3) 1 79
(R A Fahey) *prom: hdwy to chse wnr 1/2-way: rdn 2f out: drvn over 1f out: kpt on ins fnl f* **7/1**
2026 **3** *½* **Shadowtime**[3] 4333 4-8-11 **67**............................ RobertWinston 9 73
(Miss Tracy Waggott) *hld up towards rr: hdwy 3f out: rdn wl over 1f out: styd on wl u.p ins fnl f* **11/2**[2]
1660 **4** *½* **Paraguay (USA)**[20] 3736 6-9-6 **76**........................ EdwardCreighton 15 81+
(Mrs D J Sanderson) *in tch: pushed along and outpcd 1/2-way: hdwy 2f out: sn rdn and n.m.r: swtchd lft over 1f out: kpt on ins fnl f: nrst fin* **6/1**[3]
2004 **5** *1 ¼* **Tarzan (IRE)**[19] 3770 3-9-2 **80**............................ RoystonFfrench 3 80
(M Johnston) *chsd ldrs: rdn along and outpcd over 3f out: kpt on u.p appr fnl f* **8/1**
0006 **6** *¾* **Nevada Desert (IRE)**[10] 4104 9-8-10 **69**............ MichaelJStainton(3) 11 69
(R M Whitaker) *chsd ldrs on inner: rdn along over 2f out: drvn over 1f out and sn wknd* **12/1**
5200 **7** *2 ¼* **Tiger Dream**[18] 3825 4-8-12 **73**..............................(p) AmyRyan(5) 4 68
(K A Ryan) *dwlt: sn in tch: rdn along 3f out: drvn 2f out: kpt on same pce* **12/1**
0031 **8** *½* **Danehillsundance (IRE)**[14] 3941 5-9-4 **74**....................(t) TedDurcan 7 68
(D H Brown) *prom: rdn along wl over 2f out and sn wknd* **5/1**[1]
0600 **9** *16* **Blue Spinnaker (IRE)**[23] 3656 10-8-9 **72**............ JamesPSullivan(7) 10 29
(M W Easterby) *dwlt: a towards rr* **25/1**
0460 **10** *3 ¾* **Minority Report**[32] 3353 9-8-9 **72**............................ NSLawes(7) 14 20
(D Nicholls) *s.i.s: a in rr* **20/1**
00 **11** *3 ½* **Ansells Pride (IRE)**[87] 1684 6-10-0 **84**............................ TomEaves 8 24
(B Smart) *dwlt: sn in tch on outer: pushed along and hung lft bnd 4f out: wknd over 2f out* **16/1**
403 **12** *10* **Blue Charm**[8] 4144 5-8-8 **69**............................ JamesO'Reilly(5) 12 —
(I W McInnes) *rrd s and lost many l: a wl bhd* **20/1**

1m 44.84s (-2.76) **Going Correction** -0.20s/f (Firm) **12** Ran SP% **117.1**
WFA 3 from 4yo+ 8lb
Speed ratings (Par 105): **105,104,103,103,101 101,98,98,82,78 75,65**
toteswingers: 1&2 £9.60, 1&3 £9.80, 2&3 £12.30. CSF £52.98 CT £295.63 TOTE £9.30: £2.70, £2.90, £2.20; EX 63.80.
Owner P Taylor **Bred** Wardstown Stud Ltd **Trained** Denton, Co Durham

FOCUS
As the betting suggested this was a wide-open handicap in which six of them had already been successful over the track. It paid to be near the pace as it was run at an even gallop. Sound form for the grade.
Danehillsundance(IRE) Official explanation: jockey said gelding had no more to give
Blue Charm Official explanation: jockey said gelding reared in the stalls

4401 LEVY BOARD H'CAP 1m 1f 207y
4:55 (4:58) (Class 4) (0-85,85) 3-Y-O £5,180 (£1,541; £770; £384) **Stalls** High

Form RPR
4131 **1** **Honimiere (IRE)**[8] 4139 3-9-0 **78** 6ex............................ RobertWinston 8 88+
(G A Swinbank) *trckd ldrs: hdwy 3f out: n.m.r and swtchd lft 2f out: rdn to ld over 1f out and styd on strly* **5/4**[1]
0-45 **2** *2 ¼* **Maybeme**[45] 2937 3-8-4 **68** oh4 ow2............................ RoystonFfrench 5 71
(N Bycroft) *hld up: hdwy over 2f out: sn rdn: kpt on u.p ins fnl f* **22/1**
2311 **3** *1 ½* **Amazing Blue Sky**[5] 4230 3-8-7 **71** 6ex.................. SilvestreDeSousa 3 71
(Mrs R A Carr) *led: rdn along 3f out: drvn 2f out: hdd over 1f out and kpt on same pce* **7/2**[2]
321 **4** *shd* **Sanctuary**[47] 2843 3-9-0 **78**............................ TomEaves 6 78
(B Smart) *trckd ldrs: hdwy over 2f out and sn rdn: drvn over 1f out and kpt on same pce* **5/1**
2020 **5** *¾* **Union Island (IRE)**[19] 3780 3-9-7 **85**............................ PhillipMakin 1 83
(K A Ryan) *cl up: chal 3f out: sn rdn and ev ch tl drvn wl over 1f out and grad wknd* **4/1**[3]

2m 5.16s (-1.84) **Going Correction** -0.20s/f (Firm) **5** Ran SP% **107.7**
Speed ratings (Par 102): **99,97,96,95,95**
toteswingers: 1&2 £17.20 CSF £24.82 TOTE £1.80: £1.30, £3.70; EX 24.70.
Owner Mrs J Porter & Mrs David Parkinson **Bred** Peter Collier **Trained** Melsonby, N Yorks

FOCUS
Only five runners with the late withdrawal of Cornish Castle, who refused to enter the stalls, but there was still plenty of recent form on hand for this handicap, which was run at an even gallop. The form is unconvincing with the runner-up 6lb wrong.

4402 DOROTHY LAIRD MEMORIAL TROPHY LADIES RACE STKS (HANDICAP STAKES) 1m 1f 207y
5:30 (5:31) (Class 6) (0-65,64) 3-Y-O+ £2,729 (£806; £403) **Stalls** High

Form RPR
6000 **1** **Monfils Monfils (USA)**[2] 4345 7-10-3 **62**........................ MissVBarr(5) 15 73
(R E Barr) *mde all: rdn clr wl over 1f out: styd on wl u.p fnl f* **12/1**
/003 **2** *2 ¼* **Tivers Song (USA)**[55] 2608 5-9-5 **45**....................(b) SoniaEaton 9 51
(John A Harris) *hld up towards rr: hdwy on wd outside 2f out and sn rdn: drvn to chsewnr and hung rt ins fnl f: kpt on* **20/1**
5656 **3** *1* **General Tufto**[7] 4171 4-10-9 **63**....................(b) MissEJJones 6 67
(C Smith) *hld up towards rr: gd hdwy 3f out: rdn to chse ldrs over 1f out: drvn and edgd rt ins fnl f: kpt on* **11/1**
0650 **4** *nk* **Bivouac (UAE)**[17] 3863 5-10-5 **59**............................ MrsCBartley 8 62
(G A Swinbank) *chsd wnr rdn along over 2f out: drvn over 1f out: kpt on same pce* **10/1**
0460 **5** *¾* **Hucking Heat (IRE)**[21] 3721 5-10-5 **64**................(p) MissRKneller(5) 11 66+
(R Hollinshead) *in tch: lost pl 3f out: gd hdwy whn nt clr run on inner over 1f out and again ent fnl f: swtchd lft and rdn: fin strly* **16/1**
0060 **6** *1 ¼* **Coole Dodger (IRE)**[13] 3983 4-10-3 **57**........................ MissLEllison 13 56
(B Ellison) *midfield: hdwy on inner to chse ldrs over 3f out: rdn 2f out: drvn and n.m.r over 1f out: one pce* **16/1**
0012 **7** *nse* **Gala Sunday (USA)**[14] 3943 9-10-4 **58**..............(bt) MissSBrotherton 16 57
(M W Easterby) *trckd ldrs: hdwy 3f out: rdn along 2f out: drvn wl over 1f out and kpt on same pce* **7/2**[1]
02B2 **8** *hd* **Whipma Whopma Gate (IRE)**[11] 4071 4-9-12 **52**....... KellyHarrison 12 51
(D Carroll) *chsd ldrs: effrt 3f out: rdn 2f out: drvn and edgd rt over 1f out: one pce* **11/2**[2]
6002 **9** *1 ¾* **Rossini's Dancer**[11] 4034 4-10-0 **59**....................(p) MrsVFahey(5) 4 54
(R A Fahey) *hld up towards rr: hdwy 3f out: rdn and edgd rt wl over 1f out: sn swtchd lft and no imp appr fnl f* **6/1**[3]
6-10 **10** *1 ¼* **Bright Sparky (GER)**[84] 623 6-9-5 **50**..........(bt) MissJoannaMason(5) 3 43
(M W Easterby) *s.i.s and bhd tl sme late hdwy* **28/1**
4444 **11** *½* **Hurricane Thomas (IRE)**[29] 3450 5-9-3 **48**.......(v) MissPhillipaTutty(5) 7 40
(R A Fahey) *a in rr* **6/1**[3]
4000 **12** *1 ¼* **Bestowed**[15] 3919 4-9-9 **49**............................ JosephineBruning 2 38
(M C Chapman) *chsd ldeing pair: rdn along 3f out: sn wknd* **66/1**
6543 **13** *1 ¼* **Wannarock (IRE)**[24] 3609 4-9-1 **46**............................ RachelKing(5) 1 33
(M C Chapman) *chsd ldrs on outer: rdn along over 3f out and sn wknd* **18/1**
00-0 **14** *4 ½* **Intavac Boy**[35] 3233 8-9-0 **45**............................ MissERamstrom(5) 10 23
(S P Griffiths) *midfield: lost pl 3f out and sn bhd* **100/1**
600P **15** *15* **Jarvo**[14] 3943 8-9-4 **49**..............................(p) MissCLWhitehead(5) 14 —
(I W McInnes) *dwlt: a in rr* **80/1**
60-0 **16** *4 ½* **Scotty's Future (IRE)**[66] 2263 11-9-2 **47**.................... MissDLenge(5) 5 —
(A Berry) *dwlt: a in rr: swtchd wd over 2f out and sn bhd* **66/1**

2m 5.32s (-1.68) **Going Correction** -0.20s/f (Firm) **16** Ran SP% **121.7**
Speed ratings (Par 101): **98,96,95,95,94 93,93,93,91,90 90,89,88,84,72 69**
toteswingers: 1&2 £48.10, 1&3 £28.60, 2&3 £48.60. CSF £243.83 CT £2717.26 TOTE £14.60: £2.80, £4.40, £2.40, £2.20; EX 376.50.
Owner Northumbria Leisure Ltd & B Morton **Bred** Douglas McIntyre **Trained** Seamer, N Yorks
■ Stewards' Enquiry : Miss E Ramstrom one-day ban: used whip when out of contention (Aug 13)
Sonia Eaton one-day ban: careless riding (Aug 11)
Miss E J Jones one-day ban: careless riding (Aug 13)

FOCUS
This was a low grade-handicap confined to lady riders and not for the first time on the card the winner made all the running. It was run at a sound gallop. The form is fairly sound.

4403 JOURNAL LADIES DAY NEXT 12 AUGUST STKS (H'CAP) 1m 4f 16y
6:00 (6:03) (Class 5) (0-70,70) 3-Y-O+ £3,238 (£963; £481; £240) **Stalls** High

Form RPR
212 **1** **Summer Lodge**[18] 3814 6-9-11 **70**....................(p) FrederikTylicki(3) 4 76
(J A Glover) *prom: chsd clr ldr after 2f: hdwy and cl up over 3f out: sn rdn to chal and hung rt: drvn to ld wl over 1f out and sn edgd rt: hrd drvn ins fnl f and hld on grimly* **11/4**[1]
-003 **2** *shd* **Tender Moments**[11] 4034 5-8-10 **52** oh1............................ TomEaves 8 58
(B Smart) *chsd ldng pair: hdwy over 3f out: rdn over 2f out: drvn to chse wnr ins fnl f: kpt on wl u.p: jst failed* **14/1**
-006 **3** *¾* **Fossgate**[25] 3561 8-8-10 **52** oh2............................ RoystonFfrench 9 57
(J D Bethell) *hld up in midfield: hdwy 4f out: effrt on outer over 2f out and sn rdn: drvn to chse ldng pair ins fnl f: sn hung rt and no ex towards fin* **10/1**
4-05 **4** *1 ¾* **Simple Jim (FR)**[28] 3486 5-8-10 **52**........................ SilvestreDeSousa 10 54
(J Hetherton) *hld up in tch: hdwy 4f out: rdn to chse ldrs over 2f out: drvn over 1f out and kpt on same pce* **9/2**[2]
-010 **5** *1 ¾* **Piverina (IRE)**[21] 3714 4-8-10 **52** oh1............................ TonyHamilton 6 51
(Miss J A Camacho) *hld up in rr: hdwy 3f out: rdn 2f out: drvn and no imp fnl f* **9/1**
0000 **6** *1* **Lady Anne Nevill**[28] 3486 5-8-7 **52** oh7.................... KellyHarrison(3) 12 50?
(C W Fairhurst) *hld up in rr: hdwy 3f out: rdn 2f out: kpt on: nvr nr ldrs* **50/1**
0421 **7** *½* **Credential**[7] 4170 7-8-5 **52** oh4............................ PaulPickard(5) 3 49+
(John A Harris) *sn led and clr at fast pce: jnd and rdn along 3f out: drvn and n.m.r 2f out: hdd over 1f out and wkng whn n.m.r ent fnl f* **13/2**[3]
0000 **8** *2 ¼* **Able Dara**[8] 4139 6-8-10 **52** oh7............................ DuranFentiman 11 45?
(N Bycroft) *a towards rr* **40/1**
0-50 **9** *53* **John Dillon (IRE)**[125] 623 5-9-2 **58**........................(v) PaulMulrennan 7 —
(P C Haslam) *chsd ldrs: rdn along 4f out: sn wknd and bhd* **33/1**
40/0 **10** *shd* **Lady Calido (USA)**[81] 1834 4-9-0 **56**............................ SebSanders 5 —
(Sir Mark Prescott) *midfield: effrt over 4f out: sn rdn and wknd* **10/1**

2m 36.48s (-4.42) **Going Correction** -0.20s/f (Firm) **10** Ran SP% **100.4**
Speed ratings (Par 103): **106,105,105,104,103 102,102,100,—,—**
toteswingers: 1&2 £4.80, 1&3 £5.70, 2&3 £13.70. CSF £31.10 CT £203.09 TOTE £3.10: £1.20, £3.70, £2.50; EX 25.60 Place 6: £56.82 Place 5: £36.21.
Owner Paul J Dixon **Bred** Seymour Cohn **Trained** Babworth, Notts
■ Stewards' Enquiry : Royston Ffrench caution: used whip with excessive force

FOCUS
Just a run-of-the-mill handicap which was weakened at the start by the withdrawal of Shaylee, who refused to enter the stalls. The gallop was furious thanks to Credential, who understandably weakened in the final furlong.
Credential Official explanation: jockey said gelding suffered interference in the straight
John Dillon(IRE) Official explanation: jockey said gelding had no more to give
T/Plt: £77.90 to a £1 stake. Pool: £60,756.46. 568.62 winning tickets. T/Qpdt: £17.30 to a £1 stake. Pool: £4,527.12. 193.21 winning tickets. JR

3099 GOODWOOD (R-H)
Tuesday, July 28

OFFICIAL GOING: Good (8.3)
Rail from 6f on lower bend to winning post moved out 6yards increasing distances by 15yds; top bend dolled out 4yds increasing distances by 8yds.
Wind: Brisk, mostly against Weather: Fine but cloudy

4404 PAUL GOES THE EXTRA MILE STKS (HERITAGE H'CAP) 1m 1f 192y
2:10 (2:11) (Class 2) 4-Y-O+
£31,155 (£9,330; £4,665; £2,335; £1,165; £585) **Stalls** High

Form RPR
3420 **1** **Drumfire (IRE)**[19] 3781 5-9-10 **107**............................ JimmyFortune 11 115
(M Johnston) *hld up in abt 10th: taken to outer and prog over 2f out: hrd rdn to ld narrowly 1f out: asserted last 75yds* **8/1**
-266 **2** *½* **Sweet Lightning**[17] 3873 4-8-3 **86** ow1............................ MartinDwyer 4 93+
(W R Muir) *hld up in last pair: looking for room fr 3f out: stl last ent fnl 2f: gd prog jst over 1f out: r.o to snatch 2nd last stride* **11/2**[1]
0-11 **3** *nse* **Royal Destination (IRE)**[23] 3656 4-8-7 **90**............................ DaleGibson 7 97+
(J Noseda) *trckd ldng quartet: effrt to ld over 2f out: hrd rdn and hdd narrowly 1f out: kpt on but lost 2nd last stride* **8/1**
4362 **4** *1 ¼* **William Blake**[4] 4261 4-8-0 **83**............................ FrancisNorton 9 87+
(M Johnston) *ldng trio: lost pl 3f out and squeezed out immediately after: rdn to press ldrs fr 2f out: styd on but nt pce to chal* **7/1**[3]
6-55 **5** *1* **Alfathaa**[24] 3639 4-9-5 **102**............................ RHills 10 104
(W J Haggas) *lw: hld up in last pair: effrt on outer 2f out: styd on fr over 1f out: nt pce to threaten ldrs* **6/1**[2]

-004 **6** *nk* **Lang Shining (IRE)**[17] [3872] 5-9-2 **99** .... RyanMoore 6 100+
(Sir Michael Stoute) *lw: hld up in abt 10th: nt clr run fr 3f out to over 1f out: prog to chse ldrs ent fnl f: checked briefly sn after: kpt on same pce* **9/1**

7 *1 3/4* **Bravely Fought (IRE)**[27] [3517] 4-8-11 **94** .... KLatham 2 92
(Sabrina J Harty, Ire) *hld up in midfield: prog on outer 3f out: chal and upsides 2f out: wknd jst over 1f out* **16/1**

8 *2 1/2* **Charminamix (IRE)**[38] [3180] 6-8-1 **84** .... NickyMackay 8 77
(A J Martin, Ire) *hld up in last quartet: effrt towards outer over 2f out: hanging rt and no prog wl over 1f out: n.d after* **18/1**

-340 **9** *nk* **Dona Alba (IRE)**[59] [2475] 4-8-7 **90** .... EddieAhern 5 86+
(J L Dunlop) *hld up in midfield: prog on outer to chal over 2f out: edgd rt and nt qckn over 1f out: eased fnl f* **16/1**

-513 **10** *1* **Australia Day (IRE)**[25] [3586] 6-9-1 **98** .... RichardHughes 1 93+
(P R Webber) *mounted on crse and taken down early: led at brisk pce: shkn up and hdd over 2f out: steadily fdd: n.m.r 1f out and eased* **8/1**

0-63 **11** *1 3/4* **Moyenne Corniche**[12] [4002] 4-9-4 **101** .... HayleyTurner 14 94+
(M L W Bell) *lw: prom on inner: trapped bhd rivals fr 3f out: grad lost pl fr 2f out: eased whn no ch fnl f* **20/1**

0152 **12** *1 1/2* **Dark Prospect**[21] [3705] 4-8-2 **85** ....(p) ChrisCatlin 3 69
(M A Jarvis) *swtg: ldng trio tl rdn and steadily wknd fr wl over 2f out* **33/1**

1560 **13** *2 1/2* **Unbreak My Heart (IRE)**[17] [3873] 4-8-9 **92** .... PaulHanagan 12 71
(R A Fahey) *trckd ldrs: rdn and steadily wknd fr over 2f out* **12/1**

0650 **14** *3 3/4* **Blythe Knight (IRE)**[24] [3639] 9-9-2 **99** .... GrahamGibbons 13 70
(J J Quinn) *hld up in midfield on inner: rdn and dropped to rr wl over 2f out: sn no ch* **33/1**

2m 6.92s (-1.08) **Going Correction** +0.125s/f (Good) **14** Ran SP% **120.9**
Speed ratings (Par 109): **109,108,108,107,106 106,105,103,102,102 100,99,97,94**
toteswingers: 1&2 £12.50, 1&3 £16.40, 2&3 £7.40. CSF £50.67 CT £369.20 TOTE £10.70: £3.60, £2.40, £3.20; EX 62.00 Trifecta £878.20 Pool: £1,542.88 1.30 - winning units..
Owner Kennet Valley Thoroughbreds Iv **Bred** Epona Bloodstock Ltd **Trained** Middleham Moor, N Yorks

FOCUS
A high-class handicap run at a solid gallop thanks to Australia Day, who was soon in front and gradually tacked across from the widest stall, before weakening in the straight. A personal best from Drumfire,who enjoyed a clearer run than most.

NOTEBOOK
Drumfire(IRE), in contrast to the fast-finishing runner-up, enjoyed one continuous run in the straight after being switched towards the outer around two furlongs out, and he stayed on well. The winner was a faller in the 2007 totesport Mile here only his only previous try in a handicap, and this represented a drop in grade after facing some stiff tasks lately, including a Group 3 last time. This was a very smart effort under top weight off a mark of 107, and a return to pattern company probably awaits. It's interesting to note his stable's last winner of this race, Crosspeace in 2006, followed up later in the week in the Glorious Stakes, which was then a Listed contest, and Drumfire holds an entry in that same contest, although it's now a Group 3. (op 10-1)
Sweet Lightning got going too late after being denied a clear run for much of the straight. Having been held up in an unpromising position by Dwyer, who put up 1lb overweight, the gelding only had two of three behind when still trying to negotiate a clear passage over a furlong out, before finishing strongly. (op 6-1 tchd 5-1 and 13-2 in places)
Royal Destination(IRE) ◆, the winner of two races over 1m this year, the first a maiden and then a handicap off 82, was travelling better than most in the straight, but he was in front plenty soon enough (around two furlongs out) and would probably have preferred to get a lead for longer, especially as he was up in trip. He remains progressive but on this evidence he'll be well suited by a return to shorter. (op 7-1 tchd 17-2 and 9-1 in places)
William Blake, a stablemate of the winner, looked unlucky not to finish quite a bit closer as he lost a handy position around three furlongs out when squeezed up between rivals, possibly as a result of becoming briefly outpaced. He recovered his momentum admirably and ran on, but the damage was already done. (op 8-1)
Alfathaa was set quite a bit to do and had to wait for a run, even though he had been taken towards the outer in good time, but in truth he simply failed to muster the required speed once under pressure. (tchd 7-1)
Lang Shining(IRE), held up towards the inside for much of the way, didn't get a clear run in the straight, continually having to be switched, but at the same time didn't look totally comfortable on the track. He would have finished closer granted a better trip. Official explanation: jockey said horse was denied a clear run (op 10-1)
Bravely Fought(IRE), bidding for a hat-trick following wins over this sort of trip in his native Ireland, made a big move towards the outside early in the straight, which was plenty soon enough, and unsurprisingly couldn't sustain his run. (tchd 18-1 and 20-1 in places)
Charminamix(IRE) is a little better than he showed considering he didn't get the best of runs through and was inclined to hang right, not handling the track, when his rider attempted to switch him left. (op 20-1 tchd 16-1)
Dona Alba(IRE) was reported to have suffered interference in running. Official explanation: jockey said filly suffered interference in running (op 20-1)
Moyenne Corniche ideally wants soft ground but Hayley Turner reported the colt was denied a clear run. Official explanation: jockey said colt was denied a clear run (tchd 16-1)

4405 BETFAIR GORDON STKS (GROUP 3) 1m 4f
2:45 (2:47) (Class 1) 3-Y-O

£39,739 (£15,064; £7,539; £3,759; £1,883; £945) **Stalls** Low

Form RPR

21 **1** **Harbinger**[83] [1793] 3-9-0 96 .... RyanMoore 4 116+
(Sir Michael Stoute) *trckd ldrs: effrt to ld over 2f out: wl in command fr over 1f out: rdn out fnl f* **11/4**[1]

2111 **2** *1 3/4* **Firebet (IRE)**[19] [3780] 3-9-0 107 .... PaulHanagan 1 110+
(R A Fahey) *lw: hld up in rr: prog on outer fr 3f out: sn rdn: chsd wnr over 1f out: kpt on but no imp* **3/1**[2]

1 **3** *nk* **Urban Poet (USA)**[12] [4014] 3-9-0 0 .... GregFairley 7 109+
(M Johnston) *w'like: str: lw: led at modest pce to over 7f out: dropped to 3rd 1/2-way: trapped bhd rivals 3f out and nt pce to get out: styd on again to take 3rd 1f out: gaining on runner-up fin* **6/1**

1442 **4** *2* **Tactic**[19] [3778] 3-9-0 105 .... RHills 3 106
(J L Dunlop) *swtg: ldng trio: jnd ldr 5f out: disp tl hdd over 2f out: one pce fr over 1f out* **7/1**

-200 **5** *1 1/4* **Montaff**[39] [3087] 3-9-0 106 ....(v[1]) DarryllHolland 5 104
(M R Channon) *plld hrd: hld up tl prog to trck ldrs 1/2-way: pushed along over 4f out and rn in snatches after: dropped to rr 2f out: kpt on last 150yds* **16/1**

3656 **6** *shd* **Heliodor (USA)**[10] [4090] 3-9-0 104 .... RichardHughes 2 104
(R Hannon) *hld up in last: sme prog fr 3f out: nt pce to trble ldrs fr over 1f out: pushed along ins fnl f* **50/1**

5301 **7** *1/2* **Big Bound (USA)**[12] [4020] 3-9-0 100 .... JimmyFortune 6 103
(J H M Gosden) *trckd ldr's slow pce tl led over 7f out: jnd 5f out: rdn and hdd over 2f out: grad fdd* **25/1**

-234 **8** *shd* **Masterofthehorse (IRE)**[30] [3438] 3-9-0 0 .... PhilipRobinson 8 103
(Miss D Mountain) *hld up in rr: effrt on outer 3f out: nt qckn and no prog 2f out: fdd over 1f out* **4/1**[3]

2- **9** *7* **Swindler (IRE)**[384] [3853] 3-9-0 0 .... WilliamBuick 9 92
(A M Balding) *t.k.h: in tch: dropped to last wl over 2f out: wknd* **16/1**

2m 39.98s (1.58) **Going Correction** +0.125s/f (Good) **9** Ran SP% **116.0**
Speed ratings (Par 110): **99,97,97,96,95 95,95,95,90**
toteswingers: 1&2 £2.70, 1&3 £4.10, 2&3 £4.70. CSF £11.24 TOTE £3.80: £1.50, £1.70, £1.90; EX 12.70 Trifecta £70.70 £1,671.16 - 17.00 winning units..
Owner Highclere Thoroughbred Racing (Adm. Rous) **Bred** Mrs A K H Ooi **Trained** Newmarket, Suffolk

FOCUS
A traditional St Leger Trial whose winners boast a good record in the final Classic, with three having gone on to take that race this century. This was a muddling renewal, the field finishing compressed, but Harbinger looked better than the bare form.

NOTEBOOK
Harbinger ◆, representing Sir Michael Stoute, who had been responsible for three of the previous eight winners, improved that statistic with a decisive success. Lightly raced, this colt built on his debut when taking a 1m2f maiden at Chester in May (beating a subsequent dual winner), but had been absent since having suffered a muscle tear in his quarters. Sent off favourite, he moved up to chase the leaders soon after taking the top turn and went to the front a fair way from home. He kept galloping despite flashing his tail, and never looked like being beaten. His trainer reckons he will come on for the run and will now send him for the Great Voltigeur, after which a decision will be made about the St Leger, although he is not totally convinced that he is the type for the latter race. The only negative aspect of the race was the modest time, but that was due to the pace slowing appreciably before halfway, plus the runners faced a strong wind in the straight. (op 5-2 tchd 7-2 and 4-1 in places)
Firebet(IRE), a smart, progressive sort who is effective at 1m-1m2f, was stepping up in trip but ran his race and seemed to get the extra distance. He was within half a length of the winner over 2f out but his rider was already at work and, although he never gave up, the winner always had his measure. He will probably be aimed for a Group 2 in Baden-Baden next. (op 7-2 tchd 4-1 in places)
Urban Poet(USA) ◆, a $2,900,000 yearling and half-brother to seven winners including the high-class American dirt performer Pulpit, had been an easy winner on his sole start over 1m3f on fast ground. This was a big step up in class but, after setting the pace, his rider steadied the gallop and conceded the lead before halfway. He stayed on really well in the straight as if he will get further, and it may have been better if he had kept up the gallop from the front. (tchd 11-2)
Tactic, a Group 3-placed C&D winner, has been racing over further and was given a positive ride. He was quite keen early but his rider did not want to be exposed in front, although he kept close tabs on whoever was leading. He was unable to pick up as well as the principals but kept galloping and the longer trip of the St Leger should be in his favour. (op 12-1 tchd 14-1 in places)
Montaff, second in the Lingfield Derby Trial, had a lot to find with Masterofthehorse on Epsom Derby form. He did not run badly in the first-time visor, but looks held at this level and may have to go to abroad to find success. (op 25-1)
Heliodor(USA) has not really been able to make an impression at Listed level this season and this step up in trip and grade was unlikely to make things easier. He kept on without ever really being involved. (tchd 40-1)
Big Bound(USA) is a keen sort and went to the front once the pace dropped before halfway. He led until about the quarter-mile pole but then had nothing more to offer. Perhaps this longer trip found him out and a drop back to 1m2f looks on the cards.
Masterofthehorse(IRE), third in the Derby and fourth in the Irish Derby, has since left Aidan O'Brien. He was held up off the pace but tended to lug in under pressure in the straight and never threatened. (tchd 7-2)
Swindler(IRE), runner-up to Soul City on only his start at Newmarket over a year ago, a race from which eight of the 11 runners have all won at least once since, is bred to be a middle-distance horse. However, this was a stiff ask on his return to action and, although he looked fit enough, he did not help himself by being keen early on. He can be expected to do better with this run under his belt, albeit at a lower level. (op 12-1)

4406 BETFAIR CUP (REGISTERED AS THE LENNOX STKS) (GROUP 2) 7f
3:25 (3:26) (Class 1) 3-Y-O+

£87,993 (£33,356; £16,693; £8,323; £4,169; £2,092) **Stalls** High

Form RPR

03-0 **1** **Finjaan**[87] [1675] 3-8-9 116 .... TPO'Shea 9 114+
(M P Tregoning) *hld up in 5th gng wl: plld out and prog over 1f out: drvn and r.o to ld last 150yds: a holding runner-up* **5/1**[3]

1032 **2** *1/2* **Balthazaar's Gift (IRE)**[17] [3846] 6-9-2 111 .... AdamKirby 3 115
(C G Cox) *stdd s: hld up in last pair: plld out and prog 2f out: drvn to press wnr last 100yds: r.o but nvr gng to get past* **25/1**

2101 **3** *1* **Regal Parade**[17] [3846] 5-9-2 107 .... AdrianTNicholls 4 113
(D Nicholls) *trckd ldng trio: rdn 3f out: prog to ld over 1f out: hdd and outpcd last 150yds* **16/1**

0544 **4** *1 1/2* **Dream Eater (IRE)**[17] [3841] 4-9-2 111 ....(t) WilliamBuick 8 109
(A M Balding) *t.k.h: led 1f: lost pl on inner over 2f out: waiting for run over 1f out: kpt on fnl f: no ch* **16/1**

5-00 **5** *nk* **Express Wish**[31] [3398] 5-9-2 107 .... RichardHughes 5 108
(J Noseda) *stdd s: t.k.h: hld up in last trio: hld on to tl asked for effrt over 1f out: styd on same pce: n.d* **33/1**

-101 **6** *3/4* **Ouqba**[41] [3011] 3-8-9 114 .... RHills 6 103
(B W Hills) *s.s and rousted along early: in tch in last trio: taken to outer and shkn up 3f out: no rspnse: no ch after: plugged on fnl f* **6/1**

1143 **7** *1* **J J The Jet Plane (SAF)**[18] [3819] 5-9-2 119 .... KShea 2 103
(M F De Kock, South Africa) *b: trckd ldr over 4f out and sn upsides: led over 2f out: rdn and hdd over 1f out: wknd and eased* **4/1**[2]

1142 **8** *3 1/4* **Main Aim**[18] [3819] 4-9-2 121 .... RyanMoore 1 94
(Sir Michael Stoute) *led after 1f: pushed along whn pressed over 3f out: hdd u.p over 2f out: sn btn and eased* **6/5**[1]

1m 26.46s (-0.94) **Going Correction** +0.125s/f (Good)
WFA 3 from 4yo+ 7lb **8** Ran SP% **115.0**
Speed ratings (Par 115): **110,109,108,106,106 105,104,100**
toteswingers: 1&2 £21.00, 1&3 £16.20, 2&3 £16.60. CSF £112.60 TOTE £7.10: £2.10, £4.10, £4.00; EX 140.20 Trifecta £542.00 Pool: £2,051.02 - 2.80 winning units..
Owner Hamdan Al Maktoum **Bred** Shadwell Estate Company Limited **Trained** Lambourn, Berks

FOCUS
This 7f Group 2 is usually pretty competitive and often falls to an in-form or improving type. Three-year-olds have slightly the better record, although successes have been fairly evenly spread amongst that age group, four and five-year-olds. This year's line-up looked interesting in that it pitched some progressive types against some seasoned older horses. A bit of a messy renewal with the form pair from the July Cup finishing seventh and eighth, and this is pretty ordinary form for the grade.

NOTEBOOK
Finjaan, not seen since finishing ninth in 2000 Guineas, partly due to his stable having been closed down for a period, had finished a close third in the Dewhurst last year. He had also won the Molecomb on this corresponding day last season and had reportedly been working well. He travelled well into the race and found enough for pressure to hold off the runner-up. The Hungerford Stakes at Newbury looks a likely target but he may revert to sprinting before too long, in which case the Betfred Sprint Cup could come into the equation. (op 8-1)

Balthazaar's Gift(IRE) is best known as a Group-class sprinter but stays 7f. He has been running well since joining his current trainer after a spell in Dubai and ran with plenty of credit again, chasing the winner throughout the final furlong. On this evidence there may be another Group race to be won with him. (op 22-1)

Regal Parade has really improved in the last year, winning the Ayr Gold Cup, a conditions race and a Listed contest. This was another step up, even though after coming to have every chance he was unable to respond to the late challenges. He is in the Betfred Sprint Cup but the City of York Stakes at the Ebor meeting looks a possible target for him. (op 20-1)

Dream Eater(IRE), who has given the impression that a drop to 7f would suit, ran a fine race having never been far away. He is not easy to place but looks more than capable of taking a Listed event if things fall right. (op 20-1)

Express Wish, a C&D winner on soft ground, has been struggling for form this season but the return here produced something of a revival. He could be one to bear in mind for a race on a sharp track and easier ground. (op 40-1)

Ouqba, winner of the Jersey Stakes, had a bit to find with Finjaan on previous form and did not help his chance by missing the break. He had to come wide and never reached the front rank and his rider reported he moved badly throughout. he was subsequently reported as lame by the vet. Official explanation: jockey said colt moved poorly throughout; vet said colt returned lame near-fore (tchd 13-2)

J J The Jet Plane(SAF), a top-class South African sprinter, had finished third in the July Cup and fourth in Golden Jubilee, and connections believed this longer trip would suit. He was ridden positively and never let the favourite get too far ahead, but ultimately that may have left him with nothing in reserve for the finish, as he faded late on. He is now to join Richard Hannon after a disagreement between his owners and Mike de Kock. (op 9-2 tchd 5-1 in places)

Main Aim, a progressive sort with the best form coming into this, having beaten J J The Jet Plane when second in July Cup and had Dream Eater behind when fourth in Queen Anne. He was quite free early and after a furlong he took over in front, but he looked in trouble at the quarter-mile pole and dropped away, being eased when his chance had gone. His rider reported that the colt hit his head on the stalls and that he ran flat - possibly the race came too soon - and he will be given a break before being aimed at the Betfred Sprint Cup. Official explanation: jockey said colt hit its head on starting stalls (op 11-10 tchd Evens and 5-4, 10-11 in places)

4407 BETFAIR MOLECOMB STKS (GROUP 3) 5f

4:00 (4:02) (Class 1) 2-Y-O

£34,062 (£12,912; £6,462; £3,222; £1,614; £810) **Stalls** Low

Form				RPR
1151	**1**		**Monsieur Chevalier (IRE)**[10] 4089 2-9-0 0 RichardHughes 10 (R Hannon) *lw: stdd s: dropped in drom wd draw and hld up in last: stl there 2f out: prog but only 6th 1f out: qcknd through rivals to ld last 75yds: impressive* **10/11**[1]	108+
310	**2**	1 1/4	**Mister Manannan (IRE)**[42] 2995 2-9-0 0 AdrianTNicholls 8 (D Nicholls) *led over 3f out: crossed to nr side sn after 1/2-way: drvn and kpt on wl fr over 1f out: hdd and outpcd fnl 75yds* **8/1**[2]	101
1533	**3**	1	**Archers Road (IRE)**[10] 4089 2-9-0 0 RyanMoore 11 (M R Channon) *racd on wd outside: nt able to go early pce: rdn and prog fr 2f out: styd on steadily to take 3rd last strides* **8/1**[2]	97
2606	**4**	hd	**Star Rover (IRE)**[10] 4089 2-9-0 0 PaulDoe 7 (P D Evans) *gd spd: chsd ldr 3f out: rdn and hld 1f out: lost 2 pls fnl 100yds but kpt on* **25/1**	96
4311	**5**	3/4	**Bould Mover**[25] 3559 2-9-0 0 DarryllHolland 5 (R Curtis) *chsd ldrs: rdn wl over 1f out: kpt on ins fnl f: nvr enough pce to chal* **14/1**	93
1224	**6**	1/2	**Reignier**[19] 3779 2-9-0 0 AndrewElliott 3 (K R Burke) *lw: gd spd over 1f: lost pl sn after: hrd rdn 1/2-way: clsd u.p over 1f out: kpt on one pce* **11/1**[3]	92
1242	**7**	3 1/4	**Soccer (USA)**[20] 3742 2-9-0 0 (t) RichardKingscote 9 (Tom Dascombe) *sn dropped to rr on outer: rdn bef 1/2-way: keeping on steadily but no real ch whn hmpd jst ins fnl f* **25/1**	82+
1105	**8**	2 1/4	**Here Now And Why (IRE)**[10] 4089 2-9-0 0 NCallan 6 (K A Ryan) *racd towards outer: chsd ldrs: drvn 2f out: wknd jst over 1f out* **50/1**	72
102	**9**	1	**Mdawee (IRE)**[18] 3805 2-9-0 0 JimCrowley 1 (Tom Dascombe) *racd against nr side rail: led to over 3f out: nt hold position fr 1/2-way: wknd over 1f out* **33/1**	68
2311	**10**	1	**Iver Bridge Lad**[25] 3583 2-9-0 0 MarcHalford 4 (J Ryan) *sn struggling to go the pce: u.p in rr by 1/2-way: no prog* **8/1**[2]	65
0411	**11**	2 1/2	**Totally Invincible (IRE)**[18] 3805 2-8-11 0 RichardMullen 2 (E S McMahon) *unable to hold pl and dropped to rr against nr side rail after 2f: sltly hmpd 1/2-way: no ch after* **16/1**	53

58.24 secs (-0.16) **Going Correction** +0.125s/f (Good) **11 Ran SP% 119.2**

Speed ratings (Par 104): **106,104,102,102,100 100,94,91,89,88 84**

toteswingers: 1&2 £4.00, 1&3 £2.60, 2&3 £9.90. CSF £8.38 TOTE £1.90: £1.20, £2.90, £2.20; EX 11.30 Trifecta £82.40 Pool: £1,937.11 - 17.39 winning units..

Owner Mrs Valerie Hubbard & Ian Higginson **Bred** Tally-Ho Stud **Trained** East Everleigh, Wilts

■ Stewards' Enquiry : Richard Hughes one-day ban: careless riding (Aug 11)

FOCUS

A solid renewal of this Group 3 contest run, as usual, at a very strong pace.

NOTEBOOK

Monsieur Chevalier(IRE) followed up his Super Sprint success from ten days earlier with another visually remarkable effort, his sixth win from seven career starts. As per usual, he was well out the back early on and, racing in last place, was soon around seven lengths off the pace, but his terrific finishing effort was once again in evidence and he weaved between horses in the latter stages to ultimately get on top in good time and win comfortably. By no means sure to train on, it's no surprise his connections want to get as much out of him as possible this season and it's not out of the question he could return to Goodwood for Friday's Richmond Stakes. In the longer term, it's a shame he's not in the Nunthorpe, but he's entered in the Gimcrack and the Middle Park, and the Mill Reef is also an option. He shapes as though he'll get another furlong okay, but Richard Hughes made a good point after the Super Sprint, noting that jockeys tend to ride more of a race over 6f and this colt might not find the leaders stopping as quickly when upped in trip. (op Evens tchd 11-10 in a place)

Mister Manannan(IRE) ◆ was suffering from sore shins when disappointing in the Windsor Castle at Royal Ascot, but this was much better. He showed the sort of speed he displayed when winning his maiden impressively at Pontefract, and kept on best of those who were handy, but the winner was much too good late on. He has an entry in the Gimcrack, but his trainer describes him as still backward and weak and doesn't want to over-race him this year. (tchd 9-1 and 10-1 in places)

Archers Road(IRE) was having his 11th start and must be at least on a par with the winner in terms of toughness, but he was held by that rival on recent Super Sprint form. Racing out wide throughout from his high draw, he lacked the early speed of some of these but finished quite well and ran about as well as could have been expected. Ryan Moore reported the colt hung left-handed. Official explanation: jockey said colt hung left-handed (op 12-1)

Star Rover(IRE) is another supremely tough individual and he ran a cracker on his tenth start of the campaign. (op 40-1)

Bould Mover cost only 3,000gns but he's progressed to a very useful level and ran well following a couple of wins in minor company. (op 10-1 tchd 9-1)

Reignier showed good speed to sit about fourth after a furlong or so, but he didn't seem to handle the undulations and soon lost his place, before keeping on all too late. He had good Group-race form coming into this, most notably when runner-up (ahead of today's winner, albeit that one was hampered) in the Norfolk, and can be given another chance. (op 12-1)

Soccer(USA) is a likeable individual but lacked the speed of some of these and looks ready for 6f. (op 20-1)

Iver Bridge Lad ran nowhere near the form he showed to win a Listed race over 5f at Sandown on his previous start and seemingly didn't appreciate this vastly different track. (op 9-1)

4408 DETICA SUMMER STKS (H'CAP) 1m 6f

4:35 (4:36) (Class 2) (0-105,104) 3-Y-O+

£12,462 (£3,732; £1,866; £934; £466; £234) **Stalls** Low

Form				RPR
-302	**1**		**Manyriverstocross (IRE)**[18] 3822 4-9-0 **90** RyanMoore 3 (A King) *settled wl in rr: plenty to do 4f out: sustained prog on outer fr 3f out: clsd 1f out: drvn ahd last 100yds: a jst holding on* **5/1**[1]	99
11-0	**2**	hd	**Precision Break (USA)**[86] 1696 4-9-1 **91** MartinDwyer 4 (P F I Cole) *hld up in last trio: plenty to do 4f out: sustained prog on outer fr 3f out: drvn to chal fnl f: pressed wnr: jst hld* **20/1**	100
2156	**3**	1 1/4	**Drill Sergeant**[17] 3874 4-10-0 **104** GregFairley 14 (M Johnston) *led at decent pce: breather 1/2-way: rdn and hdd on inner over 2f out: battled bk gamely to ld over 1f out: v tired and hdd last 100yds* **14/1**	111
4120	**4**	3/4	**Yes Mr President (IRE)**[24] 3620 4-8-13 **89** NCallan 13 (M Johnston) *lw: pressed ldrs: rdn over 2f out: wnt 2nd briefly 1f out: no ex fnl 150yds* **11/2**[2]	95
2131	**5**	1/2	**Cool Strike (UAE)**[18] 3822 3-7-12 **88** (v) NickyMackay 12 (A M Balding) *t.k.h: prog to trck ldrs after 5f: cl up on inner 2f out: nt qckn over 1f out: one pce* **6/1**[3]	93
3305	**6**	1	**Rajeh (IRE)**[18] 3826 6-8-12 **88** LiamJones 1 (J L Spearing) *lw: t.k.h: wl plcd: chsd ldrs and rdn over 4f out: kpt on and cl enough in 5th over 2f out: one pce after* **8/1**	92
0165	**7**	3/4	**Hindu Kush (IRE)**[22] 3700 4-9-11 **101** AdrianTNicholls 8 (D Nicholls) *prom 4f: dropped to midfield after: rdn and in tch over 3f out: nt qckn over 2f out: kpt on same pce* **20/1**	104
00-4	**8**	1	**Camps Bay (USA)**[59] 2471 5-9-7 **97** JimCrowley 6 (Mrs A J Perrett) *settled in rr: u.p and wl off the pce over 4f out: nt clr run briefly 3f out: kpt on fnl 2f: no ch* **12/1**	99
1015	**9**	2	**Quai D'Orsay**[17] 3874 3-8-7 **97** RHills 2 (M Johnston) *trckd ldr: effrt to ld gng strly over 2f out: hdd & wknd over 1f out* **8/1**	96+
00-0	**10**	3 1/4	**Bureaucrat**[9] 2706 7-8-12 **88** EddieAhern 10 (P J Hobbs) *lw: dwlt: towards rr: rdn and wl off the pce over 4f out: nvr on terms w ldrs after* **16/1**	82
04-0	**11**	nk	**Candle**[15] 3510 6-8-9 **85** oh2 HayleyTurner 5 (T R George) *sn trckd ldrs: rdn in cl 4th over 2f out: wknd over 1f out* **33/1**	79
5344	**12**	25	**Sugar Ray (IRE)**[17] 3874 5-9-11 **101** (vt) LDettori 11 (Saeed Bin Suroor) *t.k.h: stdd into midfield after 4f: lost tch w ldrs 4f out: threw in the towel sn after: eased fnl 2f: t.o* **11/1**	60
-00	**13**	3	**Rock Ascot (URU)**[10] 4090 5-9-3 **93** GeorgeBaker 9 (G L Moore) *hld up in rr: wknd 4f out: t.o* **66/1**	48
40-6	**14**	65	**Waldvogel (IRE)**[159] 616 5-9-13 **103** DaneO'Neill 7 (L M Cumani) *a in last trio: wknd over 4f out: t.o* **17/2**	—

3m 1.19s (-2.41) **Going Correction** +0.125s/f (Good)

WFA 3 from 4yo+ 14lb **14 Ran SP% 121.6**

Speed ratings (Par 109): **111,110,110,109,109 108,108,107,106,104 104,90,88,51**

toteswingers: 1&2 £22.60, 1&3 £18.60, 2&3 £36.40. CSF £110.53 CT £1335.23 TOTE £6.20: £2.50, £6.00, £5.00; EX 127.10 TRIFECTA Not won..

Owner Mrs M C Sweeney **Bred** Crone Stud Farms Ltd **Trained** Barbury Castle, Wilts

FOCUS

The pace was strong, helping those held up, and this was a good race. Solid form, the winner turning around Newmarket form with the fifth.

NOTEBOOK

Manyriverstocross(IRE) proved suited by this step back up in trip and reversed recent July course placings with Cool Strike. He was still a long way off the third-placed finisher early in the straight, but responded really well to pressure and reeled that rival in, as well finding enough to hold off the runner-up's sustained challenge on his outside. He'll now be aimed at the Ebor and a 4lb penalty should help him make the cut. In the longer term, he's already been schooled over hurdles and promises to make a useful recruit to jumping. (op 7-1)

Precision Break(USA) raced even further back than the winner - he was last of all early - but produced a sustained effort on the outside and stayed on really well, although he was possibly always just held. A progressive middle-distance/staying performer last year, he lost a shoe on his reappearance over 1m4f and this was a fine effort on only his second start of the campaign. Evidently still improving, he's in the Ebor but is no sure thing to make the cut. (op 16-1)

Drill Sergeant did well to finish so close considering he set a fast pace, and the front two came from well back. A smart effort under top weight. (op 10-1)

Yes Mr President(IRE) proved suited by the return to this trip and ran a good race in defeat, only tiring late on having been handily placed throughout. (op 13-2)

Cool Strike(UAE) was unable to confirm recent Newmarket placings with today's winner on 3lb worse terms and was seemingly not as well suited by the step up to 1m6f as that rival. (tchd 7-1 and 15-2 in places)

Rajeh(IRE) seemed to have the race run to suit and a little better could have been expected. He's proving frustrating this season. (op 12-1)

Hindu Kush(IRE), successful in a weak Listed race in Ireland earlier in the year, didn't look particularly well treated on this first try in a handicap. (op 14-1)

Camps Bay(USA) was looking to stay on from a long way back when checked in his run early in the straight and that cost him vital momentum. Although not unlucky, he couldn't have been expected to recover and is worth another chance.

Quai D'Orsay looked a non-stayer when upped to this trip for the first time in a Listed handicap at York on his previous start and confirmed that impression, travelling strongly in the straight before finding less than had looked likely. (op 9-1)

Sugar Ray(IRE) was keen early and offered little under pressure. Last year's Duke of Edinburgh winner for Sir Michael Stoute, he has proved frustrating since joining his current yard and may only take an interest these days when allowed a soft lead. Frankie Dettori reported that the gelding was unsuited by the track. Official explanation: jockey said gelding was unsuited by the track (op 8-1)

Waldvogel(IRE), an Ebor entrant, was always out the back. His rider reported that the gelding lost his action coming down the hill. Official explanation: jockey said colt lost its action coming down the hill (op 14-1 tchd 8-1)

4409 TATLER SUMMER SEASON STKS (H'CAP) 1m

5:10 (5:13) (Class 3) (0-90,90) 3-Y-O+ **£12,952** (£3,854; £1,926; £962) **Stalls** High

Form				RPR
6215	**1**		**Marajaa (IRE)**[20] 3752 7-9-8 **84** ChrisCatlin 20 (W J Musson) *hld up in rr: clsd on ldng gp fr 3f out and looking for room gng wl: gap appeared jst over 1f out: qcknd and led last 100yds: rdn out* **12/1**	94+

1114 **2** ¾ **Mister Dee Bee (IRE)**[19] 3780 3-9-6 **90**.......................... MichaelHills 15 96
(B W Hills) *lw: bec unsettled in stalls: led: gng strly w pack trying to cl 2f out: styd on wl but hdd and outpcd last 100yds* **11/2**[1]

1-04 **3** 1½ **The Which Doctor**[13] 3988 4-9-11 **87**.......................... RyanMoore 17 93+
(J Noseda) *swtg: hld up in midfield on inner: trckd ldrs fr 3f out: trying for gap up inner after: wnt 2nd briefly 1f out: appeared hmpd sn after: one pce* **8/1**[3]

3006 **4** nse **Salient**[6] 4211 5-9-2 **78**.......................... KirstyMilczarek 18 85+
(M J Attwater) *sn trckd ldng pair: squeezed for room fr jst over 2f out whn disputing 2nd: styd on same pce fnl f* **20/1**

0554 **5** ¾ **Sohcahtoa (IRE)**[6] 4210 3-9-6 **90**.......................... RichardHughes 6 91+
(R Hannon) *stdd s: hld up wl in rr: tried for run on inner fr over 2f out and repeatedly nowhere to go: styd on wl whn in the clr fnl f* **14/1**

3110 **6** shd **Eastern Empire**[40] 3049 3-9-5 **89**.......................... EddieAhern 11 90
(J W Hills) *lw: pressed ldrs: disp 2nd fr over 2f out and hanging rt: nt qckn over 1f out: one pce after* **9/1**

-013 **7** ½ **Wellington Square**[26] 3523 4-9-8 **84**.......................... GeorgeBaker 16 86
(H Morrison) *hld up in midfield: trcking ldrs fr 3f out and looking for room: gap appeared jst over 1f out but nt pce to deliver a chal* **13/2**[2]

1314 **8** 2 **Bold Cross (IRE)**[24] 3628 6-9-4 **80**.......................... PaulFitzsimons 3 77
(E G Bevan) *wl in rr: effrt on outer and sme prog 2f out: kpt on but nt pce to threaten* **50/1**

2023 **9** nk **Mujood**[20] 3752 6-9-8 **87**.......................... KevinGhunowa(3) 10 83
(Eve Johnson Houghton) *mostly chsd ldr: tight for room fr over 2f out: unable to hold pl and squeezed out jst over 1f out* **12/1**

5100 **10** 1¼ **Ellemujie**[24] 3639 4-10-0 **90**.......................... MartinDwyer 19 84+
(D K Ivory) *stdd s: hld up wl in rr: wnt for ambitious run up inner fr over 2f out and nowhere to go: one pce and n.d whn in the clr fnl f* **11/1**

2122 **11** 3¼ **Woodcote Place**[24] 3628 6-9-13 **89**.......................... JimCrowley 12 75
(P R Chamings) *restless stalls: hld up towards rr: hmpd 1/2-way and off the pce after: effrt on outer over 2f out: no prog over 1f out: wknd* **14/1**

1312 **12** 3 **Sunnyside Tom (IRE)**[24] 3615 5-9-9 **85**.......................... PaulHanagan 2 64
(R A Fahey) *racd wd in midfield: prog and on terms w ldrs fr 1/2-way: nt qckn 2f out: wknd jst over 1f out* **16/1**

1-00 **13** 1 **Willow Dancer (IRE)**[24] 3639 5-9-12 **88**..........................(p) AdamKirby 4 65
(W R Swinburn) *racd wd: hld up in midfield: effrt over 2f out and in tch w ldrs: wknd jst over 1f out* **25/1**

5510 **14** 11 **I Confess**[24] 3628 4-9-4 **80**..........................(b) PaulDoe 7 32
(P D Evans) *pressed ldrs: rdn over 3f out: sn lost pl and btn: t.o* **50/1**

-261 **15** 2½ **Mount Hadley (USA)**[24] 3615 5-9-6 **82**.......................... HayleyTurner 9 28
(G A Butler) *trckd ldrs: rdn over 2f out: sn lost pl: eased whn no ch over 1f out: t.o* **14/1**

0-03 **16** 6 **The Snatcher (IRE)**[85] 1731 6-9-10 **86**.......................... JimmyFortune 1 18
(R Hannon) *swtg: a wl in rr: eased whn no ch fnl 2f: t.o* **33/1**

0300 **17** 2¼ **Bencoolen (IRE)**[53] 2669 4-9-13 **89**.......................... AdrianTNicholls 13 16
(D Nicholls) *bec unsettled in stalls: a wl in rr: eased fnl 2f: t.o* **14/1**

-006 **U** **South Cape**[3] 4293 6-9-4 **85**..........................(p) MartinLane(5) 8 —
(G L Moore) *b: t.k.h in midfield: 11th whn stmbld and uns rdr 1/2-way* **20/1**

1m 39.7s (-0.20) **Going Correction** +0.125s/f (Good)
WFA 3 from 4yo+ 8lb **18 Ran SP% 126.3**
Speed ratings (Par 107): **106,105,103,103,102 102,102,100,100,98 95,92,91,80,78 72,69,—**
toteswingers: 1&2 £23.20, 1&3 £24.80, 2&3 £10.00. CSF £72.37 CT £420.99 TOTE £17.50: £3.60, £2.10, £2.20, £5.30; EX 111.10 Trifecta £1361.80 Pool: £2,024.30 - 1.10 winning units..
Owner John D Jacques **Bred** Shadwell Estate Company Limited **Trained** Newmarket, Suffolk
■ Stewards' Enquiry : Eddie Ahern four-day ban: careless riding (Aug 11-14)

FOCUS
A good and highly competitive handicap with as usual a big field and only 12lb covering them. A high draw has not necessarily been essential in recent runnings, with half of the last ten winners having come from a single-figure draw. However, on this occasion the high numbers prevailed with the first four all drawn 15 and above. The winner was back to his best with a pesonal best from the second and the next two close to their marks, but it was a messy race and several shaped better than the bare form.

NOTEBOOK
Marajaa(IRE) suffered from a lack of an opening, but when he did get some daylight he swept through and the race was over even before he hit the front. He was 6lb above his last winning mark but had proved he handled the track behind Mujood here in May. Also, since then he had run well in a handicap at Newmarket that has worked out really well, with now five of the first seven scoring next time out. He may stay here for the totesport Mile on Friday, where he will have a 3lb penalty, depending on how he comes out of this contest. (tchd 14-1)
Mister Dee Bee(IRE) ran a terrific race from the front and did not deserve to be beaten, but had no chance once the winner was in the clear. A three-time winner at up to 1m2f on fast ground earlier in the season, this was a drop in grade after he had been beaten in a heritage handicap last time. He clearly remains in good heart and compensation awaits, providing the handicapper does not react too strongly. The Cambridgeshire is the long-term target. (tchd 13-2 in places)
The Which Doctor had been well beaten on his only previous try here and was 3lb above his last winning mark. He tracked the leading group on the inner and got a relatively clear passage up the rail but could not quicken inside the final furlong. (tchd 9-1)
Salient, a regular in this type of contest on this track, took a similar route to the third but got involved in some buffeting over a furlong out before staying on again. He has not scored since winning over C&D in May 2008 but is now 8lb lower and will be suited by more cut in the ground. (op 16-1)
Sohcahtoa(IRE) ◆ was the eyecatcher of the race, apart from the winner. Held up off the pace he did not get much room on the rail over a furlong out but came through well in the last furlong. This spoilt his perfect record on the track but he is one to bear in mind, especially if returning here. (op 20-1)
Eastern Empire, another to have gained both his previous wins here, was another to run well under a fairly positive ride. He only tired in the closing stages but may just need the handicapper to ease him a little before scoring again. (op 10-1)
Wellington Square is lightly raced but had won here over 7f and stays 1m2f. Despite being 5lb above his last winning mark, he ran well to get into contention from off the pace before his effort flattened out late on. (tchd 7-1 in places)
Bold Cross(IRE), a multiple winner at this trip but making his first appearance on this track, was doing his best work late without ever getting into contention. (tchd 100-1 in places)
Mujood loves this track and had narrowly beaten the winner here early in the season and at Newmarket since. He ran well as usual but his positive running style was not helped by his middle draw which meant he had to do a lot of running to hold his place and meant he was vulnerable to the late challengers. He was beginning to struggle when short of room over a furlong out but may have another chance on his favourite track as he has three other engagements. (tchd 14-1 in places)
Ellemujie was looking for a run up the rail when his path was blocked and he had to switch, otherwise he would have been a little closer (op 14-1)
Woodcote Place probably lost his chance when getting upset in the stalls.
Sunnyside Tom(IRE) likes to race up with the pace but had to run wide from his outside stall and could never reach the front rank.
Mount Hadley(USA) was another one short of room at a vital stage but he was eased in the last furlong or so as if something was amiss. (op 16-1)
Bencoolen(IRE) reportedly lost his action. Official explanation: jockey said gelding lost its action (op 11-1)

4410 EUROPEAN BREEDERS' FUND SELSEY MAIDEN STKS (C&G) 6f
5:45 (5:47) (Class 2) 2-Y-O **£12,952** (£3,854; £1,926; £962) **Stalls** Low

Form RPR

52 **1** **Lowdown (IRE)**[14] 3957 2-9-0 **0**.......................... GregFairley 1 90+
(M Johnston) *lw: racd against nr side rail: mde all: stretched clr fr 2f out: at least 3 l ahd 1f out: rdn out and nvr in any danger* **2/1**[1]

23 **2** 1¼ **Red Badge (IRE)**[15] 3920 2-9-0 **0**.......................... RichardHughes 3 86+
(R Hannon) *lw: racd against nr side rail: mostly chsd wnr: hrd rdn over 2f out: sn outpcd: at least 3 l down over 1f out: drew clr of rest and grad clsd fnl f* **6/1**[3]

23 **3** 7 **George Benjamin**[17] 3875 2-9-0 **0**.......................... AdrianTNicholls 6 64
(D Nicholls) *lw: prom: disp 2nd pl fr 1/2-way: rdn over 2f out: sn outpcd: lft wl bhd by ldng pair fr over 1f out* **13/2**

4 1 **Aetos** 2-9-0 **0**.......................... PatDobbs 8 61
(M P Tregoning) *swtg: gd sort: t.k.h: hld up in midfeld: wl outpcd fr 2f out: plugged on* **10/3**[2]

5 1¼ **One Good Emperor (IRE)** 2-9-0 **0**.......................... SteveDrowne 9 58
(J R Best) *settled in last trio tl prog on outer to join chsers 1/2-way: outpcd 2f out: no ch after* **25/1**

6 hd **Ilston Lord (IRE)** 2-9-0 **0**.......................... MartinDwyer 5 60+
(M P Tregoning) *w'like: dwlt: struggling in last trio: wl bhd 2f out: styd on ins fnl f* **28/1**

7 1½ **Viking Dancer** 2-9-0 **0**.......................... WilliamBuick 4 52
(A M Balding) *w'like: unf: dwlt: rn green in last pair: nvr a factor: plugged on late* **11/1**

8 1 **Machine Gun Kelly (IRE)** 2-9-0 **0**.......................... RyanMoore 2 49
(G L Moore) *w'like: s.i.s: spd 2f: sn lost pl: struggling in rr over 2f out* **14/1**

03 **9** 3 **Sheer Force (IRE)**[18] 3792 2-9-0 **0**.......................... JimCrowley 7 40
(W J Knight) *unf: plld hrd: hld up in midfield: wknd rapidly over 1f out* **8/1**

1m 12.35s (0.15) **Going Correction** +0.125s/f (Good) **9 Ran SP% 117.4**
Speed ratings (Par 100): **104,102,93,91,90 89,87,86,82**
toteswingers: 1&2 £3.20, 1&3 £3.70, 2&3 £5.10. CSF £14.78 TOTE £3.30: £1.40, £2.10, £2.50; EX 15.50 Trifecta £34.90 Pool: £2,024.30 - 10.36 winning units. Place 6: £142.73 Place 5: £54.55.
Owner Sheikh Hamdan Bin Mohammed Al Maktoum **Bred** A Stroud And J Hanly **Trained** Middleham Moor, N Yorks

FOCUS
A maiden that should produce some winners.

NOTEBOOK
Lowdown(IRE) ◆ made full use of stall one. Soon in front against the stands'-side rail, this Shamardal colt gradually wound up the pace and lengthened impressively in the closing stages, drawing nicely clear and, although the runner-up made some late headway, there was a big gap back to the remainder. According to connections he has been quite a keen type, but he's well regarded and is expected to stay 7f-plus provided he continues to go the right way. One to keep on side. (op 5-2 tchd 11-4 and 3-1 in places)
Red Badge(IRE) ◆ ran his best race so far. He was being niggled along by about halfway, but gradually responded and there was much to like about the way he closed on the winner inside the final furlong, just as that rival was pulling away from the rest. He appeals as one to be with next time, either in another maiden or a nursery. (tchd 13-2)
George Benjamin was no match whatsoever for the front pair, but he had shown ability prior to this and helps give the form a solid look. Nurseries are now an option. (op 5-1)
Aetos, a 72,000gns half-brother to, among others, 7f juvenile winner Nizhoni Dancer, didn't help his chance by racing keenly. A big gamble throughout the day, he looked a nice type in the paddock and it's hoped he'll settle better next time. (op 4-1 tchd 9-2 and 5-1 in places)
One Good Emperor(IRE) ◆, a half-brother to dual 6f-7f winner Laddies Poker Two, was easy to back but showed definite signs of ability and this was an encouraging debut. He made a short-lived effort at about halfway, before tiring, and should improve.
Ilston Lord(IRE) ◆ cost only 7,000gns but he shaped with some promise. He was basically very green and should improve. (op 22-1)
Viking Dancer ◆, who looked inexperienced, should do much better in time. (op 8-1)
Sheer Force(IRE) was disappointing, running too keen early and then dropping away. (op 9-1 tchd 10-1)
T/Jkpt: Not won. T/Plt: £367.50 to a £1 stake. Pool: £264,789.97. 525.95 winning tickets. T/Qpdt: £142.60 to a £1 stake. Pool: £12,204.14. 63.31 winning tickets. JN

4390 GALWAY (R-H)
Tuesday, July 28
OFFICIAL GOING: Soft to heavy (heavy in places on chase course)

4412a TOTE GALWAY MILE EUROPEAN BREEDERS FUND H'CAP (PREMIER HANDICAP) 1m 100y
7:00 (7:02) 3-Y-O+
£81,689 (£25,961; £12,368; £4,213; £2,854; £1,495)

RPR

1 **Rock And Roll Kid (IRE)**[30] 3433 4-8-13 **97**.......................... DEMullins(5) 3 105+
(Anthony Mullins, Ire) *trckd ldrs: rdn to ld over 2f out: sn clr: styd on wl* **6/1**[1]

2 2 **Maundy Money**[18] 3829 6-9-0 **93**.......................... CO'Donoghue 16 97
(David Marnane, Ire) *sn trckd ldr in 2nd: t.k.h: rdn over 2f out: sn no imp: kpt on wout matching wnr* **11/1**

3 shd **Bobs Pride (IRE)**[30] 3439 7-9-1 **94**.......................... PJSmullen 5 98
(D K Weld, Ire) *mid-div: impr into 4th fr 2f out: no imp and kpt on u.p wout threatening fnl f* **9/1**[3]

4 ½ **Wigwam Willie (IRE)**[41] 3034 7-8-10 **89**..........................(tp) WJSupple 10 92
(K A Ryan) *mid-div: clsr in 7th fr 2f out: sn no imp u.p and kpt on wout threatening* **10/1**

5 ½ **Marias Dream (IRE)**[12] 4031 7-8-5 **89**.......................... GFCarroll(5) 4 91
(J G Coogan, Ire) *mid-div: hdwy into 3rd fr 2f out: sn no imp u.p and kpt on* **12/1**

6 1¼ **Kaitlins Joy (IRE)**[13] 3990 4-8-7 **89**.......................... PBBeggy(3) 14 88
(Patrick Martin, Ire) *sn mid-div: hdwy in 11th fr 2f out: kpt on wl u.p wout threatening* **11/1**

7 shd **Rose Hip (IRE)**[12] 4031 5-8-6 **85**.......................... CDHayes 1 84
(Joseph G Murphy, Ire) *towards rr: hdwy into 8th fr 2f out: kpt on wout threatening u.p* **14/1**

8 ½ **Castle Bar Sling (USA)**[30] 3433 4-8-13 **92**.......................... WMLordan 15 90
(T J O'Mara, Ire) *mid-div: 7th 3f out: dropped to 9th 2f out: sn no imp and kpt on same pce u.p* **14/1**

9 *1* **Miranda's Girl (IRE)**[22] 3699 4-9-0 93...............................(p) RPCleary 17 88
(Thomas Cleary, Ire) *prom: sn 3rd: dropped to 5th 2f out: sn no imp u.p*
6/1[1]

10 *2* **Belle's Ridge**[12] 4031 5-9-3 96...............................(b[1]) WJLee 13 87
(Timothy Doyle, Ire) *towards rr: nt clr run early stages: no imp and kpt on wout threatening fr over 2f out*
14/1

11 *hd* **Dedo (IRE)**[30] 3435 4-9-1 94... DPMcDonogh 18 84
(Kevin Prendergast, Ire) *sn trckd ldrs in 6th: no imp u.p fr bef st*
7/1[2]

12 *½* **Pires**[12] 3142 5-8-12 91.. FMBerry 2 80
(A J Martin, Ire) *towards rr: no imp fr under 3f out*
16/1

13 *1* **Monteriggioni (IRE)**[12] 4031 7-8-12 101.................. DCByrne[(10)] 11 88
(John Geoghegan, Ire) *towards rr: no imp fr over 2f out*
20/1

14 *hd* **Royal Power (IRE)**[41] 3014 6-8-10 94........................ ShaneFoley[(5)] 12 81
(D Nicholls) *nvr bttr than mid-div*
25/1

15 *1¾* **Celtic Dane (IRE)**[12] 4031 5-9-2 98.......................... CPGeoghegan[(3)] 6 81
(Kevin Prendergast, Ire) *sn mid-div: no imp fr over 2f out*
12/1

16 *4½* **Bashkirov**[29f] 6640 4-9-3 106....................................... RPWalsh[(10)] 9 79
(Luke Comer, Ire) *sn led: hdd over 2f out: wknd*
66/1

17 *2½* **Settigano (IRE)**[283] 6831 6-9-9 102...............................(p) MJKinane 7 69
(Michael Joseph Fitzgerald, Ire) *trckd ldrs: 4th 3f out: wknd u.p fr over 2f out*
16/1

18 *28* **Six Of Hearts**[39] 3091 5-9-2 95...(p) KJManning 8 1
(Cecil Ross, Ire) *mid-div best: dropped towards rr 1/2-way: sn no imp: t.o*
20/1

1m 57.02s (6.82) **18** Ran SP% **138.8**
CSF £76.76 CT £642.87 TOTE £6.10: £1.90, £3.40, £2.10, £2.50; DF 100.30.
Owner Barry Connell **Bred** Barry Connell **Trained** Gowran, Co Kilkenny

NOTEBOOK

Wigwam Willie(IRE) goes well with cut in the ground and was not beaten far in the end, although he never threatened to trouble the winner.

Royal Power(IRE) handled soft ground in the distant past but is better known for his exploits on fast and failed to make an impact.

4413 - 4416a (Foreign Racing) - See Raceform Interactive

[4404]GOODWOOD (R-H)

Wednesday, July 29

OFFICIAL GOING: Good

Rail from 6f on lower bend to winning post moved out 6yards increasing distances by 15yds; top bend dolled out 4yds increasing distances by 8yds.
Wind: Strong, mostly against Weather: Overcast becoming brighter

4417 RANGE ROVER BEST OF BRITISH GOODWOOD STKS (H'CAP) 2m 5f

2:10 (2:10) (Class 2) (0-95,95) 3-Y-O+

£31,155 (£9,330; £4,665; £2,335; £1,165; £585) **Stalls** Far side

Form RPR

1142 **1** **Sweetheart**[19] 3793 5-8-1 72.. LiamJones 2 83
(Jamie Poulton) *hld up in rr: rapid prog fr 12f out to join ldrs over 9f out: wnt 2nd over 4f out: led 3f out: rdn and steadily drew clr fnl 2f*
8/1[3]

-212 **2** *3¾* **Tyrrells Wood (IRE)**[39] 3143 4-9-5 **90**.......................... TPQueally 7 98
(T G Mills) *a in ldng quartet: wnt 2nd over 6f out: led 5f out and sn clr w 2 others: drvn over 3f out: sn hdd: plugged on but no ch w wnr fr over 1f out*
15/2[2]

-221 **3** *2* **Swingkeel (IRE)**[28] 3510 4-9-5 **90**................................. JimmyFortune 4 96+
(J L Dunlop) *lw: hld up wl in rr: stl in last pair over 4f out: rapid prog on inner sn after: wnt 3rd bhd clr ldng pair wl over 1f out: grad clsd on runner-up: hopeless task*
11/2[1]

2-16 **4** *1¾* **Woolfall Treasure**[43] 2994 4-9-4 **89**.............................. RyanMoore 17 93+
(G L Moore) *swtg: hld up towards rr: pushed along and n.m.r over 3f out: prog over 2f out: styd on wl to take 4th wl ins fnl f*
8/1[3]

4042 **5** *½* **Alnwick**[11] 4092 5-8-4 75.. AlanMunro 16 79
(P D Cundell) *hld up wl in rr: sme prog fr 3f out: swtchd rt over 2f out: hdwy after: kpt on fnl f: nvr able to strike a blow*
20/1

2-04 **6** *¾* **Absolut Power (GER)**[11] 4092 8-8-4 75......................... MartinDwyer 20 78
(J A Geake) *sn prom in chsng gp: 5th and rdn over 4f out: nvr on terms w ldrs but kpt on steadily u.p*
33/1

0-02 **7** *4½* **Always Bold (IRE)**[21] 3728 4-9-1 **86**............................ PaulHanagan 8 85
(D McCain Jnr) *lw: mostly in midfield: 11th and rdn over 4f out: plugged on fnl 3f but nvr remotely on terms*
14/1

0332 **8** *nk* **Relative Strength (IRE)**[19] 3797 4-8-6 77...................(v) WilliamBuick 5 76
(A M Balding) *hld up wl in rr: sme prog 8f out: rdn on outer over 3f out: w chsng gp over 2f out but no ch: wknd*
20/1

020/ **9** *5* **Shore Thing (IRE)**[38] 4572 6-7-11 71.............................. DavidProbert[(3)] 9 65
(C R Egerton) *prom in chsng gp: 6th and rdn over 4f out: no imp after: wknd 2f out*
40/1

0014 **10** *5* **Kasban**[19] 3793 5-8-3 74 ow2...(tp) RoystonFfrench 19 64
(Ian Williams) *hld up wl in rr: no prog over 4f out: nvr on terms after: only passed wkng and eased rivals*
28/1

-111 **11** *nk* **Markington**[34] 3313 6-8-2 76 ow5...............................(b) WilliamCarson[(3)] 11 66
(P Bowen) *slowly away: wl in rr: last and hanging to centre of crse 4f out: passed wkng and eased rivals fr over 2f out*
10/1

362/ **12** *½* **Last Flight (IRE)**[11] 6421 5-8-2 73...................................(b) LukeMorris 15 64
(P Bowen) *hld up in rr early: midfield fr 1/2-way: struggling u.p over 4f out: nt on terms w ldrs after*
9/1

5213 **13** *2½* **Swordsman (GER)**[11] 4092 7-8-0 71.......................... CatherineGannon 3 66+
(C Gordon) *disp ld tl led after 4f: hdd 5f out but clr w 2 rivals: steadily lost tch: heavily eased over 1f out*
25/1

-051 **14** *17* **Som Tala**[32] 3390 6-9-10 **95**.. LDettori 13 88+
(M R Channon) *w ldrs tl stdd after 4f: led chsng pack after: rdn and no imp 4f out: stl in chsng gp but wl btn 2f out: heavily eased over 1f out*
14/1

0 **15** *nse* **Sufad**[187] 271 4-8-4 75... HayleyTurner 1 46
(T D McCarthy) *prom in chsng gp: u.p in 7th 5f out: wknd rapidly 3f out: t.o*
100/1

6452 **16** *1½* **Valdan (IRE)**[19] 3809 5-7-11 75.................................. AndrewHeffernan[(7)] 18 45
(P D Evans) *hld up wl in rr: stl there whn nt clr run over 3f out to over 2f out: no prog: t.o*
40/1

4461 **17** *1* **Aaim To Prosper (IRE)**[11] 4092 5-8-9 **80**.....................(v) DarryllHolland 14 49
(M R Channon) *slowly away: a wl in rr: no prog 4f out: t.o*
20/1

1-06 **18** *10* **Casual Garcia**[14] 3986 4-8-2 73 ow2...............................(b) ChrisCatlin 12 33
(Sir Mark Prescott) *disp ld 4f: chsd ldr to over 6f out: sn u.p and losing grnd: wkng whn hmpd 3f out: t.o*
25/1

0-30 **19** *3½* **Baddam**[43] 2994 7-9-5 **90**..(p) RichardHughes 6 47
(Ian Williams) *nvr beyond midfield: dropped in rr over 5f out: no ch after: eased over 2f out: t.o*
14/1

4m 28.38s (-4.72) **Going Correction** +0.125s/f (Good) **19** Ran SP% **122.7**
Speed ratings (Par 109): **113,111,110,110,109 109,107,107,105,104 103,103,102,96,96 95,95,91,90**
toteswingers: 1&2 £6.20, 1&3 £5.00, 2&3 £4.40 CSF £57.35 CT £367.34 TOTE £6.30: £1.60, £2.00, £2.00, £2.80; EX 43.70 Trifecta £96.20 Pool: £2015.05 - 15.50 winning units..

Owner R W Huggins **Bred** Darley **Trained** Lewes, E Sussex

■ Stewards' Enquiry : Alan Munro two-day ban: careless riding (Aug 12-13)

FOCUS

A cracking marathon handicap, run at a solid gallop. Few got into it from off the pace, but the markets leaders still filled the first four places.

NOTEBOOK

Sweetheart proved an exception to those making an impact from off the pace and her rider's decision to move her nearer to the leaders, just as the gallop was being steadied a little with 7f to run, proved a winning move. She was right in the firing line prior to being asked for maximum effort passing the 3f marker and maintained a relentless gallop to the line. The runner-up did not go down without a fight, but she probably idled somewhat in front and was always holding that rival where it mattered. Her trainer does very well with this type of staying horse and this, her third win on the level since reverting from hurdling, rates a career-best display. The extra distance made all the difference to this game mare, as she stays 3m over jumps, and a likely rise in the weights will help her chances of getting a run in the Cesarewitch later in the year. (op 15-2 tchd 7-1 in places)

Tyrrells Wood(IRE) put in a brave effort and there should be no questioning his attitude, despite the fact he has now found one too good on four of his last five outings. He emerges with credit for rallying as he did considering he helped force the pace, and certainly deserves a change of fortune. This was his first run in new ownership and he is now set to join Jane Chapple-Hyam. (tchd 7-1 and 8-1 in places)

Swingkeel(IRE) ◆ came into this 7lb higher than when winning on the AW 28 days earlier. He got going all too late from way off the pace, but his rider should not be overly criticised as this is a confirmed hold-up horse. He is no doubt still on an upward curve and can be placed to find compensation sooner rather than later. (op 7-1 tchd 15-2 and 8-1 in places)

Woolfall Treasure, 3lb lower then when sixth in the Ascot Stakes in June, was another who stayed on too late in the day. He has now done more than enough in his last two runs to suggest he would be effective under a more positive ride at around this trip. (op 10-1)

Alnwick was back up to a career-high mark and ran a sound race over this stiffer test, but never threatened to play a part in the finish. He helps to set the level, though. He was later found to have finished distressed and his rider picked up a two-day ban for careless riding. Official explanation: vet said gelding returned distressed

Absolut Power(GER) ran close enough to his last-time-out form with Alnwick and is fairly treated at present, but this trip stretched him.

Always Bold(IRE) was not disgraced, but again left the impression a distance further than 2m stretches his stamina.

Relative Strength(IRE) is consistent and plugged on over this much longer trip but looks worth dropping back to 2m. (op 18-1 tchd 16-1)

Markington, bidding for a four-timer, did not fare too well with the tape start but is normally held up in any case. It was really the 5lb overweight he carried that hampered his cause. (tchd 9-1)

4418 VEUVE CLICQUOT VINTAGE STKS (GROUP 2) 7f

2:45 (2:47) (Class 1) 2-Y-O

£45,416 (£17,216; £8,616; £4,296; £2,152; £1,080) **Stalls** High

Form RPR

12 **1** **Xtension (IRE)**[43] 2993 2-9-0 0.. AdamKirby 2 110+
(C G Cox) *hld up in last trio: shkn up and looked in trble on inner over 2f out: plld out wd over 1f out: swooping run to ld last 100yds: edgd rt but sn clr*
7/2[1]

3 **2** *1¼* **Mata Keranjang (USA)**[25] 3648 2-9-0 0........................... MartinDwyer 8 106
(P F I Cole) *w'like: str: trckd ldrs: prog fr 2f out: gd burst to ld 1f out and looked likely wnr: swamped by wnr last 100yds*
14/1

4113 **3** *1½* **Corporal Maddox**[24] 3667 2-9-0 0....................................... JimCrowley 10 104+
(A P Jarvis) *hld up bhd ldrs: waiting for run over 2f out: eased out jst over 1f out: styd on to take 3rd but nt pce to trble ldng pair*
8/1

4210 **4** *½* **Big Audio (IRE)**[19] 3817 2-9-0 0...................................... RichardHughes 7 101
(R Hannon) *lw: led: set stdy pce to 1/2-way: drvn and hdd 1f out: outpcd*
7/1

1132 **5** *1* **Roi De Vitesse (IRE)**[19] 3817 2-9-0 0............................ JamesMillman 5 100+
(B R Millman) *hld up in tch on inner: clsd on ldrs over 2f out: nt clrest of runs after: kpt on same pce fnl f*
14/1

14 **6** *½* **She's A Character**[40] 3086 2-8-11 0................................ PaulHanagan 6 94
(R A Fahey) *trckd ldr: pushed along 3f out: stl wl there but u.p whn bmpd over 1f out: fdd fnl f*
16/1

1 **7** *hd* **Dreamspeed (IRE)**[26] 3584 2-9-0 0................................. WilliamBuick 1 97
(A M Balding) *lw: mostly in last on outer: rdn and struggling 3f out: no prog tl styd on ins fnl f*
11/2[3]

221 **8** *½* **Chaperno (USA)**[18] 3875 2-9-0 0... LDettori 9 97+
(Saeed Bin Suroor) *trckd ldng pair on inner: trying for gap fr 2f out: forced way through and bmpd rival over 1f out: looked real threat but effrt petered out v tamely fnl f*
4/1[2]

1 **9** *3¼* **Ishtar Gate (USA)**[41] 3052 2-9-0 0.................................... AlanMunro 4 87
(P F I Cole) *stdd s: wl in tch: drvn and struggling on inner over 2f out: wknd over 1f out*
16/1

514 **10** *1½* **Lucky General (IRE)**[19] 3817 2-9-0 0.............................. RyanMoore 3 84
(R Hannon) *a in last trio: shkn up and no prog 3f out: pushed along and wl btn 2f out*
9/1

1m 27.46s (0.06) **Going Correction** +0.125s/f (Good) **10** Ran SP% **116.3**
Speed ratings (Par 106): **104,102,100,100,99 98,98,97,94,92**
toteswingers: 1&2 £13.20, 1&3 £8.20, 2&3 £24.70 CSF £53.31 TOTE £3.90: £1.70, £4.20, £2.70; EX 56.80 Trifecta £358.70 Pool: £1406.03 - 2.90 winning units..

Owner Brighthelm Racing **Bred** Paul McCartan **Trained** Lambourn, Berks

FOCUS

With the winners of the Chesham and Woodcote, and runners-up from the Coventry and Superlative Stakes taking each other on, coupled with some less experienced but very promising maiden winners in the line-up, this looked a decent renewal of this Group 2 contest, and it produced a taking winner.

NOTEBOOK

Xtension(IRE), a winner here on his debut, had found Canford Cliffs much too speedy for him in the Coventry, but had run on best of all to take second, and the step up to 7f here looked sure to see him to better effect. Held up out the rear, he got a little outpaced early in the straight, but once switched wide a furlong and a half out he really found his stride and he finished off his race in tremendous fashion. He was well on top at the line and looks the type that will always be seen at his best in a strongly run race, and the uphill finish on the Rowley Mile course should suit him ideally if connections decide to go to the Dewhurst in the autumn. Still relatively inexperienced and described by his rider as a big baby, there is still better to come from him. No winner of this race has gone on to take the 2000 Guineas since Mister Baileys, although the 2004 winner Shamardal did go on to take the French Guineas the following year. Regarding the first colts' Classic, the bookmakers' initial reaction was to trim the price of Canford Cliffs, which was understandable given his superiority over Xtension at Ascot, but leaving Clive Cox's charge largely unchanged at 25-1 seemed a little generous, especially given that a mile looks sure to suit him, while Richard Hannon's colt is by no means certain to appreciate a longer distance. One wonders how long he will remain in his current ownership, though. (op 4-1 tchd 9-2 in places)

Mata Keranjang(USA) had finished third in a Listed race for unraced two-year-olds on his debut and that form had been given a serious boost when the runner-up went and won the Group 2 Prix Robert Papin next time out. The question was whether he'd be suited by the step up to 7f. In the event he ran a fine race, hitting the front a furlong out before the winner flew by late on. He clearly got the trip but is not short of speed either, and the Solario Stakes could fit the bill, while the Champagne Stakes looks another obvious target. (op 12-1)

Corporal Maddox, running for Alan Jarvis in place of the warned off Karl Burke, promised to be suited by this longer trip having found the drop back to 5f against him last time out. From the best draw, he hugged the rail all the way into the straight, but then had to wait for a gap to appear. Switched out wide a furlong out, the winner crossed in front of him slightly as he was beginning his move, and he gave the impression that had he enjoyed a clear run he might have finished a little closer. (tchd 17-2 and 10-1 in places)

Big Audio(IRE) didn't handle Newmarket last time but ran a solid race here having been given a good ride from the front. He simply looks a little short of this level. (op 13-2 tchd 15-2 in places)

Roi De Vitesse(IRE) edged towards the inside rail in the straight and a gap never really came for him. Whether he would have been good enough to take it had it arrived must be open to question, though. (op 12-1 tchd 16-1)

She's A Character, the only filly in the field, was towards the front throughout and ran a sound race. She should find things easier back against her own sex.

Dreamspeed(IRE) had impressed in coming from last to first to win his maiden at Sandown, but repeating the trick in this company proved too difficult. He already shapes as though he needs a mile, and he could yet make his mark in Pattern company over that trip. (op 5-1 tchd 6-1 in places)

Chaperno(USA) travelled well in behind the leader but found little off the bridle, so a drop back to 6f might be in order. (op 11-2)

Ishtar Gate(USA) had plenty to find at this level and wasn't up to it. (op 20-1)

Lucky General(IRE) was forced wide from his low draw and didn't look happy on the track. (tchd 10-1)

4419 BGC SUSSEX STKS (GROUP 1) — 1m

3:25 (3:25) (Class 1) 3-Y-O+

£170,310 (£64,560; £32,310; £16,110; £8,070; £4,050) **Stalls** High

Form					RPR
-442	**1**		**Rip Van Winkle (IRE)**[25] 3640 3-8-13 128 .... JMurtagh 2 (A P O'Brien, Ire) *swtg: pressed ldr: led wl over 3f out: drew at least 2 l clr 2f out: galloped on strly w one reminder ins fnl f: impressive*	**6/4**[1]	131
1414	**2**	2 ½	**Paco Boy (IRE)**[19] 3819 4-9-7 124 .... RichardHughes 7 (R Hannon) *lw: hld up in 6th: stdy prog fr 3f out: chsd wnr wl over 1f out: sn hrd rdn: r.o to draw clr of rest but no imp*	**7/2**[3]	126
1-11	**3**	*4*	**Ghanaati (USA)**[40] 3088 3-8-10 119 .... RHills 5 (B W Hills) *trckd ldng pair: chsd wnr over 3f out: rdn and wanting to hang rt 2f out: no imp: sn lost 2nd: wl btn fnl f*	**2/1**[2]	112
1114	**4**	*1 ¼*	**Forgotten Voice (IRE)**[13] 4002 4-9-7 112 .... LDettori 8 (J Noseda) *swtg: stdd s: hld up in last pair and wl off the pce: rdn and struggling 3f out: prog over 1f out: styd on to take 4th ins fnl f*	**16/1**	114
-031	**5**	*1 ¼*	**Lord Shanakill (USA)**[24] 3669 3-8-13 118 .... JimCrowley 6 (A P Jarvis) *lw: trckd ldng trio: wnt 3rd over 3f out: rdn and outpcd fr over 2f out: n.d after: fin lame*	**12/1**	109
0121	**6**	*2 ¾*	**Beacon Lodge (IRE)**[45] 2953 4-9-7 114 .... AdamKirby 3 (C G Cox) *hld up in 5th: effrt 3f out: drvn into 4th briefly over 1f out: wknd fnl f*	**33/1**	105
2323	**7**	*7*	**Mia's Boy**[42] 3014 5-9-7 105 .... RyanMoore 1 (C A Dwyer) *hld up in last pair: a wl off the pce: bhd fnl 3f*	**50/1**	89
3000	**8**	*33*	**Malibu Bay (USA)**[6] 4253 3-8-13 102 .... SMLevey 4 (A P O'Brien, Ire) *drvn to ld: hanging in front and u.p: hdd & wknd wl over 3f out: t.o*	**100/1**	—

1m 37.16s (-2.74) **Going Correction** +0.125s/f (Good)
WFA 3 from 4yo+ 8lb — **8** Ran SP% **115.0**
Speed ratings (Par 117): **118,115,111,110,109 106,99,66**
toteswingers: 1&2 £2.00, 2&3 £1.80, 1&3, not won. CSF £7.21 TOTE £3.00: £1.30, £1.80, £1.10; EX 8.60 Trifecta £16.30 Pool: £12602.13 - 569.76 winning units..

Owner Mrs John Magnier, M Tabor & D Smith **Bred** Roberto Brogi **Trained** Ballydoyle, Co Tipperary

FOCUS

Despite a lack of 2000 Guineas winners, this was still a compelling Sussex and it saw the Classic generation gain another success in the race - their seventh success in the last eleven years. Their was a strong gallop on thanks to the pacemaking Malibu Bay, but he folded earlier than had surely been planned and that makes Rip Van Winkle's display all the more impressive. A good renewal, and the form looks solid with Paco Boy finishing a clear second-best. Rip Van Winkle is rated the best winner since Rock Of Gibraltar in 2002.

NOTEBOOK

Rip Van Winkle(IRE) was surely left in front sooner than had been planned for a horse who has been held up in each of his races since being awarded the race on his debut last season. With this being a drop back in trip, however, the more prominent tactics worked the oracle and he ran on powerfully to repel challengers down the home straight, finally getting his head in front at the top level. His attitude when asked to win the race was very pleasing and this sharp mile proved little bother to him, although the suspicion remains that 1m2f is his optimum. Since 1989 only Zafonic (1993) and Giant's Causeway (2000) came into the race with a higher RPR than the 129 Rip Van Winkle achieved when finishing a clear second-best to Sea The Stars in the Eclipse on his previous start. Along with last week's King George hero Conduit, he is yet another to pay this year's 2000 Guineas and Derby winner a big compliment. His performance also confirms the three-year-old colts to be an outstanding bunch this year and they will probably continue to dominate throughout the year. It must also be remembered that he suffered another last-minute scare with Aidan O'Brien reporting the previous day that the colt had a slight problem with his hind hoof and the first time he had trotted since was going down to the start. O'Brien also went down to the start, highlighting the worries connections had, and so the best of this colt could still be forthcoming. He may stick to 1m in the short term, with the Queen Elizabeth II Stakes his likely next target. Longer term, surely the Breeders' Cup will come into the equation, and Coral clipped him into 6/1 for the Classic. (op 13-8 tchd 7-4 and 2-1 in places)

Paco Boy(IRE) had Hughes back on top after flashing home all too late in the July Cup last time, and had taken the Lennox Stakes last year on his only previous run at the track. He was given his usual waiting ride and moved up travelling powerfully as normal nearing 2f out. The winner had gone beyond recall, but he showed his true colours and ran on to finish nicely clear of the rest, giving the form a solid look. A return to France to defend the Prix De la Foret over 7f - which is his optimum distance - looks on the cards and then a trip to Santa Anita for the Breeders' Cup Mile could also figure. He would very likely bump into another of the crack three-year-olds in the latter, however. (tchd 10-3 and 4-1 in places)

Ghanaati(USA) looked brilliant when taking the 1000 Guineas and the Coronation Stakes on her two previous runs this term. Fillies have a good record in the race, as advertised by Soviet Song in recent years, but no filly of her age had won this since Marling in 1992. She was stepping up into unknown territory taking on the colts for the first time and did little wrong through the race despite wanting to hang a little right under pressure, but simply found the first pair too strong. It is most unlikely any other female in training would have fared as well, however, so her connections must be commended for having a crack and can still rest assured they have the top filly around. She also still has few miles on the clock and promises to enjoy stepping up to 1m2f, so there should still be another Group 1 prize for her this year. Her rider later reported she felt a little flat. (tchd 5-2)

Forgotten Voice(IRE) ◆ had lost his unbeaten record when flopping in a conditions race on easy ground 13 days earlier. This was a bold move by his connections, but he confirmed himself a Group performer with a taking display. It could be that he was a little flattered as he was held up out the back and ran on strongly without ever threatening for a place, but it was a career-best effort and a drop in grade should really see him back to winning ways. (op 20-1)

Lord Shanakill(USA) showed his true worth when an excellent third in the St James's Palace Stakes and took the Group 1 Prix Jean Prat earlier this month. He was a bit tight for room on the rail around 2f out, but the gap was big enough if he had the speed to go through it and he ran a little below par. He finished second in the Vintage Stakes on this card last year, so the track should not have been to blame and it may be that running somewhat freely through the early parts was the issue. His rider later reported his mount had slipped a little at the start and that he finished slightly lame behind, but was not using it as an excuse. Official explanation: trainer said colt was lame behind (tchd 11-1 and 14-1 in places)

Beacon Lodge(IRE) readily took a Group 3 over the trip at Chantilly 45 days earlier and this was too stiff an ask for him. He also looks ideally suited by 7f and should show up a lot more prominently when eased in grade again.

Mia's Boy came from a similar position to Forgotten Voice, but lacked anything like the change of gear displayed by that rival and was another for whom this level of competition was all too much. (tchd 40-1)

4420 RACING UK STKS (HERITAGE H'CAP) — 1m 4f

4:00 (4:02) (Class 2) (0-105,98) 3-Y-O

£37,386 (£11,196; £5,598; £2,802; £1,398; £702) **Stalls** Low

Form					RPR
6013	**1**		**Classic Vintage (USA)**[19] 3822 3-8-13 **90** .... JimCrowley 9 (Mrs A J Perrett) *lw: shoved along early and reminder after 100yds: sn gng bttr in midfield: cruising bhd ldrs 3f out w rest all u.p: led 2f out: sn drvn and edgd rt: kpt on wl enough*	**11/1**	103+
1-23	**2**	*2 ¾*	**State Banquet (USA)**[23] 3695 3-8-7 **84** .... SteveDrowne 13 (H Morrison) *chsd ldrs: pushed along fr 1/2-way: effrt u.p over 3f out: kpt on to chse wnr ins fnl f: jst clung on for 2nd*	**18/1**	90
-216	**3**	*hd*	**Becausewecan (USA)**[25] 3618 3-8-1 **78** .... RoystonFfrench 12 (M Johnston) *moved poorly to post: prom: effrt to ld 3f out: hdd u.p 2f out: kpt on to battle for 2nd fnl f*	**20/1**	84
0131	**4**	*shd*	**Cosmic Sun**[19] 3826 3-9-0 **91** .... PaulHanagan 5 (R A Fahey) *settled midfield: rdn and prog fr wl over 3f out: tried to cl fr 2f out: kpt on to press for a pl fnl f*	**14/1**	97+
1121	**5**	*4 ½*	**Akmal**[19] 3827 3-9-2 **93** .... RHills 15 (J L Dunlop) *prom: chsng ldrs fr over 3f out: rdn and nt qckn over 2f out: fdd over 1f out*	**11/1**	92
1645	**6**	*2 ¼*	**Too Much Trouble**[20] 3778 3-9-7 **98** .... DarryllHolland 11 (M R Channon) *hld up in rr: wdst of all bnd whn last 5f out: sn rdn: hanging rt fr 4f out: fnlly styd on fr 2f out: nrst fin*	**16/1**	93
-112	**7**	*hd*	**Chiberta King**[41] 3051 3-8-11 **88** .... WilliamBuick 18 (A M Balding) *hld up towards rr: rdn 4f out: nt on terms w ldrs after: kpt on fr over 1f out: n.d*	**9/1**[3]	83
1023	**8**	*nk*	**Sabotage (UAE)**[3] 4340 3-9-4 **95** .... NCallan 1 (M Johnston) *dwlt: hld up towards rr: rdn and effrt over 3f out: rchd 7th 2f out but nt on terms: no imp after*	**8/1**[2]	89
2211	**9**	*1 ¼*	**Matraash (USA)**[34] 3307 3-9-2 **93** .... TPO'Shea 17 (M Johnston) *lw: mostly trckd ldr: led 5f out: shkn up and hdd 3f out: hanging bdly and wknd sn after*	**14/1**	85
0003	**10**	*2 ¾*	**Fin Vin De Leu (GER)**[21] 3728 3-8-0 **77** .... AndrewMullen 4 (M Johnston) *chsd ldrs tl lost pl u.p over 4f out: sn wl in rr: plugged on again late*	**66/1**	65
1025	**11**	*1*	**Topolski (IRE)**[41] 3051 3-8-12 **89** .... GregFairley 16 (M Johnston) *led to 5f out: wknd over 3f out*	**14/1**	75
01-1	**12**	*¾*	**Braveheart Move (IRE)**[84] 1792 3-8-9 **86** .... SebSanders 8 (Sir Mark Prescott) *bit bkwd: swtg: hld up in midfield: tried to make prog 4f out: u.p whn hmpd 3f out: no ch after: wknd*	**3/1**[1]	71+
1213	**13**	*5*	**Barwell Bridge**[41] 3051 3-9-1 **92** .... JamesDoyle 3 (S Kirk) *a wl in rr: last pair whn hmpd over 4f out: rdn and no prog after*	**25/1**	69
5011	**14**	*25*	**Norwegian Dancer (UAE)**[19] 3808 3-8-10 **87** .... StephenDonohoe 2 (E S McMahon) *moved poorly to post: dwlt: a wl in rr: u.p and wkng over 4f out: t.o*	**33/1**	24

2m 36.52s (-1.88) **Going Correction** +0.125s/f (Good) — **14** Ran SP% **107.0**
Speed ratings (Par 106): **111,109,109,108,105 104,104,104,103,101 100,100,96,80**
toteswingers: 1&2 £33.40, 1&3 £44.40, 2&3 £33.30 CSF £141.08 CT £2410.43 TOTE £11.70: £4.00, £4.50, £6.90; EX 130.30 Trifecta £1253.10 Part won. Pool: £1693.41 - 0.60 winning units..

Owner R & P Scott A & J Powell Gallagher Stud **Bred** Gallagher's Stud **Trained** Pulborough, W Sussex

FOCUS

A quality handicap for three-year-olds, although the top-weight weighed in at 7lb below the ceiling for the race. Solid form amongst the princiapls, and a race which should work out. It was run at a good gallop.

NOTEBOOK

Classic Vintage(USA) had run well to finish third in a race dominated by the pace horses at Newmarket last time, and the form had been given a boost by the runner-up, who won the 1m6f handicap here on Tuesday. The stronger gallop suited him this time and he travelled noticeably well throughout. Switched to challenge at the intersection, he quickened up well and, although not doing a lot in front, ran out a comfortable winner. A big horse, he'll make a hurdler one day, but for the time being the Melrose is likely to be the aim, while his connections see him as a stayer in the making next year. (op 10-1)

State Banquet(USA), one of the least experienced runners in the line-up, was stepping up to 1m4f for the first time and improved for the greater test of stamina. Despite being on and off the bridle, he kept finding for pressure to record a personal best, and a more galloping track ought to suit him in future. (op 20-1 tchd 16-1)

Becausewecan(USA) ◆, who is quite a keen-going sort and was always towards the fore, did best of the Mark Johnston-trained quintet. He boxed on well in the straight and, although unable to hold off the closers, indicated that he remains a well-handicapped horse. Still relatively unexposed over this trip, he can win a similar race. (op 18-1)
Cosmic Sun ◆ has been steadily progressive this term and promises to improve again when stepped up to a longer trip than this. He's by Helissio and his dam won over 2m, so he isn't short of stamina. (op 16-1 tchd 12-1)
Akmal was dropping back in distance having won over 1m6f last time, but he was 2lb worse off with Classic Vintage for a half-length beating at Salisbury on his previous start and was unable to reverse that form. (op 12-1)
Too Much Trouble has not cut it at Pattern level and was running in a handicap for the first time. Slowly away and held up in last place, he was brought widest into the straight and proved almost unrideable, hanging badly to his right from half a mile out. A more conventional track will be in his favour but he doesn't look entirely straightforward. Official explanation: jockey said colt hung badly right-handed (op 20-1)
Chiberta King was disappointing, failing to run up to his Royal Ascot form with Cosmic Sun. Official explanation: jockey said gelding hung left-handed off the top bend (tchd 10-1)
Sabotage(UAE), who holds a Great Voltigeur entry, was another to fail to land a blow. Perhaps the race came too soon for him following his outing at Ascot on Sunday. (op 11-1)
Matraash(USA) didn't seem to get home over this longer trip. (op 12-1)
Fin Vin De Leu(GER) found the competition too hot. (tchd 100-1 in places)
Topolski(IRE) dropped out tamely having made the running to the turn into the straight. He'd been given a break to prepare him specifically for this race after Royal Ascot, so this has to go down as a disappointing run. (op 11-1 tchd 16-1 in places)
Braveheart Move(IRE) was all the rage beforehand. A St Leger entrant, he'd impressed in winning at Chester back in May and looked to be well ahead of the handicapper on a mark of just 86. He proved desperately disappointing though, looking in trouble as they swung into the straight before being hampered 3f out. This was not his true form, but he has a bit to prove now. (op 7-2 tchd 4-1 in a place)
Barwell Bridge Official explanation: jockey said colt suffered interference in running

4421 MARKEL INTERNATIONAL MAIDEN FILLIES' STKS — 6f

4:35 (4:36) (Class 2) 2-Y-O — **£12,952** (£3,854; £1,926; £962) **Stalls** Low

Form				RPR
	1		**Beyond Desire** 2-9-0 0 ... NCallan 8 — (M A Jarvis) *w'like: str: athletic: lw: fast away: mde all: dictated stdy pce to 1/2-way: pushed along and only one rival over 1f out: shkn up last 150yds: styd on wl* **2/1**[1]	88+
	2	1 ¼	**Nimue (USA)** 2-9-0 0 ... MartinDwyer 1 — (P F I Cole) *w'like: scope: lw: t.k.h: hld up bhd ldrs: wnt 2nd 2f out: rdn over 1f out: tried to press wnr and drew clr of rest: a safely hld* **7/2**[2]	84+
	3	5	**Damietta (USA)** 2-9-0 0 ... LDettori 9 — (Saeed Bin Suroor) *athletic: wnt rt s: hld up in last trio: prog on outer to chse ldrs 2f out: sn wl outpcd* **5/1**[3]	69+
	4	1 ¼	**Bonheurs Art (IRE)** 2-9-0 0 ... MichaelHills 7 — (B W Hills) *unf: hld up in last trio: outpcd fr 2f out: pushed along and kpt on fnl f* **12/1**	66+
	5	2 ¼	**First Term** 2-9-0 0 ... RichardHughes 5 — (R Hannon) *unf: scope: pressed wnr: rdn over 2f out: lost 2nd sn after: wknd over 1f out: eased fnl f* **10/1**	59+
	6	½	**Specialising** 2-9-0 0 ... EdwardCreighton 4 — (M R Channon) *leggy: scope: settled last trio: rdn sn after 1/2-way and struggling: kpt on* **33/1**	57
63	7	3 ¼	**So Surreal (IRE)**[14] 3987 2-9-0 0 ... RyanMoore 2 — (G L Moore) *cl up tl rdn and wknd 2f out* **7/1**	48
	8	3 ¼	**Mystic Millie (IRE)** 2-9-0 0 ... AdamKirby 6 — (C G Cox) *leggy: scope: prom tl rdn and wknd jst over 2f out* **9/1**	38

1m 13.23s (1.03) **Going Correction** +0.125s/f (Good) **8** Ran SP% **114.4**
Speed ratings (Par 97): **98,96,89,88,85 84,80,75**
toteswingers: 1&2 £2.70, 1&3 £2.50, 2&3 £3.90 CSF £8.99 TOTE £2.80: £1.40, £1.50, £1.90; EX 10.30 Trifecta £33.20 Pool: £617.55 - 13.76 winning units..
Owner Clipper Logistics **Bred** Pinnacle Bloodstock **Trained** Newmarket, Suffolk

FOCUS
A good fillies' maiden which saw the first pair come nicely clear. The form should work out.

NOTEBOOK
Beyond Desire ◆ made all to open her account at the first time of asking and enhanced her yard's decent record in the race. She broke well to get across to the stands' rail and set an average pace. She found the required change of gear when asked to win the race, despite showing signs of greenness, and was always holding the runner-up. She holds entries in the Lowther and Cheveley Park so is clearly well regarded by her shrewd trainer, which was also highlighted by the fact she started favourite. This looks very much her trip at present on breeding and improvement is assured, so she rates one to follow. (tchd 9-4 and 7-4 in places)
Nimue(USA), who cost $310,000, also holds some big-race entries and was fancied to make a winning start. She was the only one to give the winner a serious race, but spoilt her chance by refusing to settle through the early parts. This experience will not be lost on her and she should soon land her maiden before going on to better things. (op 9-2 tchd 11-2)
Damietta(USA), a half-sister to juvenile winners, did not help her chances by going out to her right from the stalls and it took time for the penny to drop. She was keeping on when the race was effectively over and ought to know a lot more next time. (op 11-2 tchd 9-2)
Bonheurs Art(IRE) ◆ cost £90,000 and her dam has already thrown up three speedy juvenile winners. She holds an entry in the Cheveley Park Stakes and was surprisingly easy to back for this racecourse bow. As it transpired she proved too green to do herself full justice, but should improve a deal with this experience behind her. (op 17-2 tchd 8-1)
First Term showed well through the early parts, but was done with soon after 2f out and the run looked to be needed. (op 8-1)
Specialising is bred to enjoy racing over further than this and lacked the pace to get seriously involved. She is one to side with when stepping up in trip. (op 40-1)
So Surreal(IRE) should find her niche in handicaps. (op 9-1 tchd 6-1)
Mystic Millie(IRE) should benefit from the experience and leave this firmly behind in time. (tchd 17-2 and 10-1)

4422 COUNTRY LIFE MAGAZINE EUROPEAN BREEDERS' FUND FILLIES' AND MARES' STKS (H'CAP) — 1m 1f

5:10 (5:10) (Class 2) (0-100,88) 3-Y-O+
£12,462 (£3,732; £1,866; £934; £466; £234) **Stalls** High

Form				RPR
-112	1		**Alsace Lorraine (IRE)**[18] 3843 4-9-13 84 ... JamieSpencer 15 — (J R Fanshawe) *t.k.h early: trckd ldrs: disp 2nd fr 2f out: hanging u.p over 1f out: r.o ins fnl f to ld last 50yds* **9/2**[1]	92+
1123	2	nk	**Full Of Love (IRE)**[11] 4088 3-9-1 81 ... MichaelHills 3 — (B W Hills) *racd wd: hld up towards rr: stdy prog over 2f out: rdn to dispute 2nd over 1f out: r.o but jst hld by wnr* **11/2**[2]	86
0-04	3	nse	**Club Tahiti**[11] 4088 3-9-5 85 ... EddieAhern 2 — (R Charlton) *hld up in rr: taken to outer and prog 2f out: drvn and clsd on ldrs fr 1f out: r.o last 100yds: jst hld* **13/2**[3]	90
3055	4	shd	**Tottie**[4] 4328 3-9-8 88 ... (b[1]) JimCrowley 9 — (Mrs A J Perrett) *trckd ldng pair on inner: led 3f out: over a l up and gng strly 2f out: rdn 1f out: wknd and hdd last 50yds* **15/2**	93
640-	5	¾	**My Aunt Fanny**[305] 6276 4-10-0 85 ... LPKeniry 1 — (A M Balding) *t.k.h: hld up in rr: stl there and pushed along 2f out: taken to outer and rdn over 1f out: stl 10th ent fnl f: r.o: gaining fin* **33/1**	90
5011	6	nk	**Romany Princess (IRE)**[7] 4211 4-10-3 88 6ex ... RichardHughes 14 — (R Hannon) *lw: hld up towards rr: trying to make prog over 2f out but n.m.r: hdwy on inner over 1f out: cl up bhd ldrs whn nowhere to go last 75yds* **9/2**[1]	95+
20-0	7	½	**Such Optimism**[18] 3870 3-9-5 85 ... RichardKingscote 6 — (R M Beckett) *trckd ldrs: rdn and lost pl jst over 2f out: struggling: styd on again ins fnl f* **50/1**	86
5603	8	nk	**Atabaas Allure (FR)**[15] 3941 3-9-0 80 ... RoystonFfrench 12 — (M Johnston) *led 1f: styd on ldng trio: rdn to dispute 2nd 2f out: nt qckn 1f out: fdd* **11/1**	81
3065	9	1	**Trumpet Lily**[32] 3400 4-9-12 83 ... AlanMunro 11 — (J G Portman) *hld up in midfield: nowhere to go over 2f out and dropped to rr: stl there 1f out: pushed along and styd on steadily fnl f: no ch* **33/1**	84+
122	10	hd	**Ocean Transit (IRE)**[11] 4088 4-9-10 81 ... JamesDoyle 13 — (R J Price) *t.k.h: led after 1f: rdn and hdd 3f out: n.m.r and lost pl 2f out: btn after: plugged on* **16/1**	81
20	11	2	**Qalahari (IRE)**[42] 3016 3-9-7 87 ... TPO'Shea 7 — (D J Coakley) *hld up in last: shkn up and no prog 3f out: nvr on terms after: taken out wd and plugged on fnl f* **33/1**	81
4120	12	1 ½	**Perfect Friend**[4] 4326 3-8-13 79 ... NCallan 10 — (S Kirk) *wl pl tl nt qckn and lost pl 2f out: rdn and wknd over 1f out* **18/1**	69
2464	13	7	**Fanditha (IRE)**[18] 3870 3-9-3 83 ... RyanMoore 8 — (R Hannon) *s.i.s and pushed along early: nvr gng wl in rr: bhd fr 3f out* **11/1**	58
220-	14	18	**Fantasy Princess (USA)**[293] 6599 4-9-7 78 ... LDettori 4 — (G A Butler) *t.k.h: wnt prom after 2f: lost pl 3f out: sn wknd: t.o* **20/1**	15

1m 56.31s (0.01) **Going Correction** +0.125s/f (Good)
WFA 3 from 4yo 9lb **14** Ran SP% **120.2**
Speed ratings (Par 96): **104,103,103,103,102 102,102,101,101,100 99,97,91,75**
toteswingers: 1&2 £3.10, 1&3 £7.90, 2&3 £7.40 CSF £26.79 CT £167.87 TOTE £4.90: £2.20, £1.70, £2.60; EX 15.00 Trifecta £73.30 Pool: £1238.94 - 12.50 winning units..
Owner Merry Fox Stud Limited **Bred** 6c Stallions Ltd **Trained** Newmarket, Suffolk

FOCUS
Not the classiest fillies' race for the grade, but it was certainly competitive. There were the usual hard-luck stories and with a blanket finish the form needs treating with a degree of caution. It has been rated through the second and third.

NOTEBOOK
Alsace Lorraine(IRE) stuck her head out where it mattered and got back to winning ways under a very strong ride. She found the gaps coming at the right time on the inside and showed a very honest attitude when asked to win the race. She has now won three of her four outings as a 4yo (finished second on the other) and has developed into a very likeable filly. This was also the longest trip she has encountered to date and she promises to be even better suited by a step up to 1m2f. (op 4-1 tchd 5-1 in places)
Full Of Love(IRE) ◆ had to make her challenge wide of the pack due to her low draw and ran a career-best race on this return to a suitably quicker surface. She only just lost out, despite having to cover more ground than the winner, and this lightly-raced filly should soon be placed to go in again. (op 5-1 tchd 6-1)
Club Tahiti, stepping up a furlong, was another forced to race wide from her low draw yet that dictated she missed any trouble. She stayed on nicely and ran right up to her last-time-out form with the runner-up on identical terms. (op 8-1)
Tottie had first-time blinkers replacing cheekpieces and put a up bold show. She got a dream run against the far rail and was the one to catch passing the furlong marker, but failed to sustain her effort where it mattered most. This was a lot more like it, on just her second outing in a handicap, but her optimum trip has yet to be established. (op 7-1 tchd 9-1)
My Aunt Fanny ◆ fared best of those who came from well off the pace and turned in a very pleasing return from a 305-day layoff, although she looked fit enough. She also ideally wants a stiffer test so looks one to keep on side next time out. (tchd 40-1 in places)
Romany Princess(IRE) ◆ shouldered top weight under her penalty. She got no run on the inside from the 2f pole and finished with plenty left in the tank. It would not be surprising to see her out again soon in a bid for compensation. Official explanation: jockey said filly was denied a clear run (op 13-2)
Such Optimism, whose yard won the race last year, hit a flat spot before keeping on again and posted a much more encouraging display. She could come on again for the run and now looks ready to tackle a bit further. (op 40-1 tchd 66-1 in places)
Atabaas Allure(FR) gained both her previous wins on Polytrack but is getting better on turf. She was unable to make the running with Ocean Transit in the race but did not drop away until late on. A drop back in grade will benefit her. (op 10-1 tchd 9-1)
Trumpet Lily was another who found nowhere to go in the straight and this is best forgiven. Official explanation: jockey said filly was denied a clear run
Qalahari(IRE) Official explanation: jockey said filly lost its action
Fanditha(IRE) Official explanation: jockey said filly suffered interference in running
Fantasy Princess(USA) looked fit enough for this first run in 293 days but offered very little after racing keenly. Official explanation: jockey said filly lost its action

4423 EBF KENNELS CLASSIFIED STKS — 7f

5:45 (5:47) (Class 2) 3-Y-O+
£12,462 (£3,732; £1,866; £934; £466; £234) **Stalls** High

Form				RPR
5-26	1		**Axiom**[42] 3014 5-9-4 94 ... LDettori 6 — (L M Cumani) *lw: dwlt: wl in rr: pushed along fr 1/2-way: prog fr over 2f out: drvn and r.o to ld last 100yds* **4/1**[2]	102
34-0	2	½	**Moynahan (USA)**[76] 2015 4-9-4 95 ... AlanMunro 14 — (P F I Cole) *swtg: dwlt: wl in rr: hmpd on inner 5f out: prog fr over 2f out: stl only 8th 1f out: r.o wl to take 2nd nr fin* **20/1**	101
1000	3	1	**Proclaim**[21] 3747 3-8-11 95 ... (b[1]) RoystonFfrench 13 — (M Johnston) *lw: chsd ldr's str pce: clsd to ld 2f out: hdd u.str.p last 100yds* **9/1**	95+
0630	4	hd	**Spanish Bounty**[19] 3818 4-9-4 93 ... EddieAhern 17 — (J G Portman) *dwlt: sn in midfield: gng wl 3f out: prog 2f out: drvn and styd on fr over 1f out: nt quite pce to chal* **20/1**	98
3050	5	1 ¼	**Something (IRE)**[4] 4330 7-9-4 95 ... AndrewMullen 12 — (D Nicholls) *prom on inner: effrt in 3rd whn hmpd wl over 1f out: disp 2nd 1f out: hld whn hit rail ins fnl f* **12/1**	97+
1100	6	2	**Mister Hardy**[19] 3818 4-9-4 95 ... PaulHanagan 7 — (R A Fahey) *towards rr: trying to make prog fr over 2f out: styd on fr over 1f out: nt pce to threaten* **14/1**	89
1305	7	1 ½	**Saucy Brown (IRE)**[25] 3628 3-8-11 93 ... RichardHughes 15 — (R Hannon) *prom: rdn 2f out: carried hd high and nt qckn: eased whn btn last 100yds* **7/1**	82

2020 **8** *nse* **Celtic Sultan (IRE)**[18] 3846 5-9-4 92 .... MickyFenton 5 85
(T P Tate) *dwlt: drvn up to ld and set str pce: hdd 2f out: wknd ins fnl f* **25/1**

10- **9** *shd* **Purissima (USA)**[284] 6818 3-8-8 95 .... RyanMoore 16 79+
(Sir Michael Stoute) *hld up towards rr: n.m.r 5f out: hmpd on inner wl over 2f out: nvr rcvrd: kpt on fnl f* **3/1**[1]

0230 **10** *½* **Mujood**[1] 4409 6-9-4 87 .... KevinGhunowa 1 83
(Eve Johnson Houghton) *nvr gng wl on outer towards rr: plugged on fnl 2f: nvr really a factor* **25/1**

1600 **11** *shd* **Baby Strange**[12] 4037 5-9-4 91 .... JimCrowley 9 83
(D Shaw) *hld up in rr: nt clr run fr over 2f out to over 1f out: one pce whn in the clr after* **33/1**

-300 **12** *1* **Clifton Dancer**[40] 3091 4-9-1 92 .... RichardKingscote 3 77
(Tom Dascombe) *a in rr: taken to outer and no real prog 2f out: plugged on* **40/1**

20-1 **13** *½* **King's Wonder**[61] 2434 4-9-4 91 .... MartinDwyer 11 79
(W R Muir) *prom: rdn over 2f out: edgd lft u.p and carried hd high: sn wknd* **6/1**[3]

00-4 **14** *1½* **Perfect Flight**[74] 2078 4-9-1 90 .... KirstyMilczarek 8 72
(M Blanshard) *trckd ldrs tl lost pl over 2f out: sn wknd* **16/1**

0000 **15** *25* **Grand Vista**[14] 3988 5-9-4 86 .... (t) AdamKirby 2 7
(G L Moore) *reluctant to enter stalls: rel to r and lft at least 20 l: nvr rcvrd* **100/1**

1m 26.75s (-0.65) **Going Correction** +0.125s/f (Good)
WFA 3 from 4yo+ 7lb **15** Ran SP% **125.6**
Speed ratings (Par 109): **108,107,106,106,104 102,100,100,100,99 99,98,98,96,67**
toteswingers: 1&2 £20.80, 1&3 £11.00, 2&3 £42.60 CSF £89.83 TOTE £4.60: £2.10, £5.90, £3.50; EX 93.50 TRIFECTA Not won. Place 6: £59.73 Place 5: £32.08.
Owner DIC Racing Syndicate **Bred** Cheveley Park Stud Ltd **Trained** Newmarket, Suffolk
■ Stewards' Enquiry : Royston Ffrench three-day ban: careless riding (Aug 12-14)

FOCUS
With 14 of the 16 runners rated between 90 and 95 (the exceptions being the mid-80s rated Mujood and Grand Vista), this had the look of race framed for the benefit of the bookmakers, but the winner was nicely backed and justified the support with a slightly cosy success. The form looks pretty solid.

NOTEBOOK
Axiom was suited by the decent gallop because he was dropping back from a mile and the ground was again a slight concern, as he's undoubtedly at his best with cut. He coped well with conditions, though, and came through with his challenge up the inside rail before switching out approaching the furlong marker and running on strongly. There is more to come from him, especially on softer ground. (op 9-2)
Moynahan(USA) ran no sort of race on his reappearance but this was far more encouraging. He didn't get the best of runs as he was hampered on the bend at the top of the straight and was also short of room inside the final quarter mile, so in the circumstances he did well to take second. He has not been the luckiest in his career to date but clearly retains plenty of ability. (op 16-1)
Proclaim bounced back to form for the application of blinkers for the first time. Considering that they went a good gallop up front and he was in the thick of the action throughout he did well to hang on for third, but a slightly more patient ride might have reaped its reward. (op 10-1 tchd 12-1)
Spanish Bounty is an inconsistent sort and he had his stamina to prove over this trip. He was travelling as well as anything two and a half furlongs out but he didn't look to put it all in once put under pressure. He looks one for the in-running layers. (op 16-1)
Something(IRE) is another with an inconsistent profile. On the rail throughout, he was slightly hampered on a couple of occasions but a gap came for him in the closing stages and he wasn't good enough to take advantage.
Mister Hardy put behind him a couple of below-par efforts in top handicaps. He endured a bit of rough passage and didn't run at all badly in the circumstances. (op 12-1 tchd 11-1)
Saucy Brown(IRE) travelled nicely in behind the leaders but he didn't fancy it at all once the stick came out. He's another for the in-running brigade to get stuck into. (op 14-1)
Celtic Sultan(IRE) was reported to have hit his head on the stalls but it didn't stop him too much and he was soon making the running at a really good clip. Ultimately, though, he went too fast and simply set it up for those more patiently ridden. Official explanation: jockey said gelding hit its head as stalls opened (tchd 33-1 in places)
Purissima(USA), who holds a Group 1 entry, was making a belated seasonal reappearance. Badly hampered at the top of the bend into the straight, she got shuffled back in the pack and was then hampered again, by the winner this time, around 2f out. As a result not a lot should be read into this performance. Official explanation: jockey said filly suffered interference in runing (op 4-1 tchd 9-2 in places)
Mujood, making a quick reappearance having run here 24 hours earlier, had little chance of adopting his usual prominent role from the worst draw of all. (op 20-1 tchd 33-1 in places)
Baby Strange was denied a clear run from over 2f out and shouldn't be judged too harshly. (tchd 40-1 in places)
King's Wonder stuck his head in the air as soon as things got serious and didn't want to know. He needs to lead to be seen at his best, but he clearly retains some mental issues. (tchd 5-1)
T/Jkpt: £44,804.30 to a £1 stake. Pool: £63,104.75. 1.00 winning ticket. T/Plt: £86.70 to a £1 stake. Pool: £272,891.56. 2,295.75 winning tickets. T/Qpdt: £18.30 to a £1 stake. Pool: £12,915.48. 521.60 winning tickets. JN

4194 LEICESTER (R-H)
Wednesday, July 29

OFFICIAL GOING: Soft (the last race was abandoned (8.45) due to lack of medical cover on-course after a jockey was injured in the previous race)
Wind: Fresh behind Weather: Raining

4424 EBF LUTTERWORTH MAIDEN STKS — 5f 218y
6:00 (6:06) (Class 4) 2-Y-O **£4,857** (£1,445; £722; £360) **Stalls** Low

Form — RPR

0 **1** **Royal Box**[23] 3692 2-9-3 0 .... PatDobbs 10 74
(R Hannon) *led: rdn: edgd lft and hdd over 1f out: rallied to ld ins fnl f: r.o* **18/1**

00 **2** *nk* **West Leake Star (IRE)**[6] 4219 2-9-3 0 .... RobertWinston 9 73
(B W Hills) *trckd ldrs: led over 1f out: rdn: edgd lft and hdd ins fnl f: r.o* **14/1**

3 *3¼* **Iptkaar (USA)** 2-8-5 0 .... DebraEngland(7) 1 58
(C E Brittain) *sn outpcd: swtchd rt wl over 3f out: r.o ins fnl f: nrst fin* **14/1**

0 **4** *½* **Boquito (IRE)**[61] 2430 2-9-3 0 .... JerryO'Dwyer 2 62
(Miss Amy Weaver) *chsd ldrs: rdn over 1f out: styng on same pce whn edgd rt ins fnl f* **20/1**

3 **5** *¾* **Royal Etiquette (IRE)**[18] 3867 2-9-3 0 .... TPQueally 4 60
(H J L Dunlop) *chsd wnr tl rdn over 1f out: no ex ins fnl f* **11/10**[1]

6 *nk* **Glen Shiel (USA)** 2-9-3 0 .... AndrewElliott 8 59
(M Johnston) *chsd ldrs: rdn over 2f out: no ex fnl f* **15/2**[3]

0 **7** *1½* **Gold Rules**[18] 3875 2-9-3 0 .... DaneO'Neill 5 54
(L M Cumani) *chsd ldrs: rdn over 2f out: wknd fnl f* **7/2**[2]

6 **8** *10* **Verona Lad**[12] 4041 2-9-3 0 .... SJCraine 3 24
(Jennie Candlish) *sn pushed along in rr: lost tch 1/2-way* **33/1**

9 *nk* **Kingsdine (IRE)** 2-9-3 0 .... TGMcLaughlin 7 23
(M S Saunders) *s.s: outpcd* **40/1**

10 *10* **Alfalevva** 2-9-3 0 .... SamHitchcott 6 —
(M R Channon) *mid-div: sn pushed along: wknd 1/2-way* **14/1**

1m 15.9s (2.90) **Going Correction** +0.45s/f (Yiel) **10** Ran SP% **117.0**
Speed ratings (Par 96): **98,97,93,92,91 91,89,75,75,62**
toteswingers: 1&2 £9.80, 1&3 £14.10, 2&3 £9.30 CSF £238.90 TOTE £25.40: £4.30, £5.20, £4.70; EX 448.60.
Owner The Queen **Bred** The Queen **Trained** East Everleigh, Wilts
■ Stewards' Enquiry : Pat Dobbs caution: careless riding; two-day ban: used whip in incorrect place (Aug 12-13)

FOCUS
Ground changed to soft all round just before racing, after persistent rain throughout the afternoon so conditions very testing, especially for these inexperienced juveniles in what was not a strong maiden by any means.

NOTEBOOK
Royal Box had clearly taken a big step forward from his Windsor debut, where he was too green to do himself justice and, bred to appreciate this stiffer test of stamina, he fared considerably better, staying on grittily to edge out the runner-up with the pair coming nicely clear. His dam was a multiple winner over 1m-9f so this colt is likely to want further than this in time and he proved here that soft ground was no hindrance. (op 16-1 tchd 20-1)
West Leake Star(IRE) had shown promise on his second start and he travelled particularly well towards the middle of the track before just being outstayed in the closing stages. He is improving with every start and he's qualified for a mark now. (op 10-1 tchd 16-1)
Iptkaar(USA) got going late in the day, finishing well from a long way back and this was an encouraging debut. (op 12-1)
Boquito(IRE) shaped with more promise than at Goodwood on his debut, where he was too green to do himself justice. (op 22-1 tchd 25-1)
Royal Etiquette(IRE), who was dropping back in trip, had every chance but was made to look a bit one-paced when coming under pressure and he needs stepping back up in trip (from a family of stayers). He's likely to prove this run all wrong. (op 5-4)
Glen Shiel(USA) is bred to come into his own over further and given his pedigree the softening of the ground may not have helped him, so he's entitled to improve considerably on this. (op 7-1)

4425 SHANGTON (S) STKS — 7f 9y
6:35 (6:35) (Class 5) 3-Y-O **£2,590** (£770; £385; £192) **Stalls** Low

Form — RPR

55 **1** **Jenny's Pride (IRE)**[18] 3862 3-8-4 0 .... DavidProbert(3) 4 53
(John A Harris) *chsd ldrs: rdn to ld 1f out: sn hung lft: styd on* **7/1**

5236 **2** *1¼* **Blue Noodles**[21] 3729 3-9-3 66 .... TPQueally 8 60
(Ollie Pears) *chsd ldrs: rdn over 2f out: edgd lft ins fnl f: styd on* **11/2**[3]

0P60 **3** *½* **Sirjosh**[7] 4202 3-8-12 60 .... (t) NeilChalmers 7 53
(D Donovan) *hld up: hdwy u.p over 1f out: hung lft ins fnl f: r.o: nt rch ldrs* **16/1**

0043 **4** *1¼* **Spring Secret**[15] 3946 3-8-12 57 .... LukeMorris 18 50
(B Palling) *chsd ldrs: rdn 1/2-way: hung lft ins fnl f: styd on same pce* **9/2**[2]

0005 **5** *2* **Handcuff**[7] 4196 3-8-12 49 .... JerryO'Dwyer 15 45
(J Gallagher) *led: rdn and hdd 1f out: hung lft ins fnl f: wknd towards fin* **33/1**

3206 **6** *1* **Come On Buckers (IRE)**[2] 4372 3-8-12 62 .... TGMcLaughlin 2 42
(E J Creighton) *hld up: hdwy 1/2-way: rdn and hung rt over 2f out: styd on same pce appr fnl f* **14/1**

010 **7** *nse* **Kinigi (IRE)**[8] 4172 3-8-10 56 ow5 .... SPRyan(7) 1 47
(R A Harris) *s.i.s: hld up: hdwy 1/2-way: rdn over 2f out: no ex fnl f* **14/1**

3050 **8** *11* **Tidal Force (USA)**[26] 3577 3-8-12 65 .... SebSanders 17 14
(P F I Cole) *s.i.s: hdwy over 4f out: sn rdn: wknd over 2f out* **4/1**[1]

6064 **9** *1¾* **Buckle Up**[7] 4196 3-8-12 41 .... SaleemGolam 12 9
(D K Ivory) *chsd ldrs tl rdn and wknd over 2f out* **20/1**

2005 **10** *nk* **Mr Flannegan**[26] 3577 3-8-12 55 .... DaneO'Neill 11 8
(H Candy) *sn pushed along in rr: wknd 1/2-way* **15/2**

0 **11** *2¼* **Targs (IRE)**[14] 3975 3-8-12 0 .... JamieMackay 13 2
(Peter Grayson) *s.i.s: outpcd* **66/1**

000 **12** *nk* **Hello Sunshine**[82] 1840 3-8-12 42 .... CatherineGannon 3 2
(T J Pitt) *hld up: hdwy 1/2-way: sn rdn: wknd over 2f out* **50/1**

465 **13** *3¼* **Cash In The Attic**[27] 3541 3-8-7 45 .... SamHitchcott 14 —
(M R Channon) *prom: rdn 1/2-way: sn wknd* **14/1**

0050 **14** *2¾* **Yellow River (USA)**[52] 2737 3-8-2 42 .... (e) SophieDoyle(5) 5 —
(E J Creighton) *mid-div: rdn and wknd 1/2-way* **50/1**

1m 29.91s (3.71) **Going Correction** +0.45s/f (Yiel) **14** Ran SP% **116.8**
Speed ratings (Par 100): **96,94,94,92,90 89,89,76,74,74 71,71,67,64**
toteswingers: 1&2 £15.90, 2&3 £34.10 CSF £42.03 TOTE £9.10: £2.80, £1.50, £6.40; EX 43.20.The winner was bought in for 5,500gns.
Owner Nigel O'Sullivan **Bred** John Doyle **Trained** Eastwell, Leics

FOCUS
Poor stuff even for this grade and most of these had questions to answer regarding the ground. Not form to be positive about.

4426 SNOWED UNDER H'CAP — 1m 1f 218y
7:10 (7:11) (Class 4) (0-80,80) 3-Y-O+ **£4,731** (£1,416; £708; £354; £176) **Stalls** High

Form — RPR

2626 **1** **Cry Alot Boy**[18] 3864 6-9-4 70 .... PatCosgrave 6 79
(K A Morgan) *s.s: hld up: plld hrd: rdn over 2f out: hdwy over 1f out: led ins fnl f: styd on u.p* **11/1**

5-32 **2** *2* **Nbhan (USA)**[25] 3644 3-9-0 76 .... DaneO'Neill 8 81+
(L M Cumani) *chsd ldrs: led 2f out: rdn and edgd lft over 1f out: hdd ins fnl f: edgd rt: styd on same pce* **2/1**[1]

130 **3** *1* **Timocracy**[20] 3761 4-9-11 77 .... AndrewElliott 5 80
(T D Walford) *led 1f: chsd ldr: rdn over 2f out: styd on same pce ins fnl f* **4/1**[2]

-236 **4** *nse* **Tropical Blue**[18] 3861 3-8-12 74 .... (v[1]) SamHitchcott 4 77
(Jennie Candlish) *pushed along early: sn trcking ldrs and racd keenly: rdn over 3f out: outpcd over 2f out: rallied over 1f out: styng on whn hmpd ins fnl f: jst failed to get 3rd* **11/2**[3]

4061 **5** *3* **Can Can Star**[18] 3864 6-9-7 80 .... DebraEngland(7) 7 77
(A W Carroll) *hld up: hdwy over 4f out: led over 3f out: hdd 2f out: wknd ins fnl f* **7/1**

3140 **6** *18* **Buddy Holly**[30] 3461 4-9-3 76 .... (v) CharlesEddery(7) 3 37
(Pat Eddery) *awkward leaving stalls: led after 1f: hdd over 3f out: sn rdn: wknd over 1f out* **7/1**

2455 **7** *22* **Shady Gloom (IRE)**[26] 3573 4-9-9 75 .... DO'Donohoe 2 —
(K A Ryan) *chsd ldrs: rdn and hung rt over 3f out: wknd over 2f out* **22/1**

0-16 **8** *11* **Agapanthus (GER)**[33] 3361 4-9-6 72 .... TPQueally 13 —
(B J Curley) *hld up: rdn and wknd over 3f out* **25/1**

The Form Book, Raceform Ltd, Compton, RG20 6NL

-103 9 17 **Snowed Under**[36] 3235 8-9-11 **80**........................... WilliamCarson(3) 11 —
(J D Bethell) *hld up: wknd over 3f out* **7/1**
2m 14.37s (6.47) **Going Correction** +0.45s/f (Yiel)
WFA 3 from 4yo+ 10lb 9 Ran SP% **122.7**
Speed ratings (Par 105): **92,90,89,89,87 72,55,46,32**
toteswingers: 1&2 £5.40, 1&3 £13.00, 2&3 £3.00 CSF £35.56 CT £110.79 TOTE £15.30: £3.20, £1.50, £1.10; EX 60.80.
Owner D S Cooper **Bred** Ridgecourt Stud **Trained** Newmarket, Suffolk

FOCUS
They were virtually walking in the closing stages of this fair 1m2f handicap. The form looks sound enough though, rated around those in the frame behind the winner.

4427 EBF SWITHLAND MEDIAN AUCTION MAIDEN FILLIES' STKS 5f 218y
7:45 (7:47) (Class 5) 2-Y-O **£3,561** (£1,059; £529; £264) **Stalls** Low

Form RPR
1 **Waltz Around (IRE)** 2-9-0 0........................... SebSanders 13 70
(C E Brittain) *chsd ldrs: rdn over 2f out: edgd rt and r.o to ld wl ins fnl f* **10/3**[1]
2 3/4 **Lexi's Layla (IRE)** 2-9-0 0........................... CatherineGannon 2 68
(D M Simcock) *dwlt: outpcd: hdwy over 1f out: rdn to ld ins fnl f: sn hdd: r.o* **6/1**[3]
66 3 3 **Dixi Heights**[23] 3692 2-9-0 0........................... PatCosgrave 9 59
(J R Boyle) *sn prom: led over 2f out: rdn over 1f out: hdd and no ex ins fnl f* **15/2**
4 2 1/4 **Green Community (USA)** 2-9-0 0........................... RobertWinston 11 52
(E F Vaughan) *sn pushed along in rr: hdwy 1/2-way: rdn over 1f out: wknd ins fnl f* **7/1**
06 5 1 **Boogie Waltzer**[6] 4239 2-8-11 0........................... WilliamCarson(3) 12 49
(S C Williams) *trckd ldrs: plld hrd: outpcd over 3f out: swtchd rt over 2f out: hdwy over 1f out: wknd ins fnl f* **28/1**
5 6 2 1/4 **Kildangan Girl**[46] 2914 2-8-11 0........................... DavidProbert(3) 14 43
(W R Muir) *led: hdd over 2f out: sn rdn: wknd fnl f* **9/2**[2]
7 2 **Derval (IRE)** 2-9-0 0........................... DO'Donohoe 4 37
(K A Ryan) *plld hrd and prom: jnd ldr over 3f out: rdn and wknd over 1f out* **9/2**[2]
8 nk **Miss Wendy** 2-9-0 0........................... SaleemGolam 7 36
(M H Tompkins) *sn outpcd* **16/1**
0 9 3 **Mooinooi**[33] 3337 2-9-0 0........................... AndrewElliott 8 27
(T D Walford) *sn pushed along and prom: wknd over 2f out: bhd whn hung rt over 1f out* **8/1**
1m 17.39s (4.39) **Going Correction** +0.45s/f (Yiel) 9 Ran SP% **118.4**
Speed ratings (Par 91): **88,87,83,80,78 75,73,72,68**
toteswingers: 1&2 £3.70, 1&3 £14.80, 2&3 £4.80 CSF £24.29 TOTE £3.90: £1.60, £2.50, £3.00; EX 21.70.
Owner Saif Ali **Bred** Rabbah Bloodstock Limited **Trained** Newmarket, Suffolk

FOCUS
Those with experience hadn't shown a great deal previously, so it was no surprise that this was dominated by two newcomers.

NOTEBOOK
Waltz Around(IRE), who caught the eye in the paddock, is sprint-bred. She looked quite professional, breaking well and showing good early speed, and although she took time to pick up once initially coming under pressure, she gradually got stronger through the final furlong and was going on nicely at the finish. She has the potential to be pretty useful. (op 4-1 tchd 3-1)
Lexi's Layla(IRE) shaped with tons of promise despite being edged out close home. She burst on to the scene approaching the furlong marker and came nicely clear of the third. (op 8-1)
Dixi Heights looked a big player when taking over 2f out but her effort petered out somewhat in the closing stages and she looks more of a nursery type, for which she is now qualified. (op 8-1 tchd 9-1 and 6-1)
Green Community(USA) kept on well and wasn't knocked about when her chance was gone in the final furlong. She looked quite green under pressure and is the type to come on plenty for this. (tchd 8-1)
Boogie Waltzer showed her best form so far and it may be that this slower ground helped. (op 25-1 tchd 33-1)
Derval(IRE) showed good speed early, albeit racing a little too freely, before dropping away and there is clearly something there for connections to work with. (op 11-2 tchd 9-1)

4428 QUORN H'CAP 5f 218y
8:15 (8:15) (Class 5) (0-70,70) 3-Y-O+ **£2,914** (£867; £433; £216) **Stalls** Low

Form RPR
522 1 **Big Boom**[8] 4183 4-8-8 **52**........................... PatCosgrave 2 72
(M Quinn) *a.p: rdn to ld over 1f out: c clr fnl f* **11/4**[1]
400- 2 5 **Witchry**[259] 7286 7-9-6 **64**........................... TPQueally 1 68
(A G Newcombe) *hld up: hdwy u.p and hung rt over 2f out: styd on same pce fnl f* **33/1**
2550 3 1 **Captain Kallis (IRE)**[2] 4374 3-8-12 **61**...........................(t) SebSanders 14 61+
(D J S Ffrench Davis) *chsd ldrs: rdn over 2f out: wknd ins fnl f* **16/1**
004 4 1 1/4 **Don Pele (IRE)**[8] 4167 7-9-10 **68**...........................(p) RobertWinston 8 65
(R A Harris) *chsd ldr tl led over 3f out: rdn and hdd over 1f out: wknd ins fnl f* **16/1**
0346 5 hd **Dualagi**[18] 3866 5-8-13 **57**........................... NeilChalmers 9 53
(M R Bosley) *mid-div: rdn over 2f out: hdwy over 1f out: no ex ins fnl f* **25/1**
1505 6 1 1/4 **Xpres Maite**[16] 3928 6-9-5 **70**...........................(b) AndrewYoxall(7) 7 62
(S R Bowring) *hld up: rdn over 2f out: styd on fnl f: nt trble ldrs* **14/1**
6000 7 1 **Polar Annie**[8] 4167 4-9-12 **70**........................... TGMcLaughlin 18 59
(M S Saunders) *led: hdd over 3f out: rdn over 1f out: sn wknd* **28/1**
3543 8 1/2 **River Dee (IRE)**[15] 3939 3-8-7 **59**........................... DavidProbert(3) 15 45
(D Donovan) *prom: outpcd over 3f out: hdwy u.p over 1f out: wknd fnl f* **9/1**
0 9 nk **Whiteoak Lady (IRE)**[22] 3713 4-9-6 **67**........................... MarcHalford(3) 6 53
(J L Spearing) *chsd ldrs: rdn over 2f out: wknd fnl f* **10/1**
4-00 10 1 **Flashy Photon**[33] 3347 4-9-9 **67**........................... DaneO'Neill 5 50
(H Candy) *s.i.s: hld up: rdn 1/2-way: n.d* **14/1**
5040 11 6 **Caustic Wit (IRE)**[37] 3208 11-8-4 **55**........................... JakePayne(7) 10 19
(M S Saunders) *in rr whn hmpd sn after s: hdwy over 2f out: wknd over 1f out* **50/1**
604 12 nk **Castano**[14] 3983 5-8-13 **60** ow2...........................(p) JamesMillman(3) 17 23
(B R Millman) *prom: rdn over 2f out: wknd over 1f out: eased* **4/1**[2]
51/3 13 3 1/2 **Moral Duty (USA)**[13] 4023 4-9-7 **65**........................... LukeMorris 3 17
(J S Moore) *sn drvn along in rr: lost tch fr 1/2-way* **7/1**[3]
0424 U **Towy Boy (IRE)**[21] 3743 4-8-8 **55**...........................(v) JackMitchell(3) 11 —
(I A Wood) *awkward leaving stalls: uns rdr sn after* **14/1**
1m 15.17s (2.17) **Going Correction** +0.45s/f (Yiel)
WFA 3 from 4yo+ 5lb 14 Ran SP% **122.2**
Speed ratings (Par 103): **103,96,95,93,93 91,90,89,89,87 79,79,74,—**
toteswingers: 1&2 £6.90, 2&3 £34.90, 1&3 not won. CSF £113.85 CT £1304.29 TOTE £4.70: £1.60, £11.20, £2.10; EX 159.80 Place 6: £287.68 Place 5: £32.95.
Owner Andy Viner **Bred** Whitsbury Manor Stud **Trained** Newmarket, Suffolk

FOCUS
A big field spread right across the track but the first two came stands' side. The winner looks to be improving though.

4429 COLD NEWTON H'CAP 1m 60y
() (Class 5) (0-70,) 3-Y-O £

T/Jkpt: £164.40 to a £1 stake. Pool: £60229.86. 267.40 winning tickets. T/Plt: £3.20 to a £1 stake. Pool: £7966.48. 1809.24 winning tickets. CR

3539 REDCAR (L-H)
Wednesday, July 29

OFFICIAL GOING: Good to firm changing to good to firm (good in places) after race 6 (5.00)
Wind: fresh 1/2 behind Weather: overcast, rain race 3 onwards

4430 EUROPEAN BREEDERS' FUND MAIDEN STKS 6f
2:05 (2:26) (Class 5) 2-Y-O **£3,753** (£1,108; £554) **Stalls** Centre

Form RPR
5 1 **Bond Fastrac**[37] 3226 2-9-3 0........................... PJMcDonald 3 80+
(G R Oldroyd) *mde all: styd on strly fnl f: readily* **16/1**
02 2 2 1/4 **Elusive Sue (USA)**[28] 3495 2-8-12 0........................... TonyHamilton 1 68+
(R A Fahey) *trckd wnr: effrt over 2f out: rdn and kpt on same pce ins fnl f* **5/6**[1]
0 3 1 3/4 **Suzi's A Smartlady (IRE)**[14] 3987 2-8-12 0........................... AndrewElliott 15 63
(M Johnston) *chsd ldrs: kpt on same pce appr fnl f* **13/2**[2]
4 1 **Chushka** 2-8-12 0........................... TomEaves 2 60
(B Smart) *s.s: t.k.h: sn trcking ldrs: kpt on same pce fnl 2f* **11/1**
05 5 3 1/4 **Kahail (USA)**[27] 3546 2-9-3 0...........................(t) PhilipRobinson 7 55
(Miss D Mountain) *chsd ldrs: rdn over 2f out: sn outpcd* **17/2**[3]
0 6 1 1/2 **Kookie**[11] 4100 2-8-12 0........................... PhillipMakin 9 46
(R E Barr) *s.s: styd on fnl 2f: nrst fin* **100/1**
0 7 hd **Magic Millie (IRE)**[6] 4226 2-8-5 0........................... JamesPSullivan(7) 5 45
(J Hetherton) *prominenmt: wknd over 1f out* **28/1**
0 8 nk **Star Cruiser (USA)**[43] 2997 2-9-3 0........................... DavidAllan 14 49
(T D Easterby) *chsd ldrs: hung rt and wknd over 1f out* **100/1**
9 4 **Fireflash (IRE)** 2-9-3 0........................... PaulMulrennan 8 37
(Mrs A Duffield) *mid-div: drvn over 2f out: nvr nr ldrs* **16/1**
10 nk **Both Ends Burning (IRE)** 2-8-12 0........................... PAspell 13 31
(J S Wainwright) *s.s: racd stands' side: nvr on terms* **125/1**
40 11 3 1/2 **Reallymissgreeley (USA)**[35] 3262 2-8-12 0........................... TedDurcan 4 21
(K A Ryan) *mid-div: sn drvn along: lost pl over 2f out* **16/1**
12 6 **Patricks Lodge** 2-9-3 0........................... GrahamGibbons 16 8
(J D Bethell) *s.s: a bhd* **33/1**
0 13 hd **Green Shoots**[18] 3858 2-8-12 0........................... PatrickMathers 12 2
(M E Sowersby) *in rr: bhd fnl 2f* **200/1**
14 nk **Royal Cheer** 2-8-12 0........................... SilvestreDeSousa 10 1
(Mrs A Duffield) *in rr: bhd fnl 2f* **10/1**
1m 10.13s (-1.67) **Going Correction** -0.20s/f (Firm) 14 Ran SP% **123.1**
Speed ratings (Par 94): **103,100,97,96,92 90,89,89,84,83 78,70,70,70**
toteswingers: 1&2 £6.40, 1&3 £11.10, 2&3 £2.90 CSF £30.21 TOTE £22.60: £4.10, £1.20, £2.10; EX 51.60.
Owner R C Bond **Bred** Bond Thoroughbred Corporation **Trained** Brawby, N Yorks
■

FOCUS
A maiden lacking strength in depth, with one third of the field making their racecourse debuts, and the market not giving many clues either. Not many got into it from behind.

NOTEBOOK
Bond Fastrac had showed some promise when he made his debut at Wolverhampton last month, and clearly had come on plenty for that as he made most of the running, and in the end ran out a convincing winner. He should improve for this and can go in again.
Elusive Sue(USA) had no excuses in second place, as although most of her pedigree is about speed she looked quite one-paced and might be worth stepping up in trip. She is still in good hands to do better. (op 10-11 tchd 11-10)
Suzi's A Smartlady(IRE) kept on in third place without really troubling the winner. This was her first try on turf and she can improve. (op 15-2)
Chushka did best of the newcomers and should improve in time. (tchd 12-1)
Kahail(USA) Official explanation: jockey said colt was unsuited by the good to firm (firm in places) ground
Reallymissgreeley(USA) proved very disappointing once again. One of the first to come off the bridle, she was eased when beaten inside the final furlong. She clearly showed ability on her debut at Haydock and could be on a good mark for nurseries if her trainer can get her back to form.
Official explanation: jockey said filly never travelled (tchd 14-1)

4431 BUY YOUR TICKETS ON-LINE @ REDCARRACING.CO.UK H'CAP 1m 2f
2:40 (3:01) (Class 5) (0-70,69) 3-Y-O+ **£2,590** (£770; £385; £192) **Stalls** Low

Form RPR
2313 1 **Singora Lady (IRE)**[30] 3451 4-9-1 **54**........................... TonyCulhane 6 63
(P T Midgley) *hld up in rr gd hdwy and hmpd over 2f out: hung lft and led 1f out: drew clr* **5/1**[2]
-354 2 3 1/4 **King's Counsel (IRE)**[6] 4230 3-8-11 **60**........................... PJMcDonald 14 63+
(J Hetherton) *drvn to ld: hdd 1f out: no ex* **20/1**
-150 3 1/2 **Strong Storm (USA)**[79] 1928 3-9-6 **69**........................... ShaneKelly 12 71
(J Noseda) *s.i.s: hdwy over 3f out: swtchd rt over 2f out: kpt on fnl f* **9/2**[1]
020 4 1/2 **Spartan Prince (USA)**[54] 2667 3-8-12 **64**...........................(t) NeilBrown(3) 4 65
(T D Barron) *in rr: hdwy on ins over 3f out: styd on fnl f* **15/2**
6561 5 3/4 **Whaston (IRE)**[16] 3911 4-9-2 **55**...........................(v) GrahamGibbons 8 54
(J D Bethell) *sn trcking ldrs: kpt on one pce fnl 2f* **11/2**[3]
6140 6 4 **Trouble Mountain (USA)**[18] 3864 12-9-3 **56**...........................(bt) DaleGibson 13 47
(M W Easterby) *in rr div: drvn 4f out: nvr on terms* **10/1**
-543 7 3/4 **Waterloo Corner**[29] 3486 7-8-13 **52**...........................(v) PaulMulrennan 9 42
(R Craggs) *drvn to chse ldrs: wknd over 1f out* **6/1**
004S 8 1/2 **Neon Blue**[16] 3911 8-8-7 **51**...........................(p) AmyRyan(5) 3 40
(R M Whitaker) *s.s: sme hdwy on outside over 2f out: sn wknd* **20/1**
4005 9 6 **Jebel Tara**[23] 3689 4-9-13 **66**...........................(b) SilvestreDeSousa 10 43
(A D Brown) *racd wd: t.k.h: sn trcking ldrs: lost pl and hmpd over 2f out* **6/1**
2200 10 9 **Transmission (IRE)**[112] 1192 4-9-12 **65**........................... TomEaves 7 24
(B Smart) *mid-div: pushed along over 5f out: lost pl over 2f out: eased* **20/1**

The Form Book, Raceform Ltd, Compton, RG20 6NL

000- **11** 37 **Instructor**[424] 2591 8-9-9 **67**.................... MichaelO'Connell(5) 2 —
(C A Mulhall) *chsd ldrs: lost pl over 3f out: sn bhd and eased: wl t.o* **80/1**

2m 5.22s (-1.88) **Going Correction** -0.20s/f (Firm)
WFA 3 from 4yo+ 10lb **11 Ran SP% 115.2**
Speed ratings (Par 103): **99,96,96,95,95 91,91,90,86,78 49**
toteswingers: 1&2 £15.00, 1&3 £4.70, 2&3 £18.80 CSF £103.05 CT £481.57 TOTE £4.50: £1.60, £5.90, £1.80; EX 122.90.
Owner M McGinn **Bred** Mick McGinn **Trained** Westow, N Yorks
■ Stewards' Enquiry : Michael O'Connell one-day ban: used whip with excessive force (Aug 12)
Shane Kelly four-day ban: careless riding (Aug 12-15)

FOCUS
This was no more than a modest handicap with a lot of the runners having questions to answer. It was run at a good gallop, though, and the form is sound.

4432 CARIBBEAN CARNIVAL DAY - 8TH AUGUST RATING RELATED MAIDEN STKS 7f
3:15 (3:36) (Class 5) 3-Y-0+ **£2,590** (£770; £385; £192) **Stalls** Centre

Form RPR
564- **1** **Ishiadancer**[250] 7403 4-9-5 64.................... DavidAllan 8 64
(E J Alston) *mde virtually all: hld on wl* **8/1**[2]
0202 **2** ½ **Peaceful Rule (USA)**[9] 4143 3-9-1 68.................... FrancisNorton 3 63
(D Nicholls) *sn chsng ldrs: chal over 2f out: no ex wl ins fnl f* **4/6**[1]
02-5 **3** 1 **Pacific Bay (IRE)**[9] 4131 3-8-12 65.................... TonyHamilton 2 57
(R A Fahey) *sn chsng ldrs: effrt over 2f out: styd on same pce fnl f* **8/1**[2]
6-06 **4** ½ **Granny McPhee**[18] 3856 3-8-9 68.................... KellyHarrison(3) 5 56
(A Bailey) *w ldrs: hung bdly lft and kpt on fnl f* **17/2**[3]
0604 **5** shd **Feet Of Fury**[25] 3625 3-8-12 57.................... PaulMulrennan 7 55
(W M Brisbourne) *mid-div: effrt over 2f out: kpt on fnl f* **16/1**
604- **6** hd **Magic Haze**[312] 6109 3-9-1 60.................... PhillipMakin 10 58
(Miss S E Hall) *hld up in midfield: effrt over 2f out: kpt on fnl f* **40/1**
-500 **7** 2¾ **Virtuality (USA)**[57] 2579 4-9-5 55.................... TomEaves 4 50
(B Smart) *t.k.h: sn trcking ldrs: drvn over 2f out: edgd rt and wknd over 1f out* **33/1**
0-4 **8** 10 **Unconsoled**[14] 3975 3-8-12 55.................... GrahamGibbons 1 20
(J Hetherton) *w ldrs: wknd qckly over 1f out* **33/1**
626 **9** 1 **Moon Money (IRE)**[13] 4014 3-9-1 59.................... SilvestreDeSousa 6 21
(K A Ryan) *sn in rr: reminders after 2f: sn bhd* **8/1**[2]
500- **10** 23 **Boy Racer (IRE)**[394] 3555 4-9-8 64.................... DanielTudhope 9 —
(C J Teague) *in rr: lost pl 3f out: sn wl bhd* **50/1**

1m 23.46s (-1.04) **Going Correction** -0.20s/f (Firm)
WFA 3 from 4yo 7lb **10 Ran SP% 120.0**
Speed ratings (Par 103): **97,96,95,94,94 94,91,79,78,52**
toteswingers: 1&2 £2.90, 1&3 £4.30, 2&3 £2.10 CSF £13.90 TOTE £10.00: £1.90, £1.10, £1.60; EX 18.50.
Owner Racing Shares Nuppend **Bred** Southern Seafoods **Trained** Longton, Lancs

FOCUS
Not a strong maiden by any stretch of the imagination. The winner probably just ran to form.

4433 BODDINGTONS REDCAR STRAIGHT-MILE CHAMPIONSHIP STKS (QUALIFIER) (H'CAP) 1m
3:50 (4:11) (Class 4) (0-85,85) 3-Y-0 **£4,857** (£1,445; £722; £360) **Stalls** Centre

Form RPR
32-1 **1** **Applause (IRE)**[23] 3696 3-9-4 **82**.................... ShaneKelly 2 97+
(J Noseda) *w ldrs: led gng easily best over 2f out: rdn clr 1f out: eased towards fin* **3/1**[2]
2644 **2** 2¾ **Wannabe King**[12] 4056 3-9-7 **85**.................... TedDurcan 8 93
(D R Lanigan) *led 1f: effrt over 2f out: edgd rt and styd on same pce fnl f* **6/1**[3]
6004 **3** 1½ **Canwinn (IRE)**[19] 3816 3-9-7 **85**....................(v) TonyCulhane 3 90
(M R Channon) *trckd ldrs: effrt over 2f out: styd on same pce* **3/1**[2]
-614 **4** 2¼ **Glowing Praise**[18] 3868 3-9-2 **80**.................... GrahamGibbons 6 79
(E S McMahon) *stl had hood on whn stalls opened: s.s: hdwy to chse ldrs after 3f: effrt over 2f out: one pce* **5/2**[1]
-560 **5** 3½ **Striker Torres (IRE)**[62] 2406 3-8-10 **74**.................... TomEaves 7 65
(B Smart) *t.k.h in rr: effrt over 2f out: nvr a factor* **20/1**
5461 **6** 1¼ **Olympic Dream**[34] 3316 3-8-8 **75**.................... FrederikTylicki(3) 1 63
(R A Fahey) *hdwy to ld after 1f: hdd over 2f out: wknd over 1f out* **7/1**
0154 **7** 5 **Jimwil (IRE)**[20] 3790 3-8-11 **75**....................(b) PhillipMakin 5 52
(M Dods) *hld up in rr: shkn up over 2f out: no rspnse: eased ins fnl f* **16/1**

1m 35.21s (-2.79) **Going Correction** -0.20s/f (Firm) **7 Ran SP% 116.0**
Speed ratings (Par 102): **105,102,100,98,95 93,88**
toteswingers: 1&2 £3.80, 1&3 £2.30, 2&3 £4.80 CSF £21.81 CT £58.10 TOTE £3.00: £1.90, £2.00; EX 15.60.
Owner M Tabor, D Smith & Mrs J Magnier **Bred** John M Weld **Trained** Newmarket, Suffolk

FOCUS
An interesting handicap for the grade that might just prove quite strong form in time. It was run at an even pace and the form is rated around the second and third.
Glowing Praise Official explanation: jockey said gelding missed the break due to blindfold being difficult to release

4434 THE COMMITMENTS PERFORMING ON SATURDAY 29TH AUGUST CLAIMING STKS 1m 2f
4:30 (4:51) (Class 6) 3-Y-0+ **£2,047** (£604; £302) **Stalls** Low

Form RPR
2531 **1** **Tufton**[18] 3854 6-9-6 74.................... FrederikTylicki(3) 6 76
(R A Fahey) *hld up in midfield: smooth hdwy over 3f out: led over 2f out: rdn clr 1f out* **7/4**[1]
2413 **2** 6 **Lucayan Dancer**[18] 3854 9-9-10 66.................... FrancisNorton 7 65
(D Nicholls) *mid-div: drvn 4f out: hdwy over 2f out: styd on to take 2nd appr fnl f: no ch w wnr* **5/1**
30B0 **3** 1¼ **All In The Red (IRE)**[3] 4351 4-9-7 69....................(p) ShaneKelly 2 60
(A Crook) *s.i.s: hdwy over 2f out: styd on wl ins fnl f* **20/1**
6205 **4** 1 **Ming Vase**[3] 4351 7-9-3 50.................... PaulMulrennan 3 54
(P T Midgley) *chsd ldrs: edgd lft over 1f out: kpt on same pce* **14/1**
-15 **5** 2 **Heroes**[13] 2773 5-9-10 76....................(tp) TedDurcan 4 57
(Tim Vaughan) *dwlt: in rr: hdwy on ins 4f out: swtchd rt over 1f out: nvr nr ldrs* **9/2**[3]
11-0 **6** 6 **La Columbina**[123] 999 4-9-3 77....................(p) SilvestreDeSousa 1 38
(G A Harker) *chsd ldrs: drvn 4f out: wknd over 1f out* **3/1**[2]
0050 **7** nk **Super King**[73] 603 8-9-0 35.................... LeeVickers(3) 11 37
(A D Brown) *hld up in midfield: effrt over 3f out: nvr a factor* **200/1**
6400 **8** 3¼ **Son Of Monsieur**[14] 3974 3-8-6 54 ow1.................... PJMcDonald 10 29
(G R Oldroyd) *in rr: nvr a factor* **100/1**
0504 **9** 4 **Picture Frame**[28] 3501 5-8-12 55.................... PatrickDonaghy(5) 9 22
(J T Stimpson) *in rr: drvn 5f out: nvr on terms* **33/1**
-660 **10** 4 **Prince Samos (IRE)**[14] 3974 7-9-6 59.................... DaleGibson 8 17
(C A Mulhall) *led 3f: chsd ldr: drvn 4f out: lost pl over 2f out* **50/1**
0454 **11** 4½ **Gold Maha**[48] 2838 3-7-11 52.................... JamieKyne(5) 5 —
(M E Sowersby) *w ldr: led after 3f: hdd over 2f out: ducked lft and sn lost pl* **20/1**

2m 5.88s (-1.22) **Going Correction** -0.20s/f (Firm)
WFA 3 from 4yo+ 10lb **11 Ran SP% 118.8**
Speed ratings (Par 101): **96,91,90,89,87 83,82,80,76,73 70**
toteswingers: 1&2 £2.80, 1&3 £10.10, 2&3 £11.90 CSF £10.42 TOTE £2.70: £1.30, £1.90, £3.40; EX 8.80.
Owner G Brogan **Bred** Gainsborough Stud Management Ltd **Trained** Musley Bank, N Yorks

FOCUS
An ordinary claimer run at an even gallop thanks to Gold Maha, before that one faded tamely in the final couple of furlongs. The winner did not need to be at his best with his main rivals disappointing.

4435 SAVE OUR STEEL FAMILY FUNDAY - 9TH AUGUST H'CAP 1m
5:00 (5:22) (Class 6) (0-65,62) 3-Y-0+ **£1,942** (£578; £288; £144) **Stalls** Centre

Form RPR
1242 **1** **Ninth House (USA)**[16] 3924 7-9-6 **55**....................(t) SilvestreDeSousa 4 67
(Mrs R A Carr) *mid-div: hdwy over 2f out: led jst ins fnl f: drvn out* **13/2**[2]
3322 **2** ¾ **Wiseman's Diamond (USA)**[18] 3862 4-9-1 **55**.................... PaulPickard(5) 11 65
(P T Midgley) *w ldrs: led over 3f out: hdd jst ins fnl f: no ex* **7/1**[3]
-000 **3** 1¾ **Lujano**[41] 3070 4-9-10 **59**.................... TonyHamilton 6 65
(Ollie Pears) *w ldrs towards far side: kpt on same pce fnl f* **33/1**
3504 **4** ½ **Jord (IRE)**[7] 4191 5-8-10 **48**.................... FrederikTylicki(3) 7 53
(J A Glover) *chsd ldrs: kpt on same pce appr fnl f* **8/1**
0253 **5** shd **Efidium**[3] 4346 11-9-6 **60**.................... JamieKyne(5) 5 65
(N Bycroft) *dwlt: in rr: hdwy 2f out: styd on wl ins fnl f* **8/1**
1520 **6** ½ **Aussie Blue (IRE)**[12] 4046 5-9-10 **59**.................... PaulQuinn 8 63
(R M Whitaker) *chsd ldrs: kpt on same pce appr fnl f* **12/1**
2213 **7** nk **King Pin**[18] 3857 4-9-13 **62**.................... PaulMulrennan 19 65
(Miss Tracy Waggott) *hld up in rr stands' side: hdwy over 2f out: kpt on fnl f* **11/2**[1]
0000 **8** 2 **Emperor's Well**[29] 3490 10-8-9 **51**....................(b) JamesPSullivan(7) 12 49
(M W Easterby) *in tch: one pce fnl 3f* **40/1**
3300 **9** 6 **Business Class (BRZ)**[9] 4140 4-9-13 **62**.................... FrancisNorton 15 47
(D Nicholls) *chsd ldrs: rdn over 2f out: sn lost pl* **16/1**
0040 **10** 2½ **Fyodorovich (USA)**[26] 3558 4-9-2 **51**.................... PAspell 16 30
(J S Wainwright) *rrd s: nvr on terms* **50/1**
0006 **11** ¾ **Cross Of Lorraine (IRE)**[36] 3234 6-9-0 **49**....................(b) PJMcDonald 18 26
(J Wade) *prom: rdn 3f out: sn lost pl* **33/1**
000- **12** 1½ **Mundo's Magic**[290] 6681 5-8-10 **50**....................(t) BMcHugh(5) 17 24
(N Wilson) *mid-div stands' side: rdn 3f out: nvr a factor* **33/1**
1152 **13** 1¼ **Lady Florence**[9] 4140 4-9-9 **58**.................... PhilipRobinson 13 29
(A B Coogan) *led tl over 3f out: lost pl over 1f out* **11/2**[1]
-000 **14** 2¼ **Boy Dancer (IRE)**[24] 3653 6-9-7 **56**.................... GrahamGibbons 14 22
(J J Quinn) *in rr: sn pushed along: nvr on terms* **20/1**
0300 **15** 1¼ **Desert Ben (IRE)**[7] 4191 6-9-6 **55**.................... TomEaves 1 18
(C Grant) *hld up in rr: nvr on terms* **33/1**
6300 **16** 12 **King Of The Moors (USA)**[18] 3863 6-9-12 **61**....................(p) PhillipMakin 3 —
(R C Guest) *hld up in rr far side: sme hdwy 4f out: lost pl over 2f out: eased whn bhd* **12/1**
0033 **17** 6 **Rowaad**[18] 3863 4-9-0 **49**....................(v) TedDurcan 10 —
(A E Price) *w ldrs: lost pl 3f: eased whn bhd* **16/1**

1m 36.09s (-1.91) **Going Correction** -0.20s/f (Firm) **17 Ran SP% 126.9**
Speed ratings (Par 101): **101,100,98,98,97 97,97,95,89,86 85,84,83,80,79 67,61**
toteswingers: 1&2 £12.60, 1&3 £66.40, 2&3 £61.20 CSF £49.87 CT £1443.71 TOTE £8.00: £2.10, £2.10, £7.40, £2.30; EX 69.50.
Owner Michael Hill **Bred** Juddmonte Farms Inc **Trained** Huby, N Yorks

FOCUS
A big field for this low-grade handicap which as expected was run at a good gallop; all 17 elected to race down the centre of the track. Solid form for the grade.
Lady Florence Official explanation: trainer's rep said, regarding running, that the filly was unsuited by the fast early pace

4436 GORACING.CO.UK H'CAP 6f
5:35 (5:58) (Class 6) (0-65,65) 3-Y-0+ **£1,942** (£578; £288; £144) **Stalls** Centre

Form RPR
1040 **1** **Just Sam (IRE)**[7] 4191 4-9-0 **58**.................... BMcHugh(5) 15 72
(R E Barr) *chsd ldrs stands' side: led over 1f out: hld on wl* **20/1**
2230 **2** ¾ **Who's Shirl**[32] 3381 3-8-7 **54**.................... KellyHarrison(3) 12 65
(C W Fairhurst) *towards rr stands' side: hdwy 2f out: edgd rt: styd on to take 2nd towards fin* **14/1**
0663 **3** 1¾ **Redwater River**[7] 4191 5-8-8 **52**....................(b) DeanHeslop(5) 14 58
(Mrs R A Carr) *led tl over 1f out: kpt on same pce* **8/1**[3]
2224 **4** 2¾ **Soto**[25] 3612 6-9-3 **63**....................(b) JamesPSullivan(7) 2 60
(M W Easterby) *chsd ldrs far side: hrd rdn and hung bdly lft 1f out: wknd towards fin* **6/1**[2]
6003 **5** nk **Kalhan Sands (IRE)**[9] 4136 4-9-9 **62**.................... GrahamGibbons 8 58
(J J Quinn) *chsd ldrs: kpt on same pce fnl 2f* **10/1**
0434 **6** 1¾ **Sheik'N'Knotsterd**[27] 3539 4-8-13 **57**.................... MarkCoumbe(5) 4 48
(J F Coupland) *w ldr: fdd appr fnl f* **16/1**
4064 **7** nk **Sunley Sovereign**[6] 4225 5-8-9 **48** ow2....................(p) PaulMulrennan 18 38
(Mrs R A Carr) *mid-div: hdwy 2f out: nvr nr ldrs* **8/1**[3]
0006 **8** ½ **Half A Crown (IRE)**[15] 3938 4-8-10 **49** ow3....................(b[1]) PhillipMakin 1 37
(M Dods) *in rr far side: hdwy over 2f out: nvr nr ldrs* **12/1**
-364 **9** 1¼ **Ursus**[20] 3765 4-9-1 **54**.................... SilvestreDeSousa 3 38
(C R Wilson) *slipped s: hdwy over 2f out: nvr a factor* **5/1**[1]
1434 **10** ¾ **Forever's Girl**[140] 804 3-9-5 **63**.................... PJMcDonald 13 44
(G R Oldroyd) *in rr div: nvr a factor* **22/1**
0-20 **11** nk **Exopuntia**[18] 3859 3-8-8 **55**.................... MichaelJStainton(3) 7 35
(R M Whitaker) *in rr: sn drvn along: hung lft over 1f out: nvr on terms* **20/1**
2434 **12** shd **Where's Reiley (USA)**[12] 4061 3-9-4 **65**.................... NeilBrown(3) 6 44
(T D Barron) *mid-div: lost pl 2f out* **9/1**
60-5 **13** hd **Liteup My World (USA)**[15] 3939 3-9-3 **61**.................... TomEaves 17 40
(B Ellison) *a in rr* **18/1**
001 **14** ½ **Greek Secret**[15] 3938 6-9-0 **58**.................... JamesO'Reilly(5) 5 36
(J O'Reilly) *a in rr* **12/1**
0000 **15** 2½ **Fitzwarren**[36] 3234 8-8-7 **46**....................(v) DuranFentiman 11 16
(A D Brown) *chsd ldrs: lost pl 2f out* **100/1**
0060 **16** 7 **Angle Of Attack (IRE)**[30] 3445 4-9-2 **55**....................(p) DanielTudhope 19 —
(A D Brown) *w ldrs stands' side: lost pl over 1f out: eased ins fnl f* **33/1**
340R **R** **Johnston's Glory (IRE)**[65] 2312 5-9-10 **63**....................(p) ShaneKelly 16 —
(E J Alston) *ref to r: tk no part* **16/1**

33/0 **P** **Glencairn Star**[7] 4192 8-9-12 **65**.......................... TonyHamilton 20 —
(F Watson) *in rr stands' side: p.u over 1f out* **50/1**
1m 10.43s (-1.37) **Going Correction** -0.20s/f (Firm)
WFA 3 from 4yo+ 5lb **18** Ran SP% **131.1**
Speed ratings (Par 101): **101,100,97,94,93 91,90,90,88,87 87,87,86,86,82 73,—,—**
Place 6: £53.34 Place 5: £38.03 CSF £277.61 CT £2460.57 TOTE £32.10: £6.50, £3.40, £2.70, £2.10; EX 538.50.
Owner P Cartmell **Bred** John J Carroll **Trained** Seamer, N Yorks
FOCUS
Another low-grade but competitive 6f handicap to close the card. The gallop was strong and the form looks sound.
Ursus Official explanation: jockey said gelding slipped on leaving stalls
Glencairn Star Official explanation: jockey said gelding lost its action
T/Plt: £14.70 to a £1 stake. Pool: £51,898.80. 2,574.16 winning tickets. T/Qpdt: £6.90 to a £1 stake. Pool: £3,202.40. 341.40 winning tickets. WG

4243 SANDOWN (R-H)
Wednesday, July 29

OFFICIAL GOING: Good (good to firm in places; 8.7)
Home bend at mid configuration adding about 5yards to all race distances, false rail at 3f pole.
Wind: Brisk across Weather: Overcast

4437 AIR CHARTER SERVICE APPRENTICE H'CAP 1m 2f 7y
5:50 (5:51) (Class 5) (0-70,70) 4-Y-0+ **£3,238** (£963; £481; £240) **Stalls** High

Form RPR
1402 **1** **Agilete**[39] 3151 7-9-6 **69**.......................... SimonPearce(3) 10 76
(J Pearce) *trckd ldrs and t.k.h off mod pce 3f: stdd 5f out: hdwy over 2f out and sn squeezed through to chse ldrs: rdn to ld jst ins fnl f: hld on wl* **9/1**
6621 **2** *1* **Dragon Slayer (IRE)**[9] 4158 7-9-2 **67** 6ex.......... TobyAtkinson(5) 5 72
(John A Harris) *s.i.s: hld up towards rr tl drvn over 2f out: styd on wl fr over 1f out and kpt on ins fnl f to go 2nd cl home but nt rch wnr* **9/4**[1]
2301 **3** *3/4* **Ross Moor**[7] 4207 7-9-4 **64** 6ex.......... Louis-PhilippeBeuzelin 8 68
(Mike Murphy) *s.i.s: in rr tl drvn and hdwy on outside over 2f out: pressed ldrs over 1f out and kpt on ins fnl f* **9/2**[2]
0000 **4** *2 1/4* **Classical Rhythm (IRE)**[4] 4300 4-8-9 **55**.......... AmyBaker 2 54
(J R Boyle) *t.k.h and chsd ldr off mod pce 3f: drvn to ld ins fnl 2f: hdd jst ins fnl f: wknd fnl 100yds* **8/1**[3]
0-04 **5** *1 1/4* **Harting Hill**[86] 1728 4-8-0 **51** oh1.......... KatiaScallan(5) 6 48
(M P Tregoning) *chsd ldrs and t.k.h off mod pce 3f: rdn and effrt whn edgd rt ins fnl 2f: wknd fnl f* **9/2**[2]
3/00 **6** *1 3/4* **New World Order (IRE)**[21] 3734 5-9-0 **60**.......... MCGeran 7 53
(Mrs S Leech) *led at mod pce 1st 3f: rdn and hdd ins fnl 2f and one pce whn hmpd on ins sn after: wknd fnl f* **10/1**
60-0 **7** *1/2* **Zaif (IRE)**[86] 1750 6-9-7 **70**.......... BillyCray(3) 4 62
(D J S Ffrench Davis) *in tch: hdwy 5f out: chsd ldrs over 3f out: sn no imp hung rt and wknd over 1f out* **28/1**
1124 **8** *2 1/4* **Theocritus (USA)**[18] 3847 4-9-5 **70**.......... (b) ChrisHough(5) 1 58
(D M Simcock) *s.i.s: rr and ken hold of mod pce 3f: rapis hdwy on outside 5f out to press ldrs 3f out: sn rdn: edgd rt and wknd qckly 2f out* **9/2**[2]
2m 11.2s (0.70) **Going Correction** +0.15s/f (Good) **8** Ran SP% **119.0**
Speed ratings (Par 103): **103,102,101,99,98 97,97,95**
toteswingers: 1&2 £1.60, 1&3 £8.30, 2&3 £1.40 CSF £30.93 CT £107.58 TOTE £9.30: £2.10, £1.40, £1.30; EX 19.50.
Owner S & M Supplies (Aylsham) Ltd **Bred** J W Parker And Lavington Stud **Trained** Newmarket, Suffolk
■ Stewards' Enquiry : Simon Pearce two-day ban: careless riding (Aug 12-13)
FOCUS
This was a modest handicap and the form is a bit muddling. The winner is rated to his best.

4438 MICHAEL WRIGHT RACING CLAIMING STKS 1m 14y
6:20 (6:20) (Class 5) 4-Y-0+ **£3,238** (£963; £481; £240) **Stalls** High

Form RPR
300 **1** **Saltagioo (ITY)**[43] 3008 5-9-2 83.......... DarryllHolland 3 70
(M Botti) *in tch: hdwy fr 3f out: disp ld and rdn ins fnl 2f: def advantage appr fnl f: drvn out* **4/1**[3]
3416 **2** *nk* **Fremen (USA)**[27] 3525 9-9-2 82.......... AdrianTNicholls 8 69
(D Nicholls) *s.i.s: hld up in rr: hdwy on ins 2f out: n.m.r appr fnl f: sn rdn: qcknd ins fnl f and styd on to go 2nd cl home: nt quite get up* **5/2**[2]
4220 **3** *1 1/2* **Elna Bright**[4] 4293 4-8-12 80.......... RichardEvans(5) 6 67
(P D Evans) *in tch: hdwy 3f out: disp ld ins fnl 2f tl appr fnl f: styd chsng wnr tl wknd into 3rd cl home* **2/1**[1]
66-5 **4** *3/4* **Persian Storm (GER)**[64] 634 5-9-3 103.......... GeorgeBaker 2 65
(G L Moore) *plld hrd and chsd ldr after 2f: rdn and ev ch 2f out: one pce fimal f* **4/1**[3]
006- **5** *1 1/4* **Womaniser (IRE)**[257] 7310 5-8-13 44.......... PaulDoe 1 58
(T Keddy) *s.i.s: hld up in rr tl shkn up and stdy hdwy fnl f: fin wl but nvr in contention* **25/1**
0000 **6** *nk* **Cordell (IRE)**[47] 2891 4-9-7 75.......... JimmyFortune 4 65
(R Hannon) *led: rdn and hdd ins fnl 2f: wknd fnl f* **10/1**
0020 **7** *4* **Dichoh**[14] 3977 6-9-0 67.......... (v) FergusSweeney 5 49
(M Madgwick) *chsd ldr 2f: wknd ins fnl 2f* **14/1**
1m 43.92s (0.62) **Going Correction** +0.15s/f (Good) **7** Ran SP% **121.5**
Speed ratings (Par 103): **102,101,100,99,98 97,93**
toteswingers: 1&2 £4.00, 2&3 £2.20, 1&3 not won. CSF £15.70 TOTE £5.90: £2.50, £1.90; EX 12.70.Elna Bright was claimed by B. R. Johnson for £17000. Saltagioo was claimed by I. A. Wood for £15000.
Owner Op - Center **Bred** Az Ag Francesca **Trained** Newmarket, Suffolk
FOCUS
This seemed a decent event of its type, as it contained a couple of useful yardsticks in claiming company. However, they all finished in a bit of a heap, so the form might turn out to be run of the mill. The fifth is the likely key to the standard.
Saltagioo(ITY) Official explanation: trainer said, regarding apparent improvement in form, that the horse appreciated being ridden by a more experienced jockey

4439 EUROPEAN BREEDERS' FUND MAIDEN STKS 7f 16y
6:55 (6:57) (Class 4) 2-Y-0 **£5,180** (£1,541; £770; £384) **Stalls** High

Form RPR
1 **Azmeel** 2-9-3 0.......... JimmyFortune 3 85+
(J H M Gosden) *s.i.s: hld up in rr: stdy hdwy on outside fr 2f out: shkn up and qcknd fnl f to ld fnl 50yds: won gng away* **10/11**[1]
04 **2** *1 1/4* **Deauville Post (FR)**[13] 4006 2-9-3 0.......... RyanMoore 6 77
(R Hannon) *trckd ldr: drvn to take slt ld 2f out: narrowly hdd sn after: styd chalng tl edgd lft: bmpd and led again 1f out: hdd and outpcd fnl 50yds* **2/1**[2]
0 **3** *1 3/4* **White Devil**[26] 3584 2-9-3 0.......... WilliamBuick 4 73
(A M Balding) *chsd ldrs and plld hrd: drvn to ld ins fnl 2f: u.p whn bmpd and hdd 1f out: sn no ex and one pce* **33/1**
0 **4** *2 1/4* **Flying Destination**[16] 3920 2-9-3 0.......... PaulDoe 5 67
(W J Knight) *in tch: pushed along 2f out: rdn and styd on fr over 1f out but nvr gng pce to rch ldng trio fnl f* **40/1**
6 **5** *1 1/4* **Pebblesonthebeach**[18] 3867 2-9-3 0.......... GeorgeBaker 2 64
(J W Hills) *s.i.s: in rr: hdwy fr 2f out: edgd rt over 1f out: edgd lft and kpt on fnl f but nvr gng pce to get into contention* **20/1**
6 *2 3/4* **Cloudy City (USA)** 2-9-3 0.......... GregFairley 10 57
(M Johnston) *led: drvn and tried to qckn 3f out: hdd 2f out: wknd over 1f out* **7/1**[3]
7 *2 1/2* **Greek Key (IRE)** 2-9-3 0.......... JamieSpencer 1 51
(M L W Bell) *s.i.s: t.k.h in rr: mod prog fr over 1f out* **11/1**
0 **8** *3* **Mrs Puff (IRE)**[117] 1090 2-8-12 0.......... JamesDoyle 8 38
(P D Evans) *chsd ldrs: rdn 3f out: wknd ins fnl 2f* **66/1**
00 **9** *1* **Campaigner**[48] 2839 2-9-3 0.......... SteveDrowne 7 41
(J W Hills) *in tch: rdn 3f out: wknd 2f out: btn whn hmpd over 1f out* **80/1**
1m 30.02s (0.52) **Going Correction** +0.15s/f (Good) **9** Ran SP% **119.4**
Speed ratings (Par 96): **103,101,99,97,95 92,89,86,85**
toteswingers: 1&2 £1.10, 1&3 £11.50, 2&3 £13.20 CSF £2.88 TOTE £2.10: £1.20, £1.20, £4.80; EX 3.40.
Owner M Al-Qatami & K M Al-Mudhaf **Bred** Elsdon Farms **Trained** Newmarket, Suffolk
FOCUS
There were not many that one could fancy seriously in this maiden, but it still looked a decent event.
NOTEBOOK
Azmeel ◆, the first foal of a quite useful 7f/1m winner in Ireland, had clearly been showing something at home, as he was well backed and holds two Group 2 entries this season. A lengthy, scopey sort that was wearing a cross noseband, he did not get away too quickly but travelled strongly and won in tidy fashion once getting to the front. He is bound to progress for this effort and possibly justify some of the entries he holds. (tchd 11-10 and 6-5 in a place)
Deauville Post(FR) ◆ had improved with each run and has the physical make-up to keep progressing. Always close up, he was in the ideal place to collect his first success but was claimed close to home by a classy looking opponent. His time will come. (op 9-4 tchd 7-4 and 5-2 in a place)
White Devil ◆, wearing a noseband, has some size about him and looks sure to develop with maturity. He improved a lot on his first run, which had come over this course and distance, and is making good progress. (op 20-1)
Flying Destination, noticeably smaller than the first three home, finished in eyecatching style after coming under pressure 3f out. He can make his mark at a slightly lower level, possibly over further.
Pebblesonthebeach was not subjected to a hard time throughout the latter stages (he edged a little left once in the clear) and could develop into a fair handicapper if maintaining the promise he is showing. (op 25-1)
Cloudy City(USA), who is by Giant´s Causeway out of a Graded-winning mare in America, does not hold any big-race entries but looks a lovely big type. Quickly away, possibly a shade too fast, he started to falter three out and was beaten by the 2f pole. He can be given another chance, however. (tchd 13-2 and 8-1)
Greek Key(IRE), out of a dam who was a useful 6f winner,only showed a modicum of promise for the future after looking green early. (tchd 10-1 and 12-1)

4440 DRIVERS JONAS H'CAP 1m 14y
7:30 (7:32) (Class 4) (0-80,80) 3-Y-O **£4,857** (£1,445; £722; £360) **Stalls** High

Form RPR
0 **1** **The Happy Hammer (IRE)**[12] 4056 3-8-4 **61**.......... MartinDwyer 2 64
(E V Stanford) *t.k.h: led 1f: styd trcking ldr: drvn to chal fr 2f out and stl upsides u.p fr 1f out: kpt on wl in driving fin to ld last stride* **14/1**
31 **2** *shd* **Negotiation (IRE)**[107] 1255 3-9-9 **80**.......... JimmyFortune 4 83
(J H M Gosden) *s.i.s: hld up in rr: pushed along and hdwy over 2f out: drvn to chal 1f out: slt advantage in driving fin fnl 110yds: ct last stride* **5/4**[1]
1043 **3** *nk* **Spring Adventure**[16] 3921 3-9-5 **76**.......... (v) RyanMoore 1 78
(E A L Dunlop) *led after 1f and set mod pce 3f: grad qcknd pce fr 3f out and continued to keep slt ld: hdd in driving fin fnl 110yds and no ex cl home* **2/1**[2]
2644 **4** *1* **Red Suede Shoes**[19] 3800 3-8-11 **68**.......... HayleyTurner 6 70+
(B R Millman) *trckd ldrs: shkn up whn nt clr run fr over 1f out and ins fnl f: edgd lft and kpt on cl home but nt rcvr* **12/1**
0-00 **5** *nk* **Swift Chap**[18] 3868 3-9-6 **77**.......... AlanMunro 5 76
(B R Millman) *in rr: drvn along fr 3f oit: styd on fnl f and clsng nr fin but nvr gng pce to chal* **9/2**[3]
1m 44.53s (1.23) **Going Correction** +0.15s/f (Good) **5** Ran SP% **110.3**
Speed ratings (Par 102): **99,98,98,97,97**
CSF £32.54 TOTE £12.50: £3.50, £1.40; EX 39.70.
Owner D D C One **Bred** Rathbarry Stud **Trained** Newmarket, Suffolk
■ Eugene Stanford's first winner.
FOCUS
With only a handful of runners lining up for this fair-looking handicap, this appeared a muddling affair.
Red Suede Shoes ◆ Official explanation: jockey said gelding was denied a clear run

4441 EPSOM TRAINERS OPEN DAY 2ND AUGUST FILLIES' H'CAP 1m 1f
8:05 (8:05) (Class 5) (0-75,75) 3-Y-O+ **£3,230** (£963, £481; £240) **Stalls** High

Form RPR
5212 **1** **Candy Ride (IRE)**[32] 3408 3-9-7 **75**.......... RyanMoore 8 80
(E A L Dunlop) *trckd ldrs: pushed along to ld ins 2f: rdn whn strly chal fr over 1f out: jst hld on in driving fin ins fnl f: edgd rt cl home: all out* **15/8**[1]
2202 **2** *hd* **Luck Will Come (IRE)**[11] 4085 5-9-9 **73**...... Louis-PhilippeBeuzelin(5) 2 79
(H J Collingridge) *in tch: hdwy on outside fr 4f out: rdn to chal 1f out: upsides in driving fin thrght fnl f: edgd rt cl home and jst failed* **4/1**[2]
243 **3** *1/2* **Seasonal Cross**[26] 3581 4-8-12 **57**.......... HayleyTurner 1 62
(S Dow) *s.i.s: hld up in rr: hdwy on outside fr 2f out: drvn and qcknd to chal ins fnl f: kpt on in driving fin tl edgd rt and no ex cl home* **9/2**[3]
3200 **4** *1 1/4* **Lady Brora**[11] 4085 4-9-13 **72**.......... LPKeniry 3 74
(A M Balding) *chsd ldr: rdn to chal ins fnl 2f tl 1f out: wknd ins fnl f* **17/2**
2015 **5** *nk* **Hip Hip Hooray**[23] 3695 3-9-1 **69**.......... JimCrowley 6 72+
(L A Dace) *in tch: drvn and hdwy over 1f out: styng on whn nt clr run ins fnl f: styd on cl home but nt rcvr* **17/2**
4511 **6** *nk* **Caster Sugar (USA)**[13] 4010 3-9-1 **69**.......... JimmyFortune 4 69
(R Hannon) *led: rdn pushed along ins fnl 3f: hdd ins fnl 2f: wkng n.m.r on ins fnl f* **9/2**[3]

3650 7 ¾ **Hallingdal (UAE)**[9] 4150 4-9-8 **67** .... TPO'Shea 5 66
(J J Bridger) *s.i.s: hld up in rr: pushed along and styd on fr over 1f out but nvr gng pce to get competitive* **20/1**

1m 58.47s (2.17) **Going Correction** +0.15s/f (Good)
WFA 3 from 4yo+ 9lb **7** Ran SP% **117.0**
Speed ratings (Par 100): **96,95,95,94,94 93,93**
toteswingers: 1&2 £2.90, 1&3 £4.00, 2&3 £6.20 CSF £10.00 CT £29.53 TOTE £3.40: £1.80, £2.70; EX 11.50.
Owner Rick Barnes **Bred** Grangecon Stud **Trained** Newmarket, Suffolk

FOCUS
The early pace was nothing special, so the whole field were only covered by a few lengths passing the winning post, which should mean this is unreliable form. The front pair both posted slight personal bests.
Hip Hip Hooray Official explanation: jockey said filly was denied a clear run

4442 DRIVERS JONAS WON'T WAIT FURLONG H'CAP 1m 6f
8:35 (8:37) (Class 4) (0-80,78) 3-Y-O £4,857 (£1,445; £722; £360) **Stalls** High

Form RPR
0-02 **1** **Royal Diamond (IRE)**[12] 4045 3-8-11 **66** .... StephenDonohoe 2 75
(Sir Mark Prescott) *in rr: hdwy 4f out: rdn to chse ldrs fr 3f out: drvn to ld 1f out: styd on strly ins fnl f* **6/1**[3]

1253 **2** 2½ **Ermyn Lodge**[34] 3300 3-8-6 **61** .... (v[1]) FergusSweeney 5 66
(P M Phelan) *chsd ldrs: chal fr 3f out and stl upside u.p 1f out: styd on for 2nd fnl 110yds but no ch w wnr* **10/1**

4112 **3** ¾ **Strathcal**[26] 3587 3-9-9 **78** .... SteveDrowne 4 82
(H Morrison) *chsd ldr 4f: styd front rn and slt ld 3f out and kpt it u.p tl hdd 1f out: wknd into 3rd fnl 110yds* **3/1**[2]

0-40 **4** ½ **Sir Freddie**[72] 2126 3-9-0 **69** .... JimmyFortune 3 72
(Lady Herries) *trckd ldr after 4f: led 6f out: hdd 3f out: sn one pce: styd on aain ins fnl f but ever a threat* **14/1**

3522 **5** 7 **Longboat Key**[15] 3940 3-9-5 **74** .... (b) GregFairley 8 68
(M Johnston) *led tl hdd 6f out: wknd over 2f out* **9/1**

-031 **6** 2½ **Harlestone Snake**[47] 2881 3-9-7 **76** .... RyanMoore 1 66
(J L Dunlop) *hld up in rr: pushed along and sme hdwy fr 3f out: nvr in contention and btn 2f out* **11/10**[1]

056 **7** 2 **Warrants Attention (IRE)**[20] 3791 3-8-8 **63** .... LPKeniry 7 50
(A M Balding) *t.k.h: chsd ldrs to 3f out: sn wknd* **40/1**

0003 **8** ¾ **Blue Tango (IRE)**[15] 3954 3-8-10 **65** .... (b[1]) JimCrowley 6 51
(Mrs A J Perrett) *t.k.h to 1/2-way: a towards rr* **20/1**

3m 6.17s (-0.43) **Going Correction** +0.15s/f (Good) **8** Ran SP% **119.9**
Speed ratings (Par 102): **107,105,105,104,100 99,98,97**
toteswingers: 1&2 £5.90, 1&3 £3.80, 2&3 £4.80 CSF £66.24 CT £218.21 TOTE £6.70: £1.90, £2.40, £1.40; EX 99.70 Place 6: £31.55 Place 5: £17.47.
Owner E B Rimmer-Osborne House **Bred** Moyglare Stud Farm Ltd **Trained** Newmarket, Suffolk

FOCUS
This was a modest handicap. The unexposed winner was up 8lb on his form over shorter.
Harlestone Snake Official explanation: jockey said gelding hung right
T/Plt: £39.40 to a £1 stake. Pool: £56,382.84. 1,042.33 winning tickets. T/Qpdt: £8.40 to a £1 stake. Pool: £6,235.82. 548.70 winning tickets. ST

4443 - 4448a (Foreign Racing) - See Raceform Interactive

[4231] EPSOM (L-H)
Thursday, July 30

OFFICIAL GOING: Good (good to soft in places; overall 7.8, far side 7.7, stands' side 8.1)
Rails at inner configuration and distances as advertised.
Wind: Fresh, against Weather: Bright and breezy

4449 BETFAIR APPRENTICE TRAINING SERIES H'CAP 1m 4f 10y
5:55 (5:56) (Class 5) (0-70,73) 4-Y-O+ £3,238 (£963; £481; £240) **Stalls** Centre

Form RPR
4230 **1** **Calculating (IRE)**[12] 4092 5-8-3 **50** .... TobyAtkinson(3) 8 55
(M D I Usher) *stdd s: hld up wl off the pce: rdn and c towards stands' side st: edgd rt over 2f out: styd on wl to ld ins fnl f: all out* **9/2**[3]

0660 **2** ½ **Princess Flame (GER)**[61] 2493 7-9-5 **63** .... KylieManser 2 67
(B G Powell) *hld up wl off the pce: rdn and styd far side st: chsd ldr over 2f out: ev ch ins fnl f: kpt on* **16/1**

4652 **3** 1¼ **Tecktal (FR)**[7] 4235 6-8-8 **52** .... DebraEngland 7 54
(P M Phelan) *sn led: allowed to go clr after 2f: 8 l clr 6f out: c stands' side st: rdn over 2f out: hdd ins fnl f: no ex* **9/2**[3]

2333 **4** nk **Watson's Bay**[7] 4235 4-9-5 **68** .... KierenFox(5) 3 70
(P Howling) *stdd s: hld up wl off the pce: styd far side st: rdn 3f out: pressed ldrs ent fnl f: kpt on same pce fnl 100yds* **11/4**[1]

2040 **5** 3¼ **Star Choice**[16] 3950 4-9-4 **62** .... (v) SimonPearce 4 58
(J Pearce) *stdd s: hld up wl in rr: styd far side st: pushed along and hdwy 3f out: nvr trbld ldrs* **10/1**

66-3 **6** 7 **Recalcitrant**[24] 3675 6-8-5 **49** oh3 .... RosieJessop 5 34
(S Dow) *led briefly: chsd ldr after: c towards stands' side and rdn over 3f out: lost 2nd wl over 2f out: wknd 2f out: eased ins fnl f* **10/1**

1103 **7** ½ **Maybe I Wont**[10] 4139 4-9-6 **64** .... (p) JPHamblett 1 48
(Lucinda Featherstone) *prom in main gp: c towards stands' side and rdn st: wknd over 2f out: wl btn and eased ins fnl f* **10/1**

6151 **R** **Inspirina (IRE)**[7] 4235 5-9-10 **73** 6ex .... BarryAdams(5) 9 —
(R Ford) *ref to r* **4/1**[2]

2m 43.4s (4.50) **Going Correction** +0.375s/f (Good) **8** Ran SP% **116.2**
Speed ratings (Par 103): **100,99,98,98,96 91,91,—**
toteswingers: 1&2 £6.70, 1&3 £4.80, 2&3 £11.50 CSF £72.03 CT £343.50 TOTE £6.10: £1.70, £3.80, £2.00; EX 89.30.
Owner Brian Rogan **Bred** Darley **Trained** Upper Lambourn, Berks
■ Stewards' Enquiry : Kylie Manser one-day ban: excessive use of the whip (Aug 13)

FOCUS
The track avoided much of the rain of the previous day, with only 5mm falling overnight. However, 3mm at lunchtime eased the ground to Good, Good to Soft in places. The wind was in the faces of the runners in the straight. A modest apprentices' handicap over the Derby distance in which the key race appeared to be a handicap run here last week. With the first three there reopposing, the winner of that race Inspirina refused to come out when the gates opened and took no part. The riders had a difference of opinion in the straight with three sticking to the inside and the remaining four coming to the stands' rail. In the end, there was little in it, but the winner came up the stands' side. Muddling and weak form.
Star Choice Official explanation: jockey said gelding had a breathing problem

4450 FEDERATION OF BLOODSTOCK AGENTS CLAIMING STKS 1m 2f 18y
6:25 (6:27) (Class 5) 3-Y-O+ £3,238 (£963; £481; £240) **Stalls** Low

Form RPR
3411 **1** **What's Up Doc (IRE)**[32] 3245 8-9-7 **72** .... IanMongan 7 79
(Mrs T J Hill) *led at stdy gallop: qcknd over 3f out: narrowly hdd 2f out: hanging lft but rallied gamely to ld ins fnl f: styd on wl* **5/2**[2]

1106 **2** 1¾ **Ahlawy (IRE)**[33] 3374 6-9-11 **86** .... (bt) DavidProbert(3) 1 83
(F Sheridan) *chsd wnr tl upsides 4f out: pushed along to ld narrowly 2f out: rdn ent fnl f: hdd ins fnl f: no ex and btn fnl 75yds* **9/2**

4002 **3** 3½ **Dhania (IRE)**[17] 3919 3-8-2 **62** .... (b) JPFahy(7) 2 67
(R A Teal) *t.k.h: trckd ldrs: nt clr run on inner and swtchd rt jst over 2f out: sn rdn and outpcd by ldrs: wl hld fnl f* **20/1**

51 **4** 2½ **Slip**[22] 3740 4-9-11 **80** .... PatCosgrave 4 68
(J R Boyle) *hld up wl in tch: hdwy over 3f out: shkn up to chse ldng pair over 2f out: rdn 2f out: hld hd high and fnd nil: wl btn fnl f* **4/1**[3]

2331 **5** 1 **King Supreme (IRE)**[13] 4042 4-9-11 **81** .... (b) PatrickHills(3) 5 69
(R Hannon) *trckd ldrs: pressed ldrs over 5f out: rdn and nt qckn over 3f out: sn struggling: wl btn fnl 2f* **11/8**[1]

00-0 **6** 4½ **Mr Deal**[8] 4206 3-8-9 **54** .... GregFairley 3 51?
(Eve Johnson Houghton) *stdd s: hld up in last pair: rdn 3f out: sn strugglling and lost tch* **50/1**

0000 **7** 11 **I Certainly May**[55] 2675 4-8-12 **42** .... RosieJessop(7) 6 29
(S Dow) *s.i.s: a bhd: rdn and struggling 4f out: wl bhd fnl 3f* **80/1**

2m 13.22s (3.52) **Going Correction** +0.375s/f (Good)
WFA 3 from 4yo+ 10lb **7** Ran SP% **116.8**
Speed ratings (Par 103): **100,98,95,93,93 89,80**
toteswingers: 1&2 £2.50, 1&3 £7.80, 2&3 £6.80 CSF £14.44 TOTE £3.50: £1.90, £2.30; EX 15.70.What's Up Doc was claimed by Mr B Pollock for £11,000.
Owner M B Clarke **Bred** James J Monaghan **Trained** Aston Rowant, Oxon

FOCUS
The usual mixed range of abilities in this claimer, but this was a better-than-average race of its type with three of the runners having marks in the 80s. The form is rated around the front pair but is dubious as the race was slowly run.
King Supreme(IRE) Official explanation: trainer said, regarding running, that the colt was unsuited by then uneven pace

4451 TOTEQUADPOT MAIDEN STKS 7f
7:00 (7:00) (Class 4) 2-Y-O £4,533 (£1,348; £674; £336) **Stalls** Low

Form RPR
043 **1** **Universal Circus**[10] 4152 2-8-12 0 .... SamHitchcott 3 76
(M R Channon) *chsd ldrs: rdn and hdwy over 3f out: nt clr run and swtchd rt over 1f out: sn squeezed between horses and chal ldr: led ins fnl f: r.o wl* **7/2**[3]

62 **2** ½ **Fine Sight**[13] 4041 2-9-3 0 .... PatDobbs 2 80
(R Hannon) *led: rdn and edging rt over 1f out: hdd ins fnl f: kpt on same pce fnl 100yds* **11/10**[1]

0 **3** 1 **Lethal Combination (USA)**[12] 4093 2-9-3 0 .... TonyCulhane 1 77
(W J Haggas) *s.i.s: sn outpcd in last pl: hdwy over 3f out: chsd ldng trio and hanging lft 3f out: swtchd rt over 1f out: wnt 3rd jst ins fnl f: stiil hanging lft but kpt on wl: nt quite rch ldrs* **14/1**

60 **4** 7 **Gold Diamond (USA)**[22] 3750 2-9-3 0 .... GregFairley 4 60
(M Johnston) *w ldr: rdn over 3f out: stl ev ch whn bmpd over 1f out: sn btn: wknd fnl f* **5/2**[2]

56 **5** 8 **Whiepa Snappa (IRE)**[14] 4006 2-9-3 0 .... IanMongan 5 40
(P M Phelan) *outpcd in last pair: c wd over 3f out: edgd lft and no hdwy 3f out: wl btn whn eased ins fnl f* **20/1**

0 **6** 11 **Tiger Hawk (USA)**[22] 3750 2-9-3 0 .... (b[1]) PatCosgrave 6 12
(S A Callaghan) *awkward leaving stalls and dwlt: sn in midfield: pushed along and struggling 4f out: wl bhd 3f out* **66/1**

1m 25.26s (1.96) **Going Correction** +0.375s/f (Good) **6** Ran SP% **111.3**
Speed ratings (Par 96): **103,102,101,93,84 71**
toteswingers: 1&2 £1.10, 1&3 £6.20, 2&3 £4.10 CSF £7.64 TOTE £5.20: £2.10, £1.40; EX 8.80.
Owner Steve Fisher **Bred** Wansdyke Farms Limited **Trained** West Ilsley, Berks
■ Stewards' Enquiry : Sam Hitchcott one-day ban: careless riding (Aug 13)

FOCUS
All the runners in this maiden had previous racecourse experience, but it was fairly uncompetitive as they bet 14-1 bar three. The front three set the level.

NOTEBOOK
Universal Circus had put up some fair efforts in maidens at this trip, generally progressing with racing, and handled the track well. She had to wait for a gap between the favourites over a furlong out but, once in the clear, found plenty for pressure to get up in the last 50 yards. She should not be too badly treated in nurseries now. (op 4-1)
Fine Sight, a half-brother to the temperamental Highland Glen, had run well on his second start over 7f on easy ground and, for much of the way, looked like justifying favouritism. However, after opening up an advantage over a furlong out, he had nothing left to repel the late surge of the winner. (op 6-5 tchd 5-4)
Lethal Combination(USA) was the eyecatcher of the race. He had been slowly away and well beaten in a Newmarket maiden earlier in the month and was at the back early. However, he began to run on once in the straight, despite not handling the track, and finished on the heels of the principals. He should have learnt a fair amount from this. (op 16-1 tchd 12-1)
Gold Diamond(USA), held in a couple of 7f Newmarket maidens, tried to lead early but could not get ahead of the favourite. He came under pressure over 2f out, but the response was disappointing and he ended up well beaten. (op 11-4 tchd 3-1)
Whiepa Snappa(IRE) was always out the back but at least qualifies for handicaps now. (op 14-1)
Tiger Hawk(USA), who was tailed off last on his debut, did a little better in the first-time blinkers but looks very moderate. (op 40-1 tchd 33-1)

4452 TOTEEXACTA FILLIES' H'CAP 7f
7:30 (7:33) (Class 5) (0-75,75) 3-Y-O+ £3,238 (£963; £481; £240) **Stalls** Low

Form RPR
4046 **1** **Koraleva Tectona (IRE)**[21] 3787 4-9-11 **73** .... PaulEddery 6 79
(Pat Eddery) *mde all: t.k.h and set stdy gallop: pushed along and qcknd jst over 3f out: clr ent fnl f: eased towards fin* **5/1**[3]

3610 **2** 1½ **Turning Top (IRE)**[22] 3752 3-9-6 **75** .... PatDobbs 1 74+
(S A Callaghan) *hld up wl in tch: nt clr run 3f out tl swtchd lft 2f out: hdwy on inner to chse wnr 1f out: kpt on wl but nvr able to chal* **11/2**

-000 **3** 1¼ **Danzadil (IRE)**[17] 3917 3-7-7 **55** oh2 .... CharlesEddery(7) 8 51
(R A Teal) *t.k.h: chsd ldrs: rdn 3f out: kpt on same pce u.p fnl f* **40/1**

-006 **4** 1½ **Dove Mews**[43] 3033 3-9-4 **73** .... HayleyTurner 10 65
(M L W Bell) *chsd wnr: rdn 3f out: drvn and unable qck 2f out: lost 2nd 1f out: one pce after* **10/1**

0213 **5** shd **All For You (IRE)**[21] 3789 3-9-1 **70** .... PatCosgrave 5 61
(M Botti) *t.k.h: hld up wl in tch: effrt 2f out: rdn and unable qck over 1f out: kpt on same pce fnl f* **5/2**[2]

4421 **6** *nk* **Support Fund (IRE)**[14] 4009 5-9-12 **74** ShaneKelly 2 67
(Eve Johnson Houghton) *mounted on crse: t.k.h: hld up in last trio: hdwy towards outer wl over 2f out: rdn and no imp 2f out: nvr pce to threaten ldrs* **9/4**[1]

0604 **7** *hd* **Polemica (IRE)**[9] 4179 3-8-7 **62** WilliamBuick 4 52
(E A L Dunlop) *stdd s: hld up in rr: effrt on outer ent fnl 2f: kpt on but nvr pce to threaten ldrs* **7/1**

-405 **8** *7* **Mamlakati (IRE)**[21] 3789 3-9-3 **75** PatrickHills(3) 9 46
(R Hannon) *stdd s: plld hrd: chsd ldrs over 5f out: rdn wl over 2f out: edgd rt and wknd 2f out* **25/1**

1564 **9** *3* **Berrymead**[16] 3945 4-8-10 **63** ow7 AnnStokell(5) 3 29
(Miss A Stokell) *stdd s: plld hrd: hld up in last trio: struggling and rdn 3f out: sn wl btn* **28/1**

1m 25.76s (2.46) **Going Correction** +0.375s/f (Good)
WFA 3 from 4yo+ 7lb **9** Ran SP% **122.7**
Speed ratings (Par 100): **100,98,96,95,95 94,94,86,83**
toteswingers: 1&2 £7.00, 1&3 £103.30, 2&3 £45.70 CSF £34.15 CT £1023.92 TOTE £5.60: £1.80, £2.10, £11.00; EX 38.80.
Owner Pat Eddery Racing (Ramruma) **Bred** Cathal Ryan **Trained** Nether Winchendon, Bucks
■ Stewards' Enquiry : Paul Eddery She has been waiting for this ground but has also been a bit disappointing this year. - Paul Eddery, jockey

FOCUS
A fairly competitive fillies' handicap but the early pace was slow, emphasised by the fact that the time was half a second slower than the preceding juvenile contest, making it difficult to come from behind, and the bare form looks unreliable. The winner is rated to form but was allowed a very easy lead.
Berrymead Official explanation: jockey said filly ran too freely

4453 PCL WHITEHALL SECURITY H'CAP — 1m 114y
8:05 (8:05) (Class 4) (0-80,79) 3-Y-O **£5,180** (£1,541; £770; £384) **Stalls** Low

Form RPR
011 **1** **Desire To Excel (IRE)**[26] 3608 3-9-9 **79** NCallan 2 81
(P F I Cole) *mde all: rdn ent fnl 2f: kpt on wl u.p fnl f* **1/1**[1]

6016 **2** *3/4* **Hel's Angel (IRE)**[16] 3941 3-9-3 **73** PatCosgrave 4 73+
(Mrs A Duffield) *stdd s: t.k.h: hld up trcking ldrs: hemmed in and nt enough room fr 3f out: bumping match w 3rd 1f out: fnlly in the clr and chsd wnr ins fnl f: r.o but nvr able to chal* **11/4**[2]

-210 **3** *1 1/4* **Tilos Gem (IRE)**[44] 3008 3-9-8 **78** RoystonFfrench 1 75
(M Johnston) *chsd wnr: effrt and rdn 3f out: drvn and edgd lft jst ins fnl f: lost 2nd and btn fnl 100yds* **3/1**[3]

4-64 **4** *65* **Kattar**[34] 3349 3-8-1 **60** AhmedAjtebi(3) 3 —
(D M Simcock) *t.k.h: hld up in tch: rdn and lost tch qckly 3f out: t.o and virtually p.u fnl f* **10/1**

1m 49.75s (3.65) **Going Correction** +0.375s/f (Good) **4** Ran SP% **110.8**
Speed ratings (Par 102): **98,97,96,38**
CSF £4.16 TOTE £1.90; EX 3.40.
Owner H R H Sultan Ahmad Shah **Bred** Glending Bloodstock **Trained** Whatcombe, Oxon

FOCUS
Just a small field for this three-year-old handicap, but still a tight contest and it produced a pretty good race. The winner made all and it is doubtful he had to improve, but the second was possibly unlucky in this messy race.

4454 TOTESWINGER H'CAP — 6f
8:35 (8:35) (Class 4) (0-80,77) 3-Y-O **£5,180** (£1,541; £770; £384) **Stalls** High

Form RPR
531 **1** **Fyelehk (IRE)**[7] 4237 3-8-0 **59** DavidProbert(3) 6 69
(B R Millman) *taken down early: chsd ldr: rdn to ld wl over 1f out: kpt on wl and a holding runner up fnl f* **5/2**[1]

4404 **2** *1/2* **My Kingdom (IRE)**[21] 3771 3-9-7 **77** (t) GeorgeBaker 5 85
(H Morrison) *hld up in midfield: hdwy 3f out: ev ch 2f out: drvn over 1f out: r.o but a hld* **3/1**[2]

5322 **3** *3 1/4* **Halaak (USA)**[7] 4237 3-8-4 **63** AhmedAjtebi(3) 2 61
(D M Simcock) *t.k.h: hld up in tch: nt clr run over 2f out tl over 1f out: sn rdn: kpt on to go 3rd ins fnl f: no ch w ldng pair* **8/1**

0131 **4** *3/4* **Rocket Rob (IRE)**[7] 4231 3-9-3 **73** 6ex HayleyTurner 3 69
(S A Callaghan) *hld up in last pl: swtchd rt 2f out: drvn and effrt on outer over 1f out: no imp and wl hld fnl f* **7/2**[3]

4-02 **5** *1 1/4* **Corton Charlemagne (IRE)**[79] 1969 3-8-4 **63** WilliamCarson(3) 1 55
(Rae Guest) *bucking leaving stalls: hld up towards rr: hmpd and snatched up bnd over 3f out: hdwy on inner over 2f out: chsng ldrs whn nt clr run and shuffled bk over 1f out: no ch w ldrs fnl f* **14/1**

0052 **6** *1* **Mazzola**[7] 4231 3-9-0 **70** TonyCulhane 4 58
(M R Channon) *led: rdn and hdd wl over 1f out: wknd ent fnl f* **7/2**[3]

6365 **7** *2* **Red Rossini (IRE)**[57] 2602 3-8-12 **68** PatDobbs 7 50
(R Hannon) *in tch: rdn over 2f out: sn struggling: no ch fnl f* **14/1**

1m 10.54s (1.14) **Going Correction** +0.375s/f (Good) **7** Ran SP% **122.5**
Speed ratings (Par 102): **107,106,102,101,99 98,95**
toteswingers: 1&2 £2.80, 1&3 £5.80, 2&3 £5.90 CSF £11.37 TOTE £3.70: £1.90, £2.50; EX 14.80 Place 6: £109.91, Place 5: £43.35.
Owner The Links Partnership **Bred** Camogue Stud Ltd **Trained** Kentisbeare, Devon

FOCUS
A modest sprint, but fairly well contested with the first and second from a couple of sprints run a week previously renewing rivalry. The winner confirmed Folkestone form with the third.
T/Plt: £580.90 to a £1 stake. Pool: £47,548.72. 59.75 winning tickets. T/Qpdt: £46.60 to a £1 stake. Pool: £6,270.10. 99.40 winning tickets. SP

4417 GOODWOOD (R-H)
Thursday, July 30

OFFICIAL GOING: Good changing to good (good to soft in places) after race 3 (3.25) changing to good to soft after race 4 (4.00)
Rail from 6f on lower bend to 3.5f moved out 6yds increasing distances by 15yds; top bend dolled out 4yds increasing distances by 8yds.
Wind: Mostly moderate, against Weather: Changeable, heavy downpour after race 3

4455 SUMMER VASE STKS (HERITAGE H'CAP) — 1m 1f 192y
2:10 (2:10) (Class 2) 3-Y-O
£37,386 (£11,196; £5,598; £2,802; £1,398; £702) **Stalls** High

Form RPR
1062 **1** **Roman Republic (FR)**[21] 3780 3-9-0 **94** NCallan 14 105
(M Johnston) *prom: trckd ldng trio fr 1/2-way: smooth effrt towards outer to ld over 2f out: drvn over 1f out: edgd lft fnl f: hld on wl* **9/2**[2]

-102 **2** *3/4* **Sopranist**[13] 4058 3-9-5 **99** JimmyFortune 9 108
(J H M Gosden) *dwlt: hld up in rr: carried hd to one side but stdy prog fr 3f out: styng on to chal for 2nd whn bmpd jst ins fnl f: carried lft after: r.o to take 2nd nr fin* **14/1**

1133 **3** *1/2* **Mirrored**[26] 3639 3-9-3 **97** RyanMoore 11 105
(Sir Michael Stoute) *hld up towards rr: stdy prog gng wl fr 3f out: chsd wnr wl over 1f out: edgd lft u.p jst ins fnl f: hld after: lost 2nd nr fin* **7/2**[1]

1615 **4** *1 1/2* **River Captain (IRE)**[42] 3049 3-9-2 **96** EddieAhern 7 101
(S Kirk) *swtg: hld up and sn in last pair: prog fr 3f out bhd eventual 2nd and 3rd: drvn and styd on fr over 1f out: tk 4th nr fin* **10/1**

1231 **5** *nk* **Sandor**[26] 3644 3-8-10 **90** RichardMullen 16 95
(P J Makin) *t.k.h: trckd ldrs: rdn over 2f out: kpt on fr over 1f out: nvr able to chal* **20/1**

5126 **6** *3/4* **Hyades (USA)**[42] 3049 3-8-12 **92** TPQueally 17 95
(H R A Cecil) *lw: s.i.s and rousted along early: towards rr whn shkn up 3f out: prog over 2f out but hanging: edgd lft over 1f out: no imp on ldrs after* **8/1**[3]

2-00 **7** *2* **Ra Junior (USA)**[19] 3873 3-9-0 **94** (b[1]) LDettori 5 94
(B J Meehan) *dwlt: hld up in last pair: effrt on wd outside over 2f out: sme prog u.p over 1f out: nvr rchd ldrs* **40/1**

3122 **8** *1/2* **Set The Trend**[35] 3298 3-9-2 **96** WilliamBuick 12 95
(A M Balding) *lw: sn restrained to rr: taken to wd outside and effrt 3f out: prog u.p over 2f out: chsd ldrs and edgd rt over 1f out: wknd fnl f* **12/1**

4121 **9** *3 1/2* **Dome Rocket**[14] 4008 3-7-12 **81** (p) DavidProbert(3) 6 73
(W J Knight) *trckd ldrs: effrt on outer 3f out: no real prog u.p 2f out: fdd* **20/1**

2515 **10** *3/4* **Changing The Guard**[21] 3780 3-8-8 **88** PaulHanagan 4 79
(R A Fahey) *b: plld hrd: prom: disp 2nd 3f out: wknd wl over 1f out* **12/1**

116 **11** *hd* **Alpen Glen**[27] 3586 3-8-13 **93** RoystonFfrench 3 83
(M Johnston) *hld up in midfield in abt 8th: drvn on outer over 2f out: no real prog or imp* **16/1**

5010 **12** *1 1/4* **Alazeyab (USA)**[19] 3873 3-9-7 **101** RHills 13 89
(M A Jarvis) *lw: prom: effrt and cl up on inner over 2f out: wknd over 1f out* **20/1**

5131 **13** *5* **Geneva Geyser (GER)**[28] 3543 3-8-5 **85** LukeMorris 1 63
(J M P Eustace) *lw: sn trckd ldr: cl enough over 2f out: sn wknd rapidly* **50/1**

310 **14** *3/4* **Midnight Cruiser (IRE)**[19] 3840 3-8-13 **93** RichardHughes 15 70
(R Hannon) *nvr beyond midfield: lost pl on inner 3f out: wl in rr after* **40/1**

1400 **15** *1 1/4* **Takaatuf (IRE)**[21] 3780 3-8-5 **85** TPO'Shea 10 60
(M Johnston) *hld up in midfield: lost pl 3f out: last pair 2f out: eased* **20/1**

0011 **16** *1 1/4* **Fastnet Storm (IRE)**[39] 3189 3-8-7 **87** MickyFenton 2 59
(T P Tate) *led to over 2f out: wknd rapidly* **14/1**

2m 7.18s (-0.82) **Going Correction** +0.15s/f (Good) **16** Ran SP% **121.1**
Speed ratings (Par 106): **109,108,108,106,106 105,104,103,101,100 100,99,95,94,93 92**
toteswingers: 1&2 £9.00, 1&3 £3.30, 2&3 £5.70 CSF £59.03 CT £250.53 TOTE £5.80: £1.80, £2.80, £1.70, £2.20; EX 72.30 Trifecta £114.20 Pool: £1667.49 - 10.80 winning units..
Owner Sheikh Hamdan Bin Mohammed Al Maktoum **Bred** Famille Niarchos **Trained** Middleham Moor, N Yorks
■ Stewards' Enquiry : N Callan one-day ban: careless riding (Aug 13)

FOCUS
There was 5mm of rain overnight and a further 4mm in a heavy shower before racing. The time was just over two seconds outside standard and the ground still appeared to be riding close to the official description of good. Another change of identity for this race, traditionally a very strong 3yo handicap. This year's running appeared no exception. The pace was reasonable without being overly strong and there were no real hard-luck stories, so the form should hold up. The fourth is a pretty solid guide.

NOTEBOOK
Roman Republic(FR) was runner-up at Newmarket on his latest start, for which he went up 3lb, and the form had been boosted by winner Firebet's good second in the Gordon Stakes on Tuesday. Always well placed before striking the front plenty soon enough, he edged left under pressure but displayed a very gritty attitude to hold on. Maturing now and likely to improve again, he will get 1m4f but this could prove his best trip. (op 5-1 tchd 11-2 in places)
Sopranist was one of the least experienced in the line-up and was having just his fourth start. He came from further back than the winner and secured second close home after being carried to his left by Mirrored. He is still on the upgrade, but his head carriage was a slight cause for concern. (op 16-1)
Mirrored was keen through the early parts but was well placed from halfway. He went after the winner when that one burst clear but edged left and could not quicken. His jockey had to stop riding in the last couple of strides as the colt ran out of room behind the winner, but for which he may have held second. He saw out the extra 2f well enough. (tchd 4-1)
River Captain(IRE), back over perhaps his best trip after tackling a mile at Royal Ascot, was ridden differently than in previous runs this year and stayed on from the rear in the straight without reaching the leaders.
Sandor, who is tough and progressive, came off the bridle earlier than most but kept responding without quite possessing the pace to land a blow. (tchd 22-1, 25-1 in places)
Hyades(USA) was a place behind River Captain in the Britannia at Ascot. Well drawn right on the inside, he improved up the rail in the straight but edged off it and could make no further inroads late on. (tchd 15-2)
Ra Junior(USA) did best of those drawn low, staying on down the outside if never promising to reach the principals. He came here with something to prove, albeit after a light campaign so far, and ran a mildly encouraging race in the first-time headgear. The handicapper has given him a chance and he saw out this longer trip well enough. (op 33-1)
Set The Trend appeared to be running out of stamina late on after threatening to make the frame a furlong out. He handled the conditions on only his second run on turf. (op 9-1)
Dome Rocket ran respectably off a 5lb higher mark than when winning a slowly run Epsom race. (op 25-1)
Changing The Guard failed to settle and raced much more prominently than in recent outings, including when three places behind Roman Republic at Newmarket. He weakened quickly below the distance. (op 14-1 tchd 16-1 in places)

4456 AUDI STKS (REGISTERED AS THE KING GEORGE STAKES) (GROUP 3) — 5f
2:45 (2:45) (Class 1) 3-Y-O+
£39,739 (£15,064; £7,539; £3,759; £1,883; £945) **Stalls** Low

Form RPR
53-0 **1** **Kingsgate Native (IRE)**[40] 3140 4-9-0 116 RyanMoore 2 123
(Sir Michael Stoute) *racd against nr side rail: trckd ldrs: gap appeared and decisive burst of spd to ld over 1f out: sn clr: impressive* **7/1**[3]

5001 **2** *2 3/4* **Total Gallery (IRE)**[22] 3747 3-8-10 108 RichardHughes 1 113+
(J S Moore) *hld up wl in rr: gng wl 1/2-way and looking for room: swtchd to nr side over 1f out: r.o wl to take 2nd last 100yds: no ch w wnr* **16/1**

1113 **3** *1 1/2* **Inxile (IRE)**[32] 3434 4-9-0 108 AdrianTNicholls 3 108
(D Nicholls) *hld up bhd ldrs towards nr side: gng v strly 1/2-way: rdn and nt qckn over 1f out: styd on against nr side rail to snatch 3rd nr fin* **8/1**

3251 **4** *shd* **Borderlescott**[19] 3848 7-9-0 112 PatCosgrave 16 108+
(R Bastiman) *gd spd and on terms w ldrs: tried to get across but stl racd towards outer: disp ld wl over 1f out: outpcd after* **9/4**[1]

-000 **5** *shd* **Dandy Man (IRE)**[44] 2991 6-9-0 100 (t) LDettori 6 107
(Saeed Bin Suroor) *racd towards nr side: w ldrs: led 1/2-way: hdd and outpcd over 1f out* **16/1**

6166 **6** *1* **Rowe Park**[4] 4341 6-9-0 104 SteveDrowne 11 104
(Mrs L C Jewell) *swtg: racd on outer in rr: drvn and styd on fr over 1f out: no ch* **28/1**

10 **7** *nk* **Spin Cycle (IRE)**[44] 2991 3-8-10 106 RichardMullen 8 103
(B Smart) *wl in rr: pushed along bef 1/2-way: styd on towards outer fr over 1f out: n.d* **33/1**

0000 **8** *nse* **Equiano (FR)**[20] 3819 4-9-0 109 MichaelHills 10 102+
(B W Hills) *fluffed s: wl in rr on outer: jst abt last 1/2-way: prog over 1f out: kpt on: no ch* **14/1**

2044 **9** *hd* **Reverence**[10] 4135 8-9-0 102 EddieAhern 5 102
(E J Alston) *hld up in rr: swtchd towards nr side jst over 1f out: nudged along and styd on steadily: nvr on terms* **40/1**

0-41 **10** *1* **Sugar Free (IRE)**[40] 3145 3-8-7 100 WMLordan 13 95
(T Stack, Ire) *racd towards outer: chsd ldrs: drvn and kpt on same pce fr over 1f out* **16/1**

20-0 **11** *2 1/4* **Moorhouse Lad**[89] 1676 6-9-0 110 TomEaves 12 90
(B Smart) *b.hind: trckd ldrs and racd towards outer: lost pl and btn wl over 1f out* **12/1**

05-0 **12** *nk* **Fat Boy (IRE)**[89] 1676 4-9-0 106 JimmyFortune 15 89
(P W Chapple-Hyam) *s.i.s: racd on outer: wl in rr: last trio 1/2-way: nvr a factor* **20/1**

101 **13** *1/2* **Ialysos (GR)**[26] 3638 5-9-5 109 GMosse 14 92
(L M Cumani) *gd spd and on terms w ldrs but racd on outer: nrly upsides wl over 1f out: wknd fnl f* **6/1**[2]

0340 **14** *1/2* **Matsunosuke**[19] 3844 7-9-0 104 LukeMorris 9 85
(A B Coogan) *a wl in rr: last trio 1/2-way: nvr gng the pce* **66/1**

3064 **15** *3 1/2* **Siren's Gift**[40] 3145 5-8-11 90 (b) WilliamBuick 18 70
(A M Balding) *racd on outer: gd spd and w ldrs to 1/2-way: wknd rapidly over 1f out* **33/1**

4526 **16** *11* **Jargelle (IRE)**[40] 3145 3-8-7 97 AlanMunro 7 30
(K A Ryan) *racd towards nr side rail: disp ld to 1/2-way: wknd rapidly: t.o* **66/1**

5206 **17** *4 1/2* **Rievaulx World**[19] 3848 3-8-10 98 NCallan 4 17
(K A Ryan) *racd against nr side rail: disp ld to 1/2-way: wknd rapidly: t.o* **66/1**

57.96 secs (-0.44) **Going Correction** +0.25s/f (Good)
WFA 3 from 4yo+ 4lb **17** Ran SP% **121.7**
Speed ratings (Par 113): **113,108,106,106,105 104,103,103,103,101 98,97,96,96,90 72,65**
toteswingers: 1&2 £25.00, 1&3 £9.20, 2&3 £37.20 CSF £104.85 TOTE £7.20: £2.70, £4.30, £1.90; EX 113.30 Trifecta £755.40 Pool: £6737.42 - 6.60 winning units..
Owner Cheveley Park Stud **Bred** Peter McCutcheon **Trained** Newmarket, Suffolk

FOCUS
This looked a good Group 3 contest but the draw seemed to play a big part, with the first three finishers emerging from the three lowest stalls. The pace was predictably strong and they raced middle to stands' side. Kingsgate Native is rated back to his best.

NOTEBOOK
Kingsgate Native(IRE) ◆, a dual Group 1 winner when trained by John Best, had proved infertile at stud and was sent back into training with Sir Michael Stoute. He didn't show much on his return to the track in the Golden Jubilee, but that run clearly brought him on significantly and he was a decisive winner, bursting clear when switched on to the near rail inside the final two furlongs, having travelled enthusiastically. It needs pointing out that he was favourably drawn, and the runner-up didn't get much of a run in behind, but this still represented a return to something like his best form. All things considered this was a most encouraging performance, and he looks a leading contender for the Nunthorpe, a race he won as a juvenile, before running third last year when the race was staged on the July course. (tchd 8-1)
Total Gallery(IRE) ◆, upped in grade after winning a 3yo handicap off 103 at Newmarket's July meeting, ran a big race in defeat and was probably unlucky not to finish closer. The way he travelled was quite taking, moving into contention really easily off the strong pace, but he was denied a clear run until switched left, back towards the near rail a furlong out. By that time the winner had already committed and he faced a hopeless task with that rival, but he still finished well for second. It's a shame he's not in the Nunthorpe as he would have been worth his place in the line-up. (op 20-1)
Inxile(IRE), like the runner-up, travelled well for a long way but was forced to wait for a run. He found some room over a furlong out and kept on well, but he had no chance with the winner. Successful twice in Listed company this year, and first past the post in a French Group 3, he looks to have further improvement in him. He'll now be aimed at the Flying Five at the Curragh. (op 9-1)
Borderlescott won a Listed race from a favourable draw at Chester on his previous start, but he has yet to recapture his very best form so far this year. This was a creditable effort as he showed his usual early speed and kept on to fare best of those drawn in a double-figure stall. (op 11-4 tchd 3-1 in places)
Dandy Man(IRE), third in this last year, seemed to have his chance and ran a respectable race but he's a very difficult horse to win this these days. (tchd 14-1)
Rowe Park ran okay but simply didn't look good enough and he hasn't really gone on as one might have hoped since winning at this level in 2007. (op 33-1)
Spin Cycle(IRE) had no obvious excuse and basically wasn't good enough. (op 25-1)
Equiano(FR) ◆ has struggled since winning last year's King's Stand for a different yard, but he's better than this result implies. He basically lost his winning chance with a very slow start after appearing to stumble as the gates opened, but made good headway to move into a threatening position inside the final two furlongs, before understandably getting tired. Official explanation: jockey said colt slipped leaving stalls (op 16-1)
Reverence isn't up to this grade any more. (op 50-1)
Sugar Free(IRE), a recent Listed winner at Ayr, showed speed but was soon put in her place. (op 12-1)
Moorhouse Lad, returning from three months off, stepped up on the form he showed on his reappearance but was still below his best.
Ialysos(GR) had no easy task under a 5lb penalty for his recent Group 3 success at Sandown and a high draw probably wasn't ideal, but he could still have been expected to fare better. (tchd 11-2)

4457 COUTTS GOODWOOD CUP (GROUP 2) 2m

3:25 (3:25) (Class 1) 3-Y-O+

£56,770 (£21,520; £10,770; £5,370; £2,690; £1,350) **Stalls** Low

Form RPR

20-2 **1** **Schiaparelli (GER)**[21] 3781 6-9-7 115 LDettori 3 119
(Saeed Bin Suroor) *lw: trckd ldng pair: clsd to ld over 4f out: at least 3 l clr 3f out: coaxed along tl rdn out whn pressed last 150yds* **6/4**[1]

-320 **2** *1* **Mourilyan (IRE)**[147] 772 5-9-7 112 RyanMoore 7 117
(G L Moore) *lw: dwlt: hld up in last trio: gd prog fr over 4f out to chse wnr wl over 2f out: hrd rdn and hanging rt but clsd to 1 l down 150yds out: no imp after* **5/1**[2]

3350 **3** *12* **The Betchworth Kid**[33] 3390 4-9-7 100 HayleyTurner 8 103
(M L W Bell) *hld up in last: gd prog on outer fr 4f out to go 3rd 2f out: no ch w ldng pair and lft further bhd fr over 1f out* **33/1**

1-11 **4** *5* **Caracciola (GER)**[40] 3143 12-9-7 105 EddieAhern 9 97
(B W Hills) *mostly trckd ldr to 5f out: chsd wnr 4f out to wl over 2f out: wknd* **11/1**

-144 **5** *4* **Enroller (IRE)**[21] 3781 4-9-7 110 MartinDwyer 4 92
(W R Muir) *hld up in 7th: prog 7f out to disp 4th over 4f out: drvn and no imp 3f out: wknd over 2f out* **13/2**[3]

1230 **6** *11* **Friston Forest (IRE)**[19] 3874 5-9-7 108 TedDurcan 2 79
(Saeed Bin Suroor) *b: lw: hld up in 6th: clsd on ldrs 5f out: gng wl enough over 3f out: sn shkn up and fnd nil: eased over 1f out* **14/1**

-260 **7** *3/4* **Centennial (IRE)**[42] 3048 4-9-7 108 (b) JimmyFortune 1 78
(J H M Gosden) *trckd clr ldng trio: clsd fr 5f out: drvn and wknd over 2f out: sn bhd: eased* **12/1**

114- **8** *9* **Askar Tau (FR)**[285] 6817 4-9-7 102 RichardMullen 10 67
(M P Tregoning) *dwlt: hld up in last trio: pushed along 7f out: struggling 5f out: sn wl bhd* **13/2**[3]

1114 **9** *16* **Judgethemoment (USA)**[26] 3642 4-9-7 96 MichellePayne 5 48
(Jane Chapple-Hyam) *hld up in 5th: rdn 6f out: wknd rapidly 4f out: t.o* **40/1**

0-54 **10** *15* **Tungsten Strike (USA)**[63] 2409 8-9-7 100 (v) JimCrowley 6 30
(Mrs A J Perrett) *led: spreadeagled field after 4f: stl clr over 5f out: hdd & wknd rapidly over 4f out: sn t.o* **16/1**

3m 25.18s (-3.82) **Going Correction** +0.25s/f (Good) **10** Ran SP% **117.3**
Speed ratings (Par 115): **119,118,112,110,108 102,102,97,89,82**
toteswingers: 1&2 £3.00, 1&3 £16.80, 2&3 £34.50 CSF £8.90 TOTE £2.10: £1.10, £1.90, £11.00; EX 10.60 Trifecta £326.80 Pool: £7818.14 - 17.70 winning units..
Owner Godolphin **Bred** Gestut Karlshof **Trained** Newmarket, Suffolk

FOCUS
No Yeats to enjoy this year and this did not look a vintage Goodwood Cup, but the winner is a class act and the first two finished clear. Schiaparelli is rated to his best. The pace was strong and the form should hold up, although a couple of these were below par.

NOTEBOOK
Schiaparelli(GER) was a four-times Group 1 winner when trained in Germany, all of them over 1m4f, and he demonstrated his versatility with a nice performance on his first try over 2m. Keen early on, he soon settled in third place, some way behind Tungsten Stike and Caracciola. He moved smoothly to the front early in the straight and, although the runner-up briefly threatened him, he always had a bit left in the tank and won with something to spare. Well suited by cut in the ground, his target is the Grosser Preis Von Baden in early September, a race in which he was a beaten favourite as a 3yo, and should he run very well there then consideration would be given to the Arc. Godolphin completed the Grosser Preis-Arc double with Marienbard seven years ago. (op 7-4 tchd 2-1 in places)
Mourilyan(IRE), last in action in Dubai in March when trained by Herman Brown, is back with his former handler. Held up a good way off the pace, he made rapid progress in the straight and went after the winner with more than two furlongs left. He momentarily looked like getting to him entering the last but slightly ducked in behind and was just held from that point. Connections were understandably delighted with the run and York's Lonsdale Cup will be his next outing, rather than carrying top weight in the Ebor. (op 15-2)
The Betchworth Kid was another to come from the rear, but although he moved past several floundering rivals in the straight to go third he had only a distant view of the pair ahead of him. He will also head to York, in his case for the Ebor in which he has 9st. (tchd 40-1 and 50-1 in places)
Caracciola(GER)'s winning run came to an end on this rise in grade, as he attempted to become the oldest ever European pattern-race winner. Moved to the Barry Hills yards with Nicky Henderson currently suspended, he chased the clear leader, himself some way clear of the remainder, but could not counter when the winner went for home and weakened in the last 2f. He needs further and faster ground, and a trip to Japan in September may still be on the cards. (op 8-1)
Enroller(IRE) could never move out of midfield and finished a good deal further behind Schiaparelli than he had in Newmarket's Princess of Wales's Stakes, when both were demoted for causing interference. He stayed 1m7f last year but did not get home here and perhaps he simply failed to handle the track. (op 6-1 tchd 7-1 and 15-2 in places)
Friston Forest(IRE), the winner's stablemate, was another who failed to make his presence felt, although he was going well enough when the race really warmed up. He could not turn around York form with Caracciola despite a 3lb pull for a short head. (op 12-1 tchd 20-1)
Centennial(IRE) was the only one of these to run behind Yeats in the Gold Cup at Ascot, where he failed to last the 2m4f. Returning to Goodwood for the first time since winning last August's Great Voltigeur Stakes over 1m4f, and with blinkers back on in place of a visor, he was close enough entering the straight but did not seem to stay. (tchd 11-1)
Askar Tau(FR) landed five successive handicaps last year, rising nearly 40lb in the weights, before the run ended with a fourth to Caracciola in the Cesarewitch. Gelded since he was last seen, and making a belated seasonal bow, his yard having suffered with the virus, he looked fit enough but was in trouble at the back of the field with 6f to run and failed to pick up. He is better than this. (op 8-1)
Judgethemoment(USA), the Ascot Stakes winner, had the lowest BHA rating of these and he was beaten a good way out. He needs faster ground. (op 33-1)
Tungsten Strike(USA) was running in this event for the fifth successive year, with his second to Yeats 12 months ago his best placing. He missed Ascot to be kept fresh for this, but after setting a strong pace in the second-time visor, clear for a time, he stopped very quickly once headed by the winner. (op 12-1)

4458 MOET HENNESSY FILLIES' STKS (REGISTERED AS THE LILLIE LANGTRY STAKES) (GROUP 3) 1m 6f

4:00 (4:03) (Class 1) 3-Y-O+

£39,739 (£15,064; £7,539; £3,759; £1,883; £945) **Stalls** Low

Form RPR

-562 **1** **Sevenna (FR)**[41] 3103 4-9-6 85 TPQueally 4 102
(H R A Cecil) *dwlt: trckd ldrs: rdn to go 2nd over 3f out: clsd to ld over 2f out: sn in command: drvn and kpt on wl enough fr over 1f out* **12/1**

-031 **2** *1 1/2* **Cassique Lady (IRE)**[45] 2974 4-9-6 102 RyanMoore 8 99
(Mrs L Wadham) *hld up in 7th: rdn and prog jst over 3f out: disp 2nd fr wl over 1f out: no imp on wnr but kpt on* **9/2**[2]

-122 **3** *nk* **Victoria Montoya**[26] 3642 4-9-6 89 WilliamBuick 1 99
(A M Balding) *lw: pressed ldr: led over 4f out and tried to kick on: hdd over 2f out and sn outpcd: kpt on wl u.p though lost 2nd nr fin* **9/2**[2]

3522 **4** *1 1/2* **Princess Taylor**[12] 4094 5-9-6 97 AlanMunro 6 97
(M Botti) *trckd ldrs: rdn to go 3rd 3f out: disp 2nd wl over 1f out: no ex fnl f* **8/1**[3]

2212 **5** *1 3/4* **Lady Artemisia (IRE)**[12] 4103 3-8-6 82 HayleyTurner 3 94
(M L W Bell) *hld up in 8th: rdn and prog on outer over 3f out: nrly on terms w plcd horses wl over 1f out: fdd fnl f* **16/1**

44 **6** *3* **Suailce (IRE)**[33] 3413 4-9-6 0 (b) JimmyFortune 5 90
(D K Weld, Ire) *dwlt: hld up in 6th: rdn and effrt over 3f out: sn no prog: btn fnl 2f* **3/1**[1]

5-36 **7** *5* **Presbyterian Nun (IRE)**[41] 3103 4-9-6 90 RichardMullen 9 83
(J L Dunlop) *hld up in last: lft bhd over 3f out: rdn over 2f out: no real prog* **33/1**

-243 **8** *18* **Starfala**[26] 3619 4-9-6 100 LDettori 2 58
(P F I Cole) *lw: mde most to over 4f out: sn btn: eased 2f out: t.o* **9/2**[2]

2241 **9** *23* **Dolly Penrose**[12] 4078 4-9-6 86 TonyCulhane 7 26
(M R Channon) *trckd ldrs tl wknd rapidly wl over 3f out: t.o* **12/1**

3m 6.55s (2.95) **Going Correction** +0.475s/f (Yiel)
WFA 3 from 4yo+ 14lb **9** Ran SP% **114.9**
Speed ratings (Par 110): **110,109,108,108,107 105,102,92,79**
toteswingers: 1&2 £10.60, 1&3 £11.40, 2&3 £5.10 CSF £64.90 TOTE £15.20: £3.50, £1.80, £1.70; EX 80.60 Trifecta £947.00 Pool: £1663.78 - 1.30 winning units..
Owner Gestut Ammerland **Bred** Gestut Ittlingen & Arial Bloodstock **Trained** Newmarket, Suffolk

FOCUS
The going was changed to good, good to soft in places before this race, and then changed to good to soft all over immediately afterwards, following 4mm of rain within the space of an hour. This looked a pretty weak fillies' Group 3 and the form is ordinary for the grade. Improved form from the winner.

NOTEBOOK
Sevenna(FR) is officially rated only 85, but the rain arrived just in time for her and she relished conditions, keeping on strongly having come under pressure early in the straight. This has to be rated as a much-improved performance, but it would still probably be unwise to get carried away and connections suggested they might look for a suitable race in Germany, where she ought to get similarly easy going. (op 16-1 tchd 10-1)
Cassique Lady(IRE), the winner of a Listed race over 1m3f at Warwick on her previous start, confirmed placings from that contest with Princess Taylor on this step up in trip but didn't seem to run up to her official mark of 102. (op 7-2)
Victoria Montoya, runner-up in a weak 2m Listed race on her previous start, is a dour stayer and proved unsuited by this drop in trip. She committed for home in good time, with her rider no doubt keen to make use of her stamina, and she seemed to handle the ground okay, but she couldn't get away from her rivals. Once headed, she kept on well and ought to do better back over further. (op 13-2)
Princess Taylor couldn't reverse recent Haydock or Warwick placings with Classique Lady and didn't seem to run up to her absolute best. She has form on an easy surface, but all her wins have been gained on fast ground. (op 10-1 tchd 11-1)
Lady Artemisia(IRE) didn't run too badly considering she had a bit to find at this level, but the easy ground probably didn't suit. (op 25-1)
Suailce(IRE) looked to have a fine chance with conditions very much in her favour, but she proved disappointing. She was possibly a little short of room when first trying to produce a challenge, but she soon gave up and this was a tame performance. (op 9-4 tchd 2-1 and 10-3)
Starfala was soon beaten once coming under pressure and seemed totally unsuited by the ground. Official explanation: jockey said filly was unsuited by the good to soft ground (tchd 4-1 and 5-1)

4459 XL INSURANCE STKS (HERITAGE H'CAP) 7f
4:35 (4:36) (Class 2) (0-105,102) 3-Y-O
£24,924 (£7,464; £3,732; £1,868; £932; £468) **Stalls** High

Form RPR

1102 **1** **Suruor (IRE)**[19] 3839 3-8-12 93 JimmyFortune 12 101
(D M Simcock) *hld up in abt 7th: prog on inner over 2f out: clsd on ldrs over 1f out: led ent fnl f: drvn out* **9/2**[2]

-120 **2** *¾* **Shamwari Lodge (IRE)**[22] 3747 3-8-13 94 RichardHughes 8 100+
(R Hannon) *hld up in last quartet: prog whn nt clr run 2f out: nt clr run over 1f out and swtchd ins: got through and r.o to take 2nd last strides* **4/1**[1]

2400 **3** *hd* **Akhenaten**[22] 3747 3-8-11 92 TonyCulhane 16 97
(M R Channon) *t.k.h early: pressed ldr: rdn to ld over 1f out: hdd ent fnl f: styd on same pce u.p* **12/1**

5164 **4** *shd* **Deadly Encounter (IRE)**[26] 3643 3-7-12 79 PaulHanagan 13 84
(R A Fahey) *pressed ldng pair: u.p fr wl over 2f out: kpt on and cl up after: nvr quite pce to chal* **14/1**

2000 **5** *2* **Enact**[22] 3747 3-8-4 85 WilliamBuick 6 84+
(Sir Michael Stoute) *hld up in last quartet on outer: rdn and prog fr 3f out: clsd on ldrs jst over 1f out: wknd fnl 150yds* **12/1**

0116 **6** *½* **Kyllachy Star**[20] 3816 3-8-9 90 MartinDwyer 7 88
(R A Fahey) *lw: hld up in last quartet: pushed along 1/2-way: u.p and no prog over 2f out: plld out wd and 10th 1f out: styd on* **8/1**[3]

0-01 **7** *½* **Brae Hill (IRE)**[33] 3375 3-8-11 92 HayleyTurner 15 89
(M L W Bell) *led at gd pce: hdd over 1f out: wknd fnl f* **9/2**[2]

1505 **8** *1 ¼* **Dark Mischief**[26] 3622 3-8-10 91 DaneO'Neill 4 84
(H Candy) *hld up in abt 8th: u.p over 2f out: no prog* **16/1**

6633 **9** *nk* **Khor Dubai (IRE)**[19] 3839 3-9-3 98 (v) LDettori 10 90
(Saeed Bin Suroor) *hld up in 6th: effrt over 2f out: rdn and fnd nil over 1f out: wknd fnl f* **8/1**[3]

20-2 **10** *nk* **Prime Spirit (IRE)**[12] 4077 3-9-0 95 TomEaves 14 87
(B Smart) *plld hrd early: prom in 5th: rdn wl over 2f out: losing pl whn squeezed out and hmpd over 1f out* **12/1**

3202 **11** *13* **Servoca (CAN)**[26] 3622 3-8-8 89 (t) MichaelHills 5 46
(B W Hills) *t.k.h early: hld up in last: hanging and no prog whn shkn up 3f out: t.o* **25/1**

3160 **12** *20* **Jobe (USA)**[43] 3011 3-9-0 95 (p) NCallan 11 —
(K A Ryan) *lw: dwlt: t.k.h early and sn trckd ldng trio: cl up on inner whn reminder over 2f out: ref to r properly and virtually plld himself up* **14/1**

1m 28.98s (1.58) **Going Correction** +0.475s/f (Yiel) **12** Ran SP% **124.7**
Speed ratings (Par 106): **109,108,107,107,105 104,104,102,102,102 87,64**
toteswingers: 1&2 £6.20, 1&3 £17.90, 2&3 £17.00 CSF £24.19 CT £214.96 TOTE £6.30: £2.40, £2.00, £4.50; EX 30.50 Trifecta £579.80 Part won. Pool: £783.52 - 0.10 winning units..
Owner Dr Marwan Koukash **Bred** Shadwell Estate Company Limited **Trained** Newmarket, Suffolk

FOCUS
A decent 3yo handicap run at a fair pace considering the conditions. Solid form with the third a good guide.

NOTEBOOK
Suruor(IRE), just denied by the progressive Secret Society in a similar race at Ascot on his previous start, gained compensation off a 5lb higher mark. He showed a good attitude to take a narrow gap between rivals in the closing stages, and although the runner-up looked slightly unlucky, this was still a very useful effort. The plan now is the totesport Challenge Cup back at Ascot on September 26. (op 7-1)
Shamwari Lodge(IRE) was suited by this step back up in trip and was probably an unlucky loser. Held up well out the back, she gradually responded to pressure in the straight, but was denied a clear run over two furlongs out, and again had her path blocked around a furlong from the finish. She finished well once finally in the clear and was closing on the winner at the line. (op 5-1 tchd 11-2, 6-1 in places)
Akhenaten was a little keen early but he had his chance. He doesn't look easy to win with but has plenty of ability and gives the impression he will show his best form when ridden patiently off a strong gallop. (op 16-1)
Deadly Encounter(IRE) was produced with every chance and ran well, but he wasn't quite good enough. The ground might have been a little easier than ideal. Official explanation: vet said gelding had been struck into (op 12-1 tchd 16-1 in places)

Enact ◆ was not ideally drawn and she came wide into the straight. She looked a threat about a furlong out but couldn't sustain her run and gave the impression she might be worth another try over 6f. (op 14-1)
Kyllachy Star kept on gradually in the straight, despite not getting the best of runs, but he never looked like winning. (op 17-2 tchd 15-2)
Brae Hill(IRE) should not have minded the ease in the ground and he had his chance from the front but couldn't confirm recent Chester placings with Deadly Encounter, proving held off a 5lb higher mark. (tchd 5-1)
Dark Mischief seemed unsuited by this step up to 7f. (op 20-1)
Khor Dubai(IRE) found less than had looked likely. Official explanation: jockey said colt was unsuited by the good to soft ground
Prime Spirit(IRE) had conditions to suit but failed to confirm the promise he showed in a small-field conditions race on his belated reappearance. It's possible this came too soon, but he was still disappointing. (op 8-1)
Servoca(CAN) Official explanation: jockey said colt lost its action
Jobe(USA) looked held against the rail in the straight when he started to look particularly awkward under pressure around two furlongs out, and his jockey was soon unable to ride him out. Official explanation: jockey said gelding hung right-handed into the running rail approaching the furlong marker (op 16-1 tchd 11-1)

4460 EUROPEAN BREEDERS' FUND NEW HAM MAIDEN FILLIES' STKS 7f
5:10 (5:13) (Class 2) 2-Y-O **£12,952** (£3,854; £1,926; £962) **Stalls** High

Form RPR

22 **1** **Water Biscuit**[20] 3820 2-9-0 0 LDettori 10 79
(B J Meehan) *lw: chsd ldrs: prog fr 2f out on outer: led 1f out: styd on wl fnl 100yds* **4/1**[2]

4 **2** *1 ½* **Ghazwah**[20] 3820 2-9-0 0 RHills 12 75
(J H M Gosden) *lw: trckd ldrs: gng easily over 2f out: chal over 1f out: upsides ent fnl f: outpcd last 100yds* **9/2**[3]

0 **3** *1 ½* **Whipperway (IRE)**[10] 4147 2-9-0 0 JimmyFortune 9 72
(M R Channon) *leggy: unf: hld up in midfield: pushed along over 2f out: prog over 1f out: shkn up and styd on wl to take 3rd ins fnl f* **25/1**

2 **4** *1* **Laureldean Spirit (IRE)**[20] 3823 2-9-0 0 PaulHanagan 14 69
(R A Fahey) *athletic: t.k.h early: trckd ldrs: shkn up and nt qckn over 1f out: styd on again ins fnl f* **9/4**[1]

5 *¾* **Pink Symphony** 2-9-0 0 MartinDwyer 7 69+
(P F I Cole) *w'like: scope: tall: t.k.h: hld up wl in rr: brought to outer in st: nudged along and styd on in taking style fnl 2f: nvr nrr* **8/1**

5 **6** *1* **Saafia (USA)**[14] 4001 2-9-0 0 TPO'Shea 13 65
(M Johnston) *lengthy: pressed ldr: upsides fr 2f out tl wknd 1f out* **14/1**

4 **7** *1 ¼* **Candleshoe (IRE)**[10] 4147 2-9-0 0 RyanMoore 1 62
(R Hannon) *lw: chsd ldrs: disputing 3rd whn brought to r alone against nr side rail: hanging fr 2f out: nt on terms fnl f* **7/1**

0 **8** *nse* **Paleo (IRE)**[13] 4047 2-9-0 0 RichardHughes 16 61
(R Hannon) *racd freely: mde most: jnd 2f out: hdd & wknd 1f out* **12/1**

9 *½* **Leitzu (IRE)** 2-9-0 0 TonyCulhane 6 60+
(M R Channon) *w'like: str: dwlt: t.k.h early: hld up in rr: pushed along 2f out: kpt on one pce: nvr on terms* **50/1**

5 **10** *1* **Calatrava Cape (IRE)**[20] 3810 2-9-0 0 EddieAhern 2 58
(J L Dunlop) *stdd s: hld up in last: pushed along over 2f out: nvr nr ldrs: do bttr* **16/1**

0 **11** *2 ¾* **Rosa Gurney (IRE)**[58] 2563 2-9-0 0 SteveDrowne 8 51
(J R Best) *w'like: leggy: dwlt: t.k.h: hld up in rr: pushed along and no prog 3f out* **66/1**

12 *5* **Nom De La Rosa (IRE)** 2-9-0 0 TedDurcan 15 38
(G L Moore) *w'like: leggy: chsd ldrs tl lost pl rapidly 3f out: sn bhd* **40/1**

13 *32* **Miss Chaumiere** 2-9-0 0 HayleyTurner 3 —
(M L W Bell) *w'like: str: b.hind: wl in rr: ended up alone in centre st: sn bhd: t.o* **40/1**

1m 31.63s (4.23) **Going Correction** +0.475s/f (Yiel) **13** Ran SP% **125.0**
Speed ratings (Par 97): **94,92,90,89,88 87,86,85,85,84 81,75,38**
toteswingers: 1&2 £4.60, 1&3 £17.60, 2&3 £36.90 CSF £22.79 TOTE £3.40: £1.40, £2.20, £7.70; EX 20.40 Trifecta £423.70 Pool: £629.85 - 1.10 winning units..
Owner Lady Rothschild **Bred** The Rt Hon Lord Rothschild **Trained** Manton, Wilts

FOCUS
A decent maiden dominated by fillies with previous racecourse experience. Although the time in the rain-affected conditions was over seven seconds outside standard, this looked a good field on looks and several winners should come out of it. The winner sets the level.

NOTEBOOK
Water Biscuit had been runner-up on both her previous two starts, each over 6f at Newmarket, and that represented the best form on offer. She came under pressure 3f out here before delivering a good run down the outer to lead inside the last and score decisively. Like on her second start she gave a flash of the tail, but that is just a quirk and nothing to be unduly concerned about. She is by a sprinter but there is plenty of stamina on the dam's side and the seventh furlong was not a problem to her. A step up to Listed company is likely to be next. (op 7-2 tchd 3-1)
Ghazwah ◆ travelled well, and although she could not race on with Water Biscuit inside the last she finished considerably closer to that filly than she had on her debut at Newmarket. She should not be long in getting off the mark, perhaps back on better ground. (tchd 5-1, 6-1 in places)
Whipperway(IRE) did not show a great deal first time out at Windsor but she was staying on at the end that evening. The extra furlong here suited her well and again she was doing her best work late. (tchd 28-1)
Laureldean Spirit(IRE), runner-up at York on her debut, is very well regarded and was a little disappointing after pulling too hard early on. She was keeping on again near the finish and should soon get off the mark. (op 3-1 tchd 7-2)
Pink Symphony ◆, a Montjeu filly who is closely related to the high-class Fantasia, did best of the debutantes. She was going on close home without being given at all a hard time and looks a surefire maiden winner. (op 10-1)
Saafia(USA), the Hamdan Al Maktoum second string, was in the firing line until weakening inside the last and improved on what she showed first time out at Doncaster. (op 11-1 tchd 16-1 in places)
Candleshoe(IRE), drawn on the outside, came right over to the stands' side in the straight, but she hung through the last quarter mile and was never on terms with the main bunch, who took the conventional inside line. She had finished ahead of today's third when they made their respective debuts at Windsor. (op 12-1)
Paleo(IRE) showed pace first time up at Newbury and it was a similar story here, although she did not quite get home over this extra furlong in this rain-softened ground. (tchd 10-1 and 14-1, 16-1 in places)
Leitzu(IRE), a half-sister to 1m4f winners, was keeping on in encouraging fashion at the end. (op 100-1 tchd 40-1)

Calatrava Cape(IRE) should leave this form behind over further in time. (op 14-1)

4461 CHARLTON STKS (H'CAP) 5f

5:45 (5:47) (Class 3) (0-90,90) 4-Y-O+ **£12,952** (£3,854; £1,926; £962) **Stalls** Low

Form				RPR
1510	**1**		**Blue Jack**[10] 4135 4-9-6 **89**..........................(b) MartinDwyer 5 (W R Muir) *racd against nr side rail: wl in rr: rdn and gd prog fr over 1f out: led gp ins fnl f: r.o wl and overall ldr last strides* **9/1**[3]	99
1212	**2**	*nk*	**Feelin Foxy**[8] 4189 5-8-6 **75**.......................... AlanMunro 24 (J G Given) *taken down early: pressed far side ldr: led 1/2-way: clr of rest fr over 1f out: overall ldr ins fnl f: hdd last strides* **16/1**	84+
0130	**3**	*¾*	**Invincible Lad (IRE)**[40] 3149 5-9-0 **83**.......................... RichardHughes 8 (E J Alston) *s.s: mostly last nr side but racd against rail: gd prog jst over 1f out: r.o to snatch 3rd nr fin: 2nd of 15 in gp* **12/1**	89
6505	**4**	*½*	**Indian Trail**[4] 4341 9-9-5 **88**..........................(v) FrancisNorton 2 (D Nicholls) *lw: trckd nr side ldrs and racd against rail: cruising 2f out: brought to chal jst over 1f out: hung rt and fnd nil: 3rd of 15 in gp* **7/1**[1]	93
011	**5**	*½*	**Le Toreador**[30] 3491 4-9-0 **83**..........................(t) NCallan 6 (K A Ryan) *lw: racd on outer of nr side: wl on terms: disp ld 1f out: no ex ins fnl f: 4th of 15 in gp* **16/1**	86+
-006	**6**	*¾*	**Northern Bolt**[16] 3956 4-8-8 **77**.......................... TedDurcan 22 (D Nicholls) *chsd far side ldrs: rdn and styd on to go 2nd of gp ins fnl f: no ch w ldr* **20/1**	77
0001	**7**	*nk*	**Highland Harvest**[16] 3945 5-8-4 **73**.......................... TPO'Shea 3 (Jamie Poulton) *chsd ldrs nr side and racd against rail: nt qckn over 1f out: kpt on ins fnl f: 5th of 15 in gp* **33/1**	72
2012	**8**	*hd*	**Luscivious**[5] 4311 5-8-6 **75**.......................... RichardKingscote 18 (J A Glover) *racd on outer nr side: cl up: u.p fr 2f out: kpt on wl but nvr quite able to chal: 6th of 15 in gp* **25/1**	73
1040	**9**	*hd*	**Total Impact**[13] 4069 6-9-0 **83**.......................... PaulHanagan 10 (R A Fahey) *racd nr side in midfield: effrt to chse ldrs 1f out: nt clr run but nvr pce to chal: 7th of 15 in gp* **8/1**[2]	83+
0304	**10**	*hd*	**Good Gorsoon (USA)**[6] 4273 4-8-13 **82**.......................... MichaelHills 7 (B W Hills) *swtg: racd towards outer nr side: w ldrs: upsides jst over 1f out: bmpd jst ins fnl f: wknd: 8th of 15 in gp* **20/1**	79
4560	**11**	*½*	**Methaaly (IRE)**[28] 3529 6-8-9 **78**..........................(be) RichardMullen 20 (M Mullineaux) *lw: awkward s: last of far side gp: prog but nt clr run 2f out: r.o ins fnl f: 3rd of 8 in gp* **66/1**	73
0000	**12**	*½*	**Piscean (USA)**[4] 4341 4-9-7 **90**.......................... AdamKirby 9 (T Keddy) *racd nr side: nvr beyond midfield: kpt on fnl f: nt pce to threaten: 9th of 15 in gp* **20/1**	83
0000	**13**	*¾*	**Northern Fling**[4] 4353 5-9-2 **85**.......................... AndrewMullen 16 (D Nicholls) *racd on outer of nr side: nvr on terms w ldrs: 10th of 15 in gp* **25/1**	75
3103	**14**	*nse*	**Our Piccadilly (IRE)**[7] 4232 4-8-9 **78**.......................... EddieAhern 23 (W S Kittow) *dwlt: in rr of far side gp: styd on ins fnl f: no ch: 4th of 8 in gp* **10/1**	68
5220	**15**	*½*	**Vhujon (IRE)**[41] 3122 4-9-5 **88**.......................... TomEaves 11 (P D Evans) *swtg: racd nr side: wl in rr: nvr pce to threaten ldrs: 11th of 15 in gp* **40/1**	76
0110	**16**	*hd*	**Mandurah (IRE)**[4] 4341 5-9-6 **89**.......................... AdrianTNicholls 1 (D Nicholls) *led nr side: rdn 2f out: hdd and squeezed out 1f out: wknd: 12th of 15 in gp* **8/1**[2]	77
156	**17**	*nk*	**Equuleus Pictor**[12] 4099 5-9-1 **87**.......................... JackDean(3) 25 (J L Spearing) *lw: led far side to 1/2-way: wknd fnl f: 5th of 8 in gp* **16/1**	74
3005	**18**	*½*	**Little Pete (IRE)**[21] 3784 4-9-4 **87**.......................... LPKeniry 19 (A M Balding) *unruly to post: racd far side: nvr on terms w ldrs: 6th of 8 in gp* **16/1**	72
5404	**19**	*nk*	**Steelcut**[13] 4043 5-8-6 **75**.......................... RoystonFfrench 17 (R A Fahey) *swtg: racd on outer of nr side: nvr on terms w ldrs: fdd fnl f: 13th of 15 in gp* **50/1**	59
5120	**20**	*shd*	**Alfresco**[47] 2929 5-8-9 **78**..........................(b) JimCrowley 26 (J R Best) *chsd far side ldrs but nvr on terms: no ch over 1f out: 7th of 8 in gp* **33/1**	61
0241	**21**	*hd*	**Rocker**[7] 4232 5-8-11 **80** 6ex.......................... RyanMoore 4 (G L Moore) *wl in rr nr side: rdn and no prog 2f out: 14th of 15 in gp* **8/1**[2]	63
4040	**22**	*½*	**Dazed And Amazed**[46] 2946 5-8-12 **81**.......................... SteveDrowne 21 (R Hannon) *racd far side: nvr on terms w ldrs: 8th of 8 in gp* **33/1**	62
2143	**23**	*1 ¾*	**Incomparable**[132] 901 4-8-9 **78**.......................... TPQueally 13 (J A Glover) *racd towards outer nr side: a in rr: 15th of 15 in gp* **66/1**	53

59.32 secs (0.92) **Going Correction** +0.375s/f (Good) **23** Ran SP% **134.3**
Speed ratings (Par 107): **107,106,105,104,103 102,102,101,101,101 100,99,98,98,97 97,96,95,95,95 94,94,91**
toteswingers: 1&2 £86.60, 1&3 £36.20, 2&3 £59.60 CSF £132.62 CT £1801.34 TOTE £15.20: £3.40, £2.50, £3.30, £2.40; EX 418.10 TRIFECTA Not won. Place 6: £119.37 Place 5: £59.48.
Owner Martin P Graham **Bred** Miss S N Ralphs **Trained** Lambourn, Berks
■ Stewards' Enquiry : Francis Norton caution: careless riding

FOCUS

The field split into two groups and there was very little between the far-side group and those on the stands' side. That said, just like in the earlier Group 3 over this trip, bang on the rail was the place to be for those on the stands' side. The form is rated around the winner and third.

NOTEBOOK

Blue Jack still had plenty of ground to make up over a furlong out but he had the benefit of the stands' rail and ran on really strongly, getting nicely on top on his side and finding just enough to hold a challenger on the opposite side of the track. He's held in high regard by his trainer, who is considering races like the Portland and the Ayr Gold Cup, and Willie Muir even mentioned the Prix de l'Abbaye as a possible target if this gelding continues to progress. (op 12-1)

Feelin Foxy was given a positive ride on the far side and pulled clear of her seven rivals on that part of the track, but was just denied by a runner on the stands' side. A fine run in defeat.

Invincible Lad(IRE) looked to be last of all in the stands'-side bunch for much of the way but he raced against the favoured rail and finished really strongly to get up for an unlikely third. He's well suited by a strong pace and could pick up a decent contest when things fall right. (op 10-1)

Indian Trail probably wouldn't have appreciated the easing in the ground but he still ran well. As usual he travelled very strongly, but if anything he was ridden closer to the pace than ideal and he was vulnerable to the strong finishers who had sat further back, although that said, he didn't help his chance by continually hanging right. Official explanation: jockey said gelding hung right-handed (op 15-2 tchd 8-1)

Le Toreador ◆, bidding for a hat-trick off a mark only 3lb higher than for the first of his two recent wins, was always handy on the near side but raced away from the favoured rail and couldn't sustain his challenge. This was a creditable effort in defeat and he remains a sprinter to keep on side.

Northern Bolt hasn't won since 2007 and he was comfortably held on the far side of the track, albeit he was second best in that eight-strong group. (op 25-1)

Highland Harvest ran with credit off a mark 4lb higher than when winning over 6f at Brighton on his previous start. (tchd 25-1 in places)

Luscivious is probably better than he showed considering stall 18 was far from ideal and he raced well away from the favoured rail. (op 20-1)

Total Impact was disappointing considering he was only 1lb higher than when winning this race last year, but even though he's a son of Pivotal his overall record suggests this ground probably wasn't in his favour. (op 7-1)

Methaaly(IRE) finished well on the far side of the track after being blocked in his run when first trying to pick up.

Piscean(USA) had won his previous three starts at this track, but this easy ground might not have been ideal. (op 25-1)

Mandurah(IRE) showed good speed to lead the near-side bunch but couldn't sustain his effort. (op 9-1)

Rocker, carrying a penalty for his recent Epsom success, had a good draw but ran well below form and was reported to have never been travelling. Official explanation: jockey said gelding was never travelling (op 9-1, tchd 10-1 in places)

T/Jkpt: Not won. T/Plt: £118.10 to a £1 stake. Pool: £256,286.05. 1,584.08 winning tickets. T/Qpdt: £23.50 to a £1 stake. Pool: £12,719.95. 400.10 winning tickets. JN

3678 MUSSELBURGH (R-H)

Thursday, July 30

OFFICIAL GOING: Good (good to firm in places)

The ground was changed ahead of racing, but it looked much slower than the official version, on the slow side, especially down the back straight.

Wind: Fresh, half against Weather: Cloudy, bright

4462 RACING UK HORSERACING IN YOUR HOME AMATEUR RIDERS' H'CAP 1m 5f

6:10 (6:10) (Class 6) (0-65,62) 4-Y-O+ **£2,498** (£774; £387; £193) **Stalls** High

Form				RPR
4440	**1**		**Hurricane Thomas (IRE)**[2] 4402 5-10-0 **48**.......... MissPhillipaTutty(7) 5 (R A Fahey) *in tch: hdwy on ins to ld over 2f out: hld on wl fnl f* **9/2**[2]	55
1222	**2**	*nk*	**Mystified (IRE)**[14] 3444 6-10-12 **53**..........(tp) MrSDobson 1 (R F Fisher) *led to over 2f out: sn rdn: rallied ins fnl f: jst hld* **7/1**	60
-051	**3**	*1 ¾*	**Toshi (USA)**[12] 2783 7-11-1 **56**.......... MrsCBartley 6 (J S Goldie) *hld up: effrt and swtchd lft 3f out: kpt on u.p ins fnl f* **5/2**[1]	60
0060	**4**	*1*	**Call Of Duty (IRE)**[16] 3943 4-10-9 **57**.......... MissNSayer(7) 7 (Mrs Dianne Sayer) *t.k.h: trckd ldrs: effrt and ev ch over 2f out: one pce fnl f* **15/2**	60
1510	**5**	*5*	**Dimashq**[4] 4350 7-10-10 **51**.......... MrSWalker 10 (P T Midgley) *hld up: hdwy and in tch 1/2-way: effrt and ev ch over 2f out: wknd fnl f* **5/1**[3]	46
00-2	**6**	*1 ¾*	**Goldan Jess (IRE)**[18] 3594 5-10-0 **46**.......... ColmMcCormack(5) 12 (P A Kirby) *midfield: pushed along over 2f out: nvr able to chal* **7/1**	38
66/0	**7**	*5*	**Great Quest (IRE)**[17] 3927 7-10-4 **52**.......... MissRebeccaSparkes(7) 3 (James Moffatt) *hld up: rdn over 3f out: nvr rchd ldrs* **50/1**	37
0340	**8**	*4*	**Merrion Tiger (IRE)**[4] 4350 4-11-0 **62**.......... MrMEnnis(7) 2 (A G Foster) *prom tl rdn and wknd over 1f out* **20/1**	41
020/	**9**	*½*	**The Buck (IRE)**[45] 2987 6-10-3 **49**.......... MrTRDavid(5) 4 (John Joseph Murphy, Ire) *chsd ldrs: pushed along over 4f out: wknd 3f out* **20/1**	27
45/5	**10**	*5*	**Sea Cove**[26] 3617 9-9-13 **45**.......... MissECSayer(5) 11 (Mrs Dianne Sayer) *hld up: rdn over 3f out: sn btn* **50/1**	16
-340	**P**		**Always Best**[42] 3068 5-10-4 **45**.......... MissLHorner 9 (R Allan) *bhd: drvn and struggling over 3f out: sn btn: p.u and dismntd ins fnl f* **33/1**	—

2m 51.6s (-0.40) **Going Correction** -0.225s/f (Firm) **11** Ran SP% **116.6**
Speed ratings (Par 101): **92,91,90,90,87 85,82,80,80,77** —
toteswingers: 1&2 £6.10, 1&3 £2.90, 2&3 £2.70 CSF £33.23 CT £94.86 TOTE £6.00: £2.00, £2.60, £2.00; EX 42.00.
Owner N D Tutty **Bred** P D Savill **Trained** Musley Bank, N Yorks
■ Philippa Tutty's first Flat winner.
■ Stewards' Enquiry : Mr S Dobson four-day ban: excessive use of the whip without allowing mount time to respond (Aug 13-14, 19, 24)

FOCUS

A modest 45-62 amateur riders' handicap run at a sound pace. The form is sound enough, rated around the third.

Always Best Official explanation: vet said gelding was lame on his off fore

4463 EUROPEAN BREEDERS' FUND MAIDEN STKS 5f

6:45 (6:47) (Class 5) 2-Y-O **£3,885** (£1,156; £577; £288) **Stalls** Low

Form				RPR
2	**1**		**Living It Large (FR)**[35] 3292 2-9-3 0.......... TonyHamilton 6 (R F Fisher) *cl up: rdn 2f out: led ins fnl f: kpt on wl* **6/4**[2]	69+
0	**2**	*½*	**Pink Lemonade (IRE)**[46] 2956 2-8-12 0.......... PJMcDonald 3 (John Joseph Murphy, Ire) *chsd ldrs: drvn 2f out: chsd wnr ins fnl f: r.o* **22/1**	62
2035	**3**	*1 ½*	**Dower Glen**[30] 3478 2-8-7 0..........(b[1]) PatrickDonaghy(5) 5 (I Semple) *sn w ldrs: led 1/2-way: hung lft and hdd ins fnl f: one pce* **6/1**[3]	57
05	**4**	*2 ¾*	**Chilean Fizz**[22] 3726 2-8-12 0.......... SilvestreDeSousa 4 (Mrs A Duffield) *cl up: drvn 1/2-way: one pce over 1f out* **33/1**	47+
050	**5**	*1 ¼*	**Grace Jicaro**[14] 4018 2-8-7 0.......... DeanHeslop(5) 7 (Mrs L Williamson) *sn outpcd and drvn bhd ldng gp: edgd rt 1/2-way: no imp* **80/1**	42
4	**6**	*1 ¾*	**Bahraj (USA)**[17] 3910 2-8-12 0.......... AndrewElliott 8 (M Johnston) *led to 1/2-way: rdn and wknd over 1f out* **1/1**[1]	36
	7	*¾*	**Lady Laurem** 2-8-12 0.......... DuranFentiman 1 (D A Nolan) *s.s: outpcd thrght* **100/1**	33

61.64 secs (1.24) **Going Correction** 0.0s/f (Good) **7** Ran SP% **113.8**
Speed ratings (Par 94): **90,89,86,82,80 77,76**
toteswingers: 1&2 £4.50, 1&3 £1.60, 2&3 £16.30 CSF £30.29 TOTE £2.20: £1.10, £4.30; EX 36.00.
Owner Des Johnston **Bred** Sunny Days Limited **Trained** Ulverston, Cumbria
■ Stewards' Enquiry : P J McDonald two-day ban: excessive use of the whip (Aug 13-14)

FOCUS

A weak maiden with little depth went to the only colt pitted against six fillies.

NOTEBOOK

Living It Large(FR), runner-up to the useful Colonel Mak over 6f at Hamilton, made very hard work of it and just held on. He should be seen to better effect in nurseries back over further. (op 2-1 tchd 9-4 and 11-4 in a place)

Pink Lemonade(IRE), beaten a total of about sixty lengths in three starts in Ireland, misbehaved behind the stalls. After showing plenty of speed, she stuck to her guns, but was just denied. (op 20-1 tchd 18-1)

Dower Glen, blinkered for the first time on her sixth start, took it up but came off a straight line and didn't see it out. She looks regressive. (op 9-2, tchd 7-1 in a place)

Chilean Fizz, well beaten in a Catterick seller on her previous starts, seemed to show improved form but her proximity underlines how weak the overall level of form is. (tchd 40-1)

Grace Jicaro, who gave problems leaving the paddock, had finished well beaten in selling company on her last two starts. She casts another doubt about the value of the form. (op 40-1)
Bahraj(USA) had led much of the way before finishing fourth on her debut over 6f at Ayr. Pushed sideways at the start, she soon showed ahead but dropped right out. This was too bad to be true. (op 11-10 tchd 6-5 and 11-8 in a place)

4464 EDINBURGH EVENING NEWS H'CAP — 5f
7:15 (7:15) (Class 4) (0-80,80) 3-Y-O+ — **£6,476** (£1,927; £963; £481) **Stalls** Low

Form — RPR
1256 **1** **Efistorm**[13] 4069 8-9-6 **80** ... BMcHugh(5) 3 — 88
(C R Dore) *sn pushed along in midfield: hdwy over 1f out: led ins fnl f: r.o* **15/2**
5506 **2** ½ **Miss Daawe**[4] 4355 5-8-6 **61** oh2 ... PJMcDonald 7 — 67
(B Ellison) *cl up: led over 1f out to ins fnl f: kpt on* **14/1**
3105 **3** ½ **Requisite**[2] 4399 4-9-3 **72** ... (v) SilvestreDeSousa 2 — 76
(I A Wood) *hld up: n.m.r over 2f out: hdwy over 1f out: edgd lft and r.o ins fnl f* **4/1**[2]
1021 **4** 1 **Blue Tomato**[13] 4036 8-9-3 **77** ... (p) PatrickDonaghy(5) 9 — 78
(Miss L A Perratt) *dwlt: hld up: hdwy over 1f out: r.o: nrst fin* **11/1**
0364 **5** ½ **Discanti (IRE)**[37] 3236 4-9-6 **75** ... (t) DuranFentiman 1 — 74
(T D Easterby) *trckd ldrs: n.m.r briefly over 1f out: one pce ins fnl f* **14/1**
2355 **6** 1 **Wicked Wilma (IRE)**[6] 4283 5-7-13 **61** oh1 ... CharlotteKerton(7) 5 — 56
(A Berry) *in tch on outside: effrt and ev ch over 1f out: no ex ins fnl f* **9/1**
600- **7** ¾ **Killer Class**[265] 7222 4-8-7 **67** ... GaryBartley(5) 6 — 60+
(J S Goldie) *hld up: nt clr run fr 2f out to ins fnl f: nt rcvr* **22/1**
1112 **8** ½ **Secret Venue**[6] 4289 3-8-10 **69** ... TonyHamilton 4 — 60
(Jedd O'Keeffe) *led to over 1f out: sn no ex* **9/4**[1]
2020 **9** hd **Sandwith**[5] 4311 6-9-5 **74** ... GrahamGibbons 8 — 64
(A G Foster) *w ldr to over 1f out: wkng whn n.m.r ins fnl f* **5/1**[3]

59.75 secs (-0.65) **Going Correction** 0.0s/f (Good)
WFA 3 from 4yo+ 4lb — **9** Ran SP% **115.2**
Speed ratings (Par 105): **105,104,103,101,101 99,98,97,97**
toteswingers: 1&2 £22.40, 1&3 £7.40, 2&3 £18.80 CSF £104.92 CT £483.19 TOTE £10.70: £2.40, £3.90, £1.60; EX 185.90.
Owner Sean J Murphy **Bred** E Duggan And D Churchman **Trained** Cowbit, Lincs

FOCUS
A tight knit 61-80 sprint handicap and they seemed to go very fast, the two pacesetters occupied the last two places in the end. The winner is rated to this year's best, with the second a slight doubt.
Killer Class Official explanation: jockey said filly was denied a clear run
Secret Venue Official explanation: trainer said, regarding running, that the gelding had been suffering from having several quick runs recently and had lost a right fore shoe

4465 RACING UK THE UK'S BEST RACECOURSES LIVE (S) STKS — 1m 1f
7:45 (7:45) (Class 6) 4-Y-0+ — **£1,942** (£578; £288; £144) **Stalls** High

Form — RPR
5466 **1** **Masterofceremonies**[17] 3923 6-9-3 57 ... (p) PJMcDonald 11 — 70
(James Moffatt) *s.i.s: bhd: hdwy over 2f out: led appr fnl f: drvn out* **8/1**
525 **2** 1¾ **Red Skipper (IRE)**[25] 3653 4-8-7 58 ... BMcHugh(5) 9 — 61
(N Wilson) *trckd ldrs: effrt and ev ch over 1f out: one pce ins fnl f* **11/2**[3]
6654 **3** 2 **Papa's Princess**[17] 3911 5-8-8 52 ow1 ... DanielTudhope 4 — 53
(J S Goldie) *mde most to appr fnl f: kpt on same pce ins fnl f* **17/2**
5513 **4** 2¼ **Keisha Kayleigh (IRE)**[34] 3350 6-8-9 67 ... NeilBrown(3) 8 — 52
(B Ellison) *hld up: hdwy on ins whn nt clr run over 2f out: swtchd lft over 1f out: kpt on fnl f: no imp* **6/5**[1]
0004 **5** nk **Bourse (IRE)**[5] 4313 4-8-12 55 ... (b) DuranFentiman 2 — 51
(A G Foster) *t.k.h: in tch tl rdn and one pce fr 2f out* **14/1**
-000 **6** hd **Jamieson Gold (IRE)**[25] 3653 6-8-12 60 ... (p) TonyHamilton 5 — 51
(Miss L A Perratt) *w ldr: rdn over 2f out: sn one pce* **40/1**
0146 **7** 4½ **King Of Legend (IRE)**[13] 4034 5-8-10 55 ... (t) IJBrennan(7) 6 — 46
(A G Foster) *t.k.h: hld up: effrt over 2f out: edgd rt and sn wknd* **16/1**
41-0 **8** ¾ **Zennerman (IRE)**[19] 3851 6-8-9 62 ... KellyHarrison(3) 3 — 39
(W M Brisbourne) *t.k.h: trckd ldrs tl edgd rt and wknd over 1f out* **9/2**[2]
6040 **9** 5 **Ducal Regancy Duke**[4] 4347 5-9-0 32 ow2 ... (v) DNolan 10 — 30
(C J Teague) *trckd ldrs to 2f out: sn rdn and wknd* **100/1**
006- **10** 3¾ **Smart Pick**[32] 5045 6-8-2 45 ... DeanHeslop(5) 1 — 15
(Mrs L Williamson) *midfield on outside: struggling over 2f out: sn wknd* **100/1**

1m 52.67s (-2.03) **Going Correction** -0.225s/f (Firm) — **10** Ran SP% **117.6**
Speed ratings (Par 101): **100,98,96,94,94 94,90,89,85,81**
toteswingers: 1&2 £5.90, 1&3 £12.20, 2&3 £11.50 CSF £51.92 TOTE £9.50: £2.30, £2.10, £2.40; EX 67.00.The winner was bought by Paul Murphy for £11,000.
Owner Alan Macleod **Bred** C J Hill **Trained** Cartmel, Cumbria

FOCUS
A low-grade seller with the favourite meeting traffic problems and the winner coming from last to first. The form looks sound enough.

4466 TOTESWINGER H'CAP — 7f 30y
8:20 (8:21) (Class 5) (0-70,68) 3-Y-O+ — **£3,238** (£963; £481; £240) **Stalls** High

Form — RPR
-003 **1** **Morocchius (USA)**[24] 3683 4-8-6 **51** ... (p) BMcHugh(5) 11 — 62
(Miss J A Camacho) *hld up in midfield: rdn over 2f out: hdwy and swtchd lft over 1f out: edgd rt and kpt on wl fnl f to ld nr fin* **8/1**
5645 **2** nk **Zabeel Tower**[4] 4346 6-9-12 **66** ... (p) TonyHamilton 7 — 76
(R Allan) *hld up in tch: hdwy to ld appr fnl f: kpt on: hdd cl home* **10/3**[1]
3441 **3** 1 **Kargan (IRE)**[25] 3655 4-9-9 **63** ... GrahamGibbons 10 — 70
(A G Foster) *hld up: rdn over 2f out: effrt over 1f out: r.o ins fnl f* **4/1**[2]
0331 **4** 3 **Nufoudh (IRE)**[24] 3683 5-8-13 **56** ... KellyHarrison(3) 1 — 55
(Miss Tracy Waggott) *w ldr: led over 2f out to appr fnl f: sn no ex* **14/1**
0540 **5** hd **Sands Of Barra (IRE)**[19] 3851 6-8-10 **55** ... AmyRyan(5) 6 — 54
(I W McInnes) *midfield: drvn over 2f out: kpt on fnl f: no imp* **14/1**
-236 **6** ¾ **Finsbury**[10] 4134 6-9-7 **61** ... DanielTudhope 8 — 58
(J S Goldie) *hld up: pushed along over 2f out: no imp fr over 1f out* **4/1**[2]
2023 **7** 3½ **Liberty Trail (IRE)**[30] 3480 3-9-2 **68** ... (b[1]) GaryBartley(5) 4 — 52
(I Semple) *led to over 2f out: rallied and ev ch over 1f out: wknd ent fnl f* **16/1**
0505 **8** ½ **Boss Hog**[10] 4140 4-8-10 **50** ... PJMcDonald 5 — 36
(P T Midgley) *hld up: rdn over 2f out: nvr on terms* **12/1**
0021 **9** ¾ **Only A Splash**[12] 4105 5-8-12 **52** ... SilvestreDeSousa 3 — 36
(Mrs R A Carr) *t.k.h: trckd ldrs tl rdn and wknd over 1f out* **7/1**[3]
-000 **10** 3½ **Shunkawakhan (IRE)**[25] 3655 6-9-3 **60** ... NeilBrown(3) 9 — 34
(Miss L A Perratt) *hld up: drvn over 2f out: sn btn* **50/1**
0-00 **11** 10 **Forrest Star**[35] 3296 4-8-4 **49** ... PatrickDonaghy(5) 2 — —
(Miss L A Perratt) *prom: rdn over 2f out: hung lft and sn wknd* **100/1**

1m 28.1s (-2.20) **Going Correction** -0.225s/f (Firm)
WFA 3 from 4yo+ 7lb — **11** Ran SP% **116.5**
Speed ratings (Par 103): **103,102,101,98,97 97,93,92,91,87 76**
toteswingers: 1&2 £10.60, 1&3 £12.00, 2&3 £5.80 CSF £34.46 CT £124.61 TOTE £11.40: £2.90, £1.80, £1.70; EX 43.30.
Owner Lee Bolingbroke Currie & Partners **Bred** E And D Enterprises **Trained** Norton, N Yorks
■ Stewards' Enquiry : Graham Gibbons one-day ban: careless riding (Aug 13)
B McHugh four-day ban: excessive use of the whip (Aug 13-16)

FOCUS
A modest 49-66 handicap run at a strong pace. Solid form for the grade.

4467 BEST HORSERACING ON SKY CHANNEL 432 H'CAP — 5f
8:50 (8:51) (Class 6) (0-65,71) 3-Y-0+ — **£2,266** (£674; £337; £168) **Stalls** Low

Form — RPR
1212 **1** **Ingleby Star (IRE)**[6] 4283 4-9-12 **71** 6ex ... (p) GaryBartley(5) 2 — 79
(N Wilson) *trckd ldrs: led over 1f out: hrd pressed ins fnl f: hld on wl* **7/4**[1]
0435 **2** nk **Angelofthenorth**[8] 4192 7-8-3 **46** oh1 ... KellyHarrison(3) 9 — 53
(C J Teague) *towards rr: hdwy to dispute ld ins fnl f: kpt on: jst hld* **7/1**
0104 **3** 1½ **Princess Charlmane (IRE)**[8] 4192 6-8-13 **53** ... (p) DNolan 5 — 55
(C J Teague) *led to over 1f out: kpt on same pce ins fnl f* **12/1**
4114 **4** ½ **Rocketball (IRE)**[27] 3570 4-9-6 **65** ... DeanHeslop(5) 3 — 65
(Mrs L Williamson) *prom: drvn 2f out: nt qckn fnl f* **9/4**[2]
4244 **5** ¾ **Dubai To Barnsley**[13] 4036 4-8-13 **53** ... DuranFentiman 6 — 50
(D A Nolan) *trckd ldrs: effrt over 1f out: n.m.r ins fnl f: one pce* **9/1**
0-00 **6** 2½ **Barley Bree (IRE)**[26] 3611 4-8-6 **46** ... SilvestreDeSousa 4 — 34
(Mrs A Duffield) *towards rr: drvn 1/2-way: sme hdwy over 1f out: no imp and eased ins fnl f* **13/2**[3]
0506 **7** 2½ **Blazing Heights**[17] 3909 6-9-4 **58** ... DanielTudhope 8 — 37
(J S Goldie) *bhd: drvn 1/2-way: nvr able to chal* **9/1**
0006 **8** ½ **Mr Rooney (IRE)**[41] 3111 6-7-13 **46** ... CharlotteKerton(7) 7 — 23
(A Berry) *towards rr: struggling 1/2-way: nvr on terms* **25/1**
0-00 **9** 4½ **Town And Gown**[10] 4136 4-8-7 **47** ... PJMcDonald 1 — 8
(J S Goldie) *rrd s: nvr on terms* **40/1**

59.80 secs (-0.60) **Going Correction** 0.0s/f (Good) — **9** Ran SP% **126.9**
Speed ratings (Par 101): **104,103,101,100,99 95,91,90,83**
toteswingers: 1&2 £5.00, 1&3 £5.00, 2&3 £12.10 CSF £16.99 CT £126.04 TOTE £2.90: £1.30, £2.10, £3.20; EX 20.20 Place 6: £118.22, Place 5: £75.25.
Owner Renaissance Racing **Bred** Pat Cosgrove **Trained** Flaxton, N Yorks

FOCUS
A 46-71 sprint handicap. The time was good for the grade and the form is sound.
Dubai To Barnsley Official explanation: jockey said gelding was denied a clear run
Town And Gown Official explanation: jockey said filly reared as the stalls opened
T/Plt: £208.70 to a £1 stake. Pool: £50,627.09. 177.08 winning tickets. T/Qpdt: £36.90 to a £1 stake. Pool: £6,264.70. 125.50 winning tickets. RY

4061 NOTTINGHAM (L-H)
Thursday, July 30

OFFICIAL GOING: Heavy
Wind: Light against Weather: Heavy rain clearing prior to race 1, becoming brighter

4468 EBF MANNY BERNSTEIN MAIDEN FILLIES' STKS — 6f 15y
2:05 (2:06) (Class 5) 2-Y-O — **£3,885** (£1,156; £577; £288) **Stalls** High

Form — RPR
0 **1** **Fairy Promises (USA)**[19] 3858 2-9-0 0 ... RobertWinston 1 — 75+
(Pat Eddery) *racd alone in centre: mde all: shkn up over 1f out: styd on wl* **13/2**[3]
2 3 **Bintalwaadi** 2-9-0 0 ... DO'Donohoe 7 — 66+
(E A L Dunlop) *racd stands' side: s.i.s: sn prom: chsd wnr over 2f out: rdn over 1f out: edgd lft and styd on same pce fnl f* **9/1**
52 **3** 13 **Gundaroo**[19] 3858 2-9-0 0 ... ShaneKelly 11 — 27
(J L Dunlop) *racd stands' side: chsd wnr tl rdn and edgd lft over 2f out: sn wknd* **4/9**[1]
4 hd **Casey's Rebel (IRE)** 2-9-0 0 ... JerryO'Dwyer 6 — 26
(M G Quinlan) *s.s and wnt lft s: hdwy 1/2-way: rdn: edgd lft and wknd over 2f out* **40/1**
5 5 **Gracelightening** 2-8-11 0 ... FrederikTylicki(3) 9 — 11
(Paul Green) *racd stands' side: sn pushed along and prom: wknd 1/2-way* **11/2**[2]

1m 21.34s (6.44) **Going Correction** +0.65s/f (Yiel) — **5** Ran SP% **110.4**
Speed ratings (Par 91): **83,79,61,61,54**
CSF £54.00 TOTE £6.90: £2.70, £3.30; EX 26.10.
Owner K Abdulla **Bred** Millsec Limited **Trained** Nether Winchendon, Bucks

FOCUS
Two came well clear in this opening fillies' maiden, which was hit by eight non-runners owing to the bad ground. The favourite flopped and the first two came clear. Not an easy race to rate.

NOTEBOOK
Fairy Promises(USA), well beaten in a fast-ground maiden over C&D on debut, raced alone in the centre of the course and always looked in control from 2f out. She seemed to handle the ground, but there is no question she will be just as effective on a better surface and there should be more to come. (op 10-1 tchd 12-1)
Bintalwaadi, a half-sister to a 1m2f winner in Italy, is by Barathea and showed promise on this debut. She was clear of the rest and should benefit from a seventh furlong in time. (op 9-2 tchd 11-1)
Gundaroo, runner-up in a C&D maiden last time, was nowhere near as effective in this heavy ground and failed to run her race, just holding on for third. This was hugely disappointing, but she probably deserves another chance and may fare better in nurseries. (op 1-2 tchd 2-5)
Casey's Rebel(IRE), half-sister to a couple of 1m winners, was soon outpaced and should fare better on quicker ground. (tchd 33-1)
Gracelightening, a daughter of Reset representing an in-form yard, showed little and was quickly beaten. (op 7-1 tchd 5-1)

4469 MANNY BERNSTEIN FREEPHONE 0800 821821 H'CAP — 5f 13y
2:40 (2:40) (Class 5) (0-75,72) 3-Y-0+ — **£2,590** (£770; £385; £192) **Stalls** High

Form — RPR
3642 **1** **Jilly Why (IRE)**[6] 4281 8-8-10 **60** ... (b) FrederikTylicki(3) 2 — 73
(Paul Green) *mid-div: hdwy to chse ldr 1/2-way: rdn to ld over 1f out: r.o* **10/3**[2]
3032 **2** 2¾ **Cape Royal**[6] 4268 9-9-6 **70** ... (bt) KevinGhunowa(3) 6 — 73
(J M Bradley) *led: rdn and hdd over 1f out: styd on same pce* **7/1**
1533 **3** 3¼ **Weet A Surprise**[6] 4283 4-8-6 **60** ... (v) AlexEdwards(7) 10 — 51
(J W Unett) *prom: outpcd over 3f out: hung lft and r.o ins fnl f* **11/1**

0142 **4** *1 ¼* **Top Bid**[7] 4225 5-8-11 **61**..(b) KellyHarrison(3) 3 48
(T D Easterby) *rrd s: bhd: hdwy and edgd rt 1/2-way: sn rdn: styd on same pce fnl f* **3/1**[1]
0126 **5** *1 ¼* **Flying Applause**[7] 4225 4-9-6 **70**....................(bt) RussellKennemore(3) 8 52
(S R Bowring) *chsd ldrs: outpcd 3f out: n.d after* **12/1**
0353 **6** *nk* **Green Park (IRE)**[2] 4399 6-9-11 **72**..............................(b) DNolan 9 53
(D Carroll) *hld up: rdn 3f out: n.d* **4/1**[3]
2226 **7** *1 ¾* **Northern Empire (IRE)**[16] 3945 6-9-4 **65**......................(p) ChrisCatlin 5 40
(F Jordan) *chsd ldrs: rdn and wknd over 1f out* **40/1**
3225 **8** *½* **Tartatartufata**[19] 3860 7-9-5 **66**..............................(b[1]) PaulMulrennan 7 39
(J G Given) *chsd ldrs: rdn 1/2-way: wknd over 1f out* **9/1**
4501 **9** *1 ¼* **Rough Rock (IRE)**[9] 4182 4-8-10 **57** 6ex..................... JerryO'Dwyer 12 26
(C A Dwyer) *sn pushed along in rr: no ch fr 1/2-way* **20/1**
0163 **10** *½* **Dragon Flame (IRE)**[12] 4099 6-9-11 **72**.......................... ShaneKelly 11 39
(M Quinn) *chsd ldrs: rdn over 3f out: wknd 1/2-way* **16/1**

63.80 secs (2.80) **Going Correction** +0.65s/f (Yiel) **10** Ran SP% **119.7**
Speed ratings (Par 103): **103,98,93,91,89 88,86,85,83,82**
toteswingers: 1&2 £11.20, 1&3 £14.50, 2&3 £6.90 CSF £27.95 CT £240.40 TOTE £4.30: £1.40, £2.60, £4.40; EX 31.80.
Owner Paul Green (Oaklea) **Bred** K And Mrs Cullen **Trained** Lydiate, Merseyside

FOCUS
The main action took place down the centre of the track here and Jilly Why ultimately got well on top of the front-running Cape Royal. The form is rated around the runner-up.
Top Bid Official explanation: jockey said gelding was slowly away

4470 MANNY BERNSTEIN CREDIT BETTING H'CAP — 2m 9y
3:15 (3:15) (Class 6) (0-60,62) 3-Y-O **£2,047** (£604; £302) **Stalls** Low

Form RPR
0062 **1** **Winterbrook King**[2] 4397 3-8-4 **49** ow3....................... MarcHalford(3) 8 64
(J R Best) *hld up: hdwy over 2f out: bmpd and led over 1f out: sn rdn: styd on wl* **14/1**
0431 **2** *3 ¼* **Strikemaster (IRE)**[10] 4142 3-9-1 **62** 6ex..................... LanceBetts(5) 11 73
(B Ellison) *s.i.s: hld up: hdwy over 3f out: led 2f out: sn rdn: hung lft and hdd: no ex fnl f* **11/8**[1]
-022 **3** *17* **Kidson (USA)**[10] 4142 3-8-4 **51**.............................. MatthewDavies(5) 7 42
(George Baker) *hld up: hdwy over 3f out: led over 2f out: sn rdn and hdd: wkng whn hung rt fr over 1f out* **7/2**[2]
0-00 **4** *8* **Highams Park (IRE)**[66] 2323 3-8-4 **46** oh1...................... SaleemGolam 6 27
(J G Portman) *prom: rdn over 3f out: wknd over 2f out* **100/1**
-041 **5** *nk* **Seminal Moment**[9] 4175 3-8-11 **56** 6ex.................. FrederikTylicki(3) 14 37
(J G Given) *chsd ldr tl led 4f out: rdn and hdd over 2f out: sn wknd* **13/2**[3]
3003 **6** *4 ½* **Dark Oasis**[10] 4142 3-8-4 **53**............................. AndrewHeffernan(7) 13 28
(M C Chapman) *hld up: hdwy over 3f out: sn rdn: hung lft and wknd over 2f out* **16/1**
-331 **7** *8* **Astroleo**[16] 3954 3-8-11 **53**.. NickyMackay 4 19
(M H Tompkins) *chsd ldrs tl rdn and wknd over 2f out* **15/2**
-024 **8** *14* **Fongoli**[11] 2635 3-8-10 **52**..(v) StephenDonohoe 5 1
(B G Powell) *s.i.s: sn pushed along and prom: led over 13f out: rdn and hdd 4f out: wknd over 2f out* **11/1**
-000 **9** *6* **Cooper Island Kid (USA)**[9] 4178 3-8-13 **55**..................... ShaneKelly 1 —
(P W D'Arcy) *led: hdd over 13f out: chsd ldrs: rdn over 3f out: sn wknd* **100/1**
0255 **10** *12* **Pure Crystal**[12] 2866 3-8-10 **52**.................................(b) JerryO'Dwyer 9 —
(M G Quinlan) *hld up: reminders over 6f out: wknd over 3f out* **20/1**

3m 48.92s (18.62) **Going Correction** +0.90s/f (Soft) **10** Ran SP% **117.0**
Speed ratings (Par 98): **89,87,78,74,74 72,68,61,58,52**
toteswingers: 1&2 £7.90, 1&3 £11.70, 2&3 £2.80 CSF £33.63 CT £87.59 TOTE £18.40: £3.50, £1.40, £1.50; EX 51.40.
Owner Fielden Racing **Bred** Mrs S C Greenfield **Trained** Hucking, Kent

FOCUS
The front pair came a long way clear in this staying handicap. Surprising improvement from the winner but the form seems sound enough.

4471 MANNY BERNSTEIN EARLY PRICES H'CAP — 1m 2f 50y
3:50 (3:50) (Class 4) (0-85,82) 3-Y-O+ **£7,771** (£2,312; £1,155; £577) **Stalls** Low

Form RPR
-106 **1** **Puzzlemaster**[66] 2341 3-9-1 **79**.................................... JerryO'Dwyer 3 89
(M Botti) *a.p: chsd ldr over 2f out: rdn to ld over 1f out: sn hung lft: styd on wl: eased ins fnl f* **4/1**[3]
0030 **2** *6* **Best Prospect (IRE)**[14] 4003 7-9-12 **80**.........................(t) ShaneKelly 8 79
(M Dods) *hld up: hdwy over 2f out: trckd ldr on bit over 1f out: rdn and wknd ins fnl f* **10/3**[2]
3 **3** *1* **Persian Peril**[5] 4315 5-10-0 **82**.................................... RobertWinston 7 79
(G A Swinbank) *trckd ldr: racd keenly: rdn over 2f out: sn outpcd* **6/4**[1]
6200 **4** *¾* **Hurlingham**[14] 4003 5-9-9 **77**.....................................(b) PaulMulrennan 5 73
(M W Easterby) *led: rdn and hdd over 1f out: wknd fnl f* **7/1**
3420 **5** *nk* **Rosbay (IRE)**[20] 3826 5-9-13 **81**................................ StephenDonohoe 1 76
(T D Easterby) *hld up: outpcd over 3f out: swtchd rt and r.o ins fnl f: nt trble ldrs* **6/1**

2m 19.56s (7.86) **Going Correction** +0.90s/f (Soft)
WFA 3 from 4yo+ 10lb **5** Ran SP% **109.9**
Speed ratings (Par 105): **104,99,98,97,97**
CSF £17.17 TOTE £5.50: £2.90, £1.50; EX 18.50.
Owner Norcroft Park Stud **Bred** Norcroft Park Stud **Trained** Newmarket, Suffolk

FOCUS
Nearly half of those originally declared were non-runners in this modest handicap. With the favourite disappointing it is hard to know how literally to take this form.

4472 MANNY BERNSTEIN DEBIT CARD BETTING MEDIAN AUCTION MAIDEN STKS — 1m 75y
4:25 (4:27) (Class 6) 3-4-Y-O **£2,729** (£806; £403) **Stalls** Low

Form RPR
0560 **1** **Illusive Spirit (IRE)**[49] 2845 3-9-3 68....................... RobertHavlin 1 70
(J H M Gosden) *chsd ldrs: led over 2f out: rdn and edgd rt over 1f out: r.o* **7/2**[3]
0 **2** *¾* **Lilly Royal (IRE)**[7] 4246 3-8-12 0............................... NeilChalmers 11 63
(B Palling) *s.i.s: hld up: hdwy over 2f out: rdn over 1f out: chsd wnr and eded lft ins fnl f: r.o* **33/1**
60- **3** *2* **Group Leader (IRE)**[330] 5609 3-9-3 0....................... AdrianMcCarthy 10 64
(J R Jenkins) *chsd ldrs: rdn and ev ch over 2f out: nt clr run and swtchd lft ins fnl f: styd on same pce* **50/1**
5 **4** *1* **Landofthefourones (USA)**[13] 4057 3-9-3 0.................. GeorgeBaker 5 61
(D R Lanigan) *prom: racd keenly: rdn 1/2-way: no ex ins fnl f* **5/4**[1]
6-66 **5** *9* **Chateauneuf (IRE)**[17] 3921 3-8-12 58........................ RobertWinston 4 36
(B W Hills) *sn led: hdd over 2f out: wknd fnl f* **9/2**
6 **6** *3* **Herecomethegirls** 3-8-12 0.. ChrisCatlin 3 29
(M L W Bell) *s.i.s: hld up: rdn and wknd over 2f out* **3/1**[2]
0- **7** *4* **Largem**[331] 5590 3-9-3 0... StephenDonohoe 9 25
(J R Jenkins) *s.i.s: hld up: rdn over 2f out: sn hung lft and wknd* **16/1**
00- **8** *21* **Mythical Thrill**[287] 6759 3-9-3 0................................. PaulMulrennan 8 —
(J G Given) *chsd ldr: rdn over 3f out: wknd over 2f out* **33/1**

1m 55.95s (10.35) **Going Correction** +0.90s/f (Soft) **8** Ran SP% **123.6**
Speed ratings (Par 101): **84,83,81,80,71 68,64,43**
toteswingers: 1&2 £19.90, 1&3 £14.20, 2&3 £19.30 CSF £108.42 TOTE £6.00: £1.20, £4.30, £5.80; EX 106.50.
Owner G Strawbridge & Ptnrs **Bred** Bryan Ryan **Trained** Newmarket, Suffolk

FOCUS
This was a weak maiden, with the favourite disappointing. It has been rated around the winner.

4473 HEDGE WITH MANNY BERNSTEIN H'CAP — 1m 75y
5:00 (5:01) (Class 5) (0-75,75) 3-Y-O+ **£2,590** (£770; £385; £192) **Stalls** Low

Form RPR
2104 **1** **Focail Eile**[26] 3637 4-9-5 **66**................................ StephenDonohoe 12 77
(J Ryan) *hld up: hdwy u.p and hung lft over 1f out: styd on to ld wl ins fnl f* **16/1**
5451 **2** *¾* **Kindest**[12] 4079 3-9-4 **73**.. GeorgeBaker 8 80+
(C F Wall) *hld up in tch: led over 2f out: rdn and edgd lft over 1f out: hdd and unable qck wl ins fnl f* **2/1**[2]
3000 **3** *3* **Marning Star**[6] 4262 4-9-7 **68**..................................(t) SaleemGolam 10 70
(Ian Williams) *chsd ldrs: rdn and ev ch over 2f out: no ex fnl f* **50/1**
43 **4** *¾* **Full Victory (IRE)**[13] 4064 7-9-7 **68**........................... RobertHavlin 5 68
(R A Farrant) *hld up: hdwy over 2f out: sn rdn and hung lft: styd on same pce fnl f* **8/1**
0-04 **5** *¾* **Ela Gorrie Mou**[10] 4151 3-7-10 **56** oh9.......... Louis-PhilippeBeuzelin(5) 7 53
(T T Clement) *chsd ldrs: rdn and ev ch over 2f out: wknd ins fnl f* **15/8**[1]
0161 **6** *5* **West End Lad**[19] 3863 6-9-11 **75**..................(b) RussellKennemore(3) 1 62
(S R Bowring) *led: rdn and hdd over 2f out: wknd over 1f out* **10/1**
-000 **7** *5* **Stand In Flames**[21] 3789 4-9-1 **65**........................ FrederikTylicki(3) 9 41
(Pat Eddery) *hld up: hdwy over 3f out: rdn and ev ch over 2f out: hung lft and wknd over 1f out* **12/1**
605 **8** *14* **Addiena**[20] 3800 5-9-1 **62**.. NeilChalmers 2 5
(B Palling) *hld up: rdn over 2f out: sn wknd* **20/1**
6-15 **9** *14* **Gassin**[26] 3624 3-9-3 **72**.. ChrisCatlin 11 —
(M L W Bell) *s.i.s: sn prom: rdn and ev ch over 2f out: sn wknd* **10/1**
445 **10** *¾* **Olive Green (USA)**[48] 2885 3-9-5 **74**......................... RobertWinston 4 —
(Pat Eddery) *dwlt: hld up: racd keenly: rdn over 3f out: sn wknd and eased* **6/1**[3]

1m 52.1s (6.50) **Going Correction** +0.90s/f (Soft)
WFA 3 from 4yo+ 8lb **10** Ran SP% **132.0**
Speed ratings (Par 103): **103,102,99,98,97 92,87,73,59,59**
toteswingers: 1&2 £8.00, 1&3 £31.10, 2&3 £20.50 CSF £54.73 CT £1733.00 TOTE £20.70: £4.00, £1.50, £9.90; EX 76.30 Place 6: £861.57 Place 5: £103.79 .
Owner Cathal Fegan **Bred** D Robb **Trained** Newmarket, Suffolk

FOCUS
This was a moderate handicap. The form is rated through the placed horses.
Addiena Official explanation: jockey said mare hung right in straight
T/Plt: £1,202.30 to a £1 stake. Pool: £43,234.79. 26.25 winning tickets. T/Qpdt: £76.20 to a £1 stake. Pool: £3,533.10. 34.30 winning tickets. CR

4474 - 4477a (Foreign Racing) - See Raceform Interactive

4219 BATH (L-H)
Friday, July 31

OFFICIAL GOING: Good (good to firm in places; 7.7)
Wind: Light, across. Weather: Light rain

4478 HIGOS INSURANCE CHIPPING SODBURY MAIDEN AUCTION STKS — 5f 161y
6:05 (6:06) (Class 5) 2-Y-O **£3,885** (£1,156; £577; £288) **Stalls** Centre

Form RPR
1 **Wisecraic** 2-8-11 0.. RichardKingscote 6 80+
(Tom Dascombe) *bhd: pushed along over 2f out: hdwy over 1f out: led jst ins fnl f: r.o wl* **11/10**[1]
264 **2** *3 ¾* **Emma Jean Lass (IRE)**[8] 4221 2-8-6 0.......................... LukeMorris 8 59
(J S Moore) *chsd ldrs: rdn and ev ch 1f out: one pce* **11/1**
0 **3** *2 ¾* **Primo De Vida (IRE)**[8] 4219 2-9-2 0................................ AdamKirby 2 60
(R M Beckett) *led: rdn and hdd over 1f out: no ex ins fnl f* **25/1**
4 **4** *3* **Little Brazilien**[95] 1569 2-8-4 0................................ JosedeSouza 10 38
(P F I Cole) *w ldrs: led over 1f out tl jst ins fnl f: wknd* **5/1**[3]
0 **5** *1 ½* **Madam Isshe**[7] 4265 2-8-4 0...................................... NickyMackay 9 33+
(M S Saunders) *sn outpcd: kpt on fnl f: n.d* **80/1**
24 **6** *hd* **Cool Valentine**[22] 3767 2-8-11 0.................................. ChrisCatlin 5 40
(A M Balding) *w ldrs: rdn and ev ch over 1f out: wknd fnl f* **11/4**[2]
00 **7** *1* **Dudley**[39] 3218 2-8-4 0.. MatthewDavies(5) 1 34
(J G Portman) *prom: rdn over 2f out: wknd over 1f out* **66/1**
0 **8** *shd* **Moonraker's Choice (IRE)**[28] 3576 2-8-11 0.................. PatDobbs 7 36
(R Hannon) *bhd: rdn over 2f out: sn struggling* **10/1**
0 **9** *9* **Catchanova (IRE)**[25] 3692 2-8-11 0.......................... StephenCarson 4 7
(Eve Johnson Houghton) *s.i.s: sn hld up in tch: wknd wl over 1f out* **33/1**
10 *12* **Sputnik One (IRE)** 2-8-9 0...................................... SimonWhitworth 11 —
(J S Moore) *s.s: outpcd* **50/1**

1m 11.13s (-0.07) **Going Correction** -0.075s/f (Good) **10** Ran SP% **119.9**
Speed ratings (Par 94): **97,92,88,84,82 82,80,80,68,52**
toteswingers: 1&2 £5.30, 1&3 Not won, 2&3 £28.60. CSF £15.49 TOTE £2.00: £1.10, £2.80, £5.10; EX 17.30.
Owner L Mann, S Briddon, N Attenborough **Bred** Darley **Trained** Lambourn, Berks

FOCUS
No strength in depth to this race but the winner made an impressive start and should improve for the experience. The runner-up is the best guide to the level.

NOTEBOOK
Wisecraic ◆, a 14,000 euros purchase, looks to possess enough ability to go up several grades after an impressive winning debut, which looked anything but certain at halfway. Despite being backed to the exclusion of any other runner, he was immature, and was bustled along at halfway, following a tardy start. However, he found a fine turn of foot when pulled to the outside and won with plenty in hand. There are plenty of winners in his pedigree and his dam, Belle Genius won the Group One Moyglare Stud Stakes over 7f. Despite his sire producing generally speedy horses, he will benefit for a 6f trip. He has been given a Mill Reef entry and is also in the Tattersalls Ireland Sales Stakes at Fairyhouse on August 22, both over that trip. (op 11-8)
Emma Jean Lass(IRE), rated only 68, was staying on and produced a career best. Nurseries should give her a chance of getting off the mark. (tchd 12-1)
Primo De Vida(IRE) was much sharper than on his debut and will win a small race judged on this, although 6f might be the limit at present. (op 20-1)

Little Brazilien ran in the same style as on her debut, and races too keenly. She would be interesting over a little further, if she settles better. (op 4-1)

Madam Isshe ran a fine race and left her debut run behind. She looked sure to finish well behind at halfway, but picked up in some style late on and would be interesting over a full 6f. (op 66-1)

Cool Valentine was up with the pace, but doesn't appear to have a finishing kick. He is now qualified for nurseries. (op 3-1)

Dudley, a cheap purchase, has some ability and is another that can try his hand in nurseries.

4479 OAK UNDERWRITING (S) STKS — 5f 161y

6:35 (6:37) (Class 5) 3-Y-0+ — **£3,238** (£963; £481; £240) **Stalls** Centre

Form — RPR

0400 **1** **Cwmni**[27] 3632 3-8-1 47 ... DavidProbert(3) 4 — 53+
(B Palling) *hld up towards rr: swtchd rt over 2f out: nt clr run: rdn and hdwy over 1f out: str run to ld nr fin* — **33/1**

0 **2** ½ **Compton Classic**[9] 4203 7-9-5 70 ... (p) GeorgeBaker 17 — 62
(J R Boyle) *hld up in mid-div: smooth prog over 2f out: led over 1f out: sn rdn and edgd lft: hdd nr fin* — **5/1**[2]

6664 **3** ¾ **Rockfield Lodge (IRE)**[7] 4268 4-8-11 57 ... KevinGhunowa(3) 6 — 55
(R A Harris) *a.p: rdn and ev ch over 1f out: swtchd rt ins fnl f: kpt on* — **6/1**[3]

2225 **4** ½ **Outer Hebrides**[10] 4183 8-9-0 55 ... (v) SophieDoyle(5) 10 — 58
(J M Bradley) *towards rr: hdwy over 2f out: rdn 1f out: kpt on towards fin* — **12/1**

3422 **5** 2¼ **Duke Of Milan (IRE)**[17] 3948 6-9-0 58 ... (v) RichardKingscote 11 — 45
(Tom Dascombe) *hld up towards rr: swtchd rt and hdwy wl over 1f out: rdn ent fnl f: one pce* — **3/1**[1]

3005 **6** 1½ **Mr Forthright**[15] 3994 5-9-0 46 ... (p) LukeMorris 13 — 40
(J M Bradley) *s.i.s: in rr: pushed along and hdwy on outside 2f out: rdn and no further prog fnl f* — **12/1**

1305 **7** 1½ **Bertie Southstreet**[9] 4203 6-9-5 63 ... (p) PatDobbs 8 — 40
(Karen George) *a.p: led 3f out: rdn and hdd over 1f out: sn wknd* — **7/1**

006 **8** 4½ **Brazilian Brush (IRE)**[27] 3632 4-9-0 44 ... (t) AdamKirby 7 — 20
(J M Bradley) *prom: rdn 2f out: wkng whn n.m.r over 1f out* — **25/1**

0020 **9** ¾ **Supreme Speedster**[31] 3471 5-9-0 49 ... SimonWhitworth 15 — 17
(A G Newcombe) *hld up in rr: rdn wl over 1f out: nvr nr ldrs* — **20/1**

1-00 **10** ¾ **Sky High Kid (IRE)**[8] 4223 3-8-9 63 ... TPO'Shea 9 — 14
(M R Channon) *hld up in mid-div: nt clr run briefly over 1f out: sn lost pl* — **8/1**

5000 **11** 6 **Marina Walk**[28] 3580 3-8-4 51 ... NickyMackay 2 — —
(H Morrison) *w ldr: rdn over 2f out: wknd wl over 1f out* — **16/1**

0-00 **12** 1¼ **Pappoose**[23] 3743 4-8-9 45 ... ChrisCatlin 1 — —
(H Candy) *led: hdd 3f out: wknd 2f out* — **16/1**

056- **13** 1½ **Our Wee Girl (IRE)**[223] 7738 3-8-4 59 ... RichardThomas 5 — —
(Miss Tor Sturgis) *awkward leaving stalls: sn mid-div: wknd over 2f out* — **14/1**

0000 **14** hd **Bilboa**[27] 3632 4-8-11 41 ... (p) RussellKennemore(3) 12 — —
(J M Bradley) *prom: ev ch wl over 1f out: wknd qckly* — **66/1**

0300 **15** 20 **Hamaasy**[101] 1438 8-9-0 45 ... TravisBlock 3 — —
(G A Ham) *a in rr: eased whn no ch over 1f out* — **40/1**

1m 11.0s (-0.20) **Going Correction** -0.075s/f (Good)
WFA 3 from 4yo+ 5lb — **15** Ran SP% **128.9**
Speed ratings (Par 103): **98,97,96,95,92 90,88,82,81,80 72,71,69,68,42**
toteswingers: 1&2 £39.50, 1&3 £39.50, 2&3 £7.30. CSF £196.13 TOTE £47.80: £9.80, £2.40, £2.60; EX 1406.30.There was no bid for the winner. Compton Classic was the subject to a friendly claim.

Owner Flying Eight Partnership **Bred** Exors Of The Late Mrs M M Palling **Trained** Tredodridge, Vale Of Glamorgan

FOCUS
A surprise result in a low-level race full of disappointing horses. The fourth is the best guide to the form.

Cwmni Official explanation: trainer's rep said, regarding the improved form shown, filly got upset in the preliminaries at Nottingham

Sky High Kid(IRE) Official explanation: jockey said gelding was denied a clear run

Our Wee Girl(IRE) Official explanation: vet said filly lost a right fore shoe

4480 HIGOS INSURANCE WELLS MEDIAN AUCTION MAIDEN STKS — 1m 3f 144y

7:10 (7:14) (Class 5) 3-5-Y-0 — **£3,367** (£1,002; £500; £250) **Stalls** Low

Form — RPR

1 **Sheshali (IRE)**[52] 5499 5-9-10 0 ... GeorgeBaker 2 — 74+
(Evan Williams) *hld up towards rr: pushed along and hdwy over 3f out: rdn over 2f out: led ins fnl f: styd on* — **9/2**[2]

6 **2** 1¼ **Reset City**[15] 4022 3-8-4 0 ... KevinGhunowa(3) 11 — 67
(A B Haynes) *hld up in tch: hrd rdn to ld 2f out: hdd ins fnl f: nt qckn cl home* — **25/1**

2223 **3** 3¼ **Astrodiva**[21] 3827 3-8-7 73 ... NickyMackay 13 — 61
(M H Tompkins) *sn chsng ldr: ev ch 2f out: sn rdn: one pce fnl f* — **6/5**[1]

465 **4** hd **Sana Abel (IRE)**[39] 3214 3-8-7 72 ... TPO'Shea 6 — 61
(M A Jarvis) *s.i.s: hld up in rr: rdn over 3f out: sme hdwy over 2f out: styd on ins fnl f* — **5/1**[3]

0 **5** 1¾ **Double Whammy**[57] 2640 3-8-12 0 ... LukeMorris 8 — 63
(Jamie Poulton) *s.i.s: hld up towards rr: pushed along 3f out: rdn and styd on fr over 1f out: n.d* — **16/1**

00 **6** 3 **La Polka**[64] 2395 3-8-4 0 ... DavidProbert(3) 9 — 53
(H Morrison) *hld up in mid-div: lost pl over 4f out: n.d after* — **12/1**

5 **7** 2½ **Cecily Parsley**[29] 3538 3-8-7 0 ... TravisBlock 12 — 49
(H Morrison) *led: hdd 2f out: wknd over 1f out* — **12/1**

50 **8** 6 **Whiterocks**[11] 4145 3-8-12 0 ... RichardKingscote 7 — 44
(M R Channon) *prom: pushed along over 3f out: rdn and wknd over 2f out* — **50/1**

9 4 **Recurring Dream** 3-8-7 0 ... PatDobbs 5 — 32
(P J Hobbs) *s.i.s: in rr: rdn and short-lived effrt over 2f out* — **14/1**

0060 **10** 41 **Bright Wire (IRE)**[36] 3303 3-8-12 48 ... AdamKirby 10 — —
(M Madgwick) *prom: pushed along briefly over 8f out and over 6f out: rdn and wknd wl over 2f out* — **80/1**

2m 30.64s (0.04) **Going Correction** +0.10s/f (Good)
WFA 3 from 5yo 12lb — **10** Ran SP% **115.3**
Speed ratings (Par 103): **103,102,100,99,98 96,95,91,88,61**
toteswingers: 1&2 £10.50, 1&3 £1.70, 2&3 £8.20. CSF £101.44 TOTE £5.70: £1.60, £4.30, £1.10; EX 161.60.

Owner Edwards, Swinnerton, Babb, Howell **Bred** His Highness The Aga Khan's Studs S C **Trained** Llancarfan, Vale Of Glamorgan

FOCUS
Three were withdrawn at the start, due to bad behaviour at the stalls, before the start of this weak maiden. There is little solid to go on with the sixth and seventh arguably the best guides.

4481 HIGOS INSURANCE H'CAP — 1m 2f 46y

7:40 (7:42) (Class 4) (0-80,78) 3-Y-0 — **£6,476** (£1,927; £963; £481) **Stalls** Low

Form — RPR

30-1 **1** **Point Of Light**[6] 4320 3-8-3 60 ... ChrisCatlin 4 — 72+
(Sir Mark Prescott) *led early: chsd ldr over 7f out: pushed along over 4f out: led over 2f out: rdn over 1f out: drvn out* — **7/4**[1]

3010 **2** ¾ **Rumble Of Thunder (IRE)**[63] 2432 3-9-4 78 ... DavidProbert(3) 7 — 88
(D W P Arbuthnot) *chsd ldr: led 8f out tl over 2f out: rdn and swtchd rt over 1f out: rallied ins fnl f: styd on* — **8/1**

01 **3** 1¼ **Dangerous Midge (USA)**[33] 3425 3-9-6 77 ... NickyMackay 1 — 85
(B J Meehan) *hld up: prog on ins 7f out: pushed along over 2f out: rdn wl over 1f out: styd on one pce ins fnl f* — **3/1**[2]

2104 **4** nk **Dreamwalk (IRE)**[36] 3307 3-9-7 78 ... (v[1]) GeorgeBaker 10 — 85
(R M Beckett) *s.i.s: hld up in rr: stdy prog over 4f out: rdn wl over 1f out: styd on one pce ins fnl f* — **25/1**

6201 **5** 1½ **Ethics Girl (IRE)**[21] 3803 3-8-13 70 ... PatDobbs 6 — 74
(John Berry) *hld up in mid-div: lost pl over 6f out: hdwy over 2f out: rdn over 1f out: one pce* — **10/1**

-004 **6** ½ **Master Fong (IRE)**[14] 4058 3-9-3 74 ... WilliamBuick 9 — 77
(B W Hills) *hld up in tch: lost pl over 5f out: c wd st: sme prog on outside over 1f out: rdn and no imp ins fnl f* — **6/1**[3]

00-5 **7** 2¾ **Marju King (IRE)**[48] 2930 3-9-2 73 ... TravisBlock 3 — 70
(W S Kittow) *hld up in tch: lost pl bnd over 4f out: rdn and rallied on outside over 2f out: wknd ins fnl f* — **8/1**

1-05 **8** 27 **Spiritual Treasure (USA)**[32] 3466 3-9-0 71 ... (t) AdamKirby 8 — 14
(M A Magnusson) *sn led: hdd 8f out: rdn and wknd over 2f out: eased whn no ch fnl f* — **40/1**

321 **9** 4½ **Voortrekker**[39] 3228 3-9-2 73 ... TPO'Shea 5 — —
(D J Coakley) *hld up: hdwy over 7f out: lost pl 5f out: lost tch fnl 2f* — **9/1**

2m 9.70s (-1.30) **Going Correction** +0.10s/f (Good) — **9** Ran SP% **123.2**
Speed ratings (Par 102): **109,108,107,107,105 105,103,81,78**
toteswingers: 1&2 £4.90, 1&3 £2.00, 2&3 £17.00. CSF £18.46 CT £42.90 TOTE £2.80: £1.40, £2.40, £1.70; EX 21.00.

Owner Syndicate 2007 **Bred** Watership Down Stud **Trained** Newmarket, Suffolk

FOCUS
A fair handicap with a winner who looks well handicapped at present. He can do better with the third running to his previous form.

Voortrekker Official explanation: jockey said gelding was never travelling

4482 OAK FILLIES' H'CAP — 1m 5y

8:15 (8:16) (Class 4) (0-80,80) 3-Y-0+ **£6,308** (£1,888; £944; £472; £235) **Stalls** Low

Form — RPR

2352 **1** **Perfect Class**[16] 3981 3-8-8 66 ... LukeMorris 10 — 73
(C G Cox) *stdd s: hld up towards rr: pushed along over 2f out: hdwy over 1f out: rdn and squeezed through to ld wl ins fnl f: drvn out* — **6/1**[3]

4011 **2** hd **Desert Kiss**[20] 3843 4-9-13 77 ... AdamKirby 8 — 85
(W R Swinburn) *hld up in tch: rdn on outside over 1f out: ev ch ins fnl f: r.o* — **7/2**[1]

031 **3** 1¾ **Flying Valentino**[34] 3408 5-9-13 77 ... PatDobbs 1 — 81
(Ian Williams) *a.p: rdn to ld jst over 1f out: hdd wl ins fnl f: no ex: jst hld on for 3rd* — **7/1**

-026 **4** nse **Chatanoogachoochoo**[7] 4266 4-9-1 65 ... RichardKingscote 4 — 69
(M Hill) *hld up in rr: rdn over 1f out: str run wl ins fnl f: jst failed to take 3rd* — **14/1**

3215 **5** ½ **Sparkling Crystal (IRE)**[20] 3870 3-9-3 75 ... ChrisCatlin 7 — 76
(B W Hills) *led: hdd over 4f out: pushed along over 2f out: rdn over 1f out: one pce ins fnl f* — **8/1**

1215 **6** ½ **You've Been Mowed**[27] 3637 3-8-3 64 ... DavidProbert(3) 5 — 63
(R J Price) *a.p: chsd ldr over 2f out: rdn over 1f out: ev ch ins fnl f: one pce* — **15/2**

610 **7** ¾ **So Blissful (IRE)**[36] 3320 3-9-4 76 ... WilliamBuick 3 — 78+
(T G Mills) *hld up in rr: pushed along over 3f out: rdn and hdwy 1f out: styng on whn nt clr run wl ins fnl f* — **7/1**

3431 **8** 1¼ **Evening Sunset (GER)**[15] 4013 3-8-7 65 ... TPO'Shea 9 — 60
(M R Channon) *chsd ldr: led over 4f out: rdn and hdd jst over 1f out: wknd wl ins fnl f* — **5/1**[2]

5342 **9** ¾ **Sunceleb (IRE)**[26] 3660 3-9-0 72 ... TravisBlock 2 — 65
(H Morrison) *hld up towards rr: pushed along over 3f out: rdn over 1f out: nt clr run briefly ins fnl f: n.d* — **14/1**

1m 40.62s (-0.18) **Going Correction** +0.10s/f (Good)
WFA 3 from 4yo+ 8lb — **9** Ran SP% **114.4**
Speed ratings (Par 102): **104,103,102,102,101 101,100,99,98**
toteswingers: 1&2 £4.90, 1&3 £9.50, 2&3 £6.60. CSF £27.02 CT £150.78 TOTE £6.30: £2.30, £1.90, £2.60; EX 22.30.

Owner The Perfect Partnership **Bred** Cheveley Park Stud Ltd **Trained** Lambourn, Berks

FOCUS
A tight fillies' handicap which produced a close finish. The runner-up is improving and the third is rated to form.

So Blissful(IRE) Official explanation: jockey said filly was denied a clear run

4483 HIGOS INSURANCE CORSHAM H'CAP — 5f 11y

8:45 (8:45) (Class 5) (0-75,75) 3-Y-0 — **£3,885** (£1,156; £577; £288) **Stalls** Centre

Form — RPR

3156 **1** **Speak The Truth (IRE)**[30] 3506 3-8-8 67 ... (p) MatthewDavies(5) 5 — 71
(J R Boyle) *hld up and bhd: pushed along over 2f out: rdn and hdwy on outside over 1f out: r.o to ld nr fin* — **11/1**

2062 **2** ½ **Avrilo**[8] 4223 3-8-2 56 oh8 ... NickyMackay 6 — 58
(M S Saunders) *chsd ldrs: rdn to ld 1f out: hdd nr fin* — **11/1**

5-40 **3** 1¾ **Battle**[85] 1814 3-9-3 71 ... TravisBlock 4 — 67
(H Morrison) *a.p: ev ch over 1f out: rdn fnl f: no ex towards fin* — **15/2**[3]

3303 **4** 1 **Riflessione**[16] 3989 3-9-2 73 ... (p) KevinGhunowa(3) 2 — 65
(R A Harris) *chsd ldrs: pushed along over 2f out: rdn over 1f out: one pce* — **11/1**

1131 **5** 1½ **Mythical Blue (IRE)**[8] 4223 3-9-0 71 6ex ... DavidProbert(3) 10 — 58
(J M Bradley) *half-rrd s: sn rcvrd: w ldr over 3f out: led 2f out: rdn and hdd 1f out: wknd wl ins fnl f* — **5/4**[1]

0330 **6** 3¼ **Evelyn May (IRE)**[11] 4148 3-9-7 75 ... ChrisCatlin 1 — 50
(B W Hills) *wnt lft s: led: hdd 2f out: rdn and wknd over 1f out* — **8/1**

0526 **7** *1 ¾* **Mazzola**[1] 4454 3-9-2 **70**.. TPO'Shea 3 39
(M R Channon) *s.i.s whn rdr sltly late removing blindfold: hld up in rr: pushed along over 2f out: rdn over 1f out: no rspnse* **7/2**[2]
62.01 secs (-0.49) **Going Correction** -0.075s/f (Good) **7** Ran SP% **114.5**
Speed ratings (Par 100): **100,99,96,94,92 87,84**
toteswingers: 1&2 £13.60, 1&3 £12.80, 2&3 £14.70. CSF £118.55 CT £965.77 TOTE £8.00: £3.10, £5.40; EX 170.50 Place 6 £465.10, Place 5 £238.65..
Owner Inside Track Racing Club **Bred** Gerard Mulligan **Trained** Epsom, Surrey

FOCUS
A fair sprint handicap with the runner-up performing above herself from 8lb out of the handicap. The winner is the best guide.
Mythical Blue(IRE) Official explanation: jockey said gelding reared as the stalls opened and ran too free
T/Plt: £828.60 to a £1 stake. Pool: £41,830.22. 36.85 winning tickets. T/Qpdt: £117.30 to a £1 stake. Pool: £5,106.31. 32.20 winning tickets. KH

4455 GOODWOOD (R-H)
Friday, July 31

OFFICIAL GOING: Good (8.2)
Top bend rail out 4yards increasing distances by 8yards.
Wind: medium, across Weather: bright

4484 COUTTS GLORIOUS STKS (GROUP 3) 1m 4f
2:10 (2:10) (Class 1) 4-Y-0+
£39,739 (£15,064; £7,539; £3,759; £1,883; £945) **Stalls** Low

Form RPR
-436 **1** **Illustrious Blue**[41] 3139 6-9-0 107.. JimCrowley 5 114
(W J Knight) *stdd s: hld up in last pl: plld out and rdn 3f out: chsd ldr over 1f out: led ins fnl f: rdn out* **9/1**

-012 **2** *nk* **Warringah**[20] 3874 4-9-0 105.. RyanMoore 6 114
(Sir Michael Stoute) *swtg: led: pushed along over 3f out: rdn ent fnl 2f: battled on wl tl hdd and no ex ins fnl f* **7/2**[1]

2050 **3** *1 ¾* **Halicarnassus (IRE)**[6] 4329 5-9-0 110.. TPO'Shea 10 111
(M R Channon) *t.k.h: chsd ldrs: pushed along over 4f out: rdn over 3f out: edgd lft and one pce ent fnl f* **12/1**

4201 **4** *1* **Drumfire (IRE)**[3] 4404 5-9-0 107.. JimmyFortune 3 110
(M Johnston) *hld up towards rr: effrt on inner 3f out: nt clr run wl over 1f out tl swtchd lft over 1f out: styd on fnl f: unable to rch ldrs* **4/1**[2]

0043 **5** *3* **Unleashed (IRE)**[40] 3190 4-9-0 102.. TPQueally 1 105
(H R A Cecil) *lw: dwlt: sn in tch in midfield: effrt to chse ldr 3f out tl over 1f out: wknd u.p ent fnl f* **16/1**

-003 **6** *1* **Basaltico (IRE)**[155] 699 5-9-0 110.. C-PLemaire 7 103
(L M Cumani) *lw: hld up in tch in midfield: lost pl and towards rr over 3f out: rdn and no hdwy whn nt clr run over 2f out: swtchd lft over 1f out: nvr threatened ldrs* **9/2**[3]

0-50 **7** *½* **Muhannak (IRE)**[125] 1013 5-9-0 112.. GeorgeBaker 9 102
(R M Beckett) *hld up in midfield early: dropped towards rr over 5f out: hdwy and rdn 3f out: keeping on same pce whn edgd rt u.p over 1f out: no ch w ldrs after* **14/1**

5065 **8** *19* **Indian Days**[22] 3781 4-9-0 105.. RichardHughes 4 72
(J G Given) *hld up towards rr: hdwy into midfield 5f out: rdn and struggling over 2f out: no ch and eased ins fnl f* **15/2**

0261 **9** *2 ¼* **Crime Scene (IRE)**[13] 4090 6-9-0 113.. LDettori 2 68
(Saeed Bin Suroor) *chsd ldr: rdn over 3f out: drvn and lost 2nd 3f out: wkng whn hmpd over 1f out: wl btn and eased ins fnl f* **4/1**[2]

2m 37.22s (-1.18) **Going Correction** -0.025s/f (Good) **9** Ran SP% **122.4**
Speed ratings (Par 113): **102,101,100,99,97 97,96,84,82**
toteswingers: 1&2 £8.60, 1&3 £22.00, 2&3 £9.20 CSF £43.14 TOTE £10.60: £2.00, £1.80, £3.80; EX 38.90 Trifecta £430.50 Pool: £1629.02 - 2.80 winning units..
Owner Mr & Mrs I H Bendelow **Bred** B J And Mrs Crangle **Trained** Patching, W Sussex
■ Stewards' Enquiry : Jimmy Fortune two-day ban: careless riding (Aug 14-15)

FOCUS
This was the race's second year as a Group 3 event and it was certainly an open heat, though in all truth probably no better than a Listed contest. They went just a sensible gallop. Course specialist Illustrious Blue produced a slight personal best.

NOTEBOOK
Illustrious Blue, something of a course specialist, ultimately came out on top. Although without a win in well over two years coming into this, he had been running with credit this season, finishing sixth in the Group 2 Hardwicke Stakes latest, and he capitalised on this drop back down in grade. Held up through the early stages, he was full of running with half a mile to run and closed rapidly on the leaders approaching the two-pole. He took a while to master the game runner-up, but got there in the end and six of his eight career wins have now come as this venue. The 6yo, who was registering a first victory over 1m4f, was also returning to something like his best and his next start may come in the Bosphorus Cup in Turkey next month. (op 12-1 tchd 8-1)
Warringah, a well-beaten 13th in the St Leger on his one previous venture into Group company, has definitely improved this term, being narrowly denied in a 1m6f Listed handicap at York last time, having earlier bolted up off a mark of 91, and he took another step forward here. A horse who seems to enjoy bowling along, allowing him a chance to put his fine, long stride to good use, he gradually wound up the tempo and had all bar the winner in trouble with a furlong to run, but was unable to quicken on close home. There is more to come from this scopey sort who should benefit from a step back up in trip. (tchd 3-1)
Halicarnassus(IRE), another who goes well at this track, was out again quickly having run poorly at York just six days earlier and this was more of a true reflection of what he is capable of. He stayed on willingly back in third, having been one of the first under pressure, and deserves to get his head in front again. (op 16-1)
Drumfire(IRE), back up to Group company on this quick reappearance (yard completed same double with Crosspeace in 2006), stays this trip and he ran on having been switched over a furlong out, but never looked in with a shout of winning. He has returned to his best form. (tchd 5-1 and 11-2 in places)
Unleashed(IRE), one place behind Drumfire when third in a Listed prize at Pontefract last time, held every chance from two out, but could find no extra from a furlong out and faded.
Basaltico(IRE), who ran a couple of fair races for Herman Brown in Dubai earlier in the year, looked an interesting contender on this debut for Luca Cumani and was backed beforehand. However, he was a beaten horse with three to run and could only plug on at the one pace having briefly been short of room. He may do better next time, especially if stepped back up in trip. (op 6-1 tchd 7-1 and 15-2 in places)
Muhannak(IRE), winner of last season's Breeders' Cup Marathon, had been off since finishing well beaten in the Dubai World Cup, and never got into it. (op 12-1 tchd 11-1 in places)
Indian Days was disappointing considering he ran so well in the Princess Of Wales´s Stakes last time. (op 10-1)
Crime Scene(IRE), back to form when winning a 1m2f Listed contest at Newbury last time, was already beaten when hampered and clearly dislikes this track, failing to beat a rival in three visits here now. His trainer later reported the course did not suit. Official explanation: trainer said gelding was unsuited by the track (tchd 11-2 and 6-1 in places)

4485 ROLF GROUP STEWARDS' SPRINT STKS (H'CAP) 6f
2:45 (2:45) (Class 2) 3-Y-0+
£18,693 (£5,598; £2,799; £1,401; £699; £351) **Stalls** Low

Form RPR
1210 **1** **Johannes (IRE)**[21] 3825 6-9-0 **82**.. TonyHamilton 22 96
(R A Fahey) *racd on far side: chsd ldrs: rdn to ld overall over 1f out: styd on strly* **12/1**

41 **2** *1 ½* **Northern Dare (IRE)**[14] 4069 5-9-8 **90** 3ex........................ JimCrowley 19 100
(D Nicholls) *racd on far side: towards rr: hdwy u.p 2f out: chsd wnr ins fnl f: r.o but nvr gng to rch wnr: 2nd of 9 in gp* **7/1**[3]

30 **3** *1 ½* **Jaconet (USA)**[28] 3582 4-8-13 **86**........................(b) DeanHeslop(5) 24 91
(T D Barron) *racd on far side: overall ldr tl over 1f out: kpt on same pce fnl f: 3rd of 9 in gp* **33/1**

2200 **4** *shd* **Vhujon (IRE)**[1] 4461 4-9-6 **88**.. RichardHughes 12 93+
(P D Evans) *on toes: racd on stands' side: stdd and swtchd lft s: bhd: hdwy and rdn over 1f out: hung rt but r.o wl fnl f: nt rch ldrs: 1st of 13 in gp* **50/1**

2002 **5** *¾* **Harrison George (IRE)**[5] 4353 4-9-8 **90**........................ RyanMoore 3 93+
(R A Fahey) *racd on stands' side: bhd: nt clr run over 2f out: hdwy u.p over 1f out: r.o wl fnl f: nt rch ldrs: 2nd of 13 in gp* **6/1**[1]

5020 **6** *1* **Bond City (IRE)**[6] 4330 7-9-4 **89**........................ DavidProbert(3) 23 89
(G R Oldroyd) *swtg: racd on far side: bhd: rdn over 2f out: styd on u.p fnl f: nvr trbld ldrs: 4th of 9 in gp* **33/1**

5036 **7** *nk* **Phantom Whisper**[21] 3802 6-9-2 **87**........................ JamesMillman(3) 21 86
(B R Millman) *racd on far side: in tch: rdn ent fnl 2f: kpt on same pce and no imp after: 5th of 9 in gp* **20/1**

6046 **8** *nk* **Peter Island (FR)**[8] 4232 6-9-2 **84**........................(b) AlanMunro 10 82
(J Gallagher) *lw; racd on stands' side: led that gp: rdn 2f out: pressing wnr over 1f out: wknd fnl 100yds: 3rd of 13 in gp* **40/1**

1330 **9** *½* **Artistic License (IRE)**[7] 4273 4-9-1 **83**........................ TonyCulhane 7 79
(M R Channon) *racd on stands' side: bhd: hdwy over 1f out: hung rt but kpt on wl fnl f: nvr trbld ldrs: 4th of 13 in gp* **33/1**

5054 **10** *nse* **Indian Trail**[1] 4461 9-9-6 **88**..(v) LDettori 8 84
(D Nicholls) *racd on stands' side: stdd and swtchd lft s: hld up towards rr: hdwy 1/2-way: chsd ldr gng wl 2f out: rdn ent fnl f: sn edgd rt and fnd nil: 5th of 13 in gp* **10/1**

4361 **11** *½* **Spirit Of Sharjah (IRE)**[8] 4236 4-9-5 **87** 3ex........................ TPO'Shea 13 82
(Miss J Feilden) *on toes: racd on stands' side: swtchd lft after s: towards rr: hdwy to chse ldrs 1/2-way: rdn 2f out: no imp fnl f: 6th of 13 in gp* **20/1**

0000 **12** *hd* **Van Bossed (CAN)**[5] 4341 4-9-4 **86**........................ FrancisNorton 15 80
(D Nicholls) *racd on far side: bhd: hdwy u.p over 1f out: kpt on fnl f: nvr trbld ldrs: 6th of 9 in gp* **16/1**

206 **13** *1 ¼* **Pawan (IRE)**[36] 3318 9-9-1 **88**........................(b) AnnStokell(5) 2 78
(Miss A Stokell) *racd on stands' side: towards rr: rdn and effrt 2f out: kpt on same pce: 7th of 13 in gp* **33/1**

3222 **14** *¾* **Everymanforhimself (IRE)**[38] 3236 5-9-10 **92**........................(b) NCallan 17 80
(K A Ryan) *lw: racd on far side: in tch: rdn over 2f out: drvn and wknd over 1f out: 7th of 9 in gp* **12/1**

3425 **15** *1* **Parisian Pyramid (IRE)**[23] 3747 3-9-9 **95**........................ AdrianTNicholls 4 81
(D Nicholls) *lw: racd on stands' side: chsd ldr tl 2f out: sn hung rt u.p: wknd fnl f: 8th of 13 in gp* **8/1**

0351 **16** *nk* **Sunrise Safari (IRE)**[5] 4353 6-9-0 **85** 3ex........................(v) FrederikTylicki(3) 14 69
(R A Fahey) *taken down early: racd on stands' side: swtchd lft after s: chsd ldrs: rdn over 2f out: wknd over 1f out: 9th of 13 in gp* **13/2**[2]

102 **17** *½* **Filligree (IRE)**[35] 3347 4-9-3 **85**.. JimmyFortune 5 68
(Rae Guest) *racd on stands' side: hld up in rr: pushed along and swtchd rt jst over 2f out: rdn and edgd lft 2f out: no prog: 10th of 13 in gp* **12/1**

0050 **18** *¾* **Little Pete (IRE)**[1] 4461 4-9-6 **88**..(v) LPKeniry 6 69
(A M Balding) *racd on stands' side: a towards rr: swtchd rt and rdn jst over 2f out: sn rdn and no prog: 11th of 13 in gp* **25/1**

5600 **19** *nk* **Methaaly (IRE)**[1] 4461 6-8-12 **80**........................(be) RichardMullen 11 60
(M Mullineaux) *racd on stands' side: awkward leaving stalls and slowly away: sn rcvrd and chsng ldrs: drvn over 2f out: wknd wl over 1f out: 12th of 13 in gp* **40/1**

1630 **20** *1 ¼* **Fault**[48] 2928 3-9-7 **93**..(t) MickyFenton 18 70
(Stef Liddiard) *lw: racd on far side: chsd ldr: rdn 3f out: wknd u.p 2f out: wl btn ins fnl f: 8th of 9 in gp* **25/1**

0-05 **21** *1 ¼* **Hurricane Spirit (IRE)**[21] 3795 5-9-6 **88**........................ SteveDrowne 9 60
(J R Best) *lw: racd on stands' side: a towards rr: n.d: 13th of 13 in gp* **25/1**

-000 **22** *3 ¼* **Burnwynd Boy**[7] 4273 4-9-3 **85**.. GrahamGibbons 20 47
(D Nicholls) *racd on far side: chsd ldrs tl 1/2-way: wknd wl over 1f out: wl bhd and eased ins fnl f: 9th of 9 in gp* **40/1**

1m 10.61s (-1.59) **Going Correction** -0.025s/f (Good)
WFA 3 from 4yo+ 5lb **22** Ran SP% **131.4**
Speed ratings (Par 109): **109,107,105,104,103 102,102,101,101,101 100,100,98,97,96 95,95,94,93,91 90,85**
toteswingers: 1&2 £22.10, 1&3 £382.50, 2&3 £103.40 CSF £83.36 CT £1690.59 TOTE £16.80: £4.20, £2.20, £9.20, £10.60; EX 145.10 Trifecta £2075.60 Part won. Pool: £2804.92 - 0.70 winning units..
Owner John Nicholls Ltd/David Kilburn **Bred** Blue Bloodstock Limited **Trained** Musley Bank, N Yorks

FOCUS
A consolation race for those who missed the cut in the Stewards´ Cup. The field split into two, with the first three home coming from the far-side group, and racing as close as possible to either rail proved a significant advantage. The winner is rated close to his best old form.

NOTEBOOK
Johannes(IRE) was back over his ideal trip and, although the ground was not as quick as he would ideally like, he had a favourable high draw and bagged a good position tracking the leader on the far rail, before going to the front approaching the final furlong and keeping onwell to win a shade comfortably. He was smart at two but struggled with the handicapper afterwards, and a return to form has coincided with a switch to the Fahey stable. Even after being reassessed for this he should remain competitive, but he undoubtedly benefited from a good draw here. (op 14-1 tchd 16-1 in places)
Northern Dare(IRE) came here at the top of his game having won at Pontefract last time out andran well considering he raced more towards the outside of the far-side group. Softer ground would have suited him even better. (tchd 15-2 and 8-1 in places)
Jaconet(USA) showed good speed to take them along on the far side and didn´t fall away after being headed. An easy 6f is well within her stamina and she boasts a decent strike-rate, but the handicapper probably just about has her measure for the time being.

The Form Book, Raceform Ltd, Compton, RG20 6NL

Vhujon(IRE) is a hold-up type who likes the leaders to go off fast and set it up for him. He had the race run to suit but still did very well as he was drawn in the middle of the track, raced in the stands´-side group and hung right across the track from two furlongs out, so that in the end he finished on the outer of the far-side group. He can win off his current mark.

Harrison George(IRE) had a good draw in stall three and was held up right out the back, but crucially he bagged the stands´-side rail. He didn´t come off it throughout the race and really motored home inside the final furlong and a half, showing its benefit. (op 7-1 tchd 8-1 in places)

Bond City(IRE) was held up towards the back of the far-side group and challenged out wide, which was not the best place to be. Softer ground would have been more to his liking. (tchd 40-1 in places)

Phantom Whisper didn´t get the clearest of runs on the far-side rail but kept on well once in the clear. He´s well handicapped on his form from this time last year, and is already due to be dropped another 2lb, but whether he showed enough to be of interest next time is open to question. (op 16-1)

Peter Island(FR) is a speedy front-runner and had no trouble getting over from stall ten to make the running on the stands´ side. With the rail to help, he took some overhauling, but he´s probably more effective in a slightly lower grade. (op 33-1)

Artistic License(IRE) didn´t run too badly considering she was held up towards the outside of the stands´-side group and was carried right by the hanging Vhujon. She finished up racing up the middle, which was no advantage.

Indian Trail, making a quick reappearance after finishing fourth in the 5f handicap here the previous day, travelled strongly in behind the pace on the stands´ side but found little under pressure. He´s better over 5f these days, and quick ground is essential, too. (tchd 11-1)

Spirit Of Sharjah(IRE) was drawn in the middle and raced on the wide outside of the stands´-side group, so had his excuses. (op 22-1 tchd 25-1)

Parisian Pyramid(IRE), one of only two three-year-olds in the field, wasn´t able to lead on the stands´ side and tended to hang right. The handicapper looks to be keeping up with his progress. Official explanation: jockey said gelding hung right throughout (op 9-1)

Sunrise Safari(IRE) couldn´t repeat his effort at Pontefract five days earlier and may have had too much use made of him, or maybe the track didn´t suit. (op 15-2 tchd 8-1 in places)

Little Pete(IRE) Official explanation: jockey said gelding hung right

4486 TOTESPORT MILE (HERITAGE H'CAP) 1m

3:25 (3:26) (Class 2) 3-Y-O+

£93,465 (£27,990; £13,995; £7,005; £3,495; £1,755) **Stalls** High

Form				RPR
6030	**1**		**Laa Rayb (USA)**[21] 3818 5-9-6 **105**.....(b1) JimmyFortune 8 (M Johnston) *slowly away: towards rr: swtchd to rails and gd hdwy fr 4f out: swtchd lft over 2f out: sn drvn to ld: clr ent fnl f: kpt on strly* **25/1**	116
1L40	**2**	2 1/4	**Spectait**[27] 3628 7-8-9 **94**..... JimCrowley 16 (Jonjo O'Neill) *mid-div: struggling to hold pl 4f out: hdwy u.p over 2f out: styd on to chse wnr jst ins fnl f but a hld* **9/1**	100
0003	**3**	3/4	**Docofthebay (IRE)**[58] 2606 5-8-12 **97**.....(p) RyanMoore 3 (J A Osborne) *s.i.s: bhd: squeezed up on rails over 3f out: hdwy over 2f out: sn rdn: styd on fnl f* **22/1**	101+
2402	**4**	shd	**Webbow (IRE)**[20] 3872 7-8-0 **90**..... Louis-PhilippeBeuzelin(5) 12 (N Tinkler) *lw: hld up towards rr: hdwy over 2f out: rdn whn nt clr run over 1f out: fin strly: jst failed to snatch 3rd* **10/1**	94
6460	**5**	nk	**Lovelace**[44] 3014 5-9-10 **109**..... JamieSpencer 4 (M Johnston) *hld up bhd: hdwy on rails jst over 2f out: rdn whn stopped briefly over 1f out: styd on fnl f* **14/1**	112+
-441	**6**	1	**Acrostic**[27] 3639 4-9-1 **100**..... C-PLemaire 6 (L M Cumani) *lw: hld up towards rr: rdn in center 2f out: styd on wl fnl f: nrst fin* **13/2[2]**	101+
3112	**7**	nk	**Cloudy Start**[22] 3783 3-9-1 **108**..... TPQueally 21 (H R A Cecil) *chsd ldrs: rdn to ld over 2f out: sn hdd: wknd ins fnl f* **6/1[1]**	106
3100	**8**	2 3/4	**Extraterrestrial**[27] 3639 5-8-10 **98**..... FrederikTylicki(3) 20 (R A Fahey) *lw: mid-div: hdwy over 3f out: effrt over 2f out: fdd ent fnl f* **8/1[3]**	92
2310	**9**	1/2	**Kavachi (IRE)**[44] 3014 6-8-6 **91**..... RichardMullen 19 (G L Moore) *s.i.s: sn mid-div: rdn to chse ldrs over 2f out: one pce fnl f* **10/1**	84
5/35	**10**	1 1/4	**Court Masterpiece**[34] 3398 9-9-8 **107**..... GrahamGibbons 10 (J J Quinn) *nvr bttr than mid-div* **20/1**	97
0100	**11**	1 1/4	**Tartan Gigha (IRE)**[20] 3872 4-8-9 **94**..... GregFairley 17 (M Johnston) *chsd ldrs: rdn and ev ch over 2f out: wknd over 1f out* **16/1**	81
24	**12**	3/4	**Huzzah (IRE)**[27] 3639 4-9-0 **99**..... MichaelHills 7 (B W Hills) *lw: hld up towards rr: rdn over 2f out: prog over 1f: no further imp ins fnl f* **16/1**	84
3010	**13**	3 1/2	**Horatio Carter**[6] 4297 4-8-8 **93**.....(p) NCallan 14 (K A Ryan) *in tch: effrt 3f out: wknd fnl f* **40/1**	70
0140	**14**	2 1/4	**Benandonner (USA)**[21] 3818 6-8-12 **97**..... TonyHamilton 13 (R A Fahey) *chsd ldrs: rdn over 3f out: wknd 2f out* **28/1**	69
4001	**15**	1	**Dubai's Touch**[21] 3796 5-8-8 **93** 3ex.....(b) RoystonFfrench 5 (M Johnston) *lw: a towards rr* **11/1**	63
0600	**16**	3/4	**Jack Junior (USA)**[18] 3928 5-8-9 **94**..... FrancisNorton 15 (D Nicholls) *lw: led: rdn and hdd over 2f out: wknd over 1f out* **50/1**	62
0220	**17**	2 3/4	**Crackdown (IRE)**[6] 4297 3-8-9 **102**..... AlanMunro 2 (M Johnston) *kpt wd tl jnd main gp after nrly 4f: mid-div: rdn and hdwy 3f out: wknd 2f out* **25/1**	62
0506	**18**	1/2	**Vitznau (IRE)**[29] 3536 5-9-3 **102**..... RichardHughes 22 (R Hannon) *lw: mid-div: hdwy 3f out: rdn 2f out: sn wknd* **16/1**	63
0064	**19**	2 3/4	**Joseph Henry**[21] 3818 7-8-10 **95**..... AdrianTNicholls 9 (D Nicholls) *prom: rdn and ev ch over 2f out: wknd over 1f out* **33/1**	49

1m 37.34s (-2.56) **Going Correction** -0.025s/f (Good)

WFA 3 from 4yo+ 8lb **19** Ran **SP%** **127.2**

Speed ratings (Par 109): **111,108,108,107,107 106,106,103,103,101 100,99,96,94,93 92,89,89,86**

toteswingers: 1&2 £74.00, 1&3 £39.40, 2&3 £50.50 CSF £224.51 CT £5125.98 TOTE £38.90: £7.60, £2.60, £4.20, £3.00; EX 537.60 Trifecta £3464.10 Part won. Pool: £4681.28 - 0.30 winning units..

Owner Sheikh Ahmed Al Maktoum **Bred** Darley **Trained** Middleham Moor, N Yorks

FOCUS

Traditionally the draw has played a huge role in deciding the result of this valuable handicap, with those berthed in the highest stalls holding a big advantage, but while the bare stats didn't hold up this year, the advantage of racing on the inside rail was once again highlighted. The pace was strong which suited those who had been ridden patiently. A solid renewal with few hard-luck stories.

NOTEBOOK

Laa Rayb(USA) had not been at his best this year but had slipped 12lb in the ratings as a result. Blinkered for the first time on this return to a mile, he had an ordinary draw in stall eight, but his rider settled him out the back and crossed over to the inside rail as soon as possible. As the field swung into the straight, he found those in front of him edging off the rail, providing him with a dream run to make up a few places with little effort. The only time he had to move off the rail was when switched out to pass the tiring leader, and in a flash he was past and back on the rail to finish his race strongly. He undoubtedly enjoyed the run of the race and got all the breaks, but it is not as if he wasn't worthy of respect on his best form, which the headgear clearly helped him recapture.

Spectait, who won this race back in 2006, ran well considering he was on and off the bridle for much of the way, got crowded and was eventually forced to challenge wide. He had no chance with the winner but ran a creditable race to beat the rest, and the Cambridgeshire was mentioned as his autumn target. (op 8-1 tchd 10-1 in places and 11-1 in a place)

Docofthebay(IRE), who didn't take part in the Hunt Cup after being unruly, had cheekpieces on for only the second time in his career. Poorly drawn in stall three, his rider dropped him out towards the rear and got over to the inside rail. The race was run to suit him with the leaders going off too quick, and the gaps did open up for him, but the winner had too many guns. He is clearly well handicapped on his best form but perhaps he's not up to performing quite at that level now. (op 25-1)

Webbow(IRE), who was officially 4lb well in at the weights, was towards the rear and looking for room two furlongs out. Denied a clear run again approaching the furlong marker, he finished well once in the clear, confirming his recent improvement. He has never been in better form. (op 11-1 tchd 12-1)

Lovelace, another drawn low and held up at the back of the field, was last turning into the straight, at which point his rider took him to the rail. In contrast to his stablemate Laa Rayb, though, the gaps didn't open up for him and he found himself trapped behind a horses until well inside the last. He did make up some late ground once in the clear but it was all far too late and it's fair to say he shaped better than his finishing position. (tchd 16-1)

Acrostic ◆ is one to take from the race as he was drawn low and ended up racing up racing wide throughout. He also had his challenge delayed by being stuck behind horses inside the final two furlongs, so in the circumstances he did very well to finish where he did. He remains one to be interested in for a big handicap. (op 8-1)

Cloudy Start, one of only two three-year-olds in the field, had a great draw but had a bit to prove back in handicap company off a mark of 108. In making the most of his draw and chasing the leader on the rail, though, he ended up going too fast early, and he paid for his efforts late on. That said, he did by far the best of the pace horses and rates better than his finishing position suggests. (op 7-1)

Extraterrestrial had a good draw and not too many excuses. Softer ground would have suited him, though. (tchd 9-1)

Kavachi(IRE), who didn't get much luck in running in the Hunt Cup, was a little disappointing as he had a good draw and, having avoided trouble, failed to find much off the bridle. (tchd 11-1)

Huzzah(IRE), fifth in this race last year from stall 16, wasn't as fortunate with the draw this time around. (op 18-1)

Crackdown(IRE) was stuck out wide throughout from his low draw and shouldn't be judged too harshly. (tchd 20-1 in places)

Vitznau(IRE) Official explanation: jockey said horse lost it's action

4487 RICHMOND STKS (GROUP 2) (C&G) 6f

4:00 (4:00) (Class 1) 2-Y-O

£45,416 (£17,216; £8,616; £4,296; £2,152; £1,080) **Stalls** Low

Form				RPR
11	**1**		**Dick Turpin (IRE)**[20] 3865 2-9-0 0..... RichardHughes 4 (R Hannon) *str: scope: lw: led for 2f: rdn to ld again 2f out: drvn ent fnl f: stormed clr fnl 100yds: r.o strly* **6/5[1]**	108+
21	**2**	3	**Buzzword**[18] 3920 2-9-0 0..... LDettori 1 (Saeed Bin Suroor) *str: swtg: in tch in midfield: edging rt looking for run whn bdly bmpd and lost pl over 1f out: hdwy on stands' rail ins fnl f: r.o wl to go 2nd last strides: no ch w wnr* **9/2[3]**	102+
0411	**3**	hd	**Stargaze (IRE)**[8] 4221 2-9-0 0..... WilliamBuick 9 (A M Balding) *prom: rdn and ev ch 2f out tl nt pce of wnr ins fnl f: lost 2nd last strides* **20/1**	96
52	**4**	1 3/4	**Lucky Like (FR)**[14] 4073 2-9-0 0..... FrancisNorton 10 (E J O'Neill) *t.k.h: hld up towards rr: hdwy and rdn 2f out: one pce and no imp ins fnl f* **33/1**	91
315	**5**	3/4	**Ghostwing**[22] 3779 2-9-0 0..... TonyHamilton 5 (R A Fahey) *chsd ldrs: shkn up 2f out: rdn and hld hd awkwardly over 1f out: outpcd fnl f* **20/1**	89
140	**6**	nk	**Nosedive**[22] 3779 2-9-0 0..... RyanMoore 8 (W J Haggas) *swtg: stdd s: hld up in rr: rdn 2f out: swtchd lft over 1f out: kpt on but nvr nr ldrs* **16/1**	88
14	**7**	nk	**Moran Gra (USA)**[45] 2993 2-9-0 0..... WMLordan 7 (Ms Joanna Morgan, Ire) *s.i.s: t.k.h: hld up towards rr: rdn over 2f out: nvr pce to threaten ldrs* **14/1**	87
223	**8**	hd	**Rakaan (IRE)**[45] 2993 2-9-0 0..... JamieSpencer 2 (B J Meehan) *stdd s: hld up towards rr: hdwy over 2f out: chsng ldrs whn edgd lft u.p and bmpd over 1f out: no prog after* **11/4[2]**	86
3115	**9**	3	**Bould Mover**[3] 4407 2-9-0 0..... GrahamGibbons 3 (R Curtis) *swtg: w ldr tl led after 2f: hdd 2f out: wknd u.p over 1f out* **25/1**	77

1m 11.31s (-0.89) **Going Correction** -0.025s/f (Good) **9** Ran **SP%** **119.2**

Speed ratings (Par 106): **104,100,99,97,96 96,95,95,91**

toteswingers: 1&2 £1.80, 1&3 £5.80, 2&3 £9.90 CSF £6.80 TOTE £2.00: £1.20, £1.60, £3.00; EX 8.10 Trifecta £53.80 Pool: £1913.36 - 26.30 winning units..

Owner John Manley **Bred** John McEnery **Trained** East Everleigh, Wilts

FOCUS

This isn't the race it used to be, recent winners going on to achieve very little, but Dick Turpin may be about to change that. Admittedly this wouldn't have been the strongest of Group 2's, especially in the absence of Showcasing, but the winner was impressive. Overall the race is rated close to recent averages.

NOTEBOOK

Dick Turpin(IRE) ◆ did it in most impressive fasion, going on again with 2f to run and powering clear inside the final 100 yards. Deeply impressive in winning both his maiden at Windsor and a novice event at Salisbury last time, this tall, scopey individual looks more than just a 2yo and will almost certainly benefit from another furlong, though whether he will have enough stamina to make it at the top level over 1m remains to be seen. Regardless, he looks a horse to keep on side and may well be given a short break now before reappearing in the big 7f sales race at the Curragh, a contest the yard won last year with Soul City. (op Evens tchd 5-4)

Buzzword, easy winner of a Windsor maiden and backed beforehand, was hampered by Rakaan when trying to come with a run and can be rated better than the bare form. He stayed on well inside the final furlong, having been switched back to the rail, and just managed to get up for second. A son of Pivotal, his dam was a 1m2f winner and he is obviously going to benefit from a rise in distance. (op 7-1)

Stargaze(IRE), on a hat-trick following two minor wins, narrowly scoring in a 5f novice event at Bath last time, was backed at large odds beforehand and showed bright speed widest of all. He couldn't race on with the winner, but stuck on best he could, just losing second close home, and clearly had no problem with the extra furlong. Genuine quick ground is thought to suit best and it will be the Mill Reef next. (op 33-1 tchd 16-1)

Lucky Like(FR) had run both races in France prior to this, finishing fifth in a Listed event for newcomers on debut before narrowly failing in 6f maiden last time, and he was far from disgraced on this first start in Britain, staying on again having been outpaced. He should find an ordinary maiden. (tchd 25-1)
Ghostwing, easy winner of an Ayr maiden who finished a well-beaten fifth behind Arcano in the July Stakes at Newmarket, didn't look overly happy under strong pressure and could only find the one pace. (op 25-1)
Nosedive, fourth in the Norfolk prior to disappointing on his first try at 6f in the July Stakes, was held up last of all and made a little late headway when switched right, but never looked like reaching a challenging position. (tchd 14-1)
Moran Gra(USA), fourth to Canford Cliffs at Ascot, wasn't the quickest away and then proceeded to race keen. He didn't pick up for pressure, keeping on at the just the one pace, and failed to confirm the promise he showed at Ascot. (op 12-1 tchd 16-1 and 18-1 in a place)
Rakaan(IRE), one place ahead of Moran Gra at the Royal meeting, was trying to stay on when short of room, but he made no real progress inside the final furlong and would have been no better than fourth anyway. Maybe connections should give him a confidence-boost in a maiden now. (op 10-3 tchd 7-2)
Bould Mover, fifth in the Molecomb three days earlier, showed bright early speed on the rail, but was readily brushed aside and weakened from a furlong out.

4488 RSA NURSERY STKS (H'CAP) 7f
4:35 (4:35) (Class 2) 2-Y-O £12,952 (£3,854; £1,926; £962) Stalls High

Form RPR

21 **1** **Black Snowflake (USA)**[28] 3571 2-9-2 **86** .... LDettori 11 93+
(Saeed Bin Suroor) *hld up towards rr: looking for run but n.m.r towards inner over 2f out: nt clr run and switching to outer over 1f out: stl plenty to do ent fnl f: str run to ld last strides* **7/2**[1]

421 **2** *nk* **Gunner Lindley (IRE)**[14] 4041 2-9-0 **84** .... MichaelHills 16 87+
(B W Hills) *t.k.h: hld up in tch: rdn and hdwy over 1f out: drvn to ld ins fnl f: hdd last strides* **8/1**[3]

1304 **3** *nk* **Raine's Cross**[20] 3865 2-9-7 **91** .... JimCrowley 10 93+
(P Winkworth) *str: lw: hld up in rr: looking for run but n.m.r over 2f out: nt clr run and switching to outer over 1f out: r.o strly fnl f: nt quite rch ldrs* **20/1**

421 **4** *3/4* **Contract Caterer (IRE)**[30] 3494 2-8-11 **81** .... JimmyFortune 19 81
(Pat Eddery) *lw: in tch: rdn and ev ch over 1f out tl wknd and lost 2 pls fnl 75yds* **9/2**[2]

212 **5** *hd* **Coloursoftheglen (IRE)**[7] 4271 2-8-8 **83**... Louis-PhilippeBeuzelin(5) 18 83
(Tom Dascombe) *hld up towards rr: hdwy on inner over 3f out: chsd ldrs and rdn 2f out: kpt on same pce u.p ins fnl f* **9/1**

13 **6** *1/2* **Jairzihno**[15] 4000 2-8-5 **78** .... MarcHalford(3) 2 76
(J R Best) *s.i.s: hld up bhd: hdwy on inner over 2f out: swtchd lft 1f out: chsng ldrs and swtchd rt ins fnl f: kpt on* **25/1**

316 **7** *nse* **The Human League**[22] 3782 2-9-2 **86** .... TonyCulhane 8 84
(M R Channon) *s.i.s: hld up in midfield: rdn and hdwy over 2f out: chsd ldrs 1f out: kpt on same pce u.p fnl 100yds* **16/1**

341 **8** *3/4* **Suffolk Punch (IRE)**[29] 3522 2-9-1 **85** .... LPKeniry 15 81
(A M Balding) *lw: t.k.h: hld up wl in tch: rdn to ld over 1f out: drvn and hdd ins fnl f: edgd lft u.p and wknd fnl 100yds* **8/1**[3]

10 **9** *1* **Marsh Warbler**[45] 2993 2-9-1 **85** .... RoystonFfrench 12 79
(M Johnston) *racd in midfield: pushed along 4f out: outpcd and towards rr 3f out: rdn 1f out: r.o but nvr pce to threaten ldrs* **14/1**

013 **10** *2* **Ingleby Spirit**[36] 3311 2-9-0 **87** .... FrederikTylicki(3) 1 76
(R A Fahey) *hld up in rr: rdn 3f out: hdwy on inner over 1f out: kpt on but nr nr ldrs* **28/1**

630 **11** *1/2* **Imperial Warrior**[18] 3920 2-8-6 **76** .... SteveDrowne 20 64
(H Morrison) *hld up in midfield: rdn and unable qck over 2f out: no prog after* **18/1**

003 **12** *1/2* **Avow (USA)**[13] 4080 2-8-5 **75** ....(b) AdrianMcCarthy 6 61
(J S Moore) *swtg: on toes: t.k.h: chsd ldrs tl wknd u.p over 1f out* **66/1**

3122 **13** *shd* **Tres Coronas (IRE)**[21] 3821 2-8-2 **77** .... DeanHeslop(5) 13 63
(T D Barron) *slowly itnto stride: hld up in midfield: hmpd and stmbld 5f out: rdn and hanging rt 2f out: no hdwy* **11/1**

2314 **14** *hd* **Rock Of Love (IRE)**[21] 3821 2-9-7 **91** .... GregFairley 17 77
(M Johnston) *chsd ldr tl led 5f out: drvn over 2f out: hdd over 1f out: wknd fnl f* **12/1**

3322 **15** *1 1/2* **Going French (IRE)**[10] 4163 2-7-12 **71** ow1........ KellyHarrison(3) 7 53
(R Curtis) *a in rr: rdn and no rspnse over 3f out* **40/1**

1005 **16** *1/2* **Flyinflyout**[15] 3993 2-8-5 **75** .... EdwardCreighton 9 65+
(M R Channon) *t.k.h: hld up in rr: rdn and edging rt looking for run over 2f out: sme hdwy but stl plenty to do whn bdly hmpd and snatched up 1f out: no ch after* **33/1**

1305 **17** *25* **King's Approach (IRE)**[33] 3424 2-9-0 **84** .... RichardHughes 5 2
(R Hannon) *led for 2f: styd handy tl wknd qckly over 2f out: eased fnl f: t.o* **33/1**

1m 28.1s (0.70) **Going Correction** -0.025s/f (Good) 17 Ran SP% 128.3
Speed ratings (Par 100): **95,94,94,93,93 92,92,91,90,88 87,87,87,86,85 84,55**
toteswingers: 1&2 £6.70, 1&3 £16.60, 2&3 £46.10 CSF £30.29 CT £519.35 TOTE £3.60: £1.50, £2.00, £6.00, £2.00; EX 22.10 Trifecta £1228.70 Pool: £2158.60 - 1.30 winning units..
Owner Godolphin **Bred** Grapestock Llc **Trained** Newmarket, Suffolk

FOCUS
They went no more than a fair gallop in what looked a wide-open nursery. The winner had a fair bit in hand and the form should work out.

NOTEBOOK
Black Snowflake(USA) swooped late to deny Gunner Lindley, just as he had done when winning his maiden at Haydock last month. Up to 7f for the first time, he looked fairly treated for this step into nurseries, considering his Middle Park/Royal Lodge entries, and was understandably made favourite. Held up in midfield, he was beginning to run on when short of room over 2f out and then briefly denied a clear run, but really found his stride once switched out and rattled home in the final 100 yards. On this evidence he should stay 1m, despite having tons of speed in his pedigree, though it wouldn't surprise to see connections, who have their juveniles in top form at present, stick to this trip with him for the time being. A Listed race is likely to be next on the agenda. (op 9-2)
Gunner Lindley(IRE) appreciated the step up to 7f when winning a minor maiden last time and he was 2lb better off with the winner on earlier Haydock form. He hit the front inside the final furlong and looked set to score, but couldn't hold on. This son of Medicean should stay 1m in time and remains capable of better. (op 15-2)
Raine's Cross has run down the field behind Richard Hannon's trio of top juveniles on his last three starts, latterly finishing fourth behind Dick Turpin at Salisbury, and he ran a big race on this handicap debut. Coming from further back than the winner, he had nowhere to go from three out to two out and ended up challenging widest of all, but couldn't stay on well enough in the final 100 yards. This was a really good effort under joint-top weight. (tchd 22-1)
Contract Caterer(IRE), easy winner of a weak maiden at Catterick last time, held a nice position just in behind the leaders and came to hold every chance from a furlong out, but could find no extra in the final 100 yards. (op 6-1 tchd 13-2)
Coloursoftheglen(IRE), runner-up at Newmarket on his recent handicap debut, was 2lb higher here and ran every bit as well in what was a stronger race. (op 10-1)
Jairzihno looked in need of this trip when third in a 6f novice race at Doncaster last time and he made some late headway against the inner having got a bit behind following a slow start. (op 20-1)
The Human League finished sixth behind the smart-looking Awzaan at Newmarket last time and he ran well on this nursery debut/step up to 7f, keeping on for strong pressure down the outside.
Suffolk Punch(IRE) dominated throughout when winning at Epsom last time, but he couldn't lead in this more competitive race and got knocked wide at the first bend. He raced keenly and, having come to hit the front over a furlong out, was headed and faded in the final 150 yards. His rider reported that he hung left and he can probably be rated a shade better than the bare form. Official explanation: jockey said colt hung left (tchd 7-1)
Marsh Warbler ran better than he had done in the Coventry last time, running on late having been outpaced, and he remains capable of better as he goes up to 1m. (tchd 16-1)
Tres Coronas(IRE) didn't enjoy the smoothest of runs. He was reported to have run too free, clipped heels and stumbled. Official explanation: jockey said gelding ran too free, clipped heels and stumbled 5 1/2f out (op 9-1)
Rock Of Love(IRE) stopped quickly having been passed over a furlong out.
Flyinflyout was in the process of making late headway when badly hampered and eased a furlong out. He could make no further headway. (op 50-1 tchd 25-1)
King's Approach(IRE) was reported to have stopped quickly. Official explanation: jockey said colt stopped quickly (op 25-1)

4489 OAK TREE STKS (GROUP 3) (F&M) 7f
5:10 (5:10) (Class 1) 3-Y-O+
£36,900 (£13,988; £7,000; £3,490; £1,748; £877) Stalls High

Form RPR

1-03 **1** **Summer Fete (IRE)**[14] 4052 3-8-9 **102** .... RichardMullen 5 104
(B Smart) *b.hind: stdd s: t.k.h: hld up bhd: hdwy over 2f out: swtchd lft and rdn over 1f out: r.o strly to ld fnl 50yds* **9/1**

1034 **2** *1 1/4* **Select (IRE)**[20] 3892 3-8-9 **100** .... AlanMunro 12 101
(P W Chapple-Hyam) *t.k.h: chsd ldrs: rdn effrt 2f out: kpt on u.p fnl f: wnt 2nd towards fin* **25/1**

-633 **3** *hd* **Please Sing**[44] 3016 3-8-9 **100** .... EdwardCreighton 2 100
(M R Channon) *hld up in rr: rdn over 2f out: hdwy and swtchd lft ent fnl f: r.o wl to go 3rd nr fin* **12/1**

4-06 **4** *nk* **Red Dune (IRE)**[20] 3846 4-9-2 **97** .... LDettori 9 103
(M A Jarvis) *led: rdn jst over 2f out: battled on gamely tl hdd fnl 50yds: lost 2 pls nr fin* **16/1**

-200 **5** *1* **Lessing (FR)**[65] 4-9-2 **0** .... C-PLemaire 7 100
(X-Thomas Demeaulte, France) *fly-jmpd leaving stalls: hld up in rr: hdwy towards inner 2f out: squeezed between horses ins fnl f: r.o: nt rch ldrs* **12/1**

1266 **6** *1/2* **San Sicharia (IRE)**[23] 3749 4-9-5 **0** ....(p) WMLordan 11 102+
(Ms Joanna Morgan, Ire) *s.i.s: sn in midfield: chsng ldrs over 1f out: n.m.r and swtchd lft ins fnl f: r.o but nvr able to chal ldrs* **8/1**[3]

1604 **7** *hd* **King's Starlet**[27] 3641 3-8-9 **92** .... SteveDrowne 13 95
(H Morrison) *t.k.h: chsd ldrs: rdn and hanging rt fr 2f out: unable qck u.p: wknd fnl 75yds* **25/1**

0013 **8** *nse* **Greenisland (IRE)**[7] 4259 3-8-9 **94** .... RobertHavlin 6 95
(H Morrison) *chsd ldr: rdn over 2f out: kpt on tl lost 2nd ins fnl f: wknd fnl 75yds* **28/1**

3615 **9** *6* **Penny's Gift**[23] 3749 3-9-0 **107** .... RichardHughes 3 84
(R Hannon) *lw: hld up in tch in midfield: rdn and unable qck ent fnl 2f: wl btn fnl f* **4/1**[2]

-621 **10** *nk* **Golden Stream (IRE)**[36] 3320 3-8-9 **101** .... RyanMoore 4 78
(Sir Michael Stoute) *towards rr: rdn and effrt on outer 3f out: no prog: wl btn fnl f* **2/1**[1]

4660 **11** *2* **Infamous Angel**[21] 3824 3-8-9 **97** .... JimCrowley 1 73
(R Hannon) *wnt lft s: hld up in rr: rdn and no prog 3f out: wl btn fnl f* **40/1**

-460 **12** *1/2* **Royal Confidence**[44] 3012 4-9-2 **103** .... MichaelHills 8 78+
(B W Hills) *chsd ldrs: rdn and keeping on same pce whn hmpd over 1f out: no ch after* **12/1**

1101 **13** *1/2* **Cosmopolitan**[13] 4088 4-9-2 **91** .... JimmyFortune 10 70+
(J H M Gosden) *chsd ldrs: rdn and unable qck whn hmpd and lost pl 2f out: no ch after* **9/1**

1m 26.08s (-1.32) **Going Correction** -0.025s/f (Good)
WFA 3 from 4yo 7lb 13 Ran SP% **127.0**
Speed ratings (Par 113): **106,104,104,104,102 102,102,102,95,94 92,91,91**
toteswingers: 1&2 £40.20, 1&3 £18.90, 2&3 £41.10 CSF £229.45 TOTE £13.30: £3.50, £7.10, £3.50; EX 339.30 Trifecta £1335.30 Part won. Pool: £1804.58 - 0.10 winning units..
Owner H E Sheikh Rashid Bin Mohammed **Bred** Darley **Trained** Hambleton, N Yorks
■ Stewards' Enquiry : Richard Mullen one-day ban: careless riding (Aug 14)

FOCUS
Not a particularly strong Group 3 fillies' event, for all that it was competitive, and for the eighth time in the last ten years it went the way of a 3yo. Ordinary but sound form for the grade.

NOTEBOOK
Summer Fete(IRE), a smart 2yo who bounced back from a poor effort on unsuitably quick ground in the Nell Gwyn when finishing third in a good conditions race at Newbury last time, had clearly come on appreciably for that run and she showed a nice change of pace to get well on top close home. This slower ground ideally suits the daughter of Pivotal and, though the form is nothing special, she is lightly raced and remains capable of better. (op 12-1 tchd 14-1)
Select(IRE) has been running above expectations in minor Listed contests, finishing fourth at Deauville latest, so this has to go down as a career-best effort. She held every chance from two out and stuck on well, but in the end was no match for the winner. (op 20-1)
Please Sing is showing herself to be a very consistent filly and this represented another step forward. Third in the Listed Sandringham handicap at Royal Ascot last time, she came home strongly on this return to 7f and this former Group 2 winner should pick up another pattern prize before long. (tchd 11-1)
Red Dune(IRE), fourth in this a year ago, set the fractions under Dettori and returned to something like her best. She was given a confidence-boosting outing at Chester last time, having broken blood vessels on her reappearance, and can probably win a Listed race assuming she continues to go the right way. (op 12-1)
Lessing(FR), a winner at Maisons-Laffitte last time, ran well considering she got behind having fly-jumped leaving the stalls. She stayed on well from over a furlong out, squeezing between runners with her challenge, and looks capable of winning another race at Listed level back home. (tchd 14-1)
San Sicharia(IRE), who had a few of these behind, including the runner-up, when winning at Lingfield earlier in the season, was outclassed in the Falmouth Stakes last time and she ran well under her 3lb penalty on this return to Group 3 level. The first-time cheekpieces didn't do her any harm. (op 14-1)
King's Starlet ran really well when fourth in a Listed contest at Sandown last time and she again did okay considering she had a fair bit to find on ratings. (op 40-1)
Greenisland(IRE) has been progressing well, finishing third in a Listed contest at Ascot last week, and she ran well for a long way on this step up to Group company. (op 33-1)
Penny's Gift held leading form claims, but she was unable to obtain a good position from her draw, racing further back than she likes to, and never really threatened to come with a challenge. She was shouldering a 5lb Group 2 winner's penalty, but should still have done better. (op 9-2 tchd 5-1 in places)

Golden Stream(IRE) made all when winning a Listed prize at Warwick last time and she was unable to race handily from her berth in stall four. She challenged widest of all, but like Penny's Gift, never looked like coming with a winning run. (op 5-2 tchd 11-4 in places)
Royal Confidence was staying on when hampered by the winner. (op 10-1 tchd 14-1)
Cosmopolitan was under pressure and going nowhere when badly hampered over 2f out. Official explanation: jockey said filly suffered interference in running (op 10-1 tchd 17-2)

4490 TURF CLUB STKS (H'CAP) 5f
5:45 (5:45) (Class 3) (0-95,95) 3-Y-O

£12,462 (£3,732; £1,866; £934; £466; £234) **Stalls** Low

Form RPR

2152 **1** **Noble Storm (USA)**[21] 3806 3-9-6 **94** .... GrahamGibbons 3 103
(E S McMahon) *dwlt: sn rcvrd and chsd ldr after 1f: led over 1f out and sn rdn 2 l clr hld on nr fin* **9/2**[3]

2112 **2** *hd* **Mattamia (IRE)**[13] 4099 3-9-0 **91** .... JamesMillman(3) 1 99
(B R Millman) *lw: chsd ldr for 1f: rdn 2f out: no hdwy tl r.o strly fnl 150yds: pressing wnr nr fin: jst hld* **12/1**

5524 **3** *½* **Green Beret (IRE)**[22] 3784 3-9-6 **94** .... JimmyFortune 5 100
(J H M Gosden) *lw: chsd ldrs: rdn and hang rt over 2f out: chsd wnr 1f out tl fnl 75yds: kpt on u.p* **4/1**[2]

1-10 **4** *½* **Master Of Disguise**[48] 2934 3-9-7 **95** .... PhilipRobinson 7 100+
(C G Cox) *b: on toes: towards rr: pushed along and hdwy on outer ent fnl 2f: rdn over 1f out: kpt on ins fnl f but nt pce to rch ldrs* **3/1**[1]

2151 **5** *1 ½* **La Zamora**[41] 3166 3-8-0 **79** .... DeanHeslop(5) 10 78
(T D Barron) *swtg: s.i.s: sn in tch: rdn and effrt 2f out: no imp fnl f* **7/1**

30-5 **6** *hd* **Ginobili (IRE)**[21] 3802 3-9-7 **95** ....(b) MickyFenton 2 94
(Stef Liddiard) *lw: t.k.h: in tch: swtchd rt and rdn over 1f out: unable qck and no imp fnl f* **33/1**

2302 **7** *1 ¾* **Titus Andronicus (IRE)**[16] 3973 3-8-13 **87** .... RichardHughes 4 79
(K A Ryan) *taken down early: led: rdn 2f out: hdd over 1f out: wknd fnl f: eased towards fin* **14/1**

2132 **8** *1 ¼* **Strictly**[8] 4244 3-8-6 **80** .... RyanMoore 6 68+
(Sir Michael Stoute) *bhd: hdwy wl over 1f out: swtchd lft jst over 1f out: nt clr run thrght fnl f: no ch* **5/1**

1004 **9** *1 ¼* **Sloop Johnb**[16] 3973 3-8-8 **82** .... TonyHamilton 8 65
(R A Fahey) *b.hind: stdd s and sn swtchd lft: nvr gng wl in rr: rdn and no rspnse 2f out* **16/1**

57.99 secs (-0.41) **Going Correction** -0.025s/f (Good) **9** Ran SP% **115.5**
Speed ratings (Par 104): **102,101,100,100,97 97,94,92,90**
toteswingers: 1&2 £10.00, 1&3 £7.30, 2&3 £6.70 CSF £56.76 CT £235.09 TOTE £6.40: £2.00, £2.80, £1.90; EX 81.20 Trifecta £320.70 Pool: £1516.90 - 3.50 winning units. Place 6: £1471.22 Place 5: £457.28.
Owner R L Bedding **Bred** Brereton C Jones **Trained** Lichfield, Staffs

FOCUS
This decent sprint handicap featured a few improving sorts and should throw up some winners in the coming weeks. The form is rated around the winner to his best.

NOTEBOOK
Noble Storm(USA), second in a similar race at Chester last time out, got to race off the same mark here. After showing up well throughout, he responded well to pressure to hold off the late challenge of Mattamia, who had the benefit of the favoured stands' rail in the closing stages. The winner has been steadily progressive this season having been dropped back to the minimum trip, but a five or six pound rise for this will potentially leave him in the twilight zone if he cannot hack it back in Listed company. (op 11-2 tchd 6-1)
Mattamia(IRE) was denied his favoured front-running role but was never too far off the pace, and crucially he had the advantage of the rail. It was no great surprise to see him finish his race out strongly having initially looked held, but the bare form might flatter him. (op 9-1 tchd 17-2)
Green Beret(IRE) never looked entirely happy on the track, hanging right from some way out. It is to his credit that he stayed in contention the whole way and he should remain of interest in similar company. Jimmy Fortune reported that the gelding hung right. Official explanation: jockey said gelding hung right (op 7-2 tchd 9-2 in places)
Master Of Disguise was interesting back over the minimum trip, but he was stuck out wide all the way, which was not where the best ground was, and in the circumstances he was far from disgraced. He's another who's worth giving another chance to. (op 9-2)
La Zamora, who sweated up beforehand and had the worst of the draw, faded after showing early pace. She might have to dominate to be seen at her best. (op 6-1 tchd 9-2)
Ginobili(IRE), who is a keen-going sort, was highly tried at two and as a result began this campaign off a mark of 98. He was 3lb lower here but on this evidence needs further help from the handicapper. (op 25-1)
Titus Andronicus(IRE), who put the pace to the race, couldn't hold them off in this better contest off a career-high mark. His rider later reported that he'd moved poorly throughout. Official explanation: jockey said gelding moved poorly throughout
Strictly found a wall of horses in front of her as she tried to mount a challenge in the closing stages. She shaped better than her finishing position suggests and will be suited by a return to a stiffer track. Ryan Moore reported that the filly was denied a clear run. Official explanation: jockey said filly was denied a clear run (tchd 9-2)
Sloop Johnb has struggled off marks in the 80s and took little interest here having been dropped in from his wide draw.
T/Jkpt: Not won. T/Plt: £979.80 to a £1 stake. Pool: £268,773.28. 200.23 winning tickets. T/Qpdt: £118.70 to a £1 stake. Pool: £14,518.34. 90.50 winning tickets. SP

4074 HAYDOCK (L-H)
Friday, July 31

OFFICIAL GOING: 6f - good to soft (good in places; 7.9); remainder - heavy (6.9)
The first time the new inner sprint track had been used and it was riding much faster than the main track. Distances on round course increased by 25yds.
Wind: Virtually nil. Weather: Overcast

4491 FREE £25 BET AT CORBETTSPORTS.COM H'CAP 1m 6f
6:10 (6:11) (Class 5) (0-70,69) 3-Y-O **£3,238** (£963; £481; £240) **Stalls** Low

Form RPR

3134 **1** **Deauville Flyer**[21] 3827 3-9-7 **69** .... RobertWinston 3 82+
(T D Easterby) *trckd ldrs: hdwy 5f out: chsd ldr over 3f out: rdn to chal over 2f out: drvn over 1f out: styd on to ld ent fnl f: drvn out* **9/4**[1]

-653 **2** *½* **Crocus Rose**[8] 4229 3-9-0 **62** .... JimmyQuinn 4 74+
(H J L Dunlop) *trckd ldr: hdwy to ld over 5f out: rdn 3f out: jnd and drvn 2f out: hdd ent fnl f: rallied and ev ch tl no ex last 75yds* **5/2**[2]

0-63 **3** *6* **Theola (IRE)**[40] 3192 3-9-6 **68** .... SaleemGolam 8 72
(M H Tompkins) *trckd ldrs: rdn along and outpcd over 4f out: styd on u.p fr 2f out: kpt on ins fnl f: no ch w front pair* **7/1**

6635 **4** *4* **Gosforth Park**[25] 3687 3-8-2 **57** ow2........................ JohnCavanagh(7) 6 55
(M Brittain) *trckd ldrs: hdwy over 4f out: rdn over 3f out: sn drvn and plugged on same pce* **10/3**[3]

604 **5** *8* **Rebel Prince (IRE)**[54] 2742 3-8-2 **50** .... CatherineGannon 7 37
(M G Quinlan) *hld up in rr: hdwy over 3f out: rdn along wl over 2f out: sn no imp* **8/1**

0003 **6** *11* **Inside Knowledge (USA)**[8] 4230 3-8-2 **50** oh2........................ JamieMackay 5 21
(G Woodward) *towards rr: rapid hdwy appr 1/2-way and sn prom: rdn along over 4f out and sn wknd* **14/1**

6000 **7** *10* **Hit The Switch**[16] 3976 3-7-10 **51** ow1........................ JamesPSullivan(7) 2 8
(Patrick Morris) *led: rdn along and hdd over 5f out: sn wknd* **33/1**

3m 14.1s (9.80) **Going Correction** +0.70s/f (Yiel) **7** Ran SP% **115.6**
Speed ratings (Par 100): **100,99,96,94,89 83,77**
toteswingers: 1&2 £1.80, 1&3 £10.20, 2&3 £7.90. CSF £8.39 CT £32.51 TOTE £3.80: £1.90, £1.80; EX 8.20.
Owner Mr And Mrs J D Cotton **Bred** Harts Farm And Stud **Trained** Great Habton, N Yorks

FOCUS
The going on the new inner sprint track was good to soft, good in places and the original outer Flat track was heavy. A couple of progressive sorts in an ordinary handicap. The pace was only moderate and the field tacked over to the stands' side in the straight. The runner-up to his latest form sets the standard.
Inside Knowledge(USA) Official explanation: jockey said gelding ran too free early on

4492 PAULINE DAVIES BELATED BIRTHDAY MAIDEN AUCTION STKS 6f
6:45 (6:45) (Class 5) 2-Y-O **£3,238** (£963; £481; £240) **Stalls** High

Form RPR

1 **Petougg** 2-8-11 0........................ LiamJones 2 76+
(W Jarvis) *trckd ldng pair: hdwy over 2f out and sn chal: rdn to ld appr fnl f: kpt on* **13/2**[3]

0334 **2** *1 ¾* **Regardless**[21] 3807 2-7-11 0........................(v[1]) BillyCray(7) 4 64
(Mrs G S Rees) *led: jnd 2f out: rdn: hung lft and hdd appr fnl f: sn drvn and kpt on* **10/3**[2]

3 *4* **Search For The Key (USA)** 2-9-2 0........................ JimmyQuinn 1 64+
(P F I Cole) *wnt lft s and s.i.s: hdwy to chse ldrs 1/2-way: rdn over 2f out and kpt on same pce appr fnl f* **7/4**[1]

56 **4** *½* **Fibs And Flannel**[49] 2893 2-8-13 0........................ RobertWinston 6 59+
(T D Easterby) *in tch: hdwy to chse ldrs 1/2-way: rdn along over 2f out: drvn and one pce fr over 1f out* **13/2**[3]

63 **5** *9* **Sweet Mirasol (IRE)**[36] 3292 2-8-9 0 ow1........................ StephenDonohoe 7 28
(K A Ryan) *cl up: rdn along wl over 2f out and sn wknd* **10/3**[2]

000 **6** *4 ½* **Stanley Bridge**[37] 3263 2-8-8 0........................ SladeO'Hara(5) 8 19
(A Berry) *a in rr* **50/1**

1m 13.63s (-0.87) **Going Correction** -0.275s/f (Firm) **6** Ran SP% **111.1**
Speed ratings (Par 94): **94,91,86,85,73 67**
toteswingers: 1&2 £5.30, 1&3 £4.30, 2&3 £1.20. CSF £27.54 TOTE £9.70: £4.20, £2.40; EX 40.00.
Owner E Randall, N Rich & GB Turnbull Ltd **Bred** Mrs C J Tribe **Trained** Newmarket, Suffolk

FOCUS
An uncompetitive maiden and one that took less winning than seemed likely beforehand with the two market leaders disappointing. The early gallop was not a strong one and the form is limited, with the runner-up the best guide. The official time suggested the ground was nearer good on this new track.

NOTEBOOK
Petougg, a gelded half-brother to a multiple 6f-7f winner, travelled strongly under restraint on this racecourse debut and did enough when asked for an effort to win an uncompetitive event in workmanlike fashion. He should stay 7f and, although this is not strong form, he may do better in ordinary nursery company. (op 4-1 tchd 7-1)
Regardless is a reliable sort who had the run of the race and seemed to give it her best shot in the first-time visor. She's a good guide to this form but, although she pulled clear of the remainder, is likely to remain vulnerable to the better sorts in this grade. (tchd 3-1 and 7-2)
Search For The Key(USA) holds a host of big race entries but, even allowing for his apparent greenness, it was disappointing he couldn't fare better in a race of this nature on this debut. He should improve but it'll be surprising if he's anything out of the ordinary. (op 11-4)
Fibs And Flannel, upped in distance, had something to find on previous evidence and was readily left behind by the principals in the closing stages but he wasn't unduly knocked about and will be of more interest in run-of-the-mill nurseries. (op 8-1 tchd 11-2)
Sweet Mirasol(IRE) looked to have strong prospects back on his latest Hamilton form but she dropped out very tamely in the closing stages. Genuinely quick ground may suit better but she looks one to tread carefully with next time. (tchd 7-2 in places)

4493 JEREMY AND ADELE CARR 40TH BIRTHDAY NURSERY 6f
7:20 (7:21) (Class 4) 2-Y-O **£5,504** (£1,637; £818; £408) **Stalls** High

Form RPR

11 **1** **Kaptain Kirkup (IRE)**[36] 3311 2-9-7 **90** .... PhillipMakin 7 96+
(M Dods) *t.k.h: trckd ldrs on ins: effrt and nt clr run 2f out: hdwy and hmpd 1f out: swtchd lft and rdn ins fnl f: styd on to ld nr fin* **6/4**[1]

3652 **2** *hd* **Gillburg (USA)**[15] 4017 2-8-1 **70** ....(b[1]) SilvestreDeSousa 6 72
(K A Ryan) *led: rdn and qcknd over 2f out: edgd lft over 1f out: sn drvn: hdd and no ex towards fin* **11/4**[2]

414 **3** *2* **Kylladdie**[32] 3452 2-8-8 **77** .... DNolan 2 73
(T P Tate) *cl up: rdn 2f out and ev ch: drvn and edgd lft ent fnl f: kpt on same pce* **11/4**[2]

403 **4** *1 ½* **Bitter Honey**[13] 4075 2-7-13 **68** ow1........................ JimmyQuinn 5 60
(Mrs G S Rees) *s.i.s: hdwy 4f out: cl up over 2f out: sn rdn and wknd over 1f out* **9/1**

150 **5** *5* **Strike Shot**[13] 4089 2-8-9 **78** .... PaulMulrennan 1 55
(W R Muir) *cl up on outer: rdn along 2f out and sn wknd* **7/1**[3]

1m 13.39s (-1.11) **Going Correction** -0.275s/f (Firm) **5** Ran SP% **115.8**
Speed ratings (Par 96): **96,95,93,91,84**
toteswingers: 1&2 £4.00, 1&3 not won, 2&3 not won CSF £6.35 TOTE £2.60: £1.60, £1.60; EX 8.30.
Owner Kevin Kirkup **Bred** David Barry **Trained** Denton, Co Durham

FOCUS
Not the strongest of races for the money and one in which the gallop was only reasonable (about a quarter of a second quicker than the previous event) but the winner is a fair bit better than this form suggests.

NOTEBOOK
Kaptain Kirkup(IRE) ◆ maintained his unbeaten record on this nursery debut but looks a fair bit better than the bare form suggests, as he was trapped in a pocket until the gap appeared in the last 150yds. He's already very useful, is open to further progress and his long-term objective is the Listed Redcar Two-Year-Old Trophy in early October. (tchd 15-8 in places)
Gillburg(USA), with first-time blinkers replacing cheekpieces, had the run of the race against the stands' rail and, while he was clearly flattered by his proximity to a winner who didn't see daylight till late on, this represented his best effort. He should be able to pick up an ordinary nursery in the north. (tchd 7-2 in places)
Kylladdie, gelded since his previous (below-par) start, had the rub of things and was not disgraced, despite edging off a true line, on this nursery debut. Easier ground may suit better but he'll have to improve to win a similar event from this mark. (tchd 7-2 in places)

Bitter Honey, the only filly in the field, was not disgraced on this nursery debut after getting restless in the stalls and then making a tardy start. She may do better over 5f in lesser company. (tchd 10-1)
Strike Shot, from a yard among the winners, proved disappointing on this first venture into nursery company. He may do better over 5f but has not really progressed since his maiden win at this track. (op 13-2 tchd 6-1)

4494 ST HELENS H'CAP — 6f
7:50 (7:51) (Class 4) (0-80,78) 3-Y-O — £5,504 (£1,637; £818; £408) Stalls High

Form — RPR
0413 1 **Medicean Man**[14] 4044 3-9-3 **74** ... StephenDonohoe 9 — 84+
(J R Gask) *trckd ldrs: swtchd lft and hdwy to ld over 1f out: sn rdn and kpt on wl fnl f* — **9/2**[2]
1045 2 *1* **Doc Jones (IRE)**[11] 4148 3-8-11 **73** ... RichardEvans(5) 12 — 78
(P D Evans) *hld up in tch: swtchd lft and hdwy over 2f out: rdn to chse wnr ent fnl f: sn edgd lft: kpt on* — **10/1**
-003 3 *½* **Cook's Endeavour (USA)**[15] 4019 3-9-4 **75** ... PhillipMakin 1 — 78
(K A Ryan) *led: rdn along 2f out: drvn and hdd over 1f out: kpt on u.p ins fnl f* — **4/1**[1]
4014 4 *½* **Francis Walsingham (IRE)**[39] 3219 3-9-3 **74** ... RobertWinston 11 — 75
(H Morrison) *trckd ldrs: hdwy 1/2-way: rdn wl over 1f out: sn drvn and kpt on u.p ins fnl f* — **17/2**
1053 5 *¾* **Grissom (IRE)**[6] 4309 3-8-11 **75** ... BillyCray(7) 2 — 74
(A Berry) *chsd ldrs on outer: effrt over 2f out: sn rdn and ch whn edgd lft over 1f out: sn drvn and kpt on same pce* — **14/1**
3201 6 *shd* **Arachnophobia (IRE)**[16] 3982 3-9-7 **78** ... PaulEddery 7 — 77
(Pat Eddery) *cl up: rdn along 2f out: drvn and wknd appr fnl f* — **15/2**
0414 7 *1½* **Ben's Dream (IRE)**[11] 4148 3-8-13 **70** ... (t) NeilChalmers 6 — 64
(A M Balding) *chsd ldrs: rdn along 2f out: sn drvn and no imp* — **7/1**[3]
61 8 *shd* **Imperial House**[41] 3175 3-8-13 **70** ... SamHitchcott 5 — 64
(M R Channon) *s.i.s: a in rr* — **8/1**
0010 9 *2½* **Lucky Dan (IRE)**[5] 4343 3-8-10 **67** ... SilvestreDeSousa 4 — 53
(Paul Green) *t.k.h: chsd ldrs on wd outisde: rdn along over 2f out and sn wknd* — **17/2**
6000 10 *¾* **Caranbola**[8] 4227 3-8-12 **76** ... JohnCavanagh(7) 10 — 59
(M Brittain) *dwlt: a outpcd in rr* — **20/1**

1m 13.35s (-1.15) **Going Correction** -0.275s/f (Firm) — 10 Ran SP% **115.1**
Speed ratings (Par 102): **96,94,94,93,92 92,90,90,86,85**
toteswingers: 1&2 £12.90, 1&3 £1.30, 2&3 £10.50. CSF £48.24 CT £198.79 TOTE £5.10: £1.60, £3.50, £1.40; EX 60.10.
Owner Miss K M Dobb **Bred** Barry Taylor **Trained** Sutton Veny, Wilts

FOCUS
A fair handicap run at a decent gallop and marginally the quickest time of the evening over this trip.
Ben's Dream(IRE) Official explanation: trainer's rep had no explanation for the poor form shown

4495 CHESHIRE OAKS DESIGNER OUTLET FILLIES' H'CAP — 1m 2f 95y
8:20 (8:21) (Class 5) (0-75,73) 3-Y-O+ — £3,238 (£963; £481; £240) Stalls Low

Form — RPR
1606 1 **Supaverdi (USA)**[13] 4085 4-10-0 **73** ... RobertWinston 3 — 84
(H Morrison) *mde all: jnd and rdn 2f out: drvn ent fnl f and styd on strly* — **7/2**[2]
3042 2 *3* **Punch Drunk**[15] 4004 3-9-1 **70** ... (p) PaulMulrennan 8 — 75
(J G Given) *trckd ldrs: hdwy 3f out: chal 2f out and sn rdn: drvn and ev ch whn hung lft ent fnl f: sn one pce* — **9/4**[1]
216 3 *1¾* **Drum Dragon**[11] 4143 3-9-4 **73** ... SaleemGolam 7 — 74
(M H Tompkins) *hld up in rr: hdwy 3f out: rdn to chse ldrs wl over 1f out: sn drvn and one pce appr fnl f* — **8/1**
0 4 *1½* **Takizada (IRE)**[24] 3718 4-9-9 **68** ... JimmyQuinn 5 — 66
(J R Gask) *trckd ldrs: rdn along and outpcd over 3f out: kpt on u.p appr fnl f* — **11/1**
5204 5 *½* **Rio Guru (IRE)**[6] 4328 4-9-13 **72** ... SamHitchcott 2 — 69
(M R Channon) *hld up in tch: effrt on inner over 3f out: rdn along over 2f out and sn one pce* — **6/1**
2450 6 *3* **Grethel (IRE)**[17] 3943 5-8-2 **54** oh7 ... BillyCray(7) 6 — 45
(A Berry) *t.k.h: chsd ldrs: rdn along and outpcd over 3f out: sn swtchd lft and drvn: n.d* — **12/1**
5623 7 *8* **La Rosa Nostra**[24] 3721 4-9-13 **72** ... (tp) StephenDonohoe 1 — 47
(W R Swinburn) *cl up on inner: rdn along 3f out: drvn 2f out and sn wknd* — **4/1**[3]

2m 23.18s (10.18) **Going Correction** +0.70s/f (Yiel)
WFA 3 from 4yo+ 10lb — 7 Ran SP% **114.4**
Speed ratings (Par 100): **96,93,92,91,90 88,81**
toteswingers: 1&2 £2.90, 1&3 £3.60, 2&3 £8.80. CSF £11.84 CT £56.93 TOTE £5.30: £2.60, £1.70; EX 18.90.
Owner Ben & Sir Martyn Arbib **Bred** Arbib Bloodstock Partnership **Trained** East Ilsley, Berks

FOCUS
An ordinary handicap in which the gallop was on the steady side. The runner-up rather threw it away while the third ran just about his best race on turf.

4496 TURFTV H'CAP — 1m 30y
8:55 (8:56) (Class 5) (0-70,68) 3-Y-O+ — £3,238 (£963; £481; £240) Stalls Low

Form — RPR
2235 1 **Royal Premium**[27] 3616 3-8-4 **53** ... (v) CatherineGannon 7 — 62
(Mrs G S Rees) *t.k.h: a.p: hdwy to ld 2f out: sn rdn and edgd lft over 1f out: drvn ins fnl f and kpt on* — **11/1**
4114 2 *1¼* **Montiboli (IRE)**[5] 4346 4-9-8 **68** ... (p) AmyRyan(5) 2 — 76
(K A Ryan) *trckd ldrs on inner: hdwy 3f out: rdn over 2f out: drvn to chse wnr ins fnl f: kpt on* — **8/1**[3]
0-31 3 *1* **Feeling Fresh (IRE)**[20] 3852 4-9-5 **60** ... SilvestreDeSousa 1 — 66
(Paul Green) *hld up in rr: hdwy 3f out: rdn to chse ldrs wl over 1f out: drvn ent fnl f and kpt on* — **11/1**
152 4 *nk* **Tanforan**[14] 4046 7-9-3 **65** ... BillyCray(7) 12 — 70
(B P J Baugh) *hld up towards rr: hdwy over 3f out: rdn over 2f out: kpt on appr fnl f: nrst fin* — **14/1**
0061 5 *shd* **Natural Rhythm (IRE)**[11] 4144 4-8-13 **54** 6ex ... (b) RobertWinston 9 — 59
(Mrs R A Carr) *led: rdn along 3f out: hdd 2f out: sn drvn and kpt on same pce* — **11/1**
0032 6 *5* **Pitbull**[5] 4351 6-9-1 **56** ... (p) JimmyQuinn 11 — 49
(Mrs G S Rees) *s.i.s and bhd tl sme late hdwy* — **4/1**[2]
-243 7 *1¼* **Tamasou (IRE)**[18] 3911 4-9-6 **66** ... MarkCoumbe(5) 10 — 56
(Garry Moss) *chsd ldrs: rdn along 3f out: drvn 2f out and sn wknd* — **7/2**[1]
-131 8 *6* **Tom Tower (IRE)**[14] 4046 5-9-10 **68** ... NeilBrown(3) 8 — 45
(A C Whillans) *t.k.h: cl up: effrt 3f out: sn rdn and wknd 2f out* — **4/1**[2]
0000 9 *3* **Fulford**[8] 4225 4-8-4 **52** ... (v[1]) JohnCavanagh(7) 5 — 22
(M Brittain) *chsd ldrs: rdn along over 3f out and sn wknd* — **50/1**
06 10 *3½* **Tres Froide (FR)**[34] 3378 4-9-10 **65** ... PhillipMakin 13 — 27
(N Tinkler) *towards rr: effrt and sme hdwy over 3f out: sn rdn and wknd* — **8/1**[3]
000- 11 *1¼* **Kool Katie**[302] 6409 4-8-8 **49** oh2 ... LiamJones 3 — 8
(Mrs G S Rees) *a towards rr* — **40/1**

1m 50.62s (6.82) **Going Correction** +0.70s/f (Yiel)
WFA 3 from 4yo+ 8lb — 11 Ran SP% **120.5**
Speed ratings (Par 103): **93,91,90,90,90 85,84,78,75,71 70**
toteswingers: 1&2 £26.60, 1&3 £30.40, 2&3 £10.10. CSF £98.54 CT £1007.01 TOTE £14.20: £3.80, £3.30, £3.10; EX 183.00 Place 6 £104.52, Place 5 £70.98..
Owner P B J Racing **Bred** Mr And Mrs R J Hall **Trained** Sollom, Lancs

FOCUS
The bend out of the back straight was moved, adding 25yds to the original distance of this race. A modest handicap run at a fair gallop in the conditions and the form is sound but ordinary.
Royal Premium Official explanation: trainer had no explanation for the apparent improvement in form shown
Natural Rhythm(IRE) Official explanation: jockey said gelding hung left in the straight
T/Plt: £128.20 to a £1 stake. Pool: £43,524.80. 247.72 winning tickets. T/Qpdt: £16.90 to a £1 stake. Pool: £4,938.83. 215.00 winning tickets. JR

4314 NEWMARKET (R-H)
Friday, July 31

OFFICIAL GOING: Good (good to soft in places; 8.0)
Stands' side track used.
Wind: Light, across. Weather: Cloudy with sunny spells

4497 H2O TOWERGATE E B F MAIDEN STKS — 6f
5:55 (5:55) (Class 4) 2-Y-O — £5,180 (£1,541; £770; £384) Stalls Low

Form — RPR
2 1 **Taajub (IRE)**[21] 3792 2-9-3 0 ... RHills 11 — 89+
(W J Haggas) *a.p: chsd ldr over 3f out: led over 2f out: rdn and edgd lft 1f out: r.o wl* — **8/11**[1]
324 2 *2¼* **Arabian Pride**[36] 3311 2-9-3 0 ... EddieAhern 2 — 79
(D M Simcock) *led: hdd over 2f out: sn rdn: styd on same pce fnl f* — **10/3**[2]
0 3 *½* **Electric City (IRE)**[9] 4200 2-8-7 0 ... NicolPolli(5) 1 — 73+
(M G Quinlan) *chsd ldrs: rdn over 1f out: hung rt ins fnl f: styd on* — **66/1**
4 *3* **New Christmas (USA)** 2-9-3 0 ... MartinDwyer 12 — 69
(B J Meehan) *s.s: hdwy over 4f out: rdn over 2f out: wknd fnl f* — **10/1**[3]
5 *hd* **Ice Viking (IRE)** 2-9-3 0 ... PatCosgrave 4 — 68
(J G Given) *s.i.s: hdwy 1/2-way: sn rdn: outpcd wl over 1f out: styd on ins fnl f* — **20/1**
6 *¾* **Kona Coast** 2-9-3 0 ... (b[1]) TedDurcan 7 — 66+
(J H M Gosden) *s.s: pushed along early: rdn over 2f out: r.o ins fnl f: nvr nrr* — **10/1**[3]
6 7 *nse* **Maldon Prom (IRE)**[7] 4272 2-9-3 0 ... JerryO'Dwyer 6 — 66
(C A Dwyer) *hld up: hdwy 1/2-way: rdn and edgd lft over 1f out: wknd fnl f* — **33/1**
8 *½* **Fardyieh** 2-8-12 0 ... KShea 3 — 59
(C E Brittain) *chsd ldr tl over 3f out: rdn whn nt clr run over 1f out: sn wknd* — **16/1**
9 *4½* **Al Barq (IRE)** 2-8-9 0 ... WilliamCarson(3) 9 — 46
(Miss D Mountain) *s.i.s: a in rr: rdn over 2f out: sn wknd* — **66/1**
0 10 *1* **The Ducking Stool**[41] 3167 2-8-12 0 ... DarryllHolland 5 — 43
(H J Collingridge) *hld up: rdn over 2f out: sn wknd* — **50/1**
11 *4½* **Gabriel's Spirit (IRE)** 2-9-3 0 ... DaneO'Neill 10 — 34
(Miss Amy Weaver) *hld up: a in rr: rdn over 2f out: sn wknd* — **33/1**

1m 15.27s (2.77) **Going Correction** +0.20s/f (Good) — 11 Ran SP% **120.6**
Speed ratings (Par 96): **89,86,85,81,81 80,80,79,73,72 66**
toteswingers: 1&2 £1.50, 1&3 £23.60, 2&3 £38.90. CSF £3.06 TOTE £1.80: £1.10, £1.50, £8.20; EX 3.60.
Owner Hamdan Al Maktoum **Bred** Rabbah Bloodstock Limited **Trained** Newmarket, Suffolk

FOCUS
There was probably not a great deal of strength in depth in the opening maiden but the two market leaders filled the first two positions and the form looks solid enough, rated through the runner-up.

NOTEBOOK
Taajub(IRE) looked inexperienced but ran a promising race when second as joint favourite in a similar race at Ascot on debut. He set a decent standard, attracted a flood of support throughout the day and did the job in smooth style. Always moving well just off the pace, he made up the ground easily and only had to be pushed out to win with a fair bit in hand. He is a good-looking son of Exceed And Excel and his multiple big-race entries suggest he is expected to be competing at a much higher level in the future. (tchd 10-11)
Arabian Pride dictated a steady pace and stuck to his task quite well but never looked like he was going to give the winner a scare in the closing stages. He was closely matched with Taajub on form and has run a respectable race but his profile is consistent rather than progressive and he could continue to find life tough against less-exposed types. (op 5-1 tchd 11-4)
Electric City(IRE) was always towards the rear at 100-1 on her debut at Lingfield the previous week, but caught the eye flashing home from off the pace here and seems to have improved significantly for her initial experience.
New Christmas(USA) was a bit coltish in the paddock but found some rhythm in the race and shaped with some promise on his debut. He is a half-brother to the stable's useful maiden Skadrak and turf/dirt winners at up to 1m in the US. A selection of big-race entries suggest he is well thought of and he could take a fair step forward next time. (op 8-1)
Ice Viking(IRE) showed a glimmer of ability on debut and should have learned quite a bit from the experience. (tchd 16-1)
Kona Coast had blinkers applied for his first start but plugged on quite well after missing the break. (tchd 8-1 and 11-1)

4498 NGK SPARK PLUGS FILLIES' H'CAP — 1m 4f
6:25 (6:25) (Class 5) (0-70,68) 3-Y-O+ — £3,885 (£1,156; £577; £288) Stalls Centre

Form — RPR
5-20 1 **Teeky**[50] 2858 3-9-2 **68** ... RHills 1 — 83+
(J H M Gosden) *hld up: hdwy over 3f out: led over 2f out: styd on strly* — **9/2**[2]
-406 2 *6* **Jenny Soba**[9] 4193 6-9-4 **58** ... DarryllHolland 3 — 63
(Lucinda Featherstone) *hld up: hdwy to chse wnr over 2f out: sn rdn: no ex fnl f* — **16/1**
3000 3 *6* **Alittlemoreflair**[30] 3511 3-8-1 **53** ... (v[1]) DO'Donohoe 4 — 48
(J Pearce) *s.i.s: sn pushed along in rr: hdwy 3f out: rdn and edgd lft over 1f out: wknd fnl f* — **50/1**
4466 4 *1¾* **Sphere (IRE)**[43] 3073 4-9-8 **62** ... (t) DaneO'Neill 6 — 55
(J R Fanshawe) *hld up: hdwy over 2f out: rdn and hung lft over 1f out: wknd fnl f* — **9/1**
-560 5 *11* **Chanrossa (IRE)**[32] 3462 3-8-12 **64** ... EddieAhern 11 — 39
(E A L Dunlop) *prom: rdn over 2f out: wknd over 1f out* — **25/1**

-000 **6** 3 1/4 **Itsy Bitsy**[11] 4158 7-8-2 **49** oh4 .... TobyAtkinson(7) 8 19
(W J Musson) *hld up: rdn over 5f out: nvr nrr* **33/1**

6052 **7** *hd* **Welsh Anthem**[8] 4224 3-8-13 **65** .... (b) MartinDwyer 7 34
(W R Muir) *prom: chsd ldr 5f out: led 3f out: sn rdn and hdd: wknd over 1f out* **9/2**[2]

-055 **8** 3/4 **Bushy Dell (IRE)**[24] 3721 4-9-8 **67** .... AmyBaker(5) 2 35
(Miss J Feilden) *mid-div: hdwy over 5f out: rdn and ev ch over 2f out: sn wknd* **16/1**

2350 **9** 2 1/2 **Granary Girl**[9] 4193 7-8-12 **59** .... SimonPearce(7) 12 23
(J Pearce) *hld up: sme hdwy over 2f out: sn wknd* **11/1**

453 **10** 3 1/2 **Jabroot (IRE)**[17] 3951 3-8-13 **65** .... (p) PatCosgrave 13 24
(M A Jarvis) *mid-div: rdn over 4f out: wknd over 2f out* **4/1**[1]

0631 **11** 7 **Proficiency**[14] 4071 4-9-5 **59** .... (b) TedDurcan 5 6
(T D Walford) *prom: rdn over 5f out: wknd over 3f out* **7/1**[3]

400 **12** 9 **Maid Of Stone (IRE)**[14] 4057 3-8-5 **57** .... KirstyMilczarek 10 —
(D R C Elsworth) *sn led: rdn and hdd 3f out: wknd 2f out* **20/1**

40 **13** 40 **Rose Row**[4] 4378 5-10-0 **68** .... IanMongan 9 —
(Mrs Mary Hambro) *chsd ldr 7f: rdn and wknd over 3f out* **12/1**

2m 33.01s (0.11) **Going Correction** +0.20s/f (Good)
WFA 3 from 4yo+ 12lb **13** Ran SP% **120.2**
Speed ratings (Par 100): **107,103,99,97,90 88,88,87,86,83 79,73,46**
toteswingers: 1&2 £17.30, 1&3 £277.70, 2&3 £187.60. CSF £71.57 CT £3187.96 TOTE £5.30: £2.00, £4.30, £18.30; EX 84.60.

Owner George Strawbridge **Bred** George Strawbridge **Trained** Newmarket, Suffolk

FOCUS
A fair fillies' handicap run at a decent pace and rated through the runner-up to this year's form. The field raced down the centre-to-far side in the straight and the field finished well strung out. The two market leaders both disappointed, which casts a bit of a shadow over the form, but the winner was very impressive.

Granary Girl Official explanation: jockey said mare was never travelling
Jabroot(IRE) Official explanation: vet said filly was in a distressed state after the race
Proficiency Official explanation: trainer had no explanation for the poor form shown
Rose Row Official explanation: jockey said mare ran flat

4499 WALKER TRANSPORT NOVICE STKS 7f
7:00 (7:00) (Class 4) 2-Y-O **£6,476** (£1,927; £963; £481) **Stalls** Low

Form RPR

3 **1** **Poet's Voice**[23] 3750 2-8-12 0 .... LDettori 4 103+
(Saeed Bin Suroor) *plld hrd: trckd ldr tl swtchd centre 6f out and led that trio: led overall over 1f out: hung lft and pushed clr fnl f: eased towards fin: impressive* **4/9**[1]

01 **2** 10 **Pallantes Cross**[42] 3106 2-9-0 0 .... NCallan 1 78
(M Johnston) *led: lft to r alone far side 6f out: rdn: edgd rt and hdd over 1f out: wknd ins fnl f* **15/2**[3]

3 **3** *nk* **Cockney Class (USA)**[21] 3794 2-8-12 0 .... JamieSpencer 3 75
(B J Meehan) *trckd ldr: swtchd centre 6f out: rdn over 1f out: wknd ins fnl f* **7/2**[2]

4 1 1/4 **Zaahy (USA)** 2-8-9 0 .... AlanMunro 2 69
(P W Chapple-Hyam) *prom: swtchd centre and chsd ldr of that gp tl shkn up over 2f out: edgd lft and wknd over 1f out* **14/1**

1m 27.68s (1.98) **Going Correction** +0.20s/f (Good) **4** Ran SP% **109.9**
Speed ratings (Par 96): **96,84,84,82**
CSF £4.49 TOTE £1.50; EX 3.90.

Owner Godolphin **Bred** Darley **Trained** Newmarket, Suffolk

FOCUS
A fascinating contest with the winner scoring in good style. The pace was sound and the time was just under four seconds above standard.

NOTEBOOK
Poet's Voice was a promising third when an easy 6-1 chance in an above-average course-and-distance maiden on his debut last month. He had a bit to find on figures but attracted relentless support and absolutely slammed his rivals. The big, powerful son of Dubawi was always travelling easily and showed a sharp turn of foot to sprint clear approaching the final furlong. He looks a very exciting prospect and holds a raft of high-profile entries, including the Middle Park, Royal Lodge and Derby. (op 8-13 tchd 8-11 in a place and 4-6 in places)
Pallantes Cross was tailed off on his debut but looked a different horse when accounting for a better-fancied stablemate Mister Angry (who won his next two starts) under a trailblazing ride on good to firm over 7f at Musselburgh. He set the pace against the far rail while the others plotted their course down the middle, but had no answer to the winner's devastating burst. It is hard to say whether the slow ground has inconvenienced him, but he has clearly run into a very useful type and could easily bounce back in a less-gruelling event next time. (op 11-2)
Cockney Class(USA) did not look entirely comfortable on the slow ground but will be worth another chance to confirm the promise of his third behind a pair of well-regarded fellow newcomers in a similar race at Ascot on debut last month. (op 4-1 tchd 10-3)
Zaahy(USA) cost $105,000 and had been catching the eye of work-watchers. He faced a stiff task on his debut and ran a bit green but showed a decent attitude to keep battling away. He is a relatively late-foaled half-brother to winners in US and South Africa, who should stay a bit further in time. (op 8-1)

4500 GL EVENTS H'CAP 6f
7:30 (7:30) (Class 3) (0-90,87) 3-Y-O+ **£9,066** (£2,697; £1,348; £673) **Stalls** Low

Form RPR

0402 **1** **Esteem Machine (USA)**[20] 3845 5-9-5 **81** .... LDettori 6 90+
(R A Teal) *hld up: hdwy and nt clr run over 1f out: swtchd rt: r.o to ld wl ins fnl f* **6/1**[3]

2050 **2** 1/2 **Silver Wind**[6] 4333 4-9-4 **80** .... (v) NCallan 11 87
(P D Evans) *chsd ldr tl led over 1f out: sn rdn and edgd lft: hdd wl ins fnl f* **6/1**[3]

3060 **3** 3/4 **Diriculous**[36] 3318 5-9-9 **85** .... (b[1]) JamesDoyle 7 90
(T G Mills) *a.p: racd keenly: rdn and ev ch over 1f out: no ex towards fin* **20/1**

-500 **4** 3/4 **Seamus Shindig**[47] 2941 7-9-2 **85** .... AmyScott(7) 8 87+
(H Candy) *chsd ldrs: nt clr run and lost pl over 1f out: r.o ins fnl f* **7/1**

0132 **5** 1 1/2 **River Kirov (IRE)**[4] 4387 6-8-9 **78** .... TobyAtkinson(7) 10 75
(M Wigham) *hld up in tch: rdn over 1f out: no ex ins fnl f* **8/1**

0-21 **6** 2 1/2 **Baunagain (IRE)**[22] 3787 4-9-11 **87** .... JamieSpencer 1 76
(P W Chapple-Hyam) *led: rdn: hung rt and hdd over 1f out: wknd ins fnl f* **9/2**[2]

2554 **7** 2 1/4 **Valatrix (IRE)**[22] 3789 4-9-2 **78** .... TedDurcan 9 60
(C F Wall) *hld up: rdn over 2f out: wknd and eased fnl f* **16/1**

10/0 **8** *nk* **La Voile Rouge**[32] 3469 4-9-6 **82** .... TPQueally 3 63
(R M Beckett) *prom: rdn and wknd over 1f out* **33/1**

2112 **9** *nk* **Pumpkin**[7] 4273 3-9-2 **83** .... RyanMoore 4 63
(Sir Michael Stoute) *chsd ldrs: rdn over 2f out: wknd over 1f out* **2/1**[1]

1m 13.83s (1.33) **Going Correction** +0.20s/f (Good)
WFA 3 from 4yo+ 5lb **9** Ran SP% **117.3**
Speed ratings (Par 107): **99,98,97,96,94 91,88,87,87**
toteswingers: 1&2 £9.90, 1&3 £27.10, 2&3 £23.10. CSF £42.48 CT £684.73 TOTE £4.90: £1.60, £1.90, £4.10; EX 48.70.

Owner M Vickers **Bred** Mindy Hodges Powell **Trained** Ashtead, Surrey

FOCUS
A good handicap but the two most prominent in the betting disappointed, which makes the form look a bit suspect. Otherwise though, the form looks straightforward, rated around those in the frame behind the winner.

NOTEBOOK
Esteem Machine(USA) did well to snatch second after blowing the start at Ascot last time. He made life difficult for himself by starting slowly again but he gradually weaved his way into a threatening position, and pounced late to win with a bit more to spare than the margin suggests. He is a bit better on Polytrack and his style makes him a bit of a risky one, but he is a formidable force at this level on turf when things go his way and his versatility regarding ground is a bonus. (op 9-2)
Silver Wind hit the front approaching the final furlong and looked like landing a gamble but was just picked off close home. He has managed just one win in his last 16 starts but the return to 6f seems to have galvanised him and he looked very willing under pressure. (op 11-1 tchd 11-2)
Diriculous seemed to have lost the plot this season but first-time blinkers have spurred him back to action and he probably run right up to his best turf form. He is potentially well treated off his current turf rating, and could be a major player if the headgear works again next time. (tchd 16-1)
Seamus Shindig did not get the best of runs but stayed on strongly and posted his best effort since returning to action in May. He was a triple 6f winner last summer and has slipped back to a tempting mark. Official explanation: jockey said gelding was denied a clear run (op 13-2 tchd 6-1)
River Kirov(IRE) saw plenty of daylight out wide and could never get into the thick of things. (op 15-2 tchd 7-1)
Baunagain(IRE) had looked better than ever for his new yard in three runs this season but he put in a tame effort under forcing tactics and carried his head awkwardly in the closing stages. He has gone close on slow ground in the past, which suggests something may have been amiss here. (op 4-1 tchd 5-1)
Pumpkin finished a close second over course and distance in her bid for a hat-trick last week but was driven along some way out in this race and found very little for pressure. Official explanation: trainer's rep said gelding was unsuited by the good, good to soft in places ground (op 9-4 tchd 5-2)

4501 TALK DIAGEO H'CAP 7f
8:05 (8:05) (Class 4) (0-85,82) 4-Y-O+ **£5,180** (£1,541; £770; £384) **Stalls** Low

Form RPR

0030 **1** **Without Prejudice (USA)**[21] 3825 4-9-3 **76** .... (v[1]) RyanMoore 6 88
(J Noseda) *trckd ldrs: racd keenly: led over 1f out: sn rdn: edgd rt ins fnl f: jst hld on* **13/2**

21-4 **2** *nk* **Choiseau (IRE)**[17] 3956 4-9-7 **80** .... AlanMunro 13 91
(Pat Eddery) *chsd ldrs: rdn over 1f out: hung lft ins fnl f: r.o* **5/1**[3]

3-12 **3** 1/2 **Cape Rock**[21] 3795 4-9-4 **77** .... PaulDoe 8 87
(W J Knight) *led: rdn and hdd over 1f out: r.o* **4/1**[1]

2036 **4** 3 1/2 **Last Sovereign**[63] 2434 5-9-9 **82** .... LDettori 3 82
(Jane Chapple-Hyam) *s.i.s: hld up: hdwy over 1f out: r.o: nt rch ldrs* **9/2**[2]

0040 **5** *hd* **Aflaam (IRE)**[18] 3928 4-9-6 **79** .... TolleyDean 14 79
(P Howling) *hld up: rdn over 1f out: hung lft and r.o ins fnl f: nt rch ldrs* **11/1**

1-00 **6** *nse* **Rum Jungle**[42] 3116 5-9-5 **78** .... DaneO'Neill 7 78
(H Candy) *chsd ldr: rdn over 1f out: styd on same pce ins fnl f* **8/1**

0406 **7** 3 1/4 **Cornus**[55] 2695 7-9-4 **77** .... (p) JamesDoyle 2 68
(J A Glover) *s.i.s: hld up: nt clr run over 1f out: n.d* **20/1**

1530 **8** 3/4 **Highly Regal (IRE)**[9] 4211 4-9-4 **77** .... (b) NCallan 4 66
(R A Teal) *hld up in tch: rdn over 2f out: wknd and eased ins fnl f* **20/1**

0403 **9** 3/4 **Orpen Wide (IRE)**[31] 3353 7-9-6 **82** .... (bt) LeeVickers(3) 12 69
(M C Chapman) *chsd ldrs: rdn over 2f out: wknd over 1f out* **25/1**

6340 **10** 8 **Grey Boy (GER)**[21] 3812 8-8-9 **68** .... ShaneKelly 10 33
(A W Carroll) *mid-div: rdn 1/2-way: wknd over 1f out* **25/1**

-022 **11** 2 1/2 **Orlando's Tale (USA)**[15] 4019 4-9-4 **77** .... JamieSpencer 1 35
(J R Fanshawe) *hld up in tch: rdn over 2f out: sn wknd* **11/2**

1m 26.2s (0.50) **Going Correction** +0.20s/f (Good) **11** Ran SP% **120.2**
Speed ratings (Par 105): **105,104,104,100,99 99,96,95,94,85 82**
toteswingers: 1&2 £9.00, 1&3 £6.20, 2&3 £4.90. CSF £37.69 CT £150.68 TOTE £8.90: £2.80, £2.10, £1.90; EX 67.50.

Owner C Fox & J Wright **Bred** Castlemartin Stud And Skymarc Farm **Trained** Newmarket, Suffolk

FOCUS
A reasonable handicap run at a fair pace and the time was decent. The first two were relatively unexposed and the third is a solid yardstick, so it looks good form for the grade could work out.

4502 ROUTE VK H'CAP 1m
8:35 (8:36) (Class 4) (0-80,86) 3-Y-O+ **£5,180** (£1,541; £770; £384) **Stalls** Low

Form RPR

0511 **1** **Credit Swap**[7] 4262 4-9-13 **86** 6ex .... TobyAtkinson(7) 4 96+
(M Wigham) *hld up: hdwy over 1f out: rdn and hung rt ins fnl f: r.o to ld towards fin* **11/4**[1]

2506 **2** *nk* **Will He Wish**[11] 4144 13-9-4 **70** .... IanMongan 15 79
(S Gollings) *hld up: hdwy over 2f out: led over 1f out: sn rdn: hdd towards fin* **22/1**

534 **3** 3/4 **Jake The Snake (IRE)**[30] 3509 8-9-5 **76** .... AmyBaker(5) 8 83
(A W Carroll) *plld hrd and prom: stdd and lost pl 6f out: hdwy over 1f out: sn rdn: r.o* **8/1**

-354 **4** *nse* **Raaeidd (IRE)**[13] 4102 3-9-6 **80** .... LDettori 6 85
(M A Jarvis) *hld up in tch: rdn over 1f out: ev ch ins fnl f: unable qckn nr fin* **7/2**[2]

4614 **5** 3 **King Columbo (IRE)**[14] 4060 4-9-4 **70** .... DarryllHolland 10 70
(Miss J Feilden) *led: hdd over 6f out: remained handy: rdn and ev ch over 1f out: no ex ins fnl f* **11/2**

-61P **6** 1/2 **Sonny Parkin**[35] 3357 7-9-0 **73** .... (v) SimonPearce(7) 12 72
(J Pearce) *dwlt: hld up: hdwy over 1f out: no ex ins fnl f* **14/1**

3204 **7** 1 1/2 **Billberry**[10] 4181 4-8-9 **61** oh1 .... (tp) AlanMunro 9 56
(S C Williams) *plld hrd and prom: rdn over 1f out: wknd ins fnl f* **11/1**

3000 **8** 3 **Bustan (IRE)**[9] 4211 10-9-12 **78** .... PatCosgrave 3 66
(G C Bravery) *chsd ldrs: rdn over 2f out: wknd over 1f out* **33/1**

6-61 **9** 9 **Northern Jem**[14] 4060 5-9-11 **77** .... JamieSpencer 11 44
(Jane Chapple-Hyam) *led over 6f out: hdd 1/2-way: led again over 2f out: rdn and hdd over 1f out: wknd fnl f* **4/1**[3]

0060 **10** 3 1/2 **Aviso (GER)**[125] 999 5-9-13 **79**.. TPQueally 2 37
(B J Curley) *awkward leaving stalls: hld up: plld hrd: hdwy over 5f out: led 1/2-way: rdn and hdd over 2f out: wknd wl over 1f out* **33/1**

1m 42.59s (2.59) **Going Correction** +0.20s/f (Good)
WFA 3 from 4yo+ 8lb **10** Ran SP% **120.6**
Speed ratings (Par 105): **95,94,93,93,90 90,88,85,76,73**
toteswingers: 1&2 £22.90, 1&3 £3.40, 2&3 £34.40. CSF £70.39 CT £450.14 TOTE £4.00: £1.70, £4.70, £1.90; EX 74.30 Place 6 £92.76, Place 5 £72.48..
Owner Your Golf Travel Ltd **Bred** Jeremy Green And Sons **Trained** Newmarket, Suffolk

FOCUS
A fair handicap but it was weakened by a number of withdrawals. Several took a keen grip off the slow early pace and there was an exciting finish. The winner and third set a reasonable standard.
T/Plt: £273.70 to a £1 stake. Pool: £75,899.06. 202.40 winning tickets. T/Qpdt: £23.60 to a £1 stake. Pool: £4,187.80. 131.30 winning tickets. CR

4276 THIRSK (L-H)

Friday, July 31

OFFICIAL GOING: Good (9.2)
Wind: moderate 1/2 behind Weather: fine

4503 PICKERING CASTLE CLAIMING STKS 7f
2:05 (2:08) (Class 4) 2-Y-O **£4,338** (£1,291; £645; £322) **Stalls** Low

Form RPR
5542 **1** **Alphacino**[9] 4188 2-9-0 0..(p) HayleyTurner 14 66
(P C Haslam) *swvd rt s: swtchd lft after s: t.k.h towards rr: hdwy on outside over 2f out: hung lft and led appr fnl f: kpt on wl* **7/1**[3]

4316 **2** 1 **Mary Helen**[9] 4188 2-8-4 0.. LiamJones 10 54+
(W M Brisbourne) *in rr div: hdwy over 2f out: hung lft and hmpd over 1f out: kpt on to take 2nd ins fnl f: nt rch wnr* **9/2**[1]

4 **3** 1 3/4 **Patachou**[13] 4101 2-8-4 0.. SaleemGolam 9 49+
(Rae Guest) *swtchd lft s: sn chsng ldrs: nt clr run over 1f out: kpt on to take 3rd ins fnl f* **5/1**[2]

5436 **4** 3 **Gulf Punch**[4] 4371 2-8-9 0.. AndrewMullen 1 47
(M F Harris) *s.s: in rr: hrd rdn and styd on fnl 2f: nt rch ldrs* **11/1**

5 **5** shd **Drinking Buddy**[13] 4101 2-8-9 0..............................(t) PaulMulrennan 5 46
(K A Ryan) *chsd ldrs: hmpd over 1f out: sn wknd* **14/1**

0055 **6** 2 1/4 **Dispol Antonio (IRE)**[9] 4190 2-8-10 0..............................(v) PhillipMakin 13 42
(P T Midgley) *chsd ldrs: led 2f out: hdd: hmpd and wknd appr fnl f* **9/1**

4650 **7** 1 1/2 **Prettiest Star (IRE)**[9] 4190 2-8-9 0.. PJMcDonald 8 37
(K A Ryan) *gave problems s: w ldr: led 3f out: hdd 2f out: sn wknd* **18/1**

000 **8** 1/2 **Seldom Seen Kid (IRE)**[14] 4067 2-9-0 0.. DavidAllan 11 41
(T D Easterby) *hld up in midfield: rdn and outpcd 3f out: hdwy over 1f out: nvr nr ldrs* **11/1**

00 **9** 1/2 **Maiwand**[9] 4188 2-8-1 0.. JimmyQuinn 7 27+
(Sir Mark Prescott) *chsd ldrs: rdn and outpcd over 2f out* **25/1**

6 **10** 7 **Drews Lane**[13] 4080 2-8-6 0..(t) JackDean(3) 12 17
(W G M Turner) *in rr: sn drvn along* **15/2**

6 **11** nk **Otterton**[28] 3572 2-8-11 0.. DuranFentiman 3 18
(R Hollinshead) *s.i.s: a in rr* **16/1**

5 **12** 1/2 **Kwami Biscuit**[9] 4188 2-8-11 0.. SilvestreDeSousa 4 22+
(G A Harker) *led tl hdd 3f out: wknd over 1f out* **9/1**

006 **13** 8 **Foricherforpoorer**[11] 4138 2-8-7 0.. PaulQuinn 2 —
(N Tinkler) *in rr: bhd fnl 3f* **100/1**

14 3 1/4 **Mizair Nouvair (IRE)** 2-8-12 0.. AndrewElliott 6 —
(J R Weymes) *swvd rt s: sn bhd* **66/1**

1m 30.47s (3.27) **Going Correction** +0.25s/f (Good) **14** Ran SP% **119.9**
Speed ratings (Par 96): **91,89,87,84,84 81,80,79,78,70 70,69,60,57**
toteswingers: 1&2 £2.30, 1&3 £3.60, 2&3 £7.40 CSF £37.95 TOTE £5.40: £1.80, £2.50, £2.90; EX 21.40.Patachou was claimed by K. Old for £5000.
Owner S A B Dinsmore **Bred** P Taplin & Mike Channon Bloodstock Ltd **Trained** Middleham Moor, N Yorks
■ Stewards' Enquiry : Andrew Mullen four-day ban: excessive use of the whip (Aug 14-17)

FOCUS
A very ordinary claimer run at a fair pace. The ground looked to be riding on the easy side of good and the time was just under six seconds outside standard. Very modest form.

NOTEBOOK
Alphacino was the most experienced runner having had seven previous starts. Claimed out of Mick Channon's yard after the latest of them, and fitted with first-time cheekpieces, he was slotted in from his wide draw before coming with a sweeping run down the outside in the home straight. He hung left all the time, inconveniencing some opponents and looking less than straightforward, but won pretty easily. (op 6-1 tchd 11-2)
Mary Helen, successful in a Yarmouth seller, was the only previous winner in the line-up. She was slightly tightened up by the winner but it did not affect the result, although she was closing at the line. Some headgear might not come amiss. (tchd 5-1)
Patachou lacked the experience of the first two, having finished fourth at Ripon on her only previous start. She kept staying on over this longer trip but hung and looked less than easy for her rider. She was claimed. (op 9-2 tchd 4-1)
Gulf Punch, the top-rated here on official adjusted figures, was well held on her debut for this yard on Fibresand four days earlier. She missed the break after rearing as the stalls were about to open and always had a lot to do if she was to reach the principals, although she did finish well after switching off the rail. Official explanation: jockey said filly missed the break (op 9-1)
Drinking Buddy improved on what he showed in a Ripon seller over 6f on his debut but could not reverse the form with Patachou. He was already held when he was hampered over a furlong out. Official explanation: jockey said gelding hung right-handed throughout (op 16-1)
Dispol Antonio(IRE) showed briefly ahead before fading inside the last. (op 12-1)

4504 BYLAND ABBEY H'CAP 7f
2:40 (2:40) (Class 5) (0-70,73) 3-Y-O+ **£4,338** (£1,291; £645; £322) **Stalls** Low

Form RPR
-066 **1** **Apollo Shark (IRE)**[45] 2998 4-9-11 **67**.. PaulMulrennan 13 77
(J Howard Johnson) *prom: effrt over 2f out: styd on to ld jst ins fnl f: hld on wl* **9/2**[1]

1533 **2** 3/4 **Violent Velocity (IRE)**[11] 4140 6-9-4 **67**.. IJBrennan(7) 7 75
(J J Quinn) *hld up in rr: hdwy over 2f out: chal jst ins fnl f: no ex* **5/1**[2]

6241 **3** 2 1/4 **Tuxedo**[10] 4181 4-9-12 **73** 6ex.. ByronMoorcroft(5) 5 75
(P W Hiatt) *in rr: hdwy over 2f out: styd on fnl f* **8/1**

-035 **4** 1/2 **Sea Salt**[6] 4312 6-8-11 **58**.. BMcHugh(5) 14 59
(R E Barr) *chsd ldrs: led 2f out: hdd jst ins fnl f: kpt on same pce* **17/2**

1300 **5** 1/2 **Woodsley House (IRE)**[11] 4134 7-9-11 **70**.. NeilBrown(3) 1 69
(A G Foster) *stdd s: hld up in rr: hdwy whn attempted to bite rival 1f out: styd on: nt rch ldrs* **13/2**

0050 **6** 1 3/4 **Pacific Pride**[21] 3828 6-9-13 **69**.. PhillipMakin 12 63
(J J Quinn) *chsd ldrs: one pce fnl 2f* **25/1**

1-30 **7** nk **Smalljohn**[45] 2998 3-9-0 **70**..(v) RichardOliver(7) 10 61
(B Smart) *chsd ldrs: one pce fnl 2f* **22/1**

16-4 **8** 3 1/4 **Devinius (IRE)**[56] 2661 4-9-6 **62**.. PJMcDonald 2 47
(G A Swinbank) *hld up in midfield: effrt on ins over 2f out: one pce whn n.m.r ins fnl f* **25/1**

3-00 **9** shd **Nuit Sombre (IRE)**[11] 4140 9-10-0 **70**..............................(p) SilvestreDeSousa 4 55
(G A Harker) *led tl 2f out: sn wknd* **16/1**

0006 **10** 1 1/4 **Dorn Dancer (IRE)**[7] 4281 7-9-4 **65**.. AmyRyan(5) 11 46
(W M Brisbourne) *hld up towards rr: hdwy on outside over 2f out: no imp whn threatened 1f out* **14/1**

005- **11** 3/4 **Micky Mac (IRE)**[266] 7228 5-9-2 **58**.. DanielTudhope 3 37
(C J Teague) *chsd ldrs: edgd lft and wknd over 1f out* **33/1**

4144 **12** 2 3/4 **Maison Dieu**[20] 3851 6-9-5 **61**.. DavidAllan 6 33
(E J Alston) *a in rr* **6/1**[3]

0601 **13** 5 **Moonage Daydream (IRE)**[11] 4140 4-9-7 **63** 6ex..............................(b) DNolan 8 21
(T D Easterby) *in rr: sn drvn along: rdn and hung lft 2f out: no ch whn eased ins fnl f* **8/1**

1m 29.25s (2.05) **Going Correction** +0.25s/f (Good)
WFA 3 from 4yo+ 7lb **13** Ran SP% **122.7**
Speed ratings (Par 103): **98,97,94,94,93 91,91,87,87,85 84,81,76**
toteswingers: 1&2 £7.00, 1&3 £12.00, 2&3 £3.50 CSF £25.97 CT £187.40 TOTE £6.90: £2.40, £2.30, £3.50; EX 38.50.
Owner Transcend Bloodstock LLP **Bred** Churchtown House Stud **Trained** Billy Row, Co Durham

FOCUS
An open handicap run at a strong pace, but the time did not compare too favourably with the opening 2yo claimer. Modest but straightforward form.
Moonage Daydream(IRE) Official explanation: jockey said gelding hung right-handed throughout

4505 NATTRASS CONSTRUCTION MAIDEN STKS 1m
3:15 (3:18) (Class 4) 3-Y-O+ **£5,634** (£1,676; £837; £418) **Stalls** Low

Form RPR
-440 **1** **Royal Defence (IRE)**[59] 2571 3-9-0 77.. AhmedAjtebi(3) 13 76
(D Nicholls) *chsd ldrs: led over 1f out: kpt on wl* **9/1**[3]

432 **2** 2 1/4 **Truly Asia (IRE)**[13] 4097 3-9-3 78.. SebSanders 15 71
(R Charlton) *trckd ldrs: led over 2f out: sn rdn: hdd over 1f out: styd on same pce* **8/13**[1]

60- **3** 1 3/4 **Dalesway**[296] 6580 3-8-12 0.. BMcHugh(5) 12 66
(R A Fahey) *gave problems at s: chsd ldrs: kpt on fnl 2f* **14/1**

0-36 **4** 6 **Alacity (IRE)**[20] 3876 3-8-12 40.. SilvestreDeSousa 6 47
(N Bycroft) *led after 1f: hdd over 2f out: wknd and eased ins fnl f* **33/1**

50- **5** 1 1/4 **Queens Flight**[224] 7726 3-8-12 0.. SaleemGolam 10 44
(Tom Dascombe) *chsd ldrs: fdd over 1f out* **33/1**

0 **6** 2 1/2 **Doctor Of Music (IRE)**[7] 4276 3-9-3 0.. PhillipMakin 14 43+
(B Smart) *mid-div: hdwy over 3f out hmpd over 1f out: nvr nr ldrs* **80/1**

0 **7** 1 1/4 **Emiratesdotcom**[16] 3984 3-9-3 0.. AndrewElliott 17 40
(M Johnston) *mid-div: hung lft 2f out: nvr a factor* **20/1**

8 1/2 **Step Into Sunshine (USA)** 3-8-12 0.. LiamJones 8 34
(M Johnston) *s.i.s: hdwy into midfield over 4f out: wknd 2f out* **16/1**

0 **9** 1/2 **Clanachy**[25] 3680 3-8-12 0.. AndrewMullen 11 33
(A G Foster) *led 1f: chsd ldrs: wknd 2f out* **150/1**

6 **10** 1/2 **Beat The Shower**[7] 4276 3-9-3 0.. PaulMulrennan 5 36
(P D Niven) *in rr: sme hdwy 2f out: nvr on terms* **50/1**

6 **11** nk **Meml**[25] 3690 3-8-12 0.. PJMcDonald 3 31
(J D Bethell) *s.i.s: a towards rr* **50/1**

54 **12** 2 **King Of Eden (IRE)**[22] 3764 3-9-3 0.. DavidAllan 9 31
(E J Alston) *mid-div: hdwy on ins to chse ldrs over 3f out: wknd 2f out* **14/1**

0 **13** 3/4 **Blastie**[83] 1888 4-9-11 0.. DuranFentiman 4 29
(T D Walford) *a towards rr* **33/1**

14 3/4 **Day Of The Eagle (IRE)** 3-9-3 0.. HayleyTurner 1 27
(L M Cumani) *in rr: sn drvn along* **7/1**[2]

15 5 **Italian Dame** 3-9-0 0 ow2.. PAspell 7 12
(J R Turner) *mid-div: outpcd and lost pl 3f out* **100/1**

1m 42.83s (2.73) **Going Correction** +0.25s/f (Good)
WFA 3 from 4yo+ 8lb **15** Ran SP% **124.0**
Speed ratings (Par 105): **96,93,92,86,84 82,81,80,80,79 79,77,76,75,70**
toteswingers: 1&2 £2.20, 1&3 £18.00, 2&3 £5.90 CSF £14.42 TOTE £13.20: £1.40, £1.10, £3.90; EX 18.40.
Owner Mrs C C Regalado-Gonzalez **Bred** Joseph Rogers **Trained** Sessay, N Yorks

FOCUS
A very modest maiden in which the first three finished clear. Nothing got into it from the rear and the form is a bit dubious.
Doctor Of Music(IRE) Official explanation: jockey said gelding hung left-handed throughout
Emiratesdotcom Official explanation: jockey said gelding hung left-handed throughout

4506 DEEPDALE SOLUTIONS FILLIES' H'CAP 1m 4f
3:50 (3:51) (Class 5) (0-70,74) 3-Y-O **£4,338** (£1,291; £645; £322) **Stalls** Low

Form RPR
60-1 **1** **Upton Seas**[27] 3610 3-8-11 **58**.. AndrewElliott 5 67+
(M W Easterby) *hld up in mid-div: effrt 3f out: led over 1f out: styd on strly: readily* **6/1**[3]

0440 **2** 4 1/2 **Madamlily (IRE)**[14] 4068 3-9-6 **67**.. PaulMulrennan 8 69
(J J Quinn) *hld up: hdwy 8f out: sn trcking ldrs: smooth hdwy to ld over 2f out: hdd over 1f out: no ex* **16/1**

4313 **3** 2 3/4 **Bollin Judith**[28] 3575 3-8-13 **60**.. DavidAllan 9 58
(T D Easterby) *chsd ldrs: edgd lft and one pce over 1f out* **5/1**[2]

6060 **4** 2 **Katie Girl**[16] 3976 3-7-9 **49** oh2..(p) BillyCray(7) 6 43
(Mrs G S Rees) *in rr: hdwy 7f out: chsng ldrs over 3f out: hung lft and one pce fnl 2f* **80/1**

6023 **5** 2 3/4 **Dispol Diva**[16] 3976 3-9-2 **63**..(v) PhillipMakin 4 53
(P T Midgley) *in rr: hdwy over 3f out: one pce fnl 2f* **12/1**

5000 **6** 3/4 **Goswick**[51] 2802 3-8-4 **51**.. AndrewMullen 10 40
(Micky Hammond) *drvn along to chse ldrs: rn wd bnd after 2f: lost pl over 2f out* **100/1**

5000 **7** nse **Knock Three Times (IRE)**[29] 3541 3-7-13 **49** oh4........ DominicFox(3) 7 38
(W Storey) *hld up in rr: hung bdly lft 2f out: nvr a factor* **100/1**

4563 **8** 2 1/2 **Musical Maze**[13] 4074 3-9-0 **61**.. DuranFentiman 1 46
(W M Brisbourne) *hld up in mid-div: effrt over 3f out: wknd 2f out* **14/1**

-455 **9** 12 **Petella**[14] 4039 3-8-7 **54**.. PJMcDonald 11 20
(C W Thornton) *sn chsng ldr: lost pl 2f out: bhd whn eased ins fnl f* **16/1**

-511 **10** 13 **Alicante**[10] 4178 3-9-13 **74** 6ex.. SebSanders 2 19
(Sir Mark Prescott) *led: qcknd over 4f out: hdd over 2f out: sn lost pl: bhd whn eased ins fnl f* **8/11**[1]

2m 38.97s (2.77) **Going Correction** +0.25s/f (Good) **10** Ran SP% **118.2**
Speed ratings (Par 97): **100,97,95,93,92 91,91,89,81,73**
toteswingers: 1&2 £12.20, 1&3 £4.40, 2&3 £10.80 CSF £96.76 CT £517.99 TOTE £6.20: £1.80, £4.30, £1.70; EX 128.80.

Owner Stephen Curtis & Eric Brook **Bred** S J Curtis - Park Farm Stud **Trained** Sheriff Hutton, N Yorks

FOCUS

They went very hard to the first bend in this ordinary fillies' handicap before the pace settled down. The proximity of the fourth and the poor showing of the favourite lend doubts to this form, but Upton Seas is on the upgrade.

Dispol Diva Official explanation: jockey said filly was never travelling

Alicante Official explanation: trainer's rep had no explanation for the poor form shown

4507 PETER BELL MEMORIAL H'CAP 6f

4:25 (4:25) (Class 4) (0-85,85) 3-Y-O+ **£5,634** (£1,257; £1,257; £418) **Stalls** High

Form RPR

0321 **1** **Sudden Impact (IRE)**[14] 4043 4-9-12 **85**..................(e) PaulMulrennan 3 95
(Paul Green) *chsd ldrs: styd on to ld last 150yds* **7/1**

1230 **2** *1 ½* **Red Cape (FR)**[5] 4353 6-9-8 **81**.......................... AndrewElliott 10 86
(Mrs R A Carr) *chsd ldrs: rdn over 2f out: kpt on ins fnl f* **3/1**[2]

0521 **2** *dht* **Cape Vale (IRE)**[10] 4167 4-9-9 **85** 6ex.......................... AhmedAjtebi(3) 7 90
(D Nicholls) *led: rdn over 1f out: hdd and no ex ins fnl f* **11/4**[1]

3520 **4** *4 ½* **John Keats**[11] 4134 6-8-10 **69**.......................... DanielTudhope 6 60
(J S Goldie) *in rr: hdwy on wd outside over 1f out: nvr rchd ldrs* **12/1**

3053 **5** *nk* **Solar Spirit (IRE)**[14] 4069 4-9-2 **82**..........................(v[1]) IJBrennan(7) 5 72
(J J Quinn) *trckd ldrs: effrt over 2f out: one pce* **11/2**[3]

0265 **6** *shd* **Errigal Lad**[4] 4387 4-9-9 **82**..........................(p) PhillipMakin 8 72
(K A Ryan) *dwlt: hdwy over 2f out: kpt on fnl f* **7/1**

0006 **7** *1 ¾* **Inter Vision (USA)**[20] 3877 9-9-7 **80**.......................... DavidAllan 2 64
(A Dickman) *in rr: nvr on terms* **9/1**

1560 **8** *5* **All The Nines (IRE)**[17] 3956 3-9-3 **81**.......................... HayleyTurner 9 49
(Mrs D J Sanderson) *chsd ldrs: lost pl over 1f out* **16/1**

6503 **9** *2* **Bahamian Lad**[29] 3529 4-9-1 **74**.......................... PJMcDonald 4 36
(R Hollinshead) *dwlt: hdwy on outside to chse ldrs 3f out: lost pl over 1f out* **20/1**

1m 11.66s (-1.04) **Going Correction** +0.125s/f (Good)
WFA 3 from 4yo+ 5lb **9** Ran SP% **120.4**
Speed ratings (Par 105): **111,109,109,103,102 102,100,93,90**
TOTE £7.00: £2.60.
Owner Terry Cummins **Bred** Owen Bourke **Trained** Lydiate, Merseyside

FOCUS

A fair handicap which few got into. The first three came clear in a decent time given the conditions and the form should stand up well in similar company. The winner is rated back to her best.

4508 HELMSLEY APPRENTICE H'CAP 6f

5:00 (5:00) (Class 5) (0-70,69) 3-Y-O+ **£4,338** (£1,291; £645; £322) **Stalls** High

Form RPR

0410 **1** **Downhill Skier (IRE)**[102] 1413 5-9-7 **62**.......................... KierenFox 4 70
(W M Brisbourne) *hld up: hdwy to ld over 2f out: styd on wl ins fnl f* **8/1**

0606 **2** *1 ¼* **Imperial Sword**[15] 4015 6-9-6 **64**..........................(b) JanWilson(3) 6 68
(T D Barron) *hld up: effrt and nt clr run over 2f out: swtchd lft: styd on to chse wnr 1f out: no ex* **4/1**[3]

-000 **3** *1 ½* **Uace Mac**[7] 4281 5-8-8 **57**.......................... TerenceFury(8) 9 56
(N Bycroft) *hld up: hdwy on ins to join ldrs 3f out: kpt on same pce fnl f* **9/1**

2022 **4** *½* **Hits Only Jude (IRE)**[4] 4374 6-9-6 **69**.......................... NeilFarley(8) 2 67
(D Carroll) *chsd ldrs on outer: outpcd over 2f out: edgd rt and kpt on appr fnl f* **7/4**[1]

6633 **5** *2 ¾* **Redwater River**[2] 4436 5-8-11 **52**..........................(b) AlexEdwards 1 41
(Mrs R A Carr) *chsd ldrs on outer: wknd fnl f* **10/3**[2]

6150 **6** *6* **All You Need (IRE)**[31] 3490 5-8-13 **54**..........................(p) BarryAdams 7 24
(R Hollinshead) *w ldrs: led 3f out: sn hdd: wknd over 1f out* **12/1**

00-0 **7** *¾* **Nabra**[197] 175 5-8-9 **50** oh5.......................... AnthonyBetts 8 17
(M Brittain) *led tl 3f out: wknd 2f out* **33/1**

400- **8** *1* **Lujiana**[330] 5638 4-9-3 **58**.......................... SamuelDrury 5 22
(M Brittain) *chsd ldrs: lost pl over 1f out* **20/1**

1m 13.82s (1.12) **Going Correction** +0.125s/f (Good) **8** Ran SP% **115.9**
Speed ratings (Par 103): **97,95,93,92,89 81,80,78**
toteswingers: 1&2 £5.80, 1&3 £9.80, 2&3 £7.70 CSF £40.56 CT £299.89 TOTE £8.30: £2.20, £1.90, £3.00; EX 34.10 Place 6: £50.68 Place 5: £28.82.
Owner Miss P D Insull **Bred** Swettenham Stud **Trained** Great Ness, Shropshire

FOCUS

A weak race for apprentice riders who had not ridden more than five winners. The time was over two seconds slower than the the preceding 68-85 handicap and this is not form to rate positively. The winner looks the best guide to the form.

T/Plt: £89.80 to a £1 stake. Pool: £40,921.91. 332.59 winning tickets. T/Qpdt: £28.20 to a £1 stake. Pool: £2,847.80. 74.50 winning tickets. WG

4509 - (Foreign Racing) - See Raceform Interactive

4474 GALWAY (R-H)

Friday, July 31

OFFICIAL GOING: Hurdle & flat courses - soft; chase course - soft to heavy changing to soft to heavy on all courses after race 2 (5.40)

4510a ARTHUR'S DAY H'CAP (PREMIER HANDICAP) 1m 4f

6:50 (6:50) 3-Y-O+ **£41,082** (£12,053; £5,742; £1,956)

RPR

1 **Drunken Sailor (IRE)**[33] 3439 4-8-9 82..........................(bt) PBBeggy(3) 8 85
(Paul W Flynn, Ire) *cl up in 3rd: impr to chal 2f out: led appr st: edgd clr 1f out: strly pressed clsng stages: all out* **9/2**[1]

2 *nk* **Rajik (IRE)**[4] 4391 4-8-12 89..........................(t) CO'Farrell(7) 10 92+
(C F Swan, Ire) *hld up towards rr: last 1/2-way: 7th and hdwy ent st: r.o strly ins fnl f: nrest at fin* **16/1**

3 *1 ¼* **Taralga (IRE)**[13] 4111 4-8-12 82.......................... DJMoran 2 83
(S J Treacy, Ire) *led: rdn and strly pressed fr 3f out: hdd appr st: kpt on u.p ins fnl f* **5/1**[2]

4 *shd* **Aliyfa (IRE)**[15] 4033 3-9-7 103.......................... MJKinane 12 104
(John M Oxx, Ire) *a.p: 2nd 1/2-way: rdn to chal fr 3f out: 3rd appr st: kpt on u.p* **13/2**[3]

5 *2* **South Wing (IRE)**[64] 2427 5-8-12 82.......................... KLatham 9 80
(Eoin Griffin, Ire) *trckd ldrs: 6th 1/2-way: rdn fr 3f out: 5th into st: kpt on same pce* **16/1**

6 *nk* **Tin Town Boy (IRE)**[2] 4443 8-7-13 74..........................(t) ShaneFoley(5) 6 71
(H Rogers, Ire) *mid-div: 7th after 1/2-way: 5th and hdwy 3f out: 4th 2f out: no imp st* **13/2**[3]

7 *8* **Sesenta (IRE)**[45] 2994 5-9-10 94.......................... JMurtagh 11 78
(W P Mullins, Ire) *trckd ldrs: 5th 1/2-way: mod 4th 3f out: sn u.p: 6th and no imp ent st* **9/2**[1]

8 *2 ½* **King Royal (IRE)**[19] 3899 4-8-9 79.......................... DMGrant 4 59
(Patrick J Flynn, Ire) *mid-div: lost pl after 1/2-way: no imp fr 3f out* **9/1**

9 *hd* **Shela House**[20] 3879 5-8-7 82.......................... DEMullins(5) 1 62
(J H Culloty, Ire) *in rr of mid-div: 8th 4f out: rdn fr 3f out: no imp fr bef st* **14/1**

10 *¾* **The Last Hurrah (IRE)**[19] 3897 9-8-11 81..........................(b) WJSupple 7 60
(Mrs John Harrington, Ire) *chsd ldrs in 4th: rdn 4f out: sn wknd* **12/1**

11 *dist* **Rayhani (USA)**[8] 4247 6-9-3 87.......................... FMBerry 5 —
(D Nicholls) *s.i.s and a towards rr: t.o st* **25/1**

2m 52.09s (8.99)
WFA 3 from 4yo+ 12lb **11** Ran SP% **119.7**
CSF £78.72 CT £379.52 TOTE £4.90: £1.80, £4.60, £2.00; DF 129.60.
Owner J J Keogh **Bred** Cyril Kiernan **Trained** Colehill, Co. Longford

■ Stewards' Enquiry : P B Beggy two-day ban: used whip with excessive frequency without allowing mount time to respond (Aug 15-16)

4225 DONCASTER (L-H)

Saturday, August 1

OFFICIAL GOING: Soft (good to soft in places; 6.9)

Races over 1m2f and 1m4f were approximately 12 yards longer than usual after rail movements.

Wind: Light across Weather: Overcast and rain

4514 FAYE BLYTH H'CAP 5f

2:05 (2:05) (Class 5) (0-70,68) 3-Y-O **£3,238** (£963; £481; £240) **Stalls** High

Form RPR

6252 **1** **La Capriosa**[6] 4355 3-9-2 **63**.......................... RobertWinston 2 69+
(J A Glover) *cl up: rdn to ld over 1f out: clr ent fnl f* **10/11**[1]

0 **2** *1 ¾* **Sea Crest**[28] 3611 3-8-7 **61**.......................... JohnCavanagh(7) 1 61
(M Brittain) *s.i.s and bhd: swtchd outside and hdwy 1/2-way: sn rdn and styd on strly ins fnl f: nrst fin* **25/1**

333 **3** *2 ¼* **Imaginary Diva**[34] 3428 3-9-3 **64**.......................... AdrianMcCarthy 4 56
(G G Margarson) *in tch: hdwy and cl up 1/2-way: rdn wl over 1f out and kpt on same pce* **7/1**[3]

3320 **4** *1 ¼* **Diamond Blade**[42] 3175 3-8-9 **56**.......................... TonyHamilton 3 43
(T D Easterby) *hld up in rr: hdwy to chse ldrs 2f out: sn rdn and kpt on same pce appr fnl f* **8/1**

3440 **5** *1 ¼* **Dispol Kylie (IRE)**[17] 3973 3-9-6 **67**.......................... ShaneKelly 8 50
(P T Midgley) *led: rdn along and jnd 2f out: hdd over 1f out and sn wknd* **13/2**[2]

6334 **6** *12* **You'relikemefrank**[40] 3229 3-8-3 **50** oh3 ow1..........(p) RoystonFfrench 6 —
(J Balding) *cl up: rdn along over 2f out: sn drvn and wknd* **11/1**

0215 **7** *11* **Chris's Jem**[9] 4244 3-9-7 **68**.......................... EddieAhern 7 —
(J R Jenkins) *trckd ldrs: smooth hdwy 1/2-way: effrt 2f out: sn rdn and btn: eased* **15/2**

63.36 secs (2.86) **Going Correction** +0.55s/f (Yiel) **7** Ran SP% **113.3**
Speed ratings (Par 100): **99,96,92,90,88 69,51**
toteswingers: 1&2 £8.50, 1&3 £1.30, 2&3 £2.30 CSF £26.90 CT £107.47 TOTE £1.90: £1.30, £10.20; EX 28.80 Trifecta £83.90 Pool: £435.81 - 3.84 winning units..
Owner Paul J Dixon **Bred** Slatch Farm Stud **Trained** Babworth, Notts

FOCUS

Following overnight rain the ground was changed to soft, good to soft in places. The winning rider in the first reported that they were getting through the ground well enough. This was just a modest sprint handicap.

Chris's Jem Official explanation: jockey said filly was unsuited by the soft ground

4515 SOCIETY LIFESTYLE AND LEISURE MAGAZINE MAIDEN AUCTION STKS 6f

2:40 (2:43) (Class 4) 2-Y-O **£4,857** (£1,445; £722; £360) **Stalls** High

Form RPR

1 **Bagamoyo** 2-8-11 0.......................... EddieAhern 9 82+
(J R Fanshawe) *dwlt: sn in tch: hdwy over 2f out: effrt to ld 1f out: rdn ent fnl f and kpt on wl* **7/1**

2 *1 ¾* **Lutine Charlie (IRE)** 2-8-11 0.......................... MickyFenton 7 77+
(P Winkworth) *dwlt: sn in midfield: swtchd outside and hdwy over 2f out: rdn over 1f out: chsd wnr ins fnl f: edgd rt and one pce last 100yds* **25/1**

0 **3** *4 ½* **Mexican Milly (IRE)**[107] 1298 2-8-4 0.......................... PaulEddery 13 56
(B W Hills) *led: rdn along over 2f out: hdd 1/2f out: sn drvn and wknd ent fnl f* **14/1**

66 **4** *nk* **Royal Record**[9] 4226 2-8-5 0 ow1.......................... RichardMullen 2 56
(M Brittain) *cl up on outer: rdn to chal wl over 1f out: sn drvn and wknd ent fnl f* **16/1**

66 **5** *2 ¼* **Venture Girl (IRE)**[63] 2503 2-8-3 0.......................... KellyHarrison(3) 8 51
(T D Easterby) *in tch: hdwy to chse ldrs 1/2-way: rdn over 2f out: sn one pce* **25/1**

6 *6* **Admiral Cochrane (IRE)** 2-8-4 0.......................... Louis-PhilippeBeuzelin(5) 5 36
(W Jarvis) *cl up: rdn along over 2f out: grad wknd* **8/1**

30 **7** *nse* **Newton Circus**[25] 3715 2-8-11 0.......................... RobertWinston 10 37
(R Hannon) *a in midfield* **5/1**[1]

525 **8** *¾* **Rio Caribe (IRE)**[70] 2258 2-8-11 0.......................... DanielTudhope 11 35
(T D Walford) *chsd ldrs: rdn along 1/2-way: sn wknd* **5/1**[1]

9 *1* **Cracking Lass (IRE)** 2-8-8 0.......................... TonyHamilton 12 29
(R A Fahey) *s.i.s: a in rr* **7/1**

0 **10** *nk* **Shercon (IRE)**[35] 3376 2-8-7 0 ow1.......................... MichaelJStainton(3) 3 30
(N Tinkler) *a towards rr* **100/1**

00 **11** *1 ½* **Woodhouse Mill (IRE)**[36] 3337 2-8-8 0 ow2.......................... FergusSweeney 4 24
(N Tinkler) *a towards rr* **100/1**

12 *¾* **Al Khawarezmi** 2-9-2 0.......................... RoystonFfrench 1 30
(M Johnston) *sn rdn along and a in rr* **11/2**[2]

4 **13** *3 ½* **Ella Grace (USA)**[49] 2914 2-8-3 0 ow2.......................... LeeTopliss(7) 14 13
(R A Fahey) *cl up: rdn along 1/2-way: sn wknd* **6/1**[3]

14 *30* **Bahamian Sun (IRE)** 2-8-8 0..........................(t) RossAtkinson(5) 6 —
(Tom Dascombe) *sn rdn along and a in rr* **12/1**

1m 16.86s (3.26) **Going Correction** +0.55s/f (Yiel) **14** Ran SP% **129.0**
Speed ratings (Par 96): **100,97,91,91,88 80,80,79,77,77 75,74,69,29**
toteswingers: 1&2 £66.20, 2&3 £29.50, 1&3 not won. CSF £184.97 TOTE £10.00: £2.80, £5.60, £4.30; EX 259.00 TRIFECTA Not won..
Owner Chippenham Lodge Stud Limited **Bred** Chippenham Lodge Stud Ltd **Trained** Newmarket, Suffolk

FOCUS

An ordinary maiden. Those with previous experience had not shown a great deal and it was one of the newcomers who emerged on top.

NOTEBOOK

Bagamoyo, soon tracking the pace after a slightly tardy start, moved smoothly to the front and ran on well to assert. His dam's four previous foals all won, the best of them being fair handicapper Brief Goodbye, and he should improve, as he was still a little green here. (tchd 15-2)

Lutine Charlie(IRE), like the winner, was a little slow to break. He picked up well down the outside going to the final furlong but was always being held. Sprint-bred, this looks his trip and he should know more next time. (tchd 20-1)

Mexican Milly(IRE) had not run since finishing down the field on her debut at the Craven meeting in April. She showed good pace up the stands' side and kept on for third after the winner pounced. (op 12-1 tchd 11-1)

Royal Record drawn on the outside, ran a nice race and seemed suited by the return to this trip after a try over 7f last time. She can now run in nurseries. (op 12-1)

Venture Girl(IRE), who gave trouble at the stalls, showed more than she had on her first two starts and looks ready for a step up to 7f now. (op 20-1)

Admiral Cochrane(IRE) is a half-brother to several winners, most of them abroad. He showed up well towards the outside before being outpaced by the principals in the last quarter mile. (op 14-1)

Newton Circus ran as if something was amiss on Polytrack last time and this was a better effort, although he never threatened the leaders. (tchd 9-2 and 11-2)

Rio Caribe(IRE) was the subject of support, but after showing pace on this step up in trip, he dropped away rather tamely. (op 11-1)

Cracking Lass(IRE) took a deal of persuading to enter the stalls and came out of them slowly, but she did shape with a bit of promise. A half-sister to three winners, notably Tagula Sunrise, she will have learned from the experience. (op 8-1)

4516 SUSAN HULME BIRTHDAY CONDITIONS STKS — 6f

3:15 (3:17) (Class 3) 3-Y-0+

£7,477 (£2,239; £1,119; £560; £279; £140) Stalls High

Form — RPR

-030 **1** **Zidane**[42] 3141 7-8-13 102 .... EddieAhern 11 105
(J R Fanshawe) *dwlt and rr: swtchd rt and gd hdwy 2f out: rdn to chse ldr over 1f out: led ins fnl f and kpt on* 15/2[3]

-120 **2** ¾ **Eisteddfod**[35] 3405 8-9-7 102 .... (b) MickyFenton 3 111
(P F I Cole) *led: rdn along over 2f out and sn hdd: drvn and rallied ins fnl f: kpt on wl towards fin* 25/1

6-20 **3** hd **Ancien Regime (IRE)**[22] 3819 4-9-4 108 .... RichardMullen 8 107
(Saeed Bin Suroor) *towards rr: swtchd rt and hdwy 2f out: rdn over 1f out: styd on strly ins fnl f* 9/2[2]

23-4 **4** ¾ **War Artist (AUS)**[14] 4087 6-8-13 115 .... ShaneKelly 10 100
(J M P Eustace) *trckd ldrs on outer: smooth hdwy to ld 2f out: rdn over 1f out: hdd ins fnl f and wknd* 5/6[1]

1325 **5** 1 ¾ **Pretty Bonnie**[14] 4096 4-8-3 85 .... Louis-PhilippeBeuzelin(5) 2 89
(A E Price) *prom: rdn along 2f out: drvn over 1f out and kpt on same pce* 25/1

3053 **6** 6 **Peace Offering (IRE)**[15] 4059 9-9-2 104 .... FergusSweeney 9 78
(D Nicholls) *prom: rdn along 2f out: sn drvn and wknd* 10/1

3500 **7** 1 ¾ **First Order**[21] 3855 8-8-10 75 ow2 .... (v) AnnStokell(5) 5 71
(Miss A Stokell) *t.k.h: chsd ldrs tl rdn over 2f out and sn wknd* 100/1

0-06 **8** 12 **Galeota (IRE)**[15] 4059 7-9-2 94 .... RobertWinston 4 34
(R Hannon) *in tch on outer: rdn along over 2f out and sn btn* 12/1

4-50 **9** 2 **Adorn**[49] 2928 3-8-4 100 .... RoystonFfrench 7 19
(J Noseda) *cl up: rdn along over 2f out: sn wknd and eased* 14/1

1m 15.77s (2.17) **Going Correction** +0.55s/f (Yiel)
WFA 3 from 4yo+ 4lb — **9** Ran SP% **116.6**
Speed ratings (Par 107): **107,106,105,104,102 94,92,76,73**
toteswingers: 1&2 £16.30, 1&3 £6.90, 2&3 £48.10 CSF £169.79 TOTE £7.60: £1.90, £3.10, £1.70; EX 79.40 Trifecta £503.40 Part won. Pool: £680.32 - 0.53 winning units..
Owner Jan and Peter Hopper **Bred** Mrs J P Hopper And Mrs E M Grundy **Trained** Newmarket, Suffolk

FOCUS

A decent conditions sprint in which the field raced some way from the rail.

NOTEBOOK

Zidane, whose yard has returned to form, was winning for the first time since taking the Abernant at Newmarket in April last year. He had not shown a great deal this season, but he tracked the favourite through on the stands' side and, striking the front inside the last, held on well, despite showing a high head carriage. Smart though he is, things need to go his way and he would not be one to back for a follow-up. Official explanation: trainer said, regarding the improved form shown, that he could not explain the poor run at Ascot (op 5-1)

Eisteddfod appreciated the return to soft conditions and, having led until the favourite eased past, he rallied tenaciously for second. (op 16-1)

Ancien Regime(IRE), who lost his action when last in the July Cup, faced a more realistic task. Held up in rear, he hung a little, but came through late for third. He may not prove easy to place but would not mind faster ground. (op 7-2 tchd 11-2)

War Artist(AUS) had 10lb in hand on these terms and everything looked to be going according to plan as he made smooth progress to strike the front. Tiring inside the last, he could not hold off the winner and was relegated two further places late on. He was in front plenty soon enough in these unsuitably soft conditions, and can start to make up for lost time back on a sound surface. (op 13-8)

Pretty Bonnie had ground conditions to suit and ran well in the face of a stiff task at the weights. Official explanation: jockey said filly hung right (tchd 20-1)

Peace Offering(IRE), who has done all his winning over the minimum trip, had not tackled 6f since October 2006. He finished well adrift of the five in front of him. (op 8-1)

Galeota(IRE), a winner of four of his five previous starts here, was buffeted leaving the stalls and could never get into it. (op 11-1 tchd 15-2)

Adorn is another who looks best suited to a sound surface, but she is yet to prove she has trained on. (op 12-1 tchd 16-1)

4517 SAXTON MEE H'CAP — 1m 2f 60y

3:50 (3:51) (Class 2) (0-100,98) 3-Y-0+

£12,462 (£3,732; £1,866; £934; £466; £234) Stalls Low

Form — RPR

1230 **1** **Hillview Boy (IRE)**[22] 3826 5-9-0 80 .... DanielTudhope 10 92+
(J S Goldie) *hld up and bhd: hdwy and swtchd lft over 2f out: rdn wl over 1f out: str run to ld ent fnl f: sn clr* 6/1[3]

4412 **2** 2 ¾ **Shaloo Diamond**[16] 4003 4-9-1 84 .... MichaelJStainton(3) 9 90
(R M Whitaker) *trckd ldrs: hdwy 3f out: sn chal and rdn to ld wl over 1f out: sn drvn and edgd lft: hdd ent fnl f and kpt on same pce* 11/4[1]

-023 **3** nse **Safari Sunup (IRE)**[14] 4091 4-9-13 93 .... RobertWinston 8 99
(P Winkworth) *a.p: effrt 3f out: cl up 2f out: sn rdn and ev ch tl drvn and one pce ent fnl f* 6/1[3]

501 **4** 4 ½ **Mull Of Dubai**[49] 2932 6-10-0 94 .... MickyFenton 4 91
(T P Tate) *hld up in rr: hdwy 3f out: rdn and ch 2f out: sn drvn and wknd over 1f out* 10/1

2265 **5** nk **Sahrati**[22] 3822 5-9-7 87 .... (p) EddieAhern 1 83
(D R C Elsworth) *led: rdn along 3f out: drvn and hdd 2f out: grad wknd* 9/2[2]

004 **6** 1 ¾ **Red Jade**[25] 3705 4-8-11 82 .... RossAtkinson(5) 7 75
(A P Jarvis) *chsd ldrs: rdn along 3f out: drvn over 2f out and sn wknd* 10/1

4406 **7** 17 **Humble Opinion**[8] 4274 7-9-4 84 .... RoystonFfrench 2 43
(A King) *trckd ldrs: hdwy and cl up 3f out: rdn to ld briefly 2f out: sn hdd & wknd* 20/1

12-0 **8** 1 **Full Toss**[37] 3298 3-9-9 98 .... ShaneKelly 5 55
(R Hannon) *t.k.h: prom: rdn along 4f out and sn wknd* 11/1

3-06 **9** 4 **Jaser**[14] 4091 4-9-8 88 .... RichardMullen 6 37
(P W Chapple-Hyam) *hld up towards rr: hdwy over 4f out: cl up 3f out: sn rdn and wknd* 15/2

2m 16.83s (5.63) **Going Correction** +0.625s/f (Yiel)
WFA 3 from 4yo+ 9lb — **9** Ran SP% **116.5**
Speed ratings (Par 109): **102,99,99,96,95 94,80,80,76**
toteswingers: 1&2 £2.30, 2&3 £5.40 CSF £23.08 CT £104.49 TOTE £8.40: £2.20, £1.90, £1.80; EX 31.20 TRIFECTA Not won..
Owner Connor & Dunne **Bred** John Coleman **Trained** Uplawmoor, E Renfrews

FOCUS

Not a strong handicap for the class. The pace was only moderate and, after the field had tacked over to the stands' side in the home straight, it turned into a bit of a sprint through the last two and a half furlongs.

NOTEBOOK

Hillview Boy(IRE) ◆ raced keenly in rear, before making rapid headway when switched to the wide outside. He cut down the two leaders to win going away and looks to be on the upgrade. As his knee action hinted, he proved well at home in the ground and he could follow the path of his stablemate Nanton, who won this race a year ago before finishing second in the Cambridgeshire. (tchd 7-1)

Shaloo Diamond won in the mud here over 1m4f two runs back before finding the in-form Plaisterer too good over course and distance last time. Another 4lb higher, he worked his way to the rail in the straight and injected some pace going to the two pole. He could not hold off the winner, but stuck on to just hold second and remains in form. (op 4-1 tchd 5-2)

Safari Sunup(IRE) was always towards the fore and went after the runner-up when that one kicked for home, sticking on willingly and almost getting past him on the line. (op 7-1 tchd 11-2)

Mull Of Dubai had today's winner behind when winning a valuable York ladies' race last time over 1m4f. Put up 5lb for that, and again held up in rear, he improved to have his chance but could not quicken when the pace lifted and was well held in fourth. (op 8-1)

Sahrati set the modest pace and was readily left behind once collared. (op 13-2 tchd 4-1)

Red Jade remains below his best and a 2lb drop since his last run did not have much effect. (op 13-2 tchd 6-1)

Humble Opinion had been dropped 5lb since his last start amd was down in trip, but he faded tamely after being in the firing line when the pace quickened. He is better on faster ground. (op 16-1 tchd 25-1)

Full Toss, who was keen in the early stages, was outpaced when the pace picked up and steadily left behind. (op 9-1 tchd 12-1)

Jaser's rider was looking down at his mount in the closing stages as if something may have been amiss. Official explanation: jockey said colt hung violently right (op 7-1)

4518 SAXTON MEE YORKSHIRE H'CAP — 1m 4f

4:25 (4:26) (Class 4) (0-85,85) 3-Y-0 — £4,857 (£1,445; £722; £360) Stalls Low

Form — RPR

0312 **1** **Red Cadeaux**[25] 3721 3-9-6 84 .... ShaneKelly 9 94
(E A L Dunlop) *hld up in tch: hdwy 3f out: rdn to chse ldr wl over 1f out: chal ent fnl f: drvn and styd on wl to ld last 100yds* 8/1

1644 **2** ½ **Advisor (FR)**[16] 4008 3-8-12 76 .... RobertWinston 2 85
(M L W Bell) *trckd ldrs on inner: swtchd rt and hdwy on bit 3f out: led over 2f out: rdn over 1f out: jnd and drvn ent fnl f: hdd and no ex last 100yds* 6/1[3]

2132 **3** 5 **Mr Freddy (IRE)**[14] 4102 3-8-8 72 .... TonyHamilton 6 73
(R A Fahey) *hld up towards rr: hdwy over 3f out: rdn to chse ldr wl over 1f out: drvn and n.m.r on inner over 1f out: sn swtchd rt and kpt on same pce* 6/1[3]

1-40 **4** 1 ¼ **Worth A King'S**[30] 3535 3-8-4 73 .... Louis-PhilippeBeuzelin(5) 7 72
(Sir Michael Stoute) *hld up in rr: hdwy on inner 4f out: rdn to chse ldrs wl over 1f out: sn drvn and no imp* 40/1

2331 **5** 5 **Times Up**[25] 3707 3-9-7 85 .... EddieAhern 8 76
(J L Dunlop) *chsd ldrs: rdn along 3f out: drvn over 2f out and grad wknd* 7/2[2]

-401 **6** 10 **Devotion To Duty (IRE)**[64] 2447 3-9-6 84 .... PaulEddery 4 59
(B W Hills) *chsd ldng pair: hdwy to ld 3f out: sn rdn and hdd over 2f out: sn drvn and wknd* 20/1

11- **7** 2 ¾ **Alcalde**[298] 6561 3-9-4 82 .... RoystonFfrench 5 53
(M Johnston) *chsd ldr: rdn along over 3f out: wknd over 2f out* 15/8[1]

-0PP **8** 4 ½ **Captain Imperial (IRE)**[9] 4229 3-8-8 72 .... MickyFenton 3 35
(T P Tate) *led: rdn along and hdd 3f out: sn wknd* 66/1

-120 **9** 1 ¼ **Lively Fling (USA)**[72] 2208 3-9-6 84 .... RichardMullen 10 45
(J H M Gosden) *a towards rr* 20/1

562 **10** 29 **Golden Rock (IRE)**[47] 2981 3-8-12 76 .... (v[1]) FergusSweeney 1 —
(R Charlton) *hld up: a towards rr* 12/1

2m 41.98s (6.88) **Going Correction** +0.625s/f (Yiel) — **10** Ran SP% **117.8**
Speed ratings (Par 102): **102,101,98,97,94 87,85,82,81,62**
toteswingers: 1&2 £52.10, 1&3 £12.90, 2&3 £12.80 CSF £53.54 CT £312.95 TOTE £9.60: £2.70, £2.20, £2.00; EX 55.00 Trifecta £350.50 Pool: £810.10 - 1.71 winning units..
Owner R J Arculli **Bred** Foursome Thoroughbreds **Trained** Newmarket, Suffolk

FOCUS

The rain came down heavily before this event, a decent three-year-old handicap. The conditions placed the emphasis on stamina and the field was well stretched out at the finish.

Times Up Official explanation: jockey said gelding was unsuited by the soft ground
Captain Imperial(IRE) Official explanation: jockey said colt hung left
Lively Fling(USA) Official explanation: jockey said gelding was unsuited by the soft ground
Golden Rock(IRE) Official explanation: jockey said colt ran too freely

4519 ADAM BOTT EASTWOOD CONSULTANCY ACCOUNTANTS MAIDEN STKS — 1m 2f 60y

4:55 (4:58) (Class 5) 3-4-Y-0 — £3,238 (£963; £481; £240) Stalls Low

Form — RPR

04 **1** **Do The Strand (IRE)**[24] 3751 3-9-0 0 .... RobertWinston 9 87
(B W Hills) *chsd ldrs: hdwy over 3f out: led over 2f out: rdn wl over 1f out: drvn ins fnl f and kpt on gamely* 5/1[3]

2 **2** ½ **Troopingthecolour**[49] 2930 3-9-0 0 .... RichardMullen 10 86
(J H M Gosden) *trckd ldrs: hdwy over 3f out: rdn to chse wnr 2f out: drvn ent fnl f: kpt on* 11/4[1]

3 **7** *Deportment* 3-8-9 0 EddieAhern 7 74+
(J R Fanshawe) *hld up: gd hdwy on inner 4f out: trckd ldrs whn hmpd 3f out: sn swtchd rt and rdn: styd on to take 3rd ins fnl f* **18/1**
662 **4** *2 ¼* **Outrageous Request**[96] 1573 3-9-0 83 PaulEddery 15 67
(Pat Eddery) *midfield: hdwy 3f out: rdn to chse ldrs 2f out: drvn and kpt on same pce fr over 1f out* **7/2**[2]
06 **5** *nk* **Primera Vista**[15] 4057 3-9-0 0 FergusSweeney 6 67
(L M Cumani) *in tch: hdwy 3f out: chsd ldrs 2f out: kpt on same pce* **28/1**
50- **6** *1 ¼* **King's Song (IRE)**[280] 6977 3-8-9 0 Louis-PhilippeBeuzelin(5) 16 64
(Sir Michael Stoute) *stdd s and hld up towards rr: hdwy over 3f out: rdn along 2f out: no imp fr over 1f out* **15/2**
3 **7** *shd* **Mustakmil (IRE)**[26] 3690 3-9-0 0 RoystonFfrench 13 64
(E A L Dunlop) *towards rr: hdwy over 4f out: rdn to chse ldrs over 2f out: sn drvn and no imp* **18/1**
33 **8** *4 ½* **Acquavella**[16] 4014 3-8-9 0 TonyHamilton 3 50
(R A Fahey) *chsd ldrs: rdn along 3f out: wknd 2f out* **6/1**
9 *nse* **Country Road (IRE)** 3-9-0 0 AdrianMcCarthy 1 55
(P W Chapple-Hyam) *chsd ldr: hdwy and cl up over 3f out: rdn over 2f out: sn drvn and wknd* **6/1**
3 **10** *14* **Rapid Desire (IRE)**[56] 2723 3-8-10 0 ow1 DNolan 11 23
(J R Weymes) *a towards rr* **50/1**
45 **11** *4* **Anessia**[15] 4066 3-8-4 0 RossAtkinson(5) 5 14
(Tom Dascombe) *a towards rr* **66/1**
0-03 **12** *4 ½* **Galley Slave (IRE)**[14] 516 4-9-6 43 (b) LeeVickers(3) 4 10
(M C Chapman) *led: clr 1/2-way: rdn along over 3f out: sn hdd & wknd* **100/1**
13 *3 ¾* **Mathaaq** 3-9-0 0 ShaneKelly 8 —
(M A Jarvis) *chsd ldrs to 1/2-way: sn lost pl and bhd* **14/1**
-606 **14** *16* **Zelos Diktator**[25] 3708 3-9-0 48 (v¹) MickyFenton 14 —
(J G Given) *chsd ldrs on outer: rdn along over 3f out and sn wknd* **100/1**
15 *¾* **Katya Kabanova** 3-8-6 0 MichaelJStainton(3) 2 —
(J R Fanshawe) *dwlt: a bhd* **28/1**
16 *¾* **Princeofthedesert** 3-9-0 0 SJCraine 12 —
(G Woodward) *dwlt: a bhd* **100/1**

2m 17.5s (6.30) **Going Correction** +0.625s/f (Yiel)
WFA 3 from 4yo 9lb **16** Ran SP% **136.4**
Speed ratings (Par 103): **99,98,93,91,90 89,89,86,86,75 71,68,65,52,51 51**
toteswingers: 1&2 £6.30, 1&3 £23.50, 2&3 £8.80 CSF £21.10 TOTE £5.90: £2.30, £1.90, £5.10; EX 26.40 Trifecta £148.10 Pool: £506.56 - 2.53 winning units. Place 6: £296.80 Place 5: £181.29.
Owner Suzanne & Nigel Williams **Bred** Kildare Racing Syndicate **Trained** Lambourn, Berks

FOCUS
A fair maiden run at a reasonable pace and the time compared favourably with the earlier Class 2 handicap.
Deportment ◆ Official explanation: jockey said filly was denied a clear run
T/Plt: £669.80 to a £1 stake. Pool: £69,276.09. 75.50 winning tickets. T/Qpdt: £20.90 to a £1 stake. Pool: £5,584.25. 197.60 winning tickets. JR

4484 GOODWOOD (R-H)

Saturday, August 1

OFFICIAL GOING: Good changing to soft after race 1 (1.55)
Going was changed to soft after the first race, following persistent rain, but appeared to be riding more like good to soft.
Wind: Moderate, mostly against Weather: Misty, rain, miserable

4520 BLUESQUAREPOKER.COM STKS (H'CAP) 1m 3f
1:55 (1:56) (Class 3) (0-90,88) 3-Y-O

£12,462 (£3,732; £1,866; £934; £466; £234) **Stalls** Low

Form RPR
1210 **1** **Eastern Aria (UAE)**[23] 3780 3-9-7 88 GregFairley 15 101
(M Johnston) *trckd ldng pair: prog to ld over 2f out: clr over 1f out: styd on wl* **14/1**
144 **2** *2 ¼* **Citizenship**[15] 4045 3-8-5 72 (t) WilliamBuick 11 81
(Ian Williams) *t.k.h: sn hld up in midfield: 8th over 4f out: gd prog on outer 3f out: chsd wnr 1f out: r.o but no imp* **25/1**
411 **3** *2 ¾* **Lady Luachmhar (IRE)**[14] 4074 3-9-1 82 PaulHanagan 10 86
(R A Fahey) *swtg: t.k.h: trckd ldrs: 4th over 4f out: rdn over 2f out: kpt on same pce* **11/2**[2]
2163 **4** *1 ¾* **Becausewecan (USA)**[3] 4420 3-8-11 78 NCallan 16 79
(M Johnston) *led to over 2f out: grad fdd* **9/2**[1]
0-01 **5** *½* **Itlaaq**[64] 2432 3-8-11 78 TPO'Shea 9 79+
(J L Dunlop) *lw: hld up wl in rr: 13th over 4f out and wl off the pce: gd prog on outer fr 3f out: styd on: nrst fin* **7/1**
2-10 **6** *1* **Natural Flair (USA)**[90] 1701 3-9-0 81 JimmyFortune 14 80
(P W Chapple-Hyam) *trckd ldr to over 2f out: fdd over 1f out* **20/1**
4012 **7** *3* **Thin Red Line (IRE)**[28] 3618 3-9-6 87 JamieSpencer 5 81
(E A L Dunlop) *wl in tch: 5th over 4f out: wknd over 1f out* **8/1**
03-3 **8** *nk* **Navajo Nation (IRE)**[29] 3566 3-8-5 72 MartinDwyer 2 65
(B J Meehan) *hld up wl in rr: 14th and shkn up over 4f out: sme prog over 3f out but nvr on terms w ldng gp* **33/1**
5600 **9** *3* **Aurorian (IRE)**[23] 3780 3-9-1 82 RichardHughes 12 70
(R Hannon) *trckd ldrs: 6th over 4f out: wknd u.p 2f out* **14/1**
1-53 **10** *3 ¼* **Jedi**[87] 1792 3-9-2 83 RyanMoore 1 66
(Sir Michael Stoute) *lw: hld up in rr: 11th and plenty to do over 4f out: nvr on terms* **13/2**[3]
3360 **11** *11* **Princability (IRE)**[72] 2189 3-8-7 74 SamHitchcott 4 38
(M R Channon) *lw: a towards rr: 11th over 4f out: hrd rdn and no prog 3f out: wknd* **100/1**
1403 **12** *2 ¾* **Blaise Tower**[50] 2884 3-8-10 77 SteveDrowne 8 36
(G L Moore) **25/1**
4 **13** *½* **Zarinski (IRE)**[44] 3051 3-9-7 88 MJKinane 13 46
(Jim Best) *lw: hld up in midfield: 7th over 4f out: sn wknd and bhd* **9/1**
1200 **14** *5* **Dubai Crest**[44] 3051 3-9-4 85 JimCrowley 7 35
(Mrs A J Perrett) *hld up towards rr: 10th over 4f out: lost tch w ldrs sn after* **14/1**
4030 **15** *3 ¼* **Guestofthenation (USA)**[8] 4280 3-8-7 74 (b¹) JimmyQuinn 3 18
(M Johnston) *dwlt: a last: wl bhd 4f out* **28/1**

2m 27.83s (-0.47) **Going Correction** +0.075s/f (Good) **15** Ran SP% **120.3**
Speed ratings (Par 104): **104,102,100,99,98 98,95,95,93,91 83,81,80,77,74**
toteswingers: 1&2 £60.10, 1&3 £15.60, 2&3 £34.60 CSF £336.58 CT £2163.07 TOTE £16.30: £4.50, £8.40, £2.20; EX 434.70 TRIFECTA Not won..
Owner Sheikh Hamdan Bin Mohammed Al Maktoum **Bred** Darley **Trained** Middleham Moor, N Yorks

FOCUS
This race was run in a combination of mist and rain, which limited visibility. It was a decent contest, although the pace didn't seem that strong, unsurprisingly given the conditions, and those who raced handy seemed at an advantage. The form is best not taken too literally and is limited by the proximity of the runner-up.

NOTEBOOK
Eastern Aria(UAE) was always well placed and stayed on strongly after committing for home early in the straight. Mark Johnston revealed afterwards he has always considered this daughter of Halling to be a decent-ground filly, but she handled these conditions well (the going probably wasn't terrible, it being the first race of the day) and was a convincing winner. She was obviously well suited by the slight step up in trip, having struggled in a hot 1m2f handicap at the July course last time, and this was by some way a career-best performance. (tchd 12-1)
Citizenship, dropped in trip, did well to stay on from off the modest pace considering he was keen for much of the way in about mid-division, and he clearly benefited from the fitting of a tongue-tie for the first time. His knee action suggests the soft ground suited and he should have more to offer if he can settle better, provided of course the breathing aid continues to have a positive effect. (op 33-1)
Lady Luachmhar(IRE) had no easy task off a 7lb higher mark than when winning a much lesser race at Haydock on her debut for this stable, and she didn't help her chance by racing keenly for much of the way. She kept on in the straight but never looked a threat and needs to learn to settle better. (op 7-1)
Becausewecan(USA) enjoyed a soft time up front, and the easy ground was also very much in his favour, but he couldn't sustain his challenge in the straight. His third over this course and distance earlier in the week, when he was noted to have moved poorly to post, probably took the edge off him. (op 6-1)
Itlaaq, 8lb higher than when winning over just short of 1m2f around here two months earlier, looked to be given too much to do and only ran on when the race was as good as over. (tchd 8-1)
Natural Flair(USA), who had been given three months off having come back stiff from her last run at Newmarket, has won on easy ground and was always well placed, so better could have been expected. (tchd 16-1)
Thin Red Line(IRE) was well below form, even allowing for being stuck out a little wide for most of the journey, and this ground probably wasn't to his liking. He can be given another chance under more suitable conditions. (tchd 15-2 and 17-2, 9-1 in places)
Aurorian(IRE) is proving difficult to place and didn't seem suited by the trip or the ground. (op 25-1)
Jedi was another set a lot to do, but even so, he simply didn't pick up in the straight. This was a very disappointing return from nearly three months off, especially considering he won his maiden on heavy ground. (op 11-2)
Zarinski(IRE) had been sold by the Aga Khan and moved from John Oxx's yard since running fourth in the King George V Handicap at Royal Ascot, and this was a bitterly disappointing debut for his new connections. Perhaps he wants better ground. (op 8-1)

4521 BLUE SQUARE PREMIER STKS (REGISTERED AS THE THOROUGHBRED STAKES) (LISTED RACE) 1m
2:30 (2:31) (Class 1) 3-Y-O

£28,385 (£10,760; £5,385; £2,685; £1,345; £675) **Stalls** High

Form RPR
12- **1** **Zacinto**[322] 5889 3-9-0 107 RyanMoore 4 107+
(Sir Michael Stoute) *lw: hld up in last trio: cl enough and cruising 3f out: prog over 2f out: rdn to ld ins fnl f: hld on* **5/2**[1]
0-23 **2** *hd* **Hartley**[21] 3846 3-9-0 101 PhilipRobinson 9 107
(J D Bethell) *led to 5f out: pressed ldr: effrt again to ld narrowly jst over 2f out: hdd ins fnl f: battled on wl* **12/1**
3026 **3** *½* **Pure Poetry (IRE)**[46] 2992 3-9-4 109 RichardHughes 7 110
(R Hannon) *trckd ldrs: 4th over 3f out: grabbed nr side rail over 2f out but nt qckn and lost pl sltly: styd on ins fnl f* **7/1**
-216 **4** *¾* **Four Winds**[44] 3050 3-9-0 101 JamieSpencer 8 104
(M L W Bell) *lw: hld up in last pair: prog on outer 3f out: rdn to press ldrs 1f out: no ex* **11/2**
-451 **5** *¾* **Donativum**[28] 3649 3-9-4 113 LDettori 2 106
(Saeed Bin Suroor) *hld up in last trio: prog to go 3rd over 3f out: chal 2f out: wknd fnl f* **5/1**[3]
6101 **6** *1 ¾* **Brief Encounter (IRE)**[22] 3816 3-9-0 96 WilliamBuick 5 98
(A M Balding) *lw: prom early: lost pl 5f out: 7th and struggling 3f out: plugged on* **16/1**
0104 **7** *2* **Ocean's Minstrel**[21] 3846 3-9-4 102 JerryO'Dwyer 1 98
(J Ryan) *pressed ldr: led 5f out to jst over 2f out: fdd over 1f out* **16/1**
4-41 **8** *1 ¾* **Gallagher**[30] 3536 3-9-0 114 MartinDwyer 6 90
(B J Meehan) *lw: prom: cl up in abt 4th over 2f out: wknd over 1f out* **9/2**[2]
0232 **9** *9* **Ashram (IRE)**[15] 4052 3-9-0 110 (v) AhmedAjtebi 3 69
(Saeed Bin Suroor) *stdd s: hld up in last: rdn and effrt whn hmpd jst over 2f out: sn wknd* **8/1**

1m 41.3s (1.40) **Going Correction** +0.375s/f (Good) **9** Ran SP% **121.9**
Speed ratings (Par 108): **108,107,107,106,105 104,102,100,91**
toteswingers: 1&2 £9.50, 1&3 £5.50, 2&3 £14.60 CSF £37.24 TOTE £3.70: £1.60, £2.90, £2.30; EX 50.10 Trifecta £425.60 Pool: £1208.06 - 2.10 winning units..
Owner K Abdulla **Bred** Juddmonte Farms Ltd **Trained** Newmarket, Suffolk
■ Stewards' Enquiry : William Buick six-day ban (includes three deferred days): careless riding (Aug 15-17, 19, 22-23)

FOCUS
Though visibility was once again limited, time may show that this was a good Listed race, with the winner and third dropping down from Group 2 and Group 1 company respectively. The field came across to the stands' side in the straight. The winner did not need to match his juvenile form, while the runner-up is rated as having improved 5lb on his juvenile form, with the third and fourth to their marks.

NOTEBOOK
Zacinto ◆ had been off since finishing second to Westphalia in the Champagne Stakes as Doncaster last September, but he boasts quite a reputation and, though widely expected to come on for this outing, his class saw him through. Relatively weak in the market despite looking fit and well, he had already shown himself to be effective in soft ground and, having hit the front inside the final furlong, kept on well to just do enough, earning extra plaudits as he challenged wide of the favoured stands' rail. He appeared to travel strongly throughout and Ryan Moore commented that he was still green under pressure, so it is reasonable to expect considerable improvement from this, especially on better ground. A horse of considerable promise, his trainer will be in no hurry with him and it shall be fascinating to see where he goes next, with connections expecting him to stay 1m2f. (op 11-4 tchd 7-2)
Hartley was taken on for the lead by Ocean's Minstrel yet kept finding when headed by the winner and was edging back at him as they hit the line. Third in a Listed event open to older horses at Chester last time, he is clearly progressing fast and can find a race at this level. (op 20-1)
Pure Poetry(IRE), runner-up in a Listed contest over course and distance two starts back, finished seventh and sixth in the 2000 Guineas and St James's Palace Stakes respectively either side of that effort and gives the form a solid look. He stayed on well, having moved on to the rail, just lacking that vital acceleration under his 4lb penalty, and is another capable of winning again at this level. (op 8-1)
Four Winds, back down to 1m having finished sixth in the Hampton Court last time, made ground to challenge widest of all and was close enough if good enough over a furlong out, but he couldn't quicken on. The ground was probably softer than he likes it. (op 11-1)

Donativum, who scraped home in a 1m Listed event at Deauville last time, needed to have stepped forward to take this under a penalty and he simply wasn't good enough. He lacked a change of gear in the ground, which was as soft as he would want it. (op 4-1 tchd 11-2 in places)

Brief Encounter(IRE) has been largely progressive and bounced back from a slightly disappointing effort at Royal Ascot when taking a competitive handicap off a mark of 90 at Newmarket last time. This was easily his toughest test to date, though, and he could only plug on at the one pace, having been pretty much the first under pressure. (tchd 12-1)

Ocean's Minstrel, another carrying a 4lb penalty, had finished just behind Hartley at Chester last time and he failed to run his race on this softer ground. (op 25-1)

Gallagher, a classy juvenile who confirmed the promise of his Jersey Stakes fourth when winning a 7f conditions event at Newmarket last time, had stamina to prove on this first crack at 1m, but he was beaten before that became an issue. Official explanation: trainer said colt was unsuited by the soft ground (tchd 5-1)

Ashram(IRE) is proving to be frustrating for his new connections and he was already looking in trouble when hampered by Brief Encounter. (op 9-1)

4522 BLUE SQUARE NASSAU STKS (GROUP 1) 1m 1f 192y

3:05 (3:06) (Class 1) 3-Y-O+

£113,540 (£43,040; £21,540; £10,740; £5,380; £2,700) **Stalls** High

Form RPR

2123 **1** **Midday**[20] 3896 3-8-10 118 TPQueally 1 120
(H R A Cecil) *lw: sn trckd ldng trio: grabbed nr side rail in st: rdn and prog to ld 2f out: styd on wl to draw clr fnl f* **11/2**[3]

5434 **2** 2 1/4 **Rainbow View (USA)**[24] 3749 3-8-10 114 JimmyFortune 9 116
(J H M Gosden) *hld up in 6th: effrt on outer over 3f out and sn pushed along: prog 2f out: chsd wnr over 1f out: no imp fnl f* **5/2**[1]

5311 **3** 1/2 **Moneycantbuymelove (IRE)**[45] 3016 3-8-10 106 JamieSpencer 4 115
(M L W Bell) *hld up in 9th: prog 3f out: rdn and clsng in 6th 2f out: wnt 3rd fnl f: one pce* **17/2**

3511 **4** 2 1/4 **Barshiba (IRE)**[14] 4094 5-9-5 110 PaulHanagan 5 110
(D R C Elsworth) *led rdn and hdd over 3f out: rallied and disp 2nd briefly wl over 1f out: sn outpcd: kpt on fnl f* **14/1**

4331 **5** nk **High Heeled (IRE)**[8] 4287 3-8-10 114 MichaelHills 8 109
(B W Hills) *hld up in 8th: pushed along and struggling over 3f out: kpt on fr over 1f out: n.d* **8/1**

13-5 **6** 2 1/2 **Katiyra (IRE)**[35] 3412 4-9-5 114 MJKinane 10 106
(John M Oxx, Ire) *lw: trckd ldng pair: effrt on outer to chal and upsides 2f out: wknd jst over 1f out: tired and eased ins fnl f* **7/2**[2]

-122 **7** 5 **Heaven Sent**[24] 3749 6-9-5 114 RyanMoore 3 94
(Sir Michael Stoute) *hld up in 5th: rdn and no prog 3f out: sn wl btn* **8/1**

03-5 **8** 3 1/2 **Saphira's Fire (IRE)**[28] 3619 4-9-5 103 MartinDwyer 2 87
(W R Muir) *t.k.h: sn restrained to rr: last 1/2-way: nvr on terms fnl 3f* **50/1**

-313 **9** 3 1/4 **Spacious**[24] 3749 4-9-5 113 LDettori 6 81
(J R Fanshawe) *lw: trckd ldr: led over 3f out to 2f out: wknd rapidly sn after* **11/1**

0105 **10** 7 **Nashmiah (IRE)**[21] 3846 3-8-10 101 NCallan 7 67
(C E Brittain) *mostly in 7th tl rdn and wknd over 4f out: t.o* **50/1**

2m 9.42s (1.42) **Going Correction** +0.375s/f (Good)
WFA 3 from 4yo+ 9lb **10** Ran SP% **117.8**
Speed ratings (Par 117): **109,107,106,105,104 102,98,95,93,87**
toteswingers: 1&2 £4.40, 1&3 £10.20, 2&3 £5.50 CSF £19.84 TOTE £5.20: £1.80, £1.50, £4.00; EX 21.30 Trifecta £423.90 Pool: £11514.87 - 20.10 winning units..
Owner K Abdulla **Bred** Juddmonte Farms Ltd **Trained** Newmarket, Suffolk

FOCUS

This has gone to some top-notch fillies' in the last ten years, Crimplene, Islington, Russian Rhythm, Alexander Goldrun, Ouija Board and Peeping Fawn being about the pick of them, but there didn't seem to be a standout performer in this field. It had looked to be one of the more open renewals, but the three-year-olds, responsible for seven of the last ten winners, dominated by having the first three home. The winner is rated to her Oaks form with the runner-up close to her juvenile form.

NOTEBOOK

Midday's participation had been in the balance on account of the softening ground, but she handled it more than adequately. Boasting the best piece of form in this line-up, her narrow second to Sariska in the Epsom Oaks, she could be excused a below-par showing in the Irish version when unsuited by the heavy ground and this performance signalled a return to something near her best. Chasing the early speed, she really began to hit top stride against the rail from 2f out and appeared to quicken into the lead. She was always going to take some catching having gone clear, and stayed on strongly for pressure to win with a good bit in hand. There is no doubting she is just as good at this trip as she is 1m4f and it wouldn't surprise to see her end up in the Breeders' Cup Filly & Mare Turf later in the year. (op 13-2 tchd 7-1)

Rainbow View(USA) continues to run well without reward. She might not have lived up to her high billing, having been a top-notch 2yo, but she is slowly getting better with each run and the softer ground here was undoubtedly a help. Well behind the winner in the Oaks, she ran really well when third in the Coronation and finished a close-up fourth behind Goldikova in the Falmouth last time. This represented another step forward, staying on to chase the winner from over a furlong out, but she was unable to stay on as strongly in the final furlong. She enjoys some give in the ground and is sure to find a suitable opening at some stage this season. (op 3-1 tchd 7-2 in places)

Moneycantbuymelove(IRE) was taking a huge jump in class but she already had a course and distance win to her name and is bred to cope with the softer ground. A filly on the up, she began to close from three out, having travelled well, and stayed on for pressure, but never got close enough to seriously threaten the winner. All her best form has come on a faster surface, but she seems fairly versatile with regards to distance as well, and it would be a surprise were she not to pick up a Group prize at some stage in the latter part of the season. (op 10-1 tchd 12-1)

Barshiba(IRE) has always been a very smart filly on her day and seems to be as good as ever this season, definitely improving for the step up to 1m4f. A filly who is blind in one eye, she came into this in search of a hat-trick, having landed the Lancashire Oaks followed by a Listed race at Newmarket, and she raced enthusiastically in the lead. She was readily left behind by the winner, but kept digging in and stayed on right the way to the line, comfortably faring best of the older brigade. (op 12-1 tchd 11-1)

High Heeled(IRE) had ground to make up on a couple of these, having finished third in the Oaks and just over five lengths behind Barshiba at Haydock, and she capitalised on the drop in grade when winning a Listed event at York last time. She never got into it, though, having been held up, and could only keep on at the one pace for pressure. On this evidence a return to 1m4f is going to suit.

Katiyra(IRE), expected to have come on for her reappearance effort in the Pretty Polly Stakes at the Curragh, had her chance if good enough, but began to tire from over a furlong out and was eased inside the final furlong. This was disappointing and she has yet to show she's gone on from three to four. (op 9-2)

Heaven Sent, fourth in this a year ago, showed herself to be as good as ever when runner-up in the Falmouth last time, but the ground wouldn't really have been to her liking and she failed to run to anything like her best. She was reported to have been unsuited by the ground. Official explanation: trainer's rep said mare was unsuited by the soft ground (op 7-1)

Saphira's Fire(IRE), not far behind in the Lancashire Oaks, had never run on ground any worse than good before and she was always expected to struggle. (tchd 40-1)

Spacious has won on both previous starts with cut in the ground and she followed her Windsor Forest victory by finishing third in the Falmouth. The return to 1m2f looked in her favour and she was driven to the lead 3f out, but stopped worryingly quickly approaching the final furlong and was another who evidently didn't run her race. Official explanation: jockey said filly lost its action (op 15-2 tchd 7-1)

Nashmiah(IRE) was always going to struggle on this return to Group 1 level and she finished tailed off. (op 66-1 tchd 40-1)

4523 BLUESQUARE.COM STEWARDS' CUP (HERITAGE H'CAP) 6f

3:40 (3:40) (Class 2) 3-Y-O+

£62,310 (£18,660; £9,330; £4,670; £2,330; £1,170) **Stalls** Low

Form RPR

5024 **1** **Genki (IRE)**[7] 4297 5-9-1 96 SteveDrowne 10 109
(R Charlton) *chsd nr side ldrs: 4th and clsng 1/2-way: led gp on outer over 1f out: styd on wl to take overall ld last 100yds* **14/1**

3100 **2** 1 **Evens And Odds (IRE)**[42] 3141 5-9-0 98 WilliamCarson(3) 16 108
(D Nicholls) *lw: chsd far side ldrs in abt 6th: prog on outer 2f out: styd on to ld gp nr fin* **33/1**

0141 **3** 3/4 **Knot In Wood (IRE)**[7] 4330 7-9-6 106 3ex BMcHugh(5) 11 114
(R A Fahey) *chsd ldng pair nr side: 2nd 1/2-way: chal 2f out: chsd wnr over 1f out: kpt on: 2nd of 12 in gp* **10/1**[3]

2-64 **4** hd **Markab**[42] 3141 6-9-4 99 PatCosgrave 13 106+
(H Candy) *racd alone in centre: overall ldr: crossed to far side 2f out: clr of gp over 1f out: wknd and hdd last 100yds: 2nd of 14 in gp* **15/2**[1]

0241 **5** 2 1/4 **Mac Gille Eoin**[30] 3524 5-9-2 97 3ex JimCrowley 14 97
(J Gallagher) *sn crossed to nr side: led gp but wl off far side pce: clr w 2 rivals sn after 1/2-way: hdd and one pce over 1f out* **25/1**

4150 **6** 3/4 **Valery Borzov (IRE)**[7] 4330 5-9-9 104 (v) FrancisNorton 15 101
(D Nicholls) *wl off the pce far side: gd prog on outer fr 1/2-way: chsng ldrs 1f out: no ex: 3rd of 14 in gp* **16/1**

00-0 **7** 3/4 **Brave Prospector**[42] 3141 4-9-5 100 (t) JamieSpencer 6 95
(P W Chapple-Hyam) *sn virtually t.o nr side: gd prog fr over 2f out: kpt on fnl f: n.d: 4th of 12 in gp* **25/1**

0010 **8** 3/4 **Striking Spirit**[7] 4330 4-8-12 96 3ex AhmedAjtebi(3) 27 89
(D Nicholls) *disp ld far side tl overall ldr c across 2f out: fdd fnl f: 4th of 14 in gp* **20/1**

1 **9** nk **Biniou (IRE)**[14] 4099 6-9-3 98 3ex RichardHughes 9 90
(R M H Cowell) *lw: hld up nr side and wl off the pce in last pair: gd prog jst over 1f out: nvr nrr: 5th of 12 in gp* **9/1**[2]

2613 **10** nk **Enderby Spirit (GR)**[24] 3747 3-9-2 101 3ex TomEaves 3 92
(B Smart) *lw: midfield on nr side in abt 7th: nt on terms w ldrs fr 1/2-way: 6th of 12 in gp* **25/1**

0600 **11** hd **Hitchens (IRE)**[36] 3351 4-9-3 101 NeilBrown(3) 5 91
(T D Barron) *racd nr side: towards rr against rail: wl off the pce 1/2-way: plugged on: 7th of 12 in gp* **33/1**

-605 **12** 1/2 **Prohibit**[42] 3141 4-9-4 99 JimmyFortune 8 87
(J H M Gosden) *chsd nr side ldrs in abt 6th: nt on terms fr 1/2-way: no ch after: 8th of 14 in gp* **20/1**

1602 **13** nse **Buachaill Dona (IRE)**[36] 3351 6-9-6 101 JimmyQuinn 24 89
(D Nicholls) *chsd ldng trio on far side: no imp over 1f out: btn after: 5th of 14 in gp* **14/1**

4104 **14** hd **Fol Hollow (IRE)**[6] 4341 4-9-1 96 AndrewMullen 21 84
(D Nicholls) *wl in rr far side and nvr on terms: plugged on: 6th of 14 in gp* **33/1**

2012 **15** 1 1/4 **Tamagin (USA)**[15] 4037 6-9-10 105 (p) SebSanders 20 89
(J Pearce) *taken down early: disp ld far side tl overall ldr c across 2f out: sn wknd: 7th of 14 in gp* **20/1**

5100 **16** 1/2 **Thebes**[7] 4297 4-8-12 93 3ex GregFairley 28 75
(M Johnston) *disp ld far side tl overall ldr c across 2f out: sn wknd: 8th of 14 in gp* **14/1**

4000 **17** 1 **Beaver Patrol (IRE)**[22] 3818 7-9-5 100 (b) TPQueally 23 79
(Eve Johnson Houghton) *hld up in last trio nr side: wl off the pce 1/2-way: nvr a factor: 9th of 12 in gp* **33/1**

4105 **18** 1 **Judd Street**[28] 3638 7-9-8 103 (v) RyanMoore 4 79
(Eve Johnson Houghton) *lw: hld up nr side: a wl off the pce: 9th of 12 in gp* **33/1**

4510 **19** 2 1/4 **Global City (IRE)**[24] 3747 3-9-3 102 (t) LDettori 25 70
(Saeed Bin Suroor) *hld up in rr far side: effrt 1/2-way: nvr on terms: 10th of 14 in gp* **25/1**

2136 **20** 1 **Advanced**[42] 3141 6-9-3 98 NCallan 17 63
(K A Ryan) *racd far side: in midfield and nvr on terms: 11th of 14 in gp* **20/1**

2202 **21** nk **Barney McGrew (IRE)**[7] 4330 6-9-3 98 PhillipMakin 7 62
(M Dods) *taken down early: sn in last trio on nr side: nvr on terms: 10th of 12 in gp* **16/1**

2105 **22** hd **Jimmy Styles**[35] 3405 5-9-7 102 (p) PhilipRobinson 22 66
(C G Cox) *chsd far side ldrs but nvr on terms: wknd fnl f: 12th of 14 in gp* **16/1**

4000 **23** nk **Orpsie Boy (IRE)**[7] 4297 6-9-1 96 (v) StephenDonohoe 19 59
(N P Littmoden) *sn last on far side: nvr a factor: 13th of 14th in gp* **40/1**

-401 **24** nk **Sonny Red (IRE)**[21] 3844 5-9-4 99 3ex AdrianTNicholls 26 61
(D Nicholls) *s.s: racd far side: a wl in rr: last of 14 in gp* **9/1**[2]

-400 **25** 3 3/4 **Osiris Way**[22] 3802 7-8-13 94 TPO'Shea 2 44
(P R Chamings) *chsd nr side ldr to 1/2-way: sn wknd rapidly: 11th of 12 in gp* **33/1**

2100 **26** 2 1/4 **Fishforcompliments**[15] 4037 5-9-3 98 (b) PaulHanagan 1 40
(R A Fahey) *chsd ldrs nr side in abt 5th: u.p and wkng 1/2-way: last of 12 in gp* **20/1**

1m 12.28s (0.08) **Going Correction** +0.25s/f (Good)
WFA 3 from 4yo+ 4lb **26** Ran SP% **139.7**
Speed ratings (Par 109): **109,107,106,106,103 102,101,100,100,99 99,98,98,98,96 96,94,93,90,89 88,88,87,87,82 79**
toteswingers: 1&2 £213.40, 1&3 £56.00, 2&3 £358.00 CSF £432.35 CT £4829.47 TOTE £13.00: £3.00, £13.10, £2.80, £4.60; EX 1201.80 Trifecta £18778.50 Pool: £63440.93 - 2.50 winning units..
Owner Ms Gillian Khosla **Bred** Rathbarry Stud **Trained** Beckhampton, Wilts

FOCUS

One of the most prestigious sprint handicaps of the season, but this year's race seemed more difficult to solve than ever. For a start, going on the soft side was vastly different from the good ground that prevailed when these horses were declared two days earlier, yet there were only a couple of non-runners. Also, a thick mist covered most of the straight course, severely restricting viewing, and it's impossible to know exactly how the race unfolded. What's clear from the result is the draw played little part, and there seemed no particular track bias. The field split into two main groups, although one runner raced alone up the centre of the track early on. Through the opening stages those on the far side, along with the lone challenger up the middle, seemed to be well ahead of the near-side bunch, but as they emerged from the gloom inside the final furlong, it was a runner from the stands'-side group who was in front, albeit he had edged towards the centre late on. The form is rated at face value with the third the best guide.

NOTEBOOK

Genki(IRE), off the pace through the early stages in his group, was soon a long way behind some of those on the opposite side of the track, but he obviously picked up well and was already a couple of lengths clear of his bunch when coming back into view over half a furlong out, and ultimately got on top decisively overall. Other than a poor run in the Wokingham (when fancied) on his second outing of the season, he had been in good form since returning from over a year off the track, including when fourth in a big 7f handicap at Ascot the previous weekend, and this represented a career best. Ground on the soft side was a bit of a question mark, but as it turned out he seemed to really appreciate the conditions, which isn't a total surprise considering he's had some physical problems in the past. The Ayr Gold Cup is a possible target, but his trainer is also keen to look at Listed and Group races, and the Dubai Carnival is also an option next year.

Evens And Odds(IRE), reported to have lost his action when well behind a few of these in the Wokingham on his previous start, returned to form, faring best of those on the far side of the track. He handled the softish ground well and connections will now consider the Ayr Gold Cup.

Knot In Wood(IRE) is having a tremendous season, winning a Group 3 at Newcastle in June and a competitive handicap at York on his latest start, and he ran another terrific race. He was 1lb well in under his penalty, but this is still the highest mark he has contested a handicap off and it was a smart effort on ground he likes. His connections are thinking about aiming him at the Taby Sprint in Sweden next month as he'll avoid a penalty in that contest, and the Ayr Gold Cup is another option. (op 14-1)

Markab ◆, off the same mark as when ahead of most of these in the Wokingham, ran a big race in defeat considering he was asked to race alone up the centre of the track for much of the way and was the overall leader, having gone off plenty quick enough, when edging across to the far-side group by about 2f out. He only tired late on and will be one to consider for the Ayr Gold Cup. (op 17-2 tchd 9-1, 10-1 in places)

Mac Gille Eoin, 3lb higher than when winning a four-runner race at Epsom on his previous start, showed good speed to lead the near-side group after tacking across from stall 14, but this ground might have been softer than ideal and he couldn't sustain his challenge.

Valery Borzov(IRE), 1lb wrong, raced further back than is often the case, despite having a visor re-fitted, but he finished quite well to take third on the far side. (op 20-1 tchd 14-1)

Brave Prospector was soon detached in last on the near side of the track, and must have been a long way off the overall lead, but he evidently finished with a quite a rattle. (tchd 33-1)

Striking Spirit ◆ had excuses. He was 3lb wrong, seemingly found the ground softer than ideal, and probably went off too quick.

Biniou(IRE), the winner of both his starts in 5f handicaps this year, was 4lb well in under the penalty he picked up for his recent Newmarket victory. However, having been set plenty to do, it's possible he was denied a clear run, as he was still well behind on the near side, just as the winner was making his challenge. He can be given another chance. (op 11-1 tchd 12-1 in places)

Enderby Spirit(GR), 3lb higher than his new mark under his penalty, didn't make much progress on the near side, although it's impossible to know what sort of trip he had when the runners were out of view.

Hitchens(IRE) almost certainly wouldn't have appreciated the rain.

Prohibit is another who probably didn't appreciate the easy ground. (op 16-1)

Buachaill Dona(IRE) was below the form he showed when runner-up in the Gosforth Park Cup on his most recent start, and was disappointing. (tchd 16-1 in places)

Tamagin(USA) can be excused this below-par run considering he was taken on for the lead by Striking Spirit and Thebes, and the ground might not have been ideal either. (tchd 25-1)

Global City(IRE) Official explanation: jockey said colt was unsuited by the soft ground

Jimmy Styles Official explanation: jockey said gelding was unsuited by the soft ground

Sonny Red(IRE) was 1lb well in under the penalty picked up for his 5f win at Ascot, and this ground shouldn't have been a problem, but he's yet to win beyond the minimum trip. (op 10-1 tchd 8-1, 11-1 in places)

Osiris Way Official explanation: jockey said gelding hing right throughout

4524 BLUE SQUARE EBF MAIDEN STKS (C&G) 7f

4:15 (4:17) (Class 2) 2-Y-O **£12,952** (£3,854; £1,926; £962) **Stalls** High

Form	Pos	Dist	Horse	Jockey	RPR
5	1		**Stags Leap (IRE)**[10] 4209 2-9-0 0	RyanMoore 8	81
			(R Hannon) *cl 4th 1/2-way: led and rdn 1f out: kpt on wl* **6/1**[2]		
23	2	¾	**Yarra River**[16] 4006 2-9-0 0	WilliamBuick 5	79
			(A M Balding) *cl 6th 1/2-way: styd on to take 2nd ins fnl f: a hld* **15/2**		
2	3	½	**Poor Prince**[29] 3584 2-9-0 0	PhilipRobinson 3	78
			(C G Cox) *swtg: in ld 1/2-way: u.p and disputing 2nd 1f out: kpt on* **13/2**[3]		
	4	hd	**Destination Aim** 2-9-0 0	LDettori 6	77
			(Saeed Bin Suroor) *w'like: scope: trcking ldrs in 5th 1/2-way: pushed along and keeping on same pce fnl f* **9/1**		
	5	½	**Love Delta (USA)** 2-9-0 0	GregFairley 9	76
			(M Johnston) *leggy: wl in rr 1/2-way: rdn and styng on wl fnl f: nrst fin* **10/1**		
	6	2¾	**Music Maestro (IRE)** 2-9-0 0	SteveDrowne 4	69
			(B W Hills) *lengthy: scope: last pair 1/2-way: off the pce 1f out: pushed along and keeping on fnl 100yds* **33/1**		
	7	½	**Gomrath (IRE)** 2-9-0 0	SamHitchcott 10	68
			(M R Channon) *w'like: bit bkwd: midfield and in tch 1/2-way: off the pce in rr gp fnl f* **25/1**		
	8	2½	**Invincible Soul (IRE)** 2-9-0 0	RichardHughes 7	62
			(R Hannon) *str: in rr 1/2-way: nt on terms in rr gp 1f out* **14/1**		
	9	1¼	**Bin Shamardal (IRE)** 2-9-0 0	MichaelHills 11	59
			(B W Hills) *lengthy: midfield 1/2-way: off the pce in rr 1f out* **20/1**		
2	10	hd	**Texan Star (IRE)**[15] 4048 2-9-0 0	JimmyFortune 2	58
			(J H M Gosden) *cl 3rd 1/2-way: wl in rr 1f out* **13/8**[1]		
3	11	3½	**Akula (IRE)**[18] 3957 2-9-0 0	TPQueally 1	49
			(M H Tompkins) *w'like: athletic: last pair 1/2-way: detached in last 1f out: keeping on fnl f* **12/1**		
0	12	nse	**Fancy Star**[15] 4048 2-9-0 0	SebSanders 12	54+
			(B W Hills) *chsng ldr 1/2-way: wkng and being eased ent fnl f* **25/1**		

1m 30.88s (3.48) **Going Correction** +0.375s/f (Good) **12 Ran SP% 126.3**

Speed ratings (Par 100): **95,94,93,93,92 89,89,86,84,84 80,80**

toteswingers: 1&2 £11.60, 1&3 £11.60, 2&3 £4.60 CSF £51.60 TOTE £7.80: £2.40, £2.70, £2.10; EX 70.60 Trifecta £598.10 Part won. Pool: £808.36 - 0.10 winning units..

Owner Mrs J Wood **Bred** P McCartan & Paddy Twomey **Trained** East Everleigh, Wilts

FOCUS

Visibility had worsened before this contest, the runners probably only being in view for less than half the race. This was a fair juvenile maiden, nothing more, and those with previous experience dominated.

NOTEBOOK

Stags Leap(IRE) ◆, a Derby entry who was given a nice introduction at Sandown the previous week, seemed well suited by this slower ground and stayed on well having hit the front around a furlong out. The step up to 1m will suit this son of Refuse To Bend and he looks to have bright future. (op 10-1 tchd 11-1)

Yarra River had posted two fair placed efforts at Windsor and Epsom and this was probably his best run yet. He ran on well inside the final furlong and now looks ready for 1m. (op 5-1)

Poor Prince, runner-up to a fair sort on his debut at Sandown, could have done without the rain, but he still ran well until deep inside the final furlong, in the end just holding on for third. He shows enough speed to suggest 6f will not be a problem. (tchd 5-1)

Destination Aim, a son of Dubai Destination who is in the Gimcrack, came out best of the newcomers. He was edging nearer with every stride at the line and should come on for the outing, suggesting a standard maiden should be his for the taking. (op 6-1)

Love Delta(USA), a US-bred whose sales price dropped to 100,000gns at the breeze-ups, stayed on well from over a furlong out, having been one of the first under pressure, and like most juveniles from the yard, he should come on markedly for the run. (op 9-1 tchd 8-1)

Music Maestro(IRE), an already gelded son of Oratorio, put in some good late work and should be wiser next time. (op 25-1)

Invincible Soul(IRE), a tall, good-looking son of Invincible Spirit, made 160,000 euros as a yearling but he looked too green to do himself justice on this racecourse debut. (op 12-1 tchd 10-1)

Texan Star(IRE) had run so encouragingly behind a useful-looking sort on his debut at Newbury but this was disappointing. The ground shouldn't have been a problem and he now has something to prove. (op 7-2 tchd 4-1 in places)

Fancy Star Official explanation: jockey said saddle slipped

4525 BLUESQUARE.COM NURSERY (H'CAP) 6f

4:50 (4:50) (Class 2) 2-Y-O **£12,952** (£3,854; £1,926; £962) **Stalls** Low

Form	Pos	Dist	Horse	Jockey	RPR
0431	1		**Bluie**[29] 3572 2-7-13 66	FrancisNorton 7	78+
			(D Nicholls) *pressed ldr 4f out: in ld ent fnl f: rdn out and wl in command* **3/1**[2]		
41	2	1½	**Layla's Hero (IRE)**[16] 4011 2-8-4 71	AdrianTNicholls 6	79
			(D Nicholls) *lw: s.i.s: cl up in centre 4f out: chsng wnr ent fnl f and clr of rest: no imp* **11/4**[1]		
360	3	¾	**Pintura**[22] 3792 2-8-0 67	JimmyQuinn 11	72
			(M R Channon) *towards rr but in tch in centre 4f out: chsng clr ldng pair 1f out: clsd on runner-up last 100yds* **25/1**		
4565	4	5	**The Shuffler**[10] 4208 2-7-9 65	DavidProbert(3) 10	55
			(G L Moore) *wl in rr in centre 4f out: modest 4th ent fnl f: no imp* **33/1**		
01	5	1¾	**Coolree Star (IRE)**[12] 4153 2-8-8 75	WilliamBuick 1	60
			(J A Glover) *overall ldr in centre 4f out: off the pce and no ch fnl f* **33/1**		
3012	6	nk	**Florio Vincitore (IRE)**[11] 4173 2-9-2 83	EdwardCreighton 5	67
			(E J Creighton) *chsd ldng pair in centre 4f out: wl off the pce fnl f* **25/1**		
0550	7	1½	**Leleyf (IRE)**[14] 4089 2-8-8 75	SamHitchcott 13	55
			(M R Channon) *chsd ldrs in centre 4f out: wl off the pce fnl f* **16/1**		
4032	8	2¼	**Antonius Moris (IRE)**[15] 4063 2-9-4 85	RichardSmith 9	58
			(Tom Dascombe) *towards rr in centre 4f out: wl bhd ent fnl f* **14/1**		
4401	9	1½	**Running Mate (IRE)**[15] 4062 2-8-10 77	JimmyFortune 12	45
			(J H M Gosden) *lw: in tch on wd outside 4f out: wl in rr fnl f* **11/2**[3]		
212	10	1¼	**Ballodair (IRE)**[15] 4035 2-9-0 81	PaulHanagan 2	46
			(R A Fahey) *racd nr side: nvr on terms w ldrs: wl bhd fnl f* **11/2**[3]		
2150	11	2¾	**Palisades Park**[14] 4089 2-9-4 85	RyanMoore 4	41
			(R Hannon) *racd nr side: nvr on terms w ldrs: wl bhd fnl f* **8/1**		
51	12	13	**Slice (IRE)**[31] 3500 2-8-13 80	NCallan 3	—
			(Eve Johnson Houghton) *lw: dwlt: racd nr side: a bhd: t.o* **12/1**		

1m 13.66s (1.46) **Going Correction** +0.25s/f (Good) **12 Ran SP% 127.4**

Speed ratings (Par 100): **100,98,97,90,88 87,85,82,80,78 75,57**

toteswingers: 1&2 £18.10, 1&3 £4.40, 2&3 £18.70 CSF £12.23 CT £182.11 TOTE £4.10: £1.90, £1.70, £7.20; EX 15.00 Trifecta £75.90 Pool: £698.20 - 6.80 winning units..

Owner The Three K's **Bred** P Baugh **Trained** Sessay, N Yorks

FOCUS

There was once again limited viewing and the field tended to come more down the middle of the track. Dandy Nicholls has dominated this nursery in recent years, winning the last three runnings, and he again showed his affinity for this race by training a one-two.

NOTEBOOK

Bluie, who made all when winning a seller over this trip at Haydock last time, was soon up on the speed and had gone clear by the time they came back into view a furlong out. This son of Ishiguru is clearly progressing fast, but he will need to continue to do so, as things are only going to get tougher. (op 9-2 tchd 5-1)

Layla's Hero(IRE), ready winner of a 5f Hamilton maiden, appeared to be the better fancied of the pair and he stayed on right the way to the line, but was always being held by his stable companion. (tchd 7-2 and 4-1 in places)

Pintura didn't progress in three starts in maidens, but he was always likely to fare better once handicapping and stayed on well inside the final furlong to finish on the heels of the front pair. A step up to 7f wouldn't go amiss on this evidence. (op 22-1)

The Shuffler is coming down the weights and ran well enough to suggest he will pick up a lower-grade race at some stage.

Coolree Star(IRE), narrow winner of a Yarmouth seller last week, showed bright speed to lead down the centre of the track, but had been readily brushed aside by the time they came back into view. Official explanation: jockey said gelding hung right

Florio Vincitore(IRE) has been in good form on the all-weather but this run seemed to confirm he is not yet as effective on turf. (op 20-1)

Running Mate(IRE) should have done better considering he won in heavy ground last time. (op 9-2)

Slice(IRE) Official explanation: jockey said colt was never travelling

4526 BLUESQUARECASINO.COM APPRENTICE STKS (H'CAP) 1m 1f

5:25 (5:25) (Class 3) (0-90,89) 4-Y-0+ **£12,952** (£3,854; £1,926; £962) **Stalls** High

Form	Pos	Dist	Horse	Jockey	RPR
3000	1		**Bencoolen (IRE)**[4] 4409 4-9-5 89	NSLawes(5) 9	99
			(D Nicholls) *hld up in last pair: rdn and prog on outer fr 3f out: disp ld over 1f out: battled on wl to gain upper hand last 75yds* **14/1**		
0143	2	¾	**Mountain Pride (IRE)**[8] 4261 4-9-4 88	MatthewDavies(5) 12	97
			(J L Dunlop) *lw: hld up in last pair: stdy prog towards inner fr 3f out: rdn to dispute ld over 1f out: nt qckn last 75yds* **9/2**[2]		
3233	3	3¾	**Effigy**[8] 4262 5-8-8 78	AmyScott(5) 2	79
			(H Candy) *lw: sn prom: led on outer over 3f out: rdn and hdd over 1f out: one pce* **7/2**[1]		
3460	4	4½	**Cape Hawk (IRE)**[22] 3796 5-9-4 83	PatrickHills 3	75
			(R Hannon) *lw: hld up in midfield: effrt over 3f out: tried to cl on ldrs 2f out: sn no imp* **9/1**		
602	5	1¾	**Kaleo**[23] 3769 5-8-6 76	RosieJessop(5) 13	65
			(S Dow) *hld up in midfield on inner: effrt and in tch wl over 2f out: sn btn* **8/1**		

0103 **6** *5* **Thunder Gorge (USA)**[10] 4211 4-8-5 **75** ow1............ JPHamblett(5) 14 54
(Mouse Hamilton-Fairley) *plld hrd early: hld up bhd ldrs: rdn over 3f out: sn lft bhd* **11/1**

2-10 **7** *1 1/2* **Mohathab (IRE)**[91] 1673 4-9-0 **82**............................ MCGeran(3) 6 58
(J R Boyle) *hld up in last trio: u.p and no prog over 3f out: n.d after* **9/1**

-114 **8** *3* **Shavansky**[21] 3840 5-9-7 **86**............................ JamesMillman 4 56
(B R Millman) *plld hrd early: prom: chal over 3f out: btn over 2f out: wknd and eased fnl f* **6/1[3]**

-522 **9** *2 1/2* **Visions Of Johanna (USA)**[15] 4042 4-9-0 **79**...............(p) NeilBrown 11 44
(R A Fahey) *led 2f: led again briefly 4f out: rdn and wknd 3f out* **8/1**

5153 **10** *hd* **Stravella (IRE)**[28] 3627 4-8-8 **78**............................ JPFahy(5) 7 42
(R M Beckett) *towards rr: u.p and struggling 4f out: sn bhd* **12/1**

-000 **11** *38* **Alan Devonshire**[29] 3586 4-8-6 **76**............................ AshleyMorgan(5) 1 —
(M H Tompkins) *plld way through to ld after 2f: hdd and dropped out rapidly 4f out: t.o* **25/1**

2m 0.27s (3.97) **Going Correction** +0.375s/f (Good) **11** Ran SP% **123.5**
Speed ratings (Par 107): **97,96,93,89,87 83,81,79,76,76 42**
CSF £79.82 CT £284.17 TOTE £19.00: £4.60, £2.20, £2.00; EX 91.30 Trifecta £526.50 Part won. Pool: £711.58 - 0.30 winning units. Place 6: £238.11 Place 5: £45.96 .
Owner Eamon Maher **Bred** Darley **Trained** Sessay, N Yorks

FOCUS
Visibility was much better than in the earlier races on the card. The pace seemed pretty good considering the conditions and those held up looked to be at an advantage. They all raced middle to far side in the track, but off the rail. The form is best rated around the first two.

NOTEBOOK
Bencoolen(IRE) didn't look an obvious one beforehand, having lost his action around here last time, and he had failed to beat a rival on his only other start at Goodwood. However, the easy ground clearly suited and he was a game winner, proving far more resolute under pressure than the runner-up. This was his first success since being bought out of Roger Charlton's yard for 32,000gns last October, and he can avoid a penalty if turned out before being reassessed. (op 11-1 tchd 10-1)
Mountain Pride(IRE), suited by the strong pace, looked the likeliest winner over a furlong out, but his attitude was far from convincing when strongly challenged late on, as he carried his head a little proud and had his tongue hanging out. (op 4-1 tchd 7-2)
Effigy is enduring a frustrating run but it's hard to fault this effort as, although unable to sustain his challenge, he still fared best of those who raced handy, and this trip might have stretched him as well. (op 6-1 tchd 13-2)
Cape Hawk(IRE) ran disappointingly but probably just didn't stay the trip. (op 8-1)
Kaleo had conditions to suit and could have been expected to fare better, but he's yet to win since coming over from Germany. (op 15-2)
Shavansky came into this in pretty good form but on a faster surface. He did not help hi cause by being too free early and was struggling a long way from home. Official explanation: jockey said gelding was unsuited by the soft ground (op 7-1 tchd 8-1)
Alan Devonshire Official explanation: jockey said gelding ran too free
T/Jkpt: Not won. T/Plt: £182.30 to a £1 stake. Pool: £257,469.69. 1,030.95 winning tickets. T/Qpdt: £24.60 to a £1 stake. Pool: £14,455.34. 434.70 winning tickets. JN

4034 HAMILTON (R-H)
Saturday, August 1

OFFICIAL GOING: Good to soft changing to soft after race 3 (7.40)
Normal configuration and all distances as advertised. The first five winners made all the running.
Wind: Fresh, half behind Weather: Overcast

4527 CHAMPAGNE COCKTAILS AT HAMILTON PARK NOVICE STKS 1m 65y
6:40 (6:40) (Class 4) 2-Y-O **£4,533** (£1,348) **Stalls** High

Form RPR
211 **1** **Mister Angry (IRE)**[17] 3971 2-9-6 0............................ PaulMulrennan 2 87+
(M Johnston) *mde all: drew clr fr 1/2-way: v easily* **1/50[1]**

0000 **2** *25* **Kerolad (IRE)**[8] 4286 2-8-12 0............................ DuranFentiman 1 24
(N Wilson) *chsd wnr: pushed along 1/2-way: sn struggling* **18/1[2]**

1m 54.65s (6.25) **Going Correction** +0.525s/f (Yiel) **2** Ran SP% **103.3**
Speed ratings (Par 96): **89,64**
TOTE £1.05.
Owner The Originals **Bred** Darley **Trained** Middleham Moor, N Yorks

FOCUS
A totally one-sided affair.

NOTEBOOK
Mister Angry(IRE) could not be seriously opposed and duly made all to score in little more than an exercise canter. He stays well and remains a very useful prospect. (tchd 1-40)
Kerolad(IRE) had no chance on previous form, as he had been beaten long distances on all four of his outings, and this proved to be just the case as he was struggling to keep tabs on the winner from halfway. (op 20-1 tchd 16-1)

4528 AVIA SIGNS (S) STKS 1m 65y
7:10 (7:12) (Class 6) 3-4-Y-O **£2,388** (£705; £352) **Stalls** High

Form RPR
1605 **1** **Ask Dan (IRE)**[6] 4348 3-9-0 58............................(p) PhillipMakin 6 61
(M Dods) *mde all: clr over 3f out: rdn over 2f out: hld on wl fnl f* **5/1[3]**

1014 **2** *1 1/4* **San Silvestro (IRE)**[12] 4144 4-9-7 62...............(p) SilvestreDeSousa 3 60
(Mrs A Duffield) *sn bhd: pushed along 1/2-way: effrt on outside 3f out: edgd rt: chsd wnr ins fnl f: r.o* **7/4[2]**

0063 **3** *3/4* **Hettie Hubble**[21] 3852 3-8-4 46 ow7............................ DTDaSilva(7) 1 53
(D W Thompson) *in tch: hdwy to chse wnr over 2f out: lost 2nd and no ex ins fnl f* **28/1**

0401 **4** *2 1/4* **Castlebury (IRE)**[6] 4351 4-9-7 60............................ PaulMulrennan 5 53
(G A Swinbank) *chsd wnr to over 2f out: sn outpcd: no imp fnl f* **1/1[1]**

-000 **5** *11* **Dark Velvet (IRE)**[14] 4105 3-8-4 55............................ DuranFentiman 4 14
(E J Alston) *chsd ldrs tl rdn and wknd fr 3f out* **33/1**

1m 53.26s (4.86) **Going Correction** +0.525s/f (Yiel)
WFA 3 from 4yo 7lb **5** Ran SP% **109.4**
Speed ratings (Par 101): **96,94,94,91,80**
toteswingers: 1&2 £4.40 CSF £14.04 TOTE £5.40: £2.30, £1.50; EX 14.30.There was no bid for the winner.
Owner Andrew Tinkler **Bred** Darley **Trained** Denton, Co Durham

FOCUS
A weak seller and it is doubtful whether the winner had to improve much.

4529 MACGREGOR FLOORING COMPANY H'CAP 1m 3f 16y
7:40 (7:40) (Class 6) (0-60,64) 3-Y-O+ **£2,266** (£674; £337; £168) **Stalls** High

Form RPR
0030 **1** **Shifting Gold (IRE)**[55] 2742 3-8-8 **57**............................(b) AmyRyan(5) 2 67
(K A Ryan) *mde all: rdn over 2f out: edgd rt over 1f out: hld on wl fnl f* **14/1**

-061 **2** *3/4* **Amazing King (IRE)**[12] 4156 5-9-13 **64**............ RussellKennemore(3) 5 72
(P A Kirby) *prom: rdn over 3f out: hdwy over 1f out: kpt on fnl f: hld towards fin* **3/1[2]**

2333 **3** *1 1/4* **Dontpaytheferryman (USA)**[6] 4351 4-9-0 **51**......... FrederikTylicki(3) 1 57
(R A Fahey) *in tch: hdwy and cl up 1/2-way: effrt over 2f out: edgd rt: one pce over 1f out* **2/1[1]**

02B **4** *2 3/4* **Hawkit (USA)**[19] 3911 8-9-8 **56**............................ PaulMulrennan 4 58
(P Monteith) *hld up: pushed along 3f out: hdwy over 1f out: no imp fnl f* **14/1**

6U3- **5** *3 3/4* **Ulysees (IRE)**[273] 7132 10-8-9 **48**............................ JamieKyne(5) 8 43
(I Semple) *hld up: rdn 3f out: nvr able to chal* **14/1**

0633 **6** *2 1/2* **Tillietudlem (FR)**[15] 4039 3-8-2 **46** oh1............................ DuranFentiman 6 37
(J S Goldie) *midfield: drvn and outpcd over 4f out: n.d after* **8/1**

0500 **7** *4 1/2* **Sharp Sovereign (USA)**[6] 4348 3-9-1 **59**...............(b[1]) PJMcDonald 3 42
(I Semple) *dwlt: sn cl up: rdn and wknd fr 3f out* **14/1**

64 **8** *13* **Berriedale**[33] 3454 3-8-10 **54**............................ SilvestreDeSousa 7 15
(Mrs A Duffield) *hld up: drvn over 4f out: sn struggling* **7/2[3]**

0400 **9** *17* **Oh Landino (GER)**[27] 3654 4-8-12 **46** oh1............................ PhillipMakin 9 —
(P Monteith) *chsd ldrs tl rdn and wknd fr 3f out* **50/1**

2m 32.18s (6.58) **Going Correction** +0.525s/f (Yiel)
WFA 3 from 4yo+ 10lb **9** Ran SP% **120.3**
Speed ratings (Par 101): **97,96,95,93,90 89,85,76,63**
toteswingers: 1&2 £11.30, 1&3 £4.70, 2&3 £2.90 CSF £58.33 CT £125.22 TOTE £14.70: £3.50, £1.60, £1.40; EX 95.90.
Owner Hambleton Racing Ltd VIII **Bred** Watership Down Stud **Trained** Hambleton, N Yorks

FOCUS
A modest handicap, run at a fair pace set by the winner who is rated back to his AW form from earlier in the year. Front runners did well through the card.
Berriedale Official explanation: jockey said filly was unsuited by the soft ground

4530 EUROPEAN BREEDERS' FUND FILLIES' H'CAP 5f 4y
8:10 (8:11) (Class 4) (0-85,81) 3-Y-O+ **£6,799** (£2,023; £1,011; £505) **Stalls** Centre

Form RPR
1210 **1** **Impressible**[22] 3806 3-9-6 **80**............................ PaulMulrennan 2 96
(E J Alston) *mde all: rdn over 1f out: drew clr fnl f* **10/3[2]**

1053 **2** *4 1/2* **Requisite**[2] 4464 4-8-12 **72**............................(v) FrederikTylicki(3) 3 71
(I A Wood) *w wnr: rdn and edgd rt over 1f out: one pce fnl f* **3/1[1]**

001 **3** *1/2* **Evna (USA)**[11] 4174 3-8-7 **67**............................ DuranFentiman 1 65
(R A Fahey) *trckd ldrs: effrt 2f out: kpt on same pce fnl f* **4/1[3]**

3501 **4** *1/2* **Red Kyte**[25] 3704 3-9-0 **74**............................(p) SilvestreDeSousa 8 70
(K A Ryan) *midfield on outside: rdn over 2f out: edgd rt: no ex fnl f* **5/1**

0350 **5** *1 1/4* **Joyeaux**[8] 4281 7-8-0 **62** oh2............................ JamieKyne(5) 7 53
(Ollie Pears) *dwlt: bhd tl styd on fnl f: nvr rchd ldrs* **13/2**

3100 **6** *1 1/2* **Rothesay Dancer**[12] 4135 6-9-7 **81**............................ KellyHarrison(3) 6 67
(J S Goldie) *hld up: hdwy over 1f out: n.d* **8/1**

00-0 **7** *1 1/4* **Killer Class**[2] 4464 4-8-10 **67**............................ DanielTudhope 4 48
(J S Goldie) *midfield: rdn and hung rt over 1f out: sn no imp* **8/1**

5000 **8** *9* **Wibbadune (IRE)**[21] 3860 5-8-6 **63**............................ PJMcDonald 9 12
(D Shaw) *prom tl rdn and wknd fr 2f out* **33/1**

61.18 secs (1.18) **Going Correction** +0.30s/f (Good)
WFA 3 from 4yo+ 3lb **8** Ran SP% **123.2**
Speed ratings (Par 102): **102,94,94,93,91 88,86,72**
toteswingers: 1&2 £3.90, 1&3 £7.80, 2&3 £2.10 CSF £15.09 CT £42.95 TOTE £5.60: £2.00, £1.40, £2.00; EX 18.30.
Owner Mr & Mrs G Middlebrook **Bred** Mr & Mrs G Middlebrook **Trained** Longton, Lancs

FOCUS
A decent fillies-only sprint. The form is not easy to assess, but the winner impressed and her performance has been taken at something like face value.
Rothesay Dancer Official explanation: jockey said mare was unsuited by the soft ground

4531 RACING UK MAIDEN STKS 6f 5y
8:40 (8:42) (Class 5) 3-Y-O+ **£2,590** (£770; £385; £192) **Stalls** Centre

Form RPR
4232 **1** **Cheyenne Red (IRE)**[6] 4343 3-9-3 65............................ PhillipMakin 3 67
(M Dods) *mde all: drvn over 1f out: hld on gamely fnl f* **2/1[2]**

323 **2** *hd* **Hightime Heroine (IRE)**[23] 3764 3-8-12 75............................ PaulMulrennan 7 61
(J Noseda) *cl up: effrt over 1f out: kpt on fnl f: jst hld* **4/6[1]**

-656 **3** *1/2* **Quick Gourmet**[43] 3108 3-8-5 51............................ DTDaSilva(7) 2 60
(J A McShane) *plld hrd: in tch: effrt and edgd rt over 1f out: r.o fnl f* **25/1**

60 **4** *13* **There We Go (IRE)**[6] 4347 3-9-3 0............................ PJMcDonald 12 23
(G A Swinbank) *bhd: outpcd 1/2-way: hdwy over 1f out: no ch w first three* **50/1**

03 **5** *hd* **Noble Attitude**[15] 4066 3-8-12 0............................ DanielTudhope 1 18
(N Tinkler) *bhd: drvn over 2f out: nvr rchd ldrs* **33/1**

5 **6** *1 3/4* **Camomile**[17] 3975 3-8-12 0............................ SilvestreDeSousa 9 12
(K A Ryan) *spd centre tl wknd fr 2f out* **12/1[3]**

0403 **7** *3/4* **Trade Price (GR)**[33] 3449 3-8-12 51............................ PatrickDonaghy(5) 11 15
(I Semple) *in tch centre tl wknd over 2f out* **28/1**

0 **8** *4* **Mister Biscuit (USA)**[8] 4277 3-8-12 0............................ LanceBetts(5) 4 2
(Miss L A Perratt) *bhd: drvn 1/2-way: nvr on terms* **50/1**

2-00 **9** *nk* **Hosanna**[12] 4134 3-8-7 60............................ JamieKyne(5) 10 —
(J Barclay) *spd centre tl wknd fr 2f out* **50/1**

60 **10** *4 1/2* **Star Addition**[28] 3611 3-9-0 0............................ FrederikTylicki(3) 8 —
(E J Alston) *in tch tl wknd fr 2f out* **66/1**

11 *21* **Old Firm** 3-9-3 0............................(t) DuranFentiman 5 —
(D A Nolan) *s.i.s: sn wl bhd* **33/1**

1m 15.12s (2.92) **Going Correction** +0.30s/f (Good)
WFA 3 from 4yo+ 4lb **11** Ran SP% **121.6**
Speed ratings (Par 103): **92,91,91,73,73 71,70,64,64,58 30**
toteswingers: 1&2 £1.10, 1&3 £6.90, 2&3 £7.10 CSF £3.53 TOTE £3.50: £1.10, £1.10, £3.90; EX 5.40.
Owner The Westerners **Bred** Crandon Park Stud **Trained** Denton, Co Durham
■ Stewards' Enquiry : Paul Mulrennan caution: used whip with excessive frequency

FOCUS
A fair maiden that was run at a decent enough pace with the first three finishing well clear of the remainder. The winner is probably the best guide to the form.

4532 HAMILTON-PARK.CO.UK H'CAP (FINAL QUALIFIER FOR THE SCOTTISH TROPHY HANDICAP SERIES) 1m 1f 36y
9:10 (9:10) (Class 5) (0-75,75) 3-Y-O+ £3,238 (£963; £481; £240) Stalls High

Form RPR
3423 1 **Casino Night**[6] 4345 4-9-2 70 AndrewHeffernan(7) 7 80
(F P Murtagh) *prom: drvn over 3f out: rallied to ld appr fnl f: hld on wl towards fin* 9/2
14 2 nk **Hippolytus**[21] 3864 4-9-6 72 JamieKyne(5) 2 81
(J J Quinn) *hld up: hdwy over 2f out: edgd rt: ev ch ins fnl f: hld cl home* 4/1[3]
0434 3 6 **Primo Way**[15] 4040 8-8-10 57 DuranFentiman 8 53
(D A Nolan) *hld up: hdwy to ld over 2f out: hdd appr fnl f: sn outpcd* 33/1
0-31 4 7 **Doon Haymer (IRE)**[15] 4040 4-9-12 73 PhillipMakin 6 54
(I Semple) *prom: pushed along 1/2-way: no imp fr over 2f out* 3/1[1]
0003 5 ½ **Goodbye Mr Bond**[28] 3624 9-9-7 68 PJMcDonald 4 48
(E J Alston) *in tch: smooth hdwy and ev ch over 2f: wknd fnl f* 8/1
652B 6 9 **Talk Of Saafend (IRE)**[19] 3911 4-9-3 64 PaulMulrennan 5 24
(P Monteith) *hld up: hdwy 3f out: wknd 2f out* 12/1
-005 7 5 **Naomh Geileis (USA)**[172] 490 4-10-0 75 SilvestreDeSousa 1 24
(M Johnston) *chsd ldr tl rdn and wknd over 2f out* 16/1
5331 8 2¾ **Shy Glance (USA)**[42] 3150 7-9-5 71 LanceBetts(5) 9 14
(P Monteith) *led to over 2f out: sn rdn and wknd* 11/1
330- 9 9 **Resounding Glory (USA)**[143] 6250 4-9-10 74 FrederikTylicki(3) 11 —
(R A Fahey) *trckd ldrs tl wknd fr 3f out* 7/2[2]
2m 3.74s (4.04) **Going Correction** +0.525s/f (Yiel) **9** Ran SP% **121.4**
Speed ratings (Par 103): **103,102,97,91,90 82,78,75,67**
toteswingers: 1&2 £5.50, 1&3 £14.30, 2&3 £25.80 CSF £24.20 CT £543.65 TOTE £5.60: £1.70, £1.80, £4.80; EX 32.00 Place 6: £14.18 Place 5: £13.50.
Owner Barry Robson **Bred** Kingsmead Breeders **Trained** Low Braithwaite, Cumbria

FOCUS
A tight handicap, run at a good pace. A personal best from the winner to turn around latest running with the favourite.
Doon Haymer(IRE) Official explanation: jockey said gelding was never travelling
Resounding Glory(USA) Official explanation: jockey said gelding finished distressed
T/Plt: £17.60 to a £1 stake. Pool: £46,784.39. 1,931.20 winning tickets. T/Qpdt: £8.70 to a £1 stake. Pool: £6,356.70. 539.40 winning tickets. RY

4300 LINGFIELD (L-H)
Saturday, August 1

OFFICIAL GOING: Turf course - good to soft changing to soft after race 1 (5.55) all-weather - standard
Wind: light behind Weather: overcast and raining

4533 TOTEPLACEPOT APPRENTICE H'CAP 7f 140y
5:55 (6:01) (Class 6) (0-65,65) 3-Y-O+ £2,047 (£604; £302) Stalls Centre

Form RPR
6622 1 **Whotsit (IRE)**[5] 4389 3-8-8 54 (b) LauraPike(2) 8 66
(Miss Amy Weaver) *crossed to stands rails and sn led: clr over 1f out: rdn and in command after* 9/2[2]
2 3½ **Blue Turk**[99] 1499 4-9-0 55 ChrisHough(4) 14 59
(J R Boyle) *chsd ldrs on stands' side: plugged on fr 2f out: wnt 2nd ins fnl f: no ch w wnr* 8/1
0243 3 1¼ **Resentful Angel**[17] 3983 4-9-12 63 (b) TobyAtkinson 2 64+
(Pat Eddery) *one of pair racing on far side: swtchd rt fr 1/2-way: wnt 2nd but hanging bdly rt: no imp on wnr: hung lft and lost 2nd ins fnl f* 7/2[1]
0052 4 3¼ **Cardinal**[14] 4105 4-9-5 58 SPRyan(2) 13 51+
(R A Harris) *midfield: rdn over 2f out: plodded on wout threatening* 9/2[2]
5634 5 shd **Ishibee (IRE)**[26] 3671 5-8-7 48 (p) RyanClark(4) 12 41
(J J Bridger) *prom: rdn over 2f out: one pce in fnl f* 16/1
-400 6 nk **Turfwolke (GER)**[68] 2330 4-9-4 59 AlexEdwards(4) 10 51
(Mrs H S Main) *wnt bdly lft s: sn cl up: rdn over 2f out: wl hld after* 33/1
0406 7 ½ **Wavertree Warrior (IRE)**[44] 3076 7-9-2 53 (b) HollyHall 1 44
(N P Littmoden) *one of two racing alone far side: nvr nr ldrs: plugged on fnl 2f* 8/1
3356 8 1¼ **Tignello (IRE)**[22] 3800 4-9-4 59 HarryBentley(4) 11 46
(G L Moore) *prom but drvn along: fdd over 2f out* 11/2[3]
0040 9 3¼ **Mystic Touch**[27] 3662 3-8-12 56 (p) DavidKenny 4 34
(Miss E C Lavelle) *s.s: nvr on terms* 25/1
1400 10 ½ **Avoca Dancer (IRE)**[14] 4082 6-9-0 55 (v) NatashaEaton(4) 16 33
(Karen George) *chsd ldrs tl rdn and fdd over 2f out* 14/1
-400 11 2 **Mount Ella**[54] 2776 3-8-6 54 BarryAdams(4) 17 26
(J R Boyle) *struggling in rr after 3f: hanging lft after* 25/1
0630 12 3 **Charles Darwin (IRE)**[22] 3800 6-10-0 65 CharlesEddery 7 31
(M Blanshard) *s.s: sn rcvrd to chse wnr: fdd rapidly over 2f out* 16/1
3500 13 7 **Jessica Wigmo**[38] 3269 6-8-5 46 oh1 JakePayne(4) 9 —
(A W Carroll) *swtchd rt after s: sn rdn in midfield: no ch over 2f out* 25/1
0200 14 1½ **Divine White**[67] 2353 6-8-13 50 JosephineBruning 3 —
(G P Enright) *t.o fnl 2f* 66/1
060- 15 5 **Good Queen Best**[304] 6392 3-8-6 54 RyanPowell(4) 18 —
(B De Haan) *sn rdn: a bhd: t.o fnl 2f* 66/1
000 16 ¾ **Tallulah Sunrise**[22] 3811 4-8-8 49 MarieLequarre(4) 15 —
(M D I Usher) *t.o fnl 2f* 40/1
1m 34.17s (1.87) **Going Correction** +0.275s/f (Good)
WFA 3 from 4yo+ 7lb **16** Ran SP% **134.5**
Speed ratings (Par 101): **101,97,96,93,92 92,92,90,87,87 85,82,75,73,68 67**
toteswingers: 1&2 £17.00, 1&3 £4.20, 2&3 £10.40 CSF £42.66 CT £155.11 TOTE £5.60: £1.40, £2.90, £1.80, £1.50; EX 61.70.
Owner Miss A Weaver **Bred** Michael J Woodlock **Trained** Newmarket, Suffolk

FOCUS
The ground was much softer than that on which the runners had been declared so caution should be exercised when assessing this meeting. The stands' rail was heavily favoured through the card. The winner rates a personal best.

4534 TOTESWINGER MEDIAN AUCTION MAIDEN STKS 7f 140y
6:25 (6:30) (Class 6) 2-Y-O £2,047 (£604; £302) Stalls Centre

Form RPR
65 1 **Agony And Ecstasy**[23] 3785 2-8-12 0 RichardKingscote 15 69
(R M Beckett) *sn led: rdn over 1f out: a holding chalr fnl f* 14/1
4 2 1¼ **Dr Finley (IRE)**[18] 3957 2-9-3 0 RichardHughes 17 71
(M L W Bell) *chsd ldrs: n.m.r fr over 2f out: sustained chal fnl f: swtchd lft wl ins fnl f: kpt on* 9/4[2]
0 3 2½ **Puteri (IRE)**[15] 4055 2-8-12 0 PhilipRobinson 1 61+
(M A Jarvis) *one of pair racing far side: grad tacked over fr 1/2-way: chsd ldrs: hld by wnr 1f out: kpt on to snatch 3rd* 12/1
52 4 shd **Joe Packet**[19] 3920 2-9-3 0 SaleemGolam 4 65+
(J G Portman) *prom: rdn 2f out: nt qckn 1f out: lost 3rd nr fin* 8/1
3 5 1¼ **Kensei (IRE)**[34] 3420 2-9-3 0 SebSanders 12 63
(R M Beckett) *chsd ldrs: n.m.r 2f out: rdn and btn over 1f out* 2/1[1]
00 6 4½ **Rodrigo De Freitas (IRE)**[16] 4006 2-9-3 0 PatCosgrave 6 52
(J R Boyle) *s.s: tacked rt after s: sn chsng ldrs: drvn over 2f out: wknd over 1f out* 66/1
0 7 1¾ **Rose Alba (IRE)**[22] 3810 2-8-12 0 JimCrowley 13 43
(J L Dunlop) *midfield: rdn 1/2-way: rn green: btn 2f out* 10/1
0 8 3¾ **Chandrayaan**[12] 4152 2-9-3 0 TGMcLaughlin 8 40
(E A L Dunlop) *plld hrd: sn tacked rt to main gp: pushed along 4f out: btn wl over 2f out* 20/1
9 14 **Masterful Act (USA)** 2-9-3 0 RichardThomas 14 9
(J R Best) *s.s: a labouring: t.o over 2f out* 66/1
0 10 1½ **Book Of Truth (USA)**[10] 4209 2-9-0 0 AhmedAjtebi(3) 9 5
(D M Simcock) *unbalanced most of way: chsd ldrs tl fdd over 2f out: t.o* 20/1
11 1¾ **Harry Paget (IRE)** 2-9-3 0 SteveDrowne 11 1
(J R Best) *s.s: struggling in rr 1/2-way: t.o over 1f out* 25/1
12 6 **Power Series (USA)** 2-9-3 0 RobertHavlin 18 —
(J H M Gosden) *s.s: rn green and kpt hanging lft: t.o wl over 1f out* 6/1[3]
13 11 **Fine Lace (IRE)** 2-8-12 0 FrankieMcDonald 5 —
(D J S Ffrench Davis) *s.s: one of pair racing on far side: t.o over 2f out* 100/1
0 14 6 **Double Rollover**[10] 4194 2-9-3 0 (b[1]) MartinDwyer 10 —
(W R Muir) *prom but sn urged along: reluctant: eased 2f out: t.o* 66/1
1m 35.46s (3.16) **Going Correction** +0.275s/f (Good) **14** Ran SP% **131.8**
Speed ratings (Par 92): **95,93,91,91,89 85,83,79,65,64 62,56,45,39**
toteswingers: 1&2 £16.70, 1&3 £52.50, 2&3 £12.60 CSF £48.00 TOTE £18.50: £4.00, £1.60, £4.20; EX 85.00.
Owner Miss Rachel Tregaskes **Bred** Downfield Cottage Stud **Trained** Whitsbury, Hants

FOCUS
Quite a few of these youngsters would not have encountered such testing conditions at home over this distance and those with experience came to the fore.

NOTEBOOK
Agony And Ecstasy had two advantages over the majority of the field in that she had the benefit of two races, despite them being on faster ground, and she also got the stands rail and that combination, plus a willing attitude was enough. She'll get 1m on this evidence. (op 16-1)
Dr Finley(IRE) was one who had raced under these conditions on his debutover 7f at Yarmouth and again showed promise. However, he doesn't do things quickly and didn't get much room when getting fully motivated throughout the final furlong and was never quite going to reach the winner. He gives the impression he might need a slightly stiffer test. (op 5-2 tchd 2-1)
Puteri(IRE) did really well on her second start having run on soft ground at Newmarket on her debut in the middle of July. She was at a big disadvantage from the draw and raced virtually alone until joining the main bunch at halfway but was still on the outside. She stayed on willingly and should win any average maiden on this performance. (tchd 11-1)
Joe Packet didn't quite get home, which seemed a surprise judged on his run over 6f at Windsor last time but he will be of interest in nurseries around this distance now he can get a mark. (op 15-2 tchd 7-1)
Kensei(IRE) might be a bit better than this as he didn't get a great deal of room from over a furlong out and wasn't knocked about when he couldn't win. (op 11-4)
Rodrigo De Freitas(IRE) was on the pace and ran his best of three races so far which make him an interesting candidate for nurseries around this distance.
Rose Alba(IRE) got tired on this testing ground but has ability.
Chandrayaan was pretty keen and in the circumstances ran with some credit. (tchd 25-1)

4535 KAY HEGARTY 70TH BIRTHDAY SURPRISE H'CAP 7f
6:55 (6:59) (Class 5) (0-75,75) 3-Y-O £3,238 (£963; £481; £240) Stalls High

Form RPR
6152 1 **Secret Hero**[8] 4267 3-8-11 65 (b[1]) RichardHughes 10 76
(R Hannon) *slowly away: clsd to ld wl over 4f out: sn bagged stands rail: jnd 1f out: hung on gamely u.p* 9/4[1]
1643 2 hd **Hi Shinko**[9] 4223 3-9-1 69 TGMcLaughlin 11 79
(B R Millman) *prom: wnt 2nd 3f out: rnged level 1f out: hrd rdn and btn on nod* 13/2[2]
-651 3 4½ **Learo Dochais (USA)**[7] 4303 3-9-7 75 PhilipRobinson 9 73
(M A Jarvis) *t.k.h: a pressing ldrs: rdn over 1f out: one pce and no imp after* 9/4[1]
0-00 4 ¾ **Champion Girl (IRE)**[57] 2685 3-8-4 58 FrankieMcDonald 13 54
(D Haydn Jones) *led and keen: hdd wl over 4f out: btn 1f out: kpt on one pce* 12/1
5300 5 6 **Protiva**[46] 3005 3-8-2 56 oh1 JamieMackay 4 36
(Karen George) *racd on outside: immediately rdn: hopeleslly outpcd 1/2-way: plugged on* 50/1
5001 6 hd **Peper Harow (IRE)**[22] 3815 3-8-3 57 NeilChalmers 8 36
(M D I Usher) *t.k.h in midfield: rdn and btn over 1f out: wkng fnl f* 16/1
1235 7 4½ **Hellbender (IRE)**[8] 4267 3-9-2 70 JamesDoyle 12 37
(S Kirk) *bhd and rdn: lost tch over 2f out* 12/1
5-55 8 2 **Captain Flasheart (IRE)**[106] 1317 3-8-5 62 WilliamCarson(3) 3 24
(S C Williams) *s.s and swtchd rt: a struggling in rr* 15/2[3]
40-4 9 10 **Kingsgate Storm (IRE)**[205] 85 3-9-3 71 SteveDrowne 7 —
(J R Best) *rdn and struggling after 3f: eased over 1f out: t.o* 25/1
-050 10 3 **Piccolinda**[10] 4202 3-8-4 58 MartinDwyer 6 —
(W R Muir) *sn rdn: nvr gng wl: btn over 2f out: t.o and eased over 1f out* 12/1
1m 26.37s (3.07) **Going Correction** +0.45s/f (Yiel) **10** Ran SP% **121.4**
Speed ratings (Par 100): **100,99,94,93,86 86,81,79,67,64**
toteswingers: 1&2 £6.00, 1&3 £1.50, 2&3 £7.80 CSF £18.62 CT £37.65 TOTE £3.60: £1.20, £2.50, £1.60; EX 18.50.
Owner Carmel Stud **Bred** Carmel Stud **Trained** East Everleigh, Wilts

FOCUS
Once again the stands rail was important to the success of Secret Hero. Ordinary form.

4536 TOTEEXACTA H'CAP 6f
7:25 (7:27) (Class 6) (0-65,65) 3-Y-O+ £2,388 (£705; £352) Stalls High

Form RPR
0004 1 **Regal Royale**[10] 4203 6-9-6 58 (v) JamieMackay 9 70+
(Peter Grayson) *led after 2f: rdn clr over 1f out: styd on strly* 20/1

3533 **2** 1 ½ **Dr Wintringham (IRE)**[14] 4082 3-8-12 **54**.................. RichardHughes 14 58
(Karen George) *bhd: rdn 1/2-way: gd prog over 1f out and swtchd rt: fin full of running: gave herself too much to do* **15/2**[2]

6206 **3** ¾ **Cheshire Rose**[78] 2046 4-9-7 **59**..................................(p) WilliamBuick 3 62
(A M Hales) *grad tacked rt to r promly: drvn and outpcd by wnr over 1f out: lost 2nd ins fnl f* **22/1**

5621 **4** 3 **Mr Skipiton (IRE)**[11] 4183 4-9-10 **62**......................... TGMcLaughlin 11 55+
(B J McMath) *bhd: prog and hrd rdn 2f out: plugged on ins fnl f: n.d* **2/1**[1]

3002 **5** hd **Realt Na Mara (IRE)**[26] 3691 6-9-5 **57**.........................(p) TravisBlock 16 49
(H Morrison) *chsd ldrs for 4f: rdn and btn wl over 1f out* **9/1**

3413 **6** 1 ¼ **Stamford Blue**[8] 4268 8-9-6 **65**...(b) SPRyan(7) 6 53
(R A Harris) *prom tl rdn and btn wl over 1f out* **8/1**[3]

006 **7** ½ **Kingsgate Castle**[17] 3983 4-9-7 **59**.............................(b) SteveDrowne 4 46
(Miss Gay Kelleway) *immediately drvn: chsd ldrs 4f: sn btn* **12/1**

4662 **8** shd **Vanadium**[7] 4305 7-8-12 **57**.. JemmaMarshall(7) 7 43
(G L Moore) *s.s: passed sme floundering rivals fnl 2f: no ch w ldrs* **12/1**

0020 **9** 1 **Wooden King (IRE)**[64] 2458 4-9-1 **53**............................. JimCrowley 17 36
(M S Saunders) *immediately rdn: led 2f: wknd wl over 2f out* **9/1**

5661 **10** nk **Dynamo Dave (USA)**[9] 4238 4-9-0 **52**.........................(b) RobertHavlin 18 34
(M D I Usher) *swishing tail gng to s: prom tl 1/2-way: btn 2f out* **16/1**

101 **11** 2 **Bohobe (IRE)**[12] 4154 4-9-3 **58**.......................... WilliamCarson(3) 12 34
(Rae Guest) *sn bhd: btn wl over 2f out* **10/1**

03 **12** ¾ **Reigning Monarch (USA)**[15] 4051 6-8-12 **50**.........(b) SaleemGolam 10 23
(Miss Z C Davison) *t.k.h early: midfield: rdn and struggling 1/2-way* **20/1**

0000 **13** ¾ **Bonne**[5] 4380 4-9-8 **60**...(b) PaulFitzsimons 1 31
(Miss J R Tooth) *s.s: nt keen in rr* **40/1**

0600 **14** 1 ½ **Bold Rose**[15] 4061 3-8-13 **60**...(p) LeeNewnes(5) 8 25
(M D I Usher) *drvn and struggling 1/2-way* **33/1**

1m 14.0s (2.80) **Going Correction** +0.45s/f (Yiel)
WFA 3 from 4yo+ 4lb **14** Ran SP% **125.8**
Speed ratings (Par 101): **99,97,96,92,91 90,89,89,87,87 84,83,82,80**
toteswingers: 1&2 £44.30, 1&3 £53.20, 2&3 £51.10 CSF £161.39 CT £3460.65 TOTE £24.60: £3.80, £3.40, £5.50; EX 446.20.
Owner S Kamis And Mrs S Grayson **Bred** Cheveley Park Stud Ltd **Trained** Formby, Lancs

FOCUS
The pattern of the first three races continued with the stands' rail position being pivotal for success for the final race of the evening on turf. Modest form.

4537 TOTEPOOL AT TOTESPORT.COM EBF MAIDEN STKS 5f (P)
7:55 (7:55) (Class 5) 2-Y-O £3,335 (£992; £495; £247) Stalls High

Form RPR

202 **1** **Piccadilly Filly (IRE)**[17] 3987 2-8-12 0..................... EdwardCreighton 5 93+
(E J Creighton) *rdn and sn blitzed 7 l clr: nvr looked in slest danger fr wl over 1f out* **3/1**[2]

2 **2** 7 **Bush Tucker (IRE)**[19] 3918 2-9-3 0................................... JimCrowley 7 73+
(P Winkworth) *sn shkn up in rr: hdwy on outside ent st: kpt on wl to snatch 2nd: nvr win sight of wnr* **7/4**[1]

0 **3** ½ **Tatawor (IRE)**[22] 3792 2-9-3 0...................................... MartinDwyer 1 71
(M P Tregoning) *10 l 3rd at 1/2-way: wnt poor 2nd ins fnl f: relegated 3rd cl home* **16/1**

55 **4** 3 **Key Breeze**[9] 4233 2-9-3 0... RobertHavlin 4 60
(J H M Gosden) *v free to post: chsd long ldr tl jst ins fnl f: no ex* **7/1**

0334 **5** shd **Val C**[10] 4208 2-8-12 0.. LukeMorris 8 55
(N P Littmoden) *towards rr and wl bhd ldng pair: no ch fnl 2f* **16/1**

6 1 ¼ **Dusty Spirit** 2-9-0 0.. JackDean(3) 3 55
(W G M Turner) *last away and sn rdn: rn green: no ch fr 1/2-way* **40/1**

50 **7** hd **Athwaab**[38] 3271 2-8-12 0... TPO'Shea 2 49
(E A L Dunlop) *nvr bttr than midfield and off pce: rdn and no ex 2f out* **8/1**

2222 **8** hd **Listillo (USA)**[5] 4379 2-9-3 0... RichardHughes 6 54
(H J L Dunlop) *midfield and keen early: wl off pce of ldng pair: rdn over 2f out: wl btn whn hung rt and lost action clsng stages* **4/1**[3]

58.46 secs (-0.34) **Going Correction** 0.0s/f (Stan) 2y crse rec **8** Ran SP% **119.2**
Speed ratings (Par 94): **102,90,90,85,85 83,82,82**
toteswingers: 1&2 £2.10, 1&3 £29.60, 2&3 £8.30 CSF £9.11 TOTE £4.00: £1.50, £1.20, £3.30; EX 10.20.
Owner The Ultimate Racing Fraternity **Bred** Stock Vale Ltd **Trained** Mill Hill, London NW7

FOCUS
This was an absolute rout for Piccadilly Filly.

NOTEBOOK
Piccadilly Filly(IRE) hadn´t got home when showing pace over 6f in three previous starts - possibly unsuited by going right-handed at Kempton - but acted well here when tiring last time. She is getting stronger and it would have been hard to say she wouldn´t have had the momentum to beat these with another furlong, but it seems speed is her game although the handicapper might not give her respite if she goes into nurseries as this was a smart time. (op 4-1)
Bush Tucker(IRE) made things hard by taking a keen hold then sitting out the back and coming wide. Nothing finished better, as he did on debut at Windsor and he looks nailed on to be suited by a sixth furlong. (op 13-8)
Tatawor(IRE) tried to go the pace but was never going to get near the winner and was outpaced inside the last. However this was a much better effort than on debut over 6f at Ascot although that looks a more realistic distance.
Key Breeze was dropping back to the minimum trip after two attempts at 6f but trying to keep tabs on the winner did for him. (op 11-2 tchd 15-2)
Val C might drop a couple of pounds for this which might make nurseries more attractive. (op 20-1)
Listillo(USA) had finished second in his four previous races, three of which were from July 13. He didn´t handle the bend and showed little. He might have had enough for the moment. Official explanation: jockey said colt hung right and lost its action in the closing stages (op 5-1)

4538 BET TOTEPOOL ON 0800 221 221 H'CAP 1m 2f (P)
8:25 (8:25) (Class 6) (0-55,54) 3-Y-0+ £2,388 (£705; £352) Stalls Low

Form RPR

0 **1** **Denton (NZ)**[25] 3710 6-9-2 **50**..(t) PatCosgrave 8 64+
(J R Gask) *sn led at modest pce: qcknd clr whn drvn over 1f out: sn in command: eased ins fnl f* **4/1**[1]

0000 **2** 2 ¾ **Our Kes (IRE)**[8] 4269 7-9-4 **52**.. JimmyQuinn 13 55
(P Howling) *bhd: hdwy over 2f out: c wd in 7th and racd awkwardly st: fin strly to go 2nd ins fnl f: flattered by proximity to eased wnr* **5/1**[3]

-560 **3** ½ **Touch Of Style (IRE)**[157] 669 5-9-2 **50**......................... RobertHavlin 12 52
(T D McCarthy) *chsd ldrs: pushed along over 2f out: kpt on ins fnl f: no ch w wnr* **9/1**

000 **4** 1 **Cyber Space**[30] 3549 5-8-13 **52**....................................... NicolPolli(5) 5 52
(B J McMath) *settled midfield: rdn over 2f out: plugged on to go 4th ins fnl f* **33/1**

0565 **5** 1 ½ **Inquisitress**[130] 948 5-8-13 **47**...................................... NeilChalmers 10 44
(J J Bridger) *bhd: hdwy and edgd rt over 1f out: styd on gamely* **14/1**

000 **6** nk **Empire Seeker (USA)**[44] 3077 4-9-1 **49**.........................(p) JimCrowley 6 45
(Mrs H S Main) *cl up: rdn 3f out: ev ch of 2nd tl no ex over 1f out* **4/1**[1]

0003 **7** shd **Platoche (IRE)**[14] 4084 4-9-3 **51**.. WilliamBuick 1 47
(G A Butler) *midfield: rdn over 2f out: n.d after* **6/1**

0503 **8** nk **Play Up Pompey**[23] 3769 7-8-12 **46**.................................. SebSanders 11 41
(J J Bridger) *a towards rr: rdn and btn over 2f out* **9/2**[2]

00-0 **9** 1 **King's Fable (USA)**[19] 3927 6-9-6 **54**........................(p) TGMcLaughlin 14 47
(Karen George) *last away and rdn: struggling in last 3f out* **14/1**

500- **10** ¾ **Hurstpierpoint (IRE)**[9] 4910 4-9-1 **49**............................. RichardHughes 4 41
(M G Rimell) *prom: rdn over 2f out: stl ev ch of 2nd 1f out: lost pl qckly ins fnl f: eased* **11/1**

-200 **11** 1 ¾ **Chinese Profit**[24] 3735 4-9-4 **52**... LukeMorris 2 40
(G C Bravery) *t.k.h and prom: drvn over 3f out: wknd rapidly ent fnl f* **20/1**

2m 8.57s (1.97) **Going Correction** 0.0s/f (Stan) **11** Ran SP% **128.5**
Speed ratings (Par 101): **92,89,89,88,87 87,87,86,86,85 84**
toteswingers: 1&2 £6.40, 1&3 £12.40, 2&3 £17.10 CSF £26.53 CT £180.90 TOTE £5.60: £1.90, £2.30, £4.20; EX 39.50 Place 6: £84.40 Place 5: £64.65.
Owner Horses First Racing Limited **Bred** Windsor Park Stud Ltd **Trained** Sutton Veny, Wilts

FOCUS
This was a moderate handicap. The winner made all at a steady pace for an impressive win.
T/Plt: £129.70 to a £1 stake. Pool: £67,818.88. 381.43 winning tickets. T/Qpdt: £28.40 to a £1 stake. Pool: £6,239.80. 162.50 winning tickets. IM

4497 NEWMARKET (R-H)
Saturday, August 1

OFFICIAL GOING: Good (8.4)
Stands' side track used.
Wind: Light across Weather: Overcast

4539 SPORTINGBET.COM FILLIES' NURSERY 6f
2:10 (2:11) (Class 2) 2-Y-O £12,952 (£3,854; £1,926; £962) Stalls High

Form RPR

6222 **1** **She's Ok (IRE)**[5] 4385 2-8-5 **74**....................................... ChrisCatlin 8 79
(C E Brittain) *racd centre: mid-div: swtchd rt and hdwy over 1f out: rdn to ld ins fnl f: hung lft: r.o* **12/1**

31 **2** hd **Snow Fairy (IRE)**[24] 3745 2-9-7 **90**................................... AdamKirby 18 94+
(E A L Dunlop) *racd stands' side: hld up: swtchd lft and hdwy over 1f out: rdn and hung lft ins fnl f: r.o wl* **8/1**[1]

5141 **3** 1 ¼ **Fleeting Echo**[14] 4081 2-8-6 **75**................................... RichardThomas 1 76
(R Hannon) *overall ldr in centre: rdn over 1f out: hdd and unable qck ins fnl f* **12/1**

10 **4** hd **Bahati (IRE)**[9] 4245 2-8-13 **82**................................. FrankieMcDonald 2 82
(J G Portman) *s.s: racd centre: hld up: hdwy over 1f out: r.o* **14/1**

3221 **5** hd **Miss Lesley**[12] 4147 2-8-9 **78**.. KShea 15 77
(D K Ivory) *racd stands' side: chsd ldrs: rdn over 1f out: edgd lft ins fnl f: r.o* **10/1**[3]

0310 **6** 1 ¼ **Lady Pattern (IRE)**[23] 3782 2-9-0 **83**................................ IanMongan 10 79
(P W D'Arcy) *racd stands' side: chsd ldrs: rdn and hung lft over 1f out: styd on same pce* **16/1**

21 **7** nk **Silver Grey (IRE)**[23] 3767 2-8-9 **78**................................ RobertHavlin 16 73+
(R Ingram) *racd stands' side: prom: rdn over 2f out: outpcd over 1f out: r.o towards fin* **11/1**

321 **8** ¾ **Exotic Beauty**[49] 2907 2-9-2 **85**...................................... DarryllHolland 4 78
(M R Channon) *racd centre: mid-div: hdwy 2f out: sn rdn and edgd lft: hung rt and no ex ins fnl f* **17/2**[2]

4561 **9** hd **Angel Of Fashion (IRE)**[16] 4017 2-8-5 **74**......................... LiamJones 6 66
(B W Hills) *racd centre: plld hrd: w ldrs: rdn and ev ch over 1f out: styd on same pce* **8/1**[1]

0631 **10** 2 ¼ **Quaker Parrot**[16] 3993 2-8-6 **75**.............................. RichardKingscote 3 60
(Tom Dascombe) *racd centre: w ldr tl rdn over 2f out: wknd fnl f* **16/1**

021 **11** shd **Six Diamonds**[49] 2906 2-8-5 **74**...................................... NickyMackay 11 59
(H Morrison) *racd centre: chsd ldrs: rdn and hung rt over 1f out: wknd fnl f* **20/1**

5106 **12** ½ **Bell's Ocean (USA)**[22] 3821 2-8-5 **74**............................ KirstyMilczarek 9 57
(J Ryan) *racd centre: hld up: hdwy and hung rt over 1f out: no imp ins fnl f* **20/1**

351 **13** ½ **Tom Folan**[14] 4076 2-8-3 **72**...(p) HayleyTurner 14 54
(H J Collingridge) *racd stands' side: stdd s: hld up: nt clr run over 1f out: n.d* **16/1**

10 **14** ¾ **Reach For The Sky (IRE)**[14] 4089 2-8-6 **75** ow1.............. PatDobbs 13 55
(R Hannon) *racd stands' side: hld up: hdwy over 2f out: wknd fnl f* **16/1**

443 **15** ½ **Bathwick Xaara**[29] 3576 2-8-3 **72**....................................... SaleemGolam 5 50
(J G Portman) *uns rdr and bolted to post: racd centre: prom: rdn over 1f out: wknd fnl f* **16/1**

1500 **16** ½ **Azif**[46] 2995 2-8-12 **81**... DaneO'Neill 12 58
(Miss Gay Kelleway) *racd stands' side: chsd ldr tl rdn over 2f out: wknd fnl f* **33/1**

3261 **17** nk **Velvet Band**[27] 3658 2-8-6 **75**.. AlanMunro 17 51
(P F I Cole) *led stands' side: rdn and wknd over 1f out* **12/1**

431 **18** 9 **Refuse To Wait (IRE)**[56] 2721 2-8-9 **78**............................ TedDurcan 7 27
(T D Easterby) *racd centre: mid-div: rdn 1/2-way: wknd 2f out* **16/1**

1m 13.28s (0.78) **Going Correction** +0.075s/f (Good) **18** Ran SP% **127.7**
Speed ratings (Par 97): **97,96,95,94,94 92,92,91,91,88 88,87,86,85,85 84,84,72**
toteswingers: 1&2 £19.40, 1&3 £68.00, 2&3 £26.10 CSF £105.36 CT £1241.45 TOTE £14.40: £2.70, £2.40, £3.80, £4.80; EX 78.70 Trifecta £259.50 Pool: £ - 350.70 - 1.00 winning units..
Owner Saeed Manana **Bred** Victor Stud Bloodstock Ltd **Trained** Newmarket, Suffolk

FOCUS
The ground had dried out since the previous evening and was officially changed to good. A big field for this competitive-looking fillies' nursery and a wide-open race, as the betting market testified. The field raced in two groups in the early stages, although they converged up the centre of the track in the final furlong.

NOTEBOOK
She's Ok(IRE) had been runner-up on her previous three starts but was dropping in trip for this handicap debut, having been beaten over 7f at the beginning of the week. She was held up behind the leaders and then did not come down the hill particularly well, but found her stride once meeting the rising ground. Despite carrying her head a trifle high, she stuck on under pressure to hold off the fast-finishing runner-up. She will now be aimed at the Watership Down Sales race. (tchd 14-1)
Snow Fairy(IRE) ◆ looked a little unlucky, as she tracked the leader on the stands' side but found the overall leaders racing more towards the centre of the track. She wandered across to join them when making her challenge and was closing on the winner all the way to the line. She looks progressive and should gain compensation at a similar level. (op 9-1)
Fleeting Echo ran a good race, having been in the leading group on the far side for most of the way. She looks a typically consistent type from the yard and may have more to offer. (op 10-1)

Bahati(IRE) ◆ had made a promising debut at Newbury but had been too keen in a Listed race over 7f the previous week. She took a while to load, but once the race began she travelled strongly in the rear before running on well in the closing stages. She has plenty of ability and, although she may not quite up to justifying a Fillies' Mile entry, looks one to bear in mind for the big fillies' nurseries later in the season.
Miss Lesley has been improving with experience and ran another decent race having been held up on the stands' side. She faded a little in the closing stages but only narrowly missed out on the places. (op 14-1)
Lady Pattern(IRE), who had beaten today's runner-up when that filly made her debut, showed up for a long way but had nothing in reserve for the climb to the line. (tchd 20-1)
Silver Grey(IRE) was another one to note. Held up in the stands' side group, she appeared to flounder on the run down into the dip, despite having won at Epsom on her previous start. She found her stride again up the hill and finished quite strongly, giving the impression she will improve again from this. (op 12-1 tchd 10-1)
Exotic Beauty chased the leaders in the far-side group throughout and kept on up the hill without quickening. She may be best back on fast ground. (op 9-1 tchd 10-1)
Angel Of Fashion(IRE) had struck form on her nursery debut last time, but was 7lb higher in a higher grade, and in the circumstances ran well under a positive ride. (op 10-1)
Refuse To Wait(IRE) Official explanation: trainer's rep said filly showed signs of coming into season

4540 SPORTINGBET.COM H'CAP 7f
2:45 (2:45) (Class 3) (0-90,85) 3-Y-O **£9,066** (£2,697; £1,348; £673) **Stalls** High

Form RPR
-324 **1** **Glen Molly (IRE)**[42] 3163 3-9-5 **81** DarryllHolland 1 96
(B W Hills) *hld up: hdwy over 1f out: rdn to ld ins fnl f: r.o wl* **11/2**[1]
155 **2** 2 ¼ **Imaam**[21] 3868 3-9-1 **77** RHills 7 86
(J L Dunlop) *chsd ldr tl led over 2f out: rdn: hung lft and hdd ins fnl f: styd on same pce* **8/1**[2]
1422 **3** 1 **Sir Isaac**[44] 3062 3-9-2 **78** KirstyMilczarek 13 87+
(W J Haggas) *hld up: hdwy over 2f out: nt clr run and lost pl over 1f out: hung lft and r.o ins fnl f: nt rch ldrs* **11/2**[1]
1430 **4** hd **Laudatory**[50] 2890 3-9-7 **83** (t) AdamKirby 8 89
(W R Swinburn) *hld up: hdwy u.p over 1f out: hung lft and r.o ins fnl f: nt rch ldrs* **16/1**
2612 **5** 1 ¼ **Invincible Isle (IRE)**[15] 4056 3-9-2 **78** IanMongan 2 80
(H R A Cecil) *hld up in tch: racd keenly: rdn and ev ch over 1f out: no ex ins fnl f* **11/2**[1]
2332 **6** 1 **Star Links (USA)**[10] 4210 3-9-7 **83** PatDobbs 4 83
(R Hannon) *prom: rdn over 1f out: edgd lft and no ex fnl f* **12/1**[3]
3-10 **7** ½ **Mabait**[36] 3347 3-9-6 **82** DaneO'Neill 6 80
(L M Cumani) *mid-div: hdwy over 2f out: rdn over 1f out: styd on same pce* **20/1**
2055 **8** 1 ¾ **Al Sabaheya**[21] 3843 3-9-5 **81** ChrisCatlin 14 75
(C E Brittain) *racd alone tl jnd main gp over 5f out: chsd ldrs: rdn over 1f out: hung lft and wknd fnl f* **20/1**
-514 **9** nk **Lujeanie**[24] 3738 3-8-13 **75** KShea 11 68
(D K Ivory) *hld up: rdn over 1f out: n.d* **16/1**
-310 **10** 2 ¼ **Diapason (IRE)**[19] 3921 3-8-10 **72** RichardKingscote 5 59
(Tom Dascombe) *chsd ldrs: rdn over 2f out: edgd rt over 1f out: wknd fnl f* **25/1**
0142 **11** 4 **Jack Cool (IRE)**[15] 4064 3-9-7 **83** AlanMunro 9 59
(P W Chapple-Hyam) *prom: rdn over 2f out: wknd wl over 1f out* **11/2**[1]
143- **12** 6 **Spanish Cygnet (USA)**[332] 5615 3-9-9 **85** GeorgeBaker 12 45
(Mrs A J Perrett) *stdd s: hld up: hdwy 2f out: wknd over 1f out* **20/1**
40-0 **13** 14 **Amber Sunset**[22] 3804 3-9-0 **76** LukeMorris 3 —
(J Jay) *led: rdn and hdd over 2f out: sn wknd* **66/1**
10 **14** ¾ **Secret Witness**[72] 2198 3-9-1 **77** (v[1]) TedDurcan 10 —
(J Noseda) *s.s: hld up: rdn over 2f out: no rspnse: sn wknd and eased* **12/1**[3]

1m 25.38s (-0.32) **Going Correction** +0.075s/f (Good) **14** Ran SP% **119.4**
Speed ratings (Par 104): **104,101,100,100,98 97,96,94,94,92 87,80,64,63**
toteswingers: 1&2 £8.90, 1&3 £5.50, 2&3 £21.30 CSF £44.48 CT £264.26 TOTE £6.60: £2.10, £3.20, £2.40; EX 62.20 Trifecta £294.00 Part won. Pool: £397.30 - 0.50 winning units..
Owner John C Grant **Bred** Noel O'Callaghan **Trained** Lambourn, Berks

FOCUS
A good, competitive handicap that often falls to an improving type and in which those at the head of the market have a good record. That proved again the case and the form looks reasonably rated around the placed horses.

NOTEBOOK
Glen Molly(IRE), the well-backed joint favourite, found plenty up the hill and came away from her rivals for a decisive success. She came into this with some solid form and is suited by some ease in the ground, although she handles fast. (tchd 6-1)
Imaam was given a positive ride and continued his progression with another good effort, although he had no chance with the winner. (op 12-1)
Sir Isaac had finished ahead of today's runner-up when second at Sandown on his penultimate start. He was held up more towards the stands' side and looked beaten before staying on well in the closing stages, although he would have struggled to trouble the winner. (op 15-2)
Laudatory had finished well behind the placed horses at Sandown but performed better this time. However, he appeared to get a tow into the race from the third, which might have helped him. (op 12-1)
Invincible Isle(IRE) ran another decent race, but her best efforts have been on faster ground and she could not respond to the challengers after having every chance. (op 5-1)
Star Links(USA) is a pretty consistent performer who stays further, acts on most ground and appeared to run his race again. He is probably the best guide to the level. (op 9-1)
Mabait tracked the leaders throughout but could not pick up enough to mount a serious challenge. This was his first try at 7f this season and he is likely to be dropping back in trip on this evidence. (op 16-1 tchd 25-1)
Jack Cool(IRE), dropping back from a mile, chased the leaders but did not pick up under pressure. His record suggests that a flat track suits him best. (op 6-1 tchd 5-1)
Secret Witness Official explanation: jockey said gelding had no more to give

4541 ADNAMS H'CAP 1m 2f
3:20 (3:20) (Class 3) (0-90,90) 3-Y-O+ **£9,066** (£2,697; £1,348; £673) **Stalls** Centre

Form RPR
241/ **1** **Broomielaw**[715] 4568 5-9-12 **88** HayleyTurner 6 105+
(E A L Dunlop) *a.p: lft chsng ldr in centre turning for home: edgd lft fr over 2f out: rdn over 1f out: styd on to ld wl ins fnl f* **7/1**
011 **2** nk **Laaheb**[15] 4058 3-9-3 **88** RHills 4 104+
(M A Jarvis) *chsd ldr tl wnt far side and led that gp turning for home: led overall wl over 2f out: rdn and hung rt over 1f out: hdd wl ins fnl f* **4/6**[1]
6011 **3** 5 **Mick's Dancer**[21] 3847 4-9-0 **76** DarryllHolland 5 83
(W R Muir) *led: wnt towards centre turning for home: hung lft fr 3f out: sn rdn and hdd: wknd wl ins fnl f* **6/1**[3]
50-1 **4** 6 **Hollins**[25] 3705 5-9-0 **76** TedDurcan 3 72
(Micky Hammond) *prom: chsd ldr far side turning for home: rdn and wknd over 2f out* **16/1**
-150 **5** 1 ¼ **Falcativ**[28] 3620 4-10-0 **90** DaneO'Neill 1 83
(L M Cumani) *hld up and bhd: wnt far side turning for home: rdn over 2f out: sn wknd* **5/1**[2]
6030 **6** 82 **Dar Es Salaam**[14] 4091 5-9-2 **78** GeorgeBaker 2 —
(J S Goldie) *hld up and bhd: wnt far side turning for home: rdn over 3f out: sn wknd: virtually p.u ins fnl f* **20/1**

2m 4.33s (-1.17) **Going Correction** +0.075s/f (Good)
WFA 3 from 4yo+ 9lb **6** Ran SP% **114.1**
Speed ratings (Par 107): **107,106,102,97,96 31**
toteswingers: 1&2 £1.80, 1&3 £5.60, 2&3 £1.10 CSF £12.55 TOTE £7.20: £3.00, £1.10; EX 15.80.
Owner Lady Ferguson **Bred** Biddestone Stud **Trained** Newmarket, Suffolk

FOCUS
Another good handicap and, despite the relatively small turnout, the field split in the straight before coming together over 2f out. The time was decent and the front pair look reasonably well handicapped with the runner-up the best guide.

NOTEBOOK
Broomielaw had not been seen for almost two years but was a decent, progressive colt then. He had been gelded during his extended break, was pretty fit for this and attracted market support. He tracked the third for much of the way and was slightly crossed by the favourite in the dip, but found for pressure up the hill to eventually wear him down. He is quite talented and could prove reasonably handicapped, although he may need a while to get over this. The Cambridgeshire is the target if he can be kept in one piece. (op 10-1)
Laaheb was strong in the market, was again ridden positively and travelled well enough. However, despite running his race, the winner proved too strong for him. This was only his fourth start and there is more to come. (op 8-11 tchd 8-13 and 4-5 in places)
Mick's Dancer is progressing and made sure it was a decent gallop. He could not find an extra in the last quarter-mile but it was no disgrace to be beaten by a pair of unexposed, potentially useful performers. (op 15-2 tchd 8-1)
Hollins was a market drifter and, although he tracked the runner-up throughout, was left behind at the business end. He was 6lb higher that when scoring on his previous start and may not be quite up to this grade yet. (op 11-1)
Falcativ was sweating and got stirred up going to the start, effectively losing his race before it had begun. (op 9-2 tchd 6-1)
Dar Es Salaam was eased in the closing stages and dismounted after the line as if something was amiss. (op 16-1 tchd 25-1)

4542 SPORTINGBET.COM EBF MAIDEN FILLIES' STKS 7f
3:55 (3:59) (Class 4) 2-Y-O **£5,180** (£1,541; £770; £384) **Stalls** High

Form RPR
1 **Seta** 2-9-0 0 DaneO'Neill 6 95+
(L M Cumani) *hld up in tch: led 2f out: rdn clr fnl f* **11/8**[1]
3 **2** 8 **Dyna Waltz**[15] 4055 2-9-0 0 NickyMackay 3 73
(J H M Gosden) *chsd ldr tl led 1/2-way: hdd 2f out: wknd fnl f* **7/4**[2]
3 ½ **Moonline Dancer (FR)** 2-9-0 0 PatDobbs 7 72
(R Hannon) *chsd ldrs: ev ch 2f out: rdn and hung rt over 1f out: wknd fnl f* **25/1**
4 1 ¼ **Rare Malt (IRE)** 2-9-0 0 HayleyTurner 15 69
(Miss Amy Weaver) *s.s: sn mid-div: rdn over 2f out: sn outpcd* **28/1**
5 ¾ **Tipperary Boutique (IRE)** 2-9-0 0 TedDurcan 5 67
(B W Hills) *s.i.s: sn chsng ldrs: rdn over 2f out: wknd fnl f* **20/1**
6 1 ½ **Quality Mover (USA)** 2-9-0 0 DarryllHolland 1 63
(D M Simcock) *hld up: shkn up over 2f out: n.d* **16/1**
0 **7** 1 ¾ **Jean Jeannie**[41] 3187 2-9-0 0 LiamJones 4 59
(W J Haggas) *led: racd keenly: hdd 1/2-way: wknd over 1f out* **12/1**[3]
00 **8** nse **Precious Coral (IRE)**[14] 4093 2-9-0 0 (t) SaleemGolam 14 59
(S A Callaghan) *hld up: rdn over 2f out: n.d* **80/1**
0 **9** ¾ **Astronomer's Dream**[15] 4055 2-9-0 0 LPKeniry 2 57
(E F Vaughan) *prom: rdn over 2f out: wknd sn after: in rr whn hmpd ins fnl f* **80/1**
10 1 **Queen Of Wands** 2-9-0 0 AlanMunro 9 54
(J L Dunlop) *s.i.s: a in rr: detached 1/2-way* **25/1**
11 1 ¼ **Silk Runner (IRE)** 2-9-0 0 ChrisCatlin 13 51
(J W Hills) *hld up: wknd over 2f out* **40/1**
12 11 **Satwa Excel** 2-9-0 0 KirstyMilczarek 12 24
(E A L Dunlop) *hld up: rdn and wknd over 2f out: hung rt over 1f out* **20/1**
13 4 ½ **Albeed** 2-9-0 0 RHills 10 12+
(J L Dunlop) *hld up in tch: plld hrd: wknd over 2f out* **12/1**[3]
0 **14** 6 **Sparkling Crown**[5] 4385 2-9-0 0 RobertHavlin 11 —
(J Ryan) *hld up: a in rr: wknd over 2f out* **66/1**

1m 28.3s (2.60) **Going Correction** +0.075s/f (Good) **14** Ran SP% **126.8**
Speed ratings (Par 93): **88,78,78,76,76 74,72,72,71,70 68,56,51,44**
toteswingers: 1&2 £2.00, 1&3 £11.80, 2&3 £8.20 CSF £3.58 TOTE £2.40: £1.40, £1.30, £3.10; EX 4.90.
Owner Miss Sarah J Leigh **Bred** Sarah J Leigh And Robin S Leigh **Trained** Newmarket, Suffolk

FOCUS
This fillies' maiden usually falls to a representative of one of the major local yards, although John Dunlop has trained the winner twice in the last ten years and was represented by a pair of newcomers. The whole field raced towards the far side. Only two were really fancied though, they went 12/1 bar the pair and the market proved correct.

NOTEBOOK
Seta ◆ ran away with this in the manner of a Group-class performer in the making. A half-sister to five winners, including the useful Gravitas, from the family of Gossamer and Barathea, she clearly knew her job and travelled nicely just behind the leaders before taking over inside the last quarter-mile. She quickly opened up an advantage and extended it all the way to the line, without being fully extended. She has a Fillies' Mile entry and appeals as the type who could take in the Prestige Stakes at Goodwood at the end of next month (which connections won with Gossamer) en-route. She has been quoted at a not particularly generous 10/1 for next season's 1000 Guineas. (op 11-4 tchd 3-1)
Dyna Waltz, out of the French 1000 Guineas winner Valentine Waltz, was deposed as favourite by the winner. She improved on her debut over course and distance in that she came through to lead inside the last 3f and held on for second, but caught a tartar in the winner and should not be too long in winning her maiden. (op 13-8 tchd 6-4)
Moonline Dancer(FR), a 160,000gns half-sister to four winners, has a couple of Group 1 entries and showed up pretty well from the start and stuck on in the wake of the winner in the closing stages. She should come on for the run, as runners from this stable often do, and can win a similar contest. (op 14-1)
Rare Malt(IRE), a cheaply bought filly, put up an eyecatching effort, staying on from well off the pace to make the frame. She should benefit from this debut. (op 33-1 tchd 25-1)
Tipperary Boutique(IRE), a 90,000 euros filly with a middle-distance pedigree, was a market drifter but ran a nice race without being given too hard a time. She will be better over longer trips in time. (op 14-1)
Quality Mover(USA), a $140,000 filly with a Fillies' Mile entry, did best of the rest, staying on steadily at the finish and is yet another who looks to have a future. (op 14-1 tchd 12-1)

Albeed was keen early and never got into contention. She ended up on the outside of the pack and was allowed to come home in her own time once her chance had gone. (op 8-1)

4543 SPORTINGBET.COM EBF CONDITIONS STKS 1m
4:30 (4:30) (Class 2) 4-Y-O+

£12,462 (£3,732; £1,866; £934; £466; £234) Stalls High

Form RPR

05 1 **Bushman**16 4002 5-8-9 100 DarryllHolland 2 109+
(D M Simcock) *trckd ldrs: nt clr run 2f out: swtchd lft: shkn up to ld over 1f out: r.o wl: eased nr fin* 13/23

3035 2 4 **Kay Gee Be (IRE)**21 3872 5-8-9 91 AlanMunro 8 99
(W Jarvis) *chsd ldr tl led 3f out: rdn and hdd over 1f out: styd on same pce* 16/1

3-25 3 shd **Cesare**21 3841 8-8-9 118 HayleyTurner 4 99
(J R Fanshawe) *hld up: hdwy over 2f out: n.m.r over 1f out: sn rdn: styd on same pce* 8/111

0160 4 2 **Cadre (IRE)**45 3014 4-8-9 95 NickyMackay 6 94
(J H M Gosden) *prom: racd keenly: pushed along over 3f out: led over 1f out: sn rdn: edgd rt and hdd: wknd ins fnl f* 11/1

-010 5 4 1/2 **Jack Dawkins (USA)**29 3586 4-8-9 95 IanMongan 5 83
(H R A Cecil) *hld up: rdn over 2f out: sn hung lft and wknd* 14/1

-300 6 2 **Stubbs Art (IRE)**7 4297 4-8-9 103 KShea 7 78
(M F De Kock, South Africa) *hld up: racd keenly: hdwy over 4f out: rdn over 1f out: sn hung rt and wknd* 9/1

20-0 7 15 **Mutajarred**14 4090 5-8-9 104 (b1) RHills 1 59
(W J Haggas) *led: hdd 3f out: rdn whn n.m.r wl over 1f out: sn wknd and eased* 6/12

1m 41.06s (1.06) **Going Correction** +0.075s/f (Good) 7 Ran SP% 116.4
Speed ratings (Par 109): **97,93,92,90,86 84,69**
toteswingers: 1&2 £9.40, 1&3 £2.40, 2&3 £4.20 CSF £98.64 TOTE £7.40: £2.70, £5.50; EX 92.70.
Owner Khalifa Dasmal **Bred** Darley **Trained** Newmarket, Suffolk
■ Stewards' Enquiry : Alan Munro caution: used whip without giving mount time to respond

FOCUS
A good conditions stakes, close to Listed standard judged on the official ratings of the participants, and again they raced towards the far side. The winner looks back to his best with the runner-up setting the level.

NOTEBOOK
Bushman goes well on good and easy ground and has been running well without a great deal of success in mainly Group and Listed company this season. However, everything fell right for him this time and, getting a gap over a furlong out, he picked up strongly up the hill and quickly settled matters. This will help his confidence and the Cambridgeshire could be on the agenda, but much depends on how the Handicapper reacts. (op 8-1 tchd 10-1)
Kay Gee Be(IRE) has been campaigned mainly in handicaps on fast ground, some over longer trips. He showed up throughout and, although no match for the winner in the closing stages, kept going to hold off the favourite.
Cesare stood out on that basis of those figures but has not been at his best of late. He came to have his chance inside the last quarter-mile but could not pick up as well as the winner and was then held off for the runner-up spot. He may be one to go cautiously with in the short-term. (tchd 4-5 in places)
Cadre(IRE) has run in a couple of good handicaps recently and finished well beaten in the Royal Hunt Cup. He appeared to have every chance but could not find an extra gear in the closing stages. He will not prove easy to place in the short-term. (tchd 12-1)
Jack Dawkins(USA) was held up at the back but got rather outpaced soon after halfway and only stayed on past beaten rivals. (op 12-1 tchd 16-1)
Stubbs Art(IRE) had the blinkers left off but has not shown much in two starts back in this country. Although slipping in the weights, he looks a shadow of the horse who was places in two Guineas last season. (op 12-1)
Mutajarred appreciates cut in the ground and was dropping back in trip. He ran freely in front in the first-time blinkers and stopped pretty quickly once headed. Official explanation: vet said gelding bled from the nose (tchd 8-1 in places)

4544 SPORTINGBET H'CAP 1m 4f
5:05 (5:05) (Class 4) (0-85,85) 4-Y-O+ £5,180 (£1,541; £770; £384) Stalls Centre

Form RPR

3-60 1 **Coeur De Lionne (IRE)**16 4003 5-8-12 74 HayleyTurner 1 84
(E A L Dunlop) *hld up: wnt far side ent st: hdwy 7f out: chsd ldr over 5f out: led that gp over 3f out: rdn to ld overall over 1f out: styd on u.p* 18/1

3114 2 2 **Run For Ede's**6 4340 5-8-9 74 JackDean(3) 3 81
(P M Phelan) *hld up: wnt far side ent st: hdwy over 6f out: rdn over 1f out: styd on* 5/22

5640 3 1/2 **Force Group (IRE)**22 3822 5-8-8 70 TedDurcan 4 76
(M H Tompkins) *chsd ldrs: wnt far side ent st: chal over 3f out: rdn over 1f out: styd on* 11/23

2-04 4 1/2 **Mubrook (USA)**29 3564 4-9-6 82 DaneO'Neill 2 87
(L M Cumani) *prom: wnt far side ent st: rdn over 3f out: outpcd over 2f out: r.o u.p ins fnl f* 11/23

1002 5 hd **Clear Reef**14 4098 5-9-4 80 (p) KShea 8 85
(Jane Chapple-Hyam) *led and sn clr: wnt towards centre ent st: rdn and hdd over 1f out: sn hung lft and no etxra* 13/2

6211 6 2 1/2 **Sir Boss (IRE)**11 4169 4-9-9 85 ChrisCatlin 6 86
(D E Cantillon) *hld up: wnt far side ent st: hdwy over 2f out: rdn over 1f out: no ex ins fnl f* 15/81

0000 7 9 **Rowan Rio**8 4269 4-8-4 66 LiamJones 9 52
(W J Haggas) *chsd clr ldr tl wnt far side and led that gp ent st: hdd over 3f out: wknd over 2f out* 16/1

2m 33.41s (0.51) **Going Correction** +0.075s/f (Good) 7 Ran SP% 118.6
Speed ratings (Par 105): **101,99,99,99,98 97,91**
toteswingers: 1&2 £8.00, 1&3 £12.50, 2&3 £4.70 CSF £66.12 CT £294.93 TOTE £22.20: £4.80, £2.00; EX 94.70 Place 6: £375.26 Place 5: £110.31.
Owner The Lamprell Partnership **Bred** Hawthorn Villa Stud **Trained** Newmarket, Suffolk

FOCUS
A relatively ordinary handicap and weakened by the absence of the 2007 winner Invasian. It produced something of a surprise result and is not the most solid form, with the third and fourth rated to their recent marks.
Clear Reef Official explanation: jockey said horse hung both ways

4545 WIN AT SPORTINGBET.COM H'CAP 1m 4f
5:40 (5:41) (Class 5) (0-70,72) 3-Y-O £3,885 (£1,156; £577; £288) Stalls Centre

Form RPR

0012 1 **The Last Don (IRE)**11 4175 3-9-11 72 TedDurcan 6 81+
(D R Lanigan) *sn led: rdn and hdd over 2f out: edgd rt over 1f out: rallied to ld ins fnl f: r.o* 6/12

0-23 2 hd **Broughtons Paradis (IRE)**48 2950 3-8-8 55 ChrisCatlin 3 64
(W J Musson) *hld up: hdwy over 2f out: rdn ins fnl f: r.o* 16/1

-202 3 1 1/4 **Jachol (IRE)**12 4157 3-8-8 55 RHills 1 62
(W J Haggas) *sn chsng ldr: led over 2f out: rdn over 1f out: hdd and unable qck ins fnl f* 3/11

-662 4 1 1/2 **Incendo**31 3511 3-9-7 68 LPKeniry 4 73
(J R Fanshawe) *hld up: hdwy over 2f out: rdn over 1f out: styd on same pce ins fnl f* 3/11

-346 5 1/2 **Theologist (IRE)**63 2479 3-9-7 68 GeorgeBaker 8 72
(Mrs A J Perrett) *prom: rdn over 2f out: styd on same pce fnl f* 8/13

05-0 6 1 1/4 **Tomintoul Star**99 1488 3-8-12 59 IanMongan 10 61
(H R A Cecil) *hld up: hdwy and nt clr run over 1f out: sn rdn: edgd lft and no imp ins fnl f* 10/1

1105 7 3/4 **Taste The Wine (IRE)**21 3861 3-9-7 68 DarryllHolland 7 69
(J S Moore) *hld up: hdwy and nt clr run over 1f out: sn lost pl: n.d after* 17/2

004 8 1 **Stormy Morning**16 4022 3-9-3 64 AdamKirby 2 63
(W R Swinburn) *chsd ldrs: rdn over 2f out: sn hung lft: wknd ins fnl f* 14/1

0-04 9 1/2 **Caught On Camera**24 3741 3-8-8 55 HayleyTurner 9 53
(M L W Bell) *chsd ldrs: rdn over 1f out: wknd ins fnl f* 14/1

0-00 10 4 1/2 **Sircozy (IRE)**26 3693 3-8-9 56 ow1 KShea 11 47
(S C Williams) *hld up: rdn over 2f out: sn wknd* 11/1

2m 34.96s (2.06) **Going Correction** +0.075s/f (Good) 10 Ran SP% 122.6
Speed ratings (Par 100): **96,95,95,94,93 92,92,91,91,88**
toteswingers: 1&2 £9.30, 1&3 £3.90, 2&3 £10.90 CSF £101.70 CT £350.84 TOTE £6.40: £2.10, £4.50, £1.60; EX 90.30.
Owner P Brosnan **Bred** Tally-Ho Stud **Trained** Newmarket, Suffolk

FOCUS
A moderate handicap in which the runners came more towards the stands' side in the straight, although about half a dozen horses wide of the rail. The winner can rate higher with the third to recent form and the fiifth and sixth in line with their maiden form.
T/Plt: £447.50 to a £1 stake. Pool: £99,295.35. 161.95 winning tickets. T/Qpdt: £44.10 to a £1 stake. Pool: £4,822.25. 80.90 winning tickets. CR

4503 THIRSK (L-H)
Saturday, August 1

OFFICIAL GOING: Good to soft (soft in places; 8.3)
Wind: light 1/2 behind Weather: persistent morning rain, becoming overcast with rain again race 7.

4546 EUROPEAN BREEDERS' FUND MAIDEN STKS 5f
1:45 (1:46) (Class 4) 2-Y-O £5,504 (£1,637; £818; £408) Stalls High

Form RPR

4230 1 **Ignatieff (IRE)**7 4327 2-9-3 0 DuranFentiman 7 80
(Mrs L Stubbs) *mde all: rdn clr fnl f* 4/12

2 4 **Taborcillo** 2-8-12 0 DeanHeslop(5) 5 66
(T D Barron) *chsd wnr: kpt on same pce fnl f* 16/1

0 3 5 **Autocracy**9 4243 2-9-3 0 TonyCulhane 1 48
(W J Haggas) *dwlt: sn chsng ldrs: drvn over 2f out: hung lft and wknd over 1f out* 8/111

4 1 1/2 **Kalahari Desert (IRE)** 2-9-3 0 PaulQuinn 2 42
(R M Whitaker) *s.s: sn chsng ldrs: wknd 1f out* 33/1

45 5 1 **Perfect Blossom**36 3337 2-8-12 0 PatrickMathers 3 34
(I W McInnes) *chsd ldrs: hung lft and wknd over 1f out* 14/1

6 2 1/4 **Wing Forward (IRE)** 2-8-5 0 BillyCray(7) 4 26
(A Berry) *s.s: swtchd rt after s: a outpcd and in rr* 100/1

7 1/2 **Sharp Shoes** 2-9-3 0 SilvestreDeSousa 8 29+
(Mrs A Duffield) *chsd ldrs: lost pl over 1f out* 14/1

8 nk **Piccola Stella (IRE)** 2-8-9 0 FrederikTylicki(3) 9 23
(R M H Cowell) *chsd ldrs: wknd 2f out* 13/23

61.90 secs (2.30) **Going Correction** +0.325s/f (Good) 8 Ran SP% 114.4
Speed ratings (Par 96): **94,87,79,77,75 72,71,70**
toteswingers: 1&2 £12.00, 1&3 £1.40, 2&3 £7.50 CSF £63.45 TOTE £5.40: £1.70, £4.40, £1.02; EX 110.00.
Owner P G Shorrock **Bred** Holborn Trust Co **Trained** Norton, N Yorks

FOCUS
The ground was described as good to soft, soft in places (GoingStick reading of 8.3), but the divots were flying and it looked like the runners were going in quite deep, especially towards the middle of the track.

NOTEBOOK
Ignatieff(IRE), the most exposed runner in the field after seven starts and with an official rating of 70, made all the running up the stands' rail and drew clear in the final furlong, despite wanting to hang to his left. It may be that the stands' rail was the place to be, given he didn't seem to be going into the ground quite as deeply as those racing wider, which means he could be a touch flattered, and his exposed profile suggests the opposition wasn't that great anyway. (op 5-1)
Taborcillo, who looked green going to post, made a very pleasing introduction, especially given that his pedigree suggests further will suit in time, and he can be expected to improve on this. (op 20-1 tchd 25-1)
Autocracy holds some big-race entries and is clearly held in some regard, but he looked a bit exposed out wide and just didn't find anything when coming under pressure. Given he is by Green Desert, this ground may not have been ideal and it's likely he's a good deal better than he was able to show here. (tchd 4-5)
Kalahari Desert(IRE) shaped encouragingly, travelling quite well, and although he could never land a blow, there looks to be something to work with. (tchd 28-1)
Perfect Blossom disappointed but this was her first try on soft ground and she's worth another chance on that basis alone. Official explanation: jockey said filly was unsuited by the good to soft, soft in places ground (op 9-1)
Sharp Shoes Official explanation: jockey said colt was unsuited by the good to soft, soft in places ground

4547 HERTEL NURSERY 5f
2:20 (2:20) (Class 3) 2-Y-O £8,159 (£2,428; £1,213; £606) Stalls High

Form RPR

441 1 **Midnight Martini**38 3263 2-8-9 77 DavidAllan 7 83+
(T D Easterby) *in rr: hdwy over 2f out: led jst ins fnl f: hld on towards fin* 9/22

0230 2 nk **Tillys Tale**21 3871 2-7-13 72 ow2 PaulPickard(5) 3 75
(P T Midgley) *w ldrs: no ex towards fin* 11/1

0010 3 2 **Eternal Instinct**14 4089 2-8-9 82 GaryBartley(5) 8 78
(J S Goldie) *trckd ldrs: dropped bk after 2f: effrt over 1f out: hung lft and styd on ins fnl f* 5/13

42 4 1/2 **Goodbye Earl (IRE)**8 4282 2-7-13 74 BillyCray(7) 6 68
(A Berry) *led tl 2f out: hmpd and swtchd lft 1f out: kpt on wl* 9/1

644 5 nk **Senate Majority**45 3032 2-7-12 66 DuranFentiman 9 59
(T D Easterby) *sn outpcd and in rr: hdwy over 1f out: styd on towards fin* 15/2

2102 **6** *shd* **Kingdom Of Light**[21] 3871 2-9-4 **89**........................... FrederikTylicki(3) 2 81
(J Howard Johnson) *w ldrs: led and edgd rt 2f out: hdd jst ins fnl f: no ex* **5/1**[3]
2201 **7** *5* **Mijas Playa**[11] 4165 2-8-6 **81**........................... AndrewHeffernan(7) 5 55
(C A Dwyer) *chsd ldrs: lost pl over 1f out* **8/1**
4210 **8** *1 1/4* **Social Grace**[14] 4089 2-8-7 **75**........................... GrahamGibbons 11 45
(D H Brown) *mid-div: effrt over 2f out: wknd over 1f out* **3/1**[1]
006 **9** *16* **Alfalasteeni**[14] 4075 2-7-12 **66** oh21........................... (b[1]) PaulQuinn 10 —
(Ian Williams) *dwlt: sn detached in last: bhd fnl 2f* **80/1**
61.47 secs (1.87) **Going Correction** +0.325s/f (Good) **9** Ran SP% **119.0**
Speed ratings (Par 98): **98,97,94,93,93 92,84,82,57**
toteswingers: 1&2 £7.90, 1&3 £5.00, 2&3 £12.70 CSF £54.40 CT £262.06 TOTE £5.30: £1.70, £3.00, £1.70; EX 53.50.
Owner D A West **Bred** Helescane Stud **Trained** Great Habton, N Yorks

FOCUS
The impression from the first race was that the stands' rail may have been the place to be but that wasn't borne out here.

NOTEBOOK
Midnight Martini came clear to fight out the finish down the middle of the track with the runner-up, and just edged it on the line. Held up and looking a touch outpaced early, she made good headway once switched wide and although she had a good tussle with Tilly's Tale in the closing stages, her rider always looked as though he was confident of getting the job done. The form of her maiden win has been boosted by the runner-up winning since so she looked quite reasonably treated for this nursery bow and so it proved. She is progressive and handles soft ground well. (tchd 4-1)
Tillys Tale is much more exposed than the winner, having already run seven times, but ran much better than at York last time, where she was a fair way behind Kingdom Of Light, and it may be that she is suited by testing conditions. Strictly speaking, she may have won had her rider Paul Pickard not put up 2lb overweight. (op 12-1)
Eternal Instinct travelled well off the pace but couldn't find the gears to challenge the front two and perhaps she is in the grip of the assessor now she is 8lb higher than when winning a Musselburgh nursery in July. (op 9-2)
Goodbye Earl(IRE) had the early speed to bag the rail but couldn't sustain her effort and is vulnerable in whatever company she races in now, having had ten chances. (op 11-1)
Senate Majority kept on quite well from well back and wasn't knocked about in the closing stages. (op 7-1)
Kingdom Of Light, tackling slow ground for the first time, was drawn out wide but showed good pace to race on the speed towards the middle of the track and ended up on the stands' rail but dropped away in the final half-furlong. (op 4-1)

4548 POOLEY BRIDGE H'CAP 1m
2:55 (2:55) (Class 5) (0-75,75) 3-Y-O+ **£4,274** (£1,271; £635; £317) **Stalls** Low

Form RPR
4060 **1** **Mozayada (USA)**[23] 3763 5-9-1 **62**........................... DavidAllan 6 71
(M Brittain) *mid-div: hdwy over 2f out: led appr fnl f: hld on towards fin* **40/1**
2421 **2** *nk* **Ninth House (USA)**[3] 4435 7-9-0 **61** 6ex........................... (t) SilvestreDeSousa 14 69
(Mrs R A Carr) *in rr: hdwy 3f out: sn chsng ldrs: styd on wl towards fin: jst hld* **11/2**[2]
2641 **3** *nse* **Rosko**[36] 3353 5-9-7 **68**........................... J-PGuillambert 5 76
(B Ellison) *prom: effrt over 2f out: kpt on wl fnl f* **4/1**[1]
3363 **4** *2* **Kalasam**[18] 3943 5-8-10 **64**........................... JamesPSullivan(7) 3 67
(M W Easterby) *hld up in rr: hdwy over 2f out: kpt on same pce fnl f* **8/1**
3460 **5** *nse* **Inside Story (IRE)**[7] 4333 7-9-6 **67**........................... (b) PJMcDonald 7 70
(C R Dore) *hld up in rr: hdwy 3f out: styd on same pce fnl f* **20/1**
5300 **6** *4 1/2* **Count Ceprano (IRE)**[11] 4181 5-9-7 **68**........................... CatherineGannon 8 61
(C R Dore) *s.i.s: hdwy over 2f out: nvr nr ldrs* **16/1**
0030 **7** *1 1/4* **Mujaadel (USA)**[21] 3847 4-10-0 **75**........................... PaulMulrennan 2 65
(D Nicholls) *led tl hdd & wknd appr fnl f* **10/1**
0544 **8** *1 3/4* **Steel Stockholder**[8] 4284 3-8-6 **60**........................... AndrewElliott 1 46
(M Brittain) *s.i.s: drvn to sn chse ldrs: wknd over 1f out* **10/1**
6600 **9** *1 3/4* **Silver Hotspur**[7] 4333 5-9-1 **69**........................... DebraEngland(7) 9 51
(C R Dore) *rrd s: hld up in rr: effrt over 2f out: hung lft: wknd over 1f out* **33/1**
2000 **10** *nk* **Tiger Dream**[4] 4400 4-9-12 **73**........................... (p) TonyCulhane 4 54
(K A Ryan) *chsd ldrs: wknd over 1f out* **13/2**[3]
-030 **11** *2 3/4* **Celtic Step**[7] 4333 5-9-11 **75**........................... (p) FrederikTylicki(3) 10 50
(P D Niven) *mid-div: hdwy on wd outside over 2f out: lost pl over 1f out* **7/1**
2230 **12** *10* **Kildare Sun (IRE)**[36] 3331 7-9-0 **66**........................... (p) JamieKyne(5) 12 18
(J Mackie) *mid-div: drvn over 3f out: sn lost pl: eased whn bhd* **9/1**
600 **13** *4 1/2* **French Art**[15] 4046 4-9-6 **67**........................... DO'Donohoe 11 9
(N Tinkler) *chsd ldrs: wknd 2f out: bhd whn eased* **16/1**
1m 43.15s (3.05) **Going Correction** +0.50s/f (Yiel)
WFA 3 from 4yo+ 7lb **13** Ran SP% **122.4**
Speed ratings (Par 103): **104,103,103,101,101 97,95,94,92,92 89,79,74**
toteswingers: 1&2 £35.70, 1&3 £28.80, 2&3 £3.90 CSF £196.73 CT £1090.07 TOTE £61.80: £12.00, £1.90, £2.00; EX 167.70.
Owner Mel Brittain **Bred** Shadwell Farm LLC **Trained** Warthill, N Yorks
■ Stewards' Enquiry : Debra England caution: used whip when out of contention

FOCUS
A strong pace to this handicap thanks to Mujaadel, who travelled well on the front end for a long way but ultimately set this up for the hold-up horses. Sound form.
Mozayada(USA) Official explanation: trainer's rep had no explanation for the improved form shown
Count Ceprano(IRE) Official explanation: jockey said gelding missed the break
Kildare Sun(IRE) Official explanation: jockey said gelding was never travelling
French Art Official explanation: jockey said gelding had a breathing problem

4549 EKOSGEN H'CAP 1m
3:30 (3:33) (Class 3) (0-90,89) 3-Y-O+ **£8,159** (£2,428; £1,213; £606) **Stalls** Low

Form RPR
3403 **1** **Moheebb (IRE)**[14] 4102 5-9-3 **78**........................... (b) SilvestreDeSousa 9 92
(Mrs R A Carr) *in rr: gd hdwy and swtchd outside 2f out: r.o strly to ld ins fnl f: readily* **6/1**[2]
2364 **2** *1 3/4* **Gala Casino Star (IRE)**[14] 4104 4-9-5 **83**........................... FrederikTylicki(3) 3 93+
(R A Fahey) *pushed along to chse ldrs: led appr fnl f: hdd and no ex ins fnl f* **9/2**[1]
-524 **3** *2 3/4* **Observatory Star (IRE)**[38] 3265 6-9-3 **78**........................... (tp) DavidAllan 14 82
(T D Easterby) *chsd ldrs: drvn and outpcd over 4f out: kpt on fnl 2f* **17/2**
3403 **4** *nk* **Boy Blue**[35] 3391 4-9-6 **81**........................... DaleGibson 5 84
(P Salmon) *a chsng ldrs: styd on same pce appr fnl f* **12/1**
1240 **5** *2 1/4* **Grazeon Gold Blend**[21] 3877 6-9-4 **79**........................... (p) GrahamGibbons 16 77
(J J Quinn) *in rr: kpt on fnl 2f: nvr rchd ldrs* **20/1**
0066 **6** *1/2* **Nevada Desert (IRE)**[4] 4400 9-8-9 **70** oh1........................... (p) DO'Donohoe 8 67
(R M Whitaker) *mid-div: outpcd over 4f out: kpt on fnl 2f: nvr nr ldrs* **25/1**
1300 **7** *1/2* **Fesko**[14] 4104 3-8-12 **80**........................... AndrewElliott 2 76+
(M Johnston) *sn drvn along to chse ldrs: led 5f out: hdd & wknd appr fnl f* **22/1**
0400 **8** *4* **Maze (IRE)**[25] 3706 4-9-9 **84**........................... PaulMulrennan 6 70
(B Smart) *hld up towards rr: hdwy over 2f out: wknd over 1f out* **18/1**
0013 **9** *3* **Flawed Genius**[21] 3872 4-9-9 **89**........................... (t) AmyRyan(5) 13 68
(K A Ryan) *dwlt: hdwy on ins 3f out: wknd over 1f out* **9/1**
5502 **10** *1/2* **Ilie Nastase (FR)**[14] 4104 5-9-6 **86**........................... (b) JamieKyne(5) 10 64+
(D Nicholls) *led 3f: chsd ldrs: wknd over 1f out* **6/1**[2]
-501 **11** *1/2* **Keys Of Cyprus**[14] 4104 7-9-4 **79**........................... PaulQuinn 1 56
(D Nicholls) *chsd ldrs: wknd 2f out* **7/1**[3]
1505 **12** *nk* **Spinning**[14] 4104 6-9-1 **81**........................... (b) DeanHeslop(5) 12 57
(T D Barron) *s.i.s: a in rr* **16/1**
3310 **13** *12* **Mohtashem (IRE)**[22] 3816 3-9-6 **88**........................... J-PGuillambert 4 37
(Sir Michael Stoute) *mid-div: lost pl over 3f out: bhd and eased 2f out* **7/1**[3]
1m 42.66s (2.56) **Going Correction** +0.50s/f (Yiel)
WFA 3 from 4yo+ 7lb **13** Ran SP% **124.1**
Speed ratings (Par 107): **107,105,102,102,99 99,98,94,91,91 90,90,78**
toteswingers: 1&2 £9.50, 1&3 £13.00, 2&3 £9.60 CSF £33.55 CT £245.68 TOTE £7.50: £2.40, £1.90, £3.20; EX 48.00.
Owner Michael Hill **Bred** Hascombe And Valiant Studs **Trained** Huby, N Yorks

FOCUS
A strongly run handicap. The winner is rated back to the form of his Haydock win.

NOTEBOOK
Moheebb(IRE) is ideally suited by a strongly run race on soft ground over this trip, and Ruth Carr's gambled-on 5yo got everything he needed as Fesko and Ilie Nastase cut each other's throats by setting a blistering gallop. He was hard under the pump and a long way back turning into the straight but, as those up front began to founder, he set sail down the wide outside to pass rival after rival and storm clear in the final furlong. This has to go down as nigh-on a career-best effort from the gelding but, although ultimately impressive, the race was teed up to perfection for him, so it may be wise not to get too carried away. (op 9-1)
Gala Casino Star(IRE) didn't get the strong pace he needs at Ripon last time but this was much more his cup of tea and he ran a fine race in second, with the headgear left off this time. He ideally wants slightly better ground but, on this evidence, his turn looks to be coming round again, while he has won off this mark before. (op 13-2)
Observatory Star(IRE) made sustained headway down the outside in the straight and made a bold bid to follow up his victory in this race 12 months ago, but just came up short. Still, given he was 3lb higher in what looked a stronger renewal, and he was drawn wide, this was a really good effort in the circumstances. (op 8-1 tchd 9-1)
Boy Blue kept on, having raced in touch with the pace early, so he deserves plenty of credit. But he looks in the grip of the assessor. (op 10-1)
Grazeon Gold Blend still has to prove he is as effective over this trip as shorter and this run was inconclusive, given he was never able to land a blow, having been dropped out from his wide draw. He kept on well enough but the feeling remains that the handicapper has the better of the argument at the moment. (op 14-1)
Nevada Desert(IRE) wasn't disgraced and isn't one to write off completely, despite his advancing years. (op 14-1)
Fesko did well to last as long as she did, given the strong pace she set. (op 12-1)
Keys Of Cyprus Official explanation: trainer's rep had no explanation for the poor form shown

4550 WEATHERBYS BLOODSTOCK INSURANCE MAIDEN FILLIES' STKS 7f
4:05 (4:06) (Class 4) 3-Y-O+ **£5,569** (£1,657; £828; £413) **Stalls** Low

Form RPR
60 **1** **Cils Blancs (IRE)**[64] 2446 3-8-11 0........................... FrederikTylicki(3) 13 63
(B Smart) *trckd ldrs: led over 2f out: styd on wl* **12/1**
3505 **2** *1 3/4* **Silk Gallery (USA)**[15] 4046 4-9-6 50........................... (t) DavidAllan 11 60
(E J Alston) *trckd ldrs: effrt over 2f out: styd on same pce ins fnl f* **16/1**
6-30 **3** *1/2* **Equinine (IRE)**[14] 4097 3-9-0 68........................... TonyCulhane 10 56
(B W Hills) *towards rr: drvn over 4f out: hdwy over 2f out: kpt on same pce fnl f* **6/4**[2]
224 **4** *2 1/4* **Global Conquest (IRE)**[29] 3569 3-9-0 79........................... SilvestreDeSousa 12 50
(Pat Eddery) *in rr: drvn over 4f out: hdwy over 2f out: nvr rchd ldrs* **11/8**[1]
0 **5** *3 1/4* **Needy McCredie**[8] 4276 3-9-0 0........................... PAspell 8 41
(J R Turner) *mid-div: hdwy over 2f out: wknd over 1f out* **33/1**
0-40 **6** *3/4* **Unconsoled**[3] 4432 3-9-0 55........................... CatherineGannon 7 39
(J Hetherton) *w ldrs: wknd fnl f* **40/1**
4 **7** *3/4* **Pure Heir (USA)**[36] 3352 3-8-9 0........................... DeanHeslop(5) 3 37
(T D Barron) *trckd ldrs: outpcd over 4f out: wknd 2f out* **9/1**[3]
0 **8** *4 1/2* **Ex Gracia**[23] 3764 3-9-0 0........................... PJMcDonald 5 25
(K A Ryan) *prom: lost pl over 4f out* **20/1**
9 *1 3/4* **Argent Avia** 3-9-0 0........................... AndrewElliott 6 20
(M Brittain) *s.s: a in rr* **50/1**
0/00 **10** *1 3/4* **Viola Rosa (IRE)**[35] 3379 4-9-6 40........................... J-PGuillambert 1 19
(J G Given) *led tl over 2f out: lost pl over 1f out* **66/1**
11 *hd* **Spartan Princess (IRE)** 3-8-7 0........................... JohnCavanagh(7) 4 15
(M Brittain) *sn in rr* **25/1**
1m 30.49s (3.29) **Going Correction** +0.50s/f (Yiel)
WFA 3 from 4yo 6lb **11** Ran SP% **123.1**
Speed ratings (Par 102): **101,99,98,95,92 91,90,85,83,81 81**
toteswingers: 1&2 £20.10, 1&3 £4.60, 2&3 £5.20 CSF £170.83 TOTE £18.40: £3.40, £3.60, £1.10; EX 165.80.
Owner Mrs Julie Martin **Bred** Imortal Partnership **Trained** Hambleton, N Yorks

FOCUS
They were quite well strung out in this modest fillies' maiden. The third and fourth were below their best.

4551 ROE HEAD H'CAP 2m
4:40 (4:41) (Class 5) (0-75,70) 4-Y-O+ **£4,274** (£1,271; £635; £317) **Stalls** Low

Form RPR
0143 **1** **Miss Keck**[18] 3940 5-9-2 **65**........................... PJMcDonald 8 73
(G A Swinbank) *trckd ldr: led 3f out: sn hdd: swtchd rt over 1f out: styd on wl to ld jst ins fnl f* **7/1**[3]
-021 **2** *2 1/4* **Black Or Red (IRE)**[11] 4168 4-9-2 **65**........................... (b) CatherineGannon 9 70
(I A Wood) *hld up in rr: hdwy to trck ldrs 9f out: led over 2f out: sn rdn and hung bdly lft: hdd ins fnl f* **7/4**[1]
1606 **3** *1 1/4* **Danzatrice**[18] 3940 7-9-2 **68**........................... FrederikTylicki(3) 10 72+
(C W Thornton) *hld up in rr: hdwy over 2f out: kpt on fnl f* **10/1**
3242 **4** *1* **Jackday (IRE)**[32] 3486 4-9-0 **63**........................... GrahamGibbons 5 65
(T D Easterby) *hld up in mid-div: hdwy to trck ldrs over 3f out: kpt on same pce appr fnl f* **5/1**[2]
30/0 **5** *1* **Secret Ploy**[23] 3788 9-9-2 **70**........................... JamieKyne(5) 7 71
(H Morrison) *led: reluctant and hrd drvn bnd after 6f: hdd 3f out: one pce* **15/2**

5510 **6** *6* **Squirtle (IRE)**[5] 4388 6-8-5 **59** PaulPickard(5) 1 53
(W M Brisbourne) *hld up in midfield: lost pl over 5f out: sme hdwy over 1f out: nvr a factor* **8/1**

6035 **7** *3/4* **Sir Sandicliffe (IRE)**[21] 3850 5-8-9 **63** DeanHeslop(5) 4 56
(W M Brisbourne) *hld up in mid-div: hdwy over 4f out: sn chsng ldrs: wknd fnl f* **14/1**

3-24 **8** *4 1/2* **Unawatuna**[28] 3617 4-8-4 **60** IJBrennan(7) 2 48
(Mrs K Walton) *trckd ldrs: t.k.h: drvn 6f out: lost pl over 3f out* **15/2**

6500 **9** *1 1/4* **King In Waiting (IRE)**[6] 4350 6-9-3 **66** (vt[1]) TonyCulhane 6 52
(J Hetherton) *hld up in rr: swtchd outside and hdwy 5f out: lost pl over 3f out* **40/1**

3-00 **10** *12* **River Danube**[78] 2044 6-8-10 **59** DavidAllan 3 31
(T J Fitzgerald) *sn trcking ldrs: lost pl over 2f out: bhd whn eased* **33/1**

3m 41.74s (8.94) **Going Correction** +0.50s/f (Yiel) **10** Ran SP% **121.3**
Speed ratings (Par 103): **97,95,95,94,94 91,90,88,88,82**
toteswingers: 1&2 £3.60, 1&3 £12.10, 2&3 £5.30 CSF £20.45 CT £129.58 TOTE £7.40: £2.50, £1.40, £2.90; EX 26.90.
Owner Alan Wright **Bred** The Woodhaven Stud **Trained** Melsonby, N Yorks
■ Stewards' Enquiry : Catherine Gannon caution: careless riding

FOCUS
Not a strong gallop, unsurprisingly in the conditions, but the form looks straightforward enough.

4552 WHITBY H'CAP STKS (LADIES' RACE) 6f
5:15 (5:17) (Class 6) (0-55,55) 3-Y-0+ **£2,873** (£891; £445; £222) **Stalls** High

Form RPR

002 **1** **Titus Gent**[24] 3743 4-10-4 **52** MissGAndrews(3) 4 69
(J Ryan) *chsd ldrs: led 1f out: sn wnt clr: v readily* **14/1**

0620 **2** *3 1/2* **It's A Mans World**[31] 3505 3-10-1 **55** (v) MissKellyBurke(5) 18 60
(K M Prendergast) *chsd ldrs: led 2f out: hdd 1f out: edgd lft and no ex* **16/1**

0060 **3** *2 1/4* **Half A Crown (IRE)**[3] 4436 4-10-1 **46** (bt) MissLHorner 3 45
(M Dods) *racd w 1 other exclusively far side: clr that side over 2f out: styd on same pce fnl f* **12/1**

0-10 **4** *1 3/4* **Sea Land (FR)**[17] 3983 5-10-9 **54** MissLEllison 5 47
(B Ellison) *mid-div: hdwy 2f out: kpt on ins fnl f* **15/2**[3]

3625 **5** *1 3/4* **Ingleby Princess**[5] 4375 5-10-8 **53** MissSBrotherton 16 41
(T D Barron) *in tch: hdwy over 2f out: kpt on same pce appr fnl f* **3/1**[1]

1500 **6** *1* **Foreign Rhythm (IRE)**[6] 4355 4-9-10 **48** MissCharlotteHolmes(7) 17 32
(N Tinkler) *in tch: kpt on same pce fnl 2f* **25/1**

0033 **7** *1/2* **Circle Dance (IRE)**[9] 4225 4-10-8 **53** (v) MrsMMorris 7 36
(D Shaw) *chsd ldrs: one pce fnl 2f* **9/1**

0-00 **8** *1* **Sorrel Point**[30] 3548 6-9-10 **46** oh1 (t) MissMHugo(5) 2 26
(H J Collingridge) *racd far side: edgd rt into centre over 2f out: nvr rchd ldrs* **50/1**

3 **9** *2 1/4* **Minnola**[14] 4105 4-10-10 **55** MissEJJones 12 27
(Rae Guest) *w ldrs: lost pl over 2f out* **7/1**[2]

0-40 **10** *2 3/4* **Mormeatmic**[46] 3002 6-9-10 **46** oh1 (b) MissJoannaMason(5) 11 10
(M W Easterby) *w ldrs: wknd 2f out* **25/1**

0050 **11** *hd* **Obe One**[21] 3852 9-9-8 **46** oh1 MissDLenge(7) 20 9
(A Berry) *racd towards stands' side: nvr a factor* **33/1**

500 **12** *2 3/4* **Qualitas**[11] 4174 3-9-13 **55** MissPhillipaTutty(7) 14 8
(M W Easterby) *w ldrs: wknd 2f out* **33/1**

-305 **13** *1/2* **Chin Wag (IRE)**[12] 4133 5-10-9 **54** (v) MrsCBartley 19 6
(J S Goldie) *a towards rr* **8/1**

0U04 **13** *hd* **Coconut Moon**[8] 4281 7-9-8 **46** MissSarahRichardson(7) 15 —
(A Berry) *led tl hdd 2f out: sn wknd* **14/1**

00-0 **15** *nk* **Gems Star**[41] 3193 3-10-1 **50** MissADeniel 6 —
(J J Quinn) *a towards rr* **33/1**

-000 **16** *1/2* **Warners Bay (IRE)**[26] 3683 4-9-10 **46** oh1 MissRBastiman(5) 1 —
(R Bastiman) *chsd one other exclusively far side: lost tch over 2f out* **16/1**

5405 **17** *1/2* **Sands Of Barra (IRE)**[2] 4466 6-10-3 **55** (b) MissHBethell(7) 9 3
(I W McInnes) *w ldrs: lost pl 2f out* **12/1**

-054 **18** *7* **Tilerium's Dream (IRE)**[82] 1926 3-10-1 **55** (p) MrsVFahey(5) 13 —
(K A Ryan) *in rr: bhd fnl 2f* **12/1**

1m 15.79s (3.09) **Going Correction** +0.325s/f (Good)
WFA 3 from 4yo+ 4lb **18** Ran SP% **137.0**
Speed ratings (Par 101): **92,87,84,82,79 78,77,76,73,69 69,65,64,64,64 63,63,53**
toteswingers: 1&2 £63.90, 1&3 £30.60, 2&3 £64.60 CSF £230.96 CT £2889.35 TOTE £18.50: £3.60, £3.40, £3.70, £2.60; EX 390.60 Place 6: £51.49 Place 5: £40.24 .
Owner G Wilson **Bred** Heather Raw **Trained** Newmarket, Suffolk

FOCUS
Quantity over quality here, and a weak handicap for lady riders in which most had plenty to prove. Three went over to the far side, although Sorrel Point ended up coming back across towards the middle. A personal best from the winner with the runner-up the best guide.
Circle Dance(IRE) Official explanation: jockey said gelding lost its action
T/Plt: £66.00 to a £1 stake. Pool: £59,043.46. 652.07 winning tickets. T/Qpdt: £21.40 to a £1 stake. Pool: £3,734.00. 129.00 winning tickets. WG

4553 - 4556a (Foreign Racing) - See Raceform Interactive

[3846] CHESTER (L-H)
Sunday, August 2

OFFICIAL GOING: Good (good to soft in places) changing to good after race 3 (3.30)
Course at innermost configuration, all distances as advertised and no false rail in use.
Wind: Light, across

4557 EUROPEAN BREEDERS' FUND MAIDEN STKS 7f 2y
2:20 (2:20) (Class 4) 2-Y-O **£5,180** (£1,541; £770; £384) **Stalls** Low

Form RPR

2 **1** **Prompter**[23] 3794 2-9-3 0 HayleyTurner 5 85+
(M L W Bell) *mde all: shkn up 1f out: pushed out and r.o wl fnl f: a in full control* **8/11**[1]

5 **2** *2* **Tominator**[16] 4041 2-9-3 0 ChrisCatlin 4 77
(R Hollinshead) *trckd ldrs: wnt 2nd 2f out: pushed along over 1f out: nt pce of wnr fnl f* **25/1**

3 **3** *1/2* **Realisation (USA)**[16] 4041 2-9-3 0 GregFairley 2 76
(M Johnston) *in tch: chsd ldrs wl over 2f out: rdn over 1f out: styd on ins fnl f: nt quite pce to mount serious chal* **13/8**[2]

6 **4** *8* **Jimmy The Poacher (IRE)**[23] 3823 2-9-3 0 GrahamGibbons 7 58+
(T D Easterby) *bmpd s: in tch: niggled along after 1f: rdn over 2f out: kpt on but nt trble front trio fnl f* **12/1**

0 **5** *3 1/4* **Arkellion**[65] 2430 2-9-3 0 PaulHanagan 1 48
(P D Evans) *racd keenly: towards rr: sme hdwy and pushed along over 2f out: nvr able to get on terms w ldrs* **28/1**

65 **6** *1 3/4* **Number One Guy**[30] 3584 2-9-3 0 SebSanders 10 44
(M H Tompkins) *hld up: pushed along over 2f out: hung lft over 1f out: nvr able to chal* **10/1**[3]

0 **7** *1/2* **Sam Jicaro**[45] 3064 2-8-12 0 DeanHeslop(5) 3 42
(Mrs L Williamson) *missed break: bhd: pushed along over 2f out: nvr on terms* **100/1**

5 **8** *3/4* **Black Sapphire**[16] 4055 2-8-12 0 JerryO'Dwyer 9 35
(Miss Amy Weaver) *bustled along to sn chse wnr: rdn and lost 2nd 2f out: wknd over 1f out* **25/1**

0 **9** *13* **Lord Wheathill**[16] 4041 2-9-3 0 NeilChalmers 6 8
(Mrs L Williamson) *wnt rt s: racd keenly in tch: hung rt most of way: wnt wd and lost grnd wl over 2f out: sn bhd* **100/1**

00 **10** *4 1/2* **Lighterman**[8] 4307 2-9-3 0 ShaneKelly 11 —
(E J Alston) *chsd ldrs: pushed along 3f out: wknd over 2f out* **80/1**

60 **11** *1/2* **Port Hill**[16] 4041 2-9-3 0 LiamJones 8 —
(W M Brisbourne) *midfield tl wknd 3f out* **100/1**

1m 26.42s (-0.08) **Going Correction** -0.075s/f (Good) **11** Ran SP% **128.1**
Speed ratings (Par 96): **97,94,94,85,81 79,78,77,63,57 57**
toteswinger: 1&2 £7.40, 1&3 £1.02, 2&3 £10.90 CSF £32.23 TOTE £2.10: £1.20, £3.40, £1.10; EX 39.10.
Owner The Royal Ascot Racing Club **Bred** Mr & Mrs G Middlebrook **Trained** Newmarket, Suffolk
■ A first winner as a sire for Motivator, the 2005 Epsom Derby hero.

FOCUS
An ordinary maiden in which it proved hard to make up ground, and those dropped in from high draws had no chance.

NOTEBOOK
Prompter, a Champagne Stakes and Royal Lodge entrant, confirmed the promise he showed when second in a six-runner race on his debut at Ascot. He was a little bit on edge at the start and got warm down his neck but, after enjoying the run of the race out in front, he was always doing enough in the straight under mainly hands-and-heels riding, looking to win with something to spare. He still has some way to go to justify his lofty entries, however, and won't make much appeal in anything better than a novice event or nursery for the time being. (tchd Evens)
Tominator, always close up but a bit keen, kept on in the straight without ever looking likely to reel in the winner. He's quite well regarded and this represented significant improvement on his debut effort, as he was able to reverse form from that Haydock race with Realisation.
Realisation(USA)raced just off the pace, having been unable to make full use of stall two, and can be given another chance considering it was difficult to make up ground. (op 5-2)
Jimmy The Poacher(IRE) was never a threat after being squeezed out at the start but he again showed ability and looks the type to keep improving with racing. (op 14-1 tchd 11-1)
Arkellion, gelded since showing next to nothing for a different trainer at Goodwood two months earlier, offered more hope this time, despite racing a little keenly. He was too inexperienced to take advantage of the inside stall, but wasn't given a hard time once held and is open to further improvement. (op 33-1 tchd 25-1)
Number One Guy ◆ couldn't build on the form he showed at Sandown last time, but his draw was a major disadvantage. Although never a threat, he again showed ability and is one to keep in mind for nurseries. (op 12-1 tchd 8-1)
Lord Wheathill Official explanation: jockey said gelding hung right
Lighterman ◆ had little chance from stall 11 and was duly well held, but he's one to keep in mind for handicaps next season. He's a sizeable individual who has plenty of filling out to do and, according to his trainer, he is now likely to be put away until next year, when he should come back much stronger. (tchd 66-1)

4558 FREE RACE REPLAYS AT RACINGUK.COM NURSERY 6f 18y
2:55 (2:55) (Class 4) 2-Y-O **£5,180** (£1,541; £770; £384) **Stalls** Low

Form RPR

4011 **1** **Diamond Laura**[13] 4138 2-9-0 **80** SilvestreDeSousa 4 82
(Mrs R A Carr) *in tch: sn niggled along: hdwy on outside to ld 1f out: r.o* **7/2**[3]

452 **2** *3/4* **Capacity (IRE)**[15] 4075 2-8-9 **75** GregFairley 6 75
(M Johnston) *in rr: effrt and hdwy on inner 2f out: str chal over 1f out: nt quite pce of wnr ins fnl 100yds* **7/1**

1323 **3** *1* **Transfixed (IRE)**[12] 4165 2-8-3 **69** CatherineGannon 2 66
(P D Evans) *led: edgd rt u.p wl over 1f out: hdd 1f out: nt qckn cl home* **5/2**[2]

313 **4** *1 3/4* **Tukitinyasok (IRE)**[15] 4086 2-9-7 **87** PaulHanagan 1 79
(R F Fisher) *chsd ldrs: wnt 2nd over 2f out: rdn to chal over 1f out: no ex fnl 75yds* **2/1**[1]

10 **5** *12* **Brambleberry**[30] 3583 2-9-0 **87** MarieLequarre(7) 3 43
(Tom Dascombe) *pressed ldr tl over 2f out: wknd over 1f out* **25/1**

0312 **6** *2* **Michaelmas Daisy**[23] 3807 2-7-12 **67** KellyHarrison(3) 7 17+
(Miss Amy Weaver) *sn pushed along in rr: rdn whn outpcd and bhd 2f out: eased whn wl btn ins fnl f* **8/1**

1m 14.72s (0.92) **Going Correction** -0.075s/f (Good) **6** Ran SP% **111.6**
Speed ratings (Par 96): **90,89,87,85,69 66**
toteswinger: 1&2 £5.20, 1&3 £1.60, 2&3 £3.90 CSF £26.61 CT £68.72 TOTE £3.80: £1.90, £3.40; EX 21.00.
Owner Middleham Park Racing XXXII **Bred** Paul Sweeting **Trained** Huby, N Yorks

FOCUS
In the opener, a 7f contest, nothing got involved from off the pace, but it was the opposite story in this nursery, with the leaders looking to go off too fast.

NOTEBOOK
Diamond Laura, claimed out of David Evans' yard for £13,000 after winning over 5f at Beverley on her latest outing, had already shown herself to be equally effective over this trip when landing a claimer at Wolverhampton two starts back, and she readily completed a hat-trick on this rise in grade. Held up through the early stages, the strong pace suited her and she picked up well in the straight, despite having to challenge four wide. This was her fourth win of the campaign and she's progressing into a pretty useful filly. (tchd 4-1)
Capacity(IRE), making his nursery debut after showing ability in maidens, got a good run through against the inside rail in the straight but couldn't take advantage. He still needs to learn to battle. (op 11-2)
Transfixed(IRE) was hassled for the lead by Brambleberry through the first couple of furlongs and basically seemed to do too much racing early on. (tchd 3-1)
Tukitinyasok(IRE), dropped in trip, tracked the pace for much of the way and looked the likeliest winner when produced with every chance in the straight, but he didn't pick up as expected. This shorter trip shouldn't have been a problem and it was disappointing he couldn't get by Transfixed. Official explanation: jockey said gelding hung right-handed (op 5-2 tchd 11-4 in places)
Brambleberry was left behind in the straight after being stuck out a little wide trying to keep tabs on the early leader. She looks poorly handicapped but will come down in the weights now. (op 20-1)

The Form Book, Raceform Ltd, Compton, RG20 6NL

Michaelmas Daisy was well below form, even allowing for being heavily eased once short of room inside the final furlong. Official explanation: jockey said filly ran flat (op 7-1 tchd 13-2)

4559 FLIGHT CENTRE CHESTER QUEENSFERRY STKS (LISTED RACE) 6f 18y
3:30 (3:30) (Class 1) 3-Y-O+

£22,708 (£8,608; £4,308; £2,148; £1,076; £540) **Stalls** Low

Form RPR

0213 **1** **Doncaster Rover (USA)**[15] 4087 3-8-10 103 PhillipMakin 1 108+
(D H Brown) *n.m.r and lost pl sn after s: in rr: hdwy whn nt clr run wl over 1f out: qcknd up through gap to chal ins fnl f: led fnl 50yds* **11/10**[1]

1404 **2** ½ **Sohraab**[22] 3848 5-9-0 100 GrahamGibbons 4 108
(H Morrison) *broke wl: chsd ldrs: effrt to ld ins fnl f: hdd fnl 50yds* **7/2**[2]

562 **3** 1 ½ **City Dancer (IRE)**[43] 3145 3-8-5 95 PJMcDonald 7 97+
(A Berry) *hld up: nt clr run wl over 1f out: effrt ins fnl f: styd on wl towards fin: nt pce to get to front pair* **10/1**

1600 **4** *nk* **Carcinetto (IRE)**[22] 3846 7-8-9 98 CatherineGannon 3 98+
(P D Evans) *midfield: pushed along 2f out: nt qckn over 1f out: nt clr run ins fnl f: styd on: nt pce of ldrs* **33/1**

20-0 **5** *nk* **Beckermet (IRE)**[148] 781 7-9-0 108 ChrisCatlin 8 101
(R F Fisher) *sn chsd ldr: upsides fr 3f out: rdn and str chal over 1f out: no ex fnl 75yds* **16/1**

2303 **6** ½ **Hoh Hoh Hoh**[22] 3848 7-9-0 104 SebSanders 5 99
(R J Price) *chsd ldrs: rdn over 1f out: styd on same pce fnl 100yds* **11/2**[3]

4054 **7** 1 ½ **Angus Newz**[16] 4059 6-8-9 92 (v) FrancisNorton 11 90
(M Quinn) *bustled along to ld and sn crossed over to bag rail: rdn over 1f out: hdd ins fnl f: sn wknd* **18/1**

0000 **8** 5 **Tournedos (IRE)**[7] 4341 7-9-0 93 PaulHanagan 6 79
(D Nicholls) *sqeezed out jst after s: hld up: pushed along and outpcd over 1f out* **28/1**

1m 13.55s (-0.25) **Going Correction** -0.075s/f (Good)
WFA 3 from 4yo+ 4lb **8** Ran SP% **111.9**
Speed ratings (Par 111): **98,97,95,94,94 93,91,85**
toteswinger: 1&2 £1.50, 1&3 £3.60, 2&3 £4.10 CSF £4.68 TOTE £1.90: £1.10, £1.70, £2.50; EX 5.20.
Owner P Holling I Raeburn S Halsall S Bolland **Bred** Coffeepot Stable **Trained** Maltby, S Yorks

FOCUS
Just a fair Listed contest and it was run at an overly strong pace, suiting those held up. The form is ordinary for the grade but reasonably sound, with those in the frame behind the winner close to their marks.

NOTEBOOK
Doncaster Rover(USA) ◆ was unable to get a handy position from stall one, but that turned out to be no bad thing considering the quick gallop, and he was given a fine ride by Makin, who recovered the situation by keeping his mount towards the inside and simply biding his time. A gap duly opened for this War Chant colt around a furlong out and he stayed on well, ultimately looking to win with something to spare. He won the Lily Agnes on his only previous start at Chester and this track obviously suits. He is progressing into a very smart sprinter and the plan now is to go for the Group 3 Phoenix Sprint Stakes at the Curragh, followed by a Group 2 at Baden Baden. He's also in the Haydock Sprint Cup. (op 13-8 tchd 7-4 in places)
Sohraab, possibly unlucky over 5f around here on his previous start, emerges with real credit considering he fared best of those who raced handy. (tchd 4-1)
City Dancer(IRE) was immediately out the back after starting slowly, but the strong pace suited and she followed the winner through for a never-nearer third. This was only her tenth start, and just her third try at 6f, so there could be more to come. (op 7-1)
Carcinetto(IRE) was denied a clear run in the closing stages and, although not unlucky, she would have finished a little closer with a better trip. (tchd 28-1)
Beckermet(IRE), off the track since March, couldn't sustain his run after going off quickly. This was an encouraging enough return, though, and he should come on for the run. (op 14-1)
Hoh Hoh Hoh didn't have an ideal draw and was not at his best. (op 7-2)
Angus Newz had to use up plenty of energy to lead from stall 11 and lost several places when tiring inside the final furlong. (op 14-1)

4560 HALLIWELL JONES BMW GRAN TURISMO MILE (H'CAP) 7f 122y
4:05 (4:07) (Class 3) (0-95,91) 3-Y-O+ **£10,037** (£2,986; £1,492; £745) **Stalls** Low

Form RPR

0001 **1** **Invincible Force (IRE)**[7] 4360 5-9-11 88 6ex (b) SilvestreDeSousa 6 98+
(Paul Green) *mde all: pushed along 3f out: shook off nrest rival over 1f out: gd advantage ent fnl f: eased cl home* **9/1**

5040 **2** 1 **Dixey**[20] 3928 4-9-13 90 PhilipRobinson 5 95
(M A Jarvis) *bmpd s: chsd ldrs: rdn whn chsng clr front pair wl over 1f out: styd on to take 2nd ins fnl f: nt rch eased down wnr* **12/1**

-035 **3** *shd* **Brasingaman Hifive**[43] 3154 4-8-13 76 DaleGibson 1 81
(Mrs G S Rees) *midfield: nt clr run over 2f out: hdwy over 1f out: r.o u.p ins fnl f* **10/1**

0500 **4** ½ **Opus Maximus (IRE)**[16] 4037 4-9-9 86 GregFairley 4 90+
(M Johnston) *bmpd s: towards rr: hdwy on outside 2f out: rdn over 1f out: r.o and clsd at fin* **7/2**[1]

5100 **5** ½ **I Confess**[5] 4409 4-8-12 80 (b) RichardEvans[(5)] 2 83
(P D Evans) *in tch: rdn over 1f out and edgd sltly lft: styd on same pce fnl f* **10/1**

6441 **6** 2 ¾ **Mastership (IRE)**[8] 4310 5-9-9 91 (p) JamieKyne[(5)] 12 87
(J J Quinn) *swtchd lft s: hld up: hdwy whn nt clr run over 2f out and again over 1f out: nvr got to ldrs* **12/1**

1120 **7** 1 ¼ **Glenridding**[8] 4333 5-8-11 74 (p) J-PGuillambert 10 67
(J G Given) *pressed wnr tl rdn over 1f out: wknd ins fnl f: eased whn btn nr fin* **20/1**

2405 **8** 1 **Daaweitza**[7] 4353 6-8-13 76 TomEaves 8 66
(B Ellison) *bhd: sn pushed along: rdn over 4f out: kpt on steadily fnl f wout troubling ldrs* **14/1**

-354 **9** 3 ¾ **Stevie Thunder**[23] 3796 4-9-11 88 (t) SebSanders 3 69
(Ian Williams) *towards rr: hdwy over 3f out: rdn 2f out: wknd over 1f out* **9/2**[2]

3310 **10** *shd* **Bold Marc (IRE)**[8] 4333 7-9-3 80 AndrewElliott 9 60
(A P Jarvis) *midfield: pushed along and lost pl over 3f out: n.d after* **33/1**

6532 **11** 12 **Fathsta (IRE)**[71] 2266 4-9-13 90 FrancisNorton 11 40
(D Nicholls) *midfield: pushed along over 3f out: wknd wl over 1f out* **6/1**[3]

0231 **12** 44 **Captain Jacksparra (IRE)**[15] 4083 5-9-2 79 PaulHanagan 7 —
(K A Ryan) *chsd ldrs: pushed along and wknd 3f out* **9/1**

1m 32.78s (-1.02) **Going Correction** -0.075s/f (Good) **12** Ran SP% **122.6**
Speed ratings (Par 107): **102,101,100,100,99 97,95,94,91,91 79,35**
toteswinger: 1&2 £25.10, 1&3 £24.70, 2&3 £33.80 CSF £116.25 CT £1131.33 TOTE £6.00: £2.80, £3.80, £4.00; EX 65.40 Trifecta £492.10 Part won. Pool: £665.06 - 0.20 winning units..
Owner Terry Cummins **Bred** Robert Wilson **Trained** Lydiate, Merseyside
■ Stewards' Enquiry : Richard Evans three-day ban: failed to ride out for fourth place (Aug 16-17, 19)

FOCUS
A decent handicap in which the winner made all and looks the best guide to the form.

The Form Book, Raceform Ltd, Compton, RG20 6NL

NOTEBOOK
Invincible Force(IRE) ◆ produced quite a taking effort considering he was hassled for the lead for much of the way by Glenridding, who ended up dropping away, and with the pair clear early on, it seemed certain that they had gone off too fast. However, this Invincible Spirit gelding kept on really well for pressure and was eventually eased down in the final strides. Although carrying a penalty for his recent success at the Curragh, he was still 6lb below his highest winning mark and he must have a big chance of completing the hat-trick. Later on, his trainer is keen to run him in the Ayr Gold Cup. (op 7-1 tchd 6-1)
Dixey fared best of those who raced off the pace, although a few of her rivals didn't enjoy the best of trips and it would be unwise to get carried away, as she simply doesn't look that well handicapped. (op 8-1)
Brasingaman Hifive, dropped in trip, had to wait for a run turning into the straight but wasn't an unlucky loser. (tchd 12-1)
Opus Maximus(IRE) ◆ is a fair bit better than he showed as he was unable to make use of his low draw and got going far too late after having to challenge very wide in the straight. (tchd 6-1 in places)
I Confess has only ever won on the Polytrack at Lingfield. (op 14-1)
Mastership(IRE), carrying a penalty for his recent win at Newcastle, was dropped in from stall 12 and was continually denied a clear run against the rail from the home bend through to the straight. He was probably unlucky not to finish quite a bit closer but he is most certainly not one to make excuses for. (tchd 9-1 in places)
Stevie Thunder was out the back before making a brief effort roundign the home turn. He seems best suited by a mare galloping track. (op 5-1 tchd 4-1)
Captain Jacksparra(IRE) Official explanation: jockey said gelding hung right

4561 BET MULTIPLES - BETDAQ H'CAP 1m 4f 66y
4:35 (4:35) (Class 4) (0-85,81) 3-Y-O+ **£5,828** (£1,734; £866; £432) **Stalls** Low

Form RPR

6063 **1** **Destinys Dream (IRE)**[23] 3809 4-8-12 68 KellyHarrison[(3)] 8 77
(Miss Tracy Waggott) *hld up: hdwy 2f out: burst through to ld ins fnl f: r.o* **12/1**

2044 **2** 1 ½ **Distinctive Image (USA)**[11] 4197 4-9-11 78 ChrisCatlin 2 84
(R Hollinshead) *bhd: hdwy 3f out: rdn to chse ldrs over 1f out: styd on to take 2nd towards fin: nt pce of wnr* **8/1**[2]

1240 **3** ¾ **I'm In The Pink (FR)**[22] 3847 5-9-3 70 PaulHanagan 4 75
(P D Evans) *chsd ldrs: effrt over 3f out: wnt 2nd 2f out: rdn and chal over 1f out: lost 2nd and no ex towards fin* **9/1**[3]

151R **4** 3 **Inspirina (IRE)**[3] 4449 5-9-6 73 TonyHamilton 1 73
(R Ford) *hld up: hdwy over 3f out: rdn 2f out: led over 1f out: hdd ins fnl f: wknd ins fnl 100yds* **7/2**[1]

4200 **5** 2 ½ **King Fingal (IRE)**[23] 3826 4-9-11 78 GrahamGibbons 7 74
(J J Quinn) *hld up: hdwy over 3f out: outpcd over 2f out: no imp after* **7/2**[1]

0050 **6** 2 ¾ **Robby Bobby**[7] 4340 4-10-0 81 GregFairley 5 73
(M Johnston) *chsd ldr: led over 3f out: rdn and hdd over 1f out: wknd ins fnl f* **7/2**[1]

-530 **7** 11 **Prelude**[23] 3809 8-8-9 62 LiamJones 3 36
(W M Brisbourne) *in tch: hdwy 4f out: chal 3f out: wknd wl over 1f out* **8/1**[2]

100/ **8** 24 **Baskerville**[10] 6690 6-9-0 67 SebSanders 9 3
(Mrs L Williamson) *led: hdd over 3f out: wknd over 2f out* **14/1**

00-4 **9** 19 **Bajan Parkes**[30] 3573 6-9-12 79 ShaneKelly 6 —
(E J Alston) *in tch: rdn and lost pl over 4f out: eased and dropped away over 3f out* **22/1**

2m 37.38s (-2.52) **Going Correction** -0.075s/f (Good) **9** Ran SP% **117.6**
Speed ratings (Par 105): **105,104,103,101,99 98,90,74,62**
toteswinger: 1&2 £10.50, 1&3 £17.50, 2&3 £5.90 CSF £105.54 CT £914.89 TOTE £12.40: £2.80, £3.10, £2.30; EX 79.90.
Owner H Conlon **Bred** Sean Burke **Trained** Spennymoor, Co Durham

FOCUS
A fair handicap run at a reasonable pace. The third is rated to previous course form and looks the best guide.

4562 BETDAQ THE BETTING EXCHANGE H'CAP 1m 2f 75y
5:10 (5:10) (Class 5) (0-75,73) 3-Y-O **£4,435** (£1,309; £655) **Stalls** High

Form RPR

621 **1** **Vita Mia**[24] 3776 3-8-8 60 CatherineGannon 6 68
(P D Evans) *sn led: rdn over 1f out: styd on wl and in command fnl f* **8/1**

1466 **2** 2 ¾ **Veroon (IRE)**[18] 3976 3-9-2 68 (p) J-PGuillambert 3 71
(J G Given) *broke wl: chsd wnr thrght: rdn over 1f out: no imp ins fnl f* **11/1**

0344 **3** 3 **Wee Sonny (IRE)**[27] 3697 3-9-4 70 RichardKingscote 11 67
(Tom Dascombe) *hld up: hdwy 2f out: styd on ins fnl f: tk 3rd cl home: nvr able to rch front 2* **8/1**

0053 **4** ½ **Moon Lightning (IRE)**[9] 4284 3-9-1 67 JerryO'Dwyer 10 63
(M H Tompkins) *midfield: hdwy 3f out: chsd ldrs over 2f out: one pce fnl 100yds* **11/1**

4532 **5** ½ **Hypnotic Gaze (IRE)**[7] 4348 3-8-5 62 JamieKyne[(5)] 8 57+
(J Mackie) *hld up: hdwy on outside over 3f out: chsd ldrs over 2f out: no ex ins fnl f* **11/4**[1]

00-3 **6** 5 **Game Roseanna**[16] 4042 3-8-3 60 DeanHeslop[(5)] 12 46
(W M Brisbourne) *bhd: pushed along 2f out: nvr able to get to ldrs* **40/1**

4-26 **7** *hd* **Bessie Lou (IRE)**[36] 3379 3-9-7 73 SilvestreDeSousa 1 58
(K A Ryan) *racd keenly: chsd ldrs: rdn over 4f out: wknd 2f out: eased whn wl btn ins fnl f* **6/1**[2]

5305 **8** 4 ½ **Kristopher James (IRE)**[15] 4074 3-8-3 55 PaulHanagan 9 32
(W M Brisbourne) *chsd ldrs: n.m.r 3f out: outpcd 2f out: wl btn over 1f out* **20/1**

0040 **9** 1 **Duke Of Normandy (IRE)**[15] 4074 3-8-2 54 FrancisNorton 4 29
(B P J Baugh) *racd keenly in midfield: lost pl 4f out: n.d after* **25/1**

0414 **10** 15 **Uncle Brit**[12] 4171 3-9-0 66 SebSanders 13 12
(Sir Mark Prescott) *midfield: reminders 7f out: rdn and hdwy to chse ldrs 5f out: wknd over 2f out* **8/1**

-041 **11** 1 ½ **Carter**[37] 3336 3-8-10 62 LiamJones 7 5
(W M Brisbourne) *racd keenly: chsd ldrs: rdn over 3f out: wknd over 2f out* **7/1**[3]

030 **12** 41 **Castle Myth (USA)**[9] 4279 3-8-3 55 ow1 ChrisCatlin 2 —
(B Ellison) *hld up: pushed along 4f out: lost tch 3f out: t.o* **33/1**

5630 **P** **Musical Maze**[2] 4506 3-8-9 61 DuranFentiman 5 —
(W M Brisbourne) *bhd: sn smething amiss: p.u 7f out* **16/1**

2m 11.27s (-0.93) **Going Correction** -0.075s/f (Good) **13** Ran SP% **123.3**
Speed ratings (Par 100): **100,97,95,95,94 90,90,86,86,74 72,40,—**
toteswinger: 1&2 £13.90, 1&3 £18.50, 2&3 £20.60 CSF £92.07 CT £742.41 TOTE £11.20: £3.40, £3.30, £3.10; EX 170.70 Place 6: £1,103.15 Place 5: £955.98..
Owner Countess Of Lonsdale **Bred** Lady Lonsdale **Trained** Pandy, Monmouths

FOCUS
A modest 3yo handicap in which the first pair dominated throughout. The third is getting back to somewhere near his best.

Bessie Lou(IRE) Official explanation: jockey said filly lost its action
Castle Myth(USA) Official explanation: jockey said gelding lost its action
T/Plt: £441.60 to a £1 stake. Pool: £99,241.78. 164.05 winning tickets. T/Qpdt: £102.30 to a £1 stake. Pool: £6,305.83. 45.60 winning tickets. DO

4086 **NEWBURY** (L-H)

Sunday, August 2

OFFICIAL GOING: Good (good to soft in places; 7.6)
Rail realignment increased advertised distances on round course by about 33yards.
Wind: Virtually nil Weather: Sunny spells

4563 BATHWICK TYRES AMATEUR RIDERS' H'CAP — 1m 2f 6y
1:35 (1:35) (Class 5) (0-70,70) 3-Y-0+ — **£2,498** (£774; £387; £193) **Stalls** Low

Form — RPR

5042 **1** **Recession Proof (FR)**[9] 4269 3-10-7 **70** .... MrJohnEnnis(5) 10 86+
(S A Callaghan) *trckd ldr: swtchd rt 3f out: rdn to ld 2f out: pushed 8l clr over 1f out: eased fnl 50yds* **7/2**[1]

0020 **2** *5* **Debdene Bank (IRE)**[61] 2580 6-10-0 **56** .... MissCBlakey(7) 5 58
(Mrs Mary Hambro) *rr: stdy prog fr 3f out: swtchd rt 2f out: styd on to take 2nd cl home but nvr any ch w eased down wnr* **16/1**

4053 **3** *½* **Peter Grimes (IRE)**[16] 4054 3-10-3 **66** .... MrJoshuaMoore(5) 9 67
(H J L Dunlop) *chsd ldrs: rdn 3f out: briefly chsd easy wnr ins fnl f but no ch: lost 2nd cl home* **9/2**[3]

2451 **4** *¾* **Don Pietro**[10] 4220 6-10-11 **67** .... MissCBoxall(7) 15 66
(R Curtis) *plld hrd chsd ldrs and stl t.k.h 5f out: led over 3f out: hdd 2f out: one pce and dropped bk to 4th ins fnl f* **16/1**

15-0 **5** *½* **It's Josr**[13] 4149 4-10-6 **55** .... (b) MrSWalker 14 53
(I A Wood) *led tl hdd 3f out: one pce u.p fr over 1f out* **16/1**

3600 **6** *1 ¾* **Randama Bay (IRE)**[8] 4321 4-11-0 **68** .... MrCMartin(5) 13 63
(I A Wood) *in tch: rdn to chse ldrs fr 4f out: one pce fnl 2f* **14/1**

2131 **7** *4* **Iceman George**[16] 4054 5-10-7 **61** .... (b) MrBMMorris(5) 6 48
(D Morris) *in tch: rdn to chse ldrs 4f out: outpcd fr 3f out* **4/1**[2]

0250 **8** *½* **Artreju (GER)**[9] 4269 6-10-1 **57** .... MissKLoftus(7) 1 43
(P Butler) *t.k.h in rr towards outside: sme hdwy 3f out: nvr gng pce to rch ldrs and sn btn* **50/1**

035 **9** *¾* **Lytham (IRE)**[20] 3923 8-10-7 **56** .... MrSDobson 4 40
(A W Carroll) *rr: rdn and sme prog fr 3f out: nvr gng pce to get into contention* **8/1**

06/0 **10** *1 ¼* **Lady Romanov (IRE)**[9] 4263 6-10-6 **60** .... (p) MissMBryant(5) 2 42
(P Butler) *a towards rr* **66/1**

1236 **11** *½* **Blockley (USA)**[9] 4269 5-10-10 **66** .... MrJHodson(5) 8 47
(Ian Williams) *nvr travelling in rr* **14/1**

200- **12** *2 ¼* **Top Ticket (IRE)**[112] 6898 4-11-0 **70** .... MrDTStratton(7) 16 46
(D E Pipe) *stdd s: a in rr* **16/1**

0200 **13** *¾* **Binnion Bay (IRE)**[8] 4321 8-10-1 **55** .... (p) MrAshleyBird(5) 3 30
(J J Bridger) *racd towards outside a in rr* **33/1**

1310 **14** *2 ¾* **Hatch A Plan (IRE)**[13] 4150 8-10-9 **58** .... MissFayeBramley 7 27
(Mouse Hamilton-Fairley) *chsd ldrs: rdn over 3f out: sn wknd* **20/1**

0011 **15** *4 ½* **Gallego**[8] 4321 7-10-12 **66** .... MrMPrice(5) 12 26
(R J Price) *stdd s: a in rr* **14/1**

2m 13.38s (4.58) **Going Correction** +0.30s/f (Good)
WFA 3 from 4yo+ 9lb — **15** Ran SP% **126.2**
Speed ratings (Par 103): **93,89,88,88,87 86,83,82,82,81 80,78,78,76,72**
toteswinger: 1&2 not won, 1&3 £6.30, 2&3 not won. CSF £62.56 CT £269.17 TOTE £5.80: £2.20, £8.20, £2.30; EX 110.10.
Owner Martin M Dempsey **Bred** N P Bloodstock Ltd & Morton Bloodstock **Trained** Newmarket, Suffolk

FOCUS
The rail was moved out from 1m out to the 5f bend by 12 metres, which added an extra 30 metres to round-course distances. After a dry morning the official going was amended to good, good to soft in places. They went a fair gallop in this ordinary handicap for amateur riders. Nothing got into it from the rear and the third and fourth set the level of the form.

4564 AJC PREMIER EBF MAIDEN STKS (DIV I) — 6f 8y
2:10 (2:11) (Class 4) 2-Y-0 — **£4,857** (£1,445; £722; £360) **Stalls** High

Form — RPR

1 **Quadrille** 2-9-3 0 .... RichardHughes 7 89+
(R Hannon) *trckd ldrs: shkn up to ld over 1f out: c clr ins fnl f: easily* **7/4**[1]

3 **2** *4* **Chips O'Toole (IRE)**[10] 4219 2-9-3 0 .... MartinDwyer 3 76+
(B J Meehan) *narrow led: pushed along and hdd over 1f out: no ch w wnr ins fnl f but styd on for wl hld but clr 2nd* **9/4**[2]

3 *4* **Mr Corby (IRE)** 2-9-3 0 .... TonyCulhane 5 64+
(M R Channon) *hld up towards rr: styd on fnl 2f to take n.d 3rd nr fin* **9/1**

50 **4** *1* **Captain Bluebird (IRE)**[15] 4093 2-9-3 0 .... JimmyQuinn 2 61
(D Donovan) *t.k.h chsd ldrs: wnt 3rd over 1f out: wknd ins fnl f and dropped bk to 4th nr fin* **33/1**

05 **5** *3 ¾* **Mountrath**[31] 3522 2-9-3 0 .... AdamKirby 4 50
(B R Johnson) *broke wl stdd rr sn after: reminder 2f out: kpt on for 5th ins fnl f* **33/1**

6 *1 ¼* **Hooligan Sean** 2-9-3 0 .... FergusSweeney 8 46
(H Candy) *slowly away: rcvrd to chse ldrs 1/2-way: wknd fr 2f out* **3/1**[3]

7 *hd* **Pearl Of Kent (IRE)** 2-8-12 0 .... PaulDoe 1 40
(P D Evans) *w ldr over 3f: sn rdn: wknd ins fnl 2f* **20/1**

8 *5* **Queen's Grace** 2-8-12 0 .... SteveDrowne 10 25
(H Morrison) *rdn 1/2-way: green and a bhd* **11/1**

1m 15.34s (2.34) **Going Correction** +0.475s/f (Yiel) — **8** Ran SP% **121.1**
Speed ratings (Par 96): **103,97,92,91,86 84,84,77**
toteswinger: 1&2 £1.10, 1&3 £24.60, 2&3 £2.30 CSF £6.25 TOTE £2.90: £1.50, £1.40, £1.80; EX 5.00.
Owner The Queen **Bred** The Queen **Trained** East Everleigh, Wilts

FOCUS
They raced down the centre of the track in this maiden. The race certainly lacked strength in depth.

NOTEBOOK
Quadrille ◆ won nicely and looks to have a bright future. Out of a smart mare at 1m-1m2f, herself a half-sister to Ribblesdale winner Phantom Gold, he is a half-brother to winning miler/hurdler Hunting Tower. After tracking the pace set by the runner-up he cleared right away in the last furlong, proving much too good for some admittedly ordinary opposition. It was noticeable that he blew quite a bit afterwards so he will strip fitter for the run. His trainer holds him in high regard but has no particular race in mind for his next outing, although he is likely to step him up to 7f. (op 2-1 tchd 5-2)
Chips O'Toole(IRE) was third in only a modest race on his debut at Bath. He ran better here and finished clear of the others, but the winner was ultimately much too good. (tchd 2-1)
Mr Corby(IRE), out of a half-sister to Cheveley Park Stakes winner Capricciosa, is a half-brother to a couple of winning sprinters. He made late gains into third on this debut without being given too hard a time and should derive plenty of benefit from this initial experience. (op 10-1)
Captain Bluebird(IRE) did not show much on his first two starts, but had been the subject of support on his debut. He ran a bit better here and can now switch to nurseries if required. (op 28-1)
Mountrath, another having his third run, appears exposed as modest. (op 40-1)
Hooligan Sean comes from a good family that Henry Candy knows well and may improve in time. He ran green on this debut and, after improving at halfway, was quickly left behind again. (op 4-1)
Pearl Of Kent(IRE), whose dam was a winning miler, showed pace for 4f. (tchd 16-1)
Queen's Grace is a half-sister to good handicapper April Fool from a fine family, being out of a smart sprinter who was a half-sister to July Cup winner Sakhee's Secret. She was green first time and trailed throughout, but should be capable of considerably better, although she will need to be. (op 12-1)

4565 GRUNDON RECYCLE NURSERY — 7f (S)
2:45 (2:47) (Class 4) 2-Y-0 — **£3,885** (£1,156; £577; £288) **Stalls** High

Form — RPR

0040 **1** **Desert Auction (IRE)**[15] 4089 2-9-6 **86** .... RichardHughes 9 87+
(R Hannon) *in tch: nt clr run and swtchd lft 2f out: styng on to chal whn pushed lft over 1f out: rdn and qcknd to ld fnl 100yds: jst hld on* **11/2**[3]

000 **2** *nse* **Gold Fix (IRE)**[16] 4047 2-7-13 **65** oh1 ow1 .... JimmyQuinn 3 66
(M R Channon) *in tch: hdwy over 2f out: chalng whn pushed lft and lost momentum over 1f out: rallied and str run ins fnl f: jst failed* **18/1**

662 **3** *¾* **Maoi Chinn Tire (IRE)**[30] 3572 2-7-12 **64** oh4 .... LukeMorris 14 63
(J S Moore) *hld up in rr: stdy hdwy fr 2f out: hung lft over 1f out and led jst ins fnl f: hdd fnl 100yds: one pce cl home* **4/1**[2]

5034 **4** *2 ¼* **Ever So Bold**[45] 3072 2-8-2 **68** .... KirstyMilczarek 13 61
(W R Muir) *in rr: hdwy and hung lft 2f out and again whn chalng over 1f out: fdd fnl 100yds* **33/1**

2101 **5** *1 ¼* **Jehu**[11] 4190 2-9-2 **82** .... TonyCulhane 6 72+
(M R Channon) *broke wl: t.k.h and stdd rr: hdwy 3f out: clsng on ldrs whn hmpd and lost pl 2f out: rallied and kpt on again fnl f* **12/1**

01 **6** *nk* **Butch And Sundance**[12] 4176 2-9-3 **83** .... MartinDwyer 7 73+
(B J Meehan) *s.i.s: in rr: rdn along over 2f out: styd on fr over 1f out: fin wl but nvr gng pce to rch ldrs* **8/1**

0101 **7** *½* **Avon River**[37] 3340 2-9-4 **84** .... RyanMoore 8 74+
(R Hannon) *led tl narrowly hdd 3f out: styd upsides and stl chalng whn hit over hd w whip and hmpd over 1f out: nt rcvr and sn btn* **7/1**

5653 **8** *2 ¾* **Two Kisses (IRE)**[39] 3256 2-8-1 **72** .... Louis-PhilippeBeuzelin(5) 5 53+
(B G Powell) *chsd ldrs: rdn and n.m.r 2f out: wknd over 1f out* **14/1**

651 **9** *hd* **Giulietta Da Vinci**[11] 4194 2-8-9 **75** .... DaneO'Neill 2 60+
(R Hannon) *trckd ldrs: slt ld 3f out: rdn and hmpd over 1f out: nt rcvr and sn wknd* **7/2**[1]

5240 **10** *nse* **Just The Tonic**[10] 4226 2-8-7 **73** .... SamHitchcott 12 59+
(M R Channon) *t.k.h: pressed ldrs: upsides 3f out: rdn over 2f out: one pce whn hmpd wl over 1f out: sn btn* **33/1**

10 **11** *¾* **Meglio Ancora**[43] 3138 2-9-7 **87** .... PatCosgrave 15 66+
(J G Portman) *in rr: hdwy 3f out: chsng ldrs whn hmpd and wknd 2f out:* **20/1**

051 **12** *1* **Danger Mulally**[24] 3785 2-8-8 **74** .... WilliamBuick 11 54+
(A M Balding) *t.k.h: trckd ldrs: rdn whn bdly hmpd 2f out and sn wknd* **20/1**

034 **13** *¾* **Fire And Stone (IRE)**[35] 3420 2-8-4 **70** .... RichardSmith 16 45
(Tom Dascombe) *chsd ldrs 5f* **25/1**

12 **14** *5* **Decree Absolute (USA)**[34] 3452 2-8-8 **74** ow1 .... PaulFitzsimons 10 36
(Miss J R Tooth) *chsd ldrs: rdn 3f out: sn btn* **14/1**

1m 28.64s (2.94) **Going Correction** +0.475s/f (Yiel) — **14** Ran SP% **126.8**
Speed ratings (Par 96): **102,101,101,98,97 96,96,93,92,92 91,90,89,84**
toteswinger: 1&2 £19.90, 1&3 £23.90, 2&3 not won. CSF £97.90 CT £461.03 TOTE £10.30: £3.00, £7.80, £2.30; EX 247.20.
Owner A J Ilsley, K T Ivory & G Battocchi **Bred** J Kilpatrick **Trained** East Everleigh, Wilts
■ Stewards' Enquiry : Kirsty Milczarek two-day ban: careless riding (Aug 16-17)

FOCUS
An open nursery in which they came down the middle. There was quite a bit of trouble and this is muddling form.

NOTEBOOK
Desert Auction(IRE), one of three runners in the race for Richard Hannon, was upped in trip after finishing in midfield behind stablemate Monsieur Chevalier in the Super Sprint here. Held up in touch, he was briefly short of room over 2f out then was the last of several to suffer in a chain reaction caused by the third, finding himself carried towards the far rail just as he was coming with his run. He ran on well when straightened up and won on the nod, proving well suited by the 7f. (op 8-1 tchd 9-1)
Gold Fix(IRE) was making her nursery debut after three unplaced runs in maidens, all at this venue. She travelled well towards the far side of the bunch and, after being carried slightly left in the trouble, ran on to miss out by a whisker. Official explanation: jockey said filly suffered interference in running (op 22-1 tchd 25-1)
Maoi Chinn Tire(IRE) seemed set to win after striking the front on the near side but drifted markedly to his left and was collared inside the last. He was 4lb out of the weights and this was a decent effort, but it is to be hoped he does not repeat his wayward tendencies. (op 5-1 tchd 11-2)
Ever So Bold was left in second place inside the last but could only stick on at the one pace. This was a fair run on his first try at beyond 5f, but he did not quite see it out.
Jehu was 6lb higher than when winning at Catterick. He was staying on late and looks to need 1m now. (tchd 14-1)
Butch And Sundance, a Yarmouth maiden winner, was another to make late progress without getting into it. He does not look a straightforward ride. (op 15-2 tchd 9-1)
Avon River, the winner's stablemate, ran better than the bare form indicates as he was in the firing line when carried to his left. Official explanation: jockey said colt suffered interference in running (op 5-1)
Giulietta Da Vinci, another from the Hannon yard, was severely inconvenienced by the third wandering entering the last furlong. (op 5-1)
Just The Tonic, from the same yard as the runner-up and fifth, was perhaps the worst affected in the shemozzle as she was on Maoi Chinn Tire's immediate left when he started to drift. (op 40-1)
Danger Mulally showed speed, but had just come under pressure when getting squeezed out in bunching 2f from home. (op 16-1)

4566 EUROPEAN BREEDERS' FUND CHALICE STKS (LISTED RACE) (F&M) — 1m 4f 5y
3:20 (3:20) (Class 1) 3-Y-0+
£22,708 (£8,608; £4,308; £2,148; £1,076; £540) **Stalls** Low

Form — RPR

103 **1** **Polly's Mark (IRE)**[12] 4166 3-8-5 87 .... WilliamBuick 2 104
(C G Cox) *hld up in tch: hdwy whn bmpd over 3f out: styd on to ld jst ins fnl 2f: hung rt u.p ins fnl f: rdn out* **16/1**

232 **2** *1* **Fallen In Love**[29] 3619 3-8-5 102 SteveDrowne 3 102+
(J L Dunlop) *trckd ldrs: nt clr run on ins and edgd rt over 3f out: stl hld in and n.m.r 2f out: swtchd rt and hdwy over 1f out: styd on to chse wnr ins fnl f but a hld* **5/2**[2]

-105 **3** *6* **Rosaleen (IRE)**[9] 4259 4-9-5 98 MartinDwyer 1 95
(B J Meehan) *rr: pushed along 5f out: hmpd over 3f out: styd on to take wl hld 3rd fnl f* **16/1**

41 **4** *2 1/4* **Queen Of Pentacles (IRE)**[46] 3025 3-8-5 86 AlanMunro 4 89
(J Noseda) *t.k.h in rr: hdwy and drvn along 3f out: styd on same pce for wl hld 4th fnl f* **10/1**

240- **5** *5* **Arthur's Girl**[270] 7193 4-9-2 102 JimmyFortune 8 81
(J H M Gosden) *chsd ldrs: led over 3f out: hdd jst ins fnl 2f: sn wknd* **8/1**[3]

216 **6** *1* **Ainia**[15] 4088 4-9-2 76 JimCrowley 7 79
(D M Simcock) *in rr but in tch: pushed along to trck ldrs ins fnl 3f: sn rdn: wknd 2f out* **33/1**

5-60 **7** *1 1/4* **Si Belle (IRE)**[33] 3493 4-9-2 93 RichardHughes 6 77
(Rae Guest) *led tl hdd over 3f out: sn btn* **33/1**

5261 **8** *3/4* **Phillipina**[16] 4066 3-8-6 104 ow1 RyanMoore 9 77
(Sir Michael Stoute) *in rr and pushed along over 4f out: hdwy to press ldrs 3f out: wknd qckly 2f out* **5/4**[1]

0305 **9** *3 1/4* **Kaabari (USA)**[16] 4052 3-8-5 80 JimmyQuinn 5 71
(C E Brittain) *chsd ldrs tl hmpd 3f out: sn wknd* **66/1**

2m 36.56s (1.06) **Going Correction** +0.30s/f (Good)
WFA 3 from 4yo 11lb **9** Ran SP% **112.4**
Speed ratings (Par 111): **108,107,103,101,98 97,97,96,94**
toteswinger: 1&2 £3.10, 1&3 £25.30, 2&3 £29.80 CSF £54.17 TOTE £24.70: £3.00, £1.30, £3.40; EX 114.00.
Owner Wickham Stud **Bred** Glashare House Stud **Trained** Lambourn, Berks

FOCUS
A fair Listed race on paper, and the first two came clear, but with the favourite below par the form is ordinary for the grade and none too solid, with the runner-up the best guide.

NOTEBOOK
Polly's Mark(IRE), third in a Ffos Las handicap last time, had a good deal to find on these terms. She held on well after striking the front, despite edging to her right, and saw out the 1m4f well enough. This will have done her handicap mark no good and she may step up to Group 3 company now. (op 25-1)
Fallen In Love was arguably unlucky, as she was denied a run up the rail for around a furlong, losing valuable momentum. She was out after the winner with just under 2f to run, but was always being held. She handled the easier ground well but has now made the frame on all four of her starts this year without winning. (op 9-4)
Rosaleen(IRE) was another slightly trapped on the rail but that could not be used as an excuse. She ran on late for third and can revert to more prominent tactics now she has proved that she stays this far.
Queen Of Pentacles(IRE), in the same ownership as the second, lacked the experience of her opponents having run just twice. Taking a big step up in class after winning a Polytrack maiden, she was keen in the first part of the race. She improved down the outer in the straight but was left trailing by the principals in the final quarter mile. (tchd 9-1)
Arthur's Girl was runner-up in the Ribblesdale last year when trained by Geoff Wragg. Making her belated reappearance, she showed ahead for a time in the straight before fading. She should come on for this but may not be easy to place this year. (tchd 15-2)
Ainia had no realistic chance on these terms but she ran a creditable race in the circumstances. (tchd 40-1)
Phillipina enjoyed a confidence-boosting maiden win last time, but she was a bitter disappointment on this return to a higher grade, weakening tamely after challenging with 3f to run. (tchd 11-8)
Kaabari(USA), the rider reported that the filly suffered interference in running. Official explanation: , the rider reported that the filly suffered interference in running.

4567 BLACKMORE BUILDING CONTRACTORS H'CAP 5f 34y
3:55 (3:56) (Class 4) (0-85,88) 3-Y-O+ £4,857 (£1,445; £722; £360) Stalls High

Form RPR

2431 **1** **The Tatling (IRE)**[10] 4222 12-8-13 77 JackDean(3) 10 86
(J M Bradley) *s.i.s: rr: hdwy 2f out: n.m.r 1f out and ins fnl f: shkn up and qcknd wl to ld cl home* **10/1**

0664 **2** *nk* **Kingswinford (IRE)**[10] 4227 3-8-9 73 RyanMoore 2 80
(P D Evans) *chsd ldrs: rdn 2f out: styd on to chal 1f out: led fnl 110yds: hdd cl home* **10/3**[1]

5000 **3** *1 3/4* **Ebraam (USA)**[24] 3784 6-9-9 84 TolleyDean 12 86+
(P Howling) *stdd: swtchd lft to outside fr 2f out: styng on whn nt clr run ins fnl f: rdr dropped reins fnl 50yds: fin wl* **12/1**

1230 **4** *1/2* **The Jobber (IRE)**[7] 4341 8-9-10 85 DaneO'Neill 7 85
(M Blanshard) *chsd ldrs: drvn to chal 1f out and ev ch jst ins fnl f: outpcd fnl 110yds* **13/2**

0400 **5** *1/2* **Dazed And Amazed**[3] 4461 5-9-6 81 RichardHughes 3 79
(R Hannon) *broke wl and sn grabbed ld on stands rail: rdn 2f out: hdd fnl 110yds: sn wknd* **9/1**

0003 **6** *1* **Even Bolder**[22] 3845 6-8-10 71 StephenCarson 8 65+
(E A Wheeler) *hld up in rr but in tch: nt clr run fr 2f out tl ins fnl f: gng on cl home but nt rcvr* **14/1**

-220 **7** *shd* **Ivory Silk**[22] 3845 4-9-1 76 SteveDrowne 6 70
(J R Gask) *outpcd towards rr 1/2-way: kpt on ins fnl f but nvr a threat* **9/2**[2]

0322 **8** *3 1/4* **Bertoliver**[10] 4232 5-9-6 81 JimCrowley 9 63
(Tom Dascombe) *pressed ldr and upsides fr 1/2-way tl 1f out: wknd ins fnl f* **5/1**[3]

3204 **9** *2 3/4* **Robin The Till**[22] 3859 3-8-2 66 oh2 RichardThomas 1 37
(R Hannon) *chsd ldrs bur sn hanging lft: wknd over 1f out* **22/1**

20 **10** *2 1/4* **Wotashirtfull (IRE)**[57] 2704 4-9-7 82 (v) PatCosgrave 11 46
(J R Boyle) *chsd ldrs: rdn over 2f out: wknd over 1f out* **9/1**

63.06 secs (1.66) **Going Correction** +0.475s/f (Yiel)
WFA 3 from 4yo+ 3lb **10** Ran SP% **119.1**
Speed ratings (Par 105): **105,104,101,100,100 98,98,93,88,85**
toteswinger: 1&2 £10.40, 1&3 £14.50, 2&3 £10.70 CSF £44.34 CT £425.59 TOTE £9.70: £2.10, £2.10, £4.10; EX 85.80.
Owner J M Bradley **Bred** Patrick J Power **Trained** Sedbury, Gloucs

FOCUS
A fair sprint handicap where they raced next to the stands' rail. The race got a bit messy and is best rated through the runner-up ata length off his juvenile best.
Ebraam(USA) Official explanation: jockey said gelding was denied a clear run
Dazed And Amazed Official explanation: jockey said gelding hung left in the final furlong
Even Bolder ◆ Official explanation: jockey said gelding was denied a clear run

4568 AJC PREMIER EBF MAIDEN STKS (DIV II) 6f 8y
4:25 (4:28) (Class 4) 2-Y-O £4,857 (£1,445; £722; £360) Stalls High

Form RPR

00 **1** **Avongate**[10] 4219 2-9-3 0 RyanMoore 5 78
(R Hannon) *mde all: drvn and hld on wl thrght fnl f* **8/1**

5 **2** *1/2* **Tasmeem (IRE)**[16] 4062 2-9-3 0 RHills 10 78+
(B W Hills) *trckd ldrs: drvn to chse wnr fr over 1f out: styd on wl thrght fnl f but a jst hld* **15/8**[1]

6 **3** *5* **Quinner (IRE)**[9] 4265 2-9-3 0 (t) PaulDoe 1 62
(P D Evans) *chsd ldrs: rdn and ev ch fr 2f out: dropped bk to 3rd and wknd fnl f* **16/1**

4 *1* **Imperial Delight** 2-9-3 0 DaneO'Neill 8 59
(H Candy) *in rr: hdwy and swtchd lft to outside 2f out: nvr quite gng pce to chal: wknd ins fnl f* **7/2**[2]

5 *1* **Firehawk** 2-9-3 0 PatCosgrave 3 56+
(J G Portman) *slowly away: green in rr: sn drvn along: mod prog fr over 1f out* **16/1**

6 *nk* **Trewarthenick** 2-9-3 0 WilliamBuick 2 55
(A M Balding) *green and pushed along in rr: reminders 1/2-way: swtchd lft to outside over 2f out: sn rdn: mod prog ins fnl f* **4/1**[3]

00 **7** *3 1/2* **Private Olley**[25] 3745 2-9-3 0 AdamKirby 6 44
(J Akehurst) *chsd ldrs tl wknd qckly 1f out* **16/1**

0 **8** *7* **Musical Delight**[60] 2599 2-9-3 0 AlanMunro 4 23
(A P Jarvis) *chsd ldrs tl wknd qckly ins fnl 2f* **33/1**

1m 15.83s (2.83) **Going Correction** +0.475s/f (Yiel) **8** Ran SP% **108.7**
Speed ratings (Par 96): **100,99,92,91,90 89,84,75**
toteswinger: 1&2 £2.70, 1&3 £3.40, 2&3 £5.90 CSF £20.49 TOTE £6.50: £2.10, £1.50, £3.60; EX 13.30.
Owner D J Deer **Bred** D J Deer **Trained** East Everleigh, Wilts

FOCUS
This was run about half a second slower than the first division. Unlike that contest, they raced down the rail this time. The first two came clear, but this was probably a weak maiden for the track.

NOTEBOOK
Avongate, another from the Hannon yard, showed little on his first two starts, but he put the experience gained to good use and made every yard. He held on tenaciously but does not look in the same league as Quadrille, winner of division one for the stable. (op 13-2 tchd 6-1)
Tasmeem(IRE) went after the winner over a furlong out and closed the gap without quite getting there. He had veered badly on his debut in heavy ground at Nottingham and this was much more encouraging. He gave the impression he has more to offer and should find an ordinary race. (op 11-4 tchd 3-1)
Quinner(IRE), well held on soft ground on his debut last week, showed more here until fading inside the final furlong. He might appreciate some fast ground. (op 20-1)
Imperial Delight, out of a sister to the high-class 1m2f performer Stage Gift, made modest late gains after being switched wide and is entitled to learn from this. (op 4-1)
Firehawk, in the same ownership as the third, missed the break badly but was picking up quite well when it was all over. Related to several sprint winners, he can leave this running behind. (op 12-1)
Trewarthenick was distinctly green and showed little, but this half-brother to decent sprinters Coconut Penang and Milbag is another who should do better in time. (op 5-1)

4569 W R MACKINNON FILLIES' H'CAP 1m 2f 6y
5:00 (5:00) (Class 5) (0-75,73) 3-Y-O £2,590 (£770; £385; £192) Stalls Low

Form RPR

-100 **1** **It's Dubai Dolly**[45] 3047 3-9-7 73 MartinDwyer 8 79
(A J Lidderdale) *mde all: hrd rdn thrght fnl f and hld on wl* **25/1**

000 **2** *1 1/4* **Regal Blush**[25] 3751 3-8-10 62 WilliamBuick 2 65
(A M Balding) *trckd ldrs: rdn 2f out: styd on u.p fnl f to take 2nd fnl 75yds but a jst hld by wnr* **25/1**

2211 **3** *nk* **Air Maze**[10] 4224 3-9-6 72 StephenDonohoe 5 75
(Sir Mark Prescott) *chsd wnr: rdn 2f out: no imp fnl f and lost 2nd fnl 75yds* **3/1**[1]

64 **4** *1* **Eurotanz (IRE)**[13] 4150 3-8-11 63 SteveDrowne 14 64
(H Morrison) *chsd ldrs: pushed along 2f out: rdn and styd on same pce fr over 1f out* **9/1**

0610 **5** *2 1/4* **Mejala (IRE)**[29] 3627 3-9-6 72 RHills 16 68+
(J L Dunlop) *t.k.h: bmpd over 4f out: carried hd awkwardly fr 3f out: hung lft and nt keen fr 2f out but styd on ins fnl f* **8/1**

6063 **6** *1* **Triple Cee (IRE)**[10] 4224 3-8-8 60 EdwardCreighton 7 54
(M R Channon) *chsd ldrs: rdn fr over 3f out: wknd over 1f out* **10/1**

2304 **7** *1 1/4* **Salybia Bay**[32] 3511 3-8-10 62 RichardHughes 15 54
(R Hannon) *in tch: edgd rt over 4f out: rdn and hdwy to chse ldrs over 2f out: wknd over 1f out* **11/2**[2]

0-40 **8** *3/4* **Full Of Nature**[15] 4085 3-9-6 72 GeorgeBaker 13 62
(S Kirk) *stdd s and swtchd lft s: rr tl rdn and hdwy on outside over 2f out: sme prog fnl f* **25/1**

0-00 **9** *1 3/4* **Matilda Poliport**[16] 4057 3-9-1 67 AdamKirby 10 54
(W R Swinburn) *in rr: hdwy 4f out: chsd ldrs 3f out: wknd fr 2f out* **20/1**

1525 **10** *1* **Fong's Alibi**[10] 4224 3-8-12 64 (p) LPKeniry 6 49
(J S Moore) *in tch: hdwy to chse ldrs 4f out: rdn: hung lft and wknd fr over 2f out* **14/1**

543 **11** *hd* **Bow To No One (IRE)**[17] 4022 3-9-4 70 AlanMunro 12 54
(A P Jarvis) *rr: rdn along towards outside over 3f out: nvr in contention* **18/1**

-412 **12** *1 1/2* **Royal Superlative**[23] 3803 3-9-0 73 JPFahy(7) 4 54
(R M Beckett) *hld up in rr: sme hdwy 4f out: wknd 3f out* **6/1**[3]

333- **13** *3/4* **Colangnik (USA)**[243] 7524 3-9-6 72 RyanMoore 11 52
(J R Best) *nvr bttr than mid-div: rdn 3f out: sn wknd* **11/1**

0600 **14** *3 1/2* **Efficiency**[22] 3868 3-9-6 72 DaneO'Neill 3 45
(M Blanshard) *rr: hdwy into mid-div over 3f out: sn rdn: wknd qckly over 2f out* **28/1**

540 **15** *25* **Spirit Of The Glen**[52] 2847 3-8-8 60 PaulDoe 1 —
(Jamie Poulton) *rdn after s: a in rr* **50/1**

2m 11.81s (3.01) **Going Correction** +0.30s/f (Good) **15** Ran SP% **126.8**
Speed ratings (Par 97): **99,98,97,96,95 94,93,92,91,90 90,89,88,85,65**
toteswinger: 1&2 not won, 1&3 £39.10, 2&3 not won. CSF £540.67 CT £2434.77 TOTE £23.50: £5.40, £7.00, £2.40; EX 181.70 Place 6: £97.76 Place 5: £45.74..
Owner Exors Of The Late Mrs Kath Cox **Bred** R G Percival **Trained** Eastbury, Berks

FOCUS
Just a modest fillies' handicap. The winner made all, setting only a modest pace, and the next three home were all in the first four throughout too. The form is suspect and has not been rated too positively.
Full Of Nature Official explanation: jockey said filly missed the break
Spirit Of The Glen Official explanation: jockey said filly was never travelling
T/Jkpt: Not won. T/Plt: £83.50 to a £1 stake. Pool: £69,729.44. 609.43 winning tickets. T/Qpdt: £41.60 to a £1 stake. Pool: £4,341.55. 77.10 winning tickets. ST

4570 - 4573a (Foreign Racing) - See Raceform Interactive

4553 GALWAY (R-H)

Sunday, August 2

OFFICIAL GOING: Chase course - soft; remainder - yielding

4574a CONNACHT TRIBUNE CENTENARY H'CAP — 7f

4:00 (4:02) 3-Y-0+ **£56,883** (£16,689; £7,951; £2,708)

RPR

1 **Fit The Cove (IRE)**[3] 4474 9-8-10 86 5ex (t) WJSupple 11 — 91
(H Rogers, Ire) *led: strly pressed and jnd ins fnl f: styd on wl to be jst in front on line* **10/1**

2 shd **Ask Jack (USA)**[52] 2871 5-8-9 85 (p) CDHayes 16 — 90
(Joseph G Murphy, Ire) *mid-div: prog fr under 3f out: 3rd and rdn bef st: chal in 2nd and on terms ins fnl f: styd on wl: jst failed* **16/1**

3 hd **Maundy Money**[5] 4412 6-9-3 93 CO'Donoghue 12 — 97
(David Marnane, Ire) *trckd ldrs: clsr in 2nd under 3f out: rdn in 2nd bef st: chal between horses fnl f: struck on hd by rival rdr's whip: kpt on wl: jst failed* **9/2**[1]

4 2 ½ **Castle Bar Sling (USA)**[5] 4412 4-9-2 92 WMLordan 2 — 90
(T J O'Mara, Ire) *towards rr: rdn in 12th bef st: sn no imp: kpt on wl wout threatening* **16/1**

5 nk **Funatfuntasia**[24] 3834 5-8-9 85 WJLee 9 — 82
(Ms Joanna Morgan, Ire) *trckd ldrs: 5th and rdn bef st: kpt on same pce fr over 1f out* **14/1**

6 1 ½ **Hard Rock City (USA)**[17] 4027 9-8-8 89 DEMullins(5) 1 — 82
(M J Grassick, Ire) *in rr of mid-div: rdn in 13th bef st: sn no imp: kpt on wout threatening* **14/1**

7 ¾ **Majestic Times (IRE)**[7] 4360 9-8-4 80 oh1 (b) DJMoran 6 — 71
(Liam McAteer, Ire) *chsd ldrs: 7th and rdn bef st: kpt on same pce fr over 1f out* **28/1**

8 nk **Firey Red (IRE)**[11] 4216 3-9-4 100 PJSmullen 7 — 88
(D K Weld, Ire) *mid-div best: rdn in 8th bef st: sn no imp and kpt on same pce* **6/1**[2]

9 3 **Tajneed (IRE)**[8] 4330 6-9-4 94 AdrianTNicholls 8 — 76
(D Nicholls) *prom: dropped to 6th bef st: sn no ex* **9/2**[1]

10 nk **The Tooth Fairy (IRE)**[15] 4108 3-8-2 89 GFCarroll(5) 4 — 68
(Michael Mulvany, Ire) *mid-div: 11th bef st: sn no imp u.p* **7/1**[3]

11 1 ½ **Seachantach (USA)**[11] 4216 3-9-4 100 (bt) KJManning 3 — 75
(J S Bolger, Ire) *sn prom on outer: 4th bef st: sn wknd* **9/1**

12 ¾ **Senators Alibi**[5] 4414 11-7-13 80 oh3 (t) BACurtis(5) 14 — 55
(T J O'Mara, Ire) *towards rr: sme hdwy on inner early st: sn no ex u.p* **22/1**

13 ½ **Just For Mary**[13] 4135 5-8-10 86 RPCleary 13 — 60
(Daniel Mark Loughnane, Ire) *towards rr: hdwy on outer over 3f out: rdn in 9th bef st: sn no ex* **10/1**

14 1 **Impossible Dream (IRE)**[21] 3898 5-9-7 102 ShaneFoley(5) 10 — 73
(A Kinsella, Ire) *mid-div: rdn and wknd fr under 3f out* **33/1**

R **Patio**[62] 2554 4-9-2 92 (b[1]) FMBerry 5 — —
(David Marnane, Ire) *ref to r* **20/1**

1m 29.95s (-1.65)
WFA 3 from 4yo+ 6lb **15 Ran SP% 131.9**
CSF £167.28 CT £618.83 TOTE £13.10: £4.10, £7.10, £1.90; DF 357.00.
Owner Brendan Smith **Bred** Daniel McLorey **Trained** Ardee, Co. Louth

NOTEBOOK
Tajneed(IRE) tracked the leaders until weakening on the climb towards the straight. (op 5/1 tchd 11/2)

4575 - 4576a (Foreign Racing) - See Raceform Interactive

3892 DEAUVILLE (R-H)

Saturday, August 1

OFFICIAL GOING: Turf course - good to soft; all-weather - standard

4577a PRIX BEACHCOMBER HOTELS DINAROBIN (UNRACED FILLIES) (STRAIGHT) — 6f

2:40 (2:43) 2-Y-0 **£11,650** (£4,660; £3,495; £2,330; £1,165)

RPR

1 **Yamam** 2-9-0 MGuyon 7 — 89
(A Fabre, France)

2 nse **Courchevel (IRE)** 2-9-0 SMaillot 9 — 89
(Robert Collet, France)

3 2 **Miss Tara (FR)** 2-9-0 DBoeuf 10 — 83
(W Baltromei, Germany)

4 ¾ **Tierra Luna (IRE)** 2-9-0 CSoumillon 6 — 81
(Y De Nicolay, France)

5 ¾ **On Verra (IRE)** 2-9-0 TThulliez 1 — 78
(F Doumen, France) **44/1**[1]

6 ¾ **Minimalist** 2-9-0 SPasquier 5 — 76
(Mme C Head-Maarek, France)

7 6 **Hill Tribe** 2-9-0 MarcHalford 4 — 58
(J R Best) *prom: 3rd and pushed along 2 1/2f out: rdn and one pce fr over 1 1/2f out* **50/1**[2]

8 nk **Mixfeeling (IRE)** 2-9-0 OPeslier 8 — 57
(C Laffon-Parias, France)

9 hd **Cup Cake (FR)** 2-9-0 IMendizabal 12 — 57
(Mme Pia Brandt, France)

10 1 ½ **Sunrise (FR)** 2-9-0 AlexisBadel 11 — 52
(Mme R-W Allen, France)

0 **Green Ridge (FR)** 2-9-0 GMasure 2 — —
(J Van Handenhove, France)

0 **She Say'S** 2-9-0 C-PLemaire 3 — —
(J-C Rouget, France)

1m 10.9s (-0.30) **12 Ran SP% 4.2**
PARI-MUTUEL: WIN 6.30; PL 2.80, 3.20, 5.10; DF 31.10.
Owner Muteb Bin Abdullah **Bred** Janus Bloodstock Inc & G Lugon **Trained** Chantilly, France

NOTEBOOK
Hill Tribe was well placed during the early part of the race but began to drop out of contention from the two-furlong marker.

4578a PRIX DE PSYCHE BEACHCOMBER HOTELS ROYAL PALM (GROUP 3) (FILLIES) — 1m 2f

3:15 (3:16) 3-Y-0 **£38,835** (£15,534; £11,650; £7,767; £3,883)

RPR

1 **Board Meeting (IRE)**[48] 2952 3-8-11 ACrastus 4 — 111
(E Lellouche, France) *in tch in 4th: 3rd st: pushed along and r.o over 1 1/2f out: rdn to ld over 1f out: jst hld runner up cl home* **22/5**[3]

2 shd **Proportional**[83] 1918 3-8-11 SPasquier 3 — 111
(Mme C Head-Maarek, France) *mid-div: 5th and running on st: cl 3rd 1 1/2f out: chal fnl f: ev ch ins fnl f: jst hld cl home* **9/5**[1]

3 2 ½ **Plumania**[48] 2952 3-8-11 OPeslier 2 — 106
(A Fabre, France) *hld up: disputing last st: pushed along 2f out: hdwy fr 1 1/2f out: wnt 3rd cl home* **27/10**[2]

4 shd **One Clever Cat (IRE)**[27] 3668 3-8-11 FPrat 5 — 106
(T Clout, France) *hld up: disputing last st: styd on steadily fr 1 1/2f out: jst missed 3rd* **79/10**

5 hd **Shalanaya (IRE)**[44] 3-8-11 CSoumillon 6 — 105
(M Delzangles, France) *racd in 2nd: led over 2f out to over 1f out: styd on tl lost pl cl home* **32/5**

6 ¾ **Rex Regina (IRE)**[37] 3330 3-8-11 C-PLemaire 8 — 104
(J-C Rouget, France) *hld up: 6th on ins st: pushed along and wnt 4th briefly 1 1/2f out: n.d* **12/1**

7 2 ½ **Norderney (GER)**[29] 3604 3-8-11 AStarke 1 — 99
(P Schiergen, Germany) *racd in 3rd: pushed along 3 1/2f out: 4th and u.p st: sn btn* **28/1**

8 15 **Pas Mure (IRE)**[70] 3-8-11 MBarzalona 7 — 69
(F Head, France) *led to over 2f out: eased* **27/10**[2]

2m 5.00s (-5.20) **8 Ran SP% 144.2**
PARI-MUTUEL: WIN 5.40; PL 1.50, 1.10, 1.20; DF 6.90.
Owner Ecurie Wildenstein **Bred** Dayton Investments Ltd **Trained** Lamorlaye, France

NOTEBOOK
Board Meeting(IRE), for whom a strong pace enabled her to show her true form, which she had not had when she last ran in the Diane. Held up in the early stages, she came with a well-timed run to take the lead in the dying stages of the race. It was a game effort and she will now be aimed at the Prix Vermeille at Longchamp next month.
Proportional hadn't been out for nearly three months and put up a decent effort. She was well placed throughout and had the lead by the furlong marker but was just run out of things as the race came to an end. This race will have done her a lot of good and she is now to be aimed at the Prix de la Nonette here later in the month.
Plumania had finished ahead of the winner in the Diane but was well beaten on this occasion. Sixth in the early stages, she was one paced when things quickened up and never looked like getting on terms with the principals. Connections feel she might be better suited by a longer trip.
One Clever Cat(IRE) was given a waiting race and was putting in her best work at the finish. She only failed by a short head to take third place, which she would have done if not given so much to do in the straight.

4577 DEAUVILLE (R-H)

Sunday, August 2

OFFICIAL GOING: Turf course - soft; all-weather - standard

4579a PRIX DE CABOURG JOCKEY-CLUB DE TURQUIE (GROUP 3) — 6f

2:55 (2:57) 2-Y-0 **£38,835** (£15,534; £11,650; £7,767; £3,883)

RPR

1 **Zanzibari (USA)**[23] 2-8-11 MGuyon 3 — 107
(A Fabre, France) *racd in 2nd: pushed along 2 1/2f out: rdn and nt qckn 1 1/2f out: styd on u.p to ld 100yds out: r.o wl* **3/1**[2]

2 1 ½ **Sorciere (IRE)**[29] 3648 2-8-8 CSoumillon 5 — 99
(C Lerner, France) *led to 100yds out: no ex* **6/5**[1]

3 1 **Lixirova (FR)**[23] 2-8-8 DBoeuf 1 — 96
(D Smaga, France) *last to ins fnl f: kpt on* **7/1**

4 snk **Boltcity (FR)**[23] 2-8-11 C-PLemaire 2 — 99
(J-C Rouget, France) *disp 3rd: pushed along 2 1/2f out: disputing last ins fnl f: kpt on clsng stages* **4/1**[3]

5 nk **Wonderfilly (FR)**[7] 4366 2-8-8 SPasquier 4 — 95
(P Demercastel, France) *disp 3rd on outside: hdwy to dispute 2nd and ev ch appr fnl f: wknd 100yds out* **12/1**

1m 11.7s (0.50) **5 Ran SP% 110.6**
PARI-MUTUEL: WIN 3.20; PL 1.30, 1.50,; SF 10.10.
Owner Sheikh Mohammed **Bred** Mme A Fabre **Trained** Chantilly, France

NOTEBOOK
Zanzibari(USA), a fine-looking colt, he looked outpaced one and a half out but then ran on gamely inside the final furlong to win with something in hand. He had always been handy and reversed form with the fourth in his previous race. There are no real plans for the moment as his trainer feels the Morny might come a little soon, and they may possibly wait for Longchamp in September.
Sorciere(IRE) had an outside draw and was gradually brought across to take the lead on the rail after a furlong and a half. The filly looked to have the race in her grasp at the furlong marker but she didn't keep up the impetus until the line. Beaten by a better one on the day, she will probably race against fillies next time out, possibly in the Prix du Calvados.
Lixirova(FR), dropped out last in the early stages, was brought with a run on the outside and was putting in her best work at the finish. Not given too hard a time by her jockey, she will next be seen out in the Prix Morny.
Boltcity(FR), a strong colt, was a little disappointing considering his previous form. Waited with, he was outpaced from the 2f marker and just stayed on in the final stages. He is better than his performance suggests.

4580a PRIX ROTHSCHILD (EX PRIX D'ASTARTE) (GROUP 1) (FILLIES) (STRAIGHT) — 1m (R)

3:35 (3:37) 3-Y-0+ **£138,689** (£55,485; £27,743; £13,859; £6,942)

RPR

1 **Goldikova (IRE)**[25] 3749 4-9-0 OPeslier 7 — 124+
(F Head, France) *sn trcking pcemaker in 2nd: led 2f out: pushed 4l clr 1f out: eased last strides* **5/4**[1]

2 1 ½ **Elusive Wave (IRE)**[44] 3088 3-8-7 C-PLemaire 5 — 118
(J-C Rouget, France) *racd in 4th or 5th on ins: swtchd rt 2f out: wnt 2nd 1f out: styd on wl but nvr nr wnr* **7/1**[3]

3 3 **Proviso**[46] 3012 4-9-0 .... SPasquier 8 112
(A Fabre, France) *hld up in rr: hdwy and swtchd rt 1 1/2f out: str run between rivals to take 3rd last 50yds* **20/1**

4 ½ **Sahpresa (USA)**[49] 2953 4-9-0 .... CSoumillon 1 111+
(Rod Collet, France) *midfield on ins: kpt on u.p fnl 1 1/2f* **16/1**

5 ¾ **Eva's Request (IRE)**[25] 3749 4-9-0 .... TThulliez 6 109
(M R Channon) *racd in 3rd: disp 2nd 1 1/2f out to 1f out: one pce* **33/1**

6 ¾ **Reggane**[44] 3088 3-8-7 .... GMosse 2 107
(A De Royer-Dupre, France) *towards rr on ins: rdn over 1 1/2f out: kpt on at one pce* **9/2**[2]

7 snk **Lady Marian (GER)**[127] 1011 4-9-0 .... LDettori 4 107
(Saeed Bin Suroor) *hld up in rr: kpt on at one pce down outside fr 2f out* **10/1**

8 2 **Lahaleeb (IRE)**[44] 3088 3-8-7 .... DarryllHolland 11 102
(M R Channon) *midfield on outside: rdn over 2f out: no qckn* **16/1**

9 2½ **Danse Grecque (USA)**[66] 2428 4-9-0 .... ACrastus 9 97
(E Lellouche, France) *a towards rr* **25/1**

10 5 **Testama (FR)**[49] 2953 5-9-0 .... JAuge 3 85
(J De Roualle, France) *a in rr* **66/1**

11 nse **Only Green (IRE)**[21] 3908 3-8-7 .... (b) DBonilla 12 84
(F Head, France) *set str pce: rdn 2 1/2f out: hdd 2f out: wknd* **80/1**

12 ½ **Homebound (USA)**[63] 2521 3-8-7 .... IMendizabal 10 83
(J-C Rouget, France) *in tch: rdn over 2f out: sn btn* **17/2**

1m 35.7s (-5.30) **Going Correction** -0.30s/f (Firm)
WFA 3 from 4yo+ 7lb **12** Ran SP% **120.8**
Speed ratings: **114,112,109,109,108 107,107,105,102,97 97,97**
PARI-MUTUEL: WIN 1.90 (coupled with Only Green) 3.40; PL 1.30, 1.90, 5.90; DF 6.20.
Owner Wertheimer & Frere **Bred** Wertheimer Et Frere **Trained** France
■ Stewards' Enquiry : T Thulliez 300euro fine: careless riding

NOTEBOOK
Goldikova(IRE) put up a totally outstanding performance and had this Group 1 race sewn up by the 3f marker. Early on she had settled behind her pacemaker, who did a fine job. She took command a little over two out and then quickened impressively to be in an unassailable lead at the furlong marker, then just cruised to the line. She proved on this occasion she had definitely trained on and more Group 1 races look at her mercy. The next one will be the Prix Jacques Le Marois and the Breeders' Cup is the final target before she goes to stud. In between connections will be having a look at the Moulin de Longchamp, Queen Elizabeth II Stakes and the Sun Chariot.
Elusive Wave(IRE) was the only three-year-old in the first five and this Classic winner ran well up to expectations. She was behind the leading group early on but couldn't quicken like the winner at the two-furlong marker but was staying on at the end. She acts well on the straight course at Deauville and her trainer felt that this was the best performance of her career to date. She is in the Prix Maurice de Gheest and also the Matron and Sun Chariot Stakes.
Proviso put up a much better performance on a course that suits, having won a Group race on the track as a two-year-old. Held up towards the tail of the field in the early stages, she ran on really well in the final furlong, and if she holds this kind of form another Group race may come her way.
Sahpresa(USA) put up the best performance of her career to date and was running on at the finish. Connections may now have a look at the Prix Quincey over the straight mile later in the month, and she has also been entered in the Sun Chariot Stakes.
Eva's Request(IRE) was well away and in third place on the rail for much of the race, but she could only stay on at one pace throughout the final furlong and a half.
Lady Marian(GER) raced on the outside of the pack and mid-division before staying on one paced. The outing will have done her a power of good and she will be back at Deauville later in the month, as the Prix Jean Romanet is her next target.
Lahaleeb(IRE) raced on the outside of the field and had every chance halfway through the race, but just stayed on one paced throughout the final 2f.

4581a PRIX D'ENGLESQUEVILLE (CLAIMER) (C&G) (ALL-WEATHER) 7f 110y
4:40 (4:47) 3-Y-O **£10,194** (£4,077; £3,058; £2,039; £1,019)

RPR

1 **Key To The Stars (IRE)**[25] 3-8-5 .... WSaraiva(8) 73
(S Wattel, France)

2 1 **Diamond Twister (USA)**[17] 4004 3-9-2 .... MarcHalford 74
(J R Best) *racd in 2nd tl led 3f out: hdd 100yds out: no ex* **27/1**[1]

3 1 **Palmeral (IRE)**[308] 3-8-10 .... MickaelForest(3) 68
(J-C Rouget, France)

4 ¾ **Vera's Moscou (IRE)**[19] 3-9-2 .... TThulliez 69
(N Clement, France)

5 nk **Coronelli (FR)**[29] 3-8-9 .... CSoumillon 61
(C Lerner, France)

6 ¾ **Pure Land (FR)**[23] 3-8-9 .... DBonilla 60
(Mme E Augonnet, France)

7 hd **Stricke (FR)**[58] 3-8-13 .... FPrat 63
(Mme C Head-Maarek, France)

8 2 **Gold Music (FR)**[35] 3-9-4 .... EBureller 63
(J-L Pelletan, France)

9 2 **Piste Perdue**[89] 3-8-9 .... OPeslier 49
(Robert Collet, France)

10 15 **L'Arcobaleno (FR)** 3-8-9 .... (b) JVictoire 12
(J Rossi, France)

0 **Karanga (FR)**[19] 3-9-3 .... SPasquier —
(A Lyon, France)

0 **Royal Ranger (FR)** 3-9-2 .... GMasure —
(F-X De Chevigny, France)

1m 32.4s (92.40) **12** Ran SP% **3.6**
PARI-MUTUEL: WIN 10.40; PL 2.80, 6.20, 1.90; DF 108.40.
Owner E Pokrovsky & Mlle I Pinguet **Bred** Skymarc Farm Inc **Trained** France

NOTEBOOK
Diamond Twister(USA) made much of the running but couldn't hold the eventual winner inside the final furlong. It was a decent effort from this 27/1 chance.

4128 DUSSELDORF (R-H)
Sunday, August 2

OFFICIAL GOING: Good

4582a HENKEL-TROPHY (GROUP 2) 1m
3:05 (3:13) 3-Y-O+ **£38,835** (£10,194; £10,194; £3,883)

RPR

1 **King Of Sydney (USA)**[84] 1915 3-9-0 .... ASuborics 2 111
(Mario Hofer, Germany) *hld up in last: hdwy down outside to ld 150yds out: r.o wl* **16/5**[3]

2 ¾ **Aspectus (IRE)**[36] 3416 6-9-6 .... AStarke 3 109
(T Mundry, Germany) *a cl up: disp ld 1 1/2f out to 150yds out: one pce* **6/4**[1]

2 dht **Querari (GER)**[14] 4129 3-9-0 .... EPedroza 5 108
(A Wohler, Germany) *racd in 2nd: disp ld 1 1/2f out to 150yds out: one pce* **17/10**[2]

4 1¾ **Tertullus (FR)**[31] 6-9-6 .... EspenSki 6 105
(Rune Haugen, Norway) *hld up: hdwy on outside to press ldr appr fnl f: no ex* **68/10**

5 5 **Mharadono (GER)**[36] 3416 6-9-6 .... FilipMinarik 8 93
(P Hirschberger, Germany) *led to 1 1/2f out: wknd* **43/5**

6 1¼ **Four Dancers (GER)**[653] 6324 4-9-6 .... MSuerland 4 91
(Frau E Mader, Germany) *a bhd* **99/10**

1m 37.7s (-3.46)
WFA 3 from 4yo+ 7lb **6** Ran SP% **133.3**
(including 10 Euro stake): WIN 42; PL 17, 8 (A), 7 (Q); SF 53 (A),50 (Q).
Owner Hoffmeister & Hermann-Schmitt **Bred** E Melynk **Trained** Germany

4583a HENKEL PREIS DER DIANA (GERMAN OAKS) (GROUP 1) (FILLIES) 1m 3f
4:25 (4:33) 3-Y-O **£223,301** (£87,379; £43,689; £24,272; £9,709)

RPR

1 **Night Magic (GER)**[30] 3604 3-9-2 .... KKerekes 13 110
(W Figge, Germany) *mde all: drvn 6 l clr over 1f out: easily* **6/1**

2 4½ **Soberania (GER)**[42] 3201 3-9-2 .... MDemuro 12 101
(A Wohler, Germany) *towards rr: hdwy to go modest 2nd over 1 1/2f out: no ch w wnr* **28/1**

3 ½ **Andrea (GER)**[30] 3604 3-9-2 .... WMongil 6 100
(H Blume, Germany) *in rr tl kpt on fnl 2f* **45/1**

4 1 **Serienhoehe (IRE)**[42] 3-9-2 .... AStarke 5 99
(P Schiergen, Germany) *9th early: styd on at one pce down ins fnl 2f* **39/10**[2]

5 1 **Near Galante (GER)**[30] 3604 3-9-2 .... EPedroza 2 97
(A Wohler, Germany) *racd in 5th: one pce fnl 2f* **41/1**

6 ¾ **Nina Celebre (IRE)**[21] 3-9-2 .... FilipMinarik 9 96
(P Schiergen, Germany) *hld up in rr: sme late hdwy down outside* **37/1**

7 3 **All Annalena (IRE)**[21] 3-9-2 .... JiriPalik 14 91
(Andreas Lowe, Germany) *midfield: rdn and btn over 2f out* **19/1**

8 hd **Sworn Pro (GER)**[30] 3604 3-9-2 .... AHelfenbein 7 90
(Mario Hofer, Germany) *a towards rr* **153/10**

9 1¼ **Bolivia (GER)**[28] 3670 3-9-2 .... ASuborics 8 88
(W Hickst, Germany) *racd in 2nd: pushed along 4f out: wknd under 2f out* **53/10**[3]

10 ¾ **Forever Nadine (GER)**[25] 3-9-2 .... HGrewe 4 87
(Andreas Lowe, Germany) *midfield: rdn and wknd 2f out* **25/1**

11 10 **Quillaja (GER)**[30] 3604 3-9-2 .... THellier 10 70
(W Hickst, Germany) *a bhd* **163/10**

12 3½ **Anjella (GER)**[56] 2757 3-9-2 .... ADeVries 3 64
(J Hirschberger, Germany) *racd in 4th: wknd over 2f out* **189/10**

13 30 **Celimene (IRE)**[49] 2952 3-9-2 .... YLerner 1 13
(C Lerner, France) *racd in 3rd: wknd over 2f out* **11/10**[1]

2m 15.34s (34.18) **13** Ran SP% **134.6**
WIN 70; PL 24, 75, 76; SF 1337.
Owner Stall Salzburg **Bred** Gestut Etzean **Trained** Germany

LA TESTE DE BUCH (R-H)
Sunday, August 2

OFFICIAL GOING: Soft

4584a CRITERIUM DU BEQUET (LISTED RACE) 6f
3:00 (12:00) 2-Y-O **£26,699** (£10,680; £8,010; £5,340; £2,670)

RPR

1 **Chantilly Creme (USA)**[28] 3667 2-8-13 .... RonanThomas 6 98
(R Gibson, France) **27/10**[1]

2 ¾ **Virginia Hall**[12] 4173 2-8-13 .... J-BEyquem 5 96
(Sir Mark Prescott)

3 2½ **Evaporation (FR)**[44] 2-8-13 .... GBenoist 8 88
(C Laffon-Parias, France)

4 1½ **Blue Panis (FR)**[28] 3667 2-9-2 .... THuet 2 87
(F Chappet, France)

5 1½ **Bellaside (IRE)** 2-8-13 .... J-LMartinezTejera 3 79
(E Leon Penate, Spain)

6 2 **Mon Nono (IRE)**[46] 3044 2-9-2 .... DMichaux 1 76
(Mlle A Imaz-Ceca, France)

7 8 **Foresta (FR)**[19] 3967 2-8-13 .... JMartin 7 49
(B De Montzey, France)

8 4 **M'Oubliez Pas (USA)**[28] 2-8-13 .... FBlondel 4 37
(J-C Rouget, France)

1m 12.1s (72.10) **8** Ran SP% **27.0**
(including 1 Euro stake): WIN 3.70; PL 1.60, 1.40, 1.60; DF 5.60.
Owner L B Robbins **Bred** Azalea Stables **Trained** Lamorlaye, France

NOTEBOOK
Virginia Hall, always well up, went to the head of affairs at the entrance to the straight and looked the likely winner, but in the end she couldn't hold the challenge of the winner, who had previously been runner-up in a Group 3 event.

KLAMPENBORG
Sunday, August 2

OFFICIAL GOING: Good to firm

4585a SCANDINAVIAN OPEN CHAMPIONSHIP (GROUP 3) 1m 4f
3:25 (12:00) 3-Y-O+ **£38,961** (£12,987; £6,494; £3,896; £2,597)

RPR

1 **Peas And Carrots (DEN)**[35] 6-9-4 .... FJohansson 10 101
(L Reuterskiold Jr, Sweden) **19/10**[1]

2 ½ **Chinese Mandarin (USA)**[308] 6-9-4 .... LennartHammer-Hansen 2 100
(E Van Doorn, Sweden) **2/1**[2]

3 ¾ **Luca Brasi (FR)**[31] 5-9-2 ManuelMartinez 3 97
(F Castro, Sweden) **7/1**
4 ¾ **Django (SWE)**[308] 6-9-2 MLarsen 5 96
(Jessica Long, Denmark) **54/10**[3]
5 1 ½ **Classical World (USA)**[35] 4-9-2 AnnNielsen 4 93
(T Christensen, Denmark) **25/1**
6 hd **St Jean Cap Ferrat**[30] 3578 4-9-2 (b) NicolajStott 9 93
(S Jensen, Denmark) **12/1**
7 ½ **Marron (DEN)**[770] 5-9-2 RSchistl 11 92
(S Jensen, Denmark) **30/1**
8 2 **Alnitak (USA)**[31] 8-9-2 (b) FDiaz 8 89
(B Olsen, Denmark) **25/1**
9 4 **Itsagroom (SWE)**[357] 4918 4-9-2 DinaDanekilde 7 83
(Karola Larsson, Sweden) **23/1**
10 5 **Volo Cat (FR)**[31] 5-9-2 JacobJohansen 1 75
(B Olsen, Denmark) **27/1**
11 6 **Dan Tucket**[35] 4-9-2 KAndersen 6 65
(B Olsen, Denmark) **31/1**

2m 29.8s (1.00) **11** Ran SP% **125.4**
WIN: 2.86, PL: 1.36, 1.46, 2.19 SF 6.80.
Owner O Zawawi **Bred** Havreholms Stutteri **Trained** Sweden

LES LANDES
Sunday, August 2
OFFICIAL GOING: Good to soft

4586a ENTWHISTLE'S OF GOREY FISH & CHIPS H'CAP 5f 110y
3:05 (3:10) 3-Y-0+ **£1,000** (£550; £300)

RPR
1 **High Voltage**[14] 8-10-12 (tp) VinceSlattery 4 —
(Mrs J L Le Brocq, Jersey) **2/1**[2]
2 shd **Top Pursuit**[14] 7-8-12 PaulQuinn 3 —
(Ms V S Lucas, Jersey) **4/1**
3 6 **Toggle**[14] 5-9-3 MattieBatchelor 5 —
(Ms V S Lucas, Jersey) **4/1**
4 2 **Majestical (IRE)**[14] 7-9-5 AntonyProcter 7 —
(J S O Arthur, Jersey) **1/1**[1]
5 8 **Perfect Portrait**[14] 9-8-9 (b) KylieManser 6 —
(Mrs A Malzard, Jersey) **15/2**
6 3 **Highland Flight**[14] 11-9-10 AmyBaker 8 —
(J S O Arthur, Jersey) **2/1**[2]
7 4 **Rope Bridge (IRE)**[476] 4-10-0 MrRJKirk 1 —
(Mrs J L Le Brocq, Jersey) **12/1**
P **Talamahana**[10] 4222 4-9-3 (v) EmmettStack 2 —
(A B Haynes) **11/4**[3]

1m 10.0s (70.00) **8** Ran SP% **202.8**

Owner Mrs J L Le Brocq **Bred** D P Martin **Trained** St Peters, Jersey

4587a LES LANDES H'CAP 1m 6f
4:50 (5:01) 3-Y-0+ **£1,000** (£550; £300)

RPR
1 **Crystal Reign (IRE)**[14] 4-10-10 EmmettStack 7 —
(Mrs J L Le Brocq, Jersey) **10/3**[3]
2 10 **Snow Lark**[14] 11-8-9 PaulQuinn 5 —
(Ms V S Lucas, Jersey) **11/4**[2]
3 hd **Hassadin**[59] 2635 3-10-12 VinceSlattery 3 —
(A B Haynes) **10/3**[3]
4 3 ½ **Silver Silence (JPN)**[14] 8-10-8 (tp) AntonyProcter 2 —
(J S O Arthur, Jersey) **7/4**[1]
5 5 **Cronkyvoddy**[14] 8-9-9 KylieManser 4 —
(Mrs A Malzard, Jersey) **9/2**
6 3 ½ **Slickdalay (IRE)**[90] 5-10-8 (b) AdamJones 6 —
(Mrs A Malzard, Jersey) **10/1**

3m 35.0s (215.00)
WFA 3 from 4yo+ 13lb **6** Ran SP% **136.5**

Owner A Le Brocq & Messrs Le Brocq **Bred** Holborn Trust Co **Trained** St Peters, Jersey

4342 CARLISLE (R-H)
Monday, August 3
OFFICIAL GOING: Good (good to soft in places) changing to good after race 4 (7.15)
Rail on Old Stable Bend moved out 5m from inside running line but impact on distances not quantified.
Wind: moderate 1/2 against Weather: overcast, breezy

4588 LLOYD MINI 50TH BIRTHDAY LADY AMATEUR RIDERS' H'CAP 7f 200y
5:45 (5:46) (Class 5) (0-70,75) 3-Y-0+ **£2,498** (£774; £387; £193) **Stalls** High

Form RPR
4021 1 **Moody Tunes**[8] 4344 6-10-11 **75** 6ex MissLEBurke(5) 3 85
(A P Jarvis) *chsd ldrs: edgd rt bnd over 4f out: styd on strly* **8/1**
0000 2 3 ¼ **Emperor's Well**[5] 4435 10-9-1 **51** MissJoannaMason(5) 15 54
(M W Easterby) *prom: outpcd over 4f out: hdwy to chse ldrs over 2f out: styd on to take 2nd ins fnl f: no imp* **12/1**
3320 3 3 **Silly Gilly (IRE)**[14] 4140 5-9-9 **59** MissVBarr(5) 9 55
(R E Barr) *w ldrs: kpt on same pce appr fnl f* **11/2**[1]
-524 4 ½ **Rain Stops Play (IRE)**[45] 3092 7-9-0 **50** oh2 MissJRRichards(5) 11 44
(N G Richards) *trckd ldrs: t.k.h: hmpd bnd over 4f out: kpt on same pce fnl 2f* **8/1**
4506 5 ¾ **Grethel (IRE)**[3] 4495 5-9-5 **50** oh3 MrsCBartley 1 43
(A Berry) *in rr: hdwy and swtchd outside over 2f out: kpt on: nt rch ldrs* **14/1**
00-0 6 hd **Second Reef**[23] 3852 7-9-0 **50** oh5 MissHCuthbert(5) 13 42
(T A K Cuthbert) *mid-div: hdwy over 2f out: one pce* **100/1**
421 7 3 **Winrob**[10] 4279 3-9-2 **57** MissCJMacmahon(3) 16 42
(Patrick Morris) *chsd ldrs: wknd appr fnl f* **7/1**[3]
3616 8 nk **Not Now Lewis (IRE)**[9] 4313 5-9-9 **57** MissGAndrews(3) 5 42
(F P Murtagh) *in tch: effrt on outer 3f out: edgd rt over 1f out: one pce* **9/1**
0000 9 ½ **Oddsmaker (IRE)**[65] 2499 8-9-7 **57** (t) MissAngelaBarnes(5) 12 41
(M A Barnes) *mde most tl wl over 1f out: grad wknd* **20/1**
-000 10 hd **Wednesdays Boy (IRE)**[14] 4144 6-9-5 **50** (p) MissADeniel 6 33
(P D Niven) *in rr: sn drvn along: kpt on fnl 2f: nvr on terms* **16/1**
3204 11 6 **Know By Now**[45] 3120 3-9-12 **69** MissKECooper(5) 4 38
(T P Tate) *chsd ldrs: hmpd and lost pl bnd: over 4f out: sn bhd* **12/1**
0-00 12 4 ½ **Uhuru Peak**[23] 3863 8-9-7 **52** (bt) MissSBrotherton 10 11
(M W Easterby) *in tch: lost pl over 1f out* **12/1**
000 13 1 ¾ **Rainbow Zest**[8] 4351 6-9-13 **58** MissLHorner 2 13
(W Storey) *s.i.s: hdwy on wd outside 4f out: lost pl 2f out* **50/1**
0-00 14 hd **Scotty's Future (IRE)**[6] 4402 11-8-12 **50** oh3 MissSarahRichardson(7) 17 4
(A Berry) *stl had hood on whn stalls opened: s.v.s: a bhd* **100/1**
105- 15 ¾ **Wizard Of Us**[380] 779 9-9-0 **50** oh2 MissMMullineaux(5) 14 3
(M Mullineaux) *dwlt: a in rr* **22/1**
2306 16 ¾ **Carpe Diem**[27] 3710 4-9-5 **55** ow2 (p) MrsVFahey(5) 8 6
(R A Fahey) *in rr: effrt on outside over 3f out: sn lost pl* **6/1**[2]

1m 44.03s (4.03) **Going Correction** +0.375s/f (Good)
WFA 3 from 4yo+ 7lb **16** Ran SP% **123.1**
Speed ratings (Par 103): **94,90,87,87,86 86,83,83,82,82 76,71,70,69,69 68**
toteswingers: 1&2 £37.40, 1&3 £8.40, 2&3 £31.20 CSF £97.53 CT £608.54 TOTE £7.00: £1.80, £3.30, £1.50, £2.70; EX 141.70.
Owner Geoffrey Hamilton **Bred** Llety Stud **Trained** Middleham Moor, N Yorks
■ Alan Jarvis's first winner since taking over at Spigot Lodge from his son-on-law Karl Burke, who has been banned.
■ Stewards' Enquiry : Miss L E Burke three-day ban: careless riding (Aug 19, 24, 29)

FOCUS
The running rail on the old stable bend was moved out 5m from the inside running line. These amateurs varied significantly in riding ability and this is form to treat with a little caution. The pace seemed strong and they were all over the track in the straight, with the main action taking place up the middle. Modest form, clouded by the sixth, with the winner rated to last year's best.
Rainbow Zest Official explanation: jockey said gelding had a breathing problem
Scotty's Future(IRE) Official explanation: jockey said gelding missed the break after difficult removing the blindfold

4589 NIGEL BROWN FROM ASPATRIA 50TH BIRTHDAY CLAIMING STKS 7f 200y
6:15 (6:17) (Class 6) 3-Y-O **£2,047** (£604; £302) **Stalls** High

Form RPR
5266 1 **Diggeratt (USA)**[14] 4140 3-8-7 **73** PaulHanagan 3 70
(R A Fahey) *led 1f: chsd ldrs: hdwy on ins to ld over 2f out: hung bdly lft: styd on fnl f* **5/6**[1]
405 2 3 ½ **Jill Le Brocq**[25] 3764 3-8-6 **50** (b[1]) PJMcDonald 1 61
(M Dods) *trckd ldrs: upsides over qf out: kpt on same pce* **16/1**[3]
0506 3 13 **Hawkleaf Flier (IRE)**[55] 2790 3-8-2 **47** (b[1]) DuranFentiman 2 27
(T D Easterby) *dwlt: hdwy to chse ldrs after 3f: wknd over 1f out* **10/1**[2]
-000 4 1 ¾ **Our Apolonia (IRE)**[16] 4105 3-8-0 **45** BillyCray(7) 4 28
(A Berry) *dwlt: outpcd and lost pl after 3f: sme hdwy over 2f out: wknd appr fnl f* **50/1**
4-0 5 ½ **Artesium**[38] 3336 3-7-12 **55** JamesPSullivan(7) 6 25
(Patrick Morris) *led after 1f: hdd and sltly hmpd over 2f out: wknd over 1f out* **25/1**

1m 44.25s (4.25) **Going Correction** +0.375s/f (Good) **5** Ran SP% **75.3**
Speed ratings (Par 98): **93,89,76,74,74**
CSF £4.27 TOTE £1.20: £1.10, £2.20; EX 4.00.
Owner J A Rattigan **Bred** Hobby Horse Farm Inc **Trained** Musley Bank, N Yorks
■ Just Five was withdrawn (6/4, very unruly in stalls). Deduct 40p in the £ under R4.
■ Stewards' Enquiry : Paul Hanagan caution: careless riding

FOCUS
This claimer was weakened by the late withdrawal of Just Five. The time was slow and this is unconvincing form.

4590 CARLISLE LIVING MAIDEN AUCTION STKS 5f 193y
6:45 (6:46) (Class 5) 2-Y-O **£2,590** (£770; £385; £192) **Stalls** High

Form RPR
1 **Mr Grinch (IRE)** 2-8-13 **0** PhillipMakin 7 70
(M Dods) *dwlt: stdy hdwy over 2f out: led 1f out: hld on towards fin* **10/1**
0 2 hd **Jozafeen**[28] 3686 2-8-4 **0** GregFairley 4 61
(R Bastiman) *in rr: drvn over 2f out: hdwy and c wd appr fnl f: upsides ins fnl f: no ex nr fin* **11/1**
0 3 3 ¼ **Coolella (IRE)**[17] 4067 2-8-1 **0** JamieKyne(5) 1 53
(J R Weymes) *chsd ldrs: hmpd and lost pl over 3f out: hdwy over 2f out: kpt on same pce fnl f* **18/1**
426 4 2 ¼ **Saint Sebastian (IRE)**[20] 3937 2-8-10 **0** GrahamGibbons 3 50
(E S McMahon) *chsd ldrs: wknd ins fnl f* **11/4**[1]
5 3 **Pavement Games** 2-8-5 **0** FrancisNorton 11 36
(R C Guest) *dwlt: in rr: kpt on fnl 2f: nvr nr ldrs* **28/1**
052 6 2 ½ **Clever Molly (IRE)**[18] 4011 2-8-4 **0** PaulQuinn 5 28
(E J Alston) *chsd ldr: bdly hmpd on ins and lost pl over 3f out: hdwy and nt clr run appr fnl f: sn wknd* **4/1**[3]
02 7 ½ **Pink Lemonade (IRE)**[4] 4463 2-8-4 **0** PaulHanagan 10 26
(John Joseph Murphy, Ire) *led: edgd lft over 2f out: hdd & wknd 1f out* **10/3**[2]
8 2 ¾ **I'm Super Too (IRE)** 2-8-11 **0** PJMcDonald 8 25
(G A Swinbank) *s.i.s: hdwy to chse ldrs 3f out: hung rt and lost pl over 1f out* **11/2**
4063 9 ¾ **Lord's Seat**[8] 4342 2-8-9 **0** TomEaves 6 21
(A Berry) *mid-div: drvn 3f out: lost pl over 1f out* **40/1**
10 4 **Antonius Park (IRE)** 2-8-0 **0** MartinLane(5) 2 5
(Rodger Sweeney, Ire) *trckd ldrs: chal over 1f out: sn wknd* **20/1**

1m 16.99s (3.29) **Going Correction** +0.375s/f (Good) **10** Ran SP% **118.5**
Speed ratings (Par 94): **93,92,88,85,81 78,77,73,72,67**
toteswingers: 1&2 £19.60, 1&3 £25.70, 2&3 £47.70 CSF £112.91 TOTE £13.20: £2.70, £3.60, £3.70; EX 102.00.
Owner M J K Dods **Bred** Bluegate Stud **Trained** Denton, Co Durham

FOCUS
This looked a modest juvenile maiden and the first two came from well off the pace, suggesting the early gallop might have been overly quick. They raced towards the stands' side in the straight.

NOTEBOOK
Mr Grinch(IRE), a 12,500gns already gelded half-brother to a few middle-distance winners, did well to make a winning debut considering he was noticeably green and had to concede weight all round. Although soon niggled along after starting slowly, he gradually got the idea and picked up nicely on the rising ground in the straight. He showed a good attitude when strongly challenged late on and, although this form probably doesn't amount to much, this was a pleasing start considering he's bred to want further. (tchd 9-1)

Jozafeen stepped up massively on the form she showed on her debut at Ripon, pulling clear of the remainder in second. (op 8-1)
Coolella(IRE) was slightly checked in her run about 3f out, but it made no difference to her finishing position. She's going the right way. (op 20-1)
Saint Sebastian(IRE) has yet to confirm the ability he showed at Leicester on his second start and has now been a beaten favourite on his last three outings. He's probably little better than selling class. (tchd 7-2)
Pavement Games, a £3,800 first foal of a winner over 6f and 1m3f, looked as though the run would bring her on but she showed ability keeping on late after missing the break. (op 25-1 tchd 33-1)
Clever Molly(IRE) is a fair bit better than her finishing position suggests. She was badly hampered by Pink Lemonade against the near rail entering the straight, just as she was beginning to aim for an ambitious gap, and she was then blocked in her run again a furlong out. (op 9-2 tchd 5-1)
Pink Lemonade(IRE) had to be niggled to hold the lead from an early stage and never looked happy. (op 9-2 tchd 3-1)
I'm Super Too(IRE), already gelded, attracted support on his debut but looked as though the run would do him good and ruined his chance by hanging right in the straight. (op 13-2 tchd 5-1)

4591 EDINBURGH WOOLLEN MILL H'CAP — 6f 192y
7:15 (7:15) (Class 4) (0-85,84) 3-Y-O — **£6,476** (£1,927; £963; £481) **Stalls** High

Form — RPR
4335 **1** **Inheritor (IRE)**30 3643 3-9-2 **79** .... TomEaves 6 — 87
(B Smart) *trckd ldrs: led over 1f out: hld on wl* — **9/2**
4111 **2** 1 1/2 **Legal Legacy**38 3341 3-9-3 **80** .... PhillipMakin 1 — 84
(M Dods) *trckd ldrs: chal over 1f out: no ex wl ins fnl f* — **3/1**1
5316 **3** hd **Kammaan**24 3804 3-9-1 **78** .... PhilipRobinson 3 — 81
(M A Jarvis) *in rr: effrt on outer over 2f out: chal towards centre jst ins fnl f: kpt on same pce* — **7/2**2
1001 **4** 2 1/4 **Spinners End (IRE)**9 4326 3-9-7 **84** .... AndrewElliott 4 — 81
(A P Jarvis) *led: qcknd over 3f out: hrd rdn and edgd lft 2f out: sn hdd: wknd towards fin* — **10/1**
4514 **5** 2 1/2 **Rising Kheleyf (IRE)**14 4140 3-8-10 **73** .... PJMcDonald 5 — 64
(G A Swinbank) *chsd ldrs: wknd fnl f* — **15/2**
3164 **6** 1 1/2 **Kersivay**35 3455 3-8-12 **75** .... TonyHamilton 8 — 62
(Ollie Pears) *mid-div: styd to r upsides over 1f out: wknd jst ins fnl f* — **33/1**
0455 **7** 11 **Lakeman (IRE)**9 4309 3-8-7 **70** ....(v1) GregFairley 2 — 27
(B Ellison) *chsd ldrs: lost pl over 1f out: sn bhd* — **16/1**
5022 **8** 1 1/4 **Fathey (IRE)**8 4346 3-8-2 **65** .... PaulHanagan 7 — 19
(R A Fahey) *restless in stalls: s.s: bhd: sme hdwy over 2f out: wknd over 1f out: sn bhd* — **4/1**3

1m 29.28s (2.18) **Going Correction** +0.375s/f (Good) — **8** Ran SP% **115.1**
Speed ratings (Par 102): **102,100,100,97,94 92,80,78**
toteswingers: 1&2 £3.10, 1&3 £5.80, 2&3 £3.40 CSF £18.56 CT £52.36 TOTE £5.60: £1.80, £1.60, £1.60; EX 25.80.
Owner Richard Page **Bred** Dominic O'Neill And Julie White **Trained** Hambleton, N Yorks

FOCUS
Following this race the ground was changed to good. This was a fair handicap for the grade with slight personal bests from the first two. They gradually edged towards the stands' side in the straight and the winner had the benefit of the rail late on.
Fathey(IRE) Official explanation: jockey said gelding missed the break

4592 BEADLE & HILL H'CAP — 6f 192y
7:45 (7:46) (Class 4) (0-85,84) 4-Y-O+ — **£4,727** (£1,406; £702; £351) **Stalls** High

Form — RPR
1305 **1** **Captain Macarry (IRE)**31 3560 4-9-3 **80** ....(v) TomEaves 4 — 96
(B Smart) *chsd ldrs: styd on to ld ins fnl f: drew clr* — **12/1**
0600 **2** 3 3/4 **Billy Dane (IRE)**23 3872 5-9-1 **83** .... JamieKyne(5) 10 — 89
(F P Murtagh) *trckd ldr: effrt over 2f out: led over 1f out: edgd rt and hdd ins fnl f: no imp* — **6/1**3
5014 **3** 2 1/2 **Smarty Socks (IRE)**9 4310 5-9-7 **84** .... TonyCulhane 11 — 83+
(P T Midgley) *detached in last: hdwy over 2f out: kpt on: nvr rchd ldrs* — **7/1**
0061 **4** 3 **Timber Treasure (USA)**8 4346 5-8-5 **73** 6ex........ MartinLane(5) 6 — 64
(Paul Green) *hld up in midfield: effrt on outside over 2f out: kpt on fnl f: nvr a threat* — **7/1**
4243 **5** nk **Ancient Cross**48 2998 5-7-10 **66** ....(bt) JamesPSullivan(7) 1 — 56
(M W Easterby) *in rr: effrt on outside over 2f out: nvr nr ldrs* — **3/1**1
2106 **6** 3 **Miss Glitters (IRE)**33 3509 4-8-13 **76** .... TravisBlock 8 — 58
(H Morrison) *drvn early in rr: sme hdwy over 2f out: wknd over 1f out* — **7/2**2
646 **7** 6 **Jewelled Dagger (IRE)**45 3097 5-9-5 **82** ....(b) PaulHanagan 9 — 48
(I Semple) *led tl hdd over 1f out: sn wknd* — **14/1**
0204 **8** 1 3/4 **Hiccups**8 4344 9-8-11 **74** .... PhillipMakin 7 — 35
(M Dods) *hld up in midfield: effrt on outside over 2f out: lost pl over 1f out* — **9/1**
30 **9** 8 **Navajo Joe (IRE)**67 2402 4-8-6 **69** ....(bt) GrahamGibbons 2 — 8
(R Johnson) *chsd ldrs: lost pl over 2f out* — **25/1**

1m 28.51s (1.41) **Going Correction** +0.375s/f (Good) — **9** Ran SP% **114.7**
Speed ratings (Par 105): **106,101,98,95,95 91,84,82,73**
toteswingers: 1&2 £8.80, 1&3 £8.00, 2&3 £9.70 CSF £81.45 CT £551.56 TOTE £16.50: £3.70, £2.70, £2.30; EX 108.70.
Owner Anthony D Gee **Bred** Humphrey Okeke **Trained** Hambleton, N Yorks

FOCUS
A fair handicap run at a very strong pace. They raced middle to far side in the straight. The winner is inconsistent but this form has been rated at face value.

4593 CHAMPAGNE LANSON H'CAP — 1m 3f 107y
8:15 (8:16) (Class 6) (0-60,60) 3-Y-O+ — **£2,047** (£604; £302) **Stalls** Low

Form — RPR
5505 **1** **Golden Future**12 4193 6-9-3 **49** .... TomEaves 6 — 58
(P D Niven) *w ldr: led after 3f: qcknd 4f out: kpt on wl fnl f* — **8/1**2
0254 **2** 1 1/4 **Shekan Star**20 3943 7-9-5 **51** .... PaulHanagan 10 — 58
(K G Reveley) *hld up in midfield: drvn and hdwy 3f out: styd on to take 2nd towards fin* — **4/1**1
0- **3** hd **Summercove (IRE)**18 4025 4-8-8 **47** ....(b) JamesPSullivan(7) 9 — 54
(John Joseph Murphy, Ire) *hld up towards rr: hdwy on ins over 3f out: styd on fnl f* — **8/1**2
3534 **4** 3/4 **Cheers For Thea (IRE)**17 4068 4-9-9 **55** .... DavidAllan 2 — 60
(T D Easterby) *chsd ldrs: wnt 2nd after 4f: chal over 2f out: one pce fnl f* — **4/1**1
5050 **5** 4 **Key Of Fortune (IRE)**69 2350 3-8-10 **52** .... FrancisNorton 5 — 51
(Jennie Candlish) *trckd ldrs: effrt over 2f out: wknd fnl f* — **8/1**2
46 **6** 3/4 **Louisa (GER)**8 4345 5-9-12 **58** .... TonyHamilton 7 — 56
(P Monteith) *led 3f: chsd ldrs: one pce fnl 2f* — **10/1**3
1150 **7** 2 1/4 **World Of Choice (USA)**21 3923 4-9-12 **58** ....(b) DaleGibson 1 — 52
(M W Easterby) *hld up in mid-div: drvn over 3f out: no imp* — **12/1**
0006 **8** 6 **Lady Anne Nevill**6 4403 5-8-11 **46** oh1........ KellyHarrison(3) 8 — 31
(C W Fairhurst) *in rr: drvn over 3f out: nvr on terms* — **14/1**
04-4 **9** 3/4 **Gulnaz**13 4170 4-8-7 **46** oh1........ BillyCray(7) 3 — 29
(Mrs G S Rees) *in rr: effrt over 3f out: hung lft and lost pl over 1f out* — **22/1**
0-04 **10** 7 **Kames Park (IRE)**31 3561 7-10-0 **60** .... PhillipMakin 4 — 32
(R C Guest) *s.i.s: effrt on outside over 2f out: sn wknd* — **8/1**2

2m 29.99s (6.89) **Going Correction** +0.375s/f (Good)
WFA 3 from 4yo+ 10lb — **10** Ran SP% **112.2**
Speed ratings (Par 101): **89,88,87,87,84 83,82,77,77,72**
toteswingers: 1&2 £13.30, 1&3 £5.30, 2&3 £7.20 CSF £36.85 CT £231.14 TOTE £9.80: £2.90, £2.00, £2.10; EX 37.80.
Owner The Little Ice Club **Bred** Larksborough Stud Limited **Trained** Barton-le-Street, N Yorks
■ Drumadoon Bay was withdrawn (14/1, very unruly in stalls). R4 applies, deduct 5p in the £.

FOCUS
A very moderate handicap but the form is sound.

4594 DEBENHAMS H'CAP — 5f 193y
8:45 (8:45) (Class 6) (0-60,60) 3-Y-O — **£2,047** (£604; £302) **Stalls** High

Form — RPR
6202 **1** **It's A Mans World**2 4552 3-8-8 **55** ....(v) BMcHugh(5) 3 — 65
(K M Prendergast) *dwlt: in rr: hdwy on outside over 2f out: bmpd over 1f out: led ins fnl f: styd on wl* — **2/1**1
0666 **2** 2 1/4 **Two Turtle Doves (IRE)**20 3939 3-8-13 **55** .... GregFairley 8 — 58
(M Mullineaux) *chsd ldrs: kpt on to take 2nd ins fnl f: no ex* — **16/1**
3060 **3** 3 3/4 **Lucky Buddha**26 3729 3-8-13 **55** .... TonyHamilton 10 — 46
(Jedd O'Keeffe) *hld up: effrt over 2f out: kpt on same pce fnl f* — **10/1**
0000 **4** 2 1/4 **Bold Bomber**29 3651 3-8-8 **50** .... SilvestreDeSousa 6 — 34
(Paul Green) *mid-div: hdwy and edged lft over 1f out: one pce* — **6/1**3
0050 **5** 1/2 **Port Ronan (USA)**20 3938 3-8-1 **48** ....(p) JamieKyne(5) 1 — 30
(J S Wainwright) *chsd ldrs: kpt on same pce over 1f out* — **16/1**
5210 **6** 1/2 **Hawkeyethenoo (IRE)**13 4171 3-8-7 **56** ....(b) JamesPSullivan(7) 5 — 37
(M W Easterby) *chsd ldrs: led over 2f out: hdd ins fnl f: wknd* — **4/1**2
5650 **7** 5 **Scotch And Soda (IRE)**17 4070 3-8-8 **50** .... PJMcDonald 9 — 15
(Jedd O'Keeffe) *mid-div: effrt over 2f out: nvr on terms* — **33/1**
6000 **8** hd **Fitzolini**26 3727 3-9-4 **60** ....(p) TomEaves 2 — 24
(A D Brown) *led tl over 2f out: lost pl over 1f out* — **20/1**
0003 **9** 1 1/2 **Meydan Groove**18 4016 3-7-11 **46** oh1........ MatthewLawson(7) 4 — 5
(R Johnson) *in rr: sme hdwy on outside over 2f out: lost pl over 1f out* — **12/1**
-064 **10** 9 **Nino Zachetti (IRE)**16 4105 3-8-5 **47** .... PaulQuinn 7 — —
(E J Alston) *chsd ldrs: lost pl over 1f out: sn bhd* — **7/1**

1m 15.09s (1.39) **Going Correction** +0.20s/f (Good) — **10** Ran SP% **116.4**
Speed ratings (Par 98): **98,95,90,87,86 85,79,78,76,64**
toteswingers: 1&2 £9.40, 1&3 £6.80, 2&3 £28.90 CSF £37.94 CT £272.14 TOTE £3.00: £1.40, £4.90, £3.20; EX 40.30 Place 6: £278.77 Place 5: £117.41.
Owner Alchemy Bloodstock **Bred** Cheveley Park Stud Ltd **Trained** Sellack, H'fords
■ Stewards' Enquiry : Silvestre De Sousa two-day ban: used whip without giving mount time to respond (Aug 17, 19)

FOCUS
A dire sprint handicap in which they raced middle to stands' side in the straight. It was quite strongly run and the form is sound.
T/Plt: £319.10 to a £1 stake. Pool: £56,467.95. 129.15 winning tickets. T/Qpdt: £389.30 to a £1 stake. Pool: £4,840.10. 9.20 winning tickets. WG

4100 RIPON (R-H)
Monday, August 3

OFFICIAL GOING: Good (7.7)
Rail on bend from back straight to home straight moved out from innermost position but impact on distances not quantified.
Wind: Virtually nil Weather: Dry and sunny

4595 E B F CHILDREN'S DAY MAIDEN STKS — 6f
2:15 (2:17) (Class 5) 2-Y-O — **£4,209** (£1,252; £625; £312) **Stalls** Low

Form — RPR
3342 **1** **Makbullet**12 4187 2-9-0 0........ FrederikTylicki(3) 1 — 79+
(J Howard Johnson) *trckd ldr: hdwy 1/2-way: led 2f out: rdn clr appr fnl f: styd on* — **7/4**1
62 **2** 3 3/4 **Mad Millie (IRE)**10 4278 2-8-12 0........ GrahamGibbons 2 — 63+
(J Hetherton) *wnt bdly rt s: sn led: rdn along and hdd 2f out: sn drvn and kpt on: no ch w wnr* — **4/1**3
20 **3** 2 **We'll Deal Again**24 3823 2-8-10 0........ JamesPSullivan(7) 8 — 62
(M W Easterby) *towards rr: hdwy over 2f out: rdn wl over 1f out: styd on appr fnl f: nrst fin* — **7/1**
4 **4** 1 3/4 **Cross Key (IRE)**16 4100 2-8-12 0........ PaulHanagan 7 — 52
(R A Fahey) *midfield and rdn along 1/2-way: swtchd lft 2f out: styd on appr fnl f: nrst fin* — **7/1**
06 **5** 3/4 **Dinkys Diamond (IRE)**9 4308 2-8-12 0........ LanceBetts(5) 5 — 54
(B Ellison) *chsd ldng pair: rdn along over 2f out: sn drvn and plugged on same pce* — **100/1**
6 1 **Lava Lamp (GER)** 2-9-3 0........ GregFairley 6 — 51
(M Johnston) *hmpd s and sn rdn along: a towards rr* — **16/1**
7 1/2 **Royal Holiday (IRE)** 2-9-3 0........ TomEaves 9 — 50
(B Ellison) *chsd ldrs: rdn along 1/2-way: sn drvn and wknd 2f out* — **50/1**
6 **8** 2 3/4 **Al Adham**11 4233 2-9-3 0........ TedDurcan 4 — 42
(Saeed Bin Suroor) *hmpd s: sn swtchd lft and hdwy to trck ldrs: swtchd rt and effrt to chse ldng pair 1/2-way: rdn 2f out: sn edgd rt and wknd qckly over 1f out* — **7/2**2
6 **9** nk **Labretella (IRE)**7 4383 2-8-12 0........ TPQueally 10 — 36
(M H Tompkins) *s.i.s: a in rr* — **12/1**
0 **10** hd **Newtons Cradle (IRE)**24 3823 2-9-3 0........ TonyHamilton 3 — 40
(J Howard Johnson) *hmpd s: a in rr* — **100/1**

1m 14.16s (1.16) **Going Correction** +0.025s/f (Good) — **10** Ran SP% **118.1**
Speed ratings (Par 94): **93,88,85,83,82 80,80,76,75,75**
toteswingers: 1&2 £2.30, 1&3 £4.50, 2&3 £6.90 CSF £10.24 TOTE £2.60: £1.10, £1.60, £2.70; EX 10.20 Trifecta £50.20 Pool: £656.51 - 9.67 winning units..
Owner Transcend Bloodstock LLP **Bred** Longdon Stud Ltd **Trained** Billy Row, Co Durham

FOCUS
A modest juvenile maiden, run at a sound pace. Improved form from the winner.

NOTEBOOK
Makbullet was again well backed and rewarded his supporters at the fifth attempt. He took it up nearing the 2f marker and soon had matters in control. This is his optimum trip and he ought to be high on confidence now, but will need to improve in order to win a nursery, as the handicapper really knows all about him. (op 11-4)
Mad Millie(IRE) bounced out and grabbed the stands' rail, setting a nice pace. She was outclassed by the winner, but kept on resolutely and is a fair performer. A stiffer 6f will probably prove ideal in the short term and she now qualifies for nurseries. (tchd 7-2 and 9-2)

We'll Deal Again ◆ took time to settle and was running on too late in the day from off the pace. A more positive ride on this drop back in distance would have likely suited better and he should fare better now he has the option of nurseries. (op 8-1 tchd 9-1)

Cross Key(IRE) was ridden to get the extra furlong and again looked green. She should go forward for the experience and needs one more run before becoming eligible for the nursery route. (op 6-1 tchd 11-2)

Al Adham did not really act around Epsom on his debut, but this switch to a more conventional track failed to do the trick and he dropped out tamely nearing the final furlong. Perhaps the run came too soon. Official explanation: jockey said colt had no more to give (tchd 5-1)

4596 ALISTAIR AND JOANNE'S WEDDING DAY (S) H'CAP 5f

2:45 (2:46) (Class 6) (0-65,64) 3-Y-O **£2,590** (£770; £385; £192) **Stalls** Low

Form RPR

4300 **1** **Theta Wave (USA)**[23] 3859 3-9-4 **61** .... NCallan 4 68
(J R Gask) *midfield: pushed along 1/2-way: hdwy 2f out: swtchd rt and rdn wl over 1f out: drvn and styd on ent fnl f: sn hung rt and kpt on to ld last stride* **9/2**[3]

500 **2** *shd* **Red Cell (IRE)**[44] 3176 3-8-4 **52** .... (b) AmyRyan(5) 5 59
(I W McInnes) *chsd ldrs: rdn wl over 1f out: swtchd rt and drvn ent fnl f and ev ch tl no ex last stride* **25/1**

4144 **3** *nk* **Simple Rhythm**[33] 3506 3-9-4 **64** .... FrederikTylicki(3) 7 70
(J G Given) *cl up: led 1/2-way: rdn over 1f out: drvn ins fnl f: hdd and no ex towards fin* **10/3**[1]

00-0 **4** *1* **Gee Gina**[30] 3611 3-8-1 **49** .... PaulPickard(5) 8 51
(P T Midgley) *chsd ldrs: rdn along 2f out: drvn over 1f out: kpt on u.p ins fnl f* **40/1**

4604 **5** *¾* **Compton Ford**[21] 3926 3-9-3 **60** .... (v[1]) PhillipMakin 1 59
(M Dods) *led: pushed along and hdd 1/2-way: sn rdn: drvn wl over 1f out and kpt on same pce* **9/2**[3]

-064 **6** *¾* **Zelos Girl (IRE)**[36] 3428 3-9-5 **62** .... (e) SaleemGolam 10 59
(Rae Guest) *wnt rt s and in rr: rdn along and hdwy over 2f out: styd on appr fnl f: nrst fin* **16/1**

-604 **7** *¾* **Equinity**[29] 3663 3-8-5 **48** .... (t) GregFairley 9 42
(J Pearce) *chsd ldrs: rdn along 2f out: kpt on same pce* **14/1**

304 **8** *1 ¼* **Africa's Star (IRE)**[23] 3853 3-8-12 **55** .... (p) TonyHamilton 6 44
(M Dods) *prom: rdn along over 2f out and sn wknd* **15/2**

3013 **9** *1 ¼* **What A Fella**[14] 4137 3-8-4 **47** .... SilvestreDeSousa 11 32
(Mrs A Duffield) *hmpd s and a towards rr* **4/1**[2]

0500 **10** *2 ¾* **Yellow River (USA)**[5] 4425 3-7-13 **45** .... (t) DominicFox(3) 2 20
(E J Creighton) *s.i.s and a in rr* **66/1**

0-00 **11** *3 ¾* **Adozen Dreams**[8] 4343 3-8-7 **55** .... (p) JamieKyne(5) 13 16
(N Bycroft) *a in rr* **50/1**

6060 **12** *1 ¼* **Pressed For Time (IRE)**[29] 3663 3-8-10 **53** .... (tp) EdwardCreighton 14 10
(E J Creighton) *midfield: effrt and in tch on outer 1/2-way: sn rdn and wknd* **40/1**

-604 **13** *2 ¼* **Wrens Hope**[33] 3498 3-8-2 **45** .... JimmyQuinn 12 —
(N Bycroft) *dwlt: a in rr* **20/1**

60.54 secs (-0.16) **Going Correction** +0.025s/f (Good) 13 Ran SP% **120.7**

Speed ratings (Par 98): **102,101,101,99,98 97,96,94,92,87 81,79,76**

toteswingers: 1&2 £20.30, 1&3 £5.80, 2&3 £22.10 CSF £122.07 CT £429.56 TOTE £6.90: £2.20, £7.30, £1.70; EX 140.70 TRIFECTA Not won..There was no bid for the winner.

Owner For Sale **Bred** John Hawkins **Trained** Sutton Veny, Wilts

FOCUS

This was run at a solid pace and the form looks fair for the grade with the first three coming clear.

What A Fella Official explanation: jockey said gelding was unsuited by the undulating track

4597 WEATHERBYS BLOODSTOCK INSURANCE H'CAP 1m 1f 170y

3:15 (3:16) (Class 4) (0-85,84) 3-Y-O+ **£4,731** (£1,416; £708; £354; £176) **Stalls** High

Form RPR

4031 **1** **Moheebb (IRE)**[2] 4549 5-10-0 **84** 6ex .... (b) PJMcDonald 5 97
(Mrs R A Carr) *hld up towards rr: hdwy over 4f out: trckd ldrs over 2f out: swtchd lft and rdn over 1f out: styd on to ld jst ins fnl f: sn clr* **7/1**

051 **2** *3* **Demolition**[10] 4288 5-10-0 **84** .... (p) DanielTudhope 7 91
(N Wilson) *in tch: hdwy to trck ldrs over 4f out: effrt 3f out: rdn to chal 2f out: drvn and led briefly over 1f out: hdd jst ins fnl f and kpt on same pce* **6/1**[3]

5565 **3** *2 ¼* **Bavarian Nordic (USA)**[11] 4229 4-9-4 **74** .... SilvestreDeSousa 10 76
(Mrs A Duffield) *trckd ldrs: hdwy 4f out: effrt over 2f out: sn rdn to chal and evch tl drvn ent fnl f and wknd* **9/2**[1]

1400 **4** *1 ¼* **Templetuohy Max (IRE)**[23] 3847 4-9-2 **72** .... (v) JimmyQuinn 11 72
(J D Bethell) *chsd ldng pair on inner: hdwy 3f out: swtchd lft and rdn over 2f out: sn drvn and wknd appr fnl f* **20/1**

4205 **5** *nk* **Rosbay (IRE)**[4] 4471 5-9-11 **81** .... (b[1]) DavidAllan 9 80
(T D Easterby) *t.k.h: hld up: hdwy on inner and in tch 1/2-way: swtchd lft and effrt over 3f out: rdn to chse ldrs over 2f out: sn drvn wknd appr fnl f* **8/1**

2126 **6** *1 ¼* **Society Venue**[31] 3563 4-9-4 **74** .... TonyHamilton 6 70
(Jedd O'Keeffe) *led and sn clr: pushed along 3f out: rdn and jnd 2f out: sn drvn: hdd & wknd appr fnl f* **15/2**

3054 **7** *2* **Amanda Carter**[38] 3333 5-9-8 **81** .... FrederikTylicki(3) 1 73
(R A Fahey) *hld up in midfield: hdwy on outer 3f out: rdn to chse ldrs wl over 1f out: drvn appr fnl f and wknd* **8/1**

1210 **8** *8* **Joinedupwriting**[45] 3121 4-8-9 **65** oh3 .... TonyCulhane 4 40
(R M Whitaker) *a towards rr* **14/1**

0150 **9** *½* **Stevie Gee (IRE)**[9] 4310 5-10-0 **84** .... RobertWinston 2 58
(G A Swinbank) *dwlt and hld up in rr: hdwy 4f out: rdn along 3f out and nvr nr ldrs* **9/1**

1036 **10** *¾* **Crime Writer (USA)**[12] 4210 3-8-12 **77** .... RoystonFfrench 8 50
(M Johnston) *chsd clr ldr: rdn along over 3f out and sn wknd* **5/1**[2]

-300 **11** *85* **Moves Goodenough**[18] 4003 6-9-7 **80** .... NeilBrown(3) 3 —
(A G Foster) *towards rr: rdn along and bhd 1/2-way: sn lost tch and eased over 2f out* **33/1**

2m 3.98s (-1.42) **Going Correction** +0.025s/f (Good)

WFA 3 from 4yo+ 9lb 11 Ran SP% **120.0**

Speed ratings (Par 105): **106,103,101,100,100 99,97,91,91,90 22**

toteswingers: 1&2 £6.30, 1&3 £7.20, 2&3 £5.80 CSF £49.75 CT £214.15 TOTE £6.50: £3.20, £2.40, £2.10; EX 29.10 Trifecta £70.10 Pool: £446.34 - 4.71 winning units..

Owner Michael Hill **Bred** Hascombe And Valiant Studs **Trained** Huby, N Yorks

■ Stewards' Enquiry : Daniel Tudhope caution: used whip down the shoulder in the forehand position

FOCUS

A fair handicap, run at a good pace. Sound form with a clear personal best from Moheebb.

Moves Goodenough Official explanation: jockey said gelding lost it's action turning into the st

4598 ARMSTRONG MEMORIAL H'CAP 6f

3:45 (3:45) (Class 3) (0-95,92) 3-Y-O+

£9,346 (£2,799; £1,399; £700; £349; £175) **Stalls** Low

Form RPR

2302 **1** **Red Cape (FR)**[3] 4507 6-9-0 **81** .... AndrewElliott 4 91
(Mrs R A Carr) *mde all: rdn along over 1f out: styd on strly ins fnl f* **7/2**[1]

-630 **2** *1 ½* **Viking Spirit**[9] 4330 7-9-9 **90** .... (t) ShaneKelly 3 95
(W R Swinburn) *dwlt and sn pushed along in midfield: hdwy over 2f out: swtchd rt and rdn wl over 1f out: styd on strly ins fnl f: nt rch wnr* **12/1**

2632 **3** *¾* **Kerrys Requiem (IRE)**[9] 4309 3-9-4 **89** .... TonyCulhane 1 91+
(M R Channon) *hld up in rr: hdwy 2f out: rdn over 1f out: styd on ins fnl f: nrst fin* **10/1**

0100 **4** *1 ¾* **Bel Cantor**[8] 4353 6-8-9 **79** .... (p) KellyHarrison(3) 11 76
(W J H Ratcliffe) *dwlt and swtchd to r alone far side: sn prom: rdn along over 2f out: drvnover 1f out and sn one pce* **20/1**

364 **5** *nk* **Atlantic Story (USA)**[23] 3877 7-9-8 **89** .... (b) DaleGibson 8 85
(M W Easterby) *cl up: rdn along 2f out: drvn over 1f out and grad wknd* **13/2**[3]

5362 **6** *nk* **Capucci**[35] 3469 4-8-13 **80** .... (t) GrahamGibbons 7 75
(J J Quinn) *dwlt and hld up in rr: hdwy 2f out: rdn over 1f out: kpt on ins fnl f: nrst fin* **7/1**

0623 **7** *1 ¾* **Tabaret**[23] 3877 6-9-11 **92** .... TonyHamilton 6 82
(R M Whitaker) *chsd ldrs: swtchd lft and effrt 2f out: sn rdn and wknd ent fnl f* **10/1**

0206 **8** *½* **Bond City (IRE)**[3] 4485 7-9-6 **87** .... PJMcDonald 5 75
(G R Oldroyd) *towards rr: sme hdwy on outer over 2f out: rdn wl over 1f out: n.d* **7/1**

0000 **9** *8* **Malcheek (IRE)**[9] 4333 7-8-6 **73** .... DavidAllan 9 35
(T D Easterby) *prom: rdn along over 3f out and sn wknd* **16/1**

5631 **10** *¾* **Mister Laurel**[9] 4309 3-8-12 **83** .... PaulHanagan 2 42
(R A Fahey) *chsd ldng pair: rdn along 1/2-way: sn wknd* **5/1**[2]

000 **11** *14* **Ajigolo**[23] 3877 6-9-2 **83** .... DanielTudhope 10 —
(N Wilson) *a in rr: lost tch and eased over 1f out* **33/1**

1m 12.12s (-0.88) **Going Correction** +0.025s/f (Good)

WFA 3 from 4yo+ 4lb 11 Ran SP% **116.7**

Speed ratings (Par 107): **106,104,103,100,100 99,97,96,86,85 66**

toteswingers: 1&2 £13.00, 1&3 £6.90, 2&3 £30.10 CSF £46.69 CT £312.09 TOTE £4.00: £1.70, £3.80, £2.50; EX 55.40 Trifecta £425.40 Pool: £574.99 - 1.00 winning units..

Owner Middleham Park Racing LVI **Bred** Gilles And Mrs Forien **Trained** Huby, N Yorks

FOCUS

A fair sprint, run at a sound pace and all bar Bel Cantor stayed near side. The winner had the run of things but the form should work out.

NOTEBOOK

Red Cape(FR) was well backed on this return from just a three-day break and gave his stable a quick-fire double. He won the battle for the lead and dug really deep when asked to win the race. This uncomplicated sprinter is suited by a sharp test over this trip and continues in grand form, despite being kept busy. A trip to Haydock on Saturday night is now on the cards for him and his trainer will also look at the Great St Wilfrid back here later in the month as a possible target, but already has Excusez Moi for that. (op 4-1)

Viking Spirit ◆ found the winner gone beyond recall when coming out of the pack, yet appreciated the drop in class and his turn could well be nearing once more. (op 11-1)

Kerrys Requiem(IRE) needs things to fall right in her races, but she was simply given too much to do here. There is no doubt a race in her off this sort of mark, but she is not one to completely rely on. (op 8-1)

Bel Cantor was certainly not disgraced considering he went solo on the far side and deserves credit. (op 18-1)

Atlantic Story(USA) produced just the same pace when it mattered, but ran fairly again and a stiffer test over this trip should see him get closer. (op 7-1 tchd 9-1)

Capucci failed to convince he wants this shorter trip. (op 17-2)

Mister Laurel, who slammed Kerrys Requiem last time out, never looked that happy and posted a tame effort from his 7lb higher mark. Official explanation: trainer's rep had no explanation for the poor form shown (op 9-2)

Ajigolo Official explanation: vet said horse finished lame

4599 DESTINATION HARROGATE MAIDEN STKS 1m 4f 10y

4:15 (4:16) (Class 5) 3-Y-O+ **£2,914** (£867; £433; £216) **Stalls** High

Form RPR

4342 **1** **My Chestnut Girl (USA)**[28] 3674 3-8-12 72 .... TPQueally 2 81
(H R A Cecil) *trckd ldrs: smooth hdwy over 3f out and sn cl up on bit: led 2f out and sn clr: easily* **4/1**[2]

5-4 **2** *7* **Leulahleulahlay**[103] 1464 3-9-3 0 .... RoystonFfrench 7 75
(M Johnston) *trckd ldng pair: hdwy on inner and cl up 4f out: rdn along 3f out: drvn 2f out and kpt on same pce: no ch w wnr* **14/1**

3 *3* **Laazim (USA)**[33] 3-9-3 85 .... GregFairley 6 70
(M Johnston) *trckd ldr: hdwy to ld over 4f out: rdn along 3f out: drvn and hdd 2f out: wknd over 1f out* **4/1**[2]

6-4 **4** *4* **Nakoma (IRE)**[8] 4347 7-9-9 0 .... TomEaves 11 59
(B Ellison) *trckd ldrs on inner: pushed along and sltly outpcd over 3f out: swtchd lft and rdn over 2f out: kpt on appr fnl f: n.d* **50/1**

262 **5** *2 ¼* **Cotillion**[10] 4270 3-9-3 82 .... NCallan 3 60
(W J Haggas) *s.i.s and reminders s: sn trcking ldrs on outer: effrt 4f out: rdn along 3f out: drvn over 2f out and sn wknd* **10/11**[1]

6 *hd* **Duke Of Burgundy (FR)**[484] 6-10-0 0 .... ShaneKelly 5 60
(Jennie Candlish) *dwlt: sn in midfield: effrt 4f out: rdn along over 3f out and sn no imp* **33/1**

6-30 **7** *5* **Cherish The Moment (IRE)**[96] 1611 3-9-3 72 .... MichaelHills 12 52
(B W Hills) *led: rdn along and ejaded over 4f out: sn wknd* **13/2**[3]

0 **8** *1 ½* **Informal Affair**[28] 3690 3-9-3 0 .... JimmyQuinn 8 49
(J D Bethell) *dwlt: t.k.h: a in rr* **66/1**

50 **9** *1 ½* **East Of The Sun (IRE)**[50] 2943 3-9-3 0 .... MickyFenton 9 47
(T P Tate) *nvr bttr than midfield* **66/1**

10 *6* **Steel Giant (USA)**[33] 3519 4-10-0 0 .... SJCraine 1 37
(J J Lambe, Ire) *a in rr* **100/1**

11 *64* **Mistic Academy (IRE)**[29] 4-9-6 0 .... FrederikTylicki(3) 10 —
(Miss J E Foster) *dwlt: a in rr: lost tch 4f out and wl bhd fnl 3f* **150/1**

12 *27* **Haunting** 3-8-12 0 .... GrahamGibbons 13 —
(A G Foster) *dwlt: t.k.h: a in rr* **100/1**

2m 36.82s (0.12) **Going Correction** +0.025s/f (Good)

WFA 3 from 4yo+ 11lb 12 Ran SP% **122.9**

Speed ratings (Par 103): **100,95,93,90,89 89,85,84,83,79 37,19**

toteswingers: 1&2 £7.20, 1&3 £3.90, 2&3 £6.10 CSF £58.63 TOTE £4.70: £1.60, £2.60, £1.80; EX 46.70 Trifecta £136.90 Pool: £696.06 - 3.76 winning units..

Owner Malih L Al Basti **Bred** Monticule **Trained** Newmarket, Suffolk

FOCUS
A modest maiden which took little winning as the favourite failed to run his race. An improved effort from My Chestnut Girl even so.
Cotillion Official explanation: vet said colt had a breathing problem
Mistic Academy(IRE) Official explanation: jockey said saddle slipped

4600 TONY TYMON MEMORIAL H'CAP 1m 4f 10y
4:45 (4:47) (Class 5) (0-70,69) 3-Y-O+ **£2,914** (£867; £433; £216) **Stalls** High

Form RPR
0063 **1** **Fossgate**[6] 4403 8-8-9 **50**........................(b[1]) RoystonFfrench 9 58
(J D Bethell) *trckd ldrs: hdwy to ld 3f out: rdn clr wl over 1f out: styd on strly* **3/1**[1]
4000 **2** *3 3/4* **Regal Lyric (IRE)**[28] 3689 3-8-13 **65**........................ MickyFenton 7 67
(T P Tate) *hld up in rr: hdwy on outer 3f out: rdn to chse ldng pair wl over 1f out: sn drvn and kpt on ins fnl f: no ch w wnr* **11/2**[3]
3 *1/2* **Choctaw Nation**[25] 3838 5-9-10 **65**........................ NCallan 6 66
(J J Lambe, Ire) *hld up in rr: hdwy on outer over 3f out: rdn to chse wnr and hung rt wl over 1f out: sn drvn and kpt on same pce* **7/1**
4444 **4** *7* **Veronicas Boy**[8] 4348 3-8-6 **58**........................ JimmyQuinn 3 48
(G M Moore) *hld up in tch: rdn along and outpcd over 3f out: styd on u.p fr wl over 1f out: nt rch ldrs* **7/1**
6-50 **5** *shd* **Moonwalking**[66] 2445 5-9-3 **58**........................ TonyHamilton 5 48
(Jedd O'Keeffe) *prom: rdn along 4f out and sltly outpcd: kpt on u.p fnl 2f* **8/1**
2035 **6** *1 1/2* **Andorn (GER)**[24] 3809 5-9-5 **63**........................ RussellKennemore(3) 10 50
(P A Kirby) *t.k.h: cl up on inner: led 1/2-way: rdn along 4f out: hdd 3f out: sn drvn and wknd 2f out* **13/2**
1022 **7** *6* **Promise Maker (USA)**[12] 4193 4-9-3 **63**........................ AmyRyan(5) 2 41
(T D Walford) *slt ld to 1/2-way: cl up tl rdn along over 3f out and grad wknd* **7/2**[2]
50-0 **8** *7* **Wild Fell Hall (IRE)**[11] 4229 6-9-9 **64**........................ SilvestreDeSousa 1 30
(J Hetherton) *cl up on outer: rdn along 4f out: drvn 3f out and sn wknd* **33/1**
0-06 **9** *27* **Masking Baldini (IRE)**[27] 3707 5-8-8 **52** oh5 ow2.... FrederikTylicki(3) 8 —
(J Hetherton) *hld up in rr: hdwy on inner 4f out: rdn along over 3f out and sn wknd* **100/1**

2m 38.02s (1.32) **Going Correction** +0.025s/f (Good)
WFA 3 from 4yo+ 11lb **9** Ran SP% **116.0**
Speed ratings (Par 103): **96,93,93,88,88 87,83,78,60**
toteswingers: 1&2 £7.10, 1&3 £4.10, 2&3 £7.50 CSF £19.97 CT £106.32 TOTE £4.00: £1.80, £2.50, £2.10; EX 25.00 Trifecta £23.40 Pool: £501.72 - 15.83 winning units..
Owner Mrs James Bethell **Bred** Mrs P A Clark **Trained** Middleham Moor, N Yorks
■ Stewards' Enquiry : Russell Kennemore one-day ban: used whip with excessive force (Aug 17)

FOCUS
A modest handicap, rated through the runner-up. Fossgate registered his third win in the race over the last four years.

4601 LEVY BOARD H'CAP 5f
5:15 (5:16) (Class 4) (0-85,83) 3-Y-O **£4,857** (£1,445; £722; £360) **Stalls** Low

Form RPR
-104 **1** **Doctor Parkes**[51] 2915 3-9-6 **82**........................ ShaneKelly 8 89
(E J Alston) *cl up: effrt 2f out: sn rdn to ld and edgd lft wl over 1f out: drvn and edgd lft ent fnl f: kpt on wl towards fin* **7/1**
06-6 **2** *nk* **La Brigitte**[68] 2373 3-9-4 **83**........................ FrederikTylicki(3) 4 89
(J A Glover) *towards rr: hdwy 2f out: rdn over 1f out: styd on to chal ins fnl f and ch whn drvn and nt qckn last 75yds* **16/1**
035 **3** *1 1/2* **Excellent Show**[44] 3173 3-9-4 **80**........................ RoystonFfrench 9 81
(B Smart) *cl up on outer: rdn along 2f out: drvn over 1f out: kpt on u.p ins fnl f* **11/1**
5002 **4** *shd* **Lucky Art (USA)**[12] 4192 3-8-9 **71**........................ SilvestreDeSousa 6 71+
(Mrs R A Carr) *cl up: rdn along whn hmpd and lost pl 2f out: sn swtchd rt and rdn: drvn and kpt on ins fnl f* **9/2**[2]
4-04 **5** *1 1/4* **Go Go Green (IRE)**[12] 4189 3-9-5 **81**........................ RobertWinston 5 77
(D H Brown) *led: rdn along 1/2-way: drvn 2f out and sn hdd: grad wknd* **5/1**[3]
0454 **6** *1/2* **Rowayton**[26] 3747 3-9-7 **83**........................ JimmyQuinn 1 77+
(J D Bethell) *chsd ldrs on inner whn hmpd after 1f: effrt and hmpd 2f out: sn swtchd rt and rdn: kpt on ins fnl f* **5/2**[1]
0016 **7** *1 1/4* **Mullglen**[9] 4309 3-9-0 **76**........................(b[1]) DavidAllan 3 65+
(T D Easterby) *trckd ldrs: effrt on inner whn nt clr run and hmpd 2f out: sn rdn and btn* **15/2**
3406 **8** *3/4* **Tagula Breeze (IRE)**[11] 4227 3-8-9 **74**........................(p) NeilBrown(3) 7 61
(I W McInnes) *dwlt and wnt rt s: a in rr* **14/1**
1-00 **9** *6* **Albertine Rose**[17] 4069 3-9-6 **82**........................ NCallan 2 47
(W R Muir) *chsd ldrs: rdn along whn n.m.r 2f out and sn wknd* **14/1**

59.72 secs (-0.98) **Going Correction** +0.025s/f (Good) **9** Ran SP% **115.2**
Speed ratings (Par 105): **108,107,105,104,102 102,100,98,89**
toteswingers: 1&2 £22.50, 1&3 £8.80, 2&3 £31.60 CSF £109.91 CT £1223.78 TOTE £6.50: £2.30, £3.90, £4.00; EX 69.70 Trifecta £329.60 Pool: £445.45 - 0.53 winning units. Place 6: £ 45.99 Place 5: £29.50.
Owner Joseph Heler **Bred** Joseph Heler **Trained** Longton, Lancs

FOCUS
A fair 3yo sprint, run at a sound pace. The winner looks the best guide and some of these are better than the bare form.
Rowayton Official explanation: jockey said filly was denied a clear run
T/Plt: £65.70 to a £1 stake. Pool: £76,996.55. 854.64 winning tickets. T/Qpdt: £19.90 to a £1 stake. Pool: £4,883.35. 181.20 winning tickets. JR

4377 WINDSOR (R-H)
Monday, August 3

OFFICIAL GOING: Good to firm (firm in places)
Rail realignment increased distances of races of a mile and over by 15yards.
Wind: Light, behind Weather: Fine but cloudy

4602 BOLLINGER CHAMPAGNE CHALLENGE SERIES H'CAP (GENTLEMAN AMATEURS') (IN ASSOC WITH DAILY TELEGRAPH) 1m 3f 135y
6:00 (6:00) (Class 5) (0-75,80) 3-Y-O+ **£2,637** (£811; £405) **Stalls** Low

Form RPR
3402 **1** **Maslak (IRE)**[8] 4350 5-10-13 **70**........................ MrPCollington(3) 5 79
(P W Hiatt) *led 1f: stdd: prog to ld over 4f out: rdn and pressed fr 2f out: kpt on wl* **10/3**[2]
3221 **2** *3/4* **Falcon Rock (IRE)**[7] 4378 4-11-7 **80** 6ex........................ MrJohnEnnis(5) 11 88
(S A Callaghan) *hld up in tch: gng eaasily bhd ldrs over 2f out: rdn to chal and upsides over 1f out: nt qckn* **5/6**[1]
0323 **3** *hd* **Mustajed**[13] 4169 8-10-9 **68**........................ MrPMillman(5) 13 75
(B R Millman) *hld up in last: prog on wd outside 3f out: chal 2f out: urged along and nt qckn over 1f out* **8/1**[3]
026 **4** *9* **Apache Fort**[45] 3114 6-10-2 **56** oh1........................(b) MrSWalker 1 48
(T Keddy) *hld up in rr: effrt 3f out: chsd ldng trio over 1f out: no imp: fdd fnl f* **8/1**[3]
-600 **5** *1/2* **Crossbow Creek**[40] 3266 11-11-7 **75**........................ MrMRimell 10 66
(M G Rimell) *dwlt: hld up in last pair: outpcd fr wl over 2f out: kpt on ins fnl f* **25/1**
/604 **6** *1 1/2* **Captain Oats (IRE)**[30] 3631 6-9-13 **60** oh8 ow4........................ MrKFord(7) 8 49
(Mrs P Ford) *s.s: rcvrd and sn prom: chsd ldr 6f out to over 4f out: grad wknd over 2f out* **50/1**
0505 **7** *8* **Wicksy Creek**[10] 4269 4-9-9 **56** oh11........................(t) MrMMarris(7) 7 31
(G C Bravery) *plld hrd and racd v wd early: led after 1f to over 4f out: wknd over 2f out* **66/1**
-100 **8** *7* **State General (IRE)**[54] 2829 3-10-1 **71**........................ MrRBirkett(5) 3 34
(Miss J Feilden) *prom: lost pl over 3f out: wknd over 2f out* **11/1**

2m 32.92s (3.42) **Going Correction** -0.125s/f (Firm)
WFA 3 from 4yo+ 11lb **8** Ran SP% **115.5**
Speed ratings (Par 103): **83,82,82,76,76 75,69,65**
totewingers: 1&2 £1.30, 1&3 £1.50, 2&3 £3.00 CSF £6.47 CT £18.75 TOTE £4.20: £1.50, £1.30, £1.60; EX 7.20.
Owner Clive Roberts **Bred** Shadwell Estate Company Limited **Trained** Hook Norton, Oxon

FOCUS
Stands' rail dolled out five yards at 6f down to a yard at winning post. Top bend dolled out nine yards from innermost line adding 15 1/2 yards to races over a mile and over. The field was cut to eight after five withdrawals in a race that already lacked any depth. Modest but straightforward form.

4603 EBF PREMIER LEAGUE MAIDEN FILLIES' STKS 6f
6:30 (6:30) (Class 4) 2-Y-O **£5,569** (£1,657; £828; £413) **Stalls** High

Form RPR
32 **1** **Seeking Dubai**[10] 4257 2-9-0 0........................ RyanMoore 2 79
(E F Vaughan) *trckd ldng pair: led over 1f out: rdn out and in command fnl f* **11/4**[1]
2 *1 1/2* **Adele Blanc Sec (FR)** 2-9-0 0........................ RichardKingscote 8 75
(Tom Dascombe) *sn trckd ldng trio: shkn up on inner 2f out: styd on fnl f to take 2nd last stride* **9/2**[2]
24 **3** *shd* **Zubova**[10] 4257 2-9-0 0........................ RichardHughes 3 74
(R Hannon) *led and sn crossed fr outside draw to nr side rail: edgd lft and hdd over 1f out: one pce* **11/2**[3]
0 **4** *3* **Pose (IRE)**[21] 3918 2-9-0 0........................ PatDobbs 1 65
(R Hannon) *chsd ldrs in 6th: pushed along 2f out: kpt on steadily fr over 1f out* **25/1**
5 *1* **Love And Devotion** 2-9-0 0........................ LDettori 15 62+
(Saeed Bin Suroor) *wnt rt s: in tch in 7th: pushed along 2f out: kpt on steadily: nvr nrr* **9/1**
20 **6** *1 1/2* **Bideeya (USA)**[24] 3810 2-9-0 0........................ SebSanders 4 58
(C E Brittain) *pressed ldr to 2f out: fdd fnl f* **25/1**
7 *shd* **Pin Cushion** 2-9-0 0........................ MartinDwyer 5 57+
(B J Meehan) *dwlt: sn in midfield in 8th: pushed along 2f out: kpt on steadily: n.d* **13/2**
44 **8** *nk* **Yurituni**[25] 3772 2-9-0 0........................ DarryllHolland 7 57
(Eve Johnson Houghton) *trckd ldng quartet: shuffled along 2f out: grad outpcd* **16/1**
0 **9** *1* **In The Slips (USA)**[19] 3979 2-9-0 0........................ WilliamBuick 12 54
(P F I Cole) *a in same pl on inner: reminder over 1f out: kpt on: no imp on ldrs* **50/1**
10 *nk* **Madame Boot (FR)** 2-9-0 0........................ FergusSweeney 10 53
(P J Makin) *a in same pl: shkn up over 2f out: no imp* **66/1**
11 *1 1/4* **Houda (IRE)** 2-9-0 0........................ PatCosgrave 9 49
(J G Portman) *s.s: off the pce in last quintet: pushed along over 2f out: kpt on steadily fnl f* **100/1**
12 *1* **Oak Leaves** 2-9-0 0........................ JimCrowley 6 46
(J G Portman) *s.s: a in last quintet: taken wdst of all 1/2-way: no prog* **66/1**
13 *1 3/4* **Weeping Willow (IRE)** 2-9-0 0........................ JimmyFortune 16 41+
(J H M Gosden) *dwlt and hmpd s: a in last quartet: nvr a factor* **11/2**[3]
14 *1 3/4* **Rosiliant (IRE)** 2-9-0 0........................ AdamKirby 13 35
(C G Cox) *a wl in rr: struggling by 1/2-way* **33/1**
15 *1 1/4* **Have More** 2-9-0 0........................ NickyMackay 11 32
(B J Meehan) *a in last quintet: wd fr 1/2-way: sn n.d* **100/1**

1m 12.55s (-0.45) **Going Correction** -0.125s/f (Firm) **15** Ran SP% **122.4**
Speed ratings (Par 93): **98,96,95,91,90 88,88,88,86,86 84,83,80,78,76**
toteswingers: 1&2 £5.70, 1&3 £2.20, 2&3 £8.10 CSF £14.01 TOTE £3.80: £1.70, £2.50, £2.60; EX 21.30.
Owner Nabil Mourad **Bred** M E Wates **Trained** Newmarket, Suffolk

FOCUS
Some decent pedigrees here and some smart entries to go with them. However, it might be wise to exercise caution until more is known about the race in which three fillies from the unfavoured outside draw had the pace to get over to dominate on the stands' side. The form is just fairly useful.

NOTEBOOK
Seeking Dubai, who has the Watership Down Stud Sales entry at Ascot on September 25, had shown more than enough to win a race of this type having finished third and second on her two outings. On the second of them at Ascot she had beaten Zubova around two lengths and there was marginally less between them here, with little excuse for the latter. She will get further. (op 4-1 tchd 9-2 in a place)
Adele Blanc Sec(FR), from a yard with a fine line in juvenile form, made a solid debut and is another that will stay a bit further, although she'll win over this trip now she knows what's required. (op 4-1 tchd 5-1 in places)
Zubova, who holds a Fillies' Mile entry, will appreciate a longer trip, but the Ascot Group 1 is light years from this form. (op 6-1)
Pose(IRE) was another to show good pace with the first and second to get over from a poor draw and this was a much better effort than last time over 5f and she might be worth a try back at the minimum. (op 20-1)
Love And Devotion was green from the stalls and wasn't given a hard time and is well worth a second glance next time in similar grade. (op 17-2 tchd 10-1)
Bideeya(USA) was yet another to have the pace to get over but ultimately paid for it. Her two previous runs were over 7f and she'll get a nursery mark after this. (op 20-1)
Pin Cushion can win a race judged on this debut from a moderate draw. From a yard whose youngsters always improve, she wasn't given a hard time and has ability. (op 15-2 tchd 6-1)
Yurituni was moving up from 5f to 6f and wasn't knocked about when fading. A nursery beckons. (op 12-1)

Weeping Willow(IRE), a full sister to Deposer, never got back from a bad bump from Love And Devotion at the stalls. This is best forgotten. (op 7-1 tchd 8-1)

4604 SPORTINGBET.COM H'CAP 5f 10y
7:00 (7:00) (Class 5) (0-70,69) 3-Y-O+ £2,729 (£806; £403) Stalls High

Form RPR
1121 1 Solemn[10] 4268 4-9-1 63....(b) DavidProbert(3) 5 74
(J M Bradley) chsd ldrs and wl in tch: effrt towards outer over 1f out: drvn ahd ent fnl f: styd on wl 7/2[2]
2304 2 1 Espy[17] 4051 4-9-8 67.... JimmyFortune 15 75
(S Kirk) trckd ldrs: gng easily towards nr side 2f out: rdn to chal over 1f out and upsides: nt qckn ins fnl f 12/1
0364 3 nse Gwilym (GER)[21] 3917 6-9-4 63.... MartinDwyer 8 70
(D Haydn Jones) disp ld: hrd rdn over 1f out: hdd ent fnl f: one pce 20/1
0525 4 shd Triple Dream[20] 3959 4-9-1 60....(p) SteveDrowne 2 67+
(J M Bradley) hld up towards rr: effrt and nt clr run briefly over 1f out: rdn and styd on wl fnl f: too much to do 20/1
0212 5 nk Sister Clement (IRE)[7] 4380 3-9-6 68.... RichardHughes 6 73
(R Hannon) trckd ldrs: hrd rdn and nt qckn over 1f out: kpt on ins fnl f: a hld 13/8[1]
1220 6 1 1/2 Matterofact (IRE)[10] 4268 6-9-2 68.... JakePayne(7) 3 69
(M S Saunders) dwlt: wl in rr in abt 12th: prog on wd outside fr 1/2-way: rdn to chal over 1f out: no ex fnl f 20/1
-040 7 1/2 Heaven[18] 3998 4-9-10 69.... RyanMoore 7 68
(P J Makin) wl in rr in abt 10th: pushed along 2f out: rdn and styd on ins fnl f: n.d 11/1
636 8 1/2 Step It Up (IRE)[18] 3998 5-9-0 59.... PatCosgrave 14 56
(J R Boyle) wl in tch in midfield: rdn over 1f out: one pce and no imp on ldrs 25/1
0434 9 1/2 Peopleton Brook[25] 3775 7-8-8 58....(t) RossAtkinson(5) 16 53
(B G Powell) lost pl against rail over 3f out and wl in rr: rdn and prog on fnl f: n.d 20/1
0036 10 1/2 Digital[10] 4268 12-9-2 61....(v) ChrisCatlin 1 54
(M R Channon) sn outpcd in last: sme prog 2f out: nvr on terms 33/1
1364 11 nse Brandywell Boy (IRE)[18] 3998 6-9-2 61.... SebSanders 11 54
(D J S Ffrench Davis) racd against nr side rail: pressed ldng pair: upsides fr 1/2-way to over 1f out: wknd 25/1
-551 12 1 Rondeau (GR)[12] 4203 4-9-10 69.... JimCrowley 10 59
(P R Chamings) pressed ldrs: hrd rdn 2f out: sn lost pl and btn 9/1[3]
4356 13 1 1/4 Fromsong (IRE)[21] 3917 11-9-3 67.... JamesO'Reilly(5) 9 52
(D K Ivory) taen down early: disp ld to over 2f out: sn lost pl and btn 20/1
4436 F Romantic Queen[133] 936 3-9-1 68....(t[1]) MatthewDavies(5) 13 —
(George Baker) stmbld and fell sn after s 66/1

59.26 secs (-1.04) **Going Correction** -0.125s/f (Firm)
WFA 3 from 4yo+ 3lb 14 Ran SP% **122.3**
Speed ratings (Par 103): **103,101,101,101,100 98,97,96,95,95 95,93,91,—**
toteswingers: 1&2 £11.90, 1&3 £12.20, 2&3 £5.70 CSF £37.35 CT £774.97 TOTE £4.90: £2.00, £3.20, £2.80; EX 65.00.
Owner E A Hayward **Bred** Cheveley Park Stud Ltd **Trained** Sedbury, Gloucs

FOCUS
A tight handicap. Straightforward from with another step forward from the winner.

4605 PREMIER LEAGUE CREATING CHANCES H'CAP 1m 67y
7:30 (7:30) (Class 4) (0-85,85) 3-Y-O+ £5,180 (£1,541; £770; £384) Stalls High

Form RPR
041 1 Prince Of Johanne (IRE)[79] 2081 3-8-12 76.... RyanMoore 5 84
(J Noseda) dwlt: hld up in 5th: pushed along and looked in trble over 3f out: taken to outer and drvn 2f out: prog to press ldr 1f out: edgd ahd last 75yds 13/8[1]
1202 2 1/2 Tinshu (IRE)[21] 3921 3-8-12 76.... AdamKirby 8 83
(D Haydn Jones) sn settled bhd ldng pair: effrt 2f out: prog to ld over 1f out: hrd rdn and hanging lft but r.o: hdd last 75yds 10/3[3]
0615 3 2 3/4 Can Can Star[5] 4426 6-9-2 80.... DebraEngland(7) 9 82
(A W Carroll) dwlt: hld up in last: rdn on inner over 2f out: kpt on same pce fr over 1f out: no threat to ldng pair 20/1
1050 4 1 1/2 Global[23] 3868 3-9-5 83.... RichardHughes 4 80
(R Hannon) sn led: reminders 1/2-way: drvn and hdd over 1f out: sn btn 9/1
0023 5 3/4 Striding Edge (IRE)[14] 4149 3-8-7 71.... MartinDwyer 6 67
(W R Muir) hld up in 4th: rdn and prog to chal 2f out: wknd jst over 1f out 15/2
0442 6 2 Dear Maurice[14] 4149 5-9-4 75....(v) SebSanders 2 67
(E A L Dunlop) mostly trckd ldr: chal fr over 3f out: nrly upsides wl over 1f out: sn wknd 5/2[2]

1m 42.81s (-1.89) **Going Correction** -0.125s/f (Firm)
WFA 3 from 4yo+ 7lb 6 Ran SP% **116.3**
Speed ratings (Par 105): **104,103,100,99,98 96**
toteswingers: 1&2 £1.80, 1&3 £9.20, 2&3 £7.80 CSF £7.82 CT £76.09 TOTE £2.90: £2.20, £1.90; EX 10.50.
Owner M Tabor, Mrs Susan Roy, M Green **Bred** T J Rooney And Corduff Stud **Trained** Newmarket, Suffolk

■ Stewards' Enquiry : Adam Kirby one-day ban: excessive use of whip (Aug 17)

FOCUS
A weak race for a class four contest and the form is a bit muddling, but the winner is going the right way.

4606 SPORTINGBET.COM MAIDEN STKS 1m 2f 7y
8:00 (8:04) (Class 5) 3-4-Y-O £2,729 (£806; £403) Stalls Low

Form RPR
1 Assabiyya (IRE) 3-8-12 0.... LDettori 3 81+
(Saeed Bin Suroor) led 4f: trckd ldng pair sn after: plld out and effrt 3f out: rdn to ld over 1f out: pushed out fnl f 5/1
44 2 2 1/2 Laughing Boy (IRE)[27] 3703 3-9-3 0.... DaneO'Neill 2 81
(L M Cumani) t.k.h: cl up tl plld way through to ld 6f out: drvn and hdd over 1f out: readily hld fnl f 9/4[2]
42-3 3 1 1/4 Kansai Spirit (IRE)[26] 3751 3-9-3 80.... JimmyFortune 13 78
(J H M Gosden) prom: pressed ldr 1/2-way: hanging bdly lft fnl 3f: nt qckn 2f out: kpt on 7/4[1]
4- 4 4 Opera Wings[241] 7561 3-8-12 0.... RyanMoore 14 65
(Sir Michael Stoute) dwlt: sn in tch in midfield: effrt to chse ldrs 3f out: rdn and fnd nil 2f out: wknd 9/2[3]
00 5 1 Sea Lavender[39] 3297 3-8-12 0.... FergusSweeney 11 63+
(R Charlton) hld up: in rr tl wnt 9th over 4f out: outpcd 3f out: shuffled along and kpt on steadily: nvr nr ldrs 33/1
0- 6 7 Pezula[291] 6759 3-8-12 0.... SteveDrowne 1 49
(R T Phillips) reluctant to enter stalls: in tch in midfield: outpcd fr 3f out: n.d after: plugged on 66/1
0 7 nk Cottonfields (USA)[79] 2081 3-9-3 0.... JimCrowley 6 53
(Mrs H S Main) hld up in last trio: lft bhd fr over 3f out: passed wkng rivals fnl 2f 22/1
500 8 1/2 Grand Pere[7] 4381 3-8-12 0.... RichardEvans(5) 5 52
(P D Evans) chsd ldrs: pushed along to cl over 3f out: rdn and no prog over 2f out: wknd rapidly and wandered over 1f out 40/1
00 9 3/4 Errol Flynn (IRE)[42] 3207 3-9-0 0....(p) KevinGhunowa(3) 15 51
(R A Harris) chsd ldng quartet: hrd rdn over 2f out: wkng whn checked over 1f out 66/1
44 10 2 Park Melody (IRE)[41] 3250 3-8-12 0.... MartinDwyer 4 42
(B J Meehan) prom tl wknd rapidly over 2f out 16/1
0 11 3 1/4 Sula Dream[14] 4151 3-8-10 0.... SimonPearce(7) 8 40
(J Pearce) a wl in rr: rdn and wknd 3f out 150/1
0-6 12 3 1/2 Mid Wicket (USA)[63] 2551 3-9-3 0.... ChrisCatlin 9 33
(Mouse Hamilton-Fairley) hld up in last: pushed into 11th briefly over 2f out: sn wknd 33/1

2m 6.97s (-1.73) **Going Correction** -0.125s/f (Firm) 12 Ran SP% **124.2**
Speed ratings (Par 103): **101,99,98,94,94 88,88,87,87,85 82,80**
toteswingers: 1&2 £2.30, 1&3 £3.20, 2&3 £1.70 CSF £16.91 TOTE £6.00: £1.60, £1.30, £1.40; EX 21.90.
Owner Godolphin **Bred** Darley **Trained** Newmarket, Suffolk

FOCUS
The market got this maiden right with the first four in the betting filling the frame. A nice start from the winner but not much strength in depth.

4607 OAKLEY COURT H'CAP 6f
8:30 (8:32) (Class 5) (0-75,75) 3-Y-O+ £2,729 (£806; £403) Stalls High

Form RPR
002- 1 Tagula Night (IRE)[248] 7465 3-9-5 74....(vt) AdamKirby 7 84
(W R Swinburn) disp 2nd bhd clr ldr: rdn and clsd to ld over 1f out: drvn clr 20/1
2021 2 1 1/2 Patavium Prince (IRE)[41] 3243 6-9-10 75.... DaneO'Neill 13 80
(Miss Jo Crowley) disp ld bhd clr ldr: clsd to chal over 1f out: chsd wnr after but sn outpcd 10/1
1245 3 nk Sweet Gale (IRE)[18] 4019 5-9-3 73.... Louis-PhilippeBeuzelin(5) 6 77+
(Mike Murphy) hld up: wl in rr and plenty to do over 2f out: gd prog on outer fr over 1f out: styd on and nrly snatched 2nd 8/1
5143 4 nk Dressed To Dance (IRE)[13] 4167 5-9-7 75....(b) KevinGhunowa(3) 11 78
(R A Harris) chsd ldng trio: rdn and nt on terms fr 2f out: kpt on one pce fr over 1f out 8/1
5353 5 shd Memphis Man[7] 4387 6-9-3 73.... RichardEvans(5) 1 76+
(P D Evans) hld up wl in rr: taken to wd outside 1/2-way: rdn over 2f out: tried to cl over 1f out: kpt on same pce 10/1
0501 6 3/4 Kyle (IRE)[14] 4154 5-9-8 73.... RyanMoore 15 73
(C R Dore) chsd ldrs: rdn and nt on terms over 2f out: kpt on against nr side rail fr over 1f out: n.d 5/1[1]
40/1 7 shd Matuza (IRE)[35] 3459 6-9-5 70.... LPKeniry 10 70
(P R Chamings) chsd ldrs: rdn and fnd nil 2f out: one pce and no imp over 1f out 16/1
4003 8 2 Magical Speedfit (IRE)[20] 3945 4-9-6 71.... ChrisCatlin 8 65
(G G Margarson) hld up in rr: taken to outer 1/2-way: effrt over 2f out: no imp on ldrs over 1f out 40/1
6521 9 shd Sarah's Art (IRE)[112] 1248 6-9-3 68....(t) PatCosgrave 4 61
(Stef Liddiard) hld up in last trio: nudged along fr 2f out: swtchd to inner over 1f out: kpt on: nvr nr ldrs 12/1
0322 10 1/2 Cape Royal[4] 4469 9-9-4 72....(bt) JackDean(3) 16 64
(J M Bradley) led: clr after 2f: wknd and hdd over 1f out 6/1[2]
3124 11 nk Bateleur[18] 3995 5-9-2 67.... SamHitchcott 12 58
(M R Channon) t.k.h: chsd ldrs: no prog 2f out: wknd jst over 1f out 12/1
0026 12 hd Dvinsky (USA)[26] 3738 8-9-3 68....(b) IanMongan 2 58+
(P Howling) hld up and swtchd to r against nr side rail: a wl in rr 20/1
4050 13 1 1/2 Mamlakati (IRE)[4] 4452 3-9-6 75.... JimCrowley 14 60
(R Hannon) nvr bttr than midfield: no progrss over 2f out: wknd fnl f 20/1
0264 14 1/2 Balata[18] 4019 4-9-5 70.... TGMcLaughlin 5 54
(B R Millman) mostly midfield: effrt on outer over 2f out: wknd rapidly over 1f out 15/2[3]

1m 11.63s (-1.37) **Going Correction** -0.125s/f (Firm)
WFA 3 from 4yo+ 4lb 14 Ran SP% **121.1**
Speed ratings (Par 103): **104,102,101,101,100 100,98,98,97,96 96,94,92,91**
toteswingers: 1&2 £52.60, 1&3 £52.30, 2&3 £27.40 CSF £200.67 CT £1794.17 TOTE £23.40: £6.30, £3.90, £3.50; EX 226.10 Place 6: £57.59 Place 5: £48.96.
Owner Hodgson, Hufford, Moss & Papworth **Bred** Carpet Lady Partnership **Trained** Aldbury, Herts

FOCUS
Some old sweats here who the handicapper knows well, but he had to guess with the winner. Not many got into it and the form is ordinary.
T/Jkpt: £60,322.40 to a £1 stake. Pool: £84,961.14. 0.50 winning tickets. T/Plt: £48.50 to a £1 stake. Pool: £98,548.15. 1,483.26 winning tickets. T/Qpdt: £27.90 to a £1 stake. Pool: £7,405.50. 195.80 winning tickets. JN

4608 - (Foreign Racing) - See Raceform Interactive

4570 CORK (R-H)
Monday, August 3

OFFICIAL GOING: Yielding (yielding to soft in places) changing to soft after race 3 (3.35)

4609a LADBROKES GIVE THANKS STKS (GROUP 3) (F&M) 1m 4f
4:05 (4:05) 3-Y-O+ £56,873 (£16,679; £7,941; £2,699)

RPR
1 Tamarind (IRE)[16] 4112 3-8-10 89.... CO'Donoghue 7 105+
(A P O'Brien, Ire) chsd ldrs: 4th 1/2-way: rdn to ld 2f out: strly pressed: kpt on wl fr 1f out to assert fnl f 20/1
2 1 1/2 Perfect Truth (IRE)[59] 2672 3-8-10 104.... JMurtagh 5 103
(A P O'Brien, Ire) trckd ldrs in 3rd: rdn to chal 2f out: no ex in 2nd ins fnl f: kpt on same pce 4/1[3]
3 3/4 Beauty O' Gwaun (IRE)[22] 3896 3-8-13 104.... MJKinane 8 105
(John M Oxx, Ire) hld up towards rr: hdwy in 5th 3f out: rdn to 3rd 1 1/2f out: no ex fnl f: kpt on same pce 6/1
4 3 Dance Pass (IRE)[45] 3132 3-8-10 98.... PJSmullen 3 97
(D K Weld, Ire) hld up towards rr: 6th 1/2-way: rdn into 4th 2f out: no ex over 1f out: kpt on same pce 11/1

5 4 **Roman Empress (IRE)**[22] 3896 3-8-10 93 SMLevey 6 91
(A P O'Brien, Ire) *led: rdn and hdd 2f out: sn no ex* **14/1**

6 ½ **Magen's Star (IRE)**[19] 3990 4-9-7 97 WJLee 9 90
(T Stack, Ire) *chsd ldr in 2nd: rdn 3f out: no ex over 2f out* **11/4**[2]

7 22 **Beach Bunny (IRE)**[11] 4253 4-9-7 113 CDHayes 4 55
(Kevin Prendergast, Ire) *settled bhd ldrs: 5th 1/2-way: rdn 4f out: wknd to rr ent st* **15/8**[1]

2m 40.39s (-7.51)
WFA 3 from 4yo 11lb **7 Ran SP% 115.5**
CSF £99.17 TOTE £30.00: £5.90, £2.10; DF 31.90.
Owner Mrs John Magnier **Bred** Barronstown Stud **Trained** Ballydoyle, Co Tipperary

FOCUS
The winner has been rated as recording a personal best, with the runner-up and third below their best.

NOTEBOOK
Tamarind(IRE) looked one of the first ones beaten before turning out of the back straight, but she found plenty of reserves of stamina to win this contest. Tracking the early lead set by her stable companion, she was being pushed along to maintain her position over half a mile out but she began to stay on again from early in the straight, kept up that momentum to lead a furlong and a half out and maintained that gallop all the way to the line. Coming after winning a very bad Tipperary maiden, this was a decent performance from a filly that appreciates soft ground and should have little difficulty stepping up in trip. (op 14/1)
Perfect Truth(IRE) came back to something like her best on ground she may not have appreciated. Always close to the pace, she came under pressure to mount a challenge early in the straight but didn't seem to really pick up to any degree until she was headed by the winner. She ran on pretty well inside the last but couldn't make any impression. (op 7/2)
Beauty O' Gwaun(IRE) had something to prove after her very disappointing effort in the Irish Oaks and redeemed her reputation somewhat. Held up off the pace, she was being ridden to close early in the straight and picked up to some degree as she came up on the outside with every chance over a furlong out, but her run flattened out quite quickly. (op 5/1)
Dance Pass(IRE) appeared not to stay on the ground. Pat Smullen gave her a very patient ride and she came up on the outside with a short-lived effort inside the final two furlongs before tiring.
Roman Empress(IRE) acted as the pacemaker before she was headed inside the final two furlongs. (op 12/1)
Magen's Star(IRE), stepping out of handicaps for the first time, was found out on her first start in this company. She settled in second and travelled well until coming under pressure early in the straight. (op 7/2)
Beach Bunny(IRE) ran no race at all and was beaten turning into the straight. She eventually came home in her own time. Official explanation: jockey said filly never travelled (op 9/4)

4610 - 4616a (Foreign Racing) - See Raceform Interactive

4187
CATTERICK (L-H)
Tuesday, August 4

OFFICIAL GOING: Good (good to firm in places; 8.4) (meeting abandoned after race 5 (4.20) due to unsafe ground)
Rail in home straight moved out 2.5 metres Both bends dolled out 1m but impact distances not quantified.
Wind: Light, behind Weather: Overcast

4617 CATTERICKBRIDGE.CO.UK (S) STKS 1m 7f 177y
2:20 (2:21) (Class 6) 3-5-Y-O **£2,047** (£604; £302) **Stalls** Low

Form RPR

30-0 1 **Carlton Mac**[47] 3068 4-9-8 42 (p) FrancisNorton 11 46
(N Bycroft) *hld up towards rr: stdy hdwy on outer 3f out: rdn along wl over 1f out: styd on to ld ent fnl f: sn drvn and hung lft: jst hld on* **13/2**

2 hd **Tubby Littlejohns (IRE)**[16] 5-9-3 0 RichardEvans(5) 4 46
(B J Llewellyn) *s.i.s: hdwy into midfield 1/2-way: gd hdwy 3f out: swtchd lft and effrt over 1f out: rdn to chal ent fnl f: sn edgd lft and ev ch: n.m.r whn rdr dropped whip last 50yds: no ex* **8/1**

0-00 3 4 **Art Gallery**[31] 3617 5-9-1 37 DTDaSilva(7) 10 41
(D W Thompson) *cl up: effrt 3f out and sn rdn along: led 2f out: drvn and hdd ent fnl f: sn edgd lft and one pce* **14/1**

0000 4 3 **Autumn Charm**[14] 4170 4-9-3 40 DNolan 6 32
(Lucinda Featherstone) *trckd ldrs on inner: hdwy 4f out: rdn over 2f out: sn drvn and ev ch tl wknd ent fnl f* **33/1**

0000 5 2½ **Just Oscar (GER)**[24] 3851 5-9-8 46 DavidAllan 1 34
(W M Brisbourne) *midfied: hdwy over 5f out: rdn to chse ldrs over 2f out: sn drvn and no imp* **9/1**

000 6 hd **Indigo Belle (IRE)**[4] 3614 3-8-2 32 (v) SilvestreDeSousa 5 29
(Mrs A Duffield) *chsd ldrs: rdn along 3f out: drvn 2f out and sn wknd* **22/1**

0050 7 21 **Ernies Keep**[55] 2802 3-8-4 39 DominicFox(3) 2 9
(W Storey) *led: rdn along over 3f out: drvn and hdd 2f out: sn wknd* **125/1**

2206 8 3½ **Dream In Blue**[19] 3997 4-9-8 60 (b[1]) ShaneKelly 7 5
(J A Osborne) *in tch: hdwy to chse ldrs 6f out: rdn along 3f out: drvn 2f out and sn wknd* **9/4**[1]

00- 9 52 **Classic Dancer**[229] 7713 4-9-3 0 NCallan 3 —
(Jane Chapple-Hyam) *trckd ldrs: rdn along over 4f out and sn wknd* **6/1**[3]

3000 10 1 **One Tou Many**[28] 3714 4-9-0 42 (v[1]) KellyHarrison(3) 9 —
(C W Fairhurst) *a in rr: bhd fnl 4f* **5/1**[2]

000- 11 118 **Franali (IRE)**[255] 7425 3-7-12 45 ow1 JamieKyne(5) 8 —
(R F Fisher) *a in rr: wl bhd fr 1/2-way* **16/1**

3m 34.03s (2.03) **Going Correction** -0.025s/f (Good)
WFA 3 from 4yo+ 15lb **11 Ran SP% 116.8**
Speed ratings (Par 101): **93,92,90,89,88 88,77,75,49,49** —
toteswingers: 1&2 £8.00, 1&3 £14.70, 2&3 £14.60. CSF £56.39 TOTE £7.40: £2.70, £3.20, £3.40; EX 62.20.There was no bid for the winner.
Owner S D Rose **Bred** N Bycroft **Trained** Brandsby, N Yorks

FOCUS
This was a truly awful contest, sub-banded form.

4618 WEATHERBYS BANK MAIDEN STKS 7f
2:50 (2:53) (Class 5) 2-Y-O **£3,238** (£963; £481; £240) **Stalls** Low

Form RPR

23 1 **Bonfire Knight**[18] 4067 2-9-3 0 (t) GrahamGibbons 7 67+
(J J Quinn) *trckd ldng pair: effrt over 2f out: rdn to ld over 1f out: drvn ins fnl f: kpt on wl towards fin* **7/4**[1]

005 2 1 **William Arnold**[34] 3494 2-9-0 46 KellyHarrison(3) 3 63
(C W Fairhurst) *led 3f: cl up on outer: rdn 2f out: drvn and ev ch ent fnl f: sn edgd lft and no ex last 50yds* **250/1**

3 ½ **Decimus Meridius (IRE)** 2-9-0 0 FrederikTylicki(3) 6 62+
(J Howard Johnson) *sn outpcd and pushed along: rn green and rdn along 1/2-way: hdwy wl over 1f out: styd on strly ins fnl f* **9/4**[2]

4 nk **Greyfriarschorista** 2-9-3 0 GregFairley 4 61
(M Johnston) *chsd ldrs: rdn along over 2f out and sn cl up: ev ch ent fnl f: sn drvn and wknd last 75yds* **9/2**[3]

50 5 2½ **Bustard Bay (IRE)**[13] 4194 2-9-3 0 TPQueally 2 55
(J G Given) *s.i.s: reminders after s and sn in tch: hdwy on inner 3f out: rdn and cl up 2f out: sn drvn and wknd appr fnl f* **28/1**

06 6 1¾ **Tribal Myth (IRE)**[13] 4194 2-9-3 0 NCallan 1 51
(K A Ryan) *cl up on inner: led 4f out: rdn 2f out: drvn and hdd over 1f out: hld whn n.m.r ent fnl f: sn wknd* **18/1**

0 7 1½ **Pleasant Day (IRE)**[10] 4314 2-9-3 0 MartinDwyer 5 47
(B J Meehan) *a towards rr: rdn along and outpcd fr 1/2-way* **9/2**[3]

8 5 **Lady Pacha** 2-8-12 0 TomEaves 8 29
(T J Pitt) *sn outpcd and a bhd* **40/1**

1m 28.82s (1.82) **Going Correction** -0.025s/f (Good) **8 Ran SP% 115.0**
Speed ratings (Par 94): **88,86,86,85,83 81,79,73**
toteswingers: 1&2 £10.30, 1&3 £2.80, 2&3 £20.80. CSF £455.38 TOTE £2.80: £1.10, £8.30, £1.10; EX 84.30.
Owner Ross Harmon **Bred** Wyck Hall Stud Ltd **Trained** Settrington, N Yorks
■ Stewards' Enquiry : Kelly Harrison caution: careless riding

FOCUS
This looked no more than a modest maiden and the huge run of 46-rated performer William Arnold, who was sent off at 250/1, seemed to confirm it wasn't much of a race. The winner could afford to be below form.

NOTEBOOK
Bonfire Knight looked ready for the step back up to 7f when finishing third over 6f at Pontefract last time and in the end he stayed on too strongly for his rivals, going on over a furlong out and battling on bravely. He may have more to offer in nurseries. (op 2-1 tchd 5-2)
William Arnold produced this effort from out of nowhere. He had finished nearer last than first on all three previous starts, including over C&D last time, but he seemed to enjoy being up on the pace this time and kept finding having been headed to hold on for second. A small race at a lower level should come his way. (op 200-1)
Decimus Meridius(IRE), a brother to useful 1m winner Windsor Palace, holds a Derby entry and this effort very much suggested he needs further. Soon outpaced and running green, he stayed on strongly from over a furlong out and was closing at the line. He should learn a lot from this and can win a maiden. (op 5-2 tchd 2-1)
Greyfriarschorista, whose dam was a winner at up to 1m1f, showed enough ability to suggest he will find a race if improving, which he is entitled to. (op 4-1 tchd 7-2)
Bustard Bay(IRE), who reared over backwards before the start, was given early reminders to chase the early pace and didn't run badly considering all these factors. He looks sure to do better in nurseries. (op 20-1)
Pleasant Day(IRE) was always struggling and failed to improve on his debut effort. (op 13-2 tchd 7-1)

4619 WEATHERBYS BLOODSTOCK INSURANCE H'CAP 1m 5f 175y
3:20 (3:20) (Class 4) (0-85,82) 3-Y-O+ **£5,180** (£1,541; £770; £384) **Stalls** Low

Form RPR

12 1 **Saga De Tercey (FR)**[9] 4345 4-9-10 78 NCallan 3 85+
(G A Swinbank) *set stdy pce: qcknd 3f out: rdn 2f out: drvn and hdd ent fnl f: rallied to ld again nr fin* **13/8**[1]

6301 2 shd **Bergonzi (IRE)**[27] 3728 5-9-3 74 FrederikTylicki(3) 1 81
(J Howard Johnson) *trckd wnr: effrt over 2f out: rdn over 1f out: led ent fnl f: sn drvn: hdd and no ex nr line* **9/2**[2]

1243 3 2¼ **Phoenix Flight (IRE)**[18] 4038 4-10-0 82 SebSanders 2 86+
(Sir Mark Prescott) *trckd ldrs on inner: rdn along and sltly outpcd over 2f out: styd on u.p ins fnl f* **7/1**[3]

2051 4 nk **Harry The Hawk**[12] 4229 5-9-7 75 GrahamGibbons 9 79
(T D Walford) *trckd ldrs: effrt 3f out: swtchd rt and rdn over 1f out and sn ev ch tl drvn ent fnl f and kpt on same pce* **8/1**

112 5 ¾ **Chookie Hamilton**[18] 4038 5-9-3 76 JamieKyne(5) 6 79
(I Semple) *trckd ldng pair: hdwy to chse wnr after 5f: effrt and cl up 5f out: rdn along 3f out: drvn and ev ch 2f out: wknd over 1f out* **7/1**[3]

0620 6 3¼ **Eijaaz (IRE)**[39] 3350 8-8-13 67 SilvestreDeSousa 4 65
(G A Harker) *hld up in rr: effrt and sme hdwy 3f out: sn rdn and no imp fnl 2f* **12/1**

3460 7 ¾ **Black Dahlia**[19] 4003 4-8-13 67 PJMcDonald 5 64
(J A Glover) *hld up towards rr: effrt and sme hdwy 3f out: sn rdn and nvr a factor* **22/1**

1344 8 2 **That'll Do Nicely (IRE)**[29] 3679 6-8-13 67 TomEaves 7 61
(N G Richards) *hld up: hdwy 4f out: rdn to chse ldrs 2f out: sn hung lft and wknd* **12/1**

3m 6.29s (2.69) **Going Correction** -0.025s/f (Good) **8 Ran SP% 112.1**
Speed ratings (Par 105): **91,90,89,89,89 87,86,85**
toteswingers: 1&2 £2.70, 1&3 £2.90, 2&3 £4.50. CSF £8.44 CT £37.98 TOTE £2.30: £1.20, £1.50, £2.10; EX 9.90.
Owner Andrew Dick, Brian Dunn & Philip Holden **Bred** Haras De Tercey **Trained** Melsonby, N Yorks

FOCUS
This was a fair staying handicap. The winner made all at a steady pace, with the runner-up always in second. The winner can rate higher faced with a true test.

4620 NEXT FRIDAY'S LADIES NIGHT H'CAP 5f 212y
3:50 (4:20) (Class 5) (0-75,72) 3-Y-O+ **£2,914** (£867; £433; £216) **Stalls** Low

Form RPR

6335 1 **Redwater River**[4] 4508 5-8-1 52 (b) DeanHeslop(5) 3 61
(Mrs R A Carr) *hld up: gd hdwy 2f out: rdn to ld ent fnl f: kpt on wl towards fin* **6/1**[3]

6021 2 ½ **Mandalay King (IRE)**[11] 4285 4-9-9 69 PJMcDonald 10 76
(Mrs Marjorie Fife) *sn outpcd and bhd: gd hdwy wl over 1f out: rdn and styd on to chal ins fnl f: drvn and nt qckn towards fin* **7/2**[1]

2400 3 1 **Bonnie Prince Blue**[11] 4285 6-9-10 70 (b) PaulQuinn 4 74
(D Nicholls) *in tch: swtchd rt and hdwy 2f out: rdn to chal ent fnl f: drvn and no ex towards fin* **12/1**

60-1 4 3 **Bedloe's Island (IRE)**[46] 3125 4-9-2 62 FrancisNorton 8 56+
(N Bycroft) *chsd ldrs: hdwy 1/2-way: cl up 2f out: sn rdn and ev ch tl drvn and one pce ent fnl f* **5/1**[2]

1330 5 1¼ **Ryedane (IRE)**[34] 3497 7-8-13 59 (b) DavidAllan 9 49
(T D Easterby) *in tch: hdwy and wd st: effrt whn nt clr run wl over 1f out: kpt on ins fnl f* **14/1**

6311 6 hd **Grimes Faith**[135] 919 6-9-0 65 (p) AmyRyan(5) 1 55
(K A Ryan) *midfield: effrt and nt clr run wl over 1f out: rdn and kpt on ins fnl f* **17/2**

01U6 7 1¾ **Buy On The Red**[29] 3681 8-9-4 71 (b) NSLawes(7) 2 55
(D Nicholls) *led: rdn along 2f out: sn drvn and hdd 1f out: wknd* **12/1**

-015 8 nk **Real Diamond**[20] 3973 3-9-3 72 JamieKyne(5) 11 55+
(A Dickman) *towards rr on outer: effrt over 2f out and sn rdn: nt clr run wl over 1f out and swtchd lft: kpt on: n.d* **18/1**

0210 **9** 1/2 **Only A Splash**[5] 4466 5-8-6 **52** SilvestreDeSousa 6 33
(Mrs R A Carr) *chsd ldrs: wd st: rdn whn hmpd 2f out and sn btn* **12/1**

-000 **10** 1 **Chosen One (IRE)**[12] 4225 4-9-0 **60** TomEaves 5 38+
(B Smart) *chsd ldrs: hdwy whn hmpd wl over 1f out: nt rcvr* **9/1**

6540 **11** 2 1/2 **Istiqdaam**[11] 4285 4-9-3 **63** DaleGibson 12 33
(M W Easterby) *hld up: a bhd* **22/1**

-000 **12** hd **Braille**[7] 4399 4-9-6 **66** GrahamGibbons 7 36
(T D Walford) *cl up: rdn along over 2f out: sn drvn and wknd over 1f out* **25/1**

1m 12.76s (-0.84) **Going Correction** -0.025s/f (Good)
WFA 3 from 4yo+ 4lb **12** Ran SP% **116.9**
Speed ratings (Par 103): **104,103,102,98,96 96,93,93,92,91 88,87**
toteswingers: 1&2 £4.70, 1&3 £9.90, 2&3 £7.00. CSF £26.78 CT £250.35 TOTE £7.60: £2.60, £1.70, £3.40; EX 34.60.
Owner David W Chapman **Bred** Cheveley Park Stud Ltd **Trained** Huby, N Yorks
■ Stewards' Enquiry : Paul Quinn two-day ban: careless riding (Aug 19, 22)

FOCUS
This race was delayed by half an hour, the course having to pass an inspection as the ground on the bend racing away from the stands seemed unsafe. The runners were advised to come stands' side for the remainder of the races. A strongly run race and a step up from the winner under different tactics.
Bedloe's Island(IRE) Official explanation: jockey said saddle slipped

4621 HORSERACE BETTING LEVY BOARD CLAIMING STKS 5f 212y
4:20 (4:50) (Class 5) 3-Y-O+ **£2,590** (£770; £385; £192) **Stalls** Low

Form RPR

0403 **1** **Rasaman (IRE)**[13] 4192 5-9-4 80 (v[1]) AmyRyan(5) 9 87
(K A Ryan) *chsd ldr: hdwy and wd st to stands' rail: rdn to ld wl over 1f out and sn clr* **11/2**

0035 **2** 4 **High Curragh**[8] 4372 6-9-6 76 (p) NCallan 7 72
(K A Ryan) *led: wd st: rdn along and hdd wl over 1f out: kpt on same pce u.p ins fnl f* **3/1[3]**

0615 **3** 1 3/4 **Turnkey**[18] 4069 7-9-12 84 FrancisNorton 1 72+
(D Nicholls) *hld up towards rr: hdwy 2f out: rdn and styd on wl fnl f: nrst fin* **2/1[1]**

0065 **4** 1 1/4 **Louisiade (IRE)**[95] 1655 8-8-9 43 (p) KellyHarrison(3) 2 54
(M C Chapman) *chsd ldrs: rdn along over 2f out: sn drvn and kpt on same pce* **28/1**

4500 **5** 5 **Paint Stripper**[47] 3066 4-8-8 42 DominicFox(3) 10 37
(W Storey) *chsd ldrs: rdn along over 2f out and n.d* **100/1**

6-64 **6** nk **Ava's World (IRE)**[19] 4012 5-7-13 40 AndrewHeffernan(7) 8 31
(Peter Grayson) *chsd ldrs: hdwy 3f out: rdn over 2f out and sn wknd* **125/1**

-051 **7** 1 1/2 **Stonehaugh (IRE)**[64] 2531 6-9-4 74 FrederikTylicki(3) 11 41
(J Howard Johnson) *midfield on outer: rdn along 2f out and nvr a factor* **5/2[2]**

0442 **8** 2 1/2 **One More Round (USA)**[12] 4238 11-8-12 60 (b) TomEaves 4 24
(P D Evans) *hld up: a in rr* **16/1**

0300 **9** 4 **Bold Account (IRE)**[14] 4172 3-8-9 45 (p) GregFairley 3 12
(Garry Moss) *chsd ldng pair: rdn along 3f out and sn wknd* **40/1**

0460 **U** **Actabou**[19] 4016 4-8-6 43 (b[1]) BMcHugh(5) 5 —
(F P Murtagh) *dwlt: a in rr: stmbld and uns rdr 2f out* **50/1**

1m 12.88s (-0.72) **Going Correction** -0.025s/f (Good)
WFA 3 from 4yo+ 4lb **10** Ran SP% **117.8**
Speed ratings (Par 103): **103,97,95,93,87 86,84,81,75,—**
toteswingers: 1&2 £4.40, 1&3 £3.60, 2&3 £2.70. CSF £22.27 TOTE £6.70: £1.10, £1.60, £1.80; EX 28.80 Place 6 £28.02, Place 5 £3.95.The winner was claimed by Paul Moulton for £15,000.
Owner Royston Vasey **Bred** Rasana Partnership **Trained** Hambleton, N Yorks

FOCUS
The usual mixed range of abilities in this claimer, but pretty competitive with not much between the top four on adjusted official marks and they bet 16/1 bar that quartet. The runners came stands' side in the straight and the time was only fractionally slower than the preceding handicap. However, Actabou appeared to slip at around the quarter-mile pole, raising further concerns over the surface. Slightly dubious form with the winner back to his best.

4622 TELEPHONE 01748 810165 TO BOOK CORPORATE HOSPITALITY CLAIMING STKS 1m 3f 214y
() (Class 6) 3-Y-O+ £

4623 BOOK NOW FOR SATURDAY 19TH SEPTEMBER H'CAP 7f
() (Class 6) (0-65,) 3-Y-O £

4624 GORACING.CO.UK H'CAP 5f
() (Class 6) (0-60,) 3-Y-O+ £

T/Plt: £15.40 to a £1 stake. Pool: £65,267.18. 3,081.16 winning tickets. T/Qpdt: £2.30 to a £1 stake. Pool: £5,075.10. 1,591.30 winning tickets. JR

4263 CHEPSTOW (L-H)
Tuesday, August 4

OFFICIAL GOING: Heavy (meeting abandoned after race 2 (2.40) due to waterlogged ground)
Heavy rain, more than 10mm in total, changed the going from good to soft (soft in places) to heavy, and further rain during racing led to abandonment.
Wind: Nil Weather: Raining

4625 SUNSHINE RADIO H'CAP 1m 4f 23y
2:10 (2:11) (Class 6) (0-60,60) 3-Y-O+ **£2,072** (£616; £308; £153) **Stalls** Low

Form RPR

00/3 **1** **Picot De Say**[17] 3798 7-8-12 **47** RichardThomas 4 58+
(C Roberts) *hld up towards rr: stdy hdwy over 4f out: led jst over 2f out: pushed out fnl f* **11/2[2]**

005 **2** 2 **Inchando (FR)**[11] 4263 5-8-12 **52** MCGeran(5) 5 57
(A W Carroll) *hld up in mid-div: hdwy over 5f out: ev ch wl over 2f out: sn rdn: styd on same pce fnl f* **20/1**

000- **3** 2 1/2 **Bathwick Man**[16] 4278 4-9-3 **52** (tp) StephenDonohoe 11 53
(D E Pipe) *led: rdn and hdd jst over 2f out: one pce appr fnl f* **7/2[1]**

0105 **4** 4 **Mossmann Gorge**[12] 4235 7-8-12 **50** (p) KevinGhunowa(3) 15 45
(A Middleton) *hld up in tch: wnt 2nd over 5f out: ev ch 3f out: sn rdn: wknd over 1f out* **8/1**

6200 **5** 3 **Oronsay**[27] 3739 4-8-9 **47** (t) AndreaAtzeni(3) 6 38
(B R Millman) *t.k.h towards rr: hdwy over 5f out: rdn and wknd over 2f out* **16/1**

-450 **6** 13 **Kokkokila**[48] 3029 5-9-10 **59** (p) RichardHughes 3 30
(Lady Herries) *hld up in rr: hdwy over 3f out: sn rdn: wknd wl over 2f out* **7/1[3]**

6-24 **7** 2 3/4 **Bert's Memory**[13] 4193 5-9-2 **51** SJCraine 13 18
(Jennie Candlish) *hld up in tch: rdn over 3f out: sn wknd* **16/1**

8 22 **Seader (USA)**[16] 2424 4-9-10 **59** DaneO'Neill 17 —
(Tim Vaughan) *prom: 2nd whn pushed along over 5f out: rdn and wknd 4f out* **8/1**

006 **9** 5 **Giant Sequoia (USA)**[8] 4373 5-9-11 **60** (t) VinceSlattery 16 —
(A J Chamberlain) *a in rr: no ch fnl 4f* **50/1**

0630 **10** 1 1/4 **Little Sark (IRE)**[20] 3986 4-9-2 **51** (p) JamieSpencer 14 —
(P D Evans) *prom tl wknd over 4f out* **12/1**

-504 **11** hd **Great View (IRE)**[25] 3798 10-9-6 **55** (v) KirstyMilczarek 2 —
(Mrs A L M King) *s.i.s: hdwy on ins 7f out: rdn and wknd over 5f out* **10/1**

60-0 **12** 16 **Aaman (IRE)**[54] 2856 3-8-12 **58** LPKeniry 1 —
(E F Vaughan) *t.k.h in tch: lost pl after 5f: bhd and rdn over 5f out: sn struggling* **12/1**

-005 **13** 109 **Lady Oaksey**[21] 3951 3-8-9 **55** FergusSweeney 8 —
(W S Kittow) *prom tl wknd over 4f out: eased whn no ch fnl 3f* **20/1**

2m 53.86s (14.86) **Going Correction** +1.275s/f (Soft)
WFA 3 from 4yo+ 11lb **13** Ran SP% **120.1**
Speed ratings (Par 101): **101,99,98,95,93 84,82,68,64,64 63,53,—**
toteswingers: 1&2 £29.50, 1&3 £6.10, 2&3 £20.30 CSF £114.64 CT £444.90 TOTE £5.80: £2.80, £7.60, £1.70; EX 173.20 Trifecta £205.90 Part won. Pool: £278.31 - 0.30 winning units..
Owner Irish Legend Racing Team **Bred** Henry And Mrs Rosemary Moszkowicz **Trained** Coedkernew, Newport

FOCUS
Heavy rain, more than 10mm in total, changed the going from good to soft (soft in places) to heavy and two of the non-runners in this opener were because of unsuitable ground. The time was 20 seconds slower than standard. The winner is rtaed somewhere near his old Flat form.
Oronsay Official explanation: jockey said filly ran too freely
Little Sark(IRE) Official explanation: jockey said gelding was unsuited by the heavy ground
Aaman(IRE) Official explanation: jockey said colt was unsuited by the heavy ground

4626 LINDLEY CATERING MEDIAN AUCTION MAIDEN FILLIES' STKS 5f 16y
2:40 (2:40) (Class 5) 2-Y-O **£2,719** (£809; £404; £202) **Stalls** Centre

Form RPR

5600 **1** **Monte Mayor One**[27] 3733 2-9-0 58 DaneO'Neill 1 65
(D Haydn Jones) *broke wl: led: hdd over 1f out: sn rdn: rallied to ld wl ins fnl f: r.o wl* **16/1**

2 **2** 1 3/4 **Lexi's Layla (IRE)**[6] 4427 2-9-0 0 JamieSpencer 5 59
(D M Simcock) *t.k.h early: chsd wnr: led over 1f out: sn hrd rdn: hdd wl ins fnl f: no ex* **6/4[2]**

32 **3** 2 3/4 **L'Enchanteresse (IRE)**[10] 4331 2-9-0 0 HayleyTurner 4 49
(M L W Bell) *t.k.h early in last: wnt 3rd 3f out: rdn over 1f out: no rspnse* **10/11[1]**

0 **4** 10 **Avon Krystal**[15] 4147 2-9-0 0 RichardHughes 3 19+
(R Hannon) *s.i.s: sn hld up in 3rd: last 3f out: nudged along and struggling over 1f out* **8/1[3]**

65.49 secs (6.19) **Going Correction** +1.025s/f (Soft) **4** Ran SP% **109.4**
Speed ratings (Par 91): **91,88,83,67**
CSF £40.21 TOTE £16.50; EX 49.80 Place 6 £45.20, Place 5 £20.92.
Owner R Phillips **Bred** Mrs D J Hughes **Trained** Efail Isaf, Rhondda C Taff

FOCUS
This has the look of a "heavy-ground shock" about it. The form is very hard to assess and is rated negatively.

NOTEBOOK
Monte Mayor One had looked ordinary in four previous maidens, one of them on good to soft ground. She looked beaten as the runner-up swept to the front, but her one pace was enough to regain the lead as her rival failed to put the race to bed. Dane O'Neill, describing her as a "tough little filly", felt that her experience was a big plus but the result would probably have been very different had conditions been less exacting.
Lexi's Layla(IRE) had shown ability in one previous race, and the fact that it was run on soft ground appeared significant in the prevailing conditions, but she failed to finish the job off, She can be given another chance in less desperate ground, with a return to 6f an obvious option. (tchd 11-8 and 13-8)
L'Enchanteresse(IRE) had shown considerable promise in her two previous races and, while one of them was on ground with some cut in it, the state of the track was nothing like this. She still looks likely to find a race in faster conditions. (op Evens tchd 11-10)
Avon Krystal is by the sprinter Avonbridge, but there is middle-distance stamina on her dam's side. If she is to show anything, it will probably be in nurseries at 7f plus. (op 15-2)

4627 LINDLEY CATERING NURSERY 6f 16y
() (Class 5) 2-Y-O £

4628 LINDLEY CATERING (S) STKS 1m 14y
() (Class 6) 3-Y-O+ £

4629 LINDLEY CATERING FILLIES' H'CAP 1m 14y
() (Class 5) (0-75,) 3-Y-O+ £

4630 WEST COAST MARKETS H'CAP 7f 16y
() (Class 3) (0-95,) 3-Y-O+ £

4631 SUNSHINE RADIO MAIDEN STKS 7f 16y
() (Class 5) 3-Y-O+ £

4632 LINDLEY CATERING H'CAP (LADIES RACE) 1m 14y
() (Class 5) (0-70,) 3-Y-O+ £

T/Jkpt: £3,491.90 to a £1 stake. Pool: £81,150. 16.50 winning tickets. T/Plt: £132.70 to a £1 stake. Pool: £77,9686. 428.79 winning tickets. KH

4633 - 4636a (Foreign Racing) - See Raceform Interactive

4579 DEAUVILLE (R-H)
Tuesday, August 4

OFFICIAL GOING: Turf course - good; all-weather - standard

4637a PRIX DU CERCLE (LISTED RACE) 5f
2:55 (2:55) 3-Y-O+ **£25,243** (£10,097; £7,573; £5,049; £2,524)

RPR

1 **Stern Opinion (USA)**[273] 7187 4-9-0 SPasquier 5 112
(P Bary, France) **66/10[1]**

2 1 1/2 **Peace Camp (USA)**[24] 3892 3-8-7 .... JVictoire 8 102
(A Fabre, France)
3 nk **Cadeau For Maggi**[61] 4-9-0 .... MGuyon 9 106
(H-A Pantall, France)
4 nse **Masta Plasta (IRE)**[24] 3848 6-9-4 .... TThulliez 3 110
(D Nicholls) *prom: disputing ld 1/2-way: led 2f out to 1f out: no ex fnl 100yds* **7/1**[2]
5 shd **Aiboa (IRE)**[23] 3908 3-8-11 .... CSoumillon 1 104
(L A Urbano-Grajales, France)
6 nk **Treasure (FR)**[27] 3-8-7 .... C-PLemaire 2 99
(Mme C Head-Maarek, France)
7 nk **Lisselan Castle (USA)**[65] 4-9-0 ....(b) GMasure 6 103
(Mme J Bidgood, Spain)
8 1 1/2 **Sacho (GER)**[46] 3202 11-9-4 .... WMongil 11 102
(W Kujath, Germany)
9 1/2 **Contest (IRE)**[23] 3908 5-9-4 ....(b) FJohansson 10 100
(C Theodorakis, Greece)
10 1 1/2 **Skyteam (FR)**[46] 3202 5-9-0 ....(p) DBoeuf 13 91
(Mme C Head-Maarek, France)
0 **Dramatic Turn**[360] 4881 5-8-10 .... OPeslier 12 —
(Mme J Bidgood, Spain)
0 **Best Joking (GER)**[46] 3202 4-8-10 ....(b) GMosse 4 —
(W Hefter, Germany)

55.90 secs (-1.60)
WFA 3 from 4yo+ 3lb **12** Ran SP% **25.7**
PARI-MUTUEL: WIN 7.60; PL 2.80, 2.60, 3.00; DF 28.00.
Owner K Abdulla **Bred** Juddmonte Farms **Trained** Chantilly, France

NOTEBOOK
Masta Plasta(IRE) showed up well for a long way but didn't quite see it out.

[3944] BRIGHTON (L-H)
Wednesday, August 5

OFFICIAL GOING: Good to firm (8.3)
Wind: Nil Weather: Hot and sunny

4638 THE WINDMILL AT RUSTINGTON E B F MAIDEN STKS 6f 209y
2:30 (2:30) (Class 5) 2-Y-O **£4,037** (£1,208; £604; £302; £150) **Stalls Low**

Form RPR
46 1 **Jutland**[14] 4209 2-9-3 0 .... GregFairley 1 78+
(M Johnston) *mde virtually all: shkn up 1/2-way: rn green and wanting to hang lft fnl 2f: rdn to assert fnl 100yds* **7/2**[2]
56 2 1 1/2 **Luminous Star (USA)**[11] 4323 2-9-3 0 .... SebSanders 7 72
(R M Beckett) *t.k.h in last pair: effrt down centre 1/2-way: jnd wnr and edgd lft briefly 1f out: nt qckn fnl 100yds* **11/1**
52 3 1/2 **Interakt**[34] 3522 2-8-12 0 .... DarryllHolland 4 66
(M R Channon) *sn pressing wnr: rdn over 1f out: ev ch 1f out: kpt on same pce* **1/1**[1]
0 4 2 1/4 **Hellenio**[14] 4194 2-9-3 0 .... ChrisCatlin 5 65
(S C Williams) *racd freely in midfield: rdn over 2f out: btn over 1f out: kpt on ins fnl f*
5 1 1/2 **Caribou Island** 2-9-0 0 .... AhmedAjtebi(3) 2 62+
(Saeed Bin Suroor) *last away: sn rcvrd to press ldrs: rn green and edging lft fnl 2f: one pce* **9/2**[3]
05 6 nk **Rezwaan**[22] 3957 2-9-3 0 .... TPO'Shea 3 60
(E A L Dunlop) *cl up: rdn and n.m.r briefly 3f out: btn 2f out* **33/1**
0 7 1/2 **Beyond The City (USA)**[33] 3584 2-9-3 0 .... RyanMoore 6 59
(R Hannon) *last pair: pushed along after 2f: n.d fr 1/2-way* **8/1**

1m 22.26s (-0.84) **Going Correction** -0.25s/f (Firm) **7** Ran SP% **113.8**
Speed ratings (Par 94): **94,92,91,89,87 87,86**
toteswingers: 1&2 £9.90, 1&3 £2.80, 2&3 £1.02. CSF £39.47 TOTE £4.00: £2.10, £2.90; EX 35.70.
Owner Sheikh Hamdan Bin Mohammed Al Maktoum **Bred** Darley **Trained** Middleham Moor, N Yorks

FOCUS
Not a strong maiden and the form is limited, but the winner might leave this behind..

NOTEBOOK
Jutland built on the promise of his first two runs to make all the running. Greg Fairley was allowed to set just steady fractions early, resulting in many of his rivals racing keenly, and although he wanted to hang left throughout the final couple of furlongs, he repelled the challenge of Interakt and Luminous Star to assert again in the final half furlong. He is clearly held in quite high regard given his Royal Lodge entry but Mark Johnston said afterwards that he'd be unlikely to go for anything quite so fancy and the step up to 1m on a more conventional track ought to bring about further improvement. (op 4-1 tchd 3-1)
Luminous Star(USA)disappointed a touch at Salisbury last time but this was a big step back in the right direction and, although he looked uneasy on the track, he mounted a big challenge a furlong out only to find the winner too strong. He's now qualified for a mark and should be placed to advantage soon. (op 14-1 tchd 10-1)
Interakt was a little keen early but had every chance and there can't be many excuses. She may well do better on a more conventional track but doesn't look to be progressing. (op 5-4 tchd 6-4)
Hellenio was quite keen early and couldn't maintain a significant challenge. He looks more of a long-term project. (op 66-1 tchd 50-1)
Caribou Island looked as though the run would bring him on plenty in the parade ring and, after travelling with some promise, he looked very green when coming under pressure. He might not be one of the yard's better juveniles but wasn't cheap at 160,000euros and he ought to come on plenty for this experience, both mentally and physically. (op 4-1 tchd 7-2 and 5-1)

4639 CORRINGHAM CLUB NURSERY 5f 59y
3:00 (3:00) (Class 5) 2-Y-O **£3,532** (£1,057; £528; £264; £131) **Stalls Low**

Form RPR
363 1 **Radio City**[14] 4208 2-9-0 69 .... SebSanders 5 71
(R M Beckett) *midfield: rdn and effrt whn sltly impeded 2f out: edgd lft: hrd rdn to ld ins fnl f: jst hung on* **7/2**[1]
2356 2 shd **Vilnius**[15] 4165 2-8-3 58 .... ChrisCatlin 2 60
(M R Channon) *midfield: effrt whn n.m.r and swtchd rt over 1f out: drvn and str run fnl f: jst failed* **4/1**[2]
0216 3 1 1/2 **Craicattack (IRE)**[33] 3559 2-9-7 76 .... LPKeniry 3 72
(J S Moore) *chsd clr ldr: clsd and impeded whn edgd rt 2f out: led over 1f out: hdd ins fnl f: no ex fnl 75yds* **17/2**
566 4 1 1/4 **Watch Chain (IRE)**[11] 4318 2-8-0 55 .... NickyMackay 10 47
(M H Tompkins) *towards rr: rdn 1/2-way: kpt on ins fnl f: unable to chal* **16/1**
0505 5 3/4 **Grace Jicaro**[6] 4463 2-7-9 53 oh8 .... DavidProbert(3) 1 42
(Mrs L Williamson) *chsd ldng pair: sltly impeded 2f out: fnd nthing over 1f out and put hd in air* **33/1**
535 6 1/2 **Oasis Jade**[16] 4147 2-9-0 69 .... RyanMoore 7 56+
(G L Moore) *hmpd sn after s: plld hrd in rr: effrt 1/2-way: rdn and btn 2f out* **4/1**[2]
1452 7 nk **Lucky Mellor**[22] 3952 2-8-11 71 ....(b[1]) JamesO'Reilly(5) 4 57+
(D K Ivory) *tore off in 5 l ld: edgd rt 2f out: hdd and racd v awkwardly over 1f out: sn gave up: eased cl home* **8/1**
5526 7 dht **Point To Prove**[14] 4208 2-9-2 71 .... TPQueally 8 57
(Miss Amy Weaver) *last and rdn and struggling 1/2-way* **12/1**
6643 9 5 **Safari Camp (IRE)**[44] 3203 2-7-12 53 .... LukeMorris 6 21
(P Winkworth) *midfield: rdn and sltly impeded 2f out: n.d after* **15/2**[3]
6000 10 hd **Silvee**[16] 4147 2-7-9 55 .... NicolPolli(5) 9 22
(J J Bridger) *reluctant to go to s: towards rr and racing awkwardly: struggling 1/2-way and hanging lft* **40/1**

62.11 secs (-0.19) **Going Correction** -0.25s/f (Firm) **10** Ran SP% **114.6**
Speed ratings (Par 94): **91,90,88,86,85 84,83,83,75,75**
toteswingers: 1&2 £4.50, 1&3 £5.30, 2&3 £5.60. CSF £17.05 CT £108.77 TOTE £4.10: £1.60, £2.00, £3.00; EX 26.30 Trifecta £123.10 Pool: £224.66 - 1.35 winning units..
Owner Clipper Logistics **Bred** Baroness Bloodstock & Redmyre Bloodstock **Trained** Whitsbury, Hants
■ Stewards' Enquiry : James O'Reilly two-day ban: careless riding (Aug 19, 22)
Chris Catlin two-day ban: careless riding (Aug 19, 22)

FOCUS
Not a strong nursery with topweight Craicattack rated just 76 and the fact that the exposed Vilnius was an unfortunate loser suggests the form isn't anything to get excited about. The pace was strong, though, as Lucky Mellor went tearing off, lit up by the first-time blinkers, and the picture changed dramatically entering the final furlong.

NOTEBOOK
Radio City made his bid for glory down the outside. He looked to have the prize in the bag until Vilnius got clear and flew home to get within a short head at the line. He saw this out well though having been posted wide for much of the race and although he's probably no more than a handicapper in the long term, he shapes as though he'll get a bit further. (op 10-3 tchd 3-1and 4-1 in places)
Vilnius has been coming up short in nurseries of marks in the low 60s but the handicapper had given her a chance by dropping her to 58 and it was only fate that prevented her taking advantage. Trapped in a pocket up the inside and travelling well, her rider was forced to wait for an opening but by the time it came the winner had got first run on her, which ultimately proved crucial. She is clearly capable of winning off this sort of mark. (op 5-1)
Craicattack(IRE) had every chance before not having the pace of the front two in the final furlong. This wasn't a bad run and he looks reasonably treated. (op 8-1 tchd 13-2)
Watch Chain(IRE) made some late headway down the outside but he was always badly positioned from his wide draw and can do better. (op 20-1)
Grace Jicaro looked all at sea on the track at times so she did well to keep on.
Oasis Jade was a bit disappointing on this nursery debut and could never get in a blow. (op 3-1)
Lucky Mellor Official explanation: trainer said colt was unsuited by the good to firm ground

4640 DRINK IN BRIGHTON (S) H'CAP 1m 3f 196y
3:30 (3:31) (Class 6) (0-55,56) 3-Y-O+ **£1,942** (£578; £288; £144) **Stalls High**

Form RPR
6044 1 **Fleur De'Lion (IRE)**[13] 4224 3-8-3 50 .... DavidProbert(3) 14 57
(S Kirk) *cl up: pushed along 3f out: led over 1f out: sn clr* **8/1**
0004 2 2 1/2 **Classical Rhythm (IRE)**[7] 4437 4-9-6 53 .... TPQueally 11 56+
(J R Boyle) *cl up: n.m.r and swtchd rt over 1f out and outpcd briefly: kpt on to go 2nd ins fnl f: nt rch wnr* **12/1**
4505 3 1/2 **Special Chapter (IRE)**[20] 4021 4-8-12 45 .... SebSanders 16 47
(A B Haynes) *prom: rdn 2f out: wnt 2nd over 1f out: edgd lft: relegated 3rd and nt qckn ins fnl f* **25/1**
6 4 1/2 **Ocean Of Peace (FR)**[19] 4053 6-9-5 52 .... GeorgeBaker 5 53
(M R Bosley) *bhd: effrt over 2f out: kpt on ins fnl f: hanging lft and reluctant: unable to chal* **25/1**
0064 5 hd **Turner's Touch**[22] 3950 7-9-1 48 ....(b) RyanMoore 15 49
(G L Moore) *s.v.s: rdn and reluctant 4f out: hung lft but fnlly styd on ins fnl f: no ch w ldrs: dismounted sn after fin* **5/1**[2]
3450 6 1/2 **Barbirolli**[14] 4193 7-9-0 47 .... LukeMorris 3 47
(W M Brisbourne) *bhd: rdn to pass btn horses fnl f: unable to chal* **17/2**
3030 7 1 **Spring Quartet**[71] 2350 3-8-5 49 ....(v) PaulEddery 9 48
(Pat Eddery) *dwlt: shkn up after 4f: effrt 4f out: no imp fnl 2f* **16/1**
4501 8 1 **Kochanski (IRE)**[8] 4397 3-8-12 56 6ex .... GregFairley 13 53
(M Johnston) *set modest pce: rdn and hdd over 1f out: qckly lost pl* **7/2**[1]
5066 9 2 **Heart Of Tuscany**[14] 4206 3-8-11 55 ....(p) JimCrowley 2 49
(W J Knight) *plld hrd in rr: effrt 4f out: sn no imp* **12/1**
0304 10 nse **April's Daughter**[13] 4220 4-9-1 51 .... JamesMillman(3) 8 45
(B R Millman) *midfield: drvn 4f out: btn over 2f out* **9/1**
0060 11 6 **Royal Arthur**[13] 4241 3-8-4 48 ow3 ....(p) ChrisCatlin 10 32
(L A Dace) *w ldr tl 1/2-way: sn lost pl* **66/1**
5520 12 1 1/4 **Art Value**[16] 4156 4-8-5 45 ....(p) TobyAtkinson(7) 7 27
(M Wigham) *plld v hrd: nvr bttr than midfield* **11/2**[3]
0360 13 3/4 **Desert Lover (IRE)**[25] 3851 7-8-8 46 .... NicolPolli(5) 6 27
(A M Hales) *plld hrd: chsd ldrs tl lost pl 3f out* **33/1**
5-00 14 30 **Percys Corismatic**[22] 3946 3-8-5 49 .... TPO'Shea 1 —
(J Gallagher) *struggling 1/2-way: t.o 3f out: sn eased* **100/1**

2m 32.62s (-0.08) **Going Correction** -0.25s/f (Firm)
WFA 3 from 4yo+ 11lb **14** Ran SP% **120.3**
Speed ratings (Par 101): **90,88,88,87,87 87,86,85,84,84 80,79,79,59**
toteswingers: 1&2 £18.20, 1&3 £10.80, 2&3 £22.10. CSF £96.12 CT £2303.24 TOTE £8.90: £3.30, £5.00, £8.40; EX 132.00 TRIFECTA Not won..There was no bid for the winner.
Owner Mrs John Lee **Bred** Paget Bloodstock **Trained** Upper Lambourn, Berks

FOCUS
A very sedate pace to this1m4f selling handicap in which the field were well grouped half a mile out, so the form wouldn't be bombproof, and the first three home all raced close to the pace throughout.
Classical Rhythm(IRE) Official explanation: jockey said gelding was denied a clear run
Turner's Touch Official explanation: jockey said gelding stopped quickly
Barbirolli Official explanation: jockey said gelding was denied a clear run
Art Value Official explanation: jockey said gelding ran too freely
Desert Lover(IRE) Official explanation: jockey said gelding ran too freely

4641 JOHN SMITH'S BRIGHTON MILE CHALLENGE TROPHY (H'CAP) 7f 214y
4:00 (4:00) (Class 4) (0-80,80) 3-Y-O+
£16,099 (£4,825; £2,415; £1,203; £603; £304) **Stalls Low**

Form RPR
0061 1 **My Gacho (IRE)**[20] 4019 7-9-5 75 ....(v) J-PGuillambert 13 88
(M Johnston) *mde all: drvn over 1f out: only had one serious chalr fnl f: hld on gamely: all out* **20/1**

2203 **2** *shd* **Elna Bright**[7] 4438 4-9-8 **78** .... SebSanders 14 90
(B R Johnson) *hld up in last trio: rdn and gd prog 2f out: swtchd rt and chsd wnr over 1f out: styd on u.p: jst hld* **16/1**

-125 **3** *4½* **Driven (IRE)**[75] 2243 4-9-3 **73** .... JimCrowley 15 75
(Mrs A J Perrett) *hld up in rr: effrt over 2f out: r.o cl home: snatched mod 3rd nr fin: too much to do* **7/1**[3]

3140 **4** *shd* **Bold Cross (IRE)**[8] 4409 6-9-10 **80** .... PaulFitzsimons 8 82
(E G Bevan) *bhd: rdn 1/2-way: kpt on to duel for mod 3rd ins fnl f: nt rch ldrs* **16/1**

0006 **5** *1* **Hustle (IRE)**[19] 4064 4-9-10 **80** .... GeorgeBaker 10 79
(Miss Gay Kelleway) *trckd ldrs: rdn 3f out: no ch w ldng pair over 1f out: plugged on* **10/1**

6023 **6** *hd* **Twilight Star (IRE)**[13] 4236 5-9-7 **77** .... DarryllHolland 7 76
(R A Teal) *chsd wnr tl rdn and wknd 1f out* **12/1**

6114 **7** *1* **Marvo**[14] 4211 5-9-7 **77** .... RyanMoore 16 74
(M H Tompkins) *last at 1/2-way: passed btn horses and fin wl: unable to chal* **5/1**[1]

2300 **8** *1* **Purus (IRE)**[34] 3523 7-9-7 **77** .... DaneO'Neill 5 71
(R A Teal) *midfield: shkn up over 3f out: sn btn* **25/1**

4260 **9** *¾* **Bere Davis (FR)**[20] 3996 4-8-10 **73** .... AndrewHeffernan(7) 9 66
(P D Evans) *cl up: drvn 3f out: no ex and racing awkwardly over 1f out* **25/1**

0013 **10** *1* **Arthur's Edge**[11] 4293 5-9-2 **72** .... SteveDrowne 11 62
(B Palling) *t.k.h early: prom on outside: drvn over 3f out: sn lost pl* **12/1**

1324 **11** *¾* **Burns Night**[16] 4143 3-9-2 **79** .... (b[1]) GregFairley 6 68
(M Johnston) *immediately rdn in midfield: n.d fr 1/2-way* **13/2**[2]

-212 **12** *hd* **Uncle Fred**[42] 3274 4-9-7 **80** .... DavidProbert(3) 12 68
(P R Chamings) *immediately drvn and sn cl up: wknd 3f out* **5/1**[1]

4216 **13** *3* **Support Fund (IRE)**[6] 4452 5-9-4 **74** .... ShaneKelly 1 55
(Eve Johnson Houghton) *slowly away: a bhd* **20/1**

0160 **14** *5* **April Fool**[20] 3996 5-9-4 **74** .... (v) RichardThomas 4 44
(J A Geake) *drvn 1/2-way: sn btn: eased over 1f out* **50/1**

0313 **15** *1½* **Flying Valentino**[5] 4482 5-9-7 **77** .... TPO'Shea 3 43
(Ian Williams) *chsd ldrs over 5f: eased whn btn: t.o* **14/1**

1m 32.57s (-3.43) **Going Correction** -0.25s/f (Firm)
WFA 3 from 4yo+ 7lb **15 Ran SP% 121.3**
Speed ratings (Par 105): **107,106,102,102,101 101,100,99,98,97 96,96,93,88,86**
toteswingers: 1&2 £46.10, 1&3 £36.60, 2&3 £20.40. CSF £293.55 CT £1561.31 TOTE £25.30: £6.50, £3.40, £3.40; EX 384.40 Trifecta £212.70 Part won. Pool: £287.51 - 0.40 winning units..
Owner Grant Mercer **Bred** Mount Coote Stud **Trained** Middleham Moor, N Yorks

FOCUS
Brighton's most valuable race of the year so very competitive but in the end two came clear.
Elna Bright Official explanation: vet said gelding lost two shoes

4642 SOUTH EAST LEISURE GROUP H'CAP 7f 214y
4:30 (4:30) (Class 5) (0-70,70) 3-Y-O **£3,280** (£981; £490; £245; £122) **Stalls Low**

Form RPR

3001 **1** **Cheam Forever (USA)**[29] 3708 3-9-4 **67** .... RichardKingscote 1 75+
(R Charlton) *pressed ldr: led after 3f: kpt on wl ins fnl f: cosily* **4/1**[1]

-000 **2** *¾* **Jazacosta (USA)**[55] 2845 3-9-5 **68** .... JimCrowley 6 74
(Mrs A J Perrett) *hanging bdly lft tl rchd far rails: wnt 2nd ins fnl f and kpt on u.p: a hld* **5/1**[2]

215 **3** *1½* **Shared Moment (IRE)**[12] 4279 3-8-13 **62** .... (p) TPO'Shea 8 65
(J Gallagher) *detached last early: clsd 3f out: hanging lft but plugged on ins fnl f: snatched 3rd but unable to chal* **11/2**[3]

2-63 **4** *hd* **Good For Her**[32] 3630 3-9-4 **67** .... DaneO'Neill 4 69
(J L Dunlop) *taken down early: led 3f: pressed wnr tl rdn and nt qckn ins fnl f: lost 3rd fnl strides* **4/1**[1]

3610 **5** *7* **Athania (IRE)**[12] 4262 3-9-6 **69** .... (v) RichardMullen 3 55
(A P Jarvis) *nvr bttr than midfield: rdn and finding nthing whn n.m.r over 1f out* **14/1**

-553 **6** *nk* **Astrobrava**[32] 3610 3-8-2 **51** .... NickyMackay 10 37
(M H Tompkins) *towards rr: wl btn fnl 2f* **8/1**

2503 **7** *shd* **Jewelled Reef (IRE)**[26] 3803 3-8-10 **59** .... ShaneKelly 9 44
(Eve Johnson Houghton) *bhd early: effrt 2f out: drvn over 1f out: one pce and sn btn* **14/1**

-060 **8** *2* **Lennie Briscoe (IRE)**[95] 1670 3-8-13 **62** .... JamesDoyle 11 43
(S Kirk) *chsd ldrs 5f: edgd lft and put hd in air fnl f* **12/1**

0560 **9** *5* **Bounty Reef**[13] 4224 3-7-13 **51** oh3 .... DavidProbert(3) 5 20
(P D Evans) *chsd ldrs over 5f: sn btn* **33/1**

5-05 **10** *6* **Waahej**[40] 3357 3-9-3 **66** .... DarryllHolland 2 21
(P W Hiatt) *chsd ldrs tl 1/2-way: sn racing awkwardly: eased whn btn fnl f* **12/1**

1m 33.84s (-2.16) **Going Correction** -0.25s/f (Firm) **10 Ran SP% 114.8**
Speed ratings (Par 100): **100,99,97,97,90 90,90,88,83,77**
toteswingers: 1&2 £7.30, 1&3 £4.70, 2&3 £5.30. CSF £23.30 CT £111.97 TOTE £3.40: £1.50, £2.40, £1.70; EX 28.40 Trifecta £130.20 Pool: £443.50 - 2.52 winning units..
Owner H R H Sultan Ahmad Shah **Bred** Robert W McCann Et Al **Trained** Beckhampton, Wilts

FOCUS
The front four finished a long way clear and the form looks solid enough for the grade.
Waahej Official explanation: trainer's rep said gelding was unsuited by the good to firm ground

4643 SOUND LONDON H'CAP 5f 213y
5:00 (5:00) (Class 6) (0-55,55) 3-Y-O **£2,590** (£770; £385; £192) **Stalls Low**

Form RPR

4-20 **1** **Mandhooma**[15] 4183 3-8-12 **53** .... PaulDoe 1 63
(P W Hiatt) *drvn along to dispute ld for 2f: in front after: only had one danger fnl f and kpt finding plenty* **16/1**

0235 **2** *½* **Dancing Welcome**[16] 4155 3-8-8 **49** .... (b) LukeMorris 4 57
(J M Bradley) *dwlt: bhd and a drvn along: styd on to go 2nd over 1f out: swtchd rt and tried to chal: kpt on but a hld* **8/1**[3]

00-0 **3** *2¾* **Short Cut**[53] 2918 3-8-8 **49** .... (t) ShaneKelly 5 48
(S Kirk) *prom: rdn over 1f out: one pce after* **15/2**[2]

0060 **4** *nk* **Clear Hand**[11] 4324 3-8-6 **47** .... (b) RichardSmith 6 45
(B R Millman) *cl up: drvn 2f out: hung rt and then lft and no ex fnl f* **25/1**

0004 **5** *2¼* **Bermondsey Bob (IRE)**[11] 4304 3-8-7 **48** .... FrankieMcDonald 11 39
(J L Spearing) *bhd: nvr on an even keel: kpt on ins fnl f despite hanging lft* **9/1**

0032 **6** *1¼* **Cindy Incidentally**[21] 3975 3-8-7 **48** .... (b) MickyFenton 7 35
(Miss Gay Kelleway) *w ldng pair over 3f: rdn and no ex over 1f out* **20/1**

633 **7** *½* **Abhainn (IRE)**[32] 3632 3-8-5 **49** .... DavidProbert(3) 13 34
(B Palling) *midfield on outside: rdn and hung lft 1/2-way: n.d after* **7/1**[1]

0-40 **8** *1* **Miss Pusey Street**[89] 1840 3-8-9 **50** .... TPO'Shea 9 32
(J Gallagher) *prom tl 1/2-way* **20/1**

4256 **9** *nk* **Louie's Lad**[13] 4231 3-8-10 **51** .... (p) RichardKingscote 3 32
(J J Bridger) *w wnr for 2f: prom tl wl over 1f out: curled up tamely ins fnl f* **7/1**[1]

4000 **10** *1¾* **La Gifted**[18] 4105 3-8-10 **51** .... ChrisCatlin 12 27
(M R Channon) *nvr bttr than midfield: btn wl over 1f out* **17/2**

3002 **11** *nk* **Lily Jicaro (IRE)**[22] 3947 3-8-11 **52** .... NeilChalmers 10 27
(Mrs L Williamson) *midfield: drvn 1/2-way: sn btn* **11/1**

0000 **12** *2¾* **Thefillyfromepsom**[26] 3815 3-8-10 **51** ow1 .... IanMongan 2 17
(P M Phelan) *midfield: struggling over 1f out: eased fnl f* **50/1**

0042 **13** *1¼* **Call Me Courageous (IRE)**[16] 4155 3-8-9 **50** .... (v[1]) SteveDrowne 15 12
(A B Haynes) *struggling fr 1/2-way* **15/2**[2]

0033 **14** *7* **Tricky Trev (USA)**[22] 3947 3-8-9 **50** .... (t) JamesDoyle 16 —
(S Curran) *chsd ldrs tl drvn 1/2-way: eased fnl f: t.o* **8/1**[3]

5340 **15** *2¾* **Elusive Ronnie (IRE)**[30] 3671 3-8-11 **52** .... (p) LPKeniry 14 —
(R A Teal) *bhd fr 1/2-way: eased fnl f: t.o* **28/1**

69.52 secs (-0.68) **Going Correction** -0.25s/f (Firm) **15 Ran SP% 124.3**
Speed ratings (Par 98): **94,93,89,89,86 84,83,82,82,79 79,75,74,64,61**
toteswingers: 1&2 £24.00, 1&3 £37.30, 2&3 £16.50. CSF £133.20 CT £731.65 TOTE £25.40: £7.10, £3.30, £3.20; EX 156.10 TRIFECTA Not won. Place 6 £1,643.56, Place 5 £441.73.
Owner Mrs Rosemary Gasson **Bred** Shadwell Estate Company Limited **Trained** Hook Norton, Oxon

FOCUS
A very modest handicap which continued the theme of front-runners doing well at the meeting.
Bermondsey Bob(IRE) Official explanation: jockey said gelding hung left in the final furlong
T/Jkpt: Not won. T/Plt: £1,576.60 to a £1 stake. Pool: £68,097.78. 31.53 winning tickets. T/Qpdt: £220.40 to a £1 stake. Pool: £5,392.38. 18.10 winning tickets. IM

3977 **KEMPTON (A.W)** (R-H)
Wednesday, August 5

OFFICIAL GOING: Standard
Wind: Light, behind Weather: Fine but cloudy, humid

4644 WEATHERBYS BLOODSTOCK INSURANCE APPRENTICE H'CAP (ROUND 8) 1m 3f (P)
6:05 (6:06) (Class 4) (0-85,85) 4-Y-O+ **£4,727** (£1,406; £702; £351) **Stalls High**

Form RPR

1002 **1** **Balnagore**[21] 3977 5-8-6 **70** .... JPFahy(3) 2 79
(J L Dunlop) *pressed ldr after 2f: led 3f out and sn drew abt 4 l clr: idled and hd high fr over 1f out: cajoled along wout use of whip to hold on* **5/1**[2]

-604 **2** *½* **Dance The Star (USA)**[42] 3273 4-9-10 **85** .... Louis-PhilippeBeuzelin 4 93+
(D M Simcock) *stdd s: hld up in last pair: nt clr run briefly wl over 2f out: prog to chse clr wnr wl over 1f out: clsd u.p: nt qckn last 75yds* **11/10**[1]

2500 **3** *2½* **Mista Rossa**[42] 3273 4-8-7 **68** .... (b[1]) MCGeran 10 72
(H Morrison) *trckd ldng trio: rdn 3f out and nt qckn: styd on fr over 1f out to take 3rd ins fnl f* **13/2**[3]

1000 **4** *3¼* **Stand Guard**[84] 1990 5-9-7 **82** .... JackDean 6 80
(P Howling) *hld up in 7th: rdn 3f out: prog to go 3rd over 1f out to ins fnl f: wknd* **8/1**

0-00 **5** *½* **Zaif (IRE)**[7] 4437 6-8-6 **70** .... TobyAtkinson(3) 1 68
(D J S Ffrench Davis) *hld up in last pair: taken to wd outside and rdn 3f out: no prog tl plugged on fnl f* **33/1**

106 **6** *nk* **Majehar**[25] 3869 7-8-3 **69** .... DavidKenny(5) 5 66
(A G Newcombe) *hld up in 5th: hrd rdn and nt qckn over 2f out: n.d after: plugged on fnl f* **20/1**

1052 **7** *1* **Polish Power (GER)**[18] 4084 9-9-0 **75** .... SophieDoyle 8 70
(J S Moore) *hld up in 6th: rdn over 3f out: struggling and no prog over 2f out* **16/1**

3315 **8** *nk* **King Supreme (IRE)**[6] 4450 4-9-1 **81** .... CharlesEddery(5) 7 76
(R Hannon) *trckd ldr 2f: 3rd after: rdn wl over 2f out: losing pl whn squeezed out 1f out* **10/1**

2400 **9** *8* **Wind Flow**[21] 3977 5-8-8 **72** .... (p) SimonPearce(3) 3 53
(C A Dwyer) *drvn to ld: hdd 3f out: wknd rapidly wl over 1f out* **12/1**

2m 21.22s (-0.68) **Going Correction** +0.025s/f (Slow) **9 Ran SP% 119.1**
Speed ratings (Par 105): **103,102,100,98,98 97,97,96,91**
toteswingers: 1&2 £1.30, 1&3 £7.20, 2&3 £2.50. CSF £11.22 CT £37.40 TOTE £7.50: £1.70, £1.40, £2.20; EX 14.00.
Owner Mrs Simon Boscawen **Bred** Mrs S A Lloyd **Trained** Arundel, W Sussex

FOCUS
A strong pace looked guaranteed but that was not to be the case as it took over a furlong for Wind Flow to get into gear and take up the proceedings to set just a fair gallop.

4645 KEMPTON FOR WEDDINGS H'CAP 1m (P)
6:35 (6:36) (Class 6) (0-65,65) 3-Y-O+ **£2,047** (£604; £302) **Stalls High**

Form RPR

4200 **1** **Hits Only Cash**[23] 3929 7-8-10 **57** .... (p) SimonPearce(7) 9 64
(J Pearce) *t.k.h: hld up in midfield: rdn over 2f out: stdy prog on outer over 1f out: clsd on ldrs fnl f: led post* **33/1**

0422 **2** *nse* **Feasible**[28] 3735 4-9-6 **60** .... TPQueally 12 67
(J G Portman) *mounted on crse: keen early: trckd ldr after 3f: drvn ahd over 1f out: hrd pressed on all sides fnl f: hdd post* **4/1**[1]

0000 **3** *nk* **Millfield (IRE)**[41] 3322 6-9-11 **65** .... WilliamBuick 10 71+
(P R Chamings) *c out slowly and abt 7 l bhd rest: fierce hold and midfield after 3f: hrd rdn and prog 2f out: clsd on ldr fnl f: jst hld* **6/1**[3]

2-20 **4** *nk* **One Oi**[53] 2924 4-9-3 **57** .... MartinDwyer 4 63+
(D W P Arbuthnot) *t.k.h: hld up towards rr: rdn over 2f out: prog jst over 1f out: styd on on wl fnl f: nrst fin* **10/1**

5011 **5** *hd* **Sovereignty (JPN)**[28] 3735 7-9-3 **62** .... SophieDoyle(5) 14 67
(D K Ivory) *t.k.h: trckd ldr 3f: styd cl up on inner: drvn and effrt over 1f out: chal ins fnl f: no ex last 50yds* **9/2**[2]

2450 **6** *1* **Confide In Me**[11] 4300 5-9-5 **59** .... (tp) JimCrowley 3 62
(G A Butler) *sn restrained to last pair: brought wdst of all over 2f out: gd prog over 1f out: styng on fin: nvr nr enough to chal* **8/1**

00-0 **7** *½* **Leptis Magna**[21] 3980 5-9-3 **57** .... StephenDonohoe 13 59
(T E Powell) *prom: rdn to chal 2f out: upsides over 1f out: nt qckn ent fnl f: wknd last 75yds* **33/1**

520- **8** *1½* **Candy Rose**[287] 6899 4-9-6 **60** .... PatDobbs 5 58+
(M P Tregoning) *hld up in last trio: stl there over 2f out: prog over 1f out: styng on fin but no ch* **25/1**

0005 **9** *3* **Sign Of The Cross**[16] 4144 5-9-11 **65** .... LPKeniry 1 56
(C R Dore) *hld up in rr fr worst draw: nt qckn over 2f out: plugged on fnl f: no ch* **16/1**

0000 **10** *shd* **Royal Island (IRE)**[11] 4305 7-9-2 **56** .... VinceSlattery 2 47
(M G Quinlan) *hld up in last pair: shuffled along fnl 2f: nvr nr ldrs* **80/1**

5563 **11** *nk* **Takitwo**[57] 2794 6-9-3 **57** .... SimonWhitworth 7 47
(P D Cundell) *hld up in rr: nudged along fnl 2f: nvr nr ldrs* **16/1**

5560 **12** *hd* **Sew'N'So Character (IRE)**[21] 3983 8-9-7 **61**............ KirstyMilczarek 6 51
(M Blanshard) *t.k.h: hld up in midfield on wd outside: lost pl over 2f out: n.d after* **16/1**

0063 **13** *1* **Fifty (IRE)**[11] 4305 4-9-4 **58**............ RichardHughes 11 46
(R Hannon) *led at stdy pce: hdd & wknd rapidly over 1f out* **7/1**

0062 **14** *6* **The Grey One (IRE)**[23] 3929 6-9-1 **58**............(p) KevinGhunowa(3) 8 32
(J M Bradley) *t.k.h: prom: lost pl 2f out: wknd rapidly over 1f out* **10/1**

1m 41.16s (1.36) **Going Correction** +0.025s/f (Slow) **14** Ran SP% **122.9**
Speed ratings (Par 101): **94,93,93,93,93 92,91,90,87,87 86,86,85,79**
toteswingers: 1&2 £37.70, 1&3 £120.70, 2&3 £4.10. CSF £161.56 CT £940.84 TOTE £33.10: £6.80, £2.00, £2.50; EX 309.60.
Owner Oceana racing **Bred** G S Shropshire **Trained** Newmarket, Suffolk

FOCUS
Not much early pace on in this open handicap thus resulting a blanket finish.
Millfield(IRE) Official explanation: jockey said gelding ran too freely
The Grey One(IRE) Official explanation: trainer said gelding finished distressed

4646 DIGIBET MEDIAN AUCTION MAIDEN STKS 7f (P)
7:05 (7:05) (Class 5) 2-Y-O **£2,590** (£770; £385; £192) **Stalls** High

Form RPR

0242 **1** **Astonishment (IRE)**[16] 4152 2-9-3 77............ RyanMoore 11 76
(S Kirk) *trckd ldng pair: shkn up over 2f out: plld out and led wl over 1f out: styd on wl enough fnl f and in command* **8/11**[1]

6 **2** *1 ½* **Sea Dubai**[38] 3420 2-9-3 0............ RichardHughes 3 72
(R Hannon) *trckd ldng trio and racd wd: effrt to chal over 2f out: styd on to taken 2nd ins fnl f: no imp wnr* **7/1**[3]

04 **3** *½* **Edgewater (IRE)**[11] 4323 2-9-3 0............ MartinDwyer 7 71
(B J Meehan) *trckd ldr: chal over 2f out: chsd wnr over 1f out to ins fnl f: kpt on* **15/2**

0 **4** *2* **Winged (IRE)**[19] 4055 2-8-12 0............ WilliamBuick 9 61
(B W Hills) *s.i.s: bustled along to chse ldng quartet: effrt on inner 2f out: drvn and kpt on to take 4th nr fin* **25/1**

6 **5** *½* **Epic (IRE)**[34] 3522 2-9-3 0............ GregFairley 8 65
(M Johnston) *led: edgd lft fr over 2f out: hdd wl over 1f out: grad fdd* **9/2**[2]

00 **6** *nse* **First Cat**[42] 3270 2-9-3 0............ PatDobbs 4 65
(R Hannon) *sn in 6th: pushed along 1/2-way: clsd grad on ldrs fr 2f out: reminder 1f out: styd on encouragingly* **25/1**

0 **7** *8* **Knockback (IRE)**[13] 4219 2-9-3 0............ JimCrowley 5 45
(P R Chamings) *allowed to s slowly: hld up in last and wl off the pce: reminder 2f out whn wl bhd: passed wkng rivals* **66/1**

0 **8** *1* **Refuse To Tell**[34] 3546 2-9-3 0............ ChrisCatlin 2 42
(C E Brittain) *a abt same pl: pushed along by 1/2-way: lft wl bhd fr 3f out: t.o* **50/1**

00 **9** *4 ½* **Book Of Truth (USA)**[4] 4534 2-9-3 0............ FergusSweeney 6 31
(D M Simcock) *a in last trio: pushed along bef 1/2-way: lft wl bhd fr 3f out: t.o* **66/1**

10 *1 ½* **Typical Female** 2-8-12 0............ JamesDoyle 10 22
(A B Haynes) *pushed along in 7th bef 1/2-way: wknd wl over 2f out: t.o* **33/1**

11 *23* **Federal Reserve** 2-9-3 0............ LPKeniry 1 —
(M Madgwick) *t.k.h in last trio: wknd 3f out: sn wl t.o* **80/1**

1m 27.47s (1.47) **Going Correction** +0.025s/f (Slow) **11** Ran SP% **117.2**
Speed ratings (Par 94): **92,90,89,87,86 86,77,76,71,69 43**
toteswingers: 1&2 £2.70, 1&3 £2.40, 2&3 £5.90. CSF £5.97 TOTE £1.60: £1.10, £1.90, £1.60; EX 5.60.
Owner Mrs Barbara Facchino **Bred** Barouche Stud (ire) Ltd **Trained** Upper Lambourn, Berks

FOCUS
A decent pace, and those with previous experience dominated. The race has been rated around the principals.

NOTEBOOK
Astonishment(IRE) set a fair standard and only had to reproduce a similar level to get off the mark. Tracking the leaders until taking it up 2f out, he ran on well to run out a comfortable winner. (op 5-6 tchd 10-11 in a place)
Sea Dubai ran better than the bare form suggests at Salisbury on debut after a poor start and this was an encouraging performance. He was never far behind the winner but just lacked his pace when asked, although he stayed on well enough in the closing stages. (op 6-1)
Edgewater(IRE) left his debut run far behind when fourth last time and this was another step in the right direction. He held every chance at the two-furlong marker but was soon outpaced by the winner before getting run out of second towards the finish. He should find a nursery within his compass. (op 8-1 tchd 17-2)
Winged(IRE) never got competitive after an untidy start on her debut, but this was a step in the right direction. Although never going to threaten the principals, she stuck on well enough. (op 20-1)
Epic(IRE), who made most of the running, could find an opportunity in nurseries. (tchd 5-1)
First Cat shaped with promise. (op 20-1 tchd 16-1)

4647 DIGIBET.COM NURSERY 6f (P)
7:35 (7:35) (Class 4) 2-Y-O **£3,885** (£1,156; £577; £288) **Stalls** High

Form RPR

21U0 **1** **Kurtanella**[39] 3396 2-9-7 **80**............ RichardHughes 2 83
(R Hannon) *settled in last trio: wound up fr wl over 2f out: taken out wd and prog over 1f out: str run to ld last 75yds and immediately eased: cleverly* **6/1**[3]

2400 **2** *nk* **Ginger Grey (IRE)**[14] 4208 2-8-5 **64**............ MartinDwyer 8 66
(S A Callaghan) *trckd ldrs: produced between rivals to ld jst over 1f out: drvn and styd on: hdd and hld last 75yds* **6/1**[3]

006 **3** *1* **Candyfloss Girl**[13] 4219 2-7-10 **58**............ DavidProbert(3) 6 57
(H J L Dunlop) *fractious preliminaries: trckd ldng pair: effrt to chal on inner 2f out: tail whirling furiously: kpt on* **9/1**

2565 **4** *1* **Tucker's Law**[19] 4063 2-8-12 **71**............ FergusSweeney 3 67
(B R Millman) *pressed ldr: led briefly over 1f out: nt qckn: fdd tamely ins fnl f* **50/1**

0334 **5** *1 ¼* **Zinjbar (USA)**[21] 3978 2-8-11 **70**............ RyanMoore 9 62
(C E Brittain) *towards rr on inner: rdn and prog fr 2f out to chse ldrs 1f out: one pce ins fnl f* **2/1**[1]

030 **6** *hd* **Nave (USA)**[19] 4067 2-8-6 **65**............ GregFairley 5 57
(M Johnston) *dwlt: last pair: rdn over 2f out: kpt on fr over 1f out: n.d* **4/1**[2]

304 **7** *2 ¾* **Hill Of Miller (IRE)**[19] 4062 2-9-2 **75**............ JimmyFortune 4 59
(Rae Guest) *mde most to over 1f out: wknd fnl f* **12/1**

035 **8** *2 ¼* **Kakapuka**[13] 4219 2-9-2 **75**............ KirstyMilczarek 1 52
(Mrs A L M King) *racd wd: prom: u.p over 2f out: wknd wl over 1f out* **12/1**

400 **9** *5* **Evergreen Dancer (IRE)**[30] 3692 2-8-4 **63**............ WilliamBuick 7 25
(J R Best) *dwlt: in tch in rr tl wknd over 2f out* **10/1**

1m 13.88s (0.78) **Going Correction** +0.025s/f (Slow) **9** Ran SP% **118.3**
Speed ratings (Par 96): **95,94,93,77,75 75,71,68,62**
toteswingers: 1&2 £3.50, 1&3 £3.70, 2&3 £5.00. CSF £42.89 CT £328.14 TOTE £5.50: £1.60, £1.80, £2.60; EX 41.90.
Owner Mrs Philip Snow **Bred** The National Stud **Trained** East Everleigh, Wilts

FOCUS
A decent nursery run at a good pace. The winner produced a step up but the next two seem to anchor the form.

NOTEBOOK
Kurtanella unseated in the Albany Stakes and failed to run a race in a Listed contest at Newmarket last time, but got in here on a fair enough mark. Held up at the back, she was switched out to start her surge up the straight, and finished with a decent turn of foot to win going away. She looks a sharp filly who should hold her own when stepped back up in class. (op 11-2 tchd 13-2 in a place)
Ginger Grey(IRE) bounced back to form with a fine display after a couple of disappointing efforts, including when tried in blinkers. Tracking the leaders until taking the advantage entering the final furlong, he was just run out of it by a filly with a touch of class and if repeating this should break his duck. (op 7-1 tchd 11-2)
Candyfloss Girl ran with plenty of credit - a sustained effort from the two-furlong marker only saw her give best well inside the final furlong. She got a bit wound up in the preliminaries and swished her tail when asked for her effort but nonetheless stuck to her task well. (op 13-2)
Tucker's Law can be forgiven for his run on heavy ground last time. After racing prominently for much of the way he lacked the pace to keep tabs on the principals. He does not look particularly well handicapped.
Zinjbar(USA) was disappointing as he was well fancied but could never get competitive. (op 11-4)
Evergreen Dancer(IRE) Official explanation: jockey said colt hung left

4648 DIGIBET CASINO MAIDEN STKS 1m (P)
8:05 (8:07) (Class 5) 3-Y-O+ **£2,590** (£770; £385; £192) **Stalls** High

Form RPR

0 **1** **Fanunalter**[108] 1392 3-9-3 0............ DarryllHolland 3 90+
(M Botti) *last early fr wd draw: prog rnd outside of rivals bnd over 4f out to 3f out: gng strly over 2f out: chsd ldr wl over 1f out: hrd rdn and r.o wl to ld last 100yds: promising* **12/1**

2 *½* **Dhaawiah (USA)** 3-8-12 0............ LDettori 5 80+
(Saeed Bin Suroor) *nt that wl away but sn trckd ldrs: qcknd impressively to ld 2f out: rn green and hung rt in front: hdd last 100yds* **11/4**[2]

2 **3** *5* **Expressive**[79] 2142 3-8-12 0............ RyanMoore 7 68
(Sir Michael Stoute) *trckd ldrs: poised to chal over 2f out: sn rdn and outpcd: wnt 3rd jst over 1f out: no ch w ldng pair* **2/1**[1]

4 **4** *1* **El Libertador (USA)**[13] 4246 3-9-3 0............ StephenCarson 14 71
(E A Wheeler) *led to over 6f out: led again wl over 2f out: hdd 2f out and easily outpcd* **10/1**

0-3 **5** *nk* **Silverglas (IRE)**[96] 1638 3-9-3 0............ PatDobbs 10 70+
(M P Tregoning) *dwlt: wl in rr: stl there over 2f out: pushed along and decent prog over 1f out: kpt on wl fnl f: do bttr* **16/1**

0 **6** *¾* **Ultimate Respect (USA)**[13] 4246 3-9-3 0............ GregFairley 1 68
(M Johnston) *cl up: poised bhd ldrs over 2f out: sn drvn and outpcd: one pce after* **22/1**

05 **7** *2* **Weekend Away (IRE)**[26] 3813 3-9-3 0............ JamesDoyle 6 63
(S Kirk) *towards rr: sme prog on inner 2f out but outpcd: plugged on same pce fnl f* **66/1**

2204 **8** *nk* **Makaam (USA)**[33] 3590 3-9-3 86............ TPO'Shea 2 63
(M P Tregoning) *towards rr: shkn up over 2f out: sn outpcd: sme prog fr over 1f out: nvr on terms* **7/1**[3]

9 *4 ½* **Whatagoodcatch (IRE)**[46] 3182 3-8-12 73............ RichardHughes 8 47
(R Hannon) *settled wl in rr: jst pushed along fr over 2f out: nvr remotely on terms w ldrs: eased nr fin* **12/1**

2-00 **10** *1 ½* **Deo Valente (IRE)**[46] 3159 4-9-7 67............ KevinGhunowa(3) 9 48
(J M Bradley) *taken down early and walked to post: sweating: w ldrs: upsides over 2f out: wknd rapidly wl over 1f out* **66/1**

0 **11** *3* **Dayanara (USA)**[30] 3696 3-8-12 0............ PhilipRobinson 4 36
(C G Cox) *last bef 1/2-way and sn pushed along: nvr a factor* **66/1**

P53 **12** *1* **Kimberley Rocks (IRE)**[9] 4381 3-8-12 0............ JimCrowley 12 34
(R M Beckett) *nt that wl away: rchd midfield by 1/2-way: cl up on inner over 2f out: wknd over 1f out* **20/1**

222- **13** *nk* **Hay Fever (IRE)**[376] 4367 3-9-3 79............ ShaneKelly 11 38
(Eve Johnson Houghton) *wl in tch: poised bhd ldrs over 2f out: effrt sn after: wknd rapidly over 1f out* **8/1**

4400 **14** *26* **Kings On The Roof**[16] 4155 3-9-3 49............ GeorgeBaker 13 —
(G C Bravery) *led over 6f out to wl over 2f out: wknd rapidly: t.o* **125/1**

1m 38.85s (-0.95) **Going Correction** +0.025s/f (Slow)
WFA 3 from 4yo 7lb **14** Ran SP% **128.3**
Speed ratings (Par 103): **105,104,99,98,98 97,95,95,90,89 86,85,84,58**
toteswingers: 1&2 £15.40, 1&3 £16.90, 2&3 £1.60. CSF £46.48 TOTE £16.60: £3.70, £2.10, £1.60; EX 83.50.
Owner Scuderia Rencati Srl **Bred** Azienda Agricola Francesca **Trained** Newmarket, Suffolk

FOCUS
An interesting maiden run at just a fair pace until the straight where the front pair eventually drew clear to record a decent time. They could be a couple of very decent prospects.
Kings On The Roof Official explanation: jockey said colt hung badly left throughout

4649 THAMES MATERIALS LONDON MILE H'CAP (LONDON MILE QUALIFIER) 1m (P)
8:35 (8:37) (Class 4) (0-85,83) 3-Y-O **£4,727** (£1,406; £702; £351) **Stalls** High

Form RPR

21- **1** **Musleh (USA)**[299] 6621 3-9-3 **79**............ LDettori 9 92+
(Saeed Bin Suroor) *led after 1f: mde rest: shkn up and 2 l clr 2f out: kpt up to work but wl in command after: eased nr fin* **5/2**[1]

3406 **2** *2 ¾* **Roar Of Applause**[11] 4296 3-9-0 **79**............(b) DavidProbert(3) 2 85
(B J Meehan) *sn prom: chsd wnr over 3f out: upsides wl over 2f out: rdn and nt qckn sn after: clr of rest but no ch over 1f out* **20/1**

-301 **3** *1* **Assail**[21] 3980 3-8-13 **75**............ TravisBlock 11 79
(H Morrison) *led 1f: prom: rdn over 3f out and lost pl: drvn bk into 3rd wl over 1f out: plugged on* **9/2**[2]

21-6 **4** *nk* **Audemar (IRE)**[78] 2148 3-8-13 **75**............ JamieSpencer 4 78+
(E F Vaughan) *rrd s: hld up in last: stl there on inner over 2f out: drvn and gd prog over 1f out: styd on and nrly snatched 3rd* **20/1**

2524 **5** *¾* **Gaily Noble (IRE)**[34] 3543 3-9-7 **83**............ RyanMoore 3 84
(A B Haynes) *cl up on outer: wnt 3rd 3f out: no imp on ldng pair over 2f out: one pce after* **11/1**

51-1 **6** *1* **Cut And Thrust (IRE)**[203] 158 3-8-11 **73**............ PhilipRobinson 6 72
(M A Jarvis) *s.i.s: in tch: nt qckn over 2f out: shovelled along and one pce after* **12/1**

2106 **7** *nse* **Sam Sharp (USA)**[19] 4058 3-9-4 **80** TPQueally 1 79
(H R A Cecil) *racd wd in midfield: drvn wl over 2f out: sn outpcd: plugged on again fnl f* **12/1**

1611 **8** *shd* **Cool Hand Jake**[42] 3274 3-9-5 **81** FergusSweeney 8 79
(P J Makin) *nvr bttr than midfield: rdn and nt on terms w ldrs over 2f out: plugged on fnl f* **9/2**[2]

01-6 **9** *nse* **Shooting Party (IRE)**[54] 2890 3-9-2 **78** RichardHughes 7 76+
(R Hannon) *hld up wl in rr: shkn up over 2f out: no prog* **20/1**

31-0 **10** *2* **Officer In Command (USA)**[93] 1751 3-9-4 **80** LukeMorris 10 73
(J S Moore) *nvr gng wl and a in rr: urged along and struggling over 3f out* **28/1**

-12 **11** *1* **Satwa Gold (USA)**[125] 1082 3-9-7 **83** JimmyFortune 12 74
(E A L Dunlop) *hld up towards rr on inner: outpcd fr over 2f out: n.d after: fdd* **10/1**[3]

0361 **12** *1* **Cruikadyke**[11] 4322 3-9-7 **83** MartinDwyer 5 72
(P F I Cole) *t.k.h early: chsd wnr 6f out to over 3f out: sn rdn: grad wknd fnl 2f* **14/1**

1m 38.93s (-0.87) **Going Correction** +0.025s/f (Slow) **12** Ran SP% **122.1**
Speed ratings (Par 102): **105,102,101,100,100 99,99,99,99,97 96,95**
toteswingers: 1&2 £12.20, 1&3 £2.60, 2&3 £33.40. CSF £63.65 CT £227.83 TOTE £3.50: £1.70, £6.00, £1.90; EX 64.80.
Owner Godolphin **Bred** Nesco II Limited **Trained** Newmarket, Suffolk

FOCUS
A decent handicap run at a good pace.
Sam Sharp(USA) Official explanation: jockey said colt hung left

4650 THAMES MATERIALS H'CAP — 1m 3f (P)
9:05 (9:10) (Class 5) (0-75,73) 3-Y-O — **£2,590** (£770; £385; £192) **Stalls** High

Form RPR

3610 **1** **Haafhd Time (IRE)**[11] 4325 3-8-6 **58** RichardKingscote 9 64
(Tom Dascombe) *cl up: prog to go 2nd 3f out: rdn to chal 2f out: styd on wl to ld last 100yds* **17/2**

00 **2** *1* **Lady Rusty (IRE)**[19] 4050 3-9-3 **69** JimCrowley 8 73
(P Winkworth) *hld up in abt 7th: sme prog and 5th over 2f out: sn drvn: styd on fr over 1f out on outer to snatch 2nd on post* **11/1**

4224 **3** *nse* **Bagber**[25] 3869 3-9-7 **73** RyanMoore 4 77
(H J L Dunlop) *nt that wl away but sn rcvrd: led after 2f: drvn over 2f out: hdd last 100yds: lost 2nd on post* **15/2**

2343 **4** *3 1/4* **Demeanour (USA)**[14] 4206 3-9-5 **71** (v[1]) JimmyFortune 13 69
(E A L Dunlop) *t.k.h: prom: wnt 3rd over 2f out: sn drvn: no imp over 1f out: one pce after* **6/1**[3]

05-0 **5** *1 3/4* **Causeway King (USA)**[21] 3980 3-9-0 **66** DaneO'Neill 3 61
(A King) *rn in snatches in midfield: rdn 4f out: gng bttr 3f out: rdn again and fnd nil over 2f out: kpt on fnl f* **16/1**

0-42 **6** *nse* **Qelaan (USA)**[102] 1515 3-9-7 **73** TPO'Shea 5 68
(M P Tregoning) *led 2f: chsd ldr: rdn 4f out: lost pl 3f out: grad fdd fnl 2f* **12/1**

004 **7** *1 1/2* **Madison Park (IRE)**[14] 4205 3-9-4 **70** (vt[1]) TPQueally 12 63
(H R A Cecil) *v s.i.s and drvn to catch up rest: last tl prog on inner over 2f out: chsd ldrs over 1f out: one pce after* **9/2**[2]

0063 **8** *3/4* **Bedarra Boy**[21] 3985 3-7-13 **54** DavidProbert[(3)] 1 46+
(D W P Arbuthnot) *dwlt: hld up in 10th: c v wd bnd over 3f out and lost grnd: nowhere nr ldrs over 2f out: rdn and kpt on: nrst fin* **20/1**

1-56 **9** *shd* **Scene Two**[13] 4229 3-9-6 **72** (v[1]) JamieSpencer 11 63
(L M Cumani) *hld up in abt 9th: sme prog 3f out: rdn and nt on terms w ldrs over 2f out: fdd fnl f* **3/1**[1]

066- **10** *7* **Great Bounder (CAN)**[254] 7434 3-9-1 **67** GeorgeBaker 6 46
(J R Best) *hld up in last pair: shkn up and no prog 3f out: sn no ch* **25/1**

02-5 **11** *5* **Rock Relief (IRE)**[14] 4206 3-9-0 **66** StephenDonohoe 7 37
(Sir Mark Prescott) *trckd ldrs: rdn wl over 3f out: wknd wl over 2f out* **10/1**

6306 **12** *12* **Mellow Mixture**[32] 3630 3-9-2 **68** RichardHughes 10 19
(S Kirk) *mostly in last trio: rdn and no rspnse wl over 2f out: sn wknd and eased: t.o* **16/1**

0000 **13** *33* **Angelica's Art (IRE)**[27] 3776 3-8-7 **59** (b[1]) MartinDwyer 2 —
(B J Meehan) *dwlt: rushed arnd on outside of rivals to go 3rd after 3f: wknd rapidly 4f out: sn wl t.o* **66/1**

2m 20.1s (-1.80) **Going Correction** +0.025s/f (Slow) **13** Ran SP% **126.7**
Speed ratings (Par 100): **107,106,106,103,102 102,101,100,100,95 92,83,59**
toteswingers: 1&2 £27.70, 1&3 £21.80, 2&3 £13.80. CSF £102.91 CT £753.56 TOTE £12.40: £3.60, £4.60, £2.40; EX 201.10 Place 6 £16.73, Place 5 £13.86.
Owner Mrs Maureen Coxon **Bred** Gainsborough Stud Management Ltd **Trained** Lambourn, Berks

FOCUS
An open handicap run at a steady pace.
T/Plt: £28.80 to a £1 stake. Pool: £57,882.03. 1,465.15 winning tickets. T/Qpdt: £10.40 to a £1 stake. Pool: £6,352.80. 448.10 winning tickets. JN

4306 NEWCASTLE (L-H)
Wednesday, August 5

OFFICIAL GOING: Good to firm (firm in places; 8.6)
False rail in place from 1m to 6.5f on stands' side rail.
Wind: Fresh, half against Weather: Fine and sunny, very warm

4651 EAGA ELECTRICAL SERVICES NURSERY — 7f
2:20 (2:20) (Class 4) 2-Y-O — **£3,784** (£1,132; £566; £283) **Stalls** Centre

Form RPR

41 **1** **Azizi**[14] 4201 2-9-3 **75** RHills 3 90+
(W J Haggas) *hld up: effrt over 2f out: rdn: hung lft and led appr fnl f: forged clr: eased towards fin* **4/5**[1]

436 **2** *4 1/2* **William Morgan (IRE)**[25] 3875 2-8-5 **63** PaulHanagan 1 65
(R A Fahey) *led: qcknd over 3f out: hdd appr fnl f: no ex* **9/1**

0002 **3** *6* **Gold Fix (IRE)**[3] 4565 2-8-5 **63** RoystonFfrench 2 50
(M R Channon) *sn chsng ldrs: reminders 3f out: wl outpcd fnl 2f* **3/1**[2]

0222 **4** *7* **Desert Forest (IRE)**[21] 3971 2-8-12 **70** PhillipMakin 5 39
(J Howard Johnson) *chsd ldr: drvn 3f out: hung lft and lost pl over 1f out* **5/1**[3]

1m 25.59s (-3.11) **Going Correction** -0.325s/f (Firm) **4** Ran SP% **107.2**
Speed ratings (Par 96): **104,98,92,84**
toteswingers: 1&2 £3.80. CSF £7.91 TOTE £1.60; EX 6.40.
Owner Hamdan Al Maktoum **Bred** Shadwell Estate Company Limited **Trained** Newmarket, Suffolk

FOCUS
Two non-runners arguably made this a tougher-looking contest to work out than it had originally seemed, but two of the remaining four proved to be a league above their rivals. Despite the small field the form has a solid look to it.

NOTEBOOK
Azizi confirmed the promise he showed on his debut with an easy win at short odds on Lingfield's Polytrack last time. Punters were keen to be with him again but he looked in a bit of trouble early before powering through in the latter stages. He is bred to be a superstar, so it is slightly interesting to note that Lahaleeb took this race last season before going on to bigger and better things. (tchd 4-6 and 5-6 in a place)
William Morgan(IRE), who showed a bit of promise in 6f maidens, was always to the fore and came right away from the other two with the winner, which suggests he will be shedding his maiden tag sooner rather than later. (op 7-1 tchd 10-1)
Gold Fix(IRE), who was just beaten in a competitive nursery at Newbury the previous Sunday, failed to get competitive and was readily left behind. (tchd 10-3)
Desert Forest(IRE) has been finishing second quite a lot but managed to break that sequence here, and in truth never looked like playing a part. However, he has some size about him and should make up into a 3yo. Official explanation: jockey said gelding was unsuited by the good to firm, firm in places ground (tchd 11-2)

4652 LOCKTON INSURANCE BROKERS MEDIAN AUCTION MAIDEN STKS — 6f
2:50 (2:52) (Class 5) 2-Y-O — **£2,590** (£770; £385; £192) **Stalls** High

Form RPR

44 **1** **Hoof It**[12] 4286 2-9-3 0 DavidAllan 5 66
(M W Easterby) *trckd ldr: led over 2f out: rdn 1f out: kpt on wl* **3/1**[1]

60 **2** *1 1/2* **Blue Avon**[12] 4278 2-8-12 0 PaulHanagan 10 57
(R A Fahey) *led tl over 2f out: kpt on same pce fnl f* **33/1**

3 *hd* **Benny The Bear** 2-9-3 0 RoystonFfrench 6 62+
(James Moffatt) *dwlt: hld up in rr: nt clr run over 2f out tl over 1f out: styd on wl: no ex wl ins fnl f* **20/1**

4 *1* **Empressofboogie** 2-8-12 0 PhillipMakin 4 53+
(M Dods) *chsd ldrs: effrt 2f out: kpt on same pce* **7/1**[3]

5 **5** *4 1/2* **Lucky Traveller**[42] 3262 2-9-3 0 AlanMunro 8 44
(T D Easterby) *mid-div: effrt over 2f out: sn outpcd* **14/1**

04 **6** *3 1/2* **French Seventyfive**[39] 3376 2-9-3 0 DuranFentiman 3 34
(T D Walford) *gave problems in stalls: sn drvn along on outside: hdwy over 2f out: lost pl over 1f out* **8/1**

0 **7** *hd* **Fireflash (IRE)**[7] 4430 2-9-3 0 SilvestreDeSousa 7 33
(Mrs A Duffield) *chsd ldrs: drvn and outpcd over 2f out: sn lost pl* **5/1**[2]

8 *1/2* **Golden Emperor (IRE)** 2-9-3 0 PJMcDonald 1 32
(G A Swinbank) *hld up in rr: hdwy over 2f out: wknd over 1f out* **18/1**

1m 15.43s (0.23) **Going Correction** -0.325s/f (Firm) **8** Ran SP% **84.9**
Speed ratings (Par 94): **85,83,82,81,75 70,70,69**
toteswingers: 1&2 £8.00, 1&3 £7.70, 2&3 £27.40. CSF £53.24 TOTE £3.10: £1.20, £4.70, £4.20; EX 46.30.
Owner A Chandler & L Westwood **Bred** Bond Thoroughbred Corporation **Trained** Sheriff Hutton, N Yorks

FOCUS
A weak maiden. Burgau Royal, who had got worked up before running last time, got down to the start but was withdrawn after getting upset in the stalls (2/1, deduct 30p in the £ under R4).

NOTEBOOK
Hoof It, back down in trip, had shaped nicely in a couple of maidens, and got a first win under his belt after staying on strongly throughout the final furlong. A move into handicaps seems likely. (op 4-1 tchd 9-2)
Blue Avon, who is related to winners, had not shown a great deal in the past, so this was a big improvement after bagging the rail and leading. She would be interesting in nurseries if given a low mark. (op 28-1)
Benny The Bear, a sprint-bred gelding, kept on well despite looking green. This was a promising start to his career. (op 14-1)
Empressofboogie, a half-sister to the very useful sprinter Empress Jain and another winner, was not given a hard ride inside the final furlong and shaped better than her position suggests. (op 6-1 tchd 8-1)
French Seventyfive, a fair fourth at Doncaster last time when starting at 100/1, showed a bit of promise again after misbehaving in the stalls, and can win a race of some description in time. (op 11-2)
Fireflash(IRE), who was beaten over 14 lengths on his debut last time, received plenty of support in the market but failed to justify punters enthusiasm about him. (op 16-1)

4653 EAGA SHOWERSMART H'CAP — 5f
3:20 (3:20) (Class 5) (0-75,72) 3-Y-O — **£2,978** (£886; £442; £221) **Stalls** High

Form RPR

4544 **1** **Angelo Poliziano**[10] 4343 3-9-1 **66** (b) SilvestreDeSousa 2 74
(Mrs A Duffield) *chsd ldrs: led on outer over 1f out: edgd rt ins fnl f: rdn out* **11/1**

3215 **2** *1 1/2* **Noodles Blue Boy**[29] 3704 3-9-7 **72** PaulHanagan 3 75
(Ollie Pears) *trckd ldrs: effrt over 2f out: styd on same pce fnl f* **6/1**

0024 **3** *1/2* **Lucky Art (USA)**[2] 4601 3-9-3 **71** NeilBrown[(3)] 6 72+
(Mrs R A Carr) *trckd ldrs: nt clr and lost pl over 2f out tl over 2f out: styd on wl ins fnl f* **5/2**[1]

2145 **4** *nk* **Dispol Grand (IRE)**[12] 4289 3-9-4 **69** PhillipMakin 8 69
(P T Midgley) *w ldrs on ins: kpt on same pce appr fnl f* **9/2**[2]

004 **5** *3/4* **Arjemis**[12] 4276 3-7-13 **57** JamesPSullivan[(7)] 9 54+
(C R Wilson) *chsd ldrs on ins: outpcd and n.m.r 2f out: kpt on fnl f: nt clr run towards fin* **11/1**

65-0 **6** *1* **Blow Your Mind**[36] 3484 3-8-9 **60** (v[1]) DavidAllan 5 53
(Karen McLintock) *sn outpcd and drvn along in last: hdwy on outside over 1f out: nvr rchd ldrs* **22/1**

1533 **7** *hd* **Musical Bridge**[13] 4231 3-9-1 **71** DeanHeslop[(5)] 4 64
(Mrs L Williamson) *chsd ldrs: drvn 3f out: n.m.r over 1f out: one pce* **6/1**

0-62 **8** *3/4* **Residency (IRE)**[15] 4174 3-9-0 **65** RoystonFfrench 7 55
(B Smart) *led tl over 2f out: fdd appr fnl f* **11/2**[3]

2416 **9** *1/2* **Piste**[12] 4289 3-9-5 **70** PJMcDonald 1 58
(Miss T Jackson) *w ldrs: led over 2f out: hdd over 1f out: sn wknd* **20/1**

60.05 secs (-0.65) **Going Correction** -0.325s/f (Firm) **9** Ran SP% **116.5**
Speed ratings (Par 100): **92,89,88,88,87 85,85,84,83**
toteswingers: 1&2 £9.10, 1&3 £8.20, 2&3 £3.80. CSF £75.98 CT £221.31 TOTE £13.30: £3.00, £1.60, £1.70; EX 97.40.
Owner Middleham Park Racing XXVIII **Bred** Bumble Bs, C Liesack & Mrs S Nicholls **Trained** Constable Burton, N Yorks

FOCUS
Plenty of these could be given a chance, so this form should be fairly sound for the level.
Arjemis Official explanation: jockey said filly was denied a clear run

4654 EAGA HEAT (S) STKS — 6f
3:50 (3:50) (Class 6) 3-Y-O+ — **£1,942** (£578; £288; £144) **Stalls** High

Form RPR

0354 **1** **Sea Salt**[5] 4504 6-9-2 **55** SilvestreDeSousa 5 62+
(R E Barr) *hld up: hdwy over 2f out: styd on to ld last 75yds* **7/1**

-530 **2** *nk* **Darcey**[14] 4198 3-8-7 70 PaulHanagan 12 56
(R A Fahey) *mde most tl hdd and no ex wl ins fnl f* **10/3**[2]

2244 **3** *1 1/4* **Soto**[7] 4436 6-8-9 63 (v[1]) JamesPSullivan(7) 3 57
(M W Easterby) *w ldrs on outside: upsides over 1f out: kpt on same pce ins fnl f* **5/1**

0005 **4** *nse* **Captain Royale (IRE)**[13] 4225 4-8-11 46 (p) PaulPickard(5) 7 57
(Miss Tracy Waggott) *t.k.h: w ldrs: kpt on same pce ins fnl f* **33/1**

2040 **5** *1 1/2* **Hiccups**[2] 4592 9-9-2 74 PhillipMakin 11 52+
(M Dods) *hld up: effrt on ins over 1f out: kpt on: nt rch ldrs* **3/1**[1]

0600 **6** *2* **Steel Blue**[8] 4399 9-8-11 57 (p) AmyRyan(5) 4 46
(R M Whitaker) *hld up: hdwy over 2f out: one pce* **18/1**

5553 **7** *3/4* **Ice Planet**[16] 4133 8-8-11 60 DeanHeslop(5) 13 43
(Mrs R A Carr) *w ldrs on ins: one pce appr fnl f* **7/2**[3]

0600 **8** *nk* **Bentley**[21] 3972 5-9-2 49 (v) RoystonFfrench 1 42
(J G Given) *chsd ldrs on outside: wknd over 1f out* **50/1**

0460 **9** *3/4* **Secret Dubai (IRE)**[15] 4183 4-8-9 55 (bt) KristinStubbs(7) 8 40
(Mrs L Stubbs) *s.s: hdwy on ins over 2f out: lost pl over 1f out* **28/1**

-000 **10** *nk* **Recoil (IRE)**[10] 4344 4-8-13 42 (b) NeilBrown(3) 10 39
(R Johnson) *chsd ldrs: one pce fnl 2f* **200/1**

0400 **11** *1 1/2* **Fyodorovich (USA)**[7] 4435 4-9-2 51 (b) PAspell 6 34
(J S Wainwright) *chsd ldrs: drvn over 2f out: wknd over 1f out* **50/1**

00-0 **12** *28* **Frill A Minute**[10] 4346 5-8-6 33 PatrickDonaghy(5) 9 —
(Miss L C Siddall) *chsd ldrs: lost pl over 32f out: sn bhd: t.o* **200/1**

0 **13** *1/2* **Mareva**[21] 3975 3-8-7 0 PJMcDonald 2 —
(Ollie Pears) *dwlt: in rr on outer: sme hdwy 3f out: lost pl over 1f out: sn bhd: t.o* **125/1**

1m 13.68s (-1.52) **Going Correction** -0.325s/f (Firm)
WFA 3 from 4yo+ 4lb **13** Ran SP% **116.8**
Speed ratings (Par 101): **97,96,94,94,92 90,89,88,87,87 85,48,47**
toteswingers: 1&2 £6.00, 1&3 £6.40, 2&3 £4.40. CSF £29.30 TOTE £8.80: £2.60, £1.40, £2.00; EX 33.30.The winner was bought in for 5,000gns. Soto was subject to a friendly claim.
Owner Brian Morton **Bred** D R Tucker **Trained** Seamer, N Yorks
■ Stewards' Enquiry : Amy Ryan caution: used whip down shoulder in the forehand position

FOCUS
This was a bunch of mostly disappointing and/or out-of-form horses, so this was a proper low-grade event.

4655 EAGA INSULATION RATING RELATED MAIDEN STKS 1m 3y(S)
4:20 (4:20) (Class 5) 3-Y-O+ **£3,154** (£944; £472; £236; £117) **Stalls** Centre

Form RPR

-524 **1** **West With The Wind (USA)**[32] 3630 3-8-12 68 AlanMunro 1 70
(P W Chapple-Hyam) *trckd ldrs: effrt over 3f out: led over 1f out: drvn out* **9/1**

3242 **2** *2 1/2* **Starla Dancer (GER)**[10] 4347 3-8-12 70 PaulHanagan 5 64
(R A Fahey) *led tl 4f out: rallied over 1f out: styd on to take 2nd towards fin* **11/4**[2]

0340 **3** *1/2* **Steel Trade**[13] 4230 3-9-1 68 DavidAllan 7 66
(M Brittain) *dwlt: hdwy 4f out: sn chsng ldrs: kpt on same pce fnl f* **12/1**

0024 **4** *shd* **Indian Violet (IRE)**[12] 4275 3-9-1 69 AdrianTNicholls 4 66
(P F I Cole) *hld up: effrt over 3f out: kpt on same pce appr fnl f* **11/2**

0-24 **5** *nk* **Kessraa (IRE)**[15] 4180 3-9-1 70 TonyCulhane 8 65
(M R Channon) *sn drvn along in rr: hdwy 2f out: kpt on same pce: nvr able to chal* **16/1**

024 **6** *5* **Nisaal (IRE)**[19] 4046 4-9-1 70 (t) IJBrennan(7) 6 54
(J J Quinn) *trckd ldrs: effrt over 2f out: wknd over 1f out* **5/1**[3]

4-22 **7** *shd* **Storming Sioux**[48] 3061 3-8-12 70 RHills 3 50
(W J Haggas) *w ldr: led 4f out: hdd over 1f out: sn lost pl* **9/4**[1]

1m 40.03s (-3.37) **Going Correction** -0.325s/f (Firm)
WFA 3 from 4yo 7lb **7** Ran SP% **113.1**
Speed ratings (Par 103): **103,100,100,99,99 94,94**
toteswingers: 1&2 £4.80, 1&3 £12.50, 2&3 £6.50. CSF £33.20 TOTE £9.70: £4.20, £2.00; EX 39.40.
Owner Miss K Rausing **Bred** Lady Olivia At North Cliff Llc **Trained** Newmarket, Suffolk

FOCUS
This was a competitive maiden, with only 2lb between the whole field on official ratings.
Storming Sioux Official explanation: trainer's rep said the filly was unsuited by the good to firm, firm in places going

4656 EAGA RENEWABLES APPRENTICE H'CAP 1m 3y(S)
4:50 (4:50) (Class 6) (0-60,66) 3-Y-O+ **£2,072** (£616; £308; £153) **Stalls** Centre

Form RPR

3222 **1** **Wiseman's Diamond (USA)**[7] 4435 4-9-8 55 PaulPickard 3 70
(P T Midgley) *chsd ldrs: wnt 2nd over 3f out: led over 1f out: drew clr* **9/4**[1]

-401 **2** *7* **Zaplamation (IRE)**[11] 4313 4-9-5 55 IJBrennan(3) 2 54
(J J Quinn) *hld up in midfield: hdwy over 2f out: styd on fnl f: tk modest 2nd nr line* **9/2**[3]

0644 **3** *hd* **Georgie Bee**[37] 3451 3-8-10 50 JamesPSullivan 13 48
(T D Walford) *hld up in tch: hdwy over 2f out: kpt on to take modest 2nd jst ins fnl f: lost 2nd last strides* **11/4**[2]

0023 **4** *2* **Byron Bay**[11] 4313 7-8-12 48 ow1 (p) GarryWhillans(3) 9 42
(R Johnson) *t.k.h: led: clr over 4f out: hdd over 1f out: one pce* **10/1**

463 **5** *1* **Carragold**[43] 3237 3-8-11 54 JohnCavanagh(3) 7 46
(M Brittain) *s.i.s: sn drvn along: sme hdwy 3f out: nvr a factor* **20/1**

6-02 **6** *1 3/4* **Benitez Bond**[9] 4376 4-8-11 49 AnthonyBetts(5) 4 37
(G R Oldroyd) *chsd ldrs: one pce fnl 2f* **11/1**

245 **7** *5* **Darfour**[23] 3911 5-9-9 59 NSLawes(3) 1 35
(J S Goldie) *in rr: drvn over 3f out: nvr on terms* **11/1**

0-60 **8** *27* **Dolly No Hair**[47] 3124 4-9-4 51 AshleyMorgan 5 —
(N Wilson) *rrd s: hld up in rr: hdwy on outside over 3f out: lost pl over 1f out: eased and sn bhd: t.o* **25/1**

6000 **9** *21* **Lunar Storm (IRE)**[57] 2785 5-8-12 45 JPHamblett 8 —
(Mrs R A Carr) *in rr: sn drvn along: bhd fnl 3f: t.o* **20/1**

06-0 **10** *3 1/4* **Resolute Defender (IRE)**[11] 4312 4-9-1 48 ByronMoorcroft 12 —
(R Johnson) *led early: chsd ldrs: wknd 3f out: sn bhd: eased appr fnl f: t.o* **66/1**

1m 40.98s (-2.42) **Going Correction** -0.325s/f (Firm)
WFA 3 from 4yo+ 7lb **10** Ran SP% **116.2**
Speed ratings (Par 101): **99,92,91,89,88 87,82,55,34,30**
toteswingers: 1&2 £3.20, 1&3 £2.80, 2&3 £4.40. CSF £11.91 CT £29.03 TOTE £3.00: £1.40, £1.90, £1.50; EX 13.90.
Owner D I Perry **Bred** Hatta Bloodstock International **Trained** Westow, N Yorks

FOCUS
The leader went very hard early and the whole field was spread out at wide intervals for much of the contest.
Dolly No Hair Official explanation: jockey said gelding was unsuited by the good to firm, firm in places going and had reared as the stalls opened
Lunar Storm(IRE) Official explanation: jockey said gelding was unsuited by the good to firm, firm in places going

4657 WARMSURE H'CAP 7f
5:20 (5:20) (Class 5) (0-75,74) 3-Y-O+ **£2,901** (£868; £434; £217; £108) **Stalls** Centre

Form RPR

5332 **1** **Violent Velocity (IRE)**[5] 4504 6-8-13 67 IJBrennan(7) 11 78+
(J J Quinn) *hld up in rr: smooth hdwy 2f out: str run to ld last 75yds: readily* **5/2**[1]

5250 **2** *3/4* **Compton's Eleven**[13] 4236 8-9-7 68 TonyCulhane 1 75
(M R Channon) *mid-div: effrt over 2f out: chsng ldrs over 1f out: styd on same pce ins fnl f* **16/1**

1220 **3** *hd* **Hansomis (IRE)**[32] 3612 5-8-12 66 ow1 GarryWhillans(7) 5 72
(B Mactaggart) *w ldr: led over 1f out: hrd rdn whn hdd and no ex ins fnl f* **14/1**

6663 **4** *1* **Jonny Lesters Hair (IRE)**[35] 3496 4-9-9 70 DavidAllan 2 74
(T D Easterby) *trckd ldrs: t.k.h: effrt 2f out: kpt on same pce* **5/1**[3]

0303 **5** *1 1/2* **Leonid Glow**[20] 4015 4-9-12 73 PhillipMakin 3 73
(M Dods) *hld up in rr: effeort and edgd lft over 1f out: nt clr run: kpt on ins fnl f* **14/1**

3005 **6** *1 1/4* **Woodsley House (IRE)**[5] 4504 7-9-5 69 NeilBrown(3) 8 65
(A G Foster) *rrd s: in rr: drvn over 2f out: kpt on fnl f* **10/1**

0640 **7** *1 1/4* **Sunley Sovereign**[7] 4436 5-8-8 55 oh6 (p) SilvestreDeSousa 10 48
(Mrs R A Carr) *hld up: hdwy 3f out: sn chsng ldrs: wknd 1f out* **8/1**

0446 **8** *1/2* **Avontuur (FR)**[12] 4285 7-8-11 63 DeanHeslop(5) 6 55
(Mrs R A Carr) *led tl over 1f out: sn fdd* **7/1**

2435 **9** *3 3/4* **Fortunate Flame**[64] 2578 3-8-12 65 AlanMunro 7 46
(K A Ryan) *w ldrs: lost pl over 1f out* **9/2**[2]

1m 26.64s (-2.06) **Going Correction** -0.325s/f (Firm)
WFA 3 from 4yo+ 6lb **9** Ran SP% **115.3**
Speed ratings (Par 103): **98,97,96,95,94 92,91,90,86**
toteswingers: 1&2 £10.10, 1&3 £6.40, 2&3 £20.30. CSF £45.78 CT £472.70 TOTE £3.30: £1.60, £4.00, £2.90; EX 32.10 Place 6 £58.50, Place 5 £36.68.
Owner Mrs S Quinn **Bred** Miss Jill Finegan **Trained** Settrington, N Yorks
■ Stewards' Enquiry : Garry Whillans one-day ban: excessive use of the whip (Aug 19)

FOCUS
Quite a range of abilities were on show in this handicap, so the form will probably be unreliable.
Fortunate Flame Official explanation: trainer's rep said gelding was unsuited by the good to firm, firm in places going
T/Plt: £22.30 to a £1 stake. Pool: £52,179.54. 1,701.08 winning tickets. T/Qpdt: £7.20 to a £1 stake. Pool: £3,871.68. 394.15 winning tickets. WG

4349 PONTEFRACT (L-H)
Wednesday, August 5

OFFICIAL GOING: Good (good to firm in places; 8.0)
Wind: Virtually nil Weather: Cloudy

4658 BOLLINGER CHAMPAGNE CHALLENGE SERIES H'CAP (FOR GENTLEMAN AMATEUR RIDERS) 1m 2f 6y
2:10 (2:10) (Class 5) (0-75,76) 3-Y-O+ **£3,747** (£1,162; £580; £290) **Stalls** Low

Form RPR

0421 **1** **Recession Proof (FR)**[3] 4563 3-10-10 76 6ex MrJohnEnnis(5) 2 95
(S A Callaghan) *set stdy pce: rdn and qcknd clr 2f out: easily* **15/8**[1]

3046 **2** *9* **Locum**[16] 4150 4-10-6 65 MrDJEustace(7) 5 66
(M H Tompkins) *midfield: hdwy over 4f out: chsd ldrs 2f out: swtchd rt and rdn over 1f out: kpt on fnl f* **16/1**

1223 **3** *nk* **Safebreaker**[75] 2237 4-10-10 67 (p) MrJoshuaMoore(5) 6 67
(K A Ryan) *trckd ldrs: hdwy 3f out: rdn wl over 1f out: kpt on ins fnl f* **9/1**[3]

1550 **4** *1 3/4* **Fell Pack**[14] 4193 5-10-4 56 (p) MrSDobson 4 53
(J J Quinn) *trckd ldrs on inner: effrt 2f out: swtchd rt and rdn over 1f out: kpt on same pce ins fnl f* **17/2**[2]

3005 **5** *nk* **Allformary**[15] 4171 3-9-12 66 MrJNewman(7) 8 62
(B Smart) *cl up: rdn along over 2f out: drvn and wknd over 1f out* **50/1**

2120 **6** *1/2* **Dechiper (IRE)**[10] 4345 7-10-12 71 MrTSpeke(7) 9 66
(R Johnson) *midfield on inner: swtchd rt and hdwy wl over 1f out: sn rdn and no imp* **33/1**

3634 **7** *1/2* **Kalasam**[4] 4548 5-10-7 64 MrJakeGreenall(5) 3 58
(M W Easterby) *t.k.h: trckd wnr on inner: rdn along over 2f out: sn drvn and wknd over 1f out* **12/1**

4436 **8** *3 1/2* **Johnston's Baby (IRE)**[25] 3847 7-10-5 60 MrTRDavid(3) 7 47
(E J Alston) *chsd ldrs: rdn along 3f out: drvn 2f out and sn wknd* **14/1**

5064 **9** *2 3/4* **We'Re Delighted**[43] 3235 4-10-10 69 MrLStrong(7) 13 51
(T D Walford) *s.i.s: a towards rr* **50/1**

3531 **10** *3/4* **Bavarica**[12] 4269 7-10-10 67 MrRBirkett(5) 14 47
(Miss J Feilden) *hld up: a in rr* **9/1**[3]

/520 **11** *3 1/2* **Astronomical (IRE)**[13] 4229 7-10-7 64 MrStephenHarrison(5) 12 37
(R Hollinshead) *midfield: rdn along over 3f out: sn wknd* **33/1**

606- **12** *4* **Good Cause (IRE)**[429] 2667 8-9-11 54 oh4 DaleSwift(5) 1 19
(Mrs S Lamyman) *midfield: rdn along 5f out: sn wknd* **100/1**

6211 **13** *1* **Umverti**[19] 4068 4-11-0 73 MrSebSpencer(7) 10 36
(N Bycroft) *dwlt: t.k.h: a in rr* **9/1**[3]

6015 **14** *5* **Torch Of Freedom (IRE)**[131] 981 4-11-0 71 MrBMMorris(5) 15 24
(Sir Mark Prescott) *a towards rr* **12/1**

0/00 **15** *5* **Parisian Dream**[32] 3628 5-11-7 73 MrSWalker 11 16
(T J Pitt) *hld up: hdwy on outer to chse ldrs over 4f out: rdn along over 3f out and sn wknd* **16/1**

2m 16.23s (2.53) **Going Correction** +0.15s/f (Good)
WFA 3 from 4yo+ 9lb **15** Ran SP% **119.9**
Speed ratings (Par 103): **95,87,87,86,85 85,85,82,80,79 76,73,72,68,64**
toteswingers: 1&2 £16.20, 1&3 £4.40, 2&3 £33.80. CSF £33.70 CT £229.14 TOTE £2.70: £1.20, £5.90, £2.50; EX 55.50.
Owner Martin M Dempsey **Bred** N P Bloodstock Ltd & Morton Bloodstock **Trained** Newmarket, Suffolk
■ Stewards' Enquiry : Dale Swift caution: used whip when out of contention
Mr J Newman four-day ban: failed to ride out for 5th place (Aug 19, 21, 24, 29)

FOCUS
There was only 1mm of rain overnight and the going remained Good, Good to Firm in places. A modest amateurs' event and they didn't go that quick early.

4659 FAMILY FUNDAY ON SUNDAY 16TH AUGUST MAIDEN STKS 6f
2:40 (2:41) (Class 4) 2-Y-O £4,533 (£1,348; £674; £336) Stalls Low

Form RPR
1 **Atlantis Star** 2-9-3 0 TedDurcan 1 88+
(Saeed Bin Suroor) *trckd ldrs: smooth hdwy on inner 2f out: sn led and qcknd clr: easily* **11/4**[1]
66 2 6 **Raleigh Quay (IRE)**[32] 3613 2-9-0 0 FrederikTylicki(3) 3 65
(Micky Hammond) *cl up: led after 2f: rdn and hung rt home bnd 2f out: sn hdd and drvn: kpt on one pce* **18/1**
0 3 1 3/4 **Demonstrative (USA)**[34] 3546 2-9-3 0 NCallan 5 60
(M Johnston) *led 2f: cl up: rdn along over 2f out: sn drvn and kpt on same pce* **3/1**[2]
4 shd **Nizaa (USA)** 2-9-3 0 MichaelHills 7 59+
(B W Hills) *bdly hmpd s and bhd: hdwy 2f out: styd on ins fnl f: nrst fin* **11/4**[1]
23 5 1 **Miss Taken (IRE)**[8] 4398 2-8-12 0 DNolan 4 51
(D Carroll) *chsd ldrs: rdn along 2f out: sn one pce* **4/1**[3]
6 4 **Transmit (IRE)** 2-9-3 0 GrahamGibbons 6 44
(T D Easterby) *sltly bmpd and wnt bdly rt s: sn chsng ldrs: rdn along 3f out and sn wknd* **25/1**
7 4 1/2 **Scooby Dee** 2-8-9 0 MichaelJStainton(3) 2 26
(R M Whitaker) *a in rr* **20/1**

1m 18.44s (1.54) **Going Correction** +0.15s/f (Good) **7** Ran SP% **112.2**
Speed ratings (Par 96): **95,87,84,84,83 77,71**
toteswingers: 1&2 £7.40, 1&3 £2.20, 2&3 £8.60. CSF £47.56 TOTE £3.10: £1.80, £6.10; EX 39.10.
Owner Godolphin **Bred** Highclere Stud **Trained** Newmarket, Suffolk

FOCUS
An interesting maiden won in impressive style. The form is rated around the second and third.

NOTEBOOK
Atlantis Star, who's by Cape Cross out of a Dubai Millennium mare and cost 200,000gns, was soon travelling well on the inside behind the pace, quickened up in good style to draw away in the straight and looks a useful recruit. The bare form is held down a little by the more experienced runner-up, but he won eased down and will deserve respect when upped in class. Another furlong shouldn't bother him. (tchd 5-2 and 3-1)
Raleigh Quay(IRE) had shown only moderate ability in his first two starts, but his previous experience was useful in this company and he took them along until the winner quickened past. It was a sound effort and nurseries should offer more opportunities. (op 16-1 tchd 20-1)
Demonstrative(USA), too green on his debut, showed a lot more this time, but the best of him won't be seen until next year. (op 9-2)
Nizaa(USA) wasn't knocked about and should come on a lot for this debut. Bred to get a lot further next year, in the shorter term he should appreciate a step up to 7f. Official explanation: jockey said colt suffered interference at the start (op 3-1 tchd 7-2)
Miss Taken(IRE) was up in class here and came up short. She is now eligible for a mark, though, and should be more of a force in nurseries. (tchd 9-2 in a place)

4660 HEAVEN LAP DANCING BAR PONTEFRACT H'CAP 1m 4y
3:10 (3:10) (Class 5) (0-75,72) 3-Y-O £3,885 (£1,156; £577; £288) Stalls Low

Form RPR
-403 1 **Flying Silks (IRE)**[18] 4079 3-8-11 62 RobertHavlin 1 74+
(J R Gask) *stdd s: sn trcking ldrs on inner: smooth hdeway 3f out: swtchd rt and effrt 2f out: rdn to ld ent fnl f and styd on wl* **5/2**[1]
5541 2 2 1/2 **Play It Sam**[19] 4070 3-9-4 69 (t) AdamKirby 7 75+
(W R Swinburn) *trckd ldng pair: hdwy 3f out: led 2f out and sn rdn: drvn and hdd ent fnl f: kpt on same pce* **11/4**[2]
-005 3 5 **Trumpstoo (USA)**[16] 4143 3-9-7 72 TonyHamilton 4 67
(R A Fahey) *in tch: hdwy 3f out: rdn along 2f out: drvn wl over 1f out and sn no imp* **15/2**[3]
45-4 4 1/2 **Battle Royal (IRE)**[12] 4277 3-8-12 63 TomEaves 8 57
(B Smart) *led: rdn along over 3f out: hdd 2f out and sn wknd* **8/1**
405 5 3 **Brockfield**[30] 3690 3-8-9 60 FrancisNorton 3 47
(M Brittain) *hld up towards rr: effrt and sme hdwy over 2f out: sn rdn and nvr a factor* **9/1**
0540 6 4 1/2 **Toby Tyler**[40] 3341 3-9-2 67 RobertWinston 6 43
(P T Midgley) *hld up in rr: hdwy on outer 1/2-way: rdn to chse ldrs over 2f out: sn edgd lft and wknd* **10/1**
06-0 7 1/2 **Ay Tay Tate (IRE)**[109] 1361 3-8-11 62 GrahamGibbons 9 37
(D Shaw) *hld up: a in rr* **9/1**
3-56 8 16 **Heading East (IRE)**[18] 4074 3-9-4 69 NCallan 2 —
(K A Ryan) *t.k.h: cl up: rdn along wl over 2f out: sn wknd and eased fnl f* **12/1**

1m 45.96s (0.06) **Going Correction** +0.15s/f (Good) **8** Ran SP% **114.9**
Speed ratings (Par 100): **105,102,97,97,94 89,89,73**
toteswingers: 1&2 £2.20, 1&3 £4.30, 2&3 £4.70. CSF £9.62 CT £43.76 TOTE £3.30: £1.20, £1.40, £2.20; EX 8.80.
Owner Coffen Construction **Bred** Ennistown Stud **Trained** Sutton Veny, Wilts

FOCUS
Some improving sorts lined up here and the race was run at a decent pace.
Toby Tyler Official explanation: jockey said gelding hung left in home straight

4661 BIG FELLAS & SILKS NIGHTCLUB PONTEFRACT H'CAP 1m 4f 8y
3:40 (3:40) (Class 3) (0-90,90) 3-Y-O+
£9,346 (£2,799; £1,399; £700; £349; £175) Stalls Low

Form RPR
/001 1 **High Ambition**[40] 3350 6-8-8 73 FrederikTylicki(3) 3 83
(R A Fahey) *dwlt: hld up in rr: tk clsr order 3f out: hdwy on inner 2f out: swtchd rt and rdn to chal ent fnl f: sn led and styd on wl towards fin* **10/3**[2]
5043 2 2 **Resplendent Light**[26] 3826 4-9-11 87 NCallan 5 94
(W R Muir) *trckd ldrs on inner: swtchd rt and hdwy 2f out: rdn to ld 1 1/2f out: drvn and hdd ins fnl f: kpt on one pce* **3/1**[1]
3315 3 2 1/4 **Cyborg**[18] 4092 5-9-5 81 RobertHavlin 1 84
(D R C Elsworth) *hld up in tch: hdwy 4f out: effrt to chse ldng pair over 2f out: rdn to chal over 1f out and ev ch tl drvn and one pce ins fnl f* **6/1**
5320 4 6 **Jabal Tariq**[26] 3822 4-9-7 83 MichaelHills 6 76
(B W Hills) *set stdy pce: qcknd over 3f out: rdn and qcknd again over 2f out: hdd 1 1/2f out: sn drvn and wknd ent fnl f* **10/1**
4122 5 4 **Shaloo Diamond**[4] 4517 4-9-5 84 MichaelJStainton(3) 4 71+
(R M Whitaker) *t.k.h: trckd ldrs: effrt 3f out: sn rdn and wknd wl over 1f out* **3/1**[1]
5000 6 6 **Night Crescendo (USA)**[10] 4340 6-10-0 90 (p) TedDurcan 7 67
(Mrs A J Perrett) *cl up: rdn along over 3f out: wknd over 2f out* **5/1**[3]

2m 40.32s (-0.48) **Going Correction** +0.15s/f (Good) **6** Ran SP% **113.1**
Speed ratings (Par 107): **107,105,104,100,97 93**
toteswingers: 1&2 £2.80, 1&3 £3.90, 2&3 £4.60. CSF £13.93 TOTE £4.40: £2.30, £2.30; EX 12.40.
Owner G H Leatham **Bred** A B Phipps **Trained** Musley Bank, N Yorks

FOCUS
A decent handicap but they only went an ordinary pace early, although the overall time was reasonable, and arguably that suited the winner.

NOTEBOOK
High Ambition was stepping up in trip from 1m2f. Ridden with plenty of patience, he quickened up well between horses in the straight and looks one to keep on-side now that he has found his calling over middle distances. He's lightly raced as a result of missing the 2008 campaign, and he's only had five starts for Fahey, so there are plenty of reasons to expect him to progress further. He should make a hurdler in time. (op 3-1)
Resplendent Light was well placed throughout tracking the leader and had no excuses. He simply ran into a well-handicapped and progressive rival. He has dropped 9lb since the beginning of the season but remains on a mark 5lb higher than when last successful. (tchd 4-1)
Cyborg is a galloper who stays further than this so a steadily run race on this turning track was not ideal. He was left behind when the first two quickened away. (op 13-2 tchd 5-1)
Jabal Tariq enjoyed the run of the race out in front, setting nothing likes a strong gallop, but didn't make the most of it. He is easing to a good mark and will be interesting either on softer ground or back on Polytrack. (op 11-1)
Shaloo Diamond raced too keenly and as a result had nothing left for the finish. He's another with a preference for soft ground. (op 7-2 tchd 11-4 and 4-1 in places)
Night Crescendo(USA) reserves his best for Ascot and dropped away before the home turn. Official explanation: jockey said gelding had no more to give (tchd 11-2)

4662 CHAPLINS CLUB H'CAP 5f
4:10 (4:10) (Class 5) (0-75,75) 3-Y-O+ £4,533 (£1,348; £674; £336) Stalls Low

Form RPR
0000 1 **King Of Swords (IRE)**[14] 4191 5-8-5 56 (p) AndrewElliott 2 66
(N Tinkler) *chsd ldrs on inner: hdwy 2f out: rdn over 1f out: styd on to chal ent fnl f: sn drvn and led last 100yds* **22/1**
6006 2 nk **Namir (IRE)**[8] 4399 7-9-6 71 (vt) GrahamGibbons 9 80
(D Shaw) *in tch: hdwy 2f out: rdn over 1f out: drvn to chal ins fnl f: nt qckn nr fin* **6/1**
0521 3 1/2 **Blessed Place**[12] 4283 9-7-13 57 (t) BillyCray(7) 1 64
(D J S Ffrench Davis) *chsd ldr: hdwy to ld 1/2-way and sn rdn: drvn and hdd ins fnl f: no ex last 75yds* **17/2**
0224 4 3 **Hits Only Jude (IRE)**[5] 4508 6-9-4 69 DNolan 6 65
(D Carroll) *chsd ldrs: rdn along 1/2-way: kpt on u.p appr fnl f: nrst fin* **11/1**
0-00 5 shd **Avertuoso**[16] 4141 5-9-5 70 TomEaves 11 66
(B Smart) *s.i.s and in rr: hdwy on inner: wl over 1f out: sn rdn and kpt on ins fnl f: nrst fin* **20/1**
0144 6 3/4 **Sir Nod**[16] 4141 7-9-4 74 BMcHugh(5) 3 67
(Miss J A Camacho) *dwlt and towards rr: gd hdwy to chse ldrs 1/2-way: effrt and n.m.r wl over 1f out: sn swtchd rt and rdn: no imp ins fnl f* **9/2**[2]
06 7 1 3/4 **Molly Two**[67] 2472 4-8-12 63 RobertWinston 7 50
(L A Mullaney) *chsd ldng pair: rdn along and edgd lft 2f out: sn drvn and grad wknd* **16/1**
6160 8 1 1/2 **Mr Wolf**[29] 3706 8-9-8 73 TonyHamilton 5 55
(J J Quinn) *led to 1/2-way: cl up tl rdn wl over 1f out and sn wknd* **4/1**[1]
5300 9 1 1/2 **Kheylide (IRE)**[8] 4399 3-8-10 67 DominicFox(3) 10 43
(Mrs D J Sanderson) *in tch: rdn along 1/2-way: sn wknd* **40/1**
6004 10 1 1/4 **Lord Of The Reins (IRE)**[10] 4355 5-9-2 70 FrederikTylicki(3) 4 42
(J G Given) *chsd ldrs: rdn along 2f out: sn drvn and wknd over 1f out* **5/1**[3]
0601 11 3 1/2 **Bravely (IRE)**[11] 4311 5-9-10 75 TedDurcan 12 34
(T D Easterby) *in tch on wd outside: rdn along 2f out: sn wknd* **15/2**

64.28 secs (0.98) **Going Correction** +0.15s/f (Good)
WFA 3 from 4yo+ 3lb **11** Ran SP% **117.2**
Speed ratings (Par 103): **98,97,96,91,91 90,87,85,82,80 75**
toteswingers: 1&2 £32.40, 1&3 £24.90, 2&3 £13.50. CSF £145.69 CT £1253.87 TOTE £24.30: £5.30, £2.60, £2.80; EX 203.60.
Owner P Alderson & J Raybould **Bred** Maurice G McAuley **Trained** Langton, N Yorks
■ Stewards' Enquiry : Graham Gibbons caution: excessive use of the whip

FOCUS
A competitive sprint run at a good, strong early pace, in which a low draw proved an advantage.

4663 MATTY BOWN VETERANS H'CAP 1m 4y
4:40 (4:40) (Class 4) (0-80,80) 6-Y-O+ £6,476 (£1,927; £963; £481) Stalls Low

Form RPR
0232 1 **Exit Smiling**[22] 3941 7-9-8 79 NCallan 6 88
(P T Midgley) *trckd ldrs: hdwy 3f out: rdn to chal over 1f out: led ent fnl f: sn drvn and kpt on wl* **6/1**[2]
0-20 2 nk **Motafarred (IRE)**[26] 3796 7-9-4 78 FrederikTylicki(3) 5 86
(Micky Hammond) *led: rdn along 2f out: drvn and hdd ent fnl f: rallied gamely u.p: no ex towards fin* **6/1**[2]
0005 3 2 3/4 **Collateral Damage (IRE)**[22] 3941 6-9-2 73 (t) DNolan 17 75
(T D Easterby) *trckd ldrs: hdwy over 2f out: rdn wl over 1f out: kpt on u.p ins fnl f* **16/1**
0352 4 shd **Ours (IRE)**[19] 4070 6-8-8 70 (p) BMcHugh(5) 15 72
(John A Harris) *midfield: hdwy on outer 2f out: rdn wl over 1f out: kpt on u.p ins fnl f: nrst fin* **7/1**
0025 5 1/2 **Commando Scott (IRE)**[19] 4072 8-9-1 72 PatrickMathers 10 73
(I W McInnes) *in tch: hdwy 3f out: rdn wl over 1f out: sn drvn and kpt on same pce* **33/1**
6365 6 1 **Veiled Applause**[40] 2103 6-9-9 80 GrahamGibbons 11 78
(J J Quinn) *hld up in rr: gd hdwy on inner wl over 1f out: sn rdn and kpt on ins fnl f: nrst fin* **12/1**
1000 7 hd **Champain Sands (IRE)**[20] 4019 10-8-4 61 AndrewMullen 7 59+
(E J Alston) *s.i.s and bhd: hdwy wl over 1f out: rdn and styng on whn n.m.r ins fnl f: sn swtchd lft and kpt on wl towards fin* **25/1**
0666 8 hd **Nevada Desert (IRE)**[4] 4549 9-8-9 69 (t) MichaelJStainton(3) 13 66
(R M Whitaker) *chsd ldr: effrt 3f out: rdn along 2f out: sn wknd* **20/1**
0035 9 shd **Goodbye Mr Bond**[4] 4532 9-8-11 68 TedDurcan 1 65
(E J Alston) *nvr bttr than midfield* **17/2**
6604 10 1/2 **Paraguay (USA)**[8] 4400 6-9-2 76 DominicFox(3) 12 72+
(Mrs D J Sanderson) *nvr bttr than midfield* **13/2**[3]
00-6 11 2 3/4 **Hartshead**[10] 4346 10-8-13 70 AndrewElliott 2 60
(W Storey) *chsd ldng pair: rdn along 3f out: drvn 2f out and sn wknd* **25/1**
0000 12 2 1/2 **Major Magpie (IRE)**[10] 4346 7-9-2 73 TomEaves 4 57
(M Dods) *t.k.h: hld up in midfield: effrt and sme hdwy 3f out: rdn along 2f out and sn btn* **8/1**

051- **13** *21* **Active Asset (IRE)**[438] 2394 7-9-0 **71** .... TonyHamilton 3 7
(J A Glover) *a towards rr: rdn along 3f out: bhd and eased wl over 1f out* **25/1**

3101 **14** *3/4* **Betteras Bertie**[37] 3457 6-8-11 **68** .... RobertWinston 8 —
(M Brittain) *dwlt: t.k.h and hld up in rr: sme hdwy on outer 1/2-way: sn wknd and bhd whn eased over 1f out* **11/2**[1]

1m 45.85s (-0.05) **Going Correction** +0.15s/f (Good) **14** Ran SP% **124.2**
Speed ratings: **106,105,102,102,102 101,101,100,100,100 97,95,74,73**
toteswingers: 1&2 £10.50, 1&3 £18.40, 2&3 £26.00. CSF £40.23 CT £580.39 TOTE £5.50: £2.40, £3.20, £4.70; EX 42.10.
Owner Peter Mee **Bred** Mrs D O Joly **Trained** Westow, N Yorks

FOCUS
An open-looking handicap run at just a fair gallop.
Betteras Bertie Official explanation: trainer's rep said, regarding running, that the gelding ran too free

4664 KEITH HAMMILL MEMORIAL H'CAP — 6f
5:10 (5:13) (Class 5) (0-75,74) 3-Y-O **£3,238** (£963; £481; £240) **Stalls** Low

Form RPR

6113 **1** **Mister Tinktastic (IRE)**[28] 3727 3-9-4 **71** .... (p) TomEaves 7 84
(M Dods) *mde all: rdn clr over 1f out: styd on strly* **5/1**[2]

0264 **2** *6* **Oriental Rose**[28] 3729 3-8-13 **66** .... DanielTudhope 2 60
(G M Moore) *cl up on inner: effrt 2f out and sn rdn: drvn to chse wnr wl over 1f out: sn no imp* **9/1**

2122 **3** *hd* **Northern Flyer (GER)**[22] 3939 3-8-13 **66** .... GrahamGibbons 10 59+
(J J Quinn) *hld up in rr: hdwy on outer 1/2-way: rdn to chse ldrs over 1f out: kpt on ins fnl f: nrst fin* **7/2**[1]

0023 **4** *1/2* **Merry Diva**[13] 4227 3-9-3 **73** .... JackMitchell(3) 9 65
(C F Wall) *chsd ldrs on outer: rdn along over 2f out: sn drvn and kpt on same pce* **7/2**[1]

5014 **5** *2 1/2* **Red Kyte**[4] 4530 3-9-7 **74** .... (p) NCallan 5 58
(K A Ryan) *prom: rdn to chse wnr wl over 1f out: sn drvn and wknd* **9/1**

1-04 **6** *1* **Wotatomboy**[93] 1720 3-8-7 **60** ow1 .... TonyHamilton 4 41
(R M Whitaker) *chsd ldrs: rdn along over 2f out and sn btn* **18/1**

1624 **7** *1 3/4* **Go Alone (IRE)**[16] 4131 3-9-3 **70** .... RobertWinston 8 45
(G A Swinbank) *chadsed ldrs: rdn along over 2f out: sn drvn and wknd* **9/1**

5503 **8** *9* **Captain Kallis (IRE)**[7] 4428 3-8-8 **61** .... (t) TedDurcan 6 7
(D J S Ffrench Davis) *a towards rr* **16/1**

4050 **9** *1* **Whatyouwoodwishfor (USA)**[13] 4227 3-9-0 **70** .... FrederikTylicki(3) 1 13
(R A Fahey) *a towards rr* **11/2**[3]

0000 **10** *9* **Irish Saint (IRE)**[40] 1926 3-8-2 **55** oh2 .... (v[1]) DaleGibson 3 —
(T J Pitt) *chsd ldrs to 1/2-way: sn lost pl and bhd* **66/1**

1m 18.0s (1.10) **Going Correction** +0.15s/f (Good) **10** Ran SP% **119.1**
Speed ratings (Par 100): **98,90,89,89,85 84,82,70,68,56**
toteswingers: 1&2 £10.50, 1&3 £3.70, 2&3 £8.50. CSF £50.62 CT £183.60 TOTE £6.40: £1.80, £3.00, £1.80; EX 51.80 Place 6 £165.67, Place 5 £86.65.
Owner Andrew Tinkler **Bred** R G Levin **Trained** Denton, Co Durham

FOCUS
A modest sprint handicap.
T/Plt: £57.50 to a £1 stake. Pool: £64,476.24. 817.57 winning tickets. T/Qpdt: £12.60 to a £1 stake. Pool: £4,240.00. 248.75 winning tickets. JR

4383 YARMOUTH (L-H)
Wednesday, August 5

OFFICIAL GOING: Good
Back straight rail moved out by 3.5m.
Wind: Fresh, against Weather: Cloudy

4665 GEORGE DARLING MEMORIAL APPRENTICE H'CAP — 7f 3y
5:50 (5:51) (Class 5) (0-70,65) 4-Y-O+ **£2,849** (£847; £423; £211) **Stalls** High

Form RPR

2016 **1** **Takaamul**[34] 3548 6-8-9 **55** .... RyanClark(5) 4 62
(K A Morgan) *hld up: racd keenly: hdwy 1/2-way: rdn to ld wl ins fnl f: r.o* **5/1**

35U1 **2** *nk* **Many Welcomes**[25] 3851 4-8-12 **56** .... KierenFox(3) 3 62
(B P J Baugh) *unruly in stalls: rdr late removing hood: s.s: hdwy over 2f out: sn rdn: ev ch ins fnl f: r.o* **9/2**[3]

0603 **3** *1/2* **Straight Face (IRE)**[11] 4312 5-8-11 **52** .... (b) RichardRowe 1 57
(Miss Gay Kelleway) *chsd ldrs: rdn over 1f out: r.o* **9/1**

606 **4** *nk* **Colombard (IRE)**[43] 3241 4-8-0 **46** oh1 .... AlexEdwards(5) 5 50
(Patrick Morris) *a.p: led 2f out: sn rdn: hdd and unable qck ins fnl f* **22/1**

2311 **5** *1/2* **Global Village (IRE)**[21] 3983 4-9-5 **65** .... ChrisHough(5) 7 68+
(Miss D Mountain) *prom: lost pl 1/2-way: hdwy over 1f out: rdn and hung lft ins fnl f: r.o* **11/4**[1]

0040 **6** *1/2* **Hilltop Legacy**[15] 4183 6-8-11 **52** .... HollyHall 2 53
(J R Jenkins) *hld up: racd keenly: hdwy 2f out: styd on same pce ins fnl f* **25/1**

6150 **7** *3 1/2* **My Flame**[75] 2223 4-8-11 **57** .... DannyBrock(5) 6 49
(J R Jenkins) *led: hdd 2f out: sn rdn: wknd ins fnl f* **12/1**

0003 **8** *4 1/2* **Norcroft**[9] 4375 7-8-10 **51** .... (v) LauraPike 9 31
(Mrs C A Dunnett) *chsd ldr tl rdn over 2f out: wknd wl over 1f out* **4/1**[2]

34- **9** *5* **Mugeba**[363] 4779 8-8-9 **50** .... JosephineBruning 8 16
(C A Dwyer) *hld up in tch: rdn and wknd over 2f out* **22/1**

1m 29.01s (2.41) **Going Correction** +0.025s/f (Good) **9** Ran SP% **111.7**
Speed ratings (Par 103): **87,86,86,85,85 84,80,75,69**
toteswingers: 1&2 £1.50, 1&3 £25.90, 2&3 £11.80. CSF £25.93 CT £191.80 TOTE £5.10: £1.90, £1.60, £2.50; EX 22.90.
Owner K A Morgan **Bred** Shadwell Estate Company Limited **Trained** Newmarket, Suffolk

FOCUS
This apprentice handicap was run at an average pace the field shunned the stands' side rail. The first six were closely bunched at the finish.

4666 MOULTON NURSERIES MAIDEN AUCTION STKS — 7f 3y
6:20 (6:20) (Class 6) 2-Y-O **£2,590** (£770; £385; £192) **Stalls** High

Form RPR

1 **The Starboard Bow** 2-8-11 0 .... SaleemGolam 8 78
(S Kirk) *plld hrd and prom: rdn and hung rt over 1f out: r.o to ld post* **20/1**

40 **2** *nse* **Keyta Bonita (IRE)**[9] 4385 2-8-4 0 .... LiamJones 1 71
(M G Quinlan) *led: rdn over 1f out: hung rt ins fnl f: hdd post* **8/1**[3]

03 **3** *4 1/2* **Llandovery**[29] 3715 2-8-9 0 .... EdwardCreighton 5 65
(P J McBride) *chsd ldrs: rdn over 2f out: hung lft and no ex ins fnl f* **12/1**

4 **4** *1* **Iron Condor**[16] 4152 2-8-7 0 .... WilliamCarson(3) 4 63
(J M P Eustace) *s.i.s: hdwy to chse ldr over 4f out: rdn over 2f out: styd on same pce appr fnl f* **9/1**

00 **5** *3 1/4* **Anchorage Boy (USA)**[16] 4152 2-8-11 0 .... PatCosgrave 6 56
(Miss Amy Weaver) *sn pushed along in rr: bhd and drvn 1/2-way: styd on ins fnl f* **150/1**

5 **6** *1/2* **Wanchai Whisper**[15] 4176 2-8-3 0 .... JimmyQuinn 2 47
(W J Haggas) *trckd ldrs: plld hrd: chal 2f out: sn rdn: wknd ins fnl f* **11/4**[2]

4 **7** *5* **Enjoyment**[13] 4226 2-8-6 0 .... HayleyTurner 3 37
(M L W Bell) *hld up: racd keenly: hdwy over 2f out: rdn and wknd over 1f out* **1/1**[1]

60 **8** *19* **The Frying Pan (IRE)**[16] 4152 2-8-6 0 .... DO'Donohoe 7 —
(Dr J D Scargill) *sn pushed along in rr: wknd 1/2-way* **125/1**

1m 29.59s (2.99) **Going Correction** +0.025s/f (Good) **8** Ran SP% **111.7**
Speed ratings (Par 92): **83,82,77,76,72 72,66,44**
toteswingers: 1&2 £33.80, 1&3 £27.00, 2&3 £16.80. CSF £160.60 TOTE £13.40: £4.40, £1.90, £3.10; EX 201.70.
Owner C Wright & The Hon Mrs J M Corbett **Bred** Stratford Place Stud **Trained** Upper Lambourn, Berks

FOCUS
A moderate juvenile maiden. The first pair were clear and the form looks sound if fairly modest.

NOTEBOOK
The Starboard Bow was the sole newcomer in attendance and proved good enough to make a winning start, despite doing just about everything wrong in the race. He ran green to post and took a keen pull through the early parts, but as the race developed he began to find his feet. He motored home inside the final furlong to just mow down the runner-up at the line and can only improve for this experience. He is also bred to be more effective over middle-distances in due course so this rates a promising effort. (op 22-1 tchd 16-1)
Keyta Bonita(IRE) looked like making just about all of the running, but was mugged near the finish. This was a lot more like it from her and she now has the option of nurseries, so should be placed to gain compensation before that long. (op 13-2 tchd 9-1)
Llandovery battled on for third, but may need a quicker surface to really shine. He now qualifies for nurseries. (op 14-1)
Iron Condor lacked a gear change, but still posted another sufficient effort and will be more interesting when going handicapping over longer distances. (op 7-1 tchd 12-1)
Wanchai Whisper, well backed, spoilt any chance of staying the extra furlong by refusing to settle. (op 9-2)
Enjoyment ran no sort of race at all and this was simply too bad to be true. Official explanation: trainer had no explanation for the poor form shown (op 5-6 tchd 8-11and 11-10 in a place)

4667 ROBERT GREEN MEMORIAL (S) H'CAP — 1m 3y
6:50 (6:51) (Class 6) (0-65,59) 4-Y-O+ **£1,942** (£578; £288; £144) **Stalls** High

Form RPR

0000 **1** **Broughtons Silk**[15] 4179 4-8-9 **47** .... EdwardCreighton 8 60
(W J Musson) *s.i.s: hld up: hdwy and edgd lft 3f out: led 2f out: sn edgd rt: drvn clr fnl f* **11/1**

004 **2** *5* **Sotik Star (IRE)**[29] 3717 6-9-7 **59** .... JimmyQuinn 9 63+
(K A Morgan) *hld up: hdwy over 3f out: nt clr run and lost pl over 2f out: swtchd lft and n.m.r wl over 1f out: styd on u.p: no ch w wnr* **9/1**

0-30 **3** *3/4* **Signora Frasi (IRE)**[44] 3208 4-9-0 **55** .... RussellKennemore(3) 1 55
(A G Newcombe) *hld up: hdwy over 2f out: rdn over 1f out: styd on same pce fnl f* **13/2**[2]

2605 **4** *1 1/4* **Al Rayanah**[9] 4376 6-9-2 **54** .... (b[1]) SaleemGolam 14 51
(G Prodromou) *s.i.s: hld up: hdwy over 2f out: rdn over 1f out: no etxra fnl f* **12/1**

-000 **5** *8* **Union Jack Jackson (IRE)**[20] 4023 7-8-7 **45** .... (b) DO'Donohoe 2 24
(John A Harris) *chsd ldrs: rdn over 2f out: hmpd and wknd over 1f out* **66/1**

2223 **6** *1* **Sion Hill (IRE)**[9] 4389 8-9-0 **55** .... (p) KellyHarrison(3) 6 31
(John A Harris) *led: rdn and hdd over 2f out: wknd over 1f out* **5/2**[1]

3604 **7** *1/2* **Maddy**[22] 3961 4-8-3 **46** .... (p) MatthewDavies(5) 4 21
(George Baker) *w ldr tl led over 2f out: sn rdn and hdd: wknd over 1f out* **10/1**

060 **8** *3 1/2* **Rock Tech**[37] 3460 4-8-12 **50** .... AdrianMcCarthy 5 17
(J R Jenkins) *s.i.s: sn in mid-div: rdn 1/2-way: hmpd and nrly fell 3f out: sn wknd* **100/1**

0000 **9** *2 3/4* **Space Pirate**[22] 3949 4-8-7 **45** .... (b[1]) LiamJones 13 6
(J Pearce) *sn pushed along in rr: wknd over 3f out* **28/1**

3060 **10** *3 1/4* **Bigfanofthat (IRE)**[28] 3732 4-9-2 **57** .... (bt[1]) AndreaAtzeni(3) 7 10
(M D Squance) *prom: rdn over 2f out: sn wknd* **9/1**

00-4 **11** *3/4* **Domesday (UAE)**[16] 4158 8-8-0 **45** .... JosephineBruning(7) 15 —
(T T Clement) *mid-div: rdn 1/2-way: sn wknd* **16/1**

4544 **12** *6* **Tabulate**[16] 4146 6-8-7 **45** .... HayleyTurner 12 —
(P Howling) *hld up: rdn and wknd over 3f out: eased fnl f* **12/1**

0034 **13** *1 3/4* **Quick Off The Mark**[25] 3862 4-8-12 **50** .... PatCosgrave 11 —
(J G Given) *chsd ldrs tl rdn and wknd wl over 1f out: eased ins fnl f* **17/2**[3]

1m 40.53s (-0.07) **Going Correction** +0.025s/f (Good) **13** Ran SP% **117.1**
Speed ratings (Par 101): **101,96,95,94,86 85,84,81,78,75 74,68,66**
toteswingers: 1&2 £42.10, 1&3 £21.80, 2&3 £15.50. CSF £103.57 CT £725.87 TOTE £15.50: £4.00, £3.80, £1.90; EX 169.40.There was no bid for the winner.
Owner Broughton Thermal Insulation **Bred** Broughton Bloodstock **Trained** Newmarket, Suffolk
■ Stewards' Enquiry : Edward Creighton three-day ban: careless riding (Aug 19, 22-23)

FOCUS
There was a fair pace on in this weak handicap and the first four came nicely clear.
Broughtons Silk Official explanation: trainer said, regarding the apparent improvement in form shown, that the filly had possibly strengthened since her last run and had benefitted from wearing a noseband.
Sion Hill(IRE) Official explanation: jockey said gelding ran flat

4668 BANHAM POULTRY H'CAP — 6f 3y
7:20 (7:24) (Class 5) (0-70,67) 3-Y-O+ **£2,978** (£886; £442; £221) **Stalls** High

Form RPR

-061 **1** **Capone (IRE)**[13] 4225 4-9-11 **65** .... HayleyTurner 8 79+
(Garry Moss) *hld up: hdwy to ld over 1f out: sn edgd rt: r.o wl: eased nr fin* **5/2**[2]

4-53 **2** *2 1/4* **Fantasy Gladiator**[40] 3362 3-9-9 **67** .... DO'Donohoe 6 73
(R M H Cowell) *s.i.s: outpcd: hdwy over 1f out: no ch w wnr* **14/1**

004 **3** *1 1/4* **Mansii**[15] 4182 4-8-9 **52** .... (t) AndreaAtzeni(3) 7 55
(P J McBride) *prom: rdn over 1f out: styd on same pce ins fnl f* **9/1**[3]

221 **4** *2 1/2* **Big Boom**[7] 4428 4-9-5 **59** 6ex .... PatCosgrave 1 54
(M Quinn) *led: hdd over 4f out: rdn over 2f out: wknd ins fnl f* **1/1**[1]

5010 **5** *1 3/4* **Rough Rock (IRE)**[6] 4469 4-8-13 **53** .... JimmyQuinn 5 42
(C A Dwyer) *chsd ldrs: rdn over 2f out: sn edgd lft: wknd fnl f* **12/1**

56-0 **6** *1 1/4* **Sheriff's Silk**[146] 823 5-8-12 **55** .... (b) RussellKennemore(3) 2 40
(Paul Mason) *w ldr tl led over 4f out: rdn and hdd over 1f out: wknd fnl f* **40/1**

0062 7 10 **Gone'N'Dunnett (IRE)**[15] 4182 10-8-3 **46**...............(v) WilliamCarson[(3)] 3 —
(Mrs C A Dunnett) *chsd ldrs: rdn 1/2-way: wknd 2f out* **16/1**

1m 13.9s (-0.50) **Going Correction** +0.025s/f (Good)
WFA 3 from 4yo+ 4lb **7** Ran SP% **111.3**
Speed ratings (Par 103): **104,101,99,96,93 92,78**
toteswingers: 1&2 £9.60, 1&3 £5.50, 2&3 £13.00. CSF £33.51 CT £261.05 TOTE £3.70: £1.90, £4.40; EX 39.80.
Owner Brooklands Racing **Bred** S J Macdonald **Trained**

FOCUS
A moderate sprint, run at a fair pace.

4669 FIRSTBET.COM 0800 230 0800 £50 MATCHED BET CLAIMING STKS 1m 2f 21y
7:50 (7:50) (Class 6) 3-Y-O **£2,201** (£655; £327; £163) **Stalls** Low

Form RPR

0404 1 **Bubses Boy**[16] 4157 3-8-8 54..................................... HayleyTurner 6 61
(M L W Bell) *led over 8f out: rdn and hdd over 2f out: rallied to ld and hung rt ins fnl f: r.o* **3/1**[2]

-330 2 ¾ **Tiger Flash**[32] 3644 3-9-4 73.....................................(b[1]) SebSanders 1 70
(W J Haggas) *s.i.s: sn prom: led 2f out: rdn over 1f out: edgd rt and hdd ins fnl f: kpt on* **6/4**[1]

0000 3 8 **Kingaroo (IRE)**[9] 4375 3-9-0 56.............................. PatCosgrave 2 50
(Garry Moss) *hld up: rdn over 4f out: wnt 3rd ins fnl f: n.d* **20/1**

5630 4 nk **Valkyrie (IRE)**[39] 3383 3-8-6 50 ow4......................(p) MarkCoumbe[(5)] 3 46
(N P Littmoden) *s.i.s: outpcd: hdwy u.p and hung lft over 2f out: n.d* **7/2**[3]

6530 5 3½ **Charismatic Lady**[19] 4068 3-8-11 62.......................... JimmyQuinn 5 39
(M Botti) *led: hdd over 8f out: chsd ldr tl led over 2f out: sn hdd: wknd fnl f* **5/1**

040 6 33 **Double Moon**[33] 3590 3-8-10 59.............................. DO'Donohoe 4 —
(George Baker) *prom: rdn over 4f out: wknd over 2f out: t.o* **16/1**

2m 9.40s (-1.10) **Going Correction** -0.15s/f (Firm) **6** Ran SP% **114.5**
Speed ratings (Par 98): **98,97,91,90,87 61**
toteswingers: 1&2 £1.20, 1&3 £7.00, 2&3 £3.90. CSF £8.19 TOTE £3.60: £2.30, £1.40; EX 11.00.The winner was claimed by Paul Howling for £5,000.
Owner C A Gershinson **Bred** Messinger Stud Ltd **Trained** Newmarket, Suffolk

FOCUS
This moderate claimer was run at a fair pace and it saw a tight finish between the first pair.

4670 FREEBETS AT THEBOOKIESOFFERS.CO.UK H'CAP 1m 6f 17y
8:20 (8:20) (Class 5) (0-75,72) 3-Y-O+ **£2,978** (£886; £442; £221) **Stalls** High

Form RPR

-021 1 **Royal Diamond (IRE)**[7] 4442 3-9-3 **72** 6ex.......................... SebSanders 7 84+
(Sir Mark Prescott) *hld up: plld hrd: hdwy 1/2-way: chsd ldr over 3f out: sn rdn: led over 1f out: styd on gamely* **4/6**[1]

6440 2 nk **Royal Premier (IRE)**[9] 4388 6-8-11 **53** oh3...................(v) JimmyQuinn 3 65
(H J Collingridge) *sn chsng ldr: pushed along over 5f out: led over 3f out: rdn and hdd over 1f out: stl ev ch ins fnl f: styd on gamely* **10/1**[3]

4-33 3 8 **Valvigneres (IRE)**[85] 1966 4-10-0 **70**.......................... TGMcLaughlin 6 71
(E A L Dunlop) *sn pushed along to ld then set stdy pce: qcknd over 4f out: hdd over 3f out: sn rdn: styd on same pce fnl 2f* **4/1**[2]

0425 4 3¼ **Piper's Song (IRE)**[15] 4169 6-9-5 **61**.......................... SJCraine 5 57
(Patrick Morris) *prom: rdn over 3f out: wknd over 2f out* **12/1**

0306 5 ½ **Trachonitis (IRE)**[13] 4235 5-9-13 **69**.......................... AdrianMcCarthy 4 65
(J R Jenkins) *s.i.s: hld up: hdwy over 3f out: rdn and wknd over 1f out* **10/1**[3]

000- 6 22 **Sir Jake**[474] 1459 5-8-11 **53** oh8.......................... LiamJones 2 18
(T T Clement) *chsd ldrs: rdn over 4f out: wknd 3f out* **28/1**

3m 17.74s (10.14) **Going Correction** -0.15s/f (Firm)
WFA 3 from 4yo+ 13lb **6** Ran SP% **109.3**
Speed ratings (Par 103): **65,64,60,58,58 45**
toteswingers: 1&2 £2.90, 1&3 £1.30, 2&3 £4.60. CSF £7.83 TOTE £1.60: £1.10, £3.20; EX 8.60 Place 6 £224.26, Place 5 £99.20.
Owner E B Rimmer-Osborne House **Bred** Moyglare Stud Farm Ltd **Trained** Newmarket, Suffolk

FOCUS
This staying handicap had gone the way of a progressive 3yo in two of the past three years and Royal Diamond kept up the trend.
T/Plt: £1,158.40 to a £1 stake. Pool: £54,035.03. 34.05 winning tickets. T/Qpdt: £67.50 to a £1 stake. Pool: £5,642.30. 61.85 winning tickets. CR

4671 - 4684a (Foreign Racing) - See Raceform Interactive

4637 DEAUVILLE (R-H)
Wednesday, August 5
OFFICIAL GOING: Turf course - good; all-weather - standard

4685a PRIX DE TOURGEVILLE (LISTED RACE) (C&G) (ROUND) 1m (R)
3:10 (3:11) 3-Y-O **£26,699** (£10,680; £8,010; £5,340; £2,670)

RPR

1 **Spring Of Fame (USA)**[27] 3783 3-8-11 .... LDettori 7 111+
(Saeed Bin Suroor) *cl 2nd: led 1/2-way: pushed along st: rdn and 2 l clr 1 1/2f out: qcknd wl clr fnl f: eased nr fin* **6/5**[1]

2 3 **Mantoro (GER)**[32] 3649 3-8-11 .... GMosse 3 102
(A De Royer-Dupre, France)

3 ½ **Portus Blendium (USA)**[65] 2561 3-8-11 .... CSoumillon 8 101
(C Laffon-Parias, France)

4 ½ **Saphir River (FR)**[19] 3-8-11 .... YLerner 4 99
(C Lerner, France)

5 ½ **Polarix**[32] 3649 3-8-11 .... MGuyon 6 98
(H-A Pantall, France)

6 shd **Accord Secret (FR)**[135] 942 3-8-11 .... C-PLemaire 5 98
(J-C Rouget, France)

7 1 **Randonneur (USA)**[28] 3-8-11 .... ACrastus 1 96
(E Lellouche, France)

8 ½ **Gaelic Silver (FR)**[151] 3-8-11 .... IMendizabal 2 94
(J-C Rouget, France)

1m 40.3s (-0.70) **8** Ran SP% **45.5**
PARI-MUTUEL: WIN 2.20; PL 1.30, 1.70, 1.70; DF 6.80.
Owner Godolphin **Bred** Brushwood Stable **Trained** Newmarket, Suffolk

NOTEBOOK
Spring Of Fame(USA), smartly into his stride, settled into second place early on and moved sweetly into the lead rounding the final turn. Quickening things up early in the straight, he pulled out a lead of several lengths by the two-furlong marker and totally dominated the final stages. He was in a different class to the other seven runners and looks more than capable of winning a Group 3 event over this distance. He could come back for the Prix Quincey at the end of the month.

4584 LA TESTE DE BUCH (R-H)
Wednesday, August 5
OFFICIAL GOING: Good

4686a PRIX ANDRE LACOUR (MAIDEN) (C&G) 1m
2:30 (12:00) 2-Y-O **£6,796** (£2,718; £2,039; £1,359; £680)

RPR

1 **Ivory Land (FR)**[29] 2-8-11 .... CNora 79
(R Martin Sanchez, Spain)

2 ½ **Zarly (FR)** 2-8-11 .... F-XBertras 78
(F Rohaut, France)

3 2½ **Carmen's Boy (FR)** 2-8-11 .... OTrigodet 72
(C Baillet, France)

4 ½ **Tussian Bere (FR)**[24] 3934 2-8-11 .... J-BEyquem 71
(E J O'Neill) *prominent, stayed on under pressure from 1f out*

5 3 **Elrond (IRE)** 2-8-11 64
(Unknown)

6 8 **Poisson Pilote (FR)** 2-8-11 47
(Unknown)

7 4 **Frederi (FR)** 2-8-11 38
(Unknown)

8 ¾ **Loudeacien (FR)** 2-8-11 36
(Unknown)

9 8 **Singapore Gift (FR)** 2-8-11 19
(Unknown)

10 1½ **Buttermilk (IRE)** 2-8-11 15
(Unknown)

1m 42.48s (102.48) **10** Ran
.
Owner E Fierro **Bred** Z Hakam **Trained** Spain
■ Stewards' Enquiry : J-B Eyquem 100euro fine: whip abuse

4478 BATH (L-H)
Thursday, August 6
OFFICIAL GOING: Good changing to good to soft after race 4 (7.30) changing to soft after race 5 (8.05)
Wind: Nil Weather: Overcast, raining after Race 4

4687 JOHN SMITH'S APPRENTICE H'CAP 1m 3f 144y
5:55 (5:55) (Class 5) (0-75,74) 3-Y-O **£2,590** (£770; £385; £192) **Stalls** Low

Form RPR

0-11 1 **Point Of Light**[6] 4481 3-9-8 **72** 6ex.......................... RosieJessop 4 85+
(Sir Mark Prescott) *sn led: set stdy pce: qcknd clr over 3f out: pushed out fnl f* **4/5**[1]

5-22 2 1½ **Blue Nymph**[23] 3951 3-9-10 **74**.......................... JPFahy 2 82
(R M Beckett) *hld up in tch: hdwy to chse wnr over 2f out: hrd rdn over 1f out: styd on same pce* **4/1**[2]

2400 3 8 **Sounds Of Jupiter (IRE)**[71] 2371 3-8-12 **65**.......................... LauraPike[(3)] 3 59
(D M Simcock) *led early: chsd ldr tl over 6f out: prom: rdn over 2f out: wknd over 1f out* **4/1**[2]

0403 4 17 **Lucy's Perfect**[54] 2909 3-8-2 **55** oh9.......................... DavidKenny[(3)] 5 21
(B R Millman) *prom tl rdn and wknd over 2f out* **16/1**[3]

3004 5 2¼ **Mrs Slocombe (IRE)**[29] 3740 3-8-7 **60**.......................... RichardRowe[(3)] 6 22
(Mrs N S Evans) *t.k.h: prog to chse wnr over 6f out: rdn and lost 2nd over 2f out: sn wknd* **33/1**

01-0 6 1¾ **Tombov (FR)**[33] 3636 3-9-10 **74**.......................... TobyAtkinson 1 33
(A King) *a in rr: pushed along over 3f out: rdn and no ch wl over 1f out* **16/1**[3]

2m 34.14s (3.54) **Going Correction** +0.30s/f (Good) **6** Ran SP% **110.3**
Speed ratings (Par 100): **100,99,93,82,80 79**
toteswingers: 1&2 £1.10, 1&3 £1.02, 2&3 £1.10. CSF £4.12 TOTE £1.90: £1.40, £1.90; EX 3.30.
Owner Syndicate 2007 **Bred** Watership Down Stud **Trained** Newmarket, Suffolk

FOCUS
The ground dried out during the morning and then eased due to afternoon rain and was good at the start of racing, although possibly riding on the dead side. A weakish apprentices' handicap in which several had questions to answer. The winner again created a good impression.

4688 JOHN SMITH'S EXTRA SMOOTH MAIDEN AUCTION FILLIES' STKS 5f 161y
6:25 (6:27) (Class 6) 2-Y-O **£2,201** (£655; £327; £163) **Stalls** Centre

Form RPR

1 **Music Show (IRE)** 2-8-12 0.......................... TonyCulhane 6 80+
(M R Channon) *towards rr: pushed along 4f out: hdwy over 2f out: led jst ins fnl f: pushed out* **6/1**

452 2 2½ **Zelos Dream (IRE)**[10] 4383 2-7-13 0.......................... DavidProbert[(3)] 8 59
(Rae Guest) *chsd ldrs: led over 1f out: rdn and hdd jst ins fnl f: nt qckn* **10/3**[1]

00 3 1¾ **Freddie's Girl (USA)**[17] 4147 2-8-1 0.......................... TobyAtkinson[(7)] 13 59+
(Stef Liddiard) *n.m.r sn after s: in rr: hdwy on wd outside wl over 1f out: rdn and kpt on same pce fnl f* **20/1**

6 4 ¾ **Fair Nella**[17] 4147 2-8-8 0.......................... FergusSweeney 14 56
(J G Portman) *mid-div: pushed along and hdwy on outside over 2f out: rdn and one pce fnl f* **4/1**[2]

5 2 **Miss Zooter (IRE)** 2-7-13 0.......................... JPFahy[(7)] 2 47
(R M Beckett) *dwlt: sn hld up in mid-div: hdwy over 2f out: rdn over 1f out: one pce* **8/1**

00 6 1½ **Dimaire**[30] 3715 2-8-4 0.......................... JamieMackay 15 40
(D Haydn Jones) *prom: led over 2f out: edgd lft and hdd over 1f out: sn rdn: wknd fnl f* **22/1**

2004 7 6 **Pherousa**[12] 4302 2-8-2 **66**.......................... FrancisNorton 12 18
(M Blanshard) *prom: ev ch over 2f out: wknd over 1f out* **12/1**

0500 8 1¾ **Dolly Will Do**[22] 3987 2-7-13 **45**.......................... KellyHarrison[(3)] 5 12
(N P Mulholland) *s.i.s: outpcd in rr: rdn 3f out: swtchd rt wl over 1f out: nvr nr ldrs* **100/1**

9 2½ **L'Isle Joyeuse** 2-8-2 0.......................... FrankieMcDonald 10 —
(P Winkworth) *prom: n.m.r over 2f out: rdn and wknd wl over 1f out* **33/1**

05 10 2 **Madam Isshe**[6] 4478 2-8-4 0 ow1.......................... KevinGhunowa[(3)] 4 —+
(M S Saunders) *chsd ldr: hung rt sn after s: lost 2nd 3f out: wknd 2f out: sddle slipped* **40/1**

6 **11** *2 ¼* **Miss Kitty Grey (IRE)**[12] 4302 2-8-8 0........................ TGMcLaughlin 9 —
(J R Boyle) *a towards rr* **20/1**

0 **12** *1 ¼* **Polish Steps (IRE)**[38] 3458 2-8-8 0........................ PaulEddery 11 —
(J A Osborne) *s.i.s: pushed along 3f out: a in rr* **25/1**

44 **13** *1* **Little Brazilien**[6] 4478 2-8-4 0........................ JosedeSouza 3 —
(P F I Cole) *prom tl pushed along and wknd over 2f out* **5/1**[3]

00 **14** *4 ½* **Truly Magic**[28] 3786 2-8-5 0 ow1........................ EdwardCreighton 1 —
(H J L Dunlop) *led: hdd over 2f out: sn wknd* **25/1**

1m 12.85s (1.65) **Going Correction** +0.05s/f (Good) **14** Ran SP% **120.8**
Speed ratings (Par 89): **91,87,85,84,81 79,71,69,66,63 60,58,57,51**
toteswingers: 1&2 £6.10, 1&3 £41.70, 2&3 £18.20. CSF £23.49 TOTE £7.90: £2.40, £1.80, £7.60; EX 41.60.
Owner Jaber Abdullah **Bred** Darley **Trained** West Ilsley, Berks

FOCUS
A modest maiden that was open to one of the inexperienced fillies improving to beat the more exposed runners. That turned out to be the case. There is better to come from the winner.

NOTEBOOK
Music Show(IRE) came through to strike the front inside the final furlong and win comfortably, despite showing signs of greenness. A half-sister to the useful 1m2f winner Fantasia Girl, but with plenty of other winners at shorter trips in her pedigree, she has more size and scope than most of these and holds a Cheveley Park Stakes entry. Presumably she will be aimed at something better after this. (tchd 7-1)
Zelos Dream(IRE) was backed into favourite on this fourth start and appeared to have every chance but found the winner too good. She beat the remainder well enough so should be up to winning a similar contest before long. (op 11-2)
Freddie's Girl(USA) did well to reach the placings, having been drawn high and ended up racing widest of all. She reversed previous form with the fourth and now qualifies for nurseries. (op 16-1)
Fair Nella was another drawn high and was always struggling to get to the leading group. She had beaten the third at Windsor previously, so better could have been expected. (op 7-2)
Miss Zooter(IRE), a relatively cheaply bought sister to the multiple winner Raza Cab, made a promising debut despite having missed the break and will appreciate a bit further. (tchd 9-1)
Dimaire, dropping in trip after fading over 7f last time, ran well until tiring inside the last and may be worth dropping back to the minimum now she is qualified for handicaps. (op 25-1)
Madam Isshe Official explanation: jockey said saddle slipped
Little Brazilien was disappointing considering the promise she had shown previously and the fact that she had a low draw. (tchd 11-2)

4689 FREEBETS.CO.UK PREMIER LEAGUE FREE BETS (S) STKS 5f 11y
6:55 (6:56) (Class 6) 2-Y-O **£1,942** (£578; £288; £144) **Stalls** Centre

Form RPR

6335 **1** **Mister Hughie (IRE)**[13] 4282 2-9-2 70........................ TonyCulhane 8 69+
(M R Channon) *towards rr: pushed along over 3f out: hdwy over 2f out: shkn up to ld towards fin* **1/1**[1]

4225 **2** *nk* **True Red (IRE)**[16] 4165 2-8-8 60........................ DavidProbert[(3)] 1 60
(B R Millman) *led: hrd rdn and hdd towards fin* **7/2**[2]

60 **3** *5* **Aegean Destiny**[65] 2563 2-8-11 0........................ FrancisNorton 5 42
(R Hannon) *a.p: rdn wl over 1f out: edgd lft and wknd ins fnl f* **6/1**[3]

060 **4** *7* **Miss Roma (IRE)**[10] 4370 2-8-8 0........................ KevinGhunowa[(3)] 4 17
(R A Harris) *w ldr: rdn 2f out: wknd over 1f out* **33/1**

0 **5** *1 ½* **Bury St Edmunds**[26] 3867 2-9-2 0........................ TGMcLaughlin 6 16
(A G Newcombe) *hld up and bhd: pushed along and struggling wl over 2f out* **80/1**

0056 **6** *shd* **That'Lldonowthen (IRE)**[10] 4384 2-9-2 58........................(p) LukeMorris 3 16
(J S Moore) *chsd ldrs: rdn and wkng whden edgd rt over 1f out* **14/1**

7 *9* **Lady Avon** 2-8-6 0........................ RossAtkinson[(5)] 2 —
(W G M Turner) *wnt lft s: outpcd* **20/1**

0430 **8** *4 ½* **Xaara Star (IRE)**[10] 4384 2-8-11 59........................(b) FergusSweeney 7 —
(Eve Johnson Houghton) *prom tl rdn and wknd over 2f out* **15/2**

63.75 secs (1.25) **Going Correction** +0.05s/f (Good) **8** Ran SP% **113.9**
Speed ratings (Par 92): **92,91,83,72,69 69,55,48**
toteswingers: 1&2 £1.10, 1&3 £1.40, 2&3 £5.20. CSF £4.47 TOTE £1.80: £1.10, £1.40, £1.90; EX 3.50.Winner bought in for 8,500gns.
Owner Liam Mulryan **Bred** Mcmac Syndicate **Trained** West Ilsley, Berks

FOCUS
An indication that the afternoon rain had got into the ground was that the field came to the stands' side for the first time on the night and the going was officially changed to Good To Soft. An ordinary seller, and although several had form in this grade much of the interest centred around those dropping to this level for the first time. The first two came clear.

NOTEBOOK
Mister Hughie(IRE) had shown fair ability in maidens and his official mark was much the best of those with ratings. Given a confident ride by Tony Culhane, who was completing a double, he was held up early before moving up to join issue entering the last furlong. He looked held for a few strides but his rider did not panic and nudged him into the lead near the finish to score a shade cheekily. Clearly better than the usual winner in this grade, it was no surprise connections had to go to 8,500gns to retain him. (op 5-6 tchd 4-5)
True Red(IRE) has plenty of experience and was runner-up for the fourth time in nine starts. She did nothing wrong though, and in fact was pretty game and deserves to pick up a little race, as she was clear of the remainder. (op 9-2 tchd 5-1)
Aegean Destiny, another dropping in grade, ran reasonably well although eventually left behind by the principals. She was also dropping in trip and, as she is bred to appreciate further rather than shorter, may do better in handicaps over longer trips. (op 15-2)
Miss Roma(IRE), another dropping in grade, gave trouble in the stalls, something she has done before, and was too keen early as a result. (op 28-1 tchd 25-1)
Xaara Star(IRE) had finished in front of the third at Folkestone in June but seems to have regressed of late, with blinkers on her two most recent starts not seeming to help. (op 8-1 tchd 9-1)

4690 FREEBETS.CO.UK PREMIERSHIP FREE BETS CLAIMING STKS 5f 161y
7:30 (7:30) (Class 6) 3-Y-O+ **£1,942** (£578; £288; £144) **Stalls** Centre

Form RPR

3161 **1** **Swinbrook (USA)**[10] 4372 8-8-9 74........................ SPRyan[(7)] 4 81
(R A Harris) *hld up in tch: swtchd lft over 1f out: led jst ins fnl f: sn edgd rt: rdn and r.o wl* **9/4**[2]

1434 **2** *3 ¼* **Dressed To Dance (IRE)**[3] 4607 5-8-10 75........(b) KevinGhunowa[(3)] 8 67
(R A Harris) *hld up: hdwy over 2f out: ev ch jst ins fnl f: sn rdn: one pce* **1/1**[1]

6311 **3** *½* **Obe Gold**[15] 4192 7-9-9 83........................(v) FrancisNorton 2 75
(Miss D Mountain) *w ldr: led over 1f out tl jst ins fnl f: no ex* **11/2**[3]

3060 **4** *3 ½* **Ghost Dancer**[26] 3866 5-9-2 62........................(p) LukeMorris 7 56
(J M Bradley) *t.k.h early: a.p: ev ch over 1f out: hrd rdn and wknd ins fnl f* **11/1**

603P **5** *1* **Talamahana**[4] 4586 4-8-9 47........................(v) TGMcLaughlin 1 46
(A B Haynes) *led: hdd over 1f out: rdn and wknd fnl f* **40/1**

0056 **6** *12* **Mr Forthright**[6] 4479 5-8-13 46........................(p) JackDean[(3)] 6 12
(J M Bradley) *hld up and bhd: rdn over 2f out: toiling over 1f out* **28/1**

0060 **7** *3 ¼* **Captain Peachey**[21] 4023 3-8-6 36........................(b[1]) DavidProbert[(3)] 5 —
(B R Millman) *hld up and bhd: rdn over 2f out: sn struggling* **50/1**

1m 12.64s (1.44) **Going Correction** +0.275s/f (Good)
WFA 3 from 4yo+ 4lb **7** Ran SP% **112.3**
Speed ratings (Par 101): **101,96,96,91,90 74,69**
toteswingers: 1&2 £1.10, 1&3 £2.20, 2&3 £1.10. CSF £4.65 TOTE £3.00: £1.80, £1.50; EX 5.70.Swinbrook was the subject of a friendly claim.
Owner Mrs Ruth M Serrell **Bred** Bill Bronstad **Trained** Earlswood, Monmouths

FOCUS
A fair claimer in which three stood out based on their official marks and they completely dominated the market.

4691 FREEBETS.CO.UK FREE FOOTBALL BETS H'CAP 1m 5y
8:05 (8:06) (Class 5) (0-75,75) 3-Y-O **£2,719** (£809; £404; £202) **Stalls** Low

Form RPR

3622 **1** **Carbon Hoofprint**[48] 3115 3-9-7 75........................ FergusSweeney 7 85+
(P J Makin) *led: bit slipped through mouth and hdd over 4f out: led over 2f out: edgd rt jst over 1f out: pushed out* **7/4**[1]

-302 **2** *2 ½* **Mr Udagawa**[12] 4321 3-9-2 70........................ RichardKingscote 8 74
(R M Beckett) *chsd ldr: led over 4f out tl over 2f out: rdn and swtchd lft jst over 1f out: no imp* **10/3**[2]

-400 **3** *1 ¾* **Full Of Nature**[4] 4569 3-9-1 72........................ DavidProbert[(3)] 6 72
(S Kirk) *s.s: sn rcvrd and prom: rdn over 1f out: one pce* **5/1**[3]

0204 **4** *2 ½* **Sunny Future (IRE)**[13] 4267 3-9-0 68........................ TGMcLaughlin 4 62
(M S Saunders) *hld up: hdwy over 3f out: rdn and wknd over 1f out* **14/1**

4566 **5** *2* **Quinsman**[26] 3868 3-8-12 66........................ LukeMorris 5 56
(J S Moore) *hld up in last: pushed along over 2f out: rdn wl over 1f out: no rspnse* **7/1**

-606 **6** *4* **Davids Matador**[47] 3159 3-9-0 68........................ FrancisNorton 3 49
(Eve Johnson Houghton) *hld up: hdwy over 2f out: sn pushed along: wknd over 1f out* **6/1**

7 *19* **Cheetah Beetah**[43] 3286 3-7-11 56 oh11........................ NicolPolli[(5)] 2 —
(H S Howe) *prom tl rdn and wknd jst over 2f out: struggling whn hung lft over 1f out* **50/1**

1m 45.98s (5.18) **Going Correction** +0.525s/f (Yiel) **7** Ran SP% **111.5**
Speed ratings (Par 100): **95,92,90,88,86 82,63**
toteswingers: 1&2 £2.90, 1&3 £1.10, 2&3 £8.70. CSF £7.27 CT £22.21 TOTE £2.90: £1.50, £2.50; EX 6.10.
Owner The Billinomas **Bred** Newsells Park Stud **Trained** Ogbourne Maisey, Wilts

FOCUS
A modest but tight-knit 3yo handicap run in heavy rain, but it went very much as the market suggested.

4692 E.B.F./FREEBETS.CO.UK FREE BETS FILLIES' H'CAP 5f 11y
8:35 (8:37) (Class 5) (0-75,75) 3-Y-O+ **£3,238** (£963; £481; £240) **Stalls** Centre

Form RPR

3302 **1** **Diane's Choice**[14] 4222 6-8-2 56........................(e) DavidProbert[(3)] 4 63
(Miss Gay Kelleway) *hld up in 3rd: rdn over 1f out: led ins fnl f: r.o wl* **7/4**[1]

0000 **2** *2* **Wibbadune (IRE)**[5] 4530 5-8-9 63........................ KellyHarrison[(3)] 5 62
(D Shaw) *broke wl: sn stdd into last pl: rdn and r.o to take 2nd cl home: nt trble wnr* **8/1**

2206 **3** *1* **Matterofact (IRE)**[3] 4604 6-9-3 68........................ TGMcLaughlin 6 64
(M S Saunders) *led: hdd ins fnl f: sn rdn: one pce* **2/1**[2]

/0-0 **4** *½* **Littlemisssunshine (IRE)**[61] 2712 4-9-2 67........(p) FergusSweeney 8 61
(J S Moore) *w ldr: ev ch over 1f out: one pce ins fnl f* **5/2**[3]

64.74 secs (2.24) **Going Correction** +0.275s/f (Good)
WFA 3 from 4yo+ 3lb **4** Ran SP% **109.4**
Speed ratings (Par 100): **93,89,88,87**
toteswingers: 1&2 £13.50 CSF £13.60 TOTE £2.40; EX 10.20 Place 6: £6.51, Place 5: £5.01.
Owner The Dark Side **Bred** Green Pastures Farm **Trained** Exning, Suffolk

FOCUS
The going was changed to soft before this race. A weak fillies' sprint, this became much less competitive with the withdrawal of half the field, mostly due to the softening ground. Not form to take too positively.
T/Plt: £4.20 to a £1 stake. Pool: £38,726.48. 6,574.85 winning tickets. T/Qpdt: £1.80 to a £1 stake. Pool: £3,256.82. 1,299.90 winning tickets. KH

4638 BRIGHTON (L-H)
Thursday, August 6

OFFICIAL GOING: Firm (good to firm in places; 8.3)
Bend moved out 3metres to the 3f marker but impact on distances not quantified.
Wind: almost nil Weather: very hot and sunny

4693 TOTESPORTCASINO.COM MAIDEN AUCTION STKS 6f 209y
2:30 (2:30) (Class 5) 2-Y-O **£3,154** (£944; £472; £236; £117) **Stalls** Low

Form RPR

3 **1** **Bab At The Bowster (IRE)**[13] 4257 2-8-8 0........................ LiamJones 2 74+
(W J Haggas) *racd keenly: prom: rdn to ld 2f out: in command ins fnl f* **8/13**[1]

0 **2** *2 ¼* **Pastello**[20] 4055 2-8-10 0........................ JamieSpencer 4 70
(R Hannon) *drvn in detached last: cajoled to cl over 1f out: racd w awkward hd carriage and waving tail after: hung lft: wnt 2nd ins fnl f: n.g.t* **14/1**

3 *¾* **Saint Thomas (IRE)** 2-9-2 0........................ TPQueally 6 74
(J A Osborne) *stdd s: detached in 5th: rdn 1/2-way: drvn to chal 1f out: nt qckn after* **33/1**

45 **4** *1 ¼* **Dream Spinner**[28] 3786 2-8-13 0........................ JimCrowley 1 68
(J L Dunlop) *slt ld 5f: drvn and one pce over 1f out* **5/1**[3]

052 **5** *shd* **Chairman Pat (USA)**[19] 4080 2-9-1 76........................ RichardKingscote 3 70
(Tom Dascombe) *chsd ldrs: rdn 1/2-way: outpcd over 1f out: plugged on again ins fnl f* **9/2**[2]

3000 **6** *1* **French Connexion (IRE)**[19] 4089 2-8-4 65........................ LukeMorris 5 56
(J S Moore) *plld hrd: pressed ldrs over 4f: rdn and sn outpcd: plugged on ins fnl f* **50/1**

1m 23.22s (0.12) **Going Correction** -0.10s/f (Good) **6** Ran SP% **108.3**
Speed ratings (Par 94): **95,92,91,90,90 88**
toteswingers: 1&2 £2.70, 1&3 £3.60, 2&3 £6.20. CSF £9.97 TOTE £1.50: £1.20, £3.40; EX 8.40.
Owner Findlay & Bloom **Bred** Raymond P Doyle **Trained** Newmarket, Suffolk

FOCUS
This was an ordinary maiden which is tentatively rated around the winner, fourth and fifth.

NOTEBOOK
Bab At The Bowster(IRE) set the standard, having made a promising debut over 7f at Ascot, and she kept finding for pressure under a strong ride. The extra furlong was clearly a help and she may well go on to do better still in nurseries. (op 4-7 tchd 4-6 in places and 8-11 in a place)

Pastello improved markedly on her debut effort, keeping on well having been slow to get going. A small race should come her way at some stage. (tchd 12-1)
Saint Thomas(IRE), whose yard is more than capable of producing one to win at the first attempt, came through to challenge over a furlong out and ran really well considering he was completely dismissed in the market. (op 25-1)
Dream Spinner showed plenty of early speed and, though ultimately well held, he is the type to fare better in low-grade nurseries. (op 15-2)
Chairman Pat(USA), who has an official rating of 76, was one of the first beaten and failed to run his race. (op 4-1)

4694 TOTESPORTGAMES.COM FILLIES' H'CAP 6f 209y
3:00 (3:00) (Class 5) (0-70,69) 3-Y-0+ **£3,154** (£944; £472; £236; £117) **Stalls** Low

Form RPR
1520 **1** **Lady Florence**[8] 4435 4-9-5 **61**........................ LPKeniry 6 71
(A B Coogan) *2nd tl led over 2f out: qcknd clr wl over 1f out: racing lazily and edging lft w rdr brndishing whip fnl f: a looked like winning* **5/2**[2]
0100 **2** 1 ¾ **Ocean Countess (IRE)**[35] 3551 3-8-8 **56**........................(v) LiamJones 3 59
(Miss J Feilden) *chsd ldrs: rdn and effrt whn gap clsd on her 2f out: swtchd rt and lost momentum: wnt 2nd 100yds out: nt rch wnr* **13/2**
0001 **3** 1 ¾ **Goodbye Cash (IRE)**[23] 3948 5-8-13 **55**........................ PaulDoe 1 56
(P D Evans) *kpt hanging rt: racd keenly: led tl over 2f out: rdn and no imp over 1f out: lost 2nd fnl 100yds* **11/4**[3]
3335 **4** 2 ½ **Ivory Lace**[35] 3523 8-9-13 **69**........................ JimCrowley 5 63
(S Woodman) *chsd ldrs: rdn 2f out: wl hld fnl f* **2/1**[1]
05-0 **5** 12 **Sparkling Suzie**[12] 4324 3-8-9 **57**........................ LukeMorris 4 16
(J S Moore) *last and rdn 1/2-way: sn struggling: eased fnl f* **14/1**

1m 21.92s (-1.18) **Going Correction** -0.10s/f (Good)
WFA 3 from 4yo+ 6lb **5** Ran SP% **108.6**
Speed ratings (Par 100): **102,100,98,95,81**
toteswingers: 1&2 £10.00. CSF £17.21 TOTE £3.60: £1.80, £2.90; EX 13.60.
Owner A B Coogan **Bred** The National Stud **Trained** Soham, Cambs

FOCUS
A moderate handicap best rated around the placed horses. A personal best from the winner.
Goodbye Cash(IRE) Official explanation: jockey said mare hung right
Sparkling Suzie Official explanation: trainer's rep said filly was unsuited by the track

4695 BET IN-PLAY AT TOTESPORT.COM H'CAP 5f 213y
3:30 (3:30) (Class 5) (0-75,75) 3-Y-0 **£3,154** (£944; £472; £236; £117) **Stalls** Low

Form RPR
-602 **1** **Fleeting Star (USA)**[11] 4338 3-9-4 **72**........................(v) TPQueally 1 81+
(J Noseda) *taken down early: cl up and keen: rdn to ld wl over 1f out: sn clr and gng best: readily* **8/11**[1]
4434 **2** 2 ¼ **Raimond Ridge (IRE)**[22] 3989 3-9-2 **70**........................ ChrisCatlin 6 72
(M R Channon) *t.k.h: rdn and effrt 2f out: cajoled into 2nd ins fnl f: no ch w wnr* **10/1**
6102 **3** *nk* **Turning Top (IRE)**[7] 4452 3-9-7 **75**........................ JamieSpencer 3 76
(S A Callaghan) *led tl rdn and hdd wl over 1f out: drvn and plugged on: wl hld fnl f* **3/1**[2]
0240 **4** *shd* **Rio Royale (IRE)**[41] 3347 3-9-7 **75**........................(p) JimCrowley 4 76
(Mrs A J Perrett) *cl up: rdn over 2f out: one pce and wl hld over 1f out* **8/1**[3]
3650 **5** 6 **Red Rossini (IRE)**[7] 4454 3-9-0 **68**........................ DaneO'Neill 5 49
(R Hannon) *pressed ldrs: rdn 3f out: wknd wl over 1f out: edgd rt and eased ins fnl f* **16/1**

69.48 secs (-0.72) **Going Correction** -0.10s/f (Good) **5** Ran SP% **109.0**
Speed ratings (Par 100): **100,97,96,96,88**
toteswingers: 1&2 £6.40. CSF £8.63 TOTE £1.70: £1.10, £3.00; EX 6.80.
Owner The Searchers **Bred** Jilsie's Gigalo Stables Inc Et Al **Trained** Newmarket, Suffolk

FOCUS
The runners came stands' side in this low-grade sprint handicap. The form is rated around those in the frame behind the winner, who did not have to match her Ascot running.

4696 TOTESPORT.COM BRIGHTON CHALLENGE CUP (H'CAP) 1m 3f 196y
4:00 (4:00) (Class 4) (0-80,80) 3-Y-0+
£12,384 (£3,712; £1,858; £926; £464; £234) **Stalls** High

Form RPR
000 **1** **Eton Fable (IRE)**[34] 3564 4-9-1 **71**........................(p) TravisBlock 13 79
(W J H Ratcliffe) *led and 4l clr: rdn 4f out: hdd over 1f out: battled bk to ld again ins fnl f: had smething in hand* **22/1**
0011 **2** ½ **Halfway House**[14] 4241 3-8-7 **74** ow1........................ JamieSpencer 6 81
(M L W Bell) *t.k.h and bhd early: clsd after 4f: 2nd 4f out: led over 1f out: drvn and hdd ins fnl f: nt qckn* **2/1**[1]
5220 **3** ¾ **Step This Way (USA)**[55] 2895 4-9-7 **77**........................ RoystonFfrench 15 83
(M Johnston) *prom: drvn and outpcd over 1f out: racd w awkward hd carriage but styd on again ins fnl f* **7/1**
015 **4** 2 ¾ **Epsom Salts**[27] 3814 4-8-8 **67**........................ JackDean(3) 7 69+
(P M Phelan) *midfield: rdn and lost pl and outpcd over 2f out: kpt on wl ins fnl f* **6/1**[2]
2-24 **5** 1 **Outlandish**[41] 3343 6-9-6 **76**........................ TedDurcan 2 76
(Miss E C Lavelle) *s.s: nvr bttr than midfield: effrt over 2f out: rdn and no imp fnl 2f* **12/1**
3334 **6** 1 ½ **Watson's Bay**[7] 4449 4-8-13 **69**........................ PaulDoe 12 67
(P Howling) *stdd s: plld hrd in rr: effrt 4f out: fdd over 1f out: edgd lft* **7/1**
0645 **7** ¾ **Capable Guest (IRE)**[19] 4091 7-9-6 **76**........................ TPO'Shea 11 72
(M R Channon) *bhd: rdn 4f out: n.d after: wanted to hang lft fnl f* **11/1**
6101 **8** ¾ **Free Tussy (ARG)**[47] 3158 5-8-10 **66**........................(bt) LPKeniry 4 61
(G L Moore) *racd freely and chsd ldrs: rdn 2f out: sn btn: hanging lft fnl f* **20/1**
30-0 **9** 2 **Indicible (FR)**[140] 82 5-9-6 **76**........................ DaneO'Neill 10 68
(A King) *plld hrd early: bhd: nvr gng wl fr 1/2-way: labouring in last over 2f out* **40/1**
3055 **10** 1 ¾ **Soundbyte**[21] 4007 4-8-9 **65**........................ JimCrowley 8 54
(J Gallagher) *cl up: rdn 4f out: btn wl over 1f out* **13/2**[3]
4520 **11** ¾ **Valdan (IRE)**[8] 4417 5-8-12 **75**........................ AndrewHeffernan(7) 1 63
(P D Evans) *prom: hmpd on rails 5f out: lost pl wl over 1f out* **12/1**

2m 32.34s (-0.36) **Going Correction** -0.10s/f (Good)
WFA 3 from 4yo+ 11lb **11** Ran SP% **121.2**
Speed ratings (Par 105): **97,96,96,94,93 92,92,91,90,89 88**
toteswingers: 1&2 £12.80, 1&3 £25.30, 2&3 £3.70. CSF £66.83 CT £366.29 TOTE £30.00: £6.00, £1.10, £2.90; EX 126.10 Trifecta £214.10 Part won. Pool: £289.43 - 0.20 winning units..
Owner The Gathering **Bred** Andrew Christy **Trained** Newmarket, Suffolk
■ Stewards' Enquiry : Royston Ffrench two-day ban: careless riding (Aug 22-23)
Jamie Spencer one-day ban: used whip with excessive frequency without giving gelding time to respond (Aug 22)

FOCUS
This was a competitive handicap run at a fair clip. The winner and third are the best guides to the form.

4697 TOTESPORTBINGO.COM H'CAP 7f 214y
4:30 (4:32) (Class 6) (0-60,60) 3-Y-0+ **£2,590** (£770; £385; £192) **Stalls** Low

Form RPR
6-36 **1** **Recalcitrant**[7] 4449 6-8-9 **46**........................ JamieSpencer 7 55
(S Dow) *led 2f: chsd clr ldr tl led again over 1f out: rdn and got first run on rivals: kpt on wl* **4/1**[1]
0500 **2** ½ **Gifted Heir (IRE)**[10] 4389 5-8-2 **46** oh1........................ NatashaEaton(7) 6 54
(A Bailey) *dwlt: sn rcvrd: bhd: pushed along 2f out: styd on stoutly ins fnl f: too much to do* **50/1**
0-00 **3** 1 ½ **Prince Valentine**[31] 3671 8-8-11 **48**........................(p) LPKeniry 5 52
(G L Moore) *plld v hrd in midfield: rdn and kpt on to go 3rd wl ins fnl f: nvr looked like winning* **12/1**
4143 **4** ¾ **Landucci**[23] 3948 8-9-9 **60**........................(p) JamesDoyle 9 63
(S Curran) *t.k.h in midfield: effrt 2f out: wnt 2nd ins fnl f: one pce and lost two pls last 100yds* **5/1**[2]
4036 **5** 1 **Jonnie Skull (IRE)**[19] 3783 3-8-0 **51**........................(vt) CarolineKelly(7) 10 51
(P S McEntee) *taken down early: plld hrd: led after 2f: dashed clr: 4 l ahd 3f out: hdd over 1f out: lost 2nd ins fnl f: fin weakly* **16/1**
1530 **6** *hd* **Golden Prospect**[12] 4305 5-9-5 **56**........................ LiamJones 2 56
(J W Hills) *rrd and lost 6 l s: effrt and hung rt fnl f: wl hld whn checked cl home* **13/2**[3]
3045 **7** 2 ¾ **Shavoulin (USA)**[20] 4071 5-8-11 **48**........................ ChrisCatlin 1 42
(P W Hiatt) *pressed ldrs: drvn over 2f out: btn wl over 1f out* **4/1**[1]
1U00 **8** 1 ¼ **Annes Rocket (IRE)**[12] 4321 4-8-13 **55**........................ GabrielHannon(5) 4 46
(J C Fox) *plld hrd: bhd: prog 1/2-way: wknd over 1f out: hung lft and eased* **14/1**
00-0 **9** 12 **Street Diva (USA)**[107] 1417 4-9-3 **54**........................ SimonWhitworth 8 17
(R Curtis) *t.k.h: pressed ldrs over 6f: eased fnl f* **28/1**
0432 **10** 4 ½ **Astroangel**[23] 3946 5-9-3 **54**........................(p) TedDurcan 3 7
(M H Tompkins) *bhd: brief effrt halfwaqy: struggling wl over 1f out: eased fnl f* **4/1**[1]

1m 35.75s (-0.25) **Going Correction** -0.10s/f (Good)
WFA 3 from 4yo+ 7lb **10** Ran SP% **115.7**
Speed ratings (Par 101): **97,96,95,94,93 93,90,89,77,72**
toteswingers: 1&2 £31.30, 1&3 £9.10, 2&3 £54.10. CSF £195.71 CT £2200.08 TOTE £5.70: £2.00, £8.20, £2.80; EX 227.30 TRIFECTA Not won..
Owner T Staplehurst **Bred** T Staplehurst **Trained** Epsom, Surrey

FOCUS
A moderate but competitive handicap, although the form looks muddling with the first two improving on recent form.
Golden Prospect Official explanation: jockey said gelding was denied a clear run
Astroangel Official explanation: jockey said mare was never travelling and lost her action coming up the hill; trainer's rep said mare was in season

4698 RINA TAIRO JEWELLERY BRIGHTON BELLE LADY RIDERS' H'CAP 1m 1f 209y
5:00 (5:01) (Class 5) (0-70,70) 3-Y-0+ **£3,038** (£949; £474; £237; £118) **Stalls** High

Form RPR
1240 **1** **Theocritus (USA)**[8] 4437 4-10-5 **70**........................ MissHayleyMoore(5) 1 79
(D M Simcock) *towards rr: effrt on outside over 2f out: styd on to ld wl ins fnl f: kpt on stoutly* **11/4**[2]
0000 **2** ¾ **Eastern Gift**[20] 4060 4-10-10 **70**........................ MissEJJones 10 77
(Miss Gay Kelleway) *midfield and hld up bhd front rnk who were gng too fast: clsd to ld wl over 1f out: ct and nt qckn wl ins fnl f: outbattled* **7/1**
0235 **3** 3 ¼ **Strike Force**[23] 3950 5-9-7 **58**........................ MissALHutchinson(5) 2 59
(Miss J Feilden) *bhd: clsd grad fnl 2f: wnt mod 3rd ins fnl f: no ch w ldrs* **9/4**[1]
2500 **4** 1 ½ **Artreju (GER)**[4] 4563 6-9-4 **57**........................ MissKLoftus(7) 5 55
(P Butler) *plld frntically in rr: 15 l last at 1/2-way: effrt 2f out: kpt on fnl f: nvr able to chal* **14/1**
3000 **5** 1 ¾ **It's My Day (IRE)**[24] 3919 4-9-4 **55**........................ MissCAllen(5) 4 49
(C Gordon) *plld hrd: led 3f: wkng whn hung lft ins fnl f: nt run on* **22/1**
1000 **6** 3 **Solent Ridge (IRE)**[12] 4322 4-10-10 **70**........................(p) MrsSMoore 3 58
(J S Moore) *led after 3f: hdd wl over 1f out: fin v weakly fnl f* **12/1**
1600 **7** ½ **Corlough Mountain**[95] 1710 5-9-2 **51** oh1........................ MissZoeLilly(3) 7 38
(P Butler) *t.k.h in midfield: wknd over 2f out* **22/1**
000- **8** 5 **Shape Shifter (USA)**[369] 4636 3-8-10 **56** oh1 ow5........ MissJFerguson(5) 8 33
(J R Best) *chsd ldrs: rdn over 3f out: sn struggling* **12/1**
1300 **9** 1 **Western Roots**[62] 2675 8-9-13 **64**........................ MissMBryant(5) 11 39
(P Butler) *racd freely: w ldrs tl fdd over 2f out* **16/1**
0-56 **10** 18 **Silver Blue (IRE)**[36] 3504 6-9-0 **53**........................ MissGMorris(7) 9 —
(W K Goldsworthy) *bhd: t.o fnl 4f: eased sn after* **16/1**
064 **U** **Granny McPhee**[8] 4432 3-9-13 **68**........................ MissLHorner 6 —
(A Bailey) *reluctant to leave stall: leapt in air and uns rdr* **13/2**[3]

2m 3.53s (-0.07) **Going Correction** -0.10s/f (Good)
WFA 3 from 4yo+ 9lb **11** Ran SP% **125.8**
Speed ratings (Par 103): **96,95,92,91,90 87,87,83,82,68** —
toteswingers: 1&2 £5.20, 1&3 £2.50, 2&3 £5.00. CSF £24.58 CT £51.54 TOTE £4.00: £1.60, £2.60, £1.50; EX 25.00 Trifecta £245.20 Part won. Pool: £331.41 - 0.52 winning units. Place 6: £31.29 Place 5: £22.21.
Owner Dr Marwan Koukash **Bred** Allen E Paulson Living Trust **Trained** Newmarket, Suffolk

FOCUS
They went a good clip in this lady riders' handicap. The form is probably modest.
T/Plt: £57.50 to a £1 stake. Pool: £55,586.13. 704.63 winning tickets. T/Qpdt: £28.50 to a £1 stake. Pool: £3,906.72. 101.40 winning tickets. IM

4237 FOLKESTONE (R-H)
Thursday, August 6

OFFICIAL GOING: Good to firm (firm in places) (overall 8.2; round course - 8.3; straight course - 8.2; stands' side 8.0; far side 8.3)
Wind: Nil Weather: Warm amd sultry

4699 LADBROKES.COM MEDIAN AUCTION MAIDEN STKS 7f (S)
5:30 (5:33) (Class 5) 2-Y-0 **£2,729** (£806; £403) **Stalls** Low

Form RPR
04 **1** **Come On Safari (IRE)**[14] 4219 2-9-0 0........................ JackMitchell(3) 5 80+
(P Winkworth) *wnt rt and stdd s: hld up in rr: hdwy 2f out: swtchd sharply rt over 1f out: ev ch 1f out: pushed along hands and heels to ld fnl 100yds: r.o wl* **3/1**[1]

5 **2** 1 1/2 **Onyx Of Arabia (IRE)**[10] 4377 2-9-3 0.......................... MartinDwyer 10 75
(B J Meehan) *wnt rt s: sn rcvrd and pressing ldr: rdn to ld wl over 1f out: hdd and no ex fnl 100yds* **3/1**[1]

644 **3** 4 **Orsett Lad (USA)**[15] 4200 2-9-3 77.......................... SteveDrowne 8 65
(J R Best) *racd keenly: led: rdn and hanging rt fr 2f out: hdd wl over 1f out: outpcd by ldng pair fnl f* **4/1**[2]

05 **4** 2 **Spanish Duke (IRE)**[19] 4080 2-9-3 0.......................... LDettori 7 60
(J L Dunlop) *sltly hmpd and stdd s: t.k.h: hld up in tch: rdn 2f out: keeping on same pce whn carried sltly rt over 1f out: sn wl outpcd* **4/1**[2]

0 **5** 3/4 **Red Amy**[20] 4055 2-8-12 0.......................... J-PGuillambert 9 53
(M L W Bell) *stdd s: plld hrd: hld up in rr: rdn and effrt 2f out: sn wanting to hang rt and outpcd: plugged on fnl f* **7/1**[3]

605 **6** 3/4 **Riffelalp (IRE)**[50] 3027 2-8-12 58.......................... StephenCarson 2 51
(Eve Johnson Houghton) *hld up in tch: sltly short of room on stands' rail wl over 1f out: sn drvn and btn* **66/1**

7 4 1/2 **Stratton Banker (IRE)** 2-9-3 0.......................... SaleemGolam 4 45
(S C Williams) *wnt rt s: t.k.h and sn chsng ldrs: rdn 2f out: wknd qckly over 1f out: no ch fnl f* **18/1**

4550 **8** 6 **Master Mylo (IRE)**[26] 3842 2-9-3 59.......................... RichardThomas 1 30
(Mrs L C Jewell) *t.k.h: hld up in tch towards rr: rdn and struggling 3f out: wl bhd fnl 2f* **16/1**

9 2 3/4 **Arnie Guru** 2-8-10 0.......................... KierenFox(7) 11 23
(M J Attwater) *wnt rt s: styd wd: in tch tl rdn and wknd qckly 2f out: wl bhd fnl f* **33/1**

1m 26.49s (-0.81) **Going Correction** -0.275s/f (Firm) **9** Ran SP% **118.1**
Speed ratings (Par 94): **93,91,86,84,83 82,77,70,67**
toteswingers: 1&2 £2.10, 1&3 £2.20, 2&3 £2.30. CSF £12.28 TOTE £3.90: £1.30, £1.40, £1.90; EX 16.30.
Owner Rupert Williams **Bred** J Quigley **Trained** Chiddingfold, Surrey

FOCUS
This looked a weak maiden, with the majority having already run, but none having shown any form above the mundane. The winner is one to keep an eye on.

NOTEBOOK
Come On Safari(IRE) had stepped up on his debut outing when finishing fourth in a Bath maiden two weeks prior to this and, on that form, he appeared to have place prospects at least in this weaker contest. He was held up off the pace in the early stages, before making eyecatching progress at halfway, and, once he was switched sharply right to make his challenge, he comfortably overhauled the runner-up to score with a bit in hand. (op 7-2)
Onyx Of Arabia(IRE) had shown some ability on his only previous start, taking fifth after a slow break in a Windsor maiden, and the majority of two-year-olds from his stable improve from their initial appearance. He almost certainly did take a step forward, but it was not vast and after figuring prominently from the outset, vying with the third from the start, he could offer no great resistance when the winner went past him. (op 7-2)
Orsett Lad(USA) seemingly set the standard, albeit a modest one, having finished fourth in his last two races, both on Polytrack. His official rating of 77 looked high for what he had acheived, however, and he had a bit to prove switching back to turf. He ran another solid race, breaking quicky and contesting the lead for more than half the journey, but he was left behind at the business end of the race. Official explanation: jockey said colt hung right (op 9-2)
Spanish Duke(IRE) came here off a disappointing second outing, having pulled too hard when well backed over this distance at Lingfield, but the fact that he had been supported on each of his two runs suggested that connections had reason to expect better than he had so far revealed. They had booked Frankie Dettori to take the mount, and once again the colt was supported, but the change of jockey made little difference to his display, as he ran in snatches, by turns tugging for his head and dropping the bit, before coming home a disappointing fourth. Official explanation: jockey said colt was unsuited by the track (op 7-2 tchd 9-2)
Red Amy, ninth of 13 in a race contested by newcomers at Newmarket three weeks previously, fared a little better here, without threatening to take a major hand in proceedings. (op 9-1)

4700 LADBROKES.COM H'CAP 7f (S)
6:05 (6:06) (Class 5) (0-75,75) 3-Y-O **£2,729** (£806; £403) **Stalls** Low

Form RPR
2253 **1** **My Best Bet**[13] 4267 3-8-12 **71**.......................... MCGeran(5) 3 78
(M R Channon) *s.i.s: towards rr: hdwy 1/2-way: rdn and edgd rt over 1f out: drvn to chse ldr ent fnl f: styd on wl u.p to ld fnl 50yds* **11/2**[3]

5051 **2** 3/4 **Bea Menace (USA)**[14] 4240 3-9-2 **70**..........................(b) LDettori 8 75
(P F I Cole) *led and grad crossed to stands' rail: rdn over 1f out: drvn fnl f: hdd and no ex fnl 50yds* **4/1**[2]

50-5 **3** 5 **Golden Rosie (IRE)**[54] 2917 3-9-5 **73**..........................[1] SteveDrowne 1 65
(B W Hills) *wnt rt s: sn chsng ldr: rdn 2f out: lost 2nd and drvn ent fnl f: sn wknd* **4/1**[2]

2603 **4** 1 **Safari Guide**[12] 4303 3-9-2 **70**.......................... IanMongan 2 59
(P Winkworth) *towards rr: hdwy to chse ldng trio and rdn over 3f out: no imp fnl 2f* **15/2**

-442 **5** 5 **Aurora Sky (IRE)**[21] 4010 3-9-5 **73**.......................... J-PGuillambert 5 48
(J Akehurst) *nvr gng wl: sn pushed along in rr: racd awkwardly and lost tch over 3f out* **3/1**[1]

2004 **6** 17 **Admiral Sandhoe (USA)**[15] 4202 3-9-2 **70**.......................... TPQueally 6 —
(Mrs A J Perrett) *nvr gng wl towards rr: rdn and struggling 1/2-way: wl bhd fnl 2f* **16/1**

4002 **7** 5 **King's Sabre**[22] 3982 3-9-2 **70**.......................... MartinDwyer 7 —
(W R Muir) *taken down early: chsd ldrs: rdn and struggling 1/2-way: sn bhd: t.o* **7/1**

1m 25.0s (-2.30) **Going Correction** -0.275s/f (Firm) **7** Ran SP% **110.5**
Speed ratings (Par 100): **102,101,95,94,88 69,63**
toteswingers: 1&2 £3.50, 1&3 £2.60, 2&3 £2.80. CSF £25.70 CT £91.39 TOTE £7.20: £2.50, £2.60; EX 27.60.
Owner Phil Jen Racing **Bred** Phil Jen Racing **Trained** West Ilsley, Berks

FOCUS
No superstars in this contest, with the top weight after a withdrawal rated just 73. Several in the line-up had solid recent form to their credit, however, and, with more than one runner having shown a preference for setting a decent gallop, a decent pace seemed guaranteed. The overall form is modest with the winner to the best view of his earlier form.
Aurora Sky(IRE) Official explanation: trainer's rep said, regarding the poor form shown, filly was unable to dominate and was unsuited by the good to firm, firm in places ground
King's Sabre Official explanation: jockey said gelding hung right

4701 EBF LADBROKES.COM MAIDEN STKS 6f
6:35 (6:36) (Class 5) 2-Y-O **£3,723** (£1,108; £553; £276) **Stalls** Low

Form RPR
43 **1** **Marine Spirit (GER)**[19] 4093 2-9-3 0.......................... LDettori 3 84+
(Saeed Bin Suroor) *s.i.s: hdwy to ld after 1f: mde rest: pushed along over 1f out: in command fnl f: comf* **5/6**[1]

2 2 1/2 **Subtefuge** 2-8-12 0.......................... TPQueally 1 71
(H R A Cecil) *led for 1f: chsd wnr after: rdn and rn geen over 1f out: kpt on fnl f but no ch w wnr* **4/1**[3]

55 **3** 1/2 **Love Match**[20] 4047 2-8-12 0.......................... SteveDrowne 6 69
(R Charlton) *racd in midfield: hdwy and chsng ldrs over 2f out: chsd ldng pair 2f out: rdn and unable qckn over 1f out: kpt on fnl f but no ch w wnr* **7/2**[2]

4 7 **Cuts Both Ways (USA)** 2-9-3 0.......................... TedDurcan 4 53
(P F I Cole) *chsd ldrs tl rdn 2f out: sn wl outpcd and wl btn fnl f* **12/1**

5 3 1/2 **Persian Heroine (IRE)** 2-8-12 0.......................... DaneO'Neill 7 38
(J L Dunlop) *s.i.s: rn green and a in rr: rdn and no prog 2f out: wl bhd fnl f* **14/1**

6 nk **Ellen Vannin (IRE)** 2-8-12 0.......................... StephenCarson 9 37
(Eve Johnson Houghton) *a in rr: rdn and no prog 2f out: wl btn whn swtchd rt 1f out* **50/1**

7 2 3/4 **Generoso (USA)** 2-9-3 0.......................... SaleemGolam 8 33
(S C Williams) *dwlt: a last trio: lost tch 2f out: wl btn whn edgd lft 1f out* **66/1**

1m 11.51s (-1.19) **Going Correction** -0.275s/f (Firm) **7** Ran SP% **114.6**
Speed ratings (Par 94): **96,92,92,82,78 77,73**
toteswingers: 1&2 £1.40, 1&3 £1.10, 2&3 £5.30. CSF £4.59 TOTE £1.80: £1.30, £1.80; EX 5.50.
Owner Godolphin **Bred** Gestut Auenquelle **Trained** Newmarket, Suffolk

FOCUS
Not the strongest maiden ever staged, but it was made more interesting by the presence of a clutch of nicely-bred newcomers from high-profile stables. The third looks the best guide to the level.

NOTEBOOK
Marine Spirit(GER) lined up having taken third in a fair maiden at Newmarket 19 days previously, but the level he had reached that day was hardly out of the ordinary and his performance then had not indicated he had made an especially large leap forward from his so-so debut outing at Goodwood. He appeared to improve markedly here, though, quickly establishing a lead after a slowish start and, racing perhaps three horse widths from the far side rail, making all the remaining running to score decisively. (op 10-11 tchd Evens and 4-5)
Subtefuge, from a stable that has been doing well with its two-year-olds this summer, comes from a highly productive family at this sort of distance and is out of a mare successful over 6f at three. He posted an encouraging debut performance, giving the winner a decent run for his money despite showing signs of greenness and a tendency to hang, and, if any of these has a significant amount of progress to come, it is probably him. (op 5-1)
Love Match had encountered easy ground on both her earlier starts, finishing fifth in reasonable maidens at Doncaster and Newbury, and there had to be a chance that a faster surface would bring about some improvement on those two mildly encouraging, but hardly scintillating, efforts. It is hard to be certain if she did take a step forward, but it seems unlikely, and, consequently, she is probably the best marker to the form, as she was never too far off the pace and kept on gamely even when her chance of winning was gone. (op 3-1)
Cuts Both Ways(USA) hails from a yard whose juveniles have been in fine form over recent weeks and, as he is by a smart stallion, Johannesburg, successful in own his first season on the racecourse, and out of mare who won at two in the US, he is bred to make his mark as a youngster. He ran a fair race, although it would not be sensible to get carried with the standard he achieved, and, in finishing fourth, he did enough to suggest that there are prizes to be won with him, even if handicaps eventually prove his ideal medium. (op 14-1)
Persian Heroine(IRE), by the classy older miler Intikhab from a mare whose best efforts came over 1m4f as a three-year-old, has the beeding of a relatively long-term prospect, although the form of her juvenile stablemates this summer indicated she was worth considering if encouraging betting moves occurred. There was not a great deal of support for her, however, and she ran as might have been expected, finding the pace too hot in the early stages, but coming home quite pleasingly, albeit a good distance behind the winner. (tchd 12-1)

4702 LADBROKES.COM FILLIES' H'CAP 6f
7:05 (7:05) (Class 5) (0-70,68) 3-Y-O+ **£2,729** (£806; £403) **Stalls** Low

Form RPR
6345 **1** **Ishibee (IRE)**[5] 4533 5-8-6 **48**..........................(p) MarcHalford(3) 7 54
(J J Bridger) *trckd ldrs: rdn and effrt to ld over 1f out: drvn ent fnl f: hld on gamely thrght fnl f* **11/2**

21 **2** 1/2 **Namu**[31] 3671 6-9-7 **60**..........................(p) DaneO'Neill 2 64
(Miss T Spearing) *t.k.h: hld up wl in tch in last pair: hdwy over 1f out: rdn to chal jst ins fnl f: r.o but a jst hld* **2/1**[1]

3465 **3** 2 1/4 **Dualagi**[8] 4428 5-9-4 **57**.......................... J-PGuillambert 1 54
(M R Bosley) *t.k.h: hld up wl in tch: nt clr run over 2f out tl ent fnl f: sn drvn and kpt on but nvr pce to chal ldrs* **3/1**[2]

0-00 **4** 1 3/4 **Black Moma (IRE)**[80] 2130 5-9-0 **53**.......................... SteveDrowne 8 45
(J R Boyle) *led: rdn 2f out: hdd over 1f out: wknd u.p jst ins fnl f* **16/1**

5240 **5** 1 **Rhapsilian**[40] 3407 5-9-1 **54**..........................(v) RobertHavlin 4 42
(J R Jenkins) *stdd s: t.k.h: hld up in tch in last pair: hdwy to chse ldrs 2f out: shkn up jst over 1f out: rdn and fnd nil 1f out: sn btn* **10/3**[3]

4000 **6** 1 3/4 **Mount Ella**[5] 4533 3-8-11 **54**.......................... MartinDwyer 6 37
(J R Boyle) *w ldr tl rdn and lost pl 2f out: rr whn n.m.r on stands' rail over 1f out: wl btn after* **8/1**

1m 12.05s (-0.65) **Going Correction** -0.275s/f (Firm)
WFA 3 from 5yo+ 4lb **6** Ran SP% **113.8**
Speed ratings (Par 100): **93,92,89,87,85 83**
toteswingers: 1&2 £1.80, 1&3 £4.00, 2&3 £2.80. CSF £17.34 CT £38.57 TOTE £6.70: £2.80, £1.70; EX 14.50.
Owner J J Bridger **Bred** Ambersham Stud **Trained** Liphook, Hants

FOCUS
A weak fillies' handicap, with the top weight rated 68 and several of the runners struggling for form. The winner is rated in line with her winter best.
Mount Ella Official explanation: jockey said filly was unsuited by the good to firm, firm in places ground

4703 HOBBS PARKER TELECOM H'CAP 1m 7f 92y
7:40 (7:40) (Class 5) (0-70,65) 3-Y-O+ **£3,070** (£906; £453) **Stalls** Low

Form RPR
0621 **1** **Winterbrook King**[7] 4470 3-8-5 **52** 6ex.......................... MarcHalford(3) 8 58
(J R Best) *hld up in last trio: chsd ldrs and pushed along over 4f out: nt clr run jst over 2f out tl wl over 1f out: swtchd lft jst over 1f out: sn drvn and ev ch: led fnl 100yds: hld on wl* **15/8**[1]

-204 **2** shd **Honorable Endeavor**[56] 2866 3-8-11 **55**..........................(v) NickyMackay 5 61
(E F Vaughan) *trckd ldrs: pushed along 4f out: rdn to chse ldr wl over 1f out: led over 1f out: hdd fnl 100yds: edgd lft but kpt on wl towards fin: jst hld* **8/1**

3-25 **3** 4 **Tobago Bay**[67] 2519 4-9-10 **57**..........................(b) DominicFox(3) 9 58
(Miss Sheena West) *sn bustled along to ld: rdn 3f out: drvn and hdd over 1f out: one pce fnl f* **11/4**[2]

-066 **4** 1 1/4 **Perception (IRE)**[12] 4319 3-9-7 **65**.......................... SteveDrowne 2 64
(R Charlton) *wiith ldr early: sn settled in midfield: effrt to chse ldrs on outer over 2f out: hung lft u.p over 1f out: sn btn* **5/1**

021 **5** 4 **Saxona (IRE)**[33] 3617 5-10-0 **58**.......................... MartinDwyer 7 54
(Ian Williams) *chsd ldr after 1f: shkn up 4f out: rdn wl over 2f out: lost 2nd wl over 1f out: sn wknd: eased wl ins fnl f* **7/2**[3]

/0-0 **6** *47* **Debord (FR)**[50] 3029 6-9-1 **45** .... IanMongan 1 —
(Jamie Poulton) *racd in last trio: reminders over 6f out: rdn and lost tch 4f out: t.o* **40/1**

000 **7** *78* **Rony Dony (IRE)**[19] 4083 5-9-1 **45** .... (t) DaneO'Neill 4 —
(M E Rimmer) *plld hrd: prom early: stdd and in last pl after 2f: rdn over 6f out: sn toiling bdly: hopelessly t.o fnl 3f* **66/1**

3m 24.18s (-5.52) **Going Correction** -0.275s/f (Firm)
WFA 3 from 4yo+ 14lb **7** Ran SP% **115.4**
Speed ratings (Par 103): **103,102,100,100,98 72,31**
toteswingers: 1&2 £4.20, 1&3 £1.60, 2&3 £4.60. CSF £18.34 CT £40.82 TOTE £3.10: £1.80, £2.60; EX 17.90.
Owner Fielden Racing **Bred** Mrs S C Greenfield **Trained** Hucking, Kent

FOCUS
A moderate staying contest and they finished well strung out.

4704 CHERYL IRELAND AND HER FILLIES' H'CAP — 1m 1f 149y
8:15 (8:15) (Class 5) (0-70,67) 3-Y-0+ **£2,729** (£806; £403) **Stalls** Centre

Form RPR

5204 **1** **Rosy Dawn**[12] 4300 4-9-0 **51** .... MarcHalford(3) 9 56
(J J Bridger) *mde all: rdn over 2f out: hrd rdn and hrd pressed over 1f out: battled on wl and hld on gamely fnl f* **11/2**[3]

-605 **2** *½* **Aphrodite's Rock**[43] 3278 3-9-3 **65** .... KylieManser(5) 8 69+
(Miss Gay Kelleway) *dwlt: racd in last trio: hdwy on outer 2f out: chsd ldrs over 1f out: r.o but edgd rt u.p ins fnl f: wnt 2nd nr fin* **12/1**

0000 **3** *½* **Onenightinlisbon (IRE)**[12] 4305 5-9-9 **57** .... RobertHavlin 12 60
(J R Boyle) *chsd ldrs: wnt 2nd 2f out tl over 1f out: ev ch ent fnl f: no ex fnl 100yds: lost 2nd nr fin* **15/2**

000 **4** *1½* **Haling Park (UAE)**[16] 4180 3-8-12 **55** .... SteveDrowne 5 56+
(G L Moore) *hld up in tch towards rr: pushed along 4f out: hdwy to chse ldrs on inner over 1f out: swtchd lft 1f out: 5th and keeping on whn squeezed and hmpd ins fnl f: one pce after* **12/1**

5554 **5** *¾* **Jewelled**[20] 4071 3-9-9 **66** .... DaneO'Neill 1 65
(J W Hills) *chsd ldrs: rdn to chse wnr over 1f out: ev ch and drvn 1f out: 4th and wkng whn bmpd ins fnl f* **7/2**[1]

3555 **6** *nse* **Carmela Maria**[20] 4053 4-9-10 **58** .... SaleemGolam 6 56
(S C Williams) *towards rr: rdn 4f out: hdwy u.p on inner over 1f out: styd on fnl f but nvr trbld ldrs* **5/1**[2]

/640 **7** *2¾* **Action Girl**[17] 4151 4-10-0 **62** .... IanMongan 3 55
(R M H Cowell) *s.i.s: detached in last pl tl 7f out: hdwy on outer over 2f out: no imp u.p fr over 1f out* **12/1**

-026 **8** *nk* **Rock Art (IRE)**[16] 4179 3-9-10 **67** .... MartinDwyer 2 59
(B J Meehan) *chsd wnr tl 2f out: wknd u.p over 1f out: wl hld fnl f* **7/1**

0-00 **9** *5* **Ma Patrice**[48] 3100 3-7-12 **46** .... AmyBaker(5) 10 28
(T D McCarthy) *s.i.s: t.k.h: hld up in rr: effrt on outer over 2f out: hung lft and no prog fnl 2f* **33/1**

5-50 **10** *2¾* **Pointillist (IRE)**[39] 3425 3-9-8 **65** .... TPQueally 11 42
(R M Beckett) *in tch: rdn over 2f out: wknd qckly wl over 1f out: wl btn fnl f* **7/1**

2m 2.13s (-2.77) **Going Correction** -0.275s/f (Firm)
WFA 3 from 4yo+ 9lb **10** Ran SP% **117.1**
Speed ratings (Par 100): **100,99,99,98,97 97,95,94,90,88**
toteswingers: 1&2 £23.00, 1&3 £12.40, 2&3 £12.60. CSF £69.67 CT £499.83 TOTE £5.70: £1.70, £3.30, £3.20; EX 55.90 Place 6: £80.10, Place 5: £55.29.
Owner Gayler William Chambers **Bred** Overbury Stallions Ltd **Trained** Liphook, Hants

FOCUS
Few of these had ever managed a victory, with several still struggling to notch a first-three placing, and it can only be described as a low-grade fillies' event. The winner looks the best guide to the form with the time good for the grade.

4491 HAYDOCK (L-H)
Thursday, August 6

OFFICIAL GOING: 6f course - good to firm (8.0); remainder - 1m to winning post: good to soft; winning post to 1m: good
Rail realignment increased advertised distances on round course by 10yards.
Inner straight track used.
Wind: light 1/2 against Weather: fine but overcast and warm

4705 JAMES EDWARDS LAND ROVER MAIDEN AUCTION STKS — 1m 30y
2:10 (2:11) (Class 5) 2-Y-0 **£3,238** (£963; £481; £240) **Stalls** Low

Form RPR

43 **1** **Diamond Duchess (IRE)**[14] 4226 2-8-8 0 .... RobertWinston 7 72
(D R Lanigan) *chsd ldrs: wnt 2nd 3f out: led jst ins fnl f: hld on towards fin* **9/4**[1]

44 **2** *nk* **Music Of The Moor (IRE)**[47] 3170 2-8-13 0 .... MickyFenton 4 76
(T P Tate) *trckd ldrs: effrt over 3f out: hung bdly lft: swtchd ins and ev ch ins fnl f: no ex: bit plld through mouth* **7/2**[3]

5 **3** *3¼* **Mark Anthony (IRE)**[13] 4286 2-8-11 0 ow2 .... NCallan 2 67
(K A Ryan) *t.k.h: led: wandered over 1f out: hdd jst ins fnl f: sn wknd* **7/1**

022 **4** *2* **Brunette (IRE)**[36] 3507 2-8-8 75 .... EddieAhern 1 60
(R Hannon) *w ldr: reminders over 4f out: one pce fnl 2f* **3/1**[2]

0 **5** *6* **Storm Command (IRE)**[9] 4396 2-8-9 0 .... TomEaves 6 48
(B Smart) *mid-div: sn drvn along: outaced and lost pl over 5f out: no threat after* **66/1**

06 **6** *nse* **Young Firth**[12] 4307 2-8-9 0 .... PaulMulrennan 3 47
(J R Norton) *mid-div: outpcd over 5f out* **100/1**

7 *5* **Land Of Plenty (IRE)** 2-8-6 0 .... AlanMunro 5 33
(M Johnston) *sn outpcd and in rr* **10/1**

04 **8** *16* **Smog (IRE)**[13] 4265 2-8-13 0 .... SebSanders 8 5
(B J Meehan) *w ldrs: lost pl over 2f out: bhd whn eased: sddle slipped* **16/1**

9 *3¾* **Big Buzz (IRE)** 2-8-9 0 .... DuranFentiman 9 —
(Mrs L Stubbs) *s.i.s: sn bhd and drvn along* **33/1**

1m 45.0s (1.20) **Going Correction** 0.0s/f (Good) **9** Ran SP% **110.9**
Speed ratings (Par 94): **94,93,90,88,82 82,77,61,57**
toteswingers: 1&2 £2.90, 1&3 £4.00, 2&3 £4.90. CSF £9.55 TOTE £2.90: £1.30, £1.30, £2.00; EX 12.50.
Owner Saif Ali **Bred** R N Auld **Trained** Newmarket, Suffolk

FOCUS
A modest maiden for the track, rated around the front pair and the sixth.

NOTEBOOK
Diamond Duchess(IRE), stepping up in trip again, sat close to the pace and kept on much straighter than most of her rivals to gain her first victory. A half-sister to winners, she holds entries in a couple of sales races at the end of the season, so one would imagine that she will be aimed towards one of those events. (op 5-2 tchd 2-1)

Music Of The Moor(IRE), gelded since his last run, tracked the pace and came through to look a big danger, but he started to hang (the bit ended up slipping through his mouth) and took his time to get close to the winner. It would appear that he is not a straightforward ride. (op 9-2)

Mark Anthony(IRE), whose jockey was carrying 2lb overweight, only showed a modicum of promise on his debut but did better here, even after again failing to settle in front. A big type who looks to have a knee action, there is more improvement to come. (op 12-1)

Brunette(IRE), back on turf after two fair efforts on the all-weather, is a leggy sort who proved to be one paced in the latter stages. She looks sure to be stronger with time. (op 5-2)

Storm Command(IRE) stayed on but was never dangerous. (op 80-1)

Land Of Plenty(IRE) was very weak in the market, and those who were happy to lay him on the exchanges were proved right as he never got involved. (op 11-2)

Smog(IRE), well beaten in two previous outings, was up with the leaders until his jockey started to ease him in the home straight. It was reported afterwards that the saddle had slipped. Official explanation: jockey said saddle slipped

Big Buzz(IRE), whose sales price rose significantly to 12,000gns as a yearling, was lively in the paddock and failed to make any impact in the race after starting slowly. (op 50-1)

4706 EBF HATTONS TRAVEL NOVICE FILLIES' STKS — 6f
2:40 (2:41) (Class 4) 2-Y-0 **£6,476** (£1,927; £963; £481) **Stalls** High

Form RPR

421 **1** **Farmers Wish (IRE)**[13] 4265 2-9-0 70 .... NCallan 3 81
(J L Spearing) *led: shkn up and qcknd over 1f out: edgd lft ins fnl f: jst hld on* **6/4**[1]

2 *nse* **Catbells (IRE)** 2-8-6 0 .... NeilChalmers 4 73+
(A Bailey) *chsd ldrs: styd on wl ins fnl f: jst failed* **11/4**[3]

1 **3** *¾* **Dark Eyes (IRE)**[14] 4219 2-8-12 0 .... EddieAhern 2 77
(D J Coakley) *trckd ldr: t.k.h: effrt 2f out: no ex ins fnl f* **13/8**[2]

4 *14* **Ed's A Red** 2-7-13 0 .... BillyCray(7) 1 29
(A Berry) *wnt lft s: drvn and outpcd 3f out: lost tch over 1f out* **50/1**

1m 16.28s (1.78) **Going Correction** -0.025s/f (Good) **4** Ran SP% **106.7**
Speed ratings (Par 93): **87,86,85,67**
CSF £5.74 TOTE £2.50; EX 7.30.
Owner D J Oseman **Bred** Frank Moynihan **Trained** Kinnersley, Worcs

FOCUS
Some nice fillies have taken this in the past, so the winner is probably one to follow, although it was a shame to see a fairly valuable contest attract only four runners. A tricky race to assess but the form has been rated positively.

NOTEBOOK
Farmers Wish(IRE) had shown a steady level of form in three previous runs, including a win last time, and did just enough here to hold on from a strong-finishing newcomer. Many winners of this race have gone on to contest the Dick Poole Fillies' Stakes, a Listed event at Salisbury, so it would not be a surprise to see her turn up for that contest. (op 15-8)

Catbells(IRE), a half-brother to the useful 2yo 6f winner Exhibition, showed a really good attitude on her first racecourse experience and was closing on the winner with every stride. A maiden looks a formality. (op 3-1)

Dark Eyes(IRE) appeared to cause a shock on her debut, considering her starting price, but proved that success was no fluke by running well again. (op 11-8)

Ed's A Red did not break from the stalls very smartly and was left behind, after making some ground up, by the leading three once they quickened up. (op 25-1)

4707 NETFLIGHTS.COM H'CAP — 6f
3:10 (3:10) (Class 5) (0-70,69) 3-Y-0 **£3,238** (£963; £481; £240) **Stalls** High

Form RPR

2113 **1** **Sarasota Sunshine**[20] 4061 3-9-7 **69** .... (b) NCallan 6 75+
(N P Littmoden) *mid-div: hdwy over 1f out: hrd rdn and styd on wl to ld last strides* **9/2**[2]

1320 **2** *nk* **Rio Cobolo (IRE)**[10] 4392 3-9-2 **64** .... (v) SilvestreDeSousa 8 69
(Paul Green) *chsd ldrs: led ins fnl f: edgd lft: hdd nr fin* **9/2**[2]

02 **3** *1¾* **Sea Crest**[5] 4514 3-8-13 **61** .... AlanMunro 5 61
(M Brittain) *dwlt: hdwy on outside to chse ldrs over 2f out: styd on same pce fnl f* **8/1**

-066 **4** *1½* **Viking Awake (IRE)**[52] 2970 3-8-11 **59** .... (t) PaulMulrennan 1 54
(J W Unett) *chsd ldrs on oter: kpt on same pce appr fnl f* **40/1**

4000 **5** *1¾* **Diddums**[24] 3924 3-9-7 **69** .... EddieAhern 7 58
(J W Hills) *w ldrs: led 2f out: hdd and fdd ins fnl f* **12/1**

2252 **6** *½* **Inthawain**[107] 1437 3-8-10 **58** .... DuranFentiman 2 46
(N Wilson) *led tl 2f out: one pce* **20/1**

2431 **7** *¾* **Minturno (USA)**[17] 4131 3-9-6 **68** .... (p) SebSanders 3 53+
(Mrs A Duffield) *hld up in rr: nt clr run and swtchd outside over 1f out: nvr a factor* **11/2**[3]

0100 **8** *1¼* **Lucky Dan (IRE)**[6] 4494 3-9-5 **67** .... (e[1]) RobertWinston 9 48+
(Paul Green) *t.k.h in rr: sme hdwy and nt clr run 1f out: nvr on terms* **10/1**

0013 **9** *50* **Evna (USA)**[5] 4530 3-9-5 **67** .... PaulHanagan 4 —
(R A Fahey) *chsd ldrs: lost pl and eased over 1f out: sn bhd: t.o: dead* **11/4**[1]

1m 13.74s (-0.76) **Going Correction** -0.025s/f (Good) **9** Ran SP% **113.5**
Speed ratings (Par 100): **104,103,101,99,96 96,95,93,26**
toteswingers: 1&2 £3.80, 1&3 £5.60, 2&3 £8.40. CSF £24.60 CT £155.32 TOTE £6.30: £1.90, £1.80, £2.10; EX 25.10.
Owner Franconson Partners **Bred** London Thoroughbred S'Vces Ltd & West Bl **Trained** Newmarket, Suffolk

FOCUS
A fairly exposed bunch lined up for this modest sprint on the new inner course. Slight improvement from the winner.

Lucky Dan(IRE) Official explanation: jockey said gelding was denied a clear run

4708 HATTONS SOLICITORS H'CAP — 1m 30y
3:40 (3:40) (Class 3) (0-95,93) 3-Y-0 **£8,095** (£2,408; £1,203; £601) **Stalls** Low

Form RPR

1421 **1** **Tiger Reigns**[40] 3394 3-8-12 **84** .... PhillipMakin 1 94+
(M Dods) *trckd ldrs: nt clr run over 2f out: styd on wl appr fnl f: led wl ins fnl f: hld on* **3/1**[2]

4111 **2** *nk* **Cyflymder (IRE)**[33] 3643 3-9-5 **91** .... EddieAhern 7 99
(R Hannon) *chsd ldrs on outer: led 2f out: hdd last 50yds* **6/1**

12 **3** *nk* **Mull Of Killough (IRE)**[56] 2855 3-9-3 **89** .... RobertWinston 5 96
(J L Spearing) *dwlt: hld up in rr: stdy hdwy 3f out: nt clr run and swtchd outside over 1f out: styd on wl ins fnl f* **5/2**[1]

-322 **4** *3¼* **Happy Anniversary (IRE)**[14] 4228 3-8-12 **84** .... SebSanders 2 84
(Mrs D J Sanderson) *slowly into streide: hdwy on ins over 4f out: sn hrd drvn and outpcd: kpt on fnl 2f* **13/2**

0020 **5** *3* **Deadly Secret (USA)**[49] 3049 3-9-4 **90** .... PaulHanagan 3 83
(R A Fahey) *t.k.h: trckd ldrs: chal over 2f out: wknd over 1f out* **4/1**[3]

3650 **6** *1¼* **Mishrif (USA)**[49] 3049 3-9-7 **93** .... NCallan 6 83
(J R Jenkins) *w ldrs: chal 2f out: sn wknd* **20/1**

-230 7 3 1/4 **Toledo Gold (IRE)**[14] 4227 3-8-7 **79** ow1 DavidAllan 4 61
(E J Alston) *t.k.h: led tl 2f out: sn wknd: eased ins fnl f* **16/1**
1m 43.55s (-0.25) **Going Correction** 0.0s/f (Good) 7 Ran SP% **111.8**
Speed ratings (Par 104): **101,100,100,97,94 92,89**
toteswingers: 1&2 £3.50, 1&3 £2.40, 2&3 £2.80. CSF £20.15 CT £49.14 TOTE £3.90: £2.20, £2.30; EX 19.90.
Owner Joe Buzzeo **Bred** Richard Green And New England Stud **Trained** Denton, Co Durham

FOCUS
A good little handicap. Most of these have looked promising or were on an upward curve, so the form should be reliable, although it should be noted that some of them did not always have the smoothest of passages. The winner is rated slightly better than the bare form.

NOTEBOOK
Tiger Reigns, who had also run the progressive Firebet close this season, had been raised 3lb for winning last time and pulled quite hard just behind the leader here. His rider was forced to sit and suffer for a while as the race took shape, but once in the clear he showed a really good attitude to fight his way to the front up the inside rail. (op 10-3 tchd 11-4 and 7-2)
Cyflymder(IRE) was brought with what seemed a well-timed challenge 2f out, but he could not hold off the winner in the final strides. It was another fine effort since joining the Richard Hannon stable. (op 5-1)
Mull Of Killough(IRE) is a nice-looking type with scope and looked unlucky not to get through when his jockey wanted to make his bid. Forced wide, he had every chance thereafter but could not poke his nose to the front. (op 11-4 tchd 3-1)
Happy Anniversary(IRE) is extremely consistent and added another sound effort to her collection. (tchd 8-1)
Deadly Secret(USA), who finished second to the previous week's Goodwood winner Roman Republic at Doncaster two starts previously, had been gelded since his last effort and did not help his chance here by taking a good grip. (op 6-1)
Mishrif(USA), well beaten in the Britannia on his handicap debut last time, dropped away after looking dangerous two furlongs out. (op 14-1)
Toledo Gold(IRE), beaten 31 lengths on his previous outing, was on his toes before the off and got to the lead easily. (op 14-1)

4709 FRONTLINE BATHROOMS H'CAP 1m 3f 200y
4:10 (4:10) (Class 4) (0-80,85) 3-Y-O £5,504 (£1,637; £818; £408) Stalls Centre

Form RPR
0144 1 **Excelsior Academy**[12] 4319 3-8-10 **73** Louis-PhilippeBeuzelin(5) 6 82
(B J Meehan) *in rr: drvn over 5f out: hdwy on outer over 2f out: swtchd ins and nt clr run appr fnl f: burst through between horses to ld last 100yds: readily* **20/1**
442 2 1 1/4 **Citizenship**[5] 4520 3-9-0 **72** (t) NCallan 4 79
(Ian Williams) *mid-div: pushed along 4f out: styd on to ld 2f out: hdd and no ex ins fnl f* **4/1**[2]
0-31 3 1/2 **Going For Gold**[35] 3527 3-9-5 **77** EddieAhern 5 83
(R Charlton) *s.i.s: hdwy on wd outside over 1f out: chsng ldrs whn hung lft over 1f out: styd on same pce ins fnl f* **6/1**
5152 4 1 1/2 **Embsay Crag**[19] 4074 3-8-11 **76** IJBrennan(7) 10 80
(Mrs K Walton) *led tl over 1f out: one pce* **14/1**
3431 5 2 1/4 **Royal Trooper (IRE)**[13] 4280 3-9-2 **77** FrederikTylicki(3) 1 77
(J G Given) *hld up in midfield: outpcd over 2f out: swtchd to outside over 1f out: kpt on* **8/1**
6442 6 1/2 **Advisor (FR)**[5] 4518 3-8-13 **76** LanceBetts(5) 3 75
(M L W Bell) *hld up in midfield: nt clr run over 3f out: sn chsng ldrs: wknd over 1f out* **11/4**[1]
22-1 7 3 1/2 **Choral Festival**[23] 3951 3-9-3 **75** SebSanders 9 69
(Sir Mark Prescott) *hdwy on outer to chse ldrs 7f out: wnt 2nd over 2f out: edgd lft and sn wknd* **11/2**[3]
220 8 2 **Sweet Hollow**[14] 4229 3-8-12 **70** PaulMulrennan 2 60
(C G Cox) *chsd ldrs: drvn over 4f out: lost pl 2f out* **16/1**
14 9 1 1/2 **Whooshka (USA)**[33] 3627 3-9-6 **78** AlanMunro 7 66
(P W Chapple-Hyam) *chsd ldrs: lost pl over 2f out* **10/1**
2m 32.21s (-0.99) **Going Correction** 0.0s/f (Good) 9 Ran SP% **113.8**
Speed ratings (Par 102): **103,102,101,100,99 99,96,95,94**
toteswingers: 1&2 £17.50, 1&3 £24.30, 2&3 £4.50. CSF £97.07 CT £549.95 TOTE £30.30: £5.30, £1.90, £2.00; EX 147.40.
Owner Lady Laidlaw Of Rothiemay **Bred** Lady Halifax **Trained** Manton, Wilts

FOCUS
This was a decent handicap for the grade that featured plenty of horses coming into the race in good heart. The form is not as strong as it might have been with the sixth and seventh rather blowing out and the winner a surprise improver.
Whooshka(USA) Official explanation: trainer's rep said filly made a noise

4710 SAINTSRLFC.COM H'CAP 1m 2f 95y
4:40 (4:42) (Class 5) (0-70,69) 3-Y-O+ £3,238 (£963; £481; £240) Stalls Low

Form RPR
4021 1 **Agilete**[8] 4437 7-9-7 **69** SimonPearce(7) 14 81+
(J Pearce) *hld up towards rr: smooth hdwy over 2f out: led 2f out: sn clr: pushed out* **7/1**[2]
1406 2 1 **Trouble Mountain (USA)**[8] 4431 12-9-1 **56** (t) DaleGibson 13 63
(M W Easterby) *mid-div: hdwy over 2f out: styd on wl fnl f: nt rch wnr* **25/1**
6010 3 3/4 **Ibrox (IRE)**[32] 3654 4-9-12 **67** SilvestreDeSousa 2 73
(A D Brown) *in rr: sn drvn along: gd hdwy on outside over 2f out: styd on ins fnl f* **8/1**[3]
252 4 2 3/4 **Red Skipper (IRE)**[7] 4465 4-8-12 **58** BMcHugh(5) 9 58
(N Wilson) *uns rdr leaving paddock and briefly rn loose: prom: hdwy over 2f out: kpt on same pce appr fnl f* **11/2**[1]
4605 5 2 1/4 **Hucking Heat (IRE)**[9] 4402 5-9-9 **64** (p) MickyFenton 3 60
(R Hollinshead) *s.i.s: hdwy 4f out: kpt on one pce fnl 2f* **7/1**[2]
0-56 6 nk **Noche De Reyes**[11] 4351 4-8-13 **54** DavidAllan 12 50
(E J Alston) *hld up in rr: hdwy over 2f out: kpt on wl fnl f* **22/1**
0326 7 1 **Pitbull**[6] 4496 6-9-1 **56** (p) SebSanders 10 50
(Mrs G S Rees) *s.s: hdwy over 3f out: hung lft: nvr nr ldrs* **7/1**[2]
00-0 8 1/2 **Kool Katie**[6] 4496 4-8-9 **50** oh3 AndrewElliott 17 43+
(Mrs G S Rees) *in rr: hmpd over 2f out: kpt on: nvr on terms* **66/1**
5445 9 1/2 **Shanavaz**[22] 3976 3-8-4 **54** ow1 AdrianTNicholls 8 46
(Mrs G S Rees) *s.i.s: in rr: hmpd over 2f out: swtchd outside over 1f out: kpt on: nvr nr ldrs* **12/1**
3066 10 6 **Gamesters Lady**[33] 3631 6-8-9 **50** DuranFentiman 15 30
(W M Brisbourne) *chsd ldrs: drvn over 5f out: wknd over 1f out* **25/1**
2054 11 2 3/4 **Ming Vase**[8] 4434 7-8-9 **50** PaulMulrennan 7 25
(P T Midgley) *prom: effrt over 2f out: edgd lft and lost pl over 1f out* **14/1**
600 12 nk **Tobago Reef**[26] 3851 5-8-2 **50** oh3 (p) BillyCray(7) 11 25
(C W Moore) *chsd ldrs on outer: lost pl over 2f out* **50/1**
05 13 5 **Plenilune (IRE)**[12] 4313 4-9-2 **57** AlanMunro 4 22
(M Brittain) *mid-div: lost pl 3f out* **16/1**
5040 14 1 3/4 **Susurrayshaan**[38] 3454 3-7-11 **52** ow2 (v) Louis-PhilippeBeuzelin(5) 6 14
(Mrs G S Rees) *led: wnt clr over 3f out: hdd 2f out: sn lost pl: eased ins fnl f* **28/1**
-005 15 5 **Dustry (IRE)**[17] 4149 3-9-4 **68** EddieAhern 5 20
(R Hannon) *iun tch: wknd over 1f out: bhd whn eased ins fnl f* **9/1**
43-0 16 6 **Highland Love**[90] 1845 4-9-9 **67** FrederikTylicki(3) 16 8
(J T Stimpson) *chsd ldrs on outer: lost pl 2f out: bhd whn eased ins fnl f* **14/1**
6-00 17 3/4 **Blues Minor (IRE)**[24] 3924 4-9-8 **63** (b) SJCraine 1 2
(M Mullineaux) *chsd ldrs: lost pl over 3f out* **66/1**
2m 14.43s (1.43) **Going Correction** 0.0s/f (Good)
WFA 3 from 4yo+ 9lb 17 Ran SP% **121.3**
Speed ratings (Par 103): **103,102,101,99,97 96,96,95,90 88,88,84,83,79 74,73**
toteswingers: 1&2 £35.70, 1&3 £9.60, 2&3 £29.20. CSF £179.05 CT £1438.43 TOTE £7.50: £2.20, £5.40, £2.70, £1.90; EX 112.10 Place 6: £117.66 Place 5: £77.65.
Owner S & M Supplies (Aylsham) Ltd **Bred** J W Parker And Lavington Stud **Trained** Newmarket, Suffolk

FOCUS
There was a right mixture of ages and abilities in this. The pace looked sound but some of the horses involved in the finish looked far from enthusiastic under pressure. Sound form.
Kool Katie Official explanation: jockey said filly suffered interference in running
T/Plt: £88.60 to a £1 stake. Pool: £57,354.82. 472.26 winning tickets. T/Qpdt: £23.50 to a £1 stake. Pool: £4,259.56. 134.09 winning tickets. WG

4437 SANDOWN (R-H)
Thursday, August 6

OFFICIAL GOING: Good to firm changing to good after race 3 (6.45) changing to good to soft after race 4 (7.20).
Home bend at outermost configuration. Home straight dolled out about 5yds adding about 8yards to advertised distances on round course.
Wind: Moderate, against Weather: Overcast, drizzle turning to rain by race 3.

4711 BUY A RACING POST YEARLING BONUS CANDIDATE MAIDEN FILLIES' STKS 5f 6y
5:40 (5:43) (Class 5) 2-Y-O £3,238 (£963; £481; £240) Stalls High

Form RPR
02 1 **Excellent Day (IRE)**[14] 4243 2-9-0 0 DarryllHolland 1 75
(M R Channon) *trckd ldng quartet on outer: prog 2f out: edgd rt but led 1f out: drvn out to hold on* **4/1**[2]
0503 2 hd **More Lashes (USA)**[11] 4349 2-9-0 0 WilliamBuick 9 74
(M G Quinlan) *trckd ldrs and racd against far rail: nt clr run fr 2f out tl got out jst ins fnl f: r.o to take 2nd nr fin and press wnr* **20/1**
432 3 hd **Waveband**[14] 4233 2-9-0 75 JimmyFortune 10 74
(M Johnston) *racd against far rail: led but pressed fr the s: edgd lft jst over 1f out: sn hdd and nt qckn: lost 2nd last strides* **1/1**[1]
53 4 2 1/2 **Admirable Duchess**[12] 4323 2-9-0 0 JimCrowley 8 65
(D J S Ffrench Davis) *pressed ldng pair to 1/2-way: lost pl u.p: kpt on again ins fnl f* **11/1**
3334 5 1 1/2 **La Fortunata**[21] 3993 2-9-0 73 AdrianMcCarthy 6 59
(J R Jenkins) *w ldr to jst over 1f out: wknd* **14/1**
6 3/4 **Ruthie Babe** 2-9-0 0 MichaelHills 5 56
(W J Haggas) *dwlt: hld up in 7th: sme prog on outer over 1f out: nt on terms whn one light reminder ins fnl f* **8/1**
2 7 5 **Memory And Magic (USA)**[28] 3772 2-9-0 0 PhilipRobinson 2 38
(C G Cox) *dwlt and wnt lft s: sn detached in last: nvr a factor* **15/2**[3]
0 8 2 1/4 **Hope'N'Reason (USA)**[22] 3987 2-9-0 0 ShaneKelly 7 30
(D M Simcock) *hld up in 6th: wknd rapidly over 1f out: eased* **100/1**
62.17 secs (0.57) **Going Correction** +0.075s/f (Good) 8 Ran SP% **113.6**
Speed ratings (Par 91): **98,97,97,93,90 89,81,78**
toteswingers: 1&2 £11.20, 1&3 £2.00, 2&3 £7.40. CSF £75.22 TOTE £4.50: £1.40, £3.90, £1.10; EX 146.00.
Owner Jaber Abdullah **Bred** Richard Hall **Trained** West Ilsley, Berks

FOCUS
Rain began to fall in the hour before racing, though it had made little impact on the ground for this first race. The pace was good but nothing came from too far back to get involved. The winner built on her previous course form.

NOTEBOOK
Excellent Day(IRE), runner-up over course and distance last month, went one better with a workmanlike win, but there did not appear to be any future stars in the line-up so she will have to improve a lot to justify her Lowther Stakes entry. (op 5-1 tchd 11-2)
More Lashes(USA) is gradually inching towards a first success and, while she was well beaten over 6f last time, she was reported to have "run flat" that day and a return to an extra furlong should suit. (op 18-1)
Waveband has yet to finish out of the first four in four outings but yet again was not quite good enough to win. Effective over 6f or a stiff 5f, she is capable of winning a routine maiden over either trip but would be equally at home in nurseries. (op 11-10 tchd 11-8 in a place)
Admirable Duchess has done well in three maidens and acquitted herself well on this first effort at 5f after tackling 6f in the first two. She can win a nursery and might yet sneak a lesser maiden if kept to that route instead. (tchd 10-1 and 12-1)
La Fortunata has a lot of early pace and would be more effective on a less testing course. She might yet win a run-of-the-mill maiden at one of the smaller venues, but her pace would stand her in particularly good stead in a 5f nursery on an easy track. (op 16-1 tchd 12-1)
Ruthie Babe, a £90,000 yearling by the Australian speedster Exceed And Excel out of a sprinter, is bred to be quick and this nippy-looking sort looked fit for her debut if lacking the scope of others. Her stable had high hopes that she would make a decent early sort, but she has taken longer than expected to get her onto the track and there should be some improvement. (op 5-1 tchd 9-1)
Memory And Magic(USA) had shown promise on her debut but missed the break and never got going. She can be given another chance in an ordinary maiden. Official explanation: jockey said filly was slowly away and hung left (op 8-1 tchd 7-1)

4712 BOYZONE CLASSIC H'CAP 5f 6y
6:15 (6:19) (Class 4) (0-80,80) 3-Y-O £4,857 (£1,445; £722; £360) Stalls High

Form RPR
-031 1 **Golden Destiny (IRE)**[14] 4244 3-9-7 **78** (p) JimmyFortune 5 85+
(P J Makin) *pressed ldr: led 1/2-way and gng bttr than the rest: hrd rdn fnl f but nvr seriously chal* **15/8**[1]
-000 2 1 **Lucky Leigh**[40] 3389 3-9-9 **80** DarryllHolland 6 83
(M R Channon) *chsd ldrs: rdn 2f out: styd on to take 2nd ins fnl f: no imp on wnr* **11/1**
1305 3 3/4 **Amosite**[14] 4231 3-9-0 **71** (v) ShaneKelly 7 72
(J R Jenkins) *racd against far rail: led to 1/2-way: chsd wnr tl ins fnl f: one pce* **16/1**

6260 **4** *shd* **Cut The Cackle (IRE)**[17] 4148 3-9-8 **79** .... JimCrowley 2 79
(P Winkworth) *wnt lft s: sn in tch: rdn on outer 2f out: tried to chal for 2nd 1f out: one pce* **4/1**[2]

2040 **5** *¾* **Robin The Till**[4] 4567 3-8-7 **64** .... WilliamBuick 3 62
(R Hannon) *settled in last pair: swtchd to wd outside and rdn 2f out: tried to chal for 2nd fnl f: one pce* **14/1**

010- **6** *½* **Especially Special (IRE)**[307] 6441 3-9-5 **76** .... JamesDoyle 4 72
(S Kirk) *trckd ldng pair: rdn 2f out: stl pressing for 2nd ins fnl f: wknd tamely last 100yds* **5/1**[3]

6434 **7** *nk* **All Spin (IRE)**[26] 3845 3-8-3 **65** .... MatthewDavies(5) 1 60
(A P Jarvis) *s.s: a in last pair: shkn up 2f out: plugging on but no ch whn nowhere to go nr fin* **4/1**[2]

61.61 secs (0.01) **Going Correction** +0.075s/f (Good) **7 Ran SP% 112.3**
Speed ratings (Par 102): **102,100,99,99,97 97,96**
toteswingers: 1&2 £2.50, 1&3 £4.30, 2&3 £9.60. CSF £23.10 TOTE £2.50: £1.60, £4.10; EX 15.50.
Owner H J W Davies P Spencer-Jones M H Holland **Bred** Yeomanstown Stud **Trained** Ogbourne Maisey, Wilts

FOCUS
Once again the main contenders raced handily.

4713 WATCH RACING UK ON SKY CHANNEL 432 MAIDEN STKS 1m 14y
6:45 (6:50) (Class 5) 2-Y-O **£3,238** (£963; £481; £240) **Stalls High**

Form RPR

2 **1** **High Twelve (IRE)**[15] 4209 2-9-3 0 .... JimmyFortune 1 89+
(J H M Gosden) *led after 1f: mde rest: pushed clr fr jst over 2f out: in n.d fr over 1f out* **2/7**[1]

2 *3¼* **Corsica (IRE)** 2-9-3 0 .... RoystonFfrench 2 79
(M Johnston) *chsd wnr over 6f out: lugging lft and green whn rdn over 2f out: n.d fr over 1f out: hld on for 2nd* **15/2**[2]

0 **3** *1¼* **Valiant Knight (FR)**[13] 4258 2-9-3 0 .... RichardHughes 4 76
(R Hannon) *led 1f: sn chsd ldng pair: shkn up over 2f out: one pce after* **16/1**

4 *hd* **Guidecca Ten** 2-9-3 0 .... WilliamBuick 3 76+
(A M Balding) *s.s: hld up in last and wl off the pce: effrt 3f out: kpt on fr over 1f out: n.d* **20/1**

5 *3¾* **Jibrrya** 2-9-3 0 .... DarryllHolland 5 67
(M R Channon) *hld up in 4th: shkn up and no prog over 2f out: wknd fnl f* **14/1**[3]

0 **6** *21* **Set In Ice**[14] 4219 2-9-3 0 .... JamesDoyle 6 21
(Mark Gillard) *t.k.h early: hld up in 5th: dropped to last 3f out: sn t.o* **200/1**

1m 45.49s (2.19) **Going Correction** +0.25s/f (Good) **6 Ran SP% 107.3**
Speed ratings (Par 94): **99,95,94,94,90 69**
toteswingers: 1&2 £1.10, 1&3 £2.10, 2&3 £2.70. CSF £2.57 TOTE £1.30: £1.02, £3.00; EX 2.90.
Owner Thomas Barr **Bred** Grangecon Stud **Trained** Newmarket, Suffolk

FOCUS
A race containing several juveniles of some potential, but the winner looks exceptional and there is more to come from him.

NOTEBOOK
High Twelve(IRE) ♦ was always comfortable in setting a decent gallop and the way he lengthened when asked made him look a high-class performer in the making. A step up in class is on the cards for this good-looking, well-grown sort. Trainer John Gosden, revealing that the initial plan was not to make the running but delighted that Jimmy Fortune had opted to do so, reported that he had improved since his debut and that he expects him to improve again. He will be given a break until September and then has a choice of select targets including the Champagne Stakes, Royal Lodge and Tattersalls Million, with Gosden confirming that he is "very much up to that quality". (op 3-10)

Corsica(IRE), a 48,000gns Cape Cross newcomer out of a French miler, travelled keenly but showed his inexperience off the bridle. The winner was far too good, but he has scope and this first run will have done him a lot of good. (op 8-1 tchd 17-2)

Valiant Knight(FR), a 115,000euro Night Shift colt out of a French winner up to 1m4f, should stay further as he matures. The 1m suited him better than the 7f of his debut and he stepped up considerably, just being nudged out to make sure of third, and there should be even better to come. (op 12-1)

Guidecca Ten ♦, by the top-class Peintre Celebre out of a winner at 1m2f and 1m4f in France, is a half-brother to a triple winner at 1m2f and 1m4f in Italy, so his stamina screams middle distances. In the circumstances, this 45,000gns yearling made a most encouraging debut, looking better as the race went on, and he is an interesting long-term prospect. (op 16-1)

Jibrrya cost 140,000gns a yearling, and this Motivator colt out of a maiden juvenile looks as if he needs more time to grow into his frame. However, he has the scope to do better as he strengthens. (tchd 12-1)

Set In Ice, closely related to several winners at 7f and 1m, has not shown much in two races to date and was taking on far too much here. (op 100-1 tchd 80-1)

4714 DAYTONA AT SANDOWN PARK H'CAP 1m 14y
7:20 (7:23) (Class 5) (0-75,70) 3-Y-0+ **£3,238** (£963; £481; £240) **Stalls High**

Form RPR

-046 **1** **Compton Blue**[42] 3299 3-9-2 **63** .... RichardHughes 6 70
(R Hannon) *led 1f: styd cl up: rdn over 2f out: prog again over 1f out: led last 150yds* **15/2**[3]

0060 **2** *1* **Pegasus Lad (USA)**[20] 4040 3-9-5 **66** .... RoystonFfrench 4 70
(M Johnston) *cl up: effrt to ld jst over 2f out: drvn 1 l ahd wl over 1f out: hdd and nt qckn last 150yds* **9/1**

6500 **3** *1¼* **Hallingdal (UAE)**[8] 4441 4-9-12 **66** .... TPO'Shea 10 68
(J J Bridger) *dwlt: hld up in 8th: looking for room over 2f out: stl wl in rr over 1f out: prog after to take 3rd ins fnl f: nvr able to chal* **10/1**

0155 **4** *1* **Hip Hip Hooray**[8] 4441 3-9-8 **69** .... DarryllHolland 2 68
(L A Dace) *dwlt: hld up in last trio: effrt on outer over 2f out: prog over 1f out: kpt on fnl f: nt pce to threaten* **9/2**[1]

0346 **5** *½* **Justcallmehandsome**[12] 4321 7-9-4 **63** ....(v) SophieDoyle(5) 3 62
(D J S Ffrench Davis) *hld up in 7th on outer: prog over 2f out: drvn to go 2nd briefly wl over 1f out: wknd ins fnl f* **9/1**

-000 **6** *1¾* **Dancer's Legacy**[17] 4150 4-9-9 **63** .... JimmyFortune 1 58
(J R Boyle) *dwlt: hld up in last and wl off the pce: effrt on outer over 2f out: sme prog u.p over 1f out: no hdwy fnl f* **12/1**

0155 **6** *dht* **Miss Mujanna**[20] 4060 4-9-5 **66** .... BarryAdams(7) 9 61
(J Akehurst) *hld up on inner in 6th: rdn 2f out: no prog and no threat to ldrs* **14/1**

-350 **8** *shd* **King's La Mont (IRE)**[80] 2126 3-9-9 **70** .... JimCrowley 8 63
(Mrs A J Perrett) *cl up: rdn and lost pl 2f out: nvr on terms w ldrs after* **9/2**[1]

2600 **9** *2½* **Wunder Strike (USA)**[17] 4149 3-8-12 **59** .... WilliamBuick 11 46
(J R Boyle) *a in last trio: rdn and no real prog wl over 2f out* **25/1**

4634 **10** *1* **By Command**[15] 4207 4-9-13 **67** .... MichaelHills 7 53
(J W Hills) *disp ld after 1f to jst over 2f out: wknd wl over 1f out* **11/2**[2]

4404 **11** *1¾* **Pippbrook Gold**[14] 4236 4-9-9 **68** .... MatthewDavies(5) 5 50
(J R Boyle) *disp ld after 1f tl jst over 2f out: n.m.r sn after: wknd* **15/2**[3]

1m 45.48s (2.18) **Going Correction** +0.25s/f (Good)
WFA 3 from 4yo+ 7lb **11 Ran SP% 114.4**
Speed ratings (Par 103): **99,98,96,95,95 93,93,93,90,89 88**
toteswingers: 1&2 £19.90, 1&3 £26.70, 2&3 £28.80. CSF £71.21 CT £690.59 TOTE £8.10: £2.50, £3.20, £3.40; EX 105.20.
Owner Godfrey Wilson **Bred** Caroline Wilson **Trained** East Everleigh, Wilts

FOCUS
Continuing rain changed the ground to good following the preceding race and it was amended again to "good to soft" after this one. They went just a fair gallop but every horse had a chance from its racing position.

4715 APRES-SKI CHRISTMAS PARTY NIGHTS H'CAP 1m 2f 7y
7:55 (7:56) (Class 3) (0-90,85) 3-Y-O **£7,771** (£2,312; £1,155; £577) **Stalls High**

Form RPR

3113 **1** **Amazing Blue Sky**[9] 4401 3-8-6 **70** .... LiamJones 1 77
(Mrs R A Carr) *sn led: drew 6 l clr after 4f: stl 4 l up 3f out: hrd rdn over 1f out: jst lasted* **9/1**

0411 **2** *shd* **Sequillo**[14] 4242 3-9-0 **78** .... RichardHughes 5 85+
(R Hannon) *stdd s: hld up in last trio: nt clr run briefly 2f out: prog over 1f out: drvn and styd on to take 2nd last strides: jst failed* **3/1**[2]

5421 **3** *nk* **Almuktahem**[22] 3984 3-9-2 **80** ....(v) TPO'Shea 4 86
(Sir Michael Stoute) *chsd wnr: rdn wl over 2f out: clsng grad whn lost action sltly 100yds out: lost 2nd last strides* **11/4**[1]

-120 **4** *2½* **Sehoy (USA)**[82] 2077 3-9-7 **85** .... JimmyFortune 6 86+
(J H M Gosden) *stdd s: hld up in last trio: effrt on inner over 2f out: one pce and no imp on ldrs* **6/1**

3-20 **5** *1* **Akbabend**[81] 2104 3-9-0 **78** .... RoystonFfrench 7 77
(M Johnston) *chsd ldng pair: rdn wl over 2f out: no imp wl over 1f out: fdd* **16/1**

0554 **6** *3¼* **Tottie**[8] 4422 3-9-7 **85** ....(b) JimCrowley 3 78
(Mrs A J Perrett) *hld up in 4th: stl looked to be gng easily over 2f out: rdn wl over 1f out and fnd nil: btn after* **7/2**[3]

-164 **7** *9* **Smart Endeavour (USA)**[45] 3220 3-9-4 **82** ....(t) ShaneKelly 2 57
(W R Swinburn) *hld up in last trio: rdn and wknd 3f out: sn t.o* **11/1**

2m 11.84s (1.34) **Going Correction** +0.25s/f (Good) **7 Ran SP% 112.4**
Speed ratings (Par 104): **104,103,103,101,100 98,91**
toteswingers: 1&2 £4.60, 1&3 £3.30, 2&3 £2.20. CSF £34.87 TOTE £9.00: £3.20, £2.40; EX 28.30.
Owner David W Chapman **Bred** Hong Kong Breeders Club **Trained** Huby, N Yorks

FOCUS
With the rain unrelenting, the going was changed again to "good to soft", with fast-ground performers now at a disadvantage.

NOTEBOOK
Amazing Blue Sky is from an in-form stable and he put up a heroic performance under an excellent ride, with Jones confirming that the soft lead had played into his hands and that he had been able to get a breather into him turning for home. The number of times this big, scopey front-runner has attracted the comment "gamely" recently speaks for itself, and connections believe that he will continue to improve. (op 14-1 tchd 8-1)

Sequillo, who only just failed to complete his hat-trick, is inching up the weights but continues in great heart. He has to be on the short-list next time. (op 7-2 tchd 4-1)

Almuktahem, visored for the first time when scoring at Lingfield, got the extra furlong well and only just failed. He has responded well to the headgear and should not be knocked for needing it to bring out the best in him. (op 10-3 tchd 5-2)

Sehoy(USA)'s best previous runs had been on Polytrack, but he showed he can perform on turf with a respectable finish from the rear. A return to 1m4f should be in his favour. (op 7-1 tchd 9-2)

Akbabend had been reported to have unsuited by the good to soft ground last time, so it is fair to assume that the rain adversely affected his chance. (op 11-1 tchd 18-1)

Tottie again found nothing off the bridle and would probably appreciate a break. (op 11-4)

Smart Endeavour(USA) was trying a longer trip and probably failed to stay, with the rain-softened surface not helping. (op 12-1 tchd 16-1)

4716 ROBERTSON & SUMNER "STEP UP" H'CAP 1m 2f 7y
8:25 (8:27) (Class 4) (0-80,80) 3-Y-O+ **£4,857** (£1,445; £722; £360) **Stalls High**

Form RPR

0122 **1** **Wing Play (IRE)**[10] 4378 4-9-5 **72** ....(p) ShaneKelly 1 85
(H Morrison) *hld up and sn in 4th: smooth prog on outer over 2f out: led over 1f out: urged along and wl in command fnl f* **7/4**[1]

002 **2** *4½* **Mafeking (UAE)**[29] 3734 5-9-13 **80** .... ChrisCatlin 4 84
(M R Hoad) *led: shkn up over 2f out: hdd over 1f out: no ch w wnr after* **11/1**

3421 **3** *1¾* **Bomber Brown (IRE)**[17] 4151 3-8-13 **78** .... JackMitchell(3) 5 78
(P W Chapple-Hyam) *chsd ldng pair: rdn wl over 2f out: easily outpcd fr over 1f out* **11/4**[2]

0000 **4** *5* **Road To Love (IRE)**[26] 3840 6-9-10 **77** .... JimmyFortune 2 67
(M Johnston) *trckd ldr: shkn up over 2f out: wknd over 1f out* **4/1**[3]

0013 **5** *1½* **Kidlat**[63] 2641 4-9-13 **80** ....(t) JimCrowley 8 67
(B G Powell) *t.k.h early: hld up and sn in last pair: pushed along and reminder over 2f out: no rspnse* **8/1**

0-0 **6** *nk* **Bid For Glory**[40] 3378 5-9-10 **77** .... DarryllHolland 7 63
(H J Collingridge) *hld up in last pair: rdn wl over 2f out: no prog and struggling after* **10/1**

2m 13.18s (2.68) **Going Correction** +0.25s/f (Good)
WFA 3 from 4yo+ 9lb **6 Ran SP% 111.6**
Speed ratings (Par 105): **99,95,94,90,88 88**
toteswingers: 1&2 £6.00, 1&3 £1.10, 2&3 £7.10. CSF £21.07 CT £49.41 TOTE £2.50: £1.60, £3.60; EX 15.90 Place 6: £64.86, Place 5: £47.64.
Owner Watching Brief **Bred** Churchtown House Stud **Trained** East Ilsley, Berks

FOCUS
A modest handicap for the track but reasonable form for the grade, with the second and fourth potentially well treated.

T/Plt: £48.90 to a £1 stake. Pool: £45,834.10. 683.03 winning tickets. T/Qpdt: £34.00 to a £1 stake. Pool: £3,196.12. 69.40 winning tickets. JN

[4665] YARMOUTH (L-H)

Thursday, August 6

OFFICIAL GOING: Good (good to firm in places in straight; str: 7.7, bstr:7.3)
Back straight rail moved out by 3.5m.
Wind: Almost nil Weather: Fine and sunny

4717 EUROPEAN BREEDERS' FUND MAIDEN STKS — 6f 3y
2:20 (2:21) (Class 5) 2-Y-O — **£4,163** (£1,246; £623; £311) **Stalls** High

Form — RPR

443 **1** — **Excellent Guest**[13] 4258 2-9-3 80 — RyanMoore 3 — 80
(G G Margarson) *mde all: shkn up over 2f out: edgd rt over 1f out: rdn out* — **8/13**[1]

2 4 — **Serhaal (IRE)** 2-9-3 0 — RHills 5 — 68+
(Sir Michael Stoute) *s.i.s: sn prom: chsd wnr over 4f out: shkn up over 2f out: nt clr run over 1f out: styd on same pce* — **7/4**[2]

3 6 — **Rock Of Eire** 2-9-0 0 — AlanCreighton(3) 4 — 50
(E J Creighton) *w wnr to over 4f out: sn pushed along: wknd over 1f out* — **40/1**

4 11 — **Firefly Mustique** 2-9-3 0 — DO'Donohoe 1 — 17
(George Baker) *outpcd* — **20/1**[3]

1m 14.49s (0.09) **Going Correction** -0.275s/f (Firm) — 4 Ran SP% **105.5**
Speed ratings (Par 94): **88,82,74,60**
CSF £1.80 TOTE £1.70; EX 1.90.
Owner John Guest **Bred** John Guest Racing Ltd **Trained** Newmarket, Suffolk

FOCUS
An uncompetitive maiden, rated around the winner, but not a race to draw any firm conclusions from.

NOTEBOOK
Excellent Guest put his course experience to good use as he made his fourth start a winning one, although the time was almost exactly 3secs above standard. Third in a 7f Ascot maiden two weeks earlier, he was dropped back in trip here, set the tempo from the stalls and was never headed. It wasn't merely a training exercise, however, as Moore gave him several cracks with the whip inside the final furlong just to make sure he got the job done. The Handicapper has him assessed at 80 and the inference is that he would need to improve to defy that mark. He certainly won't find life as straightforward as this in nursery company. (op 8-11 tchd 1-2)
Serhaal(IRE), who cost 240,000gns as a foal, was exceptionally novicey in the paddock, repeatedly hollering and looking ill at ease. He was green, too, in the race and finished his race with a somewhat high head carriage; whether that was just inexperience or not, time will tell. (op 6-4 tchd 2-1)
Rock Of Eire's pedigree suggests that this would be his minimum trip with the dam having won over 1m4f-1m6f. He was soon ridden and may improve as he matures and steps up in distance. (tchd 50-1)
Firefly Mustique, led from the sales ring unsold at 48,000gns, is out of a dam who has produced a clutch of winners. He was another to be noisy in the preliminaries and was unable to go with them from the stalls, perhaps down to greenness as much as anything. (op 16-1)

4718 BET365 BEST ODDS GUARANTEED ON EVERY RACE MAIDEN H'CAP — 6f 3y
2:50 (2:50) (Class 6) (0-65,65) 3-Y-O+ — **£2,201** (£655; £327; £163) **Stalls** High

Form — RPR

-000 **1** — **Straboe (USA)**[33] 3637 3-8-2 45 — WilliamCarson(3) 1 — 53+
(S C Williams) *mde all: rdn and hung rt over 1f out: styd on* — **11/1**

66-0 **2** 2 — **Dance Club (IRE)**[16] 4179 3-9-5 59 — HayleyTurner 9 — 61
(W Jarvis) *awkward leaving stalls: hld up: hdwy u.p over 1f out: edgd lft ins fnl f: wnt 2nd post: nt rch wnr* — **12/1**

4232 **3** nk — **Choisharp (IRE)**[31] 3676 3-9-11 65 — JerryO'Dwyer 6 — 66
(M Botti) *hld up: hdwy over 2f out: rdn to chse wnr over 1f out: styd on same pce ins fnl f: lost 2nd post* — **11/4**[1]

6640 **4** ½ — **Abu Derby (IRE)**[16] 4174 3-9-8 62 — (t) PatCosgrave 4 — 61
(J G Given) *chsd wnr 2f: remained handy: rdn over 1f out: styd on same pce* — **33/1**

504 **5** 1½ — **Migliori**[15] 4199 3-9-6 60 — RyanMoore 8 — 55
(Rae Guest) *prom: rdn over 2f out: styd on same pce fnl f* — **9/2**[2]

-000 **6** shd — **Sorrel Point**[5] 4552 6-8-9 45 — (t) KirstyMilczarek 5 — 39
(H J Collingridge) *s.i.s: hld up: hdwy over 1f out: one pce ins fnl f* — **11/1**

0450 **7** ¾ — **Wicklewood**[17] 4155 3-8-5 45 — (v) PaulQuinn 13 — 37
(Mrs C A Dunnett) *chsd ldrs: rdn over 2f out: styng on same pce whn nt clr run ins fnl f* — **25/1**

6000 **8** shd — **Sonhador**[24] 3926 3-9-0 54 — (b[1]) StephenDonohoe 10 — 46
(G Prodromou) *prom: racd keenly: trckd wnr 4f out tl rdn over 1f out: no ex ins fnl f* — **33/1**

43-3 **9** 2¾ — **Clerical (USA)**[36] 3506 3-9-5 59 — RichardMullen 7 — 42
(R M H Cowell) *prom: rdn over 2f out: hung lft over 1f out: wknd fnl f* — **9/2**[2]

6442 **10** ½ — **Silca Meydan**[155] 758 3-9-9 63 — SamHitchcott 12 — 44
(M R Channon) *hld up: rdn over 2f out: a in rr* — **9/1**[3]

600- **11** 11 — **Safaseef (IRE)**[295] 6735 4-9-2 52 — JimmyQuinn 11 — —
(K A Morgan) *s.s: a in rr: wknd over 2f out* — **12/1**

0U54 **12** 47 — **Always The Sun**[17] 4155 3-8-5 45 — DO'Donohoe 3 — —
(P Leech) *s.i.s: a in rr: wknd over 2f out: eased fnl f* — **25/1**

1m 12.56s (-1.84) **Going Correction** -0.275s/f (Firm)
WFA 3 from 4yo+ 4lb — 12 Ran SP% **118.7**
Speed ratings (Par 101): **101,98,97,97,95 95,94,94,90,89 75,12**
toteswingers: 1&2 £71.00, 1&3 £19.30, 2&3 £8.80. CSF £130.10 CT £475.67 TOTE £12.50: £2.80, £4.10, £1.70; EX 339.40.
Owner Brigid & Damian Hennessy-Bourke **Bred** Darley **Trained** Newmarket, Suffolk
■ Stewards' Enquiry : William Carson caution: excessive use of the whip

FOCUS
A very moderate event and the form is limited, with the third the best guide.
Straboe(USA) Official explanation: trainer said, regarding the apparent improvement shown, gelding was a late foal, would appear to be strengthening and today apparently benefited from a drop in trip and being raced on faster ground
Always The Sun Official explanation: jockey said filly lost its action

4719 BBC RADIO NORFOLK (S) STKS — 1m 3y
3:20 (3:20) (Class 6) 3-Y-O — **£1,942** (£578; £288; £144) **Stalls** High

Form — RPR

00-0 **1** — **Molly The Witch (IRE)**[17] 4145 3-8-12 60 — HayleyTurner 7 — 59
(M P Tregoning) *trckd ldrs: racd keenly: led 1f out: rdn out* — **15/2**

0000 **2** 1½ — **Count On Guest**[14] 4241 3-9-3 55 — (t) JimmyQuinn 1 — 60
(G G Margarson) *chsd ldr tl led 1/2-way: rdn and hdd 1f out: styd on same pce ins fnl f* — **14/1**

3000 **3** ¾ — **Rose Cheval (USA)**[19] 4079 3-8-12 62 — SamHitchcott 2 — 53
(M R Channon) *prom: outpcd over 3f out: hdwy over 1f out: styd on u.p* — **16/1**

5456 **4** 2 — **Extracurricular (USA)**[16] 4177 3-8-9 57 — AndreaAtzeni(3) 5 — 48
(M Botti) *hld up: hdwy over 1f out: nt rch ldrs* — **11/2**[3]

0012 **5** ¾ — **Guga (IRE)**[10] 4373 3-9-8 61 — DO'Donohoe 11 — 57
(George Baker) *s.i.s: hdwy 1/2-way: edgd lft and no ex ins fnl f* — **7/2**[2]

060 **6** hd — **Special Cuvee**[13] 4279 3-9-8 62 — RyanMoore 6 — 56
(A B Haynes) *hld up: rdn over 2f out: hung lft over 1f out: nt trble ldrs* — **6/1**

0500 **7** nse — **Sairaam (IRE)**[17] 4142 3-8-12 56 — StephenDonohoe 8 — 46
(C Smith) *mid-div: rdn over 2f out: nt clr run over 1f out: nt trble ldrs* — **33/1**

-000 **8** nse — **Yeoman Of England (IRE)**[16] 4183 3-9-3 55 — GeorgeBaker 9 — 51
(C F Wall) *chsd ldrs: rdn over 1f out: no ex* — **20/1**

0564 **9** 2¼ — **King's Masque**[16] 4177 3-9-3 61 — RichardMullen 3 — 45
(W R Muir) *hld up: rdn over 2f out: no rspnse* — **3/1**[1]

2066 **10** 7 — **Come On Buckers (IRE)**[8] 4425 3-9-0 62 — AlanCreighton(3) 10 — 29
(E J Creighton) *led: hung lft: hdd 1/2-way: wknd over 1f out: eased ins fnl f* — **33/1**

0000 **11** 8 — **Dolores Ortiz (IRE)**[17] 4157 3-8-9 57 — (v[1]) WilliamCarson(3) 4 — 4
(S C Williams) *s.i.s: hdwy over 5f out: rdn and wknd over 2f out* — **20/1**

1m 39.19s (-1.41) **Going Correction** -0.275s/f (Firm) — 11 Ran SP% **116.6**
Speed ratings (Par 98): **96,94,93,91,91 90,90,90,88,81 73**
toteswingers: 1&2 £19.50, 1&3 £22.00, 2&3 £41.40. CSF £99.57 TOTE £7.60: £2.00, £5.20, £3.40; EX 134.30.Winner was bought by W. Musson for 9,400gns. Guga was bought by Dr. D. Newland for £5,000.
Owner A E Oppenheimer **Bred** Hascombe And Valiant Studs **Trained** Lambourn, Berks

FOCUS
A typically poor seller best rated around the first two.
Guga(IRE) Official explanation: jockey said colt was unsuited by the good, good to firm in places ground
Come On Buckers(IRE) Official explanation: jockey said gelding hung left

4720 BENNETTS ELECTRICAL FILLIES' H'CAP — 1m 3y
3:50 (3:54) (Class 5) (0-75,75) 3-Y-O — **£2,978** (£886; £442; £221) **Stalls** High

Form — RPR

5521 **1** — **Surprise Party**[16] 4179 3-9-1 69 — GeorgeBaker 6 — 82+
(C F Wall) *hld up: hdwy over 2f out: led and edgd rt over 1f out: rdn clr ins fnl f* — **5/2**[1]

525 **2** 3½ — **Miss Sophisticat**[17] 4151 3-9-2 70 — (p) RyanMoore 2 — 72
(W J Knight) *led: rdn and hdd over 1f out: styd on same pce* — **9/2**[3]

6250 **3** ½ — **Act Green**[19] 4096 3-9-5 73 — HayleyTurner 1 — 74
(M L W Bell) *sn trcking ldr: racd keenly: rdn and ev ch over 1f out: styd on same pce* — **8/1**

4310 **4** 1¾ — **Evening Sunset (GER)**[6] 4482 3-8-13 67 — SamHitchcott 7 — 64
(M R Channon) *prom: racd keenly: rdn over 2f out: styd on same pce appr fnl f* — **25/1**

1243 **5** nk — **Bombina**[15] 4198 3-9-7 75 — RichardMullen 5 — 71
(P W Chapple-Hyam) *chsd ldrs: gng wl enough whn hmpd over 1f out: sn rdn and wknd* — **3/1**[2]

0361 **6** 4½ — **Chadwell Spring (IRE)**[29] 3741 3-8-9 63 — (p) JimmyQuinn 8 — 49
(Miss J Feilden) *prom: rdn over 2f out: wknd over 1f out* — **7/1**

1340 **7** 1 — **Ballet Dancer (IRE)**[21] 4008 3-9-3 71 — (t) RHills 4 — 54
(M A Jarvis) *s.i.s and n.m.r s: hld up: rdn over 2f out: wknd over 1f out* — **14/1**

20-0 **8** 9 — **Tamarah**[17] 4151 3-9-4 75 — (t) WilliamCarson(3) 9 — 38
(Miss D Mountain) *s.i.s: hld up: rdn and hung lft over 2f out: sn wknd* — **50/1**

0650 **9** 10 — **Viva La Vida**[69] 2432 3-9-3 71 — PatCosgrave 3 — 11
(J Ryan) *hld up: racd keenly: pushed along 1/2-way: sn lost tch* — **20/1**

1m 37.73s (-2.87) **Going Correction** -0.275s/f (Firm) — 9 Ran SP% **112.6**
Speed ratings (Par 97): **103,99,99,97,96 92,91,82,72**
toteswingers: 1&2 £5.00, 1&3 £4.70, 2&3 £8.00. CSF £13.24 CT £76.28 TOTE £2.90: £1.30, £1.90, £2.30; EX 14.40.
Owner The Leap Year Partnership **Bred** Farmers Hill Stud **Trained** Newmarket, Suffolk

FOCUS
A modest fillies' handicap rated around the placed horses. The winner remains progressive.

4721 MRKING.CO.UK H'CAP — 1m 1f
4:20 (4:20) (Class 6) (0-65,64) 3-Y-O+ — **£2,072** (£616; £308; £153) **Stalls** Low

Form — RPR

3616 **1** — **Crystal Feather**[69] 2461 3-9-2 59 — HayleyTurner 11 — 66
(E F Vaughan) *chsd ldrs: led 2f out: rdn and hdd 1f out: rallied to ld wl ins fnl f: r.o* — **9/1**[3]

6563 **2** ½ — **General Tufto**[9] 4402 4-9-13 62 — (b) KirstyMilczarek 9 — 68
(C Smith) *trckd ldrs: racd keenly: led 1f out: rdn and hdd wl ins fnl f* — **12/1**

3131 **3** ¾ — **Singora Lady (IRE)**[8] 4431 4-9-11 60 6ex — RyanMoore 3 — 64
(P T Midgley) *s.i.s: hld up: pushed along 1/2-way: hdwy u.p over 1f out: edgd lft and styd on: nt rch ldrs* — **5/4**[1]

400 **4** ½ — **King Of Connacht**[20] 4054 6-9-2 54 — (p) AndreaAtzeni(3) 2 — 57
(M Wellings) *hld up: hdwy over 2f out: nt clr run and swtchd rt over 1f out: hmpd ins fnl f: r.o* — **7/1**[2]

3100 **5** nk — **Mick Is Back**[10] 4389 5-9-12 61 — (v) GeorgeBaker 4 — 64
(G G Margarson) *hld up: hdwy 3f out: rdn over 1f out: hung lft ins fnl f: r.o* — **18/1**

0300 **6** 1½ — **King's Ransom**[38] 3450 6-10-0 63 — PatCosgrave 10 — 62
(S Gollings) *s.i.s: rcvrd to ld over 7f out: rdn and hdd 2f out: no ex ins fnl f* — **33/1**

-006 **7** nse — **Sitwell**[20] 4054 3-9-7 64 — RichardMullen 1 — 63
(J R Fanshawe) *hld up: hdwy u.p over 1f out: nt rch ldrs* — **9/1**[3]

40 **8** 2½ — **Applesnap (IRE)**[34] 3581 4-9-6 55 — (b) JerryO'Dwyer 6 — 49
(Miss Amy Weaver) *led: hdd over 7f out: remained handy: rdn over 2f out: wknd fnl f* — **25/1**

1230 **9** 1 — **Inch Lodge**[22] 3977 7-9-2 54 — (t) WilliamCarson(3) 8 — 45
(Miss D Mountain) *chsd ldrs: rdn over 1f out: wknd ins fnl f* — **10/1**

6 **10** 1½ — **Forced Opinion (USA)**[135] 944 4-9-10 59 — JimmyQuinn 7 — 47
(K A Morgan) *s.i.s: hld up: hdwy 2f out: wknd fnl f* — **10/1**

1m 53.7s (-2.10) **Going Correction** -0.275s/f (Firm)
WFA 3 from 4yo+ 8lb — 10 Ran SP% **114.9**
Speed ratings (Par 101): **98,97,96,96,96 94,94,92,91,90**
toteswingers: 1&2 £5.20, 1&3 £3.40, 2&3 £3.20. CSF £109.58 CT £230.43 TOTE £10.10: £2.40, £2.50, £1.30; EX 69.90.
Owner Featherbed Ladies **Bred** Whitsbury Manor Stud **Trained** Newmarket, Suffolk

FOCUS
A moderate handicap that was steadily run and not the most solid. The third is rated to form.

4722 YARMOUTH STADIUM H'CAP 1m 3f 101y
4:50 (4:50) (Class 6) (0-65,65) 3-Y-O £2,072 (£616; £308; £153) Stalls Low

Form RPR
-232 1 **Broughtons Paradis (IRE)**[5] 4545 3-8-8 55 AndreaAtzeni(3) 6 68+
(W J Musson) *hld up in tch: nt clr run and swtchd lft over 3f out: led over 1f out: r.o wl* **2/1**[1]
6062 2 4 **Galiotto (IRE)**[17] 4156 3-8-6 50 KirstyMilczarek 1 58+
(C F Wall) *hld up: hdwy whn hmpd and lost pl over 3f out: rallied over 1f out: r.o: wnt 2nd post* **7/2**[2]
5003 3 shd **Twist Again (IRE)**[16] 4178 3-8-12 56 JimmyQuinn 2 62
(P Howling) *s.i.s: sn prom: led over 4f out: rdn and hdd over 1f out: styd on same pce: lost 2nd post* **15/2**
356 4 3 3/4 **Screaming Brave**[16] 4178 3-9-3 61 RyanMoore 9 61
(M R Channon) *hld up: hdwy over 3f out: rdn and hung lft over 1f out: styd on same pce ins fnl f* **9/1**
006 5 1/2 **Any Given Moment (IRE)**[47] 3168 3-8-13 57 RichardMullen 11 56
(D M Simcock) *s.i.s: hld up: pushed along 5f out: hdwy u.p over 2f out: hung lft over 1f out: no imp* **9/2**[3]
0201 6 9 **Fisadara**[43] 3260 3-9-7 65 KShea 4 48
(Jane Chapple-Hyam) *led early: chsd ldr: rdn over 2f out: wknd fnl f* **9/1**
0052 7 11 **Mymateeric**[16] 4178 3-8-8 52 (b) DO'Donohoe 12 17
(J Pearce) *hld up: hdwy over 4f out: wknd over 2f out* **18/1**
-000 8 1 1/4 **Vin De Rose**[17] 4157 3-7-9 46 oh1 JosephineBruning(7) 3 9
(John A Harris) *sn led: hdd over 4f out: wknd 3f out* **80/1**
00-4 9 5 **Tuppenny Piece**[36] 3508 3-9-4 62 (t) StephenDonohoe 7 16
(W R Swinburn) *prom: pushed along 5f out: wknd wl over 3f out* **25/1**

2m 26.33s (-2.37) **Going Correction** -0.275s/f (Firm) 9 Ran SP% **115.8**
Speed ratings (Par 98): **97,94,94,91,90 84,76,75,71**
toteswingers: 1&2 £3.10, 1&3 £5.70, 2&3 £6.30. CSF £8.95 CT £42.53 TOTE £3.20: £1.10, £1.90, £2.60; EX 8.70 Place 6: £59.21 Place 5: £41.10.
Owner Broughton Thermal Insulation **Bred** Mount Coote Stud **Trained** Newmarket, Suffolk
■ Stewards' Enquiry : K Shea three-day ban: careless riding (Aug 22-24)

FOCUS
A moderate handicap and the first three pulled clear. The form looks fair for the grade.
Tuppenny Piece Official explanation: jockey said filly lost its action
T/Jkpt: Not won. T/Plt: £94.50 to a £1 stake. Pool: £53,408.16. 412.47 winning tickets. T/Qpdt: £29.20 to a £1 stake. Pool: £3,427.96. 86.70 winning tickets. CR

4723 - 4725a (Foreign Racing) - See Raceform Interactive

4249 LEOPARDSTOWN (L-H)
Thursday, August 6

OFFICIAL GOING: Good changing to good to yielding after race 1 (5.40)

4726a DEBUTANTE STKS (GROUP 2) (FILLIES) 7f
7:10 (7:13) 2-Y-O £72,572 (£21,213; £10,048; £3,349)

RPR
1 **Lillie Langtry (IRE)**[48] 3086 2-8-12 JMurtagh 6 107+
(A P O'Brien, Ire) *hld up in last: clsr in 4th 2f out: sn asked to qckn: led ins fnl f: styd on wl* **2/5**[1]
2 1 3/4 **Devoted To You (IRE)**[9] 4413 2-8-12 CO'Donoghue 3 101
(A P O'Brien, Ire) *chsd ldrs in 3rd: rdn to ld under 1f out: sn hdd: kpt on same pce* **9/2**[2]
3 nk **Elusive Galaxy (IRE)**[41] 3366 2-8-12 KLatham 4 100
(G M Lyons, Ire) *hld up in 5th: rdn along and outpcd in last 3f out: 5th 1 1/2f out: kpt on fnl f* **10/1**[3]
4 nk **Gold Bubbles (USA)**[41] 3366 2-8-12 95 (p) KJManning 1 99
(J S Bolger, Ire) *led: rdn fr 2f out: hdd under 1f out: no ex* **18/1**
5 4 **Famous (IRE)**[28] 3832 2-8-12 94 JAHeffernan 2 89
(A P O'Brien, Ire) *chsd ldr in 2nd: rdn ent st: wknd fr 2f out* **16/1**
6 10 **Alshahbaa (IRE)**[21] 4028 2-8-12 DPMcDonogh 5 64
(Kevin Prendergast, Ire) *chsd ldrs in 4th: rdn and no imp fr 2 1/2f out* **16/1**

1m 29.63s (0.93) **Going Correction** 0.0s/f (Good) 6 Ran SP% **115.7**
Speed ratings: **94,92,91,91,86 75**
CSF £2.83 TOTE £1.30: £1.10, £2.10; DF 1.90.
Owner Michael Tabor **Bred** K B Lynch **Trained** Ballydoyle, Co Tipperary

FOCUS
There was a steady pace here and the trio of Ballydoyle runners helped ensure the winner had plenty of room when needed. It is hard to think the bare form is any better than this, although the winner remains a nice type and won with a bit in hand.

NOTEBOOK
Lillie Langtry(IRE) won at Naas prior to finishing second in the Albany Stakes at Royal Ascot. The step up in trip was expected to suit and, after being held up in rear, she made headway in the straight and won in good style, having had questions to answer over a furlong out. She picked up well to lead inside the final furlong and was going away at the finish. The Group 1 Moyglare Stud Stakes at the Curragh is a likely target and her performance here prompted some firms to make her favourite for the 1,000 Guineas, with Boylesports and William Hill going 6-1 and 7-1 respectively from 8-1 and Paddy Power 13-2 from 8-1. Going 1m should not present any problems. (op 8/15)
Devoted To You(IRE), a stablemate of the winner, had come good at her third attempt at Galway nine days previously when scoring by nine lengths, and she acquitted herself well, tracking the leaders and getting to the front under a furlong out before being headed and outpaced by the winner. She is another who will appreciate going further.
Elusive Galaxy(IRE), runner-up in a 6f Listed event at the Curragh following a debut win over 6f here, was held up before being ridden and briefly outpaced on the final bend. Only fifth over a furlong out, she ran on quite well to snatch third close home.
Gold Bubbles(USA), three-quarters of a length behind Elusive Galaxy at the Curragh, won her maiden over 6f here in April. Wearing cheekpieces for the first time, she made the running and only gave best under a furlong out. (op 14/1)
Famous(IRE), fourth in the same Listed event contested by Elusive Galaxy and Gold Bubbles at the Curragh before winning a maiden over this course and trip in good style, raced in second place but was unable to raise her effort over the last two furlongs. (op 14/1)
Alshahbaa(IRE), a good winner of a 6f Curragh maiden on heavy ground in May, had proved no match for another Ballydoyle filly, Cabaret, in a Group 3 over course and distance last month. Fifth into the straight, she could make no impression from two furlongs out and was eased when all hope had gone. (op 14/1)

4727 - 4729a (Foreign Racing) - See Raceform Interactive

4693 BRIGHTON (L-H)
Friday, August 7

OFFICIAL GOING: Good to soft
Bend dolled out 5m to 3f marker but impact on distances not quantified.
Wind: Almost nil

4730 180 BETS - BRIGHTON ROCKS SPEED POKER CHALLENGE MAIDEN H'CAP 6f 209y
2:30 (2:30) (Class 6) (0-65,65) 3-Y-O+ £2,901 (£868; £434; £217; £108) Stalls Low

Form RPR
0006 1 **Jeremiah (IRE)**[30] 3743 3-9-12 64 JamesDoyle 4 70
(J G Portman) *trckd ldrs: rdn to chal over 1f out: kpt on to ld nr fin* **9/1**
0-03 2 nse **Short Cut**[2] 4643 3-8-11 49 (t) RichardSmith 9 55
(S Kirk) *t.k.h: chsd ldr: rdn to ld over 1f out: hdd nr fin* **8/1**
5604 3 2 **Forty Thirty (IRE)**[26] 2220 3-9-5 57 DaneO'Neill 14 57
(Miss Sheena West) *led tl hdd over 1f out: kpt on but nt pce of first 2* **9/2**[2]
-040 4 1 1/4 **Eleanor Eloise (USA)**[38] 3471 5-9-1 50 AndreaAtzeni(3) 7 49
(J R Gask) *trckd ldrs: styd on one pce fr over 1f out* **9/2**[2]
0-04 5 5 **Salamon**[21] 4066 3-9-3 55 (t) GeorgeBaker 6 39
(P F I Cole) *nvr bttr than mid-div* **9/1**
5356 6 1 1/4 **Mr Rev**[30] 2879 6-9-0 49 (b) JackDean(3) 13 31
(J M Bradley) *mid-div: effrt over 2f out but nvr nr to chal* **16/1**
0252 7 1 1/4 **Sermons Mount (USA)**[15] 4240 3-9-2 54 NeilChalmers 5 31
(Mouse Hamilton-Fairley) *slowly away: sn mid-div: wknd wl over 1f out* **7/2**[1]
0005 8 2 1/4 **Flute Magic**[16] 4199 3-9-8 60 (bt[1]) FergusSweeney 10 31
(W S Kittow) *hld up towards rr: short of room wl over 1f out and nvr on terms* **12/1**
0-50 9 2 **Perez Prado (USA)**[27] 3863 4-9-13 59 (t) LiamJones 2 26
(W Jarvis) *hld up: sme hdwy in centre over 2f out: sn btn* **7/1**[3]
6-00 10 6 **Academy Of War (USA)**[28] 3813 3-9-3 55 LukeMorris 11 4
(J M Bradley) *stdd s: in rr: rdn and wknd over 1f out* **40/1**

1m 24.42s (1.32) **Going Correction** +0.20s/f (Good)
WFA 3 from 4yo+ 6lb 10 Ran SP% **118.2**
Speed ratings (Par 101): **100,99,97,96,90 89,87,85,82,75**
toteswinger: 1&2 £9.10, 1&3 £11.90, 2&3 £15.30. CSF £80.02 CT £380.57 TOTE £11.20: £2.80, £2.70, £2.40; EX 81.60 TRIFECTA Not won..
Owner M J Vandenberghe **Bred** Eddie Fox **Trained** Compton, Berks
■ Stewards' Enquiry : James Doyle three-day ban: excessive use of the whip without giving mount time to respond (Aug 22-24)

FOCUS
Six hours of overnight rain saw the ground changed from the advertised firm, good to firm in places to good to soft all round on the third day of the meeting, although riders in the first race thought it was only just on the easy side of good. There were a host of non-runners through the card, including half a dozen in the opener. This maiden handicap was run at a good pace, and as expected the runners came over to the stands' side in the straight. Nothing got into it from the back. The form is very modest with the winner rated back to his best of this season's level.
Sermons Mount(USA) Official explanation: trainer said gelding was unsuited by the good to soft going

4731 180BETS.COM - FOR DARTS, RACING AND POKER CLAIMING STKS 7f 214y
3:00 (3:00) (Class 6) 3-Y-O+ £2,072 (£616; £308; £153) Stalls Low

Form RPR
0006 1 **Cordell (IRE)**[9] 4438 4-9-8 75 DaneO'Neill 5 70
(R Hannon) *mde all: responded wl whn chal over 1f out: r.o* **5/2**[2]
6202 2 1 3/4 **Northern Desert (IRE)**[31] 3717 10-8-12 57 (p) JamesDoyle 7 56
(S Curran) *s.i.s: hld up: hdwy 2f out: ev chwhn wnt 2nd 1f out: kpt on* **4/1**[3]
6-54 3 2 3/4 **Persian Storm (GER)**[9] 4438 5-9-8 103 GeorgeBaker 6 60
(G L Moore) *t.k.h: trckd wnr: ev ch whn hrd rdn over 1f out: one pce after: lame* **5/4**[1]
06 4 1 3/4 **Flying Gazebo (IRE)**[13] 4322 3-8-9 0 LukeMorris 4 50
(J S Moore) *in tch tl outpcd over 1f out* **12/1**
0200 5 3/4 **Dichoh**[9] 4438 6-8-13 67 (v) JackDean(3) 8 48
(M Madgwick) *trckd ldrs: outpcd over 2f out: rdn and sn btn* **10/1**
6-00 6 12 **Evianne**[24] 3949 5-8-6 36 DO'Donohoe 3 10
(P W Hiatt) *prom: rdn over 3f out: rallied 2f out: sn wknd* **100/1**

1m 37.51s (1.51) **Going Correction** +0.20s/f (Good)
WFA 3 from 4yo+ 7lb 6 Ran SP% **110.8**
Speed ratings (Par 101): **100,98,95,93,93 81**
toteswinger: 1&2 £9.10, 1&3 £11.90, 2&3 £15.30. CSF £12.47 TOTE £2.90: £1.80, £2.40; EX 14.10 Trifecta £31.30 Pool: £418.18 - 9.86 winning units..Cordell was claimed by Roger Ingram for £16,000.
Owner Mrs J Wood **Bred** Scea Haras De La Poterie **Trained** East Everleigh, Wilts

FOCUS
With the favourite well below par this claimer did not take a great deal of winning. The form is rated around the winner.
Persian Storm(GER) Official explanation: vet said gelding finished lame on his right fore

4732 180POKER.COM (S) STKS 5f 213y
3:30 (3:30) (Class 6) 3-Y-O+ £1,942 (£578; £288; £144) Stalls Low

Form RPR
6445 1 **Carmenero (GER)**[22] 4005 6-9-2 70 (p) SebSanders 8 56
(W R Muir) *mid-div: short of room 2f out: swtchd rt to stands' rail: sustained run u.p to ld post:* **8/11**[1]
-400 2 nse **Miss Pusey Street**[2] 4643 3-8-7 50 LukeMorris 12 50
(J Gallagher) *led: rdn wl over 1f out: kpt on: hdd post* **14/1**
0450 3 1 1/4 **Star Strider**[13] 4305 5-8-13 55 (b) DavidProbert(3) 4 52
(Miss Gay Kelleway) *hld up: hdwy 2f out: kpt on u.p to 3rd post* **5/1**[2]
0053 4 nse **Boldinor**[15] 4238 6-9-2 45 GeorgeBaker 3 52
(M R Bosley) *a.p: chal over 1f out: nt qckn and lost 3rd post* **8/1**[3]
6403 5 3 3/4 **Briannsta (IRE)**[8] 854 7-9-2 45 (b) RichardThomas 10 40
(J E Long) *in tch tl rdn and wknd appr fnl f* **33/1**
5505 6 7 **Geoffdaw**[24] 3948 4-9-2 55 (v) PaulDoe 9 17
(P D Evans) *a towards rr and lost tch fr wl over 1f out* **9/1**
5206 7 nk **Scruffy Skip (IRE)**[17] 4183 4-9-2 50 (v) TGMcLaughlin 11 16
(Mrs C A Dunnett) *trckd ldr tl wknd over 1f out* **12/1**

0014 8 6 **Pintano**[15] 4238 4-9-4 51 ....(t) JackDean(3) 1 2
(J M Bradley) *prom: rdn 3f out: wknd wl over 1f out* **25/1**

1m 11.29s (1.09) **Going Correction** +0.20s/f (Good)
WFA 3 from 4yo+ 4lb 8 Ran SP% **116.8**
Speed ratings (Par 101): **100,99,98,98,93 83,83,75**
toteswinger: 1&2 £6.10, 1&3 £2.40, 2&3 £11.90. CSF £13.69 TOTE £1.80: £1.10, £2.80, £1.70; EX 16.20 Trifecta £90.20 Pool: £362.27 - 2.97 winning units..The winner was sold to C R Dore for 11,500gns. Miss Pusey Street was claimed by Sheena West for £6,000.
Owner Middleham Park Racing XXXVIII **Bred** Graf And Grafin Von Stauffenberg **Trained** Lambourn, Berks
■ Stewards' Enquiry : Luke Morris caution: excessive use of the whip

FOCUS
A weakish seller, rated through the runner-up. The time was not bad compared to the following handicap.

4733 180CASINO.COM BRIGHTON ROCKET H'CAP 5f 213y
4:00 (4:00) (Class 4) (0-80,78) 3-Y-O+
£6,231 (£1,866; £933; £467; £233; £117) Stalls Low

Form RPR
4042 1 **My Kingdom (IRE)**[8] 4454 3-9-6 77 ....(t) GeorgeBaker 1 89
(H Morrison) *w.w: gd hdwy 2f out: led appr fnl f: sn clr* **11/4**[1]
0010 2 2 1/4 **Highland Harvest**[8] 4461 5-9-6 73 .... RobertHavlin 14 82+
(Jamie Poulton) *mid-div: hdwy whn hmpd over 1f out: r.o wl to go 2nd ins fnl f* **9/2**[2]
2001 3 1 1/4 **Desperate Dan**[22] 3998 8-9-8 78 ....(v) DavidProbert(3) 13 80
(A B Haynes) *trckd ldrs: rdn and one pce ins fnl f* **10/1**
0212 4 nse **Patavium Prince (IRE)**[4] 4607 6-9-5 75 .... AndreaAtzeni(3) 12 77
(Miss Jo Crowley) *in tch: rdn whn short of room appr fnl f: rallied and r.o ins fnl f* **6/1**[3]
4-05 5 1/2 **Too Tall**[42] 3341 3-8-13 70 ....(b[1]) DaneO'Neill 9 69
(L M Cumani) *s.i.s: bhd tl r.o ins fnl f: nvr nrr* **6/1**[3]
0012 6 nk **Billy Red**[29] 3775 5-9-0 67 ....(b) FergusSweeney 4 66
(J R Jenkins) *led tl hdd over 1f out: fdd ins fnl f* **14/1**
1000 7 nk **Gift Horse**[22] 3995 9-9-6 73 ....(p) PaulDoe 3 71
(P D Evans) *s.i.s: in rr tl rdn and hdwy over 1f out: nvr nrr* **12/1**
0006 8 nk **Choreography**[33] 3659 6-9-4 71 ....(p) RichardThomas 5 68
(Jim Best) *s.i.s: nvr on terms* **20/1**
5000 9 1 **First Order**[6] 4516 8-9-3 75 ....(v) AnnStokell(5) 8 69
(Miss A Stokell) *chsd ldrs tl wknd fnl f* **25/1**
61-6 10 4 **Shamrock Lady (IRE)**[22] 4009 4-9-10 77 .... LPKeniry 10 58
(J Gallagher) *mid-div: pushed along 1/2-way: bhd fnl 2f* **16/1**
4010 11 6 **Sam's Cross (IRE)**[15] 4236 4-8-13 66 ....(bt) LiamJones 15 28
(J J Bridger) *s.i.s: a bhd* **22/1**
6006 12 nk **Lesley's Choice**[23] 3973 3-9-6 77 .... SimonWhitworth 7 37
(R Curtis) *trckd ldr to 1/2-way: wkng whn bmpd over 1f out* **66/1**

1m 10.48s (0.28) **Going Correction** +0.20s/f (Good)
WFA 3 from 4yo+ 4lb 12 Ran SP% **117.2**
Speed ratings (Par 105): **106,103,101,101,100 100,99,99,98,92 84,84**
toteswinger: 1&2 £5.50, 1&3 £4.40, 2&3 £15.40. CSF £13.49 CT £109.39 TOTE £3.20: £1.30, £1.90, £3.60; EX 20.20 Trifecta £101.30 Pool: £287.62 - 2.10 winning units..
Owner Wood Street Syndicate V **Bred** Irish National Stud **Trained** East Ilsley, Berks

FOCUS
A fair sprint handicap, run in a time only 0.6secs faster than the preceding seller. One or two of these met trouble but the form looks sound enough overall with the winner on the up.
Highland Harvest Official explanation: jockey said gelding was denied a clear run
First Order Official explanation: jockey said gelding ran too free
Lesley's Choice Official explanation: jockey said gelding suffered interference in running

4734 MCDONNELL RACING H'CAP 1m 1f 209y
4:30 (4:31) (Class 6) (0-60,66) 3-Y-O £2,590 (£770; £385; £192) Stalls High

Form RPR
6353 1 **Squad**[22] 4010 3-9-2 58 .... PaulDoe 7 64
(S Dow) *hld up in rr: hdwy 2f out: rdn to ld ins fnl f: drvn out* **7/1**[3]
4263 2 1 1/4 **Beaubrav**[18] 4157 3-9-4 60 ....(t) SebSanders 8 63
(P W D'Arcy) *led after 3f: rdn and hdd ins fnl f* **7/2**[1]
0046 3 3 1/4 **Join Up**[14] 4279 3-8-6 48 .... LiamJones 5 48+
(W M Brisbourne) *hld up towards rr: hdwy whn nt clr run 2f out: swtchd lft and r.o to go 3rd ins fnl f* **20/1**
0344 4 1/2 **Kyle Of Bute**[15] 4240 3-8-4 46 .... DO'Donohoe 2 42
(J L Dunlop) *t.k.h: a.p: kpt on one pce ins fnl 2f* **10/1**
0354 5 3/4 **Primo Dilettante**[24] 3949 3-8-12 57 .... DavidProbert(3) 6 51
(W J Knight) *hld up in mid-div: effrt whn n.m.r 2f out: one pce after* **4/1**[2]
0600 6 5 **Dalrymple (IRE)**[30] 3741 3-8-7 49 .... LPKeniry 3 33
(M Madgwick) *led for 3f: rdn over 2f out: wknd over 1f out* **25/1**
3422 7 1 3/4 **Rose Of Coma (IRE)**[33] 3661 3-8-11 53 .... MickyFenton 10 34
(Miss Gay Kelleway) *chsd ldrs tl wknd wl over 1f out* **8/1**
4415 8 5 **Fire King**[11] 4378 3-9-4 60 .... RobertHavlin 15 31
(J A Geake) *t.k.h: trckd ldrs: rdn 3f out: wknd over 1f out* **7/1**[3]
1305 9 6 **Second To Nun (IRE)**[28] 3803 3-9-3 59 .... FergusSweeney 4 18
(Jean-Rene Auvray) *mid-div: wknd over 1f out: eased* **14/1**
6030 10 11 **Aboukir**[16] 4196 3-9-3 59 .... GeorgeBaker 16 —
(P F I Cole) *slowly away: a in rr* **16/1**
0-00 11 16 **Dannios**[27] 3863 3-9-3 59 ....(b[1]) DaneO'Neill 11 —
(L M Cumani) *mid-div: rdn 1/2-way: sn bhd: t.o* **8/1**

2m 5.01s (1.41) **Going Correction** +0.20s/f (Good) 11 Ran SP% **119.7**
Speed ratings (Par 98): **102,101,98,98,97 93,92,88,83,74 61**
toteswinger: 1&2 £6.50, 1&3 £19.90, 2&3 £15.60. CSF £32.29 CT £479.71 TOTE £8.40: £2.30, £1.80, £4.90; EX 31.60 Trifecta £303.50 Pool: £488.17 - 1.19 winning units..
Owner Classics P'ship, Devine, Snell & Chua **Bred** Juddmonte Farms Ltd **Trained** Epsom, Surrey

FOCUS
A moderate handicap in which the pace was not strong. The runner-up is the best guide to the form, which is sound but limited.
Rose Of Coma(IRE) Official explanation: jockey said filly was denied a clear run
Aboukir Official explanation: jockey said gelding had no more to give

4735 HIGGIDY H'CAP 1m 3f 196y
5:00 (5:02) (Class 6) (0-65,64) 3-Y-O+ £2,590 (£770; £385; £192) Stalls High

Form RPR
1241 1 **Penang Cinta**[24] 3950 6-10-0 64 .... PaulDoe 7 72+
(P D Evans) *a in tch: swtchd rt to stands' rail 2f out: r.o to ld jst ins fnl f: sn clr* **11/8**[1]
3320 2 3 3/4 **Barodine**[14] 4263 6-9-4 54 .... GeorgeBaker 5 56
(R J Hodges) *hld up: effrt whn hit rail over 2f out: styd on to go 2nd ins fnl f* **4/1**[2]
0024 3 1 1/4 **Bari Bay**[60] 2772 3-8-6 53 .... FergusSweeney 4 53
(J W Mullins) *hld up in rr: effrt over 2f out: styd on one pce* **11/1**[3]
-010 4 nk **Dot's Delight**[17] 4170 5-8-13 49 .... LukeMorris 3 49
(M G Rimell) *t.k.h in mid-div: hdwy to trck ldrs 1/2-way: carried lft fr over 1f out: no ex fnl f* **14/1**
24 5 1 3/4 **Casablanca Minx (IRE)**[18] 4156 6-9-0 50 ....(b) MickyFenton 11 47
(Miss Gay Kelleway) *mid-div: rdn to ld over 2f: hung bdly lft fr over 1f out: hdd jst ins fnl f and wknd* **4/1**[2]
/0-0 6 9 **Spartan Dance**[64] 2634 5-8-13 49 .... RichardThomas 8 31
(J A Geake) *trckd ldr: outpcd 3f out: nvr on terms after* **20/1**
0-00 7 4 **Improper (USA)**[67] 2551 3-8-0 47 ow2 .... FrankieMcDonald 10 23
(Mouse Hamilton-Fairley) *trckd ldrs tl wknd 3f out* **16/1**
-036 8 3/4 **Silver Surprise**[13] 4301 5-8-9 45 .... LPKeniry 9 20
(J J Bridger) *led tl hdd over 2f out: wknd qckly* **16/1**

2m 36.04s (3.34) **Going Correction** +0.20s/f (Good)
WFA 3 from 4yo+ 11lb 8 Ran SP% **113.6**
Speed ratings (Par 101): **96,93,92,92,91 85,82,82**
toteswinger: 1&2 £2.20, 1&3 £3.90, 2&3 £3.80. CSF £6.79 CT £40.67 TOTE £2.50: £1.20, £1.40, £2.00; EX 8.40 Trifecta £15.40 Pool: £345.33 - 16.52 winning units..
Owner Trevor Gallienne **Bred** Mrs A K H Ooi **Trained** Pandy, Monmouths

FOCUS
A very ordinary handicap. The winner is in fine form and this was his best effort for a couple of years.
Dot's Delight Official explanation: jockey said mare hung left
Casablanca Minx(IRE) Official explanation: jockey said mare hung left
Silver Surprise Official explanation: jockey said mare had no more to give

4736 SPEARMINT RHINO ROUGE BRIGHTON H'CAP 5f 59y
5:30 (5:30) (Class 6) (0-60,56) 3-Y-O+ £2,590 (£770; £385; £192) Stalls Low

Form RPR
0005 1 **Maggie Kate**[24] 3947 4-8-13 48 ....(b) RobertHavlin 7 58
(R Ingram) *mid-div: hdwy whn short of room and swtchd rt jst ins fnl f: drvn to ld post* **14/1**
140 2 nse **Green Lagonda (AUS)**[22] 3998 7-9-6 55 .... PaulDoe 5 64
(P D Evans) *trckd ldr: led 3f out: hrd rdn fr over 1f out: hdd post* **4/1**[1]
6023 3 1 1/4 **Miss Firefly**[22] 3994 4-9-5 54 .... SamHitchcott 11 59
(R J Hodges) *a in tch: hrd rdn over 1f out: r.o fnl f* **6/1**[3]
2560 4 1 1/4 **Louie's Lad**[2] 4643 3-8-13 51 ....(p) LPKeniry 4 51
(J J Bridger) *led tl hdd 3f out: styd centre of crse: one pce fnl f* **10/1**
5640 5 1 1/4 **Berrymead**[8] 4452 4-9-2 56 .... AnnStokell(5) 13 52
(Miss A Stokell) *s.i.s: hdwy in centre of crse over 1f out: nt qckn fnl f* **12/1**
3036 6 nk **Lithaam (IRE)**[17] 4182 5-9-0 52 ....(p) JackDean(3) 6 47
(J M Bradley) *chsd ldrs tl wknd fnl f* **13/2**
0020 7 nk **Lily Jicaro (IRE)**[2] 4643 3-9-0 52 .... NeilChalmers 3 45
(Mrs L Williamson) *in tch: rdn to chse ldrs 2f out: wknd fnl f* **11/1**
0060 8 3/4 **Metropolitan Chief**[16] 4203 5-8-10 45 ....(p) TGMcLaughlin 14 37
(P Burgoyne) *s.i.s: hdwy over 1f out: wknd ins fnl f* **20/1**
0500 9 1/2 **Monsieur Reynard**[27] 3860 4-9-2 54 .... DavidProbert(3) 10 44
(J M Bradley) *towards rr: rdn 2f out: nvr a danger* **11/2**[2]
5031 10 3 1/4 **Joss Stick**[24] 3947 4-9-4 56 .... MarcHalford(3) 2 34
(J J Bridger) *in tch: rdn 2f out: wknd fnl f* **8/1**
0500 11 2 **Thumberlina**[18] 4155 3-8-7 45 ....(v) LiamJones 15 15
(Mrs C A Dunnett) *s.i.s: hdwy after 2f: n.m.r on stands' rail over 2f out: n.d after* **20/1**

63.11 secs (0.81) **Going Correction** +0.20s/f (Good)
WFA 3 from 4yo+ 3lb 11 Ran SP% **115.4**
Speed ratings (Par 101): **101,100,98,96,94 94,93,92,91,86 83**
toteswinger: 1&2 £13.30, 1&3 £12.70, 2&3 £6.60. CSF £68.03 CT £375.69 TOTE £15.70: £4.80, £1.50, £2.50; EX 108.40 TRIFECTA Not won. Place 6: £44.50, Place 5: £10.46..
Owner Tommy Tighe **Bred** F L Mallaghan **Trained** Epsom, Surrey
■ Stewards' Enquiry : Paul Doe three-day ban: excessive use of the whip (Aug 22-24)

FOCUS
An open but very modest sprint. Ordinary form for the grade.
Thumberlina Official explanation: jockey said filly was denied a clear run
T/Plt: £80.70 to a £1 stake. Pool: £68,158.87. 616.43 winning tickets. T/Qpdt: £5.00 to a £1 stake. Pool: £4,505.45. 656.40 winning tickets. JS

4705 HAYDOCK (L-H)
Friday, August 7

OFFICIAL GOING: 6f course - good to firm (9.1); remainder - good (8.4)
Rail realignment increased advertised distances on round course by 10yards.
Inner straight track used.
Wind: Light, half-against. Weather: fine and sunny

4737 BET ONLINE AT CORBETTSPORTS.COM PJA APPRENTICE SERIES H'CAP 1m 3f 200y
5:50 (5:50) (Class 5) (0-75,75) 4-Y-O+ £3,238 (£963; £481; £240) Stalls Low

Form RPR
6512 1 **Trip The Light**[36] 3532 4-9-10 75 ....(v) FrederikTylicki 4 84
(R A Fahey) *trckd ldrs: drvn 3f out: led over 1f out: idled ins fnl f: drvn out* **10/3**[2]
4014 2 1/2 **Drawn Gold**[28] 3809 5-8-8 59 .... RussellKennemore 2 67
(R Hollinshead) *led 1f: chsd ldr: led 3f out tl over 1f out: styd on same pce ins fnl f* **10/1**
0211 3 1 3/4 **Agilete**[1] 4710 7-9-11 75 12ex .... SimonPearce(5) 1 86
(J Pearce) *hld up in rr: hdwy on ins over 3f out: chsng ldrs and rdn over 1f out: kpt on same pce* **4/1**[3]
4-16 4 nk **Beau Fighter**[63] 2678 4-9-7 72 .... JackMitchell 3 77
(C F Wall) *trckd ldrs: swtchd outside and outpcd 2f out: kpt on wl ins fnl f* **5/2**[1]
5-02 5 4 **Mae Cigan (FR)**[17] 4169 6-8-7 61 .... MCGeran(3) 6 60
(M Blanshard) *hld up towards rr: effrt 3f out: nvr a factor* **5/1**
2104 6 2 1/4 **Red Wine**[29] 3761 10-9-0 72 .... JonathanHinch(7) 7 67
(J A Glover) *s.i.s: hdwy over 4f out: sn drvn and no imp* **16/1**
1-06 7 3/4 **Orkney (IRE)**[49] 3095 4-8-13 64 ....(p) NeilBrown 5 58
(Miss J A Camacho) *led after 1f: hdd 3f out: wknd over 1f out* **12/1**

2m 31.77s (-1.43) **Going Correction** -0.025s/f (Good) 7 Ran SP% **111.0**
Speed ratings (Par 103): **103,102,101,101,98 97,96**
toteswingers: 1&2 £4.00, 1&3 £1.90, 2&3 £7.40. CSF £33.12 TOTE £4.10: £2.10, £4.20; EX 22.50.
Owner The Matthewman One Partnership **Bred** Darley **Trained** Musley Bank, N Yorks

FOCUS
A fair handicap for the grade which was run at a fair pace despite the small field. The form should work out.

Orkney(IRE) Official explanation: trainer said gelding lost a front shoe

4738 E B F HAYDOCK PARK PONY CLUB MAIDEN STKS 6f

6:20 (6:23) (Class 5) 2-Y-O **£3,885** (£1,156; £577; £288) **Stalls** Low

Form				RPR
	1		**Khattaab (USA)** 2-9-3 0 ... RobertWinston 6 (B W Hills) *t.k.h: trckd ldrs: smooth hdwy to ld appr fnl f: pushed wl clr: easily* **3/1[2]**	90+
565	**2**	7	**Durham Reflection (IRE)**[23] 3971 2-9-3 62 ... PaulMulrennan 2 (J Howard Johnson) *mde most tl appr fnl f: no ch w wnr* **22/1**	66
2	**3**	3 ¾	**Call To Arms (IRE)**[38] 3487 2-9-3 0 ... GregFairley 5 (M Johnston) *swvd rt s: t.k.h: sn trcking ldrs: chal over 2f out: rdn and wknd 1f out* **4/11[1]**	55
	4	5	**Revelator (IRE)** 2-9-3 0 ... AndrewElliott 3 (A P Jarvis) *chsd ldrs: wknd appr fnl f* **20/1[3]**	40
00	**5**	5	**Sandy Toes**[69] 2467 2-9-0 0 ... FrederikTylicki(3) 1 (J A Glover) *reluctant to go to post: w ldr: sn pushed along: lost pl over 1f out* **50/1**	25

1m 14.51s (0.01) **Going Correction** -0.15s/f (Firm) **5** Ran SP% **109.4**
Speed ratings (Par 94): **93,83,78,72,65**
toteswingers: 1&2 £10.70. CSF £39.10 TOTE £3.60: £1.50, £6.50; EX 87.90.

Owner Hamdan Al Maktoum **Bred** W S Farish & Martha F Gerry **Trained** Lambourn, Berks

FOCUS

An uncompetitive maiden that saw an easy winner who looks sure to rate higher. The form is rated around the second.

NOTEBOOK

Khattaab(USA) ◆ went in at the first time of asking. He proved easy to back, but looked the part going to post and shaped even better in the race itself, winning easily. He proved green early on, but the penny dropped from halfway and he was cantering just off the leaders 2f out. He eventually powered clear when asked to win the race and had plenty left in the tank passing the finish. This quick ground was to his liking and he looks to have a very bright future, with another furlong or so likely to suit ideally before the year is out. He holds entries in the Champagne, Royal Lodge and the Dewhurst Stakes so it will be fascinating to see where he pitches up next. (tchd 7-2 and 4-1 in places)

Durham Reflection(IRE) showed his best form to date on this drop back in distance and for the quicker ground. He is steadily progressing, this looks his optimum distance and a move into nurseries now seems a good option. (op 14-1)

Call To Arms(IRE) proved all the rage, but failed to even master the more exposed runner-up. He showed an undesirable head carriage through the early parts and ran keen. His finishing effort was then blunted and this was too bad to be true. It may have been the quicker surface which failed to suit and he probably now needs an extra furlong, but this still leaves him with everything to prove. (op 8-15)

Revelator(IRE) cost 30,000euros and is bred to enjoy a stiffer test. He showed his inexperience and a step up to 7f should suit ideally. (op 12-1)

Sandy Toes, despite needing encouragement to get to the start, broke a lot better on this return from a 69-day break and posted his most encouraging effort so far. However, although he now qualifies for nurseries, a drop back to 5f looks the right move in the short term and he is only moderate. (op 33-1)

4739 COUNTRYWIDE FREIGHT NURSERY 6f

6:55 (6:57) (Class 4) (0-80,80) 2-Y-O **£5,504** (£1,637; £818; £408) **Stalls** Low

Form				RPR
412	**1**		**Layla's Hero (IRE)**[6] 4525 2-8-12 **71** ... PhillipMakin 3 (D Nicholls) *hld up in rr: effrt 2f out: str run to ld appr fnl f: drvn clr* **5/4[1]**	80+
3342	**2**	3	**Regardless**[7] 4492 2-8-6 **65** ... (v) FrancisNorton 8 (Mrs G S Rees) *gave problems leaving paddock: t.k.h: led tl appr fnl f: no ch w wnr* **9/1[3]**	65
351	**3**	3 ¾	**Our Dream Queen**[17] 4163 2-9-1 **74** ... RobertWinston 2 (B W Hills) *hld up towards rr: effrt over 2f out: kpt on same pce appr fnl f* **5/1[2]**	63
313	**4**	1 ¼	**Maison Brillet (IRE)**[21] 4035 2-9-4 **80** ... FrederikTylicki(3) 4 (J Howard Johnson) *chsd ldrs on outer: drvn 3f out: sn outpcd: kpt on ins fnl f* **9/1[3]**	65
155	**5**	½	**Dancing Red Devil (IRE)**[12] 4357 2-9-4 **77** ... PaulMulrennan 1 (Paul Green) *trckd ldrs: drvn 3f out: wknd over 1f out* **16/1**	61
2515	**6**	1	**Military Call**[16] 4195 2-9-0 **73** ... RichardMullen 9 (E S McMahon) *t.k.h: trckd ldrs: effrt over 2f out: hung lft and wknd fnl f* **5/1[2]**	54
0310	**7**	nk	**Wigan Lane**[27] 3842 2-8-11 **70** ... PaulHanagan 7 (R A Fahey) *w ldr: rdn over 2f out: edgd lft and wknd fnl f* **14/1**	50
0004	**8**	16	**Countrywide Ice (IRE)**[20] 4076 2-7-12 **57** oh4 ... (b) DuranFentiman 6 (K A Ryan) *s.i.s: swvd rt after s: hdwy to chse ldrs after 2f: wknd over 1f out: heavily eased* **50/1**	—

1m 13.92s (-0.58) **Going Correction** -0.15s/f (Firm) **8** Ran SP% **112.3**
Speed ratings (Par 96): **97,93,88,86,85 84,83,62**
toteswingers: 1&2 £2.90, 1&3 £2.20, 2&3 £8.20. CSF £13.05 CT £42.25 TOTE £2.30: £1.10, £2.90, £1.90; EX 16.30.

Owner Dr Marwan Koukash **Bred** Epona Bloodstock Ltd **Trained** Sessay, N Yorks

FOCUS

A fair nursery, run at a sound pace. The winner proved far too strong and the form looks solid.

NOTEBOOK

Layla's Hero(IRE) proved far too good for his rivals on this quick reappearance. He was given plenty of time to find his feet and came to the leaders full of running at the two-furlong pole. He quickened up readily when hitting the front and came right away, shaping as though he relished this return to much quicker ground. The handicapper will now punish him, as he was already due to race from a 3lb higher mark, but he looks just the sort his trainer excels with. He could take in the valuable sales race over this trip at York later this month and would be entitled to respect there. (tchd 11-8)

Regardless, who played up in the preliminaries, finished second in a first-time visor over course and distance last time when racing from the front. She again had her own way out in front and found one too good, but has to be considered a little unfortunate to have bumped into the progressive winner. She is versatile as regards underfoot conditions, deserves to find an opening and rates the benchmark. (op 11-1)

Our Dream Queen got off the mark in the first ever Flat race to be run at Ffos Las 17 days previously and looked fairly treated for this nursery bow. She was staying on at the same pace without ever threatening and ran well enough, but left the impression the ground was quicker than she cares for. (op 11-2 tchd 6-1)

Maison Brillet(IRE) got outpaced and kept on bravely for fourth, but appears in need of further respite from the handicapper. (op 11-1 tchd 12-1)

Dancing Red Devil(IRE) proved very easy to back on this step up in trip and nursery debut. She posted a somewhat laboured effort on this return to much quicker ground and it is hard to gauge whether she really got the trip. (op 7-1)

Military Call, back on fast ground, provided a limited response after moving nicely through the first half of the race and will need to settle better before getting closer off this mark. (op 6-1 tchd 4-1)

4740 MTB GROUP CLAIMING STKS 1m 2f 95y

7:25 (7:25) (Class 5) 3-4-Y-O **£3,238** (£963; £481; £240) **Stalls** Low

Form				RPR
0350	**1**		**Applaude**[12] 4350 4-9-3 67 ... (b[1]) RobertWinston 5 (G A Swinbank) *chsd ldrs: hdwy to chal 2f out: kpt on wl to ld post* **7/1[3]**	75
-222	**2**	nse	**Graceful Descent (FR)**[18] 4139 4-9-2 69 ... PaulHanagan 4 (R A Fahey) *chsd ldrs: drvn over 4f out: led 2f out: hrd rdn: hdd last stride* **6/4[1]**	74
21-4	**3**	2	**Kind Heart**[14] 4280 3-8-13 79 ... StephenDonohoe 2 (Sir Mark Prescott) *led: qcknd over 4f out: hdd 2f out: one pce appr fnl f* **13/8[2]**	76
6006	**4**	5	**Randama Bay (IRE)**[5] 4563 4-9-7 68 ... RichardMullen 6 (I A Wood) *w ldrs: drvn over 4f out: sn outpcd: edgd lft and wknd 2f out* **11/1**	66
4062	**5**	2 ¼	**Highland Storm**[20] 3588 3-8-6 63 ... (p) FrancisNorton 1 (B N Pollock) *dwlt: hld up: effrt on inner over 4f out: lost pl over 2f out* **10/1**	55

2m 13.28s (0.28) **Going Correction** -0.025s/f (Good)
WFA 3 from 4yo 9lb **5** Ran SP% **108.0**
Speed ratings (Par 103): **106,105,104,100,98**
toteswingers: 1&2 £4.90. CSF £17.40 TOTE £7.30: £2.60, £1.40; EX 13.20.Applaude was claimed by John A. Harris for £8,000.

Owner Guy Reed **Bred** G Reed **Trained** Melsonby, N Yorks

■ Stewards' Enquiry : Paul Hanagan two-day ban: excessive use of the whip (Aug 22-23)

Robert Winston two-day ban: excessive use of the whip (Aug 22-23)

FOCUS

A modest claimer in which first pair came clear in a bobbing finish. The winner was still 5lb off last year's best, with the runner-up probably the best guide.

4741 CHESHIRE OAKS DESIGNER OUTLET H'CAP 1m 30y

8:00 (8:00) (Class 4) (0-80,80) 3-Y-O **£5,504** (£1,637; £818; £408) **Stalls** Low

Form				RPR
3562	**1**		**Harriet's Girl**[14] 4284 3-8-11 **70** ... AndrewElliott 6 (A P Jarvis) *trckd ldrs: effrt on outside 4f out: styd on to ld jst ins fnl f: kpt on wl* **7/2[2]**	77
-000	**2**	½	**Goliaths Boy (IRE)**[55] 2935 3-9-7 **80** ... PaulHanagan 5 (R A Fahey) *chsd ldng pair: effrt over 3f out: styd on to ld appr fnl f: sn hdd: no ex fnl 50yds* **10/3[1]**	86
3115	**3**	3 ¾	**Aldaado (IRE)**[34] 3608 3-9-3 **76** ... PhillipMakin 3 (M Dods) *chsd ldrs: drvn 5f out: kpt on to r upsides appr fnl f: edgd lft and one pce* **5/1[3]**	73
-414	**4**	1	**Chief Red Cloud (USA)**[23] 3980 3-8-7 **66** ... RichardMullen 7 (A P Jarvis) *hld up in last: effrt on ins over 3f out: swtchd rt ins fnl f: one pce* **6/1**	61
1443	**5**	1 ¼	**Postman**[18] 4143 3-8-13 **72** ... RoystonFfrench 2 (B Smart) *mde most: hdd over 1f out: sn fdd* **8/1**	64+
2215	**6**	12	**Eastern Warrior**[16] 4211 3-9-4 **77** ... RobertWinston 4 (J W Hills) *t.k.h: sn w ldr: hung lft and lost pl over 1f out: eased* **10/3[1]**	41

1m 43.28s (-0.52) **Going Correction** -0.025s/f (Good) **6** Ran SP% **110.4**
Speed ratings (Par 102): **101,100,96,95,94 82**
toteswingers: 1&2 £3.10, 1&3 £7.90, 2&3 £3.70. CSF £14.94 TOTE £4.60: £2.50, £2.30; EX 18.70.

Owner Joe Sankey & Ray Bailey **Bred** J Sankey **Trained** Middleham Moor, N Yorks

FOCUS

The two leaders went off too quick here and that set it up the the first pair, who came clear. Probably ordinary form for the grade.

4742 JILL AND MARIA BIRTHDAY H'CAP 1m 6f

8:30 (8:30) (Class 5) (0-70,69) 4-Y-O+ **£3,238** (£963; £481; £240) **Stalls** Low

Form				RPR
0-05	**1**		**Leyte Gulf (USA)**[11] 4388 6-8-4 **52** ... RoystonFfrench 3 (C C Bealby) *hld up in rr: hdwy 7f out: nt clr run and swtchd rt over 1f out: led jst ins fnl f: kpt on wl* **16/1**	61
-050	**2**	1	**Ameeq (USA)**[20] 3721 7-9-7 **69** ... RichardMullen 6 (Dr R D P Newland) *trckd ldrs: effrt on ins over 2f out: upsides over 1f out: kpt on same pce ins fnl f* **7/1[3]**	77
2301	**3**	1 ¼	**Calculating (IRE)**[8] 4449 5-8-2 **50** ... DuranFentiman 4 (M D I Usher) *hld up towards rr: hdwy over 4f out: sn chsng ldrs: led 1f out: sn hdd: kpt on same pce* **7/2[1]**	56
6/00	**4**	1 ¼	**Great Quest (IRE)**[8] 4462 7-8-4 **52** ... PaulHanagan 7 (James Moffatt) *hld up in rr: effrt over 4f out: nt clr run over 2f out tl swtchd outside over 1f out: styd on ins fnl f* **14/1**	56
/002	**5**	1 ¾	**John Forbes**[14] 4288 7-8-12 **65** ... LanceBetts(5) 5 (B Ellison) *led tl over 1f out: sn fdd* **6/1[2]**	67
4445	**6**	1 ¼	**Puy D'Arnac (FR)**[20] 4078 6-9-3 **65** ... RobertWinston 2 (G A Swinbank) *hld up in midfield: smooth hdwy over 2f out: led over 1f out: sn hdd & wknd* **7/2[1]**	65
6333	**7**	3 ¾	**Solas Alainn (IRE)**[20] 4098 4-9-1 **63** ... (v[1]) GregFairley 8 (M Johnston) *chsd ldr: drvn over 3f out: lost pl over 1f out* **7/2[1]**	58
0/0-	**8**	2	**Tora Petcha (IRE)**[19] 7695 6-8-3 **56** ... PatrickDonaghy(5) 1 (B D Leavy) *hld up in rr: effrt over 3f out: rdn and wknd over 2f out* **20/1**	48
06/5	**9**	78	**Lilymay**[36] 3527 9-7-10 **51** oh5 ow1 ... BillyCray(7) 9 (B P J Baugh) *sn chsng ldrs: drvn 8f out: sn lost pl: t.o 3f out: virtually p.u* **50/1**	—

3m 4.15s (-0.15) **Going Correction** -0.025s/f (Good) **9** Ran SP% **112.7**
Speed ratings (Par 103): **99,98,97,97,96 95,93,92,47**
toteswingers: 1&2 £5.80, 1&3 £13.00, 2&3 £5.20. CSF £119.80 CT £484.62 TOTE £22.70: £4.50, £2.30, £1.30; EX 185.50 Place 6 £129.81, Place 5 £30.47..

Owner Robert Jenkinson **Bred** Paradigm Thoroughbred Inc **Trained** Barrowby, Lincs

FOCUS

A moderate staying handicap, but there was a solid pace on and the form should work out, although several of these are regressive. The winner is rated back to last year's turf form.

T/Plt: £117.90 to a £1 stake. Pool: £45,932.31. 284.20 winning tickets. T/Qpdt: £7.70 to a £1 stake. Pool: £4,911.70. 468.90 winning tickets. WG

4533 LINGFIELD (L-H)

Friday, August 7

OFFICIAL GOING: Turf course - good to soft (good in places) changing to good to soft after race 1 (2.10); all-weather course - standard

Wind: Light, against Weather: Very overcast

4743 SINGAPORE TURF CLUB MAIDEN STKS — 1m 6f
2:10 (2:10) (Class 5) 3-Y-O+ **£2,590** (£770; £385; £192) **Stalls** High

Form RPR

5333 1 **Bernie The Bolt (IRE)**[28] 3793 3-9-0 75 .... WilliamBuick 2 85
(A M Balding) trckd ldng pair: pushed along over 4f out: wnt 2nd over 3f out: rdn to cl on ldr: led jst over 1f out: kpt on wl **13/8**[2]

2202 2 2 3/4 **Gibb River (IRE)**[31] 3707 3-9-0 82 ....(b[1]) JamieSpencer 4 81
(P W Chapple-Hyam) led: drew 4 l clr 4f out: rdn and hung rt over 3f out: fnd little for press: hdd jst over 1f out: sn btn **5/4**[1]

0452 3 23 **Dark Quest**[31] 3703 3-8-9 74 .... RichardHughes 1 44+
(J L Dunlop) chsd ldr: pushed along over 4f out: lost 2nd over 3f out: btn 2f out: eased fr over 1f out **4/1**[3]

4 4 20 **De Soto**[29] 3791 8-9-13 0 ....(t) TedDurcan 3 21
(P R Webber) s.s: in tch in last tl wknd over 3f out: t.o **16/1**

3m 14.32s (4.32) **Going Correction** +0.45s/f (Yiel)
WFA 3 from 5yo+ 13lb 4 Ran SP% **108.4**
Speed ratings (Par 103): **105,103,90,78**
CSF £4.04 TOTE £2.50; EX 5.40.
Owner B P McGuire **Bred** John Munnelly **Trained** Kingsclere, Hants

FOCUS
An ordinary, uncompetitive maiden where the first pair came a long way clear of the disappointing third. The winner may not have had to improve that much.

4744 EAST GRINSTEAD COURIER AND OBSERVER H'CAP — 1m 3f 106y
2:40 (2:40) (Class 5) (0-70,70) 3-Y-O+ **£3,070** (£906; £453) **Stalls** High

Form RPR

5023 1 **Shesha Bear**[16] 4207 4-9-10 63 ....(b) RichardHughes 1 69
(W R Muir) prom: chsd ldr over 2f out: rdn to ld 1f out: kpt on wl **5/1**[2]

-050 2 1 1/4 **Whisky Galore**[56] 2892 3-9-7 70 .... WilliamBuick 7 74
(C G Cox) dwlt: last pair: urged along 1/2-way: stl last pair 3f out and reluctant u.p: prog on outer jst over 2f out: hanging but styd on to take 2nd last strides **15/2**

0322 3 hd **Persian Memories (IRE)**[15] 4241 3-9-2 65 .... EddieAhern 8 68
(J L Dunlop) trckd ldr: clsd to ld jst over 3f out: rdn 2f out: hdd and nt qckn 1f out: lost 2nd last strides **9/4**[1]

2420 4 2 1/2 **Bramalea**[14] 4269 4-9-12 65 .... JimCrowley 6 64
(B W Duke) t.k.h: cl up: effrt to dispute 2nd over 2f out: nt qckn over 1f out: fdd ins fnl f **8/1**

250 5 3 1/2 **Drum Major (IRE)**[30] 3737 4-10-0 67 .... PatCosgrave 2 60
(G L Moore) wl in tch: bustled along over 4f out: 6th and chsng ldrs over 3f out: rdn and no imp over 2f out **16/1**

550 6 1 1/4 **Adnams**[18] 4145 3-9-4 67 .... TedDurcan 12 58
(C F Wall) dropped in to last fr wd draw: prog into midfield 5f out: 7th and in tch over 3f out: sn rdn and no hdwy **11/2**[3]

030 7 4 **Sahara Sunshine**[16] 4207 4-9-8 61 .... IanMongan 4 45
(Mrs L J Mongan) s.i.s: hld up in rr: lost tch w ldng gp 4f out: effrt on outer over 2f out: no prog over 1f out **20/1**

5530 8 2 1/4 **Uig**[17] 4169 8-8-13 52 .... KirstyMilczarek 3 32
(H S Howe) hld up towards rr: lost tch w ldng gp 4f out: effrt u.p 3f out: sn no prog **16/1**

6420 9 2 1/2 **Cayman Sky**[46] 3222 3-8-8 64 ....(b) CharlesEddery[(7)] 5 40
(R Hannon) sn in rr: lost tch w ldng gp 4f out: effrt u.p on inner over 2f out: sn wknd **9/1**

-400 10 shd **Am I Blue**[56] 2881 3-8-12 61 ....(b[1]) ShaneKelly 9 37
(H J L Dunlop) sn prom on outer: rdn over 4f out: lost pl and btn wl over 2f out: wknd **33/1**

4400 11 6 **Brad's Luck (IRE)**[22] 4004 3-8-8 57 .... SteveDrowne 11 23
(M Blanshard) nvr bttr than midfield: lost tch w ldng gp 4f out: struggling wl in rr 3f out **16/1**

0-06 12 17 **Mr Deal**[8] 4450 3-8-3 52 ....(b[1]) RichardKingscote 13 —
(Eve Johnson Houghton) led: clr 1/2-way: hdd & wknd jst over 3f out: eased: t.o **40/1**

2m 35.59s (4.09) **Going Correction** +0.45s/f (Yiel)
WFA 3 from 4yo+ 10lb 12 Ran SP% **123.5**
Speed ratings (Par 103): **103,102,101,100,97 96,93,92,90,90 85,73**
toteswinger: 1&2 £10.90, 1&3 £2.60, 2&3 £5.90. CSF £43.50 CT £110.33 TOTE £5.90: £1.80, £2.50, £1.50; EX 48.40.
Owner Joe Bear Racing **Bred** Beechgrove Stud Farm Ltd & Catridge Farm Stud **Trained** Lambourn, Berks
■ Stewards' Enquiry : Charles Eddery three-day ban: excessive use of the whip and when out of contention (Aug 22-24)

FOCUS
A handicap for horses who had yet to win in 2009 and it almost goes without saying this was a modest contest. The pace seemed fair and the form seems sound enough, if limited.

4745 SURREY MIRROR H'CAP — 1m 2f
3:10 (3:11) (Class 6) (0-65,65) 3-Y-O+ **£2,047** (£604; £302) **Stalls** Low

Form RPR

2131 1 **Love In The Park**[13] 4300 4-10-0 65 .... PatCosgrave 14 75+
(R Brotherton) settled towards rr: pushed along over 4f out: gd prog fr 3f out to chal 2f out: led over 1f out: kpt on wl nr fin **3/1**[1]

046 2 1 1/2 **Red Reef**[15] 4224 3-9-1 61 .... EddieAhern 4 68
(D J Coakley) hld up in midfield: prog jst over 3f out to chal over 2f out: w wnr over 1f out: no ex ins fnl f **9/1**

0600 3 6 **Filun**[14] 4263 4-9-6 57 .... IanMongan 6 52
(A Middleton) hld up in rr: pushed up to go prom after 4f: effrt on outer to ld over 2f out: hdd over 1f out: sn wknd **25/1**

4-00 4 2 1/4 **Rehabilitation**[18] 4150 4-9-9 60 ....(tp) ShaneKelly 7 51
(W R Swinburn) mde most to over 2f out: steadily wknd fnl 2f **20/1**

-004 5 2 1/4 **Carbon Print (USA)**[21] 4054 4-9-5 56 .... TedDurcan 13 42
(P R Webber) heavily restrained s: hld up in last pair: urged along and no rspnse 3f out: plugged on fnl 2f: no ch **4/1**[2]

6020 6 nse **Heartsease**[15] 4224 3-8-12 58 .... RichardKingscote 3 44
(J G Portman) prom: rdn and cl up wl over 2f out: steadily wknd **7/1**

5345 7 1 **Vinces**[13] 4300 5-9-12 63 .... KirstyMilczarek 12 47
(T D McCarthy) t.k.h early: trckd ldr 3f: styd prom: chal and upsides wl over 2f out: sn wknd **11/2**[3]

3230 8 1 1/4 **Clipperdown (IRE)**[32] 3675 8-9-8 62 ....(t) AlanCreighton[(3)] 8 43
(E J Creighton) s.i.s: plld hrd and hld up in last trio: rdn and no real prog over 3f out **16/1**

50-0 9 1 3/4 **A Dream Come True**[11] 4389 4-9-5 61 .... JamesO'Reilly[(5)] 1 39
(D K Ivory) t.k.h: hld up wl in rr: last pair and struggling over 3f out: no ch after **16/1**

-660 10 shd **Kayfiar (USA)**[23] 3985 3-9-1 61 ....(b[1]) RichardHughes 5 39
(P F I Cole) chsd ldr after 3f: reminders 5f out: wknd over 2f out **11/1**

0026 11 2 3/4 **Mayfair's Future**[25] 3929 4-9-3 54 .... JimCrowley 2 26
(J R Jenkins) prom: rdn to chal 3f out: wknd rapidly over 2f out: eased over 1f out **11/1**

-602 12 32 **Top Seed (IRE)**[131] 1014 8-10-0 65 .... TonyCulhane 10 —
(M S Tuck) a wl in rr: losing tch in last pair over 3f out: t.o **14/1**

2m 14.76s (4.26) **Going Correction** +0.45s/f (Yiel)
WFA 3 from 4yo+ 9lb 12 Ran SP% **126.6**
Speed ratings (Par 101): **100,98,94,92,90 90,89,88,87,87 84,59**
toteswinger: 1&2 £8.00, 1&3 £27.80, 2&3 £72.60. CSF £33.26 CT £602.26 TOTE £4.30: £1.70, £2.90, £9.10; EX 46.00.
Owner Arthur Clayton **Bred** New England Stud And Partners **Trained** Elmley Castle, Worcs

FOCUS
A modest handicap. The first two came clear and the form has been rated at something like face value.
Kayfiar(USA) Official explanation: jockey said colt had no more to give

4746 THISISSURREYTODAY.CO.UK NOVICE STKS — 5f (P)
3:40 (3:41) (Class 5) 2-Y-O **£3,885** (£1,156; £577; £288) **Stalls** High

Form RPR

105 1 **Brambleberry**[5] 4558 2-9-0 87 .... RichardKingscote 1 86
(Tom Dascombe) led to over 3f out: rdn 2f out: clsd to ld again 150yds out: drvn out **10/1**

2 1/2 **Elusive Trader (USA)** 2-8-9 0 .... RichardHughes 4 79
(R Hannon) dwlt: trckd ldng pair: rdn 2f out: styd on to take 2nd wl ins fnl f: a jst hld **13/2**

30 3 2 **Lady Royal Oak (IRE)**[51] 3015 2-8-7 0 ....(t) WilliamBuick 3 70
(M Botti) t.k.h early: led over 3f out: 2 l clr 2f out: wknd and hdd 150yds out **7/2**[3]

2310 4 nk **Farmer Giles (IRE)**[29] 3782 2-9-2 88 .... JamieSpencer 5 84+
(M L W Bell) hanging rt thrght: hld up in 4th: v wd bnd 2f out and lost all ch: r.o ins fnl f **6/5**[1]

1 5 2 1/2 **Schoolboy Champ**[48] 3152 2-9-2 0 .... JerryO'Dwyer 2 69
(Patrick Morris) dwlt: a in last pair: rdn and struggling 1/2-way: n.d after **10/3**[2]

59.30 secs (0.50) **Going Correction** -0.025s/f (Stan) 5 Ran SP% **113.2**
Speed ratings (Par 94): **95,94,91,90,86**
toteswinger: 1&2 £13.70. CSF £66.88 TOTE £10.30: £3.40, £3.50; EX 35.50.
Owner Grant Thornton Racing Club **Bred** Highclere Stud **Trained** Lambourn, Berks

FOCUS
A fair novice event, even though it was a bit of a surprise to see Brambleberry back in winning form. The form is slightly messy with the favourite below par.

NOTEBOOK
Brambleberry had offered nothing in a Chester nursery only five days earlier, but in fairness that was over 6f and, racing off a harsh-looking 87 that day, she used up plenty of energy early under an apprentice. This drop in trip and return to Polytrack - the course and distance she won her maiden over - proved ideal, and so did a positive ride, with the results of some of the later races on the card suggesting those who raced handy might have been at an advantage. She's clearly pretty useful, and the handicapper may not have been too far out in his original assessment of her after all, but it remains to be seen whether she can reproduce this sort of form on turf. (tchd 11-1)
Elusive Trader(USA), a 160,000gns purchase out of a high-class triple winner at around 1m at in the US, shaped nicely on his debut. He recovered from a sluggish start and kept on in the straight, pulling clear of all bar the determined winner. It will be disappointing if he can't win a maiden soon. (op 7-1 tchd 6-1)
Lady Royal Oak(IRE) is a filly with a terrific amount of natural speed, but she's very headstrong and her rider had little choice but to let her stride on after fighting her for about a furlong. She unsurprisingly burnt herself out, with the first-time tongue-tie not really doing the trick. She'll be decent if learning to settle, but that looks a fair way off. (op 3-1 tchd 11-4)
Farmer Giles(IRE) ruined his chance by continually hanging right and completely failing to handle the bend into the straight. In the circumstances he did well to finish so close and he's evidently pretty useful, but his waywardness was disconcerting. He seemingly needs a straight course, or is worth a go right-handed. Official explanation: jockey said colt hung right throughout (op 11-8 tchd 6-4)
Schoolboy Champ ran nowhere near the form he showed when winning a fair Haydock maiden at odds of 33/1 on his debut and was bitterly disappointing. Official explanation: jockey said gelding failed to handle the final bend; trainer said gelding scoped badly (op 4-1)

4747 CHIPSTEAD FILLIES' (S) STKS — 6f (P)
4:10 (4:11) (Class 6) 2-Y-O **£2,047** (£604; £302) **Stalls** Low

Form RPR

6 1 **Ramamara (IRE)**[92] 1802 2-8-12 0 .... EddieAhern 7 66+
(P D Evans) trckd ldr: rdn to chal 2f out: led over 1f out: drvn and kpt on wl to draw clr fnl f **15/8**[1]

U005 2 4 **New York Lights (IRE)**[16] 4201 2-8-7 54 .... LeeNewnes[(5)] 8 54
(M D I Usher) led: drvn and hdd over 1f out: plugged on and jst hld on for 2nd **16/1**

4056 3 shd **Mind The Monarch**[24] 3952 2-8-12 60 .... WilliamBuick 1 54
(R A Teal) settled in tch: chsd ldng pair on inner 2f out: looked dangerous jst over 1f out: rdn to dispute 2nd ent fnl f: fnd nil **6/1**

2 4 nse **Rescent**[11] 4384 2-8-12 0 .... SaleemGolam 9 54+
(Rae Guest) chsd ldrs: pushed along 1/2-way: hrd rdn to dispute 3rd 2f out: nt qckn and sn btn: kpt on nr fin **3/1**[2]

6565 5 4 1/2 **Aintwogrand (IRE)**[11] 4384 2-8-12 60 .... TonyCulhane 2 40
(M R Channon) sn trckd ldng pair: rdn 2f out: wknd over 1f out **10/3**[3]

0 6 7 **Lake Nakuru**[55] 2914 2-8-12 0 .... KirstyMilczarek 6 19
(H S Howe) dwlt: a in last pair: shkn up 3f out: sn wknd and bhd **33/1**

0025 7 nk **Steeley Flyer**[24] 3958 2-8-12 52 .... PatCosgrave 3 18
(P D Evans) a in last pair: rdn and lost tch 1/2-way **14/1**

1m 12.68s (0.78) **Going Correction** -0.025s/f (Stan) 7 Ran SP% **112.6**
Speed ratings (Par 89): **93,87,87,87,81 72,71**
toteswinger: 1&2 £6.90, 1&3 £3.80, 2&3 £10.60. CSF £32.29 TOTE £3.10: £1.80, £5.00; EX 38.40.The winner was bought in for 7,600gns.
Owner Raymond N R Auld **Bred** R N Auld **Trained** Pandy, Monmouths

FOCUS
A weak seller for juvenile fillies. The winner did it well for the grade.

NOTEBOOK
Ramamara(IRE) won well and is possibly slightly better than this level. She had shown ability on her debut in a 5f maiden at Chester three months earlier and took full advantage of this drop in grade. She was bought in for 7,600gns and should do well in the short term, possibly off a light weight in a nursery comapny, but she lacks size. (op 2-1 tchd 9-4, 5-2 in places)

New York Lights(IRE), dropped in trip, had his chance from the front but was no match whatsoever for the winner. (op 14-1)
Mind The Monarch offered very little and looks flattered by her official mark. (op 15-2)
Recent failed to build on the form she showed when runner-up on her debut and proved disappointing. (op 5-2 tchd 9-4)

4748 "MAKING LOCAL MATTER" MORE H'CAP 6f (P)
4:40 (4:40) (Class 6) (0-60,60) 3-Y-O+ **£2,047** (£604; £302) **Stalls** Low

Form RPR
0003 **1** **Hatman Jack (IRE)**[64] 2630 3-9-0 **55**...(p) JimCrowley 12 64
(B G Powell) *mde virtually all: drvn at least a l up over 1f out: kpt on wl* **18/1**
424U **2** *1 ¾* **Towy Boy (IRE)**[9] 4428 4-9-4 **55**...(v) PatCosgrave 4 59
(I A Wood) *awkward s: prom: wnt 2nd jst over 2f out: drvn and no imp on wnr fr over 1f out* **12/1**
6064 **3** *nk* **Colombard (IRE)**[2] 4665 4-8-13 **50**... SJCraine 3 53
(Patrick Morris) *settled in rr: sme prog on inner 1/2-way: 7th and in tch 2f out: rdn and prog to take 3rd ins fnl f and pressed runner-up nr fin* **12/1**
6610 **4** *1 ½* **Dynamo Dave (USA)**[6] 4536 4-8-10 **52**...(b) LeeNewnes(5) 2 50
(M D I Usher) *chsd ldrs: drvn to dispute 4th 2f out: nt qckn over 1f out: one pce* **14/1**
5150 **5** *¾* **Great Knight (IRE)**[27] 3866 4-9-6 **57**... RichardHughes 8 53
(S Kirk) *pressed wnr to jst over 2f out: stl chalng for 2nd fnl f: wknd last 100yds* **5/1**[3]
0406 **6** *hd* **Davids Mark**[32] 3671 9-9-1 **52**... TonyCulhane 11 47+
(J R Jenkins) *stdd s: racd wd and hld up wl in rr: lost tch w ldrs over 2f out: pushed along and prog over 1f out: kpt on* **11/1**
5505 **7** *nk* **Freepressionist**[17] 4172 3-9-2 **57**... WilliamBuick 1 50
(R A Teal) *settled in midfield on inner: effrt to dispute 4th 2f out: no prog 1f out: fdd* **8/1**
-550 **8** *2 ½* **Dark Camellia**[24] 3946 4-9-6 **57**...(b[1]) EddieAhern 6 43
(H J L Dunlop) *s.s: in tch in rr: prog u.p to dispute 4th 2f out: wknd jst over 1f out* **10/1**
060 **9** *shd* **Kingsgate Castle**[6] 4536 4-9-8 **59**...(v[1]) IanMongan 9 45+
(Miss Gay Kelleway) *hmpd after 1f and dropped to rr: lost tch w ldng gp over 2f out: no ch* **7/2**[1]
042 **10** *6* **Crystal B Good (USA)**[34] 3625 3-9-4 **59**... SteveDrowne 7 25
(J R Best) *a in rr: u.p and struggling 1/2-way: sn lost tch* **9/2**[2]
6666 **11** *17* **Blushing Maid**[22] 3995 3-9-0 **60**... NicolPolli(5) 10 —
(H S Howe) *prom on outer whn sddle slipped after 2f: allowed to coast home* **16/1**

1m 12.03s (0.13) **Going Correction** -0.025s/f (Stan)
WFA 3 from 4yo+ 4lb **11** Ran SP% **118.8**
Speed ratings (Par 101): **98,95,95,93,92 92,91,88,88,80 57**
toteswinger: 1&2 £17.10, 1&3 £34.90, 2&3 £24.60. CSF £219.57 CT £2751.17 TOTE £18.70: £4.90, £4.20, £3.60; EX 187.80.
Owner B G Powell **Bred** Hyde Park Stud **Trained** Upper Lambourn, Berks
■ Stewards' Enquiry : Nicol Polli two-day ban: careless riding (Aug 22-23)

FOCUS
Just as in the two previous Polytrack races on the card, it paid to sit handy. Sound if limited form.
Dark Camellia Official explanation: jockey said filly was slowly away
Kingsgate Castle Official explanation: jockey said gelding suffered suffered interference shortly after the start
Crystal B Good(USA) Official explanation: jockey said filly suffered interference shortly after the start
Blushing Maid Official explanation: jockey said saddle slipped

4749 BLINDLEY HEATH H'CAP 7f (P)
5:10 (5:12) (Class 6) (0-60,60) 3-Y-O **£2,047** (£604; £302) **Stalls** Low

Form RPR
00-0 **1** **Desert Streak (FR)**[64] 2640 3-9-4 **60**... EddieAhern 1 64+
(C G Cox) *trckd ldrs: effrt over 1f out: led ent fnl f: jst hld on* **3/1**[1]
5400 **2** *nk* **Baby Josr**[30] 3741 3-9-4 **60**...(vt) PatCosgrave 6 63
(I A Wood) *dwlt: sltly hmpd over 5f out and again 4f out: drvn in 9th 2f out: gd prog on outer fnl f: styd on to snatch 2nd post* **16/1**
0542 **3** *nse* **Vamos (IRE)**[21] 4061 3-9-1 **57**... SteveDrowne 2 60+
(J R Gask) *hld up bhd ldrs: pushed along in 6th over 2f out: rdn on outer and r.o fnl f: nvr gng to get there in time* **11/2**[3]
0-00 **4** *¾* **Sultans Way (IRE)**[22] 4010 3-9-4 **60**... JosedeSouza 7 61
(P F I Cole) *t.k.h: hld up in tch: chsd ldrs 2f out: rdn and styd on fnl f: jst lacked pce to chal* **25/1**
4000 **5** *½* **Azharia**[35] 3580 3-9-2 **58**...(b[1]) RichardHughes 11 57+
(R Hannon) *stdd s: hld up in last: stl there over 2f out: rapid prog wl over 1f out: chsd ldrs ins fnl f: no ex last 75yds: too much to do* **14/1**
0545 **6** *2 ½* **If Only**[81] 2132 3-9-2 **58**... TonyCulhane 13 51
(J Jay) *relucant to go out on to crse: restrained in rr: sltly hmpd 4f out: prog on outer over 2f out: lost grnd bnd sn after: kpt on fnl f* **6/1**
05 **7** *nk* **Artesium**[4] 4589 3-8-13 **55**... SJCraine 5 47
(Patrick Morris) *pressed ldr: rdn to ld 2f out: hdd ent fnl f: wknd rapidly* **33/1**
-000 **8** *3 ½* **Zim Ho**[13] 4304 3-9-3 **59**... JimCrowley 12 41
(J Akehurst) *led to 2f out: stl cl up on inner jst over 1f out: wknd rapidly* **25/1**
006- **9** *¾* **Hekaaya (IRE)**[290] 6879 3-8-8 **57**... KatiaScallan(7) 3 37
(M P Tregoning) *a wl in rr: lost tch w ldng gp over 2f out: n.d after* **14/1**
3040 **10** *2 ¾* **Order Order**[59] 2797 3-9-3 **59**...(v) TravisBlock 9 32
(H J L Dunlop) *prom: 3rd over 2f out: wknd rapidly over 1f out* **16/1**
0026 **11** *2* **Motor Home**[24] 3946 3-9-2 **58**... WilliamBuick 14 26
(A M Balding) *in tch in midfield: u.p and struggling 3f out: wknd wl over 1f out* **5/1**[2]
0400 **12** *1 ¾* **Ridgeway Silver**[15] 4238 3-8-10 **57**... LeeNewnes(5) 10 20
(M D I Usher) *midfield whn stmbld over 5f out: sltly hmpd 4f out: struggling in rr over 2f out* **66/1**
0-36 **13** *32* **One Cool Mission (IRE)**[14] 4267 3-9-0 **56**...(t) RichardKingscote 4 —
(Tom Dascombe) *dwlt: a in rr: wknd and eased over 2f out: t.o* **12/1**
-635 **P** **Miss Tikitiboo (IRE)**[55] 2918 3-9-3 **59**... IanMongan 8 —
(E F Vaughan) *prom whn p.u 4f out* **9/1**

1m 25.31s (0.51) **Going Correction** -0.025s/f (Stan) **14** Ran SP% **126.3**
Speed ratings (Par 98): **96,95,95,94,94 91,90,86,86,82 80,78,42,—**
toteswinger: 1&2 £15.00, 1&3 £7.10, 2&3 £15.60. CSF £57.01 CT £267.48 TOTE £3.90: £1.60, £5.80, £2.10; EX 69.30 Place 6: £7,799.29, Place 5: £2,467.26..
Owner H E Sheikh Sultan Bin Khalifa Al Nahyan **Bred** Sh Sultan Bin Khalifa Al Nahyan **Trained** Lambourn, Berks

FOCUS
The track seemed to be favouring pace horses in the three previous Polytrack races on the card, but the leaders looked to overdo it a touch this time. Limited form but the winner should do better.
Desert Streak(FR) Official explanation: trainer said, regarding the apparent improved form shown, that he had no explanation as this was the colt's first run from his yard
Motor Home Official explanation: jockey said gelding ran flat
Ridgeway Silver Official explanation: jockey said filly was hampered by an injured horse
One Cool Mission(IRE) Official explanation: jockey said filly had moved poorly
T/Plt: £1,841.60 to a £1 stake. Pool: £51,717.35. 20.50 winning tickets. T/Qpdt: £404.20 to a £1 stake. Pool: £3,495.85. 6.40 winning tickets. JN

4462 MUSSELBURGH (R-H)
Friday, August 7

OFFICIAL GOING: Good to firm (7.5)
Bottom bend rail moved out 1.5m but impact on distances not quantified.
Wind: Very light, across. Weather: Overcast

4750 BUY A RACING POST YEARLING BONUS CANDIDATE (S) STKS 7f 30y
6:00 (6:00) (Class 5) 3-Y-O+ **£2,590** (£770; £385; £192) **Stalls** High

Form RPR
4162 **1** **Fremen (USA)**[9] 4438 9-9-3 82... AdrianTNicholls 2 73+
(D Nicholls) *trckd ldrs: hdwy to ld over 2f out: sn pushed clr* **1/12**[1]
0006 **2** *5* **Jamieson Gold (IRE)**[8] 4465 6-8-12 60...(p) TomEaves 5 50
(Miss L A Perratt) *led: hdd over 3f out and sn rdn: chsd wnr 2f out: sn drvn and kpt on same pce* **12/1**[2]
0006 **3** *2 ¾* **Welcome Approach**[32] 3678 6-8-12 47... TonyHamilton 3 43
(J R Weymes) *dwlt: sn chsng ldng pair: rdn along over 3f out: drvn 2f out and kpt on same pce* **18/1**[3]
0000 **4** *1 ½* **Reddy Ronnie (IRE)**[30] 3730 5-8-5 43... JamesPSullivan(7) 4 39
(D W Thompson) *cl up: led over 3f out: sn rdn and hdd over 2f out: sn wknd* **33/1**
0-00 **5** *2 ¼* **Mangano**[33] 3655 5-8-8 39 ow1... SladeO'Hara(5) 1 34
(A Berry) *a in rr* **50/1**

1m 28.71s (-1.59) **Going Correction** -0.15s/f (Firm) **5** Ran SP% **110.2**
Speed ratings (Par 103): **103,97,94,92,89**
CSF £2.14 TOTE £1.10: £1.02, £2.90; EX 2.30.There was no bid for the winner.
Owner Miss C King Mrs A Seed Ms Finola Devaney **Bred** Flaxman Holdings Ltd **Trained** Sessay, N Yorks

FOCUS
An uncompetitive seller and a straight forward task for Fremen who did not need to be anywhere near his best.

4751 PDM H'CAP 1m
6:30 (6:30) (Class 5) (0-75,74) 3-Y-O+ **£3,885** (£1,156; £577; £288) **Stalls** High

Form RPR
0/0- **1** **Rookwith (IRE)**[29] 3835 9-8-2 **55** oh3...(v) BACurtis(5) 7 62+
(T G McCourt, Ire) *hld up in rr: hdwy on inner over 2f out: drvn ins fnl f: squeezed through and kpt on to ld nr line* **16/1**
2404 **2** *nse* **Grand Diamond (IRE)**[33] 3656 5-9-2 **64**...(p) DanielTudhope 2 71
(J S Goldie) *led: pushed along and hdd wl over 2f out: cl up: drvn ent fnl f and rallied to ld again last 100yds: hdd and nt qckn nr line* **9/1**[3]
6543 **3** *¾* **Papa's Princess**[8] 4465 5-8-4 **55** oh3... KellyHarrison(3) 1 60
(J S Goldie) *cl up: led wl over 2f out: rdn over 1f out: drvn ent fnl f: hdd and no ex last 100yds* **16/1**
0162 **4** *1 ½* **Hel's Angel (IRE)**[8] 4453 3-9-4 **73**... SilvestreDeSousa 3 73
(Mrs A Duffield) *t.k.h: chsd ldrs: rdn along wl over 2f out: drvn over 1f out: sn one pce* **11/4**[1]
4212 **5** *shd* **Ninth House (USA)**[6] 4548 7-8-13 **61** 6ex... PJMcDonald 4 62
(Mrs R A Carr) *hld up: hdwy on outer 3f out: rdn to chse ldrs 2f out: drvn over 1f out and one pce ins fnl f* **3/1**[2]
6452 **6** *2* **Zabeel Tower**[8] 4466 6-9-4 **66**...(p) TonyHamilton 8 62
(R Allan) *trckd ldrs: effrt and n.m.r over 2f out: sn lost pl and swtchd outside: drvn and no imp appr fnl f* **3/1**[2]
4302 **7** *½* **Willyn (IRE)**[25] 3911 4-8-7 **55** oh1...(v[1]) TomEaves 5 50
(J S Goldie) *cl up: rdn along 3f out: wknd over 2f out* **11/1**
04-0 **8** *9* **Distant Sun (USA)**[18] 4134 5-9-7 **74**... BMcHugh(5) 6 48
(Miss L A Perratt) *hld up: a in rr* **16/1**

1m 41.59s (0.39) **Going Correction** -0.15s/f (Firm)
WFA 3 from 4yo+ 7lb **8** Ran SP% **112.6**
Speed ratings (Par 103): **92,91,91,89,89 87,87,78**
toteswingers: 1&2 £27.20, 1&3 £63.10, 2&3 £29.70. CSF £144.59 CT £2348.37 TOTE £18.20: £4.30, £3.50, £5.30; EX 190.10.
Owner James Gogarty **Bred** Yeomanstown Stud Syndicate **Trained** Stamullen, Co Meath
■ The first winner in Britain for apprentice Ben Curtis.
■ Stewards' Enquiry : B A Curtis two-day ban: excessive use of the whip (Aug 21-22)
Daniel Tudhope caution: used whip down the shoulder in the forehand position

FOCUS
A competitive handicap run at an even gallop and it produced a cracking finish. The form makes sense at face value but the market leaders disappointed which raises doubts.
Hel's Angel(IRE) Official explanation: jockey said saddle slipped

4752 NAIRN'S OATCAKES CONDITIONS STKS 5f
7:05 (7:05) (Class 3) 2-Y-O **£7,771** (£2,312; £1,155; £577) **Stalls** Low

Form RPR
2111 **1** **Singeur (IRE)**[13] 4327 2-8-12 86... DanielTudhope 6 89+
(R Bastiman) *in tch: hdwy 1/2-way: effrt on outer over 1f out: sn rdn and qcknd ent fnl f to ld last 100yds* **15/8**[1]
010 **2** *1 ½* **Raddy 'Ell Pauline (IRE)**[30] 3748 2-8-10 90... SilvestreDeSousa 4 82
(K A Ryan) *cl up on inner: effrt wl over 1f out and sn: rdn: drvn to ld briefly ins fnl f: sn hdd and no ex towards fin* **4/1**[3]
1 **3** *hd* **Falasteen (IRE)**[56] 2893 2-9-1 0... AdrianTNicholls 3 86
(D Nicholls) *in tch: hdwy 1/2-way: swtchd rt and rdn to chal over 1f out: ev ch tl drvn and nt qckn ins fnl f* **9/4**[2]
6020 **4** *1* **High Spice (USA)**[13] 4295 2-8-10 80... GrahamGibbons 7 77
(R M H Cowell) *cl up: led 2f out and sn rdn: drvn ent fnl f: sn hdd & wknd* **8/1**
1 **5** *1 ¾* **Monalini (IRE)**[126] 1097 2-9-1 0... TomEaves 2 76
(B Smart) *sn rdn along and a in rr* **10/1**
24 **6** *3* **Goodbye Earl (IRE)**[6] 4547 2-8-7 74... PJMcDonald 5 57
(A Berry) *sn led: rdn along and hdd 2f out: sn wknd* **14/1**
4 **7** *1 ¼* **Kristen Jane (USA)**[12] 4342 2-8-7 0... TonyHamilton 1 53
(Miss L A Perratt) *dwlt: t.k.h: a in rr* **100/1**

58.40 secs (-2.00) **Going Correction** -0.35s/f (Firm) **7** Ran SP% **113.4**
Speed ratings (Par 98): **102,99,99,97,94 90,88**
toteswingers: 1&2 £2.40, 1&3 £1.10, 2&3 £1.70. CSF £9.66 TOTE £2.60: £1.20, £2.80; EX 11.80.
Owner Ms M Austerfield **Bred** Patrick Cassidy **Trained** Cowthorpe, N Yorks

FOCUS
An interesting conditions stakes run at a good gallop, and it should throw up a few winners in the coming weeks. Fairly solid form and the winner could rate higher still.

NOTEBOOK
Singeur(IRE) is progressing nicely as the season goes on, and once again showed a determined attitude to run out an easy winner. A return to York for another nursery could be on the cards for him before a tilt at the valuable two year-old trophy at Redcar later in the season, and he clearly bounces off the fast ground. (tchd 5-2 in a place)
Raddy 'Ell Pauline(IRE) was soon ridden along on her first try at 5f and kept on well close home. She should be placed to good effect before the end of the season, especially when back up to 6f. (op 11-4)
Falasteen(IRE), who was a winner on his debut at York, also showed promise here on quicker ground. Still looking green he should continue to progress, but will have to if he is going to take up his entry in the Gimcrack. (op 3-1)
Monalini(IRE) ran better than his finishing position suggested. He was badly outpaced, before running on well on his first start since early April. (op 8-1 tchd 15-2)
Goodbye Earl(IRE) soon weakened after showing early speed, and she will find easier assignments than this. (op 25-1)

4753 INVESTEC INVESTMENT BANKING H'CAP 5f
7:35 (7:35) (Class 4) (0-85,85) 3-Y-0+ **£6,476** (£1,927; £963; £481) **Stalls** Low

Form RPR
2422 **1** **Raccoon (IRE)**[21] 4036 9-8-11 **72**........ PJMcDonald 1 81
(Mrs R A Carr) *chsd ldrs on inner: rdn over 1f out: styd on strly ins fnl f to ld fnl 50yds* **12/1**
0-53 **2** 3/4 **Hypnosis**[35] 3565 6-9-3 **78**........ TonyHamilton 9 84
(N Wilson) *sn led: rdn along 2f out: drvn and edgd rt ins fnl f: hdd and no ex fnl 50yds* **11/1**
0035 **3** hd **Nickel Silver**[41] 3372 4-9-1 **76**........(b) TomEaves 11 82
(B Smart) *wnt rt s: sn cl up: rdn over 1f out and ev ch: drvn ins fnl f and no ex last 50yds* **10/1**
0631 **4** shd **The Nifty Fox**[16] 4189 5-9-2 **77**........ DavidAllan 7 82
(T D Easterby) *chsd ldrs: effrt wl over 1f out and sn rdn: drvn and edgd lft ins fnl f: nt qckn last 100yds* **5/1**[2]
3025 **5** hd **Speedy Senorita (IRE)**[35] 3565 4-8-8 **69** ow1........ GrahamGibbons 2 74
(J J Quinn) *cl up: rdn and sltly outpcd over 1f out: swtchd lft and drvn ins fnl f: kpt on* **20/1**
0066 **6** 1/2 **Northern Bolt**[8] 4461 4-9-2 **77**........ AdrianTNicholls 4 80
(D Nicholls) *bhd: gd hdwy on inner over 1f out: rdn and styd on strly ins fnl f: nrest at fin* **10/1**
1006 **7** 3/4 **Rothesay Dancer**[6] 4530 6-9-3 **81**........ KellyHarrison(3) 5 81
(J S Goldie) *towards rr: hdwy 1/2-way: rdn to chse ldrs over 1f out: sn drvn and no imp* **20/1**
115 **8** hd **Le Toreador**[8] 4461 4-9-3 **83**........(t) AmyRyan(5) 6 82
(K A Ryan) *in midfield: hdwy 2f out: rdn whn n.m.r over 1f out and sn swtchd rt: drvn and no imp ins fnl f* **9/4**[1]
00-0 **9** 4 **Hadaf (IRE)**[27] 3844 4-9-10 **85**........ DaleGibson 3 70
(M P Tregoning) *dwlt and squeezed out s: swtchd rt and hdwy 1/2-way: swtchd lft and rdn wl over 1f out: nvr a factor* **7/1**[3]
0254 **10** 3/4 **Kyzer Chief**[13] 4311 4-8-5 **66** oh1........(p) SilvestreDeSousa 10 48
(R E Barr) *cl up: rdn along 2f out and sn wknd* **18/1**
0214 **11** 43 **Blue Tomato**[8] 4464 8-8-11 **77**........(p) BMcHugh(5) 8 —
(Miss L A Perratt) *a in rr* **10/1**

57.99 secs (-2.41) **Going Correction** -0.35s/f (Firm) **11** Ran SP% **118.0**
Speed ratings (Par 105): **105,103,103,103,103 102,101,100,94,93 24**
toteswingers: 1&2 £26.80, 1&3 £33.80, 2&3 £26.80. CSF £137.49 CT £1394.69 TOTE £13.20: £5.20, £4.10, £2.90; EX 89.30.
Owner P D Savill **Bred** P D Savill **Trained** Huby, N Yorks
■ Stewards' Enquiry : Amy Ryan caution: prematurely eased an unplaced horse

FOCUS
Another competitive sprint handicap which was run at a good gallop thanks to the runner-up. Sound form, rated at face value.
Hadaf(IRE) Official explanation: jockey said colt ran flat
Blue Tomato Official explanation: jockey said gelding bled from the nose

4754 BERNARD HUNTER CRANE HIRE H'CAP 5f
8:10 (8:13) (Class 6) (0-65,65) 3-Y-0+ **£2,590** (£770; £385; £192) **Stalls** Low

Form RPR
1043 **1** **Princess Charlmane (IRE)**[8] 4467 6-8-12 **53**........(p) DanielTudhope 2 61
(C J Teague) *mde all: rdn clr over 1f out: hung rt ins fnl f: kpt on* **11/2**[3]
600- **2** nk **Yorke's Folly (USA)**[294] 6791 8-8-6 **47** oh1 ow1........ PJMcDonald 7 54
(C W Fairhurst) *hld up in rr: swtchd lft after 1f: hdwy on inner over 1f out: sn rdn and chsd wnr ins fnl f: kpt on wl towards fin* **10/1**
4352 **3** 3 1/2 **Angelofthenorth**[8] 4467 7-8-4 **48**........ KellyHarrison(3) 1 42
(C J Teague) *trckd ldrs: hdwy 2f out: swtchd rt and rdn to chse wnr appr fnl f: sn drvn and one pce* **3/1**[2]
0306 **4** 2 **Strensall**[33] 3657 12-8-10 **51**........ SilvestreDeSousa 3 38
(R E Barr) *chsd ldrs: rdn along and n.m.r over 1f out: sn btn* **17/2**
5062 **5** 1 **Miss Daawe**[8] 4464 5-9-2 **57**........ TomEaves 4 41
(B Ellison) *dwlt: sn pushed along: hdwy and cl up 1/2-way: rdn wl over 1f out and sn btn* **11/10**[1]
6 1 **Frisky Queen (IRE)**[16] 4214 3-7-12 **47** oh1 ow1........ BACurtis(5) 8 27
(T G McCourt, Ire) *in tch: hdwy on outer to chal 2f out: sn rdn and wknd over 1f out* **16/1**

58.75 secs (-1.65) **Going Correction** -0.35s/f (Firm)
WFA 3 from 4yo+ 3lb **6** Ran SP% **113.5**
Speed ratings (Par 101): **99,98,92,89,88 86**
toteswingers: 1&2 £8.20, 1&3 £1.50, 2&3 £3.60. CSF £55.01 CT £193.80 TOTE £5.50: £1.80, £4.80; EX 58.30.
Owner M N Emmerson **Bred** James And Joe Brannigan **Trained** Station Town, Co Durham
■ Stewards' Enquiry : Kelly Harrison caution: careless riding

FOCUS
A small field for this moderate sprint handicap, in which half of the field had won over course and distance. The pace was sound enough and the winner bounced back to last month's C&D form.
Miss Daawe Official explanation: jockey said mare was never travelling

4755 SURE PUBLIC RELATIONS H'CAP 1m 4f 100y
8:40 (8:41) (Class 6) (0-65,65) 3-Y-0+ **£2,590** (£770; £385; £192) **Stalls** High

Form RPR
340- **1** **Mister Fizzbomb (IRE)**[238] 7039 6-9-7 **58**........(b) GrahamGibbons 7 72
(T D Walford) *mde all: sn clr: rdn wl over 2f out: drvn ent fnl f and styd on wl* **9/2**[2]
0612 **2** 2 1/2 **Amazing King (IRE)**[6] 4529 5-9-10 **64**........ LeeVickers(3) 9 74
(P A Kirby) *trckd ldrs: hdwy over 2f out and sn rdn: chsd wnr wl over 1f out: drvn ent fnl f and no imp* **13/8**[1]
0-05 **3** 5 **Bed Fellow (IRE)**[10] 3023 5-8-9 **46** oh1........ TonyHamilton 6 48
(P Monteith) *chsd wnr: rdn along wl over 2f out: drvn wl over 1f out and sn one pce* **40/1**
0-02 **4** 1/2 **Ballade De La Mer**[21] 4039 3-8-0 **48**........ AndrewMullen 5 49
(A G Foster) *in tch: rdn along 3f out: drvn over 2f out and n.d* **14/1**
0051 **5** 1 1/2 **Sporting Gesture**[12] 4350 12-8-10 **54** 6ex........ JamesPSullivan(7) 8 53
(M W Easterby) *nvr bttr than midfield* **9/2**[2]
1425 **6** 1 3/4 **Ifatfirst (IRE)**[12] 4345 6-10-0 **65**........ DanielTudhope 4 61
(J S Goldie) *hld up: a towards rr* **6/1**[3]
40 **7** 1 1/4 **Berriedale**[6] 4529 3-8-6 **54**........ SilvestreDeSousa 3 48
(Mrs A Duffield) *hld up: effrt and sme hdwy 3f out: rdn over 2f out and sn wknd* **7/1**
8 1 1/2 **A Chailin Mo Chroi (IRE)**[91] 1856 4-8-5 **47**........(v[1]) BACurtis(5) 2 39
(T G McCourt, Ire) *in tch: effrt over 3f out: sn rdn and wknd over 2f out* **50/1**
4550 **9** hd **Petella**[7] 4506 3-8-6 **54**........ PJMcDonald 1 45
(C W Thornton) *a in rr* **33/1**

2m 42.07s (0.07) **Going Correction** -0.15s/f (Firm)
WFA 3 from 4yo+ 11lb **9** Ran SP% **115.3**
Speed ratings (Par 101): **93,91,88,87,86 85,84,83,83**
toteswingers: 1&2 £3.40, 1&3 £11.60, 2&3 £11.50. CSF £12.06 CT £254.93 TOTE £5.60: £1.80, £1.10, £4.80; EX 20.20 Place 6 £1,884.06, Place 5 £1,833.67..
Owner S Enwright **Bred** Remora Bloodstock Ltd **Trained** Sheriff Hutton, N Yorks

FOCUS
A run-of-the-mill 46-65 handicap, which was run at an even gallop. Very few landed any sort of blow. The winner is rated close to his best.
T/Plt: £925.10 to a £1 stake. Pool: £40,349.94. 31.84 winning tickets. T/Qpdt: £84.00 to a £1 stake. Pool: £4,328.40. 38.10 winning tickets. JR

4539 NEWMARKET (R-H)
Friday, August 7

OFFICIAL GOING: Good to soft (soft in places; 6.6)
Far side track used for both days of the meeting.
Wind: Almost nil. Weather: Overcast

4756 JULY COURSE MAIDEN STKS 7f
5:40 (5:41) (Class 4) 2-Y-0 **£5,180** (£1,541; £770; £384) **Stalls** High

Form RPR
1 **Al Zir (USA)** 2-9-3 0........ LDettori 10 93+
(Saeed Bin Suroor) *s.i.s: sn rcvrd to ld: shkn up over 1f out: r.o strly: eased fnl 50yds: impressive* **15/8**[1]
2 4 **Awesome Act (USA)** 2-9-3 0........ ShaneKelly 3 79+
(J Noseda) *a.p: chsd wnr 2f out: sn ev ch: no ex ins fnl f* **14/1**
3 3 1/4 **Munsarim (IRE)** 2-9-3 0........ RHills 5 71+
(J L Dunlop) *s.i.s: hdwy 1/2-way: rdn and hung rt fr over 1f out: styd on same pce* **5/2**[2]
4 1 1/4 **Togiak (IRE)** 2-9-3 0........ TPQueally 8 68
(E A L Dunlop) *hld up: pushed along 1/2-way: swtchd lft and hdwy over 1f out: no imp fnl f* **66/1**
5 nk **Snoqualmie Star** 2-8-12 0........ NCallan 7 62+
(D R C Elsworth) *hld up: rdn over 2f out: nt trble ldrs* **28/1**
6 shd **Sabander Bleue (IRE)** 2-9-3 0........ ChrisCatlin 1 67
(M R Channon) *led early: chsd wnr tl rdn over 2f out: wknd over 1f out* **66/1**
7 nk **Treble Jig (USA)** 2-9-3 0........ RyanMoore 14 66+
(Sir Michael Stoute) *stdd s: hld up: stl last 1/2-way: styd on fr over 1f out: n.d* **13/2**[3]
8 shd **Tesslam** 2-9-3 0........ PhilipRobinson 12 66
(M A Jarvis) *chsd ldrs tl wknd over 1f out* **16/1**
9 1 1/2 **Times Ahead (USA)** 2-9-3 0........ AdrianMcCarthy 2 62
(P W Chapple-Hyam) *s.i.s: hdwy 1/2-way: wknd over 1f out* **80/1**
10 nse **Hayek** 2-9-3 0........ AlanMunro 6 62
(W Jarvis) *hld up: rdn over 2f out: wknd over 1f out* **33/1**
11 1/2 **Activate** 2-9-3 0........ HayleyTurner 4 61
(M L W Bell) *hld up in tch: rdn and wknd over 1f out* **14/1**
12 4 **Whistle Blower** 2-9-3 0........ MichaelHills 11 51
(J H M Gosden) *prom: rdn over 2f out: sn wknd* **10/1**
13 2 1/4 **Rum King (USA)** 2-9-0 0........ PatrickHills(3) 13 45
(R Hannon) *s.i.s: hld up: rdn over 2f out: wknd over 1f out* **33/1**
14 3 **Red Eddie** 2-9-3 0........ JimmyQuinn 9 38
(B J Meehan) *mid-div: lost pl 1/2-way: sn bhd* **33/1**

1m 27.87s (2.17) **Going Correction** +0.275s/f (Good) **14** Ran SP% **121.5**
Speed ratings (Par 96): **98,93,89,88,87 87,87,87,85,85 85,80,77,74**
toteswingers: 1&2 £11.30, 1&3 £1.80, 2&3 £9.00. CSF £29.65 TOTE £2.70: £1.40, £3.50, £1.60; EX 38.40.
Owner Godolphin **Bred** Jacks Or Better Farm Inc **Trained** Newmarket, Suffolk

FOCUS
A fascinating maiden for newcomers, involving a number of contenders with high-profile entries from top yards. The pace was steady and the time was over four seconds above standard, but the winner was very impressive.

NOTEBOOK
Al Zir(USA) travelled smoothly under a front-running ride and quickened up well to hammer his rivals and land a huge gamble. He was slightly awkward leaving the stalls, but the rest of this performance was highly professional and he looks a very useful prospect. He is a half-brother to high-class winners in US and was a $1.6m sales topper at Fasig-Tipton in March. He currently holds an entry in the Dewhurst. (op 5-2 tchd 13-8)
Awesome Act(USA), a third foal of a 1m2f-winning half-sister to Machiavellian and Coup De Genie, was a bit keen in the early stages but kept going and pulled clear of the rest. This was a promising effort, particularly as he was weak in the market. He is engaged in all the right races, including the Dewhurst and Royal Lodge. (op 10-1 tchd 16-1)
Munsarim(IRE) was matched at 11-1 on the exchanges in the morning, but sent off at 5-2. He never really posed a threat, but was stuck out wide for most of the way and did manage to stay on in the closing stages. He should improve for the run and is a half-brother to the smart 6f-7f performer Munaddam. (tchd 7-2)
Togiak(IRE) looked green and was niggled along at an early stage, but weaved his way through some potential traffic problems and has shown ability for a relatively cheap 45,000gns breeze-up purchase. It will be interesting to see how he develops, as his sire is a stamina influence, but his dam is a good producer of sprinters/milers. (op 100-1)
Snoqualmie Star has done well taking on the colts for a yard not noted for debut winners. She is a half-sister to the stable's smart pair Snoqualmie Girl and Snoqualmie Boy. (op 33-1 tchd 25-1)

Treble Jig(USA) was a bit revved up and looked very inexperienced, but managed to find a reasonable finishing effort. He could improve most for the initial run and is out of a 1m2f winner in France, who was later top-class in the US. (op 8-1 tchd 5-1)

4757 RACING UK SKY 432 (S) STKS 7f
6:10 (6:15) (Class 5) 2-Y-O **£3,238** (£963; £481; £240) **Stalls** High

Form RPR
0653 **1** **Flashy Lover (IRE)**[20] 4101 2-8-8 60 .... ChrisCatlin 3 57
(M R Channon) *plld hrd: led 6f out: rdn over 2f out: edgd lft and styd on wl* **13/2**[3]
6063 **2** *nk* **Glen Lass**[24] 3958 2-8-9 55 ow1 .... (p) NCallan 12 57
(J S Moore) *a.p: chal over 2f out: sn rdn: hung lft fnl f: styd on* **9/2**[2]
P041 **3** *1 ¼* **Arken Lad**[11] 4384 2-9-4 0 .... (p) JimmyQuinn 1 63
(D Donovan) *plld hrd: trckd ldrs: rdn over 1f out: edgd lft and styd on same pce fnl f* **15/2**
4 *1 ¼* **Miss Whippy** 2-8-8 0 .... JamieSpencer 6 50+
(M L W Bell) *stdd s: hld up and swished tail thrght: pushed along 1/2-way: swtchd rt and hdwy over 1f out: sn rdn and hung lft: styd on reluctantly* **9/2**[2]
4365 **5** *1 ¼* **Flapjack**[13] 4302 2-8-8 69 .... RyanMoore 10 47
(R Hannon) *led 1f: chsd ldrs: chal over 2f out: sn rdn: no ex fnl f* **10/3**[1]
04 **6** *¾* **Steel My Heart (IRE)**[18] 4153 2-8-5 0 .... DominicFox(3) 13 45
(Miss D Mountain) *s.i.s: hld up: hdwy over 2f out: rdn over 1f out: styng on same pce whn hung lft ins fnl f* **33/1**
0 **7** *nk* **The Great Husk (IRE)**[48] 3160 2-8-13 0 .... AlanMunro 8 49
(J S Moore) *chsd ldrs: rdn over 2f out: no ex fnl f* **25/1**
00 **8** *4* **Walnut Rise**[18] 4152 2-8-8 0 .... TedDurcan 2 34
(M H Tompkins) *sn pushed along: a in rr* **16/1**
4 **9** *¾* **Casey's Rebel (IRE)**[8] 4468 2-8-8 0 .... JerryO'Dwyer 7 32
(M G Quinlan) *prom: rdn over 2f out: wknd over 1f out* **14/1**
10 *4 ½* **Al Zaeem** 2-8-13 0 .... TPQueally 11 26
(Miss D Mountain) *s.s: hdwy into mid-div: 5f out: rdn 1/2-way: wknd over 2f out* **16/1**

1m 30.38s (4.68) **Going Correction** +0.275s/f (Good) **10** Ran SP% **109.8**
Speed ratings (Par 94): **84,83,82,80,79 78,78,73,72,67**
toteswingers: 1&2 £, 1&3 £, 2&3 £. CSF £32.16 TOTE £7.20: £2.20, £1.70, £2.30; EX 31.00.The winner was bought in for £3,600.
Owner Mrs T Burns **Bred** Rathasker Stud **Trained** West Ilsley, Berks
■ Lochbroom Sunset was withdrawn (12/1, unruly in stalls). Deduct 5p in the 3 under R4.

FOCUS
An average seller, weakened by the withdrawal of two of the main form contenders and rated around the principals. It was run at a very steady pace and the form looks suspect.

NOTEBOOK
Flashy Lover(IRE), who had struggled to get home over 6f recently, took a fierce hold and probably wasted quite a bit of energy stepped up to 7f. She did remarkably well to repel the finishers and get off the mark at the fifth attempt. The form does not amount to much and she will probably face stiffer opposition wherever she goes next time, but if she learns to settle better, she should be capable of improvement. (tchd 5-1 and 7-1)
Glen Lass ran a solid race behind a rival with a 5lb higher official mark. She had not built on her debut promise and looked up against it, but seems to have found a bit extra with cheekpieces applied. (op 9-1 tchd 4-1)
Arken Lad, under a penalty, found this tougher than the 6f Yarmouth seller in which he carried his head high and scrambled home last week. However, he did keep grinding away on the far side after racing keenly and seemed to put in a fairly resolute display. (op 7-1 tchd 9-1)
Miss Whippy shaped with some promise on this debut, despite displaying an incredible propeller movement in her tail. She was quite a rare runner at this level for the stable, but is a 38,000gns half-sister to some useful winners and should benefit from the experience. (op 7-2 tchd 5-1)
Flapjack moved ominously into contention, but her stamina seemed to crack on her first try at this trip. A return to sprinting on quicker ground will suit. (op 7-2 tchd 4-1)

4758 WHITEHOT PROPERTY NURSERY 7f
6:45 (6:46) (Class 4) 2-Y-O **£5,180** (£1,541; £770; £384) **Stalls** High

Form RPR
01 **1** **Clarietta**[22] 4001 2-8-13 77 .... TedDurcan 11 86+
(J L Dunlop) *chsd ldr: led over 1f out: edgd rt ins fnl f: rdn out* **9/4**[1]
31 **2** *¾* **Audacity Of Hope**[65] 2610 2-8-12 76 .... EdwardCreighton 8 83+
(P J McBride) *hld up: hdwy over 2f out: rdn to chse wnr over 1f out: r.o* **4/1**[2]
0344 **3** *3 ¼* **Dashing Doc (IRE)**[14] 4271 2-9-0 78 .... JamieSpencer 10 77
(D R C Elsworth) *s.i.s: hdwy over 4f out: led over 2f out: rdn and hdd over 1f out: no ex ins fnl f* **6/1**
0041 **4** *2 ½* **Keen Bidder**[14] 4271 2-8-2 66 .... JimmyQuinn 2 59
(D M Simcock) *hld up: racd keenly: rdn: swtchd lft and hdwy over 1f out: nt trble ldrs* **5/1**[3]
015 **5** *1 ¾* **Cultured Pride (IRE)**[27] 3842 2-8-13 77 .... RyanMoore 3 65
(R Hannon) *chsd ldrs: rdn over 2f out: hung lft over 1f out: sn wknd* **12/1**
463 **6** *2 ¼* **Knockenduff**[14] 4278 2-8-3 67 .... ChrisCatlin 9 50
(M R Channon) *hld up in tch: rdn over 2f out: wknd over 1f out* **16/1**
056 **7** *2 ¼* **Bubbly Braveheart (IRE)**[35] 3584 2-8-9 73 .... AlanMunro 1 50
(A Bailey) *mid-div: rdn over 2f out: edgd lft and wknd over 1f out* **40/1**
1050 **8** *1 ¾* **Queen's Hawk**[16] 4195 2-8-12 76 .... TPQueally 4 49
(D J Coakley) *prom: rdn over 2f out: wknd over 1f out* **33/1**
21 **9** *3 ½* **Atacama Crossing (IRE)**[73] 2358 2-9-6 84 .... MichaelHills 6 48
(B W Hills) *led: hdd over 2f out: rdn and wknd wl over 1f out* **13/2**
61 **10** *1 ¾* **Professor John (IRE)**[24] 3944 2-9-7 85 .... HayleyTurner 5 45
(M L W Bell) *hld up: racd keenly: rdn over 2f out: sn wknd* **20/1**

1m 27.72s (2.02) **Going Correction** +0.275s/f (Good) **10** Ran SP% **118.8**
Speed ratings (Par 96): **99,98,94,91,89 87,84,82,78,76**
toteswingers: 1&2 £4.80, 1&3 £6.70, 2&3 £5.20. CSF £11.07 CT £48.25 TOTE £3.50: £1.60, £2.20, £2.00; EX 12.20.
Owner Bluehills Racing Limited **Bred** Hesmonds Stud Ltd **Trained** Arundel, W Sussex

FOCUS
A competitive nursery, involving five last-time-out-winners. It was run at a very steady tempo and the first two pulled clear of the third who was some way ahead of the rest. The form could be rated 3lb higher.

NOTEBOOK
Clarietta was a big mover in the morning and justified the support by winning in decent style. Always well positioned near the steady pace, she showed plenty of determination to see off a queue a challengers at the furlong pole and was value for more than the winning margin suggests. She sidestepped a Group 3 entry the following day and also holds an entry in the Group 1 Fillies' Mile at Ascot, so is clearly well regarded. This win was off a mark of 77, but she should continue to climb the ranks and looks a nice prospect. (op 6-4 tchd 11-8 and 5-2 in places)
Audacity Of Hope, a quite impressive winner of a 6f Ripon maiden last time, stayed on resolutely down the near side and has taken another step forward. He seems to have a good attitude, is equally effective on fast and slow ground and should be able to win more races. (op 11-2 tchd 7-2)
Dashing Doc(IRE) was well supported and had every chance but could not match the first two. This was a solid effort behind a pair of progressive types, but he does look a bit short of gears at this trip. (op 11-1)
Keen Bidder compromised his chance by taking a strong hold and was probably a bit below the form of his course-and-distance win off 6lb lower on slow ground two weeks ago. He could resume his progress in a more strongly run race next time. (op 7-1)
Cultured Pride(IRE) raced near the pace but did not find a great deal for pressure. She has been well held in two nurseries since getting up late in a Goodwood fillies' maiden and may continue to find life tough against improving rivals. (tchd 14-1)

4759 TURFTV BETTING SHOP SERVICE H'CAP 1m 2f
7:15 (7:16) (Class 5) (0-75,74) 3-Y-O+ **£3,885** (£1,156; £577; £288) **Stalls** Centre

Form RPR
256 **1** **Lord Theo**[24] 3960 5-9-3 63 .... RyanMoore 10 75
(N P Littmoden) *chsd ldr to 1/2-way: remained handy tl led overall over 2f out: hung rt fnl f: drvn out* **8/1**
6023 **2** *3 ¼* **Seventh Cavalry (IRE)**[27] 3869 4-9-5 65 .... TedDurcan 5 70
(A King) *s.i.s: hld up: hdwy 2f out: rdn to go 2nd ins fnl f: nt rch wnr* **5/1**[2]
6-40 **3** *3 ¼* **Devinius (IRE)**[7] 4504 4-9-2 62 .... NCallan 7 61
(G A Swinbank) *hld up in tch: chsd wnr 2f out: sn rdn and hung rt: wknd wl ins fnl f* **9/1**
-062 **4** *7* **Mount Hermon (IRE)**[28] 3811 5-9-13 73 .... (b) HayleyTurner 1 58
(H Morrison) *hld up: hdwy over 3f out: rdn: hung rt and wknd over 1f out* **9/2**[1]
0520 **5** *20* **Bookiebasher Babe (IRE)**[17] 4179 4-9-3 63 .... JerryO'Dwyer 12 8
(M Quinn) *chsd ldr tl racd alone fr over 7f out: led over 3f out: rdn and hdd over 2f out: sn wknd* **14/1**
0050 **6** *1 ¼* **Spensley (IRE)**[29] 3761 3-8-9 69 .... Louis-PhilippeBeuzelin(5) 2 11
(J R Fanshawe) *prom: rdn over 4f out: sn wknd* **18/1**
-065 **7** *shd* **Dubburg (USA)**[74] 2332 4-9-3 63 .... ChrisCatlin 3 5
(W J Musson) *hld up: hdwy over 4f out: rdn and wknd over 2f out* **7/1**
2-00 **8** *5* **Black Rain**[27] 3840 4-10-0 74 .... JamieSpencer 4 6
(M Wigham) *hld up in tch: chsd ldr 1/2-way: gng wl enough 3f out: carried hd fr side to side and sn lost pl* **11/2**[3]
4000 **9** *3 ¼* **Old Romney**[18] 4150 5-9-8 68 .... KirstyMilczarek 6 —
(P Howling) *led: hdd over 3f out: wknd 2f out* **33/1**
043 **10** *2 ½* **Everaard (USA)**[44] 3279 3-8-9 64 .... AlanMunro 11 —
(D R C Elsworth) *prom: rdn over 3f out: wknd over 2f out* **7/1**
61P6 **11** *7* **Sonny Parkin**[7] 4502 7-9-13 73 .... (b) TPQueally 8 —
(J Pearce) *s.i.s: hld up: wknd over 2f out* **16/1**

2m 7.40s (1.90) **Going Correction** +0.275s/f (Good)
WFA 3 from 4yo+ 9lb **11** Ran SP% **117.1**
Speed ratings (Par 103): **103,100,97,92,76 75,75,71,68,66 60**
toteswingers: 1&2 £6.60, 1&3 £32.20, 2&3 £10.80. CSF £47.55 CT £372.27 TOTE £8.90: £3.10, £2.10, £3.10; EX 52.10.
Owner Mrs Karen Graham **Bred** Mike Perkins **Trained** Newmarket, Suffolk

FOCUS
A modest looking handicap. Six of the runners had been beaten more than seven lengths on their latest start and this is probably not form to view too positively. The pace was reasonable and they finished well strung out.
Black Rain Official explanation: vet said gelding was lame

4760 NEWMARKET NIGHTS CONDITIONS STKS 1m 2f
7:50 (7:50) (Class 3) 3-Y-O **£9,969** (£2,985; £1,492; £747; £372) **Stalls** Centre

Form RPR
2-33 **1** **Prince Siegfried (FR)**[12] 4367 3-9-0 111 .... LDettori 4 111+
(Saeed Bin Suroor) *mde all: rdn and hung lft over 1f out: styd on wl* **5/4**[1]
2005 **2** *3 ¼* **Montaff**[10] 4405 3-9-0 106 .... (v) RyanMoore 2 104
(M R Channon) *chsd wnr: rdn over 2f out: hung lft over 1f out: styng on same pce whn hung rt fnl f* **11/2**[3]
2100 **3** *2* **Native Ruler**[49] 3087 3-9-0 105 .... TPQueally 3 100+
(H R A Cecil) *chsd ldrs: lost pl over 6f out: hdwy over 2f out: sn rdn and edgd lft: no ex fnl f* **7/4**[2]
0024 **4** *13* **Fullback (IRE)**[13] 4296 3-9-0 89 .... TedDurcan 5 74
(J S Moore) *awkward leaving stalls: prom: rdn over 3f out: wknd 2f out* **25/1**
415- **5** *4 ½* **Almiqdaad**[314] 6267 3-9-0 97 .... RHills 1 65
(M A Jarvis) *hld up: hdwy over 6f out: rdn and wknd over 2f out* **7/1**

2m 6.90s (1.40) **Going Correction** +0.275s/f (Good) **5** Ran SP% **112.5**
Speed ratings (Par 104): **105,102,100,90,86**
toteswingers: 1&2 £6.90. CSF £8.84 TOTE £2.00: £1.20, £2.40; EX 8.00.
Owner Godolphin **Bred** Haras Saint Pair Du Mont **Trained** Newmarket, Suffolk

FOCUS
A hot conditions event, three of the runners held an official rating between 104 and 111. A slight personal best from the winner, with the second to his Goodwood latest and the third 15lb off his Dante level.

NOTEBOOK
Prince Siegfried(FR) was narrowly beaten in the Group 1 Criterium International on heavy ground at Saint-Cloud on his final start at two for Andrew Balding. He got back near those heights when third in a Group 2 over 1m2f on good to soft at Maisons-Laffitte last month on his second run for Godolphin. He had strong form claims and the deluge the previous night was very much in his favour. He travelled fluently out in front under a shrewd Frankie Dettori ride, lengthened well when hitting the rising ground and ran his rivals into submission. He is a very classy and likeable type who should be able to strike in Group company. (op 6-4 tchd 7-4)
Montaff has had a bit of a chequered career. He posted a smart effort when splitting Age Of Aquarius and Father Time in the Lingfield Derby Trial on reappearance before finishing down the field at Epsom and in the King Edward VII Stakes at Royal Ascot. Things got back on track when fifth to Harbinger in the Gordon Stakes at Goodwood and he has run another respectable race with the headgear reapplied here. He is useful when on song but may just be too to high for handicaps and not quite good enough in better company. (op 7-1 tchd 4-1)
Native Ruler has always had a big reputation, was not beaten far in the Dante in May and probably didn't get home over 1m4f in the King Edward VII Stakes last time. He had fair claims on the pick of his form, back down in trip, but wandered around when pressure was applied and gave the impression he couldn't cope with the sapping ground. He is worth another chance on a sound surface next time. (op 13-8 tchd 2-1)
Fullback(IRE) faced a stiff task at the weights and was never a factor. He will face much more realistic opportunities, but has been difficult to place since his all-weather maiden win last September and a current handicap mark of 89 is probably near the ceiling of his ability. (op 16-1 tchd 14-1)

Almiqdaad posed a brief threat approaching the three furlong marker but could not sustain his effort against some smart opponents on return from 314 days off. This was not a very encouraging return, but he was progressive in three outings as a juvenile, culminating with a fifth in what was a non-vintage renewal of the Royal Lodge. He has a good physique, should be sharper next time and could still develop into a useful three-year-old on fast ground. (op 8-1 tchd 11-2)

4761 NEWMARKETRACECOURSES.CO.UK H'CAP 6f

8:20 (8:20) (Class 4) (0-85,83) 3-Y-O+ **£5,828** (£1,734; £866; £432) **Stalls** High

Form RPR

0502 **1** **Silver Wind**[7] 4500 4-9-7 **78**............(v) NCallan 8 88
(P D Evans) *mde all: rdn and hung lft fr over 1f out: all out* **2/1**[2]

1106 **2** *hd* **Zowington**[14] 4273 7-9-7 **81**............(v) WilliamCarson(3) 6 90
(S C Williams) *trckd ldrs: rdn to chse wnr and hung lft fr over 1f out: r.o* **14/1**

0010 **3** *4* **Klynch**[15] 4227 3-9-8 **83**............(b) JamieSpencer 2 79
(B J Meehan) *hld up: hdwy 1/2-way: rdn and hung rt over 1f out: styng on same pce whn hmpd ins fnl f* **12/1**

2205 **4** *1* **Indian Skipper (IRE)**[13] 4322 4-9-2 **73**............(p) TedDurcan 9 69+
(M H Tompkins) *s.i.s: hld up: rdn whn hmpd over 1f out: nvr trbld ldrs* **12/1**

-422 **5** *1 3/4* **Belle Des Airs (IRE)**[16] 4198 3-9-7 **82**............ GeorgeBaker 5 69
(R M Beckett) *racd keenly: trckd wnr tl rdn and n.m.r over 1f out: hung lft and wknd fnl f* **7/4**[1]

50-0 **6** *1* **Muftarres (IRE)**[14] 4273 4-9-3 **74**............ HayleyTurner 1 59
(G A Butler) *hld up: rdn over 2f out: sn hung lft: wknd fnl f* **9/1**

0255 **7** *6* **Orange Pip**[64] 2637 4-9-7 **78**............ RyanMoore 4 43
(R Hannon) *plld hrd: trckd ldrs: hmpd over 1f out: sn wknd and eased* **7/1**[3]

1m 14.15s (1.65) **Going Correction** +0.275s/f (Good)
WFA 3 from 4yo+ 4lb **7 Ran SP% 114.2**
Speed ratings (Par 105): **100,99,94,93,90 89,81**
toteswingers: 1&2 £6.90, 1&3 £8.10, 2&3 £9.70. CSF £29.01 CT £269.02 TOTE £3.30: £1.90, £4.00; EX 32.40 Place 6 £57.79, Place 5 £48.17..
Owner Silver Wind Partnership **Bred** W H R John And Partners **Trained** Pandy, Monmouths
■ Stewards' Enquiry : William Carson three-day ban: careless riding (Aug 22-24)
Jamie Spencer 23-day ban (takes into account previous offences; five days deferred): careless riding (Aug 21, 23-25, 28-Sep 10)

FOCUS
A reasonable sprint handicap, although the runner-up was rated 4lb below the ceiling of the grade. It was a rough race and the first two both ran diagonally in the closing stages. The winner only needed to repeat his previous week's C&D form.
T/Jkpt: £8,816.70 to a £1 stake. Pool: £12,417.90. 1.00 winning ticket. T/Plt: £70.70 to a £1 stake. Pool: £65,055.84. 670.88 winning tickets. T/Qpdt: £11.20 to a £1 stake. Pool: £4,817.60. 315.65 winning tickets. CR

4762 - 4765a (Foreign Racing) - See Raceform Interactive

4336 ASCOT (R-H)

Saturday, August 8

OFFICIAL GOING: Straight course - good ; round course - good to soft (good in places) (overall 9.5; straight course 10.0; round course 9.1)
An easy win for Ireland in the Shergar Cup, helped by a treble for Richard Hughes.
Wind: virtually nil Weather: sunny

4766 BARCLAYS SHERGAR CUP DASH STKS (H'CAP) 5f

1:10 (1:12) (Class 2) (0-105,102) 3-Y-O+
£17,230 (£6,034; £2,758; £2,152; £1,897; £1,379) **Stalls** Low

Form RPR

5020 **1** **Group Therapy**[13] 4341 4-9-10 **98**............ FJohansson 4 109
(N P Littmoden) *plld hrd early: travelled wl: trckd ldrs: led jst ins fnl f: shkn up and r.o wl* **9/1**

6020 **2** *1 1/2* **Buachaill Dona (IRE)**[7] 4523 6-9-13 **101**............ HUchida 3 107
(D Nicholls) *s.i.s: towards rr: rdn over 2f out: hdwy over 1f out: kpt on wl fnl f: wnt 2nd nr fin* **7/1**

641 **3** *nk* **Judge 'n Jury**[13] 4341 5-9-13 **101**............(t) AlanMunro 10 106
(R A Harris) *prom: rdn to take narrow advantage over 1f out: hdd jst ins fnl f: kpt on same pce* **7/2**[2]

1040 **4** *shd* **Fol Hollow (IRE)**[7] 4523 4-9-9 **97**............ HayleyTurner 6 102
(D Nicholls) *trckd ldrs: nt clr run and swtchd rt over 2f out: sn rdn: kpt on same pce fnl f* **11/2**[3]

3030 **5** *1 1/2* **Cheveton**[14] 4330 5-9-7 **95**............ GMosse 8 94
(R J Price) *hld up: hdwy 3f out: sn rdn: one pce fnl f* **10/3**[1]

2200 **6** *nk* **Captain Dunne (IRE)**[19] 4135 4-9-11 **99**............ AStarke 7 97
(T D Easterby) *led: rdn and hdd over 1f out: one pce after* **16/1**

0000 **7** *1 1/4* **Orpsie Boy (IRE)**[7] 4523 6-9-1 **92**............(b) AhmedAjtebi(3) 5 86
(N P Littmoden) *towards rr: rdn over 2f out: no imp* **16/1**

1100 **8** *shd* **Mandurah (IRE)**[9] 4461 5-9-0 **88**............ DarryllHolland 9 81
(D Nicholls) *prom: rdn over 2f out: wknd over 1f out: n.m.r whn snatched up ins fnl f* **10/1**

0-56 **9** *9* **Ginobili (IRE)**[8] 4490 3-9-1 **92**............(b) JAHeffernan 2 53
(Stef Liddiard) *dwlt bdly: nvr rcvrd* **16/1**

60.20 secs (-0.30) **Going Correction** +0.175s/f (Good)
WFA 3 from 4yo+ 3lb **9 Ran SP% 109.9**
Speed ratings (Par 109): **109,106,106,105,103 103,101,100,86**
toteswingers: 1&2 £14.70, 1&3 £6.80, 2&3 £2.90. CSF £64.99 CT £247.08 TOTE £10.50: £2.20, £2.20, £1.50; EX 61.60 Trifecta £166.90 Pool: £886.43 - 3.93 winning units..
Owner Franconson Partners **Bred** Stratford Place Stud **Trained** Newmarket, Suffolk
■ Jimmy Ryan (20/1) was withdrawn after unseating Richard Hughes and running loose.

FOCUS
A good, competitive sprint, and solid form. There was a decent pace on and, unsurprisingly, the main action developed close to the stands' rail.

NOTEBOOK
Group Therapy landed his first win since 2007 and did the job readily. He was not disgraced over course and distance last time and only just lost out here on his penultimate outing as well, so clearly enjoys the track. He was a bit free early on, but the generous tempo helped and he sealed the race with a neat turn of foot at the furlong pole. His confidence should be high now and this 5f specialist could head to the Curragh for a valuable sprint later this term. (tchd 17-2)
Buachaill Dona(IRE), who got warm beforehand, disappointed in last week's Stewards' Cup and had not shone in two previous runs at this venue. He got markedly outpaced early on over this sharper test, but finished strongly from off the pace and this was much more like it from him. He is not the easiest to predict, but it would be a surprise were he not to go one better before the season is out.
Judge 'n Jury was 3lb higher than when taking the Hong Kong Sprint over course and distance 13 days earlier and, while he failed to confirm that form with the winner, ran another solid race on a track he loves. His deserves credit as he was drawn wide and rates the benchmark. (op 10-3 tchd 3-1)
Fol Hollow(IRE) had his chance on this return to his optimum trip. He ran close to his Stewards' Cup form with stable-companion Buachaill Dona and course-and-distance form with Judge 'N Jury. (op 13-2 tchd 5-1)
Cheveton, very well backed for this return to the minimum, got taken off his feet through the early parts and that cost him. This is the second run in succession that he has taken too long to find his stride and it may now be that he needs a stiffer test. With that in mind, it would not be surprising to see him go close if heading to the Portland Handicap at Doncaster next month, a race in which he finished a close fifth last term. (op 9-2 tchd 5-1)
Captain Dunne(IRE) pinged out and showed natural early speed. He was done with before the business end, but this was a lot better than his two previous outings. (tchd 18-1)

4767 TITANIC QUARTER SHERGAR CUP CLASSIC (H'CAP) 1m 4f

1:45 (1:45) (Class 2) (0-100,96) 3-Y-O
£17,230 (£6,034; £2,758; £2,152; £1,897; £1,379) **Stalls** High

Form RPR

1031 **1** **Polly's Mark (IRE)**[6] 4566 3-9-8 **90** 3ex............ RichardHughes 8 103
(C G Cox) *t.k.h: hld up: snatched up on rails 3f out: hdwy 2f out: nt clr run whn swtchd lft over 1f out: led ent fnl f: qcknd up wl: pushed out* **5/2**[1]

1120 **2** *3* **Chiberta King**[10] 4420 3-9-6 **88**............ JAHeffernan 5 96
(A M Balding) *in tch: wnt 2nd 3f out: sn rdn: led briefly over 1f out: kpt on but nt pce of wnr* **7/1**

0230 **3** *1/2* **Sabotage (UAE)**[10] 4420 3-10-0 **96**............ MNarredu 7 103
(M Johnston) *hld up bhd: swtchd wd to center for effrt over 2f out: styd on ent fnl f* **8/1**

2130 **4** *1 1/4* **Barwell Bridge**[10] 4420 3-9-9 **91**............ GMosse 6 96
(S Kirk) *hld up: rdn and stdy prog fr 2f out: styd on fnl f: nvr threatened ldrs* **8/1**

0150 **5** *2* **Quai D'Orsay**[11] 4408 3-10-0 **96**............ HUchida 9 98
(M Johnston) *trckd ldrs: rdn over 2f out: sn one pce* **10/1**

0112 **6** *hd* **Alanbrooke**[15] 4260 3-9-12 **94**............(b) DarryllHolland 1 95
(M Johnston) *led after 1f: rdn over 2f out: hdd over 1f out: fdd ins fnl f* **6/1**[3]

2312 **7** *nk* **Mabuya (UAE)**[28] 3840 3-9-1 **83**............ AStarke 3 84
(P J Makin) *t.k.h: led for 1f: trckd ldr tl rdn over 3f out: styd chsng ldrs tl fdd fnl f* **7/2**[2]

-130 **8** *nk* **Holyrood**[63] 2715 3-9-4 **86**............ HayleyTurner 2 87
(Sir Michael Stoute) *in tch: rdn 3f out: sn one pce: fdd fnl f* **14/1**

2m 33.86s (1.36) **Going Correction** +0.30s/f (Good) **8 Ran SP% 115.6**
Speed ratings (Par 106): **107,105,104,103,102 102,102,101**
toteswinger: 1&2 £7.70, 1&3 £2.30, 2&3 £20.40. CSF £20.82 CT £122.23 TOTE £3.10: £1.60, £2.70, £2.60; EX 21.80 Trifecta £146.90 Pool: £1,340.62 - 6.75 winning units..
Owner Wickham Stud **Bred** Glashare House Stud **Trained** Lambourn, Berks

FOCUS
A decent 3yo handicap. Solid form with the winner confirming her recent improvement.

NOTEBOOK
Polly's Mark(IRE) ran well above this mark when taking a Listed event against her own sex six days earlier and so was theoretically "well in" here under her 3lb penalty. She confirmed that previous effort to be no fluke with a comfortable success and relished the way the race was run. She made smooth headway from off the pace, under a well-judged ride, and was in no danger after taking it up near the furlong marker. She will now have to go back up in class, but there should be more to come. A Group 2 at Longchamp on Arc day is reportedly her big target. (op 9-4, tchd 11-4 in places)
Chiberta King, placed at the Royal Meeting on his only previous outing over course and distance, stayed on stoutly for second. He ran right up to his last-time-out Goodwood form with the third and fourth. He just looks held by the Handicapper now, but could be the sort to benefit from a further step up in trip and can still gain reward for his consistency. (op 8-1)
Sabotage(UAE)'s rider Malesh Narredu is a leading kockey in India. Also placed on his only previous run over course and distance, he took time to hit top gear and was staying on too late in the day. He performed right up to his recent level and looks a horse that needs more use made of him over this trip. He could also be worth a try over a longer distance. (op 10-1)
Barwell Bridge, yet another placed over course and distance on his only previous visit to the track, was just behind the two in front of him at Goodwood last time out. He did little wrong here, but the Handicapper now looks to have his measure. (op 12-1)
Quai D'Orsay hit a flat spot down the home straight before staying on with some purpose again. It is not hard to see why connections ran him over further the last twice. He needs to be ridden more aggressively over this trip and can find another race this term.
Alanbrooke was dropping back from 2m and, while he had his own way out in front, really wants further now. (op 4-1, tchd 13-2 in places)
Mabuya(UAE) ran a big race at the track on his previous outing and looked a player, off 2lb higher, back against his own age group. He simply spoilt his chance of getting home by refusing to settle, however. (op 9-2 tchd 5-1)
Holyrood, with the visor abandoned, was returning from a 63-day break and produced a limited effort when push came to shove. He has something to prove at present. (tchd 12-1)

4768 LES AMBASSADEURS CLUB SHERGAR CUP MILE (H'CAP) 1m (R)

2:20 (2:20) (Class 2) (0-100,100) 4-Y-O+
£17,230 (£6,034; £2,758; £2,152; £1,897; £1,379) **Stalls** High

Form RPR

-010 **1** **We'll Come**[35] 3639 5-9-12 **100**............(b) RichardHughes 2 113
(M A Jarvis) *hld up: hdwy 2f out: squeezed through narrow gap on rails over 1f out: led ent fnl f: r.o strly: readily* **8/1**

4-02 **2** *4 1/2* **Moynahan (USA)**[10] 4423 4-9-9 **97**............ GMosse 12 100
(P F I Cole) *hld up: swtchd lft 2f out: sn rdn to cl on ldrs: styd on but no ch w wnr* **9/2**[1]

0001 **3** *1 1/2* **Bencoolen (IRE)**[7] 4526 4-9-6 **94**............ DarryllHolland 1 93
(D Nicholls) *hld up: swtchd lft 2f out: sn rdn and hdwy: styd on wl fnl f: wnt 3rd fnl strides* **9/1**

1000 **4** *hd* **Tartan Gigha (IRE)**[8] 4486 4-9-5 **93**............ FJohansson 4 92
(M Johnston) *in tch: rdn 2f out: styd on ent fnl f: lost 3rd fnl strides* **16/1**

0033 **5** *3* **Docofthebay (IRE)**[8] 4486 5-9-10 **98**............(p) HayleyTurner 6 90
(J A Osborne) *hld up: rdn over 2f out: sme late prog: nvr a danger* **9/2**[1]

1610 **6** *2 3/4* **Dunn'o (IRE)**[52] 3014 4-9-8 **96**............ NCallan 3 82
(C G Cox) *led after 2f: rdn whn edgd lft and hdd ent fnl f: wknd* **11/2**[2]

05 **7** *1 1/4* **Glow Star (SAF)**[148] 5-9-7 **95**............ MNarredu 9 78
(G L Moore) *in tch: rdn wl over 2f out: sn one pce* **12/1**

0010 **8** *1/2* **Dubai's Touch**[8] 4486 5-9-8 **99**............(b) AhmedAjtebi(3) 11 80
(M Johnston) *led for 2f: trckd ldr: swtchd lft for effrt over 2f out: hung lft and wknd fnl f out* **7/1**[3]

0130 **9** *1* **Mahadee (IRE)**[52] 3014 4-9-10 **98**............(b) HUchida 7 77
(C E Brittain) *trckd ldrs: rdn to chal over 2f out: wknd over 1f out* **16/1**

-211 **10** *10* **City Of The Kings (IRE)**[28] 3872 4-9-7 **95**.................... JAHeffernan 10 51
(G A Harker) *trckd ldrs: rdn over 3f out: sn btn* **11/2**[2]

1m 41.23s (0.53) **Going Correction** +0.30s/f (Good) **10** Ran SP% **120.2**
Speed ratings (Par 109): **109,104,103,102,99 97,95,95,94,84**
toteswinger: 1&2 £9.80, 1&3 £48.00, 2&3 £9.20. CSF £45.36 CT £346.61 TOTE £10.70: £2.70, £2.20, £3.40; EX 58.30 Trifecta £502.30 Pool: £1,038.65 - 1.53 winning units..
Owner Stephen Dartnell **Bred** J A And P Duffy **Trained** Newmarket, Suffolk

FOCUS
A strong handicap, run at a decent pace. The winner had the run of the race and this is probably not form to get carried away with.

NOTEBOOK
We'll Come is a very frustrating performer and needs things to go his way, but there is little doubt about his talent when the mood strikes him. It was little surprise that Richard Hughes got him to travel sweetly out the back and his response when getting the gap on the rail down the home straight was immediate. He has now won two of his last three races, both when ridden confidently, and Hughes looks tailor-made for this imposing five-year-old. It must rate a career-best effort, but whether he will reproduce it next time is the worry and the Handicapper will now have his say as well. (tchd 9-1)
Moynahan(USA) ◆, back up a furlong, found the winner far too strong when hitting top gear but produced another decent effort and is obviously back in top form. He looks worth a more positive ride now and his turn should not be far off. (op 13-2, tchd 7-1 in places)
Bencoolen(IRE) was 5lb higher than when scoring over slightly further on softer ground at Goodwood a week previously. He made his move widest of all in the home straight and ideally wants a stiffer test, so this was another solid effort in defeat. (op 15-2 tchd 7-1)
Tartan Gigha(IRE) bounced back to something like his previous best, but the Handicapper looks in charge of him. (op 14-1)
Docofthebay(IRE) lost out by getting too far back through the early parts and, for all his talent, has become very hard to win with. (op 5-1 tchd 11-2)

4769 SODEXO PRESTIGE SHERGAR CUP STAYERS (H'CAP) 2m
2:55 (2:55) (Class 2) (0-100,100) 4-Y-0+

£17,230 (£6,034; £2,758; £2,152; £1,897; £1,379) **Stalls** High

Form RPR
4610 **1** **Aaim To Prosper (IRE)**[10] 4417 5-8-9 **81** oh2......................(v) NCallan 3 88
(M R Channon) *mid-div: rdn 3f out: no imp tl styd on wl fr 2f out: led ins fnl f: drvn out* **8/1**
1204 **2** *1 ¼* **Yes Mr President (IRE)**[11] 4408 4-9-0 **89**.................. AhmedAjtebi(3) 7 94
(M Johnston) *prom: led after 4f: rdn over 2f out: no ex whn hdd ins fnl f* **7/2**[1]
-020 **3** *1 ¾* **Always Bold (IRE)**[10] 4417 4-8-13 **85**......................... HUchida 10 88
(D McCain Jnr) *led for 4f: trckd ldrs: rdn and edgd lft fr over 2f out: styd on same pce* **10/1**
-100 **4** *hd* **Keenes Day (FR)**[42] 3390 4-9-6 **92**.................................. FJohansson 9 95+
(M Johnston) *trckd ldrs: lost pl sltly 3f out: rdn and nt best of runs on rails fr 2f out: squeezed up and stopped jst ins fnl f: swtchd lft: fin wl* **9/2**[2]
-660 **5** *1 ¼* **Bulwark (IRE)**[28] 3874 7-9-4 **90**.. MNarredu 4 92
(Ian Williams) *hld up: rdn and stdy prog fr over 2f out: nvr trbld ldrs* **14/1**
2410 **6** *3* **Dolly Penrose**[9] 4458 4-9-0 **86**....................................... AStarke 11 84
(M R Channon) *mid-div: lost pl and rdn 3f out: styd on same pce fnl 2f* **10/1**
10-5 **7** *¾* **Gee Dee Nen**[121] 1007 6-9-6 **92**................................. DarryllHolland 8 89
(Jim Best) *hld up: rdn wl over 2f out: little imp* **6/1**[3]
-540 **8** *2 ½* **Tungsten Strike (USA)**[9] 4457 8-9-9 **95**........................... AlanMunro 2 89
(Mrs A J Perrett) *trckd ldrs: wnt 2nd 1/2-way: rdn 3f out: wkng whn short of room over 1f out* **11/1**
0 **9** *3* **Macorville (USA)**[14] 4329 6-10-0 **100**................................... GMosse 6 90
(G M Moore) *in tch: rdn 3f out: wknd over 1f out* **10/1**
0310 **10** *5* **Overrule (USA)**[13] 4340 5-9-2 **88**................................. RichardHughes 5 72
(B Ellison) *hld up: rapid hdwy to sit 3rd 5f out: rdn wl over 2f out: wknd over 1f out* **7/1**

3m 36.96s (7.96) **Going Correction** +0.30s/f (Good) **10** Ran SP% **120.6**
Speed ratings (Par 109): **92,91,90,90,89 88,87,86,85,82**
toteswinger: 1&2 £10.10, 1&3 £17.00, 2&3 £8.80. CSF £37.46 CT £292.30 TOTE £9.90: £3.00, £2.00, £3.20; EX 54.80 Trifecta £829.50 Pool: £1,177.10 - 1.05 winning units..
Owner CGA Racing Partnership 2 **Bred** Stephanie Hanly **Trained** West Ilsley, Berks
■ Stewards' Enquiry : N Callan caution: careless riding

FOCUS
A wide-open renewal of this staying prize. Surprisingly there was just a steady pace on until halfway and the form should be treated with some caution. There should be more to come from the winner on his old form.

NOTEBOOK
Aaim To Prosper(IRE) got up late on, despite racing from 2lb out of the handicap. He failed to enjoy 2m5f last time out, but had won on his penultimate outing over this distance off 3lb lower. There was a good deal to like about his attitude when asked for maximum effort and the recent application of the visor has clearly helped his cause. There may be more improvement to come at this trip, despite a likely rise in the weights. Official explanation: trainer said, regarding the apparent improvement in form, gelding was unused to a flag start and consequently dwelt; thereafter, having used his energy to regain his position, the gelding failed to stay the 2m5f trip (op 10-1)
Yes Mr President(IRE) put some pace into the race when going to the front down the far side, and only got reeled in by the winner late on. He just found a stouter stayer on the day, but remains in good heart and deserves another winning turn. (tchd 9-2)
Always Bold(IRE), well in front of the winner over further at Goodwood last time, led on sufferance through the early parts. He kept on gamely without threatening down the home straight and this is more his sort of trip, but the race did not pan out to his needs. (op 9-1)
Keenes Day(FR) ◆ was the eyecatcher. He moved sweetly through the race on the inside of runners, but got no run coming to the two-furlong pole. When he got in the clear, it was all too late, but he finished with purpose and a similar race is within his compass when things go more his way. (tchd 5-1)
Bulwark(IRE), with the visor left off, stayed on stoutly without landing a serious blow, but the race was hardly run to suit. (tchd 12-1)
Dolly Penrose another who would have been much better suited by a truly-run race. (op 12-1)
Gee Dee Nen, last year's winner, was not suited by being held up off the steady pace. (op 7-1 tchd 11-2)

4770 MICHAEL PAGE INTERNATIONAL SHERGAR CUP CHALLENGE (H'CAP) 1m 4f
3:30 (3:30) (Class 2) (0-100,98) 4-Y-0+

£17,230 (£6,034; £2,758; £2,152; £1,897; £1,379) **Stalls** High

Form RPR
0502 **1** **Press The Button (GER)**[16] 4247 6-9-5 **89**.................. RichardHughes 2 98
(J R Boyle) *led for 4f: trckd ldrs: swtchd lft 2f out: sn rdn to ld: kpt on: rdn out* **11/1**
0006 **2** *½* **Night Crescendo (USA)**[3] 4661 6-9-4 **88**.............................. NCallan 3 96
(Mrs A J Perrett) *cl up: rdn over 2f out: squeezed through to dispute cl 2nd ent fnl f: styd on to take 2nd and clsng on wnr towards fin* **8/1**
0004 **3** *½* **Heron Bay**[21] 4091 5-9-10 **94**.. HayleyTurner 9 101
(C F Wall) *slowly away: sn mid-div: rdn over 3f out: swtchd lft 2f out: hung rt but styd on to chse wnr ent fnl f: lost 2nd towards fin* **7/1**
3624 **4** *1 ¼* **William Blake**[11] 4404 4-9-1 **85**.. AlanMunro 10 90
(M Johnston) *trckd ldrs: rdn to ld over 2f out: hdd over 1f out: kpt on same pce* **7/2**[1]
4-51 **5** *nk* **Conquisto**[36] 3564 4-9-7 **91**.. JAHeffernan 5 96
(C G Cox) *hld up: rdn wl over 2f out: no imp tl styd on fnl f* **9/2**[3]
2502 **6** *1* **Mystery Star (IRE)**[13] 4340 4-9-7 **94**............................ AhmedAjtebi(3) 7 98+
(M H Tompkins) *in tch: effrt 3f out: kpt chsng tl wknd ins fnl f* **4/1**[2]
0415 **7** *1* **King Charles**[14] 4315 5-9-11 **95**... MNarredu 4 96
(E A L Dunlop) *hld up: rdn wl over 2f out: no imp* **12/1**
41 **8** *5* **Remember Ramon (USA)**[15] 4274 6-9-2 **86**.................. DarryllHolland 6 79+
(J R Gask) *trckd ldr: led after 4f: rdn and hdd over 2f out: remained cl 3rd tl bdly hmpd on rails ent fnl f: nt rcvr* **15/2**
3350 **9** *8* **Buddhist Monk**[42] 3390 4-9-2 **86**.................................(t) FJohansson 8 67
(Ian Williams) *awkward in stalls: a last* **14/1**

2m 33.38s (0.88) **Going Correction** +0.30s/f (Good) **9** Ran SP% **118.5**
Speed ratings (Par 109): **109,108,108,107,107 106,105,102,97**
toteswinger: 1&2 £22.30, 1&3 £11.50, 2&3 £14.50. CSF £97.73 CT £669.45 TOTE £8.00: £2.20, £2.50, £2.90; EX 64.40 Trifecta £850.70 Part won. Pool: £1,148.72 - 0.30 winning units..
Owner Brian McAtavey **Bred** Gestut Sommerberg **Trained** Epsom, Surrey

FOCUS
A good handicap in which it paid to race handily. The bare form looks sound enough with the runner-up the best guide.

NOTEBOOK
Press The Button(GER) finished second to Dancourt over 1m2f when trying to make all 16 days earlier and looked set for a repeat of those tactics when leading from the gates. Hughes was happy to let others past him after the first 2f or so, however, and it proved to be a winning decision. He hit the front going strongly in between the final 2f and it was soon apparent he had the race in safe keeping. This rates the his best perfomance away from the all-weather and it would probably be a good move to turn him out under a penalty, should connections be able to find a suitable opportunity. (op 9-1 tchd 7-1)
Night Crescendo(USA) has developed into a fiendishly hard horse to predict, but he is a triple winner at the course and this was a notable return to form. He had the cheekpieces left off and ran to the line here, but one would not bet on a repeat next time. (op 9-1)
Heron Bay, back up in distance, reared just before the gates flew back and was then slowly away. He proved a difficult ride as he went in snatches, but showed he is more than capable of success from this mark when in the mood. (tchd 13-2 and 8-1)
William Blake was suited by racing near the pace and had his chance, but a drop in trip/grade now looks best for him. Official explanation: jockey said gelding hung right (op 9-2 tchd 5-1)
Conquisto had been upped 7lb for his Doncaster win 36 days previously and proved popular in the betting ring. He failed to get competitive from off the pace, but this race was not run to suit and he is still worth a chance to prove he is up to this sort of mark. (op 4-1)
Mystery Star(IRE) just lost out over course and distance 13 days earlier, but dropped out tamely here after looking set to make a bold bid coming to the 2f marker. (op 9-2)
Remember Ramon(USA) got hampered in the home straight and is better than the bare form, but was held at that stage. (tchd 8-1)

4771 DUBAI DUTY FREE SHERGAR CUP SPRINT (H'CAP) 6f
4:05 (4:05) (Class 2) (0-100,95) 3-Y-0

£17,230 (£6,034; £2,758; £2,152; £1,897; £1,379) **Stalls** Low

Form RPR
-403 **1** **Noverre To Go (IRE)**[35] 3622 3-9-7 **88**.........................(t) HayleyTurner 5 98
(Tom Dascombe) *chsd ldrs: rdn 2f out: chal ent fnl f: led towards fin: drvn out* **5/1**[2]
61-4 **2** *hd* **Tropical Paradise (IRE)**[22] 4052 3-9-11 **92**.............. JAHeffernan 11 101
(P Winkworth) *mid-div: hdwy 3f out: rdn to ld over 1f out: kpt on whn hdd towards fin* **9/1**
-420 **3** *2 ¾* **Able Master (IRE)**[77] 2279 3-9-11 **92**............................... HUchida 7 92
(B Smart) *hld up: rdn over 2f out: little imp tl r.o fnl f: snatched 3rd fnl stride: nrst fin* **16/1**
2443 **4** *shd* **Five Star Junior (USA)**[35] 3622 3-9-12 **93**...................... FJohansson 9 93
(Mrs L Stubbs) *hld up: hdwy over 2f out: sn rdn: kpt on same pce fnl f* **15/2**
3400 **5** *nk* **Never Lose**[21] 4088 3-9-10 **91**... AlanMunro 2 90
(C E Brittain) *s.i.s: sn mid-div: rdn and hung rt fr 2f out: styd on ins fnl f* **9/1**
1-00 **6** *¾* **Run For The Hills**[31] 3747 3-9-9 **90**.................................. NCallan 6 87
(J H M Gosden) *prom: rdn and ev ch 2f out: one pce fnl f* **4/1**[1]
0003 **7** *2 ¼* **Proclaim**[10] 4423 3-10-0 **95**.......................................(b) MNarredu 1 84
(M Johnston) *broke wl: led: rdn and hdd over 1f out: sn wknd* **13/2**[3]
6300 **8** *1* **Favourite Girl (IRE)**[29] 3824 3-9-11 **95**........................ AhmedAjtebi(3) 8 81
(T D Easterby) *chsd ldrs: rdn 2f out: wknd fnl f* **12/1**
6323 **9** *1 ¼* **Kerrys Requiem (IRE)**[5] 4598 3-9-8 **89**.............................. GMosse 12 71
(M R Channon) *hld up: hdwy over 2f out: sn rdn: wknd fnl f* **4/1**[1]
0640 **10** *4 ½* **Smokey Ryder**[52] 3033 3-9-8 **89**.. AStarke 4 57
(R A Harris) *a outpcd in rr* **22/1**

1m 14.06s (-0.34) **Going Correction** +0.175s/f (Good) **10** Ran SP% **119.7**
Speed ratings (Par 106): **109,108,105,104,104 103,100,99,97,91**
toteswinger: 1&2 £9.70, 1&3 £16.10, 2&3 £29.80. CSF £50.88 CT £695.53 TOTE £5.70: £1.80, £2.60, £4.60; EX 55.10 Trifecta £1019.40 Pool: £1,377 - 1 winning unit. Place 6: £734.40 Place 5: £293.46.
Owner Duddy Duffy Heeney McBride **Bred** Gestut Gorlsdorf **Trained** Lambourn, Berks
■ Stewards' Enquiry : H Uchida nine-day ban: excessive use of the whip (Aug 22-30)

FOCUS
A wide-open 3yo sprint handicap. A step forward for the winner and the form could be rated a bit higher.

NOTEBOOK
Noverre To Go(IRE) just got the better of a bobbing finish to open his account for the season at the third time of asking. He took a little time to settle, but once pulled off the rail he found plenty and was always getting there. This was his first success on turf (scored off 1lb higher on the all-weather) and he has few miles on the clock, so it wouldn't be surprising to see him go on from this. (op 6-1)
Tropical Paradise(IRE) ◆, back down in trip, was never far away from her wide draw and showed the benefit of her comeback run at Newbury 22 days earlier. She refused to go down lightly when the winner came to her and there should be more improvement to come as she is a fresh horse. (op 8-1)
Able Master(IRE) fared best of those to come from behind and returned to something like his best form on this return from a 77-day break. He is entitled to come on for the run. His Japanese rider picked up a nine-day whip ban.
Five Star Junior(USA) came into this having been freshened up by a 35-day absence and ran a sound race, but just looks held by the Handicapper. (op 6-1)
Never Lose was not the best away, but stayed on strongly to post a fair effort on ground that would have been lively enough. She is also happiest over another furlong. (op 12-1 tchd 8-1)
Run For The Hills was returning from a month away from the track and paid for refusing to settle through the early parts. (tchd 5-1)

Kerrys Requiem(IRE) was backing up quickly after being set plenty to do at Ripon earlier this week. She was drawn widest of all, which did not help, and again raced out the back, but her finishing effort suggests the run came too soon. (op 11-2)
T/Plt: £597.60 to a £1 stake. Pool: £123,245.61. 150.53 winning tickets. T/Qpdt: £147.80 to a £1 stake. Pool: £7,134.76. 35.70 winning tickets. TM

4131 AYR (L-H)

Saturday, August 8

OFFICIAL GOING: Good to firm (good in places; 7.3)
An all-sprint card.
Wind: Light across Weather: Overcast and showers

4772 CHAMPAGNE G H MUMM GRAND CRU APPRENTICE H'CAP 6f
5:50 (5:51) (Class 5) (0-70,67) 3-Y-O+ **£3,885** (£1,156; £577; £288) **Stalls** High

Form RPR
6062 **1** **Imperial Sword**[8] 4508 6-9-7 **64**....(b) JanWilson(5) 7 72
(T D Barron) *midfield: effrt and in tch over 2f out: swtchd rt and rdn wl over 1f out: styd on strly ins fnl f to ld nr line* **15/2**[3]
0230 **2** *hd* **Liberty Trail (IRE)**[9] 4466 3-9-6 **67**.... RossSmith(5) 5 73
(I Semple) *cl up: effrt to ld 2f out: rdn over 1f out: hdd and nt qckn nr fin* **16/1**
-313 **3** *nk* **Feeling Fresh (IRE)**[8] 4496 4-9-3 **60**.... RyanClark(5) 6 66+
(Paul Green) *s.i.s and bhd: hdwy over 2f out: rdn wl over 1f out: str run ins fnl f: jst failed* **7/2**[1]
U040 **4** *2 ¾* **Coconut Moon**[7] 4552 7-8-9 **47** oh2.... BillyCray 9 44
(A Berry) *chsd ldrs: swtchd lft and rdn wl over 1f out: kpt on same pce ins fnl f* **25/1**
0300 **5** *½* **Thunder Bay**[19] 4136 4-9-2 **59**....(p) LeeTopliss(5) 8 55
(R A Fahey) *led: rdn along and hdd 2f out: sn drvn and kpt on same pce* **12/1**
4101 **6** *½* **Downhill Skier (IRE)**[8] 4508 5-9-8 **65**.... KierenFox(5) 1 59
(W M Brisbourne) *towards rr and sn rdn along: hdwy over 2f out: kpt on same pce u.p fr over 1f out* **6/1**[2]
2061 **7** *3 ¼* **Botham (USA)**[23] 4016 5-9-8 **60**.... PaulPickard 10 44
(J S Goldie) *in tch: rdn along over 2f out and no hdwy* **6/1**[2]
0-41 **8** *1 ½* **Hitches Dubai (BRZ)**[35] 3611 4-9-11 **66**.... NSLawes(3) 11 45
(D Nicholls) *chsd ldrs: rdn along over 2f out and sn wknd* **7/2**[1]
-000 **9** *6* **Forrest Star**[9] 4466 4-8-4 **47** oh2.... AdamCarter(5) 4 7
(Miss L A Perratt) *prom on wd outside: rdn along 1/2-way: sn wknd* **50/1**
36-0 **10** *13* **Almost Married (IRE)**[81] 2158 5-9-4 **56**.... AndrewHeffernan 2 —
(J S Goldie) *in tch: pushed along 1/2-way: sn rdn and wknd* **10/1**

1m 10.92s (-2.68) **Going Correction** -0.475s/f (Firm)
WFA 3 from 4yo+ 4lb **10 Ran SP% 113.3**
Speed ratings (Par 103): **98,97,97,93,93 92,88,86,78,60**
toteswingers: 1&2 £19.70, 1&3 £5.60, 2&3 £10.20. CSF £116.00 CT £491.02 TOTE £10.00: £2.50, £4.20, £1.70; EX 94.40.
Owner Mrs Margaret Wilson **Bred** David John Brown **Trained** Maunby, N Yorks
■ Stewards' Enquiry : Billy Cray two-day ban; excessive use of the whip (Aug 22-23)

FOCUS
This opening apprentice contest was run at a generous pace early on, and two of those involved in the close finish arrived late on the scene. Straightforward form.
Thunder Bay Official explanation: jockey said gelding lost an offside front shoe

4773 CHAMPAGNE G.H. MUMM CORDON ROUGE CLAIMING STKS 5f
6:20 (6:20) (Class 6) 2-Y-O **£2,047** (£604; £302) **Stalls** High

Form RPR
623 **1** **Melody In The Mist (FR)**[23] 4011 2-9-2 **80**.... PhillipMakin 5 69+
(T D Barron) *mde all: rdn along wl over 1f out: drvn ins fnl f and kpt on towards fin* **4/7**[1]
040 **2** *1* **Sands Of Dee (USA)**[60] 2788 2-8-9 **63**.... TonyHamilton 3 58
(R A Fahey) *cl up: pushed along over 2f out: rdn to chal wl over 1f out: drvn and ch whn wandered ins fnl f: no ex towards fin* **9/2**[2]
5 **3** *1 ½* **Luv U Noo**[11] 4398 2-8-11 0.... GaryBartley(5) 4 60
(A P Jarvis) *dwlt: t.k.h and sn chsng ldng pair: rdn along 2f out: drvn and one pce ent fnl f* **10/1**
0353 **4** *4 ½* **Dower Glen**[9] 4463 2-8-10 **64**....(b) TomEaves 2 37
(I Semple) *t.k.h: trckd ldrs: effrt over 2f out: sn rdn and btn* **11/2**[3]
00 **5** *6* **Somewhere Else**[14] 4308 2-8-3 0.... BillyCray(7) 1 16
(A Berry) *in tch: rdn along 1/2-way: sn wknd* **50/1**

59.22 secs (-0.88) **Going Correction** -0.475s/f (Firm) **5 Ran SP% 108.3**
Speed ratings (Par 92): **88,86,84,76,67**
CSF £3.34 TOTE £1.70: £1.10, £2.20; EX 4.30.
Owner P D Savill **Bred** Ballykilbride Stud **Trained** Maunby, N Yorks

FOCUS
An ordinary juvenile claimer on by the pre-race clear form choice.

NOTEBOOK
Melody In The Mist(FR)'s backers had a few anxious moments prior to collecting. Breaking smartly, she had to be rousted briefly 2f from home to hold the runner-up at bay, but Phillip Makin was able to revert to a hands and heels ride close home. A mark of 80 probably flatters her slightly, and the drop to this class, rather than taking in nurseries, was a sensible move. She can find another of these if getting away as well. (op 8-11)
Sands Of Dee(USA), gelded since last seen 60 days earlier, responded well to urgings to keep the winner honest. There should be a small northern nursery in him. (op 7-2)
Luv U Noo gifted her rivals 2l at the start. She didn't do badly given the energy expended to recover the lost ground. She had shown some good early speed at Beverley on debut and might have a seller in her over a sharper 5f, if breaking on terms next time. (op 8-1)
Dower Glen's best efforts have been over stiffer 5f courses, and also, worryingly, all back in May. She has now failed in blinkers the last twice and can't be backed with any confidence right now. (op 6-1)
Somewhere Else was the first beaten and has nothing to offer. (op 66-1 tchd 40-1)

4774 CHAMPAGNE G.H. MUMM CUVEE R. LALOU E B F MAIDEN STKS 6f
6:50 (6:51) (Class 5) 2-Y-O **£4,015** (£1,194; £597; £298) **Stalls** High

Form RPR
3 **1** **Sunnandaeg**[14] 4307 2-9-3 0.... PhillipMakin 8 84+
(I Semple) *trckd ldng pair: hdwy on inner to ld 2f out: rdn clr over 1f out: styd on wl* **5/2**[2]
2 *4 ½* **Happy Dubai (IRE)** 2-9-3 0.... TomEaves 2 70
(B Smart) *cl up on outer: chal 1/2-way: rdn along 2f out and ev ch tl drvn and one pce appr fnl f* **8/1**[3]
0 **3** *8* **Kai Broon (IRE)**[14] 4307 2-8-10 0.... AndrewHeffernan(7) 5 46
(Miss Lucinda V Russell) *in tch: rdn along 1/2-way: swtchd lft 2f out and kpt on u.p ins fnl f to take 3rd nr fin* **25/1**
322 **4** *¾* **Yeadon**[12] 4370 2-9-3 81.... TonyHamilton 7 44
(R A Fahey) *led and sn hanging lft: pushed along 1/2-way: rdn: rdr dropped reins and rdn 2f out: sn wknd: lost 3rd nr fin* **8/11**[1]
0 **5** *3 ¼* **Daphne Du Maurier (IRE)**[26] 3910 2-8-11 0 ow6.... RossSmith(7) 6 35
(I Semple) *s.i.s: sn chsng ldrs: rdn along 1/2-way and sn wknd* **66/1**
6 **6** *1* **Wing Forward (IRE)**[7] 4546 2-8-5 0.... BillyCray(7) 3 26
(A Berry) *s.i.s: a in rr* **66/1**
7 *2* **Classlin** 2-8-7 0.... GaryBartley(5) 4 20
(J S Goldie) *towards rr: rdn along 1/2-way: sn bhd* **12/1**

1m 11.46s (-2.14) **Going Correction** -0.475s/f (Firm) **7 Ran SP% 112.1**
Speed ratings (Par 94): **95,89,78,77,73 71,69**
toteswingers: 1&2 £2.00, 1&3 £9.30, 2&3 £2.50. CSF £20.90 TOTE £3.50: £1.70, £3.00; EX 19.10.
Owner A Gauley **Bred** C C And Mrs D J Buckley **Trained** Carluke, S Lanarks

FOCUS
This was run in a time just over half a second slower than the opener. The winner impressed but the favourite disappointed.

NOTEBOOK
Sunnandaeg could have travelled with more restraint early on, so the fact he was able to burst clear and run out an easy winner either marks this out as a maiden with no strength-in-depth or his effort as a bit above average. His next run will reveal plenty. (op 3-1 tchd 10-3)
Happy Dubai(IRE) looked well but was edgy in the preliminaries. Swerving left out of the stalls exacerbated his disadvantageous draw, and he was another to run keenly in the opening fractions. He kept on determinedly after the winner had sailed past, though, albeit at the one speed, and posted a pleasing debut which can be built on, if he goes about his business more calmly next time. (op 10-1 tchd 7-1)
Kai Broon(IRE) still looks to be learning, but was able to deprive the disappointing favourite of a place finish late on. (tchd 20-1)
Yeadon got away best of anything, Tony Hamilton had his hands full preventing the colt from hanging away from his excellent draw into the centre of the course and the response when headed a furlong out was negligible. Already the recipient of a wind operation and wearing a crossed noseband here, he still looks like a horse with his share of problems. His rider reported that the colt hung left. Official explanation: jockey said colt hung badly left throughout (tchd 4-5)

4775 MJD & SONS (SCAFFOLDING) LTD CLAIMING STKS 6f
7:20 (7:20) (Class 5) 3-Y-O+ **£2,590** (£770; £385; £192) **Stalls** High

Form RPR
6153 **1** **Turnkey**[4] 4621 7-9-5 84.... AdrianTNicholls 5 80
(D Nicholls) *dwlt: sn trcking ldrs: hdwy and nt clr run 2f out: sn swtchd lft: rdn over 1f out: kpt on ins fnl f to ld last 75yds* **15/8**[1]
3050 **2** *hd* **Mutamared (USA)**[51] 3066 9-9-5 80....(t) TonyHamilton 8 79
(K A Ryan) *sn trcking ldrs: effrt 2f out: nt clr run over 1f out: squeezed through and rdn to ld ins fnl f: drvn and hdd last 75yds: kpt on* **4/1**[3]
0114 **3** *nk* **Dream Express (IRE)**[14] 4312 4-9-0 67.... PhillipMakin 7 73+
(M Dods) *hld up in tch: hdwy 2f out: rdn over 1f out: swtchd rt ent fnl f and kpt on wl towards fin* **3/1**[2]
0162 **4** *1* **Stellite**[19] 4133 9-8-6 68.... GaryBartley(5) 2 67
(J S Goldie) *chsd ldr: led after 2f: rdn along 2f out: drvn over 1f out: hdd ins fnl f and one pce* **5/1**
0000 **5** *4 ½* **Tarus (IRE)**[28] 3853 5-7-11 40.... BillyCray(7) 6 45
(A Berry) *led 2f: cl up: rdn wl over 2f out: drvn and wknd wl over 1f out* **66/1**
3050 **6** *4 ½* **Chin Wag (IRE)**[7] 4552 5-8-4 52....(b[1]) PaulPickard(5) 10 36
(J S Goldie) *dwlt: a in rr* **16/1**
045- **7** *½* **Yorkshire Blue**[280] 7131 10-8-9 59.... DanielTudhope 9 34
(J S Goldie) *hld up: a in rr* **8/1**

1m 10.87s (-2.73) **Going Correction** -0.475s/f (Firm)
WFA 3 from 4yo+ 4lb **7 Ran SP% 114.9**
Speed ratings (Par 103): **99,98,98,97,91 85,84**
toteswingers: 1&2 £2.60, 1&3 £2.40, 2&3 £3.10. CSF £9.88 TOTE £3.10: £1.90, £2.70; EX 11.10.Dream Express was claimed by Paul Howling for £10,000.
Owner Middleham Park Racing Xxiii **Bred** Mrs E M Charlton **Trained** Sessay, N Yorks

FOCUS
Four defections from this contest included two with realistic chances in Blue Tomato and Charles Parnell. The race was framed by Stellite and Tarus's trailblazing antics, and the winning time was just faster than that of the opener. The front pair were probably not at their best.

4776 CHAMPAGNE G.H. MUMM ROSE H'CAP 6f
7:50 (7:50) (Class 4) (0-85,85) 3-Y-O **£4,857** (£1,445; £722; £360) **Stalls** High

Form RPR
3450 **1** **Blown It (USA)**[19] 4134 3-8-7 71 ow1.... TomEaves 2 77
(I Semple) *hld up: hdwy to trck ldrs 2f out: effrt and nt clr run over 1f out and again jst ins fnl f: squeezed through and rdn last 100yds: kpt on to ld nr fin* **12/1**
0620 **2** *nk* **Lucky Numbers (IRE)**[13] 4338 3-9-6 84.... SilvestreDeSousa 1 89
(Paul Green) *chsd ldr: hdwy to chal 2f out: sn rdn and edgd rt over 1f out: drvn to ld ent fnl f: hdd and no ex nr line* **3/1**[2]
1131 **3** *1* **Mister Tinktastic (IRE)**[3] 4664 3-8-13 77 6ex....(p) PhillipMakin 3 79
(M Dods) *led: rdn along 2f out: drvn over 1f out: hdd ent fnl f and sn edgd lft: no ex last 100yds* **4/6**[1]
0535 **4** *1 ½* **Grissom (IRE)**[8] 4494 3-8-9 73.... DanielTudhope 5 70
(A Berry) *hld up in tch: hdwy on outer over 2f out: sn rdn to chal and ev ch tl drvn ent fnl f and sn one pce* **6/1**[3]
13-P **5** *5* **The Magic Of Rio**[202] 207 3-9-0 85.... AndrewHeffernan(7) 4 66
(Peter Grayson) *chsd ldng pair: rdn along and lost pl 1/2-way: bhd after* **25/1**

1m 10.06s (-3.54) **Going Correction** -0.475s/f (Firm) **5 Ran SP% 110.8**
Speed ratings (Par 102): **104,103,102,100,93**
toteswingers: 1&2 £12.10. CSF £46.86 TOTE £10.60: £2.60, £1.80; EX 71.90.
Owner D G Savala **Bred** H & W Thoroughbreds & Adrian Regan **Trained** Carluke, S Lanarks

FOCUS
Strange to talk about the gaps having to come in a five-runner event, but the outcome of the feature race on the card (the fastest of the night over the 6f trip) was determined by the winner being able to thread between the placed horses inside the final furlong. The quickest of the four C&D times. The winner probably did not have to improve much on his early-season form.
Blown It(USA) ◆ Official explanation: trainer's rep said, regarding the improved form shown, gelding benefited from the removal of cheek pieces

4777 NMT PLANT LTD H'CAP 5f
8:20 (8:20) (Class 6) (0-65,67) 3-Y-O **£2,388** (£705; £352) **Stalls** High

Form RPR
05-2 **1** **Igoyougo**[51] 3063 3-9-1 **59**.... SilvestreDeSousa 2 73
(G A Harker) *cl up: rdn and slt ld 2f out: drvn ent fnl f: edgd lft and kpt on wl* **15/8**[1]

0021 **2** 2 1/4 **Arriva La Diva**[19] 4137 3-8-7 **51**........................ TonyHamilton 1 57
(J J Quinn) *led: rdn along and hdd 2f out: drvn and ev ch tl wknd ins fnl f*
7/2[3]

2321 **3** 2 1/4 **Cheyenne Red (IRE)**[7] 4531 3-9-9 **67**........................ PhillipMakin 5 65
(M Dods) *dwlt and hld up in rr: hdwy over 2f out: rdn wl over 1f out: kpt on ins fnl f: n.d*
2/1[2]

0456 **4** 1 1/2 **Moneysupermarket (IRE)**[13] 4343 3-8-11 **55**............ DanielTudhope 4 47
(Patrick Morris) *a towards rr*
11/1

4030 **5** nk **Trade Price (GR)**[7] 4531 3-8-7 **51** ow1........................(v[1]) TomEaves 3 42
(I Semple) *in tch: effrt to chse ldng pair over 2f out: sn rdn and no imp*
11/1

000 **6** 9 **Maigh Eo (IRE)**[40] 3464 3-8-9 **53**........................ AdrianTNicholls 6 12
(Patrick Morris) *chsd ldrs: rdn along 1/2-way: sn wknd*
25/1

57.96 secs (-2.14) **Going Correction** -0.475s/f (Firm) **6** Ran SP% **110.9**
Speed ratings (Par 98): **98,94,90,88,87 73**
toteswingers: 1&2 £1.60, 1&3 £1.50, 2&3 £1.30. CSF £8.60 TOTE £2.90: £1.70, £1.80; EX 6.30.
Owner Miss K Watson **Bred** Karen Watson **Trained** Thirkleby, N Yorks

FOCUS

Only two of the sextet were ever meaningfully involved in this modest but strongly-run sprint. The clear pick of the three C&D times and good form for the grade.

4778 MUMM DE CRAMANT H'CAP 5f

8:50 (8:52) (Class 6) (0-65,65) 3-Y-O+ **£2,047** (£604; £302) **Stalls** High

Form RPR

6445 **1** **Andrasta**[19] 4136 4-8-11 **50**........................ AdrianTNicholls 3 55
(A Berry) *led 1f: cl up on outer: rdn to ld wl over 1f out: sn edgd rt: drvn ins fnl f and hld on wl*
16/1

0130 **2** 3/4 **What A Fella**[5] 4596 3-8-5 **47**........................(p) SilvestreDeSousa 6 48
(Mrs A Duffield) *midfield: hdwy 2f out: sn rdn and styng on whn edgd rt ent fnl f: sn drvn to chse wnr: no imp towards fin*
9/2[3]

5400 **3** 1 1/4 **Fern House (IRE)**[13] 4346 7-8-0 **46** oh1........................(b) BillyCray(7) 2 44+
(Bruce Hellier) *s.i.s and bhd: hdwy 2f out: sn rdn and styd on strly ins fnl f*
50/1

5060 **4** 3/4 **Blazing Heights**[9] 4467 6-9-2 **55**........................(v[1]) DanielTudhope 10 50
(J S Goldie) *midfield: hdwy 2f out: swtchd lft and styng on wl whn n.m.r ent fnl f: sn swtchd lft and kpt on*
12/1

0035 **5** hd **Kalhan Sands (IRE)**[10] 4436 4-9-7 **60**........................ TonyHamilton 1 54
(J J Quinn) *in rr and sn rdn along: hdwy wl over 1f out: swtchd lft and rdn appr fnl f: styd on wl towards fin*
11/1

6 **6** shd **Frisky Queen (IRE)**[1] 4754 3-7-13 **48** oh1 ow2................ KierenFox(7) 5 41
(T G McCourt, Ire) *in rr: hdwy over 2f out: rdn to chse ldrs whn swtchd rt over 1f out: sn drvn and kpt on: nrst fin*
28/1

0-00 **7** nk **Blakeshall Diamond**[59] 2811 4-8-6 **50** oh1 ow4......... MarkCoumbe(5) 7 43
(A J Chamberlain) *cl up whn hmpd after 1f: prom tl rdn along 2f out and grad wknd*
28/1

4500 **8** 1 **Howards Tipple**[23] 4016 5-8-10 **49**........................ TomEaves 4 38
(I Semple) *midfield: effrt and hdwy wl over 1f out: rdn and n.m.r appr fnl f: sn no imp*
11/1

34 **9** 3/4 **Grudge**[15] 4283 4-9-9 **65**........................ KellyHarrison(3) 12 52
(Ollie Pears) *dwlt: sn cl up on inner and hmpd after 1f: sn led: rdn and hdd wl over 1f out: sn drvn and wknd appr fnl f*
5/2[1]

1226 **10** 3/4 **Toy Top (USA)**[15] 4283 6-9-5 **58**........................(b) PhillipMakin 8 42
(M Dods) *cl up: edgd rt after 1f: rdn along 2f out and ev ch: sn drvn and wknd appr fnl f*
3/1[2]

-000 **11** 2 1/2 **Town And Gown**[9] 4467 4-8-2 **46** oh1........................ PaulPickard(5) 9 21
(J S Goldie) *cl up whn hmpd after 1f and lost pl: swtchd lft and hdwy whn nt clr run over 1f out and again ent fnl f: no ch after*
40/1

446 **12** 2 **Just Joey**[25] 3947 5-8-1 **47**........................(be) AndrewHeffernan(7) 11 15+
(J R Weymes) *cl up whn hmpd after 1f: chsd ldrs tl rdn along and wkng whn bdly hmpd over 1f out: bhd after*
12/1

58.70 secs (-1.40) **Going Correction** -0.475s/f (Firm)
WFA 3 from 4yo+ 3lb **12** Ran SP% **121.0**
Speed ratings (Par 101): **92,90,88,87,87 87,86,85,83,82 78,75**
toteswingers: 1&2 £25.80, 1&3 £40.40, 2&3 £36.80. CSF £86.24 CT £3572.64 TOTE £20.30: £4.50, £2.10, £12.60; EX 172.30 Place 6: £73.55, Place 5: £29.58..
Owner A B Parr **Bred** Peter Barclay **Trained** Cockerham, Lancs
■ Stewards' Enquiry : Kieren Fox five-day ban: careless riding (Aug 22-26)

FOCUS

The largest field of the evening contested a moderate and very rough sprint handicap. The form is rated around the placed horses.

Grudge Official explanation: jockey said gelding hung left

T/Plt: £133.80 to a £1 stake. Pool: £39,119.36. 213.40 winning tickets. T/Qpdt: £38.70 to a £1 stake. Pool: £3,513.90. 67.15 winning tickets. JR

4737 HAYDOCK (L-H)

Saturday, August 8

OFFICIAL GOING: 5f & 6f - good to firm (9.0) remainder - good (good to firm in places; 8.4)

Rail realignment increased distances on round course by 16yards. Inner straight 6f course used.

Wind: Nil Weather: Fine

4779 TURFTV.CO.UK H'CAP 1m 30y

2:10 (2:10) (Class 2) (0-100,98) 3-Y-O+ **£14,571** (£4,335; £2,166; £1,082) **Stalls** Low

Form RPR

2404 **1** **Balcarce Nov (ARG)**[21] 4077 4-10-0 **98**........................ MickyFenton 11 108
(T P Tate) *hld up: hdwy over 3f out: sn hung lft: wnt 2nd over 1f out: r.o to nose ahd towards fin*
66/1

6002 **2** nse **Billy Dane (IRE)**[5] 4592 5-8-13 **83**........................(p) RobertWinston 2 93
(F P Murtagh) *led: rdn and carried hd awkwardly over 2f out: hdd narrowly towards fin but r.o for press*
11/1

5004 **3** 2 **Opus Maximus (IRE)**[6] 4560 4-9-2 **86**........................ JoeFanning 8 91
(M Johnston) *trckd ldrs: effrt to try and chal 2f out: nt qckn ins fnl f* **11/2**[3]

0022 **4** 1 3/4 **Flipando (IRE)**[37] 3530 8-9-10 **97**........................ NeilBrown(3) 6 98
(T D Barron) *hld up: hdwy 3f out: rdn 2f out: styd on ins fnl f but nt pce to get to ldrs*
7/1

15 **5** 1 1/2 **Angel Rock (IRE)**[56] 2933 4-9-1 **85**........................(p) JimmyFortune 5 83
(M Botti) *trckd ldrs: pushed along 3f out: styd on same pce fr over 1f out*
9/2[1]

012 **6** 1 1/4 **One Way Or Another (AUS)**[29] 3796 6-9-8 **92**........ StephenDonohoe 14 87
(J R Gask) *hld up: hdwy 3f out: rdn to chse ldrs over 1f out: no real imp and one pce fnl 100yds*
5/1[2]

4213 **7** 3 3/4 **Cobo Bay**[14] 4310 4-9-7 **91**........................(v[1]) LDettori 3 77
(K A Ryan) *s.i.s: sn in tch: rdn over 2f out: no imp on ldrs: wl btn ins fnl f*
7/1

3-00 **8** 3 1/4 **Bolodenka (IRE)**[133] 997 7-9-3 **94**........................ FrazerWilliams(7) 9 73
(R A Fahey) *missed break: bhd: pushed along 4f out: kpt on steadily fr over 1f out: nvr on terms w ldrs*
40/1

116 **9** 2 **Lowther**[50] 3116 4-9-7 **91**........................ NeilChalmers 7 65
(A Bailey) *midfield: pushed along over 2f out: edgd lft fr over 1f out: nvr a danger*
15/2

000 **10** 4 **Ansells Pride (IRE)**[11] 4400 6-8-10 **80**........................ TomEaves 12 45
(B Smart) *prom: hung lft fr 4f out: wknd 3f out*
25/1

0011 **11** 3 1/2 **The Osteopath (IRE)**[44] 3312 6-9-10 **94**........................ PhillipMakin 4 51
(M Dods) *midfield: rdn 3f out: sn outpcd: wknd 1f out*
8/1

535- **12** 18 **Silver Rime (FR)**[316] 6249 4-9-2 **86**........................ RoystonFfrench 10 —
(Miss L A Perratt) *prom: pushed along over 2f out: sn wknd*
33/1

1m 41.61s (-2.19) **Going Correction** -0.20s/f (Firm) **12** Ran SP% **117.2**
Speed ratings (Par 109): **102,101,99,98,96 95,91,88,86,82 78,60**
toteswingers: 1&2 £62.10, 1&3 £50.10, 2&3 £15.60. CSF £664.08 CT £4692.14 TOTE £67.90: £12.50, £3.30, £2.50; EX 399.90 TRIFECTA Not won..
Owner Mrs Fitri Hay **Bred** Firmamento **Trained** Tadcaster, N Yorks
■ Stewards' Enquiry : Robert Winston caution: careless riding

FOCUS

Following a dry night, the ground on the sprint course was described as good to firm, while on the round course it was good, good to firm in places. An open-looking handicap, but when the declarations were made the ground was on the easy side, and so a number found conditions quicker than they would have liked. That probably helps to explain the shock result. The runner-up is the key to the form.

NOTEBOOK

Balcarce Nov(ARG) travelled well out the back, was brought with his challenge wide and just edged out the long-time leader on the line. Fifth in an Argentine Group 1 last autumn, he ran well in his first two starts in Dubai in the spring but didn't handle the dirt in the UAE Derby and probably found the combination of soft ground and lack of race-fitness against him on his first start for his current stable last month. Back on quick ground, he showed his true ability, and while his price would suggest little had been expected, he does hold a Group 2 entry, suggesting connections have faith that he can make it in Pattern company over here. (op 50-1)

Billy Dane(IRE), who had the cheekpieces back on for the first time this year, set a good gallop out in front and was only just denied. He takes his racing well and likes fast ground, so the drying conditions were definitely in his favour. (op 12-1)

Opus Maximus(IRE) represented Mark Johnston, who had sent out two of the previous four winners of this race. He's another who takes plenty of racing and, just six days after putting in a solid effort at Chester, he ran another sound race in defeat. He's on a mark he should be able to win off. (op 6-1 tchd 13-2 in places)

Flipando(IRE) had conditions to suit and, given a patient ride as usual, came through and passed some rivals late on. He could never threaten the first two, though, and his current mark is higher than he has ever won off.

Angel Rock(IRE), wearing cheekpieces for the first time, is a steadily progressive miler but has a preference for softer ground and the drying conditions were against him. He's one to bear in mind for when the weather turns again. (op 7-1)

One Way Or Another(AUS) has been in good form of late but he'd never previously run on ground this quick and perhaps he, too, will be more effective back on an easier surface. (op 6-1)

Cobo Bay is another who was brought here in search of a bit of cut but found the ground going against him. (tchd 6-1)

Ansells Pride(IRE) Official explanation: jockey said gelding hung left

The Osteopath(IRE) Official explanation: jockey said gelding was unsuited by the good (good to firm in places) ground

4780 TOTEPOOL ROSE OF LANCASTER STKS (GROUP 3) 1m 2f 95y

2:40 (2:41) (Class 1) 3-Y-O+

£36,900 (£13,988; £7,000; £3,490; £1,748; £877) **Stalls** Centre

Form RPR

2-06 **1** **Jukebox Jury (IRE)**[35] 3640 3-8-8 **109**........................ RoystonFfrench 5 119
(M Johnston) *prom: dropped to midfield over 5f out: pushed along over 3f out: rallied to chse ldrs over 1f out: r.o to ld ins fnl 75yds: wl on top at fin*
6/1

-020 **2** 1 1/4 **Campanologist (USA)**[30] 3781 4-9-3 **115**........................ LDettori 2 117
(Saeed Bin Suroor) *trckd ldrs: rdn to ld 2f out: hdd ins fnl 75yds: hld after*
9/4[1]

1140 **3** 1 **Duncan**[30] 3781 4-9-3 **119**........................ JimmyFortune 1 115
(J H M Gosden) *hld up: hdwy over 2f out: rdn to chse ldr wl over 1f out: lost 2nd and nt qckn ins fnl f*
10/3[2]

6663 **4** 1/2 **Traffic Guard (USA)**[21] 4090 5-9-3 **113**........................ MickyFenton 9 114
(P F I Cole) *s.i.s: hld up: hdwy over 2f out: rdn to chse ldrs over 1f out: styd on ins fnl f: nt quite pce to chal*
12/1

1262 **5** 4 **Staying On (IRE)**[28] 3882 4-9-3 **110**........................(t) ShaneKelly 7 107
(W R Swinburn) *racd keenly: prom: rdn over 2f out: outpcd over 1f out*
9/1

0-00 **6** 1 1/2 **Supaseus**[13] 4352 6-9-3 **105**........................ RobertWinston 6 104
(H Morrison) *racd keenly and hung rt most of way: led: rdn and hdd 2f out: wknd ins fnl f*
40/1

5-13 **7** 7 **Tranquil Tiger**[36] 3585 5-9-3 **114**........................(b) EddieAhern 8 90
(H R A Cecil) *prom: n.m.r briefly after 100yds: sn lost pl and dropped to rr: hdwy 6f out: rdn over 2f out: wknd over 1f out*
9/2[3]

-441 **8** 18 **Philatelist (USA)**[150] 801 5-9-3 **105**........................ RobertHavlin 3 56
(M A Jarvis) *hld up: rdn over 2f out: sn dropped away*
16/1

2m 9.95s (-3.05) **Going Correction** -0.20s/f (Firm)
WFA 3 from 4yo+ 9lb **8** Ran SP% **112.3**
Speed ratings (Par 113): **113,112,111,110,107 106,100,86**
toteswingers: 1&2 £4.80, 1&3 £4.60, 2&3 £1.90. CSF £19.19 TOTE £6.60: £1.80, £1.20, £1.70; EX 17.90 Trifecta £17.20 Pool: £844.70 - 36.30 winning units..
Owner A D Spence **Bred** Paul Nataf **Trained** Middleham Moor, N Yorks

FOCUS

Three-year-olds had taken six of the previous eight runnings of this Group 3 and, with evidence already pointing to this year's Classic generation being a strong bunch, Jukebox Jury's success only went to confirm that impression. This was a decent renewal with the runner-up probably the best guide.

NOTEBOOK

Jukebox Jury(IRE), last year's Royal Lodge winner, needed his comeback run from injury but shaped with a good deal more promise when sixth in what can now be safely called a red-hot Eclipse last time out. Down in grade and in receipt of a nice weight allowance from the older horses, his stamina saw him through off a good early gallop, and there's every chance he'll appreciate a step up to 1m4f this autumn. He's in the Great Voltigeur, but strangely doesn't hold an entry in the St Leger. (op 11-2 tchd 7-1)

Campanologist(USA) ran a sound race with conditions to suit, leaving behind his disappointing effort at Newmarket, but was unable to concede the weight to the three-year-old. This is as good as he is. (op 5-2 tchd 3-1 in a place)

Duncan had the race run to suit with a contested lead up front, and he settled a lot better than at Newmarket. He stays further than this too, so had things set up for him to challenge late, but couldn't quite muster the pace. Perhaps he needs a break as he's been on the go since the spring. (tchd 3-1 and 4-1)
Traffic Guard(USA) challenged nearest the stands' rail in the straight, which was probably not an advantage, as the best ground appeared to be up the middle. He's well up to winning at this level at his best, but has a poor strike-rate. (tchd 11-1 and 14-1)
Staying On(IRE) likes to make the running but was denied his own way in front by the keen-going Supaseus, and neither did each other any favours. (op 8-1 tchd 15-2)
Supaseus Official explanation: jockey said helding hung right throughout
Tranquil Tiger settled pretty well off the decent gallop but found little under pressure. He tends to be found out when he ventures out of Listed company and it was the same story this time. (op 5-1)

4781 TOTESCOOP6 STKS (HERITAGE H'CAP) 1m 2f 95y
3:15 (3:20) (Class 2) (0-105,104) 3-Y-0+
£40,501 (£12,129; £6,064; £3,035; £1,514; £760) **Stalls** Centre

Form RPR
-162 **1** **Libel Law**[23] 4020 3-8-10 **99** LDettori 16 111
(M A Jarvis) *in tch: effrt to ld over 1f out: r.o wl fnl f: wl in control towards fin* **6/1**[3]
2400 **2** *2 1/4* **Nanton (USA)**[14] 4297 7-8-13 **93** DanielTudhope 7 101
(J S Goldie) *hld up: rdn and hdwy over 1f out: r.o to take 2nd towards fin: nt pce to rch wnr* **16/1**
-000 **3** *nk* **Laterly (IRE)**[28] 3873 4-8-9 **89** MickyFenton 2 96
(T P Tate) *racd keenly: a.p: rdn to ld over 2f out: hdd over 1f out: styd on same pce ins fnl f* **25/1**
2211 **4** *shd* **Dancourt (IRE)**[16] 4247 3-8-2 **91** RoystonFfrench 13 98
(Sir Michael Stoute) *racd keenly in midfield: pushed along 3f out: hdwy over 2f out: styd on ins fnl f: nt quite pce of ldrs* **5/2**[1]
-043 **5** *1 1/4* **The Which Doctor**[11] 4409 4-8-7 **87** ShaneKelly 8 92
(J Noseda) *hld up: rdn and hdwy over 1f out: r.o and gd prog towards fin* **14/1**
4340 **6** *shd* **Re Barolo (IRE)**[28] 3873 6-9-8 **102** JimmyFortune 11 106
(M Botti) *racd keenly in midfield: pushed along 2f out: hdwy over 1f out: styd on ins fnl f: nt pce to get to ldrs* **8/1**
5020 **7** *shd* **Ilie Nastase (FR)**[7] 4549 5-8-2 **85** (p) AndreaAtzeni(3) 6 89
(D Nicholls) *t.k.h: trckd ldrs: rdn to chal 2f out: no ex fnl 100yds* **22/1**
304- **8** *5* **Alfie Flits**[127] 6106 7-9-10 **104** RobertWinston 10 99
(G A Swinbank) *hld up: pushed along and sme hdwy over 2f out: nvr on terms w ldrs* **33/1**
0146 **9** *1 1/4* **Charlie Cool**[13] 4352 6-9-5 **99** AndrewElliott 9 91
(Mrs R A Carr) *in tch: rdn over 2f out: wknd fnl f* **16/1**
3421 **10** *3 3/4* **Summer Gold (IRE)**[14] 4328 5-8-3 **83** DaleGibson 4 68
(E J Alston) *midfield: rdn 2f out: wknd over 1f out* **14/1**
2662 **11** *1/2* **Sweet Lightning**[11] 4404 4-8-9 **89** EddieAhern 12 73
(W R Muir) *hld up: pushed along 3f out: no imp: wl btn 1f out* **4/1**[2]
0200 **12** *1* **Kandidate**[50] 3089 7-9-9 **103** LPKeniry 17 85
(C E Brittain) *midfield: effrt and sme hdwy to chse ldrs 3f out: wknd over 2f out* **40/1**
0022 **13** *2* **Cheshire Prince**[14] 4315 5-8-13 **93** LiamJones 1 72
(W M Brisbourne) *led: rdn and hdd over 2f out: wknd over 1f out* **22/1**
-500 **14** *4* **Bon Spiel**[133] 1004 5-9-6 **100** JamieSpencer 15 71
(L M Cumani) *prom: rdn to chal over 2f out: hung lft and wknd wl over 1f out* **28/1**
/20- **15** *8* **Cold Quest (USA)**[273] 7244 5-9-0 **94** RobertHavlin 5 50
(Miss L A Perratt) *fly-jmpd leaving stalls: a bhd* **50/1**

2m 10.42s (-2.58) **Going Correction** -0.20s/f (Firm)
WFA 3 from 4yo+ 9lb **15 Ran SP% 122.4**
Speed ratings (Par 109): **111,109,108,108,107 107,107,103,102,99 99,98,96,93,87**
toteswingers: 1&2 £20.70, 1&3 £37.40, 2&3 £84.10. CSF £90.78 CT £2257.22 TOTE £6.40: £2.50, £4.10, £8.20; EX 138.60 Trifecta £2520.80 Pool: £26,570.89 - 7.80 winning units..
Owner Sheikh Ahmed Al Maktoum **Bred** Darley **Trained** Newmarket, Suffolk

FOCUS
This valuable heritage handicap was run in a time just 0.47sec slower than the earlier Group 3 race. A clear personal best from the winner with the solid runner-up a good guide.

NOTEBOOK
Libel Law was the least-exposed runner in the line-up, having had just the four previous starts, and was running in a handicap for the first time after competing in Group company earlier in the campaign. A son of Kingmambo, he relished the drying ground, showed a nice turn of foot to take over in front and ran on in taking style. He'll be rated in the mid 100s after this, so a step up to Listed company can be expected.
Nanton(USA) was back over a more suitable trip and returned to his best in a race run to suit. He stayed on strongly from the back of the field, but the unexposed winner had simply gone beyond recall. He remains capable in these types of events, granted ground on the fast side.
Laterly(IRE) probably finds this trip on the short side, so in the circumstances he ran a sound race, especially as he had to accept a position behind the leader, rather than out in front, as he prefers. (op 20-1)
Dancourt(IRE) was strong in the market beforehand on his hat-trick bid, but the ground was much quicker than when he'd been declared and, while he won on good to firm at Sandown, the suspicion is that this son of Cadeaux Genereux will be much happier getting his toe in a bit. He remains of interest for the Cambridgeshire, with autumn ground likely to bring about improvement. (op 11-4 tchd 3-1 in places)
The Which Doctor was trying a new trip and seemed to stay well enough, having been ridden patiently. Now connections know that there isn't an issue with stamina perhaps he'll be ridden a bit more positively in future. (op 12-1)
Re Barolo(IRE), representing an in-form yard, appeared to have his chance but wasn't good enough. (op 12-1 tchd 14-1)
Ilie Nastase(FR), wearing cheekpieces for the first time, drifted towards the far side as he tired in the closing stages while the main action unfolded up the centre. He won over an extended 1m1f when trained in France, but this trip probably just stretches him a touch. (tchd 20-1)
Alfie Flits had a tough task under top weight on his return a 127-day break. He's entitled to come on for it. (op 28-1 tchd 25-1)
Sweet Lightning was brought to have his chance but dropped out tamely and it's possible his hard race at Goodwood 11 days earlier had left its mark. Official explanation: jockey said gelding ran flat (op 5-1 tchd 7-2)

4782 JOHN AND ALISON FITZGIBBONS ANNIVERSARY NURSERY 5f
3:50 (3:54) (Class 2) 2-Y-0 **£11,333** (£3,372; £1,685; £841) **Stalls** Centre

Form RPR
12 **1** **Skylla**[23] 4000 2-9-7 **82** JerryO'Dwyer 4 90+
(J R Holt) *mde all: rdn over 1f out: r.o wl fnl furlong and a in command* **3/1**[1]
31 **2** *2 1/2* **Duchess Dora (IRE)**[95] 1764 2-9-3 **78** GrahamGibbons 5 77
(J J Quinn) *chsd wnr thrght: rdn and nt qckn over 1f out: kpt on but no imp fnl f* **3/1**[1]
3500 **3** *nk* **Shibhan**[12] 4383 2-8-6 **67** LiamJones 8 65
(C E Brittain) *in rr: pushed along and outpcd 3f out: hdwy 2f out: styd on to chal for pls fnl f but nt pce of wnr* **15/2**
0303 **4** *1/2* **Olympic Ceremony**[14] 4306 2-8-9 **70** RobertWinston 2 66
(R A Fahey) *prom: rdn over 1f out: kpt on same pce fnl f* **13/2**[3]
342 **5** *1 1/4* **Bossy Kitty**[14] 4327 2-8-7 **68** EddieAhern 7 60
(N Tinkler) *in tch: rdn over 2f out: one pce fr over 1f out* **10/3**[2]
310 **6** *nk* **Duke Of Rainford**[17] 4195 2-7-9 **59** oh6 (t) AndreaAtzeni(3) 9 50
(Ian Williams) *got upset in stalls: hld up: rdn 2f out: no imp* **14/1**
4010 **7** *nk* **Gertmegalush (IRE)**[14] 4327 2-9-1 **76** RoystonFfrench 1 65
(J D Bethell) *missed break: bhd: rdn over 1f out: nvr able to get on terms* **8/1**

60.37 secs (-0.73) **Going Correction** -0.275s/f (Firm) **7 Ran SP% 116.0**
Speed ratings (Par 100): **94,90,89,88,86 86,85**
toteswingers: 1&2 £2.50, 1&3 £5.50, 2&3 £5.80. CSF £12.63 CT £60.67 TOTE £3.60: £2.00, £2.60; EX 10.40.
Owner Facts & Figures **Bred** Bearstone Stud **Trained** Peckleton, Leics

FOCUS
Three of the previous eight winners of this nursery had defied top weight, and Skylla continued their good record. She showed improved form.

NOTEBOOK
Skylla got a bit warm beforehand and was on her toes before going in the stalls, but she has bags of speed and once the gates opened was quickly into her stride. The rest never got near her and she ran out a clear winner. She was only narrowly denied over 6f last time, but this looks her trip and her trainer now plans to give her a break before bringing her back next month for a Listed race. (op 5-2 tchd 7-2 in places)
Duchess Dora(IRE), who hadn't been seen since winning her maiden at Catterick back in May, held on in a tight finish for second, but she could never really get to grips with the winner, who was clearly let in lightly. Hopefully, there is some improvement to come because, on this evidence, it would seem the handicapper wasn't far off in his assessment of her. (tchd 4-1 tchd 9-2 in places)
Shibhan challenged more towards the far rail so might not have been on the best ground, but she has not found the drop back to the minimum trip helping her and looks to want a return to 6f. (op 12-1 tchd 7-1)
Olympic Ceremony was held on his nursery debut over 6f on easy ground and didn't improve for a drop back to 5f on a quicker surface. (op 15-2 tchd 8-1)
Bossy Kitty, who got a bit warm beforehand, ran well in defeat on her handicap debut at York but failed to build on that effort. Official explanation: jockey said filly was unsuited by the good to firm ground (op 4-1)
Duke Of Rainford had a tough task from 6lb out of the weights and played up in the stalls. (tchd 11-1)
Gertmegalush(IRE) looks to have issues as he missed the break badly and seemed far from keen to race early on. Official explanation: jockey said gelding was reluctant to race (tchd 13-2)

4783 DUKE OF LANCASTER'S OWN YEOMANRY H'CAP 6f
4:25 (4:26) (Class 5) (0-70,71) 3-Y-0+ **£4,857** (£1,445; £541; £541) **Stalls** Centre

Form RPR
0032 **1** **Medici Time**[39] 3491 4-9-3 **62** (v) GrahamGibbons 7 76
(T D Easterby) *racd keenly: w ldr: led 4f out: travelled strly thrght: shkn up 1f out: r.o wl and a in command* **8/1**
-250 **2** *2 1/2* **Jack Rackham**[91] 1885 5-9-8 **67** (v) RoystonFfrench 9 73
(B Smart) *led: hdd 4f out: racd in 2nd pl after: rdn over 2f out: kpt on u.p but nt pce of wnr* **16/1**
1655 **3** *3/4* **Elijah Pepper (USA)**[37] 3529 4-9-7 **69** NeilBrown(3) 10 73+
(T D Barron) *in rr: rdn over 2f out: hdwy to chse ldrs over 1f out: styd on u.p fnl f but nvr threatened wnr* **17/2**
0611 **3** *dht* **Capone (IRE)**[3] 4668 4-9-12 **71** 6ex RobertWinston 6 75
(Garry Moss) *hld up: hdwy 3f out: rdn to chse ldrs over 1f out: kpt on u.p: nt pce to mount serious chal* **15/8**[1]
06-1 **5** *2 1/4* **Onebidkintymill (IRE)**[38] 3505 4-9-6 **65** MickyFenton 8 61
(R Hollinshead) *midfield: rdn and hung lft over 1f out: one pce fnl f* **13/2**[3]
6421 **6** *9* **Jilly Why (IRE)**[9] 4469 8-9-7 **66** (b) JamieSpencer 13 34
(Paul Green) *in rr: rdn over 2f out: nvr able to get on terms w ldng bunch* **5/1**[2]
1265 **7** *1 1/4* **Flying Applause**[9] 4469 4-9-6 **68** (bt) AndreaAtzeni(3) 11 32
(S R Bowring) *bmpd s: hld up: rdn over 3f out: nvr on terms* **11/1**
3246 **8** *1 1/4* **Atlantic Beach**[28] 3855 4-9-6 **68** JackMitchell(3) 2 28
(J Hetherton) *chsd ldrs: pushed along 3f out: rdn over 2f out: wknd over 1f out* **11/1**
4100 **9** *1* **Volito**[43] 3342 3-9-3 **66** EddieAhern 4 22
(Jonjo O'Neill) *prom: lost pl 3f out: sn rdn: n.d after* **25/1**
1000 **10** *hd* **Sea Rover (IRE)**[15] 4285 5-9-11 **70** DaleGibson 12 26
(M Brittain) *prom: pushed along over 2f out: wknd over 1f out* **14/1**

1m 12.26s (-2.24) **Going Correction** -0.275s/f (Firm)
WFA 3 from 4yo+ 4lb **10 Ran SP% 119.5**
Speed ratings (Par 103): **103,99,98,98,95 83,82,80,79,78**
PL: Medici Time £2.60 Jack Rackham £4.10 Capone £0.60 Elijah Pepper £1.40. TRICAST: MT-JR-C £170.91 MT-JR-EP £562.49. toteswingers: MT&JR £15.40, MT&C £2.80, MT&EP £5.50, JR&C £5.50, JR&EP £11.50. CSF £130.10 TOTE £10.20; EX 82.80.
Owner Mrs C A Hodgetts **Bred** Mrs Fiona Denniff **Trained** Great Habton, N Yorks

FOCUS
Just as in the nursery earlier on the card, early speed won the day here. Sound form, with a personal best from the winner.
Onebidkintymill(IRE) Official explanation: jockey said gelding was unsuited by the good to firm ground
Jilly Why(IRE) Official explanation: jockey said mare was unsuited by the good to firm ground
Sea Rover(IRE) Official explanation: jockey said horse lost its action 2f out

4784 RACING UK H'CAP 6f
5:00 (5:01) (Class 3) (0-95,92) 3-Y-0+ **£9,714** (£2,890; £1,444; £721) **Stalls** Centre

Form RPR
2220 **1** **Everymanforhimself (IRE)**[8] 4485 5-9-11 **92** (v) JamieSpencer 6 103
(K A Ryan) *hld up: hdwy over 2f out: drvn over 1f out: r.o to ld wl ins fnl f: wl on top at fin* **7/1**
3021 **2** *1 1/2* **Red Cape (FR)**[5] 4598 6-9-6 **87** 6ex AndrewElliott 8 93
(Mrs R A Carr) *in tch: effrt to chal 1f out: styd on to take 2nd towards fin: wl hld by wnr* **7/2**[1]
0120 **3** *1/2* **First In Command (IRE)**[13] 4360 4-9-0 **81** (t) ShaneKelly 9 86
(Daniel Mark Loughnane, Ire) *towards rr: hdwy to chse ldrs 3f out: rdn to chal fr 1f out: nt qckn ins fnl 100yds* **8/1**
1261 **4** *nk* **Aye Aye Digby (IRE)**[15] 4273 4-9-11 **92** FergusSweeney 7 96
(H Candy) *chsd ldrs: wnt 2nd 3f out: rdn to ld over 1f out: hdd wl ins fnl f: no ex towards fin* **9/2**[2]
3110 **5** *1* **Novellen Lad (IRE)**[32] 3706 4-9-5 **86** EddieAhern 12 86
(E J Alston) *midfield: hdwy to chse ldrs over 2f out: chal 1f out: one pce fnl 75yds* **9/2**[2]

5500 **6** ¾ **Wyatt Earp (IRE)**[13] 4353 8-8-11 **78** DaleGibson 10 76
(P Salmon) *towards rr: effrt over 1f out: styd on but nt pce to chal ldrs* **20/1**

-335 **7** 1 **Kashimin (IRE)**[59] 2814 4-8-13 **80** RobertWinston 3 75
(G A Swinbank) *hld up in rr: pushed along 2f out: kpt on fnl f: nvr able to rch chalng position* **16/1**

3320 **8** nk **Legal Eagle (IRE)**[13] 4341 4-8-10 **80** NeilBrown(3) 1 74
(Paul Green) *led: rdn and hdd over 1f out: wknd ins fnl f* **16/1**

0414 **9** 6 **Dancing Maite**[13] 4353 4-9-0 **84** AndreaAtzeni(3) 2 59
(S R Bowring) *prom: pushed along over 2f out: wknd over 1f out* **11/2**[3]

6000 **10** 12 **Supermassive Muse (IRE)**[60] 2782 4-8-13 **80**.....(p) GrahamGibbons 4 16
(E S McMahon) *prom tl wknd 2f out* **33/1**

1m 11.79s (-2.71) **Going Correction** -0.275s/f (Firm) **10** Ran SP% **117.0**
Speed ratings (Par 107): **107,105,104,103,102 101,100,99,91,75**
toteswingers: 1&2 £4.50, 1&3 £13.60, 2&3 £8.10. CSF £31.86 CT £203.40 TOTE £6.80: £2.40, £1.60, £3.20; EX 32.90.
Owner J Duddy B McDonald & A Heeney **Bred** Denis McDonnell **Trained** Hambleton, N Yorks

FOCUS
A competitive sprint. Straightforward form judged around the front pair.

NOTEBOOK
Everymanforhimself(IRE) is a consistent sort, granted his conditions, and the drying ground was certainly in his favour here. Held up, but not too far off the gallop, the gelding came through under a strong ride inside the last and finally got his reward for some solid efforts this term. The Ayr Gold Cup is the plan providing the ground is suitable, but a rise in the weights will probably leave him vulnerable again, as it must be remembered that this was just his third success in his last 28 starts. (op 6-1)
Red Cape(FR), carrying a penalty for his Ripon win, was never too far away on a track suited to his style of running. In great form at present, he's been pencilled in for the Great St Wilfrid at Ripon next Saturday. (op 10-3 tchd 4-1 in places)
First In Command(IRE) has been getting bogged down in the mud back home this year but has run well on quicker ground over here. Despite being by Captain Rio, a fast surface is clearly the key to him, as his form figures of 021123 on good to firm reveals. (op 11-1 tchd 12-1 in places)
Aye Aye Digby(IRE), on the other hand, prefers a bit of dig, so connections will no doubt have been disappointed to see the ground dry out so much since the declaration stage. He didn't run badly in the circumstances. (op 5-1)
Novellen Lad(IRE), who found the ground too soft at Pontefract last time, sweated up beforehand, but he's done that before and won. He raced on the stands' side of the group, though, which was probably no advantage, and didn't quite have it at the finish. (op 5-1 tchd 6-1)
Wyatt Earp(IRE) hasn't been in much form recently and, although he's now dropped to a lower mark than when last successful, there wasn't really enough in this effort to encourage support next time. (tchd 22-1)
Kashimin(IRE) was slowly away and struggled to get involved on this speed-favouring track. (op 18-1)
Dancing Maite was beaten off quickly and his rider eased him right down in the closing stages, so all may not have been well. (op 13-2)

4785 BUY A RACING POST YEARLING BONUS CANDIDATE H'CAP 1m 6f
5:30 (5:30) (Class 3) (0-95,92) 3-Y-O **£11,527** (£3,430; £1,714; £856) **Stalls** Low

Form RPR

2211 **1** **Stanstill (IRE)**[14] 4299 3-9-2 **87** RobertWinston 1 94
(G A Swinbank) *slipped coming out of stalls: racd keenly: prom: rdn over 2f out: led over 1f out: edgd rt ins fnl f: styd on* **5/2**[2]

2120 **2** 1 **Interdiamonds**[14] 4299 3-8-3 **74** JoeFanning 4 79
(M Johnston) *racd keenly: a.p: rdn to draw upsides over 2f out: nt qckn over 1f out: kpt on u.p ins fnl f* **11/2**

1132 **3** nk **Final Victory**[16] 4248 3-9-0 **85** LPKeniry 3 90
(A M Balding) *led: rdn whn pressed over 2f out: hdd over 1f out: styd on same pce ins fnl f* **11/4**[3]

221 **4** ¾ **Spiekeroog**[31] 3731 3-8-9 **80** EddieAhern 2 84
(H R A Cecil) *racd keenly: hld up in rr: effrt 2f out: kpt on ins fnl f: nvr quite able to land a serous blow* **13/8**[1]

3m 5.21s (0.91) **Going Correction** -0.20s/f (Firm) **4** Ran SP% **108.7**
Speed ratings (Par 104): **89,88,88,87**
toteswingers: 1&2 £8.10 CSF £14.33 TOTE £2.70; EX 12.90 Place 6: £171.23 Place 5: £28.23.
Owner The Twopin Partnership **Bred** E J Daly **Trained** Melsonby, N Yorks

FOCUS
Despite the small field this was a tight affair. They went an ordinary gallop early on and the race turned into something of a sprint. Probably form to take fairly positively despite the muddling nature of the race.

NOTEBOOK
Stanstill(IRE) took a grip early but he won last time at Ascot after racing keenly, and, challenging nearest the centre of the track in the closing stages, found plenty under pressure to edge ahead. He wandered about a bit once in front, but the race was in safe keeping by then and it made no difference. This was not a proper test at the trip but it looks to suit him and, given the narrowness of victory, he could well go in again, as the handicapper will once again be restricted in the amount he can put him up in the weights. (op 9-4)
Interdiamonds got a lot closer to Stanstill than she did at Ascot last time, but was unable to reverse the form despite being 6lb better off at the weights and getting the jump on him inside the final 3f. (op 6-1 tchd 5-1)
Final Victory, who was coltish and got a bit warm beforehand, took them along and, in theory, was best placed when the dash for the line began. He might not want to go this far, though, and could benefit from a drop back to 1m4f, a trip over which he recorded his best effort so far in a hot little handicap at Salisbury in June. (op 9-4)
Spiekeroog showed that stamina is his strong suit when scoring over this trip at Catterick last time, so the way this race was run wouldn't have suited him at all. He may well turn this form around in a stronger-run race. (op 9-4 tchd 5-2 in places)
T/Jkpt: Not won. T/Plt: £278.40 to a £1 stake. Pool: £113,554.65. 297.75 winning tickets. T/Qpdt: £30.20 to a £1 stake. Pool: £5,621.57. 137.65 winning tickets. DO

4743 LINGFIELD (L-H)
Saturday, August 8

OFFICIAL GOING: Turf course - good (good to soft in places); all-weather - standard
Wind: nil Weather: very warm amd muggy

4786 HAPPY BIRTHDAY HELEN MAIDEN STKS 6f
5:40 (5:44) (Class 5) 3-Y-O+ **£2,729** (£806; £403) **Stalls** High

Form RPR

04 **1** **Sutton Veny (IRE)**[18] 4164 3-8-12 0 PatCosgrave 12 70
(J R Gask) *led tl wl over 3f out: styd pressing ldr: rdn 2f out led again narrowly ins fnl f: hld on wl* **25/1**

652 **2** shd **Present Alchemy**[14] 4324 3-9-3 74 TravisBlock 11 75
(H Morrison) *w wnr tl led wl over 3f out: rdn and edgd lft over 1f out: hdd narrowly ins fnl f: a jst hld after* **9/2**[2]

2 **3** 3¾ **Major Lawrence (IRE)**[29] 3813 3-9-3 0 RichardHughes 9 63
(J Noseda) *chsd ldng pair: rdn over 2f out: hrd drvn and no imp fr over 1f out* **1/2**[1]

62 **4** 1 **Mata Hari Blue**[17] 4199 3-8-12 0 J-PGuillambert 8 55
(J R Holt) *chsd ldrs: rdn 2f out: hrd drvn and kpt on same pce fr over 1f out* **12/1**[3]

U **5** ½ **Louise Sauvage**[14] 4324 3-8-12 0 RichardThomas 13 53
(M D I Usher) *wnt rt s and s.i.s: hdwy into midfield but stl wl off the pce 4f out: rdn and swtchd lft 2f out: kpt on fnl f: nvr trbld ldrs* **100/1**

0/0 **6** nk **So Glamorous**[18] 4180 4-8-9 0 SimonPearce(7) 15 53
(C F Wall) *s.i.s: racd wl off the pce in midfield: rdn 2f out: kpt on fnl f: nvr trbld ldrs* **25/1**

7 5 **Poppanan (USA)** 3-9-3 0 TonyCulhane 2 41
(S Dow) *s.i.s and swtchd rt s: bhd: rdn over 2f out: kpt on fnl f: nvr nr ldrs* **40/1**

0 **8** 2½ **Early Morning Rain (IRE)**[45] 3278 3-8-9 0...........(e[1]) DavidProbert(3) 6 28
(Rae Guest) *swtchd rt s: wl bhd: sme modest hdwy u.p over 2f out: nvr nr ldrs* **25/1**

0 **9** shd **Public Image**[60] 2795 3-8-12 0 SimonWhitworth 4 28
(Jamie Poulton) *s.i.s and swtchd rt s: wl bhd: sme modest hdwy fnl f: nvr nr ldrs* **100/1**

40 **10** shd **Spring Bridge (IRE)**[14] 4303 3-9-3 0 FrankieMcDonald 7 33
(Mrs L C Jewell) *a towards rr: rdn 3f out: nvr nr ldrs* **100/1**

11 2¼ **Keibla Spirit** 3-8-12 0 PaulDoe 3 20
(R Ingram) *swtchd rt s: a wl bhd* **100/1**

36 **12** 1¼ **Bobble Rock (IRE)**[18] 4180 3-9-0 0 MarcHalford(3) 17 21
(J R Best) *a wl bhd: rdn and no prog 3f out* **33/1**

13 1½ **Copper Sovereign** 7-9-0 0 NathanAlison(7) 1 18
(Jamie Poulton) *swtchd rt s: a wl bhd* **50/1**

14 ¾ **Captain Teddo** 3-9-3 0.............................(t) TGMcLaughlin 10 14
(R Ingram) *s.i.s: a wl bhd* **66/1**

-200 **15** 5 **Alpha Tauri (USA)**[30] 3764 3-9-3 74...........................(b[1]) IanMongan 14 —
(H R A Cecil) *chsd ldrs tl wknd rapidly over 2f out: virtually p.u ins fnl f* **12/1**[3]

1m 11.06s (-0.14) **Going Correction** +0.025s/f (Good)
WFA 3 from 4yo+ 4lb **15** Ran SP% **124.6**
Speed ratings (Par 103): **101,100,95,94,93 93,86,83,83,83 80,78,76,75,68**
toteswingers: 1&2 £12.00, 1&3 £4.10, 2&3 £1.40. CSF £132.94 TOTE £48.40: £8.10, £1.60, £1.02; EX 307.40.
Owner The Sutton Veny Syndicate **Bred** Rathbarry Stud **Trained** Sutton Veny, Wilts

FOCUS
An uncompetitive maiden in which they were well strung out from a very early stage and the front two filled those positions throughout. The form is rated around the runner-up and fourth.

4787 10% CASHBACK AT CORAL.CO.UK H'CAP 6f
6:10 (6:14) (Class 5) (0-75,74) 3-Y-O+ **£3,070** (£906; £453) **Stalls** High

Form RPR

5140 **1** **Lujeanie**[7] 4540 3-9-5 **72**.................................(p) RichardHughes 2 80
(D K Ivory) *stdd and swtchd rt s: hdwy into midfield over 4f out: swtchd lft and hdwy over 1f out: edgd rt u.p fnl f: led fnl 100yds: rdn out* **6/1**[3]

3535 **2** ½ **Memphis Man**[5] 4607 6-9-10 **73** PaulDoe 15 81
(P D Evans) *taken down early: stdd s: hld up bhd: swtchd lft and hdwy ent fnl f: r.o wl to go 2nd nr fin: nt quite rch wnr* **9/2**[2]

0144 **3** hd **Luminous Gold**[19] 4154 4-9-9 **72** AlanMunro 1 79
(C F Wall) *in tch: rdn to chal 2f out: led over 1f out: hdd and unable qck fnl 100yds* **8/1**

5016 **4** nk **Kyle (IRE)**[5] 4607 5-9-10 **73** DarryllHolland 14 79
(C R Dore) *hld up bhd: swtchd lft and hdwy between horses jst ins fnl f: r.o but nt quite rch ldrs* **4/1**[1]

0030 **5** ½ **Make My Dream**[16] 4225 6-9-4 **67** PatCosgrave 6 71
(J Gallagher) *chsd ldrs: rdn 2f out: drvn ent fnl f: kpt on same pce fnl 100yds* **12/1**

4006 **6** 2¼ **Imperial Djay (IRE)**[21] 4105 4-8-6 **55** oh8.............(p) AdrianMcCarthy 11 52
(J R Holt) *bmpd s: in tch: rdn and unable qck over 1f out: swtchd lft jst ins fnl f: kpt on same pce after* **20/1**

100 **7** 1¼ **Westwood**[56] 2929 4-9-5 **71** DavidProbert(3) 8 64
(D Haydn Jones) *taken down early: uns rdr and galloped loose to s: awkward leaving stalls: sn rcvrd to chse ldrs: wnt 2nd 3f out: ev ch and rdn wl over 1f out: wknd ins fnl f* **10/1**

350 **8** 2½ **Punching**[58] 2852 5-9-2 **65** TravisBlock 13 50
(C R Dore) *stdd s: hld up in rr: rdn and effrt wl over 1f out: no hdwy* **8/1**

3014 **9** 2½ **Hillside Lad**[16] 4223 3-9-0 **67**................................(p) J-PGuillambert 7 43
(R M Beckett) *sn bustled along to ld and crossed to stands' rail: rdn and hdd over 1f out: wknd fnl f* **9/1**

0300 **10** 13 **Kipchak (IRE)**[18] 4181 4-9-10 **73**..............................(p) IanMongan 9 9
(C R Dore) *walked to s: t.k.h: hld up towards rr: lost tch and nt pushed 2f out: wl btn after* **9/1**

000 **11** ¾ **Kelamon**[33] 3694 5-9-0 **63** SaleemGolam 4 —
(S C Williams) *chsd ldr tl 3f out: edgd rt and wknd qckly u.p over 1f out: eased ins fnl f* **22/1**

1m 10.87s (-0.33) **Going Correction** +0.025s/f (Good)
WFA 3 from 4yo+ 4lb **11** Ran SP% **120.6**
Speed ratings (Par 103): **103,102,102,101,101 98,96,93,89,72 71**
toteswingers: 1&2 £6.60, 1&3 £10.60, 2&3 £8.10. CSF £34.08 CT £226.56 TOTE £8.10: £2.50, £1.70, £2.10; EX 38.10.
Owner K T Ivory **Bred** K T Ivory **Trained** Radlett, Herts

FOCUS
Some inconsistent sorts on show in a pretty modest handicap, but the pace was strong and the hold-up horses burst onto the scene in the final furlong. Straightforward form.
Hillside Lad Official explanation: jockey said gelding stopped quickly
Kipchak(IRE) Official explanation: jockey said gelding hung right

4788 DAVID WARD HAPPY RETIREMENT H'CAP 6f
6:40 (6:43) (Class 4) (0-85,84) 3-Y-O **£4,857** (£1,445; £722; £360) **Stalls** High

Form RPR

0564 **1** **Son Of The Cat (USA)**[52] 3028 3-9-7 **84**.....................(t) DarryllHolland 5 94
(B Gubby) *sn niggled along and outpcd in last: hdwy jst over 2f out: led and edgd rt over 1f out: pushed clr ent fnl f: easily* **6/1**[3]

6642 **2** 5 **Kingswinford (IRE)**[6] 4567 3-8-10 **73** RichardHughes 4 67
(P D Evans) *led narrowly tl 4f out: led again 2f out: rdn and hdd over 1f out: sltly hmpd ent fnl f: no ch w wnr after* **13/8**[2]

5311 **3** 1 **Fyelehk (IRE)**[9] 4454 3-7-13 **65** DavidProbert(3) 6 56
(B R Millman) *taken down early: w ldrs: ev ch and wanting to edgd lft over fr 2f out: nt pce of wnr ent fnl f: wl btn after* **1/1**[1]

0444 **4** 3 ½ **Top Town Girl**[12] 4380 3-8-11 **74** SebSanders 1 54
(R M Beckett) *w ldr tl led narrowly 4f out: hdd 2f out: sn wknd: wl btn fnl f* **8/1**

1m 10.5s (-0.70) **Going Correction** +0.025s/f (Good) 4 Ran SP% **113.5**
Speed ratings (Par 102): **105,98,97,92**
toteswingers: 1&2 £7.90. CSF £16.69 TOTE £7.70; EX 20.00.
Owner Brian Gubby **Bred** Andover Stable Llc **Trained** Bagshot, Surrey
■ Coconut Shy (12/1) was withdrawn on vet's advice. Deduct 5p in the 3 under R4.
■ Stewards' Enquiry : Darryll Holland caution: careless riding

FOCUS
The most valuable race of the evening, but just four runners, three of whom took each other on for the lead. Probably not form to take too literally, with the winner not having to improve much.
Fyelehk(IRE) Official explanation: jockey said gelding ran too free

4789 HAPPY DAYS MEDIAN AUCTION MAIDEN STKS 1m 2f (P)
7:10 (7:10) (Class 6) 3-4-Y-O **£2,729** (£806; £403) **Stalls** Low

Form RPR
254 **1** **Kefalonia (USA)**[47] 3228 3-8-12 67 SebSanders 5 71
(B W Hills) *mde all: clr fr 9f out: 15l clr 4f out: stl wl clr and rdn over 1f out: tiring fnl f but a jst gng to hold on* **13/2**
6224 **2** nk **Some Sunny Day**[29] 3803 3-8-12 70 RichardHughes 1 71
(H Morrison) *chsd wnr thrght: stl 10 l down and rdn over 2f out: clsd u.p fnl f but nvr quite gng to get there* **7/2**[2]
2223 **3** ¾ **Pyrus Time (IRE)**[33] 3674 3-9-3 74 DaneO'Neill 2 74
(J S Moore) *t.k.h: prom in main gp: wnt modest 3rd and rdn over 2f out: clsd u.p fnl f but nvr quite gng to get there* **3/1**[1]
00 **4** 2 ½ **Beat Companion**[22] 4057 3-9-3 0 PatCosgrave 10 69
(P Howling) *t.k.h: hld up in rr: rdn and hdwy into modest 4th over 2f out: kpt u.p but nvr gng to rch wnr* **14/1**
4243 **5** nk **Buckie Boy (IRE)**[37] 3549 3-9-3 73 (v[1]) IanMongan 8 68
(H R A Cecil) *s.i.s and sn rdn along: bhd: rdn and effrt over 2f out: racd awkwardly u.p over 1f out: kpt on reluctantly: nvr able to chal* **4/1**[3]
6 nk **Satwa Moon (USA)** 3-9-3 0 DO'Donohoe 9 68+
(E A L Dunlop) *hld up in rr: nudged along on outer bnd 2f out: hdwy and edging lft over 1f out: shkn up and r.o ins fnl f: eased towards fin* **14/1**
6022 **7** 1 ¼ **Layer Cake**[32] 3718 3-9-3 72 SimonWhitworth 4 65
(J W Hills) *t.k.h: hld up in main gp: rdn and effrt on inner jst over 2f out: kpt on but nvr able to chal* **6/1**
8 7 **Rainiers Girl** 3-8-12 0 TGMcLaughlin 6 46
(R A Teal) *t.k.h: hld up in main gp: rdn and struggling over 3f out: wl btn fnl 2f* **66/1**
9 4 ½ **Jezza** 3-9-3 0 DarryllHolland 7 42
(Karen George) *prom in main gp: rdn 3f out: wknd jst over 2f out* **20/1**
00- **10** 12 **Miss Jodarah (USA)**[318] 6205 3-8-12 0 SteveDrowne 3 13
(J R Best) *racd in main gp tl dropped to last and rdn over 4f out: sn lost tch* **50/1**

2m 7.25s (0.65) **Going Correction** +0.075s/f (Slow) 10 Ran SP% **116.4**
Speed ratings (Par 101): **100,99,99,97,96 96,95,90,86,76**
toteswingers: 1&2 £10.10, 1&3 £2.50, 2&3 £3.50. CSF £29.07 TOTE £5.90: £1.90, £1.60, £1.40; EX 18.20.
Owner K Abdulla **Bred** Juddmonte Farms Inc **Trained** Lambourn, Berks

FOCUS
A very modest maiden, which was gifted to Seb Sanders and Kefalonia. Shaky form, rated around the second and third.

4790 COPS & ROBBERS EXCLUSIVE TO CORAL SHOPS MAIDEN STKS 1m (P)
7:40 (7:44) (Class 5) 2-Y-O **£2,729** (£806; £403) **Stalls** High

Form RPR
46 **1** **Kavak**[25] 3957 2-9-3 0 DarryllHolland 9 83
(M Botti) *hld up in tch: hdwy to chse ldr 2f out: led jst over 1f out: racd awkwardly and hung lft after but stormed clr fnl f: easily* **12/1**
0 **2** 4 ½ **Navy List (FR)**[14] 4314 2-9-0 0 AhmedAjtebi(3) 1 73
(Saeed Bin Suroor) *dwlt: sn pushed along and hdwy to ld after 1f: rdn wl over 1f out: hdd jst over 1f out: sn wl outpcd by wnr* **10/1**[3]
4 **3** ¾ **Advertisement (USA)**[13] 4336 2-9-3 0 TPQueally 2 72+
(J Noseda) *chsd ldrs: rdn and unable qck on inner over 1f out: nt clr run and swtchd rt jst ins fnl f: no imp after* **1/2**[1]
0 **4** ½ **Kinky Afro (IRE)**[70] 2494 2-8-12 0 StephenDonohoe 4 65
(J S Moore) *towards rr: hdwy 3f out: rdn and outpcd 2f out: rallied and styd on ins fnl f: no ch w wnr* **28/1**
034 **5** nk **Aattash (IRE)**[34] 3652 2-9-3 75 TonyCulhane 7 69
(M R Channon) *t.k.h: hld up in midfield: rdn and hung lft wl over 1f out: kpt on same pce fr over 1f out* **14/1**
6 nse **James Barrymore** 2-9-3 0 RichardHughes 6 69+
(R Hannon) *awkward leaving stalls and s.i.s: hld up in rr: hdwy over 2f out: nt clr run and swtchd rt wl over 1f out: styd on steadily fnl f: nvr trbld ldrs* **14/1**
24 **7** 6 **Cafe Greco**[28] 3867 2-9-3 0 SteveDrowne 12 55
(P J Makin) *led for 1f: chsd ldr after tl 2f out: sn drvn and wknd qckly over 1f out* **11/2**[2]
50 **8** 6 **Comedy Act**[37] 3522 2-9-3 0 SebSanders 3 41
(Sir Mark Prescott) *a in last trio: rdn over 3f out: struggling over 2f out and sn bhd* **40/1**
0 **9** ½ **Little Meadow (IRE)**[43] 3344 2-8-12 0 SaleemGolam 5 35
(Miss J Feilden) *in tch in midfield: rdn and struggling over 2f out: wl bhd fnl f* **100/1**
10 47 **Superhoops** 2-9-3 0 TGMcLaughlin 8 —
(H S Howe) *s.i.s: a bhd: rdn and lost tch 4f out: t.o fnl 2f* **66/1**

1m 38.36s (0.16) **Going Correction** +0.075s/f (Slow) 10 Ran SP% **120.5**
Speed ratings (Par 94): **102,97,96,96,95 95,89,83,83,36**
toteswingers: 1&2 £8.60, 1&3 £3.90, 2&3 £4.70. CSF £125.55 TOTE £17.30: £2.20, £2.60, £1.10; EX 69.10.
Owner Grundy Bloodstock Limited **Bred** Grundy Bloodstock Srl **Trained** Newmarket, Suffolk

FOCUS
This didn't have much strength in depth. Improved form from the impressive winner but the favourite disappointed.

NOTEBOOK
Kavak sprinted clear of his rivals in the final furlong. Despite wanting to hang left all the way through the final furlong, the son of Dubawi quickened clear in impressive style. This was his first run on Polytrack and it clearly suited him much better than the soft ground he disappointed on at Yarmouth last time (when well backed). Connections clearly think a fair bit of him and he holds an entry in the Timeform Million race at Newmarket later in the season. (op 9-1)
Navy List(FR) didn't show much promise on debut, but this was a big step forward. He kept on well, having raced on the pace throughout, and he will win races if maintaining this progress. (tchd 12-1)
Advertisement(USA) had a nice position in behind the pace, but lacked a change of gear when the pace quickened in the straight and, although he kept on, this was a bit disappointing. He probably needs a more galloping track to show his best. Official explanation: jockey said colt hung left (op 4-6)
Kinky Afro(IRE) showed next to nothing at Newbury on debut, but this was more encouraging. She travelled quite well in midfield before keeping on for pressure in the straight. An entry in the Fillies' Mile looks ambitious, but she clearly has ability and looks to be going forward. (op 40-1)
Aattash(IRE), who was very keen to post and free in the race itself, didn't have a great trip out wide and ran reasonably in the circumstances. (op 16-1)
James Barrymore kept on well in the closing stages and will come on plenty for this. (op 12-1)

4791 HOLLOW LANE H'CAP 7f (P)
8:10 (8:12) (Class 5) (0-70,70) 3-Y-O+ **£3,070** (£906; £453) **Stalls** Low

Form RPR
-412 **1** **Regeneration (IRE)**[12] 4375 3-9-6 **64** RichardHughes 8 72+
(S A Callaghan) *plld hrd early: hld up in midfield: rdn and effrt over 1f out: hrd drvn ins fnl f: str run to ld nr fin* **15/8**[1]
4-02 **2** hd **Art Market (CAN)**[66] 2598 6-9-6 **58** IanMongan 6 66
(Miss Jo Crowley) *chsd ldrs: rdn to chse ldr 2f out: hrd rdn to ld ins fnl f: r.o tl hdd nr fin* **9/1**
5040 **3** ¾ **Idle Power (IRE)**[23] 4009 11-9-13 **65** PatCosgrave 7 71
(J R Boyle) *t.k.h: hld up wl in tch: rdn and chsd ldng trio over 1f out: kpt on u.p fnl f* **12/1**
5632 **4** ½ **Brooksby**[14] 4322 3-9-12 **70** (b) PatDobbs 5 72
(R Hannon) *chsd ldr: rdn over 3f out: lost 2nd 2f out: kpt on u.p and pressing ldrs ins fnl f: no ex fnl 50yds* **12/1**
550 **5** 2 **Satwa Star (IRE)**[17] 4199 3-9-11 **69** DO'Donohoe 3 68+
(E A L Dunlop) *stdd after s: t.k.h: hld up wl in rr: nt clr run over 1f out: hdwy 1f out: r.o wl ins fnl f: nt rch ldrs* **14/1**
4332 **6** ½ **Cativo Cavallino**[21] 4082 6-9-7 **62** NataliaGemelova(3) 2 60
(J E Long) *dwlt: towards rr: nt clr run over 1f out: pushed along and hdwy ent fnl f: r.o but nvr pce to rch ldrs* **7/1**[2]
0003 **7** ½ **Hereford Boy**[17] 4203 5-9-10 **62** TPQueally 13 58
(D K Ivory) *towards rr: rdn wl over 3f out: hdwy on outer over 1f out: kpt on fnl f: nvr able to rch ldrs* **10/1**
430- **8** 1 ¼ **Boho Chic**[311] 6389 3-9-3 **66** MatthewDavies(5) 9 57
(George Baker) *sn led: rdn 2 l clr 2f out: hdd ins fnl f: wknd qckly fnl 100yds* **20/1**
00-0 **9** nse **Dawson Creek (IRE)**[118] 155 5-9-11 **63** SebSanders 14 56
(B Gubby) *chsd ldrs on outer: rdn and unable qck jst over 2f out: plugged on same pce after* **12/1**
0003 **10** hd **Danzadil (IRE)**[9] 4452 3-8-2 **53** CharlesEddery(7) 4 43
(R A Teal) *s.i.s: a towards rr: rdn 3f out: kpt on same pce u.p fr over 1f out* **20/1**
3602 **11** 2 ¾ **Ever Cheerful**[17] 4202 8-9-10 **62** (p) SteveDrowne 10 47
(A B Haynes) *chsd ldrs: rdn over 2f out: wknd qckly over 1f out* **8/1**[3]
0500 **12** ½ **Sapphire Prince (USA)**[18] 4181 3-9-9 **70** MarcHalford(3) 12 51
(J R Best) *s.i.s and swtchd rt s: a bhd* **12/1**
0606 **13** 2 ¼ **Imperial Skylight**[16] 4237 3-9-6 **64** TonyCulhane 1 39
(M R Channon) *in tch in midfield: rdn and effrt on inner wl over 1f out: sn wknd* **20/1**
4040 **14** 15 **Blackwater Fort (USA)**[39] 3476 3-8-9 **53** ow1 StephenDonohoe 11 —
(J Gallagher) *s.i.s: alway bhd: struggling and rdn 4f out: wl bhd fnl 2f* **50/1**

1m 24.69s (-0.11) **Going Correction** +0.075s/f (Slow)
WFA 3 from 5yo+ 6lb 14 Ran SP% **131.2**
Speed ratings (Par 103): **103,102,101,101,99 98,97,96,96,96 93,92,89,72**
toteswingers: 1&2 £5.30, 1&3 £8.60, 2&3 £23.50. CSF £20.04 CT £180.74 TOTE £3.20: £1.80, £3.20, £4.30; EX 27.80 Place 6: £67.01, Place 5: £56.18..
Owner Tamdown Group Limited **Bred** Tally-Ho Stud **Trained** Newmarket, Suffolk

FOCUS
A strong pace to this 7f handicap. Sound form with the unexposed winner stepping forward.
Satwa Star(IRE) Official explanation: jockey said gelding was denied a clear run
T/Plt: £357.40 to a £1 stake. Pool: £45,705.16. 93.35 winning tickets. T/Qpdt: £125.90 to a £1 stake. Pool: £4,033.40. 23.70 winning tickets. SP

4756 NEWMARKET (R-H)
Saturday, August 8

OFFICIAL GOING: Good (good to soft in places)
Wind: Nil Weather: Fine and sunny

4792 PERFORMANCE AND VALUE-GERMAN THOROUGHBRED MAIDEN FILLIES' STKS (DIV I) 7f
1:25 (1:25) (Class 4) 2-Y-O **£4,857** (£1,445; £722; £360) **Stalls** Low

Form RPR
1 **Eolith** 2-9-0 0 JimCrowley 11 83
(W J Knight) *hld up: hdwy over 2f out: rdn over 1f out: edgd lft ins fnl f: r.o to ld post* **12/1**
62 **2** shd **Pollenator (IRE)**[16] 4239 2-9-0 0 PatDobbs 12 83
(R Hannon) *wnt rt s: chsd ldrs: rdn to ld over 1f out: hung lft ins fnl f: hdd post* **10/3**[2]
3 2 ¾ **Hibaayeb** 2-9-0 0 PhilipRobinson 3 76
(C E Brittain) *chsd ldr tl rdn over 1f out: styd on same pce* **16/1**
6 **4** ½ **Battlemaiden (IRE)**[15] 4257 2-9-0 0 TedDurcan 7 75
(Saeed Bin Suroor) *led: rdn and hdd over 1f out: hung lft and no ex ins fnl f* **5/2**[1]
5 shd **Zahoo (IRE)** 2-9-0 0 RHills 5 75+
(J L Dunlop) *hld up: rdn over 2f out: hdwy over 1f out: no imp ins fnl f* **17/2**
4 **6** 1 ¾ **Carioca (IRE)**[23] 4001 2-9-0 0 SebSanders 2 70
(M Botti) *prom: rdn over 1f out: no ex fnl f* **4/1**[3]
7 1 ¾ **Dubai Media (CAN)** 2-9-0 0 TPQueally 6 66
(D M Simcock) *prom: rdn over 2f out: wkng whn hung lft ins fnl f* **12/1**
8 ¾ **Forethought** 2-9-0 0 JimmyQuinn 10 64
(P Howling) *s.i.s: hld up: effrt over 2f out: edgd lft and wknd over 1f out* **80/1**
9 3 ¾ **Katehari (IRE)** 2-9-0 0 RichardMullen 4 55
(A M Balding) *hld up in tch: rdn over 2f out: wknd over 1f out* **33/1**
10 ½ **Tallawalla (IRE)** 2-9-0 0 EdwardCreighton 1 53
(M R Channon) *hld up: rdn 1/2-way: wknd over 1f out* **66/1**
11 ½ **Copper Penny** 2-9-0 0 DaneO'Neill 8 52
(D R Lanigan) *hld up: rdn over 2f out: edgd lft and wknd over 1f out* **18/1**

12 *10* **Tiger Girl** 2-9-0 0 .... SteveDrowne 9 27
(R Charlton) *s.i.s: hld up: rdn: hung rt and wknd fr over 2f out* **18/1**

1m 27.64s (1.94) **Going Correction** +0.225s/f (Good) **12** Ran SP% **119.6**
Speed ratings (Par 93): **97,96,93,93,93 91,89,88,83,83 82,71**
toteswinger: 1&2 £15.90, 1&3 £60.00, 2&3 £8.70. CSF £52.06 TOTE £18.80: £4.50, £1.80, £4.90; EX 94.20.
Owner Mrs Alison Ruggles **Bred** Mrs A R Ruggles **Trained** Patching, W Sussex

FOCUS
The last three winners of this fillies' maiden all went on to score at Listed level at this very least and the most well known of them was Passage Of Time, who subsequently landed a Group 1. This year's form doesn't look anything special, with the runner-up the best guide, but there should still be a few winners to emerge. The winning time was 0.97 seconds quicker than the second division won by Tabassum. The main action took place up the centre of the track.

NOTEBOOK
Eolith is a half-sister to 1m6f winner Eventide, but she has clearly inherited plenty of speed from Pastoral Pursuits. Not without support in the market, she made a very pleasing debut, getting up on the line without being given an unnecessarily hard ride. She deserves to try something better now. (op 16-1)
Pollenator(IRE) looked the likeliest winner once she had got the better of the Godolphin filly, but she was caught in the final stride. She pulled clear of the rest and should soon be winning. Nurseries are now an option, but it would be no surprise if she sticks to maiden company. (op 3-1 tchd 7-2)
Hibaayeb, a half-sister to quite useful 6f juvenile winner May Meeting, out of a dual 7f-1m scorer, was no match for the front pair but still showed plenty of ability. There ought to be better to come. (op 14-1)
Battlemaiden(IRE), from a stable who operated at a 42 per cent strike-rate with their juveniles during July, seemed to enjoy a soft enough lead but she was soon in trouble once coming under pressure, hanging slightly left and failing to pick up. She had shaped quite nicely over 6f at Ascot on her debut, when not given a particularly hard time, but she failed to build on that performance. (op 10-3)
Zahoo(IRE), a half-sister to quite useful 1m4f winner Tactic, out of 1m2f scorer, is entered in the Fillies' Mile. She was held up early and never featured but should do better in time, particularly over further next season. (op 5-1 tchd 9-1)
Carioca(IRE) was below the form she showed at Doncaster on her debut, although she displayed quite a fluent action and ground that seemed to riding quite tacky probably didn't suit. She is well regarded but is considered to be on the weak side and may need more time. (op 11-2 tchd 6-1)

4793 RACING UK SKY 432 H'CAP — 2m 24y
1:55 (1:56) (Class 3) (0-90,84) 3-Y-O+ **£9,066** (£2,697; £1,348; £673) **Stalls** Centre

Form | | | | RPR
0212 **1** **Perfect Shot (IRE)**[28] 3861 3-8-10 **81** .... TedDurcan 2 89+
(J L Dunlop) *hld up: hdwy over 2f out: led over 1f out: hung lft and drvn clr ins fnl f* **3/1**[1]
6063 **2** *3 ½* **Danzatrice**[7] 4551 7-8-12 **68** .... PaulHanagan 8 72
(C W Thornton) *hld up: hdwy over 2f out: rdn to chse wnr fnl f: no imp* **16/1**
1-03 **3** *1 ½* **Dulcie**[22] 4045 3-8-4 **75** .... RichardMullen 3 77
(M H Tompkins) *hld up: n.m.r and hdwy over 1f out: styd on wl to go 3rd post: nt rch ldrs* **14/1**
043- **4** *nk* **Ragamuffin Man (IRE)**[162] 6934 4-9-5 **75** ....(v) JimCrowley 6 77
(W J Knight) *led: racd keenly: rdn and hdd over 1f out: edgd lft and no ex fnl f: lost 3rd post* **8/1**
645/ **5** *7* **Thunder Rock (IRE)**[27] 5920 7-9-12 **82** ....(p) RichardKingscote 4 75
(Jonjo O'Neill) *mid-div: hdwy over 3f out: rdn over 1f out: wknd fnl f* **16/1**
11 **6** *3 ½* **Pseudonym (IRE)**[25] 3940 7-8-13 **69** ....(t) J-PGuillambert 10 58
(M F Harris) *mid-div: hdwy 5f out: rdn over 1f out: sn wknd* **8/1**
0025 **7** *11* **Clear Reef**[7] 4544 5-9-10 **80** ....(p) KShea 1 56
(Jane Chapple-Hyam) *hld up: hdwy over 2f out: rdn and wknd over 1f out* **7/1**[3]
2130 **8** *3 ¼* **Swordsman (GER)**[10] 4417 7-9-0 **70** .... IanMongan 9 42
(C Gordon) *chsd ldrs: pushed along over 4f out: wknd over 1f out: eased ins fnl f* **15/2**
5225 **9** *11* **Longboat Key**[10] 4442 3-7-13 **73** ....(b) DavidProbert(3) 7 32
(M Johnston) *chsd ldr: rdn over 3f out: wknd 2f out* **4/1**[2]
25/5 **10** *61* **Alessano**[17] 4212 7-10-0 **84** .... GeorgeBaker 5 —
(G L Moore) *prom: rdn over 3f out: wknd over 2f out: virtually p.u fnl f: dismntd after crossing line* **11/1**

3m 29.36s (2.36) **Going Correction** +0.225s/f (Good)
WFA 3 from 4yo+ 15lb **10** Ran SP% **118.3**
Speed ratings (Par 107): **103,101,100,100,96 95,89,87,82,51**
toteswinger: 1&2 £15.00, 1&3 £6.20, 2&3 £36.00. CSF £54.31 CT £592.87 TOTE £3.40: £1.50, £3.80, £2.90; EX 25.60.
Owner Sir Philip Wroughton **Bred** David Jamison Bloodstock **Trained** Arundel, W Sussex

FOCUS
A fair staying handicap and they seemed to go a reasonable gallop, but the time was over eight seconds above standard, suggesting the ground was pretty tacky. They tended to race up the centre of the track in the straight, although the winner eventually ended up far side. The form is rated around those in the frame behind the winner.

NOTEBOOK
Perfect Shot(IRE) travelled as well as anything and found plenty to run out a most decisive winner, despite displaying a slightly awkward head carriage and, not for the first time, hanging left under pressure. This first try at 2m suited and he's progressing into a very useful stayer. (op 4-1)
Danzatrice, given a patient ride as usual, stayed on quite well for second and ran her race; she was simply beaten by a more progressive rival. (op 10-1)
Dulcie took an age to pick up, not being helped when slightly short of room over a furlong out, before finally running on quite well past tiring rivals to grab third near the line. Seemingly all she does is stay, so a more positive ride might suit better. (op 10-1)
Ragamuffin Man(IRE), reported by his jockey to have felt wrong throughout when pulled up over hurdles in February, ran respectably on this return to the Flat. He didn't help his chance by racing keenly in front early on, though, and lost third place in the final strides after getting tired. (op 14-1)
Thunder Rock(IRE), a winner over hurdles and fences since he was last seen on the Flat in 2006, didn't shape as though about to add to his tally back on the level. (op 11-1 tchd 10-1)
Pseudonym(IRE) was chasing a hat-trick but proved disappointing, possibly not enjoying the ground. (tchd 7-1 and 9-1)
Longboat Key was quite well backed but he dropped away, having kept the early leader honest. (op 7-1)
Alessano was dismounted after crossing the line and something looked amiss. (op 8-1 tchd 7-1)

4794 CHAMPIONSHIP KICK OFF WITH SKY BET H'CAP — 1m 2f
2:25 (2:27) (Class 2) (0-100,99) 3-Y-O+ **£12,952** (£3,854; £1,926; £962) **Stalls** Centre

Form | | | | RPR
14 **1** **Whispering Gallery**[29] 3826 3-8-12 **92** .... RHills 6 106+
(M Johnston) *mde all: rdn over 1f out: sn hung lft: styd on wl* **11/4**[2]
4211 **2** *2 ¼* **Recession Proof (FR)**[3] 4658 3-7-13 **82** 12ex........ DavidProbert(3) 9 91
(S A Callaghan) *chsd ldrs: rdn over 1f out: edgd lft and styd on same pce ins fnl f: wnt 2nd towards fin* **13/8**[1]
5030 **3** *½* **Alarazi (IRE)**[50] 3089 5-9-10 **95** .... TPQueally 1 103
(T G Mills) *s.i.s: hld up: racd keenly: hdwy: nt clr run and swtchd lft over 1f out: rdn ins fnl f: styd on same pce: lost 2nd towards fin* **20/1**
0-36 **4** *2 ¼* **Scuffle**[98] 1667 4-10-0 **99** .... SteveDrowne 5 103
(R Charlton) *hld up: rdn over 2f out: hdwy over 1f out: edgd lft ins fnl f: nt trble ldrs* **10/1**
3123 **5** *1 ½* **Vainglory (USA)**[15] 4261 5-9-2 **87** .... RichardMullen 8 88
(D M Simcock) *hld up: rdn over 2f out: edgd lft and styd on ins fnl f: nvr nr ldrs* **8/1**
/130 **6** *nk* **Bugaku**[21] 4091 4-9-1 **91** .... Louis-PhilippeBeuzelin(5) 3 91
(Sir Michael Stoute) *chsd wnr tl over 8f out: remained handy: rdn over 2f out: wknd over 1f out* **12/1**
3112 **7** *1 ¾* **Yirga**[16] 4242 3-8-5 **85** ....(t) TedDurcan 2 81
(Saeed Bin Suroor) *hld up: hdwy over 2f out: sn rdn: wknd over 1f out* **5/1**[3]
5000 **8** *4* **Weald Park (USA)**[14] 4296 3-8-10 **90** ....(v[1]) PatDobbs 7 78
(R Hannon) *chsd wnr over 8f out tl rdn and wknd over 1f out* **25/1**

2m 7.88s (2.38) **Going Correction** +0.225s/f (Good)
WFA 3 from 4yo+ 9lb **8** Ran SP% **117.9**
Speed ratings (Par 109): **99,97,96,95,93 93,92,88**
toteswinger: 1&2 £1.20, 1&3 £25.20, 2&3 £5.70. CSF £7.91 CT £72.11 TOTE £4.10: £1.10, £1.40, £4.40; EX 9.00 TRIFECTA Not won..
Owner Sheikh Hamdan Bin Mohammed Al Maktoum **Bred** Darley **Trained** Middleham Moor, N Yorks

FOCUS
A good handicap but they seemed to go just an ordinary pace with the winner stepping up on his debut win. They raced middle to far side in the straight.

NOTEBOOK
Whispering Gallery defied a mark of 92, despite edging left under pressure, although he was allowed the run of the race. Considering this was only his third start, it's not unreasonable to expect more improvement and he can be given another chance to prove he will stay further (beaten favourite over 1m4f last time). He looks all over a Dubai Carnival type. (op 4-1)
Recession Proof(FR), by no means for the first time, was noticeably sweating, but he still posted a decent effort behind the progressive winner under his double penalty for two wins in amateur races. (op 15-8 tchd 2-1 in places)
Alarazi(IRE) looked a big threat when looming up in behind the winner going as well as anything inside the final 2f, but he had been keen early on and his exertions seemed to tell when he produced only a short-lived challenge once in the clear. His chance wasn't helped when Whispering Gallery carried him left late on, but he basically just couldn't sustain his run. (op 14-1 tchd 12-1)
Scuffle, returning from over three months off, was a little keen early and could find only the one pace under pressure. She is struggling this season. (op 8-1 tchd 12-1)
Vainglory(USA) only ran on when the race was as good as over. (op 15-2 tchd 6-1)
Bugaku failed to pick up, possibly not handing the tacky going, and might do better back on Polytrack or quick turf. (op 10-1)
Yirga was turned over at odds of 2-5 in a three-runner race at Folkestone last time and this was another disappointing effort. He might want better ground. Official explanation: jockey said colt had no more to give (op 6-1 tchd 13-2 and 7-1 in places)

4795 SKYBET.COM SWEET SOLERA STKS (GROUP 3) (FILLIES) — 7f
3:00 (3:00) (Class 1) 2-Y-O
£28,385 (£10,760; £5,385; £2,685; £1,345; £675) **Stalls** Low

Form | | | | RPR
1 **Long Lashes (USA)**[43] 3366 2-8-12 0 .... TedDurcan 2 107+
(Saeed Bin Suroor) *a.p: led and hung rt over 1f out: rdn and hung lft ins fnl f: r.o* **2/1**[1]
21 **2** *1* **Blue Maiden**[14] 4318 2-8-12 85 .... EdwardCreighton 4 104
(P J McBride) *s.i.s: hld up: rdn over 2f out: hdwy u.p over 1f out: styd on* **66/1**
1 **3** *1 ½* **Sent From Heaven (IRE)**[24] 3979 2-8-12 0 .... MichaelHills 10 100
(B W Hills) *s.i.s: hld up: hdwy 2f out: rdn over 1f out: styd on same pce ins fnl f* **11/2**[3]
312 **4** *¾* **Snow Fairy (IRE)**[7] 4539 2-8-12 94 .... JimCrowley 7 98
(E A L Dunlop) *hld up in tch: nt clr run and lost pl over 2f out: swtchd lft and hdwy over 1f out: sn rdn: styd on* **9/1**
014 **5** *1* **Gallic Star (IRE)**[16] 4245 2-8-12 93 .... DaneO'Neill 9 95
(M R Channon) *a.p: rdn over 1f out: styd on same pce* **6/1**
13 **6** *2 ¼* **Chachamaidee (IRE)**[50] 3086 2-8-12 0 .... TPQueally 3 90
(H R A Cecil) *plld hrd: led 6f out: rdn and hdd over 1f out: wknd ins fnl f* **7/2**[2]
12 **7** *nk* **Blue Angel (IRE)**[15] 4272 2-8-12 90 .... PatDobbs 8 89
(R Hannon) *hld up: rdn over 2f out: n.d* **33/1**
1014 **8** *1 ¾* **Jira**[14] 4295 2-8-12 96 .... KShea 5 85
(C E Brittain) *mid-div: rdn over 1f out: wknd fnl f* **16/1**
0103 **9** *2 ¼* **Bikini Babe (IRE)**[16] 4245 2-8-12 94 .... RHills 1 79
(M Johnston) *led 1f: remained w ldr tl rdn 2f out: wknd over 1f out* **16/1**
01 **10** *12* **Admire The View (IRE)**[15] 4278 2-8-12 87 .... SebSanders 6 49
(D R Lanigan) *chsd ldrs: rdn and wknd over 1f out* **20/1**

1m 25.9s (0.20) **Going Correction** +0.225s/f (Good) **10** Ran SP% **116.2**
Speed ratings (Par 101): **107,105,104,103,102 99,99,97,94,80**
toteswinger: 1&2 £28.80, 1&3 £1.80, 2&3 £30.30. CSF £173.62 TOTE £3.00: £1.40, £9.90, £1.80; EX 121.40 Trifecta £464.80 Part won. Pool: £628.16 - 0.60 winning units..
Owner Godolphin **Bred** Robert V La Penta & Nocholas P **Trained** Newmarket, Suffolk

FOCUS
Recent winners of this juvenile fillies' Group 3 include Soviet Song, Maids Causeway and Rainbow View. It's hard to pin down the exact worth of this year's race, but despite a modest early pace, and the presence of a 66-1 shot in second, it still looked a decent contest and the form should prove reliable. The clock seems to support that view - much quicker than both divisions of the juvenile fillies' maiden - although the race was hand timed. The main action was up the middle of the track.

NOTEBOOK
Long Lashes(USA) ◆, bought privately out of Jessica Harrington's yard after winning a 6f Listed race at the Curragh on her debut, has joined a stable in superb form with their juveniles and showed she has gone the right way with a decisive, if unspectacular, success. The modest early gallop was hardly conducive to an impressive performance and she did all that was asked of her, despite still looking inexperienced. There was talk beforehand that she might be coming into season, but whatever the case, she clearly wasn't affected. The winner is still available at 25-1 for the 1000 Guineas with Coral and Totesport, but her connections are keen to campaign her in Dubai early next year, with the UAE 1000 Guineas and Oaks mentioned as likely targets. In light of that, it's difficult to fancy her for the Newmarket Classic at this stage, even though the new racing surface at Meydan might be more forgiving than a traditional dirt track. Her more immediate aim is apparently the Group 1 Moyglare Stud Stakes at the Curragh. (op 9-4)

Blue Maiden was not afforded any respect in the market, but she had shown plenty of ability in reasonable company on her first two starts, both over 6f, including when winning a maiden here last time, and she belied her big odds with a fine run in second. It was no surprise to see her improve for the step up in trip considering she is quite stoutly bred, and she showed herself to be very useful, keeping on well from a fair way back. She'll get even further this year, before no doubt appreciating middle-distances next season, and her connections have every right to look for a similar race again next time.
Sent From Heaven(IRE) ◆, an impressive winner at Kempton on her debut, started slowly and was left with a bit too much to do. She kept on steadily, despite on occasions flashing her tail, but could never muster the required speed and gave the impression she can do better still. (op 6-1 tchd 13-2)
Snow Fairy(IRE) was left with an impossible task inside the final 2f. She was still last with no room to make a move when the race got serious and she got going too late once switched all the way across to the far rail. (op 10-1)
Gallic Star(IRE), reported to have been denied a clear run when one place behind Bikini Babe in a Sandown Listed race on her previous start, ran okay without proving herself up to this level. (op 7-1)
Chachamaidee(IRE), a 6f maiden winner on her debut before running third in the Albany Stakes at Royal Ascot, pulled far too hard over this extra furlong, despite the fitting of a cross-noseband. If connections persevere over this sort of trip, she is likely to need a patient ride off a much stronger pace. (op 10-3 tchd 3-1)

4796 SKY BET FOR ALL YOUR FOOTBALL BETTING (HERITAGE H'CAP) 7f
3:35 (3:36) (Class 2) (0-105,102) 3-Y-O+
£24,924 (£7,464; £3,732; £1,868; £932; £468) **Stalls** Low

Form RPR
61 **1** **Jeninsky (USA)**[16] 4228 4-8-8 **86** .... TedDurcan 3 95
(Rae Guest) *chsd ldrs: nt clr run over 1f out: swtchd rt: rdn and r.o to ld wl ins fnl f* **33/1**
4105 **2** ½ **Signor Peltro**[14] 4297 6-9-4 **96** .... DaneO'Neill 7 108+
(H Candy) *hld up: nt clr run and swtchd rt over 1f out: r.o wl ins fnl f: nt rch wnr* **7/1**
5-21 **3** ½ **Splendorinthegrass (IRE)**[22] 4057 3-8-10 **94** .... JimCrowley 1 99+
(R Charlton) *chsd ldr tl led over 1f out: sn rdn: hdd wl ins fnl f* **6/1**[3]
1360 **4** ¾ **Advanced**[7] 4523 6-9-5 **97** .... MichaelHills 4 102
(K A Ryan) *trckd ldrs: rdn over 1f out: styd on same pce towards fin* **25/1**
20-1 **5** ¾ **Big Noise**[35] 3628 5-8-10 **93** .... Louis-PhilippeBeuzelin(5) 13 96
(Dr J D Scargill) *hld up: hdwy over 1f out: rdn and edgd lft ins fnl f: styd on* **8/1**
3000 **6** ¾ **Dhaular Dhar (IRE)**[14] 4297 7-9-4 **96** .... GeorgeBaker 6 97
(J S Goldie) *hld up: hdwy over 1f out: sn rdn: styd on* **25/1**
0000 **7** *nk* **Southandwest (IRE)**[101] 1607 5-8-5 **83** .... JimmyQuinn 8 83
(J S Moore) *hld up: racd keenly: hdwy and nt clr run over 2f out: rdn over 1f out: styd on* **50/1**
6201 **8** *1* **Castles In The Air**[14] 4293 4-9-0 **92** .... PaulHanagan 11 89
(R A Fahey) *chsd ldrs: rdn over 1f out: no ex ins fnl f* **10/1**
12-0 **9** *nk* **Al Khaleej (IRE)**[14] 4330 5-9-10 **102** .... SebSanders 14 98+
(E A L Dunlop) *s.i.s: hld up: pushed along over 2f out: r.o ins fnl f: nvr any ch* **5/1**[2]
002 **10** ½ **Noble Citizen (USA)**[37] 3524 4-8-12 **90** .... RichardMullen 5 85
(D M Simcock) *led: rdn and hdd over 1f out: wknd wl ins fnl f* **20/1**
1526 **11** 1½ **Taqdeyr**[14] 4297 4-9-8 **100** .... PhilipRobinson 10 91
(M A Jarvis) *hld up: racd keenly: effrt over 1f out: edgd rt and no ex ins fnl f* **9/2**[1]
0330 **12** *shd* **Eastern Hills**[29] 3825 4-7-12 **76** oh4 .... KirstyMilczarek 2 69+
(J S Wainwright) *hld up: hdwy over 1f out: hmpd ins fnl f: nt rcvr* **66/1**
4416 **13** *hd* **Mastership (IRE)**[6] 4560 5-8-13 **91** ....(p) TPQueally 12 81+
(J J Quinn) *hld up: hdwy and nt clr run over 1f out: n.d* **16/1**
6046 **14** *9* **Masai Moon**[35] 3628 5-8-11 **92** ow2 .... JamesMillman(3) 15 58
(B R Millman) *prom tl rdn and wknd over 1f out* **16/1**
-501 **15** 3½ **Musaalem (USA)**[36] 3567 5-9-6 **98** .... RHills 9 54
(W J Haggas) *broke wl: plld hrd: stdd and lost pl 6f out: hdwy 1/2-way: wkng whn hmpd wl over 1f out* **8/1**

1m 26.2s (0.50) **Going Correction** +0.225s/f (Good)
WFA 3 from 4yo+ 6lb **15** Ran SP% **123.6**
Speed ratings (Par 109): **106,105,104,104,103 102,101,100,100,99 98,98,97,87,83**
toteswinger: 1&2 £73.70, 1&3 £25.60, 2&3 £11.00. CSF £243.29 CT £1648.90 TOTE £38.20: £8.90, £3.30, £2.50; EX 268.70 Trifecta £549.60 Part won. Pool: £742.80 - 0.10 winning units..
Owner J M Beever **Bred** Dr R And Mrs Smiser West & Mr And Mrs M **Trained** Newmarket, Suffolk
■ Stewards' Enquiry : Dane O'Neill three-day ban: careless riding (Aug 22-24)

FOCUS
They raced towards the far side and the early pace seemed just steady, meaning those drawn low, as well as the prominent racers, were at an advantage. Not form to rate too positively but the winner recorded another personal best and the runner-up is a solid guide.

NOTEBOOK
Jeninsky(USA) was well positioned from a favourable draw and, although briefly blocked in her run over a furlong out, she ran on well when in the clear to defy a 5lb rise for her recent Doncaster success. This was a career-best performance and she's evidently improving, but plenty went her way. (op 25-1)
Signor Peltro ◆ was given too much to do and looked an unlucky loser. Stall seven didn't seem a bad draw, but he raced quite a way off the pace and, initially denied a clear run when trying to pick up, just got going too late once switched out wide. (op 15-2 tchd 8-1 in places)
Splendorinthegrass(IRE), a nine-length maiden winner over 1m here on his previous start, didn't look to have any excuses. He was always nicely placed from a favourable draw and travelled; a couple of his rivals were just too strong. (op 13-2 tchd 8-1)
Advanced ran better than in the Stewards' Cup the previous week, but still wasn't good enough. (op 20-1)
Big Noise ◆, 4lb higher than when winning at Leicester on his previous start, fared best of those from a double-figure stall, and second-best of the hold-up horses. This was a good effort considering he would have preferred a stronger pace. (op 11-1)
Dhaular Dhar(IRE) ◆ is gradually dropping back to a feasible mark and he didn't run badly considering the race was not really run to suit him.
Southandwest(IRE), returning from over three months off, didn't get the race run to suit and was a bit keen early. (op 100-1)
Al Khaleej(IRE) didn't build on the form he showed on his return from an absence over 6f at York, but it will be easy enough to give him another chance. A high draw was no help and he never featured after missing the break and being dropped in off the steady pace. (op 9-2)
Noble Citizen(USA) will be one to be with when he returns to an artificial surface. He's just not the same horse on turf, especially tacky going. (tchd 16-1)
Taqdeyr, who was reported to have run too free when one place behind Signor Peltro in a big handicap over this trip at Ascot on his previous start, was again keen, with the lack of pace clearly not suiting him. (op 11-2)
Eastern Hills, 4lb out of the handicap, is a bit better than he showed, as he was badly hampered against the far rail when keeping on.
Mastership(IRE), just as at Chester six days earlier, didn't get much of a run.
Musaalem(USA) was far too keen and looked in trouble when meeting all sorts of interference over a furlong out. Official explanation: jockey said gelding hung badly right from the start

4797 PERFORMANCE AND VALUE-GERMAN THOROUGHBRED MAIDEN FILLIES' STKS (DIV II) 7f
4:10 (4:11) (Class 4) 2-Y-O **£4,857** (£1,445; £722; £360) **Stalls** Low

Form RPR
1 **Tabassum (IRE)** 2-9-0 0 .... RHills 7 80+
(Sir Michael Stoute) *led 6f out to 5f out: rdn to ld again over 1f out: hung rt ins fnl f: r.o* **9/2**[2]
2 1¾ **Huroof (IRE)** 2-9-0 0 .... TedDurcan 9 76+
(Saeed Bin Suroor) *s.i.s: hld up: hdwy over 2f out: rdn over 1f out: sn hung rt: r.o* **5/1**[3]
3 ¾ **Meeznah (USA)** 2-9-0 0 .... DaneO'Neill 6 74+
(D R Lanigan) *s.i.s: hld up: shkn up over 2f out: hdwy over 1f out: edgd rt and r.o ins fnl f* **33/1**
4 **4** *nk* **Duty And Destiny (IRE)**[22] 4055 2-9-0 0 .... SebSanders 10 73
(B J Meehan) *chsd ldrs: led 5f out: rdn: hdd and hung rt over 1f out: no ex ins fnl f* **13/2**
5 ¾ **Ruler Of My Heart (IRE)** 2-9-0 0 .... RichardKingscote 11 71
(Tom Dascombe) *chsd ldrs: rdn over 2f out: hung lft over 1f out: no ex fnl f* **4/1**[1]
6 2¾ **Dancing Queen (IRE)** 2-9-0 0 .... PaulHanagan 3 64
(M A Magnusson) *hld up: shkn up over 2f out: styd on ins fnl f: nvr nrr* **14/1**
7 *1* **Desert Liaison** 2-9-0 0 .... TPQueally 5 62
(J Noseda) *trckd ldrs: shkn up over 1f out: wknd fnl f* **6/1**
5 **8** 1½ **Emirates Hills**[15] 4257 2-9-0 0 .... JimCrowley 8 58
(E F Vaughan) *prom: rdn over 1f out: wknd fnl f* **9/1**
9 ½ **Miniyamba (IRE)** 2-9-0 0 .... KShea 4 57
(J L Dunlop) *plld hrd: led 1f: lost pl over 4f out: bhd fr 1/2-way* **22/1**
05 **10** ½ **Golden Pippin**[14] 4318 2-9-0 0 .... PatDobbs 1 56
(R Hannon) *plld hrd and prom: rdn over 2f out: wknd wl over 1f out* **50/1**
11 *2* **Maany (USA)** 2-9-0 0 .... PhilipRobinson 2 51
(M A Jarvis) *hld up: rdn over 2f out: wknd wl over 1f out* **10/1**

1m 28.61s (2.91) **Going Correction** +0.225s/f (Good) **11** Ran SP% **117.5**
Speed ratings (Par 93): **92,90,89,88,87 84,83,81,81,80 78**
toteswinger: 1&2 £3.20, 1&3 £18.80, 2&3 £31.40. CSF £26.78 TOTE £3.50: £1.60, £2.60, £9.80; EX 30.10.
Owner Hamdan Al Maktoum **Bred** Shadwell Estate Company Limited **Trained** Newmarket, Suffolk

FOCUS
This second division of the fillies' maiden was the slowest of four 7f races on the card, including 0.97 seconds off Eolith's time in the first leg. They raced all over the place late on, with the main action middle to near side but the first three shaped well.

NOTEBOOK
Tabassum(IRE), the first foal of a lightly raced 6f two-year-old winner, created a nice impression on this debut, although the final time suggests she was allowed a pretty soft time in a share of the lead. Whatever, though, she's from the leading British yard and is evidently pretty useful, so a rise in class surely awaits. (op 3-1)
Huroof(IRE), who is out of a 7f-1m2f winner, showed plenty of ability on her debut. From a stable with a host of nice juveniles, she should be hard to beat next time. (op 6-1)
Meeznah(USA), a $120,000 half-sister to quite useful 1m winner Shahin, out of a useful dual middle-distance scorer, got the idea late on and finished well from a fair way back against the stands' rail. She should go on from this and, in the longer time, benefit from significantly further next year. (tchd 40-1)
Duty And Destiny(IRE), just as on her debut over course and distance, was ponied to the start but she proved reluctant to go into the stalls. In the race itself she was disappointing, failing to pick up despite having been ideally placed, and she has plenty to prove. (op 7-1 tchd 8-1)
Ruler Of My Heart(IRE), an 80,000euros half-sister to Al Namix, a Listed winner over 1m-1m2f in France, was sent off favourite for her debut but wasn't quite up to the task. She hung left once coming under pressure, possibly not handling the tacky going, and that cost her any chance she might have had. (op 5-1 tchd 7-1)
Dancing Queen(IRE) ◆ was easy to back but kept on gradually and is open to plenty of improvement. (op 11-1)
Desert Liaison might do better when her stable's juveniles hit form. (tchd 5-1)

4798 ROYAL BRITISH LEGION POPPY MAIDEN STKS 1m 4f
4:40 (4:42) (Class 4) 3-Y-O+ **£5,180** (£1,541; £770; £384) **Stalls** Centre

Form RPR
2 **1** **Manifest**[31] 3751 3-9-1 0 .... TPQueally 4 107+
(H R A Cecil) *hld up: hdwy over 5f out: led on bit 3f out: c clr fr over 1f out: canter* **4/7**[1]
3- **2** *19* **Count Of Tuscany (USA)**[281] 7106 3-9-1 0 .... JimCrowley 2 71
(Mrs A J Perrett) *s.i.s: hld up: hdwy 4f out: rdn to chse wnr over 2f out: wknd over 1f out* **15/2**[3]
62 **3** *4* **Sally Forth**[30] 3791 3-8-10 0 .... SteveDrowne 6 60
(R Charlton) *chsd ldr to 1/2-way: sn rdn and lost pl: wknd 3f out* **20/1**
3-33 **4** 1¾ **Ebiayn (FR)**[63] 2710 3-9-1 82 .... RHills 5 62
(M A Jarvis) *led over 3f out: sn rdn: wknd over 2f out* **5/2**[2]
5 3¼ **Beat The Devil** 3-9-1 0 .... PaulHanagan 3 57
(T R George) *prom: chsd ldr 1/2-way: led over 3f out: sn rdn and hdd: wknd over 2f out* **33/1**
52 **U** **Princess Aliuska**[50] 3120 4-9-0 0 .... GihanArnolda(7) 7 —
(Mrs S Lamyman) *uns rdr leaving stalls* **66/1**

2m 33.95s (1.05) **Going Correction** +0.225s/f (Good)
WFA 3 from 4yo 11lb **6** Ran SP% **113.2**
Speed ratings (Par 105): **105,92,89,88,86** —
toteswinger: 1&2 £1.70, 1&3 £3.10, 2&3 £3.80. CSF £5.79 TOTE £1.70: £1.20, £2.90; EX 5.30.
Owner K Abdulla **Bred** Juddmonte Farms Ltd **Trained** Newmarket, Suffolk

FOCUS
A mightily impressive performance from Manifest with the runner-up the best guide for now.

4799 BBAG-SALES.DE E B F FILLIES' H'CAP 1m
5:10 (5:11) (Class 4) (0-80,80) 3-Y-O+ **£5,180** (£1,541; £770; £384) **Stalls** Low

Form RPR
4401 **1** **Flapper (IRE)**[15] 4284 3-8-0 **61** .... AmyScott(7) 7 76
(J W Hills) *mde all: rdn clr and hung rt fr over 1f out: r.o wl* **6/1**
4512 **2** *6* **Kindest**[9] 4473 3-9-8 **76** .... GeorgeBaker 1 77
(C F Wall) *hld up: rdn over 2f out: hdwy over 1f out: edgd rt and no imp ins fnl f* **9/4**[1]
1446 **3** ¾ **At A Great Rate (USA)**[22] 4050 3-9-9 **77** .... TPQueally 4 76
(H R A Cecil) *hld up: hdwy u.p over 1f out: styd on same pce ins fnl f* **11/2**
0-00 **4** 1¼ **Izzibizzi**[21] 4088 4-10-0 **75** ....(p) KirstyMilczarek 8 71
(E A L Dunlop) *hld up: outpcd 2f out: styd on u.p ins fnl f: n.d* **16/1**

110 **5** *nk* **Miss Christophene (IRE)**[74] 2356 3-9-4 **72**.................... JimmyQuinn 6 67+
(Mrs S Lamyman) *prom: chsd wnr 6f out: tl rdn over 2f out: nt clr run and lost pl over 1f out: kpt on towards fin* **20/1**
6100 **6** *3/4* **So Blissful (IRE)**[8] 4482 3-9-8 **76**.................................... MichaelHills 9 70
(T G Mills) *chsd ldrs: rdn over 2f out: wknd fnl f* **5/1**[3]
633 **7** *4* **Repetischa (IRE)**[44] 3297 3-9-4 **72**.................................... JimCrowley 3 56
(E A L Dunlop) *chsd wnr 2f: remained handy: rdn over 1f out: wknd fnl f* **8/1**
0514 **8** *2 1/4* **Volochkova (USA)**[14] 4317 3-9-4 **77**...........(t) Louis-PhilippeBeuzelin(5) 5 56
(J R Fanshawe) *hld up: hdwy over 2f out: rdn over 1f out: wknd ins fnl f: virtually p.u nr fin* **9/2**[2]
1m 42.42s (2.42) **Going Correction** +0.225s/f (Good)
WFA 3 from 4yo 7lb **8** Ran SP% **117.0**
Speed ratings (Par 102): **96,90,89,88,87 86,82,80**
toteswinger: 1&2 £4.10, 1&3 £6.00, 2&3 £3.80. CSF £20.45 CT £80.28 TOTE £6.30: £2.20, £1.20, £2.10; EX 16.10 Place 6: £178.15 Place 5: £52.85.
Owner Abbott Racing Partners **Bred** Celbridge Estates Ltd **Trained** Upper Lambourn, Berks

FOCUS
A fair fillies' handicap which is rated at close to face value through the placed horses. They tended to race up the middle of the track.
Repetischa(IRE) Official explanation: jockey said filly stopped quickly
T/Plt: £115.70 to a £1 stake. Pool: £82,143.15. 517.92 winning tickets. T/Qpdt: £27.50 to a £1 stake. Pool: £5,873.78. 158.00 winning tickets. CR

4430 REDCAR (L-H)
Saturday, August 8

OFFICIAL GOING: Good to firm (9.9)
Wind: light, half behind Weather: fine

4800 REDCAR RACECOURSE CONFERENCE & EVENTS VENUE (S) STKS 6f
2:05 (2:05) (Class 6) 2-Y-O **£2,047** (£604; £302) **Stalls** High

Form RPR
0 **1** **Kapelad Junior (IRE)**[16] 4219 2-8-11 0.................................. PaulEddery 2 59
(Pat Eddery) *chsd ldrs: swtchd outside 2 f out: hung rt and styd on to ld last 150yds* **9/1**[3]
2400 **2** *1* **Just The Tonic**[6] 4565 2-8-6 71.. ChrisCatlin 6 51
(M R Channon) *chsd ldrs: effrt 2f out: no ex ins fnl f* **5/6**[1]
55 **3** *1* **Drinking Buddy**[8] 4503 2-8-11 0.................................... PJMcDonald 10 53
(K A Ryan) *led: edgd lft over 1f out: hdd and no ex ins fnl f* **10/1**
0005 **4** *1/2* **Cygnet Committee (IRE)**[19] 4138 2-7-13 41.....(b[1]) JamesPSullivan(7) 7 47
(J S Wainwright) *in rr: hdwy 2f out: edgd lft and styd on ins fnl f* **100/1**
6500 **5** *1/2* **Prettiest Star (IRE)**[8] 4503 2-8-6 50......................... SilvestreDeSousa 5 45
(K A Ryan) *w ldr: kpt on same pce fnl f* **10/1**
55 **6** *nk* **Wijikura (IRE)**[13] 4349 2-8-11 0.................................... PaulMulrennan 9 49
(J J Quinn) *dwlt: sn trcking ldrs: effrt 2f out: kpt on same pce* **7/2**[2]
0000 **7** *3* **Seldom Seen Kid (IRE)**[8] 4503 2-8-11 53.............(b[1]) DuranFentiman 1 40+
(T D Easterby) *chsd ldrs on outer: wkng whn hmpd 1f out* **33/1**
0044 **8** *9* **Menediva**[19] 4138 2-8-5 48 ow2.................................. WilliamCarson(3) 3 20+
(L A Mullaney) *chsd ldrs: lost pl over 1f out: heavily eased* **40/1**
60 **9** *2 3/4* **Wallgate**[74] 2360 2-8-6 0.. AndrewMullen 8 —
(Miss J A Camacho) *w ldr: lost pl over 1f out* **40/1**
0060 **10** *2* **Foricherforpoorer**[8] 4503 2-8-3 0.........................(v[1]) KellyHarrison(3) 12 —
(N Tinkler) *s.i.s: t.k.h in rr: bhd fnl 2f* **100/1**
00 **11** *8* **Calders**[17] 4187 2-8-8 0 ow7.. SladeO'Hara(5) 11 —
(A Berry) *in rr: sn drvn along: bhd fnl 2f* **100/1**
1m 12.37s (0.57) **Going Correction** -0.05s/f (Good) **11** Ran SP% **115.7**
Speed ratings (Par 92): **94,92,91,90,90 89,85,73,69,67 56**
toteswingers: 1&2 £2.10, 1&3 £5.70, 2&3 £3.70. CSF £16.53 TOTE £8.40: £2.20, £1.10, £2.30; EX 23.50.The winner was bought in for 5,500gns.
Owner Mrs S White & Mrs J McCarlie **Bred** G W Robinson **Trained** Nether Winchendon, Bucks
■ Stewards' Enquiry : Chris Catlin caution:careless riding
Slade O'Hara one-day ban: used whip when out of contention (Aug 25)

FOCUS
An average seller. The winner stepped up by 12lb with the fourth the key to the level.

NOTEBOOK
Kapelad Junior(IRE), soon in trouble over five and a half furlongs at Bath on his debut, had clearly learned a good deal from that effort and he benefited from the slight rise in distance, staying on too strongly for the favourite. There may well be more to come in low-grade nurseries and he should appreciate the step up to 7f. (op 8-1)
Just The Tonic, officially rated 71, showed some fair form earlier in the season and was expected to capitalise on this drop in grade. She had her chance, but the winner saw it out the better. (op 5-4)
Drinking Buddy had plenty of use of made of him on this drop in trip and led into the final furlong, but he was always going to be vulnerable to a finisher and could find no extra late on. (op 8-1 tchd 11-1)
Cygnet Committee(IRE) made some late headway in the first-time blinkers and the 41-rated performer recorded easily her best effort. (tchd 80-1)
Prettiest Star(IRE) is not progressing and this further drop in grade failed to yield a better effort. (op 9-1 tchd 14-1)
Wijikura(IRE) has his chance and simply couldn't quicken. (op 11-4 tchd 5-2)
Wallgate Official explanation: jockey said filly lost its action

4801 BODDINGTONS REDCAR STRAIGHT-MILE CHAMPIONSHIP H'CAP (QUALIFIER) 1m
2:35 (2:36) (Class 3) (0-90,88) 3-Y-0+ **£7,771** (£2,312; £1,155; £577) **Stalls** High

Form RPR
20 **1** **Just Bond (IRE)**[98] 1684 7-9-5 **81**.......................... SilvestreDeSousa 5 89
(G R Oldroyd) *hld up: smooth hdwy over 2f out: led over 1f out: wnt rt ins fnl f: hld on wl* **12/1**
5243 **2** *1/2* **Observatory Star (IRE)**[7] 4549 6-9-2 **78**.................(tp) PaulMulrennan 4 85
(T D Easterby) *hld up: hdwy over 2f out: chal over 1f out: upsides whn crowded ins fnl f: no ex* **5/1**[2]
1-15 **3** *2* **Emirates Sports**[17] 4210 3-9-4 **87**.................................... WilliamBuick 3 88
(Saeed Bin Suroor) *hld up: hdwy to trck ldrs 4f out: effrt and edgd lft over 1f out: kpt on same pce* **6/1**[3]
0130 **4** *nk* **Flawed Genius**[7] 4549 4-9-7 **88**.......................................(t) AmyRyan(5) 7 89
(K A Ryan) *s.s: hdwy on wd outside 5f out: sn chsng ldrs: hung lft over 1f out: kpt on same pce* **9/1**
2111 **5** *nk* **Mountain Cat (IRE)**[50] 3110 5-9-0 **76**............................ PJMcDonald 6 77
(G A Swinbank) *trckd ldrs: led 2f out: hdd over 1f out: kpt on same pce* **5/1**[2]
562 **6** *1 1/2* **Reel Buddy Star**[42] 3378 4-8-11 **73**.................................(p) ChrisCatlin 2 70
(G M Moore) *chsd ldrs: fdd appr fnl f* **11/1**
2310 **6** *dht* **Pride Of Kings**[14] 4296 3-9-3 **86**.. GregFairley 8 82
(M Johnston) *w ldr: led over 2f out: sn hdd: fdd fnl f* **6/1**[3]
-202 **8** *1 1/4* **Motafarred (IRE)**[3] 4663 7-8-13 **78**.........................(v[1]) FrederikTylicki(3) 9 72
(Micky Hammond) *chsd ldrs: drvn over 2f out: wknd over 1f out* **3/1**[1]
2300 **9** *3 1/2* **Toledo Gold (IRE)**[2] 4708 3-8-8 **77**............................ AndrewMullen 1 62
(E J Alston) *t.k.h: led tl over 2f out: lost pl over 1f out* **20/1**
1m 36.15s (-1.85) **Going Correction** -0.05s/f (Good)
WFA 3 from 4yo+ 7lb **9** Ran SP% **117.7**
Speed ratings (Par 107): **107,106,104,104,103 102,102,101,97**
toteswingers: 1&2 £7.80, 1&3 £19.90, 2&3 £2.70. CSF £72.25 CT £404.05 TOTE £15.80: £3.60, £1.70, £1.70; EX 58.90.
Owner R C Bond **Bred** Schwindibode Ag **Trained** Brawby, N Yorks

FOCUS
This was a fair handicap for the grade although it was a bit of a muddling race.

NOTEBOOK
Just Bond(IRE), still 3lb higher than when winning at Musselburgh earlier in the season, never got into the race at Thirsk last time, but he had been given a nice break and returned with an improved effort. He made ground with the minimum of fuss and, having got the front over a furlong out, battled on well to just do enough. This was the highest mark he has won off on turf. (op 20-1)
Observatory Star(IRE) has been running well without suggesting he is up to winning off this mark, but this was a good effort considering he was a bit crowded inside the final furlong. (op 4-1 tchd 11-2)
Emirates Sports has recorded both wins on the all-weather and he looked ready for the step up to 1m when finishing fifth over 7f at Sandown last time. He came through to challenge and had every chance but was unable to quicken. (op 5-1 tchd 13-2)
Flawed Genius has never been easy to win with and he hung under pressure from over a furlong out. He is probably too high in the weights. (op 8-1 tchd 10-1)
Mountain Cat(IRE) has raced up the weights this year, winning his last three starts, and he was running from a mark 5lb higher than when scoring at Musselburgh in June. He went on two out, but his stint in front didn't last long and he was brushed aside in the end. (op 9-2 tchd 11-2)
Pride Of Kings has twice disappointed off this mark now and looks to have lost his form. (op 15-2 tchd 8-1)
Motafarred(IRE) failed to run his race in the first-time visor. (op 9-2 tchd 5-1)

4802 SAVE OUR STEEL FAMILY FUNDAY TOMORROW H'CAP 7f
3:10 (3:11) (Class 4) (0-80,79) 3-Y-0+ **£5,180** (£1,541; £770; £384) **Stalls** High

Form RPR
0300 **1** **Mujaadel (USA)**[7] 4548 4-9-6 **72**................................(p) AndrewMullen 8 80
(D Nicholls) *sn chsng ldrs: led and qcknd over 2f out: hung lft: styd on fnl f* **15/2**
2050 **2** *1* **Kiwi Bay**[29] 3825 4-9-12 **78**.. PJMcDonald 2 83
(M Dods) *sn trcking ldrs: effrt 2f out: styd on same pce ins fnl f* **8/1**
4616 **3** *1/2* **Olympic Dream**[10] 4433 3-8-13 **74**.............................. FrederikTylicki(3) 3 76
(R A Fahey) *hld up: hdwy 2f out: kpt on wl fnl f* **11/2**
0301 **4** *nk* **Without Prejudice (USA)**[8] 4501 4-9-13 **79**.................(v) WilliamBuick 5 82
(J Noseda) *trckd ldrs: effrt 2f out: kpt on same pce* **10/3**[1]
1144 **5** *1/2* **Summer Dancer (IRE)**[14] 4333 5-9-9 **75**.......................... PaulMulrennan 4 76
(P T Midgley) *hld up: effrt 2f out: edgd lft: kpt on same pce appr fnl f* **5/1**[3]
0060 **6** *3/4* **Inter Vision (USA)**[8] 4507 9-9-11 **77**.......................... SilvestreDeSousa 6 76
(A Dickman) *t.k.h: trckd ldrs: rdn over 2f out: fdd 1f out* **4/1**[2]
0033 **7** *1 1/4* **Cook's Endeavour (USA)**[8] 4494 3-9-3 **75**........................ ChrisCatlin 1 69
(K A Ryan) *led tl over 2f out: wknd fnl f* **5/1**[3]
1m 23.52s (-0.98) **Going Correction** -0.05s/f (Good)
WFA 3 from 4yo+ 6lb **7** Ran SP% **112.7**
Speed ratings (Par 105): **103,101,101,100,100 99,98**
toteswingers: 1&2 £7.70, 1&3 £4.70, 2&3 £11.40. CSF £73.87 CT £442.76 TOTE £9.20: £5.10, £5.50; EX 81.60.
Owner W R B Racing 49 **Bred** Lawrence Goichman **Trained** Sessay, N Yorks

FOCUS
A modest handicap and Andrew Mullen deserves the plaudits for an enterprising ride. Overall the form is straightforward.
Inter Vision(USA) Official explanation: jockey said gelding ran too free

4803 SAY NO MORE SAY TRANSMORE NURSERY 6f
3:45 (3:46) (Class 3) 2-Y-O **£7,123** (£2,119; £1,059; £529) **Stalls** High

Form RPR
603 **1** **Pintura**[7] 4525 2-8-10 **68**... ChrisCatlin 11 72
(M R Channon) *s.i.s: hdwy over 2f out: str run fnl f: led nr fin* **7/2**[1]
5331 **2** *3/4* **Flaneur**[14] 4306 2-9-3 **75**..(b) PJMcDonald 9 77
(T D Easterby) *led tl over 2f out: led over 1f out: hdd and no ex nr fin* **8/1**
430 **3** *nse* **Flow Chart (IRE)**[13] 4349 2-8-2 **65**................................ DeanHeslop(5) 2 67
(T D Barron) *mid-div: hdwy on outer over 2f out: chal jst ins fnl f: no ex nr fin* **20/1**
500 **4** *2* **Uddy Mac**[16] 4226 2-7-12 **59** oh3 ow3........................... KellyHarrison(3) 5 55
(N Bycroft) *sn outpcd and in rr: hdwy 2f out: styd on ins fnl f* **10/1**
014 **5** *3/4* **Haltela (IRE)**[23] 4000 2-9-6 **78**..................................(b[1]) WilliamBuick 12 71
(K A Ryan) *s.i.s: sn chsng ldrs: led over 2f out: wnt lft and hdd over 1f out: sn fdd* **10/1**
0500 **6** *1 1/4* **Charity Fair**[14] 4306 2-7-9 **56** oh8.................................. DominicFox(3) 8 46
(A Berry) *s.s: hdwy and hung lft over 2f out: kpt on: nvr nr ldrs* **100/1**
1335 **7** *2* **Oondiri (IRE)**[14] 4327 2-8-8 **66**...................................... DuranFentiman 13 50
(T D Easterby) *t.k.h: trckd ldrs: hung lft and lost pl over 1f out* **20/1**
01 **8** *1* **Eight Hours**[124] 1158 2-8-3 **61**... GregFairley 1 42
(R A Fahey) *mid-div: sn drvn along: hdwy over 2f out: upsides appr fnl f: sn wknd* **5/1**[2]
041 **9** *1 3/4* **Cian Rooney (IRE)**[13] 4349 2-9-2 **74**......................... SilvestreDeSousa 6 49
(Mrs A Duffield) *t.k.h: trckd ldrs: lost pl over 1f out* **6/1**[3]
2100 **10** *nse* **Itsthursdayalready**[21] 4089 2-9-7 **79**............................ PaulMulrennan 4 54
(J G Given) *chsd ldrs: wknd over 1f out* **9/1**
5540 **11** *8* **Clear Ice (IRE)**[25] 3937 2-8-1 **59**................................... AndrewMullen 7 10
(D Nicholls) *rr-div: reminders after 2f: sn drvn along: bhd fnl 2f* **12/1**
1m 10.91s (-0.89) **Going Correction** -0.05s/f (Good) **11** Ran SP% **110.7**
Speed ratings (Par 98): **103,102,101,99,98 96,93,92,90,90 79**
toteswingers: 1&2 £2.10, 1&3 £12.60, 2&3 £13.50. CSF £26.40 CT £367.74 TOTE £3.90: £1.50, £2.30, £6.50; EX 39.90 TRIFECTA Not won..
Owner R Bastian **Bred** Dulverton Equine **Trained** West Ilsley, Berks
■ Novay Essjay (9/1, unruly in stalls) was withdrawn. R4 applies, deduct 10p in the £.
■ Stewards' Enquiry : P J McDonald one-day ban: excessive use of the whip (Aug 22)

FOCUS
This had the look of quite a competitive nursery and the form looks sound. The winner franked the good nursery he ran in at Goodwood.

NOTEBOOK
Pintura, who ran a much-improved race when third at Goodwood on his recent handicap debut (runner-up won on Friday night), didn't look suited by these faster conditions and was never travelling that well after a slow start, but he eventually found his stride and came home strongly to get up deep inside the final furlong. He looks to be crying out for 7f and is clearly progressing. (op 9-2)

Flaneur, raised 8lb for winning at Newcastle last month, was soon in front and wouldn't give in when headed, battling on and just getting the better of Flow Chart for second, but he couldn't fend off the winner. (op 15-2)
Flow Chart(IRE) was always likely to improve once sent handicapping and he came through to take the lead inside the final furlong, but couldn't see it out as strongly as the winner and just lost second on the line. (tchd 22-1)
Uddy Mac, racing from 3lb out of the handicap and carrying 3lb overweight, stayed on late to register easily her best effort. On this evidence a step back up to 7f will suit. (op 12-1 tchd 14-1)
Haltela(IRE), a winner at York on his second start, took a backward step last time when a well-beaten fourth at Doncaster and he didn't get home here in the first-time blinkers. (tchd 12-1)
Cian Rooney(IRE), a winner at York on his second start, took a backward step last time when a well-beaten fourth at Doncaster and he didn't get home here in the first-time blinkers. (tchd 5-1 and 13-2)

4804 MARKET CROSS JEWELLERS CLAIMING STKS 1m 1f
4:20 (4:20) (Class 6) 4-Y-0+ £2,047 (£604; £302) Stalls Low

Form			Horse	Jockey	RPR
-305	1		**Baltimore Jack (IRE)**[51] 3070 5-9-1 56 (T D Walford) *led: qcknd 3f out: styd on wl: drvn rt out* **17/2**	DuranFentiman 10	67
4132	2	2	**Lucayan Dancer**[10] 4434 9-9-5 66 (D Nicholls) *trckd ldrs: drvn 3f out: styd on same pce ins fnl f* **9/4**[1]	PaulEddery 1	67
00-6	3	1 1/4	**Roman History (IRE)**[44] 3314 6-8-7 48 (Miss Tracy Waggott) *chsd wnr: chal over 3f out: kpt on same pce fnl f* **25/1**	(p) GregFairley 9	52
4300	4	1/2	**Pianoforte (USA)**[13] 4344 7-8-5 53 (E J Alston) *hld up in rr: hdwy and nt clr run over 2f out: kpt on wl fnl f* **12/1**	(b) AndrewMullen 8	49
0604	5	1/2	**Royal Fantasy (IRE)**[13] 4351 6-8-7 63 (N Tinkler) *hld up in midfield: stdy hdwy 4f out: nt clr run over 2f out: kpt on ins fnl f* **5/1**[3]	(p) KellyHarrison(3) 2	53
5400	6	3/4	**Wovoka (IRE)**[14] 4312 6-9-6 80 (K A Ryan) *s.s: hld up in rr: hdwy on ins over 4f out: nt clr run fr over 2f out: one pce* **5/2**[2]	AmyRyan(5) 5	66
6/0-	7	5	**Reflective Glory (IRE)**[11] 193 5-8-10 42 ow4 (J S Wainwright) *chsd ldrs: rdn over 3f out: lost pl over 1f out* **100/1**	(p) PAspell 3	40
034	8	1 1/4	**Awaken**[37] 3755 8-8-4 47 ow2 (Miss Tracy Waggott) *hld up in tch: drvn to chse ldrs over 3f out: lost pl over 2f out* **16/1**	PatrickMathers 4	31
1-06	9	2 1/4	**La Columbina**[10] 4434 4-8-8 72 (G A Harker) *hld up in midfield: hdwy and swtchd outside over 2f out: edgd lft and sn wknd* **8/1**	(v) PaulMulrennan 6	30
5-30	10	18	**Glamoroso (IRE)**[176] 537 4-8-5 41 (A Kirtley) *s.i.s: detached in last: bhd and drvn 5f out: sn t.o* **50/1**	ChrisCatlin 7	—

1m 52.68s (-0.32) **Going Correction** -0.05s/f (Good) **10** Ran SP% **118.0**
Speed ratings (Par 101): **99,97,96,95,95 94,90,89,87,71**
toteswingers: 1&2 £5.50, 1&3 £30.40, 2&3 £15.00. CSF £28.12 TOTE £9.90: £2.60, £1.30, £4.90; EX 32.10.
Owner D Swales **Bred** P Monagnan And J Collins And G Dillon **Trained** Sheriff Hutton, N Yorks

FOCUS
Quite a competitive claimer on paper but the sixth and ninth, who were best in, disappointed. The winner had the run of things.

4805 WEDDING RECEPTIONS @ REDCAR RACECOURSE MEDIAN AUCTION MAIDEN STKS 7f
4:50 (4:50) (Class 5) 3-4-Y-0 £2,590 (£770; £385; £192) Stalls High

Form			Horse	Jockey	RPR
2	1		**Ordoney (IRE)**[15] 4276 4-9-9 0 (L M Cumani) *trckd ldrs: led over 2f out: edgd rt fnl f: jst hld on* **4/6**[1]	WilliamBuick 7	79+
-323	2	nse	**Helieorbea**[33] 3680 3-9-3 70 (T D Easterby) *w ldrs: chal over 1f out: jst failed* **2/1**[2]	DuranFentiman 8	76
	3	10	**Towthorpe** 3-9-3 0 (M Brittain) *led tl over 2f out: hung lft and wknd appr fnl f* **14/1**	PaulMulrennan 4	49
00	4	1 1/4	**Blastie**[8] 4505 4-9-9 0 (T D Walford) *chsd ldrs: drvn 3f out: sn wl outpcd* **25/1**	PJMcDonald 1	48
0	5	3/4	**Severio (IRE)**[15] 4277 3-8-12 0 (A P Jarvis) *sn chsng ldrs: rdn and outpcd 3f out* **9/1**[3]	ChrisCatlin 3	39
40-0	6	3/4	**Consequence**[15] 4277 3-9-0 39 (A Dickman) *chsd ldrs: rdn and hung lft over 2f out: grad wknd* **40/1**	FrederikTylicki(3) 6	42
0-60	7	5	**Avonlini**[28] 3859 3-8-5 48 (B P J Baugh) *sn outpcd and in rr: reminders after 2f* **40/1**	JemmaMarshall(7) 9	23
0	8	6	**Spartan Storm (IRE)**[30] 3764 3-8-10 0 (M Brittain) *dwlt: sme hdwy on wd outside after 2f: hung lft and sn lost pl* **33/1**	JohnCavanagh(7) 2	12

1m 23.01s (-1.49) **Going Correction** -0.05s/f (Good)
WFA 3 from 4yo 6lb **8** Ran SP% **121.7**
Speed ratings (Par 103): **106,105,94,93,92 91,85,78**
toteswingers: 1&2 £1.60, 1&3 £3.70, 2&3 £4.80. CSF £2.33 TOTE £1.60: £1.02, £1.10, £3.40; EX 2.80.
Owner Sheikh Mohammed Obaid Al Maktoum **Bred** Mrs Mary Coonan **Trained** Newmarket, Suffolk

FOCUS
The 'big two' came clear and produced good form for the track, although this was a very weak maiden overall.

4806 BUY YOUR TICKETS ON-LINE @ REDCARRACING.CO.UK H'CAP 1m 6f 19y
5:20 (5:22) (Class 6) (0-60,57) 3-Y-0+ £1,942 (£578; £288; £144) Stalls Low

Form			Horse	Jockey	RPR
4500	1		**Harcas (IRE)**[27] 3499 7-9-8 **54** (M Todhunter) *trckd ldrs: led 4f out: styd on u.p: nvr really threatened* **22/1**	(v1) PJMcDonald 1	63
0-26	2	1	**Goldan Jess (IRE)**[9] 4462 5-8-11 **46** ow1 (P A Kirby) *prom: wnt 2nd over 3f out: kpt on: nvr able to chal* **9/1**	LeeVickers(3) 4	54
-100	3	1 1/2	**Bright Sparky (GER)**[11] 4402 6-8-11 **48** (M W Easterby) *s.i.s: hld up in rr: hdwy on wd outside over 3f out: kpt on to take 3rd ins fnl f* **40/1**	(vt1) SladeO'Hara(5) 13	54
0000	4	1 1/4	**Knock Three Times (IRE)**[8] 4506 3-7-11 **45** (W Storey) *in tch: hdwy to take 3rd 3f out: kpt on one pce* **50/1**	DominicFox(3) 6	49
/P41	5	1/2	**Patavium (IRE)**[17] 4193 6-8-11 **50** (E W Tuer) *hld up in rr: hdwy on ins over 3f out: kpt on: nvr rchd ldrs* **10/1**	JamesPSullivan(7) 12	53
0/0-	6	1	**Oniz Tiptoes (IRE)**[11] 1017 8-8-13 **45** (J S Wainwright) *mid-div: effrt 4f out: kpt on: nvr a threat* **10/1**	(p) PAspell 5	47
2222	7	3/4	**Mystified (IRE)**[9] 4462 6-9-4 **55** (R F Fisher) *drvn early to chse ldrs: effrt 4f out: one pce* **5/1**[1]	(tp) PatrickDonaghy(5) 8	56
3153	8	3 3/4	**Rosewin (IRE)**[24] 3974 3-8-9 **54** (A Dickman) *mid-div: lost pl over 6f out: sme hdwy 3f out: hung lft and no imp whn eased over 1f out* **10/1**	ChrisCatlin 11	50
6362	9	1/2	**Terenzium (IRE)**[30] 3760 7-8-13 **48** (Micky Hammond) *in rr: pushed along 6f out: nvr a factor* **6/1**[2]	(p) FrederikTylicki(3) 16	43
3240	10	1	**Tae Kwon Do (USA)**[39] 3482 3-8-10 **55** (Miss J A Camacho) *swtchd lft s: mid-div: effrt 4f out: nvr on terms* **8/1**	PaulMulrennan 10	49
4340	11	1/2	**Cripsey Brook**[13] 4350 11-9-1 **52** (K G Reveley) *s.i.s: a towards rr* **7/1**[3]	(b) AmyRyan(5) 7	45
60-0	12	13	**Mcqueen (IRE)**[41] 2445 9-9-8 **57** (B D Leavy) *led: hdd 10f out: lost pl over 3f out: bhd whn eased* **16/1**	RussellKennemore(3) 2	32
041	13	6	**Looks The Business (IRE)**[36] 3594 8-9-8 **54** (A B Haynes) *w ldr: led 10f out tl 4f out: lost pl over 2f out: bhd whn eased* **7/1**[3]	WilliamBuick 3	20
000/	14	3/4	**English Archer**[648] 6558 6-8-13 **45** (A Kirtley) *t.k.h in midfield: lost pl over 2f out: bhd whn eased* **50/1**	GregFairley 15	10

3m 1.12s (-3.58) **Going Correction** -0.05s/f (Good)
WFA 3 from 5yo+ 13lb **14** Ran SP% **120.9**
Speed ratings (Par 101): **108,107,106,105,105 105,104,102,102,101 101,93,90,90**
toteswingers: 1&2 £54.90, 1&3 £60.50, 2&3 £46.20. CSF £205.64 CT £7676.29 TOTE £29.20: £6.40, £3.80, £4.70; EX 312.20 Place 6: £386.64 Place 5: £275.68.
Owner Mr & Mrs Ian Hall **Bred** N Hartery **Trained** Orton, Cumbria

FOCUS
This was a competitive low-grade staying handicap. Sound if limited form.
Rosewin(IRE) Official explanation: jockey said filly hung left throughout
Looks The Business(IRE) Official explanation: jockey said gelding had no more to give
T/Plt: £245.70 to a £1 stake. Pool: £50,818.99. 150.95 winning tickets. T/Qpdt: £43.10 to a £1 stake. Pool: £2,630.40. 45.10 winning tickets. WG

4685 DEAUVILLE (R-H)
Friday, August 7

OFFICIAL GOING: Turf course - soft; all-weather - standard

4807a PRIX DE CREVECOEUR (UNRACED COLTS & GELDINGS) (ROUND) 1m (R)
12:50 (12:52) 2-Y-0 £11,650 (£4,660; £3,495; £2,330; £1,165)

		Horse	Jockey	RPR
1		**Planteur (IRE)** 2-9-2 (E Lellouche, France)	ACrastus	83
2	1/2	**Wealthy (IRE)** 2-8-10 (A Fabre, France)	MBarzalona(6)	82
3	3	**Twinlight (FR)** 2-8-10 (G Cherel, France)	FPrat(6)	75
4	1/2	**Philander** 2-9-2 (E J O'Neill) *racd in 9th: swtchd outside 1 1/2f out: styd on steadily fr over 1f out* **28/1**[1]		74
5	1 1/2	**Trajectory** 2-9-2 (D Smaga, France)		71
6	shd	**Marine Officer (USA)** 2-9-2 (J-C Rouget, France)		71
7	1/2	**Dubawi Junior (IRE)** 2-9-2 (J-C Rouget, France)		70
8	3	**Anaxis (FR)** 2-9-2 (C Laffon-Parias, France)		63
9	1/2	**Casa Battlo (FR)** 2-9-2 (Robert Collet, France)	OPeslier	62
10	3/4	**Ustilago (GER)** 2-9-2 (W Baltromei, Germany)		60
0		**Cacao Bey (FR)** 2-9-2 (P Chevillard, France)		—
0		**Gosse De Sevres (FR)** 2-9-2 (Ron Caget, France)		—
0		**Abou Selem (FR)** 2-9-2 (J-L Pelletan, France)		—

1m 45.5s (4.50) **13** Ran SP% **3.4**
PARI-MUTUEL (Including 1 Euro stake): WIN 14.10; PL 3.40, 1.70, 8.80;DF 26.70.
Owner Ecurie Wildenstein **Bred** Dayton Investments Ltd **Trained** Lamorlaye, France

4808 - (Foreign Racing) - See Raceform Interactive

ARLINGTON PARK (L-H)
Saturday, August 8

OFFICIAL GOING: Good

4809a ARLINGTON MILLION XXVII (GRADE 1) (TURF) 1m 2f
10:42 (10:45) 3-Y-0+
£408,333 (£136,111; £68,056; £34,028; £20,417; £13,611)

		Horse	Jockey	RPR
1		**Gio Ponti (USA)**[28] 4-9-0 (Christophe Clement, U.S.A) *settled disputing 5th, strong run from 3f out, led approaching straight, soon ridden, ran on well* **6/4**[1]	RADominguez 6	122+
2	1 1/4	**Just As Well (USA)**[28] 6-9-0 (Jonathan Sheppard, U.S.A) *held up, last 3f out, headway over 2f out, edged to outside & 7th straight, ran on under pressure to take 2nd last strides* **191/10**	EBaird 3	119
3	hd	**Stotsfold**[51] 3085 6-9-0 (W R Swinburn) *held up in touch, close 6th straight, went 2nd 1f out, driven & lost 2nd last strides* **29/1**	AdamKirby 4	119
4	6	**Cima De Triomphe (IRE)**[35] 3640 4-9-0 (L M Cumani) *held up, last on outside & bore out straight, stayed on one pace final f* **84/10**	C-PLemaire 8	107
5	1 1/4	**Einstein (BRZ)**[56] 7-9-0 (Helen Pitts-Blasi, U.S.A) *disputed 2nd early, 4th half-way, close 5th on outside straight, one pace* **3/1**[2]	JRLeparoux 1	105
6	nse	**Mr. Sidney (USA)**[35] 5-9-0 (William Mott, U.S.A) *raced in 4th, went 3rd half-way, 2nd over 3f out, led briefly just inside final 2f, close 3rd straight, soon beaten* **67/10**	(b) KDesormeaux 5	104
7	1/2	**Gloria De Campeao (BRZ)**[83] 2117 6-9-0 (P Bary, France) *raced in 2nd behind clear leader, 4th & driven on inside straight, soon beaten* **113/10**	TJPereira 7	103

8 3/4 **Presious Passion (USA)**[35] 6-9-0 ....(b) ETrujillo 2 102+
(Mary Hartmann, U.S.A) *led, soon 8 lengths clear, rivals closed up from half-way, headed just inside final 2f, 2nd straight, soon weakened* **49/10**[3]

2m 4.19s (2.55) **8** Ran SP% **122.0**
PARI-MUTUEL: WIN 5.00; PL (1-2) 3.40, 11.80;SHOW (1-2-3) 2.60, 6.80, 9.80; SF 72.20.
Owner Castleton Lyons Farm **Bred** Kilboy Estate **Trained** USA

NOTEBOOK
Gio Ponti(USA), winner of the Grade 1 Man o'War last time out, has developed into a top performer on the grass. He appreciated the decent gallop and quickened up well between horses on the home turn before staying on strongly up the straight. He's won on fast ground and with ease, and is effective between 1m and 1m3f, and a step up in trip to 1m4f for the Breeders' Cup Turf ought not to be a problem.
Stotsfold, winner of a French Group 3 last time, had been training well prior to the race and his prominent effort came as no surprise to connections. It wouldn't be a surprise to see him back pot-hunting in the US following this fine effort.
Cima De Triomphe(IRE) was disappointing, never getting involved from off the pace despite the good gallop. Given how well the Eclpise form has been working out, this was a surprisingly tame effort.

SAINT-MALO (L-H)
Saturday, August 8

OFFICIAL GOING: Soft

4810a PRIX VINCENT DE GOURNAY (MAIDEN) (FILLIES) 1m 1f
5:30 (12:00) 3-Y-O **£6,311** (£2,524; £1,893; £1,262; £631)

Form	Pos	Dist	Horse	Jockey	RPR
	1		**In The Mist**[121] 3-9-0 (F Head, France)	AMalenfant 7	80
	2	1	**Dame Anouska (IRE)**[20] 4130 3-9-0 (E J O'Neill) *tracked front-running winner, tried to challenge approaching final f, ran on same pace (9/2)* **9/2**[1]	JAuge 3	78
	3	1	**Belondine (FR)**[21] 3-8-12 (Y De Nicolay, France)	JBensimon 11	74
	4	3	**Camille's Secret (FR)** 3-8-9 (R Gibson, France)	10	65
	5	3/4	**Sweetner (FR)** 3-8-9 (C Rouget, France)	1	63
	6	hd	**Glimmer**[42] 3417 3-8-12 (H-A Pantall, France)	9	66
	7	2 1/2	**Maricath (FR)**[35] 3-8-12 (C Lotoux, France)	8	60
	8	1/2	**Deauville Royale** 3-8-9 (S Wattel, France)	2	56
	9	shd	**Karta (IRE)**[109] 1423 3-8-9 (H-A Pantall, France)	4	56
	10	4	**Carousel Lady (FR)** 3-8-9 (D Sepulchre, France)	6	48

1m 52.5s (112.50) **10** Ran SP% **18.2**
PARI-MUTUEL: WIN 2.60; PL 1.20, 1.60, 1.80; DF 4.90.
Owner J Wigan & G Strawbridge **Bred** Britton House Stud **Trained** France

4424 LEICESTER (R-H)
Sunday, August 9

OFFICIAL GOING: Heavy (soft in places; 6.4)
Wind: Nil Weather: Cloudy with sunny spells

4811 E B F LEICESTERSHIRE AND RUTLAND LIFE MAIDEN STKS 7f 9y
2:20 (2:20) (Class 4) 2-Y-O **£5,180** (£1,541; £770; £384) **Stalls** Low

Form	Pos	Dist	Horse	Jockey	RPR
42	1		**Hoss Cartwright (IRE)**[15] 4307 2-9-3 0 (J Howard Johnson) *mde all: rdn and hung rt over 1f out: r.o* **10/3**[2]	PaulHanagan 2	73+
	2	nk	**King's Parade** 2-9-3 0 (Sir Michael Stoute) *a.p: rdn to chse wnr over 1f out: edgd rt: r.o* **5/1**	NCallan 4	72+
00	3	3	**Killusty Fancy (IRE)**[24] 4006 2-9-3 0 (D J S Ffrench Davis) *chsd wnr tl rdn over 1f out: styd on same pce* **100/1**	StephenDonohoe 5	65
00	4	3/4	**Thewinnatakesitall**[29] 3858 2-8-9 0 (H J Evans) *hld up: plld hrd: hdwy over 1f out: nt rch ldrs* **28/1**	KevinGhunowa(3) 9	58
	5	1 1/4	**Crunched** 2-9-3 0 (M L W Bell) *prom: rdn over 2f out: styd on same pce appr fnl f* **16/1**	PatCosgrave 8	60
0	6	1	**Lost Cause**[15] 4314 2-9-3 0 (R Charlton) *hld up: hdwy over 1f out: wknd ins fnl f* **7/2**[3]	DarryllHolland 6	57
	7	nk	**Groove Master** 2-9-3 0 (A King) *hld up: rdn 1/2-way: n.d* **12/1**	FergusSweeney 7	57
0	8	1	**Greek Key (IRE)**[11] 4439 2-9-3 0 (M L W Bell) *s.i.s: hld up: hdwy 3f out: wkng whn hung rt over 1f out* **11/1**	HayleyTurner 1	54
	9	6	**Ebony Boom (IRE)** 2-9-3 0 (H R A Cecil) *s.i.s: rn green thrght: pushed along in rr: hdwy over 2f out: sn wknd* **3/1**[1]	TPQueally 3	39

1m 29.97s (3.77) **Going Correction** +0.20s/f (Good) **9** Ran SP% **113.3**
Speed ratings (Par 96): **86,85,82,81,79 78,78,77,70**
toteswinger: 1&2 £3.10, 1&3 £31.50, 2&3 £42.80. CSF £19.99 TOTE £4.60: £1.80, £1.90, £20.90; EX 14.40.
Owner J Howard Johnson **Bred** Sir E J Loder **Trained** Billy Row, Co Durham

FOCUS
An average maiden, run at an ordinary pace. The first pair came clear and the third/fourth put the form into perspective.

NOTEBOOK
Hoss Cartwright(IRE) hed his maiden tag at the third attempt and he made every yard. He got the run of things and it would be a surprise were he to confirm this form with the runner-up should they ever meet again, but there was plenty to like about the way he went about his business all the same. He has scope and can build on this in nurseries. (op 3-1 tchd 7-2)
King's Parade ♦, whose yard like to start off an above-average juvenile in this race, was the only one to give the winner a race and made him pull out all the stops. It looked as though he may prevail shortly after the furlong marker, but making up ground was not easy here and that also means he deserves extra credit. He is a half-brother to a juvenile winner at this trip, should not be long in winning and could be smart. (op 4-1 tchd 11-2)
Killusty Fancy(IRE) puts the overall form into some perspective, but has now improved with each of his three outings and he evidently enjoys cut underfoot. Nurseries are now an option. (op 150-1)
Thewinnatakesitall, up in distance, also came into this with the benefit of two previous outings and experience was an advantage to her here. This was her most encouraging display to date, on a totally contrasting surface, and she too now qualifies for nurseries. (op 50-1)
Crunched fared the best of the two from his stable despite looking the second string and his pedigree suggesting the trip would be plenty far enough at this stage. He took time to get going, but left the clear impression he would get closer next time. (tchd 14-1)
Lost Cause failed to improve on his debut effort at Newmarket 15 days earlier and should benefit for a return to less demanding ground. (op 9-2)
Ebony Boom(IRE) has a stamina-laden pedigree and headed the betting on his racecourse bow. He proved far too green to do himself justice though and looks to need more time. (op 10-3)

4812 FEDERATION OF SMALL BUSINESSES (S) STKS 7f 9y
2:50 (2:52) (Class 5) 3-4-Y-O **£2,590** (£770; £385; £192) **Stalls** Low

Form	Pos	Dist	Horse	Jockey	RPR
0000	1		**Stand In Flames**[10] 4473 4-8-11 61 (Pat Eddery) *chsd ldr tl led 1/2-way: rdn over 1f out: r.o: eased nr fin* **10/3**[2]	DarryllHolland 9	63
0330	2	1 1/4	**La Belle Joannie**[22] 4084 4-8-11 46 (S Curran) *hld up: hdwy over 2f out: chsd wnr over 1f out: styd on* **12/1**	JamesDoyle 1	60
2362	3	5	**Blue Noodles**[11] 4425 3-9-1 65 (Ollie Pears) *led: hung rt and hdd 1/2-way: sn rdn: wknd ins fnl f* **13/8**[1]	TPQueally 11	55
0-50	4	hd	**Cadeaux Fax**[15] 4322 4-9-2 52 (B R Millman) *prom: swtchd rt 1/2-way: sn rdn: wknd ins fnl f* **14/1**	TGMcLaughlin 2	51
4506	5	1 1/4	**Zeffirelli**[57] 2921 4-9-2 53 (M Quinn) *chsd ldrs: rdn 1/2-way: wknd fnl f* **6/1**[3]	PatCosgrave 3	48
4056	6	1/2	**Feeling Stylish (IRE)**[34] 3685 3-8-5 45 (N Tinkler) *mid-div: rdn 1/2-way: outpcd over 2f out: n.d after* **14/1**	JimmyQuinn 8	40
600	7	3/4	**Monte Mayor Eagle**[19] 4172 3-8-5 46 (D Haydn Jones) *s.i.s: rdn 1/2-way: sme hdwy over 1f out: n.d* **14/1**	JamieMackay 10	38
6060	8	5	**Songful (IRE)**[20] 4155 3-8-5 46 (Pat Eddery) *s.i.s: pushed along over 2f out: n.d* **20/1**	PaulHanagan 4	25
0/00	9	11	**Days Of Thunder (IRE)**[13] 4372 4-8-13 38 (B R Summers) *prom: rdn 1/2-way: wknd over 2f out* **100/1**	KevinGhunowa(3) 12	—
0	10	8	**Legnani**[34] 3685 3-8-5 65 (George Baker) *dwlt: outpcd* **25/1**	(v1) DO'Donohoe 6	—
0	11	11	**Slumdog (IRE)**[14] 4354 4-8-11 0 (Garry Moss) *hld up: rdn 1/2-way: sn wknd* **50/1**	MarkCoumbe(5) 7	—

1m 27.38s (1.18) **Going Correction** +0.20s/f (Good)
WFA 3 from 4yo 6lb **11** Ran SP% **114.7**
Speed ratings (Par 103): **101,99,93,93,92 91,90,85,72,63 50**
toteswinger: 1&2 £7.90, 1&3 £1.90, 2&3 £3.90. CSF £40.04 TOTE £4.80: £1.80, £2.60, £1.30; EX 46.70.The winner was sold to George Baker for 5,200gns. Blue Noodles was claimed by P. D. Evans for £6,000.
Owner Chris Hardy **Bred** Chris E Hardy **Trained** Nether Winchendon, Bucks

FOCUS
They raced towards the stands' side in this weak affair and it was another race where two pulled clear.
Stand In Flames Official explanation: trainer's rep said, regarding the apparent improvement in form shown, that this was a drop in trip and a drop in class

4813 FSB "THE LEADING BUSINESS ORGANISATION" H'CAP 1m 1f 218y
3:20 (3:20) (Class 5) (0-70,70) 3-Y-O **£3,885** (£1,156; £577; £288) **Stalls** High

Form	Pos	Dist	Horse	Jockey	RPR
042	1		**Vivachi (IRE)**[20] 4145 3-9-0 **70** (R M Beckett) *trckd ldr: plld hrd: led over 1f out: rdn clr* **15/8**[1]	JPFahy(7) 2	78
034	2	4 1/2	**Mayolynn (USA)**[25] 3984 3-9-2 **65** (H R A Cecil) *sn led: rdn and hdd over 1f out: no ex fnl f* **9/4**[2]	(v1) TPQueally 1	64
0-50	3	3 1/2	**Major Value**[17] 4246 3-8-8 **57** (C G Cox) *chsd ldrs: rdn over 3f out: wknd over 1f out* **3/1**[3]	PaulHanagan 4	49
662	4	12	**Arashi**[24] 4022 3-9-4 **67** (Lucinda Featherstone) *plld hrd and prom: rdn over 3f out: wknd 2f out* **4/1**	(p) TGMcLaughlin 3	35

2m 11.54s (3.64) **Going Correction** +0.325s/f (Good) **4** Ran SP% **110.6**
Speed ratings (Par 100): **98,94,91,82**
CSF £6.49 TOTE £2.90; EX 6.90.
Owner Trevor Stewart & Anthony Stroud **Bred** Roland H Alder **Trained** Whitsbury, Hants

FOCUS
Each of these 3yos were maidens making their handicap debuts. There was no real pace on early and the form is worth treating with a degree of caution, but the best horse still won.

4814 LEICESTER MERCURY FAMILY FUN DAY H'CAP 7f 9y
3:50 (3:50) (Class 2) (0-100,92) 3-Y-O
£12,462 (£3,732; £1,866; £934; £466; £234) **Stalls** Low

Form	Pos	Dist	Horse	Jockey	RPR
552	1		**Imaam**[8] 4540 3-8-8 **79** (J L Dunlop) *mde all: rdn over 1f out: r.o wl* **10/3**[2]	RHills 3	87+
1111	2	1 1/4	**Rafta (IRE)**[16] 4281 3-7-12 **76** (T T Clement) *s.i.s: sn prom: rdn to chse wnr over 1f out: styd on same pce ins fnl f* **10/3**[2]	JosephineBruning(7) 7	81
1166	3	1/2	**Kyllachy Star**[10] 4459 3-9-4 **89** (R A Fahey) *trckd ldrs: plld hrd: rdn over 1f out: styd on same pce ins fnl f* **13/2**[3]	(p) PaulHanagan 2	92
1422	4	7	**Sunshine Always (IRE)**[22] 4095 3-8-10 **81** (W J Haggas) *stdd s: hld up: swtchd rt and hdwy over 2f out: rdn over 1f out: wknd and eased ins fnl f* **9/4**[1]	HayleyTurner 5	73
00-	5	1 1/4	**Kings Troop**[289] 6946 3-8-7 **85** (H R A Cecil) *s.i.s: hld up: plld hrd: rdn and swtchd rt over 2f out: sn wknd* **20/1**	CharlesEddery(7) 4	67
5400	6	nse	**Viva Ronaldo (IRE)**[52] 3049 3-9-0 **92** (R A Fahey) *awkward leaving stalls: hld up: swtchd rt over 5f out: rdn and outpcd whn swtchd lft 2f out: n.d* **20/1**	TimothyAyres(7) 1	74
2510	7	nk	**El Loco Uno (USA)**[42] 3431 3-9-1 **86** (H R A Cecil) *plld hrd: trckd wnr tl rdn and wknd over 1f out* **8/1**	TPQueally 6	67

1m 26.37s (0.17) **Going Correction** +0.20s/f (Good) **7** Ran SP% **110.9**
Speed ratings (Par 106): **107,105,105,97,95 95,95**
toteswinger: 1&2 £14.10, 1&3 £13.50, 2&3 £13.90. CSF £13.91 TOTE £4.20: £2.50, £1.80; EX 16.30.
Owner Hamdan Al Maktoum **Bred** Shadwell Estate Company Limited **Trained** Arundel, W Sussex

FOCUS
A fair 3yo handicap and they again came to the stands' rail. The winner dictated.

NOTEBOOK
Imaam bagged the rail and made all in ready fashion. He had his rivals in trouble coming to the furlong marker and the ground held no fears, but everything went his way. (op 4-1 tchd 9-2)
Rafta(IRE) was another 6lb higher and kept on gamely for second. This was another improved run in defeat and she is not weighted out of winning again just yet. (tchd 3-1)

Kyllachy Star, a previous heavy-ground winner, ran a sound enough race in the first-time cheekpieces and remains in good form. He helps to set the level as the handicapper looks to have his measure. (op 5-1)
Sunshine Always(IRE) was forced to make his challenge wide of runners and never seriously looked like getting involved. The return to 1m looks on the cards for him. (op 5-2 tchd 2-1)
El Loco Uno(USA), after refusing to settle, looked unsuited by the ground and appears in need of respite from the handicapper.

4815 FSB "FIGHTING RED TAPE" H'CAP — 1m 1f 218y
4:20 (4:20) (Class 4) (0-85,83) 4-Y-0+ **£4,857** (£1,445; £722; £360) **Stalls** High

Form				RPR
303	1		**Charlie Tokyo (IRE)**[33] 3705 6-9-6 **82**........(v) PaulHanagan 7 (R A Fahey) *chsd ldr: led 2f out: rdn over 1f out: styd on gamely* **4/1**[2]	88
303	2	hd	**Rangefinder**[24] 4003 5-9-5 **81**........RHills 6 (L M Cumani) *trckd ldrs: racd keenly: rdn to chse wnr over 1f out: edgd rt: ev ch ins fnl f: styd on* **11/4**[1]	87
5134	3	nk	**Keisha Kayleigh (IRE)**[10] 4465 6-8-4 **66**........HayleyTurner 5 (B Ellison) *s.s: hld up: swtchd lft over 2f out: hdwy over 1f out: r.o wl* **6/1**[3]	71
-530	4	2	**Suzi Spends (IRE)**[15] 4328 4-9-5 **81**........JimmyQuinn 2 (H J Collingridge) *hld up: hdwy over 2f out: sn rdn: edgd rt and styd on same pce ins fnl f* **15/2**	82
0/0-	5	7	**Sadler's Star (GER)**[61] 96 6-8-7 **69**........FergusSweeney 3 (A King) *s.i.s: sn prom: rdn over 2f out: wknd over 1f out* **9/1**	56
240	6	nk	**Magic Echo**[15] 4328 5-9-7 **83**........DarryllHolland 4 (M Dods) *hld up: hdwy 2f out: sn rdn and wknd* **4/1**[2]	69
-560	7	4	**Mr Hichens**[58] 2891 4-9-3 **79**........(v[1]) TGMcLaughlin 1 (Karen George) *sn led: clr 1/2-way: rdn and hdd 2f out wknd over 1f out* **9/1**	57

2m 9.87s (1.97) **Going Correction** +0.325s/f (Good) **7 Ran SP% 112.7**
Speed ratings (Par 105): **105,104,104,103,97 97,93**
toteswinger: 1&2 £2.60, 1&3 £3.80, 2&3 £3.60. CSF £14.96 TOTE £4.70: £2.40, £2.00; EX 8.50.
Owner Stanley Yu **Bred** J Donnelly **Trained** Musley Bank, N Yorks

FOCUS
A fair handicap, run at an average pace.
Magic Echo Official explanation: jockey said mare lost its action

4816 FEDERATION OF SMALL BUSINESSES "BUSINESS ENTERPRISE" H'CAP — 1m 60y
4:50 (4:50) (Class 5) (0-75,71) 3-Y-0+ **£3,885** (£1,156; £577; £288) **Stalls** High

Form				RPR
1041	1		**Focail Eile**[10] 4473 4-10-0 **71**........StephenDonohoe 8 (J Ryan) *chsd ldrs: swtchd lft over 2f out: rdn over 1f out: edgd rt and r.o to ld nr fin* **5/2**[1]	77
0146	2	nk	**Very Well Red**[24] 3996 6-9-13 **70**........PatCosgrave 2 (P W Hiatt) *led: rdn over 1f out: edgd lft ins fnl f: hdd nr fin* **16/1**	75
0606	3	1 1/4	**Coole Dodger (IRE)**[12] 4402 4-8-12 **55**........PaulHanagan 3 (B Ellison) *trckd ldr: racd keenly: rdn and hung rt fr over 1f out: styd on same pce wl ins fnl f* **11/2**	57
3524	4	nse	**Ours (IRE)**[4] 4663 6-9-13 **70**........(p) DarryllHolland 4 (John A Harris) *s.i.s: hld up: hdwy over 2f out: rdn and hung rt over 1f out: swtchd lft ins fnl f: styd on* **11/4**[2]	72
0645	5	8	**Stanley Goodspeed**[17] 4236 6-9-9 **66**........RHills 5 (J W Hills) *hld up: rdn: hung rt and wknd over 1f out* **7/1**	50
4350	6	3 1/4	**Fortunate Flame**[4] 4657 3-9-1 **65**........HayleyTurner 7 (K A Ryan) *prom: rdn over 3f out: wknd wl over 1f out* **9/2**[3]	41
3006	7	11	**Count Ceprano (IRE)**[8] 4548 5-9-9 **66**........FergusSweeney 1 (C R Dore) *hld up: shkn up over 2f out: wknd and eased over 1f out* **12/1**	17

1m 46.85s (1.75) **Going Correction** +0.325s/f (Good)
WFA 3 from 4yo+ 7lb **7 Ran SP% 114.9**
Speed ratings (Par 103): **104,103,102,102,94 91,80**
toteswinger: 1&2 £8.90, 1&3 £4.40, 2&3 £15.20. CSF £41.45 CT £203.28 TOTE £3.80: £2.00, £4.00; EX 26.00 Place 6 £72.14, Place 5 £20.51..
Owner Cathal Fegan **Bred** D Robb **Trained** Newmarket, Suffolk

FOCUS
This was yet another race in which it proved hard to make up ground from off the pace and the first four came clear.
Coole Dodger(IRE) Official explanation: jockey said gelding was hanging right
Ours(IRE) Official explanation: jockey said gelding suffered interference in the home straight
Count Ceprano(IRE) Official explanation: jockey said gelding was unsuited by the ground
T/Plt: £22.70 to a £1 stake. Pool: £51,415.40. 1,647.23 winning tickets. T/Qpdt: £19.20 to a £1 stake. Pool: £3,166.40. 121.60 winning tickets. CR

4800 REDCAR (L-H)
Sunday, August 9

OFFICIAL GOING: Good to firm (9.7)
Wind: Light, half-behind. Weather: fine and sunny

4817 EUROPEAN BREEDERS' FUND MAIDEN FILLIES' STKS — 7f
2:10 (2:11) (Class 5) 2-Y-O **£3,885** (£1,156; £577; £288) **Stalls** High

Form				RPR
	1		**Siyaadah** 2-9-0 0........RoystonFfrench 14 (Saeed Bin Suroor) *in rr and sn pushed along: gd hdwy to ld over 2f out: styd on wl* **4/1**[3]	82+
3	2	1 3/4	**Cash Queen Anna (IRE)**[23] 4047 2-9-0 0........WilliamBuick 15 (B W Hills) *chsd ldrs: kpt on same pce appr fnl f* **11/4**[2]	78
	3	nk	**Boogie Diva** 2-8-11 0........AndreaAtzeni(3) 4 (M Botti) *s.s: hdwy on outside 3f out: chsd ldrs over 1f out: kpt on wl* **16/1**	78+
3	4	4 1/2	**Iptkaar (USA)**[11] 4424 2-9-0 0........ChrisCatlin 13 (C E Brittain) *in rr: hdwy over 2f out: styd on fnl f* **15/2**	66
2	5	2 1/4	**Aquarius Star (IRE)**[12] 4396 2-9-0 0........PaulEddery 8 (Pat Eddery) *chsd ldrs: sn drvn along: rdn 3f out: sn outpcd* **9/4**[1]	60
23	6	1 1/2	**Izuizorizuain't (IRE)**[24] 4018 2-9-0 0........JoeFanning 3 (K A Ryan) *chsd ldrs: wknd over 1f out* **20/1**	57
5	7	nk	**Hedgerow (IRE)**[16] 4278 2-9-0 0........DanielTudhope 11 (A Dickman) *chsd ldrs: led 3f out: sn hdd: wknd over 1f out* **50/1**	56
0	8	2	**Buzz Bird**[16] 4278 2-9-0 0........PhillipMakin 2 (T D Barron) *chsd ldrs: wknd over 1f out* **50/1**	51
06	9	1 1/4	**Kookie**[11] 4430 2-8-11 0........FrederikTylicki(3) 10 (R E Barr) *in rr and drvn along: nvr on terms* **50/1**	48
00	10	nk	**Ellies Image**[41] 3468 2-9-0 0........TonyHamilton 6 (B P J Baugh) *chsd ldrs: lost pl 3f out* **100/1**	47
	11	1 3/4	**Lost In The Forest** 2-9-0 0........TomEaves 16 (A P Jarvis) *prom: rdn and lost pl over 2f out* **40/1**	43
0	12	4 1/2	**Keenes Royale**[24] 4001 2-9-0 0........(t) PaulMulrennan 7 (P C Haslam) *led tl hdd & wknd 3f out* **22/1**	36+
	13	3/4	**Infinity World** 2-9-0 0........PJMcDonald 5 (G R Oldroyd) *s.i.s: hdwy on outer 3f out: hung lft and lost pl over 1f out* **100/1**	30
00	14	6	**Magic Millie (IRE)**[11] 4430 2-8-7 0........AndrewHeffernan(7) 9 (J Hetherton) *s.i.s: in rr and pushed along: bhd fnl 2f* **100/1**	15
0	15	3 1/4	**Both Ends Burning (IRE)**[11] 4430 2-9-0 0........PAspell 12 (J S Wainwright) *in rr: bhd fnl 2f* **100/1**	6

1m 22.75s (-1.75) **Going Correction** -0.275s/f (Firm) **15 Ran SP% 116.5**
Speed ratings (Par 91): **99,97,96,91,88 87,86,84,83,82 80,75,74,67,64**
toteswinger: 1&2 £4.10, 1&3 £17.90, 2&3 £13.40. CSF £13.74 TOTE £4.60: £1.50, £1.80, £5.00; EX 18.20.
Owner Godolphin **Bred** Lofts Hall Stud **Trained** Newmarket, Suffolk

FOCUS
There was 3mm of water applied to the course after yesterday's racing to maintain the good to firm conditions. A decent pace in what was probably an above average maiden but won in a good time. The form is rated around the time and the runner-up.

NOTEBOOK
Siyaadaha 110,000gns filly by Shamardal out of the useful US stakes winner River Belle, made a very encouraging debut. She was a little slowly away and was soon being nudged along but moved through the field quite sweetly to take up proceedings over 2f out. She was only kept up to her work in what was quite a taking display. Goldolphin have many juveniles at the moment and she shapes as though she would be one of the better types. She holds entries in the Watership Down Stud Sales and the Tattersalls Timeform Fillies and, with Royston Ffrench most impressed with this performance, she looks capable of making her presence felt when upped in class.\n
Cash Queen Anna(IRE) came up against a couple of useful looking prospects on debut at Newbury over 6f. She was close enough to the pace but was one of the first to be ridden along. She stayed on well enough without ever threatening to get to the winner. She is going the right way and looks uncomplicated. (op 5-2)
Boogie Diva completely missed the break but she steadily recovered and stayed on to press the runner-up entering the final furlong. A pleasing effort, and if she can build upon this experience she can be found an opportunity with the yard in good form. (op 20-1 tchd 25-1)
Iptkaar(USA) was struggling at the rear at quite an early stage and was doing most of her good work towards the end, although never going to threaten. She looks as though a step up in trip would suit and holds an entry for the Group 1 Fillies' Mile which would seem slightly optimistic. (op 8-1)
Aquarius Star(IRE) was again well supported throughout the morning after her encouraging debut but was disappointing, having been under pressure from a fair way out and never having the pace to get on terms. She has ability after being well backed on both starts now. (tchd 2-1)

4818 REDCAR CRICKET CLUB (S) STKS — 1m 2f
2:40 (2:41) (Class 6) 3-5-Y-0 **£2,047** (£604; £302) **Stalls** Low

Form				RPR
-006	1		**Miss Ferney**[23] 4068 5-8-10 45........PaulPickard(5) 2 (A Kirtley) *t.k.h in rr: pushed along and hdwy over 5f out: led 3f out: drvn clr* **66/1**	59+
105	2	5	**Jeronimo Joe**[19] 4177 3-9-3 59........PhillipMakin 4 (A B Haynes) *dwlt: in rr: drvn and outpcd over 3f out: styd on to take 2nd over 1f out: no ch w wnr* **10/3**[2]	61
0204	3	3 3/4	**Lady Valentino**[24] 4021 5-8-12 50........(t) RussellKennemore(3) 8 (B D Leavy) *chsd ldrs: one pce fnl 2f* **7/2**[3]	43
00-0	4	3 3/4	**Mundo's Magic**[11] 4435 5-9-1 48........BMcHugh(5) 1 (N Wilson) *chsd ldrs: effrt 3f out: wknd over 1f out* **14/1**	41
	5	5	**Shanghai Star (IRE)**[16] 4290 5-9-12 74........MAPhillips 6 (Irene J Monaghan, Ire) *hld up: effrt over 3f out: sn rdn and no imp* **3/1**[1]	37
50	6	7	**I See Nice Sea**[73] 2415 3-8-6 0........TonyHamilton 7 (Ollie Pears) *chsd ldrs: effrt over 3f out: hung lft and wknd 2f out* **13/2**	13
0434	7	3/4	**Lomica**[12] 4397 3-8-6 48........(p) RoystonFfrench 3 (Miss J A Camacho) *led: t.k.h: hdd 3f out: wknd and eased over 1f out* **5/1**	11
3006	8	9	**Antipodean (UAE)**[49] 3192 3-8-11 46........PaulMulrennan 5 (P T Midgley) *chsd ldrs: drvn 4f out: lost pl over 2f out: sn bhd* **25/1**	—

2m 4.66s (-2.44) **Going Correction** -0.275s/f (Firm)
WFA 3 from 5yo 9lb **8 Ran SP% 112.3**
Speed ratings (Par 101): **98,94,91,88,84 78,77,70**
toteswinger: 1&2 £18.90, 1&3 £23.20, 2&3 £3.10. CSF £266.75 TOTE £63.80: £5.20, £1.70, £1.20; EX 165.10.There was no bid for the winner.
Owner Mrs P J Taylor-Garthwaite **Bred** K And P J Garthwaite **Trained** Houghton-le-Spring, Tyne & W

FOCUS
A weak seller with some in-and-out horses. It was run at a fair gallop and the second looks the best guide.
Lomica Official explanation: jockey said filly ran too free

4819 SAVE OUR STEEL H'CAP — 1m
3:10 (3:13) (Class 6) (0-60,60) 3-Y-O **£2,047** (£604; £302) **Stalls** High

Form				RPR
0000	1		**Tropical Duke (IRE)**[14] 4348 3-8-5 **52**........LanceBetts(5) 13 (R E Barr) *chsd ldrs: wnt 2nd over 2f out: styd on to ld nr fin* **14/1**	55
2063	2	hd	**Jiggalong**[16] 4279 3-9-3 **59**........TPO'Shea 11 (Jane Chapple-Hyam) *in rr: hdwy over 2f out: wnt 3rd 1f out: styd on strly: jst failed* **4/1**[1]	62
00-0	3	nk	**Melkatant**[26] 3939 3-8-4 **46** oh1........AndrewMullen 10 (N Bycroft) *in rr: hdwy 2f out: kpt on wl ins fnl f* **40/1**	48
2351	4	shd	**Royal Premium**[9] 4496 3-8-9 **58**........(v) BillyCray(7) 17 (Mrs G S Rees) *led: drvn 3 l clr over 2f out: hdd towards fin* **11/2**[2]	60
3234	5	1 1/2	**Paint Splash**[16] 4279 3-8-4 **51**........DeanHeslop(5) 3 (T D Barron) *in rr: hdwy over 2f out: kpt on fnl f* **6/1**[3]	49
2340	6	1 3/4	**Lyric Art (USA)**[43] 3381 3-9-3 **59**........RichardMullen 5 (B Smart) *t.k.h towards rr: hdwy on outside over 2f out: kpt on same pce appr fnl f* **8/1**	53
5553	7	2 1/4	**Chichen Daawe**[26] 3942 3-8-7 **49**........TomEaves 9 (B Ellison) *chsd ldrs: wknd appr fnl f* **8/1**	38
0-50	8	1 1/2	**Aven Mac (IRE)**[16] 4284 3-8-6 **48**........(p) GregFairley 15 (N Bycroft) *dwlt: hdwy over 2f out: nvr nr ldrs* **18/1**	33
-000	9	1 3/4	**Lady Dinsdale (IRE)**[20] 4155 3-8-4 **46**........KirstyMilczarek 14 (T Keddy) *mid-div: kpt on fnl 2f: nvr a factor* **25/1**	27
0540	10	2 1/4	**Tilerium's Dream (IRE)**[8] 4552 3-8-10 **52**........JoeFanning 6 (K A Ryan) *chsd ldr: wknd over 1f out* **18/1**	28
0403	11	1 1/2	**Off Hand**[26] 3936 3-8-4 **46** oh1........(b) DuranFentiman 19 (T D Easterby) *chsd ldrs: wknd 2f out* **20/1**	18
0400	12	shd	**Waltzalong (IRE)**[20] 4142 3-8-4 **49**........KellyHarrison(3) 16 (T D Easterby) *in rr div: sme hdwy over 2f out: nvr on terms* **33/1**	21

00-0 **13** *16* **Are Can (USA)**[51] 3120 3-8-10 **52**...............(p) PAspell 4 —
(J S Wainwright) *chsd ldrs: hung lft and lost pl over 2f out: eased fnl f* **40/1**

660 **14** *1 1/4* **Yashkur**[20] 4151 3-8-13 **55**............... ChrisCatlin 8 —
(C E Brittain) *in rr: eased whn no ch ins fnl f* **16/1**

4340 **15** *6* **Piccolo Express**[22] 4079 3-8-11 **53**............... RoystonFfrench 18 —
(B P J Baugh) *in rr: eased whn bhd ins fnl f* **16/1**

3330 **16** *nk* **Lady Dunhill (IRE)**[170] 621 3-8-9 **51**............... TonyHamilton 7 —
(E W Tuer) *mid-div: lost pl over 3f out: bhd whn eased ins fnl f* **20/1**

17 *4 1/2* **Saorocain (IRE)**[49] 3194 3-8-12 **54**...............(v[1]) AdrianTNicholls 1 —
(Mrs John Harrington, Ire) *chsd ldrs on outer: wkng whn rdr dropped whip 2f out: eased whn bhd ins fnl f* **16/1**

1m 36.89s (-1.11) **Going Correction** -0.275s/f (Firm) 17 Ran SP% **127.9**
Speed ratings (Par 98): **94,93,93,93,91 90,87,86,84,82 80,80,64,63,57 57,52**
toteswinger: 1&2 £18.50, 1&3 £118.80, 2&3 £56.90. CSF £66.46 CT £2267.81 TOTE £17.40: £4.70, £1.70, £7.40, £1.50; EX 125.30.
Owner Mrs R E Barr **Bred** George Ward **Trained** Seamer, N Yorks

FOCUS
The top two in the market were withdrawn which made this a rather competitive heat. It was run at an ordinary pace.
Saorocain(IRE) Official explanation: jockey said filly had no more to give

4820 THE COMMITMENTS PERFORMING HERE - SATURDAY 29TH AUGUST H'CAP 6f
3:40 (3:42) (Class 4) (0-85,82) 3-Y-O **£5,180** (£1,541; £770; £384) **Stalls** High

Form RPR

6413 **1** **Ingleby Lady**[25] 3973 3-9-6 **81**............... PhillipMakin 2 89+
(T D Barron) *dwlt: t.k.h: sn trcking ldrs: led over 2f out: styd on strly: readily* **6/4**[1]

5620 **2** *2 3/4* **Come And Go (UAE)**[23] 4044 3-9-2 **77**............... PJMcDonald 5 76
(G A Swinbank) *w ldrs on ins: rdn over 2f out: kpt on same pce* **5/1**[3]

4350 **3** *nk* **Desert Falls**[23] 4044 3-9-3 **78**...............(t) TonyHamilton 3 76
(R M Whitaker) *mde most tl over 3f out: sn rdn: styd on same pce* **8/1**

2642 **4** *3/4* **Oriental Rose**[4] 4664 3-8-5 **66**............... ChrisCatlin 1 62
(G M Moore) *w ldrs on outside: rdn over 2f out: kpt on same pce* **5/1**[3]

2641 **5** *24* **Brierty (IRE)**[16] 4289 3-9-7 **82**............... DanielTudhope 4 1
(D Carroll) *unruly in stalls: trckd ldrs: wknd over 1f out: heavily eased* **3/1**[2]

69.81 secs (-1.99) **Going Correction** -0.275s/f (Firm) 5 Ran SP% **109.4**
Speed ratings (Par 102): **102,98,97,96,64**
CSF £9.15 TOTE £2.20: £1.30, £2.90; EX 8.50.
Owner Dave Scott **Bred** Hellwood Stud Farm **Trained** Maunby, N Yorks

FOCUS
Only five runners but quite a tight little handicap run at a fair pace.
Brierty(IRE) Official explanation: jockey said filly was never travelling

4821 REDCAR RACECOURSE SUPPORTING TEES VALLEY INDUSTRY CLAIMING STKS 1m
4:10 (4:10) (Class 6) 3-4-Y-O **£2,047** (£604; £302) **Stalls** High

Form RPR

2661 **1** **Diggeratt (USA)**[6] 4589 3-8-5 73............... TonyHamilton 2 72
(R A Fahey) *trckd ldrs: wnt 2nd 2f out: rdn to ld 1f out: styd on wl* **10/11**[1]

-015 **2** *2 1/2* **Fortunate Bid (IRE)**[22] 4079 3-8-13 73............... RoystonFfrench 3 74
(Mrs L Stubbs) *w ldr: led over 2f out: hung rt and hdd 1f out: no ex* **11/4**[2]

00-0 **3** *4* **Tina's Best (IRE)**[39] 3496 4-8-12 70............... TomEaves 4 57
(E J Alston) *swvd rt s: t.k.h in last: effrt over 2f out: kpt on same pce* **13/2**

4030 **4** *15* **Carnival Dream**[40] 3490 4-8-9 52...............(p) SladeO'Hara(5) 5 23
(H A McWilliams) *led tl over 2f out: sn wknd* **25/1**

4014 **5** *4 1/2* **Castlebury (IRE)**[8] 4528 4-9-3 64............... PJMcDonald 1 16
(G A Swinbank) *stmbld bdly s: sn chsng ldrs: lost pl over 2f out: sn bhd* **9/2**[3]

1m 35.85s (-2.15) **Going Correction** -0.275s/f (Firm)
WFA 3 from 4yo 7lb 5 Ran SP% **114.4**
Speed ratings (Par 101): **99,96,92,77,73**
CSF £3.92 TOTE £1.70: £1.10, £1.60; EX 3.50.
Owner J A Rattigan **Bred** Hobby Horse Farm Inc **Trained** Musley Bank, N Yorks

FOCUS
A small field for this claimer but a decent pace was set.
Castlebury(IRE) Official explanation: jockey said gelding stumbled on leaving the stalls

4822 WEDDING RECEPTIONS @ REDCAR RACECOURSE MAIDEN H'CAP 1m 2f
4:40 (4:41) (Class 5) (0-75,74) 3-Y-O+ **£2,590** (£770; £385; £192) **Stalls** Low

Form RPR

540/ **1** **Bollin Dolly**[698] 5300 6-8-12 **58**............... TonyHamilton 4 70+
(T D Easterby) *trckd ldrs: led 1f out: drvn clr* **20/1**

44B **2** *3 3/4* **Northside Prince (IRE)**[27] 3911 3-8-10 **65**............... PJMcDonald 13 69
(G A Swinbank) *trckd ldrs: led over 2f out: hdd and no ex 1f out* **8/1**

3-23 **3** *1* **Alqaffay (IRE)**[33] 3707 4-10-0 **74**............... RichardMullen 12 76
(J H M Gosden) *mid-div: hdwy over 3f out: styd on fnl 2f* **4/1**[2]

2003 **4** *1 1/2* **Oskari**[19] 4171 4-8-9 **55**............... PaulMulrennan 3 54
(P T Midgley) *chsd ldrs: one pce fnl 2f* **16/1**

0355 **5** *3 1/2* **Nut Hand (IRE)**[26] 3954 3-8-0 **55** oh5............... DuranFentiman 2 47
(T D Easterby) *w ldr: led 6f out tl over 2f out: wknd fnl f* **33/1**

6-00 **6** *nk* **Markadam**[37] 3561 3-8-1 **56**............... AndrewMullen 1 47
(Miss S E Hall) *hld up in rr: reminders 4f out: styd on appr fnl f: nrst fin* **33/1**

5455 **7** *1 1/2* **Flora's Pride**[38] 3545 5-8-6 **55** oh1............... KellyHarrison(3) 14 43
(K G Reveley) *in rr: drvn 4f out: kpt on fnl 2f: nvr on terms* **33/1**

0052 **8** *1/2* **Diamond Lass (IRE)**[35] 3653 4-8-13 **62**............... FrederikTylicki(3) 9 49
(R A Fahey) *in rr: drvn 4f out: nvr nr ldrs* **13/2**[3]

23-3 **9** *1* **Talayeb**[102] 1603 4-9-12 **72**............... TPO'Shea 8 57
(M P Tregoning) *hld up in rr: effrt over 3f out: nvr a factor* **7/2**[1]

-560 **10** *2 1/4* **Heading East (IRE)**[4] 4660 3-8-9 **69**...............(p) AmyRyan(5) 10 50
(K A Ryan) *led tl 6f out: wknd over 1f out* **50/1**

-344 **11** *1 1/2* **Kapsiliat (IRE)**[22] 4085 3-9-2 **71**............... RoystonFfrench 5 49
(J Noseda) *towards rr: drvn 4f out: nvr a factor* **7/1**

3542 **12** *1/2* **King's Counsel (IRE)**[11] 4431 3-7-12 **60**............... AndrewHeffernan(7) 11 37
(J Hetherton) *sn chsng ldrs: drvn 4f out: lost pl over 2f out* **14/1**

2364 **13** *2 1/4* **Tropical Blue**[11] 4426 3-9-5 **74**...............(v) JoeFanning 15 46
(Jennie Candlish) *in rr: drvn 4f out: nvr on terms* **10/1**

0 **14** *10* **Lady Rose Anne (IRE)**[14] 4350 4-9-5 **65**............... PhillipMakin 6 17
(T D Barron) *in midfield: drvn 4f out: sn lost pl: bhd whn eased ins fnl f* **18/1**

2m 3.69s (-3.41) **Going Correction** -0.275s/f (Firm)
WFA 3 from 4yo+ 9lb 14 Ran SP% **121.6**
Speed ratings (Par 103): **102,99,98,97,94 93,92,92,91,89 88,88,86,78**
toteswinger: 1&2 £39.30, 1&3 £24.70, 2&3 £9.30. CSF £167.54 CT £786.82 TOTE £27.50: £7.00, £3.50, £1.90; EX 318.50.
Owner Sir Neil Westbrook **Bred** Sir Neil And Lady Westbrook **Trained** Great Habton, N Yorks

FOCUS
Not a lot of strength in this open handicap with stamina doubts surrounding the favourite. It was run at a good pace in a respectable time.
Kapsiliat(IRE) Official explanation: jockey said filly was unsuited by the good to firm ground

4823 WIN A VIP DAY OUT @ REDCARRACING.CO.UK H'CAP 6f
5:10 (5:13) (Class 6) (0-60,62) 3-Y-O+ **£2,047** (£604; £302) **Stalls** High

Form RPR

0401 **1** **Just Sam (IRE)**[11] 4436 4-9-3 **62**............... IJBrennan(7) 2 71
(R E Barr) *mde all: rdn over 1f out: hld on wl* **15/2**[3]

0345 **2** *3/4* **Elkhorn**[24] 4015 7-9-0 **52**...............(b) TomEaves 7 59
(Miss J A Camacho) *chsd ldrs: kpt on same pce wl ins fnl f* **9/1**

05-0 **3** *nk* **Micky Mac (IRE)**[9] 4504 5-9-2 **57**............... FrederikTylicki(3) 1 63
(C J Teague) *chsd ldrs: edgd rt ins fnl f: kpt on same pce* **16/1**

0330 **4** *1 1/4* **Circle Dance (IRE)**[8] 4552 4-9-0 **52**...............(v) PhillipMakin 4 55+
(D Shaw) *in rr: hdwy 2f out: styng on same pce whn nt clr run and bmpd wl ins fnl f: eased nr fin* **12/1**

021 **5** *nk* **Titus Gent**[8] 4552 4-9-7 **59**............... KirstyMilczarek 9 60+
(J Ryan) *hld up: hdwy over 2f out: styng on same pce whn bmpd wl ins fnl f* **5/1**[1]

0054 **6** *nse* **Captain Royale (IRE)**[4] 4654 4-8-3 **46**...............(p) PaulPickard(5) 6 47
(Miss Tracy Waggott) *chsd ldrs: no ex ins fnl f* **17/2**

6046 **7** *1 1/2* **Conjecture**[18] 4191 7-9-5 **57**............... GregFairley 15 53
(R Bastiman) *w ldrs: fdd appr fnl f* **6/1**[2]

0042 **8** *1 1/2* **Distant Vision (IRE)**[37] 3570 6-8-7 **50**............... PatrickDonaghy(5) 20 41+
(H A McWilliams) *s.s: hdwy over 2f out: kpt on same pce* **18/1**

3314 **9** *1 1/4* **Nufoudh (IRE)**[10] 4466 5-8-13 **54**............... KellyHarrison(3) 3 41
(Miss Tracy Waggott) *restless in stalls: s.i.s: sn chsng ldrs: wknd over 1f out* **14/1**

0635 **10** *hd* **Dalarossie**[24] 4016 4-9-3 **55**............... PaulMulrennan 13 41
(E J Alston) *mid-div: kpt on fnl 2f* **16/1**

3000 **11** *3/4* **Desert Ben (IRE)**[11] 4435 6-9-0 **52**...............(v[1]) TonyHamilton 8 36
(C Grant) *chsd ldrs: fdd over 1f out* **40/1**

0563 **12** *nk* **Sardan Dansar (IRE)**[16] 4281 3-8-5 **47**............... RoystonFfrench 14 30
(Mrs A Duffield) *in tch: effrt over 2f out: sn btn* **10/1**

0-0 **13** *1 1/4* **Just Spike**[24] 4016 6-8-6 **51**............... JemmaMarshall(7) 12 30
(B P J Baugh) *in rr div: nvr on terms* **20/1**

0003 **14** *nk* **Uace Mac**[9] 4508 5-8-9 **54**............... TerenceFury(7) 5 32
(N Bycroft) *chsd ldrs: lost pl over 2f out* **18/1**

0-00 **15** *3/4* **Chosen Forever**[19] 4171 4-9-5 **57**...............(p) PJMcDonald 18 33
(G R Oldroyd) *mid-div: lost pl over 2f out* **20/1**

4346 **16** *1 1/2* **Sheik'N'Knotsterd**[11] 4436 4-9-3 **55**............... ChrisCatlin 11 26
(J F Coupland) *in rr: bhd fnl 2f* **33/1**

5525 **17** *3/4* **Admiral Bond (IRE)**[152] 794 4-9-3 **60**............... LanceBetts(5) 10 28
(G R Oldroyd) *mid-div: lost pl over 2f out* **16/1**

-406 **18** *1* **Unconsoled**[8] 4550 3-8-1 **50**............... AndrewHeffernan(7) 19 15
(J Hetherton) *chsd ldrs: lost pl over 2f out* **80/1**

1m 10.3s (-1.50) **Going Correction** -0.275s/f (Firm)
WFA 3 from 4yo+ 4lb 18 Ran SP% **131.0**
Speed ratings (Par 101): **99,98,97,95,95 95,93,91,89,89 88,88,86,86,85 83,82,80**
toteswinger: 1&2 £17.60, 1&3 £34.50, 2&3 £47.60. CSF £73.98 CT £1090.55 TOTE £9.50: £2.10, £2.10, £6.50, £2.30; EX 103.80 Place 6 £56.07, Place 5 £27.98..
Owner P Cartmell **Bred** John J Carroll **Trained** Seamer, N Yorks

FOCUS
A modest affair but a competitive handicap run at a fair pace with the front three always up in the firing line.
Nufoudh(IRE) Official explanation: jockey said gelding boiled over in the stalls
T/Jkpt: Not won. T/Plt: £84.10 to a £1 stake. Pool: £59,931.63. 520.15 winning tickets. T/Qpdt: £12.60 to a £1 stake. Pool: £4,054.20. 236.30 winning tickets. WG

4602 WINDSOR (R-H)
Sunday, August 9

OFFICIAL GOING: Good (good to firm in places; 8.1)
Rail realignment increased advertised distances on round course by about 25yards.
Wind: Almost nil. Weather: Sunny, warm

4824 BRITISH RACING SCHOOL APPRENTICE H'CAP 1m 67y
2:30 (2:31) (Class 5) (0-70,70) 4-Y-O+ **£2,729** (£806; £403) **Stalls** High

Form RPR

-056 **1** **Cool Ebony**[20] 4149 6-9-10 **70**............... DavidProbert 3 77
(P J Makin) *trckd ldrs: rdn over 2f out: prog to ld over 1f out: hrd pressed fnl f: kpt on wl* **5/1**[3]

1524 **2** *1/2* **Tanforan**[9] 4496 7-8-12 **65**............... KierenFox(7) 7 71
(B P J Baugh) *chsd ldrs: prog 2f out: rdn to press wnr jst over 1f out: kpt on fnl f: a hld* **8/1**

3115 **3** *1 1/4* **Global Village (IRE)**[4] 4665 4-9-2 **65**............... WilliamCarson(3) 4 68
(Miss D Mountain) *hld up in last: rdn over 2f out: sme prog over 1f out: kpt on to take 3rd ins fnl f* **5/2**[1]

623 **4** *1 1/4* **Pretty Officer (USA)**[54] 3004 4-8-0 **53**............... DannyBrock(7) 6 53
(Rae Guest) *towards rr: brought wdst of all fr 4f out: rdn to chse ldrs over 1f out: kpt on same pce* **9/2**[2]

-006 **5** *1 1/2* **Poppy Dean (IRE)**[138] 945 4-8-2 **51** oh2..... Louis-PhilippeBeuzelin(3) 2 48
(J G Portman) *led after 1f: rdn over 2f out: hdd & wknd over 1f out* **33/1**

0-03 **6** *1 1/4* **Petomic (IRE)**[39] 3504 4-8-4 **57** ow1............... RichardFelton(7) 5 51
(M Hill) *s.i.s: sn midfield: rdn on outer 2f out: no prog over 1f out: wknd fnl f* **16/1**

4222 **7** *3/4* **Feasible**[4] 4645 4-8-9 **60**............... MatthewDavies(5) 1 52
(J G Portman) *chsd ldr after 2f: hrd rdn over 2f out: wknd over 1f out* **9/2**[2]

6340 **8** *shd* **By Command**[3] 4714 4-9-7 **67**............... PatrickHills 8 59
(J W Hills) *in tch towards rr: rdn over 2f out: plugging on but btn whn nt clr run ent fnl f* **9/1**

3540 **9** *hd* **Magnitude**[26] 3960 4-9-0 **65**....(b) TobyAtkinson(5) 10 57
(M E Rimmer) *led 1f: sn 3rd: rdn over 2f out: cl enough over 1f out: wknd* **11/1**

00-0 **10** *1* **White Ledger (IRE)**[44] 3331 10-8-0 **51** oh6.... SimonPearce(5) 9 40
(R E Peacock) *snatched up after 1f: lost further grnd after 2f: wl in rr after: struggling in last 2f out* **66/1**

1m 45.55s (0.85) **Going Correction** -0.075s/f (Good) **10** Ran SP% **121.4**
Speed ratings (Par 103): **92,91,90,89,87 86,85,85,85,84**
toteswinger: 1&2 £8.50, 1&3 £2.90, 2&3 £2.90. CSF £46.73 CT £125.68 TOTE £6.00: £2.00, £2.40, £1.80; EX 31.20 Trifecta £114.60 Pool: £252.59 - 1.63 winning units..
Owner Wedgewood Estates **Bred** Wedgewood Estates **Trained** Ogbourne Maisey, Wilts

FOCUS
Following a dry night the going had quickened up to good, good to firm in places. Just an ordinary handicap and there were plenty in with a shout two furlongs out.

4825 STAINLESS WIRE LTD MAIDEN AUCTION STKS 6f
3:00 (3:02) (Class 5) 2-Y-O **£2,729** (£806; £403) **Stalls** High

Form RPR

4 **1** **Marcus Cicero (IRE)**[39] 3500 2-8-13 0.... JimCrowley 2 78
(P Winkworth) *sn prom on outer: effrt to ld wl over 1f out: edgd rt to nr side rail: drvn and styd on wl* **9/2**[3]

2 **2** *1 ½* **Baby Dottie**[32] 3745 2-8-4 0.... LukeMorris 4 65
(P M Phelan) *sn midfield: pushed along bef 1/2-way: rdn and prog over 2f out: chsd wnr over 1f out: no imp fnl f* **7/2**[2]

3 *hd* **Sunraider (IRE)** 2-9-1 0.... MichaelHills 10 81+
(B W Hills) *rn green in midfield: nt clr run on inner fr over 2f out: no ch whn gap appeared jst over 1f out: pushed along and r.o wl fnl f* **13/8**[1]

0 **4** *nk* **My Sister**[47] 3248 2-8-1 0.... DavidProbert(3) 5 63
(M D I Usher) *dwlt: towards rr: rdn and prog on outer fr 2f out: chsd ldng pair ins fnl f: kpt on but lost 3rd nr fin* **20/1**

5 *1 ¼* **Caldermud (IRE)** 2-8-12 0.... SteveDrowne 7 67
(J R Best) *s.s: hld up in last quartet: gd prog on wd outside fr 2f out: nt pce of ldrs fnl f but kpt on* **25/1**

40 **6** *2* **Apostle Of Rome (IRE)**[23] 4048 2-8-10 0.... RichardKingscote 11 59
(Tom Dascombe) *in tch in midfield: n.m.r briefly 2f out: outpcd fr over 1f out but kpt on steadily* **22/1**

56 **7** *2 ½* **Ballachulish**[17] 4243 2-8-12 0.... DaneO'Neill 6 54
(H Candy) *pressed ldrs: upsides over 2f out: wknd over 1f out* **20/1**

00 **8** *¾* **Mrs Puff (IRE)**[11] 4439 2-7-13 0.... Louis-PhilippeBeuzelin(5) 8 44
(P D Evans) *towards rr: shkn up over 2f out: nvr on terms w ldrs* **40/1**

33 **9** *2 ¾* **Kathindi (IRE)**[18] 4200 2-8-10 0.... LPKeniry 13 41
(J S Moore) *disp ld: narrow advantage over 2f out to wl over 1f out: hrd rdn and wknd* **9/1**

00 **10** *nse* **Email Exit (IRE)**[19] 4176 2-8-12 0.... AlanMunro 12 43
(C F Wall) *dwlt: sn cl up on inner: eased off rail 2f out: no prog over 1f out: wknd* **40/1**

11 *1 ¼* **Vito Volterra (IRE)** 2-9-1 0.... TonyCulhane 9 42
(J R Best) *hld up in last quartet: shuffled along and no prog 2f out* **33/1**

63 **12** *10* **Quinner (IRE)**[7] 4568 2-8-11 0....(t) PaulDoe 14 8
(P D Evans) *disp ld against nr side rail to over 2f out: wknd rapidly over 1f out* **14/1**

13 *1 ½* **Seeking Stardom** 2-8-9 0.... TedDurcan 16 —
(P M Phelan) *s.s: rn green in last quartet: wl bhd fnl 2f* **40/1**

14 *8* **Zeloca (IRE)** 2-8-4 0.... RichardThomas 3 —
(Mrs L C Jewell) *s.i.s: a in last quartet: t.o* **100/1**

1m 13.19s (0.19) **Going Correction** -0.075s/f (Good) **14** Ran SP% **124.1**
Speed ratings (Par 94): **95,93,92,92,90 88,84,83,80,79 78,64,62,52**
toteswinger: 1&2 £3.50, 1&3 £2.10, 2&3 £2.70. CSF £18.89 TOTE £5.40: £1.70, £1.90, £1.30; EX 22.20 Trifecta £18.40 Pool: £200.64 - 8.03 winning units..
Owner Kennet Valley Thoroughbreds VIII **Bred** Knockainey Stud **Trained** Chiddingfold, Surrey

FOCUS
Not a bad race for the class of contest with the winner putting up an improved effort and the third looking unlucky.

NOTEBOOK
Marcus Cicero(IRE) had shown plenty of promise on his debut at Chepstow despite running green and stepped up on that effort here. He played up beforehand but did little wrong in the race itself, breaking well from his wide draw and securing a handy position before quickening when given the office. The unlucky in-running favourite is the one that will go into most notebooks, but there was plenty to like about the way he scored, and he'll be interesting when stepped up in class. (op 6-1 tchd 4-1)
Baby Dottie finished second to a very useful sort at Lingfield on her debut and looked to hold sound claims. She had her chance approaching the furlong pole but hung in behind the winner and was held thereafter. (tchd 4-1 and 9-2 in a place)
Sunraider(IRE), a half-brother to 7f winner Always Be True, holds a Middle Park entry and was sent off favourite to make a winning debut. Keen and throwing his head about in the early stages, he met quite a bit of trouble in running in the straight and by the time he got daylight the winner had flown. He showed signs of inexperience here and had looked as though he would benefit from the run beforehand, so there should be plenty of improvement to come. Being by Namid, though, perhaps easier ground will suit him ideally. Official explanation: jockey said colt was denied a clear run (op 7-4 tchd 15-8 and 2-1 in places)
My Sister improved on her debut when finishing in mid-division in a Newbury maiden, and she gives the impression that, despite being by Royal Applause, she'll be suited by a longer trip than this. Her half-brother Greyfriars Abbey, who was by Fasliyev, won at up to 1m4f.
Caldermud(IRE), who challenged widest of all, is a half-brother to a couple of winners over 1m plus. A big, backward sort, this was a pleasing debut and he looks sure to come on plenty for the run. (op 20-1)
Apostle Of Rome(IRE) couldn't cope with the soft ground at Newbury last time but this was more encouraging. He'll be of more interest in nurseries and on breeding should appreciate stepping up in distance. (op 25-1 tchd 20-1)
Quinner(IRE) Official explanation: jockey said colt hung left

4826 E B F OSSIE & HUTCH MEMORIAL CONDITIONS STKS 6f
3:30 (3:30) (Class 3) 2-Y-O **£7,512** (£2,235; £1,117; £557) **Stalls** High

Form RPR

5140 **1** **Lucky General (IRE)**[11] 4418 2-8-12 **97**.... RichardHughes 5 93+
(R Hannon) *t.k.h early: led at mod pce to over 3f out: pushed along 2f out: effrt to ld again jst over 1f out: sn clr w hd high* **11/8**[2]

0 **2** *2 ¼* **Starwatch**[14] 4336 2-8-7 0.... MarcHalford(3) 2 82
(J J Bridger) *chsd ldng trio: rdn wl over 2f out and struggling: styd on to take 2nd ins fnl f: no threat to wnr* **50/1**

2210 **3** *4* **Chaperno (USA)**[11] 4418 2-8-9 **98**....(v[1]) AhmedAjtebi(3) 3 72
(Saeed Bin Suroor) *t.k.h early: trckd ldr: led over 3f out: 2 l clr and gng strly 2f out: hdd jst over 1f out and wknd v tamely* **4/5**[1]

6066 **4** *1 ½* **Little Perisher**[30] 3805 2-8-12 **88**.... AlanMunro 1 67
(A P Jarvis) *chsd ldng pair: shkn up 2f out: wknd over 1f out* **10/1**[3]

5 *3 ½* **Caramelita** 2-7-9 0.... DannyBrock(7) 4 47
(J R Jenkins) *a last and rn green: wl off the pce over 2f out* **40/1**

1m 13.67s (0.67) **Going Correction** -0.075s/f (Good) **5** Ran SP% **111.2**
Speed ratings (Par 98): **92,89,83,81,77**
CSF £39.71 TOTE £2.30: £1.10, £6.00; EX 59.20.
Owner Mrs J Wood **Bred** K Molloy **Trained** East Everleigh, Wilts

FOCUS
They didn't go a great pace early here and the winning time was 0.48sec slower than the preceding maiden. Not form to be positive about.

NOTEBOOK
Lucky General(IRE) got worked up beforehand and didn't look at home on the track at Goodwood last time, but he was better behaved here and the drop back to sprinting worked for him. He was plenty keen enough through the early stages but quickened past the disappointing Godolphin colt a furlong out and went on to win easily. With the outsider finishing second the value of the form is open to question, but hopefully it'll have done his confidence some good, and the valuable Weatherbys Insurance Sales race at Doncaster over an extended 6f is now the plan for him, with the Mill Reef also a possible target a week later. (op 7-4)
Starwatch, who showed little on his debut at Ascot, had a tough task on the book but showed much improved form to take second. A half-brother to a couple of winners at up to 1m6f, he's bred to want a lot further than this in time, but he's clearly not short of speed. (op 40-1)
Chaperno(USA), who had a visor on for the first time, looked the one to beat on his Vintage Stakes effort and the drop back to 6f promised to be bang up his street. However, he found little off the bridle at Goodwood and it was the same story here, and he looks one to avoid for the time being. (op 8-11 tchd 10-11 and evens in places)
Little Perisher was an early two-year-old and hasn't progressed since May. (op 9-1 tchd 8-1)
Caramelita, a daughter of a juvenile 6f winner, is bred to be speedy, but she was up against it in this company on her debut. (op 50-1)

4827 SPORTINGBET.COM H'CAP 1m 2f 7y
4:00 (4:00) (Class 4) (0-85,84) 3-Y-O **£5,180** (£1,541; £770; £384) **Stalls** Low

Form RPR

2000 **1** **Dubai Crest**[8] 4520 3-9-6 **83**.... JimCrowley 3 90
(Mrs A J Perrett) *hld up in 5th: disputing last 2f out but cl enough: prog over 1f out: got through to press ldr ent fnl f: drvn ahd last 75yds* **13/2**

0353 **2** *½* **Call It On (IRE)**[36] 3644 3-9-7 **84**.... MichaelHills 5 90
(M H Tompkins) *sn led and dictated stdy pce: rdn 2f out: fought off nrest rivals jst over 1f out: edgd lft fnl f: hdd last 75yds* **5/1**[3]

1 **3** *¾* **Mary Goodnight**[20] 4145 3-9-2 **79**.... ShaneKelly 4 84
(J Noseda) *hld up in 6th: awkward bnd 6f out: prog on outer over 3f out: tried to chal fr 2f out: nt qckn 1f out: kpt on* **9/2**[2]

5321 **4** *1* **North Cape (USA)**[58] 2892 3-8-11 **74**.... DaneO'Neill 1 77
(H Candy) *sn trckd ldr: rdn over 2f out: lost 2nd and btn 1f out* **10/3**[1]

1 **5** *nk* **Warpedsenseofhumor (FR)**[118] 1245 3-9-0 **77**.... IanMongan 7 79
(H R A Cecil) *trckd ldng pair: rdn and nt qckn on inner 2f out: kpt on same pce after: nvr able to chal* **6/1**

2511 **6** *shd* **Hollow Green (IRE)**[13] 4382 3-8-10 **78**.... Louis-PhilippeBeuzelin(5) 6 80
(P D Evans) *hld up in last: taken to wd outside and effrt 3f out: clsd over 1f out: kpt on same pce after* **8/1**

4410 **7** *8* **History Lesson**[15] 4299 3-9-7 **84**.... RichardHughes 2 70
(R Hannon) *sn settled in 4th: reminders 4f out and no rspnse: dropped to rr 2f: eased fnl f* **5/1**[3]

2m 7.27s (-1.43) **Going Correction** -0.075s/f (Good) **7** Ran SP% **113.3**
Speed ratings (Par 102): **102,101,101,100,99 99,93**
toteswinger: 1&2 £11.30, 1&3 £10.70, 2&3 £4.80. CSF £37.74 TOTE £7.80: £3.60, £2.80; EX 57.80.
Owner A D Spence **Bred** Bearstone Stud **Trained** Pulborough, W Sussex

FOCUS
This looked an open contest.
Dubai Crest Official explanation: trainer said, regarding the apparent improvement in form shown, gelding was never able to challenge from a poor draw last time
History Lesson Official explanation: jockey said colt had no more to give

4828 ASSURANT SOLUTIONS UK MAIDEN FILLIES' STKS 1m 2f 7y
4:30 (4:31) (Class 5) 3-Y-O+ **£2,729** (£806; £403) **Stalls** Low

Form RPR

64 **1** **Tinaar (USA)**[14] 4337 3-8-11 0.... DaneO'Neill 11 78+
(G A Butler) *hld up in midfield: plld off rail towards outer fr 3f out: rdn and prog 2f out: wnt 2nd over 1f out: led ins fnl f: styd on wl* **3/1**[3]

3-43 **2** *1 ½* **Heritage Coast (USA)**[47] 3250 4-9-6 **78**.... SteveDrowne 8 75
(H Morrison) *led: rdn 2f out against nr side rail: hdd and one pce ins fnl f* **2/1**[1]

2 **3** *2 ½* **Samaaha**[23] 4066 3-8-11 0.... TedDurcan 10 70
(Saeed Bin Suroor) *trckd ldrs: nt clr run briefly on inner over 2f out: outpcd over 1f out: kpt on* **9/4**[2]

00 **4** *4 ½* **Mediterranean Sea (IRE)**[72] 2433 3-8-4 0.... DannyBrock(7) 9 61?
(J R Jenkins) *hld up in rr: outpcd fr 3f out: pushed along and styd on steadily to take 4th ins fnl f* **80/1**

00 **5** *1 ½* **Sanctum**[53] 3025 3-8-6 0.... Louis-PhilippeBeuzelin(5) 5 58
(Dr J D Scargill) *mostly in midfield: pushed along over 3f out: sn outpcd: kpt on fnl 2f* **80/1**

063 **6** *½* **Phantom Ridge (IRE)**[20] 4145 3-8-11 **70**.... RichardHughes 3 64+
(R Hannon) *s.s: sn wl in tch: prog 4f out: chsd wnr 3f out: sn rdn: lost 2nd over 1f out: wknd and eased* **7/1**

7 *1 ½* **Silk And Satin (USA)** 3-8-11 0.... IanMongan 1 54
(H R A Cecil) *cl up: effrt to dispute 2nd over 2f out: wknd over 1f out* **8/1**

00 **8** *5* **Through The Forest (USA)**[17] 4246 3-8-11 0.... ShaneKelly 4 44
(W R Swinburn) *a in rr: shkn up 4f out: lost tch fr 3f out* **33/1**

00-0 **9** *3 ¼* **Lily Of The Nile (UAE)**[76] 2323 3-8-8 **40**....(v[1]) DavidProbert(3) 2 38
(J G Portman) *dwlt: sn trckd ldr: wknd and hanging lft fr 3f out* **50/1**

10 *4 ½* **Miss Totnes**[46] 5-9-6 0.... RichardThomas 6 29
(M Hill) *s.s: a in rr: rdn 4f out: sn bhd* **66/1**

5- **P** **La Cortezana**[496] 1119 5-9-6 0.... AlanMunro 12 —
(A P Jarvis) *wnt rt s: detached in last tl p.u over 6f out: dismntd* **33/1**

2m 8.04s (-0.66) **Going Correction** -0.075s/f (Good)
WFA 3 from 4yo+ 9lb **11** Ran SP% **124.5**
Speed ratings (Par 100): **99,97,95,92,91 90,89,85,82,79** —
toteswinger: 1&2 £2.70, 1&3 £2.20, 2&3 £2.10. CSF £9.88 TOTE £4.80: £1.70, £1.40, £1.50; EX 14.00 Trifecta £48.60 Pool: £386.32 - 5.88 winning units..
Owner Fawzi Abdulla Nass **Bred** Robert S Evans **Trained** Newmarket, Suffolk

FOCUS
Not a strong maiden.

4829 ST JOHN AMBULANCE TEXT "DONATE" TO 85010 H'CAP 5f 10y
5:00 (5:04) (Class 5) (0-75,75) 3-Y-O **£2,729** (£806; £403) **Stalls High**

Form RPR
25 **1** **Corton Charlemagne (IRE)**[10] 4454 3-8-6 **63**......... WilliamCarson(3) 5 72
(Rae Guest) *prom: drvn ahd over 1f out: hrd pressed after: edgd lft but hld on wl* **7/1**
1561 **2** *1* **Speak The Truth (IRE)**[9] 4483 3-8-9 **68**..............(p) MatthewDavies(5) 1 73
(J R Boyle) *stdd s: hld up in last trio: prog on wd outside fr 2f out: rdn to press wnr fnl f: nt qckn and hld nr fin* **5/1**[2]
065 **3** *1* **Chandika**[15] 4324 3-8-4 **58**.. LukeMorris 6 59
(C G Cox) *cl up against nr side rail: chal over 1f out: nt qckn fnl f* **9/2**[1]
0622 **4** *½* **Avrilo**[9] 4483 3-8-2 **56** oh1.................................... RichardThomas 4 56
(M S Saunders) *hld up in tch: effrt 2f out: pressed wnr over 1f out: fdd ins fnl f* **6/1**[3]
3333 **5** *1¼* **Imaginary Diva**[8] 4514 3-8-8 **62**.................................... DaneO'Neill 8 57
(G G Margarson) *hld up in last trio: prog over 1f out to chse ldrs ent fnl f: no ex* **7/1**
0415 **6** *1* **Keep Dancing (IRE)**[13] 4380 3-8-12 **69**..............(p) DavidProbert(3) 9 61
(A M Balding) *hld up in last trio: effrt against nr side rail whn no room over 2f out and again 2f out: no real prog whn in the clr fnl f* **5/1**[2]
150 **7** *nk* **Love You Louis**[83] 2140 3-9-7 **75**..................................(b) ShaneKelly 3 65
(J R Jenkins) *awkward s: rcvrd to ld after 1f: hdd & wknd over 1f out* **16/1**
050 **8** *1¾* **Calypso Girl (IRE)**[17] 4237 3-7-13 **58**.......... Louis-PhilippeBeuzelin(5) 2 42
(P D Evans) *racd on outer: in tch: rdn 2f out: no prog and btn over 1f out* **9/1**
1106 **9** *4½* **Baby Queen (IRE)**[33] 3704 3-8-10 **64**......................... J-PGuillambert 7 32
(B P J Baugh) *led 1f: sn pushed along: lost pl and wknd 2f out* **10/1**

59.80 secs (-0.50) **Going Correction** -0.075s/f (Good) **9 Ran SP% 115.8**
Speed ratings (Par 100): **101,99,97,97,95 93,92,90,82**
toteswinger: 1&2 £8.30, 1&3 £9.70, 2&3 £4.20. CSF £41.98 CT £177.23 TOTE £9.10: £2.80, £2.00, £2.20; EX 61.40 Trifecta £283.30 Pool: £650.89 - 1.70 winning units. Place 6 £49.64, Place 5 £25.38..
Owner Cheval Ct,Alexander,Bottriell,Guest&LKP **Bred** Tony Hirschfeld & L K Piggott **Trained** Newmarket, Suffolk

FOCUS
They went a good gallop throughout in this 5f dash and the form looks sound for the grade.
Keep Dancing(IRE) Official explanation: jockey said filly was denied a clear run
T/Plt: £102.00 to a £1 stake. Pool: £63,811.16. 456.43 winning tickets. T/Qpdt: £47.20 to a £1 stake. Pool: £3,732.10. 58.40 winning tickets. JN

4807 DEAUVILLE (R-H)
Sunday, August 9

OFFICIAL GOING: Turf course - good to soft; all-weather - standard

4837a PRIX MAURICE DE GHEEST (GROUP 1) 6f 110y(S)
3:30 (3:29) 3-Y-O+ **£138,689** (£55,485; £27,743; £13,859; £6,942)

RPR
1 **King's Apostle (IRE)**[30] 3819 5-9-2 .... RyanMoore 7 117
(W J Haggas) *a cl up in middle: led 150yds out: drvn out* **7/1**
2 *½* **Mariol (FR)**[28] 3908 6-9-2 .... C-PLemaire 10 116
(Robert Collet, France) *hld up in middle: hdwy 2f out: r.o to take 2nd 50yds out* **50/1**
3 *hd* **Lesson In Humility (IRE)**[30] 3824 4-8-13 .... AndrewElliott 9 112
(A P Jarvis) *pressed ldr in middle: led on outside jst over 2f out to 150yds out: one pce clsng stages* **8/1**
4 *nk* **Varenar (FR)**[48] 3231 3-8-12 .... CSoumillon 4 116
(A De Royer-Dupre, France) *5th on rails' side early: edgd to middle over 2f out: r.o u.p fnl f: nrest at fin* **25/1**
5 *hd* **Sayif (IRE)**[71] 2485 3-8-12 .... JamieSpencer 8 115
(P W Chapple-Hyam) *led gp in middle: overall ldr at 1/2-way: hdd jst over 2f out: kpt on steadily* **40/1**
6 *1½* **Dunkerque (FR)**[48] 3231 4-9-2 ....(p) DBoeuf 11 110
(Mme C Head-Maarek, France) *cl up in middle tl outpcd 1/2-way: drvn and hdwy on outside wl over 1f out: nvr able to chal* **40/1**
7 *nk* **Tiza (SAF)**[28] 3908 7-9-2 ....(p) GMosse 12 109
(A De Royer-Dupre, France) *cl up in middle: 4th appr fnl f: no ex* **11/1**
8 *2½* **Serious Attitude (IRE)**[30] 3824 3-8-8 .... EddieAhern 1 99
(Rae Guest) *chsd ldr on rails' side: rdn and btn 2f out* **11/2**[3]
9 *hd* **Asset (IRE)**[50] 3141 6-9-2 ....(b) LDettori 5 101
(Saeed Bin Suroor) *s.s: stl last on rails 1f out: nvr a factor* **8/1**
10 *1½* **Naaqoos**[91] 1917 3-8-12 .... DBonilla 3 98
(F Head, France) *sn led rails' gp: rdn and wknd wl over 1f out* **5/2**[1]
11 *1½* **African Rose**[30] 3819 4-8-13 .... SPasquier 6 89
(Mme C Head-Maarek, France) *hld up on rails' side: btn wl over 1f out* **9/2**[2]
12 *1½* **Delvita (FR)**[28] 3908 5-8-13 .... OPeslier 2 85
(J-V Toux, France) *pressed ldr on rails' side tl wkng 1/2-way* **33/1**

1m 15.7s (-1.50) **Going Correction** +0.225s/f (Good)
WFA 3 from 4yo+ 4lb **12 Ran SP% 118.8**
Speed ratings: **117,116,116,115,115 113,113,110,110,108 107,105**
PARI-MUTUEL: WIN 14.80; PL 5.30, 9.80, 4.30; DF 314.80.
Owner Bernard Kantor **Bred** Wentworth Racing **Trained** Newmarket, Suffolk
■ Stewards' Enquiry : Jamie SpencerE 75euro fine: whip abuse

FOCUS
With its distinctly unconventional 6.5f trip and a winner's prize of less than £140,000, the Prix Maurice de Gheest has not always attracted the strongest field in the European Group 1 calendar, and this year's running once again looked below par, even bearing in mind that top level sprints – if that is what this race is – are sometimes a mixed bag. Just three of this field of 12 had previously tasted success at the highest level, and further questions can be asked about the strength of this form, with the riders splitting into two groups of six shortly after the start, and the first three home, as well as the fifth, sixth and seventh all coming from the group that raced down the centre of the track.

NOTEBOOK
King's Apostle(IRE) graduated out of handicap company at the end of his four-year-old career, but had yet to set the world alight in four starts since in Group company, but ran his best race last time out, when he was an unlucky fifth after getting caught up in scrimmaging in the July Cup. Although his chances were done no favours that time, and with the form subsequently taking a knock, he did not have a profile that screamed 'future Group 1 winner'. All credit, therefore, to him and his connections for getting a top level win, but you can't help but feel his name will become another on the increasing list of over-achievers to have won this, as opposed to the select few top class sprinters like Marchand D'Or and Anabaa. We should know more after next month's Betfred Sprint Cup, which should prove more of a test. The Prix de la Foret at the beginning of October might also come in for consideration.
Mariol(FR) had finished behind Tiza, Delvita and Dunkerque in three Group 3 starts earlier in the season, and he was only tenth in this race 12 months earlier, so his performance doesn't do a lot for the value of the form. He did, however, put up a display that suggests that a step back up in trip will suit, having finished well after being towards the rear. He finished third in the Prix de Meautry last year and will no doubt race in the same event again later in the month.
Lesson In Humility(IRE) is having a fine year. She finished third in the Golden Jubilee Stakes – well ahead of King's Apostle – from a poor draw two starts ago. Connections reported her to have thrived since her most recent start, and she showed good battling qualities here, having been ridden from fully 3f out. No doubt the Haydock Sprint will be considered if she comes out of this race well.
Varenar(FR) finished best of the half dozen who raced on the stands' side. He had plenty to find with a lot of these and it was also questionable whether a drop back to this trip would suit this half-brother to Visindar. It was no surprise to see him doing his best work late on, and having been forced to check slightly when his rider started to make headway, not to mention racing on the unfavoured part of the track, he was perhaps a little unlucky here. He is worth another try over a similar trip, and if conditions fell in his favour, it would not be the biggest shock to see him reverse form with those who finished in front of him. He certainly looks to be a colt going the right way, and an outing in the Meautry looks on the cards.
Sayif(IRE)'s trainer Peter Chapple-Hyam has been having a good time of it with his three-year-olds this season. This was the toughest task he has faced since finishing second in last season's Middle Park Stakes, but he acquitted himself as well as could be expected. His rider was fined for abusive use of the whip.
Dunkerque(FR) has been running well around this trip in Group 3 company. He kept on without troubling those in front of him. He ran his race.
Tiza(SAF) has won twice in lesser company this season. He fared worst of those who raced down the middle and filled a similar position as in the last two years.
Serious Attitude(IRE), having lost her unbeaten record when failing to stay in the Guineas, bounced back to winning ways when beating Lesson In Humility in Listed company at York last time. Her stall one berth did not do last season's Cheveley Park Stakes winner any favours, and she was eased when beaten.
Asset(IRE), having been steadied at the start, had plenty to do late on. His rider's decision to come up the rail may not have helped, but he would have been unlikely to trouble the principals wherever he came from.
Naaqoos had looked like he was destined for the top last year, when victory in the Prix Jean-Luc Lagardere stretched his unbeaten run to four. He has now failed to get his head in front in four starts as a three-year-old, and had little to give late on after racing keenly early.
African Rose, the third Group 1 winner in the line-up, was never on terms. She was eased when beaten and was subsequently found to have bled during the race.This was her final start in a 13-race career, which saw her win three times and make the frame on a further five occasions.
Delvita(FR) has been racing over the minimum trip in Listed company. She dropped away tamely, upped in distance and grade.

4370 SOUTHWELL (L-H)
Monday, August 10

OFFICIAL GOING: Standard
Wind: Light across Weather: Overcast

4838 LADIES DAY BOOK ON LINE MAIDEN STKS 1m 3f (F)
2:15 (2:16) (Class 5) 3-Y-O+ **£4,209** (£1,252; £625; £312) **Stalls Low**

Form RPR
525 **1** **Ottoman Empire (FR)**[88] 2002 3-8-9 0................................ TedDurcan 6 91+
(D R Lanigan) *mde all: rdn over 1f out: edgd lft ins fnl f: styd on wl: eased nr fin* **15/8**[1]
2 **2** *1½* **Brief Look**[60] 2847 3-8-4 0... JimmyQuinn 13 84+
(H R A Cecil) *chsd ldrs: outpcd 2f out: rallied ins fnl f: r.o: wnt 2nd nr fin* **9/4**[2]
6255 **3** *nk* **Monetary Fund (USA)**[24] 4045 3-8-9 72.........................(t) ShaneKelly 8 88
(G A Butler) *chsd wnr: rdn 2f out: styd on same pce ins fnl f: lost 2nd nr fin* **12/1**
4304 **4** *16* **Favours Brave**[59] 2881 3-8-9 69.................................... RobertWinston 10 61
(Mrs S Lamyman) *chsd ldrs: rdn over 3f out: wknd over 2f out* **15/2**
5 **5** *2* **Oneofapear (IRE)**[41] 3485 3-8-9 0.................................. PJMcDonald 3 57
(G A Swinbank) *hld up: lost pl 1/2-way: n.d after* **100/1**
6 *2¾* **Knight's Victory (IRE)** 3-8-9 0.................................... GregFairley 5 53
(M Johnston) *sn pushed along in rr: hdwy u.p over 4f out: wknd 3f out* **7/1**[3]
60 **7** *7* **Beat The Shower**[10] 4505 3-8-9 0................................ PaulMulrennan 4 41
(P D Niven) *mid-div: rdn over 4f out: sme hdwy over 3f out: sn wknd* **100/1**
562- **8** *4½* **Desert Vision**[247] 7583 5-9-5 79... DaleGibson 1 33
(M W Easterby) *trckd ldrs: racd keenly: rdn and wknd over 3f out* **14/1**
9 *2½* **Fred Kennet**[103] 4-9-5 0.. AdamKirby 12 29
(M Salaman) *s.s: outpcd* **50/1**
5 **10** *1¼* **Eloise**[19] 4205 3-8-4 0.. ChrisCatlin 9 22
(Sir Mark Prescott) *mid-div: sn pushed along: wknd 4f out* **28/1**
30 **11** *22* **Rapid Desire (IRE)**[9] 4519 3-8-4 0......................... SilvestreDeSousa 7 —
(J R Weymes) *dwlt: outpcd* **66/1**

2m 23.42s (-4.58) **Going Correction** -0.10s/f (Stan)
WFA 3 from 4yo+ 10lb **11 Ran SP% 113.1**
Speed ratings (Par 103): **112,110,110,99,97 95,90,87,85,84 68**
toteswinger: 1&2 £1.70, 1&3 £7.40, 2&3 £6.60. CSF £5.71 TOTE £3.30: £1.70, £1.20, £3.10; EX 5.90 Trifecta £34.60 Pool: £390.31 - 8.33 winning units..
Owner Plantation Stud **Bred** S C E A Haras De La Perelle **Trained** Newmarket, Suffolk

FOCUS
A well above-average maiden for the track, the winner setting a good standard. The first three came well clear.

4839 DOCTOR STEPHEN WROE HALF CENTURY MAIDEN AUCTION STKS 6f (F)
2:45 (2:47) (Class 4) 2-Y-O £3,885 (£1,156; £577; £288) Stalls Low

Form RPR
0 **1** **Royal Holiday (IRE)**[7] 4595 2-8-9 0 TomEaves 3 69
(B Ellison) *chsd ldrs: outpcd over 3f out: hdwy u.p over 1f out: r.o to ld post* **7/1**[3]
2 **2** ½ **Duster**[19] 4200 2-8-8 0 SteveDrowne 5 66
(H Morrison) *chsd ldr: rdn over 1f out: styd on u.p to ld nr fin: hdd post* **8/11**[1]
00 **3** nse **Stef And Stelio**[37] 3613 2-8-10 0 ShaneKelly 7 68
(G A Butler) *chsd ldrs: rdn to ld 1f out: hdd nr fin* **20/1**
4 ¾ **Cape Kimberley** 2-8-9 0 PaulMulrennan 4 65
(J G Given) *led: rdn and hdd 1f out: unable qck nr fin* **14/1**
2003 **5** 9 **Mr Smithson (IRE)**[27] 3952 2-8-4 70 ow1 LanceBetts(5) 2 38
(B Ellison) *chsd ldrs: rdn over 2f out: wknd over 1f out* **9/2**[2]
03 **6** 7 **Coolella (IRE)**[7] 4590 2-8-4 0 ChrisCatlin 6 12
(J R Weymes) *chsd ldrs: sn pushed along: wknd 1/2-way* **9/1**
0 **7** 11 **Nicaldani**[38] 3576 2-8-3 0 JimmyQuinn 1 —
(M Blanshard) *s.i.s: hld up: rdn 1/2-way: sn wknd* **100/1**
00 **8** nk **Sancho Panza**[33] 3750 2-8-8 0 MickyFenton 8 —
(Miss J Feilden) *sn pushed along in rr: wknd 1/2-way* **33/1**

1m 17.33s (0.83) **Going Correction** -0.10s/f (Stan) **8 Ran SP% 113.9**
Speed ratings (Par 96): **90,89,89,88,76 66,52,51**
toteswinger: 1&2 £2.70, 1&3 £8.70, 2&3 £4.10. CSF £12.36 TOTE £10.60: £1.80, £1.10, £4.60; EX 21.10 Trifecta £437.20 Part won. Pool: £590.85 - 0.43 winning units..
Owner Joan Turner & William Gibson **Bred** E Tynan **Trained** Norton, N Yorks

FOCUS
A modest juvenile maiden. The runner-up was probably below his debut form and this may not be a race to be with.

NOTEBOOK
Royal Holiday(IRE) improved significantly on the form he showed on his debut at Ripon a week earlier. He struggled to lay up with the pace for much of the way and still looked held passing the final-furlong pole, but he finally got going once switched towards the stands' rail, out of the kickback. Ordinary nurseries probably await and he might stay 7f. (op 9-1)
Duster, keener than ideal early on, didn't build on the form he showed when first time up in a 7f Lingfield maiden, and that race is not working out. (tchd 10-11 and evens in place)
Stef And Stelio improved significantly on his two turf efforts. He now has the option of nurseries. (op 12-1)
Cape Kimberley, a £10,000 purchase, knew his job and showed good speed, before not quite getting home. He displayed a bit of knee action and might not appreciate quick turf. (tchd 11-1)
Mr Smithson(IRE) ran poorly on this step up to 6f, clearly failing to see out the trip. (op 13-2)

4840 SOUTHWELL RACECOURSE FOR CONFERENCES H'CAP 1m 4f (F)
3:15 (3:15) (Class 3) (0-90,90) 3-Y-O+ £10,037 (£2,986; £1,492; £745) Stalls Low

Form RPR
0442 **1** **Distinctive Image (USA)**[8] 4561 4-9-6 82 ChrisCatlin 7 101
(R Hollinshead) *hld up: hdwy over 4f out: rdn over 2f out: led wl over 1f out: sn clr: styd on strly* **8/1**
0-33 **2** 8 **Kensington Oval**[17] 4274 4-9-10 86 JimmyFortune 10 92
(Sir Michael Stoute) *dwlt: sn prom: chsd ldr over 5f out: rdn over 2f out: styd on same pce appr fnl f* **3/1**[1]
3135 **3** 1½ **Kingsdale Orion (IRE)**[23] 4102 5-8-8 75 LanceBetts(5) 8 78
(B Ellison) *hld up: hdwy over 4f out: rdn over 2f out: styd on same pce* **10/1**
0506 **4** 2½ **Robby Bobby**[8] 4561 4-10-0 90 GregFairley 5 89
(M Johnston) *chsd ldrs: led over 8f out: rdn and hdd wl over 1f out: sn wknd* **6/1**[3]
0461 **5** 2¾ **Jadalee (IRE)**[23] 4098 6-8-13 75 (p) ShaneKelly 4 70
(G A Butler) *s.i.s: sn pushed along in rr: hdwy 7f out: rdn over 3f out: wknd over 2f out* **8/1**
0560 **6** 1 **Dunaskin (IRE)**[58] 2932 9-9-6 82 TomEaves 3 75
(B Ellison) *prom: lost pl over 7f out: n.d after* **16/1**
32U **7** 6 **Lochiel**[17] 4274 5-9-11 87 PJMcDonald 9 71
(G A Swinbank) *hld up: hdwy 1/2-way: rdn and wknd over 3f out* **5/1**[2]
1- **8** ¾ **Ella**[395] 3929 5-10-0 90 RobertWinston 6 73
(G A Swinbank) *racd keenly: led 1f: chsd ldrs: rdn over 3f out: sn wknd* **10/1**
0021 **9** 1½ **Crimson Mitre**[14] 4373 4-8-10 72 LPKeniry 2 52
(J Jay) *chsd ldrs: lost pl 1/2-way: wknd over 4f out* **17/2**
4-00 **10** 1½ **Candle**[13] 4408 6-9-6 82 PaulMulrennan 1 60
(T R George) *led after 1f: hdd over 8f out: rdn and wknd over 4f out* **25/1**

2m 36.62s (-4.38) **Going Correction** -0.10s/f (Stan) **10 Ran SP% 116.6**
Speed ratings (Par 107): **110,104,103,102,100 99,95,95,94,93**
toteswinger: 1&2 £4.30, 1&3 £17.60, 2&3 £9.00. CSF £32.24 CT £247.10 TOTE £8.90: £1.90, £1.60, £3.60; EX 42.80 Trifecta £216.60 Part won. Pool: £292.77 - 0.43 winning units..
Owner Stevenson Leadbeater & Hollinshead **Bred** Juddmonte Farms Inc **Trained** Upper Longdon, Staffs

FOCUS
A decent handicap for the track, run at a good pace, although the leaders looked to get a breather in at about halfway. The form is rated around the third.

NOTEBOOK
Distinctive Image(USA) ◆ ran out an impressive winner on his first start on Fibresand. A son of Mineshaft who had always looked better on Polytrack than turf, it was no surprise he handled the surface so well. He struggled to lay up early, possibly not facing the kickback, but is a strong stayer, so the decent early gallop suited, and he bounded clear once in the open in the straight. When getting a strong pace to chase on an artificial surface, he is clearly very useful. (op 9-1)
Kensington Oval is a disappointing sort, but in fairness he may have been unsuited by the Fibresand, and he was up against a colt who is clearly very useful on the surface. It could be hurdling for him this winter. (op 4-1)
Kingsdale Orion(IRE) ran okay without improving for the switch to Fibresand. (op 12-1 tchd 16-1)
Robby Bobby, 12lb higher than on turf, managed to get a breather in down the back straight but he was left behind when the race really got going. (op 7-1)
Jadalee(IRE), 4lb higher than when winning over 1m6f at Newmarket on his previous start, ran below his best on this switch to Fibresand. (tchd 7-1)
Dunaskin(IRE) was well below the form he showed when runner-up at this track last November. **Ella** won her last two starts on heavy ground in 2008, but it had been over a year since she was last seen and she offered little tried on Fibresand for the first time. (op 7-1)

4841 MEMBERSHIP OF SOUTHWELL GOLF CLUB RACING H'CAP 7f (F)
3:45 (3:45) (Class 4) (0-80,78) 3-Y-O £5,180 (£1,541; £770; £384) Stalls Low

Form RPR
0016 **1** **Elusive Fame (USA)**[14] 4374 3-9-1 72 (b) GregFairley 9 78
(M Johnston) *s.i.s: sn prom: led 5f out: rdn clr over 1f out: eased nr fin* **7/2**[2]
1236 **2** 1¼ **Iron Out (USA)**[17] 4284 3-8-10 67 MickyFenton 3 70
(R Hollinshead) *chsd ldrs: outpcd over 5f out: hdwy u.p 2f out: r.o: nt rch wnr* **9/2**[3]
-006 **3** nk **Perfect Citizen (USA)**[58] 2926 3-9-7 78 (tp) AdamKirby 8 80
(W R Swinburn) *s.i.s: sn pushed along in rr: hrd rdn 1/2-way: hdwy over 1f out: r.o* **8/1**
1210 **4** 3 **Swiss Art (IRE)**[17] 4284 3-9-3 74 SilvestreDeSousa 1 68
(Mrs R A Carr) *sn pushed along in rr: hdwy 1/2-way: rdn over 1f out: edgd lft and no ex fnl f* **10/3**[1]
4550 **5** 3 **Lakeman (IRE)**[7] 4591 3-8-13 70 TomEaves 4 56
(B Ellison) *sn outpcd: stl last over 1f out: sme late hdwy* **16/1**
3221 **6** ½ **Dance And Dance (IRE)**[167] 663 3-9-7 78 LPKeniry 2 62
(E F Vaughan) *chsd ldrs: rdn over 2f out: wknd over 1f out* **5/1**
2156 **7** shd **You've Been Mowed**[10] 4482 3-8-0 64 AndrewHeffernan(7) 5 48
(R J Price) *led: hdd 5f out: outpcd over 3f out: n.d after* **10/1**
2223 **8** ½ **Andean Margin (IRE)**[74] 2406 3-9-4 75 DaleGibson 7 58
(M W Easterby) *chsd ldrs: rdn over 2f out: wknd over 1f out* **9/1**

1m 29.29s (-1.01) **Going Correction** -0.10s/f (Stan) **8 Ran SP% 116.2**
Speed ratings (Par 102): **101,99,99,95,92 91,91,91**
toteswinger: 1&2 £4.20, 1&3 £9.40, 2&3 £8.00. CSF £20.04 CT £117.96 TOTE £4.00: £1.60, £1.80, £2.80; EX 25.90 Trifecta £233.20 Part won. Pool: £283.64 - 0.10 winning units..
Owner Mark Johnston Racing Ltd **Bred** Summer Wind Farm **Trained** Middleham Moor, N Yorks

FOCUS
A fair handicap for the track, and sound form.

4842 SOUTHWELL-RACECOURSE.CO.UK H'CAP 5f (F)
4:15 (4:15) (Class 3) (0-95,86) 3-Y-O+ £9,066 (£2,697; £1,348; £673) Stalls High

Form RPR
0120 **1** **Luscivious**[11] 4461 5-9-9 85 (p) GrahamGibbons 1 93
(J A Glover) *led 4f out: shkn up over 1f out: jst hld on* **7/4**[1]
5560 **2** shd **Figaro Flyer (IRE)**[24] 4051 6-8-5 67 JimmyQuinn 3 75
(P Howling) *trckd ldrs: rdn to chse wnr 2f out: r.o* **9/2**[2]
5056 **3** 2¼ **Xpres Maite**[12] 4428 6-9-10 86 (b) RobertWinston 6 86
(S R Bowring) *sn outpcd: edgd lft 3f out: r.o ins fnl f: nt trble ldrs* **11/2**[3]
060 **4** 4 **Pawan (IRE)**[10] 4485 9-9-4 85 (b) AnnStokell(5) 4 71
(Miss A Stokell) *s.i.s: outpcd: sme late hdwy* **9/2**[2]
2250 **5** 2 **Tartatartufata**[11] 4469 7-9-2 78 (v) PaulMulrennan 5 56
(J G Given) *led 1f: chsd wnr tl rdn 1/2-way: wknd over 1f out* **8/1**
400 **6** 6 **Stoneacre Lad (IRE)**[21] 4135 6-9-4 80 (b) JamieMackay 7 37
(Peter Grayson) *chsd ldrs: rdn 1/2-way: edgd lft and wknd over 1f out* **13/2**

58.79 secs (-0.91) **Going Correction** 0.0s/f (Stan)
WFA 3 from 5yo+ 3lb **6 Ran SP% 112.6**
Speed ratings (Par 107): **107,106,103,96,93 84**
toteswinger: 1&2 £2.50, 1&3 £2.50, 2&3 £4.60. CSF £9.92 TOTE £2.40: £1.90, £2.70; EX 9.20.
Owner Paul J Dixon & Brian Morton **Bred** R J Turner **Trained** Babworth, Notts

FOCUS
A disappointing turnout numerically but this was still a fair sprint handicap. Straightforward form.

NOTEBOOK
Luscivious was able to dominate and always looked like holding on, even though the winning margin was just a short-head. He's now won his last two starts on Fibresand. The plan now is to go for a £12,000 handicap over 6f at Wolverhampton on Monday. (op 2-1)
Figaro Flyer(IRE) pulled clear of the remainder and this was a good effort in defeat. His form figures over this course and distance read 212312. (op 7-2)
Xpres Maite was outpaced for most of the way before running on all too late. He's better over further. (op 7-1 tchd 8-1)
Pawan(IRE) was given early reminders and never featured. This was disappointing considering he defied a mark of 91 over this course and distance earlier in the year. (op 11-2)
Tartatartufata had conditions to suit and is on a good mark, so better could have been expected. (op 10-1 tchd 12-1)

4843 LADIES DAY 16TH AUGUST H'CAP 6f (F)
4:45 (4:46) (Class 5) (0-70,69) 3-Y-O+ £2,590 (£770; £385; £192) Stalls Low

Form RPR
0025 **1** **Realt Na Mara (IRE)**[9] 4536 6-9-11 69 (p) SteveDrowne 3 81
(H Morrison) *chsd ldrs: led over 3f out: edgd rt over 2f out: rdn out* **5/1**[3]
-053 **2** 1½ **Yankee Storm**[14] 4374 4-9-10 68 RobertWinston 8 75
(M Quinn) *a.p: rdn to chse wnr 2f out: styd on same pce ins fnl f* **3/1**[1]
0000 **3** 3¼ **Guildenstern (IRE)**[34] 3722 7-9-5 63 JimmyQuinn 7 60
(P Howling) *sn outpcd: hdwy over 1f out: wnt 3rd wl ins fnl f: nvr nrr* **25/1**
3440 **4** ¾ **Elusive Warrior (USA)**[84] 2133 6-8-13 62 (p) JamesO'Reilly(5) 6 56
(A J McCabe) *chsd ldrs: rdn over 2f out: styd on same pce appr fnl f* **8/1**
6021 **5** 2 **First Blade**[20] 4172 3-8-8 56 (b) FrankieMcDonald 2 44
(S R Bowring) *s.i.s: hdwy over 3f out: sn rdn: styd on same pce fnl 2f* **5/1**[3]
4050 **6** hd **Tri Chara (IRE)**[18] 4225 5-9-5 63 (p) AdamKirby 10 50
(R Hollinshead) *chsd ldrs: rdn over 2f out: wknd over 1f out* **8/1**
0000 **7** 1½ **A Big Sky Brewing (USA)**[14] 4374 5-9-6 69 DeanHeslop(5) 5 51
(T D Barron) *sn outpcd: sme hdwy over 1f out: n.d* **20/1**
2100 **8** ½ **Only A Splash**[6] 4620 5-8-0 51 JamesPSullivan(7) 1 32
(Mrs R A Carr) *prom: n.m.r over 4f out: rdn over 2f out: wknd wl over 1f out* **20/1**
5000 **9** 4 **Cool Sands (IRE)**[14] 4374 7-9-5 63 (v) MickyFenton 4 31
(J G Given) *s.i.s: outpcd* **28/1**
-405 **10** 11 **Good Humoured**[26] 3989 3-8-12 60 PaulMulrennan 9 —
(Sir Mark Prescott) *led: hdd over 3f out: rdn and wknd wl over 1f out* **9/2**[2]

1m 15.95s (-0.55) **Going Correction** -0.10s/f (Stan)
WFA 3 from 4yo+ 4lb **10 Ran SP% 115.6**
Speed ratings (Par 103): **99,97,92,91,89 88,86,86,80,66**
toteswinger: 1&2 £3.40, 1&3 £21.90, 2&3 £15.90. CSF £19.02 CT £347.99 TOTE £5.60: £2.00, £1.60, £5.80; EX 18.70 TRIFECTA Not won. Place 6: £15.99, Place 5: £12.09..
Owner H Morrison **Bred** J C Condon **Trained** East Ilsley, Berks

FOCUS
A modest sprint handicap in which the lead was contested, but the pace still didn't seem overly strong. Straightforward form.
First Blade Official explanation: jockey said gelding would not face the kickback
Good Humoured Official explanation: jockey said gelding stopped very quickly
T/Plt: £27.50 to a £1 stake. Pool: £56,268.86. 1,490.76 winning tickets. T/Qpdt: £26.40 to a £1 stake. Pool: £4,056.70. 113.60 winning tickets. CR

[4546]THIRSK (L-H)

Monday, August 10

OFFICIAL GOING: Good (good to soft in places; 8.6)

Wind: Virtually nil Weather: Overcast and showers

4844 EUROPEAN BREEDERS' FUND MAIDEN STKS 5f

6:00 (6:02) (Class 5) 2-Y-O £4,274 (£1,271; £635; £317) **Stalls** High

Form				RPR
52	1		**Take Ten**[58] 2907 2-9-3 0 ... JoeFanning 12 (M Johnston) *sn led: rdn along and hdd wl over 1f out: drvn ins fnl f and rallied to ld nr fin* **3/1**[1]	70
4205	2	*nk*	**Bronze Beau**[73] 2435 2-9-3 65 ... TGMcLaughlin 8 (Mrs L Stubbs) *prom: effrt and cl up 1/2-way: rdn to ld over 1f out: drvn ins fnl f: hdd and no ex nr fin* **16/1**	69
	3	*3*	**Durham Express (IRE)** 2-9-3 0 ... PhillipMakin 14 (M Dods) *hld up in midfield: effrt 2f out and n.m.r: swtchd lft over 1f out and styd on wl fnl f* **7/1**[3]	58+
0526	4	*¾*	**Clever Molly (IRE)**[7] 4590 2-8-12 57 ... DanielTudhope 1 (E J Alston) *wnt rt s: in tch on outer: hdwy to chse ldrs 2f out: sn rdn and one pce appr fnl f* **12/1**	50
35	5	*¾*	**So Bazaar (IRE)**[16] 4307 2-9-3 0 ... PJMcDonald 13 (G A Swinbank) *chsd ldrs: rdn along 2f out: sn drvn and no imp* **9/2**[2]	53
005	6	*2*	**Kirkby's Gem**[25] 4011 2-8-5 50 ... BillyCray(7) 6 (A Berry) *bmpd s: in tch: swtchd wd and rdn 2f out: sn no imp* **80/1**	41
	7	*1 ¼*	**Croft Bridge** 2-9-3 0 ... TonyHamilton 5 (M Dods) *a towards rr* **50/1**	41
6	8	*nk*	**Dusty Spirit**[9] 4537 2-9-0 0 ... JackDean(3) 7 (W G M Turner) *sn rdn along and a towards rr* **33/1**	40
0430	9	*1 ¼*	**Tarrants Way**[23] 4076 2-9-3 57 ... PaulEddery 10 (Jennie Candlish) *prom: rdn along over 1/2-way: grad wknd* **66/1**	35
	10	*nk*	**Baze Mac** 2-8-12 0 ... SilvestreDeSousa 16 (N Bycroft) *prom: rdn along 1/2-way: sn wknd* **66/1**	29
	11	*5*	**Shegarrdi** 2-9-0 0 ... NeilBrown(3) 3 (K A Ryan) *s.i.s: a bhd* **25/1**	16
	12	*4 ½*	**On Holiday** 2-8-7 0 ... BMcHugh(5) 15 (M W Easterby) *v.s.a: green and a bhd* **50/1**	—

61.02 secs (1.42) **Going Correction** +0.275s/f (Good) **12** Ran SP% **84.2**

Speed ratings (Par 94): **99,98,93,92,91 88,86,85,83,83 75,67**

toteswinger: 1&2 £3.10, 1&3 £2.30, 2&3 £7.10. CSF £20.91 TOTE £3.00: £1.20, £3.50, £1.50; EX 19.70.

Owner Sheikh Hamdan Bin Mohammed Al Maktoum **Bred** Whitsbury Manor Stud And Mrs M E Slade **Trained** Middleham Moor, N Yorks

FOCUS

After morning rain, the ground was officially eased, but it looked only just on the easy side of good on the straight track. A modest maiden made even weaker when the favourite Dubawi Heights had to be withdrawn after giving problems in the stalls and getting her head under the gates (6/4F, deduct 40p in the £.) Straightforward but modest form.

NOTEBOOK

Take Ten, back after a two-month break, grabbed the favoured stands' side rail. After being headed, he battled back well to gain the upper hand near the line. Nurseries now presumably beckon. (op 7-2)

Bronze Beau, having his sixth start and officially rated 65, went a neck up only to miss out near the line. (op 14-1 tchd 12-1)

Durham Express(IRE) is the one to take out of the race. A gelded son of Acclamation, he has size and scope. Well backed to make a winning debut, he had to switch wide for a run after being waited with in mid-field. He stayed on in pleasing fashion and should improve and make his mark. (op 14-1)

Clever Molly(IRE), having her fifth start and rated just 57, was at a disadvantage having to race wide from the worst of the draw. (op 10-1 tchd 14-1)

So Bazaar(IRE), dropping back in trip on his third start, is now qualified for nurseries and on breeding will appreciate a return to further. (tchd 5-1)

Kirkby's Gem, rated just 50 and forced to race wide on his fourth start, wasn't beaten far and emphasises the low-grade nature of the race. (op 66-1)

4845 OTTERINGTON SHORTHORN (S) H'CAP 1m

6:30 (6:31) (Class 6) (0-65,62) 3-Y-0+ £2,978 (£886; £442; £221) **Stalls** Low

Form				RPR
5050	1		**Funky Munky**[42] 3448 4-9-7 55 ... PJMcDonald 6 (G A Swinbank) *trckd ldrs: hdwy 3f out: led wl over 1f out: jnd and drvn ent fnl f: kpt on gamely u.p towards fin* **15/2**	71
0031	2	*1 ¼*	**Morocchius (USA)**[11] 4466 4-9-1 54 ... (p) BMcHugh(5) 4 (Miss J A Camacho) *hld up in midfield: hdwy 1/2-way: effrt to chse wnr over 1f out: rdn to chal ent fnl f: sn drvn and ev ch tl one pce last 100yds* **9/2**[2]	67
4050	3	*4 ½*	**Sands Of Barra (IRE)**[9] 4552 6-8-13 52 ... AmyRyan(5) 10 (I W McInnes) *hld up and bhd: hdwy on outer over 2f out: rdn to chse ldrs and edgd lft over 1f out: sn one pce* **16/1**	55
3060	4	*3 ¼*	**Carpe Diem**[7] 4588 4-9-5 53 ... (v) TonyHamilton 12 (R A Fahey) *sn prom: effrt 3f out: rdn to ld over 2f out: hdd wl over 1f out: sn drvn and wknd* **12/1**	48
0025	5	*1 ½*	**Spin Again (IRE)**[28] 3924 4-10-0 62 ... AdrianTNicholls 5 (D Nicholls) *hld up towards rr: hdwy over 2f out: sn rdn and no imp fr wl over 1f out* **4/1**[1]	54
4000	6	*2*	**Fyodorovich (USA)**[5] 4654 4-9-1 49 ... PAspell 15 (J S Wainwright) *hld up in rr: gd hdwy on inner over 2f out: rdn to chse ldrs wl over 1f out: sn no imp* **25/1**	36
1-00	7	*2 ½*	**Zennerman (IRE)**[11] 4465 6-9-11 59 ... (b) GrahamGibbons 3 (W M Brisbourne) *dwlt: hdwy and in tch 1/2-way: rdn along over 2f out and sn wknd* **10/1**	40
2535	8	*2 ½*	**Efidium**[12] 4435 11-9-9 60 ... NeilBrown(3) 11 (N Bycroft) *nvr nr ldrs* **13/2**[3]	36
-600	9	*2 ½*	**Dolly No Hair**[5] 4656 4-9-3 51 ... PaulEddery 2 (N Wilson) *led: rdn along 3f out: sn hdd & wknd* **33/1**	21
3000	10	*2*	**King Of The Moors (USA)**[12] 4435 6-9-11 59 ... PhillipMakin 1 (R C Guest) *chsd ldrs on inner: rdn along 3f out: sn drvn and wknd* **9/1**	24
-410	11	*3*	**Whispering Spirit (IRE)**[14] 4375 3-9-7 62 ... SilvestreDeSousa 13 (Mrs A Duffield) *midfield: towards rr fr 1/2-way* **12/1**	20
6005	12	*5*	**Portrush Storm**[15] 4344 4-9-7 55 ... (b) DanielTudhope 9 (D Carroll) *chsd ldrs: rdn along 3f out: drvn and wknd over 2f out* **12/1**	—
5040	13	*3*	**Picture Frame**[12] 4434 5-9-1 54 ... (p) PatrickDonaghy(5) 8 (J T Stimpson) *s.i.s: a in rr* **22/1**	—
6600	14	*12*	**Flying Bantam (IRE)**[14] 4376 8-8-9 50 ... (b[1]) JohnCavanagh(7) 17 (J R Norton) *a towards rr* **40/1**	—
6-00	15	*5*	**Short Sharp Shock**[34] 3710 3-8-13 54 ... TomEaves 18 (J Mackie) *chsd ldrs: rdn along 3f out and sn wknd* **40/1**	—

1m 42.02s (1.92) **Going Correction** +0.275s/f (Good)

WFA 3 from 4yo+ 7lb **15** Ran SP% **127.3**

Speed ratings (Par 101): **101,99,95,92,90 88,86,83,81,79 76,71,68,56,51**

toteswinger: 1&2 £5.70, 1&3 £18.90, 2&3 £25.90 CSF £41.13 CT £545.96 TOTE £9.50: £2.60, £2.00, £4.40; EX 53.10.There was no bid for the winner.

Owner The Twelve Munkys **Bred** Mrs S Corbett **Trained** Melsonby, N Yorks

FOCUS

A routine 45-62 selling handicap and the ground looked more good to soft in the back straight. The front pair came clear and may be a little better than the grade.

Funky Munky Official explanation: trainer said, regarding apparent improvement in form, that the gelding had appreciated the drop in class and its first run in a seller.

4846 BEATRICE STEPHENSON MEMORIAL H'CAP 1m

7:00 (7:00) (Class 5) (0-75,75) 3-Y-O £4,274 (£1,271; £635; £317) **Stalls** Low

Form				RPR
3441	1		**Diamond Daisy (IRE)**[27] 3939 3-8-12 66 ... SilvestreDeSousa 2 (Mrs A Duffield) *trckd ldrs on inner: hdwy to chse ldr over 3f out: led 2f out: drvn ent fnl f: styd on wl towards fin* **6/1**[3]	72
4300	2	*½*	**Green Agenda**[17] 4262 3-9-7 75 ... JoeFanning 3 (M Johnston) *s.i.s: gd hdwy on inner 3f out: rdn to chse ldng pair ent fnl f: sn swtchd rt and drvn: styd on wl: jst hld* **11/2**[2]	80+
0PP0	3	*1*	**Captain Imperial (IRE)**[9] 4518 3-9-0 68 ... MickyFenton 5 (T P Tate) *led: rdn along and hdd 2f out: sn drvn and ev ch tl wknd ins fnl f* **16/1**	71
5440	4	*1 ¼*	**Steel Stockholder**[9] 4548 3-8-5 59 ... GregFairley 7 (M Brittain) *prom: pushed along 3f out and sltly outpcd: hdwy 2f out: rdn to chse ldrs whn edgd lft appr fnl f: kpt on same pce* **7/1**	59
3-10	5	*4 ½*	**Ykikamoocow**[33] 3727 3-9-0 68 ... PJMcDonald 11 (G A Harker) *a.p: rdn along over 2f out and grad wknd* **16/1**	57
5420	6	*nk*	**King's Counsel (IRE)**[1] 4822 3-7-13 60 ... AndrewHeffernan(7) 8 (J Hetherton) *chsd ldrs: rdn along wl over 2f out and sn btn* **10/1**	49
00-2	7	*½*	**Safari Song (IRE)**[17] 4277 3-9-5 73 ... TomEaves 10 (B Smart) *towards rr: effrt on outer over 2f out: sn rdn and nvr a factor* **5/1**[1]	61
2022	8	*2 ¼*	**Peaceful Rule (USA)**[12] 4432 3-9-4 72 ... AdrianTNicholls 9 (D Nicholls) *chsd ldrs: effrt 3f out: rdn over 2f out: sn drvn and wknd* **5/1**[1]	54
6-20	9	*3 ¼*	**Gordy Bee (USA)**[24] 4057 3-9-4 72 ... PaulEddery 1 (Pat Eddery) *midfield: rdn along over 3f out and sn wknd* **5/1**[1]	47
2-05	10	*8*	**Premier Angel (USA)**[187] 391 3-8-7 61 ... TonyHamilton 4 (Ollie Pears) *a in rr* **22/1**	18

1m 43.03s (2.93) **Going Correction** +0.275s/f (Good) **10** Ran SP% **117.4**

Speed ratings (Par 100): **96,95,94,93,88 88,87,85,82,74**

toteswinger: 1&2 £6.30, 1&3 £28.20, 2&3 £16.70. CSF £39.29 CT £506.57 TOTE £6.60: £2.40, £2.60, £5.10; EX 46.30.

Owner John and Elaine Culf and John Gatenby **Bred** Thomas F Brennan & Holborn Trust Co Ltd **Trained** Constable Burton, N Yorks

FOCUS

A wide-open event run at a strong pace and again the time suggested it was good to soft in the back straight. The time was slower than for the seller and this is ordinary form for the grade.

4847 BLACK SHEEP BREWERY MAIDEN AUCTION STKS 7f

7:30 (7:35) (Class 5) 2-Y-O £4,274 (£1,271; £635; £317) **Stalls** Low

Form				RPR
3	1		**Our Joe Mac (IRE)**[17] 4286 2-8-12 0 ... PaulHanagan 2 (R A Fahey) *trckd ldrs: hdwy over 2f out: led on bit over 1f out: clr ins fnl f* **10/11**[1]	86+
233	2	*4*	**George Benjamin**[13] 4410 2-8-9 68 ... AdrianTNicholls 5 (D Nicholls) *led: rdn along and jnd over 2f out: hdd over 1f out: sn drvn and kpt on same pce* **4/1**[2]	68
2	3	*½*	**Forshour**[34] 3715 2-8-9 0 ... GrahamGibbons 7 (E S McMahon) *prom: effrt over 2f out and sn rdn: drvn over 1f out and kpt on same pce* **17/2**[3]	67
00	4	*1 ¾*	**No Quarter (IRE)**[16] 4307 2-8-9 0 ... DanielTudhope 8 (A Dickman) *midfield: hdwy 3f out: rdn to chse ldrs 2f out: drvn and kpt on same pce appr fnl f* **50/1**	62
5	5	*1 ¼*	**Boss's Destination**[15] 4342 2-9-1 0 ... PJMcDonald 11 (G A Swinbank) *hld up towards rr: hdwy over 2f out: kpt on appr fnl f: nrst fin* **25/1**	65
	6	*1 ¾*	**Quite Sparky** 2-8-9 0 ... MickyFenton 4 (T P Tate) *s.i.s: hdwy in midfield 3f out: sn rdn along and n.d* **20/1**	55+
	7	*3 ¾*	**Bintalaleumydarlin (IRE)** 2-8-7 0 ... JoeFanning 12 (M Johnston) *prom: rdn along 1/2-way: wknd over 2f out* **16/1**	44
	8	*9*	**Arlequin** 2-8-9 0 ... JamieSpencer 13 (J D Bethell) *s.i.s: a in rr* **14/1**	23
6	9	*2 ¾*	**Emerald Glade (IRE)**[16] 4331 2-8-7 0 ... DuranFentiman 3 (T D Easterby) *a towards rr* **20/1**	14
	10	*1*	**Princess Neenee (IRE)** 2-8-7 0 ... (t) SilvestreDeSousa 9 (Paul Green) *s.i.s: a in rr* **20/1**	12+
	11	*1 ½*	**Frontline Boy (IRE)** 2-8-9 0 ... AndrewElliott 1 (A P Jarvis) *midfield: rdn along 1/2-way: sn wknd* **66/1**	10+
60	12	*3 ½*	**Verona Lad**[12] 4424 2-8-12 0 ... PaulMulrennan 10 (Jennie Candlish) *a bhd* **100/1**	4+
	13	*¾*	**Vittachi** 2-8-9 0 ... JimmyQuinn 14 (J D Bethell) *s.i.s: a in rr* **80/1**	—
0	P		**Ochilview Warrior (IRE)**[25] 4011 2-8-9 0 ... GregFairley 6 (R Bastiman) *chsd ldrs: hung bdly rt and v wd home turn: sn p.u* **80/1**	—

1m 29.78s (2.58) **Going Correction** +0.275s/f (Good) **14** Ran SP% **120.5**

Speed ratings (Par 94): **96,91,90,88,87 85,81,70,67,66 64,60,60,—**

toteswinger: 1&2 £1.10, 1&3 £4.20, 2&3 £4.50. CSF £3.70 TOTE £1.90: £1.10, £1.70, £2.40; EX 4.30.

Owner A Long **Bred** Castlefarm Stud **Trained** Musley Bank, N Yorks

FOCUS

Plenty of deadwood in this maiden auction event but a winner of real potential. Not form to get carried away with otherwise.

NOTEBOOK

Our Joe Mac(IRE), third behind a Godolphin winner in an above average maiden at York, travelled strongly. Shaken up to take charge a furlong out, he soon went clear. He achieved a RPR of 79 at York, so can hardly expect a nursery mark under 80. Whatever mark he is given, he will be well worth keeping on the right side. (op Evens tchd 11-10)

George Benjamin, who gave problems entering the stalls, was having his fourth start and already has a mark of 68. He is the guide to the overall value of the form. (op 6-1)

Forshour, runner-up behind a wide-margin winner on his debut at Wolverhampton, again showed ability, but will need another outing to qualify for nurseries. (op 9-1 tchd 10-1)

No Quarter(IRE), on his toes beforehand, put a poor effort at Newcastle on his second start behind him and evidently appreciated going left-handed. (op 40-1 tchd 33-1)

Boss's Destination, outpaced over five on his debut at Carlisle, showed a fair bit more and will appreciate a mile in time. (op 33-1 tchd 20-1)

Quite Sparky showed ability, staying on in his own time after a sluggish start. He will know a lot more next time. (op 16-1 tchd 14-1)

4848 CALVERTS CARPETS H'CAP — 2m

8:00 (8:04) (Class 6) (0-65,65) 4-Y-O+ — **£2,978** (£886; £442; £221) **Stalls** Low

Form — RPR

4361 **1** **Baan (USA)**[14] 4388 6-9-7 **65** ... JimmyQuinn 4 — 70
(H J Collingridge) *trckd ldrs: hdwy 3f out: chsd ldr 2f out: rdn to chal wl over 1f out: drvn ent fnl f: edgd lft and kpt on u.p to ld last strides* **4/1**[1]

-400 **2** *hd* **Front Rank (IRE)**[46] 3291 9-8-2 **46** ... DuranFentiman 5 — 51
(Mrs Dianne Sayer) *sn led: rdn along 3f out: drvn wl over 1f out: styd on gamely ins fnl f tl hdd and no ex last strides* **25/1**

5200 **3** *½* **Fistral**[40] 3499 5-8-5 **49** ... PaulHanagan 10 — 53
(P D Niven) *hld up: hdwy in midfield 1/2-way: effrt to chse ldrs over 2f out and sn rdn: drvn over 1f out: styng on whn n.m.r and swtchd rt wl ins fnl f: kpt on towards fin* **10/1**

360- **4** *½* **Abstract Folly (IRE)**[282] 6957 7-9-5 **63** ... JamieSpencer 12 — 67
(J D Bethell) *hld up and bhd: hdwy 4f out: effrt to chse ldrs on outer over 2f out: sn rdn and edgd lft wl over 1f out: kpt on u.p ins fnl f* **8/1**[3]

5430 **5** *4* **Wannarock (IRE)**[13] 4402 4-7-9 **46** oh1 ... JosephineBruning(7) 3 — 45
(M C Chapman) *chsd ldrs: rdn along on inner 3f out: wkng and hld whn hung bdly rt wl over 1f out* **14/1**

-054 **6** *1 ¾* **Simple Jim (FR)**[13] 4403 5-8-6 **50** ... SilvestreDeSousa 1 — 47
(J Hetherton) *prom: effrt 4f out: rdn along 3f out: drvn over 2f out and grad wknd* **4/1**[1]

2-55 **7** *nk* **Wotchalike (IRE)**[13] 3444 7-8-5 **49** ... (p) PJMcDonald 11 — 45
(Miss S Johnstone) *prom: rdn along 4f out: drvn 3f out and grad wknd* **17/2**

5/50 **8** *1 ¾* **Sea Cove**[11] 4462 9-7-13 **46** oh1 ... DominicFox(3) 6 — 40
(Mrs Dianne Sayer) *hld up in rr: sme hdwy over 2f out: kpt on: nvr a factor* **50/1**

-060 **9** *nse* **Rocknest Island (IRE)**[42] 3444 6-8-2 **46** oh1 ... (p) AndrewMullen 8 — 40
(P D Niven) *chsd ldrs: rdn along over 3f out: sn drvn and wknd over 2f out* **33/1**

035/ **10** *14* **Top Rocker**[517] 3840 5-7-11 **48** oh1 ow2 ... JamesPSullivan(7) 13 — 25
(E W Tuer) *a in rr* **18/1**

3-3 **11** *2* **Pinewood Legend (IRE)**[25] 1439 7-8-2 **46** oh1 ... AndrewElliott 2 — 21
(P D Niven) *a towards rr* **8/1**[3]

4-64 **12** *23* **Feeling Peckish (USA)**[8] 3609 5-7-12 **49** oh1 ow3(t) AndrewHeffernan(7) 7 — —
(M C Chapman) *chsd ldrs to 1/2-way: sn wknd* **33/1**

5106 **13** *18* **Squirtle (IRE)**[9] 4551 6-9-0 **58** ... TGMcLaughlin 9 — —
(W M Brisbourne) *hld up towards rr: pushed along 1/2-way: rdn on inner whn hmpd bnd over 4f out: sn bhd* **6/1**[2]

3m 38.53s (5.73) **Going Correction** +0.275s/f (Good) **13** Ran SP% **119.7**
Speed ratings (Par 101): **96,95,95,95,93 92,92,91,91,84 83,71,62**
toteswinger: 1&2 £16.70, 1&3 £22.20, 2&3 £23.40. CSF £115.10 CT £950.01 TOTE £4.50: £2.10, £7.60, £2.70; EX 166.20.

Owner Greenstead Hall Racing Ltd **Bred** Shadwell Farm Inc **Trained** Exning, Suffolk

■ Stewards' Enquiry : Andrew Heffernan four-day ban: careless riding (Aug 24-27)

FOCUS
A modest 46-65 stayers' handicap, weakened by the absence of hat-trick seeking Spiders Star. The pace looked sound but the time was very slow, confirming that the ground was good to soft in the back straight. There was a bunch finish.

4849 THE CARPENTERS ARMS FELIXKIRK H'CAP — 5f

8:30 (8:32) (Class 4) (0-85,85) 3-Y-O — **£5,569** (£1,657; £828; £413) **Stalls** High

Form — RPR

0243 **1** **Lucky Art (USA)**[5] 4653 3-8-7 **71** ... SilvestreDeSousa 3 — 78
(Mrs R A Carr) *cl up on outer: pushed along over 2f out: rdn to ld wl over 1f out: edgd rt and drvn ins fnl f: hung lft and hld on towards fin* **11/4**[1]

412- **2** *½* **Sirenuse (IRE)**[373] 4648 3-9-2 **80** ... TomEaves 8 — 85
(B Smart) *t.k.h: cl up: led over 2f out: rdn and hdd wl over 1f out: drvn and kpt on ins fnl f* **14/1**

0160 **3** *hd* **Mullglen**[7] 4601 3-8-10 **74** ... (b) DuranFentiman 10 — 78
(T D Easterby) *chsd ldrs: pushed along and sltly outpcd 2f out: sn rdn and styd on strly ins fnl f* **8/1**

1316 **4** *1* **Hysterical Lady**[45] 3355 3-8-8 **72** ... AdrianTNicholls 7 — 72
(D Nicholls) *trckd ldrs: smooth hdwy 2f out: nt clr run and swtchd outside over 1f out: sn rdn and kpt on same pce ins fnl f* **8/1**

1020 **5** *nk* **Dark Lane**[33] 3747 3-9-4 **82** ... PaulHanagan 5 — 81
(R A Fahey) *j. awkwardly and in rr: hdwy wl over 1f out: sn rdn and styd on ins fnl f: nrst fin* **5/1**[3]

0-00 **6** *½* **Blades Princess**[73] 2443 3-9-1 **79** ... GrahamGibbons 4 — 77
(E S McMahon) *hld up: hdwy wl over 1f out: rdn and kpt on ins fnl f: nrst fin* **20/1**

1454 **7** *2 ¼* **Dispol Grand (IRE)**[5] 4653 3-8-5 **69** ... JoeFanning 6 — 58
(P T Midgley) *cl up: rdn along over 2f out: sn drvn and wknd over 1f out* **12/1**

4124 **8** *6* **Devil You Know (IRE)**[35] 3688 3-9-5 **83** ... EddieAhern 2 — 51
(D R C Elsworth) *wnt lft s: bhd: swtchd wd and hdwy 2f out: sn rdn and btn* **9/2**[2]

1501 **9** *7* **Glamorous Spirit (IRE)**[31] 3806 3-9-4 **85** ... KevinGhunowa(3) 9 — 28
(R A Harris) *led: rdn along 1/2-way: sn hdd & wknd* **5/1**[3]

60.61 secs (1.01) **Going Correction** +0.275s/f (Good) **9** Ran SP% **119.5**
Speed ratings (Par 102): **102,101,100,99,98 98,94,84,73**
toteswinger: 1&2 £15.10, 1&3 £12.10, 2&3 £18.20. CSF £45.81 CT £284.69 TOTE £4.30: £1.60, £4.90, £1.90; EX 71.70 Place 6 £155.53, Place 5 £94.73..

Owner Brian Morton **Bred** Gaines-Gentry Thoroughbreds **Trained** Huby, N Yorks

FOCUS
A competitive 69-85 sprint handicap run at a very strong pace. Sound form, and the winner was still a few pounds off his 2yo best.

Glamorous Spirit(IRE) Official explanation: jockey said filly had a breathing problem

T/Jkpt: Not won. T/Plt: £27.10 to a £1 stake. Pool: £63,420.27. 1,705.00 winning tickets. T/Qpdt: £9.60 to a £1 stake. Pool: £4,763.23. 366.25 winning tickets. JR

[4824] WINDSOR (R-H)

Monday, August 10

OFFICIAL GOING: Good to firm (good in places; 8.8)
Rail realignment increased distances of races of a mile and over by 25yards.
Wind: Moderate across Weather: Overcast

4850 SPORTINGBET.COM FILLIES' AUCTION NURSERY — 6f

5:50 (5:51) (Class 5) 2-Y-O — **£2,729** (£806; £403) **Stalls** High

Form — RPR

0216 **1** **Fly Silca Fly (IRE)**[16] 4306 2-8-10 **74** ... MCGeran(5) 9 — 78
(M R Channon) *s.i.s: in rr tl swtchd to outer and hdwy 2f out: str run u.p to ld wl ins fnl f: hung rt cl home: hld on wl* **16/1**

210 **2** *nk* **Silver Grey (IRE)**[9] 4539 2-9-3 **76** ... RobertHavlin 13 — 79
(R Ingram) *chsd ldrs tl hung lft and outpcd 2f out: rallied and r.o again over 1f out: str run ins fnl f and clsng on ldr whn hung lft again nr fin* **7/2**[1]

3613 **3** *1 ½* **Any Day (IRE)**[25] 3993 2-8-5 **71** ... JPFahy(7) 8 — 70
(R M Beckett) *chsd ldr: chal 2f out and led sn after: hdd wl ins fnl f: btn whn n.m.r cl home* **10/1**

100 **4** *½* **Reach For The Sky (IRE)**[9] 4539 2-8-12 **71** ... DaneO'Neill 15 — 68+
(R Hannon) *chsd ldrs tl rdn and outpcd 2f out: styd on again fnl f: gng on cl home* **16/1**

1104 **5** *½* **Anjomarba (IRE)**[20] 4165 2-9-7 **80** ... TolleyDean 7 — 76
(W G M Turner) *chsd ldr: drvn to chal 2f out: stl wl there 1f out: wknd ins fnl f* **12/1**

01 **6** *nk* **Right Rave (IRE)**[14] 4383 2-8-8 **67** ... EdwardCreighton 11 — 62
(P J McBride) *in rr: rdn 3f out: hdwy fr 2f out: kpt on fnl f but nvr gng pce to rch ldrs* **9/2**[2]

1060 **7** *¾* **Bell's Ocean (USA)**[9] 4539 2-8-12 **71** ... JerryO'Dwyer 1 — 63
(J Ryan) *hdwy 1/2-way on outside: drvn to chal 2f out: wknd ins fnl f* **16/1**

2642 **8** *1 ¾* **Emma Jean Lass (IRE)**[10] 4478 2-8-12 **71** ... LukeMorris 14 — 58
(J S Moore) *chsd ldrs: rdn and one pce whn n.m.r on ins 2f out: nvr in contention after* **12/1**

210 **9** *3 ¼* **Gwynedd (IRE)**[31] 3807 2-8-13 **72** ... RichardMullen 10 — 49
(E S McMahon) *led tl hdd jst ins fnl 2f: wknd qckly sn after* **11/1**

3233 **10** *hd* **Transfixed (IRE)**[8] 4558 2-8-5 **69** ... Louis-PhilippeBeuzelin(5) 3 — 47+
(P D Evans) *chsd ldrs: rdn to chal on outer 2f out: wknd sn after* **15/2**[3]

4402 **11** *1 ¾* **Folletta (IRE)**[19] 4195 2-8-13 **72** ... RichardHughes 4 — 44
(R Hannon) *s.i.s: in rr: no ch whn reminder and flashed tail over 1f out* **9/1**

630 **12** *14* **So Surreal (IRE)**[12] 4421 2-9-2 **75** ... GeorgeBaker 12 — 5
(G L Moore) *in tch to 1/2-way* **20/1**

1m 12.4s (-0.60) **Going Correction** -0.25s/f (Firm) **12** Ran SP% **117.4**
Speed ratings (Par 91): **94,93,91,90,90 89,88,86,82,81 79,60**
toteswinger: 1&2 £28.60, 1&3 £11.20, 2&3 £42.50. CSF £70.63 CT £615.04 TOTE £19.80: £5.10, £1.70, £3.50; EX 112.70.

Owner Aldridge Racing Partnership **Bred** Glenlogan Park Stud **Trained** West Ilsley, Berks

FOCUS
A modest, but competitive fillies' nursery. There was a fair pace set early on and the main action developed down the centre of the home straight, with the first seven beings quite closely covered at the finish.

NOTEBOOK
Fly Silca Fly(IRE) was patiently ridden and came home to score in determined fashion. She failed to run her race when a beaten favourite at Newcastle last time, but was very free to post there and the more patient tactics suited here. She displayed a pretty willing attitude once given a few smacks and is clearly versatile as regards going.
Silver Grey(IRE) didn't enjoy the undulations of the July course at Newmarket nine days earlier, but was 2lb lower here and proved popular. She fared best of those to race handily and was not beaten far, but shaped as though she ideally wants a stiffer finish over this trip. Official explanation: jockey said filly hung left (tchd 3-1 and 4-1)
Any Day(IRE) travelled best of all until feeling the pinch between the final two furlongs and failed to see out this longer trip like the first pair. She remains in good form, helps to set the standard, and can be found one of these back over a stiff 5f.
Reach For The Sky(IRE) was down in grade and ran much better as a result, but looked to find it too sharp a test as she got going far too late. (tchd 14-1)
Anjomarba(IRE), who got warm beforehand, again showed natural early speed and ran her race back over the extra furlong, but seems held by the handicapper. (op 11-1 tchd 14-1)
Right Rave(IRE) was making her debut in this sphere after a ready success in a moderate Yarmouth maiden and was stepping back up in trip. She got the distance, but went in snatches early on and may have found things a bit lively underfoot. (tchd 5-1and 6-1 in a place)

4851 EBF SPORTINGBET.COM MAIDEN STKS — 6f

6:20 (6:23) (Class 4) 2-Y-O — **£5,180** (£1,541; £770; £384) **Stalls** High

Form — RPR

44 **1** **Gene Autry (USA)**[17] 4258 2-9-3 0 ... RichardHughes 5 — 83+
(R Hannon) *trckd ldrs: slt ld ins fnl 2f: rdn whn strly chal thrght fnl f: asserted and in command fnl 30yds* **4/6**[1]

4 **2** *¾* **Bonheurs Art (IRE)**[12] 4421 2-8-12 0 ... MichaelHills 4 — 76+
(B W Hills) *trckd ldrs tl chal fr 2f out: stl upsides and rdn thrght fnl f: outpcd fnl 30yds* **11/4**[2]

002 **3** *7* **Bush Master**[19] 4201 2-9-3 66 ... PatDobbs 3 — 60
(R Hannon) *led tl hdd ins fnl 2f: outpcd by ldng duo over 1f out but stl an easy 3rd* **10/1**[3]

0 **4** *3* **Bojangles Andrews**[16] 4314 2-9-0 0 ... PatrickHills(3) 6 — 51
(B G Powell) *chsd ldrs: rdn 3f out and sn no ch w ldng trio: styd on same pce for 4th fnl 2f* **40/1**

5 *1 ¼* **Accountable** 2-9-3 0 ... GeorgeBaker 7 — 47+
(B G Powell) *s.i.s: green in rr early: hdwy and wandered on outside over 2f out: nvr in contention* **25/1**

6 *4 ½* **Richboy** 2-9-3 0 ... IanMongan 1 — 34
(Mrs L J Mongan) *unruly for stalls entry: slowly away and green: mod prog fnl f* **20/1**

7 *3* **Aunty Betty (IRE)** 2-8-12 0 ... VinceSlattery 8 — 20
(M S Tuck) *s.i.s: green and a in rr* **33/1**

8 *hd* **Young Simon** 2-9-3 0 ... AdrianMcCarthy 10 — 24
(G G Margarson) *mid-div 3f: sn wknd* **25/1**

0 **9** *3 ½* **Alfalevva**[12] 4424 2-9-3 0 ... ChrisCatlin 9 — 13
(M R Channon) *in tch early: sn rdn and bhd* **28/1**

1m 12.0s (-1.00) **Going Correction** -0.25s/f (Firm) **9** Ran SP% **117.0**
Speed ratings (Par 96): **96,95,85,81,80 74,70,69,65**
toteswinger: 1&2 £1.10, 1&3 £2.70, 2&3 £2.60. CSF £2.30 TOTE £1.80: £1.02, £1.70, £2.50; EX 2.50.

Owner Mrs J K Powell **Bred** Rankin, Freeman & McClinton **Trained** East Everleigh, Wilts

FOCUS
This maiden had the look of a match between the two clear market leaders and the pair duly dominated. Good form from the front two.

NOTEBOOK

Gene Autry(USA) made it third time lucky and rewarded strong support, but made heavy weather of going so. Dropping back from 7f, he showed good early pace and again travelled nicely. His response when pressed by the runner-up was somewhat limited, however, and he was all out close home. It may be this ground was quicker than he ideally cares for and he is held in some regard by connections - who believe he will make into a nice 3yo - but the nursery route looks best for him at present. (op 8-11 tchd 8-13)

Bonheurs Art(IRE) ran distinctly green on debut, in what looked a good maiden against her own sex 12 days earlier. She was a lot more professional this time and gave the winner a real fright, but really lacked that rival's resolution as he came towards her when pulling off the rail inside the final furlong. The winner has more size about him, however, so it is too soon to be questioning her temperament and she is well up to taking one of these. Her Group 1 entry is too ambitious, though. (tchd 3-1 in places)

Bush Master put it up to his winning stable companion early on, but proved free and that blunted his finishing effort. He rates the best guide for the form and should find his feet in nurseries.

Bojangles Andrews was well held but is steadily going the right way.

Accountable, a place behind her more experienced stablemate, should know a lot more next time.

4852 SPORTINGBET.COM H'CAP 1m 67y

6:50 (6:50) (Class 4) (0-85,85) 3-Y-O+ £4,857 (£1,445; £722; £360) Stalls High

Form RPR

6442 **1** **Wannabe King**[12] 4433 3-9-5 **85**..................(p) TedDurcan 10 97
(D R Lanigan) *trckd ldrs: drvn to ld ins fnl 2f: in command whn hung rt ins fnl f* **4/1**[2]

4604 **2** *3* **Cape Hawk (IRE)**[9] 4526 5-9-9 **82**..................(v[1]) RichardHughes 9 88
(R Hannon) *led tl hdd ins fnl 2f: no ch w wnr whn hung lft ins fnl f* **4/1**[2]

0405 **3** *3/4* **Aflaam (IRE)**[10] 4501 4-9-4 **77**.................. TolleyDean 1 81+
(P Howling) *t.k.h in rr: hdwy on outside over 2f out: rdn and styd on to take 3rd fnl f but nvr any ch w wnr* **16/1**

5001 **4** *1/2* **Northern Spy (USA)**[32] 3770 5-9-2 **75**.................. TPQueally 2 78
(S Dow) *in tch: rdn and kpt on fr 2f out but nvr gng pce to get into contention* **8/1**[3]

300/ **5** *4* **Farleigh House (USA)**[359] 5-9-12 **85**.................. DarryllHolland 5 79+
(Sir Mark Prescott) *hld up in rr: styd on under hand riding fr over 1f out: fin wl* **8/1**[3]

/35- **6** *nk* **Ektimaal**[534] 679 6-9-12 **85**.................. DO'Donohoe 7 78
(E A L Dunlop) *in tch: rdn over 2f out: nvr rchd ldrs and wknd over 1f out* **20/1**

41 **7** *1 1/4* **Clientele (USA)**[15] 4354 3-9-2 **82**.................. NCallan 8 71
(M Johnston) *t.k.h: chsd ldr: rdn and effrt over 2f out: sn btn* **5/2**[1]

1000 **8** *1 1/4* **Lodi (IRE)**[25] 4019 4-9-3 **76**..................(t) JimCrowley 6 63
(J Akehurst) *rdn and hung bdly lft fr 3f out: a in rr* **28/1**

610 **9** *2 1/4* **Mount Hadley (USA)**[13] 4409 5-9-9 **82**..................(b) AlanMunro 4 64
(G A Butler) *chsd ldrs: rdn 3f out: sn wknd* **11/1**

1m 43.52s (-1.18) **Going Correction** +0.025s/f (Good)
WFA 3 from 4yo+ 7lb **9** Ran SP% **113.2**
Speed ratings (Par 105): **106,103,102,101,97 97,96,94,92**
toteswinger: 1&2 £2.20, 1&3 £27.00, 2&3 £9.30. CSF £19.95 CT £227.19 TOTE £4.50: £1.50, £1.60, £3.50; EX 18.80.
Owner Saif Ali & Saeed H Altayer **Bred** Chippenham Lodge Stud Ltd **Trained** Newmarket, Suffolk

FOCUS
A fair handicap, run at a sound pace. A biggish step forward from the winner.
Farleigh House(USA) Official explanation: jockey said, regarding running and riding, that his orders were to drop the gelding out and stay on the inner, adding that he was unable to drop it out, but it ran free round the top bend and, when asked for its effort passing the junction, stayed on one paced.

4853 GOTRINIDADANDTOBAGO.COM H'CAP 6f

7:20 (7:20) (Class 3) (0-95,94) 3-Y-O+ £7,771 (£2,312; £1,155; £577) Stalls High

Form RPR

431 **1** **Olynard (IRE)**[21] 4148 3-9-1 **88**.................. RichardKingscote 12 97
(R M Beckett) *fly-jmpd s: sn rcvrd to trck ldrs towards outside: pushed along to ld ins fnl f: styd on strly* **9/2**[1]

1004 **2** *1/2* **Bel Cantor**[7] 4598 6-8-5 **77**..................(p) KellyHarrison(3) 3 85
(W J H Ratcliffe) *t.k.h: trckd ldr tl led 2f out: hdd ins fnl f: kpt on but nt pce of wnr* **20/1**

0040 **3** *1/2* **The Galloping Shoe**[17] 4273 4-8-8 **77** ow1.................. TPQueally 9 83
(J Noseda) *towards rr tl hdwy 3f out: chsd ldrs fr 2f out: styd on ins fnl f but nvr quite gng pce of ldng duo* **9/1**

2004 **4** *3 1/4* **Vhujon (IRE)**[10] 4485 4-9-5 **88**.................. RichardHughes 4 84
(P D Evans) *s.i.s: sn in tch: hdwy on ins whn n.m.r over 1f out: swtchd lft and r.o fnl f but nvr gng pce to rch ldrs* **9/2**[1]

4000 **5** *3/4* **Osiris Way**[9] 4523 7-9-7 **90**.................. JimCrowley 5 84
(P R Chamings) *chsd ldrs: rdn over 2f out: wknd fnl f* **16/1**

0460 **6** *nk* **Peter Island (FR)**[10] 4485 6-8-13 **82**..................(v) ChrisCatlin 11 75
(J Gallagher) *led tl hdd 2f out: wknd fnl f* **10/1**

0360 **7** *nk* **Phantom Whisper**[10] 4485 6-8-13 **85**.................. JamesMillman(3) 13 77
(B R Millman) *in tch: n.m.r towards ins over 1f out: swtchd lft and hdwy fnl f: kpt on cl home* **7/1**[3]

5100 **8** *1 3/4* **Princess Valerina**[79] 2271 5-9-1 **84**.................. DaneO'Neill 10 70
(D Haydn Jones) *in rr tl mod late hdwy* **33/1**

6-00 **9** *3 1/4* **Pearly Wey**[31] 3802 6-9-11 **94**.................. PhilipRobinson 6 70
(C G Cox) *s.i.s: a towards rr* **10/1**

4021 **10** *1/2* **Esteem Machine (USA)**[10] 4500 5-9-3 **86**.................. JimmyFortune 7 60
(R A Teal) *s.i.s: a towards rr* **8/1**

6302 **11** *18* **Viking Spirit**[7] 4598 7-9-7 **90**..................(t) ShaneKelly 2 6
(W R Swinburn) *chsd ldrs over 3f* **5/1**[2]

1m 11.31s (-1.69) **Going Correction** -0.25s/f (Firm)
WFA 3 from 4yo+ 4lb **11** Ran SP% **118.4**
Speed ratings (Par 107): **101,100,99,95,94 93,93,91,86,86 62**
toteswinger: 1&2 £20.60, 1&3 £49.60, 2&3 £38.90. CSF £95.79 CT £798.65 TOTE £5.70: £2.30, £4.90, £3.20; EX 116.80.
Owner R Roberts **Bred** Redmyre Bloodstock & John Cullinan **Trained** Whitsbury, Hants

FOCUS
This was a good and competitive sprint handicap. It was run at a solid pace and a high draw was an advantage. A personal best from the winner with the second a solid guide.

NOTEBOOK

Olynard(IRE) scored nicely from a low draw over course and distance three weeks earlier and followed that up from a 6lb higher mark. He fared better with the draw this time, but still made his challenge towards the outer of the pack and again proved a bit free early on. He is clearly progressing and a likely higher mark may not be enough to scupper him in his quest for the hat-trick. (tchd 5/1 in places)

Bel Cantor ran a respectable race at Ripon on his previous outing and confirmed his current wellbeing with a solid effort in defeat here. He deserves extra credit, as he was not left alone in front and refused to go down without a fight nearing the business end. A return to easier ground can see him back to winning ways. (op 16-1)

The Galloping Shoe, whose rider put up 1lb overweight, finished well from off the pace on the outside of runners. He is evidently not straightforward, as he got warm beforehand and refused to settle early on, but clearly has it in him to defy this sort of mark when in the mood. A stiffer 6f should also prove more to his liking. (op 14-1)

Vhujon(IRE) again finished well and ran close to his recent level, despite not getting the best of passages. He finds it hard to get his head in front. (op 6-1)

Esteem Machine(USA) Official explanation: jockey said gelding was slowly away

Viking Spirit, who finished in front of the runner-up when running well at Ripon a week earlier. He was not well drawn, but was beaten too far out for comfort. He was reported to have bled from the nose. Official explanation: vet said gelding bled from the nose (op 6-1)

4854 SPORTINGBET.COM MAIDEN STKS 1m 67y

7:50 (7:51) (Class 5) 3-Y-O+ £2,729 (£806; £403) Stalls High

Form RPR

4200 **1** **Beauchamp Xerxes**[33] 3751 3-9-3 100.................. RichardHughes 10 85
(G A Butler) *mde all: awkward bnd 6f out: drvn along fr over 2f out: styd on strly fr over 1f out* **6/5**[1]

4 **2** *2* **Awesome Surprise (USA)**[51] 3168 3-8-12 0.................. TPQueally 6 75
(J Noseda) *in tch: hdwy 3f out: rdn and wnt bdly lft 2f out: styd on wl to go 2nd ins fnl f but no ch w wnr* **7/2**[2]

44 **3** *3* **El Libertador (USA)**[5] 4648 3-9-3 0.................. StephenCarson 2 73
(E A Wheeler) *t.k.h early: trckd wnr and pushed out bnd 6f out: drvn and effrt over 2f out: no imp over 1f out: wknd and lost 2nd ins fnl f* **9/2**[3]

-0 **4** *4 1/2* **One Cool Dream**[46] 3297 3-8-12 0.................. ShaneKelly 11 57
(W R Swinburn) *s.i.s: trckd ldrs: rdn 3f out: wknd fr 2f out* **14/1**

5 *3/4* **Mydy Easy (USA)** 3-9-3 0.................. AlanMunro 7 60
(P W Chapple-Hyam) *chsd ldrs: rdn and hung lft over 2f out: sn btn* **11/1**

6 *1/2* **Ban Garda (IRE)**[311] 6456 3-8-12 0.................. LPKeniry 4 54
(J S Moore) *in rr and drvn along over 2f out: sme prog fnl f* **16/1**

7 *4* **Be Kind** 3-8-12 0.................. DarryllHolland 5 45
(Karen George) *s.i.s: green and in rr tl mod prog fnl f* **40/1**

04 **8** *1/2* **Countrystyle Lass (IRE)**[14] 4381 3-8-12 0.................. IanMongan 9 43
(P Winkworth) *a in rr* **20/1**

9 *8* **Legend Of Greece (IRE)**[399] 3803 3-9-3 0.................. LukeMorris 8 29
(Mrs N Smith) *chsd ldrs: rdn: green and wknd over 3f out* **33/1**

000- **10** *6* **Welsh Passion**[317] 6273 3-8-12 25.................. DaneO'Neill 1 10
(D Haydn Jones) *wd bnd over 4f out: a in rr* **80/1**

1m 44.55s (-0.15) **Going Correction** +0.025s/f (Good) **10** Ran SP% **118.1**
Speed ratings (Par 103): **101,99,96,91,90 90,86,85,77,71**
toteswinger: 1&2 £1.10, 1&3 £2.70, 2&3 £3.60. CSF £5.23 TOTE £2.40: £1.30, £1.60, £1.80; EX 4.90.
Owner Erik Penser **Bred** E Penser **Trained** Newmarket, Suffolk

FOCUS
An ordinary maiden overall, but the winner is a smart colt. He probably ran to his earlier maiden form.
Awesome Surprise(USA) Official explanation: jockey said filly was carried wide up the straight

4855 BEST OF BARBADOS H'CAP 1m 3f 135y

8:20 (8:20) (Class 5) (0-75,74) 3-Y-O+ £2,729 (£806; £403) Stalls Low

Form RPR

-111 **1** **Point Of Light**[4] 4687 3-8-9 **66**.................. ChrisCatlin 7 73+
(Sir Mark Prescott) *trckd ldr: pushed along 3f out: drvn to ld 2f out: styd on strly fnl f: readily* **8/13**[1]

1100 **2** *2* **Eseej (USA)**[17] 4288 4-10-0 **74**.................. DarryllHolland 4 78
(P W Hiatt) *led: t.k.h: rdn and hdd 2f out: rallied fnl f but nvr any ch w wnr* **20/1**

0023 **3** *2 1/2* **Dhania (IRE)**[11] 4450 3-8-3 **60**..................(b) LukeMorris 8 60
(R A Teal) *t.k.h: stdd in rr but in tch: hdwy over 3f out: styd on to go 3rd over 1f out but nvr any ch w ldng duo* **20/1**

3333 **4** *3* **Bolanderi (USA)**[21] 4150 4-9-10 **70**.................. RichardHughes 1 65
(Andrew Turnell) *hld up in rr: drvn over 2f out: sme prog fnl f but nvr anywhere nr ldrs* **6/1**[3]

345 **5** *shd* **Little Prudence**[32] 3791 3-8-9 **73**.................. JPFahy(7) 6 67
(R M Beckett) *in rr early: hdwy to chse ldrs 7f out: rdn 3f out: wknd ins fnl 2f* **20/1**

211 **6** *shd* **Vita Mia**[8] 4562 3-8-4 **66** 6ex.................. Louis-PhilippeBeuzelin(5) 5 60
(P D Evans) *in rr: rdn over 4f out: styd on over 1f out and kpt on ins fnl f but nvr anywhere nr ldrs* **9/2**[2]

03/5 **7** *2 1/2* **Enthusius**[207] 168 6-8-9 **55** oh5.................. LPKeniry 3 45
(G L Moore) *chsd ldrs to 3f out: wknd over 2f out* **33/1**

3233 **8** *14* **Mustajed**[7] 4602 8-9-5 **68**.................. JamesMillman(3) 2 34
(B R Millman) *rdn 5f out: a in rr* **10/1**

2m 28.63s (-0.87) **Going Correction** +0.025s/f (Good)
WFA 3 from 4yo+ 11lb **8** Ran SP% **120.7**
Speed ratings (Par 103): **103,101,100,98,97 97,96,86**
toteswinger: 1&2 £9.10, 1&3 £11.50, 2&3 £35.30. CSF £21.30 CT £155.26 TOTE £1.60: £1.10, £5.10, £5.10; EX 25.40 Place 6 £22.08, Place 5 £8.06..
Owner Syndicate 2007 **Bred** Watership Down Stud **Trained** Newmarket, Suffolk

FOCUS
This was a fair handicap for the class. The winner was a stone well in and did not need to match his latest improved Bath form. Oveall the form is a bit muddling.
T/Plt: £36.10 to a £1 stake. Pool: £73,655.90. 1,488.44 winning tickets. T/Qpdt: £13.40 to a £1 stake. Pool: £5,999.24. 330.10 winning tickets. ST

3923 WOLVERHAMPTON (A.W) (L-H)

Monday, August 10

OFFICIAL GOING: Standard
Wind: Almost nil Weather: Shower after race 2

4856 EUROPEAN BREEDERS' FUND MAIDEN STKS 5f 216y(P)

2:30 (2:31) (Class 5) 2-Y-O £4,209 (£1,252; £625; £312) Stalls Low

Form RPR

3 **1** **Dahakaa**[78] 2295 2-9-3 0.................. PhilipRobinson 4 79+
(M A Jarvis) *mde all: swvd bdly rt wl over 1f out: continued to hang rt: rdn and flashed tail ins fnl f: edgd lft towards fin: r.o* **5/4**[1]

2 *1 1/4* **Wellmarked (IRE)** 2-9-3 0..................(t) EddieAhern 7 71
(John A Quinn, Ire) *sn prom: rdn wl over 1f out: ev ch ins fnl f: kpt on* **7/1**[3]

60 **3** *2 1/2* **Maldon Prom (IRE)**[10] 4497 2-9-3 0.................. JerryO'Dwyer 6 64
(C A Dwyer) *hld up in tch: hung lft jst over 2f out: rdn and ev ch ins fnl f: one pce* **9/1**

002 **4** *nk* **West Leake Star (IRE)**[12] 4424 2-9-3 74.................. WilliamBuick 5 63+
(B W Hills) *hld up: sn towards rr: swtchd rt over 3f out: rdn and hdwy whn edgd lft over 1f out: kpt on same pce ins fnl f* **2/1**[2]

055 **5** *2¼* **Kahail (USA)**[12] 4430 2-9-3 65........................(t) SaleemGolam 1 56
(Miss D Mountain) *a.p: rdn and ev ch 1f out: wknd ins fnl f* **12/1**

000 **6** *6* **Campaigner**[12] 4439 2-9-3 46........................ LiamJones 10 38
(J W Hills) *hld up: sn bhd: sme prog 3f out: sn pushed along and wknd* **66/1**

0 **7** *3* **Sovereign Secure (IRE)**[17] 4286 2-8-12 0........ RoystonFfrench 11 24
(Lee Smyth, Ire) *sn w wnr: ev ch over 2f out: pushed along and wknd wl over 1f out* **66/1**

0 **8** *5* **Dencolstina**[61] 2800 2-8-9 0........................ FrederikTylicki(3) 3 9
(Joss Saville) *s.i.s: in rr: pushed along and struggling over 2f out* **66/1**

05 **9** *2* **Summa Cum Laude**[23] 4100 2-8-12 0........................ PatCosgrave 2 3
(Mrs A Duffield) *mid-div: pushed along 4f out: wknd wl over 2f out* **16/1**

00 **10** *2* **Woodenitbenice**[42] 3468 2-8-12 0........................ LukeMorris 8 —
(D Shaw) *sn outpcd* **200/1**

0 **11** *19* **Sixbox**[74] 2401 2-8-7 0........................ MartinLane(5) 9 —
(D Shaw) *hld up in mid-div: lost pl 3f out: lost tch fnl 2f* **66/1**

1m 14.6s (-0.40) **Going Correction** -0.10s/f (Stan) **11** Ran SP% **120.3**
Speed ratings (Par 94): **98,96,93,92,89 81,77,70,68,65 40**
toteswinger: 1&2 £5.00, 1&3 £3.90, 2&3 £19.40. CSF £11.54 TOTE £2.40: £1.10, £1.70, £3.10; EX 10.50.
Owner Sheikh Ahmed Al Maktoum **Bred** Darley **Trained** Newmarket, Suffolk

FOCUS
An uncompetitive maiden. The wayward winner was much the best on the day and can rate higher.

NOTEBOOK
Dahakaa, a promising third on his debut at Newmarket, did well to win considering he swerved badly right off the final bend and flashed his tail when initially coming under pressure. Up to 6f for the first time, he travelled comfortably in the lead and the fact he still managed to win with a fair bit in hand suggests he is a potentially useful performer, assuming his waywardness was a one-off. (op Evens tchd 11-8 in places)
Wellmarked(IRE), a half-brother to multiple AW winner Chjimes, was wearing a tongue tie for this debut and has already been gelded. He ran a race full of promise, being run down by the winner inside the final furlong, and natural progress should see him winning a small race. (op 11-1 tchd 12-1)
Maldon Prom(IRE) just held on for third and is a likely type for nurseries. (op 12-1)
West Leake Star(IRE), the main danger to the favourite, was unable to obtain a prominent early position and soon found himself well adrift of the pace. He made some late headway down the straight, finishing up on the inside, but never posed any sort of threat. (op 5-2)
Kahail(USA) is another likely to fare a bit better in low-grade handicaps. (op 11-1)
Summa Cum Laude Official explanation: jockey said filly had no more to give

4857 GREAT OFFERS AT WOLVERHAMPTON-RACECOURSE.CO.UK (S) STKS 1m 4f 50y(P)
3:00 (3:00) (Class 6) 3-Y-O+ **£2,047** (£604; £302) **Stalls Low**

Form RPR

2653 **1** **New England**[28] 3923 7-9-12 58........................ LukeMorris 4 63
(W M Brisbourne) *hld up towards rr: hdwy 3f out: sn rdn: led ent fnl f: r.o* **10/3**[1]

3215 **2** *hd* **Terminate (GER)**[18] 4220 7-9-12 60........................(t) WilliamBuick 3 63
(Ian Williams) *hld up in mid-div: swtchd rt and hdwy 4f out: rdn to ld wl over 1f out: hdd ent fnl f: r.o* **4/1**[2]

-010 **3** *¾* **Captain Flack**[30] 3861 3-9-1 59........................(b) KirstyMilczarek 7 61
(J A R Toller) *hld up in rr: pushed along 4f out: swtchd rt and hdwy over 2f out: rdn over 1f out: tk 3rd wl ins fnl f: edgd lft: kpt on* **8/1**

0-00 **4** *2¼* **Desert Leader (IRE)**[34] 3721 8-9-4 52........................ DavidProbert(3) 2 53
(W M Brisbourne) *hld up in tch: nt clr run over 2f out: rdn wl over 1f out: one pce* **28/1**

244 **5** *1¼* **Bernabeu (IRE)**[11] 838 7-9-7 57........................ JamesDoyle 1 51
(S Curran) *led early: prom: rdn wl over 1f out: wknd ins fnl f* **10/1**

5324 **6** *1½* **Nawamees (IRE)**[17] 4263 11-9-12 65........................(p) PaulDoe 8 53
(P D Evans) *chsd ldr after 1f: led wl over 2f out: hdd wl over 1f out: sn rdn: wknd ins fnl f* **9/2**[3]

2200 **7** *8* **Jackie Kiely**[17] 4264 8-9-7 51........................(t) PatCosgrave 11 36
(R Brotherton) *hld up towards rr: pushed along and effrt over 3f out: rdn and wknd over 2f out* **14/1**

236- **8** *3¼* **Berrynarbor**[353] 5216 4-9-2 55........................ FergusSweeney 12 25
(A G Newcombe) *a in rr* **12/1**

9 *29* **My Condor (IRE)**[20] 8-9-7 0........................ EddieAhern 9 —
(D McCain Jnr) *sn led: hdd wl over 2f out: sn eased* **28/1**

001/ **10** *73* **Billich**[717] 4786 6-9-7 75........................ LiamJones 6 —
(S W Hall) *hld up in tch: pushed along and wknd wl over 1f out: sn eased* **7/1**

2m 40.43s (-0.67) **Going Correction** -0.10s/f (Stan)
WFA 3 from 4yo+ 11lb **10** Ran SP% **115.2**
Speed ratings (Par 101): **98,97,97,95,95 94,88,86,67,18**
toteswinger: 1&2 £3.40, 1&3 £13.50, 2&3 £4.60. CSF £16.25 TOTE £3.30: £1.90, £1.50, £2.80; EX 21.00.There was no bid for the winner. Terminate was claimed by Alan Berry for £6,000.
Owner Bould & Walker Racing **Bred** Darley **Trained** Great Ness, Shropshire

FOCUS
This was a competitive seller. The front pair were close to their marks.
Desert Leader(IRE) Official explanation: jockey said gelding was denied a clear run
Nawamees(IRE) Official explanation: jockey said gelding lost its shoe

4858 WOLVERHAMPTON-RACECOURSE.CO.UK NURSERY 7f 32y(P)
3:30 (3:33) (Class 4) 2-Y-O **£4,533** (£1,348; £674; £336) **Stalls High**

Form RPR

31 **1** **Bahamian Music (IRE)**[16] 4307 2-9-0 75........................ PaulHanagan 6 78+
(R A Fahey) *hld up in mid-div: pushed along over 3f out: hdwy 2f out: sn rdn: led ins fnl f: r.o* **5/2**[1]

0354 **2** *nk* **Dolphin Rock**[14] 4371 2-8-4 65........................ LiamJones 3 67
(Mrs G S Rees) *hld up in tch: pushed along over 2f out: chsd ldr wl over 1f out: sn carried sltly lft: rdn and ev ch ins fnl f: r.o* **14/1**

0421 **3** *1¼* **Silver Symphony (IRE)**[54] 3027 2-9-7 82........................ EddieAhern 2 81
(P F I Cole) *led: rdn and edgd lft over 1f out: hdd ins fnl f: nt qckn* **3/1**[2]

41 **4** *hd* **Sultan's Choice**[19] 4188 2-7-9 59 oh3........................ DavidProbert(3) 4 58
(P D Evans) *a.p: swtchd rt jst over 2f out: rdn wl over 1f out: sn swtchd lft: kpt on towards fin* **5/1**[3]

1366 **5** *1* **Saxby (IRE)**[19] 4195 2-8-7 68........................ TPO'Shea 5 65+
(M R Channon) *hld up towards rr: nt clr run briefly on ins over 2f out: rdn and hdwy wl over 1f out: sn hung rt: nt clr run ins fnl f: nvr able to chal* **7/1**

5230 **6** *½* **Fasilight**[17] 4271 2-8-8 72........................ AndreaAtzeni(3) 1 67
(M Botti) *chsd ldr over 1f: wnt 2nd again 3f out: edgd rt over 1f out: fdd wl ins fnl f* **8/1**

4353 **7** *17* **Petrocelli**[72] 2467 2-9-0 75........................(b) PaulFitzsimons 10 28
(A J McCabe) *s.i.s: hdwy to chse ldr over 5f out: rdn and lost 2nd 3f out: wknd 2f out* **11/1**

015 **8** *8* **Dixie Bright (USA)**[25] 4000 2-9-3 78........................ J-PGuillambert 8 12
(J G Given) *hld up in rr: wknd 3f out* **20/1**

0606 **9** *¾* **Blue Bond**[20] 4173 2-7-12 59 oh14........................ DuranFentiman 9 —
(P T Midgley) *s.i.s: in rr: pushed along 4f out: sn struggling: eased over 1f out* **100/1**

1m 29.84s (0.24) **Going Correction** -0.10s/f (Stan) **9** Ran SP% **114.6**
Speed ratings (Par 96): **94,93,92,92,90 90,70,61,60**
toteswinger: 1&2 £7.30, 1&3 £2.20, 2&3 £8.10. CSF £38.71 CT £110.07 TOTE £3.50: £1.30, £4.90, £1.50; EX 37.30.
Owner R A Fahey **Bred** Genesis Green Stud Ltd **Trained** Musley Bank, N Yorks

FOCUS
This was no more than a modest nursery. The winner built on his Newcastle win.

NOTEBOOK
Bahamian Music(IRE), winner of a 7f Newcastle maiden last time, looked open to further improvement on this nursery debut and she came through strongly under pressure to get up inside the final furlong. On this evidence she may be suited by the step up to 1m. (op 9-4 tchd 2-1)
Dolphin Rock ran a lot better than he had done on his nursery debut at Southwell and was clearly well suited by the Polytrack surface. He is bred to be suited by an additional furlong. (op 12-1)
Silver Symphony(IRE), winner of a 7f maiden at Kempton last time, ran really well under top weight on this nursery debut. She should prove just as effective back at 6f. (tchd 7-2)
Sultan's Choice was up in grade having won a 7f seller at Catterick last time and she ran well from 3lb out of the handicap, sticking on right the way to the line. (op 13-2)
Saxby(IRE) would have been involved in the finish but for meeting more than his share of trouble in running. The step up to 7f seemed to suit and he can be rated better than the bare form. Official explanation: jockey said colt was denied a clear run (op 11-1)
Fasilight looked a big danger off the home bend, but could find no extra inside the final furlong. (op 7-1)

4859 STAY AT THE WOLVERHAMPTON HOLIDAY INN H'CAP 7f 32y(P)
4:00 (4:00) (Class 5) (0-70,70) 3-Y-O+ **£3,885** (£1,156; £577; £288) **Stalls High**

Form RPR

05-2 **1** **Kyleene**[20] 4164 3-9-8 70........................ WilliamBuick 8 78
(J Noseda) *s.i.s: hld up towards rr: swtchd rt and hdwy jst over 2f out: hrd rdn wl over 1f out: swtchd rt ins fnl f: r.o u.str.p to ld last strides* **9/2**[3]

0-01 **2** *hd* **Desert Streak (FR)**[3] 4749 3-9-4 66 6ex........................ EddieAhern 6 74
(C G Cox) *hld up in mid-div: hdwy 3f out: rdn to ld ins fnl f: hdd last strides* **10/3**[2]

0006 **3** *nk* **Obe Royal**[19] 4202 5-9-13 69........................(v) PaulDoe 2 78
(P D Evans) *hld up towards rr: hdwy over 2f out: rdn 1f out: ev ch wl ins fnl f: kpt on* **12/1**

0255 **4** *1* **Commando Scott (IRE)**[5] 4663 8-9-6 65........................ FrederikTylicki(3) 4 71
(I W McInnes) *hld up in tch: rdn to ld over 1f out: hdd ins fnl f: nt qckn* **3/1**[1]

030 **5** *hd* **Fol Liam**[49] 3225 3-9-3 65........................(p) AndrewMullen 11 69
(A J McCabe) *s.i.s: hld up in rr: rdn and hdwy wl over 1f out: kpt on ins fnl f* **12/1**

3321 **6** *3½* **Ugenius**[14] 4375 5-9-6 62........................ TonyCulhane 3 58
(Mrs C A Dunnett) *a.p: ev ch wl over 1f out: sn rdn: wknd ins fnl f* **8/1**

0403 **7** *1¼* **Dhhamaan (IRE)**[28] 3929 4-9-2 58........................(b) AndrewElliott 12 51
(Mrs R A Carr) *chsd ldr: led over 3f out: rdn and hdd over 1f out: wknd ins fnl f* **15/2**

0000 **8** *1* **Royal Challenge**[24] 4072 8-9-9 65........................ PatrickMathers 10 55
(I W McInnes) *hld up: sn towards rr: pushed along over 3f out: n.d* **40/1**

000- **9** *13* **Roman Maze**[296] 6826 9-9-9 65........................ JamesDoyle 5 20
(W M Brisbourne) *hld up in mid-div: pushed along and wknd over 2f out* **33/1**

2010 **10** *2¼* **Romantic Verse**[14] 4374 4-9-6 65........................ MichaelJStainton(3) 1 14
(S Curran) *led: hdd over 3f out: wknd over 2f out* **25/1**

6-0 **11** *32* **Dream Rainbow**[45] 3354 4-9-4 60........................(v[1]) PatCosgrave 9 —
(Joss Saville) *s.i.s: a towards rr: eased whn no ch fnl 2f* **50/1**

1m 28.73s (-0.87) **Going Correction** -0.10s/f (Stan)
WFA 3 from 4yo+ 6lb **11** Ran SP% **115.7**
Speed ratings (Par 103): **100,99,99,98,98 94,92,91,76,74 37**
toteswinger: 1&2 £4.60, 1&3 £9.50, 2&3 £9.20. CSF £18.91 CT £171.38 TOTE £4.30: £1.50, £1.80, £3.40; EX 17.70.
Owner Lordship Stud **Bred** Snailwell Stud Co Ltd **Trained** Newmarket, Suffolk

FOCUS
This was a modest handicap but the form is fair for the grade with the front pair unexposed.

4860 ENJOY THE LUCKY 7 GROUP OFFER MAIDEN STKS 5f 20y(P)
4:30 (4:33) (Class 5) 3-Y-O **£3,238** (£963; £481; £240) **Stalls Low**

Form RPR

30 **1** **Island Legend (IRE)**[94] 1840 3-9-0 0........................ DavidProbert(3) 13 73
(J M Bradley) *mde all: clr whn rdn jst over 1f out: r.o wl* **16/1**

2 *4½* **South African (USA)** 3-8-12 0........................ EddieAhern 11 52
(M A Magnusson) *s.i.s: sn prom: chsd wnr wl over 2f out: rdn and edgd lft jst over 1f out: no imp* **9/2**[2]

00 **3** *1½* **Running Flush (USA)**[31] 3813 3-9-3 0........................ J-PGuillambert 9 51
(J R Gask) *hld up in mid-div: rdn and hdwy jst over 1f out: kpt on ins fnl f* **14/1**

5526 **4** *¾* **Majestic Lady (IRE)**[20] 4164 3-8-12 58........................ WilliamBuick 4 44
(B W Hills) *hld up in tch: rdn over 2f out: edgd lft over 1f out: one pce* **10/3**[1]

4420 **5** *2¼* **Silca Meydan**[4] 4718 3-9-3 63........................ SamHitchcott 7 41
(M R Channon) *s.i.s: in rr: pushed along over 3f out: hdwy on ins wl over 1f out: sn rdn: nvr trbld ldrs* **5/1**[3]

6 *¾* **Almatlaie (USA)**[295] 6844 3-8-12 0........................ FergusSweeney 8 33
(J W Unett) *t.k.h: chsd wnr tl wl over 2f out: wknd fnl f* **18/1**

60- **7** *nk* **No Nightmare (USA)**[256] 7458 3-8-7 0........................ MartinLane(5) 3 32
(A P Jarvis) *hld up in tch: wknd over 2f out* **25/1**

6-0 **8** *½* **Hanta Yo (IRE)**[51] 3161 3-9-3 0........................ PatCosgrave 2 35
(J R Gask) *hld up towards rr: hdwy on ins over 2f out: rdn jst over 1f out: no further prog* **8/1**

00 **9** *4½* **Francis Albert**[32] 3764 3-9-3 0........................ LiamJones 10 19
(M Mullineaux) *s.i.s: a towards rr* **25/1**

0 **10** *1* **Clever Omneya (USA)**[19] 4199 3-8-12 0........................ TonyCulhane 5 10
(J R Jenkins) *s.i.s: a towards rr* **10/1**

11 *4* **Duke Of Bothwell (USA)** 3-9-0 0........................ FrederikTylicki(3) 1 1
(R A Fahey) *dwlt: outpcd* **9/2**[2]

00 **12** *¾* **By The Wind (IRE)**[139] 947 3-9-0 0........................ LeeVickers(3) 6 —
(T J Etherington) *hld up in tch: n.m.r and lost pl over 3f out: bhd fnl 2f* **100/1**

0 **13** 2¾ **Orpen Lady**[31] 3813 3-8-12 0....... PaulFitzsimons 12 —
(J M Bradley) *prom tl pushed along and wknd over 2f out* **66/1**

61.46 secs (-0.84) **Going Correction** -0.10s/f (Stan) **13** Ran SP% **124.3**
Speed ratings (Par 100): **102,94,92,91,87 86,85,85,77,76 69,68,64**
toteswinger: 1&2 £16.80, 1&3 £27.90, 2&3 £10.40. CSF £88.39 TOTE £24.40: £6.10, £1.70, £4.20; EX 50.40.

Owner J M Bradley **Bred** Jerome Casey **Trained** Sedbury, Gloucs

FOCUS
This was a typically weak 3yo-plus sprint maiden. Guessy form, with the winner apparently a big improver.

Clever Omneya(USA) Official explanation: jockey said filly reared leaving stalls

4861 CARLSBERG EXPORT H'CAP — 1m 1f 103y(P)
5:00 (5:02) (Class 6) (0-60,60) 4-Y-O+ — **£2,388** (£705; £352) **Stalls** Low

Form — RPR

0/00 **1** **Lady Calido (USA)**[13] 4403 4-8-13 **55**....... (b[1]) PatCosgrave 13 65
(Sir Mark Prescott) *sn led: hrd rdn over 2f out: edgd lft to ins rail over 1f out: drvn out* **25/1**

4004 **2** 1¼ **King Of Connacht**[4] 4721 6-8-12 **54**....... (p) LiamJones 8 61
(M Wellings) *hld up towards rr: pushed along and hdwy over 2f out: rdn and wnt 2nd ins fnl f: nt rch wnr* **5/1**[2]

0340 **3** 1 **Quick Off The Mark**[5] 4667 4-9-2 **58**....... (t) J-PGuillambert 11 63
(J G Given) *led early: chsd wnr: rdn 2f out: lost 2nd ins fnl f: kpt on same pce* **15/2**

350 **4** 3 **Lytham (IRE)**[8] 4563 8-9-0 **56**....... FergusSweeney 5 55
(A W Carroll) *hld up towards rr: pushed along and sme prog over 2f out: styd on to take 4th wl ins fnl f: nt trble ldng trio* **8/1**

5052 **5** shd **Waterside (IRE)**[33] 3740 10-9-4 **60**....... (t) JamesDoyle 10 58
(S Curran) *hld up in rr: pushed along over 2f out: hdwy over 1f out: styd on fnl f: nrst fin* **13/2**[3]

0464 **6** 1¾ **Stoic Leader (IRE)**[25] 3655 9-8-12 **54**....... RoystonFfrench 4 49
(R F Fisher) *hld up in mid-div: rdn over 2f out: wknd wl over 1f out* **10/1**

1153 **7** 2 **Rowan Lodge (IRE)**[15] 4344 7-8-11 **56**....... (b) FrederikTylicki(3) 7 47
(Ollie Pears) *hld up in tch: wnt 3rd 2f out: sn rdn: edgd lft over 2f out: wknd fnl f* **5/2**[1]

0-06 **8** 2½ **Marino Prince (FR)**[40] 3501 4-8-5 **47**....... (p) WilliamBuick 1 32
(T Wall) *a in rr* **25/1**

34/4 **9** 2¼ **Barndeh (IRE)**[50] 3194 6-8-8 **50**....... (p) TonyCulhane 9 31
(Lee Smyth, Ire) *prom: pushed along over 2f out: rdn and wkng whn hmpd on ins over 1f out* **10/1**

0660 **10** 9 **Gamesters Lady**[4] 4710 6-8-1 **50**....... KierenFox(7) 3 12
(W M Brisbourne) *hld up towards rr: pushed along over 4f out: sn struggling* **11/1**

535/ **11** 15 **Itcanbedone Again (IRE)**[756] 3595 10-8-2 **51**....... AlexEdwards(7) 12 —
(J W Unett) *prom tl wknd over 3f out* **33/1**

1m 59.72s (-1.98) **Going Correction** -0.10s/f (Stan) **11** Ran SP% **118.6**
Speed ratings (Par 101): **104,102,102,99,99 97,95,93,91,83 70**
toteswinger: 1&2 £22.90, 1&3 £20.90, 2&3 £5.90. CSF £144.77 CT £1056.25 TOTE £22.40: £6.80, £2.20, £2.20; EX 188.50.

Owner Lordship Stud **Bred** Lordship Stud **Trained** Newmarket, Suffolk

FOCUS
This was a low-grade handicap. Modest but sound form.

4862 NAME A RACE TO ENHANCE YOUR BRAND APPRENTICE H'CAP 2m 119y(P)
5:30 (5:30) (Class 6) (0-65,65) 4-Y-O+ — **£2,388** (£705; £352) **Stalls** Low

Form — RPR

0/ **1** **Tiger Tee (IRE)**[299] 4757 4-8-5 **46** oh1....... DavidKenny 8 53
(John A Quinn, Ire) *hld up in rr: stdy prog over 3f out: pushed along over 2f out: rdn to ld and edgd lft wl over 1f out: drvn out* **10/1**

0350 **2** ½ **Sir Sandicliffe (IRE)**[9] 4551 5-9-3 **61**....... KierenFox(3) 10 67
(W M Brisbourne) *s.i.s: hld up in rr: rdn and hdwy 2f out: hung lft over 1f out: styd on u.p ins fnl f* **7/1**

0-05 **3** nk **Dee Cee Elle**[50] 2517 5-8-6 **47**....... AmyScott 4 53
(D Burchell) *hld up towards rr: pushed along and hdwy 2f out: c wd st: edgd lft and styd on ins fnl f* **8/1**

-050 **4** 3¼ **Lilac Wine**[60] 2127 6-8-7 **48**....... NSLawes 6 50
(D J S Ffrench Davis) *hld up in tch: lost pl 7f out: sn pushed along: hdwy 2f out: rdn whn nt clr run and swtchd rt jst over 1f out: styd on one pce ins fnl f* **25/1**

0350 **5** ½ **Swords**[14] 4373 7-8-13 **54**....... CharlesEddery 3 56
(R E Peacock) *a.p: wnt 2nd over 3f out: led 2f out: hdd and carried lft wl over 1f out: sn rdn: wknd wl ins fnl f* **9/2**[2]

2000 **6** 2½ **Snowberry Hill (USA)**[32] 3760 6-8-7 **53**....... RyanClark(5) 5 52
(Lucinda Featherstone) *hld up: sn in tch: chsd ldr over 6f out tl over 3f out: rdn over 2f out: wknd wl over 1f out* **8/1**

1306 **7** ¾ **Rare Coincidence**[25] 3291 8-9-7 **62**....... (p) IJBrennan 1 60
(R F Fisher) *led: wl clr after 3f tl 5f out: rdn and hdd 2f out: wkng whn edgd rt ins fnl f* **11/4**[1]

04-4 **8** 11 **Dark Energy**[20] 4169 5-9-5 **63**....... SPRyan(3) 9 47
(R A Harris) *hld up towards rr: hdwy on ins 8f out: rdn over 2f out: sn wknd* **11/2**[3]

00-6 **9** 8 **Mean Machine (IRE)**[20] 4170 7-8-0 **46** oh1....... AlexEdwards(5) 7 21
(J W Unett) *hld up in mid-div: wknd over 5f out* **40/1**

0 **10** 3 **Vertueux (FR)**[11] 3593 4-9-10 **65**....... (p) RichardRowe 2 36
(A W Carroll) *chsd ldr tl over 6f out: wknd over 3f out* **25/1**

3m 41.12s (-0.68) **Going Correction** -0.10s/f (Stan) **10** Ran SP% **114.2**
Speed ratings (Par 101): **97,96,96,95,94 93,93,88,84,82**
toteswinger: 1&2 £16.60, 1&3 £14.00, 2&3 £10.20. CSF £74.81 CT £589.68 TOTE £11.80: £2.70, £2.20, £3.20; EX 113.30 Place 6: £92.31, Place 5: £57.11..

Owner Thomas C Farrell **Bred** Airlie Stud **Trained** Blackmiller Hill, Co. Kildare

FOCUS
This was a weak staying handicap. A bit of a messy race but the runner-up looks a sound enough guide.

T/Plt: £109.20 to a £1 stake. Pool: £55,298.59. 369.66 winning tickets. T/Qpdt: £22.40 to a £1 stake. Pool: £4,231.40. 139.60 winning tickets. KH

4863 - 4866a (Foreign Racing) - See Raceform Interactive

4786 LINGFIELD (L-H)
Tuesday, August 11

OFFICIAL GOING: Standard
Wind: nil Weather: sunny

4867 100 ACRE WOODS MEDIAN AUCTION MAIDEN STKS — 1m 4f (P)
2:30 (2:31) (Class 5) 3-5-Y-0 — **£2,729** (£806; £403) **Stalls** Low

Form — RPR

1 **Sheila's Castle**[34] 5-9-6 0....... JamesDoyle 3 63
(S Regan) *hld up towards rr: hdwy to chse ldrs over 2f out: rdn to ld over 1f out: styd on wl to draw clr fnl f* **16/1**

2002 **2** 3 **Deuce**[29] 3923 3-8-9 60....... (b) RobertWinston 7 58
(Eve Johnson Houghton) *in tch: squeezed for room and lost pl bnd 9f out: nvr gng wl after and sn niggled along: rdn over 4f out: hdwy over 2f out: rn wd bnd 2f out: chsd wnr 1f out: looked reluctant and wl hld after* **15/8**[2]

3 7 **Awani**[79] 2301 3-8-9 0....... RichardKingscote 9 47
(E F Vaughan) *wnt rt s: chsd ldr after 1f: led over 2f out: rdn 2f out: hdd over 1f out: wknd qckly fnl f* **7/1**[3]

0/ **4** 1½ **Red Army Commander (IRE)**[726] 4539 4-9-11 0....... RobertHavlin 1 49
(J A Geake) *v s.i.s: bhd: stl last over 1f out: r.o past btn horses fnl f: nvr trbld ldrs* **50/1**

000- **5** 1¾ **My Les**[318] 6282 3-8-6 44....... MarcHalford(3) 5 42
(J R Best) *racd in last pair: niggled along 8f out: rdn 5f out: no prog tl styd on past btn horses fnl f: nvr trbld ldrs* **50/1**

6 **6** 1¾ **Love Call (IRE)**[16] 4337 3-8-9 0....... HayleyTurner 4 39
(W R Muir) *t.k.h: hld up wl in tch: rdn and wknd jst over 2f out* **10/1**

06 **7** ½ **Dramatic Jewel (USA)**[24] 4084 3-9-0 0....... SebSanders 8 43
(J W Hills) *chsd ldrs: rdn 3f out: wknd qckly u.p over 1f out* **25/1**

2403 **8** 2¾ **Mt Kintyre (IRE)**[22] 4151 3-9-0 75....... TPQueally 6 39
(M H Tompkins) *sn pushed along to ld after 1f: rdn and hdd over 2f out: wknd qckly u.p over 1f out* **5/4**[1]

000- **9** 3 **Julie Mill (IRE)**[309] 6534 3-8-2 30....... JPFahy(7) 2 29
(R A Teal) *awkward leaving stalls: t.k.h: sn rcvrd and led for 1f: chsd ldrs after tl wknd u.p 3f out* **80/1**

2m 32.34s (-0.66) **Going Correction** -0.05s/f (Stan)
WFA 3 from 4yo+ 11lb **9** Ran SP% **115.7**
Speed ratings (Par 103): **100,98,93,92,91 90,89,87,85**
toteswinger: 1&2 £3.00, 1&3 £5.60, 2&3 £4.80. CSF £46.11 TOTE £9.80: £2.90, £1.50, £2.30; EX 28.90 Trifecta £436.30 Part won. Pool: £589.72 - 0.43 winning units..

Owner N Trevithick **Bred** Ian Murray Tough **Trained** Snetterton, Norfolk
■ Sean Regan's first Flat winner.

FOCUS
A weak older-horse maiden and a two-horse race according to the market, though neither was able to collect. No strength in depth.

4868 OWL NURSERY — 5f (P)
3:00 (3:02) (Class 5) 2-Y-O — **£3,885** (£1,156; £577; £288) **Stalls** High

Form — RPR

3360 **1** **Six Wives**[17] 4327 2-9-0 **71**....... JamesDoyle 9 75
(J A Glover) *taken down early: chsd ldrs: hdwy to chse ldr over 2f out: edgd rt u.p ent fnl f: styd on to ld towards fin: hld on* **16/1**

352 **2** hd **Admin (IRE)**[54] 3072 2-9-0 **78**....... JPFahy(7) 1 82+
(R M Beckett) *racd in midfield: hdwy 2f out: rdn and carried sltly rt ent fnl f: drvn and r.o wl fnl 100yds: wnt 2nd nr fin: nt quite get to wnr* **2/1**[1]

4520 **3** ½ **Lucky Mellor**[6] 4639 2-8-9 **71**....... (b) JamesO'Reilly(5) 10 72
(D K Ivory) *led: rdn 2f out: kpt on wl tl edgd lft u.p and hdd towards fin: lost 2nd nr fin* **12/1**

4205 **4** 2 **Yawary**[18] 4271 2-8-6 **63**....... ChrisCatlin 6 57
(C E Brittain) *sn outpcd towards rr: hdwy u.p jst over 1f out: chsd ldng trio ins fnl f: kpt on but nt pce to rch ldrs* **12/1**

200 **5** 3¼ **Do More Business (IRE)**[24] 4080 2-8-10 **67**....... IanMongan 8 51+
(P M Phelan) *s.i.s: sn outpcd in rr: styd on past btn horses fnl f: nvr trbld ldrs* **14/1**

510 **6** shd **Tom Folan**[10] 4539 2-9-1 **72**....... (p) SebSanders 5 54
(H J Collingridge) *s.i.s: towards rr: rdn and effrt 2f out: no prog over 1f out* **7/1**[3]

511 **7** ½ **Mahiki**[28] 3952 2-9-0 **71**....... HayleyTurner 2 51
(S A Callaghan) *racd in midfield: hung rt bnd jst over 2f out: no prog u.p over 1f out* **9/1**

2220 **8** 1 **Reddy To Star (IRE)**[24] 4089 2-9-7 **78**....... PhilipRobinson 4 55
(C G Cox) *chsd ldrs: struggling u.p over 2f out: wl btn over 1f out* **9/2**[2]

5654 **9** shd **The Shuffler**[10] 4525 2-8-4 **61**....... RoystonFfrench 3 37
(G L Moore) *taken down early: restless in stalls: sn outpcd in rr: nvr a factor* **8/1**

13 **10** 1¼ **Annia Galeria (IRE)**[22] 4153 2-8-2 **62**....... DavidProbert(3) 7 34
(C A Dwyer) *chsd ldr tl over 2f out: wknd qckly over 1f out* **20/1**

58.99 secs (0.19) **Going Correction** -0.05s/f (Stan) **10** Ran SP% **117.8**
Speed ratings (Par 94): **96,95,94,91,86 86,85,83,83,81**
toteswinger: 1&2 £12.30, 1&3 £43.20, 2&3 £7.70. CSF £48.78 CT £428.65 TOTE £18.00: £5.40, £1.10, £4.50; EX 79.90 Trifecta £348.10 Part won. Pool: £470.54 - 0.43 winning units..

Owner Sexy Six Partnership **Bred** Cheveley Park Stud Ltd **Trained** Babworth, Notts

FOCUS
A fair nursery and there was no hanging about. A wide stall was no handicap with the two highest-drawn horses finishing in the first three. The form looks solid.

NOTEBOOK
Six Wives, held in a couple of classier nurseries on turf since beaten less than a length off 1lb higher over course and distance last month, was never far away and put in a sustained effort to hit the front in the shadow of the past. The evidence seems to be that she is more effective on Polytrack than on turf. (op 14-1)

Admin(IRE) ◆, making his handicap and sand debuts and runner-up to a classy sort at Warwick last time, was very well supported earlier in the day and may have been a bit unlucky, as he couldn't go the early pace and was wide off the home bend. His strong late effort only just failed and his winning turn is probably merely delayed. (op 9-4 tchd 5-2 in a place)

Lucky Mellor, who virtually bolted in first-time blinkers at Brighton last time, has shown his best form so far on Fibresand and was meeting Mahiki on the same terms as when beaten a short head by her at Southwell last month. He showed smart early speed to soon lead from the outside stall and tried his hardest to hang on, but he was swamped by the front pair in the dying strides. There will be another day for him. (op 16-1)

Yawary, down to the minimum trip for the first time on this sand debut, was taken off her feet early before staying on late and a return to further is needed. (op 14-1)

Do More Business(IRE), twice well beaten over 7f after being narrowly denied over this trip on his debut in a Goodwood seller, was backed at big prices. However, he couldn't go the early pace and was still just about last passing the furlong pole before finishing strongly. It may be that 6f will prove to be his optimum trip. (op 25-1)

Tom Folan, well beaten when not enjoying the clearest of runs in a hot fillies' nursery at Newmarket last time, gave away vital ground at the start and, although she ran on late, there was no way back from that. (op 9-1 tchd 10-1)
Mahiki, up 2lb in her bid for a hat-trick after winning twice over this trip on the Southwell Fibresand, was a big drifter on the exchanges earlier in the day. Keen enough in the first half of the contest, she was very awkward rounding the home bend and looks to need a return to a straight track. Official explanation: jockey said filly did not handle the final bend (op 7-1)
Reddy To Star(IRE) Official explanation: jockey said colt hung left

4869 ARCH MAIDEN FILLIES' STKS 6f (P)
3:30 (3:31) (Class 5) 2-Y-O **£2,729** (£806; £403) **Stalls** Low

Form RPR
6 1 **Transvaal Sky**[25] 4047 2-9-0 0 RichardKingscote 2 81+
(Tom Dascombe) *mde all: shkn up jst over 2f out: rdn and drew clr over 1f out: in n.d fnl f: easily* **11/4**[2]
03 2 4 ½ **Amtaar**[27] 3979 2-9-0 0 SebSanders 9 67
(C E Brittain) *chsd ldrs: rdn and wd bnd jst over 2f out: outpcd by wnr over 1f out: kpt on fnl f to go 2nd wl ins fnl f: no ch w wnr* **9/1**
3 hd **Shimmering Moment (USA)** 2-9-0 0 JimCrowley 1 66
(A P Jarvis) *in tch in midfield: pushed along over 4f out: rdn over 2f out: outpcd by wnr over 1f out: kpt on fnl f to go 3rd nr fin: no ch w wnr* **12/1**
4 nk **Tia Juana (IRE)** 2-9-0 0 LDettori 8 65
(Saeed Bin Suroor) *chsd wnr: rdn and nt pce of wnr over 1f out: lost 2 pls wl ins fnl f* **13/8**[1]
00 5 4 ½ **Delta Sky (IRE)**[19] 4226 2-9-0 0 TPQueally 4 52
(Miss Amy Weaver) *stdd s: hld up in rr: rdn and unable qck over 2f out: wknd wl over 1f out* **50/1**
6 ½ **La Ville Lumiere (USA)** 2-9-0 0 RoystonFfrench 5 50+
(Saeed Bin Suroor) *v.s.a: sn wl detached in last pl: clsd and in tch 3f out: rdn and wknd wl over 1f out* **9/1**
7 4 ½ **Decency (IRE)** 2-9-0 0 HayleyTurner 3 37
(E A L Dunlop) *stdd s: hld up in tch: hdwy to chse ldrs over 2f out: rdn over 2f out: sn btn: edgd rt ins fnl f* **9/2**[3]
0 8 4 ½ **Dancealot Lady (USA)**[18] 4265 2-9-0 0 LukeMorris 7 23
(P Winkworth) *in tch in midfield: rdn and struggling over 2f out: wl bhd over 1f out* **66/1**

1m 12.38s (0.48) **Going Correction** -0.05s/f (Stan) 8 Ran SP% **114.1**
Speed ratings (Par 91): **94,88,87,87,81 80,74,68**
toteswinger: 1&2 £3.20, 1&3 £6.70, 2&3 £5.00. CSF £27.41 TOTE £3.70: £1.40, £1.40, £3.10; EX 19.20 Trifecta £82.40 Pool: £666.22 - 5.98 winning units..
Owner Findlay & Bloom **Bred** Charlock Farm Stud **Trained** Lambourn, Berks

FOCUS
Not the most competitive of maidens though it did feature a couple of interesting newcomers. However, the first two home both had previous racecourse experience. An improved effort from the winner.

NOTEBOOK
Transvaal Sky, sixth over this trip on her Newbury debut when looking in need of further, attracted good market support earlier in the day. Soon disputing the lead, she kicked into a significant advantage off the home bend and fairly bounded clear. Her trainer has a wonderful touch with his juveniles and she looks a filly with a future. She should get further. (tchd 5-2)
Amtaar, the only one of these with previous experience of sand having run well from a moderate draw over a furlong further at Kempton last time, found herself drawn wider than ideal again here but she ran her race having had every chance. She should be able to find an ordinary contest when the cards fall better for her. (tchd 8-1)
Shimmering Moment(USA), a $280,000 half-sister to a couple of winners in the US including the high-class Coast Guard, came off the bridle in the middle of the field at halfway, but responded to pressure to stay on for a creditable third. Entries in both the Cheveley Park and Fillies' Mile suggest she is held in high regard and, whilst they are probably optimistic targets, she should be able to win races. (op 16-1 tchd 11-1)
Tia Juana(IRE), a 50,000euros half-sister to five winners including the 2000 Guineas winner Island Sands, looked very much the stable's main hope in this and she raced alongside the winner for a long way, but she appeared to race a little green off the final bend and there was nothing more to come. She doesn't look one of the stable's stars, but may still have learnt a bit from this. (op 7-4 tchd 15-8 in a place)
La Ville Lumiere(USA), a stable-companion of the beaten favourite, closely related to winners in France and the US, fell out of the stalls and was soon tailed off, but she is bred to come into her own over middle distances so is likely to leave this debut effort well behind in due course. Official explanation: jockey said filly missed the break (op 10-1 tchd 11-1)

4870 GOPHER H'CAP 6f (P)
4:00 (4:00) (Class 4) (0-85,85) 3-Y-O+ **£5,828** (£1,734; £866; £432) **Stalls** Low

Form RPR
13-6 1 **Prescription**[19] 4228 4-9-11 85 SebSanders 2 101
(Sir Mark Prescott) *hld up in midfield: rdn and hdwy 2f out: str run u.p to ld fnl 100yds: sn clr: readily* **13/8**[1]
-106 2 3 ¼ **Al Gillani (IRE)**[32] 3795 4-9-11 85 GeorgeBaker 9 91
(J R Boyle) *in tch in midfield: hdwy to chse ldrs over 2f out: rdn wl over 1f out: ev ch ins fnl f: nt pce of wnr fnl 100yds* **8/1**
0041 3 ½ **Regal Royale**[10] 4536 6-8-6 66 oh2 (v) JamieMackay 4 70
(Peter Grayson) *sn rdn along to chse ldr: hmpd 5f out: ev ch 2f out: rdn to ld over 1f out: hdd and nt pce of wnr fnl 100yds* **25/1**
2602 4 1 ¼ **Forest Dane**[26] 3995 9-8-1 68 JPFahy(7) 5 68
(Mrs N Smith) *short of room sn after s: hld up in rr: rdn and effrt over 1f out: styd on ins fnl f: nvr trbld ldrs* **13/2**[3]
02 5 ¾ **Ravi River (IRE)**[132] 1065 5-9-6 80 PatCosgrave 1 78
(J R Boyle) *broke wl: sn chsd ldrs: rdn along over 4f out: kpt on same pce u.p fnl 2f* **16/1**
016 6 1 **For Life (IRE)**[44] 3422 7-8-10 73 NataliaGemelova(3) 8 68
(J E Long) *sn crossed to rail and led: rdn and hdd over 1f out: wknd ins fnl f* **8/1**
4166 7 hd **Halsion Chancer**[36] 3691 5-9-7 81 RobertWinston 3 75
(J R Best) *t.k.h: hld up in midfield: n.m.r 5f out: rdn and unable qck jst over 2f out: no prog after* **5/1**[2]
1036 8 1 ¼ **Ray Of Joy**[22] 4148 3-9-5 83 LDettori 7 73
(J R Jenkins) *hmpd sn after s: bhd: effrt and rdn on inner over 1f out: no real prog* **8/1**
0506 9 2 ¼ **Lastroarofdtiger (USA)**[29] 3928 3-8-11 75 JimCrowley 6 58
(A P Jarvis) *hmpd sn after s: bhd: effrt on outer 2f out: sn no hdwy and wl btn* **12/1**

1m 10.84s (-1.06) **Going Correction** -0.05s/f (Stan)
WFA 3 from 4yo+ 4lb 9 Ran SP% **118.8**
Speed ratings (Par 105): **105,100,100,98,97 96,95,94,91**
toteswinger: 1&2 £4.40, 1&3 £8.50, 2&3 £15.10. CSF £16.08 CT £245.25 TOTE £2.70: £1.30, £3.20, £5.00; EX 13.50 Trifecta £428.00 Part won. Pool: £578.42 - 0.96 winning units..
Owner Cheveley Park Stud **Bred** Cheveley Park Stud Ltd **Trained** Newmarket, Suffolk
■ Stewards' Enquiry : Natalia Gemelova two-day ban: careless riding (Aug 25-26)

FOCUS
A competitive sprint handicap run at a strong pace. A biggish step forward from the winner.
Ray Of Joy Official explanation: jockey said filly was hampered leaving stalls

4871 ROO H'CAP 7f (P)
4:30 (4:32) (Class 4) (0-80,78) 3-Y-O+ **£5,828** (£1,734; £866; £432) **Stalls** Low

Form RPR
1306 1 **Pha Mai Blue**[15] 4378 4-9-0 65 PatCosgrave 1 73
(J R Boyle) *chsd ldrs: rdn ent fnl 2f out: drvn ent fnl f: styd on wl to ld wl ins fnl f: all out* **10/1**
1150 2 nk **Shaded Edge**[17] 4293 5-9-5 70 HayleyTurner 7 77
(D W P Arbuthnot) *chsd ldr: rdn jst over 2f out: ev ch ins fnl f: kpt on* **8/1**
0334 3 hd **Autumn Blades (IRE)**[15] 4386 4-9-11 76 RobertWinston 4 83
(A Bailey) *dwlt: sn pushed up to trck ldrs: shkn up and hanging lft over 1f out: rdn and nt qckn jst ins fnl f: fnlly consented to run on towards fin* **6/1**[3]
0064 4 ½ **Salient**[14] 4409 5-9-13 78 PaulDoe 2 83
(M J Attwater) *led: rdn 2f out: hrd drvn 1f out: hdd wl ins fnl f: lost 2 pls towards fin* **5/2**[1]
2640 5 1 ½ **Balata**[8] 4607 4-9-5 70 TGMcLaughlin 9 71
(B R Millman) *taken down early: dropped in bhd sn after s: rdn and effrt jst over 2f out: drvn and one pce fr over 1f out* **14/1**
6-64 6 1 ¼ **Perfect Act**[183] 470 4-9-7 72 PhilipRobinson 6 70+
(C G Cox) *t.k.h: hld up in tch in rr: rdn and carried wd bnd 2f out: sn drvn and kpt on same pce after* **10/1**
530 7 ½ **Fiefdom (IRE)**[26] 4019 7-9-8 73 PatrickMathers 3 70
(I W McInnes) *in tch in midfield: rdn 3f out: kpt on same pce fnl 2f* **16/1**
31- 8 25 **Monsieur Fillioux (USA)**[240] 7674 3-9-3 74 GeorgeBaker 8 3
(J R Fanshawe) *in tch tl stdd to last trio 5f out: rdn 2f out: sn eased and virtually p.u fr wl over 1f out* **7/2**[2]

1m 25.61s (0.81) **Going Correction** -0.05s/f (Stan)
WFA 3 from 4yo+ 6lb 8 Ran SP% **106.9**
Speed ratings (Par 105): **93,92,92,91,90 88,88,59**
toteswinger: 1&2 £9.50, 1&3 £10.20, 2&3 £5.90. CSF £68.78 CT £335.32 TOTE £12.80: £2.80, £1.80, £2.00; EX 101.50 Trifecta £215.10 Pool: £308.24 - 1.06 winning units..
Owner Bluefriar Construction Ltd **Bred** Chippenham Lodge Stud Ltd **Trained** Epsom, Surrey

FOCUS
A fair handicap, though slightly weakened when Pegasus Again had to be withdrawn after getting wedged under the front gate of his stall (5/1, deduct 15p in the £ under R4). The principals were close to their marks.
Monsieur Fillioux(USA) Official explanation: vet said gelding was lame behind

4872 TIGGER H'CAP 1m (P)
5:00 (5:01) (Class 5) (0-70,70) 3-Y-O **£3,238** (£963; £481; £240) **Stalls** High

Form RPR
1003 1 **Kiss A Prince**[27] 3982 3-9-5 68 JimCrowley 4 75
(D K Ivory) *in tch: reminder over 3f out: rdn to chse ldng trio over 2f out: swtchd rt and drvn ent fnl f: led fnl 100yds: r.o wl* **5/1**[2]
0050 2 1 ¼ **Leelu**[24] 4085 3-8-6 55 HayleyTurner 12 59
(D W P Arbuthnot) *taken down early: chsd ldr over 6f out: rdn to ld wl over 1f out: drvn over 1f out: hdd and one pce fnl 100yds* **10/1**
6444 3 1 ¾ **Red Suede Shoes**[13] 4440 3-9-5 68 MichaelHills 5 68
(B R Millman) *chsd ldng pair: rdn ent fnl 2f out: nt pce of ldng pair ins fnl f: kpt on* **4/1**[1]
4140 4 3 ¼ **Uncle Brit**[9] 4562 3-9-3 66 SebSanders 10 59
(Sir Mark Prescott) *dwlt: sn rdn along and hdwy to ld after 1f: rdn and hdd wl over 1f out: btn and hung rt ins fnl f* **11/2**[3]
6006 5 1 ¾ **Woolston Ferry (IRE)**[27] 3982 3-9-7 70 ChrisCatlin 6 59
(David Pinder) *towards rr: rdn on outer 3f out: no real hdwy: wnt modest 5th ins fnl f: nvr trbld ldrs* **12/1**
066- 6 ¾ **Rosco Flyer (IRE)**[293] 6910 3-9-4 67 PatCosgrave 3 54
(J R Boyle) *s.i.s: sn pushed along in rr: rdn 3f out: no hdwy tl styd on ins fnl f: nvr trbld ldrs* **6/1**
-460 7 ½ **Majd Aljazeera**[20] 4206 3-8-6 58 (t) AndreaAtzeni(3) 11 44
(D M Simcock) *a towards rr: rdn 4f out: nvr trbld ldrs* **25/1**
1230 8 nk **Dark Ranger**[18] 4284 3-8-13 62 RobertHavlin 1 47
(T J Pitt) *broke wl: chsd ldrs early: steadily lost pl and in last trio over 4f out: rdn and no imp over 2f out* **5/1**[2]
0640 9 2 **Give Us A Song (USA)**[36] 3672 3-9-1 64 LPKeniry 8 44
(J S Moore) *hld up towards rr: hdwy into midfield over 3f out: rdn and struggling over 2f out: wl hld fnl 2f* **50/1**
6040 10 4 ½ **Rockabout (IRE)**[32] 3803 3-8-11 60 ShaneKelly 2 30
(B J Meehan) *dwlt: sn pushed along and hdwy to chse ldrs: rdn and wknd jst over 2f out: sn bhd* **16/1**
000- 11 7 **Yaldas Girl (USA)**[365] 4926 3-8-10 59 RobertWinston 7 13
(J R Best) *plld hrd: sn led: hdd after 1f: chsd ldrs untl lost pl over 4f out: bhd fnl 3f* **16/1**

1m 37.78s (-0.42) **Going Correction** -0.05s/f (Stan) 11 Ran SP% **117.4**
Speed ratings (Par 100): **100,98,97,93,92 91,90,90,88,83 76**
toteswinger: 1&2 £9.90, 1&3 £6.70, 2&3 £7.50. CSF £54.22 CT £224.72 TOTE £7.50: £2.10, £3.00, £1.80; EX 49.70 Trifecta £255.70 Part won. Pool: £345.63 - 0.95 winning units. Place 6: £135.46, Place 5: £61.23..
Owner A Pryer **Bred** Baroness, Magnusson, Myriade, Redmyre **Trained** Radlett, Herts

FOCUS
An ordinary three-year-old handicap run at a solid pace and the front three pulled clear. Not many got into the race.
T/Plt: £128.70 to a £1 stake. Pool: £72,213.95. 409.45 winning tickets. T/Qpdt: £22.30 to a £1 stake. Pool: £5,386.30. 178.70 winning tickets. SP

4750 MUSSELBURGH (R-H)
Tuesday, August 11

OFFICIAL GOING: Good (good to soft in places; 7.0)
Wind: Fresh, half-against.

4873 SCOTTISH RACING APPRENTICE H'CAP 1m 6f
5:40 (5:40) (Class 6) (0-65,65) 4-Y-O+ **£2,590** (£770; £385; £192) **Stalls** High

Form RPR
335 1 **Dramatic Solo**[17] 4325 4-9-5 63 (b) MartinLane(3) 2 70
(A P Jarvis) *mde all: clr 1/2-way: rdn and qcknd 3f out: styd on strly* **7/1**[3]
5112 2 2 ½ **Zefooha (FR)**[40] 3544 5-9-3 63 JamesPSullivan(5) 3 67
(T D Walford) *trckd ldrs: chsd wnr after 4f: rdn along 3f out: drvn 2f out and no imp fnl f* **7/2**[2]

/50- **3** ½ **English City (IRE)**[24] 5415 6-8-7 51 ow1 .... SladeO'Hara(3) 1 54
(Mrs L B Normile) *hld up towards rr: hdwy 3f out: swtchd lft and effrt 2f out: sn rdn and kpt on to chal for 2nd appr fnl f: drvn and kpt on same pce* **7/1**[3]

-554 **4** 2 **Kyber**[43] 3444 8-8-7 51 .... GaryBartley(3) 5 51
(J S Goldie) *chsd ldrs: hdwy 3f out and sn rdn: drvn 2f out and sn one pce* **7/1**[3]

0525 **5** 6 **Lets Roll**[28] 3940 8-9-5 65 .... PaulPickard(5) 4 57
(C W Thornton) *hld up in rr: effrt and rdn along over 5f out: drvn over 3f out and nvr a factor* **7/2**[2]

4113 **6** ½ **Master Nimbus**[16] 4350 9-9-4 64 .... IJBrennan(5) 7 55
(J J Quinn) *trckd ldrs: pushed along over 4f out: rdn 3f out: drvn and hdwy over 2f out: sn edgd rt and wknd* **11/4**[1]

0/6P **7** 9 **Humourous (IRE)**[40] 3266 7-9-3 58 ....(bt) NeilBrown 6 36
(B Storey) *a in rr: bhd fnl 4f* **66/1**

3m 6.11s (0.81) **Going Correction** +0.15s/f (Good) **7 Ran SP% 110.1**
Speed ratings (Par 101): **103,101,101,100,96 96,91**
toteswinger: 1&2 £3.60, 1&3 £5.90, 2&3 £5.10. CSF £29.21 TOTE £10.90: £5.10, £2.50; EX 36.70.
Owner Malih L Al Basti **Bred** Matthews Breeding And Racing Ltd **Trained** Middleham Moor, N Yorks

FOCUS
A modest handicap confined to apprentices. The winner was granted an easy lead and was closely matched with the runner-up on Redcar form, where both were behind today's beaten favourite.
Master Nimbus Official explanation: jockey said gelding had a breathing problem

4874 RACING UK CLAIMING STKS 1m 4f 100y
6:10 (6:10) (Class 5) 3-Y-0+ £2,590 (£770; £385; £192) Stalls High

Form RPR

6240 **1** **Birkside**[18] 4288 6-10-0 71 .... PhillipMakin 8 68
(Miss L A Perratt) *trckd ldrs: smooth hdwy 3f out and sn cl up: led on bit wl over 1f out: shkn up ent fnl f and styd on* **1/1**[1]

6443 **2** 1 **Regent's Secret (USA)**[25] 4040 9-9-7 55 ....(p) DanielTudhope 6 59
(J S Goldie) *hld up towards rr: effrt on inner 3f out: sn rdn along: n.m.r 2f out: swtchd lft over 1f out: styd on u.p ins fnl f: nt rch wnr* **11/4**[2]

0006 **3** ¾ **Run Free**[15] 4375 5-8-11 46 .... BMcHugh(5) 3 53
(N Wilson) *led: rdn along over 3f out: hdd 2f out and sn drvn: kpt on u.p fnl f* **10/1**

4/0- **4** 1½ **Swift Sailing (USA)**[26] 4032 8-9-0 55 ....(t) RobbieEgan(7) 4 55
(Patrick Allen, Ire) *hld up towards rr: hdwy 3f out: rdn 2f out: kpt on same pce* **7/1**[3]

0300 **5** 7 **Graycliffe (IRE)**[11] 3383 3-8-8 58 .... SilvestreDeSousa 5 42
(Patrick Morris) *trckd ldrs: rdn along 3f out: drvn and wknd 2f out* **12/1**

6 15 **Wyn Dixie (IRE)**[30] 10-9-5 0 .... PJMcDonald 7 18
(B Storey) *cl up: rdn along over 3f out and sn wknd* **66/1**

0/ **7** 60 **Por Chablis (IRE)**[1159] 2428 10-9-2 37 .... AndrewElliott 2 —
(P J Lally, Ire) *a bhd: t.o fnl 3f* **66/1**

2m 45.58s (3.58) **Going Correction** +0.15s/f (Good)
WFA 3 from 5yo+ 11lb **7 Ran SP% 108.9**
Speed ratings (Par 103): **94,93,92,91,87 77,37**
toteswinger: 1&2 £1.10, 1&3 £3.70, 2&3 £2.70. CSF £3.40 TOTE £1.90: £1.10, £1.20; EX 3.20.
Owner Ken McGarrity **Bred** Pendley Farm **Trained** East Kilbride, South Lanarks

FOCUS
A fairly modest claimer. The winner did not need to match his recent best.

4875 BUY A RACING POST YEARLING BONUS CANDIDATE NURSERY 5f
6:40 (6:40) (Class 5) 2-Y-0 £3,885 (£1,156; £577; £288) Stalls Low

Form RPR

2301 **1** **Ignatieff (IRE)**[10] 4546 2-9-7 77 .... DuranFentiman 5 83+
(Mrs L Stubbs) *qckly away: mde all: rdn over 1f out: kpt on strly ins fnl f* **5/1**

01 **2** 1 **Star Promise**[15] 4370 2-8-13 74 .... DeanHeslop(5) 1 76
(T D Barron) *trckd ldrs on inner: effrt 2f out: sn swtchd rt and rdn to chal ent fnl f: ev ch tl drvn and nt qckn last 100yds* **7/2**[1]

420 **3** 1¾ **Mercers Row**[18] 4282 2-9-1 71 .... DanielTudhope 2 67
(A Dickman) *hld up in rr: hdwy 2f out: swtchd rt and rdn to chse ldrs ent fnl f: kpt on* **9/1**

634 **4** nk **Lady Lube Rye (IRE)**[17] 4327 2-8-6 67 .... BMcHugh(5) 3 62
(N Wilson) *chsd ldrs: effrt and n.m.r over 1f out: sn rdn and kpt on same pce ins fnl f* **4/1**[2]

2302 **5** hd **Tillys Tale**[10] 4547 2-9-2 77 .... PaulPickard(5) 7 71
(P T Midgley) *cl up: rdn and ev ch wl over 1f out: sn drvn and wknd ins fnl f* **9/2**[3]

606 **6** 7 **Emeralds Spirit (IRE)**[18] 4278 2-8-4 60 .... PaulHanagan 6 29
(J R Weymes) *t.k.h: chsd ldrs: rdn along 2f out and sn wknd* **28/1**

21 **7** 6 **Patch Patch**[16] 4342 2-9-0 70 .... PhillipMakin 8 17
(M Dods) *chsd ldrs on outer: rdn along 2f out and sn wknd* **7/2**[1]

61.53 secs (1.13) **Going Correction** +0.15s/f (Good) **7 Ran SP% 112.7**
Speed ratings (Par 94): **96,94,91,91,90 79,70**
toteswinger: 1&2 £2.50, 1&3 £8.90, 2&3 £6.60. CSF £22.11 CT £150.65 TOTE £6.20: £2.90, £2.50; EX 25.10.
Owner P G Shorrock **Bred** Holborn Trust Co **Trained** Norton, N Yorks

FOCUS
An ordinary nursery, but it looked competitive with three last-time-out winners in the line-up. Improved form from the winner.

NOTEBOOK
Ignatieff(IRE) had taken eight goes to break his duck, finally notching a breakthrough success on testing ground at Thirsk ten days earlier, and in order to register back-to-back successes he needed to prove he was equally effective on the slightly faster surface here. He was quickly away and into his stride, making smartly for the stands' rail, and he made virtually all the running to score decisively. As at Thirsk, he was quickly away and into his stride, making smartly for the stands' rail, and he made virtually all the running from that advantageous position to score decisively. (op 6-1 tchd 13-2)
Star Promise had notched a visually impressive success on Southwell's Fibresand on her last start. She ran well, without demonstrating for sure that she is either well-treated or entirely straightforward, as, despite making ground in the closing stages, she held her head slightly high and, perhaps showing her greenness after just two previous starts, seemed to wander a little off a true line. (op 5-1 tchd 6-1)
Mercers Row, still a maiden but with a fair course-and-distance second to his credit, again showed he performs well at this venue, making late progress to take third, but his effort did not scream imminent future scorer all the same for that. (op 8-1)
Lady Lube Rye(IRE) has been admirably consistent, winning at Redcar in April and posting solid efforts from around her current mark on her last few outings, so, although she does not seem especially well-handicapped, she at least acts a useful marker to the overall form. (op 7-2)
Tillys Tale ran reasonably well, figuring prominently early on, but she faded inside the final furlong and may eventually prove better on quicker ground. (tchd 4-1)
Emeralds Spirit(IRE), no closer than sixth in four starts including this, never threatened to make a major impact and appears to need some help from the handicapper if she is to notch a success in this grade. (op 25-1)
Patch Patch had made all to get off the mark, on only his second start, in a Carlisle maiden 16 days previously. That race was far from strong, but he looked feasibly treated on a mark of 70 and his stable has been going well in recent weeks. Given his profile, then, he was disappointing, but he was stuck out wide from the start, having been drawn eight, so that can be used in his defence. (tchd 4-1)

4876 EAST LOTHIAN COUNCIL H'CAP 1m
7:10 (7:11) (Class 6) (0-65,64) 3-Y-0+ £2,590 (£770; £385; £192) Stalls High

Form RPR

604- **1** **Social Rhythm**[284] 7112 5-9-0 50 .... PJMcDonald 6 59
(A C Whillans) *hld up in rr: hdwy 3f out: in tch 2f out: sn swtchd outside and rdn over 1f out: str run to ld ins fnl f and kpt on* **16/1**

0062 **2** ¾ **Jamieson Gold (IRE)**[4] 4750 6-9-5 55 ....(p) TonyHamilton 8 62
(Miss L A Perratt) *in tch: hdwy over 2f out: rdn to chse ldrs over 1f out: drvn and kpt on wl fnl f* **16/1**

4042 **3** shd **Grand Diamond (IRE)**[4] 4751 5-10-0 64 ....(p) DanielTudhope 9 71
(J S Goldie) *a.p: led 2f out and sn rdn: drvn ent fnl f: edgd rt and sn hdd: kpt on gamely* **7/2**[1]

0142 **4** 1½ **San Silvestro (IRE)**[10] 4528 4-9-12 62 ....(p) SilvestreDeSousa 1 66
(Mrs A Duffield) *hld up in midfield: hdwy on outer over 2f out: rdn over 1f out and sn ev ch tl drvn and one pce ins fnl f* **9/2**[2]

6255 **5** 1¾ **Ingleby Princess**[10] 4552 5-9-2 52 .... PhillipMakin 3 52
(T D Barron) *hld up towards rr: hdwy over 2f out: sn rdn and kpt on ins fnl f: nrst fin* **9/1**

0020 **6** 4 **Rossini's Dancer**[14] 4402 4-9-8 58 ....(p) PaulHanagan 12 48
(R A Fahey) *cl up: effrt 3f out and sn rdn: drvn and ev ch tl wknd wl over 1f out* **7/1**[3]

7 5 **Grand Minstrel (IRE)**[20] 4216 5-8-6 49 .... RobbieEgan(7) 11 28
(P J Lally, Ire) *in tch on inner: hdwy to chse ldrs over 2f out: drvn wl over 1f out and sn wknd* **33/1**

6-60 **8** 1¾ **Lady Norlela**[28] 3942 3-8-2 45 ....(t) DuranFentiman 10 19
(T J Fitzgerald) *a bhd* **80/1**

4000 **9** ¾ **Millie's Rock (IRE)**[75] 2389 4-9-12 62 .... TomEaves 4 35
(K A Ryan) *trckd ldrs: effrt 3f out: rdn over 2f out and sn wknd* **20/1**

416- **10** 2 **Malguru**[377] 4540 5-8-12 55 ....(b[1]) AndrewHeffernan(7) 5 23
(J A McShane) *led: rdn along 3f out: hdd 2f out and sn wknd* **9/1**

5433 **11** 23 **Papa's Princess**[4] 4751 5-8-10 51 .... GaryBartley(5) 2 —
(J S Goldie) *stmbld bdly in stalls and v.s.a: a t.o* **7/2**[1]

1m 42.29s (1.09) **Going Correction** +0.15s/f (Good)
WFA 3 from 4yo+ 7lb **11 Ran SP% 115.8**
Speed ratings (Par 101): **100,99,99,97,95 91,86,85,84,82 59**
toteswinger: 1&2 £38.10, 1&3 £16.50, 2&3 £9.60. CSF £238.35 CT £1104.06 TOTE £18.50: £3.90, £4.40, £1.60; EX 248.80.
Owner Mrs L M Whillans **Bred** A And B Fairfields **Trained** Newmill-On-Slitrig, Borders

FOCUS
A moderate, but wide-open handicap. Sound form.
Rossini's Dancer Official explanation: jockey said gelding finished distressed
Papa's Princess Official explanation: jockey said mare anticipated start, hit its nose on the gate and slipped over

4877 SUBSCRIBE ONLINE AT RACINGUK.COM (S) STKS 5f
7:40 (7:40) (Class 6) 3-Y-0+ £1,942 (£578; £288; £144) Stalls Low

Form RPR

4221 **1** **Raccoon (IRE)**[4] 4753 9-9-5 72 .... PJMcDonald 1 69
(Mrs R A Carr) *cl up on inner: effrt 2f out and sn ev ch: rdn and qcknd to ld ins fnl f: kpt on* **9/4**[2]

1666 **2** ½ **Fivefootnumberone (IRE)**[25] 4043 3-9-2 76 ....(v) GrahamGibbons 5 67
(J J Quinn) *cl up on outer: effrt to ld wl over 1f out: drvn and hdd ins fnl f: nt qckn towards fin* **11/2**[3]

0604 **3** ¾ **Blazing Heights**[3] 4778 6-9-0 55 ....(v) DanielTudhope 2 59
(J S Goldie) *hld up on heels of ldng trio: swtchd outside and effrt wl over 1f out: sn rdn and ev ch tl drvn and nt qckn wl ins fnl f* **25/1**

2121 **4** 1½ **Ingleby Star (IRE)**[12] 4467 4-9-0 75 ....(p) GaryBartley(5) 3 59
(N Wilson) *led: rdn along and hdd wl over 1f out: ev ch tl drvn and wknd ins fnl f* **4/5**[1]

60.75 secs (0.35) **Going Correction** +0.15s/f (Good)
WFA 3 from 4yo+ 3lb **4 Ran SP% 105.6**
Speed ratings (Par 101): **103,102,101,98**
toteswinger: 1&2 £6.10. CSF £12.49 TOTE £2.70; EX 10.30.There was no bid for the winner.
Owner P D Savill **Bred** P D Savill **Trained** Huby, N Yorks

FOCUS
An above-average race of its type which produced a thrilling finish, with all four of the runners entering the final furlong line abreast. The proximity of the third is a concern.

4878 RACING UK SKY 432 H'CAP 7f 30y
8:10 (8:11) (Class 5) (0-75,75) 3-Y-0+ £3,885 (£1,156; £577; £288) Stalls High

Form RPR

1445 **1** **Summer Dancer (IRE)**[3] 4802 5-9-13 75 .... PhillipMakin 9 83+
(P T Midgley) *hld up in rr: swtchd lft and hdwy wl over 1f out: nt clr run appr fnl f: squeezed through and qcknd to ld last 100yds* **5/2**[1]

1624 **2** 1¼ **Stellite**[3] 4775 9-9-1 68 .... GaryBartley(5) 8 73+
(J S Goldie) *trckd ldrs on inner: effrt 2f out and nt clr run: swtchd lft and effrt whn hmpd ins fnl f: rdn and styd on wl towards fin* **7/2**[3]

3010 **3** ½ **Optical Illusion (USA)**[26] 4015 5-8-9 57 .... PaulHanagan 7 60
(R A Fahey) *hld up: hdwy over 2f out: rdn to chse ldrs over 1f out: drvn and kpt on ins fnl f* **7/1**

4526 **4** shd **Zabeel Tower**[4] 4751 6-9-6 68 ....(v) TonyHamilton 5 71
(R Allan) *led 2f: cl up on inner tl rdn to ld again wl over 1f out: drvn ent fnl f: hdd and no ex last 100yds* **3/1**[2]

-500 **5** nse **Doric Echo**[17] 4333 3-9-6 74 .... TomEaves 1 75
(B Smart) *chsd ldrs: effrt 3f out: sn rdn and kpt on same pce ent fnl f* **14/1**

0000 **6** nk **Shunkawakhan (IRE)**[12] 4466 6-8-9 57 ....(p) PJMcDonald 3 59
(Miss L A Perratt) *sn led: rdn along 3f out: drvn 2f out: sn hdd and grad wknd* **28/1**

0440 **7** ½ **Dig Deep (IRE)**[33] 3787 7-9-6 68 ....(t) GrahamGibbons 6 69
(J J Quinn) *hld up towards rr: hdwy over 2f out and sn rdn: drvn over 1f out: nt qckn ins fnl f* **8/1**

04-0 **8** *1* **Obe Brave**[16] 4361 6-8-7 **60**.....(p) BMcHugh(5) 4 58
(Lee Smyth, Ire) *chsd ldrs: rdn over 2f out: drvn and n.m.r over 1f out: sn wknd* **20/1**

1m 30.7s (0.40) **Going Correction** +0.15s/f (Good)
WFA 3 from 5yo+ 6lb **8** Ran SP% **114.3**
Speed ratings (Par 103): **103,101,101,100,100 100,99,98**
toteswinger: 1&2 £2.20, 1&3 £5.30, 2&3 £6.10. CSF £11.46 CT £52.49 TOTE £4.10: £1.50, £1.10, £1.80; EX 11.60.
Owner The Howarting's Partnership **Bred** Eddie O'Leary **Trained** Westow, N Yorks

FOCUS
A modest and tricky handicap, not well run. The form is rated through the runner-up.

4879 TOTEEXACTA H'CAP 7f 30y
8:40 (8:42) (Class 6) (0-65,62) 3-Y-O £2,590 (£770; £385; £192) **Stalls** High

Form RPR

-1R4 **1** **Dark Moment**[26] 4013 3-9-3 **58**.....(p) DanielTudhope 2 65
(A Dickman) *hld up in midfield: nt clr run over 2f out: chsd wnr 1f out: styd on wl to ld nr fin* **9/2**[3]

01 **2** *½* **Ms Sophie Eleanor (USA)**[18] 4276 3-9-7 **62**..... PhillipMakin 6 68
(T D Barron) *led qcknd 4f out: rdn ins fnl f: hdd nr fin* **85/40**[2]

601 **3** *2* **Cils Blancs (IRE)**[10] 4550 3-9-4 **59**..... TomEaves 4 59
(B Smart) *chsd ldrs: effrt 3f out: kpt on same pce appr fnl f* **7/4**[1]

0-00 **4** *½* **Gems Star**[10] 4552 3-8-6 **47**..... GrahamGibbons 7 46
(J J Quinn) *trckd ldrs: effrt on ins 3f out: kpt on same pce* **14/1**

-606 **5** *1 ½* **More Tea Vicar (IRE)**[42] 3485 3-8-2 **50**..... JamesPSullivan(7) 1 45
(Patrick Morris) *swtchd rt s: hld up detached in last: kpt on fnl 3f: nt rch ldrs* **33/1**

-000 **6** *2 ¼* **Hosanna**[10] 4531 3-9-0 **55**..... PaulHanagan 3 44
(J Barclay) *chsd ldrs: effrt 3f out: wknd over 1f out* **25/1**

-660 **7** *12* **Meydan Style (USA)**[110] 1481 3-8-6 **47** ow2.....(p) PJMcDonald 8 3
(J Balding) *t.k.h: trckd ldr: wknd over 2f out: sn bhd* **16/1**

05-0 **8** *2* **Hindford Oak Sioux**[25] 4066 3-8-9 **55**..... DeanHeslop(5) 9 6
(Mrs L Williamson) *unruly stalls: s.i.s: effrt on outer over 3f out: sn bhd* **12/1**

1m 32.68s (2.38) **Going Correction** +0.15s/f (Good) **8** Ran SP% **113.6**
Speed ratings (Par 98): **92,91,89,88,86 84,70,68**
toteswinger: 1&2 £2.70, 1&3 £2.50, 2&3 £1.10. CSF £14.28 CT £22.16 TOTE £4.90: £1.30, £1.10, £1.70; EX 15.60 Place 6 £148.65, Place 5 £34.83..
Owner Construction Crew Racing Partnership **Bred** Wilderbrook Stud **Trained** Sandhutton, N Yorks

FOCUS
A modest handicap, with more than half the field looking exposed and/or over-rated, but a clutch had the potential to show more than previously. It was only steadily run.
Gems Star Official explanation: vet said gelding finished distressed
T/Plt: £198.40 to a £1 stake. Pool: £52,006.02. 191.28 winning tickets. T/Qpdt: £63.00 to a £1 stake. Pool: £6,306.42. 74.00 winning tickets. JR

4468 NOTTINGHAM (L-H)
Tuesday, August 11

OFFICIAL GOING: Good to soft
Bottom bend moved out 2m from 1m to 4f marker increasing distances on Round course by about 9 yards.
Wind: Light, half-against. Weather: Sunny

4880 JOHN SMITH'S APPRENTICE H'CAP 1m 2f 50y
5:25 (5:26) (Class 6) (0-65,62) 4-Y-O+ £1,942 (£578; £216; £216) **Stalls** Low

Form RPR

01 **1** **Denton (NZ)**[10] 4538 6-9-6 **58**.....(t) SimonPearce 7 74+
(J R Gask) *led early: chsd ldr: led on bit wl over 2f out: sn edgd lft: shkn up and drew clr 1f out: pushed out* **6/4**[1]

1030 **2** *3 ¾* **Maybe I Wont**[12] 4449 4-9-10 **62**..... JPHamblett 11 68
(Lucinda Featherstone) *hld up in tch: chsd wnr wl over 1f out: sn rdn: no imp* **15/2**

3003 **3** *1 ¾* **Jiminor Mack**[22] 4158 6-8-7 **45**.....(p) DeclanCannon 6 47
(W J H Ratcliffe) *hld up in tch: rdn 3f out: one pce fnl 2f* **12/1**

5632 **3** *dht* **General Tufto**[5] 4721 4-9-7 **62**.....(b) HollyHall(3) 8 64
(C Smith) *t.k.h towards rr: hdwy whn swtchd rt 2f out: sn rdn: one pce fnl f* **4/1**[2]

5 **5** *1 ½* **Crazy Bold (GER)**[23] 1651 6-8-7 **45**..... TobyAtkinson 3 44
(A W Carroll) *t.k.h in mid-div: pushed along 3f out: rdn 2f out: one pce* **5/1**[3]

4210 **6** *2 ¼* **Credential**[14] 4403 7-9-0 **52**.....(p) AshleyMorgan 2 47
(John A Harris) *sn led: hdd wl over 2f out: sn rdn: nt clr run and swtchd rt 2f out: sn wknd* **11/1**

0430 **7** *10* **Athboy Auction**[45] 3381 4-8-11 **49**.....(t) RosieJessop 9 24
(H J Collingridge) *s.s: hld up in rr: hdwy on ins over 3f out: rdn and wknd 2f out* **22/1**

005 **8** *6* **Abbeygate**[48] 3269 8-8-0 **45**..... TraceyAddey(7) 4 8
(T Keddy) *hld up towards rr: rdn and struggling wl over 2f out* **66/1**

2m 15.6s (3.90) **Going Correction** +0.425s/f (Yiel) **8** Ran SP% **110.3**
Speed ratings (Par 101): **101,98,96,96,95 93,85,80**
Place: General Tufto £0.80, Jiminor Mack £1.80; Tricast: D/MIW/GT £17.16, D/MIW/JM £44.61. toteswinger: 1&2 £2.70, 1&3 (D/GT) £0.80 (D/JM) £2.60, 2&3 (MIW/GT) £2.90, (MIW/JM) £3.70. CSF £12.46 TOTE £2.00: £1.10, £1.70; EX 14.50.
Owner Horses First Racing Limited **Bred** Windsor Park Stud Ltd **Trained** Sutton Veny, Wilts
■ Stewards' Enquiry : Simon Pearce two-day ban: careless riding (Aug 25-26)

FOCUS
This apprentice handicap, run at a fair pace, was won by an above-average type for the grade. Sound form overall.

4881 JOHN SMITH'S EXTRA COLD H'CAP 1m 75y
5:55 (5:57) (Class 4) (0-80,80) 3-Y-O+ £4,727 (£1,406; £702; £351) **Stalls** Low

Form RPR

0003 **1** **Marning Star**[12] 4473 4-8-13 **67**.....(t) SaleemGolam 6 76
(Ian Williams) *w ldr: led 6f out: qcknd clr 3f out: rdn 2f out: drvn out* **9/1**[3]

0642 **2** *½* **Handsome Falcon**[14] 4400 5-9-2 **73**..... FrederikTylicki(3) 7 81
(R A Fahey) *a.p: chsd wnr over 2f out: rdn wl over 1f out: kpt on towards fin* **2/1**[2]

4310 **3** *2* **Faithful Ruler (USA)**[148] 850 5-9-5 **80**..... FrazerWilliams(7) 5 83
(R A Fahey) *hld up towards rr: hdwy 2f out: kpt on same pce fnl f* **16/1**

0411 **4** *nk* **Focail Eile**[2] 4816 4-9-9 **77** 6ex..... AdamKirby 8 80
(J Ryan) *sn stdd into mid-div: hrd rdn and hdwy over 2f out: one pce ins fnl f* **7/4**[1]

1 **5** *3 ¾* **Laafet**[21] 4180 4-9-8 **76**..... JimmyQuinn 10 70
(K A Morgan) *led 2f: chsd wnr tl rdn over 2f out: wknd over 1f out* **12/1**

6000 **6** *2 ¾* **Blue Spinnaker (IRE)**[14] 4400 10-9-1 **69**..... DaleGibson 1 57
(M W Easterby) *hld up in mid-div: pushed along 3f out: wknd 2f out* **16/1**

6000 **7** *4* **Silver Hotspur**[10] 4548 5-8-6 **65**..... SimonPearce(5) 3 44
(C R Dore) *hld up towards rr: pushed along over 2f out: no rspnse* **33/1**

0100 **8** *½* **Saa'Ida (IRE)**[25] 4050 3-8-13 **74**..... NCallan 4 51
(C E Brittain) *chsd ldrs: rdn 3f out: wknd wl over 1f out* **12/1**

2600 **9** *nk* **Follow The Flag (IRE)**[53] 3112 5-8-8 **69**..... DeclanCannon(7) 2 46
(A J McCabe) *s.s: hld up in rr: pushed along 3f out: sn struggling* **20/1**

1-20 **10** *1 ¾* **Hyde Lea Flyer**[73] 2495 4-9-7 **75**..... TPO'Shea 9 48
(E S McMahon) *hld up in mid-div: pushed along and edgd lft over 3f out: sn wknd* **16/1**

1m 47.77s (2.17) **Going Correction** +0.425s/f (Yiel)
WFA 3 from 4yo+ 7lb **10** Ran SP% **120.4**
Speed ratings (Par 105): **106,105,103,103,99 96,92,92,91,90**
toteswinger: 1&2 £3.80, 1&3 £11.60, 2&3 £7.10. CSF £28.27 CT £299.06 TOTE £12.00: £2.70, £1.20, £4.70; EX 43.80.
Owner N Martin **Bred** P And Mrs A G Venner **Trained** Portway, Worcs

FOCUS
A fair handicap. The form makes a fair bit of sense and has been rated at face value.
Saa'Ida(IRE) Official explanation: jockey said filly had no more to give
Follow The Flag(IRE) Official explanation: jockey said gelding was slowly away

4882 JOHN SMITH'S NO NONSENSE H'CAP 1m 6f 15y
6:25 (6:25) (Class 3) (0-90,86) 3-Y-O+ £7,771 (£2,312; £1,155; £577) **Stalls** Low

Form RPR

-102 **1** **Rotative**[20] 4197 4-9-7 **79**..... AdamKirby 2 89
(W R Swinburn) *hld up in last: pushed along 4f out: hrd rdn and hdwy over 1f out: led jst ins fnl f: styd on* **9/4**[2]

2-13 **2** *2* **Hada Men (USA)**[20] 4197 4-9-4 **76**..... WilliamBuick 4 83
(L M Cumani) *hld up in tch: wnt 2nd 7f out: rdn over 2f out: led jst over 1f out tl jst ins fnl f: nt qckn* **15/8**[1]

-460 **3** *2 ¾* **Kudu Country (IRE)**[32] 3827 3-8-1 **72**..... JimmyQuinn 3 75
(T P Tate) *led: hrd rdn 2f out: hdd jst over 1f out: one pce* **7/2**[3]

-006 **4** *1 ½* **Red Kestrel (USA)**[32] 3826 4-9-9 **86**..... AmyRyan(5) 1 87
(K A Ryan) *chsd ldr 7f: prom: rdn 3f out: btn over 1f out* **7/2**[3]

3m 8.65s (3.65) **Going Correction** +0.425s/f (Yiel)
WFA 3 from 4yo+ 13lb **4** Ran SP% **110.0**
Speed ratings (Par 107): **106,104,103,102**
CSF £6.91 TOTE £3.80; EX 5.60.
Owner Pendley Farm **Bred** Pendley Farm **Trained** Aldbury, Herts

FOCUS
A disappointing turnout numerically and the top weight was 4lb below the ceiling of 90. Despite the small field, the pace seemed reasonable. The first two matched their Leciester running but the next two were unproven at the trip.

NOTEBOOK
Rotative didn´t travel with any great fluency and looked in trouble when niggled along before the straight, but she was given a determined ride by Adam Kirby and gradually responded to pressure ultimately to win decisively after getting on top inside the final furlong. Quite a sizeable filly who is clearly a strong stayer, this step up in trip suited and she should have no problems getting even further. (op 3-1)
Hada Men(USA) had his chance if good enough but the tacky going might not have suited. (op 7-4 tchd 2-1)
Kudu Country(IRE), who lost his action last time, was allowed a soft time up front and had ground to suit, but he failed to prove his stamina. (op 9-2)
Red Kestrel(USA) had offered some promise on two of his three starts for this yard, but he was disappointing. He may have been unsuited by both the trip and the ground. (op 11-4)

4883 E B F JOHN SMITH'S NOVICE STKS 6f 15y
6:55 (6:56) (Class 5) 2-Y-O £3,885 (£1,156; £577; £288) **Stalls** High

Form RPR

0512 **1** **Perfect Ch'l (IRE)**[31] 3865 2-8-9 81..... FrancisNorton 5 81
(I A Wood) *w ldr: led over 1f out: sn rdn: r.o* **12/1**

555 **2** *hd* **Marafong**[15] 4385 2-8-12 66..... AmirQuinn 1 83
(Miss J Feilden) *hld up in rr: outpcd over 4f out: rdn 2f out: hdwy jst over 1f out: hrd rdn fnl f: r.o* **80/1**

1 **3** *3 ¼* **Waltz Around (IRE)**[13] 4427 2-8-11 0..... NCallan 6 73
(C E Brittain) *hld up in tch: pushed along 2f out: wnt 2nd jst over 1f out: sn rdn: one pce ins fnl f* **10/1**

01 **4** *4 ½* **Flipping**[24] 4075 2-9-4 84..... FergusSweeney 4 66
(W S Kittow) *prom: rdn jst over 1f out: wknd fnl f* **6/1**[3]

1 **5** *4 ½* **Petougg**[11] 4492 2-9-2 0..... AlanMunro 3 51
(W Jarvis) *prom: rdn jst over 1f out: wknd fnl f* **9/2**[2]

1 **6** *1 ½* **Dorback**[45] 3403 2-9-4 0..... DaneO'Neill 2 48
(H Candy) *led: rdn and hdd over 1f out: wknd fnl f* **8/11**[1]

1m 17.36s (2.46) **Going Correction** +0.05s/f (Good) **6** Ran SP% **108.4**
Speed ratings (Par 94): **85,84,80,74,68 66**
toteswinger: 1&2 £14.20, 1&3 £7.70, 2&3 £33.10. CSF £345.76 TOTE £11.30: £5.40, £18.30; EX 361.70.
Owner Paddy Barrett **Bred** Glencarrig Stud **Trained** Upper Lambourn, Berks

FOCUS
Not an easy race to assess but it has been taken at face value. The bare form is held down by the proximity of the 66-rated runner-up, and a time 1.32 seconds slower than the following nursery won by the 68-rated Ginger Ted.

NOTEBOOK
Perfect Ch'l(IRE) looks better than this result implies. For a start, she raced handily throughout (the other pace horses dropped away) and also forfeited the favoured near-side rail in the closing stages when inclined to hang slightly to her left. Considering she changed her legs a couple of times as well, it seems this tacky going didn´t really suit, but she still displayed a most willing attitude. She had already shown herself to be pretty useful when second to subsequent Richmond Stakes winner Dick Turpin in a similar event at Salisbury on her previous start and clearly continues to go the right way. Her main aim is the Watership Down Stud Sales race at Ascot in September, but before then she may go for a novice event at Newcastle. (op 8-1 tchd 14-1)
Marafong may well have been flattered as he sat well off a pace that looked pretty strong through the early stages, and raced tight against the stands´ rail for much of the way, which was a big advantage judged on the evidence of the next race.
Waltz Around(IRE) didn´t build on the form she showed when winning on her debut at Leicester and looks only fair. (op 8-1)
Flipping created a good impression when winning his maiden on quite testing ground at Haydock, but he had 6lb to find with today´s winner on official figures. (op 9-1)
Petougg, who won just an ordinary maiden at Haydock on his debut, was caught very wide when trying to make his move and that was probably a major disadvantage. Official explanation: jockey said gelding lost its action (op 11-2 tchd 4-1)

Dorback was strongly supported to follow up his Windsor maiden success (race worked out well), but he stopped quickly after matching strides with the winner early on. He was a little keen, but it was still disappointing he finished so tamely. Henry Candy said the colt lost his action, but even so the trainer was apparently still baffled by this performance. Official explanation: jockey said colt lost its action: vet said colt scoped dirty (tchd 4-6 and 4-5 in places)

4884 JOHN SMITH'S EXTRA SMOOTH NURSERY 6f 15y

7:25 (7:25) (Class 5) (0-75,75) 2-Y-O £2,590 (£770; £385; £192) Stalls High

Form RPR

5010 **1** **Ginger Ted (IRE)**[20] 4195 2-9-0 **68** .... J-PGuillambert 15 76
(R C Guest) *racd stands' side: hld up and bhd: rdn and hdwy jst over 1f out: swtchd lft ent fnl f: led last 100yds: r.o wl* **20/1**

6522 **2** *3 1/2* **Gillburg (USA)**[11] 4493 2-9-5 **73** ....(b) NCallan 12 71
(K A Ryan) *led stands' side: rdn and hdd over 1f out: kpt on to take 2nd post* **13/2**[2]

334 **3** *shd* **Look Whos Next**[29] 3918 2-9-2 **70** .... TPO'Shea 9 67+
(E S McMahon) *racd stands' side: hld up and bhd: hdwy over 2f out: rdn to ld jst over 1f out: hdd last 75yds: lost 2nd post* **12/1**

6623 **4** *nse* **Maoi Chinn Tire (IRE)**[9] 4565 2-8-6 **60** .... LukeMorris 13 57+
(J S Moore) *sltly hmpd s: towards rr on stands' side: rdn and hdwy 2f out: kpt on one pce ins fnl f* **2/1**[1]

353 **5** *3 1/4* **Gasparilla (IRE)**[62] 2800 2-7-13 **53** oh2 ow1 .... AndrewMullen 14 40
(A J McCabe) *hld up in tch on stands' side: rdn wl over 1f out: wknd ins fnl f* **25/1**

153 **6** *4 1/2* **On The Bounty**[20] 4195 2-9-3 **74** .... FrederikTylicki(3) 5 48
(R A Fahey) *w ldrs on stands' side: rdn and wknd over 1f out* **13/2**[2]

460 **7** *shd* **Pepi Royal (IRE)**[22] 4147 2-8-13 **67** .... PaulEddery 10 41
(Pat Eddery) *w ldr on stands' side: wknd jst over 2f out* **18/1**

0541 **8** *1 1/4* **Rosedale**[20] 4195 2-8-6 **60** .... AdrianMcCarthy 1 30+
(J A R Toller) *chsd ldr on far side: rdn over 2f out: led that gp over 1f out: sn edgd rt: wknd fnl f* **14/1**

6445 **9** *1* **Senate Majority**[10] 4547 2-8-11 **65** .... TedDurcan 7 32
(T D Easterby) *hld up in tch on stands' side: wknd over 1f out* **9/1**[3]

363 **10** *7* **Lairy (IRE)**[25] 4063 2-8-1 **55** .... FrankieMcDonald 3 1+
(M F Harris) *hld up in last far side gp: rdn 3f out: wknd over 1f out: 2nd of 4 in gp* **50/1**

6541 **11** *1 1/4* **Drumpellier (IRE)**[24] 4101 2-8-9 **63** .... TonyCulhane 2 5+
(P T Midgley) *led far side tl over 1f out: sn wknd: fin 3rd of 4 in gp* **20/1**

324 **12** *11* **Cuthbert (IRE)**[24] 4080 2-9-4 **72** .... AlanMunro 4 —+
(W Jarvis) *chsd ldrs on far side: rdn over 2f out: wknd over 1f out: fin last of 4 in gp* **9/1**[3]

1m 16.04s (1.14) **Going Correction** +0.05s/f (Good) **12** Ran SP% **115.0**
Speed ratings (Par 94): **94,89,89,89,84 78,78,77,75,66 64,50**
toteswinger: 1&2 £33.00, 1&3 £45.10, 2&3 £7.90. CSF £135.57 CT £1664.04 TOTE £28.40: £6.30, £2.10, £2.10; EX 167.80.

Owner Shaun Taylor **Bred** T Counihan **Trained** Stainforth, S Yorks

FOCUS

A modest nursery, although the winning time was 1.32 seconds quicker than the earlier novice event won by the 81-rated Perfect Ch´I. The first two raced close to the rail.

NOTEBOOK

Ginger Ted(IRE) switched left in order to find a clear run inside the final furlong. He picked up nicely, again showing a liking for soft ground, but this is form to treat with caution. Official explanation: trainer said, regarding apparent improvement in form, that the gelding appeared to benfit from the removal of cheek pieces. (op 16-1)

Gillburg(USA), like the winner, raced almost exclusively against the stands´ rail. He can have no excuse. (op 7-1 tchd 11-2)

Look Whos Next ◆ fared best of those who raced away from the rail - he was quite wide in the main group - and emerges with a deal of credit. (op 11-1)

Maoi Chinn Tire(IRE) is holding his form well and looks up to winning a similar event. (op 9-4)

Gasparilla(IRE), 2lb out of the handicap, was well drawn and had her chance.

4885 JOHN SMITH'S EXTRA SMOOTH CISWO CONDITIONS STKS 5f 13y

7:55 (7:55) (Class 3) 3-Y-0+

£7,477 (£2,239; £1,119; £560; £279; £140) Stalls High

Form RPR

10 **1** **Biniou (IRE)**[10] 4523 6-8-11 102 .... JamieSpencer 4 111
(R M H Cowell) *hld up: hdwy 2f out: rdn to ld and edgd rt 1f out: r.o wl* **7/4**[1]

3300 **2** *2 1/4* **Wi Dud**[56] 2991 5-8-11 105 .... NCallan 7 103
(K A Ryan) *stmbld s: trckd ldng pair: rdn and chsd wnr ins fnl f: no imp* **7/4**[1]

0540 **3** *nk* **Angus Newz**[9] 4559 6-8-9 92 ....(v) FrancisNorton 5 100
(M Quinn) *led: rdn and hdd over 1f out: n.m.r briefly ins fnl f: nt qckn* **8/1**[3]

2304 **4** *2* **Masta Plasta (IRE)**[7] 4637 6-9-0 106 .... AdrianTNicholls 1 98
(D Nicholls) *w ldr: rdn to ld over 1f out: sn hdd: n.m.r ins fnl f: fdd* **5/2**[2]

604 **5** *3/4* **Pawan (IRE)**[1] 4842 9-8-9 85 ow3 ....(b) AnnStokell(5) 3 95?
(Miss A Stokell) *in rr: niggled along after 1f: rdn wl over 1f out: nvr trbld ldrs* **40/1**

0 **6** *16* **Turbo Shandy**[17] 4324 6-8-11 0 .... AndrewMullen 2 34
(D Burchell) *sn pushed along in rr: rdn over 2f out: sn struggling* **200/1**

60.17 secs (-0.83) **Going Correction** +0.05s/f (Good) **6** Ran SP% **115.3**
Speed ratings (Par 107): **108,104,103,100,99 73**
toteswinger: 1&2 £1.10, 1&3 £3.20, 2&3 £2.30. CSF £5.32 TOTE £2.60: £1.40, £1.90; EX 5.60.

Owner Stennett, Dasmal, Rix, Barr, Mrs Penney **Bred** Kilfrush And Knocktoran Studs **Trained** Six Mile Bottom, Cambs

FOCUS

A good conditions contest. Unlike in the two previous straight track races, there seemed no real bias towards the stands´ rail. The form is rated around the winenr and third and is typically messy.

NOTEBOOK

Biniou(IRE) had 3lb to find with Wi Dud on official figures, but he´s a far more willing individual than that rival and was a tidy winner. He was inclined to lug left late on, but was always doing enough to gain his third success from four starts this year. (op 6-4 tchd 2-1)

Wi Dud was the best off at the weights but he´s an extremely hard horse to win with - last success came as a two-year-old - and he again came up short. Not one to be following. (op 3-1)

Angus Newz took the field along against the stands´ rail and has her chance, but she had plenty to find with the front two at the weights. (op 10-1 tchd 11-1)

Masta Plasta(IRE) was held by Wi Dud on their Temple Stakes running but better could still have been expected. Official explanation: jockey said gelding boiled over (op 9-4 tchd 11-4 and 3-1 in places)

Pawan(IRE), below form at Southwell the previous day, ran about as well as could have been expected. (op 33-1)

4886 JOHN SMITH'S H'CAP 5f 13y

8:25 (8:26) (Class 5) (0-70,70) 3-Y-0+ £2,590 (£770; £385; £192) Stalls High

Form RPR

6224 **1** **Guto**[21] 4183 6-8-8 **57** .... KellyHarrison(3) 4 66
(W J H Ratcliffe) *a.p: rdn wl over 1f out: led towards fin: r.o wl* **17/2**[3]

4036 **2** *1* **Lake Chini (IRE)**[22] 4141 7-8-11 **57** ....(b) DaleGibson 9 62+
(M W Easterby) *hld up in mid-div: niggled along over 3f out: hdwy 1f out: nt clr run wl ins fnl f: r.o to take 2nd post* **11/1**

2063 **3** *nse* **Cheshire Rose**[10] 4536 4-8-13 **59** ....(p) WilliamBuick 1 64
(A M Hales) *chsd ldr: rdn jst over 1f out: led ins fnl f: hdd towards fin* **14/1**

2260 **4** *hd* **Northern Empire (IRE)**[12] 4469 6-9-2 **62** ....(p) JimmyQuinn 11 66
(F Jordan) *hld up and bhd: nt clr run over 1f out: swtchd lft and hdwy ent fnl f: r.o towards fin* **25/1**

0050 **5** *1/2* **Sofinella (IRE)**[26] 3999 6-8-5 **51** oh6 .... LukeMorris 3 53
(A W Carroll) *led: rdn and hdd ins fnl f: no ex towards fin* **40/1**

4513 **6** *1/2* **Russian Rocket (IRE)**[20] 4204 7-9-4 **64** .... TGMcLaughlin 13 65
(Mrs C A Dunnett) *a.p on stands' rail: rdn over 1f out: nt qckn ins fnl f* **8/1**[2]

02 **7** *nk* **Compton Classic**[11] 4479 7-9-0 **63** ....(p) JackMitchell(3) 12 63+
(J R Boyle) *trckd ldrs: nt clr run fnl f: nvr able to chal* **17/2**[3]

0062 **8** *1/2* **Namir (IRE)**[6] 4662 7-9-4 **69** ....(bt[1]) Louis-PhilippeBeuzelin(5) 10 67
(H J Evans) *hld up in mid-div: no hdwy fnl f* **9/2**[1]

2201 **9** *1/2* **Select Committee**[14] 4399 4-9-1 **61** ....(v) JamieSpencer 2 57+
(J J Quinn) *swtchd rt sn after s: hld up in rr: swtchd lft ins fnl f: sn nt clr run: nvr nrr* **9/2**[1]

3116 **10** *nk* **Grimes Faith**[7] 4620 6-9-0 **65** ....(p) AmyRyan(5) 8 60
(K A Ryan) *hld up in mid-div: pushed along and hdwy over 2f out: sn rdn: wknd wl ins fnl f* **17/2**[3]

500- **11** *3/4* **Wavertree Princess (IRE)**[299] 6765 4-8-13 **59** .... TedDurcan 6 51
(C F Wall) *hld up and bhd: pushed along over 1f out: nvr trbld ldrs* **20/1**

1105 **12** *1/2* **Highland Warrior**[17] 4311 10-9-10 **70** .... TonyCulhane 5 60
(P T Midgley) *a in rr* **16/1**

0002 **13** *2* **Wibbadune (IRE)**[5] 4692 5-9-0 **60** .... AdamKirby 14 43
(D Shaw) *hld up in mid-div on stands' rail: pushed along over 2f out: wknd 1f out* **16/1**

61.91 secs (0.91) **Going Correction** +0.05s/f (Good) **13** Ran SP% **116.9**
Speed ratings (Par 103): **94,92,92,92,91 90,89,89,88,87 86,85,82**
toteswinger: 1&2 £12.10, 1&3 £28.70, 2&3 £18.50. CSF £94.19 CT £1337.84 TOTE £10.20: £2.30, £3.60, £3.70; EX 54.50 Place 6 £1,431.30, Place 5 £1,096.62..

Owner W J H Ratcliffe **Bred** H B Hughes **Trained** Newmarket, Suffolk

FOCUS

A number of these were denied clear runs and this is form to treat with caution. The race is rated aorund the principals.

Lake Chini(IRE) ◆ Official explanation: jockey said gelding was denied a clear run
Namir(IRE) Official explanation: jockey said gelding was denied a clear run
Select Committee Official explanation: jockey said gelding was denied a clear run

T/Plt: £577.70 to a £1 stake. Pool: £53,536.10. 67.64 winning tickets. T/Qpdt: £155.80 to a £1 stake. Pool: £4,592.32. 21.80 winning tickets. KH

4396 BEVERLEY (R-H)

Wednesday, August 12

OFFICIAL GOING: Good (8.2)

Wind: Light, half against Weather: Sunny and dry

4887 JOURNAL CLAIMING STKS 7f 100y

2:10 (2:11) (Class 5) 3-Y-0+ £2,590 (£770; £385; £192) Stalls High

Form RPR

0005 **1** **Union Jack Jackson (IRE)**[7] 4667 7-8-7 37 ....(v) KellyHarrison(3) 11 52
(John A Harris) *trckd ldrs on inner: hdwy wl over 1f out: swtchd lft and rdn ent fnl f: sn led and kpt on wl* **50/1**

2435 **2** *1* **Ancient Cross**[9] 4592 5-9-8 66 ....(t) AndrewElliott 1 62+
(M W Easterby) *hld up in rr: hdwy over 2f out: effrt over 1f out and sn rdn: swtchd rt and squeezed through ent fnl f: styd on wl* **5/1**[3]

0352 **3** *1/2* **High Curragh**[8] 4621 6-9-12 75 .... NCallan 9 64
(K A Ryan) *led: rdn along 2f out: drvn over 1f out: hdd ins fnl f: wknd towards fin* **4/1**[2]

5206 **4** *3/4* **Aussie Blue (IRE)**[14] 4435 5-9-12 59 ....(p) J-PGuillambert 5 62
(R M Whitaker) *in tch: hdwy over 2f out: effrt and nt clr run wl over 1f out: swtchd lft: rdn and squeezed through to chse ldng pair ent fnl f: sn drvn and nt qckn* **11/1**

0434 **5** *7* **Bertie Vista**[35] 3730 4-9-8 57 ....(b) DNolan 10 41
(T D Easterby) *chsd ldrs: effrt on inner whn nt clr run wl over 1f out: sn rdn and no imp* **7/1**

5136 **6** *nk* **Kabis Amigos**[42] 3496 7-9-8 70 ....(b) TonyHamilton 6 40
(Ollie Pears) *t.k.h: chsd ldr: effrt 2f out: sn rdn and wknd appr fnl f* **7/2**[1]

0060 **7** *nse* **Cross Of Lorraine (IRE)**[14] 4435 6-9-2 47 ....(b) PJMcDonald 3 34
(J Wade) *s.i.s and bhd: swtchd outside and rdn over 2f out: styd on wl fnl f: nrst fin* **33/1**

5050 **8** *nk* **Boss Hog**[13] 4466 4-9-2 50 .... LeeEnstone 8 33
(P T Midgley) *chsd ldrs: rdn along over 2f out: wknd over 1f out* **16/1**

0000 **9** *1* **Grey Gurkha**[18] 4313 8-9-2 42 .... DanielTudhope 4 31
(I W McInnes) *s.i.s and in rr tl styd on fnl 2f: nt rch ldrs* **100/1**

6004 **10** *shd* **Crocodile Bay (IRE)**[16] 4375 6-9-1 55 ....(b) MarkCoumbe(5) 14 35+
(John A Harris) *towards rr whn sltly hmpd and sddle slipped after 1f: no ch after* **10/1**

460U **11** *nk* **Actabou**[8] 4621 4-8-6 43 ow1 ....(b) BMcHugh(5) 15 25
(F P Murtagh) *a towards rr* **40/1**

00-0 **12** *4 1/2* **Jellytot (USA)**[19] 1259 6-8-7 44 ow1 .... PatrickMathers 13 10
(I W McInnes) *in tch: rdn along 3f out and sn wknd* **50/1**

0050 **13** *3 1/2* **Portrush Storm**[2] 4845 4-8-5 55 ....(b) DuranFentiman 7 —
(D Carroll) *t.k.h: chsd ldrs: rdn along wl over 2f out and sn wknd* **11/1**

5000 **14** *shd* **Makshoof (IRE)**[20] 4225 5-9-5 60 ....(p) FrederikTylicki(3) 12 16
(I W McInnes) *a towards rr* **14/1**

/00- **15** *1/2* **Fuel Cell (IRE)**[325] 4966 8-9-7 37 .... JamesO'Reilly(5) 16 18
(I W McInnes) *a in rr* **100/1**

1m 32.42s (-1.38) **Going Correction** -0.15s/f (Firm) **15** Ran SP% **121.0**
Speed ratings (Par 103): **101,99,99,98,90 90,90,89,88,88 88,82,78,78,78**
toteswinger: 1&2 £53.50, 1&3 £28.90, 2&3 £5.20. CSF £284.56 TOTE £56.20: £10.90, £2.40, £1.90; EX 582.80.

Owner Mrs A E Harris **Bred** Tom Foley **Trained** Eastwell, Leics

■ Stewards' Enquiry : Andrew Elliott one-day ban: careless riding (Aug 26)

FOCUS

The first four came clear in this large-field claimer. There was a shock result.

Union Jack Jackson(IRE) Official explanation: trainer said, regarding apparent improvement in form, that the gelding was better suited by the shorter trip and has been recovering from a virus.
Cross Of Lorraine(IRE) Official explanation: jockey said gelding missed the break
Crocodile Bay(IRE) Official explanation: jockey said saddle slipped

4888 E B F GO FIND MAIDEN STKS 7f 100y
2:40 (2:44) (Class 4) 2-Y-O **£5,018** (£1,493; £746; £372) **Stalls** High

Form RPR
52 **1** **Tominator**[10] 4557 2-9-3 0 GrahamGibbons 6 79+
(R Hollinshead) *cl up on inner: led 3f out: pushed clr over 1f out: styd on strly* **7/2**[2]
2 5 **Gritstone** 2-9-0 0 FrederikTylicki(3) 7 66
(R A Fahey) *midfield: hdwy on outer 3f out: rdn over 1f out: styd on wl fnl f: no ch w wnr* **9/1**[3]
5 **3** 1 3/4 **Love Delta (USA)**[11] 4524 2-9-3 0 NCallan 12 62
(M Johnston) *t.k.h: chsd ldng pair and hung lft bnd over 4f out: sn stdd and swtchd ins: chsd wnr 2f out and sn rdn: drvn and one pce fr over 1f out* **4/6**[1]
4 1 1/4 **Muwalla** 2-9-3 0 J-PGuillambert 8 62+
(C E Brittain) *dwlt and towards rr: hdwy over 2f out: swtchd lft and rdn wl over 1f out: kpt on ins fnl f: nrest* **16/1**
00 **5** nse **Moonlight Blaze**[33] 3823 2-9-0 0 KellyHarrison(3) 5 59
(C W Fairhurst) *towards rr: hdwy over 2f out: swtchd rt and rdn over 1f out: nrst fin* **50/1**
00 **6** 8 **Escape Artist**[15] 4396 2-9-3 0 DuranFentiman 9 40
(T D Easterby) *hld up in towards rr: sme hdwy over 2f out: sn rdn and no imp* **33/1**
00 **7** 1/2 **Eeny Mac (IRE)**[18] 4307 2-9-3 0 FrancisNorton 4 39
(N Bycroft) *chsd ldrs: rdn along over 2f out: grad wknd* **66/1**
8 3/4 **Robens Rock (IRE)** 2-9-3 0 RichardKingscote 1 37
(A B Haynes) *qckly away and t.k.h in ld: edgd lft bnd over 4f out: hdd 3f out: sn rdn and wknd fnl 2f* **14/1**
0 **9** 3 1/4 **Ainthegorgeous**[15] 4396 2-9-3 0 PJMcDonald 10 30
(P T Midgley) *a towards rr* **50/1**
5 **10** 1/2 **Dahes (IRE)**[63] 2813 2-9-3 0 TomEaves 13 29
(B Smart) *midfield: pushed along 1/2-way: sn wknd* **20/1**
11 1/2 **Alotago (IRE)** 2-8-12 0 AndrewMullen 3 22
(D Nicholls) *s.i.s: a in rr* **40/1**
12 3 3/4 **Gadobout Dancer** 2-8-12 0 PatrickMathers 11 14
(I W McInnes) *s.i.s: a in rr* **50/1**
13 1 **I'Lldoit** 2-9-3 0 PaulQuinn 2 16
(G A Harker) *s.i.s: green and a bhd* **50/1**

1m 33.17s (-0.63) **Going Correction** -0.15s/f (Firm) **13** Ran SP% **124.2**
Speed ratings (Par 96): **97,91,89,87,87 78,78,77,73,72 72,68,66**
toteswinger: 1&2 £5.20, 1&3 £1.60, 2&3 £4.50. CSF £34.13 TOTE £5.00: £1.50, £2.20, £1.10; EX 37.20.
Owner Mrs Susy Haslehurst **Bred** Mrs S L Brimble **Trained** Upper Longdon, Staffs

FOCUS
Probably quite an informative maiden in which the front five came a long way clear of the rest.

NOTEBOOK
Tominator, who had finished runner-up at a big price at Chester earlier this month, is bred to have appreciated this stiffer test and his jockey did the right thing in riding him so positively. In front after a couple of furlongs, he gradually turned the screw on reaching the home straight and just went further and further clear. He will stay much further than this and is likely to be given a break now before taking the nursery route. (tchd 100-30 and 4-1)
Gritstone, a 70,000gns colt whose dam was a multiple winning juvenile sprinter before enjoying success in the US, raced wide in the middle of the field early before staying on in encouraging fashion up the home straight. He had no chance with the winner, but got up to pip the favourite for second and this gives him something to build on. (op 6-1)
Love Delta(USA), a Royal Lodge entry who looked as though he would benefit from a stiffer test when fifth over slightly shorter on his Goodwood debut at the start of the month, did himself no good at all by taking a fierce hold early and he threatened to go straight on at the first bend. His rider then managed to tuck him in behind the leading pair, but not surprisingly when he was asked for his effort up the hill the response was limited. He is better than this and it is too early to write him off. Official explanation: jockey said colt failed to handle the bend (op Evens)
Muwalla, a 32,000gns half-brother to a winning pointer, was given plenty to do but he eventually stayed on to finish a respectable fourth and is likely to come on for this. (op 20-1 tchd 12-1)
Moonlight Blaze also stayed on from the middle of the field late and pulled clear of the others. This was his best effort so far and nurseries now become an option. (op 66-1)
Robens Rock(IRE), a 77,000gns brother to two winners over 1m2f and a half-brother to a high-class miler in the US, showed up for a fair way before tiring. He was weak in the market beforehand which suggested the run was needed and it would be no surprise to see him fare better next time. Official explanation: trainer said colt was unsuited by the track (op 9-1)
Dahes(IRE) Official explanation: jockey said colt hung right

4889 HULL DAILY MAIL MAIDEN AUCTION STKS 5f
3:15 (3:15) (Class 5) 2-Y-O **£3,561** (£1,059; £529; £264) **Stalls** High

Form RPR
1 **Theymistim** 2-8-13 0 TomEaves 3 80+
(Mrs L Stubbs) *in rr and sn pushed along: swtchd outside and hdwy 1/2-way: str run fr over 1f out: rdn and hung bdly rt ins fnl f: sn led and kpt on strly* **12/1**
0 **2** 3 3/4 **Lieu Day Louie (IRE)**[19] 4282 2-8-11 0 DanielTudhope 6 64
(N Wilson) *trckd ldrs: hdwy over 1f out: rdn to ld briefly ins fnl f: sn hdd and kpt on same pce* **12/1**
4 **3** 1 **Peter's Follie**[16] 4383 2-8-8 0 RichardKingscote 7 57
(Tom Dascombe) *led: rdn along 2f out: drvn over 1f out: hdd jst ins fnl f: kpt on same pce u.p* **3/1**[1]
556 **4** hd **Wijikura (IRE)**[4] 4800 2-8-11 0 (v[1]) GrahamGibbons 9 60
(J J Quinn) *hmpd s and towards rr: hdwy after 2f: rdn to chse ldrs over 1f out: sn drvn and no imp ent fnl f* **11/2**[2]
2324 **5** 1/2 **Orpen Arms (IRE)**[48] 3292 2-8-7 64 ow3 TonyHamilton 1 55+
(R A Fahey) *chsd ldrs on wd outside: rdn along wl over 1f out: n.m.r ins fnl f: kpt on* **3/1**[1]
5024 **6** 3/4 **Daisy Brown**[15] 4398 2-8-4 57 AndrewElliott 14 52+
(N Tinkler) *trckd ldrs on inner: effrt and nt clr run wl over 1f out: rdn and kpt on ins fnl f* **13/2**[3]
0000 **7** hd **Daft Lad**[29] 3937 2-8-11 54 ow2 (v) DNolan 13 54
(L A Mullaney) *chsd ldrs on inner: rdn along 2f out: drvn: edgd rt and wknd appr fnl f* **25/1**
8 nk **Lady Compton** 2-8-4 0 GregFairley 11 46+
(R Bastiman) *bmpd s: green and sn pushed along in rr: hdwy wl over 1f out: nt clr run appr fnl f: sn swtchd rt and styd on towards fin* **12/1**
56 **9** 1 1/2 **Nabrina (IRE)**[34] 3762 2-8-1 0 ow4 JohnCavanagh(7) 8 45
(M Brittain) *wnt rt s: cl up tl rdn along 2f out and sn wknd* **14/1**
00 **10** 3/4 **Tulip Explosion**[16] 4370 2-8-8 0 PatrickMathers 2 42
(D Shaw) *a towards rr* **50/1**
06 **11** 8 **Selina Rio**[15] 4398 2-8-4 0 DuranFentiman 5 9
(L A Mullaney) *chsd ldrs on outer: rdn along 2f out and sn wknd* **66/1**
0 **12** 2 1/2 **Derval (IRE)**[14] 4427 2-8-6 0 FrancisNorton 12 2
(K A Ryan) *cl up: rdn along 2f out and sn wknd* **10/1**

65.01 secs (1.51) **Going Correction** +0.10s/f (Good) **12** Ran SP% **124.9**
Speed ratings (Par 94): **91,85,83,83,82 81,80,80,77,76 63,59**
toteswinger: 1&2 £13.50, 1&3 £10.90, 2&3 £6.30. CSF £153.85 TOTE £15.30: £3.70, £3.50, £1.60; EX 184.00.
Owner Mrs L Stubbs **Bred** Cheveley Park Stud Ltd **Trained** Norton, N Yorks

FOCUS
A modest maiden auction event in which the usual bias towards those drawn high didn't materialise.

NOTEBOOK
Theymistim, a 10,000gns half-brother to four winners, three of them as juveniles, looked to face a stiff task on his debut from his low draw and his chances looked even more remote as he seemed to have a real problem keeping up in the early stages. He was also forced to make his effort widest off all, but despite the negatives he produced a devastating turn of foot down the outside to score despite edging away to his right inside the last furlong. A May foal, he is held in high regard and may now be aimed at the Listed Harry Rosebery Stakes at Ayr next month. (op 10-1)
Lieu Day Louie(IRE) was backed into from 66/1 into 11/1 at one stage, despite having shown nothing when 100/1 for his Thirsk debut. The gamble proved justified too, as he was always close to the pace and briefly looked like winning a furlong out until the winner engaged the afterburner. He obviously has the ability to win a race like this, but he won't be available at such monster odds in the near future. (op 66-1 tchd 11-1)
Peter's Follie, a fair fourth on her Yarmouth debut last month, is bred to stay much further so the stiffer track would have helped. She did well to get across to bag the inside rail early and had every chance, but was done for foot late on. She looks worth a try over 6f. (op 7-2)
Wijikura(IRE), unplaced in his first three outings including in a seller last time, came from the middle of the field to hold every chance and this was a better effort in the first-time visor, but he doesn't have much in the way of scope. (op 6-1 tchd 5-1)
Orpen Arms(IRE) had the best form coming into this, though the return to the minimum trip and the lowest stall were concerns. She was close enough if good enough throughout and her draw cannot really be blamed as the winner made his effort even wider. (op 7-2)
Daisy Brown, not disgraced in a couple of modest events over course and distance the last twice, had the plum draw but she was repeatedly denied a run against the inside rail from over a furlong out and she would have finished closer otherwise. Official explanation: jockey said filly was denied a clear run (op 6-1)

4890 WBX.COM H'CAP 2m 35y
3:45 (3:46) (Class 4) (0-85,75) 3-Y-O+ **£5,180** (£1,541; £770; £384) **Stalls** High

Form RPR
0030 **1** **Fin Vin De Leu (GER)**[14] 4420 3-9-2 **75** NCallan 4 82
(M Johnston) *led: stdd pce 1/2-way: pushed along and qcknd over 3f out: rdn clr 2f out: drvn ins fnl f and kpt on gamely* **4/1**[2]
2424 **2** 1 1/2 **Jackday (IRE)**[11] 4551 4-8-13 **62** JamieKyne(5) 5 67
(T D Easterby) *hld up in tch: hdwy on inner over 2f out: sn rdn to chse wnr fr wl over 1f out: drvn ins fnl f and kpt on: nt rch wnr* **4/1**[2]
11 **3** 2 **Spiders Star**[39] 3609 6-8-11 **60** PaulPickard(5) 3 63
(S G West) *hld up in rr: hdwy on outer 3f out: rdn to chse ldng pair over 1f out: sn drvn and kpt on* **3/1**[1]
1431 **4** 3/4 **Miss Keck**[11] 4551 5-9-11 **69** PJMcDonald 6 71
(G A Swinbank) *prom: effrt 3f out: rdn along 2f out: sn drvn and kpt on same pce* **4/1**[2]
16 **5** 1 1/4 **Pseudonym (IRE)**[4] 4793 7-9-11 **69** (t) J-PGuillambert 1 69
(M F Harris) *hld up in tch: effrt and hdwy 3f out: rdn 2f out: sn drvn and no imp fr over 1f out* **9/2**[3]
1323 **6** 3 3/4 **Princess Rainbow (FR)**[25] 4078 4-9-13 **71** FrancisNorton 2 67
(Jennie Candlish) *chsd wnr: rdn along 3f out: drvn wl over 1f out and grad wknd* **10/1**

3m 36.22s (-3.58) **Going Correction** -0.15s/f (Firm)
WFA 3 from 4yo+ 15lb **6** Ran SP% **112.3**
Speed ratings (Par 105): **102,101,100,99,99 97**
toteswinger: 1&2 £5.20, 1&3 £3.50, 2&3 £2.40. CSF £20.07 TOTE £5.20: £3.40, £2.50; EX 22.70.
Owner R M F Curry **Bred** Newsells Park Stud Ltd **Trained** Middleham Moor, N Yorks

FOCUS
A small field, but a tight staying handicap. The winner dictated.
Princess Rainbow(FR) Official explanation: jockey said filly had no more to give

4891 RAWFIELD H'CAP 5f
4:20 (4:23) (Class 4) (0-85,84) 3-Y-O+ **£5,180** (£1,541; £770; £384) **Stalls** High

Form RPR
3645 **1** **Discanti (IRE)**[13] 4464 4-8-13 **73** DuranFentiman 14 84
(T D Easterby) *trckd ldrs on inner: hung lft 1/2-way: hdwy over 1f out: rdn to ld appr fnl f: drvn and kpt on towards fin* **9/1**[3]
0-14 **2** 1/2 **Bedloe's Island (IRE)**[8] 4620 4-8-5 **65** oh3 FrancisNorton 6 74
(N Bycroft) *chsd ldng pair: effrt whn nt clr run and swtchd lft appr fnl f: sn rdn and kpt on to chal ins fnl f: nt qckn towards fin* **8/1**[2]
2561 **3** 1 3/4 **Efistorm**[13] 4464 8-9-3 **82** BMcHugh(5) 11 85
(C R Dore) *in tch: hdwy to chse ldrs and n.m.r over 1f out: sn rdn and kpt on ins fnl f* **6/1**[1]
0003 **4** 1 1/4 **Ebraam (USA)**[10] 4567 6-9-7 **84** JackDean(3) 3 82
(P Howling) *hld up in rr: hdwy on outer wl over 1f out: sn rdn and edgd rt ent fnl f: sn drvn and kpt on* **10/1**
0013 **5** 1 1/4 **Desperate Dan**[5] 4733 8-9-4 **78** (p) NCallan 2 72
(A B Haynes) *in tch: hdwy to chse ldrs 2f out: rdn and n.m.r over 1f out and ins fnl f: no ex towards fin* **9/1**[3]
2140 **6** shd **Sands Crooner (IRE)**[34] 3784 6-9-5 **79** (v) J-PGuillambert 12 73
(J G Given) *slt bump s: sn trcking ldrs: hdwy on bit and cl up over 1f out: ev ch tl rdn and wknd ins fnl f* **14/1**
1004 **7** nse **Baybshambles (IRE)**[15] 4399 5-8-7 **70** KellyHarrison(3) 5 63
(R E Barr) *towards rr: hdwy wl over 1f out: sn rdn and kpt on ins fnl f: nt rch ldrs* **8/1**[2]
0005 **8** 1 **Stolt (IRE)**[53] 3149 5-9-7 **81** PJMcDonald 9 71
(N Wilson) *dwlt: hld up and t.k.h: hdwy over 1f out: rdn and n.m.r ent fnl f: n.d* **10/1**
1120 **9** 1/2 **Tyrannosaurus Rex (IRE)**[23] 4135 5-9-5 **79** GrahamGibbons 8 73+
(D Shaw) *hld up: hdwy 2f out: chsd ldrs whn n.m.r appr fnl f: sn rdn and nt clr run ins fnl f: eased* **6/1**[1]
0000 **10** 1 **Van Bossed (CAN)**[12] 4485 4-9-9 **83** AndrewMullen 7 67
(D Nicholls) *chsd ldrs: rdn along 2f out: swtchd rt and drvn wl over 1f out: sn wknd* **10/1**

5600 **11** ¾ **Divine Spirit**23 4141 8-8-10 **70** TomEaves 10 52+
(M Dods) *hld up: hdwy on inner wl over 1f out: rdn and styng on whn hmpd ent fnl f: no ch after* **16/1**

00-0 **12** 2 **Loch Jipp (USA)**19 4285 4-9-1 **75** (b1) PAspell 4 49
(J S Wainwright) *cl up: led 2f out: sn rdn: edgd rt and hdd over 1f out: sn wknd* **33/1**

4060 **13** 3¼ **Tagula Breeze (IRE)**9 4601 3-8-8 **74** (b1) FrederikTylicki(3) 1 37
(I W McInnes) *sn led: rdn along 1/2-way: hdd 2f out and sn drvn: hung rt and wknd over 1f out* **40/1**

4606 **14** 116 **Chjimes (IRE)**16 4387 5-9-6 **80** TonyHamilton 13 —
(C R Dore) *stmbld bdly s: a wl bhd and virtually p.u fnl f* **22/1**

63.37 secs (-0.13) **Going Correction** +0.10s/f (Good)
WFA 3 from 4yo+ 3lb **14** Ran SP% **120.3**
Speed ratings (Par 105): **105,104,101,99,97 97,97,95,94,93 91,88,83,—**
toteswinger: 1&2 £15.50, 1&3 £10.50, 2&3 £10.90. CSF £77.78 CT £488.40 TOTE £11.20: £3.40, £3.10, £2.30; EX 105.30.
Owner The Lapin Blanc Racing Partnership **Bred** Glending Bloodstock **Trained** Great Habton, N Yorks

FOCUS
A competitive sprint run at a frantic pace.
Divine Spirit Official explanation: jockey said gelding was denied a clear run
Chjimes(IRE) Official explanation: jockey said gelding stumbled leaving stalls and lost its action

4892 EAST RIDING MAIL H'CAP 1m 1f 207y
4:50 (4:52) (Class 5) (0-70,68) 3-Y-O £3,238 (£963; £481; £240) Stalls High

Form RPR

4662 **1** **Veroon (IRE)**10 4562 3-9-7 **68** (p) J-PGuillambert 3 71
(J G Given) *dwlt: sn trcking ldrs: hdwy and cl up 6f out: effrt 3f out: rdn 2f out: led over 1f out: drvn ins fnl f and hld on wl* **6/1**2

0000 **2** ¾ **What A Day**27 4004 3-8-8 **55** GrahamGibbons 1 56
(J J Quinn) *t.k.h: chsd ldrs: effrt 2f out and sn rdn: drvn over 1f out: squeezed through to chal ins fnl f: no ex towards fin* **12/1**

450 **3** ½ **Merchant Man**17 4347 3-8-10 **57** (b1) PJMcDonald 7 57
(J D Bethell) *dwlt: sn chsng ldrs: rdn along and outpcd 3f out: hdwy u.p over 1f out: drvn and kpt on ins fnl f* **20/1**

6443 **4** ½ **Georgie Bee**7 4656 3-8-3 **50** DuranFentiman 4 49
(T D Walford) *hld up in tch: hdwy over 3f out: rdn to chse ldrs 2f out: drvn and ch ent fnl f: wknd last 100yds* **15/2**3

0-11 **5** ½ **Upton Seas**12 4506 3-9-6 **67** AndrewElliott 9 67+
(M W Easterby) *sn chsng ldrs on inner: rdn along 3f out: drvn wl over 1f out: kpt on u.p ins fnl f* **5/4**1

3403 **6** 1½ **Steel Trade**7 4655 3-9-7 **68** NCallan 5 63
(M Brittain) *s.i.s and bhd: hdwy over 2f out: rdn over 1f out: kpt on wl u.p ins fnl f: nrst fin* **9/1**

0604 **7** nk **Katie Girl**12 4506 3-7-11 **49** oh4 (p) JamieKyne(5) 8 43
(Mrs G S Rees) *s.i.s: a in rr* **16/1**

5036 **8** ¾ **Digger Derek (IRE)**17 4348 3-9-4 **65** TonyHamilton 2 58
(R A Fahey) *sn led: rdn along 3f out: drvn and hdd wl over 1f out: sn wknd* **8/1**

04-6 **9** 1 **Magic Haze**14 4432 3-8-10 **60** FrederikTylicki(3) 6 51
(Miss S E Hall) *in tch: rdn along over 4f out and sn wknd* **14/1**

2m 5.87s (-1.13) **Going Correction** -0.15s/f (Firm) **9** Ran SP% **116.6**
Speed ratings (Par 100): **98,97,97,96,96 95,94,94,93**
toteswinger: 1&2 £6.90, 1&3 £18.00, 2&3 £28.60. CSF £75.38 CT £1352.56 TOTE £5.70: £1.50, £3.40, £5.20; EX 101.10.
Owner Danethorpe Racing Partnership **Bred** C M Farrell **Trained** Willoughton, Lincs

FOCUS
An ordinary handicap, run at a modest pace.
Upton Seas ◆ Official explanation: jockey said filly was denied a clear run

4893 FINDAPROPERTY H'CAP 1m 4f 16y
5:20 (5:21) (Class 6) (0-65,64) 3-Y-O+ £2,590 (£770; £385; £192) Stalls High

Form RPR

24/0 **1** **Mexican Bob**33 3811 6-9-13 **60** RichardKingscote 6 70
(C E Longsdon) *trckd ldrs: hdwy 3f out: rdn over 2f out: chsd clr ldr over 1f out: hrd drvn ins fnl f: styd on wl to ld nr fin* **10/1**

40-1 **2** ¾ **Mister Fizzbomb (IRE)**5 4755 6-9-12 **64** 6ex (b) JamieKyne(5) 10 73
(T D Walford) *led 1f: cl up tl led again over 3f out and sn rdn clr: drvn ent fnl f: hdd and no ex nr fin* **3/1**1

2542 **3** 2 **Shekan Star**9 4593 7-9-4 **51** PJMcDonald 2 57+
(K G Reveley) *hld up in rr: hdwy on inner over 2f out: nt clr run and hmpd over 1f out: swtchd lft to wd outside and styd on u.p ins fnl f: nrst fin* **15/2**

2255 **4** ½ **Fenners (USA)**17 4350 6-9-3 **50** DaleGibson 7 55
(M W Easterby) *hld up towards rr: hdwy over 2f out: rdn to chse ldrs over 1f out: drvn and kpt on ins fnl f* **10/1**

3314 **5** ¾ **Dazzling Begum**16 4388 4-9-4 **51** (p) GregFairley 4 55
(J Pearce) *hld up towards rr: hdwy over 3f out: rdn over 2f out: drvn and chsd ldng pair ent fnl f: no imp* **12/1**

0032 **6** 2¾ **Tender Moments**15 4403 5-9-7 **54** TomEaves 8 53
(B Smart) *trckd ldrs: effrt over 3f out and sn rdn: drvn 2f out and grad wknd* **15/2**

0105 **7** 2 **Piverina (IRE)**15 4403 4-9-3 **50** TonyHamilton 5 46
(Miss J A Camacho) *hld up: a towards rr* **16/1**

100/ **8** hd **Sonic Anthem (USA)**71 7146 7-9-0 **50** LeeVickers(3) 11 46
(B D Leavy) *in tch on inner: hdwy 3f out: rdn along 2f out and sn wknd* **33/1**

3-03 **9** 1 **Sagarich (FR)**19 4269 5-9-8 **55** NCallan 12 49
(M G Quinlan) *cl up: led after 1f: rdn along 4f out: hdd over 3f out: sn wknd* **8/1**

5504 **10** 3¾ **Fell Pack**7 4658 5-9-9 **56** (p) GrahamGibbons 3 44
(J J Quinn) *dwlt: sn trcking ldrs: effrt to chse ldng pair 3f out: sn rdn along: drvn 2f out and sn wknd* **11/2**2

00-4 **11** shd **Amical Risks (FR)**16 4382 5-9-2 **49** FrancisNorton 1 37
(W J Musson) *a in rr* **7/1**3

2m 38.61s (-2.29) **Going Correction** -0.15s/f (Firm) **11** Ran SP% **122.2**
Speed ratings (Par 101): **101,100,99,98,98 96,95,95,94,91 91**
toteswinger: 1&2 £9.00, 1&3 £14.10, 2&3 £7.40. CSF £41.71 CT £249.39 TOTE £11.00: £3.10, £1.60, £2.50; EX 55.00 Place 6 £177.27, Place 5 £68.79.
Owner First Chance Racing **Bred** First Chance Racing **Trained** Sezincote, Gloucs
■ Stewards' Enquiry : Jamie Kyne one-day ban: careless riding (Aug 26)

FOCUS
A modest handicap, run at an ordinary pace.
Piverina(IRE) Official explanation: jockey said filly was denied a clear run
Amical Risks(FR) Official explanation: jockey said gelding was denied a clear run and had no more to give
T/Plt: £157.30 to a £1 stake. Pool: £51,317.70. 238.11 winning tickets. T/Qpdt: £86.50 to a £1 stake. Pool: £3,076.80. 26.30 winning tickets. JR

4527 HAMILTON (R-H)
Wednesday, August 12

OFFICIAL GOING: Good to soft (good in places; 8.4)
Wind: Fresh, half behind Weather: Mainly fine

4894 "HANDS AND HEELS" APPRENTICE H'CAP (ROUND 4 OF THE HAMILTON PARK APPRENTICE RIDER SERIES) 6f 5y
5:50 (5:51) (Class 6) (0-65,61) 3-Y-O+ £2,266 (£674; £337; £168) Stalls Low

Form RPR

0610 **1** **Botham (USA)**4 4772 5-10-0 **60** JamesPSullivan 7 69
(J S Goldie) *trckd ldrs: swtchd outside over 1f out: r.o to ld last 75yds* **9/2**2

0633 **2** 1¼ **Hettie Hubble**11 4528 3-8-10 **46** DTDaSilva 8 50
(D W Thompson) *dwlt: sn chsng ldrs on outside: led over 1f out: hdd and no ex wl ins fnl f* **13/2**3

6563 **3** ¾ **Quick Gourmet**11 4531 3-9-6 **59** NSLawes(3) 10 61
(J A McShane) *w ldrs on outer: kpt on same pce ins fnl f* **9/2**2

4040 **4** ½ **Strathmore (IRE)**23 4141 5-9-2 **55** TimothyAyres(7) 2 56
(R A Fahey) *in rr: hdwy over 2f out: styd on same pce ins fnl f* **7/2**1

0 **5** ½ **Grand Minstrel (IRE)**1 4876 5-9-0 **49** MatthewLawson(3) 1 48
(P J Lally, Ire) *led tl over 1f out: kpt on same pce* **20/1**

3641 **6** 1¼ **Scrapper Smith (IRE)**17 4343 3-9-8 **61** GarryWhillans(3) 6 55+
(A C Whillans) *chsd ldrs: hdwy over 2f out: continually denied clr run: swtchd rt wl ins fnl f: no ch* **7/1**

3000 **7** ¾ **Fantasy Fighter (IRE)**21 4204 4-8-10 **45** IJBrennan(3) 3 38
(J J Quinn) *t.k.h: w ldrs: one pce fnl f* **9/1**

0540 **8** 1¾ **Highly Acclaimed**19 4279 3-8-11 **50** (v1) DavidKenny(3) 5 36
(Mrs A Duffield) *w ldrs: one pce appr fnl f* **11/1**

000 **9** 4 **Mission Impossible**27 3999 4-9-9 **60** SamuelDrury(5) 4 35
(P C Haslam) *hood removed v late: dwlt: a in rr* **22/1**

0-00 **10** 1¾ **James Street (IRE)**38 3655 6-8-13 **45** AndrewHeffernan 9 14
(Peter Grayson) *chsd ldrs: drvn over 2f out: sn wknd* **33/1**

1m 15.22s (3.02) **Going Correction** +0.375s/f (Good)
WFA 3 from 4yo+ 4lb **10** Ran SP% **114.8**
Speed ratings (Par 101): **94,92,91,90,90 88,87,85,79,77**
toteswinger: 1&2 £6.80, 1&3 £4.10, 2&3 £2.90. CSF £32.30 CT £125.63 TOTE £3.70: £1.30, £2.60, £1.90; EX 35.80.
Owner J S Morrison **Bred** France Weiner & Neal Hayias **Trained** Uplawmoor, E Renfrews

FOCUS
After 3mm of rain the ground remained good to soft, good in places. A personal best from Botham.
Botham(USA) Official explanation: trainer said, regarding apparent improvement in form, that he had no explanation for the poor run last time but added that the gelding was a course specialist.

4895 RACING UK AUCTION NURSERY 6f 5y
6:20 (6:20) (Class 4) 2-Y-O £4,209 (£1,252; £625; £312) Stalls Low

Form RPR

4311 **1** **Bluie**11 4525 2-9-0 **73** AdrianTNicholls 7 79+
(D Nicholls) *mde all: rdn and edgd lft over 1f out: styd on strly* **11/10**1

0111 **2** 2¼ **Diamond Laura**10 4558 2-9-13 **86** 6ex SilvestreDeSousa 1 85
(Mrs R A Carr) *stmbld s: sn chsng ldrs: edgd rt over 1f out: no imp* **4/1**2

242 **3** ¾ **Cherry Bee**47 3337 2-8-10 **69** JoeFanning 3 66
(M Johnston) *chsd ldrs: edgd lft over 1f out: kpt on same pce* **5/1**3

063 **4** 2¾ **High Rolling**23 4138 2-8-7 **66** ow1 DavidAllan 2 55
(T D Easterby) *w ldrs: rdn and outpcd appr fnl f* **20/1**

410 **5** ¾ **Whispered Times (USA)**41 3542 2-9-4 **77** PhillipMakin 6 64
(P C Haslam) *chsd ldrs: drvn over 2f out: edgd lft and wknd over 1f out* **8/1**

0145 **6** 1 **Miami Gator (IRE)**40 3572 2-7-13 **63** ow3 MartinLane(5) 8 47
(A P Jarvis) *sn outpcd on outside: sn drvn along: nvr a factor* **10/1**

5330 **7** ½ **Cambuslang (IRE)**18 4306 2-8-2 **61** PaulHanagan 5 43
(I Semple) *dwlt: towards rr: outpcd over 2f out: nvr a factor* **20/1**

1m 15.01s (2.81) **Going Correction** +0.375s/f (Good) **7** Ran SP% **114.0**
Speed ratings (Par 96): **96,93,92,88,87 86,85**
toteswinger: 1&2 £1.40, 1&3 £2.60, 2&3 £2.70. CSF £5.67 CT £14.35 TOTE £1.80: £1.40, £1.90; EX 5.00.
Owner The Three K's **Bred** P Baugh **Trained** Sessay, N Yorks

FOCUS
An interesting nursery, in which the seven runners had been successful eight times already between them. It should throw up plenty of future winners as well.

NOTEBOOK
Bluie landed the hat-trick in good style. He looks uncomplicated and although the handicapper is set to have his say, he is in the right hands to progress. He should have no problem scoring again. (op Evens tchd 5-4)
Diamond Laura ran a gallant race, after getting out paced early she kept on well up the hill. Life will not be easy off her current mark, but with such a willing attitude she should continue to pay her way for her in-form yard. (op 7-2)
Cherry Bee has been consistent in all four starts so far, and should be able to get her head in front very soon. She can progress when stepped up in trip. (op 9-2)
High Rolling is another who continues to improve with every start and should be able to get competitive off a similar mark before the season is out. (op 33-1)
Whispered Times(USA) didn't travel that well down the hill and remains better than the bare result suggests. (op 14-1)

4896 E B F CAPTAIN J.C. STEWART FILLIES' H'CAP 1m 65y
6:55 (6:55) (Class 3) (0-95,89) 3-Y-O+ £11,009 (£3,275; £1,637; £817) Stalls High

Form RPR

0306 **1** **Medici Pearl**19 4287 5-9-10 **87** DavidAllan 5 92
(T D Easterby) *dwlt: stdy hdwy over 3f out: effrt over 1f out: r.o wl to ld wl ins fnl f* **4/1**3

2103 **2** nk **Just Lille (IRE)**17 4339 6-9-12 **89** (p) SilvestreDeSousa 1 93
(Mrs A Duffield) *led: hung lft and hdd last 75yds: no ex* **3/1**2

52B6 **3** 1¼ **Talk Of Saafend (IRE)**11 4532 4-8-0 **70** oh7 IJBrennan(7) 7 71
(P Monteith) *hld up towards rr: nt clr run on ins over 2f out: squeezed through appr fnl f: kpt on same pce* **25/1**

311 **4** 1¼ **Honimiere (IRE)**15 4401 3-9-1 **85** RobertWinston 4 83
(G A Swinbank) *chsd ldrs: effrt over 3f out: styd on fnl f* **11/4**1

3000 **5** ½ **Fesko**11 4549 3-8-8 **78** JoeFanning 3 75
(M Johnston) *chsd ldr: chal over 3f out: fdd fnl 150yds* **9/1**

1553 **6** shd **Celtic Lynn (IRE)**20 4228 4-8-13 **76** PhillipMakin 8 73
(M Dods) *dwlt: hld up in rr: effrt over 2f out: kpt on: nvr nr to chal* **8/1**

1 7 1 1/4 **Wood Fairy**[19] 4277 3-8-2 **72**.......................... PaulHanagan 6 66
(R A Fahey) *chsd ldrs: nt clr run on ins fr over 2f out tl fdd jst ins fnl f* **11/2**

1m 50.57s (2.17) **Going Correction** +0.375s/f (Good)
WFA 3 from 4yo+ 7lb 7 Ran SP% **112.0**
Speed ratings (Par 104): **104,103,102,101,100 100,99**
toteswinger: 1&2 £3.70, 1&3 £22.40, 2&3 £12.70. CSF £15.70 CT £255.33 TOTE £5.50: £3.10, £2.20; EX 16.40.
Owner Ryedale Partners No 3 **Bred** Larkwood Stud **Trained** Great Habton, N Yorks

FOCUS
A competitive fillies' handicap, which was run at a sound pace thanks to the runner up. The runner-up looks the best guide.

NOTEBOOK
Medici Pearl enjoyed the drop in class to record her first victory since last September. She is plying her trade off a career-high mark but should be able to score again, especially if there's plenty of give in the ground, softer the better for the five year-old. (op 5-1)
Just Lille(IRE), who was looking for her fourth course success, battled on gamely all the way to the line and although she's off her highest ever mark, she should continue to pay her way. (op 100-30 tchd 4-1)
Talk Of Saafend(IRE), who's last four wins have come in claiming company when trained by Richard Hannon, ran well from 7lb out of the handicap, and should be placed to good effect in the coming weeks. (op 20-1)
Honimiere(IRE) was looking for her fourth success this season but the drop back in trip didn't suit. She got out paced before staying on in the final furlong, and should be able to score again when stepped back up to 10f. (op 7-2 tchd 4-1)
Wood Fairy, having only her second start ran respectably for a long way, the experience will not have been lost on her. (op 4-1 tchd 7-2)

4897 RIVA RESTAURANT CLAIMING STKS 1m 65y
7:30 (7:30) (Class 6) 3-Y-O+ £2,388 (£705; £352) Stalls High

Form RPR
1621 1 **Fremen (USA)**[5] 4750 9-9-13 **81**.......................... AdrianTNicholls 7 88
(D Nicholls) *s.i.s: hdwy and swtchd ins over 3f out: led over 2f out: drvn clr 1f out: eased towards fin* **5/2**[2]
5635 2 6 **Bold Indian (IRE)**[26] 4034 5-8-10 **52**.......................... PaulHanagan 3 57
(I Semple) *hld up in rr: hdwy over 2f out: wnt 2nd appr fnl f: no ch w wnr* **12/1**
0000 3 2 1/2 **Tiger Dream**[11] 4548 4-9-8 **70**.......................... (p) AmyRyan(5) 4 68
(K A Ryan) *chsd ldrs: led 3f out: sn hdd: one pce* **8/1**
0211 4 3 3/4 **Moody Tunes**[9] 4588 6-9-8 **71**.......................... MartinLane(5) 6 60
(A P Jarvis) *hld up towards rr: hdwy 4f out: hung rt over 2f out: nvr trbld ldrs* **9/4**[1]
400 5 2 3/4 **Middlemarch (IRE)**[18] 4293 9-8-8 **69**.......................... (p) GaryBartley(5) 2 39
(J S Goldie) *in rr: drvn over 3f out: wandered: kpt on fnl 2f: nvr on terms* **11/2**[3]
450 6 3/4 **Darfour**[7] 4656 5-8-3 **59**.......................... (v[1]) JamesPSullivan(7) 1 35
(J S Goldie) *chsd ldrs: reminders after 2f: one pce fnl 3f* **25/1**
6051 7 16 **Ask Dan (IRE)**[11] 4528 3-8-10 **58**.......................... (p) PhillipMakin 9 5
(M Dods) *led tl 3f out: lost pl 2f out: bhd whn eased ins fnl f* **8/1**
0/0- 8 9 **Abbey Express**[31] 3551 4-8-8 **50** ow2.......................... (t) SladeO'Hara(5) 5 —
(M A Barnes) *chsd ldr: chal over 5f out: wknd over 2f out: eased ins fnl f* **100/1**
0/0 9 32 **Por Chablis (IRE)**[1] 4874 10-8-10 **37**.......................... (b) SilvestreDeSousa 8 —
(P J Lally, Ire) *chsd ldrs: sn drvn along: hung rt over 4f out: sn lost pl: t.o 2f out* **125/1**

1m 50.62s (2.22) **Going Correction** +0.375s/f (Good)
WFA 3 from 4yo+ 7lb 9 Ran SP% **110.3**
Speed ratings (Par 101): **103,97,94,90,88 87,71,62,30**
toteswinger: 1&2 £3.90, 1&3 £4.40, 2&3 £11.50. CSF £29.54 TOTE £3.10: £1.70, £2.60, £2.80; EX 32.10.
Owner Miss C King Mrs A Seed Ms Finola Devaney **Bred** Flaxman Holdings Ltd **Trained** Sessay, N Yorks

FOCUS
In the end it was only an ordinary claimer after a couple of horses ran well below par. It was run at a very sound pace thanks to recent course-and-distance seller winner Ask Dan, who folded tamely in the final couple of furlongs. The runner-up is the best guide to the form.

4898 TOTESWINGER H'CAP 1m 4f 17y
8:05 (8:05) (Class 5) (0-70,68) 3-Y-O+ £3,238 (£963; £481; £240) Stalls High

Form RPR
40-0 1 **Jordan's Light (USA)**[27] 1690 6-8-7 **53**.......................... JamesPSullivan(7) 7 64+
(P Monteith) *hld up towards rr: hdwy on ins 4f out: nt clr run over 2f out: styd on strly fnl f: led last 75yds* **16/1**
0604 2 1 **Call Of Duty (IRE)**[13] 4462 4-8-12 **56**.......................... SladeO'Hara(5) 9 62
(Mrs Dianne Sayer) *hld up towards rr: hdwy 4f out: led over 1f out: no ex and hdd towards fin* **9/2**[1]
02B4 3 1 3/4 **Hawkit (USA)**[11] 4529 8-8-10 **54**.......................... MartinLane(5) 1 58
(P Monteith) *trckd ldrs: chal over 3f out: styd on same pce fnl f* **12/1**
0301 4 3/4 **Shifting Gold (IRE)**[11] 4529 3-8-7 **62**.......................... (b) AmyRyan(5) 6 64
(K A Ryan) *bmpd s: hdwy to join ldr 9f out: led 4f out tl over 1f out: edgd lft and kpt on same pce* **13/2**
0412 5 1 3/4 **Love In The West (IRE)**[29] 3936 3-8-8 **58** ow1.......................... RobertWinston 8 58
(G A Swinbank) *chsd ldrs: pushed along 6f out: kpt on one pce fnl 3f: nvr a threat* **6/1**[3]
466 6 1/2 **Louisa (GER)**[9] 4593 5-9-2 **55**.......................... DavidAllan 4 54
(P Monteith) *in rr: effrt on outside over 3f out: one pce* **12/1**
31-5 7 1 **Prince Rhyddarch**[26] 4038 4-9-9 **65**.......................... NeilBrown(3) 5 62
(I Semple) *swvd rt s: towards rr: reminders over 5f out: kpt on fnl 2f: nvr a factor* **5/1**[2]
0116 8 1/2 **Forrest Flyer (IRE)**[17] 4350 5-10-0 **67**.......................... PhillipMakin 3 63
(I Semple) *t.k.h: trckd ldrs: one pce fnl 2f* **7/1**
2010 9 21 **New Tricks**[33] 3809 3-9-4 **68**.......................... (b) PaulHanagan 10 31
(I Semple) *led tl 4f out: lost pl over 2f out: sn bhd: t.o* **5/1**[2]

2m 42.69s (4.09) **Going Correction** +0.375s/f (Good)
WFA 3 from 4yo+ 11lb 9 Ran SP% **112.9**
Speed ratings (Par 103): **101,100,99,98,97 97,96,96,82**
toteswinger: 1&2 £34.80, 1&3 £33.00, 2&3 £8.30. CSF £84.56 CT £903.27 TOTE £16.50: £3.50, £1.20, £4.60; EX 137.10.
Owner Mrs C Jordan & Mrs A Jordan **Bred** Lantern Hill Farm Llc **Trained** Rosewell, Midlothian
■ Stewards' Enquiry : Slade O'Hara caution: careless riding

FOCUS
A run of the mill handicap, run at a fast pace and it produced a thrilling finish. Sound form for the grade.

4899 BUONA NOTTE H'CAP 5f 4y
8:35 (8:36) (Class 5) (0-75,74) 3-Y-O+ £3,238 (£963; £481; £240) Stalls Low

Form RPR
0036 1 **The Bear**[23] 4136 6-7-13 **56**.......................... AndrewHeffernan(7) 4 66
(Miss L A Perratt) *led tl over 1f out: kpt on wl to ld nr fin* **8/1**
6400 2 nk **Sunley Sovereign**[7] 4657 5-7-12 **55** oh7.......................... (b) JamesPSullivan(7) 8 64
(Mrs R A Carr) *w ldrs: led over 1f out: edgd rt: hdd towards fin* **10/1**
2240 3 1 1/4 **Artsu**[26] 4069 4-9-9 **73**.......................... PhillipMakin 6 78
(M Dods) *t.k.h: trckd ldrs: nt clr run fr 2f out tl edgd lft jst ins fnl f: r.o: nt rch 1st 2* **10/3**[2]
4040 4 1 3/4 **Steelcut**[13] 4461 5-9-10 **74**.......................... PaulHanagan 7 72
(R A Fahey) *w ldrs: kpt on same pce fnl f* **8/1**
3241 5 1 1/4 **Hotham**[17] 4355 6-9-2 **71**.......................... GaryBartley(5) 1 65
(N Wilson) *s.s: hdwy over 2f out: kpt on: nvr nr ldrs* **3/1**[1]
1U60 6 nk **Buy On The Red**[8] 4620 8-9-7 **71**.......................... (b) AdrianTNicholls 2 64
(D Nicholls) *chsd ldrs: drvn over 2f out: kpt on same pce appr fnl f* **9/1**
5441 7 1/2 **Angelo Poliziano**[7] 4653 3-9-4 **71** 6ex.......................... (b) SilvestreDeSousa 3 62
(Mrs A Duffield) *dwlt: hdwy over 2f out: kpt on: nvr trbld ldrs* **7/2**[3]
6/0- 8 4 **Glenluji**[439] 2576 4-8-10 **60**.......................... DavidAllan 9 36
(J S Goldie) *w ldrs: drvn and outpcd over 2f out: sn lost pl* **50/1**

61.37 secs (1.37) **Going Correction** +0.375s/f (Good)
WFA 3 from 4yo+ 3lb 8 Ran SP% **113.6**
Speed ratings (Par 103): **104,103,101,98,96 96,95,89**
toteswinger: 1&2 £10.40, 1&3 £8.20, 2&3 £8.10. CSF £82.03 CT £317.83 TOTE £9.60: £2.40, £3.00, £1.20; EX 37.80 Place 6 £89.02, Place 5 £48.09.
Owner Cincinnati Club **Bred** P G Airey And R R Whitton **Trained** East Kilbride, South Lanarks

FOCUS
An ordinary sprint run at a sound pace and the race developed down the middle of the track. A modest handicap for the grade, with the second 7lb wrong.
T/Plt: £183.50 to a £1 stake. Pool: £50,899.27. 202.41 winning tickets. T/Qpdt: £74.50 to a £1 stake. Pool: £4,330.60. 43.00 winning tickets. WG

4321 SALISBURY (R-H)
Wednesday, August 12

OFFICIAL GOING: Good to firm changing to good to firm (firm in places) after 4.05 (race 4)
Rail dolled out 5yards from 6.5f to wining post.
Wind: Moderate, ahead Weather: Bright

4900 E B F MOLSON COORS MAIDEN STKS 6f
2:30 (2:32) (Class 4) 2-Y-O £4,695 (£1,397; £698; £348) Stalls High

Form RPR
2 1 **Mon Cadeaux**[18] 4318 2-9-3 0.......................... WilliamBuick 1 89+
(A M Balding) *lengthy: scope: lw: sn trcking ldr: led 3f out: drvn clr ins fnl 2f: comf* **9/4**[1]
2 3 **Dafeef** 2-9-3 0.......................... LDettori 8 80+
(Saeed Bin Suroor) *w'like: scope: s.i.s: in rr: hdwy on outside 3f out: rdn: green and hung lft ins fnl 2f: chsd wnr and hung rt over 1f out: styd on same pce ins fnl f* **9/2**[3]
3 1/2 **Folly Bridge** 2-8-12 0.......................... SteveDrowne 9 74+
(R Charlton) *lengthy: unf: s.i.s: mid-div: hdwy over 2f out: styd on wl to take 3rd ins fnl f and clsng on 2nd but no ch w wnr* **40/1**
4 1/2 **King Of Windsor (IRE)** 2-9-3 0.......................... SebSanders 2 77+
(R M Beckett) *w'like: tall: s.i.s: hld up in rr: hdwy towards outside over 2f out: styd on fnl f and gng on cl home but nvr nr wnr* **20/1**
24 5 1 1/2 **Cansili Star**[26] 4041 2-9-3 0.......................... PhilipRobinson 7 73
(M A Jarvis) *w'like: tall: s.i.s: wnt 2nd and rdn 2f out: nvr any ch w wnr and lost 2nd over 1f out: sn btn* **8/1**
4 6 1 3/4 **Gallant Eagle (IRE)**[62] 2844 2-9-3 0.......................... RyanMoore 12 67+
(S Kirk) *bit bkwd: in rr: pushed along ins fnl 3f: sme late prog but nvr gng wl enough to get into contention* **5/2**[2]
02 7 nse **Carnaby Street (IRE)**[16] 4377 2-9-3 0.......................... JamieSpencer 5 67+
(R Hannon) *str: lw: led tl j. path and hdd 3f out: flyj. again ins fnl 2f and no ch whn faltered ins fnl f* **9/2**[3]
8 6 **Wet Feet** 2-9-3 0.......................... JimCrowley 10 49
(P R Chamings) *str: s.i.s: sn chsng ldrs: wknd ins fnl 2f* **50/1**
9 3/4 **Skyflight** 2-8-12 0.......................... FergusSweeney 3 42+
(Eve Johnson Houghton) *leggy: unruly stalls: chsd ldrs 4f* **100/1**
10 8 **Draco Boy** 2-9-3 0.......................... GeorgeBaker 13 23
(Andrew Turnell) *leggy: scope: bit bkwd: a in rr* **100/1**
11 1 3/4 **Bathwick Gold (IRE)** 2-9-3 0.......................... EdwardCreighton 4 18
(P D Evans) *str: bit bkwd: slowly away: wnt lft s: v green and a wl bhd* **50/1**
0 12 hd **Lilyannabanana**[60] 2919 2-8-12 0.......................... CatherineGannon 11 12
(P D Evans) *w'like: s.i.s: sn rcvrd to chse ldrs 2f: wknd qckly over 3f out* **100/1**

1m 14.81s (0.01) **Going Correction** -0.175s/f (Firm) 12 Ran SP% **120.9**
Speed ratings (Par 96): **92,88,87,86,84 82,82,74,73,62 60,60**
toteswinger: 1&2 £5.10, 1&3 £11.30, 2&3 £17.90. CSF £12.76 TOTE £3.20: £1.40, £1.80, £5.80; EX 18.40.
Owner Mick and Janice Mariscotti **Bred** Stourbank Stud **Trained** Kingsclere, Hants

FOCUS
This was probably a fair maiden.

NOTEBOOK
Mon Cadeaux won in the style of a useful performer. A close second at Newmarket on debut (modest race for the course/hampered), he looked sure to have come on for that initial outing and took over after Carnaby Street jumped the bath at halfway. Clear inside the two, he stretched out in quite taking style and it would come as no surprise to see him take his chance in something a bit better next time. He holds an entry in next months Mill Reef Stakes, though that may be flying too high at this stage. (op 4-1 tchd 9-2 in a place)
Dafeef, a half-brother to useful 1m winner Mutamasshi, moved well off the pace and closed travelling well, but he couldn't quicken on with the winner. His yard is going really well at present and he should improve for the exeprience. (op 5-2 tchd 7-1)
Folly Bridge, a daughter of Avonbridge, ran a race full of promise, chasing the pace throughout and staying on well inside the final furlong to take third. She should come on a good deal for this outing and can find something similar. (op 33-1)
King Of Windsor(IRE), a brother to useful 7f/1m winner Suruor, was representing a yard which has won this race twice in the recent years and he kept on nicely for hands and heels riding inside the final furlong. (op 33-1)

Cansili Star, who failed to get home over 7f at Haydock last time, couldn't quicken on this drop in trip. Official explanation: jockey said colt was unsuited by the good to firm ground (op 6-1 tchd 5-1)

Gallant Eagle(IRE), who caught the eye of many when fourth over 6f on debut at Newbury, never got into this having been held up and hung under pressure. This effort leaves him with a bit to prove. (tchd 15-8)

Carnaby Street(IRE) was in trouble soon after he jumped the path, which clearly put him on edge as he fly-jumped again inside the final 2f. He deserves another chance. Official explanation: jockey said colt was unsuited by the good to firm ground (op 7-1)

Bathwick Gold(IRE) Official explanation: jockey said colt was slowly away

4901 CARMEN WINES NURSERY — 6f 212y

3:00 (3:01) (Class 5) 2-Y-O — **£3,238** (£963; £481; £240) **Stalls** Centre

Form — RPR

41 **1** **Frozen Power (IRE)**[20] [4233] 2-9-3 **81**.......... LDettori 1 — 92+
(Saeed Bin Suroor) *lw: in tch: hdwy and wnt sharply rt 2f out: led sn after: drvn along ins fnl f: styd on wl* **8/11**[1]

016 **2** 2 ½ **Butch And Sundance**[10] [4565] 2-9-5 **83**.......... JamieSpencer 5 — 83
(B J Meehan) *lw: in rr: swtchd sharply lft and hdwy over 2f out: rdn to chse wnr and hung rt 1f out: styd on but nvr any ch* **16/1**

1010 **3** 1 ¼ **Avon River**[10] [4565] 2-9-6 **84**.......... RyanMoore 2 — 81
(R Hannon) *in rr: swtchd lft to outside and hdwy fr 2f out: styd on fnl f but nvr gng pce to rch ldng duo* **10/1**[3]

233 **4** 1 ½ **Nina Rose**[32] [3858] 2-8-7 **71**.......... WilliamBuick 3 — 64
(C G Cox) *in tch: styng on whn bdly hmpd 2f out: kpt on again fnl f* **10/1**[3]

2201 **5** ½ **Janeiro (IRE)**[16] [4385] 2-9-4 **87**.......... RossAtkinson(5) 7 — 79
(Tom Dascombe) *swtg: chsd ldrs: rdn over 2f out: wknd fnl f* **7/1**[2]

3035 **6** 2 ½ **Thomas Baines (USA)**[20] [4243] 2-7-11 **66**.. Louis-PhilippeBeuzelin(5) 10 — 52+
(M L W Bell) *lw: t.k.h: chsd ldrs: rdn 2f out: btn whn hmpd on ins appr fnl f* **11/1**

2556 **7** ½ **Pullyourfingerout (IRE)**[19] [4271] 2-8-2 **66**.......... FrankieMcDonald 8 — 50
(B G Powell) *chsd ldr: led 3f out: hdd ins fnl 2f: wknd and hung rt appr fnl f* **25/1**

0050 **8** 4 ½ **Flyinflyout**[12] [4488] 2-8-8 **72**.......... EdwardCreighton 9 — 45+
(M R Channon) *s.i.s: in rr but in tch: sltly hmpd 2f out: nvr in contention after* **20/1**

004 **9** hd **Mnarani (IRE)**[61] [2875] 2-8-8 **72**.......... LPKeniry 4 — 45
(J S Moore) *hmpd 2f out: a bhd* **50/1**

5160 **10** 1 **Underworld Dandy**[21] [4190] 2-8-1 **65**.......... CatherineGannon 11 — 35
(P D Evans) *led tl hdd 3f out: wknd fr 2f out* **66/1**

1355 **11** 41 **Boga (IRE)**[60] [2907] 2-8-1 **65**.......... RichardThomas 6 — —
(R J Hodges) *pressed ldrs 3f: wkng whn hmpd 2f out: no ch whn hmpd again over 1f out: eased: t.o* **50/1**

1m 28.48s (-0.52) **Going Correction** -0.175s/f (Firm) — **11** Ran SP% **116.8**

Speed ratings (Par 94): **95,92,90,89,88 85,85,79,79,78 31**

toteswinger: 1&2 £4.50, 1&3 £2.30, 2&3 £11.60. CSF £13.50 CT £73.96 TOTE £1.70: £1.10, £4.20, £2.60; EX 14.80.

Owner Godolphin **Bred** Rathbarry Stud **Trained** Newmarket, Suffolk

■ Stewards' Enquiry : L Dettori three-day ban (reduced from four days on appeal): careless riding (Aug 26-28)

FOCUS

A modest nursery that went the way of the red-hot favourite.

NOTEBOOK

Frozen Power(IRE) took over approaching the final furlong and stayed on well to score. Narrow winner of a 6f Epsom maiden last time, he needed this seventh furlong as he was outpaced at halfway when the tempo increased. He got there in plenty of time, though, cutting up several of his rivals in the process, and was good value for the win. (op 6-5)

Butch And Sundance, a Yarmouth maiden winner who got going too late on his recent nursery debut, was again ridden under restraint, but picked up well when switched to the outside and chased the winner hard, but was never getting to him. He looks well worth a shot at 1m now.

Avon River, one place behind the runner-up at Newbury, ran to form back in third but doesn't look up to winning off his current mark. (op 8-1)

Nina Rose looked open to improvement on this nursery debut, especially as she was stepping up to 7f for the first time, and she ran well considering she was badly hampered by the winner. (op 9-1)

Janeiro(IRE) improved for the step up to 7f when winning at Yarmouth last time, but he needed to have progressed to make an impact off a mark of 87 on this nursery debut and he wasn't up to it. (op 5-1 tchd 9-2)

Thomas Baines(USA) was already in trouble when hampered. (op 9-1 tchd 17-2)

Pullyourfingerout(IRE) was beaten quickly once headed. (tchd 20-1)

Mnarani(IRE) Official explanation: jockey said gelding was denied a clear run

4902 GOLDRING SECURITY SERVICES PEMBROKE CUP (H'CAP) — 1m

3:35 (3:36) (Class 4) (0-85,83) 3-Y-O — **£4,857** (£1,445; £722; £360) **Stalls** Centre

Form — RPR

-654 **1** **Marching Time**[60] [2935] 3-9-7 **83**.......... RyanMoore 2 — 92+
(Sir Michael Stoute) *lw: hld up in rr: hdwy on outside 3f out to ld 2f out: drvn and hld to one side 1f out: kpt on wl* **11/8**[1]

2-26 **2** 2 ¾ **Wilfred Pickles (IRE)**[83] [2210] 3-9-1 **77**.......... (t) JimCrowley 7 — 79
(Mrs A J Perrett) *trckd ldr tl slt ld 5f out tl over 3f out: styd disputing 2nd and chsd wnr fnl f but a wl hld* **8/1**

-421 **3** 1 **Block Party**[16] [4381] 3-9-4 **80**.......... JamieSpencer 9 — 80
(R Charlton) *sn led: c wd and narrowly hdd 5f out tl led again over 3f out: hdd 2f out: sn rdn: styd on same pce fr over 1f out* **5/2**[2]

5050 **4** nse **Ballyalla**[41] [3537] 3-9-1 **77**.......... WilliamBuick 4 — 76
(R Hannon) *awkward s: in rr: rdn and outpcd 3f out: styd on u.p fnl f to press for readily hld 3rd cl home* **16/1**

-304 **5** nk **All About You (IRE)**[60] [2926] 3-9-6 **82**.......... SebSanders 8 — 81
(W J Haggas) *chsd ldrs: rdn over 2f out: styd on same pce fr over 1f out* **6/1**[3]

4-01 **6** ½ **Directorship**[20] [4246] 3-9-7 **83**.......... LPKeniry 3 — 81
(P R Chamings) *lw: towards rr: rdn and hdwy fr 2f out: nvr rchd ldrs and one pce fr over 1f out* **10/1**

-620 **7** 8 **Levitation (IRE)**[26] [4050] 3-8-11 **73**.......... FergusSweeney 6 — 51
(W S Kittow) *chsd ldrs: rdn 3f out: wknd 2f out* **20/1**

1m 43.2s (-0.30) **Going Correction** -0.175s/f (Firm) — **7** Ran SP% **115.8**

Speed ratings (Par 102): **94,91,90,90,89 89,81**

toteswinger: 1&2 £3.70, 1&3 £1.20, 2&3 £2.90. CSF £13.88 CT £25.73 TOTE £2.00: £1.70, £3.60; EX 14.30.

Owner K Abdulla **Bred** Juddmonte Farms Ltd **Trained** Newmarket, Suffolk

FOCUS

An ordinary handicap won in good style by Marching Time.

4903 EUROPEAN BREEDERS' FUND UPAVON FILLIES' STKS (LISTED RACE) — 1m 1f 198y

4:05 (4:06) (Class 1) 3-Y-O+

£28,385 (£10,760; £5,385; £2,685; £1,345; £675) **Stalls** High

Form — RPR

-312 **1** **Ave**[19] [4287] 3-8-7 106 ow2.......... RyanMoore 10 — 104
(Sir Michael Stoute) *trckd ldrs: led 2f out: wnt rt to far rail over 1f out: pushed out: readily* **5/4**[1]

-415 **2** 1 ¼ **Splashdown**[25] [4094] 3-8-9 102.......... WilliamBuick 7 — 104
(L M Cumani) *lw: in tch: rdn along over 2f out: styd on wl fr over 1f out and sn chsng wnr: kpt on but a readily hld* **4/1**[2]

-331 **3** 3 **Sterling Sound (USA)**[17] [4337] 3-8-5 79.......... TPO'Shea 1 — 94
(M P Tregoning) *lw: in rr: rdn and hung rt 2f out: styd on fr over 1f out and kpt on fnl f but nvr anywhere nr ldng duo* **20/1**

0026 **4** nk **Syvilla**[25] [4094] 4-9-0 89.......... WilliamCarson 6 — 93
(Rae Guest) *sn chsng ldr: rdn over 2f out: lost 2nd and swtchd lft over 1f out: wknd sn after* **33/1**

361- **5** 2 ¼ **Cape Amber (IRE)**[329] [6034] 4-9-0 107.......... SebSanders 2 — 89
(R M Beckett) *t.k.h: sn led: hdd 2f out: wknd appr fnl f* **9/2**[3]

50-3 **6** 1 **Sweet Lilly**[19] [4287] 5-9-0 105.......... EdwardCreighton 3 — 87
(M R Channon) *nvr travelling in rr: drvn along fr over 4f out: mod prog fr over 1f out* **7/1**

7 1 ¾ **Wymering File (IRE)**[68] 4-9-0 0.......... NKNicolaou 8 — 83
(Petros Petroutsios, Cyprus) *broke wl: stdd in rr: rdn 3f out and nvr any ch* **10/1**

0-14 **8** 1 ¼ **Cosmea**[51] [3213] 4-9-0 81.......... FergusSweeney 4 — 81
(A King) *chsd ldrs: rdn and wknd qckly 2f out* **25/1**

2m 5.99s (-3.91) **Going Correction** -0.175s/f (Firm)

WFA 3 from 4yo+ 9lb — **8** Ran SP% **115.8**

Speed ratings (Par 108): **108,107,104,104,102 101,100,99**

toteswinger: 1&2 £2.30, 1&3 £5.00, 2&3 £11.10. CSF £6.30 TOTE £2.00: £1.20, £1.50, £3.60; EX 6.40.

Owner Plantation Stud **Bred** Plantation Stud **Trained** Newmarket, Suffolk

FOCUS

This Listed prize was run at a fair gallop and the Classic generation dominated.

NOTEBOOK

Ave won in quite ready fashion, going to the front inside the two and quickly racing clear. Runner-up to High Heeled in this company at York last time, she was faced with lesser opposition on this occasion and she confirmed herself to be a most progressive filly. The step up to middle-distances has enabled her to take her form to another level and connections will no doubt be keen to try and win a Group contest with her now. (op 11-10 tchd 10-11, 11-8 in places)

Splashdown, already a winner at this level earlier in the season, failed to stay 1m4f last time and she ran much better on this drop in trip, staying on to chase the winner without ever looking likely to seriously shake her up. She remains capable of better. (op 6-1 tchd 7-1)

Sterling Sound(USA) stayed on well inside the final furlong to just snatch third. Winner of a minor maiden at Ascot last time, that victory has clearly done her confidence the world of good and she now has some valuable black type to her name. (op 25-1)

Syvilla looked up against it facing a few unexposed sorts and she ran as well as could have been expected, coming out best of the older generation.

Cape Amber(IRE), officially the highest-rated runner in the field, raced keenly in a clear lead and was always likely to tire on this return from around an 11-month absence. She still ran respectably for a long way, though, and can probably win again at this level if going the right way. (op 5-1 tchd 11-2)

Sweet Lilly, one place behind the winner at York on her belated reappearance, never really looked happy and made only limited late headway. Official explanation: trainer said mare was in season (tchd 13-2)

Wymering File(IRE), the top filly in Cyprus who has been successful in eight of her 12 starts from 5f-1m4f, was making her turf debut and offered little immediate promise, fading for pressure inside the final quarter mile. She is due to join Irish trainer Michael Grassick now, but evidently needs to raise her game. (op 8-1)

4904 CHAMPAGNE JOSEPH PERRIER H'CAP — 1m 1f 198y

4:40 (4:41) (Class 5) (0-70,70) 3-Y-O+ — **£3,238** (£963; £481; £240) **Stalls** High

Form — RPR

3260 **1** **Wilbury Star (IRE)**[23] [4149] 3-9-9 **70**.......... (b[1]) PatrickHills(3) 10 — 78
(R Hannon) *in tch: hdwy 3f out: led appr fnl 2f: pushed out ins fnl f* **8/1**[3]

6440 **2** 1 **Oriental Girl**[40] [3581] 4-9-7 **59**.......... (v[1]) MarcHalford(3) 4 — 65
(J A Geake) *in tch but bustled along 4f out: styd on wl fr 2f out and kpt on ins fnl f to take 2nd cl home but no imp on wnr* **9/1**

4302 **3** nk **Streets Apart (USA)**[26] [4054] 4-10-0 **63**.......... (p) AdamKirby 1 — 68
(W R Swinburn) *lw: led after 1f: narrowly hdd appr fnl 2f: styd disputing 2nd and hung rt u.p 1f out: lost 2nd cl home* **6/1**[2]

-520 **4** nk **Silent Act (USA)**[23] [4156] 3-9-0 **58**.......... JimCrowley 6 — 63+
(Mrs A J Perrett) *s.i.s: in rr: stl plenty to do whn hdwy over 1f out: styd on strly fnl f: fin wl to take 3rd nr fin* **17/2**

5006 **5** ¾ **Dream On Connie**[27] [4010] 3-9-0 **63**.......... (t) Louis-PhilippeBeuzelin(5) 11 — 66
(W J Knight) *in tch: chsd ldrs and rdn 3f out: styng on same pce whn hmpd 1f out: no imp after* **6/1**[2]

6-60 **6** 2 ¼ **Champagne Fizz (IRE)**[18] [4305] 3-9-4 **62**.......... EdwardCreighton 9 — 61
(Miss Jo Crowley) *chsd ldr after 1f: rdn over 3f out: dropped bk to cl 3rd over 2f out: wknd fnl f* **20/1**

0002 **7** 1 **Regal Blush**[10] [4569] 3-9-4 **62**.......... WilliamBuick 13 — 59
(A M Balding) *led 1f: styd chsng ldrs: rdn and n.m.r over 2f out: sn swtchd lft and sme hdwy: nvr rchd ldrs and wknd fnl f* **11/4**[1]

0025 **8** hd **Sixties Swinger (USA)**[37] [3674] 3-9-6 **64**.......... (t) PhilipRobinson 8 — 60
(M A Jarvis) *chsd ldrs: drvn to chal over 2f out: styd front rnk tl over 1f out: wknd ins fnl f* **8/1**[3]

-055 **9** 3 **Carte D'Oro (IRE)**[49] [3279] 3-9-5 **63**.......... SebSanders 7 — 53
(R M Beckett) *in rr: edgd lft and sme prog over 2f out: nvr in contention and sn wknd* **14/1**

0050 **10** 7 **Lady Oakesy**[8] [4625] 3-8-11 **55**.......... FergusSweeney 3 — 31
(W S Kittow) *a towards rr* **33/1**

0030 **11** ½ **Paul's Pet**[35] [3735] 4-9-4 **53**.......... TPO'Shea 2 — 28
(Karen George) *s.i.s: in rr: mod prog on outside whn edgd lft over 2f out and sn wknd* **12/1**

2m 11.18s (1.28) **Going Correction** -0.175s/f (Firm)

WFA 3 from 4yo 9lb — **11** Ran SP% **120.0**

Speed ratings (Par 103): **87,86,85,85,85 83,82,82,79,74 73**

toteswinger: 1&2 £14.80, 1&3 £5.80, 2&3 £10.50. CSF £79.72 CT £470.22 TOTE £9.80: £3.40, £3.30, £1.50; EX 73.70.

Owner John Tobin, Ian Higginson & Fergus Carey **Bred** Rathasker Stud **Trained** East Everleigh, Wilts

■ Stewards' Enquiry : Adam Kirby two-day ban: careless riding (Aug 26-27)

FOCUS
This was a low-grade handicap.
Paul's Pet Official explanation: jockey said gelding lost its action

4905 AXMINSTER CARPETS APPRENTICE H'CAP (WHIPS SHALL BE CARRIED BUT NOT USED) 6f 212y
5:10 (5:10) (Class 5) (0-70,68) 3-Y-0+ **£3,238** (£963; £481; £240) **Stalls** Centre

Form RPR
356 **1** **Getcarter**[62] 2849 3-9-11 **68** .... CharlesEddery[(3)] 3 84
(R Hannon) *lw: in tch: hdwy 3f out: led ins fnl 2f: hung lft to stands' side thrght fnl f but a in command* **4/1**[1]
00 **2** *4 ½* **Cheap Street**[25] 4082 5-9-12 **60** .... RosieJessop 6 66
(J G Portman) *in tch: hdwy over 2f out: sn pushed along: styd on to chse wnr ins fnl f but nvr any ch* **12/1**
4064 **3** *2 ¼* **Bahkov (IRE)**[29] 3939 3-8-12 **57** .... AlexEdwards[(5)] 12 55
(Andrew Turnell) *chsd ldrs wnt 2nd over 1f out but nvr any ch w wnr: sn wknd and lost 2nd ins fnl f* **13/2**
-000 **4** *1* **Flashy Photon**[14] 4428 4-10-0 **62** .... AmyScott 10 59
(H Candy) *in rr: pushed along and hdwy fr 2f out: styd on fnl f but nvr in contention* **8/1**
2520 **5** *1* **Sermons Mount (USA)**[5] 4730 3-8-9 **54** .... RyanClark[(5)] 7 47
(Mouse Hamilton-Fairley) *in tch: pushed along fr 3f out: styd on same pce fnl 2f* **5/1**[2]
0200 **6** *½* **Wooden King (IRE)**[11] 4536 4-8-13 **52** .... (p) JakePayne[(5)] 5 45
(M S Saunders) *led: rdn: hdd and hung lft fr ins fnl 2f: wknd over 1f out* **12/1**
3050 **7** *nk* **Nun Today (USA)**[21] 4202 3-8-7 **47** .... (p) DeclanCannon 11 37
(Karen George) *chsd ldrs: rdn and faltered 5f out: styd on through btn horses fnl f* **12/1**
2000 **8** *1 ¾* **Divine White**[11] 4533 6-8-11 **48** .... LauraPike[(3)] 4 36
(G P Enright) *chsd ldrs: ev ch 2f out: hung lft and wknd over 1f out* **33/1**
-002 **9** *½* **Hold The Star**[86] 2141 3-9-9 **63** .... (v[1]) TobyAtkinson 8 47
(E F Vaughan) *in tch early: styd alone on far rail and no ch fr over 2f out* **13/2**
046 **10** *3 ¼* **Akabar**[18] 4324 3-9-4 **58** .... (b[1]) JPFahy 1 34
(R M Beckett) *s.i.s: sn pressing ldrs: ev ch over 2f out: hung lft and wknd qckly over 1f out* **6/1**[3]

1m 28.96s (-0.04) **Going Correction** -0.175s/f (Firm)
WFA 3 from 4yo+ 6lb **10** Ran SP% **114.7**
Speed ratings (Par 103): **93,87,85,84,83 82,82,80,79,75**
toteswinger: 1&2 £13.70, 1&3 £7.80, 2&3 £17.80. CSF £52.05 CT £312.21 TOTE £4.40: £1.80, £4.10, £2.80; EX 50.10 Place 6 £37.04, Place 5 £18.44.
Owner Mrs J K Powell **Bred** C R Mason **Trained** East Everleigh, Wilts

FOCUS
This apprentices' handicap was dominated by Getcarter.
T/Plt: £33.60 to a £1 stake. Pool: £62,912.52. 1,363.01 winning tickets. T/Qpdt: £15.10 to a £1 stake. Pool: £3,434.40. 167.55 winning tickets. ST

4711 SANDOWN (R-H)
Wednesday, August 12

OFFICIAL GOING: Good (good to firm in places; 8.6)
Home bend at mid-configuration and home straight dolled out 5yards adding about 5yards to race distances on round course.
Wind: Light, against Weather: Overcast

4906 SHEENGATE PUBLISHING MAIDEN STKS 5f 6y
5:30 (5:30) (Class 5) 2-Y-O **£3,238** (£963; £481; £240) **Stalls** High

Form RPR
4532 **1** **Bridge Valley**[19] 4265 2-9-3 73 .... RichardHughes 5 78+
(R Hannon) *last of main gp and pushed along after 2f: plld out wd and gd prog over 1f out: rdn to ld last 150yds: sn wl in command* **10/3**[3]
425 **2** *1 ¼* **Key Art (IRE)**[18] 4331 2-9-3 77 .... LDettori 9 73
(J Noseda) *racd against far rail: led: stretched on over 1f out: hdd and outpcd last 150yds* **11/4**[2]
3 *2 ¼* **Felsham** 2-9-3 0 .... DaneO'Neill 2 65
(H Candy) *cl up: rdn to chse ldr briefly over 1f out: sn outpcd* **9/2**
6 **4** *nk* **Admiral Cochrane (IRE)**[11] 4515 2-9-3 0 .... JimmyFortune 7 64
(W Jarvis) *racd against far rail: trckd ldrs: effrt to dispute 2nd briefly over 1f out: sn wl outpcd* **14/1**
00 **5** *1 ¾* **Joan's Legacy**[18] 4323 2-8-12 0 .... RichardSmith 4 53
(J C Fox) *in tch: effrt and nt squeezed for room over 1f out: wknd fnl f* **66/1**
6 *3 ½* **Freeforaday (USA)** 2-9-3 0 .... SteveDrowne 6 45
(J R Best) *chsd ldr to over 1f out: wknd rapidly* **16/1**
7 *40* **Annacaboe (IRE)** 2-8-12 0 .... RichardThomas 3 —
(Mrs L C Jewell) *dwlt: rel to r and sn t.o* **100/1**
5 **U** **Wellington Fair**[46] 3402 2-9-0 0 .... DavidProbert[(3)] 1 —
(C G Cox) *swvd lft and uns rdr sn after s* **9/4**[1]

62.53 secs (0.93) **Going Correction** +0.20s/f (Good) **8** Ran SP% **113.7**
Speed ratings (Par 94): **100,98,94,93,91 85,21,—**
toteswinger: 1&2 £1.70, 1&3 £6.80, 2&3 £3.70. CSF £12.80 TOTE £4.90: £1.50, £1.10, £1.90; EX 9.00.
Owner D J Deer **Bred** D J And Mrs Deer **Trained** East Everleigh, Wilts

FOCUS
Only four were really considered in this maiden.

NOTEBOOK
Bridge Valley was the most experienced runner in the race but was dropping in trip having run all his previous races over 6f and 7f. He struggled to go the early pace, but his stamina kicked in over a furlong out and he swept past his rivals to win somewhat cosily. This should act as a confidence booster but it will be no surprise to see him back over 6f before long, probably in nurseries. (op 11-4)
Key Art(IRE) made the running nearest the rail and looked in charge entering the final furlong. However, he was run down late by the strong-finishing winner. He looks capable of winning a race at this trip, possibly on a flatter track. (op 5-2 tchd 3-1 and 100-30 in places)
Felsham, a half-brother to the stable's Oldjoesaid, was making his debut but it was interesting to see that the trainer met him at the start and he was loaded using a blanket. He was quickly enough away and raced up with the pace throughout, but could not pick up in the closing stages. Although clearly not the most straightforward, he has ability and should be able to go on from this. (tchd 5-1)
Admiral Cochrane(IRE) had shown some promise over 6f, on soft ground, on his debut and built on that, despite the different conditions. He had his chance inside the last two furlongs, but couldn't find an extra gear. (op 16-1)
Joan's Legacy, who had been well held in 6f maidens prior to this, tends to limit the form. However, she now qualifies for handicaps, which should improve her chances of success. (op 100-1 tchd 50-1)
Wellington Fair who was drawn in stall one, tried to go back the way he had come to the start and decanted his rider after 50 yards, in the process ending the chance of Annacaboe who tried to follow him. This can be regarded as an aberration rather than a sign of quirkiness. (op 3-1)

4907 WATCH RACING UK ON SKY CHANNEL 432 H'CAP 5f 6y
6:00 (6:02) (Class 4) (0-80,80) 4-Y-0+ **£4,857** (£1,445; £722; £360) **Stalls** High

Form RPR
-041 **1** **Royal Intruder**[15] 4414 4-9-3 **74** .... RichardHughes 10 81+
(S Donohoe, Ire) *hld up in last quartet: looking for room fr 2f out: squeezed through ent fnl f: r.o to ld post* **11/4**[1]
360 **2** *nse* **Step It Up (IRE)**[9] 4604 5-8-4 **61** oh2 .... FrankieMcDonald 4 68
(J R Boyle) *chsd ldrs: rdn over 1f out: prog to ld ins fnl f: kpt on wl: hdd post* **25/1**
30-4 **3** *hd* **Handsome Cross (IRE)**[20] 4232 8-9-1 **72** .... JimmyFortune 5 78+
(W J Musson) *hld up in 8th: prog over 1f out: squeezed through ent fnl f: drvn and r.o: jst hld* **11/2**[2]
3640 **4** *½* **Brandywell Boy (IRE)**[9] 4604 6-8-4 **61** .... RichardThomas 6 65
(D J S Ffrench Davis) *disp 2nd pl: drvn to ld 1f out: hdd and one pce ins fnl f* **16/1**
1450 **5** *¾* **Golden Dixie (USA)**[22] 4167 10-8-10 **70** .... KevinGhunowa[(3)] 8 71
(R A Harris) *awkward s: chsd ldrs: rdn over 2f out: nvr much room fr over 1f out but kpt on pressing* **25/1**
0060 **6** *hd* **Gentle Guru**[16] 4380 5-9-3 **74** .... SteveDrowne 1 75
(R T Phillips) *s.i.s: hld up in last quartet: rdn and wdst of all 2f out: prog to chse ldrs 1f out: kpt on same pce* **16/1**
5205 **7** *½* **Kyllachy Storm**[27] 3995 5-9-1 **72** .... DarryllHolland 12 71+
(R J Hodges) *s.i.s: hld up in last quartet: trapped on inner fr 2f out: last ent fnl f: pushed along and r.o: fin on heels of ldrs* **9/1**
0532 **8** *nse* **Requisite**[11] 4530 4-9-1 **72** .... (v) DaneO'Neill 9 71
(I A Wood) *s.i.s: settled in last quartet: shkn up and effrt on outer 2f out: kpt on same pce and nvr able to chal* **8/1**
000 **9** *2 ½* **Elhamri**[37] 3694 5-9-6 **77** .... JamesDoyle 7 71+
(S Kirk) *mostly chsd ldr: led briefly jst over 1f out: wkng whn no room and snatched up 100yds out* **10/1**
5213 **10** *nse* **Blessed Place**[7] 4662 9-8-1 **61** oh4 .... DavidProbert[(3)] 2 50
(D J S Ffrench Davis) *racd wd: led to jst over 1f out: wknd ins fnl f* **14/1**
0036 **11** *¾* **Even Bolder**[10] 4567 6-9-0 **71** .... StephenCarson 13 58+
(E A Wheeler) *hld up bhd ldrs on inner: nt clr run fr 2f out to 1f out: keeping on at one pce whn hmpd and snatched up 100yds out* **13/2**[3]
3000 **12** *2 ¼* **Commander Wish**[23] 4141 6-8-5 **62** .... (p) NeilChalmers 11 41
(Lucinda Featherstone) *racd against far rail: disp 2nd pl to over 1f out: wknd rapidly fnl f* **18/1**

61.87 secs (0.27) **Going Correction** +0.20s/f (Good) **12** Ran SP% **117.0**
Speed ratings (Par 105): **105,104,104,103,102 102,101,101,97,97 96,92**
toteswinger: 1&2 £30.20, 1&3 £3.30, 2&3 £48.90. CSF £81.16 CT £357.63 TOTE £3.20: £1.50, £7.80, £1.30; EX 127.60.
Owner Mrs Anna McDwyer **Bred** Farmers Hill Stud **Trained** Cootehill Road, Co. Cavan

FOCUS
This fair sprint has been won by some subsequently decent performers and had fallen to high-drawn horses on each of the four previous renewals. It did so again, but this was quite a rough race and there were several hard-luck stories.
Kyllachy Storm Official explanation: jockey said gelding was denied a clear run
Elhamri Official explanation: jockey said gelding suffered interference in running
Even Bolder Official explanation: jockey said gelding was denied a clear run

4908 CHAMPAGNE LANSON MEDIAN AUCTION MAIDEN STKS 7f 16y
6:35 (6:38) (Class 5) 2-Y-O **£3,238** (£963; £481; £240) **Stalls** High

Form RPR
3 **1** **Al Ghazal (USA)**[37] 3692 2-9-3 0 .... LDettori 1 83+
(Saeed Bin Suroor) *trckd ldrs: pushed along on outer 3f out: prog 2f out: rdn to ld jst over 1f out: styd on wl* **1/1**[1]
2 *1 ¼* **Champagne Style (USA)** 2-9-3 0 .... TedDurcan 7 78+
(B J Meehan) *dwlt: sn trckd ldrs: pushed along 2f out: nt qckn over 1f out: styd on wl fnl f to take 2nd last strides* **25/1**
5 **3** *nk* **Ultravox (USA)**[26] 4048 2-9-3 0 .... JamieSpencer 10 77
(B J Meehan) *prom: chsd ldr 4f out: hrd rdn to chal over 1f out: chsd wnr fnl f but sn hld: lost 2nd last strides* **9/4**[2]
03 **4** *1* **White Devil**[14] 4439 2-9-3 0 .... LPKeniry 4 75
(A M Balding) *led over 5f out: rdn 2f out: hdd and one pce jst over 1f out* **8/1**[3]
5 *4* **Henry San (IRE)** 2-9-3 0 .... DaneO'Neill 9 65
(A King) *chsd ldrs: shkn up and outpcd over 2f out: plugged on same pce after* **50/1**
6 *¾* **Kerchak (USA)** 2-9-3 0 .... JimmyFortune 5 63
(W Jarvis) *dwlt: off the pce in last trio and rn green: effrt over 2f out: disp 6th over 1f out: plugged on: nvr on terms* **33/1**
0 **7** *½* **Mahjong Girl**[33] 3810 2-8-9 0 .... JackMitchell[(3)] 8 57+
(R M Beckett) *stdd s: hld up in 8th: nt clr run over 2f out and again over 1f out: kpt on but no ch* **66/1**
8 *1* **Finest Reserve (IRE)** 2-9-3 0 .... TonyCulhane 6 59+
(M R Channon) *dwlt: rn green and sn detached in last: wl bhd 1/2-way: shkn up and styd on fr over 2f out: nrst fin* **66/1**
00 **9** *3* **Our Boy Barrington (IRE)**[46] 3395 2-9-3 0 .... RichardHughes 11 52
(R Hannon) *led to over 5f out: prom after: stl cl up over 1f out: wknd rapidly* **25/1**
10 *3* **Krymian** 2-9-3 0 .... RyanMoore 2 44+
(Sir Michael Stoute) *dwlt: rn green and pushed along over 4f out: nvr on terms after: wknd over 1f out* **8/1**[3]
11 *nk* **Dinkie Short** 2-9-3 0 .... DarryllHolland 3 43
(W R Muir) *sn wl in rr: dropped to last and wl bhd over 2f out* **66/1**

1m 30.62s (1.12) **Going Correction** +0.125s/f (Good) **11** Ran SP% **120.1**
Speed ratings (Par 94): **98,96,96,95,90 89,89,87,84,81 80**
toteswinger: 1&2 £6.70, 1&3 £1.50, 2&3 £11.40. CSF £36.98 TOTE £2.50: £1.10, £5.30, £1.40; EX 36.20.
Owner Godolphin **Bred** Darley **Trained** Newmarket, Suffolk

FOCUS
There were several expensive and/or well-entered sorts in this maiden, but all four previous winners of this contest had run once prior to scoring here, so experience seemed likely to play an important part.

NOTEBOOK

Al Ghazal(USA) justified favouritism, having made a promising debut in a Windsor maiden that is working out; four of those behind having scored since. His rider took his time before making his challenge but the colt asserted inside the final furlong and should go on from this. He has a fair way to go though, if he is to live up to entries in races such as the Dewhurst and Royal Lodge. (tchd 10-11 and 5-4 tchd 11-8 in a place)

Champagne Style(USA) ◆ is a half-brother to winners on both dirt and turf in the US. Although appearing to be the stable second-string, he was never far off the pace and stayed on well in the closing stages despite appearing in need of the experience. He should be sharper next time. (op 20-1)

Ultravox(USA), the better-fancied stable companion of the runner-up, was backed against the favourite and was given a positive ride. He had his chance but could not find any extra in the final furlong. (op 100-30 tchd 2-1)

White Devil, all three of whose appearances have been over course and distance, made a bold bid from the front but was headed inside the last furlong and was run out of the places late on. He is quite a keen sort and may be seen to best effect on a sharper track. (op 15-2 tchd 7-1)

Kerchak(USA), related to a winner in the US, was noted keeping on quite nicely from the back and should come on for the experience. (op 25-1)

Our Boy Barrington(IRE) showed up for a long way before fading quite quickly in the last furlong. He has done that on both starts over this trip and, now qualified for handicaps, he will be of interest if dropped in trip and racing in that grade. (op 20-1)

Krymianshould know a lot more next time, having looked quite green.\n (tchd 12-1)

4909 NEWLIFE FOUNDATION FOR DISABLED CHILDREN H'CAP — 7f 16y

7:10 (7:12) (Class 3) (0-90,86) 3-Y-O — **£7,771** (£2,312; £1,155; £577) **Stalls** High

Form — RPR

4223 **1** **Sir Isaac**[11] 4540 3-9-1 **78** ... KirstyMilczarek 1 — 87
(W J Haggas) *mde all: urged along whn pressed 2f out: kpt on wl fnl f: pushed out* — **4/1**[2]

6262 **2** ¾ **Hail Promenader (IRE)**[18] 4326 3-9-5 **82** ... MichaelHills 5 — 89
(B W Hills) *a chsng wnr: rdn to try to cl over 2f out: pressing after but a hld fnl f* — **9/1**

3101 **3** ¾ **Broad Cairn**[21] 4210 3-9-7 **84** ... SteveDrowne 8 — 94+
(R Charlton) *hld up in 7th: effrt on wd outside 2f out: rdn jst over 1f out: styd on to take 3rd ins fnl f: too much to do* — **11/2**[3]

1265 **4** ½ **Militarist (USA)**[18] 4316 3-9-9 **86** ... JimmyFortune 6 — 90
(J H M Gosden) *chsd ldng pair: rdn and nt qckn 2f out: no real imp after: kpt on but lost 3rd ins fnl f* — **7/1**

1553 **5** 1 ¼ **Thousand Miles (IRE)**[21] 4210 3-9-6 **83** ... RyanMoore 10 — 83
(P W Chapple-Hyam) *hld up in 5th: rdn 2f out: hanging and nt qckn over 1f out: kpt on ins fnl f* — **13/2**

5132 **6** nse **Peking Prince**[18] 4296 3-9-8 **85** ... (v) WilliamBuick 4 — 85
(A M Balding) *hld up in 6th: shkn up on outer and nt qckn 2f out: lost pl sn after: nt clr run ent fnl f: kpt on nr fin* — **3/1**[1]

-124 **7** 2 ¾ **Maswerte (IRE)**[25] 4095 3-9-5 **82** ... DaneO'Neill 9 — 75
(L M Cumani) *chsd ldng trio: rdn over 2f out: nt qckn and lost pl over 1f out: fdd* — **9/1**

5030 **8** 2 ½ **Key Signature**[20] 4228 3-9-2 **79** ... (b) LDettori 7 — 65
(Pat Eddery) *mostly last: brief effrt on inner over 2f out: no prog over 1f out: wknd* — **12/1**

1m 30.05s (0.55) **Going Correction** +0.125s/f (Good) — **8** Ran SP% **113.9**
Speed ratings (Par 104): **101,100,99,98,97 97,94,91**
toteswinger: 1&2 £9.60, 1&3 £4.10, 2&3 £11.10. CSF £38.93 CT £198.35 TOTE £4.40: £1.80, £3.20, £1.90; EX 36.40.
Owner Mr & Mrs R Scott **Bred** Mr & Mrs R & P Scott **Trained** Newmarket, Suffolk

FOCUS

A decent-looking 3yo handicap and several of the previous winners of the corresponding race had gone on to better things. The pace was not that strong and was only 0.57secs faster than the preceding juvenile maiden.

NOTEBOOK

Sir Isaac had been running pretty well all season and had previous experience of this track. He had finished third in a handicap at Newmarket, and the two horses from that race to have run since had both won, so it was unsurprising he was supported in the market. He jumped well from his outside draw and got the better of a brief tussle for the lead with the eventual runner-up. Dictating the gallop from then on, his rider kicked over two furlongs out and was always holding the remainder from that point. This was only his seventh start and further progression seems likely. (op 9-2 tchd 5-1 in a place)

Hail Promenader(IRE) again ran his race and looks a good guide to the level of the form. He conceded the early advantage to the winner, but never let that rival get too far ahead and made his challenge in the last quarter-mile, although was always being held. He looks high enough in the weights now, but might benefit from a return to slightly easier ground. (op 11-1 tchd 12-1)

Broad Cairn did best of those held up off the pace. He was still at the rear when the race began in earnest over two furlongs out, but stayed on quite well and was gradually reeling in the principals as the line approached. He has won at 1m and would have preferred a stiffer test at this trip. (tchd 5-1)

Militarist(USA) tracked the leading pair throughout and stuck to his task under pressure. The drop in trip seemed to help a little but he might be worth trying from the front. (op 8-1 tchd 13-2)

Thousand Miles(IRE) was 5lb better off with the third for just over two lengths compared with their running here in July but could not reverse the placings. He is another 1m winner and looked to be caught out for a change of gear when the pace quickened. (op 8-1 tchd 6-1)

Peking Prince had just lost out in a heritage handicap at Ascot last time when the visor was fitted for the first time but he could not pick up from the back as those at the head of affairs quickened. He was not done any favours by the third when trying to make his effort but his recent record suggests that a decent gallop and possibly a straight track suits him best. (op 11-4 tchd 7-2)

4910 BUY A RACING POST YEARLING BONUS CANDIDATE H'CAP — 1m 2f 7y

7:45 (7:46) (Class 4) (0-80,80) 3-Y-O — **£4,857** (£1,445; £722; £360) **Stalls** High

Form — RPR

0112 **1** **Brett Vale (IRE)**[62] 2865 3-9-6 **77** ... SebSanders 2 — 91
(Sir Mark Prescott) *trckd ldr after 1f: led jst over 2f out: rdn clr fr over 1f out: unchal* — **3/1**[2]

4112 **2** 6 **Sequillo**[6] 4715 3-9-7 **78** ... RichardHughes 9 — 80+
(R Hannon) *dwlt: hld up in last trio: trapped on inner over 2f out: stl there as wnr wnt clr over 1f out: prog after: tk 2nd ins fnl f: no ch* — **7/4**[1]

-005 **3** ½ **Swift Chap**[14] 4440 3-9-1 **75** ... JamesMillman(3) 8 — 76
(B R Millman) *cl up: nt clr run over 2f out: rdn to chse wnr over 1f out: no imp: lost 2nd ins fnl f* — **8/1**

3600 **4** 1 ¾ **Princability (IRE)**[11] 4520 3-9-0 **71** ... TonyCulhane 3 — 69
(M R Channon) *hld up in last pair: shkn up on outer over 2f out: sn nt qckn: kpt on to take 4th ins fnl f* — **33/1**

4520 **5** 1 ½ **Night Lily (IRE)**[26] 4054 3-8-9 **66** ... (t) LPKeniry 1 — 61
(J Jay) *cl up on outer: rdn to dispute 3rd 2f out: nt qckn over 1f out: lost pl and n.d after* — **22/1**

0-50 **6** nk **Silver Print (USA)**[19] 4275 3-9-1 **72** ... AdamKirby 4 — 66
(W R Swinburn) *hld up in last trio: shkn up on outer over 2f out: nt qckn and no imp: fdd ins fnl f* — **9/1**

4100 **7** 1 ¼ **London Bridge**[55] 3051 3-9-9 **80** ... JimmyFortune 5 — 71
(J H M Gosden) *led to jst over 2f out: wknd over 1f out* — **11/2**[3]

1322 **8** ¾ **Sumani (FR)**[21] 4206 3-8-10 **67** ... IanMongan 6 — 57
(S Dow) *trckd ldr 1f: styd cl up on inner: n.m.r over 2f out: wknd over 1f out* — **10/1**

2m 9.23s (-1.27) **Going Correction** +0.125s/f (Good) — **8** Ran SP% **114.2**
Speed ratings (Par 102): **110,105,104,103,102 101,100,100**
toteswinger: 1&2 £1.10, 1&3 £9.40, 2&3 £6.10. CSF £8.63 CT £35.79 TOTE £4.50: £1.70, £1.30, £2.10; EX 9.60.
Owner G D Waters **Bred** Mrs O Murtagh **Trained** Newmarket, Suffolk

FOCUS

An ordinary 3yo handicap that often falls to an improving type and did so again

4911 ISINGLASS H'CAP — 1m 6f

8:15 (8:15) (Class 4) (0-80,79) 3-Y-O — **£4,857** (£1,445; £722; £360) **Stalls** High

Form — RPR

2532 **1** **Ermyn Lodge**[14] 4442 3-8-6 **62** ... (v) FergusSweeney 2 — 69
(P M Phelan) *pushed up to ld after 2f: mde rest: drvn 2f out: jnd ins fnl f: styd on stoutly last 100yds* — **8/1**

2061 **2** ¾ **Dice (IRE)**[37] 3674 3-9-2 **72** ... JamieSpencer 8 — 78
(L M Cumani) *trckd ldng trio: effrt over 2f out: hrd rdn to go 2nd over 1f out: jnd wnr ins fnl f: nt qckn last 100yds* — **5/1**[2]

3511 **3** 2 ¼ **Curacao**[18] 4325 3-9-9 **79** ... JimCrowley 10 — 82+
(Mrs A J Perrett) *hld up in last pair: reminder over 2f out: stl only 8th over 1f out: drvn and r.o fnl f to take 3rd nr fin: hopeless task* — **11/2**[3]

3121 **4** nk **Sherman McCoy**[18] 4319 3-9-6 **79** ... JamesMillman(3) 4 — 81
(B R Millman) *hld up in 6th: shkn up over 2f out: wandering and nt qckn: styd on fnl f: tk 4th nr fin* — **4/1**[1]

1050 **5** ½ **Taste The Wine (IRE)**[11] 4545 3-8-11 **67** ... RichardHughes 7 — 69
(J S Moore) *hld up in 7th: rdn on wd outside 3f out: prog u.p 2f out: wnt 3rd 1f out: no imp on ldng pair: lost 2 pls nr fin* — **12/1**

036 **6** 3 ¼ **Miss Doodle**[19] 4270 3-8-5 **61** ... WilliamBuick 5 — 58
(Eve Johnson Houghton) *prom: lost pl 3f out: shkn up over 2f out: steadily fdd fr over 1f out* — **20/1**

-563 **7** 1 **Moresco**[18] 4319 3-9-3 **73** ... AdamKirby 6 — 69
(W R Swinburn) *led 2f: chsd wnr to 3f out: u.p and btn after: wknd over 1f out* — **7/1**

0122 **8** ½ **Devil To Pay**[18] 4325 3-9-6 **76** ... TedDurcan 9 — 71
(J L Dunlop) *settled in 8th: rdn 3f out: no prog and struggling 2f out* — **4/1**[1]

0050 **9** nk **Admirable Duque (IRE)**[18] 4325 3-9-2 **72** ... JamesDoyle 3 — 67
(D J S Ffrench Davis) *wl in tch: prog 5f out: chsd wnr 3f out: hrd rdn and no imp 2f out: wknd rapidly over 1f out* — **33/1**

65 **10** 15 **Supernoverre (IRE)**[27] 4008 3-9-3 **73** ... IanMongan 11 — 47
(P Howling) *a in last trio: wknd over 2f out: t.o* — **28/1**

3m 7.44s (0.84) **Going Correction** +0.125s/f (Good) — **10** Ran SP% **114.5**
Speed ratings (Par 102): **102,101,100,100,99 97,97,97,96,88**
toteswinger: 1&2 £8.30, 1&3 £10.40, 2&3 £6.30. CSF £45.74 CT £239.85 TOTE £10.10: £2.90, £2.30, £1.80; EX 66.30 Place 6 £29.90, Place 5 £17.83.
Owner Ermyn Lodge Stud & Heatherwold Stud **Bred** Horizon Bloodstock Limited **Trained** Epsom, Surrey

■ Stewards' Enquiry : Jamie Spencer two-day ban: used whip with excessive frequency down shoulder in forehand without giving colt time to respond (Aug 26-27)

FOCUS

A fair handicap.

T/Jkpt: £13,814.50 to a £1 stake. Pool: £48,642.62. 2.50 winning tickets. T/Plt: £19.80 to a £1 stake. Pool: £54,151.69. 1,993.87 winning tickets. T/Qpdt: £7.00 to a £1 stake. Pool: £6,361.80. 665.20 winning tickets. JN

4717 YARMOUTH (L-H)

Wednesday, August 12

OFFICIAL GOING: Good (7.9)

Back straight rail and bottom bend moved out by 3.5m but impact on distances not quantified.

Wind: Virtually nil Weather: overcast, muggy

4912 MANNY BERNSTEIN FREEPHONE 0800 821 821 (S) STKS — 5f 43y

2:20 (2:20) (Class 6) 2-Y-O — **£1,942** (£578; £288; £144) **Stalls** High

Form — RPR

56 **1** **Prince Fortune**[17] 4342 2-8-12 0 ... TGMcLaughlin 2 — 66+
(Mrs L Stubbs) *stdd s: hld up towards rr: hdwy 3f out: led and edgd rt wl over 1f out: rdn clr 1f out: kpt on wl* — **14/1**

516 **2** ¾ **Italian Tom (IRE)**[35] 3742 2-9-4 70 ... HayleyTurner 3 — 69
(S A Callaghan) *in tch: hdwy to press ldrs whn sltly hmpd wl over 1f out: sn chsng wnr and drvn: no imp tl kpt on fnl 50yds* — **11/8**[1]

4554 **3** 3 ¾ **Masked Dance (IRE)**[26] 4063 2-8-12 70 ... (v[1]) RichardMullen 4 — 50
(K A Ryan) *led: hdd and rdn wl over 1f out: sn hung rt and looked reluctant: wl outpcd by ldng pair fnl f* — **10/3**[2]

0500 **4** 1 ¼ **Avec Moi**[16] 4383 2-8-7 50 ... AdrianMcCarthy 6 — 40
(Mrs C A Dunnett) *chsd ldr: rdn ent fnl 2f: sn outpcd by ldrs: wl btn 1f out: plugged on* — **25/1**

0566 **5** 1 ¼ **That'Ldonowthen (IRE)**[6] 4689 2-8-12 58 ... LukeMorris 1 — 41+
(J S Moore) *chsd ldrs: rdn and pressing ldrs whn nt clr run and swtchd lft wl over 1f out: sn drvn and outpcd by ldrs* — **12/1**

640 **6** 8 **Bathwick Gino**[62] 2861 2-8-12 59 ... SamHitchcott 5 — 12
(P D Evans) *sn rdn along in rr: no ch fnl 2f* — **18/1**

0343 **7** ¼ **Southwark Newshawk**[16] 4383 2-8-7 59 ... LiamJones 8 — 6
(Mrs C A Dunnett) *chsd ldrs: rdn 1/2-way: wknd u.p 2f out: wl btn over 1f out* — **11/2**[3]

8 nse **Kankan Prince (IRE)** 2-8-12 0 ... TPQueally 7 — 11
(M G Quinlan) *v.s.a: a bhd: nvr a factor* — **12/1**

0 **9** 13 **Angela Jones**[16] 4384 2-8-7 0 ... SaleemGolam 9 — —
(D K Ivory) *sn outpcd in rr: nvr a factor: t.o* — **100/1**

63.65 secs (1.45) **Going Correction** +0.125s/f (Good) — **9** Ran SP% **112.7**
Speed ratings (Par 92): **93,91,85,83,81 69,68,68,47**
toteswinger: 1&2 £4.30, 1&3 £7.70, 2&3 £1.70. CSF £32.83 TOTE £11.60: £4.50, £1.20, £1.40; EX 38.10 Trifecta £170.40 Pool: £338.53 - 1.47 winning units..The winner was bought in for £6,600. Italian Tom was claimed by C. R. Dore for £5,000.
Owner D M Smith **Bred** Biddestone Stud **Trained** Norton, N Yorks

FOCUS

Run-of-the-mill selling form. The pace was decent.

NOTEBOOK

Prince Fortune had shown precious little in two previous outings and a drop into the basement grade proved just the ticket. He moved through smoothly to take it up well over a furlong out and quickly assert from the well backed Italian Tom. The second has already won a race in this grade so the form isn't too bad for the level and the winner looks to be going the right way. (tchd 12-1 and 16-1)

Italian Tom(IRE) was very strongly backed throughout the day but having made good headway to get into a challenging position, he didn't have the turn of foot of the winner. He kept on well to come clear of the rest and ran his race, but he is vulnerable to an improver, even in this company. (op 13-8 tchd 5-4)

Masked Dance(IRE) ran with the choke out a touch in the first time visor but to his credit he kept on well in the closing stages having looked initially like he might drop right away. He's not progressing though which has to be a concern for connections. (op 7-2 tchd 4-1)

Avec Moi, a pretty exposed 50-rated performer, kept on at the one pace and connections will do well to find a race for her. (op 22-1)

That'Lldonowthen(IRE) has now been beaten in selling company on five of his six starts and looks to have an even bleaker future. (op 16-1)

4913 MANNY BERNSTEIN HEDGING SERVICE MAIDEN FILLIES' STKS 6f 3y

2:50 (2:52) (Class 5) 3-Y-O **£2,719** (£809; £404; £202) **Stalls High**

Form RPR

0- **1** **Brushing**[329] 6030 3-8-7 0 AshleyMorgan(7) 3 71
(M H Tompkins) *t.k.h: hld up in tch: hdwy over 2f out: rdn to chal over 1f out: led jst ins fnl f: pushed out hands and heels: r.o wl* **50/1**

43 **2** 1/2 **Miss Frangipane (IRE)**[18] 4324 3-9-0 0 TPQueally 6 69
(J Noseda) *disp ld tl led and shkn up wl over 1f out: rdn over 1f out: hdd jst ins fnl f: unable qck and hld after* **3/1**[2]

03 **3** 2 3/4 **Farncombe (IRE)**[102] 1671 3-9-0 0 RHills 10 60
(M P Tregoning) *disp ld tl wl over 1f out: sn edgd lft u.p: nt pce of ldng pair fnl f: kpt on* **15/8**[1]

6 **4** 1 1/2 **Eliza Doolittle**[62] 2862 3-9-0 0 HayleyTurner 8 55+
(J R Fanshawe) *hld up wl in tch: rdn ent fnl 2f: unable qck u.p wl over 1f out: kpt on fnl f to go 4th nr fin: nvr pce to threaten ldrs* **9/2**[3]

30- **5** hd **Prowl**[320] 6240 3-9-0 0 DO'Donohoe 2 55
(E A L Dunlop) *t.k.h: chsd ldrs: rdn wl over 1f out: edgd lft ent fnl f: sn wknd* **7/1**

0- **6** shd **Freeing**[233] 7769 3-9-0 0 KirstyMilczarek 5 54
(J A R Toller) *wnt rt s: sn wl in tch: rdn and unable qck 2f out: plugged on same pce fr over 1f out* **25/1**

00 **7** 2 1/4 **Fortezza**[21] 4199 3-9-0 0 ChrisCatlin 7 47
(C F Wall) *s.i.s: in tch: hdwy 1/2-way: pressing ldrs and rdn ent fnl 2f: wknd over 1f out* **16/1**

8 1 1/4 **Teia Tephi** 3-9-0 0 AdrianMcCarthy 4 43
(P W Chapple-Hyam) *awkward leaving stalls and s.i.s: t.k.h: hld up in tch in last pl: rdn wl over 1f out: no prog and wl hld after* **8/1**

1m 14.9s (0.50) **Going Correction** +0.125s/f (Good) **8** Ran SP% **113.3**

Speed ratings (Par 97): **101,100,96,94,94 94,91,89**

toteswinger: 1&2 £38.60, 1&3 £21.30, 2&3 £1.20. CSF £192.29 TOTE £84.40: £11.20, £1.10, £1.30; EX 239.20 TRIFECTA Not won..

Owner Dullingham Park **Bred** Dullingham Park **Trained** Newmarket, Suffolk

FOCUS

An ordinary-looking fillies' maiden.

4914 MANNY BERNSTEIN EARLY PRICE SERVICE H'CAP 7f 3y

3:25 (3:27) (Class 5) (0-75,75) 3-Y-O+ **£2,590** (£770; £385; £192) **Stalls High**

Form RPR

6020 **1** **Registrar**[22] 4183 7-8-8 **54** oh1 (p) SaleemGolam 1 61
(Mrs C A Dunnett) *t.k.h: chsd ldrs: rdn 2f out: drvn over 1f out: chsd ldr 1f out: kpt on to ld towards fin* **10/1**

2034 **2** nk **Mudhish (IRE)**[41] 3548 4-9-7 **67** (b) HayleyTurner 4 75
(C E Brittain) *w ldr and travelling strly: led over 1f out: shkn up ent fnl f: rdn: pricked ears and idled ins fnl f: hdd towards fin* **13/2**[3]

0306 **3** 3/4 **Sahaal (USA)**[25] 4097 3-9-9 **75** (t) RHills 5 77
(M P Tregoning) *led narrowly tl rdn and hdd over 1f out: kpt on u.p ins fnl f* **10/3**[1]

0000 **4** 1/2 **Gift Horse**[5] 4733 9-9-8 **73** (p) RichardEvans(5) 2 76
(P D Evans) *t.k.h: hld up in last trio: rdn and effrt 2f out: drvn to chse ldrs over 1f out: kpt on ins fnl f* **11/1**

1352 **5** 2 **Captainrisk (IRE)**[53] 3156 3-9-7 **73** (v) JerryO'Dwyer 3 68
(Mrs C A Dunnett) *t.k.h: pressed ldrs: rdn over 2f out: drvn and outpcd over 1f out: one pce fnl f* **8/1**

000 **6** 2 **Buxton**[27] 4009 5-9-13 **73** (t) RobertHavlin 7 65
(R Ingram) *in tch in midfield: rdn over 2f out: no prog u.p fnl 2f* **12/1**

0410 **7** 3 1/2 **Pressing Matters (IRE)**[28] 3982 3-9-5 **74** (p) AndreaAtzeni(3) 8 54
(M Botti) *hld up in last trio: rdn 2f out: no hdwy and wl hld after* **5/1**[2]

2502 **8** nse **Compton's Eleven**[7] 4657 8-9-8 **68** ChrisCatlin 9 50
(M R Channon) *stdd s: hld up in last trio: rdn and no rspnse wl over 1f out: wl btn fnl f* **5/1**[2]

1106 **9** 1 1/2 **Just Timmy Marcus**[78] 2365 3-8-13 **65** LiamJones 6 41
(B P J Baugh) *in tch in midfield: rdn over 2f out: wknd wl over 1f out* **10/1**

1m 27.9s (1.30) **Going Correction** +0.125s/f (Good)

WFA 3 from 4yo+ 6lb **9** Ran SP% **115.1**

Speed ratings (Par 103): **97,96,95,95,92 90,86,86,84**

toteswinger: 1&2 £13.00, 1&3 £14.80, 2&3 £5.70. CSF £72.98 CT £266.65 TOTE £10.80: £3.40, £2.60, £1.50; EX 85.90 Trifecta £264.80 Pool: £357.86 - 0.50 winning units..

Owner The Smart Syndicate **Bred** Cheveley Park Stud Ltd **Trained** Hingham, Norfolk

FOCUS

Mostly exposed performers in this ordinary handicap.

Just Timmy Marcus Official explanation: trainer said gelding was unsuited by the good ground

4915 MANNY BERNSTEIN CREDIT BETTING CLAIMING STKS 7f 3y

3:55 (3:57) (Class 6) 2-Y-O **£1,942** (£578; £288; £144) **Stalls High**

Form RPR

603 **1** **Ibmab**[16] 4384 2-8-11 62 TGMcLaughlin 6 67+
(Mrs L Stubbs) *racd in midfield: hdwy on far side 3f out: rdn and ev ch jst over 2f out: led and edgd rt over 1f out: styd on wl to draw clr fnl f* **11/2**[3]

6 **2** 4 1/2 **Tanto Quanto (IRE)**[22] 4163 2-9-11 0 (b[1]) RichardMullen 7 70
(W R Muir) *chsd ldr tl rdn to ld jst over 2f out: hdd over 1f out: nt pce of wnr ins fnl f: hld on for 2nd* **33/1**

06 **3** 1 **Tiger Hawk (USA)**[13] 4451 2-8-3 0 (b) HayleyTurner 4 45
(S A Callaghan) *towards rr: rdn 3f out: no hdwy: stl 12th and edging rt over 1f out: r.o u.p fnl f to snatch 3rd on line: nvr trbld ldrs* **16/1**

45 **4** nse **Zaffature**[28] 3979 2-8-13 0 AndreaAtzeni(3) 3 58
(M Botti) *in tch in midfield: effrt and rdn over 2f out: chsd ldng pair and edgd lft jst over 1f out: no imp after: lost 3rd on line* **5/1**[2]

0030 **5** 2 1/2 **Avow (USA)**[12] 4488 2-9-5 72 (b) LukeMorris 14 55
(J S Moore) *chsd ldrs: rdn and effrt over 2f out: hrd rdn and wknd over 1f out* **9/2**[1]

0406 **6** 3/4 **Durham Town (IRE)**[16] 4377 2-9-5 62 TPQueally 10 53
(D K Ivory) *awkward leaving stalls and s.i.s: bhd: hdwy 4f out: drvn and chsng ldrs 2f out: sn no imp and wl hld after* **12/1**

0 **7** 3 3/4 **Al Barq (IRE)**[12] 4497 2-8-7 0 ow1 JerryO'Dwyer 1 32
(Miss D Mountain) *chsd ldrs: rdn and chsd ldng pair over 1f out: wknd ent fnl f* **20/1**

0 **8** shd **Noverre Over There (IRE)**[16] 4385 2-9-1 0 MickyFenton 9 39
(M E Rimmer) *s.i.s: sn rcvrd and chsng ldrs: rdn 3f out: struggling over 2f out and wl btn after* **33/1**

3310 **9** 3 **Highcliffe Bridge (IRE)**[19] 4271 2-8-8 56 RobertHavlin 2 25
(N P Littmoden) *in tch: rdn wl over 2f out: drvn and wknd wl over 1f out* **9/1**

00 **10** 1 3/4 **Restyle**[23] 4147 2-8-10 0 (p) SaleemGolam 13 23
(D K Ivory) *chsd ldrs: rdn 3f out: wknd qckly u.p over 2f out* **66/1**

00 **11** 1 1/2 **High Resolution**[21] 4209 2-8-11 0 LiamJones 8 20
(S C Williams) *led tl hdd jst over 2f out: sn struggling: wl btn over 1f out* **17/2**

000 **12** 10 **Walnut Rise**[5] 4757 2-8-1 0 ow2 AshleyMorgan(7) 11 —
(M H Tompkins) *a towards rr: struggling 1/2-way: wl bhd and eased ins fnl f* **33/1**

3204 **13** 1 1/2 **Musiara**[27] 4018 2-8-2 53 ChrisCatlin 5 —
(M R Channon) *s.i.s: sn rcvrd and in tch: rdn 3f out: wknd qckly over 2f out: wl bhd and eased ins fnl f: t.o* **9/1**

000 **14** 9 **Woodface**[18] 4331 2-9-1 46 (bt[1]) RHills 15 —
(B J Meehan) *a in rr: strugging bdly 1/2-way: wl bhd and eased ins fnl f: t.o* **10/1**

0 **15** 7 **Sputnik One (IRE)**[12] 4478 2-8-11 0 (p) SamHitchcott 12 —
(J S Moore) *sn struggling in rr: reminder 5f out: toiling bdly fr 1/2-way: t.o and eased ins fnl f* **40/1**

1m 28.8s (2.20) **Going Correction** +0.125s/f (Good) **15** Ran SP% **120.9**

Speed ratings (Par 92): **92,86,85,85,82 81,77,77,74,72 70,58,57,46,38**

toteswinger: 1&2 £17.70, 1&3 £21.60, 2&3 £104.50. CSF £190.70 TOTE £5.60: £2.00, £6.20, £5.90; EX 129.00 TRIFECTA Not won..Tiger Hawk was claimed by K. M. Prendergast for £4,000.

Owner L Woolams **Bred** Bambi Bloodstock **Trained** Norton, N Yorks

FOCUS

A weak claimer.

NOTEBOOK

Ibmab, who was a little unlucky in selling company at this track last time, made no mistake to win in fairly emphatic style. Put in on a reasonable looking mark, he was stepping up in trip here but having travelled smoothly, he was produced on the far side to strike for home over a furlong out and he saw it out really well. Although this juvenile isn't anything out of the ordinary, he got this done in good style and looks to be going forward as he gains experience. (op 9-2)

Tanto Quanto(IRE), quickly dropped in grade after showing little first time up and fitted with blinkers, fared a deal better here and the way he travelled offers hope he'll be able to find a race at some point. (tchd 28-1)

Tiger Hawk(USA) put in some good late work from off the pace to finish encouragingly.

Zaffature didn't run too badly on her first try on turf but her effort flattened out in the final furlong. (op 9-2)

Avow(USA)'s handicap mark looks very flattering on this evidence, for although he travelled well towards the stands side, his finishing effort was very one-paced. (tchd 4-1)

Durham Town(IRE) Official explanation: jockey said gelding hung right throughout

Musiara Official explanation: jockey said filly suffered interference shortly after start

Woodface Official explanation: jockey said colt never travelled

Sputnik One(IRE) Official explanation: jockey said colt never travelled

4916 MANNY BERNSTEIN "GIVES GUARANTEED ODDS" H'CAP 1m 3y

4:30 (4:30) (Class 6) (0-65,65) 3-Y-O+ **£1,942** (£578; £288; £144) **Stalls High**

Form RPR

0462 **1** **Astrodonna**[22] 4179 4-9-7 **65** AshleyMorgan(7) 2 78
(M H Tompkins) *hld up in rr: hdwy on outer over 2f out: jnd ldrs gng wl over 1f out: pushed into ld ent fnl f: sn pushed clr: comf* **5/1**[3]

0003 **2** 4 **Onenightinlisbon (IRE)**[6] 4704 5-9-6 **57** RobertHavlin 11 60
(J R Boyle) *hld up in tch: rdn 2f out: styd on u.p to chse wnr ins fnl f: no imp* **9/1**

0000 **3** 1 1/2 **Kaystar Ridge**[25] 4082 4-8-9 **46** JerryO'Dwyer 14 46
(D K Ivory) *hld up in rr: rdn 2f out: no hdwy tl r.o ins fnl f to snatch 3rd on line: no ch w wnr* **33/1**

0645 **4** shd **Dudley Docker (IRE)**[18] 4321 7-9-13 **64** LiamJones 5 64
(T T Clement) *stdd after s: hld up in tch: pushed along and effrt over 1f out: racd awkwardly and one pce fnl f: lost 3rd on line* **14/1**

644 **5** 1 1/2 **Eurotanz (IRE)**[10] 4569 3-9-5 **63** TravisBlock 1 58
(H Morrison) *chsd ldng pair tl wnt 2nd jst over 2f out: edgd rt u.p over 1f out: lost 2nd over 1f out: wknd ins fnl f* **9/2**[2]

0001 **6** nse **Broughtons Silk**[7] 4667 4-9-2 **53** 6ex ChrisCatlin 7 49
(W J Musson) *w.w in midfield: rdn and effrt 2f out: edgd lft u.p and wknd fnl f* **7/4**[1]

2 **7** hd **Blue Turk**[11] 4533 4-9-5 **56** PatCosgrave 13 51
(J R Boyle) *stdd s: hld up in tch: nt clr run and shuffled bk over 2f out: drvn over 1f out: swtchd lft ins fnl f: nvr pce to trble ldrs* **15/2**

0100 **8** hd **Night Knight (IRE)**[39] 3637 3-9-7 **65** (v) HayleyTurner 3 59
(M L W Bell) *t.k.h: hld up in rr: n.m.r 2f out: sn drvn: no real hdwy whn n.m.r again ins fnl f: nvr able to chal* **16/1**

0000 **9** 3/4 **Rony Dony (IRE)**[6] 4703 5-8-9 **46** oh1 MickyFenton 6 39
(M E Rimmer) *led: sn clr: c to stands' rail 5f out: rdn wl over 1f out: hdd ent fnl f: wknd ins fnl f* **66/1**

0450 **10** 9 **Shavoulin (USA)**[6] 4697 5-8-11 **48** (b) LukeMorris 8 19
(P W Hiatt) *chsd ldr tl jst over 2f out: struggling u.p 2f out: eased whn wl btn ins fnl f* **12/1**

1m 41.73s (1.13) **Going Correction** +0.125s/f (Good)

WFA 3 from 4yo+ 7lb **10** Ran SP% **117.7**

Speed ratings (Par 101): **99,95,93,93,91 91,91,91,90,81**

toteswinger: 1&2 £7.00, 1&3 £20.50, 2&3 £30.00. CSF £49.93 CT £1382.55 TOTE £6.20: £2.30, £3.40, £11.30; EX 33.60 Trifecta £207.40 Pool: £280.29 - 0.10 winning units..

Owner Mystic Meg Limited **Bred** Mystic Meg Limited **Trained** Newmarket, Suffolk

FOCUS

A low-grade handicap in which the field went a decent clip and ended up congregating towards the stands' rail.

Shavoulin(USA) Official explanation: jockey said gelding hung right

4917 MANNY BERNSTEIN "PAYS DOUBLE RESULT" H'CAP — 1m 3f 101y
5:00 (5:01) (Class 5) (0-70,72) 3-Y-O — **£2,590** (£770; £385; £192) **Stalls** Low

Form — RPR

1111 **1** **Point Of Light**[2] 4855 3-9-11 **72** 6ex .... ChrisCatlin 1 87+
(Sir Mark Prescott) *mde all: pushed along and drew clr w runner up wl over 2f out: rdn 2f out: styd on wl fnl f* **2/5**[1]

0-00 **2** *1 1/4* **Royal Bet (IRE)**[87] 2105 3-8-2 **49** .... HayleyTurner 8 61
(M L W Bell) *t.k.h: chsd ldrs: wnt 2nd wl over 2f out: sn clr w wnr but hanging bdly lft after: swtchd rt jst ins fnl f: stl hanging and one pce fnl 100yds* **15/2**[2]

-640 **3** *8* **Khayar (IRE)**[22] 4178 3-8-7 **61** .... AshleyMorgan(7) 6 59
(M H Tompkins) *stdd s: t.k.h hld up in last pair: swtchd rt and rdn over 2f out: chsd clr ldng pair 2f out: sn no prog and wl btn fnl f* **10/1**[3]

0520 **4** *3/4* **Mymateeric**[6] 4722 3-8-5 **52** ....(v) LiamJones 7 49
(J Pearce) *hld up in last pl: hdwy on outer over 3f out: rdn and unable qck wl over 2f out: wl btn 2f out* **20/1**

0214 **5** *7* **Diktalina**[21] 4206 3-8-9 **56** .... TPQueally 5 41
(W R Muir) *chsd wnr tl wl over 2f out: sn drvn and struggling: wl btn fnl 2f* **12/1**

0010 **6** *13* **Hi Fling**[22] 4178 3-9-2 **63** ....(b) RobertHavlin 2 26
(B J Meehan) *in tch: effrt and rdn 3f out: drvn and btn over 2f out: wl bhd and eased ins fnl f* **18/1**

2m 29.83s (1.13) **Going Correction** +0.125s/f (Good) **6 Ran SP% 110.0**
Speed ratings (Par 100): **100,99,93,92,87 78**
toteswinger: 1&2 £2.00, 1&3 £3.10, 2&3 £6.40. CSF £3.77 CT £10.60 TOTE £1.40: £1.50, £2.00; EX 3.90 Trifecta £26.60 Pool: £476.86 - 13.25 winning units..
Owner Syndicate 2007 **Bred** Watership Down Stud **Trained** Newmarket, Suffolk

FOCUS
An uncompetitive handicap.

4918 MANNY BERNSTEIN INDEPENDENT BOOKMAKERS H'CAP — 1m 2f 21y
5:35 (5:35) (Class 5) (0-70,70) 3-Y-O — **£2,590** (£770; £385; £192) **Stalls** Low

Form — RPR

0424 **1** **Mykingdomforahorse**[27] 4004 3-9-5 **68** .... ChrisCatlin 2 70+
(M R Channon) *chsd ldrs: n.m.r 3f out tl swtchd rt and forced way out 2f out: rdn to chal ent fnl f: kpt on u.p to ld towards fin* **9/4**[2]

3-30 **2** *hd* **Navajo Nation (IRE)**[11] 4520 3-9-5 **68** .... RHills 8 70
(B J Meehan) *chsd ldr tl led 3f out: rdn 2f out: drvn and hrd pressed ent fnl f: kpt on tl hdd and no ex towards fin* **2/1**[1]

4021 **3** *3 3/4* **Playful Asset (IRE)**[39] 3629 3-8-11 **65** .... AmyBaker(5) 3 59
(P Howling) *hld up in tch: rdn and unable qck over 2f out: plugged on u.p to go 3rd wl ins fnl f: nt pce to threaten ldng pair* **15/2**

20-0 **4** *3/4* **Noordhoek Kid**[86] 2126 3-9-7 **70** ....(bt[1]) MickyFenton 1 63
(C R Egerton) *dwlt: sn pushed along to ld: hdd and rdn 3f out: styd chsng ldr tl wknd u.p 1f out* **12/1**

2560 **5** *1 1/4* **Hypnotist (UAE)**[48] 3321 3-9-7 **70** .... HayleyTurner 9 60
(C E Brittain) *chsd ldrs: rdn whn barging match w rival 2f out: wknd jst over 1f out* **8/1**

4541 **6** *6* **Chantilly Dancer (IRE)**[57] 3005 3-8-0 **52** .... AndreaAtzeni(3) 7 30
(M Quinn) *hld up in last pair: pushed along and hdwy 4f out: rdn over 2f out: sn struggling: wl btn fnl f* **6/1**[3]

0400 **7** *3/4* **Duke Of Normandy (IRE)**[10] 4562 3-8-5 **54** .... LiamJones 6 31
(B P J Baugh) *hld up in last pair: effrt on inner 3f out: no hdwy over 2f out: wl btn fnl f* **20/1**

2m 11.18s (0.68) **Going Correction** +0.125s/f (Good) **7 Ran SP% 113.7**
Speed ratings (Par 100): **102,101,98,98,97 92,91**
toteswinger: 1&2 £1.80, 1&3 £2.80, 2&3 £4.40. CSF £7.09 CT £26.37 TOTE £2.50: £1.50, £2.00; EX 8.90 Trifecta £23.40 Pool: £228.98 - 7.23 winning units. Place 6 £79.14, Place 5 £56.70.
Owner C C Buckley **Bred** Hunscote House Farm Stud **Trained** West Ilsley, Berks
■ Stewards' Enquiry : Chris Catlin one-day ban: careless riding (Aug 26)

FOCUS
Just an ordinary pace to this handicap but the form looks solid enough with the two market leaders dominating the finish.
Duke Of Normandy(IRE) Official explanation: jockey said gelding had no more to give
T/Plt: £65.10 to a £1 stake. Pool: £51,258.71. 574.46 winning tickets. T/Qpdt: £51.70 to a £1 stake. Pool: £3,262.75. 46.70 winning tickets. SP

4919 - 4922a (Foreign Racing) - See Raceform Interactive

4671
GOWRAN PARK (R-H)
Wednesday, August 12

OFFICIAL GOING: Good (good to yielding in places)

4923a IRISH STALLION FARMS EUROPEAN BREEDERS' FUND HURRY HARRIET STKS (LISTED RACE) — 1m 1f 100y
7:20 (7:21) 3-Y-O+ — **£26,861** (£7,881; £3,754; £1,279)

RPR

1 **Chinese White (IRE)**[91] 1996 4-9-6 107 .... PJSmullen 5 116+
(D K Weld, Ire) *trckd ldrs: 5th 1/2-way: hdwy in 3rd travelling wl 2f out: 2nd 1 1/2f out: rdn to chal 1f out: styd on to ld last 100yds: kpt on wl* **15/8**[1]

2 *1 1/2* **Roman Empress (IRE)**[9] 4609 3-8-12 93 .... JAHeffernan 8 111
(A P O'Brien, Ire) *led: rdn 1 1/2f out: chal 1f out: hdd last 100yds and no ex: kpt on same pce* **14/1**

3 *6* **She's Our Mark**[20] 4253 5-9-11 106 .... DMGrant 11 104
(Patrick J Flynn, Ire) *chsd ldrs: 6th 1/2-way: rdn 2f out: styd on to 3rd under 1f out: no imp on ldrs: kpt on same pce* **5/2**[2]

4 *3/4* **Festival Princess (IRE)**[55] 3082 4-9-6 102 .... FMBerry 4 97
(Mrs John Harrington, Ire) *mid-div: 8th 1/2-way: rdn in 7th 2f out: no imp in 5th 1f out: kpt on same pce fnl f* **11/2**[3]

5 *2* **Choose Me (IRE)**[17] 4358 3-8-12 92 .... DPMcDonogh 7 93
(Kevin Prendergast, Ire) *hld up towards rr: rdn in 9th 2f out: styd on to mod 6th 1f out: kpt on same pce fnl f* **16/1**

6 *3* **Timabiyra (IRE)**[31] 3894 3-8-12 96 ....(p) MJKinane 6 87
(John M Oxx, Ire) *hld up towards rr: rdn and no imp 2f out: sme late hdwy fnl f* **13/2**

7 *1/2* **Crossing**[20] 4253 8-9-6 95 .... KJManning 10 86
(William J Fitzpatrick, Ire) *chsd ldrs: 3rd 1/2-way: rdn in 4th 2f out: no imp in 3rd over 1f out: wknd fnl f* **33/1**

8 *3/4* **Wanna (IRE)**[37] 3700 3-8-12 88 .... WMLordan 2 84
(T Stack, Ire) *chsd ldrs: 4th 1/2-way: rdn in 5th 2f out: no ex 1 1/2f out: kpt on one pce* **25/1**

9 *3* **Dollar Chick (IRE)**[45] 3433 5-9-6 86 ....(p) CO'Donoghue 9 78
(Noel Meade, Ire) *in rr of mid-div: rdn in 8th and no imp 2f out: kpt on one pce* **50/1**

10 *5 1/2* **Cristal Island (IRE)**[13] 4475 3-8-12 93 .... DEMullins 1 67
(Thomas Mullins, Ire) *chsd ldr in 2nd: rdn over 2f out: no ex and sn wknd* **50/1**

11 *15* **Always Be True (IRE)**[31] 3894 3-8-12 92 ....(b[1]) JMurtagh 3 36
(David Wachman, Ire) *towards rr early: sn in mid-div: 7th 1/2-way: wknd over 3f out* **8/1**

2m 1.16s (-5.84)
WFA 3 from 4yo+ 8lb **11 Ran SP% 126.4**
CSF £32.85 TOTE £3.40: £1.50, £3.00, £1.90; DF 39.30.
Owner Lady O'Reilly **Bred** Skymarc Farm & Castlemartin St **Trained** The Curragh, Co Kildare

FOCUS
The winner put up a nice effort to pick up the leader and go clear, but she was the clear form pick beforehand. The runner-up has been rated to her best.

NOTEBOOK
Chinese White(IRE) justified her market position and underlined her official assessment of 107 when she recorded her third career win, her second over this course and distance. Connections admitted the lack of a recent run was a slight concern for the lightly raced Dalakhani filly, winner of the Listed McCalmont Stakes here last year. She had encountered some slight problems and had only been in training a month, so there should be improvement to come. She travelled ominously well throughout before taking over from long-time leader Roman Empress a furlong down and she stuck to her task well. Dermot Weld has an autumn campaign in mind and the Prix de l'Opera on Arc day is a possible target. (op 7/4 tchd 9/4)
Roman Empress(IRE) made the favourite battle when she seized the initiative and the sole Ballydoyle representative clearly appreciated this better ground and the drop in class.
She's Our Mark had defeated Chinese White when they clashed last May over this course and distance and was fancied to follow up last month's Curragh Listed and Leopardstown Group 3 victories. Conditions, though, favoured Dermot Weld's filly on this occasion who was 8lb better off with Pat Flynn's mare. She never looked like getting involved and more ease in the ground might have helped her cause. (op 3/1 tchd 9/4)
Festival Princess(IRE) is best suited by some ease in the ground and she was also struggling early in the straight to go about her business when asked a question. (op 7/1)
Crossing Official explanation: trainer said mare ran below par and blew hard post race, adding that she is nearing 120 days pregnant and will now retire from racing
Always Be True(IRE) Official explanation: jockey said filly weakened quickly in the home straight and may have resented the application of blinkers

4924 - 4926a (Foreign Racing) - See Raceform Interactive

4887
BEVERLEY (R-H)
Thursday, August 13

OFFICIAL GOING: Good (8.7)
Wind: Virtually nil Weather: Sunny periods

4927 HOLD YOUR CHRISTMAS PARTY HERE (S) H'CAP — 1m 4f 16y
2:10 (2:10) (Class 6) (0-60,60) 3-Y-O+ — **£2,428** (£722; £361; £180) **Stalls** High

Form — RPR

4506 **1** **Barbirolli**[8] 4640 7-8-9 **47** .... PaulPickard(5) 2 51
(W M Brisbourne) *prom: effrt and cl up over 4f out: led 2f out: rdn over 1f out: drvn ins fnl f and kpt on* **6/1**[2]

5010 **2** *3/4* **Kochanski (IRE)**[8] 4640 3-8-12 **56** .... GregFairley 7 59
(M Johnston) *dwlt: sn in tch: hdwy to trck ldrs 1/2-way: effrt over 2f out: swtchd rt and rdn over 1f out: styd on u.p ins fnl f* **4/1**[1]

5105 **3** *3/4* **Dimashq**[14] 4462 7-9-3 **50** .... PhillipMakin 1 51
(P T Midgley) *hld up: stdy hdwy on outer over 3f out: effrt to chse wnr wl over 1f out: rdn to chal ent fnl f: sn drvn and one pce* **13/2**[3]

3343 **4** *nk* **Saffron's Son (IRE)**[16] 4397 3-8-8 **52** ....(b) PaulMulrennan 12 53
(P T Midgley) *hld up towards rr: smooth hdwy 3f out: rdn to chse ldrs over 1f out: kpt on ins fnl f* **7/1**

245 **5** *3 1/4* **Casablanca Minx (IRE)**[6] 4735 6-8-12 **50** ....(b) JamieKyne(5) 6 46
(Miss Gay Kelleway) *hld up towards rr: hdwy on outer 3f out: bmpd over 2f out and sn rdn: styd on ins fnl f: nt rch ldrs* **17/2**

04S0 **6** *1* **Neon Blue**[15] 4431 8-8-9 **47** ....(p) AmyRyan(5) 5 41
(R M Whitaker) *prom: rdn along over 3f out: grad wknd* **16/1**

3400 **7** *nk* **Cripsey Brook**[5] 4806 11-9-5 **52** .... PaulHanagan 8 46
(K G Reveley) *hld up towards rr: hdwy 3f out: effrt to swtch lft and bmpd 2f out: sn btn* **15/2**

0-01 **8** *1 3/4* **Carlton Mac**[9] 4617 4-9-4 **51** 6ex ....(p) FrancisNorton 10 42
(N Bycroft) *trckd ldrs on inner: rdn along 3f out: sn wknd* **10/1**

4063 **9** *hd* **York Cliff**[20] 4264 11-9-3 **50** .... LiamJones 9 41
(W M Brisbourne) *chsd ldrs: rdn along over 4f out and sn wknd* **14/1**

-300 **10** *3/4* **Glamoroso (IRE)**[5] 4804 4-8-13 **46** oh1 .... AndrewElliott 4 35
(A Kirtley) *led: rdn along over 3f out: hdd 2f out and sn wknd* **66/1**

0006 **11** *1 3/4* **Itsy Bitsy**[13] 4498 7-8-13 **46** oh1 ....(p) RobertWinston 3 33
(W J Musson) *dwlt: a bhd* **11/1**

2m 39.75s (-1.15) **Going Correction** -0.175s/f (Firm)
WFA 3 from 4yo+ 11lb **11 Ran SP% 113.9**
Speed ratings (Par 101): **96,95,95,94,92 91,91,90,90,89 88**
toteswingers: 1&2 £5.90, 1&3 £9.60, 2&3 £3.80 CSF £29.15 CT £160.37 TOTE £6.80: £2.90, £1.60, £2.70; EX 29.60.There was no bid for the winner.
Owner Mark Brisbourne **Bred** Gainsborough Stud Management Ltd **Trained** Great Ness, Shropshire

FOCUS
This was a weak selling handicap. It is doubtful if the winner had to match this year's best.

4928 E B F BEVERLEY ANNUAL BADGEHOLDERS MAIDEN FILLIES' STKS — 5f
2:40 (2:40) (Class 4) 2-Y-O — **£5,018** (£1,493; £746; £372) **Stalls** High

Form — RPR

44 **1** **Tarita (IRE)**[21] 4243 2-9-0 0 .... FrancisNorton 4 74
(R Hannon) *chsd ldng pair: hdwy 2f out: rdn ent fnl f: qcknd to ld last 100yds and sn clr* **7/2**[2]

2 *1 3/4* **Moorhouse Girl** 2-9-0 0 .... PhillipMakin 8 68
(D H Brown) *dwlt: hdwy 1/2-way: chsd ldrs over 1f out: sn rdn and styd on strly ins fnl f* **6/1**

642 **3** *1* **My Mandy (IRE)**[30] 3937 2-9-0 69 .... AdrianTNicholls 9 64
(Ian Williams) *chsd ldr: hdwy 2f out: rdn to chal over 1f out: drvn to ld briefly ins fnl f: sn hdd & wknd* **9/4**[1]

46 **4** *1 1/2* **Bahraj (USA)**[14] 4463 2-9-0 0 .... GregFairley 10 59
(M Johnston) *led: rdn along over 2f out: drvn ent fnl f: sn hdd & wknd* **11/2**[3]

0 **5** *2 3/4* **Scooby Dee**[8] 4659 2-8-11 0 .... MichaelJStainton(3) 6 49
(R M Whitaker) *chsd ldrs: rdn along 2f out and grad wknd* **33/1**

6 *4 1/2* **Laureldean Desert** 2-9-0 0 .... PaulHanagan 1 33+
(R A Fahey) *towards rr: sme hdwy 2f out: n.d* **11/2**[3]

00 **7** 2 1/4 **Moonlight Babe (USA)**[43] 3495 2-9-0 0........................ DanielTudhope 3 25
(I W McInnes) *a in rr* **100/1**

8 1/2 **Charmaxjoanne** 2-8-9 0........................ PatrickDonaghy(5) 5 23
(P C Haslam) *sn outpcd and a in rr* **33/1**

455 **9** 2 3/4 **Perfect Blossom**[12] 4546 2-9-0 62........................ PatrickMathers 11 13
(I W McInnes) *chsd ldrs: rdn along 1/2-way: sn wknd* **10/1**

62.06 secs (-1.44) **Going Correction** -0.30s/f (Firm) **9** Ran SP% **114.0**
Speed ratings (Par 93): **99,96,94,92,87 80,77,76,71**
toteswingers: 1&2 £6.30, 1&3 £1.40, 2&3 £3.00 CSF £24.13 TOTE £4.40: £1.10, £2.30, £1.50; EX 24.30.
Owner De La Warr Racing **Bred** Brian Walsh **Trained** East Everleigh, Wilts

FOCUS
They went a decent clip in what was a modest fillies' maiden. The third anchors the level.

NOTEBOOK
Tarita(IRE), who chased the early pace, relished the stiff finish this course provided and got well on top inside the final furlong. She is going to appreciate a step back up in trip before long and should have more to offer in nurseries. (op 4-1)
Moorhouse Girl, whose dam has produced a couple of very speedy sorts, comes from a yard that does well with their juveniles and she ran a race full of promise, keeping on having been outpaced to take second. She should be sharper next time and can win a standard maiden. (op 7-1 tchd 11-2)
My Mandy(IRE), officially rated 69, had finished second over the C&D last time and she set the standard. However, she probably did too much too soon in tracking the early pace-setter and could find no extra inside the final furlong. (tchd 11-4)
Bahraj(USA) again showed good speed from the gate, but she was always likely to leave herself vulnerable at the business end and faded having been headed inside the final furlong. She is now qualified for nurseries. (op 9-2 tchd 6-1)
Laureldean Desert, who is quite a late foal, comes from a decent family and she should leave this form behind in time. (op 7-1 tchd 9-2)

4929 JOHN BOTTOMLEY "LIFETIME IN RACING" FILLIES' H'CAP 5f
3:15 (3:19) (Class 5) (0-70,70) 3-Y-0+ **£2,914** (£867; £433; £216) **Stalls** High

Form RPR

0255 **1** **Speedy Senorita (IRE)**[6] 4753 4-9-1 68........................ IJBrennan(7) 9 76
(J J Quinn) *wnt rt s: sn cl up: led over 2f out: rdn ent fnl f: kpt on wl towards fin* **8/1**[3]

3505 **2** nk **Joyeaux**[12] 4530 7-9-0 60........................ PaulHanagan 6 67+
(Ollie Pears) *towards rr: pushed along 1/2-way: hdwy wl over 1f out and sn rdn: drvn and styd on ent fnl f: swtchd rt and hrd drvn last 100yds: hit in face by wnr's whip nr fin: jst hld* **12/1**

2521 **3** nk **La Capriosa**[12] 4514 3-9-5 68........................ RobertWinston 14 73
(J A Glover) *sltly checked s: sn chsng ldrs: effrt over 1f out and sn rdn: drvn ins fnl f and nt qckn nr fin* **4/1**[1]

2400 **4** 1 1/4 **Bahamian Ballad**[20] 4281 4-8-5 51 oh4........................(v) JimmyQuinn 13 52
(J D Bethell) *trckd ldrs: hdwy 2f out: rdn over 1f out: ev ch and drvn ins fnl f: sn edgd rt: one pce* **14/1**

3556 **5** 1/2 **Wicked Wilma (IRE)**[14] 4464 5-8-8 59........................ SladeO'Hara(5) 5 59
(A Berry) *towards rr: hdwy 2f out: rdn and styng on ent fnl f whn nt clr run and swtchd lft: kpt on* **11/1**

4460 **6** 1 3/4 **Just Joey**[5] 4778 5-7-12 51 oh4........................(be) AndrewHeffernan(7) 17 44
(J R Weymes) *led: rdn along and hdd over 2f out: drvn over 1f out: wkng whn n.m.r ins fnl f* **20/1**

3021 **7** shd **Diane's Choice**[7] 4692 6-8-11 62 6ex........................(e) JamieKyne(5) 16 55
(Miss Gay Kelleway) *chsd ldrs on inner: rdn wl over 1f out: wknd appr fnl f* **15/2**[2]

5202 **8** nk **Mey Blossom**[27] 4072 4-9-5 70........................(p) AmyRyan(5) 15 62
(R M Whitaker) *stmbld bdly s: hdwy to chse ldrs 1/2-way: rdn over 1f out and sn one pce* **4/1**[1]

5006 **9** 1 1/2 **Foreign Rhythm (IRE)**[12] 4552 4-8-5 51 oh4........................ AndrewElliott 8 37
(N Tinkler) *in rr: rdn along 1/2-way: sme late hdwy* **40/1**

0030 **10** shd **Darcy's Pride (IRE)**[18] 4355 5-8-8 54........................(t) TonyHamilton 2 40
(P T Midgley) *wnt lft s: a towards rr* **22/1**

060 **11** 1/2 **Molly Two**[8] 4662 4-8-12 63........................(v[1]) PaulPickard(5) 11 47
(L A Mullaney) *wnt lft s: sn prom: rdn along wl over 1f out and sn wknd* **20/1**

5-05 **12** 3/4 **Metal Guru**[38] 3677 5-8-10 59........................(p) RussellKennemore(3) 12 41
(R Hollinshead) *chsd ldrs: rdn along over 2f out and sn wknd* **9/1**

-006 **13** 8 **Barley Bree (IRE)**[14] 4467 4-8-5 51 oh6........................ PaulQuinn 10 4
(Mrs A Duffield) *s.i.s: a bhd* **66/1**

61.94 secs (-1.56) **Going Correction** -0.30s/f (Firm)
WFA 3 from 4yo+ 3lb **13** Ran SP% **113.4**
Speed ratings (Par 100): **100,99,99,97,96 93,93,92,90,90 89,88,75**
toteswingers: 1&2 £21.90, 1&3 £6.60, 2&3 £7.80 CSF £87.77 CT £452.71 TOTE £10.30: £2.40, £3.20, £2.00; EX 120.80.
Owner F D C Racing Club **Bred** R McEnery And Vincent Millett **Trained** Settrington, N Yorks

FOCUS
This had looked a competitive fillies' sprint handicap, but very few got into it. A repeat of her recent form was probably enough for the winner.

4930 GEORGE KILBURN MEMORIAL H'CAP 1m 1f 207y
3:50 (3:51) (Class 3) (0-90,90) 3-Y-0+ **£7,641** (£2,273; £1,136; £567) **Stalls** High

Form RPR

0053 **1** **Bazergan (IRE)**[75] 2468 4-9-7 85........................(tp) DebraEngland(7) 9 93
(C E Brittain) *trckled ldrs: smmoth hdwy on inner over 2f out: rdn to ld over 1f out: hdd ent fnl f: sn drvn and edgd lft: rallied to ld again nr line* **7/1**

2140 **2** nse **Granston (IRE)**[61] 2933 8-10-0 85........................ JimmyQuinn 3 93
(J D Bethell) *trckd ldr: effrt and cl up over 2f out: sn rdn: drvn to ld ent fnl f: edgd rt wl ins fnl f: hdd and no ex nr line* **12/1**

512 **3** 1 3/4 **Demolition**[10] 4597 5-9-13 84........................(p) DanielTudhope 1 88
(N Wilson) *trckd ldrs: hdwy over 2f out: rdn to chse ldng pair over 1f out: drvn and no imp ins fnl f* **7/1**

2055 **4** 1/2 **Rosbay (IRE)**[10] 4597 5-9-8 79........................ DavidAllan 5 82
(T D Easterby) *led: rdn along over 2f out: drvn and hdd over 1f out: grad wknd* **10/1**

212 **5** 3/4 **Jo'Burg (USA)**[22] 4207 5-9-4 80........................ MartinLane(5) 6 82+
(Lady Herries) *hld up in rr: rdn along over 3f out: drvn 2f out: styd on ins fnl f: nrst fin* **6/1**[3]

2004 **6** 1/2 **Hurlingham**[14] 4471 5-9-4 75........................(t) PaulMulrennan 8 76
(M W Easterby) *chsd ldrs: rdn along over 2f out: drvn over 1f out and sn one pce* **16/1**

2222 **7** 1 **Snow Dancer (IRE)**[41] 3573 5-8-5 67........................(p) PatrickDonaghy(5) 7 66
(H A McWilliams) *hld up in rr: effrt and sme hdwy over 2f out: sn rdn and nvr a factor* **14/1**

0311 **8** 1 **Moheebb (IRE)**[10] 4597 5-10-5 90 6ex........................(b) RobertWinston 10 87
(Mrs R A Carr) *hld up in midfield: effrt and hdwy over 2f out: sn rdn and no imp fr over 1f out* **7/2**[1]

5311 **9** 8 **Tufton**[15] 4434 6-9-4 75........................ PaulHanagan 4 56
(R A Fahey) *in tch: rdn along 3f out: sn wknd* **9/2**[2]

2-00 **10** 2 1/2 **Pedasus (USA)**[120] 1295 3-8-2 68........................(t) FrancisNorton 11 44
(T Keddy) *midfield on inner: rdn along 3f out and sn wknd* **28/1**

44 **11** 12 **Addikt (IRE)**[30] 3941 4-9-6 77........................ PaulQuinn 2 29
(G A Harker) *hld up: a in rr: rdn along wl over 2f out: sn bhd and eased fnl f* **14/1**

2m 4.06s (-2.94) **Going Correction** -0.175s/f (Firm)
WFA 3 from 4yo+ 9lb **11** Ran SP% **119.1**
Speed ratings (Par 107): **104,103,102,102,101 101,100,99,93,91 81**
toteswingers: 1&2 £26.40, 1&3 £17.60, 2&3 £25.20 CSF £89.12 CT £616.84 TOTE £7.20: £2.30, £4.90, £2.30; EX 111.90.
Owner Saeed Manana **Bred** Darley **Trained** Newmarket, Suffolk

FOCUS
A fair handicap in which the first foiur were always prominent. The form is rated around the runner-up.

NOTEBOOK
Bazergan(IRE), who hadn't tasted victory in handicap prior to today, was down to a new career-low mark and came through to take a narrow lead inside the two. He couldn't shake the runner-up, though, and was headed inside the final furlong, but stuck out a willing neck under Debra England and just shaded it in a bobbing finish. (op 8-1)
Granston(IRE) ran no sort of race in a really competitive handicap at York last time, but he had earlier been in good form and came right back to his best. He looked the winner when edging ahead once again, but couldn't hold on. (op 16-1)
Demolition has been in good form and he kept on back in third to register another credible effort. He may win again once returned to 1m4f. (op 11-2)
Rosbay(IRE), going without the blinkers this time, is slipping back to a fair mark and may soon be able to capitalise. (tchd 11-1)
Jo'Burg(USA), 5lb higher than when a clear second at Sandown last time, was closing steadily inside the final furlong, but never threatened to win the race. (tchd 13-2)
Hurlingham held obvious claims under a 6lb penalty, despite having to shoulder a big weight, but he was under strong pressure and beaten with two to run. (tchd 11-1)
Addikt(IRE) quickly lost his position and was the first beaten. (op 11-1)

4931 RACING UK ON SKY 432 NURSERY 7f 100y
4:25 (4:26) (Class 5) (0-75,75) 2-Y-0 **£3,238** (£963; £481; £240) **Stalls** High

Form RPR

0423 **1** **Whippers Love (IRE)**[22] 4190 2-9-0 68........................ J-PGuillambert 12 78
(M Johnston) *mde all: rdn and qcknd clr over 2f out: rdn appr last and kpt on wl* **7/1**[2]

331 **2** 3/4 **Aquarian Spirit**[19] 4308 2-9-7 75........................ PaulHanagan 4 83
(R A Fahey) *wnt lft s: sn trcking ldrs: hdwy 3f out: rdn to chse wnr wl over 1f out: drvn and kpt on ins fnl f: nt rch wnr* **7/4**[1]

0052 **3** 5 **William Arnold**[9] 4618 2-7-12 55 oh6 ow3........................ KellyHarrison(3) 5 51
(C W Fairhurst) *in tch: hdwy wl over 2f out: swtchd ins and rdn over 1f out: kpt on ins fnl f: nrst fin* **7/1**[2]

3162 **4** hd **Mary Helen**[13] 4503 2-8-3 57........................ LiamJones 8 53
(W M Brisbourne) *hld up towards rr: hdwy over 2f out: swtchd rt and rdn over 1f out: styd on ins fnl f: nrst fin* **10/1**

5421 **5** 1 1/2 **Alphacino**[13] 4503 2-9-1 69........................(p) RobertWinston 2 61
(P C Haslam) *stdd s and hld up in rr: hdwy on outer wl over 2f out: rdn to chse ldrs wl over 1f out: edgd rt and one pce appr last* **16/1**

500 **6** 1 1/2 **Captain Cool (IRE)**[80] 2324 2-8-6 60........................ FrancisNorton 1 50+
(R Hannon) *in rr: hdwy on outer over 2f out: rdn and styng on whn hmpd over 1f out: kpt on ins fnl f: nt rch ldrs* **16/1**

536 **7** 3/4 **Brinscall**[68] 2699 2-8-7 61........................ AdrianTNicholls 11 48
(T D Easterby) *cl up: rdn along wl over 2f out: sn drvn and wknd wl over 1f out* **14/1**

364 **8** 1/2 **Gulf Punch**[13] 4503 2-8-5 59........................ JamieMackay 6 45
(M F Harris) *chsd ldng pair: rdn along wl over 2f out: grad wknd* **33/1**

6542 **9** 1 1/4 **Sejanus**[17] 4371 2-9-2 73........................ NeilBrown(3) 7 56
(K A Ryan) *chsd ldrs on inner: rdn along wl over 2f out: sn wknd* **9/1**[3]

050 **10** 1 **Countrymans Dream**[59] 2963 2-8-0 54 oh6 ow2........................ JimmyQuinn 10 35
(J R Weymes) *dwlt: a in rr* **100/1**

5532 **11** 9 **Storm Hawk (IRE)**[22] 4190 2-9-2 70........................ PaulEddery 3 29
(Pat Eddery) *sltly hmpd s and rr: hdwy and in tch 1/2-way: sn rdn and btn* **7/1**[2]

000 **12** 3/4 **Maiwand**[13] 4503 2-7-12 52 oh7........................ PaulQuinn 9 10
(Mrs R A Carr) *a in rr* **50/1**

1m 32.21s (-1.59) **Going Correction** -0.175s/f (Firm) **12** Ran SP% **117.3**
Speed ratings (Par 94): **102,101,95,95,93 91,90,90,88,87 77,76**
toteswingers: 1&2 £5.70, 1&3 £8.10, 2&3 £5.20 CSF £19.15 CT £92.89 TOTE £9.60: £2.40, £1.40, £2.60; EX 22.60.
Owner Crone Stud Farms Ltd **Bred** Jim McCormack **Trained** Middleham Moor, N Yorks

FOCUS
This moderate nursery was dominated throughout by Whippers Love. Decent form, with the first pair clear.

NOTEBOOK
Whippers Love(IRE) had been worn down late on each of his last two starts, but galloped on relentlessly on this occasion and always looked to be doing enough inside the final furlong. This represented an improved effort and he remains capable of better still.
Aquarian Spirit, winner of a 7f maiden at Newcastle last time, ran well off a mark of 75 on this nursery debut and should benefit from the step up to 1m sooner rather than later. (op 2-1 tchd 9-4)
William Arnold, second at 250/1 in a 7f Catterick maiden last time, showed that was no fluke by finishing third, especially considering he was 6lb out of the handicap and his rider was putting up 2lb overweight. He was a bit adrift of the front pair, but should find an opening at some point. (op 8-1)
Mary Helen finished fast and would have snatched third in a few more strides. She has been doing well at a lower level and looks well worth a try over 1m now. (op 16-1)
Alphacino, winner of a 7f claimer at Thirsk last time, didn't seem to improve for the slight rise in trip. (op 14-1)
Captain Cool(IRE) can be rated a bit better than the bare form as he was keeping on when hampered over 1f out. (op 14-1)

4932 RACING AGAIN BANK HOLIDAY WEEKEND H'CAP (FOR AMATEUR RIDERS) 1m 100y
5:00 (5:01) (Class 6) (0-65,65) 4-Y-0+ **£2,186** (£677; £338; £169) **Stalls** High

Form RPR

2221 **1** **Wiseman's Diamond (USA)**[8] 4656 4-10-7 58........................ MrSWalker 7 70
(P T Midgley) *in tch: hdwy over 2f out: rdn to chse ldrs over 1f out: styd on to ld ins fnl f* **7/4**[1]

2000 **2** 2 **Transmission (IRE)**[15] 4431 4-10-4 **62**........................ MrJNewman(7) 9 70
(B Smart) *t.k.h: chsd ldr: rdn along over 2f out: drvn to ld over 1f out: hdd ins fnl f and kpt on same pce* **33/1**

6063 **3** 3/4 **Coole Dodger (IRE)**[4] 4816 4-10-4 **55**........................ MissLEllison 11 61
(B Ellison) *t.k.h early in midfield: effrt and n.m.r 2f out: swtchd rt and rdn over 1f out: squeezed through ins fnl f and styd on wl towards fin* **10/1**

0002 **4** 1/2 **Emperor's Well**[10] 4588 10-9-7 **49**..................(b) MissJoannaMason(5) 15 54
(M W Easterby) *chsd ldrs on inner: hdwy over 2f out: rdn and ev ch over 1f out: kpt on same pce ins fnl f* **7/1**[3]

62 **5** shd **Josephine Malines**[19] 4313 5-9-9 **51**........................(p) MrBMMorris(5) 5 56
(Mrs A Duffield) *hld up: hdwy over 3f out: rdn to chse ldrs wl over 1f out: kpt on ins fnl f: nrst fin* **17/2**

6504 **6** 1 **Bivouac (UAE)**[16] 4402 5-10-7 **58**........................ MrsCBartley 14 60
(G A Swinbank) *led: rdn along over 2f out: hdd over 1f out: wknd ins fnl f* **9/1**

3203 **7** nk **Silly Gilly (IRE)**[10] 4588 5-10-3 **59**........................ MissVBarr(5) 10 61
(R E Barr) *t.k.h early in midfield: effrt and nt clr run over 2f out: sn swtchd lft and rdn: kpt on ins fnl f: nt rch ldrs* **11/1**

5065 **8** 3 1/2 **Grethel (IRE)**[10] 4588 5-9-10 **47**........................ MissLHorner 17 41
(A Berry) *towards rr: swtchd wd to stands rail 3f out and sme hdwy: sn rdn and nvr nr ldrs* **22/1**

303 **9** 2 **Salerosa (IRE)**[19] 4333 4-10-7 **65**........................ MrOJMurphy(7) 8 54
(Mrs A Duffield) *chsd ldrs: rdn over 2f out: drvn and wknd over 1f out* **5/1**[2]

-000 **10** 2 1/4 **Uhuru Peak**[10] 4588 8-9-10 **52**........................(bt) MrJakeGreenall(5) 4 36
(M W Easterby) *chsd ldrs: rdn along over 2f out: wknd over 1f out* **25/1**

630/ **11** 3 1/2 **Chicamia**[684] 5803 5-9-4 **46** oh1........................ MissMMullineaux(5) 3 22
(M Mullineaux) *dwlt: a in rr* **50/1**

0040 **12** 1 **Bernix**[23] 4170 7-9-6 **50**........................(p) MissLWilson(7) 2 24
(N Tinkler) *a in rr* **66/1**

1040 **13** 6 **Director's Chair**[27] 4054 4-10-8 **64**........................(p) MrRBirkett(5) 6 24
(Miss J Feilden) *dwlt: a in rr* **25/1**

00P0 **14** 3 **Jarvo**[16] 4402 8-9-2 **46** oh1........................(b) MissCLWhitehead(7) 13 —
(I W McInnes) *in rr: swtchd wd to stands rail 3f out: a bhd* **66/1**

1m 45.93s (-1.67) **Going Correction** -0.175s/f (Firm) **14** Ran SP% **123.4**
Speed ratings (Par 101): **101,99,98,97,97 96,96,92,90,88 85,84,78,75**
toteswingers: 1&2 £22.10, 1&3 £7.60, 2&3 £65.70 CSF £83.95 CT £488.17 TOTE £2.70: £1.30, £9.20, £3.60; EX 95.80 Place 6: £49.55 Place 5: £31.86.
Owner D I Perry **Bred** Hatta Bloodstock International **Trained** Westow, N Yorks

FOCUS
This was a low-grade handicap but not bad for its type and the form reads sound.
T/Jkpt: Not won. T/Plt: £48.50 to a £1 stake. Pool: £58,095.89. 874.14 winning tickets. T/Qpdt: £15.60 to a £1 stake. Pool: £3,442.93. 162.28 winning tickets. JR

4625 CHEPSTOW (L-H)
Thursday, August 13

OFFICIAL GOING: Good (8.1)
Wind: nil Weather: Sunny

4933 LINDLEY CATERING MEDIAN AUCTION MAIDEN STKS 6f 16y
5:50 (5:50) (Class 5) 2-Y-O **£2,719** (£809; £404; £202) **Stalls** Centre

Form RPR

0 **1** **Magnus Thrax (USA)**[63] 2844 2-9-3 0........................ RichardHughes 7 76+
(R Hannon) *a.p: rdn to ld over 1f out: r.o wl* **6/4**[2]

635 **2** 1 1/2 **Could It Be Magic**[16] 4396 2-9-0 70........................(p) JackDean(3) 3 72
(W G M Turner) *led: hdd wl over 1f out: sn rdn: kpt on same pce ins fnl f* **14/1**[3]

46 **3** 3/4 **Vanishing Grey (IRE)**[47] 3396 2-8-12 0........................ JamieSpencer 5 64
(B J Meehan) *hld up in tch: led wl over 1f out: sn rdn and hdd: no ex ins fnl f* **1/1**[1]

0 **4** 1 1/2 **Carnaval Court (IRE)**[20] 4257 2-8-12 0........................ LPKeniry 6 60+
(A M Balding) *w ldr tl pushed along over 2f out: rdn and wknd wl over 1f out* **16/1**

0 **5** 3 1/2 **Ridgeway Sapphire**[27] 4047 2-8-7 0........................ LeeNewnes(5) 11 49
(M D I Usher) *hld up in tch: pushed along 3f out: wkng whn hung lft 2f out* **50/1**

0 **6** 3 3/4 **Il Portico**[27] 4048 2-9-3 0........................ ChrisCatlin 10 43
(M R Channon) *hld up towards rr: pushed along and hdwy over 2f out: wknd over 1f out* **66/1**

7 1 3/4 **Starry Mount** 2-9-3 0........................ FergusSweeney 9 38
(A B Haynes) *hld up in mid-div: pushed along over 3f out: sn wknd* **50/1**

3 **8** nk **The Cardinal's Hat (FR)**[92] 1981 2-9-3 0........................(t) LukeMorris 8 37
(P Winkworth) *mid-div: rdn over 3f out: sn bhd* **14/1**[3]

0 **9** 3 3/4 **Carnival Time (IRE)**[38] 3692 2-9-3 0........................(b[1]) StephenCarson 4 26
(C G Cox) *sn prom: wknd wl over 2f out* **40/1**

00 **10** 1/2 **Captain Blake (IRE)**[120] 1275 2-9-3 0........................ PaulDoe 1 24
(P D Evans) *s.i.s: a in rr* **80/1**

11 15 **Knowledgeable** 2-9-3 0........................ NeilChalmers 2 —
(B Palling) *s.i.s: outpcd* **66/1**

1m 11.19s (-0.81) **Going Correction** -0.20s/f (Firm) **11** Ran SP% **119.8**
Speed ratings (Par 94): **97,95,94,92,87 82,80,79,74,73 53**
toteswingers: 1&2 £3.90, 1&3 £1.50, 2&3 £3.70 CSF £22.53 TOTE £2.50: £1.10, £2.40, £1.10; EX 21.40.
Owner Michael Pescod **Bred** Super Fine Farm **Trained** East Everleigh, Wilts

FOCUS
Just a modest juvenile maiden. The second sets the level.

NOTEBOOK
Magnus Thrax(USA) came home to reward strong support and get off the mark at the second attempt. The winner performed modestly when finishing tenth on debut at Newbury in June, but that was in one of the best juvenile maidens run so far this term and he had clearly improved during his time off the track. He was available at as big as 4/1 on the morning of the race, but strong and sustained support saw him vying for favouritism and he didn't disappoint. He was a lot better away from the gates and, while taking time to hit top gear when asked for his effort, it was clear inside the final furlong he would win. This looks very much his trip on breeding, and with the likelihood of more to come it will be interesting to see how the handicapper rates this. (op 13-8)
Could It Be Magic was offered a mark of 70 after his previous run at Beverley and ran his race from the front here, so is the most sensible guide for this form. He could be deemed as being somewhat flattered, but it is worth remembering he began this year in the Brocklesby and may be an improver. (tchd 16-1)
Vanishing Grey(IRE)'s previous Newmarket sixth in Listed company was far better form than anything her rivals here had achieved. She ultimately paid for running freely early on and now has something to prove. (op 6-5)
Carnaval Court(IRE) looked much in need of her debut experience at Ascot 20 days earlier and again looked green here. She finished nicely though after hitting a flat spot and ought to progress as she becomes more streetwise. (op 18-1)

4934 LINDLEY GROUP (S) STKS 1m 4f 23y
6:20 (6:20) (Class 6) 3-Y-O **£1,942** (£578; £288; £144) **Stalls** Low

Form RPR

0655 **1** **Primera Rossa**[16] 4397 3-8-7 42........................ LukeMorris 9 49
(J S Moore) *hld up in tch: rdn to ld over 1f out: all out* **14/1**

5633 **2** shd **Tesserae**[50] 3260 3-8-7 60........................ FergusSweeney 4 49
(A B Haynes) *chsd ldr: led 3f out: rdn over 2f out: hdd over 1f out: ev ch ins fnl f: r.o* **3/1**[1]

0003 **3** 1 **Soul Singer**[24] 4146 3-8-12 52........................ SaleemGolam 5 52
(J G Portman) *s.i.s: sn prom: rdn and swtchd lft wl over 1f out: kpt on ins fnl f* **8/1**[3]

-600 **4** 3/4 **Blazing Buck**[22] 4196 3-8-12 63........................ TolleyDean 7 51
(A W Carroll) *hld up and bhd: pushed along and hdwy on outside whn rdr dropped whip over 2f out: sn continued to hang lft: one pce ins fnl f* **9/1**

500 **5** nse **Whiterocks**[13] 4480 3-8-7 60........................ MCGeran(5) 3 51
(M R Channon) *hld up: sme prog on ins over 3f out: rdn 2f out: sn swtchd rt: styd on towards fin* **8/1**[3]

0560 **6** 1 1/4 **Warrants Attention (IRE)**[15] 4442 3-8-12 61........................ LPKeniry 8 49
(A M Balding) *hld up in tch: rdn over 2f out: fdd wl ins fnl f* **3/1**[1]

50 **7** 2 3/4 **Eloise**[3] 4838 3-8-7 0........................ HayleyTurner 6 39
(Sir Mark Prescott) *prom early: rn in snatches and sn mid-div: rdn over 5f out: short-lived effrt over 2f out* **7/2**[2]

0 **8** 3 **First Maid**[22] 4205 3-8-7 0........................ ChrisCatlin 1 35
(A B Haynes) *hld up in rr: rdn 4f out: sn struggling* **66/1**

0000 **9** 1 **Maison D'Or**[52] 3215 3-8-12 42........................ RobertHavlin 2 38
(R Ingram) *led: hdd 3f out: rdn and wknd wl over 1f out* **33/1**

2m 38.03s (-0.97) **Going Correction** -0.20s/f (Firm) **9** Ran SP% **115.5**
Speed ratings (Par 98): **95,94,94,93,93 92,91,89,88**
toteswingers: 1&2 not won, 1&3 not won, 2&3 £1.80 CSF £56.00 TOTE £21.30: £4.20, £1.10, £1.80; EX 139.60.There was no bid for the winner.
Owner Miss D L Wisbey & R J Viney **Bred** Miss D L Wisbey **Trained** Upper Lambourn, Berks

FOCUS
A very weak 3yo seller. Muddling form, with the third the best guide.

4935 LINDLEY STADIA MAIDEN STKS (H'CAP) 2m 2f
6:50 (6:50) (Class 6) (0-65,64) 3-Y-O+ **£2,266** (£674; £337; £168) **Stalls** Low

Form RPR

0563 **1** **Follow The Dream**[19] 4301 6-9-0 **50**........................ ChrisCatlin 6 57
(Karen George) *hld up towards rr: hdwy on ins whn swtchd rt 3f out: led 2f out: drvn out fnl f: styd on wl* **5/1**

0052 **2** 4 **Inchando (FR)**[9] 4625 5-8-11 **52**........................ MCGeran(5) 5 55
(A W Carroll) *hld up in mid-div: lost pl 11f out: swtchd rt and hdwy 3f out: rdn to chal wl over 1f out: sn edgd lft: one pce ins fnl f* **9/2**[3]

0- **3** 1 1/2 **Cold Mountain (IRE)**[32] 5027 7-9-0 **50** oh2..............(p) RichardHughes 3 51
(J W Mullins) *t.k.h early in tch: rdn wl over 3f out: ev ch 2f out: one pce fnl f* **7/2**[1]

060 **4** 3/4 **Trempari**[19] 4301 6-9-0 **50** oh1........................(b[1]) FergusSweeney 4 51
(Mike Murphy) *led: edgd lft over 2f out: rdn and hdd 2f out: sn btn* **14/1**

054 **5** 1/2 **Strategic Princess (IRE)**[30] 3951 3-8-3 **57**........................ JosedeSouza 9 57
(P F I Cole) *hld up in mid-div: nt clr run on ins bnd over 5f out: hdwy over 4f out: rdn and cl 2nd whn hmpd over 2f out: swtchd rt over 1f out: one pce fnl f* **4/1**[2]

-002 **6** 2 3/4 **Hill Of Clare (IRE)**[20] 4264 7-8-9 **50** oh5........................ AmyBaker(5) 1 47
(G H Jones) *hld up in rr: hdwy on outside over 4f out: rdn and ev ch 3f out: wknd over 1f out* **16/1**

400- **7** 7 **Morestead (IRE)**[13] 5631 4-9-0 **50** oh2........................ HayleyTurner 12 39
(B G Powell) *hld up towards rr: pushed along 4f out: struggling 3f out* **11/1**

-004 **8** 7 **Highams Park (IRE)**[14] 4470 3-8-3 **57** oh7 ow5........... SaleemGolam 2 39
(J G Portman) *t.k.h early: a.p: chsd ldr over 5f out tl pushed along over 3f out: wknd wl over 2f out* **40/1**

0-00 **9** 48 **Extreme Pleasure (IRE)**[36] 3739 4-9-5 **55**........................ SebSanders 11 —
(W J Knight) *hld up in tch: hung lft over 4f out: rdn and wknd over 3f out: eased over 2f out* **6/1**

03-0 **10** 35 **Fly With The Stars (USA)**[30] 3960 4-10-0 **64**..............(t) SteveDrowne 7 —
(A B Haynes) *reminder after s: sn chsng ldr: lost 2nd over 5f out: sn wknd: eased whn no ch over 3f out* **20/1**

4m 1.63s (-1.97) **Going Correction** -0.20s/f (Firm)
WFA 3 from 4yo+ 18lb **10** Ran SP% **119.4**
Speed ratings (Par 101): **96,94,93,93,93 91,88,85,64,48**
toteswingers: 1&2 £6.90, 1&3 £1.70, 2&3 £3.40 CSF £28.56 CT £90.47 TOTE £4.20: £1.50, £1.70, £1.70; EX 26.60.
Owner Miss Karen George **Bred** Miss Karen George **Trained** Higher Eastington, Devon

FOCUS
A typically weak maiden handicap and it is doubtful if the winner had to improve much. The pace was not strong form.

4936 HEATHCOTES OUTSIDE MEDIAN AUCTION MAIDEN STKS 7f 16y
7:20 (7:25) (Class 5) 3-5-Y-O **£3,238** (£963; £481; £240) **Stalls** Centre

Form RPR

20 **1** **Poppet's Lovein**[18] 4337 3-8-12 0........................ RobertHavlin 7 76
(A B Haynes) *hld up in tch: pushed along to ld over 1f out: rdn ins fnl f: r.o* **16/1**

-533 **2** 1 3/4 **Manere Bay**[27] 4060 4-9-4 65........................ TedDurcan 5 73
(J L Dunlop) *hld up in tch: ev ch over 1f out: sn rdn: nt qckn ins fnl f* **3/1**[2]

633 **3** 3 **Milldown Story**[23] 4164 3-8-12 69........................ FergusSweeney 6 63
(B R Millman) *chsd ldr: led over 2f out: rdn and hdd over 1f out: one pce* **8/1**[3]

2 **4** 3 3/4 **Criticize (USA)**[89] 2081 3-9-3 0........................ RichardHughes 1 58
(R Charlton) *dwlt: shkn up and hdd over 2f out: wknd wl over 1f out* **8/15**[1]

0 **5** 10 **Red Willow**[19] 4324 3-8-9 0........................ NataliaGemelova(3) 2 26
(J E Long) *towards rr: reminder after 1f: hdwy over 3f out: wknd 2f out* **100/1**

6 shd **Diamond Paula (IRE)** 3-8-12 0........................ PaulDoe 9 26
(P D Evans) *s.s: hld up in rr: prog over 3f out: wknd over 2f out* **33/1**

1m 22.16s (-1.04) **Going Correction** -0.20s/f (Firm)
WFA 3 from 4yo 6lb **6** Ran SP% **111.2**
Speed ratings (Par 103): **97,95,91,87,75 75**
toteswingers: 1&2 £3.00, 1&3 £5.90, 2&3 £1.60 CSF £61.82 TOTE £10.30: £2.50, £1.40; EX 58.00.
Owner Graham Robinson **Bred** G And Mrs Robinson **Trained** Limpley Stoke, Bath

FOCUS
A modest maiden, run at a fair pace. The winner built on her debut effort but the third and fourth were disappointing.
Criticize(USA) Official explanation: jockey said gelding ran too freely
Red Willow Official explanation: jockey said filly hung badly right

4937 LINDLEY CATERING 1ST CHOICE FOR CONFERENCES MAIDEN H'CAP 6f 16y
7:50 (7:53) (Class 6) (0-65,65) 3-Y-O **£2,266** (£674; £337; £168) **Stalls** Centre

Form RPR
-445 **1** **Quiquillo (USA)**[28] 4004 3-9-4 **62**.. PaulDoe 8 70
(P D Evans) *a.p: carried lft over 2f out: bmpd wl over 1f out: sn rdn: led jst ins fnl f: edgd rt to stands' rail: drvn out* **10/1**
2352 **2** *1 ¼* **Dancing Welcome**[8] 4643 3-8-5 **49**..............................(b) LukeMorris 10 53
(J M Bradley) *towards rr: rdn 3f out: hdwy wl over 1f out: swtchd lft ins fnl f: kpt on* **6/1**[2]
0604 **3** *½* **Clear Hand**[8] 4643 3-8-4 **48** ow1..................................(b) RichardSmith 1 50
(B R Millman) *chsd ldrs: rdn whn bmpd and carried lft 2f out: kpt on ins fnl f* **20/1**
032 **4** *1* **Short Cut**[6] 4730 3-8-2 **49**..(t) DavidProbert[(3)] 6 48
(S Kirk) *hld up in tch: rdn and nt qckn ins fnl f* **9/2**[1]
5030 **5** *½* **Jewelled Reef (IRE)**[8] 4642 3-9-1 **59**......................... StephenCarson 9 57+
(Eve Johnson Houghton) *s.i.s: hld up in rr: swtchd rt towards stands' rail over 3f out: carried lft 2f out: hdwy fnl f: rdn and r.o towards fin* **16/1**
3665 **6** *½* **My Best Man**[20] 4268 3-8-11 **55**..................................(t) TGMcLaughlin 4 51
(B R Millman) *hld up in mid-div: pushed along 3f out: hdwy 2f out: rdn and one pce ins fnl f* **12/1**
0405 **7** *nk* **Robin The Till**[7] 4712 3-9-6 **64**.................................... RichardHughes 14 59
(R Hannon) *hld up towards rr: stdy prog whn swtchd lft over 2f out: rdn over 1f out: no ex towards fin* **15/2**
5045 **8** *¾* **Migliori**[7] 4718 3-9-2 **60**.. SebSanders 13 53
(Rae Guest) *prom: led jst over 2f out: hdd jst ins fnl f: one pce* **7/1**[3]
0055 **9** *nk* **Handcuff**[15] 4425 3-8-4 **48**.. HayleyTurner 2 40
(J Gallagher) *a.p towards far side: rdn and ev ch over 1f out: wknd wl ins fnl f* **16/1**
0000 **10** *nk* **La Gifted**[8] 4643 3-8-7 **51**... ChrisCatlin 3 42
(M R Channon) *mid-div: lost pl 3f out: kpt on u.p fnl f: n.d* **20/1**
6662 **11** *nk* **Two Turtle Doves (IRE)**[10] 4594 3-8-11 **55**.................... RobertHavlin 5 45+
(M Mullineaux) *hld up towards rr: pushed along and sme hdwy 1f out: nvr trbld ldrs* **15/2**
0050 **12** *2 ¼* **Flute Magic**[6] 4730 3-9-2 **60**.......................................(bt) LPKeniry 15 43
(W S Kittow) *led after 1f: hung bdly lft and hdd jst over 2f out: wknd over 1f out* **22/1**
0056 **13** *2 ¼* **Rosie Two**[21] 4223 3-8-4 **51** ow2.............................. KevinGhunowa[(3)] 16 26
(W S Kittow) *led 1f: prom on stands' rail: rdn and hung bdly lft wl over 1f out: sn wknd* **25/1**
2000 **14** *1 ¾* **Charlietoo**[61] 2917 3-9-7 **65**... PaulFitzsimons 7 35
(E G Bevan) *hld up in tch: pushed along over 3f out: wkng whn hmpd jst over 2f out* **25/1**
-600 **15** *1* **Cruise Control**[20] 4267 3-8-8 **52**.................................... JamesDoyle 12 19
(R J Price) *hld up in mid-div: hdwy 3f out: hung lft 2f out: sn wknd* **25/1**
5000 **16** *6* **Yellow River (USA)**[10] 4596 3-7-13 **46** oh1..............(t) DominicFox[(3)] 11 —
(E J Creighton) *v awkward and s.s: a in rr* **80/1**

1m 11.28s (-0.72) **Going Correction** -0.20s/f (Firm) **16** Ran SP% **123.7**
Speed ratings (Par 98): **96,94,93,92,91 91,90,89,89,88 88,85,82,80,78 70**
toteswingers: 1&2 not won, 1&3 £26.50, 2&3 not won CSF £63.38 CT £1255.21 TOTE £11.00: £2.20, £1.80, £5.30, £1.80; EX 93.30.
Owner Diamond Racing Ltd **Bred** Hyperion Bloodstock **Trained** Pandy, Monmouths

FOCUS
Another maiden handicap, this time for 3yo sprinters. Limited form. The second, third and fourth all ran in the same Brighton race last week.
Flute Magic Official explanation: jockey said gelding hung badly left throughout
Cruise Control Official explanation: jockey said gelding hung left

4938 GREEN'S OF ST JAMES H'CAP 1m 14y
8:20 (8:23) (Class 6) (0-55,55) 3-Y-0+ **£2,266** (£674; £337; £168) **Stalls** Centre

Form RPR
5332 **1** **Dr Wintringham (IRE)**[12] 4536 3-8-13 **55**................... RichardHughes 5 66+
(Karen George) *hld up in rr: hdwy and swtchd lft over 1f out: rdn to ld ins fnl f: r.o wl* **9/2**[2]
-504 **2** *1* **Cadeaux Fax**[4] 4812 4-9-3 **52**.................................... TGMcLaughlin 14 61
(B R Millman) *hld up in tch: led wl over 1f out: sn rdn: hdd ins fnl f: nt qckn* **11/1**
-642 **3** *nk* **King's Icon (IRE)**[40] 3637 4-9-2 **51**............................... SteveDrowne 6 59
(M Wigham) *stdd sn after s: hld up in mid-div: hdwy wl over 1f out: sn hrd rdn: nt qckn ins fnl f* **4/1**[1]
6046 **4** *2* **Captain Oats (IRE)**[10] 4602 6-8-13 **48**......................... PaulFitzsimons 4 51
(Mrs P Ford) *hld up in tch: rdn and ev ch 2f out: one pce fnl f* **25/1**
0140 **5** *hd* **Red Current**[17] 4376 5-9-0 **52**................................. KevinGhunowa[(3)] 16 55
(R A Harris) *hld up in mid-div: hdwy over 3f out: led over 2f out tl wl over 1f out: rdn and one pce fnl f* **16/1**
3500 **6** *¾* **Libre**[17] 4389 9-9-2 **51**..(p) TolleyDean 10 52
(F Jordan) *hld up towards rr: hdwy 3f out: pushed along and carried hd high over 1f out: rdn and no imp ins fnl f* **16/1**
4044 **7** *shd* **Master Mahogany**[50] 3258 8-9-4 **53**............................. HayleyTurner 12 54
(R J Hodges) *w ldr: ev ch over 2f out: rdn and btn over 1f out* **17/2**
2200 **8** *2* **Amber Ridge**[17] 4389 4-9-2 **51**.................................. CatherineGannon 11 47
(B P J Baugh) *led: rdn and hdd over 2f out: wknd jst over 1f out* **16/1**
506 **9** *2 ¼* **Lordship (IRE)**[23] 4181 5-9-4 **53**................................. LukeMorris 9 44
(A W Carroll) *t.k.h early in tch: pushed along 3f out: rdn and wknd 2f out* **16/1**
0065 **10** *1 ¼* **Poppy Dean (IRE)**[4] 4824 4-9-0 **49**.............................. JamesDoyle 8 37
(J G Portman) *prom tl wknd 3f out* **14/1**
0620 **11** *1* **The Grey One (IRE)**[8] 4645 6-9-1 **50**...........................(p) LPKeniry 3 36
(J M Bradley) *hld up in mid-div: rdn and wknd wl over 1f out* **16/1**
050 **12** *1* **Bermacha**[30] 3949 4-9-4 **53**... RichardThomas 13 37
(J E Long) *hld up in tch: pushed along over 3f out: losing pl whn n.m.r wl over 2f out* **50/1**
5-05 **13** *2 ¼* **It's Josr**[11] 4563 4-9-3 **55**......................................(b) DavidProbert[(3)] 2 34
(I A Wood) *w ldrs tl rdn and wknd wl over 2f out* **14/1**
2254 **14** *nk* **Outer Hebrides**[13] 4479 8-9-1 **55**..............................(v) AmyBaker[(5)] 17 33
(J M Bradley) *hld up towards rr: pushed along and short-lived effrt 3f out* **12/1**
0561 **15** *14* **Eye For The Girls**[24] 4155 3-8-13 **55**.............................. ChrisCatlin 7 —
(M R Channon) *hld up towards rr: short-lived effrt 3f out* **8/1**[3]
00 **16** *22* **Vanilla Bally (ISR)**[24] 4158 4-8-12 **52**...................... MatthewDavies[(5)] 15 —
(George Baker) *s.i.s: in rr: pushed along 4f out: struggling 3f out* **25/1**

1m 34.22s (-1.98) **Going Correction** -0.20s/f (Firm)
WFA 3 from 4yo+ 7lb **16** Ran SP% **128.2**
Speed ratings (Par 101): **101,100,99,97,97 96,96,94,92,91 90,89,86,86,72 50**
toteswingers: 1&2 £14.30, 1&3 £7.50, 2&3 £20.80 CSF £55.64 CT £232.44 TOTE £6.20: £1.60, £3.00, £1.50, £7.10; EX 82.70 Place 6: £55.47, Place 5: £50.45.
Owner Mrs Isabel Fraser **Bred** Peter Molony **Trained** Higher Eastington, Devon

FOCUS
A weakish handicap, run at a solid pace. There were doubts over most of these but the winer looked a bit better than the bare form.
Bermacha Official explanation: jockey said filly was unsuited by track
It's Josr Official explanation: jockey said gelding hung righ
Vanilla Bally(ISR) Official explanation: jockey said filly lost her action
T/Plt: £34.40 to a £1 stake. Pool: £44,296.75. 937.71 winning tickets. T/Qpdt: £15.30 to a £1 stake. Pool: £3,387.13. 162.90 winning tickets. KH

4651 NEWCASTLE (L-H)
Thursday, August 13

OFFICIAL GOING: Good to firm (firm in places; 8.6)
Entire one mile straight dolled out by 3yards on stands' side.
Wind: light, half against Weather: fine

4939 WBX.COM BRITISH BASED BETTING NOVICE STKS 7f
6:00 (6:02) (Class 4) 2-Y-O **£4,533** (£1,348; £674; £336) **Stalls** High

Form RPR
1 **1** **Spying**[16] 4396 2-9-5 0.. SilvestreDeSousa 2 91+
(Mrs A Duffield) *unruly s: w ldr: t.k.h: shkn up to ld over 2f out: rdn clr fnl f* **4/7**[1]
1 **2** *3 ½* **Bow Beaver (USA)**[73] 2526 2-8-13 0............................ FrederikTylicki[(3)] 3 79
(J Howard Johnson) *led tl over 2f out: kpt on same pce appr fnl f* **11/4**[2]
3 *1 ½* **Al Naouwee (USA)** 2-8-9 0.. TomEaves 4 69
(B Smart) *trckd ldrs: lost pl and hung lft over 2f out: kpt on fnl f* **8/1**[3]
4 *1 ¼* **Think Its All Over (USA)** 2-8-9 0.................................... DNolan 1 65
(T P Tate) *green to post: swvd rt s: sn chsng ldrs: wl outpcd over 4f out: styd on fnl f* **10/1**
00 **5** *25* **Dencolstina**[3] 4856 2-8-0 0.. JamesPSullivan[(7)] 6 —
(Joss Saville) *free to post: s.s: hld up detached in last: drvn over 2f out: sn lost pl and bhd: t.o* **200/1**

1m 26.5s (-2.20) **Going Correction** -0.375s/f (Firm) **5** Ran SP% **111.0**
Speed ratings (Par 96): **97,93,91,89,61**
toteswinger: 1&2 £1.10. CSF £2.45 TOTE £1.60: £1.10, £1.40; EX 2.70.
Owner Evelyn Duchess Of Sutherland **Bred** Evelyn Duchess Of Sutherland **Trained** Constable Burton, N Yorks

FOCUS
After selective watering in the morning, the going was good to firm, firm in places. The opening race was an intriguing novice event. The two market leaders had both shown reasonable form when winning on debut. They dominated the race, but there was also some promise from a couple of newcomers. The form is rated through the runner-up.

NOTEBOOK
Spying gave some problems at the start, but travelled enthusiastically through the race and showed a good turn of foot to power clear and justify sustained support. He was a bit keen, but kept on strongly to land a gamble in a decent-looking Beverley maiden on debut, and has taken a step forward. He is out of a sister to Bahamian Bounty and closely related to La Neige, a Group 3 runner-up at 6f. There could be more to come from this classy prospect and he holds an entry in the Racing Post Trophy. (op 11-10)
Bow Beaver(USA) justified market confidence when making all in a 5f Carlisle auction maiden on debut in June. The same tactics were adopted here and he put in a fairly professional display, but he had no answer to the finishing burst of the winner. (op 7-4)
Al Naouwee(USA) attracted support in the morning and shaped with quite a bit of promise on his debut. He moved well for a long way, but veered left when pressure was applied, before staying on again. He should have learned a lot from this initial experience in a fairly hot contest. (op 7-1)
Think Its All Over(USA) was slowly away and ran very green, but seemed to get the hang of things late. He is a 55,000euro foal, out of an unraced mare from a very successful family, and holds entries in the Racing Post Trophy and Derby, so has clearly been doing some good work at home. (op 11-1 tchd 9-1)

4940 WBX.COM FOR FOOTBALL BETTING FILLIES' H'CAP 7f
6:30 (6:30) (Class 5) (0-75,74) 3-Y-O **£3,238** (£963; £481; £240) **Stalls** High

Form RPR
0265 **1** **She's In The Money**[20] 4284 3-8-8 **64**........................ FrederikTylicki[(3)] 1 73+
(R A Fahey) *stdd s and sn swtchd rt: effrt on ins over 1f out: swtchd lft over 1f out: str run to ld last 100yds: drvn clr* **4/1**[2]
0605 **2** *2 ¼* **Sanvean (IRE)**[22] 4198 3-9-0 **67**.................................... TonyCulhane 8 70
(M R Channon) *chsd ldrs: wnt 2nd over 2f out: upsides jst ins fnl f: sn outpcd by wnr* **11/2**
0512 **3** *4* **Bea Menace (USA)**[7] 4700 3-9-3 **70**...........................(b) JimmyQuinn 4 62
(P F I Cole) *led: qcknd over 4f out: hdd ins fnl f: sn wknd* **9/4**[1]
0336 **4** *¾* **Sweet Possession (USA)**[18] 4338 3-8-11 **64**.................. AndrewElliott 6 54
(A P Jarvis) *t.k.h in rr: effrt over 2f out: kpt on same pce: nvr nr ldrs* **8/1**
1624 **5** *½* **Hel's Angel (IRE)**[6] 4751 3-9-7 **74**........................... SilvestreDeSousa 2 63
(Mrs A Duffield) *in rr: sn pushed along: hdwy on outside over 3f out: one pce fnl 2f* **9/2**[3]
0005 **6** *8* **Cashleen (USA)**[33] 3859 3-8-8 **61**..................................(p) TomEaves 7 28
(K A Ryan) *chsd ldrs: reminders over 2f out: lost pl 2f out* **12/1**
0150 **7** *7* **Real Diamond**[9] 4620 3-9-5 **72**...................................... PhillipMakin 3 20
(A Dickman) *t.k.h: trckd ldrs: lost pl over 2f out: eased whn bhd ins fnl f* **12/1**

1m 25.44s (-3.26) **Going Correction** -0.375s/f (Firm) **7** Ran SP% **110.8**
Speed ratings (Par 97): **103,100,95,95,94 85,77**
toteswingers: 1&2 not won, 1&3 £1.02, 2&3 £1.60 CSF £24.28 CT £57.09 TOTE £7.10: £2.80, £1.90; EX 25.80.
Owner Cavan Pickering & Stewart Whitehead **Bred** Hermes Services Ltd **Trained** Musley Bank, N Yorks

FOCUS
A fair handicap. It was run at a steady tempo and was a race of wildly changing fortunes. The winner did it well and the second is the guide to the form.

4941 WBX.COM LOW COMMISSION-NO PREMIUM CHARGE H'CAP 1m 3y(S)
7:00 (7:01) (Class 4) (0-80,80) 3-Y-O+ **£6,476** (£1,927; £963; £481) **Stalls** High

Form RPR
626 **1** **Reel Buddy Star**[5] 4801 4-9-5 **73**.................................. DanielTudhope 9 86
(G M Moore) *mde all: qcknd over 2f out: rdn clr fnl f: eased towards fin* **3/1**[1]

2125 **2** *4 ½* **Ninth House (USA)**[6] 4751 7-8-10 **64**....................(t) SilvestreDeSousa 2 66
(Mrs R A Carr) *in rr: hdwy on outside over 2f out: chsd wnr over 1f out: no imp* **5/1**[2]

6153 **3** *1* **Intersky Charm (USA)**[40] 3615 5-8-12 **66**.................... TonyCulhane 10 66
(R M Whitaker) *chsd ldrs: effrt over 2f out: kpt on same pce* **5/1**[2]

6413 **4** *1 ¼* **Rosko**[12] 4548 5-9-2 **70**.. TomEaves 6 67
(B Ellison) *hld up in midfield: effrt 3f out: kpt on: nvr a threat* **3/1**[1]

0640 **5** *1 ½* **We'Re Delighted**[8] 4658 4-9-1 **69**.................................. DuranFentiman 4 62
(T D Walford) *s.s: hdwy over 2f out: kpt on fnl f: nvr nr ldrs* **12/1**

0506 **6** *¾* **Pacific Pride**[13] 4504 6-9-0 **68**.. PhillipMakin 5 60
(J J Quinn) *t.k.h: w wnr: rdn over 2f out: wknd ins fnl f* **14/1**

1206 **7** *¾* **Dechiper (IRE)**[8] 4658 7-8-11 **70**.................................. DeanHeslop(5) 1 60
(R Johnson) *chsd ldrs on outside: drvn 3f out: wknd over 1f out* **9/1**

-000 **8** *hd* **Mesbaah (IRE)**[19] 4333 5-8-10 **67**............................ FrederikTylicki(3) 7 56
(R A Fahey) *chsd ldrs: sn drvn along: outpcd and lost pl over 2f out* **8/1**[3]

0000 **9** *7* **Santiago Atitlan**[19] 4310 7-9-12 **80**................................ TonyHamilton 8 53
(P Monteith) *s.i.s: in rr: drvn over 2f out: sn lost pl* **22/1**

1m 39.27s (-4.13) **Going Correction** -0.375s/f (Firm) **9** Ran SP% **123.2**
Speed ratings (Par 105): **105,100,99,98,96 96,95,95,88**
toteswingers: 1&2 £2.20, 1&3 £2.10, 2&3 £2.10 CSF £19.60 CT £76.33 TOTE £4.30: £1.20, £2.30, £2.70; EX 26.30.

Owner J W Armstrong & M J Howarth **Bred** M Pennell **Trained** Middleham Moor, N Yorks

FOCUS
A fair handicap. The winner made all and this is probably not the most solid piece of form.

4942 BET WBX MOBILE @ M.WBX.COM H'CAP 5f
7:30 (7:30) (Class 6) (0-65,65) 3-Y-O £2,201 (£655; £327; £163) **Stalls** High

Form RPR

5-21 **1** **Igoyougo**[5] 4777 3-9-7 **65** 6ex.................................. SilvestreDeSousa 2 74+
(G A Harker) *w ldrs: swtchd rt after 100yds: led over 1f out: kpt on u.p fnl f* **8/11**[1]

0045 **2** *1 ¾* **Arjemis**[8] 4653 3-8-13 **57**.. PAspell 5 60
(C R Wilson) *s.i.s: hdwy 2f out: styd on to take 2nd wl ins fnl f* **18/1**

4405 **3** *hd* **Dispol Kylie (IRE)**[12] 4514 3-9-7 **65**........................... PaulMulrennan 4 67
(P T Midgley) *led: swtchd rt after 100yds: hdd over 1f out: kpt on same pce* **16/1**

0-04 **4** *1 ¼* **Gee Gina**[10] 4596 3-8-0 **49**... PaulPickard(5) 1 47
(P T Midgley) *chsd ldrs on outside: styd on same pce fnl 2f* **20/1**

5022 **5** *1 ¼* **Future Gem**[22] 4191 3-8-10 **54** ow1..........................(p) DanielTudhope 10 47
(A Dickman) *sn chsng ldrs: kpt on same pce fnl 2f* **8/1**[2]

3503 **6** *nse* **Iachimo**[18] 4343 3-8-2 **51**..(p) MartinLane(5) 9 44
(A P Jarvis) *mid-div: effrt over 2f out: kpt on fnl f: nvr nr ldrs* **14/1**

2362 **7** *½* **Fasliyanne (IRE)**[77] 2394 3-9-0 **63**..............................(b) AmyRyan(5) 6 54
(K A Ryan) *sn chsng ldrs: one pce fnl 2f* **8/1**[2]

0-00 **8** *1 ½* **Soviet Rhythm**[65] 2786 3-8-11 **55**................................... PhillipMakin 7 41+
(M Dods) *in rr: drvn over 2f out: nvr a factor* **20/1**

0403 **9** *shd* **Bees River (IRE)**[39] 3663 3-8-8 **52**............................(v) AndrewElliott 8 37
(A P Jarvis) *s.i.s: in rr: nt clr run 1f out: nvr on terms* **12/1**[3]

-P00 **10** *3 ¾* **Oceanic Dancer (IRE)**[117] 1359 3-8-3 **52**...................... JamieKyne(5) 3 24
(Patrick Morris) *chsd ldrs: lost pl over 1f out* **50/1**

59.30 secs (-1.40) **Going Correction** -0.375s/f (Firm) **10** Ran SP% **117.1**
Speed ratings (Par 98): **96,93,92,90,88 88,88,85,85,79**
toteswingers: 1&2 £14.50, 1&3 £2.60, 2&3 £14.50 CSF £16.28 CT £129.91 TOTE £1.50: £1.10, £4.70, £3.70; EX 14.60.

Owner Miss K Watson **Bred** Karen Watson **Trained** Thirkleby, N Yorks

FOCUS
A modest handicap run at a decent pace. The winner confirmed his Ayr improvement and the form is rated around the third.

Soviet Rhythm Official explanation: jockey said filly was denied a clear run
Bees River(IRE) Official explanation: jockey said filly was denied a clear run

4943 BET WBX.COM FOR BETTER ODDS H'CAP 1m 2f 32y
8:00 (8:00) (Class 6) (0-65,65) 3-Y-O £2,331 (£693; £346; £173) **Stalls** Centre

Form RPR

0442 **1** **Addison De Witt**[16] 3976 3-8-11 **55**..............................(v) PaulHanagan 10 58
(Micky Hammond) *trckd ldrs: t.k.h: styd on to ld last 75yds: hld on* **3/1**[1]

5530 **2** *¾* **Chichen Daawe**[4] 4819 3-7-12 **49**..................................... IJBrennan(7) 7 50+
(B Ellison) *hld up in midfield: hdwy over 2f out: kpt on wl ins fnl f: no ex nr fin* **9/1**

0-50 **3** *shd* **Shadows Lengthen**[87] 2131 3-8-11 **55**.............................(b[1]) DaleGibson 13 56
(M W Easterby) *t.k.h: sn trcking ldrs: effrt and hung lft 2f out: led jst ins fnl f: sn hdd and no ex* **7/1**

3050 **4** *½* **Kristopher James (IRE)**[11] 4562 3-8-11 **55**...................... LiamJones 5 55
(W M Brisbourne) *t.k.h: trckd ldr: upsides 5f out: narrow ld over 3f out tl jst ins fnl f: kpt on same pce* **12/1**

5000 **5** *¾* **Sharp Sovereign (USA)**[12] 4529 3-8-11 **55**.................... PhillipMakin 2 54
(I Semple) *trckd ldrs: t.k.h: outpcd over 3f out: styd on one pce fnl 2f* **12/1**

-046 **6** *shd* **Acclaim To Fame (IRE)**[24] 4156 3-7-13 **49** ow1.......... MartinLane(5) 12 46
(A P Jarvis) *set stdy pce: hdd over 2f out: remained upsides: kpt on same pce ins fnl f* **5/1**[3]

6052 **7** *nk* **Aphrodite's Rock**[7] 4704 3-9-7 **65**................................. TomEaves 11 63
(Miss Gay Kelleway) *t.k.h dropped towards rr: hdwy on outside over 2f out: kpt on: nt rch ldrs* **9/2**[2]

-022 **8** *1 ½* **Moggy (IRE)**[27] 4065 3-8-10 **54**..................................... TonyHamilton 3 49
(G A Harker) *towards rr: kpt on fnl 2f: nvr a threat* **10/1**

06-0 **9** *½* **K'Gari (USA)**[18] 4354 3-8-2 **46** oh1.......................... SilvestreDeSousa 1 40
(B Ellison) *trckd ldrs: rdn over 3f out: one pce fnl 2f* **12/1**

0400 **10** *½* **Susurrayshaan**[7] 4710 3-8-6 **50**..................................(p) FrancisNorton 9 43
(Mrs G S Rees) *hld up in rr: hdwy over 2f out: wknd fnl f* **33/1**

3660 **11** *4* **Sydney Cove (IRE)**[18] 4348 3-7-10 **47** oh1 ow1..... JamesPSullivan(7) 8 32
(R Allan) *s.s: tk fierce hold: jnd ldrs 7f out: wknd 2f out* **33/1**

2m 13.65s (1.75) **Going Correction** -0.20s/f (Firm) **11** Ran SP% **120.4**
Speed ratings (Par 98): **85,84,84,83,83 83,83,81,81,81 77**
toteswingers: 1&2 £2.00, 1&3 not won, 2&3 not won CSF £31.77 CT £176.72 TOTE £5.50: £1.50, £3.50, £2.90; EX 37.40.

Owner Peter J Davies **Bred** J H Widdows **Trained** Middleham Moor, N Yorks

FOCUS
A weak handicap; the field had managed just one win between them in a total of 83 runs. The pace was very steady, several took a fierce hold and they finished in a heap. The form looks very suspect.

4944 WBX.COM FOR ANTE POST BETTING H'CAP 1m 2f 32y
8:30 (8:30) (Class 6) (0-52,52) 3-Y-O+ £2,072 (£616; £308; £153) **Stalls** Centre

Form RPR

0061 **1** **Miss Ferney**[4] 4818 5-8-11 **51** 6ex................................... PaulPickard(5) 2 60+
(A Kirtley) *hld up in rr: smooth hdwy on outer over 2f out: led appr fnl f: styd on wl* **15/2**[3]

0032 **2** *¾* **Tivers Song (USA)**[16] 4402 5-8-8 **46**....................(b) FrederikTylicki(3) 12 50
(John A Harris) *mid-div: hdwy over 4f out: styd on fnl f: tk 2nd nr fin* **4/1**[1]

-040 **3** *½* **Caught On Camera**[12] 4545 3-8-8 **52**............................ PaulHanagan 11 55
(M L W Bell) *mid-div: drvn 5f out: hdwy and nt clr run over 2f out: sn chsng ldrs: kpt on same pce fnl f* **9/2**[2]

0463 **4** *hd* **Join Up**[6] 4734 3-8-4 **48**.. DuranFentiman 14 53+
(W M Brisbourne) *hld up in midfield: hdwy whn nt clr run over 2f out tl over 1f out: styd on wl ins fnl f* **10/1**

0045 **5** *1 ½* **Bourse (IRE)**[14] 4465 4-9-3 **52**.....................................(b) AndrewMullen 8 52
(A G Foster) *chsd ldrs: edgd rt and upsides appr fnl f: kpt on same pce* **20/1**

2B20 **6** *1* **Whipma Whopma Gate (IRE)**[16] 4402 4-9-2 **51**................ DNolan 16 49
(D Carroll) *in rr: hdwy and nt clr run over 2f out: kpt on: nvr rchd ldrs* **11/1**

0-63 **7** *1 ¼* **Roman History (IRE)**[5] 4804 6-8-13 **48**..............(p) SilvestreDeSousa 15 43
(Miss Tracy Waggott) *in rr: effrt over 2f out: styd on fnl f* **14/1**

0052 **8** *1 ½* **Altos Reales**[23] 4170 5-9-0 **49**.. PaulMulrennan 5 41
(J G Given) *prom: effrt and n.m.r over 2f out: chsng ldrs and hung rt over 1f out: kpt on same pce* **8/1**

340 **9** *shd* **Awaken**[5] 4804 8-8-12 **47**.. PhillipMakin 1 39
(Miss Tracy Waggott) *in rr: effrt over 2f out: hmpd ins fnl f: kpt on wl* **33/1**

4242 **10** *2 ¼* **Den Maschine**[29] 3974 4-8-12 **52**..................................(p) MartinLane(5) 3 39
(B N Pollock) *chsd ldrs: hung rt and wknd fnl f* **8/1**

0-40 **11** *2 ½* **Park's Prodigy**[44] 3486 5-9-0 **49**.................................. TonyHamilton 7 31
(G A Harker) *chsd ldrs: wkng whn n.m.r ins fnl f* **17/2**

0000 **12** *2* **Flashy Max**[48] 3331 4-8-12 **47**.. AndrewElliott 4 25
(Jedd O'Keeffe) *led: drvn over 5f out: hdd & wknd appr fnl f* **50/1**

000 **13** *1 ¾* **Annes Sound (IRE)**[21] 4224 3-7-13 **50**................... JamesPSullivan(7) 13 25
(Patrick Morris) *s.i.s: t.k.h in rr: sme hdwy on ins over 2f out: nvr on terms* **100/1**

-556 **14** *2 ½* **Jelly Mo**[24] 4158 4-8-11 **46**.. LiamJones 10 16
(W M Brisbourne) *chsd ldrs: drvn over 3f out: hmpd and lost pl 2f out* **33/1**

5430 **15** *7* **Waterloo Corner**[15] 4431 7-9-3 **52**.................................(p) TomEaves 6 8
(R Craggs) *chsd ldrs: drvn over 5f out: lost pl over 2f out* **20/1**

2m 9.44s (-2.46) **Going Correction** -0.20s/f (Firm)
WFA 3 from 4yo+ 9lb **15** Ran SP% **125.1**
Speed ratings (Par 101): **101,100,100,99,98 97,96,95,95,93 91,90,88,86,81**
toteswingers: 1&2 £1.90, 1&3 not won, 2&3 £11.90 CSF £36.26 CT £157.93 TOTE £9.00: £3.80, £2.00, £1.50; EX 35.90 Place 6: £16.29, Place 5: £14.83.
Owner Mrs P J Taylor-Garthwaite **Bred** K And P J Garthwaite **Trained** Houghton-le-Spring, Tyne & W

FOCUS
A low-grade handicap, but it did involve a last-time-out winner and several others who had been placed on their latest start. The pace was solid, the winner was fairly impressive and there were a few hard-luck stories. Sound form.
Altos Reales Official explanation: jockey said mare hung right in final furlong
Den Maschine Official explanation: jockey said gelding hung right in final furlong
T/Plt: £39.60 to a £1 stake. Pool: £42,552.31. 784.18 winning tickets. T/Qpdt: £9.40 to a £1 stake. Pool: £4,053.33. 316.80 winning tickets. WG

4900 SALISBURY (R-H)
Thursday, August 13

OFFICIAL GOING: Good to firm (firm in places; 8.7) changing to good to firm after race 1 (1.55)
Wind: Virtually nil Weather: Bright

4945 TENON RECOVERY MAIDEN AUCTION STKS (DIV I) 6f 212y
1:55 (1:55) (Class 5) 2-Y-O £2,914 (£867; £433; £216) **Stalls** Centre

Form RPR

0 **1** **Dromore (IRE)**[22] 4200 2-8-8 0...................................... DavidProbert(3) 1 75
(A M Balding) *leggy: scope: trckd ldrs: drvn to chal over 2f out: rdn and slt ld fnl 100yds: hld on wl* **17/2**

524 **2** *½* **Joe Packet**[12] 4534 2-8-9 81... TPQueally 4 72
(J G Portman) *trckd ldrs: chal 2f out: slt ld u.p 1f out: narrowly hdd fnl 100yds: styd on same pce* **7/2**[2]

00 **3** *3 ½* **Ashkalara**[21] 4226 2-8-6 0.. KirstyMilczarek 6 60
(H S Howe) *w ldr: led after 2f: rdn 3f out: narrowly hdd 2f out: styd wl there tl wknd fnl 110yds* **20/1**

65 **4** *nse* **Pebblesonthebeach**[15] 4439 2-8-13 0................................... SebSanders 5 67
(J W Hills) *s.i.s: in rr tl hdwy over 3f out: slt ld u.p 2f out: hdd 1f out: wknd ins fnl f* **8/1**

6 **5** *½* **Lenkiewicz**[50] 3277 2-8-4 0.. RichardThomas 8 57
(B R Millman) *prssed ldrs: rdn 3f out: styd wl there tl wknd fnl f* **50/1**

0 **6** *hd* **Valkov**[31] 3925 2-8-4 0.. RichardKingscote 9 56
(Tom Dascombe) *leggy: led 2f: styd pressing ldrs: rdn over 2f out: wknd over 1f out* **25/1**

05 **7** *1* **High Holborn (IRE)**[20] 4258 2-9-2 0............................... JamieSpencer 14 67+
(B J Meehan) *lw: in rr: rdn over 3f out: styd on u.p fr 2f out: no imp and hung rt fr over 1f out* **9/2**[3]

8 *1* **Green Earth (IRE)** 2-9-2 0.. JimCrowley 7 63+
(Mrs A J Perrett) *w'like: bit bkwd: s.i.s: in rr: pushed along and hdwy fr 2f out: styd on ins fnl f but nvr anywhere nr ldrs* **14/1**

5 **9** *1 ¼* **Themanforacrisis (IRE)**[33] 3867 2-8-13 0............................ RyanMoore 10 57
(R M Beckett) *lw: chsd ldrs: rdn over 3f out: wknd 3f out* **10/3**[1]

10 *¾* **Jubail (IRE)** 2-8-9 0.. FergusSweeney 15 51
(A King) *str: bit bkwd: in rr tl sme prog over 2f out: no imp fnl f* **50/1**

00 **11** *1* **Expensive Legacy**[29] 3979 2-8-4 0...................................... HayleyTurner 2 44
(H J L Dunlop) *chsd ldrs over 4f* **33/1**

12 *10* **Pollan Bay (IRE)** 2-8-9 0.. JamesDoyle 12 24
(S Kirk) *w'like: bit bkwd: s.i.s: a in rr* **33/1**

13 14 **Red Farasi (IRE)** 2-8-9 0 .... JerryO'Dwyer 11 —
(B W Duke) *w'like: early spd: bhd fr 1/2-way* **66/1**

1m 28.62s (-0.38) **Going Correction** -0.175s/f (Firm) **13** Ran SP% **114.1**
Speed ratings (Par 94): **95,94,90,90,89 89,88,87,85,85 83,72,56**
toteswingers: 1&2 £7.90, 1&3 £48.70, 2&3 £16.60 CSF £33.70 TOTE £11.60: £3.50, £1.60, £5.90; EX 43.90.
Owner I G Burbidge **Bred** Mount Eaton Stud **Trained** Kingsclere, Hants

FOCUS
After 4mm of rain overnight the ground was riding better than the previous day, according to the jockeys. A fair maiden in which debutants have a reasonable record but none of that group was particularly fancied. The first two came clear but this is fairly modest maiden form for the track.

NOTEBOOK
Dromore(IRE), a 14,000gns half-brother to four winners including the top-class Storming Home, had showed promise after missing the break on his debut on Polytrack and the experience had been positive, as he chased the leaders before being produced on the outside and proved strongest in the closing stages. He should go on from this but much depends on what mark the handicapper gives him. (op 9-1 tchd 11-1)
Joe Packet set the standard and, although he was slightly edgy beforehand, ran his race. He tracked the leaders and looked the most likely winner when going on over 1f out, only to be worn down late on. He will have a difficult task in handicaps off his current marks so may be best kept to maiden company. (op 100-30)
Ashkalara stepped up considerably on her two previous efforts under a positive ride. She is out of an unraced sister to Ashkalani, and could be interesting in handicaps now she qualifies for a mark. (op 16-1)
Pebblesonthebeach is another who now qualifies for handicaps having shown ability on all three starts. He looked likely to play a more prominent role when first arriving on the scene, but could not maintain his effort in the last furlong. He is bred to stay middle-distances so a step up in trip could be on the cards. (op 9-1 tchd 10-1)
Lenkiewicz had not run since finishing last on her debut over 5f here in June. She has clearly improved in the meantime as she was always in the front rank and kept going under pressure, and is another who will appreciate longer trips in time.
Valkov was well beaten on her debut on Polytrack but ran an interesting race, being up with the leaders until losing her place over 2f out before running on again in the closing stages. She gave the impression she is capable of building on this. (op 16-1)
High Holborn(IRE) was well supported but failed to really build on his modest previous form, although at least now qualifies for a mark. (op 6-1)
Green Earth(IRE), from a family of middle-distance performers, was the best backed of the newcomers and did best of that group, showing minor promise in staying on from the rear in the latter part of the race. (tchd 12-1)
Themanforacrisis(IRE), for whom Ryan Moore was an eyecatching booking, was under pressure 3f out and could only keep on at the one speed. Maybe the ground was faster than ideal. (tchd 11-4)

4946 TENON RECOVERY MAIDEN AUCTION STKS (DIV II) 6f 212y
2:30 (2:31) (Class 5) 2-Y-O £2,914 (£867; £433; £216) **Stalls** Centre

Form RPR

024 **1** **Many A Slip**[35] 3785 2-8-9 0 .... RyanMoore 13 76
(J L Dunlop) *s.i.s: sn rcvrd and in tch: pushed along and hdwy over 2f out: slt ld appr fnl f: hrd drvn and hld on gamely thrght fnl f* **9/2**[2]

02 **2** *hd* **Magic Lantern**[29] 3979 2-8-8 0 .... RichardHughes 1 75
(R Hannon) *lw: broke wl fr outside draw and sn led: pushed along over 2f out: hdd appr fnl f: styd chalng wnr tl no ex last strides* **4/5**[1]

53 **3** *4* **Bandear (IRE)**[21] 4239 2-8-6 0 .... HayleyTurner 8 63
(C E Brittain) *t.k.h early: pressed ldrs and ev ch fr 3f out tl outpcd by ldng duo fnl f* **14/1**

4 *1 ¼* **One Cool Poppy (IRE)** 2-8-1 0 .... DavidProbert(3) 12 57
(H J L Dunlop) *athletic: sn in tch: chsd ldrs fr 1/2-way: rdn over 2f out: wknd ins fnl f* **20/1**

0 **5** *2 ¼* **Kingsdine (IRE)**[15] 4424 2-8-13 0 .... TGMcLaughlin 10 61
(M S Saunders) *leggy: t.k.h early: towards rr: hdwy on outsode fr 2f out: kpt on fnl f but nvr in contention* **100/1**

5 **6** *½* **Firehawk**[11] 4568 2-8-9 0 .... TPQueally 11 56
(J G Portman) *chsd ldrs: rdn and outpcd fr 3f out: styd on again fnl f* **16/1**

7 *nk* **Sundream** 2-8-4 0 .... RichardKingscote 4 50
(Tom Dascombe) *w'like: slowly away: rdn and j. path 3f out: v green u.p but sme prog fr over 1f out* **25/1**

8 *1 ¼* **Light The Way** 2-8-9 0 .... FergusSweeney 7 52
(P J Makin) *chsd ldr: rdn and upsides 2f out: wknd over 1f out* **8/1**[3]

9 *½* **Perfect Vision** 2-8-6 0 .... LukeMorris 9 47
(C G Cox) *lengthy: bit bkwd: slowly away: rdn in rr and green 4f out: mod prog fnl f* **16/1**

05 **10** *7* **City Of Rome (IRE)**[20] 4265 2-9-2 0 .... JimmyFortune 2 40
(R Hannon) *a in rr* **33/1**

05 **11** *2 ¼* **Arkellion**[11] 4557 2-8-11 0 .... PaulDoe 6 29
(P D Evans) *w'like: medium-sized: chsd ldrs 4f* **33/1**

12 *5* **Hum Again (IRE)** 2-8-13 0 .... JamesDoyle 15 19
(J S Moore) *w'like: bhd most of way* **66/1**

1m 28.18s (-0.82) **Going Correction** -0.175s/f (Firm) **12** Ran SP% **120.3**
Speed ratings (Par 94): **97,96,92,90,88 87,87,85,85,77 74,69**
toteswingers: 1&2 £2.10, 1&3 £5.70, 2&3 £4.40 CSF £8.04 TOTE £5.60: £1.70, £1.10, £3.10; EX 9.20.
Owner J L Dunlop **Bred** Whatton Manor Stud **Trained** Arundel, W Sussex

FOCUS
The second division of this maiden was run 0.44 secs faster than the first leg and produced a good battle between the market leaders, who came clear of the rest. Just fair form.

NOTEBOOK
Many A Slip had run well in a couple of maidens on similar ground and over this trip and put that experience to good use to get the better of the favourite. He settled off the pace early before being produced to lead entering the final furlong, but had to dig deep. He should not be too badly treated in handicaps. (op 7-1)
Magic Lantern had built on her debut on Polytrack last time and made a fast start from her outside draw to get over to the lead. She was a little keen early but it did not affect her too much, as she battled back well when headed and made the winner fight all the way to the line. She should not be long in getting off the mark on this evidence. (op 10-11, tchd 1-1 in a place)
Bandear(IRE) had been a well-beaten third on her previous start and, although she was comfortably held once more, she probably stepped up again. Nevertheless, she does not do much for the form.
One Cool Poppy(IRE) is a sister to a dual 6f juvenile winner but is bred to get a little further. She ran pretty well on this debut until fading in the last furlong and an easier test at this trip may enable her to build on this. (tchd 22-1)
Kingsdine(IRE), who was unfancied when well beaten on his debut on soft ground at the end of last month, showed a fair bit more on this faster surface, staying on from the rear in the last 2f. He is one to bear in mind for handicaps in due course. (op 66-1)
Sundream, a cheaply-bought half-sister to a pointer, ran on late having been out the back for much of the race. (op 20-1)

Light The Way showed plenty of pace on this debut, especially considering he is bred to get further in time. He should come on for the experience. (op 13-2 tchd 17-2)

4947 MARY WORT MEMORIAL MAIDEN STKS 6f 212y
3:05 (3:07) (Class 5) 3-4-Y-O £3,885 (£1,156; £577; £288) **Stalls** Centre

Form RPR

0-4 **1** **Netta (IRE)**[27] 4057 3-8-12 0 .... JimmyFortune 5 85+
(P J Makin) *trckd ldrs: wnt 2nd travelling wl appr fnl 2f: led over 1f out: drvn and styd on strly fnl f* **7/1**[2]

2200 **2** *3* **Ermine And Velvet**[34] 3816 3-8-12 89 .... HayleyTurner 4 77
(C E Brittain) *lw: sn slt ld: rdn over 2f out: hdd appr fnl f: one pce ins fnl f* **6/4**[1]

2 **3** *1 ¼* **Primaeval**[41] 3566 3-9-3 0 .... JamieSpencer 2 79
(J R Fanshawe) *in rr: rdn and green fr 1/2-way: hdwy 2f out: styd on to go 3rd over 1f out but stl immature and one pce ins fnl f* **6/4**[1]

0 **4** *10* **Forward Planning (USA)**[20] 4277 3-8-12 0 .... TPO'Shea 1 47
(M Johnston) *tk v t.k.h and upsides tl ins fnl 3f: wknd qckly appr fnl 2f* **12/1**[3]

5 *5* **Bahamian Mouse (IRE)** 3-8-9 0 .... DavidProbert(3) 3 33
(Andrew Turnell) *unf: in rr: rdn and green fr 1/2-way* **40/1**

4400 **6** *1 ¼* **Megasecret**[19] 4304 3-9-3 68 .... JimCrowley 8 35
(R Hannon) *w ldr to 3f out: wknd qckly sn after* **14/1**

1m 27.29s (-1.71) **Going Correction** -0.175s/f (Firm)
WFA 3 from 4yo 6lb **6** Ran SP% **109.3**
Speed ratings (Par 103): **102,98,97,85,80 78**
toteswingers: 1&2 £2.10, 1&3 £1.70, 2&3 £1.10 CSF £17.09 TOTE £7.70: £2.80, £1.40; EX 18.90.
Owner Netta Racing **Bred** Barouche Stud Ireland Ltd **Trained** Ogbourne Maisey, Wilts

FOCUS
Not the strongest of maidens but the time compared favourably with the preceding juvenile events over the same distance, being 0.89secs faster than the quicker of those two races. Tricky form to pin down, with doubts over the second and third, and the winner a big improver.

4948 EUROPEAN BREEDERS' FUND FILLIES' H'CAP 1m 4f
3:40 (3:40) (Class 4) (0-80,78) 3-Y-O+ £6,799 (£2,023; £1,011; £505) **Stalls** High

Form RPR

212 **1** **Doggerbank (IRE)**[19] 4319 3-9-4 78 .... TPQueally 3 89+
(H R A Cecil) *lw: hld up in rr: hdwy fr 3f out: rdn to ld 1f out: drvn out* **4/1**[2]

2-55 **2** *3* **Lyceana**[31] 3921 4-9-10 73 .... PhilipRobinson 1 79
(M A Jarvis) *hld up in rr: stdy hdwy on outside over 2f out: drvn to chal over 1f out: chsd wnr ins fnl f but nvr any ch* **14/1**

1421 **3** *1 ½* **Where's Susie**[36] 3739 4-9-2 65 .... RobertHavlin 9 68
(M Madgwick) *s.i.s: sn chsng ldrs: n.m.r fr ins fnl 2f: kpt on fnl f but no imp on ldng duo* **12/1**

-464 **4** *1 ½* **Piquante**[63] 2858 3-8-9 69 .... HayleyTurner 10 70
(M L W Bell) *b: lw: trckd ldrs: led 2f out: hdd and hung rt 2f out: sn btn* **9/2**[3]

631 **5** *3 ½* **Galilean Moon**[20] 4270 3-9-3 77 .... RyanMoore 6 74
(Sir Michael Stoute) *swtg: prom: chsd ldr 7f out: led ins fnl 3f: rdn and hdd 2f out: one pce and hld whn hmpd on rail ins fnl 2f* **5/2**[1]

0663 **6** *1 ½* **Lake Kalamalka (IRE)**[35] 3776 3-8-10 70 .... RichardHughes 2 63
(J L Dunlop) *in rr tl stdy hdwy fr 3f out: trckd ldrs 2f out: sn rdn: wknd fnl f* **12/1**

0110 **7** *1 ¼* **Yonder**[30] 3940 5-9-4 67 .... (b) JimCrowley 8 58
(H Morrison) *towards rr: hdwy 6f out: pressed ldrs fr 4f out: wknd ins fnl 2f* **8/1**

0360 **8** *½* **Silver Surprise**[6] 4735 5-8-6 58 oh13 .... (b[1]) MarcHalford(3) 7 48
(J J Bridger) *s.i.s: hdwy 6f out: rdn over 3f out: wknd ins fnl 2f* **100/1**

2203 **9** *17* **Step This Way (USA)**[7] 4696 4-10-0 77 .... JamieSpencer 4 40
(M Johnston) *led tl hdd ins fnl 3f: wkng whn n.m.r on ins 2f out* **15/2**

1-0 **10** *104* **Floodlit**[96] 1871 3-9-4 78 .... JimmyFortune 5 —
(J H M Gosden) *t.k.h: chsd ldrs 3f: sn bhd: t.o fnl 4f: virtually p.u fnl 3f: t.o* **14/1**

2m 35.03s (-2.97) **Going Correction** -0.175s/f (Firm)
WFA 3 from 4yo+ 11lb **10** Ran SP% **119.3**
Speed ratings (Par 102): **102,100,99,98,95 94,93,93,82,—**
toteswingers: 1&2 £12.90, 1&3 £4.70, 2&3 £31.00 CSF £60.14 CT £628.56 TOTE £3.80: £2.00, £3.80, £3.40; EX 68.60.
Owner G Schoeningh **Bred** Airlie Stud **Trained** Newmarket, Suffolk
■ Stewards' Enquiry : Hayley Turner one day: carless riding (Aug 27)

FOCUS
A fair fillies' handicap and quite a tight contest, and with one exception not much between the entire field on official marks. The pace was good and the first two came from well off the pace.
Floodlit Official explanation: jockey said filly lost her action

4949 TOTESPORT.COM SOVEREIGN STKS (GROUP 3) (C&G) 1m
4:15 (4:18) (Class 1) 3-Y-O+
£36,900 (£13,988; £7,000; £3,490; £1,748; £877) **Stalls** Centre

Form RPR

-410 **1** **Mac Love**[58] 2990 8-9-3 110 .... MickyFenton 6 116
(Stef Liddiard) *hld up in rr: hdwy on outside and travelling wl 2f out: qcknd to ld jst ins fnl f: readily* **25/1**

1242 **2** *1 ½* **Confront**[33] 3841 4-9-0 116 .... RyanMoore 2 110
(Sir Michael Stoute) *lw: led: rdn over 2f out: hdd jst ins fnl f: nt pce of wnr but kpt on for clr 2nd* **4/5**[1]

0301 **3** *2 ¾* **Laa Rayb (USA)**[13] 4486 5-9-0 112 .... (b) JimmyFortune 3 103
(M Johnston) *swtg: hld up in tch: rdn and styd on fr 2f out: hrd rdn: hung rt and fnd nil ins fnl f* **7/2**[2]

4101 **4** *1* **Khateeb (IRE)**[18] 4352 4-9-0 109 .... (t) TPO'Shea 1 101
(M A Jarvis) *lw: trckd ldr: rdn over 2f out: weaknened appr fnl f* **13/2**[3]

-302 **5** *¾* **Orizaba (IRE)**[18] 4352 3-8-7 106 .... TedDurcan 5 99
(Saeed Bin Suroor) *chsd ldrs: rdn 3f out: wknd qckly over 1f out* **11/1**

5416 **6** *2* **Without A Prayer (IRE)**[33] 3841 4-9-0 111 .... SebSanders 7 95
(R M Beckett) *broke wl: stdd towards rr but wl in tch: rdn along and no imp on ldrs fr 3f out* **9/1**

1m 40.29s (-3.21) **Going Correction** -0.175s/f (Firm)
WFA 3 from 4yo+ 7lb **6** Ran SP% **113.3**
Speed ratings: **109,107,104,103,103 101**
toteswingers: 1&2 £4.70, 1&3 £5.70, 2&3 £1.30 CSF £47.29 TOTE £17.70: £3.80, £1.20; EX 31.10.
Owner Vimal Khosla **Bred** Kingwood Bloodstock **Trained** Great Shefford, Berks

FOCUS
A fair race for the grade. Mac Love looks back to his best in confirming Diomed placings with Confront despite his penalty. The beaten horses are rated 10lb+ below their best.

NOTEBOOK
Mac Love, the outsider of the sextet, came from the back of the field to score decisively. He had beaten today's favourite when winning the Diomed Stakes, but that rival had excuses for that defeat and was 3lb better off. However, Mac Love was always travelling and, when produced, found a good turn of foot to settle the issue. He is a credit to connections, having won two Group 3s and a Listed race since November, and appears to be as good, if not better, than ever. He has a choice of the Winter Hill Stakes over 1m2f at Windsor or the Supreme Stakes over 7f at Goodwood next. (op 16-1)
Confront had apparently lost a shoe when beaten by today's winner at Epsom and was backed into odds on to reverse the placings. Wearing earplugs, he attempted to make all the running and got most of his rivals off the bit when winding up the pace from over 3f out but he had nothing left with which to repel the challenge of the winner. (op 11-10)
Laa Rayb(USA) finished second in this race last season and had shown his wellbeing when winning a valuable heritage handicap at Goodwood. He appeared to have his chance but could not find an extra gear in the closing stages. (op 3-1)
Khateeb(IRE) had beaten Orizaba at Pontefract last time and confirmed that running on 1lb better terms. He appeared a major threat to the favourite 2f out but his effort petered out from that point. (op 11-2)
Orizaba(IRE) represented the stable with the best recent record in this, but he was unable to make much impression despite running close to previous form with Khateeb. (op 12-1 tchd 14-1)
Without A Prayer(IRE) was held by most of these on recent form but even so this was a rather lacklustre effort. (tchd 10-1)

4950 RACING UK FILLIES' H'CAP — 6f
4:50 (4:50) (Class 5) (0-70,68) 3-Y-O+ — £3,238 (£963; £481; £240) Stalls High

Form — RPR
-420 1 **Lucy Brown**[17] 4380 3-9-9 **68** — RyanMoore 3 — 77
(R Hannon) *towards rr: pushed along and hdwy fr 3f out: rdn to ld appr fnl f: styd on strly* — **4/1**[1]
1104 2 *2 ¼* **Green Velvet**[75] 2492 4-9-6 **61** — TravisBlock 9 — 64
(P J Makin) *t.k.h early: chsd ldrs: rdn and styd on wl to chal over 1f out: chsd wnr fnl f: a hld but hld on wl for 2nd* — **8/1**
4653 3 *hd* **Dualagi**[7] 4702 5-9-1 **56** — JimCrowley 10 — 58
(M R Bosley) *lw: t.k.h: in tch: drvn and styd on fr 2f out: kpt on wl fnl f to press for 2nd cl home but nvr nr wnr* — **5/1**[3]
0000 4 *½* **Polar Annie**[15] 4428 4-9-11 **66** — TGMcLaughlin 4 — 67
(M S Saunders) *awkward s: in rr: hdwy on outside over 2f out: styd on fnl f and gng on cl home but nvr anywhere nr wnr* — **5/1**[3]
046- 5 *hd* **Bosamcliff (IRE)**[107] 6703 4-9-3 **63** — RichardEvans(5) 6 — 63
(P D Evans) *chsd ldrs: rdn fr 2f out: nt qcknd fnl f* — **14/1**
6660 6 *¾* **Blushing Maid**[6] 4748 3-9-1 **60** — KirstyMilczarek 7 — 57
(H S Howe) *t.k.h: trckd ldr tl led ins fnl 3f: hdd appr fnl f and sn wknd* — **12/1**
0135 7 *hd* **Wotasparkler**[23] 4167 3-9-1 **60** — MickyFenton 5 — 56
(W S Kittow) *in rr: pushed along and sme hdwy fr 2f out: styd on fnl f but nvr in contention* — **9/2**[2]
3451 8 *1 ¼* **Ishibee (IRE)**[7] 4702 5-8-9 **53** 6ex — (p) MarcHalford(3) 2 — 46
(J J Bridger) *in rr: pushed along 3f out: kpt on ins fnl f but nvr gng pce to get into contention* — **13/2**
6000 9 *1 ½* **Day In Dubai**[19] 4304 3-8-5 **50** — RichardThomas 11 — 37
(J J Bridger) *led tl hdd ins fnl 3f: wknd wl over 1f out* — **16/1**
00-0 10 *hd* **Merry May**[23] 4172 3-7-13 **47** oh2 — DavidProbert(3) 8 — 34
(S Kirk) *towards rr whn rdn over 3f out: a outpcd* — **50/1**

1m 14.68s (-0.12) **Going Correction** -0.175s/f (Firm)
WFA 3 from 4yo+ 4lb — **10** Ran SP% **118.2**
Speed ratings (Par 100): **93,90,89,89,88 87,87,85,83,83**
toteswingers: 1&2 £8.50, 1&3 £5.40, 2&3 £8.00 CSF £36.94 CT £168.28 TOTE £4.50: £1.80, £2.50, £1.90; EX 31.10.
Owner J T Brown **Bred** J T Brown **Trained** East Everleigh, Wilts
FOCUS
A modest fillies' sprint. The winner produced a step forward and the form is rated at face value.

4951 PAT BOAKES MEMORIAL H'CAP — 1m 6f 21y
5:20 (5:20) (Class 5) (0-70,70) 3-Y-O+ — £3,238 (£963; £481; £240)

Form — RPR
4034 1 **Saborido (USA)**[21] 4241 3-8-7 **62** — JimCrowley 14 — 72
(Mrs A J Perrett) *led 2f: styd trcking ldr: led again over 3f out: rdn over 2f out: styd on gamely fr over 1f out* — **8/1**
6222 2 *1 ¾* **Arab League (IRE)**[20] 4263 4-8-11 **53** — JamesDoyle 9 — 60
(R J Price) *chsd ldrs: rdn 3f out: ev ch u.p 1f out: styd on same pce ins fnl f* — **11/2**
-152 3 *nk* **Colonel Flay**[46] 3423 5-9-11 **70** — JackMitchell(3) 10 — 77
(Mrs P N Dutfield) *hld up in rr and stl last 3f out: stdy hdwy on outside sn after and styd on to chal 1f out: one pce ins fnl f* — **4/1**[2]
5516 4 *1 ½* **Murcar**[63] 2854 4-10-0 **70** — (b) PhilipRobinson 12 — 75
(C G Cox) *t.k.h: chsd ldrs and n.m.r over 2f out: rdn and styd on fnl f but nvr gng pce to get to ldng trio* — **9/2**[3]
300/ 5 *½* **Gandalf**[21] 4255 7-9-11 **67** — TPQueally 5 — 71
(Miss Amy Weaver) *in rr: hdwy and rdn 3f out: ev ch over 1f out: wknd ins fnl f* — **33/1**
1544 6 *2 ¾* **Sinbad The Sailor**[19] 4325 4-9-2 **58** — (v) RyanMoore 11 — 58
(J W Hills) *in tch: hdwy 4f out: chal over 2f out tl wl over 1f out: wknd fnl f* — **6/1**
0265 7 *3 ½* **Home**[50] 3275 4-9-1 **57** — (t) TravisBlock 3 — 52
(C Gordon) *in rr: pushed along and styd on fr 3f out but nvr in contention* — **25/1**
6210 8 *2* **Isabelonabicycle**[26] 4092 4-9-11 **70** — DavidProbert(3) 6 — 62
(A M Balding) *trckd ldrs on outside: rdn over 3f out: wknd qckly 2f out* — **10/3**[1]
0624 9 *1 ½* **Mohawk Star (IRE)**[19] 4301 8-9-8 **64** — (v) JerryO'Dwyer 2 — 54
(I A Wood) *chsd ldrs: rdn 6f out: sn towards rr: no ch fnl 3f* — **16/1**
3022 10 *21* **Samurai Warrior**[21] 4220 4-9-11 **67** — TPO'Shea 4 — 28
(Jamie Snowden) *led after 2f: hdd over 3f out: sn btn* — **20/1**

3m 2.84s (-4.56) **Going Correction** -0.175s/f (Firm)
WFA 3 from 4yo+ 13lb — **10** Ran SP% **119.5**
Speed ratings (Par 103): **106,105,104,103,103 102,100,98,98,86**
toteswingers: 1&2 £9.50, 1&3 £8.80, 2&3 £6.90 CSF £51.64 CT £206.31 TOTE £10.70: £2.10, £2.00, £1.70; EX 40.00 Place 6: £64.62 Place 5: £17.59.
Owner Tracey, Cotton, James, Slade **Bred** R D Hubbard And R Masterson **Trained** Pulborough, W Sussex
FOCUS
A fair staying handicap which was well run, and sound form. A slight personal best from the winner. There was a flip start.
T/Plt: £55.70 to a £1 stake. Pool: £51,888.86. 678.92 winning tickets. T/Qpdt: £21.00 to a £1 stake. Pool: £3,542.72. 124.75 winning tickets. ST

4906 SANDOWN (R-H)
Thursday, August 13
OFFICIAL GOING: Good (good to firm in places; round course 8.4, sprint course 8.6)
Home bend at mid-configuration and home straight dolled out 5yards adding about 5yards to race distances on round course.
Wind: Light, half against Weather: Fine, warm

4952 SANDOWN SKI CENTRE H'CAP — 5f 6y
2:20 (2:21) (Class 5) (0-75,75) 3-Y-O — £3,238 (£963; £481; £240) Stalls High

Form — RPR
1314 1 **Rocket Rob (IRE)**[14] 4454 3-9-5 **71** — LDettori 7 — 80+
(S A Callaghan) *dwlt: hld up in last: swtchd to wd outside 2f out: gd prog over 1f out to ld jst ins fnl f: shkn up and in command after* — **2/1**[1]
1-42 2 *1 ½* **Night Affair**[43] 3506 3-9-9 **75** — AdamKirby 3 — 79
(D W P Arbuthnot) *taken down early: led against far side rail: rdn 2f out: hdd jst ins fnl f: outpcd but kpt on* — **3/1**[2]
4324 3 *¾* **Edith's Boy (IRE)**[165] 722 3-8-8 **63** — JackMitchell(3) 4 — 64
(S Dow) *taken down early: racd against far rail: trckd ldrs: rdn to chal jst over 1f out: nt qckn ins fnl f and unable to pass runner-up* — **16/1**
5034 4 *2 ¾* **Leadenhall Lass (IRE)**[21] 4231 3-9-1 **67** — (p) IanMongan 1 — 58
(P M Phelan) *taken down early: chsd ldrs on outer: rdn and on terms 2f out: nt qckn over 1f out: btn after: plugged on* — **6/1**
0144 5 *¾* **Francis Walsingham (IRE)**[13] 4494 3-9-7 **73** — SteveDrowne 2 — 61
(H Morrison) *pressed ldr to jst over 1f out: wknd fnl f* — **5/1**[3]
0500 6 *1 ¼* **Mamlakati (IRE)**[10] 4607 3-9-6 **72** — DaneO'Neill 5 — 56
(R Hannon) *dwlt: a in last trio: rdn and no rspnse over 2f out: btn after* — **16/1**
3053 7 *11* **Amosite**[7] 4712 3-9-5 **71** — (v) DarryllHolland 6 — 15
(J R Jenkins) *missed break: a in last trio: rdn and btn over 2f out: wknd over 1f out: t.o* — **15/2**

61.81 secs (0.21) **Going Correction** +0.05s/f (Good) — **7** Ran SP% **112.8**
Speed ratings (Par 100): **100,97,96,92,90 88,71**
toteswingers: 1&2 £1.60, 1&3 £5.40, 2&3 £6.90 CSF £7.88 TOTE £2.50: £1.30, £1.90; EX 6.30.
Owner Bill Hinge, J Searchfield & N Callaghan **Bred** Mrs Marita Rogers **Trained** Newmarket, Suffolk
FOCUS
A fast and furious sprint. Ordinary and straightforward form.
Amosite Official explanation: jockey said gelding missed the break

4953 EUROPEAN BREEDERS' FUND MAIDEN STKS — 1m 14y
2:50 (2:51) (Class 4) 2-Y-O — £5,180 (£1,541; £770; £384) Stalls High

Form — RPR
3 1 **Waseet**[19] 4314 2-9-3 0 — RHills 4 — 88+
(J L Dunlop) *t.k.h early: pressed ldr: led 3f out: drew clr fr 2f out: easily* — **4/11**[1]
2 *4 ½* **Very Good Day (FR)** 2-9-3 0 — DarryllHolland 6 — 73+
(M R Channon) *dwlt: hld up in last pair: effrt over 2f out: shkn up and prog to go 2nd 1f out: drew clr of rest but no ch w wnr* — **14/1**
0 3 *3 ¾* **Mecox Bay (IRE)**[22] 4209 2-9-3 0 — WilliamBuick 3 — 62
(A M Balding) *t.k.h early: trckd ldng pair: shkn up over 2f out: outpcd fr wl over 1f out: kpt on to hold 3rd* — **7/1**[2]
6 4 *1* **Cloudy City (USA)**[15] 4439 2-9-3 0 — JoeFanning 1 — 60
(M Johnston) *hld up in last pair: shkn up and effrt on outer over 2f out: sn outpcd: plugged on* — **8/1**[3]
0 5 *shd* **Gordon Flash**[18] 4336 2-9-3 0 — DaneO'Neill 2 — 59
(R Hannon) *trckd ldng pair: lost pl over 2f out: sn wl outpcd and no ch: plugged on* — **33/1**
00 6 *½* **Azlak (USA)**[19] 4314 2-9-3 0 — RichardMullen 5 — 58
(C E Brittain) *led to 3f out: steadily fdd fnl 2f* — **66/1**

1m 44.46s (1.16) **Going Correction** +0.05s/f (Good) — **6** Ran SP% **108.0**
Speed ratings (Par 96): **96,91,87,86,86 86**
toteswingers: 1&2 £1.70, 1&3 £1.70, 2&3 £2.80 CSF £6.12 TOTE £1.30: £1.10, £3.40; EX 5.30.
Owner Hamdan Al Maktoum **Bred** Shadwell Estate Company Limited **Trained** Arundel, W Sussex
FOCUS
This was all about whether the heavily backed favourite was up to the expectations that punters clearly had about him. He won with a lot in hand and is rated up 8lb on his debut.
NOTEBOOK
Waseet ◆ had caught the eye on his debut at Newmarket, a race that looked like a decent contest, and was quickly away here, taking a good grip in the early stages before striding away up the hill. It was a visually impressive performance but the winning time tempers enthusiasm a little (it was the slowest at this distance of the three races to be run over 1m), although he was being eased fully half a furlong from home. The two Group 1 entries he holds are certainly warranted and he looks a smart performer at least in the making. (op 4-9 tchd 1-2 in places)
Very Good Day(FR) ◆, a fine-looking horse, stayed on much the best of the remainder after running a little green in behind the leaders. He seems sure to win any ordinary maiden if progressing and is bred to stay middle distances next season. (op 11-1)
Mecox Bay(IRE), who ran in a maiden on his debut that had already produced three individual winners, loomed up as a danger down the home straight but found little for pressure, and was very one-paced. (op 11-2 tchd 5-1)
Cloudy City(USA) looked in need of his initial outing, which was at this course, and demanded respect, as he came from a stable that has taken this event in the past with some nice sorts. Slightly slowly away, he tracked his rivals before making an effort 3f out, one that came to very little. (op 13-2 tchd 9-1 in places and 10-1 in a place)
Gordon Flash, last of eight at Ascot on his first run, represented the Richard Hannon stable, so dominant this season in the juvenile division, but he did not show a great deal again. He may want more time. (tchd 25-1)
Azlak(USA), well behind Waseet at Newmarket, did not get away too quickly but was soon leading. However, his turn in front did not last long on turning in, as he was soon left behind by the winner. (op 50-1)

4954 WATCH RACING UK ON SKY CHANNEL 432 H'CAP — 7f 16y
3:25 (3:26) (Class 3) (0-90,90) 3-Y-O+ — £7,771 (£2,312; £1,155; £577) Stalls High

Form — RPR
04-4 1 **Prime Exhibit**[27] 4064 4-9-4 **82** — SteveDrowne 12 — 94+
(R Charlton) *hld up in 6th: gng strly fr 3f out: prog to chse clr ldr over 1f out: pushed along firmly and clsd to ld last 75yds* — **17/2**
0642 2 *½* **Guilded Warrior**[21] 4236 6-9-3 **86** — Louis-PhilippeBeuzelin(5) 3 — 94
(W S Kittow) *led and sn spreadeagled field: over 3 l ahd 3f out: drvn over 1f out: collared last 75yds* — **14/1**

3610 **3** 2½ **Spirit Of Sharjah (IRE)**[13] 4485 4-9-10 **88**...................... JoeFanning 11 89
(Miss J Feilden) *hld up in 9th and off the pce: effrt on outer over 2f out: styd on u.p fr over 1f out to take 3rd ins fnl f* **10/1**

2205 **4** ½ **Thief Of Time (IRE)**[61] 2925 3-9-2 **86**.............................. WilliamBuick 4 84
(P W Chapple-Hyam) *wl in rr: effrt on wd outside over 2f out: prog u.p over 1f out: styd on to take 4th wl ins fnl f* **8/1**

210- **5** ¾ **Spate River**[306] 6663 4-9-4 **82**.............................. GeorgeBaker 8 80
(C F Wall) *chsd ldng trio: effrt over 2f out: 3rd briefly ins fnl f: one pce* **16/1**

-032 **6** ½ **Film Set (USA)**[29] 3988 3-9-6 **90**..............................(t) LDettori 6 85
(Saeed Bin Suroor) *hld up in 8th: shkn up over 2f out: hanging and no real imp over 1f out: btn after* **13/2**[3]

006U **7** ¾ **South Cape**[16] 4409 6-9-5 **83**..............................(p) PatCosgrave 9 78
(G L Moore) *chsd ldr to 3f out: styd prom on inner: shkn up over 1f out: fdd fnl f* **16/1**

2300 **8** 1¼ **Mujood**[15] 4423 6-9-5 **86**.............................. KevinGhunowa(3) 13 77
(Eve Johnson Houghton) *wl plcd in abt 5th: rdn and no prog over 2f out: sn lost pl: one pce fr over 1f out* **14/1**

-664 **9** ½ **Lindoro**[31] 3928 4-9-9 **87**..............................(tp) AdamKirby 7 77
(W R Swinburn) *trckd ldng pair: wnt 2nd 3f out: hrd rdn and no imp 2f out: wknd over 1f out* **11/1**

-211 **10** ½ **Shabib (USA)**[27] 4056 3-9-4 **88**.............................. RHills 1 74+
(B W Hills) *hld up in 7th: shkn up over 2f out: no prog: allowed to coast home whn no ch fnl f* **3/1**[1]

0130 **11** 1 **Wellington Square**[16] 4409 4-9-6 **84**.............................. DarryllHolland 5 70
(H Morrison) *taken down early: dwlt: hld up in last quartet: detached fr rest 2f out: reminder over 1f out: kpt on: nvr nr ldrs* **11/2**[2]

36-0 **12** 6 **Maxwil**[122] 585 4-9-7 **85**.............................. IanMongan 2 55
(P M Phelan) *s.s: hld up in last pair and wl off the pce: shkn up and no prog over 2f out: bhd after* **66/1**

-030 **13** ½ **The Snatcher (IRE)**[16] 4409 6-9-6 **84**.............................. DaneO'Neill 14 52
(R Hannon) *a in rr and nvr gng wl: rousted along in 10th bef 1/2-way: bhd fnl 2f* **25/1**

5020 **14** 3 **Gallantry**[29] 3988 7-8-13 **84**.............................. TobyAtkinson(7) 10 44
(P Howling) *s.i.s: a in last pair: lost tch over 2f out: bhd after* **40/1**

1m 28.54s (-0.96) **Going Correction** +0.05s/f (Good)
WFA 3 from 4yo+ 6lb **14 Ran SP% 125.7**
Speed ratings (Par 107): **107,106,103,103,102 101,100,99,98,98 97,90,89,86**
toteswingers: 1&2 £22.90, 1&3 £17.50, 2&3 £22.10 CSF £125.99 CT £1261.67 TOTE £10.20: £3.80, £4.90, £5.30; EX 204.70 TRIFECTA Not won..
Owner Beckhampton Stables Ltd **Bred** Matthews Breeding And Racing Ltd **Trained** Beckhampton, Wilts

FOCUS
Lots of these seemed capable of winning a race of this nature if at their best, so this looks quite strong handicap form for the class. The runner-up looks the best guide.

NOTEBOOK
Prime Exhibit ◆ was well beaten after a long layoff in heavy ground last time, but showed that effort had put him somewhere close to his best again, as he came through at the right time to get to the front where it mattered. He is lightly raced for his age and deserves a crack at a more valuable handicap next time. (op 9-1)
Guilded Warrior, half a length behind Spirit Of Sharjah last time, was given a positive ride from over three out, a move that almost proved victorious. He was only just denied in the final strides and ran really well. (op 12-1)
Spirit Of Sharjah(IRE) has been in really consistent form for a while, and he finished nicely in this but could not get on terms. (op 12-1 tchd 14-1)
Thief Of Time(IRE), the subject of strong market support, took a long time to hit top gear but kept on strongly inside the final half a furlong. (op 12-1 tchd 14-1)
Spate River, off the course since October last year, tracked the leaders, possibly running a little freely, and was another to take a while to fully get going. It was a fair effort after his break, however.
Film Set(USA), the top rated of these, got headed in the final strides at Lingfield on his previous start but never looked that dangerous after hanging a little. (op 5-1 tchd 4-1)
South Cape showed no ill effects from his spill last time and made some late headway up the inside rail. (op 20-1)
Shabib(USA), chasing a hat-trick, had a lot to do from a wide draw and rarely threatened. His rider reported that his mount failed to handle the bend and it was later discovered, by the racecourse vet, that the horse was lame in its off hind. Official explanation: jockey said gelding did not handle the bend (op 100-30 tchd 4-1)
Wellington Square, mounted on the course before going to post, looked tricky to say the least when his jockey wanted him to get involved and is one to have reservations about. (op 13-2)
Gallantry Official explanation: jockey said gelding missed the break

4955 BUY A RACING POST YEARLING BONUS CANDIDATE MAIDEN FILLIES' STKS 1m 14y
4:00 (4:04) (Class 5) 3-Y-O+ **£3,238** (£963; £481; £240) **Stalls** High

Form RPR

32-2 **1** **Mezenah**[18] 4337 3-8-12 79.............................. LDettori 9 78
(Saeed Bin Suroor) *mde all: shkn up 2f out: hrd pressed after: rdn and hld on fnl f* **8/13**[1]

2 ½ **Ghaneema (USA)** 3-8-12 0.............................. RHills 3 77+
(M P Tregoning) *dwlt: rcvrd to trck wnr after 2f: chal 2f out: shkn up over 1f out: pressed after but nvr quite on terms* **4/1**[2]

3 ½ **Passkey** 3-8-12 0.............................. PatCosgrave 5 76
(Sir Mark Prescott) *wl in tch: chsd ldng trio after 3f: rdn 2f out: kpt on wl to take 3rd ins fnl f and press runner-up nr fin* **6/1**[3]

0-3 **4** 1¼ **Shaaridh (USA)**[128] 1168 3-8-12 0.............................. JoeFanning 7 73
(M Johnston) *chsd wnr 2f: styd cl up: shkn up 2f out: kpt on same pce after* **12/1**

0 **5** 12 **Head First**[27] 4057 3-8-12 0.............................. RichardMullen 1 44
(W Jarvis) *dwlt and rousted along: mostly in 6th: lost tch w ldrs 3f out: tk poor 5th fnl f* **100/1**

0 **6** 1¼ **Pellinore (USA)**[68] 2710 3-8-12 0.............................. WilliamBuick 8 41
(E F Vaughan) *reluctant to enter stalls: cl up bhd ldrs tl wknd rapidly jst over 2f out* **25/1**

0-6 **7** 6 **Pezula**[10] 4606 3-8-12 0.............................. SteveDrowne 4 26
(R T Phillips) *a in last trio: bhd fr 3f out: t.o* **50/1**

8 10 **Duchess Of Alba** 4-9-5 0.............................. GeorgeBaker 6 2
(G C Bravery) *s.s: a in last trio: bhd fr 3f out: t.o* **50/1**

9 nk **Kiss 'n Tell** 3-8-12 0.............................. AdamKirby 2 2
(G L Moore) *dwlt: a in last pair: bhd fr 3f out: t.o* **33/1**

1m 43.89s (0.59) **Going Correction** +0.05s/f (Good)
WFA 3 from 4yo 7lb **9 Ran SP% 115.6**
Speed ratings (Par 100): **99,98,98,96,84 83,77,67,67**
toteswingers: 1&2 £2.00, 1&3 £2.50, 2&3 £3.40 CSF £3.16 TOTE £1.50: £1.02, £1.40, £2.00; EX 3.60.
Owner Godolphin **Bred** Gainsborough Stud Ltd **Trained** Newmarket, Suffolk

FOCUS
Much like the earlier juvenile maiden, this race centred around just one horse in the betting. A muddling race and the form has been rated a bit cautiously.
Duchess Of Alba Official explanation: jockey said filly missed the break

4956 APRES-SKI CHRISTMAS PARTY NIGHTS H'CAP 1m 14y
4:35 (4:38) (Class 4) (0-80,75) 3-Y-O **£4,857** (£1,445; £722; £360) **Stalls** High

Form RPR

5211 **1** **Surprise Party**[7] 4720 3-9-9 75 6ex.............................. GeorgeBaker 6 85+
(C F Wall) *hld up in last pair: hung lft bnd over 4f out: prog 3f out: rdn to ld narrowly jst over 1f out: sustained battle after: edgd rt nr fin: hld on* **13/8**[1]

5412 **2** nk **Play It Sam**[8] 4660 3-9-3 **69**..............................(t) AdamKirby 3 78+
(W R Swinburn) *trckd ldrs: wnt 2nd 3f out: chal over 1f out: w wnr fnl f: jst hld and nudged nr fin* **9/4**[2]

0602 **3** 2 **Pegasus Lad (USA)**[7] 4714 3-9-0 **66**.............................. JoeFanning 1 70
(M Johnston) *led after 2f: 3 l clr 1/2-way: hdd and one pce jst over 1f out* **4/1**[3]

6200 **4** 1 **Saturn Way (GR)**[28] 4010 3-9-3 **69**.............................. RichardKingscote 2 71
(P R Chamings) *t.k.h early: trckd ldrs: nt qckn in 4th 2f out: kpt on fnl f: nvr able to chal* **33/1**

0305 **5** 2¾ **Capo Regime**[20] 4275 3-9-1 **67**.............................. RichardMullen 5 62
(P Howling) *t.k.h early: hld up in last pair: rdn and struggling 3f out: sn lost tch: kpt on u.p fr over 1f out* **20/1**

2-13 **6** 9 **Farleigh**[33] 3870 3-9-8 **74**.............................. WilliamBuick 4 48
(A M Balding) *led 2f: chsd ldr to 3f out: sn wknd* **7/1**

515 **7** 11 **The Winged Assasin (USA)**[113] 1462 3-9-9 **75**.............................. IanMongan 7 22
(J Akehurst) *pushed along early to gain gd position: dropped in rr and struggling 1/2-way: t.o* **14/1**

1m 43.61s (0.31) **Going Correction** +0.05s/f (Good) **7 Ran SP% 115.7**
Speed ratings (Par 102): **100,99,97,96,93 84,73**
toteswingers: 1&2 £1.60, 1&3 £2.30, 2&3 £2.50 CSF £5.66 TOTE £2.60: £1.40, £1.60; EX 6.30.
Owner The Leap Year Partnership **Bred** Farmers Hill Stud **Trained** Newmarket, Suffolk
■ Stewards' Enquiry : George Baker two-day ban: careless riding (Aug 27-28)

FOCUS
Probably a fair handicap, which produced a really tight finish. A progressive pair pulled clear and the form seems sound enough.

4957 DAYTONA AT SANDOWN PARK H'CAP 1m 1f
5:10 (5:10) (Class 4) (0-85,85) 3-Y-O+ **£4,857** (£1,445; £722; £360) **Stalls** High

Form RPR

2015 **1** **Ethics Girl (IRE)**[13] 4481 3-8-4 **69**.............................. RichardMullen 1 81
(John Berry) *hld up in midfield: prog on outer wl over 2f out: clsd to ld 1f out: drvn and kpt on wl* **15/2**

6240 **2** ¾ **Brouhaha**[27] 4064 5-9-3 **74**.............................. RichardKingscote 2 84
(Tom Dascombe) *trckd ldng pair: wnt 2nd wl over 2f out: sn drvn: clsd to chal fnl f: pressed wnr after: a hld* **13/2**

0-22 **3** 2¼ **Mefraas (IRE)**[49] 3309 3-8-9 **74**.............................. RHills 5 79
(E A L Dunlop) *hld up in last pair: effrt jst over 2f out: prog over 1f out: wnt 3rd wl ins fnl f: too much to do* **4/1**[1]

1013 **4** ¾ **Summer Winds**[21] 4247 4-9-5 **83**..............................(b) DToole(7) 8 87
(T G Mills) *w ldr: led 4f out: under heavy press fr 2f out: hdd 1f out: unbalanced and outpcd fnl f* **5/1**[3]

0-14 **5** ½ **Latin Scholar (IRE)**[29] 3977 4-9-5 **76**.............................. DaneO'Neill 6 79
(A King) *hld up in midfield: rdn and nt qckn over 2f out: kpt on fr over 1f out: no threat* **11/2**

0200 **6** ¾ **Admiral Dundas (IRE)**[19] 4315 4-9-7 **78**..............................(b[1]) LDettori 3 79
(W Jarvis) *t.k.h early: trckd ldrs: wandering whn rdn over 2f out: tried to cl on ldrs over 1f out: one pce* **9/2**[2]

15-0 **7** 8 **Awatuki (IRE)**[17] 4378 6-8-9 **66** oh1.............................. PatCosgrave 7 50
(J R Boyle) *wl in tch tl wknd jst over 2f out* **16/1**

2103 **8** 11 **Tilos Gem (IRE)**[14] 4453 3-8-12 **77**.............................. JoeFanning 9 38
(M Johnston) *led to 4f out: rdn and wknd 3f out: sn bhd* **6/1**

0/0 **9** 13 **Canongate**[19] 4315 5-10-0 **85**.............................. GeorgeBaker 4 19
(Miss E C Lavelle) *taken down early: stdd s: hld up in last pair: wknd 3f out: t.o* **16/1**

1m 54.29s (-2.01) **Going Correction** +0.05s/f (Good)
WFA 3 from 4yo+ 8lb **9 Ran SP% 121.4**
Speed ratings (Par 105): **110,109,107,106,106 105,98,88,77**
toteswingers: 1&2 £11.70, 1&3 £9.40, 2&3 £4.90 CSF £58.33 CT £229.37 TOTE £10.40: £2.40, £1.90, £1.90; EX 74.00 Place 6: £26.12 Place 5: £18.93.
Owner The 1997 Partnership **Bred** Newsells Park Stud **Trained** Newmarket, Suffolk

FOCUS
They went 4-1 the field, so punters found it difficult to separate these handicappers. The pace looked sound and this was a fair handicap for the grade.
T/Plt: £49.60 to a £1 stake. Pool: £53,261.24. 783.59 winning tickets. T/Qpdt: £23.30 to a £1 stake. Pool: £3,572.20. 113.10 winning tickets. JN

4958 - 4961a (Foreign Racing) - See Raceform Interactive

[4723] LEOPARDSTOWN (L-H)
Thursday, August 13

OFFICIAL GOING: Good

4962a BALLYROAN STKS (GROUP 3) 1m 4f
7:25 (7:27) 3-Y-O+ **£39,126** (£11,436; £5,417; £1,805)

RPR

1 **Profound Beauty (IRE)**[28] 4033 5-9-9 108.............................. PJSmullen 3 112+
(D K Weld, Ire) *settled in 4th: hdwy travelling wl in 3rd 1 1/2f out: rdn to chal 1f out: styd on to ld last 150yds: kpt on wl* **6/4**[2]

2 1¼ **Mourayan (IRE)**[46] 3438 3-8-12 117..............................(b) MJKinane 7 109
(John M Oxx, Ire) *chsd ldr in 2nd: rdn to chal 1 1/2f out: led over 1f out: hdd last 150yds and no ex: kpt on same pce* **11/8**[1]

3 5 **Shreyas (IRE)**[56] 3082 4-9-9 110.............................. KJManning 2 101
(J S Bolger, Ire) *towards rr: pushed along st out: rdn in 5th 2f out: kpt on same pce fr over 1f out to 3rd ins fnl f: no imp on ldrs* **8/1**[3]

4 ½ **Nafaath (IRE)**[25] 4127 3-8-12 102..............................(b) DPMcDonogh 1 100
(Kevin Prendergast, Ire) *led: rdn and chal 1 1/2f out: hdd over 1f out: no ex and kpt on same pce* **20/1**

5 nk **The Bull Hayes (IRE)**[46] 3438 3-8-12 104..............................(b[1]) FMBerry 4 100
(Mrs John Harrington, Ire) *hld up in 5th: rdn in rr and no imp 2f out: kpt on one pce* **16/1**

6 8 **Stately Home (IRE)**[55] 3090 3-8-12 100 JMurtagh 6 87
(A P O'Brien, Ire) *chsd ldrs in 3rd: rdn in 4th 1 1/2f out: injured and eased ins fnl f* **10/1**

2m 30.48s (-4.82) **Going Correction** -0.075s/f (Good)
WFA 3 from 4yo+ 11lb **6** Ran SP% **113.0**
Speed ratings: **113,112,108,108,108 102**
CSF £3.98 TOTE £2.50: £1.70, £1.20; DF 3.80.
Owner Moyglare Stud Farm **Bred** Moyglare Stud Farms **Trained** The Curragh, Co Kildare

FOCUS
The runner-up has been rated back to par following an improved effort in the Irish Derby, with the winner rated to a small personal best.

NOTEBOOK
Profound Beauty(IRE), third in this event a year ago, made it three from three for the season with a smoothly achieved win. She was dropping down in distance following a Group 3 win at the Curragh and a Listed win here, both over 1m6f, and travelled well throughout before beginning her effort 2f out. Shaken up to lead inside the final furlong, she was well on top in the closing stages. The Emirates Melbourne Cup, in which she ran fifth last year, remains a possible target, although this win will effect her rating. No decision about Flemington will be made until after the weights are published early next month. The Irish Field St Leger is a more immediate target. (op 7/4)
Mourayan(IRE)'s performance when finishing third in the Irish Derby had indicated he was a St Leger type and Doncaster remains the target, despite this defeat. The ground was quicker than ideal for him and, after racing in second place, he came under pressure to lead over 1f out. He stayed on, but the winner went past him without any difficulty. Easier ground and the St Leger distance will play to his strengths. (op 11/8 tchd 6/4)
Shreyas(IRE), on a hat-trick following Listed race wins over 1m and 1m1f here, had raced over this trip only once before. She didn't fire on that occasion and the impression given here was that she didn't get the trip. Held up in rear, she was pushed along 3f out and, after making some headway under 2f out, she could make no impression on the first two inside the final furlong. (op 7/1)

4963 - 4968a (Foreign Racing) - See Raceform Interactive

5088 DEAUVILLE (R-H)
Thursday, August 13

OFFICIAL GOING: Turf course - good to soft; all-weather - standard

4969a PRIX MINERVE - SHADWELL (GROUP 3) (FILLIES) 1m 4f 110y
2:25 (2:36) 3-Y-O **£38,835** (£15,534; £11,650; £7,767; £3,883)

RPR
1 **Kalla**[46] 3442 3-8-9 MGuyon 5 104
(A Fabre, France) *racd in 3rd: 4th st: rdn under 2f out: chal towards stands' side 1 1/2f out: led 1f out: drvn out: jst hld on* **1/1**[1]
2 *shd* **Peinture Rare (IRE)**[46] 3442 3-8-9 ACrastus 2 104
(E Lellouche, France) *hld up in last: 9th st: gd hdwy between rivals to go 3rd appr fnl f: styd on u.p fnl f: jst failed* **11/1**
3 *2 1/2* **Pearlescence (USA)**[37] 3-8-9 C-PLemaire 6 100
(J-C Rouget, France) *chsd clr ldr in 2nd: led narrowly 1 1/2f out to 1f out: one pce* **12/1**
4 *nk* **Zerkeriya (IRE)**[43] 3-8-9 CSoumillon 8 99
(A De Royer-Dupre, France) *in rr: last st: stl last 1f out: fin wl down stands' rails* **73/10**[3]
5 *3/4* **Jakonda (USA)**[30] 3968 3-8-9 GMosse 9 98
(A De Royer-Dupre, France) *in rr: 8th st: kpt on towards stands' side fr over 1f out* **32/5**[2]
6 *2* **Divine Comedy (FR)**[67] 2754 3-8-9 DBoeuf 7 95
(D Smaga, France) *hld up: 6th st: rdn and one pce fnl 1 1/2f* **37/1**
7 *3* **Qertaas (IRE)**[95] 1916 3-8-9 DBonilla 3 90
(F Head, France) *racd in 7th: rdn under 2f out: one pce* **83/10**
7 *dht* **Irish Queen (FR)**[30] 3968 3-8-10 ow1 OPeslier 1 91
(H-A Pantall, France) *hld up: hdwy on ins and 5th st: one pce down centre fnl 2f* **28/1**
9 *1 1/2* **Lasting Applause (IRE)**[30] 3968 3-8-9 TThulliez 4 88
(F Doumen, France) *racd in 4th: 3rd st: wknd over 1f out* **49/1**
10 *3* **Villa Molitor (FR)**[46] 3442 3-8-9 SPasquier 10 83
(F Rohaut, France) *led: 6 l clr under 4f out: hdd 1 1/2f out: wknd* **16/1**

2m 43.3s (-3.10) **10** Ran SP% **116.3**
PARI-MUTUEL: WIN 2.00; PL 1.40, 2.60, 3.20; DF 14.60.
Owner Baroness Karin Von Ullmann **Bred** Gestut Schlenderhan **Trained** Chantilly, France

NOTEBOOK
Kalla, always well placed, she went into the lead at the furlong marker and stayed on really well. She had to be strongly ridden to hold off the runner-up inside the final furlong but will now be aimed at the Prix Vermeille. She will certainly stay the distance.
Peinture Rare(IRE) ran up to her best form on this occasion. She still had plenty to do at the halfway stage but came with a late run and only failed by a narrow margin. She has been marked down for the Prix de Royallieu on October 3rd.
Pearlescence(USA), settled in second place, went to the fore one and a half out but couldn't quicken like the winner and runner-up.
Zerkeriya(IRE) still had plenty to do rounding the final turn when taken wide. She finally made her run up the stands' rail and stayed on well, just failing to take third place.

4970a PRIX ETALON HAAFHD (ALL-WEATHER) 6f 110y
2:55 (3:07) 2-Y-O **£14,078** (£5,631; £4,223; £2,816; £1,408)

RPR
1 **Where's The Soap (FR)**[21] 4233 2-8-6 DBonilla 76
(Tom Dascombe) *racd in 3rd on ins: led 2f out: 4th whn swtchd outside and hrd drvn jst ins fnl f: drvn to ld cl home* **4/1**[1]
2 *1/2* **Shine A Line (FR)**[43] 2-8-13 MGuyon 82
(U Suter, France)
3 *2 1/2* **Otou (GER)** 2-8-9 HGrewe 71
(S Smrczek, Germany)
4 *2* **Anwilka (FR)** 2-8-9 65
(P Bary, France)
5 *2* **Russian River (FR)**[10] 2-8-6 (b) 57
(Mlle V Dissaux, France)
6 *3/4* **Sesimbra (IRE)** 2-8-6 55
(Robert Collet, France)
7 *3* **Wolumla (IRE)** 2-8-0 (6) 46
(R Pritchard-Gordon, France)

1m 21.7s (81.70) **7** Ran SP% **20.0**
PARI-MUTUEL: WIN 5.00; PL 3.00, 2.90; SF 26.50.
Owner Timeform Betfair Racing Club Partnership **Bred** Team Hogdala A B **Trained** Lambourn, Berks
■ Stewards' Enquiry : H Grewe 75euro fine: weighed out heavy

NOTEBOOK
Where's The Soap(FR), who had shown modest promise ina couple of maidens on fast ground, took to the Polytrack and the longer trip enabled her to get up near the line

4971a PRIX DE LIEUREY - SHADWELL (GROUP 3) (FILLIES) (ROUND) 1m (R)
3:25 (3:35) 3-Y-O **£38,835** (£15,534; £11,650; £7,767; £3,883)

RPR
1 **Soneva (USA)**[33] 3892 3-8-12 CSoumillon 1 108
(Y De Nicolay, France) *hld up: last but wl in tch st: moved to wd outside 2f out: hdwy over 1f out: rdn to ld ins fnl f: r.o wl* **12/5**[1]
2 *2* **Emergency**[33] 3892 3-8-12 SPasquier 2 103
(D Smaga, France) *mid-div: 7th on outside st: drvn to ld briefly jst ins fnl f: r.o same pce* **7/2**[2]
3 *1* **Wilside (IRE)**[39] 3668 3-9-2 OPeslier 6 105
(M Delzangles, France) *trckd ldr: led 2f out to jst ins fnl f: one pce* **23/5**[3]
4 *1/2* **Rosey De Megeve**[33] 3892 3-8-12 (p) C-PLemaire 5 100
(F Rohaut, France) *hld up in rr: 10th st: hdwy whn sltly hmpd appr fnl f: kpt on: nrest at fin* **44/5**
5 *3/4* **Dreamt**[18] 3-8-12 MGuyon 10 98
(A Fabre, France) *trckd ldrs: 4th st: outpcd over 1f out: kpt on u.p* **7/2**[2]
6 *snk* **Mary's Precedent (FR)**[17] 4394 3-8-13 ow1 YLerner 4 99
(C Lerner, France) *9th st: effrt on rails wl over 1f out: one pce fnl f* **19/1**
7 *shd* **Providanza (FR)**[39] 3668 3-8-12 TThulliez 12 97
(N Clement, France) *a.p: 3rd st: rdn and stl 3rd ins fnl f: one pce* **23/1**
8 *hd* **Alice De La Vis (FR)**[17] 4394 3-8-12 JVictoire 8 97
(J De Roualle, France) *8th st: nvr able to chal* **71/1**
9 *1* **Entre Deux Eaux (FR)**[67] 2757 3-9-2 IMendizabal 9 99
(Robert Collet, France) *first to show: settled in mid-div: 6th st: kpt on one pce* **23/1**
10 *1 1/2* **Sweet Hearth (USA)**[17] 4394 3-8-12 GMosse 3 91
(A De Royer-Dupre, France) *racd in 5th to st: wknd appr fnl f* **58/10**
11 *5* **Aria Di Festa (IRE)**[74] 2521 3-9-2 DVargiu 11 84
(B Grizzetti, Italy) *led to 2f out* **11/1**

1m 45.5s (4.50) **11** Ran SP% **139.7**
PARI-MUTUEL: WIN 3.40; PL 1.40, 2.70, 1.80; DF 11.30.
Owner A Curty **Bred** Mineola Farm & Dr Houchin & J W Hirshmann **Trained** France
■ Stewards' Enquiry : C Soumillon 150euro fine: weighed in heavy

NOTEBOOK
Soneva(USA) justified favouritism having been brought with a sweeping late run up the centre of the track. She had been one of the last coming into the straightand showed an excellent turn of foot to finally win with something in hand. She may well be aimed at the Prix du Moulin de Longchamp next time out.
Emergency was another who was putting in her best work at the finish but she never looked likely to peg back the winner. A mile may well be too far for her and her trainer is now thinking about a run in the 7f Prix du Pin next time out.
Wilside(IRE) was always thereabouts but failed to fend off her rivals who both came with their runs up the stands' side.
Rosey De Megeve was held up for much of the race she ran a little free and had to wait for a gap to open up. She then quickened well but could not reel in the first three.

4617 CATTERICK (L-H)
Friday, August 14

OFFICIAL GOING: Good to firm (firm in places; 9.7)
Grandstand bend moved in 1metre but impact on distances not notified.
Wind: Light across Weather: Overcast

4972 HAPPY 6TH BIRTHDAY GEORGIA AMATEUR RIDERS' H'CAP 1m 3f 214y
5:45 (5:45) (Class 5) (0-75,82) 3-Y-O+ **£2,810** (£871; £435; £217) Stalls High

Form RPR
0250 1 **Inspector Clouseau (IRE)**[35] 3809 4-10-0 66 MissKECooper(5) 8 74
(T P Tate) *led 1f styd cl up: hdwy to ld over 2f out: rdn and hdd over 1f out: rallied ins fnl f and kpt on to ld on line* **8/1**
5121 2 *shd* **Trip The Light**[7] 4737 4-10-9 75 (v) MrsVFahey(5) 13 83+
(R A Fahey) *trckd ldrs: smooth hdwy on inner 4f out: chsd wnr over 2f out: led over 1f out: 2 l up ins fnl f: hdd on line* **7/2**[1]
4340 3 *3 1/4* **Grand Art (IRE)**[20] 4332 5-10-11 72 MrSWalker 14 75
(P T Midgley) *midfield: hdwy to trck ldrs 1/2-way: effrt 3f out: rdn 2f out: sn drvn and no imp fr over 1f out* **4/1**[2]
6042 4 *3 1/2* **Call Of Duty (IRE)**[2] 4898 4-9-4 56 MissECSayer(5) 2 53+
(Mrs Dianne Sayer) *hld up: hdwy over 3f out: rdn along 2f out: styd on appr fnl f: nrst fin* **11/2**[3]
2353 5 *1 3/4* **Strike Force**[8] 4698 5-9-6 58 MissALHutchinson(5) 6 52
(Miss J Feilden) *midfield: hdwy over 3f out: rdn to chse ldrs wl over 1f out: edgd lft and no imp appr fnl f* **11/2**[3]
0001 6 *3/4* **Monfils Monfils (USA)**[17] 4402 7-10-1 67 MissVBarr(5) 4 60
(R E Barr) *prom: rdn along over 2f out: sn drvn and wknd over 1f out* **7/1**
13/ 7 *6* **Silent Lucidity (IRE)**[799] 2389 5-9-9 56 oh1 MissADeniel 7 39
(P D Niven) *nvr nr ldrs* **18/1**
5000 8 *3/4* **King In Waiting (IRE)**[13] 4551 6-10-1 62 (vt) MissLHorner 11 44
(J Hetherton) *towards rr: hdwy over 4f out: rdn over 2f out: n.d* **33/1**
00-0 9 *1 1/2* **Mycenean Prince (USA)**[63] 1131 6-9-9 61 oh11 ow5 MrCAHarris(5) 1 41
(S A Harris) *midfield: rdn along over 4f out and nvr a factor* **100/1**
0-00 10 *1/2* **Wild Fell Hall (IRE)**[11] 4600 6-9-12 64 (b) DaleSwift(5) 12 43
(J Hetherton) *sn led: rdn along 3f out: hdd over 2f out and sn wknd* **66/1**
000 11 *10* **Hunting Haze**[23] 4193 6-9-2 56 oh11 (p) MrsDWilkinson(7) 10 19
(A Crook) *a towards rr* **150/1**
0000 12 *9* **Able Dara**[17] 4403 6-11-0 82 oh11 ow26 (p) MrSebSpencer(7) 3 31
(N Bycroft) *a in rr: bhd fr 1/2-way* **100/1**
4401 13 *2 3/4* **Hurricane Thomas (IRE)**[15] 4462 5-9-4 56 oh5 MissPhillipaTutty(5) 9 —
(R A Fahey) *chsd ldrs whn stmbld bdly bnd after 3f and almost uns rdr: in tch and rdn along after drvn over 4f out: and sn wknd* **11/1**

2m 38.46s (-0.44) **Going Correction** +0.05s/f (Good) **13** Ran SP% **117.3**
Speed ratings (Par 103): **103,102,100,98,97 96,92,92,91,90 84,78,76**
toteswingers: 1&2 £4.80, 1&3 £3.80, 2&3 £8.70 CSF £35.26 CT £131.16 TOTE £11.40: £2.60, £1.50, £1.80; EX 42.40.
Owner Allan McLuckie **Bred** P Byrne, Eimear Mulhern & B Grassick **Trained** Tadcaster, N Yorks
■ Stewards' Enquiry : Miss Phillipa Tutty one-day ban: used whip when out of contention (tba)

FOCUS
No strength in depth to this amateur riders' handicap and unsurprisingly they finished well strung out. Nothing got into it from the rear and the front pair are the best guides.

4973 HAPPY BIRTHDAY DENYS SMITH (S) STKS — 7f
6:15 (6:15) (Class 6) 2-Y-O — **£2,047** (£604; £302) **Stalls** Low

Form — RPR
0023 **1** **Gold Fix (IRE)**[9] 4651 2-8-6 63 ... SamHitchcott 4 58+
(M R Channon) *in tch: hdwy 3f out: rdn along 2f out: styd on to ld appr fnl f: kpt on* **10/11**[1]
060 **2** 1 ½ **Thaliwarru**[25] 4152 2-8-11 65 ... TonyCulhane 1 58
(G G Margarson) *in tch: rdn along and outpcd 1/2-way: hdwy u.p over 1f out: swtchdlft and styd on strly ins fnl f: nt rch wnr* **5/1**[3]
60 **3** ½ **Raine Supreme**[51] 3263 2-8-6 0 ... GregFairley 6 52
(E S McMahon) *cl up: rdn along and hung rt home turn: chal 2f out and ev ch tl drvn and one pce ins fnl f* **12/1**
553 **4** 1 **Drinking Buddy**[6] 4800 2-8-11 0 ... TonyHamilton 7 54
(K A Ryan) *trckd ldrs: hdwy on inner over 2f out: sn rdn and led briefly over 1f out: sn hdd and drvn: wknd ins fnl f* **3/1**[2]
046 **5** 2 ¼ **Steel My Heart (IRE)**[7] 4757 2-8-6 0 ... NeilChalmers 8 43
(Miss D Mountain) *dwlt: sn cl up on outer: carried wd home turn: sn rdn and wknd over 1f out* **33/1**
006 **6** 3 **London Girl (IRE)**[68] 2741 2-7-13 48 ... DeclanCannon(7) 5 36
(A J McCabe) *led: rdn along over 2f out: riddr dropped reins wl over 1f out: sn hdd & wknd* **25/1**
00 **7** 66 **Double Rollover**[13] 4534 2-8-11 0 ... (b) FrancisNorton 2 —
(W R Muir) *broke wl: sn rdn along and lost pl: t.o after 2f* **28/1**
1m 29.24s (2.24) **Going Correction** +0.05s/f (Good) **7** Ran SP% **112.0**
Speed ratings (Par 92): **89,87,86,85,83 79,4**
toteswingers: 1&2 £4.20, 1&3 £2.80, 2&3 £4.70 CSF £5.57 TOTE £1.80: £1.40, £2.20; EX 6.70.There was no bid for the winner. Thaliwarru was claimed by J. R. Gask for £6000.
Owner Mrs T Burns **Bred** Rathasker Stud **Trained** West Ilsley, Berks

FOCUS
A routine seller won comfortably enough by Gold Fix.

NOTEBOOK
Gold Fix(IRE) found that the drop into selling company enabled her to get off the mark at the sixth attempt. She had been beaten just a nose in a Newbury nursery off 65 on her penultimate start and she probably didn't need to run to that level to score here. She took a while to get going but was in charge well over a furlong out and only needed pushing out to get the job done. (tchd 11-10)
Thaliwarru bombed out badly in a Yarmouth maiden last time, but this was much more encouraging as he finished his race strongly having got a bit outpaced turning into the straight. He ought to be able to find a race at this level. (op 9-2 tchd 4-1)
Raine Supreme kept on well on her first try at this trip and this should open a few doors for her. (op 17-2 tchd 7-1)
Drinking Buddy, well-backed, had every chance 2f out but weakened away rather tamely and was disappointing. (op 9-2)
Double Rollover Official explanation: jcokey said colt became unbalanced in the back straight

4974 TENNANTS FINE ART AUCTIONEERS MAIDEN STKS — 1m 3f 214y
6:50 (6:51) (Class 5) 3-Y-O+ — **£3,238** (£963; £481; £240) **Stalls** High

Form — RPR
533- **1** nse **Ascendant**[328] 6135 3-9-2 75 ... PatCosgrave 2 87+
(Sir Mark Prescott) *pushed along to take slt ld after 1f and set furious pce: rdn along 3f out: hdd and hmpd wl over 1f out: sn swtchd rt and drvn: styd on under hrd driving ins fnl f: jst failed: fin 2nd, nse: awrdd r* **10/11**[1]
-205 **2** **Akbabend**[8] 4715 3-9-2 78 ... GregFairley 5 87
(M Johnston) *led 1f: cl up: rdn along 3f out: led and hung lft wl over 1f out: sn drvn: jst hld on: fin 1st: disq & plcd 2nd* **7/4**[2]
3 28 **Minstalad**[54] 5-9-6 0 ... AnthonyBetts(7) 8 42
(G R Oldroyd) *a chsng ldng pair: rdn along and kpt on one pce fr 1/2-way* **100/1**
56 **4** 2 ¼ **Elusive Muse**[55] 3155 3-9-2 0 ... TonyHamilton 3 39
(M Dods) *chsd ldrs: rdn along over 4f out and no imp* **12/1**
00 **5** 9 **Informal Affair**[11] 4599 3-9-2 0 ... FrancisNorton 6 24
(J D Bethell) *a towards rr* **25/1**
0 **6** 3 ¼ **Mistic Academy (IRE)**[11] 4599 4-9-8 0 ... SamHitchcott 7 14
(Miss J E Foster) *a in rr* **100/1**
00 **7** 4 ½ **Skybob**[19] 4354 3-8-9 0 ... JamesPSullivan(7) 1 12
(D W Thompson) *chsd ldrs: rdn along and wknd 1/2-way* **100/1**
8 12 **Just Call Me Dave (USA)** 3-9-2 0 ... SilvestreDeSousa 4 —
(Paul Green) *a in rr* **8/1**[3]
2m 36.44s (-2.46) **Going Correction** +0.05s/f (Good)
WFA 3 from 4yo+ 11lb **8** Ran SP% **114.4**
Speed ratings (Par 103): **109,110,91,89,83 81,78,70**
toteswingers: Ascendant&Akbabend £1.10, Ascendant&3 £15.30, Akbabend &3 £8.70 CSF £2.65 TOTE £1.40: £1.02, £1.10, £22.30; EX 2.00.
Owner Cheveley Park Stud **Bred** Cheveley Park Stud Ltd **Trained** Newmarket, Suffolk

FOCUS
A particularly modest maiden which concerned only the two market leaders from the outset as they quickly opened up a huge gap on their rivals and the pair embarked on a terrific tussle all the way up the straight only to be separated by a whisker at the line. The stewards reversed the placings and the first two have been rated on the positive side.

4975 INTERNATIONAL RACECOURSE MANAGEMENT NURSERY — 5f 212y
7:20 (7:24) (Class 4) 2-Y-O — **£4,533** (£1,348; £674; £336) **Stalls** Low

Form — RPR
020 **1** **Iron Velvet (USA)**[21] 4286 2-9-0 70 ... GregFairley 11 78+
(M Johnston) *in tch: hdwy to trck ldrs over 2f out: swtchd lft and effrt over 1f out: sn rdn and styd on to ld ins fnl f* **11/2**[3]
4002 **2** 1 ¾ **Ginger Grey (IRE)**[9] 4647 2-8-8 64 ... AndrewElliott 2 66
(S A Callaghan) *trac ked ldrs: hdwy over 2f out: rdn over 1f out: led briefly ent fnl f: sn drvn and hdd: kpt on same pce* **7/1**
0442 **3** 1 **Firetrap**[19] 4342 2-8-6 62 ... SilvestreDeSousa 8 61
(Mrs A Duffield) *prom on outer: effrt over 2f out: sn rdn and ev ch tl drvn and nt qckn ins fnl f* **6/1**
5410 **4** shd **Drumpellier (IRE)**[3] 4884 2-8-2 63 ... PaulPickard(5) 3 61
(P T Midgley) *led to 1/2-way: styd cl up on inner: rdn wl over 1f out and ev ch tl drvn and no ex ins fnl f* **16/1**
3213 **5** nk **Emerald Girl (IRE)**[20] 4327 2-9-0 70 ... TonyHamilton 4 68+
(R A Fahey) *s.i.s and towards rr: swtchd rt and hdwy over 2f out: sn rdn and styd on to chse ldrs over 1f out: drvn and no imp ins fnl f* **3/1**[1]
4303 **6** hd **Flow Chart (IRE)**[6] 4803 2-8-4 65 ... (b[1]) DeanHeslop(5) 1 62
(T D Barron) *in tch on inner: hdwy 2f out: sn rdn and kpt on same pce ins fnl f* **4/1**[2]
0156 **7** 1 ¼ **Bubbelas**[30] 3971 2-9-1 71 ... GrahamGibbons 6 64
(J J Quinn) *chsd ldrs: rdn along over 2f out: drvn wl over 1f out and grad wknd* **18/1**
2100 **8** hd **Social Grace**[13] 4547 2-9-3 73 ... (p) DuranFentiman 7 66
(D H Brown) *cl up: led 1/2-way and sn rdn: drvn over 1f out: hdd ent fnl f and sn wknd* **16/1**
634 **9** nk **Silver In The Sand**[21] 4282 2-8-10 66 ... PatCosgrave 10 58
(J D Bethell) *a towards rr* **20/1**
3033 **10** 2 ¾ **Motivational (IRE)**[18] 4371 2-9-7 77 ... FrancisNorton 5 60
(D R Lanigan) *towards rr whn nt clr run and hmpd bnd over 4f out: bhd whn stmbld home turn* **8/1**
1m 14.52s (0.92) **Going Correction** +0.05s/f (Good) **10** Ran SP% **120.1**
Speed ratings (Par 96): **95,92,91,91,90 90,88,88,88,84**
toteswingers: 1&2 £2.80, 1&3 £15.80, 2&3 £11.90 CSF £45.21 CT £248.05 TOTE £6.60: £2.70, £3.00, £2.00; EX 60.90.
Owner Sheikh Hamdan Bin Mohammed Al Maktoum **Bred** Darley **Trained** Middleham Moor, N Yorks

FOCUS
Quite a competitive nursery and the pace was decent so the form should stand up. The winner is potentially a fair bit better than this.

NOTEBOOK
Iron Velvet(USA) ◆ proved his latest York maiden flop all wrong by coming home strongly to make a winning nursery debut off a mark of 70. The way he powered through the final furlong suggests another furlong is well within range and he could be a very well treated animal on this evidence. (op 6-1 tchd 5-1)
Ginger Grey(IRE) showed improved form on Polytrack last week and he transferred that back to grass with a solid effort in defeat, keeping on well up the inside, and he's close to striking if holding his form. (op 6-1 tchd 11-2)
Firetrap finished well on his nursery debut and the step back up to 6f seemed to help. (op 8-1)
Drumpellier(IRE) kept on at the one pace having been a bit keen on the front end early. (op 20-1)
Emerald Girl(IRE) got a bit outpaced towards the back and she seemed to take a bad step early in the straight which effected her momentum. She kept on down the outside in the closing stages but was never getting there and she can probably do better than she was able to show here, especially on a stiffer track. (op 100-30 tchd 4-1)
Motivational(IRE) Official explanation: jockey said colt stumbled on the bend approaching the home straight

4976 LIVE MUSIC AFTER RACING CLAIMING STKS — 5f
7:55 (7:55) (Class 6) 3-Y-O+ — **£2,388** (£705; £352) **Stalls** Low

Form — RPR
1435 **1** **Silvanus (IRE)**[28] 4036 4-8-6 66 ... (p) PatrickDonaghy(5) 8 62
(I Semple) *trckd ldng pair: hdwy 2f out: rdn to ld jst ins fnl f: kpt on* **7/1**[3]
3064 **2** 1 ¾ **Strensall**[7] 4754 12-8-11 51 ... DuranFentiman 1 56
(R E Barr) *led: rdn along over 1f out: drvn and hdd ins fnl f: kpt on same pce* **25/1**
113 **3** nk **Obe Gold**[8] 4690 7-9-7 83 ... (v) GregFairley 3 65
(Miss D Mountain) *dwlt and hmpd s: hdwy 2f out: sn rdn and styd on ins fnl f: nrst fin* **4/1**[2]
0000 **4** 1 ½ **Tournedos (IRE)**[12] 4559 7-9-8 92 ... FrancisNorton 4 61
(D Nicholls) *chsd ldr: effrt and ev ch 2f out: sn rdn and wknd appr ins fnl f* **4/9**[1]
4U0 **5** 20 **Nomoreblondes**[17] 4399 5-8-13 65 ... (p) TonyCulhane 2 —
(P T Midgley) *stmbld bdly s and rdr lost iron: a in rr* **12/1**
59.66 secs (-0.14) **Going Correction** +0.05s/f (Good)
WFA 3 from 4yo+ 3lb **5** Ran SP% **113.3**
Speed ratings (Par 101): **103,100,99,97,65**
toteswingers: 1&2 £119.80, 1&3 not won, 2&3 not won CSF £106.71 TOTE £12.70: £2.80, £5.80; EX 119.80.Silvanus was claimed by Miss M. E. Rowland for £5000.
Owner Kass Racing **Bred** Barronstown Stud And Mrs T Stack **Trained** Carluke, S Lanarks

FOCUS
A messy claimer with the two class acts flopping. Muddling form, with the runner-up the best guide.
Tournedos(IRE) Official explanation: jockey said geling lost its action
Nomoreblondes Official explanation: jockey said mare stumbled leaving the stalls and jockey lost an iron

4977 ALPHA RADIO H'CAP — 7f
8:25 (8:25) (Class 6) (0-60,62) 3-Y-O+ — **£2,388** (£705; £352) **Stalls** Low

Form — RPR
3140 **1** **Nufoudh (IRE)**[5] 4823 5-8-13 54 ... KellyHarrison(3) 6 63
(Miss Tracy Waggott) *trckd ldrs: hdwy to chse ldr 2f out and sn rdn: drvn ins fnl f: styd on to ld nr line* **11/1**
3541 **2** hd **Sea Salt**[9] 4654 6-9-5 62 6ex ... LanceBetts(5) 1 70
(R E Barr) *sn chsng ldr on inner: hdwy to ld over 2f out: rdn over 1f out: drvn ins fnl f: hdd and nt qckn nr line* **11/2**[3]
0040 **3** nk **Royal Composer (IRE)**[25] 4140 6-9-1 53 ... GrahamGibbons 2 60
(T D Easterby) *midfield: hdwy over 2f out: rdn wl over 1f out: drvn and edgd lft ins fnl f: styd on wl towards fin* **11/2**[3]
0646 **4** 1 ¼ **Mayoman (IRE)**[31] 3943 4-9-5 57 ... DNolan 12 61
(D Carroll) *chsd ldrs: effrt 2f out and sn rdn: drvn over 1f out: kpt on same pce ins fnl f* **9/2**[1]
0161 **5** ½ **Neo's Mate (IRE)**[23] 4191 3-8-11 55 ... SilvestreDeSousa 11 55+
(Paul Green) *towards rr: hdwy on outer 2f out: sn rdn: styd on ins fnl f: nt rch ldrs* **6/1**
6160 **6** 2 **Not Now Lewis (IRE)**[11] 4588 5-9-0 57 ... SladeO'Hara(5) 7 54
(F P Murtagh) *midfield: hdwy and in tch 1/2-way: effrt 2f out and sn rdn along: drvn over 1f out and no imp ins fnl f* **12/1**
0500 **7** 1 **Slip Star**[21] 4281 6-8-8 46 oh1 ... GregFairley 13 40
(T J Etherington) *chsd ldrs: rdn along over 2f out: sn drvn and grad wknd* **33/1**
0000 **8** ¾ **Hi Spec (IRE)**[18] 4376 6-8-1 46 ... (p) DeclanCannon(7) 15 38
(Miss M E Rowland) *s.i.s and bhd tl sme late hdwy* **50/1**
020 **9** hd **H Harrison (IRE)**[34] 3851 9-9-1 58 ... AmyRyan(5) 9 50
(I W McInnes) *midfield: rdn along on inner over 2f out and no hdwy* **9/1**
2006 **10** 1 **Inca Soldier (FR)**[107] 1606 6-9-3 55 ... PAspell 8 44
(S A Harris) *s.i.s: a towards rr* **25/1**
0525 **11** 9 **Party In The Park**[37] 3730 4-8-12 53 ... (b) FrederikTylicki(3) 5 18
(Miss J A Camacho) *led: rdn along and hdd over 2f out: wknd qckly* **5/1**[2]
6-00 **12** 40 **Dream Rainbow**[4] 4859 4-9-8 60 ... (t) PatCosgrave 4 —
(Joss Saville) *a in rr* **40/1**
0-00 **13** 13 **Frill A Minute**[9] 4654 5-8-3 46 oh1 ... (p) PatrickDonaghy(5) 3 —
(Miss L C Siddall) *a in rr* **100/1**
1m 27.57s (0.57) **Going Correction** +0.05s/f (Good)
WFA 3 from 4yo+ 6lb **13** Ran SP% **118.1**
Speed ratings (Par 101): **98,97,97,96,95 93,92,91,90,89 79,33,18**
toteswingers: 1&2 £22.00, 1&3 £18.90, 2&3 £12.60 CSF £67.37 CT £376.04 TOTE £13.70: £2.90, £2.60, £1.70; EX 82.00 Place 6: £260.86 Place 5: £147.48.

Owner H Conlon **Bred** Swordlestown Stud **Trained** Spennymoor, Co Durham

FOCUS

A weak handicap in which most were out of form, but it produced a good finish. Sound form.

Party In The Park Official explanation: jockey said gelding ran too free

T/Plt: £216.10 to a £1 stake. Pool: £44,141.48. 149.05 winning tickets. T/Qpdt: £81.00 to a £1 stake. Pool: £3,401.44. 31.07 winning tickets. JR

4644 KEMPTON (A.W) (R-H)

Friday, August 14

OFFICIAL GOING: Standard

Wind: Light, half behind Weather: Fine, warm

4978 ODDSCHECKER.COM H'CAP 5f (P)

6:05 (6:06) (Class 5) (0-75,75) 3-Y-O+ **£2,590** (£770; £385; £192) **Stalls** High

Form RPR

0210 1 **Silver Prelude**[24] 4182 8-8-11 **62**....(t) RyanMoore 11 73
(S C Williams) *mde all: clr after 2f: stl 3l clr jst over 1f out: all out and jst hld on* **7/4**[1]

163 2 nk **Garstang**[28] 4043 6-9-9 **74**....(b) IanMongan 7 84
(J Balding) *chsd clr wnr after 2f: grad clsd u.p fnl f: post c too sn* **4/1**[2]

5601 3 2½ **Bluebok**[23] 4204 8-8-8 **62**....(bt) JackDean(3) 2 63+
(J M Bradley) *racd wd: off the pce in midfield: wnt 3rd over 1f out: plugged on but no threat to ldng pair* **13/2**

0225 4 ½ **Lethal**[30] 3983 6-8-6 **64**.... RosieJessop(7) 5 63
(Andrew Reid) *pushed along to stay in tch bef 1/2-way: kpt on fr over 1f out: n.d: nrst fin* **11/2**[3]

-062 5 shd **Agnes Love**[23] 4204 3-8-0 **57**.... AndreaAtzeni(3) 4 56
(J Akehurst) *pushed along to stay in tch bef 1/2-way: effrt over 1f out: kpt on: nrst fin* **7/1**

0310 6 3¾ **Joss Stick**[7] 4736 4-8-3 **57** ow1.... MarcHalford(3) 12 42
(J J Bridger) *outpcd and last of main gp: nvr on terms* **14/1**

1400 7 4 **Ten Down**[80] 2359 4-9-5 **70**.... JoeFanning 6 41
(M Quinn) *chsd wnr 2f: sn struggling: wknd wl over 1f out* **12/1**

4000 8 17 **Woodcote (IRE)**[23] 4204 7-8-6 **57**.... FrankieMcDonald 3 —
(Peter Grayson) *v unsettled in stalls and completely blew the s: a t.o* **20/1**

60.36 secs (-0.14) **Going Correction** +0.025s/f (Slow)

WFA 3 from 4yo+ 3lb **8** Ran SP% **116.7**

Speed ratings (Par 103): **102,101,97,96,96 90,84,56**

toteswingers: 1&2 £2.60, 1&3 £2.20, 2&3 £3.90 CSF £8.97 CT £36.93 TOTE £2.60: £1.80, £1.60, £1.80; EX 8.30.

Owner Mrs A Shone **Bred** Bearstone Stud **Trained** Newmarket, Suffolk

FOCUS

A decent time for this modest sprint, but a strong gallop was assured with plenty who like to force the pace. Nothing got into it from the rear and the winer is rated back to his winter best.

Woodcote(IRE) Official explanation: jockey said gelding was slowly away

4979 FIND BEST THE ODDS AT ODDSCHECKER.COM MAIDEN STKS 1m 2f (P)

6:40 (6:43) (Class 4) 3-Y-O **£4,727** (£1,406; £702; £351) **Stalls** High

Form RPR

1 **Bawadi (USA)** 3-9-3 0.... LDettori 7 85+
(Saeed Bin Suroor) *dwlt: trckd ldrs: pushed along in 3rd fr 3f out: clsd to ld jst over 1f out: shkn up and in command after* **2/1**[2]

0 2 1½ **Mathaaq**[13] 4519 3-9-3 0.... ChrisCatlin 5 82
(M A Jarvis) *dwlt: sn pressed ldng pair: effrt to dispute ld jst over 3f out: hanging lft but led wl over 1f out: hdd jst over 1f out: kpt on* **22/1**

3- 3 5 **Meyyal (USA)**[294] 6944 3-9-3 0.... RHills 6 72
(B W Hills) *trckd ldrs: disp 3rd 3f out: wd bnd 2f out and lost grnd: one pce after* **5/2**[3]

043 4 1¼ **Secret Life**[62] 2930 3-9-3 **76**.... RichardHughes 3 70
(J Noseda) *trckd ldr: reminder over 6f out: disp ld jst over 3f out: hanging and hdd wl over 1f out: sn btn* **7/4**[1]

00 5 9 **Cottonfields (USA)**[11] 4606 3-9-3 0.... DO'Donohoe 1 52
(Mrs H S Main) *dropped to last and pushed along after 2f: lost tch 4f out: wl bhd after: passed one rival nr fin* **66/1**

0 6 ¾ **Secret Desert**[18] 4381 3-9-3 0.... AdamKirby 2 50
(D M Simcock) *settled in last: outpcd and pushed along 3f out: nvr on terms w ldrs after* **40/1**

0 7 11 **Morning Dress (USA)**[21] 4276 3-9-3 0.... JoeFanning 8 28
(M Johnston) *led to jst over 3f out: wknd rapidly: t.o* **14/1**

2m 7.06s (-0.94) **Going Correction** +0.025s/f (Slow) **7** Ran SP% **113.2**

Speed ratings (Par 102): **104,102,98,97,90 90,81**

toteswingers: 1&2 £6.90, 1&3 £1.20, 2&3 £10.20 CSF £36.67 TOTE £2.40: £1.20, £8.60; EX 29.10.

Owner Godolphin **Bred** Pollock Farms **Trained** Newmarket, Suffolk

FOCUS

Some interesting types in this fair maiden with just a modest level of form on display and just an ordinary pace set.

4980 TIP STAR TIPPING COMPETITION MAIDEN FILLIES' STKS 7f (P)

7:10 (7:12) (Class 4) 2-Y-O **£3,885** (£1,156; £577; £288) **Stalls** High

Form RPR

3 1 **Damietta (USA)**[16] 4421 2-9-0 0.... LDettori 3 79+
(Saeed Bin Suroor) *trckd ldr after 2f: chal 2f out: pushed firmly into ld over 1f out: shkn up and sn in command: eased last 50yds* **11/2**[3]

2 ¾ **Giants Play (USA)** 2-9-0 0.... RyanMoore 9 77+
(Sir Michael Stoute) *chsd ldrs: shkn up over 2f out: sn wnt 3rd but outpcd by ldng pair: styd on wl to take 2nd last 100yds: clsd on eased down wnr fin* **5/2**[2]

42 3 2 **Ghazwah**[15] 4460 2-9-0 0.... RHills 11 70
(J H M Gosden) *sn led: shkn up over 2f out: hdd over 1f out: sn outpcd: lost 2nd last 100yds* **4/5**[1]

4 2¾ **Taper Jean Girl (IRE)** 2-8-11 0.... AndreaAtzeni(3) 10 63
(M Botti) *pushed along in midfield after 3f: prog over 2f out: rdn to take 4th fnl f: n.d* **50/1**

5 ½ **Nafura** 2-9-0 0.... DO'Donohoe 4 62+
(Saeed Bin Suroor) *dwlt: hld up in last trio: stl last over 2f out: sme prog over 1f out: pushed along and styd on in taking style fnl f* **14/1**

6 1 **Danehill Intellect (IRE)** 2-9-0 0.... AdamKirby 1 60+
(G A Butler) *dropped in fr wd draw and hld up in last trio: slt prog 2f out: nudged along and kpt on steadily fr over 1f out* **66/1**

7 ¾ **Sandy Shaw** 2-9-0 0.... ChrisCatlin 8 58+
(J W Hills) *settled wl in rr: pushed along and kpt on steadily fnl 2f: nrst fin* **66/1**

8 shd **Flotate (USA)** 2-8-11 0.... PatrickHills(3) 2 57
(Jane Chapple-Hyam) *prom: chsd ldng pair 4f out: shkn up over 2f out: fdd wl over 1f out* **80/1**

9 ¾ **She's My Rock (IRE)** 2-9-0 0.... JamesDoyle 12 56
(S Kirk) *prom: pushed along over 3f out: steadily wknd fnl 2f* **66/1**

03 10 nk **Elizabelle (IRE)**[23] 4194 2-9-0 0.... RichardHughes 13 55+
(R Hannon) *chsd ldr 2f: styd prom: nudged along and steadily wknd fnl 2f* **14/1**

0 11 4½ **Have More**[11] 4603 2-9-0 0.... JoeFanning 7 44
(B J Meehan) *trckd ldrs: shkn up 3f out: lost pl over 2f out: steadily wknd* **100/1**

0 12 3½ **Houda (IRE)**[11] 4603 2-9-0 0.... TravisBlock 5 35
(J G Portman) *tkt.k.h early and racd wd: nvr beyond midfield: wknd 3f out* **100/1**

13 6 **Sandfairyann** 2-9-0 0.... IanMongan 14 20
(B R Johnson) *dwlt: a wl in rr: bhd fnl 2f* **33/1**

14 2¾ **Evening Glow** 2-9-0 0.... SebSanders 6 13
(C E Brittain) *reminder on outer in midfield bef 1/2-way: wknd over 2f out* **66/1**

1m 27.68s (1.68) **Going Correction** +0.025s/f (Slow) **14** Ran SP% **126.9**

Speed ratings (Par 93): **91,90,87,84,84 83,82,82,81,80 75,71,64,61**

toteswingers: 1&2 £3.10, 1&3 £1.80, 2&3 £1.30 CSF £20.57 TOTE £5.40: £2.00, £1.30, £1.10; EX 21.90.

Owner Godolphin **Bred** West Lodge Stud **Trained** Newmarket, Suffolk

FOCUS

A fair maiden for fillies run at an ordinary pace with plenty of smartly-bred newcomers which should produce a few winners. The winner is another Godolphin 2yo to go forward from its debut.

NOTEBOOK

Damietta(USA) ran with plenty of credit when getting the hang of things all too late on her debut at Goodwood. That experience held her in good stead here and she was soon tracking the leaders and went about her job well when taking the lead entering the final furlong. Connections felt she did not handle the gradients at Goodwood and that she would appreciate a flatter track. She clearly liked the surface and is progressing well with connections now eyeing a tilt at a Listed race. (op 7-2)

Giants Play(USA) ◆, an $850,000 purchase by Giants Causeway and out of the very useful mare Playful Act, was always close enough but did not pick up immediately when asked in the home straight, but she was cloing on the winner with every stride nearing the finish. She will come on for this and will no doubt do herself justice when upped in class. (tchd 9-4 and 3-1)

Ghazwah had put in a couple of solid efforts in defeat beforehand. She was soon bowling along in the lead and looked to have the winner in trouble before fading entering the final furlong. Once again this was a sound effort and she should get her head in front before long as the front three look decent fillies. (op 6-4)

Taper Jean Girl(IRE), with her yard in good form, made an encouraging debut. Although she never threatened the principals she stayed on well enough to suggest a win in this sphere is within her grasp if she builds on this effort.

Nafura, a half-sister to Group 1 winners Dubai Destination and Librettist. She caught the eye as she was held up at the back and suffered some traffic problems throughout the home straight until the final furlong, where she finished with a flourish. She did not receive too hard a race as she ran so green but it was a nice enough introduction. (tchd 12-1)

Danehill Intellect(IRE) made a promising start to her career staying on well in the home straight and will be seen in a better light when upped in trip.

4981 ODDSCHECKER.COM MEDIAN AUCTION MAIDEN STKS 7f (P)

7:45 (7:46) (Class 6) 3-5-Y-O **£2,047** (£604; £302) **Stalls** High

Form RPR

2024 1 **Arteus**[42] 3566 3-9-3 **76**.... RichardHughes 1 72
(Jane Chapple-Hyam) *trckd ldr: rdn to ld 2f out: hrd pressed fnl f: edgd rt but hld on wl* **3/1**[1]

-303 2 ½ **Equinine (IRE)**[13] 4550 3-8-12 **66**.... RHills 8 66
(B W Hills) *trckd ldng pair: effrt against far rail 2f out: sn pressing wnr: nrly upsides fnl f: hld whn tight for room briefly 75yds out* **7/2**[2]

26 3 1 **Espero (IRE)**[25] 4151 3-9-3 **79**.... ChrisCatlin 5 68
(R A Farrant) *t.k.h early: hld up in last trio: prog on outer 2f out: hrd rdn and kpt on to take 3rd ins fnl f* **7/2**[2]

4 4 ¾ **Dom Polski**[88] 2142 3-9-3 0....(t) AdamKirby 3 66
(W R Swinburn) *hld up in 6th: rdn and effrt over 2f out: prog to take 3rd briefly fnl f: one pce after* **7/2**[2]

04 5 ½ **Final Drive (IRE)**[68] 2737 3-9-0 **54**.... AlanCreighton(3) 7 65
(E J Creighton) *awkward s: hld up in last trio: plld out wdst of all 2f out and drvn: kpt on fnl f: nrst fin* **100/1**

50 6 1 **Valfurva (IRE)**[25] 4151 3-8-12 0.... WilliamBuick 4 57
(L M Cumani) *chsd ldng trio: rdn and effrt over 2f out: stl chsng over 1f out: wknd ins fnl f* **12/1**

0-6 7 2¾ **Expensive Dinner**[77] 2455 3-8-7 0.... MarkFlynn(5) 9 49
(E F Vaughan) *settled in 5th: rdn 3f out: lost pl and struggling over 2f out* **40/1**

-000 8 2 **Chasing Amy**[38] 3718 3-8-12 **50**.... IanMongan 2 44
(M G Quinlan) *led to 2f out: steadily wknd* **66/1**

9 3¾ **Camilla Knight (IRE)** 3-8-12 0.... RyanMoore 6 34
(W R Swinburn) *dwlt: a in last trio: lost tch fr 2f out* **7/1**[3]

1m 26.65s (0.65) **Going Correction** +0.025s/f (Slow) **9** Ran SP% **116.8**

Speed ratings (Par 101): **97,96,95,94,93 92,89,87,83**

toteswingers: 1&2 £2.80, 1&3 £3.00, 2&3 £2.10 CSF £13.90 TOTE £4.70: £1.60, £1.30, £1.90; EX 16.30.

Owner Norcroft Park Stud **Bred** Norcroft Park Stud **Trained** Newmarket, Suffolk

FOCUS

A weak maiden which was steadily run, and the form is modest. Muddling form.

4982 ODDSCHECKER CASINO AND POKER CLAIMING STKS 6f (P)

8:15 (8:15) (Class 6) 3-5-Y-O **£2,047** (£604; £302) **Stalls** High

Form RPR

601 1 **Whiskey Junction**[29] 3995 5-9-9 **78**.... SebSanders 10 83
(M Quinn) *led 1f: trckd ldr: led again over 2f out: drvn clr over 1f out: in n.d after* **6/4**[2]

000 2 3½ **Monte Mayor Eagle**[5] 4812 3-8-2 **46**.... JamieMackay 7 54
(D Haydn Jones) *chsd ldng pair: drvn and styd on to take 2nd over 1f out: kpt on but no imp on wnr* **28/1**

2600 3 3 **Superduper**[39] 3694 4-8-7 **77**.... RichardHughes 8 46
(R Hannon) *lost pl after 1f: sn in 5th and off the pce: drvn and kpt on to take 3rd 1f out: no ch* **4/5**[1]

4000 4 3 **Ridgeway Silver**[7] 4749 3-8-0 **57**.... FrankieMcDonald 4 33
(M D I Usher) *sn outpcd: in 7th: plugged on fnl 2f to take 4th nr fin* **28/1**

5050 5 1¼ **Freepressionist**[7] 4748 3-7-9 **57**....(b[1]) CharlesEddery(7) 6 31
(R A Teal) *racd freely: led after 1f to over 2f out: wknd rapidly fnl f* **16/1**[3]

000- **6** *5* **Umpa Loompa (IRE)**[380] 4535 5-8-8 47..................(v) AndreaAtzeni(3) 5 21
(B J McMath) *racd v awkwardly thrght: nvr on terms w ldrs: wknd rapidly over 1f out* **28/1**

0 **7** *2 ¾* **Cheetah Beetah**[8] 4691 3-7-11 44.............................. AmyBaker(5) 9 6
(H S Howe) *chsd ldrs: drvn to dispute 3rd over 2f out: sn wknd rapidly* **100/1**

0566 **8** *14* **Mr Forthright**[8] 4690 5-8-8 43..(p) JackDean(3) 1 —
(J M Bradley) *s.s: a last and sn wl bhd: t.o* **66/1**

1m 12.59s (-0.51) **Going Correction** +0.025s/f (Slow)
WFA 3 from 4yo+ 4lb **8** Ran SP% **114.3**
Speed ratings (Par 101): **104,99,95,91,89 83,79,60**
toteswingers: 1&2 £6.10, 1&3 £1.10, 2&3 £5.40 CSF £42.61 TOTE £2.70: £1.10, £5.90, £1.02; EX 39.60.
Owner Steven Astaire **Bred** Mrs I A Balding **Trained** Newmarket, Suffolk

FOCUS
A run-of-the-mill claimer run at a good pace. Suspect form, with the favourite disappointing.

4983 COMPARE ODDS AT ODDSCHECKER.COM H'CAP 1m (P)
8:45 (8:48) (Class 3) (0-95,94) 3-Y-0+
£7,352 (£2,201; £1,100; £551; £274; £138) **Stalls** High

Form RPR

21-1 **1** **Musleh (USA)**[9] 4649 3-8-12 85 6ex.............................. LDettori 7 98+
(Saeed Bin Suroor) *mde all: dictated fair pce but gng easily: shkn up and stretched 2 l clr over 1f out: in n.d after: pushed out* **8/15**[1]

0060 **2** *1 ½* **Bomber Command (USA)**[20] 4293 6-9-2 82..................(v) SebSanders 1 88
(J W Hills) *t.k.h early: hld up in tch: rdn over 1f out: wnt 2nd ent fnl f: no imp on wnr* **33/1**

1104 **3** *nk* **Soccerjackpot (USA)**[42] 3567 5-10-0 94.......................... IanMongan 10 99
(C G Cox) *trckd wnr to 1/2-way: rdn and nt qckn wl over 1f out: styd on ins fnl f* **16/1**

4304 **4** *nk* **Laudatory**[13] 4540 3-8-10 83..(t) AdamKirby 6 87
(W R Swinburn) *cl up: nt clr run over 1f out and swtchd lft: drvn and styd on ins fnl f: nrly snatched 3rd* **7/2**[2]

-010 **5** *¾* **Grand Vizier (IRE)**[28] 4060 5-9-8 88.............................. ChrisCatlin 4 91
(C F Wall) *s.i.s and rousted along in last: rapid prog to chse wnr 1/2-way: drvn 2f out: lost 2nd ent fnl f: wknd nr fin* **20/1**

-000 **6** *hd* **Easy Target (FR)**[30] 4-9-8 88.............................. RyanMoore 5 90
(G L Moore) *hld up in last trio: rdn and outpcd wl over 1f out: styd on again ins fnl f* **10/1**[3]

2-00 **7** *nk* **Full Toss**[13] 4517 3-9-0 90.............................. PatrickHills(3) 8 91
(R Hannon) *hld up in last trio: rdn and no prog 2f out: kpt on fnl f* **33/1**

5010 **8** *hd* **Tudor Key (IRE)**[20] 4296 3-9-4 91.............................. WilliamBuick 9 91
(Mrs A J Perrett) *trckd ldrs on inner: rdn and nt qckn wl over 1f out: one pce and lost pls ins fnl f* **25/1**

36-0 **9** *12* **Touching (IRE)**[118] 1353 3-9-3 90.............................. RichardHughes 3 64
(R Hannon) *t.k.h: hld up in last trio: wknd over 2f out: t.o* **25/1**

1m 38.92s (-0.88) **Going Correction** +0.025s/f (Slow)
WFA 3 from 4yo+ 7lb **9** Ran SP% **120.8**
Speed ratings (Par 107): **105,103,103,102,102 101,101,101,89**
toteswingers: 1&2 £11.40, 1&3 £4.20, 2&3 £45.40 CSF £35.54 CT £168.84 TOTE £1.60: £1.10, £6.40, £3.10; EX 35.50.
Owner Godolphin **Bred** Nesco II Limited **Trained** Newmarket, Suffolk

FOCUS
There was a delay to the start after all the horses were loaded but Nightjar had to be unloaded and subsequently withdrawn. This was a decent handicap. Another step in the right direction from the winner.

NOTEBOOK
Musleh(USA) ◆ had scored quite takingly over course and distance last week and looked potentially well treated running with a 6lb penalty. Breaking smartly with his rider steadying the pace after 3f before quickening again over the 2f marker, the race was soon put to bed. There was plenty to like about this good-looking colt, and with connections keeping him to the handicap route at present he will take all the beating, especially when he returns here. (op 4-6 tchd 8-11 and 4-5 in a place)
Bomber Command(USA) is a useful perfomer on his day on the all-weather but had completely lost his way this season which has resulted in a drop down the handicap. This was a much better effort, though, and after racing just off the pace he ran on well enough in the straight but was never a threat to the comfortable winner. He had dropped to a reasonable mark and, if repeating this performance, he can go one better.
Soccerjackpot(USA) had won a couple of all-weather handicaps earlier in the year and put in another respectable effort under top-weight. He was up against it giving so much weight to a highly progressive rival but kept on well enough to suggest he can return to winning ways. (op 14-1)
Laudatory's only defeat from three efforts on the all-weather came at the hands of no other than Ghanaati, and he once again proved his liking for this surface. Tracking the leaders, he did not receive the best of runs in the straight and had to wait for a gap to appear, running on when it did. He does not seem as good on turf but is fairly handicapped. (op 9-2)
Grand Vizier(IRE), twice a winner here, completely missed the break and was rousted along to chase the leaders after a couple of furlongs. He ran on well enough in the straight and while on a handy mark he can gain some compensation when returning here.
Easy Target(FR) put in a sound effort coming from well off the pace. (op 12-1)
Tudor Key(IRE) Official explanation: jockey said gelding hung left

4984 FIND THE BEST PRICE AT ODDSCHECKER.COM H'CAP 7f (P)
9:15 (9:18) (Class 4) (0-80,78) 3-Y-0 **£4,727** (£1,406; £702; £351) **Stalls** High

Form RPR

1-64 **1** **Audemar (IRE)**[9] 4649 3-9-4 75.............................. RichardHughes 4 83+
(E F Vaughan) *t.k.h early: trckd ldng trio: effrt 2f out: drvn to chse ldr over 1f out: styd on to ld last 75yds: jst prevailed* **7/2**[2]

11 **2** *nse* **Dukes Art**[18] 4386 3-9-6 77.............................. RyanMoore 5 85
(J A R Toller) *hld up in last trio: swtchd lft over 2f out: drvn and effrt over 1f out: r.o w wnr to dispute ld last 75yds: jst pipped* **7/4**[1]

4513 **3** *¾* **Mac's Power (IRE)**[37] 3738 3-9-4 75..............................(t) WilliamBuick 6 81+
(P J O'Gorman) *stdd s: keen early and hld up in last: swtchd to far rail over 2f out and rapid prog: led over 1f out: wknd and hdd last 75yds* **6/1**

2362 **4** *3 ¾* **Iron Out (USA)**[4] 4841 3-8-10 67.............................. ChrisCatlin 3 63
(R Hollinshead) *hld up in last trio: rdn wl over 2f out: outpcd wl over 1f out: plugged on* **6/1**

2016 **5** *shd* **Arachnophobia (IRE)**[14] 4494 3-9-7 78.............................. JamieMackay 7 74
(Pat Eddery) *hld up bhd ldng pair: effrt over 2f out: nt qckn and outpcd over 1f out: one pce after* **9/1**

0161 **6** *6* **Elusive Fame (USA)**[4] 4841 3-9-7 78 6ex..............................(b) JoeFanning 2 57
(M Johnston) *t.k.h early: sn pressed ldr: led over 2f out to over 1f out: wknd* **4/1**[3]

11-6 **7** *2 ½* **Spiritual Art**[46] 3455 3-9-5 76.............................. AdamKirby 1 49
(L A Dace) *led to over 2f out: wknd tamely over 1f out* **20/1**

1m 25.27s (-0.73) **Going Correction** +0.025s/f (Slow) **7** Ran SP% **121.9**
Speed ratings (Par 102): **105,104,104,99,99 92,89**
toteswingers: 1&2 £2.60, 1&3 £5.10, 2&3 £4.30 CSF £11.01 TOTE £4.90: £2.00, £1.90; EX 10.90 Place 6: £5.60 Place 5: £3.93.
Owner Gute Freunde Partnership **Bred** Mrs Amanda Brudenell And Mr & Mrs R A **Trained** Newmarket, Suffolk

FOCUS
A small field but a very tight handicap with a case to be made for all of the seven runners. Sound form.
T/Plt: £6.90 to a £1 stake. Pool: £48,097.16. 5,079.81 winning tickets. T/Qpdt: £1.40 to a £1 stake. Pool: £4,881.68. 2,470.56 winning tickets. JN

4563 NEWBURY (L-H)
Friday, August 14

OFFICIAL GOING: Good to firm (good in places) changing to good to firm after race 5 (3.30)
Wind: Moderate across Weather: Overcast

4985 DON DEADMAN MEMORIAL EUROPEAN BREEDERS' FUND MAIDEN STKS (DIV I) 7f (S)
1:20 (1:22) (Class 4) 2-Y-0 **£4,857** (£1,445; £722; £360) **Stalls** Centre

Form RPR

2 **1** **Pounced (USA)**[21] 4258 2-9-3 0.............................. RyanMoore 7 85+
(J H M Gosden) *lw: trckd ldr: led over 2f out: pushed along and hung bdly rt fr 1f out but a in command* **4/5**[1]

2 *3* **Markazzi** 2-9-3 0.............................. RHills 5 78+
(Sir Michael Stoute) *w'like: scope: str: in tch: hdwy 2f out: chsd wnr fnl f and kpt on encouargingly but nvr any ch* **5/2**[2]

3 *2 ½* **Cultivar** 2-9-3 0.............................. RobertWinston 12 71+
(B W Hills) *unf: scope: stdd s and hld up in rr: hdwy fr 2f out: styd on wl to go 3rd fnl f but nvr any ch w ldng duo* **20/1**

4 *2* **Averroes (IRE)** 2-9-3 0.............................. AdamKirby 3 66
(C G Cox) *w'like: chsd ldrs: drvn along fr 3f out but styd wl there tl outpcd fr over 1f out* **50/1**

5 *1* **Opera Gal (IRE)** 2-8-12 0.............................. WilliamBuick 6 59
(A M Balding) *w'like: scope: bit bkwd: t.k.h early: led tl hdd over 2f out: wknd appr fnl f* **25/1**

6 **6** *hd* **Walcot Square (IRE)**[28] 4048 2-9-3 0.............................. SteveDrowne 9 63+
(R Charlton) *w'like: in rr but in tch: n.m.r and lost position over 2f out: pushed along and styd on again ins fnl f: but nvr anywhere nr ldrs* **14/1**[3]

7 *½* **Manhattan Fox (USA)** 2-9-3 0.............................. JamieSpencer 10 62+
(B J Meehan) *w'like: scope: chsd ldrs: pusshed along over 2f out: wknd appr fnl f* **22/1**

0 **8** *½* **Invincible Soul (IRE)**[13] 4524 2-9-3 0.............................. RichardHughes 4 61
(R Hannon) *lw: in rr but in tch: hdwy to trck ldrs over 2f out: shkn up and wknd wl over 1f out* **16/1**

6 **9** *½* **Kilt Rock (IRE)**[19] 4336 2-9-3 0.............................. JamesDoyle 11 60
(T G Mills) *str: swtg: a towards rr* **33/1**

0 **10** *1 ½* **Caucus**[34] 3867 2-9-3 0.............................. ChrisCatlin 8 56
(J L Dunlop) *unf: t.k.h and sltly hmpd after 1f: a in rr* **100/1**

11 *2 ¼* **Mini Max** 2-8-7 0.............................. GabrielHannon(5) 1 45
(B W Duke) *w'like: chsd ldrs: rdn 3f out: wknd appr fnl 2f* **100/1**

1m 27.05s (1.35) **Going Correction** +0.10s/f (Good) **11** Ran SP% **116.5**
Speed ratings (Par 96): **96,92,89,87,86 86,85,84,84,82 80**
toteswingers: 1&2 £1.10, 1&3 £3.10, 2&3 £13.20 CSF £2.45 TOTE £1.70: £1.02, £1.20, £4.80; EX 3.20.
Owner Lady Rothschild **Bred** Carwell Equities Ltd **Trained** Newmarket, Suffolk

FOCUS
This had the look of a pretty decent maiden and several can leave the bare form behind.

NOTEBOOK
Pounced(USA) won in the style of a very useful juvenile. A highly promising second on his debut at Ascot, he had clearly learned from that and, having struck the front over 2f out, was soon clear. He hung right under pressure, ending up on the stands' rail, but had tons in hand and connections will no doubt look for him to take his chance in something a bit better next time. He is in the Group 2 Champagne Stakes next month, as well as the Group 1 Dewhurst and Racing Post Trophy later in the year, and it looks quite possible he will take his chance in one of those. As for next year, he has been given a 33/1 quote by VCBet for the 2,000 Guineas. (tchd 8-11)
Markazzi ◆, another entered in all the major autumn prizes, has plenty of speed in his pedigree, though his sire injects some stamina, and he made a really pleasing debut. He was never in with a chance against the winner, but kept on nicely to finish a clear second best and winning a standard maiden should prove a formality, with progress expected. (op 9-4 tchd 11-4)
Cultivar, a half-brother to high-class French performer African Rose, holds a couple of Group 1 entries and he shaped with a good deal of promise back in third. Held up, he ran on well inside the final quarter mile, albeit without looking likely to reach the front pair, and will find easier opportunities. (tchd 25-1)
Averroes(IRE), a Derby entry related to winners at 1m-1m4f, couldn't quicken against speedier types, but he stayed on right the way to the line and looks of a horse with a bright future. He cost 100,000gns and will relish the step up to 1m before long. (tchd 100-1 in places)
Opera Gal(IRE), one of only two fillies in the race, holds a Group 1 Fillies' Mile entry, but juveniles from this yard often need a run and she looks no different. Keen through the early stages, she was the leader on sufferance and hung in there best she could once headed, before eventually tiring. This was a pleasing enough start and she should find an opening against her own sex. (tchd 28-1)
Walcot Square(IRE), sixth in another useful maiden over C&D on debut, was faced with faster conditions here and ran every bit as well, staying on again having lost his position. He will benefit from an extra furlong before long. (op 16-1)
Manhattan Fox(USA), who holds a host of big-race entries, showed a bit of ability on this racecourse debut and should improve for the outing, though he will need to if he is to live up to his reputation. (op 33-1)
Invincible Soul(IRE) failed to improve on his debut effort and may be more of a nursery type.

4986 DON DEADMAN MEMORIAL EUROPEAN BREEDERS' FUND MAIDEN STKS (DIV II) 7f (S)
1:50 (1:53) (Class 4) 2-Y-0 **£4,857** (£1,445; £722; £360) **Stalls** Centre

Form RPR

1 **Najd (USA)** 2-9-3 0.............................. LDettori 11 83+
(Saeed Bin Suroor) *str: scope: in tch: pushed along and hdwy fr 2f out: pressing styng on whn carried rt ins fnl f: qcknd to ld fnl 100yds: readily* **10/3**[1]

0 **2** *hd* **Poltergeist (IRE)**[28] 4048 2-9-3 0 RichardHughes 6 83
(R Hannon) *unf: scope: in tch: pushed along over 2f out: swtchd lft wl over 1f out and styd on strly u.p thrght fnl f: gng on cl home but nt quite rch wnr* **5/1**

3 *3/4* **Esaar (USA)** 2-9-3 0 RHills 4 81
(B W Hills) *w'like: scope: trckd ldrs: pushed along 2f out: kpt on wl fnl f but nvr quite gng pce to chal ldng duo* **9/2**[3]

4 *1/2* **Harvest Dancer (IRE)** 2-9-3 0 JamieSpencer 2 79
(B J Meehan) *w'like: athletic: chsd ldrs: drvn along over 2f out: rdn to ld 1f out: hdd and no ex fnl 100yds* **7/1**

6 **5** *3/4* **Kona Coast**[14] 4497 2-9-3 0 (b) SteveDrowne 7 78
(J H M Gosden) *w'like: scope: led: rdn 2f out: hdd 1f out: hung bdly rt and hd to one side fnl f and sn fnd no ex* **16/1**

6 *1* **Never The Waiter** 2-9-3 0 DaneO'Neill 10 75+
(B J Meehan) *w'like: leggy: t.k.h early: in rr: pushed along over 2f out: hdwy over 1f out: styd on fnl f: gng on cl home* **33/1**

4 **7** *1/2* **Spa's Dancer (IRE)**[23] 4209 2-9-3 0 SebSanders 5 74
(J W Hills) *unf: scope: swtg: plld v hrd and chsd ldrs: shkn up 2f out: one pce ins fnl f* **4/1**[2]

8 *3* **Botanist** 2-9-3 0 RyanMoore 1 66+
(Sir Michael Stoute) *w'like: towards rr but in tch: pushed along: hung lft and green 2f out: n.d after* **8/1**

9 *1 1/2* **Brick Red** 2-9-3 0 WilliamBuick 3 63
(A M Balding) *w'like: scope: bit bkwd: a towards rr* **40/1**

10 *1 1/2* **Dutiful** 2-9-3 0 ChrisCatlin 9 59
(M R Channon) *w'like: bit bkwd: s.i.s: sn chsng ldrs: wknd fr 2f out* **66/1**

11 *10* **Radsky** 2-9-3 0 JamesDoyle 8 34
(J G Portman) *unf: a towards rr* **66/1**

1m 26.85s (1.15) **Going Correction** +0.10s/f (Good) **11** Ran SP% **115.8**
Speed ratings (Par 96): **97,96,95,95,94 93,92,89,87,85 74**
toteswingers: 1&2 £6.90, 1&3 £3.10, 2&3 £7.50 CSF £19.41 TOTE £4.20: £1.70, £2.40, £2.10; EX 25.00.
Owner Godolphin **Bred** Stoneside Stable **Trained** Newmarket, Suffolk

FOCUS
This was arguably the weaker of the two divisions, though the time was marginally quicker and the race should provide winners.

NOTEBOOK
Najd(USA), related to a Grade 3 winner in the US, has no big-race entries, but his yard is in top form at present and he just did enough to make a winning debut. He started to close from over 2f out and, despite being carried right inside the final furlong, appeared to quicken against the stands' rail to just prevail. This was a good start and it was particularly encouraging to hear his trainer state that he was only around 85% fit for this debut. Therefore one can expect improvement and it will be interesting to see where he goes next. He is 33/1 with Skybet for next year's 2,000 Guineas. (op 11-4 tchd 7-2 and 4-1 in a place)
Poltergeist(IRE), who travelled well for a long way until tiring in the soft ground on his debut over C&D, was backed beforehand and clearly expected to have improved for that initial outing. He may have got a little too far back, though, as by the time he was switched left, the winner had already stolen first run. He stayed on well to just miss out and should improve again, so can probably win an ordinary maiden. (op 8-1)
Esaar(USA), a son of Mr Greeley entered in all the right races, travelled nicely in behind the leaders and kept on without being given an overly hard time by his rider. This was a nice introduction and, with significant improvement likely, he is another obvious candidate to win a maiden. (op 8-1)
Harvest Dancer(IRE), a son of Danehill Dancer entered in the big juveniles contests this autumn, picked up to lead a furlong out and briefly looked the winner, but couldn't pull out any extra inside the final 100 yards. He should improve and will prove as effective back at 6f. (op 7-2)
Kona Coast, who wore blinkers for his debut when sixth over 6f at Newmarket, was made plenty of use of on this step up in trip and, having been headed, he started to hang and didn't impress with his head carriage. He is one to have reservations about. Official explanation: jockey said colt hung right-handed (tchd 18-1)
Never The Waiter ◆, entered in both the Mill Reef and the Champagne Stakes, was discarded in the market but actually ran a race full of promise. He stayed on nicely inside the final quarter mile, having been held up, and was closing with every stride as they crossed the line. Improvement should be forthcoming.
Spa's Dancer(IRE), fourth in a race that is working out well on his debut at Sandown, looked one of the more likely winners, but refused to settle and his finishing effort was always likely to suffer as a result. He may be worth another chance to confirm that initial promise. (op 5-1)
Botanist ◆, a brother to 2003 Fillies' Mile winner Red Bloom, holds the right entries, but he was too green to do himself justice on this racecourse debut, hanging left and not looking entirely sure what was required of him. He will come on appreciably for the experience and is one to be interested in next time. (tchd 9-1)

4987 MC SEAFOODS CLAIMING STKS 1m 3f 5y
2:20 (2:20) (Class 5) 3-Y-O+ £2,590 (£770; £385; £192) Stalls Low

Form RPR

5-00 **1** **Malt Or Mash (USA)**[21] 4261 5-9-12 99 RichardHughes 9 79
(R Hannon) *hld up in rr: pushed along and hdwy over 2f out: swtchd rt and hrd drvn over 1f out: styd on u.p to ld last strides* **5/4**[1]

3246 **2** *hd* **Nawamees (IRE)**[4] 4857 11-8-8 65 (p) RichardEvans(5) 2 66
(P D Evans) *led after 1f: hdd over 7f out: led again over 5f out: rdn along over 3f out: kpt on wl to keep narrow advantage fr over 2f out: stl slt ld u.p ins fnl f: ct last strides* **9/2**[2]

5040 **3** *1 3/4* **Hambledon Hill**[20] 4319 3-7-13 60 CharlesEddery(7) 8 66
(R Hannon) *slowly away: sn drvn to chse ldrs: chal fr 3f out and stl upsides 1f out: outpcd ins fnl f* **15/2**

046 **4** *7* **Boffin**[43] 3538 4-9-0 53 StephenCarson 1 52
(Eve Johnson Houghton) *in rr: hdwy to chse ldrs 4f out: sn rdn: wknd fr 2f out* **25/1**

10/1 **5** *2 1/4* **Guiseppe Verdi (USA)**[27] 4084 5-9-9 81 ChrisCatlin 5 57
(Miss Tor Sturgis) *lw: t.k.h: led 1f: styd chsng ldrs but stl t.k.h: rdn 3f out: wknd 2f out* **5/1**[3]

0520 **6** *2* **Polish Power (GER)**[9] 4644 9-9-2 75 (p) LPKeniry 7 47
(J S Moore) *in rr: rdn and sme hdwy 4f out: nvr gng pce to chal: wknd over 2f out* **11/1**

0-26 **7** *62* **Canton Road**[23] 4205 3-9-4 64 LDettori 6 —
(P F I Cole) *lw: t.k.h: led over 7f out tl over 5f out: wknd qckly fr 3f out: eased whn no ch over 2f out: t.o* **8/1**

2m 20.07s (-1.13) **Going Correction** -0.10s/f (Good)
WFA 3 from 4yo+ 10lb **7** Ran SP% **114.3**
Speed ratings (Par 103): **100,99,98,93,91 90,45**
toteswingers: 1&2 £2.90, 1&3 £5.40, 2&3 £11.10 CSF £7.13 TOTE £2.10: £1.50, £2.90; EX 9.00.
Owner A P Patey **Bred** Delahanty Stock Farm **Trained** East Everleigh, Wilts
■ Stewards' Enquiry : Richard Evans one-day ban: used whip with excessive frequency (Aug 28)

FOCUS
This wasn't a particularly strong claimer and class-act of the race Malt Or Mash got the job done, but only just. He is not the force of old, and the form is rated through the runner-up.

Canton Road Official explanation: jockey said gelding lost its action

4988 PROVIDE SECURITY H'CAP 1m 5f 61y
2:55 (2:55) (Class 3) (0-90,90) 3-Y-O+ £7,771 (£2,312; £1,155; £577) Stalls Low

Form RPR

31-0 **1** **Oasis Knight (IRE)**[120] 1303 3-8-7 **81** ow1 (v[1]) RichardHughes 8 94+
(M P Tregoning) *trckd ldrs: reminder 5f out: chal 3f out: sn led: rdn 3 l clr over 1f out: drvn out ins fnl f and nvr in any danger* **8/1**

5-21 **2** *1 3/4* **Right Stuff (FR)**[15] 1184 6-9-6 **82** RyanMoore 4 90+
(G L Moore) *lw: in rr: hdwy and n.m.r over 2f out: swtchd rt and hdwy wl over 1f out: styd on wl fnl f to take 2nd nr fin but no ch w wnr* **11/2**[3]

6313 **3** *3/4* **Zaaqya**[27] 4103 3-8-10 **84** RHills 12 91
(J L Dunlop) *hld up in rr: hdwy towards outside over 2f out: chsd wnr over 1f out but nvr any ch: one pce and lost 2nd nr fin* **4/1**[1]

1136 **4** *4 1/2* **Gloucester**[29] 4007 6-9-3 **79** SebSanders 13 79
(M J Scudamore) *hld up in rr and t.k.h: hdwy 3f out: disp 2nd over 2f out: wknd over 1f out* **16/1**

6450 **5** *2* **Capable Guest (IRE)**[8] 4696 7-9-0 **76** ChrisCatlin 6 73
(M R Channon) *in rr: drvn along 3f out: styd on fnl 2f but nvr in contention* **20/1**

1123 **6** *3/4* **Strathcal**[16] 4442 3-8-4 **78** WilliamBuick 9 74
(H Morrison) *lw: hld up in mid-div: rdn and sme prog over 3f out: nvr gng pce to rch ldrs: hung lft over 2f out and sn btn* **9/2**[2]

0/40 **7** *hd* **Takafu (USA)**[62] 2931 7-8-11 **73** LPKeniry 10 69
(W S Kittow) *chsd ldrs: rdn 4f out: wknd over 2f out* **10/1**

0-00 **8** *1* **Bureaucrat**[17] 4408 7-9-10 **86** (p) LDettori 3 81
(P J Hobbs) *in tch: pushed along and hdwy 3f out: n.m.r and wknd sn after* **12/1**

3301 **9** *nk* **Toujours Souriante**[28] 4038 3-7-9 **74** Louis-PhilippeBeuzelin(5) 5 68
(M Johnston) *chsd ldrs: rdn fr 4f out: wknd over 2f out* **8/1**

2161 **10** *1 3/4* **It's A Date**[23] 4197 4-9-9 **85** DaneO'Neill 7 77
(A King) *sn led: hdd ins fnl 3f: sn btn* **17/2**

0500 **11** *3 1/4* **Admirable Duque (IRE)**[2] 4911 3-7-13 **73** ow1 FrankieMcDonald 2 60
(D J S Ffrench Davis) *towards rr most of way* **33/1**

-265 **12** *19* **Wait For The Light**[71] 1732 5-8-10 **72** oh3 SteveDrowne 1 31
(Mrs S Leech) *chsd ldrs: wknd qckly 3f out: eased whn no ch fnl 2f* **66/1**

2m 48.33s (-3.67) **Going Correction** -0.10s/f (Good)
WFA 3 from 4yo+ 12lb **12** Ran SP% **118.2**
Speed ratings (Par 107): **107,105,105,102,101 101,100,100,100,99 97,85**
toteswingers: 1&2 £8.90, 1&3 £10.80, 2&3 £4.70 CSF £50.57 CT £205.43 TOTE £10.10: £3.20, £2.10, £2.20; EX 63.80.
Owner Lady Tennant **Bred** Deerfield Farm **Trained** Lambourn, Berks

FOCUS
This was a fair handicap for the grade. The winner produced a step up and the second also beat the older horses decisively. Sound form.

NOTEBOOK
Oasis Knight(IRE) responded well to the first-time visor. His half-brother High Accolade developed into a high-class middle-distance runner in headgear and, though this fellow is extremely unlikely to progress as far, it would come as no surprise were he to improve further. Richard Hughes, who was putting up 1lb overweight, had to give him a reminder before the straight, but he responded positively to it and was always doing enough inside the final quarter mile. He will continue down the handicap route. (op 7-1 tchd 9-1 in a place)
Right Stuff(FR), who has been running over hurdles, was 5lb higher than when winning at Kempton on his latest Flat start and he ran an improved race, staying on well in second having been a bit short of room approaching the final quarter-mile. There is more to come from him. (op 5-1)
Zaaqya, a narrow winner at the course early last month, failed to run his race off an 8lb higher mark in soft ground last time, but he was seen to better effect back under faster conditions. He didn't look in need of this trip, though, and may prove best back at 1m4f for now. (op 6-1)
Gloucester, 7lb higher than when last winning, came through to try and challenge and was close enough if good enough, but he was a beaten horse well over a furlong out, fading late on. He is in the handicapper's grip at present. (op 14-1)
Capable Guest(IRE) is on a good mark these days and he kept plodding away to take fifth. He never looked in with a chance of winning, but may well find an opening at some stage. (tchd 18-1)
Strathcal has had a good time of it of late, but the handicapper now looks in control. (op 5-1)
It's A Date, 6lb higher than when winning last time, was quickly beaten. (op 8-1)

4989 BATHWICK TYRES ST HUGH'S STKS (LISTED RACE) (FILLIES) 5f 34y
3:30 (3:30) (Class 1) 2-Y-O
£17,031 (£6,456; £3,231; £1,611; £807; £405) Stalls Centre

Form RPR

513 **1** **Sand Vixen**[20] 4295 2-8-12 96 LDettori 3 100+
(Saeed Bin Suroor) *lw: trckd ldrs: drvn and upsides thrght fnl f: asserted last stride* **7/2**[2]

12 **2** *nse* **Shamandar (FR)**[27] 4089 2-8-12 90 KirstyMilczarek 7 100+
(W J Haggas) *lw: awkrd s: s.i.s: t.k.h towards rr: hdwy and swtchd lft 2f out: narrow advantage 1f out but strly pressed: hdd ld stride* **2/1**[1]

3160 **3** *2 1/2* **Above Limits (IRE)**[27] 4089 2-8-12 89 RichardKingscote 11 91
(Tom Dascombe) *lw: led: rdn 2f out: narrowly hdd 1f out: outpcd by ldng duo ins fnl f* **15/2**

2100 **4** *1/2* **Swan Wings**[20] 4295 2-8-12 87 WilliamBuick 14 89
(A M Balding) *chsd ldrs: rdn over 2f out: styd on same pce u.p fnl f* **25/1**

216 **5** *1 3/4* **Roodle**[20] 4295 2-8-12 90 DaneO'Neill 5 83
(Eve Johnson Houghton) *chsd ldrs: rdn along 1/2-way: wknd ins fnl f* **18/1**

1501 **6** *nse* **Hairspray**[21] 4272 2-8-12 92 RyanMoore 12 83
(M R Channon) *s.i.s: in rr: hdwy 1/2-way: chsd ldrs over 1f out: wknd ins fnl f* **12/1**

01 **7** *1 3/4* **Excelling (IRE)**[20] 4302 2-8-12 0 ChrisCatlin 10 76+
(P J Makin) *lw: s.i.s: in rr: rdn and hung rt over 1f out: styd on ins fnl f gng on cl home* **6/1**[3]

8 *1/2* **Annia (IRE)**[22] 4251 2-8-12 0 LPKeniry 8 74
(David Marnane, Ire) *pressed ldrs: rdn 1/2-way: wknd fnl f* **100/1**

2103 **9** *1/2* **Avonvalley**[22] 4221 2-8-12 78 TGMcLaughlin 1 73
(M S Saunders) *fly-jmpd s: t.k.h: w ldrs tl over 1f out: wknd jst ins fnl f* **50/1**

2104 **10** *3/4* **Absolute Music (USA)**[23] 2-8-12 97 SteveDrowne 9 70
(R M H Cowell) *chsd ldrs tl wknd over 1f out* **10/1**

1530 **11** *nse* **Deal (IRE)**[20] 4295 2-8-12 88 RichardHughes 6 70+
(R Hannon) *in rr and outpcd: sme prog on ins whn bdly hmpd over 1f out: nt rcvr* **18/1**

5032 **12** *1/2* **More Lashes (USA)**[8] 4711 2-8-12 63 AdamKirby 13 68
(M G Quinlan) *chsd ldrs over 3f* **33/1**

1030 **13** *3 1/2* **Existentialist**[27] 4089 2-8-12 82.. SebSanders 2 55
(J G Portman) *chsd ldrs 3f* **40/1**
61.62 secs (0.22) **Going Correction** +0.10s/f (Good) 13 Ran SP% **121.1**
Speed ratings (Par 99): **102,101,97,97,94 94,91,90,89,88 88,87,82**
toteswingers: 1&2 £2.30, 1&3 £6.70, 2&3 £5.90 CSF £10.62 TOTE £3.80: £1.80, £1.30, £2.70; EX 8.80.
Owner Godolphin **Bred** Mrs M Campbell-Andenaes **Trained** Newmarket, Suffolk

FOCUS
The largest field in some time for this Listed contest and the 'big' two in the market drew on from the remainder. Avergae form for the grade, with good efforts from the front pair.

NOTEBOOK
Sand Vixen, an AW maiden winner who finished third in the Group 3 Princess Margaret Stakes at Ascot last time, was having her first try at 5f and she showed ample speed. Soon tracking the leaders, she travelled strongly and quickened well to lead a furlong out, but was soon passed by the runner-up. That one continued to drift left, though, and she just got up in the final stride. There is a lot to like about this daughter of Dubawi and there is no reason why she cannot continue to progress, with the Cheveley Park later in the season being her aim. (op 11-4 tchd 4-1 in places)
Shamandar(FR) may well have won had Kirsty Milczarek pulled her whip through to try and prevent her mount wandering left, especially given the narrow margin of defeat. Runner-up to Monsieur Chevalier in the Super Sprint over C&D, she wasn't the best away and raced a bit keen, but picked up really well once switched and remains a filly of potential. (tchd 15-8 and 9-4)
Above Limits(IRE), sixth in the Super Sprint, came in for support beforehand and showed plenty of pace. She was quickly brushed aside by the winner, though, and in the end could only keep on at the one pace. (op 10-1 tchd 13-2)
Swan Wings has struggled a bit since winning her maiden, but she ran pretty much to form with the winner judged on their Ascot running. She kept on right the way to the line and should be able to pick up another race at some stage this season.
Roodle, another to have run in the Princess Margaret, came under pressure over 2f out and wasn't good enough to put in a challenge. She has yet to prove she is up to pattern level, but still has some scope. (op 20-1)
Hairspray, narrow winner of a 6f conditions event at Newmarket last time, wasn't the quickest away and did her best to get into it, but couldn't race on from a furlong out.
Excelling(IRE), easy winner of a 5f maiden at Lingfield last time, was solid in the market but never really recovered from a slow start, making modest late gains. (op 8-1 tchd 17-2)
Annia(IRE) showed speed and will obviously find easier opportunities to break her duck.
Deal(IRE) was just beginning to run on when hampered against the stands' rail and would have finished a good bit closer. (op 16-1)

4990 CHRISTOPHER SMITH ASSOCIATES H'CAP 6f 8y
4:05 (4:05) (Class 4) (0-80,80) 3-Y-O **£4,857** (£1,445; £722; £360) **Stalls** Centre

Form RPR
3561 **1** **Getcarter**[2] 4905 3-8-9 **68**.. RichardHughes 8 77+
(R Hannon) *lw: stdd s: hld up in tch: trckd ldrs gng wl fr 2f out: led jst ins fnl f: pushed out: comf* **15/8**[1]
4321 **2** *1* **George Thisby**[38] 3712 3-8-11 **73** ow2.............. JamesMillman(3) 4 78
(B R Millman) *w ldr: rdn over 2f out: styd on u.p to chse wnr ins fnl f: but a readily hld* **13/2**[3]
342 **3** *1 1/2* **Raimond Ridge (IRE)**[8] 4695 3-8-6 **70**.................... MCGeran(5) 9 71
(M R Channon) *in rr: rdn over 2f out: hdwy over 1f out: styd on u.p fnl f but nvr gng pce to trble ldng duo* **12/1**
1551 **4** *1/2* **Rapid Water**[19] 4338 3-9-7 **80**.. LPKeniry 3 79
(A M Balding) *lw: led: rdn 2f out: hdd jst ins fnl f and sn wknd* **5/2**[2]
044 **5** *nk* **Fiftyfourth Street**[24] 4174 3-9-0 **73**.......................(t) SebSanders 5 71
(P J Makin) *t.k.h: in tch: rdn and outpcd ins fnl 2f: styd on again fnl f* **16/1**
6013 **6** *hd* **Bold Ring**[22] 4237 3-7-11 **61** oh1.................. Louis-PhilippeBeuzelin(5) 7 58
(E J Creighton) *fly j. s: in rr: rdn and sme prog whn nt clr run and swtchd lft 1f out: kpt on same pce ins fnl f* **16/1**
0002 **7** *hd* **Lucky Leigh**[8] 4712 3-9-7 **80**.. RyanMoore 2 77
(M R Channon) *chsd ldrs: rdn over 2f out: wknd ins fnl f* **8/1**
1m 14.07s (1.07) **Going Correction** +0.10s/f (Good) 7 Ran SP% **107.3**
Speed ratings (Par 102): **96,94,92,92,91 91,91**
toteswingers: 1&2 £3.10, 1&3 £4.40, 2&3 £6.00 CSF £12.66 CT £81.84 TOTE £2.60: £2.20, £2.70; EX 16.00.
Owner Mrs J K Powell **Bred** C R Mason **Trained** East Everleigh, Wilts

FOCUS
This was a fair sprint handicap. Straightforward form and sound enough overall.
Rapid Water Official explanation: jockey said colt was lame
Lucky Leigh Official explanation: jockey said filly hing right throughout

4991 RAMSAY V INLAND REVENUE COMMISSIONERS HL 1981 MAIDEN FILLIES' STKS 1m 2f 6y
4:35 (4:35) (Class 5) 3-Y-O+ **£3,238** (£963; £481; £240) **Stalls** Low

Form RPR
5 **1** **Arwaah (IRE)**[107] 1599 3-8-12 0.. RHills 1 98+
(M P Tregoning) *w'like: scope: tall: lw: mde all: qcknd readily clr fr 2f out: impressive* **13/8**[1]
-226 **2** *4* **Lady Francesca**[21] 4259 3-8-12 100.............................. RichardHughes 8 83
(W R Muir) *a trcking wnr: rdn over 2f out: sn easily outpcd but kpt on wl for 2nd* **2/1**[2]
3 *1* **Hajmah (IRE)** 3-8-12 0.. LDettori 4 81
(Saeed Bin Suroor) *w'like: scope: s.i.s: in rr: hdwy on outside over 3f out: clsd on ldrs and drvn 2f out: styd on same pce fr over 1f out* **9/2**[3]
-402 **4** *3/4* **Spirit Of Dubai (IRE)**[48] 3373 3-8-12 88........................ LPKeniry 7 79
(D M Simcock) *in tch: rdn over 3f out: chsd ldrs over 2f out: kpt on same pce fr over 1f out* **16/1**
3 **5** *nk* **Deportment**[13] 4519 3-8-12 0.. WilliamBuick 3 78
(J R Fanshawe) *w'like: str: swtg: trckd ldrs: pushed along ins fnl 3f: one pce fnl 2f* **10/1**
6 *2 3/4* **Benedicte (IRE)** 3-8-9 0.. AndreaAtzeni(3) 5 73
(M Botti) *w'like: in rr: rdn and sme prog over 3f out: nvr in contention and no ch fnl 2f* **33/1**
7 *21* **Stage Performance (IRE)** 3-8-12 0.............................. SebSanders 6 31
(J H M Gosden) *s.i.s: in rr: hdwy over 4f out: chsd ldrs 3f out: sn wknd* **18/1**
066 **8** *2 3/4* **Monagasque (IRE)**[53] 3228 3-8-12 47.............................. JamesDoyle 2 25
(S Kirk) *a towards rr: wl bhd fnl 2f* **100/1**
2m 6.84s (-1.96) **Going Correction** -0.10s/f (Good) 8 Ran SP% **113.8**
Speed ratings (Par 100): **103,99,99,98,98 95,79,76**
toteswingers: 1&2 £1.80, 1&3 £2.90, 2&3 £3.20 CSF £4.99 TOTE £2.70: £1.30, £1.10, £1.60; EX 6.00.
Owner Hamdan Al Maktoum **Bred** Shadwell Estate Company Limited **Trained** Lambourn, Berks

FOCUS
Probably a stronger older fillies' maiden than usual for this stage of the season, featuring some well-bred newcomers and a couple with proven ability. The early pace was modest and the front pair virtually held those positions throughout. The winner impressed but the form has not been rated positively given the lack of pace.

4992 JACK COLLING POLAR JEST APPRENTICE H'CAP 1m 1f
5:10 (5:10) (Class 5) (0-70,70) 4-Y-O+ **£2,590** (£770; £385; £192) **Stalls** Low

Form RPR
2662 **1** **Magroom**[29] 3996 5-9-2 **62**.. MCGeran 1 69
(R J Hodges) *towards rr: rdn and hdwy 3f out: one pce u.p 2f out: styd on again fnl f to ld last strides* **4/1**[1]
0002 **2** *nk* **Eastern Gift**[8] 4698 4-9-7 **70**.............................. KylieManser(3) 4 76+
(Miss Gay Kelleway) *chsd ldrs: led ins fnl 3f: rdn 3 l clr over 1f out: one pce u.p fnl f: hdd last strides* **6/1**[3]
2333 **3** *1/2* **Potentiale (IRE)**[70] 2678 5-9-5 **70**.......................(p) KierenFox(5) 6 75
(J W Hills) *hld up in rr: hdwy on outside fr 3f out: drvn to press ldrs ins fnl f: no ex cl home* **4/1**[1]
5003 **4** *nk* **Hallingdal (UAE)**[8] 4714 4-9-0 **65**.............................. RyanClark(5) 5 70
(J J Bridger) *in rr: hdwy 3f out: rdn and styd on fnl 2f: kpt on ins fnl f but nt pce to chal* **6/1**[3]
2100 **5** *3 1/4* **Merrymadcap (IRE)**[21] 4262 7-9-7 **70**........................ LeeNewnes(3) 2 67
(M Salaman) *in tch: hdwy 4f out: chsd ldrs 3f out: wknd 2f out* **9/1**
20-0 **6** *1 3/4* **Candy Rose**[9] 4645 4-8-9 **60**.............................. KatiaScallan(5) 8 54
(M P Tregoning) *t.k.h: chsd ldrs: chal over 3f out: wknd ins fnl 2f* **7/1**
2300 **7** *6* **Clipperdown (IRE)**[7] 4745 8-8-11 **62**.......................(t) DavidKenny(5) 9 42
(E J Creighton) *stdd s: in rr: hdwy on outside over 4f out: chsd ldrs 3f out: sn rdn: wknd over 2f out* **16/1**
00/5 **8** *shd* **Waziri (IRE)**[23] 3798 8-8-5 **51** oh6.............................. AmyBaker 7 31
(M Hill) *chsd ldrs: rdn and wknd 3f out* **33/1**
3001 **9** *2 3/4* **Becuille (IRE)**[31] 3960 4-9-10 **70**..................(b) Louis-PhilippeBeuzelin 3 44
(B J Meehan) *led: plld hrd: rdn 4f out: hdd & wknd ins fnl 3f* **5/1**[2]
1m 54.33s (-1.17) **Going Correction** -0.10s/f (Good) 9 Ran SP% **116.6**
Speed ratings (Par 103): **101,100,100,100,97 95,90,90,87**
toteswingers: 1&2 £5.10, 1&3 £4.50, 2&3 £5.40 CSF £28.44 CT £103.02 TOTE £4.80: £2.00, £2.50, £1.50; EX 37.90 Place 6: £5.76 Place 5: £5.10.
Owner Mrs A Hart Mrs A Hodges Mrs C Penny **Bred** Mrs M Chaworth-Musters **Trained** Charlton Mackrell, Somerset
■ Stewards' Enquiry : Kylie Manser two-day ban: used whip with excessive frequency (Aug 28-29)

FOCUS
A low-grade apprentices' handicap and the rather four rather finished on top of each other. The winner looks the best guide to this form.
T/Plt: £8.90 to a £1 stake. Pool: £58,588.44. 4,768.25 winning tickets. T/Qpdt: £6.10 to a £1 stake. Pool: £3,626.96. 436.70 winning tickets. ST

4939 NEWCASTLE (L-H)
Friday, August 14

OFFICIAL GOING: Good to firm (firm in places; 8.6)
All the races were run on the straight course. Entire one mile straight dolled out by 3yards on stands' side.
Wind: light 1/2 behind Weather: overcast, showers, rain race 3 until after race 5

4993 EBF / WATERAID MAIDEN STKS 7f
2:10 (2:11) (Class 5) 2-Y-O **£3,238** (£963; £481; £240) **Stalls** High

Form RPR
3 **1** **Right Step**[19] 4336 2-9-3 0.. AndrewElliott 5 84
(A P Jarvis) *chsd ldrs stands' side: led 2f out: styd on strly* **9/4**[1]
06 **2** *2 1/2* **Elmfield Giant (USA)**[17] 4396 2-9-3 0.............................. TonyHamilton 1 78
(R A Fahey) *chsd ldrs: sn drvn along: reminders over 3f out: styd on to chse wnr 1f out: edgd rt: no imp* **8/1**
62 **3** *4 1/2* **Jeannie Galloway (IRE)**[29] 4001 2-8-9 0.................. FrederikTylicki(3) 3 62
(A G Foster) *led tl 2f out: hung bdly rt and wknd fnl f* **5/1**[3]
4 *shd* **Sulwaan (IRE)** 2-9-3 0.. GregFairley 2 66
(M Johnston) *w ldrs: hung rt and kpt on same pce fnl f* **9/1**
2 **5** *2 1/4* **Beat The Rush**[20] 4308 2-9-3 0.. PhillipMakin 11 62
(Miss J A Camacho) *chsd ldrs stands' side: rdn over 2f out: wl hld whn hmpd 100yds out* **4/1**[2]
6 *3 1/2* **North Shadow** 2-9-3 0.. GrahamGibbons 8 52
(A D Brown) *s.i.s: sme hdwy over 2f out: nvr nr ldrs* **50/1**
06 **7** *2 3/4* **Mason Hindmarsh**[45] 3478 2-8-12 0.............................. JamieKyne(5) 9 45
(Karen McLintock) *in rr div: wandered and kpt on fnl 2f: nvr a factor* **66/1**
8 *7* **Edward Longshanks (USA)** 2-9-3 0.................. SilvestreDeSousa 12 28
(T P Tate) *s.s: sn wl bhd: sme hdwy 2f out: nvr on terms* **5/1**[3]
9 *nk* **Goodison Park** 2-8-9 0.. NeilBrown(3) 10 22
(A G Foster) *s.s: a wl bhd* **25/1**
0 **10** *3 1/2* **Mizair Nouvair (IRE)**[14] 4503 2-9-3 0.......................(v[1]) DuranFentiman 4 18
(J R Weymes) *chsd ldrs: lost pl over 2f out: sn bhd* **200/1**
11 *4* **Jack Kane** 2-8-10 0.. AndrewHeffernan(7) 7 8
(J A McShane) *dwlt: bhd fnl 3f* **50/1**
12 *10* **Bollin Andrew** 2-9-3 0.. DavidAllan 6 —
(T D Easterby) *mid-div: lost pl over 2f out: bhd whn eased ins fnl f* **33/1**
1m 26.32s (-2.38) **Going Correction** -0.375s/f (Firm) 12 Ran SP% **117.9**
Speed ratings (Par 94): **98,95,90,89,87 83,80,72,71,67 63,51**
toteswingers: 1&2 £9.50, 1&3 £2.30, 2&3 £18.80 CSF £20.49 TOTE £3.00: £1.60, £2.40, £1.90; EX 14.20 Trifecta £97.10 Pool: £200.89 - 1.53 winning units..
Owner Allen B Pope **Bred** Natton House Thoroughbreds & Mark Woodall **Trained** Middleham Moor, N Yorks

FOCUS
All the races were run on the straight course. The rail was dolled out three yards on the stands' side, all the way up the straight mile. There seemed to be something of a slow-motion finish to the opener, a modest maiden, but the time was less than a second outside the standard so it may be that they had gone off quickly early on. The ground seemed to be riding pretty fast.

NOTEBOOK
Right Step ended up near the stands' rail. He had run a promising third in a newcomers' race at Ascot on his debut, although the fourth there, Advertisement, was beaten at odds-on at Lingfield this week. Upped in trip, he stayed on stoutly after taking up the running. He jinked to his right just after the line as the false rail ended and unshipped his rider, with no harm done, although it should be noted that he had swerved under pressure on his debut. He is unlikely to take up his entry in the Acomb Stakes at York next week, but looks a decent prospect. (tchd 11-4)
Elmfield Giant(USA), a grandson of Eclipse winner Kooyonga, had shown a bit of ability on his first two starts but this was his best effort to date. He came under pressure shortly after halfway and stayed on to claim second inside the last without troubling the favourite unduly. Now eligible for nurseries, he may get a mile. (op 10-1 tchd 11-2)

Jeannie Galloway(IRE)'s Doncaster second had been boosted by the winner Clarietta's subsequent nursery win. Faced with a sounder surface here, she showed pace again but was tying up and hanging inside the last. (op 4-1)
Sulwaan(IRE) was never far from the action down the outside, but could only stick on at the same pace in the final furlong. A half-brother to several at least fair winners, mainly at up to 7f, he does not look one of the stable stars but should be up to winning a race or two. (op 8-1 tchd 10-1)
Beat The Rush stayed on strongly for second on his debut over C&D behind Aquarian Spirit, who has since finished second in a nursery. He raced closer to the pace this time, isolated near the stands' rail through the early parts, and was held in fifth when he was hampered by the weakening Jeannie Galloway inside the last. (op 9-2 tchd 5-1)
Edward Longshanks(USA), a 125,000gns yearling, is out of a half-sister to smart miler Nicholas. He showed little on this debut following a slow start, but should be accorded another chance. (op 7-1)
Goodison Park blew it at the start, but she did make a little late progress and will have learned considerably from this debut experience. (op 20-1)

4994 UTILITY TECHNOLOGY SERVICES LTD FILLIES' H'CAP — 1m 3y(S)
2:45 (2:45) (Class 5) (0-75,73) 3-Y-O — £2,978 (£886; £442; £221) **Stalls** High

Form — RPR
0146 **1** **Off Chance**[20] [4328] 3-9-7 **73** .... DuranFentiman 5 — 84
(T D Easterby) *hld up: smooth hdwy over 2f out: chal over 1f out: shkn up to ld jst ins fnl f: rdn clr* **5/2**[2]
-046 **2** *4* **Chantilly Pearl (USA)**[43] [3545] 3-8-13 **68** .... FrederikTylicki(3) 4 — 69
(J G Given) *chsd ldrs: rdn over 3f out: led over 1f out: hdd jst ins fnl f: no ex* **10/3**[3]
4411 **3** *4½* **Diamond Daisy (IRE)**[4] [4846] 3-9-6 **72** 6ex .... SilvestreDeSousa 8 — 62
(Mrs A Duffield) *chsd ldrs: effrt over 3f out: one pce appr fnl f* **15/8**[1]
5430 **4** *3* **Bow To No One (IRE)**[12] [4569] 3-9-4 **70** .... AndrewElliott 9 — 53
(A P Jarvis) *led tl over 1f out: sn fdd* **7/1**
000- **5** *9* **Accumulation (UAE)**[328] [6135] 3-7-10 **55** oh9 ow1. JamesPSullivan(7) 7 — —
(M W Easterby) *dwlt: in rr: rdn over 3f out: sn wl outpcd and bhd* **25/1**
0350 **6** *2* **Kneesy Earsy Nosey**[17] [4397] 3-7-13 **54** oh9 .... DominicFox(3) 6 — —
(Miss A Stokell) *chsd ldrs: drvn 4f out: wknd over 1f out: eased and lost 5th ins fnl f* **28/1**
500 **7** *117* **Rose Avelina**[19] [4354] 3-8-2 **54** oh9 .... (b[1]) PaulQuinn 2 — —
(I W McInnes) *swvd lft s: reluct to r: sn drvn along: lost pl over 3f out: t.o 2f out* **33/1**

1m 40.18s (-3.22) **Going Correction** -0.375s/f (Firm) — 7 Ran SP% **109.2**
Speed ratings (Par 97): **101,97,92,89,80 78,—**
toteswingers: 1&2 £1.80, 1&3 £1.30, 2&3 £1.60 CSF £10.06 CT £15.71 TOTE £3.10: £1.80, £1.50; EX 8.50 Trifecta £16.50 Pool: £400.32 - 17.95 winning units..
Owner L B Holliday **Bred** Cleaboy Farms Co **Trained** Great Habton, N Yorks

FOCUS
Only four of these could be considered in this ordinary handicap for fillies. The action took place up the dolled-off stands' rail and they finished well strung out. A personal best from the winner with the second the best guide.

4995 FASTFLOW PIPELINE SERVICES (S) STKS — 7f
3:20 (3:20) (Class 6) 3-4-Y-O — £1,942 (£578; £288; £144) **Stalls** High

Form — RPR
5302 **1** **Darcey**[9] [4654] 3-8-7 70 .... TonyHamilton 8 — 65
(R A Fahey) *trckd ldr: rdn to ld over 2f out: hung bdly lft ins fnl f: rdn clr* **13/8**[1]
0304 **2** *4* **Carnival Dream**[5] [4821] 4-8-13 52 .... (b) GregFairley 2 — 56
(H A McWilliams) *led tl over 1f out: kpt on same pce* **9/1**
-605 **3** *½* **Another Decree**[40] [3655] 4-9-4 63 .... (t) PhillipMakin 7 — 60
(M Dods) *hld up: nt clr run over 2f out: rdn and hdwy over 1f out: kpt on same pce* **8/1**[3]
3000 **4** *½* **Richo**[20] [4312] 3-8-9 75 .... (p) FrederikTylicki(3) 12 — 56
(D H Brown) *tracd stands' side: hld up: hdwy over 3f out: edgd lft: kpt on same pce fnl 2f* **7/4**[2]
0000 **5** *7* **Recoil (IRE)**[9] [4654] 4-8-13 40 .... (tp) DeanHeslop(5) 6 — 39
(R Johnson) *chsd ldrs: wknd over 1f out* **100/1**
0-00 **6** *3¼* **Home Before Dark**[27] [4105] 3-8-9 44 .... MichaelJStainton(3) 1 — 29
(R M Whitaker) *rrd s: towards rr: bhd fnl 2f* **66/1**
0-00 **7** *shd* **Mujada**[101] [1781] 4-8-6 40 .... JohnCavanagh(7) 3 — 25
(M Brittain) *in rr: sme hdwy over 2f out: sn lost pl* **50/1**
5063 **8** *½* **Hawkleaf Flier (IRE)**[11] [4589] 3-8-7 47 .... (b) DavidAllan 5 — 22
(T D Easterby) *chsd ldrs: wknd over 2f out* **14/1**
0640 **9** *9* **Nino Zachetti (IRE)**[11] [4594] 3-8-12 47 .... (p) PatrickMathers 11 — —
(E J Alston) *t.k.h: trckd ldrs: rdn and lost pl over 2f out: sn bhd* **25/1**
00 **10** *2¾* **Romantic Interlude (IRE)**[27] [4084] 3-8-7 46 .... (v) AndrewElliott 10 — —
(A P Jarvis) *sn drvn along towards rr: lost pl 3f out: sn bhd* **33/1**

1m 26.2s (-2.50) **Going Correction** -0.375s/f (Firm)
WFA 3 from 4yo 6lb — 10 Ran SP% **113.5**
Speed ratings (Par 101): **99,94,93,93,85 81,81,80,70,67**
toteswingers: 1&2 £1.60, 1&3 £1.50, 2&3 £10.90 CSF £15.82 TOTE £2.40: £1.20, £1.70, £1.80; EX 15.30 Trifecta £50.90 Pool: £440.99 - 6.40 winning units..There was no bid for the winner.
Owner R Cowie **Bred** Raymond Cowie **Trained** Musley Bank, N Yorks

FOCUS
A weak and uncompetitive seller, run in a time marginally quicker than the 2yo maiden. The winner is rated up 6lb.

4996 NORTHUMBRIAN WATER LTD H'CAP — 7f
3:55 (3:55) (Class 4) (0-85,86) 3-Y-O+ — £4,792 (£1,425; £712; £355) **Stalls** High

Form — RPR
0611 **1** **My Gacho (IRE)**[9] [4641] 7-9-10 **81** 6ex .... (v) J-PGuillambert 3 — 89
(M Johnston) *hood removed v late: sn led: hdd 2f out: rallied to ld last 50yds* **3/1**[1]
3051 **2** *½* **Captain Macarry (IRE)**[11] [4592] 4-9-12 **86** 6ex ...... (v) FrederikTylicki(3) 1 — 93
(B Smart) *led early: chsd ldr: chal over 2f out: sn led: hdd and no ex wl ins fnl f* **10/3**[2]
0-60 **3** *nk* **Hartshead**[9] [4663] 10-8-8 **68** .... DominicFox(3) 5 — 74+
(W Storey) *hld up: hdwy 2f out: styd on wl ins fnl f* **25/1**
3035 **4** *1½* **Leonid Glow**[9] [4657] 4-9-2 **73** .... PhillipMakin 7 — 75
(M Dods) *stmbld s: hld up: effrt over 2f out: kpt on same pce* **11/2**
0451 **5** *1½* **Zomerlust**[20] [4333] 7-9-12 **83** .... (v) GrahamGibbons 4 — 81
(J J Quinn) *chsd ldrs: drvn 3f out: kpt on same pce appr fnl f* **4/1**[3]
0606 **6** *nk* **Inter Vision (USA)**[6] [4802] 9-9-6 **77** .... DavidAllan 2 — 74
(A Dickman) *stall opened fractionally early: trckd ldrs: effrt over 2f out: one pce over 1f out* **7/1**
0130 **7** *8* **White Deer (USA)**[35] [3825] 5-9-8 **79** .... (v) SilvestreDeSousa 8 — 54
(G A Harker) *in rr and sn drvn along: nvr a factor: eased whn wl btn ins fnl f* **5/1**

1m 25.17s (-3.53) **Going Correction** -0.375s/f (Firm) — 7 Ran SP% **116.5**
Speed ratings (Par 105): **105,104,104,102,100 100,91**
toteswingers: 1&2 £2.40, 1&3 £22.70, 2&3 £23.60 CSF £13.76 CT £207.70 TOTE £4.20: £2.10, £1.70; EX 13.10 Trifecta £84.60 Pool: £407.35 - 3.56 winning units..
Owner Grant Mercer **Bred** Mount Coote Stud **Trained** Middleham Moor, N Yorks

FOCUS
A fair event for the grade, contested by some in-form handicappers, and the form should hold up with the winner the best guide. It produced a time inside standard. The runners raced away from the fence.
Inter Vision(USA) Official explanation: jockey said gelding anticipated the start and hit its head on the gates

4997 GOWLAND AND DAWSON LTD FILLIES' H'CAP — 6f
4:25 (4:25) (Class 5) (0-70,70) 3-Y-O — £2,978 (£886; £442; £221) **Stalls** High

Form — RPR
5510 **1** **Midnight Fantasy**[39] [3688] 3-9-7 **70** .... SaleemGolam 7 — 79
(Rae Guest) *in rr: drvn 3f out: hdwy over 1f out: styd on to ld ins fnl furlong: rdn rt out* **11/4**[2]
2302 **2** *½* **Who's Shirl**[16] [4436] 3-8-4 **56** .... KellyHarrison(3) 8 — 63
(C W Fairhurst) *chsd ldrs: styd on to take 2nd last 100yds: no ex* **5/2**[1]
0000 **3** *3½* **Caranbola**[14] [4494] 3-9-0 **70** .... JohnCavanagh(7) 6 — 66
(M Brittain) *chsd ldr: led 1f out: hdd & wknd ins fnl f* **9/1**
6424 **4** *1¼* **Oriental Rose**[5] [4820] 3-9-3 **66** .... DavidAllan 2 — 58
(G M Moore) *led tl hdd & wknd 1f out* **6/1**[3]
1060 **5** *1* **Lady Vivien**[38] [3704] 3-8-13 **65** .... (t) FrederikTylicki(3) 5 — 54
(D H Brown) *hld up: effrt 2f out: kpt on same pce* **15/2**
463 **6** *hd* **Halcyon Dancer**[21] [4277] 3-8-9 **58** .... PhillipMakin 3 — 46
(M Dods) *trckd ldrs: effrt 2f out: kpt on same pce* **6/1**[3]
3-40 **7** *7* **Exceedingly Good (IRE)**[80] [2365] 3-9-1 **64** .... GregFairley 1 — 30
(B Smart) *s.s: t.k.h: hdwy on outside to trck ldrs over 3f out: lost pl over 1f out* **16/1**

1m 13.03s (-2.17) **Going Correction** -0.375s/f (Firm) — 7 Ran SP% **111.5**
Speed ratings (Par 97): **99,98,93,92,90 90,81**
toteswingers: 1&2 £2.60, 1&3 £7.30, 2&3 £9.60 CSF £9.52 CT £49.63 TOTE £3.70: £1.80, £1.90; EX 10.60 Trifecta £95.30 Pool: £402.22 - 3.12 winning units..
Owner C J Mills **Bred** C J Mills **Trained** Newmarket, Suffolk
■ Stewards' Enquiry : Saleem Golam two-day ban: used whip with excessive frequency (Aug 28-29)

FOCUS
A very ordinary event confined to fillies. The first two came clear and the winner is rated t the form of her sand win.

4998 DAVID BENTLEY IS THE BIG 40 H'CAP — 6f
4:55 (4:55) (Class 6) (0-60,64) 3-Y-O+ — £2,201 (£655; £327; £163) **Stalls** High

Form — RPR
1R41 **1** **Dark Moment**[3] [4879] 3-9-6 **64** 6ex .... (p) FrederikTylicki(3) 3 — 71
(A Dickman) *w ldrs slt ld 1f out: jst hld on* **5/1**[2]
000 **2** *nse* **Averoo**[64] [2864] 4-8-11 **51** .... (p) NeilBrown(3) 1 — 58
(M D Squance) *s.s: in rr: hdwy over 1f out: styd on strly ins fnl f: jst failed* **13/2**[3]
3305 **3** *nk* **Ryedane (IRE)**[10] [4620] 7-9-8 **59** .... (b) DavidAllan 5 — 65
(T D Easterby) *led tl 1f out: rallied: no ex towards fin* **7/1**
0005 **4** *1¼* **Cheery Cat (USA)**[39] [3683] 5-8-9 **49** .... (p) KellyHarrison(3) 12 — 51
(J Balding) *chsd ldrs: outpcd 2f out: styd on ins fnl f* **7/1**
010 **5** *shd* **Greek Secret**[16] [4436] 6-9-1 **57** .... (b) JamesO'Reilly(5) 2 — 59
(J O'Reilly) *swtchd lft s: t.k.h: trckd ldrs: kpt on same pce appr fnl f* **16/1**
2060 **6** *¾* **Ace Of Spies (IRE)**[65] [2804] 4-9-7 **58** .... (p) SilvestreDeSousa 7 — 57
(G A Harker) *trckd ldrs: kpt on same pce fnl f* **5/1**[2]
3452 **7** *¾* **Elkhorn**[5] [4823] 7-9-1 **52** .... (b) PhillipMakin 8 — 49
(Miss J A Camacho) *hld up: effrt 2f out: kpt on same pce: nvr trbld ldrs* **5/2**[1]
0001 **8** *2¾* **Bright Falcon**[58] [3031] 4-8-8 **50** .... (bt) LanceBetts(5) 4 — 38
(J Balding) *s.s: swtchd lft to r alone far side: sn chsng ldrs: edgd rt and wknd fnl f* **14/1**
00-0 **9** *¾* **Lujiana**[14] [4508] 4-8-11 **55** .... JohnCavanagh(7) 9 — 41
(M Brittain) *in rr: rdn over 2f out: nvr a factor* **33/1**
0000 **10** *8* **Fulford**[14] [4496] 4-8-12 **49** .... (v) AndrewElliott 6 — 9
(M Brittain) *sn chsng ldrs: lost pl over 2f out* **28/1**

1m 13.31s (-1.89) **Going Correction** -0.375s/f (Firm)
WFA 3 from 4yo+ 4lb — 10 Ran SP% **119.2**
Speed ratings (Par 101): **97,96,96,94,94 93,92,89,88,77**
toteswingers: 1&2 £9.90, 1&3 £6.50, 2&3 £6.60 CSF £38.46 CT £231.50 TOTE £6.80: £2.20, £1.70, £2.50; EX 52.20 Trifecta £269.20 Part won. Pool: £363.89 - 0.43 winning units..
Owner Construction Crew Racing Partnership **Bred** Wilderbrook Stud **Trained** Sandhutton, N Yorks
■ Stewards' Enquiry : James O'Reilly caution: careless riding
Frederik Tylicki one-day ban: used whip with excessive frequency, taking into account deferred five-day suspension totalled six-day ban (Aug 28-Sep 2)

FOCUS
A tight, low-grade handicap. The third looks the best guide.

4999 LUMSDEN AND CARROLL CONSTRUCTION LTD H'CAP — 5f
5:30 (5:30) (Class 5) (0-70,71) 3-Y-O — £3,238 (£963; £481; £240) **Stalls** High

Form — RPR
51 **1** **Corton Charlemagne (IRE)**[5] [4829] 3-9-4 **69** 6ex.... FrederikTylicki(3) 1 — 77
(Rae Guest) *trckd ldrs on outer: effrt over 1f out: r.o to ld last 100yds: hld on wl* **11/8**[1]
-044 **2** *½* **Gee Gina**[1] [4942] 3-7-12 **51** oh1 ow1 .... PaulPickard(5) 5 — 57
(P T Midgley) *t.k.h: led tl over 2f out: rallied and upsides 100yds out: no ex* **7/1**
0212 **3** *2* **Arriva La Diva**[6] [4777] 3-7-12 **51** .... JamieKyne(5) 3 — 50
(J J Quinn) *w ldrs: led over 2f out: hdd 100yds out: no ex* **11/4**[2]
4540 **4** *¾* **Dispol Grand (IRE)**[4] [4849] 3-9-7 **69** .... PhillipMakin 2 — 65
(P T Midgley) *hld up: effrt 2f out: kpt on: nvr able to chal* **4/1**[3]
4340 **5** *2* **Forever's Girl**[16] [4436] 3-8-6 **59** .... LanceBetts(5) 4 — 48
(G R Oldroyd) *w ldrs: wknd 1f out* **9/1**

60.99 secs (0.29) **Going Correction** -0.375s/f (Firm) — 5 Ran SP% **111.3**
Speed ratings (Par 100): **82,81,78,76,73**
toteswingers: 1&2 £11.10, 1&3 not won, 2&3 not won. CSF £11.49 TOTE £2.60: £1.40, £2.70; EX 13.70 Place 6: £32.15 Place 5: £18.93.
Owner Cheval Ct,Alexander,Bottriell,Guest&LKP **Bred** Tony Hirschfeld & L K Piggott **Trained** Newmarket, Suffolk

FOCUS
A modest sprint handicap where the field stuck close to the rail. Three of them disputed a fast pace up front. The winner continues to impress.
T/Plt: £37.40 to a £1 stake. Pool: £54,526.89. 1,063.76 winning tickets. T/Qpdt: £8.30 to a £1 stake. Pool: £4,177.52. 372.15 winning tickets. WG

[4792] NEWMARKET (R-H)

Friday, August 14

OFFICIAL GOING: Good (8.0)

Stands' side track used for both days of the meeting.

Wind: modest, across Weather: cloudy, warm

5000 NEWMARKET NIGHTS MEDIAN AUCTION MAIDEN STKS 7f

5:25 (5:26) (Class 4) 2-Y-O **£3,885** (£1,156; £577; £288) **Stalls** Low

Form RPR

4 **1** **Destination Aim**[13] 4524 2-9-3 0.. TedDurcan 12 77+
(Saeed Bin Suroor) *chsd ldr: rdn wl over 2f out: led over 1f out: styd on strly fnl f* **1/1**[1]

2 2 ¾ **Get A Grip (IRE)** 2-9-3 0.. GeorgeBaker 17 70
(J A R Toller) *t.k.h: hld up in midfield: hdwy over 2f out: rdn to chse wnr 1f out: kpt on but no imp* **16/1**

3 1 **Inpursuitoffreedom** 2-8-12 0.. EdwardCreighton 4 63
(P J McBride) *t.k.h: hld up in midfield: rdn and hdwy over 2f out: chsd ldng pair ent fnl f: kpt on same pce* **100/1**

0 **4** 1 ¾ **Harlestone Times (IRE)**[20] 4314 2-9-3 0.................. PhilipRobinson 15 63+
(J L Dunlop) *in tch in midfield: rdn and effrt over 2f out: kpt on to go 4th ins fnl f: nvr pce to threaten ldrs* **16/1**

5 1 **Sophie's Beau (USA)** 2-9-3 0.. DarryllHolland 16 61+
(B J Meehan) *stdd s: plld hrd: hld up in rr: rdn and hdwy over 1f out: styd on steadily fnl f: nvr trbld ldrs* **25/1**

6 ½ **Affirmable** 2-8-5 0.. AmyScott(7) 9 55
(J W Hills) *in tch: swtchd lft and rdn wl over 1f out: plugged on same pce fnl f* **100/1**

00 **7** 1 **Argyll**[27] 4093 2-9-3 0.. StephenDonohoe 13 57
(J Pearce) *led: rdn 2f out: hdd over 1f out: wknd ent fnl f* **100/1**

8 ½ **Wigmore Hall (IRE)** 2-9-3 0.. JamieSpencer 2 56
(M L W Bell) *hld up in tch: effrt jst over 2f out: edgd rt and rdn over 1f out: btn ent fnl f: eased ins fnl f* **4/1**[2]

0 **9** 4 ½ **Power Series (USA)**[13] 4534 2-9-3 0.. RobertHavlin 14 45
(J H M Gosden) *chsd ldrs: rdn wl over 2f out: struggling 2f out and wl btn fr over 1f out* **20/1**

10 nk **Molon Labe (IRE)** 2-9-3 0.. MickyFenton 3 44
(T P Tate) *chsd ldrs: rdn and struggling 3f out: no ch fnl 2f* **33/1**

11 2 ½ **Rhythmic Star** 2-9-3 0.. LiamJones 1 38
(W J Haggas) *s.i.s: a towards rr: lost tch over 2f out* **25/1**

12 1 ¾ **Calm Storm (IRE)** 2-9-3 0.. TPQueally 8 33
(J Noseda) *wnt rt s and s.i.s: a bhd: no ch whn hung lft 2f out* **8/1**[3]

5 **13** hd **Holkham**[31] 3944 2-8-12 0.. MarkCoumbe(5) 11 33
(N P Littmoden) *t.k.h: wl in tch: rdn and struggling 3f out: sn hung lft and bhd fnl 2f* **100/1**

14 1 ¾ **Tewin Wood** 2-9-3 0.. PaulEddery 5 28
(M D Squance) *v.s.a: racd awkwardly and a bhd: hung lft fnl 2f* **100/1**

15 1 ¼ **Round Won (USA)** 2-9-3 0.. JimCrowley 10 25
(W J Knight) *s.i.s: a bhd: lost tch over 2f out* **20/1**

16 1 **Perceptive** 2-8-12 0.. NCallan 6 18
(J R Fanshawe) *restless stalls: awkward leaving stalls and s.i.s: bhd: struggling over 2f out: wl bhd fnl 2f* **22/1**

1m 26.88s (1.18) **Going Correction** 0.0s/f (Good) **16** Ran SP% **122.3**
Speed ratings (Par 96): **93,89,88,86,85 85,83,83,78,77 74,72,72,70,69 68**
toteswingers: 1&2 £7.40, 1&3 £38.10, 2&3 £152.30 CSF £17.57 TOTE £2.10: £1.20, £2.60, £10.30; EX 20.20.
Owner Godolphin **Bred** Darley **Trained** Newmarket, Suffolk

FOCUS
Some attractive types with scope here, but several were too green to do themselves justice, and there was much whinnying in the paddock and hanging during the race. Probably a pretty weak maiden for Newmarket.

NOTEBOOK
Destination Aim is a compact colt and gave the impression beforehand that he was ready to the job, which he duly accomplished in workmanlike fashion. One of only five in the race with previous experience, this well-related individual (mother was useful at around 1m1f in France and is out of a sister to Miesque) had shown abundant promise under hand riding on his Goodwood debut and is clearly progressing nicely. Taken out of the Gimcrack at the forfeit stage, he still holds entries for the Racing Post Trophy and the Dewhurst. (op 11-8)
Get A Grip(IRE) is only small but this 34,000gns purchase who does not have the most appealing of pedigrees buckled down to the task well, although no match for the winner. Some of those behind him might prove more progressive in future.
Inpursuitoffreedom ran surprisingly well for a potential stayer and her small stable could have a another decent prospect.
Harlestone Times(IRE) did better on this second outing and this half-brother to Harlestone Snake (won over 1m6f) may lie in handicapping over middle distances.
Sophie's Beau(USA) pulled much too hard early but kept going surprisingly well at the finish and is certainly capable of better when learning to settle. Official explanation: jockey said colt ran keen
Affirmable ran on in decent fashion, but comes from a stable who very rarely have debutant winners, and had she been strongly fancied a top jockey might have been used.
Wigmore Hall(IRE) is a strong handsome type but his mind was on other things and he didn't co-operate fully, but he certainly looks the part. (op 11-4)
Molon Labe(IRE) looks capable of better in time. (op 25-1)
Tewin Wood is already gelded and looked clueless..

5001 NGK SPARK PLUGS H'CAP 6f

5:55 (5:56) (Class 4) (0-85,85) 3-Y-O+ **£5,180** (£1,541; £770; £384) **Stalls** Low

Form RPR

5004 **1** **Seamus Shindig**[14] 4500 7-9-4 85.. AmyScott(7) 11 94
(H Candy) *racd in midfield: pushed along: hdwy and hung lft fr over 1f out: led fnl 75yds: kpt on wl* **11/2**[1]

5621 **2** nk **Silaah**[65] 2828 5-9-11 85.. AdrianTNicholls 5 93
(D Nicholls) *wnt lft s: in tch: rdn and effrt over 2f out: drvn to ld over 1f out: hdd fnl 75yds: kpt on but a jst hld after* **13/2**[3]

0364 **3** ½ **Last Sovereign**[14] 4501 5-9-6 80.. JamieSpencer 9 86
(Jane Chapple-Hyam) *racd in midfield: rdn and hdwy over 1f out: carried lft but kpt on to press ldrs ins fnl f: one pce towards fin* **8/1**

5204 **4** 1 ½ **John Keats**[14] 4507 6-8-9 69 ow2.. DanielTudhope 3 71
(J S Goldie) *stdd s: hld up in rr: rdn ent fnl 2f: no hdwy tl jst ins fnl f: styd on wl after: nt rch ldrs* **8/1**

0411 **5** ¾ **Royal Intruder**[2] 4907 4-9-1 80 6ex.. SimonPearce(5) 10 79
(S Donohoe, Ire) *stdd after s: hld up bhd: n.m.r briefly wl over 1f out: pushed along and hdwy over 1f out: styd on ins fnl f: nvr gng to rch ldrs* **11/2**[1]

453 **6** nse **Sweet Gale (IRE)**[11] 4607 5-8-13 73.. JimCrowley 12 72
(Mike Murphy) *s.i.s: sn in midfield: pushed along and hdwy 3f out: chsd ldrs and drvn over 1f out: one pce fnl f* **9/1**

0603 **7** ½ **Diriculous**[14] 4500 5-9-4 85..(b) DToole(7) 7 82
(T G Mills) *stdd after s: t.k.h: hld up in midfield: rdn and no hdwy wl over 1f out: plugged on same pce fnl f* **12/1**

1240 **8** 1 **Devil You Know (IRE)**[4] 4849 3-9-5 83..(t) DarryllHolland 6 77
(D R C Elsworth) *stdd s: t.k.h: hld up in tch: hdwy over 2f out: rdn to ld wl over 1f out: hdd over 1f out: wknd jst ins fnl f* **12/1**

0000 **9** 1 ¾ **Burnwynd Boy**[14] 4485 4-9-6 80..(b[1]) TedDurcan 1 69
(D Nicholls) *led and sn clr: hdd and rdn wl over 1f out: wknd ent fnl f* **20/1**

0102 **10** nk **Highland Harvest**[7] 4733 5-8-13 73.. RobertHavlin 2 61
(Jamie Poulton) *chsd ldr tl over 2f out: sn rdn: wknd u.p over 1f out* **6/1**[2]

440 **11** 6 **Tudor Prince (IRE)**[18] 4387 5-8-9 69 ow1.. NCallan 4 37
(A W Carroll) *dwlt: sn rcvrd to chse ldrs: rdn over 2f out: struggling 2f out: wl bhd fnl f* **14/1**

1m 12.1s (-0.40) **Going Correction** 0.0s/f (Good)
WFA 3 from 4yo+ 4lb **11** Ran SP% **117.4**
Speed ratings (Par 105): **102,101,100,98,97 97,97,95,93,93 85**
toteswingers: 1&2 £7.50, 1&3 £5.80, 2&3 £9.40 CSF £40.63 CT £292.46 TOTE £6.00: £2.30, £2.50, £2.50; EX 31.60.
Owner Henry Candy **Bred** R S A Urquhart **Trained** Kingston Warren, Oxon

FOCUS
You could run this race half a dozen times and probably get a different result on every occasion. Straightforward form.
Last Sovereign Official explanation: jockey said gelding hung both ways
Devil You Know(IRE) Official explanation: jockey said gelding hung left

5002 EUROPEAN BREEDERS' FUND MAIDEN STKS 1m

6:30 (6:30) (Class 4) 2-Y-O **£5,180** (£1,541; £770; £384) **Stalls** Low

Form RPR

3443 **1** **Dashing Doc (IRE)**[7] 4758 2-9-3 78.. PhilipRobinson 6 77
(D R C Elsworth) *chsd ldr tl rdn to ld wl over 1f out: edgd lft u.p over 1f out: styd on wl fnl f* **11/4**[1]

2 ½ **Rigidity** 2-9-3 0.. TPQueally 8 76+
(H R A Cecil) *stdd s: t.k.h: hld up in tch: rdn along over 3f out: hdwy u.p over 1f out: chsd wnr ins fnl f: kpt on wl but nvr quite gng to rch wnr* **10/3**[2]

303 **3** nk **Crystal Gale (IRE)**[29] 4001 2-8-12 70.. JimCrowley 9 70
(W J Knight) *stdd s: hld up in tch in rr: hdwy and rdn over 1f out: chsd ldrs jst ins fnl f: kpt on* **7/1**

4 nk **Mufti (IRE)** 2-9-3 0.. JamieSpencer 2 75+
(B J Meehan) *t.k.h: hld up in tch in rr: hdwy over 2f out: chsd wnr and rdn over 1f out: kpt on same pce fnl f:* **11/2**

5 4 ½ **Karamojo Bell** 2-9-3 0.. MickyFenton 4 65
(T P Tate) *stdd s: hld up in tch in rr: hdwy 4f out: chsd ldrs and rdn 2f out: wknd ent fnl f* **12/1**

6 nse **Berling (IRE)** 2-9-3 0.. TedDurcan 1 65
(J L Dunlop) *chsd ldrs: rdn and lost pl over 2f out: wknd u.p over 1f out* **5/1**[3]

7 ½ **Comradeship (IRE)** 2-9-3 0.. RobertHavlin 7 63
(J H M Gosden) *stdd s: t.k.h: hld up in tch: hdwy to chse ldrs 2f out: wknd ent fnl f* **10/1**

0 **8** 2 ¼ **Ibn Hiyyan (USA)**[40] 3652 2-9-3 0.. NCallan 3 59
(M Johnston) *sn led: hdd wl over 1f out: sn hung lft u.p and lost pl: wl bhd fnl f* **12/1**

1m 42.44s (2.44) **Going Correction** 0.0s/f (Good) **8** Ran SP% **118.8**
Speed ratings (Par 96): **87,86,86,85,81 81,80,78**
toteswingers: 1&2 £2.50, 1&3 £3.40, 2&3 £10.10 CSF £12.61 TOTE £3.60: £1.30, £1.70, £2.20; EX 13.80.
Owner J C Smith **Bred** Littleton Stud **Trained** Newmarket, Suffolk

FOCUS
A rather muddling event. The winner helps with the level.

NOTEBOOK
Dashing Doc(IRE), with five outings under his belt, was the most experienced member of the party by far and put this advantage to good use. A powerful individual (typical Elsworth type) he was sweating. This was his first attempt at 1m following a couple of decent efforts in nurseries, and he saw the trip out in good style despite tending to edge left. Now that he has got his head in front there could be more to come. (op 7-2)
Rigidity comes from an excellent family and is half-brother to the Derby second Dragon Dancer. He was a 95,000gns yearling, but looked to lack the physical scope of some of these rivals, and was a bit too keen in the early stages. He will have learned from the experience and is a potential winner. (op 7-2 tchd 4-1 and 9-2 in places)
Crystal Gale(IRE) finished third for the third time from four attempts and given that this was not an easy task she performed well in defeat. A little further would not go amiss. (op 8-1)
Mufti(IRE) was a 2000,000gns foal, and given that Meehan-trained horses usually come on a good deal for their first run, this was an encouraging start. (op 13-2)
Karamojo Bell is a good-topped sort but was a shade coltish in the paddock. Although well beaten in fifth he was not discredited. (tchd 14-1)
Berling(IRE) cost 650,000gns as a yearling but has turned out to be a disappointingly small colt and was one of the first beaten. (tchd 9-2 and 11-2)
Comradeship(IRE) cost 110,000gns and is a lovely big horse but looked a bit backward. He was given an easy time after edging left and is definitely worth another look. (op 8-1)

5003 SINGH SKIPS, THE SAFE BET H'CAP 1m

7:00 (7:00) (Class 5) (0-75,75) 3-Y-O+ **£3,885** (£1,156; £577; £288) **Stalls** Low

Form RPR

542 **1** **Kaolak (USA)**[20] 4320 3-9-9 75..(v) PhilipRobinson 17 89
(J Ryan) *mde all: clr thrght: rdn over 1f out: styd on wl* **7/2**[1]

2433 **2** 2 ½ **Seasonal Cross**[16] 4441 4-8-12 57.. TedDurcan 10 65
(S Dow) *hld up in rr: stl plenty to do and swtchd rt over 1f out: str run to go 2nd ins fnl f: no imp fnl 75yds* **10/1**

5013 **3** 1 ¼ **Arizona John (IRE)**[42] 3558 4-9-11 70.. SJCraine 7 75
(J Mackie) *rrd at s: t.k.h: hld up in midfield: swtchd rt and effrt over 2f out: hung lft over 1f out: hrd rdn and chsd wnr ent fnl f: no imp and lost 2nd ins fnl f* **20/1**

-425 **4** hd **Barliffey (IRE)**[22] 4247 4-9-12 71..(v) DarryllHolland 16 78+
(D J Coakley) *stdd s and dropped in bhd: stl last 2f out: nt clr run over 1f out tl swtchd rt 1f out: r.o wl to press for 3rd on post: nvr nr wnr* **6/1**[2]

5062 **5** 1 ½ **Will He Wish**[14] 4502 13-9-12 71.. KirstyMilczarek 2 72
(S Gollings) *hld up in midfield: hdwy 3f out: chsd ldrs and drvn over 1f out: kpt on same pce fnl f* **12/1**

2143 **6** ½ **Fajita**[21] 4275 3-9-3 69.. GeorgeBaker 3 69
(G L Moore) *hld up in midfield: rdn and nt clr run wl over 1f out: sn swtchd rt and hdwy to chse ldrs 1f out: one pce u.p after* **11/1**

0002 **7** 2 ½ **Jazacosta (USA)**[9] 4642 3-9-2 **68** JimCrowley 4 62
(Mrs A J Perrett) *hld up towards rr: rdn and effrt over 2f out: hanging lft 2f out: sn swtchd rt: no imp after* **8/1**[3]

6145 **8** 2 **King Columbo (IRE)**[14] 4502 4-9-10 **69** TPQueally 6 59
(Miss J Feilden) *prom in main gp: clsd on ldrs over 3f out: chsd wnr wl over 1f out tl ent fnl f: wknd fnl f* **10/1**

0000 **9** hd **Bustan (IRE)**[14] 4502 10-9-13 **72** (p) RobertWinston 19 61
(G C Bravery) *chsd wnr and clr of field tl wl over 1f out: sn wknd* **33/1**

1050 **10** hd **Paint The Town Red**[23] 4207 4-9-9 **71** JackMitchell(3) 9 60
(H J Collingridge) *in tch in main gp: rdn and unable qck 2f out: wknd u.p over 1f out* **20/1**

1P60 **11** nk **Sonny Parkin**[7] 4759 7-9-8 **72** (v) SimonPearce(5) 15 60
(J Pearce) *stdd s: hld up in rr: effrt on far side 2f out: n.d* **20/1**

-403 **12** 1 ¼ **Devinius (IRE)**[7] 4759 4-9-1 **60** NCallan 13 45
(G A Swinbank) *t.k.h: hld up in tch in main gp: rdn over 2f out: struggling wl over 1f out: wl btn fnl f* **14/1**

000 **13** ½ **Dinner Date**[95] 1945 7-8-6 **58** TraceyAddey(7) 8 42
(T Keddy) *swtg: t.k.h: hld up in rr: n.m.r jst over 2f out: rdn wl over 1f out: no hdwy* **40/1**

6046 **14** 9 **Millfields Dreams**[24] 4167 10-9-6 **70** MarkCoumbe(5) 12 33
(G C Bravery) *t.k.h: hld up in midfield: rdn over 2f out: unable qck whn hmpd wl over 1f out: wl btn after* **25/1**

0402 **15** hd **Tevez**[20] 4333 4-9-4 **63** (t) MickyFenton 11 26
(D Donovan) *hld up in rr: rdn and no rspnse over 2f out* **9/1**

-150 **16** 5 **Gassin**[15] 4473 3-9-4 **70** JamieSpencer 5 21
(M L W Bell) *hld up in rr: rdn and effrt 2f out: wl btn 1f out: virtually p.u ins fnl f* **14/1**

1m 39.5s (-0.50) **Going Correction** 0.0s/f (Good)
WFA 3 from 4yo+ 7lb **16** Ran SP% **128.7**
Speed ratings (Par 103): **102,99,98,98,96 96,93,91,91,91 90,89,89,80,79 74**
toteswingers: 1&2 £13.50, 1&3 £22.90, 2&3 £24.40 CSF £36.71 CT £672.09 TOTE £4.30: £1.70, £2.70, £5.20, £2.40; EX 53.80.
Owner Simon Kerr **Bred** Mr And Mrs Robert Courtney Sr Et Al **Trained** Newmarket, Suffolk

FOCUS
The time of this race was three seconds outside standard and the winner simply ground the rest into submission. Sound if limited form.
Bustan(IRE) Official explanation: jockey said gelding lost its action

5004 BURGHLEY HORSE TRIALS CONDITIONS STKS 1m 2f
7:35 (7:35) (Class 2) 3-Y-0+
£12,462 (£3,732; £1,866; £934; £466; £234) **Stalls** Centre

Form RPR
46-0 **1** **Ajhar (USA)**[139] 1004 5-9-1 103 PatDobbs 8 106
(M P Tregoning) *hld up in tch: gng wl whn nt clr run wl over 2f out: rdn and hdwy to chse ldr wl over 1f out: led ins fnl f: r.o wl* **9/2**[2]

0130 **2** 3 ¼ **Classic Punch (IRE)**[19] 4340 6-9-9 102 JamieSpencer 1 107
(D R C Elsworth) *led: rdn over 2f out: drvn and hrd pressed over 1f out: hdd ins fnl f: no ex* **6/1**

115- **3** 2 ¼ **Merchant Of Dubai**[280] 7223 4-9-1 94 RobertWinston 2 95+
(G A Swinbank) *t.k.h: chsd ldr: rdn 3f out: lost 2nd wl over 1f out: 3rd and wl hld 1f out: kpt on same pce* **9/1**

-136 **4** nse **Cape Express (IRE)**[91] 2031 4-9-1 96 PhilipRobinson 4 94+
(M A Jarvis) *sn detached in last and nt gng wl: reminder over 3f out: clsd 3f out: hdwy to dispute 3rd ent fnl f: no imp on ldrs after* **9/2**[2]

4 **5** 6 **Rugell (ARG)**[36] 3769 4-9-3 95 TPQueally 7 84
(H R A Cecil) *chsd ldr for 1f: styd handy: rdn 4f out: drvn and wknd wl over 1f out* **25/1**

4004 **6** 9 **Moon Sister (IRE)**[21] 4287 4-8-10 96 AlanMunro 9 59
(W Jarvis) *t.k.h: chsd ldrs: rdn and unable qck over 2f out: wknd qckly wl over 1f out: wl btn fnl f* **8/1**

0006 **7** 1 ½ **Stormy Summer**[38] 3714 4-9-1 49 JackMitchell 3 61?
(R W Price) *broke wl but sn pushed along and dropped to rr: rdn over 3f out: edgd lft u.p over 2f out: sn lost tch* **100/1**

10-0 **8** 4 ½ **Democrate**[42] 3585 4-9-1 105 (t) TedDurcan 5 52
(Saeed Bin Suroor) *hld up in tch on outer: rdn and effrt over 2f out: lost action wl over 1f out: sn eased* **10/3**[1]

4 **9** nse **Rendezvous (IRE)**[29] 4020 3-8-9 98 NCallan 6 55
(Sir Michael Stoute) *hld up wl in tch: rdn over 3f out: struggling bdly ent fnl 2f: wl btn and eased fnl f* **11/2**[3]

2m 3.06s (-2.44) **Going Correction** 0.0s/f (Good)
WFA 3 from 4yo+ 9lb **9** Ran SP% **115.1**
Speed ratings (Par 109): **109,106,104,104,99 92,91,87,87**
toteswingers: 1&2 £20.40, 1&3 £10.40, 2&3 £4.10 CSF £31.51 TOTE £6.40: £2.10, £2.00, £3.20; EX 37.40.
Owner Hamdan Al Maktoum **Bred** Shadwell Farm LLC **Trained** Lambourn, Berks

FOCUS
Doubts over a lot of these but the second is a sound guide and the winner is rated close to his best.

NOTEBOOK
Ajhar(USA) continued the resurgence of the Marcus Tregoning yard after their faltering start to the year and this likeable little horse scored for the third time when returning from a layoff. He is lightly raced for his age but responds well to urgings and could be in line for another success or two this year. (op 4-1 tchd 5-1)
Classic Punch(IRE) was bidding for a third win on the July course and typically tried to make all, but his attitude is often open to question and he did not put up very much resistance when tackled, but did plug on well enough to hold the rest readily. (op 8-1)
Merchant Of Dubai progressed well in the latter half of last season to win three from five and did fairly well here on a return from a 280-day absence. A step up in trip is probaby what he wants next time and he might make up into a competent hurdler. (op 8-1 tchd 10-1)
Cape Express(IRE) got a poor start and did not look that keen to find his stride, and he has been well below form on grass in his two attempts since switching his allegiance from the all-weather. (tchd 5-1)
Rugell(ARG) did not handle the track at Epsom on his English debut (previously useful in Argentina) and on this similarly awkward showing he would have done better to have stayed on the pampas. (op 16-1)
Democrate looked fit, but lost his action well before the finish after changing his legs several times and clearly has a problem. Official explanation: jockey said colt lost its action (op 7-2 tchd 3-1)
Rendezvous(IRE) sweated badly and ran a shocker. Surely his stable will not persevere with him. (op 8-1)

5005 FUTURE ELECTRICAL SERVICES FILLIES' H'CAP 7f
8:05 (8:06) (Class 3) (0-95,90) 3-Y-0+ **£9,066** (£2,697; £1,348; £673) **Stalls** Low

Form RPR
-341 **1** **Pyrrha**[20] 4317 3-9-12 **90** AlanMunro 9 107+
(C F Wall) *chsd ldrs: hdwy to ld over 2f out: clr over 1f out: r.o strly: readily* **3/1**[2]

010 **2** 3 **Iasia (GR)**[20] 4326 3-9-2 **80** TPQueally 5 89
(Jane Chapple-Hyam) *hld up in tch: pushed along over 3f otu: hdwy u.p 2f out: chsd clr wnr ent fnl f: no imp* **25/1**

4225 **3** 5 **Belle Des Airs (IRE)**[7] 4761 3-9-4 **82** RichardKingscote 6 77
(R M Beckett) *led: rdn and hdd over 2f out: outpcd by wnr wl over 1f out: 3rd and wl btn ins fnl f* **9/1**

0410 **4** shd **Shaws Diamond (USA)**[20] 4317 3-9-1 **79** NCallan 7 74
(D Shaw) *in tch: rdn over 3f out: drvn and struggling over 2f out: wl btn over 1f out* **25/1**

0461 **5** 3 **Koraleva Tectona (IRE)**[15] 4452 4-9-6 **78** PaulEddery 2 67
(Pat Eddery) *chsd ldrs: rdn over 2f out: wknd and wl btn fr over 1f out* **20/1**

010- **6** ¾ **Ballantrae (IRE)**[315] 6439 3-9-10 **88** JamieSpencer 4 73
(M L W Bell) *stdd s: hld up in last pair: rdn and lost tch qckly 2f out* **10/1**

3241 **7** ¾ **Glen Molly (IRE)**[13] 4540 3-9-12 **90** DarryllHolland 8 73
(B W Hills) *stdd s: hld up in tch: rdn and effrt jst over 2f out: sn edgd rt and wl btn* **6/4**[1]

-331 **8** 7 **Perfect Silence**[36] 3789 4-9-3 **75** PhilipRobinson 1 41
(C G Cox) *chsd ldr tl wl over 2f out: sn struggling: wl bhd fnl 2f* **9/2**[3]

43-0 **9** 2 ¼ **Spanish Cygnet (USA)**[13] 4540 3-9-6 **84** JimCrowley 3 42
(Mrs A J Perrett) *stdd s: hld up in last pair: lost tch u.p jst over 2f out* **25/1**

1m 24.08s (-1.62) **Going Correction** 0.0s/f (Good)
WFA 3 from 4yo 6lb **9** Ran SP% **118.6**
Speed ratings (Par 104): **109,105,99,99,96 95,94,86,84**
toteswingers: 1&2 £26.80, 1&3 £6.70, 2&3 £32.50 CSF £79.80 CT £601.17 TOTE £3.70: £1.70, £5.70, £2.90; EX 88.80 Place 6: £104.27 Place 5: £60.56.
Owner Lady Juliet Tadgell **Bred** Hong Kong Breeders Club **Trained** Newmarket, Suffolk

FOCUS
A decent fillies' handicap and good form for the grade.

NOTEBOOK
Pyrrha has plenty of good game efforts to her name, and despite a 6lb rise for her course win in a similar event three weeks ago, she scampered clear in the final furlong without turning a hair. The Handicapper will doubtless lash out again, but she is just the type to go well in a valuable contest, as indeed she did here two outings back when just over a length fourth in a big field. (op 11-4 tchd 5-2)
Iasia(GR) scored well under hands and heels at Warwick last time, but this was tougher and she raced rather awkwardly when setting off in vain pursuit of Pyrrha. She did beat the rest by 5l or much more however.
Belle Des Airs(IRE) was up the pace as usual but has yet to manage a win this year and had to be content with a weak third. (op 11-1 tchd 12-1)
Shaws Diamond(USA) had no hope with Pyrrha judged on their last meeting here and has only scored once from 14 attempts. (op 28-1 tchd 33-1)
Koraleva Tectona(IRE) was up in the weights after her Epsom success and could not cope. (op 16-1)
Ballantrae(IRE) would be better with more cut in the ground. (op 8-1)
Glen Molly(IRE) had her supporters but she was going up and down on the spot in the final 2f. This was most disappointing after her recent track and trip win and there looked to be no excuses. Official explanation: jockey said filly was unsuited by the good ground (op 9-4 tchd 5-2 in places)
T/Jkpt: £4,733.30 to a £1 stake. Pool: £10,000.00. 1.50 winning tickets. T/Plt: £67.50 to a £1 stake. Pool: £53,672.15. 580.17 winning tickets. T/Qpdt: £22.10 to a £1 stake. Pool: £4,378.76. 146.00 winning tickets. SP

4880 NOTTINGHAM (L-H)
Friday, August 14

OFFICIAL GOING: Good (7.5)
Bottom bend moved out 2m from 1m to 4f marker increasing distances on round course by about 9yards..
Wind: Light against Weather: Cloudy with sunny spells

5006 EUROPEAN BREEDERS' FUND MAIDEN STKS 6f 15y
2:00 (2:04) (Class 5) 2-Y-0 **£3,723** (£1,108; £553; £276) **Stalls** High

Form RPR
5 **1** **Society Rock (IRE)**[20] 4314 2-9-3 0 GeorgeBaker 8 79+
(J R Fanshawe) *hld up: plld hrd: hdwy over 2f out: led wl over 1f: hung rt 1f out: rdn out* **9/4**[1]

2 **2** ½ **Saddlers Lodge**[19] 4349 2-9-3 0 TomEaves 6 75
(G A Swinbank) *a.p: rdn to chse wnr over 1f out: edgd rt ins fnl f: r.o* **4/1**[2]

3 3 ¾ **Banks And Braes** 2-9-3 0 PatDobbs 12 63+
(R Hannon) *s.i.s: sn pushed along and hung lft: rdn over 2f out: hdwy over 1f out: nt rch ldrs* **13/2**

4 1 ½ **Sand Skier** 2-9-3 0 JoeFanning 10 59+
(M Johnston) *sn led: rdn and hdd wl over 1f out: no ex fnl f* **13/2**

5 **5** 2 ½ **Ice Viking (IRE)**[14] 4497 2-9-3 0 PatCosgrave 11 51
(J G Given) *s.i.s: hdwy over 4f out: rdn over 2f out: wknd fnl f* **6/1**[3]

6 2 ¼ **Mr Prize Fighter** 2-9-3 0 DNolan 4 45
(I W McInnes) *s.s: sn pushed along in rr: n.d* **100/1**

7 1 ¾ **Night Trade (IRE)** 2-8-9 0 RussellKennemore(3) 9 34
(Mrs D J Sanderson) *w ldrs: rdn and hung lft fr over 2f out: wknd wl over 1f out* **80/1**

04 **8** 2 **Boquito (IRE)**[16] 4424 2-9-3 0 JerryO'Dwyer 3 33
(Miss Amy Weaver) *w ldrs: rdn and hung lft 2f out: sn wknd* **25/1**

04 **9** 7 **Clan Piper**[87] 2167 2-9-3 0 RobertHavlin 1 18+
(J H M Gosden) *chsd ldrs: hung lft and wknd over 2f out* **14/1**

1m 15.88s (0.98) **Going Correction** +0.125s/f (Good) **9** Ran SP% **104.5**
Speed ratings (Par 94): **98,97,92,90,87 84,81,79,69**
toteswingers: 1&2 £2.30, 1&3 £5.50, 2&3 £3.40 CSF £9.02 TOTE £3.10: £1.10, £1.20, £2.80; EX 9.90.
Owner Simon Gibson **Bred** San Gabriel Investments **Trained** Newmarket, Suffolk

FOCUS
A modest maiden which saw the two market leaders come clear. There is more to come from the winner.

NOTEBOOK
Society Rock(IRE) got off the mark at the second attempt in fairly ready fashion. He did not have to obviously improve on the level of his Newmarket debut, but the drop back in trip proved a shrewd move and he looks a useful prospect. He did enough to suggest he would learn again for the experience and his trainer is targeting him at the Tatersalls Sales Race at Newmarket next month. (op 5-1)
Saddlers Lodge got this extra furlong well and was the only one to give the winner a serious race inside the final furlong. He can be found one of these before going into nurseries. (op 8-1 tchd 9-4)
Banks And Braes fared best of the newcomers and was allowed to come home under hands-and-heels riding after his chance became apparent. He ought to appreciate another furlong before long and should know a lot more next time. (op 8-1 tchd 10-1)

Sand Skier, a 150,000gns purchase, showed up nicely until tiring out of contention and posted an encouraging start. He should come on a bundle for this initial outing and, on breeding, is another who would appreciate stepping up in trip sooner rather than later. (op 5-1)

Ice Viking(IRE) looked a player on the strength of his debut fifth at Newmarket a fortnight earlier and was well drawn. He got warm beforehand, though, and was never travelling with any fluency through the race. This was somewhat disappointing, but easier ground and another furlong could see him in a much better light. (op 13-2 tchd 7-1)

5007 CLEANEVENT FILLIES' H'CAP — 6f 15y

2:35 (2:35) (Class 4) (0-80,78) 3-Y-O+ — **£5,180** (£1,541; £770; £384) **Stalls** High

Form — RPR

0016 **1** — **Peper Harow (IRE)**[13] 4535 3-7-13 **59** oh4 .... DavidProbert(3) 12 — 68
(M D I Usher) *s.i.s: hld up: hdwy over 2f out: led over 1f out: rdn out* **28/1**

0060 **2** 3/4 **Aunt Nicola**[23] 4198 3-8-13 **70** .... HayleyTurner 10 — 77+
(M L W Bell) *hld up in tch: nt clr run over 1f out: swtchd lft and r.o ins fnl f: nt rch wnr* **20/1**

1 **3** 3/4 **High Achieved**[20] 4324 3-9-1 **72** .... AlanMunro 3 — 76+
(P W Chapple-Hyam) *s.i.s: racd keenly: hdwy over 4f out: rdn and ev ch over 1f out: styd on same pce ins fnl f* **15/8**[1]

1243 **4** nse **Misplaced Fortune**[21] 4285 4-9-6 **73** ....(v) TomEaves 8 — 78
(N Tinkler) *chsd ldrs: led wl over 1f out: sn hdd: styd on same pce ins fnl f* **5/1**[2]

0-10 **5** 1 **Dubai Legend**[63] 2886 3-9-0 **76** .... MartinLane(5) 13 — 77
(D M Simcock) *sn pushed along in rr: hdwy and nt clr run over 1f out: swtchd lft ins fnl f: kpt on* **8/1**

00-3 **6** 2 **Queen Sally (IRE)**[21] 4266 3-8-6 **68** .... RossAtkinson(5) 6 — 62
(Tom Dascombe) *chsd ldrs: rdn 1/2-way: styd on same pce fnl f* **33/1**

2122 **7** hd **Feelin Foxy**[15] 4461 5-9-11 **78** .... PatCosgrave 11 — 73
(J G Given) *led: rdn and hdd wl over 1f out: no ex fnl f* **7/1**

2410 **8** 1 1/4 **To Be Or Not To Be**[63] 2883 4-9-9 **76** .... LukeMorris 9 — 67
(John Berry) *dwlt: hld up: hdwy and edgd lft over 1f out: wknd ins fnl f* **10/1**

2125 **9** nk **Sister Clement (IRE)**[11] 4604 3-9-0 **71** .... PatDobbs 4 — 60
(R Hannon) *hld up: racd keenly: rdn over 1f out: nvr trbld ldrs* **6/1**[3]

52-6 **10** 5 **Solitary**[23] 4198 3-9-4 **75** .... FergusSweeney 2 — 48
(H Candy) *chsd ldrs: rdn over 2f out: wknd over 1f out* **16/1**

4025 **11** 1/2 **Kheskianto (IRE)**[28] 4056 3-8-0 **64** .... JosephineBruning(7) 7 — 35
(M C Chapman) *chsd ldr: rdn 1/2-way: wknd wl over 1f out* **18/1**

0-00 **12** hd **Allexes (IRE)**[35] 3815 3-8-7 **64** .... RobertHavlin 1 — 35
(J R Boyle) *prom: lost pl whn stmbld 4f out: wknd over 2f out* **66/1**

1m 15.57s (0.67) **Going Correction** +0.125s/f (Good)
WFA 3 from 4yo+ 4lb — **12** Ran SP% **122.2**
Speed ratings (Par 102): **100,99,98,97,96 93,93,92,91,84 84,84**
toteswingers: 1&2 £59.30, 1&3 £13.30, 2&3 £11.10 CSF £493.79 CT £1596.26 TOTE £26.80: £5.40, £3.60, £1.20; EX 529.20.
Owner Mr & Mrs Richard Hames & Friends 1 **Bred** R And Mrs Hames **Trained** Upper Lambourn, Berks

FOCUS
A modest fillies' only sprint handicap, run at a sound enough pace and a high draw was an advantage. The fourth looks a sound guide but this is perhaps not the most solid form.
Solitary Official explanation: jockey said filly hung left
Allexes(IRE) Official explanation: jockey said filly stumbled

5008 KIDS COME FREE AT NOTTINGHAM RACECOURSE H'CAP — 5f 13y

3:10 (3:11) (Class 6) (0-55,57) 3-Y-O+ — **£2,047** (£604; £302) **Stalls** High

Form — RPR

0366 **1** — **Lithaam (IRE)**[7] 4736 5-8-10 **52** ....(p) DavidProbert(3) 4 — 61
(J M Bradley) *racd far side: a.p: led overall 1/2-way: rdn over 1f out: edgd rt: jst hld on* **9/1**[3]

0020 **2** nk **The Name Is Frank**[22] 4222 4-9-0 **53** ....(t) FergusSweeney 16 — 61
(Mark Gillard) *racd stands' side: chsd ldr: rdn and hung lft fr over 1f out: r.o: 1st of 9 in gp* **16/1**

3000 **3** nse **The History Man (IRE)**[29] 3999 6-8-9 **53** ....(b) PatrickDonaghy(5) 14 — 61
(B D Leavy) *racd stands' side: led that gp: rdn over 1f out: hung lft ins fnl f: r.o: lost 2nd post: 2nd of 9 in gp* **14/1**

2405 **4** 1 1/4 **Rhapsilian**[8] 4702 5-9-1 **54** ....(b[1]) HayleyTurner 5 — 57
(J R Jenkins) *racd far side: s.i.s: hld up: hdwy 2f out: rdn to chse wnr over 1f out: r.o: 2nd of 8 in gp* **16/1**

4100 **5** 1/2 **Welsh Opera**[18] 4380 4-8-13 **55** ....(t) WilliamCarson(3) 9 — 56+
(S C Williams) *racd stands' side: sn pushed along in rr: hdwy 2f out: rdn and nt clr run ins fnl f: styd on same pce: 3rd of 9 in gp* **15/2**[1]

-004 **6** 2 1/2 **Black Moma (IRE)**[8] 4702 5-9-0 **53** .... PatCosgrave 17 — 45
(J R Boyle) *racd stands' side: chsd ldrs: rdn and edged lft over 1f out: no ex ins fnl f: 4th on 9 in gp* **8/1**[2]

400 **7** nse **Sandy Par**[31] 3947 4-8-10 **52** ....(b) KevinGhunowa(3) 15 — 44
(J M Bradley) *racd stands' side: s.i.s: hdwy 2f out: sn rdn no imp fnl f: 5th of 9 in gp* **28/1**

3523 **8** 1/2 **Angelofthenorth**[7] 4754 7-8-10 **49** .... PaulHanagan 8 — 39
(C J Teague) *racd far side: chsd ldrs: rdn 1/2-way: hung rt over 1f out: styd on same pce: 3rd of 8 in gp* **9/1**[3]

405 **9** nk **Shannon Golden**[24] 4174 3-8-13 **55** .... JimmyQuinn 3 — 44
(S R Bowring) *racd far side: bhd: sme hdwy and edgd rt over 1f out: n.d: 4th of 8 in gp* **16/1**

0105 **10** 3 1/2 **Rough Rock (IRE)**[9] 4668 4-9-0 **53** .... JerryO'Dwyer 7 — 30
(C A Dwyer) *racd far side: led overall tl hdd over 3f out: rdn and wknd over 1f out: 5th of 8 in gp* **25/1**

6200 **11** 1 3/4 **Kalligal**[27] 4082 4-8-12 **51** ....(b) TolleyDean 2 — 21
(R Ingram) *racd far side: sn pushed along: a in rr: 6th of 8 in gp* **40/1**

0431 **12** 5 **Princess Charlmane (IRE)**[7] 4754 6-8-11 **57** 6ex........(p) IJBrennan(7) 1 — 9
(C J Teague) *racd far side: chsd ldr tl led overall over 3f out: hdd 1/2-way: wknd over 1f out: 7th of 8 in gp: sddle slipped* **15/2**[1]

3500 **13** 1 3/4 **Thoughtsofstardom**[28] 4059 6-8-13 **52** .... LukeMorris 10 — —
(P S McEntee) *racd stands' side: mid-div on outside of gp: hung lft and wknd 1/2-way: 6th of 9 in gp* **18/1**

3304 **14** 1 **Circle Dance (IRE)**[5] 4823 4-8-8 **52** ....(v) MartinLane(5) 11 — —
(D Shaw) *racd stands' side: hld up: hung lft and wknd 1/2-way: 7th of 9 in gp* **8/1**[2]

404 **15** hd **Efisio Princess**[27] 4082 6-9-2 **55** .... RichardThomas 12 — —
(J E Long) *racd stands' side: chsd ldrs: rdn over 3f out: wknd 2f out: 8th of 9 in gp* **9/1**[3]

0600 **16** 1 1/4 **Angle Of Attack (IRE)**[16] 4436 4-9-1 **54** .... TomEaves 6 — —
(A D Brown) *racd far side: chsd ldrs: rdn 1/2-way: wknd over 1f out: last of 8 in gp* **33/1**

0002 **17** 7 **Tenancy (IRE)**[84] 2225 5-9-1 **54** .... PAspell 13 — —
(S A Harris) *racd stands' side: chsd ldrs to 1/2-way: last of 9 in gp* **16/1**

61.56 secs (0.56) **Going Correction** +0.125s/f (Good)
WFA 3 from 4yo+ 3lb — **17** Ran SP% **123.9**
Speed ratings (Par 101): **100,99,99,97,96 92,92,91,91,85 82,74,72,70,70 68,56**
toteswingers: 1&2 £42.60, 1&3 £46.90, 2&3 £25.50 CSF £141.56 CT £2089.88 TOTE £10.30: £2.90, £3.90, £3.60, £4.10; EX 260.80.
Owner JMB Racing.co.uk **Bred** Shadwell Estate Company Limited **Trained** Sedbury, Gloucs

FOCUS
A moderate sprint. They split into two groups at first before the main action developed down the middle late on, and three came clear. The winner is rated back to his best.
The Name Is Frank Official explanation: jockey said gelding hung right-handed
Princess Charlmane(IRE) Official explanation: jockey said saddle slipped
Circle Dance(IRE) Official explanation: jockey said gelding lost its action
Efisio Princess Official explanation: jockey said mare was unsuited by today's ground

5009 CE PROPERTY SERVICES GROUP FILLIES' H'CAP — 1m 2f 50y

3:45 (3:45) (Class 4) (0-85,85) 3-Y-O — **£6,476** (£1,927; £963; £481) **Stalls** Low

Form — RPR

63-1 **1** — **Leceile (USA)**[91] 2042 3-9-0 **78** .... HayleyTurner 6 — 91+
(W J Haggas) *mde virtually all: rdn clr over 1f: eased towards fin* **7/2**[1]

0422 **2** 3 **Punch Drunk**[14] 4495 3-8-7 **71** ....(p) AlanMunro 4 — 76
(J G Given) *hld up: last over 2f out: rdn over 1f out: r.o ins fnl f: edgd lft and wnt 2nd post: no ch w wnr* **15/2**[3]

-031 **3** nk **Stan's Cool Cat (IRE)**[28] 4050 3-9-7 **85** .... JimmyQuinn 8 — 89
(P F I Cole) *hld up: hdwy u.p over 1f out: chsd wnr ins fnl f: r.o: lost 2nd post* **13/2**[2]

412 **4** 1 3/4 **Gaselee (USA)**[31] 3942 3-7-13 **68** .... MartinLane(5) 2 — 69
(Rae Guest) *chsd wnr: rdn over 2f out: lost 2nd jst ins fnl f: no ex* **9/1**

0022 **5** shd **Accede**[28] 4050 3-9-4 **82** .... PatCosgrave 3 — 83
(J G Portman) *hld up: hdwy over 3f out: rdn over 1f out: no ex fnl f* **12/1**

0-00 **6** 3 3/4 **Such Optimism**[16] 4422 3-9-0 **85** .... JPFahy(7) 5 — 78
(R M Beckett) *s.i.s: hld up: hdwy 1/2-way: rdn over 2f out: wknd over 1f out* **16/1**

0315 **7** hd **Burza**[28] 4050 3-8-5 **72** .... DavidProbert(3) 9 — 65
(J Mackie) *sn chsng ldrs: rdn over 2f out: wknd over 1f out* **13/2**[2]

0111 **8** 2 **The Last Alzao (IRE)**[31] 3943 3-8-8 **72** .... PaulHanagan 7 — 61
(R A Fahey) *prom: lost pl 1/2-way: rdn and wknd over 2f out* **7/2**[1]

3231 **9** 1 1/4 **Queen Eleanor**[27] 4085 3-9-1 **79** .... TPO'Shea 1 — 65
(J H M Gosden) *chsd ldrs: rdn over 3f out: wknd over 1f out* **10/1**

2m 11.48s (-0.22) **Going Correction** +0.125s/f (Good) — **9** Ran SP% **115.5**
Speed ratings (Par 99): **105,102,102,100,100 97,97,96,95**
toteswingers: 1&2 £3.30, 1&3 £5.70, 2&3 £7.20 CSF £30.30 CT £163.45 TOTE £3.90: £1.40, £2.20, £1.90; EX 37.10.
Owner Brian Wallace **Bred** Aaron U Jones & Marie D Jones **Trained** Newmarket, Suffolk

FOCUS
A decent and competitive handicap for the class, and good form for the grade. The winner did it in the style of a most progressive filly.
Queen Eleanor Official explanation: jockey said filly ran flat

5010 THEPADDOCKSNOTTINGHAM.CO.UK MAIDEN STKS — 1m 75y

4:15 (4:15) (Class 5) 3-Y-O — **£2,590** (£770; £385; £192) **Stalls** Low

Form — RPR

-432 **1** — **Poyle Meg**[22] 4246 3-8-5 77 ....(p) JPFahy(7) 1 — 67
(R M Beckett) *chsd ldrs: rdn to ld over 1f out: hung lft ins fnl f: styd on u.p* **11/8**[1]

30 **2** 3/4 **Mustakmil (IRE)**[13] 4519 3-9-3 0 .... HayleyTurner 3 — 70
(E A L Dunlop) *led: rdn and hdd over 1f out: unable qck towards fin* **5/1**[3]

4-06 **3** 2 1/2 **Asateer (IRE)**[100] 1793 3-9-3 87 .... TPO'Shea 2 — 64
(B W Hills) *racd keenly: sn prom: rdn and edgd lft over 1f out: styd on same pce fnl f* **15/8**[2]

60-3 **4** hd **Group Leader (IRE)**[15] 4472 3-9-3 62 .... AdrianMcCarthy 5 — 64
(J R Jenkins) *chsd ldrs: rdn over 2f out: styd on same pce fnl f* **14/1**

0 **5** 9 **Balzarine**[51] 3278 3-8-12 0 .... JimmyQuinn 8 — 37
(M Blanshard) *hld up: sme hdwy over 2f out: nvr on terms* **50/1**

- **6** 3/4 **Gearbox (IRE)** 3-9-3 0 .... PatDobbs 11 — 41+
(R Hannon) *dwlt: hld up: nvr nrr* **10/1**

00 **7** 1 1/2 **Hohrod**[23] 4199 3-9-3 0 .... LukeMorris 7 — 37
(John A Harris) *mid-div: racd keenly: rdn 1/2-way: wknd 3f out* **100/1**

06 **8** 4 1/2 **Doctor Of Music (IRE)**[14] 4505 3-9-3 0 .... TomEaves 4 — 26
(B Smart) *in rr and reminders 6f out: sme hdwy on ins 3f out: sn wknd* **33/1**

45 **9** 2 1/2 **Duke Of Urbino**[157] 796 3-9-3 0 .... PaulHanagan 6 — 20
(K A Ryan) *plld hrd: trckd ldr: rdn and wknd 2f out* **25/1**

00-0 **10** 1 1/2 **High Tensile**[19] 4354 3-8-10 37 ow1 .... LeeVickers(3) 9 — 13
(J G Given) *hld up: wknd over 3f out* **100/1**

00-0 **11** 26 **Mythical Thrill**[15] 4472 3-9-0 15 .... DavidProbert(3) 10 — —
(J G Given) *s.i.s: bhd fnl 5f: t.o* **33/1**

1m 47.82s (2.22) **Going Correction** +0.125s/f (Good) — **11** Ran SP% **123.0**
Speed ratings (Par 100): **93,92,89,89,80 79,78,73,71,69 43**
toteswingers: 1&2 £2.40, 1&3 £1.70, 2&3 £3.40 CSF £9.10 TOTE £2.40: £1.10, £1.60, £1.20; EX 14.30.
Owner Cecil Wiggins **Bred** Miss Alison Wiggins **Trained** Whitsbury, Hants

FOCUS
A moderate 3yo maiden, run at a fair pace. Muddling form, with the third disappointing.
Duke Of Urbino Official explanation: jockey said gelding had no more to give

5011 IRISH NIGHT ON TUESDAY 18TH AUGUST H'CAP — 1m 6f 15y

4:45 (4:48) (Class 6) (0-60,60) 3-Y-O — **£1,942** (£578; £288; £144) **Stalls** Low

Form — RPR

0033 **1** — **Twist Again (IRE)**[8] 4722 3-9-0 **56** .... JimmyQuinn 2 — 67+
(P Howling) *hld up: nt clr run over 4f out: hdwy: nt clr run and swtchd rt over 1f out: r.o to ld nr fin* **6/1**[3]

500- **2** nk **Transfered (IRE)**[239] 7718 3-8-5 **50** ow4 .... KevinGhunowa(3) 3 — 55
(Lucinda Featherstone) *hld up: hdwy u.p over 2f out: led over 1f out: hdd nr fin* **66/1**

-540 **3** 3 1/4 **Googoobarabajagal (IRE)**[53] 3222 3-8-8 **50** .... FergusSweeney 12 — 51
(W S Kittow) *hld up: hdwy over 2f out: sn rdn: hung lft fnl f: styd on same pce* **14/1**

004 **4** 2 **Guilin (IRE)**[53] 3205 3-8-3 **52** ow1 .... DTDaSilva(7) 6 — 50
(P F I Cole) *rdr late removing hood: s.s: bhd: hdwy over 1f out: rdn and hung lft ins fnl f: nt rch ldrs* **25/1**

0523 **5** 1 **Amethyst Dawn (IRE)**[21] 4280 3-9-4 **60** .... DNolan 8 — 57
(T D Easterby) *led and sn clr: rdn and hdd over 1f out: wknd ins fnl f* **7/1**

-036 **6** 1 1/4 **Pattern Mark**[46] 3454 3-8-11 **53** .... PaulHanagan 9 — 48
(Ollie Pears) *hld up: hdwy over 4f out: rdn over 2f out: wknd ins fnl f* **9/2**[2]

0000 7 nk **Flannel (IRE)**[18] 4373 3-8-8 **57** JPFahy(7) 16 51
(J R Fanshawe) *prom: chsd ldr 9f out: rdn over 2f out: wknd ins fnl f* **25/1**
-305 8 ½ **Windpfeil (IRE)**[24] 4178 3-9-2 **58** (b¹) TPO'Shea 5 52
(J H M Gosden) *hld up: rdn and hung lft over 2f out: sn hung rt: n.d: nt resolute* **11/1**
0340 9 1 **Arlene Phillips**[53] 3217 3-8-8 **50** ow1 PatDobbs 10 42
(R Hannon) *chsd clr ldr 5f: remained handy: rdn and wknd over 1f out* **28/1**
0036 10 ½ **Dark Oasis**[15] 4470 3-8-1 **50** JosephineBruning(7) 15 42
(M C Chapman) *sn chsng ldrs: rdn over 3f out: wknd 2f out* **25/1**
6505 11 ¾ **The Quiet Genius**[22] 4230 3-8-12 **59** PatrickDonaghy(5) 1 50
(Jedd O'Keeffe) *hld up: bhd 6f out: n.d* **25/1**
4444 12 hd **Veronicas Boy**[11] 4600 3-8-11 **56** DavidProbert(3) 4 46
(G M Moore) *prom: rdn over 2f out: wknd over 1f out* **11/1**
2042 13 10 **Honorable Endeavor**[8] 4703 3-8-13 **55** (v) HayleyTurner 11 31
(E F Vaughan) *plld hrd and prom: rdn over 2f out: sn wknd* **10/3¹**
5006 14 2½ **Luthien (IRE)**[36] 3776 3-9-2 **58** TomEaves 7 31
(W R Swinburn) *mid-div: rdn over 4f out: hung lft and wknd over 2f out* **20/1**
0415 15 8 **Seminal Moment**[15] 4470 3-8-11 **56** LeeVickers(3) 13 18
(J G Given) *hld up: hdwy 7f out: rdn and wknd over 2f out* **20/1**
0-00 16 62 **Full Blue**[30] 3976 3-8-7 **49** LukeMorris 14 —
(S C Williams) *hld up: plld hrd: wknd over 5f out* **25/1**

3m 7.37s (2.37) **Going Correction** +0.125s/f (Good) **16** Ran SP% **125.1**
Speed ratings (Par 98): **98,97,95,94,94 93,93,93,92,92 91,91,85,84,79 44**
toteswingers: 1&2 £66.10, 1&3 £25.20, 2&3 £115.50 CSF £376.27 CT £5297.34 TOTE £8.00: £1.90, £11.90, £4.00, £5.20; EX 541.90 Place 6: £115.88 Place 5: £80.17.
Owner Liam Sheridan **Bred** Michael Dalton **Trained** Newmarket, Suffolk

FOCUS
A wide-open staying 3yo handicap. Modest but sound form.
Googoobarabajagal(IRE) Official explanation: jockey said gelding was struck into
T/Plt: £516.90 to a £1 stake. Pool: £54,481.30. 76.93 winning tickets. T/Qpdt: £75.20 to a £1 stake. Pool: £3,436.40. 33.80 winning tickets. CR

CLAIREFONTAINE (R-H)
Friday, August 14

OFFICIAL GOING: Soft

5012a PRIX DU FILM "LADS ET JOCKEYS" (PRIX LIANGA) (WOMEN PROFESSIONALS) 1m
2:25 (2:25) 3-Y-O **£11,650** (£4,660; £3,495; £2,330; £1,165)

RPR
1 **Volver (IRE)**[74] 3-8-12 CelineHerissondeBeauvoir 95
(J-C Rouget, France)
2 nse **Shampagne**[36] 3783 3-9-4 CelineLaunay 101
(P F I Cole) *hld up in 6th: hdwy to go 2nd appr fnl f: styd on wl: jst failed* **13/10¹**
3 2½ **Saliyna (FR)**[50] 3330 3-9-1 BrigitteRenk 92
(J-C Rouget, France)
4 shd **Madonna Incognito (USA)**[26] 4130 3-9-1 92
(F Rohaut, France)
5 2½ **Easy Sundae (IRE)**[58] 3-9-3 88
(J E Pease, France)
6 ¾ **Ponte Di Legno (FR)**[76] 3-8-12 81
(Y De Nicolay, France)
7 8 **Mister Lux (FR)**[74] 3-8-11 62?
(C Boutin, France)

1m 40.0s (100.00) **7** Ran SP% **43.5**
PARI-MUTUEL (Including 1 Euro stake): WIN 17.10; PL 5.30, 1.70;SF 75.50.
Owner M Schwartz **Bred** Ian Fair **Trained** Pau, France

NOTEBOOK
Shampagne, on whom waiting tactics were employed, still had plenty to do coming into the straight. He quickened really well from two out and looked likely to catch the leader but finally went down on the nod by inches.

4810 SAINT-MALO (L-H)
Friday, August 14

OFFICIAL GOING: Good

5013a PRIX JEAN DE ROCHEBOUET 1m 1f
3:30 (12:00) 4-Y-O+ **£7,282** (£2,913; £2,184; £1,456; £728)

RPR
1 **Soriniere Du Lac (FR)**[30] 5-9-2 (b) ABourgeais 61
(J-L Mace, France)
2 hd **Douceur Nocturne (FR)**[265] 4-9-6 (b) FVeron 65
(H-A Pantall, France)
3 nk **Elegant Beauty (GER)**[284] 7171 4-8-11 JCabre 55
(H Blume, Germany)
4 ¾ **Russian Angel**[20] 4321 5-8-9 NEven 51
(Jean-Rene Auvray)
5 3 **Sand Du Lys (FR)** 4-9-0 GAvranche 50
(J-L Guillochon, France)
6 2 **Valse De La Tour (FR)**[109] 4-9-4 (b) AJeffrard 50
(Mme A-C Trouve, France)
7 3 **Miss Lady Kiang (FR)** 4-8-9 SBodrefaux 35
(A Rudelin, France)
8 4 **Mahie (FR)**[517] 8-8-9 FGarnier 26
(Mme O Rouleau, France)

1m 52.34s (112.34) **8** Ran
PARI-MUTUEL (including one euro stakes): WIN 6.50; PL 2.30, 1.40,2.50; DF 13.70.
Owner J-L Mace **Bred** Mme Estelle Chapeau & Ghislain Freuchet **Trained** France

NOTEBOOK
Russian Angel has been running reasonably on moderate handicaps and ran well to be beaten just over a length in this fillies' race.

5014a PRIX SOLIDOR (MAIDEN) 1m
4:00 (12:00) 2-Y-O **£6,796** (£2,718; £2,039; £1,359; £680)

RPR
1 **Impressioniste (IRE)** 2-8-11 JAuge —
(E J O'Neill) **7/5¹**
2 ½ **Cover Story (FR)** 2-8-8 GAvranche —
(E Libaud, France)
3 ½ **Royal Merit (FR)** 2-8-12 LucieVerger —
(R Lecomte, France)
4 1½ **Sailor Moon (IRE)** 2-8-12 FVeron —
(H-A Pantall, France)
5 1 **Garynella (FR)** 2-8-11 AFouassier —
(A Couetil, France)
6 ¾ **Smalkie (FR)** 2-8-12 HPaimblanc —
(G Cherel, France)
7 1 **Lily De Vauville (FR)** 2-8-8 JCabre —
(Jack Barbe, France)
8 ½ **Skimi (FR)** 2-8-11 ABernard —
(Y Fertillet, France)
9 1 **Novlime (FR)**[68] 2-8-12 JBensimon —
(J-V Toux, France)
10 4 **Compatriote (FR)** 2-8-11 LHuart —
(M Houdoin, France)
0 **Quentindemontargis (FR)** 2-8-11 DFournier —
(Mme C Madamet, France)
0 **Silver Cat** 2-8-11 MAndrouin —
(J Boisnard, France)

1m 46.94s (106.94) **12** Ran SP% **41.7**
PARI-MUTUEL: WIN 2.80; PL 1.80, 3.40, 4.70; DF 15.90.
Owner Reve De Soleil Partnership **Bred** Joe & Edel Banahan **Trained** Southwell, Notts
■ Stewards' Enquiry : A Fouassier 30euro fine: weighed in heavy
J Auge 100euro fine: careless riding

NOTEBOOK
Impressioniste(IRE) was sent off favourite on this debut and held off a trio of fillies to score.

4867 LINGFIELD (L-H)
Saturday, August 15

OFFICIAL GOING: Turf course - good to firm (8.7); all-weather - standard

5015 IDRIS MORGAN OF ELY BIRTHDAY TODAY APPRENTICE H'CAP 1m 2f (P)
5:30 (5:30) (Class 6) (0-62,60) 3-Y-O+ **£2,047** (£604; £302) **Stalls** Low

Form RPR
5655 1 **Inquisitress**[14] 4538 5-8-9 **46** KierenFox(5) 3 54
(J J Bridger) *hld up towards rr: smooth hdwy to trck ldng pair over 2f out: chsd ldr 2f out: rdn to ld 1f out: kpt on gamely* **12/1**
0463 2 ½ **Transformer (IRE)**[21] 4320 3-9-2 **57** JPFahy 14 64
(W J Knight) *chsd ldrs: wnt 2nd over 2f out: rdn to ld 2f out: clr w wnr over 1f out: hdd 1f out: kpt on but a hld after* **5/1²**
2400 3 1½ **Ready To Crown (USA)**[26] 4156 5-9-3 **49** (p) DeclanCannon 5 53
(J Mackie) *hld up in tch: rdn and effrt 2f out: kpt on u.p to go 3rd wl ins fnl f: nt pce to threaten ldrs* **10/1**
P023 4 1 **Fine Tolerance**[19] 4382 3-8-8 **54** NathanAlison(5) 8 56
(J R Boyle) *t.k.h: led for 1f: chsd ldr after tl led again over 2f out: rdn wl over 1f out: one pce after* **8/1**
5603 5 shd **Touch Of Style (IRE)**[14] 4538 5-9-4 **50** AshleyMorgan 4 52
(T D McCarthy) *hld up in tch: n.m.r and hmpd jst over 2f out: sn swtchd rt: drvn and kpt on same pce fr over 1f out* **8/1**
3005 6 2¼ **Ba Dreamflight**[32] 3943 4-8-9 **46** RyanClark(5) 10 43
(H Morrison) *chsd ldrs: rdn and unable qck over 2f out: n.m.r wl over 1f out: no imp after* **15/2**
2300 7 ½ **Inch Lodge**[9] 4721 7-10-0 **60** (t) TobyAtkinson 13 56
(Miss D Mountain) *dwlt: hld up towards rr: pushed along 4f out: rdn and effrt on outer 3f out: one pce and no imp fnl 2f* **9/2¹**
060/ 8 nk **Ringsider (IRE)**[66] 2836 8-9-9 **55** AndrewHeffernan 1 51
(R J Osborne, Ire) *s.i.s: hld up in rr: nt clr run jst over 2f out: rdn wl over 1f out: plugged on but nvr pce to threaten ldrs* **25/1**
4664 9 1 **Sphere (IRE)**[15] 4498 4-9-13 **59** (t) RosieJessop 12 53
(J R Fanshawe) *s.i.s: hld up in rr: nudged along over 1f out: kpt on fnl f: nvr trbld ldrs* **11/2³**
0030 10 shd **Bicksta**[62] 2942 3-9-2 **57** JPHamblett 7 51
(E F Vaughan) *hld up in tch: rdn over 2f out: struggling wl over 1f out* **12/1**
300/ 11 15 **Sneem's Rock**[1587] 967 8-9-0 **46** (p) SimonPearce 2 10
(P R Hedger) *t.k.h: hld up in midfield: lost pl over 2f out: wl bhd over 1f out* **16/1**
50-0 12 2 **Watch The Master**[22] 4270 3-8-10 **51** (v¹) DTDaSilva 6 11
(B I Case) *in tch tl lost pl over 3f out: wl bhd fnl 2f* **33/1**
0560 13 2½ **Poca A Poca (IRE)**[25] 4164 5-8-11 **48** (p) MatthewCosham(5) 9 3
(G C Bravery) *led after 1f: rdn and hdd over 2f out: wknd qckly: wl bhd over 1f out* **50/1**

2m 6.47s (-0.13) **Going Correction** -0.05s/f (Stan)
WFA 3 from 4yo+ 9lb **13** Ran SP% **123.3**
Speed ratings (Par 101): **98,97,96,95,95 93,93,93,92,92 80,78,76**
toteswingers: 1&2 £25.30, 1&3 £25.30, 2&3 £25.30 CSF £72.33 CT £643.72 TOTE £16.30: £3.80, £2.10, £4.00; EX 120.60.
Owner C Marshall T Wallace J J Bridger **Bred** A Saccomando **Trained** Liphook, Hants

FOCUS
A moderate apprentice handicap. Sound but limited form.

5016 MICHAEL'S HALF CENTURY CLAIMING STKS 1m (P)
6:00 (6:01) (Class 6) 3-Y-O **£2,047** (£604; £302) **Stalls** High

Form RPR
3034 1 **Head Down**[21] 4322 3-9-7 **75** RyanMoore 5 80
(R Hannon) *dwlt: sn rcvrd to chse ldng pair: wnt 2nd over 2f out: rdn to ld narrowly over 1f out: kpt on u.p fnl f* **7/2³**
6324 2 nk **Brooksby**[7] 4791 3-8-4 **70** (b) RichardThomas 10 62
(R Hannon) *led: rdn and clr w wnr wl over 1f out: hdd narrowly over 1f out: one pce and a jst hld after* **5/2²**

6611 **3** 1 1/4 **Diggeratt (USA)**[6] 4821 3-9-2 73 LDettori 1 71
(R A Fahey) *in tch: hdwy to chse ldng pair 2f out: no imp u.p tl kpt on fnl 100yds: nt pce to rch ldrs* **15/8**[1]
-206 **4** 8 **Breadstick**[54] 3209 3-8-12 69 (t) SteveDrowne 3 49
(H Morrison) *chsd ldr tl over 2f out: sn rdn and unable qck: btn over 1f out and no ch after* **10/1**
-000 **5** 1 1/4 **Academy Of War (USA)**[8] 4730 3-8-6 50 JackDean(3) 2 43
(J M Bradley) *dwlt: t.k.h: hld up in tch towards rr: rdn and effrt over 2f out: no prog and wl btn over 1f out* **66/1**
60 **6** hd **Inside Trade (IRE)**[67] 2795 3-8-2 63 (t) JPFahy(7) 8 43
(R M Beckett) *s.i.s: hld up in tch in rr: rdn and effrt over 2f out: no real hdwy and nvr nr ldrs* **16/1**
1005 **7** 1 3/4 **True Decision**[93] 2010 3-8-11 67 JamesDoyle 9 41
(S Kirk) *hld up in tch towards rr: rdn and unable qck over 3f out: no ch fnl 2f* **20/1**
6050 **8** 3/4 **Happy And Glorious (IRE)**[31] 3985 3-7-11 48 ow2 KierenFox(7) 7 32
(J W Hills) *t.k.h: hld up in tch: hdwy to chse ldrs over 2f out: struggling ent fnl 2f: wl btn after* **66/1**
0- **9** 3 **Petrafied (FR)**[36] 3890 3-8-2 67 CatherineGannon 4 23
(P J Prendergast, Ire) *in tch towards rr: rdn 3f out: sn struggling: wl btn fnl 2f* **12/1**
400 **10** 7 **Crown Affair (IRE)**[38] 3741 3-7-12 53 ow3 AmyScott(7) 6 10
(J W Hills) *v.s.a and detached in last: nvr a factor* **100/1**
-505 **11** 7 **Peal Park**[31] 3984 3-8-6 59 JamieMackay 11 —
(Karen George) *chsd ldrs tl over 2f out: sn lost pl: wl bhd fnl 2f* **66/1**

1m 37.47s (-0.73) **Going Correction** -0.05s/f (Stan) **11** Ran SP% **118.5**
Speed ratings (Par 98): **101,100,99,91,90 90,88,87,84,77 70**
toteswingers: 1&2 £1.60, 1&3 £2.30, 2&3 £1.40 CSF £12.50 TOTE £4.90: £1.60, £1.30, £1.30; EX 15.50.Head Down was claimed by Linda Jewell for £12,000. Brooksby was claimed by Luke Dace for £6,000.
Owner Jim Horgan **Bred** Hong Kong Breeders Club **Trained** East Everleigh, Wilts

FOCUS
The four runners with the highest official ratings were the only ones to figure in this claimer to any extent. The winner could have run a clear personal best, but it is more likely his rivals were not at their best.
Crown Affair(IRE) Official explanation: jockey said filly missed the break and was reluctant to race

5017 E B F BUY A RACING POST YEARLING BONUS CANDIDATE MAIDEN STKS 6f
6:30 (6:32) (Class 5) 2-Y-O £3,561 (£1,059; £529; £264) **Stalls** High

Form RPR
322 **1** **Dubai Set**[23] 4219 2-9-3 80 RyanMoore 9 78
(R Hannon) *mde all: rdn over 1f out: forged ahd ins fnl f: in command towards fin* **4/6**[1]
4 **2** 1 3/4 **Burgau Royal**[19] 4377 2-9-3 0 CatherineGannon 6 73
(M R Channon) *pressed wnr: rdn over 2f out: stl ev ch tl no ex ins fnl f* **7/1**[3]
0 **3** 2 1/4 **Machine Gun Kelly (IRE)**[18] 4410 2-9-3 0 FergusSweeney 4 66
(G L Moore) *w ldrs: rdn and outpcd by ldng pair wl over 1f out: plugged on same pce fnl f* **16/1**
4 1 1/4 **Al Dafa (USA)** 2-9-3 0 LDettori 8 65+
(Saeed Bin Suroor) *v.s.a: rn green thrght: edgd out lft over 3f out: chsd ldng trio jst over 1f out: hung rt and kpt on same pce fnl f* **2/1**[2]
00 **5** 3 1/4 **Mandarin Express**[19] 4377 2-8-12 0 GabrielHannon(5) 5 53
(B J Meehan) *s.i.s: sn rcvrd to chse ldrs: rdn over 2f out: sn struggling: no ch whn hung rt fnl f* **33/1**
00 **6** 6 **Knockback (IRE)**[10] 4646 2-9-3 0 NeilChalmers 3 35
(P R Chamings) *s.i.s: pushed along and struggling 4f out: no ch fr 1/2-way* **33/1**
7 2 1/2 **Rockweiller** 2-9-3 0 SteveDrowne 2 27
(C R Egerton) *a bhd: rdn and lost tch over 3f out: no ch after* **33/1**
0 **8** 1/2 **Fast Elaine (IRE)**[21] 4302 2-8-12 0 JamesDoyle 7 21
(Mrs L C Jewell) *s.i.s: in tch in midfield: rdn and rn green wl over 2f out: wknd u.p ent fnl 2f* **100/1**
9 2 1/2 **Until The Man (IRE)** 2-9-3 0 KirstyMilczarek 1 18
(R Ingram) *racd on outer: a towards rr: struggling fr 1/2-way* **50/1**

1m 10.24s (-0.96) **Going Correction** -0.20s/f (Firm) **9** Ran SP% **123.5**
Speed ratings (Par 94): **98,95,92,91,86 78,75,74,71**
toteswingers: 1&2 £2.00, 1&3 £5.40, 2&3 not won CSF £7.07 TOTE £1.90: £1.02, £2.30, £4.40; EX 6.50.
Owner Malih L Al Basti **Bred** Malih L Al Basti **Trained** East Everleigh, Wilts

FOCUS
Not a competitive maiden, but a useful-looking winner who basically ran to form.

NOTEBOOK
Dubai Set entered the race still on an upward curve despite four starts, and the form of last month's Bath second has been quite well advertised since. Blessed with a draw hard up against the rail, the son of Reset made no mistake, responding well when briefly joined by Burgau Royal 2f out to record an authoritative victory. He holds an entry in the Weatherbys Insurance £300,000 2-Y-O Stakes at Doncaster next month, but whilst not quite in the same league yet as some of his fellow entrants, there should still be a good nursery or minor stakes in him if his present rate of improvement is sustained. (tchd 4-7, 4-5 in a place and 8-11 in a place)
Burgau Royal stepped up on his debut effort, and looked set to give the winner a real fight of it at one stage. He has kept on to an extent after decent early speed on both tries now, and may find a small opening in a similar contest to this before too long. (op 6-1 tchd 15-2)
Machine Gun Kelly(IRE), like the winner a Doncaster entry, was another to step up on his first racecourse appearance, but at the same time he proved rather short of extra gears late on. He may ultimately need a mile to break his duck, like both his winning half-sisters. (op 20-1)
Al Dafa(USA) represented a yard that's in searing form overall right now and operating at a strike-rate of nearly 40 per cent with its juveniles this term. A Derby entrant who can list multiple Group 1 winner Crimplene among eight winning half-siblings, he looked fit and ready in the preliminaries, but betrayed signs of greenness at various stages of the race and ran around a bit late on in particular. He was not given too hard a time in defeat, and may not be too long in repaying the kindness. (op 11-4 tchd 3-1)
Fast Elaine(IRE) Official explanation: trainer said filly was unsuited by the good to firm going

5018 HOMECROFT CAVENDISH SAYS "HAPPY BIRTHDAY SIMON" (S) STKS 6f
7:00 (7:00) (Class 6) 3-Y-O+ £2,047 (£604; £302) **Stalls** High

Form RPR
16-0 **1** **Connor's Choice**[52] 3283 4-8-11 58 SimonPearce(5) 6 60
(Andrew Turnell) *stdd s: hld up in rr: hdwy over 1f out: rdn and chal between horses ins fnl f: led wl ins fnl f: r.o wl* **16/1**
4035 **2** 1 1/4 **Briannsta (IRE)**[8] 4732 7-9-2 45 RichardThomas 1 56
(J E Long) *in tch: rdn and effrt over 2f out: led over 1f out tl hdd and no ex wl ins fnl f* **28/1**
0534 **3** 2 **Boldinor**[8] 4732 6-9-2 52 J-PGuillambert 2 50
(M R Bosley) *chsd ldrs: ev ch and rdn 2f out: led wl over 1f out: sn hdd: stl ev ch tl wknd ins fnl f* **15/2**[3]
-030 **4** 1 1/4 **Boundless Applause**[42] 3632 3-8-0 39 JPFahy(7) 8 41
(I A Wood) *chsd ldrs: nt clr run and lost pl over 1f out: styd on whn in the clr fnl f: nvr able to chal* **33/1**
133 **5** nse **Obe Gold**[1] 4976 7-9-7 80 (v) KirstyMilczarek 10 50+
(Miss D Mountain) *v awkward leaving stalls and slowly away: bhd: stl plenty to do jst over 1f out: styd on fnl f: nvr nr ldrs* **1/1**[1]
0140 **6** 1/2 **Pintano**[8] 4732 4-9-7 50 (t) CatherineGannon 11 49
(J M Bradley) *led: rdn and hdd wl over 1f out: hung lft u.p: wknd fnl f* **16/1**
5050 **7** 1 **Wicksy Creek**[12] 4602 4-8-11 42 (t) MarkCoumbe(5) 3 41
(G C Bravery) *stdd s: hld up towards rr: rdn and effrt on outer wl over 1f out: plugged on fnl f: nvr trbld ldrs* **33/1**
0500 **8** 1 3/4 **Noverre To Hide (USA)**[28] 4083 3-8-12 50 SteveDrowne 7 35
(J R Best) *chsd ldrs: rdn 2f out: wknd u.p over 1f out* **14/1**
412- **9** 1 1/4 **Time For Old Time**[386] 4389 3-8-7 61 PaulDoe 12 26
(I A Wood) *chsd ldr tl 2f out: sn rdn: edging lft and wkng whn barging match w rival over 1f out: wl btn after* **7/2**[2]
0600 **10** 1/2 **Songful (IRE)**[6] 4812 3-8-7 46 JamieMackay 4 24
(Pat Eddery) *stdd s: a bhd: struggling u.p 2f out: n.d* **25/1**
0040 **11** nk **Faintly Hopeful**[187] 472 4-9-2 48 (p) TGMcLaughlin 13 28
(R A Teal) *hld up towards rr: rdn and effrt on stands' rail over 1f out: no prog* **25/1**
1505 **12** 1/2 **Great Knight (IRE)**[8] 4748 4-9-7 56 JamesDoyle 9 32+
(S Kirk) *stdd s: hld up in rr: n.m.r fr over 1f out: nvr a factor: eased wl ins fnl f* **15/2**[3]

1m 10.42s (-0.78) **Going Correction** -0.20s/f (Firm)
WFA 3 from 4yo+ 4lb **12** Ran SP% **131.2**
Speed ratings (Par 101): **97,95,92,91,90 90,88,86,84,84 83,83**
toteswingers: 1&2 £41.50, 1&3 £41.50, 2&3 £36.10 CSF £421.68 TOTE £11.20: £2.60, £6.40, £2.70; EX 430.10.There was no bid for the winner. Obe Gold was claimed by Paul Howling for £6,000.
Owner Andrew Turnell **Bred** Mrs Claire Hollowood **Trained** Broad Hinton, Wilts

FOCUS
This modest seller was won in a time 0.18 seconds slower than the juvenile maiden that preceded it. The form looks fallible, with the favourite enduring a torrid race and two longer-priced animals dominating late on. It has been rated around the third.
Obe Gold Official explanation: jockey said gelding lost its action
Wicksy Creek Official explanation: vet said gelding lost a right front shoe

5019 SC MOTOR FACTORS H'CAP 7f 140y
7:30 (7:32) (Class 6) (0-65,65) 3-Y-O+ £2,047 (£604; £302) **Stalls** Centre

Form RPR
0345 **1** **Rock Anthem (IRE)**[19] 4389 5-9-5 57 AndreaAtzeni(3) 16 72
(Mike Murphy) *hld up in rr: rdn and gd hdwy 2f ut: nt clr run jst over 1f out: swtchd lft ent fnl f: led ins fnl f and stormed clr fnl 100yds* **5/1**[3]
6221 **2** 3 1/4 **Whotsit (IRE)**[14] 4533 3-8-11 60 (b) LauraPike(7) 13 66
(Miss Amy Weaver) *sn w ldr: led wl over 4f out: rdn 2f out: kpt on tl hdd and nt pce of wnr fnl 100yds* **9/2**[2]
3326 **3** 3/4 **Cativo Cavallino**[7] 4791 6-9-10 62 NataliaGemelova(3) 1 67+
(J E Long) *in tch on outer: rdn and effrt jst over 2f out: chsd ldr over 1f out: kpt on same pce u.p* **12/1**
0-55 **4** 3/4 **Eyes Like A Hawk (IRE)**[25] 4180 3-9-3 59 (t) RichardKingscote 9 61
(Tom Dascombe) *racd in midfield: on stands' rail: hung lft fr 4f out: rdn over 2f out: kpt on same pce fnl f* **8/1**
40-5 **5** nk **Fitz**[21] 4303 3-8-13 55 JamesDoyle 14 56+
(M Salaman) *towards rr: rdn and edging lft fr 2f out: nt clr run over 1f out: styd on u.p fnl f: nvr able to rch ldrs* **20/1**
4000 **6** 3/4 **Avoca Dancer (IRE)**[14] 4533 6-9-5 54 (v) TGMcLaughlin 3 55
(Karen George) *t.k.h: hld up in tch: effrt u.p 2f out: no imp fnl f* **25/1**
2000 **7** 3/4 **Binnion Bay (IRE)**[13] 4563 8-9-0 52 (p) MarcHalford(3) 17 51
(J J Bridger) *stdd s: hld up in rr: effrt u.p on outer over 2f out: kpt on fnl f: nvr trbld ldrs* **33/1**
6620 **8** nse **Vanadium**[14] 4536 7-9-7 56 RyanMoore 11 55
(G L Moore) *hld up towards rr: rdn and effrt 2f out: no real prog* **15/2**
-104 **9** 3/4 **Hypnotic**[41] 3659 7-9-13 62 RichardThomas 10 59
(Jim Best) *chsd ldrs: wnt 2nd 4f out tl over 1f out: wknd fnl f* **4/1**[1]
0063 **10** shd **Loyal Royal (IRE)**[24] 4202 6-9-2 54 (b) JackDean(3) 6 50
(J M Bradley) *stdd s: hld up towards rr: rdn and hdwy jst over 2f out: chsd ldrs over 1f out: sn wknd* **25/1**
5U12 **11** 1/2 **Many Welcomes**[10] 4665 4-9-1 57 JemmaMarshall(7) 15 52+
(B P J Baugh) *hld up in rr: effrt 2f out: nt clr run over 1f out: rdn ent fnl f: keeping on same pce whn nt clr run and eased ins fnl f: no ch* **8/1**
0404 **12** 2 **Eleanor Eloise (USA)**[8] 4730 5-8-13 48 (b) SteveDrowne 8 44+
(J R Gask) *chsd ldrs: rdn 2f out: wkng whn hmpd ins fnl f: eased after* **20/1**
0-00 **13** 2 1/4 **Dawson Creek (IRE)**[7] 4791 5-9-6 62 JPFahy(7) 2 47
(B Gubby) *chsd ldrs on outer: rdn 1/2-way: struggling over 2f out* **33/1**
5641 **14** 8 **Montmartre (USA)**[52] 3257 3-9-9 65 FergusSweeney 18 30
(David Pinder) *led tl wl over 4f out: lost pl and bhd 3f out: wl btn and eased fnl f* **10/1**
00- **15** 3 3/4 **Monsieur Kiss Kiss**[15] 4512 3-8-10 57 MarkCoumbe(5) 7 12
(R J Osborne, Ire) *bhd on outer: rdn and hung rt over 2f out: wl bhd and eased ins fnl f* **25/1**
-000 **16** 6 **Willridge**[39] 3722 4-9-10 59 (t) CatherineGannon 5 —
(J M Bradley) *chsd ldrs: rdn and struggling over 3f out: t.o and eased fnl f* **66/1**

1m 29.97s (-2.33) **Going Correction** -0.20s/f (Firm)
WFA 3 from 4yo+ 7lb **16** Ran SP% **134.1**
Speed ratings (Par 101): **103,99,99,98,97 97,96,96,95,95 95,93,90,82,79 73**
toteswingers: 1&2 £5.10, 1&3 £6.90, 2&3 £9.60 CSF £27.68 CT £288.81 TOTE £6.10: £2.10, £1.90, £3.30, £1.90; EX 33.40.
Owner Ronald Bright **Bred** Mervyn Stewkesbury **Trained** Westoning, Beds

FOCUS
The stalls were situated in the centre of the track for this moderate contest. Several were denied clear runs but the form was sound overall.
Fitz Official explanation: jockey said colt was denied a clear run
Willridge Official explanation: jockey said gelding was never travelling

5020 DORMANS PARK H'CAP 6f
8:00 (8:00) (Class 5) (0-70,67) 4-Y-O+ £3,412 (£1,007; £504) **Stalls** High

Form RPR
3643 **1** **Gwilym (GER)**[12] 4604 6-9-3 63 HayleyTurner 14 74
(D Haydn Jones) *trckd ldrs on stands' rail: led over 1f out: rdn and r.o strly: in command whn jinked lft nr fin* **3/1**[1]

0604 **2** *1 ¾* **Ghost Dancer**[9] 4690 5-8-11 **60**..(p) JackDean(3) 9 65
(J M Bradley) *hld up towards rr on outer: hdwy over 2f out: rdn over 1f out: edgd lft ins fnl f* **10/1**

4340 **3** *5* **Peopleton Brook**[12] 4604 7-8-10 **56**..........................(t) FergusSweeney 5 45
(B G Powell) *hld up towards rr on outer: hdwy over 2f out: chsd ldrs over 1f out: wl outpcd by ldng pair fnl f: wnt 3rd nr fin* **12/1**

1240 **4** *¾* **Bateleur**[12] 4607 5-9-1 **66**.. MCGeran(5) 12 53
(M R Channon) *hld up in tch: effrt to press ldrs 2f out: wl outpcd ldng pair fnl f* **4/1**[3]

0100 **5** *2 ¼* **Sam's Cross (IRE)**[8] 4733 4-9-1 **64**.................................... MarcHalford(3) 11 44
(J J Bridger) *t.k.h: in tch: effrt and rdn 2f out: sn hung lft: wknd 1f out* **10/1**

0500 **6** *¾* **Bollin Franny**[28] 4082 5-8-2 **48** oh2.............................. RichardThomas 6 25
(J E Long) *led tl over 1f out: wknd ent fnl f* **16/1**

6300 **7** *3 ½* **Charles Darwin (IRE)**[14] 4533 6-9-4 **64**...................... SteveDrowne 10 30
(M Blanshard) *in tch in midfield: pushed along 4f out: wknd over 2f out: wl bhd fnl f* **12/1**

6104 **8** *¾* **Dynamo Dave (USA)**[8] 4748 4-8-1 **50**........................ AndreaAtzeni(3) 7 14
(M D I Usher) *sn bhd: sme late hdwy: n.d* **11/1**

0600 **9** *2 ¼* **Metropolitan Chief**[8] 4736 5-8-2 **48** oh3................(p) CatherineGannon 1 5
(P Burgoyne) *t.k.h: hld up towards rr: rdn jst over 2f out: sn wl btn* **25/1**

00 **10** *nse* **Sweet Kiss (USA)**[57] 3112 4-8-8 **54** ow1......................(v¹) JamesDoyle 3 10
(M J Attwater) *w ldrs tl wknd qckly jst over 2f out: wl btn fnl f* **20/1**

1160 **11** *1 ¾* **Super Frank (IRE)**[40] 3691 6-9-6 **66**..........................(p) J-PGuillambert 8 17
(J Akehurst) *awkward leaving stalls and slowly away: a bhd* **7/2**[2]

100 **12** *11* **Sherjawy (IRE)**[56] 3162 5-8-12 **58**..............................(b) KirstyMilczarek 4 —
(Miss Z C Davison) *in tch in midfield: struggling and rdn 1/2-way: t.o fnl f* **20/1**

69.53 secs (-1.67) **Going Correction** -0.20s/f (Firm) **12** Ran SP% **128.4**
Speed ratings (Par 103): **103,100,94,93,90 89,84,83,80,80 77,63**
toteswingers: 1&2 £9.50, 1&3 £13.00, 2&3 £42.80 CSF £36.36 CT £342.17 TOTE £3.90: £1.80, £3.90, £4.70; EX 31.00 Place 6: £217.44 Place 5: £55.34.
Owner S Kon, D Llewelyn and J Runeckles **Bred** B Krutmann **Trained** Efail Isaf, Rhondda C Taff

FOCUS
The last of three races over the straight turf 6f was also the fastest, around 0.7 seconds quicker than the maiden. The front pair grabbed the rail and pulled clear in this weakish handicap.
T/Plt: £112.20 to a £1 stake. Pool: £45,334.22. 294.93 winning tickets. T/Qpdt: £32.80 to a £1 stake. Pool: £5,977.42. 134.80 winning tickets. SP

4985 NEWBURY (L-H)

Saturday, August 15

OFFICIAL GOING: Good to firm (8.3)
Wind: Moderate across Weather: Bright intervals

5021 BATHWICK TYRES EUROPEAN BREEDERS' FUND MAIDEN FILLIES' STKS (DIV I) 6f 8y

1:30 (1:33) (Class 4) 2-Y-O **£4,857** (£1,445; £722; £360) **Stalls** Centre

Form RPR

0 **1** **Queen's Grace**[13] 4564 2-9-0 0.. SteveDrowne 1 81
(H Morrison) *leggy: w ldrs: pushed along 3f out: slt ld ins fnl 2f: drvn and styd on strly fnl f* **50/1**

2 *nk* **Jacqueline Quest (IRE)** 2-9-0 0.. TPQueally 4 80+
(H R A Cecil) *w'like: leggy: lw: trckd ldrs: chal fr ins fnl 2f: kpt on wl ins fnl f but a jst hld by wnr* **8/1**

0 **3** *2 ¼* **Pin Cushion**[12] 4603 2-9-0 0.. JamieSpencer 11 73
(B J Meehan) *str: lw: s.i.s: hld up in rr tl hdwy over 2f out: rdn to chse ldrs over 1f out: one pce ins fnl f* **4/1**[3]

4 *½* **Golden Aria (IRE)** 2-9-0 0.. RichardHughes 2 72+
(R Hannon) *lw: trckd ldrs: shkn up over 1f out: kpt on wl fnl f: should improve* **14/1**

5 *nk* **Za Za Zoom (IRE)** 2-9-0 0.. MichaelHills 8 71+
(B W Hills) *lengthy: scope: s.i.s: towards rr but in tch: hdwy fr 2f out: styd on fnl f but nvr gng pce to get into contention* **8/1**

6 *2 ¼* **Texas Queen** 2-9-0 0.. TedDurcan 9 64
(M R Channon) *leggy: chsd ldrs: rdn over 2f out: wknd fnl f* **16/1**

7 *1* **Dylanesque** 2-9-0 0.. PhilipRobinson 10 67+
(M A Jarvis) *w'like: chsd ldrs: pushed along over 2f out: wknd and no ch whn hmpd 1f out* **7/2**[2]

5 **8** *hd* **Love And Devotion**[12] 4603 2-9-0 0.............................. MickyFenton 5 61
(Saeed Bin Suroor) *w'like: scope: led after 1f: rdn and hdd ins fnl 2f: wknd appr fnl f* **5/2**[1]

9 *12* **Superior Edge** 2-9-0 0.. SebSanders 3 25
(B Palling) *led 1f: chsd ldrs to 2f out: sn wknd* **25/1**

10 *6* **Half Sister (IRE)** 2-9-0 0.. RyanMoore 6 7
(R Hannon) *w'like: rdn after s: green and a wl bhd* **14/1**

1m 14.25s (1.25) **Going Correction** +0.175s/f (Good) **10** Ran SP% **118.0**
Speed ratings (Par 93): **98,97,94,93,93 90,89,88,72,64**
toteswingers: 1&2 £56.50, 1&3 £27.10, 2&3 £9.60 CSF £414.92 TOTE £48.60: £8.40, £3.30, £1.70; EX 354.70.
Owner Miss B Swire **Bred** Miss B Swire **Trained** East Ilsley, Berks

FOCUS
Although 4mm of water was applied to the track overnight, and a fresh crosswind combined with muggy conditions had caused the course to dry out, and the jockeys believed the ground was riding firm. This fillies' maiden has thrown up several useful sorts, including Watership Down winner Salamanca and Group 1-placed Silca Chiave along with several placed at Listed level. This first leg featured only three with previous experience and one of them ran out surprise winner, showing a big step up on her debut form.

NOTEBOOK
Queen's Grace ◆ ran out a surprise winner but there was no fluke about it, as she had clearly come on from her debut and, although she scored narrowly, she may have had a bit in hand as her ears were pricked for most of the final furlong. A half-sister to April Fool from family of Sakhee's Secret, the Bahamian Bounty filly has not been the easiest at home, but that is something of a family trait. Her dam was a five-time Listed winner at 6f-7f and she may eventually reach a similar level. (op 66-1)
Jacqueline Quest(IRE) ◆, a 60,000gns first foal of a middle-distance/stayer who is a half-sister to Regime, showed plenty of promise on this debut considering on breeding the trip looked on the short side. She travelled really well into the race and ran on without being given too hard a ride, suggesting she should learn from the experience. She should not be too long getting off the mark.
Pin Cushion had finished behind the favourite on their respective debuts, but she reversed the form despite missing the break. She stayed on late and this half-sister to 6f juvenile winner Greensward out of the high-class sprinter Frizzante, is another who should not be too long in recording her initial success, although her rider reported that she hung right-handed and so may have been feeling the ground. Official explanation: jockey said filly hung right-handed (op 7-2)
Golden Aria(IRE), a 30,000 euros half-sister to City Of Tribes from a speedy family, was another to make a promising start after having looked to struggle to keep up early on. From a yard that is pre-eminent with their juveniles, she will be much better for the outing. (op 16-1)
Za Za Zoom(IRE), a half-sister to several winners at up to 1m including Genki, did not make a bad start to her career, keeping on from the rear in the last two furlongs. (op 10-1 tchd 7-1)
Texas Queen, the first foal of a half-sister to Zafeen and with plenty of juvenile talent in her pedigree, is from a yard whose juveniles are often better for the outing and she should therefore benefit from this. (op 20-1)
Dylanesque, a half-sister to Alessandro Volta but unlike that colt by a sprinter, showed some ability on this debut. However, her rider reported that she got upset in the preliminaries and, as she was near the head of the market, had clearly been showing something at home and should benefit from this outing. Official explanation: jockey said filly got upset in the preliminaries (tchd 4-1)
Love And Devotion had run green when beaten just under 6l on her debut with today's third behind. She broke well and showed in front for a long way, but when the winner went on she capitulated rather tamely. (op 11-4)

5022 USK VALLEY STUD STKS (REGISTERED AS THE WASHINGTON SINGER STAKES) (LISTED RACE) 7f (S)

2:05 (2:06) (Class 1) 2-Y-O

£17,031 (£6,456; £3,231; £1,611; £807; £405) **Stalls** Centre

Form RPR

1 **1** **Azmeel**[17] 4439 2-9-0 0.. RyanMoore 2 101+
(J H M Gosden) *w'like: scope: lw: racd centre crse tl jnd main gp 1/2-way: qcknd to ld 2f out: edgd rt fnl f but a in command: easily* **8/13**[1]

132 **2** *3 ½* **Practitioner**[28] 4086 2-9-0 87..(b¹) LDettori 3 88
(H J L Dunlop) *swtg: trckd ldrs: rdn and chsd wnr fr 2f out: edgd rt fnl f and nvr any imp* **12/1**

1 **3** *2* **Blakey's Boy**[35] 3867 2-9-0 0.. TedDurcan 6 83+
(J L Dunlop) *w'like: scope: lw: stdd s: hld up in rr: pushed along and hdwy over 2f out: hung rt and green u.p fnl f and nvr any ch w ldng duo* **8/1**[3]

1401 **4** *2 ½* **Lucky General (IRE)**[6] 4826 2-9-0 97.......................... RichardHughes 1 77
(R Hannon) *racd towards centre and w ldr tl jnd main gp 1/2-way: rdn and ev ch 2f out: wknd fnl f* **4/1**[2]

6 **5** *7* **Sabander Bleue (IRE)**[8] 4756 2-9-0 0............................ SteveDrowne 5 59
(M R Channon) *str: chsd ldrs tl wknd qckly over 2f out* **25/1**

211 **6** *4* **Farmers Wish (IRE)**[9] 4706 2-8-9 80................................ SebSanders 4 44
(J L Spearing) *t.k.h: led tl hdd 2f out: sn wknd* **14/1**

1m 25.9s (0.20) **Going Correction** +0.175s/f (Good) **6** Ran SP% **111.2**
Speed ratings (Par 102): **105,101,98,95,87 83**
toteswingers: 1&2 £2.00, 1&3 £2.00, 2&3 £3.60 CSF £9.21 TOTE £1.60: £1.20, £2.90; EX 7.80.
Owner M Al-Qatami & K M Al-Mudhaf **Bred** Elsdon Farms **Trained** Newmarket, Suffolk

FOCUS
By far the best winner of this Listed contest this century was the 2000 Guineas and Champion Stakes victor Haafhd, whilst several other winners never progressed beyond this level. Funfair Wane found his niche as a sprinter, winning two Ayr Gold Cups, while a couple ended up winning over jumps. The smallish field included a couple of unexposed winners taking on more experienced sorts. The winner impressed but the bare form is only average Listed standard.

NOTEBOOK
Azmeel, a 65,000 euros first foal of a winning half-sister to Hurricane Floyd and Al Khaleej, had been good winner on his debut over this trip and was well supported at odds-on. He cruised up to join the leaders two furlongs out and when asked to extend did so readily, drawing away for a comfortable success. A Champagne, Royal Lodge and Derby entry, he is clearly a very useful colt and should go on again from this, but quotes as short as 16-1 for the 2000 Guineas are distinctly unattractive at this juncture. (tchd 4-5)
Practitioner, a winner at 6f on fast ground and placed at this trip on soft, ran pretty well in the first-time blinkers, although proving no match for the winner. He is currently rated 87 and looks the best guide to the form. (op 14-1 tchd 8-1)
Blakey's Boy, a 40,000gns half-brother to a high-class German sprinter, was a winner on his debut over this trip on soft ground, despite running green. He ran on from the back of the field but carried his head awkwardly and looked to be feeling the ground. He has a Royal Lodge and Racing Post Trophy entry and may get a more forgiving surface in one of those races. (tchd 15-2)
Lucky General(IRE) on paper looked the benchmark off an official rating of 97. He seemed to have every chance but faded in the last furlong or so. He is a dual winner at 6f on a sound surface but has been beaten on all three tries at this trip now (although the other two were Group 2s) and a drop back in trip looks on the cards after this. (op 7-2)
Sabander Bleue(IRE), a 40,000gns half-brother to a 1m winner, had finished sixth of 14 on his debut over this trip on easy ground the previous week, and this step up in grade probably came a bit early in his career. (op 33-1 tchd 20-1)
Farmers Wish(IRE), a dual winner at 6f on fast and soft ground, was up in both trip and grade and did not get home after making the early running. (op 16-1 tchd 12-1)

5023 CGA GEOFFREY FREER STKS (GROUP 3) 1m 5f 61y

2:35 (2:37) (Class 1) 3-Y-O+

£36,900 (£13,988; £7,000; £3,490; £1,748; £877) **Stalls** Low

Form RPR

-501 **1** **Kite Wood (IRE)**[37] 3778 3-8-8 112.. LDettori 5 121
(Saeed Bin Suroor) *swtg: mde virtually all: pushed along and qcknd clr fr 2f out: edgd rt ins fnl f: easily* **11/10**[1]

0503 **2** *3 ½* **Halicarnassus (IRE)**[15] 4484 5-9-4 108.......................... AlanMunro 3 114
(M R Channon) *in tch: rdn and hdwy fr 3f out: chsd wnr over 1f out: kpt on but nvr any ch* **16/1**

3125 **3** *1 ½* **Age Of Reason (UAE)**[49] 3397 4-9-4 114.......................... TedDurcan 4 112
(Saeed Bin Suroor) *trckd ldrs: n.m.r on ins bnd 7f out: lost position 4f out: styd on wl fr 2f out to go 3rd will ins fnl f but nvr gng pce to trble wnr* **14/1**

3202 **4** *1* **Mourilyan (IRE)**[16] 4457 5-9-4 112.................................... RyanMoore 8 110
(G L Moore) *lw: in rr: pushed along and hdwy to chse ldrs fr 3f out: wnt 2nd 2f out but nvr any ch w wnr: wknd ins fnl f* **4/1**[2]

2613 **5** *4* **Dansant**[56] 3139 5-9-4 112.. EddieAhern 7 104
(G A Butler) *in tch whn hmpd and dropped in rr bnd 7f out: pushed along and sme hdwy 3f out: nvr rchd ldrs and wknd over 1f out* **11/2**[3]

-155 **6** *1 ¼* **Fiulin**[79] 2409 4-9-4 104.. RichardHughes 9 102
(M Botti) *swtg: chsd ldrs: wnt 2nd over 7f out: rdn 4f out: wknd 3f out* **14/1**

4503 **7** *¾* **Kings Gambit (SAF)**[21] 4329 5-9-4 110............................ MickyFenton 2 101
(T P Tate) *chsd ldrs: rdn to briefly take 2nd over 3f out: wknd fr 2f out* **9/1**

0036 **8** *9* **Basaltico (IRE)**[15] 4484 5-9-4 108.................................... JamieSpencer 6 88
(L M Cumani) *chsd ldrs: hmpd and dropped towards rr bnd 7f out: sme prog 4f out: wknd fr 3f out: eased whn no ch* **16/1**

2m 48.87s (-3.13) **Going Correction** -0.025s/f (Good)
WFA 3 from 4yo+ 12lb **8** Ran SP% **118.1**
Speed ratings (Par 113): **108,105,104,104,101 101,100,95**
toteswingers: 1&2 £6.10, 1&3 £4.50, 2&3 £16.30 CSF £23.07 TOTE £2.10: £1.20, £2.50, £2.60; EX 21.10 Trifecta £338.30 Pool: £731.56 - 1.60 winning units..
Owner Godolphin **Bred** Elsdon Farms **Trained** Newmarket, Suffolk
■ Stewards' Enquiry : Richard Hughes four-day ban: careless riding (Aug 29 - Sept 1st)

FOCUS
This long-established contest for middle-distance/stayers usually falls to one of the major yards with two St Leger winners in the last ten years having gone on to take this at five. This year's renewal looked a pretty tight contest judged on official ratings. Animproved effort form Kite Wood who has been rated at face value, although there are a few doubts over the form.

NOTEBOOK
Kite Wood(IRE) ◆, the sole representative of his generation, went to the front after no-one else wanted to make the running and he always looked in control from that point. He drifted towards the stands' rail in the straight - his jockey reported that the ground was too fast for him - but he had his rivals in trouble over two furlongs out and galloped on without being put under maximum pressure. He beat horses rated 108, 114 and 112 by a decent margin, looks a worthy contender for the St Leger and it will take a good one to beat him on this evidence. (op 11-8)
Halicarnassus(IRE) was trying this trip for the first time in over two years and in fact has been campaigned mainly at 1m2f of late. He has never won at this level, but does go well on fast ground and ran his race, although proving no match for Kite Wood. He might go to Turkey for the Bosphorus Cup next. (tchd 14-1 and 20-1)
Age Of Reason(UAE), the winner's stable companion was rated higher than Dettori's mount officially and was clearly not entered here as a pacemaker, which was evidenced by his rider restraining him after a quick start. He settled in the pack behind the winner and was still going well early in the straight, but could not produce a change of gar once put under pressure. (op 16-1)
Mourilyan(IRE) had finished runner-up to Godolphin's Schiaparelli on his previous start and to the same stable's Veracity on his previous attempt at 2m. He had every chance in the straight but was rather one paced, and a return to further will be in his favour, with connections probably keen to avoid runners from the winner's stable. Races such as the Jockey Club Cup and possibly even the Doncaster Cup could be on the agenda. (op 100-30, tchd 9-2 in a place)
Dansant is best known for his exploits on Polytrack but is developing into a high-class performer on turf as well. Things did not really go his way as he got rather lit up when seeing daylight at the end of the back straight before getting squeezed out shortly after. He came to have his chance in the straight but faded in the last furlong or so, and his rider reported he was unsuited by the ground. Official explanation: jockey said horse was unsuited by the good to firm ground (tchd 6-1)
Fiulin is probably not quite up to this level but ran a fair race on his return from a break. He is capable at around 1m6f to 2m and can find opportunities at a lower level with this run behind him. His rider picked up a four-day ban for causing interference leaving the back straight. (op 16-1)
Kings Gambit(SAF) was quite keen early on for this step up in trip, which did not help him get home, and he tired late on. A drop back in distance looks on the cards after this. (tchd 11-1)
Basaltico(IRE)'s rider reported that his mount was badly hampered. Official explanation: jockey said horse was badly hampered

5024 CGA HUNGERFORD STKS (GROUP 2) 7f (S)
3:10 (3:10) (Class 1) 3-Y-O+

£56,770 (£21,520; £10,770; £5,370; £2,690; £1,350) **Stalls** Centre

Form				RPR
0322	**1**		**Balthazaar's Gift (IRE)**[18] 4406 6-9-3 111 PhilipRobinson 6 (C G Cox) *stdd s: hld up in rr: hdwy between horses over 1f out: str run fnl f to ld fnl 100yds: sn clr: won gng away* **10/1**	119
1013	**2**	3	**Regal Parade**[18] 4406 5-9-3 109 AdrianTNicholls 4 (D Nicholls) *lw: chsd ldrs: wnt 2nd over 2f out: str chal ins fnl f: styd on to take 2nd fnl 100yds but nvr any ch w wnr* **12/1**	111
1221	**3**	½	**Plum Pudding (IRE)**[36] 3818 6-9-3 109 RichardHughes 10 (R Hannon) *led: rdn over 1f out: kpt slt ld tl hdd by wnr fnl 100yds and outpcd into 3rd* **7/1**[3]	109
3-12	**4**	½	**Palace Moon**[62] 2948 4-9-3 103 SteveDrowne 9 (H Morrison) *lw: plld hrd: hld up in rr: hdwy fr 3f out: drvn to chse ldrs ins fnl 2f: one pce fnl f* **13/2**[2]	108
-410	**5**	1 ¼	**Gallagher**[14] 4521 3-8-11 110 RyanMoore 7 (B J Meehan) *hld up in rr: rdn and sme hdwy over 2f out: styd on one pce fnl f* **8/1**	105
1-64	**6**	½	**Evasive**[60] 2992 3-8-11 114 LDettori 13 (Saeed Bin Suroor) *lw: chsd ldrs: rdn 2f out: wknd and edgd lft ins fnl f* **10/11**[1]	103
-005	**7**	½	**Express Wish**[18] 4406 5-9-3 105 EddieAhern 14 (J Noseda) *plld hrd: in tch: puched along over 2f out: n.m.r ins fnl 2f: eased whn no ch fnl f* **25/1**	102
1002	**8**	1 ½	**Prime Defender**[28] 4087 5-9-3 109 MichaelHills 11 (B W Hills) *chsd ldrs: rdn over 2f out: wknd over 1f out* **14/1**	98
5201	**9**	nk	**Al Muheer (IRE)**[21] 4297 4-9-3 106 (b) SebSanders 1 (C E Brittain) *lw: hld up in rr: swtchd rt and sme hdwy fr 2f out: nvr in contention and wknd 1f out* **25/1**	97

1m 25.31s (-0.39) **Going Correction** +0.175s/f (Good)
WFA 3 from 4yo+ 6lb 9 Ran SP% **120.5**
Speed ratings (Par 115): **109,105,105,104,103 102,101,100,99**
toteswingers: 1&2 £11.10, 1&3 £4.80, 2&3 £9.90 CSF £126.80 TOTE £9.70: £2.00, £3.30, £1.30; EX 68.90 Trifecta £196.60 Pool: £1488.48 - 5.60 winning units..
Owner H E Sheikh Sultan Bin Khalifa Al Nahyan **Bred** Pat Beirne **Trained** Lambourn, Berks

FOCUS
There were five non-runners due to the ground. Horses aged four have dominated this competitive Group 2 in recent seasons, and it requires a high-class horse to take it, with the last two renewals having been won by Red Evie and Paco Boy, who have both been successful in the highest grade. This year's field looked less likely to throw up something capable of scoring at that level, as most were exposed in lesser company and the majority were rated between 105 and 111. The time was the best of the three races over the trip on the day, but only a quarter of a second faster than the following handicap. The winner is rated back to his best but the form is a bit muddling.

NOTEBOOK
Balthazaar's Gift(IRE) has often run his best races with some cut in the ground, although he did win on a fast surface at Nad Al Sheba earlier in the year. He ran his best race at this level when runner-up to Finjaan in the Lennox Stakes at Goodwood and confirmed that form with the third that day Regal Parade. He did not get the clearest of runs, which may have suited as he needs plenty of cover but, when seeing daylight, he produced by far the best turn of foot to win decisively. He seems better than ever and a return to Goodwood for the Supreme Stakes or the Park Stakes at Doncaster could be suitable targets, but the Prix de la Foret was also mentioned. (op 9-1 tchd 11-1)
Regal Parade is a thoroughly likeable performer who ran his race again and had his chance. He deserves to pick up a Group race and may do so before the end of the season. (op 10-1 tchd 14-1)
Plum Pudding(IRE) is another who is better than ever this year and he was given an uncontested lead. He looked over a furlong out as if he might hold on, but he could not respond to the winner's turn of foot inside the last furlong. (op 8-1 tchd 6-1)
Palace Moon is a lightly raced but progressive performer who was stepping up in both trip and grade. He was a little keen early before settling and ran pretty well, so could make his mark at Group level. (op 8-1)
Gallagher, the other three-year-old in the line-up, ran better than he did at Goodwood on soft ground and this trip suited him better. However, he could not confirm previous form with Plum Pudding and never really got competitive. (tchd 9-1)
Evasive, a course and distance winner and since fourth in the St James's Palace as well as finishing sixth in the 2000 Guineas, was having his first start for Godolphin. He chased the leaders from the start but, when his rider got serious inside the last quarter-mile, he was soon in trouble, although he did stay on again late. It may be that ground was faster than he would ideally have wanted and his rider thought he might just have needed this. Official explanation: trainer had no explanation for the poor form shown (tchd 5-6, 6-5 and 11-10 in a place)
Express Wish finished fifth in the Lennox Stakes behind today's principals but didn't get the clearest of runs this time and failed to figure. He would prefer easier ground than this. (op 16-1)
Prime Defender had not run over this trip since scoring over it in April 2007. He appeared to have every chance but did not seem to get home. (op 11-1)
Al Muheer(IRE) is a high-class handicapper but this was a big step up in grade and he never figured. He seems to run his best turf races at Ascot. (op 20-1)

5025 CGA LADIES DAY H'CAP 7f (S)
3:45 (3:45) (Class 3) (0-95,94) 3-Y-O+

£8,723 (£2,612; £1,306; £653; £326; £163) **Stalls** Centre

Form				RPR
5-10	**1**		**Swift Gift**[57] 3091 4-9-4 91 JamieSpencer 4 (B J Meehan) *lw: hld up in rr: hdwy fr 2f out: rdn to ld 1f out: rdn out* **5/2**[1]	100+
3602	**2**	¾	**Golden Desert (IRE)**[21] 4293 5-9-2 89 TPQueally 5 (T G Mills) *trckd ldrs: drvn to chal over 1f out and stl ev ch ins fnl f: outpcd fnl 110yds* **7/1**[3]	96
0460	**3**	1 ¾	**Masai Moon**[7] 4796 5-8-13 89 JamesMillman(3) 2 (B R Millman) *lw: chsd ldr: drvn to chal fr 2f out: no ex ins fnl f* **12/1**	91
1112	**4**	½	**Cyflymder (IRE)**[9] 4708 3-9-1 94 RichardHughes 9 (R Hannon) *in tch: pushed along over 2f out: styd on u.p fnl f but nvr gng pce to rch ldrs* **5/2**[1]	93
3050	**5**	2 ¼	**Saucy Brown (IRE)**[17] 4423 3-9-0 93 RyanMoore 11 (R Hannon) *pressed ldrs: ins fnl 2f: wknd qckly fnl f* **6/1**[2]	86
0036	**6**	¾	**Spitfire**[20] 4353 4-9-1 88 PhilipRobinson 6 (J R Jenkins) *stdd s: in rr: hmpd over 3f out: swtchd rt and sme hdwy fnl f but nvr in contention* **11/1**	81
-000	**7**	¾	**Silver Guest**[35] 3877 4-8-9 82 TedDurcan 10 (M R Channon) *stdd in rr at s and t.k.h: pushed along and mod prog fnl f* **20/1**	73
120-	**8**	¾	**Orientalist Art**[482] 1513 4-9-7 94 AlanMunro 1 (P W Chapple-Hyam) *chsd ldrs: rdn and wknd 2f out* **14/1**	83
6641	**9**	shd	**Beauchamp Viceroy**[39] 3717 5-8-8 81 (p) EddieAhern 3 (G A Butler) *led tl hdd 1f out: eased whn btn ins fnl f* **17/2**	69

1m 25.56s (-0.14) **Going Correction** +0.175s/f (Good)
WFA 3 from 4yo+ 6lb 9 Ran SP% **121.9**
Speed ratings (Par 107): **107,106,104,103,101 100,99,98,98**
toteswingers: 1&2 £4.50, 1&3 £9.40, 2&3 £15.40 CSF £22.46 CT £184.67 TOTE £3.60: £1.60, £2.50, £3.90; EX 21.80 Trifecta £147.80 Pool: £499.36 - 2.50 winning units..
Owner Social and Affordable Racing Partnership **Bred** Glebe Stud And J F Dean **Trained** Manton, Wilts

FOCUS
A good handicap which in the last three seasons has fallen to an improving three-year-old, but the pair representing the Classic age group failed to make the placings. Straightforward form. The time was 0.25secs slower than the preceding Group 3.

NOTEBOOK
Swift Gift, the winner of the Victoria Cup in the Spring, ad been given a break since his defeat at Royal Ascot (when he was drawn on the wrong side and lost a shoe) and it proved beneficial. He was produced to hit the front entering the final furlong and stayed on strongly. It seems that the key to him is time between races and so he may not be seen again until the autumn, with the International Handicap at Ascot at the end of September a likely target. (op 11-4 tchd 3-1)
Golden Desert(IRE) seems well suited by Ascot and this is his trip. He has not won for over a year and is 6lb higher than his last winning mark, but he looks capable of picking up a decent handicap at this trip. (op 11-2 tchd 9-1)
Masai Moon has not won for over 13 months but often runs his race which has prevented the Handicapper from dropping him. He is edging in the right direction now, though, and this was a decent effort having been close to the pace all the way. (tchd 14-1)
Cyflymder(IRE) was a three-time winner over this trip before being beaten over 1m on easy ground last time. Now a stone higher than for the first of those wins, he ran reasonably well without ever looking likely to score. The Handicapper may have him now. (op 3-1)
Saucy Brown(IRE) has found things more difficult in good company in recent races, but he did reasonably here despite running free early on. (op 10-1)
Spitfire was held up out the back and got slightly hampered at halfway before staying on. He has won on fast ground but seems best on a slightly easier surface and could be one to bear in mind over this trip if getting his conditions. (op 9-1 tchd 8-1)
Beauchamp Viceroy won an all-weather seller over further last time and tried to make this a stiff test, but he could not sustain his effort against this stronger opposition, although his rider reported he lost his action and the vet confirmed he had been struck into. Official explanation: jcokey said gelding lost its action; vet said gelding had been struck into (op 9-1 tchd 10-1)

5026 BATHWICK TYRES EUROPEAN BREEDERS' FUND MAIDEN FILLIES' STKS (DIV II) 6f 8y
4:20 (4:21) (Class 4) 2-Y-O

£4,857 (£1,445; £722; £360) **Stalls** Centre

Form				RPR
3	**1**		**Moonline Dancer (FR)**[14] 4542 2-9-0 0 RichardHughes 7 (R Hannon) *athletic: lw: pressed ldrs: rdn to ld 1f out: hrd rdn and hung bdly lft ins fnl f: rdn out* **11/8**[1]	78
0	**2**	½	**Fardyieh**[15] 4497 2-9-0 0 PhilipRobinson 8 (C E Brittain) *unf: scope: t.k.h: towards rr: hdwy and swtchd rt over 1f out: rdn and styd on fnl f: edgd lft and styd on to chse wnr fnl 100yds but a hld* **9/1**	77+
	3	nk	**If I Were A Boy (IRE)** 2-9-0 0 JamesDoyle 6 (S Kirk) *w'like: lengthy: s.i.s: hld up in rr: hdwy whn sltly hmpd over 1f out: swtchd rt and hdwy ins fnl f: edgd lft and fin wl fnl 100yds* **14/1**	76+
0	**4**	1 ½	**Silent Secret (IRE)**[36] 3820 2-9-0 0 AlanMunro 4 (R Hannon) *str: chsd ldrs: drvn to chal over 1f out: chsd wnr ins fnl f: one pce whn hmpd on far rail fnl 110yds: nt rcvr* **11/1**	72+
0	**5**	¾	**Hill Tribe**[14] 4577 2-8-11 0 MarcHalford(3) 10 (J R Best) *w'like: leggy: sn led: rdn over 2f out: hdd 1f out: wknd ins fnl f* **28/1**	69
	6	2 ½	**Wishbone (IRE)** 2-9-0 0 HayleyTurner 5 (M G Quinlan) *unf: scope: s.i.s: t.k.h in rr: hdwy and nt clr run ins fnl 2f: swtchd lft over 1f out: styng on strly on far rail whn bdly hmpd fnl 110yds: nt rcvr and eased* **8/1**[3]	74+
0	**7**	1 ¾	**Oak Leaves**[12] 4603 2-9-0 0 TPQueally 2 (J G Portman) *w'like: leggy: chsd ldrs: rdn and ev ch fr 2f out tl wknd 1f out* **25/1**	56
	8	¾	**Born A Dancer (IRE)** 2-9-0 0 SebSanders 1 (J W Hills) *angular: bhd most of way* **12/1**	54

9 *5* **Wild Rockette** 2-9-0 0 JamieSpencer 9 39
(B J Meehan) *w'like: scope: bit bkwd: chsd ldrs: rdn 3f out: wknd 2f out* **8/1[3]**

10 *1* **Estonia** 2-9-0 0 TedDurcan 3 36
(J H M Gosden) *str: in tch: chsd ldrs 3f out: btn whn hmpd over 1f out* **11/2[2]**

11 *1 3/4* **Starstreamer (IRE)** 2-9-0 0 EddieAhern 11 31
(M P Tregoning) *w'like: str: s.i.s: a outpcd* **9/1**

1m 14.41s (1.41) **Going Correction** +0.175s/f (Good) **11 Ran SP% 129.7**
Speed ratings (Par 93): **97,96,95,93,92 89,87,86,79,78 75**
toteswingers: 1&2 £7.90, 1&3 £9.10, 2&3 £39.80 CSF £17.02 TOTE £2.50: £1.20, £3.30, £3.90; EX 22.20.
Owner Malih L Al Basti **Bred** S C E A Haras Du Ma **Trained** East Everleigh, Wilts
■ Stewards' Enquiry : Richard Hughes five-day ban: careless riding (Sept 2 -6)

FOCUS
The second division of this fillies' maiden was run 0.16secs slower than the first leg and looked the weaker division judged on future entries. The winner improved on her debut form.

NOTEBOOK
Moonline Dancer(FR) was the exception, though, having Cheveley Park and Fillies' Mile engagements, and having made a promising debut behind one of the leading fancies for next season's 1000 Guineas, Seta, at Newmarket on her debut, was a strong favourite for this. She was always in the leading group and looked set to score readily when going on over a furlong out, but she drifted left under pressure, earning her rider, who failed to change his whip hand, his second suspension of the afternoon, this time five days. This filly does not look like justifying her lofty entries on this evidence. (op 6-4 tchd 7-4)
Fardyieh, a 28,000gns half-sister to a 6f juvenile winner out of a useful 6-7f performer, had shown speed on her debut and built on that by running on late, although whether she would have made the frame but for the interference is questionable. (op 16-1)
If I Were A Boy(IRE) ◆, a 55,000gns daughter of a half-sister to a 1m2f winner in France, from family of Sun Princess and Saddlers' Hall made an encouraging debut. She was out the back until staying on from over a furlong out and finished best of all. She looks capable of going on from this. (tchd 12-1)
Silent Secret(IRE), a 30,000gns half-sister to winners at varying trips out of a smart 7f-1m performer, had started slowly and been well beaten on her debut. She looked the yard's second string on jockey bookings, but was giving her stable companion a race when that rival drifted across her and forced her rider to snatch up inside the final furlong, but for which she would probably have made the placings. (op 12-1 tchd 10-1)
Hill Tribe, a 47,000gns half-sister to winners at 1m-2m2f out of a 1m winning sister to Monsun, had shown early speed on her debut in France and did so again. She looks the sort who can make her mark in handicaps after one more start. (tchd 25-1)
Wishbone(IRE) ◆, a 30,000gns first foal of an unraced half-sister to winners at 7f-1m3f, was very unlucky on this debut as she had settled behind the leaders before making a forward move to the outside of the Hannon pair entering the final furlong. She was not done with when the winner carried the fourth across in front of her and squeezed her against the rails, otherwise she may well have been placed. She is clearly better than the official result indicates and, if none the worse, can gain compensation before long. (op 12-1)
Estonia was the main market rival to the winner, but weakened in the closing stages having shown signs of ability. (op 6-1 tchd 13-2)

5027 MIRAGE SIGNS H'CAP 1m 2f 6y
4:55 (4:55) (Class 4) (0-85,84) 3-Y-O **£4,857** (£1,445; £722; £360) **Stalls Low**

Form RPR

1310 **1** *nk* **Geneva Geyser (GER)**[16] 4455 3-9-7 **84** MickyFenton 4 88
(J M P Eustace) *swtg: led: rdn 3f out: narrowly hdd ins fnl 2f: styd chalng wnr and upsides thrght fnl f: no ex cl home: fin 2nd, nk: subs. awrdd r* **6/1**

4-24 **2** *hd* **Woodlark Island (IRE)**[133] 1130 3-8-9 **72** (v[1]) HayleyTurner 6 76
(M P Tregoning) *s.i.s: hld up in rr: pushed along and hdwy fr over 2f out: clsd on ldng duo fnl f but nvr quite get up: fin 3rd, nk & hd: plcd 2nd* **7/1**

4241 **3** *4 1/2* **Mykingdomforahorse**[3] 4918 3-8-11 **74** 6ex RichardHughes 2 70
(M R Channon) *lw: hld up in rr: sltly hmpd: rdn and outpcd over 3f out: rdn and styd on fr 2f out: nvr rch ldrs: wknd fnl f: fin 4th, plcd 3rd* **2/1[2]**

-106 **4** *2 1/4* **Natural Flair (USA)**[14] 4520 3-9-3 **80** AlanMunro 1 71
(P W Chapple-Hyam) *chsd ldrs: rdn and edgd lft over 3f out: wknd 2f out fin 5th, plcd 4th* **11/2[3]**

-113 **D** **Larkham (USA)**[43] 3578 3-9-6 **83** SebSanders 3 88
(R M Beckett) *trckd ldr: rdn to take narrow advantage ins fnl 2f: styd on u.p whn strly chal thrght fnl f: kpt on dourly: fin 1st, nk: subs. disq.* **13/8[1]**

2m 6.18s (-2.62) **Going Correction** -0.025s/f (Good) **5 Ran SP% 113.6**
Speed ratings (Par 102): **108,108,105,103,109**
CSF £11.98 TOTE £2.30: £1.50, £2.70; EX 14.30.
Owner J C Smith **Bred** Graf And Grafin Von Stauffenberg **Trained** Newmarket, Suffolk
■ Stewards' Enquiry : Hayley Turner one-day ban: used whip with excessive frequency (Aug 29)

FOCUS
A fair handicap and quite interesting despite the small field, and it produced a good finish. The pace was sound. Larkham was subsequently disqualified - prohibited substance in sample.

5028 UK HYGIENE LADIES DERBY H'CAP (FOR LADY AMATEUR RIDERS) 1m 4f 5y
5:25 (5:25) (Class 4) (0-80,80) 3-Y-O+ **£4,996** (£1,549; £774; £387) **Stalls Low**

Form RPR

4225 **1** **Just Like Silk (USA)**[29] 4058 3-9-11 **78** (t) MissSBrotherton 12 93+
(G A Butler) *lw: trckd ldrs: led over 2f out: c clr fnl f: comf* **7/2[2]**

2233 **2** *4* **Safebreaker**[10] 4658 4-9-11 **67** (p) MsKWalsh 11 73
(K A Ryan) *rr: hdwy over 3f out: styd on u.p fr 2f out to chse wnr fnl f but nvr any ch* **6/1[3]**

3034 **3** *nk* **Wiggy Smith**[23] 4247 10-10-10 **80** MissEJJones 5 85
(H Candy) *in rr: hdwy over 2f out: rdn and styd on to go 3rd ins fnl f: kpt on to press for 2nd cl home but no ch w wnr* **17/2**

313 **4** *nk* **Funday**[30] 4008 3-9-7 **79** MissHayleyMoore[(5)] 10 84+
(G L Moore) *lw: plld hrd: led 2f: styd chsng ldrs: pushed along over 2f out: styd on fnl f but nvr anywhere nr wnr* **3/1[1]**

6320 **5** *2* **Ovthenight (IRE)**[22] 3169 4-9-8 **64** (v) MissGAndrews 14 66
(Mrs P Sly) *t.k.h: led after 2f: hdd over 2f out: wknd appr fnl f* **13/2**

-111 **6** *1 1/4* **Norman The Great**[37] 3768 5-10-5 **80** RachelKing[(5)] 7 80
(A King) *hld up in rr: hdwy 3f out: swtchd rt to outside over 2f out: kpt on same pce* **13/2**

2403 **7** *13* **I'm In The Pink (FR)**[13] 4561 5-10-0 **70** MissEFolkes 9 49
(P D Evans) *s.i.s: t.k.h and sn chsng ldrs: rdn and ev ch over 2f out: wknd over 1f out* **10/1**

4021 **8** *2 1/2* **Maslak (IRE)**[12] 4602 5-10-5 **75** MissLHorner 6 50
(P W Hiatt) *rr: t.k.h: hdwy on ins over 3f out to chse ldrs over 2f out: sn wknd* **10/1**

443/ **9** *8* **Brads House (IRE)**[925] 6006 7-10-0 **75** MissSallyRandell[(5)] 4 37
(J G M O'Shea) *s.i.s: hld up in rr and a bhd* **20/1**

6/00 **10** *7* **Lady Romanov (IRE)**[13] 4563 6-9-9 **70** oh5 ow9 (p) MissMBryant[(5)] 8 21
(P Butler) *in tch: rdn to chse ldrs fr 3f out: hung lft and wknd 2f out* **33/1**

343/ **11** *1 1/4* **Misbehaviour**[27] 6797 10-9-2 **61** oh16 (p) MissZoeLilly[(3)] 3 10
(P Butler) *chsd ldrs over 1m* **33/1**

-005 **12** *3/4* **Zaif (IRE)**[10] 4644 6-9-9 **65** MissFayeBramley 13 13
(D J S Ffrench Davis) *ken hold: chsd ldrs 1m* **22/1**

000/ **13** *67* **Rocket (IRE)**[1034] 6019 8-9-0 **61** oh16 MissAWallace[(5)] 1 —
(H J Manners) *bhd fr 1/2-way: t.o fnl 2f* **66/1**

2m 35.92s (0.42) **Going Correction** -0.025s/f (Good)
WFA 3 from 4yo+ 11lb **13 Ran SP% 133.4**
Speed ratings (Par 105): **97,94,94,93,92 91,83,81,76,71 70,70,25**
toteswingers: 1&2 £8.90, 1&3 £12.70, 2&3 £15.50 CSF £26.82 CT £180.98 TOTE £4.80: £1.90, £2.70, £3.20; EX 42.80 Place 6: £154.29 Place 5: £33.65 .
Owner Future In Mind Partnership **Bred** Swettenham Stud **Trained** Newmarket, Suffolk

FOCUS
The usual mixed bag in this handicap for lady amateur riders. The early pace was steadier than normal for this sort of contest but they still finished fairly strung out. The form is rated round the second and third.
Maslak(IRE) Official explanation: jockey said gelding had been struck into
T/Plt: £328.50 to a £1 stake. Pool: £84,903.22. 188.66 winning tickets. T/Qpdt: £32.60 to a £1 stake. Pool: £6,241.20. 141.65 winning tickets. ST

5000 NEWMARKET (R-H)
Saturday, August 15

OFFICIAL GOING: Good to firm (good in places)
Wind: Fresh across Weather: Cloudy with sunny spells

5029 EBF BUY A RACING POST YEARLING BONUS CANDIDATE MAIDEN STKS 6f
1:50 (1:50) (Class 4) 2-Y-O **£5,180** (£1,541; £770; £384) **Stalls High**

Form RPR

3242 **1** **Arabian Pride**[15] 4497 2-9-3 **80** JoeFanning 7 80
(D M Simcock) *mde all: shkn up and edgd rt over 1f out: rdn out* **7/1[2]**

2230 **2** *1/2* **Rakaan (IRE)**[15] 4487 2-9-3 **102** RHills 1 79
(B J Meehan) *a.p: chsd wnr over 2f out: rdn and edgd rt over 1f out: r.o* **1/2[1]**

3 *3 1/2* **Granite Girl** 2-8-9 0 AndreaAtzeni[(3)] 6 63
(P J McBride) *prom: rdn over 2f out: styd on same pce fnl f* **50/1**

0 **4** *4* **Gabriel's Spirit (IRE)**[15] 4497 2-9-3 0 LPKeniry 4 56
(Miss Amy Weaver) *chsd wnr over 3f: sn rdn: wknd fnl f* **100/1**

5 *1* **Engulf (IRE)** 2-9-3 0 TonyCulhane 10 56+
(W J Haggas) *s.s: hld up: hdwy over 1f out: nt trble ldrs* **7/1[2]**

6 *1* **Broughtons Day** 2-9-3 0 ChrisCatlin 3 50
(W J Musson) *s.i.s: hld up: rdn over 2f out: bmpd and swvd lft 1f out: n.d* **100/1**

7 *2 1/4* **No Complaining (IRE)** 2-8-12 0 JimmyQuinn 8 38
(B J Curley) *chsd ldrs: pushed along 1/2-way: wkng whn hung lft 1f out* **33/1**

00 **8** *1 1/4* **Gessabelle**[22] 4272 2-8-5 0 (t) CarolineKelly[(7)] 9 35
(P S McEntee) *prom: rdn over 2f out: wkng whn hung lft over 1f out* **200/1**

9 *1 1/4* **Saladin's Vow (USA)** 2-9-3 0 JimCrowley 5 36
(G A Butler) *hld up: rdn over 2f out: hung lft over 1f out: a in rr* **25/1**

10 *1/2* **Tenga Venga** 2-9-3 0 AdamKirby 2 34
(P S McEntee) *stdd s: hld up: plld hrd: a in rr* **80/1**

11 *1 3/4* **Edinburgh Knight (IRE)** 2-9-3 0 DarryllHolland 11 29
(P W D'Arcy) *hld up: hdwy over 2f out: hung lft over 1f out: sn wknd* **15/2[3]**

1m 14.82s (2.32) **Going Correction** +0.05s/f (Good) **11 Ran SP% 115.9**
Speed ratings (Par 96): **86,85,80,75,74 72,69,68,66,65 63**
toteswingers: 1&2 £1.10, 1&3 £12.60, 2&3 £9.20 CSF £10.60 TOTE £9.50: £2.20, £1.02, £10.40; EX 14.40.
Owner Ahmad Al Shaikh **Bred** Whitsbury Manor Stud **Trained** Newmarket, Suffolk
■ Stewards' Enquiry : Caroline Kelly one-day ban: careless riding (Aug 29)

FOCUS
Not the most competitive of Newmarket maidens, but still a fascinating contest, with a couple with proven ability up against a couple of interesting newcomers. Experience gained the day, with the pair who had each run four times pulling clear, but still not the result most would have expected, with the odds-on favourite getting turned over. The winner is rated to form.

NOTEBOOK
Arabian Pride, who had made the frame in all four of his previous starts including when runner-up over course and distance last time, had 22lb to find with Rakaan on official ratings, but he was given a copybook front-running ride by Joe Fanning, who judged the fractions perfectly and the colt kept pulling out a bit more when the favourite came to challenge. He may go for the Tattersalls Timeform Million Sprint on the Rowley Mile next month. (op 13-2 tchd 6-1)
Rakaan(IRE), disappointing in the Richmond Stakes at Goodwood following his cracking effort behind Canford Cliffs and Xtension in the Coventry, seemed to have been found a golden opportunity. He raced prominently on the outside of the field and looked dangerous when asked for his effort entering the last two furlongs, but he could never get to the winner and was always being held in the run to the line. It looks a case of back to the drawing board, and with an official mark of 102 he is going to remain hard to place. (op 8-15 tchd 4-7)
Granite Girl, a 2,000gns half-sister to a winner in Greece, was never far away and ran on again to finish third after appearing to get outpaced. She should be found easier opportunities. (tchd 40-1)
Gabriel's Spirit(IRE)'s proximity, having finished last of 11 on his debut here last month, probably doesn't do much for those who finished behind him. (op 150-1 tchd 80-1)
Engulf(IRE) ◆ was very slowly away but was noted staying on late without being by any means knocked about. A 260,000-euros colt out of a winning half-sister to the high-class Highdown, he is entered in the Dewhurst and Racing Post Trophy and will appreciate stepping up in trip. (op 15-2 tchd 8-1)

5030 SKYSPORTS.COM/SUPER 6 FREE TO ENTER H'CAP 1m
2:20 (2:20) (Class 4) (0-85,82) 3-Y-O **£6,476** (£1,927; £963; £481) **Stalls High**

Form RPR

312 **1** **Negotiation (IRE)**[17] 4440 3-9-8 **81** RichardMullen 5 90+
(J H M Gosden) *s.i.s: hld up in tch: racd keenly: rdn over 1f out: r.o to ld nr fin* **5/1[3]**

1 **2** *nk* **Russian Jar (IRE)**[82] 2338 3-9-9 **82** GeorgeBaker 1 90
(M A Jarvis) *hld up: plld hrd: hdwy and n.m.r over 2f out: rdn to ld and hung lft over 1f out: hdd nr fin* **7/1**

1064 **3** *1/2* **Everynight (IRE)**[65] 2855 3-9-4 **80** AndreaAtzeni[(3)] 6 87
(M Botti) *led: rdn: hung rt and hdd over 1f out: hung lft ins fnl f: styd on* **4/1[2]**

11 **4** *4* **Paquerettza (FR)**[22] 4275 3-9-6 **79** DarryllHolland 2 76
(D H Brown) *chsd ldrs: rdn over 3f out: wknd ins fnl f* **4/1[2]**

2-1 **5** *4 1/2* **Suba (USA)**[73] 2607 3-9-7 **80** RHills 3 67
(L M Cumani) *chsd ldr: rdn and ev ch wl over 1f out: sn edgd lft and wknd* **7/2[1]**

15 **6** 3/4 **Adoring (IRE)**[21] 4317 3-9-9 **82** ... LiamJones 4 67
(W J Haggas) *chsd ldrs: rdn over 2f out: wknd over 1f out* **7/1**

01 **7** 7 **The Happy Hammer (IRE)**[17] 4440 3-8-4 **63** ... ChrisCatlin 7 31
(E V Stanford) *chsd ldrs: rdn over 2f out: wknd over 1f out* **10/1**

1m 39.96s (-0.04) **Going Correction** +0.05s/f (Good) **7** Ran SP% **113.0**
Speed ratings (Par 102): **102,101,101,97,92 91,84**
toteswingers: 1&2 £2.10, 1&3 £4.20, 2&3 £5.60 CSF £37.93 TOTE £7.30: £3.50, £3.00; EX 44.00 TRIFECTA Not won..
Owner H R H Princess Haya Of Jordan **Bred** Loughbrown Stud **Trained** Newmarket, Suffolk

FOCUS
A decent little handicap and although the stalls were against the stands' rail, the runners gradually made their way to race towards the far side of the track. The early pace was ordinary which caused a couple to take a hold but the form rates worth treating at face value with the third the best guide to the form.

5031 WIN £100,000 WITH SOCCER SATURDAY SUPER 6 H'CAP (FOR GREY HORSES ONLY) 6f

2:50 (2:52) (Class 4) (0-85,85) 3-Y-0+
£12,462 (£3,732; £1,866; £934; £466; £234) **Stalls** High

Form RPR

5210 **1** **Sarah's Art (IRE)**[12] 4607 6-8-7 **68** ... (t) JimCrowley 6 77
(Stef Liddiard) *hld up: hdwy over 1f out: rdn to ld ins fnl f: r.o* **8/1**[3]

1062 **2** 1/2 **Zowington**[8] 4761 7-9-6 **84** ... (v) WilliamCarson(3) 9 91
(S C Williams) *chsd ldr: rdn and edgd rt over 1f out: ev ch ins fnl f: styd on* **8/1**[3]

2040 **3** 1/2 **Billberry**[15] 4502 4-7-10 **60** ... (t) AndreaAtzeni(3) 5 65
(S C Williams) *s.i.s: hld up: hdwy over 1f out: sn rdn: r.o* **16/1**

0353 **4** 1 **Nickel Silver**[8] 4753 4-9-1 **76** ... (b) TomEaves 14 78
(B Smart) *chsd ldr tl led over 4f out: rdn over 1f out: hdd and unable qckn ins fnl f* **12/1**

1-05 **5** 1 **Cara's Request (AUS)**[58] 3055 4-9-4 **79** ... JoeFanning 11 78
(D Nicholls) *led: hdd over 4f out: chsd ldr tl rdn and edgd rt over 1f out: styd on same pce ins fnl f* **11/1**

5-5 **6** 1 **Berbice (IRE)**[10] 4680 4-8-7 **68** ... (p) PatDobbs 1 64
(S Donohoe, Ire) *hld up: swtchd rt and hdwy over 1f out: r.o: nt rch ldrs* **8/1**[3]

00-2 **7** nk **Witchry**[17] 4428 7-8-3 **64** ... JimmyQuinn 7 59
(A G Newcombe) *plld hrd and prom: rdn over 1f out: styd on same pce* **12/1**

6-60 **8** 1 1/4 **Isabella Romee (IRE)**[28] 4097 3-7-9 **65** oh9 ow2(p)
Louis-PhilippeBeuzelin(5) 12 56
(Jane Chapple-Hyam) *chsd ldrs: outpcd 2f out: sn hung rt: r.o towards fin* **50/1**

2244 **9** hd **Hits Only Jude (IRE)**[10] 4662 6-8-6 **67** ... RichardMullen 13 57
(D Carroll) *chsd ldrs: rdn over 2f out: no ex fnl f* **16/1**

0321 **10** 1/2 **Medici Time**[7] 4783 4-8-8 **69** ... (v) GrahamGibbons 17 58
(T D Easterby) *chsd ldrs: rdn over 2f out: no ex fnl f* **5/1**[1]

4503 **11** nk **Star Strider**[8] 4732 5-7-9 **59** oh5 ... (v[1]) DavidProbert(3) 8 47
(Miss Gay Kelleway) *hld up: plld hrd: rdn over 1f out: n.d* **22/1**

3400 **12** 3 1/2 **Grey Boy (GER)**[15] 4501 8-8-5 **66** ... LiamJones 3 42
(A W Carroll) *prom: rdn over 2f out: wknd over 1f out* **22/1**

0-40 **13** 3 1/4 **Kingsgate Storm (IRE)**[14] 4535 3-8-3 **68** ... ChrisCatlin 2 34
(J R Best) *mid-div: lost pl 1/2-way: no ch whn edgd lft over 1f out* **40/1**

2366 **14** 1/2 **Finsbury**[16] 4466 6-7-12 **62** ow3 ... (v[1]) KellyHarrison(3) 15 26
(J S Goldie) *s.i.s: hld up: a in rr* **15/2**[2]

6300 **15** 1 1/2 **Mogok Ruby**[61] 2980 5-9-0 **75** ... LPKeniry 4 35
(L Montague Hall) *s.i.s: hld up: a in rr* **33/1**

60-2 **16** 11 **Sir Edwin Landseer (USA)**[54] 3212 9-9-10 **85** ... GeorgeBaker 16 9
(G L Moore) *hld up in tch: rdn over 2f out: wknd and eased over 1f out* **9/1**

1m 12.3s (-0.20) **Going Correction** +0.05s/f (Good)
WFA 3 from 4yo+ 4lb **16** Ran SP% **123.3**
Speed ratings (Par 105): **103,102,101,100,99 97,97,95,95,94 94,89,85,84,82 67**
toteswingers: 1&2 £13.60, 1&3 £43.50, 2&3 £49.10 CSF £67.50 CT £1022.06 TOTE £7.90: £1.70, £2.20, £4.40, £2.50; EX 71.10.
Owner ownaracehorse.co.uk (Shefford) **Bred** Newtownbarry House Stud **Trained** Great Shefford, Berks

FOCUS
The biggest field ever assembled for this unique contest in its seven-year history. The field tended to race down the centre of the track for most of the way and the runner-up looks the best guide to the form.
Sir Edwin Landseer(USA) Official explanation: jockey said gelding was never travelling

5032 SKYBET.COM FOR ALL YOUR FOOTBALL BETTING STKS (HERITAGE H'CAP) 6f

3:25 (3:27) (Class 2) (0-105,105) 3-Y-0
£24,924 (£7,464; £3,732; £1,868; £932; £468) **Stalls** High

Form RPR

1-31 **1** **Bounty Box**[28] 4096 3-8-2 **86** ow1 ... ChrisCatlin 3 95
(C F Wall) *hld up in tch: led over 1f out: rdn and edgd lft ins fnl f: r.o* **11/4**[1]

0-05 **2** nk **Sea Of Leaves (USA)**[26] 4135 3-8-1 **88** ... KellyHarrison(3) 1 96
(J S Goldie) *hld up: hdwy over 1f out: rdn and ev ch ins fnl f: r.o* **14/1**

4203 **3** nk **Able Master (IRE)**[7] 4771 3-8-8 **92** ... JimCrowley 2 99
(B Smart) *mid-div: hdwy over 2f out: rdn and ev ch ins fnl f: styd on* **16/1**

4434 **4** 1 3/4 **Five Star Junior (USA)**[7] 4771 3-8-9 **93** ... DarryllHolland 10 94
(Mrs L Stubbs) *hld up: hdwy over 1f out: rdn and ev ch ins fnl f: no ex towards fin* **17/2**

055- **5** 3/4 **Jet D'Eau (FR)**[334] 5987 3-9-1 **99** ... (b) GeorgeBaker 8 98
(G L Moore) *hld up: rdn over 2f out: r.o wl ins fnl f: nt rch ldrs* **33/1**

0620 **6** 1/2 **Desert Icon (IRE)**[29] 4044 3-7-11 **84** ... DavidProbert(3) 16 81
(W J Knight) *chsd ldrs: led 2f out: hung lft and hdd over 1f out: styd on same pce ins fnl f* **20/1**

2-56 **7** 3/4 **Bonnie Charlie**[29] 4052 3-9-4 **102** ... PatDobbs 13 97+
(R Hannon) *hmpd s: hld up: nt clr run over 1f out: r.o ins fnl f: nvr nrr* **16/1**

6130 **8** 1 **Enderby Spirit (GR)**[14] 4523 3-9-7 **105** ... TomEaves 5 97
(B Smart) *chsd ldrs: rdn over 2f out: hmpd over 1f out: styd on same pce* **8/1**[3]

644 **9** nk **Brenin Taran**[36] 3806 3-7-13 **86** ... AndreaAtzeni(3) 4 77
(D M Simcock) *hld up: hdwy 1/2-way: rdn over 1f out: no ex ins fnl f* **20/1**

4000 **10** 3/4 **Aldermoor (USA)**[21] 4330 3-8-8 **92** ... (t) SaleemGolam 12 80
(S C Williams) *prom: rdn over 2f out: wknd ins fnl f* **20/1**

-116 **11** 1 1/2 **Sioux Rising (IRE)**[35] 3839 3-7-13 **83** ... JimmyQuinn 15 67+
(R A Fahey) *hld up: rdn over 2f out: n.d* **14/1**

4031 **12** 3/4 **Noverre To Go (IRE)**[7] 4771 3-8-10 **94** ... (t) RichardKingscote 11 75
(Tom Dascombe) *chsd ldrs: rdn whn hmpd over 1f out: sn wknd* **7/1**[2]

1600 **13** hd **Jobe (USA)**[16] 4459 3-8-8 **92** ... RobertWinston 9 73
(K A Ryan) *led 5f out: rdn and hdd 2f out: edgd rt and hmpd over 1f out: wknd ins fnl f* **25/1**

5123 **14** 1/2 **Satwa Street (IRE)**[20] 4338 3-7-5 **82** ... JosephineBruning(7) 6 61
(D M Simcock) *plld hrd: led: hdd 5f out: chsd ldrs: rdn over 1f out: wknd fnl f* **33/1**

0030 **15** 2 **Proclaim**[7] 4771 3-8-11 **95** ... (b) JoeFanning 14 68
(M Johnston) *edgd lft s: hld up: hdwy over 2f out: rdn and wknd over 1f out* **14/1**

166- **16** 7 **Frognal (IRE)**[288] 7109 3-8-7 **91** ... RobertHavlin 17 41
(B J Meehan) *hld up: effrt over 2f out: wknd over 1f out* **33/1**

1m 11.44s (-1.06) **Going Correction** +0.05s/f (Good) **16** Ran SP% **119.5**
Speed ratings (Par 106): **109,108,108,105,104 104,103,101,101,100 98,97,97,96,93 84**
toteswingers: 1&2 £9.00, 1&3 £11.30, 2&3 £28.60 CSF £37.03 CT £406.76 TOTE £3.60: £1.50, £3.40, £3.70, £2.50; EX 57.10 Trifecta £433.70 Pool: £586.20 - 1.00 winning units..
Owner John E Sims **Bred** Farmers Hill Stud **Trained** Newmarket, Suffolk

FOCUS
A red-hot three-year-old sprint handicap taken by the recent Group 1 winner King's Apostle two years ago. The field raced centre to far side and those closest to the inside rail appeared to hold a significant advantage, with the first three home starting from the three lowest stalls. The winning time was 0.86sec faster than the older horses in the preceding greys' race, so the form looks reasonable, although the draw played its part which limits confidence.

NOTEBOOK
Bounty Box ◆, one of the least exposed in the field, was 8lb higher, including the 1lb overweight, than when winning a fillies' handicap over course and distance last month. Having tracked the leaders, she hit the front a furlong out and then showed a good attitude to hold on up the hill. She is likely to go for a fillies' handicap on the Rowley Mile in early October and, if that goes well, could step up to Listed company. (tchd 3-1)
Sea Of Leaves(USA) ◆, an eyecatching fifth on her second start for the yard at Ayr last time, was held up towards the far side of the field but finished well and on this evidence she should do well for her new stable. (op 11-1)
Able Master(IRE), who was returning from a short break when third behind Noverre To Go at Ascot the previous week, had a 6lb pull and managed to turn the form around. Another to stay on well up the final climb, he is knocking on the door. (tchd 14-1)
Five Star Junior(USA), closely matched with a few of these on recent form, was held up from his double-figure draw but delivered his effort up the far rail, which would have helped him given the way the race panned out. He has held his form well since completing a four-timer on Polytrack at the start of the year and deserves to break his duck on turf. (op 10-1)
Jet D'Eau(FR) ◆, a decent two-year-old in France but making her debut for her yard after 11 months off, was an eyecatcher, as she made good late headway towards the nearside of the track well away from where the main action was unfolding. Her stable knows the time of day and will surely find the right opportunity for her. (op 66-1)
Desert Icon(IRE), who ran too badly to be true off 9lb lower at Haydock last time following his cracking effort in a hot handicap at the July meeting, ran much better here, especially as he was drawn on the nearside. However, although he showed to the fore for a long way, he did show an awkward head carriage under pressure and all still may not be quite right with him. Official explanation: jockey said gelding hung left
Bonnie Charlie, placed three times in Group company at two, had been very disappointing in his first two starts of this year and never threatened here, but he was racing on the wrong side of the track as things turned out, so this effort shouldn't be held against him.
Enderby Spirit(GR), not disgraced when tenth in the Stewards' Cup last time, was 4lb higher here. He had every chance and was racing on the favoured part of the track, so can have few excuses and it may be that he is now held off a 7lb higher mark than for his latest win. (op 9-1 tchd 10-1)
Noverre To Go(IRE) Official explanation: jockey said colt ran flat
Jobe(USA) Official explanation: jockey said gelding moved poorly

5033 OH NO RICHARD O'NEILL'S GETTING HITCHED NURSERY 5f

4:00 (4:00) (Class 4) 2-Y-O **£5,180** (£1,541; £770; £384) **Stalls** High

Form RPR

3351 **1** **Mister Hughie (IRE)**[9] 4689 2-8-10 **70** ... TonyCulhane 1 81
(M R Channon) *s.i.s: hld up: swtchd rt and hdwy over 1f out: rdn to ld and hung lft ins fnl f: r.o wl* **8/1**[3]

0210 **2** 2 **Six Diamonds**[14] 4539 2-8-11 **71** ... RobertWinston 10 75
(H Morrison) *chsd ldrs: led 2f out: rdn: hung lft and hdd ins fnl f: styd on same pce* **8/1**[3]

3345 **3** 1 **Val C**[14] 4537 2-8-5 **65** ... ChrisCatlin 2 65
(N P Littmoden) *chsd ldrs: rdn and ev ch over 1f out: styd on same pce ins fnl f* **10/1**

4210 **4** 3/4 **White Daffodil (IRE)**[48] 3430 2-8-10 **70** ... PatDobbs 3 68
(R Hannon) *hld up: hdwy over 1f out: sn rdn: no ex towards fin* **14/1**

053 **5** 1/2 **Rockabilly Rebel**[23] 4243 2-8-8 **68** ... RHills 9 64
(B W Hills) *s.i.s: hld up: hdwy 1/2-way: rdn over 1f out: edgd lft and styd on same pce fnl f* **4/1**[2]

3631 **6** nk **Radio City**[10] 4639 2-9-0 **74** ... JimCrowley 4 69
(R M Beckett) *hld up: hdwy over 1f out: sn edgd rt: no ex ins fnl f* **11/1**

2010 **7** 3 1/4 **Mijas Playa**[14] 4547 2-9-4 **81** ... DavidProbert(3) 12 64
(C A Dwyer) *chsd ldrs: rdn over 1f out: wknd fnl f* **14/1**

110 **8** 1 1/2 **Mahiki**[4] 4868 2-8-11 **71** ... DarryllHolland 6 49
(S A Callaghan) *hld up: hdwy and nt clr run over 1f out: n.d* **25/1**

41 **9** 1/2 **Electioneer (USA)**[42] 3606 2-9-2 **76** ... JoeFanning 5 52
(M Johnston) *rrd in stalls: chsd ldrs: rdn over 2f out: wknd fnl f* **2/1**[1]

6140 **10** 2 1/4 **Danzoe (IRE)**[21] 4327 2-9-4 **78** ... JimmyQuinn 8 46
(D Donovan) *chsd ldrs tl rdn and wknd over 1f out* **33/1**

061 **11** 6 **Royal Blade (IRE)**[19] 4379 2-8-13 **73** ... RichardMullen 7 19
(A P Jarvis) *led 3f: hung lft: wknd and eased over 1f out* **20/1**

59.10 secs **Going Correction** +0.05s/f (Good) **11** Ran SP% **117.9**
Speed ratings (Par 96): **102,98,97,96,95 94,89,87,86,82 73**
toteswingers: 1&2 £21.80, 1&3 £29.00, 2&3 £29.30 CSF £68.91 CT £665.73 TOTE £11.70: £3.40, £2.60, £4.80; EX 98.40.
Owner Liam Mulryan **Bred** Mcmac Syndicate **Trained** West Ilsley, Berks

FOCUS
A competitive nursery and again they raced up the centre of the track, but this time the bias towards the far side didn't materialise as although the winner was drawn in stall one, he made his effort closest to the stands' rail. Pretty sound form.

NOTEBOOK
Mister Hughie(IRE), making his nursery debut after narrowly winning a Bath seller with a little bit in hand nine days earlier, had obviously had his confidence boosted by that success. Tucked in from his low draw, he responded well to pressure when asked to make his effort on the nearside of the field and quickened up well up the hill. He should continue to do well in races like this and the hat-trick must be a possibility. (op 12-1)
Six Diamonds, who failed to see out the extra furlong in a stronger fillies' nursery here last time, raced closer to the pace than the winner and hit the front a furlong out, but although she battled back once headed, she couldn't hold off the colt. (op 12-1)

Val C, well beaten on Polytrack last time but only just over a length behind Radio City in a Sandown nursery before that, was 9lb better off with that rival here. She was never far off the pace towards the far side of the field and, although she remains a maiden after six attempts, she looks to have a small race in her. (op 12-1 tchd 16-1)

White Daffodil(IRE), a disappointing last of seven in a Windsor conditions event last time, was making her nursery debut and she threatened to get involved when asked for her effort up the far rail, but she couldn't maintain it. (op 12-1 tchd 10-1)

Rockabilly Rebel, who has been improving with each outing and split a couple of subsequent winners when third dropped to this trip at Sandown last month, stayed on from off the pace but was never getting there and he may need a return to 6f when ridden this way. (op 7-2)

Radio City, put up 5lb for his recent narrow Brighton success, had every chance and now looks to be in the Handicapper's grip. (op 9-1 tchd 12-1)

Mahiki, well beaten on the turning Lingfield Polytrack four days earlier following two victories over the straight 5f on the Southwell Fibresand, was keen early, but she was just starting to stay on when badly hampered over a furlong from home. It's debatable how much closer she would have been otherwise, but she may be worth another chance. (op 20-1 tchd 16-1)

Electioneer(USA), the least exposed in the field and making his nursery debut after winning a Beverley maiden last month that has worked out only fairly since, raced close to the pace early, but he received a reminder at halfway and was soon beaten. He has plenty to prove. Official explanation: jockey said colt was never travelling (tchd 7-4)

Royal Blade(IRE) Official explanation: jockey said colt lost its action

5034 NEWMARKETRACECOURSES.CO.UK H'CAP — 1m 4f

4:35 (4:35) (Class 4) (0-85,84) 3-Y-O+ — **£5,180** (£1,541; £770; £384) **Stalls** Centre

Form	Pos	Dist	Horse / Details	Jockey	RPR
3315	1		**Times Up**[14] 4518 3-9-4 **84** (J L Dunlop) *chsd ldrs: rdn and carried lft fr over 1f out tl swtchd rt ins fnl f: r.o u.p to ld post* **7/2**[2]	JimCrowley 6	95+
11-0	2	½	**Alcalde**[14] 4518 3-9-2 **82** (M Johnston) *led: rdn and hung lft fr over 1f out: hdd post* **3/1**[1]	JoeFanning 3	90
-411	3	1¾	**Turjuman (USA)**[40] 3697 4-8-11 **66** (W J Musson) *hld up: hdwy u.p over 1f out: nt rch ldrs* **7/2**[2]	ChrisCatlin 4	71+
3215	4	1¾	**Dazzling Light (UAE)**[52] 3266 4-9-9 **78** (J S Goldie) *hld up: hdwy over 3f out: rdn whn hmpd over 1f out: styd on same pce* **8/1**	DanielTudhope 9	80
10-0	5	nk	**Brave Mave**[201] 299 4-9-0 **72** (W Jarvis) *chsd ldr: rdn over 1f out: styd on same pce* **25/1**	AndreaAtzeni(3) 10	74
6403	6	1¾	**Force Group (IRE)**[14] 4544 5-9-1 **70** (M H Tompkins) *prom: rdn over 1f out: styd on same pce* **10/1**	SaleemGolam 8	69
-030	7	1	**Holden Eagle**[63] 2932 4-9-5 **74** (A G Newcombe) *prom: rdn over 2f out: styd on same pce appr fnl f* **25/1**	RichardMullen 7	72
2324	8	1¾	**Saloon (USA)**[28] 4098 5-9-0 **74** (Jane Chapple-Hyam) *swtchd rt sn after s: hld up: hdwy over 2f out: rdn and wknd over 1f out* **9/1**	(p) Louis-PhilippeBeuzelin(5) 2	69
2116	9	2	**Sir Boss (IRE)**[14] 4544 4-10-0 **83** (D E Cantillon) *hld up: rdn over 1f out: a in rr* **7/1**[3]	LPKeniry 5	75
105	10	5	**Miss Christophene (IRE)**[7] 4799 3-8-4 **70** (Mrs S Lyman) *hld up: rdn over 2f out: sn wknd* **25/1**	JimmyQuinn 11	54

2m 31.85s (-1.05) **Going Correction** +0.05s/f (Good)
WFA 3 from 4yo+ 11lb — **10** Ran SP% **123.7**
Speed ratings (Par 105): **105,104,103,102,102 100,100,99,97,94**
toteswingers: 1&2 £5.00, 1&3 £2.90, 2&3 £4.40 CSF £15.13 CT £38.82 TOTE £4.60: £1.60, £1.80, £1.50; EX 18.40.
Owner Mrs I H Stewart-Brown & M J Meacock **Bred** I Stewart-Brown And M Meacock **Trained** Arundel, W Sussex

FOCUS

An ordinary middle-distance handicap and in a race in which the early pace was only modest, the front pair were at the sharp end throughout and the form is best rated around the fourth and fifth. The field came up the centre of the track on reaching the home straight.

Alcalde Official explanation: jockey said colt hung badly left

5035 CHRIS WOTTON CUP (H'CAP) — 1m 2f

5:10 (5:15) (Class 5) (0-70,69) 3-Y-O+ — **£3,885** (£1,156; £577; £288) **Stalls** Centre

Form	Pos	Dist	Horse / Details	Jockey	RPR
561	1		**Lord Theo**[8] 4759 5-10-0 **69** (N P Littmoden) *a.p: led over 1f out: edgd lft and rdn clr* **10/1**	RobertHavlin 12	85
550	2	6	**Fantino**[22] 4284 3-8-10 **63** (J Mackie) *chsd ldrs: rdn over 1f out: styd on same pce* **8/1**	DavidProbert(3) 13	67
4020	3	¾	**Tevez**[1] 5003 4-9-5 **63** (D Donovan) *rn wout declared tongue strap: hld up: hdwy over 1f out: no imp fnl f* **14/1**	AndreaAtzeni(3) 1	65
2016	4	1¾	**Fisadara**[9] 4722 3-8-8 **63** (Jane Chapple-Hyam) *led 9f out: rdn: hung rt and hdd over 1f out: wknd fnl f* **25/1**	Louis-PhilippeBeuzelin(5) 5	62
6624	5	¾	**Incendo**[14] 4545 3-9-3 **67** (J R Fanshawe) *hld up in tch: rdn over 1f out: wknd fnl f* **13/2**[2]	GeorgeBaker 7	64
4203	6	¾	**Apotheosis**[19] 4378 4-9-10 **65** (W R Swinburn) *led 1f: chsd ldr: rdn over 1f out: wknd fnl f* **8/1**	AdamKirby 18	61
6-40	7	1¾	**Hannicean**[42] 3635 5-10-0 **69** (R W Price) *prom: rdn and wknd over 1f out* **25/1**	TomEaves 3	61
3346	8	½	**Watson's Bay**[9] 4696 4-9-11 **66** (P Howling) *s.i.s: hld up: swtchd lft and nt clr run over 2f out: rdn over 1f out: n.d* **14/1**	JimmyQuinn 6	57
6212	9	shd	**Dragon Slayer (IRE)**[17] 4437 7-9-13 **68** (John A Harris) *hld up: swtchd lft and hdwy over 2f out: sn hung lft: wknd fnl f* **7/1**[3]	DarryllHolland 4	59
6323	10	5	**General Tufto**[4] 4880 4-9-9 **64** (C Smith) *hld up: hdwy over 3f out: wknd over 1f out* **16/1**	(b) JoeFanning 16	45
1313	11	4½	**Singora Lady (IRE)**[9] 4721 4-9-6 **61** (P T Midgley) *hld up: pushed along 1/2-way: rdn: hung lft and wknd over 1f out* **14/1**	TonyCulhane 15	33
606	12	1¾	**Toballa**[60] 3004 4-8-9 **50** oh2 (P Leech) *chsd ldrs tl rdn and wknd 2f out* **40/1**	JimCrowley 9	18
0-24	13	3¾	**Garra Molly (IRE)**[148] 897 4-9-9 **64** (G A Swinbank) *hld up: rdn over 3f out: wknd over 2f out* **16/1**	RobertWinston 11	25
-033	14	½	**In Secret**[20] 4337 3-9-5 **69** (J L Dunlop) *hld up: hdwy over 2f out: hmpd sn after: wknd and eased wl over 1f out* **5/1**[1]	RichardMullen 2	29
0040	15	2½	**Risque Heights**[23] 4235 5-9-13 **68** (J R Boyle) *s.i.s: hld up: a in rr: wknd over 2f out* **20/1**	KShea 14	23
1310	16	5	**Iceman George**[13] 4563 5-9-3 **61** (D Morris) *hld up: a in rr: pushed along 6f out: rdn and wknd 3f out* **20/1**	(b) WilliamCarson(3) 10	6
0-56	17	9	**Murhee (USA)**[75] 2548 3-9-4 **68** (D R Lanigan) *mid-div: rdn over 3f out: sn wknd* **16/1**	(b[1]) ChrisCatlin 17	—

2m 4.24s (-1.26) **Going Correction** +0.05s/f (Good)
WFA 3 from 4yo+ 9lb — **17** Ran SP% **131.1**
Speed ratings (Par 103): **107,102,101,100,99 99,97,97,97,93 89,88,85,84,82 78,71**
toteswingers: 1&2 £34.60, 1&3 £12.50, 2&3 £37.50 CSF £87.51 CT £1162.01 TOTE £8.60: £2.80, £3.20, £2.70, £9.90; EX 175.40 Place 6: £205.01 Place 5: £162.13.
Owner Mrs Karen Graham **Bred** Mike Perkins **Trained** Newmarket, Suffolk
■ Stewards' Enquiry : Darryll Holland one-day ban: careless riding (Aug 29)

FOCUS

A big field and a competitive contest, but only a modest handicap, although the form looks sound enough rated around the third and fourth. The runners came down the centre of the track in the straight and again those who raced handily were very much at an advantage.
T/Jkpt: Not won. T/Plt: £140.20 to a £1 stake. Pool: £84,643.71. 440.44 winning tickets. T/Qpdt: £35.50 to a £1 stake. Pool: £5,301.14. 110.33 winning tickets. CR

4595 RIPON (R-H)

Saturday, August 15

OFFICIAL GOING: Good to firm (firm in places; 9.4)

Rail on bend from back straight to home straight moved out 5m from innermost configuration but impact on distances not quantified.

Wind: Light half behind Weather: Sunny and showers

5036 E-TECH GROUP MAIDEN AUCTION STKS — 6f

2:10 (2:11) (Class 4) 2-Y-O — **£4,533** (£1,348; £674; £336) **Stalls** Low

Form	Pos	Dist	Horse / Details	Jockey	RPR
53	1		**Mark Anthony (IRE)**[9] 4705 2-8-9 0 (K A Ryan) *qckly away: mde all: rdn over 1f out: kpt on wl* **11/4**[2]	NCallan 7	78
664	2	2½	**Royal Record**[14] 4515 2-8-6 62 (M Brittain) *wnt rt s: a chsng wnr: rdn along over 2f out: drvn over 1f out: kpt on ins fnl f: nt rch wnr* **17/2**	SilvestreDeSousa 9	67
03	3	3¾	**Mexican Milly (IRE)**[14] 4515 2-8-6 0 (B W Hills) *wnt rt s: sn chsng ldng pair: effrt whn hit on chin by opponent's whip over 2f out: sn rdn and no imp appr fnl f* **10/1**	PaulEddery 11	56
03	4	2¼	**Suzi's A Smartlady (IRE)**[17] 4430 2-8-8 0 (M Johnston) *dwlt and bmpd s: towards rr: hdwy on outer 1/2-way: rdn along 2f out: kpt on ins fnl f: nrst fin* **9/2**[3]	RoystonFfrench 10	51
0352	5	nk	**Tislaam (IRE)**[21] 4323 2-9-1 81 (M R Channon) *dwlt and sn pushed along to chse ldrs: rdn wl over 2f out: and no imp* **5/4**[1]	DaneO'Neill 8	57
5	6	1½	**Destiny's Dancer**[24] 4187 2-8-1 0 (P C Haslam) *midfield: effrt over 2f out and sn rdn: no imp* **33/1**	PatrickDonaghy(5) 4	44
460	7	2¾	**Marchin Star (IRE)**[74] 2568 2-8-9 52 (M Brittain) *a towards rr* **66/1**	DavidAllan 5	38
000	8	¾	**Woodhouse Mill (IRE)**[14] 4515 2-8-8 0 (N Tinkler) *a in rr* **100/1**	AndrewElliott 1	35
40	9	1	**Ella Grace (USA)**[14] 4515 2-8-12 0 (R A Fahey) *a towards rr* **16/1**	PaulHanagan 3	36
040	10	½	**War Wolf**[59] 3032 2-8-13 35 (T D Easterby) *a towards rr* **80/1**	DNolan 2	36

1m 12.59s (-0.41) **Going Correction** -0.175s/f (Firm) — **10** Ran SP% **121.5**
Speed ratings (Par 96): **95,91,86,83,83 81,77,76,75,74**
toteswingers: 1&2 £5.70, 1&3 £4.10, 2&3 £18.70 CSF £27.43 TOTE £4.00: £1.30, £3.40, £1.60; EX 41.20 Trifecta £273.30 Part won. Pool: £369.42 - 0.83 winning units..
Owner J Nattrass **Bred** J F Tuthill **Trained** Hambleton, N Yorks

FOCUS

The rail on the bend from the back straight to the home straight was moved out 5 metres from its innermost position. The expected rain on Friday did not materialise and a heavy shower an hour and a half before racing did not affect the ground, which had been amended slightly overnight from the advertised good to firm all round. The order of the first six in this ordinary auction maiden did not change at all in the final half mile. Improved form from the winner with the second the best guide.

NOTEBOOK

Mark Anthony(IRE) mdae all and dominated some modest opposition. He had run a better race on his second start, over 1m on easy ground, but showed his appreciation for this drop in trip on a sound surface with a comfortable success. Breaking fast and getting over to race nearest the stands' rail, although still a little way off the fence, he travelled well in front and came clear before the furlong pole, although he did wander around a bit when in command. A big, powerful colt who looks a sprinter, he should have more to offer as he strengthens up and his trainer may put him away until next year. (op 9-2)

Royal Recordc hased the winner for most of the journey and deserves credit for sticking to her task. She reversed Doncaster form on this faster ground with third home Mexican Milly. (op 11-1 tchd 12-1 in a place)

Mexican Milly(IRE) was in third place virtually throughout but was fading and on the retreat late on. She received an unintentional smack with a rival jockey's whip, but it is doubtful that had any effect on her finishing position. (op 17-2)

Suzi's A Smartlady(IRE) did not get the best of breaks and raced widest out from her high draw. She kept going to get the better of a tussle for fourth. (tchd 5-1 in a place)

Tislaam(IRE) was slow to find his stride and was in trouble from a relatively early stage. He was conceding weight all round, but set the standard on his Salisbury second last time and ought to have done better. Dane O'Neill reported that the colt was unsuited by the course. Official explanation: jockey said colt was unsuited by the undulating track (op 6-5 tchd 11-8)

Destiny's Dancer probably preferred the better underfoot conditions but did not really step up on her debut form.

5037 EUROPEAN BREEDERS' FUND FILLIES' H'CAP — 1m 1f 170y

2:45 (2:45) (Class 4) (0-80,80) 3-Y-O+ **£6,308** (£1,888; £944; £472; £235) **Stalls** High

Form	Pos	Dist	Horse / Details	Jockey	RPR
4314	1		**Kaloni (IRE)**[29] 4050 3-9-6 **76** (Mrs P Sly) *trckd ldrs: hdwy to chse ldr over 4f out: led 2 1/2f out and sn rdn: drvn over 1f out: kpt on gamely towards fin* **9/2**[3]	JerryO'Dwyer 9	89
1-46	2	nk	**Cascata (IRE)**[67] 2796 3-9-5 **75** (L M Cumani) *trckd ldrs: hdwy 3f out: rdn along 2f out: drvn to chal wnr ent fnl f: sn edgd rt and ev ch tl no ex nr fin* **11/4**[1]	DaneO'Neill 8	88
2155	3	6	**Sparkling Crystal (IRE)**[15] 4482 3-9-5 **75** (B W Hills) *led 4f: styd prom: rdn along 3f out: drvn 2f out and kpt on same pce* **12/1**	PaulEddery 6	76
1153	4	2	**Antigua Sunrise (IRE)**[21] 4328 3-9-8 **78** (R A Fahey) *trckd ldrs: hdwy 3f out: rdn along over 2f out: sn drvn and one pce appr fnl f* **7/2**[2]	PaulHanagan 5	75
1141	5	¾	**Cwm Rhondda (USA)**[44] 3550 4-9-11 **75** (P W Chapple-Hyam) *hld up in rr: hdwy on outer 3f out: rdn along 2f out: no imp fr over 1f out* **11/2**	JackMitchell(3) 2	70

0652 **6** 3 1/4 **Island Music (IRE)**[26] 4144 4-8-10 **62**............(p) JamieKyne(5) 7 51
(J J Quinn) *hld up in rr: hdwy on inner over 3f out: rdn along over 2f out and sn btn* **12/1**

030 **7** 1 1/4 **Atabaas Allure (FR)**[17] 4422 3-9-10 **80**............ RoystonFfrench 3 66
(M Johnston) *cl up: led after 4f: rdn along 3f out: sn hdd & wknd fnl 2f* **9/2**[3]

000 **8** 8 **Shosolosa (IRE)**[78] 2441 7-8-2 **56** oh7............(p) CharlotteKerton(7) 1 26
(S A Harris) *a in rr* **100/1**

2m 2.97s (-2.43) **Going Correction** -0.175s/f (Firm)
WFA 3 from 4yo+ 9lb **8** Ran SP% **117.0**
Speed ratings (Par 102): **102,101,96,95,94 92,91,84**
toteswingers: 1&2 £13.80, 1&3 £9.40, 2&3 £24.30 CSF £17.77 CT £139.60 TOTE £10.00: £1.90, £2.10, £2.20; EX 27.40 Trifecta £197.20 Part won. Pool: £266.57 - 0.43 winning units..
Owner Alan Speechley & John Watt **Bred** Niall Farrell **Trained** Thorney, Cambs

FOCUS
The first two pulled clear in this fair handicap for fillies and the form should stand up.

5038 RIPON HORN BLOWER CONDITIONS STKS 6f
3:20 (3:21) (Class 3) 2-Y-O **£6,938** (£2,076; £1,038; £519; £258) **Stalls** Low

Form RPR
3210 **1** **Exotic Beauty**[14] 4539 2-9-0 84............ PaulHanagan 4 89
(M R Channon) *mde all: rdn 2f out: drvn and hung bdly rt ins fnl f: jst hld on* **9/1**

1 **2** *shd* **Hafawa (IRE)**[55] 3187 2-9-0 0............ TPO'Shea 3 89
(M Johnston) *dwlt and towards rr: hdwy on outer 1/2-way: rdn to chal and hung rt ent fnl f: sn chal and ev ch whn carried rt last 100yds: jst failed* **7/4**[1]

1 **3** 2 1/2 **Bagamoyo**[14] 4515 2-9-5 0............ NCallan 5 86
(J R Fanshawe) *dwlt: sn trcking ldng pair: hdwy to chse wnr over 1f out: drvn and ev ch ins fnl f: hld whn n.m.r towards fin* **4/1**[3]

1213 **4** 3 **Colonel Mak**[22] 4272 2-9-0 90............ PhillipMakin 8 72
(D H Brown) *cl up: rdn 2f out and ev ch tl wknd appr fnl f* **15/8**[2]

35 **5** 8 **Irish Jugger (USA)**[49] 3395 2-9-0 0............ AndrewElliott 6 48
(A P Jarvis) *chsd ldrs: rdn along 1/2-way: sn wknd* **28/1**

51 **6** 1 3/4 **Whozthecat (IRE)**[96] 1920 2-9-0 0............ DNolan 2 43
(D Carroll) *chsd ldrs to 1/2-way: sn wknd* **8/1**

1m 11.17s (-1.83) **Going Correction** -0.175s/f (Firm) **6** Ran SP% **115.7**
Speed ratings (Par 98): **105,104,101,97,86 84**
toteswingers: 1&2 £4.30, 1&3 £2.70, 2&3 £14.50 CSF £26.29 TOTE £8.40: £2.00, £2.20; EX 32.90 Trifecta £128.60 Pool: £391.05 - 2.25 winning units..
Owner M Al-Qatami & K M Al-Mudhaf **Bred** H G And J R Dutfield **Trained** West Ilsley, Berks
■ Stewards' Enquiry : Paul Hanagan caution: careless riding and used whip with excessive frequency

FOCUS
A decent little conditions event. The finish was fought out by the two fillies in the field. Decent efforts from the first two.

NOTEBOOK
Exotic Beauty made virtually all the running and held on bravely after drifting to her right under pressure. Beaten off a mark of 85 in a Newmarket nursery last time, she found this faster surface more to her liking and did it gamely, but was perhaps a fortunate winner. (op 15-2 tchd 10-1)
Hafawa(IRE) ought to have won. Winner of a Pontefract maiden first time, she was last through the early stages here but began to pick up at halfway, despite hanging to her right. She veered to the right again going to the furlong pole before delivering her challenge to the winner, who carried her across the track in the last half-furlong. Lunging late, she needed one more stride to salvage things. She is not straightforward but looks the best long-term prospect in this field and needs at least another furlong now. (op 9-4 tchd 11-4 and 5-2 in places)
Bagamoyo won well on his Doncaster debut, and the third and fourth that day were placed behind Mark Anthony in the opening event here. He was a shade slowly away, as on his debut, but recovered to have every chance until the fillies took his measure inside the last. (tchd 7-2 and 9-2)
Colonel Mak encountered traffic problems when beaten at odds-on last time but had no obvious excuse here. He set a decent standard on his best form but was a little flat, and although he has won on fast ground he might prefer easier conditions. (op 5-2)
Irish Jugger(USA), the sole maiden in the field, Irish Jugger found things happening too quickly on this drop back in trip and was always towards the rear. (op 25-1 tchd 20-1)
Whozthecat(IRE) won well at Redcar when last seen two months ago, but he raced freely here and dropped right away in the latter stages. A drop back to 5f may suit. (op 11-2)

5039 WILLIAM HILL GREAT ST WILFRID STKS (HERITAGE H'CAP) 6f
3:55 (4:01) (Class 2) 3-Y-O+
£37,386 (£11,196; £5,598; £2,802; £1,398; £702) **Stalls** Low

Form RPR
-644 **1** **Markab**[14] 4523 6-9-3 **100**............ PatCosgrave 10 108+
(H Candy) *prom stands' side: effrt 2f out: rdn and edgd rt ins fnl f: styd on wl to ld nr line* **7/2**[1]

0120 **2** *nk* **Tamagin (USA)**[14] 4523 6-9-10 **107**............(p) StephenDonohoe 2 114
(J Pearce) *prom stands' side: edgd rt fr 1/2-way: rdn over 1f out: drvn and ev ch ins fnl f: hung rt and kpt on wl towards fin: 2nd of 10 in gp* **16/1**

3604 **3** *nse* **Advanced**[7] 4796 6-8-9 **97**............ AmyRyan(5) 17 104
(K A Ryan) *cl up far side: led that gp 2f out: rdn and overall ldr over 1f out: hdd and nt qckn nr fin: 1st of 7 in gp* **11/1**

1050 **4** 3/4 **Jimmy Styles**[14] 4523 5-9-3 **100**............ DaneO'Neill 8 104+
(C G Cox) *chsd ldrs stands' side: hdwy 2f out: rdn over 1f out and ev ch tl drvn: edgd rt and nt qckn wl ins fnl f: 3rd of 10 in gp* **11/1**

6003 **5** 2 **Ishetoo**[20] 4341 5-8-8 **96**............ JamieKyne(5) 18 94
(A Dickman) *trckd ldrs far side: hdwy over 2f out: rdn over 1f out: kpt on ins fnl f: 2nd of 7 in gp* **20/1**

6000 **6** 3/4 **Hitchens (IRE)**[14] 4523 4-9-2 **99**............ PhillipMakin 15 95
(T D Barron) *chsd ldrs far side: rdn along 2f out: styd on same pce ent fnl f: 3rd of 7 in gp* **9/1**[3]

0100 **7** *hd* **Striking Spirit**[14] 4523 4-9-3 **100**............ TPO'Shea 1 95
(D Nicholls) *overall ldr stands' side: rdn 2f out: drvn and hdd over 1f out: sn wknd: 4th of 10 in gp* **14/1**

1506 **8** 1 1/4 **Valery Borzov (IRE)**[14] 4523 5-9-6 **103**............(v) FrancisNorton 3 94+
(D Nicholls) *hld up stands' side: hdwy 2f out: sn rdn and kpt on ins fnl f: nrst fin: 5th of 10 in gp* **14/1**

0640 **9** 3/4 **Joseph Henry**[15] 4486 7-8-12 **95**............ DavidAllan 20 84
(D Nicholls) *led far side gp: rdn along 1/2-way: hdd 2f out and sn drvn: wknd appr fnl f: 3rd of 7 in gp* **16/1**

3400 **10** 1 1/4 **Matsunosuke**[16] 4456 7-9-5 **102**............ LukeMorris 16 87
(A B Coogan) *in rr far side: hdwy over 2f out: sn rdn and nt rch ldrs: 4th of 7 in gp* **33/1**

2201 **11** *nse* **Everymanforhimself (IRE)**[7] 4784 5-9-0 **97**............(v) NCallan 14 81
(K A Ryan) *chsd ldrs far side: rdn along over 2f out: sn wknd: 5th of 7 in gp* **11/1**

-000 **12** *nk* **Pearly Wey**[5] 4853 6-8-11 **94**............ PaulHanagan 12 77
(C G Cox) *stdd s and hld up in rr stands' side: sme hdwy 2f out: sn rdn and n.d: 6th of 10 in gp* **25/1**

0453 **13** 1 1/2 **Excusez Moi (USA)**[21] 4330 7-8-11 **94**............(p) SilvestreDeSousa 19 73
(Mrs R A Carr) *a in rr far side: last of 7 in gp* **6/1**[2]

6413 **14** 3/4 **Judge 'n Jury**[7] 4766 5-9-1 **101**............(t) KevinGhunowa(3) 9 77
(R A Harris) *prom stands' side: rdn along over 2f out and sn wknd: 7th of 10 in gp* **22/1**

00-0 **15** *hd* **Kostar**[49] 3405 8-8-11 **97**............ FrederikTylicki(3) 5 73
(C G Cox) *sltly hmpd s: hld up stands' side: effrt and sme hdwy over 2f out: sn rdn and btn: 8th of 10 in gp* **16/1**

0000 **16** 2 3/4 **Beaver Patrol (IRE)**[14] 4523 7-8-10 **96**............(b) JackMitchell(3) 13 63
(Eve Johnson Houghton) *in tch stands' side: rdn along 1/2-way: sn wknd: 9th of 10 in gp* **33/1**

0305 **17** 2 1/2 **Cheveton**[7] 4766 5-8-11 **94**............ DO'Donohoe 11 53
(R J Price) *a in rr stands' side: 10th of 10 in gp* **33/1**

1m 10.1s (-2.90) **Going Correction** -0.175s/f (Firm)
WFA 3 from 4yo+ 4lb **17** Ran SP% **124.3**
Speed ratings (Par 109): **112,111,111,110,107 106,106,104,103,102 102,101,99,98,98 94,91**
toteswingers: 1&2 £13.80, 1&3 £13.00, 2&3 £41.70 CSF £56.78 CT £585.93 TOTE £4.40: £1.80, £3.40, £2.70, £2.40; EX 76.60 Trifecta £1664.30 Pool: £20242.43 - 9.00 winning units..
Owner Tight Lines Partnership **Bred** Shadwell Estate Company Limited **Trained** Kingston Warren, Oxon

FOCUS
High numbers have dominated this valuable and competitive sprint in recent years, with easy conditions usually prevailing, but the ground was riding fast for the first time since 2000 and there was some doubt over which side of the track would be favoured. As expected the field immediately split into two groups, with the seven drawn highest going down the far side and the other dozen taking the stands'-side route. In the final furlong the field fanned out across the track, and with the horse in stall 10 winning from 2 and 17, and pace on both sides, there was no real draw advantage. Not many got into it and the second and third are the best guide. Markab is likely to a bit better yet.

NOTEBOOK
Markab deserved this victory after big efforts to make the frame in the Wokingham, where he was unfavourably drawn, and the Stewards' Cup in which he raced alone out in front. Drawn 10, but with only six horses to his left following three withdrawals, he took the stands'-side option and travelled noticeably strongly. Drifting towards the centre of the course, he got to the front in the last 25 yards. His trainer believes he will be equally effective over shorter and he could go for the Portland at Doncaster over 5f 140yds now. Longer term he is worth a try in Listed company. (op 9-2)
Tamagin(USA), third in this last year when trained by Kevin Ryan, was racing from a career-high mark here. He led his group, albeit some way off the fence despite being drawn 2, and edged steadily across the track as the pressure was on, ending up alongside the third whom he edged past on the line. (op 14-1)
Advanced, a former stablemate of the runner-up, has become well handicapped on his best form and the fast ground was in his favour. He got past Joseph Henry to show ahead in the far-side group and was in front overall just 25 yards from the line. (op 12-1 tchd 14-1)
Jimmy Styles has not had things go his way since a Newmarket win in May but he ran a nice race here, running on strongly in the final furlong. The cheekpieces he wore at Goodwood were left off. (op 12-1 tchd 14-1)
Ishetoo ran a better race at Ascot last time and confirmed himself in good heart, running on to finish second best in the far-side group. (op 16-1)
Hitchens(IRE), third of those drawn high, remains capable of picking up a decent prize. (op 10-1)
Striking Spirit did best of the three runners for David Nicholls, who saddled the 1-2 a year ago. (op 16-1)
Valery Borzov(IRE), runner-up last year, was two places behind Markab in the Stewards' Cup and was doing his best work at the finish here. (op 12-1)
Joseph Henry Official explanation: jockey said gelding hung left throughout
Excusez Moi(USA), winner of this four years ago when trained by Clive Brittain, came here in decent heart, but is a quirky sort and after being walked to the start he was always at the rear of the far-side septet. (tchd 11-2)
Kostar, successful in this in 2007, has been lightly raced since and failed to figure at all.

5040 BOOTHS FOOD STORES H'CAP 1m
4:30 (4:30) (Class 3) (0-90,90) 3-Y-O+ **£7,569** (£2,265; £1,132; £566; £282) **Stalls** High

Form RPR
-146 **1** **Chapter And Verse (IRE)**[21] 4315 3-8-9 **78**............ PaulEddery 6 85
(B W Hills) *trckd ldr: cl up 1/2-way: led over 2f out: rdn clr appr fnl f: styd on strly* **16/1**

2333 **2** 1 1/2 **Effigy**[14] 4526 5-9-1 **77**............ DaneO'Neill 3 81
(H Candy) *towards rr and rn wd bnd over 5f out: hdwy on outer 3f out: rdn to chse ldr 2f out: drvn and kpt on ins fnl f: nt rch wnr* **7/2**[1]

3642 **3** 3/4 **Gala Casino Star (IRE)**[14] 4549 4-9-8 **84**............ PaulHanagan 5 86
(R A Fahey) *trckd ldng pair: hdwy over 3f out: swtchd lft and rdn wl over 1f out: drvn to chse wnr ent fnl f: kpt on same pce* **4/1**[2]

0053 **4** 3 **Collateral Damage (IRE)**[10] 4663 6-8-11 **73**............(t) DavidAllan 2 68
(T D Easterby) *chsd ldrs: rdn along over 2f out: drvn wl over 1f out: kpt on same pce* **9/1**

2321 **5** *hd* **Exit Smiling**[10] 4663 7-9-8 **84**............ NCallan 10 79
(P T Midgley) *trckd ldrs on inner: effrt and n.m.r over 2f out: swtchd lft and rdn wl over 1f out: no imp fnl f* **5/1**[3]

0611 **6** 1 1/4 **Celtic Change (IRE)**[18] 4400 5-9-6 **82**............(bt) PhillipMakin 9 74
(M Dods) *dwlt: hld up in rr: hdwy 3f out: n.m.r and swtchd lft over 2f out: sn rdn and no imp* **4/1**[2]

5050 **7** *nk* **Spinning**[14] 4549 6-9-0 **79**............(b) NeilBrown(3) 1 70
(T D Barron) *s.i.s and bhd: effrt and sme hdwy 3f out: rdn over 2f out: nvr a factor* **20/1**

5220 **8** 1 **Visions Of Johanna (USA)**[14] 4526 4-9-1 **77**............ TonyHamilton 7 65
(R A Fahey) *towards rr: rn wd bnd over 5f out: nvr a factor* **14/1**

-000 **9** 1/2 **Mangham (IRE)**[90] 2101 4-9-11 **90**............(t) FrederikTylicki(3) 4 77
(D H Brown) *led: rdn along 3f out: hdd over 2f out: sn drvn and wknd wl over 1f out* **8/1**

1m 39.6s (-1.80) **Going Correction** -0.175s/f (Firm)
WFA 3 from 4yo+ 7lb **9** Ran SP% **117.3**
Speed ratings (Par 107): **102,100,99,96,96 95,95,94,93**
toteswingers: 1&2 £11.20, 1&3 £11.10, 2&3 £3.40 CSF £72.62 CT £276.01 TOTE £13.60: £2.40, £1.80, £2.40; EX 76.00 Trifecta £346.80 Part won. Pool: £468.76 - 0.60 winning units..
Owner Jack Hanson & Sir Alex Ferguson **Bred** Stuart Weld **Trained** Lambourn, Berks

FOCUS
The rain began to fall prior to this decent handicap and continued for the rest of the card. The pace was only steady and the race had a somewhat muddling look to it. The second and third are sound guides.

NOTEBOOK
Chapter And Verse(IRE) had disappointed in a couple of handicaps since a lucky maiden win, but he was down in trip here and had been eased in the weights. He kicked for home with 2f to go and held off his pursuers with a bit to spare, but did look to get first run. (op 14-1)

Effigy was not best suited by the lack of a real gallop but he was staying on at the end without reaching the winner. This consistent gelding has now been either second or third in each of his last seven starts. (op 4-1)

Gala Casino Star(IRE) was another who could have done with a stronger gallop and he ran respectably in the circumstances. He is proving difficult to win with this term and the handicapper is unlikely to drop him for this. (op 7-2)

Collateral Damage(IRE) ran creditably but is still without a win since his seasonal reappearance last year. He is 8lb lower now and is capable of taking advantage, perhaps on easier ground. (op 17-2)

Exit Smiling was 5lb higher than when winning at Pontefract and was always similarly placed. (op 7-1 tchd 9-2)

Celtic Change(IRE), shooting for a hat-trick off a 10lb higher mark than when the run started, likes to lead but missed the kick. He made a modicum of late progress without helping his rider. (op 6-1)

5041 RIPON-RACES.CO.UK MAIDEN STKS 5f

5:00 (5:01) (Class 5) 3-Y-O+ **£4,533** (£1,348; £674; £336) **Stalls** Low

Form					RPR
0-00	1		**Nabra**[15] 4508 5-8-8 41 IJBrennan(7) 4 (M Brittain) *towards rr: hdwy on outer 2f out: sn rdn and styd on wl ent fnl f to ld fnl 100yds* **16/1**		56
23	2	nk	**Sea Crest**[9] 4707 3-8-5 62 JohnCavanagh(7) 1 (M Brittain) *chsd ldrs on inner: hdwy 2f out: rdn to ld over 1f out: drvn and edgd rt ins fnl f: hdd and no ex fnl 100yds* **9/4**[1]		54
0-33	3	1 1/4	**Neva A Mull Moment (IRE)**[22] 4276 3-9-3 62 FrancisNorton 10 (D Nicholls) *chsd ldrs: hdwy 2f out: sn rdn and ev ch ent fnl f tl drvn and one pce last 100yds* **4/1**[3]		55
0005	4	3/4	**Tarus (IRE)**[7] 4775 5-8-8 40 BillyCray(7) 7 (A Berry) *led to 1/2-way: cl up: rdn and ev ch over 1f out: drvn and hld whn n.m.r fnl 100yds* **16/1**		48
3204	5	1 1/4	**Diamond Blade**[14] 4514 3-9-3 54 DavidAllan 6 (T D Easterby) *prom: rdn along 2f out: drvn and wknd over 1f out* **7/2**[2]		48
00-2	6	4	**Yorke's Folly (USA)**[8] 4754 8-9-1 48 PaulHanagan 2 (C W Fairhurst) *towards rr: rdn along 1/2-way: nvr a factor* **4/1**[3]		29
6053	7	1	**Paddy Jack**[35] 3853 4-9-6 46 (be) TonyHamilton 8 (J R Weymes) *cl up: led 1/2-way: rdn along and hdd over 1f out: wknd* **10/1**		31
600	8	hd	**Star Addition**[14] 4531 3-9-3 25 PJMcDonald 9 (E J Alston) *s.i.s: a bhd* **33/1**		29

59.98 secs (-0.72) **Going Correction** -0.175s/f (Firm)
WFA 3 from 4yo+ 3lb **8** Ran SP% **116.8**
Speed ratings (Par 103): **98,97,95,94,92 85,84,84**
toteswingers: 1&2 £7.00, 1&3 £7.50, 2&3 £3.00 CSF £53.48 TOTE £24.90: £3.80, £1.40, £1.40; EX 59.60 Trifecta £150.40 Pool: £616.17 - 3.03 winning units. Place 6: £60.91 Place 5: £18.47.
Owner Mel Brittain **Bred** Minster Stud And Bickerton Racing **Trained** Warthill, N Yorks

FOCUS
A very weak maiden and not form to rate positively. The Mel Brittain stable, successful in the race last year, enjoyed a 1-2 this time. The winner produced her best form since she was a 2yo.
Yorke's Folly(USA) Official explanation: jockey said mare was unsuited by the undulating track
T/Plt: £92.80 to a £1 stake. Pool: £66,395.94. 521.85 winning tickets. T/Qpdt: £7.60 to a £1 stake. Pool: £5,047.68. 487.06 winning tickets. JR

5048 - 5056a (Foreign Racing) - See Raceform Interactive

4969 DEAUVILLE (R-H)

Saturday, August 15

OFFICIAL GOING: Turf course - good; all-weather - standard

5057a PRISX EQUIDIA 10 ANS (PRIX DE LA VALEE D'AUGE) (LISTED RACE) 5f

2:05 (2:09) 2-Y-O **£26,699** (£10,680; £8,010; £5,340; £2,670)

			RPR
1		**Piccadilly Filly (IRE)**[14] 4537 2-8-8 EdwardCreighton 10 (E J Creighton) *mde all in centre: pushed along 1/2-way: styd on fr over 1f out: drvn out* **3/1**[1]	96
2	nk	**Angel's Pursuit (IRE)**[23] 4221 2-8-11 TThulliez 7 (R Hannon) *mid-div: pushed along and hdwy 1 1/2f out: rdn and wnt 2nd ins fnl f: fin wl: nrest at fin* **11/2**[3]	98
3	1/2	**Red Avalanche (IRE)**[28] 4089 2-8-11 IMendizabal 2 (P F I Cole) *towards rr: 8th and pushed along 1/2-way: rdn 1 1/2f out: r.o fnl f: wnt 3rd cl home* **53/10**[2]	96
4	1/2	**Kolokol (IRE)**[24] 2-8-11 CSoumillon 4 (D Prod'Homme, France)	94
5	1	**Irish Cat (IRE)**[19] 2-8-8 OPeslier 1 (Robert Collet, France)	88
6	hd	**Danny's Choice**[42] 3634 2-8-8 DBonilla 3 (R M Beckett) *mid-div: pushed along and disputing 2nd 1 1/2f out: 3rd and rdn 1f out: one pce* **44/5**	87
7	1/2	**Ladoga**[32] 3967 2-8-8 SPasquier 6 (R Gibson, France)	85
8	3	**Country Love (FR)**[12] 2-8-8 C-PLemaire 8 (David Marnane, Ire) *prom: 3rd 1/2-way: drvn 1 1/2f out: nt qckn* **35/1**	74
9	3	**Multichope (FR)**[19] 2-8-8 GBenoist 9 (C Boutin, France)	64
10	3	**Gioia (FR)**[127] 2-8-8 DBoeuf 5 (J-V Toux, France)	53

57.50 secs **10** Ran SP% **69.2**
PARI-MUTUEL: WIN 4.00; PL 1.70, 2.00, 1.80; DF 16.30.
Owner The Ultimate Racing Fraternity **Bred** Stock Vale Ltd **Trained** Mill Hill, London NW7

NOTEBOOK
Piccadilly Filly(IRE), quickly into her stride, made every yard of the running. She had a lead of several lengths at the halfway stage but then had to be hard ridden inside the final furlong when she hung a little to the left. She may be aimed at a Group 3 event over a similar distance.
Angel's Pursuit(IRE), mid-division in the early stages, came with a run on the outside and was putting in her best work at the finish, but could never quite get to the leader.
Red Avalanche(IRE) still had plenty to do at the halfway stage but was running on well up the stands' rail inside the final furlong.
Danny's Choice was smartly into his stride but was unable to quicken inside the final furlong. Although sixth, he was beaten just over two lengths.

5058a PRIX DE POMONE HARAS D'ETREHAM (GROUP 2) (F&M) 1m 4f 110y

2:35 (2:35) 3-Y-O+ **£71,942** (£27,767; £13,252; £8,835; £4,417)

			RPR
1		**Armure**[18] 4416 4-9-4 GMosse 7 (A De Royer-Dupre, France) *hld up in 6th: hdwy in centre fr over 1f out: chal fnl f: styd on to ld 100yds out: drvn out* **71/10**[3]	106
2	3/4	**Shemima**[32] 3969 4-9-4 CSoumillon 1 (A De Royer-Dupre, France) *racd in 4th: pushed along and r.o st: rdn to ld over 1f out to 100yds out: styd on* **7/10**[1]	105
3	1/2	**Tres Rapide (IRE)**[27] 4128 4-9-4 DBoeuf 2 (H-A Pantall, France) *racd in 5th: pushed along 1 1/2f out: hdwy fr over 1f out: wnt 3rd 150yds out: styd on* **10/1**	104
4	1 1/2	**Umirage**[42] 4-9-4 JVictoire 4 (H Blume, Germany) *missed break: disp last: drvn and last st: styd on fr over 1f out: wnt 4th cl home* **38/1**	102
5	nk	**Calissee (FR)**[20] 4365 5-9-4 SPasquier 3 (J De Roualle, France) *disputing last: 7th st: last over 1f out: drvn and styd on ins fnl f: jst missed 4th* **38/1**	101
6	nk	**Mahaatheer (IRE)**[95] 4-9-4 DBonilla 6 (F Head, France) *led: pushed along 1 1/2f out: hdd over 1f out: styd on tl no ex cl home* **25/1**	101
7	2	**Quetsche (USA)**[69] 2754 3-8-6 C-PLemaire 8 (J-C Rouget, France) *racd in 2nd: pushed along over 1 1/2f out: drvn and lost pl over 1f out: one pce* **13/5**[2]	98
8	1 1/2	**Winkle (IRE)**[32] 3969 4-9-4 OPeslier 5 (M Delzangles, France) *racd in 3rd to over 1f out: eased after* **7/10**[1]	96

2m 40.0s (-6.40)
WFA 3 from 4yo+ 11lb **8** Ran SP% **175.8**
PARI-MUTUEL: WIN 8.10; PL 1.80, 1.20, 2.20; DF 39.30.
Owner Haras De Saint Pair **Bred** Sarah J Leigh And Robin S Leigh **Trained** Chantilly, France

NOTEBOOK
Armure, given a beautiful ride, she came with a sweeping late run to take the advantage with 50 yards left. The filly was landing a hat-trick and is improving with every outing. Stays really well, connections are now looking at the Prix Vermeille and whatever the case she is certainly one to follow during the latter part of the season.
Shemima, never far from the lead, she took control of the race halfway up the straight and looked the likely winner at the furlong marker before her stablemate passed her well inside the final furlong. Connections will now consider races like the Prix de Royallieu for this filly.
Tres Rapide(IRE) was putting in her best work at the finish having being mid-division early on. She stayed the distance really well.
Umirage, given a waiting ride, she was hampered halfway up the straight but finished really well when in the clear.

5059a PRIX GONTAUT-BIRON HONG KONG JOCKEY-CLUB (GROUP 3) 1m 2f

3:05 (3:05) 4-Y-O+ **£38,835** (£15,534; £11,650; £7,767; £3,883)

			RPR
1		**Crossharbour**[300] 6854 5-8-9 SPasquier 4 (A Fabre, France) *cl 3rd: led 3f out: rdn and r.o 1 1/2f out: drvn out* **22/5**[3]	115
2	nk	**Adelar (GER)**[48] 3441 4-8-11 OPeslier 6 (W Baltromei, Germany) *settled towards rr: 8th st: rdn and gd hdwy fr 1 1/2f out: wnt 2nd 100yds out: nrest at fin* **24/1**	116
3	1 1/2	**Precious Boy (GER)**[20] 4364 4-8-11 ASuborics 8 (W Hickst, Germany) *prom: 3rd st: sn drvn and disputing 2nd: rdn and styd on u.p: tk 3rd fnl strides* **5/2**[1]	113
4	hd	**Blue Monday**[28] 4090 8-8-9 CSoumillon 2 (R Charlton) *led 1f: racd in 2nd: cl 4th on ins st: sn drvn and disputing 2nd: styd on at one pce to line* **12/1**	111
5	1 1/2	**The Bogberry (USA)**[111] 1551 4-8-11 GMosse 7 (A De Royer-Dupre, France) *hld up: last st: effrt on outside 1 1/2f out: styd on fnl stages: n.d* **71/10**	110
6	1	**Integral (GER)**[20] 4364 5-8-9 IMendizabal 10 (R Rohne, Germany) *hld up towards rr: 9th st: sme late hdwy but n.d* **41/1**	106
7	1 1/2	**Loup Breton (IRE)**[90] 2120 5-8-11 (p) ACrastus 3 (E Lellouche, France) *hld up: 10th st: n.d* **33/10**[2]	105
8	shd	**Mundybash**[32] 4-8-9 TThulliez 1 (N Clement, France) *mid-div: 7th st: effrt on ins 1 1/2f out: nvr in contention* **13/1**	102
9	1/2	**Mr Brock (SAF)**[28] 4113 6-8-11 DBoeuf 9 (Mme C Head-Maarek, France) *towards rr: hdwy on outside over 3f out: 5th st: drvn 2f out: one pce fr 1 1/2f out* **19/1**	103
10	2	**Unnefer (FR)**[77] 2476 4-8-9 C-PLemaire 11 (H R A Cecil) *in tch: tk clsr order appr st: 2nd st: sn pushed along: unable qck* **13/1**	97
11		**Inter Mondo (GER)**[62] 6-8-9 RPiechulek 5 (Frau M Weber, Germany) *missed break but drvn to ld after 1f: hdd 3f out: 6th and dropping bk st: t.o* **98/1**	—

2m 4.00s (-6.20) **11** Ran SP% **117.1**
PARI-MUTUEL: WIN 5.40; PL 2.20, 5.10, 1.50; DF 55.90.
Owner K Abdulla **Bred** Juddmonte Farms Ltd **Trained** Chantilly, France

NOTEBOOK
Crossharbour, who put up a fine effort considering he hadn't been out for ten months. Always well up, he took the lead coming into the straight and stayed on really well, but had to be strongly ridden to hold off the runner-up. The plan now is to run the five-year-old in the Prix Foy and he has been entered in the Arc de Triomphe. He is highly rated by his connections and jockey.
Adelar(GER) still had plenty to do coming into the straight. He took second place inside the final furlong but could never quite get to the winner.
Precious Boy(GER) was backed into favourite but never really looked like winning despite always being close up. He battled well at the end but might have been a little tired having finished second in a Group 1 race in Germany a couple of weeks before.
Blue Monday, always well up, ran on bravely up the far rail but was outpaced as the race came to a close. He would have been better suited by a softer surface
Unnefer(FR) was never far from the leaders on the outside, and although he was going well until the straight he was a spent force shortly after.

4687 BATH (L-H)

Sunday, August 16

OFFICIAL GOING: Good to firm (good in places)

Wind: Moderate, against Weather: Fine

5060 TOTEPLACEPOT MAIDEN AUCTION STKS 5f 11y

2:30 (2:30) (Class 6) 2-Y-O **£1,942** (£578; £288; £144) **Stalls** Centre

Form RPR

22 **1** **Bush Tucker (IRE)**[15] 4537 2-9-1 0 JimCrowley 3 77+
(P Winkworth) *hld up in tch: pushed along to ld over 1f out: rdn ins fnl f: r.o wl* **4/5**[1]

00 **2** 2 ½ **Gooseberry Bush**[55] 3218 2-8-4 0 ChrisCatlin 2 57
(P J Makin) *hld up: n.m.r sn after s: sn bhd: swtchd rt wl over 1f out: rdn and r.o ins fnl f: tk 2nd cl home: nt trble wnr* **14/1**

02 **3** ¾ **Morgans Choice**[22] 4302 2-8-11 0 PaulDoe 4 61
(J L Spearing) *led: rdn and hdd over 1f out: no ex and lost 2nd cl home* **5/1**[3]

4522 **4** ½ **Zelos Dream (IRE)**[10] 4688 2-8-1 64 DavidProbert(3) 5 53
(Rae Guest) *chsd ldr tl pushed along 2f out: rdn over 1f out: one pce fnl f* **3/1**[2]

0040 **5** hd **Pherousa**[10] 4688 2-8-4 61 LiamJones 1 52
(M Blanshard) *a.p: rdn and one pce fnl f* **50/1**

6 ½ **Devassa** 2-8-4 0 LukeMorris 8 50
(C G Cox) *hld up and bhd: effrt on outside over 1f out: rdn and no imp fnl f* **16/1**

62.52 secs (0.02) **Going Correction** -0.15s/f (Firm) **6** Ran SP% **111.7**

Speed ratings (Par 92): **93,89,87,87,86 85**

toteswingers: 1&2 £3.20, 1&3 £1.40, 2&3 £3.50. CSF £13.85 TOTE £1.70: £1.20, £3.30; EX 12.00 Trifecta £15.40 Pool: £266.48 - 12.73 winning units..

Owner Mrs Tessa Winkworth **Bred** Noel Brosnan **Trained** Chiddingfold, Surrey

FOCUS

An ordinary-looking maiden, weakened by a couple of non-runners.

NOTEBOOK

Bush Tucker(IRE) had some ominous form figures next to his name but showed that was not a worry with a solid display. He can make his mark in a sprint nursery. (op Evens, tchd early 5-4)

Gooseberry Bush, absent since the end of June, has plenty of size about her and stayed on well after taking a little time to get organised. She does at least have the frame to improve. Official explanation: jockey said filly was hampered leaving the stalls (op 9-1)

Morgans Choice had an easy time of it in front but could not quicken once joined. (tchd 11-2)

Zelos Dream(IRE), dropping in trip again after a fair effort at this course last time, has been consistent but never figured. (op 7-2 tchd 4-1 and 11-4)

Devassa is bred to make a speedy 2yo but her trainer said much depended on whether she behaved at the course, as she had been a bit temperamental at home. She seemed a little green but was just not good enough. (op 10-1)

5061 TOTEEXACTA MAIDEN STKS 1m 3f 144y

3:00 (3:01) (Class 5) 3-Y-O+ **£2,719** (£809; £404; £202) **Stalls** Low

Form RPR

-325 **1** **Brilliana**[29] 4085 3-8-12 74 TedDurcan 1 82+
(D R Lanigan) *mde all: pushed clr 2f out: eased considerably ins fnl f* **10/3**[3]

4 **2** 6 **Rougham**[23] 4270 3-9-3 0 LPKeniry 9 69
(A M Balding) *a.p: chsd wnr 9f out: rdn over 2f out: sn btn* **6/4**[1]

32 **3** nk **Ramora (USA)**[54] 3250 3-8-12 0 IanMongan 8 63
(H R A Cecil) *hld up in mid-div: lost pl over 4f out: hung lft fr 3f out: styd on to take 3rd towards fin: n.d* **2/1**[2]

65 **4** ¾ **Westlin' Winds (IRE)**[27] 4145 3-9-3 0 SteveDrowne 3 67
(C R Egerton) *a.p: rdn over 3f out: one pce* **8/1**

2 **5** 6 **Tubby Littlejohns (IRE)**[12] 4617 5-9-8 0 ByronMoorcroft(5) 5 57
(B J Llewellyn) *s.s: hld up: hdwy over 7f out: rdn over 2f out: wknd jst over 1f out* **16/1**

50 **6** 12 **Cecily Parsley**[16] 4480 3-8-12 0 DarryllHolland 12 31
(H Morrison) *a in rr: no ch fnl 4f* **28/1**

7 hd **Star Of Memory (FR)**[650] 5-9-6 0 AndrewHeffernan(7) 10 36
(D G Bridgwater) *w ldr over 2f: prom tl rdn and wknd 2f out* **40/1**

00/ **8** 1 ½ **Bute Street**[685] 5856 4-9-13 0 FergusSweeney 7 34
(R J Hodges) *a in rr: no ch fnl 4f* **100/1**

2m 29.99s (-0.61) **Going Correction** -0.15s/f (Firm)

WFA 3 from 4yo+ 10lb **8** Ran SP% **120.3**

Speed ratings (Par 103): **96,92,91,91,87 79,79,78**

toteswingers: 1&2 £1.80, 1&3 £2.20, 2&3 £2.00. CSF £9.23 TOTE £4.20: £1.40, £1.10, £1.40; EX 9.80 Trifecta £39.20 Pool: £316.52 - 5.97 winning units..

Owner Ms Nicola Mahoney **Bred** F Nass **Trained** Newmarket, Suffolk

FOCUS

This was a poor maiden, as only a small portion of these looked to have any chance of winning.

Ramora(USA) Official explanation: jockey said filly hung left in the straight

5062 TOTEQUADPOT H'CAP 1m 2f 46y

3:30 (3:30) (Class 4) (0-80,80) 3-Y-O+ **£4,857** (£1,445; £722; £360) **Stalls** Low

Form RPR

0113 **1** **Mick's Dancer**[15] 4541 4-9-10 76 DarryllHolland 7 85
(W R Muir) *mde all: rdn jst over 1f out: r.o* **5/1**[3]

1404 **2** 1 ¼ **Bold Cross (IRE)**[11] 4641 6-10-0 80 PaulFitzsimons 2 87
(E G Bevan) *s.i.s: hld up in rr: hdwy over 4f out: rdn and chsd wnr over 1f out: nt qckn ins fnl f* **10/1**

4331 **3** hd **Souter Point (USA)**[25] 4205 3-8-11 78 JPFahy(7) 3 84
(R Charlton) *hld up in rr: hdwy 2f out: nt clr run and swtchd lft 1f out: kpt on ins fnl f* **7/2**[1]

6153 **4** ½ **Can Can Star**[13] 4605 6-9-6 79 DebraEngland(7) 6 84
(A W Carroll) *hld up in tch: rdn wl over 1f out: nt qckn ins fnl f* **14/1**

-451 **5** 2 ¼ **Constant Cheers (IRE)**[38] 3766 6-9-9 78 DavidProbert(3) 8 79
(W R Swinburn) *chsd wnr tl pushed along over 1f out: wknd ins fnl f* **7/1**

4555 **6** 3 ¼ **Basra (IRE)**[44] 3578 6-9-13 79 IanMongan 10 74
(Miss Jo Crowley) *hld up in rr: hdwy over 2f out: rdn over 1f out: wknd fnl f* **14/1**

0-54 **7** ½ **Dove Cottage (IRE)**[20] 4378 7-9-4 70 FergusSweeney 1 64
(W S Kittow) *prom: rdn 3f out: sn wknd* **18/1**

6621 **8** nk **Magroom**[2] 4992 5-8-10 62 JimCrowley 9 55
(R J Hodges) *hld up in rr: sme prog 2f out: rdn 1f out: no rspnse* **9/2**[2]

0624 **9** 1 ¼ **Mount Hermon (IRE)**[9] 4759 5-9-7 73 (b) SteveDrowne 4 64
(H Morrison) *hld up in mid-div: wknd over 2f out* **7/1**

4310 **10** 7 **La Coveta (IRE)**[22] 4328 4-9-9 80 GabrielHannon(5) 5 58
(B J Meehan) *hld up in tch: lost pl 5f out: bhd fnl 2f* **16/1**

2m 8.06s (-2.94) **Going Correction** -0.15s/f (Firm)

WFA 3 from 4yo+ 8lb **10** Ran SP% **115.6**

Speed ratings (Par 105): **105,104,103,103,101 99,98,98,97,91**

toteswingers: 1&2 £10.80, 1&3 £4.20, 2&3 £10.30. CSF £53.63 CT £197.44 TOTE £4.70: £2.10, £3.80, £1.70; EX 52.00 TRIFECTA Not won..

Owner Perspicacious Punters Racing Club **Bred** Cheveley Park Stud Ltd **Trained** Lambourn, Berks

FOCUS

Virtually all of these had a sizeable negative against their chance of winning, so this is not a race that took a great deal of winning. As it turned out, the winner, much like the previous contest, was given the best ride.

5063 TOTESWINGER FILLIES' H'CAP 1m 5y

4:00 (4:01) (Class 5) (0-70,70) 3-Y-O+ **£2,849** (£847; £423; £211) **Stalls** Low

Form RPR

3225 **1** **Ailsa Craig (IRE)**[23] 4266 3-9-0 63 RyanMoore 15 72
(R Hannon) *hld up towards rr: pushed along and hdwy whn nt clr run jst over 2f out: swtchd lft to ins rail jst over 1f out: sn rdn: r.o to ld nr fin* **9/2**[1]

0200 **2** hd **Inis Boffin**[30] 4050 3-9-7 70 JamesDoyle 1 78
(S Kirk) *hld up in mid-div: hdwy over 1f out: rdn to ld ins fnl f: hdd nr fin* **16/1**

1462 **3** 2 ½ **Very Well Red**[7] 4816 6-9-13 70 DarryllHolland 6 74
(P W Hiatt) *a.p: rdn over 1f out: ev ch ins fnl f: no ex towards fin* **5/1**[2]

5201 **4** nk **Lady Florence**[10] 4694 4-9-8 65 LPKeniry 10 68
(A B Coogan) *led: rdn over 1f out: hdd ins fnl f: no ex* **11/1**

5261 **5** 2 ½ **Make Amends (IRE)**[38] 3777 4-9-2 62 WilliamCarson(3) 4 59
(R J Hodges) *hld up in tch: nt clr run briefly over 1f out: swtchd lft jst ins fnl f: one pce* **8/1**

-233 **6** ¾ **Monashee Rock (IRE)**[31] 3996 4-9-9 66 ChrisCatlin 7 62
(M Salaman) *in tch whn n.m.r and lost pl after 1f: hld up towards rr: hdwy on outside 2f out: rdn and wknd fnl f* **5/1**[2]

7 1 ¼ **Halcyon Princess (IRE)**[86] 2251 3-8-11 67 AndrewHeffernan(7) 9 59
(D G Bridgwater) *hld up in mid-div: nt clr run briefly over 2f out: sn pushed along: rdn and btn jst over 1f out* **66/1**

00-0 **8** hd **Heavenly Saint**[37] 3800 4-8-8 56 ow1 ByronMoorcroft(5) 14 48
(C Roberts) *hld up in tch: rdn and wknd fnl f* **50/1**

0264 **9** nk **Chatanoogachoochoo**[16] 4482 4-9-8 65 JimCrowley 12 57
(M Hill) *hld up in mid-div: hdwy on outside jst over 2f out: rdn wl over 1f out: wknd fnl f* **15/2**[3]

6504 **10** 1 **Dancing Storm**[44] 3581 6-8-13 56 FergusSweeney 13 45
(W S Kittow) *chsd ldr over 6f out tl rdn over 1f out: sn wknd* **8/1**

062 **11** 3 ¾ **Highland Lassie (IRE)**[20] 4381 3-9-2 65 JamieSpencer 3 45
(B J Meehan) *s.i.s: a in rr* **15/2**[3]

3005 **12** 2 **Protiva**[15] 4535 3-8-4 53 JamieMackay 16 28
(Karen George) *s.i.s: a in rr* **66/1**

000 **13** 1 ¼ **Tallulah Sunrise**[15] 4533 4-8-8 51 oh6 LukeMorris 11 24
(M D I Usher) *s.s: rdn 4f out: a in rr* **66/1**

0045 **14** 18 **Mrs Slocombe (IRE)**[10] 4687 3-8-3 55 DavidProbert(3) 2 —
(Mrs N S Evans) *towards rr: rdn over 4f out: no ch whn eased fnl f* **33/1**

1m 39.84s (-0.96) **Going Correction** -0.15s/f (Firm)

WFA 3 from 4yo+ 6lb **14** Ran SP% **120.9**

Speed ratings (Par 100): **98,97,95,95,92 91,90,90,90,89 85,83,82,64**

toteswingers: 1&2 £12.70, 1&3 £5.10, 2&3 £17.80. CSF £76.59 CT £386.06 TOTE £5.00: £1.90, £6.10, £2.50; EX 140.50 TRIFECTA Not won..

Owner De La Warr Racing **Bred** P J B O'Callaghan **Trained** East Everleigh, Wilts

FOCUS

A competitive handicap but it is debatable whether this will turn out to be form worth following in anything other than similar contests.

Very Well Red Official explanation: jockey said mare hung right

Highland Lassie(IRE) Official explanation: jockey said filly boiled over at the start

Protiva Official explanation: jockey said filly was never travelling

Mrs Slocombe(IRE) Official explanation: jockey said filly was never travelling

5064 EUROPEAN BREEDERS' FUND DICK HERN FILLIES' STKS (LISTED RACE) 1m 5y

4:30 (4:32) (Class 1) 3-Y-O+

£22,708 (£8,608; £4,308; £2,148; £1,076; £540) **Stalls** Low

Form RPR

3124 **1** **Annabelle's Charm (IRE)**[73] 2639 4-9-0 85 JamieSpencer 4 99
(L M Cumani) *pushed along briefly sn after s: hld up and bhd: stdy prog over 2f out: hrd rdn over 1f out: led ins fnl f: drvn out* **18/1**

6333 **2** 1 **Please Sing**[16] 4489 3-8-8 100 EdwardCreighton 8 96+
(M R Channon) *hld up: hdwy over 2f out: n.m.r over 1f out: rdn and r.o to take 2nd nr fin* **9/4**[2]

6210 **3** nk **Golden Stream (IRE)**[16] 4489 3-8-13 101 RyanMoore 7 100
(Sir Michael Stoute) *hld up in tch: led over 1f out: rdn and hdd ins fnl f: no ex and lost 2nd nr fin* **3/1**[3]

2502 **4** 1 **Damaniyat Girl (USA)**[52] 3320 3-8-8 98 (b) LiamJones 2 93
(W J Haggas) *t.k.h: a.p: kpt on same pce fnl f* **13/2**

1/2 **5** nk **Whispered Dreams (GER)**[21] 4-9-0 95 TedDurcan 1 94
(Mario Hofer, Germany) *sn led: rdn whn edgd rt and hdd over 1f out: btn whn n.m.r cl home* **16/1**

1222 **6** 1 ¼ **Balaagha (USA)**[23] 4259 3-8-8 100 TPO'Shea 6 89
(M A Jarvis) *dwlt: hld up in rr: swtchd rt to outside over 2f out: short-lived effrt over 1f out* **2/1**[1]

3050 **7** 2 ¼ **Kaabari (USA)**[14] 4566 3-8-8 75 ChrisCatlin 3 84?
(C E Brittain) *led early: chsd ldr: ev ch wl over 1f out: rdn and wknd ent fnl f* **50/1**

1m 39.6s (-1.20) **Going Correction** -0.15s/f (Firm)

WFA 3 from 4yo 6lb **7** Ran SP% **115.5**

Speed ratings (Par 108): **100,99,98,97,97 96,93**

toteswingers: 1&2 £4.60, 1&3 £6.20, 2&3 £1.80. CSF £59.92 TOTE £13.40: £5.60, £2.40; EX 79.10 Trifecta £121.10 Pool: £759.35 - 4.64 winning units..

Owner Merry Fox Stud Limited **Bred** Swordlestown Stud **Trained** Newmarket, Suffolk

FOCUS

With most of these having an official rating well over 90, this looked up to the standard you would hope to see in a Listed event.

NOTEBOOK

Annabelle's Charm(IRE), who had been running well in handicap company, was 16lb below the top-rated horse, so did not look the most obvious winner. Held up, she came with a powerful finish to win in good style, and gain that valuable black type success. Her jockey believes she will be a 10lb better horse when racing on easier ground. (op 14-1 tchd 20-1)

Please Sing won the Cherry Hinton at two but had not quite reproduced that level of form since. She looked to have a bit of a problem with the bend and met a little trouble in running just behind the winner, but stayed on well once in the clear to claim second. (op 5-2)

Golden Stream(IRE) was very disappointing in a Group 3 at Glorious Goodwood after winning a Listed race at Warwick. She looked to be going nicely up the home straight and was given every chance, but could not quicken once in front and was easily passed by Annabelle's Charm. (op 7-2)
Damaniyat Girl(USA), beaten by Golden Stream last time, stayed on up the inside rail but looked very one-paced. (op 9-1 tchd 11-1)
Whispered Dreams(GER) started off life with Godolphin, and won on her only start for them before finding her way to Mario Hofer about a year and a half later. She had been running well in this company in Germany, and did not do too badly, but appeared to hang in the latter stages. (op 10-1)
Balaagha(USA) was held on a lead rein at the start by a handler on horseback, and fell out of the stalls when they opened. She made up the ground in time to have a chance but offered little when asked to get involved. Official explanation: jockey said filly was slowly away and ran free (tchd 15-8 and 9-4 in places)
Kaabari(USA) ran better than she had done for a while but was readily held. (op 40-1)

5065 BET TOTEPOOL AT TOTESPORT.COM APPRENTICE H'CAP 5f 161y
5:00 (5:00) (Class 5) (0-75,74) 3-Y-O+ **£2,849** (£847; £423; £211) **Stalls** Centre

Form				RPR
254	**1**		**Triple Dream**[13] 4604 4-8-13 **60**......(p) JackDean 1 (J M Bradley) *hld up in tch on ins: led and edgd rt jst over 1f out: drvn out* **5/1**[1]	70
2050	**2**	3/4	**Kyllachy Storm**[4] 4907 5-9-11 **72**...... WilliamCarson 8 (R J Hodges) *a.p: rdn and ev ch ins fnl f: nt qckn* **6/1**[2]	79
1611	**3**	1/2	**Swinbrook (USA)**[10] 4690 8-9-6 **74**...... SPRyan(7) 3 (R A Harris) *hld up towards rr: hdwy 2f out: rdn jst over 1f out: r.o one pce ins fnl f* **6/1**[2]	79
0066	**4**	3/4	**Finnegan McCool**[22] 4326 3-9-1 **70**......(p) JPFahy(5) 13 (R M Beckett) *hld and bhd: hdwy over 1f out: rdn and kpt on same pce ins fnl f* **14/1**	73
2404	**5**	nk	**Bateleur**[1] 5020 5-9-2 **66**...... MCGeran(3) 2 (M R Channon) *s.i.s: sn hld up in mid-div: hdwy over 1f out: rdn and n.m.r ent fnl f: one pce* **6/1**[2]	68
0233	**6**	1 1/4	**Miss Firefly**[9] 4736 4-8-3 **55** oh1...... AshleyMorgan(5) 4 (R J Hodges) *a.p: hmpd and lost pl over 1f out: nt rcvr* **14/1**	52+
2006	**7**	1/2	**Wooden King (IRE)**[4] 4905 4-8-3 **55** oh3...... AndrewHeffernan(5) 5 (M S Saunders) *chsd ldrs: rdn to ld 2f out: edgd lft over 1f out: sn hdd: wknd wl ins fnl f* **33/1**	51
044	**8**	nk	**Don Pele (IRE)**[18] 4428 7-9-5 **66**......(p) DavidProbert 14 (R A Harris) *hld up in rr: rdn on wd outside jst over 1f out: nvr nrr* **8/1**	61
0400	**9**	3/4	**Caustic Wit (IRE)**[18] 4428 11-8-1 **55** oh2...... JakePayne(7) 11 (M S Saunders) *hld up towards rr: pushed along on outside over 2f out: nvr trbld ldrs* **40/1**	47
1000	**10**	1/2	**Bold Argument (IRE)**[26] 4167 6-9-6 **67**...... JackMitchell 6 (Mrs P N Dutfield) *s.i.s: in rr: effrt and hrd rdn 2f out: n.d* **12/1**	58
3113	**11**	nse	**Fyelehk (IRE)**[8] 4788 3-9-1 **65**...... JamesMillman 10 (B R Millman) *chsd ldr tl over 2f out: wknd over 1f out* **7/1**[3]	55
-201	**12**	3 3/4	**Mandhooma**[11] 4643 3-8-5 **58**...... RossAtkinson(3) 9 (P W Hiatt) *led: edgd rt whn rdn and hdd 2f out: wknd jst over 1f out* **14/1**	36

1m 11.52s (0.32) **Going Correction** -0.15s/f (Firm)
WFA 3 from 4yo+ 3lb **12** Ran SP% **116.2**
Speed ratings (Par 103): **91,90,89,88,87 86,85,85,84,83 83,78**
toteswingers: 1&2 £6.70, 1&3 £3.80, 2&3 £4.50. CSF £33.34 CT £186.97 TOTE £5.00: £2.20, £2.60, £2.20; EX 40.40 Trifecta £264.70 Pool: £357.82 - 0.43 winning units. Place 6 £23.60, Place 5 £14.93.
Owner J M Bradley **Bred** Hesmonds Stud Ltd **Trained** Sedbury, Gloucs

FOCUS
This was a very competitive handicap for the type of race, and the form should be sound.
T/Jkpt: Not won. T/Plt: £46.30 to a £1 stake. Pool: £64,699.06. 1,019.68 winning tickets. T/Qpdt: £27.70 to a £1 stake. Pool: £3,982.10. 106.30 winning tickets. KH

4658 PONTEFRACT (L-H)
Sunday, August 16

OFFICIAL GOING: Good to firm (8.7)
Wind: Fresh, half-behind Weather: Fine but breezy

5066 E B F HARRY & DOREEN CHAPMAN GOLDEN WEDDING ANNIVERSARY MAIDEN STKS 5f
2:10 (2:10) (Class 4) 2-Y-O **£5,828** (£1,734; £866; £432) **Stalls** Low

Form				RPR
3	**1**		**Our Jonathan**[44] 3571 2-9-3 0...... NCallan 3 (K A Ryan) *trckd ldr: led over 2f out: pushed clr ins fnl f: easily* **2/7**[1]	90+
03	**2**	6	**Licence To Till (USA)**[25] 4187 2-9-3 0...... JoeFanning 1 (M Johnston) *led tl over 2f out: no ch w wnr* **6/1**[2]	68
34	**3**	9	**Newbury Street**[25] 4187 2-9-3 0...... PaulHanagan 2 (R A Fahey) *in rr: kpt on to take modest 3rd 1f out* **9/1**[3]	39+
50	**4**	8	**Psychopathicsandra (IRE)**[37] 3805 2-8-7 45...... SladeO'Hara(5) 5 (A Berry) *s.i.s: sn chsng ldrs: wknd appr fnl f* **100/1**	2
0	**5**	3 3/4	**Sharp Shoes**[15] 4546 2-9-3 0...... SilvestreDeSousa 4 (Mrs A Duffield) *t.k.h: dropped to rr and outpcd over 2f out: sn bhd* **25/1**	—

62.13 secs (-1.17) **Going Correction** -0.20s/f (Firm) **5** Ran SP% **106.9**
Speed ratings (Par 96): **101,91,77,64,58**
CSF £2.21 TOTE £1.30: £1.02, £2.20; EX 1.90.
Owner Dr Marwan Koukash **Bred** W G M Turner **Trained** Hambleton, N Yorks

FOCUS
After a dry night the ground was pretty fast and a fresh tailwind in the straight helped these juveniles record a quick time. A good effort from the easy winner.

NOTEBOOK
Our Jonathan stood out on his debut effort, when he was trained by Bryan Smart. It was pretty straightforward, as he took a lead from the runner-up until going on two furlongs out then quickly drew clear and won with a good deal in hand. He looks sure to go on to better things, and the Flying Childers is a possibility. (op 1-3)
Licence To Till(USA) had finished third with a subsequent winner in second on his previous start and adopted the same forcing tactics on this drop in trip. However, when the winner made his move he could not respond. He now qualifies for a handicap mark and might prefer a return to an easier surface. (op 11-2)
Newbury Street had run both his previous races on soft ground, had four and a half lengths to find with the runner-up on Catterick form and was unable to match that effort. He was held up out the back early and never got involved, but at least he now qualifies for nurseries. (op 7-1 tchd 10-1)

5067 RAINBOW INTERNATIONAL H'CAP 1m 4f 8y
2:40 (2:40) (Class 3) (0-90,89) 3-Y-O+ **£9,346** (£2,799; £1,399; £700; £349; £175) **Stalls** Low

Form				RPR
1-10	**1**		**Braveheart Move (IRE)**[18] 4420 3-9-1 **86**...... SebSanders 7 (Sir Mark Prescott) *t.k.h: trckd ldrs: chal 3f out: styd on u.p to ld jst ins fnl f: hld on wl towards fin* **13/8**[1]	94
001	**2**	1/2	**Eton Fable (IRE)**[10] 4696 4-9-2 **77**......(p) TravisBlock 5 (W J H Ratcliffe) *trckd ldr: drvn to ld over 3f out: hdd jst ins fnl f: no ex* **8/1**[3]	84
0011	**3**	nk	**High Ambition**[11] 4661 6-8-13 **77**...... FrederikTylicki(3) 3 (R A Fahey) *dwlt: t.k.h towards rr: hdwy to trck ldrs 6f out: upsides over 1f out: no ex ins fnl f* **2/1**[2]	84
-004	**4**	4	**Lost Soldier Three (IRE)**[23] 4288 8-9-9 **84**...... AdrianTNicholls 1 (D Nicholls) *sn trcking ldrs: effrt over 2f out: one pce* **14/1**	84
3403	**5**	4 1/2	**Grand Art (IRE)**[2] 4972 5-8-11 **72**...... TonyCulhane 8 (P T Midgley) *hld up: hdwy to trck ldrs 6f out: drvn over 3f out: lost pl over 1f out* **8/1**[3]	65
6/	**6**	4 1/2	**Folk Tune (IRE)**[106] 4862 6-9-7 **89**...... IJBrennan(7) 2 (J J Quinn) *hld up in rr: pushed along 5f out: nvr a factor* **25/1**	75
1210	**7**	6	**Joe Jo Star**[29] 3266 7-9-3 **78**...... PaulHanagan 6 (R A Fahey) *t.k.h: led tl over 3f out: lost pl over 1f out* **8/1**[3]	54

2m 37.48s (-3.32) **Going Correction** -0.20s/f (Firm)
WFA 3 from 4yo+ 10lb **7** Ran SP% **115.3**
Speed ratings (Par 107): **103,102,102,99,96 93,89**
toteswinger: 1&2 £3.70, 1&3 £1.40, 2&3 £3.60 CSF £15.79 CT £27.20 TOTE £2.50: £1.50, £4.10; EX 16.90.
Owner Moyglare Stud Farm Ltd **Bred** Moyglare Stud Farm Ltd **Trained** Newmarket, Suffolk
■ Stewards' Enquiry : Travis Block one-day ban: used whip in the forehand position down the shoulder (Aug 30)
Seb Sanders five-day ban: used whip with excessive frequency (Aug 30-Sep 3)

FOCUS
A decent handicap. The first three came clear and this is fair form for the grade.

NOTEBOOK
Braveheart Move(IRE) was hoping to bounce back after disappointing when favourite at Goodwood on his previous start. He did so, but had to work really hard to get the better of the placed horses. He refused to give in and found a little extra inside the last furlong to settle matters. The fact that his rider picked up a five-day ban for excessive use of the whip indicates how deep he had to dig. He is in the Melrose Handicap next week, if he gets over this hard race quickly enough, but on this evidence his St Leger entry looks optimistic. (op 15-8)
Eton Fable(IRE) is a game front-runner with form on the track and ground. Instead of making the running he got a good lead from Jo Jo Star, and gave the winner a real battle, only giving best late on. He is in good form and can score again. (op 17-2 tchd 15-2)
High Ambition came into this on a hat-trick, the second of those successes being over course and distance. He came to join issue with the first two on the home turn and had every chance but could not get past. He was 10lb higher than for the first of his recent successes and he may not have finished winning yet. (op 9-4 tchd 5-2)
Lost Soldier Three(IRE) seems to have come back from a break in reasonable form and is now 4lb below his last winning mark, so may be able to capitalise in a lower grade. (op 9-1 tchd 16-1)
Grand Art(IRE) was backed but failed to play a major part. (op 12-1)
Folk Tune(IRE) used this as pipe-opener before returning to jumping. (tchd 28-1)
Joe Jo Star was also using this as pipe-opener before returning to jumping and is due to go novice chasing soon. Official explanation: trainer had no explanation for the poor form shown (op 7-1)

5068 FRONTLINE COMPLETE BATHROOM H'CAP 2m 1f 22y
3:10 (3:10) (Class 5) (0-70,71) 3-Y-O+ **£3,885** (£1,156; £577; £288) **Stalls** Low

Form				RPR
0253	**1**		**Rose Bien**[20] 4388 7-8-10 **55**......(p) AndreaAtzeni(3) 12 (P J McBride) *in rr-div: hdwy 7f out: chsng ldrs over 5f out: styd on to ld over 1f out: kpt on wl* **6/1**[2]	65
113	**2**	1	**Spiders Star**[4] 4890 6-8-13 **60**...... PaulPickard(5) 5 (S G West) *s.i.s: in rr: effrt on ins and nt clr run over 3f out: swtchd outside over 1f out: kpt on same pce fnl 75yds* **4/1**[1]	69+
0502	**3**	1 3/4	**Ameeq (USA)**[9] 4742 7-10-1 **71**...... NCallan 4 (Dr R D P Newland) *prom: effrt over 2f out: kpt on same pce fnl f* **7/1**	78
-060	**4**	3	**Casual Garcia**[18] 4417 4-9-12 **68**......(b) SebSanders 10 (Sir Mark Prescott) *hld up in rr: hdwy 6f out: drvn over 2f out: one pce appr fnl f* **11/1**	72
-211	**5**	1 1/4	**Rare Ruby (IRE)**[38] 3788 5-9-12 **68**...... JoeFanning 6 (Jennie Candlish) *trckd ldrs: led over 2f out: hdd over 1f out: sn fdd* **13/2**[3]	70
/602	**6**	2	**Celtic Carisma**[71] 2725 7-8-9 **51** oh6...... FrancisNorton 7 (K G Reveley) *hld up in rr: hdwy over 2f out: styd on fnl f: nt rch ldrs* **25/1**	51
-623	**7**	6	**Haldibari (IRE)**[69] 2766 5-9-1 **57**...... AlanMunro 3 (S Lycett) *led tl over 2f out: wknd over 1f out* **12/1**	51
0215	**8**	1/2	**Saxona (IRE)**[10] 4703 5-8-8 **55**...... MartinLane(5) 2 (Ian Williams) *prom: drvn 5f out: wknd over 1f out* **8/1**	48
0/05	**9**	10	**Secret Ploy**[15] 4551 9-9-12 **68**......(p) RobertHavlin 1 (H Morrison) *chsd ldrs: sn drvn along: lost pl over 2f out: eased 1f out* **9/1**	50
-240	**10**	1	**Unawatuna**[15] 4551 4-9-1 **57**...... TomEaves 9 (Mrs K Walton) *chsd ldrs: lost pl over 2f out* **16/1**	38
3025	**11**	1 1/2	**Tropical Bachelor (IRE)**[29] 3575 3-8-6 **67**......(p) LanceBetts(5) 11 (T J Pitt) *prom: effrt over 2f out: hung lft and sn lost pl* **16/1**	46
/004	**12**	14	**Great Quest (IRE)**[9] 4742 7-8-10 **52**...... PaulHanagan 8 (James Moffatt) *hld up in rr: hdwy on outside over 5f out: chsng ldrs over 2f out: sn lost pl: eased whn bhd ins fnl f* **9/1**	16

3m 44.55s (-5.45) **Going Correction** -0.20s/f (Firm)
WFA 3 from 4yo+ 14lb **12** Ran SP% **122.9**
Speed ratings (Par 103): **104,103,102,101,100 99,96,96,92,91 90,84**
toteswinger: 1&2 £5.40, 1&3 £7.50, 2&3 £6.30 CSF £31.38 CT £178.27 TOTE £6.50: £2.50, £2.00, £2.60; EX 36.50.
Owner PMRacing **Bred** Mrs J F Budgett **Trained** Newmarket, Suffolk
■ Stewards' Enquiry : Martin Lane two-day ban: careless riding (Aug 30-31)

FOCUS
A moderate staying handicap featuring a couple of progressive types and run at a sound pace throughout. Solid form which makes a lot of sense.

5069 E B F HIGHFIELD FARM FLYING FILLIES' STKS (LISTED RACE) 6f
3:40 (3:41) (Class 1) 3-Y-O+

£25,546 (£9,684; £4,846; £2,416; £1,210; £607) **Stalls** Low

Form RPR

1030 **1** **Mullein**22 4330 4-9-0 91 SebSanders 6 106
(R M Beckett) *hld up: hdwy on ins over 2f out: led jst ins fnl f: r.o strly* **12/1**

-211 **2** 3 ½ **Bouvardia**85 2279 3-8-11 98 TPQueally 3 95
(H R A Cecil) *trckd ldrs: effrt over 2f out: styd on to take 2nd nr fin* **15/8**1

3255 **3** ¾ **Pretty Bonnie**15 4516 4-9-0 85 StephenDonohoe 5 92
(A E Price) *mid-div: hdwy to chse ldrs over 2f out: edgd lft and kpt on ins fnl f* **20/1**

3211 **4** ½ **Sudden Impact (IRE)**16 4507 4-9-0 90 (e) SilvestreDeSousa 7 91
(Paul Green) *chsd ldrs: outpcd over 3f out: hdwy over 2f out: styd on fnl f* **7/1**3

2350 **5** ½ **Pusey Street Lady**22 4330 5-9-0 96 FrancisNorton 1 89
(J Gallagher) *led tl hdd jst ins fnl f: wknd towards fin* **11/2**2

6004 **6** 1 ¼ **Carcinetto (IRE)**14 4559 7-9-0 95 CatherineGannon 11 85
(P D Evans) *chsd ldrs: outpcd over 2f out: kpt on fnl f* **25/1**

0130 **7** *nk* **Greenisland (IRE)**16 4489 3-8-11 96 RobertHavlin 12 84
(H Morrison) *chsd ldrs on outer: one pce appr fnl f* **12/1**

5623 **8** *hd* **City Dancer (IRE)**14 4559 3-8-11 95 PJMcDonald 14 84
(A Berry) *in rr: hdwy over 2f out: chsng ldrs over 1f out: wkng whn hmpd ins fnl f* **12/1**

-500 **9** 4 ½ **Adorn**15 4516 3-8-11 95 PaulHanagan 8 69
(J Noseda) *hld up towards rr: swtchd outside and hdwy over 2f out: wknd over 1f out* **20/1**

2203 **10** ½ **Hansomis (IRE)**11 4657 5-9-0 66 NeilBrown 9 68
(B Mactaggart) *a in rr: nvr on terms* **100/1**

-064 **11** 4 ½ **Red Dune (IRE)**16 4489 4-9-0 99 NCallan 2 53
(M A Jarvis) *w ldrs: wknd appr fnl f: eased towards fin: b.b.v* **11/2**2

635- **12** 5 **Ares Choix**330 6102 3-8-11 95 J-PGuillambert 4 37
(P C Haslam) *drvn along: chsd ldrs: lost pl over 2f out: eased whn bhd ins fnl f* **40/1**

1m 14.44s (-2.46) **Going Correction** -0.20s/f (Firm)
WFA 3 from 4yo+ 3lb **12** Ran SP% **117.9**
Speed ratings (Par 108): **108,103,102,101,101 99,98,98,92,92 86,79**
toteswinger: 1&2 £6.80, 1&3 £31.90, 2&3 £15.60 CSF £32.74 TOTE £16.40: £3.70, £1.30, £7.00; EX 49.10.
Owner Landmark Racing Limited **Bred** C D S Bryce And Mrs M Bryce **Trained** Whitsbury, Hants

FOCUS
Not the strongest Listed race but competitive, with the majority of the field covered by 9lb on official ratings; several three-year-olds who were useful juveniles but had a bit to prove taking on some reliable older performers in this grade, added to the interest. They went a good gallop and it was no surprise that the winner came from off the pace. The third looks the best guide.

NOTEBOOK
Mullein, whose best form has been on Polytrack and on easy ground prior to this, was having only her second try on fast ground and second attempt in this grade. She was given a fine ride by Sanders, who settled her on the rail and got the splits when she needed them. Once the filly hit the front she burst clear to score in quite impressive style and looks capable of winning again at this level. (op 10-1)
Bouvardia picked up a couple of handicaps on fast ground in the spring but had been given a break since. She played up on the way to the start, but travelled well in the race on this first try at Listed level, only to be unable to respond when the winner arrived on the scene. An easier track might suit her better. (op 2-1 tchd 9-4 in a place)
Pretty Bonnie has won on fast ground but is better known as a filly who appreciates some cut. She had a fair bit to find with most of these on official ratings but appreciated the good gallop and stayed on under pressure to earn valuable black type, but probably blow her handicap mark in the process. (op 16-1)
Sudden Impact(IRE) has been in fine form of late and ran on to post her best effort in this grade, despite the ground being faster than she would have ideally preferred. (op 9-1)
Pusey Street Lady made the most of the running from her inside stall but came to the end of her tether when the winner went past and was run out of the placings late on. She would ideally have liked an easier surface. (op 13-2 tchd 5-1)
Carcinetto(IRE) has been busy but pretty consistent all season. She had a tough task from her high draw and only stayed on late.
Greenisland(IRE) had to race wide throughout over the shortest trip she had yet tried. (tchd 14-1)
City Dancer(IRE) has been in good form at this level of late and came to have a chance, but did not get much room inside the final furlong, otherwise she might have finished closer.
Red Dune(IRE) showed up for a fair way but reportedly bled from the nose and unsurprisingly dropped away in the closing stages. Official explanation: trainer's rep said filly bled post-race (op 9-2 tchd 6-1)

5070 NOVA DISPLAY ANNIVERSARY H'CAP 1m 4y
4:10 (4:11) (Class 3) (0-95,91) 3-Y-O

£9,346 (£2,799; £1,399; £700; £349; £175) **Stalls** Low

Form RPR

1041 **1** **Invisible Man**22 4316 3-9-4 **88** RobertHavlin 3 99+
(J H M Gosden) *trckd ldrs: nt clr run 2f out: styd on fnl f: led towards fin* **2/1**1

421 **2** *nk* **Kaolak (USA)**2 5003 3-8-11 **81** 6ex (v) FrancisNorton 2 88
(J Ryan) *led: kpt on wl fnl f: hdd towards fin* **7/2**2

3100 **3** 3 **Mohtashem (IRE)**15 4549 3-8-10 **85** Louis-PhilippeBeuzelin(5) 5 85
(Sir Michael Stoute) *stmbld s: sn chsng ldrs: drvn 3f out: styd on same pce fnl f* **14/1**

1106 **4** *shd* **Eastern Empire**19 4409 3-9-5 **89** MichaelHills 8 89
(J W Hills) *hld up in rr: effrt on outer over 2f out: kpt on same pce appr fnl f* **14/1**

4-32 **5** *nk* **Rafiqa (IRE)**36 3868 3-9-7 **91** AlanMunro 6 90
(C F Wall) *hld up in rr: effrt on ins over 3f out: n.m.r and swtchd rt over 1f out: nvr trbld ldrs* **4/1**3

3 **6** 2 ¼ **Laazim (USA)**13 4599 3-8-10 **80** JoeFanning 4 74
(M Johnston) *w ldr: drvn over 2f out: wknd appr fnl f: eased nr fin* **16/1**

0043 **7** 3 ¼ **Canwinn (IRE)**18 4433 3-9-0 **84** TonyCulhane 7 71
(M R Channon) *hld up in rr: effrt on outer over 2f out: lost pl over 1f out: eased towards fin* **10/1**

0205 **8** 3 ¼ **Deadly Secret (USA)**10 4708 3-9-4 **88** PaulHanagan 1 67
(R A Fahey) *trckd ldrs on inner: drvn over 2f out: wknd over 1f out: eased wl ins fnl f* **15/2**

1m 43.42s (-2.48) **Going Correction** -0.20s/f (Firm) **8** Ran SP% **115.6**
Speed ratings (Par 104): **104,103,100,100,100 98,94,91**
toteswinger: 1&2 £2.40, 1&3 £6.70, 2&3 £10.90 CSF £9.13 CT £74.86 TOTE £2.80: £1.30, £1.60, £4.30; EX 11.30.
Owner H R H Princess Haya Of Jordan **Bred** Darley **Trained** Newmarket, Suffolk
■ Stewards' Enquiry : Francis Norton five-day ban: used whip with excessive frequency (Aug 30-Sep 3)

FOCUS
A decent, competitive handicap run at a fair gallop. Solid form and the winner can do better still.

NOTEBOOK
Invisible Man ◆ put up a career-best performance on his previous start and won in good style off a 5lb higher mark. He travelled well behind the leaders but for a few moments early in the straight it looked as if he might not get a clear run. However, once he got the opening he picked up well and won in the manner of an improving colt. He could make up into a Cambridgeshire type if continuing to go the right way. (op 9-4)
Kaolak(USA), an all-the-way winner at Newmarket two days previously, tried to adopt the same tactics under a 6lb penalty but came up against an improving colt and it was no disgrace to lose out. He is clearly in good heart. (op 9-2)
Mohtashem(IRE) had not really gone on from his maiden win but this was better, although he could not produce a change of gear in the straight. (op 16-1)
Eastern Empire has been competing in tougher races than this but appeared to be given a fair amount to do and only ran on when the race was over. (op 12-1 tchd 10-1)
Rafiqa(IRE) was never going that well before running on and probably found the ground too quick for her. (op 3-1 tchd 9-2)
Laazim(USA) showed up for a long way before weakening. (op 20-1)
Canwinn(IRE) failed to get competitive from the rear and may need easier ground. (op 9-1 tchd 8-1)
Deadly Secret(USA) was too keen early. (op 11-1 tchd 7-1)

5071 CAROLINE LOUISE WILL YOU MARRY ME MAIDEN STKS (DIV I) 1m 4y
4:40 (4:41) (Class 4) 3-Y-O+ **£4,857** (£1,445; £722; £360) **Stalls** Low

Form RPR

1 **Life's Challenge (USA)** 3-8-10 0 GregFairley 8 78+
(M Johnston) *trckd ldrs: effrt and nt clr run over 2f out: rdn to ld over 1f out: styd on strly to forge clr ins fnl f* **13/2**3

54 **2** 7 **Landofthefourones (USA)**17 4472 3-9-1 0 TPQueally 9 66
(D R Lanigan) *trckd ldrs: shkn up 6f out: effrt 3f out: kpt on same pce over 1f out: tk modest 2nd nr fin* **9/2**2

3 **3** *hd* **El Ameen**29 4097 3-9-1 0 JoeFanning 10 65
(M Johnston) *w ldr: led over 2f out: hdd over 1f out: one pce* **2/5**1

3 **4** *shd* **Towthorpe**8 4805 3-8-8 0 JohnCavanagh(7) 5 65
(M Brittain) *led tl over 2f out: kpt on wl fnl f* **20/1**

0 **5** 8 **Fabled Dancer (IRE)**23 4276 3-9-1 0 DavidAllan 6 46
(E J Alston) *trckd ldrs: effrt 3f out: sn lost pl* **25/1**

6 5 **Convitezza** 3-8-10 0 PatrickMathers 3 29
(M E Sowersby) *s.s: hdwy and in tch over 4f out: hung lft and lost pl over 2f out* **100/1**

05 **7** 3 ¼ **Needy McCredie**15 4550 3-8-10 0 PAspell 7 21
(J R Turner) *chsd ldrs: drvn over 3f out: lost pl over 2f out* **33/1**

0 **8** 15 **Foxholes Lodge**26 4174 4-9-2 0 FrancisNorton 4 —
(J D Bethell) *in rr: drvn over 3f out: sn bhd: t.o 2f out* **66/1**

1m 44.49s (-1.41) **Going Correction** -0.20s/f (Firm)
WFA 3 from 4yo 6lb **8** Ran SP% **117.0**
Speed ratings (Par 105): **99,92,91,91,83 78,75,60**
toteswinger: 1&2 £1.50, 1&3 £1.60, 2&3 £1.70 CSF £33.41 TOTE £7.30: £1.60, £1.40, £1.02; EX 27.40.
Owner Sheikh Hamdan Bin Mohammed Al Maktoum **Bred** Fab Oak Stables **Trained** Middleham Moor, N Yorks

FOCUS
The first division of this older-horse maiden looked modest judged on limited previous form and, in the absence of Great Art, El Ameen stood out on that basis. The time was 1.07secs slower than the preceding handicap. It probably had more strength in depth than the second division and the form is rated around the runner-up.

5072 CAROLINE LOUISE WILL YOU MARRY ME MAIDEN STKS (DIV II) 1m 4y
5:10 (5:10) (Class 4) 3-Y-O+ **£4,857** (£1,445; £722; £360) **Stalls** Low

Form RPR

2232 **1** **Park Lane**30 4057 3-9-1 77 MichaelHills 4 81+
(B W Hills) *mde all: pushed wl clr over 1f out: eased towards fin* **10/11**1

-245 **2** 9 **Kessraa (IRE)**11 4655 3-9-1 68 TonyCulhane 6 56
(M R Channon) *chsd ldrs: drvn over 3f out: sn outpcd: hung lft over 1f out: kpt on to take modest 2nd nr fin* **13/2**3

5 **3** *nk* **Tripbiyah (USA)**21 4354 3-9-1 0 PJMcDonald 3 56
(G A Swinbank) *chsd wnr: drvn and clr 2nd over 2f out: wknd and lost 2nd nr fin* **15/2**

4 ½ **Freda's Rose (IRE)**23 5-8-13 0 RussellKennemore(3) 1 49
(O Brennan) *s.i.s: hld up: drvn over 2f out: styd on fnl f* **50/1**

5 15 **Sleepy Dove**65 4-9-2 0 PatrickMathers 10 13
(M E Sowersby) *s.i.s: hdwy 5f out: lost pl 2f out* **100/1**

60-3 **6** 6 **Dalesway**16 4505 3-8-12 70 FrederikTylicki(3) 5 4
(R A Fahey) *chsd ldrs: drvn 3f out: sn lost pl and bhd* **11/4**2

0 **7** 19 **Step Into Sunshine (USA)**16 4505 3-8-10 0 JoeFanning 9 —
(M Johnston) *s.i.s: sn trcking ldrs: lost pl over 2f out: sn bhd: eased* **16/1**

1m 43.91s (-1.99) **Going Correction** -0.20s/f (Firm)
WFA 3 from 4yo+ 6lb **7** Ran SP% **113.0**
Speed ratings (Par 105): **101,92,91,91,76 70,51**
toteswinger: 1&2 £1.70, 1&3 £5.40, 2&3 £3.50 CSF £7.52 TOTE £1.70: £1.10, £2.70; EX 5.20.
Owner Raymond Tooth **Bred** D J And Mrs Deer **Trained** Lambourn, Berks

FOCUS
The second leg of this mile maiden looked the weaker, despite some fair previous form on offer. The winner is probably the best guide. The time was 0.58secs faster than the previous race and just under half a second slower than the handicap over the trip.

5073 TREVOR WOODS MEMORIAL H'CAP 5f
5:40 (5:40) (Class 5) (0-70,70) 3-Y-O+ **£3,885** (£1,156; £577; £288) **Stalls** Low

Form RPR

0001 **1** **King Of Swords (IRE)**11 4662 5-8-12 **59** (p) AndrewElliott 10 67
(N Tinkler) *chsd ldrs: styd on wl ins fnl f: led nr fin* **7/1**3

0300 **2** ¾ **Darcy's Pride (IRE)**3 4929 5-8-7 **54** (t) TonyHamilton 1 59
(P T Midgley) *w ldr: led jst ins fnl f: hdd and no ex cl home* **7/1**3

6340 **3** ½ **Comptonspirit**21 4355 5-8-12 **59** J-PGuillambert 6 63
(B P J Baugh) *chsd ldrs: nt clr run and swtchd rt appr fnl f: styd on wl ins fnl f: fin strly* **5/1**1

1000 **4** *shd* **Lucky Dan (IRE)**[10] 4707 3-9-3 **66** SilvestreDeSousa 13 69
(Paul Green) *in rr: hdwy and nt clr run over 1f out: styd on wl ins fnl f: fin wl* **10/1**

4451 **5** *1 1/4* **Andrasta**[8] 4778 4-7-13 **53** CharlotteKerton(7) 9 52
(A Berry) *stall opened fractionally early: swtchd lft s: led: hdd jst ins fnl f: fdd towards fin* **16/1**

6350 **6** *1* **Dalarossie**[7] 4823 4-8-8 **55** DavidAllan 14 50
(E J Alston) *chsd ldrs on outer: kpt on same pce fnl f* **12/1**

0000 **7** *3/4* **Commander Wish**[4] 4907 6-9-1 **62** DNolan 3 54
(Lucinda Featherstone) *mid-div: effrt over 2f out: kpt on: nvr trbld ldrs* **8/1**

4203 **8** *1* **Monte Cassino (IRE)**[21] 4355 4-8-10 **62** ow2 JamesO'Reilly(5) 12 51
(J O'Reilly) *chsd ldrs: edgd lft over 2f out: wknd fnl 150yds* **7/1**[3]

10-0 **9** *2* **Azygous**[19] 4399 6-8-1 **55** JamesPSullivan(7) 2 37
(M W Easterby) *in rr: effrt on ins whn hmpd over 2f out: lost pl over 1f out* **20/1**

0010 **10** *1/2* **He's A Humbug (IRE)**[24] 4225 5-9-9 **70** (p) JoeFanning 17 50
(J O'Reilly) *chsd ldrs on outer: wknd appr fnl f* **16/1**

500 **11** *nk* **Punching**[8] 4787 5-9-2 **63** TravisBlock 8 42
(C R Dore) *mid-div: effrt on outer over 2f out: sn wknd* **14/1**

0360 **12** *10* **Digital**[13] 4604 12-8-12 **59** TonyCulhane 11 2
(M R Channon) *sn last: detached 3f out: hung lft and sn wl bhd* **6/1**[2]

62.84 secs (-0.46) **Going Correction** -0.20s/f (Firm)
WFA 3 from 4yo+ 2lb **12** Ran SP% **119.5**
Speed ratings (Par 103): **95,93,93,92,90 89,88,86,83,82 81,65**
toteswinger: 1&2 £17.50, 1&3 £8.40, 2&3 £9.80 CSF £55.90 CT £275.29 TOTE £9.10: £2.40, £2.80, £2.40; EX 92.50 Place 6 £6.32, Place 5 £6.00.
Owner P Alderson & J Raybould **Bred** Maurice G McAuley **Trained** Langton, N Yorks

FOCUS
A modest sprint handicap but a number of withdrawals made this less of a draw race than it might have been. The time was significantly slower than that recorded by the juveniles in the opening contest. Sound form.
Digital Official explanation: vet said gelding was distressed
T/Plt: £10.90 to a £1 stake. Pool: £51,612.01. 3,429.50 winning tickets. T/Qpdt: £5.30 to a £1 stake. Pool: £3,080.48. 424.78 winning tickets. WG

GRANVILLE-ST PAIR SUR MER
Saturday, August 15

OFFICIAL GOING: Good

5074a PRIX DU COTENTIN (AMATEUR RIDERS) 1m 4f
4:00 (12:00) 4-Y-0+ **£2,379** (£2,379; £1,019; £680; £340)

RPR

1 **Pole Star**[27] 11-10-3 (b) MrRHodson 63
(Ms V S Lucas, Jersey)

1 *dht* **King Tune (FR)**[743] 8-10-12 MlleAnne-SophiePacault 72
(Mme I Pacault, France)

3 *7* **Lady Sugar (FR)** 4-10-2 (p) MissMPlat 51
(Mlle M-L Mortier, France)

4 *10* **Regal Angel**[152] 501 6-10-0 MrPDetre 33
(Jean-Rene Auvray)

5 *2* **Zizou Des Fosses (FR)**[96] 7-10-3 (p) 33
(P Larbodiere, France)

6 *3* **Happy Light (FR)**[449] 10-10-0 25
(G-E Martin, France)

7 *1* **Monet's Gold**[75] 4-10-8 (b) 31
(Mme C Jung, France)

8 *3* **Top Pursuit**[13] 4586 7-10-5 MrJ-PBoisgontier 23
(Ms V S Lucas, Jersey)

9 *2* **Milouk (FR)** 4-10-0 15
(T Cambefort,)

10 *4* **Mazel Baby (FR)**[28] 6-10-0 (p) 9
(Mlle C Azzoulai, France)

0 **One Little David (GER)**[678] 9-10-3 —
(Y Fertillet, France)

0 **Corleone (FR)**[55] 7-10-3 —
(D Windrif, France)

0 **Rusee Des Ongrais (FR)** 4-10-0 —
(P Chemin, France)

0 **Idefix De Cardam (FR)** 13-10-3 —
(J R Lotout, France)

P **Cadouble (FR)**[701] 6-10-3 (b) —
(G Chaignon, France)

P **Jose Thomas (IRE)** 12-10-3 —
(Mlle V Voute, France)

16 Ran
PARI-MUTUEL (including one euro stakes): King Tune WIN 1.50, PL 1.40;Pole Star WIN 4.40, PL 3.20; Lady Sugar PL 2.80; DF 12.60.
Owner Exors of the late J-C Evain **Bred** Scea Haras De Mirande **Trained** France
Owner M Shenkin, G Shenkin, Dr I R Shenkin **Bred** Snailwell Stud Co Ltd **Trained** Jersey

5075 - (Foreign Racing) - See Raceform Interactive

4356
CURRAGH (R-H)
Sunday, August 16

OFFICIAL GOING: Soft to heavy

5076a ROYAL WHIP STKS (GROUP 2) 1m 2f
2:45 (2:46) 3-Y-0+ **£68,106** (£21,213; £10,048; £3,349; £2,233)

RPR

1 **Casual Conquest (IRE)**[24] 4253 4-9-11 121 (t) PJSmullen 2 121+
(D K Weld, Ire) *trckd ldrs in 3rd: hdwy to ld 2 1/2f out: sn chal: rdn 1 1/2f out: kpt on wl u.p fnl f to assert cl home* **8/13**[1]

2 *1 1/4* **Curtain Call (FR)**[22] 4329 4-9-8 FMBerry 6 115
(L M Cumani) *settled in 4th: hdwy to 2nd 2 1/2f out: sn chal: rdn 1 1/2f out: kpt on fnl f: no ex cl home* **15/8**[2]

3 *13* **Red Rock Canyon (IRE)**[24] 4253 5-9-8 103 JMurtagh 4 93
(A P O'Brien, Ire) *led: rdn over 3f out: hdd 2 1/2f out: sn no ex in 3rd: kpt on one pce* **14/1**[3]

4 *3/4* **Deauville Vision (IRE)**[36] 3882 6-9-5 106 (b[1]) RPCleary 5 85
(M Halford, Ire) *hld up in rr: rdn and no imp 2 1/2f out: mod 4th ins fnl f* **33/1**

5 *11* **Via Galilei (IRE)**[41] 3700 4-9-8 107 KJManning 1 66
(J S Bolger, Ire) *chsd ldr in 2nd: rdn in 4th 2 1/2f out: sn no ex and wknd* **16/1**

2m 15.74s (6.24) **Going Correction** +1.00s/f (Soft) **5** Ran SP% **112.2**
Speed ratings: **115,114,103,103,94**
CSF £2.06 TOTE £1.50: £1.10, £2.20; DF 2.50.
Owner Moyglare Stud Farm Ltd **Bred** Moyglare Stud Farm Ltd **Trained** The Curragh, Co Kildare

FOCUS
This race turned into something of a sprint, which wouldn't have necessarily suited the winner. The runner-up sets the standard.

NOTEBOOK
Casual Conquest(IRE) travelled well off what was no more than an even pace before moving through smoothly to dispute inside the final 2f and gradually asserting his superiority. He probably did no more than was required in order to win this, but it was a decent enough performance. He looks likely to take in the Irish Champion Stakes next which will be an altogether different type of contest.
Curtain Call(FR) ran right up to his mark. Fran Berry never let the winner out of his sights and travelled as well as him to mount his challenge inside the final 2f, but, despite running on well, he could do no better than get within half a length before eventually running out of steam. He's capable of winning again at a similar level. (op 9/4)
Red Rock Canyon(IRE) set the somewhat even pace before fading inside the final furlong and a half.
Deauville Vision(IRE) was struggling to compete once the pace quickened in the straight before she ran on at one pace.
Via Galilei(IRE), a very decent handicapper, was outclassed in this grade. Even so, having raced close to the pace most of the way, it was a bit disappointing the way he dropped away completely inside the final furlong. (op 12/1)

5079a PATRICK P. O'LEARY MEMORIAL PHOENIX SPRINT (GROUP 3) 6f
4:15 (4:15) 3-Y-0+ **£42,330** (£12,407; £5,902; £2,000)

RPR

1 **Girouette (IRE)**[21] 4358 4-9-1 101 PShanahan 6 103
(Tracey Collins, Ire) *trckd ldr in 2nd: impr to ld 2f out: rdn and kpt on wl fnl f: strly pressed cl home: all out and jst hld on* **5/1**[2]

2 *shd* **Perfect Polly**[7] 4832 4-9-1 100 FMBerry 3 103+
(James M Ryan, Ire) *hld up towards rr: hdwy in 6th 1 1/2f out: rdn into 5th 1f out: kpt on wl fnl f to press ldr cl home: jst failed* **8/1**

3 *1 1/4* **Icelandic**[30] 4059 7-9-4 (t) HayleyTurner 9 102
(F Sheridan) *mid-div: 7th 1/2-way: hdwy in 5th 2f out: rdn into 3rd 1f out: no ex ins fnl f and kpt on same pce* **6/1**[3]

4 *3/4* **Croisultan (IRE)**[7] 4832 3-9-1 101 CO'Donoghue 1 100
(Liam McAteer, Ire) *led: hdd 2f out: rdn and no ex over 1f out: kpt on same pce fnl f* **20/1**

5 *2* **Vocalised (USA)**[98] 1917 3-9-6 111 (t) KJManning 10 98
(J S Bolger, Ire) *chsd ldrs on outer: 4th 1/2-way: 3rd 2f out: rdn in 4th and no ex 1f out: kpt on same pce fnl f* **7/2**[1]

6 *hd* **Snaefell (IRE)**[7] 4832 5-9-7 106 (p) KLatham 5 96
(M Halford, Ire) *chsd ldrs: 5th 1/2-way: 6th 2f out: rdn and no ex over 1f out: kpt on same pce* **7/1**

7 *1 3/4* **Doncaster Rover (USA)**[14] 4559 3-9-1 PhillipMakin 4 87
(D H Brown) *chsd ldrs: 3rd 1/2-way: rdn in 4th 2f out: sn no ex* **5/1**[2]

8 *2 1/2* **Heart Shaped (USA)**[46] 3516 3-8-12 107 JMurtagh 7 76
(A P O'Brien, Ire) *hld up in rr: clsr in 7th 1 1/2f out: rdn and no imp over 1f out* **6/1**[3]

9 *1 3/4* **Gluteus Maximus (IRE)**[133] 1136 3-9-1 104 JAHeffernan 2 73
(A P O'Brien, Ire) *chsd ldrs early: 6th 1/2-way: rdn and dropped to rr 2f out: no ex* **20/1**

1m 15.28s (0.58) **Going Correction** +0.425s/f (Yiel)
WFA 3 from 4yo+ 3lb **9** Ran SP% **117.3**
Speed ratings: **113,112,111,110,107 107,104,101,99**
CSF £45.23 TOTE £6.30: £2.60, £2.40, £1.50; DF 41.60.
Owner Celbridge Estates Ltd **Bred** Celbridge Estates Ltd **Trained** The Curragh, Co Kildare

FOCUS
The front-running fourth has been rated to his best.

NOTEBOOK
Girouette(IRE) won despite the race probably not being run to suit her. She bounced quickly out of the stalls and was probably closer to the pace than was ideal, which left Pat Shanahan in the position of dictating for the second half of the race and gradually winding the pace up. In the end, the couple of lengths she got on the field inside the final furlong and a half was crucial as she just held on to win by a paper-thin margin. She is improving and this effort does show that she can be put anywhere in a race and probably has the pace for 5f. (op 6/1)
Perfect Polly was somewhat unlucky. She was held up on the stands'-side rail and eventually had to switch around the field to make her challenge. She ran on really strongly inside the last, but the post came half a stride too soon. (op 9/1)
Icelandic ran his race. He raced just off the pace and ended up making his challenge quite wide, but wasn't really good enough to get any closer. It was still a perfectly respectable effort.
Croisultan(IRE) probably put in a career-best effort as he helped to make the pace before getting outpaced by the winner inside the final 2f. He kept going well, though, and was probably coming back to an extent at the finish.
Vocalised(USA) looked as though he had every chance as he tackled this trip for the first time. He raced prominently, but was being pushed to maintain contact with the winner inside the final 2f. He couldn't get any closer and the experiment was a little inconclusive. (op 3/1)

5080a DESMOND STKS (GROUP 3) 1m
4:45 (4:45) 3-Y-0+ **£39,126** (£11,436; £5,417; £1,805)

RPR

1 **Famous Name**[36] 3882 4-9-10 117 PJSmullen 4 122+
(D K Weld, Ire) *trckd ldrs in 3rd: hdwy to ld 1 1/2f out: stretched clr fnl f: easily* **30/100**[1]

2 *4 1/2* **Three Rocks (IRE)**[28] 4123 4-9-10 108 KJManning 5 108
(J S Bolger, Ire) *hld up in rr: hdwy in 4th 1 1/2f out: rdn into 2nd 1f out: no ch w wnr: kpt on same pce* **13/2**[3]

3 *3/4* **Poet**[119] 1387 4-9-7 100 JMurtagh 1 103
(A P O'Brien, Ire) *chsd ldr in 2nd: rdn to ld 2f out: hdd 1 1/2f out: no ex in 3rd 1f out: kpt on same pce* **11/2**[2]

4 *3 1/2* **Quinmaster (USA)**[37] 3829 7-9-7 102 (t) FMBerry 2 95
(M Halford, Ire) *hld up in 4th: rdn and no imp 1 1/2f out: kpt on same pce* **25/1**

5 *4 1/2* **Man Of Iron (USA)**[50] 3414 3-9-1 93 JAHeffernan 3 85
(A P O'Brien, Ire) *led: rdn and hdd 2f out: no ex and wknd* **25/1**

1m 42.79s (0.89) **Going Correction** +0.425s/f (Yiel)
WFA 3 from 4yo+ 6lb **5** Ran SP% **113.3**
Speed ratings: **113,108,107,104,99**
CSF £3.13 TOTE £1.20: £1.10, £3.20; DF 2.20.
Owner K Abdulla **Bred** Juddmonte Farms Ltd **Trained** The Curragh, Co Kildare

FOCUS
The third sets the standard for the level of the form.

NOTEBOOK
Famous Name had little difficulty gaining his third win of the season in this Group 3. This top-class performer came close to winning the French Derby last year and the outcome here was never in doubt when he seized the initiative over a furlong and a half down. Described as very consistent all year by his trainer, who also reckons a mile is his optimum trip, the Prix Du Moulin was nominated as a possible target for the winner. (op 1/3)
Three Rocks(IRE) was having his 12th start of the current campaign. The five-time winner was held up and went in pursuit of the winner but never at any stage looked like imposing his presence. He has thrived on a busy campaign and did well again to capture the runner-up berth at the expense of Poet. (op 6/1 tchd 7/1)
Poet tracked his stable companion Man Of Iron, who set a good steady clip in the conditions, before taking over passing the 2f marker. Once the winner arrived with his run, though, the 100-rated Ballydoyle colt was soon fighting a losing battle. (op 6/1 tchd 5/1)

5081 - 5087a (Foreign Racing) - See Raceform Interactive

4363
COLOGNE (R-H)
Sunday, August 16

OFFICIAL GOING: Good

5082a RHEINLAND-POKAL (GROUP 1) 1m 4f
4:15 (4:29) 3-Y-O+ **£97,087** (£32,039; £14,563; £6,796)

RPR
1 **Wiener Walzer (GER)**[42] 3670 3-8-10 .... FJohansson 3 122
(J Hirschberger, Germany) *led after 1f: drvn 2f out: hdd narrowly wl over 1f out: battled on u.p to ld again last strides* **9/5**[1]
2 shd **Getaway (GER)**[28] 4128 6-9-6 .... ADeVries 6 122
(J Hirschberger, Germany) *trckd ldr: chal 2f out: tk narrow ld wl over 1f out: r.o: worn down last strides* **9/5**[1]
3 2 1/2 **Eastern Anthem (IRE)**[59] 3048 5-9-6 .... AhmedAjtebi 1 118+
(Saeed Bin Suroor) *hld up in rr: last and brought wd st: styd on fr over 1f out: nrest at fin* **43/10**[3]
4 2 **Schiller Danon (GER)**[42] 3-8-10 .... EPedroza 2 115
(W Hickst, Germany) *led 1f: settled in cl 3rd to st: rdn and one pce fr over 2f out: lost 3rd 100yds out* **153/10**
5 2 1/2 **Saphir (GER)**[42] 3670 3-8-10 .... FilipMinarik 4 111
(P Schiergen, Germany) *racd in 5th to st: 4th wl over 1f out: one pce* **175/10**
6 3 **Poseidon Adventure (IRE)**[16] 6-9-6 ....(b) KKerekes 7 106
(W Figge, Germany) *hld up: 6th st: brief effrt: btn 2f out* **145/10**
7 6 **Flamingo Fantasy (GER)**[28] 4128 4-9-6 .... ASuborics 5 96
(W Hickst, Germany) *cl 4th to st: btn 2f out* **39/10**[2]

2m 29.89s (-3.01)
WFA 3 from 4yo+ 10lb 7 Ran SP% **128.7**
(including ten euro stakes): WIN 28; PL 13, 12, 16: SF 57.
Owner Gestut Schlenderhan **Bred** Gestut Schlenderhan **Trained** Germany

NOTEBOOK
Eastern Anthem(IRE) was settled off the pace and, though he stayed on in the closing stages, the stable companions had already committed and had the race between them for most of the finishing straight. This was his best effort since returning from Dubai.

5057
DEAUVILLE (R-H)
Sunday, August 16

OFFICIAL GOING: Turf course - good; all-weather - standard

5084a PRIX GUILLAUME D'ORNANO (GROUP 2) 1m 2f
2:20 (2:21) 3-Y-O **£71,942** (£27,767; £13,252; £8,835; £4,417)

RPR
1 **Sri Putra**[22] 4296 3-8-11 .... LDettori 3 112
(M A Jarvis) *disp 2nd over 3f: 5th st: swtchd out wl over 1f out: drvn 1f out: qcknd to ld 80yds out: r.o wl* **9/1**
2 3/4 **Three Bodies (IRE)**[20] 4395 3-8-11 .... C-PLemaire 5 111
(P Bary, France) *hld up in rr: last st: gd hdwy appr fnl f: rdn and r.o same pce last 80yds* **6/1**[3]
3 shd **Allybar (IRE)**[21] 4367 3-8-11 .... OPeslier 1 110
(C Laffon-Parias, France) *hdwy over 4f out: 2nd st: rdn and outpcd 1 1/2f out* **9/1**
4 snk **Byword**[41] 3701 3-8-11 .... SPasquier 6 110
(A Fabre, France) *hld up in rr: 6th st: moved outside: drvn over 1f out: r.o steadily: nrest at fin* **6/4**[1]
5 shd **Vesuve (IRE)**[21] 4367 3-8-11 ....(b) ACrastus 4 110
(E Lellouche, France) *mid-div: 4th st: drvn over 1 1/2f out: r.o fnl 100yds but nvr able to chal: fin 6th: plcd 5th* **10/1**
6 shd **Debussy (IRE)**[21] 4367 3-9-2 .... JimmyFortune 7 115
(J H M Gosden) *led: hung lft u.p over 1f out: hdd 80yds out: one pce: fin 5th: disq and plcd 6th* **10/3**[2]
7 1 1/2 **Pure Poetry (IRE)**[15] 4521 3-8-11 .... RichardHughes 2 107
(R Hannon) *wnt 2nd after 3f: 3rd st: effrt on ins: 2nd over 1f out: one pce* **12/1**

2m 6.10s (-4.10) **Going Correction** -0.10s/f (Good) 7 Ran SP% **114.1**
Speed ratings: **112,111,111,111,111 111,109**
PARI-MUTUEL: WIN 19.80; PL 6.50, 2.80, 3.20; DF 53.50.
Owner H R H Sultan Ahmad Shah **Bred** Glebe Stud And Partners **Trained** Newmarket, Suffolk

NOTEBOOK
Sri Putra, dropped in just behind the leading group, was given a brilliant ride and was taken into the lead at exactly the right time. The colt went to the head of affairs in the final half furlong and then repelled several challenges. He is certainly still going the right way, and although connections are not sure about the next target, it may well be the Prix Dollar at Longchamp on October 4th. He stayed the longer distance well on this occasion and may get even further.
Three Bodies(IRE), given a waiting ride, still had plenty to do in the straight and was putting in his best work at the finish. He didn't have the best of runs and finally made his effort near the far rail. All the same it was an improved performance.
Allybar(IRE) ran up to his best form on this occasion. Always thereabouts, he challenged bravely for the lead throughout the straight and was only just pipped for second place near the line. He certainly appreciated the good ground.
Byword was the odds on favourite for this event and never really looked like winning. Dropped out last in the early stages he made progress round the final turn and was beautifully positioned for a late run up the centre but just stayed on one paced in the final stages. Inexperience played a part in his defeat.
Debussy(IRE) made a brave effort to go from pillar to post and was still going well at the head of affairs in the straight, then knuckled down to the task inside the final furlong. He was beaten under a length but was demoted from fifth place as the stewards decided he had stopped another horse obtaining the best possible prizemoney. He was giving 2kg to the rest of the field so it was an excellent effort and his jockey felt he may be best suited by a left-handed track.
Pure Poetry(IRE) has been running well this season but, after showing up early, he could not quicken when the rush to the line began. The extra quarter-mile seemed to find him out.

5085a PRIX FRANCOIS BOUTIN (LISTED RACE) (STRAIGHT COURSE) 7f
2:50 (2:51) 2-Y-O **£26,699** (£10,680; £8,010; £5,340; £2,670)

RPR
1 **Hearts Of Fire**[30] 4049 2-9-2 .... OPeslier 5 106+
(Pat Eddery) *s.i.s: sn trcking ldrs: pushed along 2f out: drvn to ld 1f out: r.o wl* **58/10**[2]
2 5 1/2 **Cadley Road (IRE)**[25] 4209 2-9-2 .... RichardHughes 4 92
(R Hannon) *pressed ldr: drvn and ev ch appr 1/2-way: sn one pce* **17/10**[1]
3 1 1/2 **Walkingonthemoon**[30] 4049 2-9-2 .... RichardKingscote 7 89
(Tom Dascombe) *led to 1f out: one pce* **13/1**[3]
4 3/4 **Beta Leo (USA)**[37] 2-8-13 .... C-PLemaire 2 84
(P Bary, France)
5 1 1/2 **Needleleaf (USA)**[39] 2-9-2 .... MGuyon 6 83
(A Fabre, France)
6 snk **Too Nice Name (FR)**[21] 2-9-2 .... GBenoist 3 83
(Robert Collet, France)
7 20 **Parisella (IRE)**[42] 2-8-13 .... GMosse 1 30
(Mario Hofer, Germany)

1m 22.7s (-5.60) 7 Ran SP% **58.9**
PARI-MUTUEL: WIN 6.80; PL 2.20, 1.20: SF 21.90.
Owner Pat Eddery Racing (Detroit) **Bred** Bearstone Stud **Trained** Nether Winchendon, Bucks

NOTEBOOK
Hearts Of Fire, who was running over 7fs for the first time, put up a most impressive performance. He was held up in the early stages and then burst through at the furlong marker to pass the post on his own. The target now is the 7f Zukunfts Trophy.
Cadley Road(IRE), smartly into his stride, he was at the head of affairs until the winner came alongside at the furlong marker. He couldn't quicken in the same style but did battle on well for second place.
Walkingonthemoon, always well up, ran a little free early on and then lost the battle for second place inside the final furlong.

5086a PRIX DU HARAS DE FRESNAY-LE-BUFFARD JACQUES LE MAROIS (GROUP 1) 1m (R)
3:25 (3:24) 3-Y-O+ **£332,854** (£133,165; £66,583; £33,262; £16,660)

RPR
1 **Goldikova (IRE)**[14] 4580 4-9-0 .... OPeslier 8 131
(F Head, France) *reluctant to load: trckd ldrs: led over 2f out: pushed along: clr whn given two slaps in fnl f: r.o strly* **1/2**[1]
2 6 **Aqlaam**[36] 3841 4-9-3 .... RHills 9 120
(W J Haggas) *pressed ldr: led over 3f out to over 2f out: rdn and sn lft bhd* **12/1**
3 5 **Virtual**[60] 3013 4-9-3 .... JimmyFortune 7 109
(J H M Gosden) *hld up: last 1/2-way: hdwy on outside to rch 3rd wl over 1f out: one pce* **20/1**
4 1 **Irian (GER)**[42] 3669 3-8-11 .... SPasquier 2 106
(J Hirschberger, Germany) *hld up: styd on one pce to rch 4th 1f out: nvr a factor* **25/1**
5 nk **Runaway**[59] 3085 7-9-3 .... TJarnet 1 106
(R Pritchard-Gordon, France) *hld up in rr: hdwy 2f out: nvr nrr than 5th* **100/1**
6 2 **Silver Frost (IRE)**[70] 2756 3-8-11 .... CSoumillon 6 101
(Y De Nicolay, France) *trckd wnr: one pce fr over 2f out* **57/10**[3]
7 snk **Never On Sunday (FR)**[60] 3013 4-9-3 .... C-PLemaire 4 101
(J-C Rouget, France) *a towards rr* **14/1**
8 6 **Gladiatorus (USA)**[61] 2990 4-9-3 .... LDettori 5 87
(Saeed Bin Suroor) *trckd ldrs tl wknd 2f out* **54/10**[2]
9 20 **Only Green (IRE)**[14] 4580 3-8-8 ....(b) DBonilla 3 38
(F Head, France) *led to over 3f out* **250/1**

1m 33.5s (-7.50) **Going Correction** -0.30s/f (Firm)
WFA 3 from 4yo+ 6lb 9 Ran SP% **121.6**
Speed ratings: **125,119,114,113,112 110,110,104,84**
PARI-MUTUEL: WIN 1.70 (coupled with Only Green); PL 1.20, 3.10, 3.90;DF 14.00.
Owner Wertheimer & Frere **Bred** Wertheimer Et Frere **Trained** France

NOTEBOOK
Goldikova(IRE), who proved tricky to load in the stalls, but did nothing wrong during the race and produced undoubtedly the best performance put up in France this season. She was in a different class to the others, was cantering throughout and just cruised into the lead at the three-furlong marker, and from then on it was a procession to the line. She needed a couple of light taps for concentration purposes and was eased in the final 50 yards. This was the filly's sixth Group 1 success and more look likely. The main objective now is a second attempt to win the Breeders' Cup Mile at Santa Anita in November. There are several options before and the most likely route is the Prix de la Foret at Longchamp on October 3rd, but the Moulin has not been totally ruled out.
Aqlaam put up a brave performance but he never had the slightest chance of catching the winner. He was well up throughout but from three out hie could not respond as the filly accelerated into an unassailable lead. Throughout the final two furlongs he stayed on well and never looked likely to lose second place. Connections are now thinking about the Queen Elizabeth II Stakes and the Breeders' Cup Mile. He is certainly an improving individual but will do well to reverse placings with the winner in the latter contest.
Virtual, considering he needs cut in the ground to show his best, put up a fine effort and he certainly acts well over a straight mile. Towards the tail of the field early on, he really began to motor from the halfway stage and was staying on well at the end without ever threatening the runner up. He may well be another to be aimed at the Queen Elizabeth II Stakes at the end of September.
Irian(GER), a German challenger, posted a fine effort and was putting in his best work at the finish after the jockey felt he was a little outpaced in the early stages.. He came with a run up the stands' rail and stayed on well to hold fourth place, doing best of the three-year-olds in the race.
Gladiatorus(USA) was well placed until the halfway stage but then never a factor. He was finally beaten over 20 lengths and is currently running way below his best form.

4837 DEAUVILLE (R-H)

Tuesday, August 11

OFFICIAL GOING: Turf course - good to soft; all-weather - standard

5088a PRIX DES ROCHES NOIRES (C&G) (ROUND) 7f 110y
12:50 (12:50) 2-Y-O £16,505 (£6,602; £4,951; £3,301; £1,650)

RPR
1 **Barbegal (USA)**[30] 2-9-0 ..... MGuyon 84
(A Fabre, France)
2 1 **Cumulus Nimbus**[24] 4080 2-9-0 ..... PatDobbs 82
(R Hannon) *racd in 3rd: pushed along over 1 1/2f out: styd on to take 2nd ins fnl f* **2/1**[1]
3 1 1/2 **Maroon Machine (IRE)**[29] 3935 2-9-0 ..... TThulliez 78
(E J O'Neill) *led: pushed along over 1 1/2f out: hdd appr fnl f: rdn and kpt on u.p* **44/5**[2]
4 snk **Tip Toe (FR)** 2-8-7 71
(F Doumen, France)
5 10 **Toc (FR)**[32] 2-8-5 ..... (6) 52
(C Boutin, France)
1m 39.6s (11.20) **5** Ran SP% **43.5**
PARI-MUTUEL (including one euro stakes): WIN 1.50; PL 1.10, 1.20; SF2.70.
Owner Sheikh Mohammed **Bred** Dapple Bloodstock **Trained** Chantilly, France

5089a PRIX DES PRAIRIES (ALL-WEATHER) 1m 4f
3:55 (4:02) 4-Y-O £12,621 (£5,049; £3,786; £2,524; £1,262)

RPR
1 **Nelson (GER)** 4-9-1 ..... OPeslier 85
(M Trybuhl, Germany)
2 1 1/2 **Natural Leader**[54] 4-8-11 ..... MGuyon 79
(H-A Pantall, France)
3 2 **Satwa Lady (FR)**[38] 4-8-8 ..... TThulliez 73
(J De Roualle, France)
4 nk **Change The World (IRE)**[80] 4-8-11 75
(S Wattel, France)
5 hd **Times Vital (IRE)**[290] 6974 4-9-1 ..... JAuge 79
(E J O'Neill) *hld up in mid-div: 7th and pulling 1/2-way: cl 7th st: rdn over 1f out: kpt on one pce* **13/1**[1]
6 2 **Tresco (FR)** 4-9-1 ..... (b) 76
(M Figge, Germany)
7 hd **Centeo (SPA)**[28] 4-8-11 71
(Mlle A De Clerck, France)
8 1/2 **Montagne Lointaine (IRE)**[40] 4-8-5 ..... (6) 71
(N Clement, France)
9 2 **Vin Royal (FR)**[302] 4-8-11 67
(E Lellouche, France)
10 3 **Khadar (GER)** 4-8-11 63
(W Baltromei, Germany)
0 **Desert Nights (IRE)**[63] 4-8-5 ..... (p)(3) —
(D Windrif, France) *cheek pieces*
0 **Lady Of La Garenne (FR)**[12] 4-8-8 ..... —
(Mlle C Azzoulai, France)
0 **Angele Fontenaille (FR)** 4-8-8 ..... —
(Mlle A Voraz, France)
2m 41.2s (161.20) **13** Ran SP% **7.1**
PARI-MUTUEL: WIN 11.20; PL 3.00, 2.00, 3.00; DF 27.30.
Owner U Zerrath **Bred** Gestut Schattauer & Stall Granum **Trained** Germany

4978 KEMPTON (A.W) (R-H)

Monday, August 17

OFFICIAL GOING: Standard
Wind: Virtually nil Weather: Bright periods

5090 DIGIBET.COM FILLIES' H'CAP 7f (P)
2:30 (2:30) (Class 4) (0-80,80) 3-Y-O £4,727 (£1,406; £702; £351) Stalls High

Form RPR
1131 1 **Sarasota Sunshine**[11] 4707 3-9-0 73 ..... (b) LDettori 9 80
(N P Littmoden) *trckd ldrs: led ins fnl 2f: rdn fnl f: hld on all out* **2/1**[1]
150 2 nse **Respite**[35] 3921 3-8-13 72 ..... MichaelHills 4 79+
(W J Haggas) *hld up in rr and racd towards outside: hdwy 2f out: styd on to chse wnr 1f out: edgd rt u.p: styd on strly cl home: jst failed* **8/1**
0020 3 2 **Beautiful Filly**[33] 3989 3-8-7 69 ..... (b) AndreaAtzeni(3) 6 70
(D M Simcock) *towards rr: pushed along 3f out: gd hdwy over 1f out: styd on to go 3rd fnl f but no impression on ldng duo* **7/1**
5600 4 2 1/2 **Calahonda**[25] 4228 3-8-11 70 ..... (p) DarryllHolland 5 65
(P W D'Arcy) *in rr but in tch: drvn along fr over 3f out: stl last whn styd on appr fnl f: gng on ins fnl f but nvr a threat* **9/1**
5614 5 hd **Russian Rave**[33] 3981 3-8-13 72 ..... TPQueally 3 66
(J G Portman) *sn chsng ldr: rdn to chal 2f out: sn outpcd but kpt on ins fnl f* **13/2**[3]
310 6 2 **Steel Free (IRE)**[25] 4228 3-9-5 78 ..... HayleyTurner 8 67
(M L W Bell) *in tch: nt: much room on ins and lost position over 3f out: sme hdwy on ins over 2f out: nvr rchd ldrs and wknd fnl f* **13/2**[3]
221 7 shd **Super Academy (USA)**[54] 3278 3-9-7 80 ..... ShaneKelly 2 69
(J A Osborne) *in tch: hdwy on outside to trck ldrs 4f out: rdn over 2f out: wknd 1f out* **14/1**
-000 8 2 3/4 **Allexes (IRE)**[3] 5007 3-8-5 64 ..... JoeFanning 10 45
(J R Boyle) *sn led: hdd ins fnl 2f: wknd over 1f out* **40/1**
1112 R **Rafta (IRE)**[8] 4814 3-8-10 76 ..... JosephineBruning(7) 1 —
(T T Clement) *ref to r* **6/1**[2]
1m 26.17s (0.17) **Going Correction** +0.10s/f (Slow) **9** Ran SP% **117.0**
Speed ratings (Par 99): **103,102,100,97,97 95,95,92,—**
toteswingers: 1&2 £4.10, 1&3 £5.80, 2&3 £15.80. CSF £19.13 CT £96.24 TOTE £2.60: £1.50, £1.60, £3.20; EX 23.30.
Owner Franconson Partners **Bred** London Thoroughbred S'Vces Ltd & West Bl **Trained** Newmarket, Suffolk

FOCUS
This was a fair fillies' handicap and the form looks sound with the winner progressive.

5091 DIGIBET.COM NURSERY 6f (P)
3:00 (3:00) (Class 4) (0-85,81) 2-Y-O £3,885 (£1,156; £577; £288) Stalls High

Form RPR
321 1 **Seeking Dubai**[14] 4603 2-9-3 77 ..... TPQueally 5 82+
(E F Vaughan) *trckd ldr: led over 2f out: drvn and styd on wl appr fnl f: readily* **7/4**[1]
5260 2 3/4 **Point To Prove**[12] 4639 2-8-7 67 ..... HayleyTurner 1 69
(Miss Amy Weaver) *t.k.h: sn chsng ldrs: drvn and styd on fr 2f out: wnt 2nd 1f out an kpt on but a hld by wnr* **20/1**
41 3 1 1/4 **Ejaab**[26] 4187 2-9-7 81 ..... RHills 4 79
(W J Haggas) *chsd ldrs: rdn and outpcd over 2f out: styd on again appr fnl f: gng on cl home but nt trble ldng duo* **9/4**[2]
01 4 hd **Royal Box**[19] 4424 2-9-1 75 ..... DaneO'Neill 2 72
(R Hannon) *s.i.s: sn rcvrd to chse ldrs: rdn over 2f out: one pce fnl f* **7/1**
21 5 1/2 **Deloria**[23] 4323 2-9-2 76 ..... LDettori 3 72
(Eve Johnson Houghton) *in rr: n.m.r over after 2f: stl plenty to do over 2f out: styd on fr over 1f out: kpt on ins fnl f but nvr a threat* **4/1**[3]
5654 6 3/4 **Tucker's Law**[12] 4647 2-8-6 69 ..... DavidProbert(3) 6 63
(B R Millman) *led tl hdd over 2f out: wknd fnl f* **14/1**
1m 14.2s (1.10) **Going Correction** +0.10s/f (Slow) **6** Ran SP% **111.1**
Speed ratings (Par 96): **96,95,93,93,92 91**
toteswingers: 1&2 £6.60, 1&3 £1.80, 2&3 £7.60. CSF £33.49 TOTE £2.50: £1.50, £5.40; EX 32.00.
Owner Nabil Mourad **Bred** M E Wates **Trained** Newmarket, Suffolk

FOCUS
Only a modest nursery but the winner looks improved.

NOTEBOOK
Seeking Dubai readily defied a mark of 77. Winner of a 6f maiden at Windsor last time, she was driven to the front over 1f out and ran on well for pressure. Stiffer tasks lie in wait and she will either contest a fillies' nursery at Doncaster next month or the Dick Poole Stakes at Salisbury next time. (op 5-2)
Point To Prove is down to a more realistic mark now and he ran easily his best race to date. The step up to 6f clearly helped and there may be more to come when he goes up to 7f for the first time. (op 25-1)
Ejaab, ready winner of a 6f maiden at Catterick last time, lost his prominent early pitch and couldn't quicken in the straight. He stayed on in the manner of a horse likely to need 7f, though, and we have still to see the best of him. (op 7-4 tchd 5-2)
Royal Box, a narrow winner at Leicester last time, was another who lacked the gears to challenge, but he kept on right the way to the line and will be helped by an extra furlong. (op 6-1 tchd 15-2)
Deloria got shuffled back early and ended up coming wide in the straight. She kept on for pressure, despite hanging, but never posed a serious threat. Official explanation: jockey said filly failed to handle the bend (op 7-2 tchd 9-2)
Tucker's Law, who was the early leader, got swamped inside the final furlong and ended up last. (op 16-1)

5092 KEMPTON.CO.UK H'CAP 7f (P)
3:30 (3:30) (Class 2) (0-100,98) 3-Y-O
£11,091 (£3,321; £1,660; £831; £414; £208) Stalls High

Form RPR
6330 1 **Khor Dubai (IRE)**[18] 4459 3-9-7 98 ..... (v) LDettori 7 103
(Saeed Bin Suroor) *trckd ldrs: rdn over 1f out: str run ins fnl f to ld fnl 50yds: kpt on strly* **7/2**[2]
21 2 nk **Penitent**[30] 4097 3-8-7 84 ..... MichaelHills 4 88
(W J Haggas) *trckd ldrs: drvn to chal fr ins fnl 2f: stl upsides ins fnl f and tk 2nd last stride but a hld by wnr* **6/4**[1]
4030 3 nse **Feeling Fab (FR)**[37] 3839 3-8-6 83 ..... JoeFanning 1 87
(M Johnston) *stdd s: plld hrd and sn chsng ldr: slt advantage fr over 4 out and styd on wl whn strly chal fr ins fnl 2f: hdd fnl 50yds: lost 2nd last stride* **10/1**
45 4 3/4 **Agente Parmigiano (IRE)**[37] 3839 3-9-4 95 ..... (t) ShaneKelly 8 97
(G A Butler) *in rr: rdn and hdwy over 1f out: styd on u.p ins fnl f: gng on cl home* **25/1**
5641 5 1 **Son Of The Cat (USA)**[9] 4788 3-9-2 93 ..... (t) DarryllHolland 2 92
(B Gubby) *chsd ldrs towards outside: rdn over 2f out: one pce fnl f* **7/1**[3]
5133 6 nse **Mac's Power (IRE)**[3] 4984 3-7-13 79 oh4 ..... (t) DavidProbert(3) 5 78
(P J O'Gorman) *hld up in rr: stl plenty to do over 1f out: sn rdn and sme prog fnl f: nvr in contention* **7/2**[2]
6506 7 1 1/2 **Mishrif (USA)**[11] 4708 3-8-12 89 ..... HayleyTurner 3 84
(J R Jenkins) *led: hdd 4f out: wknd ins fnl f* **16/1**
1m 26.52s (0.52) **Going Correction** +0.10s/f (Slow) **7** Ran SP% **115.8**
Speed ratings (Par 106): **101,100,100,99,98 98,96**
toteswingers: 1&2 £1.60, 1&3 £7.20, 2&3 £3.60. CSF £9.43 CT £46.24 TOTE £3.40: £1.40, £1.40; EX 12.80.
Owner Godolphin **Bred** K And Mrs Cullen **Trained** Newmarket, Suffolk

FOCUS
Very few got into this and it was the top weight Khor Dubai who came out on top. the third was back to his best and the sixth ran to form.

NOTEBOOK
Khor Dubai(IRE) came out on top. Disappointing off this mark at Goodwood last time, he had earlier finished a fine third in a good race at Ascot and this was a return to that sort of form. He held a nice position on the rail just in behind the speed and, having been switched, stayed on well to get up close home. (op 5-2)
Penitent, ready winner of a 7f Newmarket maiden last time, was produced to challenge two out and had every chance, but was run out of it late on by the winner. He got the better of his battle with the determined third, though, and may be worth a try at 1m. (tchd 15-8 in a place)
Feeling Fab(FR) often refuses to settle and that was again the case. She kept finding for pressure, though, sticking out a willing neck, but it wasn't enough. She has slipped to a decent mark. (tchd 14-1 in a place)
Agente Parmigiano(IRE), currently rated 8lb higher on the all-weather compared with turf, isn't the easiest to win with and he got going all too late, finishing right on the heels of the leaders. (op 16-1)
Son Of The Cat(USA), who was 9lb higher than when winning with ease at Lingfield last time (first run since being gelded), was unable to find any extra inside the final furlong. (op 8-1 tchd 10-1)

5093 TFM NETWORKS MAIDEN FILLIES' STKS 1m 4f (P)
4:00 (4:00) (Class 5) 3-Y-O+ £2,590 (£770; £385; £192) Stalls High

Form RPR
22 1 **Brief Look**[7] 4838 3-8-12 0 ..... TPQueally 4 94+
(H R A Cecil) *mde all: c easily clr in own time fr 3f out: unchal* **4/7**[1]
4654 2 5 **Sana Abel (IRE)**[17] 4480 3-8-12 72 ..... (p) RHills 3 79
(M A Jarvis) *chsd wnr: rdn over 3f out and sn no ch but styd on for clr 2nd* **14/1**

0-05 **3** *13* **Beauchamp Xenia**[94] 2051 3-8-12 68 DaneO'Neill 6 58
(H Candy) *chsd ldrs: rdn along and no ch fr 4f out: styd on to take mod 3rd ins fnl f* **12/1**

42-2 **4** *1 1/2* **Moonbeam Dancer (USA)**[118] 1430 3-8-12 74 DarrylHolland 8 56
(D M Simcock) *t.k.h: chsd ldrs: rdn 4f out and sn no ch and poor 3rd: dropped bk to 4th ins fnl f* **11/4**[2]

4-4 **5** *7* **Opera Wings**[14] 4606 3-8-12 0 HayleyTurner 2 44
(Sir Michael Stoute) *in rr: sme hdwy 5f out: nvr anywhere nr ldrs and sn rdn: lost tch fnl 3f* **10/1**[3]

0 **6** *25* **Katya Kabanova**[16] 4519 3-8-12 0 PatCosgrave 5 4
(J R Fanshawe) *rdn in rr after 4th: wl bhd sn after* **33/1**

0 **7** *3/4* **Ingenue**[28] 4145 3-8-5 0 RosieJessop(7) 1 3
(Sir Mark Prescott) *a wl bhd: lost tch fr 1/2-way* **50/1**

52U **8** *3 1/2* **Princess Aliuska**[9] 4798 4-9-1 0 GihanArnolda(7) 7 —
(Mrs S Lamyman) *s.i.s: in tch tl wknd qckly over 5f out* **25/1**

2m 33.82s (-0.68) **Going Correction** +0.10s/f (Slow)
WFA 3 from 4yo 10lb **8** Ran SP% **122.5**
Speed ratings (Par 100): **106,102,94,93,88 71,71,68**
toteswingers: 1&2 £2.70, 1&3 £3.10, 2&3 £7.90. CSF £12.46 TOTE £1.30: £1.02, £3.40, £3.80; EX 12.60.

Owner K Abdulla **Bred** Juddmonte Farms Ltd **Trained** Newmarket, Suffolk

FOCUS
Rather a weak maiden and red-hot favourite Brief Look won with ease. The level is tricky to pin down with the runner-up having disappointed since her debut.

5094 DIGIBET CASINO H'CAP 2m (P)
4:30 (4:30) (Class 4) (0-85,80) 4-Y-O+ **£4,727** (£1,406; £702; £351) **Stalls** High

Form RPR

0425 **1** **Alnwick**[19] 4417 5-9-1 **74** JoeFanning 5 83
(P D Cundell) *in rr: rdn 5f out: hdwy to go 2nd 3f out: drvn to ld over 1f out: rdn out* **9/2**[3]

130 **2** *1 1/2* **Eighteenfifty**[38] 3793 5-8-11 **70** MichaelHills 4 77
(B W Hills) *trckd ldrs: led 5f out: rdn over 2f out: hdd over 1f out: styd on u.p but a hld by wnr* **12/1**

3620 **3** *2 3/4* **Warrior Conquest**[23] 4301 4-8-2 **66** Louis-PhilippeBeuzelin(5) 1 70
(W J Knight) *towards rr but in tch: hdwy over 4f out: drvn to go 3rd over 2f out: nvr quite gng pce to chal and no imp fnl f* **5/1**

0212 **4** *1/2* **Black Or Red (IRE)**[16] 4551 4-8-7 **66** (b) FrancisNorton 2 69
(I A Wood) *in rr: hdwy over 3f out: chsd ldrs over 2f out: sn one pce* **7/2**[2]

-102 **5** *4 1/2* **Haarth Sovereign (IRE)**[26] 4212 5-9-7 **80** (tp) ShaneKelly 6 78+
(W R Swinburn) *hld up in rr: hdwy over 3f out: chsd ldrs over 2f out: wknd over 1f out* **6/1**

3320 **6** *nk* **Relative Strength (IRE)**[19] 4417 4-9-0 **76** (v) DavidProbert(3) 8 73+
(A M Balding) *chsd ldrs: n.m.r on ins and lost pl oveer 4f out: sn rdn and nvr in contention after* **11/4**[1]

330/ **7** *51* **Actodos (IRE)**[787] 2816 5-9-4 **80** JamesMillman(3) 7 16
(B R Millman) *mde most tl hdd 5f: sn wknd: t.o* **20/1**

00 **8** *1 1/4* **Sufad**[19] 4417 4-8-11 **70** DarrylHolland 3 5
(T D McCarthy) *trckd ldr: chal after 4f to 1/2-way: sn rdn: wknd 6f out: t.o* **25/1**

3m 29.43s (-0.67) **Going Correction** +0.10s/f (Slow) **8** Ran SP% **114.3**
Speed ratings (Par 105): **105,104,102,102,100 100,74,74**
toteswingers: 1&2 £8.50, 1&3 £7.40, 2&3 £11.70. CSF £55.77 CT £278.84 TOTE £6.80: £1.90, £2.70, £1.90; EX 59.60.

Owner Entre Nous and P D Cundell **Bred** Roden House Stud **Trained** Compton, Berks

FOCUS
This was a modest staying handicap and is best rated around the first three.
Actodos(IRE) Official explanation: jockey said gelding was struck into

5095 TFM NETWORKS H'CAP 1m (P)
5:00 (5:01) (Class 4) (0-80,80) 3-Y-O+ **£4,727** (£1,406; £702; £351) **Stalls** High

Form RPR

0033 **1** **Fancy Footsteps (IRE)**[33] 3980 4-8-12 **69** DavidProbert(3) 3 81
(C G Cox) *rr: hdwy 4f out: drvn to ld 1f out: sn clr: readily* **9/4**[1]

100 **2** *4* **Mohathab (IRE)**[16] 4526 4-9-12 **80** (b1) PatCosgrave 1 83
(J R Boyle) *chsd ldrs: chal over 2f out: led over 1f out: sn hdd: styd on but no ch w wnr* **7/1**

6225 **3** *1/2* **Magic Rush**[78] 2518 7-9-2 **70** LPKeniry 5 72
(Norma Twomey) *stdd s: t.k.h in rr: rdn and styd on fr 2f out: fin wl to take 3rd wl ins fnl f but nvr any ch w wnr* **10/1**

6-50 **4** *nk* **Quick Release (IRE)**[40] 3736 4-9-7 **75** DarrylHolland 7 76
(D M Simcock) *chsd ldrs: rdn over 2f out: n.m.r on ins appr fnl f: styd on again ins fnl f* **15/2**

-310 **5** *1 1/4* **Omnium Duke (IRE)**[24] 4275 3-9-0 **74** (v) MichaelHills 2 71
(J W Hills) *in rr: hdwy on outside fr 4f out: chsd ldrs and rdn 2f out: wknd ins fnl f* **9/1**

3105 **6** *1 3/4* **Carlitos Spirit (IRE)**[38] 3801 5-9-6 **77** JamesMillman(3) 8 71
(B R Millman) *led tl hdd & wknd over 1f out and sn btn* **13/2**[3]

0150 **7** *1 1/4* **Marmooq**[122] 1320 6-8-6 **67** KierenFox(7) 9 58
(M J Attwater) *in rr: stl plenty to do and rdn over 2f out: styd on fnl f* **14/1**

3660 **8** *hd* **Prince Of Thebes (IRE)**[23] 4293 8-9-11 **79** PaulDoe 4 70
(M J Attwater) *chsd ldr: chal over 3f out tl over 2f out: wknd qckly over 1f out* **9/2**[2]

1155 **9** *3* **La Diosa (IRE)**[151] 883 3-7-8 **61** oh1 RichardRowe(7) 6 45
(Mrs S Lamyman) *chsd ldrs to 1/2-way: n.d after* **25/1**

1m 40.15s (0.35) **Going Correction** +0.10s/f (Slow)
WFA 3 from 4yo+ 6lb **9** Ran SP% **116.2**
Speed ratings (Par 105): **102,98,97,97,95 94,92,92,89**
toteswingers: 1&2 £4.00, 1&3 £3.50, 2&3 £8.60. CSF £18.57 CT £132.49 TOTE £3.00: £1.40, £2.40, £2.10; EX 22.10 Place 6: £33.94 Place 5: £17.75.

Owner John And Anne Soul **Bred** Brian Dolan **Trained** Lambourn, Berks

FOCUS
This was a modest handicap but the form looks sound rated around the runner-up and fourth.

T/Plt: £34.50 to a £1 stake. Pool: £67,730.88. 1,429.61 winning tickets. T/Qpdt: £10.60 to a £1 stake. Pool: £4,506.28. 312.50 winning tickets. ST

4850 WINDSOR (R-H)
Monday, August 17

OFFICIAL GOING: Good to firm (8.5)
Wind: Moderate, behind Weather: Fine, warm

5096 EUROPEAN BREEDERS' FUND MAIDEN FILLIES' STKS 6f
5:35 (5:38) (Class 5) 2-Y-O **£3,885** (£1,156; £577; £288) **Stalls** High

Form RPR

50 **1** **Emirates Hills**[9] 4797 2-9-0 0 JimmyFortune 12 72
(E F Vaughan) *racd against nr side rail: led or disp thrght: hrd rdn fnl f: jst prevailed* **11/2**[3]

5 **2** *nse* **Filwa (IRE)**[65] 2906 2-9-0 0 RobertHavlin 4 72
(B J Meehan) *s.s: t.k.h and sn in tch: rdn and prog over 1f out: dipsuted ld fnl f but hanging lft: jst pipped* **14/1**

00 **3** *1/2* **In The Slips (USA)**[14] 4603 2-9-0 0 JosedeSouza 10 70
(P F I Cole) *w wnr: rdn 2f out: stl nrly upsides ins fnl f: no ex nr fin* **25/1**

0 **4** *1 1/2* **Nom De La Rosa (IRE)**[18] 4460 2-9-0 0 ShaneKelly 11 66
(G L Moore) *cl up: rdn 2f out: edgd lft fr over 1f out: nt qckn fnl f* **20/1**

40 **5** *3 1/4* **Candleshoe (IRE)**[18] 4460 2-9-0 0 RichardHughes 7 56+
(R Hannon) *chsd ldrs: rdn over 2f out: nt pce to get on terms fnl 2f* **15/8**[1]

64 **6** *1* **Fair Nella**[11] 4688 2-9-0 0 RichardKingscote 5 53
(J G Portman) *chsd ldrs: nt on terms fr 2f out: no imp after* **8/1**

7 *3 1/4* **Old Money** 2-9-0 0 DaneO'Neill 6 43+
(H J L Dunlop) *s.s: wl bhd in last pair: shkn up 2f out: kpt on: n.d* **20/1**

8 *1 1/4* **Theladyisatramp** 2-9-0 0 HayleyTurner 9 40
(M L W Bell) *dwlt: sn pushed along in last pair and struggling: sme prog fr 2f out: n.d* **8/1**

3 **9** *3/4* **Blue Sparkle (IRE)**[73] 2676 2-9-0 0 JimCrowley 2 37
(Mrs A J Perrett) *in tch on outer: rdn over 2f out: sn wknd* **4/1**[2]

10 *4 1/2* **No Explaining (IRE)** 2-9-0 0 TPQueally 3 24
(B J Curley) *s.s: jst in tch in rr: hanging lft fr 1/2-way: sn bhd* **25/1**

11 *6* **Jemimaville (IRE)** 2-9-0 0 TravisBlock 1 6
(G C Bravery) *reluctant to enter stalls: a wl in rr: hung bdly lft fr 1/2-way: wl bhd after* **66/1**

06 **12** *2 1/4* **Lake Nakuru**[10] 4747 2-8-9 0 AmyBaker(5) 8 —
(H S Howe) *spd to nrly 1/2-way: wknd rapidly* **200/1**

1m 11.54s (-1.46) **Going Correction** -0.275s/f (Firm) **12** Ran SP% **118.3**
Speed ratings (Par 91): **98,97,97,95,90 89,85,83,82,76 68,65**
toteswingers: 1&2 £21.90, 1&3 £16.70, 2&3 not won. CSF £71.14 TOTE £7.30: £2.30, £3.50, £4.20; EX 78.40.

Owner Ali Saeed **Bred** Red House Stud **Trained** Newmarket, Suffolk

FOCUS
The track had been watered to maintain the good to firm conditions. This was a modest fillies' maiden with just an ordinary pace being set, resulting in a tight three-way finish. The form looks fair at best but is rated conservatively around the winner.

NOTEBOOK
Emirates Hills had failed to see out the 7f last time after a fair introduction but returned to 6f seemed far more at home. Always up with the pace she showed a decent temperament when hard pressed and knuckled down well to hang on. She is from a decent sprinting family and had shown enough in her previous runs to show that a race of this nature was well within her compass. (op 5-1 tchd 6-1)

Filwa(IRE) was not particularly good coming out the stalls again but shows plenty of pace and was soon tracking the leaders. She came down the centre of the track when producing her effort and was only just held after holding every chance throughout the final furlong. Going the right way and should be capable of finding an opportunity before long. (op 12-1)

In The Slips(USA) took them along and dug deep when narrowly headed and to her credit battled on well all the way to the line. This was a much better effort than her previous two attempts and if reproducing this she can be found a little race. (op 33-1)

Nom De La Rosa(IRE) finished a long way behind Candleshoe on her debut at Goodwood but that could not have been her running as this was a much better performance. She chased the leaders but could not find the gears to get competitive but stayed on well enough. She might be worth trying back up to 7f on this evidence. (op 16-1)

Candleshoe(IRE) showed a fair standard of form when fourth over course and distance on her debut but failed to build on that effort when stepped up to 7f but after sitting behind the leaders she could not find the pace to mount a challenge. Similar conditions to her debut so this was a little disappointing. Official explanation: jockey said filly was never travelling (op 9-4)

Blue Sparkle(IRE) could never get involved from his wide draw. (op 9-2 tchd 7-2 and 5-1 in a place)

5097 DAVEY WELLINGTON 21ST BIRTHDAY CLAIMING STKS 1m 3f 135y
6:05 (6:07) (Class 6) 3-Y-O+ **£2,047** (£604; £302) **Stalls** Low

Form RPR

051- **1** **Foxhaven**[338] 5885 7-9-11 103 JimCrowley 4 79
(P R Chamings) *mostly trckd ldr: pushed into ld over 2f out: sn pressed and rdn: edgd lft u.p fnl f: hld on* **1/1**[1]

2140 **2** *nk* **Urban Space**[23] 4319 3-8-6 65 HayleyTurner 7 69
(B G Powell) *trckd ldrs: pushed along to stay in tch over 3f out: plld out and drvn over 1f out: styd on to take 2nd nr fin* **8/1**

2433 **3** *hd* **Phoenix Flight (IRE)**[13] 4619 4-9-9 82 SebSanders 3 76
(Sir Mark Prescott) *t.k.h: hld up: prog over 3f out: hrd rdn to press wnr 2f out: chalng after: hld ins fnl f: lost 2nd nr fin* **5/2**[2]

2462 **4** *nk* **Nawamees (IRE)**[3] 4987 11-9-1 65 (p) JimmyFortune 8 68
(P D Evans) *led: rdn over 3f out: hdd over 2f out: edgd lft but kpt on u.str.p fnl f* **6/1**[3]

0051 **5** *15* **The Saucy Snipe**[28] 4146 3-8-0 57 LukeMorris 5 39
(P Winkworth) *in tch: rdn 4f out: wknd rapidly over 2f out* **12/1**

00-0 **6** *3 3/4* **Still Dreaming**[54] 237 5-8-11 37 (b) JamesDoyle 1 34
(R J Price) *a last: lost tch 4f out* **100/1**

2m 29.79s (0.29) **Going Correction** -0.15s/f (Firm)
WFA 3 from 4yo+ 10lb **6** Ran SP% **112.7**
Speed ratings (Par 101): **93,92,92,92,82 79**
toteswingers: 1&2 £2.70, 1&3 £1.40, 2&3 £3.30. CSF £10.17 TOTE £1.80: £1.30, £3.40; EX 9.70.Phoenix Flight claimed by H.J. Evans for £21,000. Urban Space claimed by D. Burchell for £7,000.

Owner The Foxford House Partnership **Bred** Highclere Stud Ltd **Trained** Baughurst, Hants

FOCUS
A fair claimer but steadily run and doubts over the form, with the runner-up the best guide and the winner and third well below their best.

5098 SPORTINGBET H'CAP 5f 10y
6:35 (6:37) (Class 4) (0-85,83) 3-Y-O+ £5,180 (£1,541; £770; £384) Stalls High

Form RPR
0103 1 **Miss Chamanda (IRE)**[21] 4380 3-9-4 80 TPQueally 5 89
(P D Evans) *pressed ldr: led 1/2-way: sn at least 1l up: drvn out fnl f* 11/1
3141 2 ¾ **Rocket Rob (IRE)**[4] 4952 3-9-1 77 6ex RichardHughes 10 87+
(S A Callaghan) *hld up in rr: repeatedly denied clr run fr 2f out: fnlly got through last 100yds: fin wl to snatch 2nd on post* 7/4[1]
5613 3 shd **Efistorm**[5] 4891 8-9-8 82 SebSanders 11 88
(C R Dore) *cl up against nr side rail: plld out and effrt over 1f out: chsd wnr ins fnl f: a hld: lost 2nd post* 9/2[2]
2410 4 nk **Rocker**[18] 4461 5-9-4 78 RyanMoore 6 83
(G L Moore) *in tch towards rr: effrt over 1f out: chsng ldrs ins fnl f: nt qckn* 11/1
6250 5 nk **Ocean Blaze**[32] 3998 5-8-12 72 JimmyFortune 7 76
(B R Millman) *prom: swtchd rt and chsd wnr wl over 1f out: no imp and lost pl ins fnl f* 8/1
1550 6 1 ¼ **Misaro (GER)**[22] 4341 8-9-8 82 (b) LukeMorris 8 81
(R A Harris) *led to 1/2-way: lost pl u.p over 1f out: struggling after* 12/1
2304 7 1 ¼ **The Jobber (IRE)**[15] 4567 8-9-9 83 DaneO'Neill 2 78
(M Blanshard) *in tch: hrd rdn and nt qckn over 1f out: fdd ins fnl f* 9/1
3040 8 ½ **Good Gorsoon (USA)**[18] 4461 4-9-4 81 PatrickHills(3) 1 74
(B W Hills) *sweating: towards rr on outer: effrt 2f out: nt qckn 1f out: fdd fnl f* 6/1[3]
1-4 9 ½ **Sharp Bullet (IRE)**[91] 2140 3-9-7 83 ShaneKelly 9 74
(W R Swinburn) *dwlt: mostly in last: rdn over 1f out: no prog* 12/1

58.88 secs (-1.42) **Going Correction** -0.275s/f (Firm)
WFA 3 from 4yo+ 2lb 9 Ran SP% **122.0**
Speed ratings (Par 105): **100,98,98,97 95,93,92,92**
toteswingers: 1&2 £9.10, 1&3 £13.70, 2&3 £3.40. CSF £32.46 CT £107.51 TOTE £11.80: £2.10, £1.50, £2.30; EX 41.70.
Owner E A R Morgans **Bred** T Molan **Trained** Pandy, Monmouths

FOCUS
A fair sprint, ran at a decent pace but onlty the runner-up got into it from the rear.
Ocean Blaze Official explanation: jockey said mare hung right

5099 SUMMER CELEBRATION WITH GO WEST 29TH AUGUST FILLIES' H'CAP 1m 67y
7:05 (7:05) (Class 4) (0-85,85) 3-Y-O+ £5,180 (£1,541; £770; £384) Stalls High

Form RPR
1003 1 **Resort**[23] 4316 3-9-7 83 RyanMoore 1 91+
(Sir Michael Stoute) *mde all: mostly modest pce tl stoked it up fr over 2f out: drvn and edgd lft fnl f: unchal* 4/1[1]
2165 2 1 ¾ **Cumana Bay**[23] 4326 3-9-9 85 RichardHughes 11 88
(R Hannon) *hld up in tch: prog against rail over 2f out: chsd wnr over 1f out: kpt on but no imp* 5/1[3]
0650 3 1 ½ **Trumpet Lily**[19] 4422 4-9-13 83 JimCrowley 3 86+
(J G Portman) *t.k.h: hld up in last pair: rn into trble after 2f: stl same pl 2f out: prog and rdn over 1f out: r.o to take 3rd ins fnl f: too much to do* 7/1
0112 4 ¾ **Desert Kiss**[17] 4482 4-9-7 80 AndreaAtzeni(3) 8 79
(W R Swinburn) *t.k.h: hld up in tch: rdn over 2f out: hanging lft and nt qckn over 1f out: kpt on* 9/2[2]
0436 5 1 **Young Dottie**[25] 4236 3-8-7 69 CatherineGannon 10 65
(P M Phelan) *t.k.h: hld up towards rr: rdn wl over 2f out: plugged on one pce: no ch* 11/1
1-60 6 1 ¾ **Shamrock Lady (IRE)**[10] 4733 4-9-5 75 TPQueally 5 68
(J Gallagher) *pressed wnr: hrd rdn and nt qckn over 2f out: lost pl and fdd over 1f out* 33/1
4003 7 ¾ **Full Of Nature**[11] 4691 3-8-5 70 DavidProbert(3) 7 60
(S Kirk) *racd wd: in tch: rdn over 2f out: no prog: wknd over 1f out* 14/1
3521 8 ½ **Perfect Class**[17] 4482 3-8-8 70 LukeMorris 2 59
(C G Cox) *dwlt: keen early: dropped in frm wd draw and hld up in last pair: rdn wl over 2f out: no real prog* 7/1
-323 9 nk **Toolentidhaar (USA)**[25] 4234 5-9-3 73 GeorgeBaker 6 62
(Andrew Turnell) *t.k.h: prom: rdn over 2f out: hanging and sn lost pl* 15/2
3130 10 1 ¾ **Flying Valentino**[12] 4641 5-9-2 77 MartinLane(5) 9 62
(Ian Williams) *chsd ldrs: lost pl over 2f out: wknd over 1f out* 14/1

1m 43.48s (-1.22) **Going Correction** -0.15s/f (Firm)
WFA 3 from 4yo+ 6lb 10 Ran SP% **116.2**
Speed ratings (Par 102): **100,98,96,96,95 93,92,92,91,89**
toteswingers: 1&2 £6.40, 1&3 £9.40, 2&3 £7.60. CSF £23.81 CT £138.80 TOTE £4.70: £1.70, £2.50, £3.00; EX 16.30.
Owner Cheveley Park Stud **Bred** Cheveley Park Stud Ltd **Trained** Newmarket, Suffolk

FOCUS
A modest fillies handicap, ran at just a fair pace. The form is not the most solid although the winner ran close to her Newmarket mark.

5100 SPORTINGBET.COM MAIDEN STKS 1m 67y
7:35 (7:36) (Class 5) 3-4-Y-O £2,729 (£806; £403) Stalls High

Form RPR
2-22 1 **Jesse James (IRE)**[102] 1804 3-9-3 82 JimmyFortune 2 91
(J H M Gosden) *mde virtually all: drvn clr fr 2f out: in n.d after: r.o wl* 7/4[2]
5- 2 3 ½ **Stoic (IRE)**[318] 6438 3-9-3 0 RichardHughes 5 83
(J Noseda) *dwlt: hld up in last: effrt over 2f out: prog to go 2nd over 1f out but wnr already gone: styd on but no ch* 3/1[3]
53- 3 5 **Absinthe (IRE)**[290] 7105 3-9-3 0 ShaneKelly 3 71
(W R Swinburn) *hld up in last pair: wnt 3rd 3f out: pushed along and lft wl bhd fr 2f out* 12/1
32- 4 2 ¾ **Karoush (USA)**[441] 2673 4-9-9 0 RyanMoore 4 65
(Sir Michael Stoute) *3rd tl trckd wnr 1/2-way: rdn and cl up over 2f out: sn wknd* 11/8[1]
-000 5 4 ½ **Free Falling**[53] 3302 3-8-7 55 SophieDoyle(5) 6 50
(A J Lidderdale) *chsd wnr to 1/2-way: sn lost pl u.p* 50/1

1m 43.48s (-1.22) **Going Correction** -0.15s/f (Firm)
WFA 3 from 4yo 6lb 5 Ran SP% **113.1**
Speed ratings (Par 103): **100,96,91,88,84**
toteswingers: 1&2 £3.70 CSF £7.65 TOTE £3.20: £1.30, £2.40; EX 6.50.
Owner H R H Princess Haya Of Jordan **Bred** Castlemartin Stud And Skymarc Farm **Trained** Newmarket, Suffolk

FOCUS
An interesting little heat with three of the field making a belated return to action. An ordinary early pace but the tempo was increased as they neared the 3f marker. The form is tricky to pin down and is best rated through the winner to his Goodwood mark.

5101 SPORTINGBET.COM H'CAP 1m 2f 7y
8:05 (8:05) (Class 5) (0-75,74) 3-Y-O £2,729 (£806; £403) Stalls Low

Form RPR
2033 1 **Hawk's Eye**[52] 3357 3-9-4 71 KShea 5 86+
(M F De Kock, South Africa) *dwlt: keen early and hld up in last: smooth prog fr over 2f out: pushed into ld ent fnl f: comf* 4/1[2]
5116 2 1 ¼ **Caster Sugar (USA)**[19] 4441 3-9-1 68 RichardHughes 3 82+
(R Hannon) *hld up in midfield: clsd on ldrs over 2f out: nt clr run and swtchd lft over 1f out: kpt on to take 2nd last strides: no ch w wnr* 8/1
-160 3 hd **Featherweight (IRE)**[31] 4050 3-9-6 73 MichaelHills 7 85
(B W Hills) *trckd ldng pair: clsd 3f out: led 2f out: rdn and hdd ent fnl f: no ch w wnr: lost 2nd last strides* 6/1[3]
321 4 6 **Speed Dating**[22] 4348 3-9-0 67 SebSanders 1 68+
(Sir Mark Prescott) *led: jinked bnd over 5f out: hrd rdn over 2f out: sn hdd and btn* 5/6[1]
3500 5 7 **King's La Mont (IRE)**[11] 4714 3-9-0 67 JimCrowley 2 55
(Mrs A J Perrett) *hld up bhd ldrs: effrt and cl enough over 2f out: rdn and nt qckn: wknd over 1f out* 11/1
2153 6 2 ¼ **Shared Moment (IRE)**[12] 4642 3-8-9 62 (p) LukeMorris 8 45
(J Gallagher) *hld up in last trio: rdn and effrt 3f out: no prog 2f out: wknd over 1f out* 14/1
3060 7 1 ¾ **Mellow Mixture**[12] 4650 3-8-11 64 (t) JamesDoyle 6 44
(S Kirk) *a in last trio: struggling on outer 3f out: sn bhd* 33/1
4-50 8 17 **The Dial House**[66] 2890 3-9-7 74 ShaneKelly 4 22
(J A Osborne) *s.i.s: rcvrd to press ldr after 2f: wknd rapidly 3f out: eased: t.o* 33/1

2m 5.31s (-3.39) **Going Correction** -0.15s/f (Firm) 8 Ran SP% **120.8**
Speed ratings (Par 100): **107,106,105,101,95 93,92,78**
toteswingers: 1&2 £7.50, 1&3 £4.10, 2&3 £5.40. CSF £37.87 CT £192.39 TOTE £5.20: £1.60, £1.80, £1.80; EX 33.10 Place 6: £89.08 Place 5: £19.00.
Owner Ramsden/Mrs Ramsden/Morecombe/McVeigh **Bred** Woodcote Stud Ltd **Trained** South Africa

FOCUS
A modest handicap in which Speed Dating soon recovered from a stumble leaving the stalls to take up the running, soon being pressed and nudged along by The Dial House to set up a fair pace. The third looks the best guide to the level with the favourite not handling the track.
T/Jkpt: £15,726.50 to a £1 stake. Pool: £22,150.11. 1.00 winning ticket. T/Plt: £172.20 to a £1 stake. Pool: £72,386.14. 306.85 winning tickets. T/Qpdt: £14.50 to a £1 stake. Pool: £8,250.84. 419.10 winning tickets. JN

4856 WOLVERHAMPTON (A.W) (L-H)
Monday, August 17

OFFICIAL GOING: Standard
Wind: Light half behind Weather: Fine

5102 LADIES EVENING ON 21ST AUGUST RATING RELATED MAIDEN STKS 1m 141y(P)
2:15 (2:15) (Class 5) 3-4-Y-O £3,885 (£1,156; £577; £288) Stalls Low

Form RPR
0234 1 **Formula (USA)**[23] 4303 3-9-1 79 PatDobbs 1 82
(R Hannon) *led early: chsd ldr: led 2f out: rdn and hdd over 1f out: led towards fin: r.o* 15/2[3]
2202 2 ½ **Implication**[24] 4275 3-8-12 77 SebSanders 2 78
(E A L Dunlop) *hld up in tch: jnd ldrs over 2f out: rdn to ld over 1f out: rdr dropped whip wl ins fnl f: hdd towards fin* 9/4[2]
-322 3 nk **Nbhan (USA)**[19] 4426 3-9-1 77 NCallan 3 80
(L M Cumani) *sn led: hdd 2f out: sn rdn: nt qckn ins fnl f* 4/7[1]
-000 4 19 **Smart Tazz**[73] 2684 4-9-5 42 KevinGhunowa(3) 4 36
(S T Lewis) *hld up in last: reminder over 5f out: sme prog over 4f out: pushed along and struggling over 3f out* 100/1

1m 49.85s (-0.65) **Going Correction** -0.025s/f (Stan)
WFA 3 from 4yo 7lb 4 Ran SP% **107.2**
Speed ratings (Par 103): **101,100,100,83**
CSF £23.34 TOTE £6.50; EX 20.20.
Owner Highclere Thoroughbred Racing-SunChariot **Bred** Holtsinger Inc **Trained** East Everleigh, Wilts

FOCUS
Three fair and closely matched - if reasonably exposed - performers. The gallop was only a moderate one and the principals raced in the centre in the straight. The form is not rated too negatively, with the runner-up the best guide.

5103 BELVOIR LETTINGS H'CAP 1m 1f 103y(P)
2:45 (2:45) (Class 6) (0-60,60) 3-Y-O+ £2,388 (£705; £352) Stalls Low

Form RPR
0042 1 **King Of Connacht**[7] 4861 6-9-4 54 (p) LiamJones 7 63
(M Wellings) *hld up in mid-div: hdwy over 2f out: rdn to ld wl ins fnl f: jst hld on* 11/2[3]
6200 2 nse **The Grey One (IRE)**[4] 4938 6-9-5 58 (p) KevinGhunowa(3) 8 67
(J M Bradley) *hld up in tch: hdwy on outside over 2f out: rdn and edgd lft over 1f out: r.o towards fin: jst failed* 16/1
5344 3 nk **Cheers For Thea (IRE)**[14] 4593 4-9-5 55 (bt[1]) DavidAllan 2 63
(T D Easterby) *a.p: rdn to ld jst over 1f out: hdd wl ins fnl f: r.o* 5/1[2]
0002 4 2 ¼ **Our Kes (IRE)**[16] 4538 7-9-3 53 JimmyQuinn 12 57
(P Howling) *hld up in rr: pushed along 3f out: rdn and hdwy wl over 1f out: kpt on same pce ins fnl f* 7/1
0 5 nk **Seader (USA)**[13] 4625 4-9-6 56 ChrisCatlin 4 59
(Tim Vaughan) *hld up in mid-div: pushed along and lost pl over 5f out: rdn over 3f out: styd on fnl f: nt rch ldrs* 10/1
2001 6 1 ½ **Hits Only Cash**[12] 4645 7-9-4 59 (p) SimonPearce(5) 5 59
(J Pearce) *hld up in rr: pushed along over 4f out: rdn wl over 1f out: styd on ins fnl f: nvr nrr* 17/2
-026 7 ¾ **Benitez Bond**[12] 4656 4-8-9 52 AnthonyBetts(7) 3 50
(G R Oldroyd) *led: hdd 3f out: sn pushed along: rdn and wknd wl over 1f out* 20/1
3403 8 2 ¾ **Quick Off The Mark**[7] 4861 4-9-6 56 (t) J-PGuillambert 1 48
(J G Given) *chsd ldr: led 3f out: rdn and hdd jst over 1f out: wknd wl ins fnl f* 9/2[1]
0446 9 1 ¾ **Wellesley**[33] 3985 3-9-2 59 EddieAhern 13 48
(W R Swinburn) *prom: wkng whn n.m.r ent st wl over 1f out* 8/1

4360 **10** 3 3/4 **Johnston's Baby (IRE)**[12] 4658 7-9-7 **57**........................ TomEaves 11 38
(E J Alston) *hld up towards rr: pushed along over 2f out: sn struggling* **12/1**

400 **11** 14 **Tisifone**[59] 3100 3-9-3 **60**.. IanMongan 10 11
(C G Cox) *prom tl wknd 3f out* **22/1**

2m 1.33s (-0.37) **Going Correction** -0.025s/f (Stan)
WFA 3 from 4yo+ 7lb **11** Ran SP% **116.1**
Speed ratings (Par 101): **100,99,99,97,97 96,95,92,91,88 75**
toteswingers: 1&2 £22.90, 1&3 £8.50, 2&3 £12.70. CSF £88.59 CT £469.00 TOTE £6.10: £2.20, £6.30, £2.00; EX 84.60 Trifecta £181.10 Part won. Pool: £244.78 - 0.43 winning units..
Owner Ann Lindsay,Francis Lindsay,Jim O'Connor **Bred** B Burrough **Trained** Six Ashes, Shropshire

FOCUS
A moderate handicap run at an ordinary gallop but sound enough form. The winner and second raced in the centre in the straight.

5104 ARMY BENEVOLENT FUND - THE SOLDIERS CHARITY H'CAP 5f 216y(P)

3:15 (3:16) (Class 3) (0-95,95) 3-Y-0 **£7,569** (£2,265; £1,132; £566; £282) **Stalls Low**

Form RPR

303 **1** **Jaconet (USA)**[17] 4485 4-9-1 **86**....................................(b) PhillipMakin 2 97
(T D Barron) *a.p: pushed along 3f out: rdn and edgd rt over 1f out: led ins fnl f: r.o* **8/1**[3]

3-61 **2** 3/4 **Prescription**[6] 4870 4-9-6 **91** 6ex.................................... SebSanders 13 99+
(Sir Mark Prescott) *hld up in mid-div: hdwy on outside 2f out: c wd st: rdn jst over 1f out: kpt on same pce ins fnl f* **4/6**[1]

2060 **3** 1 **Bond City (IRE)**[14] 4598 7-9-4 **89**.................................... PJMcDonald 3 94
(G R Oldroyd) *hld up in tch: rdn and ev ch ins fnl f: nt qckn* **25/1**

6000 **4** 1 1/4 **Baby Strange**[19] 4423 5-9-0 **90**....................................... MartinLane(5) 4 91+
(D Shaw) *hld up in rr: pushed along over 2f out: hung lft wl over 1f out: r.o ins fnl f: nrst fin* **16/1**

0563 **5** 1/2 **Xpres Maite**[7] 4842 6-9-1 **86**..(b) AmirQuinn 9 85
(S R Bowring) *w ldr: ev ch over 2f out: rdn and lost 2nd wl over 1f out: sn btn* **50/1**

1201 **6** hd **Luscivious**[7] 4842 5-9-6 **91** 6ex..................................(p) GrahamGibbons 1 90
(J A Glover) *led: edgd rt and rdn over 1f out: hdd ins fnl f: fdd* **16/1**

0505 **7** 3/4 **Something (IRE)**[19] 4423 7-9-10 **95**........................(t) AdrianTNicholls 12 91
(D Nicholls) *hld up towards rr: pushed along and sme prog 2f out: rdn jst over 1f out: nvr trbld ldrs* **7/1**[2]

0502 **8** 3/4 **Mutamared (USA)**[9] 4775 9-8-13 **84**...................................(t) NCallan 11 78
(K A Ryan) *prom tl wknd over 1f out* **25/1**

0160 **9** hd **Aroundthebay**[44] 3641 3-8-12 **86**.................................... ChrisCatlin 6 79
(H J L Dunlop) *prom: lost pl over 4f out: short-lived effrt over 1f out* **33/1**

-050 **10** shd **Hurricane Spirit (IRE)**[17] 4485 5-9-5 **90**........................ JimmyQuinn 5 83
(J R Best) *s.i.s: a in rr* **28/1**

1000 **11** hd **Princess Valerina**[7] 4853 5-8-10 **84**........................ FrederikTylicki(3) 7 76
(D Haydn Jones) *a in rr* **33/1**

-216 **12** 4 1/2 **Baunagain (IRE)**[17] 4500 4-9-2 **87**.................................... EddieAhern 8 65
(P W Chapple-Hyam) *bhd fnl 4f* **20/1**

1m 13.45s (-1.55) **Going Correction** -0.025s/f (Stan)
WFA 3 from 4yo+ 3lb **12** Ran SP% **119.1**
Speed ratings (Par 107): **109,108,106,105,104 104,103,102,101,101 101,95**
toteswingers: 1&2 £1.50, 1&3 £19.40, 2&3 £9.00. CSF £12.72 CT £144.08 TOTE £7.70: £2.40, £1.10, £5.80; EX 16.80 TRIFECTA Not won..
Owner R G Toes **Bred** Team Block **Trained** Maunby, N Yorks

FOCUS
A decent handicap but only two previous winners and progressive performers were in short supply. The winner recorded a personal best with the runner-up just below his Lingfield mark. The pace was sound and the first two ended up centre to stands' side in the closing stages.

NOTEBOOK
Jaconet(USA), a much-improved sprinter in blinkers this year, had the run of the race from her good draw and did enough to post a career-best effort. She has won both starts over this course and distance and, although a further rise in the weights is likely to leave her looking vulnerable to the more unexposed sorts, she should continue to give a good account. (tchd 9-1)
Prescription, under a 6lb penalty for last week's fluent Lingfield win, looked to have solid claims and, while she ran creditably under her penalty after racing wide from her draw, it was a bit of a disappointment that she couldn't go past a more exposed rival in the straight. Nevertheless this was only her eighth career start, she is worth another try over 7f and deserves another chance. (op 8-11 tchd 4-5)
Bond City(IRE) ran well returned to Polytrack to finish a near identical distance behind the winner as he had at Goodwood at the end of last month. He's a useful sort but he has very little margin for error from his current rating.
Baby Strange, returned to sprint distances and to Polytrack, fared the best of those to come from some way off the pace but his form has been patchy since his last win and his style of racing means he remains the type that needs everything to fall just right.
Xpres Maite is a reliable yardstick on artificial surfaces and he seemed to give it his best shot back on Polytrack. He is vulnerable to the more progressive sorts from this mark but left the impression that the return to 7f would suit.
Luscivious was far from disgraced back up in trip and under a penalty for last week's Fibresand victory after hanging to his right in the closing stages. All his all-weather wins have been on that slower surface but he has little room for manoeuvre in a competitive event from this sort of mark. (op 14-1)
Something(IRE), fitted with a first-time tongue-tie, was not disgraced from his double-figure draw returned to Polytrack, and he left the impression that the return to 7f would be more to his liking. This was his first defeat in four starts on sand. (op 8-1)
Aroundthebay Official explanation: jockey said filly lost its action
Hurricane Spirit(IRE) Official explanation: jockey said horse missed the break

5105 STAY AT THE WOLVERHAMPTON HOLIDAY INN H'CAP 5f 20y(P)

3:45 (3:46) (Class 6) (0-60,60) 3-Y-0 **£2,388** (£705; £352) **Stalls Low**

Form RPR

0215 **1** **First Blade**[7] 4843 3-9-0 **56**..(b) AmirQuinn 6 64
(S R Bowring) *a.p: wnt 2nd wl over 1f out: sn rdn and edgd rt: led ins fnl f: rdn out* **3/1**[1]

3346 **2** 1 1/2 **You'relikemefrank**[16] 4514 3-8-0 **47** ow1....................(p) JamieKyne(5) 8 50
(J Balding) *swtchd lft sn after s: chsd ldrs: rdn jst over 1f out: swtchd lft ins fnl f: r.o u.p to take 2nd nr fin* **13/2**

4600 **3** 1/2 **Jolly Ranch**[25] 4223 3-8-2 **51**.. JPFahy(7) 5 52
(A G Newcombe) *w ldr: led over 3f out: hdd ins fnl f: no ex and lost 2nd nr fin* **8/1**

0136 **4** 3/4 **Bold Ring**[3] 4990 3-9-4 **60**... EdwardCreighton 4 59
(E J Creighton) *sltly hmpd s: towards rr: rdn over 1f out: hdwy fnl f: kpt on* **7/2**[2]

0-00 **5** 2 3/4 **Shirley High**[80] 2455 3-8-4 **46** oh1.................................... JimmyQuinn 3 35
(P Howling) *hld up towards rr: stdy hdwy on ins over 2f out: rdn 1f out: no imp* **20/1**

0000 **6** 1 3/4 **Chenin (IRE)**[27] 4174 3-8-4 **46** oh1.............................. FrankieMcDonald 7 28
(Peter Grayson) *w ldrs: ev ch 2f out: rdn and wknd over 1f out* **80/1**

5000 **7** 1 **Thumberlina**[10] 4736 3-8-4 **46** oh1...........................(v) AdrianMcCarthy 2 25
(Mrs C A Dunnett) *s.i.s: in rr: rdn and short-lived effrt on ins wl over 1f out* **25/1**

4566 **8** 1 1/4 **Badtanman**[28] 4137 3-7-12 **47** oh1 ow1..............(b) AndrewHeffernan(7) 1 21
(Peter Grayson) *led over 1f: rdn and wknd wl over 1f out* **11/1**

0000 **9** 4 1/2 **Hello Sunshine**[19] 4425 3-8-4 **46** oh1.................... CatherineGannon 10 4
(T J Pitt) *mid-div: pushed along over 3f out: wkng whn hung lft over 1f out* **33/1**

1302 **10** 3 **What A Fella**[9] 4778 3-8-6 **48**..(p) ChrisCatlin 9 —
(Mrs A Duffield) *s.i.s: a in rr* **4/1**[3]

62.25 secs (-0.05) **Going Correction** -0.025s/f (Stan) **10** Ran SP% **112.8**
Speed ratings (Par 98): **99,96,95,94,90 87,85,83,76,71**
toteswingers: 1&2 £6.50, 1&3 £5.20, 2&3 £8.90. CSF £21.07 CT £138.66 TOTE £4.70: £1.10, £2.90, £3.40; EX 25.10 Trifecta £381.50 Part won. Pool: £515.62 - 0.20 winning units..
Owner S R Bowring **Bred** S R Bowring **Trained** Edwinstowe, Notts

FOCUS
A moderate handicap run at a decent gallop and the placed horses rather limit the form. The winner came down the centre in the straight.

5106 SABRE MAIDEN STKS 7f 32y(P)

4:15 (4:16) (Class 4) 2-Y-0 **£3,885** (£1,156; £577; £288) **Stalls High**

Form RPR

022 **1** **Timely Jazz (IRE)**[23] 4314 2-9-3 **93**................................... EddieAhern 3 84+
(B J Meehan) *mde all: pushed clr wl over 1f out: easily* **1/4**[1]

43 **2** 5 **Logos Astra (USA)**[26] 4209 2-9-3 0...................................... TedDurcan 2 72+
(D R Lanigan) *hld up in mid-div: pushed along over 2f out: hdwy wl over 1f out: wnt 2nd ins fnl f: no ch w wnr* **9/2**[2]

6 **3** 3/4 **James Barrymore**[9] 4790 2-9-3 0...................................... PatDobbs 9 68+
(R Hannon) *hld up in tch: pushed along 2f out: rdn over 1f out: tk 3rd wl ins fnl f: one pce* **10/1**

4 **4** 1 1/2 **Green Community (USA)**[19] 4427 2-8-12 0........................ NCallan 7 59
(E F Vaughan) *chsd wnr after 1f: ev ch over 2f out: outpcd wl over 1f out: lost 2nd ins fnl f* **25/1**

00 **5** 2 3/4 **Chandrayaan**[16] 4534 2-9-3 0.................................... TGMcLaughlin 8 58
(E A L Dunlop) *hld up towards rr: hdwy on outside over 2f out: c wd st: hung lft and wknd wl over 1f out* **100/1**

00 **6** 3 1/2 **Blade Of Glory**[56] 3226 2-8-5 0...............................(v[1]) DeclanCannon(7) 4 44
(A J McCabe) *prom tl rdn and wknd wl over 1f out* **100/1**

7 nk **Temple Fair (USA)** 2-9-3 0...................................... GregFairley 1 48
(M Johnston) *prom tl wknd 2f out* **9/1**[3]

00 **8** 14 **Carlcol Girl**[21] 4385 2-8-12 0..(v) LiamJones 6 9
(Mrs C A Dunnett) *wnt lft and bmpd s: in rr: rdn over 3f out: sn struggling* **150/1**

00 **9** 2 3/4 **Kit Kat**[28] 4152 2-9-3 0... ChrisCatlin 5 7
(George Baker) *bmpd s: outpcd: sn wl in rr* **80/1**

1m 30.09s (0.49) **Going Correction** -0.025s/f (Stan) **9** Ran SP% **125.0**
Speed ratings (Par 96): **96,90,89,87,84 80,80,64,61**
toteswingers: 1&2 £2.00, 1&3 £3.50, 2&3 £3.20. CSF £2.30 TOTE £1.40: £1.02, £1.30, £3.30; EX 2.30 Trifecta £10.90 Pool: £870.57 - 58.62 winning units..
Owner Joe L Allbritton **Bred** Pier House Stud **Trained** Manton, Wilts

FOCUS
An uncompetitive maiden in which the winner was far too good for these but the form is anchored by the fifth and sixth. The pace was only ordinary and the easy winner raced against the inside rail in the straight.

NOTEBOOK
Timely Jazz(IRE), led round the paddock by two handlers, faced his easiest task to date and did not have to improve to win with plenty in hand after enjoying an easy lead on this all-weather debut. Life will be tougher from now on but the colt, who holds a Group 1 entry, remains capable of further progress. (op 4-11)
Logos Astra(USA) ◆, from a yard in good form, looked the main danger to the winner on paper but, while never looking likely to get to grips with that one, he showed more than enough without being knocked about on this all-weather debut to suggest he will be of interest in ordinary handicap company when upped to 1m. (op 4-1 tchd 5-1)
James Barrymore, who made his debut earlier this month, again showed ability at a moderate level and will be one to keep an eye on returned to 1m once qualified for a handicap mark. (tchd 12-1)
Green Community(USA) was far from disgraced on this all-weather debut but again had her limitations in this type of event and will be of more interest in ordinary handicaps in due course. (op 20-1)
Chandrayaan was not disgraced on this first run on sand. Run-of-the-mill handicaps will be the way forward with him. Official explanation: jockey said gelding did not face the kick-back (op 66-1)
Temple Fair(USA) , who is out of a Grade 1 winner in Argentina, was soundly beaten but looked and ran as though he would be all the better for this outing. He is in good hands and is entitled to improve a fair bit for this experience. (op 10-1)
Carlcol Girl Official explanation: jockey said filly never travelled

5107 RCDM - AT SELLY OAK NHS HOSPITAL H'CAP 7f 32y(P)

4:45 (4:45) (Class 4) (0-80,79) 4-Y-0+ **£5,046** (£1,510; £755; £377; £188) **Stalls High**

Form RPR

1252 **1** **Ninth House (USA)**[4] 4941 7-8-13 **71**...............................(t) PJMcDonald 5 79+
(Mrs R A Carr) *hld up in mid-div: hdwy whn swtchd rt over 1f out: rdn to ld wl ins fnl f: r.o* **11/4**[1]

0360 **2** 1 **Gazboolou**[49] 3463 5-9-2 **74**.. EddieAhern 3 79
(David Pinder) *a.p: rdn wl over 1f out: kpt on to take 2nd nr fin* **8/1**[3]

0100 **3** nk **Mark Of Meydan**[24] 4285 4-9-0 **72**.................................... PhillipMakin 10 76+
(M Dods) *hld up towards rr: c wd st: rdn and edgd lft jst over 1f out: hdwy fnl f: r.o to take 3rd last strides* **14/1**

0126 **4** nse **Chief Exec**[23] 4305 7-9-1 **73**..(b) LiamJones 11 77+
(J R Gask) *s.i.s: sn swtchd lft: hld up in rr: pushed along over 4f out: rdn and gd late hdwy on outside: jst failed to take 3rd* **17/2**

1143 **5** nk **Dream Express (IRE)**[9] 4775 4-8-12 **70**........................... IanMongan 9 73
(P Howling) *swtchd lft sn after s: hld up towards rr: hdwy over 1f out: rdn and kpt on ins fnl f* **9/1**

6634 **6** 1/2 **Jonny Lesters Hair (IRE)**[12] 4657 4-8-11 **69**...................... DavidAllan 8 71
(T D Easterby) *prom: chsd ldr over 5f out: pushed along 2f out: rdn and nt qckn fnl f* **6/1**[2]

2310 **7** hd **Captain Jacksparra (IRE)**[15] 4560 5-9-7 **79**.....................(p) NCallan 7 80
(K A Ryan) *led: rdn jst over 1f out: hdd wl ins fnl f: no ex* **12/1**

4060 **8** 1 1/4 **Cornus**[17] 4501 7-9-0 **75**...(p) FrederikTylicki(3) 2 73
(J A Glover) *a.p: rdn wl over 1f out: fdd wl ins fnl f* **12/1**

5300 **9** 1 3/4 **Fiefdom (IRE)**[6] 4871 7-9-1 **73**.. TomEaves 6 66
(I W McInnes) *hld up towards rr: rdn over 1f out: no rspnse* **22/1**

4451 **10** 1/2 **Carmenero (GER)**[10] 4732 6-8-7 **70**................................ SimonPearce(5) 1 62
(C R Dore) *hld up in mid-div on ins: pushed along and wknd wl over 1f out* **12/1**

0263 **11** *2 ¾* **Tourist**[91] 2144 4-9-6 **78**.. GrahamGibbons 4 62
(D Shaw) *sltly hmpd after nrly 1f: hld up in tch: rdn and wknd wl over 1f out* **8/1**[3]

1m 28.88s (-0.72) **Going Correction** -0.025s/f (Stan) **11** Ran SP% **117.8**
Speed ratings (Par 105): **103,101,101,101,101 100,100,98,96,96 93**
toteswingers: 1&2 £7.40, 1&3 £23.60, 2&3 £37.00. CSF £24.70 CT £270.76 TOTE £3.20: £1.50, £2.70, £4.70; EX 25.00 TRIFECTA Not won. Place 6: £113.09 Place 5: £8.55.
Owner Michael Hill **Bred** Juddmonte Farms Inc **Trained** Huby, N Yorks
■ Stewards' Enquiry : N Callan caution: careless riding

FOCUS
Mainly exposed performers in a fair handicap in which the gallop was reasonable and several finished in a heap. The winner was another to race in the centre in the straight and the runner-up uis the best guide to the form.
T/Plt: £131.10 to a £1 stake. Pool: £56,585.29. 314.91 winning tickets. T/Qpdt: £5.40 to a £1 stake. Pool: £5,604.11. 755.62 winning tickets. KH

[4912]YARMOUTH (L-H)
Monday, August 17

OFFICIAL GOING: Good to firm (8.2)
Wind: light, half behind Weather: sunny

5108 GROSVENOR CASINO GREAT YARMOUTH CLAIMING STKS 1m 2f 21y
5:20 (5:21) (Class 6) 3-4-Y-O **£2,072** (£616; £308; £153) **Stalls** Low

Form RPR

2401 **1** **Theocritus (USA)**[11] 4698 4-9-4 75.............................. JamieSpencer 2 73
(D M Simcock) *stdd s: hld up in last trio: rdn over 3f out: sn swtchd rt: hdwy to ld over 1f out: edgd lft ent fnl f: kpt on u.p* **11/10**[1]

0063 **2** *2* **Equipe De Nuit**[25] 4242 3-8-9 71................................ WilliamCarson(3) 7 71
(S C Williams) *led: rdn and hung rt 2f out: hdd over 1f out: swtchd rt ent fnl f: one pce after* **5/1**[3]

-645 **3** *2 ½* **Intikama (IRE)**[23] 4320 3-8-0 66..............................(p) AshleyMorgan(7) 3 61
(M H Tompkins) *chsd ldng pair: rdn and effrt 3f out: nt qckning u.p whn squeezed and hmpd 2f out: plugged on to regain 3rd ins fnl f* **10/1**

4214 **4** *¾* **Solo River**[54] 3259 4-8-8 62... FergusSweeney 5 53
(P J Makin) *chsd ldr: rdn jst over 3f out: keeping on one pce whn nt clr run and lost pl 2f out: kpt on same pce after* **10/3**[2]

0150 **5** *shd* **Torch Of Freedom (IRE)**[12] 4658 4-9-4 68.............. StephenDonohoe 6 62
(Sir Mark Prescott) *in tch in midfield: rdn and effrt over 3f out: edging lft over 2f out: nt qckn u.p and v one pce after* **15/2**

050 **6** *hd* **Watchoverme**[26] 4205 3-8-6 48..................................(v[1]) RichardMullen 1 58?
(J R Fanshawe) *s.i.s: reminders and reluctant after s: racd in last pl: rdn and lost tch over 3f out: fnlly consented to run on and swtchd rt ins fnl f: nvr nr ldrs* **25/1**

5000 **7** *3 ¾* **Sairaam (IRE)**[11] 4719 3-8-12 52.................................. MickyFenton 4 56
(C Smith) *stdd s: hld up in last pair: rdn and effrt on outer over 2f out: no real prog: wknd over 1f out* **66/1**

2m 10.02s (-0.48) **Going Correction** -0.20s/f (Firm)
WFA 3 from 4yo 8lb **7** Ran SP% **113.6**
Speed ratings (Par 101): **93,91,89,88,88 88,85**
toteswingers: 1&2 £2.90, 1&3 £1.30, 2&3 £7.70. CSF £6.99 TOTE £1.80: £1.10, £3.10; EX 5.70.
Owner Dr Marwan Koukash **Bred** Allen E Paulson Living Trust **Trained** Newmarket, Suffolk

FOCUS
They went just an average pace in this claimer, but the form makes some sense rated through the runner-up.

5109 GROSVENOR CASINO YARMOUTH'S PREMIER POKER ROOM MEDIAN AUCTION MAIDEN STKS 6f 3y
5:50 (5:52) (Class 6) 2-Y-O **£2,590** (£770; £385; £192) **Stalls** High

Form RPR

1 **Marrayah** 2-8-12 0.. TPO'Shea 6 80+
(M A Jarvis) *racd off the pce in midfield: hdwy over 2f out: chsd ldr and rdn over 1f out: led ins fnl f: styd on strly and sn clr* **12/1**[3]

0 **2** *2 ½* **Young Simon**[7] 4851 2-9-3 0.. MickyFenton 10 77
(G G Margarson) *led and sn clr: rdn over 1f out: hdd ins fnl f: no ch w wnr* **100/1**

0300 **3** *2 ¾* **George Baker (IRE)**[52] 3344 2-9-3 83.......................... DO'Donohoe 8 69
(George Baker) *chsd ldng pair: wnt 2nd 1/2-way: rdn jst over 2f out: lost 2nd over 1f out: wl hld fnl f* **3/1**[2]

4 *1 ½* **Via Aurelia (IRE)** 2-8-12 0...................................... RichardMullen 7 60
(J R Fanshawe) *racd off the pce in midfield: hdwy 3f out: rdn wl over 1f out: hung lft and wknd fnl f* **12/1**[3]

5 *1 ½* **Power Of Dreams (IRE)** 2-8-10 0........................ AshleyMorgan(7) 4 60
(M H Tompkins) *sn outpcd in rr: swtchd lft over 2f out: nudged along and hdwy 2f out: keeping on steadily but no ch w ldrs whn swtchd rt ins fnl f: nvr nr ldrs* **20/1**

6 *3 ½* **Buffett** 2-9-3 0.. RoystonFfrench 9 50
(L M Cumani) *sn wl outpcd in rr: nvr on terms* **20/1**

7 *¾* **Captain Clint (IRE)** 2-9-3 0.. SaleemGolam 2 47
(M H Tompkins) *sn bhd and outpcd: nvr a factor* **40/1**

8 *10* **Teeraha (IRE)** 2-8-12 0.. AlanMunro 5 12
(D Shaw) *chsd ldr tl 1/2-way: sn hung rt and wknd: t.o fnl f* **40/1**

9 *2 ¾* **Clumber Pursuits** 2-8-12 0.. AndrewElliott 1 4
(S A Harris) *sn wl outpcd in rr: t.o fr 1/2-way* **100/1**

4 **U** **New Christmas (USA)**[17] 4497 2-9-3 0.......................... JamieSpencer 3 —
(B J Meehan) *rrd and uns rdr as stalls opened* **8/13**[1]

1m 13.29s (-1.11) **Going Correction** -0.20s/f (Firm) **10** Ran SP% **118.7**
Speed ratings (Par 92): **99,95,92,90,88 83,82,69,65,—**
toteswingers: 1&2 not won, 1&3 £7.20, 2&3 £27.80. CSF £821.85 TOTE £13.20: £2.70, £10.10, £1.10; EX 355.10.
Owner Hamdan Al Maktoum **Bred** Bearstone Stud **Trained** Newmarket, Suffolk

FOCUS
The complexion of this juvenile maiden completely changed when the gambled-on New Christmas reared as the stalls opened and then jumped out without his rider on board. The form should be treated with some caution, but the winner still impressed.

NOTEBOOK
Marrayah ◆ got up late in the day to get her career off to a perfect start. She was allowed to go off at a very big price considering her connections and seeing as she is bred to make a two-year-old, but that was largely due to the presence of the favourite. She took time to get the hang of things, but moved nicely through the race and showed a decent attitude inside the final furlong. She should only go forward for the experience and, while she will get further in time, this looks her trip at present. An entry in the Watership Down Stud Sales Race at Ascot later this month may well be taken up now. (op 8-1)
Young Simon made his rivals work with a game display from the front. He is clearly going the right way and, on this evidence, is well worth dropping back to the minimum.\n
George Baker(IRE), dropped in trip, was the only danger to the favourite according to the betting and so it has to rate a missed opportunity. He has now flopped the last twice and the way he had to be ridden from an early stage here would suggest he is regressing, but perhaps he now needs all of 7f. (op 7-2 tchd 11-4)
Via Aurelia(IRE) boasts an interesting pedigree, being a half-sister to last year's Group 1 winning 2yo Zafisio and comes from a yard whose juveniles have begun to warm up in recent weeks. She proved too green to do herself full justice, but should get closer next time and has a future. (op 9-1 tchd 14-1)
New Christmas(USA) had a Monty Roberts rug on for stalls entry and was blindfolded, so obviously has an aversion to the gates. As his rider took off the hood, he reared up and came down just as the gates sprang back, exactly the moment Spencer wouldn't have wanted as he was unbalanced. This grey was backed as if defeat was not an option and he is no doubt well regarded, but will need to be put through the stalls plenty at home before he gets any better, as he was also slowly away on debut. (op 10-11tchd evens in places)

5110 GROSVENOR CASINO ROULETTE & BLACK JACK MAIDEN STKS 6f 3y
6:20 (6:20) (Class 5) 3-4-Y-O **£2,901** (£868; £434; £217; £108) **Stalls** High

Form RPR

3232 **1** **Hightime Heroine (IRE)**[16] 4531 3-8-12 75................ JamieSpencer 5 83+
(J Noseda) *mde all: nudged along drew clr wl over 1f out: v easily* **6/5**[1]

20-0 **2** *2 ¼* **Timeless Dream**[68] 2827 3-8-12 68................................... AlanMunro 2 71
(P W Chapple-Hyam) *chsd wnr: rdn 2f out: sn outpcd by wnr: kpt on same pce fnl f* **8/1**

422- **3** *4 ½* **Albaseet (IRE)**[268] 7417 3-9-3 75... TPO'Shea 1 62
(M P Tregoning) *chsd ldrs: rdn 3f out: disp 2nd pl and drvn 2f out: sn outpcd by wnr: 3rd and wl btn 1f out* **2/1**[2]

22-0 **4** *12* **Hay Fever (IRE)**[12] 4648 3-9-3 79.................................... MickyFenton 4 23
(Eve Johnson Houghton) *in tch: rdn and struggling over 3f out: wl bhd fnl 2f* **11/2**[3]

0 **5** *3 ½* **Distant Dreamer (USA)**[39] 3764 3-8-12 0.................... SaleemGolam 3 7
(Rae Guest) *s.i.s and squeezed for room sn after s: a last: rdn and lost tch 3f out: sn wl bhd* **50/1**

1m 12.03s (-2.37) **Going Correction** -0.20s/f (Firm) **5** Ran SP% **107.2**
Speed ratings (Par 103): **107,104,98,82,77**
CSF £10.51 TOTE £1.60: £1.60, £3.70; EX 8.00.
Owner Cheveley Park Stud **Bred** R O'Callaghan And D Veitch **Trained** Newmarket, Suffolk

FOCUS
A weak maiden and the winner did it easily. The runner-up to juvenile form looks the best guide.
Hay Fever(IRE) Official explanation: trainer said gelding was unsuited by the good to firm ground

5111 GROSVENOR CASINO BAR AND RESTAURANT H'CAP 1m 3y
6:50 (6:51) (Class 6) (0-65,58) 3-Y-O+ **£2,072** (£616; £308; £153) **Stalls** High

Form RPR

6423 **1** **King's Icon (IRE)**[4] 4938 4-8-13 **51**.......................(p) TobyAtkinson(7) 12 59
(M Wigham) *t.k.h: hld up in tch: hdwy jst over 2f out: rdn to ld narrowly ent fnl f: kpt on wl: edgd lft nr fin* **5/2**[1]

5002 **2** *½* **Gifted Heir (IRE)**[11] 4697 5-8-11 **49**........................... NatashaEaton(7) 5 56
(A Bailey) *hld up wl in tch: effrt over 1f out: rdn to chse ldng pair 1f out: wnt 2nd wl ins fnl f: hld towards fin* **16/1**

0-23 **3** *1 ½* **Kassuta**[27] 4179 5-9-3 **48**.. JamieSpencer 9 53+
(R M H Cowell) *racd on stands' rail tl jnd field in centre 1/2-way: prom: chsd ldr over 3f out: rdn to ld over 2f out: hdd ent fnl f: btn whn n.m.r and eased towards fin* **3/1**[2]

2305 **4** *3* **Gun For Sale (USA)**[23] 4305 4-9-5 **50**....................(t) FergusSweeney 10 47
(P J Makin) *stdd s: t.k.h: hld up towards rr: hdwy over 4f out: ev ch and rdn 2f out: sn hung lft u.p: wknd fnl f* **8/1**

4320 **5** *shd* **Astroangel**[11] 4697 5-9-2 **54**...................................(p) AshleyMorgan(7) 6 50
(M H Tompkins) *hld up in last trio: rdn and effrt wl over 1f out: kpt on u.p fnl f: nt pce to rch ldrs* **8/1**

60/0 **6** *1* **Memphis Marie**[27] 4179 5-8-11 **45**................................ JackMitchell(3) 2 39
(P J McBride) *chsd ldr tl over 3f out: wknd u.p over 1f out* **20/1**

-020 **7** *½* **Roleplay (IRE)**[26] 4202 4-9-12 **57**............................(b) MickyFenton 13 50
(J M P Eustace) *racd on stands' rail tl jnd field in centre 1/2-way: hld up in tch: rdn and no rspnse ent fnl 2f: plugged on same pce u.p fnl f* **25/1**

0051 **8** *4* **Union Jack Jackson (IRE)**[5] 4887 7-9-3 **51** 6ex....(v) KellyHarrison(3) 8 35
(John A Harris) *t.k.h: chsd ldrs: rdn and wknd qckly ent fnl 2f: wl btn fnl f* **13/2**[3]

0-00 **9** *¾* **Black Salix (USA)**[27] 4179 3-8-13 **50**............................ DO'Donohoe 7 31
(Mrs P Sly) *led tl over 2f out: sn wknd u.p: wl btn fnl f* **20/1**

6054 **10** *3 ½* **Al Rayanah**[12] 4667 6-9-7 **52**...(b) IPoullis 1 26
(G Prodromou) *stdd s and v.s.a: t.k.h: hld up in rr: rdn and hung rt over 2f out: sn lost tch* **10/1**

1m 39.82s (-0.78) **Going Correction** -0.20s/f (Firm)
WFA 3 from 4yo+ 6lb **10** Ran SP% **117.5**
Speed ratings (Par 101): **95,94,93,90,89 88,88,84,83,80**
toteswingers: 1&2 £11.00, 1&3 £4.00, 2&3 £6.90. CSF £43.07 CT £129.91 TOTE £3.20: £1.50, £5.90, £1.30; EX 45.00.
Owner A Dunmore, John Williams **Bred** C J Foy **Trained** Newmarket, Suffolk
■ Stewards' Enquiry : I Poullis three-day ban: improper use of the whip (Aug 31-Sep 2)

FOCUS
A weak handicap, but it was run at a fair pace and the form makes sense with the first three close to their marks.
Gun For Sale(USA) Official explanation: jockey said gelding hung left

5112 GROSVENORCASINOS.COM H'CAP 7f 3y
7:20 (7:20) (Class 5) (0-70,68) 3-Y-O **£2,849** (£847; £423; £211) **Stalls** High

Form RPR

6-02 **1** **Dance Club (IRE)**[11] 4718 3-8-13 **60**................................... AlanMunro 3 70
(W Jarvis) *hld up in tch: rdn and effrt 2f out: pressed ldr ent fnl f: kpt on wl u.p to ld wl ins fnl f* **13/2**[2]

4121 **2** *nk* **Regeneration (IRE)**[9] 4791 3-9-7 **68**............................. JamieSpencer 5 77
(S A Callaghan) *hld up wl in tch: effrt ent fnl 2f: rdn to ld over 1f out: drvn and hrd pressed 1f out: hdd and no ex wl ins fnl f* **2/1**[1]

-013 **3** *5* **Kuanyao (IRE)**[23] 4304 3-9-0 **61**................................... FergusSweeney 9 57
(P J Makin) *stdd s and s.i.s: t.k.h early and hld up in rr: rdn over 3f out: racd awkwardly after and no prog tl hdwy ent fnl f: kpt on to go modest 3rd towards fin: nvr nr ldrs* **2/1**[1]

4500 **4** *¾* **Wicklewood**[11] 4718 3-8-2 **49** oh4.......................................(v) PaulQuinn 2 43
(Mrs C A Dunnett) *led: rdn and hung lft 2f out: hdd over 1f out: 3rd and btn 1f out: lost 3rd towards fin* **40/1**

330 **5** *hd* **Summers Target (USA)**[22] 4338 3-9-7 **68**.................... RichardMullen 6 61
(R M H Cowell) *stdd s and s.i.s: t.k.h: hld up bhd: shkn up wl over 1f out: rdn and plugged on fnl f: n.d* **16/1**

6066 **6** *3* **Davids Matador**[11] 4691 3-9-3 **64**...................................(b[1]) TPO'Shea 1 49
(Eve Johnson Houghton) *chsd ldr tl jst over 2f out: sn drvn: wknd over 1f out* **14/1**

3060 **7** 7 **Fantasy Land (IRE)**[44] 3630 3-9-3 **64**...(t) NickyMackay 7 30
(B J Meehan) *in tch: rdn over 2f out: wknd u.p wl over 1f out: wl btn after* **28/1**

2363 **8** *hd* **Mutually Mine (USA)**[46] 3548 3-9-6 **67**...(p) MickyFenton 10 33
(Mrs P Sly) *chsd ldrs but sn niggled along: wknd u.p wl over 1f out: wl bhd fnl f* **8/1**[3]

64U **9** 7 **Granny McPhee**[11] 4698 3-8-11 **65**... NatashaEaton[(7)] 8 12
(A Bailey) *stdd s and s.i.s: alway bhd: rdn and lost tch over 2f out* **25/1**

1m 25.2s (-1.40) **Going Correction** -0.20s/f (Firm) **9** Ran SP% **113.4**
Speed ratings (Par 100): **100,99,93,93,92 89,81,81,73**
toteswingers: 1&2 £2.00, 1&3 £1.80, 2&3 £1.90. CSF £19.18 CT £35.28 TOTE £5.40: £2.60, £1.10, £1.20; EX 22.00.
Owner Dr John Fike **Bred** J Fike **Trained** Newmarket, Suffolk

FOCUS
A moderate handicap in which the first two dominated but the form looks sound.

5113 GROSVENOR CASINO JACKPOT SLOTS MAIDEN H'CAP 1m 6f 17y
7:50 (7:50) (Class 5) (0-70,67) 3-Y-O+ **£2,719** (£809; £404; £202) **Stalls** High

Form RPR

00-3 **1** **Veiled**[27] 4175 3-9-1 **66**... StephenDonohoe 9 76
(Sir Mark Prescott) *in tch: rdn and unable qckn over 4f out: last and drvn wl over 2f out: rallied and hdwy on outer ent fnl f: styd on wl u.p to ld fnl 75yds:* **9/4**[2]

-633 **2** ½ **Theola (IRE)**[17] 4491 3-8-8 **66**... AshleyMorgan[(7)] 4 75
(M H Tompkins) *chsd ldrs: chsd wnr 2f out: ev ch over 1f out: nt go past ldr tl cajoled ahd fnl 100yds: sn hdd and no ex* **15/2**

5524 **3** 2 **Penolva (IRE)**[31] 4039 3-8-5 **56**... AndrewElliott 1 62
(A P Jarvis) *racd keenly: led: rdn 3f out: hrd pressed and drvn over 1f out: hdd fnl 100yds: wknd towards fin* **7/2**[3]

-002 **4** 3¾ **Royal Bet (IRE)**[5] 4917 3-7-12 **49**... JamieMackay 6 50
(M L W Bell) *plld hrd: hld up in last pair: plld out and hdwy over 3f out: rdn 2f out: flashed tail u.p and hung lft fr over 1f out: btn jst ins fnl f* **85/40**[1]

446- **5** ¾ **Prince Zafonic**[61] 7770 6-10-0 **67**... JerryO'Dwyer 5 67
(C A Dwyer) *chsd ldr: rdn and effrt wl over 2f out: hld hd high u.p: wknd over 1f out* **16/1**

-045 **6** 2¼ **Harting Hill**[19] 4437 4-8-10 **49** oh1... TPO'Shea 3 46
(M P Tregoning) *hld up in last pl: effrt on inner 3f out: rdn and no real prog 2f out: wknd over 1f out* **11/1**

3m 3.89s (-3.71) **Going Correction** -0.20s/f (Firm)
WFA 3 from 4yo+ 12lb **6** Ran SP% **111.0**
Speed ratings (Par 103): **102,101,100,98,98 96**
toteswingers: 1&2 £3.20, 1&3 £1.80, 2&3 £3.30. CSF £18.37 CT £53.89 TOTE £2.90: £2.20, £2.20; EX 13.40 Place 6: £32.07 Place 5: £21.01.
Owner Cheveley Park Stud **Bred** Cheveley Park Stud Ltd **Trained** Newmarket, Suffolk

FOCUS
A moderate handicap, run an average pace and not easy form to pin down, although it has been treated slightly positively with the first four all relatively unexposed.
Royal Bet(IRE) Official explanation: jockey said gelding ran too free
T/Plt: £35.10 to a £1 stake. Pool: £51,459.12. 1,068.69 winning tickets. T/Qpdt: £7.10 to a £1 stake. Pool: £5,358.46. 557.30 winning tickets. SP

5114 - 5116a (Foreign Racing) - See Raceform Interactive

2293 CHATEAUBRIANT (L-H)
Monday, August 17

OFFICIAL GOING: Good

5117a PRIX DE LONGCHAMP 5f 110y
1:05 (1:06) 2-Y-O **£11,650** (£4,660; £3,495; £2,330; £1,165)

RPR

1 **Lucky Like (FR)**[17] 4487 2-9-4... JAuge 93+
(E J O'Neill) *racd in 3rd: pushed along st: led 1f out: sn clr: pushed out* **2/5**[1]

2 3 **Bad Mistone (FR)** 2-9-2... FVeron 81
(H-A Pantall, France)

3 5 **Boum Des Aigles (FR)**[82] 2-8-8... JClaudic 57
(Mme C Barande-Barbe, France)

4 1½ **Coconino (IRE)**[13] 2-9-10... 68
(C Boutin, France)

5 1½ **Hiporoi (FR)**[80] 2-9-4... 57
(M Boutin, France)

65.85 secs (65.85) **5** Ran SP% **71.4**
PARI-MUTUEL (Including 1 Euro stake): WIN 1.40; PL 1.10, 1.20; SF 2.20.
Owner Victory Racing & Partners **Bred** Paul Nataf **Trained** Southwell, Notts

NOTEBOOK
Lucky Like(FR), who finished fourth in the Richmond Stakes on his sole appearance in Britain, had a relatively straightforward task to get off the mark and picked up some good prizemoney in the process. He looks capable of making his mark at Listed level.

4730 BRIGHTON (L-H)
Tuesday, August 18

OFFICIAL GOING: Firm (8.5)
Wind: virtually nil Weather: warm and sunny

5119 EBF BUY A RACING POST YEARLING BONUS CANDIDATE MEDIAN AUCTION MAIDEN STKS 6f 209y
2:00 (2:01) (Class 5) 2-Y-O **£3,658** (£1,095; £547; £273; £136) **Stalls** Low

Form RPR

562 **1** **Luminous Star (USA)**[13] 4638 2-9-3 73... SebSanders 8 76
(R M Beckett) *stdd s and dropped in bhd: hdwy on outer over 2f out: rdn to ld narrowly over 1f out: hld on wl u.p fnl f* **6/4**[1]

2 *nk* **Pictures (IRE)** 2-8-12 0... DaneO'Neill 7 70
(L M Cumani) *hld up in tch in rr: hdwy 3f out: ev ch and rdn 2f out: kpt on wl u.p ins fnl f but a jst hld* **14/1**

02 **3** 1 **Sir Bruno (FR)**[40] 3785 2-9-3 0... DavidProbert 3 73
(B Palling) *chsd ldrs: effrt on inner 3f out: led 2f out: hdd over 1f out: stl ev ch tl no ex fnl 75yds* **13/2**[2]

42 **4** ½ **Dr Finley (IRE)**[17] 4534 2-9-3 0... PatCosgrave 6 71
(M L W Bell) *chsd ldr tl led over 2f out: sn rdn: hdd 2f out: stl ev ch tl no ex fnl 100yds* **6/4**[1]

0 **5** ½ **Constant Contact**[40] 3786 2-9-3 0... LPKeniry 9 70
(A M Balding) *in tch: rdn and unable qck wl over 1f out: no prog tl kpt on fnl 100yds: unable to chal ldrs* **12/1**[3]

00 **6** 26 **Alfalevva**[8] 4851 2-9-3 0... TonyCulhane 5 —
(M R Channon) *sn bustled along and toiling in rr: t.o and eased fnl f* **66/1**

0 **7** 4 **Federal Reserve**[13] 4646 2-9-3 0... RobertHavlin 1 —
(M Madgwick) *led tl over 2f out: wknd rapidly: virtually p.u ins fnl f: t.o* **100/1**

1m 23.16s (0.06) **Going Correction** -0.125s/f (Firm) **7** Ran SP% **110.2**
Speed ratings (Par 94): **94,93,92,91,91 61,57**
toteswingers: 1&2 £4.20, 1&3 £1.40, 2&3 £3.90 CSF £24.22 TOTE £2.50: £1.60, £3.30; EX 19.10 Trifecta £63.20 Pool: £425.31 - 4.75 winning units..
Owner Sheikh Khaled Duaij Al Sabah **Bred** Phillips Racing Partnership **Trained** Whitsbury, Hants

FOCUS
A modest juvenile maiden, run at a solid pace with the winner to recent course form.

NOTEBOOK
Luminous Star(USA) had looked somewhat uneasy on the track when second over course and distance 13 days earlier, but he handled it much better this time and completed the task in game fashion. He again ran freely under early restraint and came wide with his challenge down the home straight, but saw out the race a lot better this time. Nurseries now beckon for him and he can progress as he learns to relax through the early parts of his races. (tchd 5-4 and 13-8)
Pictures(IRE), a 15,000gns purchase, posted a very pleasing debut run and pushed the winner to the line. There was more than enough in this performance to suggest she has a future and she should prove hard to beat next time out. (op 12-1)
Sir Bruno(FR) kept on at the same pace in the home straight and posted another sound effort. He now qualifies for nurseries. (op 15-2 tchd 6-1)
Dr Finley(IRE) did his best work late on over this trip at Lingfield last time and that was the best piece of previous form on offer in this race, so it was disappointing he failed to even place. It may be that he needs to be ridden a little more patiently again in order to shine and to his credit he did keep on after being headed, so perhaps the best of him has still to come. This was also his first run away from soft ground. (tchd 7-4)
Constant Contact hit a flat spot before running on again and improved on the level of his Warwick debut. He probably already needs 1m and is one to keep an eye on. (tchd 16-1)
Federal Reserve Official explanation: jockey said gelding hung right

5120 BETDAQ.CO.UK CLAIMING STKS 6f 209y
2:35 (2:35) (Class 6) 3-Y-O+ **£1,942** (£578; £288; £144) **Stalls** Low

Form RPR

4200 **1** **Manchestermaverick (USA)**[70] 2794 4-8-11 56...(vt) TravisBlock 11 62
(H Morrison) *mde all: clr over 4f out: rdn and 2 l clr 2f out: pressed fnl 100yds: hld on wl fnl 50yds* **9/1**

522 **2** ½ **Caprio (IRE)**[22] 4386 4-9-9 79... PatCosgrave 2 73
(J R Boyle) *chsd ldrs: rdn and effrt 2f out: chsd wnr jst ins fnl f: pressed wnr fnl 100yds: no imp and hld fnl 50yds* **3/1**[2]

0013 **3** ¾ **Goodbye Cash (IRE)**[12] 4694 5-8-7 55... PaulDoe 7 55
(P D Evans) *taken down early: chsd wnr: rdn over 3f out: drvn and no imp 2f out: edgd lft and lost 2nd jst ins fnl f: plugged on same pce* **15/2**

3465 **4** ¾ **Who's Winning (IRE)**[43] 3671 8-8-11 49... SebSanders 4 57
(B G Powell) *t.k.h early: chsd ldrs: rdn and effrt on inner jst over 2f out: n.m.r jst ins fnl f: kpt on same pce after* **20/1**

3566 **5** 2 **Mr Rev**[11] 4730 6-8-10 47...(b) JackDean[(3)] 5 53
(J M Bradley) *hld up in towards rr: rdn and effrt 2f out: chsd ldrs and drvn jst over 1f out: no imp fnl f* **66/1**

6302 **6** ½ **Seneschal**[28] 4181 8-9-3 77... GeorgeBaker 8 56
(A B Haynes) *hld up in midfield: rdn and effrt 2f out: edgd lft u.p over 1f out: one pce after* **5/2**[1]

4342 **7** ½ **Dressed To Dance (IRE)**[12] 4690 5-8-9 74...(v) KevinGhunowa[(3)] 6 50
(R A Harris) *stdd s: hld up bhd: rdn and no prog over 2f out: styd on u.p ins fnl f: nvr pce to rch ldrs* **10/3**[3]

50-0 **8** 2¾ **Charlie Be (IRE)**[26] 4220 4-8-7 43... JackMitchell[(3)] 3 40
(Mrs P N Dutfield) *s.i.s: hld up in rr: rdn 3f out: n.m.r wl over 2f out: no prog and wl btn whn hung lft over 1f out* **50/1**

0050 **9** 2 **Mr Flannegan**[20] 4425 3-8-7 52... FergusSweeney 10 37
(H Candy) *chsd ldrs tl wknd u.p over 2f out: btn whn hung lft over 1f out* **33/1**

0-00 **10** 3 **Rosemarkie**[26] 4220 5-8-8 37...(p) DavidProbert 1 25
(J M Bradley) *in tch towards rr: rdn and no rspnse 3f out: wl hld fnl 2f* **66/1**

4050 **11** 9 **Batchworth Blaise**[24] 4305 6-9-1 49... StephenCarson 9 7
(E A Wheeler) *taken down early: stdd s: plld hrd and hld up in rr: btn and eased fr over 2f out* **40/1**

1m 22.4s (-0.70) **Going Correction** -0.125s/f (Firm)
WFA 3 from 4yo+ 5lb **11** Ran SP% **113.5**
Speed ratings (Par 101): **99,98,97,96,94 93,93,90,87,84 74**
toteswingers: 1&2 £6.30, 1&3 £7.30, 2&3 £3.50 CSF £33.30 TOTE £10.90: £2.30, £1.70, £1.90; EX 54.60 Trifecta £447.40 Part won. Pool: £604.66 - 0.43 winning units..Manchestermaverick was claimed by J. R. J. Naylor for £4000.
Owner D P Barrie & M J Rees **Bred** Ewi Bloodstock **Trained** East Ilsley, Berks

FOCUS
A moderate claimer with the form limited by the proximity of the fourth and fifth.
Batchworth Blaise Official explanation: jockey said gelding hung right throughout and moved badly coming down the hill

5121 BETDAQ THE BETTING EXCHANGE H'CAP 7f 214y
3:10 (3:10) (Class 6) (0-65,63) 3-Y-O **£2,590** (£770; £385; £192) **Stalls** Low

Form RPR

0413 **1** **Cavendish Road (IRE)**[26] 4240 3-9-7 **63**... DavidProbert 5 71
(W R Muir) *hld up in tch in rr: swtchd rt and hdwy over 1f out: rdn and str chal ins fnl f: r.o wl to ld fnl 50yds* **5/1**[2]

4150 **2** *nk* **Fire King**[11] 4734 3-9-2 **58**... RobertHavlin 11 65
(J A Geake) *hld up in tch towards rr: hdwy to chse ldrs gng wl over 2f out: rdn over 1f out: led ent fnl f: drvn ins fnl f: hdd and no ex fnl 50yds* **9/1**

0-1 **3** 1¾ **Orangeleg**[43] 3672 3-8-7 **52**... WilliamCarson[(3)] 13 55
(S C Williams) *in tch: rdn and effrt wl over 2f out: chsd ldng pair 1f out: kpt on same pce* **7/4**[1]

0-66 **4** 1½ **Valid Point (IRE)**[209] 230 3-8-3 **45**... JamieMackay 3 45+
(Sir Mark Prescott) *chsd ldrs: rdn and unable qck wl over 2f out: outpcd and lost pl over 2f out: nt clr run and swtchd rt jst ins fnl f: styd on fnl 100yds: nt pce to rch ldrs* **17/2**

0434 **5** ¾ **Spring Secret**[20] 4425 3-9-1 **57**... TonyCulhane 10 55
(B Palling) *chsd ldr: ev ch and rdn jst over 2f out: led over 1f out: hdd ent fnl f: wknd ins fnl f* **8/1**[3]

0600 **6** *nse* **Lennie Briscoe (IRE)**[13] 4642 3-9-3 **59**... GeorgeBaker 4 57
(S Kirk) *hld up in tch: rdn and unable qckn jst over 2f out: keeping on same pce and hld whn carried rt jst ins fnl f* **18/1**

000- **7** nk **Red Horse (IRE)**[283] 7240 3-8-10 **52**................................ PatCosgrave 2 52+
(M L W Bell) *hld up wl in tch on inner: rdn and effrt ent fnl 2f: keeping on same pce whn nt clr run 1f out: sn swtchd rt: no imp after* **12/1**

0002 **8** 7 **Count On Guest**[12] 4719 3-9-2 **58**................................(t) DaneO'Neill 7 39
(G G Margarson) *t.k.h: hld up in tch: rdn and effrt over 2f out: no hdwy: wl btn fnl f* **12/1**

-500 **9** ½ **Pointillist (IRE)**[12] 4704 3-9-6 **62**................................(p) SebSanders 6 42
(R M Beckett) *led: rdn ent fnl 2f: hdd over 1f out: sn wknd: eased whn no ch ins fnl f* **18/1**

0020 **10** nk **Hold The Star**[6] 4905 3-9-7 **63**................................(b[1]) LPKeniry 9 42
(E F Vaughan) *nvr gng wl in rr: reminders over 4f out: rdn over 3f out: lost tch and bhd fnl 2f* **18/1**

1m 34.65s (-1.35) **Going Correction** -0.125s/f (Firm) **10** Ran SP% **115.8**
Speed ratings (Par 98): **101,100,98,97,96 96,96,89,88,88**
toteswingers: 1&2 £8.50, 1&3 £3.70, 2&3 £5.60 CSF £49.09 CT £110.81 TOTE £5.20: £2.00, £2.80, £1.40; EX 32.40 Trifecta £88.00 Pool: £477.33 - 4.01 winning units..
Owner C L A Edginton **Bred** Garry Chong **Trained** Lambourn, Berks

FOCUS
An open handicap. There was a sound pace on and the form looks solid and should work out.
Hold The Star Official explanation: jockey said filly never travelled

5122 BETTINGBANTER.COM H'CAP 1m 1f 209y
3:45 (3:47) (Class 5) (0-70,68) 3-Y-0+ **£3,027** (£906; £453; £226; £112) **Stalls** High

Form RPR

12 **1** **Sceilin (IRE)**[24] 4300 5-9-4 **55**................................(t) JackMitchell(3) 4 65
(J Mackie) *hld up in tch in midfield: hdwy to chse ldr wl over 2f out: drvn over 1f out: styd on wl u.p to ld fnl 50yds* **7/2**[2]

-361 **2** 1 **Recalcitrant**[12] 4697 6-9-2 **50**................................ PaulDoe 5 58
(S Dow) *chsd ldrs: wnt 2nd over 4f out: led over 3f out: rdn and clr w wnr over 1f out: hdd and no ex fnl 50yds* **5/1**[3]

1503 **3** 3 **Strong Storm (USA)**[20] 4431 3-9-12 **68**................................ ShaneKelly 6 70
(J Noseda) *stdd s: hld up in last pl: swtchd rt and effrt over 2f out: wandered and no imp u.p over 1f out: wnt 3rd ins fnl f: nvr threatened ldrs* **9/4**[1]

353- **4** 2½ **Wester Ross (IRE)**[235] 6403 5-10-0 **62**................................ LukeMorris 8 59
(J M P Eustace) *bustled along early: hld up in midfield: rdn and hdwy jst over 3f out: chsd ldng pair and hung lft wl over 1f out: no prog: lost 3rd and wl hld ins fnl f* **11/2**

0-06 **5** 5 **Spartan Dance**[11] 4735 5-8-11 **45**................................ RichardThomas 2 32
(J A Geake) *chsd ldr tl over 4f out: rdn and lost pl over 2f out: wl hld whn hld hd high u.p over 1f out* **50/1**

0005 **6** ½ **It's My Day (IRE)**[12] 4698 4-9-4 **52**................................ LPKeniry 1 38
(C Gordon) *bustled along early: in tch in midfield: reminders over 4f out: rdn and nt qckn 3f out: hung rt and btn 2f out* **33/1**

462 **7** 5 **Red Reef**[11] 4745 3-9-7 **63**................................ DaneO'Neill 7 39
(D J Coakley) *stdd s: hld up in last pair: rdn and no rspnse 3f out: wl btn fnl 2f* **7/2**[2]

2041 **8** 1 **Rosy Dawn**[12] 4704 4-9-3 **54**................................ MarcHalford(3) 3 28
(J J Bridger) *led tl rdn and hdd over 3f out: wknd u.p jst over 2f out: wl btn and eased ins fnl f* **14/1**

2m 1.39s (-2.21) **Going Correction** -0.125s/f (Firm)
WFA 3 from 4yo+ 8lb **8** Ran SP% **118.8**
Speed ratings (Par 103): **103,102,99,97,93 93,89,88**
toteswingers: 1&2 £4.70, 1&3 £2.40, 2&3 £4.10 CSF £22.36 CT £47.99 TOTE £4.40: £1.50, £2.20, £1.30; EX 24.30 Trifecta £81.80 Pool: £958.97 - 8.67 winning units..
Owner W I Bloomfield **Bred** J S Bolger **Trained** Church Broughton , Derbys
■ Stewards' Enquiry : Jack Mitchell one-day ban: excessive use of the whip (Sep 29)

FOCUS
This moderate handicap was competitive for the class and the form looks sound. It was run at an ordinary pace but the first two pulled clear.

5123 ARMY BENEVOLENT FUND H'CAP 1m 3f 196y
4:20 (4:20) (Class 5) (0-70,67) 3-Y-0 **£3,154** (£944; £472; £236; £117) **Stalls** High

Form RPR

4003 **1** **Sounds Of Jupiter (IRE)**[12] 4687 3-9-2 **62**................................ SebSanders 3 78+
(D M Simcock) *mde all: gng much the best over 2f out: wl clr over 1f out: eased wl ins fnl f* **9/2**[3]

0-00 **2** 8 **Aaman (IRE)**[14] 4625 3-8-10 **56**................................ LPKeniry 1 58
(E F Vaughan) *chsd wnr thrght: rdn 3f out: wl outpcd 2f out: no ch w wnr but kpt on for clr 2nd* **20/1**

20 **3** 4 **Venture Capitalist**[28] 4178 3-9-3 **63**................................ DaneO'Neill 6 58
(L M Cumani) *chsd ldrs: rdn 3f out: wl outpcd over 2f out: wl btn over 1f out* **7/4**[1]

0053 **4** 1¼ **Hassadin**[16] 4587 3-7-13 **50**................................ AmyBaker(5) 4 43
(A B Haynes) *t.k.h: grad stdd towards rr after 2f: rdn and effrt 3f out: wl btn over 1f out: edgd lft fnl f* **28/1**

4220 **5** shd **Rose Of Coma (IRE)**[11] 4734 3-8-6 **52**................................ AdrianMcCarthy 8 45
(Miss Gay Kelleway) *hld up in last trio: hdwy to chse ldrs over 3f out: rdn 3f out: wl btn 2f out* **11/1**

3564 **6** 2¾ **Screaming Brave**[12] 4722 3-8-13 **59**................................ TonyCulhane 2 47
(M R Channon) *hld up in midfield: rdn and effrt on inner 3f out: sn struggling: wl btn fnl 2f* **4/1**[2]

0441 **7** ¾ **Fleur De'Lion (IRE)**[13] 4640 3-8-11 **57**................................ DavidProbert 10 44
(S Kirk) *sn pushed along in midfield: rdn 4f out: struggling u.p 3f out: wl btn fnl 2f* **5/1**

334 **8** 50 **National Monument (IRE)**[166] 767 3-9-7 **67**................................ ShaneKelly 7 —
(J A Osborne) *stdd s: hld up in last pl: lost tch and eased fr over 2f out: virtually p.u fnl f: t.o* **12/1**

2m 30.58s (-2.12) **Going Correction** -0.125s/f (Firm) **8** Ran SP% **115.4**
Speed ratings (Par 100): **102,96,94,93,93 91,90,57**
toteswingers: 1&2 £16.00, 1&3 £3.00, 2&3 £9.70 CSF £85.85 CT £214.29 TOTE £5.70: £1.70, £4.10, £1.30; EX 82.10 Trifecta £254.00 Pool: £731.29 - 2.13 winning units..
Owner Dr Marwan Koukash **Bred** Gainsborough Stud Management Ltd **Trained** Newmarket, Suffolk

FOCUS
A decidedly ordinary three-year-old handicap. It was run at an uneven pace and the first three raced in that order from the off, so not a race to rate too positively

5124 FREEBETS.CO.UK FREE BETS H'CAP 6f 209y
4:50 (4:50) (Class 5) (0-70,70) 3-Y-0+ **£3,027** (£906; £453; £226; £112) **Stalls** Low

Form RPR

3354 **1** **Ivory Lace**[12] 4694 8-9-6 **67**................................ JackMitchell(3) 12 81
(S Woodman) *bhd: hdwy and rdn on outer 3f out: led over 1f out: sn clr and in n.d fnl f: eased towards fin* **5/1**[2]

-055 **2** 4 **Too Tall**[11] 4733 3-9-5 **68**................................(b) DaneO'Neill 11 69
(L M Cumani) *bhd: hdwy over 3f out: rdn to chse ldrs over 2f out: nt pce of wnr over 1f out: wnt 2nd fnl 100yds: no ch w wnr* **5/1**[2]

3000 **3** ½ **Kipchak (IRE)**[10] 4787 4-9-12 **70**................................(p) LPKeniry 8 72
(C R Dore) *taken down early: chsd ldrs: ev ch and rdn ent fnl 2f: outpcd by wnr in 2nd over 1f out: hld hd high u.p: lost 2nd fnl 100yds* **20/1**

5400 **4** nk **Magnitude**[9] 4824 4-9-7 **65**................................(b) ShaneKelly 5 66
(M E Rimmer) *bhd: rdn and effrt over 2f out: hdwy u.p over 1f out: kpt on to press for 3rd towards fin but no ch w wnr* **25/1**

0003 **5** nse **Millfield (IRE)**[13] 4645 6-9-8 **66**................................ GeorgeBaker 3 67
(P R Chamings) *slowly away and sn detached in last: clsd and in tch over 1f out: rdn and no hdwy over 1f out: plugged on fnl f* **13/2**[3]

0060 **6** nk **Choreography**[11] 4733 6-9-10 **68**................................(p) StephenCarson 2 68+
(Jim Best) *hld up towards rr: hdwy and edging out rt looking for run over 2f out: no ch w wnr but kpt on fnl f: n.m.r nr fin: nvr nr ldrs* **9/1**

2014 **7** 2 **Lady Florence**[2] 5063 4-9-7 **65**................................ LukeMorris 10 59+
(A B Coogan) *awkward leaving stalls and s.i.s: sn pushed along to chse ldrs: rdn 4f out: drvn an dn.m.r over 1f out: wl hld after: nt clr run and swtchd rt ins fnl f* **3/1**[1]

2110 **8** 3½ **Piazza San Pietro**[27] 4203 3-9-5 **68**................................(p) SebSanders 6 51
(A B Haynes) *led for 1f: chsd ldr after tl led again over 2f out: lost 2nd over 1f out: wknd rapidly ins fnl f: eased fnl 75yds* **5/1**[2]

0260 **9** 2½ **Motor Home**[11] 4749 3-8-9 **58**................................(v[1]) DavidProbert 4 34
(A M Balding) *in tch on inner: rdn whn nt clr run and lost pl over 2f out: no ch after* **12/1**

000/ **10** 14 **Balfour House**[661] 5898 6-8-7 **51** oh6................................ CatherineGannon 7 —
(D Burchell) *s.i.s: a bhd: wl bhd fnl 2f: eased ins fnl f* **100/1**

0000 **11** 3¼ **Rony Dony (IRE)**[6] 4916 5-8-4 **51** oh6................................(b[1]) WilliamCarson(3) 1 —
(M E Rimmer) *chsd ldr tl led after 1f: hdd over 2f out: sn dropped out: wl bhd and eased ins fnl f* **80/1**

1m 21.63s (-1.47) **Going Correction** -0.125s/f (Firm)
WFA 3 from 4yo+ 5lb **11** Ran SP% **116.9**
Speed ratings (Par 103): **103,98,97,97,97 97,94,90,87,71 68**
toteswingers: 1&2 £26.20, 1&3 £14.90, 2&3 £110.20 CSF £29.14 CT £369.25 TOTE £6.20: £2.10, £2.00, £3.80; EX 41.80 Trifecta £271.50 Part won. Pool: £366.96 - 0.43 winning units..
Owner Sally Woodman J Lenaghan D Mortimer **Bred** D R Tucker **Trained** East Lavant, W Sussex
■ Stewards' Enquiry : William Carson two-day ban: careless riding (Sep 1-2)

FOCUS
This moderate handicap was run at a strong early pace and it suited the closers. The runner-up and fourth set the level and are rated close to their marks.
Motor Home Official explanation: jockey said gelding was denied a clear run

5125 FREEBETS.CO.UK PREMIER LEAGUE FREE BETS H'CAP 5f 59y
5:20 (5:21) (Class 6) (0-65,65) 3-Y-0+ **£2,460** (£732; £365; £182) **Stalls** Low

Form RPR

1402 **1** **Green Lagonda (AUS)**[11] 4736 7-9-2 **58**................................ PaulDoe 2 67
(P D Evans) *taken down early: chse ldr tl rdn to ld over 1f out: styd on wl fnl f* **11/4**[1]

1120 **2** 1¼ **Caribbean Coral**[49] 3477 10-9-6 **62**................................ GeorgeBaker 13 67+
(A B Haynes) *s.i.s: bhd: hdwy into midfield 1/2-way: kpt on u.p fnl f to go 2nd towards fin: nvr gng to rch wnr* **9/1**

0-04 **3** ½ **Littlemisssunshine (IRE)**[12] 4692 4-9-4 **65**................................(p) SophieDoyle(5) 3 68
(J S Moore) *chsd ldrs: rdn wl over 1f out: kpt on u.p fnl f but nt pce to chal wnr* **12/1**

3021 **4** ½ **Multahab**[43] 3677 10-9-4 **63**................................(t) MarcHalford(3) 11 64
(M Wigham) *chsd ldrs: c to r alone on stands' rail over 2f out: kpt on same pce u.p fnl f* **6/1**[3]

212 **5** nk **Namu**[12] 4702 6-9-4 **60**................................(p) DaneO'Neill 4 60+
(Miss T Spearing) *s.i.s: bhd: hdwy 2f out: nt clr run on inner over 1f tl swtchd lft ins fnl f: kpt on but nvr able to chal* **5/1**[2]

605 **6** 1¼ **Meikle Barfil**[26] 4222 7-8-4 **46** oh1................................(tp) LukeMorris 1 41
(J M Bradley) *in tch: hdwy to chse ldrs jst over 2f out: swtchd lft and drvn over 1f out: no ex fnl f* **50/1**

3106 **7** 2¾ **Joss Stick**[4] 4978 4-8-13 **55**................................ CatherineGannon 15 40
(J J Bridger) *bhd: nt clr run jst over 2f out: styd on fnl f: nvr trbld ldrs* **20/1**

3354 **8** nk **Cosmic Destiny (IRE)**[56] 3246 7-9-2 **63**................................ JPHamblett(5) 9 47
(E F Vaughan) *dwlt: sn in midfield: hdwy to chse ldrs 1/2-way: drvn over 1f out: wknd fnl f* **9/1**

0403 **9** ½ **Rapanui Belle**[29] 4155 3-8-2 **46** oh1................................ RichardThomas 12 29
(G L Moore) *in tch in midfield: rdn and unable qck 2f out: no imp after* **33/1**

-000 **10** ¾ **Blakeshall Diamond**[10] 4778 4-7-13 **46** oh1................................ AmyBaker(5) 10 26
(A J Chamberlain) *taken down early: towards rr: rdn along 3f out: nvr pce to threaten ldrs* **66/1**

003/ **11** hd **Tan Bonita (USA)**[130] 4-8-13 **55**................................ IvanLopez 5 34
(R J Smith) *led tl rdn and hdd over 1f: btn 1f out: eased ins fnl f* **25/1**

5604 **12** nk **Louie's Lad**[11] 4736 3-8-6 **50**................................(p) DavidProbert 14 28
(J J Bridger) *alwys towards rr: rdn and no hdwy over 2f out* **14/1**

0030 **13** 1¼ **Malapropism**[32] 4051 9-9-0 **56**................................ TonyCulhane 8 30
(M R Channon) *in tch: rdn over 2f out: wknd wl over 1f out* **16/1**

606 **14** 1¾ **Best One**[27] 4204 5-8-12 **57**................................(p) KevinGhunowa(3) 7 24
(R A Harris) *s.i.s: sn in midfield: swtchd rt and rdn over 2f out: sn wknd* **9/1**

61.54 secs (-0.76) **Going Correction** -0.125s/f (Firm)
WFA 3 from 4yo+ 2lb **14** Ran SP% **122.9**
Speed ratings (Par 101): **101,99,98,97,96 94,90,90,89,88 87,87,85,82**
toteswingers: 1&2 £9.00, 1&3 £10.40, 2&3 £23.80 CSF £27.17 CT £273.73 TOTE £3.70: £1.80, £2.70, £4.40; EX 24.50 Trifecta £154.30 Pool: £417.04 - 2.00 winning units. Place 6: £44.23 Place 5: £19.93.
Owner M D Jones **Bred** P Brain **Trained** Pandy, Monmouths

FOCUS
A typically open sprint for the class and track. It was run at a solid pace and the form looks sound for the grade.
Caribbean Coral Official explanation: jockey said gelding was denied a clear run
Namu Official explanation: jockey said mare was denied a clear run
T/Plt: £102.70 to a £1 stake. Pool: £52,899.40. 375.85 winning tickets. T/Qpdt: £15.20 to a £1 stake. Pool: £4,744.19. 229.50 winning tickets. SP

The Form Book, Raceform Ltd, Compton, RG20 6NL

[5006]NOTTINGHAM (L-H)

Tuesday, August 18

OFFICIAL GOING: Good to firm (firm in places)

Wind: Light against Weather: Cloud with sunny spells

5126 DG TAXIS FIRST PAST THE POST APPRENTICE H'CAP 1m 75y

5:30 (5:30) (Class 5) (0-75,75) 3-Y-0+ **£2,914** (£867; £433; £216) **Stalls** Low

Form RPR

-000 **1** **Zennerman (IRE)**[8] 4845 6-8-9 **59**.....(v) SPRyan(3) 3 66
(W M Brisbourne) *mde all: rdn over 1f out: styd on* **11/1**

6000 **2** ½ **Follow The Flag (IRE)**[7] 4881 5-9-8 **69**..... RichardRowe 4 75
(A J McCabe) *sn prom: lost pl over 5f out: hdwy over 1f out: chsd wnr ins fnl f: r.o* **9/1**[3]

-050 **3** 2 **Waahej**[13] 4642 3-8-6 **62**..... KierenFox(3) 7 64
(P W Hiatt) *hld up: swtchd rt over 1f out: r.o ins fnl f: nt rch ldrs* **16/1**

0- **4** nk **Belle Noverre (IRE)**[25] 4290 5-9-11 **72**.....(p) DavidKenny 2 73
(Shaun Harley, Ire) *prom: lost pl after 1f: hdwy over 4f out: rdn to chse wnr over 1f out: no ex fnl f* **10/1**

0310 **5** 1½ **Danehillsundance (IRE)**[21] 4400 5-9-8 **74**.....(t) AJSmith(5) 1 71
(D H Brown) *sn prom: sddle slipped 6f out: rdr unable to offer much help fr that point: lost pl over 3f out: styd on fnl f* **3/1**[1]

1616 **6** ¾ **West End Lad**[19] 4473 6-9-11 **75**.....(b) AndrewYoxall(3) 6 71
(S R Bowring) *chsd wnr: rdn over 3f out: no ex fnl f* **3/1**[1]

4605 **7** ½ **Inside Story (IRE)**[17] 4548 7-9-2 **66**.....(b) RyanClark(3) 8 60
(C R Dore) *plld hrd and prom: rdn over 2f out: no ex fnl f* **7/2**[2]

0305 **8** 15 **Fol Liam**[8] 4859 3-8-12 **65**.....(b) MatthewLawson 9 26
(A J McCabe) *s.s: hld up: hdwy u.p over 3f out: wknd over 1f out: eased* **10/1**

1m 47.38s (1.78) **Going Correction** +0.05s/f (Good)
WFA 3 from 5yo+ 6lb **8 Ran SP% 114.6**
Speed ratings (Par 103): **93,92,90,90,88 87,87,72**
toteswingers: 1&2 £57.90, 1&3 £33.80, 2&3 £106.60 CSF £103.98 CT £1577.78 TOTE £17.80: £5.00, £2.60, £6.00; EX 150.60.
Owner Shropshire Wolves **Bred** Eurostrait Ltd **Trained** Great Ness, Shropshire

FOCUS
A modest handicap for apprentice riders but the form looks reasonable rated around the placed horses.
Zennerman(IRE) Official explanation: trainer's rep said, regarding apparent improvement in form, that the gelding dwelt at the start last time but started promptly on this occasion and raced prominently throughout.
Danehillsundance(IRE) Official explanation: jockey said saddle slipped

5127 DG TAXIS GET YOU HOME SAFELY CLAIMING STKS 1m 1f

6:00 (6:02) (Class 6) 3-4-Y-0 **£2,266** (£674; £337; £168) **Stalls** Low

Form RPR

5250 **1** **Fong's Alibi**[16] 4569 3-8-6 62.....(p) AlanMunro 5 66
(J S Moore) *chsd ldrs: rdn over 2f out: swtchd rt ins fnl f: r.o to ld nr fin* **9/2**[2]

226- **2** ¾ **Arts Guild (USA)**[256] 7563 4-9-9 73..... ChrisCatlin 6 74
(W J Musson) *chsd ldr: rdn and ev ch fr over 1f out: unable qck nr fin* **9/2**[2]

0632 **3** hd **Equipe De Nuit**[1] 5108 3-8-13 71..... RyanMoore 1 71
(S C Williams) *led: rdn over 2f out: edgd rt fr over 1f out: hdd nr fin* **5/4**[1]

3000 **4** 19 **Eddie Boy**[33] 4004 3-8-6 57.....(v[1]) HayleyTurner 3 22
(M L W Bell) *hld up: rdn over 3f out: sn wknd* **20/1**[3]

1m 56.61s (116.61)
WFA 3 from 4yo 7lb **4 Ran SP% 85.6**
CSF £12.90 TOTE £4.20; EX 13.80.
Owner T & Mrs J Cunningham & R Frost **Bred** Darley **Trained** Upper Lambourn, Berks
■ Cornish Castle was withdrawn. Price at time of withdrawal was 3/1. Rule 4 applies to all bets - deduction 25p in the pound.
■ Stewards' Enquiry : Alan Munro one-day ban: used whip without giving filly time to respond (Sep 1)

FOCUS
A weak claimer but the winner and third ran close to their recent best.

5128 DG TAXIS FOR SPEED & COMFORT FILLIES' H'CAP 1m 2f 50y

6:30 (6:30) (Class 4) (0-80,78) 3-Y-0+ **£4,857** (£1,445; £722; £360) **Stalls** Low

Form RPR

6061 **1** **Supaverdi (USA)**[18] 4495 4-10-0 **78**..... SteveDrowne 5 89
(H Morrison) *mde all: shkn up over 1f out: styd on wl: eased nr fin* **15/8**[1]

6105 **2** 4½ **Mejala (IRE)**[16] 4569 3-8-13 **71**.....(b[1]) RHills 8 73
(J L Dunlop) *s.i.s: last and pushed along early: hdwy over 2f out: rdn over 1f out: styd on same pce: wnt 2nd post* **3/1**[3]

534 **3** shd **Insolence (USA)**[26] 4234 3-8-12 **70**..... RyanMoore 4 72
(Sir Michael Stoute) *prom: rdn over 3f out: chsd wnr over 2f out: hung lft fnl f: styd on same pce: lost 2nd post* **2/1**[2]

0050 **4** 8 **Naomh Geileis (USA)**[17] 4532 4-9-6 **70**..... RoystonFfrench 1 56
(M Johnston) *chsd wnr tl rdn over 2f out: wknd wl over 1f out* **16/1**

0411 **5** 30 **Phoenix Enforcer**[27] 4196 3-8-9 **67**.....(p) DO'Donohoe 6 —
(George Baker) *hld up: rdn and wknd over 2f out: eased fr over 1f out* **11/1**

2m 10.93s (-0.77) **Going Correction** +0.05s/f (Good)
WFA 3 from 4yo 8lb **5 Ran SP% 107.3**
Speed ratings (Par 102): **105,101,101,94,70**
CSF £7.39 TOTE £2.90: £1.30, £2.00; EX 8.30.
Owner Ben & Sir Martyn Arbib **Bred** Arbib Bloodstock Partnership **Trained** East Ilsley, Berks

FOCUS
A modest fillies' handicap, run at an uneven pace and the progressive winner dictated. The form is rated around the placed horses.

5129 DG TAXIS IS THE SAFE BET MAIDEN STKS 6f 15y

7:00 (7:03) (Class 5) 2-Y-0 **£3,399** (£758; £758; £252) **Stalls** High

Form RPR

1 **Astrophysical Jet** 2-8-12 0..... GrahamGibbons 8 78+
(E S McMahon) *s.i.s and hmpd s: hdwy over 4f out: led over 1f out: sn rdn and hung lft: r.o wl* **5/1**[2]

6 **2** 3 **Lava Lamp (GER)**[15] 4595 2-9-3 0..... RoystonFfrench 6 74
(M Johnston) *s.i.s: sn pushed along in rr: hdwy 2f out: styd on to join runner up at line* **16/1**

2 dht **Citrus Star (USA)** 2-9-3 0..... AlanMunro 7 74
(C F Wall) *edgd rt s: sn chsng ldrs: led over 2f out: rdn and hdd over 1f out: styd on same pce ins fnl f* **12/1**[3]

2 **4** ¾ **Atlaal (USA)**[23] 4336 2-9-3 0..... RHills 4 72
(M A Jarvis) *s.s: hdwy over 3f out: rdn over 1f out: styd on same pce ins fnl f* **1/4**[1]

3 **5** 2½ **Bilash**[50] 3452 2-9-3 0..... ChrisCatlin 2 64
(R Hollinshead) *sn led: rdn and hdd over 2f out: wknd ins fnl f* **16/1**

00 **6** 1½ **Regal Rave (USA)**[24] 4323 2-9-3 0..... SteveDrowne 1 60
(J R Best) *prom: rdn over 2f out: wknd fnl f* **50/1**

7 2 **Spinning Spirit (IRE)** 2-9-3 0..... RichardMullen 5 54
(J G Given) *mid-div: rdn over 2f out: wknd over 1f out* **66/1**

8 5 **Antoella (IRE)** 2-8-12 0..... SaleemGolam 10 34
(Ian Williams) *sn pushed along in rr: wknd over 2f out* **100/1**

0 **9** nk **Azzez Life**[23] 4349 2-9-3 0..... FrankieMcDonald 3 38
(R C Guest) *chsd ldr to 1/2-way: sn rdn: wkng whn n.m.r sn after* **125/1**

1m 14.32s (-0.58) **Going Correction** -0.20s/f (Firm) **9 Ran SP% 121.4**
Speed ratings (Par 94): **95,91,91,90,86 84,82,75,74**
TOTE £7.80.
Owner Ladas **Bred** Grangecon Stud **Trained** Lichfield, Staffs

FOCUS
An ordinary juvenile maiden but the form is hard to gauge with the favourite so disappointing.

NOTEBOOK
Astrophysical Jet from a yard that knows the time of day with its two-year-olds, has a decent pedigree, being by Dubawi out of a Rainbow Quest mare from a family of middle-distance stayers. Her breeding suggested she might need time and a longer trip to be seen at her best, but she made the perfect start to her racing career, chasing the pace from the start and, after quickening nicely, running out a convincing winner. (op 9-2)
Lava Lamp(GER), a half-brother to a Prix de l'Opera winner and from a stable whose youngsters can take a mighty leap forward following their first start, had shown with his debut sixth at Ripon 15 days earlier that he possesses some talent. He ran another solid race, exhibiting a pleasing attitude, but he was comfortably outpointed by the winner. (op 8-1)
Citrus Star(USA) waxs another newcomer but this time from a yard less well known for having its juveniles primed for their initial race. He showed enough to suggest he can win races, although it may not be wise to get carried away with the standard he needed to reach in order to dead-heat for second. (op 8-1)
Atlaal(USA) had started a short-priced favourite for his Ascot debut 23 days previously and, although he had been beaten into second then, he had gone down fighting against a rival who at that stage held a Gimcrack entry. This performance was therefore hugely disappointing, as, after a slow start, he never really looked comfortable and found precious little when his jockey asked him make ground at the business end of proceedings. Official explanation: jockey said colt reared on leaving stalls (op 3-10 tchd 1-3)
Bilash had been pitched into a Pontefract conditions event on his first outing, a move that suggested he is quite well regarded, but he had beaten just one of his opponents and needed to step up markedly to take this. He seemed to show some improvement here, at one stage figuring prominently, but he faded in the closing stages and may need more time. (tchd 14-1 and 20-1)

5130 DG TAXIS NOTTINGHAM'S MOST RELIABLE H'CAP 6f 15y

7:30 (7:33) (Class 3) (0-90,94) 3-Y-0 **£9,066** (£2,697; £1,348; £673) **Stalls** High

Form RPR

0005 **1** **Enact**[19] 4459 3-9-3 **84**..... RyanMoore 4 97+
(Sir Michael Stoute) *a.p: led over 1f out: rdn and r.o wl* **13/8**[1]

1400 **2** 2¾ **Bobbie Soxer (IRE)**[23] 4338 3-8-12 **79**..... TedDurcan 3 83
(J L Dunlop) *hld up: hdwy over 2f out: rdn over 1f out: styd on* **18/1**

6125 **3** hd **Invincible Isle (IRE)**[17] 4540 3-8-11 **78**..... AlanMunro 5 81
(H R A Cecil) *led 5f out: rdn and hdd over 1f out: styd on same pce ins fnl f* **11/4**[2]

4131 **4** 3¼ **Medicean Man**[18] 4494 3-8-12 **79**..... StephenDonohoe 9 72
(J R Gask) *prom: rdn over 2f out: edgd lft over 1f out: wknd ins fnl f* **7/2**[3]

6415 **5** ¾ **Brierty (IRE)**[9] 4820 3-9-1 **82**..... DNolan 6 73
(D Carroll) *chsd ldrs: rdn over 2f out: wknd fnl f* **25/1**

-151 **6** ½ **Shangani**[22] 4380 3-8-7 **81**..... AmyScott(7) 2 70
(H Candy) *wnt lft s: hld up: shkn up: sme hdwy over 1f out: nvr trbld ldrs* **7/1**

6245 **7** 10 **Rainy Night**[53] 3338 3-8-2 **69** oh3..... ChrisCatlin 7 26
(R Hollinshead) *led 1f: chsd ldr tl rdn over 2f out: wknd wl over 1f out* **25/1**

1m 12.97s (-1.93) **Going Correction** -0.20s/f (Firm) **7 Ran SP% 112.4**
Speed ratings (Par 104): **104,100,100,95,94 94,80**
toteswingers: 1&2 £8.00, 1&3 £1.30, 2&3 £7.50 CSF £31.63 CT £75.63 TOTE £2.60: £1.90, £4.10; EX 28.90.
Owner Cheveley Park Stud **Bred** Cheveley Park Stud Ltd **Trained** Newmarket, Suffolk

FOCUS
A competitive three-year-old handicap, run at a sound pace and sound enough rated around the placd horses.

NOTEBOOK
Enact, after being held up in touch for the first half of the race, burst through between rivals approaching the furlong marker and went on to score with a bit in hand. This was her easiest assignment for a while and she will be high on confidence now. (op 7-4 tchd 15-8)
Bobbie Soxer(IRE) had shown encouraging form in the spring, before putting in a couple of disappointing more recent efforts, but she bounced back to something like her best in this event, staying on resolutely without threatening the smooth winner. (op 16-1 tchd 20-1)
Invincible Isle(IRE) posted another solid performance, but the fact that she was treading water in the closing stages suggests she needs some sympathy from the handicapper if she is to get back on the winning trail in the near future. (op 100-30 tchd 7-2)
Medicean Man ran well enough, chasing the speed from the start, but he could not muster any finishing zip and, on this sort of going, may benefit from a longer trip
Brierty(IRE) looks exposed from her current rating and found the pace all too much against these rivals at these weights. (op 16-1)
Shangani, off a 4lb higher mark here, was always struggling and finished well beaten. (tchd 13-2 and 8-1)

5131 DG TAXIS THE WINNING FORECAST H'CAP 2m 9y

8:00 (8:01) (Class 6) (0-65,65) 3-Y-0 **£2,266** (£674; £337; £168) **Stalls** Low

Form RPR

0022 **1** **Deuce**[7] 4867 3-9-2 **60**.....(b) RobertWinston 6 64+
(Eve Johnson Houghton) *hld up: hdwy 5f out: led over 2f out: edgd rt ins fnl f: rdn out* **7/2**[2]

5500 **2** 1½ **Petella**[11] 4755 3-8-5 **49** ow1..... PJMcDonald 1 51
(C W Thornton) *hld up: hdwy over 2f out: sn rdn: styd on* **25/1**

0315 **3** ¾ **Drop The Hammer**[28] 4175 3-9-1 **59**..... SilvestreDeSousa 7 60
(T P Tate) *chsd ldrs: rdn 5f out: edgd rt ins fnl f: styd on* **7/1**[3]

006 **4** hd **La Polka**[18] 4480 3-9-7 **65**..... SteveDrowne 9 66
(H Morrison) *hld up: rdn 6f out: swtchd rt and hdwy over 2f out: rdn and hung lft ins fnl f: styd on* **20/1**

4041 **5** 5 **Bubses Boy**[13] 4669 3-9-1 **59**..... IanMongan 5 54
(P Howling) *hld up: hdwy over 4f out: rdn over 2f out: edgd lft and wknd ins fnl f* **8/1**

3133 **6** *1* **Bollin Judith**[18] 4506 3-8-13 **57**.. DavidAllan 8 51
(T D Easterby) *prom: rdn whn hmpd wl over 2f out: wknd over 1f out*
11/8[1]

0600 **7** *4* **Royal Arthur**[13] 4640 3-8-2 **46** oh1..........................(p) FrankieMcDonald 4 35
(L A Dace) *prom: chsd ldr 10f out: rdn over 2f out: sn hung lft: wknd over 1f out*
100/1

0603 **8** *10* **Sadaska**[35] 3962 3-8-2 **46**.. ChrisCatlin 10 23
(S C Williams) *led: rdn and hdd over 2f out: wknd over 1f out*
12/1

0625 **9** *3/4* **Highland Storm**[11] 4740 3-8-12 **59**..................(v) RussellKennemore(3) 2 35
(B N Pollock) *s.s: sn mid-div: pushed along 10f out: rdn over 6f out: wknd over 2f out*
22/1

00-5 **10** *10* **My Les**[7] 4867 3-7-13 **46** oh1....................................... AndreaAtzeni(3) 11 10
(J R Best) *chsd ldr 6f: remained handy: rdn over 4f out: wknd over 2f out*
16/1

3m 34.22s (3.92) **Going Correction** +0.05s/f (Good) **10** Ran SP% **115.5**
Speed ratings (Par 98): **92,91,90,90,88 87,85,80,80,75**
toteswingers: 1&2 £12.20, 1&3 £3.90, 2&3 £15.30 CSF £91.14 CT £583.88 TOTE £4.00: £1.70, £7.20, £1.40; EX 82.80 Place 6: £1413.34 Place 5:£155.41.
Owner Henry Marsh **Bred** Berry Racing **Trained** Blewbury, Oxon

FOCUS

A weak staying handicap for three-year-olds and not very solid, with the winner not needing to improve to score.

T/Plt: £5,424.70 to a £1 stake. Pool: £38,642.30. 5.20 winning tickets. T/Qpdt: £74.60 to a £1 stake. Pool: £5,278.52. 52.30 winning tickets. CR

4327 YORK (L-H)

Tuesday, August 18

OFFICIAL GOING: Good to firm (8.6)

Wind: moderate 1/2 behind Weather: overcast

5132 SYMPHONY GROUP STKS (HERITAGE H'CAP) 5f 89y

1:45 (1:45) (Class 2) 3-Y-0+ **£25,904** (£7,708; £3,852; £1,924) **Stalls** High

Form RPR

2020 **1** **Barney McGrew (IRE)**[17] 4523 6-9-5 **100**...................... PhillipMakin 18 108
(M Dods) *s.i.s: gd hdwy over 1f out: fin wl to ld nr fin*
14/1

4432 **2** *nk* **Hamish McGonagall**[23] 4341 4-9-4 **99**............................ DavidAllan 13 106
(T D Easterby) *lw: chsd ldr: led ins fnl f: hdd nr fin*
6/1[1]

0404 **3** *1/2* **Fol Hollow (IRE)**[10] 4766 4-9-2 **97**.................................... PaulQuinn 9 102
(D Nicholls) *overall ldr centre: hdd ins fnl f: kpt on same pce*
16/1

0406 **4** *1* **Intrepid Jack**[24] 4330 7-9-7 **102**..............................(b) EddieAhern 3 104
(H Morrison) *in rr on outer: sn drvn along: hdwy 2f out: hung lft: styd on wl fnl f*
14/1

2006 **5** *1/2* **Captain Dunne (IRE)**[10] 4766 4-9-2 **97**............................ MJKinane 16 97
(T D Easterby) *w ldrs stands' side: no ex ins fnl f*
12/1

4010 **6** *1/2* **Sonny Red (IRE)**[17] 4523 5-9-5 **100**......................... RichardHughes 20 98+
(D Nicholls) *in rr: stdy hdwy over 1f out: styng on wl at fin*
14/1

230 **7** *nk* **Tabaret**[15] 4598 6-8-9 **90**...(p) TonyHamilton 2 87
(R M Whitaker) *w ldrs on outer: kpt on same pce appr fnl f*
20/1

3002 **8** *nk* **Wi Dud**[7] 4885 5-9-3 **105**.. JPFahy(7) 1 101
(K A Ryan) *chsd ldrs on outer: kpt on same pce appr fnl f*
12/1

2100 **9** *nk* **Peak District (IRE)**[23] 4341 5-8-7 **93**............................ AmyRyan(5) 19 88
(K A Ryan) *chsd ldrs stands' side: kpt on same pce appr fnl f*
12/1

5000 **10** *1/2* **Green Manalishi**[23] 4341 8-8-11 **92**................................... NCallan 15 85
(K A Ryan) *chsd ldrs: one pce fnl 2f*
25/1

2030 **11** *hd* **River Falcon**[24] 4330 9-9-0 **95**.................................. DanielTudhope 4 88
(J S Goldie) *sn bhd: edgd lft and styd on appr fnl f*
16/1

0000 **12** *hd* **Piscean (USA)**[19] 4461 4-8-7 **88**...................................... JimmyQuinn 11 80
(T Keddy) *in rr div: kpt on fnl 2f: nvr on terms*
33/1

0540 **13** *1* **Indian Trail**[18] 4485 9-8-7 **88**......................................(v) FrancisNorton 10 76
(D Nicholls) *lw: a towards rr*
14/1

2050 **14** *1* **Cake (IRE)**[46] 3582 4-8-3 **91**.. CharlesEddery(7) 7 76
(R Hannon) *in tch: sn drvn along: hdwy 2f out: sn wknd*
33/1

0202 **15** *3 1/2* **Buachaill Dona (IRE)**[10] 4766 6-9-7 **102**................. AdrianTNicholls 14 75
(D Nicholls) *dwlt: hdwy to chse ldrs over 2f out: lost pl over 1f out: bbv*
15/2[2]

0-00 **16** *1/2* **Brave Prospector**[17] 4523 4-9-3 **98**..........................(t) JimmyFortune 17 69
(P W Chapple-Hyam) *chsd ldrs: outpcd over 2f out: lost pl over 1f out*
8/1[3]

0-20 **17** *9* **Aegean Dancer**[29] 4135 7-8-4 **85**................................ RoystonFfrench 5 24
(B Smart) *sn towards rr: wl bhd fnl 2f: lame*
12/1

62.31 secs (-1.99) **Going Correction** -0.125s/f (Firm) **17** Ran SP% **120.9**
Speed ratings (Par 109): **110,109,108,107,106 105,105,104,104,103 102,102,101,99,93 93,78**
toteswingers: 1&2 £20.30, 1&3 £67.00, 2&3 £13.60 CSF £90.01 CT £1422.60 TOTE £18.40: £3.50, £1.90, £3.60, £3.60; EX 91.90 Trifecta £1714.60 Part won. Pool: £2317.08 - 0.40 winning units..
Owner Andrew Tinkler **Bred** Mrs H B Raw **Trained** Denton, Co Durham

FOCUS

A very competitive sprint handicap run at a strong pace and the first running of the race over this intermediate trip. The field raced centre to stands' side, but the result suggested there wasn't a strong track bias and there didn't appear to be a pace bias either. The form looks sound enough rated around the third and fourth with a new best time for this still relatively new distance.

NOTEBOOK

Barney McGrew(IRE) had been beaten a long way in the Stewards' Cup last time and was well beaten in his only previous try over a distance short of 6f, but the strong pace would have been in his favour. Having been held up well off the pace towards the stands' side early, he still had plenty to do inside the final quarter-mile, but once switched to his left he produced a devastating turn of foot to hit the front close to the line. The plan now is to head for the Portland and then the Ayr Gold Cup. Official explanation: trainer had no explanation for the apparent improvement in form (op 18-1)

Hamish McGonagall, in the frame in all six of his previous starts this season, maintained that record having been put up 1lb for his narrow defeat at Ascot last time. Tracking the leaders down the centre of the track and travelling well, he took over in front around half a furlong from home and looked likely to score but he had the prize snatched from him almost on the line. Despite his string of near-misses, he doesn't seem to do very much wrong but his consistency is obviously not earning him any leniency from the Handicapper.

Fol Hollow(IRE), one of four representing the yard in this contest, has been running well this year including three victories. Still 3lb higher than for his most recent success after decent efforts in a couple of hot handicaps at Ascot, he took the field along down the centre of the track and to his credit he battled on gamely once headed inside the final furlong. He still looks capable of winning off this mark.

Intrepid Jack races almost exclusively over 6f these days so it wasn't a surprise when he came off the bridle at halfway. He did stay on well down the centre of the track late on, however, and he may be of interest back up to 6f if building on this.

Captain Dunne(IRE), unplaced three times since his narrow defeat off 2lb lower in the Investec Dash at Epsom on Derby day, was reunited with Mick Kinane for the first time since then. He showed his usual smart early speed towards the nearside, but could never get the lead on his own and he had little in reserve inside the last furlong.

Sonny Red(IRE), who ran very poorly in the Stewards' Cup after winning gamely at Ascot, was switched right off early from the stands' rail draw and he still had only a couple behind him a furlong out, but he finished very fast without ever looking like getting to the leaders. He has won on quick ground, but softer conditions seem to suit him better. Official explanation: jockey said, regarding riding, that the gelding had been a bridle horse and did not respond to the whip, adding that due to the fast early pace the gelding stayed on past beaten horses in the closing stages; trainer said, regarding running, that he did not give the jockey any instructions as he knows the gelding better than anyone (op 16-1)

Tabaret, who ran a couple of fair races last month and had the cheekpieces back on here, showed good early speed to press the leader down the centre of the track. He still had a chance a furlong out, but then weakened right out of it in the closing stages. He remains 3lb higher than for his last success in June of last year.

Wi Dud, who mainly plies his trade in Pattern company these days, ran creditably down the centre of the track having started from the lowest draw, but he is still without a win in almost three years.

Peak District(IRE) gained his only previous win on turf in Ireland in May 2007, but he was only just caught over the minimum trip off 1lb lower here in May. A confirmed front-runner, he showed good speed up the stands' rail for a long way but was never able to dominate and had run his race inside the last furlong.

Green Manalishi ◆, whose last three wins have come in Listed company, is dropping down the weights having only beaten one rival in his last three starts. He ran well for a long way and this was a little better, so another drop in the weights could make him of interest again. (op 28-1)

Buachaill Dona(IRE) was reported to have bled from the nose. Official explanation: trainer said gelding bled from the nose (op 7-1)

5133 WATCH THE LAST 2 RACES ON RACING UK ACOMB STKS (GROUP 3) 7f

2:15 (2:17) (Class 1) 2-Y-O **£29,630** (£11,205; £5,600; £2,800) **Stalls** Low

Form RPR

1 **1** **Elusive Pimpernel (USA)**[41] 3750 2-9-0 0........................ EddieAhern 7 109+
(J L Dunlop) *lw: chsd ldrs: drvn: outpcd and lost pl over 4f out: gd hdwy on outside over 1f out: fin strly to ld last strides*
7/2[2]

41 **2** *hd* **Emerald Commander (IRE)**[32] 4048 2-9-0 0.......... RichardHughes 10 109+
(R Hannon) *lw: in rr: hdwy over 2f out: styd on wl to ld last 75yds: hdd nr fin*
22/1

31 **3** *1/2* **Poet's Voice**[18] 4499 2-9-0 0.. LDettori 2 107+
(Saeed Bin Suroor) *burst out of front of stalls then reloaded: led: t.k.h: hung lft over 2f out: hdd and no ex wl ins fnl f*
7/4[1]

2332 **4** *1 1/4* **Party Doctor**[24] 4294 2-9-0 106................................ RichardKingscote 8 104
(Tom Dascombe) *lw: trckd ldrs: effrt over 2f out: kpt on same pce appr fnl f*
9/1

1 **5** *2 1/2* **Vale Of York (IRE)**[25] 4286 2-9-0 0.................................... TedDurcan 6 98+
(Saeed Bin Suroor) *hld up: hdwy 2f out: nvr trbld ldrs*
6/1[3]

32 **6** *4 1/2* **Mata Keranjang (USA)**[20] 4418 2-9-0 0.................................... NCallan 9 87
(P F I Cole) *chsd ldrs: drvn over 2f out: wknd over 1f out*
7/1

21 **7** *7* **Planet Red (IRE)**[22] 4377 2-9-0 86.. RyanMoore 5 69
(R Hannon) *hld up in mid-div: effrt 3f out: wkng whn n.m.r over 1f out*
33/1

8 *2* **Beat Surrender (FR)**[41] 3753 2-9-0 0...................................... JMurtagh 3 64
(G M Lyons, Ire) *str: chsd ldrs: lost pl over 1f out*
20/1

21 **9** *1/2* **Sea Lord (IRE)**[25] 4258 2-9-0 84... GregFairley 4 63
(M Johnston) *lw: chsd ldrs: drvn over 3f out: lost pl 2f out*
16/1

0321 **10** *12* **Take It To The Max**[42] 3702 2-9-0 89............................. JimmyFortune 1 33
(G M Moore) *chsd ldrs: drvn over 3f out: lost pl over 2f out: eased whn bhd ins fnl f*
66/1

1m 22.45s (-2.85) **Going Correction** -0.125s/f (Firm) **10** Ran SP% **114.8**
Speed ratings (Par 104): **111,110,110,108,105 100,92,90,89,76**
toteswingers: 1&2 £12.10, 1&3 £2.70, 2&3 £7.30 CSF £80.44 TOTE £4.40: £1.60, £4.40, £1.50; EX 73.60 Trifecta £564.40 Pool: £1678.08- 2.20 winning units..
Owner Windflower Overseas Holdings Inc **Bred** Windflower Overseas Holdings Inc **Trained** Arundel, W Sussex

■ Stewards' Enquiry : Eddie Ahern caution: excessive use of the whip

FOCUS

A race with a mixed recent history. It was a good renewal, with eight of the ten runners having scored last time out, and the two to have met defeat both finished runner-up at Pattern level. There was a sound gallop on, which suited the closers and the form looks decent with the solid fourth setting the level.

NOTEBOOK

Elusive Pimpernel(USA) stayed on stoutly inside the final furlong to maintain his unbeaten record. A good winner on debut at Newmarket, overcoming greenness to beat both today's placed runners, this big, scopey son of Elusive Quality again showed distinct signs of inexperience and couldn't go the early gallop. Last and ridden with over 2f to run, he slipped into a different gear once switched right and brought widest of all, putting his long, raking stride to good effect and running down his old rivals. This horse has done well to achieve what he has as a juvenile, given his size, and connections very much have an eye on next season. He is likely have one more outing, maybe in something like the Royal Lodge, as the step up to 1m is definitely going to suit. Quotes for next seasons 2000 Guineas range between 16/1 and 25/1, and he also earned a 20/1 Derby quote from VC Bet for the Derby. (op 9-2)

Emerald Commander(IRE) comes from a yard with a ridiculous amount of classy 2yos and this fellow, who was quite impressive in winning a 7f soft-ground maiden at Newbury last time, turned in another improved effort, despite looking uncomfortable on this faster surface. Another to be held up, he came with a strong challenge and hit the front deep inside the final furlong, but the winner proved too strong in the end. He is well entered up. (tchd 20-1 and 25-1)

Poet's Voice ◆, who came through front of the stalls following a malfunction and was reloaded before the start, improved on his debut effort when destroying the opposition in a novice stakes at Newmarket last time and it was easy to see why he was fancied to reverse form with Elusive Pimpernel. There was a slight doubt about him on this faster ground, being a son of Dubawi, but he travelled powerfully in front, being the last off the bridle. He started to look a little weary inside the final furlong, though, and was eventually worn down. He paid the price for going too quick, but this fine-looking individual clearly has a big engine and may show himself to be better than the bare form in time, possibly back at 6f. He returned with a cut gum, which had occured during the incident at the start, and can definitely be given another chance. (op 13-8)

Party Doctor, who is still a maiden, has twice finished placed at Listed level and he ran another big race in defeat, keeping on right the way to the line and ending up on the heels of the leaders. He should find an ordinary maiden at some stage. (tchd 10-1)

Vale Of York(IRE), a stablemate of the favourite who ran out a ready winner over course and distance on debut, made a little late headway without posing a threat to the principals. He can probably find a race at Listed level. (op 9-1)

Mata Keranjang(USA), second to Coventry runner-up Xtension in the Group 2 Vintage Stakes at Goodwood, looked vulnerable to a couple of these and he failed to reproduce his best, fading from well over a furlong out. (op 11-2 tchd 5-1)

Planet Red(IRE) came up well short on this marked rise in grade. Official explanation: jockey said colt was denied a clear run

Beat Surrender(FR), who had won at Naas on his debut, was quickly beaten.

Sea Lord(IRE) should have done better, given he looked to win what was a fair Ascot maiden last time. (op 20-1)

5134 LADBROKES GREAT VOLTIGEUR STKS (GROUP 2) (C&G) 1m 4f

2:50 (2:50) (Class 1) 3-Y-O **£82,964** (£31,374; £15,680; £7,840) **Stalls** Centre

Form				RPR
0435	**1**		**Monitor Closely (IRE)**24 4329 3-8-12 107 .... JimmyFortune 5	117
			(P W Chapple-Hyam) *led after 1f: qcknd over 4f out: styd on strly: won gng away* **28/1**	
4133	**2**	4 1/2	**Mastery**35 3970 3-9-1 111 .... LDettori 1	113
			(Saeed Bin Suroor) *led 1f: trckd wnr: drvn over 3f out: styd on same pce appr fnl f* **12/1**	
3321	**3**	1 1/4	**Father Time**60 3087 3-9-1 115 .... EddieAhern 4	111
			(H R A Cecil) *lw: hld up in rr: smooth hdwy on outside 3f out: rdn and edgd lft over 1f out: carried hd high: styd on same pce* **7/2**2	
-061	**4**	2 3/4	**Jukebox Jury (IRE)**10 4780 3-8-12 116 .... RoystonFfrench 6	104
			(M Johnston) *chsd ldrs: drvn over 3f out: stmbld over 2f out: wknd last 150yds* **5/1**3	
1003	**5**	3 1/2	**Above Average (IRE)**40 3778 3-8-12 101 .... MichaelHills 7	98
			(B W Hills) *hld up: hdwy to trck ldrs 7f: lost pl over 1f out* **66/1**	
4134	**6**	3 1/4	**Alwaary (USA)**24 4298 3-8-12 118 .... RHills 2	93
			(J H M Gosden) *swtg: in rr: t.k.h early: hdwy over 3f out: sn drvn and outpcd: lost pl over 1f out* **7/2**2	
211	**7**	12	**Harbinger**21 4405 3-8-12 112 .... RyanMoore 3	74
			(Sir Michael Stoute) *trckd ldrs: effrt over 3f out: sn drvn: wknd 2f out: eased whn bhd ins fnl f* **13/8**1	

2m 29.5s (-3.70) **Going Correction** -0.125s/f (Firm) 7 Ran SP% **111.8**

Speed ratings (Par 112): **107,104,103,101,99 96,88**

toteswingers: 1&2 £11.00, 1&3 £12.50, 2&3 £3.70 CSF £294.21 TOTE £31.00: £9.00, £3.60; EX 132.00.

Owner Lawrie Inman **Bred** Cliveden Stud Ltd **Trained** Newmarket, Suffolk

FOCUS

This appeared well up to scratch on paper, but there was no real pace on early and with the market leaders failing to really fire the form, best rated through the runner-up, looks dubious.

NOTEBOOK

Monitor Closely(IRE) has been running well without winning in decent company this year with his fourth in the Dante here in May probably his best effort. Stepping up to 1m4f for the first time, he was soon sent into the lead, which suggested that connections weren't overly worried about his stamina, but he was certainly helped by being left alone in front. Gradually winding things up once into the home straight, he had all his rivals off the bridle passing the 2f pole and he then proceeded to pull further and further clear. He would have to be supplemented for the St Leger, although he was immediately given a quote of 6/1 for the final classic. The extra distance there would obviously pose a different question and, although he certainly wasn't stopping at the finish here, he would be very unlikely to be allowed as soft a lead at Doncaster. (tchd 25-1 and 33-1)

Mastery, back down in grade after his good third in the Grand Prix de Paris, had a 3lb penalty for his Derby Italiano victory in May. From a stable in cracking form of late, he was never far off the lead but came off the bridle passing the 3f pole. To his credit he plugged on well for second, but was well and truly put in his place by the winner. He may still be allowed to take his chance at Doncaster. (tchd 14-1)

Father Time, not seen since his convincing success in the King Edward VII Stakes at Royal Ascot which earned him a 3lb penalty for this, was given a much more patient ride than the front pair. He looked like playing a part when making headway towards the nearside inside the last 3f, but then rather put his head in the air and wasn't making any impression on the front pair inside the last couple of furlongs. His trainer believed that the colt wasn't letting himself down on the ground. Official explanation: jockey said colt was unsuited by the good to firm ground (op 11-2)

Jukebox Jury(IRE), last year's Royal Lodge winner, bounced back to form when beating his elders in the Rose Of Lancaster Stakes at Haydock earlier this month. Trying this trip for the first time, he raced prominently early but was just about the first off the bridle half a mile from home and he could only stay on at one pace from that point. His stamina for the trip remains unproven. (op 11-2)

Above Average(IRE), who has struggled since winning the Sandown Classic Trial in April, was firmly put in his place by Kite Wood over an extra furlong at the Newmarket July meeting and he was the lowest-rated horse in this. He only ran here after being balloted out of the Ebor and, although he was close enough turning in, he was then made to look very one-paced.

Alwaary(USA), the highest rated in the field, had run a couple of blinders against his elders recently, chasing home the Sir Michael Stoute-trained trio in the King George last time following his luckless effort in the Princess Of Wales's Stakes at the July meeting. Back against his own age group here, a big run was expected but it failed to materialise and, having been held up early, he found very little once off the bridle. He is much better than this and perhaps he needs a bit of a break now. Official explanation: trainer said colt ran too free early (op 9-4 tchd 4-1 in a place)

Harbinger had looked a progressive colt coming into this and was stepping up in class following his win in a moderately run Gordon Stakes at Goodwood last month. However, he was just about the first beaten and was eventually eased right off over the last furlong and a half. This was too bad to be true and hopefully something will come to light to explain this dire performance. Official explanation: trainer's rep had no explanation for the poor form shown (op 2-1)

5135 JUDDMONTE INTERNATIONAL STKS (GROUP 1) 1m 2f 88y

3:25 (3:25) (Class 1) 3-Y-O+ **£340,620** (£129,120; £64,620; £32,220) **Stalls** Low

Form				RPR
-111	**1**		**Sea The Stars (IRE)**45 3640 3-8-11 133 .... MJKinane 3	131+
			(John M Oxx, Ire) *lw: hld up in last: hdwy to chse ldr over 3f out: shkn up over 1f out: rdn to ld ins fnl f: r.o* **1/4**1	
-511	**2**	1	**Mastercraftsman (IRE)**63 2992 3-8-11 122 .... JMurtagh 2	129
			(A P O'Brien, Ire) *swtg: trckd ldrs: smooth hdwy over 3f out: led wl over 2f out: hdd and no ex last 75yds* **3/1**2	
4000	**3**	32	**Set Sail (IRE)**30 4127 3-8-11 102 .... JAHeffernan 5	65
			(A P O'Brien, Ire) *chsd ldrs: chal over 4f out: wl outpcd over 2f out* **125/1**	
0302	**4**	3 1/2	**Georgebernardshaw (IRE)**15 4608 4-9-5 105 .... CO'Donoghue 1	58
			(A P O'Brien, Ire) *led: drvn over 5f out: hdd over 2f out: sn wl outpcd: wknd fnl f* **100/1**3	

2m 5.29s (-7.21) **Going Correction** -0.125s/f (Firm) course record

WFA 3 from 4yo 8lb 4 Ran SP% **106.8**

Speed ratings (Par 117): **123,122,96,93**

CSF £1.26 TOTE £1.30; EX 1.30.

Owner Christopher Tsui **Bred** Sunderland Holdings **Trained** Currabeg, Co Kildare

■ Stewards' Enquiry : J Murtagh four-day ban: used whip with excessive frequency without allowing mount time to respond (Sep 1-4)

FOCUS

Numerically this was a disappointing turnout, with the defection of Tartan Bearer leaving no home-trained runners and 100/1 shot Georgebernardshaw as the sole representative of the older generation. It was still an exciting race and the match between the big two playing out and Sea The Stars bagged his fourth Group 1 of the campaign, despite racing somewhat lazily. It was a also a personal best from Mastercraftsmen on this first run at the trip and the winner smashed the course record by 0.80 of a second. The winner is rated 3lb off his Eclipse form.

NOTEBOOK

Sea The Stars(IRE) justified odds of 1/4 but not without a few anxious moments. The first horse to complete the Guineas/Derby/Eclipse treble since Nashwan in 1989, he was happy to sit last of the four runners, and easily followed Mastercraftsman through a gap between the pacemakers when that one was taken to the front inside the 3f marker. With Kinane motionless, it seemed as though he was set for an easy victory, but the runner-up really began to open up passing the two and, having come under pressure and not responded immediately, he momentarily looked a beaten horse. However, once switched and given a couple of smacks with the whip, he engaged in overdrive and it was clear from just inside the final furlong that he was going to get up. Though visually it was his least impressive display of the season, there is no doubting the runner-up is improving all the time and is, in his own right, a top-class 1m-1m2f runner. There was also an element of laziness about his victory. As for where he goes now, it would seem the Irish Champion Stakes, where he looks likely to clash with Fame And Glory once more, is next on the agenda. That will be another big test, with Ballydoyle again sure to be mob-handed, but this son of Cape Cross, who has all the attributes one would look for in a perfect racehorse, seems sure to take all the beating in his bid for a lucrative five-timer if ground conditions are suitable, with Kinane expecting him to come on for this outing. With regard to later in the year, the Arc is a possibility, as is the Champion Stakes, but it seems as though the Breeders' Cup Classic is the race connections would most like to win. (op 1-3 in a place early)

Mastercraftsman(IRE) looked rusty when a running-on fifth in the Guineas and displayed his class with a dominant showing in a heavy-ground Irish version. A never-say-die winner of the St James's Palace Stakes at Royal Ascot, he was widely expected to improve for the step up in trip and appealed as just the type of horse to trip up the favourite. Chasing the early pace, he soon had the winner on his tail having gone to the front, but galloped on in typically relentless fashion and briefly looked in line to cause an upset. It was not to be in the end, though, the winner staying on too strongly inside the final furlong, but this performance only helped to enhance his reputation as a thoroughly likeable and top-class performer. He too has many options, with the drop back to 1m not going to be a problem, and races such as the Queen Elizabeth II at Ascot next month, Champion Stakes, and Breeders' Cup Mile are all likely to come under consideration. Johnny Murtagh was given a four-day ban for excessive use of the whip.

Set Sail(IRE) did his job as one of the pace-setters and bagged the best part of £65,00 for coming third. (tchd 100-1)

Georgebernardshaw(IRE) was the first of the pace-setters to go on and did his job, landing £32,220 for finishing fourth. (op 125-1)

5136 WATT FENCES RACECOURSE SUPPLIES STKS (NURSERY H'CAP) 6f

4:05 (4:07) (Class 2) 2-Y-O **£16,190** (£4,817; £2,407; £1,202) **Stalls** High

Form				RPR
440	**1**		**Yurituni**15 4603 2-8-0 67 .... SilvestreDeSousa 11	75+
			(Eve Johnson Houghton) *racd towards stands' side: in tch: edgd lft and hdwy over 1f out: r.o wl to ld post* **12/1**	
51	**2**	shd	**Bond Fastrac**20 4430 2-9-4 85 .... PJMcDonald 2	93
			(G R Oldroyd) *w ldr: led 2f out: hdd last strides* **12/1**	
3103	**3**	1	**Swilly Ferry (USA)**31 4081 2-9-2 83 .... MichaelHills 1	88
			(B W Hills) *hld up towards rr: hdwy over 2f out: kpt on wl fnl f* **20/1**	
3301	**4**	1 1/4	**My One Weakness (IRE)**22 4371 2-8-3 70 .... TPO'Shea 4	71
			(B Ellison) *lw: hood removed v late: s.s: hdwy outside over 2f out: styd on wl fnl f* **40/1**	
031	**5**	1/2	**Pintura**10 4803 2-8-7 74 .... TedDurcan 16	74
			(M R Channon) *lw: in rr stands' side: hdwy 2f out: styd on ins fnl f* **9/1**	
1016	**6**	hd	**Jack My Boy (IRE)**24 4294 2-9-1 82 .... JimmyFortune 6	81
			(P D Evans) *w ldrs: kpt on same pce fnl f* **20/1**	
51	**7**	1 1/4	**Lord Aeryn (IRE)**36 3910 2-8-3 70 .... PaulHanagan 17	65
			(R A Fahey) *str: lw: racd towards stands' side: hdwy over 1f out: kpt on: nt rch ldrs* **5/1**1	
2120	**8**	shd	**Ballodair (IRE)**17 4525 2-8-11 81 .... FrederikTylicki(3) 8	76+
			(R A Fahey) *chsd ldrs: kpt on same pce: hmpd over 1f out* **14/1**	
2221	**9**	1/2	**She's Ok (IRE)**17 4539 2-8-12 79 .... NCallan 14	72
			(C E Brittain) *w ldrs towards stands' side: wknd over 1f out* **7/1**2	
5004	**10**	1 1/2	**Uddy Mac**10 4803 2-7-12 65 oh8 .... JimmyQuinn 9	54
			(N Bycroft) *in rr div: sme hdwy 2f out: nvr on terms* **66/1**	
425	**11**	nk	**Bossy Kitty**10 4782 2-7-10 68 .... Louis-PhilippeBeuzelin(5) 13	56
			(N Tinkler) *towards rr stands' side: nvr nr ldrs* **28/1**	
4431	**12**	1	**Excellent Guest**12 4717 2-8-13 80 .... TPQueally 12	65
			(G G Margarson) *lw: w ldrs towards stands' side: lost pl over 1f out* **7/1**2	
3312	**13**	1 1/4	**Flaneur**10 4803 2-8-11 78 ....(b) DavidAllan 7	59
			(T D Easterby) *chsd ldrs: lost pl over 1f out* **9/1**	
0103	**14**	nk	**Eternal Instinct**17 4547 2-8-10 82 .... GaryBartley(5) 15	62
			(J S Goldie) *in rr towards stands' side: nvr on terms* **33/1**	
022	**15**	1	**Elusive Sue (USA)**20 4430 2-8-7 74 .... TonyHamilton 5	51
			(R A Fahey) *mid-div: lost pl over 2f out* **20/1**	
2102	**16**	1/2	**Step In Time (IRE)**38 3842 2-9-1 82 .... GregFairley 3	58
			(M Johnston) *led tl 2f out: sn lost pl* **8/1**3	
0664	**17**	4 1/2	**Little Perisher**9 4826 2-9-7 88 ....(v1) JimCrowley 10	50+
			(A P Jarvis) *chsd ldrs: lost pl 2f out: eased whn bhd ins fnl f* **40/1**	

1m 11.02s (-0.88) **Going Correction** -0.125s/f (Firm) 17 Ran SP% **121.9**

Speed ratings (Par 100): **100,99,98,96,96 95,94,94,93,91 91,89,88,87,86 85,79**

toteswingers: 1&2 £45.80, 1&3 £61.60, 2&3 £36.60 CSF £132.88 CT £2951.04 TOTE £15.70: £3.90, £3.30, £5.00, £7.90; EX 255.50 Trifecta £1479.60 Part won. Pool: £1999.48 - 0.86 winning units..

Owner Mrs M Findlay **Bred** Jeremy Green And Sons **Trained** Blewbury, Oxon

■ Stewards' Enquiry : Silvestre De Sousa caution: careless riding

FOCUS

A good nursery run at a decent pace and the field were spread right across the track. There was an advantage to those that raced centre to far side, but that is probably because that is where the pace was. Solid enough form.

NOTEBOOK

Yurituni, making her nursery debut after showing promise in three maidens, was very well backed earlier in the day. She was always close to the pace and, despite hanging away to her left under pressure, maintained her effort to get up almost on the line. This may have been a case of job done, but she remains lightly raced so is probably capable of winning more races and she is likely to be aimed at a fillies' nursery at Doncaster. (op 10-1)

Bond Fastrac, one of the least exposed in the field and making his nursery debut after his all-the-way win in a Redcar maiden, raced handily until taking over a furlong from home and looked like winning until mugged in the dying strides. Further progress can be expected and he shouldn't take long in regaining the winning thread.

Swilly Ferry(USA) ◆, dropped 3lb since a fair effort on his nursery debut at Lingfield, ran on from the middle of the field to snatch third and deserves credit as he came from off the pace whilst the front pair were always handy. He should be up to winning a decent nursery. (op 16-1)

My One Weakness(IRE) ◆, 7lb higher than when narrowly winning a 7f nursery on the Southwell Fibresand last time, deserves even more credit as he lost ground when awkward at the start and was then outpaced at the back of the field, but he eventually ran on strongly up the far side of the track and is one to be very interested in next time, especially back over an extra furlong. (op 50-1)

Pintura ◆ looked to need every yard of this trip and more when just getting up to beat Flaneur at Redcar last time and was 3lb worse off with that rival. He was last and outpaced from an early stage here, but stayed on well up the nearside rail without ever quite managing to land a blow. He is another to be interested in over an extra furlong.

Jack My Boy(IRE), back over his best trip after failing to stay the extra furlong last time, had won three of his previous five starts and his two defeats were in Listed company. Making his nursery debut, he ran well for a long way but his wins have all come on tracks with stiff uphill finishes. (op 18-1 tchd 16-1)

Lord Aeryn(IRE), the preferred mount of Paul Hanagan over his two stable companions, was making his nursery debut after winning an Ayr maiden that hasn't worked out particular well since. One of the least exposed in the field, he was being niggled along from a long way out before making some late progress. He is another that looks as though he will appreciate another furlong. (op 11-2)

She's Ok(IRE), 5lb higher than when narrowly winning a decent fillies' nursery at Newmarket at the start of the month, had her chance but she was racing close to the stands' rail, which was away from the main action, so it may be worth giving her another chance. (op 8-1)

5137 PATRINGTON HAVEN LEISURE PARK STKS (H'CAP) 1m 2f 88y

4:40 (4:42) (Class 2) (0-105,104) 3-Y-O+**£16,190** (£4,817; £2,407; £1,202) **Stalls** Low

Form RPR

-113 **1** **Royal Destination (IRE)**[21] 4404 4-9-2 **92**.............................. LDettori 7 105+
(J Noseda) *t.k.h: trckd ldrs: nt clr run over 2f out tl over 1f out: r.o wl to ld last strides* **5/2**[1]

3540 **2** *hd* **Stevie Thunder**[16] 4560 4-8-5 **86**.............................. MartinLane(5) 10 94
(Ian Williams) *swtg: mid-div: effrt over 2f out: styd on to ld last 50yds: hdd nr fin* **33/1**

3110 **3** *1/2* **Moheebb (IRE)**[5] 4930 5-9-1 **91**..........................(b) SilvestreDeSousa 11 98
(Mrs R A Carr) *in rr: gd hdwy on ins 4f out: led 2f out: edgd lft and hdd wl ins fnl f: no ex* **20/1**

1014 **4** *3/4* **Dream Lodge (IRE)**[23] 4352 5-9-11 **104**.................. FrederikTylicki(3) 14 109
(R A Fahey) *lw: hld up in rr: hdwy on ins whn hmpd over 3f out: keeping on wl whn nt clr run and swtchd rt wl ins fnl f* **16/1**

3400 **5** *1 1/2* **Dona Alba (IRE)**[21] 4404 4-8-12 **88**.............................. EddieAhern 15 93+
(J L Dunlop) *lw: hld up in rr: gd hdwy and nt clr run over 2f out tl swtchd outside over 1f out: styd on wl ins fnl f: nt rch ldrs* **11/1**

0 **6** *1/2* **Charminamix (IRE)**[21] 4404 6-8-9 **85** oh2.............. RichardHughes 2 88+
(A J Martin, Ire) *sn trcking ldrs: nt clr run over 2f out: kpt on same pce over 1f out* **16/1**

0003 **7** *nse* **Laterly (IRE)**[10] 4781 4-9-1 **91**.............................. MickyFenton 4 92
(T P Tate) *trckd ldrs: chal over 3f out: one pce appr fnl f* **9/1**

-100 **8** *hd* **Full Speed (GER)**[25] 4261 4-8-9 **85** oh1.................. PJMcDonald 16 86
(G A Swinbank) *lw: in rr: hdwy over 3f out: chsng ldrs 2f out: one pce* **40/1**

6423 **9** *1/2* **Gala Casino Star (IRE)**[3] 5040 4-8-9 **85** oh1.............. PaulHanagan 3 85
(R A Fahey) *chsd ldrs: styd on same pce over 1f out* **12/1**

2000 **10** *1/2* **Kandidate**[10] 4781 7-9-3 **100**.............................. DebraEngland(7) 9 99
(C E Brittain) *in rr: hdwy and nt clr run on ins 2f out: nvr nr ldrs* **33/1**

6244 **11** *2* **William Blake**[10] 4770 4-8-9 **85**.............................. JoeFanning 13 80
(M Johnston) *chsd ldrs: hrd drvn over 3f out: nt clr run over 2f out: wknd over 1f out* **7/1**[2]

4005 **12** *1/2* **Bound By Honour (SAF)**[173] 703 6-9-7 **97**.............. JimmyFortune 12 91
(G L Moore) *chsd ldrs: wknd over 1f out* **40/1**

0105 **13** *1 3/4* **Jack Dawkins (USA)**[17] 4543 4-9-4 **94**.............................. TPQueally 19 84
(H R A Cecil) *chsd ldrs: n.m.r over 1f out: sn wknd* **16/1**

0-10 **14** *2 1/2* **Yorgunnabelucky (USA)**[32] 4058 3-8-8 **92**.................. GregFairley 5 77
(M Johnston) *lw: led tl over 3f out: lost pl 2f out* **8/1**[3]

-000 **15** *5* **Ra Junior (USA)**[19] 4455 3-8-7 **91**..............................(b) TedDurcan 20 66
(B J Meehan) *s.i.s: a in rr* **16/1**

2110 **16** *7* **Matraash (USA)**[20] 4420 3-8-8 **92**.............................. TPO'Shea 8 53
(M Johnston) *chsd ldrs: led over 3f out: hdd 2f out: sn lost pl* **12/1**

20-0 **17** *17* **Cold Quest (USA)**[10] 4781 5-9-0 **90**.............................. PhillipMakin 17 17
(Miss L A Perratt) *mid-div: lost pl over 2f out: eased whn bhd ins fnl f* **100/1**

2m 9.41s (-3.09) **Going Correction** -0.125s/f (Firm)
WFA 3 from 4yo+ 8lb **17 Ran SP% 125.9**
Speed ratings (Par 109): **107,106,106,105,104 104,104,104,103,103 101,101,99,97,93 88,74**
toteswingers: 1&2 £26.20, 1&3 £14.90, 2&3 £110.20 CSF £112.33 CT £1439.29 TOTE £3.50: £1.50, £7.50, £5.20, £3.60; EX 156.10 TRIFECTA Not won. Place 6: £2481.01 Place 5: £740.86.
Owner Vimal Khosla **Bred** Miss Deirdre Barry **Trained** Newmarket, Suffolk
■ Stewards' Enquiry : Silvestre De Sousa two-day ban: careless riding (Sep 1-2)
Martin Lane four-day ban: careless riding (Sep 1-4)

FOCUS
A hugely competitive handicap. It was run at a decent clip and the form looks reasonable rated round the runner-up and fourth, despite there being hard luck stories.

NOTEBOOK
Royal Destination(IRE) ◆ did extremely well to overcome trouble in running. His bid for a hat-trick came unstuck off a 2lb lower mark at Goodwood last time, but he was ridden under more restraint on this occasion. Travelling well, he had nowhere to go from 3f out and looked unlikely to win, but once switched and in the clear, he really found top stride and just got there in time. This performance marks him down as a smart handicapper and he remains capable of better still, with this being just the sixth start of his career. (op 3-1 tchd 7-2 in places)

Stevie Thunder has long looked worth a try at this distance and he ran a much-improved race. Back on a mark just 2lb higher than when last winning, he came through over 1f out and ran on to get past Moheebb for second, but could not stay on as well as the winner.

Moheebb(IRE) had been on a roll until flopping in his bid for a hat-trick at Beverley just five days earlier, but this effort was very much in keeping with his earlier progression. He went to the front 2f out and wouldn't give in without a fight, but could find no extra in the final few strides. (op 14-1)

Dream Lodge(IRE) has really found some form again for his new yard, finishing as close-up fourth in a Listed contest at Pontefract last time, and he ran on late to record a fine effort under his big weight, despite being hampered more than once.

Dona Alba(IRE) ◆ was unlucky not to be more involved in the finish, being hampered by the runner-up when trying to come with a run 2f out. She stayed on really well to claim fifth, still registering an improved effort, but would have been right there but for the interference. (op 12-1)

Charminamix(IRE) ran pretty much to form with Donna Alba judged on their recent Goodwood efforts, though he too would have been closer but for getting stopped in his run. Official explanation: jockey said gelding was denied a clear run (tchd 20-1)

Laterly(IRE) was driven to try and lead early, but lacked the speed to get there. He didn't run too badly considering. (op 8-1)

Kandidate had all his forward momentum halted when running into the back of horses 2f out. (op 40-1)

William Blake was perhaps the worst sufferer of interference, being hampered/denied a clear run on more than one occasion. (op 15-2 tchd 8-1)

T/Jkpt: Not won. T/Plt: £1,968.90 to a £1 stake. Pool: £214,534.52. 79.54 winning tickets. T/Qpdt: £699.90 to a £1 stake. Pool: £9,505.64. 10.05 winning tickets. WG

5138 - 5140a (Foreign Racing) - See Raceform Interactive

4024 KILLARNEY (L-H)

Tuesday, August 18

OFFICIAL GOING: Good to yielding (yielding in places)

5141a VINCENT O'BRIEN MEMORIAL RUBY STKS (LISTED RACE) 1m 100y

6:50 (6:52) 3-Y-O+ **£28,441** (£8,344; £3,975; £1,354)

RPR

1 **Poet**[2] 5080 4-9-7 100.............................. SMLevey 10 106
(A P O'Brien, Ire) *trckd ldr in 2nd: rdn to chal under 3f out: led 2 1/2f out: kpt on wl fr over 1f out* **5/1**[3]

2 *1 3/4* **Four Winds**[17] 4521 3-9-1..............................(b[1]) JamieSpencer 2 102
(M L W Bell) *trckd ldrs: 4th 1/2-way: hdwy into 2nd 2f out: rdn 1 1/2f out: no imp on ldr over 1f out: kpt on same pce fnl f* **7/4**[1]

3 *nk* **Windsor Palace (IRE)**[100] 1913 4-9-7 101.............................. JPO'Brien 5 101+
(A P O'Brien, Ire) *chsd ldrs: 6th 1/2-way: rdn into 3rd 2f out: no imp over 1f out: kpt on same pce fnl f* **10/1**

4 *3/4* **Excelerate (IRE)**[375] 4832 6-9-7 106.............................. WJLee 13 100
(Edward Lynam, Ire) *towards rr: rdn into 6th 1f out: kpt on fnl f* **50/1**

5 *2* **Scarlet O'Hara (IRE)**[15] 4608 4-9-4 87.............................. PJSmullen 12 92
(D K Weld, Ire) *mid-div: rdn in 8th 2f out: styd on to 4th 1f out: no imp and kpt on same pce fnl f* **22/1**

6 *1 3/4* **Mariyca (IRE)**[303] 6847 3-8-12 92.............................. FMBerry 8 88
(John M Oxx, Ire) *mid-div: hdwy in 6th 2f out: rdn in 5th 1f out: no ex fnl f* **16/1**

7 *1 1/2* **Fergus McIver (IRE)**[33] 4033 3-9-1 105..............................(bt) KJManning 1 88
(J S Bolger, Ire) *chsd ldrs: 6th 1/2-way: rdn in 9th and no imp 2f out: kpt on one pce* **11/4**[2]

8 *1/2* **Russian Empress (IRE)**[87] 2285 5-9-4 95.............................. KLatham 9 84
(David P Myerscough, Ire) *towards rr: 10th 2f out: rdn into 7th 1f out: no imp fnl f* **50/1**

9 *shd* **Smart Coco (USA)**[100] 1911 3-8-12 100.............................. WMLordan 4 84
(T Stack, Ire) *chsd ldrs: 7th 1/2-way: rdn 2f out: sn no imp* **7/1**

10 *nk* **Impossible Dream (IRE)**[16] 4574 5-9-7 100.................. ShaneFoley 11 86
(A Kinsella, Ire) *chsd ldrs: 3rd 1/2-way: rdn in 5th and no ex 2f out: sn wknd* **50/1**

11 *5* **Finicius (USA)**[61] 3082 5-9-7 103..............................(b[1]) DPMcDonogh 6 75
(Eoin Griffin, Ire) *dwlt: a towards rr* **20/1**

12 *11* **Marquesa (USA)**[135] 1136 3-8-12 106.............................. MACleere 7 48
(David Wachman, Ire) *led: rdn and hdd 2 1/2f out: wknd under 2f out* **33/1**

13 *4 1/2* **Croi Mo Ri (IRE)**[131] 1202 4-9-7 90.............................. CDHayes 3 41
(Daniel Miley, Ire) *mid-div: wknd 3f out* **40/1**

1m 46.06s (-1.04)
WFA 3 from 4yo+ 6lb **13 Ran SP% 127.5**
CSF £14.30 TOTE £6.00: £1.80, £1.50, £4.50; DF 19.20.
Owner Derrick Smith **Bred** Meon Valley Stud **Trained** Ballydoyle, Co Tipperary
■ Stewards' Enquiry : Jamie Spencer severe caution: excessive use of the whip

FOCUS
This was probably an average race for the grade, and it's been rated around the runner-up and staying-on third.

NOTEBOOK
Poet was fully entitled to have a leading chance having run well against Famous Name at the Curragh on Sunday. He won this like an uncomplicated horse, tracking the early lead and going to the front a furlong and a half from the finish. From there he stayed on well and just looked like a racehorse compared to the runner-up. (op 6/1)

Four Winds capitulated quite ignominiously. He travelled like a good horse most of the way and looked all over a winner inside the two-furlong pole, but once asked for his effort he hung fire and didn't seem to want to know. He's certainly good enough to win a race at this level but is not one to trust on this evidence. (op 7/4 tchd 13/8)

Windsor Palace(IRE) ran a very fair race indeed and should be more effective over further. He stayed on well under pressure from mid-division without being a threat.

Excelerate(IRE) also ran a fine race after an absence of a year. As usual, he was held up for a late run and was probably close enough to do damage a furlong out before his effort flattened out inside the last. He may well be good enough to go closer in a race at this level before the season is out.

Fergus McIver(IRE) could never get in a serious blow and this trip might have been on the short side. (op 9/2 tchd 5/1)

5142 - 5144a (Foreign Racing) - See Raceform Interactive

4588 CARLISLE (R-H)

Wednesday, August 19

OFFICIAL GOING: Good to soft (soft in places; 6.8)
Wind: Moderate, half against Weather: Overcast, showers race 3 onwards

5145 LLOYD MOTOR GROUP H'CAP 5f 193y

2:05 (2:05) (Class 6) (0-55,55) 3-Y-O **£1,942** (£578; £288; £144) **Stalls** High

Form RPR

0225 **1** **Future Gem**[6] 4942 3-8-12 **53**..............................(p) FrederikTylicki(3) 6 59
(A Dickman) *mid-div: hdwy over 2f out: r.o to ld ins fnl f* **7/2**[1]

600 **2** *1 3/4* **Nimmy's Special**[36] 3955 3-8-7 **50**..............................(b[1]) SladeO'Hara(5) 8 50
(M Mullineaux) *s.i.s: hdwy 2f out: styd on to take 2nd nr fin* **66/1**

5400 **3** *nk* **Highly Acclaimed**[7] 4894 3-8-12 **50**..............................(v) FrancisNorton 11 49
(Mrs A Duffield) *chsd ldrs: led over 2f out: hdd and no ex ins fnl f* **18/1**

-000 **4** *2 1/4* **Soviet Rhythm**[6] 4942 3-9-3 **55**.............................. PhillipMakin 5 47
(M Dods) *hld up: hdwy over 2f out: styd on fnl f* **17/2**

1615 **5** *nk* **Neo's Mate (IRE)**[5] 4977 3-9-3 **55**.............................. TolleyDean 10 46
(Paul Green) *sn hld up in rr: hdwy on ins over 2f out: kpt on: nvr trbld ldrs* **7/1**[3]

2045 **6** *1* **Diamond Blade**[4] 5041 3-9-2 **54**.............................. DavidAllan 4 42
(T D Easterby) *in rr: swtchd lft and hdwy over 1f out: nvr nr ldrs* **10/1**

3343 **7** *1 3/4* **Beaux Yeux**[150] 920 3-8-11 **54**.............................. PaulPickard(5) 2 36
(P T Midgley) *s.i.s: kpt on fnl 2f: nvr nr ldrs* **8/1**

000 **8** *1 1/2* **Willent**[63] 3036 3-8-8 **46** oh1.............................. TomEaves 7 24
(Miss J A Camacho) *chsd ldrs: hung rt 2f out: wknd appr fnl f* **28/1**

0004 **9** *2 1/4* **Bold Bomber**[16] 4594 3-8-3 **48**..............................(b[1]) JohnCavanagh(7) 17 18
(Paul Green) *s.i.s: hdwy on ins 3f out: wknd appr fnl f* **16/1**

0052 **10** *nk* **Fuzzy Cat**[29] 4172 3-8-7 **50**..............................(b) DeanHeslop(5) 16 20
(T D Barron) *led after 1f: hdd over 1f out: sn lost pl* **9/2**[2]

00 **11** *nk* **Cocktail Party (IRE)**[29] 4179 3-8-12 **50**.............................. DaleGibson 15 19
(J W Hills) *t.k.h: sn trcking ldrs: wknd appr fnl f: sltly hmpd ins fnl f* **20/1**

006- **12** *3 1/2* **Shining Times (IRE)**[306] 6788 3-9-1 **53**.............................. GrahamGibbons 12 10
(P T Midgley) *led 1f: chsd ldrs: lost pl over 1f out* **18/1**

0-00 **13** 2 1/4 **Madame Jourdain (IRE)**[99] 1949 3-8-5 **50**............ CharlotteKerton(7) 1 —
(A Berry) *chsd ldrs on outer: lost pl 3f out* **80/1**
-004 **14** 8 **Gems Star**[8] 4879 3-8-2 **47**........................... IJBrennan(7) 3 —
(J J Quinn) *in rr: hung rt over 1f out: bhd whn eased ins fnl f* **18/1**
0200 **15** 1 1/2 **Lily Jicaro (IRE)**[12] 4736 3-8-9 **52** ow1..................... GaryBartley(5) 13 —
(Mrs L Williamson) *a towards rr: eased whn bhd* **22/1**
1m 17.31s (3.61) **Going Correction** +0.575s/f (Yiel) **15** Ran SP% **120.6**
Speed ratings (Par 98): **98,95,95,92,91 90,88,86,83,82 82,77,74,64,62**
toteswingers: 1&2 £34.00, 1&3 £21.00, 2&3 £105.40. CSF £281.64 CT £3690.44 TOTE £4.60: £1.40, £9.20, £7.40; EX 231.70.
Owner Coast To Coast **Bred** Genesis Green Stud Ltd **Trained** Sandhutton, N Yorks
FOCUS
This was a very moderate handicap with only four of these having previously been successful. The field came up the centre of the track, but the leaders surely went off too fast as none of the first four at halfway figured at the finish. The placed horses set the standard.
Willent Official explanation: jockey said gelding hung right-handed

5146 EUROPEAN BREEDERS' FUND MEDIAN AUCTION MAIDEN STKS 5f
2:40 (2:41) (Class 5) 2-Y-O **£3,865** (£1,141; £571) **Stalls** High

Form RPR
1 **I Am That (IRE)** 2-9-3 0.. GrahamGibbons 1 72+
(S A Callaghan) *sn trcking ldrs on outside: effrt and wnt rt over 1f out: styd on to ld ins fnl f* **8/1**[2]
025 **2** 1/2 **Dazeen**[66] 2940 2-8-12 75.. PaulPickard(5) 7 69
(P T Midgley) *s.i.s: sn trcking ldrs: effrt over 1f out: no ex towards fin* **9/4**[1]
46 **3** 3/4 **Jack Luey**[78] 2568 2-8-10 0...................................... IJBrennan(7) 2 66
(L A Mullaney) *trckd ldrs: t.k.h: led over 2f out: hdd and no ex ins fnl f* **9/1**[3]
4 **4** 2 1/2 **Kalahari Desert (IRE)**[18] 4546 2-9-0 0................. MichaelJStainton(3) 9 57
(R M Whitaker) *t.k.h: trckd ldrs: effrt over 1f out: kpt on same pce* **8/1**[2]
44 **5** 1 **Cross Key (IRE)**[16] 4595 2-8-9 0............................ FrederikTylicki(3) 8 49
(R A Fahey) *led tl hdd & wknd over 1f out* **9/4**[1]
0056 **6** 4 **Kirkby's Gem**[9] 4844 2-8-7 50.................................. SladeO'Hara(5) 3 34
(A Berry) *w ldrs: t.k.h: lost pl over 1f out* **40/1**
64.93 secs (4.13) **Going Correction** +0.575s/f (Yiel) **6** Ran SP% **96.2**
Speed ratings (Par 94): **89,88,87,83,81 75**
toteswingers: 1&2 £2.60, 1&3 £7.60, 2&3 £3.60. CSF £19.07 TOTE £5.70: £2.10, £1.70; EX 15.40.
Owner Mrs C Hassett **Bred** J L Hassett **Trained** Newmarket, Suffolk
FOCUS
An ordinary maiden, weakened further by the withdrawal of Bitter Honey who sat down in the stalls. The runners raced centre-to-far side and it was noticeable that those that raced closer to the centre of the track fared best. The form is rated around the placed horses.
NOTEBOOK
I Am That(IRE), a £19,000 two-year-old out of a half-sister to two winners including the Bunbury Cup winner Little White Lie, did well to make a winning debut here as he was the first of the sextet off the bridle, but responded well to pressure and swept down the wide outside to score. He looked as though the experience would do him good so can only go on from here. (op 9-2)
Dazeen, a bit disappointing over 6f at Doncaster last time having previously split a couple of subsequent winners over this trip at Hamilton, was returning from a short break. Settled at the back after missing a beat at the start, he ran on down the outside of the field over the last furlong or so but the newcomer was finishing even faster. Already rated 75, he may be worth a try in a nursery. (tchd 2-1 tchd 5-2 in places)
Jack Luey, a very encouraging fourth in a course-and-distance maiden in May that has since produced several winners, had been given a break since disappointing at Ripon just eight days later. Never far off the pace, he took over in front over a furlong out but was then outpaced by the front pair. He now qualifies for nurseries and could be interesting in that sphere. (op 11-1 tchd 12-1)
Kalahari Desert(IRE), beaten a fair way when fourth of eight behind a subsequent winner on his Thirsk debut at the start of the month, raced very keenly under restraint and then found little when asked for an effort. He looks one for handicaps further down the line. (op 14-1)
Cross Key(IRE), who looked green in finishing fourth in a couple of Ripon maidens, was back down to the minimum trip. She raced prominently early, but faded rather tamely from the furlong pole and has a bit to prove now. (op 11-4 tchd 3-1)

5147 KEN SCOTT 50TH BIRTHDAY CELEBRATION CLAIMING STKS 5f 193y
3:15 (3:15) (Class 5) 3-Y-O+ **£2,590** (£770; £385; £192) **Stalls** High

Form RPR
1531 **1** **Turnkey**[11] 4775 7-9-8 80.. FrancisNorton 7 85
(D Nicholls) *hmpd s: sn pushed along: hdwy 3f out: led 1f out: drew clr* **10/11**[1]
0404 **2** 7 **Steelcut**[7] 4899 5-8-13 74.................................... FrederikTylicki(3) 2 57
(R A Fahey) *w ldrs: led over 2f out: hdd 1f out: kpt on same pce* **7/2**[2]
0050 **3** 3/4 **Charles Parnell (IRE)**[23] 4372 6-9-1 70........................ DaleGibson 5 53
(M Dods) *chsd ldrs: effrt over 2f out: kpt on same pce* **8/1**
4002 **4** 1 1/2 **Sunley Sovereign**[7] 4899 5-8-10 48 ow1..................(b) PhillipMakin 1 43
(Mrs R A Carr) *chsd ldrs: one pce fnl 2f* **11/2**[3]
0500 **5** 1 1/2 **Boss Hog**[7] 4887 4-8-6 50..(b[1]) PaulPickard(5) 3 40
(P T Midgley) *led tl over 2f out: one pce* **20/1**
60U0 **6** 14 **Actabou**[7] 4887 4-8-2 43..(b) IJBrennan(7) 4 —
(F P Murtagh) *chsd ldrs: lost pl over 2f out* **50/1**
0400 **7** 6 **Ducal Regancy Duke**[20] 4465 5-8-13 34 ow1..............(b[1]) LeeEnstone 8 —
(C J Teague) *wnt lft s: sn pushed along: chsd ldrs: lost pl over 2f out: eased over 1f out* **100/1**
0006 **8** 13 **Strabinios King**[30] 4133 5-8-9 54.............................. SladeO'Hara(5) 6 —
(A Berry) *bmpd s: sn detached in last: wl bhd after 2f* **33/1**
1m 16.93s (3.23) **Going Correction** +0.575s/f (Yiel) **8** Ran SP% **111.8**
Speed ratings (Par 103): **101,91,90,88,86 68,60,42**
toteswingers: 1&2 £2.10, 1&3 £3.10, 2&3 £3.90. CSF £3.92 TOTE £1.70: £1.10, £1.30, £2.20; EX 3.80.
Owner Middleham Park Racing Xxiii **Bred** Mrs E M Charlton **Trained** Sessay, N Yorks
FOCUS
Only four of these could be given any sort of chance in this ordinary claimer and they finished very much in the order that adjusted official ratings suggested they should, although the form is not that solid. On this occasion the jockeys decided to come up the stands' rail and the winning time was 0.38 seconds faster than the earlier three-year-old handicap.

5148 STOBART GROUP & HOSPICE AT HOME H'CAP 5f
3:50 (3:51) (Class 4) (0-80,80) 3-Y-O+ **£6,476** (£1,927; £963; £481) **Stalls** High

Form RPR
4345 **1** **Captain Scooby**[27] 4227 3-8-6 67............................ MichaelJStainton(3) 9 75
(R M Whitaker) *sn drvn along in midfield: hdwy and swtchd outside 2f out: styd on to ld jst ins fnl f: edgd lft: hld on wl* **20/1**
2415 **2** 1/2 **Hotham**[7] 4899 6-8-10 71.. GaryBartley(5) 12 77
(N Wilson) *s.i.s: hdwy over 3f out: swtchd outside appr fnl f: kpt on wl towards fin* **14/1**
-142 **3** 1/2 **Bedloe's Island (IRE)**[7] 4891 4-8-6 62........................ FrancisNorton 3 66
(N Bycroft) *w ldrs: hung rt over 1f out: kpt on same pce fnl 100yds* **11/4**[1]
0666 **4** shd **Northern Bolt**[12] 4753 4-8-13 76............................... NSLawes(7) 14 80
(D Nicholls) *hood removed v late: chsd ldrs: keeping on same pce whn hmpd wl ins fnl f* **9/1**
6314 **5** hd **The Nifty Fox**[12] 4753 5-9-7 77...................................... DavidAllan 16 80
(T D Easterby) *w ldrs: led over 1f out: hdd and no ex jst ins fnl f* **7/1**[2]
0212 **6** 1 1/2 **Mandalay King (IRE)**[15] 4620 4-8-8 71.................. JohnCavanagh(7) 11 69
(Mrs Marjorie Fife) *chsd ldrs: kpt on same pce appr fnl f* **9/1**
3200 **7** 2 1/2 **Legal Eagle (IRE)**[11] 4784 4-9-3 78.............................. PaulPickard(5) 13 67
(Paul Green) *led tl hdd & wknd over 1f out* **17/2**
0-00 **8** 1 **Killer Class**[18] 4530 4-8-9 65.. TolleyDean 15 50
(J S Goldie) *in rr: hdwy on outer over 1f out: nvr nr ldrs* **40/1**
635- **9** shd **Hazelrigg (IRE)**[359] 5358 4-9-5 75.................................... LeeEnstone 7 60
(T D Easterby) *s.i.s: hdwy over 2f out: hung rt and wknd over 1f out* **16/1**
3525 **10** 1 1/4 **Bahamian Ballet**[30] 4141 7-9-1 71............................ GrahamGibbons 2 51
(E S McMahon) *chsd ldrs: lost pl over 1f out* **18/1**
1313 **11** shd **Mister Tinktastic (IRE)**[11] 4776 3-9-5 80..............(p) FrederikTylicki(3) 10 60
(M Dods) *chsd ldrs: rdn over 2f out: lost pl over 1f out* **8/1**[3]
600- **12** 1/2 **Burning Incense (IRE)**[284] 7239 6-9-9 79............................ DaleGibson 4 57
(M Dods) *a towards rr* **33/1**
30 **13** 1 3/4 **Glasshoughton**[27] 4225 6-8-13 69.................................. PhillipMakin 5 41
(M Dods) *chsd ldrs: lost pl and hmpd over 1f out* **8/1**[3]
-005 **14** 3 **Avertuoso**[14] 4662 5-8-12 68.. TomEaves 8 29
(B Smart) *chsd ldrs: sn drvn along: lost pl 2f out* **16/1**
62.82 secs (2.02) **Going Correction** +0.575s/f (Yiel)
WFA 3 from 4yo+ 2lb **14** Ran SP% **125.8**
Speed ratings (Par 105): **106,105,104,104,103 101,97,95,95,93 93,92,90,85**
toteswingers: 1&2 £53.40, 1&3 £15.70, 2&3 £14.60. CSF £283.91 CT £1052.86 TOTE £30.00: £7.20, £3.60, £1.60; EX 542.70.
Owner Paul Davies & David Horner **Bred** Hellwood Stud Farm & Paul Davies (h'Gate) **Trained** Scarcroft, W Yorks
■ Stewards' Enquiry : Lee Enstone one-day ban: careless riding (Sep 2)
FOCUS
A competitive sprint handicap in which the front six came nicely clear. Again the runners came centre-to-stands' side, but three of the first four home made their efforts more towards the centre of the track suggesting that is where the faster ground was. The form looks straightforward.

5149 RACHEL CONNELLY FROM HAWICK 18TH BIRTHDAY FILLIES' H'CAP 5f
4:25 (4:25) (Class 4) (0-80,80) 3-Y-O+ **£4,856** (£1,445; £722; £180; £180) **Stalls** High

Form RPR
0060 **1** **Rothesay Dancer**[12] 4753 6-9-6 79.............................. GaryBartley(5) 7 88
(J S Goldie) *hld up detached in last: hdwy and swtchd outside over 1f out: r.o wl to ld fnl 75yds* **16/1**
12-2 **2** 1 **Sirenuse (IRE)**[9] 4849 3-9-10 80.. TomEaves 2 85
(B Smart) *trckd ldrs: t.k.h: effrt and led jst ins fnl f: hdd and no ex fnl 75yds* **4/1**[2]
1220 **3** 1/2 **Feelin Foxy**[5] 5007 5-9-7 78.. LeeVickers(3) 1 82
(J G Given) *led: hung rt over 1f out: sn hdd: nt qckn ins fnl f* **9/2**[3]
5320 **4** 1/2 **Requisite**[7] 4907 4-9-4 72..(v) FrancisNorton 8 74
(I A Wood) *chsd ldrs: sn drvn along: upsides 1f out: kpt on same pce* **13/2**
4216 **4** dht **Jilly Why (IRE)**[11] 4783 8-8-9 66..............................(b) FrederikTylicki(3) 6 68
(Paul Green) *chsd ldrs: styd on same pce appr fnl f* **7/2**[1]
5565 **6** 2 1/4 **Wicked Wilma (IRE)**[6] 4929 5-8-6 60 oh1............................ DavidAllan 5 54
(A Berry) *chsd ldrs: drvn over 2f out: wknd jst ins fnl f* **4/1**[2]
600 **7** 5 **Molly Two**[6] 4929 4-8-1 60.. PaulPickard(5) 4 36
(L A Mullaney) *chsd ldr: drvn over 2f out: lost pl over 1f out* **16/1**
-006 **8** 6 **Blades Princess**[9] 4849 3-9-9 79.................................. GrahamGibbons 9 33
(E S McMahon) *chsd ldrs: wknd over 1f out* **15/2**
63.40 secs (2.60) **Going Correction** +0.575s/f (Yiel)
WFA 3 from 4yo+ 2lb **8** Ran SP% **117.3**
Speed ratings (Par 102): **102,100,99,98,98 95,87,77**
toteswingers: 1&2 £8.00, 1&3 £11.10, 2&3 £2.30. CSF £80.85 CT £348.94 TOTE £22.20: £2.90, £1.20, £2.20; EX 64.30.
Owner Highland Racing **Bred** Frank Brady **Trained** Uplawmoor, E Renfrews
FOCUS
A fair fillies' handicap in which they raced centre-to-stands' side, but again it did seem to be an advantage to race more towards the centre of the track. The winning time was 0.58 seconds slower than the preceding handicap and the form looks sound enough rated through the second.

5150 BRUCE BRAMHALL AMATEUR RIDERS' H'CAP 5f 193y
5:00 (5:01) (Class 6) (0-60,63) 4-Y-O+ **£1,977** (£608; £304) **Stalls** High

Form RPR
0251 **1** **Realt Na Mara (IRE)**[9] 4843 6-10-10 63 6ex.................(p) MrRPooles(7) 8 77
(H Morrison) *led 1f: chsd ldrs: led over 2f out: styd on wl* **12/1**
6101 **2** 3 **Botham (USA)**[7] 4894 5-10-9 60................................... PaulNorton(5) 10 64+
(J S Goldie) *sn bhd: swtchd rt over 1f out: styd on strly to take 2nd nr line* **15/2**[3]
0500 **3** 1 1/2 **Obe One**[18] 4552 9-10-0 46 oh1.. MrsCBartley 2 46
(A Berry) *dwlt: in rr: hdwy over 2f out: styd on to take 3rd nr fin* **66/1**
6-00 **4** nk **Westport**[44] 3678 6-10-9 60..................................... MissRBastiman(5) 13 59
(R Bastiman) *sn chsng ldrs: kpt on same pce appr fnl f* **33/1**
2443 **5** 2 3/4 **Soto**[14] 4654 6-10-13 59...(b) MrOGreenall 11 49
(M W Easterby) *chsd ldrs: one pce fnl 2f* **4/1**[2]
6000 **6** 3/4 **Avoncreek**[27] 4225 5-9-7 46 oh1.. MrOGarner(7) 14 33
(B P J Baugh) *chsd ldrs: one pce fnl 2f* **66/1**
0-06 **7** 3 1/2 **Second Reef**[16] 4588 7-9-9 46 oh1.................................. MissHCuthbert(5) 6 22
(T A K Cuthbert) *towards rr: kpt on fnl 2f: nvr a factor* **40/1**
3351 **8** 2 1/2 **Redwater River**[15] 4620 5-10-10 56.......................(b) MissSBrotherton 15 24
(Mrs R A Carr) *dwlt: in rr: sme hdwy on far side over 2f out: nvr on terms* **3/1**[1]
-104 **9** 1 **Sea Land (FR)**[18] 4552 5-10-2 53.. DaleSwift(5) 7 18
(B Ellison) *in rr: nvr a factor* **14/1**
0030 **10** 1/2 **First Swallow**[28] 4191 4-10-4 55..................................(p) MrsVFahey(5) 1 18
(R A Fahey) *restless in stalls: prom: lost pl over 4f out: hung rt 2f out* **12/1**
5005 **11** nk **Paint Stripper**[15] 4621 4-10-0 46 oh1.................................. MissLHorner 5 8
(W Storey) *in tch: lost pl over 4f out* **33/1**
0030 **12** nk **Uace Mac**[10] 4823 5-10-10 63 ow9................................ MrSebSpencer(7) 16 25
(N Bycroft) *hdwy to ld after 1f: hdd over 2f out: sn lost pl* **33/1**
5-30 **13** 1 **Mr Rio (IRE)**[32] 4082 4-10-7 58.................................... MissKellyBurke(5) 12 16
(A P Jarvis) *chsd ldrs: lost pl 2f out* **33/1**

0000 **14** *3/4* **Punta Galera (IRE)**[28] 4193 6-9-8 **47**....................(b) MissACraven[(7)] 17 3
(Paul Green) *s.s: a in rr* **22/1**

1m 17.93s (4.23) **Going Correction** +0.575s/f (Yiel) **14** Ran SP% **100.4**
Speed ratings (Par 101): **94,90,88,87,83 82,78,74,73,72 72,72,70,69**
toteswingers: 1&2 £4.70, 1&3 £40.20, 2&3 £21.80. CSF £63.89 CT £3431.28 TOTE £10.70: £3.00, £1.60, £7.20; EX 18.20 Place 6 £205.94, Place 5 £59.43.
Owner H Morrison **Bred** J C Condon **Trained** East Ilsley, Berks

FOCUS
A poor race and these amateurs were spread out all over the track. Very few ever got into it, however. The winner is rated to his previous turf best.
Redwater River Official explanation: jockey said gelding missed the break
T/Plt: £72.60 to a £1 stake. Pool: £42,549.05. 427.72 winning tickets. T/Qpdt: £15.10 to a £1 stake. Pool: £3,199.00. 155.80 winning tickets. WG

4699 FOLKESTONE (R-H)

Wednesday, August 19

OFFICIAL GOING: Good to firm (firm in places on straight course; 7.9)
Wind: Virtually nil Weather: Warm amd sunny

5151 BODY SHOP FOLKESTONE MAIDEN STKS — 1m 1f 149y
5:20 (5:20) (Class 5) 3-Y-0+ — **£2,729** (£806; £403) **Stalls** Centre

Form RPR

3353 **1** **Entreat**[32] 4085 3-8-12 73....................................(v[1]) PatDobbs 4 84
(Sir Michael Stoute) *mde all: pushed along and drew clr 3f out: in n.d fnl 2f: pushed out* **7/4[1]**

4322 **2** *8* **Truly Asia (IRE)**[19] 4505 3-9-3 77.................. FergusSweeney 1 73
(R Charlton) *hld up in tch in last pl: hdwy 3f out: rdn to chse clr wnr over 2f out: no imp and wl btn after* **9/4[2]**

0342 **3** *4 1/2* **Mayolynn (USA)**[10] 4813 3-8-12 65..........................(v) IanMongan 5 59
(H R A Cecil) *chsd wnr: rdn and nt qckn 3f out: racd awkwardly u.p and sn outpcd by wnr: lost 2nd over 2f out: wl btn fnl 2f* **6/1**

5-55 **4** *1* **Orthology (IRE)**[89] 2232 3-9-3 75.......................... JimmyQuinn 2 62
(M H Tompkins) *t.k.h: hld up in tch: hdwy on inner to chse ldrs over 4f out: rdn and outpcd 3f out: hung rt and wl btn fnl 2f* **10/1**

5 *29* **Ta Aleem** 3-8-12 0.. TPO'Shea 3 —
(M P Tregoning) *chsd ldng pair tl dropped to last over 4f out: lost tch over 2f out: eased fr over 1f out: t.o* **4/1[3]**

2m 2.33s (-2.57) **Going Correction** -0.125s/f (Firm) **5** Ran SP% **110.5**
Speed ratings (Par 103): **105,98,95,94,71**
CSF £6.00 TOTE £2.70: £1.30, £1.90; EX 7.70.
Owner Cheveley Park Stud **Bred** Cheveley Park Stud Ltd **Trained** Newmarket, Suffolk

FOCUS
A moderate maiden and not a race that can be rated too positively.
Ta Aleem Official explanation: jockey said filly lost its action 3f out

5152 HOLIDAY EXTRAS CHAMPIONS CUP H'CAP — 1m 4f
5:50 (5:50) (Class 5) (0-70,65) 3-Y-0+ — **£3,070** (£906; £453) **Stalls** Low

Form RPR

0060 **1** **Sitwell**[13] 4721 3-9-0 **61**.................................... LPKeniry 5 67
(J R Fanshawe) *racd in last trio: niggled along over 7f out: rdn to chse ldng pair 2f out: drvn to chal ldr jst ins fnl f: led fnl 75yds: styd on wl* **7/2[2]**

0522 **2** *3/4* **Ubiquitous**[23] 4382 4-9-0 **51**................................ PaulDoe 6 56
(S Dow) *trckd ldng pair: n.m.r 3f out: swtchd lft and hdwy to chse ldr over 2f out: rdn to ld over 1f out: drvn ent fnl f: hdd and no ex fnl 75yds* **3/1[1]**

0042 **3** *3 1/2* **Classical Rhythm (IRE)**[14] 4640 4-9-5 **56**............... PatCosgrave 4 55
(J R Boyle) *chsd ldr: hung lft after 2f: led over 2f out: sn rdn: hdd over 1f out: one pce fnl f* **7/2[2]**

0022 **4** *9* **Golden Games (IRE)**[47] 3575 3-9-4 **65**.................. FergusSweeney 1 50
(D C O'Brien) *t.k.h: hld up wl in tch: rdn and unable qck 2f out: sn wl outpcd by ldrs* **13/2**

0221 **5** *1 1/4* **Medieval Maiden**[74] 2708 6-9-5 **56**......................... IanMongan 7 39
(Mrs L J Mongan) *stdd after s: hld up last: hdwy 5f out: chsd ldrs 3f out: rdn 2f out: sn btn* **9/2[3]**

6 *1/2* **Theme Catcher (IRE)**[277] 4547 4-10-0 **65**.................. VinceSlattery 2 47
(G Brown) *t.k.h: hld up in last trio: dropped to last 4f out: rdn ent fnl 2f out: sn wl outpcd and no ch* **25/1**

66-0 **7** *2* **Great Bounder (CAN)**[14] 4650 3-9-0 **64**.................. MarcHalford[(3)] 8 43
(J R Best) *led: hung lft to paddock after 2f: rdn and hdd over 2f out: wknd u.p ent fnl 2f: sn bhd* **11/1**

2m 39.36s (-1.54) **Going Correction** -0.125s/f (Firm)
WFA 3 from 4yo+ 10lb **7** Ran SP% **113.1**
Speed ratings (Par 103): **100,99,97,91,90 90,88**
toteswingers: 1&2 £2.70, 1&3 £3.80, 2&3 £2.40. CSF £14.11 CT £37.92 TOTE £4.40: £3.20, £1.90; EX 19.90.
Owner Rupert Hambro & Nigel & Carolyn Elwes **Bred** Aylesfield Farms Stud Ltd **Trained** Newmarket, Suffolk

FOCUS
A moderate handicap but the step up in trip to 1m4f proved decisive for Sitwell. The form looks reasonable, backed up by the sound gallop.
Sitwell Official explanation: trainer said, regarding apparent improvement in form, that the gelding had benefited from the longer distance.
Great Bounder(CAN) Official explanation: jockey said gelding did not handle the first bend

5153 PORT LYMPNE WILD ANIMAL PARK MAIDEN AUCTION STKS — 7f (S)
6:20 (6:20) (Class 5) 2-Y-0 — **£2,729** (£806; £403) **Stalls** Low

Form RPR

3 **1** **Abriachan**[43] 3716 2-8-13 0................................ JerryO'Dwyer 3 79+
(M G Quinlan) *trckd ldrs: plld out and effrt wl over 1f out: rdn to ld ent fnl f: rdn clr ins fnl f: eased towards fin* **9/1**

232 **2** *1 1/2* **Yarra River**[18] 4524 2-9-2 81.................................... LPKeniry 6 76
(A M Balding) *disp ld: led over 2f out: rdn and edgd lft wl over 1f out: hdd ent fnl f: no ch w wnr fnl 100yds* **11/10[1]**

5 **3** *1 1/4* **Cornish Beau (IRE)**[30] 4152 2-8-11 0.......................... JimmyQuinn 4 68
(M H Tompkins) *t.k.h: hld up in tch: rdn and effrt over 1f out: kpt on to go 3rd fnl 75yds: nt pce to threaten wnr* **17/2[3]**

303 **4** *1 1/2* **Chocolate Cookie (IRE)**[23] 4379 2-8-6 74...................... PatDobbs 2 60+
(R Hannon) *disp ld tl over 2f out: stl ev ch whn barging match w rival over 1f out: wknd jst ins fnl f* **7/4[2]**

0 **5** *hd* **Chat De Soie (IRE)**[25] 4314 2-8-6 0.................... CatherineGannon 7 59
(J S Moore) *stdd s: hld up in tch in rr: rdn and unable qck jst over 2f out: kpt on ins fnl f: nvr pce to trble ldrs* **50/1**

00 **6** *2 3/4* **Dancealot Lady (USA)**[8] 4869 2-8-4 0............................ LiamJones 1 50
(P Winkworth) *chsd ldrs: rdn 3f out: struggling u.p wl over 1f out: n.d after* **80/1**

45 **7** *51* **Bramshill Lady (IRE)**[79] 2547 2-8-11 0............................ PaulEddery 5 —
(Pat Eddery) *s.i.s: hld up in tch: lost tch qckly over 2f out: virtually p.u fr over 1f out: t.o* **20/1**

1m 26.77s (-0.53) **Going Correction** -0.125s/f (Firm) **7** Ran SP% **112.5**
Speed ratings (Par 94): **98,96,94,93,92 89,31**
toteswingers: 1&2 £2.40, 1&3 £7.20, 2&3 £11.30. CSF £18.93 TOTE £11.90: £4.20, £1.10; EX 26.30.
Owner Thomas Mann **Bred** Plantation Stud **Trained** Newmarket, Suffolk

FOCUS
This was a modest maiden with not much depth but the winner progressed past those with form.

NOTEBOOK
Abriachan started favourite on his debut over 7f at Wolverhampton in early July when third to Wasami. That race hasn't worked out well, but this colt has learned from the experience. This straight track seemed to suit him better and allowed him to use his stride to cut down the leader. On pedigree and style of racing, he gives the impression that a mile won't be a problem. (op 6-1)
Yarra River may have suffered by duelling for the lead. He was bumped inside the final 2f and had nothing left. This ground was the fastest he's raced on, and he's worth another chance on easier going. (op 5-4 tchd Evens)
Cornish Beau(IRE) built on a decent debut at Yarmouth in a race that looks okay. He seems the type to do well in 1m nurseries after a bit more experience. (op 12-1)
Chocolate Cookie(IRE) had been running on over 5f but didn't really get a chance to stay this significant increase in trip. A bumping match with the runner-up didn't help, but she is worth another chance over this distance. Official explanation: jockey said filly hung right (tchd 15-8 and 13-8 in a place)
Chat De Soie(IRE) was much better than on her debut last month and might need better ground. Nurseries, perhaps over a furlong further, beckon after one more appearance.
Bramshill Lady(IRE) Official explanation: vet said filly had an irregular heartbeat

5154 10% CASHBACK AT CORAL.CO.UK H'CAP — 7f (S)
6:50 (6:51) (Class 4) (0-80,78) 3-Y-0 — **£5,180** (£1,541; £770; £384) **Stalls** Low

Form RPR

1122 **1** **Hand Painted**[30] 4148 3-9-3 **74**.............................. TravisBlock 2 80
(P J Makin) *t.k.h: trckd ldrs: rdn over 2f out: ev ch over 1f out: hrd drvn to ld ins fnl f: hld on gamely: all out* **11/4[1]**

2216 **2** *shd* **Dance And Dance (IRE)**[9] 4841 3-9-7 **78**.................. LPKeniry 3 84+
(E F Vaughan) *t.k.h: hld up in tch in rr: hdwy to trck ldrs 2f out: swtchd rt and rdn over 1f out: str chal ins fnl f: jst hld* **16/1**

6432 **3** *1/2* **Hi Shinko**[18] 4535 3-9-1 **72**................................ TGMcLaughlin 5 76
(B R Millman) *t.k.h: led: rdn and edgd rt fr 2f out: hdd ins fnl f: no ex fnl 100yds* **5/1**

2531 **4** *3/4* **My Best Bet**[13] 4700 3-8-13 **75**.............................. MCGeran[(5)] 7 77+
(M R Channon) *hld up in tch in rr: hdwy and nt clr run over 1f out tl swtchd lft ent fnl f: kpt on u.p: unable to rch ldrs* **7/1**

0452 **5** *3* **Doc Jones (IRE)**[19] 4494 3-9-3 **74**............................ PaulDoe 1 68
(P D Evans) *trckd ldrs: rdn whn short of room 1f out: drvn and outpcd 1f out: plugged on same pce after* **7/2[2]**

2140 **6** *18* **Reject**[24] 4338 3-9-1 **72**..................................... LiamJones 6 18
(W J Haggas) *t.k.h: pressed ldr: rdn over 2f out: wknd qckly over 1f out: eased ins fnl f* **9/2[3]**

5021 **7** *5* **Zebrano**[26] 4267 3-9-7 **78**.................................... AlanMunro 8 10
(Miss E C Lavelle) *t.k.h: hld up in tch: rdn 2f out: sn btn: eased fnl f* **7/1**

1m 25.94s (-1.36) **Going Correction** -0.125s/f (Firm) **7** Ran SP% **114.6**
Speed ratings (Par 102): **102,101,101,100,97 76,70**
toteswingers: 1&2 £7.40, 1&3 £3.70, 2&3 £9.30. CSF £45.97 CT £210.02 TOTE £3.90: £2.10, £5.20; EX 51.30.
Owner D A Poole **Bred** P J Makin **Trained** Ogbourne Maisey, Wilts
■ Stewards' Enquiry : T G McLaughlin caution: excessive use of the whip
Travis Block one-day ban: excessive use of the whip (Sep 2)

FOCUS
This was a fair handicap and the form looks straightforward rated around the third and fourth.

5155 COPS & ROBBERS EXCLUSIVE TO CORAL SHOPS H'CAP — 6f
7:20 (7:20) (Class 6) (0-65,65) 3-Y-0 — **£2,047** (£604; £302) **Stalls** Low

Form RPR

6040 **1** **Equinity**[16] 4596 3-8-3 **47** ow1.................................(t) TPO'Shea 2 52
(J Pearce) *in tch on stands' rail: hdwy to chal 2f out: rdn to ld over 1f out: edgd rt ins fnl f: hld on nr fin* **16/1**

-000 **2** *hd* **Sky High Kid (IRE)**[19] 4479 3-8-9 **53**.......................... AlanMunro 1 57
(M R Channon) *t.k.h: hld up in midfield on stands' rail: shkn up 2f out: n.m.r over 1f out: str run u.p ins fnl f: pressed wnr fnl 50yds: hld nr fin* **9/1**

0005 **3** *1* **Diddums**[13] 4707 3-9-7 **65**..................................... LiamJones 5 66
(J W Hills) *stdd s: hld up in midfield: shkn up 2f out: chsd ldrs and rdn hands and heels over 1f out: kpt on same pce fnl 100yds* **6/1**

3522 **4** *1/2* **Dancing Welcome**[6] 4937 3-8-5 **52**.......................(b) JackDean[(3)] 6 51
(J M Bradley) *racd in last trio: rdn over 2f out: no hdwy tl styd on wl ins fnl f: nt rch ldrs* **4/1[2]**

4002 **4** *dht* **Miss Pusey Street**[12] 4732 3-8-6 **50**.................... CatherineGannon 4 49
(P D Evans) *led: rdn and edgd rt off stands' rail 2f out: hdd over 1f out: kpt on same pce fnl f* **3/1[1]**

0020 **6** *1 1/4* **Private Passion (IRE)**[44] 3671 3-8-8 **52**.................... PaulEddery 3 47
(Pat Eddery) *bhd: rdn 3f out: styd on u.p ins fnl f: nvr trbld ldrs* **12/1**

3001 **7** *3/4* **Theta Wave (USA)**[16] 4596 3-9-6 **64**.......................... PatCosgrave 10 57
(J R Gask) *chsd ldrs: rdn to press ldr 2f out: wknd u.p fnl 100yds* **11/2[3]**

0646 **8** *2 3/4* **Zelos Girl (IRE)**[16] 4596 3-8-13 **60**..................(e) WilliamCarson[(3)] 9 44
(Rae Guest) *t.k.h: chsd ldr tl wl over 1f out: wknd u.p jst over 1f out* **12/1**

6505 **9** *1 1/2* **Red Rossini (IRE)**[13] 4695 3-9-6 **64**.......................(b[1]) PatDobbs 7 43
(R Hannon) *stdd s: hld up in last trio: rdn and effrt on outer over 1f out: no prog and wl btn fnl f* **15/2**

1m 12.63s (-0.07) **Going Correction** -0.125s/f (Firm) **9** Ran SP% **117.7**
Speed ratings (Par 98): **95,94,93,92,92 91,90,86,84**
toteswingers: 1&2 £19.90, 1&3 £11.40, 2&3 £10.20. CSF £153.56 CT £981.93 TOTE £22.40: £4.60, £4.20, £2.30; EX 194.30.
Owner Killarney Glen **Bred** Whitwell Bloodstock **Trained** Newmarket, Suffolk

FOCUS
A modest maiden and not a race to rate too positively, with the winner back to her nursery form.
Miss Pusey Street Official explanation: jockey said filly hung badly right

5156 EASTWELL MANOR H'CAP — 5f
7:50 (7:50) (Class 5) (0-75,70) 3-Y-0+ — **£3,070** (£906; £453) **Stalls** Low

Form RPR

602 **1** **Step It Up (IRE)**[7] 4907 5-8-12 **57**.............................. PatCosgrave 5 67
(J R Boyle) *chsd ldrs: wnt 2nd over 2f out: rdn to ld jst 1f out: r.o wl: eased towards fin* **6/4[1]**

0030 **2** *1 1/4* **Magical Speedfit (IRE)**[16] 4607 4-9-10 **69**.................. LiamJones 3 75
(G G Margarson) *racd off the pce in midfield: rdn and hdwy over 1f out: kpt on u.p to chse wnr wl ins fnl f: no imp fnl 75yds* **15/2**

2604 **3** ½ **Northern Empire (IRE)**[8] 4886 6-9-3 **62**........................(p) JimmyQuinn 2 66
(F Jordan) *s.i.s: bhd: swtchd rt and effrt on outer 2f out drvn to chse wnr jst ins fnl f: no imp and lost 2nd wl ins fnl f* **9/2**[3]
0300 **4** *hd* **Malapropism**[1] 5125 9-8-11 **56**.. AlanMunro 1 59
(M R Channon) *racd in last pair: outpcd over 3f out: swtchd rt and hdwy ent fnl f: styd on wl: nt rch ldrs* **11/2**
3220 **5** 1½ **Cape Royal**[16] 4607 9-9-8 **70**................................(bt) KevinGhunowa(3) 6 68
(J M Bradley) *racd keenly: led after 1f: rdn and hdd jst over 1f out: wknd ins fnl f* **4/1**[2]
0046 **6** *hd* **Black Moma (IRE)**[5] 5008 5-8-6 **51** oh1.................... FrankieMcDonald 4 48
(J R Boyle) *led for 1f: chsd ldrs tl over 2f out: wknd u.p over 1f out* **14/1**

59.29 secs (-0.71) **Going Correction** -0.125s/f (Firm) **6** Ran SP% **112.0**
Speed ratings (Par 103): **100,98,97,96,94 94**
toteswingers: 1&2 £2.90, 1&3 £4.00, 2&3 £7.70. CSF £13.42 TOTE £2.00: £1.60, £4.10; EX 17.60 Place 6 £66.23, Place 5 £53.22.
Owner The Vine Associates **Bred** David Fitzgerald **Trained** Epsom, Surrey

FOCUS
This was a moderate handicap and the winner did not have to run to his previous form, while the placed horses set the level..
Northern Empire(IRE) Official explanation: jockey said gelding missed the break
T/Plt: £204.60 to a £1 stake. Pool: £34,834.37. 124.25 winning tickets. T/Qpdt: £244.90 to a £1 stake. Pool: £4,237.30. 12.80 winning tickets. SP

4894 HAMILTON (R-H)
Wednesday, August 19

OFFICIAL GOING: Soft (good to soft in places; 7.9)
Wind: Breezy, half behind Weather: Overcast, raining

5157 EUROPEAN BREEDERS' FUND MAIDEN STKS 6f 5y
1:55 (1:56) (Class 5) 2-Y-0 **£3,885** (£1,156; £577; £288) **Stalls** Low

Form RPR
5222 **1** **Gillburg (USA)**[8] 4884 2-9-3 73..................................(b) RobertWinston 3 74
(K A Ryan) *chsd ldr: drvn over 2f out: led wl ins fnl f: r.o* **5/6**[1]
2 ½ **Colepeper** 2-9-3 0.. GregFairley 6 73
(M Johnston) *led: rdn and edgd lft 2f out: hdd and no ex wl ins fnl f* **5/2**[2]
5652 **3** 2 **Durham Reflection (IRE)**[12] 4738 2-9-3 70................. TonyHamilton 1 67
(J Howard Johnson) *chsd ldrs: outpcd over 2f out: rallied fnl f: nrst fin* **13/2**[3]
3 **4** 4 **Benny The Bear**[14] 4652 2-9-3 0...................................... PJMcDonald 5 56+
(James Moffatt) *in tch: outpcd over 3f out: sme hdwy over 1f out: n.d* **13/2**[3]
0 **5** 7 **On Holiday**[9] 4844 2-8-5 0.. JamesPSullivan(7) 2 29
(M W Easterby) *bhd and sn struggling: nvr on terms* **66/1**
0 **6** 13 **Anna's Boy**[32] 4075 2-8-10 0.. BillyCray(7) 4 —
(A Berry) *hung rt after 2f: sn wl bhd* **100/1**

1m 14.97s (2.77) **Going Correction** +0.425s/f (Yiel) **6** Ran SP% **112.3**
Speed ratings (Par 94): **98,97,94,89,80 62**
toteswingers: 1&2 £1.10, 1&3 £1.40, 2&3 £2.50. CSF £3.15 TOTE £1.80: £1.10, £1.60; EX 4.10.
Owner Highbank Syndicate **Bred** Martin Wainwright **Trained** Hambleton, N Yorks

FOCUS
A moderate maiden which would have been testing enough for these juveniles. The form is best rated around the winner and third.

NOTEBOOK
Gillburg(USA), who was well backed in the morning, looked like he was playing second fiddle to newcomer Colepeper for much of the way. To his credit, however, he kept grinding away and came up the final hill strongly to collar that one in the final 50 yards. It was his seventh start so he's fairly exposed now and his mark of 73 looks fair enough, but the way he saw this test out suggests he might have a bit of improvement in him over a little further. (op 11-10)
Colepeper ◆ is the one to take from the race as he bounced out of the gates and showed excellent speed for a long way before the lack of a run and experience probably proved his downfall in the closing stages. He comes from a yard whose juveniles nearly always come on plenty for a run and on this evidence he's a sure-fire future winner. (tchd 9-4)
Durham Reflection(IRE) kept on stoutly behind the front two but he looks vulnerable in maiden company. (op 5-1)
Benny The Bear probably didn't improve on his encouraging debut effort and could never land a blow. (op 6-1 tchd 15-2)

5158 BJORN AGAIN AT HAMILTON PARK IN SEPTEMBER H'CAP 6f 5y
2:30 (2:30) (Class 6) (0-65,70) 3-Y-0 **£2,388** (£705; £352) **Stalls** Centre

Form RPR
R411 **1** **Dark Moment**[5] 4998 3-9-12 **70** 12ex..........................(p) JamieKyne(5) 7 76
(A Dickman) *hld up: rdn over 2f out: hdwy over 1f out: edgd rt u.p ins fnl f: led nr fin* **4/1**[2]
6620 **2** *nk* **Two Turtle Doves (IRE)**[6] 4937 3-9-2 **55**........................ GregFairley 1 60
(M Mullineaux) *prom: led over 2f out: hung lft over 1f out and ins fnl f: hdd nr fin* **15/2**
2106 **3** 2¼ **Hawkeyethenoo (IRE)**[16] 4594 3-8-8 **54**...........(v1) JamesPSullivan(7) 8 52
(M W Easterby) *hld up: hdwy on outside over 2f out: rdn and edgd rt fr over 1f out: kpt on ins fnl f* **5/1**[3]
5633 **4** 1 **Quick Gourmet**[7] 4894 3-8-13 **59**........................ AndrewHeffernan(7) 2 54
(J A McShane) *t.k.h: trckd ldrs: outpcd over 2f out: rallied fnl f: no imp* **11/4**[1]
2-53 **5** 1¾ **Pacific Bay (IRE)**[21] 4432 3-9-7 **60**............................ TonyHamilton 9 49
(R A Fahey) *trckd ldrs tl rdn and no ex over 1f out* **15/2**
4564 **6** 3½ **Moneysupermarket (IRE)**[11] 4777 3-8-9 **53**.................. LanceBetts(5) 6 31
(Patrick Morris) *dwlt: bhd and drvn along: nvr able to chal* **14/1**
5400 **7** 2¾ **Jack's House (IRE)**[51] 3449 3-8-8 **52**.......................(tp) BMcHugh(5) 5 21
(Miss J A Camacho) *bhd: drvn 1/2-way: nvr on terms* **16/1**
2526 **8** 2¼ **Inthawain**[13] 4707 3-9-3 **56**.. DuranFentiman 4 18
(N Wilson) *led to over 2f out: edgd rt and wknd over 1f out* **8/1**
540 **9** 2¾ **King Of Eden (IRE)**[19] 4505 3-9-4 **57**.............................. PJMcDonald 3 10
(E J Alston) *sn bhd: struggling 1/2-way: nvr on terms* **20/1**

1m 14.95s (2.75) **Going Correction** +0.425s/f (Yiel) **9** Ran SP% **115.3**
Speed ratings (Par 98): **98,97,94,93,90 86,82,79,75**
toteswingers: 1&2 £15.40, 1&3 £2.00, 2&3 £3.60. CSF £33.95 CT £153.20 TOTE £5.20: £1.90, £2.20, £2.20; EX 39.90.
Owner Construction Crew Racing Partnership **Bred** Wilderbrook Stud **Trained** Sandhutton, N Yorks

FOCUS
Low-grade handicap form with the runner-up rated to his maiden form.
Jack's House(IRE) Official explanation: trainer said gelding did not handle the track or the soft ground

5159 DONALD STORRIE GROUP (S) STKS 5f 4y
3:05 (3:05) (Class 6) 3-Y-0+ **£2,388** (£705; £352) **Stalls** Centre

Form RPR
6006 **1** **Steel Blue**[14] 4654 9-8-6 53...(p) AmyRyan(5) 2 58
(R M Whitaker) *cl up: rdn and hung rt fr over 1f out: led ins fnl f: r.o* **3/1**[3]
0546 **2** 1 **Captain Royale (IRE)**[10] 4823 4-8-4 50.............(p) AndrewHeffernan(7) 9 54
(Miss Tracy Waggott) *midfield: drvn over 2f out: no imp tl styd on ins fnl f: tk 2nd post* **11/4**[2]
0040 **3** *nse* **Rightcar Lewis**[39] 3853 4-8-6 45.......................................(b) GregFairley 7 49
(Peter Grayson) *led over 4f out to ins fnl f: one pce* **25/1**
0404 **4** 4 **Strathmore (IRE)**[7] 4894 5-8-11 55.............................. TonyHamilton 5 39
(R A Fahey) *bhd and outpcd: hdwy over 1f out: no ch w first three* **9/4**[1]
0000 **5** 4 **Desert Ben (IRE)**[10] 4823 6-8-6 52..................................(b) JamieKyne(5) 4 25
(C Grant) *outpcd and sn t.o: hdwy over 1f out: kpt on: nvr on terms* **8/1**
0530 **6** 1½ **Paddy Jack**[4] 5041 4-8-7 46 ow1................................... MarkCoumbe(5) 3 21
(J R Weymes) *prom tl rdn and wknd over 1f out* **10/1**
0060 **7** ¾ **Mr Rooney (IRE)**[20] 4467 6-8-9 42...................................... BillyCray(7) 6 22
(A Berry) *s.i.s: bhd and sn outpcd: nvr on terms* **40/1**
0- **8** ½ **Rue Soleil**[274] 7375 5-8-6 45..(b1) PJMcDonald 1 10
(J R Weymes) *prom: drvn over 2f out: wknd over 1f out* **50/1**
0006 **9** 17 **Howards Prince**[33] 4036 6-8-11 40............................ DuranFentiman 8 —
(D A Nolan) *led to over 4f out: wknd fr 1/2-way: t.o* **80/1**

62.47 secs (2.47) **Going Correction** +0.425s/f (Yiel) **9** Ran SP% **112.1**
Speed ratings (Par 101): **97,95,95,88,82 80,78,78,50**
toteswingers: 1&2 £4.60, 1&3 £5.80, 2&3 £28.70. CSF £11.02 TOTE £4.30: £1.30, £1.60, £5.40; EX 14.30.There was no bid for the winner.
Owner Country Lane Partnership **Bred** R T And Mrs Watson **Trained** Scarcroft, W Yorks

FOCUS
A dire race but the winner probably did not need to improve on recent handicap form.
Mr Rooney(IRE) Official explanation: jockey said gelding hung right-handed throughout

5160 HAMILTON PARK SCOTTISH TROPHY SERIES FINAL (HANDICAP STKS) 1m 1f 36y
3:40 (3:41) (Class 3) 3-Y-0+ **£9,714** (£2,890; £1,444; £721) **Stalls** High

Form RPR
1140 **1** **Marvo**[14] 4641 5-9-2 **76**.. AshleyMorgan(7) 3 89+
(M H Tompkins) *hld up: smooth hdwy on outside 3f out: led over 1f out: r.o strly: eased wl ins fnl f* **9/1**
1115 **2** 1¼ **Mountain Cat (IRE)**[11] 4801 5-9-9 **76**.......................... RobertWinston 7 84
(G A Swinbank) *hld up on outside: hdwy and ch over 1f out: kpt on fnl f: nt pce of wnr* **12/1**
125 **3** ½ **Stateside (CAN)**[33] 4068 4-8-8 **61**............................. TonyHamilton 14 68
(R A Fahey) *cl up: effrt and ev ch over 1f out: kpt on same pce fnl f* **11/1**
4231 **4** 1¾ **Casino Night**[18] 4532 4-9-2 **76**........................ AndrewHeffernan(7) 11 80
(F P Murtagh) *sn in tch: effrt and drvn over 2f out: one pce fnl f* **6/1**[3]
5242 **5** 1¼ **Tanforan**[10] 4824 7-8-5 **65**.. BillyCray(7) 16 66
(B P J Baugh) *midfield on ins: effrt over 2f out: no imp fnl f* **16/1**
142 **6** *hd* **Hippolytus**[18] 4532 4-9-5 **77**.. JamieKyne(5) 5 78
(J J Quinn) *hld up: rdn 3f out: styd on fnl 2f: nvr able to chal* **4/1**[1]
0263 **7** ¾ **Shadowtime**[22] 4400 4-9-0 **67**... GregFairley 10 66
(Miss Tracy Waggott) *led after 1f to over 1f out: sn no ex* **8/1**
4343 **8** 5 **Primo Way**[18] 4532 8-8-3 **56**... DuranFentiman 6 45
(D A Nolan) *t.k.h: hld up: rdn over 2f out: n.d* **25/1**
5264 **9** *hd* **Zabeel Tower**[8] 4878 6-8-8 **68**..........................(t) JamesPSullivan(7) 8 56
(R Allan) *hld up: effrt over 2f out: sn outpcd* **20/1**
0421 **10** 2 **Petsas Pleasure**[39] 3857 3-8-4 **69**.................................. BMcHugh(5) 9 53
(Ollie Pears) *dwlt: hld up: rdn 3f out: sn btn* **14/1**
4134 **11** 2 **Rosko**[6] 4941 5-8-12 **70**.. LanceBetts(5) 13 50
(B Ellison) *t.k.h: in tch: outpcd over 3f out: sn btn* **9/2**[2]
3310 **12** 8 **Shy Glance (USA)**[18] 4532 7-9-1 **71**............................ NeilBrown(3) 12 34
(P Monteith) *led 1f: cl up tl wknd over 2f out* **25/1**
-314 **13** 7 **Doon Haymer (IRE)**[18] 4532 4-9-1 **73**..................... PatrickDonaghy(5) 4 21
(I Semple) *in tch tl rdn and wknd over 3f out* **16/1**

2m 4.53s (4.83) **Going Correction** +0.725s/f (Yiel)
WFA 3 from 4yo+ 7lb **13** Ran SP% **120.5**
Speed ratings (Par 107): **107,105,105,103,102 102,101,97,97,95 93,86,80**
toteswingers: 1&2 £49.90, 1&3 £23.00, 2&3 £15.70. CSF £110.42 CT £1203.33 TOTE £11.80: £3.40, £3.90, £3.80; EX 123.80.
Owner M P Bowring **Bred** Mystic Meg Limited **Trained** Newmarket, Suffolk

FOCUS
A modest handicap, run at an ordinary pace but the form looks sound rated around the placed horses.

NOTEBOOK
Marvo settled well towards the back of the field and, confidently ridden by young Ashley Morgan, he made stealthy headway out wide before surging clear in the final furlong to win readily. Not at his best on fast ground at Brighton last time, this five-year-old is much better suited by an easy surface (won his maiden on soft) and he was able to race off just 3lb higher than when scoring at Doncaster in June. The key to him looks to be the ground and he's one to keep on the right side of when getting his conditions. (op 11-1)
Mountain Cat(IRE) no doubt prefers it quicker, so he ran really well in the circumstances and has probably posted a career-best effort. (op 11-1 tchd 10-1)
Stateside(CAN) kept on well given she was a bit keen early and she is another who prefers better ground, so this was another decent effort. She can do better still when getting a stronger pace. (op 8-1)
Casino Night would have needed a career-best to win off this mark having been raised 6lb for her win here last time so she did perfectly well. (op 7-1 tchd 15-2)
Tanforan was a little too free early on and didn't have the smoothest of passsages up the inside.
Hippolytus likes this sort of ground but he didn't travel that well out the back, and although he made some modest late headway, this has to go down as a disappointing run. (op 11-2)
Rosko Official explanation: jockey said gelding ran flat
Shy Glance(USA) Official explanation: jockey said gelding was unsuited by the soft (good to soft places) ground

5161 MARIE CURIE CLAIMING STKS 1m 3f 16y
4:15 (4:15) (Class 6) 3-Y-0+ **£2,388** (£705; £352) **Stalls** High

Form RPR
2222 **1** **Graceful Descent (FR)**[12] 4740 4-9-3 68.......................... TonyHamilton 4 58
(R A Fahey) *chsd ldrs: pushed along 3f out: rallied and ev ch over 1f out: led ent fnl f: kpt on* **1/4**[1]
0300 **2** 1¾ **Cecina Marina**[37] 3927 6-8-5 34.. JamieKyne(5) 2 48
(Mrs K Walton) *led: jnd over 1f out: hdd ent fnl f: kpt on same pce* **20/1**[3]
2152 **3** 4½ **Terminate (GER)**[9] 4857 7-8-12 60.................................. BillyCray(7) 1 49
(A Berry) *t.k.h: pressed ldr tl rdn and outpcd fnl 2f* **4/1**[2]

-000 4 14 **Dance Sauvage**[46] 3617 6-9-3 36 PJMcDonald 3 24
(B Storey) *in tch tl rdn and wknd fr over 3f out* **33/1**
2m 37.56s (11.96) **Going Correction** +0.725s/f (Yiel) 4 Ran SP% **107.7**
Speed ratings (Par 101): **85,83,80,70**
CSF £6.57 TOTE £1.30; EX 7.60.The winner was claimed by Mr E. Nisbet for £12,000.
Owner R A Fahey **Bred** Castleton Group **Trained** Musley Bank, N Yorks
FOCUS
A very weak affair with the winner not needing to get close to his recent best and the runner-up is the best guide to the form.

5162 GRIFFITHS & ARMOUR H'CAP 1m 4f 17y
4:50 (4:50) (Class 5) (0-70,66) 3-Y-0+ **£3,238** (£963; £481; £240) **Stalls** High

Form RPR
6560 1 **Herrera (IRE)**[25] 4332 4-9-9 66 BMcHugh(5) 1 74
(R A Fahey) *hld up: hdwy over 3f out: effrt 2f out: styd on wl fnl f to ld nr fin* **9/2**[3]
3014 2 nk **Shifting Gold (IRE)**[7] 4898 3-8-9 62 (b) AmyRyan(5) 7 70
(K A Ryan) *sn led and set decent gallop: rdn 3f out: kpt on wl fnl 2f: hdd nr fin* **3/1**[1]
0-01 3 ¾ **Jordan's Light (USA)**[7] 4898 6-9-0 59 6ex JamesPSullivan(7) 3 65
(P Monteith) *hld up: hdwy over 2f out: kpt on fnl f: nrst fin* **7/2**[2]
4432 4 2½ **Regent's Secret (USA)**[8] 4874 9-8-12 55 (p) PatrickDonaghy(5) 2 57
(J S Goldie) *hld up: rdn and effrt over 2f out: kpt on fnl f: no imp* **7/1**
0631 5 4 **Fossgate**[16] 4600 8-9-3 55 (b) PJMcDonald 4 51
(J D Bethell) *hld up in tch: effrt over 3f out: hung rt and outpcd fr 2f out* **3/1**[1]
340P 6 6 **Always Best**[20] 4462 5-8-8 49 oh2 ow2 NeilBrown(3) 9 35
(R Allan) *cl up tl rdn and wknd fr 2f out* **25/1**
4666 7 8 **Louisa (GER)**[7] 4898 5-9-2 54 TonyHamilton 6 28
(P Monteith) *hld up: rdn over 3f out: wknd over 2f out* **9/1**
00/0 8 34 **English Archer**[11] 4806 6-8-9 47 oh2 GregFairley 8 —
(A Kirtley) *cl up tl rdn and wknd over 3f out: t.o* **25/1**
2m 48.14s (9.54) **Going Correction** +0.725s/f (Yiel)
WFA 3 from 4yo+ 10lb 8 Ran SP% **120.6**
Speed ratings (Par 103): **97,96,96,94,91 87,82,59**
toteswingers: 1&2 £4.10, 1&3 £3.10, 2&3 £2.50. CSF £19.58 CT £52.66 TOTE £6.50: £2.10, £1.50, £1.70; EX 22.30.
Owner Dr Anne J F Gillespie **Bred** Dr A J F Gillespie **Trained** Musley Bank, N Yorks
■ Stewards' Enquiry : Amy Ryan two-day ban: used whip down shoulder in the forehand position (Sep 2-3)
B McHugh two-day ban: excessive use of the whip (Sep 2-3)
FOCUS
A moderate handicap, run at a strong early pace. The third sets the level and the form looks sound.

5163 OFFICER AND A GENTLEMAN EVENING NEXT FRIDAY MAIDEN STKS 6f 5y
5:25 (5:26) (Class 5) 3-Y-0+ **£2,729** (£806; £403) **Stalls** Centre

Form RPR
3232 1 **Helieorbea**[11] 4805 3-9-3 75 DuranFentiman 3 73+
(T D Easterby) *prom: drvn and outpcd 1/2-way: rallied over 1f out: led ins fnl f: sn clr* **1/1**[1]
5052 2 3 **Silk Gallery (USA)**[18] 4550 4-9-1 55 (t) PJMcDonald 6 58
(E J Alston) *cl up: rdn over 1f out: ev ch ins fnl f: nt pce of wnr* **4/1**[3]
00 3 2¼ **Yes Please**[61] 3093 4-9-6 0 RobertWinston 5 56
(K A Ryan) *mde most to ins fnl f: kpt on same pce* **25/1**
06 4 1 **Ultimate Respect (USA)**[14] 4648 3-9-3 0 GregFairley 7 53
(M Johnston) *w ldrs tl rdn and outpcd appr fnl f* **9/4**[2]
0 5 2¾ **Duke Of Bothwell (USA)**[9] 4860 3-9-3 0 TonyHamilton 1 44
(R A Fahey) *bhd: rdn 1/2-way: styd on fnl f: n.d* **14/1**
60 6 13 **Our Girl Ally (IRE)**[88] 2265 3-8-5 0 BillyCray(7) 2 —
(A Berry) *trckd ldrs to 1/2-way: sn rdn and wknd: t.o* **66/1**
0-00 7 12 **Becky Quick (IRE)**[43] 3712 4-8-8 0 (b) CharlotteKerton(7) 4 —
(Bruce Hellier) *s.i.s: hld up bhd ldrs: hung rt and wknd over 2f out: t.o* **100/1**
00 8 25 **Mister Biscuit (USA)**[18] 4531 3-8-12 0 JamieKyne(5) 8 —
(Miss L A Perratt) *in tch tl rdn and wknd fr 1/2-way: t.o* **33/1**
1m 15.47s (3.27) **Going Correction** +0.425s/f (Yiel)
WFA 3 from 4yo 3lb 8 Ran SP% **116.7**
Speed ratings (Par 103): **95,91,88,86,83 65,49,16**
toteswingers: 1&2 £1.30, 1&3 £7.20, 2&3 £5.10. CSF £5.56 TOTE £1.90: £1.02, £1.40, £6.50; EX 5.80 Place 6 £49.29, Place 5 £39.69.
Owner Middleham Park Racing XXXIII **Bred** Larchwood Bloodstock **Trained** Great Habton, N Yorks
FOCUS
A weak maiden but it looks sound enough with the runner-up and fourth to their turf marks.
T/Plt: £61.10 to a £1 stake. Pool: £35,047.05. 418.53 winning tickets. T/Qpdt: £27.80 to a £1 stake. Pool: £2,570.60. 68.20 winning tickets. RY

5090 KEMPTON (A.W) (R-H)
Wednesday, August 19

OFFICIAL GOING: Standard
Wind: Moderate, half behind Weather: Sunny, very warm

5164 GREG SLARK BIRTHDAY CELEBRATION H'CAP 5f (P)
6:40 (6:40) (Class 5) (0-70,70) 3-Y-0 **£2,590** (£770; £385; £192) **Stalls** High

Form RPR
0625 1 **Agnes Love**[5] 4978 3-8-7 57 AndreaAtzeni(3) 6 64
(J Akehurst) *mde all: rdn over 1f out: edgd lft thrght fnl f: hld on wl* **7/2**[1]
6605 2 ½ **Rebecca De Winter**[37] 3926 3-8-9 63 JPFahy(7) 8 68
(David Pinder) *s.i.s: sn chsd ldng pair on inner: rdn over 1f out: wnt 2nd last 150yds and clsd on wnr: nt qckn and hld nr fin* **7/1**
5260 3 1½ **Mazzola**[19] 4483 3-9-9 70 DaneO'Neill 5 70
(M R Channon) *pressed wnr: rdn to chal over 1f out: nt qckn ent fnl f: sn lost 2nd: fdd* **7/1**
3223 4 shd **Halaak (USA)**[20] 4454 3-9-4 65 (b) DarryllHolland 1 64+
(D M Simcock) *hld up in last pair fr wd draw: rdn over 1f out: prog ent fnl f: styd on wl: nrly snatched 3rd* **6/1**
3-30 5 1¼ **Clerical (USA)**[13] 4718 3-8-12 59 ShaneKelly 3 54
(R M H Cowell) *rdn in midfield bef 1/2-way: struggling after: plugged on u.p ins fnl f* **6/1**
2150 6 nk **Chris's Jem**[18] 4514 3-9-5 66 JamesDoyle 4 60
(J R Jenkins) *chsd ldrs: rdn and nt qckn wl over 1f out: fdd* **20/1**
3-00 7 ¾ **Chosen Son (IRE)**[35] 3989 3-9-4 65 SteveDrowne 7 56
(P J O'Gorman) *nvr beyond midfield: rdn over 1f out: no prog: fdd fnl f* **4/1**[2]
5612 8 1½ **Speak The Truth (IRE)**[10] 4829 3-9-2 68 (p) MatthewDavies(5) 2 54
(J R Boyle) *settled in last fr wd draw: pushed along 1/2-way: struggling u.p and no prog over 1f out* **11/2**[3]
60.48 secs (-0.02) **Going Correction** -0.05s/f (Stan) 8 Ran SP% **115.9**
Speed ratings (Par 100): **98,97,94,94,92 92,90,88**
toteswingers: 1&2 £7.50, 1&3 £5.70, 2&3 £11.00. CSF £28.73 CT £162.99 TOTE £4.40: £1.70, £2.70, £3.40; EX 40.00.
Owner David S M Caplin **Bred** Paul Sweeting **Trained** Epsom, Surrey
■ Stewards' Enquiry : J P Fahy two-day ban: excessive use of the whip (Sep 2-3)
Andrea Atzeni five-day ban: used whip in incorrect place (Sep 2-6)
FOCUS
A modest sprint handicap and the form does not look too solid.

5165 EUROPEAN BREEDERS' FUND MAIDEN FILLIES' STKS 1m (P)
7:10 (7:12) (Class 4) 2-Y-O **£4,533** (£1,348; £674; £336) **Stalls** High

Form RPR
32 1 **Dyna Waltz**[18] 4542 2-9-0 0 NickyMackay 2 82+
(J H M Gosden) *mde virtually all: drew at least 3l clr 2f out: pushed along and nvr in serious danger after* **11/4**[2]
4 2 1 **Rare Malt (IRE)**[18] 4542 2-8-11 0 AndreaAtzeni(3) 10 78
(Miss Amy Weaver) *s.s: last pair tl prog on inner over 2f out: styd on wl to take 2nd last 150yds: clsd on wnr fin but no real threat* **14/1**
3 nk **Milnagavie** 2-9-0 0 SteveDrowne 8 77+
(R Hannon) *pushed up to press wnr for 2f: off the bridle by 1/2-way: outpcd over 2f out: kpt on wl again fr over 1f out* **25/1**
322 4 5 **Secret Queen**[40] 3810 2-9-0 85 DaneO'Neill 4 66
(B J Meehan) *t.k.h early: trckd wnr after 2f out: shkn up and no imp over 2f out: wl hld after: lost 2 pls ins fnl f: wkng rapidly nr fin* **11/10**[1]
03 5 1 **Puteri (IRE)**[18] 4534 2-9-0 0 ShaneKelly 3 64
(M A Jarvis) *racd wd towards rr: lft bhd fr 3f out: no ch whn reminders over 1f out* **6/1**[3]
0 6 shd **Leitzu (IRE)**[20] 4460 2-9-0 0 TedDurcan 7 64
(M R Channon) *chsd ldrs: pushed along fr 1/2-way: no prog and wl btn over 2f out* **10/1**
0 7 2¼ **Fine Lace (IRE)**[18] 4534 2-9-0 0 DavidProbert 5 59
(D J S Ffrench Davis) *midfield tl n.m.r 1/2-way and dropped to last: struggling fnl 3f* **80/1**
6 8 ¾ **Quality Mover (USA)**[18] 4542 2-9-0 0 DarryllHolland 1 57
(D M Simcock) *chsd ldrs: rdn wl over 3f out: sn struggling: wknd over 2f out* **8/1**
1m 40.1s (0.30) **Going Correction** -0.05s/f (Stan) 8 Ran SP% **120.5**
Speed ratings (Par 93): **96,95,94,89,88 88,86,85**
toteswingers: 1&2 £5.90, 1&3 £9.20, 2&3 £14.40. CSF £42.55 TOTE £4.50: £1.60, £3.70, £3.80; EX 47.40.
Owner George Strawbridge **Bred** George Strawbridge **Trained** Newmarket, Suffolk
FOCUS
A decent fillies' maiden which should supply a winner or two, with the winner value for more than the official margin.
NOTEBOOK
Dyna Waltz got the better of an early skirmish for the lead and kicked away from her pursuers in the straight to win more comprehensively than the eventual margin would suggest, as she was well in command as the placed fillies closed on her. She paid a big compliment to leading 1000 Guineas fancy Seta, who had beaten her by eight lengths at Newmarket at the beginning of the month. She was well at home on this surface and saw out the longer trip well, but although she is a nice prospect, her Fillies' Mile entry looks optimistic. (op 9-4 tchd 3-1)
Rare Malt(IRE), fourth to Seta and tonight's winner on her debut, ran a promising race. She was slowly away, as she had been on that debut at Newmarket, but began to run on when they reached the cutaway and she was closing down the winner at the finish. She finished closer to Dyna Waltz this time and should soon get off the mark.
Milnagavie ◆, a cheap yearling, is a half-sister to winners at up to 1m4f. After losing the battle for the lead to the winner she ran as if in need of the experience, coming off the bridle before the straight, but she was running on encouragingly in the final furlong. There are races to be won with her. (op 22-1)
Secret Queen had been placed on each of her first three starts, latterly when second to subsequent Listed race runner-up Middle Club at Newbury, but this was disappointing. She had been keen in the lead that day and she failed to settle satisfactorily here, and although she turned for home within striking distance of the winner she was soon left trailing by her and she faded out of the places late on. (op 5-4 tchd 11-8)
Puteri(IRE) did not build on her third at Lingfield on turf last time and was well held, but is now eligible for handicaps. (op 9-1)
Leitzu(IRE) shaped with a bit of promise on her debut at Glorious Goodwood but did not really improve on that, although the extra furlong should have suited. (op 14-1 tchd 16-1)
Quality Mover(USA) had shaped promisingly first time in the Newmarket race in which tonight's winner was second but she was in trouble turning for home here. (tchd 9-1)

5166 DIGIBET NURSERY 7f (P)
7:40 (7:41) (Class 5) (0-70,70) 2-Y-O **£2,590** (£770; £385; £192) **Stalls** High

Form RPR
046 1 **Russian Davis (IRE)**[23] 4370 2-8-10 59 ShaneKelly 8 67+
(R M H Cowell) *settled towards rr: 9th 1/2-way: stdy prog fr jst over 2f out: rdn to ld last 150yds: styd on wl* **16/1**
334 2 ¾ **Poppy N'Penny (IRE)**[29] 4176 2-9-0 63 KirstyMilczarek 5 69
(W J Haggas) *racd wd: wl in tch bhd ldrs: pushed along and prog over 2f out: led 1f out: sn hdd: styd on but hld* **13/2**[3]
1200 3 4 **Chicita Banana**[61] 3086 2-9-1 69 MatthewDavies(5) 11 65
(George Baker) *sn pressed ldr: rdn to ld narrowly over 2f out: hanging bdly and hdd 1f out: sn btn: fin weakly* **7/2**[1]
0414 4 2½ **Wasmi (IRE)**[32] 4081 2-9-2 65 J-PGuillambert 13 55
(C E Brittain) *led: drvn and hdd over 2f out: nt qckn: wknd fnl f* **11/2**[2]
0653 5 shd **Volatilis (IRE)**[36] 3944 2-9-3 66 GeorgeBaker 14 56
(J W Hills) *sn chsd ldng trio on inner: rdn over 2f out: no prog over 1f out: wknd fnl f* **16/1**
4430 6 nse **Bathwick Xaara**[18] 4539 2-9-0 70 JPFahy(7) 7 60
(J G Portman) *sn chsd ldng pair: rdn over 2f out: no prog over 1f out: wknd fnl f* **14/1**
3126 7 2½ **Michaelmas Daisy**[17] 4558 2-9-4 67 DaneO'Neill 12 50
(Miss Amy Weaver) *chsd ldrs: rdn in abt 5th over 2f out: sn no prog and btn: wknd fnl f* **14/1**
050 8 hd **Golden Pippin**[11] 4797 2-8-9 58 SteveDrowne 3 41
(R Hannon) *sn last and wl detached on outer: reminder and nt gng wl 3f out: passed wkng rivals fnl f* **25/1**
006 9 2¼ **Rebecca Romero**[37] 3925 2-8-8 57 ow1 DarryllHolland 4 34
(D J Coakley) *mostly in last trio: drvn and effrt over 2f out: no real prog after* **11/1**
004 10 1 **Looks Like Slim**[23] 4379 2-8-11 60 JosedeSouza 9 35
(P F I Cole) *prom 2f: lost pl qckly over 4f out: toiling in last pair 3f out* **20/1**

5552 **11** 1 1/4 **Marafong**[8] 4883 2-9-3 **66** AmirQuinn 2 38
(Miss J Feilden) *dropped in fr wd draw and hld up in last trio: urged along bef 1/2-way: no prog over 2f out: btn after* **15/2**

4002 **12** 1/2 **Just The Tonic**[11] 4800 2-8-13 **62** TedDurcan 10 32
(M R Channon) *chsd ldrs in abt 6th: rdn over 2f out: sing to lose pl whn bdly hmpd wl over 1f out: eased* **9/1**

000 **13** 1/2 **Edward Whymper**[29] 4176 2-9-0 **63** SaleemGolam 6 32
(M H Tompkins) *dwlt and awkward s: swtchd to inner and pushed up to midfield: rdn in 8th 1/2-way: wknd over 2f out* **10/1**

1m 26.84s (0.84) **Going Correction** -0.05s/f (Stan) **13** Ran SP% **123.8**
Speed ratings (Par 94): **93,92,87,84,84 84,81,81,78,77 76,75,75**
toteswingers: 1&2 £22.10, 1&3 £14.20, 2&3 £5.80. CSF £120.83 CT £473.48 TOTE £24.50: £7.80, £2.50, £1.60; EX 128.70.
Owner Stennett/Morley/Warner **Bred** Russian International Bloodstock **Trained** Six Mile Bottom, Cambs

FOCUS
A modest nursery but sound enough form. The first two were both making their debuts in this sphere and finished clear.

NOTEBOOK
Russian Davis(IRE) had plenty of ground to make up entering the straight, but he came with a strong run to cut down the leader and was nicely on top at the line. His three outings in maiden company had all been over 5f, but he improved for a trip more in keeping with his pedigree and he clearly handled the surface well. There could be more to come from him. (op 12-1)
Poppy N'Penny(IRE) was another who looked to have improved for a longer trip. Obliged to race wide, she got to the front briefly but could not hold off the colt. She was clear of the remainder and this was a solid effort. (op 6-1 tchd 15-2)
Chicita Banana was faced with a more realistic task having been down the field in the Albany at Royal Ascot last time. She made much of the running but was headed at the furlong pole and faded inside the last. She did not really see out this longer trip and was also hanging when the pressure was on, something she has done before. (op 5-1)
Wasmi(IRE) had been eased 3lb since a lacklustre effort at Wolverhampton and this was a step back in the right direction, albeit she was comfortably held in the end. (op 9-2)
Volatilis(IRE) was well drawn on the inside and saw out the extra furlong well enough but lacked a bit of pace when he needed it.
Bathwick Xaara was never far away but could not race on with the principals in the last 2f. (op 16-1)
Marafong Official explanation: jockey said colt hung right

5167 DIGIBET.COM H'CAP 6f (P)
8:10 (8:11) (Class 4) (0-80,80) 3-Y-0+ **£4,727** (£1,406; £702; £351) **Stalls** High

Form RPR

3411 **1** **Street Power (USA)**[40] 3795 4-9-12 **80** SteveDrowne 3 96+
(J R Gask) *settled in 8th: ready prog fr 2f out: led jst ins fnl f: pushed clr: comf* **6/4**[1]

5031 **2** 3 1/4 **We Have A Dream**[30] 4134 4-9-4 **72** DavidProbert 5 78
(W R Muir) *pressed ldng pair: drvn ahd over 1f out: hdd jst ins fnl f: styd on but no ch w wnr: sddle slipped* **9/1**[3]

0200 **3** 1 1/4 **Foxtrot Alpha (IRE)**[25] 4304 3-8-11 **68** LukeMorris 11 70
(P Winkworth) *settled midfield on inner: prog and cl up bhd ldng pair over 1f out: kpt on fnl f but outpcd* **16/1**

0260 **4** 3/4 **Dvinsky (USA)**[16] 4607 8-9-10 **78** (b) StephenDonohoe 10 78
(P Howling) *pressed ldng trio: rdn and nt qckn wl over 1f out: kpt on same pce after* **11/1**

0065 **5** 1 1/4 **Hustle (IRE)**[14] 4641 4-9-11 **79** GeorgeBaker 8 75
(Miss Gay Kelleway) *settled in abt 8th: effrt on inner over 2f out: sme prog over 1f out: nvr gng pce to threaten* **10/1**

5510 **6** 2 1/4 **Rondeau (GR)**[16] 4604 4-9-5 **73** DarryllHolland 4 61
(P R Chamings) *led but pressed thrght: hdd over 1f out: wknd fnl f* **14/1**

325 **7** *nk* **River Kirov (IRE)**[19] 4500 6-9-5 **80** TobyAtkinson[(7)] 7 67
(M Wigham) *trckd ldrs in 5th: gng wl enough 3f out: shkn up and fnd nil 2f out: sn lost pl and btn* **10/1**

3203 **8** *hd* **Musical Script (USA)**[181] 600 6-9-6 **74** (b) DaneO'Neill 1 61
(Mouse Hamilton-Fairley) *dwlt: mostly in last trio: effrt on inner over 2f out: nvr on terms: plugged on* **25/1**

0164 **9** 1/2 **Kyle (IRE)**[11] 4787 5-9-0 **73** SimonPearce[(5)] 6 58
(C R Dore) *settled in last trio: shuffled along fr over 2f out: nvr on terms* **20/1**

3-10 **10** 1 1/4 **Jordaura**[110] 1639 3-9-6 **77** ShaneKelly 9 58
(W R Swinburn) *a wl in rr: shkn up in 9th over 2f out: no prog* **20/1**

0042 **11** 4 1/2 **Bel Cantor**[9] 4853 6-9-6 **77** (p) KellyHarrison[(3)] 2 44
(W J H Ratcliffe) *pressed ldr to 2f out: wknd rapidly* **10/1**

1102 **12** 1 **Brunelleschi**[71] 2799 6-9-0 **75** (b) JosephineBruning[(7)] 12 39
(P L Gilligan) *dwlt and hmpd sn after s: nvr gng wl in last* **8/1**[2]

1m 11.69s (-1.41) **Going Correction** -0.05s/f (Stan)
WFA 3 from 4yo+ 3lb **12** Ran SP% **122.6**
Speed ratings (Par 105): **107,102,101,100,98 95,94,94,94,92 86,85**
toteswingers: 1&2 £4.40, 1&3 £9.70, 2&3 £32.00. CSF £15.50 CT £171.52 TOTE £2.20: £1.60, £2.60, £5.40; EX 22.40.
Owner Horses First Racing Limited **Bred** John Hawkins **Trained** Sutton Veny, Wilts
■ Stewards' Enquiry : Stephen Donohoe one-day ban: careless riding (Sep 2)

FOCUS
Just a fair handicap, but it produced a very impressive winner and the form is backed up by the placed horses running close to their marks.
We Have A Dream Official explanation: jockey said saddle slipped
Brunelleschi Official explanation: jockey said gelding suffered interference in running

5168 DIGIBET CASINO FILLIES' H'CAP 1m 3f (P)
8:40 (8:40) (Class 4) (0-80,80) 3-Y-0 **£4,727** (£1,406; £702; £351) **Stalls** High

Form RPR

200 **1** **Sweet Hollow**[13] 4709 3-8-8 **67** (b[1]) LukeMorris 1 77
(C G Cox) *hld up in 7th: smooth prog fr 3f out: led over 1f out gng easily: shkn up and readily asserted fnl f* **6/1**[3]

-201 **2** 2 1/2 **Teeky**[19] 4498 3-9-3 **76** NickyMackay 5 82+
(J H M Gosden) *chsd ldrs in 6th: pushed along 5f out: prog u.p 2f out: styd on to take 2nd ins fnl f: no ch w wnr* **2/1**[1]

0012 **3** 2 1/4 **Arcola (IRE)**[36] 3949 3-8-11 **70** DarryllHolland 8 72
(D M Simcock) *stdd s: hld up in last: sme prog 3f out: urged along to cl on ldrs over 1f out: sn outpcd and btn: plugged on* **5/1**[2]

6101 **4** 1/2 **Haafhd Time (IRE)**[14] 4650 3-8-3 **62** RichardSmith 4 63+
(Tom Dascombe) *pressed ldr: led over 3f out: drvn over 2f out: hdd over 1f out: wknd fnl f* **13/2**

002 **5** 3 **Lady Rusty (IRE)**[14] 4650 3-8-12 **71** DaneO'Neill 3 67
(P Winkworth) *pressed ldng pair: rdn to go 2nd over 3f out to over 1f out: wknd* **8/1**

0421 **6** 1 **Vivachi (IRE)**[10] 4813 3-8-10 **76** 6ex JPFahy[(7)] 9 70
(R M Beckett) *pushed up early to press ldrs: gng wl enough and disputing 3rd whn bdly hmpd 3f out and dropped to last trio: no ch after* **11/1**

00 **7** 3 3/4 **Young Americans (IRE)**[26] 4287 3-9-4 **77** JerryO'Dwyer 6 65
(M Botti) *cl up in 5th: pushed along whn hmpd 3f out: stl chsng u.p 2f out: wknd over 1f out* **25/1**

0 **8** 1 3/4 **Satisfaction Life (IRE)**[87] 2310 3-9-4 **80** AndreaAtzeni[(3)] 2 65
(M Botti) *hld up in last trio: pushed along 4f out: hung lft bnd 3f out: no prog* **25/1**

6620 **9** 3 3/4 **Nice Time (IRE)**[40] 3822 3-8-12 **71** SaleemGolam 7 50
(M H Tompkins) *a in last trio: pushed along 4f out: no prog u.p on inner over 2f out* **12/1**

1001 **10** 2 1/2 **It's Dubai Dolly**[17] 4569 3-9-5 **78** SteveDrowne 10 52
(A J Lidderdale) *led at gd pce to over 3f out: wknd rapidly* **14/1**

2m 19.1s (-2.80) **Going Correction** -0.05s/f (Stan) **10** Ran SP% **119.1**
Speed ratings (Par 99): **108,106,104,104,102 101,98,97,94,92**
toteswingers: 1&2 £5.10, 1&3 £8.10, 2&3 £3.50. CSF £18.78 CT £64.77 TOTE £8.00: £2.50, £1.50, £2.00; EX 26.20.
Owner The City & Provincial Partnership **Bred** Genesis Green Stud Ltd **Trained** Lambourn, Berks

FOCUS
A fair handicap for fillies. The pace was strong and this is probably decent form for the grade.

5169 WEATHERBYS VAT SERVICES APPRENTICE H'CAP (ROUND 9) 1m (P)
9:10 (9:10) (Class 5) (0-75,75) 3-Y-0 **£2,590** (£770; £385; £192) **Stalls** High

Form RPR

0235 **1** **Striding Edge (IRE)**[16] 4605 3-9-5 **70** MCGeran 8 75
(W R Muir) *w.w in 5th: prog over 2f out: chal over 1f out: one of three in line ent fnl f: gained advantage last 150yds* **14/1**

1-16 **2** 1 **Cut And Thrust (IRE)**[14] 4649 3-9-5 **73** (p) MatthewDavies[(3)] 6 76
(M A Jarvis) *sn prom: wnt 2nd over 3f out: led wl over 2f out: sn hrd pressed: kpt on tl hdd and no ex last 150yds* **10/3**[2]

4033 **3** *nk* **Statute Book (IRE)**[25] 4322 3-9-6 **74** LeeNewnes[(3)] 4 76
(S Kirk) *racd wd: trckd ldrs: prog to go 2nd wl over 2f out: sn chalng: upsides ent fnl f: no ex last 100yds* **20/1**

0061 **4** 3/4 **Best In Class**[28] 4202 3-9-7 **72** RossAtkinson 10 73
(Tom Dascombe) *settled in last trio: rdn and nt on terms w ldrs over 2f out: styd on over 1f out: tk 4th nr fin and nvr nrr* **7/2**[3]

031 **5** 1/2 **Flying Silks (IRE)**[14] 4660 3-9-0 **68** SimonPearce[(3)] 11 67
(J R Gask) *settled in 6th: chsd ldng trio over 2f out but nt on terms: plugged on steadily but lost 4th nr fin* **9/4**[1]

1-00 **6** 2 1/4 **Officer In Command (USA)**[14] 4649 3-9-10 **75** SophieDoyle 7 69
(J S Moore) *sn in last pair: rdn and no prog in last over 2f out: plugged on fr over 1f out: n.d* **15/2**

0461 **7** 4 1/2 **Compton Blue**[13] 4714 3-8-12 **68** CharlesEddery[(5)] 12 52
(R Hannon) *led 1f: rdn and lost pl rapidly on inner sn after 1/2-way: nvr on terms w ldrs fnl 3f* **12/1**

30 **8** 2 **Ymir**[26] 4275 3-8-0 **56** oh2 (p) KierenFox[(5)] 9 35
(M J Attwater) *chsd ldr after 2f to over 3f out: n.m.r and swtchd lft over 2f out: sn wknd* **33/1**

5124 **9** 3 **Miss Mojito (IRE)**[39] 3843 3-8-12 **66** (t) JPFahy[(3)] 1 38
(J W Hills) *s.v.s and lost abt 8l: ct up in rr after 2f: effrt on wd outside over 2f out: sn btn* **16/1**

4425 **10** 6 **Aurora Sky (IRE)**[13] 4700 3-9-3 **73** BarryAdams[(5)] 5 32
(J Akehurst) *v awkward s and lost abt 4 l: charged through to ld after 1f: hdd & wknd rapidly wl over 2f out* **16/1**

1m 39.47s (-0.33) **Going Correction** -0.05s/f (Stan) **10** Ran SP% **121.7**
Speed ratings (Par 100): **99,98,97,96,96 94,89,87,84,78**
toteswingers: 1&2 £16.70, 1&3 £38.50, 2&3 £14.50. CSF £63.10 CT £970.65 TOTE £14.70: £5.30, £2.10, £5.40; EX 128.80 Place 6 £134.60, Place 5 £49.50.
Owner Linkslade Racing and Knightley Williams **Bred** G Prendergast **Trained** Lambourn, Berks

FOCUS
An ordinary handicap, confined to apprentices with no more than 50 winners to their name. The pace was sound and the form looks solid enough, although the disappointing run of the favourite rather muddles things.
Aurora Sky(IRE) Official explanation: jockey said filly missed the break
T/Plt: £422.20 to a £1 stake. Pool: £53,330.57. 92.20 winning tickets. T/Qpdt: £51.40 to a £1 stake. Pool: £5,786.50. 83.30 winning tickets. JN

5132 YORK (L-H)
Wednesday, August 19

OFFICIAL GOING: Good to firm (8.5)
Wind: Fresh, behind Weather: Sunny

5170 RSA AND MOTABILITY STKS (H'CAP) 1m 4f
1:45 (1:46) (Class 2) (0-100,99) 3-Y-0+ **£19,428** (£5,781; £2,889; £1,443) **Stalls** Centre

Form RPR

141 **1** **Whispering Gallery**[11] 4794 3-9-3 **99** RHills 12 114+
(M Johnston) *lw: led after 1f: qcknd over 2f out: rdn clr over 1f out: styd on strly* **4/1**[2]

2-13 **2** 3 3/4 **Class Is Class (IRE)**[41] 3780 3-8-12 **94** RyanMoore 10 103+
(Sir Michael Stoute) *lw: hld up in rr: effrt whn hmpd over 3f out and sn rdn along: gd hdwy over 2f out: swtchd rt and drvn to chse ldrs over 1f out: kpt on u.p ins fnl f* **15/8**[1]

2042 **3** 1/2 **Yes Mr President (IRE)**[11] 4769 4-9-4 **90** JoeFanning 9 98
(M Johnston) *led 1f: cl up on inner: hdwy 3f out: rdn over 2f out: drvn to chse wnr over 1f out: drvn and one pce ins fnl f* **14/1**

-360 **4** 1 1/4 **Presbyterian Nun (IRE)**[20] 4458 4-9-0 **86** RichardMullen 5 92
(J L Dunlop) *midfield: hdwy and edgd lft over 4f out: rdn along 3f out: drvn to chse ldrs wl over 1f out: sn one pce* **20/1**

1124 **5** *nk* **Seeking The Buck (USA)**[39] 3873 5-9-5 **91** SebSanders 6 97
(R M Beckett) *lw: prom: chsd wnr after 4f: rdn along 3f out: drvn 2f out and kpt on same pce* **8/1**[3]

0540 **6** 1 1/2 **Amanda Carter**[16] 4597 5-8-8 **80** oh2 PaulHanagan 8 83
(R A Fahey) *lw: chsd ldrs on inner: rdn along 3f out: drvn 2f out and kpt on same pce* **33/1**

0-00 **7** 2 **Strategic Mount**[24] 4340 6-9-13 **99** (t) NCallan 13 99
(P F I Cole) *hld up in rr: hdwy whn hmpd and swtchd rt over 3f out: rdn along over 2f out: kpt on: nt rch ldrs* **50/1**

0432 **8** 3 **Resplendent Light**[14] 4661 4-9-1 **87** EddieAhern 3 82
(W R Muir) *lw: hld up towards rr: hdwy over 3f out and sn swtchd rt: rdn over 2f out: sn no imp* **17/2**

0250 **9** *1* **Topolski (IRE)**[21] 4420 3-8-6 **88** JohnEgan 4 82
(M Johnston) *hld up in midfield: effrt on inner whn hmpd bnd over 4f out: rdn and hung rt over 3f out: n.d* **20/1**

2154 **10** *3/4* **Dazzling Light (UAE)**[4] 5034 4-8-8 **80** oh2 DanielTudhope 7 72
(J S Goldie) *chsd ldrs: rdn along 3f out and grad wknd* **25/1**

2655 **11** *1 3/4* **Sahrati**[18] 4517 5-9-0 **86** (p) JimmyFortune 15 76
(D R C Elsworth) *in tch: effrt 4f out: rdn along over 3f out and sn wknd* **25/1**

0-41 **12** *4 1/2* **Coin Of The Realm (IRE)**[74] 2706 4-9-3 **89** GeorgeBaker 14 71
(G L Moore) *trckd ldrs on outer: pushed along 4f out: rdn 3f out and grad wknd* **12/1**

645 **13** *7* **Bucked Off (SAF)**[159] 5-9-6 **92** MickyFenton 2 63
(T P Tate) *dwlt: plld hrd: hld up: a in rr* **50/1**

-340 **14** *9* **Boz**[60] 3142 5-9-4 **90** (b) JamieSpencer 11 47
(L M Cumani) *hld up: a towards rr* **20/1**

2m 31.07s (-2.13) **Going Correction** 0.0s/f (Good)
WFA 3 from 4yo+ 10lb **14** Ran SP% **119.6**
Speed ratings (Par 109): **107,104,104,103,103 102,100,98,98,97 96,93,88,82**
toteswingers: 1&2 £2.60, 1&3 £9.10, 2&3 £7.50. CSF £10.28 CT £95.62 TOTE £5.40: £2.10, £1.40, £3.30; EX 14.00 Trifecta £63.60 Pool: £1,620.31 - 18.85 winning units..
Owner Sheikh Hamdan Bin Mohammed Al Maktoum **Bred** Darley **Trained** Middleham Moor, N Yorks

FOCUS
Although 4mm of water had been applied overnight, a very warm day and a strong wind meant that the ground was still riding on the fast side, but no faster than on Tuesday, according to the jockeys. A good, competitive handicap where 4yos had marginally the best recent record. It has often fallen to an improver and did so again with the winner looking up to Listed class and the runner-up capable od rating higher.

NOTEBOOK
Whispering Gallery ◆ adopted the front-running tactics that worked so well at Newmarket and, opening up a clear advantage over a furlong out, he powered home from a decent field. There were stamina doubts judged on the bare form, as his wins had been over 1m2f and his only defeat was over this course and distance, but he answered them decisively. He overcame the 7lb higher mark for his last success with ease and will go up a fair amount for this. However, it could be that his future lies in Listed or Group company after this, although a trip to Dubai will come under consideration. (op 5-1)
Class Is Class(IRE), another lightly raced but progressive three-year-old, was made a relatively short-priced favourite, despite never having tackled the trip or ground before. His breeding did not totally convince regarding the trip but the going looked more the problem, as he dropped to the rear and was being pushed along on the home turn before staying on to get second, although having no chance of catching the winner. He may not be the most straightforward ride but is clearly useful, and is in the best hands to fulfil his potential. (op 2-1 tchd 7-4)
Yes Mr President(IRE), who had form at this trip but whose best recent efforts had been over 1m6f and 2m, ran a good race considering he was 10lb above his last winning mark. He was always in the leading group and, despite staying on, could not cope with his stable companion. He ran in this because he did not get into the Ebor, but looks the sort that will have a sound chance in the Mallard Handicap at Doncaster, back over a longer distance. (op 12-1)
Presbyterian Nun(IRE), who has been placed at Listed level over this trip but had not won since her juvenile days, ran her best race of the season having been dropped 10lb in the last 11 months. She looks reasonably treated for similar handicaps, but it will be no surprise to see her attempting to pick up more black type against her own sex before the end of the season. (tchd 25-1 in a place)
Seeking The Buck(USA) missed most of 2008 but has been in decent form since his return, scoring twice over 1m2f. He ran well on only this second try at 1m4f, responding to pressure until weakening inside the last furlong.
Amanda Carter had conditions to suit and ran well, despite being 2lb out of the handicap and stepping up in grade. If she can repeat this effort in lesser company, she should be able to end a losing run that now extends back over a year.
Strategic Mount ◆ had been lightly raced and well beaten so far this season, but had decent form in Listed company last year and had eased in the weights. He looked fit and put up a fair effort having missed the break and, if this signals a return to form, could be interesting back at Ascot, a course where he has gained his last two successes.
Resplendent Light, like the runner-up, came from well off the pace but after seeming likely to figure in the placings, his effort flattened out late on. He might prefer the ground a little easier than this. (op 12-1)
Topolski(IRE) had form on fast going at this trip but this is the second time he has not appeared to run to his best on this course, as he was one of the first off the bridle before staying on in his own time. He was below par at Goodwood last time as well, and needs to show something of a return to form before he can be supported again. Official explanation: jockey said gelding suffered interference (tchd 25-1)
Dazzling Light(UAE), another racing from out of the weights, was in total 6lb above his last winning mark. He ran reasonably well but looks in the Handicapper's grip at present. Official explanation: jockey said filly ran flat (op 20-1)
Coin Of The Realm(IRE), lightly raced but having gained both his wins at this trip, had taken a similar contest at Epsom Derby meeting. Absent since and 5lb higher this time, he showed up for a long way, if a little free, and can be expected to do better with this outing having blown away the cobwebs. (op 11-1)

5171 WEATHERBYS INSURANCE LONSDALE CUP (GROUP 2) 2m 88y
2:15 (2:15) (Class 1) 3-Y-O+ **£79,478** (£30,128; £15,078; £7,518; £3,766) **Stalls** Low

Form RPR

14-0 **1** **Askar Tau (FR)**[20] 4457 4-9-1 102 (v[1]) RyanMoore 4 110
(M P Tregoning) *hld up in rr: hdwy over 4f out: effrt and nt clr run over 2f out: sn chal: rdn to ld over 1f out and styd on wl* **5/2**[2]

1563 **2** *1 1/4* **Drill Sergeant**[22] 4408 4-9-1 105 JoeFanning 3 109
(M Johnston) *led 1f: cl up tl led again over 6f out: rdn along 3f out: hdd 2f out and sn drvn: kpt on u.p ins fnl f* **15/8**[1]

3-40 **3** *3 3/4* **Royal And Regal (IRE)**[96] 2056 5-9-1 109 NCallan 2 104
(M A Jarvis) *lw: trckd ldng pair: smooth hdwy over 3f out: edgd rt over 2f out and sn led on bit: rdn and hdd over 1f out: drvn and wknd ent fnl f* **7/2**[3]

-300 **4** *13* **Baddam**[21] 4417 7-9-1 85 SaleemGolam 6 88
(Ian Williams) *cl up: led after 1f: pushed along appr 1/2-way: rdn and hdd over 6f out: drvn along 4f out and sn outpcd* **25/1**

1445 **5** *29* **Enroller (IRE)**[20] 4457 4-9-1 109 RichardHughes 5 54
(W R Muir) *lw: trckd ldrs: hdwy whn n.m.r and swtchd rt bnd over 4f out: sn rdn and ch wl over 2f out: sn drvn and wknd* **4/1**

3m 30.63s (-3.87) **Going Correction** 0.0s/f (Good) **5** Ran SP% **109.4**
Speed ratings (Par 115): **109,108,106,100,85**
toteswingers: 1&2 £3.70. CSF £7.50 TOTE £2.90: £1.80, £1.50; EX 5.10.
Owner Nurlan Bizakov **Bred** Gestut Zoppenbroich & Aerial Bloodstock **Trained** Lambourn, Berks

FOCUS
A poor event for the class, featuring only two Group-race winners (Royal And Regal and Enroller), and at Group 3 level at that. In reality this looked no more than a Listed race in quality. The early pace was only fair, but Drill Sergeant upped the tempo from the end of the back straight and the overall time was decent.

NOTEBOOK
Askar Tau(FR) was a most progressive staying handicapper last term but ran no sort of race at Goodwood on his reappearance. He'd apparently worked well in a visor at home since, though, and the headgear seemed to do the trick on this return to a more conventional track. Held up in rear, he came under pressure early in the straight, but he loves quick ground and stays well, and once squeezed between runners two and a half furlongs out, outbattled the strong-travelling Royal And Regal and ran on strongly. He's in the Melbourne Cup, and that could be a possibility as he's likely to get his ground out there, but whether he'll have the pace for that race is open to question. The other big target is the Prix du Cadran, but the question there would be whether conditions would be quick enough for him, and the competition will certainly be a lot tougher. (tchd 9-4)

Drill Sergeant kept the leader company and kicked on plenty soon enough. He couldn't get away from his main rivals, though, and looked to be held in third until rallying to retake second late on. He's a consistent sort, but no more than a Listed-class animal. The Doncaster Cup is likely to be his next target. (op 9-4)

Royal And Regal(IRE), returning from a three-month break, was keen through the early stages but entered the straight going better than anything. He looked all over the winner when hitting the front but, when challenged, soon threw in the towel. Perhaps he got to the front too soon, but he certainly didn't fancy the battle much, and backed out quickly. It's worth remembering that he broke a blood-vessel at the Dante meeting here in May.

Baddam took them along at an ordinary gallop and got the run of things for much of the way, but once Drill Sergeant injected some pace into the race he began to struggle. He was beaten before the entrance to the straight and is struggling this season. (tchd 20-1)

Enroller(IRE), for whom the ground was a worry as he prefers to get his toe in, was forced wide on the turn into the straight and struggled to pick up under pressure. Official explanation: jockey said colt hung right throughout and lost its action closing stages (op 7-2 tchd 9-2 in a place)

5172 IRISH THOROUGHBRED MARKETING GIMCRACK STKS (GROUP 2) (C&G) 6f
2:50 (2:50) (Class 1) 2-Y-O **£82,964** (£31,374; £15,680; £7,840) **Stalls** High

Form RPR

21 **1** **Showcasing**[48] 3546 2-8-12 0 JimmyFortune 4 116+
(J H M Gosden) *lw: hld up in rr and t.k.h: shkn up and hdwy 2f out: rdn to ld over 1f out: kpt on wl fnl f* **2/1**[1]

21 **2** *2* **Taajub (IRE)**[19] 4497 2-8-12 87 RHills 3 109
(W J Haggas) *cl up: led over 2f out: sn rdn and hdd over 1f out: kpt on u.p ins fnl f* **16/1**

1511 **3** *1/2* **Monsieur Chevalier (IRE)**[22] 4407 2-8-12 108 RichardHughes 8 108+
(R Hannon) *lw: towards rr: pushed along and outpcd after 2f: hdwy over 2f out: swtchd lft and hdwy wl over 1f out: sn rdn and edgd rt ins fnl f: kpt on: nrst fin* **5/2**[2]

41 **4** *1 1/4* **Mr David (USA)**[32] 4093 2-8-12 0 JamieSpencer 2 103
(B J Meehan) *swtg: trckd ldrs on outer: hdwy over 2f out: sn rdn and one pce* **9/1**

5112 **5** *1 1/4* **Orpen Grey (IRE)**[41] 3779 2-8-12 114 RichardKingscote 7 100
(Tom Dascombe) *wnt lft s: sn led: pushed along and hdd over 2f out: sn rdn wknd: hld whn n.m.r ins fnl f* **11/4**[3]

1133 **6** *4* **Corporal Maddox**[21] 4418 2-8-12 106 JimCrowley 6 88
(A P Jarvis) *chsd ldrs: rdn along over 2f out and sn wknd* **20/1**

69.28 secs (-2.62) **Going Correction** -0.275s/f (Firm) 2y crse rec **6** Ran SP% **109.2**
Speed ratings (Par 106): **106,103,102,101,99 94**
toteswingers: 1&2 £5.10, 1&3 £1.90, 2&3 £4.50. CSF £30.42 TOTE £3.70: £2.20, £4.70; EX 28.30 Trifecta £97.30 Pool: £11,680.25 - 88.75 winning units..

Owner K Abdulla **Bred** Juddmonte Farms Ltd **Trained** Newmarket, Suffolk

FOCUS
This well-established 2yo contest has not fallen to any future stars since Rock Of Gibraltar scored in 2001, although Conquest did go on to win the Stewards' Cup and a Group 3 as a four-year-old. This season's line-up looked interesting and included a couple of proven performers, plus several stepping up in grade after winning their maidens. The third is the best guide, being rated a fraction below form.

NOTEBOOK
Showcasing ◆ was a well-backed favourite to beat his more experienced rivals and duly justified support with an emphatic success. A brother to Bouvardia and a half-brother to Camacho, he had been narrowly beaten by Arcano on his debut and was then the easy winner of a maiden on his second start. He struggled to go the early pace but picked up well when asked and, asserting over a furlong out, established himself as a major contender for the title of leading sprint juvenile. The tailwind enabled him to break the previous juvenile course record in the process. He was quoted at 14/1 and longer for the 2000 Guineas, but his rider did not exude confidence about his ability to get much further and his pedigree suggests that he may not last that trip. Like his sire, it would be no surprise if he was campaigned purely as a sprinter in 2010. In the short-term though, he has entries in the Mill Reef, Middle Park and Dewhurst, with the Group 1 Middle Park looking the best option. (tchd 9-4 in places)

Taajub(IRE) ◆, another relatively inexperienced performer stepping up in grade, had done little wrong and had beaten a subsequent winner in his maiden. The fast ground was an unknown, but he handled it well enough and travelled smoothly when going to the front. However, he could not respond when the winner ranged alongside, although he was always holding on for second. He will now be aimed at the £300,000 Weatherbys Insurance sales race at Doncaster next month, and on this effort is sure to be a leading contender for that. (tchd 18-1)

Monsieur Chevalier(IRE) had gained six wins in seven starts including the Super Sprint and Molecomb, but his only previous defeat was at this level. In the past he had looked as if this extra furlong would suit but he was struggling to go the pace at halfway - something he has appeared to do before though - before running on to take the minor placing. He failed to trouble front pair though and, although his jockey was inclined to blame the fast ground, it looks as if he will need to avoid progressive sorts from now on if he is to resume winning ways, although connections were talking in terms of the Middle Park as the target. He will be kept on the go but eventually this tough and genuine sort should make a reasonably priced commercial sire. Official explanation: jockey said colt was unsuited by the good to firm ground (op 9-4)

Mr David(USA), fourth on his debut in Windsor maiden before winning next time over this trip on good ground, ran creditably on this step up in grade. He had to race on the outside of the field but showed plenty of pace and is the type that will be better for the experience. He has the same big entries as the winner though, and the Mill Reef might be the best option. With his pedigree there is every chance he could eventually end up racing in the USA. (op 10-1 tchd 8-1)

Orpen Grey(IRE), a dual winner over 5f and 6f before upped in grade when second to Arcano in July Stakes - form which had earned him the highest official rating - was however encountering fast ground for the first time. He made the running but had little to offer when taken on and might have found the going too fast; he certainly did not run up to his previous mark judged on a line through today's winner and Arcano. Official explanation: jockey said colt ran too free (tchd 3-1 in places)

Corporal Maddox, the winner of the Woodcote Stakes, had run well in Group company since. He was dropping back in trip and did not have the pace of the others in the last quarter-mile. (tchd 25-1)

5173 TOTESPORT EBOR (HERITAGE H'CAP) 1m 6f

3:25 (3:31) (Class 2) 3-Y-0+

£130,851 (£39,186; £19,593; £9,807; £4,893; £2,457) **Stalls** Low

Form RPR

-120 **1** **Sesenta (IRE)**[19] 4510 5-8-8 **94**........................ GFCarroll(5) 16 102
(W P Mullins, Ire) *midfield: hdwy over 3f out: effrt on outer 2f out: rdn to chse ldrs over 1f out: styd on wl u.p ins fnl f to ld last 50yds: hld on wl* **25/1**

2 **2** *hd* **Changingoftheguard (IRE)**[60] 3180 3-9-0 **107**.................. JMurtagh 7 117+
(A P O'Brien, Ire) *w'like: scope: dwlt and hld up towards rr: hdwy on inner 4f out: nt clr run and swtchd rt over 1f out: sn rdn to chse ldrs and n.m.r ent fnl f: swtchd lft and drvn: styd on: jst hld* **15/8**[1]

-101 **3** *3/4* **Hits Only Vic (USA)**[39] 3874 5-9-6 **101**........................ DNolan 10 108
(D Carroll) *hld up in midfield: hdwy on inner 4f out: swtchd rt and rdn to chse ldrs wl over 1f out: styng on whn bmpd ent fnl f: swtchd rt and styd on wl towards fin* **16/1**

4002 **4** *shd* **Nanton (USA)**[11] 4781 7-8-12 **93**........................ DanielTudhope 3 100+
(J S Goldie) *hld up in rr: hdwy whn nt clr run 3f out: swtchd rt and rdn along over 2f out: n.m.r over 1f out: styd on strly ins fnl f: nrst fin* **40/1**

0122 **5** *nse* **Warringah**[19] 4484 4-9-10 **105**........................ RyanMoore 1 112
(Sir Michael Stoute) *lw: cl up: led after 1f: jnd 3f out and sn rdn: drvn clr over 1f out: hrd rdn and edgd rt ins fnl f: hdd and no ex last 50yds* **17/2**[2]

3021 **6** *1/2* **Manyriverstocross (IRE)**[22] 4408 4-8-13 **94** 4ex........ JamieSpencer 20 100
(A King) *trckd ldrs: hdwy to chse ldng pair 4f out: rdn along wl over 2f out: drvn and chsd ldr over 1f out: ev ch tl no ex wl ins fnl f* **12/1**

3503 **7** *nk* **The Betchworth Kid**[20] 4457 4-9-5 **100**........................ HayleyTurner 11 106
(M L W Bell) *hld up and bhd: effrt whn bmpd over 3f out and sn swtchd to inner: hdwy over 2f out: nt clr run and swtchd rt over 1f out: rdn whn n.m.r and swtchd lft ins fnl f: styng on whn n.m.r nr fin* **33/1**

231/ **8** *3/4* **Deutschland (USA)**[20] 3907 6-9-5 **100**........................ MJKinane 19 105
(W P Mullins, Ire) *trckd ldrs on outer: hdwy 4f out: rdn along to chse ldrs over 2f out: edgd lft and drvn over 1f out: kpt on same pce ins fnl f* **14/1**

-523 **9** *4 1/2* **Magicalmysterytour (IRE)**[39] 3874 6-9-5 **100**.......... RichardHughes 17 98
(W J Musson) *hld up towards rr: hdwy over 3f out: rdn along over 2f out: nt rch ldrs* **20/1**

0-60 **10** *hd* **Waldvogel (IRE)**[22] 4408 5-9-3 **103**.............. Louis-PhilippeBeuzelin(5) 2 101
(L M Cumani) *lw: trckd ldrs on inner: hdwy over 4f out: rdn along 3f out: drvn over 2f out and wknd over 1f out* **50/1**

04-0 **11** *3/4* **Siberian Tiger (IRE)**[49] 3142 4-9-4 **99**....................(p) JimmyFortune 21 96
(A J Martin, Ire) *hld up in rr: sme hdwy 4f out: rdn along over 2f out: n.d* **66/1**

2111 **12** *3 1/2* **Red Merlin (IRE)**[46] 3620 4-9-6 **101**....................(v) PhilipRobinson 15 93
(C G Cox) *midfield: hdwy and in tch 4f out: rdn along 3f out: drvn over 2f out and sn btn* **9/1**[3]

1205 **13** *3/4* **Record Breaker (IRE)**[24] 4340 5-9-4 **99**..................(b) RoystonFfrench 5 90
(M Johnston) *led 1f: trckd ldr tl hdwy to chal 2f out: sn rdn and ev ch tl drvn wl over 1f out and wknd* **25/1**

0510 **14** *1/2* **Som Tala**[21] 4417 6-9-0 **95**........................ TonyCulhane 14 85
(M R Channon) *chsd ldrs: rdn along over 3f out and sn wknd* **50/1**

1445 **15** *1 1/2* **Ladies Best**[39] 3873 5-8-13 **94**........................ NCallan 12 82
(B Ellison) *a towards rr: swtchd lft and rdn over 3f out: nvr a factor* **25/1**

1-02 **16** *7* **Precision Break (USA)**[22] 4408 4-8-10 **91**.................... PaulHanagan 8 69
(P F I Cole) *lw: chsd ldrs: rdn along over 3f out and sn wknd* **9/1**[3]

4160 **17** *2 3/4* **Dansili Dancer**[46] 3620 7-9-7 **102**........................ AdamKirby 4 77
(C G Cox) *chsd ldng pair: rdn along over 4f out and sn wknd* **28/1**

-141 **18** *2 1/4* **Desert Sea (IRE)**[46] 3642 6-9-1 **96**........................ SebSanders 18 67
(D W P Arbuthnot) *hld up: effrt and sme hdwy 3f out: rdn along over 2f out and nvr a factor* **16/1**

0-40 **19** *1* **Camps Bay (USA)**[22] 4408 5-9-2 **97**........................(b1) JimCrowley 13 67
(Mrs A J Perrett) *a towards rr* **33/1**

2m 57.52s (-2.68) **Going Correction** 0.0s/f (Good)
WFA 3 from 4yo+ 12lb **19** Ran SP% **124.9**
Speed ratings (Par 109): **107,106,106,106,106 106,105,105,102,102 102,100,99,99,98 94,93,91,91**
toteswingers: 1&2 £40.70, 1&3 £35.30, 2&3 £10.30. CSF £65.62 CT £847.86 TOTE £31.50: £6.10, £1.40, £3.50, £8.90; EX 131.30 Trifecta £1853.50 Pool: £7,263.92 - 2.90 winning units..
Owner Michael F Carroll **Bred** Michael Carroll **Trained** Muine Beag, Co Carlow
■ Stewards' Enquiry : G F Carroll one-day ban: excessive use of the whip (Sep 2)

FOCUS

The richest handicap run on the Flat in Europe but not the cleanest of races and there were a few hard-luck stories, not least for the well-backed favourite Changingoftheguard. The form looks slightly messy and relatively ordinary for the grade.

NOTEBOOK

Sesenta(IRE) was held up alongside the favourite back in the pack, but while Murtagh went for a run up the inside in the straight, she came more towards the outside, avoided all the trouble and stayed on strongly to hold him off at the finish. Runner-up in the Ascot Stakes on her previous visit to this country, she stays particularly well, and earlier talk of her being better suited by soft ground clearly looks wide of the mark now given these two performances. Unsurprisingly her connections are now eyeing up possibilities of gaining some valuable black type with her. (op 33-1)

Changingoftheguard(IRE) ◆, whose trainer has a great record with the few three-year-olds he's run in this race - Mediterranean won in 2001, Mikado was 3rd in 2004 and Honolulu was 2nd in 2007, was a strong market favourite in his attempt to improve that record further. Although raised 12lb for his comfortable success in the Ulster Derby, there was more than a suspicion that he remained well handicapped despite racing off a mark 3lb higher than had ever been defied before in this race. He didn't help his cause by missing the break but soon recovered to race in midfield. His problems really began early in the straight as he was stuck on the inside with little room to manoeuvre, while the winner was already under maximum pressure and responding well wider out. He finally found a route through a furlong and a half out but even then had to weave his way between horses rather than enjoy a totally clear run. He came up just short but did show the sort of change of pace valuable in a staying horse, and it wasn't a surprise to see him cut to a best price of 10-1 for the St Leger on the back of this. Official explanation: jockey said colt missed the break (op 2-1 tchd 5-2 early)

Hits Only Vic(USA), who just got the better of Warringah over the course and distance last time, got a bump from the favourite as that one tried to angle out a furlong and a half out, but otherwise he had no excuses. Like the winner, he looks just as effective on fast ground as soft, despite evidence previously suggesting otherwise. The Cesarewitch is his next big target.

Nanton(USA), for whom this trip was a bit of an experiment, as he hadn't previously run beyond 1m2f. There can be no doubt about his stamina now, though, as he stayed on really well to make the frame, and that despite not enjoying a clear run. This opens up some new opportunities for him. (op 50-1)

Warringah, although carrying top weight, was officially 4lb well in following his improved effort to finish second in a Group 3 race at Goodwood last time. Still relatively unexposed, this was only his sixth start in handicap company and he ran a fine race from the front. Moore took them along at a good gallop early but steadied things rounding the turn out of the back straight before kicking on again. He was crying out for the line inside the last and in the end couldn't hold off the closers, eventually failing to place, but he actually came very close to nicking this. (op 8-1 tchd 9-1)

Manyriverstocross(IRE), who was ridden more prominently than he was at Goodwood, ran a solid race under his 4lb penalty. He's already due to go up another 1lb and remains steadily progressive. (tchd 14-1)

The Betchworth Kid ◆ was given a very patient ride as usual. In last place turning into the straight, he went for an ambitious run up the inside, following the favourite for a time, and had his path continually blocked. Only switched off it inside the last, he finished well, but could never land a blow. The stronger the pace the better it is for him, and a bit of cut usually helps, too.

Deutschland(USA), a stablemate of the winner, finished second in the Galway Hurdle last time out. He had every chance on this return to the Flat but will be more effective over a longer trip, and the Cesarewitch could be more his thing. (op 20-1)

Magicalmysterytour(IRE) didn't get the clearest of runs as he tried to make up ground from the back of the field, and he shaped better than the bare form suggests. He is likely to remain vulnerable off a three-figure mark, though. (tchd 18-1 in a place)

Waldvogel(IRE), who lost his action at Goodwood on his British debut, shaped better here, but it's questionable whether he wants the ground this quick.

Siberian Tiger(IRE), trying a longer trip and fitted with cheekpieces for the first time, made some late headway from off the pace but was never a danger and looks to need a drop in the handicap.

Red Merlin(IRE) came into the race chasing a four-timer, and he was officially 2lb well in at the weights following his success in the Old Newton Cup. The question was whether he would be as effective over this longer trip, and on this evidence it would appear not. He could well bounce back over a shorter trip, but he is now on a mark 11lb higher than when successful at Haydock. Official explanation: jockey said gelding was unsuited by the good to firm ground (op 8-1)

Record Breaker(IRE) tracked the leader into the straight but after briefly throwing down a challenge to him he cracked. 1m4f is his ideal distance. (op 22-1)

Precision Break(USA) had a 4lb pull at the weights with Manyriverstocross, who beat him narrowly at Goodwood last time, but he ran way below that form and the ground looked too quick for him. (tchd 10-1 in a place)

Desert Sea(IRE) Official explanation: trainer said gelding suffered from heat stress

5174 JULIA GRAVES ROSES STKS (LISTED RACE) 5f

4:05 (4:07) (Class 1) 2-Y-0 **£17,778** (£6,723; £3,360; £1,680) **Stalls** High

Form RPR

6064 **1** **Star Rover (IRE)**[22] 4407 2-9-0 99........................ JohnEgan 2 102
(P D Evans) *mde all: rdn 2f out: jnd and drvn ent fnl f: edgd lft and hld on gamely towards fin* **14/1**

3102 **2** *nk* **Mister Manannan (IRE)**[22] 4407 2-9-0 102.............. AdrianTNicholls 7 101
(D Nicholls) *trckd ldrs: swtchd lft and hdwy over 1f out: rdn to chal ent fnl f and ev ch tl drvn and nt qckn nr fin* **11/4**[1]

16 **3** *1 3/4* **Love Lockdown (IRE)**[52] 3436 2-9-3 0........................ JMurtagh 5 98
(G M Lyons, Ire) *on toes: wnt lft s: trckd ldrs: pushed along and edgd lft 2f out: rdn and hung rt over 1f out: styd on wl fnl f: nrst fin* **4/1**[3]

1111 **4** *1 1/2* **Singeur (IRE)**[12] 4752 2-9-0 93........................ NCallan 1 89
(R Bastiman) *trckd ldrs on outer: hdwy 2f out and sn ev ch tl rdn and wknd ent fnl f* **7/2**[2]

1406 **5** *1/2* **Nosedive**[19] 4487 2-9-0 97........................ RyanMoore 6 88
(W J Haggas) *swtg: hld up: effrt over 2f out: sn rdn and no imp* **5/1**

5333 **6** *nk* **Archers Road (IRE)**[22] 4407 2-9-0 99........................ JimmyFortune 3 86
(M R Channon) *swtg: slty hmpd s: chsd wnr: rdn along 2f out: wknd over 1f out* **11/2**

3104 **7** *5* **Farmer Giles (IRE)**[12] 4746 2-9-0 87........................ HayleyTurner 8 68
(M L W Bell) *a towards rr* **16/1**

57.33 secs (-1.97) **Going Correction** -0.275s/f (Firm) 2y crse rec **7** Ran SP% **113.5**
Speed ratings (Par 102): **104,103,100,98,97 97,89**
toteswingers: 1&2 £7.10, 1&3 £8.70, 2&3 £3.00. CSF £51.66 TOTE £14.90: £5.60, £1.90; EX 63.70 Trifecta £218.00 Pool: £825.05 - 2.80 winning units..
Owner Christy Leo **Bred** Yeomanstown Stud **Trained** Pandy, Monmouths

FOCUS

This Listed race for juveniles over the minimum trip often falls to a battle-hardened sort and there were several in the line-up again. Aided by the following wind, the time was a new juvenile course record but the form, although solid enough, is a little limited.

NOTEBOOK

Star Rover(IRE), who won his first four races beginning at Kempton in March, and has been on the go ever since, gaining a further three places in ten starts. He had finished fourth in the Molecomb (which proved the key form race) behind today's runner-up and Archers Road, but reversed that form, aided by a quick start and getting the rail. He looked likely to be headed at several stages in the last quarter-mile but refused to give in. This was thoroughly deserved and connections are thinking in terms of Redcar's Two-Year-Old Trophy at the backend. (op 12-1)

Mister Manannan(IRE) looked the one to beat on the Molecomb form, when he had today's winner and Archers Road behind. He was not done any favours when the winner rather went across his bows in the early stages, but came to have every chance entering the final furlong, only to be unable to get past the determined winner. He deserves to win one of these but may prefer easier ground, and the Flying Childers plus the Harry Rosebery at Ayr are likely to be in connections' minds. (op 9-4)

Love Lockdown(IRE), a three-time winner in Ireland at 6f on good and fast ground, including at Listed level, as a result had to give 3lb to the others on this drop in trip. He finished best of all having been out the back early and, although this was creditable effort, a return to further will be in his favour. (op 5-1 tchd 11-2 in a place)

Singeur(IRE), who had recorded four wins and a second in five starts at a lower level, had conditions in his favour and put up a decent effort on this step up in grade, especially considering he raced on the outside of the field and saw plenty of daylight. He is worth another try at this level.

Nosedive had beaten two subsequent winners on his debut over 5f and had finished fourth in the Norfolk Stakes next time, but had been held since in Group 2s at 6f. Dropping in trip, he struggled to go the early pace before running on late. (op 13-2 tchd 7-1 in a place)

Archers Road(IRE), as tough as the winner, having scored three times and been placed in seven of his 11 previous starts including third in Super Sprint and Molecomb, appeared to run his race but was on the retreat from the furlong marker. Official explanation: jockey said colt hung left (tchd 6-1)

Farmer Giles(IRE), a winner at 5f on good who acts on fast, had been held in ordinary company the last twice and had a lot to do on this step up in grade, so he probably ran as well as could be expected.

5175 WIN A TRIP TO SARATOGA RACES EBF FILLIES' STKS (H'CAP) 1m

4:40 (4:41) (Class 2) (0-100,95) 3-Y-0 **£16,190** (£4,817; £2,407; £1,202) **Stalls** Low

Form RPR

1202 **1** **Shamwari Lodge (IRE)**[20] 4459 3-9-7 **95**.................. RichardHughes 6 107+
(R Hannon) *trckd ldrs on inner: smooth hdwy over 2f out: swtchd rt and effrt to chal over 1f out: rdn and qcknd to ld last 100yds: readily* **3/1**[2]

14 **2** *1 3/4* **Paquerettza (FR)**[4] 5030 3-8-5 **79**........................ AdrianTNicholls 1 87
(D H Brown) *sn led: rdn along wl over 2f out: drvn over 1f out: hdd and no ex last 100yds* **22/1**

4235 **3** 2 **Silver Games (IRE)**[32] 4088 3-8-13 **87** RyanMoore 11 90+
(M R Channon) *in rr: hdwy over 2f out: rdn wl over 1f out: styd on wl appr fnl f: nrst fin* **8/1**

3546 **4** 2 3/4 **Seradim**[46] 3641 3-9-5 **93** EddieAhern 5 90
(P F I Cole) *lw: a.p: cl up over 3f out: rdn to chal over 2f out and ev ch tl drvn and one pce wl over 1f out: fin lame* **28/1**

3224 **5** 1 1/2 **Happy Anniversary (IRE)**[13] 4708 3-8-10 **84** JoeFanning 7 77
(Mrs D J Sanderson) *chsd ldrs: rdn along 3f out and sn outpcd: plugged on u.p fr wl over 1f out* **14/1**

-002 **6** *hd* **Vitoria (IRE)**[25] 4317 3-8-13 **87** RichardMullen 2 80
(B Smart) *in rr tl sme late hdwy* **10/1**

2150 **7** 1 1/4 **Badiat Alzaman (IRE)**[63] 3016 3-8-13 **87** JimCrowley 9 77
(D M Simcock) *swtg: midfield: hdwy on outer over 4f out: effrt and cl up 3f out: sn rdn and wknd 2f out* **20/1**

5621 **8** *hd* **Harriet's Girl**[12] 4741 3-8-0 **79** oh2 ow3 MartinLane(5) 3 68
(A P Jarvis) *midfield: hdwy on outer 1/2-way: chsd ldrs 3f out: sn rdn and wknd fnl 2f* **20/1**

2112 **9** 2 1/4 **Mo Mhuirnin (IRE)**[42] 3746 3-8-11 **85** PaulHanagan 12 69
(R A Fahey) *a towards rr* **7/1**[3]

10-2 **10** 2 1/2 **Burgundy Ice (USA)**[28] 4211 3-8-9 **83** LDettori 10 62+
(Saeed Bin Suroor) *in tch: rapid hdwy to join ldrs 5f out: cl up tl rdn along 3f out: drvn and hld whn bmpd wl over 2f out and sn in rr* **5/2**[1]

4011 **11** 3 3/4 **Flapper (IRE)**[11] 4799 3-7-11 **78** oh5 ow2 AmyScott(7) 4 48
(J W Hills) *midfield: effrt over 3f out: sn rdn and btn over 2f out* **14/1**

1123 **12** 4 1/2 **Charlotte Point (USA)**[35] 3981 3-8-11 **85** NCallan 8 45
(P F I Cole) *dwlt: a towards rr* **16/1**

1m 36.6s (-2.20) **Going Correction** 0.0s/f (Good) **12** Ran SP% **122.8**
Speed ratings (Par 103): **111,109,107,104,103 102,101,101,99,96 92,88**
toteswingers: 1&2 £13.80, 1&3 £5.90, 2&3 £25.50. CSF £75.88 CT £507.39 TOTE £4.20: £1.70, £6.20, £2.80; EX 82.80 Trifecta £1306.70 Part won. Pool: £1,765.49 - 0.90 winning units. Place 6 £37.66, Place 5 £26.40.
Owner Andrew Russell **Bred** Pier House Stud **Trained** East Everleigh, Wilts

FOCUS
The top weight weighed in 5lb below the ceiling for the race, but this looked a decent, competitive handicap for fillies. the time was good and the form looks sound, despite the majority of the principals having been well there throughout.

NOTEBOOK
Shamwari Lodge(IRE) ◆ was only 1lb higher than when an unlucky-in-running runner-up over 7f at Goodwood last time, and the step up to a mile promised to be in her favour. She travelled well tracking the leaders on the inside and quickened nicely to edge out Paqueretzza, and the impression left was that she scored with a bit in hand. There should be better to come from her and she's one to keep on-side. (op 7-2 tchd 4-1)
Paqueretzza(FR), making a quick reappearance, had a good draw in stall one and her rider made full use of it on a track that often favours those ridden positively. She ran a fine race in defeat against an improving rival. (op 20-1)
Silver Games(IRE), who had a poor draw to overcome, was settled out the back and, with the pace good, found a lot of them coming back to her at the finish. She's a consistent sort but is vulnerable off her current mark. (op 9-1)
Seradim, held in Ppattern company in her previous five starts this season, was dropping down into a handicap for the first time. Close up throughout, she had every chance, but the assessor seems to have her measure off her current mark. Official explanation: vet said filly finished lame (op 25-1)
Happy Anniversary(IRE) is another who looks to have little in hand of the handicapper off her current rating. (op 16-1)
Vitoria(IRE), who sweated up beforehand, looked to find this trip a bit too far. Her best performances to date have come over 7f. (op 16-1)
Badiat Alzaman(IRE) ended up racing wide around the turn into the straight and gave away plenty of ground in the process. Not too much should be read into this run, her first since finishing down the field at Royal Ascot.
Mo Mhuirnin(IRE)\n\x\x 's performance was certainly out of character as she's been both progressive and very consistent this term, so this down-the-field effort, albeit over a longer trip and from the widest draw, was very disappointing. There are some questions over the form of the Richard Fahey yard at the moment. (op 9-1 tchd 13-2)
Burgundy Ice(USA), Frankie Dettori's only ride of the day, was representing a stable in cracking form, but she raced keenly through the early parts, went wide around the turn into the straight and unsurprisingly failed to get home. Official explanation: jockey said filly had no more to give (op 9-4 tchd 2-1)
T/Jkpt: Not won. T/Plt: £109.00 to a £1 stake. Pool: £218,929.81. 1,465.64 winning tickets. T/Qpdt: £62.50 to a £1 stake. Pool: £9,469.74. 112.10 winning tickets. JR

5176 - 5178a (Foreign Racing) - See Raceform Interactive

4933 CHEPSTOW (L-H)
Thursday, August 20

OFFICIAL GOING: Good (good to firm in places; 8.3)
Wind: Fresh across Weather: Fine

5179 SUNSHINE RADIO APPRENTICE H'CAP 1m 14y
5:30 (5:33) (Class 6) (0-60,60) 3-Y-O+ **£2,217** (£654; £327) **Stalls** Centre

Form RPR
1434 **1** **Landucci**[14] 4697 8-9-8 **59** (p) JackMitchell 14 69
(S Curran) *s.i.s: t.k.h towards rr: stdy prog on stands' rail 3f out: pushed along over 1f out: rdn to ld wl ins fnl f: r.o* **9/1**

0525 **2** 1/2 **Waterside (IRE)**[10] 4861 10-9-4 **60** (t) DTDaSilva(5) 15 69
(S Curran) *hld up in tch: rdn to ld 2f out: hdd wl ins fnl f: r.o* **18/1**

-036 **3** 3 1/4 **Petomic (IRE)**[11] 4824 4-9-2 **56** RossAtkinson(3) 7 57
(M Hill) *led: rdn and hdd 2f out: no ex wl ins fnl f* **16/1**

1405 **4** 1 1/4 **Red Current**[7] 4938 5-8-11 **53** ow1 SPRyan(5) 17 52
(R A Harris) *hld up in mid-div: swtchd lft over 3f out: pushed along and sme hdwy over 2f out: rdn over 1f out: one pce* **12/1**

2022 **5** 3/4 **Northern Desert (IRE)**[13] 4731 10-9-7 **58** (p) WilliamCarson 5 55
(S Curran) *a.p: rdn and ev ch 2f out: wknd ins fnl f* **11/1**

5040 **6** 1/2 **Dancing Storm**[4] 5063 6-9-2 **56** RichardEvans(3) 2 52
(W S Kittow) *prom: rdn wl over 2f out: wknd wl over 1f out* **6/1**[2]

00 **7** *shd* **Just Spike**[11] 4823 6-9-0 **51** KellyHarrison 10 46
(B P J Baugh) *hld up in rr: pushed along and hdwy over 2f out: rdn over 1f out: no imp fnl f* **25/1**

0-00 **8** 1/2 **Heavenly Saint**[4] 5063 4-9-3 **57** ow2 ByronMoorcroft(3) 8 51
(C Roberts) *hld up towards rr: sme prog over 2f out: rdn over 1f out: no imp* **40/1**

0440 **9** 1 1/2 **Master Mahogany**[7] 4938 8-8-13 **53** MCGeran(3) 4 44
(R J Hodges) *hld up towards rr: rdn over 2f out: nvr trbld ldrs* **12/1**

2000 **10** 1 3/4 **Amber Ridge**[7] 4938 4-9-0 **51** (v[1]) JackDean 16 38
(B P J Baugh) *prom: rdn 3f out: sn wknd* **18/1**

04-0 **11** 2 1/4 **Miskin Flyer**[24] 4381 3-9-1 **58** DavidProbert 9 40
(B Palling) *in rr: rdn over 4f out: nvr nr ldrs* **20/1**

5042 **12** 1/2 **Cadeaux Fax**[7] 4938 4-8-10 **52** DavidKenny(5) 11 32
(B R Millman) *hld up in mid-div: rdn over 2f out: wknd over 1f out: sddle slipped* **7/2**[1]

0014 **13** 1 1/2 **Aine's Delight (IRE)**[26] 4305 3-9-0 **60** SimonPearce(3) 3 37
(Andrew Turnell) *hld up in mid-div: wknd over 2f out* **17/2**[3]

-004 **14** 3 **Rampant Ronnie (USA)**[39] 565 4-8-13 **50** RussellKennemore 6 20
(Mrs A M Thorpe) *prom tl rdn and wknd over 3f out* **40/1**

5600 **15** 3 1/4 **Poca A Poca (IRE)**[5] 5015 5-8-6 **48** (b[1]) MatthewCosham(5) 1 11
(G C Bravery) *hld up in mid-div: pushed along and struggling over 2f out* **66/1**

-033 **16** 1/2 **Super Fourteen**[45] 3693 3-8-12 **60** CharlesEddery(5) 13 21
(R Hannon) *prom tl rdn and wknd 4f out* **9/1**

1m 34.78s (-1.42) **Going Correction** -0.025s/f (Good)
WFA 3 from 4yo+ 6lb **16** Ran SP% **122.1**
Speed ratings (Par 101): **106,105,102,101,100 99,99,99,97,95 93,93,91,88,85 84**
toteswinger: 1&2 £12.60, 1&3 £26.90, 2&3 £52.20. CSF £153.16 CT £2651.69 TOTE £13.50: £1.80, £3.00, £2.80, £3.80; EX 73.10.
Owner L M Power **Bred** D J And Mrs Deer **Trained** Hatford, Oxon

FOCUS
Following some morning rain the ground was officially good (good to firm in places). Some drainage work was being started on the back straight of the Flat course, and as a result all the races were at distances of 5f-1m on the straight track. The opening race was a modest handicap. It was run at a fair pace and the field grouped towards the stands' rail. Two veterans representing the same connections fought out the finish and pulled clear of the rest. Modest form rated through the runner-up to his All-Weather form.
Cadeaux Fax Official explanation: jockey said saddle slipped
Super Fourteen Official explanation: jockey said colt lost its action

5180 WINEAUX.CO.UK MAIDEN STKS 5f 16y
6:00 (6:01) (Class 5) 2-Y-O **£2,752** (£818; £409; £204) **Stalls** Centre

Form RPR
23 **1** **Secret Millionaire (IRE)**[27] 4282 2-8-10 0 JamesPSullivan(7) 4 81
(Patrick Morris) *mde all: pushed out ins fnl f* **10/3**[2]

04 **2** 1 1/2 **Pose (IRE)**[17] 4603 2-8-12 0 PatDobbs 9 71
(R Hannon) *a.p: rdn 1f out: r.o to take 2nd last strides: nt trble wnr* **4/1**[3]

32 **3** *nse* **Chips O'Toole (IRE)**[18] 4564 2-9-3 0 NickyMackay 6 75
(B J Meehan) *chsd wnr: pushed along 2f out: rdn fnl f: no imp: lost 2nd last strides* **6/4**[1]

60 **4** 2 3/4 **Dusty Spirit**[10] 4844 2-9-0 0 JackDean(3) 8 66
(W G M Turner) *half-rrd s: sn hld up in tch: rdn wl over 1f out: one pce* **66/1**

5U **5** 3/4 **Wellington Fair**[8] 4906 2-9-3 0 (b[1]) AdamKirby 5 63+
(C G Cox) *s.s whn rdr slow to remove blindfold: bhd: pushed along over 2f out: no real prog* **4/1**[3]

6 9 **Casanova Kid** 2-9-0 0 AlanCreighton(3) 1 30
(E J Creighton) *s.i.s: outpcd* **33/1**

6 **7** 3 3/4 **Macroy**[63] 3072 2-9-3 0 TGMcLaughlin 2 17
(B R Millman) *chsd ldrs tl wknd over 2f out* **33/1**

8 18 **Taliesin** 2-9-3 0 DavidProbert 3 —
(Mrs A M Thorpe) *s.i.s: sn bdly outpcd* **25/1**

59.13 secs (-0.17) **Going Correction** -0.025s/f (Good) **8** Ran SP% **114.3**
Speed ratings (Par 94): **100,97,97,93,91 77,71,42**
toteswinger: 1&2 £2.80, 1&3 £1.10, 2&3 £2.00. CSF £16.40 TOTE £4.60: £1.20, £1.50, £1.10; EX 14.40.
Owner Rob Lloyd Racing Limited **Bred** James Delaney **Trained** Tarporley, Cheshire

FOCUS
A reasonable maiden rated around the front three.

NOTEBOOK
Secret Millionaire(IRE) produced a professional front-running performance. He finished a close second behind subsequent Group 2 Superlative Stakes runner-up Roi De Vitesse on debut and ran respectably after getting unruly at the start when third of ten at Thirsk last time. The gelded son of Kyllachy had fair form claims and this may not represent improved form, but there was plenty to like about the style of the win. He looks a bargain at £56,000 and holds an entry in the Redcar Two-Year-Old Trophy. (op 11-4)
Pose(IRE) never looked like justifying support, but stuck to her guns quite well against the near rail. She put in a very creditable effort, particularly considering she had a bit to find on form. She is steadily progressing and should not have too much trouble winning a similar race. (op 13-2 tchd 7-1)
Chips O'Toole(IRE) finished clear of the rest when chasing home a well-touted Richard Hannon-trained newcomer at Newbury on his previous run. He had solid form claims and put in a fair effort, but could not get to grips with the trailblazing winner. (tchd 11-8 ad 13-8 in a place)
Dusty Spirit reared at the start, was niggled along some way out, but did quite well to keep grinding away. His proximity casts a shadow over the form, but it is possible that something has clicked and he has taken a fair step forward.
Wellington Fair shot left exiting the stalls and unseated his rider when favourite at Sandown last time. Things did not go much more smoothly with blinkers applied here, as he forfeited around seven lengths by starting slowly. However, he did prove he has quite a bit of ability by staying on late to latch on to the leading group. If he can get his act together at the start, he could turn out to be a reasonable prospect. Official explanation: jockey said he was slow to take the blinds off (op 9-2 tchd 7-2)

5181 DOUBLE DRAGON, NATIONAL ALE OF WALES MAIDEN STKS 7f 16y
6:35 (6:35) (Class 5) 3-Y-O **£2,752** (£818; £409; £204) **Stalls** Centre

Form RPR
0 **1** **Brother Cha (IRE)**[127] 1295 3-9-3 0 PatDobbs 4 82
(M G Quinlan) *t.k.h early: a.p: led over 1f out: sn rdn: r.o wl* **13/8**[2]

2263 **2** 1 **Luc Jordan**[30] 4180 3-9-3 76 AdamKirby 3 79
(L M Cumani) *hld up and bhd: stdy hdwy over 2f out: rdn over 1f out: r.o u.p to take 2nd wl ins fnl f: nt trbld wnr* **6/5**[1]

5-40 **3** 2 1/4 **Casting Couch (IRE)**[72] 2795 3-8-12 70 DavidProbert 1 68
(B W Hills) *led: rdn and hdd over 1f out: no ex and lost 2nd wl ins fnl f* **6/1**[3]

00 **4** 10 **Croeso Ynol**[30] 4164 3-8-12 0 TGMcLaughlin 2 41
(J L Spearing) *prom: pushed along over 2f out: wknd wl over 1f out* **33/1**

0 **5** *nk* **Rare Bet**[100] 1956 3-8-9 0 JackDean(3) 8 40
(W G M Turner) *hld up: rdn 2f out: sn struggling* **100/1**

02 **6** 2 1/4 **Lilly Royal (IRE)**[21] 4472 3-8-12 0 NeilChalmers 7 34
(B Palling) *hld up: pushed along and bhd fnl 3f* **11/1**

1m 23.2s **Going Correction** -0.025s/f (Good) **6** Ran SP% **110.1**
Speed ratings (Par 100): **99,97,95,83,83 80**
toteswinger: 1&2 £1.02, 1&3 £2.40, 2&3 £2.60. CSF £3.73 TOTE £3.20: £1.70, £1.10; EX 3.60.
Owner Exors of The Late Cathal M Ryan **Bred** Cathal Ryan **Trained** Newmarket, Suffolk

FOCUS
A fair maiden. The three main contenders finished a long way clear of the rest and the form has been rated around the runner-up and third for now.

5182 CELTIC PRIDE, WALES' NEW PREMIUM ALE H'CAP 7f 16y
7:05 (7:05) (Class 4) (0-85,82) 3-Y-O+ £5,180 (£1,541; £770; £384) Stalls Centre

Form RPR
4400 1 **Dig Deep (IRE)**[9] 4878 7-8-10 68 (t) JamieKyne(5) 3 77
(J J Quinn) *hld up and bhd: rdn and hdwy over 1f out: r.o to ld nr fin* 16/1
2021 2 shd **Indian Art (IRE)**[48] 3577 3-9-10 82 PatDobbs 7 89
(R Hannon) *hld up: hdwy over 2f out: sn rdn: led wl ins fnl f: hdd nr fin* 5/1[2]
-123 3 1 1/2 **Cape Rock**[20] 4501 4-9-11 78 (p) AdamKirby 9 83+
(W J Knight) *hld up: rdn and hdwy 2f out: carried rt ins fnl f: kpt on same pce: tk 3rd post: b.b.v* 2/1[1]
205 4 shd **Catalan Bay (AUS)**[24] 4386 5-9-6 73 (t) ChrisCatlin 2 77
(J R Gask) *led: rdn 1f out: edgd rt and hdd wl ins fnl f: nt qckn* 7/1
0130 5 1 1/2 **Arthur's Edge**[15] 4641 5-9-5 72 NeilChalmers 10 72
(B Palling) *a.p on stands' rail: rdn and edgd lft over 1f out: carried rt ins fnl f: one pce* 13/2
0210 6 shd **My Learned Friend (IRE)**[26] 4293 5-9-9 76 DavidProbert 6 76
(A M Balding) *hld up in tch: rdn 2f out: one pce* 6/1[3]
5222 7 1/2 **Ken's Girl**[27] 4266 5-8-12 70 SimonPearce(5) 1 69
(W S Kittow) *chsd ldr tl rdn over 2f out: wknd over 1f out* 8/1
0460 8 nk **Millfields Dreams**[6] 5003 10-8-12 70 (p) MarkCoumbe(5) 8 68
(G C Bravery) *hld up in rr: pushed along whn swtchd lft over 3f out: rdn over 2f out: nvr trbld ldrs* 25/1
3026 9 4 **Seneschal**[2] 5120 8-9-10 77 TGMcLaughlin 5 64
(A B Haynes) *hld up: pushed along 3f out: bhd fnl 2f* 20/1

1m 22.07s (-1.13) **Going Correction** -0.025s/f (Good)
WFA 3 from 4yo+ 5lb 9 Ran SP% 115.7
Speed ratings (Par 105): **105,104,103,103,101 101,100,100,95**
toteswinger: 1&2 £14.90, 1&3 £12.50, 2&3 £2.60. CSF £94.14 CT £234.95 TOTE £18.50: £5.30, £1.90, £1.70; EX 164.10.
Owner Roberts Green Whittall-Williams Savidge **Bred** Sir Eric Parker **Trained** Settrington, N Yorks

FOCUS
A competitive handicap run at a fair pace. They split into two groups and finished in a bit of a bunch. There is a slight doubt over the value of the form, with the runner-up being rated as having posted a small personal best.
Cape Rock Official explanation: vet said gelding had bled from the nose
Arthur's Edge Official explanation: jockey said gelding suffered interference in running

5183 FELINFOEL BREWERY H'CAP 5f 16y
7:40 (7:40) (Class 3) (0-90,85) 3-Y-O+ £7,771 (£2,312; £1,155; £577) Stalls Centre

Form RPR
650 1 **Tony The Tap**[25] 4341 8-9-8 84 DavidProbert 4 93
(W R Muir) *hld up and bhd: rdn and hdwy over 1f out: led wl ins fnl f: r.o* 10/3[2]
654 2 3/4 **Godfrey Street**[28] 4222 6-8-5 70 (p) KellyHarrison(3) 7 76
(A G Newcombe) *a.p on stands' rail: ev ch whn rdn and edgd lft jst ins fnl f: kpt on* 16/1
204 3 nk **Kay Two (IRE)**[34] 4069 7-9-4 85 (p) JamieKyne(5) 2 90
(R J Price) *led: rdn and hdd wl over 1f out: kpt on ins fnl f* 11/2[3]
1203 4 3/4 **First In Command (IRE)**[12] 4784 4-9-5 81 (t) RPCleary 1 83
(Daniel Mark Loughnane, Ire) *hld up in tch: led wl over 1f out: rdn and hdd wl ins fnl f: no ex: sddle slipped* 11/4[1]
4311 5 hd **The Tatling (IRE)**[18] 4567 12-9-2 81 JackDean(3) 3 83
(J M Bradley) *hld up in tch: pushed along whn nt clr run briefly over 1f out: one pce ins fnl f* 6/1
1030 6 1/2 **Our Piccadilly (IRE)**[21] 4461 4-9-2 78 AdamKirby 6 78
(W S Kittow) *hld up in tch: rdn over 1f out: one pce* 6/1
4525 7 1 **Doc Jones (IRE)**[1] 5154 3-8-10 79 ow5 RichardEvans(5) 5 75
(P D Evans) *hld up in tch: rdn 2f out: one pce* 7/1
4003 8 10 **Fern House (IRE)**[12] 4778 7-7-11 66 oh21 (b) CharlotteKerton(7) 8 26
(Bruce Hellier) *s.v.s: a wl in rr* 100/1

58.81 secs (-0.49) **Going Correction** -0.025s/f (Good)
WFA 3 from 4yo+ 2lb 8 Ran SP% 113.1
Speed ratings (Par 107): **102,100,100,99,98 98,96,80**
toteswinger: 1&2 £21.80, 1&3 £3.90, 2&3 £11.70. CSF £52.26 CT £285.81 TOTE £3.90: £1.20, £5.30, £1.90; EX 62.10.
Owner K J Mercer & Mrs S Mercer **Bred** K J Mercer **Trained** Lambourn, Berks

FOCUS
A decent handicap. They finished in a bit of a heap and it might not be the most solid of form, but it could work out.

NOTEBOOK
Tony The Tap took a while to get going, as he often does, but eventually flashed home down the centre of the track to win with something in hand. His style makes him a bit of a risky one to follow, but he hit form with back-to-back wins last autumn and should have a decent chance of following up. (op 3-1 tchd 7-2)
Godfrey Street blasted along against the near rail and did well to hang on for second, after drifting markedly left in the closing stages. He is an eight-time winner but has had plenty of peaks and troughs in his career and would not be certain to reproduce this effort next time. (tchd 20-1)
Kay Two(IRE) put in a decent pacesetting bid down the centre of the track. He is just 1lb higher than his last success and seven of his last eight wins have been between the months of August and October. He could be one to follow this autumn. (op 9-2)
First In Command(IRE) tracked the pace down the middle of the course. It looked like he might land a big gamble when hitting the front at the furlong pole, but he could not sustain his effort. It was reported that the saddle slipped. Official explanation: jockey said saddle slipped (op 9-2 tchd 5-2)
The Tatling(IRE) was the hard-luck story of the race. He travelled stylishly into contention, but his path was blocked at a crucial stage and he could not regain momentum. (op 11-2)
Fern House(IRE) Official explanation: jockey said gelding was very slowly away

5184 WEST COAST MARKETS H'CAP 5f 16y
8:10 (8:10) (Class 6) (0-65,65) 3-Y-O+ £2,388 (£705; £352) Stalls Centre

Form RPR
-043 1 **Littlemisssunshine (IRE)**[2] 5125 4-9-9 65 (p) AdamKirby 12 73+
(J S Moore) *hld up in mid-div: swtchd lft and hdwy over 1f out: rdn to ld nr fin* 5/1[2]
5000 2 nk **Monsieur Reynard**[13] 4736 4-8-5 52 MCGeran(5) 7 59
(J M Bradley) *hld up: hdwy and c towards stands' side over 3f out: carried hd high and edgd lft over 1f out: sn rdn: led cl home: hdd nr fin* 16/1
0041 3 3/4 **Spic 'n Span**[38] 3926 4-9-2 58 (b) ChrisCatlin 10 62+
(R A Harris) *led: clr over 3f out: pushed along and ct cl home* 14/1
3661 4 3/4 **Lithaam (IRE)**[6] 5008 5-9-1 57 6ex (p) DavidProbert 13 59
(J M Bradley) *hld up towards rr: nt clr run and swtchd lft 2f out: rdn and hdwy jst over 1f out: kpt on towards fin* 6/1[3]
6013 5 1/2 **Bluebok**[6] 4978 8-9-3 62 (bt) JackDean(3) 1 62
(J M Bradley) *a.p: rdn wl over 1f out: kpt on same pce ins fnl f* 12/1
4021 6 1 1/4 **Green Lagonda (AUS)**[2] 5125 7-9-3 64 6ex RichardEvans(5) 16 59
(P D Evans) *hld up in tch: rdn on stands' rail 2f out: one pce fnl f* 3/1[1]
0-05 7 nk **Wreningham**[30] 4182 4-8-13 58 JackMitchell(3) 5 52
(M D Squance) *prom: c rt towards stands' rail over 3f out: rdn wl over 1f out: sn edgd rt: one pce fnl f* 11/1
4136 8 1/2 **Stamford Blue**[19] 4536 8-9-1 64 (b) SPRyan(7) 9 56
(R A Harris) *hld up in mid-div: rdn and no hdwy fnl 2f* 12/1
0200 9 hd **Supreme Speedster**[20] 4479 5-8-2 47 KellyHarrison(3) 11 39
(A G Newcombe) *hld up towards rr: pushed along over 2f out: carried lft wl over 1f out: n.d* 66/1
060 10 1/2 **Best One**[2] 5125 5-8-12 57 (v[1]) KevinGhunowa(3) 15 47
(R A Harris) *prom: rdn over 2f out: wkng whn edgd lft 1f out* 25/1
0-00 11 1 1/4 **Street Diva (USA)**[14] 4697 4-8-4 51 AmyBaker(5) 14 36
(A B Haynes) *s.i.s: outpcd: nvr nrr* 66/1
60 12 1 1/4 **Charlie Delta**[50] 3505 6-9-0 56 (p) LukeMorris 2 37
(R A Harris) *stmbld s: sn hld up in mid-div: rdn and wknd over 2f out* 20/1
606 13 1 1/2 **Fyodor (IRE)**[35] 3994 8-9-1 62 (v) SimonPearce(5) 17 37
(P D Evans) *bhd: pushed along on stands' rail wl over 2f out: no rspnse* 12/1
6656 14 1 **My Best Man**[7] 4937 3-8-11 55 (t) TGMcLaughlin 8 27
(B R Millman) *sn bhd* 20/1
0355 15 2 3/4 **Kalhan Sands (IRE)**[12] 4778 4-8-13 60 JamieKyne(5) 4 22
(J J Quinn) *rrd and s.s: a in rr* 14/1
16 nk **Catch Roy (IRE)**[17] 4613 3-8-6 50 (t) RPCleary 3 11
(Daniel Mark Loughnane, Ire) *s.i.s: a towards rr* 25/1

58.95 secs (-0.35) **Going Correction** -0.025s/f (Good)
WFA 3 from 4yo+ 2lb 16 Ran SP% 126.8
Speed ratings (Par 101): **101,100,99,98,97 95,94,94,93,92 90,88,86,84,80 80**
toteswinger: 1&2 £38.70, 1&3 £23.70, 2&3 £38.70. CSF £79.09 CT £1082.08 TOTE £6.40: £1.80, £3.30, £2.70, £1.90; EX 218.20 Place 6: £51.54, Place 5: £12.38.
Owner Albert Conneally **Bred** Swordlestown Stud **Trained** Upper Lambourn, Berks
■ Stewards' Enquiry : Adam Kirby one-day ban: used whip without giving filly time to respond (Sep 3)

FOCUS
An ordinary sprint handicap. It was run at a furious pace and there was an exciting finish. The winner has progressed with each run for her current yard but this is not form to be too positive about.
T/Plt: £121.00 to a £1 stake. Pool: £41,644.87. 251.12 winning tickets. T/Qpdt: £13.60 to a £1 stake. Pool: £5,126.99. 277.70 winning tickets. KH

4449 EPSOM (L-H)
Thursday, August 20

OFFICIAL GOING: Good to firm (good in places; overall 8.8; home straight: stands' side 9.0, far side 8.6)
The rail was dolled out from the mile pole to the winning post, adding approximiately 10yds to all distances.
Wind: Strong, half against Weather: Fine

5185 LADIES' DERBY H'CAP (FOR LADY AMATEUR RIDERS) 1m 4f 10y
5:15 (5:18) (Class 4) (0-80,78) 4-Y-O+ £4,996 (£1,549; £774; £387) Stalls Centre

Form RPR
154 1 **Epsom Salts**[14] 4696 4-9-13 67 MissSBrotherton 7 76
(P M Phelan) *hld up wl off the pce: prog after 1/2-way: wnt 2nd 4f out: clsd on ldr 2f out: rdn to ld narrowly 1f out: hld on wl* 2/1[1]
611 2 nk **Lord Theo**[5] 5035 5-10-7 75 6ex MrsEmmaLittmoden 11 84
(N P Littmoden) *hld up wl off the pce: prog into 4th st: sn 3rd and clsd on ldng pair: pushed along to chal 1f out: w wnr after: jst hld last 100yds* 10/3[2]
351 3 2 3/4 **Dramatic Solo**[9] 4873 4-9-4 63 (b) MissKellyBurke(5) 6 67
(A P Jarvis) *disp clr ld tl def advantage 7f out: 5 l ahd st: reeled in fr 2f out: hdd and no ex 1f out* 7/1
4624 4 9 **Nawamees (IRE)**[3] 5097 11-9-11 65 (p) MissEFolkes 3 55
(P D Evans) *hld up wl off the pce: last and wl bhd st: plugged on fnl 2f: no ch* 12/1
0014 5 4 1/2 **Sky Quest (IRE)**[27] 4269 11-9-6 65 MissMHugo(5) 8 48
(J R Boyle) *hld up wl off the pce: 5th st: no real prog fnl 3f* 20/1
0331 6 1 **Simonside**[25] 4345 6-10-2 70 MissLEllison 4 51
(B Ellison) *hld up wl off the pce: 7th and rdn st: nvr on terms* 9/2[3]
1002 7 12 **Eseej (USA)**[10] 4855 4-10-6 74 MissEJJones 5 36
(P W Hiatt) *disp ld and clr of rest tl sed to lose grnd 7f out: 3rd and wkng st: t.o* 8/1
320 8 15 **Sri Kuantan (IRE)**[54] 3399 5-10-10 78 (t) MissCharmaineO'Neill 2 16
(R C Guest) *s.s: rcvrd to chse clr ldng pair and sn clr of rest: lost pl over 4f out: 6th and wkng st: t.o* 20/1

2m 39.02s (0.12) **Going Correction** -0.10s/f (Good) 8 Ran SP% 115.4
Speed ratings (Par 105): **95,94,92,86,83 83,75,65**
toteswinger: 1&2 £2.20, 1&3 £4.70, 2&3 £4.60. CSF £8.79 CT £36.25 TOTE £2.80: £1.50, £1.10, £2.20; EX 9.20.
Owner The Epsom Racegoers **Bred** Heatherwold Stud **Trained** Epsom, Surrey

FOCUS
A fair handicap comprising three previous winners. The pace was sound and the first three finished a long way clear of the remainder. The form looks straightforward to rate, with the winner rated to his best all-weather form.
Eseej(USA) Official explanation: jockey said gelding hung badly right

5186 NONSUCH CLAIMING STKS 1m 2f 18y
5:50 (5:53) (Class 5) 3-Y-O+ £3,238 (£963; £481; £240) Stalls Low

Form RPR
025 1 **Kaleo**[19] 4526 5-9-9 74 DarryllHolland 7 80
(S Dow) *mde all: abt 4 l clr st: rdn over 2f out: kpt on* 5/2[2]
1062 2 2 1/4 **Ahlawy (IRE)**[21] 4450 6-9-10 80 (bt) AndreaAtzeni(3) 3 80
(F Sheridan) *cl up: clr in 2nd fr 6f out: abt 4 l down st: rdn 3f out: hanging and clsd slowly: nvr able to chal* 15/8[1]
6300 3 14 **Quince (IRE)**[52] 3461 6-9-5 71 (v) TedDurcan 5 48
(J Pearce) *last and nvr gng wl: wnt 4th st: tk modest 3rd 2f out: no ch w ldng pair: eased last 100yds* 7/2[3]

0002 **4** *4* **Keeptheboatafloat (USA)**[120] 1453 3-9-0 86............ MartinLane(5) 2 44
(A P Jarvis) *cl up tl racd v awkwardly fr 6f out: 3rd and struggling st: continued to move poorly and sn bhd* **5/1**

4356 **5** *10* **Daring Racer (GER)**[37] 3949 6-8-13 52..................(p) PaulDoe 4 10
(Mrs L J Mongan) *cl up tl lost grnd after 4f: dropped to last and struggling st: sn wl bhd* **11/1**

2m 7.02s (-2.68) **Going Correction** -0.10s/f (Good)
WFA 3 from 5yo+ 8lb **5** Ran SP% **110.6**
Speed ratings (Par 103): **106,104,93,89,81**
toteswinger: 1&2 £2.40. CSF £7.65 TOTE £2.30: £1.50, £1.60; EX 5.30.
Owner John Robinson and Derek Stubbs **Bred** Gestut Hof Ittlingen **Trained** Epsom, Surrey

FOCUS
An uncompetitive claimer in which a moderate gallop increased around 4f out. The first two pulled clear in the straight. It has been rated around the runner-up.

5187 CHAMPAGNE LANSON NURSERY 7f
6:25 (6:25) (Class 4) 2-Y-O **£5,180** (£1,541; £770; £384) **Stalls** Low

Form RPR

2330 **1** **Transfixed (IRE)**[10] 4850 2-8-4 68.................... CatherineGannon 4 70
(P D Evans) *chsd ldr: rdn 2f out: no imp and looked hld tl styd on ins fnl f to ld nr fin* **6/1**

3665 **2** *nk* **Saxby (IRE)**[10] 4858 2-8-3 67.................... JoeFanning 1 68
(M R Channon) *led: gng bttr than rivals fr 2f out: rdn fnl f: worn down nr fin* **11/8**[1]

1U01 **3** *nk* **Kurtanella**[15] 4647 2-9-7 85.................... DaneO'Neill 2 85
(R Hannon) *hld up in last: shkn up over 2f out: no prog tl styd on ins fnl f: gaining fin* **5/2**[2]

1436 **4** *1 1/2* **Merseyside Star (IRE)**[26] 4327 2-7-13 68.............. MartinLane(5) 5 65
(A P Jarvis) *stdd s: hld up in 3rd: cl up on inner fr over 2f out: rdn and nt qckn over 1f out: one pce after* **11/4**[3]

1m 24.61s (1.31) **Going Correction** -0.10s/f (Good) **4** Ran SP% **111.6**
Speed ratings (Par 96): **88,87,87,85**
CSF £15.11 TOTE £7.90; EX 11.50.
Owner Mrs I M Folkes **Bred** Rathasker Stud **Trained** Pandy, Monmouths

FOCUS
Not a strong race for the money and a moderate gallop means the form is not entirely reliable.

NOTEBOOK
Transfixed(IRE) is a tough and durable type - like so many from this yard - and she showed a determined attitude to notch her fourth win. She did have the run of the race, but she should not be going up too much for this and can continue to give it her best shot after reassessment. (op 5-1)
Saxby(IRE), better than the bare form of his previous start, had an easy time of it in front and went close to justifying the market support. He was suited by the way things panned out here but he may be able to pick up a similar event from this mark. (op 15-8)
Kurtanella ◆, a dual-sprint winner, ran creditably over this longer trip, albeit in a race that was more a test of speed than stamina. She may be a little better than the bare form suggests against two rivals that were ideally placed throughout, and she looks the type to win over 6f in a strongly run event. (op 2-1 tchd 15-8)
Merseyside Star(IRE) didn't see his race out as well as his rivals on this first start over 7f, even in a race that wasn't a true test of stamina. He left the impression a drop back to 6f on a flatter track in a more truly run race will suit him better. (op 3-1)

5188 CHALK LANE H'CAP 7f
6:55 (6:56) (Class 5) (0-75,79) 3-Y-O+ **£3,885** (£1,156; £577; £288) **Stalls** Low

Form RPR

3321 **1** **Violent Velocity (IRE)**[15] 4657 6-8-13 71.................. IJBrennan(7) 4 81+
(J J Quinn) *trckd ldrs: 5th st: waiting for room fr over 2f out: squeezed through ent fnl f to ld last 100yds: pushed out* **4/1**[2]

4451 **2** *3/4* **Summer Dancer (IRE)**[9] 4878 5-10-0 79 6ex.............. JoeFanning 2 87+
(P T Midgley) *stdd s: plld hrd and hld up: 7th st: shkn up bhd ldrs 2f out: plld out jst over 1f out: r.o to snatch 2nd on post* **11/4**[1]

5002 **3** *hd* **Napoletano (GER)**[35] 4009 8-8-12 63....................(p) PaulDoe 5 70
(S Dow) *pressed ldr: led 2f out: sn pressed: hdd and outpcd last 100yds: lost 2nd post* **9/2**[3]

1163 **4** *1 3/4* **Another Try (IRE)**[43] 3732 4-8-6 62.................. MartinLane(5) 6 65
(A P Jarvis) *cl up: 4th on outer st: effrt to press ldrs over 2f out: one pce fnl f* **7/1**

4040 **5** *3/4* **Pippbrook Gold**[14] 4714 4-9-0 65.................... PatCosgrave 1 66
(J R Boyle) *prom: 3rd st: rdn over 2f out: stl cl up jst over 1f out: outpcd fnl f* **9/1**

3000 **6** *hd* **Purus (IRE)**[15] 4641 7-9-3 75.................... JPFahy(7) 10 75+
(R A Teal) *blindfold late off and missed break: hld up in last: wl off the pce st: rdn and sme prog over 2f out: nvr able to get on terms w ldrs* **10/1**

3-32 **7** *4 1/2* **Azure Mist**[64] 3021 4-8-7 65.................... AshleyMorgan(7) 11 53
(M H Tompkins) *t.k.h: led: shkn up and hdd 2f out: wknd tamely fnl f* **6/1**

1500 **8** *9* **Resplendent Nova**[30] 4181 7-9-3 68.................... IanMongan 7 32
(P Howling) *hld up: 8th and wl off the pce st: no prog: t.o* **20/1**

0006 **9** *nk* **Mount Ella**[14] 4702 3-7-11 56 oh7..................(b[1]) AndreaAtzeni(3) 3 19
(J R Boyle) *cl up tl 6th and losing pl u.p st: sn bhd: t.o* **25/1**

1m 23.02s (-0.28) **Going Correction** -0.10s/f (Good)
WFA 3 from 4yo+ 5lb **9** Ran SP% **119.3**
Speed ratings (Par 103): **97,96,95,93,93 92,87,77,77**
toteswinger: 1&2 £2.80, 1&3 £7.30, 2&3 £3.70. CSF £16.03 CT £52.26 TOTE £4.80: £1.40, £1.50, £1.70; EX 11.90.
Owner Mrs S Quinn **Bred** Miss Jill Finegan **Trained** Settrington, N Yorks

FOCUS
A fair handicap run at just an ordinary gallop and the first six finished in a heap. The runner-up has been rated to the best of his old form, but the race did not really play to his strengths and he may do bit better again back up north, while the third has been rated close to his latest C&D effort.

5189 ASHLEY ROAD H'CAP 1m 114y
7:30 (7:30) (Class 4) (0-85,91) 3-Y-O **£5,180** (£1,541; £770; £384) **Stalls** Low

Form RPR

4421 **1** **Wannabe King**[10] 4852 3-9-13 91 6ex..................(p) TedDurcan 1 99+
(D R Lanigan) *cl up on inner: 3rd st: looking for way through fr 2f out: squeezed through fnl f: shkn up to ld last 75yds* **10/3**[2]

2300 **2** *1/2* **Emirates Roadshow (USA)**[42] 3780 3-9-7 85.............. LDettori 7 90
(Saeed Bin Suroor) *pressed ldr: led 2f out: rdn and pressed over 1f out: kpt on: hdd and outpcd last 75yds* **1/1**[1]

4062 **3** *1/2* **Roar Of Applause**[15] 4649 3-9-2 80..................(b) DarryllHolland 4 84
(B J Meehan) *hld up last: prog on outer 2f out: rdn to chal and looked dangerous 1f out: nt qckn* **10/1**

3326 **4** *3/4* **Star Links (USA)**[19] 4540 3-9-5 83.................... DaneO'Neill 6 85+
(R Hannon) *hld up in 6th: last and pushed along 2f out: plld out and rdn fnl f: r.o to take 4th last stride: no ch* **17/2**[3]

4463 **5** *shd* **At A Great Rate (USA)**[12] 4799 3-8-12 76.................... IanMongan 5 78
(H R A Cecil) *trckd ldrs: cl 5th st: rdn over 2f out: stl pressing ldrs over 1f out: one pce fnl f* **14/1**

0020 **6** *3/4* **Johnmanderville**[26] 4296 3-8-10 79.................. MartinLane(5) 3 79
(A P Jarvis) *led: rdn and hdd 2f out: fdd ins fnl f* **14/1**

3002 **7** *8* **Green Agenda**[10] 4846 3-8-11 75.................... JoeFanning 8 57
(M Johnston) *cl up on outer: 4th st: rdn and wknd 2f out* **10/1**

1m 44.27s (-1.83) **Going Correction** -0.10s/f (Good) **7** Ran SP% **115.1**
Speed ratings (Par 102): **104,103,103,102,102 101,94**
toteswinger: 1&2 £1.60, 1&3 £4.40, 2&3 £3.70. CSF £7.15 CT £27.84 TOTE £4.40: £1.90, £1.50; EX 7.00.
Owner Saif Ali & Saeed H Altayer **Bred** Chippenham Lodge Stud Ltd **Trained** Newmarket, Suffolk
■ Stewards' Enquiry : Ian Mongan three-day ban: failed to ride out for 4th place (Sep 3, 4, 6)

FOCUS
A reasonable handicap, but another moderately run race which suited the prominent racers. The runner-up is the guide to the form, with the third being rated to his latest All-Weather effort.
Roar Of Applause Official explanation: jockey said gelding hung left

5190 SHEPHERD'S WALK H'CAP 1m 114y
8:00 (8:01) (Class 5) (0-75,75) 4-Y-O+ **£3,885** (£1,156; £577; £288) **Stalls** Low

Form RPR

1336 **1** **Sarah Park (IRE)**[27] 4262 4-9-9 75.................... LDettori 14 84
(B J Meehan) *trckd ldr: led 2f out: rdn and pressed ins fnl f: r.o wl nr fin* **5/1**[3]

0022 **2** *1 1/4* **Eastern Gift**[6] 4992 4-9-7 73.................... GeorgeBaker 9 79
(Miss Gay Kelleway) *hld up in rr: 12th st: stdy prog on outer over 2f out: chsd wnr ins fnl f: tried to chal but no imp last 100yds* **10/1**

4413 **3** *1/2* **Kargan (IRE)**[21] 4466 4-8-4 63.................... AndrewHeffernan(7) 7 68
(R A Farrant) *t.k.h: hld up bhd ldrs: 5th st: got through to chse wnr over 1f out tl ins fnl f: one pce* **11/1**

0014 **4** *2* **Northern Spy (USA)**[10] 4852 5-9-9 75.................... DarryllHolland 1 75
(S Dow) *prom: 3rd st: rdn to dispute 2nd over 1f out: hld whn checked ent fnl f: one pce* **9/2**[2]

3465 **5** *1* **Justcallmehandsome**[14] 4714 7-8-4 61..................(v) SophieDoyle(5) 10 59
(D J S Ffrench Davis) *hld up: 13th st: rdn on outer over 2f out: styd on fr over 1f out: nrst fin* **25/1**

4621 **6** *1/2* **Astrodonna**[8] 4916 4-8-12 71 6ex.................... AshleyMorgan(7) 13 68
(M H Tompkins) *dwlt: hld up: last but in tch st: effrt on outer 2f out: shkn up over 1f out: styd on: nvr nrr* **14/1**

0311 **7** *nk* **Ogre (USA)**[35] 4005 4-9-8 74..................(t) PaulDoe 3 70
(P D Evans) *dwlt: hld up: 10th st: swtchd to inner 2f out: shkn up and kpt on: n.d* **4/1**[1]

2344 **8** *1/2* **Murrin (IRE)**[71] 2824 5-9-3 69.................... JoeFanning 15 64
(T G Mills) *hld up in midfield: 8th st: rdn and no prog over 2f out: one pce and edging lft over 1f out* **16/1**

0006 **9** *1 1/2* **Dancer's Legacy**[14] 4714 4-8-9 61.................... PatCosgrave 5 53
(J R Boyle) *chsd ldrs: 4th st: rdn to dispute 2nd over 1f out: sn wknd* **33/1**

0061 **10** *1/2* **Cordell (IRE)**[13] 4731 4-9-7 73.................... RobertHavlin 11 63
(R Ingram) *mde most to 2f out: wknd over 1f out* **20/1**

1253 **11** *3/4* **Driven (IRE)**[15] 4641 4-9-7 73.................... JimCrowley 8 62+
(Mrs A J Perrett) *t.k.h: hld up in midfield: plld hrd downhill over 4f out: 9th st: sn rdn and no prog: hanging lft and one pce fnl 2f* **5/1**[3]

06 **12** *4* **Bid For Glory**[14] 4716 5-9-5 71.................... TedDurcan 6 50
(H J Collingridge) *chsd ldrs: 6th st: lost pl 2f out: btn after* **20/1**

0/16 **13** *1* **Expensive Problem**[42] 3766 6-9-5 71.................... IvanLopez 4 48
(R J Smith) *towards rr: 11th st: btn whn sltly hmpd 2f out* **14/1**

0506 **14** *4* **Evident Pride (USA)**[112] 1621 6-9-6 72.................... IanMongan 2 40
(B R Johnson) *hld up in midfield: 7th st: rdn and struggling whn hmpd 2f out: bhd and eased after* **11/1**

1m 44.52s (-1.58) **Going Correction** -0.10s/f (Good) **14** Ran SP% **132.8**
Speed ratings (Par 103): **103,101,101,99,98 98,97,96,95 95,91,90,87**
toteswinger: 1&2 £12.30, 1&3 £20.30, 2&3 £28.30. CSF £57.74 CT £569.88 TOTE £7.60: £2.60, £3.80, £4.10; EX 101.10 Place 6: £75.45, Place 5: £51.35..
Owner Mrs J & D E Cash **Bred** George S O'Malley **Trained** Manton, Wilts
■ Stewards' Enquiry : Paul Doe three-day ban: careless riding (Sep 3, 4, 6)

FOCUS
A fair handicap run at a reasonable gallop and the majority of those held up were at a disadvantage. Straightforward form to rate with the runner-up rated to his recent best and the third and fourth rated a length off their marks.
T/Plt: £112.80 to a £1 stake. Pool: £39,628.05. 256.35 winning tickets. T/Qpdt: £53.50 to a £1 stake. Pool: £3,492.40. 48.30 winning tickets. JN

5015 LINGFIELD (L-H)
Thursday, August 20

OFFICIAL GOING: Standard
Wind: Fresh Weather: Overcast

5191 BUY A RACING POST YEARLING BONUS CANDIDATE MAIDEN STKS (DIV I) 7f (P)
1:30 (1:30) (Class 5) 2-Y-O **£3,238** (£963; £481; £240) **Stalls** Low

Form RPR

03 **1** **Lethal Combination (USA)**[21] 4451 2-9-3 0.............. TonyCulhane 9 76
(W J Haggas) *sn led: mde rest: rdn wl over 1f out: kpt on wl and a holding runner-up fnl f* **1/1**[1]

2 *1/2* **Resuscitator (USA)** 2-9-3 0.................... FergusSweeney 10 75
(Mrs H S Main) *sn chsng wnr: rdn and pressing wnr wl over 1f out: unable qck and a hld fnl f* **66/1**

3 *1 1/4* **Shaayeq (IRE)** 2-9-3 0.................... PatDobbs 3 72
(M P Tregoning) *chsd ldng trio: wnt 3rd wl over 1f out: swtchd rt jst over 1f out: one pce fnl f* **4/1**[2]

030 **4** *2 1/4* **Sheer Force (IRE)**[23] 4410 2-9-3 74.................... JimCrowley 7 66
(W J Knight) *t.k.h: hld up wl in tch: effrt and edging lft u.p wl over 1f out: sltly hmpd over 1f out: kpt on same pce fnl f* **5/1**[3]

0 **5** *nk* **Another Magic Man (USA)**[55] 3344 2-9-3 0.......... RobertWinston 11 65
(J R Best) *t.k.h: sn chsng ldng pair: rdn and unable qck wl over 1f out: edgd rt over 1f out: one pce fnl f* **50/1**

00 **6** *1/2* **Greek Key (IRE)**[11] 4811 2-9-3 0.................... HayleyTurner 1 64+
(M L W Bell) *hld up wl in tch on inner: rdn and effrt wl over 1f out: edgd rt and no imp fr over 1f out* **25/1**

7 *1 1/4* **Loaded** 2-9-3 0.................... LukeMorris 8 61
(P Winkworth) *s.i.s: in tch in last trio: effrt on outer bnd 2f out: no imp fr over 1f out* **25/1**

8 nk **Shabak Hom (IRE)** 2-9-3 0 PatCosgrave 2 60
(D M Simcock) *s.i.s: rn green in last trio: pushed along over 4f out: rdn jst over 2f out: one pce and no prog after* **25/1**

0 9 3/4 **Satwa Son (IRE)**[41] 3792 2-9-3 0 StephenDonohoe 4 58
(E A L Dunlop) *t.k.h: trckd ldrs: rdn and lost pl over 2f out: n.d fnl 2f* **14/1**

4 10 11 **Cuts Both Ways (USA)**[14] 4701 2-9-3 0 JoeFanning 5 31
(P F I Cole) *bhd: rdn and struggling over 4f out: swtchd wd over 3f out: sn lost tch and wl bhd fnl 2f* **10/1**

1m 25.21s (0.41) **Going Correction** -0.075s/f (Stan) **10** Ran SP% **117.4**
Speed ratings (Par 94): **94,93,92,89,89 88,87,86,85,73**
toteswingers: 1&2 £15.30, 1&3 £2.10, 2&3 £34.60. CSF £116.62 TOTE £1.90: £1.10, £14.00, £1.30; EX 62.90 TRIFECTA Not won..

Owner Findlay & Bloom **Bred** Indian Creek **Trained** Newmarket, Suffolk

FOCUS
A moderate Polytrack maiden made a little more interesting by the presence of a small contingent of nicely-bred unraced colts. The fourth helps set the level.

NOTEBOOK
Lethal Combination(USA) had stepped up considerably from his debut effort when finishing third over this distance at Epsom three weeks prior to this but, while that form suggested he set the standard here, it was not an especially demanding one. The fact that he won with a little to spare, staying on well after being prominent from the outset, indicates that, while he should go on to score again at some stage, those behind almost certainly have only limited ability. (op 10-11 tchd 11-10 in a place)

Resuscitator(USA), with a less-than-eyecatching pedigree and from a small yard not known for its exploits with juveniles, was another who raced up with the pace and he did enough in taking second to encourage his connections to believe he can beak his duck in ordinary company.

Shaayeq(IRE), representing a stable emerging gradually from a long period in the doldrums, has a smart pedigree, being by Classic winner Dubawi out of a mare who won on her first appearance over this distance as a juvenile. He too chased the pace from the start and, although he could not muster sufficient finishing zip to trouble the first two, he made a solid start to his career and should improve with racing. (op 5-1)

Sheer Force(IRE) has an official rating of 74, based presumably on his third over 6f at Ascot in July, but he had run well below that level on his only subsequent outing at Goodwood and he had a bit to prove. This effort was reasonable enough, even if it did not indicate his BHA mark is justified, but on this evidence he will need to be found a weak contest in order to get his head in front in a maiden. (op 9-2)

Another Magic Man(USA), slowly into his stride when a well-beaten ninth of 12 in Fokestone maiden on his debut, improved on that performance without striking as the type to make a major impact in the near future.

Greek Key(IRE) had shown a little debut promise when seventh in a fair maiden at Sandown in July, but then disappointed after a slow start in very testing ground at Leicester on his second outing. He seemed better suited to this surface and may even have posted his best effort to date, but he will need to progress considerably on anything shown so far, or obtain a favourable rating, if he is to notch a first success.

5192 BUY A RACING POST YEARLING BONUS CANDIDATE MAIDEN STKS (DIV II) 7f (P)
2:05 (2:06) (Class 5) 2-Y-0 **£3,238** (£963; £481; £240) **Stalls** Low

Form RPR

00 1 **Pleasant Day (IRE)**[16] 4618 2-9-3 0 (b[1]) DaneO'Neill 10 79+
(B J Meehan) *chsd ldrs: wnt 2nd gng wl 3f out: led jst over 2f out: rdn clr over 1f out: comf* **9/1**

35 2 3 3/4 **Kensei (IRE)**[19] 4534 2-9-3 0 GeorgeBaker 5 69+
(R M Beckett) *hld up in tch: rdn and effrt jst over 2f out: chsd clr wnr over 1f out: no imp* **1/1**[1]

44 3 3 **Iron Condor**[15] 4666 2-9-3 0 LukeMorris 6 60
(J M P Eustace) *dwlt: sn pushed along and hdwy to chse ldr after 1f tl 3f out: rdn and hung rt bnd jst over 2f out: outpcd over 1f out and wl btn after* **11/2**[2]

0 4 nk **Ebony Boom (IRE)**[11] 4811 2-9-3 0 IanMongan 2 60
(H R A Cecil) *led for 1f: in tch tl lost pl and rdn over 2f out: edgd rt and kpt on fnl f to press for 3rd nr fin: no ch w ldng pair* **6/1**[3]

05 5 2 3/4 **Red Amy**[14] 4699 2-8-12 0 HayleyTurner 8 48
(M L W Bell) *s.i.s: sn swtchd lft and pushed along: a towards rr: rdn over 2f out: no ch fr wl over 1f out* **8/1**

0 6 4 **Masterful Act (USA)**[19] 4534 2-9-3 0 RobertWinston 7 44+
(J R Best) *dwlt: a in rr: rdn and struggling 3f out: no ch fnl 2f* **50/1**

0 7 2 **Lanizza**[61] 3167 2-9-3 0 (b[1]) StephenDonohoe 3 37
(E A L Dunlop) *dwlt: rcvrd to ld after 1f: hdd jst over 2f out: wknd qckly over 1f out* **8/1**

1m 25.03s (0.23) **Going Correction** -0.075s/f (Stan) **7** Ran SP% **113.9**
Speed ratings (Par 94): **95,90,87,86,83 79,76**
toteswingers: 1&2 £3.70, 1&3 £6.30, 2&3 £2.40. CSF £18.40 TOTE £14.10: £5.40, £1.20; EX 27.60 Trifecta £108.70 Pool: £501.11 - 3.41 winning units..

Owner Jaber Abdullah **Bred** Patrick J Gleeson **Trained** Manton, Wilts

FOCUS
This looked weaker than the first division, with no tastily-bred unraced runners in the line-up, and those that had raced had shown form of only a moderate standard. It has been rated around the balance of the runner-up's form.

NOTEBOOK
Pleasant Day(IRE), already gelded and from a yard which has seen a few of its two-year-olds disappoint in recent days, was attempting to put a moderate recent run at Catterick behind him. He was fitted with first-time blinkers here, though, and they seemed to do the trick, as, after chasing the pace from the start, he made an eyecatching move on the home turn and quickened away in the straight to score decisively. (op 10-1 tchd 11-1)

Kensei(IRE) had made an encouraging start to his career, finishing third at Salisbury in June, but he had been turned over as a short-priced favourite on his second run, in muddy conditions, at this course at the beginning of this month. He ran better here than he had on that testing ground, making progress from midfield to take second in the straight, but did not really convince that he will progress sufficiently to take an average maiden. (op 11-10 tchd 11-8 in a place)

Iron Condor had not set the world alight in his two previous starts, finishing fourth on both occasions, but those efforts suggested he has the ability to win races at some stage and that - on admittedly limited evidence - he is consistent in his performance. That being the case, he is probably the best marker for the overall form, as he had a clean run throughout but was just not good enough. (op 13-2 tchd 5-1)

Ebony Boom(IRE), who has a stout pedigree and looks the type to improve with age, had disappointed when market leader for his Leicester debut over this distance on heavy ground 11 days previously. He improved on that modest effort here, figuring in the vanguard from the outset, but does not look any great shakes on his two outings so far. (op 5-1)

Red Amy, the only filly in either of the two divisions of this event, had pulled far too hard for her own good when a modest fifth of nine on her previous start. She was less inclined to tug this time, indeed she seemed to get outpaced in mid-race, but, being by Hawk Wing out of a middle-distance mare, appears more likely to thrive over longer trips as a three-year-old. (op 15-2 tchd 7-1)

5193 EDENBRIDGE MAIDEN FILLIES' STKS 7f (P)
2:40 (2:41) (Class 5) 3-Y-O+ **£3,561** (£1,059; £529; £264) **Stalls** Low

Form RPR

2 1 **Dhaawiah (USA)**[15] 4648 3-8-12 0 LDettori 7 89+
(Saeed Bin Suroor) *chsd ldrs: wnt 2nd over 3f out: led over 2f out: pushed clr over 1f out: in command and pushed along fnl f: eased towards fin* **2/11**[1]

3 2 3/4 **Passkey**[7] 4955 3-8-12 0 StephenDonohoe 2 80+
(Sir Mark Prescott) *hld up wl in tch: hdwy to chse ldng pair wl clr of rest wl over 2f out: rdn over 1f out: wnt 2nd fnl 100yds: kpt on* **9/2**[2]

00 3 3/4 **Tenteare**[61] 3168 3-8-12 0 IanMongan 12 78
(H R A Cecil) *s.i.s: sn chsng ldrs: led over 3f out: hdd over 2f out: hung rt bnd jst over 2f out: edgd lft and flashed tail u.p over 1f out: kpt on same pce fnl f: lost 2nd fnl 100yds* **25/1**

0 4 9 **Keibla Spirit**[12] 4786 3-8-12 0 RobertHavlin 5 54
(R Ingram) *plld hrd: hld up in tch: rdn and outpcd by ldng trio over 2f out: n.d after* **50/1**

U5 5 1 3/4 **Louise Sauvage**[12] 4786 3-8-12 0 NeilChalmers 3 49
(M D I Usher) *stdd s: hld up in midfield: rdn and wl outpcd over 2f out: no ch fnl 2f* **33/1**

02 6 4 1/2 **Betony (USA)**[30] 4180 3-8-12 0 HayleyTurner 11 37
(M L W Bell) *stdd and dropped in bhd after s: swtchd rt and pushed along wl over 2f out: sn no ch w ldrs: nvr on terms* **10/1**[3]

6- 7 nse **Anasy (USA)**[258] 7561 3-8-12 0 LPKeniry 6 37
(T Keddy) *led for 1f: chsd ldrs tl rdn and wl outpcd over 2f out: no ch fnl 2f* **33/1**

0- 8 1 3/4 **Rumramah (USA)**[337] 6030 3-8-12 0 PatCosgrave 1 32
(D M Simcock) *s.i.s: in tch towards rr: rdn and wl outpcd wl over 2f out: no ch whn rn green bnd 2f out* **20/1**

0 9 12 **Mumtaz Begum**[30] 4180 4-9-0 0 NataliaGemelova[(3)] 9 —
(J E Long) *s.i.s: sn detached in last pl: rdn over 4f out: t.o fr over 2f out* **66/1**

00-0 10 14 **Miss Jodarah (USA)**[12] 4789 3-8-12 35 (b[1]) RobertWinston 10 —
(J R Best) *chsd ldr: led 1f tl over 5f out: hdd over 3f out: sn dropped out: t.o fnl 2f: virtually p.u fnl f* **33/1**

1m 23.98s (-0.82) **Going Correction** -0.075s/f (Stan)
WFA 3 from 4yo 5lb **10** Ran SP% **132.8**
Speed ratings (Par 100): **101,100,99,89,87 81,81,79,66,50**
toteswingers: 1&2 £1.60, 1&3 £7.00, 2&3 £10.20. CSF £1.90 TOTE £1.30: £1.02, £1.40, £8.50; EX 2.40 Trifecta £25.50 Pool: £783.42 - 22.72 winning units..

Owner Godolphin **Bred** Shadwell Farm LLC **Trained** Newmarket, Suffolk

FOCUS
A fillies' maiden lacking strength in depth, but it featured a clutch of well-bred three-year-olds with promising form in the book. There was little pace early but the form doesn't look too bad with the winner looking better than the bare result suggests.

5194 MARSH GREEN NURSERY 5f (P)
3:15 (3:15) (Class 4) (0-85,85) 2-Y-O **£5,180** (£1,541; £770; £384) **Stalls** High

Form RPR

2102 1 **Six Diamonds**[5] 5033 2-8-7 71 RobertWinston 2 81+
(H Morrison) *chsd ldr tl led wl over 2f out: rdn and clr jst ins fnl f: eased nr fin* **5/2**[2]

3601 2 2 1/4 **Six Wives**[9] 4868 2-8-13 77 6ex JamesDoyle 4 78
(J A Glover) *taken down early: chsd ldrs: drvn to chse wnr over 1f out: kpt on same pce fnl f* **9/1**

3522 3 1 3/4 **Admin (IRE)**[9] 4868 2-8-7 78 JPFahy[(7)] 5 73
(R M Beckett) *in tch: rdn and unable qck over 1f out: kpt on to go 3rd fnl 100yds: nvr pce to trble wnr* **11/10**[1]

3562 4 1/2 **Vilnius**[15] 4639 2-7-12 62 CatherineGannon 6 55
(M R Channon) *sn bhd and niggled along: swtchd rt jst over 2f out: no hdwy u.p tl kpt on ins fnl f to go 4th towards fin: nvr trbld ldrs* **10/1**

1051 5 3/4 **Brambleberry**[13] 4746 2-9-7 85 RichardKingscote 1 75
(Tom Dascombe) *led tl wl over 2f out: drvn and lost 2nd over 2f out: wknd jst ins fnl f* **7/1**[3]

1505 6 2 3/4 **Strike Shot**[20] 4493 2-8-12 76 (p) ShaneKelly 3 56
(W R Muir) *a in last pair: rdn and no prog 2f out: wl btn fnl f* **16/1**

58.35 secs (-0.45) **Going Correction** -0.075s/f (Stan) 2y crse rec **6** Ran SP% **113.7**
Speed ratings (Par 96): **100,96,93,92,91 87**
toteswingers: 1&2 £2.30, 1&3 £1.60, 2&3 £2.40. CSF £24.45 TOTE £3.90: £1.60, £2.60; EX 14.80.

Owner A J Struthers Mrs J Scott Mrs F Woodd **Bred** Mrs S F Dibben **Trained** East Ilsley, Berks

FOCUS
Only a small field for this nursery, but none in the line-up could be entirely discounted, and all bar one had run really well on their latest start. This race could have been rated too high but the winner's Newmarket form is solid and the runner-up appears to have built on her recent course win.

NOTEBOOK
Six Diamonds had shown she is competitive off her current mark of 71 when taking second over this distance at Newmarket just five days prior to this. In order to win she had to prove she was equally effective on an artificial surface but, after getting a nice lead from Brambleberry in the early stages, she shot to the front on the home turn and was never in danger of defeat thereafter. (op 3-1 tchd 100-30)

Six Wives, already twice a winner on Polytrack having collected at Wolverhampton and over this track and trip, was attempting to shrug off a 6lb penalty for her narrow defeat of Admin nine days previously. She was worse off at the weights with that rival - and the betting suggested she would find it hard to confirm the form - but she did and this appears to be another improved effort from a filly whose stable has upped a gear since a new trainer was appointed. (op 13-2 tchd 14-1)

Admin(IRE) could mathematically be credited with a gently progressive profile, his most recent run resulting in a second behind Six Wives over this course and distance, and he was 6lb better off at the weights for a head defeat. He finished further behind that rival here, though, and having been sent off favourite more than once, is becoming rather expensive to follow. (op 6-4 tchd 10-11and 13-8 in places)

Vilnius had notched her only previous success in a Catterick seller, but she had posted a string of solid efforts in nurseries since that victory and had been third from a 2lb higher mark at York in July. She again ran creditably, without quite threatening to make the first three, and is quite consistent for one with limited ability. (op 9-1 tchd 12-1)

Brambleberry was obliged to give weight away to all her rivals, even though she had been eased a couple of pounds in the ratings since making no better than fifth in a Chester nursery in July, and that looked to provide her with a tough task. It proved too much and, after making the early running, she was swamped in the closing stages. (op 6-1)

Strike Shot does not look unfairly treated on his very best form, as he had been taking on some smart types since landing a maiden at Haydock in May, but his stable has been generally out of sorts recently and he appeared to run a bit flat here. Official explanation: jockey said colt suffered interference at start (op 12-1 tchd 11-1)

5195 COLEMANS HATCH FILLIES' H'CAP — 1m 2f (P)

3:50 (3:50) (Class 5) (0-70,70) 3-Y-O+ — **£3,885** (£1,156; £577; £288) **Stalls** Low

Form — RPR

2242 **1** **Some Sunny Day**[12] 4789 3-9-5 **69** .... TravisBlock 9 — 74+
(H Morrison) *led tl over 7f out: chsd ldr tl 3f out: stl wl in tch and rdn 2f out: hung bdly rt u.p fnl f but kpt on to ld nr fin* **4/1**[1]

3246 **2** *hd* **Lunar River (FR)**[26] 4300 6-9-10 **66** .... (t) FergusSweeney 6 — 70
(David Pinder) *s.i.s: hld up in rr: hdwy towards inner wl over 1f out: rdn to chal ins fnl f: led fnl 50yds: hdd nr fin* **11/2**[2]

3-60 **3** *nse* **Yvonne Evelyn (USA)**[40] 3869 4-9-4 **60** .... GeorgeBaker 11 — 64
(J R Gask) *s.i.s: bhd: gd hdwy on outer to ld over 7f out: rdn 2f out: kpt on wl tl hdd and no ex fnl 50yds* **15/2**

0030 **4** *½* **Full Of Nature**[3] 5099 3-9-6 **70** .... JamesDoyle 5 — 73
(S Kirk) *t.k.h: hld up wl in tch: rdn jst over 2f out: hdwy u.p jst over 1f out: chsng ldrs and carried rt ins fnl f: kpt on* **16/1**

2433 **5** *1 ¼* **Resentful Angel**[19] 4533 4-9-0 **63** .... TobyAtkinson(7) 1 — 64
(Pat Eddery) *s.i.s: hld up bhd: hmpd bnd 9f out: reminder over 4f out: hung lft and nt clr run wl over 1f out: sn swtchd rt: hdwy 1f out: styng on but hld whn nt clr run towards fin* **13/2**[3]

635 **6** *nse* **Ebony Eyes**[28] 4234 3-9-2 **66** .... JimCrowley 14 — 66+
(W J Knight) *s.i.s: hld up in rr: rdn over 2f out: hdwy u.p ent fnl f: styd on wl: nt rch ldrs* **10/1**

4006 **7** *2* **Turfwolke (GER)**[19] 4533 4-8-6 **55** .... AlexEdwards(7) 7 — 51
(Mrs H S Main) *t.k.h: chsd ldr tl over 7f out: styd handy: rdn and unable qck on inner over 1f out: kpt on same pce fnl f* **33/1**

0-10 **8** *1* **Madam President**[97] 2052 4-9-9 **70** .... (t) MartinLane(5) 3 — 64
(W R Swinburn) *hld up in tch in midfield: rdn and effrt on outer whn jostled wl over 1f out: kpt on same pce fnl f* **10/1**

0032 **9** *1 ¼* **Onenightinlisbon (IRE)**[8] 4916 5-9-2 **58** .... PatCosgrave 12 — 50
(J R Boyle) *chsd ldrs: rdn and ev ch ent fnl 2f: wknd u.p 1f out* **10/1**

0-00 **10** *1 ¼* **A Dream Come True**[13] 4745 4-9-7 **68** .... JamesO'Reilly(5) 8 — 57
(D K Ivory) *t.k.h: hld up towards rr: rdn wl over 2f out: no prog and btn fnl 2f* **33/1**

4204 **11** *nk* **Bramalea**[13] 4744 4-9-7 **63** .... DaneO'Neill 10 — 52
(B W Duke) *t.k.h: hld up wl in tch: hdwy to chse ldrs 3f out: rdn and unable qck whn jostled wl over 1f out: no hdwy after* **13/2**[3]

6400 **12** *½* **Action Girl**[14] 4704 4-9-4 **60** .... (p) DarryllHolland 2 — 48
(R M H Cowell) *hld up towards rr: dropped to last pl and rdn 3f out: no prog fnl 2f* **14/1**

3616 **13** *½* **Chadwell Spring (IRE)**[14] 4720 3-9-4 **68** .... (p) RichardKingscote 13 — 55
(Miss J Feilden) *t.k.h: chsd ldrs tl wnt 2nd 3f out tl jst over 2f out: wknd qckly over 1f out* **16/1**

2m 6.39s (-0.21) **Going Correction** -0.075s/f (Stan)
WFA 3 from 4yo+ 8lb — **13** Ran SP% **125.4**
Speed ratings (Par 100): **97,96,96,96,95 95,93,92,91,90 90,90,89**
toteswingers: 1&2 £6.30, 1&3 £7.70, 2&3 £12.90. CSF £26.29 CT £164.25 TOTE £3.70: £1.80, £2.30, £3.10; EX 29.00 TRIFECTA Not won..
Owner Miss B Swire **Bred** Miss B Swire **Trained** East Ilsley, Berks
■ Stewards' Enquiry : Travis Block three-day ban: careless riding (Sep 3-4, 6)

FOCUS
This looked a seriously complex puzzle, with a sizeable field of closely-matched fillies. The form looks modest with the runner-up pretty exposed at this sort of level.
Action Girl Official explanation: jockey said filly suffered interference in back straight

5196 FOREST ROW CONDITIONS STKS — 6f (P)

4:25 (4:25) (Class 2) 3-Y-O+ — **£12,952** (£3,854; £1,926; £962) **Stalls** Low

Form — RPR

-203 **1** **Ancien Regime (IRE)**[19] 4516 4-9-0 105 .... LDettori 3 — 97+
(Saeed Bin Suroor) *mde all: rdn and drew clr over 1f out: styd on wl fnl f* **6/4**[1]

1050 **2** *1 ½* **Judd Street**[19] 4523 7-9-7 102 .... (v) ShaneKelly 6 — 97+
(Eve Johnson Houghton) *hld up in tch in midfield: lost pl and rdn jst over 2f out: nt clr run and swtchd rt 1f out: r.o fnl f to go 2nd nr fin: no ch w wnr* **20/1**

22-0 **3** *nk* **Cat Junior (USA)**[145] 1008 4-9-0 115 .... (t) DarryllHolland 7 — 89+
(B J Meehan) *dwlt: sn niggled along in last trio: pushed along and hdwy on outer 3f out: drvn and edgd lft over 1f out: chsd clr wnr fnl 100yds: no imp and lost 2nd nr fin* **7/2**[3]

1202 **4** *½* **Eisteddfod**[19] 4516 8-9-3 103 .... (b) GeorgeBaker 8 — 90
(P F I Cole) *pressed wnr: ev ch whn hung rt bnd ent fnl 2f: sn lost 2nd and one pce after* **10/1**

254- **5** *½* **Corrybrough**[341] 5891 4-9-0 110 .... DaneO'Neill 5 — 86+
(H Candy) *dwlt: rcvrd to chse ldrs over 4f out: rdn to chse clr wnr wl over 1f out: no imp and lost 3 pls fnl 100yds* **5/2**[2]

6432 **6** *½* **Louphole**[29] 4203 7-9-0 64 .... RobertHavlin 2 — 84?
(J R Jenkins) *stdd s: hld up in rr: rdn and effrt whn nt clr run over 1f out tl 1f out: kpt on same pce and no imp fnl f* **66/1**

0-10 **7** *1 ¼* **King's Wonder**[22] 4423 4-9-0 90 .... JimCrowley 4 — 80
(W R Muir) *chsd ldrs: racd awkwardly and unable qck bnd jst over 2f out: no prog fr over 1f out* **25/1**

4000 **8** *4 ½* **Matsunosuke**[5] 5039 7-9-7 109 .... LPKeniry 1 — 73
(A B Coogan) *hld up in last pair: rdn and effrt on inner wl over 1f out: no prog and wl btn fnl f* **16/1**

69.87 secs (-2.03) **Going Correction** -0.075s/f (Stan) course record **8** Ran SP% **115.9**
Speed ratings (Par 109): **110,108,107,106,106 105,103,97**
toteswingers: 1&2 £7.50, 1&3 £2.90, 2&3 £14.50. CSF £36.21 TOTE £2.10: £1.10, £3.90, £1.40; EX 35.50 Trifecta £194.00 Pool: £734.40 - 2.80 winning units..
Owner Godolphin **Bred** Deer Forest Stud **Trained** Newmarket, Suffolk

FOCUS
Decent prize-money attracted an interesting field and, while not all the runners were in obviously blinding form, the majority had something in their records to recommend them to punters. The form looks a bit muddling and the winner didn't need to be at his best to score.

NOTEBOOK
Ancien Regime(IRE) has not always looked straightforward, often hanging and sometimes taking a very strong hold, but he is a winner at Group 3 level and possesses plenty of raw ability. He was given a beautifully forthright ride by Frankie Dettori here, breaking smartly, grabbing a position close to the inside rail, and making virtually all the running without ever being given the chance to wander off a true line. (op 5-4)
Judd Street, three times a course winner on this surface, including at this distance, had shown by landing a Listed prize at Salisbury in June that he is still a very able performer. He had to give weight away to all bar one of is rivals, which looked a big ask but, astutely partnered by Shane Kelly, he made stealthy progress on the wide outside in the home straight to pass several tiring rivals. (tchd 25-1)
Cat Junior(USA) came here with easily the highest official rating, but his 115 mark was earned for races at 1m or longer on turf, and this greater test of speed, staged on an artificial surface, meant he was facing a very different set of circumstances. He ran well in defeat, however, staying on in the closing stages while others were fading, and, on this evidence, he might be worth another try on this surface, even if a step back up in distance would probably help him. (op 13-2 tchd 7-1)
Eisteddfod, two of whose 11 career victories have been achieved over this trip on Polytrack, had beaten Ancien Regime on soft ground at Doncaster at the beginning of the month. He faced a tough task on official ratings, nonetheless, not being assisted by having to carry a penalty for a class 3 victory at Kempton in March, and he performed as well as could be expected for an eight-year-old, chasing the pace from the outset but finding the first three too strong in the closing stages. (op 8-1)
Corrybrough developed into a smart sprinter as a three-year-old, winning at Listed level and then holding his own against Group 1 company, and, while this was his first race of the season and his initial try on Polytrack, he looked a worthy contender. His trainer warned beforehand that he might need the race though, as he is a big horse who had suffered an injury in the spring, and he ran like a horse in need of the outing, mounting a short-lived challenge off the home turn but fading inside the final furlong. (op 9-4 tchd 2-1)

5197 HARTFIELD H'CAP — 5f (P)

5:00 (5:01) (Class 4) (0-85,84) 3-Y-O+ — **£6,476** (£1,927; £963; £481) **Stalls** High

Form — RPR

00 **1** **Wotashirtfull (IRE)**[18] 4567 4-9-5 **80** .... (p) PatCosgrave 8 — 89
(J R Boyle) *led: rdn and c towards centre wl over 1f out: hdd narrowly ins fnl f: rallied gamely to ld on post* **7/2**[2]

632 **2** *nse* **Garstang**[6] 4978 6-8-13 **74** .... (b) IanMongan 7 — 83
(J Balding) *chsd ldrs: rdn to chal over 1f out: led narrowly ins fnl f tl hdd on post* **7/4**[1]

6060 **3** *3* **Chjimes (IRE)**[8] 4891 5-9-9 **84** .... LPKeniry 6 — 82
(C R Dore) *sn niggled along in last pl: rdn and hdwy 2f out: chsd ldng pair jst ins fnl f: no imp* **9/2**[3]

2050 **4** *1 ¾* **Pocket's Pick (IRE)**[36] 3989 3-8-9 **72** .... (b[1]) FergusSweeney 10 — 64
(G L Moore) *w ldr tl jst over 2f out: outpcd u.p wl over 1f out: btn jst over 1f out* **12/1**

3-P5 **5** *2 ¾* **The Magic Of Rio**[12] 4776 3-9-3 **80** .... JamieMackay 4 — 62
(Peter Grayson) *chsd ldrs tl lost pl 1/2-way: no prog u.p wl over 1f out: no ch fnl f* **16/1**

004- **6** *2 ½* **Asaint Needs Brass (USA)**[357] 5422 3-9-6 **83** .... RobertWinston 9 — 56
(J R Best) *in tch towards rr: hung rt bnd and bhd jst over 2f out: no ch after* **8/1**

58.08 secs (-0.72) **Going Correction** -0.075s/f (Stan)
WFA 3 from 4yo+ 2lb — **6** Ran SP% **101.5**
Speed ratings (Par 105): **102,101,97,94,89 85**
toteswingers: 1&2 £1.80, 1&3 £2.70, 2&3 £1.90. CSF £8.10 CT £16.02 TOTE £3.70: £3.70, £1.20; EX 7.50 Trifecta £20.70 Pool: £195.96 - 7.00 winning units. Place 6: £12.81, Place 5: £9.29.
Owner M Khan X2 **Bred** Luke O'Reilly **Trained** Epsom, Surrey

FOCUS
Just a run-of-the-mill sprint handicap, weakened considerably by the absence of two of the 48-hour declarations and the late withdrawal of Fromsong, and few in the line-up had any recent form worth shouting about. Straightforward form to rate, with the winner rated to his best and the runner-up rated close to his latest Kempton effort.
Wotashirtfull(IRE) Official explanation: trainer said, regarding apparent improvement in form, that the gelding appeared to benefit from the removal of visor.
Asaint Needs Brass(USA) Official explanation: jockey said colt hung right on bend
T/Plt: £24.10 to a £1 stake. Pool: £33,122.68. 999.54 winning tickets. T/Qpdt: £13.50 to a £1 stake. Pool: £2,815.82. 153.80 winning tickets. SP

5170 YORK (L-H)

Thursday, August 20

OFFICIAL GOING: Good to firm (8.6)
The rail had been moved out three yards from 1m1f to the entrance to the home straight and that added seven yards to distances of 1m and over.
Wind: Fresh 1/2 behind Weather: Overcast and breezy

5198 DBS £300000 ST LEGER YEARLING STKS — 6f

1:45 (1:47) (Class 2) 2-Y-O

£147,720 (£59,100; £29,550; £14,760; £7,380; £7,380) **Stalls** High

Form — RPR

4411 **1** **Midnight Martini**[19] 4547 2-8-6 84 .... DavidAllan 13 — 89
(T D Easterby) *w ldr: led over 1f out: hld on towards fin* **18/1**

020 **2** *nk* **Carnaby Street (IRE)**[8] 4900 2-8-11 0 .... EddieAhern 18 — 93
(R Hannon) *lw: trckd ldrs: upsides on wl ins fnl f: no ex nr fin* **50/1**

2 **3** *nk* **Sole Power**[25] 4357 2-8-11 0 .... PJSmullen 7 — 92
(Edward Lynam, Ire) *chsd ldrs: hmpd over 1f out: kpt on wl ins fnl f* **16/1**

1033 **4** *¾* **Swilly Ferry (USA)**[2] 5136 2-8-11 83 .... MichaelHills 14 — 90
(B W Hills) *in rr: hdwy over 2f out: kpt on wl fnl f* **20/1**

13 **5** *½* **Falasteen (IRE)**[13] 4752 2-8-11 90 .... AdrianTNicholls 19 — 89
(D Nicholls) *led tl over 1f out: kpt on same pce* **16/1**

232 **6** *½* **Red Badge (IRE)**[23] 4410 2-8-11 82 .... RyanMoore 8 — 89+
(R Hannon) *lw: mid-div: hdwy over 2f out: nt clr run: swtchd lft wl ins fnl f: fin full of running* **11/1**

1026 **7** *½* **Kingdom Of Light**[19] 4547 2-8-11 88 .... FrederikTylicki 4 — 86
(J Howard Johnson) *w ldrs towards far side: one pce fnl f* **33/1**

1131 **8** *½* **Sir Parky (IRE)**[33] 4086 2-9-0 94 .... RichardHughes 20 — 87
(R Hannon) *lw: mid-div and sn drvn along: hdwy over 2f out: hung lft: one pce whn sltly hmpd ins fnl f* **9/1**[3]

231 **9** *2 ½* **Bonfire Knight**[16] 4618 2-8-11 76 .... GrahamGibbons 9 — 77
(J J Quinn) *in tch: wl outpcd over 2f out: styd on wl fnl f* **66/1**

4121 **10** *¾* **Layla's Hero (IRE)**[13] 4739 2-8-11 83 .... JamieSpencer 6 — 75+
(D Nicholls) *chsd ldrs: drvn over 2f out: no imp whn nt clr run over 1f out: eased fnl strides* **9/1**[3]

4132 **11** *1 ½* **Di Stefano**[48] 3583 2-8-11 97 .... JimmyFortune 15 — 70
(M R Channon) *mid-div: sn drvn along: nvr a factor* **7/1**[2]

210 **12** *1* **Alrasm (IRE)**[65] 2993 2-8-11 87 .... RHills 1 — 67
(M A Jarvis) *lw: chsd ldrs on outside: wknd appr fnl f* **11/1**

0162 **13** *4* **Butch And Sundance**[8] 4901 2-8-11 81 .... (b[1]) MartinDwyer 10 — 55
(B J Meehan) *sn bhd: nvr on terms* **25/1**

2 **14** *1* **Kings Bayonet**[30] 4176 2-8-11 0 TPQueally 11 52
(H R A Cecil) *sn outpcd and in rr* **18/1**
3155 **15** *2 1/2* **Ghostwing**[20] 4487 2-8-11 97 (p) PaulHanagan 5 44
(R A Fahey) *sn in rr and drvn along* **14/1**
15 **16** *2 3/4* **Schoolboy Champ**[13] 4746 2-8-11 80 MJKinane 17 36
(Patrick Morris) *hld up towards rr: nvr a factor* **66/1**
3421 **17** *1 1/2* **Makbullet**[17] 4595 2-8-11 80 PhillipMakin 2 32
(J Howard Johnson) *a towards rr* **66/1**
3060 **18** *nse* **Kirsty's Boy (IRE)**[33] 4089 2-8-11 82 DO'Donohoe 16 31
(J S Moore) *sn detached in rr* **100/1**
15 **19** *nk* **Monalini (IRE)**[13] 4752 2-8-11 83 TomEaves 3 30
(B Smart) *a in rr: bhd fnl 2f* **40/1**
1 **U** **Rodrigo De Torres**[26] 4331 2-8-11 0 NCallan 12 78+
(A P Jarvis) *lw: chsd ldrs: effrt over 2f out: hung lft: 9th and wl hld whn bdly hmpd and uns rdr nr line* **3/1**[1]

1m 10.9s (-1.00) **Going Correction** -0.225s/f (Firm) **20** Ran SP% **124.5**
Speed ratings (Par 100): **97,96,96,95,94 93,93,92,89,88 86,84,79,78,74 71,69,69,68,—**
toteswingers: 1&2 £172.30, 1&3 £62.10, 2&3 £111.90. CSF £761.67 TOTE £20.20: £4.70, £13.00, £5.30; EX 1931.40 TRIFECTA Not won..
Owner D A West **Bred** Helescane Stud **Trained** Great Habton, N Yorks
■ Stewards' Enquiry : Ryan Moore eight-day ban: careless riding (Sep 3-10)

FOCUS
This richly-endowed sales race attracted the usual mixed bag of juveniles, with none obviously fitting the usual trends required to succeed coming into the race, though plenty were open to improvement. It was a good-looking field on paddock inspection and as the gates opened the runners elected to shun the stands' rail, congregating in the centre of the track. The form looks unlikely to prove that strong, with the fourth helping to set the level.

NOTEBOOK
Midnight Martini deserves real credit considering no filly had been successful since the inaugural running of this race in 1998 and she was the only female in attendance. Never far away from what proved to be a decent draw, she found the required extra gear when kicking for home nearing the final furlong. Her honest attitude counted for plenty nearing the business end and she just held off the runner-up at the line. She came into this with a progressive profile having won a moderate Carlisle maiden in June and then a nursery off a mark of 77 at Thirsk on her previous outing 19 days previously. This was her first run on ground this quick and it clearly helped bring about this much-improved display. It was also just her second outing over the extra furlong and that also suited, though she was tying up near the finish so may not prove as happy over a stiffer 6f at present, despite being related to winners over further. While this event has thrown up two Group 1 winners in its history so far, and two other winners at Group level, this daughter of Night Shift still has to convince she is up to maintaining the trend (holds no big-race entries at present) as the overall form looks average. That is not to say there is still some more to come from her, however, and a try at Listed company could be on the cards. (op 16-1)
Carnaby Street(IRE), representing last year's winning connections, motored home inside the final furlong but the line came that bit too soon. He looked the stable's third string on jockey bookings, but had to be forgiven his latest effort at Salisbury when jumping a cross-section and is clearly an improving sprinter.
Sole Power, an Irish challenger, bumped into the smart Walk On Bye on debut and then ran second to a very promising sort in Listed company. He threw down the biggest challenge to the winner inside the final furlong, but could not get past, try as he might, and lost second in the dying strides. Despite being a maiden he rates the most positive benchmark for the form and should make up into a smart sprinter as he matures.
Swilly Ferry(USA) finished strongly at this meeting two days earlier and did so again, but his effort earlier in the week came in nursery company off a mark of 83 so he does not do a great deal for the form. That said he is evidently a tough sort in decent heart at present. (tchd 22-1)
Falasteen(IRE) led the field down the middle of the track and kept on gamely when headed by the winner. He is the sort his trainer does so well with, so remains one to keep on side. (op 20-1)
Red Badge(IRE) lacked the natural pace to race handily through the early stages, but showed a good attitude and finished with plenty left in the tank. He went left near the finish, however, and tightened up Rodrigo De Torres, which caused that rival to clip heels and unseat his rider before the line. Jockey Ryan Moore was later handed an eight-day ban for careless riding. (op 10-1)
Kingdom Of Light showed decent early speed on the far side and ran an improved race, but still has to really prove he gets this longer distance.
Sir Parky(IRE) faced a stiff task considering no penalised runner has ever taken this event. He is not easy to place now. (op 8-1)
Bonfire Knight was never a serious threat, but finished with purpose after being outpaced and wasn't suited by this drop back in trip. He is one to side with when stepping back up a furlong.
Layla's Hero(IRE) Official explanation: jockey said, regarding riding, that he stopped riding momentarily due to interference taking place in front of him
Di Stefano set the standard on his last two placings in Listed company and seemed likely to appreciate the step up to this trip. He put in a laboured display after being ridden to get the trip, though, and was keeping on too late before finding a bit of trouble at the furlong marker. This leaves him with something to prove. (op 15-2)
Alrasm(IRE) was last seen running down the field in the Coventry Stakes, but he was edgy beforehand and posted a tame effort on the far side. He was later reported to have been unsuited by the ground. Official explanation: jockey said colt was unsuited by the good to firm ground (tchd 12-1)
Ghostwing, who had finished fifth in Group races the last twice, looked thoroughly disinterested in the first-time cheekpieces and has to rate very disappointing. Official explanation: jockey said colt never travelled (tchd 16-1 in a place)
Rodrigo De Torres was very well backed on the strength of his taking debut success over C&D 26 days earlier, despite that form not looking strong. No juvenile had won this on the back of one run in the past, however, and it was experience that probably found him out here as he was beaten before being hampered. His big-race entries suggest that he is not one to be writing off yet. (op 100-30 tchd 7-2 and 4-1 in places)

5199 JAGUAR CARS LOWTHER STKS (GROUP 2) (FILLIES) 6f
2:15 (2:20) (Class 1) 2-Y-O
£56,770 (£21,520; £10,770; £5,370; £2,690; £1,350) **Stalls** High

Form RPR
161 **1** **Lady Of The Desert (USA)**[26] 4295 2-8-12 104 MartinDwyer 8 112+
(B J Meehan) *trckd overall ldr stands' side: led over 2f out: shkn up 1f out: sn qcknd clr* **13/8**[1]
1 **2** *3* **Beyond Desire**[22] 4421 2-8-12 0 NCallan 4 103+
(M A Jarvis) *lw: swtchd centre after 1f: trckd ldrs: led centre over 2f out: edgd rt and wnt overall 2nd 1f out: kpt on but no ch w wnr* **10/3**[2]
05 **3** *2 1/4* **Dubawi Heights**[27] 4272 2-8-12 0 JMurtagh 10 96
(S A Callaghan) *lw: overall ldrs stands' side: hdd over 2f out: kpt on same pce fnl f* **40/1**
1 **4** *2 1/2* **Puff (IRE)**[36] 3987 2-8-12 0 SebSanders 7 89
(R M Beckett) *chsd ldrs: swtchd centre after 1f: drvn over 2f out: kpt on same pce* **14/1**
136 **5** *1 1/4* **Chachamaidee (IRE)**[12] 4795 2-8-12 98 TPQueally 6 85
(H R A Cecil) *in rr stands' side: styd on fnl 2f: nvr nr ldrs* **17/2**
24 **6** *7* **Gold Bubbles (USA)**[14] 4726 2-8-12 0 (p) KJManning 1 64
(J S Bolger, Ire) *chsd ldrs far side: drvn over 2f out: lost pl over 1f out* **8/1**[3]
101 **7** *nk* **Rose Blossom**[49] 3528 2-8-12 91 PaulHanagan 9 63
(R A Fahey) *lw: t.k.h: trckd ldrs: swtchd centre after 1f: led that gp over 3f out: hdd over 2f out: wknd over 1f out* **8/1**[3]
3540 **8** *4 1/2* **Little Scotland**[43] 3748 2-8-12 90 AlanMunro 5 50
(T D Easterby) *chsd ldrs centre: drvn over 2f out: wknd over 1f out* **33/1**
0102 **9** *1 1/4* **Raddy 'Ell Pauline (IRE)**[13] 4752 2-8-12 86 RyanMoore 12 46
(K A Ryan) *chsd ldrs stands' side: outpcd over 3f out: wknd 2f out* **25/1**
6344 **10** *2 1/4* **Lady Lube Rye (IRE)**[9] 4875 2-8-12 67 DuranFentiman 2 39
(N Wilson) *led far side gp tl over 3f out: lost pl over 1f out* **150/1**
622 **11** *1 1/4* **Mad Millie (IRE)**[17] 4595 2-8-12 68 SilvestreDeSousa 11 35
(J Hetherton) *chsd ldrs stands' side: lost pl over 2f out: edgd lft and sn bhd* **100/1**
2 **12** *13* **Nimue (USA)**[22] 4421 2-8-12 0 RichardHughes 3 —+
(P F I Cole) *gave problems in stalls: hld up centre: lost pl over 1f out: sn heavily eased* **12/1**

69.34 secs (-2.56) **Going Correction** -0.225s/f (Firm) 2y crse rec **12** Ran SP% **119.2**
Speed ratings (Par 103): **108,104,101,97,96 86,86,80,78,75 73,56**
toteswingers: 1&2 £2.80, 1&3 £22.40, 2&3 £32.30. CSF £6.52 TOTE £2.90: £1.50, £1.90, £9.30; EX 8.30 Trifecta £758.00 Pool: £1,639.09 - 1.60 winning units..
Owner Jaber Abdullah **Bred** Rabbah Bloodstock Llc **Trained** Manton, Wilts

FOCUS
Not a great deal of depth to this Group 2, but it produced a very smart performance from a filly who is well up to the standard of recent winners. The field split into two fairly loose groups early on, with five remaining near the stands' rail, although some of those who raced down the centre came over to the rail in the latter stages. The pace was strong and the winning time was only fractionally outside the 2yo track record set by Showcasing the previous day. The form looks solid with the winner, who looks more of a sprinter than a miler, impressing, and the second and third posting improved efforts.

NOTEBOOK
Lady Of The Desert(USA) was taken to race down the stands' side and she always travelled strongly, given a lead by the third. She was in front in her group before halfway and quickened away in taking style in the last quarter mile to slam her field and emulate her dam, who won this race in 2001. Her only defeat in four starts now came in the Queen Mary at the Royal meeting, where she was probably second best on merit but paid for trying to race with the American speedball Jealous Again, and she got back on track upped to 6f at Ascot in the Princess Margaret. She is now a general 10/1 shot for next year's Stan James 1000 Guineas, and connections believe that she will stay the mile. The last Lowther winner to take the Guineas was Russian Rhythm in 2002/03, who had also won the Princess Margaret. Lady Of The Desert's autumn target will be the Cheveley Park Stakes at Newmarket, and she will take plenty of beating. (op 15-8 tchd 2-1)
Beyond Desire lacked the experience of the favourite having won a maiden at Glorious Goodwood on her only previous start. She ran a fine race, showing prominently near the centre before edging over towards the rail in fruitless pursuit of the winner. Connections are ready to take on Lady Of The Desert again in the Cheveley Park and there is further improvement in her. (op 3-1 tchd 7-2)
Dubawi Heights, withdrawn from her last intended start at Thirsk when trying to break out from the stalls, could not race on with the winner in the last 2f but kept going for a most creditable third. She may have been a little flattered by racing on the favoured stands' rail, but this was still a useful effort. She may try to win a maiden now, which ought to be a formalilty. (op 50-1)
Puff(IRE) ran well, sticking on for fourth having raced with the centre-field group before, like the runner-up, making for the stands' side in the latter stages. She had won a Polytrack maiden on her sole previous start and this was a fine effort upped in grade. (op 16-1)
Chachamaidee(IRE), who pulled too hard upped to 7f last time, stayed on from the rear after a slightly slow start here and could be worth trying again over the longer trip. (op 9-1 tchd 8-1)
Gold Bubbles(USA) was fourth to ante-post Guineas favourite Lillie Langtry last time and she did not build on that form here, but she was trapped on the outside of the centre group from her low draw and that looked a disadvantage. (op 9-1 tchd 10-1)
Rose Blossom finished a place behind Lady Of The Desert in the Queen Mary and has since landed a minor event at Haydock. After being switched to race down the centre of the track, she showed early pace here but was labouring and well held in the last 2f. (op 7-1)
Nimue(USA), runner-up to Beyond Desire on her debut at Goodwood, dropped away tamely and was eased right down inside the final furlong. She is better than she showed. Official explanation: jockey said filly never travelled and felt amiss (tchd 11-1 and 14-1)

5200 ADDLESHAW GODDARD STKS (HERITAGE H'CAP) 1m
2:50 (2:52) (Class 2) 3-Y-0+
£32,380 (£9,635; £4,815; £2,405) **Stalls** Low

Form RPR
1-10 **1** **Roaring Forte (IRE)**[26] 4297 4-9-0 99 JMurtagh 14 111
(W J Haggas) *lw: led tl 4f out: led over 1f out: edgd rt ins fnl f: hld on wl: uns rdr pulling up* **8/1**[3]
0100 **2** *2* **Alazeyab (USA)**[21] 4455 3-8-9 100 RHills 5 106
(M A Jarvis) *lw: w wnr: led 4f out tl over 1f out: styd on same pce ins fnl f* **20/1**
4416 **3** *nse* **Acrostic**[20] 4486 4-9-1 100 RichardHughes 11 107
(L M Cumani) *trckd ldrs: styd on wl ins fnl f: no ex towards fin* **5/1**[2]
4024 **4** *4 1/2* **Webbow (IRE)**[20] 4486 7-8-3 93 Louis-PhilippeBeuzelin(5) 7 89
(N Tinkler) *lw: s.i.s: hdwy 6f out: chsng ldrs over 3f out: nt clr run 2f out: kpt on one pce* **10/1**
-364 **5** *nse* **Scuffle**[12] 4794 4-8-12 97 SteveDrowne 8 93+
(R Charlton) *mid-div: effrt over 3f out: styd on wl fnl f* **20/1**
-555 **6** *3/4* **Alfathaa**[23] 4404 4-9-2 101 TPO'Shea 13 95
(W J Haggas) *rr-div: hdwy stands' side 3f out: styd on: nt rch ldrs* **20/1**
0335 **7** *1/2* **Docofthebay (IRE)**[12] 4768 5-8-13 98 (p) TPQueally 9 91
(J A Osborne) *hld up in rr: hdwy over 3f out: sn chsng ldrs: one pce fnl 2f* **20/1**
0352 **8** *1* **Kay Gee Be (IRE)**[19] 4543 5-8-7 92 AlanMunro 6 83
(W Jarvis) *chsd ldrs: fdd fnl f* **25/1**
4605 **9** *3* **Lovelace**[20] 4486 5-9-10 109 JamieSpencer 16 92+
(M Johnston) *hld up in rr: hdwy over 2f out: nt clr run over 1f out: nvr a factor* **8/1**[3]
3230 **10** *3/4* **Mia's Boy**[22] 4419 5-9-6 105 JimmyFortune 15 87
(C A Dwyer) *in rr: hdwy 4f out: lost pl over 1f out* **16/1**
1460 **11** *1/2* **Charlie Cool**[12] 4781 6-8-11 96 (t) SilvestreDeSousa 17 76
(Mrs R A Carr) *in rr: drvn 4f out: nvr on terms* **33/1**
0224 **12** *nk* **Flipando (IRE)**[12] 4779 8-8-11 96 PhillipMakin 10 76
(T D Barron) *in rr: sme hdwy over 1f out: nvr on terms* **20/1**
1000 **13** *hd* **Extraterrestrial**[20] 4486 5-8-12 97 PaulHanagan 3 76
(R A Fahey) *mid-div: hdwy over 3f out: lost pl 2f out* **25/1**
240 **14** *1 1/4* **Huzzah (IRE)**[20] 4486 4-8-13 98 MichaelHills 18 74
(B W Hills) *trckd ldrs on outer: t.k.h: lost pl over 2f out* **25/1**
1000 **15** *2 1/2* **Fishforcompliments**[19] 4523 5-8-7 95 (p) FrederikTylicki(3) 19 65
(R A Fahey) *chsd ldrs: wknd over 1f out* **50/1**
/120 **16** *1* **Captain Brilliance (USA)**[26] 4297 4-9-2 101 SebSanders 1 69
(J Noseda) *lw: chsd ldrs: wknd over 1f out* **12/1**
1333 **17** *1* **Mirrored**[21] 4455 3-8-9 100 RyanMoore 2 64
(Sir Michael Stoute) *trckd ldrs: rdn 3f out: sn btn* **4/1**[1]
5400 **18** *nse* **Wise Dennis**[27] 4261 7-8-12 97 MJKinane 12 62
(A P Jarvis) *a towards rr* **50/1**

-265 19 2 ½ **Patrician's Glory (USA)**[49] 3536 3-8-12 **103**................ MickyFenton 20 61
(T P Tate) *a in rr: hung rt and bhd fnl 2f* **40/1**

1m 36.65s (-2.15) **Going Correction** +0.175s/f (Good)
WFA 3 from 4yo+ 6lb **19** Ran SP% **126.2**
Speed ratings (Par 109): **117,115,114,110,110 109,109,108,105,104 103,103,103,102,99 98,97,97,95**
toteswingers: 1&2 £46.30, 1&3 £11.20, 2&3 £36.30. CSF £161.68 CT £917.46 TOTE £8.90: £2.40, £5.70, £2.20, £2.60; EX 225.30 Trifecta £2470.20 Part won. Pool: £3,338.12 - 0.50 winning units..
Owner Flying Tiger Partnership **Bred** Grangecon Stud **Trained** Newmarket, Suffolk

FOCUS
A strong race featuring mostly exposed handicappers. There was a solid enough gallop on but nothing got seriously involved from off the pace and the first three were always to the fore. The field also elected to come down the middle of the home straight and avoid the far rail.

NOTEBOOK
Roaring Forte(IRE) was a bitter disappointment at Ascot last month but he showed his true colours again here under his usual aggressive tactics, and ran out a gutsy winner. He helped cut out the pace and did well to get across from his wide stall. His response when asked to quicken up 2f out was immediate and that move proved to be a winning one. Although two of his three previous wins were over 7f, this step up in trip looked to make the difference to him and he is no doubt a Pattern performer in the making. There are no solid plans for him, but a step up in class may beckon. (op 17-2 tchd 9-1)

Alazeyab(USA) fared best of the three-year-olds and returned to his best after two below-par efforts over further on his two previous outings. He too cut out the running and was certainly at an advantage in doing so, but he still kept on resolutely when headed by the winner to hold on for second. He is high enough in the weights, but the Cambridgeshire should be right up his street.

Acrostic took time to settle but still had his chance and posted a solid effort in defeat, reversing form with those in front of him at Goodwood last time out. He probably prefers a stiffer test over this trip and is another for whom the Cambridgeshire will surely come into serious consideration. (tchd 11-2)

Webbow(IRE), in front of Acrostic at Goodwood 20 days earlier, was 3lb higher and did not help his cause with a tardy start. He still confirmed his current wellbeing with a decent effort and did best of those coming from off the pace. He goes really well here and rates a decent benchmark. (tchd 11-1)

Scuffle, 2lb lower, kept on at the same pace down the home straight and would very probably have fared better under a more prominent ride on this drop in trip. It was still another encouraging effort considering it was her second run back from a break and she is probably capable of defying this mark.

Alfathaa was again given plenty to do and he stayed on well down the near side, but the race hardly unfolded to his liking. He is not proving easy to get right, but remains in decent form and is another who will enjoy returning to a stiffer test. (op 16-1)

Docofthebay(IRE) also stayed on strongly from way off the pace and this was better, but he remains one to avoid for win-only betting. (op 25-1)

Kay Gee Be(IRE) was never far away from a good draw, but proved free and that blunted his finished effort. A drop in grade can see him fare better.

Lovelace, who got no run at Goodwood last time, again got going all too late from off the pace and deserves to be ridden more positively in his races.

Huzzah(IRE) Official explanation: jockey said colt ran too free

Captain Brilliance(USA) also flopped in the same race as Roaring Forte at Ascot last month, when hanging, and he was 3lb higher for this. It was his first outing over this extra furlong, but he was beaten before stamina came into play and something may have gone amiss with him. (op 14-1)

Mirrored simply failed to quicken when asked for maximum effort and probably needs more use made of him over a sharp 1m, but this was very disappointing all the same. Official explanation: trainer's rep had no explanation for the poor form shown (op 9-2 tchd 5-1 in a place)

Patrician's Glory(USA) Official explanation: jockey said colt hung right

5201 DARLEY YORKSHIRE OAKS (GROUP 1) (F&M) 1m 4f
3:25 (3:26) (Class 1) 3-Y-O+

£175,987 (£66,712; £33,387; £16,647; £8,339; £4,185) **Stalls** Centre

Form				RPR
3-21	**1**		**Dar Re Mi**[54] 3412 4-9-7 114 .... JimmyFortune 4 (J H M Gosden) *trckd ldrs: smooth hdwy 3f out: rdn to ld jst ins fnl f: hld on wl* **11/2**[2]	119
4111	**2**	¾	**Sariska**[39] 3896 3-8-11 120 .... JamieSpencer 6 (M L W Bell) *lw: hld up towards rr: hdwy 4f out: sn chsng ldrs: rdn over 1f out: styd on same pce ins fnl f* **4/11**[1]	118
6652	**3**	1 ½	**Roman Empress (IRE)**[8] 4923 3-8-11 93 .... JAHeffernan 5 (A P O'Brien, Ire) *lw: trckd ldr: chal over 2f out: sn rdn: styd on same pce fnl f* **40/1**	115
5114	**4**	1	**Barshiba (IRE)**[19] 4522 5-9-7 110 .... RyanMoore 3 (D R C Elsworth) *lw: led: rdn 2f out: kpt on wl: hdd jst ins fnl f: no ex* **12/1**	114
51	**5**	7	**Tamarind (IRE)**[17] 4609 3-8-11 105 .... JMurtagh 2 (A P O'Brien, Ire) *leggy: chsd ldrs: effrt 4f out: sn rdn wknd over 1f out* **11/1**[3]	103
3-50	**6**	6	**Saphira's Fire (IRE)**[19] 4522 4-9-7 100 .... MartinDwyer 1 (W R Muir) *lw: hld up in last: drvn over 3f out: nvr on terms* **50/1**	93

2m 30.98s (-2.22) **Going Correction** +0.175s/f (Good)
WFA 3 from 4yo+ 10lb **6** Ran SP% **109.1**
Speed ratings (Par 117): **114,113,112,111,107 103**
toteswingers: 1&2 £1.40, 1&3 £11.10, 2&3 £4.70. CSF £7.49 TOTE £5.00: £2.60, £1.02; EX 11.20.
Owner Lord Lloyd-Webber **Bred** Watership Down Stud **Trained** Newmarket, Suffolk
■ Stewards' Enquiry : Jimmy Fortune one-day ban: used whip in incorrect place (Sep 3)

FOCUS
This did not appear a vintage renewal of this Group 1 event, with Look Here and last year's winner Lush Lashes perhaps the most notable absentees. The way looked clear for Sariska to emulate the likes of User Friendly, Ramruma and Alexandrova in adding Yorkshire's version to her Epsom and Curragh Oaks victories, but instead the warm favourite became the sixth Epsom heroine since 1997 - the others were Reams Of Verse, Shahtoush, Love Divine, Kazzia, Casual Look and Eswarah - to be beaten here. It has been rated as an ordinary renewal, with the runner-up rated to her Musidora form.

NOTEBOOK
Dar Re Mi sat in fourth spot in a race run at a solid pace and was going better than Sariska at the two pole. She got past the long-time leader Barshiba entering the last and, staying on strongly, was always holding the favourite. This notably game and genuine filly was runner-up to Lush Lashes in this event a year ago when it was switched to the July course, and had gained Group 1 honours last time in the Pretty Polly at the Curragh. She appreciated the return to 1m4f here and will now head for the the Prix Vermeille, in which she was no match for Zarkava last year, and where she could well meet the brilliant Prix de Diane winner Stacelita this time round. Should things go her way there are ambitious autumn plans for her, with the Arc, the Breeders' Cup Filly and Mare Turf and a very valuable distaff race in Japan all possibilities for this admirable filly. (op 5-1 tchd 6-1 in a place)

Sariska, settled in fifth and seemingly travelling well, came off the bridle with over 2f to run and it quickly became apparent that she was in trouble. Still only fourth approaching the final furlong, she stayed on for Spencer's driving and reached the winner's quarters, but that was as close as she got. There had been a bit of doubt over her participation here before the track was watered and it certainly looks as if she is best with some cut, her incredibly easy Irish Oaks win having come in heavy ground, but she won the Musidora here on similarly fast going and connections were reluctant to blame the conditions, and it later emerged that she had come into season. This was her first run against older horses, and she came up against a very tough four-year-old who was too strong on the day. She may still go for the Arc if the ground is suitable, but would need to be supplemented. Official explanation: trainer said filly was heavily in season (tchd 2-5 and 1-3 in a place)

Roman Empress(IRE), the outsider of the O'Brien pair, had acted as pacemaker when fifth to Tamarind two runs back. She ran an honest race and relished the return to this trip. This half-sister to Derby runner-up The Great Gatsby falls a little short at this level but is a fine broodmare prospect. (op 50-1)

Barshiba(IRE) faced a stiff task against the big guns, but she seemed to appreciate the return to 1m4f after finishing fourth in the Nassau and she battled on well alongside the rail until being headed a furlong or so out.

Tamarind(IRE)'s Cork win came in soft ground when Beach Bunny, who had been short-headed by Dar Re Mi in the Pretty Polly, ran no race in last place. On this sounder surface in much stronger company, she was in trouble with more than 3f to run. She looks to lack scope. (op 14-1)

Saphira's Fire(IRE) continues to fly too high and was struggling in rear once in line for home.

5202 EUROPEAN BREEDERS' FUND GALTRES STKS (LISTED RACE) 1m 4f
4:05 (4:05) (Class 1) 3-Y-O+ **£23,704** (£8,964; £4,480; £2,240) **Stalls** Centre

Form				RPR
3-2	**1**		**Tanoura (IRE)**[67] 2960 3-8-8 101 .... MJKinane 4 (John M Oxx, Ire) *leggy: athletic: hld up in midfield: hdwy on outside to trck ldrs over 5f out: wnt 2nd 1f out: styd on to ld last 75yds* **3/1**[2]	109
1-14	**2**	½	**Leocorno (IRE)**[63] 3047 3-8-8 100 .... RyanMoore 7 (Sir Michael Stoute) *lw: trckd ldrs: t.k.h: led over 2f out: hdd and no ex wl ins fnl f* **11/4**[1]	108
2124	**3**	3 ½	**Flame Of Gibraltar (IRE)**[33] 4094 3-8-8 102 .... TPQueally 2 (H R A Cecil) *lw: hld up in rr: effrt on outside over 3f out: styd on same pce appr fnl f* **8/1**	102+
-605	**4**	nk	**Snoqualmie Girl (IRE)**[70] 2846 3-8-8 93 .... MickyFenton 5 (D R C Elsworth) *hld up in midfield: effrt and swtchd lft over 3f out: kpt on same pce fnl 2f* **40/1**	102
5224	**5**	shd	**Princess Taylor**[21] 4458 5-9-4 96 .... AlanMunro 3 (M Botti) *trckd ldr: led over 3f out: sn hdd: kpt on same pce fnl 2f* **10/1**	102
2322	**6**	1 ½	**Fallen In Love**[18] 4566 3-8-8 102 .... SteveDrowne 9 (J L Dunlop) *lw: trckd ldrs: led 3f out: ssn hdd: one pce* **7/2**[3]	99
2430	**7**	hd	**Starfala**[21] 4458 4-9-4 100 .... EddieAhern 6 (P F I Cole) *mid-div: outpcd and lost pl over 2f out: kpt on wl fnl f* **20/1**	99
4333	**8**	4	**Uvinza**[33] 4094 3-8-8 100 .... JamieSpencer 10 (W J Knight) *lw: led: qcknd over 4f out: hdd over 3f out: wknd 2f out* **14/1**	93
0456	**9**	1 ¼	**Storyland (USA)**[25] 4340 4-9-4 88 .... KirstyMilczarek 1 (W J Haggas) *stl had hood on whn stalls opened: s.s: in rr: drvn over 4f out: nvr on terms* **14/1**	91

2m 32.64s (-0.56) **Going Correction** +0.175s/f (Good)
WFA 3 from 4yo+ 10lb **9** Ran SP% **114.6**
Speed ratings (Par 111): **108,107,105,105,105 104,103,101,100**
toteswingers: 1&2 £2.20, 1&3 £5.70, 2&3 £5.70. CSF £11.59 TOTE £3.60: £1.70, £1.50, £2.10; EX 11.60 Trifecta £72.30 Pool: £1,901.76 - 19.46 winning units..
Owner H H Aga Khan **Bred** Hh Aga Khan's Studs Sc **Trained** Currabeg, Co Kildare

FOCUS
An open running of this fillies' Listed prize, which is a race that often goes the way of a tough and consistent performer. It was a steadily run race, but the first pair came nicely clear and the form still looks sound. It has been rated around the third to her Ribblesdale effort and the fifth to her form.

NOTEBOOK
Tanoura(IRE) deservedly came out on top and was given a well-judged ride by the evergreen Mick Kinane. She proved free when going down by a short-head in a Group 3 at Cork, which was by far her best effort so far, and again took time to settle here. That was due to the lack of early pace, though, and her jockey proved wise to it as he moved her up to hold a prominent position on the turn for home. She took time to hit top gear when the race became serious 3f out, but the further she went the better she looked and she was always going to master the runner-up where it mattered. This was just her second outing at the trip and her first run on ground this quick, so she is clearly a versatile sort. With so few miles on the clock there really ought to be some more to come and a step back up to Group company is now firmly on the cards. (op 11-4 tchd 100-30 in places)

Leocorno(IRE) is another lightly raced filly and was also having her second outing over this distance, having finished fourth in the Ribblesdale when last seen. She too had run freely on her previous start and did so again here, probably down to the moderate early fractions. She still came through to hit the front and held every chance, but simply looked to get outstayed by the winner. She stays the distance, but still seems to be learning her trade and it could be that she is crying out for a drop back to 1m2f. Her pedigree backs that up and it would also allow her the chance to race off a stronger pace. Connections will be very happy with this as she now picks up that all-important black type, but the best of her is probably still to come. (op 3-1 tchd 100-30 and 7-2 in places)

Flame Of Gibraltar(IRE) was two places ahead of the runner-up in the Ribblesdale. She disappointed on her subsequent start, however, and proved very easy to back on this first outing for 33 days. She ultimately shaped as though a stronger pace would have been much more to her liking and this was a step back in the right direction. (op 7-1 tchd 9-1)

Snoqualmie Girl(IRE) was returning from a 70-day break and was ridden to get the trip on this first run beyond 1m2f. She ran with much more encouragement, hitting a flat spot down the centre of the track before keeping on again, and probably ran very close to her previous best. (op 33-1)

Princess Taylor confirmed her last-time-out form with Starfala and did not perform badly considering she would have preferred a stronger pace to chase. She deserves to find another opening.

Fallen In Love, whose stable won the race in 2007, put some real pace into the race around 3f out. She failed to sustain it, though, and was headed not long after, ultimately performing some way below her recent best. (op 4-1 tchd 3-1)

Starfala could have done with a more truly run race on this drop back in trip and was keeping on too late from off the pace.

Uvinza had finished one place behind Princess Talyor and one in front of Flame Of Gibraltar at Newmarket last time out, so it was surprising to see her at such big odds. However, she dropped out tamely after dictating the pace and failed to run her race. (op 20-1)

Storyland(USA) faced a tall order on this step out of handicap company and her cause was made even tougher by the blindfold being taken off after the gates sprung back. Her effort thereafter was most limited, though. (op 16-1)

5203 EVENTMASTERS STKS (H'CAP) 5f
4:40 (4:41) (Class 2) (0-100,99) 3-Y-O **£16,190** (£4,817; £2,407; £1,202) **Stalls** High

Form RPR
1521 **1** **Noble Storm (USA)**[20] 4490 3-9-6 **98** GrahamGibbons 13 109
(E S McMahon) *lw: chsd ldr: led 1f out: rdn and edgd lft: hld on wl towards fin* **9/2**[1]
2-3 **2** ½ **Rain Delayed (IRE)**[56] 3325 3-9-7 **99** JMurtagh 9 108
(G M Lyons, Ire) *chsd ldrs: chal 1f out: crowded ins fnl f: no ex nr fin* **11/2**[2]
5260 **3** 2 **Jargelle (IRE)**[21] 4456 3-9-3 **95** RyanMoore 6 97
(K A Ryan) *led overall in centre: hdd 1f out: kpt on same pce* **16/1**
1122 **4** hd **Mattamia (IRE)**[20] 4490 3-8-13 **94** JamesMillman(3) 8 95+
(B R Millman) *lw: chsd ldrs: outpcd over 2f out: styd on wl fnl f* **8/1**[3]
5243 **5** hd **Green Beret (IRE)**[20] 4490 3-9-3 **95** (v[1]) JimmyFortune 11 96
(J H M Gosden) *lw: chsd ldrs: kpt on same pce appr fnl f* **9/2**[1]
6202 **6** 1 **Lucky Numbers (IRE)**[12] 4776 3-8-7 **85** (b[1]) SilvestreDeSousa 5 82
(Paul Green) *chsd ldrs: kpt on same pce appr fnl f* **14/1**
0010 **7** 2 ¾ **Bajan Tryst (USA)**[25] 4338 3-8-0 **83** (p) Louis-PhilippeBeuzelin(5) 2 70
(K A Ryan) *chsd ldrs on outer: wknd appr fnl f* **66/1**
434- **8** 2 **Go Nani Go**[339] 5969 3-8-7 **85** RichardMullen 7 65
(B Smart) *hld up in rr: styd on fnl 2f: nvr nr ldrs* **33/1**
0020 **9** nk **Lucky Leigh**[6] 4990 3-8-2 **80** PaulHanagan 14 59
(M R Channon) *chsd ldrs stands' side: wknd over 1f out* **25/1**
2101 **10** 1 ¼ **Impressible**[19] 4530 3-8-12 **90** EddieAhern 3 64
(E J Alston) *chsd ldrs centre: fdd fnl f* **8/1**[3]
6300 **11** nk **Fault**[20] 4485 3-8-13 **91** (vt[1]) MickyFenton 15 64
(Stef Liddiard) *lw: in rr stands' side* **20/1**
0104 **12** ¾ **Bahamian Babe**[33] 4099 3-8-10 **88** JamieSpencer 12 59
(M L W Bell) *in tch stands' side: outpcd over 2f out: sn btn* **10/1**
3000 **13** ½ **Favourite Girl (IRE)**[12] 4771 3-9-0 **92** DavidAllan 1 61
(T D Easterby) *mid-div on outer: lost pl over 2f out* **16/1**
3020 **14** 3 **Titus Andronicus (IRE)**[20] 4490 3-8-7 **85** AlanMunro 4 43
(K A Ryan) *dwlt: a in rr* **20/1**
1515 **15** ½ **La Zamora**[20] 4490 3-8-2 **80** oh1 MartinDwyer 10 36
(T D Barron) *dwlt: sn drvn along: a in rr* **12/1**

57.38 secs (-1.92) **Going Correction** -0.225s/f (Firm) **15** Ran SP% **127.0**
Speed ratings (Par 106): **106,105,102,101,101 99,95,92,91,89 89,88,87,82,81**
toteswingers: 1&2 £5.50, 1&3 £24.10, 2&3 £24.00. CSF £27.83 CT £390.17 TOTE £5.60: £2.30, £2.60, £6.40; EX 37.20 Trifecta £1221.40 Pool: £2,145.74 - 1.30 winning units.Place 6: £111.21, Place 5: £8.92..
Owner R L Bedding **Bred** Brereton C Jones **Trained** Lichfield, Staffs
■ Stewards' Enquiry : Graham Gibbons caution: careless riding.
J Murtagh caution: used whip down shoulder.

FOCUS
A cracking 3yo sprint, and strong and very solid form for the grade. Nothing got into it from off a scorching pace, which was set by Jargelle down the centre. The fourth and fifth set the level.

NOTEBOOK
Noble Storm(USA) was never far from the speed near the stands' fence and he got the better of a fine tussle with the runner-up, asserting close home. Put up to a career-high mark of 98 after his win at Glorious Goodwood, he is a most progressive young sprinter and is well worth another try in Listed company - he was behind Jargelle and Rain Delayed in Triple Aspect's race at Sandown on his one previous try in that grade - with the Beverley Bullet at the end of the month his immediate target. Group 3 races will soon be on his agenda too and he is well worth keeping on the right side. (op 6-1)
Rain Delayed(IRE) had won a little race at Tipperary since his Sandown effort and he ran a big race here, just finding the favourite too strong in the final 50 yards after the pair had been locked together for more than a furlong. He was conceding a pound to the winner and is another promising sprinter with Listed/Group 3 pretensions, well at home on a sound surface. (op 7-1)
Jargelle(IRE) showed blazing pace on this first venture into handicap company and stuck on to hold third after the first two had raced on from her. She had been below par on her previous two starts and this was better. (tchd 18-1)
Mattamia(IRE) could never really get involved, but he was running on near the rail when it was all over. He was a pound better off with Noble Storm for a head beating at Goodwood but had led that day and could not get to the front in this event. (op 9-1)
Green Beret(IRE) was fitted with a first-time visor and he ran close to his Goodwood form with Noble Storm and Mattamia, just lacking the pace of the principals late on. (tchd 5-1)
Lucky Numbers(IRE), fitted with blinkers for the first time, ran a solid race on this first try over the minimum trip since the spring. A stiffer 5f will suit him.
Bajan Tryst(USA) ran a lot better than he had at Ascot.
Go Nani Go was running on when it was all over on this seasonal bow.
Impressible was hit with a 10lb rise for her Haydock win, where she had made all. Back on a sound surface, she could not dominate with the likes of Jargelle in the field and she faded after chasing the pace for 4f. (tchd 9-1)
Titus Andronicus(IRE) Official explanation: jockey said gelding moved poorly throughout
T/Jkpt: Not won. T/Plt: £315.60 to a £1 stake. Pool: £230,327.92. 532.70 winning tickets. T/Qpdt: £9.80 to a £1 stake. Pool: £15,626.58. 1,171.06 winning tickets. WG

5012 CLAIREFONTAINE (R-H)
Thursday, August 20

OFFICIAL GOING: Good to soft

5204a GRAND PRIX L'AFTER FOOT (PRIX DES ROSELYS) (CLAIMER) 1m 6f 110y
4:05 (4:06) 4-Y-0+ **£8,738** (£3,495; £2,621; £1,748; £874)

RPR
1 **Cloudor (FR)**[9] 7-9-2 ACrastus 59
(P Demercastel, France)
2 1 **Greenwich Meantime**[134] 591 9-8-11 JAuge 53
(E J O'Neill) *midfield on outside: hrd rdn and nt qckn in 6th 2f out: styd on wl between horses ins fnl f but no ch w easy wnr* **23/5**[1]
3 1 **Andrei Roublev (USA)**[9] 8-8-11 C-PLemaire 51
(D Windrif, France)
4 nse **Beaubahhare (FR)**[144] 4-9-4 (b) 58
(J-P Delaporte, France)
5 ¾ **High Court (FR)**[33] 5-9-4 57
(P Lefevre, France)
6 1 **Mustalainen (FR)**[50] 5-8-8 46
(Mme R-W Allen, France)
7 nk **Tori Parry (FR)**[9] 6-9-1 (b) 53
(Y Fouin, France)
8 2 **Lisselan Catcher (IRE)**[67] 4-8-11 46
(Mme J Bidgood, Spain)
9 1 ½ **Landolino (FR)** 4-8-11 44
(J-M Lefebvre, France)
10 10 **Prince Rodrigue (FR)** 5-8-11 31
(Y Rougegrez, France)
0 **Caphe Sabrina (FR)**[21] 4-8-8 —
(J-Y Beaurain, France)
0 **Galix Du Val (FR)** 4-8-11 —
(P Duval, France)

3m 17.6s (197.60) **12** Ran SP% **17.9**
PARI-MUTUEL (including 1 Euro stake): WIN 6.00; PL 2.20, 2.70, 2.30;DF 20.20.
Owner Ecurie Bader SCEA **Bred** Scea Ecurie Bader **Trained** France
■ Stewards' Enquiry : J Auge 200euro fine: whip abuse

4557 CHESTER (L-H)
Friday, August 21

OFFICIAL GOING: Good to firm (8.2)
Wind: Light, across Weather: Sunny intervals

5205 SPORTINGBET.COM MAIDEN FILLIES' STKS 1m 2f 75y
1:55 (1:55) (Class 5) 3-Y-0+ **£4,047** (£1,204; £601; £300) **Stalls** High

Form RPR
-432 **1** **Heritage Coast (USA)**[12] 4828 4-9-6 78 SteveDrowne 6 58
(H Morrison) *mde all: rdn over 1f out: all out towards fin: jst hld on* **4/5**[1]
0-00 **2** hd **Kool Katie**[15] 4710 4-9-6 45 CatherineGannon 2 58
(Mrs G S Rees) *prom: lost pl 7f out: tried to prog whn n.m.r briefly wl over 1f out: sn rallied: r.o strly ins fnl f: gaining and tk 2nd at fin* **40/1**
2233 **3** nse **Astrodiva**[21] 4480 3-8-5 72 AshleyMorgan(7) 3 58
(M H Tompkins) *hld up: hdwy 5f out: rdn to chse wnr over 1f out: r.o ins fnl f: gaining on wnr but lost 2nd at fin* **5/2**[2]
0 **4** 1 ¼ **Silk And Satin (USA)**[12] 4828 3-8-12 0 (t) TPQueally 4 55
(H R A Cecil) *a.p: rdn to chal over 1f out: nt qckn ins fnl f* **15/2**[3]
330 **5** 5 **Acquavella**[20] 4519 3-8-12 71 TonyHamilton 1 45
(R A Fahey) *hld up: niggled along 6f out: outpcd over 2f out* **8/1**
0 **6** 1 ¾ **Laura Land**[68] 2943 3-8-12 0 PatCosgrave 5 42
(W M Brisbourne) *hld up: hdwy 7f out: sn w wnr: rdn and lost 2nd over 1f out: wknd fnl f* **66/1**

2m 13.56s (1.36) **Going Correction** +0.15s/f (Good)
WFA 3 from 4yo 8lb **6** Ran SP% **110.9**
Speed ratings (Par 100): **100,99,99,98,94 93**
toteswinger: 1&2 £7.90, 1&3 £1.10, 2&3 £11.80. CSF £34.20 TOTE £2.00: £1.30, £4.20; EX 36.00.
Owner Britannia Thoroughbreds **Bred** Juddmonte Farms Inc **Trained** East Ilsley, Berks
■ Stewards' Enquiry : Catherine Gannon two-day ban: used whip in incorrect place (Sep 4, 6)

FOCUS
A moderate contest but it produced a driving finish with the first three crossing the line in a bunch. The runner-up looks the best guide to the level.

5206 GLOBAL TRAVEL GROUP H'CAP 7f 2y
2:30 (2:31) (Class 3) (0-95,95) 3-Y-O+ **£9,462** (£2,832; £1,416; £708; £352) **Stalls** Low

Form RPR
6111 **1** **My Gacho (IRE)**[7] 4996 7-9-6 **88** 6ex (v) J-PGuillambert 5 96
(M Johnston) *chsd ldrs: rdn to take 2nd over 1f out: r.o to ld wl ins fnl f: wl on top at fin* **6/1**[3]
1005 **2** 1 ½ **I Confess**[19] 4560 4-8-11 **79** (b) CatherineGannon 11 83
(P D Evans) *chsd ldr: led over 2f out: rdn over 1f out: hdd wl ins fnl f: hld fnl strides* **25/1**
4003 **3** nk **Akhenaten**[22] 4459 3-9-5 **92** TonyCulhane 7 93
(M R Channon) *trckd ldrs: rdn to take 3rd over 1f out: r.o ins fnl f: clsng on runner-up at fin* **6/1**[3]
0303 **4** 1 ½ **Feeling Fab (FR)**[4] 5092 3-8-10 **83** DarryllHolland 2 84+
(M Johnston) *dwlt: in tch: effrt over 1f out: styd on ins fnl f: one pce fnl 50yds* **3/1**[1]
1105 **5** nse **Novellen Lad (IRE)**[13] 4784 4-9-3 **85** AlanMunro 9 84
(E J Alston) *midfield: rdn and sme hdwy to chse ldrs over 1f out: kpt on ins fnl f* **12/1**
1200 **6** 1 **Desert Dreamer (IRE)**[27] 4293 8-8-9 **82** ow2 RichardEvans(5) 3 81+
(P D Evans) *midfield: nt clr run wl over 1f out and again appr fnl f: edgd rt ins fnl f: nvr able to get to ldrs* **12/1**
0000 **7** ¾ **Kings Point (IRE)**[27] 4293 8-9-3 **85** AndrewMullen 4 79
(D Nicholls) *trckd ldrs: rdn wl over 1f out: one pce ins fnl f* **11/1**
500 **8** hd **Esoterica (IRE)**[27] 4297 6-8-12 **85** (v) GaryBartley(5) 12 79
(J S Goldie) *in rr: rdn over 1f out: nvr able to chal* **33/1**
0123 **9** shd **Barons Spy (IRE)**[26] 4353 8-9-5 **87** StephenDonohoe 10 80
(R J Price) *dwlt: towards rr: rdn over 1f out: no real hdwy* **14/1**
-000 **10** nk **Bolodenka (IRE)**[13] 4779 7-9-10 **92** TonyHamilton 6 84
(R A Fahey) *hld up: rdn over 1f out: nvr on terms w ldrs: nt clr run whn no imp towards fin* **18/1**
4250 **11** ½ **Parisian Pyramid (IRE)**[21] 4485 3-9-1 **95** NSLawes(7) 13 84
(D Nicholls) *in rr: rdn over 1f out: nvr on terms w ldrs* **20/1**
5320 **12** 29 **Fathsta (IRE)**[19] 4560 4-9-8 **90** FrancisNorton 8 3
(D Nicholls) *led: hdd 2f out: wknd qckly wl over 1f out* **5/1**[2]

1m 26.29s (-0.21) **Going Correction** +0.15s/f (Good)
WFA 3 from 4yo+ 5lb **12** Ran SP% **117.4**
Speed ratings (Par 107): **107,105,104,103,103 102,101,100,100,100 99,66**
toteswinger: 1&2 £9.80, 1&3 £4.80, 2&3 £68.40. CSF £149.58 CT £956.13 TOTE £5.00: £2.10, £7.00, £2.50; EX 161.70.
Owner Grant Mercer **Bred** Mount Coote Stud **Trained** Middleham Moor, N Yorks

FOCUS
The pace was sound enough yet those racing near the lead dominated from start to finish. The first two, who were prominent throughout, are rated to form.

NOTEBOOK
My Gacho(IRE) could not get an easy lead, but that did not matter as he tracked the leaders parked a couple wide throughout, and when the leader kicked for home he readily covered that move and had plenty in reserve to stay on strongly at the finish. He was the lesser fancied of the Mark Johnston pair, stepping up in class in his bid for a four-timer under a penalty, but he did it in the manner of a horse at the top of his game. (op 5-1 tchd 9-2 and 13-2 in places)
I Confess broke smartly to get to the front rank and disputed the lead one off the rail before kicking for home 2f out, a move that nearly paid dividends until he was reeled in by an in-form rival close home. This was a sterling effort from the Lingfield Polytrack specialist. (tchd 22-1)
Akhenaten has been running well in tougher company and is suited by a strong pace over this trip, but he had to settle for racing two-wide in the third wave of horses and could never quite make up the deficit. (op 11-2)

Feeling Fab(FR) was backed into favouritism but did not get the run of the race. She can take a strong hold and is effective from the front, but dwelt at the start, which meant she could not take advantage of her inside draw, and was fighting a losing battle thereafter. She was keeping on once again but could find no room and carried her head awkwardly in the closing stages. (op 4-1)
Novellen Lad(IRE) has a generally progressive profile but could get no nearer than three off the rail on the first turn and ran as well as he could in the circumstances. (tchd 11-1)
Desert Dreamer(IRE) has been below his best recently and did not have enough early pace to take advantage of his favourable draw. (tchd 14-1)
Fathsta(IRE) Official explanation: jockey said gelding finished distressed

5207 SURRENDA-LINK NURSERY — 7f 2y

3:05 (3:05) (Class 3) 2-Y-O **£9,066** (£2,697; £1,348; £673) **Stalls** Low

Form — RPR

5003 **1** **Shibhan**[13] 4782 2-8-1 **68** .... FrancisNorton 1 — 70
(C E Brittain) *trckd ldrs: n.m.r and lost pl over 5f out: hdwy over 1f out: r.o to come through between horses to ld 75yds out: rdn out* **13/2**[2]

3301 **2** ½ **Transfixed (IRE)**[1] 5187 2-8-7 **74** 6ex........ CatherineGannon 7 — 75
(P D Evans) *led: rdn and hrd pressed fr over 1f out: hdd 75yds out: r.o gamely but jst hld after* **10/1**

610 **3** *nk* **Professor John (IRE)**[14] 4758 2-9-0 **81**........ TPQueally 2 — 81
(M L W Bell) *trckd ldrs: rdn over 1f out: r.o towards fin: clsng at fin* **8/1**

3542 **4** *shd* **Dolphin Rock**[11] 4858 2-7-12 **65**........ DuranFentiman 6 — 65
(Mrs G S Rees) *a.p: rdn to chal over 1f out: nt qckn towards fin* **8/1**

4212 **5** 3¼ **Gunner Lindley (IRE)**[21] 4488 2-9-7 **88**........ DarryllHolland 5 — 80
(B W Hills) *midfield: niggled along 6f out: hdwy over 3f out: rdn over 2f out: kpt on and edgd lft ins fnl f: nt pce to chal ldng bunch* **11/10**[1]

5500 **6** 2 **Leleyf (IRE)**[20] 4525 2-8-8 **75**........ TonyCulhane 3 — 62
(M R Channon) *racd keenly: hld up: effrt whn nt clr run 1f out: nvr able to get to ldrs* **7/1**[3]

4310 **7** 1½ **Refuse To Wait (IRE)**[20] 4539 2-8-9 **76**........ DavidAllan 9 — 59
(T D Easterby) *trckd ldrs: wnt 2nd over 5f out: rdn over 2f out: lost 2nd over 1f out: sn wknd* **25/1**

5006 **8** *nk* **Charity Fair**[13] 4803 2-7-9 **65** oh17........ DominicFox(3) 4 — 47
(A Berry) *in rr: outpcd over 1f out: nvr on terms w ldrs* **66/1**

603 **9** 9 **Lady Lefroy (IRE)**[34] 4100 2-7-12 **65** oh2........ SilvestreDeSousa 10 — 25
(R A Fahey) *in rr: sn niggled along: outpcd over 2f out* **16/1**

1m 27.48s (0.98) **Going Correction** +0.15s/f (Good) **9** Ran SP% **116.0**
Speed ratings (Par 98): **100,99,99,98,95 92,91,90,80**
toteswinger: 1&2 £10.10, 1&3 £9.50, 2&3 £15.50. CSF £69.38 CT £533.54 TOTE £7.70: £2.40, £2.40, £2.10; EX 90.40.
Owner Saeed Manana **Bred** Richard C J Manning **Trained** Newmarket, Suffolk

FOCUS
Quite a valuable and competitive nursery run at a decent pace, and when Transfixed kicked for home from the final turn, soon all bar the winner were on the stretch. The winner is rated to his pre-race mark but the form could go a little higher.

NOTEBOOK
Shibhan, breaking from the inside stall, had to bide her time in mid-division trapped against the rail, but that was to her advantage as she avoided the early pace and was the only one travelling comfortably when the leaders kicked for home, so when a gap opened in the straight she readily burst through. She had been struggling to find a trip, having been outpaced at 5f and weakening on her previous attempt at this distance, but with hold-up tactics 7f around here proved ideal. (op 8-1 tchd 17-2)
Transfixed(IRE) had a hard time of it in winning at Epsom yesterday evening, and put up another game effort under a penalty. Breaking smartly, she got the lead on the rail before kicking on from the home turn, a move that immediately had everything under pressure, unfortunately including herself before too long. However, she is thoroughly genuine and kept on again at the finish. (tchd 11-1)
Professor John(IRE) was beginning to feel the pressure even before the drive for home, but he did make some late progress to suggest that this trip is within his compass, though probably at a different track. (op 10-1)
Dolphin Rock was technically 2lb well in on his all-weather form and, racing against the rail, ran well enough to suggest he acts on turf as well, despite his high head carriage. (op 11-1)
Gunner Lindley(IRE) was well fancied after his narrow defeat in a competitive Goodwood nursery last time, but he had to be niggled from an early stage, raced wide throughout and did not look happy around this track. Official explanation: trainer's rep had no explanation for the poor form shown (op 10-11)
Leleyf(IRE) never got competitive enough to put her stamina over this longer trip to the test, and she might be in the grip of the Handicapper at present. (op 8-1)

5208 AXON RESOURCING EBF COMBERMERE FILLIES' CONDITIONS STKS — 6f 18y

3:40 (3:40) (Class 2) 2-Y-O **£12,616** (£3,776; £1,888; £944; £470) **Stalls** Low

Form — RPR

1 **1** **Walk On Water**[28] 4257 2-9-1 0........ TPQueally 5 — 94+
(H R A Cecil) *racd keenly: w ldr: led over 1f out: r.o wl and pushed clr ins fnl f: impressive* **10/11**[1]

2161 **2** 4 **Fly Silca Fly (IRE)**[11] 4850 2-9-1 74........ AlanMunro 1 — 80
(M R Channon) *led: pushed along 2f out: hdd over 1f out: nt pce of wnr and no ch fnl f* **8/1**[3]

1112 **3** 1¾ **Diamond Laura**[9] 4895 2-9-1 85........ SilvestreDeSousa 3 — 75+
(Mrs R A Carr) *stmbld s: trckd ldrs: rdn 2f out: kpt on fnl f but nt pce to trble front 2* **9/4**[2]

1055 **4** 2 **Crown (IRE)**[29] 4245 2-9-4 92........ FrancisNorton 6 — 72
(R Hannon) *chsd ldrs: rdn and wl outpcd over 1f out* **10/1**

2 **5** 1¾ **Catbells (IRE)**[15] 4706 2-8-12 0........ NeilChalmers 7 — 61
(A Bailey) *hld up: rdn over 1f out: nvr able to chal* **14/1**

4 **6** 13 **Ed's A Red**[15] 4706 2-8-12 0........ BillyCray 2 — 22
(A Berry) *a pushed along and bhd: wl outpcd fnl 2f* **100/1**

1m 14.51s (0.71) **Going Correction** +0.15s/f (Good) **6** Ran SP% **111.0**
Speed ratings (Par 97): **101,95,93,90,88 71**
toteswinger: 1&2 £2.30, 1&3 £1.30, 2&3 £2.50. CSF £9.00 TOTE £1.80: £1.10, £3.50; EX 8.20.
Owner Bloomsbury Stud **Bred** Bloomsbury Stud **Trained** Newmarket, Suffolk

FOCUS
A decent contest dominated by the two pacesetters. The runner-up dictates the level of the form.

NOTEBOOK
Walk On Water did not want to set the pace but readily tracked the leader and for a couple of strides she was just caught out as the pace quickened, but she was soon back into a rhythm and strode clear to win impressively. From a successful family in New Zealand and Australia at trips up to 1m, she is bred to excel as a juvenile but looks classy enough to progress. The form of her debut success at Ascot is working out well and she should continue to improve, especially on fast ground. (tchd 4-5)
Fly Silca Fly(IRE) readily seized the lead, racing keenly against the rail, tried to quicken clear from the home turn and beat off all bar a superior winner. She had plenty to find on official ratings but is making steady progress this summer and ran right up to form. (op 9-1)
Diamond Laura stumbled out of the stalls and immediately lost a couple of lengths, and though she soon regained her composure to track the leaders, she began to feel the pressure from the home turn. She stumbled at the start at Hamilton on her previous outing as well but still managed to finish second, and once again ran up to form despite the sluggish start. Official explanation: jockey said filly stumbled leaving stalls (op 11-4 tchd 3-1)
Crown(IRE) has been highly tried of late so this looked an easier opportunity, however she raced freely, hung right around the final bend and did not stay. (op 7-1 tchd 11-1 in places)
Catbells(IRE) was taking a step up in class from her debut second earlier this month but was never a threat. (op 12-1 tchd 16-1)
Ed's A Red had finished more than 14 lengths behind Catbells on her debut last time and, although finishing a length closer this time, was thoroughly outclassed. (op 125-1)

5209 SURRENDA-LINK H'CAP — 1m 2f 75y

4:15 (4:16) (Class 3) (0-90,90) 3-Y-O **£8,831** (£2,643; £1,321; £660; £329) **Stalls** High

Form — RPR

1524 **1** **Embsay Crag**[15] 4709 3-8-0 **76**........ IJBrennan(7) 2 — 83+
(Mrs K Walton) *prom: settled to trck ldrs 7f out: nt clr run and swtchd rt over 1f out: r.o to chal ins fnl f: led fnl stride* **8/1**

3310 **2** *shd* **Clerk's Choice (IRE)**[43] 3780 3-9-0 **83**........ AlanMunro 9 — 88+
(W Jarvis) *hld up towards rr: rdn and hdwy on outside 2f out: r.o to chal ins fnl f: battled gamely in driving fin of hds* **16/1**

0110 **3** *shd* **Fastnet Storm (IRE)**[22] 4455 3-9-3 **86**........ SilvestreDeSousa 3 — 91
(T P Tate) *prom: led over 2f out: rdn over 1f out: hrd pressed ins fnl f: hdd fnl stride* **9/2**[1]

0110 **4** *hd* **Norwegian Dancer (UAE)**[23] 4420 3-9-4 **87**........ FrancisNorton 7 — 92
(E S McMahon) *trckd ldrs: rdn to chal fr over 1f out: r.o: hld fnl strides in fin of hds* **14/1**

0002 **5** *nk* **Goliaths Boy (IRE)**[14] 4741 3-8-10 **82**........ FrederikTylicki(3) 1 — 86
(R A Fahey) *in tch: dropped to midfield over 5f out: prog over 1f out: chal ins fnl f: nt qckn cl home in fin of hds* **12/1**

1060 **6** 1¾ **Sam Sharp (USA)**[16] 4649 3-8-9 **78**........ TPQueally 8 — 79
(H R A Cecil) *midfield: rdn over 1f out: styd on and edgd lft ins fnl f: nt pce to rch front 5* **16/1**

4000 **7** 2 **Takaatuf (IRE)**[22] 4455 3-9-1 **84**........ J-PGuillambert 5 — 81
(M Johnston) *hld up: rdn over 1f out: styd on but nt pce to chal* **9/1**

64-4 **8** 1½ **Watergate (IRE)**[27] 4316 3-9-4 **87**........ StephenDonohoe 11 — 81
(Sir Mark Prescott) *s.i.s: bhd: u.p 1f out: kpt on but unable to get to ldrs* **9/1**

0205 **9** ½ **Union Island (IRE)**[24] 4401 3-9-0 **83**........ DarryllHolland 6 — 76
(K A Ryan) *bhd: pushed along over 2f out: kpt on fnl f but unable to get to ldrs* **20/1**

2423 **10** ¾ **Decision**[28] 4270 3-8-13 **82**........(p) PhilipRobinson 4 — 73
(C G Cox) *led: hdd over 2f out: sn rdn: wknd ins fnl f* **6/1**[2]

2315 **11** *nk* **Sandor**[22] 4455 3-9-7 **90**........ PatCosgrave 12 — 80
(P J Makin) *midfield: rdn and hdwy over 3f out: no imp on ldrs: wknd fnl f* **15/2**

4213 **12** 13 **Almuktahem**[15] 4715 3-9-0 **83**........(v) PhillipMakin 10 — 47
(Sir Michael Stoute) *racd keenly: trckd ldrs: moved upsides to chal 3 wd 3f out: rdn over 2f out: wknd qckly wl over 1f out* **7/1**[3]

2m 10.44s (-1.76) **Going Correction** +0.15s/f (Good) **12** Ran SP% **118.7**
Speed ratings (Par 104): **113,112,112,112,112 111,109,108,107,107 107,96**
toteswinger: 1&2 £33.50, 1&3 £11.40, 2&3 £24.00. CSF £129.15 CT £651.80 TOTE £10.50: £3.30, £5.00, £2.20; EX 198.30.
Owner Keep The Faith Partnership **Bred** Mrs Glenda Swinglehurst **Trained** Middleham Moor, N Yorks
■ Stewards' Enquiry : Alan Munro one-day ban: used whip without giving gelding time to respond (Sep 4)

FOCUS
This had the look of a competitive handicap and the front five were covered by around half a length. The form looks decent and sound enough, rated around the trio close behind the first two.

NOTEBOOK
Embsay Crag, always going nicely on the rails just in behind the speed, had next to no weight to carry with his rider's claim and, having been switched right in the straight, he just found enough to score. A course and distance winner earlier in the season, he was 11lb higher here and has clearly improved since then. (op 9-1)
Clerk's Choice(IRE), 6lb higher than when beating useful handicapper Dancourt at Sandown in June, bounced back from a dismal effort at Newmarket last time, keeping on right the way to the line and just missing out.
Fastnet Storm(IRE) had to go too quick when bidding for a hat-trick at Goodwood last time and connections were happy enough for him track the pace. He went on before the straight and battled right the way to the line, just holding on for third. (op 5-1 tchd 4-1)
Norwegian Dancer(UAE), another to have run poorly at Goodwood last time when bidding for a hat-trick, held every chance in the straight and kept on, but was just run out of it. (op 9-1 tchd 8-1)
Goliaths Boy(IRE), back to form when second over 1m at Haydock last time, ran just as well on this step back up in trip, finishing right in the mix without being able to quicken. (op 8-1)
Sam Sharp(USA) ran a more encouraging race, staying on late. (op 14-1 tchd 20-1)
Takaatuf(IRE) couldn't lead as he likes to and got going too late. (op 12-1 tchd 14-1)
Watergate(IRE) was never travelling and looked unhappy on the track. (op 8-1 tchd 10-1)
Union Island(IRE) Official explanation: jockey said colt was unsuited by the good to firm ground
Almuktahem raced too keenly and failed to last home. (op 8-1 tchd 6-1)

5210 BOLLINGER CHAMPAGNE CHALLENGE SERIES H'CAP (FOR GENTLEMAN AMATEUR RIDERS) — 1m 4f 66y

4:50 (4:50) (Class 5) (0-75,73) 3-Y-O+ **£3,903** (£1,210; £605; £302) **Stalls** Low

Form — RPR

2332 **1** **Safebreaker**[6] 5028 4-10-10 **67**........(p) MrJoshuaMoore(5) 7 — 71
(K A Ryan) *midfield: rdn and hdwy over 2f out: led wl ins fnl f: jst hld on* **7/2**[1]

5061 **2** *shd* **Barbirolli**[8] 4927 7-9-13 **53** 6ex........ MrPCollington(3) 4 — 58
(W M Brisbourne) *in tch: effrt over 1f out: r.o strly fnl 100yds: jst failed* **9/1**

0142 **3** ¾ **Drawn Gold**[14] 4737 5-10-4 **61**........ MrStephenHarrison(5) 9 — 64
(R Hollinshead) *led: slowed pce after 3f: pushed along 2f out: hdd wl ins fnl f: nt qckn cl home* **11/2**[2]

0462 **4** 1¼ **Locum**[16] 4658 4-10-6 **65**........ MrDJEustace(7) 6 — 66
(M H Tompkins) *hld up: went into midfield 7f out: hdwy 2f out: styd on to chse ldrs 1f out: one pce cl home* **15/2**

121 **5** 1½ **Summer Lodge**[24] 4403 6-11-7 **73**........ MrMSeston 5 — 71
(J A Glover) *racd keenly: a.p: rdn over 1f out: no ex fnl 100yds* **15/2**

0-12 **6** 1¼ **Mister Fizzbomb (IRE)**[9] 4893 6-10-8 **67**........ MrMKing(7) 11 — 63+
(T D Walford) *trckd ldrs: pushed along 1f out: kpt on same pce ins fnl f* **6/1**[3]

0526 **7** ½ **Thorny Mandate**[42] 3809 7-9-13 **54**........ MrBenBrisbourne(3) 3 — 50
(W M Brisbourne) *racd keenly: hld up: effrt and swtchd lft over 1f out: one pce ins fnl f* **7/1**

0005 **8** 1¾ **Desert Hawk**[32] 4158 8-9-13 **54** oh9........(b) MrHarryChalloner(3) 10 — 47
(W M Brisbourne) *hld up: hdwy into midfield after 4f: rdn over 1f out: no imp on ldrs* **50/1**

4312 **9** *2 ¾* **Sand Repeal (IRE)**[43] 3774 7-10-2 **59**............................ MrRBirkett(5) 8 47
(Miss J Feilden) *in rr: rdn over 1f out: nvr on terms w ldrs* **13/2**

-004 **10** *2* **Desert Leader (IRE)**[11] 4857 8-9-13 **54** oh9............... MrJohnEnnis(3) 2 39
(W M Brisbourne) *prom: rdn 2f out: wknd over 1f out* **20/1**

0630 **11** *5* **York Cliff**[8] 4927 11-9-9 **54** oh4.. MrLWard(7) 1 31
(W M Brisbourne) *hld up: hmpd jst after 3f: shuffled bk to rr over 7f out: n.d after* **33/1**

2m 40.96s (1.06) **Going Correction** +0.15s/f (Good) **11** Ran SP% **120.9**
Speed ratings (Par 103): **102,101,101,100,99 98,98,97,95,94 90**
toteswinger: 1&2 £7.80, 1&3 £6.00, 2&3 £11.00. CSF £36.46 CT £175.01 TOTE £4.40: £1.70, £2.50, £2.60; EX 51.20 Place 6: £142.18, Place 5: £83.88..
Owner Hambleton Racing Ltd X **Bred** Gainsborough Stud Management Ltd **Trained** Hambleton, N Yorks

■ Stewards' Enquiry : Mr L Ward six-day ban: used whip when out of contention (Sep 7, 8, 15, 22, 25, 29)
Mr Joshua Moore one-day ban: excessive use of the whip (Sep 7)

FOCUS
This was an open handicap and the runner-up is probably the best guide to the form.
T/Plt: £405.50 to a £1 stake. Pool: £55,774.28. 100.40 winning tickets. T/Qpdt: £51.90 to a £1 stake. Pool: £3,714.00. 52.90 winning tickets. DO

4945 SALISBURY (R-H)
Friday, August 21

OFFICIAL GOING: Good (8.4)
Wind: Mild breeze Weather: Sunny

5211 RACING UK LADY RIDERS' H'CAP — 1m
4:45 (4:46) (Class 5) (0-70,65) 3-Y-O+ **£3,123** (£968; £484; £242) **Stalls** Centre

Form RPR

3451 **1** **Rock Anthem (IRE)**[6] 5019 5-10-1 **63** 6ex................ MissSLWatson(7) 6 77
(Mike Murphy) *s.i.s: patiently rdn towards rr: smooth prog fr over 3f out: led ent fnl f: r.o strly: readily* **11/4**[1]

666- **2** *6* **Cape Cobra**[440] 2846 5-10-0 **60**................................... MissVCartmel(5) 5 60
(H Morrison) *racd keenly: prom: led over 4f out tl over 1f out: nt pce of ready wnr* **5/1**[3]

2615 **3** *1 ¾* **Make Amends (IRE)**[5] 5063 4-10-0 **62**..................... MissKClark(7) 3 58
(R J Hodges) *sn swtchd to far rails: travelled wl trcking ldrs: rdn over 1f out: nt qckn* **7/2**[2]

5004 **4** *shd* **Artreju (GER)**[15] 4698 6-9-6 **54**.................................. MissKLoftus(7) 9 50
(P Butler) *hld up bhd: hdwy whn nt clr run wl over 1f out: r.o wl fnl f: nrst fin* **12/1**

1350 **5** *4* **Wotasparkler**[8] 4950 3-9-13 **60**.................................. MissGAndrews 11 46
(W S Kittow) *in tch: hdwy to chal over 2f out: led briefly over 1f out: sn hung lft and fdd* **7/1**

5030 **6** *7* **Play Up Pompey**[20] 4538 7-9-5 **46** oh1.................... MissFayeBramley 4 16
(J J Bridger) *nvr bttr than mid-div* **20/1**

0300 **7** *2* **Never Sold Out (IRE)**[52] 3473 4-9-2 **50**........... MissLauraThomas(7) 10 16
(J G M O'Shea) *a towards rr* **20/1**

0P65 **8** *6* **Magic Warrior**[77] 2675 9-9-0 **46** oh1........... MissSarah-JaneDurman(5) 8 —
(J C Fox) *s.i.s: a towards rr* **16/1**

3000 **9** *1 ½* **Western Roots**[15] 4698 8-10-0 **60**........................... MissMBryant(5) 2 9
(P Butler) *trckd ldrs: chal over 3f out: wknd 2f out* **33/1**

0006 **10** *18* **Solent Ridge (IRE)**[15] 4698 4-10-10 **65**...................(p) MrsSMoore 1 —
(J S Moore) *led tl over 4f out: wknd over 2f out: t.o* **8/1**

1m 44.25s (0.75) **Going Correction** -0.05s/f (Good)
WFA 3 from 4yo+ 6lb **10** Ran SP% **115.2**
Speed ratings (Par 103): **94,88,86,86,82 75,73,67,65,47**
toteswinger: 1&2 £3.20, 1&3 £2.60, 2&3 £5.30. CSF £15.84 CT £48.54 TOTE £2.40: £1.20, £2.40, £2.10; EX 13.40.
Owner Ronald Bright **Bred** Mervyn Stewkesbury **Trained** Westoning, Beds

FOCUS
A fast gallop early in this handicap confined to lady amateurs. The winner is close to his best with the runner-up doing better for his new yard.

5212 TURFTV MAIDEN AUCTION STKS — 6f
5:20 (5:21) (Class 5) 2-Y-O **£3,238** (£963; £481; £240) **Stalls** High

Form RPR

5 **1** **Theladyinquestion**[50] 3534 2-8-6 0.. LPKeniry 7 78+
(A M Balding) *a.p: led 2f out: sn rdn: in command and r.o wl fnl f* **6/1**[3]

4 **2** *1 ½* **King Of Windsor (IRE)**[9] 4900 2-8-13 0............... RichardKingscote 8 80
(R M Beckett) *prom: rdn and ev ch over 1f out: kpt on but a hld by wnr ins fnl f* **5/6**[1]

04 **3** *nk* **Silent Secret (IRE)**[6] 5026 2-8-8 0....................................... TravisBlock 5 74
(R Hannon) *mid-div: hdwy over 2f out: sn rdn: kpt on fnl f* **11/4**[2]

4 *3 ¾* **Ferris Wheel (IRE)** 2-8-6 0.. JosedeSouza 9 61
(P F I Cole) *led tl over 2f out: one pce fnl f* **25/1**

04 **5** *2 ¼* **My Sister**[12] 4825 2-8-4 0.. RichardSmith 4 52
(M D I Usher) *chsd ldrs: rdn wl over 2f out: edgd lft over 1f out: one pce after* **16/1**

00 **6** *½* **Catchanova (IRE)**[21] 4478 2-8-11 0............................(t) StephenCarson 6 58
(Eve Johnson Houghton) *hld up: swtchd lft whn rdn 2f out: little imp* **100/1**

003 **7** *½* **Freddie's Girl (USA)**[15] 4688 2-7-11 **65**.................... RichardRowe(7) 11 49
(Stef Liddiard) *chsd ldrs: rdn over 3f out: one pce fnl 2f* **14/1**

00 **8** *3 ¾* **Madj's Baby**[42] 3810 2-8-6 0...................................... GregFairley 13 40
(H S Howe) *sn pushed along in mid-div: wknd jst over 1f out* **40/1**

9 *11* **Dreamy Eyed (IRE)** 2-8-6 0 ow3............................... JackMitchell(3) 12 10
(Mrs P N Dutfield) *a bhd* **25/1**

10 *6* **Novillero** 2-8-11 0.. SamHitchcott 1 —
(J C Fox) *s.i.s: a towards rr* **100/1**

06 **11** *1 ¾* **Mactrac**[79] 2599 2-8-13 0.. PatrickHills(3) 3 —
(R Hannon) *a towards rr* **50/1**

1m 14.89s (0.09) **Going Correction** -0.05s/f (Good) **11** Ran SP% **122.1**
Speed ratings (Par 94): **97,95,94,89,86 85,85,80,65,57 55**
toteswinger: 1&2 £2.30, 1&3 £3.60, 2&3 £1.60. CSF £11.52 TOTE £8.30: £2.00, £1.20, £1.30; EX 13.90.
Owner D H Caslon & Mildmay Racing **Bred** Middle Park Stud Ltd **Trained** Kingsclere, Hants

FOCUS
A modest maiden. The winner can rate higher and the form makes sense rated around the placed horses.

NOTEBOOK
Theladyinquestion ◆ was not knocked about on her encouraging debut at Newbury and that experience was not lost on her. A robust filly, she should do even better over further and it will be surprising if she does not find more opportunities. (op 5-1)
King Of Windsor(IRE), who had shaped well on his debut here last week, took the eye in the paddock and did nothing wrong in the race but simply found the winner too good. There is surely a race for him, possibly over another furlong. (op 5-4)
Silent Secret(IRE) is getting the hang of the things, but still needs to settle better. She kept on well in the closing stages and with nurseries now an option her turn awaits. (op 7-2 tchd 4-1)
Ferris Wheel(IRE) has physical scope and will come on for the run. She has an entry in the Redcar Two-Year-Old Trophy, which might be an interesting option. (tchd 20-1)
My Sister was not disgraced but probably needs further.
Freddie's Girl(USA) looked as if she might benefit from the assistance of a more experienced jockey. (op 9-1)

5213 RACING UK NURSERY — 1m
5:55 (5:55) (Class 5) (0-75,75) 2-Y-O **£3,238** (£963; £481; £240) **Stalls** Centre

Form RPR

006 **1** **First Cat**[16] 4646 2-9-2 **70**.. PatDobbs 7 74+
(R Hannon) *hld up towards rr: rdn 3f out: sme prog whn swtchd lft 2f out: styng on whn swtchd lft again over 1f out: str run ins fnl f: drifted rt: led fnl stride* **20/1**

065 **2** *shd* **Flaming Miracle**[27] 4323 2-9-4 **72**.. LPKeniry 12 76
(A M Balding) *trckd ldr: led travelling wl jst under 2f out: rdn ent fnl f: ct whn bmpd fnl stride* **9/2**[2]

565 **3** *1 ½* **Whiepa Snappa (IRE)**[22] 4451 2-8-6 **63**.................. JackMitchell(3) 11 63
(P M Phelan) *racd keenly: trckd ldr: rdn over 3f out: kpt on gamely to chal wl over 1f out: kpt on but no ex ins fnl f* **5/1**[3]

4636 **4** *1 ¼* **Knockenduff**[14] 4758 2-8-7 **61**.................................. SamHitchcott 13 59
(M R Channon) *mid-div: rdn 3f out: hdwy over 1f out: styd on* **14/1**

431 **5** *2 ¼* **Diamond Duchess (IRE)**[15] 4705 2-9-7 **75**................... TedDurcan 1 68
(D R Lanigan) *in tch: effrt over 2f out: edgd rt over 1f out: wknd ins fnl f* **3/1**[1]

0003 **6** *5* **Sixpenny Moon (USA)**[37] 3978 2-8-8 **62**......................... TravisBlock 6 44
(R Hannon) *sme late prog but mainly towards rr* **14/1**

454 **7** *shd* **Dream Spinner**[15] 4693 2-9-4 **72**.. GregFairley 3 54
(J L Dunlop) *trckd ldr: rdn and ev ch over 2f out tl wl over 1f out: wknd* **7/1**

0525 **8** *½* **Chairman Pat (USA)**[15] 4693 2-9-6 **74**................. RichardKingscote 10 54
(Tom Dascombe) *led: rdn and hdd wl over 1f out: sn wknd* **12/1**

0224 **9** *2 ¾* **Brunette (IRE)**[15] 4705 2-9-4 **72**........................... RichardHughes 5 46
(R Hannon) *rdn over 3f out: a towards rr* **5/1**[3]

0664 **10** *1 ¾* **Wing Of Faith**[30] 4195 2-8-8 **62**............................. StephenCarson 8 33
(S Kirk) *in tch: tk clsr order 4f out: sn rdn: wknd over 1f out* **25/1**

000 **11** *1* **Vadition (IRE)**[59] 3249 2-7-11 **58** oh7 ow6......................... KierenFox(7) 4 26
(J J Bridger) *a towards rr* **100/1**

0000 **12** *6* **Silvee**[16] 4639 2-8-0 **54** oh3 ow2....................................... RichardThomas 2 9
(J J Bridger) *a towards rr* **100/1**

1m 45.48s (1.98) **Going Correction** -0.05s/f (Good) **12** Ran SP% **120.6**
Speed ratings (Par 94): **88,87,86,85,82 77,77,77,74,72 71,65**
toteswinger: 1&2 £25.90, 1&3 £28.10, 2&3 £7.40. CSF £107.83 CT £536.65 TOTE £19.50: £4.70, £2.10, £2.30; EX 137.50.
Owner R Barnett **Bred** W And R Barnett Ltd **Trained** East Everleigh, Wilts

■ Stewards' Enquiry : Pat Dobbs one-day ban: careless riding (Sep 4)

FOCUS
Regular nursery form best rated around the third, fourth and fifth.

NOTEBOOK
First Cat was racing with his head cocked to one side, but that could well be because he is blind in his off eye. He was going nowhere and looked uncomfortable for most of the race, but he suddenly found his stride inside the final furlong and came with a storming run to snatch the verdict, despite edging slightly right. His previous effort had been encouraging, and the extra furlong today was obviously essential. Official explanation: trainer said, regarding apparent improvement in form, that the gelding is improving with every run and appreciated the step up to a mile. (tchd 25-1)
Flaming Miracle ◆ is a strong individual and on the upgrade. He came under heavy pressure in the closing stages, but even that could not quite lift him home. He should go close over a similar trip next time and his stable remains in fine form. (op 6-1 tchd 4-1)
Whiepa Snappa(IRE) seems to be improving but is a bit too keen at present and 1m1f may currently be stretching his stamina. He should be winning before too long. (tchd 7-1)
Knockenduff, whose stable have a good record in this race, could not build on that but was not disgraced. (op 11-1 tchd 16-1)
Diamond Duchess(IRE) hit a flat spot soon after halfway and then went right when trying to stay on again. The heavy rain before racing may not have helped.
Chairman Pat(USA) has had his chances, but has yet to show much resolve in the closing stages. (op 11-1 tchd 16-1)
Brunette(IRE) attracted market support but spoiled any chance by hanging persistently right. She continues to look a tricky ride. (op 7-1)

5214 WEATHERBYS BANK STONEHENGE STKS (LISTED RACE) — 1m
6:25 (6:25) (Class 1) 2-Y-O
£17,031 (£6,456; £3,231; £1,611; £807; £405) **Stalls** Centre

Form RPR

2104 **1** **Big Audio (IRE)**[23] 4418 2-9-2 **107**........................ RichardHughes 5 101
(R Hannon) *mde all: led field to stands' side rails over 3f out: rdn whn hrd pressed fr 2f out: drifted rt ins fnl f: hld on gamely* **4/1**[3]

431 **2** *hd* **Dubai Miracle (USA)**[30] 4200 2-8-13 **88**.................... HayleyTurner 7 98
(D M Simcock) *trckd ldrs: rdn to press wnr fr 2f out: ev ch thrght fnl f: carried sltly rt towards fin: jst hld* **25/1**

211 **3** *1* **Black Snowflake (USA)**[21] 4488 2-8-13 **92**..................... LDettori 4 95+
(Saeed Bin Suroor) *trckd ldrs: short of room over 3f out: swtchd rt wl over 2f out: sn rdn: cl 3rd and kpt on but nt pce to mount chal ins fnl f* **6/4**[1]

3043 **4** *¾* **Raine's Cross**[21] 4488 2-8-13 **94**................................... JimCrowley 1 94
(P Winkworth) *hld up: effrt over 2f out: kpt on same pce* **10/1**

10 **5** *1* **Dreamspeed (IRE)**[23] 4418 2-8-13 0.......................... WilliamBuick 2 92
(A M Balding) *trckd wnr: rdn wl over 2f out: one pce fr over 1f out* **5/2**[2]

0401 **6** *2* **Desert Auction (IRE)**[19] 4565 2-8-13 **91**........................ PatDobbs 8 87
(R Hannon) *t.k.h: hld up: bmpd wl over 2f out: sn rdn: nt pce to get on terms* **20/1**

1 **7** *½* **The Starboard Bow**[16] 4666 2-8-13 0.............................. LPKeniry 6 86
(S Kirk) *racd keenly bhd ldrs: short of room 3f out: sn rdn: one pce fr over 1f out* **25/1**

5131 **8** *7* **Toga Tiger (IRE)**[37] 3978 2-8-13 **88**............................. TedDurcan 3 71+
(M R Channon) *s.i.s: hld up: beginning effrt whn squeezed out 3f out: nvr able to get on terms after* **28/1**

1m 44.33s (0.83) **Going Correction** -0.05s/f (Good) **8** Ran SP% **113.6**
Speed ratings (Par 102): **93,92,91,91,90 88,87,80**
toteswinger: 1&2 £10.20, 1&3 £1.70, 2&3 £8.60. CSF £93.90 TOTE £4.60: £1.30, £4.90, £1.10; EX 64.20.
Owner Michael Pescod **Bred** Stephen Sullivan **Trained** East Everleigh, Wilts

■ Stewards' Enquiry : Richard Hughes 16-day ban: 2 for careless riding; 14 days (4-days deferred) under totting-up procedure (Sep 7-18)
L Dettori two-day ban: careless riding (Sep 4, 6)

FOCUS
Standard Listed form and the fourth sets the level.

NOTEBOOK
Big Audio(IRE) won the Chesham at Royal Ascot and was not disgraced in a Group 2 last time. The switch to 1m combined with his battling attitude stood him in very good stead. He looked held inside the final furlong, but would not give up and mastered the runner-up on the line. (op 3-1)
Dubai Miracle(USA) ◆, a well-grown colt, was making his debut on grass and he ran a blinder. His physical appearance suggests that he will maintain improvement and he is a very good prospect. (op 28-1)
Black Snowflake(USA) is a strong colt who had two paddock handlers. He overcame traffic problems in a big field nursery at Goodwood last time, but failed to do so here. He had to shift right in a quick manoeuvre 3f out and was always fighting a losing battle thereafter. He confirmed form with Raine's Cross and there is probably a good race to\n\x\x be had with him. (tchd 11-8 and 13-8)
Raine's Cross ran well enough without looking a live contender in the final furlong. Although he comes from a sprinting family, he seemed reasonably happy over 1m. (op 8-1)
Dreamspeed(IRE) is a strong, attractive sort who looked particularly well. He was behind Big Audio last time and never looked like getting his revenge. (op 4-1)
The Starboard Bow pulled hard, as he did when winning at Yarmouth last time and was outclassed here. (tchd 28-1)

5215 BH.QMS LTD INDUSTRIAL CONTRACTING SERVICES MAIDEN STKS — 1m 1f 198y
6:55 (6:57) (Class 5) 3-4-Y-O — **£3,885** (£1,156; £577; £288) **Stalls** High

Form — RPR
5 **1** **Paisley**[34] 4097 3-8-12 0 ... WilliamBuick 3 — 77+
(L M Cumani) *trckd ldr: led wl over 2f out: wandered rt then lft u.p fr over 1f out but a in command: drvn out* **15/8**[1]
-233 **2** *1* **Alqaffay (IRE)**[12] 4822 4-9-11 74 ... RobertHavlin 5 — 77
(J H M Gosden) *led: rdn and hdd wl over 2f out: 1 l down whn hmpd over 1f out and jst ins fnl f but nvr finding enough to get bk on terms* **9/4**[2]
0 **3** *3 ½* **Day Of The Eagle (IRE)**[21] 4505 3-9-3 0 ... LPKeniry 6 — 70
(L M Cumani) *hld up: rdn and hdwy over 2f out: wnt 3rd over 1f out: styd on same pce* **33/1**
4 *9* **Bowsers Beau** 3-9-3 0 ... RichardHughes 1 — 52
(M P Tregoning) *in tch: hdwy to chal over 3f out: wknd over 1f out* **9/4**[2]
40 **5** *½* **Lady's Art (FR)**[129] 1269 3-8-12 0 ... JimCrowley 7 — 46
(E F Vaughan) *trckd ldr: effrt 3f out: wknd over 1f out* **9/1**[3]
0/4 **6** *½* **Red Army Commander (IRE)**[10] 4867 4-9-11 0 ... RichardThomas 2 — 50
(J A Geake) *in tch: rdn 4f out: wknd 2f out* **33/1**
00- **7** *7* **Coeur Brule (FR)**[282] 7289 3-9-1 0 ow5 ... EdwardSibbick(7) 4 — 41
(Edgar Byrne) *a in last pair* **100/1**

2m 9.86s (-0.04) **Going Correction** -0.05s/f (Good)
WFA 3 from 4yo 8lb — 7 Ran SP% **113.2**
Speed ratings (Par 103): **98,97,94,87,86 86,80**
toteswinger: 1&2 £1.10, 1&3 £8.20, 2&3 £7.80. CSF £6.27 TOTE £3.10: £1.50, £1.50; EX 7.00.
Owner Fittocks Stud **Bred** Fittocks Stud **Trained** Newmarket, Suffolk

FOCUS
Ordinary maiden form, rated around the runner-up. The winner should do better.

5216 WEATHERBYS BANK H'CAP — 1m 4f
7:30 (7:30) (Class 4) (0-85,84) 3-Y-O — **£4,857** (£1,445; £722; £360) **Stalls** High

Form — RPR
411 **1** **Acquisition**[46] 3687 3-9-0 77 ... IanMongan 7 — 87
(H R A Cecil) *trckd ldr: led over 3f out: rdn 2f out: styd on wl fnl 100yds: rdn out* **10/3**[2]
2343 **2** *1 ¼* **Non Dom (IRE)**[27] 4299 3-9-0 77 ... SteveDrowne 5 — 85
(H Morrison) *trckd ldrs: rdn over 2f out: chal over 1f out: no ex fnl 100yds* **7/2**[3]
-404 **3** *¾* **Worth A King'S**[20] 4518 3-8-9 72 ... WilliamBuick 1 — 79
(Sir Michael Stoute) *hld up in last trio: pushed along 5f out: rdn over 3f out: hdwy 2f out: styd on same pce* **16/1**
1204 **4** *3 ¼* **Sehoy (USA)**[15] 4715 3-9-7 84 ... RobertHavlin 4 — 86
(J H M Gosden) *hld up in last trio: trckd ldrs 3f out: nt clr run briefly whn rdn over 1f out: one pce fnl f* **7/1**
1324 **5** *1 ½* **Solar Graphite (IRE)**[27] 4299 3-8-10 73 ... RichardHughes 3 — 72
(J L Dunlop) *hld up in last trio: hdwy to trck ldrs over 4f out: rdn over 3f out: nt pce to mount chal: fading whn hung into rail ins fnl f* **3/1**[1]
0112 **6** *nk* **Halfway House**[15] 4696 3-9-2 79 ... HayleyTurner 2 — 78
(M L W Bell) *hld up last: hdwy and cl enough 4f out: sn rdn: nt clrest of runs but nvr pce to mount chal* **10/1**
1334 **7** *7* **Cry For The Moon (USA)**[29] 4248 3-9-4 81 ... JimCrowley 8 — 69
(Mrs A J Perrett) *t.k.h: trckd ldrs: effrt 3f out: squeezed up 2f out: sn wknd* **9/1**
2314 **8** *6* **Shemoli**[41] 3861 3-9-0 77 ... TedDurcan 6 — 55
(M A Jarvis) *led tl over 3f out: sn rdn: wknd over 2f out* **11/1**

2m 36.12s (-1.88) **Going Correction** -0.05s/f (Good) — 8 Ran SP% **116.1**
Speed ratings (Par 102): **104,103,102,100,99 99,94,90**
toteswinger: 1&2 £4.40, 1&3 £8.20, 2&3 £16.60. CSF £15.75 CT £161.90 TOTE £3.90: £1.60, £1.60, £5.40; EX 18.10.
Owner K Abdulla **Bred** Juddmonte Farms Ltd **Trained** Newmarket, Suffolk

FOCUS
An open handicap and a good race for the grade. The form looks sound with the first three possible improvers and the fourth setting the standard.
Solar Graphite(IRE) Official explanation: jockey said gelding hung right-handed into rail

5217 WESTOVER GROUP H'CAP — 1m 6f 21y
8:00 (8:00) (Class 5) (0-70,70) 3-Y-O+ — **£3,238** (£963; £481; £240)

Form — RPR
6532 **1** **Crocus Rose**[21] 4491 3-8-11 65 ... RichardHughes 11 — 74+
(H J L Dunlop) *mid-div tl lost pl and swtchd lft 5f out: hdwy over 3f out: chalng whn bmpd over 2f out: rdn to ld jst ins fnl f: asserted towards fin* **9/4**[1]
3465 **2** *¾* **Theologist (IRE)**[20] 4545 3-8-13 67 ... JimCrowley 12 — 75
(Mrs A J Perrett) *trckd ldrs: rdn to ld 2f out: sn hrd pressed: hdd jst ins fnl f: no ex* **3/1**[2]
1523 **3** *¾* **Colonel Flay**[8] 4951 5-9-11 70 ... JackMitchell(3) 3 — 77
(Mrs P N Dutfield) *hld up bhd: swtchd to center and hdwy fr over 3f out: rdn and ev ch whn edgd rt over 2f out: no ex ins fnl f* **3/1**[2]
-004 **4** *10* **The Composer**[31] 4168 7-8-10 52 oh7 ... LPKeniry 6 — 45
(M Blanshard) *mid-div: rdn over 3f out: little imp on ldrs but styd on to go 4th ins fnl f* **18/1**
00-0 **5** *1* **Top Ticket (IRE)**[19] 4563 4-9-11 67 ... (p) WilliamBuick 13 — 59
(D E Pipe) *trckd ldr: led after 2f: hdd after 3f: trckd ldr: led over 4f out: rdn and hdd over 2f out: steadily fdd* **20/1**
0504 **6** *5* **Lilac Wine**[11] 4862 6-8-5 52 oh4 ... (b[1]) RossAtkinson(5) 8 — 37
(D J S Ffrench Davis) *towards rr: rdn over 4f out: sn swtchd to r alone in center: styd on same pce wout ever threatening* **25/1**
5-00 **7** *10* **Lady Maya**[25] 4382 4-8-10 52 oh7 ... RichardKingscote 2 — 23
(P Henderson) *hld up towards rr: hdwy over 4f out: rdn and ev ch wl over 2f out: sn wknd* **40/1**
05 **8** *7* **Drum Major (IRE)**[14] 4744 4-9-9 65 ... SteveDrowne 5 — 26
(G L Moore) *mid-div tl wknd 2f out* **10/1**[3]
3600 **9** *13* **Silver Surprise**[8] 4948 5-8-7 52 oh7 ... (b) MarcHalford(3) 7 — —
(J J Bridger) *towards rr: hdwy over 5f out: wknd over 2f out* **50/1**
3234 **10** *1* **Regal Angel**[6] 5074 6-9-5 61 ... HayleyTurner 9 — 2
(Jean-Rene Auvray) *hld up towards rr: gd hdwy to trck ldrs after 5f: rdn and ev ch over 3f out: wknd qckly* **14/1**
6/0- **11** *6* **Go Free**[64] 1267 8-8-8 53 oh7 ow1 ... RussellKennemore(3) 1 — —
(J G M O'Shea) *prom: led after 3f tl over 4f out: sn wknd* **20/1**
-000 **12** *3 ½* **Improper (USA)**[14] 4735 3-7-12 52 oh7 ... NickyMackay 4 — —
(Mouse Hamilton-Fairley) *led for 2f: chsd ldrs tl wknd qckly 4f out* **66/1**

3m 5.49s (-1.91) **Going Correction** -0.05s/f (Good)
WFA 3 from 4yo+ 12lb — 12 Ran SP% **121.1**
Speed ratings (Par 103): **103,102,102,96,95 93,87,83,75,75 71,69**
toteswinger: 1&2 £2.60, 1&3 £1.90, 2&3 £3.00. CSF £8.43 CT £20.91 TOTE £3.30: £1.70, £1.50, £1.30; EX 10.00 Place 6: £16.10, Place 5: £12.11.
Owner When Harry Met Rosie Partnership **Bred** Biddestone Stud **Trained** Lambourn, Berks
■ Stewards' Enquiry : Ross Atkinson four-day ban: used whip with excessive frequency (Sep 4, 6-8)

FOCUS
No strength in depth here with half the field out of the handicap. The winner is progressing with a slight personal best from the runner-up.
T/Plt: £16.80 to a £1 stake. Pool: £36,394.23. 1,579.74 winning tickets. T/Qpdt: £19.10 to a £1 stake. Pool: £4,025.10. 155.40 winning tickets. TM

4952 SANDOWN (R-H)
Friday, August 21

OFFICIAL GOING: Good to firm changing to good after race 4 (3.50)
Wind: Moderate ahead Weather: Bright intervals

5218 ORLEANS NURSERY — 5f 6y
2:05 (2:06) (Class 4) 2-Y-O — **£3,885** (£1,156; £577; £288) **Stalls** High

Form — RPR
312 **1** **Duchess Dora (IRE)**[13] 4782 2-8-13 80 ... JamieKyne(5) 5 — 84+
(J J Quinn) *chsd ldrs: drvn to ld 1f out: sn in command: readily* **9/4**[1]
0023 **2** *2 ¼* **Bush Master**[11] 4851 2-8-7 69 ... PatDobbs 3 — 64
(R Hannon) *in rr but in tch: pushed along and hdwy 2f out: edgd rt ins fnl f and styd on to go 2nd wl nr fin but no ch w wnr* **8/1**
2252 **3** *½* **True Red (IRE)**[15] 4689 2-8-0 62 ... DavidProbert 6 — 56
(B R Millman) *chsd ldr: rdn 2f out: no imp on wnr fnl f and lost 2nd nr fin* **10/3**[3]
5624 **4** *1* **Vilnius**[1] 5194 2-8-3 65 ow3 ... ChrisCatlin 1 — 55
(M R Channon) *in rr but in tch: rdn fr 1/2-way: styd on fnl f but nvr gng pce to press ldng trio* **9/2**
1500 **5** *2 ½* **Palisades Park**[20] 4525 2-9-7 83 ... RichardHughes 4 — 69+
(R Hannon) *hld up in rr but in tch: nt clr run and swtchd lft over 1f out: swtchd rt and prog on rail whn hmpd ins fnl f: nt rcvr* **11/4**[2]
6001 **6** *nk* **Monte Mayor One**[17] 4626 2-8-6 68 ... JamieMackay 2 — 48
(D Haydn Jones) *led tl hdd 1f out: edgd rt u.p ins fnl f and sn wknd* **16/1**

62.55 secs (0.95) **Going Correction** +0.10s/f (Good) — 6 Ran SP% **115.7**
Speed ratings (Par 96): **96,92,91,90,86 85**
toteswinger: 1&2 £3.50, 1&3 £1.80, 2&3 £5.00. CSF £21.24 TOTE £3.20: £1.70, £2.70; EX 24.60.
Owner The Clay Family **Bred** Glending Bloodstock **Trained** Settrington, N Yorks

FOCUS
There was a downpour of 3mm before the first race but the going remained on the fast side. The rail was dolled out five or six yards from the far side on the sprint track. This fair nursery produced a convincing winner with the form rated around the runner-up and fourth.

NOTEBOOK
Duchess Dora(IRE) travelled well in behind the pace and, as soon as she got a gap between horses inside the final 2f, always looked like winning. She'd not been able to cope with the speedy Skylla at Haydock last time but this stiffer track suited her better and she was able to find the necessary improvement. (tchd 5-2, 11-4 in a place)
Bush Master, who was dropping back to the minimum trip having shown speed over 6f and 7f, was given a more patient ride this time and ran a sound race on his handicap debut. (op 7-1 tchd 13-2)
True Red(IRE) likes to lead and ran another good race from the front, but she could have done without Monte Mayor One pestering her on the front end. (op 4-1 tchd 9-2)
Vilnius briefly threatened to throw down a challenge out wide but it came to nothing and perhaps this race came too soon after her exertions the previous day. (op 6-1)
Palisades Park, who was dropping in class, didn't get much luck in running when looking for a way through from the rear. He shaped better than his finishing position suggests but looks likely to remain vulnerable in this sort of company off his current mark. Official explanation: vet said colt was found to be lame (op 100-30)
Monte Mayor One, another making her handicap debut, also likes to front-run, but the ground might have been on the quick side for her. (op 12-1 tchd 11-1)

5219 FURNITURE VILLAGE 20TH BIRTHDAY H'CAP — 5f 6y
2:40 (2:40) (Class 5) (0-75,74) 3-Y-O+ — **£3,238** (£963; £481; £240) **Stalls** High

Form — RPR
021 **1** **Step It Up (IRE)**[2] 5156 5-8-9 63 6ex ... JackMitchell(3) 4 — 76
(J R Boyle) *trckd ldr: led over 3f out: pushed along fnl f: kpt on wl: readily* **7/4**[1]
653 **2** *1 ½* **Chandika**[12] 4829 3-8-5 58 ... LukeMorris 9 — 65
(C G Cox) *chsd ldrs: chsd wnr 2nd and swtchd lft over 1f out then hung lft: styd on ins fnl f but nvr any ch w wnr* **10/1**
1211 **3** *2* **Solemn**[18] 4604 4-9-2 67 ... (b) DavidProbert 2 — 67
(J M Bradley) *chsd ldrs: rdn 2f out: styd on fnl f but nvr gng pce to get nr wnr* **10/3**[2]
0606 **4** *nk* **Gentle Guru**[9] 4907 5-9-9 74 ... SebSanders 3 — 73
(R T Phillips) *in rr: pushed along over 2f out: styd on wl fnl f but nvr gng pce to get into contention* **10/1**
30 **5** *¾* **Reigning Monarch (USA)**[20] 4536 6-8-1 57 oh6 ow2(b) RossAtkinson(5) 8 — 53
(Miss Z C Davison) *in rr: pidden 1/2-way: styd on fnl f but nvr in contention* **50/1**
0360 **6** *nk* **Even Bolder**[9] 4907 6-9-6 71 ... StephenCarson 6 — 66
(E A Wheeler) *trckd ldrs: rdn ins fnl 2f: edgd lft ins fnl f and sn btn* **11/2**[3]

000 7 1/2 **Sherjawy (IRE)**[6] 5020 5-8-7 58 (b) KirstyMilczarek 5 51
(Miss Z C Davison) *led tl hdd over 3f out: wknd over 1f out* **33/1**
0-43 8 2 1/2 **Handsome Cross (IRE)**[9] 4907 8-9-7 72 ChrisCatlin 1 56
(W J Musson) *a outpcd* **7/1**
61.66 secs (0.06) **Going Correction** +0.10s/f (Good)
WFA 3 from 4yo+ 2lb **8** Ran SP% **110.4**
Speed ratings (Par 103): **103,100,97,96,95 95,94,90**
toteswinger: 1&2 £2.90, 1&3 £1.30, 2&3 £2.90. CSF £19.12 CT £50.06 TOTE £2.50: £1.10, £1.80, £1.70; EX 15.30.
Owner The Vine Associates **Bred** David Fitzgerald **Trained** Epsom, Surrey

FOCUS
It paid to race fairly handily in this modest handicap. The winner is rated to the ebst of his winter form backed up by the runner-up.
Even Bolder Official explanation: jockey said gelding hung left

5220 EUROPEAN BREEDERS' FUND MAIDEN STKS 7f 16y
3:15 (3:17) (Class 4) 2-Y-O **£5,180** (£1,541; £770; £384) **Stalls** High

Form RPR
1 **Private Story (USA)** 2-9-3 0 PatDobbs 9 80+
(R Hannon) *chsd ldr tl dropped bk to cl 3rd over 2f out: qcknd to chse ldr again over 1f out: styd on strly ins fnl f to ld nr fin: won gng away* **25/1**
03 2 1/2 **Valiant Knight (FR)**[15] 4713 2-9-3 0 RichardHughes 10 79
(R Hannon) *led: rdn and styd on wl fr 2f out: hdd and outpcd cl home* **9/4**[1]
3 3/4 **Mufarrh (IRE)** 2-9-3 0 TPO'Shea 8 79+
(J L Dunlop) *in rr: pushed along 3f out: pushed along and hdwy fr 2f out: swtchd lft appr fnl f and rn green: styd on strly cl home* **5/1**[3]
4 2 3/4 **Goolagong (IRE)** 2-8-12 0 SebSanders 2 65
(R M Beckett) *chsd ldrs: rdn to chse ldr over 2f out: tl over 1f out and no imp: wknd ins fnl f* **7/2**[2]
0 5 3 1/4 **Viking Dancer**[24] 4410 2-9-3 0 DavidProbert 3 62
(A M Balding) *towards rr: rdn over 3f out and sme prog: kpt on u.p fnl 2f: styd on cl home* **7/1**
6 1 3/4 **Magnetic Force (IRE)** 2-9-3 0 ShaneKelly 5 58
(Sir Michael Stoute) *in rr: rdn over 3f out: sme prog fr over 1f out: styd on cl home* **10/1**
04 7 shd **Flying Destination**[23] 4439 2-9-3 0 ChrisCatlin 6 58
(W J Knight) *in rr: pushed along fr 3f out: styd on fnl 2f but nvr anywhere nr ldrs* **12/1**
8 nse **Oasis Dancer** 2-9-3 0 FergusSweeney 11 57
(R M Beckett) *chsd ldrs: rdn over 3f out: wknd ins fnl 2f* **22/1**
9 nse **Inside Track (IRE)** 2-9-3 0 TedDurcan 7 57
(B J Meehan) *chsd ldrs: rdn over 4f out: n.m.r and wknd 2f out* **25/1**
0 10 2 **Green Earth (IRE)**[8] 4945 2-9-3 0 AdamKirby 1 52
(Mrs A J Perrett) *in rr towards outside: mod prog fnl 2f* **12/1**
0 11 1 **Red Eddie**[14] 4756 2-9-3 0 NickyMackay 4 50
(B J Meehan) *chsd ldrs: rdn over 3f out: wknd over 2f out* **33/1**
1m 31.69s (2.19) **Going Correction** +0.225s/f (Good) **11** Ran SP% **121.6**
Speed ratings (Par 96): **96,95,94,91,87 85,85,85,85,83 82**
toteswinger: 1&2 £18.80, 1&3 £15.30, 2&3 £4.30. CSF £81.08 TOTE £28.60: £5.90, £1.40, £1.70; EX 150.60.
Owner Malih L Al Basti **Bred** Gail Peters Beitz **Trained** East Everleigh, Wilts

FOCUS
A fair maiden with the runner-up rated a minor improver.

NOTEBOOK
Private Story(USA), an American-bred 130,000euros purchase as a yearling, is apparently a laid-back individual at home and not a great deal was expected of him on his debut, hence his 25-1 SP, but he clearly boasts plenty of ability as he overcame his inexperience to wear down his stable companion close home. One of the Goffs Million races is apparently his big aim. (op 22-1 tchd 16-1)
Valiant Knight(FR) is progressing with racing and tried to make all the running. He had the run of the race but was cut down by his more talented stablemate close home, and he's likely to go the nursery route now. (op 100-30 tchd 7-2)
Mufarrh(IRE) ◆, who holds some big-race entries, is probably the one to take from the race, as he was very green and was looking about all over the place when asked to go about his business. He ran on really strongly without being given a hard time and can only improve for this experience. A maiden should be a formality before he steps up in class. Official explanation: jockey said colt was denied a clear run (op 8-1)
Goolagong(IRE) was caught out wide rounding the bend into the straight. A 105,000gns daughter of Giant's Causeway, she travelled up well two and a half furlongs out but could then find only the one pace. (op 11-4)
Viking Dancer, who looked to face an easier task than on his debut at Goodwood, was a little disappointing but will be of more interest once he goes handicapping. (op 10-1)
Magnetic Force(IRE) was weak in the market and looked in need of the run beforehand. His dam won over 1m4f and he should do better in time over further. (op 7-1)
Flying Destination is now eligible for a mark and should do better in handicaps.

5221 FURNITURE VILLAGE CELEBRATION H'CAP 1m 14y
3:50 (3:52) (Class 3) (0-90,90) 3-Y-O+ **£7,771** (£2,312; £1,155; £577) **Stalls** High

Form RPR
1- 1 **Bab Al Salam (USA)**[315] 6620 3-8-12 81 TedDurcan 2 89+
(Saeed Bin Suroor) *sn trcking ldrs: drvn and styd on to ld jst ins fnl f: rdn out* **9/2**[1]
0054 2 hd **Isphahan**[28] 4262 6-9-3 80 (v) DavidProbert 12 88
(A M Balding) *in rr: hdwy on outside over 2f out: rdn and edgd rt over 1f out: styd on wl fnl f: clsng on wnr nr fin but a jst hld* **16/1**
2003 3 1 1/2 **Light From Mars**[49] 3567 4-9-10 90 JamesMillman(3) 14 95
(B R Millman) *chsd ldrs: drvn to take slt ld over 1f out: sn hdd outpcd ins fnl f* **7/1**[2]
36-2 4 1 1/4 **Rainbow Mirage (IRE)**[161] 834 5-9-12 89 SebSanders 9 91
(E S McMahon) *s.i.s: in rr: hdwy on outside over 2f out: edgd lft and chal 1f out: sn one pce* **20/1**
0116 5 1 **Romany Princess (IRE)**[23] 4422 4-9-12 89 RichardHughes 5 90+
(R Hannon) *hld up in rr: hdwy and n.m.r 2f out: styd on fnl f but nvr gng pce to rch ldrs* **9/2**[1]
0644 6 nk **Salient**[10] 4871 5-9-1 78 KirstyMilczarek 8 77+
(M J Attwater) *chsd ldrs: rdn 2f out: hmpd 1f out: styd on again cl home* **20/1**
261 7 2 **Reel Buddy Star**[8] 4941 4-8-11 79 6ex JamieKyne(5) 6 73
(G M Moore) *chsd ldr: rdn to chal fr 3f out tl over 1f out: wknd and hung lft ins fnl f* **12/1**
2151 8 1/2 **Marajaa (IRE)**[24] 4409 7-9-13 90 ChrisCatlin 16 83+
(W J Musson) *hld up towards rr: stdy hdwy and n.m.r ins fnl 2f and over 1f out: nudged along and styd on strly fnl f but nvr in contention* **14/1**
0000 9 1 1/2 **Southandwest (IRE)**[13] 4796 5-9-5 82 LukeMorris 11 71
(J S Moore) *in rr: styd on fnl 2f: gng on cl home* **25/1**
4125 10 2 1/2 **Resurge (IRE)**[28] 4261 4-9-10 87 FergusSweeney 13 71
(W S Kittow) *led: rdn 3f out: kpt slt ld tl hdd over 1f out: wkng whn hmpd on rails ins fnl f* **15/2**[3]
6103 11 3 1/2 **Spirit Of Sharjah (IRE)**[8] 4954 4-9-11 88 TPO'Shea 17 70+
(Miss J Feilden) *in tch: hdwy on ins over 2f out: n.m.r whn styng on over 1f out: hmpd ins fnl f: nt rcvr and eased* **20/1**
1000 12 1 3/4 **Ellemujie**[24] 4409 4-9-7 89 JamesO'Reilly(5) 15 61
(D K Ivory) *in rr: sme hdwy on ins over 2f out: nvr gng pce to get into contention* **8/1**
0100 13 nk **Tudor Key (IRE)**[7] 4983 3-9-5 88 ShaneKelly 7 59
(Mrs A J Perrett) *chsd ldrs: rdn over 2f out: wkng whn hmpd over 1f out* **50/1**
00-5 14 1 **Kings Troop**[12] 4814 3-9-2 85 IanMongan 3 54
(H R A Cecil) *chsd ldrs: wkng whn hmpd ins fnl 2f* **50/1**
0411 15 20 **Gold Express**[32] 4149 6-9-3 80 NickyMackay 10 3
(P J O'Gorman) *a in rr* **15/2**[3]
1m 43.62s (0.32) **Going Correction** +0.225s/f (Good)
WFA 3 from 4yo+ 6lb **15** Ran SP% **125.8**
Speed ratings (Par 107): **107,106,105,104,103 102,100,100,98,96 92,91,90,89,69**
toteswinger: 1&2 £5.90, 1&3 £22.60, 2&3 £18.50. CSF £77.03 CT £522.40 TOTE £5.50: £2.20, £3.80, £3.10; EX 104.20.
Owner Godolphin **Bred** Darley **Trained** Newmarket, Suffolk

FOCUS
A competitive handicap but rather messy, although the runner-up appears to have run to his mark and is the best guide.

NOTEBOOK
Bab Al Salam(USA) had not been seen since winning a maiden on his debut on the Polytrack last October, but he crept in at the bottom of the weights in this handicap and, with his stable in flying form, it was no surprise to see him sent off favourite. His rider did well to bag a good early position from his wide draw, but he didn't pick up immediately when coming under pressure and had to dig deep, but he kept finding and he can surely only improve for this second career start. He could well develop into the right sort for the Dubai Carnival providing he progresses. (tchd 11-2)
Isphahan, second in this race last year, ran on strongly from off the pace despite hanging right, and once again came up slightly short. He won off a 5lb higher mark last autumn, though, so should remain competitive once reassessed.
Light From Mars, who seems to like this course, had a good position throughout tracking the leader on the rail. He had to wait for a gap to appear between horses, but it came soon enough and he had no real excuse. (op 8-1)
Rainbow Mirage(IRE) hadn't run since March so this was a good effort in the circumstances. Best with some cut, the drop of rain that had hit the track no doubt helped him a bit.
Romany Princess(IRE) found the gaps coming too late to throw down a meaningful challenge. She'd have been in the mix for the places with a clear run, but her style of running will always leave her vulnerable to trouble. (tchd 4-1 and 5-1)
Salient saved ground racing on the inside for much of the race before switching out to challenge. He had his chance but looks held off his current mark. Official explanation: jockey said gelding suffered interference in running (op 25-1)
Marajaa(IRE) didn't enjoy much luck as he tried to challenge from off the pace, and he can be forgiven this effort. (op 10-1)
Resurge(IRE) Official explanation: jockey said gelding lost a near-fore shoe
Spirit Of Sharjah(IRE) Official explanation: jockey said gelding was denied a clear run
Tudor Key(IRE) Official explanation: jockey said gelding suffered interference in running

5222 CAPITAL GROUP RECRUITMENT MAIDEN FILLIES' STKS 1m 14y
4:25 (4:26) (Class 5) 3-Y-O **£3,238** (£963; £481; £240) **Stalls** High

Form RPR
2-2 1 **Flora Trevelyan**[114] 1605 3-9-0 0 AdamKirby 7 87+
(W R Swinburn) *trckd ldr: led ins fnl 3f: c clr over 2f out: v easily* **4/5**[1]
3630 2 9 **Chicora (USA)**[68] 2942 3-9-0 67 RobertHavlin 6 66
(J H M Gosden) *led tl ins fnl 3f: briefly lost 2nd 2f out but sn chsng easy wnr and nvr any ch* **4/1**[2]
3 3 3/4 **Parallel (IRE)** 3-9-0 0 NickyMackay 4 57+
(J H M Gosden) *slowly away: awkward bnd whn hdwy 4f out: chsd easy wnr briefly 2f out: sn dropped bk to wl hld 3rd* **4/1**[2]
4 9 **Intimar (IRE)**[152] 3-9-0 0 IvanLopez 3 37
(R J Smith) *in 3rd tl rdn lost tch and continually flashed tail fnl 3f* **14/1**
5 1/2 **Choosy Floosy** 3-8-7 0 TobyAtkinson(7) 2 36
(Pat Eddery) *slowly away: a wl bhd* **12/1**[3]
1m 44.88s (1.58) **Going Correction** +0.225s/f (Good) **5** Ran SP% **109.9**
Speed ratings (Par 97): **101,92,88,79,78**
toteswinger: 1&2 £3.10. CSF £4.31 TOTE £1.70: £1.10, £2.00; EX 3.30.
Owner Pendley Farm **Bred** Pendley Farm **Trained** Aldbury, Herts

FOCUS
The going was changed to good from good to firm before this ordinary maiden.The winner did not need to improve to score, with the runner-up looking exposed as modest.
Choosy Floosy Official explanation: jockey said filly was slowly away

5223 HAMPTON COURT H'CAP 1m 2f 7y
5:00 (5:00) (Class 4) (0-80,83) 3-Y-O **£5,180** (£1,541; £770; £384) **Stalls** High

Form RPR
0046 1 **Master Fong (IRE)**[21] 4481 3-9-5 73 AdamKirby 6 76
(B W Hills) *trckd ldrs: hrd rdn and squeezed through between horses ins fnl f to ld cl home* **5/1**[2]
6040 2 1/2 **Nawaadi (USA)**[98] 2060 3-9-6 74 TPO'Shea 2 76
(J H M Gosden) *chsd ldr: rdn over 3f out: slt ld 2f out: hrd rdn fnl f: hdd and no ex cl home* **7/1**[3]
0-50 3 2 1/2 **Marju King (IRE)**[21] 4481 3-9-2 70 FergusSweeney 1 67
(W S Kittow) *in rr but in tch: rdn over 2f out: styd on to take 3rd ins fnl f but no ch w ldng pair* **12/1**
4443 4 1 3/4 **Red Suede Shoes**[10] 4872 3-9-0 68 ChrisCatlin 3 62
(B R Millman) *chsd ldrs: rdn to chal fr ins fnl 2f: edgd rt u.p ins fnl f: sn wknd* **14/1**
1121 5 3 1/4 **Brett Vale (IRE)**[9] 4910 3-10-1 83 6ex SebSanders 5 70
(Sir Mark Prescott) *mde most tl rdn and hdd 2f out: wknd over 1f out* **4/9**[1]
2m 10.76s (0.26) **Going Correction** +0.225s/f (Good) **5** Ran SP% **112.8**
Speed ratings (Par 102): **107,106,104,103,100**
toteswinger: 1&2 £10.60. CSF £36.32 TOTE £6.50: £2.70, £2.60; EX 36.50 Place 6: £53.27, Place 5: £20.58..
Owner Mrs Barbara James **Bred** Keatly Overseas Ltd **Trained** Lambourn, Berks
■ Stewards' Enquiry : Adam Kirby £140 fine: whip did not comply with Instruction H8

FOCUS
A fair handicap and the form appears sopund although the favourite disappointed.
T/Plt: £181.00 to a £1 stake. Pool: £50,006.54. 201.66 winning tickets. T/Qpdt: £75.20 to a £1 stake. Pool: £3,445.80. 33.90 winning tickets. ST

5102 WOLVERHAMPTON (A.W) (L-H)

Friday, August 21

OFFICIAL GOING: Standard changing standard to fast after race 2 (7.10)

Wind: Light half behind, becoming nil Weather: Fine

5224 ENJOY A PITCHER OF PIMM'S CLAIMING STKS 7f 32y(P)

6:40 (6:43) (Class 5) 2-Y-O £3,238 (£963; £481; £240) Stalls High

Form RPR

500 1 **Dear Mr Fantasy (IRE)**34 4080 2-9-0 58 PatCosgrave 5 61
(J W Hills) *s.i.s: sn hld up in tch: pushed along over 2f out: rdn wl over 1f out: led wl ins fnl f: r.o* 11/1

454 2 nk **Zaffature**9 4915 2-8-11 0 DarryllHolland 9 57
(M Botti) *hld up towards rr: pushed along over 3f out: swtchd lft and hdwy over 2f out: led wl over 1f out: sn rdn: hung rt 1f out: hdd wl ins fnl f: r.o* 7/2[2]

000 3 3/4 **High Resolution**9 4915 2-8-7 0 WilliamCarson(3) 7 54
(S C Williams) *hld up: hdwy over 3f out: c wd and rdn wl over 1f out: kpt on ins fnl f* 10/1

6406 4 1 **Bathwick Gino**9 4912 2-8-8 59 PaulDoe 8 50
(P D Evans) *hld up in rr: rdn and hdwy wl over 1f out: kpt on same pce u.p fnl f* 25/1

000 5 2 1/4 **Double Rollover**7 4973 2-8-7 0 (p) AlanMunro 4 43
(W R Muir) *led: hdd over 2f out: rdn and hdd wl over 1f out: wknd ins fnl f* 40/1

0231 6 1 **Gold Fix (IRE)**7 4973 2-8-6 68 JimmyQuinn 12 43+
(M R Channon) *bhd: pushed along whn n.m.r over 3f out: rdn and hdwy 1f out: sn hung bdly lft: nvr trbld ldrs* 4/5[1]

640 7 hd **Gulf Punch**8 4931 2-8-7 59 JamieMackay 2 41
(M F Harris) *w ldr: led over 2f out: rdn and hdd wl over 1f out: wknd ins fnl f* 8/1[3]

000 8 2 **Woodenitbenice**11 4856 2-8-0 0 ow1 MartinLane(5) 3 34
(D Shaw) *s.i.s: sn hld up in tch: pushed along and wknd over 2f out* 100/1

00 9 9 **Mizair Nouvair (IRE)**7 4993 2-8-0 0 (v) AndrewHeffernan(7) 10 14
(J R Weymes) *hld up in tch: lost pl over 4f out: bhd and hmpd over 3f out: sn lost tch* 100/1

0 P **Rock Of Behistun (IRE)**30 4200 2-8-8 0 DominicFox(3) 6 —
(P L Gilligan) *prom tl wnt lame over 3f out: p.u and dismntd over 2f out* 50/1

1m 30.46s (0.86) **Going Correction** -0.175s/f (Stan) 10 Ran SP% 116.5
Speed ratings (Par 94): **88,87,86,85,83 81,81,79,69,—**
toteswinger: 1&2 £6.70, 1&3 £29.30, 2&3 £9.80. CSF £48.41 TOTE £10.70: £3.70, £1.30, £2.70; EX 63.40.
Owner Christopher Wright & Mrs J A Wright **Bred** Stratford Place Stud **Trained** Upper Lambourn, Berks
■ Stewards' Enquiry : Darryll Holland caution: careless riding

FOCUS
A dreadfully weak claimer and the form is devalued by the very disappointing effort of form choice Gold Fix, who was in trouble a long way out. The pace wasn't very strong and a few were quite keen as the field bunched up.

NOTEBOOK
Dear Mr Fantasy(IRE) was always close to the pace and battled on bravely up the straight to repel the challenge of the runner-up. He had looked regressive in turf maidens since his encouraging first run, but the combination of a drop in class and switch to Polytrack enabled him to step up. (op 12-1)
Zaffature came from further back and was only just edged out in the closing stages. She can win a weak race. (op 11-4 tchd 5-2)
High Resolution, who was well backed at double figure odds, proved a completely different animal from the one that was beaten 19l in a Yarmouth claimer last time. He travelled well in midfield, boxing on gamely without being able to reel in the winner. (op 16-1 tchd 22-1)
Bathwick Gino came from miles back to post a career best on his first try at this trip. (op 33-1)
Double Rollover dropped away after racing in the front-rank early on.
Rock Of Behistun(IRE) Official explanation: jockey said colt lost its action

5225 GALA CASINO WOLVERHAMPTON CASINO MAGIC H'CAP 5f 216y(P)

7:10 (7:12) (Class 6) (0-60,60) 3-Y-O+ £2,388 (£705; £352) Stalls Low

Form RPR

3050 1 **Bertie Southstreet**21 4479 6-9-7 60 (v[1]) DarryllHolland 7 70
(Karen George) *mde all: clr whn rdn wl over 1f out: jst hld on* 12/1

0630 2 nse **Loyal Royal (IRE)**6 5019 6-9-0 56 (b) JackDean(3) 5 65
(J M Bradley) *s.i.s: hld up in mid-div: hdwy 2f out: rdn and r.o ins fnl f: jst failed* 9/1

2100 3 nk **Dickie Le Davoir**35 4072 5-9-3 56 (v) PatCosgrave 8 61+
(John A Harris) *s.i.s: hld up towards rr: hdwy on ins whn hmpd over 1f out: sn swtchd rt: r.o towards fin: fin 4th: plcd 3rd* 13/2[3]

334 4 2 1/4 **Poppy's Rose**28 4281 5-9-4 57 TGMcLaughlin 1 58
(I W McInnes) *hld up in tch on ins: swtchd rt over 2f out: rdn and chsd wnr wl over 1f out: sn hung lft: no ex and lost 2nd wl ins fnl f: fin 3rd and disqualified: plcd 4th* 11/4[1]

4345 5 1 **Bertie Vista**9 4887 4-9-4 57 (p) DuranFentiman 3 55
(T D Easterby) *prom: chsd wnr briefly wl over 1f out: sn carried lft: wknd ins fnl f* 17/2

02-5 6 2 1/4 **The City Kid (IRE)**231 14 6-9-2 60 GabrielHannon(5) 10 51
(G D Blake) *hld up in mid-div: swtchd lft and sme hdwy on ins over 1f out: rdn whn swtchd lft ins fnl f: nvr trbld ldrs* 22/1

305 7 3/4 **Cactus Curtsey**26 4337 3-9-4 60 (t) GeorgeBaker 4 48
(J R Fanshawe) *hld up in tch: pushed along over 2f out: wknd over 1f out* 9/2[2]

4000 8 1/2 **Mafaheem**31 4183 7-9-2 55 (b) StephenDonohoe 11 42
(A B Haynes) *s.i.s: hld up towards rr: hrd rdn and hung lft wl over 1f out: n.d* 16/1

5050 9 nk **Great Knight (IRE)**6 5018 4-9-3 56 AlanMunro 2 42
(S Kirk) *hld up in tch: wknd over 2f out* 10/1

4030 10 1 **Dhhamaan (IRE)**11 4859 4-9-5 58 (b) PJMcDonald 12 41
(Mrs R A Carr) *hld up in mid-div on outside: forced wd over 2f out: c wd st: sn hung bdly lft: n.d after* 12/1

6-00 11 shd **Ay Tay Tate (IRE)**16 4660 3-8-12 59 MartinLane(5) 9 41
(D Shaw) *a in rr* 40/1

4060 12 1 1/2 **Bahamian Bliss**30 4203 4-9-7 60 PaulDoe 6 38
(J A R Toller) *a in rr* 18/1

6200 13 1 1/4 **Gioacchino (IRE)**30 4191 4-9-1 57 KevinGhunowa(3) 13 31
(R A Harris) *chsd wnr tl rdn wl over 1f out: sn wknd* 33/1

1m 13.8s (-1.20) **Going Correction** -0.175s/f (Stan)
WFA 3 from 4yo+ 3lb 13 Ran SP% 124.1
Speed ratings (Par 101): **101,100,97,97,96 93,92,91,91,89 89,87,86**
toteswinger: 1&2 £25.30, 1&3 £38.90, 2&3 £4.90. CSF £118.28 CT £781.27 TOTE £10.10: £3.90, £3.00, £2.40; EX 155.40.
Owner Mrs Isabel Fraser **Bred** B Whitehouse **Trained** Higher Eastington, Devon
■ Stewards' Enquiry : Stephen Donohoe two-day ban: careless riding (Sep 4, 6)

FOCUS
A low-grade handicap which was effectively won at the start. The winner is rated in line with this year's form with the runner-up to his mark.
Dhhamaan(IRE) Official explanation: jockey said gelding hung left

5226 BEST HAT COMPETITION FILLIES' (S) STKS 5f 20y(P)

7:45 (7:46) (Class 5) 2-Y-O £2,729 (£806; £403) Stalls Low

Form RPR

56 1 **Wanchai Whisper**16 4666 2-8-12 0 LiamJones 3 66+
(W J Haggas) *s.i.s: hld up: hdwy on ins whn nt clr run over 2f out: rdn to ld ent fnl f: sn clr: r.o wl* 5/2[1]

5005 2 5 **Prettiest Star (IRE)**13 4800 2-8-12 49 (p) StephenDonohoe 2 48
(K A Ryan) *led: rdn wl over 1f out: hdd ent fnl f: sn btn* 9/1

000 3 3/4 **Tulip Explosion**9 4889 2-8-12 0 PaulEddery 6 45
(D Shaw) *n.m.r and bmpd s: t.k.h towards rr: hdwy wl over 1f out: kpt on ins fnl f* 33/1

3100 4 shd **Wigan Lane**14 4739 2-9-1 67 FrederikTylicki(3) 8 51
(R A Fahey) *wnt rt and bmpd s: mid-div: pushed along over 2f out: rdn wl over 1f out: kpt on fnl f: jst failed to take 3rd* 10/3[2]

2246 5 3/4 **Reel Credit Crunch**72 2800 2-8-5 65 (b[1]) AndrewHeffernan(7) 13 42
(I W McInnes) *chsd ldrs on outside: c wd st: rdn and hung lft 1f out: one pce* 7/1

3535 6 1 1/4 **Gasparilla (IRE)**10 4884 2-8-12 50 AndrewMullen 5 38
(A J McCabe) *wnt lft and bmpd s: prom: pushed along over 2f out: rdn wl over 1f out: sn wknd* 5/1[3]

500 7 shd **Cariad Coch**91 2226 2-8-12 0 TGMcLaughlin 11 37
(Mrs L Stubbs) *outpcd: rdn over 3f out: nvr nrr* 20/1

6404 8 2 1/2 **Mrs Jones And Me (IRE)**25 4370 2-8-12 58 (b[1]) FrankieMcDonald 9 28
(P T Midgley) *prom: pushed along over 2f out: wknd wl over 1f out* 16/1

0066 9 3/4 **London Girl (IRE)**7 4973 2-8-5 48 (p) DeclanCannon(7) 4 26
(A J McCabe) *chsd ldrs on ins: wnt 2nd over 2f out: rdn wl over 1f out: sn wknd* 25/1

6354 10 1 3/4 **Acting Elegant**25 4384 2-8-12 52 PaulDoe 10 19
(P D Evans) *sn outpcd* 12/1

000 11 8 **Nidamar**81 2541 2-8-12 0 PJMcDonald 12 —
(Mrs R A Carr) *prom tl wknd 2f out* 66/1

62.27 secs (-0.03) **Going Correction** -0.175s/f (Stan) 11 Ran SP% 117.4
Speed ratings (Par 91): **93,85,83,83,82 80,80,76,75,72 59**
toteswinger: 1&2 £4.70, 1&3 £20.40, 2&3 £39.20. CSF £24.86 TOTE £4.00: £1.40, £2.70, £9.50; EX 30.20.The winner was sold to David Evans for 11,500gns. Wigan Lane was claimed by Paul Howling for £6,000.
Owner M S Bloodstock Ltd **Bred** Mike Smith **Trained** Newmarket, Suffolk

FOCUS
A fillies' seller and not form to be getting excited about. The pace was fast and furious and that set things up for the closers.

NOTEBOOK
Wanchai Whisper was slow from the gates and was stuck at the back of the field early, but that probably worked in her favour as they were going too quick up front. Having got a split up the inside rail, she swept past the runner-up to win as she liked. The drop back in trip suited her well – she pulled her chance away over 7f last time – and this represented a drop in class. She is open to improvement, but sprinting looks her game as she travels well off a strong pace. (op 3-1 tchd 100-30)
Prettiest Star(IRE) did well to hold on for second having set such a searching pace. On this evidence, she ought to be able to find a race. (tchd 17-2 and 10-1)
Tulip Explosion didn't get the clearest of runs towards the back of the field and put in enough decent late work to suggest she's not a lost cause. (op 28-1)
Wigan Lane found the pace too hot and although she made late headway, she couldn't get into it and needs stepping up to 6f. (op 11-4 tchd 7-2)
Reel Credit Crunch looked one paced in the closing stages and isn't improving. (op 17-2)

5227 G4S IN PARTNERSHIP WITH IFORCE H'CAP 1m 4f 50y(P)

8:15 (8:15) (Class 5) (0-70,70) 3-Y-O+ £3,885 (£1,156; £577; £288) Stalls Low

Form RPR

400 1 **Rose Row**21 4498 5-9-5 65 GeorgeBaker 9 71
(Mrs Mary Hambro) *hld up in mid-div: stdy hdwy over 3f out: chalng whn edgd lft over 1f out: led ent fnl f: rdn out* 20/1

3460 2 3/4 **Watson's Bay**6 5035 4-9-6 66 PatCosgrave 7 71+
(P Howling) *s.i.s: hld up and bhd: hdwy on outside over 2f out: c wd st: rdn ins fnl f: edgd lft wl ins fnl f: styd on: nt rch wnr* 7/2[1]

3-00 3 2 **Highland Love**15 4710 4-9-2 65 FrederikTylicki(3) 4 67
(J T Stimpson) *racd keenly: a.p: led 2f out: sn rdn: hdd ent fnl f: no ex and lost 2nd towards fin* 20/1

3040 4 nk **Smooth As Silk (IRE)**25 4373 4-9-2 62 (b[1]) SebSanders 1 64
(C R Egerton) *hld up towards rr: hdwy on ins whn n.m.r briefly 2f out: sn swtchd rt: hrd rdn over 1f out: one pce ins fnl f* 10/1

6003 5 1/2 **Filun**14 4745 4-9-2 65 AndreaAtzeni(3) 5 66
(A Middleton) *hld up in mid-div: hdwy over 2f out: rdn jst over 1f out: one pce* 8/1

6152 6 3 3/4 **Graylyn Ruby (FR)**36 4007 4-9-10 70 AlanMunro 8 65
(J Jay) *hld up towards rr: pushed along over 2f out: rdn over 1f out: nvr nr ldrs* 11/2[3]

4000 7 9 **Wind Flow**16 4644 5-9-10 70 (v) DarryllHolland 10 50
(C A Dwyer) *w ldr: led after 2f: rdn and hdd 2f out: sn wknd* 10/1

6531 8 1 1/2 **New England**11 4857 7-9-4 64 6ex LiamJones 6 42
(W M Brisbourne) *hld up in mid-div: pushed along over 3f out: bhd fnl 2f* 5/1[2]

-000 9 3 **Allanit (GER)**163 798 5-9-10 70 JerryO'Dwyer 2 43
(B J Curley) *t.k.h: led 2f: chsd ldr: ev ch over 2f out: sn rdn and wknd* 8/1

0605 10 4 **Flying Squad (UAE)**120 1479 5-9-5 65 JamieMackay 12 32
(M F Harris) *a in rr* 33/1

04 11 13 **Takizada (IRE)**21 4495 4-9-5 65 JimmyQuinn 3 11
(J R Gask) *hld up in tch: wknd wl over 2f out* 8/1

2m 37.23s (-3.87) **Going Correction** -0.175s/f (Stan) 11 Ran SP% 118.3
Speed ratings (Par 103): **105,104,103,102,102 100,94,93,91,88 79**
toteswinger: 1&2 £20.80, 1&3 £54.80, 2&3 £22.90. CSF £87.63 CT £1460.69 TOTE £16.00: £3.60, £1.70, £4.20; EX 92.00.
Owner Mrs Richard Hambro **Bred** Cotswold Stud **Trained** Bourton-on-the-Hill, Gloucs

FOCUS
A modest handicap in which the pace was good which makes the form look sound, if limited, rated around the first two.

5228 BEST DRESSED COUPLE COMPETITION MEDIAN AUCTION MAIDEN STKS 1m 141y(P)
8:45 (8:45) (Class 6) 3-4-Y-O £2,047 (£604; £302) Stalls Low

Form RPR
2 1 **Golden Button (IRE)**27 4303 4-9-5 0 SebSanders 3 77+
(Sir Mark Prescott) *mde all: set stdy pce: qcknd over 2f out: rdn and r.o wl ins fnl f* 13/8[1]
23 2 1 3/4 **Expressive**16 4648 3-8-7 0 Louis-PhilippeBeuzelin(5) 6 73
(Sir Michael Stoute) *a.p: rdn and ev ch jst over 1f out: nt qckn ins fnl f* 2/1[2]
6 3 1/2 **Satwa Moon (USA)**13 4789 3-9-3 0 StephenDonohoe 1 77
(E A L Dunlop) *s.i.s: sn prom: pushed along over 2f out: rdn and ev ch over 1f out: nt qckn ins fnl f* 7/2[3]
4 4 **Tiddliwinks** 3-9-0 0 FrederikTylicki(3) 12 67
(K A Ryan) *s.i.s: hdwy over 6f out: rdn over 2f out: wknd wl over 1f out* 33/1
0220 5 3/4 **Layer Cake**13 4789 3-9-3 69 SimonWhitworth 9 66
(J W Hills) *hld up towards rr: hdwy over 2f out: rdn wl over 1f out: sn wknd* 6/1
0 6 7 **Jezza**13 4789 3-9-3 0 TGMcLaughlin 7 50
(Karen George) *hld up and bhd: rdn and short-lived effrt on ins over 2f out* 66/1
004 7 2 **Champion Girl (IRE)**20 4535 3-8-12 55 JamieMackay 11 40
(D Haydn Jones) *t.k.h: w wnr tl rdn over 2f out: wkng whn hung rt and rn wd ent st wl over 1f out* 40/1
P 8 3 1/2 **The Coach**45 3718 3-9-3 0 NeilChalmers 8 37
(T Wall) *hld up and bhd: pushed along over 3f out: sn struggling* 100/1
6 9 2 3/4 **Diamond Paula (IRE)**8 4936 3-8-12 0 PaulDoe 4 26
(P D Evans) *s.i.s: in rr: pushed along and struggling over 3f out* 50/1
5 10 1 1/4 **Silvertown Boy**87 2364 3-9-3 0 PJMcDonald 10 28
(H A McWilliams) *t.k.h in mid-div: bhd fnl 3f* 100/1

1m 49.34s (-1.16) **Going Correction** -0.175s/f (Stan)
WFA 3 from 4yo 7lb 10 Ran SP% 118.8
Speed ratings (Par 101): **98,96,96,92,91 85,83,80,78,77**
toteswinger: 1&2 £1.10, 1&3 £2.40, 2&3 £2.20. CSF £5.15 TOTE £3.30: £1.30, £1.10, £1.60; EX 6.90.
Owner William Charnley & Tweenhills Racing **Bred** Glashare House Stud **Trained** Newmarket, Suffolk

FOCUS
No depth to this maiden and the form horses dominated. The form is not solid and somewhat muddling.

5229 G4S IN PARTNERSHIP WITH NYK LOGISTICS H'CAP 1m 141y(P)
9:15 (9:15) (Class 6) (0-60,60) 3-Y-O+ £2,388 (£705; £352) Stalls Low

Form RPR
42 1 **Sotik Star (IRE)**16 4667 6-9-7 58 JimmyQuinn 9 67+
(K A Morgan) *s.i.s: sn hld up in mid-div: nt clr run fr over 3f out: hdwy wl over 1f out: hrd rdn to ld ins fnl f: drvn out* 11/2[2]
01 2 nk **Atacama Sunrise**50 3551 3-9-2 60 DO'Donohoe 5 68+
(J Pearce) *hld up towards rr: hdwy on outside over 2f out: c v wd st: led wl over 1f out: sn rdn: hung lft 1f out: hdd ins fnl f: r.o* 9/1
0202 3 1 1/2 **Debdene Bank (IRE)**19 4563 6-9-7 58 GeorgeBaker 11 63
(Mrs Mary Hambro) *hld up in mid-div: hdwy on outside 3f out: c wd st: rdn and edgd lft 1f out: nt qckn* 6/1[3]
2002 4 4 1/2 **The Grey One (IRE)**4 5103 6-9-4 58 (p) KevinGhunowa(3) 3 53
(J M Bradley) *hld up in tch: rdn over 2f out: wknd fnl f* 4/1[1]
4506 5 1/2 **Confide In Me**16 4645 5-9-7 58 (bt[1]) SebSanders 8 52
(G A Butler) *hld up in mid-div: hdwy 6f out: rdn and wnt 2nd briefly 2f out: wkng whn n.m.r jst over 1f out* 6/1[3]
0001 6 1/2 **Zennerman (IRE)**3 5126 6-8-11 55 (v) SPRyan(7) 6 47
(W M Brisbourne) *a.p: wnt 2nd 6f out: led 3f out: hdd wl over 1f out: wknd fnl f* 4/1[1]
4000 7 2 3/4 **Novastasia (IRE)**31 4179 3-8-13 60 (p) AndreaAtzeni(3) 12 46
(W R Swinburn) *hld up towards rr: rdn on ins over 2f out: nvr nr ldrs* 33/1
1233 8 1/2 **Aggbag**25 4376 5-8-10 54 DeclanCannon(7) 7 39
(Miss M E Rowland) *hld up in tch: lost pl 3f out: rdn and bhd fnl 2f* 12/1
4000 9 1 **Herbert Crescent**109 1734 4-9-1 55 FrederikTylicki(3) 2 38
(Ollie Pears) *led early: chsd ldr to 6f out: prom tl rdn and wknd wl over 1f out* 25/1
3000 10 1 1/2 **Ardent Prince**154 898 6-9-5 56 AndrewMullen 13 35
(A J McCabe) *stdd s: hld up in rr: rdn over 2f out: struggling whn nt clr run and swtchd lft over 1f out* 28/1
0-30 11 10 **Well Of Echoes**68 2942 3-9-2 60 PatCosgrave 10 16
(J A Glover) *sn led: hdd 3f out: wknd wl over 1f out: eased fnl f* 25/1

1m 48.68s (-1.82) **Going Correction** -0.175s/f (Stan)
WFA 3 from 4yo+ 7lb 11 Ran SP% 115.7
Speed ratings (Par 101): **101,100,99,95,94 94,92,91,90,89 80**
toteswinger: 1&2 £10.80, 1&3 £7.80, 2&3 £15.90. CSF £50.60 CT £313.44 TOTE £7.50: £2.20, £3.30, £2.80; EX 85.80 Place 6: £225.83, Place 5: £73.57.
Owner J D M Stables **Bred** Holborn Trust Co **Trained** Newmarket, Suffolk

FOCUS
Quite a competitive low-grade handicap and the pace was honest. The form looks sound with the first two possibly better than the bare form and the third the best guide to the level.
T/Plt: £782.90 to a £1 stake. Pool: £62,097.53. 57.90 winning tickets. T/Qpdt: £57.30 to a £1 stake. Pool: £7,200.89. 92.90 winning tickets. KH

5198 YORK (L-H)
Friday, August 21

OFFICIAL GOING: Good to firm (8.5)
Wind: Fresh across Weather: Sunny periods

5230 SKY BET MELROSE STKS (HERITAGE H'CAP) 1m 6f
1:45 (1:45) (Class 2) (0-105,97) 3-Y-O £32,380 (£9,635; £4,815; £2,405) Stalls Low

Form RPR
1215 1 **Akmal**23 4420 3-9-3 93 RHills 3 105
(J L Dunlop) *lw: hld up in tch on inner: hdwy over 4f out: chsd ldr 3f out: effrt to chal wl over 1f out: rdn to ld ins fnl f: kpt on wl* 8/1[3]
1126 2 3/4 **Alanbrooke**13 4767 3-9-3 93 (b) JoeFanning 11 104
(M Johnston) *dwlt: sn trcking ldr: hdwy to ld 4f out: rdn along wl over 2f out: drvn and hdd ins fnl f: kpt on gamely u.p* 12/1
3331 3 hd **Bernie The Bolt (IRE)**14 4743 3-8-4 80 WilliamBuick 9 91
(A M Balding) *hld up: hdwy over 5f out: effrt on outer and in tch over 2f out: rdn to chse ldrs wl over 1f out: drvn ins fnl f and kpt on wl* 20/1
1314 4 1/2 **Cosmic Sun**23 4420 3-9-2 92 PaulHanagan 4 102+
(R A Fahey) *in tch: hdwy to chse ldrs 4f out: rdn along over 2f out: drvn over 1f out: kpt on same pce ins fnl f* 9/2[1]
2022 5 2 1/4 **Gibb River (IRE)**14 4743 3-8-2 78 AdrianMcCarthy 1 85
(P W Chapple-Hyam) *lw: hld up towards rr: hdwy over 3f out: rdn along over 2f out: drvn and kpt on fnl f: nrst fin* 20/1
0131 6 1 **Classic Vintage (USA)**23 4420 3-9-7 97 JimCrowley 7 102
(Mrs A J Perrett) *lw: trckd ldrs: effrt over 3f out: rdn over 2f out: sn drvn and kpt on same pce* 9/2[1]
4211 7 1/2 **Penang Princess**57 3300 3-8-0 83 JPFahy(7) 13 88
(R M Beckett) *lw: chsd ldrs: styd far side home st and rdn along over 3f out: drvn and one pce fnl 2f* 8/1[3]
-101 8 1 3/4 **Braveheart Move (IRE)**5 5067 3-9-2 92 6ex RyanMoore 2 94
(Sir Mark Prescott) *hld up: hdwy over 4f out: rdn to chse ldrs 3f out: drvn over 2f out and sn wknd* 13/2[2]
1323 9 1 1/2 **Final Victory**13 4785 3-8-9 85 EddieAhern 10 85
(A M Balding) *chsd ldrs: effrt over 3f out: rdn along over 2f out: sn drvn and grad wknd* 16/1
1304 10 6 **Barwell Bridge**13 4767 3-9-0 90 JamesDoyle 14 82
(S Kirk) *chsd ldrs: rdn along over 3f out: wknd wl over 2f out* 25/1
4315 11 13 **Royal Trooper (IRE)**15 4709 3-8-1 77 MartinDwyer 6 51
(J G Given) *a in rr* 33/1
6456 12 15 **Too Much Trouble**23 4420 3-9-6 96 JimmyFortune 12 49
(M R Channon) *in tch: hdwy to chse ldrs over 4f out: rdn over 3f out and sn wknd* 12/1
1-02 13 22 **Alcalde**6 5034 3-8-6 82 (b[1]) RoystonFrench 5 4
(M Johnston) *led: rdn along and hdd over 4f out: styd far side home st: sn wknd and eased fnl 2f* 10/1

2m 58.47s (-1.73) **Going Correction** +0.075s/f (Good) 13 Ran SP% 118.6
Speed ratings (Par 106): **107,106,106,106,104 104,104,103,102,98 91,82,70**
toteswinger: 1&2 £11.50, 1&3 £16.50, 2&3 £43.80. CSF £94.05 CT £1857.18 TOTE £9.20: £2.20, £4.50, £5.20; EX 112.00 Trifecta £1378.60 Part won. Pool £1,862.98 - 0.40 winning units..
Owner Hamdan Al Maktoum **Bred** Shadwell Estate Company Limited **Trained** Arundel, W Sussex
■ Stewards' Enquiry : R Hills caution: used whip down shoulder in forehand position.
J P Fahy six-day ban: excessive use of the whip (Sep 4-9)
William Buick one-day ban: excessive use of the whip (Sep 4)

FOCUS
As always, this fiercely competitive handicap was full of progressive and solid handicappers, and even those beaten are ones to keep on-side. Only two years previously, the now Group 1 winner Ask finished second to Trick Or Treat, who herself went on to Group 3 success. Looking even further back, subsequent Ascot Gold Cup placer Distinction only managed third in 2002. There did not look any hard luck stories on this quick ground and the form looks good the first three all running close to previous marks.

NOTEBOOK
Akmal deserves plenty of credit considering it had been quite a while since a horse managed to carry over nine stone to victory in this. Representing a stable that has a fine record in the contest, he moved well throughout and pulled out plenty when asked. The same connections took this with Tawqeet in 2007, who eventually went on to be successful in Australia, so one would imagine Akmal has more to offer. (op 11-1)
Alanbrooke is really well bred for this sort of trip but has been an inconsistent performer for most of the season. He was given a good lead by his stablemate Alcalde and kept on relentlessly to the line, losing little in defeat. Staying distances suit him best.
Bernie The Bolt(IRE) got off the mark last time but could not quite get on terms with the first two after being held up. It was still a decent effort, albeit getting plenty of weight, and he remains capable of better in handicaps. (tchd 16-1)
Cosmic Sun has been in great heart all season and is a tough customer. He did not move that well to post but ran his customary good race and has let very few people down this year. (op 5-1)
Gibb River(IRE), who was behind Bernie The Bolt last time when tried in blinkers, was fractious in the stalls and did not get away quickly. He became outpaced over 2f out but did stay on well to catch the eye.
Classic Vintage(USA), stepping up in distance, finished in front of Akmal and Cosmic Sun at Goodwood last time, but the combination of a big weight and new trip appeared to find him out. (op 11-2)
Penang Princess, returning from an absence, was taken to the far rail on turning in and stayed there to make her bid alone. That did not seem a big disadvantage to her and she kept on really well.
Braveheart Move(IRE), making a swift reappearance, was once again very keen in the early stages and can make bigger improvement when learning to settle. (op 11-2)
Alcalde dropped right away after running too keen in first-time blinkers Official explanation: jockey said colt ran too free (op 9-1)

5231 SKY BET STRENSALL STKS (GROUP 3) 1m 208y
2:15 (2:18) (Class 1) 3-Y-O+
£56,770 (£21,520; £10,770; £5,370; £2,690; £1,350) Stalls Low

Form RPR
4210 1 **Palavicini (USA)**64 3050 3-8-12 107 EddieAhern 2 112
(J L Dunlop) *t.k.h: trckd ldrs: hdwy 3f out: effrt 2f out and sn rdn: edgd lft and stydon ent fnl f to ld last 100yds* 8/1
0144 2 1 **Dream Lodge (IRE)**3 5137 5-9-5 104 PaulHanagan 5 110
(R A Fahey) *lw: led: styd alone on far rail in home st and sn pushed along: rdn wl over 2f out: drvn over 1f out: hdd and no ex last 100yds* 16/1
-261 3 4 1/2 **Perfect Stride**63 3089 4-9-5 113 RyanMoore 3 100
(Sir Michael Stoute) *lw: t.k.h early: trckd ldrs: hdwy on outer 3f out and sn cl up: rdn along 2f out and ev ch tl drvn and one pce ent fnl f* 7/2[2]
3011 4 1 1/2 **Spring Of Fame (USA)**16 4685 3-8-12 110 LDettori 4 97
(Saeed Bin Suroor) *lw: sn prom: cl up 1/2-way: rdn along wl over 2f out and ev ch tl drvn and wknd appr fnl f* 9/2[3]
1144 5 1 **Forgotten Voice (IRE)**23 4419 4-9-5 113 JimmyFortune 6 95
(J Noseda) *hld up: hdwy 3f out: rdn to chse ldrs over 2f out: sn drvn and btn wl over 1f out* 9/4[1]
-052 6 1/2 **Lord Admiral (USA)**29 4253 8-9-5 108 (v[1]) MJKinane 7 94
(Charles O'Brien, Ire) *hld up in rr: hdwy 3f out: rdn over 2f out: sn drvn and no imp* 16/1
220 7 2 **Russian Sage (SAF)**146 1012 5-9-5 116 KShea 8 90
(M F De Kock, South Africa) *trckd ldrs: hdwy on outer over 3f out: rdn along wl over 2f out and sn wknd* 9/2[3]

1m 51.06s (-0.94) **Going Correction** +0.075s/f (Good)
WFA 3 from 4yo+ 7lb 7 Ran SP% 112.2
Speed ratings (Par 113): **107,106,102,100,99 99,97**
toteswinger: 1&2 £13.10, 1&3 £5.10, 2&3 £9.70. CSF £112.45 TOTE £9.00: £3.50, £4.70; EX 103.30 Trifecta £623.30 Part won. Pool £842.31 - 0.60 winning units..

Owner Windflower Overseas Holdings Inc **Bred** Windflower Overseas Holdings Inc **Trained** Arundel, W Sussex

FOCUS

A valuable Group 3 prize and a race that used to be run at a different fixture here later in the season. This was a messy contest, however, as the early pace was modest and then six of the seven runners decided to come up the centre of the track, but the runner-up stayed tight against the inside rail and the way he performed strongly suggests that there was no disadvantage in staying on the inside. The form is best rated around the runner-up to the best of his handicap marks.

NOTEBOOK

Palavicini(USA) had been given a break since a modest effort in the Hampton Court at Royal Ascot, though he was hampered there and he had looked a consistent and progressive colt before that. Although keen enough early, he was soon settled and travelled well in a handy position. He started off amongst the larger group that came up the centre of the track once into the straight, but after coming off the bridle inside the last 3f, he found plenty and despite hanging away to his left to join the runner-up from over 1f out, forged his way to the front well inside the last furlong. The absence since Ascot had obviously not done him any harm and there is probably plenty more to come from him. (op 11-1)

Dream Lodge(IRE) was making a quick reappearance after his decent effort in a 1m2f handicap here on Tuesday, but he was facing much stiffer company and was the lowest rated in the field. However, he was given a fine ride by Paul Hanagan, who soon had him bowling along in front, and decided there was no disadvantage in staying alone on the inside once in the straight. It was obvious from some way out that he was keeping pace with his rivals in the centre of the field and he was very unfortunate that one emerged from the pack to mow him down. The problem is that he may well have been flattered by the way the race was run and might have jeopardised his handicap mark.

Perfect Stride, given a short break since his battling success in the Wolferton Handicap at Royal Ascot, came off the bridle passing the 3f pole and, though he had every chance a furlong later, then had nothing more to offer. He was 6lb well in with the winner at these weights and 9lb well in with the runner-up, so wasn't at his very best. (tchd 4-1)

Spring Of Fame(USA), representing the stable that took this race three times between 2003 and 2007, took a while to find his form after joining Godolphin from Mikael Magnusson, but he had looked good in winning his previous two starts over 1m, especially when bolting up in a Deauville Listed race last time. His rider decided to come up the centre of the track after turning in and the majority of his rivals followed him, but once challenged on both sides he had nothing left from over a 1f out. It may be that 1m suits him better and it would be interesting to see him back on an artificial surface. (op 4-1)

Forgotten Voice(IRE), dropping in class following his decent fourth behind Rip Van Winkle in the Sussex Stakes, was attempting beyond 1m for the first time, but he was making hard work of it from some way out and wouldn't have won at any trip. This was a flat performance. (op 2-1 tchd 5-2)

Lord Admiral(USA), without a win since March of last year but seemingly returning to form of late, had a first-time visor replacing the usual blinkers but it failed to have much of an effect and he never threatened. (op 14-1 tchd 12-1)

Russian Sage(SAF), not seen since bleeding from the nose in the Dubai Sheema Classic at Nad Al Sheba in March, looked awkward when asked for his effort and could never get involved. He has plenty of questions to answer now. (op 6-1)

5232 SKY BET CITY OF YORK STKS (LISTED RACE) 7f

2:50 (2:50) (Class 1) 3-Y-O+ **£16,334** (£16,334; £4,480; £2,240) **Stalls** Low

Form				RPR
5444	**1**		**Dream Eater (IRE)**[24] 4406 4-9-0 109..........(t) WilliamBuick 11 *(A M Balding) trckd ldrs: smooth hdwy over 2f out and sn cl up: rdn to ld ent fnl f and sn hung lft: drvn and edgd rt last 100yds: jnd on line* **7/1**	113
2422	**1**	dht	**Confront**[8] 4949 4-9-0 116.......... RyanMoore 12 *(Sir Michael Stoute) lw: trckd ldrs: hdwy on wd outside over 2f out: rdn and ev ch over 1f out: drvn ent fnl f and styd on wl to join ldr on line* **3/1**[2]	113+
4600	**3**	¾	**Royal Confidence**[21] 4489 4-8-9 102.......... MichaelHills 7 *(B W Hills) prom: hdwy 3f out: rdn and cl up 2f out: drvn and ev ch ent fnl f tl edgd rt and no ex last 50yds* **40/1**	106
1212	**4**	shd	**Secret Society**[27] 4297 3-8-9 104.......... HayleyTurner 9 *(M L W Bell) lw: hld up towards rr: smooth hdwy over 2f out and sn trcking ldrs: swtchd rt and rdn over 1f out: drvn and ev ch ins fnl f: n.m.r and snatched up nr fin* **9/2**[3]	109+
30-2	**5**	1 ½	**Huntdown (USA)**[55] 3398 3-8-9 111.......... LDettori 10 *(Saeed Bin Suroor) lw: hld up in tch: hdwy to chse ldrs over 2f out and sn rdn: drvn wl over 1f out and kpt on same pce* **5/2**[1]	105
4041	**5**	dht	**Balcarce Nov (ARG)**[13] 4779 4-9-0 103.......... MickyFenton 4 *(T P Tate) in tch: swtchd towards far rail in st and hdwy to trck ldrs 3f out: rdn over 2f out: drvn over 1f out and kpt on same pce ins fnl f* **20/1**	107
00	**7**	1	**Pointing North (SAF)**[183] 609 5-9-0 105.......... RichardMullen 2 *(B Smart) prom: hdwy 3f out: rdn to ld 2f out: drvn and hdd ent fnl f: wknd* **25/1**	104
-466	**8**	nk	**Tombi (USA)**[35] 4037 5-9-0 103.......... EddieAhern 8 *(J Howard Johnson) towards rr: pushed along 3f out: rdn over 1f out: kpt on u.p appr fnl f: nt rch ldrs* **25/1**	103
0-05	**9**	1 ½	**Beckermet (IRE)**[19] 4559 7-9-0 103.......... RoystonFfrench 5 *(R F Fisher) led: rdn along 3f out: drvn and hdd 2f out: sn wknd* **33/1**	99
1114	**10**	nk	**Abbondanza (IRE)**[102] 1929 6-9-0 108..........(p) TomEaves 6 *(I Semple) sn pushed along and cl up: rdn over 3f out: wknd over 2f out* **16/1**	98
00-3	**11**	1	**Battle Paint (USA)**[146] 1006 5-9-0 103..........(t) JimmyFortune 1 *(J H M Gosden) bit bkwd: hld up: swtchd lft towards far rail in home st: hdwy 3f out: rdn along 2f out and sn wknd* **22/1**	96
/350	**12**	½	**Court Masterpiece**[21] 4486 9-9-0 105.......... GrahamGibbons 3 *(J J Quinn) a towards rr: rdn along and outpcd fnl 2f* **20/1**	94

1m 23.15s (-2.15) **Going Correction** +0.075s/f (Good)
WFA 3 from 4yo+ 5lb **12** Ran SP% **117.1**
Speed ratings (Par 111): **115,115,114,114,112 112,111,110,109,108 107,107**WIN: Confront £1.90, Dream Eater £3.70. PL: C £1.70, DE £2.10, Royal Confidence £8.90. EX: C-DE £15.20, DE-C £12.90. CSF: C-DE £10.57, DE-C £12.57. Toteswinger: C-DE £5.00, C-RC £29.10, DE-RC £26.60. TRIFECTA: C-DE-RC £395.00, DE-C-RC £240.40. 27.

Owner K Abdulla **Bred** Juddmonte Farms Ltd **Trained** Newmarket, Suffolk

FOCUS

This race has been a struggle for 3yos in the past (Priors Lodge was the last to win in 2001), so the older generation have held the upper hand. Plenty came through to hold every chance as the race developed, and the judge could not separate the two who crossed the line together. The form makes sense on figures but is not totally convincing, although Confont and the third ran to their marks.

NOTEBOOK

Dream Eater(IRE) has been running in some very good Group races this season, so arguably deserved to find a race of this nature on his best efforts. He did not take a strong hold this time, as he has done in the past, and battled on well when asked to quicken despite edging both ways under pressure. However, those sideways movements may have cost him outright victory. (op 15-2)

Confront, who had earplugs in again, looked to have a hard task from a wide draw and he more or less came home alone closet to the stands' side rail. Considering he was under hard pressure over 2f out, this was a commendable effort. He has an entry in the Celebration Mile, so one would imagine that he may head to Goodwood. (op 15-2)

Royal Confidence, the only filly in the line-up, had run fairly well in Group company this season so was entitled to be thereabouts. She appeared to run her race without proving good enough. The entry she holds in the Group 1 Sun Chariot Stakes looks a little optimistic at this stage. (tchd 50-1)

Secret Society travelled better than most for much of the home straight, so his final effort was slightly disappointing without being below par (he was hampered 20 yards from the line and may have finished third with a clear passage). Big field, strongly run contests are probably his ideal conditions. (tchd 4-1)

Huntdown(USA) promised plenty on his seasonal return but was below par here. He hit a flat spot at halfway and made little impact. (op 9-4 tchd 11-4)

Balcarce Nov(ARG) caused an upset when winning at Haydock on his previous outing, but showed that was no fluke with a solid run. He put his head down when asked to make his bid and looks a real professional. (op 9-4 tchd 11-4)

Pointing North(SAF), having his first outing for this trainer, was really keen after his absence and found little off the bridle. A Group 1 winner in his native South Africa, he may be at his best when returned to front-running duties.

5233 COOLMORE NUNTHORPE STKS (GROUP 1) 5f

3:25 (3:25) (Class 1) 2-Y-O+

£136,248 (£51,648; £25,848; £12,888; £6,456; £3,240) **Stalls** High

Form				RPR
2514	**1**		**Borderlescott**[22] 4456 7-9-11 108.......... NCallan 2 *(R Bastiman) in tch towards centre: hdwy 2f out: swtchd rt and rdn over 1f out: str run to ld wl ins fnl f* **9/1**	121
0331	**2**	nk	**Benbaun (IRE)**[54] 3434 8-9-11 111..........(v) JoeFanning 11 *(K A Ryan) wnt lft s: sn overall ldr stands' rail: rdn along over 1f out: edgd lft and hdd wl ins fnl f: kpt on* **25/1**	120
211	**3**	1 ¼	**Radiohead**[64] 3046 2-8-1 109..........(t) MartinDwyer 9 *(B J Meehan) lw: bmpd s and towards rr: gd hdwy 2f out: rdn over 1f out: styd on strly ins fnl f* **9/2**[2]	108
1310	**4**	hd	**Tax Free (IRE)**[66] 2991 7-9-11 111.......... AdrianTNicholls 1 *(D Nicholls) cl up centre: effrt 2f out: sn rdn and ev ch tl drvn ent fnl f and kpt on same pce* **12/1**	115
1-10	**5**	shd	**Amour Propre**[66] 2991 3-9-9 114.......... DaneO'Neill 3 *(H Candy) lw: cl up centre: effrt 2f out: sn rdn and ev ch tl drvn ent fnl f and grad wknd* **6/1**[3]	115
3-01	**6**	1	**Kingsgate Native (IRE)**[22] 4456 4-9-11 119.......... RyanMoore 7 *(Sir Michael Stoute) lw: in tch towards centre: hdwy to chse ldrs 2f out and sn rdn: drvn over 1f out: no imp ins fnl f* **5/2**[1]	111
0005	**7**	1 ¼	**Dandy Man (IRE)**[22] 4456 6-9-11 106..........(t) LDettori 10 *(Saeed Bin Suroor) lw: carried lft s: in tch: hdwy 2f out: sn swtchd rt and rdn: kpt on ins fnl f* **14/1**	107
0000	**8**	nse	**Equiano (FR)**[22] 4456 4-9-11 109.......... MichaelHills 12 *(B W Hills) chsd ldrs towards stands' rail: rdn along 2f out: grad wknd* **18/1**	106
0-00	**9**	¾	**Moorhouse Lad**[22] 4456 6-9-11 105.......... JimCrowley 8 *(B Smart) chsd ldrs centre: rdn along wl over 1f out: drvn and one pce appr fnl f* **25/1**	104
1010	**10**	hd	**Ialysos (GR)**[22] 4456 5-9-11 109.......... JimmyFortune 4 *(L M Cumani) hld up and towards rr tl sme late hdwy* **16/1**	103
3136	**11**	2	**Look Busy (IRE)**[32] 4135 4-9-8 103.......... SladeO'Hara 17 *(A Berry) dwlt and towards rr: rdn along and sme hdwy 1/2-way: nvr a factor: sddle slipped* **20/1**	93
0-60	**12**	½	**Mythical Flight (SAF)**[66] 2991 6-9-11 112.......... KShea 5 *(S g Tarry, South Africa) chsd ldrs centre: rdn along over 2f out: sn wknd* **28/1**	94
4002	**13**	1 ½	**Captain Gerrard (IRE)**[41] 3848 4-9-11 105.......... TomEaves 14 *(B Smart) bmpd s: chsd ldrs towards stands' rail: rdn along over 2f out and grad wknd* **33/1**	89
20-3	**14**	1 ½	**Excellerator (IRE)**[48] 3621 3-9-6 98..........(vt[1]) DO'Donohoe 15 *(George Baker) wnt lft s and rr: rdn along 2f out: sn hung lft: a bhd* **80/1**	80
-010	**15**	7	**Art Connoisseur (IRE)**[42] 3819 3-9-9 119.......... HayleyTurner 6 *(M L W Bell) a towards rr: rdn along over 2f out and no hdwy: sn eased: sddle slipped* **18/1**	58
130-	**16**	17	**Mythical Border (USA)**[322] 6441 3-9-6 104.......... WilliamBuick 16 *(J Noseda) a towards rr: outpcd and bhd fnl 2f* **80/1**	—

57.50 secs (-1.80) **Going Correction** +0.075s/f (Good)
WFA 2 from 3yo 24lb 3 from 4yo+ 2lb **16** Ran SP% **123.1**
Speed ratings: **117,116,114,114,114 112,110,110,109,108 105,104,102,100,88 61**
toteswinger: 1&2 £28.90, 1&3 £10.10, 2&3 £22.50. CSF £225.16 TOTE £11.30: £3.10, £5.60, £2.60; EX 198.50 Trifecta £855.90 Pool: £6,708.61 - 5.80 winning units..

Owner James Edgar & William Donaldson **Bred** James Clark **Trained** Cowthorpe, N Yorks

■ Stewards' Enquiry : Adrian T Nicholls one-day ban: used whip down shoulder in forehand position (Sep 4)

FOCUS

This year's Nunthorpe field looked well up to scratch, despite only one overseas challenger. Five of the 16 runners were previous Group 1 winners, one had been successful at Grade 1 level in South Africa and the last two winners of the race lined up again. The contest was given added spice with a representative from the 2yo generation which had won the race twice since 1992, including Kingsgate Native the last time it was staged here two years ago. However this year's renewal proved a triumph for the veterans with a 7yo beating an 8yo. The field raced centre to stands' side, but the result suggested there was no great bias. The winner is probably the best guide to the form.

NOTEBOOK

Borderlescott, winner of this race last year when it was run at Newmarket, despite that win still had a bit to find with a few of these on official ratings, but he had probably run even better than it looked when fourth behind Kingsgate Native from a disadvantageous draw at Goodwood last time. Well backed beforehand, he was always close to the pace in the group that came down the centre of the track and found enough when asked to force his head in front where it mattered. This victory showed that last year's win was no fluke and it does seem that he comes to life at this time of year. He is better than he has ever been at the age of seven and may now be aimed at the Abbaye and then possibly Hong Kong. (op 11-1)

Benbaun(IRE), who ended a lengthy losing run when successful at the Curragh in his most recent outing in June, showed dazzling early pace down the stands' rail and it looked for a long time was though he might win, but he had the prize snatched from him in the dying strides. Winner of the 2007 Prix de l'Abbaye at Longchamp plus six Group 3 races and a Listed contest at the Curragh, it seems amazing that he has never won at above Class 3 level in Britain. He may renew rivalry with the winner in the Abbaye.

Radiohead ◆, who ran out a decent winner of the Norfolk Stakes at Royal Ascot despite getting badly hampered, was fancied by many on this first start since to make the most of his big weight allowance. However, he gave himself plenty to do and in a race where the front pair were always handy, that proved too much of a handicap. He did run on very strongly over the last 2f to snatch third and he will be very interesting when stepped up to 6f. The Middle Park is a possibility. (op 4-1)

Tax Free(IRE) had been beaten a long way in the King's Stand last time, but he has never run well in three tries at Ascot. He has winning form here, though, and ran a blinder having been up there with the pace towards the far side of the field from the off. Already the winner of 14 races, he owes nothing to anyone. (tchd 11-1)
Amour Propre, very progressive until a modest effort in the King's Stand, had been given a short break since then. Another to show smart speed out in the centre of the track from the start, this was much better and this lightly raced colt can still make it to the top as a sprinter. (tchd 7-1)
Kingsgate Native(IRE), winner of this race for John Best as a juvenile in 2007, bounced back to form on his second start since failing at stud at Goodwood last month. He had every chance out in the centre of the track and appeared to run his race with few excuses. He can still win more Group sprints. (op 11-4 tchd 3-1 and 100-30)
Dandy Man(IRE), third behind Kingsgate Native in this two years ago, but without a win since April 2007 and behind that rival and Borderlescott at Goodwood last time, took a strong hold early despite the strong pace. He had his chance, but wasn't good enough and it's hard to see him winning a race at this level now. (op 16-1)
Equiano(FR), fourth behind Borderlescott in this race at Newmarket last year, has mainly been disappointing since joining his current yard after winning last season's King's Stand. He showed good speed towards the nearside, but never really looked like figuring. (op 20-1)
Moorhouse Lad, disappointing in three outings, including behind Kingsgate Native at Goodwood last time, since finishing runner-up in the Prix de l'Abbaye last October, ran well for a long way and this was a bit better. (op 33-1)
Ialysos(GR) took too long to get into stride and probably needs a drop in class and a stiffer track. (op 20-1)
Look Busy(IRE) could never get into the race following a tardy start. Official explanation: jockey said saddle slipped (op 33-1)
Art Connoisseur(IRE) appeared to disappoint again on this first outing over the minimum trip since winning at Newmarket on his second start at two. However, his rider looked very uncomfortable from a long way out. Official explanation: jockey said saddle slipped (op 16-1)

5234 RACING POST YEARLING BONUS CONVIVIAL MAIDEN STKS 6f
4:05 (4:06) (Class 2) 2-Y-O **£16,190** (£4,817; £2,407; £1,202) **Stalls** High

Form RPR
1 **Businessman** 2-9-3 0 ... JoeFanning 1 83+
(M Johnston) *w'like: lengthy: scope: mde most: rdn 2f out: hung bdly lft ent fnl f: sn drvn and kpt on wl* **13/2**
20 2 1 1/4 **Noble Greek (USA)**[43] 3779 2-9-3 0 ... RobertWinston 7 79
(J R Best) *str: cl up: effrt 2f out and sn rdn: drvn over 1f out and ev ch tl no ex wl ins fnl f* **3/1**[1]
3 nse **Dherghaam (IRE)** 2-9-3 0 ... RHills 6 79+
(E A L Dunlop) *leggy: attractive: hld up in tch: smooth hdwy to trck ldrs over 2f out: swtchd lft and effrt to chal over 1f out: sn rdn and ev ch tl nt qckn wl ins fnl f* **4/1**[3]
4 shd **Hanson'D (IRE)** 2-9-3 0 ... NCallan 4 79+
(K A Ryan) *athletic: lw: chsd ldrs on outer: effrt 2f out: sn rdn and ev ch tl drvn ins fnl f and one pce* **7/2**[2]
5 3 1/4 **Arry's Orse** 2-9-3 0 ... TomEaves 5 69+
(B Smart) *w'like: scope: lw: dwlt and bhd: hdwy 2f out: styd on appr fnl f: nrst fin* **11/2**
0 6 nk **Frontline Boy (IRE)**[11] 4847 2-9-3 0 ... AndrewElliott 3 68
(A P Jarvis) *w'like: cl up: rdn along over 2f out: drvn and edgd lft over 1f out: grad wknd* **40/1**
0 7 1 **Beat Baby (IRE)**[41] 3875 2-9-3 0 ... RoystonFfrench 2 65
(J Howard Johnson) *chsd ldrs: rdn along over 2f out: drvn and edgd lft over 1f out: sn wknd* **11/1**
0 8 9 **Cracking Lass (IRE)**[20] 4515 2-8-12 0 ... PaulHanagan 8 33
(R A Fahey) *leggy: s.i.s: a in rr* **10/1**
9 2 1/2 **Taeping (IRE)** 2-9-3 0 ... MickyFenton 9 30
(R Hollinshead) *leggy: chsd ldrs: rdn along over 2f out and sn wknd* **16/1**

1m 12.73s (0.83) **Going Correction** +0.075s/f (Good) **9** Ran SP% **121.7**
Speed ratings (Par 100): **97,95,95,95,90 90,89,77,73**
toteswinger: 1&2 £3.90, 1&3 £5.10, 2&3 £3.80. CSF £27.87 TOTE £6.30: £2.50, £1.60, £2.10; EX 20.00 Trifecta £94.00 Pool: £660.59 - 5.20 winning units..
Owner Sheikh Hamdan Bin Mohammed Al Maktoum **Bred** Providence Stud **Trained** Middleham Moor, N Yorks

FOCUS
A couple of very good horses have taken this contest in the recent past, but generally the winners have been a little disappointing. The 2009 version did not look a particularly strong renewal, although there were three newcomers in the first four, all of whom could go on from this.

NOTEBOOK
Businessman, the first foal of an unraced half-sister to Kandidate, saw his sales price rise to 105,000gns this year after being sold for 90,000gns as a foal. He does not look overly big and won despite hanging badly left across the course from his early centre-track position. The fact that he does not hold any fancy entries helps to make the form look only average. (op 11-2 tchd 7-1)
Noble Greek(USA), down the field in the Group 2 July Stakes last time, travelled sweetly before finding little for pressure. He was soundly held. (op 9-2)
Dherghaam(IRE) went nicely on his debut but could not finish his run off. He is entitled to come on for the effort. (tchd 9-2)
Hanson'D(IRE) ◆, who holds Dewhurst and Racing Post Trophy engagements, is very well bred, as he is a half-brother to Carry On Katie, who won the Cheveley Park Stakes in 2003. Green early, he took a while to hit top gear and was far from disgraced. His was one of the most promising debuts. (op 4-1 tchd 5-1)
Arry's Orse cost £92,000 at the breeze-up sales and has entries in the Mill Reef, Middle Park and Two-Year-Old Trophy at Redcar. Slowly away, this big sort took a while to sort himself out before staying on strongly inside the final 2f. (op 9-2)
Frontline Boy(IRE) showed a lot of pace and was not disgraced.

5235 COLLINGWOOD TEAM SERVICE KNAVESMIRE STKS (H'CAP) 2m 88y
4:40 (4:40) (Class 3) (0-95,95) 4-Y-O+ **£16,190** (£4,817; £2,407; £1,202) **Stalls** Low

Form RPR
2213 1 **Swingkeel (IRE)**[23] 4417 4-9-2 90 ... JimmyFortune 16 104+
(J L Dunlop) *hld up towards rr: hdwy 5f out: trckd ldrs 2f out: swtchd rt and rdn over 1f out: styd on to ld ins fnl f* **5/2**[1]
121 2 2 **Saga De Tercey (FR)**[17] 4619 4-8-9 83 ow1 ... NCallan 3 92
(G A Swinbank) *trckd ldrs: hdwy 4f out: led 3f out: rdn along 2f out: drvn over 1f out: edgd and hdd ins fnl f: kpt on same pce* **8/1**
6101 3 1 3/4 **Aaim To Prosper (IRE)**[13] 4769 5-8-10 84 ... (v) RyanMoore 15 91
(M R Channon) *midfield: hdwy and in tch over 6f out: effrt on inner to chse ldrs wl over 2f out: rdn wl over 1f out and ev ch tl drvn and one pce ins fnl f* **10/1**
4212 4 1 **Hawk Mountain (UAE)**[27] 4332 4-8-10 84 ... GrahamGibbons 2 90
(J J Quinn) *lw: in tch: hdwy 4f out: cl up 3f out: sn rdn and ev ch tl drvn appr fnl f and kpt on same pce* **6/1**[2]
5143 5 3/4 **Gordonsville**[28] 4260 6-8-9 83 ... DanielTudhope 17 88
(J S Goldie) *hld up towards rr: hdwy on outer 3f out: rdn along to chse ldrs 2f out: sn drvn and no imp ins fnl f* **12/1**
3012 6 2 3/4 **Bergonzi (IRE)**[17] 4619 5-8-3 77 ... PaulHanagan 13 79
(J Howard Johnson) *cl up: led after 3f: hdd 1/2-way and styd prom: rdn 3f out and cl up tl drvn 2f out and grad wknd* **25/1**
0-50 7 9 **Gee Dee Nen**[13] 4769 6-9-1 89 ... JoeFanning 7 80
(Jim Best) *midfield: hdwy 4f out: rdn along 3f out: sn drvn and n.d* **22/1**
6053 8 hd **Inchnadamph**[27] 4332 9-8-8 82 ... (t) RobertWinston 11 73
(T J Fitzgerald) *lw: trckd ldrs: pushed along and hdwy 4f out: rdn 3f out: sn drvn and grad wknd fnl 2f* **14/1**
00-4 9 2 **Downing Street (IRE)**[40] 3532 8-8-3 77 oh4 ow1 ... (v) AndrewElliott 8 65
(Jennie Candlish) *s.i.s: a towards rr* **40/1**
4062 10 nk **Snoqualmie Boy**[28] 4274 6-8-13 87 ... MickyFenton 5 75
(T P Tate) *lw: hld up towards rr: sme hdwy on inner over 3f out: nvr a factor* **28/1**
-132 11 2 **Hada Men (USA)**[10] 4882 4-8-2 76 ... MartinDwyer 14 62
(L M Cumani) *a towards rr* **9/1**
0041 12 1/2 **Valmari (IRE)**[56] 3343 6-8-12 86 ... (b) TomEaves 4 71
(C E Brittain) *midfield: hdwy and in tch 6f out: rdn to chse ldrs 4f out: drvn over 3f out and sn wknd* **28/1**
2030 13 nk **Step This Way (USA)**[8] 4948 4-8-6 80 ... RoystonFfrench 9 65
(M Johnston) *led 3f: prom tl rdn along over 4f out and sn wknd* **40/1**
1140 14 nk **Judgethemoment (USA)**[22] 4457 4-9-7 95 ... KShea 6 79
(Jane Chapple-Hyam) *lw: trckd ldrs: effrt over 4f out: rdn 3f out and sn wknd* **7/1**[3]
3500 15 27 **Buddhist Monk**[13] 4770 4-8-11 85 ... (tp) EddieAhern 12 37
(Ian Williams) *lw: t.k.h: prom tl led 1/2-way: rdn along 4f out: sn hdd & wknd* **20/1**

3m 32.26s (-2.24) **Going Correction** +0.075s/f (Good) **15** Ran SP% **124.6**
Speed ratings (Par 107): **108,107,106,105,105 103,99,99,98,98 97,96,96,96,83**
toteswinger: 1&2 £7.80, 1&3 £7.60, 2&3 £17.70. CSF £20.66 CT £179.17 TOTE £3.30: £1.60, £3.10, £3.10; EX 26.30 Trifecta £176.00 Pool: £2,022.18 - 8.50 winning units. Place 6: £3,376.81, Place 5: £522.35..
Owner Mrs M E Slade **Bred** R J Cornelius **Trained** Arundel, W Sussex
■ Stewards' Enquiry : K Shea two-day ban: used whip when out of contention (Sep 4, 6)

FOCUS
A competitive staying handicap to end the meeting, but despite what seemed a generous pace there were several still in with a shout coming to the final quarter-mile. The form looks solid with more to come from the winner and the third and fourth close to recent marks. The field came centre-to-stands' side on reaching the home straight.

NOTEBOOK
Swingkeel(IRE), who was 16lb higher than when last successful on turf, though he did win off 7lb lower on Polytrack two starts ago, had run well off this mark over 5f further at Goodwood last time when ridden to get the trip, though connections believed that he wasn't quite right then. Held up early, he moved into contention starting up the home straight and maintained his effort to hit the front inside the last furlong. He is now likely to head straight for the Cesarewitch and he must have a big chance there. (op 11-4)
Saga De Tercey(FR) ◆, a winner twice from three starts on the Flat after making a successful racecourse debut in a Huntingdon bumper, was 5lb higher, including the overweight, than when scrambling home just ahead of Bergonzi at Catterick last time. Upped in trip, he was always close to the pace and had every chance, but was just run out of it. Still lightly raced having not seen the racecourse until March, he looks a nice staying prospect.
Aaim To Prosper(IRE), successful in his last two tries over this trip, albeit on softer ground, was 3lb higher than when scoring at Ascot earlier in the month. He came though to hold every chance entering the last 2f and just lacked a vital turn of foot when it mattered. He remains in good form and a return to easier conditions should see him winning again. (op 11-1)
Hawk Mountain(UAE), who has been very consistent for well over a year now, was 1lb higher than when runner-up over course and distance last month. He was never too far off the pace and this was another decent effort, especially as he was keen enough early despite the good pace. (op 11-2)
Gordonsville, back to a mark just 1lb higher than for his last win, threatened to get into it on the nearside halfway up the home straight but then couldn't find any more. He does look better over slightly shorter.
Bergonzi(IRE), a short head behind Saga De Tercey at Catterick last time and 2lb better off, made much of the early running and remained close up until his stamina appeared to give out inside the last couple of furlongs. He has won off a much higher mark in his younger days, but this trip on such a galloping track may just be beyond him.
Hada Men(USA), twice held on an easy surface since getting of the mark on quick ground, was trying this trip for the first time and was 1lb well in compared with his new mark. He never got into the race from off the pace, however, and is surely better than this. Perhaps a drop back to 1m4f is needed. (op 17-2)
Judgethemoment(USA), twice well held in Pattern company since completing a hat-trick in the 2m4f Ascot Stakes at the royal meeting, dropped away over the last 3f and seems to have lost his form for the time being. (op 9-1 tchd 10-1)
Buddhist Monk Official explanation: jockey said gelding ran too free
T/Jkpt: Not won. T/Plt: £1,840.30 to a £1 stake. Pool: £227,150.56. 90.10 winning tickets. T/Qpdt: £13.20 to a £1 stake. Pool: £16,644.36. 926.83 winning tickets. JR

5236 - 5239a (Foreign Racing) - See Raceform Interactive

[5083] DEAUVILLE (R-H)
Friday, August 21

OFFICIAL GOING: Standard

5240a PRIX DE LA LOUVIERE (ALL-WEATHER) 6f 110y
12:45 (12:47) 2-Y-O **£16,505** (£6,602; £4,951; £3,301; £1,650)

RPR
1 **Evaporation (FR)**[19] 4584 2-8-10 ... OPeslier 90
(C Laffon-Parias, France)
2 1 **Yamam**[20] 4577 2-8-10 ... MGuyon 87
(A Fabre, France)
3 hd **Country Love (FR)**[6] 5057 2-8-7 ... C-PLemaire 84
(David Marnane, Ire) *led to ins fnl f: lost 2nd cl home* **30/1**[2]
4 3/4 **Where's The Soap (FR)**[8] 4970 2-8-10 ... DBonilla 85
(Tom Dascombe) *trckd ldr in 3rd: angling out whn n.m.r 1 1/2f out and dropped bk to 5th: swtchd lft 1f out: styd on fnl f* **10/1**[1]
5 3/4 **Irish Cat (IRE)**[6] 5057 2-8-10 ... (p) GMosse 83
(Robert Collet, France)
6 2 1/2 **As Speed (FR)** 2-8-10 ... CSoumillon 76
(P Khozian, France)

1m 21.0s (81.00) **6** Ran SP% **12.3**
PARI-MUTUEL (including one euro stakes): WIN 4.90; PL 1.60, 1.30; SF 9.70.
Owner Wertheimer & Frere **Bred** Wertheimer Et Frere **Trained** Chantilly, France

NOTEBOOK
Where's The Soap(FR), a winner here earlier in the month, was short of room when she needed it and when she got going again could not reach the first three.

[5060]BATH (L-H)

Saturday, August 22

OFFICIAL GOING: Firm (9.7)

Wind: Virtually nil Weather: Cloudy

5241 BATH ALES HOP POLE NOVICE STKS 5f 161y

5:15 (5:15) (Class 4) 2-Y-O **£3,950** (£1,175; £587; £293) **Stalls** Centre

Form RPR

1 **1** **Music Show (IRE)**[16] 4688 2-8-8 0 TonyCulhane 5 93+
(M R Channon) *hld up in rr but in tch: stdy hdwy on outside over 2f out to ld over 1f out: edgd lft and c clr 1f out: easily* **4/5**[1]

61 **2** 3 1/4 **Ramamara (IRE)**[15] 4747 2-8-6 64 CatherineGannon 2 77
(P D Evans) *tke ken hold early: chsd ldr: led 3f out: rdn 2f out: hdd over 1f out: sn no ch w wnr but styd on for clr 2nd* **16/1**

2420 **3** 2 3/4 **Soccer (USA)**[25] 4407 2-8-13 94 (t) RichardSmith 4 75
(Tom Dascombe) *trckd ldrs: drvn to chal ins fnl 2f: no ex over 1f out and sn btn* **2/1**[2]

1030 **4** 1 1/4 **Avonvalley**[8] 4989 2-8-10 78 TGMcLaughlin 3 68
(M S Saunders) *chsd ldrs: rdn over 2f out: wknd 1f out* **10/1**[3]

0300 **5** 5 **Existentialist**[8] 4989 2-8-13 79 DavidProbert 1 55
(J G Portman) *dwlt: sn led: hdd 3f out: sn rdn: wknd wl over 1f out* **14/1**

69.73 secs (-1.47) **Going Correction** -0.325s/f (Firm) **5** Ran SP% **110.5**

Speed ratings (Par 96): **96,91,88,86,79**

CSF £14.46 TOTE £1.90: £1.10, £5.10; EX 6.60.

Owner Jaber Abdullah **Bred** Darley **Trained** West Ilsley, Berks

FOCUS

A reasonable novice event.

NOTEBOOK

Music Show(IRE) ◆ looks an above-average filly. She was last of all for much of the way but quickened up readily in the straight, confirming the promise she showed when winning over course and distance on her debut. This Cheveley Park entrant deserves her chance in Pattern company. (tchd 10-11)

Ramamara(IRE) beat little of note in a seller on the Polytrack last time, but she had looked better than a plater that day and confirmed that impression in this tougher company, running above her official mark of 64. She seems quite a tough filly, typical of an Evans-trained runner.

Soccer(USA) was dropped in grade after contesting the Molecomb Stakes on his latest start, but he ran below his official rating of 94. His response under pressure was disappointing and he remains winless since his debut. (op 9-4 tchd 15-8)

Avonvalley looked to have conditions to suit but she was another to underperform. (op 12-1 tchd 9-1)

Existentialist has a regressive profile. (tchd 16-1)

5242 BATH ALES SALAMANDER MAIDEN STKS 1m 5y

5:45 (5:45) (Class 5) 3-Y-O+ **£2,687** (£799; £399; £199) **Stalls** Low

Form RPR

3063 **1** **Sahaal (USA)**[10] 4914 3-9-3 75 (t) GeorgeBaker 2 80
(M P Tregoning) *hld up in tch: trckd ldr over 2f out: rdn to chal jst ins fnl f: grad asserted cl home* **5/2**[3]

2 nk **Bended Knee** 3-8-12 0 FrankieMcDonald 6 74
(H Candy) *plld hrd and led: shkn up and green ins fnl 2f: hld on ins fnl f tl worn down cl home* **14/1**

-262 **3** 6 **Wilfred Pickles (IRE)**[10] 4902 3-9-3 78 (t) SebSanders 5 65
(Mrs A J Perrett) *hld up in rr: pushed along and hdwy fr 3f out: chsd ldng duo 2f out: sn no imp: wknd fnl f* **2/1**[2]

3522 **4** 2 1/4 **Papyrian**[50] 3590 3-9-3 78 (b) AlanMunro 8 59
(W Jarvis) *in rr tl hdwy on outside fr 3f out: chsd ldrs and rdn 2f out: wknd over 1f out* **13/8**[1]

00 **5** 2 1/4 **Fortina's Boy (USA)**[110] 1730 3-9-3 0 (t) AdamKirby 1 54
(W R Swinburn) *in rr: rdn and effrt on ins over 2f out: nvr rchd ldrs and sn btn* **16/1**

06 **6** 5 **Turbo Shandy**[11] 4885 6-9-9 0 VinceSlattery 7 43
(D Burchell) *s.i.s: sme hdwy towards outside 3f out: sn rdn: wknd 2f out* **25/1**

0040 **7** 2 1/2 **Jay Gee Wigmo**[43] 3800 4-9-9 43 TolleyDean 4 37
(A W Carroll) *chsd ldrs: rdn over 3f out and sn wknd* **40/1**

8 1 3/4 **Castlefish (IRE)**[1035] 6111 5-9-9 0 DavidProbert 3 33
(D Burchell) *plld hrd early: chsd ldrs 5f* **40/1**

1m 39.72s (-1.08) **Going Correction** -0.15s/f (Firm)

WFA 3 from 4yo+ 6lb **8** Ran SP% **121.3**

Speed ratings (Par 103): **99,98,92,90,88 83,80,78**

toteswingers: 1&2 £14.70, 1&3 £1.40, 2&3 £4.70 CSF £37.53 TOTE £3.80: £1.20, £1.70, £1.30; EX 42.80.

Owner Hamdan Al Maktoum **Bred** Shadwell Farm LLC **Trained** Lambourn, Berks

FOCUS

An ordinary maiden in which the third and fourth-placed finishers clearly ran well below their respective official marks. The winning time was 1.26 seconds slower than the following handicap won by a horse rated 66 and the form is rated through the winner to his previous best.

Fortina's Boy(USA) Official explanation: jockey said colt was unsuited by the firm ground

5243 BATH ALES SWAN H'CAP 1m 5y

6:15 (6:15) (Class 4) (0-80,80) 3-Y-O+ **£4,727** (£1,406; £702; £351) **Stalls** Low

Form RPR

4514 **1** **Don Pietro**[20] 4563 6-8-12 66 (p) TonyCulhane 7 75
(R Curtis) *trckd ldrs: awkward bnd ins fnl 5f: rdn to chse wnr fnl f: styd on to ld fnl 30yds: hld on wl* **16/1**

6221 **2** nk **Carbon Hoofprint**[16] 4691 3-9-6 80 FergusSweeney 9 87+
(P J Makin) *t.k.h: sn chsng ldr: chalng whn awkward and pushed wd bnd ins fnl 5f: sn rcvrd and styd 2nd: led ins fnl 2f: and sn rdn: hdd fnl 30yds: kpt on wl but a jst hld* **10/3**[1]

0011 **3** 3/4 **Cheam Forever (USA)**[17] 4642 3-8-12 72 SteveDrowne 3 77+
(R Charlton) *t.k.h: sn led: awkward and wd bnd ins fnl 5f: rdn and hdd ins fnl 2f: one pce tl rallied ins fnl f and styd on again cl home* **4/1**[2]

3421 **4** shd **Dingaan (IRE)**[37] 3996 6-9-12 80 DavidProbert 1 86
(A M Balding) *stdd s and hld up in rr: hdwy on outside fr 2f oit: styd on u.p fnl f: no ex whn hung lft cl home* **10/3**[1]

0052 **5** 1 1/2 **I Confess**[1] 5206 4-9-6 79 (b) RichardEvans(5) 8 82
(P D Evans) *chsd ldrs: awkward bnd ins fnl 5f: styd chsng ldrs tl outpcd 2f out: styd on again ins fnl f tl one pce and hmpd cl home* **13/2**[3]

6230 **6** 2 3/4 **La Rosa Nostra**[22] 4495 4-9-4 72 AdamKirby 2 68
(W R Swinburn) *in rr: rdn over 2f oit: nvr gng pce to get into contention* **13/2**[3]

0000 **7** 2 **Champain Sands (IRE)**[17] 4663 10-8-7 61 oh1 CatherineGannon 10 52
(E J Alston) *in rr and awkward bnd ins fnl 5f: rdn 3f out: effrt to chse ldrs ins fnl 2f: wknd over 1f out* **14/1**

1036 **8** 9 **Thunder Gorge (USA)**[21] 4526 4-9-6 74 LPKeniry 4 44
(Mouse Hamilton-Fairley) *plld hrd: sn chsng ldrs: awkward bnd ins fnl 5f: wknd fr 3f out* **12/1**

1m 38.46s (-2.34) **Going Correction** -0.15s/f (Firm)

WFA 3 from 4yo+ 6lb **8** Ran SP% **113.1**

Speed ratings (Par 105): **105,104,103,103,102 99,97,88**

toteswingers: 1&2 £15.60, 1&3 £3.40, 2&3 £15.70 CSF £67.32 CT £260.66 TOTE £18.70: £3.50, £1.70, £1.30; EX 124.70.

Owner Mrs Joanna Hughes **Bred** B N And Mrs Toye **Trained** Lambourn, Berks

■ Stewards' Enquiry : David Probert one-day ban: careless riding (Sep 6)

FOCUS

A fair, competitive handicap run at a sound gallop and the form makes sense rated around the winner and fourth.

Carbon Hoofprint Official explanation: jockey said gelding failed to handle the bottom bend

5244 BATH ALES GEM H'CAP 1m 3f 144y

6:45 (6:45) (Class 4) (0-80,80) 3-Y-O+ **£4,727** (£1,406; £702; £351) **Stalls** Low

Form RPR

1005 **1** **Merrymadcap (IRE)**[8] 4992 7-9-2 68 LPKeniry 2 74
(M Salaman) *mde all: rdn and styd on strly fr over 2f out: unchal* **7/1**

1044 **2** 1 1/2 **Dreamwalk (IRE)**[22] 4481 3-9-2 78 (v) SebSanders 1 82
(R M Beckett) *s.i.s: hld up in rr but in tch: trckd ldrs 3f out: chsd wnr and rdn 2f out: styd on but sn no imp* **6/4**[1]

0-00 **3** 6 **Kevkat (IRE)**[35] 4091 8-10-0 80 SteveDrowne 3 73
(D E Pipe) *t.k.h: trckd wnr: rdn 3f out: lost 2nd 2f out and sn wknd* **15/2**

6602 **4** 1/2 **Princess Flame (GER)**[23] 4449 7-8-12 64 CatherineGannon 5 57
(B G Powell) *chsd ldrs: rdn: bmpd and lost footing on bnd over 3f out: no ch fr 2f out but styd on again fnl f* **3/1**[2]

3334 **5** 5 **Bolanderi (USA)**[12] 4855 4-9-2 68 (b[1]) GeorgeBaker 6 52
(Andrew Turnell) *hld up in rr but in tch: hdwy whn bmpd bnd over 3f out: drvn to dispite 2nd u.p 2f out: sn wknd* **4/1**[3]

2m 31.42s (0.82) **Going Correction** -0.15s/f (Firm)

WFA 3 from 4yo+ 10lb **5** Ran SP% **109.3**

Speed ratings (Par 105): **91,90,86,85,82**

CSF £17.81 TOTE £6.20: £3.00, £1.30; EX 20.50.

Owner Mrs N L Young **Bred** Wickfield Farm Partnership **Trained** Upper Lambourn, Berks

■ Stewards' Enquiry : George Baker two-day ban: careless riding (Sep 6-7)

FOCUS

An ordinary handicap and form to treat with caution as the winner was allowed to set a steady pace.

Bolanderi(USA) Official explanation: jockey said gelding had no more to give

5245 BATH ALES WELLINGTON H'CAP 5f 161y

7:15 (7:15) (Class 4) (0-85,85) 3-Y-O **£4,792** (£1,425; £712; £355) **Stalls** Centre

Form RPR

0311 **1** **Golden Destiny (IRE)**[16] 4712 3-9-4 82 (p) SebSanders 1 102
(P J Makin) *mde all: c readily clr fr over 1f out: unchal* **9/4**[1]

0604 **2** 8 **White Shift (IRE)**[27] 4338 3-8-9 80 JPFahy(7) 5 73
(P Howling) *chsd wnr thrght: rdn along 3f out: easily outpcd fr over 1f out but kpt on for wl hld 2nd* **6/1**[3]

423 **3** 1 1/2 **Raimond Ridge (IRE)**[8] 4990 3-8-5 74 ow4 MCGeran(5) 2 62
(M R Channon) *racd in 3rd thrght: rdn 3f out: easily outpcd fr over 1f out* **8/1**

3155 **4** 1/2 **Affluent**[35] 4099 3-9-7 85 SteveDrowne 3 71
(R Charlton) *t.k.h: racd in 4th thrght: rdn and outpcd fr 2f out* **9/4**[1]

6251 **5** 3/4 **Captain Carey**[75] 2774 3-9-3 81 TGMcLaughlin 4 64
(M S Saunders) *a last: rdn 3f out and sme prog over 2f out: nvr on terms* **11/4**[2]

68.85 secs (-2.35) **Going Correction** -0.325s/f (Firm) **5** Ran SP% **113.6**

Speed ratings (Par 102): **102,91,89,88,87**

CSF £16.06 TOTE £2.80: £1.20, £3.90; EX 17.80.

Owner H J W Davies P Spencer-Jones M H Holland **Bred** Yeomanstown Stud **Trained** Ogbourne Maisey, Wilts

FOCUS

This looked a fair sprint handicap, but Golden Destiny was in a league of her own and should rate much higher.

Captain Carey Official explanation: jockey said gelding was unsuited by the firm ground

5246 BATH ALES SPA H'CAP 1m 5f 22y

7:45 (7:45) (Class 6) (0-55,55) 3-Y-O+ **£1,942** (£578; £288; £144) **Stalls** High

Form RPR

410 **1** **Looks The Business (IRE)**[14] 4806 8-9-5 53 FergusSweeney 9 61
(A B Haynes) *led after 3f: rdn and hdd 2f out: rallied gamely fnl f to ld fnl 50yds: all out* **6/1**[3]

3202 **2** shd **Barodine**[15] 4735 6-9-4 52 GeorgeBaker 10 59
(R J Hodges) *in tch: hdwy over 2f out: drvn to chal fnl 50yds: no ex last strides and hung lft cl home* **5/1**[2]

3604 **3** 2 **Annambo**[40] 3923 9-9-7 55 (p) SebSanders 13 60+
(Andrew Reid) *in tch: smooth hdwy to ld 2f out: sn rdn: kpt slt ld tl hdd fnl 50yds: hld whn hmpd cl home* **10/1**

0104 **4** 2 3/4 **Dot's Delight**[15] 4735 5-9-1 49 LPKeniry 5 49
(M G Rimell) *in rr: hdwy 1/2-way: chsd ldrs and rdn over 2f out: wknd appr fnl f* **20/1**

03 **5** 1 1/4 **Precious Citizen (USA)**[28] 4300 4-9-3 51 SteveDrowne 8 49
(J R Gask) *chsd ldrs: drvn to chal 2f out: wknd qckly jst ins fnl f* **4/1**[1]

6453 **6** hd **Le Corvee (IRE)**[50] 3594 7-8-11 50 MCGeran(5) 11 48
(A W Carroll) *in rr: rdn and hdwy over 2f out: styd on same pce* **12/1**

1054 **7** nk **Mossmann Gorge**[18] 4625 7-8-11 48 (p) KevinGhunowa(3) 7 46
(A Middleton) *chsd ldrs: rdn 3f out: wknd ins fnl 2f* **12/1**

0545 **8** 1 1/2 **Amwell Brave**[46] 3714 8-8-12 46 TolleyDean 12 41
(J R Jenkins) *in rr: hdwy on outside over 2f out: nvr rchd ldrs and sn btn* **20/1**

0306 **9** 3 1/4 **Bob's Your Uncle**[44] 3774 6-8-8 49 JPFahy(7) 6 40
(J G Portman) *s.i.s: in rr: hdwy on wd outside over 4f out: rdn 3f out: wknd 2f out* **8/1**

5255 **10** 8 **Lady Jinks**[33] 4146 4-9-1 49 TonyCulhane 14 28
(R J Hodges) *bhd most of way* **16/1**

5500 **11** 3 **Flowerbud**[59] 3275 4-8-12 46 FrankieMcDonald 4 20
(G A Ham) *chsd ldrs to 3f out:* **28/1**

656- **P** **Trevian**[38] 4635 8-9-1 **49**..(vt) TravisBlock 1 —
(Tim Vaughan) *led 3f: styd chsng ldrs tl lost action 3f out and sn p.u* **4/1**[1]

2m 52.01s (0.01) **Going Correction** -0.15s/f (Firm) **12** Ran SP% **125.4**
Speed ratings (Par 101): **93,92,91,90,89 89,88,88,86,81 79,—**
toteswingers: 1&2 £5.50, 1&3 £15.60, 2&3 £6.30 CSF £37.32 CT £307.91 TOTE £6.30: £3.10, £2.20, £3.20; EX 30.90 Place 6: £60.53 Place 5: £35.20.
Owner Mould, Harrold, Drewett & Drewett **Bred** Mrs M O'Callaghan **Trained** Limpley Stoke, Bath
■ Stewards' Enquiry : Fergus Sweeney two-day ban: careless riding (Sep 6-7)

FOCUS
A moderate but competitive handicap best rated around the first three.
Amwell Brave Official explanation: jockey said gelding slipped on the bend
Bob's Your Uncle Official explanation: trainer said gelding was unsuited by the firm ground
Lady Jinks Official explanation: jockey said filly was upset by the preliminaries
T/Plt: £36.40 to a £1 stake. Pool: £38,517.02. 771.55 winning tickets. T/Qpdt: £17.00 to a £1 stake. Pool: £5,919.59. 257.36 winning tickets. ST

5205 CHESTER (L-H)

Saturday, August 22

OFFICIAL GOING: Good to firm (firm in places; 8.4)
Wind: Almost nil Weather: Fine

5247 TOTEPLACEPOT H'CAP 5f 16y

2:25 (2:26) (Class 4) (0-85,85) 3-Y-O+ **£5,828** (£1,734; £866; £432) **Stalls** Low

Form RPR

3220 **1** **Bertoliver**[20] 4567 5-9-6 **81**.. PhilipRobinson 2 90
(Tom Dascombe) *mde all: rdn ins fnl f: kpt up to work towards fin* **3/1**[1]

150 **2** *1* **Le Toreador**[15] 4753 4-9-8 **83**..................................(t) SilvestreDeSousa 8 88
(K A Ryan) *trckd ldrs: rdn 2f out: wnt 2nd ins fnl f: styd on: nt quite pce to get to wnr* **15/2**

6134 **3** *1* **Tyfos**[26] 4387 4-9-2 **77**.. LukeMorris 1 78
(W M Brisbourne) *chsd wnr: rdn over 1f out: lost 2nd ins fnl f: nt qckn* **5/1**[3]

506 **4** *1 ¼* **Misaro (GER)**[5] 5098 8-9-2 **82**....................................(v) RichardEvans(5) 5 79
(R A Harris) *chsd ldrs: rdn 2f out: kpt on but nt pce to chal* **20/1**

0000 **5** *½* **Supermassive Muse (IRE)**[14] 4784 4-9-2 **77**........(p) GrahamGibbons 4 72
(E S McMahon) *chsd ldrs: rdn 2f out: styd on same pce fnl f* **9/1**

1303 **6** *nk* **Invincible Lad (IRE)**[23] 4461 5-9-9 **84**................................ ShaneKelly 7 78+
(E J Alston) *midfield: rdn ins fnl f: kpt on: nvr able to chal* **9/2**[2]

0400 **7** *nk* **Total Impact**[23] 4461 6-9-2 **82**... BMcHugh(5) 11 75+
(R A Fahey) *hld up: hdwy on outside over 1f out: styd on: nt pce to get to ldrs* **16/1**

1200 **8** *nk* **Tyrannosaurus Rex (IRE)**[10] 4891 5-8-12 **78**............... MartinLane(5) 6 70
(D Shaw) *towards rr: pushed along over 2f out: kpt on ins fnl f: nt pce to chal* **8/1**

1406 **9** *hd* **Sands Crooner (IRE)**[10] 4891 6-9-3 **78**.........................(v) TPQueally 13 69
(J G Given) *missed break: sn pushed along in rr: kpt on u.p towards fin: nvr able to chal* **50/1**

4031 **10** *1* **Rasaman (IRE)**[18] 4621 5-9-6 **81**................................(v) DanielTudhope 9 69+
(J S Goldie) *rrd s: bhd: shkn up 1f out: continually denied a run ins fnl f: eased whn no ch towards fin* **20/1**

5010 **11** *1 ¼* **Glamorous Spirit (IRE)**[12] 4849 3-9-5 **85**............... KevinGhunowa(3) 3 68
(R A Harris) *s.i.s: n.m.r after 100yds: racd in midfield: rdn over 2f out: wknd fnl f* **15/2**

60.77 secs (-0.23) **Going Correction** +0.10s/f (Good)
WFA 3 from 4yo+ 2lb **11** Ran SP% **121.9**
Speed ratings (Par 105): **105,103,101,99,99 98,98,97,97,95 93**
toteswinger: 1&2 £5.70, 1&3 £4.40, 2&3 £8.90. CSF £26.44 CT £115.08 TOTE £3.90: £1.70, £3.00, £2.30; EX 27.80 Trifecta £365.80 Pool: £741.54 - 1.50 winning units..
Owner Mrs A Shone **Bred** Pillar To Post Racing **Trained** Lambourn, Berks

FOCUS
A total of 3mm of water was applied to the straight the previous night but the ground remained good to firm, with the two furlongs after the winning post into the bend on the back straight closer to firm. The running rail had been moved out a little more since the previous day. Very few got involved in this 5f handicap, with the pace holding up well.
Rasaman(IRE) Official explanation: jockey said gelding was denied a clear run

5248 TOTEPOOL CHESTER STKS (H'CAP) (LISTED RACE) 1m 5f 89y

2:55 (2:55) (Class 1) (0-110,108) 3-Y-O+ **£22,708** (£8,608; £4,308; £2,148; £1,076; £540) **Stalls** Low

Form RPR

0121 **1** **Munsef**[27] 4340 7-9-8 **105**.. EddieAhern 10 110
(Ian Williams) *midfield: hdwy over 3f out: led over 1f out: sn pressed: a doing enough towards fin* **5/1**[2]

5026 **2** *½* **Mystery Star (IRE)**[14] 4770 4-8-11 **94** oh1.......................... TedDurcan 6 98
(M H Tompkins) *hld up: hdwy 2f out: rdn to go 2nd and mount str chal over 1f out: almost upsides ins fnl f: hld towards fin* **11/1**

2303 **3** *½* **Sabotage (UAE)**[14] 4767 3-8-2 **96**........................... SilvestreDeSousa 4 101+
(M Johnston) *chsd ldrs: nt clr run over 1f out: effrt and swtchd lft to chal ent fnl f: r.o: nt qckn towards fin* **15/8**[1]

0360 **4** *1 ¾* **Basaltico (IRE)**[7] 5023 5-9-11 **108**................................ JimmyFortune 5 109
(L M Cumani) *hld up: rdn 2f out: hdwy over 1f out: chsd ldrs ins fnl f: styd on but nt quite pce to chal front trio* **12/1**

1004 **5** *1* **Keenes Day (FR)**[14] 4769 4-8-11 **94** oh1...................... J-PGuillambert 7 93+
(M Johnston) *bhd: rdn over 1f out: styd on u.p ins fnl f: nt pce to rch ldrs* **15/2**

0220 **6** *nk* **Cheshire Prince**[14] 4781 5-8-11 **94** oh1............................... LukeMorris 2 94+
(W M Brisbourne) *in tch: lost pl whn nt clr run over 1f out: sn rdn: kpt on ins fnl f: nvr able to chal* **12/1**

-600 **7** *1 ¼* **Si Belle (IRE)**[20] 4566 4-8-11 **94** oh4.............................. NickyMackay 3 91
(Rae Guest) *hld up: rdn and hdwy over 1f out: no imp fnl f* **40/1**

5021 **8** *¾* **Press The Button (GER)**[14] 4770 6-8-11 **94** oh2................. SJCraine 8 90+
(J R Boyle) *prom: nt clr run over 1f out: sn lost pl and rdn: failed to pick up and one pce after* **14/1**

0435 **9** *4 ½* **Unleashed (IRE)**[22] 4484 4-9-5 **102**................................... TPQueally 11 91
(H R A Cecil) *prom: effrt to chal 4f out: led over 2f out: hdd over 1f out: sn wknd* **7/1**[3]

1650 **10** *3 ¾* **Hindu Kush (IRE)**[25] 4408 4-9-1 **98**........................... AdrianTNicholls 9 82
(D Nicholls) *sn led: rdn and hdd over 2f out: wknd over 1f out* **8/1**

2m 51.7s (-1.50) **Going Correction** +0.10s/f (Good)
WFA 3 from 4yo+ 11lb **10** Ran SP% **119.6**
Speed ratings (Par 111): **108,107,107,106,105 105,104,104,101,99**
toteswinger: 1&2 £10.60, 1&3 £2.90, 2&3 £7.00. CSF £60.43 CT £140.88 TOTE £6.00: £2.00, £3.40, £1.30; EX 65.40 Trifecta £196.70 Pool: £691.14 - 2.60 winning units..
Owner Dr Marwan Koukash **Bred** Shadwell Estate Company Limited **Trained** Portway, Worcs

■ Stewards' Enquiry : Ted Durcan one-day ban: used whip without giving gelding time to respond (Sep 6)

FOCUS
Not a strong race for the grade and the pace fell apart and turning into the straight the closers were queueing up to make their moves. The first three finished in the same order as when they met in a heritage handicap at Ascot last month, suggesting the form is reasonably sound.

NOTEBOOK
Munsef travelled strongly into contention, kicked on once straightened up and gamely held off Mystery Star's strong challenge inside the last furlong. He hasn't looked back since taking a claimer here in June, got the longer trip well, and looks back to his best. The Melbourne Cup is being seriously considered, although the less glamorous Stockholm Cup is also a possible target. (op 11-2)
Mystery Star(IRE) was 1lb better off with the winner for a short-head defeat at Ascot, but couldn't reverse the form. He tracked him through into the straight but, try as he might, could not get by him. He remains steadily progressive, though. (op 9-1 tchd 12-1)
Sabotage(UAE), the only three-year-old in the field, was tight for room entering the straight but stayed on well under pressure to take third. Considering he never looked at home around the bends, this was a creditable effort, and he'll be far more effective back on a more galloping track. (op 5-2 tchd 11-4 in places)
Basaltico(IRE) had not enjoyed much luck in his first two starts in Britain, but this was a drop in class for him and he showed what he is capable of. He stays 2m and a Listed contest over that sort of trip could come his way this autumn, with soft ground no concern.
Keenes Day(FR) didn't handle the track and was struggling in last place down the back straight, but the leaders stopped and he finished well, as one would expect of a gelding who has won twice won over 2m-plus. (op 7-1 tchd 8-1)
Cheshire Prince, who has a good record here but has never won over this far, was brought down in a pile-up in this race last year. The way he ran suggests the trip just stretches his stamina. (op 9-1)
Press The Button(GER) raced keenly and paid for racing too close to the decent gallop. (op 12-1 tchd 11-1)

5249 TOTESCOOP6 H'CAP (HERITAGE HANDICAP) 7f 122y

3:30 (3:31) (Class 2) 3-Y-O+
£24,924 (£7,464; £3,732; £1,868; £932; £468) **Stalls** Low

Form RPR

0046 **1** **Carcinetto (IRE)**[6] 5069 7-8-6 **95**.. BMcHugh(5) 1 102
(P D Evans) *midfield: hdwy 3f out: sn rdn: r.o against inner rail to ld wl ins fnl f: kpt up to work fin* **16/1**

160 **2** *nk* **Lowther**[14] 4779 4-8-6 **90**...(e[1]) NeilChalmers 2 96
(A Bailey) *handy in chsng gp: effrt to ld wl over 1f out: hdd wl ins fnl f: hld fnl strides* **15/2**

0043 **3** *¾* **Opus Maximus (IRE)**[14] 4779 4-8-2 **86**.................... AdrianTNicholls 14 90+
(M Johnston) *hld up: hdwy on outside 2f out: chsd ldrs over 1f out: r.o ins fnl f* **17/2**

-261 **4** *hd* **Axiom**[24] 4423 5-9-2 **100**.. ShaneKelly 7 104+
(L M Cumani) *hld up bhd: rdn over 1f out: plld to outside over 1f out: hdwy ins fnl f: r.o and gaining at fin* **11/2**[2]

000 **5** *¾* **Esoterica (IRE)**[1] 5206 6-7-13 **88** ow3..........................(v) MartinLane(5) 5 90
(J S Goldie) *hld up: nt clr run 2f out: rdn over 1f out: styd on ins fnl f: nt quite get to ldrs* **25/1**

1640 **6** *nse* **Ordnance Row**[42] 3841 6-9-10 **108**.. PatDobbs 12 110
(R Hannon) *chsd ldrs: rdn and nt qckn over 1f out: r.o ins fnl f: run flattened out towards fin* **14/1**

0006 **7** *¾* **Dhaular Dhar (IRE)**[14] 4796 7-8-11 **95**...................... DanielTudhope 10 95+
(J S Goldie) *hld up: nt clr run over 1f out: rdn and r.o ins fnl f: unable to rch ldrs* **6/1**[3]

0200 **8** *1* **Celtic Sultan (IRE)**[24] 4423 5-8-8 **92**.................................. MickyFenton 3 90
(T P Tate) *led at str gallop: rdn and hdd wl over 1f out: fdd ins fnl 100yds* **5/1**[1]

6106 **9** *¾* **Dunn'o (IRE)**[14] 4768 4-8-11 **95**.................................... PhilipRobinson 13 91
(C G Cox) *chsd ldr at str gallop: lost 2nd over 2f out: wknd ins fnl f* **10/1**

5550 **10** *½* **Racer Forever (USA)**[28] 4297 6-9-5 **103**.....................(b) JimmyFortune 6 99
(J H M Gosden) *midfield: nt clr run 2f out: rdn and hdwy over 1f out: no further imp whn n.m.r wl ins fnl f* **6/1**[3]

036 **11** *1 ½* **King Jock (USA)**[55] 3433 8-9-4 **102**.................................. MichaelHills 11 93
(R J Osborne, Ire) *midfield: rdn over 1f out: sn wknd* **14/1**

0004 **12** *11* **Tartan Gigha (IRE)**[14] 4768 4-8-8 **92**............................. J-PGuillambert 9 55
(M Johnston) *handy in chsng gp: pushed along 3f out: wknd over 2f out: eased whn wl btn over 1f out* **14/1**

1m 32.91s (-0.89) **Going Correction** +0.10s/f (Good)
WFA 3 from 4yo+ 6lb **12** Ran SP% **121.7**
Speed ratings (Par 109): **108,107,106,106,106 105,105,104,103,102 101,90**
toteswinger: 1&2 £32.40, 1&3 £33.40, 2&3 £13.60. CSF £134.76 CT £1127.80 TOTE £20.10: £5.30, £3.00, £2.60; EX 154.10 TRIFECTA Not won..
Owner Mrs Sally Edwards **Bred** M A Doyle **Trained** Pandy, Monmouths
■ Stewards' Enquiry : Adrian T Nicholls two-day ban: excessive use of the whip (Sep 6-7)

FOCUS
There was a strong pace and those ridden more patiently came to the fore. A low draw also proved a big advantage and this is not form to take at face value, with the third the best guide to the level.

NOTEBOOK
Carcinetto(IRE), back in handicap company, was drawn in stall one and enjoyed the run of things, racing in midfield and saving ground bang on the rail. As they swung into the straight the leader edged off it and she tried to nip through, but the gap closed and she was momentarily held up in her run. However, as soon as they arrived at the cutaway, she was angled to the inside and saw her race out strongly. Tough as old boots, she takes her racing extremely well, and she'll no doubt be back chasing black type soon. (op 14-1 tchd 18-1)
Lowther, who won over 7f here in June, had disappointed a little since, but he bounced back to form on his return to this track and with an eyeshield fitted for the first time. Drawn well in stall two, he too benefited from racing on the rail, but his rider angled him out on the turn out of the back straight and his spot was taken by the eventual winner. Perhaps on reflection he will wish he'd stayed on the rail, as he would have been tough to pass the way the race unfolded. As it is, he came four wide into the straight and yet was only narrowly beaten. (op 8-1 tchd 9-1)
Opus Maximus(IRE) didn't enjoy the best of trips, as he raced wider than most for much of the way, having been drawn in the outside stall. He also swung widest of all into the straight, so his strong finish was pleasing, and he looks capable of winning off his current mark when things fall right. (op 10-1 tchd 8-1)
Axiom was held up at the back of the field and had his challenge delayed by being stuck behind a wall of horses entering the straight. He finished well once angled out though, and remains competitive off his new mark, although a return to easier ground will suit him. (op 4-1 tchd 6-1)
Esoterica(IRE), making a quick reappearance after finishing in midfield here the previous day, followed the winner through on the rail and had no real excuse. (op 28-1)
Ordnance Row, who won this race in 2006, was running in a handicap for the first time in over two years. It was a sound effort under his big weight considering he led the chasing pack in a race run at a strong gallop. (tchd 12-1)
Dhaular Dhar(IRE), who has such a good record here, was swinging away out the back entering the straight but got little luck in running as he tried to weave through. His style of running is always fraught with danger. (op 15-2 tchd 5-1)

Celtic Sultan(IRE) had too much use made of him. (op 11-2 tchd 13-2)

Dunn'o(IRE) paid for chasing the fast pace. (op 12-1)

Racer Forever(USA) was hampered on the turn into the straight, which didn't help his cause. (tchd 13-2 and 7-1 in places)

Tartan Gigha(IRE) Official explanation: jockey said gelding lost its action

5250 TOTEEXACTA EBF CONDITIONS STKS (C&G) 6f 18y

4:05 (4:05) (Class 2) 2-Y-O **£9,777** (£2,926; £1,463) **Stalls** Low

Form RPR

1 **1** **Quarrel (USA)**[27] 4336 2-9-1 0 .... MichaelHills 4 91+
(W J Haggas) *sn led: shkn up over 1f out: rdn ins fnl f: r.o and a looked in control* **2/1**[2]

1 **2** *1* **Atlantis Star**[17] 4659 2-9-1 0 .... TedDurcan 2 87+
(Saeed Bin Suroor) *hld up: wnt 2nd 4f out: rdn and nt qckn over 1f out: looked hld thrght fnl f* **8/11**[1]

2104 **3** *½* **Footstepsofspring (FR)**[29] 4272 2-9-1 86 .... PatDobbs 1 86+
(R Hannon) *broke wl: sn 2nd pl: dropped to rr 4f out: rdn over 1f out: kpt on same pce and nvr able to chal fnl f* **6/1**[3]

1m 15.16s (1.36) **Going Correction** +0.10s/f (Good) **3** Ran SP% **105.5**
Speed ratings (Par 100): **94,92,92**
CSF £3.83 TOTE £2.50; EX 3.20.

Owner St Albans Bloodstock LLP **Bred** Rosemont Farm Llc **Trained** Newmarket, Suffolk

FOCUS
Just the three runners for this conditions event, but a pleasing performance from the winner.

NOTEBOOK
Quarrel(USA) was taken to the front going into the first bend and made the rest of the running. Shaken up on the turn in, he held off the Godolphin colt pretty comfortably in the straight and a crack at a Pattern race beckons. He holds entries in the Champagne, Mill Reef, Middle Park and Dewhurst, so there are plenty of options open to connections, and this colt should have no trouble moving up to 7f if that's the way they decide to go. (op 7-4 tchd 13-8 in places)

Atlantis Star won impressively at Pontefract on his debut, but he holds no Group-race entries this year. Worst of the three away, he was a little keen and could never get any closer than a length behind the winner. This track didn't look much of an excuse and he probably just bumped into a better horse. (op 10-11 tchd evens in places)

Footstepsofspring(FR) has run his best races from the front but he was denied that role by the winner. More exposed than the other two, he was up against it in this company, but he's a solid performer and his performance is probably a fair guide to the level of the form. (op 9-2)

5251 TOTESPORT HOME OF POOL BETTING EBF MAIDEN STKS 7f 2y

4:40 (4:40) (Class 3) 2-Y-O **£7,317** (£2,177; £1,088; £543) **Stalls** Low

Form RPR

0 **1** **Ransom Note**[45] 3750 2-9-3 0 .... MichaelHills 5 70+
(B W Hills) *dwlt: midfield: nt much briefly after 1f: lost pl 2f out: hdwy over 1f out: c through on inner rail to ld ins fnl f: hld on gamely at fin* **3/1**[2]

03 **2** *nse* **Demonstrative (USA)**[17] 4659 2-9-3 0 .... J-PGuillambert 6 70
(M Johnston) *bhd: hdwy 2f out: rdn to chal ins fnl f: r.o: jst hld* **10/1**

64 **3** *½* **Jimmy The Poacher (IRE)**[20] 4557 2-9-3 0 .... GrahamGibbons 8 69
(T D Easterby) *in tch: pushed along over 1f out: chal ins fnl f: r.o: hld fnl strides* **14/1**

3 **4** *nk* **Mr Corby (IRE)**[20] 4564 2-9-3 0 .... TedDurcan 9 68
(M R Channon) *hld up: hdwy on outside 3f out: chsd ldrs 2f out: rdn and chal ins fnl f: nt qckn cl home* **10/1**

3 **5** *1 ¾* **Banks And Braes**[8] 5006 2-9-3 0 .... PatDobbs 7 64+
(R Hannon) *hld up: pushed along over 1f out: styd on ins fnl f: nt pce to chal ldrs* **4/1**[3]

0 **6** *¾* **Kumbeshwar**[47] 3692 2-9-3 0 .... TPQueally 1 62
(P D Evans) *led: rdn and hdd over 1f out: stl in contention ent fnl f: no ex fnl 100yds* **25/1**

00 **7** *nk* **Boycott (IRE)**[28] 4314 2-9-3 0 .... (b[1]) JimmyFortune 2 61
(J H M Gosden) *w ldr: rdn to ld over 1f out: sn edgd lft: hdd ins fnl f: no ex fnl 100yds* **14/1**

422 **8** *4* **Layla's Boy**[31] 4194 2-9-3 79 .... EddieAhern 3 51
(R A Fahey) *trckd ldrs: effrt on heels of ldrs whn n.m.r and hmpd ent fnl f: sn lost pl: n.d after* **7/4**[1]

1m 28.8s (2.30) **Going Correction** +0.10s/f (Good) **8** Ran SP% **116.7**
Speed ratings (Par 98): **90,89,89,89,87 86,85,81**
toteswinger: 1&2 £3.90, 1&3 £5.20, 2&3 £14.40. CSF £33.48 TOTE £3.80: £1.20, £3.60, £2.20; EX 33.90.

Owner H R Mould **Bred** Rabbah Bloodstock Limited **Trained** Lambourn, Berks

■ Stewards' Enquiry : Eddie Ahern 16-day ban: 2 days for careless riding; 14 days (4 days deferred for 3 months) under totting-up procedure (Sep 4-15)

FOCUS
No more than a fair maiden, but it's a race in which Barry Hills has a terrific record, and he recorded his sixth win in the last nine years with Ransom Note.

NOTEBOOK
Ransom Note, too green to do himself justice on his debut, wasn't the quickest away here, but he got a nice position on the rail, stayed there, and, when the gap opened up at the cutaway, took full advantage. He stayed on well to hold on narrowly and shapes as though he'll improve further for this second run. The bunched finish should mean the Handicapper doesn't go mad, and he could be interesting in nurseries. (tchd 7-2 and 11-4 in places)

Demonstrative(USA) was slowly away and in rear through the early stages, being pushed along and seemingly struggling, but he responded to pressure and came into contention rounding the turn widest into the straight. He got motoring in the closing stages and, only just denied, clearly appreciated the step up to 7f. A more galloping track looks sure to suit him, and nurseries are now an option. (tchd 9-1)

Jimmy The Poacher(IRE) ran on well in the closing stages to record his best effort, but he's likely to have done his handicap mark some harm in the process. A stiffer track is likely to suit him. (op 10-1 tchd 9-1)

Mr Corby(IRE), moving up a furlong, looked a big danger on the turn into the straight but was outbattled. This was a step up on his debut effort, though, and he's going the right way. (op 8-1)

Banks And Braes, who was held up out the back, ran on late, and there's more to come from him, almost certainly once he's eligible for handicaps. (op 7-2)

Kumbeshwar is going the right way. He'd clearly learned from his debut, as he made the running here, but one would imagine the best of him won't be seen until he tackles modest handicaps over middle distances next year. (op 20-1)

Boycott(IRE), blinkered for the first time, hung left under pressure, doing Layla's Boy no favours in the process. He's a half-brother to Art Connoisseur but looks moderate on the evidence of his three runs to date. (op 11-1)

Layla's Boy would not have won even with a clear run, but would have finished a good deal closer. (op 11-4)

5252 BET TOTEPOOL AT TOTESPORT.COM H'CAP 1m 7f 195y

5:10 (5:10) (Class 4) (0-85,84) 3-Y-O+ **£5,504** (£1,637; £818; £408) **Stalls** Low

Form RPR

5323 **1** **Dazinski**[28] 4325 3-8-5 75 .... NickyMackay 9 86
(M H Tompkins) *trckd ldrs: led over 2f out: dashed away over 1f out: rdn out* **10/3**[1]

6514 **2** *1 ¾* **Hawridge King**[31] 4212 7-9-3 76 .... JamesMillman[(3)] 11 85
(W S Kittow) *hld up in rr: hdwy over 2f out: wnt 2nd over 1f out: styd on ins fnl f: nt rch wnr* **14/1**

225 **3** *2 ½* **Zuwaar**[28] 4332 4-9-0 70 .... (tp) EddieAhern 1 76
(Ian Williams) *hld up: hdwy over 3f out: wnt 2nd briefly over 1f out: one pce fnl f* **4/1**[2]

0301 **4** *4* **Fin Vin De Leu (GER)**[10] 4890 3-8-7 77 .... J-PGuillambert 7 78
(M Johnston) *w ldr: chal 2f out: wknd over 1f out* **9/2**[3]

-604 **5** *1* **Wicked Daze (IRE)**[56] 3380 6-9-10 80 .... (v[1]) TedDurcan 10 83+
(K A Ryan) *trckd ldrs: dropped to midfield after 4f: n.m.r 2f out: sn lost pl: nt clr run whn no imp over 1f out: wl btn after* **12/1**

165 **6** *1 ¼* **Pseudonym (IRE)**[10] 4890 7-8-12 68 .... (t) TPQueally 8 67
(M F Harris) *midfield: pushed along over 3f out: one pce and no imp fnl 2f* **16/1**

4505 **7** *2 ½* **Capable Guest (IRE)**[8] 4988 7-9-2 72 .... JimmyFortune 4 68
(M R Channon) *hld up: pushed along 2f out: nvr on terms* **9/1**

0044 **8** *hd* **Lost Soldier Three (IRE)**[6] 5067 8-10-0 84 .... AdrianTNicholls 3 79
(D Nicholls) *trckd ldrs: pushed along 2f out: sn n.m.r: wknd wl over 1f out* **10/1**

0226 **9** *7* **My Mate Max**[44] 3788 4-9-1 71 .... (p) GrahamGibbons 6 58
(R Hollinshead) *led: pushed along 3f out: hdd over 2f out: sn n.m.r: wknd wl over 1f out* **9/1**

4366 **10** *7* **Luna Landing**[28] 4332 6-8-12 68 .... DanielTudhope 2 46
(Jedd O'Keeffe) *missed break: midfield: pushed along 4f out: sn lost pl: n.d after* **11/1**

3m 25.18s (-2.82) **Going Correction** +0.10s/f (Good)
WFA 3 from 4yo+ 14lb **10** Ran SP% **118.9**
Speed ratings (Par 105): **111,110,108,106,106 105,104,104,100,97**
toteswinger: 1&2 £4.20, 1&3 £3.80, 2&3 £12.30. CSF £52.63 CT £196.29 TOTE £4.30: £1.80, £4.40, £2.00; EX 51.80 Place 6: £214.73 Place 5: £136.39.

Owner Mrs Beryl Lockey **Bred** Darley **Trained** Newmarket, Suffolk

FOCUS
A fair handicap with a couple of progressive three-year-olds taking on their elders and it was one of them who came out on top. The pace was good and the form looks sound rated through the third.

Wicked Daze(IRE) Official explanation: jockey said gelding suffered interference in running

Luna Landing Official explanation: jockey said gelding lost a front shoe

T/Plt: £431.60 to a £1 stake. Pool: £100,007.45. 169.15 winning tickets. T/Qpdt: £77.80 to a £1 stake. Pool: £3,624.30. 34.45 winning tickets. DO

5036 RIPON (R-H)

Saturday, August 22

OFFICIAL GOING: Good to firm (8.4)
Wind: Virtually nil Weather: Fine and dry

5253 BUY A RACING POST YEARLING BONUS CANDIDATE MAIDEN STKS 6f

2:20 (2:20) (Class 5) 2-Y-O **£3,885** (£1,156; £577; £288) **Stalls** Low

Form RPR

52 **1** **Tasmeem (IRE)**[20] 4568 2-9-3 0 .... TPO'Shea 2 83+
(B W Hills) *trckd ldrs: hdwy over 2f out: rdn to ld appr fnl f: edgd rt ins fnl f and sn clr: kpt on strly* **13/8**[1]

00 **2** *3 ½* **Gold Rules**[24] 4424 2-9-3 0 .... PatCosgrave 10 73
(L M Cumani) *trckd ldrs: hdwy 1/2-way: effrt 2f out and sn ev ch tl rdn and one pce appr fnl f* **12/1**

4323 **3** *½* **Waveband**[16] 4711 2-8-12 76 .... GregFairley 5 66
(M Johnston) *cl up: effrt 1/2-way and sn led: rdn along 2f out: drvn and hdd appr fnl f: kpt on same pce* **2/1**[2]

66 **4** *6* **North Central (USA)**[58] 3310 2-9-0 0 .... FrederikTylicki[(3)] 8 53
(J Howard Johnson) *midfield: hdwy whn bmpd wl over 2f out: rdn wl over 1f out and no imp* **9/1**

56 **5** *3 ½* **Destiny's Dancer**[7] 5036 2-8-7 0 .... PatrickDonaghy[(5)] 9 38
(P C Haslam) *hld up towards rr: hdwy whn bmpd over 2f out: sn rdn and no imp* **66/1**

6 *½* **Layla's Prince (IRE)** 2-9-3 0 .... FrancisNorton 14 50+
(D Nicholls) *in rr: hdwy over 2f out: n.m.r wl over 1f out: nvr rch ldrs* **28/1**

230 **7** *2 ¼* **Saucy Girl (IRE)**[65] 3064 2-8-12 75 .... DavidAllan 1 29
(T D Easterby) *led: rdn along 1/2-way: sn hdd and grad wknd* **10/1**

0550 **8** *1* **Baby Judge (IRE)**[26] 4370 2-8-10 52 .... (b) AndrewHeffernan[(7)] 6 31
(M C Chapman) *prom: rdn along and hung lft 1/2-way: sn wknd* **125/1**

203 **9** *¾* **We'll Deal Again**[19] 4595 2-8-10 68 .... JamesPSullivan[(7)] 7 29
(M W Easterby) *dwlt and hmpd s: keen and sn swtchd rt: a in rr* **8/1**[3]

00 **10** *nk* **Buzz Bird**[13] 4817 2-8-12 0 .... PhillipMakin 13 23
(T D Barron) *midfield: n.m.r and lost pl after 2f: sn towards rr* **100/1**

40 **11** *1* **Dazakhee**[29] 4278 2-8-12 0 .... TonyHamilton 4 20
(P T Midgley) *s.i.s: a in rr* **100/1**

12 *5* **Sonofdon** 2-8-12 0 .... JamieKyne[(5)] 12 10
(C W Moore) *s.i.s: a towards rr* **100/1**

00 **13** *1 ¼* **Burtondale Boy (IRE)**[103] 1920 2-8-12 0 .... PaulPickard[(5)] 3 6
(P T Midgley) *a in rr* **50/1**

55 **14** *1 ¼* **Lucky Traveller**[17] 4652 2-9-3 0 .... DuranFentiman 11 3
(T D Easterby) *a towards rr* **66/1**

1m 12.17s (-0.83) **Going Correction** -0.125s/f (Firm) **14** Ran SP% **121.5**
Speed ratings (Par 94): **100,95,94,86,82 81,78,77,76,75 74,67,65,64**
toteswinger: 1&2 £11.20, 1&3 £1.20, 2&3 £6.90. CSF £23.16 TOTE £2.70: £1.20, £3.90, £1.40; EX 28.10 Trifecta £63.90 Pool: £241.86 - 2.80 winning units..

Owner Hamdan Al Maktoum **Bred** Max Ervine **Trained** Lambourn, Berks

■ Stewards' Enquiry : T P O'Shea caution: careless riding
Jamie Kyne caution: used whip when out of contention

FOCUS
Three drew clear in what was a modest maiden.

NOTEBOOK
Tasmeem(IRE), runner-up in a 6f Newbury maiden last time, got a nice tow through and, having led over 1f out, he stayed on well to score with quite a bit in hand. This sort of ground clearly suited the son of Acclamation and he is the type to go on to better things in nurseries. (op 15-8)

Gold Rules ◆ ran much better back on this faster ground, having disappointed on soft last time and is another now qualified for nurseries. His dam was a 1m4f winner and he is going to improve for a step up in trip, so finding a race for him shouldn't be a problem. (op 14-1)
Waveband, who is officially rated 76, looked vulnerable to something less exposed and, having shown her customary early speed, she was left well behind from 1f out. (tchd 9-4)
North Central(USA) is now qualified for an official mark and should fare better in nurseries, especially once tackling 7f. (op 10-1)
Destiny's Dancer will find opportunities at a lower level.
Layla's Prince(IRE), an already gelded son of Statue Of Liberty, shaped with some promise on this racecourse debut. (op 25-1)
We'll Deal Again was soon struggling having been slowly away and hampered at the start. (tchd 9-1)
Dazakhee Official explanation: jockey said filly hung left-handed throughout

5254 GILL HARRISON MEMORIAL APPRENTICE (S) STKS — 6f

2:50 (2:52) (Class 6) 3-4-Y-O — £2,590 (£770; £385; £192) Stalls Low

Form — RPR

3021 **1** **Darcey**[8] 4995 3-9-4 69 ... FrederikTylicki 12 — 73
(R A Fahey) *in tch stands' side: hdwy to trck ldrs 1/2-way: cl up wl over 1f out: rdn to ld appr fnl f and kpt on* **13/8**[1]

1443 **2** *2* **Simple Rhythm**[19] 4596 3-9-4 65 ... KellyHarrison 11 — 67
(J G Given) *prom stands' side: led 1/2-way: rdn wl over 1f out: hdd and drvn approachng fnl f: kpt on same pce: 2nd of 12 in gp* **4/1**[2]

0505 **3** *2 3/4* **Rio Sands**[27] 4355 4-9-7 56 ... MichaelJStainton 7 — 58
(R M Whitaker) *in tch stands' side: hdwy to chse ldrs over 2f out: sn rdn and kpt on same pce: 3rd of 12 in gp* **6/1**[3]

0600 **4** *4 1/2* **Kingsgate Castle**[15] 4748 4-9-2 58 ...(b) KylieManser(5) 2 — 43
(Miss Gay Kelleway) *midfield stands' side: hdwy 3f out: rdn to chse ldrs 2f out: sn hung lft and no imp 4th of 12 in gp* **15/2**

6000 **5** *nk* **Rossett Rose (IRE)**[29] 4279 3-8-8 48 ... JohnCavanagh(5) 5 — 37
(M Brittain) *overall ldr stands' side: rdn along and hdd 1/2-way: grad wknd: 5th of 12 in gp* **33/1**

400- **6** *1 3/4* **Faraway Sound (IRE)**[253] 7645 3-9-1 69 ... PatrickDonaghy(3) 14 — 37
(P C Haslam) *led far side gp: prom tl rdn along and kpt on same pce fnl 2f: no ch w stands' side: 1st of 3 in gp* **16/1**

0050 **7** *nk* **Paint Stripper**[3] 5150 4-9-4 42 ... JamieKyne(3) 3 — 36
(W Storey) *chsd ldrs stands' side: rdn along 1/2-way and sn wknd 6th of 12 in gp* **20/1**

0000 **8** *3/4* **Warners Bay (IRE)**[21] 4552 4-9-0 43 ... TanyaRedden(7) 9 — 33
(R Bastiman) *dwlt: a in rr stands' side: 7th of 12 in gp* **66/1**

0 **9** *nk* **Italian Dame**[22] 4505 3-8-8 0 ... JamesPSullivan(5) 13 — 28
(J R Turner) *chsd ldr far side: rdn along over 2f out and n.d: 2nd of 3 in gp* **100/1**

3506 **10** *1 1/4* **Kneesy Earsy Nosey**[8] 4994 3-8-7 39 ow1 ...(p) SeanPalmer(7) 8 — 25
(Miss A Stokell) *a towards rr stands' side: 8th of 12 in gp* **50/1**

0000 **11** *1 1/2* **Indian Diva (IRE)**[106] 1832 4-9-2 70 ... PaulPickard(5) 15 — 24
(P T Midgley) *s.i.s: a in rr far side: last of 3 in gp* **14/1**

3460 **12** *1 1/2* **Sheik'N'Knotsterd**[13] 4823 4-9-4 52 ... DeanHeslop(3) 1 — 19
(J F Coupland) *cl up stands' side: rdn along 1/2-way and sn wknd: 9th of 12 in gp* **20/1**

13 *shd* **Taguna (IRE)** 3-8-6 0 ... NoraLooby(7) 4 — 14
(M Brittain) *a in rr stands' side: 10th of 12 in gp* **66/1**

460- **14** *10* **Little Bones**[434] 3026 4-8-11 50 ... DeclanCannon(5) 6 — —
(J F Coupland) *s.i.s and a bhd: 11th of 12 in gp* **40/1**

-000 **15** *33* **Adozen Dreams**[19] 4596 3-8-6 49 ... TerenceFury(7) 10 — —
(N Bycroft) *virtually ref to r and lost many l at s: a t.o stands' side: last of 12 in gp* **100/1**

1m 11.99s (-1.01) **Going Correction** -0.125s/f (Firm) — 15 Ran SP% 118.5
WFA 3 from 4yo 3lb
Speed ratings (Par 101): **101,98,94,88,88 85,85,84,84,82 80,78,78,65,21**
toteswinger: 1&2 £2.40, 1&3 £2.00, 2&3 £4.00. CSF £6.61 TOTE £2.50: £1.40, £1.20, £2.30; EX 6.10 Trifecta £21.10 Pool: £426.63 - 14.90 winning units..The winner was bought in 5,500gns. Simple Rhythm was claimed by J Ryan for 6,000.
Owner R Cowie **Bred** Raymond Cowie **Trained** Musley Bank, N Yorks
■ Stewards' Enquiry : Kylie Manser two-day ban: careless riding (Sep 6-7)

FOCUS
The 'big two' dominated this seller and the form looks straightforward.
Adozen Dreams Official explanation: jockey said he was slow to remove blindfold and filly was slowly away

5255 WENSLEYDALE H'CAP — 1m 1f 170y

3:25 (3:26) (Class 4) (0-80,80) 3-Y-O — £6,308 (£1,888; £944; £472; £235) Stalls High

Form — RPR

4401 **1** **Royal Defence (IRE)**[22] 4505 3-9-7 80 ... FrancisNorton 3 — 85
(D Nicholls) *trckd ldrs: hdwy 3f out: swtchd lft and rdn wl over 1f out: led ent fnl f: sn drvn and edgd rt: kpt on* **5/1**[3]

1204 **2** *3/4* **Russian George (IRE)**[49] 3608 3-9-2 78 ... FrederikTylicki(3) 5 — 81
(S Gollings) *dwlt and bhd: pushed along and hdwy wl over 2f out: swtchd lft and drvn over 1f out: kpt on u.p ins fnl f* **7/2**[2]

3210 **3** *1 1/2* **Andhaar**[37] 4008 3-9-4 77 ... TPO'Shea 4 — 77
(E A L Dunlop) *cl up: led after 3f: rdn along and hdd 3f out: drvn and rallied to ld again wl over 1f out: hdd ent fnl f and one pce* **7/2**[2]

6621 **4** *hd* **Veroon (IRE)**[10] 4892 3-8-12 71 ...(p) PatCosgrave 2 — 71
(J G Given) *led 3f: cl up tl led again wl over 2f out: sn rdn and hdd wl over 1f out: sn drvn and cl up tl one pce ent fnl f* **7/4**[1]

4302 **5** *12* **Red China Blues (USA)**[27] 4344 3-8-5 64 ... DuranFentiman 1 — 40
(R E Barr) *trckd ldrs: effrt 3f out: sn rdn along and wknd 2f out* **13/2**

2m 3.19s (-2.21) **Going Correction** -0.275s/f (Firm) — 5 Ran SP% 110.8
Speed ratings (Par 102): **97,96,95,95,85**
toteswinger: 1&2 £9.30, 1&3 not won, 2&3 not won. CSF £22.21 TOTE £6.70: £2.80, £2.20; EX 26.70.
Owner Mrs C C Regalado-Gonzalez **Bred** Joseph Rogers **Trained** Sessay, N Yorks
■ Stewards' Enquiry : Francis Norton one-day ban: careless riding (Sep 6)
Pat Cosgrave caution: used whip down shoulder in forehand position

FOCUS
A competitive handicap, despite there being just the five runners, and all bar one held a chance over 1f out. The form looks ordinary for the level though, with the runner-up the best guide.

5256 DBS ST LEGER YEARLING STKS — 6f

4:00 (4:01) (Class 2) 2-Y-O
£24,620 (£9,850; £4,925; £2,460; £1,230; £1,230) Stalls Low

Form — RPR

6 **1** **Hold Your Colour (IRE)**[89] 2324 2-8-11 0 ... TPO'Shea 5 — 86+
(B J Meehan) *sn towards rr and pushed along: hdwy 1/2-way: swtchd outside and effrt 2f out: sn rdn and styd on to ld appr last: sn clr* **9/1**

2 *4* **Exceedingly Bold** 2-8-11 0 ... AdrianMcCarthy 2 — 74
(Miss Gay Kelleway) *hld up in tch: hdwy to trck ldrs 1/2-way: n.m.r and swtchd rt wl over 1f out: sn rdn and styd on ins fnl f* **25/1**

00 **3** *1/2* **Sovereign Secure (IRE)**[12] 4856 2-8-6 0 ... JamieKyne 3 — 68
(Lee Smyth, Ire) *sn led: hdd 1/2-way and styd cl up: rdn to ld again briefly wl over 1f out: sn hdd and one pce* **100/1**

02 **4** *2 3/4* **Fawley Green**[59] 3256 2-8-11 0 ... FrancisNorton 10 — 64
(W R Muir) *cl up: led 1/2-way: rdn and hdd wl over 1f out: sn drvn and wknd* **4/1**[2]

6 **5** *1 3/4* **Ruthie Babe**[16] 4711 2-8-6 0 ... LiamJones 8 — 54
(W J Haggas) *trckd ldrs: hdwy 1/2-way and sn cl up: ev ch over 2f out: sn rdn and wknd* **2/1**[1]

0300 **6** *1/2* **Powerful Pierre**[28] 4306 2-8-11 66 ... PhillipMakin 9 — 58
(Jedd O'Keeffe) *cl up: rdn alonmg 1/2-way: sn wknd* **40/1**

3034 **7** *1 1/4* **Olympic Ceremony**[14] 4782 2-8-11 69 ... FrederikTylicki 1 — 54
(R A Fahey) *prom: rdn along and lost pl 1/2-way: sn towards rr* **13/2**

564 **8** *2 3/4* **Fibs And Flannel**[22] 4492 2-8-11 64 ... DavidAllan 6 — 46
(T D Easterby) *chsd ldrs: rdn along 1/2-way: sn wknd* **12/1**

003 **9** *1 1/4* **Stef And Stelio**[12] 4839 2-8-11 71 ... TomEaves 11 — 42
(G A Butler) *prom: rdn along 1/2-way and sn wknd* **18/1**

2624 **10** *1* **Trinder**[33] 4132 2-8-11 72 ... TonyHamilton 4 — 39
(R A Fahey) *sn outpcd and a in rr* **5/1**[3]

5 **11** *hd* **Sir Louis**[36] 4067 2-8-11 0 ... StephenDonohoe 7 — 38
(R A Fahey) *dwlt and sltly hmpd s: a in rr* **12/1**

560 **12** *nse* **Ballachulish**[13] 4825 2-8-11 64 ... PatCosgrave 12 — 38
(H Candy) *in tch on wd outside: rdn along and edgd lft wl over 2f out and sn wknd* **25/1**

1m 12.68s (-0.32) **Going Correction** -0.125s/f (Firm) — 12 Ran SP% 125.1
Speed ratings (Par 100): **97,91,91,87,85 84,82,79,77,76 75,75**
toteswinger: 1&2 £35.20, 1&3 £181.10, 2&3 £85.80. CSF £224.47 TOTE £10.20: £2.80, £6.80, £22.90; EX 169.90 TRIFECTA Not won..
Owner Sangster Family & Mrs M Findlay **Bred** Trevor Reilly **Trained** Manton, Wilts

FOCUS
This wasn't a good race for the money, with none of the 11 to have raced previously managing a win.

NOTEBOOK
Hold Your Colour(IRE), well held on his debut back in May, has been gelded in the interim and, having been forced to challenge wide, he powered away with it inside the final furlong. The son of Verglas is entered in a couple of valuable sales races later in the season and deserves to take his chance in one. (op 8-1 tchd 10-1)
Exceedingly Bold, the only newcomer in the race, holds an entry in next season's Derby and made a really pleasing debut, staying on having chased the early pace. He should learn from this and can probably find a minor maiden. (op 33-1)
Sovereign Secure(IRE) had run dreadfully in two previous starts and this much-improved effort came from out of nowhere. She did race against the rail, which may have helped, but her prominent placing only underlines how modest a contest it was.
Fawley Green showed good speed before fading. He is now qualified for nurseries and may find a small race in that sphere. (op 9-2)
Ruthie Babe was clearly fancied to improve on her debut effort when sixth at Sandown, but she couldn't race on inside the final 2f. (op 5-2 tchd 11-4)
Trinder Official explanation: jockey said colt never travelled

5257 RIPON CATHEDRAL CITY OF THE DALES H'CAP — 6f

4:35 (4:35) (Class 2) (0-100,96) 4-Y-O+
£11,215 (£3,358; £1,679; £840; £419; £210) Stalls Low

Form — RPR

2101 **1** **Johannes (IRE)**[22] 4485 6-9-0 89 ... TonyHamilton 1 — 101
(R A Fahey) *trckd ldrs stands' side: hdwy to chse ldr over 2f out: rdn to ld appr fnl f: styd on* **7/2**[1]

0212 **2** *2 1/4* **Red Cape (FR)**[14] 4784 6-8-13 88 ... AndrewElliott 3 — 93
(Mrs R A Carr) *prom stands' side: effrt over 2f out: rdn over 1f out and kpt on ins fnl f: 2nd of 10 in gp* **5/1**[2]

3645 **3** *nk* **Atlantic Story (USA)**[19] 4598 7-8-12 87 ...(bt) PhillipMakin 2 — 91
(M W Easterby) *sn led stands' side: rdn clr over 2f out: drvn and hdd appr fnl f: kpt on same pce: 3rd of 10 in gp* **12/1**

0 **4** *nk* **Filligree (IRE)**[22] 4485 4-8-5 85 ... JamieKyne(5) 5 — 88+
(Rae Guest) *towards rr stands' side: hdwy 2f out: sn rdn and styd on ins fnl f: nrst fin: 4th of 10 in gp* **16/1**

3510 **5** *3/4* **Sunrise Safari (IRE)**[22] 4485 6-8-9 87 ... FrederikTylicki(3) 6 — 88
(R A Fahey) *towards rr stands' side: hdwy 2f out: swtchd rt and rdn over 1f out: kpt on ins fnl f: nrst fin: 5th of 10 in gp* **10/1**

000 **6** *nse* **Damika (IRE)**[28] 4330 6-9-3 92 ... TomEaves 4 — 93
(R M Whitaker) *chsd ldrs stands' side: rdn along 2f out: sn drvn and no imp: 6th of 10 in gp* **10/1**

0420 **7** *nse* **Bel Cantor**[3] 5167 6-8-1 79 ...(p) KellyHarrison(3) 13 — 79
(W J H Ratcliffe) *led far side pair: prom tl rdn along 2f out and sn one pce: 1st of 2 in gp* **12/1**

0035 **8** *1/2* **Ishetoo**[7] 5039 5-9-7 96 ... DavidAllan 11 — 95+
(A Dickman) *in tch stands' side: rdn along 2f out and sn no imp: 7th of 10 in gp* **8/1**[3]

5021 **9** *1 1/4* **Silver Wind**[15] 4761 4-8-9 84 ow1 ...(v) PatCosgrave 9 — 79
(P D Evans) *chsd ldrs stands' side: rdn along 2f out and sn wknd: 8th of 10 in gp* **16/1**

1000 **10** *2* **Thebes**[21] 4523 4-9-4 93 ... GregFairley 12 — 81
(M Johnston) *chsd ldr far side: rdn over 2f out and sn wknd 2nd of 2 in gp* **9/1**

0044 **11** *3/4* **Vhujon (IRE)**[12] 4853 4-8-12 87 ... StephenDonohoe 7 — 73
(P D Evans) *a towards rr stands' side: 9th of 10 in gp* **8/1**[3]

0400 **12** *shd* **Good Gorsoon (USA)**[5] 5098 4-8-6 81 ... TPO'Shea 10 — 67
(B W Hills) *chsd ldrs stands' side: rdn along over 2f out and sn wknd: 10th of 10 in gp* **20/1**

1m 10.85s (-2.15) **Going Correction** -0.125s/f (Firm) — 12 Ran SP% 121.2
Speed ratings (Par 109): **109,106,105,105,104 104,104,103,101,99 98,97**
toteswinger: 1&2 £2.90, 1&3 £13.40, 2&3 £12.30. CSF £20.50 CT £170.00 TOTE £4.20: £2.10, £2.20, £4.40; EX 13.30 Trifecta £79.40 Pool: £744.12 - 6.93 winning units..
Owner John Nicholls Ltd/David Kilburn **Bred** Blue Bloodstock Limited **Trained** Musley Bank, N Yorks
■ Stewards' Enquiry : Kelly Harrison one-day ban: failed to keep straight from stalls (Sep 6)
Greg Fairley one-day ban: failed to ride to draw (Sep 6)

FOCUS
This was a competitive sprint handicap in which all bar two of the runners stayed stands' side. It paid to be drawn low and the form is best rated through the second.

NOTEBOOK
Johannes(IRE) has been in cracking form all season (only below-par effort coming over 7f) and he stayed on strongly having hit the front 1f out to defy a 7lb rise for his Goodwood success. He has already shot up 16lb in the handicap this term, and a further rise will follow, but the way he is going, he may well be up to defying it. (op 9-2)

Red Cape(FR), another in-form sprinter, was always to the fore and kept on for strong pressure, but the winner had too many guns at the business end. (tchd 11-2)

Atlantic Story(USA) soon found himself with the lead stands' side and kept on best he could once challenged, but he couldn't race on with the winner. This all-weather specialist remains well weighted on turf and this run suggests he can pick up another race (only turf win came in 2004).

Official explanation: jockey said gelding hung right-handed final furlong; trainer said gelding lost an off-front shoe

Filligree(IRE) has been performing inconsistently and it was no surprise to see her bounce back from a moderate showing behind the winner at Goodwood last time.

Sunrise Safari(IRE), a stablemate of the winner, got going late and ran on well having been switched. (op 12-1 tchd 14-1)

Bel Cantor, 5lb lower than when winning this a year ago, led the pair on the far side and was in contention for a long way, but in the end he wasn't quite on terms with those stands' side. (tchd 14-1)

5258 COVERDALE H'CAP — 1m

5:05 (5:05) (Class 4) (0-80,79) 3-Y-O **£6,308** (£1,888; £944; £472; £235) **Stalls** High

Form — RPR

1461 **1** **Off Chance**[8] 4994 3-9-7 **79** ... DuranFentiman 3 — 87+
(T D Easterby) *hld up in tch: smooth hdwy to trck ldrs over 2f out: effrt over 1f out: shkn upto ld jst ins fnl f and kpt on* **13/8**[1]

4404 **2** 1 3/4 **Steel Stockholder**[12] 4846 3-8-2 **60** oh2 ... AndrewElliott 4 — 64
(M Brittain) *sn led: pushed along over 2f out: rdn wl over 1f out: drvn and hdd jst ins fnl f: kpt on wl u.p* **10/1**

0250 **3** 3/4 **Kheskianto (IRE)**[8] 5007 3-7-11 **62** ... AndrewHeffernan(7) 7 — 64
(M C Chapman) *trckd ldrs on inner: hdwy 3f out: rdn and ch over 1f out: sn drvn and one pce ins fnl f* **14/1**

0045 **4** hd **Tarzan (IRE)**[25] 4400 3-9-6 **78** ... GregFairley 6 — 80
(M Johnston) *trckd ldrs: hdwy 1/2-way: effrt to chal over 2f out: sn rdn and wknd over 1f out* **15/8**[2]

0462 **5** 1 **Chantilly Pearl (USA)**[8] 4994 3-8-9 **67** ... PatCosgrave 1 — 66
(J G Given) *dwlt and in rr: hdwy on outer wl over 2f out: rdn to chse ldrs over 1f out: drvn: edgd rt and one pce ins fnl f* **8/1**[3]

504 **6** 8 **Fernando Torres**[53] 3485 3-8-10 **68** ... FrancisNorton 2 — 49
(D Nicholls) *trckd ldrs: hdwy 3f out: rdn along on outer 2f out: sn drvn and wknd* **8/1**[3]

2040 **7** 2 **Know By Now**[19] 4588 3-8-7 **65** ... TPO'Shea 5 — 41
(T P Tate) *cl up: rdn along 3f out: drvn over 2f out and sn wknd* **10/1**

1m 38.71s (-2.69) **Going Correction** -0.275s/f (Firm) **7 Ran SP% 119.9**
Speed ratings (Par 102): **102,100,99,99,98 90,88**
toteswinger: 1&2 £4.70, 1&3 £10.80, 2&3 £17.60. CSF £20.26 CT £179.19 TOTE £2.30: £1.80, £4.00; EX 22.90 Trifecta £206.90 Part won. Pool of £279.62 - 0.93 winning units..
Owner L B Holliday **Bred** Cleaboy Farms Co **Trained** Great Habton, N Yorks

FOCUS
A modest handicap won in good fashion by the top weight Off Chance. There was little depth in this race and it is not form to raste too positively.

5259 WHARFEDALE MAIDEN STKS — 1m 1f 170y

5:40 (5:41) (Class 5) 3-Y-O+ **£3,885** (£1,156; £577; £288) **Stalls** High

Form — RPR

6 **1** **Knight's Victory (IRE)**[12] 4838 3-9-3 0 ... GregFairley 10 — 74
(M Johnston) *dwlt: sn trcking ldrs on inner: swtchd lft and rdn to chal over 2f out: ev ch whn edgd lft over 1f out: drvn ins fnl f and styd on wl to ld nr fin* **6/1**[3]

2553 **2** nk **Monetary Fund (USA)**[12] 4838 3-9-3 73 ... (t) PatCosgrave 9 — 73
(G A Butler) *led 3f: cl up on inner tl led again over 3f out: rdn 2f out: drvn over 1f out: hdd and no ex nr fin* **11/8**[1]

4036 **3** 1 **Steel Trade**[10] 4892 3-9-3 68 ... DavidAllan 7 — 71
(M Brittain) *s.i.s and bhd: hdwy over 3f out: swtchd lft and effrt to chse ldrs 2f out: drvn to chal ent fnl f and ev ch tl no ex last 100yds* **8/1**

2422 **4** 1 1/4 **Starla Dancer (GER)**[17] 4655 3-8-12 72 ... TonyHamilton 6 — 63
(R A Fahey) *trckd ldrs: hdwy 3f out and sn cl up: rdn along over 2f out: drvn wl over 1f out and kpt on same pce* **7/4**[2]

4 **5** 4 **Freda's Rose (IRE)**[6] 5072 5-9-3 0 ... RussellKennemore(3) 2 — 54
(O Brennan) *hld up in rr: hdwy on outer 3f out: rdn to chse ldrs 2f out: sn edgd rt and no imp* **25/1**

60 **6** 3 **Memi**[22] 4505 3-8-12 0 ... PhillipMakin 8 — 47
(J D Bethell) *in tch: rdn along over 3f out: drvn over 2f out and sn wknd* **50/1**

0 **7** 1 1/4 **Argent Avia**[21] 4550 3-8-12 0 ... AndrewElliott 1 — 44
(M Brittain) *a in rr* **50/1**

34 **8** nk **Towthorpe**[6] 5071 3-8-10 0 ... JohnCavanagh(7) 4 — 48
(M Brittain) *plld hrd: chsd ldrs tl led after 3f: rdn along and hdd over 3f out: sn wknd* **16/1**

0-03 **9** 7 **Melkatant**[13] 4819 3-8-12 47 ... AndrewMullen 3 — 27
(N Bycroft) *in tch: rdn along over 3f out and sn wknd* **33/1**

2m 4.08s (-1.32) **Going Correction** -0.275s/f (Firm)
WFA 3 from 5yo 8lb **9 Ran SP% 120.5**
Speed ratings (Par 103): **94,93,92,91,88 86,85,85,79**
toteswinger: 1&2 £3.50, 1&3 £5.90, 2&3 £3.90. CSF £15.10 TOTE £6.40: £1.80, £1.40, £2.40; EX 25.30 Trifecta £317.10 Part won. Pool £428.58 - 0.43 winning units. Place 6: £209.52 Place 5: £160.70.
Owner Sheikh Hamdan Bin Mohammed Al Maktoum **Bred** Darley **Trained** Middleham Moor, N Yorks

FOCUS
This was a fairly modest maiden and is best rated around the placed horses.
Towthorpe Official explanation: jockey said colt ran too free
T/Plt: £180.30 to a £1 stake. Pool: £58,442.48. 236.54 winning tickets. T/Qpdt: £215.90 to a £1 stake. Pool: £2,714.40. 9.30 winning tickets. JR

5218 SANDOWN (R-H)

Saturday, August 22

OFFICIAL GOING: Good to firm (8.9)
Wind: virtually nil Weather: warm, partly cloudy

5260 IVECO ATALANTA STKS (LISTED RACE) (F&M) — 1m 14y

2:10 (2:11) (Class 1) 3-Y-O+ **£22,708** (£8,608; £4,308; £2,148; £1,076; £540) **Stalls** High

Form — RPR

2111 **1** **Strawberrydaiquiri**[29] 4259 3-8-12 107 ... RyanMoore 7 — 116+
(Sir Michael Stoute) *lw: trckd ldrs: swtchd lft and effrt 2f out: rdn to ld over 1f out: clr ent fnl f: r.o strly:* **4/6**[1]

420- **2** 4 1/2 **Ada River**[322] 6476 4-9-0 100 ... WilliamBuick 8 — 101
(A M Balding) *t.k.h: hld up towards rr: rdn over 3f out: no hdwy u.p over 2f out: styng on whn swtchd lft 1f out: wnt 2nd fnl 100yds: no ch w wnr* **10/1**

1050 **3** 1 **Nashmiah (IRE)**[21] 4522 3-8-12 101 ... NCallan 3 — 103
(C E Brittain) *wnt rt s: in tch: rdn and unable qck over 3f out: no prog tl styd on and swtchd lft 1f out: wnt 3rd wl ins fnl f: no ch w wnr* **12/1**

-250 **4** 1/2 **Ahla Wasahl**[58] 3320 3-8-8 97 ... JimCrowley 6 — 98
(D M Simcock) *t.k.h: hld up in tch in rr: rdn and outpcd jst over 2f out: hdwy on inner over 1f out: kpt on past tired rivals fnl 100yds: nvr trbld ldrs* **50/1**

1302 **5** 1 1/4 **Say No Now (IRE)**[49] 3641 3-8-8 100 ... RHills 9 — 95
(D R Lanigan) *lw: led: rdn jst over 2f out: hdd over 1f out: no ch w wnr 1f out: fdd ins fnl f* **8/1**[3]

6040 **6** nk **King's Starlet**[22] 4489 3-8-8 96 ... SteveDrowne 1 — 94
(H Morrison) *pressed ldr: rdn and ev ch over 2f out: nt pce of wnr over 1f out: fdd ins fnl f* **33/1**

3332 **7** 1 1/2 **Please Sing**[6] 5064 3-8-8 100 ... AlanMunro 2 — 90
(M R Channon) *in tch: rdn and unable qck over 2f out: wl btn and edgd lft jst over 1f out* **4/1**[2]

1053 **8** 5 **Rosaleen (IRE)**[20] 4566 4-9-4 98 ... MartinDwyer 4 — 82
(B J Meehan) *carried rt and sltly hmpd s: hld up in tch in rr: rdn and struggling over 2f out: wl bhd over 1f out: eased ins fnl f* **20/1**

6-00 **9** 8 **Touching (IRE)**[8] 4983 3-8-8 86 ... (t) RichardMullen 5 — 59
(R Hannon) *hmpd s and s.i.s: hld up in tch in rr: rdn and struggling over 2f out: wl bhd over 1f out: eased ins fnl f* **66/1**

1m 41.46s (-1.84) **Going Correction** 0.0s/f (Good)
WFA 3 from 4yo 6lb **9 Ran SP% 119.0**
Speed ratings (Par 111): **109,104,103,103,101 101,99,94,86**
toteswinger: 1&2 £3.50, 1&3 £4.00, 2&3 £15.40. CSF £8.82 TOTE £1.80: £1.10, £2.30, £2.90; EX 9.90 Trifecta £111.40 Pool: £647.46 - 4.30 winning units..
Owner Mrs R J Jacobs **Bred** Newsells Park Stud Limited **Trained** Newmarket, Suffolk

FOCUS
A standard Listed race for fillies. The winner continues to improve and looks better than this level with the form behind looking sound enough.

NOTEBOOK
Strawberrydaiquiri ◆ landed the four-timer in great style. She is now three from three since stepping up to this level and came right away after taking time to hit top gear, so it rates a clear personal-best effort. She is a very straightforward and tough filly, who is also now unbeaten in two outings over course and distance and enjoys this sort of ground. She took a little more time to settle this time, so that makes her effort all the more meritorious and she looks well up to winning in Group class. Surely now is the time to step up with her, but it will very likely be as a four-year-old that she peaks (unraced at two) and connections probably have the Windsor Forest at Royal Ascot next June in mind. (tchd 4-5)

Ada River ◆ was having her first outing since running down the field in the Cambridgeshire last term. She travelled nicely off the pace and, after hitting a bit of a flat spot, ran on stoutly inside the final furlong. She has few miles on the clock for her age and, along with the winner, is the one to take from the race. (op 14-1 tchd 9-1)

Nashmiah(IRE), another three-year-old running under a penalty, was running on stoutly after getting outpaced when the tempo became really serious down the home straight. This was much better from her back on more suitable ground and she helps to set the level, but is not simple to place now. (op 14-1)

Ahla Wasahl was ridden a lot more patiently on this return from a 58-day break and step back up a furlong. She proved free early on as a result and is not easy to get right, but is clearly smart on her day. (tchd 66-1)

Say No Now(IRE) had her own way out in front when finishing second to Strawberrydaiquiri over course and distance on her previous outing and was again able to dictate as she pleased. She was done with before the final furlong and the distance she was beaten this time is another indication of how nicely the winner is progressing. (op 15-2 tchd 7-1)

King's Starlet, back up in trip, was awash with sweat but still performed very close to her previous form with old rival Say No Now and the winner. (op 28-1)

Please Sing came into this having been placed on four of her five runs so far this season. She was laboured here, however, and ran below her previous level. (op 5-1)

5261 VARIETY CLUB CHILDREN'S CHARITY SOLARIO STKS (GROUP 3) — 7f 16y

2:40 (2:41) (Class 1) 2-Y-O **£28,385** (£10,760; £5,385; £2,685; £1,345; £675) **Stalls** High

Form — RPR

153 **1** **Shakespearean (IRE)**[43] 3817 2-9-0 97 ... RHills 5 — 107+
(M Johnston) *lw: mde all: rdn jst over 2f out: styd on wl u.p fnl f* **11/2**[3]

212 **2** 1 1/4 **Buzzword**[22] 4487 2-9-0 104 ... LDettori 8 — 106+
(Saeed Bin Suroor) *lw: chsd ldr for 1f: styd chsng ldrs: nt clr run on inner over 2f out tl swtchd lft over 1f out: sn chsng wnr: drvn and kpt on same pce fnl f* **5/4**[1]

5621 **3** hd **Dubawi Phantom**[37] 4006 2-9-0 84 ... (b[1]) JimCrowley 4 — 104
(D M Simcock) *stdd s: t.k.h: hld up in rr: hdwy on inner 2f out: drvn and kpt on fnl f: nvr quite pce to chal wnr* **33/1**

1 **4** 1 **Black Spirit (USA)**[43] 3794 2-9-0 0 ... (t) AdamKirby 1 — 101
(C G Cox) *lw: t.k.h: hld up towards rr: swtchd lft and rdn 2f out: edgd rt u.p jst over 1f out: kpt on ins fnl f but nt pce to rch ldrs* **13/2**

31 **5** 1 **Simenon (IRE)**[28] 4314 2-9-0 0 ... LPKeniry 7 — 99
(A M Balding) *lw: t.k.h: hld up wl in tch: rdn and unable qck 2f out: sltly hmpd 1f out: kpt on ins fnl f but nvr pce to threaten wnr* **9/2**[2]

21 **6** nk **Prompter**[20] 4557 2-9-0 0 ... HayleyTurner 2 — 98
(M L W Bell) *chsd wnr after 1f: rdn over 2f out: unable qck and edgd lft u.p jst over 1f out: no imp fnl f* **7/1**

12 **7** 5 **Cumulus Nimbus**[11] 5088 2-9-0 0 ... RyanMoore 3 — 85
(R Hannon) *hld up in last pl: effrt and rdn on outer 2f out: no prog and wl hld fnl f* **12/1**

312 **8** 2 1/2 **Audacity Of Hope**[15] 4758 2-9-0 81 ... EdwardCreighton 6 — 79
(P J McBride) *t.k.h: hld up wl in tch: rdn and unable jst over 2f out: struggling whn edgd rt over 1f out: btn whn hmpd 1f out* **33/1**

1m 29.23s (-0.27) **Going Correction** 0.0s/f (Good) **8 Ran SP% 117.4**
Speed ratings (Par 104): **101,99,99,98,97 96,91,88**
toteswinger: 1&2 £1.80, 1&3 £28.10, 2&3 £12.00. CSF £13.18 TOTE £7.00: £1.70, £1.10, £6.60; EX 14.20 Trifecta £98.10 Pool: £1130.93 - 8.53 winning units..
Owner Sheikh Hamdan Bin Mohammed Al Maktoum **Bred** Mrs H Owen **Trained** Middleham Moor, N Yorks

FOCUS
An open renewal, but lacking a real star. There was an uneven pace on and third holds the form down.

NOTEBOOK

Shakespearean(IRE) finished a close third to Silver Grecian in the Superlative Stakes last month and paid that rival a compliment by making all in typically resolute fashion for one from his yard. The switch to front-running made all the difference to him and he clearly stays well as he relished the climbing finish. He did get very much his own way out in front, but has improved with every race since winning on debut and is no doubt progressing physically too. He is well entered up and stepping up to a mile should hold no fears for him, so the Royal Lodge at Ascot next month looks a logical next step and he should go forward again for this experience. This was also a first Group success for his first-season sire. (op 5-1 tchd 4-1)

Buzzword shaped better than the bare margin when second to Dick Turpin in the Richmond Stakes 22 days earlier and proved very popular on this drop in class. He took a keen hold to post, but settled nicely through the race and was going strongly two furlongs out. He was made to wait for his challenge just as the winner kicked on, but still held every chance and just found the stiff finish over this extra furlong far enough. He lost little in defeat. (op 11-8 tchd 6-4 in places)

Dubawi Phantom was equipped with first-time blinkers on this big step up in class. He fared best of those to come from off the pace and kept on resolutely against the rail in the home straight, posting by far his best performance to date. With an official mark of 84 he holds down the form, but is himself highly regarded and a drop into Listed company could see him back to winning ways.

Black Spirit(USA), very well backed, was last seen beating Prompter on his debut at Ascot 43 days earlier. He confirmed that form and posted an improved effort, but things did not really go his way. He was not helped by having to race wide early on and proved free. The manner in which he finished also suggested a more truly-run race is what he needs and he looks one to side next time out (op 15-2 tchd 11-2)

Simenon(IRE)'s Newmarket success 26 days earlier is working out nicely, but he was another here that proved unsuited by the way the race unfolded. He got markedly outpaced down the home straight before staying on again and looks ready to tackle another furlong now. (op 5-1)

Prompter had won nicely at Chester since just finding Black Spirit too strong on his debut at Ascot. He had every chance here, but lacked any sort of gear change and was done with before the final furlong. This ground may just have been a little lively for him. (op 6-1 tchd 9-1)

Cumulus Nimbus never threatened from off the pace in this debut in such company and found it all too hot. (op 16-1 tchd 11-1)

Audacity Of Hope was beaten off 76 in a nursery last time so this was obviously a very stiff task, but he certainly didn't help his cause by refusing to settle. Official explanation: jockey said colt ran too free

5262 DAVID HEWITT STKS (HERITAGE H'CAP) 1m 2f 7y
3:15 (3:16) (Class 2) 3-Y-O+

£31,155 (£9,330; £4,665; £2,335; £1,165; £585) **Stalls** High

Form RPR

0011 **1** **Fanjura (IRE)**[29] 4261 4-9-3 **98** LDettori 16 111+
(B W Hills) *swtg: mde all: hrd pressed and rdn jst over 2f out: forged clr over 1f out: in command fnl f: eased towards fin* **11/2**[2]

2313 **2** *nk* **Antinori (IRE)**[70] 2935 3-7-12 **92** (p) Louis-PhilippeBeuzelin(5) 8 103+
(W R Swinburn) *stdd s: t.k.h: hld up in midfield: rdn and effrt jst over 2f out: hdwy u.p over 1f out: chsd clr wnr fnl 100yds: clsng fin but nvr gng to get there* **8/1**[3]

0020 **3** *2 ¼* **Greylami (IRE)**[27] 4340 4-8-1 **89** JPFahy(7) 6 96
(T G Mills) *t.k.h: chsd ldrs: rdn and effrt jst over 2f out: chsd clr wnr over 1f out: hung rt u.p: no imp: lost 2nd fnl 100yds* **10/1**

2101 **4** *1 ¼* **Eastern Aria (UAE)**[21] 4520 3-8-7 **96** JoeFanning 9 100
(M Johnston) *chsd ldrs: rdn over 2f out: unable qck and edgd rt over 1f out: one pce fnl f* **8/1**[3]

-006 **5** *shd* **Supaseus**[14] 4780 6-9-6 **101** SteveDrowne 12 105
(H Morrison) *chsd wnr: upsides and rdn over 2f out: struggling and lost 2nd over 1f out: one pce fnl f* **12/1**

0531 **6** *1* **Bazergan (IRE)**[9] 4930 4-8-8 **89** (tp) RichardMullen 1 91
(C E Brittain) *hld up towards rr on outer: rdn and effrt jst over 2f out: hanging rt and no real prog after tl styd on ins fnl f: nvr trbld ldrs* **25/1**

0432 **7** *1* **Proponent (IRE)**[27] 4339 5-8-13 **94** AlanMunro 2 94+
(R Charlton) *stdd s: hld up wl in rr: swtchd to outer and effrt over 1f out: kpt on but nvr trbld ldrs* **16/1**

0046 **8** *nk* **Lang Shining (IRE)**[25] 4404 5-9-3 **98** RyanMoore 15 100+
(Sir Michael Stoute) *in tch in midfield: hdwy over 2f out: in tch whn nt clr run over 1f out: squeezed out and lost pl 1f out: no ch and nt pushed fnl f* **5/1**[1]

0435 **9** *1* **The Which Doctor**[14] 4781 4-8-6 **87** HayleyTurner 13 84+
(J Noseda) *lw: stdd s: hld up in rr: looking for run on inner and no room over 2f out: sme mod late hdwy: no ch* **11/1**

26-0 **10** *nk* **Pinch Of Salt (IRE)**[29] 4261 6-8-7 **88** WilliamBuick 17 85
(A M Balding) *chsd ldrs: rdn and unable qckn ent fnl 2f: wknd ent fnl f* **20/1**

15-5 **11** *1 ¼* **Almiqdaad**[15] 4760 3-8-7 **96** ow3 RHills 11 90+
(M A Jarvis) *stdd s: t.k.h: hld up towards rr: nt clr run fr wl over 2f out tl over 1f out: rdn and no prog after* **14/1**

0-00 **12** *1 ¼* **Unshakable (IRE)**[70] 2927 10-8-4 **85** PaulEddery 14 77
(Bob Jones) *b.hind: lw: hld up in midfield: rdn and unable qck over 2f out: no ch fr wl over 1f out* **33/1**

2301 **13** *½* **Hillview Boy (IRE)**[21] 4517 5-8-6 **87** JimmyQuinn 3 78+
(J S Goldie) *stdd s: hld up in rr: nt clr run on inner fr 3f out: no ch* **8/1**[3]

00/5 **14** *4 ½* **Farleigh House (USA)**[12] 4852 5-8-4 **85** JamieMackay 5 67
(Sir Mark Prescott) *t.k.h: in tch in midfield: rdn and struggling 3f out: wl hld fnl 2f* **20/1**

0062 **15** *3 ¼* **Night Crescendo (USA)**[14] 4770 6-8-8 **89** (p) JimCrowley 7 64+
(Mrs A J Perrett) *stdd s: hld up in rr: nt clr run and hmpd 2f out: no ch and eased fnl f* **25/1**

4410 **16** *nse* **Philatelist (USA)**[14] 4780 5-9-10 **105** (p) NCallan 10 80
(M A Jarvis) *in tch in midfield: rdn and unable qck over 2f out: sn struggling and wl btn over 1f out* **33/1**

2m 8.10s (-2.40) **Going Correction** 0.0s/f (Good)
WFA 3 from 4yo+ 8lb **16** Ran SP% **126.1**
Speed ratings (Par 109): **109,108,106,105,105 105,104,104,103,103 102,101,100,97,94 94**
toteswinger: 1&2 £12.40, 1&3 £17.90, 2&3 £29.60. CSF £45.93 CT £441.19 TOTE £5.10: £1.80, £2.40, £2.60, £2.20; EX 48.20 Trifecta £867.50 Pool: £57681.99 - 49.20 winning units..

Owner Terry Benson **Bred** Patrick F Kelly **Trained** Lambourn, Berks

FOCUS

A very competitive handicap, run at an uneven pace and the form is somewhat messy, with the third the best guide.

NOTEBOOK

Fanjura(IRE) got a bit warm beforehand, but that was not enough to scupper this quest for the hat-trick as he made all in ready fashion from his decent draw. He was 3lb higher than when dictating at Ascot last time and thus 8lb higher than when getting up late on over course and distance on his penultimate outing. He found a neat turn of foot when asked to win the race by his jockey, who has no peers when riding from the front, and had the race in safe keeping prior to being eased down nearing the finish, so rates value for further. The Handicapper will now make his life more difficult, but stepping up to 1m2f has been the making of this son of Marju and he should be a big player if going for the valuable John Smith's Stakes over this trip at Newbury next month. (op 6-1 tchd 5-1)

Antinori(IRE) ◆ met support on this return from a 70-day break and ran a big race considering he was the only one to get seriously involved from off the pace. He was eating up the ground in the home straight and, while he may be flattered by his proximity to the eased-down winner, he is no doubt better than the bare form. The first-time cheekpieces had a positive effect and he has developed into a most consistent three-year-old, so compensation should not be that far off. (op 10-1)

Greylami(IRE) was dropping back to his optimum trip and ran a sound race, but never looked like reversing the form of his penultimate outing over course and distance with the winner on 6lb better terms. A more positive ride over this distance now looks well worth a try.

Eastern Aria(UAE) kept on at the same pace in the home straight and did little wrong, but her latest 8lb rise in the handicap looks to have put her in the Handicapper's grip. (tchd 9-1)

Supaseus came in for some support on this drop down from a Group 3 and second run back since returning from injury. He raced just off the winner so can have no excuses, but this run could well bring him on again. (op 16-1 tchd 10-1)

Bazergan(IRE) was 4lb higher than when resuming winning ways at Beverley nine days earlier. He could have done with a stronger overall pace and was not disgraced from his moderate draw. (op 20-1)

Proponent(IRE) stayed on steadily from off the pace in a race that didn't really go his way. This trip just stretches his stamina, but he remains on a fair mark and could be an interesting one for the Cambridgeshire.

Lang Shining(IRE) was racing off the same mark as when second in this event last year. He was in with a shout prior to meeting trouble down the home straight and losing all chance. He was not given a hard time thereafter. (op 6-1)

Almiqdaad did not get a clear passage on the rail from 2f out and is better than this. (op 12-1)

Hillview Boy(IRE) got no run at all on the inside down the home straight and deserves another chance. (tchd 9-1)

Night Crescendo(USA) Official explanation: jockey said gelding was denied a clear run

5263 LIFE BUILD H'CAP 5f 6y
3:50 (3:52) (Class 2) (0-100,98) 3-Y-O+

£12,462 (£3,732; £1,866; £934; £466; £234) **Stalls** High

Form RPR

5101 **1** **Blue Jack**[23] 4461 4-9-6 **93** (b) MartinDwyer 7 102+
(W R Muir) *lw: trckd ldrs and a gng wl: hdwy to ld over 1f out: rdn ent fnl f: r.o wl* **6/1**[2]

501 **2** *1* **Tony The Tap**[2] 5183 8-9-3 **90** 6ex HayleyTurner 9 95
(W R Muir) *lw: sn towards rr: hdwy and swtchd lft over 1f out: r.o wl to go 2nd fnl 100yds: nvr quite gng to rch wnr* **9/1**

12 **3** *1* **Northern Dare (IRE)**[22] 4485 5-9-6 **93** JoeFanning 11 94
(D Nicholls) *w ldr tl led 1/2-way: rdn and hdd over 1f out: edgd lft and styd on same pce fnl f* **5/1**[1]

1-20 **4** *shd* **Macdillon**[70] 2934 3-9-3 **92** LPKeniry 12 93+
(W S Kittow) *chsd ldrs: rdn and effrt over 1f out: kpt on one pce fnl f: edgd lft u.p towards fin* **9/1**

0000 **5** *hd* **Piscean (USA)**[4] 5132 4-9-1 **88** JimmyQuinn 8 92+
(T Keddy) *s.i.s: bhd: hdwy 2f out: running on whn nt clr run and swtchd lft jst ins fnl f: swtchd lft again fnl 75yds: gng on fin* **25/1**

6040 **6** *½* **Oldjoesaid**[56] 3405 5-9-11 **98** FergusSweeney 1 97
(H Candy) *in tch in midfield: rdn and hdwy 2f out: drvn and kpt on same pce fnl f* **17/2**

0000 **7** *1* **Orpsie Boy (IRE)**[14] 4766 6-9-3 **90** (p) NCallan 5 87+
(N P Littmoden) *in tch in midfield: pushed along 3f out: nt clr run wl over 1f out tl over 1f out: styng on but hld whn nt clr run and eased towards fin* **16/1**

3230 **8** *shd* **Kerrys Requiem (IRE)**[14] 4771 3-8-12 **87** RyanMoore 3 86+
(M R Channon) *stdd after s: bhd: pushed along 1/2-way: hdwy whn hmpd and swtchd rt jst ins fnl f: keeping on but wl hld whn nt clr run and eased towards fin* **12/1**

410 **9** *¾* **Doric Lady**[35] 4096 4-8-7 **80** KirstyMilczarek 4 72
(J A R Toller) *swtg: s.i.s: bhd: rdn and effrt on outer 2f out: no prog fnl f* **25/1**

311 **10** *1 ¼* **Olynard (IRE)**[12] 4853 3-8-10 **92** JPFahy(7) 6 79
(R M Beckett) *chsd ldrs: rdn 1/2-way: struggling wl over 1f otu: btn whn sltly hmpd jst ins fnl f* **8/1**

6110 **11** *½* **Canadian Danehill (IRE)**[33] 4135 7-9-7 **94** (p) LDettori 14 80+
(R M H Cowell) *hld up in midfield on far rail: no room fr 1/2-way and lost pl: n.d after* **7/1**[3]

0-00 **12** *½* **Hadaf (IRE)**[15] 4753 4-8-10 **83** RHills 15 67
(M P Tregoning) *a towards rr: nvr trbld ldrs* **10/1**

560 **13** *9* **Ginobili (IRE)**[14] 4766 3-9-1 **90** (p) JimCrowley 2 41
(Stef Liddiard) *chsd ldrs: rdn and struggling 1/2-way: wl bhd fnl f* **50/1**

212/ **14** *½* **Jimmy Ryan (IRE)**[1547] 2079 8-9-1 **88** RobertHavlin 10 38
(T D McCarthy) *bit bkwd: taken down early: led tl 1/2-way: wknd qckly over 1f out and sn bhd* **25/1**

61.10 secs (-0.50) **Going Correction** +0.125s/f (Good)
WFA 3 from 4yo+ 2lb **14** Ran SP% **121.3**
Speed ratings (Par 109): **109,107,105,105,105 104,102,102,101,99 98,97,83,82**
toteswinger: 1&2 £7.50, 1&3 £5.80, 2&3 £12.50. CSF £57.24 CT £295.96 TOTE £5.50: £2.60, £2.70, £2.20; EX 59.40 Trifecta £567.40 Pool: £1840.40 - 2.40 winning units..

Owner Martin P Graham **Bred** Miss S N Ralphs **Trained** Lambourn, Berks

FOCUS

A decent sprint, run at a solid pace and the runner-up is the best guide to the form, although it got a bit messy in behind.

NOTEBOOK

Blue Jack followed up his Goodwood win off a 4lb higher mark and registered a fourth success of the current campaign. He was ridden more positively this time and hit the front full of running in between the final two furlongs. He quickly settled matters and is clearly a fast-improving sprinter. His rider later remarked he had hit the front too soon, so he is probably value for better than the bare margin and remains right on course for a crack at the Portland at Doncaster next month. His versatility as regards ground is also a big plus and the Ayr Gold Cup is also likely to be on his agenda, but he is yet to score over the extra furlong. (op 15-2 tchd 5-1)

Tony The Tap motored home from off the pace to give his stable a one-two. He fared best of those coming from behind so deserves some extra credit and he's clearly back in top form again. (op 11-1)

Northern Dare(IRE) did best of those to help force the pace and turned in another solid effort, rating a decent benchmark. He can go in again this season when reverting to slightly easier ground. Official explanation: jockey said gelding hung left (op 9-2)

Macdillon travelled well through the race, but lacked anything like the turn of foot displayed by the winner. He lost his action when running below par when last seen 70 days earlier and this was just his fifth career start, so he remains capable of further progression. He also could be better off back over 6f. (tchd 17-2)

Piscean(USA) ◆ was the eyecatcher. The form book will show he has run very close to his Goodwood form with the winner and was 6lb better off here, but little went his way. He had to come from behind after a tardy start and finished strongly after meeting trouble, so his turn could well be nearing again. A step back up to 6f may also now suit better as this is not the first time he has been sluggish from the gates. Official explanation: jockey said colt was denied a clear run (tchd 28-1)

Oldjoesaid wasn't helped by being housed on the outside so deserves some credit, but still looks to need respite in the weights. (op 10-1 tchd 11-1)

Orpsie Boy(IRE), in first-time cheekpieces, got hampered and is better than the bare form. He has not won over this trip since his juvenile career, though. Official explanation: jockey said gelding was denied a clear run (op 20-1)

Kerrys Requiem(IRE) wa dropped in early and proved keen. She finished with a degree of purpose after metting trouble, but remains one to tread carefully with. Official explanation: jockey was denied a clear run (op 14-1 tchd 16-1 in a place)

Canadian Danehill(IRE) was tight for room around halfway and is better than he could show. Official explanation: jockey said gelding suffered interference in runing (tchd 13-2)

Hadaf(IRE) Official explanation: jockey said colt suffered interference in running

5264 FANTASIA H'CAP — 5f 6y

4:25 (4:25) (Class 4) (0-80,80) 3-Y-O — £5,180 (£1,541; £770; £384) Stalls High

Form				RPR
1412	1		**Rocket Rob (IRE)**[5] 5098 3-9-6 **77** ... LDettori 6 (S A Callaghan) *s.i.s: bhd: hdwy over 1f out: rdn to ld ins fnl f: r.o strly* **6/4**[1]	88+
1320	2	1 ¼	**Strictly**[22] 4490 3-9-9 **80** ... RyanMoore 2 (Sir Michael Stoute) *lw: s.i.s: bhd and sn niggled along: hdwy over 1f out: carried lft 1f out: r.o to go 2nd wl ins fnl f: unable to chal wnr* **5/1**[2]	87
511	3	½	**Corton Charlemagne (IRE)**[8] 4999 3-8-11 **71** ... AndreaAtzeni(3) 7 (Rae Guest) *racd in midfield: rdn 1/2-way: hdwy over 1f out: edgd lft u.p 1f out: kpt on same pce ins fnl f* **12/1**	76
1363	4	1	**Sharpened Edge**[30] 4244 3-9-8 **79** ... WilliamBuick 9 (B Palling) *sn led: rdn 2f out: hdd ins fnl f: wknd and lost 2 pls wl ins fnl f* **7/1**	80
4162	5	1 ¼	**Cape Melody**[32] 4167 3-9-4 **75** ... TravisBlock 3 (H Morrison) *lw: sn niggled along towards rr: rdn and effrt on outer over 1f out: nvr pce to threaten ldrs* **10/1**	72
2603	6	¾	**Mazzola**[3] 5164 3-8-8 **70** ... MCGeran(5) 5 (M R Channon) *pressed ldr: ev ch and over 1f out: wknd qckly jst ins fnl f: wl hld whn hung rt towards fin* **20/1**	64
422	7	1 ¼	**Night Affair**[9] 4952 3-9-4 **75** ... MartinDwyer 8 (D W P Arbuthnot) *sn bustled along to chse ldrs: rdn 2f out: wknd ent fnl f: wl hld whn nt clr run wl ins fnl f* **6/1**[3]	65
041	8	hd	**Sutton Veny (IRE)**[14] 4786 3-8-13 **70** ... NCallan 1 (J R Gask) *sn niggled along towards rr: rdn and struggling 1/2-way: wl hld whn edgd rt ins fnl f* **25/1**	59
141	9	3 ¾	**Chasca (IRE)**[114] 1618 3-8-13 **70** ... JimCrowley 4 (Mrs A J Perrett) *chsd ldrs: shkn up and wanting to hang lft over 1f out: sn btn* **12/1**	45

61.80 secs (0.20) **Going Correction** +0.125s/f (Good) — **9** Ran SP% **116.5**
Speed ratings (Par 102): **103,101,100,98,96 95,93,93,87**
toteswinger: 1&2 £2.10, 1&3 £6.00, 2&3 £11.50. CSF £9.07 CT £66.28 TOTE £2.00: £1.30, £2.10, £2.80; EX 6.50.

Owner Bill Hinge, J Searchfield & N Callaghan **Bred** Mrs Marita Rogers **Trained** Newmarket, Suffolk

FOCUS

A fair 3yo sprint, run at a strong pace and the form looks reasonable rated around those in the frame behind the winner.

5265 MILES COMMERCIAL NURSERY — 7f 16y

4:55 (4:58) (Class 4) (0-85,84) 2-Y-O — £5,180 (£1,541; £770; £384) Stalls High

Form				RPR
246	1		**Cool Valentine**[22] 4478 2-8-9 **72** ... WilliamBuick 10 (A M Balding) *hld up in tch towards rr: hdwy to chse ldrs on rail over 1f out: rdn and wnt through gap to ld ins fnl f: r.o wl* **16/1**	79+
2421	2	2 ¼	**Astonishment (IRE)**[17] 4646 2-9-2 **79** ... LDettori 3 (S Kirk) *led: rdn 2f out: kpt on wl tl hdd and nt pce of wnr ins fnl f: hld on gamely for 2nd* **6/1**[3]	80
2102	3	hd	**Silver Grey (IRE)**[12] 4850 2-9-2 **79** ... RobertHavlin 5 (R Ingram) *hld up in tch: swtchd rt and rdn 2f out: hdwy u.p 1f out: kpt on to go 3rd wl ins fnl f* **4/1**[2]	80
1015	4	¾	**Jehu**[20] 4565 2-9-5 **82** ... NCallan 9 (M R Channon) *chsd ldrs: rdn and unable qck 2f out: edging out lft fr over 1f out: one pce ins fnl f* **16/1**	81
3106	5	2 ¾	**Lady Pattern (IRE)**[21] 4539 2-9-4 **81** ... IanMongan 8 (P W D'Arcy) *w ldr: ev ch and rdn 2f out: edgd lft u.p jst ins fnl f: wknd bdly fnl 100yds* **12/1**	73
461	6	hd	**Jutland**[17] 4638 2-9-0 **77** ... RHills 2 (M Johnston) *lw: dwlt: t.k.h: hdwy to chse ldrs over 5f out: rdn unable qck 2f out: btn whn n.m.r ins fnl f: wknd fnl 75yds* **11/4**[1]	69
31	7	4 ½	**Bab At The Bowster (IRE)**[16] 4693 2-9-0 **77** ... JoeFanning 4 (W J Haggas) *lw: t.k.h: hld up wl in tch: rdn and wanting to hang 2f out: unable qck over 1f out: btn whn short of room ins fnl f* **11/4**[1]	57+
2005	8	1	**Shark Man (IRE)**[38] 3978 2-8-13 **76** ... EdwardCreighton 6 (P J McBride) *lw: hld up towards rr: rdn 4f out: no prog: wl btn over 1f out* **50/1**	54
0103	9	2 ¼	**Avon River**[10] 4901 2-9-7 **84** ... RyanMoore 7 (R Hannon) *rrd s and s.i.s: nvr gng wl: rn wd bnd over 4f out: hanging rt and bhd fr wl over 2f out* **8/1**	56
3514	10	38	**Reeds Bay (IRE)**[57] 3340 2-9-4 **81** ... (b[1]) RichardMullen 1 (E S McMahon) *v.s.a and lost all ch s: a t.o* **28/1**	—+

1m 29.53s (0.03) **Going Correction** 0.0s/f (Good) — **10** Ran SP% **123.6**
Speed ratings (Par 96): **99,96,96,95,92 91,86,85,83,39**
toteswinger: 1&2 £19.10, 1&3 £18.70, 2&3 £6.30. CSF £115.40 CT £483.00 TOTE £25.00: £5.40, £2.00, £2.20; EX 178.70.

Owner Mick and Janice Mariscotti **Bred** Bearstone Stud **Trained** Kingsclere, Hants

FOCUS

A competitive nursery for the class, run at a sound pace.

NOTEBOOK

Cool Valentine ◆ was making his debut in this sphere after three previous outings and he got up late to win readily. He looked to get somewhat outpaced out the back through the early parts and had plenty on at the top of the home straight. As those in front of him began to tire he really found his stride, however, and stayed on stoutly against the far rail. The step up in trip worked the oracle, which was not an obvious move looking at his pedigree, and he obviously stays well. There should be more to come now, so it could be that he defies a likely higher mark next time. (op 25-1)

Astonishment(IRE) showed his 2lb rise for scoring at Kempton 17 days earlier to be a fair one and he posted a solid effort under a positive ride. (op 8-1)

Silver Grey(IRE) made a strong challenge on the outside of the pack in the home straight and had every chance. The extra furlong suited, but this was probably a little too stiff for her at present. She rates a good benchmark. (op 7-1)

Jehu can have no excuses this time, but was not disgraced and remains in fair form. (op 14-1)

Lady Pattern(IRE) was 2lb lower and failed to confirm previous Newmarket form with the third on this step up in trip, but didn't run badly considering she found it too stiff. (op 11-1 tchd 16-1)

Jutland contested a warm maiden over course and distance on his penultimate start and the form of his Brighton win last time looked better when the runner-up went in next time. He was not helped by being forced wide from his low draw here and the best of him has likely still to be seen, but his Group-race entries are far too ambitious. (op 5-1)

Bab At The Bowster(IRE) won well at Brighton 16 days previously, but was again keen and that did not help in this hotter company. She also raced somewhat awkwardly up the home straight and now has a little to prove. (op 7-4 tchd 3-1)

Reeds Bay(IRE) Official explanation: jockey said colt was reluctant to race

5266 VARIETY CLUB DIAMOND ANNIVERSARY H'CAP — 1m 2f 7y

5:25 (5:29) (Class 4) (0-80,80) 3-Y-O+ — £5,180 (£1,541; £770; £384) Stalls High

Form				RPR
411	1		**Prince Of Johanne (IRE)**[19] 4605 3-9-5 **80** ... RyanMoore 6 (J Noseda) *hld up in last trio: rdn over 3f out: drvn and hdwy on outer over 1f out: chsd ldr 1f out: hrd drvn and kpt on to ld fnl 75yds: all out* **11/4**[1]	90+
0102	2	½	**Rumble Of Thunder (IRE)**[22] 4481 3-9-5 **80** ... MartinDwyer 5 (D W P Arbuthnot) *led: clr fr 8f out: 6 l clr over 3f out: rdn 2f out: drvn and hrd pressed 1f out: hdd fnl 75yds: kpt on* **15/2**	89
21	3	1 ¼	**Ordoney (IRE)**[14] 4805 4-9-7 **76** ... WilliamBuick 7 (L M Cumani) *w'like: str: lw: chsd ldrs: chsd clr ldr 4f out: rdn and hanging rt fr wl over 2f out: clsd on ldr over 1f out: kpt on one pce ins fnl f* **7/2**[2]	82+
0232	4	1 ½	**Seventh Cavalry (IRE)**[15] 4759 4-8-12 **65** ... NCallan 2 (A King) *stdd s: hld up in last trio: hdwy 5f out: rdn over 2f out: clsd on ldr over 1f out: one pce u.p fnl f* **6/1**	68
0135	5	½	**Kidlat**[16] 4716 4-9-11 **78** ... (t) EdwardCreighton 9 (B G Powell) *hld up in midfield: dropped to rr and rdn 3f out: no prog tl plugged on u.p ins fnl f: nvr trbld ldrs* **16/1**	80
-430	6	nk	**Jawaab (IRE)**[27] 4340 5-9-7 **74** ... RichardMullen 8 (Mark Buckley) *s.i.s: hld up in last trio: rdn and no hdwy 3f out: plugged on u.p fnl f: nvr trbld ldrs* **9/2**[3]	75
000	7	¾	**Dinner Date**[8] 5003 7-8-1 **61** oh6 ... TraceyAddey(7) 1 (T Keddy) *chsd ldr tl 4f out: lost pl and dropped towards rr over 2f out: one pce after* **50/1**	61
2113	8	2 ½	**Agilete**[15] 4737 7-9-8 **80** ... SimonPearce(5) 3 (J Pearce) *hld up in midfield: clsd on ldr over 1f out: rdn ent fnl f: sn wknd* **14/1**	75

2m 9.62s (-0.88) **Going Correction** 0.0s/f (Good)
WFA 3 from 4yo+ 8lb — **8** Ran SP% **107.6**
Speed ratings (Par 105): **103,102,101,100,100 99,99,97**
toteswinger: 1&2 £4.20, 1&3 £3.00, 2&3 £6.30. CSF £20.51 CT £54.34 TOTE £2.50: £1.40, £2.00, £1.80; EX 17.00 Place 6: £49.29 Place 5: £33.58.

Owner M Tabor, Mrs Susan Roy, M Green **Bred** T J Rooney And Corduff Stud **Trained** Newmarket, Suffolk

FOCUS

An interesting handicap. It was run at a solid pace and the form looks sound and good for the grade.

T/Jkpt: £55,883.60 to a £1 stake. Pool: £157,418.59. 2.00 winning tickets. T/Plt: £35.30 to a £1 stake. Pool: £151,852.23. 3,138.87 winning tickets. T/Qpdt: £18.40 to a £1 stake. Pool: £6,875.30. 275.30 winning tickets. SP

5272 - 5273a (Foreign Racing) - See Raceform Interactive

4121

FAIRYHOUSE (R-H)

Saturday, August 22

OFFICIAL GOING: Soft (soft to heavy in places)

5274a TATTERSALLS IRELAND SALE STKS — 6f

4:20 (4:21) 2-Y-O

£142,718 (£55,339; £33,495; £18,932; £5,825; £2,912)

			RPR
1		**Dick Turpin (IRE)**[22] 4487 2-9-7 ... RichardHughes 11 (R Hannon) *trckd ldrs: travelling wl st: wnt 2nd over 1f out: pushed out to ld ins fnl f: easily* **8/15**[1]	109+
2	1 ½	**In Some Respect (IRE)**[27] 4359 2-9-2 108 ... PJSmullen 6 (Andrew Oliver, Ire) *trckd ldrs: 2nd 1/2-way: chal u.p and led over 1f out: hdd and kpt on same pce ins fnl f: no ch w wnr* **5/1**[2]	94+
3	4	**Benwilt Barney (IRE)**[17] 4678 2-9-2 ... JMurtagh 16 (John C McConnell, Ire) *trckd ldrs: rdn in mod 4th fr 2f out: sn no imp: kpt on wout threatening into 3rd ins fnl f* **12/1**	82
4	1	**Wisecraic**[22] 4478 2-9-2 ... RichardKingscote 14 (Tom Dascombe) *mid-div: wnt mod 5th under 2f out: sn no imp u.p: kpt on wout threatening into 4th ins fnl f* **6/1**[3]	79
5	¾	**Your Gifted (IRE)**[20] 4572 2-8-11 64 ... JAHeffernan 15 (P J Prendergast, Ire) *dwlt: towards rr: rdn and hdwy into 6th over 1f out: kpt on wout threatening* **50/1**	72?
6	½	**Hill Of Miller (IRE)**[17] 4647 2-9-2 ... JohnEgan 13 (Rae Guest) *towards rr: rdn to go 7th over 1f out: kpt on wout threatening* **50/1**	75
7	2	**Cavan Girl**[35] 4107 2-8-11 63 ... GFCarroll 10 (Michael Mulvany, Ire) *mid-div: 8th early: no imp u.p and kpt on same pce fr 2f out* **50/1**	64
8	½	**Craicattack (IRE)**[17] 4639 2-9-2 ... KLatham 8 (J S Moore) *trckd ldrs: 3rd 1/2-way: lost pl and no imp fr 2f out* **33/1**	68
9	1 ½	**Dancing Red Devil (IRE)**[15] 4739 2-8-11 ... (b[1]) FMBerry 9 (Paul Green) *chsd ldrs: 7th early: no imp u.p fr 2f out* **25/1**	58
10	2	**Quaestor (IRE)**[32] 4176 2-9-2 ... WJSupple 1 (Tom Dascombe) *sn led: strly pressed under 2f out: hdd and dropped to 3rd over 1f out: wknd* **33/1**	57

11 *shd* **Newpark Rio (IRE)**[20] 4572 2-9-2 77 PShanahan 4 57
(Emmanuel Hughes, Ire) *towards rr: no imp u.p st* **33/1**
12 3 **Slice (IRE)**[21] 4525 2-9-2 MJKinane 5 48
(Eve Johnson Houghton) *sn towards rr: no imp u.p st* **20/1**
13 4 **Mnarani (IRE)**[10] 4901 2-9-2 DPMcDonogh 2 36
(J S Moore) *chsd ldrs: rdn bef st: sn wknd* **33/1**
14 1 1/4 **Fait Accompli (IRE)** 2-9-2 KJManning 7 32
(Edward Lynam, Ire) *s.i.s and a towards rr* **50/1**
15 5 **Psalmson (IRE)**[5] 5114 2-9-2 RPCleary 12 17
(Emmanuel Hughes, Ire) *mid-div best: dropped towards rr and no imp st* **50/1**
16 3 **Man In Black (IRE)**[22] 4509 2-9-2 WMLordan 3 8
(David P Myerscough, Ire) *sn towards rr: nvr a factor* **50/1**
1m 15.27s (2.77) **16** Ran SP% **136.0**
CSF £3.54 TOTE £1.50: £1.10, £1.60, £2.00, £1.90; DF 3.80.
Owner John Manley **Bred** John McEnery **Trained** East Everleigh, Wilts

NOTEBOOK
Dick Turpin(IRE) retained his unbeaten record, justifying favouritism with a smoothly achieved win, following on from his Group 2 success in the Richmond Stakes at Goodwood. The soft ground was the unknown, but the Arakan colt appeared to cope with it well and, after tracking the leaders on the inside, he moved out to close travelling well in second over a furlong out. It was only a matter of time when Richard Hughes asked him to go about his business and the response was immediate, and, once in front inside the final furlong, he was eased before the finish. (op 4/6)
In Some Respect(IRE) is a 108-rated maiden who has performed well behind Alfred Nobel on a couple of occasions. He acquitted himself well on ground trainer Andrew Oliver considers unsuitable and hit the front over a furlong out. He was no match for the winner once headed, but came out of the race with his reputation enhanced. (op 9/2)
Benwilt Barney(IRE) had won an ordinary looking maiden over a slightly longer trip on soft ground at Sligo early this month. Only a fair fourth two furlongs out, he kept on quite well without troubling the first two.
Wisecraic, winner of a 5f Bath maiden on good ground on his only previous start, made headway from mid-division turning for home and kept on without ever posing a serious threat. (op 5/1)
Hill Of Miller(IRE) wasn't up to this class.
Craicattack(IRE) failed to prove himself on soft ground.
Dancing Red Devil(IRE) doesn't seem to be progressing.

5275a GALILEO EUROPEAN BREEDERS FUND FUTURITY STKS (GROUP 2) 7f
4:50 (4:50) 2-Y-O
£66,990 (£21,213; £10,048; £3,349; £2,233; £1,116)

RPR
1 **Cape Blanco (IRE)**[30] 4250 2-9-1 JMurtagh 5 108
(A P O'Brien, Ire) *mde all: rdn st: sn strly pressed: styd on best ins fnl f* **1/5**[1]
2 1 1/4 **Mister Tee**[10] 4919 2-9-1 90 KLatham 1 105
(G M Lyons, Ire) *sn racd in 5th: rdn st: clsd on inner into 2nd over 1f out: sn swtchd to chal: kpt on wout matching wnr ins fnl f* **16/1**
3 1 **King Ledley (USA)**[27] 4359 2-9-1 105 DPMcDonogh 4 103
(Kevin Prendergast, Ire) *sn towards rr in 6th: rdn st: mod 5th over 1f out: styd on to chal in 3rd ins fnl f: one pce cl home* **10/1**[2]
4 1 1/2 **Marfach (USA)**[30] 4250 2-9-1 95 (p) KJManning 3 99
(J S Bolger, Ire) *trckd ldr in 2nd: rdn st: dropped to 3rd and no imp fr over 1f out* **11/1**[3]
5 2 1/2 **Kingdom Of Munster (IRE)**[13] 4833 2-9-1 90 JAHeffernan 7 93
(A P O'Brien, Ire) *sn trckd ldrs in 3rd: pushed along appr st: 4th and no ex fr over 1f out* **25/1**
6 1 3/4 **Utrillo (IRE)**[13] 4833 2-9-1 SMLevey 6 88
(A P O'Brien, Ire) *dwlt: towards rr: no imp u.p st* **50/1**
7 4 **Moran Gra (USA)**[22] 4487 2-9-1 PJSmullen 2 78
(Ms Joanna Morgan, Ire) *sn racd in 4th pushed along fr bef st: wknd fr over 1f out* **14/1**
1m 32.59s (2.09) **7** Ran SP% **119.1**
CSF £6.40 TOTE £1.10: £1.10, £8.80; DF 6.70.
Owner Derrick Smith **Bred** Jack Ronan & Des Vere Hunt Far **Trained** Ballydoyle, Co Tipperary

FOCUS
The winner was always holding his field but the race has been rated around the third and below its usual standard.

NOTEBOOK
Cape Blanco(IRE) made it three from three by making all in this Group 2, and while he was well on top at the finish, he looked anything but a 1-5 shot for much of the way in the straight. The winning trainer's previous successes in the race include Giant's Causeway, Hawk Wing and Oratorio, and while Cape Blanco is held in high regard, this was a workmanlike performance in conditions Johnny Murtagh claimed his mount hated. Murtagh reported that the colt had hit a soft patch of ground off the bend into the straight. His Group 3 win at Leopardstown was achieved more easily when the going was described as yielding to soft, and while plans for the rest of the season are uncertain, he is one of a few Ballydoyle colts who will be considered for the Group 1 National Stakes at the Curragh next month. (op 3/10)
Mister Tee, a 90-rated maiden, had gone close on a few occasions and he justified the decision to pitch him in at this level. Held up, he began to close from two furlongs out and went second approaching the final furlong, keeping on to the line although always being held towards the finish.
King Ledley(USA), placed at this and at Group 3 level since winning the first two-year-old meeting of the season, was minus the blinkers he had worn on his previous two starts. Held up, he was ridden to close turning for home and kept on for third inside final furlong having been fifth over a furlong out. (op 8/1)
Marfach(USA), rated 95 and beaten three and a half lengths by Cape Blanco at Leopardstown last month, ran almost exactly to that form with the winner. He raced in second place but, after coming under pressure early in the straight, could find no extra from over a furlong out. (op 8/1)
Kingdom Of Munster(IRE) won his maiden on testing ground at Tipperary before finishing fourth behind Cape Blanco and Marfach at Leopardstown. Third behind another stablemate, Viscount Nelson, at Tipperary on his previous start, he tracked the leaders on the inside but was being ridden along before the straight and could make no impression from a furlong and a half out. (op 20/1)

5276 - 5277a (Foreign Racing) - See Raceform Interactive

5240
DEAUVILLE (R-H)
Saturday, August 22
OFFICIAL GOING: Turf course - good; all-weather - standard

5278a PRIX DE SAINTE-ADRESSE (CLAIMER) (ALL-WEATHER) 1m 4f
1:00 (1:01) 3-Y-O
£10,194 (£4,077; £3,058; £2,039; £1,019)

RPR
1 **L'Aventurier (FR)**[11] 3-8-12 MickaelForest(3) 73
(J De Roualle, France)
2 2 **Victorian Tycoon (IRE)**[21] 5118 3-8-11 JAuge 66
(E J O'Neill) *midfield: 6th on outside st hdwy to ld narrowly 1 1/2f out to ins fnl f: one pce* **10/1**[1]
3 *snk* **Suntil (FR)**[36] 3-9-5 FBlondel 74
(Mme C Barande-Barbe, France)
4 *hd* **Fresh Princess (FR)**[86] 3-9-5 (b) 73
(R Gibson, France)
5 1 1/2 **Flower Belle (FR)** 3-9-1 67
(Y Barberot, France)
6 3/4 **L'Impetueux (FR)**[9] 3-9-4 69
(U Suter, France)
7 3/4 **Chasse Croise (FR)**[23] 3-9-2 65
(J Bertran De Balanda, France)
8 3 **Urban Dream (FR)**[15] 3-9-4 63
(A Bonin, France)
9 5 **Ryland (SWI)** 3-8-11 48
(H-A Pantall, France)
10 2 **Piteur (FR)** 3-9-4 51
(E Leenders, France)
0 **Prime Arrival (IRE)**[88] 3-8-11 —
(Y Fouin, France)
0 **Locmaria Ker (FR)**[17] 3-8-8 (b) —
(Y Fouin, France)
2m 37.8s (157.80) **12** Ran SP% **9.1**
PARI-MUTUEL (including 1 Euro stake): WIN 30.50; PL 6.10, 3.40, 1.80;DF 37.90.
Owner D Guindon & P-N Rossier **Bred** Scea Des Bissons **Trained** France

5279a PRIX DU CALVADOS-HARAS DES CAPUCINES (GROUP 3) (FILLIES) 7f
2:05 (2:08) 2-Y-O
£38,835 (£15,534; £11,650; £7,767; £3,883)

RPR
1 **Joanna (IRE)**[69] 2-8-9 DVargiu 6 105
(B Grizzetti, Italy) *racd in 6th on outside: hdwy to ld 2f out: 1 1/2l clr jst ins fnl f: drvn out* **235/10**
2 1/2 **Virginia Hall**[20] 4584 2-8-9 J-BEyquem 5 104
(Sir Mark Prescott) *racd in 5th: hdwy to dispute ld breifly jst over 2f out: 1 1/2 l 2nd ins fnl f: styd on wl clsng stages* **14/1**
3 2 **American Nizzy (FR)**[39] 3967 2-8-9 GMosse 9 99
(Y De Nicolay, France) *hld up in rr: styd on steadily fr over 2f out to take 3rd cl home* **69/10**
4 1/2 **Heaven's Heart (IRE)**[36] 2-8-9 CSoumillon 8 98
(Y De Nicolay, France) *racd in 8th: hrd rdn in centre over 2f out: kpt on u.p to go 3rd ins fnl f: lost 3rd cl home* **66/10**
5 1 **Courchevel (IRE)**[21] 4577 2-8-9 OPeslier 7 95
(Robert Collet, France) *midfield: swtchd rt over 2f out: rdn to go 3rd 1 1/2f out: one pce fnl f* **3/1**[1]
6 *nk* **Lixirova (FR)**[20] 4579 2-8-9 DBoeuf 12 95
(D Smaga, France) *hld up in rr: hdwy down centre over 2f out: sn hrd rdn and one pce* **51/10**[2]
7 3 **Yushka (FR)**[17] 2-8-9 C-PLemaire 10 87
(P Bary, France) *hld up in 9th: nvr a factor* **15/1**
8 2 **Broken Kitten (FR)**[24] 4448 2-8-9 (p) GMillet 1 82
(T Larriviere, France) *racd in 2nd: hrd rdn and edgd rt under 2 1/2f out: wknd 2f out* **7/1**
9 2 **Mark Of Brazil (FR)**[41] 2-8-9 IMendizabal 4 77
(F Chappet, France) *racd in 3rd on ins: rdn over 2f out: sn btn* **28/1**
10 8 **Foresta (FR)**[20] 4584 2-8-9 TJarnet 3 57
(B De Montzey, France) *led to 2f out: wknd* **75/1**
11 **Rodarte**[21] 2-8-9 MDemuro 11 57
(B Grizzetti, Italy) *towards rr on outside: rdn 2 1/2f out: sn btn* **71/1**
12 **Chantilly Creme (USA)**[20] 4584 2-8-9 SPasquier 2 57
(R Gibson, France) *racd in 4th: bmpd under 2 1/2f out: sn rdn: wknd 1 1/2f out: heavily eased fnl f* **63/10**[3]
1m 22.1s (-6.20) **12** Ran SP% **116.6**
PARI-MUTUEL: WIN 24.50: PL 5.50, 4.50, 2.60; DF 139.60.
Owner Allevamento Dei Sette **Bred** Giovanni Faldatto **Trained** Italy
■ Stewards' Enquiry : D Vargiu six-day ban: whip abuse (Sep 5-10)

NOTEBOOK
Joanna(IRE), never far from the leaders in the group up the centre of the track, went to the head of affairs at the furlong marker and stayed on gamely under considerable pressure to hold the runner-up. Certainly a smart filly and connections will almost certainly enter her in the Prix Marcel Boussac at Longchamp in October. Her jockey was suspended for six days for whip abuse; the filly was hit 22 times during the seven furlongs.
Virginia Hall ran the best race of her life to date. She was always well up and looked extremely dangerous when making a forward move coming into the lastl furlong but she couldn't quite get to the winner. She completely reversed the form with an old rival and she may well be up to winning a similar race in the future.
American Nizzy(FR), towards the tail of the field early on, came up the stands' rail with her challenge and took third place well inside the final furlong.
Heaven's Heart(IRE), in mid-division in the early stages, she started her run from two out but could not sustain it and lost third place near the finish.

5280a CRITERIUM DU FONDS EUROPEEN DE L'ELEVAGE (LISTED RACE) 1m (R)
2:35 (2:35) 2-Y-O
£59,223 (£23,689; £17,767; £11,845; £5,922)

RPR
1 **Ruler Of My Heart (IRE)**[14] 4797 2-8-8 DBonilla 5 101
(Tom Dascombe) *racd in 5th: hdwy on outside ent st: led over 1f out: r.o wl* **92/10**[3]
2 2 1/2 **Maroon Machine (IRE)**[11] 5088 2-8-9 CSoumillon 6 97
(E J O'Neill) *racd in 3rd: led narrowly over 2f out to over 1f out: one pce* **53/10**[1]
3 1 1/2 **Anzas (IRE)**[35] 2-8-11 SPasquier 3 95
(R Gibson, France)
4 3 **Madiba (GER)**[55] 2-8-11 OPeslier 2 89
(J E Pease, France)
5 *nk* **Flowers In Spring (FR)**[12] 2-8-8 C-PLemaire 4 85
(David Marnane, Ire) *led to over 2f out: one pce* **13/1**
6 5 **Celestial Tryst**[30] 4226 2-8-8 J-BEyquem 1 74
(G M Moore) *last thrght* **17/2**[2]
1m 43.7s (2.70) **6** Ran SP% **43.3**
PARI-MUTUEL: WIN 10.20; PL 6.10, 3.20; SF 47.60.
Owner Timeform Betfair Racing Club Partnership **Bred** Haras D'Etreham & Pontchartrain Stud **Trained** Lambourn, Berks

NOTEBOOK

Ruler Of My Heart(IRE) was a maiden going into this race, which she completely dominated inside the final furlong. She was one but last at the halfway stage and then came charging through to take command at the furlong marker. She drew clear to win in a most impressive manner, certainly has scope for further improvement and connections may well look at the Prix d'Aumale at Chantilly.

Maroon Machine(IRE), well up from the start, looked the likely winner at the furlong marker but had nothing in hand when challenged.

Celestial Tryst, a winner at Doncaster last month, made no show on this occasion and was always behind, finishing detached.

5281a LE GALOP HERMES 3EME MANCHE (JOCKEYS COMPETITION) (ALL-WEATHER) — 1m 4f

4:25 (4:25) 4-Y-0+ **£16,990** (£6,796; £5,097; £3,398; £1,699)

RPR

1 **Bookend**[89] 5-9-0 .... SPasquier 90
(D Smaga, France)

2 *4* **Roatan**[69] 4-9-3 .... C-PLemaire 87
(P Bary, France)

3 *hd* **Secundus (GER)**[13] 4-9-0 .... DarryllHolland 83
(M Nigge, France)

4 *2* **Redesignation (IRE)**[99] 2055 4-9-0 80
(R Pritchard-Gordon, France)

5 *snk* **Green Tango (FR)**[46] 6-9-3 83
(P Van De Poele, France)

6 *nk* **Times Vital (IRE)**[11] 5089 4-9-0 .... IMendizabal 79
(E J O'Neill) *hld up in rr: styd on steadily down outside fnl 2f* **26/1**[1]

7 *3* **Brazilian Star (IRE)**[162] 4-9-0 75
(Y De Nicolay, France)

8 *snk* **Soum (GER)**[55] 3441 4-9-0 74
(C Sprengel, Germany)

9 *hd* **Naramix (FR)**[27] 5-9-0 74
(L A Urbano-Grajales, France)

10 *6* **Quanita Pierji (FR)**[15] 5-8-10 60
(E Leenders, France)

0 **Sabolienne (FR)**[27] 6-8-10 .... —
(D Sepulchre, France)

0 **Tsar De Russie (IRE)**[46] 4-9-3 ....(b) CSoumillon —
(E Lellouche, France)

2m 37.4s (157.40) **12** Ran SP% **3.7**

PARI-MUTUEL: WIN 8.00; PL 3.20, 3.90, 7.70; DF 27.00.

Owner K Abdulla **Bred** Juddmonte Farms **Trained** Lamorlaye, France

5151 FOLKESTONE (R-H)

Sunday, August 23

OFFICIAL GOING: Good to firm (firm in places on straight course; round 7.8, straight: far side 7.8, stands' side 8.4)

Wind: Fairly light, against. Weather: Warm and Sunny

5282 TOTEPLACEPOT MEDIAN AUCTION MAIDEN STKS — 5f

2:10 (2:12) (Class 5) 2-Y-O **£2,729** (£806; £403) **Stalls** Low

Form RPR

23 **1** **Monsieur Joe (IRE)**[106] 1862 2-9-3 0 .... AdamKirby 6 79+
(W R Swinburn) *trckd ldrs and a gng wl: led over 1f out: clr jst ins fnl f: easily* **11/10**[1]

6 **2** *2 1/4* **Freeforaday (USA)**[11] 4906 2-9-3 0 .... SteveDrowne 3 68
(J R Best) *restless stalls: in tch in last pair: niggled along after 1f: swtchd rt and drvn over 1f out: chsd wnr ins fnl f: no imp* **12/1**

3345 **3** *2* **La Fortunata**[17] 4711 2-8-12 68 .... AdrianMcCarthy 2 56
(J R Jenkins) *racd keenly: led: hdd and wanting to hang rt over 1f out: wknd fnl f* **7/2**[3]

0 **4** *3* **Recette**[31] 4243 2-8-12 0 .... AlanMunro 4 45
(R Ingram) *dwlt: a in rr: rdn and struggling wl over 1f out: plugged on fnl f but no ch w ldrs* **33/1**

0 **5** *2* **L'Isle Joyeuse**[17] 4688 2-8-12 0 .... JimCrowley 7 38
(P Winkworth) *chsd ldrs on outer: rdn 2f out: wknd qckly ent fnl f* **33/1**

425 **6** *3 1/2* **Bazsharani**[53] 3500 2-8-12 67 .... TPQueally 1 25
(P D Evans) *sn chsng ldr tl wl over 1f out: sn wknd: wl bhd fnl f* **5/2**[2]

60.42 secs (0.42) **Going Correction** -0.10s/f (Good) **6** Ran SP% **112.0**

Speed ratings (Par 94): **92,88,85,80,77 71**

toteswingers: 1&2 £3.50, 1&3 £1.30, 2&3 £4.60. CSF £15.79 TOTE £2.00: £1.40, £3.40; EX 10.40.

Owner Mrs Helen Checkley **Bred** Nicola And Eleanor Kent **Trained** Aldbury, Herts

FOCUS

A weak juvenile maiden.

NOTEBOOK

Monsieur Joe(IRE) had shown plenty of ability on his first two starts, but he had been off since running third at Ascot in May, when he was reported by his jockey to have hung left. He's clearly benefited from the short break, however, as he was a comfortable winner on his return to action, drawing nicely clear without his rider getting serious. He looks a nice type for nurseries. (op 11-8 tchd 6-4 in a place)

Freeforaday(USA) got a bit worked up in the stalls but he still showed ability, stepping up a good deal on the form he showed on debut. (op 10-1 tchd 9-1)

La Fortunata showed speed against the stands' rail for much of the way but she ruined her chance by continually hanging right. A right-hand rail and/or easier ground might suit better. Official explanation: jockey said, regarding running and riding, that his orders were to get to the rail and make the running, but the filly hung badly right off the rails and he was unable to ride out closing stages. (op 4-1 tchd 3-1)

Recette made some late headway after a sluggish start and probably improved a little on her debut effort. (op 22-1)

L'Isle Joyeuse looks selling class on what we've seen so far.

Bazsharani was well drawn but she dropped away tamely and ran nowhere near the form she had shown on her first three starts. (tchd 3-1)

5283 HR GO RECRUITMENT (S) STKS — 7f (S)

2:40 (2:41) (Class 6) 3-Y-O+ **£2,047** (£604; £302) **Stalls** Low

Form RPR

5314 **1** **Sir Ike (IRE)**[29] 4321 4-9-10 67 ....(tp) ShaneKelly 1 60
(W S Kittow) *chsd ldr tl led over 2f out: nudged along over 1f out: kpt on and a holding runner-up fnl f* **6/5**[1]

000/ **2** *1/2* **Insomnitas**[38] 4025 4-9-5 44 .... CatherineGannon 2 54
(Seamus Fahey, Ire) *in tch: hdwy to chse wnr over 1f out: chal ins fnl f: r.o but a hld* **20/1**

0024 **3** *1 3/4* **Cognac Boy (USA)**[40] 3946 3-9-5 56 ....(b) ChrisCatlin 5 52
(A B Haynes) *sn bhd and niggled along: hdwy on stands' rail over 1f out: chsd ldng pair 1f out: kpt on but nt pce to chal ldrs* **7/1**[3]

0352 **4** *7* **Briannsta (IRE)**[8] 5018 7-9-5 54 .... RichardThomas 4 30
(J E Long) *hld up towards rr: hdwy and rdn over 2f out: chsd ldrs ent fnl f: sn wknd* **12/1**

0-00 **5** *3 1/2* **Station Place**[29] 4305 4-9-0 53 .... StephenDonohoe 11 16
(A B Haynes) *led tl over 2f out: lost 2nd over 1f out: wknd qckly ent fnl f* **20/1**

2540 **6** *nk* **Outer Hebrides**[10] 4938 8-9-5 54 ....(v) AmyBaker(5) 9 25
(J M Bradley) *hld up towards rr on outer: pushed along and hdwy 1/2-way: rdn and btn over 1f out: no ch fnl f* **16/1**

6000 **7** *1 3/4* **Auld Arty (FR)**[54] 3476 3-9-5 67 ....(p) TPQueally 3 18
(T G Mills) *dwlt: sn rcvrd and chsng ldrs: hung rt and rdn over 1f out: fdd tamely and wl btn fnl f* **9/2**[2]

5665 **8** *2 1/4* **Mr Rev**[5] 5120 6-9-2 47 ....(b) JackDean(3) 10 9
(J M Bradley) *stdd s: hld up in rr: rdn 1/2-way: drvn and no prog wl over 1f out: wl btn fnl f* **11/1**

6-00 **9** *5* **Pinewood Lulu**[89] 2366 4-8-7 45 .... CharlotteKerton(7) 7 —
(S A Harris) *stdd s: a in rr: rdn and lost tch 2f out: wl bhd whn hung lft over 1f out* **80/1**

0-00 **10** *2 1/4* **Musigny (USA)**[36] 4083 3-9-0 58 .... AlanMunro 6 —
(W Jarvis) *t.k.h: chsd ldrs: rdn 2f out: wknd qckly over 1f out: wl bhd fnl f* **16/1**

400 **11** *16* **Spring Bridge (IRE)**[15] 4786 3-9-0 43 ....(p) FrankieMcDonald 8 —
(Mrs L C Jewell) *in tch in midfield: rdn 1/2-way: sn struggling and bhd fnl 2f: t.o* **100/1**

1m 27.62s (0.32) **Going Correction** -0.10s/f (Good)

WFA 3 from 4yo+ 5lb **11** Ran SP% **115.7**

Speed ratings (Par 101): **94,93,91,83,79 79,77,74,68,66 47**

toteswingers: 1&2 £8.30, 1&3 £4.00, 2&3 £17.60. CSF £33.57 TOTE £2.20: £1.10, £6.60, £1.60; EX 35.40 Trifecta £99.90 Part won. Pool £135.11 - 0.20 winning units..The winner was bought in for 5,200gns.

Owner Mrs Susan Arnesen **Bred** Martin Francis **Trained** Blackborough, Devon

FOCUS

A typically weak seller. They raced stands' side and a low draw seemed to be advantageous. The winner did not need to be at his best to score with the runner-up back to his old form.

5284 TOTEQUADPOT EBF MAIDEN FILLIES' STKS — 7f (S)

3:10 (3:13) (Class 5) 2-Y-O **£4,371** (£1,300; £650; £324) **Stalls** Low

Form RPR

1 **Creese** 2-9-0 0 .... TPQueally 4 80
(H R A Cecil) *wnt rt s and s.i.s: bhd: hdwy 4f out: chsd ldrs and rdn 3f out: swtchd rt over 1f out: styd on wl fnl f to ld nr fin* **20/1**

3 **2** *nk* **Hibaayeb**[15] 4792 2-9-0 0 .... PhilipRobinson 13 79
(C E Brittain) *chsd ldrs: rdn and ev ch over 1f out: led ent fnl f: kpt on wl tl hdd nr fin* **11/4**[2]

05 **3** *1* **Hill Tribe**[8] 5026 2-8-11 0 .... MarcHalford(3) 1 77
(J R Best) *led: rdn and hdd 2f out: unable qck u.p over 1f out: rallied ins fnl f: wnt 3rd nr fin* **16/1**

2 **4** *nk* **Huroof (IRE)**[15] 4797 2-9-0 0 .... TPO'Shea 12 76
(Saeed Bin Suroor) *chsd ldr: pushed along over 2f out: rdn to ld 2f out: hdd ent fnl f: no ex and lost 2 pls fnl 100yds* **13/8**[1]

44 **5** *1 1/4* **Mellifera**[39] 3987 2-9-0 0 .... AdamKirby 2 73
(W R Swinburn) *chsd ldrs: rdn and swtchd rt over 1f out: keeping on same pce whn n.m.r fnl 100yds* **15/2**

0 **6** *2 1/4* **Tallawalla (IRE)**[15] 4792 2-9-0 0 .... TonyCulhane 10 67+
(M R Channon) *hmpd s and s.i.s: bhd: hdwy and jostling match w rival jst over 2f out: swtchd rt and in tch w ldrs over 1f out: no imp fnl f* **66/1**

50 **7** *nse* **Calatrava Cape (IRE)**[24] 4460 2-9-0 0 .... ShaneKelly 5 67+
(J L Dunlop) *chsd ldrs tl wknd u.p over 1f out* **12/1**

8 *4 1/2* **Million Dollars (USA)** 2-9-0 0 .... TedDurcan 6 56
(Saeed Bin Suroor) *v.s.a: wl bhd: hdwy whn jostling match w rival jst over 2f out: wanting to hang rt and no prog fnl 2f* **6/1**[3]

000 **9** *10* **Mrs Puff (IRE)**[14] 4825 2-9-0 54 .... CatherineGannon 14 31
(P D Evans) *t.k.h: rdn and struggling 3f out: no ch fnl 2f* **66/1**

10 *12* **Areeg (IRE)** 2-9-0 0 .... AlanMunro 7 —
(W Jarvis) *t.k.h: in tch tl rdn and struggling 1/2-way: wl bhd fnl 2f: t.o* **33/1**

11 *1/2* **Lady Of Namid (IRE)** 2-9-0 0 .... StephenDonohoe 11 —
(R Curtis) *short of room sn after s: sn bhd and nvr gng pce: t.o* **100/1**

00 **12** *3/4* **Have More**[9] 4980 2-9-0 0 .... MartinDwyer 8 —
(B J Meehan) *wnt rt s: sn rcvrd and chsng ldrs: rdn and lost pl 4f out: t.o fr over 1f out* **66/1**

13 *1/2* **Posy Fossil (USA)** 2-9-0 0 .... SaleemGolam 3 —
(S C Williams) *stdd s and grad swtchd rt to r on outer: in midfield tl struggling 3f out: t.o fnl f* **40/1**

1m 27.35s (0.05) **Going Correction** -0.10s/f (Good) **13** Ran SP% **120.0**

Speed ratings (Par 91): **95,94,93,93,91 89,89,83,72,58 58,57,56**

toteswingers: 1&2 £21.60, 1&3 £54.20, 2&3 £5.30. CSF £73.41 TOTE £14.80: £4.00, £1.40, £3.50; EX 105.60 TRIFECTA Not won..

Owner Malih L Al Basti **Bred** Malih Al Basti **Trained** Newmarket, Suffolk

FOCUS

This looked a reasonable fillies' maiden; a good contest for the track. They all raced stands' side.

NOTEBOOK

Creese, the first foal of a 7f juvenile winner, displayed a pleasing attitude to make a winning debut. After a sluggish start, she came under pressure a fair way out but gradually got the idea and there was much to like about the manner in which she knuckled down near the line. There should be plenty of improvement to come and she deserves her chance in something better. (op 16-1)

Hibaayeb confirmed the promise she showed when third on her debut at the Newmarket July course but simply found one too good. She should benefit from further in time and looks well up to winning a similar race. (op 4-1)

Hill Tribe was stepped up a furlong and saw the trip out well. The bare form probably flatters her, though, as she had the best draw and raced tight against the often favoured stands'-side rail throughout. Nurseries are now an option.

Huroof(IRE) failed to build on the form she showed on her debut at the July course, which is disappointing considering the fifth-placed finisher from that race has since won a Listed race, and the eighth home has also been successful. A wide draw wasn't ideal but that can't really be used as an excuse, and she basically lacked the speed of some of these in the closing stages. She is likely to prove better suited by slightly easier ground and ought to stay further in time. (op 6-4 tchd 11-10)

Mellifera ran okay and now has the option of handicaps. (op 8-1 tchd 9-1)

Tallawalla(IRE), well behind today's runner-up on her debut, raced in an unpromising position throughout after being short of room at the start, but she travelled quite nicely and kept on, showing definite signs of ability. She can yet do better.

Calatrava Cape(IRE) is bred to appreciate a step up in trip and will be one to keep in mind for nurseries, and maybe handicaps next year. (op 9-1)

Million Dollars(USA), fitted with a sheepskin-noseband for this debut, lost several lengths with a slow start and compromised any chance she might have had of making up the lost ground by continually hanging right. Official explanation: jockey said filly missed the break (op 11-2 tchd 7-1)

5285 TOTEPOOL EBF FILLIES' H'CAP — 1m 1f 149y
3:40 (3:41) (Class 3) (0-90,85) 3-Y-O+ — **£9,714** (£2,890; £1,444; £721) **Stalls** Centre

Form — RPR

0034 **1** **Hallingdal (UAE)**[9] 4992 4-8-9 **66**.................................... RyanClark[(7)] 6 — 70
(J J Bridger) *hld up in last pl: hdwy on outer to chse ldr 2f out: edgd rt and chal over 1f out: led ins fnl f: forged ahd fnl 100yds* **8/1**

1 **2** *1 ½* **Assabiyya (IRE)**[20] 4606 3-9-13 **85**.................................... TedDurcan 7 — 86
(Saeed Bin Suroor) *sn led: rdn wl over 1f out: hrd pressed over 1f out: hdd ins fnl f: btn and eased towards fin* **4/9**[1]

0504 **3** *½* **Ballyalla**[11] 4902 3-9-4 **76**.................................... PatDobbs 2 — 76
(R Hannon) *trckd ldrs: rdn and unable qck 2f out: swtchd lft ent fnl f: kpt on same pce after* **13/2**[3]

0304 **4** *5* **Full Of Nature**[3] 5195 3-8-12 **70**.................................... LPKeniry 1 — 60
(S Kirk) *led briefly: sn chsng ldr: rdn and lost 2nd 2f out: struggling whn n.m.r over 1f out: wl hld fnl f* **11/2**[2]

2m 2.48s (-2.42) **Going Correction** -0.25s/f (Firm)
WFA 3 from 4yo 8lb — 4 Ran SP% **109.1**
Speed ratings (Par 104): **99,97,97,93**
toteswingers: 1&2 £3.40. CSF £12.67 TOTE £9.00; EX 15.00.
Owner W Wood **Bred** Darley **Trained** Liphook, Hants

FOCUS
A really poor turnout for the grade and, with the favourite running below expectations, this is weak form.

NOTEBOOK
Hallingdal(UAE) had shown her very best form over 7f on Polytrack, ideally in a strongly run race, but she was 7lb below her last winning mark and took advantage. (op 17-2 tchd 9-1)
Assabiyya(IRE) looked good when making a winning debut under similar conditions in a Windsor maiden, but this was disappointing. There seemed no obvious excuse, but surely she'll be capable of better in due course. (op 1-2)
Ballyalla was trying her furthest trip to date and ran like a non-stayer. asddasd asd had shown her very best form over 7f on Polytrack, ideally in a strongly run race, but she was 7lb below her last winning mark and took advantage. (op 6-1 tchd 7-1)
Full Of Nature dropped away tamely and offered nothing. She probably wants easier ground. (tchd 5-1 and 6-1)

5286 TOTESWINGER H'CAP — 1m 4f
4:10 (4:11) (Class 6) (0-65,68) 3-Y-O — **£2,388** (£705; £352) **Stalls** Low

Form — RPR

0031 **1** **Sounds Of Jupiter (IRE)**[5] 5123 3-9-11 **68** 6ex.............. JimCrowley 13 — 82+
(D M Simcock) *mde all: rdn clr over 1f out: in command whn edgd lft 1f out: eased towards fin* **2/1**[1]

3040 **2** *7* **Salybia Bay**[21] 4569 3-9-3 **60**.................................... PatDobbs 1 — 62
(R Hannon) *chsd ldng pair: rdn to chse wnr over 2f out: btn over 1f out: plugged on for clr 2nd* **12/1**

0233 **3** *2 ¾* **Dhania (IRE)**[13] 4855 3-9-1 **58**....................................(b) LPKeniry 12 — 56
(R A Teal) *hld up in tch: hdwy over 3f out: rdn to chse ldng pair 2f out: hld hd high u.p and sn no imp and wl hld after* **11/1**

2620 **4** *3* **Extremely So**[30] 4269 3-9-2 **59**.................................... ChrisCatlin 5 — 52+
(P J McBride) *hmpd and stdd sn after s: hld up wl bhd: hdwy over 5f out: rdn and plugged on past btn horses fnl 2f: nvr nr ldrs* **33/1**

2632 **5** *¾* **Beaubrav**[16] 4734 3-9-5 **62**....................................(t) ShaneKelly 3 — 54
(P W D'Arcy) *chsd wnr tl over 2f out: sn wknd u.p and no ch fr over 1f out* **10/1**[3]

5-06 **6** *1 ¾* **Tomintoul Star**[22] 4545 3-9-0 **57**.................................... TPQueally 8 — 46
(H R A Cecil) *hmpd s: t.k.h: hld up in midfield: shkn up over 5f out: rdn and btn wl over 2f out: no ch whn hung lft over 1f out* **8/1**[2]

0630 **7** *1 ¾* **Bedarra Boy**[18] 4650 3-8-9 **52**.................................... TPO'Shea 7 — 38
(D W P Arbuthnot) *hmpd s: sn wl bhd: rdn and styd on past btn horses fnl 2f: n.d* **50/1**

0213 **8** *6* **Playful Asset (IRE)**[11] 4918 3-9-0 **64**.................................... JPFahy[(7)] 6 — 41
(P Howling) *bmpd sn after s: racd in midfield: hdwy to chse ldrs over 4f out: rdn and wknd 3f out: wl btn fnl 2f* **20/1**

0005 **9** *13* **Academy Of War (USA)**[8] 5016 3-8-7 **50**.............. CatherineGannon 14 — 6
(J M Bradley) *stdd s: hld up wl in rr: nvr on terms* **50/1**

4233 **10** *12* **Tinkerbelle (IRE)**[59] 3303 3-8-12 **55**.................................... TedDurcan 4 — —
(J L Dunlop) *chsd ldrs: rdn and wknd qckly 3f out: virtually p.u ins fnl f: t.o* **2/1**[1]

5-05 **11** *½* **Causeway King (USA)**[18] 4650 3-9-6 **63**.............. FergusSweeney 10 — —
(A King) *t.k.h: in tch: reminder over 5f out: rdn and wkng 4f out: wl bhd fr over 2f out: t.o* **12/1**

0106 **12** *45* **Hi Fling**[11] 4917 3-9-2 **59**....................................(b) MartinDwyer 9 — —
(B J Meehan) *wnt bdly lft s: nvr looked happy: a towards rr: rdn over 5f out: lost tch 4f out: t.o fnl 3f* **28/1**

2m 36.3s (-4.60) **Going Correction** -0.25s/f (Firm) — 12 Ran SP% **125.7**
Speed ratings (Par 98): **105,100,98,96,96 94,93,89,81,73 72,42**
toteswingers: 1&2 £8.30, 1&3 £6.50, 2&3 £24.10. CSF £31.21 CT £228.30 TOTE £2.90: £1.50, £3.80, £3.20; EX 37.60 TRIFECTA Not won..
Owner Dr Marwan Koukash **Bred** Gainsborough Stud Management Ltd **Trained** Newmarket, Suffolk

FOCUS
A moderate handicap and few were ever involved. The winner was impressive although the level behind is a bit fluid.
Tinkerbelle(IRE) Official explanation: jockey said filly had no more to give

5287 TOTEEXACTA H'CAP — 7f (S)
4:40 (4:44) (Class 6) (0-60,59) 3-Y-O+ — **£2,388** (£705; £352) **Stalls** Low

Form — RPR

0133 **1** **Goodbye Cash (IRE)**[5] 5120 5-9-3 **55**.................................... TPQueally 6 — 62
(P D Evans) *s.i.s: wl bhd: stl plenty to do and rdn over 2f out: hdwy and switching rt fr 2f out: styd on wl u.p fnl f to ld nr fin* **10/3**[1]

0030 **2** *½* **Norcroft**[18] 4665 7-8-12 **50**....................................(v) AdrianMcCarthy 1 — 56
(Mrs C A Dunnett) *hld up in tch: rdn to chse ldng pair over 1f out: led jst ins fnl f hdd and no ex nr fin* **20/1**

6006 **3** *1* **Lennie Briscoe (IRE)**[5] 5121 3-9-2 **59**.................................... LPKeniry 2 — 60
(S Kirk) *t.k.h: hld up in midfield: pushed along 3f out: nt clr run and swtchd lft ent fnl f: kpt on u.p to go 3rd fnl 75yds* **8/1**

1500 **4** *1 ¼* **Deckchair**[34] 4155 3-8-6 **49**....................................(v) ChrisCatlin 7 — 47
(S Curran) *sn wl bhd: stl poor 12th 2f out: sn swtchd towards centre: styd on wl u.p fnl f: snatched 4th last strides: nvr trbld ldrs* **28/1**

4-00 **5** *hd* **Obe Brave**[12] 4878 6-9-5 **57**....................................(p) SaleemGolam 5 — 56
(Lee Smyth, Ire) *led main gp tl led overall and rdn along wl over 3f out: hrd pressed and drvn 2f out: hdd jst ins fnl f: wknd fnl 75yds* **11/2**[3]

-004 **6** *¾* **Sultans Way (IRE)**[16] 4749 3-9-2 **59**.................................... JimCrowley 8 — 54
(P F I Cole) *chsd ldrs: wnt 2nd overall wl over 3f out: ev ch and rdn ent fnl 2f: hrd drvn over 1f out: wknd fnl 75yds* **4/1**[2]

5404 **7** *2* **Fun In The Sun**[40] 3948 5-9-0 **52**.................................... StephenDonohoe 11 — 44
(A B Haynes) *sn towards rr of main gp: rdn over 3f out: plugged on u.p fnl f: nvr threatened ldrs* **18/1**

4510 **8** *3 ¾* **Ishibee (IRE)**[10] 4950 5-8-9 **50**....................................(p) MarcHalford[(3)] 3 — 32
(J J Bridger) *hld up wl in tch: rdn ent fnl 2f: edgd rt and wknd u.p over 1f out* **9/1**

0206 **9** *shd* **Private Passion (IRE)**[4] 5155 3-8-9 **52**.................................... PaulEddery 13 — 32
(Pat Eddery) *chsd ldrs: rdn 1/2-way: drvn and struggling over 2f out: wl btn fnl 2f* **16/1**

6060 **10** *24* **Imperial Skylight**[15] 4791 3-8-12 **55**....................................(v[1]) TonyCulhane 10 — —
(M R Channon) *chsd ldrs: rdn and losing pl 1/2-way: wl t.o and eased ins fnl f* **12/1**

300 **11** *¾* **Torquemada (IRE)**[182] 646 8-8-12 **50**....................................(t) LukeMorris 9 — —
(M J Attwater) *s.i.s: sn pushed along and nvr gng wl: wl bhd fnl 2f: t.o* **25/1**

1500 **12** *1 ¾* **My Flame**[18] 4665 4-9-4 **56**.................................... ShaneKelly 12 — —c
(J R Jenkins) *racd towards far side: nvr bttr than midfield overall: struggling bdly 1/2-way: t.o fnl 2f* **14/1**

0050 **13** *15* **Greystoke Prince**[62] 3211 4-9-7 **59**....................................(bt[1]) AdamKirby 14 — —c
(W R Swinburn) *racd towards far side: led overall tl wl over 3f out: sn dropped out: t.o 2f out: eased fnl f* **16/1**

1m 27.2s (-0.10) **Going Correction** -0.10s/f (Good)
WFA 3 from 4yo+ 5lb — 13 Ran SP% **123.0**
Speed ratings (Par 101): **96,95,94,92,92 91,89,85,85,57 56,54,37**
toteswingers: 1&2 £15.50, 1&3 £7.10, 2&3 £34.90. CSF £77.95 CT £409.87 TOTE £3.60: £1.60, £5.30, £3.60; EX 70.20 TRIFECTA Not won..
Owner Mrs I M Folkes **Bred** Mrs A C Peters **Trained** Pandy, Monmouths

FOCUS
A moderate handicap and weak form, little better than a seller. The main action took place towards the stands' side and the two runners who raced up the middle (My Flame and Greystone Prince) were well beaten.
Obe Brave Official explanation: jockey said gelding hung right

5288 CONCERN FOR CHERNOBYL CHILDREN H'CAP — 6f
5:10 (5:10) (Class 5) (0-75,72) 3-Y-O+ — **£3,412** (£1,007; £504) **Stalls** Low

Form — RPR

2054 **1** **Indian Skipper (IRE)**[16] 4761 4-9-10 **72**....................................(p) TedDurcan 2 — 81
(M H Tompkins) *chsd ldrs on stands' rail: rdn and effrt over 1f out: drvn to ld ins fnl f: r.o wl* **10/3**[3]

2604 **2** *1 ½* **Dvinsky (USA)**[4] 5167 8-9-5 **67**....................................(b) IanMongan 8 — 71
(P Howling) *sn pressing ldr: pushed along over 2f out: rdn to ld over 1f out: hdd ins fnl f: kpt on same pce fnl 100yds* **3/1**[2]

6024 **3** *2 ¼* **Forest Dane**[12] 4870 9-8-13 **66**.................................... SophieDoyle[(5)] 7 — 63
(Mrs N Smith) *in tch: pushed along and hdwy wl over 1f out: chsd ldrs and rdn ent fnl f: outpcd ins fnl f* **13/2**

006 **4** *nse* **Buxton**[11] 4914 5-9-8 **70**....................................(t) SteveDrowne 3 — 67
(R Ingram) *racd in last pair: swtchd rt and effrt u.p wl over 1f out: one pce and no imp after* **8/1**

0606 **5** *2 ¾* **Choreography**[5] 5124 6-9-6 **68**....................................(p) TPQueally 1 — 56
(Jim Best) *led on stands' rail: pushed along over 2f out: hdd and edgd rt over 1f out: wknd ent fnl f* **6/1**

125 **6** *1 ¾* **Namu**[5] 5125 6-8-12 **60**....................................(p) JimCrowley 5 — 42
(Miss T Spearing) *stdd s: hld up in last pair: rdn and effrt on outer over 2f out: drvn wl over 1f out: wknd ent fnl f* **9/4**[1]

1m 11.61s (-1.09) **Going Correction** -0.10s/f (Good) — 6 Ran SP% **117.6**
Speed ratings (Par 103): **103,101,98,97,94 91**
toteswingers: 1&2 £2.70, 1&3 £3.60, 2&3 £4.30. CSF £14.57 CT £61.75 TOTE £4.30: £2.00, £2.20; EX 21.00 Trifecta £176.50 Pool £310.10 - 1.30 winning units..
Owner Roalco Limited **Bred** Calley House Syndicate **Trained** Newmarket, Suffolk

FOCUS
A modest sprint handicap with the winner rated back to his best and the runner-up just below that level.
Choreography Official explanation: jockey said gelding hung right
T/Plt: £482.90 to a £1 stake. Pool: £62,786.82. 94.91 winning tickets. T/Qpdt: £152.70 to a £1 stake. Pool: £3,858.96. 18.70 winning tickets. SP

4873 MUSSELBURGH (R-H)
Sunday, August 23

OFFICIAL GOING: Good to soft (soft in places; 6.2) changing to soft after race 3 (3.20)
Wind: Light, across. Weather: Heavy showers

5289 RACING UK APPRENTICE H'CAP — 1m
2:20 (2:20) (Class 6) (0-60,59) 4-Y-O+ — **£2,590** (£770; £385; £192) **Stalls** High

Form — RPR

0312 **1** **Morocchius (USA)**[13] 4845 4-9-0 **57**....................................(p) MartinLane[(3)] 14 — 69
(Miss J A Camacho) *trckd ldrs: hdwy 3f out: cl up 2f out: sn led and rdn clr ent fnl f: kpt on* **9/2**[1]

4012 **2** *3* **Zaplamation (IRE)**[18] 4656 4-8-10 **55**.................................... IJBrennan[(5)] 1 — 60
(J J Quinn) *hld up towards rr: hdwy on inner 3f out: swtchd lft and effrt 2f out: sn rdn and styd on to chse wnr ins fnl f: sn no imp* **6/1**[2]

0000 **3** *1 ¾* **King Of The Moors (USA)**[13] 4845 6-8-11 **56**...(b[1]) JamesPSullivan[(5)] 9 — 57
(R C Guest) *t.k.h: sn led: rdn along over 2f out and sn hdd: drvn wl over 1f out: kpt on same pce u.p ins fnl f* **25/1**

2030 **4** *hd* **Silly Gilly (IRE)**[10] 4932 5-9-0 **57**.................................... SladeO'Hara[(3)] 2 — 57
(R E Barr) *cl up: effrt over 2f out: sn rdn and ev ch tl drvn over 1f out and kpt on same pce* **12/1**

0622 **5** *1* **Jamieson Gold (IRE)**[12] 4876 6-8-13 **56**....................................(p) AmyRyan[(3)] 10 — 54
(Miss L A Perratt) *dwlt: sn in midfield: hdwy to chse ldrs 3f out: rdn along 2f out and sn one pce* **12/1**

04-1 **6** *hd* **Social Rhythm**[12] 4876 5-8-11 **54**.................................... JamieKyne[(3)] 3 — 51+
(A C Whillans) *stdd s: hld up in rr: hdwy over 2f out: sn swtchd lft and rdn: styd on ins fnl f: nrst fin* **8/1**

524 **7** *shd* **Red Skipper (IRE)**[17] 4710 4-9-2 **56**....................................(v[1]) KellyHarrison 7 — 53+
(N Wilson) *hld up: pushed along: lost pl and bhd over 2f out: swtchd ins and rdn wl over 1f out: kpt on ins fnl f: nt rch ldrs* **6/1**[2]

1025 **8** *3* **Desert Hunter (IRE)**[37] 4070 6-8-11 **54**.............. PatrickDonaghy[(3)] 13 — 44
(Micky Hammond) *in tch: hdwy 3f out: rdn over 2f out and n.d* **33/1**

4600 **9** 3 ¾ **Mr Lu**[29] 4312 4-8-10 **53** GaryBartley(3) 6 34
(J S Goldie) *a in rr* **33/1**
0003 **10** 4 ½ **Lujano**[25] 4435 4-9-5 **59** FrederikTylicki 12 29
(Ollie Pears) *chsd ldrs on inner: rdn along 1/2-way and sn wknd* **8/1**
055 **11** 2 ½ **Born To Perform**[28] 4347 4-9-0 **59** PaulPickard(5) 4 23
(G A Swinbank) *racd wd: in midfield: rdn along 4f out and sn wknd* **7/1**[3]
0006 **12** *nk* **Shunkawakhan (IRE)**[12] 4878 6-9-2 **56** (p) NeilBrown 5 19
(Miss L A Perratt) *prom: rdn along over 3f out and sn wknd* **25/1**
0615 **13** 3 **Natural Rhythm (IRE)**[23] 4496 4-8-11 **54** (b) DeanHeslop(3) 8 10
(Mrs R A Carr) *chsd ldrs: rdn along 3f out: sn wknd* **12/1**

1m 43.95s (2.75) **Going Correction** +0.425s/f (Yiel) **13** Ran SP% **118.1**
Speed ratings (Par 101): **103,100,98,98,97 96,96,93,90,85 83,82,79**
toteswingers: 1&2 £5.50, 1&3 £20.10, 2&3 £44.30. CSF £28.74 CT £622.89 TOTE £4.20: £1.70, £3.00, £10.20; EX 36.50.
Owner Lee Bolingbroke Currie & Partners **Bred** E And D Enterprises **Trained** Norton, N Yorks

FOCUS
This handicap for apprentice riders was run at a sound pace and the form looks sound rated around the first two. The runners were kicking up the turf and the rain had clearly got into the ground.
Red Skipper(IRE) Official explanation: jockey said gelding hung left-handed throughout

5290 BUY A RACING POST YEARLING BONUS CANDIDATE MAIDEN AUCTION STKS 7f 30y
2:50 (2:51) (Class 6) 2-Y-O **£2,266** (£674; £337; £168) **Stalls** High

Form RPR
662 **1** **Raleigh Quay (IRE)**[18] 4659 2-8-10 66 FrederikTylicki(3) 6 70
(Micky Hammond) *trckd ldrs: hdwy over 2f out: n.m.r and rdn over 1f out: chal ent fnl f: drvn and kpt on to ld last 50yds* **11/4**[2]
02 **2** ½ **Jozafeen**[20] 4590 2-7-13 0 JamieKyne(5) 8 60
(R Bastiman) *prom: hdwy to chse ldr over 3f out: rdn to chal over 2f out: led over 1f out: sn drvn and hung lft ent fnl f: hdd and no ex last 50yds* **11/8**[1]
0 **3** 4 ½ **Golden Emperor (IRE)**[18] 4652 2-8-13 0 PJMcDonald 9 58+
(G A Swinbank) *chsd ldrs: rdn along over 2f out: drvn wl over 1f out: kpt on u.p ins fnl f* **16/1**
0 **4** ¾ **Bintalaleumydarlin (IRE)**[13] 4847 2-8-10 0 JoeFanning 10 53
(M Johnston) *sn led: rdn along 3f out: drvn and hdd over 1f out: grad wknd* **6/1**
46 **5** 8 **Ya Boy Sir (IRE)**[60] 3262 2-8-11 0 TomEaves 5 34
(I Semple) *chsd ldrs: hdwy 3f out: rdn along 2f out: sn drvn and wknd over 1f out* **33/1**
6 3 **Hotgrove Boy** 2-8-9 0 AndrewMullen 2 24
(A G Foster) *bhd tl styd on u.p fnl 2f: nvr a factor* **33/1**
004 **7** ¾ **No Quarter (IRE)**[13] 4847 2-8-12 63 DanielTudhope 4 25
(A Dickman) *in tch on outer: hdwy 3f out: rdn along over 2f out and sn wknd* **11/2**[3]
002 **8** 7 **Micky's Bird**[87] 2414 2-8-4 54 FrancisNorton 3 —
(R C Guest) *a towards rr* **8/1**
4 **9** 16 **Wing N Prayer (IRE)**[65] 3106 2-8-4 0 PaulQuinn 1 —
(A Berry) *wnt lft s: sn outpcd and bhd* **66/1**

1m 32.9s (2.60) **Going Correction** +0.425s/f (Yiel) **9** Ran SP% **122.8**
Speed ratings (Par 92): **102,101,96,95,86 82,82,74,55**
toteswingers: 1&2 £2.00, 1&3 £9.00, 2&3 £4.90. CSF £7.37 TOTE £3.80: £1.50, £1.10, £4.20; EX 8.80.
Owner S T Brankin **Bred** S O'Sullivan **Trained** Middleham Moor, N Yorks

FOCUS
This moderate juvenile maiden was run at a solid pace and the first four dominated.

NOTEBOOK
Raleigh Quay(IRE) battled it out with Jozafeen from the furlong pole and proved stronger where it mattered. He had stepped up on his first two outings when finishing second at Pontefract 18 days earlier and the step up a furlong on this softer ground worked the oracle. He will go up a few pounds for this (rated 66), but is open to further progression at the trip and should pay his way in nurseries. (op 3-1 tchd 5-2)
Jozafeen had yet to quite match the form of the winner in her two previous runs, but proved the most popular of the pair on this step up in trip. She held every chance and gave her all, but running freely early on probably cost her. She now qualifies for nurseries and can make amends. (tchd 7-4)
Golden Emperor(IRE), whose stable took this last season, put up a much more encouraging display than had been the case on debut over 6f at Newcastle. He still looked green so more improvement should be forthcoming and it wouldn't be surprising if he turned out the best of this lot, as he has scope. (op 14-1)
Bintalaleumydarlin(IRE) has some scope and she put in an improved effort from the front. She needs to learn to settle better, but ought to do so with experience. (op 7-1)
Wing N Prayer(IRE) Official explanation: jockey said filly lost an off-fore shoe

5291 DAILY RECORD GARRY OWEN H'CAP 1m 6f
3:20 (3:20) (Class 5) (0-75,74) 3-Y-O+ **£3,885** (£1,156; £577; £288) **Stalls** High

Form RPR
4456 **1** **Puy D'Arnac (FR)**[16] 4742 6-9-3 **60** PJMcDonald 3 68+
(G A Swinbank) *hld up in rr: smooth hdwy 5f out: trckd ldrs over 3f out: effrt to ld on bit 1 1/2f out: shkn up and clr ent fnl f* **4/1**[3]
1202 **2** 2 ¼ **Interdiamonds**[15] 4785 3-9-5 **74** JoeFanning 4 79
(M Johnston) *led: rdn along 3f out: hdd 1 1/2f out: sn drvn and hung lft: kpt on same pce u.p fnl f* **2/1**[1]
3-13 **3** 2 ¾ **Summer Soul (IRE)**[42] 3095 7-9-9 **71** (p) ClGillies(5) 1 72
(Miss Lucinda V Russell) *reminders after s and sn trcking ldrs: effrt over 3f out: rdn over 2f out and sltly outpcd: styd on u.p ins fnl f* **8/1**
2343 **4** *nk* **Classic Contours (USA)**[43] 3861 3-8-11 **71** JamieKyne(5) 7 72
(J J Quinn) *in tch: hdwy to trck ldrs 1/2-way: effrt 3f out: rdn and ev ch 2f out: sn drvn and hld whn n.m.r over 1f out* **5/2**[2]
1160 **5** 1 ¼ **Forrest Flyer (IRE)**[11] 4898 5-9-9 **66** PhillipMakin 2 65
(I Semple) *trckd ldr: effrt 3f out: rdn and ch over 2f out: sn drvn and hld whn n.m.r and swtchd rt over 1f out: wknd* **10/1**
256 **6** 4 ½ **Ifatfirst (IRE)**[16] 4755 6-9-5 **62** DanielTudhope 8 55
(J S Goldie) *trckd ldrs: rdn along over 3f out and sn wknd* **12/1**
6-44 **7** 28 **Nakoma (IRE)**[20] 4599 7-9-3 **60** TomEaves 5 13
(B Ellison) *prom: rdn along over 5f out: sn wknd and bhd fnl 3f* **16/1**

3m 10.01s (4.71) **Going Correction** +0.425s/f (Yiel)
WFA 3 from 5yo+ 12lb **7** Ran SP% **115.7**
Speed ratings (Par 103): **103,101,100,99,99 96,80**
toteswingers: 1&2 £2.80, 1&3 £5.20, 2&3 £3.00. CSF £12.77 CT £60.17 TOTE £4.60: £2.60, £2.20; EX 13.50.
Barrow Brook Racing **Bred** Mrs Axelle Du Verdier **Trained** Melsonby, N Yorks

FOCUS
A modest staying handicap, run at a fair pace. The winner did not match last season's form with the runner-up to his best.

5292 RACING UK SKY 432 (S) STKS 5f
3:50 (3:58) (Class 6) 2-Y-O **£1,942** (£578; £288; £144) **Stalls** Low

Form RPR
6231 **1** **Melody In The Mist (FR)**[15] 4773 2-8-12 76 PhillipMakin 5 61+
(T D Barron) *chsd ldrs: pushed along over 2f out: rdn over 1f out: swtchd rt and drvn to chal ins fnl f: styd on to ld last 75yds* **1/1**[1]
00 **2** *nse* **Micky's Knock Off (IRE)**[30] 4282 2-8-11 0 FrancisNorton 4 60
(R C Guest) *cl up: rdn over 1f out: led ent fnl f and sn drvn: hdd last 75yds: rallied gamely nr fin* **50/1**
5543 **3** ¾ **Masked Dance (IRE)**[11] 4912 2-8-8 63 (v) FrederikTylicki(3) 9 57
(K A Ryan) *sn cl up on outer: effrt 2f out: rdn and ev ch whn hung rt ent fnl f: sn drvn and kpt on* **9/2**[3]
4200 **4** ¾ **Final Ovation (IRE)**[43] 3871 2-8-11 75 GrahamGibbons 2 54
(J J Quinn) *led: rdn along 2f out: drvn and hdd ent fnl f: kpt on same pce* **5/2**[2]
0 **5** 1 ¾ **Croft Bridge**[13] 4844 2-8-11 0 TonyHamilton 6 48
(M Dods) *chsd ldrs: rdn along 2f out: sn drvn and wknd appr fnl f* **12/1**
3534 **6** 2 ¾ **Dower Glen**[15] 4773 2-8-7 62 ow1 TomEaves 1 34
(I Semple) *s.i.s: in rr tl sme hdwy over 1f out: nvr a factor* **12/1**
000 **7** 7 **Minnie Rocket**[87] 2414 2-7-13 20 JamesPSullivan(7) 7 8
(R C Guest) *a in rr* **100/1**
0 **8** 5 **Remember Dougie (IRE)**[26] 4398 2-8-3 0 ow4 SeanPalmer(7) 10 —
(A Berry) *s.i.s: a in rr* **100/1**
0 **9** 22 **Lady Laurem**[24] 4463 2-8-6 0 DuranFentiman 8 —
(D A Nolan) *dwlt: a in rr* **80/1**

62.11 secs (1.71) **Going Correction** +0.275s/f (Good) **9** Ran SP% **117.3**
Speed ratings (Par 92): **97,96,95,94,91 87,76,68,32**
toteswingers: 1&2 £10.10, 1&3 £1.90, 2&3 £15.10. CSF £65.34 TOTE £1.90: £1.10, £7.60, £1.40; EX 39.00.There was no bid for the winner.
Owner P D Savill **Bred** Ballykilbride Stud **Trained** Maunby, N Yorks

FOCUS
The ground was officially chanced to soft all over before this juvenile seller, which was run at a sound pace.

NOTEBOOK
Melody In The Mist(FR) followed up her success in a claimer at Thirsk 15 days earlier, but made very hard work of justifying favouritism. She was niggled at from an early stage and failed to travel with anything like her normal fluency. That was surely down to the different surface though and she is clearly tough as she just held on where it mattered. She was rightly dropped 4lb after her Thirsk win and will most probably be dropped again after this. (op 6-5)
Micky's Knock Off(IRE) had finished last on his previous two outings, but this drop in grade saw him prove a totally different proposition. He helped cut out the early pace and looked the most likely scorer passing the furlong pole, but wandered about in front and that allowed the winner a chance. He rallied though and so nearly got back up at the line. (op 40-1 tchd 66-1)
Masked Dance(IRE) posted an improved effort on this softer ground, but still looked far from straightforward. (op 5-1 tchd 6-1)
Final Ovation(IRE) is officially rated 75, but he has run miles below that mark in his last two outings and did so again here. This was a little better, however, and he would appreciate reverting to quicker ground. (op 3-1 tchd 9-4)
Croft Bridge was quickly dropped in grade for this second outing of his career and showed more as a result. (tchd 14-1)

5293 TOTEEXACTA H'CAP 5f
4:20 (4:24) (Class 3) (0-95,86) 3-Y-O+
£9,346 (£2,799; £1,399; £700; £349; £175) **Stalls** Low

Form RPR
3145 **1** **The Nifty Fox**[4] 5148 5-9-0 **77** DavidAllan 11 89+
(T D Easterby) *cl up: effrt over 1f out: rdn to ld appr fnl f: qcknd clr* **5/2**[1]
-040 **2** 1 ½ **Tornadodancer (IRE)**[14] 4831 6-9-6 **86** (v[1]) FrederikTylicki(3) 3 92
(T G McCourt, Ire) *cl up: stdd and lost pl after 1f: sn towards rr: pushed along and nt clr run 2f out: sn swtchd rt and rdn: hdwy and n.m.r ent fnl f: fin strly* **11/1**
5150 **3** *nk* **La Zamora**[3] 5203 3-9-0 **79** PhillipMakin 6 84+
(T D Barron) *dwlt: sn trcking ldrs: hdwy on outer wl over 1f out: rdn to chse wnr ins fnl f: sn drvn and nt qckn* **13/2**
6662 **4** *hd* **Fivefootnumberone (IRE)**[12] 4877 3-8-8 **73** (v) GrahamGibbons 9 78
(J J Quinn) *led: rdn along wl over 1f out: hdd appr fnl f and kpt on same pce* **6/1**[3]
006 **5** 2 **Stoneacre Lad (IRE)**[13] 4842 6-8-12 **75** (b) TomEaves 5 72
(Peter Grayson) *chsd ldrs: rdn along over 2f out: sn drvn and kpt on same pce* **11/1**
050 **6** 1 ½ **Stolt (IRE)**[11] 4891 5-9-3 **80** DanielTudhope 4 72
(N Wilson) *dwlt: sn chsng ldrs: rdn along wl over 2f out and sn btn* **9/2**[2]
2211 **7** ½ **Raccoon (IRE)**[12] 4877 9-8-12 **75** PJMcDonald 10 65
(Mrs R A Carr) *sn prom: rdn along wl over 1f out and sn wknd* **15/2**
0601 **8** 1 ½ **Rothesay Dancer**[4] 5149 6-9-5 **85** 6ex KellyHarrison(3) 2 70
(J S Goldie) *a in rr* **17/2**

60.90 secs (0.50) **Going Correction** +0.275s/f (Good)
WFA 3 from 4yo+ 2lb **8** Ran SP% **113.3**
Speed ratings (Par 107): **107,104,104,103,100 98,97,95**
toteswingers: 1&2 £5.20, 1&3 £4.70, 2&3 £11.00. CSF £30.75 CT £159.76 TOTE £3.30: £1.60, £3.20, £2.30; EX 27.60.
Owner Roy Peebles **Bred** Mrs Norma Peebles **Trained** Great Habton, N Yorks

FOCUS
This was a fair sprint handicap, but it was weakened by the non-runners. The winner was basically back to his best.

NOTEBOOK
The Nifty Fox, drawn widest of all, relished the underfoot conditions and ran out a ready winner under a positive ride. His two wins this term have been when the mud is flying and this was deserved. A likely rise should be enough to scupper him next time, however. (op 3-1)
Tornadodancer(IRE) likes this sort of ground. He hit a flat spot before running on strongly inside the final furlong and it is not hard to see why connections reached for the first-time visor. (op 10-1 tchd 14-1)
La Zamora, who had yet to race on this sort of ground, blew her chance at the start at York three days earlier and was again slowly away on this quick reappearance. She made her challenge more towards the centre and would've no doubt given the winner more to think about with a better break. She is still weighted to win, but now has a little to prove. (op 6-1)
Fivefootnumberone(IRE) was always in the firing line and reversed his last-time-out selling form with Raccoon. (op 13-2 tchd 7-1)
Stoneacre Lad(IRE) Official explanation: vet said horse was found to be lame left-fore
Raccoon(IRE) has had a great season, but needs better ground to shine. (op 7-1 tchd 6-1)

Rothesay Dancer, carrying a 6lb penalty, has never managed back-to-back wins, but was beaten very early on and ran no sort of race. Official explanation: jockey said mare was unsuited by the soft ground (op 7-1 tchd 9-1)

5294 SCOTTISH RACING H'CAP — 1m 4f 100y
4:50 (4:50) (Class 6) (0-65,64) 3-Y-O+ — £2,590 (£770; £385; £192) Stalls High

Form / RPR

0000 1 **Oddsmaker (IRE)**[20] 4588 8-8-10 54..........(t) AndrewHeffernan(7) 10 66
(M A Barnes) *trckd ldr: led after 4f and sn clr: rdn wl over 2f out: styd on strly fnl f* **20/1**

3233 2 4 **Grandad Bill (IRE)**[48] 3679 6-9-2 56.......... KellyHarrison(3) 8 62
(J S Goldie) *trckd ldrs: hdwy over 3f out: rdn to chse wnr wl over 1f out: sn drvn and no imp ins fnl f* **3/1**[1]

3333 3 2 1/4 **Dontpaytheferryman (USA)**[22] 4529 4-8-12 52....... FrederikTylicki(3) 7 54
(R A Fahey) *t.k.h: in tch: hdwy 3f out: rdn along over 2f out: drvn along on inner and styd on ins fnl f to take 3rd nr fin* **7/2**[2]

B206 4 shd **Whipma Whopma Gate (IRE)**[10] 4944 4-8-13 50.......... DNolan 4 52
(D Carroll) *hld up in rr: hdwy over 3f out: rdn to chse ldrs 2f out: sn drvn and one pce appr fnl f* **8/1**

-053 5 2 1/4 **Bed Fellow (IRE)**[16] 4755 5-8-8 45.......... TonyHamilton 13 43
(P Monteith) *t.k.h early: trckd ldrs: hdwy to chse wnr over 2f out and sn rdn: drvn wl over 1f out and grad wknd* **14/1**

0650 6 1 1/2 **Grethel (IRE)**[10] 4932 5-8-8 45.......... PJMcDonald 9 41
(A Berry) *towards rr: hdwy wl over 2f out: sn rdn and kpt on ins fnl f: nt rch ldrs* **20/1**

3440 7 1 3/4 **That'll Do Nicely (IRE)**[19] 4619 6-9-13 64.......... PhillipMakin 12 57
(N G Richards) *hld up in rr: hdwy wl over 2f out: sn rdn and kpt on ins fnl f: nvr rchd ldrs* **15/2**[3]

0455 8 1/2 **Bourse (IRE)**[10] 4944 4-9-0 51..........(p) AndrewMullen 6 43
(A G Foster) *hld up: hdwy over 4f out: rdn along and in tch over 2f out: sn drvn and no imp* **16/1**

2- 9 6 **Rue De Cabestan (IRE)**[33] 4185 4-8-13 57.......... IJBrennan(7) 5 40
(T G McCourt, Ire) *in midfield: hdwy over 5f out: rdn along on outer to chse ldrs 3f out: drvn and edgd rt 2f out: sn wknd* **16/1**

-040 10 nk **Kames Park (IRE)**[20] 4593 7-9-8 59.......... FrancisNorton 3 41
(R C Guest) *towards rr: swtchd outside and sme hdwy 3f out: rdn over 2f out and sn btn* **28/1**

0063 11 1 **Run Free**[12] 4874 5-8-6 48.......... BMcHugh(5) 1 29
(N Wilson) *led 4f: chsd wnr: rdn along over 3f out: sn wknd* **14/1**

0006 12 4 1/2 **Goswick**[23] 4506 3-8-3 50 ow2.......... JoeFanning 11 23
(Micky Hammond) *prom: rdn along 4f out: sn wknd* **28/1**

0000 13 3 1/4 **Boy Dancer (IRE)**[25] 4435 6-8-11 53.......... JamieKyne(5) 14 21
(J J Quinn) *a in rr* **25/1**

0005 14 4 **Sharp Sovereign (USA)**[10] 4943 3-8-7 54 ow1.......... TomEaves 2 16
(I Semple) *chsd ldrs on outer: rdn along 3f out and sn wknd* **20/1**

2m 50.14s (8.14) **Going Correction** +0.525s/f (Yiel)
WFA 3 from 4yo+ 10lb — **14** Ran SP% **120.2**
Speed ratings (Par 101): **93,90,88,88,87 86,85,84,80,80 79,76,74,72**
toteswingers: 1&2 £21.10, 1&3 £25.70, 2&3 £2.80. CSF £73.16 CT £269.94 TOTE £33.20: £7.70, £1.70, £1.70; EX 107.20.
Owner D Maloney **Bred** Margaret Conlon **Trained** Farlam, Cumbria

■ Stewards' Enquiry : Andrew Heffernan six-day ban: used whip with excessive frequency when clearly winning (Sep 6-11)

FOCUS
A moderate handicap, run at an uneven pace. The winner is flattered and the second helps to set the level backed up by the third.
Oddsmaker(IRE) Official explanation: trainer said, regarding apparent improvement in form, that the gelding was better suited by the soft ground.
Bourse(IRE) Official explanation: jockey said gelding hung right in straight

5295 TOTESWINGER H'CAP — 1m
5:20 (5:20) (Class 5) (0-70,70) 3-Y-O — £3,238 (£963; £481; £240) Stalls High

Form / RPR

5505 1 **Lakeman (IRE)**[13] 4841 3-9-4 67.......... TomEaves 3 77
(B Ellison) *in midfield: pushed along over 3f out: swtchd wd and rdn over 2f out: styd on to ld appr fnl f: sn drvn clr* **25/1**

1223 2 4 1/2 **Northern Flyer (GER)**[18] 4664 3-8-9 65.......... IJBrennan(7) 5 65+
(J J Quinn) *hld up towards rr: hdwy 3f out: effrt to chse ldrs 2f out: sn rdn and n.m.r over 1f out: swtchd lft and styd on ins fnl f* **11/4**[1]

-550 3 3/4 **Captain Flasheart (IRE)**[22] 4535 3-8-11 60.......... DavidAllan 10 58
(S C Williams) *t.k.h: in tch: hdwy 3f out: rdn to chal 2f out: led briefly over 1f out: sn hdd and drvn: kpt on same pce* **15/2**[3]

0445 4 1/2 **Pokfulham (IRE)**[49] 3659 3-8-9 58.......... DanielTudhope 1 55
(J S Goldie) *hld up in rr: hdwy 3f out: rdn and styng on whn nt clr run wl over 1f out: kpt on ins fnl f: nrst fin* **22/1**

3514 5 2 1/4 **Royal Premium**[14] 4819 3-8-7 59..........(v) FrederikTylicki(3) 11 51
(Mrs G S Rees) *trckd ldrs: hdwy 3f out: rdn to ld briefly 2f out: sn hdd: drvn and wknd appr fnl f* **11/4**[1]

6023 6 2 1/4 **Pegasus Lad (USA)**[10] 4956 3-9-6 69.......... JoeFanning 6 56
(M Johnston) *cl up: hdwy to ld 3f out and sn rdn: hdd 2f out: drvn and wknd over 1f out* **10/3**[2]

-260 7 6 **Bessie Lou (IRE)**[21] 4562 3-9-7 70.......... PhillipMakin 2 43
(K A Ryan) *prom: rdn along wl over 2f out: drvn and wkng whn edgd rt wl over 1f out* **14/1**

0053 8 1 1/4 **Trumpstoo (USA)**[18] 4660 3-9-7 70.......... TonyHamilton 7 40
(R A Fahey) *hld up in rr: sme hdwy on inner 3f out: rdn over 2f out and sn no imp* **11/1**

0606 9 6 **Clumber Place**[96] 2164 3-8-9 58.......... FrancisNorton 8 14
(R C Guest) *chsd ldrs: rdn along 3f out: sn drvn and wknd* **50/1**

500 10 2 1/2 **Viva La Vida**[17] 4720 3-9-4 67..........(v[1]) GrahamGibbons 4 17
(J Ryan) *a in rr* **28/1**

0305 11 8 **Trade Price (GR)**[15] 4777 3-7-12 52 oh2 ow1..........(p) JamieKyne(5) 9 —
(I Semple) *led: rdn along and hdd 3f out: sn wknd* **33/1**

1m 45.33s (4.13) **Going Correction** +0.525s/f (Yiel) — **11** Ran SP% **119.7**
Speed ratings (Par 100): **100,95,94,94,92 89,83,82,76,74 66**
toteswingers: 1&2 £13.30, 1&3 £23.70, 2&3 £6.40. CSF £91.14 CT £609.91 TOTE £37.20: £6.20, £1.20, £3.00; EX 138.90 Place 6 £15.66, Place 5 £6.45..
Owner The Country Stayers **Bred** Tally-Ho Stud **Trained** Norton, N Yorks

■ Stewards' Enquiry : Daniel Tudhope two-day ban: careless riding (Sep 6-7)

FOCUS
This modest handicap was run at a decent pace and the third and fourth set the standard.
T/Jkpt: Not won. T/Plt: £9.10 to a £1 stake. Pool: £70,856.09. 5,634.82 winning tickets. T/Qpdt: £3.60 to a £1 stake. Pool: £4,414.85. 891.02 winning tickets. JR

BREMEN
Sunday, August 23

OFFICIAL GOING: Good

5296a WALTHER J JACOBS-STUTENPREIS (GROUP 3) (F&M) — 1m 3f
3:35 (3:48) 3-Y-O+ — £31,068 (£9,709; £4,854; £2,913)

RPR

1 **Lady Jane Digby**[59] 3315 4-9-5.......... GregFairley 3 103
(M Johnston) *disp 2nd on ins: 3rd st: led 2f out: drvn out: jst hld on* **47/10**[2]

2 nse **Guantana (GER)**[50] 4-9-5.......... ADeVries 4 103
(J Hirschberger, Germany) *hld up in rr: moved outside 3f out: hrd rdn over 2f out: hung rt appr fnl f: r.o wl: jst failed* **13/10**[1]

3 4 1/2 **La Bamba (GER)**[50] 5-9-5.......... JBojko 8 95
(A Wohler, Germany) *hld up in rr: last st: styd on fnl 2f to take 3rd cl home* **11/1**

4 1/2 **Daveron (GER)**[50] 4-9-5.......... THellier 10 95
(A Trybuhl, Germany) *mid-div: hdwy and 7th st: rchd 3rd ins fnl f: one pce clsng stages* **67/10**

5 1 **Themelie Island (IRE)**[42] 4-9-5.......... WMongil 9 93
(A Trybuhl, Germany) *disp 4th: 5th st: 3rd over 1f out: no ex* **29/1**

6 1/2 **Goathemala (GER)**[50] 4-9-5.......... AStarke 12 92
(P Schiergen, Germany) *disp 2nd on outside: 2nd st: led briefly over 2f out to 2f out: one pce* **49/10**[3]

7 shd **Serienhoehe (IRE)**[21] 4583 3-8-10.......... KKerekes 5 92
(P Schiergen, Germany) *mid-div: hdwy and 6th st: one pce fnl 2f* **26/5**

8 1 1/2 **Stella Di Quattro**[28] 4365 5-9-5.......... RPiechulek 7 89
(Uwe Ostmann, Germany) *in rr to st: nvr a factor* **23/1**

9 7 **Dawn Dew (GER)**[14] 4-9-5.......... JiriPalik 6 77
(P Schiergen, Germany) *led to over 2f out* **30/1**

10 2 1/2 **So Pretty (GER)**[49] 3-8-10.......... ABest 1 73
(T Mundry, Germany) *disp 4th tl wkng 4f out* **40/1**

11 3/4 **Lunduv (IRE)**[28] 4365 4-9-5.......... APietsch 11 72
(C Von Der Recke, Germany) *disp 4th: 4th st: wknd over 2f out* **39/1**

2m 19.14s (139.14)
WFA 3 from 4yo+ 9lb — **11** Ran SP% **131.1**
TOTE (including 10 euro stake): WIN 57; PL 19, 15, 19; SF 204.
Owner Miss K Rausing **Bred** Miss K Rausing **Trained** Middleham Moor, N Yorks

NOTEBOOK
Lady Jane Digby followed up her success at Listed level at Newcastle with her first win in Group company, holding on by the narrowest of margins at the line.

5278 DEAUVILLE (R-H)
Sunday, August 23

OFFICIAL GOING: Turf course - good; all-weather - standard

5297a DARLEY PRIX KERGORLAY (GROUP 2) — 1m 7f
1:15 (1:15) 3-Y-O+ — £71,942 (£27,767; £13,252)

RPR

1 **Schiaparelli (GER)**[24] 4457 6-9-6.......... LDettori 1 111+
(Saeed Bin Suroor) *mde all: set even pce: accelerated on fnl turn: pushed clr fr 2f out: 6 l up ent fnl f: won pulling up* **1/5**[1]

2 3 **Mojave Moon**[35] 3-8-5.......... MGuyon 2 100
(A Fabre, France) *trckd wnr thrght: drvn 2f out: no imp but allowed to cl up fnl 100yds* **15/2**[3]

3 2 **Candy Gift (ARG)**[26] 4416 6-9-4.......... TJarnet 3 97
(T Clout, France) *hld up: last thrght: btn over 1 1/2f out* **6/1**[2]

3m 9.90s (-9.20) **Going Correction** -0.10s/f (Good)
WFA 3 from 4yo+ 13lb — **3** Ran SP% **109.4**
Speed ratings: **120,118,117**
PARI-MUTUEL (including 1 Euro stake): WIN 1.10 (coupled with Mojave Moon): SF 3.60.
Owner Godolphin **Bred** Gestut Karlshof **Trained** Newmarket, Suffolk

NOTEBOOK
Schiaparelli(GER) cantered along at the head of affairs before his jockey quickened things up coming out of the final turn. He then built up a lead of ten lengths by the furlong marker but was eased considerably in the last 100yards. He has been entered in the Arc de Triomphe and will now be aimed at the Prix Foy. (op 1/4)
Mojave Moon, was always in second position which he kept until the end. He never had any chance of catching the winner. (op 13/2)
Candy Gift(ARG) never looked like catching the winner and the runner-up and was always last of the three runners. He goes for the long-distance Prix Gladiateur at Longchamp next month. (op 11/2)

5298a DARLEY PRIX DE LA NONETTE (GROUP 3) (FILLIES) — 1m 2f
2:20 (2:23) 3-Y-O — £38,835 (£15,534; £11,650; £7,767; £3,883)

RPR

1 **Charity Belle (USA)**[33] 4166 3-9-0.......... LDettori 3 106
(J H M Gosden) *mde all: strly chal 1 1/2f out: drvn clr fnl 100yds: r.o wl* **11/1**

2 1/2 **Article Rare (USA)**[98] 2119 3-9-0..........(p) ACrastus 4 105
(E Lellouche, France) *dismntd and walked to s: trckd wnr: 3rd fr 1/2-way: ev ch on ins fr 1 1/2f out to 100yds out: one pce* **7/1**[3]

3 snk **Eclair De Lune (GER)**[29] 4334 3-9-0.......... CSoumillon 2 105
(Y De Nicolay, France) *hld up: wnt 4th bef 1/2-way: r.o down outside fr over 1f out: nrest at fin* **25/1**

4 1 1/2 **Proportional**[22] 4578 3-9-0.......... SPasquier 1 102
(Mme C Head-Maarek, France) *racd in 4th: 5th fr 1/2-way: nvr able to chal* **2/1**[2]

5 hd **Black Rose (FR)**[29] 4334 3-9-0.......... IMendizabal 6 101
(F Chappet, France) *hld up: last: rdn and c wdst 2f out: sn rdn: styd on: n.d* **25/1**

6 1/2 **Tamazirte (IRE)**[70] 2952 3-9-0.......... C-PLemaire 5 100
(J-C Rouget, France) *racd in 3rd: wnt 2nd 1/2-way: chal on outside 2f out: drvn and ev ch appr fnl f: no ex* **1/1**[1]

2m 7.30s (-2.90) **Going Correction** -0.10s/f (Good) — **6** Ran SP% **111.9**
Speed ratings: **107,106,106,105,105 104**
PARI-MUTUEL: WIN 10.20; PL 4.70, 3.20; SF 52.90.
Owner H R H Princess Haya Of Jordan **Bred** Stonerside Stable **Trained** Newmarket, Suffolk

NOTEBOOK

Charity Belle(USA) put up a very brave effort, especially as she was being moved up considerably in class following a second place in a handicap at Ffos Las. She was asked to make every yard of the running and did so bravely. She looks as if she may stay further and there are no plans for the moment, although it would be no surprise if she is entered in the Prix Vermeille.

Article Rare(USA), who had previously won a Group 3 race at this track, produced a decent performance on her first start since May. She came with a challenge up the far rail but could never quite peg back the winner. (op 13/2)

Eclair De Lune(GER), in mid-division in the early stages, had room to challenge coming into the final furlong and was putting in her best work at the end.

Proportional was disappointing and probably didn't like the ground, which was certainly on the fast side. Held up, she had room to challenge a furlong and a half out but wouldn't let herself down. She will be seen again when there is a little more cut in the ground.

5299a DARLEY PRIX MORNY (GROUP 1) (C&F) 6f

2:50 (2:53) 2-Y-O **£194,165** (£77,680; £38,840; £19,403; £9,718)

RPR

1 **Arcano (IRE)**[45] 3779 2-9-0 .... RHills 1 116
(B J Meehan) *hld up in last pl: hrd rdn 1 1/2f out: drvn and r.o to ld last strides* **9/2**[2]

2 *snk* **Special Duty**[28] 4366 2-8-11 .... SPasquier 4 113
(Mme C Head-Maarek, France) *led: drvn fnl f: ct last strides* **7/1**[3]

3 *nk* **Canford Cliffs (IRE)**[68] 2993 2-9-0 .... RichardHughes 2 115
(R Hannon) *trckd ldr: pushed along on rails 2f out: hrd rdn fnl f: kpt on same pce* **4/9**[1]

4 *nk* **Dolled Up (IRE)**[28] 4366 2-8-11 .... OPeslier 5 111
(Robert Collet, France) *racd in cl 4th: drvn fr 2f out: kpt on same pce fnl f* **40/1**

5 *hd* **Zanzibari (USA)**[21] 4579 2-9-0 .... LDettori 3 113
(A Fabre, France) *fastest away: pressed ldr fr outside: rdn 1/2-way: no ex fr dist* **9/1**

67.90 secs (-3.30) **Going Correction** -0.35s/f (Firm) **5** Ran SP% **112.4**
Speed ratings: **108,107,107,107,106**
PARI-MUTUEL: WIN 5.50; PL 2.70, 2.50; SF 22.60 (Broke all-aged course record).
Owner Hamdan Al Maktoum **Bred** Yellow Bird Syndicate **Trained** Manton, Wilts

■ Stewards' Enquiry : Richard Hughes 100euro fine: whip abuse

NOTEBOOK

Arcano(IRE) was given a waiting ride and brought with a challenge at exactly the right moment. He had to be moved right around the runner-up entering the final furlong but produced a fine turn of foot. He is certainly a colt going the right way and connections feel he will be even better suited by 7f. There are no definite plans for the moment, but races like the Dewhurst Stakes and the Prix Jean Luc Lagardere will certainly be considered in the future. He smashed the race record by 2 secs and the track record by a second. He was made favourite for next year's 2000 Guineas by most of the British bookmakers. (op 5/1)

Special Duty ran a cracker and tried to do it the hard way by making all the running. She set a blistering pace from the start and really quickened things up after halfwayg. She still looked the winner at the furlong marker but just failed in her brave attempt to make it at Group 1 level. Connections now have their eyes on the Cheveley Park Stakes at Newmarket, providing she comes out of the race in good form.

Canford Cliffs(IRE) may have been at a disadvantage by hugging the stands' rail during the final 2f. He was only beaten by under half a length and was given every possible chance but couldn't quicken inside the final furlong and maybe he wasn't quite wound up after his ten-week break following Royal Ascot. There are no plans for the moment.

Dolled Up(IRE) appeared on the scene at the furlong marker up the centre of the track. She ran on really well and was only beaten by under a length. It was a decent effort by this 5f Group winner and softer ground may well be to her advantage.

5300a PRIX JEAN ROMANET (GROUP 1) (F&M) 1m 2f

3:20 (3:23) 4-Y-O+ **£138,689** (£55,485; £27,743; £13,859; £6,942)

RPR

1 **Alpine Rose (FR)**[56] 3443 4-9-0 .... GMosse 2 116
(A De Royer-Dupre, France) *first to show: trcking her ldr after 1f: 3rd fr over 6f out to st: led 2f out: rdn out* **1/1**[1]

2 *shd* **Lady Marian (GER)**[21] 4580 4-9-0 .... LDettori 5 116
(Saeed Bin Suroor) *last st: qckly moved through on ins to chal wl over 1f out: hrd rdn fnl f: r.o wl but unable to wear down wnr* **5/2**[2]

3 *3* **La Boum (GER)**[40] 3969 6-9-0 .... TJarnet 6 110
(Robert Collet, France) *hld up: wnt 4th 1/2-way: brought wdst: drvn over 1f out: kpt on to take 3rd clsng stages* **11/1**

4 *snk* **Danse Grecque (USA)**[21] 4580 4-9-0 .... ACrastus 3 110
(E Lellouche, France) *racd in 4th: 5th st: wnt 3rd 1 1/2f out: one pce u.p fnl f* **8/1**

5 *3* **Synergy (FR)**[28] 4365 4-9-0 .... OPeslier 4 104
(Y Durepaire, Spain) *racd in 3rd: wnt up to press ldr over 6f out: 2nd st: sn one pce* **6/1**[3]

6 *15* **Nostaltir (FR)**[49] 7-9-0 .... DBoeuf 1 74
(D Prod'Homme, France) *led to 2f out* **100/1**

2m 5.50s (-4.70) **Going Correction** -0.10s/f (Good) **6** Ran SP% **113.3**
Speed ratings: **114,113,111,111,109 97**
PARI-MUTUEL: WIN 2.10 (coupled with Nostaltir); PL 1.40, 2.00; SF 6.70.
Owner Ecurie Des Monceaux, Skymarc Farm, Moussac Family **Bred** H H Aga Khan's Stud's S C **Trained** Chantilly, France

■ Stewards' Enquiry : L Dettori 100euro fine: whip abuse

NOTEBOOK

Alpine Rose(FR) settled just behind the leaders as her pacemaker went along in front. She took the lead at the 2f marker and was then joined by the runner-up. The pair had a ding-dong battle to the line and she prevailed by a short head. It was a decent performance as she had come in season two days before and she is certainly better on softer ground. There was no definite decision about the future but she has the options of the Prix Foy and the Arc, or to stay around a similar distance and be aimed at the Prix de l'Opera. Her trainer feels she will be even more of a force to be reckoned with in the future.

Lady Marian(GER), last season's Opera winner, put up a much better performance than on her previous starts for Godolphin. She was allowed to gallop along in last pace for much of the early stages, and was then brought round the turn on the inside and went in pursuit of the winner before they battled throughout the final furlong. Only beaten by a few inches, she looks back to her best form and may well go for back-to-back wins in the Opera.

La Boum(GER), as usual was waited with and came bustling along towards the end of the race. She never had a chance with the winner and the runner-up but took third place in the final 50 yards. (op 10/1)

Danse Grecque(USA) followed the winner for much of the early stages and seemed to be going well coming into the straight. She was then one paced to the line and may have been feeling the quick ground.

5301a PRIX DE SAINT JULIEN LE FAUCON (CLAIMER) (ALL WEATHER) 1m 4f

4:20 (4:21) 4-Y-O+ **£7,282** (£2,913; £2,184; £1,456; £728)

RPR

1 **Greenwich Meantime**[3] 5204 9-9-2 .... KirstyMilczarek 75
(E J O'Neill) *mde all: clr fr over 1f out: r.o strly (19/10)*

2 *2* **Miss Tonic (FR)**[166] 5-9-3 .... (b) DelphineSantiago 73
(K Borgel, France)

3 *4* **Blue Fang (IRE)**[39] 4-8-11 .... NadegeOuakli 61
(T Clout, France)

4 *1 1/2* **Have A Nice Day (GER)**[707] 5462 4-8-8 55
(S Smrczek, Germany)

5 *nk* **Atlantic King (FR)**[28] 5-9-6 67
(F Vermeulen, France)

6 *1* **The Countess**[88] 4-8-6 .... (2) 53
(J Clais, France)

7 *1 1/2* **Lettori (FR)**[36] 8-9-2 .... (b) 59
(F Bossert, France)

8 *3* **Lower Dicker (FR)**[649] 6-8-11 49
(Mlle M-L Mortier, France)

9 *3/4* **Supsonic**[14] 6-8-11 48
(R Le Gal, France)

10 *2 1/2* **Peace Of Cake (FR)**[46] 5-8-6 .... (6) 45
(Mme M-C Naim, France)

0 **Spectral (FR)**[14] 7-8-11 .... (p) —
(J Merienne, France)

0 **Baby's Memory (FR)**[998] 5-8-8 .... —
(P Vovcenko, Germany)

0 **Baie Aux Anges (FR)** 4-8-5 .... (3) —
(T Doumen, France)

2m 42.4s (162.40) **13** Ran
PARI-MUTUEL: WIN 2.90; PL 1.80, 2.80, 7.50; DF 11.00.
Owner Barlow, Crumbley & Rutherford **Bred** Juddmonte Farms **Trained** Southwell, Notts

4477 OVREVOLL (R-H)

Sunday, August 23

OFFICIAL GOING: Good

5302a MARIT SVEAAS MINNELOP (GROUP 3) 1m 1f

3:00 (12:00) 3-Y-O+ **£79,444** (£25,819; £11,917; £7,150; £4,767)

RPR

1 **Theatrical Award (NOR)**[14] 4-8-13 .... CarlosLopez 7 —
(Marianne Tveter, Norway) *held up in mid-division, headway 2f out, challenged inside final furlong, led 50yds out, ran on (12.74/1)* **127/10**

2 *1/2* **Appel Au Maitre (FR)**[35] 4128 5-9-6 .... FJohansson 8 —
(Wido Neuroth, Norway) *took keen hold, held up in mid-division, headway 4f out, ran on under pressure to lead 2f out, headed 50yds out, one pace* **1/2**[1]

3 *4* **Smart Enough**[41] 6-9-4 .... RSchistl 13 —
(F Reuterskiold, Sweden) *held up towards rear, ridden 2f out, stayed on, never nearer* **25/1**

4 *1/2* **Chicken Momo**[24] 4477 3-8-13 .... PascolinaPinto 1 —
(A Lund, Norway) *led to 2f out, kept on one pace* **23/5**[2]

5 *2* **Quilboquet (BRZ)**[21] 6-9-4 .... WilliamBuick 14 —
(L Reuterskiold Jr, Sweden) *pressed leaders, 4th straight, weakened final f* **33/1**

6 *hd* **Prince Fasliyev**[57] 3419 5-9-4 .... LennartHammer-Hansen 15 —
(Niels Petersen, Norway) *in rear til headway 3f out, close up 2f out, weakened final f* **23/1**

7 *1/2* **Tertullus (FR)**[21] 4582 6-9-4 .... EspenSki 6 —
(Rune Haugen, Norway) *held up in rear, ridden 3f out, some progress but never a factor* **20/1**

8 *2* **Volo Cat (FR)**[21] 4585 5-9-4 .... JacobJohansen 9 —
(B Olsen, Denmark) *held up in rear to straight, some late progress* **103/1**

9 *nse* **Alnitak (USA)**[21] 4585 8-9-4 .... (b) KAndersen 10 —
(B Olsen, Denmark) *prominent, ridden 3f out, soon weakened* **108/1**

10 *2 1/2* **Half Pint Bill**[41] 6-9-4 .... JosephineChini 12 —
(D Persson, Sweden) *never nearer than midfield* **98/1**

11 *nse* **Luca Brasi (FR)**[21] 4585 5-9-4 .... ManuelMartinez 2 —
(F Castro, Sweden) *tracked leader to straight, soon weakened* **41/1**

12 *1 1/2* **Peas And Carrots (DEN)**[21] 4585 6-9-6 .... EddieAhern 3 —
(L Reuterskiold Jr, Sweden) *mid-division, brief effort 3f out, soon beaten* **78/10**[3]

13 *2* **Dan Tucket**[21] 4585 4-9-4 .... FDiaz 5 —
(B Olsen, Denmark) *prominent to well over 2f out* **76/1**

14 *1 1/2* **The Pirate (DEN)**[364] 5335 6-9-4 .... P-AGraberg 4 —
(Eva Sundbye, Sweden) *raced in 3rd to straight, soon weakened* **73/1**

15 *16* **Archived (IRE)**[666] 6495 4-9-4 .... (b) MLarsen 11 —
(Are Hyldmo, Norway) *prominent to 3f out* **72/1**

1m 50.0s (0.10)
WFA 3 from 4yo+ 7lb **15** Ran SP% **128.2**
(including one krone stakes) WIN 13.74; PL 2.80, 1.20, 3.71; DF 76.80.
Owner Stall Bernadette **Bred** Johan Sohlberg **Trained** Norway

5157 HAMILTON (R-H)

Monday, August 24

OFFICIAL GOING: Heavy (soft in places; 8.0)
Wind: Light half behind Weather: Dry and sunny

5303 HAMILTON-PARK.CO.UK TWO YEAR OLD CLAIMING STKS 6f 5y

2:20 (2:28) (Class 6) 2-Y-O **£2,266** (£674; £337; £168) **Stalls** Low

Form RPR

0402 1 **Sands Of Dee (USA)**[16] 4773 2-8-8 65........................ PaulHanagan 4 66
(R A Fahey) *chsd ldr: hdwy wl over 1f out: rdn to ld ins fnl f: kpt on* **5/1**[3]

5433 **2** 3/4 **Masked Dance (IRE)**[1] 5292 2-8-10 63........................(v) PhillipMakin 5 66
(K A Ryan) *led: rdn and hung rt over 1f out: sn drvn: hdd ins fnl f and kpt on same pce* **11/2**

4264 **3** 4 **Saint Sebastian (IRE)**[21] 4590 2-8-9 64........................ GrahamGibbons 2 53
(E S McMahon) *in tch: hdwy over 2f out: rdn and n.m.r wl over 1f out: sn chsng ldng pair: drvn and no imp ent fnl f* **5/2**[2]

5201 **4** 3/4 **Pure Nostalgia (IRE)**[37] 4101 2-8-7 64........................ FrederikTylicki(3) 1 52
(J Howard Johnson) *towards rr: pushed along 1/2-way: rdn and hdwy on inner wl over 1f out: sn rdn and no imp* **6/4**[1]

0040 **5** 8 **Countrywide Ice (IRE)**[17] 4739 2-8-9 52..............(p) SilvestreDeSousa 6 27
(K A Ryan) *prom: rdn along over 2f out and sn wknd* **12/1**

6640 **6** 3/4 **Dispol Kabira**[33] 4188 2-8-4 54 ow9.................................. DTDaSilva(7) 8 26
(D W Thompson) *chsd ldrs on outer: rdn along wl over 2f out and sn wknd* **16/1**

0630 **7** 1 1/4 **Lord's Seat**[21] 4590 2-8-2 53.. BillyCray(7) 3 21
(A Berry) *s.i.s: a in rr* **50/1**

1m 15.3s (3.10) **Going Correction** +0.525s/f (Yiel) 7 Ran SP% **116.2**
Speed ratings (Par 92): **100,99,93,92,82 81,79**
toteswingers: 1&2 £2.40, 1&3 £2.60, 2&3 £2.90 CSF £33.12 TOTE £5.90: £2.40, £2.90; EX 24.00.Sands of Dee was claimed by P J. Dixon for £7000.
Owner Mrs Carol P McPhail **Bred** Mike Abraham **Trained** Musley Bank, N Yorks

FOCUS
A modest claimer in which they finished well strung out. They finished well strung out and the two market leaders were disappointing.

NOTEBOOK
Sands Of Dee(USA) headed into uncharted territory on this first try on oppressive ground. He tracked the leader for most of the way, responded gamely to pressure and eventually gained the initiative to win with a bit to spare. He gave an 80-rated rival a few anxious moments in a 5f claimer at Ayr last time on his first run since a gelding operation, and produced a likeable display to take this contest. He could be capable of further improvement on testing ground and a current mark of 63 could be within his grasp. (op 9-2 tchd 4-1)
Masked Dance(IRE) set a decent pace against the near rail and looked to have his rivals in trouble approaching the final furlong but was just overhauled in the closing stages after being backed at 1.03 in-running on the exchanges. He has been regressive and expensive to follow since a promising debut effort, but this was a decent step back in the right direction and he handled the testing ground well. It is hard to know what the form amounts to but he could be a force off a mark of 63 back in a handicap under similar conditions. (tchd 13-2)
Saint Sebastian(IRE) was a bit short of room at one stage but did not really pick when seeing daylight. This has to rate as a disappointment from the son of Group 2 heavy-ground winner Captain Rio, and he has now been beaten at short prices in his last four starts. (op 4-1)
Pure Nostalgia(IRE) forced a dead-heat dropped into a seller on soft ground just over five weeks earlier. She had reasonable form claims but was under pressure a long way out and never got involved. (op 7-4 tchd 2-1)
Countrywide Ice(IRE), faced with a tough task at the weights, raced near the pace in first-time cheekpieces but folded up quite quickly. (op 14-1)

5304 SCOTTISH RACING BUSINESS CLUB MEDIAN AUCTION MAIDEN STKS 6f 5y
2:50 (2:53) (Class 5) 3-4-Y-O **£2,590** (£770; £385; £192) **Stalls** Low

Form RPR
2302 **1** **Liberty Trail (IRE)**[16] 4772 3-9-3 68........................ TomEaves 2 65
(I Semple) *mde all: rdn and hung rt over 1f out: drvn and edgd lft ins fnl f: kpt on* **4/7**[1]

3042 **2** 1 1/4 **Carnival Dream**[10] 4995 4-9-1 52........................(b) PJMcDonald 1 56
(H A McWilliams) *trckd ldrs: effrt on inner 2f out: rdn over 1f out: swtchd rt and ev ch ent fnl f: sn drvn and no ex* **6/1**[3]

3 2 3/4 **Catchpenny** 3-8-12 0........................ PhillipMakin 5 47
(K A Ryan) *trckd ldng pair: hdwy and ev ch 2f out: sn rdn and edgd rt appr fnl f: sn btn* **3/1**[2]

606 **4** 28 **Our Girl Ally (IRE)**[5] 5163 3-8-5 0........................(t) BillyCray(7) 6 —
(A Berry) *prom on wd outside: rdn along wl over 2f out: sn wknd* **40/1**

1m 15.91s (3.71) **Going Correction** +0.525s/f (Yiel)
WFA 3 from 4yo 3lb 4 Ran SP% **105.4**
Speed ratings (Par 103): **96,94,90,53**
CSF £4.14 TOTE £1.50; EX 2.60.
Owner G L S Partnership **Bred** Clougher Partnership **Trained** Carluke, S Lanarks

FOCUS
An ordinary maiden with the winner not needing to run to his best.
Our Girl Ally(IRE) Official explanation: jockey said filly hung right

5305 NATIONAL HUNT PROSPECTS CLAIMING STKS 1m 1f 36y
3:20 (3:21) (Class 4) 3-5-Y-O **£5,180** (£1,541; £770; £384) **Stalls** High

Form RPR
3120 **1** **Sunnyside Tom (IRE)**[27] 4409 5-9-7 84........................ PaulHanagan 2 84
(R A Fahey) *mde all: jnd and rdn over 1f out: kpt on wl u.p ins fnl f* **4/5**[1]

0000 **2** 1 **Fishforcompliments**[4] 5200 5-9-7 95..............(p) FrederikTylicki(3) 4 85
(R A Fahey) *sn trcking wnr: effrt 2f out: rdn and ev ch over 1f out: drvn ins fnl f: no ex last 100yds* **11/4**[2]

3 **3** 1 **First Bay (IRE)**[29] 4347 3-9-3 0........................ PhillipMakin 6 83
(J Howard Johnson) *dwlt: sn trcking ldng pair: pushed along and outpcd 3f out: hdwy 2f out and sn rdn: styng on whn swtchd rt and ch ent fnl f: sn edgd lft and one pce* **9/2**[3]

00-0 **4** 14 **Jim Martin**[55] 3481 4-8-7 63........................ JamesPSullivan(7) 5 45
(Miss L A Perratt) *t.k.h early: trckd ldng pair: effrt 3f out: rdn along over 2f out: wknd wl over 1f out* **14/1**

2m 7.34s (7.64) **Going Correction** +1.025s/f (Soft)
WFA 3 from 4yo+ 7lb 4 Ran SP% **107.1**
Speed ratings (Par 105): **107,106,105,92**
CSF £3.18 TOTE £1.80; EX 3.20.
Owner The Sunnyside Racing Partnership **Bred** S W D McIlveen **Trained** Musley Bank, N Yorks

FOCUS
A decent claimer but difficult form to pin down. Two stablemates with official marks of 84 and 95 dominated the betting and had a sustained duel against the near rail in the straight.

5306 RACING UK H'CAP 1m 65y
3:50 (3:50) (Class 6) (0-60,60) 3-Y-O **£2,590** (£770; £385; £192) **Stalls** High

Form RPR
0234 **1** **Mohawk Ridge**[49] 3684 3-9-4 60........................ PhillipMakin 4 68
(M Dods) *hld up in tch: hdwy 3f out: cl up 2f out: rdn to ld appr fnl f and styd on strly* **3/1**[2]

6332 **2** 4 **Hettie Hubble**[12] 4894 3-8-4 53 ow5........................ DTDaSilva(7) 9 52
(D W Thompson) *hld up towards rr: hdwy over 3f out: rdn over 2f out: led briefly over 1f out: drvn and hdd appr fnl f: kpt on same pce* **5/1**[3]

-600 **3** 3 **Lady Norlela**[13] 4876 3-8-4 46 oh1........................(t) DuranFentiman 7 38
(T J Fitzgerald) *midfield: effrt over 3f out and sn rdn along: styd on u.p fnl 2f: n.d* **50/1**

0510 **4** 1/2 **Ask Dan (IRE)**[12] 4897 3-9-0 56........................(p) TomEaves 5 47
(M Dods) *led after 1f and sn clr: rdn along 3f out: drvn 2f out and sn hdd: grad wknd* **11/2**

0550 **5** 6 **Dark Echoes**[39] 4004 3-8-7 49........................ TonyHamilton 2 26
(Jedd O'Keeffe) *towards rr: hdwy 3f out and sn rdn along: kpt on u.p fr over 1f out: nvr nr ldrs* **12/1**

51 **6** 4 1/2 **Jenny's Pride (IRE)**[26] 4425 3-8-11 56........................ FrederikTylicki(3) 3 23
(John A Harris) *sn chsng clr ldr: hdwy over 3f out: rdn wl over 2f: sn drvn andwknd* **9/4**[1]

6065 **7** 3 1/4 **More Tea Vicar (IRE)**[13] 4879 3-7-13 48........................ JamesPSullivan(7) 8 7
(Patrick Morris) *s.i.s: a in rr* **18/1**

0004 **8** 5 **Our Apolonia (IRE)**[21] 4589 3-7-11 46 oh1........................(b[1]) BillyCray(7) 1 —
(A Berry) *a in rr: eased fnl f* **50/1**

0-66 **9** 7 **Elements (IRE)**[31] 4277 3-8-13 55........................ DavidAllan 10 —
(E J Alston) *chsd ldrs: rdn along over 3f out: sn wknd and bhd whn eased over 1f out* **14/1**

003 **10** 4 1/2 **Elusive Style (IRE)**[40] 3975 3-8-4 46 oh1........................ AdrianTNicholls 6 —
(S P Griffiths) *led 1f: chsd ldrs: rdn along over 3f out and sn wknd: bhd whn eased over 1f out* **16/1**

1m 55.92s (7.52) **Going Correction** +1.025s/f (Soft) 10 Ran SP% **117.2**
Speed ratings (Par 98): **103,99,96,95,89 85,81,76,69,65**
toteswingers: 1&2 £4.10, 1&3 £39.00, 2&3 £52.20 CSF £18.66 CT £624.22 TOTE £4.30: £1.80, £2.70, £13.80; EX 21.50.
Owner Doug Graham **Bred** Old Mill Stud Ltd And Oomswell Ltd **Trained** Denton, Co Durham

FOCUS
A weak-looking handicap run at a strong pace in the testing conditions. The runners had managed just three wins between them in a total of 73 starts. The winner up is rated a slight improver with the second close to her recent best.
Jenny's Pride(IRE) Official explanation: trainer had no explanation for the poor form shown
Elusive Style(IRE) Official explanation: jockey said filly had no more to give

5307 SCOTTISH RACING ON BIG SCREEN AMATEUR RIDERS' H'CAP 1m 5f 9y
4:20 (4:20) (Class 6) (0-65,64) 4-Y-O+ **£2,307** (£709; £354) **Stalls** High

Form RPR
3620 **1** **Terenzium (IRE)**[16] 4806 7-10-0 50 oh4........................(p) MrSWalker 2 59+
(Micky Hammond) *hld up in tch: hdwy 5f out: n.m.r on inner and swtchd rt over 3f out: led over 2f out and rdn clr: kpt on* **5/2**[1]

0025 **2** 1 1/2 **John Forbes**[17] 4742 7-10-12 62........................ MissLEllison 8 66
(B Ellison) *trckd ldng pair: hdwy to chse ldr 5f out: sn cl up: rdn along and sltly outpcd 3f out: drvn along over 1f out: styd on ins fnl f: tk 2nd nr fin* **5/2**[1]

4002 **3** nk **Front Rank (IRE)**[14] 4848 9-9-9 50 oh3........................ MissECSayer(5) 5 54
(Mrs Dianne Sayer) *sn led: rdn along over 3f out: hdd wl over 2f out: sn drvn and kpt on u.p: lost 2nd nr fin* **8/1**[3]

20 **4** 10 **Rudry World (IRE)**[31] 4263 6-10-2 57........................ MissMMullineaux(5) 3 47
(M Mullineaux) *hld up in rr: hdwy 3f out: rdn along 2f out: plugged on same pce: nvr a factor* **12/1**

300/ **5** 6 **Emotive**[89] 6561 6-9-9 50 oh5........................ DarylMillar(5) 6 32
(F P Murtagh) *trckd ldrs: effrt over 3f out and sn rdn: drvn over 2f out and sn wknd* **20/1**

4334 **6** shd **Edas**[29] 4345 7-10-9 64........................ MissHCuthbert(5) 1 45
(T A K Cuthbert) *hld up in rr: hdwy over 3f out: rdn to chse ldrs on wd outside 2f out: sn wknd* **8/1**[3]

-003 **7** 6 **Art Gallery**[20] 4617 5-9-12 55 oh5 ow5........................ MrJMQuinlan(7) 4 28
(D W Thompson) *chsd ldr: rdn along over 5f out: wknd wl over 3f out* **22/1**

0544 **8** 9 **Royal Flynn**[29] 4350 7-10-0 57........................(b) MrJHBrooke(7) 7 17
(Mrs K Walton) *trckd ldrs: hdwy and cl up 4f out: rdn along 3f out and sn wknd* **11/2**[2]

3m 9.09s (15.19) **Going Correction** +1.025s/f (Soft) 8 Ran SP% **111.6**
Speed ratings (Par 101): **94,93,92,86,83 82,79,73**
toteswingers: 1&2 £2.30, 1&3 £5.90, 2&3 £4.10 CSF £7.84 CT £39.52 TOTE £2.90: £1.50, £1.10, £2.50; EX 9.90.
Owner O'Sunburn Partnership **Bred** Azienda Agricola Patrizia **Trained** Middleham Moor, N Yorks

FOCUS
A modest handicap run at a very steady pace and the form looks weak with the first and third both out of the handicap.

5308 OFFICER AND A GENTLEMAN EVENING ON FRIDAY H'CAP 1m 3f 16y
4:50 (4:50) (Class 5) (0-75,74) 4-Y-O+ **£3,885** (£1,156; £577; £288) **Stalls** High

Form RPR
0-40 **1** **Bajan Parkes**[22] 4561 6-9-4 74........................ DavidAllan 3 83
(E J Alston) *early reminders: sn prom: chsd ldr after 3f: rdn along and sltly outpcd over 3f out: effrt to ld over 2f out: sn drvn clr and hung bdly rt over 1f out: hrdrdn on far rail ins fnl f: styd on wl* **4/1**[3]

0210 **2** 2 1/2 **Maslak (IRE)**[9] 5028 5-9-4 74........................ PhillipMakin 6 78
(P W Hiatt) *hld up: hdwy over 3f out: rdn to chse wnr wl over 1f out: sn drvn and styd on ins fnl f: nt rch wnr* **5/2**[2]

4550 **3** 6 **Shady Gloom (IRE)**[26] 4426 4-9-2 72........................ PaulHanagan 4 66
(K A Ryan) *led: rdn along over 3f out: edgd rt and hdd over 2f out: sn drvn and one pce fr over 1f out* **16/1**

0103 **4** 5 **Ibrox (IRE)**[18] 4710 4-8-12 68........................ SilvestreDeSousa 1 54
(A D Brown) *hld up: effrt 5f out and sn pushed along: rdn over 3f out: nvr a factor* **6/4**[1]

5031 **5** 4 1/2 **They All Laughed**[62] 3233 6-8-9 65........................ PJMcDonald 5 43
(Mrs Marjorie Fife) *trckd ldr: hdwy and cl up 3f out: sn rdn along and wknd over 2f out* **9/2**

2m 35.83s (10.23) **Going Correction** +1.025s/f (Soft) 5 Ran SP% **112.6**
Speed ratings (Par 103): **103,101,96,93,89**
CSF £14.63 TOTE £5.10: £2.50, £1.20; EX 17.10.
Owner Joseph Heler **Bred** Joseph Heler **Trained** Longton, Lancs

FOCUS
A fair handicap but several were disappointing and the winner put in a wayward performance. The time was 14 seconds outside standard and the form, rated through the runner-up, should be treated with some caution.
Bajan Parkes Official explanation: trainer was unable to offer any explanation for the apparent improvement in form.

5309 HOWARD AND NANCY MCDOWALL MEMORIAL H'CAP 5f 4y
5:20 (5:21) (Class 6) (0-60,57) 4-Y-O+ **£2,266** (£674; £337; £168) **Stalls** Low

Form RPR
0361 **1** **The Bear**[12] 4899 6-9-4 57........................ TonyHamilton 5 69
(Miss L A Perratt) *qckly away and wnt lft after s: mde all: rdn clr wl over 1f out: edgd rt and kpt on wl u.p ins fnl f* **9/2**[2]

0024 **2** 1 1/2 **Sunley Sovereign**[5] 5147 5-9-2 **55**........................(b) SilvestreDeSousa 3 62
(Mrs R A Carr) *bmpd sn after s: chsd ldrs: swtchd rt and rdn to chse wnr over 1f out: sn drvn and no imp ins fnl f* **3/1**[1]

362 **3** 3 **Lake Chini (IRE)**[13] 4886 7-9-4 **57**..................................(b) DaleGibson 2 53
(M W Easterby) *bmpd s and sn pushed along in midfield: rdn 2f out: drvn over 1f out: kpt on u.p ins fnl f: tk 3rd nr fin* **3/1**[1]

5000 **4** nk **Howards Tipple**[16] 4778 5-8-9 **48**..................................(p) TomEaves 11 43
(I Semple) *chsd ldrs: hdwy 2f out and sn rdn to chse ldng pair: drvn ins fnl f: one pce and lost 3rd nr fin* **12/1**

4515 **5** 1 3/4 **Andrasta**[8] 5073 4-9-0 **53**.. AdrianTNicholls 8 42
(A Berry) *t.k.h early: hld up: hdwy 2f out: rdn and n.m.r over 1f out: kpt on ins fnl f: nrst fin* **12/1**

0300 **6** 3/4 **First Swallow**[5] 5150 4-9-2 **55**.. PaulHanagan 12 41
(R A Fahey) *chsd ldrs: swtchd rt and rdn 2f out: sn drvn and no imp* **17/2**

0000 **7** 3/4 **Miacarla**[42] 3909 6-7-13 **45**..(t) JamesPSullivan(7) 9 28
(H A McWilliams) *chsd ldrs: rdn along 2f out: sn wknd* **33/1**

0000 **8** 1 1/4 **Prospect Court**[29] 4346 7-8-13 **57**.. JamieKyne(5) 1 36
(A C Whillans) *wnt rt s: midfield: rdn along 1/2-way: n.d* **8/1**[3]

0-00 **9** nse **George The Best (IRE)**[130] 1310 8-8-8 **50**................ FrederikTylicki(3) 7 29
(Micky Hammond) *in tch: rdn along 1/2-way: sn wknd* **22/1**

0 **10** 9 **Rue Soleil**[5] 5159 5-8-7 **46** ow1..(b) PJMcDonald 6 —
(J R Weymes) *chsd ldrs: effrt over 2f out: sn rdn and wknd* **50/1**

000 **11** 3 1/4 **Little Pandora**[31] 4281 5-8-6 **45**..(t) DuranFentiman 4 —
(L R James) *a in rr* **80/1**

00-0 **12** 7 **Take That**[145] 1061 4-8-6 **45**.. AndrewMullen 13 —
(S P Griffiths) *dwlt: a in rr* **100/1**

62.46 secs (2.46) **Going Correction** +0.525s/f (Yiel) 12 Ran SP% **116.7**
Speed ratings (Par 101): **101,98,93,93,90 89,88,86,86,71 66,55**
toteswingers: 1&2 £3.20, 1&3 £1.90, 2&3 £3.90 CSF £17.47 CT £46.79 TOTE £5.90: £1.60, £1.50, £1.40; EX 21.40 Place 6: £73.66 Place 5: £17.22.
Owner Cincinnati Club **Bred** P G Airey And R R Whitton **Trained** East Kilbride, South Lanarks
■ Stewards' Enquiry : James P Sullivan one-day ban: failed to ride to draw (Sep 7)

FOCUS
A minor handicap and not form to rate too positively.
T/Plt: £186.20 to a £1 stake. Pool: £52,210.67. 204.68 winning tickets. T/Qpdt: £26.00 to a £1 stake. Pool: £3,732.82. 106.00 winning tickets. JR

5164 KEMPTON (A.W) (R-H)
Monday, August 24

OFFICIAL GOING: Standard
Wind: Moderate, across Weather: Cloudy becoming fine

5310 LADIES DAY SATURDAY SEPTEMBER 5TH NURSERY 5f (P)
2:10 (2:12) (Class 6) (0-65,64) 2-Y-O **£2,047** (£604; £302) **Stalls** High

Form RPR

0063 **1** **Candyfloss Girl**[19] 4647 2-9-1 **58**.. DavidProbert 9 62
(H J L Dunlop) *chsd ldng trio: drvn and effrt to cl over 1f out: led last 150yds: asserted w tail swishing* **10/3**[1]

0540 **2** 1 1/2 **Papageno**[33] 4208 2-9-6 **63**.. JimCrowley 10 62
(J R Jenkins) *chsd ldng pair: effrt on inner over 1f out to chal ent fnl f: outpcd by wnr last 100yds* **17/2**

440 **3** 3/4 **Little Brazilien**[18] 4688 2-9-5 **62**..(b[1]) WilliamBuick 5 58
(P F I Cole) *chsd ldr: rdn to chal over 1f out: nt qckn and btn ins fnl f: clung on to 3rd* **8/1**

0050 **4** nse **Exceed Power**[33] 4208 2-9-0 **57**..(t) ChrisCatlin 6 53+
(D M Simcock) *dwlt: hld up in last pair: wl off the pce 2f out: rapid prog though hanging 1f out: r.o wl and nrly tk 3rd* **16/1**

130 **5** nk **Annia Galeria (IRE)**[13] 4868 2-8-11 **57**.. AndreaAtzeni(3) 7 52
(C A Dwyer) *led: hrd pressed over 1f out: hdd last 150yds: wknd nr fin* **12/1**

000 **6** hd **Precious Coral (IRE)**[23] 4542 2-9-7 **64**.. PatDobbs 12 59+
(S A Callaghan) *dwlt: hld up in last trio: wl off the pce 2f out: rapid prog on inner 1f out: running on and looked likely to grab 3rd whn snatched up nr fin* **11/2**[3]

3655 **7** 1 1/2 **Flapjack**[17] 4757 2-9-6 **63**.. RyanMoore 11 52
(R Hannon) *nvr on terms w ldrs: 6th and rdn over 1f out: no imp after* **7/2**[2]

44 **8** hd **Rightcar**[41] 3952 2-8-12 **55**.. SimonWhitworth 8 43
(Peter Grayson) *awkward s: chsd ldrs: rdn in 5th 1/2-way and nt on terms: no prog after* **20/1**

3550 **9** 9 **Boga (IRE)**[12] 4901 2-9-3 **60**.. SteveDrowne 1 15+
(R J Hodges) *t.k.h early: hld up in rr: 7th whn snatched up 1/2-way: bhd over 1f out* **40/1**

056 **10** 1 1/2 **The Midshipmaid**[59] 3337 2-8-13 **56**.. DarryllHolland 4 6+
(Lucinda Featherstone) *rousted along early: rn v wd bnd over 3f out: struggling in rr after* **8/1**

61.60 secs (1.10) **Going Correction** 0.0s/f (Stan) 10 Ran SP% **114.2**
Speed ratings (Par 92): **91,88,87,87,86 86,84,83,69,67**
toteswingers: 1&2 £8.80, 1&3 £4.70, 2&3 £14.60 CSF £31.33 CT £212.62 TOTE £3.50: £1.20, £3.20, £2.90; EX 35.10.
Owner Stephen J Buckmaster **Bred** Baroness Bloodstock **Trained** Lambourn, Berks

FOCUS
A run-of-the-mill nursery, with just two previous wins among the contestants. The runner-up sets the initial level.

NOTEBOOK
Candyfloss Girl's tail-flashing is not endearing, but it appears to be a habit rather than betraying any lack of enthusiasm, because she also did it in the paddock, at the stalls and in the unsaddling enclosure. The drop to 5f was no problem, since she had the pace to stay in touch with the two front-runners, but a return to 6f will be within her scope. (op 7-2 tchd 3-1)
Papageno had made his nursery debut off a 5lb higher mark but now he has been reassessed he is capable of getting off the mark. This was an encouraging first run on the all-weather. (op 10-1)
Little Brazilien, who was blinkered for the first time, chased the lively gallop. She again did reasonably well but is not quite living up to the promise of her debut. (op 11-2)
Exceed Power, first home of those who came from behind, has not run over 6f since his debut and looks capable of winning a Polytrack nursery if stepped back up in trip.
Annia Galeria(IRE) improved on her Polytrack debut with a solid effort from the front, but she forced a smart gallop which eventually set things up for those in pursuit of her. (op 16-1)
Precious Coral(IRE) ◆, whose previous three runs had been over longer trips, made eyecatching late headway up the rail mainly under hands and heels. She looks capable of winning a nursery, with a return to 6f likely to be in her favour. Official explanation: jockey said filly was slowly away (op 13-2 tchd 15-2)
Official explanation: jockey said filly suffered interference in running
The Midshipmaid Official explanation: jockey said filly resented the kickback

5311 PANORAMIC BAR & RESTAURANT MAIDEN STKS 6f (P)
2:40 (2:42) (Class 4) 2-Y-O **£2,520** (£2,520; £577; £288) **Stalls** High

Form RPR

1 **Haadeeth** 2-9-3 0.. RHills 7 78
(M P Tregoning) *trckd ldng pair: shkn up to chal over 1f out: narrow ld 100yds out: jnd post* **6/1**[3]

0 **1** dht **Brick Red**[10] 4986 2-9-3 0.. WilliamBuick 12 78
(A M Balding) *s.i.s: t.k.h early and hld up in midfield: plld out and prog over 1f out: drvn to chal fnl f: forced dead heat post* **12/1**

2 **3** 1 1/4 **Elusive Trader (USA)**[17] 4746 2-9-3 0.. RyanMoore 10 74
(R Hannon) *led 2f: trckd ldr: led wl over 1f out: hdd and outpcd last 100yds* **10/11**[1]

4 1 1/2 **Barlaman (USA)** 2-9-3 0.. LDettori 4 70+
(Saeed Bin Suroor) *s.s: sn in tch: shkn up and prog on outer 2f out: wnt 4th fnl f but no imp on ldrs after* **7/2**[2]

5 1/2 **Gypsy Boy (USA)** 2-9-3 0.. SimonWhitworth 6 68+
(R Curtis) *s.s: hld up in last trio: nudged along and styd on encouragingly fnl 2f: nrst fin* **20/1**

3 **6** 1 3/4 **Gold Crusher (USA)**[34] 4173 2-9-3 0.. ShaneKelly 9 63
(R M H Cowell) *cl up on inner: nrly on terms w ldrs 2f out: shkn up and nt qckn over 1f out: fdd* **14/1**

7 nse **Avenuesnalleyways (IRE)** 2-9-3 0.. SebSanders 8 63
(R M Beckett) *dwlt: t.k.h early and sn in midfield: nt qckn 2f out: no imp on ldrs after* **25/1**

8 1 3/4 **Rain On The Wind (IRE)** 2-9-3 0.. SteveDrowne 11 57
(S C Williams) *fractious preliminaries: plld fiercely: led after 2f: hdd & wknd wl over 1f out* **100/1**

9 3/4 **Maashooq** 2-9-3 0.. TPO'Shea 5 55
(M P Tregoning) *rn green and a in last trio: plugged on* **25/1**

60 **10** 2 1/2 **Motty's Gift**[63] 3218 2-9-3 0.. AdamKirby 3 48
(W R Swinburn) *rn green and a in last trio: struggling over 2f out* **100/1**

11 1 1/2 **Mount Juliet (IRE)** 2-8-12 0.. DarryllHolland 2 38
(S A Callaghan) *t.k.h early: sn prom fr wd draw: 5th over 3f out: wknd over 2f out* **66/1**

1m 13.94s (0.84) **Going Correction** 0.0s/f (Stan) 11 Ran SP% **119.2**
Speed ratings (Par 96): **94,94,92,90,89 87,87,84,83,80 78**
WIN: BR £6.40, H £3.10 PL: BR£2.80, H £1.50 ET £1.30; EX: BR/H £35.90, H/BR £37.80 CSF: BR/H £39.06, H/BR £34.47 toteswingers: Brick Red&Haadeeth £7.30, Brick Red& £4.70, Haadeth&3 £3.00.
Owner Brick Racing **Bred** Raimon Bloodstock **Trained** Kingsclere, Hants
Owner Hamdan Al Maktoum **Bred** Bolton Grange **Trained** Lambourn, Berks

FOCUS
Little experience on display, with seven debutants in the line-up and not an easy race to pin down. The early pace was modest, though the free-running Rain On The Wind, who looked a handful beforehand, soon raced up to set a better tempo.

NOTEBOOK
Haadeeth showed excellent battling qualities in the finish on this debut run. Already gelded, this £80,000 Oasis Dream half-brother to a 7f juvenile winner should continue to earn his keep. Trainer Marcus Tregoning rates him as a "nice type", reporting that he had come through everything that had been thrown at him at home. (op 17-2 tchd 11-2)
Brick Red, down the field on his debut, which had been on turf over 7f, took the drop in trip and switch to Polytrack in his stride and picked up well when pulled off the rail. William Buick says he is still backward and should improve. (op 17-2 tchd 11-2)
Elusive Trader(USA), stepping up from 5f, ran his second solid race in two attempts, both on Polytrack. Though failing to live up to market expectations here, he looks good enough to win a maiden. (op Evens tchd 11-10)
Barlaman(USA), very noisy in the paddock, made a promising debut. A son of the top-class US 7f-1m dirt performer Langfuhr and from a good winning family, he should improve enough to win races. (op 3-1)
Gypsy Boy(USA), by the US dirt winner Dixie Union and out of a winner from 6f to 1m on the same surface, shaped encouragingly without being knocked about. He is one to keep an eye on. (op 25-1)
Gold Crusher(USA) has run with credit in his three maidens and now looks ready to go close in nursery company. Official explanation: jockey said colt moved poorly throughout (op 16-1)
Avenuesnalleyways(IRE), a Bertolini half-brother to three winners up to 1m, showed ability on this debut despite finding traffic problems in the straight. He should benefit from the experience.
Rain On The Wind(IRE) Official explanation: jockey said colt ran too freely

5312 EUROPEAN BREEDERS' FUND MAIDEN STKS 1m (P)
3:10 (3:11) (Class 5) 2-Y-O **£3,561** (£1,059; £529; £264) **Stalls** High

Form RPR

4 **1** **Togiak (IRE)**[17] 4756 2-9-3 0.. TPQueally 3 81+
(E A L Dunlop) *wl plcd on outer: prog to trck ldrs over 3f out: gng easily over 2f out: chal over 1f out: narrow ld ins fnl f: r.o wl and a doing enough* **5/1**[3]

02 **2** nk **Navy List (FR)**[16] 4790 2-9-3 0.. LDettori 4 80+
(Saeed Bin Suroor) *prom: trckd ldr 1/2-way: shkn up to ld over 1f out: narrowly hdd ins fnl f: r.o but a jst hld* **7/2**[2]

3 4 **Udabaa (IRE)** 2-9-3 0.. TPO'Shea 11 71+
(M P Tregoning) *chsd ldr to 1/2-way: styd prom: outpcd by ldng trio 2f out: kpt on to take 3rd ins fnl f* **12/1**

63 **4** 1 1/2 **James Barrymore**[7] 5106 2-9-3 0.. RyanMoore 1 68
(R Hannon) *led and crossed fr wdst draw: kicked on over 2f out: hdd over 1f out: wknd ins fnl f and lost 3rd* **8/1**

5 1/2 **Sharaayeen** 2-9-3 0.. RHills 10 67+
(B W Hills) *prog fr midfield to chse ldrs 3f out: outpcd 2f out: pushed along and kpt on steadily* **13/8**[1]

6 **6** 3 1/2 **Trewarthenick**[22] 4568 2-9-3 0.. LPKeniry 13 59+
(A M Balding) *chsd ldrs: rdn and wl outpcd fr jst over 2f out: plugged on but no ch after* **20/1**

7 7 **Keleyf Byon Belief (IRE)** 2-8-12 0.. PaulFitzsimons 5 39
(Edgar Byrne) *early reminder: sn chsd ldrs: wl outpcd fr over 2f out* **80/1**

00 **8** 2 1/4 **Downtoobusiness**[33] 4201 2-9-3 0.. DarryllHolland 7 39
(Karen George) *nvr beyond midfield: rdn and wl outpcd fr over 2f out* **100/1**

9 3 1/2 **Veni Vedi Veci (IRE)** 2-8-12 0.. WilliamBuick 9 26
(A M Balding) *prom early: lost pl rapidly and in last pair 5f out: brief effrt on wd outside over 2f out: sn lft bhd* **25/1**

3 **10** shd **Rock Of Eire**[18] 4717 2-9-0 0.. AlanCreighton(3) 12 31
(E J Creighton) *chsd ldrs to 3f out: sn wknd u.p* **66/1**

3 **11** 1 1/2 **Christopher Wren (USA)**[33] 4201 2-9-3 0.. SteveDrowne 2 28+
(J R Best) *stmbld bdly s: mostly in last trio: brief effrt on outer over 2f out: sn lft wl bhd* **16/1**

04 **12** 3/4 **Hellenio**[19] 4638 2-9-3 0 .... DavidProbert 6 26
(S C Williams) *s.v.s: a wl in rr: brief effrt on inner over 2f out: sn lft wl bhd* **25/1**

13 1 1/4 **Clayton Flick (IRE)** 2-9-3 0 .... SebSanders 8 23
(A B Haynes) *t.k.h: hld up wl in rr: last 3f out: sn lft bhd by ldrs* **80/1**

1m 40.85s (1.05) **Going Correction** 0.0s/f (Stan) **13** Ran SP% **119.1**
Speed ratings (Par 94): **94,93,89,88,87 84,77,74,71,71 69,69,67**
toteswingers: 1&2 £4.10, 1&3 £10.20, 2&3 £9.50 CSF £21.63 TOTE £5.90: £1.90, £1.80, £3.30; EX 30.10.
Owner Mrs Susan Roy **Bred** John And Leslie Young **Trained** Newmarket, Suffolk

FOCUS
This looked a pretty good maiden but, following a modest gallop, which made it hard to come from too far back, the finish was dominated by two runners who had set a fair if unspectacular standard in their previous races. However, there were several behind who should do better with racing.

NOTEBOOK
Togiak(IRE) made a comfortable switch to Polytrack and, staying the 1m well, just got the better of his rival with a tenacious effort. This Racing Post Trophy entry would be flying rather high in that sort of company but he should enjoy further success at a decent level. (op 11-2 tchd 7-1)
Navy List(FR) continues to get closer with each race and is capable of finding a maiden rather than having to switch to nurseries just yet. Trainer Saeed Bin Suroor confirmed that he is still improving. (tchd 3-1)
Udabaa(IRE) ◆, a 190,000gns Alhaarth half-brother to four winners at a variety of trips, is entered for the Dewhurst, Racing Post Trophy and Royal Lodge. He benefited from racing handily in a modestly-run race but still showed some potential for juvenile staying events. Trainer Marcus Tregoning, describing him as "very big and very weak", expects him to need more time, so this was a good first attempt. (tchd 10-1)
James Barrymore has shown definite promise in three maidens. He has always looked like a nursery sort in the making and should be noted at his first attempt in that company. (op 13-2)
Sharaayeen, a fit-looking, strongly-made 85,000gns Singspiel half-brother to a sprinter and a middle-distance winner, is entered for the Racing Post Trophy and Derby. Green in the paddock, he was done for speed when the tempo stepped up, but he was staying on near the finish and looks a likely improver given a stronger gallop. (op 7-4 tchd 15-8)
Trewarthenick is not without ability but looks a nursery type in the making. (tchd 22-1)
Christopher Wren(USA) Official explanation: jockey said colt stumbled at the start

5313 EUROPEAN BREEDERS' FUND CONDITIONS STKS 1m (P)
3:40 (3:40) (Class 3) 3-Y-O+
£8,598 (£2,575; £1,287; £644; £321; £161) **Stalls** High

Form RPR

2320 **1** **Ashram (IRE)**[23] 4521 3-8-11 110 .... (v) LDettori 6 108+
(Saeed Bin Suroor) *dwlt: pushed up and sn cl up on inner and keen briefly: effrt to ld wl over 1f out: rdn and styd on wl after* **6/4[1]**

1016 **2** 1 1/4 **Brief Encounter (IRE)**[23] 4521 3-8-11 96 .... LPKeniry 5 105+
(A M Balding) *hld up in tch: pushed along over 2f out: drvn and prog over 1f out: styd on to take 2nd last 75yds: unable to chal* **4/1[3]**

0040 **3** 1 **Chantilly Tiffany**[54] 3516 5-8-12 105 .... SebSanders 1 98
(E A L Dunlop) *trckd ldrs: gng strly 3f out: effrt to chal 2f out: chsd wnr wl over 1f out: nt qckn and hld after: lost 2nd last 75yds* **9/1**

0402 **4** 1 3/4 **Dixey**[22] 4560 4-8-12 90 .... PhilipRobinson 7 93
(M A Jarvis) *led: increased the pce fr 1/2-way: hdd wl over 1f out: fdd ins fnl f* **12/1**

5060 **5** nk **Vitznau (IRE)**[24] 4486 5-9-3 100 .... RyanMoore 2 98
(R Hannon) *chsd ldrs on outer: nt qckn over 2f out: tried to rally over 1f out: fdd fnl f* **12/1**

1266 **6** 1/2 **Hyades (USA)**[25] 4455 3-8-11 91 .... TPQueally 4 96+
(H R A Cecil) *nt wl away: hld up in last: rdn and no rspnse 2f out* **7/2[2]**

0244 **7** 1 1/4 **Fullback (IRE)**[17] 4760 3-8-11 89 .... LukeMorris 3 93
(J S Moore) *trckd ldr to over 2f out: sn lost pl and btn* **20/1**

1m 38.66s (-1.14) **Going Correction** 0.0s/f (Stan)
WFA 3 from 4yo+ 6lb **7** Ran SP% **112.4**
Speed ratings (Par 107): **105,103,102,101,100 100,98**
toteswingers: 1&2 £1.90, 1&3 £2.90, 2&3 £7.50 CSF £7.38 TOTE £2.10: £1.30, £2.80; EX 9.70.
Owner Godolphin **Bred** Waterford Hall Stud **Trained** Newmarket, Suffolk

FOCUS
A good-quality race for the track, though the pace was disappointingly weak for the first 2f. The form makes sense rated through the winner.

NOTEBOOK
Ashram(IRE) missed the break and pulled too hard, but was still too quick for his rivals after Dettori made a decisive move up the inside at the cutaway 2f out. His turf form was good enough to win this, and he adapted well enough to the Polytrack in this lower grade, though he is not scaling the heights that might have been expected this season. (tchd 11-8 and 13-8, 7-4 in places)
Brief Encounter(IRE), a smart handicapper on turf, had done well in his only previous Polytrack attempt. He had 14lb to find with the winner on official figures, so it was a creditable effort. (op 7-2 tchd 3-1)
Chantilly Tiffany has been inconsistent in Group company this season, but the best of her form meant she was joint top-rated with the winner here. She ran adequately, but is generally disappointing these days. (op 12-1)
Dixey had the run of the race out in front, but still did reasonably well considering the disadvantageous terms. (op 10-1)
Vitznau(IRE) wins infrequently and was just outclassed by better rivals. (op 14-1 tchd 16-1)
Hyades(USA) would not have been suited by the slack tempo. A strongly-run 1m, or even 1m2f, will bring out the best in him, but he never looked comfortable in the rear and a return to turf should also be in his favour. Official explanation: jockey said colt was slowly away (op 4-1)
Fullback(IRE) was a bit out of his depth but did not fare too badly. (op 28-1 tchd 33-1)

5314 KEMPTON.CO.UK MEDIAN AUCTION MAIDEN STKS 1m 4f (P)
4:10 (4:10) (Class 6) 3-5-Y-O **£2,047** (£604; £302) **Stalls** Centre

Form RPR

2243 **1** **Bagber**[19] 4650 3-9-3 75 .... RyanMoore 8 82
(H J L Dunlop) *mde all: clr w runner-up over 2f out: urged along wout use of whip and a holding on* **5/4[1]**

06 **2** 2 1/4 **Bengal Tiger**[32] 4246 3-9-3 0 .... WilliamBuick 5 78
(A M Balding) *hld up in 4th: wd bnd 3f out: prog to chse wnr sn after: rdn to chal 2f out: nt qckn and hld fnl f* **6/1**

62- **3** 7 **Attainable**[334] 6205 3-8-12 0 .... JimCrowley 9 62
(Mrs A J Perrett) *trckd ldng pair: rdn over 3f out: disp 2nd briefly wl over 2f out: sn wl outpcd* **11/4[2]**

2233 **4** 2 1/2 **Pyrus Time (IRE)**[16] 4789 3-9-3 72 .... LukeMorris 7 63
(J S Moore) *hld up in last pair: effrt 3f out but sn outpcd by ldng pair: no imp after* **5/1[3]**

0-0 **5** 1 1/2 **Largem**[25] 4472 3-9-3 0 .... SimonWhitworth 2 60
(J R Jenkins) *racd wd thrght in abt 5th: lost grnd bnd 3f out: sn lft bhd: no ch whn reminder 1f out* **66/1**

0 **6** 9 **Be Kind**[14] 4854 3-8-12 0 .... DarryllHolland 4 41
(Karen George) *nvr gng that wl in last: lft bhd fr over 3f out* **20/1**

0 **7** 15 **Rainiers Girl**[16] 4789 3-8-12 0 .... LPKeniry 6 17
(R A Teal) *stdd s: t.k.h early: and hld up in 6th: reminder 5f out: lft bhd fr 4f out: t.o* **50/1**

/00- **8** 2 **Mr Plod**[255] 902 4-9-13 0 .... (p) SebSanders 1 19
(Andrew Reid) *chsd wnr to wl over 2f out: wknd rapidly and eased: t.o* **66/1**

2m 33.28s (-1.22) **Going Correction** 0.0s/f (Stan)
WFA 3 from 4yo 10lb **8** Ran SP% **111.8**
Speed ratings (Par 101): **104,102,97,96,95 89,79,77**
CSF £8.84 TOTE £2.00: £1.10, £2.40, £1.60; EX 10.40.
Owner R J McCreery & Major & Mrs R B Kennard **Bred** Stowell Hill Ltd & Major & Mrs R B Kennard **Trained** Lambourn, Berks

FOCUS
The pace was respectable, but Ryan Moore judged it perfectly and always had enough up his sleeve. The form is not that solid but looks worth a chance at this level.

5315 DAY TIME, NIGHT TIME, GREAT TIME H'CAP 1m 4f (P)
4:40 (4:40) (Class 3) (0-95,92) 3-Y-O
£7,352 (£2,201; £1,100; £551; £274; £138) **Stalls** Centre

Form RPR

051 **1** **Lethal Glaze (IRE)**[38] 4045 3-9-7 92 .... PatDobbs 3 100
(R Hannon) *chsd ldr: pushed along 4f out: u.p and no imp over 2f out: clsd grad 1f out: drvn ahd last stride* **12/1**

1634 **2** hd **Becausewecan (USA)**[23] 4520 3-8-8 79 .... RHills 1 87
(M Johnston) *led at decent pce: 3 l up and gng best over 2f out: rdn over 1f out: kpt on: hdd last stride* **3/1[2]**

3214 **3** 4 **North Cape (USA)**[15] 4827 3-8-3 74 .... FrankieMcDonald 4 76
(H Candy) *hld up in 4th: effrt over 2f out to chse ldng pair: no imp fr over 1f out* **16/1**

1 **4** 2 **Bawadi (USA)**[10] 4979 3-9-5 90 .... LDettori 7 88
(Saeed Bin Suroor) *awkward s: hld up in last pair: effrt 3f out: rdn and rchd 4th over 1f out but no prog after* **5/2[1]**

-232 **5** 1 **State Banquet (USA)**[26] 4420 3-9-0 85 .... (p) SteveDrowne 2 82
(H Morrison) *mostly in 3rd: pushed along over 4f out to dispute 2nd: grad wknd fr over 2f out* **3/1[2]**

1061 **6** 16 **Puzzlemaster**[25] 4471 3-9-1 86 .... DarryllHolland 5 57
(M Botti) *mostly in 5th: pushed along 4f out: wknd over 2f out: t.o* **11/2[3]**

610 **7** 22 **Pictorial (USA)**[45] 3822 3-8-10 81 .... RyanMoore 6 17
(Sir Michael Stoute) *a in last pair: wknd 3f out: wl t.o* **10/1**

2m 32.38s (-2.12) **Going Correction** 0.0s/f (Stan) **7** Ran SP% **116.6**
Speed ratings (Par 104): **107,106,104,102,102 91,76**
toteswingers: 1&2 £4.70, 1&3 £10.20, 2&3 £13.90 CSF £49.50 TOTE £13.00: £4.10, £2.20; EX 50.00.
Owner Nigel Morris **Bred** B Kennedy **Trained** East Everleigh, Wilts

FOCUS
The runner-up led everywhere except the line, with Hills setting a good gallop throughout and having all his rivals off the bridle turning for home. He rates as having run a slight personal best.

NOTEBOOK
Lethal Glaze(IRE) has made his way steadily up the handicap in the last year and this first run on the all-weather was in line with his progressive form on turf. Though only just getting there on the line, he won over 1m6f in his previous race and this trip is a minimum for him these days. Trainer Richard Hannon reported that he had switched him to sand because he needs "a bit of juice" in the ground on turf, something which is hard to find in the south at present.
Becausewecan(USA), sweating beforehand, deserves plaudits for a fine front-running performance, especially as he maintained a sharp tempo from the word go. Agonisingly for his connections and supporters, he did not quite make it, but Hills deserves much credit for his usual excellent judgement of pace from the front, and any criticism of his tactics for being over-forceful is way off the mark. (tchd 11-4 and 7-2)
North Cape(USA) has been doing well at 1m2f, and the step up to 1m4f did not bring about any obvious extra improvement, though he appears to stay it well enough. (tchd 20-1)
Bawadi(USA), a winner over 1m2f here on his debut, was beaten more by lack of tactical speed than the extra 2f. He never looked likely to win, and this handicap mark may prove to be on the stiff side. Official explanation: jockey said colt missed the break (op 11-4 tchd 3-1)
State Banquet(USA), with cheekpieces this time, was making his all-weather debut but failed to maintain his recent form on turf. He can do better back on grass. (tchd 11-4)
Puzzlemaster has given the impression that he should stay 1m4f but in practice did not improve for the longer trip, though he was beaten too far for that that to be the only reason for defeat. (op 8-1)

5316 BOOK KEMPTON TICKETS ON 0844 579 3008 CLASSIFIED STKS 7f (P)
5:10 (5:10) (Class 6) 3-Y-O+ **£2,047** (£604; £302) **Stalls** High

Form RPR

365 **1** **Jonnie Skull (IRE)**[18] 4697 3-8-12 55 .... (vt) TPQueally 12 59
(P S McEntee) *chsd ldng pair: rdn 2f out: styd on to take 2nd ent fnl f: narrow ld last 75yds: kpt on* **11/2[2]**

0660 **2** hd **Come On Buckers (IRE)**[18] 4719 3-8-12 55 .... EdwardCreighton 6 58
(E J Creighton) *led at decent pce: drvn over 1f out: kpt on wl u.p: hdd last 75yds* **20/1**

0-55 **3** 3/4 **Fitz**[9] 5019 3-8-12 55 .... LPKeniry 1 56+
(M Salaman) *dropped in fr wdst draw and hld up in last pair: swtchd sharply lft over 2f out and rdn: gd prog jst over 1f out: styd on to take 3rd nr fin* **11/2[2]**

0500 **4** 1/2 **Piccolinda**[23] 4535 3-8-12 55 .... (b[1]) JimCrowley 5 55
(W R Muir) *chsd ldr: rdn wl over 2f out: hld over 1f out and lost pl ent fnl f* **20/1**

P603 **5** nse **Sirjosh**[26] 4425 3-8-12 55 .... (t) JerryO'Dwyer 4 55+
(D Donovan) *dropped in fr wd draw and hld up in last pair: sme prog fr over 2f out: kpt on u.p: nvr quite rchd ldrs* **8/1**

0560 **6** 1 3/4 **Rosie Two**[11] 4937 3-8-12 48 .... IanMongan 7 50
(W S Kittow) *wl in rr: effrt on outer over 2f out: prog over 1f out: one pce fnl f* **66/1**

30 **7** 1 **Minnola**[23] 4552 4-9-3 54 .... SaleemGolam 14 50
(Rae Guest) *nvr beyond midfield: rdn bef 1/2-way: effrt on inner over 2f out but no real prog fnl 2f* **4/1[1]**

4564 **8** 2 1/4 **Extracurricular (USA)**[18] 4719 3-8-12 55 .... DarryllHolland 13 41
(S Gollings) *settled wl in rr: shkn up over 2f out: no prog over 1f out* **11/1**

5-05 **9** 3/4 **Sparkling Suzie**[18] 4694 3-8-12 55 .... LukeMorris 9 39
(J S Moore) *wl in rr: rdn 1/2-way: sme prog 2f out: no hdwy and btn over 1f out* **25/1**

2600 **10** 3/4 **Motor Home**[6] 5124 3-8-12 55 .... (v) WilliamBuick 8 37
(A M Balding) *trckd ldrs: rdn and no rspnse over 2f out: fdd over 1f out* **11/2[2]**

50-5 **11** 1/2 **Queens Flight**[24] 4505 3-8-12 53 .... RichardKingscote 11 36
(Tom Dascombe) *chsd ldrs: rdn over 2f out: wknd fr over 1f out* **13/2[3]**

0602 **12** 33 **Rockson (IRE)**[33] 4196 3-8-12 54 .... SebSanders 2 —
(Ian Williams) *prom on outer for 3f: wknd rapidly 1/2-way: t.o* **7/1**

00 13 2 3/4 **Set Em Up Mo**[187] 594 3-8-12 53 .... KirstyMilczarek 3 —
(M J Attwater) *a in rr: wknd 1/2-way: t.o* **50/1**

1m 27.55s (1.55) **Going Correction** 0.0s/f (Stan)
WFA 3 from 4yo 5lb **13** Ran SP% **128.3**
Speed ratings (Par 101): **91,90,89,89,89 87,86,83,82,81 81,43,40**
toteswingers: 1&2 £27.30, 1&3 £10.70, 2&3 £26.00 CSF £121.66 TOTE £7.40: £2.20, £8.60, £2.70; EX 134.40 Place 6: £39.46 Place 5: £16.70.
Owner Mrs Rebecca McEntee **Bred** Canice Farrell Jnr **Trained** Newmarket, Suffolk

FOCUS
A weak race, though competitive for the grade with the winner probably the best guide. They went a decent gallop, but prominent runners generally did well.
Rockson(IRE) Official explanation: jockey said filly stopped very quickly
Set Em Up Mo Official explanation: jockey said filly was never travelling
T/Plt: £30.40 to a £1 stake. Pool: £62,589.49. 1,502.27 winning tickets. T/Qpdt: £11.10 to a £1 stake. Pool: £3,666.96. 244.00 winning tickets. JN

5096 WINDSOR (R-H)

Monday, August 24

OFFICIAL GOING: Good to firm
Wind: Moderate across Weather: Cloudy

5317 EUROPEAN BREEDERS' FUND MAIDEN STKS (DIV I) 6f
2:30 (2:30) (Class 5) 2-Y-O **£3,561** (£1,059; £529; £264) **Stalls** High

Form RPR

3 1 **Sunraider (IRE)**[15] 4825 2-9-3 0 .... RobertWinston 9 83+
(B W Hills) *w ldr: led over 2f out: hung lft and narrowly hdd appr fnl f: rallied u.p and stl hanging whn led again fnl 20yds* **4/6**[1]

2 1/2 **Robinson Cruso** 2-9-3 0 .... PhilipRobinson 11 82+
(M A Jarvis) *chsd ldrs: drvn along fr 3f out: led narrowly appr fnl f: kpt on tl hdd and no ex fnl 20yds* **9/1**[3]

3 2 1/4 **Kalypso King (USA)** 2-9-3 0 .... RichardHughes 7 79+
(R Hannon) *in tch: swtchd lft and qcknd over 2f out to press ldrs fr over 1f out: nt punished whn outpcd by ldng duo fnl 100yds* **10/1**

46 4 1 1/4 **Gallant Eagle (IRE)**[12] 4900 2-9-3 0 .... JimmyFortune 5 73+
(S Kirk) *chsd ldrs: rdn 2f out: outpcd fr over 1f out* **4/1**[2]

5 3 3/4 **Swift Return** 2-9-3 0 .... SaleemGolam 4 63+
(S C Williams) *s.i.s: in rr: hdwy whn hmpd inside fnl 2f: kpt on strly cl home but nvr a threat* **100/1**

06 6 1 **Lost Cause**[15] 4811 2-9-3 0 .... FergusSweeney 8 57
(R Charlton) *t.k.h: chsd ldrs: wknd and edgd rt ins fnl 2f* **20/1**

60 7 1/2 **Kilt Rock (IRE)**[10] 4985 2-9-3 0 .... RobertHavlin 2 56
(T G Mills) *stdd s: in rr tl sme hdwy on outside 2f out: nvr gng pce to get into contention: wknd over 1f out* **66/1**

8 nk **Sternlight (IRE)** 2-9-3 0 .... RichardMullen 3 55
(E S McMahon) *s.i.s: in rr: sme prog into mid-div 1/2-way: sn bhd* **20/1**

9 1 1/2 **Dance East** 2-9-3 0 .... EddieAhern 1 45
(J Noseda) *in rr and immature: no ch whn hung lft unside fnl 2f* **14/1**

10 9 **Deely Plaza** 2-9-0 0 .... PatrickHills(3) 6 23
(R Hannon) *led tl hdd & wknd over 2f out* **50/1**

1m 11.38s (-1.62) **Going Correction** -0.225s/f (Firm) **10** Ran SP% **119.7**
Speed ratings (Par 94): **101,100,97,95,90 89,88,88,86,74**
Tote Swingers: 1&2 £2.60, 1&3 £2.10, 2&3 £11.20 CSF £7.62 TOTE £1.60: £1.02, £3.20, £2.10; EX 8.40 Trifecta £26.80 Pool: £314.00 - 8.66 winning units..
Owner Ron Young & SW Group Logistics Ltd **Bred** Lodge Park Stud **Trained** Lambourn, Berks

FOCUS
This juvenile maiden was run at a fair pace and the first four came clear. The form looks decent rated around the principals.

NOTEBOOK
Sunraider(IRE) made amends for an expensive defeat over course and distance on his debut 15 days earlier, when finding a troubled passage, and got a no-nonsense ride this time. He got himself warm beforehand and again ran a bit freely, but with the rail to help he put his previous experience to good use inside the final furlong. His Group 1 entry looks too ambitious, but there should certainly be improvement to come and he will now be aimed at the very valuable sales race at Doncaster's St Leger meeting. (op 4-5 tchd 5-6 and 10-11 in a place)
Robinson Cruso, a 100,000gns purchase, was the only one to give the winner a serious race and went down with all guns blazing. His half-sister Beach Bunny failed to find the net as a juvenile, but has progressed into a Group-race performer as she matured. This son of Footstepsinthesand is more precociously bred that his sibling, however, and this was a very pleasing introduction so he should not be long in winning. (tchd 8-1)
Kalypso King(USA) is bred to want further in time as his dam took the Musidora and finished second in the Oaks, so this was a nice debut display from him. He looks sure to come on a deal for the run and will be hard to stop next time out. (tchd 9-1)
Gallant Eagle(IRE) finished fourth in Arcano's maiden at Newbury on debut, but took a backwards step when hanging at Salisbury on his next outing. He probably ran to a similar level here, looking one paced, and has not gone on as was expected. He at least now has the option of nurseries. (op 5-1 tchd 11-2)
Swift Return was the outsider of the field at 100/1 on this racecourse bow. He turned in an eye-catching display, though, as he was given an educational ride and ran on all too late in the day after meeting trouble around 2f out. A stiffer test should suit on breeding and he is certainly one to keep an eye on. Official explanation: jockey said colt was denied a clear run
Lost Cause failed to raise his game as might have been expected for the return to less-taxing ground and lacked any sort of gear change on this drop back a furlong. He is not one to give up on as yet as he now qualifies for nurseries and now looks to need 7f. Official explanation: jockey said colt was denied a clear run (tchd 18-1)
Kilt Rock(IRE) effort on the outside of the pack proved short lived and he too now appears in need of a stiffer test. He is another who is now eligible for nurseries and looks the part, so it may be that he comes good for that switch. (op 80-1)
Sternlight(IRE) proved friendless for his debut and shaped as though the run was much needed. (op 16-1)
Dance East was never a factor from off the pace yet still showed ability when the penny eventually dropped.

5318 EUROPEAN BREEDERS' FUND MAIDEN STKS (DIV II) 6f
3:00 (3:01) (Class 5) 2-Y-O **£3,561** (£1,059; £529; £264) **Stalls** High

Form RPR

0 1 **Katehari (IRE)**[16] 4792 2-8-12 0 .... MartinDwyer 2 71
(A M Balding) *chsd ldrs: led wl over 1f out: drvn ins fnl f and kpt on: a doing enough whn strly chal cl home* **11/4**[2]

2 nk **Flip Flop (IRE)** 2-8-12 0 .... RobertWinston 5 70+
(B W Hills) *s.i.s: sn in tch: hdwy on stands' rail over 1f out: edgd lft and str run ins fnl f: fin wl but a hld by wnr* **8/1**

0 3 2 1/4 **Rockweiller**[9] 5017 2-9-3 0 .... HayleyTurner 4 69
(C R Egerton) *chsd ldrs: drvn to chal ins fnl 2f: hung lft but ev ch 1f out: wknd nr fin* **50/1**

5 4 1/2 **First Term**[26] 4421 2-8-12 0 .... RichardHughes 8 62
(R Hannon) *sn led: rdn and hdd wl over 1f out: sn hung lft: wknd ins fnl f* **11/10**[1]

5 1 1/4 **Gold Party** 2-9-3 0 .... RichardKingscote 3 63
(Tom Dascombe) *sn chsng ldrs: rdn over 2f out: one pce* **11/1**

050 6 7 **House Red (IRE)**[45] 3792 2-9-3 0 .... PaulEddery 9 42
(B W Hills) *broke wl: sn bhd and no ch fr 1/2-way* **25/1**

7 18 **Chorus Boy** 2-9-3 0 .... LiamJones 11 —
(G G Margarson) *s.i.s: swtchd lft 1/2-way: a bhd* **28/1**

02U 8 58 **Spanish Acclaim**[80] 2649 2-9-3 0 .... PatCosgrave 1 —
(J G Portman) *hung ladly lft thrght and unridable fr s: racd alone and stl showed pce for 3f: t.o* **4/1**[3]

1m 12.41s (-0.59) **Going Correction** -0.225s/f (Firm) **8** Ran SP% **123.0**
Speed ratings (Par 94): **94,93,90,89,88 78,54,—**
toteswingers: 1&2 £6.50, 1&3 £20.20, 2&3 £9.50 CSF £26.39 TOTE £3.60: £1.10, £2.60, £7.80; EX 28.10 Trifecta £334.80 Part won.Pool: £452.56 - 0.43 winning units..
Owner The Toucan Syndicate **Bred** Derick Veitch & M Tong **Trained** Kingsclere, Hants

FOCUS
The second division of the juvenile maiden was weaker than the first, even before the non-runners. The first five all had a chance of sorts inside the final furlong and the time was over a second slower than the opener. The level looks fluid and does not appear to have much depth.

NOTEBOOK
Katehari(IRE) was unfancied when weakening on debut at Newmarket 16 days earlier, but the drop back a furlong looked a wise move and the money really came for her this time. She didn't disappoint and narrowly opened her account under a strong ride. The winner's dam comes from a decent Aga Khan family and is a half-sister to Katiyra, so longer trips can be expected to suit next year. This was another indication that her stable remains in fine form. (op 6-1)
Flip Flop(IRE), whose stable took the first division with a colt by the same sire, is also bred to appreciate further in time and she very nearly made a winning start to her career. A stiffer test over this trip should prove ideal next time and the market suggested this would be needed, so she looks one to be with when reappearing. (op 6-1)
Rockweiller was never far away and stepped up very nicely on the form of his Lingfield debut nine days previously. He only gave way nearing the business end and he should be capable of finding a small maiden before plying his trade in handicaps. He is yet another who should also appreciate stepping up in trip as he matures.
First Term couldn't improve on the level of her debut in hotter company at Goodwood 26 days earlier and has now failed to really get home over this trip in both outings. With that in mind a drop back to the minimum could help, but she is now looking very much more of a nursery type. (op 6-5 tchd 5-4 and 11-8 in places)
Spanish Acclaim was having his first outing since unseating from the gates 80 days earlier and has been gelded since. He proved a nightmare from the off, hanging violently left before pulling his way to the lead down the centre and was nigh on pulled up in the end. He is clearly now one to avoid at all costs. Official explanation: jockey said gelding hung left (op 9-2 tchd 5-1)

5319 SUMMER CELEBRATION WITH GO WEST 29TH AUGUST (S) STKS 1m 67y
3:30 (3:37) (Class 6) 2-Y-O **£2,047** (£604; £302) **Stalls** High

Form RPR

4 1 **Miss Whippy**[17] 4757 2-8-7 0 .... HayleyTurner 2 56+
(M L W Bell) *flashed tail thrght: chsd ldrs: led 2f out: pushed out ins fnl f* **15/8**[1]

4 2 2 3/4 **Dontbugthebunny (USA)**[49] 3686 2-8-2 0 .... MatthewDavies(5) 5 50
(George Baker) *loose bef s: chsd ldrs on outside: rdn to chse wnr over 1f out: kpt on same pce and readily hld* **9/4**[2]

0 3 3/4 **Press To Reset**[37] 4080 2-8-12 0 .... TolleyDean 1 53
(W G M Turner) *led at mod pce: rdn over 3f out: hdd 2f out: lost 2nd over 1f out but kpt on same pce* **100/1**

05 4 1 **Bury St Edmunds**[18] 4689 2-8-12 0 .... RichardMullen 4 52+
(A G Newcombe) *chsd ldr: stl wl there whn hmpd over 2f out: rallied and styd on fr over 1f out but nvr a factor* **25/1**

0 5 1 **Al Zaeem**[17] 4757 2-8-5 0 .... (v[1]) TobyAtkinson(7) 9 49
(Miss D Mountain) *in rr: rdn and styd on fr 3f out: hung lft fr 2f out: styd on same pce fnl f* **33/1**

60 6 nk **Drews Lane**[24] 4503 2-8-6 0 ow2 .... (p) JackDean(3) 7 45
(W G M Turner) *chsd ldrs: hmpd over 2f out and swtchd lft: styd on fr over 1f out but nvr a danger* **17/2**

0 7 2 1/4 **Radsky**[10] 4986 2-8-12 0 .... PatCosgrave 14 43
(J G Portman) *s.i.s: in rr: rdn 3f out: sme hdwy fr over 1f out* **7/1**[3]

0 8 1/2 **Pollan Bay (IRE)**[11] 4945 2-8-7 0 .... SophieDoyle(5) 12 42
(S Kirk) *in rr: rdn and hung lft to centre fr 3f out: sme prog fnl f* **11/1**

00 9 1 1/2 **Fast Elaine (IRE)**[9] 5017 2-8-4 0 .... MarcHalford(3) 10 34
(Mrs L C Jewell) *in tch: rdn 3f out: wknd fr 2f out* **33/1**

0 10 hd **Just A Monkey**[42] 3920 2-8-12 0 .... TonyCulhane 13 38
(R Curtis) *a in rr* **20/1**

11 1 1/4 **Polo Springs** 2-8-2 0 .... AshleyMorgan(5) 6 31
(W G M Turner) *s.i.s: a towards rr* **20/1**

06 12 hd **Set In Ice**[18] 4713 2-8-12 0 .... FergusSweeney 3 35
(Mark Gillard) *a in rr* **66/1**

0 13 2 **Superhoops**[16] 4790 2-8-12 0 .... JoeFanning 8 31
(H S Howe) *chsd ldrs over 5f* **40/1**

1m 48.2s (3.50) **Going Correction** -0.125s/f (Firm) **13** Ran SP% **121.1**
Speed ratings (Par 92): **77,74,73,72,71 71,68,68,66,66 65,65,63**
toteswingers: 1&2 £1.10, 1&3 £15.10, 2&3 £57.30 CSF £5.54 TOTE £2.90: £1.10, £1.80, £15.30; EX 8.40 Trifecta £122.70 Pool: £486.06 - 2.93 winning units..The winner was bought in for £8,400.
Owner D W & L Y Payne **Bred** Rabbah Bloodstock Limited **Trained** Newmarket, Suffolk

FOCUS
This juvenile seller was a race where racing handily was a must as there was no real pace on early. The form still makes sense although it is slightly below par for the grade.

NOTEBOOK
Miss Whippy swished her tail violently when fifth on her debut in this class over 7f at Newmarket and did so again here on numerous occasions, even before the start. She stood out in the preliminaries, however, and after racing in the box seat proved far too strong for her rivals when asked to win the race. Her tail again propelled when she was in front, despite her rider not going for the whip, and again after passing the line so that will always be of some concern, but she ought to be well up to more success at this sort of level. (op 7-4 tchd 6-4)
Dontbugthebunny(USA) just about looked the one to beat on the form of her debut fourth at Ripon over 6f and looked sure to appreciate stepping up in trip. She didn't help her cause by proving difficult and getting loose at the start, which understandably caused her odds to lengthen, but she did not look to spend much energy in doing so. She also raced prominently and came through with her chance, but simply found the winner too strong. A drop back to slightly shorter could help and she has now clearly found her level. (op 15-8 tchd 13-8 and 5-2)
Press To Reset did well to get across and lead from the outside stall. He kept on well once headed and the class drop brought about this improved display, but he probably found the distance a little too far for him so early on in his career.

Bury St Edmunds, stepping up from 5f, helped to set the moderate early pace and shaped a little better than the bare form as he met some trouble around the 2f marker. Official explanation: jockey said colt was denied a clear run (tchd 28-1)
Al Zaeem never threatened, but did fare best of those coming from off the pace. (op 40-1)

5320 BUY A RACING POST YEARLING BONUS CANDIDATE NURSERY 1m 67y
4:00 (4:02) (Class 4) (0-85,78) 2-Y-O £3,885 (£1,156; £577; £288) Stalls High

Form RPR
2423 **1** **Cherry Bee**[12] 4895 2-8-10 **67** JoeFanning 2 72
(M Johnston) *trckd ldrs: slt advantage ins fnl 2f: edgd rt to stands' rail and styd on wl whn persistently chal thrght fnl f but on top last strides* **3/1**[2]
0652 **2** *nk* **Flaming Miracle**[3] 5213 2-9-0 **71** MartinDwyer 3 75+
(A M Balding) *slowly away and 5 lenghth bhd main gp: stdy hdwy over 4f out and trckd ldrs 3f out: qcknd to press wnr over 1f out: edgd rt and persistent chal thrght fnl f tl no ex last strides* **7/4**[1]
0345 **3** *2 ¾* **Aattash (IRE)**[16] 4790 2-9-3 **74** ChrisCatlin 6 72
(M R Channon) *disp ld tl led after 2f: rdn 3f out: hdd ins fnl 2f: outpcd fnl f* **10/1**
136 **4** *1 ¼* **Jairzihno**[24] 4488 2-9-7 **78** TonyCulhane 1 74
(J R Best) *broke ok but sn outpcd and 5 l off main gp: rdn fr 5f out and nvr traveling: edgd lft to centre crse and hdwy 2f out but nvr gng pce to get into contention* **3/1**[2]
5006 **5** *4* **Captain Cool (IRE)**[11] 4931 2-8-1 **58** CatherineGannon 5 45
(R Hannon) *chsd ldrs: rdn 3f out: no imp fr 2f out and wknd appr fnl f* **12/1**
033 **6** *2 ¾* **Llandovery**[19] 4666 2-8-8 **68** AndreaAtzeni(3) 4 49
(P J McBride) *disp ld 2f: styd chsng ldr: chal 3f out: wknd ins fnl 2f* **8/1**[3]

1m 43.83s (-0.87) **Going Correction** -0.125s/f (Firm) 2y crse rec 6 Ran SP% **114.3**
Speed ratings (Par 96): **99,98,95,94,90 87**
toteswingers: 1&2 £1.90, 1&3 £3.70, 2&3 £4.20 CSF £8.94 TOTE £3.90: £2.20, £1.70; EX 8.60.
Owner Favourites Racing IV **Bred** Mount Coote Stud **Trained** Middleham Moor, N Yorks

FOCUS
An open little nursery with the winner recording a marginal personal best. The complexion of the race changed as soon as the gates opened when the two market leaders completely fluffed the start, however, and the form needs treating with a degree of caution.

NOTEBOOK
Cherry Bee, 2lb lower, deservedly opened her account at the fifth time of asking and relished the step up to this trip. She was given a fine ride by Fanning, who was alert to the leaders duelling early and just took her back a little through the first two furlongs. He then produced her 2f out and she was always doing enough to hold off the runner-up after drifting across to the stands' rail. She looks the type to progress further now she has found her ideal trip. (op 7-2)
Flaming Miracle finished second on his nursery bow three days earlier and was reappearing quickly before the Handicapper could strike. He obviously blew his chance at the start, having been in the stalls plenty long enough, but the fact he still came there with every chance and lost out narrowly suggests he could still be weighted to win after being reassessed. (op 15-8 tchd 9-4)
Aattash(IRE) was making his debut in this sphere after four previous outings and he got an aggressive ride. He mustered only the same pace when put under pressure nearing the two-furlong pole and looks to need some respite from the Handicapper. (op 9-1 tchd 8-1)
Jairzihno, stepping up a furlong, was the other who blew the start despite breaking on terms. He was cajoled back into things turning for home, but began to race lazily again from the top of the home straight and was always held inside the final 2f. This leaves him with a deal to prove now as he was also slowly away at Goodwood on his previous start. (tchd 5-2 and 100-30 in a place)
Captain Cool(IRE) began to feel the pinch 4f out and was done with coming to the 2f marker. A drop back down in grade looks on the cards for him. (op 14-1 tchd 16-1)
Llandovery was given a positive ride over this longer distance, but was cooked before the winner drifted across him 2f out and failed to last home.

5321 HOWARD BAREHAM 40TH BIRTHDAY H'CAP 1m 2f 7y
4:30 (4:30) (Class 4) (0-85,85) 3-Y-O+ £5,180 (£1,541; £770; £384) Stalls Low

Form RPR
3664 **1** **Special Reserve (IRE)**[30] 4315 4-9-10 **80** RichardHughes 8 87
(R Hannon) *hld up in tch: smooth hdwy but hanging lft over 1f out: shkn up and qcknd smartly ins fnl f to ld fnl 20yds: cosily* **10/3**[2]
1-50 **2** *½* **Anice Stellato (IRE)**[67] 3047 3-9-0 **85** JPFahy(7) 9 91
(R M Beckett) *trckd ldrs: wnt 2nd ins fnl 2f: chalng whn carried lft ins fnl f: slt ld fnl 70yds: hdd and outpcd fnl 20yds* **11/1**
0514 **3** *½* **Emperor Court (IRE)**[52] 3578 5-9-13 **83** NCallan 7 88
(P J Makin) *led: rdn and edgd lft appr fnl f: hung lft again wl ins and hdd fnl 70yds: styd on same pce* **5/1**[3]
2004 **4** *nse* **Lady Brora**[26] 4441 4-9-1 **71** MartinDwyer 6 76
(A M Balding) *in rr: rdn over 4f out: styd on fr 2f out but hanging lft appr fnl f: styd on strly wl ins fnl f: gng on cl home* **8/1**
4060 **5** *2* **Humble Opinion**[23] 4517 7-9-8 **78** FergusSweeney 4 79
(A King) *chsd ldrs: rdn to chal over 1f out: one pce whn pushed lft and hmpd wl ins fnl f* **16/1**
0-13 **6** *3* **Serious Impact (USA)**[103] 1990 4-10-0 **84** JimmyFortune 1 79
(J H M Gosden) *in rr and on outside: rdn and sme hdwy over 2f out: nvr in contention and hanging rt whn hmpd wl ins fnl f* **1/1**[1]
-245 **7** *1 ½* **Outlandish**[18] 4696 6-9-6 **76** ChrisCatlin 3 68
(Miss E C Lavelle) *sn chsng ldr: rdn 3f out: wknd qckly ins fnl 2f* **20/1**

2m 5.98s (-2.72) **Going Correction** -0.125s/f (Firm)
WFA 3 from 4yo+ 8lb 7 Ran SP% **119.8**
Speed ratings (Par 105): **105,104,104,104,102 100,98**
toteswingers: 1&2 £5.50, 2&3 £2.80, 1&3 not won. CSF £40.64 CT £185.76 TOTE £3.80: £1.60, £3.70; EX 31.30 Trifecta £94.40 Pool: £553.83 - 4.34 winning units..
Owner Mrs J Wood **Bred** David Magnier And Cobra Bloodstock **Trained** East Everleigh, Wilts

FOCUS
A fair handicap, run at a sound pace and rated around the winner and fourth.
Emperor Court(IRE) Official explanation: jockey said horse hung left
Serious Impact(USA) Official explanation: jockey said gelding suffered interference in running

5322 10% CASH BACK AT CORAL.CO.UK MAIDEN STKS 1m 2f 7y
5:00 (5:01) (Class 5) 3-Y-O+ £2,729 (£806; £403) Stalls Low

Form RPR
1 **Zemario (IRE)** 3-9-3 0 NCallan 9 75
(M A Jarvis) *chsd ldrs: rdn over 2f out: slt ld ins fnl f: styd on gamely whn strly chal sn after: hld on wl* **5/1**[2]
-300 **2** *hd* **Cherish The Moment (IRE)**[21] 4599 3-9-3 70 RobertWinston 1 75
(B W Hills) *led: rdn 4f out: narrowly hdd ins fnl f: styd wl there and rallied to cl on wnr last strides but jst hld* **7/1**
442 **3** *1 ¼* **Laughing Boy (IRE)**[21] 4606 3-9-3 79 RichardHughes 10 73
(L M Cumani) *hld up in rr but in tch: checked over 4f out: swtchd lft and hdwy over 2f out: qcknd over 1f out to chal wnr ins fnl f: no ex and wknd nr fin* **1/2**[1]
-404 **4** *8* **Millharbour (IRE)**[53] 3538 3-9-3 67 EddieAhern 5 57
(B W Hills) *chsd ldrs: rdn and hung lft over 2f out: sn wknd* **12/1**
0/46 **5** *6* **Red Army Commander (IRE)**[3] 5215 4-9-11 0 RobertHavlin 2 45
(J A Geake) *chsd ldrs: rdn 3f out: wknd 2f out* **50/1**
0-0 **6** *2* **Stanley Rigby**[95] 2199 3-9-3 0 GeorgeBaker 4 41
(C F Wall) *a towards rr* **50/1**
7 *5* **Walls Way**[292] 5-9-8 0 MCGeran(3) 8 31
(A W Carroll) *in tch: hung lft to outside 3f out: sn rdn and wknd* **100/1**
8 *¾* **Mistoffelees** 3-9-3 0 ChrisCatlin 3 29
(L M Cumani) *s.i.s: a on rr* **20/1**
9 *6* **Sioux City Sue** 3-8-12 0 PatCosgrave 6 12
(J R Boyle) *s.i.s: a bhd* **50/1**
00 **10** *nse* **Morning Dress (USA)**[10] 4979 3-9-3 0 JoeFanning 7 17
(M Johnston) *chsd ldrs to 3f out: sn btn* **16/1**

2m 7.47s (-1.23) **Going Correction** -0.125s/f (Firm)
WFA 3 from 4yo+ 8lb 10 Ran SP% **119.7**
Speed ratings (Par 103): **99,98,97,91,86 85,81,80,75,75**
toteswingers: 1&2 £3.20, 1&3 £1.70, 2&3 £2.90 CSF £43.40 TOTE £6.00: £1.80, £2.40, £1.02; EX 45.10 Trifecta £80.40 Pool: £700.88 - 6.45 winning units..
Owner Sheikh Ahmed Al Maktoum **Bred** Darley **Trained** Newmarket, Suffolk
■ Stewards' Enquiry : Pat CosgraveJ £140 fine: passport irregularity

FOCUS
The first three came clear in this modest maiden, which was run at an average pace. The runner-up is the best guide to the level.
Stanley Rigby Official explanation: jockey said gelding suffered interference leaving the stalls

5323 CELEBRATE WITH GO WEST THIS SATURDAY H'CAP 5f 10y
5:30 (5:31) (Class 5) (0-70,70) 3-Y-O+ £2,729 (£806; £403) Stalls High

Form RPR
2205 **1** **Cape Royal**[5] 5156 9-9-8 **70** (bt) KevinGhunowa(3) 16 78
(J M Bradley) *mde all on stands' side: pushed along over 1f out: hld on wl thrght fnl f* **7/1**[2]
2063 **2** *½* **Matterofact (IRE)**[18] 4692 6-9-8 **67** TGMcLaughlin 10 73+
(M S Saunders) *in rr tl swtchd lft over 2f out: str run on far side to chse wnr ins fnl f: kpt on wl but a jst hld* **10/1**
24U2 **3** *½* **Towy Boy (IRE)**[17] 4748 4-8-10 **55** (v) NCallan 11 59
(I A Wood) *chsd ldrs: rdn and ev ch ins fnl f: kpt on but nt pce of ldng duo* **8/1**[3]
3540 **4** *nk* **Cosmic Destiny (IRE)**[6] 5125 7-8-13 **63** JPHamblett(5) 9 66
(E F Vaughan) *trckd ldrs: rdn 1/2-way: styd on wl fnl f: gng on cl home* **25/1**
6404 **5** *¾* **Brandywell Boy (IRE)**[12] 4907 6-9-1 **60** RichardThomas 14 64+
(D J S Ffrench Davis) *chsd ldrs on stands' rail: hanging ins fnl 2f but kpt on ins fnl f* **8/1**[3]
3403 **5** *dht* **Comptonspirit**[8] 5073 5-9-0 **59** J-PGuillambert 12 60
(B P J Baugh) *in tch: rdn and one pce 1/2-way: kpt on fr over 1f out: fin wl* **7/1**[2]
3004 **7** *nk* **Malapropism**[5] 5156 9-8-11 **56** (v) ChrisCatlin 5 56
(M R Channon) *chsd ldrs: rdn and ev ch towards outside over 1f out: one pce ins fnl f* **20/1**
2510 **8** *1* **Colorus (IRE)**[31] 4283 6-9-4 **66** (p) KellyHarrison(3) 8 62
(W J H Ratcliffe) *chsd ldrs: rdn 2f out: styd on same pce fnl f* **8/1**[3]
0400 **9** *1* **Heaven**[21] 4604 4-9-9 **68** JimmyFortune 4 69+
(P J Makin) *in rr tl hdwy 1/2-way: styng on whn hmpd over 1f out: nt rcvr* **8/1**[3]
2000 **10** *1 ¼* **Kalligal**[10] 5008 4-8-3 **51** oh3 MarcHalford(3) 3 39
(R Ingram) *s.i.s: in rr: rdn 3f out: hdwy on far side over 1f out: kpt on ins fnl f* **50/1**
3042 **11** *nk* **Espy**[21] 4604 4-9-8 **67** EddieAhern 2 54
(S Kirk) *in rr: plenty to do whn swtchd lft over 2f out: sme prog fnl f but nvr anywhere nr ldrs* **4/1**[1]
4000 **12** *½* **Ten Down**[10] 4978 4-9-4 **63** MartinDwyer 7 48
(M Quinn) *chsd ldrs: rdn 2f out: stl ev ch over 1f out: sn btn* **20/1**
1060 **13** *2* **Joss Stick**[6] 5125 4-8-9 **54** (t) CatherineGannon 13 32
(J J Bridger) *a outpcd* **20/1**
4050 **14** *4* **Robin The Till**[11] 4937 3-9-1 **62** RichardHughes 6 25
(R Hannon) *s.i.s and swtchd rt s: a in rr* **12/1**
03/0 **15** *3* **Tan Bonita (USA)**[6] 5125 4-8-10 **55** (t) IvanLopez 15 8
(R J Smith) *chsd ldrs to 1/2-way* **25/1**
-005 **16** *nk* **Sir Loin**[157] 896 8-8-1 **51** oh6 (v) SimonPearce(5) 1 2
(P Burgoyne) *prom: rdn and wknd fr 2f out: no ch whn hmpd over 1f out* **50/1**

58.72 secs (-1.58) **Going Correction** -0.225s/f (Firm)
WFA 3 from 4yo+ 2lb 16 Ran SP% **132.1**
Speed ratings (Par 103): **103,102,101,100,99 99,99,97,96,94 93,92,89,83,78 77**
toteswingers: 1&2 £22.60, 1&3 £15.20, 2&3 £18.70 CSF £75.01 CT £595.46 TOTE £8.70: £2.40, £2.70, £2.50, £5.60; EX 97.50 TRIFECTA Not won. Place 6: £29.75 Place 5: £22.10 .
Owner E A Hayward **Bred** D R Brotherton **Trained** Sedbury, Gloucs

FOCUS
This was a typically wide-open sprint for the class with the winner the best guide to the form. The runners were spread across the track and unsurprisingly there were plenty of chances.
T/Jkpt: £8,714.40 to a £1 stake. Pool: £12,273.91. 1.00 winning ticket. T/Plt: £81.00 to a £1 stake. Pool: £62,768.05. 565.50 winning tickets. T/Qpdt: £6.90 to a £1 stake. Pool: £5,524.00. 588.54 winning tickets. ST

4838 SOUTHWELL (L-H)
Tuesday, August 25

OFFICIAL GOING: Standard
Wind: Light across Weather: Sunshine & showers

5324 ENDURANCE RIDE AT SOUTHWELL 5TH SEPTEMBER NOVICE STKS 1m (F)
2:30 (2:30) (Class 5) 2-Y-O £4,403 (£1,310; £654; £327) Stalls Low

Form RPR
331 **1** **Mingun Bell (USA)**[47] 3786 2-9-2 83 TPQueally 5 92+
(H R A Cecil) *chsd ldr to over 5f out: remained handy: led on bit over 2f out: shkn up ins fnl f: r.o wl* **5/6**[1]
0126 **2** *3 ¾* **Florio Vincitore (IRE)**[24] 4525 2-9-2 83 EdwardCreighton 4 80
(E J Creighton) *broke wl: stdd to trck ldrs sn after s: racd keenly: rdn over 2f out: chsd wnr fnl f: styd on same pce* **6/1**[3]
0130 **3** *nk* **Ingleby Spirit**[25] 4488 2-9-2 85 PaulHanagan 2 79
(R A Fahey) *led: rdn and hdd over 2f out: styd on same pce appr fnl f* **3/1**[2]
4 *2 ¾* **Exemplary** 2-8-12 0 JoeFanning 3 69
(M Johnston) *s.i.s: sn prom: chsd ldr over 5f out: rdn and ev ch over 2f out: wknd ins fnl f* **10/1**

0104 **5** *7* **Ananda Kanda (USA)**[31] 4306 2-9-0 79.............................. TomEaves 6 56
(B Ellison) *chsd ldrs: rdn over 3f out: wknd over 2f out* **16/1**

6 **6** *22* **New World Symphony (IRE)**[70] 2997 2-8-9 0......... FrederikTylicki(3) 1 5
(J Howard Johnson) *prom tl rdn and wknd over 3f out* **33/1**

1m 43.69s (-0.01) **Going Correction** -0.075s/f (Stan) **6** Ran SP% **111.8**
Speed ratings (Par 94): **97,93,92,90,83 61**
toteswingers: 1&2 £1.60, 1&3 £1.50, 2&3 £2.20 CSF £6.43 TOTE £1.70: £1.10, £2.60; EX 7.00.
Owner Niarchos Family **Bred** Paula W Cline **Trained** Newmarket, Suffolk

FOCUS
This didn't look a bad race on paper with four of the six runners previous winners, but it was turned into a rout. The early pace seemed ordinary and the form is best rated around the placed horses.

NOTEBOOK
Mingun Bell(USA) ◆, who had beaten a subsequent Listed winner when scoring at Warwick last time, had only run on fast ground on turf before this, but being by a son of the great A P Indy gave every encouragement that he would appreciate this deeper surface. He certainly did that and he was still on the bridle when hitting the front inside the last 2f before powering right away. It remains to be seen what the form is worth, but he could hardly have won this any easier and looks ready for a step up in class now. (op 10-11 tchd Evens)
Florio Vincitore(IRE), who had shown that he could handle this surface when narrowly beaten here two starts ago, had been well beaten in his only previous try beyond 6f, but that was in the Chesham. He is bred to stay this far, however, and stayed on from off the pace all the way up the home straight, but came up against a much classier rival on the day. (op 5-1 tchd 13-2)
Ingleby Spirit, whose turf win came on soft ground, had no chance from the outside stall when stepped up to 7f in a Goodwood nursery last time. Upped in trip again here, he set the early pace against the inside rail but could only keep on at one pace after coming off the bridle turning for home. (op 7-2 tchd 4-1 and 5-2)
Exemplary, a half-brother to two winners over 1m4f in France, wasn't best away but the modest pace meant that he would soon back amongst the leading pack. He remained in the thick of the action until weakening from the furlong pole and should have benefited from this debut effort. (op 11-1 tchd 12-1 and 9-1)
Ananda Kanda(USA), whose turf victory at Haydock in May came on heavy ground, finished a tailed-off last in her only previous try beyond 6f which was on Polytrack. She was close enough on the outside of the field before getting outpaced on the home turn and she was soon left behind. Her stamina remains unproven. (op 18-1 tchd 20-1)
New World Symphony(IRE), who showed a little ability when in mid-division on his Thirsk debut, dropped right out over the last 3f and now has plenty to prove. (tchd 28-1)

5325 SOUTHWELL-RACECOURSE.CO.UK MEDIAN AUCTION MAIDEN STKS 6f (F)
3:00 (3:00) (Class 4) 2-Y-O **£4,640** (£1,370; £685) **Stalls** Low

Form RPR

1 **Circumvent** 2-9-3 0.. PaulHanagan 2 78
(P F I Cole) *chsd ldrs: led over 3f out: rdn and hung lft over 1f out: jnd ins fnl f: r.o: edgd lft nr fin* **7/1**

5 **2** *shd* **Comedy Hall (USA)**[38] 4093 2-9-3 0.................................. JoeFanning 1 78
(M Johnston) *s.i.s: hld up: hdwy 1/2-way: rdn and n.m.r over 1f out: rallied to have ev ch ins fnl f: r.o* **6/4[1]**

3 *3 1/4* **Prince Of Vasa (IRE)** 2-9-3 0.. TedDurcan 4 68
(Saeed Bin Suroor) *dwlt: plld hrd in rr: hdwy over 2f out: rdn and ev ch over 1f out: wknd wl ins fnl f* **5/1[2]**

363 **4** *1 1/4* **Belinsky (IRE)**[29] 4370 2-9-3 72... PatCosgrave 8 64
(S A Callaghan) *sn led: hdd over 3f out: rdn: edgd lft and ev ch over 1f out: wknd ins fnl f* **8/1**

4 **5** *8* **Cape Kimberley**[15] 4839 2-9-3 0.. TPQueally 3 40
(J G Given) *chsd ldrs: rdn 1/2-way: wknd over 2f out* **6/1**

635 **6** *6* **Sweet Mirasol (IRE)**[25] 4492 2-8-12 68........................... PhillipMakin 6 17
(K A Ryan) *chsd ldrs tl rdn and wknd over 2f out* **33/1**

0024 **7** *23* **West Leake Star (IRE)**[15] 4856 2-9-3 70..................... RobertWinston 5 —
(B W Hills) *prom: rdn over 3f out: sn wknd* **11/2[3]**

1m 17.14s (0.64) **Going Correction** -0.075s/f (Stan) **7** Ran SP% **112.9**
Speed ratings (Par 96): **92,91,87,85,75 67,36**
toteswingers: 1&2 £4.70, 1&3 £8.80, 2&3 £3.00 CSF £17.53 TOTE £8.10: £2.90, £1.90; EX 28.60 Trifecta £273.00 Pool: £520.34 - 1.41 winning units..
Owner The Fairy Story Partnership **Bred** Deepwood Farm Stud **Trained** Whatcombe, Oxon

FOCUS
An fair maiden with a couple of interesting newcomers taking on a few who had already shown ability. The early pace seemed solid enough but the form might take time to settle.

NOTEBOOK
Circumvent ◆, a half-brother to the dual 7f winner Seradim, is stoutly bred on the dam's side so there was the possibility that he would find this trip sharp enough on debut. The subject of market support earlier in the day, he was up there disputing the lead from the start and showed a decent attitude to keep on finding when challenged on both sides all the way up the home straight. His breeding suggests that he will improve as he goes up in trip. (op 8-1 tchd 10-1)
Comedy Hall(USA) ◆, who looked in need of the experience when fifth in a Newmarket maiden last month that has produced a couple of winners, moved into contention on the inside turning for home but became short of room for a few strides between the winner and Prince Of Vasa coming to the last furlong. He had every chance to win his race once the gap opened again, however and, although he only went down narrowly, the stewards allowed the result to stand. He has very much a US dirt pedigree and shouldn't take long in going one better. (op 15-8 tchd 11-8)
Prince Of Vasa(IRE), a 55,000gns two-year-old and a half-brother to a winning juvenile over this trip, represented a stable that boasts a fine record with its few juvenile runners here, but he was all over the place in the early stages. He did give himself every chance against the inside rail over the last couple of furlongs, but was held by the front pair in the closing stages. He doesn't look one of the stable's stars, but should come on from this and win races. (op 4-1 tchd 11-2)
Belinsky(IRE), disappointing in his only previous try at this trip, had finished a fair third over the minimum trip here since then. He helped force the pace until weakening inside the last furlong and may be worth a try in a nursery back over 5f. (op 11-2)
Cape Kimberley didn't build on his encouraging debut over course and distance earlier in the month. (op 13-2 tchd 15-2)
West Leake Star(IRE) Official explanation: jockey said colt slipped leaving stalls and lost its action

5326 GOLF SOCIETIES WELCOME AT SOUTHWELL H'CAP 6f (F)
3:30 (3:31) (Class 6) (0-60,60) 3-Y-O **£3,043** (£905; £452; £226) **Stalls** Low

Form RPR

0520 **1** **Fuzzy Cat**[6] 5145 3-8-8 **50**...(b) TomEaves 11 55
(T D Barron) *sn drvn along in rr: hdwy u.p and hung lft over 1f out: hung rt ins fnl f: styd on to ld post* **4/1[1]**

0002 **2** *nk* **Monte Mayor Eagle**[11] 4982 3-8-10 **52**........................... JamieMackay 9 56
(D Haydn Jones) *prom: rdn 1/2-way: led wl ins fnl f: hdd post* **14/1**

5264 **3** *shd* **Majestic Lady (IRE)**[15] 4860 3-8-10 **52**......................... RobertWinston 6 55
(B W Hills) *chsd ldrs: rdn over 1f out: r.o* **13/2[3]**

1036 **4** *3/4* **Pepin (IRE)**[35] 4172 3-8-12 **54**.................................... FrankieMcDonald 4 55
(D Haydn Jones) *led: rdn and hung rt over 2f out: hdd and unable qck wl ins fnl f* **12/1**

0000 **5** *6* **Dontuwishitwereso**[32] 4275 3-8-11 **53**........................(e[1]) SebSanders 13 35
(P W D'Arcy) *mid-div: hdwy u.p and hung lft over 2f out: nt trble ldrs* **17/2**

2043 **6** *3 1/4* **Denton Diva**[95] 2234 3-9-4 **60**...(v) PhillipMakin 3 31
(M Dods) *sn drvn along to chse ldr: disp ld fr 4f out tl over 2f out: wknd fnl f* **10/1**

5004 **7** *3/4* **Wicklewood**[8] 5112 3-8-5 **47**..(v) JimmyQuinn 12 16
(Mrs C A Dunnett) *s.i.s: sn outpcd: styd on ins fnl f: nvr nrr* **16/1**

0100 **8** *nk* **Kinigi (IRE)**[27] 4425 3-9-3 **59**.. ChrisCatlin 5 27
(R A Harris) *prom: rdn over 3f out: wknd 2f out* **16/1**

0420 **9** *1 1/4* **Call Me Courageous (IRE)**[20] 4643 3-8-5 **50**....(p) KevinGhunowa(3) 14 14
(R A Harris) *mid-div: rdn over 3f out: sn wknd* **16/1**

0502 **10** *4 1/2* **Leelu**[14] 4872 3-9-1 **57**.. HayleyTurner 1 7
(D W P Arbuthnot) *s.i.s: sn drvn along: sme hdwy 4f out: wknd 3f out* **5/1[2]**

4400 **11** *nk* **Transcentral**[43] 3926 3-8-6 **48**.. NeilChalmers 7 —
(T Wall) *sn outpcd* **66/1**

5430 **12** *nk* **River Dee (IRE)**[27] 4428 3-8-11 **58**................................ DeanHeslop(5) 8 6
(D Donovan) *sn outpcd* **11/1**

400- **13** *4* **Chatterszaha**[306] 6933 3-9-0 **59**............................... WilliamCarson(3) 2 —
(C Drew) *chsd ldrs: rdn 1/2-way: wknd over 2f out* **40/1**

4050 **14** *3 1/2* **Shannon Golden**[11] 5008 3-8-12 **54**.................................(t) AmirQuinn 10 —
(S R Bowring) *s.i.s: outpcd* **10/1**

1m 16.5s **Going Correction** -0.075s/f (Stan) **14** Ran SP% **123.0**
Speed ratings (Par 98): **97,96,96,95,87 83,82,81,80,74 73,73,67,63**
toteswingers: 1&2 £16.00, 1&3 £5.60, 2&3 £18.00 CSF £63.07 CT £368.32 TOTE £5.20: £2.30, £5.90, £2.40; EX 75.00 Trifecta £221.30 Part won. Pool: £299.18 - 0.63 winning units..
Owner Richard Barnes, Colin Aitken **Bred** Baroness Bloodstock **Trained** Maunby, N Yorks

FOCUS
A moderate sprint handicap, but run at a decent pace and the form looks sound enough for the grade. There wasn't much covering the front four at the line, but in a race in which not that many got into it the quartet pulled well clear of the rest.

5327 MEMBERSHIP OF SOUTHWELL GOLF CLUB CLAIMING STKS 1m 3f (F)
4:00 (4:00) (Class 5) 3-4-Y-O **£3,043** (£905; £452; £226) **Stalls** Low

Form RPR

40 **1** **Eightdaysaweek**[33] 4224 3-8-3 55.. ChrisCatlin 2 65
(S Kirk) *sn pushed along towards rr: hdwy over 6f out: rdn to ld wl over 2f out: hung lft over 1f out: hung rt u.p ins fnl f: styd on* **5/1[3]**

3501 **2** *1 1/4* **Applaude**[18] 4740 4-9-3 69...(b) PatCosgrave 5 68
(John A Harris) *prom: chsd ldr over 9f out: nt clr run and swtchd rt over 1f out: sn rdn: styd on same pce ins fnl f* **7/2[2]**

-260 **3** *4* **Canton Road**[11] 4987 3-8-6 63..(bt[1]) JoeFanning 6 59
(P F I Cole) *s.s: hdwy over 8f out: rdn over 2f out: styd on same pce* **11/1**

1-43 **4** *8* **Kind Heart**[18] 4740 3-8-11 76.. SebSanders 4 50
(Sir Mark Prescott) *led: rdn over 3f out: hdd wl over 2f out: wknd over 1f out* **5/6[1]**

6453 **5** *13* **Intikama (IRE)**[8] 5108 3-8-1 66...................................... AshleyMorgan(5) 1 23
(M H Tompkins) *sn drvn along in rr: wknd over 4f out* **16/1**

0004 **6** *shd* **Autumn Charm**[21] 4617 4-8-7 40...................................... KevinGhunowa(3) 3 18
(Lucinda Featherstone) *chsd ldr over 2f: lost pl over 7f out: wknd over 4f out* **80/1**

2m 27.08s (-0.92) **Going Correction** -0.075s/f (Stan)
WFA 3 from 4yo 9lb **6** Ran SP% **112.1**
Speed ratings (Par 103): **100,99,96,90,80 80**
toteswingers: 1&2 £2.40, 1&3 £5.60, 2&3 £4.40 CSF £22.50 TOTE £4.90: £1.90, £2.20; EX 25.10.Eightdaysaweek was claimed by Mr T R Pearson for £10,000.
Owner Christopher Wright **Bred** Stratford Place Stud **Trained** Upper Lambourn, Berks

FOCUS
An ordinary claimer and a race of changing fortunes. the winner put up an improved effort but the placed horses are far from solid.
Kind Heart Official explanation: trainer's rep had no explanation for the poor form shown

5328 BOOK ON LINE @ SOUTHWELL-RACECOURSE.CO.UK H'CAP 1m 3f (F)
4:30 (4:30) (Class 7) (0-50,51) 3-Y-O **£2,072** (£616; £308; £153) **Stalls** Low

Form RPR

500 **1** **Eloise**[12] 4934 3-8-9 **49** ow1..(b[1]) SebSanders 8 56
(Sir Mark Prescott) *chsd ldrs: led over 7f out: clr over 3f out: rdn and hung lft ins fnl f: all out* **9/1**

0300 **2** *nk* **Spring Quartet**[20] 4640 3-8-0 **47** ow1.......................(v) TobyAtkinson(7) 9 53
(Pat Eddery) *s.s and lost 11 l s: hdwy over 3f out: r.o wl ins fnl f: nt quite get to wnr* **9/4[1]**

6304 **3** *2 1/2* **Valkyrie (IRE)**[20] 4669 3-8-6 **51** ow3......................(b[1]) MarkCoumbe(5) 12 53
(N P Littmoden) *s.i.s: sn drvn along in rr: hdwy u.p over 4f out: chsd wnr over 2f out: sn hung lft: styd on* **14/1**

000- **4** *7* **Silver Sceptre (IRE)**[360] 5499 3-8-5 **45**.............................. ChrisCatlin 5 35
(W J Musson) *hld up: hdwy over 4f out: shkn up over 2f out: sn hung lft and wknd* **4/1[2]**

46 **5** *4* **Persian Tomcat (IRE)**[33] 4241 3-8-8 **48**......................... LiamJones 14 31
(Miss J Feilden) *chsd ldrs: rdn over 3f out: wknd 2f out* **10/1**

6040 **6** *6* **Katie Girl**[13] 4892 3-8-5 **45**...(p) PaulHanagan 7 18
(Mrs G S Rees) *prom: rdn over 4f out: wknd over 3f out* **18/1**

0440 **7** *10* **Just Dan**[28] 4397 3-8-2 **45**..(p) KellyHarrison(3) 6 1
(R Hollinshead) *chsd ldrs: led over 8f out: hdd over 7f out: wknd over 4f out* **22/1**

3 **8** *shd* **Awani**[14] 4867 3-8-10 **50**.. LPKeniry 2 6
(E F Vaughan) *mid-div: hdwy over 7f out: rdn over 4f out: sn wknd* **7/1[3]**

5536 **9** *16* **Astrobrava**[20] 4642 3-8-4 **49**...................................... AshleyMorgan(5) 1 —
(M H Tompkins) *prom: rdn and lost pl 6f out: wknd over 4f out* **20/1**

0-00 **10** *1/2* **Watch The Master**[10] 5015 3-8-8 **48**...............................(t) TedDurcan 10 —
(B I Case) *hld up: rdn 7f out: sn wknd* **66/1**

0-50 **11** *3 1/4* **First Hand**[200] 425 3-8-5 **45**.. DaleGibson 4 —
(M W Easterby) *led: hdd over 8f out: rdn 7f out: wknd over 4f out* **33/1**

0660 **12** *8* **Monagasque (IRE)**[11] 4991 3-8-1 **46**........................... SophieDoyle(5) 11 —
(S Kirk) *sn drvn along in rr: bhd fnl 6f* **33/1**

045 **13** *45* **Rebel Prince (IRE)**[25] 4491 3-8-7 **47**.........................(b[1]) JerryO'Dwyer 3 —
(M G Quinlan) *s.i.s: a in rr: bhd fnl 6f* **9/1**

2m 27.78s (-0.22) **Going Correction** -0.075s/f (Stan) **13** Ran SP% **120.8**
Speed ratings (Par 94): **97,96,94,89,86 82,75,75,63,63 60,55,22**
toteswingers: 1&2 £6.30, 1&3 £16.90, 2&3 £11.20 CSF £28.19 CT £295.88 TOTE £9.10: £3.50, £1.10, £5.00; EX 43.40 Trifecta £150.20 Pool: £304.55 - 1.50 winning units..
Owner Miss K Rausing **Bred** Miss K Rausing **Trained** Newmarket, Suffolk

FOCUS
A Class 7 event and this is at bad as it gets. None of the 13 runners had won before and only six had ever made the first three at any time in their career. It proved to be a messy contest too, with the second and third finding different ways to compromise their chances, and the field finished spread out all over Nottinghamshire. The early pace was ordinary and the winning time was 0.7 seconds slower than the claimer, so not a race to rate too positively.
Eloise Official explanation: trainer's rep said, regarding apparent improvement in form, that the filly was suited by the first time blinkers and the enterprising tactics.
Spring Quartet Official explanation: jockey said gelding dwelt in the stalls and was slowly away

Monagasque(IRE) Official explanation: jockey said filly resented the kickback
Rebel Prince(IRE) Official explanation: jockey said gelding never travelled

5329 SOUTHWELL GOLF CLUB LADY MEMBERS H'CAP 1m (F)
5:00 (5:04) (Class 5) (0-70,70) 3-Y-O+ **£5,051** (£1,503; £751; £375) **Stalls** Low

Form RPR
6004 1 **Calahonda**[8] [5090] 3-9-5 **70**....(e[1]) SebSanders 4 81
(P W D'Arcy) *chsd ldr: led over 5f out: rdn over 1f out: r.o* **12/1**
5244 2 *nse* **Ours (IRE)**[16] [4816] 6-9-10 **69**....(p) ChrisCatlin 9 81
(John A Harris) *dwlt: sn pushed along in rr: hdwy and edgd lft 2f out: rdn and ev ch ins fnl f: r.o* **6/1**[2]
0002 3 *4 ½* **Follow The Flag (IRE)**[7] [5126] 5-9-1 **67**.... DeclanCannon(7) 12 69
(A J McCabe) *hld up: hdwy over 2f out: rdn over 1f out: styd on same pce* **16/1**
3216 4 *1 ¼* **Ugenius**[15] [4859] 5-9-3 **62**.... TGMcLaughlin 13 61
(Mrs C A Dunnett) *hld up in tch: rdn over 1f out: styd on same pce* **10/1**
0034 5 *½* **Oskari**[16] [4822] 4-9-6 **65**.... PhillipMakin 8 63
(P T Midgley) *hld up in tch: rdn whn n.m.r wl over 1f out: styd on same pce fnl f* **3/1**[1]
0203 6 *2* **Tevez**[10] [5035] 4-8-12 **62**.... DeanHeslop(5) 2 55
(D Donovan) *sn pushed along in rr: hdwy u.p over 1f out: nt trble ldrs* **10/1**
0603 7 *hd* **Ocean Legend (IRE)**[29] [4386] 4-9-8 **67**.... JerryO'Dwyer 6 60
(Miss J Feilden) *led: hdd over 5f out: remained handy tl rdn over 1f out: wknd ins fnl f* **7/1**
050 8 *hd* **Miss Christophene (IRE)**[10] [5034] 3-9-5 **70**.... JimmyQuinn 11 61
(Mrs S Lamyman) *sn outpcd: rdn over 2f out: n.d* **8/1**
0115 9 *1 ¾* **Sovereignty (JPN)**[20] [4645] 7-8-12 **62**.... SophieDoyle(5) 3 50
(D K Ivory) *prom: rdn over 2f out: wknd over 1f out* **16/1**
60 10 *1 ¾* **Tres Froide (FR)**[25] [4496] 4-9-2 **61**.... AndrewElliott 7 45
(N Tinkler) *chsd ldrs: rdn over 2f out: sn wknd* **33/1**
006- 11 *3 ¾* **Dado Mush**[280] [7374] 6-9-11 **70**....(p) KirstyMilczarek 10 45
(T T Clement) *sn pushed along in mid-div: wkng whn nt clr run over 3f out: bhd whn hung rt over 1f out* **25/1**
0060 12 *21* **Count Ceprano (IRE)**[16] [4816] 5-9-2 **64**.... KellyHarrison(3) 5 —
(C R Dore) *got loose on the way to post: sn outpcd* **28/1**
0050 13 *hd* **Sign Of The Cross**[20] [4645] 5-9-3 **62**.... LPKeniry 1 —
(C R Dore) *prom: rdn over 3f out: wknd over 2f out* **40/1**
3-13 14 *½* **Provost**[159] [885] 5-9-7 **66**.... DaleGibson 14 —
(M W Easterby) *sn drvn along in rr: bhd fnl 3f* **13/2**[3]

1m 42.65s (-1.05) **Going Correction** -0.075s/f (Stan)
WFA 3 from 4yo+ 6lb **14 Ran SP% 126.5**
Speed ratings (Par 103): **102,101,97,96,95 93,93,93,91,89 86,65,64,64**
toteswingers: 1&2 £8.20, 1&3 £36.40, 2&3 £20.10 CSF £83.96 CT £1227.62 TOTE £13.20: £4.00, £2.50, £6.50; EX 75.90 Trifecta £439.70 Part won. Pool: £594.20 - 0.53 winning units. Place 6: £140.09, Place 5: £95.12.
Owner Gongolphin & Racing **Bred** Eurostrait Ltd **Trained** Newmarket, Suffolk

FOCUS
An ordinary handicap in which the front pair pulled nicely clear. The winner was back to form with the runner-up recording a minor personal-best.
Count Ceprano(IRE) Official explanation: jockey said gelding moved poorly
Sign Of The Cross Official explanation: jockey said gelding lost its action
T/Jkpt: Not won. T/Plt: £134.80 to a £1 stake. Pool: £89,818.82. 486.16 winning tickets. T/Qpdt: £32.70 to a £1 stake. Pool: £5,435.04. 122.63 winning tickets. CR

4772 AYR (L-H)
Wednesday, August 26

OFFICIAL GOING: Soft changing to soft (heavy in places) after race 2 (2.40)
Wind: Fresh, across Weather: Overcast

5330 CARLING LAGER EBF MAIDEN STKS 7f 50y
2:10 (2:10) (Class 4) 2-Y-O **£5,310** (£1,580; £789; £394) **Stalls** Low

Form RPR
3 1 **Tut (IRE)**[56] [3495] 2-8-7 0.... MartinLane(5) 2 73+
(A P Jarvis) *chsd ldrs: led over 2f out: hrd pressed ins fnl f: hld on wl* **6/1**[3]
2 *1 ½* **Golden Shaheen (IRE)** 2-9-3 0.... DO'Donohoe 6 74+
(Saeed Bin Suroor) *rn in snatches: prom: hdwy 2f out: ev ch ins fnl f: hld towards fin* **15/8**[2]
3 3 *3 ¾* **Weekend Millionair (IRE)**[33] [4265] 2-9-3 0.... PaulHanagan 3 65
(P D Evans) *cl up: chal over 2f out: rdn and edgd lft over 1f out: sn no ex* **7/4**[1]
4 *10* **Brootommity (IRE)** 2-8-12 0.... PhillipMakin 4 36
(I Semple) *dwlt: bhd: drvn over 2f out: sn no imp* **10/1**
0P 5 *4 ½* **Ochilview Warrior (IRE)**[16] [4847] 2-9-3 0.... DanielTudhope 7 30
(R Bastiman) *bhd on outside: rdn 3f out: sn struggling* **100/1**
56 6 *3 ¾* **Bonasera (IRE)**[56] [3495] 2-8-5 0.... BillyCray(7) 1 15
(A Berry) *led to over 2f out: sn rdn and wknd* **100/1**
0 7 *32* **Land Of Plenty (IRE)**[20] [4705] 2-8-12 0.... RoystonFfrench 5 —
(M Johnston) *towards rr: struggling over 3f out: t.o* **7/1**

1m 36.45s (3.05) **Going Correction** +0.30s/f (Good) **7 Ran SP% 109.0**
Speed ratings (Par 96): **94,92,88,76,71 67,30**
toteswingers: 1&2 £2.10, 1&3 £1.70, 2&3 £1.80 CSF £16.02 TOTE £6.90: £2.60, £1.70; EX 22.60.
Owner Hubert John Strecker **Bred** Ms Michelle Lyons **Trained** Middleham Moor, N Yorks

FOCUS
A modest maiden with the winning stepping up considerably on her debut and the third setting the standard.

NOTEBOOK
Tut(IRE), keen in the paddock, clearly learned plenty from her 5f Catterick debut. She looked a lot fitter than on her first appearance, settled well and travelled sweetly, benefiting from this step up in trip (her sire and dam were milers). There looks to be more to come if she retains her willing attitude, probably over further in time. (op 15-2 tchd 11-2)
Golden Shaheen(IRE), a 150,000gns newcomer, was immature in the paddock and green early on in the race, running in snatches in the first couple of furlongs, but once the penny dropped he travelled well and came there with every chance, without ever looking like passing the winner. Not over-big, he will come on mentally for the run, but appeared to handle the testing ground well enough despite his pedigree suggesting he may be better on a sounder surface. (op 7-4 tchd 2-1)
Weekend Millionair(IRE), stepped up in trip from a promising debut in a 6f soft-ground Chepstow maiden debut (form which was subsequently franked by the first two home), was a little disappointing. On the bridle and seemingly cantering early in the straight, he emptied quickly after making a brief challenge. He probably did too much too soon on this soft ground. The trip really should not have been an issue. (op 13-8)
Brootommity(IRE) was slowly away and ran green. She is sure to have learned a lot from this but was beaten a long way. (op 12-1)
Ochilview Warrior(IRE) did nothing to suggest he has nothing more than a modest degree of ability.
Bonasera(IRE) made much of the running before dropping away tamely. She didn't handle this step up in trip in this ground. Official explanation: jockey said filly hung right throughout (op 80-1)
Land Of Plenty(IRE) was tailed off and was wholly disappointing. The ground could be an excuse. Official explanation: jockey said filly had no more to give (op 15-2 tchd 8-1)

5331 WOODFORD RESERVE H'CAP 1m 2f
2:40 (2:40) (Class 6) (0-65,65) 3-Y-O **£2,388** (£705; £352) **Stalls** Low

Form RPR
-664 1 **Valid Point (IRE)**[8] [5121] 3-8-2 **46** oh1.... JamieMackay 2 67+
(Sir Mark Prescott) *mde virtually all: clr whn edgd lft over 1f out: eased last 100yds* **7/2**[1]
44B2 2 *2 ¾* **Northside Prince (IRE)**[17] [4822] 3-9-7 **65**.... PJMcDonald 1 70
(G A Swinbank) *prom: hdwy to dispute ld over 3f out: plugged on fr 2f out: no ch w eased down wnr* **6/1**
2023 3 *1* **Jachol (IRE)**[25] [4545] 3-8-12 **56**.... RoystonFfrench 6 59
(W J Haggas) *hld up in tch: effrt 3f out: one pce fnl 2f* **9/2**[3]
0360 4 *12* **Digger Derek (IRE)**[14] [4892] 3-9-4 **62**.... PaulHanagan 7 41
(R A Fahey) *chsd ldrs tl rdn and wknd fr over 2f out* **8/1**
0410 5 *2 ¼* **Carter**[24] [4562] 3-9-3 **61**.... TonyHamilton 9 36
(W M Brisbourne) *prom: drvn over 3f out: wknd over 2f out* **20/1**
-503 6 *nk* **Shadows Lengthen**[13] [4943] 3-8-11 **55**....(b) DaleGibson 12 29
(M W Easterby) *t.k.h in midfield: drvn 3f out: sn outpcd* **20/1**
-002 7 *2* **Sampower Rose (IRE)**[54] [3574] 3-9-4 **62**.... DavidAllan 10 32
(D Carroll) *chsd ldrs tl wknd fr 3f out* **13/2**
0300 8 *12* **Castle Myth (USA)**[24] [4562] 3-8-3 **52**.... LanceBetts(5) 3 —
(B Ellison) *towards rr: drvn after 3f: nvr on terms* **50/1**
6600 9 *1 ¾* **Sydney Cove (IRE)**[13] [4943] 3-7-10 **47** oh1 ow1.... JamesPSullivan(7) 5 —
(R Allan) *s.i.s: sn wl bhd: nvr on terms* **66/1**
0504 10 *8* **Kristopher James (IRE)**[13] [4943] 3-8-10 **54**.... LiamJones 8 —
(W M Brisbourne) *disp ld tl wknd fr 3f out* **20/1**
043 11 *8* **Dean Iarracht (IRE)**[31] [4348] 3-9-6 **64**....(v[1]) PhillipMakin 11 —
(M Dods) *bhd: struggling over 4f out: nvr on terms* **4/1**[2]
3200 12 *80* **Royal Society**[70] [3018] 3-8-11 **55**....(t) AndrewMullen 4 —
(A G Foster) *bhd: sn pushed along: struggling 1/2-way: virtually p.u in st* **20/1**

2m 14.83s (2.83) **Going Correction** +0.30s/f (Good) **12 Ran SP% 121.6**
Speed ratings (Par 98): **100,97,97,87,85 85,83,74,72,66 59,—**
toteswingers: 1&2 £4.80, 1&3 £4.60, 2&3 £3.40 CSF £22.91 CT £99.07 TOTE £5.00: £1.30, £3.00, £1.40; EX 34.60.
Owner W E Sturt - Osborne House **Bred** Pier House Stud **Trained** Newmarket, Suffolk

FOCUS
Run at a fair true pace despite the conditions, the time was run roughly a second-per-furlong slower than standard, on a par with the opening juvenile maiden. The form is best rated around the placed horses. After a sharp shower, the ground was officially changed after the race to soft, heavy in places.
Dean Iarracht(IRE) Official explanation: jockey said gelding did not face the first time visor

5332 COCA COLA H'CAP 7f 50y
3:10 (3:10) (Class 6) (0-65,65) 3-Y-O+ **£2,388** (£705; £352) **Stalls** Low

Form RPR
5032 1 **Daring Dream (GER)**[52] [3662] 4-9-5 **58**.... DanielTudhope 6 70
(J S Goldie) *trckd ldrs: led appr fnl f: drvn out* **9/2**[2]
64-1 2 *1 ¾* **Ishiadancer**[28] [4432] 4-9-11 **64**.... DavidAllan 13 71
(E J Alston) *chsd ldrs: led over 2f out: edgd lft and hdd appr fnl f: one pce ins fnl f* **10/1**
060 3 *3* **Lordship (IRE)**[13] [4938] 5-8-7 **51**.... MarkCoumbe(5) 10 50+
(A W Carroll) *hld up: nt clr run over 2f out: kpt on fnl f: no ch w first two* **7/1**[3]
020- 4 *1 ½* **Lambrini Lace (IRE)**[299] [7118] 4-9-2 **55**.... TonyHamilton 8 50
(Mrs L Williamson) *cl up: ev ch over 2f out to over 1f out: no ex fnl f* **20/1**
1000 5 *nk* **Only A Splash**[16] [4843] 5-8-5 **51**.... JamesPSullivan(7) 7 45
(Mrs R A Carr) *led to over 2f out: kpt on same pce* **9/1**
-600 6 *2 ¼* **Distant Pleasure**[40] [4070] 5-9-1 **54**....(p) PhillipMakin 3 42
(M Dods) *midfield: effrt over 2f out: no imp over 1f out* **4/1**[1]
5003 7 *2 ½* **Obe One**[7] [5150] 9-8-0 **46** oh1.... BillyCray(7) 12 27
(A Berry) *s.i.s: sn pushed along in rr: shortlived effrt over 2f out: sn no imp* **40/1**
1016 8 *shd* **Downhill Skier (IRE)**[18] [4772] 5-9-12 **65**.... LiamJones 14 46
(W M Brisbourne) *towards rr: drvn 3f out: nvr able to chal* **11/1**
0063 9 *¾* **Obe Royal**[16] [4859] 5-9-12 **65**....(b) PaulHanagan 4 44
(P D Evans) *midfield: drvn and outpcd over 2f out: sn btn* **8/1**
0-40 10 *½* **Oscar Wild**[91] [2314] 7-8-11 **50**....(p) RoystonFfrench 2 28
(I Semple) *towards rr: rdn 1/2-way: nvr on terms* **33/1**
0600 11 *2* **Cross Of Lorraine (IRE)**[14] [4887] 6-8-2 **46** oh1...(b) PatrickDonaghy(5) 9 18
(J Wade) *towards rr: drvn 1/2-way: sn btn* **16/1**
0002 12 *26* **Russian Music (USA)**[50] [3710] 4-8-10 **49**....(b) DaleGibson 5 —
(C A Mulhall) *prom tl wknd qckly over 2f out: eased whn no ch* **8/1**

1m 34.65s (1.25) **Going Correction** +0.30s/f (Good) **12 Ran SP% 116.4**
Speed ratings (Par 101): **104,102,98,96,96 93,91,90,90,89 87,57**
toteswingers: 1&2 £7.20, 1&3 £11.00, 2&3 £17.70 CSF £47.04 CT £316.60 TOTE £4.90: £1.90, £3.40, £3.20; EX 41.30.
Owner Ambrose Turnbull **Bred** Gestut Auenquelle **Trained** Uplawmoor, E Renfrews

FOCUS
An ordinary handicap run at a fair pace for the conditions, and one that few got into. The winner was back to his best with the runner-up progressing and the form looks sound.
Russian Music(USA) Official explanation: jockey said gelding had lost its action but returned sound.

5333 GUINNESS H'CAP 1m
3:40 (3:41) (Class 4) (0-80,80) 3-Y-O+ **£5,828** (£1,734; £866; £432) **Stalls** Low

Form RPR
0534 1 **Collateral Damage (IRE)**[11] [5040] 6-9-3 **70**....(t) DavidAllan 3 86+
(T D Easterby) *chsd ldrs: rdn 3f out: led over 1f out: drew clr: eased wl ins fnl f* **11/4**[1]
6242 2 *6* **Stellite**[15] [4878] 9-8-12 **70**.... GaryBartley(5) 5 70
(J S Goldie) *prom: effrt 2f out: kpt on fnl f: no ch w wnr* **22/1**
1310 3 *nk* **Tom Tower (IRE)**[26] [4496] 5-9-1 **68**.... PJMcDonald 2 68
(A C Whillans) *led: qcknd clr 1/2-way: rdn and hdd over 1f out: kpt on same pce* **12/1**
5005 4 *2* **Doric Echo**[15] [4878] 3-9-1 **74**.... RoystonFfrench 4 69
(B Smart) *prom: drvn over 3f out: one pce fnl 2f* **25/1**
0056 5 *1* **Woodsley House (IRE)**[21] [4657] 7-8-12 **68**.... NeilBrown(3) 8 61
(A G Foster) *chsd ldrs: drvn 3f out: one pce fr 2f out* **18/1**

3150 **6** 1 1/4 **High Severa (IRE)**[48] 3780 3-8-12 76 .... MartinLane(5) 6 66
(A P Jarvis) *midfield: rdn over 3f out: edgd lft 2f out: no imp* **4/1**[2]

0000 **7** 1/2 **Major Magpie (IRE)**[21] 4663 7-9-1 68 .... (p) PhillipMakin 11 57
(M Dods) *hld up: rdn over 3f out: plugged on fnl f: n.d* **28/1**

6422 **8** 1/2 **Handsome Falcon**[15] 4881 5-9-9 76 .... PaulHanagan 12 63
(R A Fahey) *midfield on outside: outpcd over 2f out: sn btn* **8/1**

4006 **9** nk **Wovoka (IRE)**[18] 4804 6-9-10 77 .... TonyHamilton 14 64
(K A Ryan) *swtchd to ins rail sn after s: hld up: rdn over 2f out: n.d* **33/1**

3045 **10** 4 1/2 **All About You (IRE)**[14] 4902 3-9-7 80 .... (b[1]) LiamJones 10 56
(W J Haggas) *bhd: rdn and hung lft 3f out: sn btn* **15/2**

4034 **11** 3/4 **Boy Blue**[25] 4549 4-9-13 80 .... DaleGibson 1 55
(P Salmon) *t.k.h: cl up tl wknd over 2f out* **6/1**[3]

440 **12** 10 **Addikt (IRE)**[13] 4930 4-9-10 77 .... PaulQuinn 9 29
(G A Harker) *bhd: drvn over 3f out: sn struggling* **40/1**

00-3 **13** 3/4 **Ella Woodcock (IRE)**[121] 1557 5-9-7 74 .... (p) DanielTudhope 7 24
(E J Alston) *hld up: struggling over 2f out: sn btn* **28/1**

0000 **14** 2 1/4 **Santiago Atitlan**[13] 4941 7-9-0 74 .... JamesPSullivan(7) 13 19
(P Monteith) *hld up: pushed along over 3f out: sn wknd* **100/1**

1m 45.15s (1.35) **Going Correction** +0.30s/f (Good)
WFA 3 from 4yo+ 6lb **14** Ran SP% **118.2**
Speed ratings (Par 105): **105,99,98,96,95 94,93,93,93,88 87,77,77,74**
toteswingers: 1&2 £8.30, 1&3 £8.10, 2&3 £6.20 CSF £71.42 CT £505.65 TOTE £3.50: £1.90, £4.60, £2.80; EX 62.70.
Owner Middleham Park Racing Xxv **Bred** Minch Bloodstock And Castletown Stud **Trained** Great Habton, N Yorks

FOCUS
Though not the Magnet Cup trial it once was, this was still a competitive handicap where the draw appeared to be a factor, with the first six home coming from stalls 3, 5, 2, 4, 8 and 6, and they all came up the far rail. The form is best rated around the placed horses.
Boy Blue Official explanation: jockey said colt hung right-handed in the final furlong.

5334 TENNENT'S LAGER H'CAP — 1m 2f
4:10 (4:10) (Class 4) (0-85,84) 3-Y-O+
£6,231 (£1,866; £933; £467; £233; £117) **Stalls** Low

Form RPR

5116 **1** **Hollow Green (IRE)**[17] 4827 3-8-11 78 .... MichaelJStainton(3) 10 88+
(P D Evans) *s.i.s: bhd: hdwy on outside to ld 2f out: drvn out fnl f* **14/1**

1225 **2** 1 1/4 **Shaloo Diamond**[21] 4661 4-10-0 84 .... TonyHamilton 8 91
(R M Whitaker) *prom: effrt 2f out: kpt on ins fnl f* **7/1**[3]

046 **3** nk **Red Jade**[25] 4517 4-9-10 80 .... PaulHanagan 6 86
(R A Fahey) *in tch: effrt over 2f out: kpt on fnl f: hld towards fin* **9/2**[1]

1353 **4** 3 1/4 **Kingsdale Orion (IRE)**[16] 4840 5-8-13 74 .... LanceBetts(5) 5 74
(B Ellison) *hld up: hdwy on outside over 2f out: no imp fnl f* **13/2**[2]

0302 **5** 1 **Best Prospect (IRE)**[27] 4471 7-9-10 80 .... (t) PhillipMakin 11 78
(M Dods) *hld up: stdy hdwy over 2f out: rdn and one pce fnl f* **12/1**

2B43 **6** 1 **Hawkit (USA)**[14] 4898 8-8-4 65 oh11 .... MartinLane(5) 12 61
(P Monteith) *hld up on outside: hdwy to chal over 2f out: rdn and no ex over 1f out* **33/1**

0554 **7** 3/4 **Rosbay (IRE)**[13] 4930 5-9-8 78 .... DavidAllan 13 75+
(T D Easterby) *prom: n.m.r and lost pl over 2f out: rallied fnl f: no imp* **9/1**

0-14 **8** nk **Hollins**[25] 4541 5-8-12 75 .... JamesPSullivan(7) 1 69
(Micky Hammond) *trckd ldrs: rdn whn n.m.r briefly over 2f out: sn no imp* **12/1**

3100 **9** 2 **Shy Glance (USA)**[7] 5160 7-8-12 71 .... NeilBrown(3) 9 61
(P Monteith) *hld up: pushed along over 2f out: nvr able to chal* **66/1**

33 **10** 1/2 **Persian Peril**[27] 4471 5-9-13 83 .... PJMcDonald 14 72
(G A Swinbank) *trckd ldrs: effrt and ev ch over 2f out: wknd fnl f* **12/1**

125 **11** 5 **Chookie Hamilton**[22] 4619 5-9-1 76 .... PatrickDonaghy(5) 4 55
(I Semple) *led to 2f out: sn rdn and btn* **20/1**

000 **12** nk **Annibale Caro**[11] 2815 7-8-9 65 .... LiamJones 7 43
(J S Goldie) *hld up towards rr: drvn 3f out: sn n.d* **20/1**

1-52 **13** 15 **Battle Planner (USA)**[54] 3564 3-9-5 83 .... RoystonFfrench 2 31
(I Semple) *midfield: lost pl over 4f out: no ch after* **10/1**

303 **14** 2 1/4 **Timocracy**[28] 4426 4-9-7 77 .... DanielTudhope 3 21
(T D Walford) *cl up: rdn whn n.m.r and lost pl over 2f out: sn btn and eased* **8/1**

2m 15.67s (3.67) **Going Correction** +0.30s/f (Good)
WFA 3 from 4yo+ 8lb **14** Ran SP% **117.9**
Speed ratings (Par 105): **97,96,95,93,92 91,90,90,89,88 84,84,72,70**
toteswingers: 1&2 £22.60, 1&3 £15.00, 2&3 £4.70 CSF £102.36 CT £520.38 TOTE £12.50: £2.80, £2.40, £2.50; EX 145.00 Trifecta £297.50 Part won. Pool: £402.10 - 0.20 winning units..
Owner Raymond N R Auld **Bred** R N Auld **Trained** Pandy, Monmouths

FOCUS
A decent handicap, run at a true clip for the conditions. The third is back to something like his reappearance form.
Rosbay(IRE) Official explanation: jockey said gelding was denied a clear run.

5335 VLADIVAR VODKA H'CAP — 6f
4:40 (4:41) (Class 5) (0-75,75) 3-Y-O
£2,914 (£867; £433; £216) **Stalls** High

Form RPR

5354 **1** **Grissom (IRE)**[18] 4776 3-8-11 72 .... BillyCray(7) 7 80
(A Berry) *trckd ldrs: led over 1f out: drvn out fnl f* **14/1**

6422 **2** 1 1/2 **Kingswinford (IRE)**[18] 4788 3-9-7 75 .... PaulHanagan 1 78
(P D Evans) *in tch: effrt 2f out: chsd wnr ins fnl f: r.o* **6/1**[3]

4454 **3** 1 1/4 **Pokfulham (IRE)**[3] 5295 3-8-4 58 .... (v) LiamJones 3 57
(J S Goldie) *cl up: ev ch over 1f out: one pce fnl f* **13/2**

3213 **4** 2 1/2 **Cheyenne Red (IRE)**[18] 4777 3-8-13 67 .... PhillipMakin 9 58
(M Dods) *in tch: rdn 2f out: kpt on same pce fnl f* **3/1**[1]

3550 **5** 3/4 **On Offer (IRE)**[32] 4309 3-9-1 69 .... (p) DavidAllan 10 58+
(T D Easterby) *dwlt: bhd: rdn 1/2-way: kpt on fnl f: n.d* **10/1**

3451 **6** 1 1/2 **Captain Scooby**[7] 5148 3-9-2 73 6ex .... MichaelJStainton(3) 8 57+
(R M Whitaker) *in tch: no room fr over 2f out to 1f out: nt rcvr* **7/2**[2]

5-30 **7** nk **Mister Fantastic**[76] 2845 3-9-2 70 .... PJMcDonald 5 53
(M Dods) *trckd ldrs tl rdn and wknd over 1f out* **11/1**

4450 **8** nk **Maggie Lou (IRE)**[35] 4198 3-9-3 74 .... (v[1]) NeilBrown(3) 4 56
(K A Ryan) *dwlt: bhd: drvn 1/2-way: nvr on terms* **20/1**

0220 **9** 4 1/2 **Fathey (IRE)**[23] 4591 3-8-13 67 .... TonyHamilton 6 35
(R A Fahey) *w ldr tl wknd over 1f out* **16/1**

10 6 **Sanjay's Choice (IRE)**[45] 3904 3-8-8 69 .... JamesPSullivan(7) 11 17
(T G McCourt, Ire) *led to over 1f out: sn wknd* **12/1**

1m 16.64s (3.04) **Going Correction** +0.525s/f (Yiel) **10** Ran SP% **117.3**
Speed ratings (Par 100): **100,98,96,93,92 90,89,89,83,75**
toteswingers: 1&2 £5.10, 1&3 £13.60, 2&3 £5.30 CSF £96.20 CT £619.84 TOTE £14.50: £3.80, £1.90, £3.60; EX 71.10.
Jim & Helen Bowers **Bred** Michael McGlynn **Trained** Cockerham, Lancs

FOCUS
An ordinary sprint handicap and they came up the stands' side for the first time. The winner recorded a personal best wit the third setting a sound level. The time was slower, particularly in comparison to the earlier races where the winners came up the far side.
On Offer(IRE) Official explanation: jockey said filly was denied a clear run.
Captain Scooby Official explanation: jockey said gelding was denied a clear run.
Sanjay's Choice(IRE) Official explanation: jockey said gelding hung left-handed throughout.

5336 MAGNER'S CIDER H'CAP — 5f
5:10 (5:11) (Class 6) (0-65,64) 3-Y-O
£2,388 (£705; £352) **Stalls** High

Form RPR

6416 **1** **Scrapper Smith (IRE)**[14] 4894 3-9-4 61 .... PJMcDonald 5 68
(A C Whillans) *hld up in tch: swtchd lft and hdwy to ld ins fnl f: r.o strly* **9/4**[2]

-620 **2** 1 1/4 **Residency (IRE)**[21] 4653 3-9-7 64 .... RoystonFfrench 6 67
(B Smart) *trckd ldrs: rdn whn n.m.r briefly ent fnl f: styd on to chse wnr towards fin* **5/1**[3]

0024 **3** nk **Miss Pusey Street**[7] 5155 3-8-7 50 .... PaulHanagan 2 51
(P D Evans) *led to over 1f out: edgd lft and kpt on u.p fnl f* **2/1**[1]

4003 **4** 3/4 **Highly Acclaimed**[7] 5145 3-8-5 48 .... (v) PaulQuinn 1 47
(Mrs A Duffield) *dwlt: hld up in tch on outside: effrt 2f out: one pce whn checked ins fnl f* **6/1**

66 **5** shd **Frisky Queen (IRE)**[18] 4778 3-8-2 45 .... LiamJones 4 43
(T G McCourt, Ire) *in tch: hdwy and ev ch over 1f out: no ex ins fnl f* **12/1**

-000 **6** 1 1/4 **Madame Jourdain (IRE)**[7] 5145 3-8-0 50 .... CharlotteKerton(7) 7 44
(A Berry) *prom: drvn 2f out: one pce fnl f* **22/1**

P000 **7** hd **Oceanic Dancer (IRE)**[13] 4942 3-7-13 49 .... JamesPSullivan(7) 3 42
(Patrick Morris) *t.k.h: cl up: led over 1f out to ins fnl f: sn no ex* **18/1**

5660 **8** 4 1/2 **Badtanman**[9] 5105 3-8-2 45 .... (b) JamieMackay 8 22
(Peter Grayson) *bhd and sn hung lft: no ch fr 1/2-way* **22/1**

63.84 secs (3.74) **Going Correction** +0.525s/f (Yiel) **8** Ran SP% **116.7**
Speed ratings (Par 98): **91,89,88,87,87 85,84,77**
toteswingers: 1&2 £2.60, 1&3 £2.10, 2&3 £3.00 CSF £14.44 CT £24.76 TOTE £3.20: £1.40, £1.70, £1.30; EX 16.40 Place 6: £133.46, Place 5: £61.10..
Owner A C Whillans **Bred** John Costello **Trained** Newmill-On-Slitrig, Borders

FOCUS
A weak sprint handicap and they finished in a heap, suggesting the form must be taken on trust, although it looks sound enough but limited on paper.
T/Jkpt: Not won. T/Plt: £258.90 to a £1 stake. Pool: £73,601.20. 207.45 winning tickets. T/Qpdt: £75.30 to a £1 stake. Pool: £5,446.23. 53.50 winning tickets. RY

4972 CATTERICK (L-H)
Wednesday, August 26

OFFICIAL GOING: Good to soft (good in places) changing to good to soft after race 1 (2.20)
Wind: Moderate 1/2 behind Weather: Persistent rain

5337 RACINGUK.TV MEDIAN AUCTION MAIDEN STKS — 5f
2:20 (2:21) (Class 6) 2-Y-O
£2,388 (£705; £352) **Stalls** Low

Form RPR

0045 **1** **Camacho Flyer (IRE)**[43] 3952 2-8-12 58 .... (v[1]) PaulPickard(5) 6 69
(P T Midgley) *chsd ldr: led 3f out: kpt on wl* **33/1**

6 **2** 1 1/4 **Glen Shiel (USA)**[28] 4424 2-9-3 0 .... GregFairley 3 65
(M Johnston) *chsd ldrs: outpcd over 1f out: kpt on wl to take 2nd wl ins fnl f* **5/2**[2]

2052 **3** 1 3/4 **Bronze Beau**[16] 4844 2-9-3 72 .... TGMcLaughlin 4 58
(Mrs L Stubbs) *chsd ldrs: kpt on same pce fnl f* **9/4**[1]

423 **4** 1 3/4 **My Mandy (IRE)**[13] 4928 2-8-12 68 .... EddieAhern 10 47
(Ian Williams) *chsd ldrs on outer: edgd lft over 1f out: eased wl ins fnl f* **4/1**[3]

246 **5** 2 1/4 **Goodbye Earl (IRE)**[19] 4752 2-8-12 71 .... TomEaves 7 39
(A Berry) *led 2f: hung rt and wknd ins fnl f* **5/1**

6 **6** 1 1/2 **Lucy Gliters**[70] 3032 2-8-12 0 .... DNolan 11 33
(T P Tate) *chsd ldrs on outside: outpcd and edgd lft over 1f out* **12/1**

040 **7** 3 1/2 **Lady Bucket**[41] 4001 2-8-12 0 .... (v[1]) PaulMulrennan 1 21
(Paul Green) *s.i.s: reminders after 1f: nvr on terms* **50/1**

054 **8** 2 1/4 **Chilean Fizz**[27] 4463 2-8-12 54 .... SilvestreDeSousa 8 19+
(Mrs A Duffield) *s.i.s: mid-div: eased fnl f* **33/1**

0 **9** 4 1/2 **Teeraha (IRE)**[9] 5109 2-8-12 0 .... GrahamGibbons 9 —
(D Shaw) *chsd ldrs on outer: hung rt and lost pl over 1f out* **80/1**

06 **10** 6 **Jigajig**[44] 3910 2-9-3 0 .... DuranFentiman 5 —
(N Wilson) *s.i.s: a bhd* **66/1**

60.68 secs (0.88) **Going Correction** +0.025s/f (Good) **10** Ran SP% **114.3**
Speed ratings (Par 92): **93,91,88,85,81 79,73,70,63,53**
toteswingers: 1&2 £14.60, 1&3 £13.90, 2&3 £2.80 CSF £111.56 TOTE £38.50: £6.90, £1.40, £1.10; EX 152.30.
Owner Peedeetee Syndicate **Bred** John Cullinan **Trained** Westow, N Yorks

FOCUS
This was a moderate juvenile maiden with the winner stepping up considerably in the headgear. The form is best treated negatively.

NOTEBOOK
Camacho Flyer(IRE), transformed by the first-time visor, galloped on relentlessly to cause something of a surprise. Officially rated just 58, he had not done much in cheekpieces on each of his last two starts, but the slower ground here definitely suited and it will be interesting to see if he goes on from this. (op 40-1 tchd 50-1)
Glen Shiel(USA), who showed a bit of promise on his debut over 6f, was soon outpaced on this drop in trip and, though he stayed on down the straight, he never looked like getting to the winner. He is the sort to do better in handicaps. (op 9-4 tchd 2-1)
Bronze Beau, although exposed, was entitled to go close on the pick of his form and he had every chance, but just couldn't quicken under pressure. (op 5-2 tchd 11-4)
My Mandy(IRE), another exposed sort, has yet to run on ground as slow as this and again came up short. (op 7-2 tchd 9-2)
Goodbye Earl(IRE), already having her 12th start of the season, showed tons of early speed, but was quickly left trailing by the winner and ended up well held. (op 13-2)
Teeraha(IRE) Official explanation: jockey said filly hung right-handed throughout

5338 ZETLAND MAIDEN STKS — 5f 212y
2:50 (2:51) (Class 5) 3-Y-O+
£2,914 (£867; £433; £216) **Stalls** Low

Form RPR

0452 **1** **Arjemis**[13] 4942 3-8-12 57 .... PAspell 1 60
(C R Wilson) *trckd ldrs: effrt over 2f out: hung rt over 1f out: led jst ins fnl f: jst hld on* **9/4**[2]

-333 **2** shd **Neva A Mull Moment (IRE)**[11] 5041 3-9-3 62 .... AdrianTNicholls 2 65
(D Nicholls) *led: edgd rt and hdd jst ins fnl f: kpt on: jst failed* **4/1**[3]

0-00 **3** 2 3/4 **Pretty Orchid**[39] 4105 4-8-10 47 (p) PaulPickard(5) 4 51
(P T Midgley) *s.i.s: detached last and drvn along: hdwy on ins over 2f out: kpt on: nt trble 1st 2* **16/1**

26-3 **4** 2 **Verinco**[35] 4199 3-9-3 73 (p) TomEaves 8 50
(B Smart) *chsd ldrs on outside: drvn over 2f out: edgd lft and fdd appr fnl f* **13/8**[1]

60-0 **5** 2 1/4 **No Nightmare (USA)**[16] 4860 3-8-12 47 PaulMulrennan 7 38
(A P Jarvis) *trckd ldrs: effrt 3f out: wknd over 1f out* **16/1**

0054 **6** 6 **Tarus (IRE)**[11] 5041 5-8-10 48 BMcHugh(5) 6 18
(A Berry) *chsd ldr: drvn over 2f out: lost pl over 1f out* **10/1**

1m 16.82s (3.22) **Going Correction** +0.55s/f (Yiel)
WFA 3 from 4yo+ 3lb **6** Ran SP% **109.7**
Speed ratings (Par 103): **100,99,96,93,90 82**
toteswingers: 1&2 £1.90, 1&3 £6.20, 2&3 £4.90 CSF £11.04 TOTE £3.00: £2.00, £2.10; EX 11.00.
Owner David Bartlett **Bred** Mrs Andrea Bartlett **Trained** Manfield, N Yorks

FOCUS
A typically weak older horse sprint maiden but the form looks straightforward rated around the first two.

5339 SWALE H'CAP — 1m 7f 177y
3:20 (3:20) (Class 5) (0-70,68) 3-Y-0+ **£3,070** (£906; £453) **Stalls** Low

Form RPR

132 **1** **Spiders Star**[10] 5068 6-9-0 59 PaulPickard(5) 2 69+
(S G West) *hld up toward rr: hdwy 7f out: effrt over 2f out: wnt 2nd over 1f out: styd on to ld towards fin* **6/4**[1]

0220 **2** 1/2 **Promise Maker (USA)**[23] 4600 4-9-8 62 GrahamGibbons 4 71
(T D Walford) *led: kpt on wl fnl 2f: hdd nr fin* **7/1**

2554 **3** 6 **Fenners (USA)**[14] 4893 6-8-7 52 oh3 BMcHugh(5) 6 54
(M W Easterby) *trckd ldrs: effrt over 4f out: one pce fnl 2f* **8/1**

3502 **4** 3 **Sir Sandicliffe (IRE)**[16] 4862 5-9-9 63 TGMcLaughlin 1 61
(W M Brisbourne) *s.s: hld up towards rr: drvn and outpcd over 3f out: kpt on fnl 2f: nvr a threat* **15/2**

5040 **5** 1 1/4 **Fell Pack**[14] 4893 5-8-6 53 IJBrennan(7) 9 50
(J J Quinn) *trckd ldrs: t.k.h: fdd appr fnl f* **4/1**[2]

0006 **6** 2 **Snowberry Hill (USA)**[16] 4862 6-8-5 52 oh2 RyanClark(7) 10 46
(Lucinda Featherstone) *trckd ldrs: t.k.h: wknd over 2f out* **22/1**

0604 **7** 32 **Casual Garcia**[10] 5068 4-10-0 68 (b) SebSanders 8 24
(Sir Mark Prescott) *hld up detached in last: hdwy over 6f out: drvn 4f out: lost pl over 2f out: sn bhd: t.o* **6/1**[3]

000 **8** 4 1/2 **Treetops Hotel (IRE)**[67] 3171 10-8-12 52 oh7 DuranFentiman 3 —
(L R James) *chsd ldr: drvn over 4f out: lost pl over 3f out: bhd whn eased over 1f out: t.o* **150/1**

3m 42.84s (10.84) **Going Correction** +0.55s/f (Yiel) **8** Ran SP% **114.7**
Speed ratings (Par 103): **94,93,90,89,88 87,71,69**
toteswingers: 1&2 £3.60, 1&3 £4.10, 2&3 £7.50 CSF £12.90 CT £63.54 TOTE £2.50: £1.30, £2.30, £2.00; EX 16.10.
Owner Miss Kate Milligan **Bred** Acrum Lodge Stud **Trained** Middleham Moor, N Yorks

FOCUS
This was just a modest staying handicap and is best rated through the third.
Casual Garcia Official explanation: trainer said gelding was unsuited by the good to soft ground

5340 RACING UK H'CAP — 7f
3:50 (3:50) (Class 4) (0-80,79) 3-Y-O **£5,180** (£1,541; £770; £384) **Stalls** Low

Form RPR

0- **1** **Conry (IRE)**[38] 4122 3-9-1 73 EddieAhern 4 84
(Patrick Morris) *hld up in rr: hdwy over 2f out: r.o to ld nr fin* **18/1**

2651 **2** nk **She's In The Money**[13] 4940 3-8-9 70 FrederikTylicki(3) 3 80
(R A Fahey) *hld up in midfield: hdwy to ld 2f out: edgd rt ins fnl f: hdd nr fin* **5/2**[1]

3202 **3** 1 3/4 **Rio Cobolo (IRE)**[20] 4707 3-8-3 66 (v) PaulPickard(5) 1 71
(Paul Green) *s.i.s: hdwy to chse ld over 2f out: edgd rt and sn hdd kpt on same pce fnl f* **12/1**

13 **4** 6 **Angel Song**[192] 562 3-9-4 76 SebSanders 6 65
(Sir Mark Prescott) *s.i.s: c stands' side and led that gp over 2f out: kpt on: nvr on terms* **7/2**[2]

4310 **5** 3 **Minturno (USA)**[20] 4707 3-8-10 68 (p) SilvestreDeSousa 11 49
(Mrs A Duffield) *s.i.s: hdwy 2f out: nvr a threat* **14/1**

-410 **6** 4 1/2 **Snow Bay**[32] 4316 3-9-7 79 TomEaves 5 48
(B Smart) *s.i.s: in rr and reminders over 4f out: c stands' side over 2f out: nvr a factor* **11/1**

6202 **7** 3/4 **Come And Go (UAE)**[17] 4820 3-9-5 77 RobertWinston 9 44
(G A Swinbank) *sn chsng ldrs: c stands' side over 2f out: sn wknd* **12/1**

5050 **8** 7 **Al Mugtareb (IRE)**[32] 4316 3-8-10 68 (b[1]) GregFairley 8 16
(M Johnston) *mde most tl over 2f out: sn wknd and eased* **14/1**

0330 **9** 2 1/4 **Cook's Endeavour (USA)**[18] 4802 3-9-2 74 (p) GrahamGibbons 2 16
(K A Ryan) *drvn to chse ldrs: edgd rt and lost pl 2f out* **9/2**[3]

1540 **10** 3 1/2 **Jimwil (IRE)**[28] 4433 3-9-1 73 (b) PaulMulrennan 10 —
(M Dods) *sn w ldrs on outer: hung rt and wknd 2f out* **33/1**

1m 29.65s (2.65) **Going Correction** +0.55s/f (Yiel) **10** Ran SP% **114.2**
Speed ratings (Par 102): **106,105,103,96,93 88,87,79,76,72**
toteswingers: 1&2 £11.30, 1&3 £26.50, 2&3 £6.50 CSF £61.73 CT £482.89 TOTE £26.90: £5.10, £1.30, £3.00; EX 94.00.
Owner Mrs S J Kelly **Bred** Shay White **Trained** Tarporley, Cheshire

FOCUS
The runners were spread across the track in the straight for this low-grade handicap. The runner-up recorded a personal best with the fairly reliable third the best guide.
Minturno(USA) Official explanation: jockey said colt was unsuited by the good to soft ground
Cook's Endeavour(USA) Official explanation: jockey said gelding was never travelling
Jimwil(IRE) Official explanation: jockey said gelding hung right-handed throughout.

5341 CATTERICKBRIDGE.CO.UK H'CAP — 5f
4:20 (4:20) (Class 6) (0-65,64) 3-Y-O+ **£2,388** (£705; £352) **Stalls** Low

Form RPR

4350 **1** **Spirit Of Coniston**[31] 4355 6-8-10 51 PaulMulrennan 6 67
(P T Midgley) *mde all far side: clr over 1f out: r.o strly* **9/1**

3-00 **2** 4 1/2 **Windjammer**[41] 3999 5-8-9 53 (v[1]) FrederikTylicki(3) 7 53
(L A Mullaney) *chsd ldrs centre: wnt 2nd over 2f out: no imp* **16/1**

6464 **3** 2 1/2 **Mayoman (IRE)**[12] 4977 4-9-1 56 DNolan 13 47+
(D Carroll) *s.i.s: in rr towards stands' side: hdwy over 1f out: kpt on ins fnl f* **7/1**

4030 **4** 3/4 **Bees River (IRE)**[13] 4942 3-8-2 50 (v) MatthewDavies(5) 11 38
(A P Jarvis) *chsd ldrs towards stands' side: one pce fnl 2f* **28/1**

2010 **5** 1 1/2 **Select Committee**[15] 4886 4-9-6 61 (v) GrahamGibbons 5 44
(J J Quinn) *hld up in rr: hdwy over 1f out: nvr nr ldrs* **3/1**[1]

2540 **6** 1 1/4 **Kyzer Chief**[19] 4753 4-9-6 64 KellyHarrison(3) 12 42
(R E Barr) *chsd ldrs outer: kpt on same pce fnl 2f* **12/1**

6-00 **7** nk **Gleaming Spirit (IRE)**[33] 4283 5-8-6 47 (v) GregFairley 3 24
(Peter Grayson) *chsd wnr towards far side: fdd fnl f* **18/1**

4606 **8** 3 **Just Joey**[13] 4929 5-8-6 47 (be) LukeMorris 8 13
(J R Weymes) *chsd ldrs: wknd over 1f out* **28/1**

06-0 **9** 2 **Shining Times (IRE)**[7] 5145 3-8-5 53 PaulPickard(5) 14 12
(P T Midgley) *in rr stands' side: nvr on terms* **50/1**

6043 **10** 3/4 **Northern Empire (IRE)**[7] 5156 6-9-7 62 (p) EddieAhern 4 18
(F Jordan) *hld up towards far side: nvr on terms* **11/2**[3]

3404 **11** 1 **Excitable (IRE)**[35] 4204 3-8-6 49 SilvestreDeSousa 1 —
(Mrs D J Sanderson) *chsd wnr far side: lost pl over 1f out* **7/2**[2]

000 **12** 2 3/4 **Molly Two**[7] 5149 4-9-4 59 RobertWinston 10 —
(L A Mullaney) *trckd ldrs outer: wknd and eased over 1f out* **18/1**

59.68 secs (-0.12) **Going Correction** +0.025s/f (Good)
WFA 3 from 4yo+ 2lb **12** Ran SP% **118.1**
Speed ratings (Par 101): **101,93,89,88,86 84,83,78,75,74 72,68**
toteswingers: 1&2 £21.70, 1&3 £14.20, 2&3 £18.20 CSF £140.73 CT £1084.30 TOTE £10.20: £3.00, £5.30, £2.60; EX 167.80.
Owner P O'Gara & N Kelly **Bred** Green Square Racing **Trained** Westow, N Yorks

FOCUS
This was a weak handicap with the winner rated to his 2008 best although little reliable in behind.
Northern Empire(IRE) Official explanation: jockey said gelding was never travelling
Excitable(IRE) Official explanation: jockey said filly finished distressed

5342 GO RACING AT REDCAR ON SATURDAY H'CAP — 1m 3f 214y
4:50 (4:50) (Class 6) (0-60,58) 3-Y-O **£2,388** (£705; £352) **Stalls** High

Form RPR

1530 **1** **Rosewin (IRE)**[18] 4806 3-8-7 52 BMcHugh(5) 1 60+
(A Dickman) *trckd ldrs: hmpd and lost pl over 4f out: hdwy and hmpd 3f out: styd on to ld last 150yds: hld on towards fin* **4/1**[2]

4421 **2** 1 **Addison De Witt**[13] 4943 3-9-0 57 (v) FrederikTylicki(3) 12 62
(Micky Hammond) *hld up in rr: hdwy over 7f out: wnt 2nd over 3f out: chal over 1f out: styd on towards fin* **13/8**[1]

4125 **3** nk **Love In The West (IRE)**[14] 4898 3-9-2 56 RobertWinston 14 60
(G A Swinbank) *racd wd: t.k.h: led tl over 7f out: led over 4f out: hdd and no ex ins fnl f* **5/1**[3]

3434 **4** 9 **Saffron's Son (IRE)**[13] 4927 3-8-12 52 (b) LeeEnstone 13 42
(P T Midgley) *dwlt: hdwy 6f out: rdn and hung lft over 2f out: wknd over 1f out* **10/1**

0102 **5** 2 3/4 **Kochanski (IRE)**[13] 4927 3-9-3 57 LukeMorris 15 43
(J R Weymes) *chsd ldrs: drvn over 3f out: wknd over 2f out* **12/1**

2400 **6** nk **Tae Kwon Do (USA)**[18] 4806 3-8-12 52 (p) TomEaves 11 37
(Miss J A Camacho) *t.k.h in rr: hdwy 6f out: hung rt and wknd over 1f out* **8/1**

00 **7** 21 **Napoletano (ITY)**[114] 1739 3-8-12 52 GrahamGibbons 3 4
(R Johnson) *hld up in rr: drvn over 3f out: sn lost pl and bhd* **20/1**

506 **8** 2 1/4 **I See Nice Sea**[17] 4818 3-9-1 55 (p) PaulMulrennan 9 3
(Ollie Pears) *hld up: effrt on ins and nt clr run over 4f out: lost pl over 3f out: sn bhd* **25/1**

-000 **9** 17 **Ready For Battle (IRE)**[31] 4348 3-8-4 51 ow2 (p) DTDaSilva(7) 5 —
(D W Thompson) *dwlt: t.k.h: sn w ldr: led over 7f out tl over 4f out: lost pl 3f out: sn bhd* **33/1**

2m 45.51s (6.61) **Going Correction** +0.55s/f (Yiel) **9** Ran SP% **114.2**
Speed ratings (Par 98): **99,98,98,92,90 90,76,74,63**
toteswingers: 1&2 £3.20, 1&3 £5.00, 2&3 £3.00 CSF £10.47 CT £31.91 TOTE £5.20: £1.40, £1.10, £1.90; EX 15.00.
Owner Major P H K Steveney **Bred** E A Bourke M R C V S **Trained** Sandhutton, N Yorks

FOCUS
This was a low-grade 3yo handicap was dominated by the first three and looks reasonable form for the grade.

5343 RACING AGAIN ON FRIDAY 4TH SEPTEMBER H'CAP — 5f 212y
5:20 (5:21) (Class 5) (0-75,74) 3-Y-O+ **£2,914** (£867; £433; £216) **Stalls** Low

Form RPR

4003 **1** **Bonnie Prince Blue**[22] 4620 6-9-6 70 (b) AdrianTNicholls 10 83
(D Nicholls) *w ldrs: c stands' side over 2f out: led appr fnl f: drew clr* **8/1**[3]

600 **2** 5 **Mr Wolf**[21] 4662 8-9-1 72 (p) IJBrennan(7) 3 69
(J J Quinn) *led: hdd appr fnl f: no ch w wnr* **10/1**

0614 **3** 1/2 **Timber Treasure (USA)**[23] 4592 5-9-7 71 (b) SilvestreDeSousa 11 66+
(Paul Green) *in rr and swtchd lft after s: hdwy and edgd rt 2f out: styd on ins fnl f* **14/1**

1000 **4** 3 3/4 **Angaric (IRE)**[82] 2658 6-8-7 64 AdamCarter(7) 8 47
(B Smart) *chsd ldrs: one pce fnl 2f* **28/1**

4152 **5** 1 1/4 **Hotham**[7] 5148 6-9-7 71 DuranFentiman 9 50
(N Wilson) *dwlt: hdwy to trck ldrs on outer over 4f out: wknd over 1f out* **9/2**[2]

0 **6** 1 **Navajo Joe (IRE)**[23] 4592 4-9-3 67 GrahamGibbons 2 43
(R Johnson) *in rr: kpt on fnl 2f: nvr a factor* **22/1**

5412 **7** 3 1/2 **Sea Salt**[12] 4977 6-9-0 64 SebSanders 7 29
(R E Barr) *chsd ldrs: lost pl over 1f out* **9/2**[2]

4-00 **8** 1 3/4 **Distant Sun (USA)**[19] 4751 5-9-7 71 TomEaves 4 30
(Miss L A Perratt) *trckd ldrs: t.k.h: effrt 3f out: lost pl over 1f out* **20/1**

2511 **9** 1 1/2 **Realt Na Mara (IRE)**[7] 5150 6-8-13 63 6ex (p) TravisBlock 1 18
(H Morrison) *dwlt: outpcd: no rspnse and lost pl over 3f out: no ch after* **13/8**[1]

1m 16.35s (2.75) **Going Correction** +0.55s/f (Yiel)
WFA 3 from 4yo+ 3lb **9** Ran SP% **113.9**
Speed ratings (Par 103): **103,96,95,90,89 87,83,80,78**
toteswingers: 1&2 £11.50, 1&3 £8.30, 2&3 £19.70 CSF £79.97 CT £1101.96 TOTE £9.30: £2.00, £3.60, £3.60; EX 70.20 Place 6: £67.12, Place 5: £47.87..
Owner Middleham Park Racing XVII **Bred** George Joseph Hicks **Trained** Sessay, N Yorks

FOCUS
Very few got into this and the winner is rated in line with his reappearance form, although he could rate higher given the margin of victory.
Realt Na Mara(IRE) Official explanation: trainer's rep said, regarding the poor form shown, that the gelding was unsuited by the good to soft ground

T/Plt: £87.10 to a £1 stake. Pool: £63,468.81. 531.55 winning tickets. T/Qpdt: £33.60 to a £1 stake. Pool: £4,158.49. 91.50 winning tickets. WG

[3785]WARWICK (L-H)

Wednesday, August 26

OFFICIAL GOING: Good to firm (good in places) changing to good after race 1 (2.30)

Wind: Fresh half-behind Weather: Light rain

5344 RACING UK NURSERY 6f

2:30 (2:31) (Class 4) (0-85,82) 2-Y-O **£5,180** (£1,541; £770; £384) **Stalls** Low

Form RPR

521 **1** **Take Ten**[16] 4844 2-8-12 **73**.................................... JoeFanning 2 90+
(M Johnston) *mde all: shkn up and r.o strly fnl f: impressive* **3/1**[2]

431 **2** 5 **Marine Spirit (GER)**[20] 4701 2-9-7 **82**.......................... TedDurcan 4 84
(Saeed Bin Suroor) *s.i.s: hld up in tch: racd keenly: rdn to chse wnr 1f out: sn outpcd* **8/11**[1]

0022 **3** 2 ¼ **Ginger Grey (IRE)**[12] 4975 2-8-3 **67**....................(p) AndreaAtzeni(3) 10 62
(S A Callaghan) *hld up: r.o ins fnl f: nvr trbld ldrs* **12/1**

2104 **4** ¾ **White Daffodil (IRE)**[11] 5033 2-8-8 **69**.......................... PatDobbs 7 62
(R Hannon) *prom: rdn 1/2-way: styd on same pce fnl 2f* **14/1**

406 **5** ¾ **Cane Cat (IRE)**[42] 3978 2-7-13 **60** oh1 ow1.................. JimmyQuinn 6 51
(A W Carroll) *trckd wnr: racd keenly: rdn over 1f out: wknd ins fnl f* **66/1**

523 **6** ½ **Gundaroo**[27] 4468 2-8-12 **73**.................................... DaneO'Neill 1 62
(J L Dunlop) *chsd ldrs: rdn over 2f out: wknd fnl f* **10/1**[3]

0030 **7** 3 ¼ **Lofthouse**[54] 3579 2-8-1 **62**.......................... CatherineGannon 9 42
(M R Channon) *hld up: a in rr: rdn and wknd wl over 1f out* **40/1**

3050 **8** 1 **King's Approach (IRE)**[26] 4488 2-9-6 **81**.................. RichardHughes 5 58
(R Hannon) *a in rr: rdn over 3f out: wknd wl over 1f out* **16/1**

1m 11.38s (-0.42) **Going Correction** -0.10s/f (Good) 2y crse rec **8** Ran SP% **116.2**
Speed ratings (Par 96): **98,91,88,87,86 85,81,80**
toteswingers: 1&2 £1.10, 1&3 £4.70, 2&3 £3.00 CSF £5.58 CT £20.37 TOTE £4.30: £1.60, £1.10, £2.70; EX 7.10.

Owner Sheikh Hamdan Bin Mohammed Al Maktoum **Bred** Whitsbury Manor Stud And Mrs M E Slade **Trained** Middleham Moor, N Yorks

FOCUS

A modest nursery in which it paid to race handily. The winner is progressive and the form looks pretty solid.

NOTEBOOK

Take Ten ◆ followed up his Thirsk maiden success pretty much as he pleased. Ridden aggressively, he relished the step up a furlong and found a neat turn of foot when asked to win the race coming to the final furlong. He has improved with every outing this term and, despite a likely hike in the weights, looks one to keep on-side this year. (op 11-4 tchd 5-2)

Marine Spirit(GER) made most when getting off the mark at Folkestone and was very well backed to go in again on this nursery bow. He was never going to get to the front after a tardy start here, however, and then took time to settle when trying to make up ground to race handily. He still came there with his chance in the home straight and simply found the winner too classy. It rates a fair effort conceding that rival 9lb and he has now found his sort of level. (op Evens tchd 11-10)

Ginger Grey(IRE), in first-time cheekpieces, fared best of those to be given waiting rides and is slightly better than the bare form. He helps to set the level, but is clearly somewhat tricky. (op 11-1 tchd 10-1)

White Daffodil(IRE), 1lb lower, failed to really see out the extra furlong on this surface but still likely ran close to her previous level. (op 11-1)

Cane Cat(IRE), 1lb out of the handicap and whose rider put up 1lb overweight, was at an advantage on racing up with the pace on this drop back a furlong. This rates just about his best effort to date. (op 50-1)

Gundaroo looked a possible on this switch to a nursery, but was very one paced in the home straight and now has it to prove. (op 9-1)

5345 GREAT OFFERS AT WARWICKRACECOURSE.CO.UK (S) STKS 5f

3:00 (3:00) (Class 6) 3-Y-0+ **£1,942** (£578; £288; £144) **Stalls** Low

Form RPR

1315 **1** **Mythical Blue (IRE)**[26] 4483 3-9-4 72.......................... DavidProbert 10 66
(J M Bradley) *chsd ldr: led 4f out to 1/2-way: rdn to ld over 1f out: edgd lft ins fnl f: r.o* **5/4**[1]

U05 **2** shd **Nomoreblondes**[12] 4976 5-9-1 65..............................(p) TonyCulhane 5 61
(P T Midgley) *chsd ldrs: led 1/2-way: rdn and hdd over 1f out: r.o* **11/1**

4000 **3** 1 ¼ **Sandy Par**[12] 5008 4-8-11 49..............................(b) KevinGhunowa(3) 2 55
(J M Bradley) *chsd ldrs: rdn over 1f out: r.o* **25/1**

5006 **4** ½ **Mamlakati (IRE)**[13] 4952 3-8-7 69.......................... PatDobbs 15 48
(R Hannon) *hld up: hdwy 1/2-way: rdn and hung lft over 1f out: r.o: nt rch ldrs* **9/1**

5050 **5** 2 ¼ **Red Rossini (IRE)**[7] 5155 3-8-12 64.......................(b) RichardHughes 7 45
(R Hannon) *s.i.s: sn pushed along in mid-div: rdn over 1f out: nt trble ldrs* **6/1**[2]

6056 **6** shd **Meikle Barfil**[8] 5125 7-9-3 45..............................(tp) JackDean(3) 4 51
(J M Bradley) *chsd ldrs: rdn over 1f out: no ex fnl f* **40/1**

0400 **7** hd **Triskaidekaphobia**[144] 1134 6-9-0 41.......................(t) PaulFitzsimons 3 44
(Miss J R Tooth) *led 1f: chsd ldrs: rdn 1/2-way: no ex fnl f* **50/1**

0002 **8** nk **Monsieur Reynard**[6] 5184 4-8-11 52.......................... MCGeran(3) 13 43+
(J M Bradley) *s.i.s and hmpd s: in rr: shkn up over 1f out: r.o ins fnl f: nvr nrr* **7/1**[3]

5036 **9** ¾ **Iachimo**[13] 4942 3-9-4 49..............................(v) RichardMullen 1 46
(A P Jarvis) *hld up: hdwy u.p over 1f out: no ex ins fnl f* **25/1**

3350 **10** 1 **Bahamian Ceilidh**[44] 3926 3-8-7 67.......................... JimmyQuinn 8 32
(B N Pollock) *s.s: outpcd: rdn over 1f out: n.d* **8/1**

4006 **11** 3 **Fizzlephut (IRE)**[82] 2682 7-9-6 52.......................... FrankieMcDonald 12 32
(Miss J R Tooth) *chsd ldrs: rdn 1/2-way: wknd wl over 1f out* **50/1**

0000 **12** 2 ¼ **Walragnek**[43] 3947 5-9-0 46..............................(v) TolleyDean 11 18
(J G M O'Shea) *hld up: rdn over 3f out: sn lost tch* **80/1**

0-00 **13** ½ **Rathmolyon**[51] 3677 4-8-11 45 ow2.......................... DaneO'Neill 9 13
(D Haydn Jones) *chsd ldrs tl rdn and wknd over 1f out* **40/1**

0050 **14** 3 ¼ **Nordic Light (USA)**[34] 4222 5-9-0 40.......................(b) StephenDonohoe 14 4
(J M Bradley) *edgd lft s: sn outpcd* **66/1**

59.28 secs (-0.32) **Going Correction** -0.10s/f (Good)
WFA 3 from 4yo+ 2lb **14** Ran SP% **119.9**
Speed ratings (Par 101): **98,97,95,95,91 91,90,90,89,87 82,79,78,73**
toteswingers: 1&2 £3.30, 1&3 £12.40, 2&3 £33.30 CSF £15.20 TOTE £2.40: £1.10, £3.00, £8.20; EX 19.60.The winner was bought in for 8,400 guineas

Owner Clifton Hunt **Bred** John O'Dowd **Trained** Sedbury, Gloucs

FOCUS

This seller was run at a decent pace and two came clear. The form is muddling and limited by the proximity of the third and sixth.

Bahamian Ceilidh Official explanation: jockey said filly was slowly away

5346 TURFTV H'CAP 1m 6f 213y

3:30 (3:31) (Class 3) (0-95,90) 3-Y-O **£7,477** (£2,239; £1,119; £560; £279) **Stalls** Low

Form RPR

1032 **1** **Just Lille (IRE)**[14] 4896 6-9-11 **90**..............................(p) JackMitchell(3) 7 93
(Mrs A Duffield) *wnt rt s: sn prom: chsd ldr over 2f out: led over 1f out: edgd rt ins fnl f: shkn up and styd on wl* **7/2**[3]

3004 **2** 1 ¼ **Baddam**[7] 5171 7-9-9 **85**..............................(vt[1]) SaleemGolam 5 86
(Ian Williams) *pushed along early to chse ldrs: rdn 4f out: styd on u.p to go 2nd wl ins fnl f* **7/1**

4251 **3** 1 **Alnwick**[9] 5094 5-9-4 **80** 6ex.......................... DaneO'Neill 1 80
(P D Cundell) *led 2f: remained w ldr tl led again 1/2-way: rdn and hdd over 1f out: no ex and lost 2nd wl ins fnl f* **7/4**[1]

1656 **4** ¾ **Pseudonym (IRE)**[4] 5252 7-8-11 **73** oh5.......................(t) FrancisNorton 2 72
(M F Harris) *hld up: hdwy u.p over 1f out: styd on: nt rch ldrs* **8/1**

/306 **5** 22 **Ermine Sea**[33] 4260 6-9-7 **83**..............................(p) MartinDwyer 4 53
(Miss H C Knight) *chsd ldr: led after 2f: hdd 1/2-way but remained w ldr tl rdn 3f out: wknd wl over 1f out* **11/4**[2]

3m 16.26s (-2.74) **Going Correction** +0.05s/f (Good) **5** Ran SP% **108.9**
Speed ratings (Par 107): **109,108,107,107,95**
toteswingers: 1&2 £5.60 CSF £24.89 TOTE £4.40: £2.60, £2.20; EX 25.60.

Owner Miss Helen Wynne **Bred** Sweetmans Bloodstock **Trained** Constable Burton, N Yorks

FOCUS

Not a bad little staying handicap, run at a sound pace but the form is limited by the proximity of the fourth from out of the handicap.

NOTEBOOK

Just Lille(IRE) took this step up in trip in her stride and defied top weight in typically game fashion. She went right out of the gates, but was soon back racing on an even keel and came there travelling best of all turning for home. The doubt then was how her stamina would hold up, especially under a big weight, but she answered every call. This was off a career-high mark, so it opens up more options for her and she has developed into a most likeable mare. (op 4-1 tchd 9-2)

Baddam raced in a first-time visor and tongue tie, but still failed to convince with his attitude. He needed to be ridden early on to keep interested and really lost out by racing lazily nearing the final bend, where he lost ground. He was running on again inside the final furlong and ran close enough to his last-time-out form in the Lonsdale Cup last week, but remains one to swerve for win-only purposes. (op 5-1)

Alnwick was penalised for his Kempton success nine days previously and he ran right up to form under an aggressive ride, but was done with before the final furlong. (op 15-8)

Pseudonym(IRE) was never going the pace to land a significant blow, but likes it here and was not at all disgraced from 5lb out of the weights on this quick reappearance. (op 10-1 tchd 7-1)

Ermine Sea helped to cut out the sound pace, but he was beaten shortly after turning into the home straight and has a little to prove at present. (op 3-1)

5347 WARWICK RACECOURSE CONDITIONS STKS 7f 26y

4:00 (4:01) (Class 3) 2-Y-O **£7,771** (£2,312; £1,155; £577) **Stalls** Low

Form RPR

51 **1** **Stags Leap (IRE)**[25] 4524 2-8-12 83.......................... RichardHughes 1 85
(R Hannon) *sn chsng ldr: led over 2f out: rdn over 1f out: r.o* **4/1**[3]

1526 **2** ½ **Avonrose**[40] 4049 2-8-7 88.......................... JoeFanning 2 79
(M Johnston) *led: edgd rt 1/2-way: hdd over 2f out: rdn over 1f out: hung rt ins fnl f: r.o* **12/1**

4114 **3** hd **Lamh Albasser (USA)**[32] 4294 2-8-12 94.......................... TedDurcan 7 84
(Saeed Bin Suroor) *chsd ldrs: edgd lft wl over 2f out: sn rdn: r.o* **7/2**[2]

0 **4** ½ **Palio Square (USA)**[33] 4286 2-8-12 0.......................... RichardMullen 4 82+
(A P Jarvis) *sn pushed along in rr: plenty to do over 1f out: r.o wl ins fnl f: nt rch ldrs* **33/1**

3410 **5** nk **Suffolk Punch (IRE)**[26] 4488 2-8-12 86.......................... WilliamBuick 3 82
(A M Balding) *chsd ldrs: rdn and hung lft 2f out: sn outpcd: r.o ins fnl f* **4/1**[3]

31 **6** ¾ **Kalam Daleel (IRE)**[91] 2376 2-8-12 0.......................... DarryllHolland 6 80
(M R Channon) *chsd ldrs: rdn over 1f out: hmpd ins fnl f f: sn hung lft and styd on same pce* **15/8**[1]

4 **7** shd **Muwalla**[14] 4888 2-8-12 0.......................... PhilipRobinson 5 79
(C E Brittain) *s.i.s: hld up: hdwy 1/2-way: hmpd and lost pl sn after: r.o ins fnl f but nvr able to rcvr* **16/1**

1m 25.57s (0.97) **Going Correction** +0.05s/f (Good) **7** Ran SP% **113.5**
Speed ratings (Par 98): **96,95,95,94,94 93,93**
toteswingers: 1&2 £4.50, 1&3 £2.30, 2&3 £5.70 CSF £47.75 TOTE £5.70: £2.50, £4.40; EX 34.90.

Owner Mrs J Wood **Bred** P McCartan & Paddy Twomey **Trained** East Everleigh, Wilts

FOCUS

An interesting event. The field were closely covered at the finish so the form looks muddling and somewhat suspect.

NOTEBOOK

Stags Leap(IRE) made most to follow up his Goodwood maiden success 25 days earlier. That came on soft ground, so the easing surface was in his favour and there was plenty to like about his attitude under pressure. A step up to 1m should hold no fears for him and further improvement cannot be ruled out. (op 5-1)

Avonrose disputed the running and ran a solid race under a strong ride, proving her flop in Listed company last time to be all wrong. The return to better ground helped her cause and she saw out the trip well, but was just outstayed by the winner. A drop back to a stiff 6f should prove ideal at present. (op 17-2 tchd 8-1)

Lamh Albasser(USA) ran poorly when searching for the hat-trick at Ascot in Listed company, but it often pays to forgive a horse a poor run on the straight track there. This was easier and he again travelled nicely through the race, but his attitude when under pressure left something to be desired as he carried his head awkwardly. On this evidence his improvement has now levelled out and he is not going to prove simple to place. (op 11-4 tchd 4-1)

Palio Square(USA) ◆ was facing a stiff task here and he really got caught out by a lack of experience. He needed to be ridden early on and ran green, but finished very nicely and rates one to take out of the race. (op 50-1)

Suffolk Punch(IRE) looked to have claims on previous form, but never looked totally happy at any stage and was shaken off near the final furlong. It may well be that he needs genuinely quick ground to shine. (tchd 9-2 and 5-1 in a place)

Kalam Daleel(IRE) won impressively, albeit at Brighton, when last seen 81 days earlier and proved popular here. He was not helped by having to race wide and took time to settle, but he was beaten before being somewhat hampered inside the final furlong. He also didn't appear the most straightforward, but that could have still been down to greenness, and he is worth another chance to prove his worth with the run now under his belt. Official explanation: jockey said colt hung left (op 9-4 tchd 5-2)

Muwalla was another who faced a difficult task and another who got found out by his lack of experience. He too finished fairly well though, and is one to become interested in when qualifying for nurseries after his next assignment. (op 20-1)

5348 KIDS COME FREE ON MONDAY MEDIAN AUCTION STKS — 1m 22y

4:30 (4:34) (Class 5) 3-5-Y-O — £2,914 (£867; £433; £216) Stalls Low

Form — RPR

66 **1** **Love Call (IRE)**[15] 4867 3-8-12 0 .... MartinDwyer 3 — 62
(W R Muir) *a.p: n.m.r over 3f out: sn chsng ldr: rdn to ld 1f out: edgd lft ins fnl f: all out* — **16/1**

-063 **2** *shd* **Asateer (IRE)**[12] 5010 3-9-3 82 .... TPO'Shea 1 — 67
(B W Hills) *sn led: rdn: wandered and carried hd high over 1f out: sn hdd and nt resolute: kpt on u.p but ref to go by* — **8/13**[1]

2205 **3** *¾* **Layer Cake**[5] 5228 3-9-3 62 .... WilliamBuick 5 — 65
(J W Hills) *hld up: hdwy over 1f out: sn rdn: r.o wl: nt rch ldrs* — **4/1**[2]

6 **4** *9* **Herecomethegirls**[27] 4472 3-8-12 0 .... HayleyTurner 7 — 38
(M L W Bell) *s.i.s: hld up: rdn over 1f out: n.d* — **7/1**[3]

00- **5** *8* **Lady Meg (IRE)**[308] 6892 3-8-12 0 .... DavidProbert 4 — 19
(B Palling) *unruly prior to s: chsd ldr tl rdn and edgd lft over 3f out: wknd 2f out* — **50/1**

00 **6** *6* **Step Into Sunshine (USA)**[10] 5072 3-8-12 0 .... JoeFanning 2 — 5
(M Johnston) *s.i.s: hdwy over 4f out: rdn and wknd over 2f out* — **25/1**

05 **7** *3½* **Balzarine**[12] 5010 3-8-12 0 .... JimmyQuinn 6 — —
(M Blanshard) *prom: rdn over 3f out: wknd over 2f out* — **28/1**

1m 41.94s (0.94) **Going Correction** +0.05s/f (Good) — **7 Ran SP% 109.6**
Speed ratings (Par 103): **97,96,96,87,79 73,69**
toteswingers: 1&2 £3.00, 1&3 £2.90, 2&3 £2.10 CSF £24.68 TOTE £12.60: £3.50, £1.10; EX 35.80.
Owner Mrs C Henley **Bred** J Connolly **Trained** Lambourn, Berks

FOCUS
A weak maiden with the runner-up nowhere near his official mark and the form anchored by the third.

5349 COME RACING ON MONDAY H'CAP — 7f 26y

5:00 (5:00) (Class 4) (0-85,84) 3-Y-0+ — £4,984 (£1,492; £746; £373; £140; £140) Stalls Low

Form — RPR

1013 **1** **Broad Cairn**[14] 4909 3-9-8 84 .... SteveDrowne 5 — 92
(R Charlton) *hld up: hdwy over 2f out: rdn to ld wl ins fnl f: r.o* — **11/4**[1]

410 **2** *¾* **Clientele (USA)**[16] 4852 3-9-6 82 .... JoeFanning 1 — 88
(M Johnston) *s.i.s: plld hrd and sn prom: rdn to ld 1f out: hdd wl ins fnl f* — **11/2**[3]

4512 **3** *½* **Summer Dancer (IRE)**[6] 5188 5-9-11 82 .... TonyCulhane 2 — 89
(P T Midgley) *hld up: plld hrd: rdn over 2f out: hdwy over 1f out: r.o* — **9/2**[2]

2006 **4** *½* **Desert Dreamer (IRE)**[5] 5206 8-9-4 80 .... RichardEvans(5) 10 — 86
(P D Evans) *s.i.s: hld up: rdn over 2f out: hdwy over 1f out: r.o wl: nt rch ldrs* — **20/1**

0003 **5** *hd* **Kipchak (IRE)**[8] 5124 4-8-13 70 .... (p) FergusSweeney 3 — 75
(C R Dore) *led: rdn and hdd 1f out: styd on same pce* — **20/1**

2-34 **5** *dht* **Burma Rock (IRE)**[47] 3812 3-9-0 76 .... DaneO'Neill 4 — 79
(L M Cumani) *hld up: hdwy over 1f out: sn rdn: r.o* — **7/1**

5540 **7** *hd* **Valatrix (IRE)**[26] 4500 4-9-2 76 .... JackMitchell(3) 14 — 81
(C F Wall) *prom: stdd into mid-div over 5f out: hdwy over 1f out: r.o* — **25/1**

0-00 **8** *2* **Amber Sunset**[25] 4540 3-8-9 74 .... WilliamCarson(3) 9 — 71
(J Jay) *hld up: hdwy u.p and swtchd rt ins fnl f: nt trble ldrs* — **33/1**

4042 **9** *1¼* **Bold Cross (IRE)**[10] 5062 6-9-9 80 .... PaulFitzsimons 6 — 76
(E G Bevan) *hld up: hdwy over 2f out: sn rdn: styd on same pce fnl f* — **6/1**

0000 **10** *2½* **Versaki (IRE)**[114] 1744 3-8-13 75 .... StephenDonohoe 7 — 62
(Ian Williams) *prom: rdn over 2f out: wknd over 1f out* — **14/1**

1502 **11** *hd* **Shaded Edge**[15] 4871 5-8-13 70 .... HayleyTurner 8 — 59
(D W P Arbuthnot) *chsd ldrs: rdn over 2f out: wknd fnl f* — **14/1**

3600 **12** *½* **Phantom Whisper**[16] 4853 6-9-9 83 .... JamesMillman(3) 13 — 70
(B R Millman) *prom: rdn over 2f out: wknd over 1f out* — **16/1**

1m 24.53s (-0.07) **Going Correction** +0.05s/f (Good)
WFA 3 from 4yo+ 5lb — **12 Ran SP% 122.5**
Speed ratings (Par 105): **102,101,100,100,99 99,99,97,95,92 92,92**
toteswingers: 1&2 £3.80, 1&3 £3.20, 2&3 £4.30 CSF £17.25 CT £68.88 TOTE £4.10: £1.50, £2.30, £1.90; EX 21.90 Place 6: £90.36, Place 5: £77.65..
Owner The Queen **Bred** The Queen **Trained** Beckhampton, Wilts

FOCUS
A competitive handicap for the grade and the form looks sound enough, rated around the third and fourth, despite the first seven home being closely covered.
T/Plt: £74.40 to a £1 stake. Pool: £60,774.33. 596.07 winning tickets. T/Qpdt: £29.40 to a £1 stake. Pool: £4,359.48. 109.40 winning tickets. CR

5350 - 5357a (Foreign Racing) - See Raceform Interactive

5330 AYR (L-H)

Thursday, August 27

OFFICIAL GOING: Soft (5.3)
Wind: Fresh, half against Weather: Overcast

5358 AYRSHIREPOST.CO.UK NURSERY — 6f

2:10 (2:13) (Class 6) (0-65,65) 2-Y-O — £2,914 (£867; £433; £216) Stalls High

Form — RPR

5630 **1** **Agent Boo**[31] 4371 2-9-1 59 .... (b[1]) GrahamGibbons 3 — 65
(E S McMahon) *trckd ldr: led over 1f out: rdn out* — **10/1**[3]

010 **2** *1½* **Eight Hours**[19] 4803 2-8-13 60 .... FrederikTylicki(3) 8 — 62
(R A Fahey) *chsd ldrs: drvn and outpcd 1/2-way: rallied to chse wnr ins fnl f: r.o* — **4/1**[2]

0060 **3** *hd* **Charity Fair**[6] 5207 2-7-11 48 .... BillyCray(7) 4 — 49
(A Berry) *dwlt: sn swtchd to stands' rail and outpcd: hung lft 2f out: styd on fnl f: nrst fin* — **10/1**[3]

446 **4** *1½* **Abbi Jicaro**[53] 3652 2-8-2 51 .... DeanHeslop(5) 11 — 47
(Mrs L Williamson) *uns rdr bef s: stdd s: hld up: outpcd 1/2-way: rallied 2f out: kpt on fnl f: n.d* — **25/1**

4423 **5** *1½* **Firetrap**[13] 4975 2-9-4 62 .... (v[1]) SilvestreDeSousa 10 — 54
(Mrs A Duffield) *led to over 1f out: sn one pce* — **5/2**[1]

3440 **6** *1* **Lady Lube Rye (IRE)**[7] 5199 2-9-2 65 .... BMcHugh(5) 12 — 54
(N Wilson) *trckd ldrs: rdn over 2f out: no ex fnl f* — **4/1**[2]

036 **7** *2¼* **Coolella (IRE)**[17] 4839 2-9-2 60 .... PJMcDonald 9 — 42
(J R Weymes) *midfield: outpcd over 2f out: n.d after* — **16/1**

000 **8** *7* **As Brave As You (IRE)**[68] 3170 2-8-4 48 ow1 .... GregFairley 6 — 9
(B Ellison) *sn pushed along in midfield: wknd fr over 2f out* — **12/1**

6050 **9** *12* **One Cool Deal (IRE)**[36] 4188 2-8-12 56 .... (b) DavidAllan 7 — —
(T D Easterby) *bhd: drvn 1/2-way: sn struggling: eased whn no ch fnl f* — **20/1**

630 **10** *25* **Quinner (IRE)**[18] 4825 2-9-6 64 .... (t) StephenDonohoe 5 — —
(P D Evans) *rrd repeatedly in stalls: sn bhd and drvn along: no ch fr 1/2-way* — **16/1**

1m 15.51s (1.91) **Going Correction** +0.125s/f (Good) — **10 Ran SP% 114.8**
Speed ratings (Par 92): **92,90,89,87,85 84,81,72,56,22**
toteswingers: 1&2 £8.60, 1&3 £11.10, 2&3 £7.60 CSF £49.05 CT £425.09 TOTE £12.60: £3.60, £2.40, £3.20; EX 63.20.
Owner Mr & Mrs E R Smith **Bred** Whitsbury Manor Stud And Csb Breeding **Trained** Lichfield, Staffs

FOCUS
The rails had been dolled out on the home bend, increasing distances on the round course by precisely 7.18 metres. The going was changed to Good to Soft before the opening contest. Very few got into this low-grade nursery. The form is solid but very limited.

NOTEBOOK
Agent Boo struck on 1f out and stayed on for pressure. Well beaten in a 7f nursery at Southwell last time, he was 3lb lower here and the first-time blinkers and drop in trip worked a treat. He remains capable of better if the headgear continues to have the desired effect. (op 11-1 tchd 12-1)
Eight Hours disappointed on his recent nursery debut, but he had earlier won a maiden at Wolverhampton and showed his true form here, keeping on to just hold second. (op 7-2 tchd 10-3)
Charity Fair is well exposed, but she was unlucky not to finish second, having been the slowest to get going. She took an age to pick up, but stayed on widest of all and may find an opening at selling level. (tchd 12-1)
Abbi Jicaro, who unshipped her rider before the off, ran her best race to date and certainly wasn't inconvenienced by the drop in trip.
Firetrap, sporting a first-time visor, took them along against the stands' rail, but was soon left trailing by the winner and again disappointed. (op 11-4 tchd 3-1)
Quinner(IRE), who banged his head leaving the stalls, was also reported to have lost a front right shoe. Official explanation: vet said colt banged its head in the stalls sustaining a cut above his eye and also lost a right foreshoe (op 12-1)

5359 BEST ODDS GUARANTEED AT VICTOR CHANDLER H'CAP — 1m 5f 13y

2:40 (2:40) (Class 6) (0-65,62) 3-Y-O+ — £2,388 (£705; £352) Stalls Low

Form — RPR

0252 **1** **John Forbes**[3] 5307 7-9-9 62 .... LanceBetts(5) 3 — 71
(B Ellison) *trckd ldrs: led 2f out: kpt on wl u.p* — **5/2**[1]

000- **2** *1¼* **Baaher (USA)**[12] 4390 5-9-2 55 .... GaryBartley(5) 1 — 62
(J S Goldie) *hld up on ins: hdwy to chse wnr appr fnl f: r.o* — **20/1**

442- **3** *4½* **No Wonga**[357] 5653 4-9-2 55 .... RichardEvans(5) 11 — 55+
(P D Evans) *hld up: hdwy on outside over 2f out: edgd lft 1f out: kpt on: nt rch first two* — **14/1**

0446 **4** *¾* **Lady Sorcerer**[31] 4388 4-9-4 52 .... (v) AndrewElliott 7 — 51
(A P Jarvis) *hld up: rdn 3f out: hdwy over 1f out: kpt on: no imp* — **11/1**

50-3 **5** *1½* **English City (IRE)**[16] 4873 6-9-4 52 .... (p) DavidAllan 2 — 49
(Mrs L B Normile) *midfield: drvn over 3f out: effrt 2f out: no imp appr fnl f* — **15/2**

05-0 **6** *½* **Wizard Of Us**[24] 4588 9-8-13 47 .... GregFairley 8 — 43
(M Mullineaux) *led to 2f out: rdn and sn no ex* — **33/1**

1-50 **7** *1¾* **Prince Rhyddarch**[15] 4898 4-9-11 62 .... FrederikTylicki(3) 9 — 55
(I Semple) *cl up: ev ch over 2f out: wknd appr fnl f* — **9/2**[2]

0326 **8** *1½* **Tender Moments**[15] 4893 5-9-4 52 .... TomEaves 4 — 43
(B Smart) *prom: drvn 3f out: no ex whn hmpd 1f out* — **16/1**

-024 **9** *¾* **Ballade De La Mer**[20] 4755 3-8-1 46 .... AndrewMullen 6 — 36
(A G Foster) *midfield: effrt over 2f out: wknd wl over 1f out* — **16/1**

6660 **10** *5* **Louisa (GER)**[8] 5162 5-9-2 50 .... PJMcDonald 10 — 32
(P Monteith) *towards rr: drvn 1/2-way: struggling fnl 3f* — **28/1**

3145 **11** *¾* **Dazzling Begum**[15] 4893 4-8-11 50 .... (p) SimonPearce(5) 14 — 31
(J Pearce) *hld up: hdwy on outside 3f out: wknd wl over 1f out* — **7/1**[3]

6320 **12** *6* **Blue Jet (USA)**[51] 3714 5-8-11 45 .... PhillipMakin 12 — 17
(R M Whitaker) *hld up: short lived effrt over 2f out: sn btn* — **16/1**

5300 **13** *23* **Prelude**[25] 4561 8-9-11 59 .... GrahamGibbons 5 — —
(W M Brisbourne) *chsd ldrs tl wknd over 2f out: eased whn no ch* — **22/1**

000- **14** *4* **Karaburan (GER)**[326] 6309 5-8-4 45 .... JamesPSullivan(7) 13 — —
(P Monteith) *towards rr: struggling over 5f out: t.o* — **100/1**

3m 0.74s (6.74) **Going Correction** +0.30s/f (Good)
WFA 3 from 4yo+ 11lb — **14 Ran SP% 120.2**
Speed ratings (Par 101): **99,98,95,95,94 93,92,91,91,88 87,84,69,67**
toteswingers: 1&2 £14.90, 1&3 £9.00, 2&3 £56.50 CSF £62.40 CT £605.74 TOTE £3.20: £1.30, £6.30, £3.90; EX 89.50.
Owner R Wagner **Bred** Northmore Stud **Trained** Norton, N Yorks

FOCUS
This was a low-grade handicap. The winner is rated to this year's form.

5360 BUY THE AYRSHIRE POST WEDNESDAY MAIDEN AUCTION STKS — 6f

3:10 (3:13) (Class 5) 2-Y-O — £2,914 (£867; £433; £216) Stalls High

Form — RPR

02 **1** **Hold On Tiger (IRE)**[73] 2963 2-8-13 0 .... PJMcDonald 4 — 75
(I Semple) *sn led: rdn 2f out: hld on wl fnl f* — **15/2**[3]

00 **2** *shd* **Lilyannabanana**[15] 4900 2-8-1 0 .... DeanHeslop(5) 11 — 68
(P D Evans) *prom: hung lft and outpcd 1/2-way: rallied and hung lft ent fnl f: kpt on wl: jst hld* — **40/1**

2 **3** *1½* **Happy Dubai (IRE)**[19] 4774 2-8-13 0 .... TomEaves 7 — 70
(B Smart) *w wnr: rdn over 2f out: kpt on same pce fnl f* — **2/1**[1]

03 **4** *3* **Electric City (IRE)**[27] 4497 2-8-4 0 .... GregFairley 6 — 52
(M G Quinlan) *chsd ldrs: drvn over 2f out: no ex over 1f out* — **9/4**[2]

03 **5** *1* **Kai Broon (IRE)**[19] 4774 2-8-8 0 .... FrederikTylicki(3) 3 — 56
(Miss Lucinda V Russell) *hld up on outside: hdwy and prom 2f out: outpcd fnl f* — **25/1**

6 *nk* **Hot Spark** 2-8-13 0 .... PhillipMakin 5 — 57+
(K A Ryan) *dwlt: hld up: outpcd over 2f out: kpt on fnl f: no imp* — **16/1**

7 *5* **Sumay Buoy (IRE)** 2-8-4 0 .... LanceBetts(5) 8 — 38+
(Mrs J C McGregor) *missed break: bhd and sn hung lft: hdwy 2f out: btn fnl f* — **100/1**

5 **8** *7* **Pavement Games**[24] 4590 2-8-4 0 .... CatherineGannon 9 — 12
(R C Guest) *t.k.h: hld up in tch: rdn over 2f out: wknd over 1f out* — **9/1**

40 **9** *¾* **Kristen Jane (USA)**[20] 4752 2-8-10 0 .... DavidAllan 12 — 16
(Miss L A Perratt) *hld up: struggling over 2f out: sn btn* — **10/1**

0 **10** *12* **Shegarrdi**[17] 4844 2-8-11 0 .... SilvestreDeSousa 13 — —
(K A Ryan) *chsd ldrs tl rdn and wknd over 2f out* — **14/1**

1m 16.2s (2.60) **Going Correction** +0.125s/f (Good) — **10 Ran SP% 114.8**
Speed ratings (Par 94): **87,86,84,80,79 79,72,63,62,46**
toteswingers: 1&2 £71.00, 1&3 £3.10, 2&3 £33.60 CSF £261.81 TOTE £6.80: £1.70, £13.70, £1.10; EX 351.70.
Owner Mrs J Penman **Bred** Patrick Hayes **Trained** Carluke, S Lanarks
■ Stewards' Enquiry : Dean Heslop caution: careless riding

FOCUS
A modest maiden. The winner improved to the tune of 7lb with the third close to his debut.
NOTEBOOK
Hold On Tiger(IRE), off since finishing second at Carlisle in June, was soon right up with the pace and had no trouble with the soft ground, striking on over 1f out and holding on well. He is the sort to go on to better things in nurseries. (tchd 7-1 and 8-1)
Lilyannabanana, who had failed to beat a horse home on two previous starts, showed dramatically improved form and was clearly transformed by the soft ground. She really ran on strongly from over 1f out, despite hanging left, and only just missed out. (op 33-1)
Happy Dubai(IRE) showed a good deal of ability when second over C&D on his debut and it was perhaps disappointing that he could only manage third. Nurseries may be the best option for him now. (op 5-2 tchd 7-4)
Electric City(IRE), third at 66/1 in a Newmarket maiden last time, was unable to build on that and the softer ground probably counted against her. (op 5-4 tchd 5-2 in a place)
Kai Broon(IRE) is now qualified for handicaps and should fare better in that sphere.
Sumay Buoy(IRE) Official explanation: jockey said colt missed the break

5361 NEW WEBSITE AT VICTORCHANDLER.COM H'CAP — 1m 1f 20y
3:40 (3:40) (Class 4) (0-85,82) 4-Y-0+ — £6,476 (£1,927; £963; £481) Stalls Low

Form — RPR
1343 **1** **Keisha Kayleigh (IRE)**[18] 4815 6-8-2 **68** .... LanceBetts(5) 2 — 76
(B Ellison) *hld up in tch: outpcd 3f out: rallied over 1f out: led wl ins fnl f: r.o* **11/4**[1]
3103 **2** ¾ **Faithful Ruler (USA)**[16] 4881 5-9-2 **80** .... FrederikTylicki(3) 3 — 87
(R A Fahey) *pressed ldr: led over 2f out: edgd lft over 1f out: hdd wl ins fnl f: r.o* **5/1**[3]
0260 **3** ½ **My Mate Mal**[33] 4312 5-8-2 **63** .... SilvestreDeSousa 5 — 68
(B Ellison) *led to over 2f out: rallied over 1f out: kpt on ins fnl f* **14/1**
2314 **4** ½ **Casino Night**[8] 5160 4-8-8 **76** .... IJBrennan(7) 8 — 80
(F P Murtagh) *prom on outside: effrt over 2f out: kpt on same pce fnl f* **3/1**[2]
3626 **5** 3¾ **Capucci**[24] 4598 4-9-5 **80** ....(t) GrahamGibbons 7 — 76
(J J Quinn) *in tch: effrt 3f out: wknd over 1f out* **8/1**
3140 **6** ½ **Doon Haymer (IRE)**[8] 5160 4-8-12 **73** ....(p) TomEaves 1 — 68
(I Semple) *chsd ldrs: outpcd over 2f out: n.d after* **8/1**
0200 **7** 2¼ **Charlie Tipple**[47] 3872 5-9-7 **82** ....(p) PhillipMakin 6 — 72
(T D Easterby) *rn in snatches: hld up in tch: outpcd fr over 2f out* **5/1**[3]

2m 1.65s (3.25) **Going Correction** +0.30s/f (Good) — 7 Ran SP% **113.9**
Speed ratings (Par 105): **97,96,95,95,92 91,89**
toteswingers: 1&2 £2.80, 1&3 £9.60, 2&3 £8.20 CSF £16.69 CT £160.05 TOTE £3.60: £1.80, £2.20; EX 15.50.
Owner Koo's Racing Club **Bred** Ronnie Boland **Trained** Norton, N Yorks
■ Stewards' Enquiry : Lance Betts one -day ban: used whip with excessive frequency (Sep 10)
FOCUS
This was a competitive heat. Straightforward form.
Charlie Tipple Official explanation: jockey said gelding was never travelling

5362 UP TO £125 FREE BET AT VICTORCHANDLER.COM H'CAP — 6f
4:10 (4:11) (Class 6) (0-60,60) 3-Y-O — £2,388 (£705; £352) Stalls High

Form — RPR
2251 **1** **Future Gem**[8] 5145 3-9-0 **59** 6ex ....(p) FrederikTylicki(3) 1 — 67
(A Dickman) *prom on outside: led over 2f out: drvn out fnl f* **7/1**
0030 **2** 1 **Kings Ace (IRE)**[72] 3010 3-9-2 **58** ....(v) AndrewElliott 4 — 62
(A P Jarvis) *cl up outside: ev ch over 2f out: kpt on fnl f* **20/1**
6002 **3** 2 **Nimmy's Special**[8] 5145 3-8-8 **50** ....(b) GregFairley 6 — 48
(M Mullineaux) *chsd ldrs: drvn over 2f out: r.o u.p fnl f* **20/1**
3322 **4** 3½ **Hettie Hubble**[3] 5306 3-8-3 **52** ow4 .... DTDaSilva(7) 5 — 39
(D W Thompson) *dwlt: hdwy 1/2-way: rdn and no imp fr over 1f out* **4/1**[2]
0006 **5** 1 **Madame Jourdain (IRE)**[1] 5336 3-8-1 **50** .... CharlotteKerton(7) 3 — 34
(A Berry) *prom: effrt over 2f out: no ex over 1f out* **66/1**
0000 **6** 2 **Fitzolini**[24] 4594 3-8-13 **55** ....(p) SilvestreDeSousa 8 — 32
(A D Brown) *led to over 2f out: sn no ex* **12/1**
500 **7** 2 **Calypso Girl (IRE)**[18] 4829 3-8-13 **55** .... StephenDonohoe 9 — 26
(P D Evans) *chsd ldrs: drvn over 2f out: sn outpcd* **10/1**
4543 **8** hd **Pokfulham (IRE)**[1] 5335 3-9-2 **58** ....(v) DanielTudhope 7 — 28
(J S Goldie) *midfield: outpcd over 2f out: sn btn* **3/1**[1]
4205 **9** 6 **Nchike**[44] 3955 3-9-4 **60** ....(p) CatherineGannon 10 — 11
(R C Guest) *cl up tl rdn and wknd fr 2f out* **20/1**
0243 **10** 2 **Miss Pusey Street**[1] 5336 3-8-8 **50** .... DavidAllan 11 — —
(P D Evans) *prom to 2f out: sn rdn and wknd* **11/2**[3]
450 **11** 2¾ **Duke Of Urbino**[13] 5010 3-8-11 **53** ....(p) TomEaves 12 — —
(K A Ryan) *dwlt: hld up: rdn over 2f out: sn wknd* **14/1**
0506 **12** 2¼ **Fifth Amendment**[38] 4131 3-9-1 **57** .... PhillipMakin 2 — —
(A Berry) *hld up: struggling 1/2-way: sn wknd* **50/1**

1m 14.6s (1.00) **Going Correction** +0.125s/f (Good) — 12 Ran SP% **114.1**
Speed ratings (Par 98): **98,96,94,89,88 85,82,82,74,71 68,65**
toteswingers: 1&2 £19.40, 1&3 £9.30, 2&3 £31.90 CSF £140.85 CT £2679.43 TOTE £5.20: £1.90, £4.70, £5.00; EX 79.60.
Owner Coast To Coast **Bred** Genesis Green Stud Ltd **Trained** Sandhutton, N Yorks
■ Stewards' Enquiry : D T Da Silva one-day ban: careless riding (Sep 10)
FOCUS
A moderate handicap. The first three raced on the outside. The winner improved again but this is not form to be too positive about.

5363 WEST SOUND & WEST FM H'CAP — 7f 50y
4:40 (4:41) (Class 4) (0-85,85) 3-Y-0+ — £6,476 (£1,927; £963; £481) Stalls Low

Form — RPR
4515 **1** **Zomerlust**[13] 4996 7-9-10 **83** ....(v) GrahamGibbons 3 — 94
(J J Quinn) *trckd ldrs: drvn over 2f out: led ins fnl f: r.o wl* **5/1**[2]
4222 **2** 1¼ **Kingswinford (IRE)**[1] 5335 3-8-11 **75** .... CatherineGannon 12 — 81
(P D Evans) *hld up on outside: hdwy over 2f out: chsd wnr ins fnl f: r.o* **10/1**
5352 **3** nk **Memphis Man**[19] 4787 6-8-10 **74** .... RichardEvans(5) 1 — 81
(P D Evans) *hld up: effrt and edgd lft over 2f out: r.o fnl f* **14/1**
41 **4** ¾ **Mutawarath (IRE)**[75] 2937 3-9-5 **83** .... J-PGuillambert 4 — 86+
(W J Haggas) *led or disp ld to ins fnl f: kpt on same pce* **11/4**[1]
406 **5** ¾ **Magic Echo**[18] 4815 5-9-8 **81** .... TomEaves 6 — 84
(M Dods) *hld up: rdn over 2f out: r.o fnl f: nrst fin* **16/1**
0005 **6** hd **Esoterica (IRE)**[5] 5249 6-9-12 **85** ....(v) DanielTudhope 5 — 87
(J S Goldie) *led or disp ld to ent fnl f: no ex* **8/1**
35-0 **7** 1¼ **Silver Rime (FR)**[19] 4779 4-9-11 **84** .... DavidAllan 14 — 83
(Miss L A Perratt) *hld up: drvn over 2f out: sn no imp* **25/1**
055 **8** 1¼ **Misphire**[35] 4228 6-9-1 **74** .... PhillipMakin 7 — 69
(M Dods) *in tch: rdn and outpcd over 2f out: no imp fnl f* **8/1**
0004 **9** ½ **Gift Horse**[15] 4914 9-8-13 **72** ....(v) StephenDonohoe 11 — 66
(P D Evans) *hld up: rdn over 2f out: nvr able to chal* **25/1**
2200 **10** nk **Fathey (IRE)**[1] 5335 3-8-3 **67** .... SilvestreDeSousa 9 — 58
(R A Fahey) *cl up tl rdn and wknd over 1f out* **25/1**
0330 **11** nse **Raptor (GER)**[63] 3312 6-9-10 **83** ....(v) AndrewElliott 10 — 76
(A P Jarvis) *bhd: drvn 1/2-way: nvr able to chal* **11/2**[3]
0603 **12** 1 **Bond City (IRE)**[10] 5104 7-9-12 **85** .... PJMcDonald 8 — 75
(G R Oldroyd) *in tch tl rdn and wknd fr 2f out* **16/1**

1m 34.46s (1.06) **Going Correction** +0.30s/f (Good)
WFA 3 from 4yo+ 5lb — **12** Ran SP% **120.0**
Speed ratings (Par 105): **105,103,103,102,101 101,99,98,97,97 97,96**
toteswingers: 1&2 £13.50 1&3 £9.30, 2&3 £19.60 CSF £53.70 CT £655.30 TOTE £6.80: £1.90, £3.00, £3.40; EX 68.60.
Owner Dawson And Quinn **Bred** The Lavington Stud **Trained** Settrington, N Yorks
■ Stewards' Enquiry : Richard Evans caution: use of whip
FOCUS
This was a fair handicap, run at a good pace. The form is rated around the second and third and the winner showed his best form since winning at York in July last year.

5364 ARMITAGE VENESTA OPEN APPRENTICE H'CAP — 1m
5:10 (5:11) (Class 6) (0-60,61) 4-Y-O+ — £2,590 (£770; £385; £192) Stalls Low

Form — RPR
0603 **1** **Lordship (IRE)**[1] 5332 5-8-6 **51** .... JakePayne(5) 6 — 64
(A W Carroll) *cl up: led 2f out: pushed clr fnl f* **13/2**
U3-5 **2** 3¼ **Ulysees (IRE)**[26] 4529 10-8-0 **47** .... SFeeney(7) 5 — 53+
(I Semple) *hld up: hdwy 2f out: chsd wnr 1f out: r.o* **20/1**
25 **3** 2¾ **Josephine Malines**[14] 4932 5-8-11 **51** ....(p) IJBrennan 11 — 51
(Mrs A Duffield) *hld up: rdn and outpcd over 2f out: hung rt and rallied over 1f out: no imp* **7/2**[1]
240 **4** 1 **Red Skipper (IRE)**[4] 5289 4-8-9 **56** ....(v) ShirleyTeasdale(7) 14 — 53
(N Wilson) *cl up: ev ch over 2f out: no ex fnl f* **14/1**
1331 **5** 2 **Goodbye Cash (IRE)**[4] 5287 5-9-4 **61** 6ex .... HollyHall(3) 9 — 54
(P D Evans) *led to 2f out: btn fnl f* **8/1**
0016 **6** 1¼ **Hits Only Cash**[10] 5103 7-9-5 **59** ....(p) SimonPearce 3 — 49
(J Pearce) *s.i.s: bhd: sme hdwy over 1f out: n.d* **12/1**
6225 **7** nk **Jamieson Gold (IRE)**[4] 5289 6-8-13 **56** ....(p) NSLawes(3) 1 — 45
(Miss L A Perratt) *midfield: effrt over 2f out: btn over 1f out* **14/1**
0426 **8** ¾ **Apache Nation (IRE)**[53] 3653 6-9-3 **57** ....(b) JamesPSullivan 12 — 44
(M Dods) *hld up: rdn 3f out: wknd over 1f out* **5/1**[2]
4330 **9** 2¾ **Papa's Princess**[16] 4876 5-8-12 **55** .... MatthewLawson(3) 13 — 36
(J S Goldie) *bhd: struggling 1/2-way: sme late hdwy: nvr on terms* **25/1**
5046 **10** 4½ **Bivouac (UAE)**[14] 4932 5-9-3 **57** .... PaulPickard 10 — 28
(G A Swinbank) *chsd ldrs tl wknd over 2f out* **6/1**[3]
0-05 **11** 2½ **Danzig Fox**[47] 3851 4-8-12 **52** .... BillyCray 8 — 17
(M Mullineaux) *in tch tl rdn and wknd over 2f out* **20/1**
5551 **12** 1¾ **Appelouse**[31] 4376 4-9-4 **58** .... DTDaSilva 7 — 19
(D W Thompson) *s.i.s: rdn over 3f out: nvr on terms* **16/1**
0000 **13** 14 **Defi (IRE)**[53] 3656 7-8-7 **52** ow7 ....(bt) RossSmith(5) 4 — —
(D A Nolan) *t.k.h: in tch: lost pl 1/2-way: sn struggling* **66/1**

1m 46.35s (2.55) **Going Correction** +0.30s/f (Good) — 13 Ran SP% **119.4**
Speed ratings (Par 101): **99,95,93,92,90 88,88,87,84,80 77,76,62**
toteswingers: 1&2 £22.20, 1&3 £10.50, 2&3 £27.00 CSF £135.13 CT £549.08 TOTE £8.40: £2.60, £7.50, £2.40; EX 150.30 Place 6: £633.65 Place 5: 214.19.
Owner Group 1 Racing (1994) Ltd **Bred** John Costello **Trained** Cropthorne, Worcs
FOCUS
This was turned into a bit of a rout by the winner.
Bivouac(UAE) Official explanation: jockey said gelding ran flat
T/Jkpt: Not won. T/Plt: £421.00 to a £1 stake. Pool: £68,958.39. 119.57 winning tickets. T/Qpdt: £31.10 to a £1 stake. Pool: £5,178.10. 123.15 winning tickets. RY

5191 LINGFIELD (L-H)
Thursday, August 27

OFFICIAL GOING: Turf course - firm (good to firm in places; 9.7); all-weather - standard
Wind: Moderate, behind Weather: Fine but cloudy

5365 HOLLOW LANE H'CAP — 1m 2f
2:20 (2:21) (Class 6) (0-65,65) 4-Y-O+ — £2,047 (£604; £302) Stalls Low

Form — RPR
3612 **1** **Recalcitrant**[9] 5122 6-8-6 **50** .... MartinDwyer 8 — 55
(S Dow) *t.k.h early: trckd ldng pair: wd bnd over 3f out: sn chsd ldr: rdn to ld jst over 2f out: all out fnl f: clung on* **15/8**[1]
-400 **2** nse **Lush (IRE)**[66] 3217 4-9-3 **61** .... RichardHughes 6 — 65
(R Hannon) *dwlt: hld up in 8th: prog on inner over 2f out: rdn over 1f out: styd on fnl f: jst failed* **16/1**
3454 **3** hd **Nassar (IRE)**[56] 3552 6-9-4 **62** ....(v) KirstyMilczarek 12 — 66
(G Prodromou) *s.v.s: hld up in last pair and wl off the pce: stdy prog over 2f out and swtchd to inner: rdn and r.o fnl f: nt qckn nr fin* **11/1**
-004 **4** 1 **Rehabilitation**[20] 4745 4-8-13 **57** ....(tp) ShaneKelly 7 — 59
(W R Swinburn) *trckd ldr: led over 3f out to jst over 2f out: nt qckn over 1f out: hld whn n.m.r nr fin* **9/1**
3450 **5** nse **Vinces**[20] 4745 5-9-4 **62** .... EddieAhern 5 — 64
(T D McCarthy) *dwlt: sn trckd ldrs: rdn and nt qckn 2f out: r.o again last 150yds: gaining fin* **5/1**[3]
6551 **6** ¾ **Inquisitress**[12] 5015 5-7-13 **50** .... KierenFox(7) 10 — 50
(J J Bridger) *dwlt: hld up in midfield: prog on outer over 2f out: chsd wnr over 1f out: looked dangerous ent fnl f: effrt petered out* **14/1**
0410 **7** 1 **Rosy Dawn**[9] 5122 4-8-7 **54** .... MarcHalford(3) 4 — 52
(J J Bridger) *led at gd pce: rdn and hdd over 3f out: styd chsng ldrs u.p: wknd fnl f* **25/1**
2100 **8** nk **Chalice Welcome**[91] 2419 6-9-1 **62** .... JackMitchell(3) 11 — 60
(N B King) *s.s: hld up in 9th: hrd rdn 3f out: prog on outer u.p 2f out: tried to cl on ldrs 1f out: fdd* **20/1**
5-01 **9** 1¼ **Kashmina**[66] 3217 4-9-7 **65** .... JamesDoyle 1 — 60
(Miss Sheena West) *t.k.h early: trckd ldng pair: rdn wl over 2f out: nt qckn and no imp wl over 1f out: fdd fnl f* **4/1**[2]
6/04 **10** 2¾ **Homebred Star**[68] 3158 8-8-2 **46** oh1 .... FrankieMcDonald 3 — 36
(G P Enright) *stdd into last pair sn after s: shkn up on inner over 2f out: blocked off wl over 1f out: no prog after* **50/1**
0405 **11** hd **Pippbrook Gold**[7] 5188 4-9-7 **65** .... PatCosgrave 2 — 54
(J R Boyle) *hld up in midfield: rdn and no prog 3f out: dropped to in rr and struggling wl over 1f out* **14/1**

2m 8.90s (-1.60) **Going Correction** -0.175s/f (Firm) — 11 Ran SP% **119.6**
Speed ratings (Par 101): **99,98,98,98,97 97,96,96,95,93 92**
toteswingers: 1&2 £7.30, 1&3 £5.10, 2&3 £14.30 CSF £36.19 CT £274.18 TOTE £2.80: £1.30, £3.40, £2.30; EX 36.30 Trifecta £159.40 Part won. Pool: £215.43 - 0.60 winning units..
Owner T Staplehurst **Bred** T Staplehurst **Trained** Epsom, Surrey

FOCUS
They finished in a bit of a bunch and this is very moderate form. The winner did not need to match his latest effort.
Pippbrook Gold Official explanation: jockey said gelding slipped approaching 3f out

5366 AURORA FIREWORKS H'CAP 1m 2f
2:50 (2:51) (Class 5) (0-75,77) 3-Y-O £3,238 (£963; £481; £240) Stalls Low

Form RPR
0331 1 **Hawk's Eye**[10] 5101 3-9-9 77 6ex PatCosgrave 7 83+
(M F De Kock, South Africa) *t.k.h early: hld up in last trio: stdy prog on outer fr over 2f out: urged along over 1f out: r.o wout use of whip to ld last 50yds* **15/8**[1]
3531 2 *hd* **Squad**[20] 4734 3-8-9 63 PaulDoe 3 66
(S Dow) *s.s: hld up in last trio: prog 4f out: effrt on outer u.p 2f out: clsd to chal ins fnl f: jst outpcd* **7/1**[3]
2601 3 *hd* **Wilbury Star (IRE)**[15] 4904 3-9-5 73 (b) RichardHughes 6 75
(R Hannon) *led 3f: styd prom: chal again 2f out: chsd ldr over 1f out: styd on and upsides last 75yds: jst outpcd* **4/1**[2]
-006 4 *hd* **Officer In Command (USA)**[8] 5169 3-9-7 75 LPKeniry 5 77
(J S Moore) *prom: rdn to ld on inner over 1f out: kpt on fnl f: hdd and lost pls last 50yds* **16/1**
2002 5 1 1/4 **Inis Boffin**[11] 5063 3-9-2 70 JamesDoyle 8 70+
(S Kirk) *hld up in rr: stdy prog over 2f out: chsd ldrs over 1f out: nt clr run but one pce anyway fnl f* **7/1**[3]
2334 6 *hd* **Pyrus Time (IRE)**[3] 5314 3-9-4 72 LukeMorris 9 71
(J S Moore) *sn prom: led after 3f and maintained ordinary pce: rdn over 2f out: hdd over 1f out: fdd last 100yds* **12/1**
0053 7 3 **Swift Chap**[15] 4910 3-9-3 74 JamesMillman(3) 11 67
(B R Millman) *trckd ldrs: nt qckn over 2f out and sn lost pl: no imp fr over 1f out* **15/2**
4620 8 2 **Red Reef**[9] 5122 3-8-9 63 EddieAhern 10 52
(D J Coakley) *trckd ldrs: rdn wl over 2f out: sn outpcd and btn* **16/1**
6624 9 *nk* **Arashi**[18] 4813 3-8-11 65 (p) DaneO'Neill 12 54
(Lucinda Featherstone) *dwlt: a in rr: rdn and easily outpcd fr over 2f out* **28/1**
000 10 *nk* **Noble Dictator**[87] 2548 3-8-8 62 RichardKingscote 2 50
(E F Vaughan) *sn hld up in midfield: outpcd and struggling over 2f out: sn no ch* **40/1**
23-6 11 3 3/4 **Naheell**[59] 3466 3-8-7 68 RichardOld(7) 1 48
(G Prodromou) *dwlt: a in rr: struggling and unbalanced over 2f out* **33/1**
2m 9.30s (-1.20) **Going Correction** -0.175s/f (Firm) **11 Ran SP% 119.8**
Speed ratings (Par 100): **97,96,96,96,95 95,92,91,90 87**
toteswingers: 1&2 £3.20, 1&3 £3.10, 2&3 £4.80 CSF £15.52 CT £49.41 TOTE £2.50: £1.10, £2.80, £1.50; EX 14.30 Trifecta £42.10 Pool: £355.13 - 6.24 winning units..
Owner Ramsden/Mrs Ramsden/Morecombe/McVeigh **Bred** Woodcote Stud Ltd **Trained** South Africa
■ Stewards' Enquiry : L P Keniry three-day ban: used whip with excessive frequency (Sep 10,11,13)

FOCUS
A modest 3yo handicap run in a time 0.40 seconds slower than the earlier 46-65 contest for older horses. A blanket finish and muddling form, rated around the second and fourth.
Noble Dictator Official explanation: trainer said gelding was unsuited by the track

5367 FELBRIDGE (S) STKS 1m 1f
3:20 (3:21) (Class 6) 3-Y-0+ £2,047 (£604; £302) Stalls Low

Form RPR
0400 1 **Simpsons Gamble (IRE)**[43] 3980 6-9-6 43 (p) LPKeniry 7 61
(R A Teal) *hld up bhd ldrs: gng easily over 2f out: prog to ld over 1f out: sn clr: readily* **20/1**
3000 2 2 3/4 **Clipperdown (IRE)**[13] 4992 8-9-3 57 (t) AlanCreighton(3) 10 55
(E J Creighton) *hld up in rr: prog on outer fr 1/2-way: chsd ldrs over 2f out: kpt on u.p fr over 1f out: tk 2nd wl ins fnl f* **14/1**
0003 3 1 **Rose Cheval (USA)**[21] 4719 3-8-8 58 TonyCulhane 12 48
(M R Channon) *trckd ldrs: effrt over 2f out: drvn and upsides over 1f out: sn outpcd by wnr: lost 2nd wl ins fnl f* **8/1**
2200 4 2 **Gasat (IRE)**[87] 2537 8-9-12 66 RichardHughes 2 55
(A B Haynes) *early reminder: sn prom on inner: 3rd over 3f out: effrt to ld over 2f out: hdd and nt qckn over 1f out: jst hld on for 4th* **4/1**[2]
600/ 5 *hd* **Iffy**[12] 5972 8-9-6 68 SteveDrowne 11 48+
(A B Haynes) *sn last and detached: wl bhd 4f out: rdn 3f out: no prog tl picked up 1f out: r.o wl nr fin* **10/1**
000- 6 *hd* **Mellifluous (IRE)**[174] 3692 4-9-1 38 FergusSweeney 8 43
(W S Kittow) *wl in rr and nt gng wl: rdn and struggling 3f out: styd on fr jst over 1f out: gng on at fin* **100/1**
0006 7 *nk* **August Days (IRE)**[36] 4196 3-8-8 47 (t) TPO'Shea 5 42
(J Pearce) *mostly in midfield: tried to cl on ldrs over 2f out: one pce fr over 1f out* **33/1**
0260 8 *hd* **Rock Art (IRE)**[21] 4704 3-8-8 63 (b[1]) MartinDwyer 14 42
(B J Meehan) *t.k.h: pressed ldr: rdn and fnd nil over 2f out: styd in tch tl wknd fnl f* **9/4**[1]
-000 9 1/2 **Kaljai (IRE)**[45] 3919 3-8-8 38 (vt[1]) FrankieMcDonald 3 41
(Mrs L C Jewell) *racd freely: led to over 2f out: styd cl up tl wknd fnl f* **100/1**
0000 10 1 1/4 **Bustan (IRE)**[13] 5003 10-9-6 70 (p) PatCosgrave 4 43
(G C Bravery) *t.k.h: trckd ldrs: cl up but nt qckn u.p over 2f out: steadily lost pl* **5/1**[3]
606 11 *nse* **Inside Trade (IRE)**[12] 5016 3-8-6 60 (t) RichardFelton(7) 6 43
(R M Beckett) *awkward s: a towards rr: tried to bridge gap to ldng gp over 2f out: sn no imp* **14/1**
-030 12 9 **Dr McFab**[84] 2634 5-9-6 48 (p) EddieAhern 13 23
(Miss Tor Sturgis) *a in rr: detached and struggling over 2f out* **12/1**
13 27 **Bertie Bacon**[14] 3-8-13 0 (p) TolleyDean 9 —
(W G M Turner) *in tch tl wknd rapidly 3f out: t.o* **66/1**
1m 54.58s (-2.02) **Going Correction** -0.175s/f (Firm)
WFA 3 from 4yo+ 7lb **13 Ran SP% 119.8**
Speed ratings (Par 101): **101,98,97,95,95 95,95,95,94,93 93,85,61**
toteswingers: 1&2 £28.30, 1&3 £18.00, 2&3 £17.30 CSF £269.61 TOTE £28.30: £5.90, £3.70, £2.70; EX 357.00 TRIFECTA Not won..There was no bid for the winner.
Owner Back 4 More Partnership **Bred** D And Mrs D Veitch **Trained** Ashtead, Surrey

FOCUS
A weak seller and not a race to be with.

5368 LASHINGS WORLD XI MEDIAN AUCTION MAIDEN STKS 6f (P)
3:50 (3:52) (Class 6) 2-Y-O £2,047 (£604; £302) Stalls Low

Form RPR
2 1 **Adele Blanc Sec (FR)**[24] 4603 2-8-12 0 RichardKingscote 10 83+
(Tom Dascombe) *disp ld at fast pce: gained upper hand over 1f out: shkn up and forged clr* **2/1**[2]
2302 2 3 1/2 **Rakaan (IRE)**[12] 5029 2-9-3 100 (b[1]) MartinDwyer 12 78
(B J Meehan) *disp ld at str pce: clr of rest 1/2-way: hdd over 1f out: btn and tired fnl f* **5/4**[1]
5 3 *nk* **One Good Emperor (IRE)**[30] 4410 2-9-3 0 RobertWinston 2 77
(J R Best) *chsd ldng pair to over 2f out: sn u.p: wnt 3rd again 1f out: clsng on tired runner-up nr fin* **20/1**
03 4 3 1/2 **Almadaa**[84] 2631 2-9-3 0 TPO'Shea 5 66
(E A L Dunlop) *chsd ldrs and in tch: wnt 3rd over 2f out but outpcd by ldng pair: fdd 1f out* **7/1**[3]
5 1 1/2 **Cat Hunter** 2-8-12 0 EddieAhern 4 57+
(Mrs A J Perrett) *s.s: sn outpcd and wl off the pce: wnt poor 6th 1/2-way: nudged along and styd on fnl 2f: encouraging debut* **33/1**
0 6 3 1/4 **Calm Storm (IRE)**[13] 5000 2-9-3 0 ShaneKelly 6 52
(J Noseda) *sn outpcd and rn green: wl off the pce bef 1/2-way: kpt on fnl 2f: no ch* **22/1**
7 2 1/2 **Foxtrot Delta (IRE)** 2-9-3 0 LukeMorris 9 44
(P Winkworth) *sn outpcd and rdn in last pair: a bhd: sme late prog* **33/1**
0 8 2 1/4 **Flotate (USA)**[13] 4980 2-8-12 0 RichardHughes 11 33
(Jane Chapple-Hyam) *outpcd: last and wl off the pce over 3f out: modest late prog* **14/1**
56 9 1/2 **Kildangan Girl**[29] 4427 2-8-12 0 SteveDrowne 3 31
(W R Muir) *chsd clr ldng quintet to 1/2-way: nvr any danger: wknd 2f out* **66/1**
6 10 1 **Casanova Kid**[7] 5180 2-9-3 0 EdwardCreighton 1 33
(E J Creighton) *s.s: sn outpcd: a struggling* **100/1**
0 11 6 **R Woody**[45] 3920 2-9-3 0 LPKeniry 7 15
(Mrs L C Jewell) *chsd ldng trio to 1/2-way: sn wknd* **100/1**
54 12 3 1/4 **Blushing (IRE)**[56] 3534 2-8-12 0 DaneO'Neill 8 —
(B J Meehan) *sn outpcd: a struggling: wknd 2f out* **25/1**
1m 11.46s (-0.44) **Going Correction** -0.20s/f (Stan) 2y crse rec **12 Ran SP% 119.3**
Speed ratings (Par 92): **94,89,88,84,82 77,74,71,70,69 61,57**
toteswingers: 1&2 £1.80, 1&3 £9.00, 2&3 £8.10 CSF £4.42 TOTE £3.50: £1.20, £1.20, £4.10; EX 5.90 Trifecta £46.60 Pool: £549.74 - 8.72 winning units..
Owner The Trial Partnership **Bred** Hubert Honore & Claire Lamotte D'Argy **Trained** Lambourn, Berks

FOCUS
Quite a good juvenile maiden but they were soon well-strung out. The pace was strong and this was a decent effort from the winner.

NOTEBOOK
Adele Blanc Sec(FR) ◆ went off quickly to help force the pace from her wide draw and kept responding to pressure in the straight. While the bare form of her 3 1/2l defeat of a rival rated 100 cannot be taken literally, she's a scopey filly who rates as potentially Pattern class. She could now be aimed at the Dick Poole conditions race at Salisbury, or a race in France. (op 6-4 tchd 9-4)
Rakaan(IRE) hasn't progressed since running third in the Coventry Stakes and didn't improve for first-time blinkers. In fairness, he used up plenty of energy to sit handy from the widest draw, and was taken on throughout, but he has now been a beaten favourite on three of his six starts and has a regressive profile. (op 6-4 tchd 6-5 and 13-8 in a place)
One Good Emperor(IRE) confirmed the promise he showed on his debut at Goodwood with another pleasing performance. He never posed a winning threat, but really got the idea late on and looks potentially useful. (op 22-1)
Almadaa ran respectably, especially as he had been off for nearly three months. Nurseries are now an option. (op 10-1)
Cat Hunter, who is out of a 1m4f winner, ran green and was not given a hard time at all. She should do better. (op 40-1)
Calm Storm(IRE) is not that big but he showed ability, stepping up on his debut performance. He was still green, looking to carry his head a little high in the face of kickback, and never posed a winning threat, but he might find his level once handicapped. (op 33-1)
Foxtrot Delta(IRE) ran as though in need of the experience and can do much better. (op 66-1)

5369 JACKSBRIDGE NURSERY 7f (P)
4:20 (4:22) (Class 5) (0-75,75) 2-Y-O £2,729 (£806; £403) Stalls Low

Form RPR
421 1 **Lucky Rave**[45] 3925 2-9-7 75 RobertWinston 4 89+
(D H Brown) *cl up: effrt 2f out: rdn to ld jst over 1f out: stormed clr* **7/2**[2]
043 2 5 **Edgewater (IRE)**[22] 4646 2-9-7 75 MartinDwyer 8 75
(B J Meehan) *trckd ldr after 2f: rdn to ld jst over 2f out to jst over 1f out: sn wl outpcd by wnr* **15/2**[3]
455 3 1 **Pastel Blue (IRE)**[43] 3987 2-9-3 71 EddieAhern 13 68
(M L W Bell) *led after 1f to jst over 2f out: nrly upsides over 1f out: sn outpcd* **10/1**
6234 4 1/2 **Maoi Chinn Tire (IRE)**[16] 4884 2-8-10 64 LukeMorris 14 61+
(J S Moore) *sn struggling in last pair: stl wl in rr over 1f out: r.o wl fnl f: gaining on plcd horses fin* **15/2**[3]
300 5 3/4 **Newton Circus**[26] 4515 2-9-5 73 RichardHughes 3 67
(R Hannon) *led 1f: styd prom: cl 4th on inner over 1f out: wknd fnl f* **20/1**
3342 6 1 **Poppy N'Penny (IRE)**[8] 5166 2-8-9 63 KirstyMilczarek 11 54+
(W J Haggas) *settled in last pair: lot to do whn effrt on inner over 2f out: no ch whn short of room over 1f out: plugged on* **15/8**[1]
000 7 3/4 **Open Glory (FR)**[41] 4047 2-8-13 67 RichardKingscote 10 57
(Tom Dascombe) *nvr beyond midfield: rdn 3f out: kpt on fr over 1f out: n.d* **20/1**
0500 8 1 1/2 **Flyinflyout**[15] 4901 2-9-1 69 TonyCulhane 2 55
(M R Channon) *dwlt: struggling and pushed along in rr over 5f out: effrt u.p over 2f out: nvr on terms* **25/1**
0006 9 2 **French Connexion (IRE)**[21] 4693 2-8-9 63 LPKeniry 9 44
(J S Moore) *nvr beyond midfield: dropped to last trio 1/2-way: struggling after* **50/1**
000 10 1 **Argyll**[13] 5000 2-8-11 65 TPO'Shea 1 43
(J Pearce) *chsd ldrs: nt qckn over 2f out: lost pl sn after: wknd fnl f* **25/1**
0150 11 1/2 **Dixie Bright (USA)**[17] 4858 2-9-5 73 (b[1]) PatCosgrave 7 50
(J G Given) *nvr beyond midfield: rdn over 3f out: wknd over 1f out* **33/1**
2204 12 23 **Baileys Vision**[41] 4035 2-9-1 69 RoystonFfrench 12 —
(M Johnston) *struggling after 2f: sn wknd: t.o* **16/1**
1m 24.71s (-0.09) **Going Correction** -0.20s/f (Stan) **12 Ran SP% 117.6**
Speed ratings (Par 94): **92,86,85,84,83 82,81,80,77,76 76,49**
toteswingers: 1&2 £3.60, 1&3 £6.20, 2&3 £9.00 CSF £26.42 CT £245.03 TOTE £4.40: £1.80, £2.60, £2.90; EX 30.90 Trifecta £206.90 Part won. Pool: £279.60 - 094 winning units..
Owner Ron Hull **Bred** Cothi Bloodstock **Trained** Maltby, S Yorks

FOCUS
A fair nursery. The winner impressed and the form should work out.

NOTEBOOK
Lucky Rave readily followed up his 6f maiden success at Wolverhampton and is now 2-2 on Polytrack. He's obviously pretty useful on this surface and his jockey suggested afterwards he would be well suited to racing in the US. (op 4-1)
Edgewater(IRE) had every chance if good enough and ran well, but the winner was simply much too good. (tchd 9-1)
Pastel Blue(IRE), upped a furlong in trip on her nursery debut, had plenty of use made of her from a wide draw and was in trouble early in the straight. (op 8-1)
Maoi Chinn Tire(IRE) had been competitive over shorter distances, so it was a surprise he got going all too late on this step up in trip. (op 10-1 tchd 7-1)
Newton Circus should have been okay over this trip judged on his breeding, but he ran like a non-stayer. (tchd 22-1)
Poppy N'Penny(IRE), due to go up 6lb following her recent second placing at Kempton, ran disappointingly, even allowing for racing in an unpromising position for much of the way, and was reported by her rider to have never been travelling. She is quite a small filly and might struggle from now on. Official explanation: jockey said filly was never travelling (op 5-2)

5370 FORD MANOR ROAD H'CAP — 6f (P)
4:50 (4:51) (Class 4) (0-80,80) 3-Y-O+ — **£5,180** (£1,541; £770; £384) **Stalls** Low

Form — RPR

02-1 **1** **Tagula Night (IRE)**[24] 4607 3-9-7 **78**....................(vt) ShaneKelly 6 — 90+
(W R Swinburn) *trckd ldr: led over 2f out and sn kicked at least 2 l clr: drvn fnl f: nvr in any real danger* — **5/1**[2]

4530 **2** *1 ¼* **Imprimis Tagula (IRE)**[44] 3956 5-9-10 **78**....................(v) RobertWinston 3 — 83
(A Bailey) *trckd ldrs: effrt over 2f out: drvn on inner to chse wnr ins fnl f: r.o but nvr able to chal* — **7/1**

064 **3** *nk* **Buxton**[4] 5288 5-9-2 **70**....................(t) RobertHavlin 10 — 74
(R Ingram) *racd wd towards rr: prog fr 1/2-way: drvn and effrt over 1f out: r.o to take 3rd ins fnl f: nvr able to chal* — **14/1**

3106 **4** *2 ¾* **Spring Green**[31] 4380 3-9-7 **78**.................... SteveDrowne 4 — 73
(H Morrison) *pressed ldrs: effrt over 2f out: disp 2nd ent fnl f: sn wknd* — **8/1**

011 **5** *½* **Whiskey Junction**[13] 4982 5-9-10 **78**.................... LPKeniry 1 — 72
(M Quinn) *led at str pce to jst over 2f out: wknd ent fnl f* — **13/2**

0-06 **6** *2 ¼* **Muftarres (IRE)**[20] 4761 4-9-2 **70**....................(tp) RichardHughes 9 — 56
(G A Butler) *settled in rr: effrt on inner over 2f out: nvr on terms w ldrs: plugged on* — **4/1**[1]

6042 **7** *hd* **Dvinsky (USA)**[4] 5288 8-9-10 **78**....................(b) IanMongan 11 — 68+
(P Howling) *hld up in last: v modest prog 2f out: stuck bhd two rivals 1f out: kpt on: nvr nr ldrs* — **20/1**

3233 **8** *nk* **Onceaponatime (IRE)**[103] 2088 4-9-4 **72**.................... AlanMunro 7 — 57
(M D Squance) *nvr beyond midfield: outpcd fr over 2f out: nvr on terms w ldrs after* — **12/1**

3204 **9** *5* **Defector (IRE)**[31] 4374 3-8-13 **70**....................(b) MartinDwyer 5 — 39
(W R Muir) *stdd s: hld up in last trio: effrt on inner whn no room over 2f out: no ch after* — **20/1**

0651 **10** *shd* **Comadoir (IRE)**[43] 3989 3-9-9 **80**.................... FergusSweeney 8 — 49
(Miss Jo Crowley) *chsd ldrs: rdn bef 1/2-way: sn struggling: no ch over 1f out* — **6/1**[3]

10-6 **11** *9* **Especially Special (IRE)**[21] 4712 3-9-3 **74**.................... EddieAhern 2 — 14
(S Kirk) *chsd ldrs tl wknd rapidly on inner over 2f out: t.o* — **11/1**

1m 10.81s (-1.09) **Going Correction** -0.20s/f (Stan)
WFA 3 from 4yo+ 3lb — **11** Ran SP% **120.1**
Speed ratings (Par 105): **99,97,96,93,92 89,89,88,82,82 70**
CSF £40.95 CT £466.73 TOTE £6.60: £2.20, £2.30, £4.40; EX 44.90 TRIFECTA Not won. Place 6: £164.20 Place 5: £73.97.
Owner Hodgson, Hufford, Moss & Papworth **Bred** Carpet Lady Partnership **Trained** Aldbury, Herts

FOCUS
A fair sprint handicap run in a good time. The winner built on his reappearance win and was value for a bit further.
Muftarres(IRE) Official explanation: jockey said colt hung badly left coming down the hill
Dvinsky(USA) Official explanation: jockey said gelding was denied a clear run
T/Plt: £87.70 to a £1 stake. Pool: £62,589.67. 520.56 winning tickets. T/Qpdt: £41.40 to a £1 stake. Pool: £3,683.90. 65.80 winning tickets. JN

5324 SOUTHWELL (L-H)
Thursday, August 27

OFFICIAL GOING: Standard
Wind: light across Weather: Sunny and dry

5371 EBF BUY A RACING POST YEARLING BONUS CANDIDATE MAIDEN STKS — 1m (F)
2:30 (2:30) (Class 5) 2-Y-O — **£4,209** (£1,252; £625; £312) **Stalls** Low

Form — RPR

62 **1** **Tanto Quanto (IRE)**[15] 4915 2-9-3 0....................(b) RichardMullen 4 — 75
(W R Muir) *mde all: rdn along wl over 1f out: drvn and edgd lft and rt ins fnl f: hung rt nr fin: hld on gamely* — **11/1**

0 **2** *hd* **Banana Republic (IRE)**[41] 4048 2-9-3 0.................... JimCrowley 5 — 75
(P F I Cole) *trckd ldrs: smooth hdwy over 2f outm chal wl over 1f out: rdn and ev ch: drvn ins fnl f: bmpd and no ex nr line* — **11/4**[2]

3 *2 ½* **Wadnaan** 2-9-3 0.................... JoeFanning 1 — 73+
(M Johnston) *s.i.s: green and in rr tl hdwy 1/2-way: swtchd wd and rdn 2f out: styd on strly ins fnl f* — **7/1**

062 **4** *¾* **Elmfield Giant (USA)**[13] 4993 2-9-3 80.................... TonyHamilton 2 — 68
(R A Fahey) *prom: effrt over 2f out: sn rdn and ev ch tl drvn and one pce ent fnl f* — **5/2**[1]

4505 **5** *3* **Hairs Vital (IRE)**[31] 4370 2-8-10 67.................... DeclanCannon(7) 3 — 61
(E J O'Neill) *chsd ldrs: rdn along over 2f out and sn one pce* — **22/1**

6 *3 ¼* **Primrose Bankes** 2-8-9 0.................... JackDean(3) 8 — 49
(W G M Turner) *chsd ldrs: rdn along over 2f out: sn one pce* — **50/1**

7 *7* **Ginger Jack** 2-9-3 0.................... TedDurcan 11 — 38
(Saeed Bin Suroor) *s.i.s: sn rdn along and rapid hdwy to go cl up after 2f: rdn alongover 2f out and sn wknd* — **3/1**[3]

0 **8** *1 ¼* **Tenga Venga**[12] 5029 2-9-3 0.................... JerryO'Dwyer 6 — 36
(P S McEntee) *midfield: rdn along 3f out: nvr a factor* — **18/1**

9 *1 ¾* **Set To Rock** 2-9-3 0.................... TPQueally 7 — 32
(J G Portman) *s.i.s: a in rr* — **40/1**

0 **10** *hd* **Man In The Mirror (IRE)**[36] 4201 2-8-10 0.......... JosephineBruning(7) 9 — 31
(P L Gilligan) *a in rr* — **150/1**

11 *21* **Don Stefano** 2-9-0 0.................... WilliamCarson(3) 10 — —
(W G M Turner) *a in rr* — **28/1**

1m 45.32s (1.62) **Going Correction** +0.025s/f (Slow) — **11** Ran SP% **119.2**
Speed ratings (Par 94): **92,91,89,88,85 82,75,74,72,72 51**
toteswingers: 1&2 £16.20, 1&3 £4.40, 2&3 £7.30 CSF £40.73 TOTE £13.70: £3.50, £1.80, £2.10; EX 58.30.
Owner Mrs J M Muir **Bred** Messrs N McSweeney & Jeff O'Callaghan **Trained** Lambourn, Berks
■ Stewards' Enquiry : Richard Mullen one-day ban: careless riding (Sep 10)

FOCUS
This would have taken some getting for these juveniles. A tricky race to assess, rated around the balance of those with experience. The first four came clear of a 67-rated performer.

NOTEBOOK
Tanto Quanto(IRE), easy to back, made all to open his account at the third time of asking. He advertised his stamina here in no uncertain terms and, although drifting right throughout the final furlong under maximum pressure, there was no faulting his attitude. He was beaten in a claimer on his previous outing so that puts this form into some perspective, but blinkers helped his cause and this was an improved display for the extra distance. (tchd 12-1)
Banana Republic(IRE), whose yard sent out a winning 2yo here earlier in the week, attracted strong support. He needed the run in hotter company at Newbury on his debut last month and was evidently fancied to relish the extra furlong. He reared momentarily in the gates, but broke sufficiently well and looked the most likely winner turning for home. He simply found the more-experienced winner too resolute where it mattered and, though that rival drifted into him, it didn't look enough to have cost him success. He has an abundance of scope and should soon be found an opening. (op 7-2)
Wadnaan ◆, a 160,000gns son of Shamardal, was clueless through the first half, but when the penny dropped he ran on most encouragingly down the home straight and is one to look out for next time. (op 5-1)
Elmfield Giant(USA) proved easy to back on this step up a furlong. He had his chance, but failed to see it out like the principals and was done with coming to the furlong marker. A drop back to 7f should suit better again, but he looks to need respite from the handicapper. (op 9-4 tchd 3-1)
Ginger Jack, representing a powerful yard that does well here, totally missed the break from the outside stall before being rushed up to race handily. That move unsurprisingly found him out, but he ought to show this initial run to be wrong as he gains more experience. (tchd 10-3)

5372 SOUTHWELL GOLF CLUB JUNIOR MEMBERS NURSERY — 5f (F)
3:00 (3:01) (Class 6) (0-65,63) 2-Y-O — **£2,729** (£806; £403) **Stalls** High

Form — RPR

5664 **1** **Watch Chain (IRE)**[22] 4639 2-8-5 **52**.................... AshleyMorgan(5) 1 — 54
(M H Tompkins) *trckd ldrs: hdwy whn bmpd 2f out: effrt on far rail to chal over 1f out: rdn to ld ins fnl f: sn drvn and edgd rt: kpt on* — **4/1**[1]

2006 **2** *nk* **Angie's Nap (USA)**[38] 4153 2-8-10 **52**....................(p) ChrisCatlin 13 — 53
(P S McEntee) *prom: effrt wl over 1f out and sn rdn: styd on to chal ent fnl f: sn drvn and edgd lft: ev ch tl no ex towards fin* — **40/1**

360 **3** *½* **Usquaebach**[90] 2444 2-8-12 **54**....................(b[1]) SebSanders 2 — 53
(S Curran) *chsd ldrs: rdn along and edgd lft 2f out: sn swtchd to far rail and strrun ins fnl f and ev ch tl no ex towards fin* — **17/2**

665 **4** *½* **Venture Girl (IRE)**[26] 4515 2-9-1 **57**.................... DuranFentiman 3 — 54
(T D Easterby) *sn outpcd and towards rr: hdwy 1/2-way: rdn 2f out: styd on strly ins fnl f: nrst fin* — **5/1**[2]

3430 **5** *1* **Southwark Newshawk**[15] 4912 2-8-13 **58**.................... WilliamCarson(3) 5 — 52
(Mrs C A Dunnett) *led: rdn along 2f out: drvn and hdd over 1f out: wknd ins fnl f* — **12/1**

5500 **6** *nk* **Baby Judge (IRE)**[5] 5253 2-8-10 **52**.................... AmirQuinn 4 — 45
(M C Chapman) *prom: rdn 2f out: led over 1f out: drvn and hdd ins fnl f: sn n.m.r and wknd* — **25/1**

0655 **7** *nk* **Princess Shamal**[31] 4383 2-9-4 **60**.................... JimCrowley 9 — 56+
(J R Jenkins) *hmpd s: midfield and pushed along 1/2-way: swtchd wd and rdn over 1f out: styd on wl fnl f: nrst fin* — **22/1**

40 **8** *½* **Rightcar**[3] 5310 2-8-13 **55**.................... TonyHamilton 8 — 45+
(Peter Grayson) *s.i.s and in rr: rdn 1/2-way: hdwy over 1f out: n.d* — **12/1**

464 **9** *1 ¼* **Yeah**[37] 4163 2-9-2 **58**.................... SJCraine 7 — 43
(Patrick Morris) *bmpd s: sn trcking ldrs: gd hdwy 1/2-way: sn chal and evch tl rdn and wknd appr fnl f* — **10/1**

400 **10** *1 ¼* **Diamond Affair (IRE)**[31] 4383 2-9-3 **59**.................... TPQueally 6 — 40
(M G Quinlan) *cl up: rdn and ev ch 2f out: drvn and wknd appr fnl f* — **7/1**[3]

4040 **11** *nk* **Mrs Jones And Me (IRE)**[6] 5226 2-9-2 **58**............(v) PaulMulrennan 12 — 38
(P T Midgley) *wnt bdly lft s: chsd ldrs: rdn along 2f out: sn wknd* — **33/1**

304 **12** *4* **Gower Sophia**[64] 3263 2-9-0 **63**....................(b[1]) JohnCavanagh(7) 11 — 28+
(M Brittain) *hmpd s: a in rr* — **12/1**

3151 **13** *5* **On The Piste (IRE)**[50] 3726 2-8-13 **60**.................... MartinLane(5) 10 — 7+
(L A Mullaney) *hmpd s: a towards rr* — **8/1**

61.20 secs (1.50) **Going Correction** +0.10s/f (Slow) — **13** Ran SP% **116.5**
Speed ratings (Par 92): **92,91,90,89,88 87,87,86,84,82 82,75,67**
toteswingers: 1&2 £33.80, 1&3 £9.70, 2&3 £65.30 CSF £181.17 CT £1338.56 TOTE £5.30: £2.00, £10.60, £3.10; EX 187.00.
Owner Miss Clare Hollest **Bred** Miss S Von Schilcher **Trained** Newmarket, Suffolk
■ Stewards' Enquiry : Seb Sanders one-day ban (Sep 10) for careless riding
Ashley Morgan caution: careless riding

FOCUS
A poor nursery. Those drawn high were at a disadvantage even before Mrs Jones And Me went left out of the gates and hampered a number of her rivals. Not a race to dwell on.

NOTEBOOK
Watch Chain(IRE) confirmed the promise of his nursery bow at Brighton 22 days previously, for which he was dropped 3lb, and opened his account at the fifth attempt. He took time to get going on the far rail, but found his feet from 2f out and was always doing enough to hold off rivals despite coming right into the centre of the track late on. That was likely down to greenness and it being the first time he had been in front in a race. He doesn't appeal as one for a follow up, though. (op 7-2)
Angie's Nap(USA) ran a big race from her high draw, but was certainly helped on that front when Mrs Jones And Me went left at the start. The first-time cheekpieces helped bring about this improved effort, but she is only a plater. (op 50-1)
Usquaebach finished with purpose against the far rail and this was a big return to form on her return from a 90-day break. She has now run both her best races over C&D. (op 12-1 tchd 8-1)
Venture Girl(IRE), making her nursery and all-weather debut, did well to finish so close considering she lacked the natural pace required on this first run over the minimum. She can be found an opening when reverting to 6f. (op 9-2 tchd 4-1 and 6-1)
Princess Shamal ran better than her finishing position suggests, as she hit a flat spot when taken to the near side before staying on with gusto all too late in the day. (op 16-1)

5373 SOUTHWELL MEDIAN AUCTION MAIDEN STKS — 6f (F)
3:30 (3:31) (Class 5) 3-4-Y-O — **£3,070** (£906; £453) **Stalls** Low

Form — RPR

-532 **1** **Fantasy Gladiator**[22] 4668 3-9-3 66.................... DO'Donohoe 8 — 77
(R M H Cowell) *trckd ldng pair: hdwy 3f out: chal 2f out: rdn over 1f out: drvn ins fnl f: kpt on to ld last 50yds* — **11/4**[2]

6333 **2** *nk* **Milldown Story**[14] 4936 3-8-12 67 ChrisCatlin 4 71
(B R Millman) *led: rdn along and jnd 2f out: drvn over 1f out: hdd and no ex last 50yds* **5/2**[1]
5503 **3** *6* **Positivity**[37] 4172 3-8-12 49 RichardMullen 3 52
(B Smart) *chsd ldrs: rdn along wl over 2f out: kpt on same pce* **7/1**
6404 **4** *3* **Abu Derby (IRE)**[21] 4718 3-8-12 61 (t) JamieKyne(5) 5 47
(J G Given) *dwlt: in rr and sn swtchd wd: hdwy 3f out: rdn 2f out: sn no imp* **8/1**
600 **5** *3* **Meydan Style (USA)**[16] 4879 3-9-3 41 (b) PaulMulrennan 1 38
(J Balding) *dwlt: a in rr* **40/1**
232 **6** *3/4* **Sea Crest**[12] 5041 3-8-5 60 JohnCavanagh(7) 6 30
(M Brittain) *in tch: rdn along 1/2-way: sn wknd* **7/2**[3]
0 **7** *6* **Teia Tephi**[15] 4913 3-8-12 0 AdrianMcCarthy 2 11
(P W Chapple-Hyam) *cl up on inner: rdn along wl over 2f out: sn drvn and wknd* **11/1**

1m 16.07s (-0.43) **Going Correction** +0.025s/f (Slow)
WFA 3 from 4yo 3lb **7 Ran SP% 111.8**
Speed ratings (Par 103): **103,102,94,90,86 85,77**
toteswingers: 1&2 £2.50, 1&3 £4.50, 2&3 £5.30 CSF £9.60 TOTE £3.70: £1.60, £1.40; EX 11.00.
Owner The Fantasy Fellowship **Bred** R S A Urquhart **Trained** Six Mile Bottom, Cambs

FOCUS
A moderate maiden in which the first pair dominated. Ordinary but sound form.

5374 DINE IN THE QUEEN MOTHER RESTAURANT H'CAP 5f (F)
4:00 (4:02) (Class 5) (0-70,70) 3-Y-0+ **£3,885** (£1,156; £577; £288) **Stalls** High

Form RPR
2241 **1** **Guto**[16] 4886 6-9-1 65 KellyHarrison(3) 5 74
(W J H Ratcliffe) *chsd ldrs: hdwy wl over 1f out and sn rdn: styd on to chal ins fnl f: edgd rt and led last 100yds* **13/2**[2]
5602 **2** *3/4* **Figaro Flyer (IRE)**[17] 4842 6-9-1 69 JPFahy(7) 13 75
(P Howling) *chsd ldr: hdwy 2f out: rdn over 1f out: styd on to ld briefly ins fnl f: sn hdd and nt qckn* **8/1**
0532 **3** *hd* **Yankee Storm**[17] 4843 4-9-7 68 FrancisNorton 12 74
(M Quinn) *chsd ldrs: hdwy 2f out: sn rdn and ev ch ins fnl f: sn drvn and nt qckn last 100yds* **9/1**
0413 **4** *2 1/4* **Spic 'n Span**[7] 5184 4-9-3 64 (b) ChrisCatlin 14 61
(R A Harris) *led: rdn along wl over 1f out: drvn: edgd rigfht and hdd ins fnl f: wknd* **15/2**[3]
0633 **5** *1 1/2* **Cheshire Rose**[16] 4886 4-8-12 59 (p) WilliamBuick 8 51
(A M Hales) *prom: rdn along wl over 1f out: sn drvn and wknd appr fnl f* **14/1**
542 **6** *3/4* **Godfrey Street**[7] 5183 6-9-4 70 (p) JamieKyne(5) 6 59+
(A G Newcombe) *stmbld s and towards rr tl styd on appr fnl f* **9/2**[1]
0210 **7** *1 1/4* **Diane's Choice**[14] 4929 6-8-11 58 (e) DavidProbert 3 43
(Miss Gay Kelleway) *towards rr: rdn along 2f out and sme hdwy: n.d* **12/1**
5320 **8** *3* **Shakespeare's Son**[37] 4183 4-9-0 61 JimCrowley 7 35
(H J Evans) *midfield: rdn along 2f out: no hdwy* **13/2**[2]
0605 **9** *1/2* **Lady Vivien**[13] 4997 3-8-13 62 SebSanders 4 34
(D H Brown) *midfield: swtchd rt and rdn along 2f out: nvr a factor* **18/1**
0126 **10** *1/2* **Billy Red**[20] 4733 5-9-6 67 (b) TPQueally 9 37
(J R Jenkins) *stmbld s: sn prom: rdn along 2f out and sn wknd* **16/1**
0003 **11** *2 1/2* **The History Man (IRE)**[13] 5008 6-8-3 55 (e) PatrickDonaghy(5) 11 16
(B D Leavy) *a in rr* **16/1**
250- **12** *2 3/4* **Megalo Maniac**[258] 7651 6-8-3 57 MarzenaJeziorek(7) 2 9
(R A Fahey) *v.s.a and a bhd* **16/1**
5136 **13** *2* **Russian Rocket (IRE)**[16] 4886 7-9-3 64 TGMcLaughlin 10 8
(Mrs C A Dunnett) *midfield: rdn along 1/2-way: sn wknd* **18/1**

59.89 secs (0.19) **Going Correction** +0.10s/f (Slow)
WFA 3 from 4yo+ 2lb **13 Ran SP% 120.3**
Speed ratings (Par 103): **102,100,100,96,94 93,91,86,85,84 80,76,73**
toteswingers: 1&2 £13.90, 1&3 £19.10, 2&3 £11.10 CSF £58.20 CT £492.00 TOTE £9.10: £2.40, £2.10, £2.90; EX 75.00.
Owner W J H Ratcliffe **Bred** H B Hughes **Trained** Newmarket, Suffolk
■ Stewards' Enquiry : J P Fahy two-day ban: used whip with excessive frequency (Sep 10-11)

FOCUS
A wide-open sprint handicap, run at a decent pace. Sound form.
Figaro Flyer(IRE) Official explanation: jockey said gelding hung badly right
Godfrey Street Official explanation: jockey said gelding stumbled leaving the stalls
Billy Red Official explanation: jockey said gelding stumbled leaving the stalls
Megalo Maniac Official explanation: jockey said gelding was slowly away

5375 MEMBERSHIP OF SOUTHWELL GOLF CLUB H'CAP 1m (F)
4:30 (4:33) (Class 3) (0-90,90) 3-Y-0+
£9,346 (£2,799; £1,399; £700; £349; £175) **Stalls** Low

Form RPR
02 **1** **Foolin Myself**[34] 4262 4-9-11 88 (b1) TPQueally 12 105
(M L W Bell) *trckd ldrs: smooth hdwy to ld 3f out: clr wl over 1f out: unchal* **7/2**[1]
5635 **2** *7* **Xpres Maite**[10] 5104 6-9-8 85 (b) AmirQuinn 14 86
(S R Bowring) *cl up: rdn along to chse wnr over 2f out: drvn wl over 1f out and kpt on same pce* **18/1**
6-24 **3** *nk* **Rainbow Mirage (IRE)**[6] 5221 5-9-12 89 SebSanders 4 89
(E S McMahon) *in tch on outer: rdn along to chse ldrs 3f out: drvn to chse wnr over 1f out: sn no imp* **11/2**[3]
5653 **4** *2 1/4* **Bavarian Nordic (USA)**[24] 4597 4-8-8 78 JPFahy(7) 9 73
(Mrs A Duffield) *sn rdn along in rr: bhd after 2f: hdwy on inner over 2f out: sn rdn and kpt on: nt rch ldrs* **16/1**
2550 **5** *1/2* **Tartan Gunna**[70] 3049 3-9-6 89 JoeFanning 10 83
(M Johnston) *s.i.s and towards rr: hdwy on outer wl over 2f out: sn rdn and kpt on same pce: nvr nr ldrs* **9/2**[2]
6410 **6** *1 1/4* **Beauchamp Viceroy**[12] 5025 5-9-7 84 (tp) WilliamBuick 7 75
(G A Butler) *trckd ldrs: effrt 3f out and sn rdn: drvn 2f out and sn wknd* **16/1**
020 **7** *1/2* **Kinsya**[50] 3752 6-9-0 82 AshleyMorgan(5) 6 72
(M H Tompkins) *a towards rr* **16/1**
1066 **8** *2* **Miss Glitters (IRE)**[24] 4592 4-8-13 76 TravisBlock 2 61
(H Morrison) *chsd ldrs on inner: rdn along 3f out and sn wknd* **14/1**
4160 **9** *1* **Mastership (IRE)**[19] 4796 5-9-8 90 (p) JamieKyne(5) 3 73
(J J Quinn) *towards rr: hdwy 1/2-way: rdn and in tch 2f out: sn drvn and no imp* **14/1**
5060 **10** *3 1/4* **Mishrif (USA)**[10] 5092 3-9-6 89 (t) ChrisCatlin 8 64
(J R Jenkins) *midfield: rdn along 1/2-way: sn lost pl and rr* **20/1**
0143 **11** *nse* **Smarty Socks (IRE)**[24] 4592 5-9-7 84 TonyHamilton 5 59
(P T Midgley) *dwlt: a in rr* **11/1**

0000 **12** *9* **Mangham (IRE)**[12] 5040 4-9-10 87 PaulMulrennan 13 41
(D H Brown) *led: rdn along and hdd 3f out: sn drvn and wknd* **16/1**
-310 **13** *2* **Captain Ellis (USA)**[47] 3839 3-9-0 83 JimCrowley 1 33
(A P Jarvis) *a towards rr* **14/1**

1m 42.28s (-1.42) **Going Correction** +0.025s/f (Slow)
WFA 3 from 4yo+ 6lb **13 Ran SP% 117.7**
Speed ratings (Par 107): **108,101,100,98,97 96,96,94,93,89 89,80,78**
toteswingers: 1&2 £18.00, 1&3 £5.20, 2&3 £16.50 CSF £68.46 CT £355.09 TOTE £4.10: £2.00, £6.20, £1.90; EX 69.60.
Owner W J Gredley **Bred** Middle Park Stud Ltd **Trained** Newmarket, Suffolk

FOCUS
This was a fair handicap which looked another wide-open affair, but the winner blew the race apart in first-time blinkers and won as he pleased. He has been rated up 7lb, with a little doubt over how literally to take this.

NOTEBOOK
Foolin Myself blew the race apart and won as he pleased. He proved popular despite being 5lb higher than when finishing second at Ascot on his previous outing last month and, in first-time blinkers, could hardly have won this any easier. He was confidently ridden on this all-weather bow and had it sewn up 2f out, belatedly delivering on the promise he showed when beating Tartan Bearer as a juvenile. He will be high on confidence and connections will surely looking to turn him out under a penalty, but it remains to be seen whether the headgear continues to have such a positive effect in the future. (tchd 4-1)
Xpres Maite was given his usual positive ride and kept gamely to his task when headed in the home straight, helping to put the form into perspective. (op 20-1)
Rainbow Mirage(IRE) was the biggest danger to the winner turning for home, but he was made to look very one-paced when that one asserted and wanted to hang throughout the final furlong. It was his first run on this surface. (op 9-2)
Bavarian Nordic(USA) had to be ridden early doors and got himself behind. Nothing finished better from off the pace, however, and again he shaped as though he is crying out for a return to further. His previous win here came over 1m4f.
Tartan Gunna shaped somewhat better than the bare form as he made a tardy start and then had to race on the outside of the pack. He should come on for this. (op 6-1 tchd 13-2)
Captain Ellis(USA) Official explanation: jockey said gelding resented the kickback

5376 PLAY GOLF BEFORE RACING AT SOUTHWELL H'CAP 2m (F)
5:00 (5:01) (Class 4) (0-80,80) 3-Y-0 **£6,476** (£1,927; £963; £481) **Stalls** Low

Form RPR
623 **1** **Sally Forth**[19] 4798 3-8-13 72 ChrisCatlin 4 83
(R Charlton) *trckd ldng pair: hdwy to trck ldr 1/2-way: cl up 5f out: led 3f out: rdn along 2f out: drvn over 1f out and styd on str fnl f* **14/1**
-033 **2** *6* **Dulcie**[19] 4793 3-8-10 74 AshleyMorgan(5) 5 78
(M H Tompkins) *hld up in tch: hdwy to trck ldng pair 1/2-way: effrt on bit to trck wnr 3f out: chal 2f out and sn shkn up: rdn over 1f out: sn edgd lft and btn* **11/4**[3]
0-31 **3** *19* **Veiled**[10] 5113 3-8-13 72 6ex SebSanders 1 53
(Sir Mark Prescott) *trckd ldr: led over 8f out: rdn along and hdd 3f out: sn drvn and wknd* **6/4**[1]
5113 **4** *24* **Curacao**[15] 4911 3-9-7 80 JimCrowley 3 32
(Mrs A J Perrett) *trckd ldrs: hung rt bnd after 6f: sn rdn along and lost pl 1/2-way: bhd after* **15/8**[2]
0360 **5** *1 1/2* **Dark Oasis**[13] 5011 3-7-9 61 oh15 JosephineBruning(7) 2 12
(M C Chapman) *led: hung rt bnd after 6f and sn rdn along: hdd over 8f out: sn lost pl and bhd* **28/1**

3m 42.05s (-3.45) **Going Correction** +0.025s/f (Slow) **5 Ran SP% 111.6**
Speed ratings (Par 102): **109,106,96,84,83**
toteswingers: 1&2 £12.00, 1&3 not won, 2&3 not won. CSF £51.85 TOTE £12.90: £3.00, £1.60; EX 33.30.
Owner The Queen **Bred** The Queen **Trained** Beckhampton, Wilts

FOCUS
Despite the low turnout this was still an interesting staying handicap for three-year-olds. The form has been rated at face value but there is a doubt, with the front pair in the market both very disappointing.
Curacao Official explanation: jockey said gelding was never travelling

5377 SOUTHWELL-RACECOURSE.CO.UK APPRENTICE H'CAP 1m 3f (F)
5:30 (5:31) (Class 6) (0-60,60) 3-Y-0+ **£2,590** (£770; £385; £192) **Stalls** Low

Form RPR
5340 **1** **Astrolibra**[44] 3949 5-9-2 53 AshleyMorgan(5) 14 65+
(M H Tompkins) *trckd ldrs: hdwy on outer 3f out: led 2f out: rdn clr appr fnl f: styd on wl* **10/1**
4260 **2** *3 3/4* **Noah Jameel**[85] 2608 7-9-10 56 DavidProbert 10 58
(A G Newcombe) *trckd ldrs: hdwy 4f out: rdn along 2f out: drvn to chse wnr over 1f out: no imp* **16/1**
0/0 **3** *1 1/2* **Tar (IRE)**[41] 4071 5-9-10 56 (v1) WilliamCarson 8 55
(John A Harris) *trckd ldr: led over 4f out: rdn along and hdd 2f out: sn drvn and kpt on same pce* **66/1**
0035 **4** *1* **King Of The Beers (USA)**[31] 4373 5-9-8 59 (p) SPRyan(5) 5 57
(R A Harris) *midfield: rdn along and lost pl over 7f out: bhd 4f out: hdwy on inner over 2f out: drvn and kpt on u.p ins fnl f: nrst fin* **6/1**[2]
6100 **5** *nk* **Sir Haydn**[50] 2830 9-8-13 52 (v) DannyBrock(7) 1 49
(J R Jenkins) *led: rdn along and hdd over 4f out: drvn along over 2f out and grad wknd* **20/1**
5051 **6** *1* **Golden Future**[24] 4593 6-9-6 52 NeilBrown 6 48
(P D Niven) *towards rr: hdwy 4f out: effrt on outer to chse ldrs over 2f out: sn rdn and no imp* **11/2**[1]
0520 **7** *1* **Altos Reales**[14] 4944 5-8-13 48 JamieKyne(3) 4 42
(J G Given) *chsd ldrs on inner: rdn along over 4f out: drvn 3f out and grad wknd* **11/2**[1]
05/6 **8** *3* **Thistle**[25] 4376 8-9-1 52 (tp) MatthewDavies(5) 9 41
(George Baker) *towards rr: hdwy 1/2-way: rdn along over 4f out: wknd 3f out* **28/1**
445- **9** *2 1/4* **Bolckow**[357] 5653 6-8-12 47 PatrickDonaghy(3) 11 32+
(J T Stimpson) *hld up: stdy hdwy on outer 1/2-way: chsd ldng pair over 3f out: rdn alongwl over 2f out and sn wknd* **8/1**[3]
3504 **10** *13* **Lytham (IRE)**[17] 4861 8-9-4 53 AmyBaker(3) 2 16
(A W Carroll) *in tch on inner: rdn along 1/2-way: sn wknd* **8/1**[3]
5600 **11** *8* **Sew'N'So Character (IRE)**[22] 4645 8-9-13 59 AndreaAtzeni 12 8
(M Blanshard) *s.i.s: a in rr* **20/1**
2006 **12** *12* **Bridgewater Boys**[83] 2656 8-9-11 60 (b) AmyRyan(3) 3 —
(T J Pitt) *s.i.s: a in rr: wl bhd fnl 3f and eased* **20/1**

2m 28.96s (0.96) **Going Correction** +0.025s/f (Slow) **12 Ran SP% 101.5**
Speed ratings (Par 101): **97,94,93,92,92 91,90,88,86,77 71,62**
toteswingers: 1&2 £18.40, 1&3 £24.10, 2&3 £60.60 CSF £104.49 CT £5959.17 TOTE £10.80: £3.10, £2.90, £11.50; EX 130.00 Place 6: £233.97 Place 5: £96.14.
Owner Mystic Meg Limited **Bred** Mystic Meg Limited **Trained** Newmarket, Suffolk
■ Credential (5/1) was withdrawn (broke out of stalls). Deduct 15p in the £ under R4.

FOCUS
A weak handicap, confined to apprentice riders. It was run at an ordinary pace and little got into it from the rear. A clear personal best from the easy winner.
T/Plt: £358.90 to a £1 stake. Pool: £59,425.16. 120.87 winning tickets. T/Qpdt: £23.90 to a £1 stake. Pool: £4,865.28. 150.54 winning tickets. JR

5013 SAINT-MALO (L-H)
Thursday, August 27

OFFICIAL GOING: Good to soft

5378a PRIX ROBERT SURCOUF (MAIDEN) (C&G) 1m 1f
11:35 (11:35) 2-Y-O £6,796 (£2,718; £2,039; £1,359; £680)

RPR
1 **Isaman** 2-8-12 ... JClaudic 74
(C Laffon-Parias, France)
2 3/4 **Tussian Bere (FR)**[22] 4686 2-9-2 ... JAuge 76
(E J O'Neill) *sn led: pushed along 2f out: rdn over 1f out: styd on: hdd 50yds out* **14/5**[1]
3 1 **Tantawangelo**[12] 2-9-2 ... IMendizabal 74
(R Pritchard-Gordon, France)
4 shd **Sam Winner (FR)** 2-9-2 ... 74
(G Cherel, France)
5 5 **Eledikris (FR)** 2-8-12 ow3 ... AFouassier 60
(A Couetil, France)
6 12 **Victory Kid (FR)** 2-8-12 ... 36
(J-V Toux, France)
7 1 **Toc (FR)**[6] 2-9-2 ... 38
(C Boutin, France)
8 6 **Letcho (FR)** 2-9-2 ... 26
(D Leblond, France)
9 10 **Ecluso (FR)** 2-8-12 ... 2
(S Guinoiseau, France)
1m 58.19s (118.19) **9** Ran SP% **26.3**
PARI-MUTUEL (Including 1 Euro stake): WIN 5.20; PL 1.30, 1.10, 1.20; DF 6.80.
Owner Mme A Cuadra-Lores **Bred** Almagro De Actividades Comerciales S A **Trained** Chantilly, France
■ Stewards' Enquiry : J Auge four-day ban: careless riding (Sep 10-13)
A Fouassier 250euro fine: weighed out heavy

NOTEBOOK
Tussian Bere(FR) has just been getting run out of things late up to now and the same thing happened here. He deserves to pick up a maiden but might need a some help, possibly from a form of headgear.

5241 BATH (L-H)
Friday, August 28

OFFICIAL GOING: Good changing to good (good to soft in places after race 3 (6.10)) changing to good to soft after race 4 (6.40)
Wind: Strong, ahead. Weather: Cloudy

5379 SPORTINGBET.COM HEROS MAIDEN AUCTION STKS 5f 161y
5:05 (5:08) (Class 5) 2-Y-O £2,590 (£770; £385; £192) Stalls Centre

Form RPR
1 **Art Scholar (IRE)** 2-8-13 0 ... PatDobbs 10 90+
(G L Moore) *broke wl: outpcd tl gd hdwy over 2f out: str run on outer to ld 1f out: sn clr: easily* **4/1**[3]
52 2 5 **Filwa (IRE)**[11] 5096 2-8-9 0 ... EddieAhern 8 68
(B J Meehan) *trckd ldrs: led jst ins fnl 2f: rdn and hdd 1f out: sn no ch w easy wnr but styd on for clr 2nd* **13/8**[1]
050 3 3 3/4 **Madam Isshe**[22] 4688 2-8-5 46 ... NickyMackay 1 51
(M S Saunders) *led tl hdd jst ins fnl 2f: sn no ch w ldng duo but styd on for clr 3rd* **66/1**
3034 4 nk **Chocolate Cookie (IRE)**[9] 5153 2-8-5 75 ... ChrisCatlin 6 49
(R Hannon) *chsd ldrs: rdn 3f out: wknd ins fnl 2f* **11/4**[2]
6530 5 1 **Two Kisses (IRE)**[26] 4565 2-8-3 69 ... CatherineGannon 3 44
(B G Powell) *chsd ldrs: rdn 1/2-way: wknd 2f out* **8/1**
000 6 3 1/4 **Truly Magic**[22] 4688 2-8-4 0 ... RichardSmith 7 33
(H J L Dunlop) *outpcd: mod prog fnl f* **50/1**
7 nk **Heligoland** 2-8-3 0 ... RichardThomas 9 31
(A G Newcombe) *slowly away and v green s: stl wl bhd 1/2-way: styd on appr fnl f: gng on cl home wout ever looking a threat* **66/1**
8 8 **Bound For Stardom** 2-8-3 0 ... FrankieMcDonald 2 2
(W S Kittow) *slowly away and rn v green: a in rr* **40/1**
22 9 3 1/4 **Lexi's Layla (IRE)**[24] 4626 2-8-12 0 ... RichardMullen 5 —
(D M Simcock) *t.k.h: chsd ldrs 3f* **5/1**
1m 12.57s (1.37) **Going Correction** +0.10s/f (Good) **9** Ran SP% **119.9**
Speed ratings (Par 94): **94,87,82,81,80 76,75,65,60**
toteswinger: 1&2 £1.90, 1&3 £35.00, 2&3 £35.00. CSF £11.35 TOTE £5.10: £1.50, £1.20, £11.80; EX 13.80.
Owner R A Green **Bred** John Ramsbottom **Trained** Lower Beeding, W Sussex

FOCUS
After 7.5mm of rain during the morning, the ground was changed to good. A strong south-westerly wind was blowing almost head on up the straight. A fair maiden run at a decent pace and it was won in impressive style by the newcomer, who looks worth a try at Listed level..

NOTEBOOK
Art Scholar(IRE), a newcomer who was backed from 8-1 into 4-1, swept into contention out wide and quickened clear. He looks potentially useful and was bought for a bargain 16,000 euros. His dam is out of a half-sister to Derby runner-up The Great Gatsby, but his sire seems to have injected plenty of speed. (op 8-1)
Filwa(IRE) was beaten just a nose over 6f at Windsor on her second start, despite starting slowly and racing keenly. She was strongly supported dropped in trip and hit the front 2f out but had no answer to the surging run of the winner. (op 2-1)
Madam Isshe, who had shown nothing in three previous starts and is rated just 46, was well beaten by the first two. It is possible that the switch to forcing tactics perked her up, but her proximity casts a shadow over the form. (op 80-1)
Chocolate Cookie(IRE), was the disappointment of the race, a she had strong claims on her eighth of 20 behind Monsieur Chevalier in a valuable 5f Newbury sales race last month and had an excuse when involved in a barging match at Folkestone last time. She raced up with the pace but was under pressure some way out and found a very negligible response. (op 5-2 tchd 7-2)
Two Kisses(IRE) improved on her early season form when close third over C&D in June but was unable to repeat that upped to 7f in a Newbury nursery last time and the return to this trip has failed to reignite her. (op 6-1)
Bound For Stardom lost all chance by starting very slowly on her debut.
Lexi's Layla(IRE) dropped away quickly on her first try on fast ground. Official explanation: jockey said filly stopped quickly (op 9-2 tchd 11-2)

5380 SPORTINGBET.COM HEROS EBF MAIDEN FILLIES' STKS 5f 11y
5:40 (5:41) (Class 5) 2-Y-O £3,561 (£1,059; £529; £264) Stalls Centre

Form RPR
463 1 **Vanishing Grey (IRE)**[15] 4933 2-9-0 87 ... EddieAhern 1 74+
(B J Meehan) *mde virtually all: rdn over 1f out: in command whn edgd rt ins fnl f* **1/1**[1]
43 2 2 3/4 **Art Summer**[34] 4302 2-9-0 0 ... RichardMullen 4 64
(D M Simcock) *wnt rt s: chsd ldrs and wnt 2nd over 2f out: styd on same pce ins fnl f* **13/2**
6 3 1 1/2 **Devassa**[12] 5060 2-9-0 0 ... LukeMorris 9 59
(C G Cox) *wnt lft s: carried rt sn after: swtchd lft to ins 3f out: hdwy 2f out and styd on to dispute 2nd 1f out: no imp on wnr and wknd cl home* **14/1**
4 4 1 **Tia Juana (IRE)**[17] 4869 2-9-0 0 ... ChrisCatlin 7 55+
(Saeed Bin Suroor) *bmpd s: carried rt sn after and detached: stl plenty to do 2f out: hdwy on outside over 1f out: kpt on ins fnl f nvr a threat* **4/1**[2]
0 5 nk **Superior Edge**[13] 5021 2-9-0 0 ... CatherineGannon 3 54
(B Palling) *chsd ldrs: rdn 1/2-way: oupced wl over 1f out* **33/1**
50 6 nk **Love And Devotion**[13] 5021 2-9-0 0 ... DO'Donohoe 5 53
(Saeed Bin Suroor) *wnt rt s: sn chsng ldrs: rdn 3f out: one pce fnl 2f* **6/1**[3]
7 14 **Grand Mary (IRE)** 2-9-0 0 ... StephenDonohoe 2 2
(P F I Cole) *chsd wnr to 1/2-way: sn btn* **14/1**
45 8 10 **Ishipink**[89] 2514 2-9-0 0 ... FergusSweeney 6 —
(R J Hodges) *bmpd s: chsd ldrs to 1/2-way: wknd qckly* **66/1**
64.05 secs (1.55) **Going Correction** +0.10s/f (Good) **8** Ran SP% **115.4**
Speed ratings (Par 91): **91,86,84,82,82 81,59,43**
toteswinger: 1&2 £1.90, 1&3 £6.10, 2&3 £18.40. CSF £8.33 TOTE £2.00: £1.10, £2.40, £5.30; EX 4.70.
Owner Andrew Rosen **Bred** Peter McCutcheon **Trained** Manton, Wilts

FOCUS
The winner stood out in this otherwise modest maiden and the form looks straightforward.

NOTEBOOK
Vanishing Grey(IRE), for whom it was fourth time lucky, had paid the price for racing too freely when beaten at Chepstow last time but set a clear standard on the form of her 2l sixth in a Newmarket Listed race in June. The 87-rated daughter of Verglas was always travelling smoothly up with the pace and bounded clear against the far rail for a comfortable success. It is hard to know what the form amounts to but she holds a stack of big-race entries and could go on to better things. (op 11-8 tchd 6-4 in places and 13-8 in a place)
Art Summer never really posed a strong threat but kept grinding away and has found some improvement on her 7l third of 11 in a Lingfield maiden auction last time. The downside to this run is that it could sabotage her handicap mark. (op 7-1 tchd 6-1)
Devassa has been reported to be a bit temperamental at home but she showed some promise in a course-and-distance maiden on her debut this month and plugged on quite gamely in what looked a tougher race here. (tchd 12-1)
Tia Juana(IRE) was sent off favourite but ran green when fourth to an impressive winner in a 6f Lingfield fillies' all-weather maiden on her debut this month. She had an interesting chance if finding expected improvement but looked very sluggish after getting hampered in the early stages before staying on late from a detached position. She is a half-sister to 2000 Guineas hero Island Sands and it is still very early days, but this was a slightly quirky display. Official explanation: jockey said filly was hampered at start
Superior Edge lasted much longer than she did on her debut. She is from a sprinting family that has done well for connections and could be a steady improver. (tchd 28-1)
Love And Devotion, who was a bit disappointing when prominent in the betting at Newbury last time, produced a similar effort here. She was always well positioned but carried her head a bit awkwardly and tried to hang left under pressure. (op 11-2 tchd 13-2)

5381 SPORTINGBET.COM HEROS (S) STKS 1m 3f 144y
6:10 (6:12) (Class 6) 3-4-Y-O £1,942 (£578; £288; £144) Stalls Low

Form RPR
0260 1 **Clovis**[10] 4300 4-9-12 62 ... (p) EddieAhern 6 61
(N P Mulholland) *in rr: stl plenty to do whn swtchd rt to outside and gd hdwy over 2f out: styd on wl to ld fnl 110yds* **12/1**
6050 2 2 **Abulharith**[55] 3636 3-8-11 63 ... LPKeniry 13 53
(R A Harris) *chsd ldrs: rdn 2f out styd on to chal ins fnl f: outpcd by wnr fnl 110yds* **15/2**
0033 3 1/2 **Soul Singer**[15] 4934 3-8-11 52 ... PatCosgrave 3 52
(J G Portman) *chsd ldrs: drvn to ld over 1f out: hdd fnl 110yds: wknd nr fin* **6/1**[3]
00-0 4 2 1/4 **Alannah (IRE)**[36] 4220 4-8-13 37 ... JackMitchell(3) 16 43
(Mrs P N Dutfield) *sn led: rdn 3f out: hdd over 1f out: wknd ins fnl f* **100/1**
6042 5 1/2 **Location**[13] 3685 3-8-11 54 ... StephenDonohoe 11 47
(P D Evans) *chsd ldrs: rdn 3f out: one pce fnl 2f* **7/2**[1]
0-04 6 1/2 **Noordhoek Kid**[16] 4918 3-8-11 67 ... (tp) WilliamBuick 15 46
(C R Egerton) *sn trcking ldr: rdn over 2f out: styd on same pce* **5/1**[2]
5053 7 1 1/4 **Special Chapter (IRE)**[23] 4640 4-9-2 45 ... FergusSweeney 5 39
(A B Haynes) *chsd ldrs: rdn over 3f out: wknd over 1f out* **10/1**
5050 8 1 1/2 **Peal Park**[13] 5016 3-8-6 47 ... NickyMackay 9 37
(Karen George) *rrd stalls: bhd: hdwy and rdn 3f out: nvr gng pce to trble ldrs* **50/1**
36-0 9 hd **Berrynarbor**[18] 4857 4-9-2 52 ... SimonWhitworth 1 36
(A G Newcombe) *s.i.s: in rr tl sme hdwy fnl 2f* **17/2**
0464 10 1 1/4 **Boffin**[14] 4987 4-9-7 51 ... StephenCarson 12 39
(Eve Johnson Houghton) *t.k.h: chsd ldrs tl n.m.r and wknd over 2f out* **11/1**
402- 11 2 **Persistent (IRE)**[8] 3687 4-9-7 50 ... (tp) DO'Donohoe 10 36
(D G Bridgwater) *mid-div on rails and no ch whn bdly squeezed ins fnl f* **25/1**
000 12 hd **Errol Flynn (IRE)**[25] 4606 3-8-11 53 ... (p) KevinGhunowa 7 35
(R A Harris) *in rr: sme prog into mid-div 3f out: sn hung lft: no ch in mid-div whn hung bdly lft ins fnl f* **25/1**
00 13 1/2 **First Maid**[15] 4934 3-8-1 0 ... AmyBaker(5) 2 29
(A B Haynes) *chsd ldrs to 1/2-way* **66/1**
14 1 1/2 **Ducal Daisey** 3-8-8 0 ow2 ... RobertHavlin 4 29
(A B Haynes) *s.i.s: bhd most of way* **33/1**
00 15 9 **Ingenue**[11] 5093 3-8-6 0 ... ChrisCatlin 8 12
(Sir Mark Prescott) *chsd ldrs tl wknd rapidly ins fnl 5f* **10/1**
2m 32.97s (2.37) **Going Correction** +0.225s/f (Good)
WFA 3 from 4yo 10lb **15** Ran SP% **124.7**
Speed ratings (Par 101): **101,99,99,97,97 97,96,95,95,94 93,92,92,91,85**
toteswinger: 1&2 £54.40, 1&3 £49.00, 2&3 £13.20. CSF £97.71 TOTE £12.90: £3.20, £2.90, £1.60; EX 75.10.The winner was sold to Mr M Hawker for 4,500gns.
Owner D J Bridger **Bred** Darley **Trained** North End, Dorset

FOCUS
An ordinary seller, but there was a very lively market and there were some wild swings in running on the exchanges. The runner-up is the best guide to the form.
Errol Flynn(IRE) Official explanation: jockey said gelding hung left-handed

5382 SPORTINGBET.COM HEROS H'CAP 1m 5f 22y
6:40 (6:41) (Class 5) (0-70,66) 3-Y-O £2,655 (£790; £394; £197) Stalls High

Form RPR
0040 1 **Stormy Morning**[27] 4545 3-9-3 **62** ChrisCatlin 11 65
(W R Swinburn) *chsd ldrs: rdn to ld over 1f out: edgd lft ins fnl f: a jst holding runner-up whn hung rt nr fin* **12/1**
6551 2 nk **Primera Rossa**[15] 4934 3-7-13 **49** SophieDoyle(5) 4 52
(J S Moore) *broke wl: t.k.h dropped to rr and rdn 6f out: stl plenty to do whn swtchd to outside and hdwy fr 2f out: str run ins fnl f: clsng on wnr but jst hld whn carried rt nr fin* **16/1**
065 3 1 1/2 **Any Given Moment (IRE)**[22] 4722 3-8-10 **55** RichardMullen 9 55
(D M Simcock) *in rr tl hdwy on outside 5f out: chsd ldrs 3f out: sn rdn: styd on same pce fnl f* **3/1**[2]
116 4 1 **Vita Mia**[18] 4855 3-9-7 **66** CatherineGannon 10 66
(P D Evans) *sn led: rdn 3f out: hdd over 1f out: styng on same pce on rail whn hmpd ins fnl f* **11/2**[3]
3223 5 1 **Persian Memories (IRE)**[21] 4744 3-9-6 **65** EddieAhern 7 62+
(J L Dunlop) *in rr: hdwy 1/2-way: rdn and outpcd over 3f out: styd on again fr 2f out: chsd ldrs over 1f out: one pce ins fnl f: eased whn hld cl home* **9/4**[1]
0505 6 nk **Taste The Wine (IRE)**[16] 4911 3-9-7 **66** LukeMorris 6 63+
(J S Moore) *chsd ldrs: rdn and outpcd 3f out: sme prog u.p whn hung lft 1f out and sn one pce* **7/1**
2145 7 1/2 **Diktalina**[16] 4917 3-8-9 **54** PatDobbs 8 50
(W R Muir) *chsd ldrs: rdn 3f out: hung lft u.p and btn 2f out: no ch w ldrs whn hmpd 1f out* **14/1**
0636 8 4 **Triple Cee (IRE)**[26] 4569 3-9-0 **59** LPKeniry 5 49
(M R Channon) *in rr: hdwy 3f out: chsd ldrs u.p over 2f out: wknd appr fnl f* **8/1**

2m 57.57s (5.57) **Going Correction** +0.225s/f (Good) **8 Ran SP% 115.0**
Speed ratings (Par 100): **91,90,89,89,88 88,88,85**
toteswinger: 1&2 £16.20, 1&3 £6.60, 2&3 £6.70. CSF £179.86 CT £725.49 TOTE £10.80: £2.60, £4.10, £2.00; EX 207.50.
Owner Rogerson, McClenaghan, Reddin & Harris **Bred** Wellsummers Stud **Trained** Aldbury, Herts
■ Stewards' Enquiry : Pat Dobbs three-day ban: careless riding (Sep 11,13-14)
Luke Morris three-day ban: careless riding (Sep 11, 13, 14)

FOCUS
It was raining heavily during this modest handicap. The ground seemed to be cutting up quite a bit and it turned into a slog. The bunch finish casts some doubt over the value of the form, which is best rated around the first two.

5383 SPORTINGBET HEROS H'CAP 5f 11y
7:10 (7:12) (Class 5) (0-70,70) 3-Y-O £2,655 (£790; £394; £197) Stalls Centre

Form RPR
-403 1 **Battle**[28] 4483 3-9-6 **69** TravisBlock 10 73
(H Morrison) *t.k.h in rr but in tch: hdwy 1/2-way: drvn to ld fnl 110yds: hld on wl* **7/2**[2]
4233 2 1/2 **Raimond Ridge (IRE)**[6] 5245 3-9-7 **70** ChrisCatlin 5 72
(M R Channon) *s.i.s: in rr: hdwy on outside over 1f out: str run ins fnl f to take 2nd cl home but a hld by wnr* **8/1**
6224 3 1 1/2 **Avrilo**[19] 4829 3-8-6 **55** NickyMackay 6 52
(M S Saunders) *chsd ldr: rdn to ld over 2f out: hdd fnl 110yds: wknd cl home* **7/1**
3034 4 1 3/4 **Riflessione**[28] 4483 3-9-7 **70** (b) LPKeniry 9 61
(R A Harris) *chsd ldrs: rdn and n.m.r 2f out: styd on again ins fnl f: nvr a threat* **17/2**
3243 5 1 1/2 **Edith's Boy (IRE)**[15] 4952 3-8-10 **62** JackMitchell(3) 4 47
(S Dow) *t.k.h: chsd ldrs: rdn 2f out: wknd fnl f* **5/1**[3]
532 6 2 **Chandika**[7] 5219 3-8-9 **58** LukeMorris 3 36
(C G Cox) *t.k.h: led tl hdd over 2f out: wknd over 1f out* **7/4**[1]
0200 7 4 **Billy Beetroot (USA)**[41] 4082 3-9-0 **63** (b) KevinGhunowa 7 27
(R A Harris) *chsd ldrs: rdn 1/2-way: sn btn* **16/1**

64.57 secs (2.07) **Going Correction** +0.425s/f (Yiel) **7 Ran SP% 115.3**
Speed ratings (Par 100): **100,99,96,94,91 88,82**
toteswinger: 1&2 £6.80, 1&3 £4.10, 2&3 £7.00. CSF £31.36 CT £185.79 TOTE £4.80: £3.10, £2.90; EX 33.10.
Owner Mr&MrsHScott-Barrett,Ben&SirMartynArbib **Bred** Lady Bland **Trained** East Ilsley, Berks

FOCUS
The ground was changed to good to soft before this minor sprint handicap. They went a decent pace and there was an exciting finish. The runner-up is the best guide to the level but the winner could rate a little higher.
Chandika Official explanation: jockey said filly was unsuited by the good to soft ground

5384 WIN AT SPORTINGBET.COM HEROS H'CAP 1m 5y
7:40 (7:40) (Class 6) (0-65,65) 3-Y-O £1,942 (£578; £288; £144) Stalls Low

Form RPR
4345 1 **Spring Secret**[10] 5121 3-8-13 **57** LukeMorris 9 61
(B Palling) *led tl rdn and hdd 3f out: rallied u.p fnl f to ld last strides* **9/1**
5545 2 nk **Jewelled**[22] 4704 3-9-7 **65** WilliamBuick 16 68
(J W Hills) *t.k.h: w ldr 6f out to 4f out: led 2f out: rdn 2 l clr wl over 1f out: hdd and no ex last strides* **5/1**[1]
2044 3 3/4 **Sunny Future (IRE)**[22] 4691 3-9-7 **65** NickyMackay 12 66
(M S Saunders) *led 3f out: hdd 2f out: one pce and nt clr run over 1f out: styd on again ins fnl f* **9/1**
1502 4 nk **Fire King**[10] 5121 3-9-0 **58** RobertHavlin 1 59+
(J A Geake) *in rr: hdwy over 2f out: rdn and styd on strly fnl f: nt rch ldrs* **5/1**[1]
0205 5 1 1/2 **Lilly Blue (IRE)**[34] 4304 3-9-1 **59** PatCosgrave 8 56
(R Brotherton) *sn drvn along: chsd ldrs 1/2-way: kpt on same pce u.p fnl f* **16/1**
0643 6 nk **Bahkov (IRE)**[16] 4905 3-8-6 **55** SimonPearce(5) 3 51
(Andrew Turnell) *in tch: rdn and sme prog on ins fr 2f out: nvr in contention* **8/1**[3]
3050 7 1 **Second To Nun (IRE)**[21] 4734 3-8-13 **57** CatherineGannon 6 51+
(Jean-Rene Auvray) *in tch: rdn and outpcd 3f out: styd on again fr over 1f out* **14/1**
0400 8 1 1/4 **Rockabout (IRE)**[17] 4872 3-9-0 **58** EddieAhern 7 49
(B J Meehan) *in rr: sme hdwy over 2f out: nvr rchd ldrs and wknd ins fnl f* **16/1**
6410 9 1 **Montmartre (USA)**[13] 5019 3-9-4 **62** FergusSweeney 4 51
(David Pinder) *chsd ldrs: rdn over 2f out: wknd over 1f out* **12/1**
6045 10 3/4 **Feet Of Fury**[30] 4432 3-8-13 **57** JamesDoyle 2 44
(W M Brisbourne) *in rr: rdn and sme prog fnl 2f* **12/1**
P530 11 3 1/2 **Kimberley Rocks (IRE)**[23] 4648 3-8-12 **63** JPFahy(7) 10 42
(R M Beckett) *in tch: rdn to chse ldrs 3f out: wknd ins fnl 2f* **14/1**
4026 12 1 3/4 **Like For Like (IRE)**[36] 4222 3-8-11 **55** TravisBlock 11 30
(R J Hodges) *chsd ldrs over 4f* **16/1**
60-0 13 1 1/4 **Good Queen Best**[27] 4533 3-8-8 **52** FrankieMcDonald 14 24
(B De Haan) *in rr: sme prog on outside 3f out: wknd and eased ins fnl 2f* **66/1**
0050 14 15 **Dustry (IRE)**[22] 4710 3-9-6 **64** (b[1]) PatDobbs 5 2
(R Hannon) *a towards rr* **15/2**[2]

1m 44.42s (3.62) **Going Correction** +0.425s/f (Yiel) **14 Ran SP% 124.1**
Speed ratings (Par 98): **98,97,96,96,95 94,93,92,91,90 87,85,84,69**
toteswinger: 1&2 £4.50, 1&3 £13.90, 2&3 £13.40. CSF £55.15 CT £432.25 TOTE £10.80: £3.10, £2.10, £4.40; EX 79.30 Place 6 £205.90, Place 5 £128.69..
Owner Flying Eight Partnership **Bred** Canary Thoroughbreds **Trained** Tredodridge, Vale Of Glamorgan

FOCUS
An ordinary handicap best rated around the first three. Not many got into it from behind and there were some more potential nightmares for in-running players. The official going was now soft.
Good Queen Best Official explanation: jockey said filly lost its action
Dustry(IRE) Official explanation: jockey said colt stumbled leaving stalls
T/Plt: £312.10 to a £1 stake. Pool: £49,217.22. 115.09 winning tickets. T/Qpdt: £102.00 to a £1 stake. Pool: £5,021.60. 36.42 winning tickets. ST

5303 HAMILTON (R-H)
Friday, August 28
5385 Meeting Abandoned - waterlogged

4993 NEWCASTLE (L-H)
Friday, August 28
OFFICIAL GOING: Good to firm (firm in places; 8.4)
Wind: Fresh, half-against. Weather: Overcast and blustery

5391 PARKLANDS GOLFCOURSE APPRENTICE H'CAP 6f
5:20 (5:20) (Class 6) (0-65,65) 3-Y-O+ £2,590 (£770; £385; £192) Stalls Low

Form RPR
3022 1 **Who's Shirl**[14] 4997 3-9-4 **59** PaulPickard 2 74
(C W Fairhurst) *w ldrs: led over 2f out: drvn clr over 1f out: kpt on wl* **11/2**[2]
5-03 2 5 **Micky Mac (IRE)**[19] 4823 5-9-5 **57** DeclanCannon 12 56
(C J Teague) *w ldrs: wnt 2nd over 2f out: kpt on: no imp* **7/1**
2021 3 nk **It's A Mans World**[25] 4594 3-9-1 **61** (v) FrazerWilliams(5) 13 59+
(K M Prendergast) *dwlt: hld up towards rr: styd on to go modest 3rd appr fnl f: kpt on: nrst fin* **10/3**[1]
4460 4 3 1/4 **Avontuur (FR)**[23] 4657 7-9-6 **61** NSLawes(3) 6 49
(Mrs R A Carr) *in rr: hdwy over 3f out: one pce fnl 2f* **7/1**
3510 5 1/2 **Redwater River**[9] 5150 5-8-11 **56** (b) NoraLooby(7) 9 42
(Mrs R A Carr) *hld up in midfield: effrt over 2f out: sn outpcd: kpt on ins fnl f* **9/1**
45-0 6 2 **Yorkshire Blue**[20] 4775 10-9-3 **55** DebraEngland 4 35
(J S Goldie) *in rr: detached 3f out: styd on fnl f* **11/1**
3000 7 shd **Kheylide (IRE)**[23] 4662 3-9-7 **62** (p) LeeNewnes 8 41
(Mrs D J Sanderson) *chsd ldrs: edgd lft 2f out: sn wknd* **16/1**
0043 8 1/2 **Mansii**[23] 4668 4-8-13 **51** (t) BillyCray 1 29
(P J McBride) *mid-div: drvn over 3f out: outpcd on inner whn nt clr run over 1f out: swtchd rt and kpt on* **10/1**
-001 9 1 **Nabra**[13] 5041 5-9-0 **55** JohnCavanagh(3) 7 30
(M Brittain) *mid-div: drvn over 3f out: hung rt and lost pl over 2f out* **33/1**
4011 10 3/4 **Just Sam (IRE)**[19] 4823 4-9-8 **65** RyanPowell(5) 10 37
(R E Barr) *led tl over 2f out: lost pl over 1f out* **6/1**[3]

1m 14.5s (-0.70) **Going Correction** -0.075s/f (Good)
WFA 3 from 4yo+ 3lb **10 Ran SP% 114.0**
Speed ratings (Par 101): **101,94,93,89,88 86,86,85,84,83**
toteswinger: 1&2 £6.00, 1&3 £3.60, 2&3 £4.60. CSF £42.71 CT £149.90 TOTE £7.00: £1.60, £2.00, £1.60; EX 54.10.
Owner Mrs Shirley France **Bred** Mrs S France **Trained** Middleham Moor, N Yorks

FOCUS
The going was on the firm side and the runners elected to edge across to the far rail. Just an ordinary sprint handicap, with not much making an impact from off the pace, and the leading two front rank throughout. That pair set the standard, although the form is a little fluid.
Mansii Official explanation: jockey said gelding never travelled
Nabra Official explanation: jockey said mare hung right-handed
Just Sam(IRE) Official explanation: trainer said filly was in season

5392 COMPLETE FOOTBALL NOVICE AUCTION STKS 6f
5:50 (5:56) (Class 4) 2-Y-O £3,885 (£1,156; £577; £288) Stalls Low

Form RPR
1 1 **Mr Grinch (IRE)**[25] 4590 2-9-6 0 PhillipMakin 5 88+
(M Dods) *t.k.h in last: hdwy over 2f out: chal over 1f out: r.o to ld towards fin* **11/4**[3]
402 2 hd **Keyta Bonita (IRE)**[23] 4666 2-8-4 73 PaulHanagan 4 71
(M G Quinlan) *led: qcknd over 3f out: jnd over 1f out: hdd nr fin* **9/4**[2]
5121 3 1 1/2 **Perfect Ch'I (IRE)**[17] 4883 2-9-2 81 FrancisNorton 6 79
(I A Wood) *reluctant to go bhd stalls: trckd ldr: shkn up over 3f out: outpcd 2f out: kpt on same pce fnl f* **7/4**[1]
0252 4 shd **Dazeen**[9] 5146 2-8-9 75 PaulMulrennan 1 72
(P T Midgley) *trckd ldrs on ins: nt clr run over 2f out tl over 1f out: styd on same pce* **5/1**

1m 15.13s (-0.07) **Going Correction** -0.075s/f (Good) **4 Ran SP% 110.5**
Speed ratings (Par 96): **97,96,94,94**
toteswinger: 1&2 £5.10. CSF £9.28 TOTE £4.20; EX 11.10.
Owner M J K Dods **Bred** Bluegate Stud **Trained** Denton, Co Durham

FOCUS
This was weakened by the withdrawals of Theymistim and Royal Record, and all four runners finished in a tight group so it's hard to know what to make of the form. On the positive side, the pace, set by Keyta Bonita, looked honest throughout and she sets the standard.

NOTEBOOK

Mr Grinch(IRE) maintained his unbeaten record. He travelled with great ease at the back of the field and, after making stealthy headway down the outside, he stuck on bravely to edge out a gutsy rival. This has to go down as a much improved effort given his Carlisle maiden win didn't look strong form, and he looks to have more improvement in him, especially over a bit further. (tchd 100-30)

Keyta Bonita(IRE) went down fighting and she handled the drop back in trip fine. Although she still hasn't won, she is showing some very useful form and a first success cannot be long in coming. (op 3-1)

Perfect Ch'I(IRE) looked as though she was going to drop out when coming under pressure but, despite hanging to her left and hampering Dazeen, she kept on well once straightened up. She is a solid yardstick, although this isn't the first time she's not looked entirely straightforward. (tchd 6-4)

Dazeen was travelling well up the rail when Perfect Ch'i impeded his progress, but even when he got racing room he couldn't go past that rival so the incident didn't have any great bearing on the result. His cruising speed should stand him in good stead back over the minimum trip and he looks good enough to win his maiden. (op 4-1 tchd 11-2 and 6-1)

5393 PHOENIX SECURITY CLAIMING STKS — 7f

6:20 (6:26) (Class 6) 2-Y-O — **£2,201** (£655; £327; £163) **Stalls** Low

Form — RPR

24 **1** **Rescent**[21] 4747 2-8-4 0 PaulHanagan 2 — 55
(Rae Guest) *chsd ldrs on inner: drvn over 3f out: nt clr run over 2f out: sn outpcd: styd on appr fnl f: str run between horses to ld cl home* **11/4**[2]

6031 **2** *hd* **Ibmab**[16] 4915 2-8-13 70 TGMcLaughlin 1 — 63
(Mrs L Stubbs) *t.k.h towards rr: hdwy 4f out: effrt over 2f out: sn rdn: styd on to chal and ld wl ins fnl f: edgd rt: no ex and hdd nr fin* **7/4**[1]

0054 **3** *½* **Cygnet Committee (IRE)**[20] 4800 2-8-6 50 (b) PJMcDonald 6 — 55
(J S Wainwright) *hld up in mid-div: smooth hdwy over 3f out: led on bit over 1f out: sn rdn: hdd wl ins fnl f* **16/1**

0 **4** *4* **Charmaxjoanne**[15] 4928 2-8-5 0 PatrickDonaghy(5) 4 — 49
(P C Haslam) *sn chsng ldrs: drvn over 3f out: chal over 2f out: wknd last 100yds* **28/1**

5 *2 ¾* **Elie Shore** 2-9-2 0 RoystonFfrench 9 — 47
(P C Haslam) *s.s and wnt bdly rt s: detached in last: kpt on fnl 2f: nt rch ldrs* **17/2**

0000 **6** *7* **Maiwand**[15] 4931 2-8-0 39 SilvestreDeSousa 5 — 13
(Mrs R A Carr) *led tl over 2f out: lost pl and hmpd over 1f out* **33/1**

4105 **7** *2 ¾* **Whispered Times (USA)**[16] 4895 2-9-7 71 (b1) PhillipMakin 8 — 27
(P C Haslam) *t.k.h: trckd ldr: led over 2f out: hdd over 1f out: sn wknd* **3/1**[3]

1m 31.06s (2.36) **Going Correction** -0.075s/f (Good) **7** Ran SP% **110.8**
Speed ratings (Par 92): **83,82,82,77,74 66,63**
toteswinger: 1&2 £1.50, 1&3 £9.20, 2&3 £3.60. CSF £7.44 TOTE £3.10: £2.00, £1.10; EX 4.90.Rescent was claimed by Mrs Ruth Carr for £6,000.

Owner C J Murfitt **Bred** C J Murfitt **Trained** Newmarket, Suffolk

■ Stewards' Enquiry : T G McLaughlin one-day ban: used whip with excessive frequency (Sep 11)

FOCUS

Not a great race for the grade but the form has a solid enough feel to it at a moderate level.

NOTEBOOK

Rescent got going late to burst between the two leaders and plunder the prize. Just as she had done at Lingfield last time, she hit a flat spot when the pace quickened, but the extra furlong here proved the making of her and she picked up strongly in the final furlong to get off the mark. Given her lack of instant acceleration, she will be seen to best effect in strongly run races and another furlong would probably see her in an even better light. (op 9-4)

Ibmab probably bettered the form of his Yarmouth selling win and he continues to progress with experience. (op 2-1 tchd 5-2)

Cygnet Committee(IRE), the most exposed runner in the field, travelled like the best horse in the race and she battled on well in the closing stages. The blinkers appear to have been the making of her and she will be able to find a race if holding this level of form.

Charmaxjoanne shaped a little better than on her debut and looks the type who can do better with time. (op 20-1)

Whispered Times(USA) was lit up by the first-time blinkers and dropped away at the business end. He is better than this. (op 100-30 tchd 5-2)

5394 GOSFORTH DECORATING & BUILDING SERVICES MAIDEN STKS — 7f

6:50 (6:57) (Class 5) 3-4-Y-O — **£3,885** (£1,156; £577; £288) **Stalls** Low

Form — RPR

0-4 **1** **Dance Card**[33] 4354 4-9-3 0 (t) PaulMulrennan 6 — 77
(A G Foster) *hld up in rr: hdwy and swtchd rt over 2f out: edgd lft and led appr fnl f: styd on wl* **16/1**

33 **2** *1 ¾* **El Ameen**[12] 5071 3-9-3 0 RoystonFfrench 10 — 75
(M Johnston) *led: hdd 2f out: styd on same pce fnl f* **9/4**[2]

42 **3** *4* **Awesome Surprise (USA)**[18] 4854 3-8-12 0 PaulHanagan 5 — 66+
(J Noseda) *chsd ldrs: drvn over 2f out: keeping on same pce whn bdly hmpd appr fnl f: kpt on to take modest 3rd last 75yds* **5/6**[1]

4 **4** *2 ¾* **Tiddliwinks**[7] 5228 3-9-3 0 SilvestreDeSousa 11 — 57
(K A Ryan) *gave problems in stalls: sn trcking ldrs: led 2f out: hdd and hmpd appr fnl f: fdd* **7/1**[3]

04 **5** *1 ½* **Fine Silk (USA)**[48] 3876 3-8-12 0 TomEaves 8 — 48
(B Smart) *t.k.h: sn trcking ldrs: outpcd over 2f out: kpt on fnl f* **28/1**

40 **6** *½* **Pure Heir (USA)**[27] 4550 3-8-12 0 PhillipMakin 7 — 46
(T D Barron) *dwlt: hdwy 3f out: kpt on fnl f* **50/1**

00 **7** *3 ¾* **Clanachy**[28] 4505 3-8-12 0 DavidAllan 13 — 36
(A G Foster) *t.k.h: trckd ldrs: lost pl over 2f out* **100/1**

8 *nse* **Tongalooma** 3-8-12 0 PAspell 1 — 36
(James Moffatt) *in rr: drvn over 3f out: hung lft: nvr on terms* **100/1**

05 **9** *17* **Duke Of Bothwell (USA)**[9] 5163 3-8-10 0 FrazerWilliams(7) 12 — —
(R A Fahey) *in rr: drvn over 3f out: lost pl over 2f out: sn bhd* **40/1**

0- **10** *8* **Cruciform (IRE)**[411] 4002 3-9-3 0 AdrianTNicholls 3 — —
(D Nicholls) *stdd s: hdwy on ins over 3f out: wknd over 2f out: eased whn bhd* **28/1**

1m 27.33s (-1.37) **Going Correction** -0.075s/f (Good)
WFA 3 from 4yo 5lb **10** Ran SP% **117.0**
Speed ratings (Par 103): **104,102,97,94,92 92,87,87,68,59**
toteswinger: 1&2 £3.80, 1&3 £5.80, 2&3 £1.10. CSF £51.20 TOTE £15.50: £2.80, £1.10, £1.10; EX 82.60.

Owner S C B Limited **Bred** Cheveley Park Stud Ltd **Trained** Haddington, East Lothian

FOCUS

Not a strong maiden by any means and the quality of the form isn't helped by Awesome Surprise, who was very disappointing despite not having the best of runs. The form is not easy to pin down.

5395 S V RUTTER H'CAP — 1m (R)

7:20 (7:27) (Class 5) (0-70,70) 3-Y-O+ — **£3,885** (£1,156; £577; £288) **Stalls** Centre

Form — RPR

3121 **1** **Morocchius (USA)**[5] 5289 4-8-10 57 (p) MartinLane(5) 1 — 64+
(Miss J A Camacho) *trckd ldrs: effrt on inner over 1f out: r.o to ld last stride* **11/4**[1]

0003 **2** *shd* **Tiger Dream**[16] 4897 4-9-7 68 (p) AmyRyan(5) 15 — 74
(K A Ryan) *trckd ldr: led over 2f out: hdd post* **10/1**[3]

0304 **3** *hd* **Silly Gilly (IRE)**[5] 5289 5-8-8 57 DeclanCannon(7) 14 — 63
(R E Barr) *chsd ldrs: hrd drvn over 2f out: styd on wl fnl f* **14/1**

2060 **4** *½* **Dechiper (IRE)**[15] 4941 7-9-12 68 GrahamGibbons 11 — 73
(R Johnson) *hld up in rr: hdwy on ins over 2f out: kpt on wl fnl f* **14/1**

2630 **5** *¾* **Shadowtime**[9] 5160 4-9-11 67 RoystonFfrench 16 — 72+
(Miss Tracy Waggott) *hld up in rr: stdy hdwy over 2f out: nt clr run jst ins fnl f: styd on wl towards fin* **8/1**[2]

000 **6** *½* **French Art**[27] 4548 4-9-6 62 AndrewElliott 17 — 64
(N Tinkler) *hld up in rr: hdwy on wd outside over 2f out: kpt on wl fnl f* **40/1**

100- **7** *1 ¾* **Nesno (USA)**[329] 6452 6-9-9 65 (p) JimmyQuinn 4 — 63
(J D Bethell) *trckd ldrs: t.k.h: kpt on same pce fnl 2f* **20/1**

2211 **8** *¾* **Wiseman's Diamond (USA)**[15] 4932 4-9-4 65 PaulPickard(5) 3 — 61+
(P T Midgley) *hld up towards rr: effrt over 2f out: nt clr run over 1f out: kpt on ins fnl f* **11/4**[1]

6 **9** *1 ¼* **Sarwin (USA)**[88] 2532 6-9-13 69 TomEaves 8 — 62
(G A Swinbank) *trckd ldrs: t.k.h: wnt 2nd over 1f out: sn wknd* **12/1**

1540 **10** *shd* **Ergo (FR)**[42] 4046 5-9-13 69 (b) PAspell 6 — 62
(James Moffatt) *trckd ldrs: t.k.h: effrt on outer over 2f out: one pce* **25/1**

10 **11** *1* **Wood Fairy**[16] 4896 3-9-8 70 PaulHanagan 9 — 60
(R A Fahey) *hld up in rr: effrt over 2f out: one pce whn nt clr run over 1f out* **8/1**[2]

435- **12** *¾* **Mandarin Spirit (IRE)**[308] 6952 9-9-12 68 PhillipMakin 10 — 56
(Miss L A Perratt) *led: hdd over 2f out: wkng whn n.m.r appr fnl f* **33/1**

1m 42.05s (-1.35) **Going Correction** -0.075s/f (Good)
WFA 3 from 4yo+ 6lb **12** Ran SP% **119.7**
Speed ratings (Par 103): **103,102,102,102,101 100,99,98,97,97 96,95**
toteswinger: 1&2 £5.90, 1&3 £3.70, 2&3 £16.00. CSF £31.48 CT £340.61 TOTE £3.70: £1.80, £3.10, £2.40; EX 37.30.

Owner Lee Bolingbroke Currie & Partners **Bred** E And D Enterprises **Trained** Norton, N Yorks

■ Stewards' Enquiry : Declan Cannon three-day ban: used whip with excessive frequency (Sep 11,13-14)

FOCUS

Quite a competitive handicap on paper with the market dominated by two in-form horses. The winner did not need to run up to his previous mark judged on the efforts of the third and fifth.

Wiseman's Diamond(USA) Official explanation: jockey said filly was denied a clear run

5396 JOHN SMITH'S H'CAP — 5f

7:50 (7:56) (Class 6) (0-55,55) 3-Y-O+ — **£2,331** (£693; £346; £173) **Stalls** Low

Form — RPR

3002 **1** **Darcy's Pride (IRE)**[12] 5073 5-9-0 54 (t) TonyHamilton 1 — 61
(P T Midgley) *mde all: kpt on wl fnl f: jst hld on* **7/1**

0242 **2** *shd* **Sunley Sovereign**[4] 5309 5-9-1 55 (b) SilvestreDeSousa 8 — 62
(Mrs R A Carr) *chsd ldr: chal over 1f out: jst failed* **11/4**[1]

0202 **3** *¾* **The Name Is Frank**[14] 5008 4-9-1 55 (t) TolleyDean 3 — 59
(Mark Gillard) *dwlt: sn trcking ldrs on ins: swtchd rt appr fnl f: kpt on wl fnl 100yds* **7/1**

4044 **4** *1* **Strathmore (IRE)**[9] 5159 5-9-1 55 PaulHanagan 10 — 55+
(R A Fahey) *in rr: hdwy whn nt clr run over 1f out: styd on wl fnl f* **11/2**[2]

/0-0 **5** *1 ¼* **Glenluji**[16] 4899 4-8-10 55 GaryBartley(5) 6 — 51
(J S Goldie) *hld up in rr: nt clr run over 1f out: kpt on wl: nt rch ldrs* **28/1**

3640 **6** *nk* **Ursus**[30] 4436 4-8-9 54 (p) JamieKyne(5) 13 — 49
(C R Wilson) *dwlt: swtchd lft s: in rr: hdwy and swtchd outside over 1f out: kpt on: nt rch ldrs* **13/2**[3]

02 **7** *1 ¼* **Red Cell (IRE)**[25] 4596 3-8-7 54 (b) AmyRyan(5) 7 — 44
(I W McInnes) *s.i.s: sn mid-div: one pce fnl 2f* **12/1**

0006 **8** *hd* **Hosanna**[17] 4879 3-8-10 52 PJMcDonald 5 — 42
(J Barclay) *chsd ldrs: kpt on same pce appr fnl f* **28/1**

4004 **9** *hd* **Bahamian Ballad**[15] 4929 4-8-9 49 (b1) JimmyQuinn 9 — 38
(J D Bethell) *t.k.h in mid-div: hdwy to trck ldrs over 2f out: one pce appr fnl f* **8/1**

0-00 **10** *2 ¼* **Lujiana**[14] 4998 4-8-5 52 JohnCavanagh(7) 11 — 33
(M Brittain) *chsd ldrs: wknd appr fnl f* **20/1**

6-00 **11** *1* **Shining Times (IRE)**[2] 5341 3-8-11 53 TomEaves 12 — 30
(P T Midgley) *a towards rr* **28/1**

5-06 **12** *4 ½* **Blow Your Mind**[23] 4653 3-8-13 55 DavidAllan 4 — 16
(Karen McLintock) *chsd ldrs: drvn over 2f out: wkng whn hmpd over 1f out: eased towards fin* **12/1**

61.18 secs (0.48) **Going Correction** -0.075s/f (Good)
WFA 3 from 4yo+ 2lb **12** Ran SP% **122.0**
Speed ratings (Par 101): **93,92,91,90,88 87,85,85,84,81 79,72**
toteswinger: 1&2 £3.10, 1&3 £2.60, 2&3 £6.40. CSF £26.11 CT £143.12 TOTE £4.90: £2.30, £1.40, £3.10; EX 23.90 Place 6 £31.65, Place 5 £18.85..

Owner T Shepherd & A Turton **Bred** Leo Cox **Trained** Westow, N Yorks

■ Stewards' Enquiry : Tolley Dean two-day ban: careless riding (Sep 11,13)

FOCUS

A moderate handicap and not a lot got into this from off the pace. The first two are rated to their recent marks.

T/Plt: £51.90 to a £1 stake. Pool: £53,146.23. 746.52 winning tickets. T/Qpdt: £5.00 to a £1 stake. Pool: £5,209.02. 762.31 winning tickets. WG

5029 NEWMARKET (R-H)

Friday, August 28

OFFICIAL GOING: Good to firm changing to good after race 1 (1.20)

Wind: Fresh, half behind Weather: Sunshine and showers

5397 STRIKING AMBITION TFR 122 EBF MAIDEN FILLIES' STKS (DIV I) — 7f

1:20 (1:21) (Class 4) 2-Y-O — **£4,857** (£1,445; £722; £360) **Stalls** High

Form — RPR

622 **1** **Pollenator (IRE)**[20] 4792 2-9-0 79 RichardHughes 9 — 86+
(R Hannon) *hld up: hdwy 2f out: led 1f out: r.o wl: hung lft towards fin* **11/2**[3]

3 **2** *3 1/4* **Boogie Diva**[19] 4817 2-9-0 0 .... MartinDwyer 10 78
(M Botti) *hld up: hdwy 1/2-way: led over 1f out: sn rdn and hdd: styd on same pce ins fnl f* **9/1**

2 **3** *3 1/4* **Qaraaba**[42] 4055 2-9-0 0 .... RHills 3 70
(J L Dunlop) *trckd ldr: led over 2f out: hdd over 1f out: wknd ins fnl f* **6/5**[1]

4 *3/4* **Miss Miracle** 2-9-0 0 .... AdamKirby 7 68
(C G Cox) *prom: rdn over 2f out: wknd over 1f out: edgd rt ins fnl f* **10/1**

6 **5** *1/2* **Touch Tone**[43] 4001 2-9-0 0 .... RobertWinston 2 67
(B W Hills) *prom: rdn over 2f out: wknd fnl f* **16/1**

6 *3/4* **Chain Of Office** 2-9-0 0 .... TonyCulhane 1 65+
(W J Haggas) *s.s: hld up: shkn up over 1f out: styd on ins fnl f: nvr nrr* **66/1**

5 **7** *1 1/4* **Nafura**[14] 4980 2-9-0 0 .... TedDurcan 6 62
(Saeed Bin Suroor) *chsd ldrs: rdn over 2f out: sn edgd lft and wknd* **5/1**[2]

8 *hd* **Fringe Success (IRE)** 2-9-0 0 .... RyanMoore 4 61+
(Sir Michael Stoute) *s.i.s: sn mid-div: rdn over 2f out: hung lft and wknd over 1f out* **14/1**

0 **9** *nk* **No Explaining (IRE)**[11] 5096 2-9-0 0 .... TPQueally 11 60
(B J Curley) *chsd ldrs: rdn over 2f out: wknd over 1f out* **150/1**

60 **10** *4* **Labretella (IRE)**[25] 4595 2-9-0 0 .... JimmyFortune 8 50
(M H Tompkins) *led: hdd over 2f out: wknd over 1f out* **100/1**

11 *nse* **Mahlak (IRE)** 2-9-0 0 .... PhilipRobinson 5 50
(C E Brittain) *s.i.s: rdn 1/2-way: wknd 2f out* **33/1**

12 *3 1/4* **Tamtara** 2-9-0 0 .... JimCrowley 12 42
(Mrs A J Perrett) *s.i.s: a in rr: rdn and wknd over 2f out* **40/1**

1m 25.17s (-0.53) **Going Correction** -0.15s/f (Firm) **12** Ran SP% **117.7**
Speed ratings (Par 93): **97,93,89,88,88 87,85,85,85,80 80,76**
toteswinger: 1&2 £4.90, 1&3 £1.40, 2&3 £4.10. CSF £52.72 TOTE £5.50: £1.70, £2.10, £1.10; EX 37.50.

Owner The Royal Ascot Racing Club **Bred** Tullamaine Castle Stud **Trained** East Everleigh, Wilts

FOCUS

There was sharp shower immediately ahead of this first race and they kicked through the top to suggest that the ground may have been a little loose, a point confirmed by one of the jockeys. Another rider was more positive about the surface calling it 'lovely'. Apart from Pollenator and one other, they finished somewhat weary, suggesting the pace was strong enough and the time was just under a second and a half beyond standard. The runner-up sets the level, rated to her debut form.

NOTEBOOK

Pollenator(IRE) was a convincing enough winner, putting her experience edge to good use, notwithstanding that she hung left near the finish. She shaped as if she'll get 1m now and her pedigree suggests she will benefit for going further as she matures. (op 9-2 tchd 7-2)

Boogie Diva was an encouraging third on debut over this trip at Redcar and produced another promising performance here. She was more street-wise for this but had no answer as the eventual winner came at her on the furlong-pole. She is entitled to come on again for this and next time should take the beating, all things considered. (op 8-1 tchd 15-2)

Qaraaba, second over course and distance on debut in the soft last month, was noted as going to post fluently but was a shade disappointing. She was notably fit for this but paddock inspection indicated that there is still some strengthening up to do behind the saddle. On breeding, she is the type to be a better three-year-old over trips of 1m 2f and upwards. (op 6-4 tchd 15-8)

Miss Miracle ◆, a well-bred filly, was a likeable individual, impressing with her athletic way of going. She flattened out on what was a by and large promising racecourse bow and should be more competitive next time. (op 12-1 tchd 9-1)

Touch Tone looked alert in the paddock but made little impression, despite having had a previous race. (op 14-1)

Chain Of Office ◆ was the eye-catcher. Slowly into stride, she made some decent late progress and it would be no surprise if she improved a fair amount for her first start.

Nafura, a half-sister to Dubai Destination, failed to build on her debut fifth at Kempton. (tchd 11-2)

Fringe Success(IRE) was given a considerate introduction and is another who can go on with this experience under her belt. (op 12-1)

5398 STRIKING AMBITION TFR 122 EBF MAIDEN FILLIES' STKS (DIV II) 7f

1:50 (1:52) (Class 4) 2-Y-O **£4,857** (£1,445; £722; £360) **Stalls** High

Form RPR

00 **1** **Paleo (IRE)**[29] 4460 2-9-0 0 .... RichardHughes 7 80
(R Hannon) *chsd ldr: led and hung lft 2f out: sn rdn: hung rt wl ins fnl f: jst hld on* **20/1**

5 **2** *nse* **Pink Symphony**[29] 4460 2-9-0 0 .... MartinDwyer 10 80
(P F I Cole) *led: rdn and hdd 2f out: sn hung lft: styng on whn carried rt wl ins fnl f: jst failed* **7/4**[1]

3 *3* **Magic Doll (USA)** 2-9-0 0 .... TedDurcan 9 72+
(Saeed Bin Suroor) *s.i.s: sn prom: rdn over 2f out: edgd lft: styd on same pce fr over 1f out* **9/1**

6 **4** *1 1/4* **Texas Queen**[13] 5021 2-9-0 0 .... TonyCulhane 4 69
(M R Channon) *trckd ldrs: racd keenly: rdn over 2f out: edgd rt over 1f out: no ex ins fnl f* **11/1**

5 **5** *1* **Snoqualmie Star**[21] 4756 2-9-0 0 .... RyanMoore 6 67
(D R C Elsworth) *hld up in tch: rdn over 2f out: styd on but nt trble ldrs* **11/4**[2]

6 *1/2* **Miss Starlight** 2-9-0 0 .... EdwardCreighton 8 66
(P J McBride) *sn pushed along in rr: rdn over 2f out: styd on but nvr trbld ldrs* **100/1**

7 *3/4* **Charpoy Cobra** 2-9-0 0 .... KirstyMilczarek 3 64
(J A R Toller) *hld up: rdn over 2f out: wknd over 1f out* **50/1**

8 *9* **Tafawut** 2-9-0 0 .... RHills 2 44+
(B W Hills) *free to post: w ldrs tl wknd and eased wl over 1f out* **4/1**[3]

9 *15* **Consider Yourself (USA)** 2-9-0 0 .... HayleyTurner 1 4
(M L W Bell) *s.s and sn given reminders: outpcd* **25/1**

1m 24.76s (-0.94) **Going Correction** -0.15s/f (Firm) **9** Ran SP% **112.9**
Speed ratings (Par 93): **99,98,95,94,92 92,91,81,64**
toteswinger: 1&2 £6.60, 1&3 £9.50, 2&3 £3.80. CSF £53.21 TOTE £22.90: £4.30, £1.20, £2.20; EX 58.10.

Owner Knockainey Stud Ltd & Partners **Bred** Miss Joan Murphy **Trained** East Everleigh, Wilts

■ Stewards' Enquiry : Richard Hughes caution: careless riding.

FOCUS

The time of this second division of the fillies' maiden was 0.41seconds quicker than the first and less than a second beyond standard. The first two improved for their debuts and the third shaped quite well.

NOTEBOOK

Paleo(IRE) and Pink Symphony pulled clear of the rest and engaged in a head-to-head battle from 2f out. The had clashed last time at Goodwood and on that occasion today's winner was two lengths adrift of her rival. She reversed that form here, showing a good attitude to just wear down Pink Symphony - and then finally come through a lengthy stewards' enquiry unscathed. The enquiry appeared no forlorn cause for the second's connections as the stewards will have considered how Paleo hung right across Pink Symphony inside the final 50 yards and appeared to carry her towards the stands' rail. However, the placings were unaltered and Paleo broke her maiden at the third attempt. She had quite a tough race here and how the Handicapper assesses her is likely to determine how competitive she'll be through the autumn.

Pink Symphony could not confirm Goodwood placings with the winner but never gave up the fight and is likely to be better over further as she matures. Assuming she comes out of this fine, it will take a good one to stop her next time. (op 2-1 tchd 13-8)

Magic Doll(USA), a half-sister to the smart miler Menokee and related to other winners, gave a most satisfactory debut display after missing the break. Not unduly knocked about, she stayed on nicely enough in the closing stages to suggest that a maiden should come her way in the near future. (op 7-1)

Texas Queen was far from disgraced on her debut over 6f at Newbury. Stepped up in trip here and from a yard whose two-year-olds tend to improve a fair amount for their racecourse bows, she was a shade keen which may have contributed to her being unable to find any extra late on. (tchd 10-1 and 12-1)

Snoqualmie Star was the paddock pick but failed to get competitive. Her pedigree hints that she'll flourish when asked to go over significantly further next year. (op 100-30 tchd 4-1)

Tafawut, who was well supported, disappointed but didn't help her chance by going to post too freely. Official explanation: jockey said filly was difficult going to post (op 7-2 tchd 9-2)

5399 BREHENY NURSERY 1m

2:20 (2:21) (Class 4) 2-Y-O **£5,180** (£1,541; £770; £384) **Stalls** High

Form RPR

4231 **1** **Whippers Love (IRE)**[15] 4931 2-8-13 **74** .... RHills 2 83+
(M Johnston) *chsd ldr tl led over 1f out: drvn out: edgd lft nr fin* **13/8**[1]

056 **2** *1* **Rezwaan**[23] 4638 2-8-3 **64** .... TPO'Shea 4 71
(E A L Dunlop) *stmbld s: sn chsng ldrs: rdn over 1f out: edgd lft ins fnl f: styd on u.p* **14/1**

042 **3** *hd* **Deauville Post (FR)**[30] 4439 2-9-5 **80** .... RichardHughes 5 86
(R Hannon) *hld up: pushed along 1/2-way: hdwy u.p on outside over 2f out: styd on* **11/4**[2]

215 **4** *3 3/4* **Missionaire (USA)**[34] 4294 2-9-7 **82** .... JimCrowley 3 80
(W J Knight) *prom: rdn over 1f out: no ex ins fnl f* **9/2**[3]

0241 **5** *6* **Many A Slip**[15] 4946 2-9-5 **80** .... RyanMoore 6 65
(J L Dunlop) *hld up: hdwy over 2f out: sn rdn: wknd fnl f* **5/1**

0560 **6** *1/2* **Bubbly Braveheart (IRE)**[21] 4758 2-8-8 **69** ....(b[1]) HayleyTurner 1 53
(A Bailey) *led and sn crossed over to stands' side rail: rdn and hdd over 1f out: sn wknd* **28/1**

0516 **7** *11* **Emma Dora (IRE)**[48] 3865 2-8-13 **74** .... DaneO'Neill 7 34
(D R C Elsworth) *chsd ldrs tl rdn and wknd over 2f out* **20/1**

1m 37.47s (-2.53) **Going Correction** -0.15s/f (Firm) 2y crse rec **7** Ran SP% **114.5**
Speed ratings (Par 96): **106,105,104,101,95 94,83**
toteswinger: 1&2 £6.80, 1&3 £2.00, 2&3 £11.10. CSF £26.25 TOTE £2.30: £1.50, £7.10; EX 26.20.

Owner Crone Stud Farms Ltd **Bred** Jim McCormack **Trained** Middleham Moor, N Yorks

FOCUS

This was run in a very decent time. Indeed, the winner took nine lengths off the previous juvenile course record. It is a race worth treating positively.

NOTEBOOK

Whippers Love(IRE) ◆ saw the race out best of these, winning in a course-record time. A winner over 7.5f at Beverley last time, he was always in the right place with the leader covered before settling matters over 1f out in straightforward fashion. He was glowing with good health in the paddock ahead of this and is worth looking out for in the weeks to come in a similar race. He was rated 74 beforehand, so nurseries should still be an option for a while, and he looks a progressive horse to remain on the right side of. (op 5-2 tchd 11-4)

Rezwaan had been uncompetitive in previous three starts, but an initial mark of 64 looked workable in nurseries, although perhaps not at a track like Newmarket. He just lost a little ground from the gates, stumbling before swiftly recovering to run a much improved race off bottom weight. He is certainly of interest in nursery company and is unlikely to go up in the weights too much for this. (op 16-1 tchd 25-1)

Deauville Post(FR) was the first off the bridle but then responded to pressure, staying on well enough. There is a race to be won with him, whether that be back in maidens (always allowing for the fact that you may bump into one at this time of the year) or in nurseries, assuming that he remains around his current mark. (op 5-2 tchd 3-1 in places)

Missionaire(USA) was burdened with top weight here, but gave a reasonable account without ever really looking as if he was coming to win the race. This followed a run when he was well beaten in Listed company at Ascot and confirmed nurseries are where he belongs for the time being. (op 100-30 tchd 3-1)

Many A Slip was unable to build on his maiden win at Salisbury. (op 4-1 tchd 11-2)

Bubbly Braveheart(IRE), first-time blinkered, ensured there was a true tempo to the race before weakening. (op 33-1)

Emma Dora(IRE), a winner over 6f, appeared not to stay 1m. (op 16-1)

5400 PROTECTAS HEALTH STEM CELL EBF MAIDEN STKS (DIV I) 7f

2:55 (2:56) (Class 4) 2-Y-O **£4,857** (£1,445; £722; £360) **Stalls** High

Form RPR

1 **Ameer (IRE)** 2-9-0 0 .... TedDurcan 10 85+
(Saeed Bin Suroor) *chsd ldrs: rdn over 1f out: r.o to ld post* **9/1**

2 **2** *hd* **Awesome Act (USA)**[21] 4756 2-9-0 0 .... ShaneKelly 7 84
(J Noseda) *hld up in tch: plld hrd: led 1/2-way: rdn and hung lft ins fnl f: edgd rt towards fin: hdd post* **4/5**[1]

3 *1 1/2* **Critical Moment (USA)** 2-9-0 0 .... RobertWinston 6 80+
(B W Hills) *hld up: hdwy 1/2-way: rdn over 1f out: r.o* **18/1**

4 *5* **Mushreq (USA)** 2-9-0 0 .... RHills 8 68
(Sir Michael Stoute) *trckd ldrs: racd keenly: rdn and ev ch over 1f out: wknd ins fnl f* **4/1**[2]

5 *1* **Primary Colors** 2-9-0 0 .... AdamKirby 12 65
(C G Cox) *chsd ldrs: rdn over 2f out: wknd fnl f* **16/1**

00 **6** *hd* **White Dart**[35] 4258 2-9-0 0 .... TonyCulhane 4 67+
(M R Channon) *stdd sn after s: hld up wl in rr: shkn up over 2f out: n.m.r over 1f out: r.o: nvr nr to chal* **66/1**

0 **7** *1/2* **Haatheq (USA)**[42] 4048 2-9-0 0 .... TPO'Shea 5 64
(J L Dunlop) *hld up: hdwy 1/2-way: rdn and wknd over 1f out* **8/1**[3]

8 *3/4* **Mr Harmoosh (IRE)** 2-9-0 0 .... RichardKingscote 1 62
(E F Vaughan) *hld up: hdwy over 4f out: rdn: hung lft and wknd over 1f out* **66/1**

00 **9** *hd* **Bun Oir (USA)**[34] 4314 2-9-0 0 .... RichardHughes 13 61
(R Hannon) *stmbld s: sn led: hdd 1/2-way: rdn over 2f out: wknd over 1f out* **25/1**

	10	nk	**Seaside Sizzler** 2-9-0 0 SebSanders 15	60
			(R M Beckett) *dwlt: sn prom: rdn over 2f out: wkng whn hung lft over 1f out* **33/1**	
00	11	1	**Noverre Over There (IRE)**[16] 4915 2-9-0 0 EdwardCreighton 9	58
			(M E Rimmer) *s.i.s: hdwy 1/2-way: sn rdn: wknd over 1f out* **150/1**	
5	12	1 1/4	**Power Of Dreams (IRE)**[11] 5109 2-9-0 0 TPQueally 3	55
			(M H Tompkins) *hld up: effrt over 2f out: wknd over 1f out* **40/1**	
	13	15	**Soho Theatre** 2-9-0 0 DaneO'Neill 2	17
			(D R C Elsworth) *s.s: outpcd* **50/1**	

1m 25.12s (-0.58) **Going Correction** -0.15s/f (Firm) **13** Ran SP% **122.6**
Speed ratings (Par 96): **97,96,95,89,88 87,87,86,86,85 84,83,66**
toteswinger: 1&2 £3.60, 1&3 £16.50, 2&3 £7.30. CSF £16.55 TOTE £9.40: £2.60, £1.10, £4.10; EX 23.30.
Owner Godolphin **Bred** E Puerari, Oceanic Blds & Charleton Blds **Trained** Newmarket, Suffolk

FOCUS
A decent-looking maiden and worth treating as such, with the first three finishing clear.

NOTEBOOK
Ameer(IRE) ◆ glowed with overall wellbeing, while leaving the impression that, physically, there is more to work on. His stable's two-year-olds have been flying and he didn't let the side down. He could improve significantly for this and his pedigree suggests that he is only likely to benefit for going further. With such a rich array of two-year-old talent at their disposal, connections are likely to know where they stand with him. He did nothing wrong here and it would be no surprise if he appeared in stakes company before the end of the season. In short, he shaped like a most promising prospect with the scope to suggest that there will be plenty to come from him. (op 7-1)
Awesome Act(USA) was keen early and Kelly spent just about the first half of this contest trying to get him to settle. As a result, he wasn't able to find the necessary to repel the winner. If he can travel more smoothly, a maiden will certainly come his way before the end of the season. (op 11-10)
Critical Moment(USA) ◆, who holds a Royal Lodge entry, impressed beforehand as a well put together colt and he showed up nicely on his debut. He ran on in taking fashion late on and a mile will be within his compass this autumn with a maiden looking there for the taking. (op 20-1)
Mushreq(USA) was another to strike as a good sort in the paddock, while his condition indicated that he will come on for this debut. Out of the Oaks winner Casual Look, it's likely he'll stay further in the future even though he weakened late on here. (tchd 7-2 and 9-2)
Primary Colors made a more than acceptable debut, while the one to note for nurseries in the future.
White Dart, who stayed on past beaten rivals. He looked well and fit for this and an eye should be kept out for him in the coming weeks. By Rakti, he is more than likely to get 1m. (tchd 100-1)
Bun Oir(USA) Official explanation: jockey said colt shortened its stride in closing stages
Seaside Sizzler Official explanation: jockey said colt ran green and hung right

5401 PROTECTAS HEALTH STEM CELL EBF MAIDEN STKS (DIV II) 7f
3:30 (3:31) (Class 4) 2-Y-O **£4,857** (£1,445; £722; £360) **Stalls** High

Form				RPR
0	1		**Treble Jig (USA)**[21] 4756 2-9-0 0 RyanMoore 5	85+
			(Sir Michael Stoute) *chsd ldrs: rdn over 1f out: r.o to ld wl ins fnl f* **5/6**[1]	
04	2	1 3/4	**Suited And Booted (IRE)**[49] 3794 2-9-0 0 RichardHughes 9	81
			(R Hannon) *led: rdn over 1f out: hung lft and hdd wl ins fnl f* **14/1**	
4	3	6	**Nizaa (USA)**[23] 4659 2-9-0 0 RHills 13	66
			(B W Hills) *chsd ldrs: rdn over 1f out: wknd ins fnl f* **6/1**[2]	
	4	1 1/4	**Pekan Star** 2-9-0 0 PhilipRobinson 2	63
			(M A Jarvis) *s.i.s: hld up in mid-div: hdwy over 2f out: sn rdn: wknd over 1f out* **16/1**	
	5	1 1/4	**Suntrap** 2-9-0 0 ShaneKelly 8	59
			(W J Knight) *hld up: hdwy over 2f out: sn rdn: wknd over 1f out* **100/1**	
	6	nk	**Best Show (IRE)** 2-9-0 0 (t) JimCrowley 11	59
			(Mrs A J Perrett) *prom: rdn over 2f out: wknd over 1f out* **66/1**	
0	7	shd	**Notice Given**[45] 3957 2-9-0 0 TPQueally 6	58
			(H R A Cecil) *chsd ldrs: rdn over 1f out: sn wknd* **13/2**[3]	
	8	3/4	**Painswick (USA)** 2-9-0 0 JimmyFortune 1	57
			(J L Dunlop) *chsd ldrs tl rdn and wknd over 1f out* **40/1**	
	9	1	**Loden** 2-9-0 0 DaneO'Neill 3	54
			(L M Cumani) *hld up: hdwy over 2f out: rdn and wknd over 1f out* **40/1**	
	10	1 1/4	**Lyric Poet (USA)** 2-9-0 0 TedDurcan 14	51
			(Saeed Bin Suroor) *s.s: rn green in rr: rdn 1/2-way: n.d* **15/2**	
	11	1 1/2	**Eltheeb** 2-9-0 0 TPO'Shea 4	47
			(J L Dunlop) *hld up: rdn 1/2-way: a in rr* **50/1**	
	12	1	**Moonbalej** 2-9-0 0 J-PGuillambert 12	48+
			(M Johnston) *prom: rdn over 2f out: sn wknd* **40/1**	
0	13	1/2	**Captain Clint (IRE)**[11] 5109 2-9-0 0 MartinDwyer 7	43+
			(M H Tompkins) *hld up: rdn 1/2-way: wknd over 2f out* **100/1**	
	14	shd	**Royal Patriot (IRE)** 2-9-0 0 TonyCulhane 10	43+
			(W J Haggas) *s.i.s: hld up: rdn whn n.m.r wl over 1f out: a in rr* **80/1**	

1m 25.0s (-0.70) **Going Correction** -0.15s/f (Firm) **14** Ran SP% **120.5**
Speed ratings (Par 96): **98,96,89,87,86 85,85,84,83,82 80,79,78,78**
toteswinger: 1&2 £6.50, 1&3 £3.70, 2&3 £6.10. CSF £14.60 TOTE £1.80: £1.10, £3.30, £1.90; EX 20.80.
Owner K Abdulla **Bred** Juddmonte Farms Inc **Trained** Newmarket, Suffolk

FOCUS
The winning time of this maiden was marginally quicker than the first division but the form is tricky to pin down, but should be sound with the first two finishing clear.

NOTEBOOK
Treble Jig(USA) ◆ was a different horse to the one who made his debut over course and distance earlier in the month. He was green on that occasion but it was clear from the manner in which he went to post here that the previous experience wasn't wasted on him. He took a good grip as he went down and then proceeded to give a professional performance to get off the mark in a time that was marginally quicker than the first division. The ground was much more to Treble Jig's liking than the soft conditions in which he'd run previously. He travelled towards the fore on the far side and gave generously when asked for his effort over 1f out. He holds plenty of fancy entries - including the Dewhurst Stakes - and connections indicated that he will have one more run this year. There is still an amount of physical development to come and he will have to be respected wherever he heads next. (op 10-11, tchd 1-1 in places)
Suited And Booted(IRE) ◆ was well beaten in an Ascot novices' race on what was his second career start but this was much more like it. He put up stirring resistance as the odds-on favourite came at him but gave way late on, losing little in defeat. He will be winning in the not too distant future, based on the fact that there was a further 6l back to the third.
Nizaa(USA) had the benefit of the stands' rail. He finished fourth of seven at Pontefract last time and was beaten just about the same distance here. (op 7-1)
Pekan Star ◆, a half-brother to a French Derby winner Blue Canari and the smart Blue Ksar, ran a race full of promise. All the indicators suggest he'll come into his own over 1m-plus. (op 14-1)
Notice Given found the soft ground not to his liking when a well-beaten favourite at Yarmouth last month but there were no such excuses here. (op 15-2)
Lyric Poet(USA), who cost $700,000 at the sales, will need to improve significantly to justify his lofty price-tag. (op 8-1)

5402 SIP-PLC.COM IDEAS, ADVICE AND CAPITAL H'CAP 1m 6f 175y
4:05 (4:06) (Class 3) (0-95,95) 3-Y-O+ **£5,882** (£5,882; £1,348; £673) **Stalls** Centre

Form				RPR
15-3	1		**Merchant Of Dubai**[14] 5004 4-9-11 **92** RobertWinston 6	101
			(G A Swinbank) *chsd ldrs: led over 3f out: rdn over 1f out: hung lft ins fnl f: jnd on post* **3/1**[2]	
2112	1	dht	**Recession Proof (FR)**[20] 4794 3-8-8 **88** RichardHughes 3	97+
			(S A Callaghan) *hld up: rdn over 2f out: hdwy over 1f out: sn swtchd rt: styd on u.p to join wnr post* **5/2**[1]	
45	3	1/2	**Rugell (ARG)**[14] 5004 4-9-0 **86** TPQueally 4	89
			(H R A Cecil) *chsd ldr: chal 3f out: rdn over 1f out: hung lft ins fnl f: unable qck nr fin* **20/1**	
1212	4	2 1/2	**Trip The Light**[14] 4972 4-8-8 **80** (v) BMcHugh(5) 8	85
			(R A Fahey) *a.p: rdn over 2f out: hung lft and nt clr run over 1f out: styd on same pce fnl f* **8/1**	
3153	5	3/4	**Cyborg**[23] 4661 5-8-13 **80** RyanMoore 9	84
			(D R C Elsworth) *hld up: hdwy 1/2-way: rdn over 2f out: hung rt over 1f out: no ex ins fnl f* **7/2**[3]	
5400	6	15	**Tungsten Strike (USA)**[20] 4769 8-9-9 **90** (p) JimCrowley 1	75
			(Mrs A J Perrett) *led: rdn and hdd over 3f out: sn wknd* **6/1**	
3150	7	1 1/4	**Royal Trooper (IRE)**[7] 5230 3-7-12 **78** oh2 JamieMackay 7	61
			(J G Given) *hld up: rdn over 2f out: hung rt and wknd wl over 1f out* **16/1**	

3m 8.42s (-2.88) **Going Correction** -0.15s/f (Firm)
WFA 3 from 4yo+ 13lb **7** Ran SP% **111.8**
Speed ratings (Par 107): **101,101,100,99,99 91,90**WIN: Merchant Of Dubai £1.70, Recession Proof £1.70. PL: MOD £1.80, RP £2.20. EX: MOD-RP £5.30, RP-MOD £4.30. CSF: MOD-RP £5.21, RP-MOD £4.86. TRICAST: MOD-RP-Rugell £59.18, RP-MOD-R £56.75. Toteswinger: MOD-RP £2.30, MOD-R £7.20, RP-R £8.90.
Owner Highland Racing 2 **Bred** A Smith **Trained** Melsonby, N Yorks.
Owner Martin M Dempsey **Bred** N P Bloodstock Ltd & Morton Bloodstock **Trained** Newmarket, Suffolk

FOCUS
A fascinating finish between a proven stayer and a progressive type, being markedly stepped up in trip, resulted in a dead heat. The fourth and fifth were close to recent marks and give the form a sound look.

NOTEBOOK
Merchant Of Dubai, third of nine over an inadequate 1m 2f here two weeks ago, was back at a more suitable distance. A four-time winner in easier underfoot conditions, he showed that he is adaptable to a faster surface, never ducking it when the going got tough in the closing strides. He came under a strong challenge from either side but would not be passed. (op 11-4 tchd 7-2)
Recession Proof(FR) ◆ effort was most commendable as he was trying this distance, having been successfully campaigned at 1m 2f this summer. He certainly proved that he gets this trip and the way he stayed on suggests that he'll actually get further. His effort was probably the most creditable as he came from off the pace, having to be switched right as Merchant Of Dubai and Rugell edged left. He is a promising young stayer and one to keep firmly in mind over the coming months. (op 11-4 tchd 7-2)
Rugell(ARG) put up a much-improved effort on what was his third English start and first at this distance. He looks like he is getting acclimatised now and hung in there, only going down by half a length to hint that he can find the winner's circle before long. (op 16-1)
Trip The Light, in the first two on each of his previous four starts, again ran well - this time in a better class of a race - to underline he remains in good order. (op 7-1)
Cyborg travelled well but found little for pressure. (op 9-2)
Tungsten Strike(USA) quickly weakened away after cutting out the early running. (op 10-1)

5403 BISHOP'S STORTFORD FOOTBALL CLUB CLAIMING STKS 7f
4:35 (4:37) (Class 5) 3-Y-O **£3,885** (£1,156; £577; £288) **Stalls** High

Form				RPR
1436	1		**Fajita**[14] 5003 3-9-3 69 (p) RyanMoore 7	74
			(G L Moore) *trckd ldrs: rdn to ld and hung rt fr over 1f out: styd on u.p* **3/1**[1]	
0064	2	1	**Dove Mews**[29] 4452 3-8-9 70 HayleyTurner 1	63
			(M L W Bell) *a.p: rdn and hung rt fr over 1f out: styd on* **6/1**	
4100	3	1	**Pressing Matters (IRE)**[16] 4914 3-9-1 73 (p) TedDurcan 6	67+
			(M Botti) *hld up: hdwy over 2f out: rdn over 1f out: r.o wl ins fnl f* **8/1**	
0020	4	1 1/4	**King's Sabre**[22] 4700 3-9-1 66 SebSanders 4	63
			(W R Muir) *led: rdn and hdd over 1f out: styd on same pce ins fnl f* **16/1**	
2404	5	3/4	**Rio Royale (IRE)**[22] 4695 3-9-0 74 (p) Louis-PhilippeBeuzelin(5) 2	65
			(Mrs A J Perrett) *chsd ldr: rdn over 2f out: no ex ins fnl f* **12/1**	
1560	6	1/2	**You've Been Mowed**[18] 4841 3-8-1 62 KellyHarrison(3) 10	49
			(R J Price) *rrd in stalls: one side of stall opened late: s.s: hld up: hdwy 1/2-way: rdn over 1f out: no ex ins fnl f* **11/2**[3]	
0644	7	1 1/4	**Roly Boy**[43] 4005 3-9-1 70 (b) RichardHughes 5	56
			(R Hannon) *hld up: rdn over 1f out: nvr trbld ldrs* **9/2**[2]	
0020	8	4 1/2	**Count On Guest**[10] 5121 3-8-7 58 (t) TPO'Shea 11	36
			(G G Margarson) *chsd ldrs: rdn over 2f out: wkng whn hung rt over 1f out* **33/1**	
3050	9	2 1/2	**Cactus Curtsey**[7] 5225 3-8-4 60 (t) MartinDwyer 8	27+
			(J R Fanshawe) *stmbld s: hld up: rdn over 2f out: n.d* **16/1**	
4000	10	1 1/4	**Maid Of Stone (IRE)**[28] 4498 3-8-9 53 ow1 DaneO'Neill 9	28
			(D R C Elsworth) *chsd ldrs: rdn over 2f out: wknd over 1f out: eased ins fnl f* **66/1**	
305	11	3/4	**Summers Target (USA)**[11] 5112 3-9-4 68 (p) JimmyFortune 13	35
			(R M H Cowell) *hld up: rdn over 2f out: hung lft and no rspnse* **10/1**	
0000	12	11	**Captain Cavendish (IRE)**[31] 2681 3-8-9 48 (p) NeilChalmers 12	—
			(A Bailey) *sn pushed along in rr: rdn and wknd over 2f out* **100/1**	

1m 25.08s (-0.62) **Going Correction** -0.15s/f (Firm) **12** Ran SP% **117.9**
Speed ratings (Par 100): **97,95,94,93,92 91,90,85,82,81 80,67**
toteswinger: 1&2 £5.70, 1&3 £8.40, 2&3 £9.60. CSF £20.57 TOTE £3.90: £1.70, £2.00, £3.30; EX 30.40.
Owner W P Flynn **Bred** Mrs Joan Langmead **Trained** Lower Beeding, W Sussex

FOCUS
An ordinary claimer that is best rated around the runner-up and fourth.
You've Been Mowed Official explanation: jockey said filly jammed its nose in stall grating and missed the break
Summers Target(USA) Official explanation: jockey said gelding was too keen going to post

5404 STRIKING AMBITION FIRST CROP YEARLINGS H'CAP 6f
5:10 (5:11) (Class 4) (0-85,83) 3-Y-O+ **£5,180** (£1,541; £770; £384) **Stalls** High

Form				RPR
1020	1		**Brunelleschi**[9] 5167 6-8-9 **75** (b) JosephineBruning(7) 4	86
			(P L Gilligan) *a.p: rdr dropped whip: edgd rt and led over 1f out: hdd briefly ins fnl f: pushed out* **28/1**	

36 **2** *1 ¼* **Sweet Gale (IRE)**[14] 5001 5-8-8 **72**.............. Louis-PhilippeBeuzelin(5) 8 79
(Mike Murphy) *hld up: hdwy over 1f out: rdn to ld briefly ins fnl f: no ex towards fin* **12/1**

0000 **3** *½* **Lodi (IRE)**[18] 4852 4-9-2 **75**.............................(t) AdamKirby 2 80
(J Akehurst) *hld up: hdwy: nt clr run and swtchd lft over 1f out: r.o* **33/1**

0210 **4** *2* **Silver Wind**[6] 5257 4-9-10 **83**.............................(v) TPQueally 16 82
(P D Evans) *chsd ldrs: rdn over 2f out: hung lft fr over 1f out: styd on same pce fnl f* **8/1**

3350 **5** *hd* **Kashimin (IRE)**[20] 4784 4-9-5 **78**.............................. RobertWinston 6 83+
(G A Swinbank) *trckd ldrs: rdn whn hmpd and lost pl over 1f out: styd on ins fnl f* **5/1**[2]

3300 **6** *2* **Eastern Hills**[20] 4796 4-8-13 **72**.............................. KirstyMilczarek 10 64
(J S Wainwright) *hld up: hdwy: hung lft and nt clr run over 1f out: r.o ins fnl f: nvr nrr* **14/1**

4200 **7** *nse* **Bel Cantor**[6] 5257 6-9-3 **79**.............................(p) KellyHarrison(3) 5 71
(W J H Ratcliffe) *led: rdn over 2f out: hdd over 1f out: no ex* **8/1**

3343 **8** *½* **Autumn Blades (IRE)**[17] 4871 4-9-3 **76**...................(b) JimmyFortune 12 66
(A Bailey) *s.i.s: hld up: rdn and hung rt fnl f: n.d* **14/1**

101 **9** *nk* **Sarah's Art (IRE)**[13] 5031 6-8-13 **72**.............................(t) JimCrowley 14 61+
(Stef Liddiard) *hld up: rdn over 1f out: n.d* **7/1**[3]

5611 **10** *hd* **Getcarter**[14] 4990 3-9-0 **76**.............................. RichardHughes 15 65+
(R Hannon) *hld up: rdn over 2f out: n.d* **7/2**[1]

0161 **11** *1 ¼* **Peper Harow (IRE)**[14] 5007 3-7-13 **64**.......................... AndreaAtzeni(3) 9 49
(M D I Usher) *hld up: rdn over 2f out: nvr trbld ldrs* **16/1**

1200 **12** *1* **Alfresco**[29] 4461 5-9-4 **77**.............................(b) TonyCulhane 11 58
(J R Best) *chsd ldr: rdn whn hmpd and wknd over 1f out* **16/1**

100 **13** *1 ½* **Maxwell Hawke (IRE)**[34] 4333 3-9-3 **79**.......................... TedDurcan 13 56
(P W Chapple-Hyam) *chsd ldrs: rdn and hung lft over 1f out: sn wknd* **16/1**

3250 **14** *1* **River Kirov (IRE)**[9] 5167 6-9-5 **78**.............................. JamieMackay 7 51
(M Wigham) *plld hrd and prom: rdn over 2f out: wknd over 1f out* **33/1**

1m 10.84s (-1.66) **Going Correction** -0.15s/f (Firm)
WFA 3 from 4yo+ 3lb **14** Ran SP% **121.6**
Speed ratings (Par 105): **105,103,102,100,99 97,97,96,95,95 94,92,90,89**
toteswinger: 1&2 £105.40, 1&3 £103.80, 2&3 £66.60. CSF £333.18 CT £10649.17 TOTE £45.40: £10.10, £4.70, £7.30; EX 367.80 Place 6: £8.25, Place 5: £6.15..
Owner Dr Susan Barnes **Bred** Dr Susan Barnes **Trained** Newmarket, Suffolk

FOCUS
A competitive handicap of its type was won in a respectable time of just over half a second outside standard. The runner-up to his best turf mark sets the level.
T/Plt: £9.10 to a £1 stake. Pool: £62,030.20. 4,936.14 winning tickets. T/Qpdt: £5.60 to a £1 stake. Pool: £3,774.94. 497.50 winning tickets. CR

4844 THIRSK (L-H)
Friday, August 28

OFFICIAL GOING: Good (8.7)
Wind: Strong behind Weather: Sunny periods and showers

5405 TURFTV H'CAP — 6f
1:30 (1:31) (Class 5) (0-75,75) 3-Y-O **£4,274** (£1,271; £635; £317) **Stalls** High

Form RPR

-160 **1** **Ishe Mac**[90] 2504 3-9-3 **74**.............................. FrancisNorton 1 81
(N Bycroft) *cl up: rdn over 1f out and ev ch: drvn ins fnl f and kpt on to ld nr fin* **18/1**

0004 **2** *nk* **Lucky Dan (IRE)**[12] 5073 3-8-9 **66**.......................... SilvestreDeSousa 10 72
(Paul Green) *midfield: hdwy over 2f out: swtchd lft and rdn to ld over 1f out: drvn ins fnl f: hdd and nt qckn nr fin* **4/1**[1]

5213 **3** *2 ½* **La Capriosa**[15] 4929 3-8-12 **69**.............................. GrahamGibbons 9 67
(J A Glover) *led: rdn along 2f out: drvn and hdd over 1f out: one pce ins fnl f* **9/2**[2]

-000 **4** *¾* **Gower Valentine**[74] 2970 3-8-13 **70**.......................... AdrianTNicholls 13 66
(D Nicholls) *chsd ldrs: effrt over 2f out and n.m.r: sn rdn and kpt on same pce appr fnl f* **12/1**

0003 **5** *2 ¼* **Caranbola**[14] 4997 3-8-11 **68**.............................. AlanMunro 8 56
(M Brittain) *towards rr: hdwy over 2f outr: sn rdn and kpt on appr fnl f: nt rch ldrs* **9/1**

0145 **6** *nk* **Red Kyte**[23] 4664 3-9-2 **73**.............................(p) NCallan 6 60
(K A Ryan) *chsd ldrs: rdn along 2f out: sn no imp* **14/1**

4501 **7** *1 ¼* **Blown It (USA)**[20] 4776 3-9-3 **74**.............................. TomEaves 3 57
(I Semple) *towards rr: pushed along 1/2-way: rdn 2f out and sme late hdwy* **10/1**

1500 **8** *¾* **Real Diamond**[15] 4940 3-8-7 **70**.............................. JamieKyne(5) 2 51
(A Dickman) *chsd ldrs on outer: rdn along over 2f out and grad wknd* **33/1**

-364 **9** *shd* **Alacity (IRE)**[28] 4505 3-8-4 **61** oh8.......................... AndrewMullen 4 42
(N Bycroft) *prom: rdn along 1/2-way: sn wknd* **80/1**

0 **10** *1* **Soul Sista (IRE)**[42] 4044 3-8-11 **68**.............................. JimmyQuinn 7 46
(J L Spearing) *a in rr* **16/1**

5404 **11** *4* **Dispol Grand (IRE)**[14] 4999 3-8-11 **68** ow1.......................... PhillipMakin 5 33
(P T Midgley) *a towards rr* **16/1**

-051 **12** *7* **Secret City (IRE)**[54] 3651 3-8-4 **61** oh2.....................(b) AndrewElliott 11 3
(R Bastiman) *dwlt: a towards rr* **13/2**[3]

301 **13** *25* **Island Legend (IRE)**[18] 4860 3-9-4 **75**.............................. DavidProbert 12 —
(J M Bradley) *cl up: rdn along over 2f out: lost action and wknd qckly wl over 1f out: sn eased and bhd* **7/1**

1m 12.33s (-0.37) **Going Correction** -0.05s/f (Good) **13** Ran SP% **118.7**
Speed ratings (Par 100): **100,99,96,95,92 91,90,89,89,87 82,73,39**
toteswinger: 1&2 £14.50, 1&3 £13.90, 2&3 £3.90. CSF £88.07 CT £404.43 TOTE £20.90: £5.60, £1.90, £1.80; EX 153.50.
Owner N Bycroft **Bred** P And Mrs J Clark **Trained** Brandsby, N Yorks

FOCUS
The ground was officially described as good, but there were a few showers around and after this opener both Neil Callan and Phillip Makin felt the going was on the soft side, whilst Adrian Nicholls said it was dead. It's true the time, like in the following straight course event, was respectable, but that can be explained by a strong tailwind. They raced stands' side, but the winner emerged from the widest stall, and it proved difficult to make up ground in this ordinary sprint handicap. The runner-up sets the level rated to the best of his previous form.

5406 GORMIRE (S) STKS — 6f
2:00 (2:00) (Class 5) 3-Y-O+ **£4,274** (£1,271; £635; £317) **Stalls** High

Form RPR

00 **1** **Whiteoak Lady (IRE)**[30] 4428 4-9-0 63.......................(b[1]) FrancisNorton 14 72+
(J L Spearing) *mde all: qcknd clr wl over 1f out: comf* **14/1**

0061 **2** *4* **Steel Blue**[9] 5159 9-9-0 53.............................(p) AmyRyan(5) 3 61
(R M Whitaker) *chsd ldrs: hdwy over 2f out: rdn and edgd rt over 1f out: kpt on underpress ins fnl f: no ch w wnr* **28/1**

0-00 **3** *shd* **Baby Rock**[111] 1890 4-8-13 60.............................. AlanMunro 4 55
(C F Wall) *prom: rdn 2f out: sn drvn to chse wnr: kpt on same pce ins fnl f* **18/1**

335 **4** *nk* **Obe Gold**[13] 5018 7-9-5 77.............................(v) JimmyQuinn 12 60
(P Howling) *stmbld and hmpd s: bhd: hdwy 2f out: swtchd lft and rdn over 1f out: styd on: nrst fin* **11/4**[2]

0503 **5** *1 ½* **Charles Parnell (IRE)**[9] 5147 6-9-5 70.......................(b) DaleGibson 8 55
(M Dods) *trckd ldrs: effrt 2f out: n.m.r over 1f out: kpt on same pce ins fnl f* **16/1**

5020 **6** *3* **Mutamared (USA)**[11] 5104 9-9-5 79.............................(t) NCallan 13 45
(K A Ryan) *wnt lft s: chsd ldrs: rdn along 2f out: sn btn* **5/2**[1]

2621 **7** *nk* **Gap Princess (IRE)**[59] 3479 5-9-0 69.......................... SilvestreDeSousa 7 39
(G A Harker) *in rr and sn rdn along: drvn over 2f out: nvr a factor* **11/2**[3]

2044 **8** *1* **John Keats**[14] 5001 6-9-5 67.............................. DanielTudhope 5 41
(J S Goldie) *in tch on outer: effrt over 2f out: sn rdn and wknd* **6/1**

-300 **9** *2* **Mr Rio (IRE)**[9] 5150 4-8-13 58.............................. AndrewElliott 9 29
(A P Jarvis) *a towards rr* **50/1**

5066 **10** *¾* **Pacific Pride**[15] 4941 6-9-5 66.............................. GrahamGibbons 11 32
(J J Quinn) *cl up: rdn along over 2f out: sn wknd* **12/1**

-000 **11** *3* **Cranworth Blaze**[56] 3569 5-8-8 44.......................(b) RoystonFfrench 2 12
(T J Etherington) *swtchd lft s and racd alone far side: a bhd* **100/1**

1m 12.46s (-0.24) **Going Correction** -0.05s/f (Good) **11** Ran SP% **116.8**
Speed ratings (Par 103): **99,93,93,93,91 87,86,85,82,81 77**
toteswinger: 1&2 £31.30, 1&3 £14.60, 2&3 £16.70. CSF £340.50 TOTE £17.20: £4.50, £6.00, £4.70; EX 235.80.The winner was bought in for 6,500gns.
Owner Leonard Kinsella **Bred** Thomas J Reid **Trained** Kinnersley, Worcs

FOCUS
A good race for the grade on paper, but just as in the opener, there was a strong tailwind and nothing got involved from off the pace. The winner looks back to her best and along with the runner-up sets the level.
Obe Gold Official explanation: jockey said gelding stumbled on leaving stalls and never travelled
Charles Parnell(IRE) Official explanation: jockey said gelding was denied a clear run
Gap Princess(IRE) Official explanation: jockey said mare moved poorly throughout

5407 EUROPEAN BREEDERS' FUND MAIDEN STKS (DIV I) — 1m
2:35 (2:36) (Class 4) 2-Y-O **£5,342** (£1,589; £794; £396) **Stalls** Low

Form RPR

5 **1** **Jibrrya**[22] 4713 2-9-3 0.............................. AlanMunro 9 78+
(M R Channon) *trckd ldrs: hdwy over 3f out: chsd ldr 2f out: sn rdn and edgd lft ent fnl f: kpt on wl u.p to ld nr fin* **12/1**

0 **2** *nk* **Manhattan Fox (USA)**[14] 4985 2-9-3 0.......................... PaulHanagan 8 77+
(B J Meehan) *cl up on outer: led 1/2-way: qcknd clr over 2f out: rdn over 1f out: drvn ins fnl f: hdd and no ex towards fin* **8/1**[3]

5 **3** *4 ½* **Gracelightening**[29] 4468 2-8-12 0.......................... SilvestreDeSousa 2 62+
(Paul Green) *chsd ldrs on inner: pushed along and lost pl after 3f: hdwy wl over 2f out: swtchd rt and rdn wl over 1f out: kpt on ins fnl f: nrst fin* **50/1**

6 **4** *4 ½* **Big Wave Bay (IRE)**[35] 4258 2-9-3 0.............................. PhillipMakin 4 58
(A P Jarvis) *towards rr: hdwy on outer over 3f out: rdn 2f out: kpt on appr fnl f: nrst fin* **16/1**

2 **5** *shd* **Corsica (IRE)**[22] 4713 2-9-3 0.............................. RoystonFfrench 6 57
(M Johnston) *led: pushed along and hdd 1/2-way: rdn along 3f out: drvn over 2f out and sn wknd* **5/4**[1]

25 **6** *1 ½* **Beat The Rush**[14] 4993 2-9-3 0.............................. TomEaves 3 54
(Miss J A Camacho) *s.i.s and t.k.h in rr: pushed along 1/2-way: hdwy on outer 2f out: kpt on ins fnl f: nvr nr ldrs* **20/1**

442 **7** *2 ¼* **Music Of The Moor (IRE)**[22] 4705 2-9-3 79.......................... MickyFenton 7 49
(T P Tate) *cl up: rdn along over 3f out: sn drvn and wknd over 2f out* **11/4**[2]

3 **8** *12* **Decimus Meridius (IRE)**[24] 4618 2-9-3 0.......................... PaulMulrennan 10 23
(J Howard Johnson) *midfield: rdn along 3f out: sn wknd* **8/1**[3]

00 **9** *10* **Captain Cash**[64] 3310 2-9-3 0.............................. DavidAllan 1 1
(T D Easterby) *dwlt: a in rr: bhd fr 1/2-way* **50/1**

10 *2* **Starmaamul** 2-9-3 0.............................. NCallan 5 —
(K A Ryan) *chsd ldrs to 1/2-way: sn wknd* **33/1**

1m 42.29s (2.19) **Going Correction** +0.10s/f (Good) **10** Ran SP% **118.5**
Speed ratings (Par 96): **93,92,88,83,83 82,79,67,57,55**
toteswinger: 1&2 £15.70, 1&3 £35.90, 2&3 £46.20. CSF £101.69 TOTE £14.90: £3.30, £2.50, £9.60; EX 60.10.
Owner Sheikh Ahmed Al Maktoum **Bred** Mrs J A Cornwell **Trained** West Ilsley, Berks

FOCUS
A fair maiden, although the winning time was 0.72 seconds slower than the second division. The first three all stepped up on previous errforts and could go on again.

NOTEBOOK
Jibrrya improved significantly on the form he showed on his debut at Sandown, in the process reversing form with Corsica. He took an age to reel in the runner-up, but showed a willing attitude and should do better with more time and distance. (op 20-1)
Manhattan Fox(USA) was given a really positive ride and looked to be holding on around a furlong out, but he was eventually pegged back. He was well clear of the remainder, stepping up a good deal on his debut performance, and looks up to winning a similar event, especially up north. (op 15-2)
Gracelightening showed nothing on her debut over 6f, but this was much better. She struggled to lay up for much of the way and was under pressure out back a fair way from the finish, but she gradually responded. (op 66-1 tchd 40-1)
Big Wave Bay(IRE) showed ability and should find his level once handicapped. (op 28-1)
Corsica(IRE) had today's winner well behind when a pleasing second on his debut at Sandown, so this was disappointing. He has quite a fluent action and this ground, on the easy side of good, probably didn't suit. The vet reported the colt finished distressed. Official explanation: vet said colt returned distressed (op 11-10 tchd Evens)
Music Of The Moor(IRE), who hung badly left when the bit slipped through his mouth last time, was well-backed but again ruined his chance by wanting to go left under pressure. He finished tamely and has plenty to prove. (op 6-1)

5408 EUROPEAN BREEDERS' FUND MAIDEN STKS (DIV II) — 1m
3:10 (3:13) (Class 4) 2-Y-O **£5,342** (£1,589; £794; £396) **Stalls** Low

Form RPR

1 **Passion For Gold (USA)** 2-9-3 0.............................. AlanMunro 1 87+
(Saeed Bin Suroor) *mde most: rdn along over 2f out: drvn over 1f out: kpt on strly fnl f* **11/4**[2]

6 **2** *5* **Super Collider**[34] 4314 2-9-3 0.............................. NCallan 9 77+
(M A Jarvis) *wnt rt s: sn chsng ldrs on outer: hdwy 1/2-way: chsd wnr over 2f out: rdn to chal and ev ch over 1f out: sn edgd lft and one pce* **8/13**[1]

3 3 1/2 **Medicinal Compound** 2-9-3 0 PhillipMakin 8 68+
(K A Ryan) *trckd ldrs: effrt and hdwy over 2f out: sn rdn and kpt on appr fnl f: bttr for r* **12/1**[3]

4 9 **Battle Study (IRE)** 2-8-10 0 DeclanCannon(7) 10 49
(A J McCabe) *in rr: pushed along over 3f out: rdn over 2f out: kpt on appr fnl f: nvr nr ldrs* **50/1**

5 1 **Pena Dorada (IRE)** 2-9-3 0 AndrewElliott 2 46
(A P Jarvis) *cl up: rdn along over 3f out and grad wknd* **20/1**

6 1 1/2 **Fusenam** 2-9-3 0 TomEaves 5 43
(Miss J A Camacho) *s.i.s: a in rr* **20/1**

6 7 2 **Transmit (IRE)**[23] 4659 2-9-3 0 DavidAllan 4 39
(T D Easterby) *t.k.h: cl up: rdn along over 2f out: drvn wl over 1f out and sn wknd* **14/1**

0 8 10 **Princess Neenee (IRE)**[18] 4847 2-8-12 0 SilvestreDeSousa 3 12
(Paul Green) *chsd ldrs on inner: rdn along 1/2-way: sn wknd* **40/1**

1m 41.57s (1.47) **Going Correction** +0.10s/f (Good) 8 Ran SP% **116.9**
Speed ratings (Par 96): **96,91,87,78,77 76,74,64**
toteswinger: 1&2 £1.10, 1&3 £1.70, 2&3 £1.70. CSF £4.70 TOTE £2.80: £1.10, £1.02, £3.30; EX 5.70.
Owner Godolphin **Bred** Mr And Mrs M Roy Jackson **Trained** Newmarket, Suffolk

FOCUS
This maiden was won by a potentially decent colt, recording a time 0.72 seconds quicker than the first division. It looked a pretty good race for the track.

NOTEBOOK
Passion For Gold(USA) ◆, looks potentially useful, having this field well strung out and recording a time quicker than the first division. He was inclined to carry his head awkwardly under pressure, but kept extending and basically just looked immature - a view backed up by Alan Munro, who is now 2-3 for Saeed Bin Suroor since 1996. Whilst he doesn't hold any fancy entries, he's bred to be pretty smart - his dam was a high class at around 1m in the US - and he deserves his chance in something better. (tchd 3-1)
Super Collider was stuck out very wide for much of the way and couldn't sustain his challenge in the straight. Even so, he still finished clear of the remainder and this probably represented an improvement on the form he showed over 7f on debut. (op 6-5 tchd 4-7)
Medicinal Compound, a £21,000 half-brother to numerous winners in France out of a winner over 1m-1m2f including in Listed company, struggled to hold his position turning into the straight, but kept on gradually and should have learnt plenty. (op 9-1)
Pena Dorada(IRE) showed up prominently early on before dropping away. (op 16-1 tchd 25-1)

5409 LIDL THIRSK STKS (H'CAP) 7f
3:45 (3:46) (Class 4) (0-80,80) 3-Y-0+ **£5,569** (£1,657; £828; £413) **Stalls** Low

Form RPR
1200 1 **Glenridding**[26] 4560 5-9-3 74 (p) AlanMunro 9 83
(J G Given) *mde all: rdn clr over 2f out: drvn ins fnl f and hld on gamely* **16/1**

0000 2 nk **Malcheek (IRE)**[25] 4598 7-8-13 70 DavidAllan 14 78
(T D Easterby) *chsd wnr: rdn along 2f out: drvn over 1f out: kpt on wl u.p ins fnl f* **25/1**

2600 3 1 **Bere Davis (FR)**[23] 4641 4-8-7 71 AndrewHeffernan(7) 13 76
(P D Evans) *midfield: hdwy over 3f out: rdn to chse ldrs 2f out: drvn and edgd lft ent fnl f: kpt on u.p towards fin* **12/1**

4100 4 1/2 **To Be Or Not To Be**[14] 5007 4-9-1 75 WilliamCarson(3) 1 79
(John Berry) *towards rr: swtchd outside and hdwy over 2f out: sn rdn and styd on wl fnl f: nrst fin* **16/1**

1020 5 nk **Turn Me On (IRE)**[49] 3825 6-9-9 80 GrahamGibbons 15 83
(T D Walford) *in tch: hdwy to chse ldrs 3f out and sn rdn: drvn wl over 1f out: kpt on same pce ins fnl f* **14/1**

3001 6 shd **Mujaadel (USA)**[20] 4802 4-9-3 74 AndrewMullen 8 77
(D Nicholls) *prom: effrt over 2f out and sn rdn: drvn over 1f out: kpt on u.p ins fnl f* **17/2**[3]

5010 7 1/2 **Keys Of Cyprus**[27] 4549 7-9-7 78 AdrianTNicholls 12 80
(D Nicholls) *midfield: hdwy wl over 2f: sn rdn: drvn over 1f out and kpt on u.p ins fnl f* **12/1**

3211 8 3/4 **Violent Velocity (IRE)**[8] 5188 6-8-13 77 6ex IJBrennan(7) 4 77
(J J Quinn) *midfield: n.m.r bnd after 3f: hdwy 3f out: rdn along over 2f out: drvn wl over 1f out: no imp appr fnl f* **3/1**[1]

6553 9 nk **Elijah Pepper (USA)**[20] 4783 4-8-6 68 DeanHeslop(5) 2 67
(T D Barron) *in rr tl sme late hdwy* **8/1**[2]

6143 10 2 1/4 **Timber Treasure (USA)**[2] 5343 5-9-0 71 FrancisNorton 10 64
(Paul Green) *dwlt: towards rr tl sme late hdwy* **12/1**

0005 11 1 **Fesko**[16] 4896 3-9-0 76 RoystonFfrench 5 66
(M Johnston) *a towards rr* **12/1**

0661 12 2 **Apollo Shark (IRE)**[28] 4504 4-9-1 72 PaulMulrennan 11 57
(J Howard Johnson) *in tch: hdwy to chse ldrs 3f out: rdn along 2f out: sn drvn and wknd* **8/1**[2]

6163 13 7 **Olympic Dream**[20] 4802 3-8-11 73 PaulHanagan 7 39
(R A Fahey) *in tch on inner: rdn along over 2f out: drvn wl over 1f out and sn wknd* **10/1**

2200 14 2 1/2 **Visions Of Johanna (USA)**[13] 5040 4-9-2 73 TonyHamilton 3 32
(R A Fahey) *a in rr* **25/1**

3523 15 1 3/4 **High Curragh**[16] 4887 6-9-1 72 NCallan 16 26
(K A Ryan) *stdd and swtchd lft s: hld up: a in rr* **14/1**

10-0 16 3 **Sadeek**[104] 2086 5-9-8 79 TomEaves 6 25
(B Smart) *a in rr* **33/1**

1m 28.49s (1.29) **Going Correction** +0.325s/f (Good)
WFA 3 from 4yo+ 5lb 16 Ran SP% **133.3**
Speed ratings (Par 105): **105,104,103,102,102 102,101,101,100,98 97,94,86,83,81 78**
toteswinger: 1&2 £116.40, 1&3 £75.60, 2&3 £93.10. CSF £397.43 CT £4945.82 TOTE £21.20: £3.80, £5.80, £4.40, £5.50; EX 569.60.
Owner Tremousser Partnership **Bred** Bolton Grange **Trained** Willoughton, Lincs

FOCUS
It was raining heavily before the off - a 15 to 20 minute shower - and considering the jockeys had already reported the ground to be riding on the soft side, it seemed quite surprising that the official going description of 'good' remained unchanged. This view is supported by a time almost four seconds slower than standard. This was a fair handicap, but it proved difficult to make up vast amounts of ground and therefore is not rated too positively, with the runner-up to previous course form.
High Curragh Official explanation: jockey said gelding ran too free

5410 PAUL SANGWIN 40TH BIRTHDAY H'CAP 2m
4:15 (4:15) (Class 4) (0-85,85) 4-Y-0+ **£5,569** (£1,657; £828; £413) **Stalls** Low

Form RPR
1212 1 **Saga De Tercey (FR)**[7] 5235 4-9-6 82 NCallan 7 89+
(G A Swinbank) *trckd ldr: effrt 3f out: rdn to ld over 2f out: drvn and kpt on strly fnl f* **11/10**[1]

43-4 2 1 1/2 **Ragamuffin Man (IRE)**[20] 4793 4-8-13 75 (v) RoystonFfrench 5 80
(W J Knight) *set stdy pce: slowed pce 1/2-way: rdn and qcknd over 3f out: hdd over 2f out: drvn over 1f out: rallied ins fnl f: kpt on* **15/2**[3]

1046 3 1 3/4 **Red Wine**[21] 4737 10-8-8 70 GrahamGibbons 8 73
(J A Glover) *hld up in rr: hdwy 5f out: effrt 3f out: rdn to chse wnr over 1f out: drvn and edgd lft ent fnl f: sn one pce* **16/1**

3611 4 2 1/2 **Baan (USA)**[18] 4848 6-8-5 67 JimmyQuinn 4 67
(H J Collingridge) *trckd ldng pair: effrt 3f out: rdn along over 2f out: drvn wl over 1f out and wknd appr fnl f* **7/1**[2]

0632 5 1 3/4 **Danzatrice**[20] 4793 7-8-6 68 PJMcDonald 2 66+
(C W Thornton) *hld up in rr: hdwy over 2f out and sn rdn: kpt on appr fnl f: nvr nr ldrs* **10/1**

4106 6 nse **Dolly Penrose**[20] 4769 4-9-9 85 SamHitchcott 6 83
(M R Channon) *t.k.h: hld up: effrt 3f out: sn rdn along to chse ldrs over 2f out: sn edgd lft and outpcd* **14/1**

104- 7 3 1/2 **Sphinx (FR)**[173] 7223 11-9-3 79 (b) DavidAllan 3 73
(E W Tuer) *t.k.h: trckd ldrs: effrt over 3f out: rdn along over 2f out: sn drvn and outpcd* **16/1**

4116 8 4 1/2 **Inchpast**[68] 3191 8-8-8 70 (b) AlanMunro 1 58
(M H Tompkins) *trckd ldrs on inner: rdn along 3f out and sn outpcd* **7/1**[2]

3m 40.06s (7.26) **Going Correction** +0.325s/f (Good) 8 Ran SP% **111.9**
Speed ratings (Par 105): **94,93,92,91,90 90,88,86**
toteswinger: 1&2 £2.90, 1&3 £5.90, 2&3 £13.10. CSF £9.34 CT £81.60 TOTE £1.90: £1.20, £2.50, £3.60; EX 10.10.
Owner Andrew Dick, Brian Dunn & Philip Holden **Bred** Haras De Tercey **Trained** Melsonby, N Yorks

FOCUS
A fair staying handicap, but a steady pace as well as rain-eased ground, resulted in a time over 15 seconds above the standard. As a result the form is not entirely solid but rated at face value for now.

5411 COLD KIRBY APPRENTICE STKS (H'CAP) 5f
4:45 (4:47) (Class 5) (0-70,69) 3-Y-0+ **£4,274** (£1,271; £635; £317) **Stalls** High

Form RPR
0600 1 **Tagula Breeze (IRE)**[16] 4891 3-9-2 69 IJBrennan(3) 4 77
(I W McInnes) *towards rr: pushed along and nt clr run over 2f out: hdwy and swtchd lft over 1f out: sn rdn and styd on ins fnl f to ld nr fin* **33/1**

340 2 1/2 **Grudge**[20] 4778 4-9-3 65 JamesO'Reilly 1 71
(Ollie Pears) *cl up: led 2f out and sn rdn: drvn ent fnl f: sn edgd rt: hdd and no ex nr fin* **16/1**

5656 3 hd **Wicked Wilma (IRE)**[9] 5149 5-8-10 58 SladeO'Hara 2 63
(A Berry) *chsd ldrs: hdwy over 1f out: sn rdn and ev ch ins fnl f: nt qckn nr fin* **9/1**

2260 4 3/4 **Toy Top (USA)**[20] 4778 6-8-10 58 (b) JamieKyne 3 61
(M Dods) *led: rdn along and hdd 2f out: drvn ent fnl f and one pce* **11/1**

3053 5 nse **Ryedane (IRE)**[14] 4998 7-8-12 60 (b) LanceBetts 11 62
(T D Easterby) *in tch: hdwy to chse ldrs 2f out: rdn over 1f out: drvn and ch ent fnl f: sn edgd lft and nt qckn* **3/1**[1]

0135 6 2 1/4 **Bluebok**[8] 5184 8-9-0 62 (bt) MCGeran 6 56
(J M Bradley) *chsd ldrs: rdn 2f out: kpt on same pce appr fnl f* **16/1**

1160 7 3 1/4 **Grimes Faith**[17] 4886 6-9-1 63 (b) AmyRyan 9 46
(K A Ryan) *chsd ldrs: rdn along 2f out: sn wknd* **6/1**[2]

2164 8 nk **Jilly Why (IRE)**[9] 5149 8-8-11 66 (b) JordanLDodd(7) 10 48
(Paul Green) *in rr: n.m.r and swtchd markedly lft to outer 2f out: nvr a factor* **8/1**

6043 9 2 **Blazing Heights**[17] 4877 6-8-12 60 (v) GaryBartley 8 34
(J S Goldie) *dwlt and swtchd rt s: a in rr* **8/1**

1144 10 8 **Rocketball (IRE)**[29] 4467 4-9-2 64 DeanHeslop 7 10
(Mrs L Williamson) *prom: rdn along over 2f out and sn wknd* **15/2**[3]

4160 11 3 1/4 **Piste**[23] 4653 3-8-13 68 AdamCarter(5) 12 2
(Miss T Jackson) *blind removed late and v.s.a: a t.o* **14/1**

59.82 secs (0.22) **Going Correction** +0.125s/f (Good)
WFA 3 from 4yo+ 2lb 11 Ran SP% **113.0**
Speed ratings (Par 103): **103,102,101,100,100 97,91,91,88,75 70**
toteswinger: 1&2 £38.80, 1&3 £30.90, 2&3 £23.60. CSF £445.42 CT £2766.60 TOTE £36.40: £7.30, £5.40, £3.40; EX 357.40 Place 6: £2,943.12, Place 5: £1,417.70..
Owner Terence Elsey **Bred** Michael And John Fahy **Trained** Catwick, E Yorks
■ Stewards' Enquiry : James O'Reilly one-day ban: used whip with excessive frequency (Sep 11)

FOCUS
A modest handicap restricted to apprentices who had not ridden more than 50 winners. The nearside rail was no advantage and the form looks sound rated around those in the frame behind the winner, but not a race to treat too positively.
Rocketball(IRE) Official explanation: jockey said gelding was unsuited by the good ground
Piste Official explanation: jockey said he was slow to remove blinds and was slowly away
T/Plt: £10,362.60 to a £1 stake. Pool: £50,393.94. 3.55 winning tickets. T/Qpdt: £263.30 to a £1 stake. Pool: £4,625.90. 13.00 winning tickets. JR

5412 - 5415a (Foreign Racing) - See Raceform Interactive

5297 DEAUVILLE (R-H)
Friday, August 28
OFFICIAL GOING: Turf course - good; all-weather - standard

5416a PRIX DE LA HUDERIE (LISTED RACE) (STRAIGHT) 7f
1:25 (1:24) 2-Y-0 **£26,699** (£10,680; £8,010; £5,340; £2,670)

RPR
1 **Frozen Power (IRE)**[16] 4901 2-9-2 OPeslier 4 102
(Saeed Bin Suroor) *disp ld tl led over 2f out: pushed out: r.o strly* **4/5**[1]

2 2 **Boltcity (FR)**[26] 4579 2-9-2 C-PLemaire 5 97
(J-C Rouget, France)

3 2 1/2 **Blue Panis (FR)**[26] 4584 2-9-2 CSoumillon 3 91
(F Chappet, France)

4 shd **Roi De Vitesse (IRE)**[30] 4418 2-9-2 JamesMillman 1 91
(B R Millman) *disp ld: pushed along 3f out: hdd over 2f out: wknd and lost 3rd cl home* **33/10**[2]

5 1/2 **Lucky Like (FR)**[11] 5117 2-9-2 JAuge 2 89
(E J O'Neill) *disp 3rd trcking ldrs: rdn and edgd rt 1 1/2f out: unable qckn* **10/1**[3]

1m 25.0s (-3.30) 5 Ran SP% **87.9**
PARI-MUTUEL: WIN 1.80; PL 1.30, 1.80; SF 5.00.
Owner Godolphin **Bred** Rathbarry Stud **Trained** Newmarket, Suffolk
■ Stewards' Enquiry : J Auge 200euro fine: whip abuse

NOTEBOOK
Frozen Power(IRE), the winner of a nursery last time, totally outclassed his rivals in this Listed race and made all the running. He quickened things up from one and a half out and coasted past the post to complete the hat-trick on this step up in grade and looks progressive. A possible target is the Group 3 Prix des Chenes at Longchamp on September 19th.
Roi De Vitesse(IRE), dropping in grade having run a couple of decent races at Group 2 level, was ridden positively in the early stages of this race on the rail, but began to feel the pace when things quickened up one and a half out. He battled on gamely and only lost third place in the final few strides.
Lucky Like(FR) got off the mark when dropped to 5½f last time but was up in both trip and class. He raced just behind the leaders, then became involved in a fight for third place during the final furlong and only missed out by a narrow margin.

4927 BEVERLEY (R-H)
Saturday, August 29
OFFICIAL GOING: Good to firm (firm in places; 9.3)
Wind: Moderate half against Weather: Sunny periods

5417 EBF DENISE MCGHEE IS 60 TODAY MAIDEN FILLIES' STKS 7f 100y
2:00 (2:00) (Class 4) 2-Y-O **£5,018** (£1,493; £746; £372) **Stalls High**

Form RPR
56 1 **Saafia (USA)**30 4460 2-9-0 0 JoeFanning 2 77+
(M Johnston) *mde all: rdn clr wl over 1f out: styd on strly* **3/1**2
0 2 5 **Whirly Dancer**49 3858 2-9-0 0 TPQueally 3 65+
(H R A Cecil) *chsd ldng pair: carried wd bnd after 3f rdn along to chse wnr wl over 1f out: drvn ins fnl f and no imp* **6/1**3
3 1¼ **Kronful** 2-9-0 0 SebSanders 5 62+
(M A Jarvis) *chsd ldrs: hdwy 3f out: rdn 2f out: styd on ins fnl f: nrst fin* **3/1**2
05 4 1¼ **Chat De Soie (IRE)**10 5153 2-9-0 0 LukeMorris 7 59
(J S Moore) *chsd ldrs on inner: hdwy 3f out: rdn along 2f out: sn one pce* **8/1**
5 ¾ **Michevious Spirit (IRE)** 2-9-0 0 NCallan 8 58+
(K A Ryan) *sn trcking wnr: rn v wd bnd after 3f: rdn over 2f out and sn wknd* **5/2**1
0 6 5 **Alotago (IRE)**17 4888 2-9-0 0 AdrianTNicholls 4 46
(D Nicholls) *dwlt: a towards rr* **33/1**
7 3½ **Light Nights (IRE)** 2-9-0 0 DavidAllan 1 38
(T D Easterby) *outpcd and bhd fr 1/2-way* **20/1**
000 8 2¼ **Moonlight Babe (USA)**16 4928 2-9-0 0 DanielTudhope 9 32
(I W McInnes) *dwlt: a in rr* **100/1**
05 9 3¾ **On Holiday**10 5157 2-8-7 0 JamesPSullivan(7) 6 24
(M W Easterby) *a towards rr* **33/1**
1m 33.34s (-0.46) **Going Correction** -0.375s/f (Firm) **9 Ran SP% 115.6**
Speed ratings (Par 93): **87,81,79,78,77 71,67,65,61**
toteswinger: 1&2 £3.40, 1&3 £2.10, 2&3 £3.30. CSF £20.49 TOTE £3.20: £1.30, £1.90, £1.50; EX 9.30.
Owner Hamdan Al Maktoum **Bred** Shadwell Farm LLC **Trained** Middleham Moor, N Yorks
FOCUS
An ordinary-looking maiden on ground that was changed to good to firm, firm in places from the original good to firm. The winner scored decisively and can do better.
NOTEBOOK
Saafia(USA) set the standard on her previous run, when she finished not far behind the talented Water Biscuit at Goodwood, and duly bolted up after being allowed an easy lead. The market weakness before the off was unfounded and she will probably now need to move into handicaps. (op 7-4)
Whirly Dancer did not show a great deal on her debut at Nottingham in July, after being slowly away, and was a little green here after leaving the stalls. However, her chance was ruined when carried wide by the fourth on the final bend, and she had no possibility of catching the winner. (op 11-2 tchd 5-1)
Kronful the first foal of a mare who won over 1m4f, took a while to find her feet and stayed on promisingly after sitting in midfield. (op 5-1 tchd 6-1)
Chat De Soie(IRE) belied her 50-1 odds at Folkestone last time when just behind a couple of 70-plus rated rivals and ran nicely again without looking a likely winner. She seems sure to stay a mile this season. (op 9-1 tchd 13-2)
Michevious Spirit(IRE) came in for market support on her debut but failed to handle the bend, which made her chances of victory slim. That said, it was still a fair effort with that in mind, and she should be mentally straighter next time. (op 3-1 tchd 100-30)

5418 BET IN-PLAY AT TOTESPORT.COM H'CAP 7f 100y
2:30 (2:30) (Class 4) (0-80,80) 3-Y-O+ **£4,857** (£1,445; £722; £360) **Stalls High**

Form RPR
6100 1 **Mount Hadley (USA)**19 4852 5-9-12 80 NCallan 4 93
(G A Butler) *trckd ldrs: smooth hdwy 2f out: swtchd lft and rdn to ld over 1f out: clr ent fnl f and styd on* **8/1**3
3503 2 3¼ **Desert Falls**20 4820 3-9-1 77 MichaelJStainton(3) 8 84+
(R M Whitaker) *chsd ldrs: hdwy on inner 2f out: rdn and nt clr run over 1f out and again ins fnl f: swtchd lft and styd on wl fnl 100yds* **12/1**
-000 3 nk **Nuit Sombre (IRE)**29 4504 9-9-0 68 (p) SilvestreDeSousa 14 72
(G A Harker) *led: rdn along wl over 2f out: drvn and hdd over 1f out: edgd rt and kpt on same pce ins fnl f* **8/1**3
6010 4 1¾ **Moonage Daydream (IRE)**29 4504 4-8-9 63 ow1 (b) DNolan 6 63
(T D Easterby) *towards rr: hdwy over 2f out: nt clr run over 1f out: sn swtchd lft and rdn: kpt on ins fnl f: nrst fin* **16/1**
2630 5 nse **Tourist**12 5107 4-9-2 75 MartinLane(5) 3 75
(D Shaw) *in tch: effrt over 2f out and sn rdn: switrcehd lft and drvn over 1f out: kpt on ins fnl f: nt rch ldrs* **12/1**
0000 6 shd **This Ones For Eddy**43 4040 4-8-10 64 PJMcDonald 11 63
(J Balding) *chsd ldng pair: rdn along over 2f out: drvn wl over 1f out and grad wknd* **12/1**
2162 7 1¼ **Dance And Dance (IRE)**10 5154 3-9-6 79 TPQueally 2 75+
(E F Vaughan) *towards rr: hdwy on outer over 2f out: rdn wl over 1f out: kpt on u.p ins fnl f: nt rch ldrs* **4/1**1
2230 8 ½ **Andean Margin (IRE)**19 4841 3-8-7 73 (b) JamesPSullivan(7) 7 68
(M W Easterby) *chsd ldr: hdwy 3f out: rdn 2f out and ev ch tl drvn and wknd over 1f out* **12/1**
6166 9 ¾ **West End Lad**11 5126 6-9-3 74 (b) RussellKennemore(3) 10 67
(S R Bowring) *dwlt: a towards rr* **7/1**2
4510 10 ½ **Carmenero (GER)**12 5107 6-9-2 70 TonyHamilton 9 62
(C R Dore) *a in rr* **14/1**
0000 11 ½ **Champain Sands (IRE)**7 5243 10-8-7 61 oh2 GrahamGibbons 13 52
(E J Alston) *dwlt and rr: effrt and sme hdwy over 2f out: sn rdn and nvr a factor* **8/1**3
4001 12 3 **Dig Deep (IRE)**9 5182 7-8-13 72 (t) JamieKyne(5) 5 55
(J J Quinn) *s.i.s: a in rr* **7/1**2
1m 30.9s (-2.90) **Going Correction** -0.375s/f (Firm)
WFA 3 from 4yo+ 5lb **12 Ran SP% 121.7**
Speed ratings (Par 105): **101,97,96,94,94 94,93,92,91,91 90,87**
toteswinger: 1&2 £18.30, 1&3 £5.10, 2&3 £9.20. CSF £103.00 CT £814.91 TOTE £11.20: £3.00, £4.70, £2.30; EX 162.10.
Owner Stef Stefanou **Bred** Gainsborough Farm Llc **Trained** Newmarket, Suffolk
FOCUS
Even though this was a modest collection of handicappers, most seemed in reasonable heart. The pace was sound but a couple of them met trouble in running and are better than their positions suggest. The winner is rated to his best British form with the runner-up setting the level.
Mount Hadley(USA) Official explanation: trainer's rep said, regarding the apparent improvement in form shown, that the Windsor race the gelding raced in last time was a more competitive affair

5419 TOTESPORTCASINO.COM STKS (HERITAGE H'CAP) 1m 1f 207y
3:00 (3:00) (Class 2) (0-105,95) 3-Y-O **£25,904** (£7,708; £3,852; £1,924) **Stalls High**

Form RPR
1014 1 **Eastern Aria (UAE)**7 5262 3-9-7 95 SilvestreDeSousa 7 105
(M Johnston) *hld up in midfield: hdwy over 2f out: rdn to chse ldrs over 1f out: styd on u.p ins fnl f to ld last 100yds* **4/1**1
3114 2 1¼ **Honimiere (IRE)**17 4896 3-8-11 85 PJMcDonald 3 93
(G A Swinbank) *trckd ldrs: smooth hdwy over 2f out: led over 1f out: shkn up ent fnl f: sn rdn: hdd and nt qckn last 100yds* **11/1**
1064 3 1¾ **Eastern Empire**13 5070 3-9-0 88 TomEaves 13 92
(J W Hills) *trckd ldrs: hdwy 3f out: rdn 2f out: swtchd rt ent fnl f and kpt on* **16/1**
-452 4 2½ **Maybeme**32 4401 3-7-12 72 oh4 AndrewMullen 10 71
(N Bycroft) *hld up in rr: hdwy 3f out: rdn along wl over 1f out: kpt on ins fnl f: nrst fin* **33/1**
2220 5 nk **Tepmokea (IRE)**77 2935 3-8-7 81 PaulHanagan 4 79
(R A Fahey) *prom: cl up 3f out: rdn to ld 2f out: drvn and hdd over 1f out: grad wknd* **11/1**
0001 6 1½ **Dubai Crest**20 4827 3-9-0 88 TPQueally 1 83
(Mrs A J Perrett) *in tch: hdwy wl over 2f out: rdn wl over 1f out: drvn and one pce appr fnl f* **14/1**
4-40 7 ¾ **Watergate (IRE)**8 5209 3-8-10 84 SebSanders 6 78
(Sir Mark Prescott) *hld up towards rr: hdwy over 2f out: sn rdn and n.d* **9/1**
23 8 ½ **Mull Of Killough (IRE)**23 4708 3-8-12 91 JamieKyne(5) 9 84
(J L Spearing) *rrd s: hdwy into midfield after 2f: rdn along over 3f out and sn wknd* **4/1**1
-100 9 ½ **Yorgunnabelucky (USA)**11 5137 3-9-2 90 JoeFanning 12 82
(M Johnston) *led 1f: prom tl led again 3f out: rdn and hdd 2f out: sn drvn and wknd* **14/1**
1160 10 ½ **Alpen Glen**30 4455 3-9-3 91 FrancisNorton 8 82
(M Johnston) *a towards rr* **7/1**2
0151 11 3 **Ethics Girl (IRE)**16 4957 3-8-1 75 JimmyQuinn 5 60
(John Berry) *a towards rr* **14/1**
4100 12 8 **Dhushan**51 3778 3-9-4 92 (b1) NCallan 11 61
(M A Jarvis) *dwlt: keen and rapdi hdwy to ld after 1f: rdn along and hdd 3f out: sn wknd* **8/1**3
2m 1.00s (-6.00) **Going Correction** -0.375s/f (Firm) course record **12 Ran SP% 119.1**
Speed ratings (Par 106): **109,108,106,104,104 103,102,102,101,101 98,92**
toteswinger: 1&2 £5.50, 1&3 £9.60, 2&3 £71.40. CSF £49.78 CT £645.04 TOTE £4.60: £1.90, £2.20, £5.30; EX 48.90.
Owner Sheikh Hamdan Bin Mohammed Al Maktoum **Bred** Darley **Trained** Middleham Moor, N Yorks
FOCUS
A lot of mainly in-form horses squared off against each other in this, so the form looks solid and it should be a race worth following.
NOTEBOOK
Eastern Aria(UAE), representing the trainer who took this race last season with Drill Sergeant, bounced back to her very best with another display of tenacity. She kept finding for her in-form rider and wore down the runner-up in the final furlong. The success paid a handsome compliment to Fanjura, who beat her comfortably at Sandown. (op 9-2 tchd 5-1)
Honimiere(IRE) gave the impression she was in the Handicapper´s grip at Hamilton over slightly shorter last time, but cruised to the lead over 2f out here and looked very likely to claim the valuable prize. However, she came up against a hardened battler and was edged out. (tchd 10-1)
Eastern Empire has been in good heart this season and was trying 1m2f for the first time. Settled towards midfield, he lacked room when wanting to get out and is value for slightly better than his beaten distance suggests. (op 14-1)
Maybeme, who finished runner-up to Honimiere when last seen, was going nowhere quickly at halfway but stayed on well past some rivals carrying a lot more weight. (op 40-1)
Tepmokea(IRE), absent since a modest run in June, was having his first run for Richard Fahey and did little wrong without making a big impression. (op 14-1 tchd 16-1)
Watergate(IRE) might be a hard ride, as he got behind before staying on steadily for really strong pressure. (op 10-1)
Mull Of Killough(IRE), who had missed plenty of recent engagements, did not show much after losing ground at the start. Official explanation: jockey said gelding reared leaving the stalls (op 3-1)
Dhushan, taking a big drop in trip and class, had the blinkers on for the first time and ran much too freely. Official explanation: jockey said colt ran too freely (op 9-1 tchd 10-1)

5420 TOTESPORT.COM BEVERLEY BULLET SPRINT STKS (LISTED RACE) 5f
3:35 (3:36) (Class 1) 3-Y-O+ **£23,704** (£8,964; £4,480; £2,240) **Stalls High**

Form RPR
-216 1 **Exceptional Art**65 3298 3-8-12 97 FrancisNorton 13 105+
(D Nicholls) *dwlt and bhd on inner: swtchd lft and around field 1/2-way: str run on outer ent fnl f: rdn and styd on wl to ld nr line* **16/1**
4042 2 hd **Sohraab**27 4559 5-9-0 102 JimmyQuinn 9 104
(H Morrison) *hld up in mid-div: sn rdn to chse ldrs: swtchd lft ent fnl f: led briefly ins fnl 50yds: hdd nr line* **7/1**2
1130 3 nk **Roker Park (IRE)**35 4330 4-9-0 95 (p) NCallan 3 103+
(K A Ryan) *hld up towards rr: hdwy wl over 1f out: rdn and styd on strly ins fnl f* **33/1**
5211 4 ½ **Noble Storm (USA)**9 5203 3-8-12 105 GrahamGibbons 16 101
(E S McMahon) *led: rdn clr appr fnl f: drvn wl ins fnl f: wknd and hdd last 50yds* **9/4**1
00 5 1¾ **Spin Cycle (IRE)**30 4456 3-8-12 104 TomEaves 12 95
(B Smart) *chsd ldrs: hdwy 2f out: rdn over 1f out: kpt on same pce ins fnl f* **7/1**2
4322 6 ½ **Hamish McGonagall**11 5132 4-9-0 100 DavidAllan 4 93
(T D Easterby) *trckd ldrs: hdwy 2f out: sn rdn and no imp ins fnl f* **7/1**2

0350 **7** *1* **Ishetoo**[7] 5257 5-9-0 95....(p) JamieKyne 7 89
(A Dickman) *towards rr: hdwy wl over 1f out: sn rdn and styd on ins fnl f: nrst fin* **25/1**

230 **8** *1 3/4* **City Dancer (IRE)**[13] 5069 3-8-7 95.... PJMcDonald 2 78
(A Berry) *midfield: hdwy on outer 2f out: sn rdn and chsd ldrs tl drvn and one pce appr fnl f* **28/1**

000 **9** *hd* **Fullandby (IRE)**[40] 4135 7-9-0 95....(b[1]) JoeFanning 10 82
(T J Etherington) *hld up: effrt wl over 1f out: sn rdn and nvr nr ldrs* **20/1**

0000 **10** *3/4* **Commander Wish**[13] 5073 6-9-0 57....(p) DNolan 11 80?
(Lucinda Featherstone) *a towards rr* **200/1**

035- **11** *1/2* **Toms Laughter**[336] 6290 5-9-0 97....(b) KevinGhunowa 15 78
(R A Harris) *dwlt: sn chsng ldrs on inner: hdwy to chse ldr over 1f out: sn drvn andwknd ins fnl f* **20/1**

3044 **12** *2* **Masta Plasta (IRE)**[18] 4885 6-9-0 105.... AdrianTNicholls 14 71
(D Nicholls) *chsd ldr: rdn along wl over 1f out: drvn and wknd appr fnl f* **15/2**[3]

3036 **13** *2 1/4* **Invincible Lad (IRE)**[7] 5247 5-9-0 84.... PaulMulrennan 5 63
(E J Alston) *sed awkwardly: a in rr* **50/1**

1000 **14** *6* **Peak District (IRE)**[11] 5132 5-9-0 92.... PaulHanagan 6 41
(K A Ryan) *prom on outer: rdn 2f out: sn wknd* **50/1**

0201 **15** *3/4* **Group Therapy**[21] 4766 4-9-0 103.... JohnEgan 8 38
(N P Littmoden) *prom: rdn along over 2f out and sn wknd* **9/1**

62.39 secs (-1.11) **Going Correction** +0.10s/f (Good)
WFA 3 from 4yo+ 2lb **15** Ran SP% **120.1**
Speed ratings (Par 111): **112,111,111,110,107 106,105,102,102,100 100,96,93,83,82**
toteswinger: 1&2 £36.90, 1&3 £53.10, 2&3 £37.90. CSF £113.04 TOTE £20.60: £5.00, £2.80, £7.90; EX 189.70 Trifecta £8758.40 Pool: £17,753.69 - 1.50 winning units..
Owner Middleham Park Racing XXVII **Bred** Mascalls Stud **Trained** Sessay, N Yorks
■ Stewards' Enquiry : Jimmy Quinn caution: used whip without giving time to respond

FOCUS

A really competitive sprint for this Listed prize, missing only stall 1 entrant Hoh Hoh Hoh, who was reported to have bruised a foot. The leaders went off hard, so it was no surprise to see the finishers get on top at the end. The runenr-up is the best guide to the level.

NOTEBOOK

Exceptional Art ◆, disappointing on the all-weather last time over a mile for Peter Chapple-Hyam, was something new altogether and his chance of victory looked close to zero as he sat almost last about two furlongs from home. However, once the acceleration kicked in, he finished fast and looked impressive. The Ayr Gold Cup is the target. (tchd 20-1)
Sohraab was not beaten far by Nunthorpe winner Borderlescott two starts previously at Chester, and weaved his way into this race up the inside rail. It always looked as if he would pick up the leader, but he had no answer to the winner as he swept to the front. (op 8-1 tchd 13-2)
Roker Park(IRE) deserved a crack at this level and was another to finish like a bullet after looking held. The fact that he started from stall three makes his run even more commendable. (op 22-1)
Noble Storm(USA) ◆ ran another impressive race despite losing places at the end. His early pace is exceptional and on a less demanding track he can win again. When everything falls right for him, he can take a Group 3 at least. (tchd 11-4)
Spin Cycle(IRE) has done most of his racing at Group level, so this obviously looked an easier assignment. He battled his way to have every chance but lacked a gear change. (tchd 6-1 and 15-2)
Hamish McGonagall must be one of the most consistent handicappers around and he can easily be given another chance after coming from a moderate stalls position. (op 9-1)
Ishetoo, wearing cheekpieces for the first time, was staying on when brought to a halt inside the final furlong. He was close to Roker Park at the time, so may have challenged for a first three position with an uninterrupted passage. (op 28-1)
Masta Plasta(IRE) seemed to have quite a lot in his favour but was on his toes beforehand and ran a lacklustre race. (op 7-1 tchd 13-2)
Invincible Lad(IRE) had loads of problems during the race and this effort can be ignored.
Group Therapy Official explanation: jockey said gelding had no more to give

5421 TOTESPORTGAMES.COM H'CAP 5f
4:10 (4:11) (Class 5) (0-75,74) 3-Y-0+ £2,849 (£847; £423; £211) Stalls High

Form RPR

0105 **1** **Select Committee**[3] 5341 4-8-10 61....(v) NCallan 13 72
(J J Quinn) *trckd ldng pair: hdwy over 1f out: qcknd to ld ins fnl f: rdn out* **13/2**[3]

0050 **2** *2 3/4* **Avertuoso**[10] 5148 5-8-7 65.... AdamCarter[(7)] 1 66
(B Smart) *s.i.s: swtchd lft and gd hdwy on outer over 1f out: str run ent fnl f: hung rt and kpt on ins fnl f* **40/1**

0040 **3** *shd* **Lord Of The Reins (IRE)**[24] 4662 5-9-0 65.... TPQueally 15 66+
(J G Given) *trckd ldrs: hdwy and swtchd rt to inner wl over 1f out: effrt and nt clr run ent fnl f: swtchd lft and rdn: kpt on* **16/1**

1446 **4** *shd* **Sir Nod**[24] 4662 7-9-7 72.... PaulHanagan 16 73
(Miss J A Camacho) *led: rdn over 1f out: drvn and hdd ins fnl f: one pce* **5/1**[2]

0431 **5** *nk* **Littlemisssunshine (IRE)**[9] 5184 4-9-3 68....(p) LukeMorris 6 68
(J S Moore) *hdwy 2f out: rdn to chse ldrs and hung lft over 1f out: drvn and kpt on same pce ins fnl f* **9/1**

1330 **6** *3 1/4* **Pickering**[60] 3488 5-9-5 70....(p) DavidAllan 5 58
(E J Alston) *stmbld s: towards rr: hdwy 2f out: sn rdn and kpt on same pce appr fnl f* **12/1**

6113 **7** *nk* **Swinbrook (USA)**[13] 5065 8-9-2 74....(v) SPRyan[(7)] 17 61+
(R A Harris) *in tch on inner: effrt whn hmpd wl over 1f out: sn rdn and kpt on ins fnl f* **13/2**[3]

551 **8** *2* **Speedy Senorita (IRE)**[16] 4929 4-9-0 72.... IJBrennan[(7)] 14 52
(J J Quinn) *cl up: rdn along 2f out: drvn and wknd over 1f out* **9/2**[1]

-000 **9** *1* **Not My Choice (IRE)**[91] 2472 4-9-2 67.... PJMcDonald 12 43
(J Balding) *chsd ldrs: effrt and cl up 1/2-way: sn rdn and wknd over 1f out* **25/1**

6001 **10** *1/2* **Tagula Breeze (IRE)**[1] 5411 3-9-2 69.... DanielTudhope 11 43+
(I W McInnes) *hld up: hdwy and nt clr run wl over 1f out: swtchd rt and rdn whn nt clr run and hmpd 1f out: nt rcvr* **7/1**

4351 **11** *3 3/4* **Silvanus (IRE)**[15] 4976 4-9-0 65.... PaulMulrennan 8 26
(P T Midgley) *prom on outer: rdn along 2f out and sn wknd* **16/1**

0010 **12** *hd* **Prince Namid**[32] 4399 7-9-5 70.... AdrianTNicholls 9 30
(D Nicholls) *cl up: rdn along and wknd qckly 1/2-way* **9/1**

63.58 secs (0.08) **Going Correction** +0.10s/f (Good)
WFA 3 from 4yo+ 2lb **12** Ran SP% **119.8**
Speed ratings (Par 103): **103,98,98,98,97 92,92,88,87,86 80,80**
toteswinger: 1&2 £37.20, 1&3 £14.30, 2&3 £47.90. CSF £236.07 CT £4008.47 TOTE £8.60: £2.80, £9.30, £5.10; EX 202.50.
Owner Which Bits Mine Syndicate **Bred** Llety Stud **Trained** Settrington, N Yorks
■ Stewards' Enquiry : T P Queally three-day ban: careless riding (Sep 13-15)

FOCUS

Not as classy as the preceding race over this trip, as the winning time showed, but what looked a highly competitive sprint was claimed in emphatic style. The form looks messy with the placed horses having struggled prior to this.
Tagula Breeze(IRE) Official explanation: jockey said gelding was denied a clear run
Prince Namid Official explanation: jockey said gelding hung left

5422 TOTESPORTBINGO.COM MAIDEN STKS 5f
4:45 (4:45) (Class 5) 3-Y-0+ £2,752 (£818; £409; £204) Stalls High

Form RPR

522 **1** **Present Alchemy**[21] 4786 3-9-3 74.... JimmyQuinn 1 89+
(H Morrison) *cl up: led over 3f out: qcknd clr wl over 1f out: unchal* **8/13**[1]

2450 **2** *9* **Rainy Night**[11] 5130 3-9-3 64.... GrahamGibbons 3 57
(R Hollinshead) *chsd ldrs: hdwy 2f out: rdn to chse wnr over 1f out: kpt on: no ch w wnr* **7/1**[3]

3 *3* **Castlecarra (IRE)** 4-8-12 0.... JamesPSullivan[(7)] 8 46+
(J Hetherton) *hld up on inner: swtchd wd and hdwy wl over 1f out: sn rdn and styd on ins fnl f: nrst fin* **40/1**

0403 **4** *1* **Rightcar Lewis**[10] 5159 4-9-0 45....(b) JamieMackay 2 38
(Peter Grayson) *chsd ldrs: rdn along 2f out: sn drvn and one pce* **33/1**

0442 **5** *1* **Gee Gina**[15] 4999 3-8-7 51.... PaulPickard[(5)] 5 34
(P T Midgley) *sn pushed along towards rr: hdwy to chse ldrs 1/2-way: sn rdn and wknd wl over 1f out* **15/2**

0505 **6** *nk* **Port Ronan (USA)**[26] 4594 3-9-3 46....(v[1]) TonyHamilton 7 38
(J S Wainwright) *s.i.s: a towards rr* **25/1**

2326 **7** *3 1/2* **Sea Crest**[2] 5373 3-8-5 60.... JohnCavanagh[(7)] 4 20
(M Brittain) *cl up: rdn along over 2f out: sn drvn and wknd* **13/2**[2]

0 **8** *3/4* **Romantic Bond**[36] 4277 3-8-12 0....(b[1]) DNolan 6 18
(T D Easterby) *chsd ldrs: rdn along 1/2-way: sn wknd* **20/1**

0546 **9** *2* **Tarus (IRE)**[3] 5338 5-8-7 48....(t) BillyCray[(7)] 9 10
(A Berry) *led: rdn along 1/2-way: sn wknd* **25/1**

62.53 secs (-0.97) **Going Correction** +0.10s/f (Good)
WFA 3 from 4yo+ 2lb **9** Ran SP% **117.4**
Speed ratings (Par 103): **111,96,91,90,88 88,82,81,78**
toteswinger: 1&2 £2.80, 1&3 £8.10, 2&3 £23.30. CSF £4.99 TOTE £1.50: £1.10, £2.00, £7.40; EX 5.60.
Owner Normandie Stud Ltd **Bred** Normandie Stud Ltd **Trained** East Ilsley, Berks
■ Stewards' Enquiry : John Cavanagh caution: careless riding

FOCUS

A really moderate maiden that the favourite could hardly have failed to win. He was impressive though and the time was very good, fractionally slower than the feature race and he could go on from this.

5423 SSANGYONG IT WORKS FOR ME "HANDS AND HEELS" APPRENTICE H'CAP 1m 1f 207y
5:15 (5:16) (Class 6) (0-65,65) 4-Y-0+ £2,266 (£674; £337; £168) Stalls High

Form RPR

P415 **1** **Patavium (IRE)**[21] 4806 6-8-4 **50**.... AdamCarter[(3)] 2 66
(E W Tuer) *chsd ldr: hdwy to ld 3f out: rdn clr 2f out: styd on strly* **11/1**

5200 **2** *6* **Astronomical (IRE)**[24] 4658 7-9-5 **62**.... DavidKenny 7 66
(R Hollinshead) *hld up in midfield: hdwy to chse ldrs over 4f out: rdn over 2f out: drvn to chse wnr over 1f out and sn no imp* **16/1**

0611 **3** *1* **Miss Ferney**[16] 4944 5-8-12 **55**.... PaulPickard 5 57
(A Kirtley) *hld up in rr: hdwy on outer over 3f out: rdn to chse ldrs 2f out: kpt on samepce appr fnl f* **7/2**[1]

4352 **4** *3 1/2* **Ancient Cross**[17] 4887 5-9-8 **65**....(t) JamesPSullivan 3 60+
(M W Easterby) *stdd s and hld up in rr: hdwy over 3f out: swtchd ins and rdn to chseldrs over 1f out: sn no imp* **7/2**[1]

0322 **5** *1 3/4* **Tivers Song (USA)**[16] 4944 5-8-4 **47**....(v[1]) TobyAtkinson 1 39
(John A Harris) *hld up towards rr: hdwy over 3f out: sn rdn and plugged on fnl 2f: nvr a factor* **9/2**[2]

2046 **6** *5* **Grey Command (USA)**[64] 3350 4-9-2 **59**.... JohnCavanagh 13 41
(M Brittain) *led: rdn along and hdd 3f out: grad wknd fnl 2f* **11/1**

-002 **7** *3 1/4* **Kool Katie**[8] 5205 4-9-3 **60**.... NSLawes 8 35
(Mrs G S Rees) *trckd ldng pair: effrt 3f out: sn rdn along and wknd 2f out* **10/1**[3]

0500 **8** *4* **Super King**[31] 4434 8-8-3 **46** oh1.... AndrewHeffernan 14 13
(A D Brown) *chsd ldrs on inner: rdn along 3f out: sn wknd* **66/1**

0000 **9** *3 1/2* **Mesbaah (IRE)**[16] 4941 5-9-3 **63**.... FrazerWilliams[(3)] 9 23
(R A Fahey) *wandered and lost pl after 4f: bhd after* **10/1**[3]

6506 **10** *3* **Grethel (IRE)**[6] 5294 5-8-3 **46** oh1.... MatthewLawson 4 —
(A Berry) *chsd ldrs tl rdn over 3f out and sn wknd* **20/1**

004 **11** *3/4* **Blastie**[21] 4805 4-8-5 **51**.... LeeTopliss[(3)] 12 4
(T D Walford) *a towards rr: bhd fnl 3f* **16/1**

0034 **12** *2 1/4* **Mccormack (IRE)**[59] 3499 7-8-0 **46** oh1.... RyanClark[(3)] 6 —
(Miss T Jackson) *a towards rr* **16/1**

0000 **13** *3/4* **Boy Dancer (IRE)**[6] 5294 6-8-10 **53**.... IJBrennan 11 —
(J J Quinn) *a in rr* **11/1**

2m 2.86s (-4.14) **Going Correction** -0.375s/f (Firm) **13** Ran SP% **129.7**
Speed ratings (Par 101): **101,96,95,92,91 87,84,81,78,76 75,73,73**
toteswinger: 1&2 £11.60, 1&3 £37.00, 2&3 £10.50. CSF £189.92 CT £762.16 TOTE £18.10: £4.40, £7.10, £2.10; EX 378.20 Place 6: £797.79, Place 5: £488.69..
Owner J A Nixon **Bred** M Channon **Trained** Great Smeaton, N Yorks

FOCUS

A moderate race full of talented, but mainly northern-based apprentices. The gallop looked good but the form is somewhat fluid, with the third the best guide.
T/Plt: £772.70 to a £1 stake. Pool: £56,974.53. 53.82 winning tickets. T/Qpdt: £72.30 to a £1 stake. Pool: £3,337.40. 34.15 winning tickets. JR

4520 GOODWOOD (R-H)
Saturday, August 29

OFFICIAL GOING: Good (good to firm in places on the round course; 8.3)
Wind: Moderate across Weather: Cloudy

5424 TOTESCOOP6 STKS (H'CAP) 6f
2:05 (2:06) (Class 3) (0-95,93) 3-Y-0+ £7,771 (£2,312; £1,155; £577) Stalls Low

Form RPR

6022 **1** **Golden Desert (IRE)**[14] 5025 5-9-10 **92**.... RyanMoore 13 109
(T G Mills) *racd centre: in tch: hdwy 2f out: styd on to ld 1f out: sn clr: readily* **4/1**[1]

0/05 **2** *3 1/4* **Hamoody (USA)**[36] 4273 5-9-6 **88**.... MartinDwyer 9 95
(P W Chapple-Hyam) *racd centre: rr tl hdwy fr 2f out: styd on to chse wnr ins fnl f but nvr any ch* **14/1**

0300 **3** *1 1/2* **Proclaim**[14] 5032 3-9-8 **93**....(v[1]) J-PGuillambert 15 95
(M Johnston) *racd centre and chse ldrs: rdn 3f out: styd on same pce fr over 1f out* **12/1**

2614 **4** *3/4* **Aye Aye Digby (IRE)**[21] 4784 4-9-10 **92**.... DaneO'Neill 8 92
(H Candy) *racd centre: rr tl hdwy fr 2f out: styd on fnl f but nvr gng pce to get into contention* **6/1**[2]

0000 **5** *1 1/4* **Pearly Wey**[14] 5039 6-9-8 **90**.................................. AdamKirby 7 86
(C G Cox) *s.i.s: racd centre: swtchd lft ins fnl 2f and r.o fnl f but nvr in contention* **10/1**[3]

3000 **6** *hd* **Mujood**[16] 4954 6-9-3 **85**..............................(b) WilliamBuick 14 80
(Eve Johnson Houghton) *tracd centre: mid-div: rdn over 3f out: styd on ins fnl f but nvr a threat* **18/1**

0005 **7** *3/4* **Osiris Way**[19] 4853 7-9-6 **88**.................................. JimCrowley 11 81
(P R Chamings) *chsd ldrs in centre of crse: rdn over 2f out: one pce fnl f* **12/1**

2020 **8** *3 1/2* **Servoca (CAN)**[30] 4459 3-9-4 **89**..............................(t) RobertWinston 6 71
(B W Hills) *racd stands' side and led that gp 1/2-way but nvr on terms w centre field gp and one pce u.p fnl 2f: 1st in gp* **25/1**

-123 **9** *nse* **Rash Judgement**[91] 2474 4-9-5 **87**.............................. FergusSweeney 2 68
(W S Kittow) *racd stands' side and chsd ldrs that side fr 1/2-way but nvr in contention w centre field gp: fin 2nd in gp* **6/1**[2]

4606 **10** *nk* **Peter Island (FR)**[19] 4853 6-8-12 **80**..............................(v) TPO'Shea 16 60
(J Gallagher) *led over all in centre gp and clr over 3f out: wknd qckly and hdd 1f out* **16/1**

0135 **11** *hd* **Desperate Dan**[17] 4891 8-8-8 **79** ow2..............................(v) JackMitchell(3) 4 59
(A B Haynes) *racd stands side gp tl hung bdly rt to centre field gp and bhd fr over 2f out* **33/1**

0-00 **12** *1* **Kostar**[14] 5039 8-9-10 **92**..............................(p) DavidProbert 1 69
(C G Cox) *racd stands' side gp and marginal ldr that gp to 1/2-way but nver on terms w centre field gp: sn wknd: fin 3rd in gp* **33/1**

0000 **13** *2 1/4* **Silver Guest**[14] 5025 4-8-11 **79**.............................. TonyCulhane 12 48
(M R Channon) *slowly inyo stride: racd centre gp: sme hdwy 2f out: sn wknd* **50/1**

0440 **14** *hd* **Vhujon (IRE)**[7] 5257 4-9-3 **85**.............................. EddieAhern 3 54
(P D Evans) *racd stands' side and chsd ldrs that gp over 3f: fin 4th in gp* **14/1**

0210 **15** *nk* **Esteem Machine (USA)**[19] 4853 5-9-4 **86**.............................. LDettori 10 54
(R A Teal) *s.i.s: racd centre gp and outpcd most of way* **14/1**

1110 **16** *1/2* **C'Mon You Irons (IRE)**[34] 4353 4-8-10 **78**.............................. IanMongan 5 44
(M R Hoad) *racd stands' side and disputed ldr that gp to 1/2-way: nvr on terms w centre gp and sn wknd fin 5th in gp* **14/1**

1m 11.42s (-0.78) **Going Correction** +0.05s/f (Good)
WFA 3 from 4yo+ 3lb **16** Ran SP% **122.5**
Speed ratings (Par 107): **107,102,100,99,98 97,96,92,92,91 91,90,87,86,86 85**
toteswinger: 1&2 £12.90, 1&3 £15.10, 2&3 £57.90. CSF £59.67 CT £636.55 TOTE £5.00: £1.60, £3.90, £3.20, £2.30; EX 75.60 Trifecta £675.60 Pool: £913.00 - 1.00 winning units..
Owner S Parker **Bred** Mervyn Stewkesbury **Trained** Headley, Surrey

FOCUS
This competitive sprint has often been won by an improving or in-form sort, although mature, battle-hardened types have a good record. In the last six seasons a single-figure draw has proved beneficial but on this occasion they split into two groups and those racing up the centre, led by the trailblazer Peter Island, dominated. The winner was impressive and could rate higher at this trip, while the third is the best guide to the level.

NOTEBOOK
Golden Desert(IRE) ◆ has been running well over 7f this season but had not run over this trip for over a year. However, the strong early pace worked in his favour, as he was able to power to the front over a furlong out and score in quite taking style. He could well follow up and connections are sure to be considering one of the big late-season sprints after this. (op 5-1 tchd 11-2)
Hamoody(USA) ◆ had won the Group 2 Richmond Stakes over course and distance as a juvenile but raced in the USA in 2007 and 2008. He was dropped to a fair-looking mark - being 6lb better off with Aye Aye Digby for less than three lengths compared with last month's Newmarket form - and staged something of a revival, coming out of the pack to chase home the winner. On this evidence he can pick up a similar handicap before the season is out. (op 11-1)
Proclaim, a three-time winner at this trip in 2009, had been held in recent starts but, 1lb below his last winning mark, had the first-time visor replacing the blinkers he had worn on recent outings. He ran quite well from his wide stall without threatening to score. (op 14-1)
Aye Aye Digby(IRE) had found some decent form dropped to this trip this year and was a course and distance winner. Racing from 4lb above his last winning mark, he stayed on when the race was all but over and would probably have preferred more ease in the ground. (op 13-2 tchd 7-1)
Pearly Wey, whose last two wins had been over course and distance and had dropped 4lb after being well held this season, raced in rear and was under pressure at halfway. He was another to keep on well in the closing stages. (op 9-1)
Mujood, who has a good record on this track but whose most recent runs have been over 7f and 1m, never got involved although he did keep on, as would have been expected from a gelding who stays further. (tchd 20-1)
Osiris Way beat Mujood in this race last season but was 6lb worse off. He ran a fair race but might prefer more cut.
Servoca(CAN) did best of those racing up the stands' side, but they had no chance with the main group in the centre.
Rash Judgement was easy to back on this return from 13 weeks off. He was also drawn low, and should do better with this run under his belt. (op 8-1)
Peter Island(FR) showed tremendous pace up the centre to race clear of the field until approaching the furlong marker.
Esteem Machine(USA) Official explanation: jockey said gelding lost its action

5425 WINDFLOWER MARCH STKS (LISTED RACE) 1m 6f
2:35 (2:36) (Class 1) 3-Y-O+

£22,708 (£8,608; £4,308; £2,148; £1,076; £540) **Stalls** Low

Form RPR

2024 **1** **Mourilyan (IRE)**[14] 5023 5-9-7 **112**.................................. RyanMoore 7 110+
(G L Moore) *hld up in rr: stdy hdwy 3f out: nt clr run and swtchd rt to ins over 1f out: qcknd to ld fnl 110yds: readily* **4/1**[3]

1223 **2** *3* **Victoria Montoya**[30] 4458 4-9-2 **93**.................................. WilliamBuick 6 101
(A M Balding) *trckd ldrs: led 4f out: rdn whn chal fr 3f out and hld on gamely u.p: tl hdd and outpcd fnl 110yds* **10/1**

1-01 **3** *1* **Oasis Knight (IRE)**[15] 4988 3-8-7 **90**..............................(v) MartinDwyer 5 103
(M P Tregoning) *in rr: rdn 7f out: rdn again and dropped further bhd 5f out: rdn: hdwy and hung rt fr 3f out: hung rt again to far rail and styd on over 1f out: kpt on ins fnl f to take 3rd but no imp on ldng duo* **14/1**

1316 **4** *1 1/4* **Classic Vintage (USA)**[8] 5230 3-8-7 **97**.................................. JimCrowley 8 101
(Mrs A J Perrett) *in tch: hdwy to trck ldrs 5f out: drvn to chal fr 3 out and stl upsides ins fnl 2f: no ex 1f out and fdd ins fnl f and lost 3rd* **8/1**

1211 **5** *1 3/4* **King Of Wands**[37] 4248 3-8-7 **100**.................................. EddieAhern 4 98+
(J L Dunlop) *chsd ldrs: qcknd to chal over 2f out: wknd appr fnl f* **9/4**[2]

13 **6** *24* **Urban Poet (USA)**[32] 4405 3-8-7 **108**.................................. LDettori 2 65
(Saeed Bin Suroor) *chsd ldr 6f: styd prom: rdn to go 2nd 4f out: nvr rcher ldr and wknd ins fnl 3f: t.o* **7/4**[1]

0125 **7** *29* **Star Of Pompey**[35] 4301 5-9-2 **56**.................................. JackMitchell 3 21
(A B Haynes) *sn led: hdd 4f out: wknd qckly 3f out: t.o* **150/1**

3m 0.71s (-2.89) **Going Correction** +0.05s/f (Good)
WFA 3 from 4yo+ 12lb **7** Ran SP% **114.7**
Speed ratings (Par 111): **110,108,107,107,106 92,75**
toteswinger: 1&2 £4.50, 1&3 £6.00, 2&3 £8.50. CSF £42.10 TOTE £5.40: £2.50, £3.40; EX 36.50 Trifecta £283.00 Pool: £420.82 - 1.10 winning units..
Owner Ramzan Kadyrov **Bred** His Highness The Aga Khan's Studs S C **Trained** Lower Beeding, W Sussex

FOCUS
This race used to be a St Leger trial but, since being opened up to older horses, it has more often than not fallen to those aged four and above, including a couple of dual winners. Two stood out on official ratings, and one of those ran out an easy winner. He did not have to run up to his Goodwood Cup form and the runner-up is probably the best guide to the level.

NOTEBOOK
Mourilyan(IRE), a winner at middle distances in Ireland and Dubai, had put up decent efforts in the Goodwood Cup and Geoffrey Freer in his last two starts, so the trip and ground did not present a problem. He had the highest official rating but had not looked the most straightforward at times, and was fitted with a sheepskin noseband for the first time. Moore took his time before getting involved and kept his mount covered up until switching to the inside rail entering the final furlong, when he soon put the issue beyond doubt. This should help his confidence and races such as the Doncaster and Jockey Club Cups could feature on his schedule, although he is likely to be returning to Dubai in the winter. (op 7-2 tchd 100-30)
Victoria Montoya is a decent filly who had gained all her wins at this trip (including over course and distance). She had been Listed and Group 3-placed on her last two starts but had a lot to find on official ratings with the winner in particular. She went on crossing the intersection and fought off the challengers on her outside, but she does not have much in the way of gears and she could not respond to the winner's late surge. This was still a fine effort and she could go for the Park Hill. Connections might consider having her covered and racing her in the early part of next season. (op 11-1)
Oasis Knight(IRE), a half-brother to High Accolade, whose finest hour was arguably on this track, had handled the step up to 1m5f and first-time visor when scoring on his previous start. He had a lot to find on the ratings here and looked hard work, but he stayed on from off the pace to take the minor placing and could make up into a decent stayer next season. (op 16-1 tchd 12-1)
Classic Vintage(USA), a decent handicapper who is effective at 1m4f, had been beaten when upped to this trip last time and again gave the impression he did not last home, having been travelling well upsides the runner-up two furlongs out.
King Of Wands, who was two wins from three starts over this trip, had gone up a stone in the handicap for his latest win and so was almost forced into trying Listed company. He was travelling well early in the straight but found disappointingly little. (op 11-4 tchd 3-1)
Urban Poet(USA) was the real disappointment of the race. A runaway winner over 1m3f on his debut, he had finished a decent third in the Group 3 Gordon Stakes here. He was stepping up in trip on his first start for Godolphin, but Dettori was hard at work soon after his mount ran a little wide on the top bend and the response was minimal. This possibly is not his track, and it's worth bearing in mind the Gordon Stakes form is not working out, but this was a tame effort from a colt connections were making few excuses for. He is another who will winter in Dubai, where he is likely to step up to 2m. Official explanation: jockey was unable to offer any explanation for the poor performance shown (op 15-8 tchd 9-4)

5426 TOTESPORT.COM CELEBRATION MILE (GROUP 2) 1m
3:10 (3:10) (Class 1) 3-Y-O+

£67,442 (£25,565; £12,794; £6,379; £3,195; £1,603) **Stalls** High

Form RPR

1202 **D** **Delegator**[74] 2992 3-8-9 **121**.................................. LDettori 5 119+
(Saeed Bin Suroor) *trckd ldrs travelling comf: shkn up and qcknd over 1f out to ld fnl 110yds: sn in command: fin 1st, 1½l: subs disq.* **4/6**[1]

12-1 **1** *1 1/2* **Zacinto**[28] 4521 3-8-9 **107**.................................. RyanMoore 2 116+
(Sir Michael Stoute) *plld hrd: trckd ldr: drvn and qcknd ins fnl 2f and chal over 1f out: slt ld ins fnl f: hdd and outpcd fnl 110yds: fin 2nd: awrdd r* **5/2**[2]

6406 **2** *hd* **Ordnance Row**[7] 5249 6-9-1 **107**.................................. DaneO'Neill 4 116
(R Hannon) *led at modest pce tl grad qcknd fr 3f out: rdn 2f out: hdd jst ins fnl f: kpt on wl to dispute 2nd fnl 110yds but nvr any ch w wnr* **33/1**

1216 **3** *1/2* **Beacon Lodge (IRE)**[31] 4419 4-9-1 **113**.................................. AdamKirby 6 115+
(C G Cox) *s.i.s: hld up in rr tl tk hold of bit and awkward 3f out: swtchd lft to outside 2f out and gd hdwy appr fnl f: fin wl but nvr any ch w wnr* **16/1**

4101 **4** *1/2* **Mac Love**[16] 4949 8-9-1 **117**.................................. MickyFenton 1 114
(Stef Liddiard) *t.k.h towards rr: stl pulling 3f out: rdn and hdwy on outside over 1f out: styd on ins fnl f but nvr any ch w wnr* **14/1**[3]

-253 **5** *1* **Cesare**[28] 4543 8-9-1 **118**.................................. EddieAhern 3 111
(J R Fanshawe) *chsd ldrs: rdn 2f out: outpcd fnl f* **16/1**

0050 **6** *4 1/2* **Smokey Oakey (IRE)**[35] 4329 5-9-1 **104**.................................. RobertWinston 7 101
(M H Tompkins) *t.k.h in rr: rdn 2f out and nvr gng pce to improve position* **66/1**

1m 41.54s (1.64) **Going Correction** +0.05s/f (Good)
WFA 3 from 4yo+ 6lb **7** Ran SP% **111.4**
Speed ratings (Par 115): **93,91,91,90,90 89,84**
toteswinger: 1&2 £1.20, 1&3 £7.30, 2&3 £9.70. CSF £2.31 TOTE £1.70: £1.30, £1.70; EX 2.50.
Owner Godolphin **Bred** Mrs P Good **Trained** Newmarket, Suffolk

FOCUS
This race often falls to a genuine Group 2 performer but has thrown up several top-notchers, including last year's winner Raven's Pass and Medicean, and the last three winners went on to score at the top level. The pace was very steady and the race developed into a two-furlong sprint and the form is best rated through the third, with the winner not needing to run to his Group 1 marks. He subs. tested positive for methylprednisolone, was disq. and his trainer fined £750

NOTEBOOK
Delegator ◆ had by far the best form, having been runner-up in the St James's Palace and 2000 Guineas, and acts on fast ground. Having his first run for Godolphin, he was tucked in behind the leader and looked as though he might have trouble getting a run halfway up the straight. However, when the leaders quickened, Dettori judged his switch to the outside perfectly and, once in the clear, his mount found plenty of speed to sweep past the leaders and score cosily. The Queen Elizabeth II Stakes is on the agenda next followed by the Breeders' Cup Mile. (op 8-11 tchd 4-5)
Zacinto ◆, whose trainer had won five of the previous nine runnings, is lightly raced, having had his problems, but was runner-up in the Champagne Stakes last season. A winner of a Listed race over course and distance this month, and supplemented for £10,000 here, he had a lot to do on official ratings with the winner. Nevertheless, he ran a fine race considering he was quite free and saw plenty of daylight early, and although no match for his market rival, he held off the remainder. He should be able to pick up a Group race before too long. (tchd 11-4 and 3-1 in a place)
Ordnance Row, in the colours of the winner's former owner, has won his share at Listed and Group 3 level but is suited by cut in the ground. He dictated the pace, however, and his rider tried to turn it into a sprint. The tactics nearly worked and his mount gave everything, only going down narrowly in the race for second. The partnership deserves full marks. (op 40-1)
Beacon Lodge(IRE) has been progressive this season at 7f and 1m but finished last in the Sussex Stakes. His best form has been with cut in the ground and, although he ran on late, being held up off a moderate gallop did not play to his strengths.
Mac Love has been in good form this season and acts on this track. However, he was up in grade, having gained both his wins this season at Group 3 level, and he was another who would not have been suited by the steady gallop, as he is best coming late off a sound pace. (tchd 12-1)

Cesare is best at Ascot but had run well here before, although he has looked to be going backwards this season. He was ridden more prominently than usual and could not pick up sufficiently when the sprint to the line began. (op 14-1)
Smokey Oakey(IRE), a Group 3 winner in 2008 who stays 1m2f, would not have been suited by either the fast surface or the lack of a true gallop. (tchd 50-1)

5427 BERRY BROTHERS AND RUDD PRESTIGE STKS (GROUP 3) 7f
3:45 (3:45) (Class 1) 2-Y-O
£28,385 (£10,760; £5,385; £2,685; £1,345; £675) Stalls High

Form RPR
13 1 **Sent From Heaven (IRE)**[21] 4795 2-9-0 0 .... RobertWinston 3 103
(B W Hills) *t.k.h: led: rdn ins fnl 2f: styd on fnl f and briefly flashed tail: jst hld on* **4/1**[2]
101 2 nse **Mudaaraah**[37] 4245 2-9-0 97 .... TPO'Shea 9 103+
(J L Dunlop) *in tch: hdwy and n.m.r 2f out: styd on and hung rt over 1f out: str run ins fnl f: squeezed between horses cl home: jst failed* **4/1**[2]
3124 3 shd **Snow Fairy (IRE)**[21] 4795 2-9-0 96 .... EddieAhern 7 103
(E A L Dunlop) *wnt lft s: t.k.h early towards rr: hdwy on outside fr 2f out: str run ins fnl f and fin strly: nt quite get up* **6/1**[3]
120 4 hd **Blue Angel (IRE)**[21] 4795 2-9-0 90 .... DaneO'Neill 6 102
(R Hannon) *bmpd s: chsd wnr 2f and again whn rdn over 2f out: styd on wl thrght fnl f to press for ld cl home but a jst hld* **33/1**
321 5 7 **Bella Swan**[50] 3820 2-9-0 84 .... AdamKirby 8 87+
(W R Swinburn) *stmbld bdly s and nrly uns rdr who qckly rcvrd: rr and t.k.h: hdwy on ins to chse ldrs over 2f out: sn no imp and wkng whn n.m.r over 1f out* **11/1**
221 6 2 **Water Biscuit**[30] 4460 2-9-0 80 .... MartinDwyer 2 80
(B J Meehan) *t.k.h early: rdn 3f out and a in rr* **14/1**
412 7 8 **Full Mandate (IRE)**[35] 4295 2-9-0 103 .... RyanMoore 4 60
(R Hannon) *chsd ldrs: rdn 3f out: btn over 2f out* **4/1**[2]
1 8 shd **Siyaadah**[20] 4817 2-9-0 0 .... LDettori 5 59
(Saeed Bin Suroor) *bmpd s: chsd wnr 5f out: rdn over 2f out: sn wknd* **3/1**[1]

1m 27.45s (0.05) **Going Correction** +0.05s/f (Good) **8 Ran SP% 117.2**
Speed ratings (Par 104): **101,100,100,100,92 90,81,81**
toteswinger: 1&2 £7.00, 1&3 £5.30, 2&3 £7.60. CSF £20.99 TOTE £5.10: £1.80, £2.10, £1.90; EX 17.70 Trifecta £24.50 Pool: £750.86 - 22.64 winning units..
Owner Triermore Stud **Bred** C O P Hanbury **Trained** Lambourn, Berks

FOCUS
This Group 3 has thrown up a couple of top-class fillies in recent seasons, Gossamer and Nannina, who both scored at Group 1 level at two and three, but the race has also produced its share of disappointments. Brian Meehan and Barry Hills were the only trainers represented to have been successful in this in the preceding ten years and the latter was responsible for the winner in what proved a desperate finish. With the first four closely matchd this does not appeal as a strong contest.

NOTEBOOK
Sent From Heaven(IRE), a winner on Polytrack over 7f on her debut, had finished third in a Group 3 last time, form which offered her a fair chance. She was given a very positive ride, set off at a good gallop and looked likely to score more decisively entering the final furlong. However, her stride began to shorten and her tail flashed under pressure but she did enough to stay in front. Her rider thinks she will be better next season and that the track might not have totally suited, but a quote of 33-1 for the 1000 Guineas looks about right at this stage. (op 7-2)
Mudaaraah ♦, a winner over 6f and 7f on fast ground, was up in grade and after being held up, really found her stride inside the final furlong and would have got there in another stride or two. She looks open to further improvement and is also 33-1 for the Guineas. (op 5-1 tchd 11-2)
Snow Fairy(IRE), a 6f winner on Polytrack, had finished runner-up in a nursery under top weight before finishing fourth, three-quarters of a length behind this winner, in a Group 3 at Newmarket. She put up another fine effort, finishing well down the outside and only just missing out, but earning valuable black type. Along with the winner she helps set the standard. (op 15-2)
Blue Angel(IRE), a winner over 7f on Polytrack, had finished a well-beaten seventh behind this winner and third in the Sweet Solera and got much closer this time, always in the leading group and staying on as if another furlong at least will be in her favour. (tchd 25-1)
Bella Swan was loaded using a blanket but stumbled and nearly unseated her rider leaving the stalls. She made headway from halfway before fading, but clearly had excuses and can be given another chance. Official explanation: jockey said filly stumbled badly on leaving the stalls (tchd 10-1 and 12-1)
Water Biscuit, who finished three-quarterrs of a length behind Bella Swan at Newmarket and had won since, could not go the pace and was unable to quite run up to that form with her old rival. (op 12-1)
Full Mandate(IRE), a winner over 6f on fast and runner-up to subsequent Lowther winner Lady Of The Desert in the Princess Margaret, was up in trip but failed to run her race, although her trainer thought the track might not have suited and her jockey reported that the filly ran too free. Official explanation: jockey said filly ran too free (op 9-2)
Siyaadah, by Shamardal out of the useful US stakes winner River Belle, had won over 7f at Redcar on her debut but was made favourite on this big step up in grade. She raced prominently early but folded pretty quickly 2f from home. She was clearly thought better than this but will need to bounce back. (op 7-2 tchd 4-1)

5428 GOODWOOD.COM MAIDEN AUCTION STKS 1m
4:20 (4:21) (Class 5) 2-Y-O
£3,238 (£963; £481; £240) Stalls High

Form RPR
1 **Notorize** 2-9-1 0 .... RichardKingscote 1 76+
(R M Beckett) *chsd ldrs on outer: drvn and styd on strly to ld over 1f out: kpt on wl cl home* **20/1**
62 2 ½ **Baltimore Clipper (USA)**[53] 3716 2-8-12 0 .... JimCrowley 9 72+
(P F I Cole) *t.k.h: chsd ldrs: hung rt: rdn and lost pl ins fnl 2f: rallied and r.o wl fnl f: gng on cl home* **9/2**[2]
64 3 1½ **Cloudy City (USA)**[16] 4953 2-8-13 0 .... J-PGuillambert 8 70
(M Johnston) *rr: rdn and hdwy fr 2f out: hung rt over 1f out: styd on ins fnl f but nvr gng pce to chal* **6/1**
5 4 ½ **Crunched**[20] 4811 2-8-11 0 .... EddieAhern 11 67
(M L W Bell) *led tl hdd over 2f out: rallied to chal again over 1f out: wknd fnl 110yds* **8/1**
04 5 nk **Kinky Afro (IRE)**[21] 4790 2-8-6 0 .... LPKeniry 5 61
(J S Moore) *chsd ldrs: rdn to chal over 1f out: wknd ins fnl f* **10/1**
0 6 1 **Dinkie Short**[17] 4908 2-8-6 0 .... MCGeran(3) 13 62
(W R Muir) *chsd ldrs: rdn along 3f out: n.m.r over 1f out: hung lft ins fnl f: kpt on cl home* **66/1**
022 7 1¼ **Magic Lantern**[16] 4946 2-8-8 78 .... WilliamBuick 2 58
(R Hannon) *stmbld and wnt rt s: sn trcking ldr: led over 2f out: rdn sn after and hdd over 1f out: wknd qckly ins fnl f* **7/4**[1]
0 8 nk **Red Barcelona (IRE)**[39] 4176 2-8-6 0 .... AshleyMorgan(5) 10 60
(M H Tompkins) *in tch: sme hdwy over 2f out: styng on same pce whn pushed lft ins fnl f* **28/1**
6 9 nk **Ilston Lord (IRE)**[32] 4410 2-8-10 0 .... DaneO'Neill 4 59+
(M P Tregoning) *s.i.s: rdn 3f out: nvr gng pce to get into contention* **11/2**[3]
0 10 1½ **Sandy Shaw**[15] 4980 2-8-8 0 .... TPO'Shea 3 53
(J W Hills) *bmpd s: racd on outer: in tch 3f out: sme hdwy whn hmpd and wknd ins fnl f* **25/1**
11 nse **Dr Mathias** 2-8-10 0 .... EdwardCreighton 6 59+
(W R Muir) *in rr: sme hdwy whn hmpd ins fnl f: nt rcvr* **66/1**
50 12 8 **Black Sapphire**[27] 4557 2-8-6 0 .... FergusSweeney 12 34
(Miss Amy Weaver) *in rr tl wnt in tch 1/2-way: sn wknd* **40/1**

1m 41.68s (1.78) **Going Correction** +0.05s/f (Good) **12 Ran SP% 121.9**
Speed ratings (Par 94): **93,92,91,90,90 89,87,87,87,85 85,77**
toteswinger: 1&2 £17.00, 1&3 £24.80, 2&3 £5.70. CSF £106.10 TOTE £28.20: £4.30, £2.00, £2.20; EX 157.10.
Owner R Roberts **Bred** Cheveley Park Stud Ltd **Trained** Whitsbury, Hants

FOCUS
All the previous winners of this race had the benefit of previous experience, and on this occasion there were just two newcomers, but one of those bucked the trend. The runner-up sets the level and the form looks reasonable if not the strongest.

NOTEBOOK
Notorize ♦, a 33,000gns half-brother to the one-time useful Hypnotic and a couple of other winners, was never far from the leaders on this debut and showed in front well over a furlong from home. He ran slightly green once there but picked up when the runner-up came to challenge and gave the impression he will have learned a fair amount from the experience. The performance is all the more meritorious because he had to overcome being drawn in the outside stall. (op 33-1)
Baltimore Clipper(USA) made his debut in a Newmarket maiden that has produced several subsequent winners and built on that at Wolverhampton. Stepping up in trip, he was a little keen in the group tracking the leaders but picked up well in the closing stages and made the winner pull out extra. He should be able to win a maiden but also qualifies for handicaps. (op 6-1)
Cloudy City(USA) ran a couple of similar races in Sandown maidens and probably helps set the standard. He ran on quite well late on and is likely to appreciate a stiffer test or a more positive ride once switched to handicaps. (op 8-1)
Crunched was right up with the pace and put up an improved effort on much faster ground than he had encountered on his debut. He has the scope to do better in time. (op 16-1)
Kinky Afro(IRE) had improved on her debut when fourth on Polytrack over this trip last time and she did not perform badly on this return to turf. She is another who now qualifies for handicaps and looks as if there is more to come once she matures. (op 9-1 tchd 12-1)
Magic Lantern, who had the form in the book and was sent off favourite. She made the running but could not pick up when challenged and faded. She does not have as much scope as some of these and does not seem to be progressing. (op 6-4 tchd 2-1)
Ilston Lord(IRE) was expected to improve for the step up in trip but was easy in the market and compromised his chance with a tardy start, although he did finish well and a stiffer test might suit. (op 9-2 tchd 4-1)

5429 GOODWOOD REVIVAL STKS (H'CAP) 7f
4:55 (4:57) (Class 5) (0-70,70) 3-Y-O+
£3,238 (£963; £481; £240) Stalls High

Form RPR
3644 1 **King's Colour**[35] 4293 4-9-5 66 .... JackMitchell(3) 5 80+
(B R Johnson) *bmpd s: hld up in rr: stdy hdwy on outside over 2f out: led 1f out: sn clr: comf* **15/2**[2]
U000 2 3¼ **Annes Rocket (IRE)**[23] 4697 4-8-10 54 .... SamHitchcott 20 62+
(J C Fox) *hdwy on ins to trck ldrs fr 3f out: n.m.r and lost position ins fnl 2f: swtchd lft over 1f out: str run ins fnl f and fin wl to take 2nd cl home but no ch w wnr* **20/1**
-200 3 hd **Gordy Bee (USA)**[19] 4846 3-9-6 69 .... PaulEddery 11 71
(Pat Eddery) *chsd ldrs: rdn over 2f out: ev ch u.p over 1f out: styd on fnl f but nvr any ch w wnr* **16/1**
0061 4 shd **Jeremiah (IRE)**[22] 4730 3-9-4 67 .... (p) JamesDoyle 19 69
(J G Portman) *chsd ldrs: rdn over 2f out: styd on ins fnl f and n.m.r but nvr any ch w wnr* **12/1**
2255 5 nk **Hobson**[58] 3548 4-9-9 67 .... RobertWinston 9 70
(Eve Johnson Houghton) *chsd ldrs: led over 2f out: sn rdn: hdd 1f out: one pce ins fnl f* **9/1**
5020 6 nk **Compton's Eleven**[17] 4914 8-9-7 68 .... MCGeran(3) 7 71
(M R Channon) *in tch: rdn to chse ldrs 2f out: styd on same pce fnl f* **16/1**
332 7 1 **Seasonal Cross**[15] 5003 4-9-0 58 .... TonyCulhane 16 58+
(S Dow) *in tch: pushed along and n.m.r 2f out: styd on same pce fnl f* **7/2**[1]
-646 8 hd **Perfect Act**[18] 4871 4-9-12 70 .... TPO'Shea 8 69
(C G Cox) *towards rr on outer whn bmpd bnd over 4f out: hdwy over 2f out: kpt on to press ldrs over 1f out: wknd ins fnl f* **12/1**
0065 9 ¾ **Grizedale (IRE)**[38] 4202 10-8-0 51 oh3 .... (tp) KierenFox(7) 6 48
(M J Attwater) *bmpd s: bhd: pushed along and hdwy fr 2f out: kpt on ins fnl f: nvr a threat* **66/1**
4610 10 nse **Compton Blue**[10] 5169 3-9-5 68 .... DaneO'Neill 18 63+
(R Hannon) *chsd ldrs: rdn over 2f out: wknd over 1f out: hld whn n.m.r ins fnl f* **8/1**[3]
0004 11 nk **Flashy Photon**[17] 4905 4-8-8 59 .... AmyScott(7) 12 55
(H Candy) *s.i.s: rr: styd on fnl 2f but nvr in contention* **12/1**
5306 12 hd **Golden Prospect**[23] 4697 5-8-11 55 .... LPKeniry 15 51+
(J W Hills) *in rr tl sme prog fnl 2f* **14/1**
3546 13 nk **Imperium**[83] 2739 8-8-7 56 .... Louis-PhilippeBeuzelin(5) 17 51
(Jean-Rene Auvray) *in tch on ins: rdn 3f out: n.m.r and wknd 2f out* **16/1**
0500 14 nk **Batchworth Blaise**[11] 5120 6-8-2 51 oh2 .... SophieDoyle(5) 1 45
(E A Wheeler) *rr: sme prog fnl 2f* **33/1**
546 15 hd **Dilli Dancer**[38] 4199 4-8-8 57 .... GabrielHannon(5) 2 51
(G D Blake) *veered rt s: a in rr* **20/1**
1500 16 1¾ **Marmooq**[12] 5095 6-9-8 66 .... IanMongan 10 55
(M J Attwater) *stmbld s: a towards rr* **33/1**
1005 17 6 **Sam's Cross (IRE)**[14] 5020 4-9-1 62 .... MarcHalford(3) 13 35
(J J Bridger) *chsd ldrs tl hmpd and wknd over 2f out* **25/1**
3000 18 shd **Love Allowed**[46] 3946 3-8-6 55 .... PaulDoe 4 25
(Jamie Poulton) *led 2f: styd chsng ldrs tl hmpd and wknd over 2f out* **50/1**
0046 19 nk **Admiral Sandhoe (USA)**[23] 4700 3-9-4 67 .... JimCrowley 14 37
(Mrs A J Perrett) *led after 2f: hdd over 2f out and sn wknd* **20/1**

1m 27.87s (0.47) **Going Correction** +0.05s/f (Good)
WFA 3 from 4yo+ 5lb **19 Ran SP% 130.0**
Speed ratings (Par 103): **99,95,95,94,94 94,93,92,92,91 91,91,91,90,90 88,81,81,81**
toteswinger: 1&2 £50.70, 1&3 £35.40, 2&3 £68.30. CSF £160.47 CT £2429.13 TOTE £9.10: £2.50, £5.50, £5.00, £3.10; EX 324.70.
Owner Tann Racing **Bred** Cheveley Park Stud Ltd **Trained** Ashtead, Surrey

FOCUS
This modest but competitive contest attracted its biggest field this century, and there was a not a lot of room for those racing towards the rail in the last couple of furlongs. The time was fractionally slower than the juvenile fillies' Group 3 earlier in the afternoon and the winner is rated an improver with those in the frame close to form despite the trouble in running.
Jeremiah(IRE) Official explanation: jockey said gelding was denied a clear run
Seasonal Cross Official explanation: jockey said filly was denied a clear run
Compton Blue Official explanation: jockey said colt was denied a clear run

Golden Prospect Official explanation: jockey said gelding was denied a clear run

5430 TURFTV IS FOR BETTING SHOPS MAIDEN STKS (H'CAP) 2m

5:30 (5:31) (Class 5) (0-70,70) 3-Y-O £3,238 (£963; £481; £240) Stalls Low

Form				RPR
002	1		**Aaman (IRE)**[11] 5123 3-8-6 53 ... LPKeniry 15	61+
			(E F Vaughan) *mde all: clr 1/2-way: styd on str fnl 3f: unchal* **12/1**	
6332	2	2 3/4	**Theola (IRE)**[12] 5113 3-9-3 69 ... AshleyMorgan(5) 6	73+
			(M H Tompkins) *rr: hdwy on outside fr 3f out: hung rt over 1f out: styd on wl fnl f to take 2nd last strides but no ch w wnr* **4/1²**	
4652	3	hd	**Theologist (IRE)**[8] 5217 3-9-9 70 ... JimCrowley 1	74
			(Mrs A J Perrett) *chsd ldrs: wnt 2nd 7f out: rdn and no imp on wnr fr 3f out: satyef on one pce and ct for 2nd last strides* **3/1¹**	
0545	4	1 3/4	**Strategic Princess (IRE)**[16] 4935 3-8-8 55 ... JosedeSouza 7	57
			(P F I Cole) *t.k.h in rr: rapid hdwy on outside fr 4f out: rdn 2f out: hung rt over 1f out and no imp on ldrs* **14/1**	
044	5	3/4	**Guilin (IRE)**[15] 5011 3-7-13 51 ... Louis-PhilippeBeuzelin(5) 11	52
			(P F I Cole) *in tch 1/2-way: styd on same pce fnl 2f* **16/1**	
-053	6	nk	**Beauchamp Xenia**[12] 5093 3-9-4 65 ... DaneO'Neill 3	66
			(H Candy) *in tch: rdn and sme hdwy 3f out: nvr rchd ldrs and sn one pce* **10/1**	
0502	7	nse	**Whisky Galore**[22] 4744 3-9-9 70 ...(v¹) IanMongan 4	71
			(C G Cox) *chsd ldrs: rdn: hung rt 2f out: sn one pce* **8/1³**	
5403	8	1 1/4	**Googoobarabajagal (IRE)**[15] 5011 3-8-4 51 oh1 ... TPO'Shea 8	50
			(W S Kittow) *rr: sme hdwy over 2f oit: styng on same pce whn hmpd over 1f out* **12/1**	
3455	9	3/4	**Little Prudence**[19] 4855 3-9-2 70 ... JPFahy(7) 9	68
			(R M Beckett) *in tch: hdwy 4f out: rdn: hung rt and wknd 2f out* **10/1**	
0064	9	dht	**La Polka**[11] 5131 3-9-4 65 ... TravisBlock 2	63
			(H Morrison) *rr: rdn and sme prog 5f out but nvr rchd ldrs* **10/1**	
5005	11	26	**Whiterocks**[16] 4934 3-8-8 55 ... SamHitchcott 5	22
			(M R Channon) *in tch: rdn 5f out: wknd fr 3f out* **40/1**	
0366	12	4	**Miss Doodle**[17] 4911 3-8-11 58 ... RobertWinston 13	20
			(Eve Johnson Houghton) *chsd wnr to 7f out: wknd 3f out* **20/1**	
0040	13	7	**Highams Park (IRE)**[9] 4935 3-7-13 51 oh6 ... SophieDoyle(5) 12	5
			(J G Portman) *in tch over 12f* **100/1**	
0600	14	10	**Bright Wire (IRE)**[29] 4480 3-8-4 51 oh5 ...(v¹) FrankieMcDonald 14	—
			(M Madgwick) *slowly away: bhd most of way* **66/1**	

3m 33.57s (4.57) **Going Correction** +0.05s/f (Good) **14 Ran SP% 121.0**
Speed ratings (Par 100): **90,88,88,87,87 87,87,86,86,86 73,71,67,62**
toteswinger: 1&2 £14.50, 1&3 £10.90, 2&3 £4.10. CSF £58.59 CT £187.63 TOTE £12.10: £4.10, £1.70, £1.80; EX 95.40 Place 6: £347.71, Place 5: £150.41..
Owner Mohammed Rashid **Bred** Darley **Trained** Newmarket, Suffolk

FOCUS
This modest staying handicap for three-year-old maidens was dominated by the front-runner. The third looks the best guide to the form, with the fifth and eighth close to recent Nottingham marks.
Miss Doodle Official explanation: jockey said filly failed to stay the trip
T/Plt: £423.70 to a £1 stake. Pool: £110,892.13. 191.04 winning tickets. T/Qpdt: £43.60 to a £1 stake. Pool: £5,803.94. 98.30 winning tickets. ST

5397 NEWMARKET (R-H)

Saturday, August 29

OFFICIAL GOING: Good (good to firm in places) changing to good to firm after race 1 (1.50)
Wind: Fresh across Weather: Cloudy

5431 EBF FAREWELL AND THANK YOU TO NICK CAMPBELL MAIDEN STKS 6f

1:50 (1:53) (Class 4) 2-Y-O £5,180 (£1,541; £770; £384) Stalls Low

Form				RPR
2	1		**Dafeef**[17] 4900 2-9-3 0 ... TedDurcan 1	87
			(Saeed Bin Suroor) *chsd ldrs: swtchd rt over 2f out: rdn and hung rt fr over 1f out: led 1f out: r.o wl* **13/8¹**	
22	2	3 1/4	**Lean Machine**[49] 3867 2-9-3 0 ... PatDobbs 11	77
			(R Hannon) *w ldr tl rdn to ld over 1f out: sn hdd: styd on same pce* **7/2²**	
	3	3/4	**Noafal (IRE)** 2-9-3 0 ... RHills 8	75+
			(M A Jarvis) *hld up: hdwy over 2f out: r.o: nt rch ldrs* **6/1**	
	4	1	**Saboteur** 2-9-3 0 ... DO'Donohoe 7	72
			(Saeed Bin Suroor) *s.s: hdwy 1/2-way: rdn and hung rt over 1f out: styd on same pce* **22/1**	
42	5	1/2	**Bonheurs Art (IRE)**[19] 4851 2-8-12 0 ... SteveDrowne 3	66
			(B W Hills) *led: rdn and hdd over 1f out: no ex ins fnl f* **9/2³**	
	6	3/4	**Guest Book (IRE)** 2-9-3 0 ... RoystonFfrench 4	68
			(M Johnston) *mid-div: sn pushed along: rdn and hung lft over 1f out: styd on* **20/1**	
	7	3 1/4	**Pirate's Song** 2-9-3 0 ... RobertHavlin 2	59
			(J A R Toller) *prom: racd keenly: rdn and wknd over 1f out* **25/1**	
	8	3/4	**Sard** 2-8-12 0 ... PhilipRobinson 10	51+
			(M A Jarvis) *hld up: swtchd rt over 1f out: r.o ins fnl f: nvr nr to chal* **16/1**	
	9	1 3/4	**Imjin River (IRE)** 2-9-3 0 ... JerryO'Dwyer 5	51
			(M H Tompkins) *s.i.s: hld up: shkn up over 2f out: styd on ins fnl f: n.d* **66/1**	
04	10	2 3/4	**Bojangles Andrews**[19] 4851 2-9-0 0 ... PatrickHills(3) 6	43
			(B G Powell) *chsd ldrs: rdn over 2f out: wknd over 1f out* **50/1**	
	11	9	**Keep Silent** 2-8-9 0 ... KellyHarrison(3) 9	11
			(W J H Ratcliffe) *hld up: a in rr: wknd 1/2-way* **100/1**	
0	12	1 1/2	**No Complaining (IRE)**[14] 5029 2-8-12 0 ... ShaneKelly 12	—
			(B J Curley) *hld up: wknd over 2f out* **40/1**	

1m 12.02s (-0.48) **Going Correction** -0.075s/f (Good) **12 Ran SP% 118.5**
Speed ratings (Par 96): **100,95,94,93,92 91,87,86,84,80 68,66**
toteswinger: 1&2 £2.90, 1&3 £5.70, 2&3 £3.00. CSF £6.58 TOTE £2.80: £1.30, £1.60, £2.40; EX 8.90.
Owner Godolphin **Bred** Shadwell Estate Company **Trained** Newmarket, Suffolk

FOCUS
This looked a decent maiden with some well-bred newcomers, but experience counted, the first two having run before. A decent effort from the winner.

NOTEBOOK
Dafeef, a good second on his Salisbury debut, was close to the pace from the start but when asked to go and win his race over a furlong from home, he put his head in the air and hung right over to the stands' rail. Fortunately for him, he still had enough forward momentum to win with a degree of authority and it may be that he was feeling the ground. An entry in a Listed contest two days after this suggested that he is thought a bit of. (tchd 6-4)
Lean Machine, runner-up in his first two starts over 7f including here on debut behind the subsequent Superlative Stakes winner Silver Grecian, had every chance having been on the pace throughout. Whether the drop to 6f was a help or a hindrance is hard to say, but he did little wrong and deserves to find a race. (op 9-2)
Noafal(IRE) ◆, a 60,000gns half-brother to three winners including the smart Corsario and the very useful Bentong, was trapped out wide, which is not always ideal, but he made some eyecatching late headway to grab third and fared best of the newcomers. He holds an entry in the Mill Reef Stakes, so is obviously thought useful. (tchd 13-2)
Saboteur ◆, a 130,000gns half-brother to the 1m2f winner Monmouthshire, had to be encouraged along at various stages, but he too did some good late work and should improve for the experience, especially over further. (tchd 20-1 and 25-1)
Bonheurs Art(IRE), clear of the third when running an odds-on shot close at Windsor last time, made much of the running but emptied rather disappointingly once headed over a furlong out. This was a step backwards and a Cheveley Park entry now looks highly optimistic. Official explanation: jockey said filly hung right (op 4-1 tchd 5-1)
Guest Book(IRE) found everything happening too quickly early, but he gradually got the hang of things and showed enough to suggest he has a future. He is by a sprinter, but there is plenty of stamina on the dam's side of his pedigree. (op 28-1)
Sard ◆ was very naughty beforehand and twice unshipped her rider before being loaded into the stalls. Once under way she ran very green, well off the pace, but showed a little but of ability late on without being knocked about. An 80,000gns half-sister to three winners including the smart Henrik, she is in the Cheveley Park and can be expected to step up significantly from this debut effort in due course. (op 14-1 tchd 18-1 and 20-1 in places)
No Complaining(IRE) Official explanation: jockey said filly was unsuited by the Good, Good to Firm in places ground

5432 CHRIS BLACKWELL MEMORIAL H'CAP 7f

2:20 (2:23) (Class 3) (0-90,87) 3-Y-O £9,066 (£2,697; £1,348; £673) Stalls Low

Form				RPR
2143	1		**Seek N' Destroy (IRE)**[63] 3375 3-9-5 83 ... RHills 7	96+
			(B W Hills) *hld up: hdwy and swtchd rt over 1f out: led 1f out: r.o wl* **5/1²**	
12	2	3	**Russian Jar (IRE)**[14] 5030 3-9-7 85 ... PhilipRobinson 2	90+
			(M A Jarvis) *trckd ldrs: racd keenly: led over 1f out: sn rdn and hdd: styd on same pce* **7/2¹**	
101	3	nk	**Elliptical (USA)**[49] 3868 3-9-9 87 ... StephenDonohoe 5	91+
			(G A Butler) *led 4f: sn rdn: outpcd over 1f out: r.o ins fnl f* **7/1**	
1112	4	1	**Legal Legacy**[26] 4591 3-9-2 80 ... PhillipMakin 6	81
			(M Dods) *chsd ldrs: rdn and ev ch over 1f out: no ex ins fnl f* **6/1³**	
-000	5	1/2	**Archie Rice (USA)**[50] 3816 3-9-9 87 ... AlanMunro 8	87
			(W Jarvis) *prom: rdn over 2f out: styd on same pce fnl f* **22/1**	
3351	6	hd	**Inheritor (IRE)**[26] 4591 3-9-4 82 ... ChrisCatlin 11	81
			(B Smart) *hld up in tch: rdn over 2f out: kpt on ins fnl f* **15/2**	
6144	7	1/2	**Glowing Praise**[31] 4433 3-9-2 80 ... RichardMullen 10	78
			(E S McMahon) *hood removed sltly late and s.i.s: hdwy to ld 3f out: rdn and hdd over 1f out: no ex ins fnl f* **12/1**	
4545	8	3/4	**Fazbee (IRE)**[52] 3734 3-8-13 77 ... ShaneKelly 4	73
			(P W D'Arcy) *hld up: hdwy over 2f out: rdn over 1f out: one pce* **20/1**	
1652	9	nk	**Cumana Bay**[12] 5099 3-9-8 86 ... PatDobbs 14	81
			(R Hannon) *hld up: rdn over 2f out: nvr trbld ldrs* **11/1**	
-641	10	1 1/4	**Audemar (IRE)**[15] 4984 3-9-1 79 ... TedDurcan 12	71+
			(E F Vaughan) *hld up: rdn over 2f out: n.d* **14/1**	
4006	11	1 3/4	**Viva Ronaldo (IRE)**[20] 4814 3-9-4 87 ... BMcHugh(5) 9	74
			(R A Fahey) *prom: rdn over 2f out: wknd over 1f out* **16/1**	
1311	12	1 3/4	**Sarasota Sunshine**[12] 5090 3-9-0 78 ...(b) SteveDrowne 13	60
			(N P Littmoden) *hld up: rdn over 2f out: a in rr* **10/1**	

1m 24.82s (-0.88) **Going Correction** -0.075s/f (Good) **12 Ran SP% 124.2**
Speed ratings (Par 104): **102,98,98,97,96 96,95,94,94,93 91,89**
toteswinger: 1&2 £3.40, 1&3 £13.00, 2&3 £6.80. CSF £24.02 CT £128.41 TOTE £6.10: £1.90, £1.80, £2.80; EX 19.40 Trifecta £45.80 Pool: £514.76 - 8.30 winning units..
Owner R J Arculli **Bred** James Waldron **Trained** Lambourn, Berks

FOCUS
A competitive and decent handicap run at an ordinary pace and the first four home raced closer to the far rail than most. The winner impressed and has more to offer.

NOTEBOOK
Seek N' Destroy(IRE) normally sets the pace or races close to it but, on this occasion, his rider was happy to drop him out. He travelled like a dream and it was only a question of how much he would find when the gaps appeared. The answer was plenty, and although he had twice been held since making all off 4lb lower at Lingfield in May, he may be capable of building on this with these tactics applied. (op 15-2)
Russian Jar(IRE) ◆, narrowly beaten off 3lb lower over 1m here a fortnight ago on his return from a break, pulled hard then, so this shorter trip was a help and he had every chance against the inside rail. Connections were concerned about the ground, so this was a decent effort and he still has scope. (op 11-4 tchd 4-1, 9-2 in a place)
Elliptical(USA) ◆, up 7lb for his soft-ground victory at Salisbury last month, ran a strange race. Having made the early running, he was headed just after halfway and looked likely to drop right out, but he then stayed on strongly again up the hill to snatch third. He was racing over a shorter trip than he had encountered before, which helps explain this effort, and he will be winning again back over further. (op 13-2 tchd 6-1)
Legal Legacy, thwarted by Inheritor in his bid for a four-timer at Carlisle last time, was 3lb better off for a length and a half and, after having held every chance, managed to turn that form around in this stronger race. (op 9-1)
Archie Rice(USA) ◆, who has struggled in handicaps so far this season, was down another 3lb here and wasn't disgraced as he raced wider than the principals. He is worth keeping an eye on if dropped in the weights again after this. (op 25-1)
Inheritor(IRE), who was well backed when returning to winning form at Carlisle last time, ran creditably, especially as he was also forced to race out wide away from the main action. (op 10-1)
Glowing Praise, who has had excuses for his two defeats since winning off 5lb lower at Leicester in June, was down to this trip for the first time since winning on his second start as a juvenile and he can be forgiven this too. His blindfold was still being removed when the gates opened causing him to lose ground, and once under way he carted himself into a prominent position. It was no surprise that those exertions eventually took their toll and he is not one to write off just yet. (op 11-1)

5433 BET365.COM NURSERY 7f

2:50 (2:52) (Class 2) 2-Y-O £12,952 (£3,854; £1,926; £962) Stalls Low

Form				RPR
2326	1		**Red Badge (IRE)**[9] 5198 2-9-0 84 ... JimmyFortune 12	92
			(R Hannon) *hld up: hdwy over 2f out: hrd rdn to ld ins fnl f: edgd lft: r.o* **10/3²**	
411	2	1/2	**Azizi**[24] 4651 2-9-1 85 ... RHills 6	92
			(W J Haggas) *hld up: hdwy 1/2-way: sn rdn: r.o* **5/4¹**	
012	3	1	**Pallantes Cross**[29] 4499 2-9-7 91 ... RoystonFfrench 9	95
			(M Johnston) *led 6f out: rdn over 1f out: edgd lft and hdd ins fnl f: styd on same pce* **25/1**	

315 **4** 1¾ **Pintura**[11] 5136 2-8-3 **73** .... AdrianMcCarthy 13 73+
(M R Channon) *hld up: hdwy over 2f out: rdn and edgd lft over 1f out: styng on same pce whn nt clr run towards fin* **9/1**[3]
016 **5** 2¾ **Right Rave (IRE)**[19] 4850 2-7-9 **68** oh1 .... AndreaAtzeni(3) 3 61
(P J McBride) *chsd ldrs: rdn over 2f out: wknd ins fnl f* **20/1**
0223 **6** ½ **Ginger Grey (IRE)**[3] 5344 2-7-6 **69** oh1 ow1 ....(p) RichardRowe(7) 5 62+
(S A Callaghan) *hld up: hdwy 1/2-way: nt clr run and lost pl over 2f out: r.o ins fnl f* **33/1**
3134 **7** ¾ **Tukitinyasok (IRE)**[27] 4558 2-9-3 **87** .... PhillipMakin 10 77
(R F Fisher) *led 1f: chsd ldrs: nt clr run 2f out: sn rdn and wknd* **18/1**
31 **8** *shd* **Damietta (USA)**[15] 4980 2-9-1 **85** .... TedDurcan 2 75
(Saeed Bin Suroor) *chsd ldrs: rdn 2f out: edgd rt and wknd fnl f* **9/1**[3]
215 **9** 1 **Deloria**[12] 5091 2-8-6 **76** .... AlanMunro 1 63
(Eve Johnson Houghton) *hld up: effrt over 2f out: wknd over 1f out* **20/1**
13 **10** 11 **Waltz Around (IRE)**[18] 4883 2-8-2 **72** ow1 .... ChrisCatlin 4 32
(C E Brittain) *chsd ldrs: rdn over 2f out: wknd over 1f out* **33/1**
612 **11** 4½ **Victoire De Lyphar (IRE)**[64] 3340 2-8-9 **79** .... ShaneKelly 8 27
(P C Haslam) *chsd ldrs tl wknd over 2f out: eased over 1f out* **16/1**

1m 24.54s (-1.16) **Going Correction** -0.075s/f (Good) **11** Ran SP% **117.9**
Speed ratings (Par 100): **103,102,101,99,96 95,94,94,93,80 75**
toteswinger: 1&2 £1.70, 1&3 £8.60, 2&3 £10.10. CSF £7.22 CT £83.62 TOTE £4.30: £1.70, £1.10, £5.20; EX 8.80 Trifecta £132.50 Pool: £580.48 - 3.24 winning units..
Owner Michael Pescod **Bred** Thomas Foy **Trained** East Everleigh, Wilts

FOCUS
A competitive nursery, although the betting suggested it was almost a two-horse race and the market was proved correct, albeit not in the order that many would have expected. The winning time was 0.28 seconds faster than the three-year-olds in the preceding handicap, so the form looks strong. The race should work out.

NOTEBOOK
Red Badge(IRE) ◆, making his nursery debut, had looked in need of this extra furlong in his recent outings and he justified that impression. His high draw wasn't ideal and, as a result, he was forced to make his effort widest of all. That makes the performance all the more creditable. He did hang away to his left under a right-hand drive inside the last furlong, but was always doing enough to hold off the favourite. Being by Captain Rio, he may improve even more for easier ground and connections believe he will get 1m. (op 3-1 tchd 7-2, 4-1 in a place)
Azizi, bidding for a hat-trick, having been hoisted up 10lb for bolting up at odds-on in a four-runner Newcastle nursery last time, stayed on strongly from off the pace and was still going forward at the line, but the winner was always holding him. On this evidence, he may need 1m now. (op 6-4 tchd 6-5, 13-8 in a place)
Pallantes Cross, making his nursery debut after being slammed by the smart Poet's Voice in a four-runner novice event here last time, was always up with the pace out wide and kept on well to the line. His mark looks only fair, but he probably has improvement left. (op 33-1)
Pintura ◆, who has been shaping as though in need of this extra furlong in his recent outings, was held up early before moving into contention coming to the last quarter-mile. He wouldn't have won, but would have finished closer but for being squeezed out between the second and third inside the last furlong. There is a nursery in him over this trip. (op 10-1 tchd 11-1)
Right Rave(IRE), who looked as though she would stay this far, despite finishing unplaced in a 6f Windsor nursery last time, wasn't disgraced from 1lb wrong. (op 25-1 tchd 28-1)
Ginger Grey(IRE) finished well from the back of the field, but has had plenty of chances and looks exposed.
Damietta(USA), making her nursery debut after getting off the mark in a Kempton Polytrack maiden, showed up for a long way against the inside rail but faded tamely inside the last furlong on this return to turf. (op 8-1)

5434 BET365 HOPEFUL STKS (LISTED RACE) 6f
3:25 (3:27) (Class 1) 3-Y-O+
£22,708 (£8,608; £4,308; £2,148; £1,076; £540) **Stalls** Low

Form RPR
-124 **1** **Palace Moon**[14] 5024 4-9-0 **107** .... SteveDrowne 1 112
(H Morrison) *hld up far side: chsd ldrs: edgd rt over 2f out: rdn to ld ins fnl f: hung lft: jst hld on* **9/4**[1]
1314 **2** *nk* **Swiss Diva**[50] 3824 3-8-6 **101** .... AlanMunro 10 106
(D R C Elsworth) *racd centre: chsd ldrs: rdn over 1f out: edgd lft: r.o* **15/2**
0504 **3** ½ **Jimmy Styles**[14] 5039 5-9-0 **100** .... PhilipRobinson 8 109
(C G Cox) *racd centre: prom: rdn over 1f out: nt clr run ins fnl f: edgd lft: r.o* **10/1**
1202 **4** *hd* **Tamagin (USA)**[14] 5039 6-9-0 **109** ....(p) StephenDonohoe 7 108
(J Pearce) *reaced centre and overall ldr: swtchd to r alone on stands' side rail 4f out: rdn and hdd over 2f out: r.o* **11/2**[3]
0301 **5** ¾ **Zidane**[28] 4516 7-9-0 **102** .... GeorgeBaker 2 109+
(J R Fanshawe) *racd far side: hld up: rdn over 2f out: hdwy over 1f out: rdn and styng on whn hmpd ins fnl f: nt rcvr* **16/1**
4105 **6** ½ **Strike The Deal (USA)**[48] 3908 4-9-0 **109** ....(v) ShaneKelly 6 104
(J Noseda) *racd centre: chsd ldrs: led overall ldr over 2f out: rdn: edgd rt and hdd ins fnl f: styd on same pce: edgd lft towards fin* **5/1**[2]
-050 **7** 3¾ **Beckermet (IRE)**[8] 5232 7-9-0 **101** .... ChrisCatlin 5 92
(R F Fisher) *racd far side: sn led that gp: hdd over 2f out: wkng whn hmpd over 1f out* **28/1**
000 **8** 3 **Pointing North (SAF)**[8] 5232 5-9-0 **105** .... RichardMullen 3 83
(B Smart) *racd far side: chsd ldr: rdn over 2f out: wknd and eased over 1f out* **16/1**
5-00 **9** ½ **Fat Boy (IRE)**[30] 4456 4-9-0 **105** ....(t) RHills 9 81
(P W Chapple-Hyam) *racd centre: chsd ldr tl lft in ld of that gp 4f out: rdn and hdd over 2f out: wknd over 1f out* **10/1**
2031 **10** 50 **Ancien Regime (IRE)**[9] 5196 4-9-0 **105** .... TedDurcan 4 —
(Saeed Bin Suroor) *racd far side: prom: rdn and lost pl over 3f out: sn bhd: eased fnl 2f* **17/2**

1m 10.33s (-2.17) **Going Correction** -0.075s/f (Good)
WFA 3 from 4yo+ 3lb **10** Ran SP% **118.5**
Speed ratings (Par 111): **111,110,109,109,108 108,103,99,98,31**
toteswinger: 1&2 £4.30, 1&3 £5.90, 2&3 £12.80. CSF £19.97 TOTE £3.30: £1.70, £2.10, £3.40; EX 22.20 Trifecta £202.10 Pool: £202.10 - 3.80 winning units..
Owner Miss B Swire **Bred** Miss B Swire **Trained** East Ilsley, Berks
■ Stewards' Enquiry : Steve Drowne three-day ban: careless riding (Sep 13-15)

FOCUS
A competitive Listed sprint, but a messy contest with the field splitting into two groups of five early, but then four of the nearside group eventually merged with those on the far side to race more towards the centre, leaving Tamagin with a solo up the stands' rail. Straightforward form, and ordinary for the grade.

NOTEBOOK
Palace Moon, who was down in class and trip following his creditable fourth in the Group 2 Hungerford Stakes last time, was very well backed beforehand. Off the pace in the far-side group, he did hang away to his left after hitting the front inside the last furlong, doing Zidane no favours, but was still the best horse on the day. He has improved since his last start, according to connections, and this ground was probably quick enough for him. He may go for the Diadem next, provided there is some cut in the ground. (op 7-2)
Swiss Diva, one of only two three-year-olds in the field and the only filly, was held up in the group that raced more towards the nearside, but she finished with quite a flourish and was catching the winner at the line. She doesn't want the ground too fast and her participation was in some doubt, so this was a fine effort. She will be winning again back on a more forgiving surface. (tchd 7-1 and 8-1)
Jimmy Styles, around a length behind Tamagin in the Great St Wilfrid and 7lb worse off, would have appreciated the drying ground. Although he needed to be niggled along in the nearside group from some way out, he stayed on very nicely up the final climb and this was a decent effort considering he was badly in at the weights with those that finished around him. (tchd 12-1)
Tamagin(USA) showed his usual bright speed against the stands' rail, but whether he was helped by being left with nothing to race against is hard to say. He should have beaten Jimmy Styles here on the form of their Great St Wilfrid encounter, so perhaps it wasn't ideal. Official explanation: jockey said gelding hung badly right (op 9-2)
Zidane, who is the sort that needs things to go his way, made a promising move towards the inside starting up the hill, but was already under strong pressure and looking held when hampered by the winner. (op 12-1 tchd 11-1)
Strike The Deal(USA), who has been performing well in Group company since finishing third in this race last year, just managed to edge out Tamagin in a conditions event on the Lingfield Polytrack in May. He had every chance in the centre of the track coming to the last furlong, but didn't seem to get up the hill. (tchd 9-2)
Pointing North(SAF) Official explanation: jockey said gelding hung right
Ancien Regime(IRE) Official explanation: jockey said colt was never travelling

5435 WT'S SNOOKER AND SPORTING CLUB MAIDEN STKS 1m
4:00 (4:03) (Class 4) 3-Y-O+ **£5,180** (£1,541; £770; £384) **Stalls** Low

Form RPR
5-2 **1** **Stoic (IRE)**[12] 5100 3-9-3 0 .... ShaneKelly 9 99+
(J Noseda) *chsd ldr tl led over 2f out: rdn and r.o wl ins fnl f* **15/8**[2]
2 2¼ **Alainmaar (FR)** 3-9-3 0 .... PhilipRobinson 4 94+
(M A Jarvis) *hld up: hdwy over 3f out: edgd lft 2f out: r.o to go 2nd wl ins fnl f: nvr nr to chal* **10/1**
0- **3** 2½ **Tafaool (IRE)**[323] 6620 3-8-12 0 .... RHills 8 83
(M P Tregoning) *prom: rdn over 2f out: chsd wnr over 1f out: styng on same pce whn lost 2nd wl ins fnl f* **6/5**[1]
2623 **4** 10 **Wilfred Pickles (IRE)**[7] 5242 3-9-3 78 ....(tp) AlanMunro 6 64
(Mrs A J Perrett) *chsd ldrs: led over 5f out: rdn and hdd over 2f out: wknd fnl f* **9/1**
5- **5** 2 **Aswaaq (IRE)**[326] 6559 3-8-12 0 .... RichardMullen 5 54+
(J L Dunlop) *hld up: nt clr run wl over 2f out: sn rdn: n.d* **6/1**[3]
6 5 **Where's Charlie** 3-9-3 0 .... KirstyMilczarek 1 47
(P Leech) *s.i.s: hld up: sme hdwy over 2f out: sn rdn and wknd* **40/1**
05 **7** 4½ **Head First**[16] 4955 3-8-12 0 .... LiamJones 3 31
(W Jarvis) *prom: lost pl over 3f out: sn bhd* **50/1**
060 **8** 14 **Toballa**[14] 5035 4-9-4 45 .... StephenDonohoe 7 —
(P Leech) *led: hdd over 5f out: rdn 1/2-way: wknd 3f out* **100/1**
0 **9** 4 **Duchess Of Alba**[16] 4955 4-8-11 0 .... RosieJessop(7) 2 —
(G C Bravery) *chsd ldrs: rdn 1/2-way: wknd 3f out* **100/1**

1m 37.14s (-2.86) **Going Correction** -0.075s/f (Good)
WFA 3 from 4yo 6lb **9** Ran SP% **120.0**
Speed ratings (Par 105): **111,108,106,96,94 89,84,70,66**
toteswinger: 1&2 £2.40, 1&3 £1.70, 2&3 £4.20. CSF £21.70 TOTE £2.80: £1.40, £2.20, £1.10; EX 18.30.
Owner Highclere Thoroughbred Racing (Gimcrack) **Bred** Darley **Trained** Newmarket, Suffolk

FOCUS
Not the most competitive of maidens for Newmarket, but a couple of interesting candidates took part. The first three pulled a long way clear of the rest. Tricky form to pin down, and the first two could be underrated.
Where's Charlie Official explanation: jockey said gelding ducked left in the dip
Toballa Official explanation: jockey said filly was unsuited by the Good to Firm ground. The trainer subsequently reported that the filly was lame and had pulled a joint

5436 LANWADES STUD SUPPORTING CAMBRIDGE VETERINARY SCHOOL H'CAP 5f
4:35 (4:36) (Class 4) (0-85,85) 3-Y-O+ **£5,180** (£1,541; £770; £384) **Stalls** Low

Form RPR
2634 **1** **Lenny Bee**[36] 4289 3-9-3 **79** .... PhillipMakin 5 89
(D H Brown) *mde all: rdn and edgd lft over 1f out: styd on* **5/1**[2]
3115 **2** 1¼ **The Tatling (IRE)**[9] 5183 12-9-4 **81** .... JackDean(3) 12 87
(J M Bradley) *hld up: hdwy over 1f out: r.o wl and swtchd lft wl ins fnl f: nt rch wnr* **12/1**
2505 **3** 1 **Ocean Blaze**[12] 5098 5-8-12 **72** .... SteveDrowne 10 74
(B R Millman) *hld up in tch: plld hrd early: rdn and edgd rt over 1f out: r.o* **16/1**
4121 **4** *nk* **Rocket Rob (IRE)**[7] 5264 3-9-9 **85** .... PatDobbs 14 86
(S A Callaghan) *s.i.s: hld up: last 1/2-way: r.o wl ins fnl f: nt rch ldrs* **7/2**[1]
1031 **5** *nk* **Miss Chamanda (IRE)**[12] 5098 3-9-8 **84** .... StephenDonohoe 6 84
(P D Evans) *chsd wnr: rdn over 1f out: no ex ins fnl f* **14/1**
4060 **6** 1¾ **Sands Crooner (IRE)**[7] 5247 6-9-2 **76** ....(v) AlanMunro 15 70+
(J G Given) *hld up: rdn over 1f out: styd on ins fnl f: nvr trbld ldrs* **14/1**
042 **7** ½ **Steelcut**[10] 5147 5-8-12 **72** .... RoystonFfrench 4 64
(R A Fahey) *chsd ldrs: rdn over 1f out: no ex ins fnl f* **20/1**
1640 **8** ½ **Kyle (IRE)**[10] 5167 5-8-8 **73** .... SimonPearce(5) 11 63
(C R Dore) *hld up: rdn 1/2-way: r.o ins fnl f: nvr nrr* **20/1**
2100 **9** 1 **Mango Music**[42] 4096 6-8-13 **76** .... AndreaAtzeni(3) 2 62
(M Quinn) *prom: rdn 1/2-way: outpcd fr over 1f out* **20/1**
0 **10** ¾ **Drifting Gold**[37] 4232 5-9-1 **75** ....(b) PhilipRobinson 3 59
(C G Cox) *prom: rdn and edgd lft over 1f out: wknd ins fnl f* **25/1**
6133 **11** *hd* **Efistorm**[12] 5098 8-9-9 **83** .... ShaneKelly 13 66
(C R Dore) *hld up: pushed along 1/2-way: n.d* **14/1**
-000 **12** 1¼ **Hadaf (IRE)**[7] 5263 4-9-8 **82** .... RHills 1 60
(M P Tregoning) *chsd ldrs: rdn over 1f out: wknd fnl f* **8/1**
6451 **13** *nk* **Discanti (IRE)**[17] 4891 4-9-3 **77** .... TedDurcan 7 54
(T D Easterby) *prom: rdn and hung lft over 1f out: sn wknd* **7/1**[3]
532 **14** 4½ **Hypnosis**[22] 4753 6-9-0 **79** .... BMcHugh(5) 9 40
(N Wilson) *mid-div: rdn and wknd over 1f out* **14/1**
6431 **P** **Gwilym (GER)**[14] 5020 6-8-8 **68** .... ChrisCatlin 8 —
(D Haydn Jones) *prom: lost action, p.u and dismntd fnl f* **14/1**

58.71 secs (-0.39) **Going Correction** -0.075s/f (Good)
WFA 3 from 4yo+ 2lb **15** Ran SP% **127.5**
Speed ratings (Par 105): **100,98,96,95,95 92,91,91,89,88 87,85,85,78,—**
toteswinger: 1&2 £14.00, 1&3 £29.50, 2&3 £42.00. CSF £63.64 CT £946.24 TOTE £6.00: £2.60, £3.00, £6.30; EX 102.90.
Owner Ron Hull **Bred** Whitsbury Manor Stud & Pigeon House Stud **Trained** Maltby, S Yorks

FOCUS
A competitive sprint handicap. The runer-up is the best guide to the form.
Efistorm Official explanation: jockey said gelding anticipated the star
Hadaf(IRE) Official explanation: jockey said colt hung right

Discanti(IRE) Official explanation: vet said gelding had bled from the nose
Gwilym(GER) Official explanation: vet said gelding had bled from the nose

5437 MICKEY FLYNN'S AMERICAN POOL H'CAP 1m 2f

5:05 (5:07) (Class 3) (0-95,95) 3-Y-0+ £9,066 (£2,697; £1,348; £673) Stalls Centre

Form RPR
112 **1** **Lord Theo**[9] 5185 5-8-12 79 .... RobertHavlin 5 86
(N P Littmoden) *a.p: rdn to ld ins fnl f: r.o* **4/1**[2]
2212 **2** ½ **Falcon Rock (IRE)**[26] 4602 4-9-2 83 .... PatDobbs 1 89+
(S A Callaghan) *hld up: hdwy over 1f out: swtchd rt ins fnl f: r.o wl* **7/2**[1]
2440 **3** *nse* **William Blake**[11] 5137 4-9-4 85 .... RoystonFfrench 3 91
(M Johnston) *chsd ldrs: led over 1f out: rdn and hdd ins fnl f: r.o* **9/2**[3]
0000 **4** 4½ **Ellemujie**[8] 5221 4-9-1 87 .... JamesO'Reilly(5) 2 84
(D K Ivory) *hld up: nt clr run over 1f out: styd on fnl f: nt trble ldrs* **16/1**
2321 **5** 1¾ **Park Lane**[13] 5072 3-8-6 81 .... SteveDrowne 4 74
(B W Hills) *trckd ldr tl led over 8f out: rdn and hdd over 1f out: wknd ins fnl f* **6/1**
0/50 **6** 1¾ **Farleigh House (USA)**[7] 5262 5-9-0 81 .... StephenDonohoe 7 71
(Sir Mark Prescott) *hld up: hdwy over 2f out: sn rdn: styng on same pce whn hmpd ins fnl f* **16/1**
4150 **7** *nse* **King Charles**[21] 4770 5-10-0 95 .... ChrisCatlin 11 85
(E A L Dunlop) *hld up: rdn over 2f out: n.d* **12/1**
1103 **8** 4 **Moheebb (IRE)**[11] 5137 5-9-12 93 .... (b) TedDurcan 8 75
(Mrs R A Carr) *s.i.s: hld up: rdn over 3f out: sme hdwy over 2f out: wknd over 1f out* **12/1**
6120 **9** ¾ **Bullet Man (USA)**[50] 3822 4-9-4 85 .... RHills 10 65
(L M Cumani) *chsd ldrs tl rdn and wknd over 2f out* **15/2**
2206 **10** 1½ **Cheshire Prince**[7] 5248 5-9-12 93 .... LiamJones 9 70
(W M Brisbourne) *led: hdd over 8f out: chsd ldr tl rdn over 2f out: hung lft over 1f out* **20/1**
2020 **11** 3½ **King Olav (UAE)**[99] 2242 4-9-5 86 .... ShaneKelly 6 56
(A W Carroll) *prom: rdn over 2f out: wknd over 1f out* **20/1**

2m 3.18s (-2.32) **Going Correction** -0.075s/f (Good)
WFA 3 from 4yo+ 8lb **11** Ran SP% **123.1**
Speed ratings (Par 107): **106,105,105,101,100 99,99,95,95,94 91**
toteswinger: 1&2 £4.80, 1&3 £4.20, 2&3 £4.40. CSF £19.41 CT £66.14 TOTE £5.40: £2.00, £1.70, £2.10; EX 19.20 Place 6: £18.75, Place 5: £14.09..
Owner Mrs Karen Graham **Bred** Mike Perkins **Trained** Newmarket, Suffolk
■ Stewards' Enquiry : Pat Dobbs two-day ban: careless riding (Sep 13-14)

FOCUS
A fair handicap, but the early pace was ordinary. The field made for the centre of the track once into the home straight. The third is a sound guide to the form.

NOTEBOOK
Lord Theo, just beaten in his hat-trick bid in a 1m4f lady amateurs' event at Epsom last time, had twice won easily over this course and distance before that, but was off a 10lb higher mark than for the second of those. He knows how to win, however, and that was the difference, for as soon as he had taken over in front passing the furlong pole, he stuck his neck out in willing fashion and wanted it more than his two main challengers. (op 9-2 tchd 5-1, 11-2 and 6-1 in places)
Falcon Rock(IRE), just beaten when favourite over further at Windsor last time, having been successful over this trip at the same track before that, was up another 3lb here. Well backed beforehand, he was switched off out the back early but took a while to respond when first put under pressure. He did stay on up the hill, having been switched to his right, but was never quite getting there and doesn't look an easy horse to get the timing right with. (op 9-2)
William Blake, whose effort at York last time when behind Moheebb can be safely ignored, was always close up and was travelling better than anything passing the 2f pole, but he again found a couple to beat him. He is without a win since scoring off 5lb lower in April of last year and it's becoming increasingly hard to make excuses for him. (op 6-1 tchd 7-1)
Ellemujie, off the same mark as when scoring at Sandown in June had been disappointing in four outings since and didn't enjoy the clearest of runs inside the last 2f before staying on when eventually in the clear. This was much better and he has now run three good races over this trip, but he still looks best over shorter.
Park Lane, the only three-year-old in the field, was making his handicap debut after easily getting off the mark at the eighth attempt in an uncompetitive Pontefract maiden last time. He soon found himself in front, but was a little keen which wasn't ideal for a colt racing beyond 1m for the first time and he had little left once headed. (op 7-1)
Farleigh House(USA), who pulled his chance away at Sandown last time, was done no favours when the runner-up switched across him a furlong out, but he was only playing for places at the time.
Bullet Man(USA), a very disappointing favourite when tailed-off over 1m4f here last month, had been running well before that, but he had also demonstrated a few quirks and this was another tame effort. (op 13-2)
T/Jkpt: £7,826.30 to a £1 stake. Pool: £49,603.83. 4.50 winning tickets. T/Plt: £32.50 to a £1 stake. Pool: £100,402.01. 2,251.32 winning tickets. T/Qpdt: £18.50 to a £1 stake. Pool: £4,207.28. 168.28 winning tickets. CR

4817 REDCAR (L-H)

Saturday, August 29

OFFICIAL GOING: Good to firm (9.7)
Wind: Fairly strong, half behind Weather: Cloudy

5438 RACING UK ON CHANNEL 432 LADY RIDERS' H'CAP 1m 2f

5:20 (5:20) (Class 5) (0-75,74) 3-Y-0+ £3,123 (£968; £484; £242) Stalls Low

Form RPR
4050 **1** **Daaweitza**[27] 4560 6-10-11 74 .... (b) MissLEllison 6 83
(B Ellison) *taken early to post: chsd ldrs: led over 3f out: hld on gamely fnl f* **9/1**
3346 **2** 1¼ **Edas**[5] 5307 7-9-10 64 .... MissHCuthbert(5) 14 70
(T A K Cuthbert) *hld up: hdwy over 3f out: effrt 2f out: styd on to chse wnr towards fin* **16/1**
3051 **3** ¾ **Baltimore Jack (IRE)**[21] 4804 5-9-8 62 .... MissJoannaMason(5) 7 67
(T D Walford) *cl up: effrt over 2f out: kpt on: lost 2nd towards fin* **10/3**[1]
5244 **4** 1¾ **Rain Stops Play (IRE)**[26] 4588 7-9-1 55 oh7 .... MissJRRichards(5) 5 56
(N G Richards) *t.k.h: hld up: hdwy over 4f out: kpt on fnl 2f: nrst fin* **20/1**
0120 **5** 2½ **Gala Sunday (USA)**[32] 4402 9-9-9 58 .... (bt) MissSBrotherton 1 54
(M W Easterby) *in tch: effrt over 2f out: one pce over 1f out* **8/1**
1322 **6** 1¼ **Lucayan Dancer**[21] 4804 9-9-10 64 .... MissERamstrom(5) 8 58
(D Nicholls) *bhd tl styd on fr 2f out: nvr able to chal* **8/1**[2]
246 **7** 3 **Nisaal (IRE)**[24] 4655 4-10-5 68 .... (p) MissADeniel 9 56
(J J Quinn) *hld up and bhd: hdwy 2f out: kpt on fnl f: n.d* **14/1**
6045 **8** 1½ **Royal Fantasy (IRE)**[21] 4804 6-9-12 61 .... (p) MissEJJones 10 46
(N Tinkler) *towards rr: hdwy over 3f out: outpcd fr 2f out* **22/1**
4661 **9** *nk* **Masterofceremonies**[30] 4465 6-9-9 65 .... (p) MissALMurphy(7) 13 49
(W M Brisbourne) *s.i.s: swtchd to ins rail sn after s: effrt over 2f out: n.d* **12/1**
0- **10** 7 **Treeko (IRE)**[36] 6511 4-9-9 65 .... MissKBannon(7) 12 35
(P A Kirby) *in tch on outside: lost pl 5f out: n.d after* **33/1**
0016 **11** 1½ **Monfils Monfils (USA)**[15] 4972 7-9-13 67 .... MissVBarr(5) 2 34
(R E Barr) *led to over 3f out: rdn and wknd over 2f out* **10/1**
1-06 **12** 1½ **West With The Wind**[51] 3761 4-10-1 69 .... MissKECooper(5) 3 33
(T P Tate) *chsd ldrs tl wknd fr 3f out* **17/2**[3]
000 **13** 6 **Shosolosa (IRE)**[14] 5037 7-9-1 55 oh10 .... MissKellyBurke(5) 4 7
(S A Harris) *hld up: rdn on outside 3f out: sn btn* **80/1**
3020 **14** ¾ **Willyn (IRE)**[22] 4751 4-9-6 55 oh2 .... MrsCBartley 11 5
(J S Goldie) *bhd: struggling 3f out: nvr on terms* **17/2**[3]
305- **15** 11 **Smirfy's Silver**[387] 4785 5-9-8 64 .... MissEGeorge(7) 15 —
(E S McMahon) *t.k.h: chsd ldrs tl wknd over 2f out* **20/1**

2m 4.81s (-2.29) **Going Correction** -0.15s/f (Firm) **15** Ran SP% **123.7**
Speed ratings (Par 103): **103,102,101,100,98 97,94,93,93,87 86,85,80,79,70**
toteswinger: 1&2 £27.10, 1&3 £5.80, 2&3 £15.40. CSF £138.26 CT £588.74 TOTE £11.30: £2.80, £5.80, £2.00; EX 278.50.
Owner Mrs Andrea M Mallinson **Bred** C Mallinson **Trained** Norton, N Yorks

FOCUS
An open-looking event and, strictly on form, few could be discounted. Riders who walked the course beforehand said the ground had no real sting in it. They went a decent pace but the form is modest and best rated around the placed horses.
Shosolosa(IRE) Official explanation: jockey said the mare hung left-handed throughout

5439 MARKET CROSS JEWELLERS MEDIAN AUCTION MAIDEN STKS 6f

5:50 (5:53) (Class 5) 2-Y-O £3,238 (£722; £722; £240) Stalls Centre

Form RPR
3 **1** **Distinctive**[35] 4331 2-8-12 0 .... TomEaves 6 78+
(B Smart) *trckd ldrs gng wl: led appr fnl f: kpt on strly ins fnl f: readily* **6/4**[1]
50 **2** 2½ **Fantastic Strike (IRE)**[56] 3613 2-9-3 0 .... JoeFanning 2 74
(M Johnston) *cl up: effrt and ev ch over 1f out: kpt on u.p fnl f* **13/2**[3]
2 *dht* **Melundy** 2-8-12 0 .... TGMcLaughlin 1 69
(Mrs L Stubbs) *dwlt: hld up: hdwy and ev ch over 1f out: kpt on u.p fnl f* **10/1**
6 **4** 3 **Shi Shan**[36] 4282 2-9-0 0 .... NeilBrown(3) 12 65
(T D Barron) *t.k.h: prom: rdn and hung rt over 1f out: one pce* **11/4**[2]
240 **5** 1¼ **Pepper Lane**[70] 3152 2-8-12 64 .... AndrewMullen 5 56
(J Hetherton) *cl up tl rdn and no ex over 1f out* **12/1**
6 *nk* **House Of Rules** 2-8-12 0 .... JamieKyne(5) 7 60+
(Miss J A Camacho) *in tch: drvn and outpcd over 2f out: kpt on fnl f* **25/1**
0 **7** 1¼ **Infinity World**[20] 4817 2-8-7 0 .... LanceBetts(5) 4 51
(G R Oldroyd) *led to over 1f out: sn no ex* **66/1**
8 1½ **All Moving Parts (USA)** 2-9-3 0 .... PAspell 11 52
(J S Wainwright) *bhd and outpcd: kpt on fnl f: n.d* **50/1**
050 **9** 2½ **Summa Cum Laude**[19] 4856 2-8-12 0 .... SilvestreDeSousa 13 39
(Mrs A Duffield) *hld up: rdn and hung lft 1/2-way: sn outpcd* **25/1**
60 **10** 3 **Emerald Glade (IRE)**[19] 4847 2-8-12 0 .... DuranFentiman 8 30
(T D Easterby) *taken early to post: bhd and outpcd: nvr on terms* **22/1**
11 11 **Check The Anchor (IRE)** 2-9-0 0 .... MichaelJStainton(3) 10 2
(N Tinkler) *missed break: a wl bhd* **25/1**
0 **12** 1½ **Clumber Pursuits**[12] 5109 2-8-7 0 .... MarkCoumbe(5) 14 —
(S A Harris) *hld up: rdn 1/2-way: sn struggling* **100/1**
13 1¾ **Timetowynagain** 2-9-0 0 .... KellyHarrison(3) 9 —
(C W Fairhurst) *bhd and sn struggling: no ch fr 1/2-way* **33/1**

1m 10.15s (-1.65) **Going Correction** -0.30s/f (Firm) **13** Ran SP% **120.1**
Speed ratings (Par 94): **99,95,95,91,90 89,87,85,82,78 63,61,59**
PL: Fantastic Strike £2.30, Melondy £2.50. Exacta: D,FS, £5.10 D,F £13.20. CSF: D,FS £5.36 D,M £8.24. toteswinger: D&FS £1.90, D&M £7.80, FS&M £15.10. TOTE £2.10: £1.20.
Owner Mr & Mrs G Middlebrook **Bred** Mr & Mrs G Middlebrook **Trained** Hambleton, N Yorks

FOCUS
Not the strongest of median auction maidens, with few in the line-up having shown form worth crowing about, but the winner scored decisively and may have more to offer.

NOTEBOOK
Distinctive set the standard, thanks to her debut third in a York maiden the previous month, and, as she had lost ground by rearing as the stalls opened that day, improvement appeared highly likely. How much she needed to progress is a moot point, as she had plenty in hand at the finish, but, after getting a nice lead for the first half-mile, she quickly asserted when asked and was well on top in the closing stages. Trainer Bryan Smart reckons she is still green, an opinion underlined by a few jinks on the way to post, and also believes she will appreciate a seventh furlong. Given some cut, she may go next for the Firth Of Clyde Stakes at Ayr. (op 7-4 tchd 15-8)
Fantastic Strike(IRE) was attempting to put a modest second run behind him - and returning after a 56-day layoff - but he had been well backed on both his starts and had shown enough on his first to indicate that he possesses sufficient talent to break his duck at some stage. He ran markedly better here than on his previous outing, which may have come a little close to his debut run, and, as he is a tall, leggy sort with some filling out still to do, he may well progress again. (op 9-2)
Melundy, bred to appreciate longer trips than this and from a stable enjoying a decent spell with its juveniles, made an encouraging debut, staying on well to share second spot and promising to go one better in the near future. (op 9-2)
Shi Shan had made a moderately promising start to his career when taking sixth after a slow start over 5f at Thirsk and the way he had stayed on in the closing stages on that occasion suggested this step up in trip would suit. He ran another sound race, figuring prominently from the outset, but did not perhaps find quite as much improvement on this second run as some might have anticipated. (op 7-2)
House Of Rules showed promise, without ever threatening to collect, and, as he looked burly and slightly backward for this debut, improvement appears a distinct possibility. (op 28-1 tchd 20-1)
Infinity World, who had cut little ice on his only previous outing, stepped up considerably on that showing, making a good deal of the running before fading over the closing stages. (op 100-1 tchd 50-1)
Summa Cum Laude Official explanation: jockey said filly hung left-handed throughout

5440 BUY YOUR TICKETS ON-LINE @ REDCARRACING.CO.UK NOVICE MEDIAN AUCTION STKS 7f

6:20 (6:21) (Class 5) 2-Y-O £3,238 (£963; £481; £240) Stalls Centre

Form RPR
2 **1** **Court Gown (IRE)**[37] 4226 2-8-8 0 .... RichardMullen 3 77+
(E S McMahon) *hld up in tch: effrt and edgd lft over 1f out: led ins fnl f: kpt on wl* **11/10**[1]
3 **2** ¾ **Al Naouwee (USA)**[16] 4939 2-8-13 0 .... TomEaves 8 80+
(B Smart) *t.k.h early: led: rdn and edgd rt over 1f out: hdd ins fnl f: r.o* **4/1**[3]
1 **3** 4½ **Gobama**[57] 3576 2-9-0 0 .... SebSanders 7 70
(J W Hills) *chsd ldrs: effrt over 2f out: outpcd over 1f out* **7/4**[2]
0 **4** 4½ **Goodison Park**[15] 4993 2-8-8 0 .... AndrewMullen 4 53
(A G Foster) *chsd ldr: rdn over 2f out: wknd over 1f out* **25/1**

The Form Book, Raceform Ltd, Compton, RG20 6NL

060 **5** 3 1/2 **Kookie**[20] 4817 2-8-5 53 KellyHarrison(3) 5 44
(R E Barr) *hld up: rdn and hung lft 2f out: sn wknd* **50/1**

1m 24.27s (-0.23) **Going Correction** -0.30s/f (Firm) 5 Ran SP% **109.8**
Speed ratings (Par 94): **89,88,83,77,73**
toteswinger: 1&2 £5.95 CSF £5.95 TOTE £2.20: £1.40, £1.80; EX 5.60.
Owner J C Fretwell **Bred** J Costello **Trained** Lichfield, Staffs

FOCUS
Despite three significant late absentees, this was an interesting two-year-old event, bringing together a previous winner and two once-raced maidens with solid first-three placings in the book. The winner did not need to step up much on her debut to score.

NOTEBOOK
Court Gown(IRE) had needed to overcome problems before filling the runner-up spot on her only previous start, pulling hard and at least twice finding trouble in running, so an improved showing looked on the cards. She duly stepped up on that debut form, being restrained early before switching left and quickening nicely to take the lead on the wide left of the field, eventually asserting snugly inside the final furlong. Trainer Ed McMahon thinks she needs time between her races at this stage of her career, so she may not be seen out again until October, but this is surely not the last time she will get her head in front. (op 11-8)
Al Naouwee(USA), representing a stable that has been quieter than normal in juvenile races so far this season but collected the previous contest on this card, had nonetheless shown promise on his only start prior to this, taking third behind a hotpot in a decent race at Newcastle. He ran well again here, grabbing an early lead, setting a decent pace and not succumbing to the winner's decisive late thrust without a fight, so it should not be long before he is found a suitable opportunity to break his duck. (op 7-2)
Gobama had made a pleasing start to her career with a victory over this trip at Salisbury and, as her trainer is not renowned for having his two-year-olds primed for first-time-out victories, it seemed possible that she would build on that performance. Third place here was therefore a little disappointing, although in mitigation it has to be noted that she was carrying a penalty and thereby giving weight to the first two. (op 13-8 tchd 15-8)
Goodison Park, well beaten after a slow start on her only previous start, broke far more quickly here. After chasing the second until halfway, however, he was the first to come under pressure, gradually fading out of contention. (op 20-1 tchd 18-1)
Kookie, whose three earlier outings had resulted in nothing better than a sixth of 14, was always towards the rear and finished well beaten. (op 40-1)

5441 BODDINGTONS REDCAR STRAIGHT-MILE CHAMPIONSHIP STKS (QUALIFIER) (H'CAP) 1m
6:50 (6:51) (Class 4) (0-80,80) 3-Y-0+ **£5,180** (£1,541; £770; £192; £192) **Stalls** Centre

Form RPR
0133 **1** **Arizona John (IRE)**[15] 5003 4-9-3 70 SJCraine 14 79
(J Mackie) *in tch: effrt over 1f out: led ins fnl f: drvn out* **12/1**[3]
2064 **2** nk **Aussie Blue (IRE)**[17] 4887 5-8-8 61 oh1 PaulQuinn 16 69
(R M Whitaker) *hld up in midfield: hdwy and cl up over 1f out: drvn and kpt on towards fin* **20/1**
2220 **3** 1 3/4 **Snow Dancer (IRE)**[16] 4930 5-8-13 66 (b[1]) PaulHanagan 5 70
(H A McWilliams) *in tch: rdn over 2f out: kpt on ins fnl f* **16/1**
0502 **4** nk **Kiwi Bay**[21] 4802 4-9-11 78 TomEaves 8 82
(M Dods) *taken early to post: t.k.h: hdwy and hung lft over 1f out: kpt on fnl f: nrst fin* **14/1**
4004 **4** dht **Templetuohy Max (IRE)**[26] 4597 4-9-2 69 (v) JimmyQuinn 12 73
(J D Bethell) *cl up: led over 2f out to ins fnl f: one pce* **14/1**
2432 **6** 1/2 **Observatory Star (IRE)**[21] 4801 6-9-13 80 (b) DavidAllan 2 82
(T D Easterby) *prom: effrt and ev ch over 1f out: no ex ins fnl f* **11/2**[1]
005 **7** 1 **Middlemarch (IRE)**[17] 4897 9-8-7 65 (v) GaryBartley(5) 18 65
(J S Goldie) *hld up: hdwy over 1f out: kpt on fnl f: nvr able to chal* **33/1**
0500 **8** hd **Spinning**[14] 5040 6-9-6 76 (b) NeilBrown(3) 19 76+
(T D Barron) *s.i.s: hld up: hdwy over 1f out: n.d* **20/1**
2521 **9** 3/4 **Ninth House (USA)**[12] 5107 7-9-0 67 (t) SilvestreDeSousa 20 65
(Mrs R A Carr) *hld up: hdwy over 1f out: nvr able to chal* **7/1**[2]
-603 **10** 1 1/2 **Hartshead**[15] 4996 10-8-12 68 DominicFox(3) 7 63
(W Storey) *hld up: drvn 3f out: no imp fr 2f out* **16/1**
1533 **11** 1/2 **Intersky Charm (USA)**[16] 4941 5-8-9 65 MichaelJStainton(3) 15 58
(R M Whitaker) *t.k.h: chsd ldrs tl no ex over 1f out* **12/1**[3]
0353 **12** 2 3/4 **Brasingaman Hifive**[27] 4560 4-9-9 76 DaleGibson 9 63
(Mrs G S Rees) *in tch: drvn over 3f out: wknd over 2f out* **12/1**[3]
3656 **13** 3 1/2 **Veiled Applause**[24] 4663 6-9-6 78 JamieKyne(5) 1 57
(J J Quinn) *in tch: rdn over 3f out: wknd fnl 2f* **12/1**[3]
-200 **14** 1 3/4 **Hyde Lea Flyer**[18] 4881 4-9-4 71 GrahamGibbons 13 46
(E S McMahon) *led to over 2f out: sn rdn and btn* **20/1**
4053 **15** 4 1/2 **Aflaam (IRE)**[19] 4852 4-9-10 77 (t) JerryO'Dwyer 3 42
(P Howling) *hld up: effrt over 2f out: sn rdn and btn* **7/1**[2]
2001 **16** 2 **Barataria**[33] 4389 7-9-3 70 SebSanders 17 30
(R Bastiman) *rrd s: hld up: rdn over 2f out: sn btn* **14/1**
2125 **17** shd **Dancing Jest (IRE)**[51] 3777 5-8-11 64 NickyMackay 6 24
(Rae Guest) *chsd ldrs to 3f out: sn rdn and btn* **16/1**
00 **18** 7 **Rainbow Zest**[26] 4588 6-8-5 61 oh7 KellyHarrison(3) 10 5
(W Storey) *rdr slow to remove blindfold whn stalls opened; slow s: a struggling* **80/1**
3000 **19** 3 1/4 **Moves Goodenough**[26] 4597 6-9-8 80 (b) DeanHeslop(5) 4 16
(A G Foster) *taken early to post: midfield: struggling 3f out: sn wknd* **33/1**

1m 35.4s (-2.60) **Going Correction** -0.30s/f (Firm) 19 Ran SP% **130.2**
Speed ratings (Par 105): **101,100,98,98,98 98,97,96,96,94 94,91,87,86,81 79,79,72,69**
PL: Templetuohy Max £2.00 Kiwi Bay £2.40. toteswinger: 1&2 £60.70, 1&3 £62.40, 2&3 £37.40. CSF £249.80 CT £3945.46 TOTE £16.00: £3.80, £5.70, £3.70; EX 212.30.
Owner Derbyshire Racing **Bred** Abergwaun Farms **Trained** Church Broughton , Derbys
■ Stewards' Enquiry : S J Craine caution: used whip with excessive frequency

FOCUS
An immensely tricky puzzle for punters to solve, with a host of closely-matched runners, housed in stalls right across the track. The whole field raced in the centre of the course and they went a decent clip. The form is ordinary but sound enough rated around the first two and the fourth.
Kiwi Bay Official explanation: jockey said gelding ran too free
Aflaam(IRE) Official explanation: vet said gelding finished distressed

5442 HOLD YOUR CHRISTMAS PARTY @ REDCAR RACECOURSE H'CAP 1m 6f 19y
7:20 (7:20) (Class 6) (0-65,63) 3-Y-0 **£2,266** (£674; £337; £168) **Stalls** Low

Form RPR
0331 **1** **Twist Again (IRE)**[15] 5011 3-9-7 63 JimmyQuinn 10 71+
(P Howling) *in tch gng wl: smooth hdwy to ld 3f out: rdn and styd on wl fnl 2f* **5/2**[1]
6403 **2** 1 1/4 **Khayar (IRE)**[17] 4917 3-9-2 58 SebSanders 1 64
(M H Tompkins) *prom: hdwy to chse wnr over 2f out: kpt on u.p fnl f* **9/2**[2]
6336 **3** 4 1/2 **Tillietudlem (FR)**[14] 4529 3-8-3 45 PaulHanagan 5 45
(J S Goldie) *chsd ldrs: rdn and ev ch 3f out: one pce fnl 2f* **8/1**
-006 **4** 3/4 **Markadam**[20] 4822 3-8-10 52 AndrewMullen 13 51
(Miss S E Hall) *hld up: outpcd over 3f out: styd on over 1f out: nrst fin* **20/1**
4503 **5** 2 1/2 **Merchant Man**[17] 4892 3-9-1 57 (b) PJMcDonald 4 52
(J D Bethell) *midfield: drvn over 3f out: no imp fnl 2f* **5/1**[3]
0004 **6** 3/4 **Knock Three Times (IRE)**[21] 4806 3-8-0 45 DominicFox(3) 6 39
(W Storey) *midfield: effrt over 3f out: one pce fnl 2f* **10/1**
0366 **7** 3 **Pattern Mark**[15] 5011 3-8-9 51 PaulMulrennan 12 41
(Ollie Pears) *hld up: effrt over 3f out: wknd ins fnl f* **5/1**[3]
0500 **8** 7 **Ernies Keep**[25] 4617 3-7-13 46 ow1 JamieKyne(5) 11 26
(W Storey) *led: clr 1/2-way: hdd 3f out: sn rdn and wknd* **66/1**
034 **9** 8 **Gwyre (IRE)**[84] 2723 3-9-2 58 DavidAllan 9 27
(T D Easterby) *dwlt: bhd: rdn 4f out: nvr on terms* **16/1**
564 **10** 7 **Elusive Muse**[15] 4974 3-8-8 50 TomEaves 2 9
(M Dods) *chsd ldr tl wknd fr 4f out* **16/1**
00- **11** 31 **Eyesore**[288] 7319 3-7-10 45 [1] CharlotteKerton(7) 3 —
(S A Harris) *plld hrd: in tch to 1/2-way: sn struggling: t.o* **100/1**
00-5 **12** 7 **Accumulation (UAE)**[15] 4994 3-8-3 45 (b[1]) DaleGibson 8 —
(M W Easterby) *bhd: lost tch 1/2-way: t.o* **50/1**

3m 3.67s (-1.03) **Going Correction** -0.15s/f (Firm) 12 Ran SP% **121.3**
Speed ratings (Par 98): **96,95,92,92,90 90,88,84,80,76 58,54**
toteswinger: 1&2 £3.10, 1&3 £5.30, 2&3 £10.40. CSF £13.46 CT £81.35 TOTE £3.70: £1.60, £2.10, £2.50; EX 16.90.
Owner Liam Sheridan **Bred** Michael Dalton **Trained** Newmarket, Suffolk

FOCUS
A modest event, with the top-weight rated just 63, but several looked out of their depth even at this low level. Not form to rate too positively and not particularly solid, with the runner-up the best guide.

5443 THE COMMITMENTS PERFORMING AFTER RACING H'CAP 6f
7:50 (7:51) (Class 6) (0-55,64) 3-Y-0+ **£2,388** (£705; £352) **Stalls** Centre

Form RPR
02 **1** **Averoo**[15] 4998 4-9-3 53 (p) SilvestreDeSousa 6 63
(M D Squance) *dwlt: hld up: gd hdwy over 1f out: led ins fnl f: r.o wl* **3/1**[1]
4520 **2** 1 1/4 **Elkhorn**[15] 4998 7-9-3 53 (b) TomEaves 5 59
(Miss J A Camacho) *in tch: led gng wl over 1f out: edgd rt and hdd ins fnl f: one pce* **7/1**
0-64 **3** hd **Imperial Echo (USA)**[89] 2531 8-8-13 52 NeilBrown(3) 9 57
(T D Barron) *midfield: effrt and swtchd rt over 1f out: kpt on ins fnl f* **14/1**
0060 **4** nk **Foreign Rhythm (IRE)**[16] 4929 4-8-11 47 JimmyQuinn 14 51
(N Tinkler) *midfield: rdn over 2f out: hdwy over 1f out: kpt on fnl f* **33/1**
0000 **5** 3 1/4 **Helping Hand (IRE)**[44] 3999 4-8-11 50 RussellKennemore(3) 4 44
(R Hollinshead) *cl up tl rdn and no ex over 1f out* **25/1**
643 **6** 1 **Colombard (IRE)**[22] 4748 4-8-10 46 oh1 SJCraine 2 37
(Patrick Morris) *midfield: effrt over 2f out: no imp over 1f out* **14/1**
0060 **7** 1 **Inca Soldier (FR)**[15] 4977 6-8-11 52 MarkCoumbe(5) 1 40
(S A Harris) *s.v.s: wl bhd tl styd on fnl 2f: nrst fin* **16/1**
2023 **8** hd **The Name Is Frank**[1] 5396 4-9-2 55 (t) MichaelJStainton(3) 8 42
(Mark Gillard) *cl up tl rdn and no ex over 1f out* **5/1**[2]
0000 **9** 1/2 **Royal Island (IRE)**[24] 4645 7-9-4 54 VinceSlattery 19 39
(M G Quinlan) *hld up: drvn over 2f out: nt pce to chal* **33/1**
0603 **10** nk **Half A Crown (IRE)**[28] 4552 4-8-10 46 oh1 (bt) PJMcDonald 15 30
(M Dods) *led to over 1f out: sn btn* **11/1**
0403 **11** 1 1/2 **Royal Composer (IRE)**[15] 4977 6-9-4 54 GrahamGibbons 17 34
(T D Easterby) *bhd and sn drvn along: nvr on terms* **13/2**[3]
465- **12** 1/2 **Lambency (IRE)**[290] 7288 6-9-3 53 DanielTudhope 16 31
(J S Goldie) *bhd and outpcd: nvr on terms* **25/1**
4600 **13** 1 1/4 **Secret Dubai (IRE)**[24] 4654 4-8-7 50 (t) KristinStubbs(7) 20 24
(Mrs L Stubbs) *bhd: shkn up over 2f out: sn no imp* **33/1**
-000 **14** 4 **Quicks The Word**[49] 3852 9-8-12 48 PaulHanagan 7 9
(T A K Cuthbert) *cl up tl rdn and wknd over 1f out* **40/1**
0460 **15** 4 1/2 **Conjecture**[20] 4823 7-9-5 55 SebSanders 10 2
(R Bastiman) *chsd ldrs tl lost pl over 2f out: eased* **15/2**

69.85 secs (-1.95) **Going Correction** -0.30s/f (Firm)
WFA 3 from 4yo+ 3lb 15 Ran SP% **125.8**
Speed ratings (Par 101): **101,99,99,98,94 93,91,91,90,90 88,87,86,80,74**
toteswinger: 1&2 £3.90, 1&3 £10.30, 2&3 £26.20. CSF £22.75 CT £269.62 TOTE £3.70: £2.10, £1.90, £3.50; EX 23.60 Place 6: £61.18, Place 5: £23.13..
Owner Troon Partnership **Bred** Mrs H Johnson Houghton & Mrs R F Johnson Hought **Trained** Newmarket, Suffolk

FOCUS
Very few in this line-up boasted consistent form, with the overall standard decidedly moderate, but they looked closely matched and the form appears straightforward rated around the runner-up and fourth.
Inca Soldier(FR) Official explanation: jockey said gelding missed the break
Conjecture Official explanation: jockey said gelding lost action
T/Plt: £102.20 to a £1 stake. Pool: £43,953.79. 313.65 winning tickets. T/Qpdt: £23.20 to a £1 stake. Pool: £4,460.92. 141.68 winning tickets. RY

5317 WINDSOR (R-H)
Saturday, August 29

OFFICIAL GOING: Good to firm (8.5)
Wind: fresh, behind Weather: partly cloudy, breezy

5444 AJA INSURE MEMBERS FEGENTRI WORLD CHAMPIONSHIP H'CAP (FOR GENTLEMAN AMATEUR RIDERS) 1m 3f 135y
5:10 (5:11) (Class 5) (0-70,67) 3-Y-0+ **£2,637** (£811; £405) **Stalls** Centre

Form RPR
0145 **1** **Sky Quest (IRE)**[9] 5185 11-11-6 63 MrlChanin 8 71
(J R Boyle) *stdd s: hld up in rr: gd hdwy on outer to ld over 2f out: rdn and hung rt over 1f out: styd on and in command fnl f* **5/1**[3]
0-00 **2** 1 1/2 **King's Fable (USA)**[28] 4538 6-10-9 52 (p) MrMWeissmeier 2 57
(Karen George) *s.i.s: hld up in tch: hdwy over 3f out: chsd wnr jst over 2f out: hung rt ent fnl f: one pce after* **11/1**
3120 **3** 2 1/2 **Sand Repeal (IRE)**[8] 5210 7-11-1 58 MrFabioLocatelli 6 59
(Miss J Feilden) *hld up in tch in midfield: hdwy to ld narrowly jst over 3f out: hdd over 2f out: nt pce of ldng pair ent fnl 2f out: plugged on one pce after* **7/2**[1]
6040 **4** 1/2 **Bolton Hall (IRE)**[9] 4168 7-10-5 48 oh3 (tp) MrFGuy 3 48
(W K Goldsworthy) *led and sn clr: hdd jst over 3f out: rdn and kpt on same pce fr over 2f out* **8/1**
0-06 **5** 2 3/4 **Still Dreaming**[12] 5097 5-10-5 48 oh3 (b) MrRBirkett 7 44
(R J Price) *s.i.s: hld up in last pair: rdn and effrt on inner jst over 3f out: no imp fnl 2f* **14/1**

-560 **6** *1 ½* **Silver Blue (IRE)**[23] 4698 6-10-8 **51** .... MrJoshuaMoore 4 44
(W K Goldsworthy) *in tch: rdn and unable qck over 3f out: n.d fnl 2f* **16/1**

-000 **7** *4 ½* **Highland River**[7] 2982 3-10-4 **57** .... MrJacobSmith 5 42
(D R C Elsworth) *t.k.h: chsd ldr tl over 3f out: rdn and wknd over 2f out:* **12/1**

360 **8** *4* **Blockley (USA)**[27] 4563 5-11-8 **65** ....(bt[1]) MrPatrickDeno 10 44
(Ian Williams) *dwlt: sn rcvrd and chsd ldrs: rdn and no rspnse over 3f out: wl bhd fnl 2f* **5/1**[3]

0423 **9** *12* **Classical Rhythm (IRE)**[10] 5152 4-10-11 **54** .... MrAJDoyle 9 12
(J R Boyle) *t.k.h: chsd ldrs: hdwy and ev ch jst over 3f out: wknd qckly over 2f out: wl bhd fnl f* **9/2**[2]

2m 29.73s (0.23) **Going Correction** -0.30s/f (Firm)
WFA 3 from 4yo+ 10lb **9** Ran SP% **113.4**
Speed ratings (Par 103): **87,86,84,84,82 81,78,75,67**
toteswinger: 1&2 £6.90, 1&3 £3.50, 2&3 £8.60. CSF £57.11 CT £215.32 TOTE £6.20: £2.00, £3.40, £2.00; EX 66.10.
Owner M C Cook **Bred** Pendley Farm **Trained** Epsom, Surrey

FOCUS
The stands' side rails in the home straight were at their normal configuration this evening. Hold-up performers filled the frame in this modest amateurs' contest with the winner probably the best guide.

5445 TOTEEXACTA NOVICE MEDIAN AUCTION STKS 6f
5:40 (5:40) (Class 5) 2-Y-O **£2,729** (£806; £403) **Stalls** High

Form RPR

612 **1** **Ramamara (IRE)**[7] 5241 2-8-11 78 .... PatCosgrave 1 80
(P D Evans) *mde all: rdn and hung lft over 1f out: styd on wl to forge clr ins fnl f* **10/3**[3]

42 **2** *2 ¼* **Burgau Royal**[14] 5017 2-8-12 0 .... CatherineGannon 5 74
(M R Channon) *chsd wnr: rdn whn carried lft over 1f out: no ex fnl 100yds* **15/8**[1]

5321 **3** *1 ¾* **Bridge Valley**[17] 4906 2-9-6 78 .... RyanMoore 6 77
(R Hannon) *hld up in tch: rdn and unable qck ent fnl 2f: plugged on to go 3rd fnl 50yds: no ch w ldng pair* **3/1**[2]

1 **4** *½* **I Am That (IRE)**[10] 5146 2-9-4 0 .... LDettori 4 73
(S A Callaghan) *chsd ldng pair: rdn and effrt jst over 2f out: nt pce of ldng pair over 1f out: wl hld fnl f: lost 3rd fnl 50yds* **5/1**

5000 **5** *4 ½* **Azif**[28] 4539 2-8-13 75 .... DavidProbert 2 55
(Miss Gay Kelleway) *hld up in tch: rdn over 2f out: sn struggling: wl hld fnl 2f* **9/1**

6 *8* **Fraamtaaztiic** 2-8-4 0 ow4 .... WilliamCarson(3) 3 25
(R J Hodges) *hmpd s: sn detached in last pl* **20/1**

1m 11.54s (-1.46) **Going Correction** -0.30s/f (Firm) **6** Ran SP% **114.3**
Speed ratings (Par 94): **97,94,91,91,85 74**
toteswinger: 1&2 £3.00, 1&3 £1.90, 2&3 £3.00. CSF £10.32 TOTE £5.30: £2.40, £1.80; EX 15.40.
Owner Raymond N R Auld **Bred** R N Auld **Trained** Pandy, Monmouths

FOCUS
Four previous winners lined up in this six-runner puzzle. The winner produced another improved effort and the form makes sense.

NOTEBOOK
Ramamara(IRE) had seen out 6f well in defeat at Bath last time, so it was not wholly surprising that a lot of use was made of her over this sharper course. She tracked over to the stands' rail having broken best, and although she drifted infield under pressure never looked like losing. She has been a marked improver since winning a Polytrack seller two runs ago, if not enough in connections' eyes to justify the 14lb hike for the Bath run. Pat Cosgrave opined that she should be able to stay a seventh furlong in due course. (op 7-2)
Burgau Royal was sent off a well-supported favourite on the strength of a decent second at Lingfield last time. That performance had betrayed a lack of late tactical speed, however, and that was exposed again here as he didn't make as much of a race of it with Ramamara as seemed likely 2f out. He was already losing the argument when carried left by the winner and can't posit that as an excuse. (op 5-2)
Bridge Valley, conceding weight all round, had posted a clear career best when dropped to the minimum for the first time at Sandown two weeks ago. Things all happened a bit too quickly for him here, notwithstanding the step back up in trip, and a return to a more exacting course would seem prudent. (op 7-2)
I Am That(IRE), friendless just before the off, always looked to be chasing the race somewhat. His debut win had come over the very different test of Carlisle's stiff 5f on good to soft, and he will be better judged granted another try over that sort of trip and course. Official explanation: jockey said colt was unsuited by the good to firm going (op 7-2)

5446 TOTEQUADPOT AUGUST STKS (LISTED RACE) 1m 3f 135y
6:10 (6:10) (Class 1) 3-Y-O+ **£22,708** (£8,608; £4,308; £2,148; £1,076) **Stalls** Centre

Form RPR

6634 **1** **Traffic Guard (USA)**[21] 4780 5-9-2 112 .... MartinDwyer 1 114
(P F I Cole) *stdd s: t.k.h: hld up in main gp: clsd on ldr 5f out: squeezed between horses to ld jst over 2f out: pushed clr over 1f out: in n.d after: eased towards fin* **3/1**[3]

1225 **2** *8* **Warringah**[10] 5173 4-9-2 109 .... RyanMoore 3 100
(Sir Michael Stoute) *chsd clr ldr: clsd 5f out: rdn to ld narrowly over 2f out: sn hdd: no ch w wnr fnl f: kpt on for 2nd* **11/8**[1]

1302 **3** *1 ¾* **Classic Punch (IRE)**[15] 5004 6-9-2 102 .... MickyFenton 4 97
(D R C Elsworth) *led and sn clr: c bk to field 5f out: rdn and hdd over 2f out: nt pce of wnr wl over 1f out: kpt on same pce u.p fnl f* **9/1**

1253 **4** *shd* **Age Of Reason (UAE)**[14] 5023 4-9-2 112 .... LDettori 2 97
(Saeed Bin Suroor) *hld up in main gp: clsd on ldr 5f out: pressed ldrs on outer and rdn 3f out: outpcd wl over 2f out: 3rd and btn whn hung rt 1f out: wnt lft and lost 3rd last stride* **2/1**[2]

0550 **5** *½* **Bushy Dell (IRE)**[29] 4498 4-8-11 65 .... CatherineGannon 5 91?
(Miss J Feilden) *hld up in last pl: clsd and in tch 5f out: rdn and outpcd over 3f out: no ch w wnr after: kpt on u.p fnl f* **100/1**

2m 23.54s (-5.96) **Going Correction** -0.30s/f (Firm) **5** Ran SP% **111.4**
Speed ratings (Par 111): **107,101,100,100,100**
CSF £7.70 TOTE £3.60: £2.20, £1.50; EX 8.70.
Owner Mrs Fitri Hay **Bred** Frank Penn And John R Penn **Trained** Whatcombe, Oxon

FOCUS
With Classic Punch likely to set an exacting pace early pace, this Listed contest looked primed for a patiently ridden winner despite the small field, and so it proved. The form is dubious, with the fifth rather close up, and the others bar the winner were all below their best.

NOTEBOOK
Traffic Guard(USA) was never higher placed than third until around 3f from home, but he found first Classic Punch and then Warringah very easy to master once sent closer and skated home to a first win in 17 runs since July 2007. Having his first run over this trip, he is likely to be kept at this sort of distance for now. No specific target has been nominated as yet, however. His owner mentioned that connections had done well to overcome some joint problems with the five-year-old, too, so there might be a little more to come if he's a significantly sounder horse now than of late. (op 4-1)
Warringah, with his rider mindful of a destructive battle ensuing with Classic Punch, wasn't asked to vie for the lead. He didn't sulk when deprived of that berth, and his limited response once relieved of his short-lived lead by the winner was more likely due to his mighty effort in the Ebor still being in his legs. He will prove better than this effort again after a longer break. (tchd 6-4)
Classic Punch(IRE), who set a strong pace and was clear for a time, retook third close home. (op 8-1 tchd 10-1)
Age Of Reason(UAE) had stayed on close home when third in the Geoffrey Freer over further last time, but his effort once produced to challenge 3f out proved disappointingly short-lived. The consistency of his efforts in the Middle East and Italy earlier in the year is just starting to desert him. Official explanation: jockey said gelding ran flat

5447 TOTEPOOL WINTER HILL STKS (GROUP 3) 1m 2f 7y
6:40 (6:40) (Class 1) 3-Y-O+
£39,739 (£15,064; £7,539; £3,759; £1,883; £945) **Stalls** Centre

Form RPR

0202 **1** **Campanologist (USA)**[21] 4780 4-9-0 114 .... LDettori 8 113
(Saeed Bin Suroor) *hld up in midfield: swtchd lft and effrt 2f out: rdn and to chal over 1f out: led fnl 100yds: kpt on* **11/10**[1]

-153 **2** *½* **Bankable (IRE)**[104] 2117 5-9-0 115 .... GeorgeBaker 4 112
(G L Moore) *stdd s: hld up in last pair: hdwy wl over 1f out: swtchd lft and rdn 1f out: pressed wnr fnl 50yds: hld nr fin* **11/2**[3]

-212 **3** *nk* **Kingdom Of Fife**[49] 3873 4-9-0 105 ....(v) RyanMoore 7 111
(Sir Michael Stoute) *chsd ldr: rdn and effrt over 2f out: led narrowly 2f out: hdd and no ex fnl 100yds* **7/2**[2]

10- **4** *¾* **Serva Jugum (USA)**[300] 7163 3-8-6 102 .... MartinDwyer 2 110
(P F I Cole) *hld up in last trio: hdwy and hmpd 2f out: chsng ldrs and n.m.r 1f out: kpt on but nvr able to chal ldrs* **25/1**

2630 **5** *1 ½* **Pure Poetry (IRE)**[13] 5084 3-8-6 109 .... EddieAhern 6 107
(R Hannon) *squeezed s and s.i.s: sn rcvrd and chsng ldrs after 1f: rdn and effrt on outer 3f out: ev ch 2f out tl wknd ins fnl f* **12/1**

2625 **6** *hd* **Staying On (IRE)**[21] 4780 4-9-0 110 ....(vt[1]) AdamKirby 5 106
(W R Swinburn) *taken down early: led: rdn wl over 2f out: drvn and hdd 2f out: wknd u.p ins fnl f* **16/1**

2014 **7** *2 ½* **Drumfire (IRE)**[29] 4484 5-9-0 111 .... JimmyFortune 3 101
(M Johnston) *chsd ldrs: pushed along 4f out: rdn and unable qck 2f out: btn whn n.m.r ins fnl f: nt pushed after* **8/1**

2-32 **8** *14* **Casilda (IRE)**[118] 1697 4-8-11 99 .... WilliamBuick 1 70
(A M Balding) *stdd s: hld up in last pl: rdn and no hdwy 3f out: eased whn wl btn fnl f* **28/1**

2m 2.44s (-6.26) **Going Correction** -0.30s/f (Firm) course record
WFA 3 from 4yo+ 8lb **8** Ran SP% **117.2**
Speed ratings (Par 113): **113,112,112,111,110 110,108,97**
toteswinger: 1&2 £1.70, 1&3 £1.40, 2&3 £4.50. CSF £7.92 TOTE £2.10: £1.10, £1.50, £1.80; EX 8.00.
Owner Godolphin **Bred** Darley **Trained** Newmarket, Suffolk

FOCUS
The 15th running of this long-established contest as a Group 3 was run at a decent tempo, but all bar one of the octet were still thereabouts with less than 2f to travel. The form looks sound enough without the front pair being at their best.

NOTEBOOK
Campanologist(USA) had raced prominently in all his recent starts, but proved entirely amenable to different tactics here and still had plenty left in the locker turning in. Frankie Dettori's post-race assertion that he had everything covered with a furlong to go tallied with the visual impression. Winless in six races since his King Edward VII Stakes win 14 months ago, this should serve the Champion Stakes entry well as a confidence booster ahead of tougher assignments this autumn. (tchd 6-5, 5-4 in places)
Bankable(IRE) was stressed to be in need of the race beforehand by his new trainer, but still posted a very pleasing effort, threading his way nicely through the traffic and evidently not missing the tongue tie of his last three runs. Available at around 33-1 for the Cambridgeshire, aspirations for him may still be a little higher than that after this performance. (op 6-1 tchd 7-1)
Kingdom Of Fife recorded a respectable first try above handicap company, just proving a little one-paced inside the last furlong. His much-improved recent efforts have been recorded when trying to make all, something Staying On stopped him doing here, and it's conjectural how often he'll get things entirely his own way at this more exalted level. (tchd 4-1)
Serva Jugum(USA), highly tried on his only two starts (both 1m) last autumn, ran a big race after his 300-day absence without completely convincing he needs the extra 2f yet. He still remains something of an open book after so few appearances, though, and would be worth a look in something a little easier than this next time dropped back in trip. (op 33-1)
Pure Poetry(IRE) faded out of it over a trip he didn't see out at Deauville last time either.
Drumfire(IRE) continues to fall a little short when stepped back up to Group company. (tchd 17-2)

5448 TOTESWINGER H'CAP 1m 67y
7:10 (7:10) (Class 4) (0-85,83) 3-Y-O+ **£5,180** (£1,156; £1,156; £384) **Stalls** High

Form RPR

223 **1** **Pegasus Again (USA)**[131] 1405 4-9-9 **78** ....(p) RobertHavlin 13 86
(T G Mills) *mde all: rdn jst over 2f out: hrd pressed ent fnl f: hld on gamely: all out* **6/1**[2]

1534 **2** *nk* **Can Can Star**[13] 5062 6-9-3 **79** .... DebraEngland(7) 11 86
(A W Carroll) *chsd ldrs: swtchd lft and hdwy to chse wnr over 1f out: ev ch fnl f: r.o but a jst hld* **8/1**

61-5 **2** *dht* **Truism**[134] 1324 3-9-8 **83** .... JimCrowley 2 89
(Mrs A J Perrett) *chsd ldrs: rdn to chse wnr jst over 2f out: ev ch ent fnl f: unable qck fnl 100yds* **5/1**[1]

2215 **4** *2* **Palacefield (IRE)**[60] 3489 3-9-5 **80** .... AlanMunro 8 81+
(P W Chapple-Hyam) *hld up towards rr: rdn and effrt over 2f out: hdwy over 1f out: styd on u.p fnl f: nt rch ldrs* **14/1**

0-50 **5** *¾* **Brief Candle**[77] 2925 3-9-8 **83** ....(t) AdamKirby 9 83+
(W R Swinburn) *hld up in last trio: rdn and hdwy on inner over 1f out: chsd ldrs ins fnl f: no imp fnl 100yds* **8/1**

0000 **6** *3* **Southandwest (IRE)**[8] 5221 5-9-11 **80** .... JimmyFortune 5 74
(J S Moore) *t.k.h: hld up in tch: hamperd after 1f: rdn and effrt over 2f out: drvn and one pce fr over 1f out* **10/1**

4500 **7** *2 ¼* **Orchard Supreme**[145] 1149 6-9-13 **82** .... RyanMoore 7 71
(R Hannon) *stdd s: hld up in last pair: shkn up and hdwy jst over 2f out: no hdwy over 1f out* **12/1**

5150 **8** *1 ¼* **The Winged Assasin (USA)**[16] 4956 3-8-13 **74** .... PatCosgrave 12 59
(J Akehurst) *hld up towards rr: rdn and effrt 2f out: hdwy towards outer ent fnl f: sn no imp* **33/1**

0031 **9** *1* **Marning Star**[18] 4881 4-9-2 **71** ....(t) EddieAhern 3 54
(Ian Williams) *chsd wnr tl jst over 2f out: wknd u.p over 1f out* **10/1**

000 **10** *½* **Black Rain**[22] 4759 4-9-3 **72** .... WilliamBuick 4 54
(M Wigham) *hld up in tch in midfield: effrt and rdn over 2f out: no prog over 1f out: wl hld fnl f* **20/1**

5600 **11** *½* **Mr Hichens**[20] 4815 4-9-3 **72** .... TPO'Shea 6 53
(Karen George) *hld up in midfield: rdn and unable qck whn short of room and hmpd over 1f out: no ch after* **8/1**

6513 **12** *2 ¾* **Learo Dochais (USA)**[28] 4535 3-8-13 74.................... PhilipRobinson 1 48
(M A Jarvis) *chsd ldrs: rdn over 2f out: sn struggling: wl btn fnl f* **13/2**[3]
110 **13** *76* **Ensnare**[38] 4207 4-8-10 65.. MickyFenton 10 —
(Ian Williams) *a bhd: lost tch over 3f out: t.o and eased fr over 1f out* **12/1**
1m 41.02s (-3.68) **Going Correction** -0.30s/f (Firm)
WFA 3 from 4yo+ 6lb **13** Ran SP% **125.6**
Speed ratings (Par 105): **106,105,105,103,102 99,97,96,95,94 94,91,15**PL: Can Can Star £3.00 Truism £3.20 Ex: Pegasus Again, Can Can Star £27.80. PA, T £19.20. CSF: PA, CCS £28.22, PA,T £19.02. Tricast: PA,CCS,T £137.39 PA,T,CCS £129.77. toteswinger: PA&CCS £5.60, PA&T £3.60, CCS&T £11.70. TOTE £8.00: £2.70, £0.0027Owner T G Mills Trifecta £Bred Stonestreet Mares Llc Trained.

FOCUS
Three pulled clear at the end of this contest, which was won in a time 0.95 seconds faster than the fillies' race that followed it. The first three were always prominent and the winner is the best guide.
Mr Hichens Official explanation: jockey said colt suffered interference in running
Ensnare Official explanation: jockey said gelding was never travelling

5449 COLIN FLETCHER 60TH BIRTHDAY FILLIES' H'CAP — 1m 67y
7:40 (7:41) (Class 5) (0-75,75) 3-Y-0+ **£2,729** (£806; £403) **Stalls** High

Form RPR
1023 **1** **Turning Top (IRE)**[23] 4695 3-9-11 75.............................. RyanMoore 2 86+
(S A Callaghan) *stdd s: hld up bhd: hdwy on inner over 2f out: led over 1f out: sn pushed clr: comf* **11/2**[2]
5241 **2** *2 ¾* **West With The Wind (USA)**[24] 4655 3-9-8 72.................. AlanMunro 8 74
(P W Chapple-Hyam) *t.k.h: chsd ldrs: rdn ent fnl f: chsd clr wnr ins fnl f: kpt on but no ch w wnr* **4/1**[1]
0-50 **3** *nk* **Margarita (IRE)**[85] 2664 3-9-4 68.................................(t) WilliamBuick 10 69
(J R Fanshawe) *hld up towards rr: pushed along 4f out: rdn and hdwy towards outer 1f out: kpt on to go 3rd on post: no ch w wnr* **10/1**
3321 **4** *nse* **Dr Wintringham (IRE)**[16] 4938 3-8-10 60..................... MartinDwyer 12 63+
(Karen George) *t.k.h: hld up in midfield: rdn and hdwy 2f out: swtchd lft jst ins fnl f: r.o but nvr a threat to wnr* **4/1**[1]
3630 **5** *nk* **Mutually Mine (USA)**[12] 5112 3-9-3 67......................... MickyFenton 6 67
(Mrs P Sly) *t.k.h: stdd after s and hld up in last pair: rdn and effrt on outer 2f out: kpt on to chal for placings fnl f: no ch w wnr* **28/1**
46-5 **6** *1 ½* **Bosamcliff (IRE)**[16] 4950 4-8-13 62.......................... RichardEvans(5) 11 59+
(P D Evans) *hld up in rr: rdn over 2f out: nt clr run and edging out lft over 1f out: styd on fnl f: nvr trbld ldrs* **16/1**
252 **7** *nse* **Miss Sophisticat**[23] 4720 3-9-6 70...........................(p) JimmyFortune 13 67
(W J Knight) *restless stalls: sn led: hdd 5f out: edgd rt u.p and wknd wl over 1f out* **7/1**[3]
6145 **8** *nk* **Russian Rave**[12] 5090 3-9-6 70.. EddieAhern 4 66
(J G Portman) *hld up in midfield on outer: rdn and hdwy to chse ldrs over 2f out: sn drvn: wknd fnl f* **14/1**
4623 **9** *½* **Very Well Red**[13] 5063 6-9-13 71.. LPKeniry 1 66
(P W Hiatt) *chsd ldrs wnt 2nd over 6f out: led 5f out: rdn over 2f out: hdd over 1f out: no ch w wnr ins fnl f: wknd fnl 100yds* **12/1**
0320 **10** *¾* **Onenightinlisbon (IRE)**[9] 5195 5-8-13 57..................... PatCosgrave 9 50+
(J R Boyle) *t.k.h: hld up in tch in midfield: rdn and effrt jst over 2f out: unable qck whn n.m.r jst over 1f out: no ch w wnr fnl f* **20/1**
0100 **11** *1 ¾* **Romantic Verse**[19] 4859 4-9-4 62...........................(b) JamesDoyle 14 51
(S Curran) *chsd ldrs: rdn and effrt 2f out: keeping on same pce and hld whn short of room 1f out* **50/1**
031- **12** *3 ¾* **Dialect**[283] 7380 3-9-10 74.. JimCrowley 7 67+
(Mrs A J Perrett) *t.k.h: hld up towards rr: hdwy over 2f out: one pce and btn whn hmpd over 1f out: sn btn and nt pushed after* **8/1**
3230 **13** *19* **Toolentidhaar (USA)**[12] 5099 5-9-13 71......................... GeorgeBaker 3 8
(Andrew Turnell) *chsd ldr tl over 6f out: styd handy tl wknd qckly 2f out: virtually p.u fnl f: sddle slipped* **25/1**
1m 41.97s (-2.73) **Going Correction** -0.30s/f (Firm)
WFA 3 from 4yo+ 6lb **13** Ran SP% **122.3**
Speed ratings (Par 100): **101,98,97,97,97 96,96,95,95,94 92,89,70**
toteswinger: 1&2 £2.80, 1&3 £21.80, 2&3 £21.00. CSF £27.27 CT £229.36 TOTE £7.30: £2.50, £2.10, £2.30; EX 28.00 Place 6: £12.70, Place 5: £6.19..
Owner Michael Tabor **Bred** Barouche Stud Ireland Ltd **Trained** Newmarket, Suffolk

FOCUS
They looked to go off quite fast in this ordinary fillies' handicap, but ultimately the winning time was the slower of the two races. The form is sound enough, with a personal best from the winner.
Onenightinlisbon(IRE) Official explanation: jockey said mare suffered interference in running
Toolentidhaar(USA) Official explanation: jockey said saddles slipped
T/Plt: £16.30 to a £1 stake. Pool: £49,098.78. 2,198.13 winning tickets. T/Qpdt: £6.70 to a £1 stake. Pool: £5,062.38. 558.55 winning tickets. SP

5450 - 5451a (Foreign Racing) - See Raceform Interactive

5042 DUNDALK (A.W) (L-H)
Saturday, August 29

OFFICIAL GOING: Standard

5452a DANEHILL DANCER TIPPERARY STKS (LISTED RACE) — 5f (P)
3:25 (3:26) 2-Y-0 **£30,021** (£8,808; £4,196; £1,429)

RPR
1 **Our Jonathan**[13] 5066 2-9-1 .... FMBerry 5 103+
(K A Ryan) *s.i.s: sn mid-div: prog to ld under 2f out: sn rdn clr: kpt on wl fnl f* **11/8**[1]
2 *1* **Rock Jock (IRE)**[34] 4359 2-9-1 98.................................... PShanahan 7 96
(Tracey Collins, Ire) *chsd ldrs: 2nd 2f out: sn rdn: kpt on same pce fnl f* **10/1**
3 *nk* **Dream Deer**[34] 4357 2-9-1 95...(b[1]) WJSupple 3 95
(P D Deegan, Ire) *chsd ldrs: rdn in 3rd over 1f out: kpt on same pce* **7/1**[3]
4 *½* **Rahya Cass (IRE)**[49] 3878 2-8-12 ....(t) WMLordan 6 90
(T Stack, Ire) *towards rr on outer: rdn and prog into 4th under 2f out: kpt on same pce fnl f* **7/1**[3]
5 *1 ¼* **Moonreach (IRE)**[23] 4723 2-9-1 .... JAHeffernan 10 89
(P D Deegan, Ire) *towards rr: swtchd to outer 2f out: sn rdn and clsd: kpt on wout threatening fnl f* **8/1**
6 *1 ¼* **Rigid Rock (IRE)**[34] 4357 2-9-1 78.................................. DMGrant 1 84
(J T Gorman, Ire) *sn led: rdn and hdd under 2f out: sn no ex* **33/1**
7 *nk* **Intapeace (IRE)**[64] 3366 2-8-12 93.................................... CDHayes 4 80
(Francis Ennis, Ire) *towards rr: no imp fr 2f out* **8/1**
8 *1 ¼* **The Mighty Atom (USA)** 2-8-12 .... MCHussey 2 76
(P J Prendergast, Ire) *hld up on inner: no imp fr 2f out* **33/1**
9 *1* **Capulet Monteque (IRE)**[20] 4830 2-8-12 90...................... WJLee 9 72
(T Stack, Ire) *chsd ldrs: rdn and no imp fr 1/2-way* **12/1**
10 *2 ½* **Invincible Vibes (IRE)**[48] 3902 2-9-1 .... KLatham 8 66
(G M Lyons, Ire) *chsd ldrs: rdn fr 2f out: sn wknd: eased cl home* **7/2**[2]
60.27 secs (60.27) **10** Ran SP% **134.2**
CSF £20.97 TOTE £2.20: £1.60, £4.00, £1.80; DF 18.40.
Owner Dr Marwan Koukash **Bred** W G M Turner **Trained** Hambleton, N Yorks
■ Stewards' Enquiry : W J Supple caution; careless riding

NOTEBOOK
Our Jonathan, easy winner of a Ponteftract maiden last time out, missed the break but showed great natural speed to recover and finished well on top on this step up in class. He looks one to keep in mind when stepped up to Group company and might do even better when ridden to use his pace. (op 6/4 tchd 7/4)

5453 - 5460a (Foreign Racing) - See Raceform Interactive

2309 BADEN-BADEN (L-H)
Saturday, August 29

OFFICIAL GOING: Good

5461a PREIS DER SPARKASSEN-FINANZGRUPPE (GROUP 3) — 1m 2f
4:00 (4:10) 4-Y-0+ **£32,039** (£13,592; £4,854; £2,913)

RPR
1 **Wiesenpfad (FR)**[104] 2113 6-9-0 .... ASuborics 9 107
(W Hickst, Germany) *mid-div: running on st: led fnl f in centre: pushed out* **17/5**[2]
2 *1* **Walzertraum (USA)**[63] 3416 4-8-11 .... SHellyn 4 102
(J Hirschberger, Germany) *prom: 5th on ins st: r.o to ld 1 1/2f out to 1f out: styd on* **31/10**[1]
3 *1* **Il Divo (GER)**[48] 4-8-11 .... JBojko 8 100
(A Wohler, Germany) *cl 2nd: pushed along early st: ev ch over 1f out: kpt on: jst hld 3rd cl home* **123/10**
4 *shd* **Liang Kay (GER)**[34] 4364 4-9-2 .... DPorcu 10 105
(Uwe Ostmann, Germany) *towards rr: pushed along in centre st: fin wl fr over 1f out: nrest at fin* **41/10**[3]
5 *hd* **Ambassador (GER)**[41] 4128 5-9-4 .... THellier 5 106
(T Mundry, Germany) *hld up on ins: pushed along 1 1/2f out: styd on fr over 1f out: nrest at fin* **22/5**
6 *¾* **Dwilano (GER)**[62] 3441 6-9-0 .... NRichter 11 101
(P Remmert, Germany) *mid-div: effrt over 1f out: styd on same pce* **19/1**
7 *nk* **Adolfina (GER)**[56] 4-8-10 .... KKerekes 3 96
(W Figge, Germany) *hld up towards outside: pushed along st: kpt on but nvr in chalng position* **147/10**
8 *½* **Duellant (IRE)**[69] 3201 4-8-11 .... AStarke 1 96
(P Schiergen, Germany) *prom on ins: 4th st: sn pushed along: unable qck fr over 1f out* **16/1**
9 *hd* **Schutzenjunker (GER)**[48] 4-9-0 .... FilipMinarik 7 99
(Uwe Ostmann, Germany) *led: pushed along st: hdd 1 1/2f out: no ex* **163/10**
10 *2* **Assahab (GER)**[34] 4364 6-8-11 .... EFrank 12 92
(U Stech, Germany) *towards rr: nvr in chalng position* **32/1**
11 *½* **Little Fighter (GER)**[22] 4808 4-8-11 ....(b) AGoritz 6 91
(J-P Carvalho, Germany) *towards rr: n.d* **19/1**
12 *1 ½* **Promesse De L'Aube (FR)**[20] 4-8-10 ....(b) JiriPalik 2 87
(P Schiergen, Germany) *prom: 3rd and pushed along st: sn one pce* **145/10**
2m 4.00s (-0.99) **12** Ran SP% **130.3**
(Including 10 Euro stake): WIN 44; PL 18, 17, 31; SF 172.
Owner Frau Heide Harzheim **Bred** Gestut Ravensberg **Trained** Germany

5204 CLAIREFONTAINE (R-H)
Saturday, August 29

OFFICIAL GOING: Good

5462a PRIX AU CHAT BLEU - DEAUVILLE (PRIX DE SAINT-FRIMBAULT) — 7f
11:45 (11:45) 3-Y-0 **£11,650** (£4,660; £3,495; £2,330; £1,165)

RPR
1 **Tamada**[24] 3-8-10 .... TThulliez 85
(N Clement, France)
2 *1 ½* **Deaufils (FR)**[81] 3-8-8 .... GBenoist 79
(X Nakkachdji, France)
3 *¾* **Polyegos (IRE)**[356] 3-8-12 .... OPeslier 81
(C Laffon-Parias, France)
4 *½* **Ebony Rose (FR)**[59] 3-9-3 ....(b) 85
(Mlle S-V Tarrou, France)
5 *½* **Riotista (IRE)**[33] 4394 3-8-8 .... JAuge 74
(E J O'Neill) *towards rr: sme hdwy fnl f but n.d* **21/1**[1]
6 *hd* **Chakacha (FR)**[91] 3-9-3 83
(D Prod'Homme, France)
7 *snk* **Aldoussa (FR)**[18] 3-8-8 73
(Mme M Bollack-Badel, France)
8 *½* **Fasina (FR)**[131] 3-8-10 74
(Mlle S-V Tarrou, France)
9 *3* **Sosua (IRE)** 3-8-10 66
(A De Royer-Dupre, France)
10 *1* **Spain Blues (FR)**[24] 3-8-10 63
(X-Thomas Demeaulte, France)
1m 22.5s (82.50) **10** Ran SP% **4.5**
PARI-MUTUEL (Including 1 Euro stake): WIN 3.80; PL 1.40, 2.10, 2.30;DF 9.30.
Owner P Goral **Bred** Ellis Stud & Bellow Hill Stud **Trained** Chantilly, France

NOTEBOOK
Riotista(IRE), a 5f winner and third in Listed company last season, has not cut much ice in two starts in France this season now. Although she was staying on here she might appreciate a drop in trip.

5464a PRIX DU 21EME ARRONDISSEMENT (PRIX DES PERVENCHES) (CLAIMER) (LADY AMATEURS) — 1m
2:20 (2:20) 4-Y-0+ **£8,738** (£3,495; £2,621; £1,748; £874)

RPR
1 **Barricado (FR)**[35] 4335 4-9-11 .... MissFayeBramley 86
(E J O'Neill) *prom: led appr st: r.o wl fnl f: readily* **53/10**[1]

2 *3* **Zariyan (FR)**[33] 6-9-11 .... MlleCNicot 79
(Mlle C Nicot, France)
3 *nk* **Bacarrita (FR)**[16] 4-9-13 .... MlleHCorcoral 80
(L A Urbano-Grajales, France)
4 *2* **Mikos (FR)**[32] 9-9-7 70
(Robert Collet, France)
5 *2* **Treize Heureux (FR)**[85] 4-9-7 65
(C Boutin, France)
6 *nk* **Queen Margot (FR)**[10] 5-9-1 59
(X Puleo, France)
7 *1* **Mezzo Forte (USA)**[72] 5-9-7 62
(J-C Rouget, France)
8 *4* **Leap Ahead (IRE)**[16] 4-10-6 66
(F Rohaut, France)

1m 37.1s (97.10) **8** Ran SP% **15.9**
PARI-MUTUEL: WIN 6.30; PL 1.90, 2.50, 1.70; DF 40.20.
Owner David Barlow **Bred** Sarl Elevage Du Haras De Bourgeauville **Trained** Southwell, Notts

NOTEBOOK
Barricado(FR), a 7f winner on fast going in the spring, had not had that sort of ground in recent starts but, back on this sounde surface, was able to take this in good style.

5463 - 5464a (Foreign Racing) - See Raceform Interactive

5417 BEVERLEY (R-H)

Sunday, August 30

OFFICIAL GOING: Home straight - good to firm; remainder - firm (good to firm in places; 10.1)
Wind: fresh 1/2 against Weather: overcast and breezy

5465 JOHN JENKINS MEMORIAL CLAIMING STKS 7f 100y

2:00 (2:00) (Class 5) 3-Y-O+ **£2,590** (£770; £385; £192) **Stalls** High

Form RPR
0125 **1** **Royal Dignitary (USA)**[58] 3568 9-9-10 85 .... AdrianTNicholls 1 72
(D Nicholls) *swtchd rt s: mde all: hld on towards fin* **5/1**[3]
2405 **2** *½* **Grazeon Gold Blend**[29] 4549 6-9-10 78 .... (p) GrahamGibbons 9 70
(J J Quinn) *chsd ldrs: effrt 3f out: chsd wnr over 1f out: kpt on towards fin* **11/4**[2]
6352 **3** *3* **Bold Indian (IRE)**[18] 4897 5-8-12 52 .... TomEaves 3 51
(I Semple) *in rr: effrt and nt clr run 2f out: styd on to take 3rd nr line* **9/1**
6000 **4** *hd* **Cross Of Lorraine (IRE)**[4] 5332 6-9-0 45 .... (b) PJMcDonald 8 52
(J Wade) *trckd ldrs: styd on same pce appr fnl f* **22/1**
6113 **5** *1* **Diggeratt (USA)**[15] 5016 3-8-4 72 .... BMcHugh(5) 2 50
(R A Fahey) *mid-div: effrt over 2f out: nt clr run and swtchd lft over 1f out: nvr rchd ldrs* **15/8**[1]
5005 **6** *6* **Boss Hog**[11] 5147 4-8-13 50 .... TonyCulhane 6 34
(P T Midgley) *in tch: wknq whn hmpd over 1f out* **14/1**
0000 **7** *1* **Royal Challenge**[20] 4859 8-8-9 56 .... NeilBrown(3) 10 30
(I W McInnes) *s.i.s: kpt on fnl 2f: nvr on terms* **22/1**
000 **8** *1 ¾* **Tump Mac**[44] 4071 5-9-1 39 .... SilvestreDeSousa 12 29
(N Bycroft) *trckd wnr: t.k.h: hung rt and lost pl over 1f out* **100/1**
0060 **9** *¾* **Antipodean (UAE)**[21] 4818 3-8-3 44 .... (b[1]) PaulPickard(5) 11 25
(P T Midgley) *prom: lost pl over 2f out* **80/1**
00 **10** *shd* **Emerald Hawk (IRE)**[58] 3566 3-9-5 0 .... (v[1]) PaulMulrennan 4 36
(D H Brown) *a in rr* **66/1**
0050 **11** *1 ½* **Machinate (USA)**[127] 1530 7-8-13 43 .... TGMcLaughlin 5 21
(W M Brisbourne) *a towards rr* **80/1**
40-0 **12** *14* **Tito (IRE)**[104] 2145 4-9-2 60 .... StephenDonohoe 7 —
(B N Pollock) *s.s: a last: bhd fnl 2f* **20/1**

1m 31.87s (-1.93) **Going Correction** -0.425s/f (Firm)
WFA 3 from 4yo+ 5lb **12** Ran SP% **113.2**
Speed ratings (Par 103): **94,93,90,89,88 81,80,78,77,77 75,59**
toteswinger: 1&2 £4.30, 1&3 £4.10, 2&3 £5.70 CSF £17.10 TOTE £5.30: £1.80, £1.60, £2.20; EX 18.70.Bold Indian was claimed by Mr I. W. McInnes £3000.
Owner Middleham Park Racing XXXVI **Bred** Bentley Smith, J Michael O'Farrell Jr , Joan Thor **Trained** Sessay, N Yorks
■ Stewards' Enquiry : B McHugh one-day ban: careless riding (Sep 13)

FOCUS
An uncompetitive claimer in which only three appeared to hold a realistic chance, and two of them dominated.

5466 EBF OLD CROSSLEYANS RUGBY CLUB MAIDEN STKS 1m 100y

2:35 (2:36) (Class 5) 2-Y-O **£3,885** (£1,156; £577; £288) **Stalls** High

Form RPR
4 **1** **Sulwaan (IRE)**[16] 4993 2-9-3 0 .... JoeFanning 7 73
(M Johnston) *trckd ldrs: t.k.h: upsides over 3f out: kpt on to ld nr fin* **11/10**[1]
65 **2** *shd* **Sabander Bleue (IRE)**[15] 5022 2-9-3 0 .... TonyCulhane 3 73
(M R Channon) *led: kpt on u.p fnl 2f: hdd nr fin* **3/1**[2]
3 *7* **Ting Ting (USA)** 2-8-12 0 .... MickyFenton 1 53+
(T P Tate) *wnt lft s: sn chsng ldrs: kpt on same pce fnl 2f* **9/2**[3]
05 **4** *1 ¾* **Storm Command (IRE)**[24] 4705 2-9-3 0 .... TomEaves 5 54
(B Smart) *t.k.h: sn trcking ldrs: one pce fnl 2f* **20/1**
5 *¾* **Danceintothelight** 2-9-3 0 .... PhillipMakin 6 52+
(K A Ryan) *s.i.s: effrt on outside 3f out: kpt on fnl f* **15/2**
0 **6** *1 ¾* **Lady Pacha**[26] 4618 2-8-12 0 .... PaulMulrennan 10 44
(T J Pitt) *sn chsng ldrs: lost pl over 1f out* **50/1**
0 **7** *4 ½* **Patricks Lodge**[32] 4430 2-9-3 0 .... GrahamGibbons 8 39
(J D Bethell) *mid-div: pushed along over 5f out: lost pl over 2f out* **28/1**
8 *nk* **Star Of Kalani (IRE)** 2-9-3 0 .... PJMcDonald 2 38
(G M Moore) *mid-div: hung lft band over 3f out: sn lost pl* **25/1**
9 *34* **Tantsor (FR)** 2-8-12 0 .... PaulPickard(5) 4 —
(P T Midgley) *s.s: rn green detached in last: lost pl 3f out: sn bhd: t.o* **40/1**

1m 46.57s (-1.03) **Going Correction** -0.425s/f (Firm) **9** Ran SP% **119.0**
Speed ratings (Par 94): **88,87,80,79,78 76,72,71,37**
toteswinger: 1&2 £1.90, 1&3 £2.50, 2&3 £3.80 CSF £4.38 TOTE £2.00: £1.10, £1.50, £1.70; EX 5.50.
Owner Hamdan Al Maktoum **Bred** Martin Francis **Trained** Middleham Moor, N Yorks
■ Stewards' Enquiry : Joe Fanning two-day ban: excessive use of the whip (Sep 13-14)
Tony Culhane two-day ban: excessive use of the whip (Sep 13-14)

FOCUS
This extended 1m on such a stiff track would have been quite a test for these juveniles, and the two market leaders duly pulled well clear of the rest.

NOTEBOOK
Sulwaan(IRE), who had finished a fair fourth in an ordinary 7f Newcastle maiden on debut, stepped up from that initial effort. Keen enough in a handy position early, he looked like winning comfortably when edging past the leader 2f from home, but was forced to dig deep when his rival rallied and won with nothing to spare. He is likely to improve again, though his pedigree would suggest this trip is right on the limit of his stamina. (op 6-5 tchd 11-8)
Sabander Bleue(IRE), well beaten in his first two starts, though the most recent was in a Newbury Listed contest, set out to make all and battled back gamely against the inside rail after the favourite headed him entering the last quarter-mile. There should be a maiden like this in him, given a decent test. (op 7-2 tchd 11-4)
Ting Ting(USA) ran creditably on this debut, having been trapped out wide from the outside stall early. A $180,000 yearling, her sire won the Belmont Stakes and she is out of a winning half-sister to the Kentucky Derby and Preakness Stakes winner War Emblem, so she is bred to be useful and there was enough here to build on. (op 11-2)
Storm Command(IRE), who seemed to find even this sort of trip inadequate at Haydock on his previous outing, showed up for a long way but lacked the speed to get competitive. He may do better in nurseries. (op 16-1 tchd 22-1)
Danceintothelight, a 95,000gns foal but only a 26,000gns two-year-old, out of a 7f winner, missed the break and proved green in the early stages, but he did show some ability once the penny dropped and can be expected to have learned from this. (op 13-2 tchd 6-1)
Lady Pacha, a half-sister to four winners at up to 1m6f, was a well-beaten last of eight on her Catterick debut, but her stamina suggested she would appreciate this stiffer test and she certainly ran much better. She looks one for handicaps over further in due course. (op 40-1 tchd 66-1)

5467 SSANGYONG SUMMER FREEZE NURSERY 5f

3:05 (3:06) (Class 4) (0-85,87) 2-Y-O **£6,476** (£1,927; £963; £481) **Stalls** High

Form RPR
3121 **1** **Duchess Dora (IRE)**[9] 5218 2-9-4 87 .... JamieKyne(5) 12 90
(J J Quinn) *w ldr: led 1f out: edgd lft: hld on towards fin* **7/2**[2]
0100 **2** *nk* **Gertmegalush (IRE)**[22] 4782 2-8-12 76 .... (b[1]) GrahamGibbons 6 78
(J D Bethell) *mid-div: hdwy on ins 2f out: styd on to chse wnr ins fnl f: kpt on towards fin* **9/1**
032 **3** *2 ½* **Licence To Till (USA)**[14] 5066 2-8-8 72 .... JoeFanning 8 65
(M Johnston) *w ldrs: kpt on same pce fnl f* **9/2**[3]
231 **4** *hd* **Secret Millionaire (IRE)**[10] 5180 2-8-10 81 .... JamesPSullivan(7) 10 73
(Patrick Morris) *led tl hdd 1f out: keeping on same pce whn sltly impeded ins fnl f* **5/2**[1]
3350 **5** *1 ¾* **Oondiri (IRE)**[22] 4803 2-7-13 63 .... DuranFentiman 1 49
(T D Easterby) *wnt lft s: t.k.h: sn trcking ldrs on wd outside: outpcd 2f out: styd on ins fnl f* **33/1**
6012 **6** *1 ¼* **Six Wives**[10] 5194 2-8-6 70 .... JamesDoyle 2 51
(J A Glover) *chsd ldrs: kpt on same pce fnl 2f* **11/1**
6244 **7** *¾* **Vilnius**[9] 5218 2-7-12 62 oh1 .... CatherineGannon 3 41
(M R Channon) *sn outpcd in rr: kpt on fnl 2f: nvr a factor* **20/1**
0035 **8** *2 ½* **Mr Smithson (IRE)**[20] 4839 2-8-0 69 ow4 .... PaulPickard(5) 9 39
(B Ellison) *prom: outpcd over 2f out: wknd over 1f out* **14/1**
6350 **9** *¾* **Gentle Beat (IRE)**[39] 4190 2-8-5 69 ow1 .... (p) PJMcDonald 7 36
(T D Easterby) *a outpcd and in rr* **25/1**
150 **10** *1 ½* **Monalini (IRE)**[10] 5198 2-9-4 82 .... TomEaves 11 44
(B Smart) *s.i.s: detached in last and sn reminders: plld wd over 2f out: nvr on terms* **14/1**
1000 **11** *3 ¾* **Social Grace**[16] 4975 2-8-5 69 .... (p) AdrianTNicholls 5 17
(D H Brown) *s.i.s: swtchd rt after s: a in rr* **16/1**

62.36 secs (-1.14) **Going Correction** -0.225s/f (Firm) **11** Ran SP% **118.1**
Speed ratings (Par 96): **100,99,95,95,92 90,89,85,84,81 75**
toteswinger: 1&2 £7.60, 1&3 £3.40, 2&3 £10.90 CSF £34.39 CT £148.52 TOTE £3.80: £1.80, £3.40, £1.50; EX 33.60.
Owner The Clay Family **Bred** Glending Bloodstock **Trained** Settrington, N Yorks

FOCUS
This was a decent and competitive nursery.

NOTEBOOK
Duchess Dora(IRE) ◆, put up 7lb for her recent Sandown success, had a great draw but still did well to win this. She didn't have much room when trying for a gap between the leader and the inside rail a furlong out, but proved very brave in going through it. She did hang away to her left when given a couple of cracks with the whip, but always had matters under control. She has yet to run a bad race and looks ready for a try in something better. (op 11-4)
Gertmegalush(IRE), who has twice fluffed the start since making all to win a York nursery off 6lb lower last month, had blinkers on for the first time and broke much better. He tracked the winner against the inside rail and ran on strongly inside the final furlong, but could never quite get to the filly. The question is whether the blinkers were the reason for him starting better, and will they have the same effect in the future? (tchd 10-1)
Licence To Till(USA), well beaten by a subsequent Listed winner in a five-runner Pontefract maiden last time, was making his nursery debut and ran well, having been handy from the off. He is still unexposed and wouldn't need to improve much to win a race like this. (op 11-2 tchd 4-1)
Secret Millionaire(IRE), making his nursery debut after getting off the mark in a Chepstow maiden, attempted the same positive tactics from his good draw and though he did his best to keep the winner hemmed in against the rail, couldn't do so and, once headed, there was little more to come. Perhaps he doesn't want the ground quite as quick as this. (op 7-2)
Oondiri(IRE), back over the minimum trip after failing to see out the extra furlong at Redcar last time, ran with credit as she confounded her poor draw by swerving out to her left exiting the stalls and was always trapped out wide.
Six Wives showed up for a long way, but it's probably significant that she has finished no worse then third in five outings on Polytrack but has been placed only once in six starts on turf. (op 12-1)

5468 BEVERLEY LIONS H'CAP 5f

3:40 (3:40) (Class 6) (0-60,60) 3-Y-O **£2,900** (£856; £428) **Stalls** High

Form RPR
4425 **1** **Gee Gina**[1] 5422 3-8-4 51 .... PaulPickard(5) 7 56
(P T Midgley) *chsd ldrs on ins: nt clr run and swtchd lft 2f out: styd on wl to ld last 50yds* **5/2**[1]
000 **2** *1* **Francis Albert**[20] 4860 3-8-10 52 .... JoeFanning 2 53
(M Mullineaux) *trckd ldr: led over 2f out: hdd wl ins fnl f* **18/1**
5056 **3** *3* **Port Ronan (USA)**[1] 5422 3-7-13 46 .... (v) JamieKyne(5) 4 36
(J S Wainwright) *s.s: outpcd in rr: hdwy and nt clr run over 1f out: swtchd outside and styd on ins fnl f* **5/1**[2]
3020 **4** *1 ¼* **What A Fella**[13] 5105 3-8-6 48 .... (p) SilvestreDeSousa 1 34
(Mrs A Duffield) *chsd ldrs on outside: hung rt over 1f out: one pce* **11/2**[3]
-400 **5** *2 ½* **Exceedingly Good (IRE)**[16] 4997 3-9-4 60 .... (v[1]) TomEaves 5 37
(B Smart) *sn trcking ldrs: effrt 2f out: wknd fnl f* **17/2**
4060 **6** *4* **Unconsoled**[21] 4823 3-8-4 46 .... (b) AdrianTNicholls 3 8
(J Hetherton) *led: edgd rt 2f out: sn hdd & wknd* **20/1**
0000 **7** *hd* **Adozen Dreams**[8] 5254 3-8-7 49 .... GrahamGibbons 9 11
(N Bycroft) *mid-div: effrt on ins over 2f out: wknd over 1f out* **20/1**

0002 **8** *6* **Sky High Kid (IRE)**[11] 5155 3-9-0 **56**.........................(v[1]) TonyCulhane 6 —
(M R Channon) *chsd ldrs: sn drvn along: lost pl wl over 1f out: eased whn bhd ins fnl f* **5/2**[1]

63.01 secs (-0.49) **Going Correction** -0.225s/f (Firm) **8** Ran SP% **114.5**
Speed ratings (Par 98): **94,92,87,85,81 75,74,65**
toteswinger: 1&2 £10.30, 1&3 £3.10, 2&3 £16.60 CSF £52.01 CT £208.84 TOTE £3.40: £1.30, £3.90, £1.70; EX 51.40.

Owner Mrs M Hills **Bred** M And S Hills **Trained** Westow, N Yorks

FOCUS
A moderate sprint handicap and little to get excited about. The winning time was 0.65 seconds slower than the nursery, which also does little for the form.

What A Fella Official explanation: jockey said gelding hung right

5469 CHARLES ELSEY MEMORIAL H'CAP 1m 4f 16y
4:15 (4:15) (Class 5) (0-75,75) 3-Y-0+ **£3,885** (£1,156; £577; £288) **Stalls** High

Form RPR

2314 **1** **Wee Charlie Castle (IRE)**[43] 4078 6-10-0 **75**.................... TomEaves 10 82+
(I Semple) *dwlt: hld up: hdwy on ins over 2f out: qcknd to ld over 1f out: hld on towards fin* **9/2**[3]

4035 **2** *nk* **Grand Art (IRE)**[14] 5067 5-9-9 **70**.................................... PaulMulrennan 8 76
(P T Midgley) *chsd ldrs: effrt over 2f out: edgd lft over 1f out: styd on ins fnl f* **5/1**

6315 **3** *1 ½* **Fossgate**[11] 5162 8-8-4 **56** oh2.......................................(b) JamieKyne(5) 1 60
(J D Bethell) *trckd ldrs: t.k.h: drvn 4f out: hung rt over 2f out: styd on same pce ins fnl f* **5/1**

0002 **4** *5* **Regal Lyric (IRE)**[27] 4600 3-8-7 **64** ow1.......................... MickyFenton 5 60
(T P Tate) *hld up in rr: effrt on outside over 2f out: kpt on fnl f: nvr nr ldrs* **10/3**[1]

-000 **5** *1 ¾* **Houri (IRE)**[53] 2493 4-8-4 **56** oh3.........................(p) PatrickDonaghy(5) 11 49
(J T Stimpson) *chsd ldrs: rdn over 2f out: wknd 1f out* **33/1**

5423 **6** *2 ½* **Shekan Star**[18] 4893 7-8-9 **56** oh3.................................... PJMcDonald 2 45
(K G Reveley) *hld up towards rr: hdwy over 5f out: edgd rt and lost pl over 1f out* **15/2**

-126 **7** *3* **Mister Fizzbomb (IRE)**[9] 5210 6-9-5 **66**................(b) GrahamGibbons 9 50
(T D Walford) *led: qcknd over 3f out: hdd & wknd over 1f out: eased towards fin* **7/2**[2]

2m 34.88s (-6.02) **Going Correction** -0.425s/f (Firm) course record
WFA 3 from 4yo+ 10lb **7** Ran SP% **111.5**
Speed ratings (Par 103): **103,102,101,98,97 95,93**
toteswinger: 1&2 £4.00, 1&3 £3.70, 2&3 £4.80 CSF £25.58 CT £112.44 TOTE £4.90: £2.30, £2.90; EX 22.30.

Owner Mrs Francesca Mitchell **Bred** Bryan Ryan **Trained** Carluke, S Lanarks

FOCUS
Just a fair handicap, weakened by the four non-runners. The early pace was strong before slackening at halfway, but they still managed to take nearly a second off the course record, which shows how quick the ground was.

5470 RACING AGAIN ON 16TH SEPTEMBER H'CAP 1m 1f 207y
4:50 (4:51) (Class 6) (0-60,60) 3-Y-0 **£2,752** (£818; £409; £204) **Stalls** High

Form RPR

6641 **1** **Valid Point (IRE)**[4] 5331 3-8-9 **51** 6ex...................... StephenDonohoe 17 59+
(Sir Mark Prescott) *drvn to sn ld: hung lft bnd and hdd over 3f out: led 2f out: edgd rt over 1f out: styd on wl: readily* **4/5**[1]

5646 **2** *1 ¾* **Screaming Brave**[12] 5123 3-8-13 **55**.............................. TonyCulhane 16 60
(M R Channon) *sn chsng ldrs: led over 3f out: hdd 2f out: hmpd and swtchd lft over 1f out: styd on same pce* **17/2**[3]

4040 **3** *1 ¾* **Black River Falls (USA)**[43] 4079 3-8-12 **54**...................(b[1]) TomEaves 3 55
(I Semple) *t.k.h: trckd ldrs on outside: outpcd and lost pl over 2f out: gd hdwy over 1f out: styd on to take 3rd ins fnl f* **33/1**

050 **4** *2* **Flying Phoebe**[37] 4270 3-8-9 **51**...................................... TGMcLaughlin 2 48
(Mrs L Stubbs) *hld up in rr: hdwy over 2f out: edgd lft and kpt on fnl f* **50/1**

-045 **5** *2* **Salamon**[23] 4730 3-8-11 **53**.. MickyFenton 14 46
(P F I Cole) *drvn to chse ldrs: one pce fnl 2f* **12/1**

2205 **6** *2 ¼* **Rose Of Coma (IRE)**[12] 5123 3-8-2 **49**................... PatrickDonaghy(5) 9 38
(Miss Gay Kelleway) *mid-div: effrt 3f out: kpt on: nvr rchd ldrs* **28/1**

4450 **7** *2 ½* **Shanavaz**[24] 4710 3-8-11 **53** ow3.................................. PaulMulrennan 12 54+
(C J Teague) *swtchd rt s: hld up towards rr: hdwy on ins over 2f out: rdn whn nt clr run over 1f out: nt rcvr* **16/1**

4434 **8** *hd* **Georgie Bee**[18] 4892 3-8-2 **49**..................................(b[1]) PaulPickard(5) 7 32
(T D Walford) *sn chsng ldrs: hung rt and wknd over 1f out* **17/2**[3]

0000 **9** *3* **Lady Dinsdale (IRE)**[21] 4819 3-8-4 **46** oh1............. SilvestreDeSousa 6 23
(T Keddy) *led early: chsd ldrs: drvn over 3f out: wknd over 1f out* **66/1**

4634 **10** *29* **Join Up**[17] 4944 3-8-8 **50**.. DuranFentiman 5 —
(W M Brisbourne) *t.k.h: trckd ldrs on outer: lost pl over 2f out: bhd whn eased ins fnl f: t.o* **14/1**

5000 **11** *½* **Rose Avelina**[16] 4994 3-7-11 **46** oh1........................ ShirleyTeasdale(7) 10 —
(I W McInnes) *s.i.s: drvn over 5f out: bhd fnl 3f: t.o* **100/1**

040 **12** *2 ¼* **Hopeful Lady**[46] 3975 3-7-13 **46** oh1................................ JamieKyne(5) 4 —
(I W McInnes) *chsd ldrs: rdn 5f out: lost pl over 3f out: sn bhd: t.o* **80/1**

0002 **13** *hd* **What A Day**[8] 4892 3-9-0 **56**..................................(p) GrahamGibbons 13 —
(J J Quinn) *mid-div: n.m.r on inner and lost pl after 2f: hdwy over 3f out: lost pl and eased over 1f out: t.o* **8/1**[2]

2m 4.80s (-2.20) **Going Correction** -0.425s/f (Firm) **13** Ran SP% **120.0**
Speed ratings (Par 98): **91,89,88,86,85 83,81,81,78,55 55,53,53**
toteswinger: 1&2 £3.80, 1&3 £12.90, 2&3 £22.90 CSF £7.81 CT £140.31 TOTE £1.90: £1.40, £2.40, £6.70; EX 9.60 Place 6: £34.96 Place 5: £18.15.

Owner W E Sturt - Osborne House **Bred** Pier House Stud **Trained** Newmarket, Suffolk

■ Stewards' Enquiry : Stephen Donohoe one-day ban: careless riding (Sep 13)

FOCUS
This race revolved around the red-hot favourite, who was carrying a 6lb penalty for his easy win in soft ground at Ayr four days earlier.

Shanavaz Official explanation: jockey said filly was denied a clear run

T/Plt: £39.30 to a £1 stake. Pool: £50,121.11. 928.91 winning tickets. T/Qpdt: £16.90 to a £1 stake. Pool: £3,350.84. 146.60 winning tickets. WG

5424 GOODWOOD (R-H)
Sunday, August 30

OFFICIAL GOING: Good to firm (8.6)
Wind: Brisk ahead Weather: Cloudy

5471 EBF CHICHESTER OBSERVER FILLIES' STKS (H'CAP) 6f
2:10 (2:10) (Class 3) (0-95,85) 3-Y-0+ **£7,771** (£2,312; £1,155; £577) **Stalls** Low

Form RPR

300 **1** **Artistic License (IRE)**[30] 4485 4-9-10 **83**........................... RyanMoore 5 93
(M R Channon) *hld up off pce tl swtchd rt to outside and stdy hdwy over 2f out: led over 1f out: pushed clr fnl f: readily* **7/2**[1]

2604 **2** *2* **Cut The Cackle (IRE)**[24] 4712 3-9-2 **78**........................... JimCrowley 4 81
(P Winkworth) *led: rdn and edgd rt ins fnl 2f: hdd over 1f out: sn no ch w wnr but styd on gamely u.p to hold 2nd thrght fnl f* **7/1**

0602 **3** *nse* **Aunt Nicola**[16] 5007 3-8-10 **72**....................................... HayleyTurner 1 75
(M L W Bell) *chsd ldrs: rdn: edgd rt and outpcd over 2f out: styd on again ins fnl f: gng on cl home but nvr any ch w wnr* **5/1**[3]

0-10 **4** *nk* **Perfect Pride (USA)**[41] 4148 3-9-9 **85**........................... AdamKirby 2 87
(C G Cox) *in rr: pushed along 2f out and no prog tl qcknd ins fnl f and fin strly* **6/1**

2002 **5** *nse* **Crystal Moments**[43] 4096 3-9-9 **85**.............................. EddieAhern 7 87
(E A L Dunlop) *chsd ldrs: rdn fr 2f out: drvn to dispute 2nd ins fnl f but nvr any ch w wnr and fdd last strides* **9/2**[2]

3306 **6** *1 ½* **Evelyn May (IRE)**[30] 4483 3-8-10 **72**............................... ChrisCatlin 6 69
(B W Hills) *plld hrd in rr: rdn over 2f out and no rspnse* **16/1**

-105 **7** *¾* **Dubai Legend**[16] 5007 3-8-13 **75**.................................. MartinDwyer 3 70
(D M Simcock) *chsd ldrs: rdn over 2f out: swtchd rt over 1f out and brief effrt: wknd fnl 110yds* **8/1**

112R **R** **Rafta (IRE)**[13] 5090 3-8-8 **77**................................ JosephineBruning(7) 8 —
(T T Clement) *styd in stalls and ref to r* **6/1**

1m 12.68s (0.48) **Going Correction** +0.125s/f (Good)
WFA 3 from 4yo 3lb **8** Ran SP% **115.1**
Speed ratings (Par 104): **101,98,98,97,97 95,94,—**
toteswinger: 1&2 £7.20, 1&3 £4.00, 2&3 £7.90 CSF £28.53 CT £122.73 TOTE £4.10: £1.30, £2.40, £1.80; EX 35.40.

Owner Wood Street Syndicate IV **Bred** Mountarmstrong Stud **Trained** West Ilsley, Berks

■ Stewards' Enquiry : Eddie Ahern four-day ban (reduced from 10 days on appeal): failed to ride out for 4th place (Sep 16-19)

FOCUS
The top weight was rated well below the ceiling of 95 and this was an ordinary fillies' handicap for the grade. They stayed stands' side, but the winner raced well away from the rail.

NOTEBOOK
Artistic License(IRE) sat last of all and still occupied that position at halfway, but she made rapid headway once asked to pick up inside the final three furlongs and sustained her challenge to draw nicely clear. This is the highest mark she has ever won off and things will be tougher against the opposite sex once she's reassessed. (op 9-2)
Cut The Cackle(IRE) has yet to win beyond 5f, and she looked to go off plenty quick enough judged by the way in which the winner powered home, so this was a good effort. (op 9-1)
Aunt Nicola took a while to pick up when first asked and seemed to compromise her chance by hanging right. She finally ran on near the line, but was never a threat. (op 9-2 tchd 11-2)
Perfect Pride(USA) made a good start to the season when defying a mark of 81 over this course and distance, but she ran poorly at Windsor last time and, although this was better, she again offered little encouragement. She didn't look particularly keen to stay in touch and, having been strongly ridden from a fair way out, only consented to run on when the race was all but over. (op 7-1 tchd 11-2)
Crystal Moments travelled quite well but found only the one pace. Her jockey stopped pushing in the final couple of strides, but for which, at a guess, she might have been fourth. Eddie Ahern received a ten-day ban for not riding out for third place. (op 7-2)
Evelyn May(IRE) was too keen. (tchd 20-1)
Rafta(IRE), for the second race in succession, stood still when the stalls opened. (tchd 11-2)

5472 EBF ALICE KEPPEL STKS (FILLIES' H'CAP) (LISTED RACE) 1m 1f 192y
2:45 (2:47) (Class 1) (0-110,102) 3-Y-0+
£22,708 (£8,608; £4,308; £2,148; £1,076; £540) **Stalls** High

Form RPR

0503 **1** **Nashmiah (IRE)**[8] 5260 3-9-5 **102**...................................... ChrisCatlin 6 106
(C E Brittain) *t.k.h: towards rr but in tch: hdwy over 2f out: pushed lft whn styng on wl over 1f out: str run u.p ins fnl f to ld cl home* **16/1**

3-11 **2** *½* **Leceile (USA)**[16] 5009 3-8-4 **87**...................................... HayleyTurner 11 90
(W J Haggas) *led: rdn and narrowly hdd 2f out: styd pressing ldr: edgd lft u.p over 1f out: styd on wl to ld again fnl 110yds: ct cl home* **9/2**[1]

-250 **3** *½* **July Jasmine (USA)**[57] 3619 3-9-2 **99**............................... RyanMoore 1 101
(Sir Michael Stoute) *chsd ldr tl drvn to take slt advantage 2f out: pushed lft u.p over 1f out: hdd and no ex fnl 110yds* **11/2**[2]

1121 **4** *¾* **Alsace Lorraine (IRE)**[32] 4422 4-8-12 **87**........................ EddieAhern 15 88+
(J R Fanshawe) *s.i.s: hld up in rr but in tch: stdy hdwy and gng wl whn hit over hd and bdly hmpd over 1f out: stl no room and swtchd rt jst ins fnl f: kpt on but nt rcvr* **9/2**[1]

1500 **5** *nk* **Badiat Alzaman (IRE)**[11] 5175 3-8-3 **86** oh2.................. MartinDwyer 8 86
(D M Simcock) *plld hrd in rr: stl plenty to do over 2f out: pushed along and kpt on fnl f: fin wl* **25/1**

40-5 **6** *1 ¾* **My Aunt Fanny**[32] 4422 4-8-11 **86**................................... LPKeniry 12 83
(A M Balding) *chsd ldrs: rdn over 2f out: styd on same pce fr over 1f out* **11/2**[2]

166 **7** *¾* **Ainia**[28] 4566 4-8-11 **86** oh10... JimCrowley 10 81
(D M Simcock) *chsd ldrs: rdn over 2f out: wknd ins fnl f* **25/1**

0-15 **8** *1* **Short Affair**[37] 4287 4-9-5 **94**...................................... DaneO'Neill 3 87
(L M Cumani) *in rr: pushed along and effrt over 2f out: nvr rchd ldrs: wknd ins fnl f* **12/1**

3313 **9** *1* **Sterling Sound (USA)**[18] 4903 3-8-10 **93**........................ PatDobbs 14 84
(M P Tregoning) *chsd ldrs: rdn over 2f out: wknd appr fnl f* **9/1**

0- **10** *2 ¼* **Class Attraction (IRE)**[14] 5083 5-9-6 **95**..................(t) JimmyFortune 9 82
(J E Hammond, France) *s.i.s: rdn 3f out: nvr gng pce to get into contention* **13/2**[3]

0264 **11** *3 ¼* **Syvilla**[18] 4903 4-9-4 **93**... WilliamCarson 4 73
(Rae Guest) *chsd ldrs: rdn over 3f out: wknd 2f out* **16/1**

2m 7.67s (-0.33) **Going Correction** +0.125s/f (Good)
WFA 3 from 4yo+ 8lb **11** Ran SP% **117.6**
Speed ratings (Par 108): **106,105,105,104,104 102,102,101,100,98 96**
toteswinger: 1&2 £19.00, 1&3 £20.60, 2&3 £5.20 CSF £86.69 CT £453.66 TOTE £21.10: £6.10, £2.00, £2.10; EX 157.00.

Owner Saeed Manana **Bred** Deerpark Stud **Trained** Newmarket, Suffolk

FOCUS
Just a fair Listed handicap for fillies'. An ordinary gallop contributed to something of a bunch finish.

NOTEBOOK
Nashmiah(IRE) was outclassed in the Nassau Stakes on her only previous try over this trip two starts back, but she ran better when third over 1m at Sandown just a week ago and stepped up on that to gain her second Listed success. As it turned out, she proved well suited by the step up in distance and was a game winner, sustaining a challenge out wide in the straight – she can get nervous when in a bunch according to connections – to get on top near the line. She might stay in training next year. (op 14-1)
Leceile(USA), 9lb higher than when winning at Nottingham, was just denied the hat-trick on this rise in class. Having set a sensible pace, she stuck on willingly when strongly challenged in the straight and is evidently still improving. Official explanation: jockey said filly hung left handed (op 4-1)
July Jasmine(USA) hasn't gone on as expected since running a pleasing second behind Midday in the Lingfield Oaks Trial, and this was just a respectable effort. She was always well placed and had no obvious excuse. (op 13-2 tchd 5-1)
Alsace Lorraine(IRE), who's entered in both the Sun Chariot and the Cambridgeshire, was trying her furthest trip to date, but her breeding suggested it wouldn't be a problem. She looked to be travelling better than most for much of the straight, but her rider took a while to get after her, arguably too long, and as a result she found trouble, being hemmed in by the eventual winner around a furlong out and hit over the head by a rival jockey's whip. In fairness, it's hard to say she was unlucky, but she has to be worth another chance. Official explanation: jockey said filly was denied a clear run (op 4-1 tchd 7-2)
Badiat Alzaman(IRE), 2lb out of the handicap, compromised her chance by racing very keenly for much of the way, but she flashed home late on from an unpromising position. She's a talented filly, but is evidently not straightforward. (tchd 28-1)
My Aunt Fanny was well held and couldn't reverse recent course placings with Alsace Lorraine. (op 15-2)
Ainia ran with credit considering she was 10lb out of the handicap.
Short Affair has now struggled in both her runs since making a winning British debut at Doncaster in June, but she probably wants ground on the soft side.
Sterling Sound(USA) was well held after racing keenly early.
Class Attraction(IRE), a French challenger, never really recovered from a slow start. (op 8-1)

5473 FEGENTRI WORLD CUP OF NATIONS STKS (AMATEUR RIDERS' H'CAP) 1m 1f
3:20 (3:21) (Class 5) (0-75,74) 3-Y-O+ **£4,684** (£1,452; £726; £363) **Stalls** High

Form RPR
3333 **1** **Potentiale (IRE)**[16] 4992 5-11-9 **71**............(p) MrMarioBaratti 3 79
(J W Hills) *in tch: hdwy to chse ldrs 4f out: led ins fnl 3f: shkn up and hld on wl thrght fnl f* **9/2**[3]
4011 **2** ½ **Theocritus (USA)**[13] 5108 4-11-12 **74**............ MrPCollington 8 81
(D M Simcock) *in rr: rdn 3f out: hdwy 2f out: styd on to chse wnr 1f out and swtchd lft ins fonal f: fin wl but a jst hld* **7/2**[2]
2640 **3** 3 **Chatanoogachoochoo**[14] 5063 4-11-3 **65**............ MrArthurHoyeau 7 65
(M Hill) *in tch: hdwy to chse ldrs over 2f out: rdn and styd on to go 3rd fnl f but nvr any ch w ldng duo* **12/1**
2120 **4** 2 **Dragon Slayer (IRE)**[15] 5035 7-11-6 **68**............ MrMWeissmeier 6 64
(John A Harris) *chsd ldrs: rdn and edgd lft ins fnl 3f: styd on same pce fnl 2f* **11/2**
/21- **5** 1¼ **Beauchamp Wizard**[380] 5049 4-11-12 **74**............ MrFabioLocatelli 2 67
(G A Butler) *chsd ldrs: rdn 3f out: wknd fnl 2f* **10/3**[1]
0000 **6** 5 **Binnion Bay (IRE)**[15] 5019 8-10-7 **55** oh5............(v) MissGAndrews 1 37
(J J Bridger) *t.k.h on outside: chsd ldrs: stl in tch whn hmpd ins fnl 3f: sn wknd* **16/1**
0000 **7** 1¼ **Trafalgar Square**[37] 4262 7-11-10 **72**............ MrAJDoyle 9 52
(M J Attwater) *s.i.s: a towards rr* **16/1**
0306 **8** 2¼ **Play Up Pompey**[9] 5211 7-10-7 **55** oh10....... MissPaulineBoisgontier 10 30
(J J Bridger) *bhd fr 1/2-way* **40/1**
2212 **9** 23 **Whotsit (IRE)**[15] 5019 3-10-6 **61**............(b) MissVRodenbusch 5 —
(Miss Amy Weaver) *led tl hdd ins fnl 3f: sn wknd* **11/2**

1m 59.98s (3.68) **Going Correction** +0.125s/f (Good)
WFA 3 from 4yo+ 7lb **9** Ran SP% **116.1**
Speed ratings (Par 103): **88,87,84,83,82 77,76,74,54**
toteswinger: 1&2 £3.70, 1&3 £8.40, 2&3 £7.50 CSF £20.79 CT £177.88 TOTE £5.80: £1.90, £1.60, £3.30; EX 18.50.
Owner J W Hills **Bred** Copperhead Stable **Trained** Upper Lambourn, Berks

FOCUS
Just a modest handicap and these amateur riders varied in ability, so this is form to treat with a little caution.

5474 SUPREME STKS (GROUP 3) 7f
3:55 (3:56) (Class 1) 3-Y-O+
£36,900 (£13,988; £7,000; £3,490; £1,748; £877) **Stalls** High

Form RPR
4063 **1** **Ordnance Row**[1] 5426 6-9-0 **107**............ RyanMoore 1 116
(R Hannon) *hld up in rr: pushed along over 2f out: str run on outside fr over 1f out: styd on to ld fnl 110yds: readily* **5/1**[3]
1420 **2** 1 **Asset (IRE)**[21] 4837 6-9-0 **114**............(b) TedDurcan 5 114
(Saeed Bin Suroor) *in rr but in tch: stdy hdwy on outside over 2f: led over 1f out and sn hung rt: hdd and outpcd fnl 110yds* **5/4**[1]
2-03 **3** hd **Cat Junior (USA)**[10] 5196 4-9-0 **115**............(t) DarryllHolland 3 113+
(B J Meehan) *t.k.h early: chsd ldrs in 3rd tl hemmed in: no room fr over 2f out and lost pl: hdwy 1f out: styng on whn crossed and swtchd lft ins fnl f: fin strly to press for 2nd cl home but nt rch wnr* **9/2**[2]
0050 **4** 2¼ **Express Wish**[15] 5024 5-9-0 **105**............ HayleyTurner 7 107
(J Noseda) *t.k.h early: chsd ldrs 4f out: drvn to chal over 2f out tl over 1f out: wknd ins fnl f* **11/2**
55-5 **5** 1½ **Jet D'Eau (FR)**[15] 5032 3-8-6 **99**............(b) FergusSweeney 2 98
(G L Moore) *in rr: n.m.r over 2f out: swtchd lft to outside over 1f out: kpt on ins fnl f but nvr a threat* **14/1**
1140 **6** 1¼ **Abbondanza (IRE)**[9] 5232 6-9-0 **104**............(v[1]) TonyHamilton 8 100
(I Semple) *unruly in stalls: drvn to ld after 1f: rdn and kpt slt advantage tl hdd & wknd over 1f out* **10/1**
0461 **7** nse **Carcinetto (IRE)**[8] 5249 7-8-11 **98**............ EddieAhern 6 96
(P D Evans) *led 1f: chsd ldr and chal 3f out: wknd ins fnl 2f* **18/1**

1m 26.09s (-1.31) **Going Correction** +0.125s/f (Good)
WFA 3 from 4yo+ 5lb **7** Ran SP% **115.7**
Speed ratings (Par 113): **112,110,110,108,106 104,104**
toteswinger: 1&2 £2.60, 1&3 £2.90, 2&3 £2.00 CSF £12.00 TOTE £5.80: £2.60, £1.60; EX 12.50.

Owner Mrs P Good **Bred** Mrs P Good **Trained** East Everleigh, Wilts

FOCUS
A reasonable Group 3, but both the early leader Abbondanza and Carcinetto went off too fast, setting this up for those waited with.

NOTEBOOK
Ordnance Row gave an almost immediate boost to the Celebration Mile form, having run third in that Group 2 contest the previous day. He had made the running around 24 hours earlier, but was sensibly waited with this time - his chance would have been ruined had he been ridden forcefully again - and he stayed on really well, having been last early. This was a very smart effort, but plenty went his way and he's a little flattered by his superiority over Cat Junior. (op 6-1 tchd 9-2)
Asset(IRE) tends to offer very little for pressure once in front and it's not difficult to argue he was committed too soon, especially considering the leaders went off so quickly. Not for the first time, he went from travelling strongly, to looking reluctant once in the lead, and he threw his chance away when hanging right. (tchd 11-8 and 6-4 in a place)
Cat Junior(USA) was handily placed early on and travelled well enough, but he lost his position when getting stuck in behind a couple of tiring rivals (Abbondanza and Carcinetto) early in the straight and was hemmed in by horses on his outside. He got no run at all and was unlucky not to finish closer, but that said, his winning record suggests it would be unwise to get carried away. Official explanation: jockey said colt was denied a clear run (op 7-2)
Express Wish has struggled since causing an upset in this race last year, when the ground was on the soft side. He moved into contention smoothly and was able to keep Cat Junior hemmed in, but his response to pressure was a let down. (op 7-1)
Jet D'Eau(FR) met some interference when trying to mount a challenge, but for which she might have finished a little closer. Formerly trained in France, she shaped nicely on her debut for this yard at the July course and can be given another chance. (op 16-1)
Abbondanza(IRE) went off too quick in a first-time visor. (op 12-1 tchd 14-1)

5475 SOUTH COAST STKS (H'CAP) 1m 1f
4:30 (4:32) (Class 4) (0-85,86) 3-Y-O **£5,180** (£1,541; £770; £384) **Stalls** High

Form RPR
4212 **1** **Kaolak (USA)**[14] 5070 3-9-7 **85**............(v) ChrisCatlin 4 96
(J Ryan) *led after 1f: drvn along 3f out: styd on strly fnl 2f* **8/1**[3]
0-35 **2** 2½ **Silverglas (IRE)**[25] 4648 3-8-7 **71**............ PatDobbs 2 77+
(M P Tregoning) *in rr tl hdwy and hmpd ins fnl 3f: styd on again fr 2f out: str run ins fnl f but nt rch wnr* **11/1**
3150 **3** nk **Burza**[16] 5009 3-8-7 **71**............ DavidProbert 8 76
(J Mackie) *chsd ldrs: rdn and one pce ins fnl 3f: kpt on again fnl f to press for 2nd but no ch w wnr* **20/1**
15 **4** nk **Suba (USA)**[15] 5030 3-9-1 **79**............ DaneO'Neill 6 83+
(L M Cumani) *in rr: hdwy whn hmpd 3f out: prog on outside whn carried bdly lft 2f out: rcvrd and r.o wl fr over 1f out: kpt on fnl f to press for 3rd but no ch w wnr* **12/1**
0063 **5** 3¼ **Perfect Citizen (USA)**[20] 4841 3-9-0 **78**............ AdamKirby 11 75
(W R Swinburn) *led 1f: styd chsng wnr: rdn and hung rt 3f out: styd chsng ldrs tl wknd fnl f* **33/1**
5605 **6** 1½ **Hypnotist (UAE)**[18] 4918 3-8-3 **67**............ MartinDwyer 10 61
(C E Brittain) *in rr: hdwy on ins fr 4f out: chsd ldrs and rdn 2f out: wknd fnl f* **25/1**
4640 **7** nk **Fanditha (IRE)**[32] 4422 3-9-3 **81**............(b[1]) RyanMoore 1 74
(R Hannon) *s.i.s: in rr: pushed along 3f out: styd on fr over 1f out: kpt on ins fnl f but nvr anywhere nr ldrs* **20/1**
3120 **8** shd **Mabuya (UAE)**[22] 4767 3-9-5 **83**............ FergusSweeney 9 76+
(P J Makin) *in tch: hdwy 3f out: hmpd over 2f out: kpt on but nvr in contention after* **3/1**[1]
443 **9** nk **El Libertador (USA)**[20] 4854 3-8-9 **73**............ LPKeniry 7 65
(E A Wheeler) *s.i.s: in rr: hdwy on ins fr 3f out: chsd ldrs over 2f out: wknd appr fnl f* **40/1**
3121 **10** 2 **Negotiation (IRE)**[15] 5030 3-9-7 **85**............ JimmyFortune 12 73+
(J H M Gosden) *chsd ldrs tl hmpd ins fnl 3f: styd chsng ldrs tl wknd ins fnl 2f* **3/1**[1]
3002 **11** 6 **Emirates Roadshow (USA)**[10] 5189 3-9-8 **86**............ TedDurcan 5 61
(Saeed Bin Suroor) *chsd ldrs: rdn 3f out: wknd 2f out: eased whn no ch fnl f* **9/2**[2]
51-0 **12** 7 **Sampi**[82] 2796 3-9-6 **84**............(t) JimCrowley 13 43+
(Mrs A J Perrett) *chsd ldrs tl bdly hmpd ins fnl 3f: nt rcvr: eased whn no ch fnl f* **25/1**
0504 **13** 1 **Global**[27] 4605 3-9-1 **82**............ PatrickHills[(3)] 3 39
(R Hannon) *in tch: reminder whn hanging lft after 3f: rdn 3f out: wknd and hung bdly lft over 2f out* **20/1**

1m 54.98s (-1.32) **Going Correction** +0.125s/f (Good) **13** Ran SP% **122.7**
Speed ratings (Par 102): **110,107,107,107,104 103,102,102,102,100 95,89,88**
toteswinger: 1&2 £19.90, 1&3 £42.40, 2&3 £56.10 CSF £85.27 CT £1767.59 TOTE £10.30: £2.40, £4.20, £5.10; EX 147.00.
Owner Simon Kerr **Bred** Mr And Mrs Robert Courtney Sr Et Al **Trained** Newmarket, Suffolk

FOCUS
A good, competitive three-year-old handicap.
Mabuya(UAE) Official explanation: jockey said colt was denied a clear run
El Libertador(USA) Official explanation: jockey said colt missed the break
Global Official explanation: jockey said colt hung left handed throughout

5476 TURFTV.CO.UK STKS (H'CAP) 7f
5:05 (5:06) (Class 2) (0-105,105) 3-Y-O+
£12,462 (£3,732; £1,866; £934; £466; £234) **Stalls** High

Form RPR
6541 **1** **Marching Time**[18] 4902 3-8-7 **91** ow1............ RyanMoore 4 98+
(Sir Michael Stoute) *hld up in rr: str run on outside fr 2f out to ld fnl 110yds: in command cl home* **11/4**[1]
1052 **2** 1¼ **Signor Peltro**[22] 4796 6-9-7 **100**............ DaneO'Neill 5 104+
(H Candy) *hld up in rr: hdwy 2f out: rdn and styd on to chal fnl 110yds: outstyd by wnr cl home* **11/4**[1]
0025 **3** nk **Harrison George (IRE)**[30] 4485 4-8-11 **90**............ TonyHamilton 11 93
(R A Fahey) *t.k.h: n.m.r and lost position on ins over 4f out: gd hdwy 2f out: styd on to press for ld appr fnl f: outpcd by ldng duo fnl 50yds* **5/1**[2]
6446 **4** ¾ **Salient**[9] 5221 5-8-0 **86** oh9............ KierenFox[(7)] 8 87
(M J Attwater) *chsd ldrs: rdn and hdwy on outside fr 3f out: slt ld appr fnl f: hdd & wknd fnl 110yds* **25/1**
-100 **5** 3 **King's Wonder**[10] 5196 4-8-11 **90**............ MartinDwyer 9 83
(W R Muir) *led: rdn over 2f out: hdd appr fnl f: sn wknd* **10/1**
0410 **6** nk **Swop (IRE)**[155] 997 6-9-5 **105**............ JPFahy[(7)] 7 97+
(L M Cumani) *in rr: pushed along and sme prog over 2f out: nvr in contention and no ch w ldrs sn after* **6/1**[3]
6422 **7** hd **Guilded Warrior**[17] 4954 6-8-5 **89**............ Louis-PhilippeBeuzelin[(5)] 2 81
(W S Kittow) *chsd ldr: rdn 3f out: wknd over 1f out* **10/1**
6304 **8** 1¾ **Spanish Bounty**[32] 4423 4-9-2 **95**............ EddieAhern 1 82
(J G Portman) *in rr: sme prog whn nt clr run over 2f out: n.d after* **20/1**
050 **9** ¾ **Glow Star (SAF)**[22] 4768 5-9-0 **93**............ FergusSweeney 3 78
(G L Moore) *chsd ldrs: rdn 3f out: wknd fr 2f out* **22/1**

36-0 **10** *7* **Talking Hands**[165] 863 3-8-10 **94**.. LPKeniry 10 60
(S Kirk) *a towards rr* **33/1**

1m 26.65s (-0.75) **Going Correction** +0.125s/f (Good)
WFA 3 from 4yo+ 5lb **10** Ran SP% **118.4**
Speed ratings (Par 109): **109,107,107,106,102 102,102,100,99,91**
toteswinger: 1&2 £2.30, 1&3 £2.80, 2&3 £3.60 CSF £9.46 CT £36.91 TOTE £3.40: £1.60, £1.40, £1.70; EX 8.80.
Owner K Abdulla **Bred** Juddmonte Farms Ltd **Trained** Newmarket, Suffolk

FOCUS

A classy handicap, and the time was very good – only 0.56 seconds slower than Ordnance Row managed in the earlier Group 3 - despite the pace looking steady for the first furlong or so.

NOTEBOOK

Marching Time ◆ didn't progress as expected at around 1m2f earlier in the season, but he proved suited by the drop to 1m when winning at Salisbury on his previous start and he coped with this further decrease in distance to defy an 8lb higher mark (including 1lb overweight). After taking a little while to really get going, he ultimately won with authority and is a smart colt in the making. (op 5-2 tchd 3-1)

Signor Peltro ◆, an unlucky loser in a similar event at the July course last time, ran well off a 4lb higher mark, finding only the progressive winner too good. A mark of 100 represented a career-high rating, and he was 15lb higher than when successful in this race last year, but he's evidently still improving. He looks an ideal type for limited handicaps at the Dubai Carnival. (tchd 5-2)

Harrison George(IRE) lost his place when short of room about half a mile out, but he stayed on well in the straight. He could find a nice race when everything falls right. (op 9-2)

Salient hasn't won since May 2008, but he ran a huge race from 9lb out of the handicap - a mark 2lb higher than when well behind Signor Peltro in this race last year

King's Wonder was given a positive ride and manage to take a length or two out of the field when upping the tempo early on, but he probably ended up going off a bit too fast. (op 14-1)

Swop(IRE), disappointing in the Lincoln when last seen in March, did little to suggest he's well handicapped, even with a 7lb claimer aboard. (op 10-1)

5477 GOODWOOD FREEPHONE 08000188191 APPRENTICE STKS (H'CAP) 6f

5:40 (5:41) (Class 5) (0-70,71) 3-Y-O+ **£3,238** (£963; £481; £240) **Stalls** Low

Form RPR

0053 **1** **Diddums**[11] 5155 3-9-0 **65**.. AmyScott(5) 7 71
(J W Hills) *in rr tl gd hdwy 2f out: led jst ins fnl f: shkn up: jst hld on* **15/2**

0600 **2** *nk* **Joss Stick**[6] 5323 4-8-7 **55** ow1.. DebraEngland(5) 3 60
(J J Bridger) *chsd ldrs tl outpcd 2f out: styd on again fnl f: fin wl but nt quite get up* **20/1**

624 **3** *1* **Mata Hari Blue**[22] 4786 3-8-11 **62**.. AshleyMorgan(5) 11 64
(J R Holt) *s.i.s: sn chsng ldrs: drvn to chal ins fnl f: one pce nr fin* **8/1**

6042 **4** *shd* **Ghost Dancer**[15] 5020 5-9-3 **60**..(p) DavidProbert 9 61
(J M Bradley) *chsd ldrs: rdn to chal 1f out and hung rt ins fnl f: styd on same pce* **5/2**[1]

1-60 **5** *3/4* **Spiritual Art**[16] 4984 3-9-5 **70**..(p) RichardRowe(5) 1 69
(L A Dace) *s.i.s: in rr: pushed along on stands' rail 2f out: styd on wl fnl f: gng on cl home* **28/1**

0050 **6** *1/2* **Sam's Cross (IRE)**[1] 5429 4-9-2 **62**.. MCGeran(3) 10 59
(J J Bridger) *chsd ldrs: rdn and styng on whn hmpd and btn ins fnl f* **15/2**

1040 **7** *1/2* **Dynamo Dave (USA)**[15] 5020 4-8-5 **51** oh3..(b) AmyBaker(5) 5 47
(M D I Usher) *sn led: rdn 2f out: hdd & wknd jst ins fnl f* **25/1**

000 **8** *1 3/4* **Sherjawy (IRE)**[9] 5219 5-8-9 **55**..(b) RossAtkinson(3) 2 45
(Miss Z C Davison) *in rr: swtchd sharply rt over 1f out: nvr gng pce to get into contention* **25/1**

0211 **9** *hd* **Step It Up (IRE)**[9] 5219 5-10-0 **71**.. JackMitchell 8 61
(J R Boyle) *chsd ldrs: str chal fr over 1f out tl wknd ins fnl f* **11/4**[2]

1600 **10** *3/4* **Super Frank (IRE)**[15] 5020 6-9-0 **64**..(p) BarryAdams(7) 4 51
(J Akehurst) *chsd ldrs: rdn 2f out: styng on one pce whn n.m.r ins fnl f: sn wknd* **13/2**[3]

6040 **11** *14* **Louie's Lad**[12] 5125 3-8-0 **51** oh3..(p) KierenFox(5) 6 —
(J J Bridger) *chsd ldrs: hmpd 2f out and sn wknd* **25/1**

1m 12.85s (0.65) **Going Correction** +0.125s/f (Good)
WFA 3 from 4yo+ 3lb **11** Ran SP% **123.0**
Speed ratings (Par 103): **100,99,98,98,97 96,95,93,93,92 73**
toteswinger: 1&2 £6.30, 1&3 £34.90, 2&3 £34.10 CSF £153.25 CT £1267.71 TOTE £7.90: £2.30, £5.40, £2.70; EX 144.30 Place 6 £96.04, Place 5 £49.91.
Owner J W Hills **Bred** J B Haggas **Trained** Upper Lambourn, Berks
■ Stewards' Enquiry : David Probert three-day ban: careless riding (Sep 13-15)

FOCUS

A modest handicap restricted to apprentices. The main action took place up the middle of the track.
Louie's Lad Official explanation: jockey said gelding suffered interference in running
T/Jkpt: Not won. T/Plt: £156.10 to a £1 stake. Pool: £74,621.91. 348.88 winning tickets. T/Qpdt: £24.90 to a £1 stake. Pool: £5,223.23. 154.80 winning tickets. ST

5108 YARMOUTH (L-H)

Sunday, August 30

OFFICIAL GOING: Good to firm (8.1)
Wind: fairly light, against Weather: sunny

5478 EBF & LOWESTOFT JOURNAL MAIDEN FILLIES STKS 6f 3y

2:20 (2:23) (Class 5) 2-Y-O **£4,289** (£1,283; £641; £320; £159) **Stalls** Centre

Form RPR

1 **Decorative (IRE)** 2-9-0 0.. PhilipRobinson 4 87+
(M A Jarvis) *t.k.h: trckd ldrs: wnt 2nd gng wl over 2f out: rdn to ld 1f out: drew clr fnl f: readily* **11/4**[1]

64 **2** *4* **Battlemaiden (IRE)**[22] 4792 2-8-11 0.. AhmedAjtebi(3) 3 75
(Saeed Bin Suroor) *led: rdn wl over 1f out: hdd 1f out: edgd rt u.p fnl f: no ch w wnr after* **4/1**[3]

6 **3** *1/2* **Wishbone (IRE)**[15] 5026 2-9-0 0.. AlanMunro 2 74
(M G Quinlan) *dwlt: t.k.h: hld up towards rr: hdwy 1/2-way: chsd ldng pair and rdn over 1f out: edgd lft and nt pce of wnr fnl f* **9/2**

0 **4** *2* **Faithful Duchess (IRE)**[51] 3820 2-9-0 0.. ShaneKelly 1 68
(E A L Dunlop) *dwlt: hld up towards rr: hdwy to chse ldrs over 2f out: rdn and plugged on same pce fr over 1f out* **66/1**

2 **5** *1 1/2* **Subtefuge**[24] 4701 2-9-0 0.. TPQueally 9 63
(H R A Cecil) *chsd ldrs: pushed along and unable qck ent fnl 2f: rdn over 1f out: wknd ent fnl f* **3/1**[2]

6 *2* **Blue Lyric** 2-9-0 0.. WilliamBuick 12 59+
(L M Cumani) *dwlt: hld up towards rr: shkn up and effrt over 2f out: swtchd rt over 1f out: no imp after* **14/1**

33 **7** *2 1/2* **Outshine**[41] 4147 2-9-0 0..(t) RichardMullen 10 50
(J H M Gosden) *hld up in tch in midfield: rdn and unable qck over 2f out: wl btn over 1f out* **7/1**

8 *1 3/4* **Chaussini** 2-9-0 0.. RobertHavlin 7 44
(J A R Toller) *dwlt: sn rcvrd and chsd ldr 4f out tl over 2f out: wknd qckly over 1f out* **25/1**

9 *shd* **Astrovenus** 2-9-0 0.. SaleemGolam 11 44
(M H Tompkins) *s.i.s: sn bhd and rdn along: lost tch fnl 2f* **100/1**

10 *3 1/2* **Whipper's Delight (IRE)** 2-8-11 0.. AndreaAtzeni(3) 8 33
(D Donovan) *dwlt: bhd: rdn along after 2f: struggling bdly 1/2-way* **66/1**

11 *4* **Interlace** 2-9-0 0.. PatCosgrave 5 21
(Sir Mark Prescott) *chsd ldr for 2f: steadily lost pl: wl bhd fnl 2f* **40/1**

12 *9* **Suzy Alexander** 2-9-0 0.. LiamJones 13 —
(G G Margarson) *dwlt: hld up in tch in midfield: rdn and struggling wl over 2f out: sn bhd* **66/1**

1m 14.07s (-0.33) **Going Correction** -0.125s/f (Firm) **12** Ran SP% **120.8**
Speed ratings (Par 94): **97,91,91,88,86 83,80,78,77,73 67,55**
toteswinger: 1&2 £4.80, 1&3 £4.80, 2&3 £6.00 CSF £13.98 TOTE £4.20: £1.50, £1.80, £2.10; EX 20.30 Trifecta £165.10 Pool: £334.79 - 1.50 winning units.
Owner Highclere Thoroughbred Racing Royal Pal **Bred** Barouche Stud (ire) Ltd **Trained** Newmarket, Suffolk

FOCUS

Plenty of these had very nice pedigrees, so this maiden may be above average and produce some nice types. The race was held up by Interlace, a sister to Feet So Fast, who had a blanket and handlers for stalls entry. Eventually she went in and showed some early speed, then weakened quickly before halfway.

NOTEBOOK

Decorative(IRE), who cost 130,000gns as a yearling, holds Cheveley Park and Fillies' Mile entries and clearly deserved them. Quickly away, this fine-looking sort was tucked in behind before being produced to win the race over a furlong out. Once the jockey asked for the effort, she shot clear and should be effective at a higher level. Connections intend taking her to the Tattersalls Timeform Fillies' 800, a race the trainer/owners won last year with the ill-fated Tiger Eye. (op 5-2 tchd 100-30)

Battlemaiden(IRE) had shown a decent level of form in two previous outings and once again did little wrong. There is little doubt she bumped into a good one. (op 9-2 tchd 7-2)

Wishbone(IRE) kept on but looked a little green and awkward. She is obviously still entitled to improve for this run. (op 4-1 tchd 7-2 and 5-1)

Faithful Duchess(IRE) ran in a hot maiden on her previous outing and caught the eye in this, staying on nicely after being just off the pace. (op 100-1 tchd 50-1)

Subtefuge found only one too good on her debut but looked very green here. Her head came up under pressure, but that may have been due to the ground and she deserves another chance. (op 9-2)

Blue Lyric stayed on steadily throughout the last two furlongs. She is bred to stay further, so this would have been an insufficient test for her. (op 12-1)

Outshine appears to be going backwards after a promising debut. (op 8-1)

5479 GREAT YARMOUTH MERCURY H'CAP 1m 3y

2:55 (2:55) (Class 6) (0-60,63) 3-Y-O+ **£2,331** (£693; £346; £173) **Stalls** Centre

Form RPR

45 **1** **Ela Gorrie Mou**[31] 4473 3-9-4 **60**.. PhilipRobinson 5 69
(T T Clement) *chsd ldrs: wnt 2nd gng wl 2f out: led over 1f out: sn rdn and hrd pressed 1f out: kpt on wl* **8/1**

4231 **2** *nk* **King's Icon (IRE)**[13] 5111 4-8-12 **55**..(p) TobyAtkinson(7) 11 63
(M Wigham) *hld up in rr: hdwy on far side 2f out: rdn to press ldrs ent fnl f: wnt 2nd fnl 50yds: kpt on* **3/1**[1]

012 **3** *3/4* **Atacama Sunrise**[9] 5229 3-9-7 **63**..(p) DO'Donohoe 1 70
(J Pearce) *hld up in midfield: rdn and effrt 2f out: ev ch and drvn ent fnl f: no ex fnl 75yds: btn whn n.m.r and eased nr fin* **9/2**[2]

3205 **4** *1* **Astroangel**[13] 5111 5-9-2 **52**..(p) RichardMullen 10 56
(M H Tompkins) *hld up in rr: nudged along and hdwy over 1f out: chsd ldrs and rdn 1f out: kpt on but nvr quite pce to chal ldrs* **16/1**

0000 **5** *3/4* **Silver Hotspur**[19] 4881 5-9-10 **60**.. TPQueally 9 63
(C R Dore) *awkward and wnt lft s: t.k.h: hld up bhd: hdwy on far side jst over 2f out: rdn to chse ldrs ent fnl f: no ex fnl 100yds* **14/1**

1002 **6** *3 3/4* **Ocean Countess (IRE)**[24] 4694 3-9-0 **56**..(v) JerryO'Dwyer 3 50
(Miss J Feilden) *pushed along briefly after s: racd in midfield: reminder 4f out: rdn and n.m.r 2f out: drvn and one pce fr over 1f out* **14/1**

0050 **7** *1* **Bromhead (USA)**[41] 4157 3-9-4 **60**..(t) SaleemGolam 6 52
(Mrs C A Dunnett) *chsd ldr tl 2f out: hrd drvn and wknd over 1f out* **25/1**

6035 **8** *2 1/4* **Sirjosh**[6] 5316 3-8-10 **55**..(vt[1]) AndreaAtzeni(3) 2 41
(D Donovan) *chsd ldrs: rdn and struggling whn stmbld jst over 2f out: no ch fr over 1f out* **7/1**

2236 **9** *3/4* **Sion Hill (IRE)**[25] 4667 8-9-5 **58**..(p) KellyHarrison(3) 7 43
(John A Harris) *led: jnd and rdn over 2f out: hdd over 1f out: wknd ent fnl f* **14/1**

0421 **10** *4 1/2* **King Of Connacht**[13] 5103 6-9-8 **58**..(p) LiamJones 8 32
(M Wellings) *bmpd s: hld up in rr: swtchd rt and rdn 2f out: sn btn: eased ins fnl f* **13/2**[3]

06-0 **11** *12* **Hekaaya (IRE)**[23] 4749 3-8-13 **55**.. RHills 12 2
(M P Tregoning) *chsd ldrs tl rdn ent fnl 2f: sn wknd* **11/1**

360 **12** *9* **Bobble Rock (IRE)**[22] 4786 3-9-1 **60**.. MarcHalford(3) 13 —
(J R Best) *bhd: rdn and strugglking 1/2-way: t.o* **33/1**

6-06 **13** *20* **Sheriff's Silk**[25] 4668 5-8-12 **51**..(b) RussellKennemore(3) 15 —
(B N Pollock) *v.s.a: a bhd: t.o and virtually p.u ins fnl f* **50/1**

1m 40.6s **Going Correction** -0.125s/f (Firm)
WFA 3 from 4yo+ 6lb **13** Ran SP% **123.1**
Speed ratings (Par 101): **95,94,93,92,92 88,87,85,84,79 67,58,38**
toteswinger: 1&2 £6.60, 1&3 £14.90, 2&3 £4.10 CSF £32.65 CT £131.10 TOTE £10.50: £3.40, £1.70, £2.50; EX 48.40 Trifecta £104.20 Pool: £225.38 - 1.60 winning units.
Owner P Charalambous **Bred** Peter Charles **Trained** Newmarket, Suffolk

FOCUS

A real mixture of ability, ages and experience took their chance, so the form looks unreliable.
Silver Hotspur Official explanation: jockey said gelding jumped awkwardly from the stalls
Hekaaya(IRE) Official explanation: jockey said filly moved badly in the latter stages
Sheriff's Silk Official explanation: jockey said gelding lost its action

5480 EDP 2 H'CAP 5f 43y

3:30 (3:31) (Class 5) (0-70,70) 3-Y-O+ **£3,154** (£944; £472; £236; £117) **Stalls** Centre

Form RPR

323 **1** **Choisharp (IRE)**[24] 4718 3-9-2 **65**..(b) JerryO'Dwyer 2 74
(M Botti) *chsd clr ldr: clsd u.p 1f out: drvn to ld fnl 75yds: eased nr fin* **7/2**[1]

2101 **2** *1* **Silver Prelude**[16] 4978 8-9-2 **63**..(t) PhilipRobinson 4 68
(S C Williams) *led and sn clr: rdn over 1f out: hdd fnl 75yds: no ex* **11/2**[3]

1100 **3** *nk* **Piazza San Pietro**[12] 5124 3-9-5 **68**.. RobertHavlin 7 72
(A B Haynes) *chsd ldrs: rdn 2f out: edgd lft u.p over 1f out: kpt on fnl f: n.m.r and swtchd lft fnl 75yds* **9/2**[2]

0302 **4** ¾ **Magical Speedfit (IRE)**[11] 5156 4-9-8 **69**.......................... LiamJones 1 70
(G G Margarson) *racd in midfield: effrt and hld hd high over 1f out: kpt on u.p but nvr quite gng to rch ldrs* **6/1**

-305 **5** 2 **Clerical (USA)**[11] 5164 3-8-1 **53**..........................(p) AndreaAtzeni(3) 3 47
(R M H Cowell) *racd off the pce in midfield: rdn over 2f out: sltly hmpd over 1f out: plugged on fnl f: nvr trbld ldrs* **9/1**

0000 **6** hd **Blakeshall Diamond**[12] 5125 4-8-1 **51** oh6................ KellyHarrison(3) 6 44
(A J Chamberlain) *taken down early: a in rr: rdn over 2f out: kpt on but nvr pce to rch ldrs* **40/1**

1630 **7** 1 ¼ **Dragon Flame (IRE)**[31] 4469 6-9-9 **70**..........................(v) ShaneKelly 10 59
(M Quinn) *bhd and sn niggled along: sme modest hdwy fnl f: nvr trbld ldrs* **11/2**[3]

0000 **8** 3 ¼ **Thumberlina**[13] 5105 3-8-2 **51** oh6.............................. AdrianMcCarthy 5 28
(Mrs C A Dunnett) *sn niggled along towards rr: n.d* **33/1**

4054 **9** 2 **Rhapsilian**[16] 5008 5-8-6 **53**.................................. WilliamBuick 9 23
(J R Jenkins) *bhd: shkn up and effrt 2f out: rdn and no rspnse over 1f out* **6/1**

62.84 secs (0.64) **Going Correction** -0.125s/f (Firm)
WFA 3 from 4yo+ 2lb **9** Ran SP% **115.1**
Speed ratings (Par 103): **89,87,86,85,82 82,80,75,71**
toteswinger: 1&2 £2.30, 1&3 £12.20, 2&3 £12.50 CSF £22.82 CT £87.69 TOTE £5.20: £1.90, £2.40, £1.50; EX 19.40 Trifecta £42.80 Pool: £362.17 - 6.26 winning units.
Owner Giuliano Manfredini **Bred** Garrett Forrest **Trained** Newmarket, Suffolk

5481 ROY AND JOAN TANNER MEMORIAL H'CAP 2m
4:05 (4:06) (Class 3) (0-95,95) 3-Y-0+ **£7,569** (£2,265; £1,132; £566) **Stalls** Centre

Form RPR
331/ **1** **Aajel (USA)**[710] 5574 5-9-9 **90**.. RHills 4 102+
(M P Tregoning) *mde all: gng much the best 3f out: pushed wl clr over 1f out: v easily* **9/2**[3]

5036 **2** 5 **Amerigo (IRE)**[57] 3642 4-10-0 **95**.......................... PhilipRobinson 3 99
(M A Jarvis) *chsd wnr: rdn 3f out: lost 2nd over 2f out: 3rd and btn over 1f out: kpt on to regain 2nd ins fnl f* **7/1**

3231 **3** ½ **Dazinski**[8] 5252 3-8-0 **81**.. NickyMackay 2 84
(M H Tompkins) *hld up in 3rd pl: rdn and effrt 3f out: chsd wnr over 2f out: btn over 1f out: lost 2nd ins fnl f* **6/4**[1]

2121 **4** 26 **Perfect Shot (IRE)**[22] 4793 3-8-7 **88**.......................... ShaneKelly 1 60
(J L Dunlop) *hld up in last pl: short-lived effrt 3f out: wl btn 2f out: eased fr over 1f out: t.o* **7/4**[2]

3m 29.44s (-5.16) **Going Correction** -0.125s/f (Firm)
WFA 3 from 4yo+ 14lb **4** Ran SP% **107.0**
Speed ratings (Par 107): **107,104,104,91**
CSF £27.58 TOTE £4.10; EX 13.40.
Owner Hamdan Al Maktoum **Bred** Shadwell Farm LLC **Trained** Lambourn, Berks

FOCUS
All of these could be given some sort of chance on their very best performances, but the winner did it easily after being allowed an uncontested lead.

NOTEBOOK
Aajel(USA), absent since September 2007 after getting a bit of a leg and gelded, got to the front quite early and kept on in relentless style to make a pleasing comeback. He does nothing quickly, seemingly, but will run his rivals into the ground. He holds an entry in the gruelling Cesarewitch, a race that does look right for him, but the owner also has Daraahem entered, so it would be a bit premature to start backing him at shortish prices. (tchd 5-1)
Amerigo(IRE) chased the winner but looked woefully one paced when asked to play a part. However, he did just enough to claim second. (op 5-1)
Dazinski could not go through with his effort after making ground up from the rear. (op 7-4)
Perfect Shot(IRE) got outpaced when the tempo increased and could never get on terms, hard though he tried. He was well beaten, so something may have been amiss. (tchd 13-8 and 15-8)

5482 EASTERN DAILY PRESS CLAIMING STKS 1m 2f 21y
4:40 (4:41) (Class 6) 3-Y-0 **£2,201** (£655; £327; £163) **Stalls** Low

Form RPR
5033 **1** **Strong Storm (USA)**[12] 5122 3-8-10 67.......................... ShaneKelly 6 59
(J Noseda) *chsd ldng pair: rdn over 2f out: drvn ent fnl f: drvn to ld and hung lft fnl 100yds: plld off rival and hdd sn after: drvn to ld again last strides: fin 1st: disq: plcd 2nd* **5/4**[1]

0250 **2** hd **Sixties Swinger (USA)**[18] 4904 3-9-5 60..................(t) PhilipRobinson 7 68
(M A Jarvis) *chsd ldr: rdn over 2f out: hrd drvn and ev ch ent fnl f: briefly short of room ins fnl f: sn lft in ld: hdd and no ex last strides: fin 2nd, hd: awrdd r* **8/1**

3302 **3** ½ **Tiger Flash**[25] 4669 3-9-1 68.. LiamJones 4 63
(W J Haggas) *t.k.h: hld up in last trio: n.m.r over 2f out: swtchd lft and effrt towards inner 2 fout: hrd drvn to chse ldrs ent fnl f: kpt on to go 3rd nr fin* **3/1**[2]

6323 **4** ¾ **Equipe De Nuit**[12] 5127 3-8-6 70.............................. TobyAtkinson(7) 10 59
(S C Williams) *led: rdn wl over 1f out: hdd fnl 100yds: no ex and lost 3 pls after* **5/1**[3]

3444 **5** ½ **Kyle Of Bute**[23] 4734 3-8-11 45.................................... TPQueally 1 56
(J L Dunlop) *t.k.h: hld up in tch: rdn and effrt over 2f out: hrd drvn and nt qckn jst over 1f out: kpt on again wl ins fnl f* **11/1**

6 6 **Broughtons Point** 3-8-5 0.. AndreaAtzeni(3) 2 41
(W J Musson) *awkward leaving stalls and s.i.s: bhd: pushed along 5f out: effrt on inner over 3f out: wknd wl over 1f out* **16/1**

0006 **7** 2 ¼ **Jacobite Prince (IRE)**[47] 3961 3-8-9 53......................(p) JerryO'Dwyer 3 38
(M H Tompkins) *t.k.h: hld up in tch in rr: rdn over 3f out: wknd u.p wl over 1f out* **28/1**

0000 **8** 20 **Vin De Rose**[24] 4722 3-8-13 40...................................... DO'Donohoe 8 —
(John A Harris) *stdd s: t.k.h: in tch in midfield: lost pl and rdn 3f out: bhd fnl 2f* **100/1**

2m 9.73s (-0.77) **Going Correction** -0.125s/f (Firm) **8** Ran SP% **115.9**
Speed ratings (Par 98): **98,97,97,96,96 91,89,73**
toteswinger: 1&2 £3.70, 1&3 £4.20, 2&3 £1.60 CSF £18.74 TOTE £8.70: £2.10, £1.20, £1.40; EX 21.20 Trifecta £39.70 Pool: £472.04 - 8.78 winning units.Strong Storm was claimed by Mr H. J. Collingridge for £7,000.
Owner Tom Ludt **Bred** Mckee Stables Inc **Trained** Newmarket, Suffolk
■ Stewards' Enquiry : Shane Kelly two-day ban: careless riding (Sep 13-14)

FOCUS
This was probably only a modest event that had a messy finish. The fact that a horse rated 45 managed a fair fifth helps to show its level.

5483 JOBS 24 H'CAP 1m 6f 17y
5:15 (5:16) (Class 6) (0-60,59) 3-Y-0+ **£2,331** (£693; £346; £173) **Stalls** High

Form RPR
0-21 **1** **Lady Hestia (USA)**[126] 1537 4-9-8 **55**.............................. RHills 4 72+
(M P Tregoning) *mde all: pushed along and drew clr 2f out: in n.d after: eased towards fin* **11/8**[1]

4566 **2** 4 ½ **Little Carmela**[104] 2123 5-9-12 **59**........................ SaleemGolam 3 65
(S C Williams) *chsd ldrs: rdn and disp 2nd 3f out: chsd clr wnr over 1f out: no imp* **10/1**

3310 **3** 2 ¾ **Astroleo**[31] 4470 3-8-7 **52**.. NickyMackay 5 54
(M H Tompkins) *chsd wnr for 2f: rdn to chse wnr again 4f out: outpcd by wnr 2f out: sn lost 2nd and wl hld after* **11/2**[3]

0103 **4** 3 **Captain Flack**[20] 4857 3-8-11 **56**..................(b) KirstyMilczarek 7 54
(J A R Toller) *hld up in tch in midfield: rdn and edgd lft 4f out: 5th and wl hld fnl 2f: plugged on to go modest 4th ins fnl f* **14/1**

001 **5** 1 ½ **Rough Sketch (USA)**[61] 3475 4-9-12 **59**......................(b) PatCosgrave 6 55
(Sir Mark Prescott) *t.k.h: hld up wl in tch: hdwy to dispute 2nd wl over 3f out: rdn and nt qckn 2f out: sn wl btn* **9/2**[2]

0506 **6** 4 ½ **Watchoverme**[13] 5108 3-8-10 **55**.................................(v) RichardMullen 1 45
(J R Fanshawe) *rel to r and early reminders: towards rr: rdn and effrt on inner 4f out: no hdwy over 3f out and wl btn after* **16/1**

6-06 **7** 17 **Muntami (IRE)**[28] 3760 8-8-12 **48**.......................... KellyHarrison(3) 12 14
(John A Harris) *hld up towards rr tl hdwy to chse ldrs 11f out: wknd 4f out: wl bhd fnl 3f: t.o* **18/1**

00-0 **8** 2 **Shape Shifter (USA)**[24] 4698 3-8-2 **47**.......................... RichardThomas 9 10
(J R Best) *hld up in rr: rdn and struggling 5f out: wl bhd fnl 3f: t.o* **40/1**

100/ **9** 4 **Zonic Boom (FR)**[30] 4906 9-8-12 **45**...........................(p) DO'Donohoe 10 2
(Heather Dalton) *stdd s: hld up in rr: struggling and rdn 5f out: t.o fnl 3f* **50/1**

00-0 **10** 16 **Renege The Joker**[138] 1273 6-8-5 **45**........................ RichardOld(7) 11 —
(S Regan) *t.k.h: chsd wnr after 2f tl 4f out: sn dropped out: t.o and eased ins fnl f* **100/1**

4402 **11** 19 **Royal Premier (IRE)**[25] 4670 6-9-11 **58**.........................(v) JimmyQuinn 8 —
(H J Collingridge) *hmpd s and sn bustled along: hld up towards rr: rdn whn hmpd and lost pl 4f out: no ch after: virtually p.u fr over 1f out: t.o* **9/1**

3m 4.85s (-2.75) **Going Correction** -0.125s/f (Firm)
WFA 3 from 4yo+ 12lb **11** Ran SP% **118.0**
Speed ratings (Par 101): **102,99,97,96,95 92,83,81,79,70 59**
toteswinger: 1&2 £3.80, 1&3 £3.20 2&3 £8.50 CSF £16.68 CT £61.80 TOTE £2.50: £1.10, £3.60, £2.10; EX 19.90 Trifecta £158.00 Part won. Pool: £213.60 - 0.54 winning units..
Owner Mr And Mrs A E Pakenham **Bred** Shadwell Farm LLC **Trained** Lambourn, Berks

FOCUS
Not many of these looked to be in good form, but they were the type of horses you would expect to see lining up in a class 6 staying handicap.

5484 BETFAIR APPRENTICE TRAINING SERIES H'CAP 1m 2f 21y
5:50 (5:50) (Class 6) (0-60,57) 4-Y-0+ **£2,331** (£693; £346; £173) **Stalls** Low

Form RPR
6234 **1** **Pretty Officer (USA)**[21] 4824 4-8-7 **53**.......................... NoelGarbutt(8) 8 59
(Rae Guest) *chsd ldr tl led 3f out: hdd narrowly 2f out: rdn over 1f out: led again fnl 100yds: styd on* **7/2**[1]

5556 **2** ½ **Carmela Maria**[24] 4704 4-9-5 **57**..............................(p) TobyAtkinson 3 62
(S C Williams) *led: rdn and hdd 3f out: rallied u.p ins fnl f: wnt 2nd towards fin: kpt on* **6/1**[2]

0000 **3** ¾ **Dinner Date**[8] 5266 7-8-9 **57**................................ TraceyAddey(10) 6 61
(T Keddy) *chsd ldrs: hdwy to join ldrs 4f out: led narrowly 2f out: rdn over 1f out: hdd fnl 100yds: no ex* **12/1**

0622 **4** 4 **Fantasy Ride**[41] 4158 7-8-9 **50**.................................. SimonPearce(3) 5 46
(J Pearce) *stdd s: hld up in rr: hdwy on inner 3f out: plugged on u.p but nvr gng pce to threaten ldrs* **7/2**[1]

0016 **5** 4 **Broughtons Silk**[18] 4916 4-8-6 **54**.............................. RosePearson(10) 4 42
(W J Musson) *stdd s: t.k.h: hld up towards rr: sme hdwy 2f out: pushed along and wknd qckly over 1f out* **13/2**[3]

022 **6** ½ **Gifted Heir (IRE)**[13] 5111 5-8-5 **51**.............................. NatashaEaton(8) 1 38
(A Bailey) *chsd ldrs: rdn and edging rt fr 3f out: wknd 2f out* **7/1**

0045 **7** ¾ **Carbon Print (USA)**[23] 4745 4-9-4 **56**.......................... RosieJessop 7 41
(P R Webber) *t.k.h: hld up in rr: rdn and effrt on outer over 3f out: struggling and wl btn fnl 2f* **7/1**

0536 **8** 21 **Generous Lad (IRE)**[65] 3348 6-8-7 **45**............................ JPHamblett 9 —
(A B Haynes) *hld up in last trio: rdn 4f out: no prog: eased fr over 1f out: t.o* **7/1**

2m 9.48s (-1.02) **Going Correction** -0.125s/f (Firm) **8** Ran SP% **117.3**
Speed ratings (Par 101): **99,98,98,94,91 91,90,73**
toteswinger: 1&2 £5.00, 1&3 £16.30, 2&3 £15.20 CSF £25.47 CT £228.37 TOTE £4.20: £1.50, £2.00, £3.30; EX 30.90 Trifecta £229.40 Part won. Pool: £310.02 - 0.62 winning units. Place 6: £30.31, Place 5: £19.34..
Owner ROA Racing Partnership VIII **Bred** Fiona Craig & Dermot Cantillon **Trained** Newmarket, Suffolk

FOCUS
A very modest event for apprentices, which featured some good riding for the type of contest. The result is probably unreliable.
T/Plt: £39.20 to a £1 stake. Pool: £59,326.98. 1,102.93 winning tickets. T/Qpdt: £17.40 to a £1 stake. Pool: £3,785.25. 160.74 winning tickets. SP

5075 CURRAGH (R-H)
Sunday, August 30

OFFICIAL GOING: Soft to heavy (heavy in places) changing to heavy after race 1 (2.15)

5486a GO AND GO ROUND TOWER STKS (GROUP 3) 6f
2:45 (2:48) 2-Y-0 **£47,402** (£13,907; £6,626; £2,257)

RPR
1 **Arctic (IRE)**[35] 4357 2-9-1 .... PShanahan 6 111+
(Tracey Collins, Ire) *a.p: led travelling easily over 2f out: sn clr: styd on strly fnl f: impressive* **11/8**[1]

2 4 ½ **Air Chief Marshal (IRE)**[35] 4359 2-9-1 112.................. JMurtagh 5 97
(A P O'Brien, Ire) *led and disp: pushed along 1/2-way: hdd over 2f out: no imp on wnr fr 1 1/2f out* **2/1**[2]

3 *1* **Sebastian Flyte**[18] 4919 2-9-1 WJSupple 2 94
(Francis Ennis, Ire) *led and disp early: rdn and hdd over 2f out: kpt on same pce in mod 3rd fnl f* **7/1**

4 *6* **Beat Surrender (FR)**[12] 5133 2-9-1 KLatham 3 76
(G M Lyons, Ire) *hld up in rr: rdn 1/2-way: mod last 2f out: wnt mod 4th fnl f* **14/1**

5 *9* **Famous Warrior (IRE)**[12] 5140 2-9-1 98 DPMcDonogh 7 49
(Kevin Prendergast, Ire) *hld up in rr: mod 4th and rdn over 2f out: no imp fnl f* **4/1**[3]

6 *15* **Wild Adventure (IRE)** 2-8-12 DMGrant 1 —
(John Joseph Murphy, Ire) *chsd ldrs: rdn 1/2-way: dropped to rr fr 2f out: trailing fnl f* **66/1**

1m 20.1s (5.40) **Going Correction** +1.00s/f (Soft) 6 Ran SP% **116.1**
Speed ratings: **104,98,96,88,76 56**
CSF £4.64 TOTE £2.00: £1.50, £1.40; DF 4.10.
Owner R A Pegum **Bred** Darley **Trained** The Curragh, Co Kildare

NOTEBOOK
Arctic(IRE) boosted his growing reputation by seeing off the opposition in impressive fashion. He made most, racing wide of his rivals, and there was only going to be one result from fully 2f out. He was travelling very easily while his rivals were under pressure and needed only one tap of the whip to keep him concentrated on the job. The winner, a son of Shamardal and a Shareef Dancer mare, is now three from three following two wins over 5f. He received quotes of 16-1 and 33-1 for the 2,000 Guineas from Ladbrokes and Victor Chandler respectively. Considering he beat Air Chief Marshal, who had run Alfred Nobel to half a length on similar ground in the Group 1 Phoenix Stakes over the same course and distance, Arctic has to be a contender for top juvenile in these parts and, on the evidence of this performance, there should be more to come. He holds plenty of big-race entries but no plans for the rest of the season have yet been made. Trainer Tracey Collins said that "he's a very smart colt and, while he handles testing conditions, we believe he won't realise his full potential until he gets better ground". (op 5/4 tchd 11/10)
Air Chief Marshal(IRE) was always close up and held every chance, but came under pressure and was unable to make any impression on the winner from well over 1f out. (op 2/1 tchd 5/2)
Sebastian Flyte, who returned from a long break to win over 7f on good ground at Gowran Park 18 days previously, raced prominently but was unable to make any impression on the winner from well over 1f out. (op 10/1)
Beat Surrender(FR), well beaten in a similar event over 7f on quick ground at York 12 days previously, was never able to get into serious contention.
Famous Warrior(IRE), winner of his maiden over this trip at Fairyhouse before winning a nursery over 1m at Killarney, was beaten over 2f out. (op 4/1 tchd 5/1)
Wild Adventure(IRE) Official explanation: jockey said filly lost a shoe in running

5487a DANCE DESIGN STKS (GROUP 3) (F&M) 1m 1f
3:15 (3:15) 3-Y-O+
£47,330 (£13,834; £6,553; £2,184)

RPR

1 **Chinese White (IRE)**[18] 4923 4-9-5 110 PJSmullen 5 112+
(D K Weld, Ire) *trckd ldrs in 3rd: led 1 1/2f out: sn rdn clr: pushed out fnl f: easily* **11/8**[1]

2 *4 1/2* **Latin Love (IRE)**[27] 4608 3-8-12 105 JMurtagh 6 102
(David Wachman, Ire) *led: rdn and hdd 1 1/2f out: drifted sltly lft 1f out: no imp on wnr* **9/4**[2]

3 *2 1/2* **Festival Princess (IRE)**[18] 4923 4-9-5 99 FMBerry 1 97
(Mrs John Harrington, Ire) *hld up towards rr: sme prog into 5th and rdn over 2f out: kpt on wout threatening ldrs to go mod 3rd fnl f* **12/1**

4 *3 1/2* **Chintz (IRE)**[50] 3882 3-8-12 99 (p) WMLordan 3 89
(David Wachman, Ire) *hld up in 5th: rdn fr 2 1/2f out: sn no imp* **16/1**

5 *hd* **Cilium (IRE)**[24] 4725 3-8-12 83 CDHayes 4 89
(Andrew Oliver, Ire) *hld up: rdn in 6th over 2f out: no imp fr 2f out* **66/1**

6 *1/2* **Deauville Vision (IRE)**[14] 5076 6-9-5 106 (p) RPCleary 7 88
(M Halford, Ire) *trckd ldr in 2nd: rdn along ent st: no imp fr 2f out* **14/1**

7 *dist* **Oh Goodness Me**[27] 4608 3-9-1 106 KJManning 2 —
(J S Bolger, Ire) *trckd ldrs: rdn in 4th 2 1/2f out: sn wknd: trailing and virtually p.u fnl f: t.o* **9/2**[3]

2m 4.10s (9.20) **Going Correction** +1.25s/f (Soft)
WFA 3 from 4yo+ 7lb 7 Ran SP% **112.8**
Speed ratings: **109,105,102,99,99 99,—**
CSF £4.48 TOTE £2.00: £1.30, £2.00; DF 4.40.
Owner Lady O'Reilly **Bred** Skymarc Farm & Castlemartin St **Trained** The Curragh, Co Kildare

FOCUS
The third and fourth give the form a solid look.

NOTEBOOK
Chinese White(IRE), a consistent dual Listed scorer who showed smart form over 1m4f last season, recorded her first Pattern-race success. She seems to have benefited from being dropped in trip this year and won in good style, tracking the leaders and beginning her effort 2f out before going to the front entering the final furlong. She quickly went clear and afterwards trainer Dermot Weld said that "she is a smart filly, always has been, and deserved to win a Group race. She will probably come back here for the Blandford Stakes next week and if she runs well then the Prix de L'Opera will be considered". (op 11/10)
Latin Love(IRE), a Listed winner over 1m on yielding ground on her previous start, had won her maiden on heavy last season. She made the running but edged briefly left when joined well over 1f out and had no answer when the winner went for home. (op 3/1 tchd 2/1)
Festival Princess(IRE), fourth behind Chinese White in a 1m1f plus Listed event at Gowran Park on her previous start, was held up in rear before making headway into the straight. She kept on for pressure and went third inside the final furlong without ever posing a serious threat. (op 8/1)
Chintz(IRE), a Group 3 winner over 7f here last season, has proved a bit disappointing this year and has yet to reach the first three in five attempts. Held up, she made some progress early in the straight but could make no impression from well over 1f out. (op 14/1)
Cilium(IRE), a maiden winner over 1m at Leopardstown on her previous start, was held up before making a forward move early in the straight which was to prove short-lived.
Oh Goodness Me Official explanation: vet said filly was found to be blowing hard post race

5488a MOYGLARE STUD STKS (GROUP 1) (FILLIES) 7f
3:45 (3:45) 2-Y-O
£143,300 (£46,213; £21,941; £7,378; £4,951; £2,524)

RPR

1 **Termagant (IRE)**[80] 2867 2-8-12 DPMcDonogh 1 110+
(Kevin Prendergast, Ire) *trckd ldrs: rdn in 3rd under 2f out: led 1 1/2f out: kpt on wl fnl f* **16/1**

2 *2 1/2* **Famous (IRE)**[24] 4726 2-8-12 95 JAHeffernan 3 104
(A P O'Brien, Ire) *led: rdn 1/2-way: hdd 1 1/2f out: kpt on same pce fnl f* **66/1**

3 *1 3/4* **Lillie Langtry (IRE)**[24] 4726 2-8-12 109 JMurtagh 7 99
(A P O'Brien, Ire) *hld up in last: rdn in 4th 2f out: wnt 3rd over 1f out: no imp on ldrs fnl f* **8/11**[1]

4 *8* **Long Lashes (USA)**[22] 4795 2-8-12 LDettori 2 79
(Saeed Bin Suroor) *trckd ldrs in 3rd: rdn in 2nd 2f out: no imp over 1f out* **5/2**[2]

5 *2* **Gile Na Greine (IRE)**[14] 5075 2-8-12 KJManning 5 74
(J S Bolger, Ire) *chsd ldrs: 4th 1/2-way: sn rdn: no imp fr 2f out* **13/2**[3]

6 *5* **Gold Bubbles (USA)**[10] 5199 2-8-12 103 (b[1]) DJMoran 6 62
(J S Bolger, Ire) *trckd ldr in 2nd: rdn over 2f out: sn wknd* **66/1**

7 *1 1/4* **Wrong Answer**[90] 2557 2-8-12 96 CDHayes 4 59
(Kevin Prendergast, Ire) *hld up in rr: rdn fr 1/2-way: no imp fr 2f out* **16/1**

1m 35.1s (8.00) **Going Correction** +1.25s/f (Soft) 7 Ran SP% **114.6**
Speed ratings: **104,101,99,90,87 82,80**
CSF £531.12 TOTE £20.90: £6.10, £10.00; DF 204.40.
Owner J Vasicek **Bred** Old Carhue Stud **Trained** Friarstown, Co Kildare

FOCUS
This Group 1 was billed as a clash between the Coolmore and Godolphin operations with Lillie Langtry and Long Lashes leading the market, but both failed to live up to expectations.

NOTEBOOK
Termagant(IRE), a winner on her only previous start over the same trip on good ground at Leopardstown in June, ran out a decisive winner, allaying trainer Kevin Prendergast's fears that she might not cope with the very testing ground. The winner tracked the leaders and began her bid 2f out, leading well over 1f out and keeping on well inside the final furlong. Plans are fluid and Prendergast hinted that the daughter of Powerscourt might be finished for the season, although the fact this win qualified her automatically for the Breeders' Cup Juvenile Fillies Turf will be discussed. Prendergast regards the Boylesports Irish 1,000 Guineas rather than the Newmarket Guineas as her likely Classic target. (op 14/1)
Famous(IRE), over six lengths behind Lillie Langtry in the Group 2 Debutante Stakes over the same trip at Leopardstown early this month, turned the tables on her stablemate here. She made the running and, after being ridden along soon after halfway, kept plugging away. (op 50/1)
Lillie Langtry(IRE), successful at Group 3 and Group 2 level, was held up in rear before making some headway over 2f out. It was soon obvious that she was labouring and, while she kept on, taking third place over 1f out, she was never travelling well enough to mount a serious challenge. Whether she was simply off the boil or disliked the heavy ground, or both, only time will tell. (op 4/5)
Long Lashes(USA), winner of a 6f Listed event here on soft ground on debut in June before joining Goldolphin and landing the Group 3 Sweet Solera Stakes over this trip on good ground at Newmarket, tracked the leaders but was done with in a hurry 2f out. The ground might have been too testing for her. Official explanation: vet said filly was found to be blowing hard post-race (op 9/4)
Gile Na Greine(IRE), a course and distance winner on soft to heavy on her debut two weeks previously, is held in high regard by her trainer. She tracked the leaders but could make no impression when asked to raise her effort 2f out. (op 11/2)

5490a HACKETTS EUROPEAN BREEDERS FUND IRISH CAMBRIDGESHIRE 1m
4:45 (4:47) 3-Y-O+
£58,349 (£18,543; £8,834; £3,009; £2,038; £1,067)

RPR

1 **Poet**[12] 5141 4-9-9 107 SMLevey(5) 17 116
(A P O'Brien, Ire) *chsd ldrs: prog to ld 2 1/2f out: rdn clr over 1f out: strly pressed fnl f: kpt on wl* **7/1**[2]

2 *nk* **Raise Your Heart (IRE)**[7] 4254 6-8-7 86 RPCleary 19 94
(Ms Joanna Morgan, Ire) *chsd ldrs: rdn and prog into 4th over 1f out: wnt 2nd ins fnl f: strly pressed wnr to line* **6/1**[1]

3 *3/4* **Worldly Wise**[18] 4921 6-8-11 90 (p) DMGrant 8 96
(Patrick J Flynn, Ire) *mid-div: rdn and prog fr 2f out: wnt 3rd ins fnl f: kpt on* **20/1**

4 *shd* **Choose Me (IRE)**[18] 4923 3-8-6 91 CDHayes 11 96
(Kevin Prendergast, Ire) *towards rr: sme prog fr 2f out: mod 9th 1 1/2f out: kpt on wout threatening fnl f* **20/1**

5 *1 1/2* **Barack (IRE)**[12] 5139 3-8-0 90 ShaneFoley(5) 25 92
(Francis Ennis, Ire) *prom: cl 2nd over 2f out: sn rdn: 2nd over 1f out: no ex fnl f* **16/1**

6 *shd* **Toraidhe (IRE)**[9] 5237 3-8-1 91 DEMullins(5) 9 92
(J S Bolger, Ire) *chsd ldrs: rdn in 5th over 2f out: no ex fr 1 1/2f out* **14/1**

7 *1 3/4* **Separate Ways (IRE)**[25] 4675 4-8-9 88 CO'Donoghue 26 86
(David Marnane, Ire) *mid-div: kpt on same pce fr 2f out* **14/1**

8 *1* **Windsor Palace (IRE)**[12] 5141 4-9-9 102 JMurtagh 16 98
(A P O'Brien, Ire) *hld up: prog fr 2f out: sn rdn: 7th 1f out: no ex* **11/1**

9 *5 1/2* **Belle's Ridge**[18] 4921 5-9-3 96 (b) WJLee 7 79
(Timothy Doyle, Ire) *mid-div: rdn in 10th 2f out: no ex fnl f* **25/1**

10 *4* **Pires**[33] 4412 5-8-11 90 JAHeffernan 18 64
(A J Martin, Ire) *chsd ldrs: no imp fr 2f out* **25/1**

11 *2 1/2* **Slieve Mish (IRE)**[24] 4727 3-8-11 96 KJManning 22 63
(J S Bolger, Ire) *chsd ldrs: no imp fr 2f out* **12/1**

12 *3/4* **Tis Mighty (IRE)**[39] 4218 6-8-6 90 (b) EJMcNamara(5) 24 57
(P J Prendergast, Ire) *in rr of mid-div: no imp fr 2f out* **20/1**

13 *nk* **Rose Hip (IRE)**[17] 4961 5-8-10 89 PJSmullen 5 55
(Joseph G Murphy, Ire) *nvr bttr than mid-div* **16/1**

14 *1* **Gluteus Maximus (IRE)**[14] 5079 3-8-8 100 JPO'Brien(7) 14 63
(A P O'Brien, Ire) *nvr bttr than mid-div* **25/1**

15 *1/2* **Dandy Boy (ITY)**[49] 3904 3-8-7 92 DPMcDonogh 15 54
(David Marnane, Ire) *nvr bttr than mid-div* **20/1**

16 *shd* **Marias Dream (IRE)**[33] 4412 7-8-5 89 GFCarroll(5) 10 51
(J G Coogan, Ire) *in rr of mid-div: rdn 1/2-way: no imp* **14/1**

17 *2* **Kyllachy Star**[21] 4814 3-8-4 89 PaulHanagan 2 46
(R A Fahey) *chsd ldrs: rdn in 5th over 2f out: no imp* **8/1**[3]

18 *2* **Steig (IRE)**[9] 5237 6-8-6 85 WJSupple 21 38
(C Moore, Ire) *mid-div: no imp fr 2f out* **14/1**

19 *6* **Amarama (IRE)**[9] 5237 4-8-11 90 RMBurke 6 29
(David P Myerscough, Ire) *chsd ldrs: wknd fr 2f out* **25/1**

20 *4* **Ballivor (IRE)**[24] 4727 6-8-6 88 PBBeggy(3) 13 18
(W T Farrell, Ire) *nvr bttr than mid-div* **16/1**

21 *4* **Gunga Din (IRE)**[35] 4360 5-8-12 91 (p) JohnEgan 1 12
(A Kinsella, Ire) *mid-div on outer: rdn 1/2-way: sn wknd* **33/1**

22 *1 1/4* **Always Be True (IRE)**[18] 4923 3-8-7 92 (p) WMLordan 12 9
(David Wachman, Ire) *in rr of mid-div: no imp fr 2f out* **25/1**

23 *1 3/4* **Wigwam Willie (IRE)**[33] 4412 7-8-11 90 (tp) NCallan 23 —
(K A Ryan) *nvr bttr than mid-div* **7/1**[2]

24 *13* **Ask Jack (USA)**[18] 4921 5-8-6 88 (p) SMGorey(3) 3 —
(Joseph G Murphy, Ire) *a towards rr* **25/1**

25 *2* **Dollar Chick (IRE)**[18] 4923 5-8-4 83 (p) DJMoran 27 —
(Noel Meade, Ire) *led: rdn and hdd 2 1/2f out: wknd* **33/1**

26 *7* **Headford View (IRE)**[15] 5045 5-9-2 95 (p) FMBerry 4 —
(James Halpin, Ire) *in rr of mid-div: no imp fr 2f out* **25/1**

27 1 1/2 **Flure De Leise (IRE)**[9] 5238 4-8-8 87.................................(p) KLatham 20 —
(Eamon Tyrrell, Ire) *a towards rr* **28/1**
1m 51.3s (9.40) **Going Correction** +1.40s/f (Soft)
WFA 3 from 4yo+ 6lb 27 Ran SP% **166.0**
Speed ratings: **109,108,107,107,106 106,104,103,98,94 91,90,90,89,88 88,86,84,78,74 70,69,67,54,52 45,44**
CSF £51.85 TOTE £10.60: £3.90, £2.10, £6.20, £6.40; DF 78.20.
Owner Derrick Smith **Bred** Meon Valley Stud **Trained** Ballydoyle, Co Tipperary
■ Stewards' Enquiry : S M Levey two-day ban: used whip with excessive force and frequency (Sep 13-14)

FOCUS
The runner-up and fourth are the guide to the level of the form.

NOTEBOOK
Poet put up a fine weight-carrying performance to credit Aidan O'Brien with a rare handicap winner. Admittedly, he doesn't have many runners in this sphere, but his rider sent the winner on over 2f out and never looked like being caught. The four-year-old is very effective on this ground and can continue to pay his way. (op 7/1 tchd 8/1)

5491a GRENZEN FLYING FIVE STKS (GROUP 3) 5f
5:15 (5:15) 3-Y-0+ **£39,126** (£11,436; £5,417; £1,805)

RPR
1 **Reverence**[31] 4456 8-9-3 .... WJSupple 7 108
(E J Alston) *led and disp: rdn 2f out: led 1 1/2f out: kpt on wl* **5/1**[3]
2 1 **Judge 'n Jury**[15] 5039 5-9-3 ....(t) KevinGhunowa 5 104
(R A Harris) *led and disp: rdn 2f out: hdd 1 1/2f out: kpt on same pce* **8/1**
3 3 1/2 **Sugar Free (IRE)**[31] 4456 3-8-12 .... WMLordan 2 88
(T Stack, Ire) *chsd ldrs: 3rd 2f out: sn rdn: no imp on ldrs over 1f out* **11/1**
4 shd **Snaefell (IRE)**[14] 5079 5-9-3 106..............................(p) JMurtagh 1 91
(M Halford, Ire) *chsd ldrs in cl 3rd: rdn 1/2-way: kpt on one pce fr 1 1/2f out* **9/2**[2]
5 1/2 **Aine (IRE)**[21] 4832 4-9-0 100.. WJLee 3 86
(T Stack, Ire) *hld up in tch: rdn fr 2f out: kpt on same pce fnl f* **12/1**
6 1/2 **Perfect Polly**[14] 5079 4-9-0 104................................ FMBerry 4 84
(James M Ryan, Ire) *hld up in tch: rdn 2f out: no imp fr 1 1/2f out* **11/4**[1]
7 4 **Look Busy (IRE)**[9] 5233 4-9-5 .... DPMcDonogh 6 75
(A Berry) *hld up in tch: rdn 1/2-way: sn wknd* **11/4**[1]
65.40 secs (4.70) **Going Correction** +1.25s/f (Soft)
WFA 3 from 4yo+ 2lb 7 Ran SP% **115.3**
Speed ratings: **112,110,104,104,103 103,96**
CSF £44.00 TOTE £6.20: £3.40, £4.30; DF 60.90.
Owner Mr & Mrs G Middlebrook **Bred** G And Mrs Middlebrook **Trained** Longton, Lancs
■ Stewards' Enquiry : W J Lee severe caution: used whip with excessive frequency

FOCUS
The front-running winner, who loves this sort of ground, has been rated to his best level since 2007.

NOTEBOOK
Reverence, with conditions deteriorating all the time, bounced back to form to record what looked a cosy success. Despite a high draw, his rider elected to race down the centre of the track. The eight-year-old held a definite advantage over 1f out and this most willing performer was nursed home under hands and heels. Remarkably for a horse of his age this was only his 36th start, and when he gets his conditions he remains a match for anyone at this level.
Judge 'n Jury ran a gallant race and, while he chased the winner home, never really threatened to get on top. He would prefer better ground but, having said that, can be placed to win before the end of the season on this type of surface. (op 9/1)
Sugar Free(IRE) fared best of the home-trained team and shaded third spot. (op 10/1)
Perfect Polly has had a busy time of it over the last few weeks, and was disappointing.

5489 - 5492a (Foreign Racing) - See Raceform Interactive

5461 BADEN-BADEN (L-H)
Sunday, August 30

OFFICIAL GOING: Good

5493a BESTWETTEN.DE GOLDENE PEITSCHE (GROUP 2) 6f
3:55 (4:08) 3-Y-0+ **£38,835** (£14,563; £5,825; £3,883)

RPR
1 **War Artist (AUS)**[29] 4516 6-9-4 .... ASuborics 2 116
(J M P Eustace) *hld up: 7th st: hdwy on outside wl over 1f out: led 150yds out: drvn out* **3/1**[2]
2 1 1/4 **Smooth Operator (GER)**[69] 3231 3-9-1 .... AHelfenbein 7 112
(Mario Hofer, Germany) *trckd ldrs: 3rd st: sn disputing ld: ev ch ins fnl f: r.o same r* **7/2**[3]
3 1 1/4 **Le Big (GER)**[35] 5-9-4 .... AStarke 1 108
(U Stoltefuss, Germany) *a.p: 4th st on ins: led wl over 1f out: sn drvn: hdd 150yds out: one pce* **20/1**
4 1 3/4 **Lesson In Humility (IRE)**[21] 4837 4-9-1 .... AndrewElliott 5 99
(A P Jarvis) *trckd ldrs: 5th st: kpt on one pce fr wl over 1f out* **11/10**[1]
5 5 **Etoile Nocturne (FR)**[57] 3650 5-9-1 .... WMongil 3 83
(W Baltromei, Germany) *pressed ldr: led after 2f to wl over 1f out: one pce* **12/1**
6 1/2 **Contat (GER)**[35] 4363 6-9-4 .... RJuracek 8 85
(P Vovcenko, Germany) *6th st on wd outside: nvr in contention* **8/1**
7 8 **Adamantinos**[91] 5-9-4 .... ADeVries 6 59
(Frau E Mader, Germany) *broke out of stall but sn returned: last st: a outpcd* **66/1**
8 2 1/2 **Glad Sky**[57] 3650 3-9-1 .... DPorcu 4 51
(M Rulec, Germany) *led 2f: 2nd st: sn wknd* **25/1**
68.06 secs (-2.23)
WFA 3 from 4yo+ 3lb 8 Ran SP% **123.7**
(including ten euro stakes): WIN 42; PL 19, 17, 22; SF 191.
Owner R Plersch **Bred** S Kirkham **Trained** Newmarket, Suffolk

NOTEBOOK
War Artist(AUS) has been running consistently without winning since coming from South Africa, including places in the Golden Jubilee and July Cup in 2008. He had not really fired this season but took this opportunity in determined fashion and might be able to build on this if this proves he is back to his best.
Lesson In Humility(IRE), placed in the Group 1 Golden Jubilee and Maurice de Gheest since winning in Ireland in June, looked to have been found a good opportunity to win at this level but for some reason did not run to those recent marks.

5416 DEAUVILLE (R-H)
Sunday, August 30

OFFICIAL GOING: Turf course - good; all-weather - standard

5494a PRIX HOTEL NORMANDY BARRIERE DEAUVILLE (ROUND) 1m (R)
1:15 (1:16) 2-Y-0 **£14,078** (£5,631; £4,223; £2,816; £1,408)

RPR
1 **Tip Toe (FR)**[19] 5088 2-8-9 .... SPasquier 92
(F Doumen, France)
2 4 **Dubawi Junior (IRE)**[23] 4807 2-8-9 .... C-PLemaire 83
(J-C Rouget, France)
3 hd **Terra Nova (FR)**[11] 2-8-12 .... OPeslier 86
(Robert Collet, France)
4 2 1/2 **Impressioniste (IRE)**[16] 5014 2-8-12 .... JAuge 81
(E J O'Neill) *broke awkwardly: racd keenly in rr early: last st: effrt 2f out: 5th and rdn 1f out: kpt on one pce* **63/10**[1]
5 1 1/2 **Une Autre Aventure (FR)**[16] 2-8-12 77
(C Boutin, France)
6 4 **Gooseley Chope (FR)**[60] 2-8-12 68
(C Boutin, France)
7 nk **Rhonaldino (GER)**[26] 2-8-6 .... (3) 65
(T Doumen, France)
1m 43.2s (2.20) 7 Ran SP% **13.7**
PARI-MUTUEL (including 1 Euro stake): WIN 3.30; PL 1.60, 1.70;SF 5.90.
Owner W Jeffcock **Bred** Haras D'Etreham **Trained** Bouce, France

NOTEBOOK
Impressioniste(IRE), a winner at Saint-Malo on his debut, found this a tougher task but did not help his cause by being too keen early.

5495a PRIX DE MEAUTRY LUCIEN BARRIERE (GROUP 3) (STRAIGHT) 6f
2:20 (2:24) 3-Y-0+ **£38,835** (£15,534; £11,650; £7,767; £3,883)

RPR
1 **Mariol (FR)**[21] 4837 6-9-1 .... C-PLemaire 8 116
(Robert Collet, France) *hld up in rr: hdwy wl over 1f out: led 130yds out: drvn clr: r.o wl* **6/4**[1]
2 2 1/2 **Contest (IRE)**[26] 4637 5-9-1 ....(b) OPeslier 10 108
(C Theodorakis, Greece) *mid-div: hdwy on far side of gp to go 3rd over 1f out: drvn to take 2nd briefly ins fnl f: one pce* **16/1**
3 1/2 **Tayseer**[51] 4-9-1 .... CSoumillon 3 106
(J E Hammond, France) *led to 130yds out: one pce* **11/2**[3]
4 1 1/2 **Blue And Gold (FR)**[26] 3-8-8 .... RMarchelli 9 98
(Mlle S-V Tarrou, France) *chsd ldrs: hrd rdn 1 1/2f out: kpt on same pce* **16/1**
5 1/2 **Aiboa (IRE)**[26] 4637 3-8-8 .... JVictoire 7 96
(L A Urbano-Grajales, France) *trckd ldr: rdn and btn 1f out* **10/3**[2]
6 2 1/2 **Blue Cayenne (FR)**[49] 3908 4-8-11 .... TJarnet 5 88
(Mlle S-V Tarrou, France) *trckd ldrs: disp 2nd 1/2-way: rdn and btn wl over 1f out* **14/1**
7 2 1/2 **Higha (FR)**[53] 3-8-8 .... SPasquier 1 80
(P Demercastel, France) *hld up in rr: nvr a factor* **12/1**
8 2 **Treasure (FR)**[26] 4637 3-8-8 .... DBoeuf 4 74
(Mme C Head-Maarek, France) *mid-div: rdn and btn wl over 1f out* **8/1**
9 3 **Isanous (FR)**[92] 2513 4-8-11 .... NCoutreau 6 64
(M Roussel, France) *trckd ldrs tl wknd over 2f out* **20/1**
10 6 **Manzila (FR)**[124] 1582 6-8-11 .... FBlondel 2 45
(Mme C Barande-Barbe, France) *a towards rr: last fr 2f out* **28/1**
68.40 secs (-2.80) **Going Correction** -0.125s/f (Firm)
WFA 3 from 4yo+ 3lb 10 Ran SP% **123.9**
Speed ratings: **113,109,109,107,106 103,99,97,93,85**
PARI-MUTUEL: WIN 3.40; PL 1.50, 4.50, 2.20; DF 39.60.
Owner Family Vidal **Bred** R Collet & S A R L Classic Breeding **Trained** Chantilly, France

NOTEBOOK
Mariol(FR), as usual was held up at the tail of the field in the early stages before coming sweetly through inside the final furlong, then quickened impressively and was in a different class to the others. A very genuine individual, who is always thereabouts in top class company, his trainer now has his eyes on either the Diadem Stakes or the Prix de la Foret.
Contest(IRE), now trained in Greece, had won a Listed race at Chantilly earlier in the year. In the early stages he was at the tail of the field with the winner and running a little free. He was brought with his run right up the centre of the track but could not quicken as well as that rival.
Tayseer, quickly into his stride, tried to make every yard of the running and looked the winner one and a half out but could do nothing when challenged at the furlong marker. He just stayed on a the same pace inside the final furlong.
Blue And Gold(FR), another one to be held up, made her effort from one and a half out. Stayed on well and won the battle for fourth position.

5496a PRIX QUINCEY LUCIEN BARRIERE (GROUP 3) (STRAIGHT) 1m (R)
2:55 (2:58) 3-Y-0+ **£38,835** (£15,534; £11,650; £7,767; £3,883)

RPR
1 **Racinger (FR)**[121] 1658 6-9-2 .... DBonilla 1 114
(F Head, France) *hld up: last to 2f out: hdwy towards outside: drvn to ld 100yds out: r.o wl* **6/1**
2 3/4 **Sahpresa (USA)**[28] 4580 4-8-13 .... CSoumillon 6 109
(Rod Collet, France) *trckd ldrs: led appr fnl f: edgd lft: drvn and hdd 100yds out: r.o* **4/1**[2]
3 3/4 **Kachgai (IRE)**[8] 6-9-0 .... IMendizabal 7 108
(Y De Nicolay, France) *hld up in rr: hdwy on outside wl over 1f out: ev ch 1f out: kpt on same pce* **14/1**
4 1 1/2 **Handsome Maestro (IRE)**[56] 3669 3-8-10 .... GMosse 3 106
(D Smaga, France) *trckd ldrs: drvn wl over 1f out: one pce fr 1f out* **10/1**
5 1 1/2 **Donativum**[29] 4521 3-8-8 .... C-PLemaire 5 100
(Saeed Bin Suroor) *led to over 3f out: ev ch over 1f out: one pce whn hmpd by 2nd appr fnl f* **4/1**[2]
6 3/4 **Golden Century (USA)**[69] 3230 3-9-1 .... MGuyon 2 106
(A Fabre, France) *trckd ldrs: rdn and wknd appr fnl f* **5/2**[1]
7 1 1/2 **Laa Rayb (USA)**[17] 4949 5-9-2 ....(b) RoystonFfrench 4 98
(M Johnston) *pressed ldr tl led over 3f out: hdd appr fnl f: wkng whn sltly hmpd 1f out* **11/2**[3]
1m 34.2s (-6.80) **Going Correction** -0.525s/f (Hard)
WFA 3 from 4yo+ 6lb 7 Ran SP% **114.0**
Speed ratings: **113,112,111,110,108 107,106**
PARI-MUTUEL: WIN 8.60; PL 3.10, 1.70; SF 26.70.

Owner Hamdan Al Maktoum **Bred** Mrs Renee Geffroy **Trained** France
■ Stewards' Enquiry : D Bonilla 200euro fine: whip abuse

NOTEBOOK
Racinger(FR) produced an excellent effort on his first run for fourth months. The five-year-old wasn't well after his last race and he was given a rest at stud but was back to his best form on this occasion. This ex-pacemaker was given a beautiful ride and he only really arrived on the scene inside the final furlong. He ran on well to beat the favourite with a little in hand and will now go for the Prix Daniel Wildenstein on October 3rd.
Sahpresa(USA), given every possible chance, made a run from one out and was just run out of things in the dying stages of this mile. A consistent filly, she deserves success at this level.
Kachgai(IRE) still had plenty to do at the halfway stage when raced just behind the runner-up. He came with his run on the wide outside and was running on well inside the final furlong.
Handsome Maestro(IRE) was always in about the same place. He looked dangerous at the furlong marker but was one paced from then on.
Donativum, smartly out of the stalls, was soon at the head of affairs. He ran a little free and seemed to hesitate at the 2f marker before running on again.
Laa Rayb(USA) was also up with the pace in the early stages and running rather free. He went into the lead two out but was then swamped by other runners, and did not show his true form on this occasion.

5497a LUCIEN BARRIERE GRAND PRIX DE DEAUVILLE (GROUP 2) 1m 4f 110y
3:30 (3:33) 3-Y-0+ **£110,680** (£42,718; £20,388; £13,592; £6,796)

RPR
1 **Jukebox Jury (IRE)**[12] 5134 3-8-6 .... RoystonFfrench 2 114
(M Johnston) *set mod pce: stdd after 4f: hdd 1/2-way: 2nd st: rdn to ld 1 1/2f out: all out* **9/4**[2]
2 *nse* **Pouvoir Absolu**[23] 4808 4-9-3 ....(b) ACrastus 5 114
(E Lellouche, France) *hld up in rr bhd slow pce: 5th st: gd hdwy on outside fr over 1f out: ev ch last strides: jst failed* **4/1**[3]
3 *2* **Kasbah Bliss (FR)**[126] 1552 7-9-3 .... TThulliez 1 111
(F Doumen, France) *trckd ldr: led 1/2-way to 1 1/2f out: one pce* **12/1**
4 *nk* **Ideal World (USA)**[23] 4808 4-9-3 .... SPasquier 4 110
(A Fabre, France) *wnt 3rd 1/2-way: 3rd st: styd on one pce fr over 1f out* **13/8**[1]
5 *3* **Inestimable**[39] 4-9-3 .... OPeslier 3 106
(A Fabre, France) *restrained bhd ldr: sn pulling: settled in 3rd: began pulling again over 7f out: 4th st: nvr able to chal* **15/2**
6 *1* **Wing Express (IRE)**[54] 5-9-3 .... CSoumillon 6 104
(J E Hammond, France) *disp 4th: last fr 1/2-way* **14/1**

2m 49.7s (3.30) **Going Correction** +0.65s/f (Yiel)
WFA 3 from 4yo+ 10lb **6 Ran SP% 115.0**
Speed ratings: **115,114,113,113,111 111**
PARI-MUTUEL: WIN 4.70; PL 2.70, 2.70; SF 20.10.
Owner A D Spence **Bred** Paul Nataf **Trained** Middleham Moor, N Yorks
■ Stewards' Enquiry : Royston Ffrench 100euro fine: whip abuse

NOTEBOOK
Jukebox Jury(IRE), the only three year old in the race, produced a really brave effort by. It wasn't the intention to take the lead but there were no other takers until the end of the back straight. He got back to the head of affairs at the 2f marker and then battled on really well to the line, winning by millimetres. His trainer has had his eyes on the Canadian International for some time but all other options will be taken into account.
Pouvoir Absolu, fifth running down the back straight, was brought with a fantastic late run up the centre of the track. He may have just taken the lead inside the final furlong but just lost out in a very close finish. Plans are not too certain for this four-year-old but he has been entered in the Prix du Cadran.
Kasbah Bliss(FR), a versatile sort, produced another fine run. He was totally unsuited by the lack of pace early on and so was taken to the lead in the back straight, where he stayed until early in the straight. he stuck on courageously to the line and just held on to third. Had been off the track for over four months and now looks right back to his best. He even surprised his trainer who will now try and win a second Prix Gladiateur with the horse.
Ideal World(USA) was probably unsuited by lack of early pace, and was virtually always in fourth place. He was asked for a final effort one and a half out but couldn't quicken and certainly didn't show his best form on this occasion. He is entered in both the Prix Foy and Arc de Triomphe.

5179 CHEPSTOW (L-H)
Monday, August 31

OFFICIAL GOING: Good (8.1)
All the races were run on the straight course.
Wind: Light across Weather: Fine

5498 E.B.F./FREEBETS.CO.UK FREE PREMIERSHIP FOOTBALL FREE BETS FILLIES' MEDIAN AUCTION MAIDEN STKS 1m 14y
2:05 (2:10) (Class 5) 2-Y-0 **£3,885** (£1,156; £577; £288) **Stalls** Centre

Form RPR
06 1 **Leitzu (IRE)**[12] 5165 2-9-0 0........................... EdwardCreighton 5 69
(M R Channon) *hld up in tch: pushed along 3f out: rdn wl over 1f out: led ins fnl f: edgd rt: pushed out* **7/1**[2]
00 2 *1 1/2* **Rose Alba (IRE)**[30] 4534 2-9-0 0........................... TPO'Shea 1 66
(J L Dunlop) *hld up in mid-div: pushed along over 2f out: rdn and hdwy wl over 1f out: r.o to take 2nd towards fin: nt trble wnr* **20/1**
44 3 *nk* **Green Community (USA)**[14] 5106 2-8-11 0........... AndreaAtzeni(3) 7 65
(E F Vaughan) *led: hdd 2f out: rdn over 1f out: kpt on ins fnl f* **9/1**[3]
00 4 *1 1/2* **Mahjong Girl**[19] 4908 2-8-11 0........................... JackMitchell(3) 2 62
(R M Beckett) *w ldr: led 2f out: rdn over 1f out: hdd ins fnl f: no ex* **14/1**
5 *3/4* **Wild Rose** 2-9-0 0........................... HayleyTurner 4 60+
(M L W Bell) *dwlt: hld up towards rr: pushed along 5f out: hdwy over 2f out: swtchd rt wl ins fnl f: one pce* **11/1**
6 *nk* **Madam Ruby (IRE)** 2-9-0 0........................... FergusSweeney 12 59+
(A King) *hld up in rr: swtchd lft over 4f out: pushed along over 3f out: rdn and sme hdwy wl over 1f out: styd on fnl f: nt rch ldrs* **25/1**
04 7 *2 1/4* **Carnaval Court (IRE)**[18] 4933 2-9-0 0........................... LPKeniry 10 54
(A M Balding) *prom: pushed along over 3f out: rdn over 2f out: wknd wl over 1f out* **9/4**[1]
8 *3 1/2* **Thousandkissesdeep (IRE)** 2-9-0 0........................... JimmyFortune 14 47
(J H M Gosden) *prom tl pushed along and wknd 2f out* **9/4**[1]
0 9 *1 1/2* **Queen Of Wands**[30] 4542 2-9-0 0........................... AdamKirby 8 43
(J L Dunlop) *hld up towards rr: pushed along over 4f out: n.d* **16/1**
05 10 *nk* **Creevy (IRE)**[55] 3715 2-9-0 0........................... PatDobbs 11 43
(S Kirk) *hld up in mid-div: pushed along over 2f out: wknd wl over 1f out* **20/1**
11 *2 3/4* **Bellaharry (IRE)** 2-9-0 0........................... TGMcLaughlin 15 37
(M Salaman) *hld up in mid-div: pushed along over 3f out: rdn and bhd over 2f out* **66/1**
5000 12 *2 1/2* **Dolly Will Do**[25] 4688 2-9-0 42........................... FrankieMcDonald 9 31
(N P Mulholland) *w ldrs tl wknd over 2f out* **80/1**
13 *6* **Anaya** 2-9-0 0........................... RichardThomas 13 18
(M R Channon) *s.i.s: a in rr* **40/1**
14 *2 1/4* **Rain In The Course** 2-9-0 0........................... CatherineGannon 6 13
(M R Channon) *a in rr* **66/1**
006 15 *3 1/4* **Smicker Smacker**[61] 3507 2-9-0 60........................... DO'Donohoe 3 6
(George Baker) *s.s: rdn over 3f out: a in rr* **100/1**

1m 38.48s (2.28) **Going Correction** +0.125s/f (Good) **15 Ran SP% 125.9**
Speed ratings (Par 91): **93,91,91,89,88 88,86,82,81,81 78,75,69,67,64**
toteswinger: 1&2 £46.00, 1&3 £21.30, 2&3 £42.20. CSF £147.50 TOTE £7.90: £2.70, £7.00, £3.70; EX 225.90.
Owner Upsan Downs Racing **Bred** Newhall Ltd **Trained** West Ilsley, Berks

FOCUS
Hard to place a value on the form of this maiden, but it is probably only modest.

NOTEBOOK
Leitzu(IRE) hadn't shown a great deal in two previous attempts over 7f and 1m. Just as in those two races, she needed to be rousted from some way out but she is clearly learning and stayed on well enough to think she will get a bit further in time. Nurseries are now an option. (op 5-1 tchd 15-2)
Rose Alba(IRE) confirmed the promise shown on debut and picked up really well from over a furlong out. This was her first attempt in three over 1m and she relished it. Her pedigree is packed with winners and she now has the nursery option to go with maidens.
Green Community(USA) ran her best race in three so is now qualified for nurseries. This was her first try at 1m and trying to force the pace was always going to be very hard. However, she showed a good attitude and with a little more restraint will stay further than this in time. (op 12-1)
Mahjong Girl was reluctant at the stalls, but built on her first two starts over 7f and in contrast to both raced on the pace. She is another that can now run in nurseries and this might be the right distance ridden more patiently. Official explanation: jockey said filly hung left handed
Wild Rose did really well on debut. She was very immature, but clearly has the right kind of engine and would have been a little closer but for finding a bit of trouble close home. There's plenty of stamina in her pedigree. (op 12-1)
Madam Ruby(IRE) made a thoroughly respectable debut without ever looking likely to make the frame. She will be more aware next time. (op 20-1)
Carnaval Court(IRE), whose two previous runs had been over 6f, was ridden positively which seemed to find out her stamina. On the plus side, she is now handicapped and will be interesting when dropped back in distance. (op 3-1)
Thousandkissesdeep(IRE) cost 140,000gns, but that wouldn't make her go faster and she was outpaced and inexperienced from halfway. She will have woken up for this. (tchd 3-1 and 100-30 in a place)
Queen Of Wands, a half-sister to the useful King Of Wands who stays well, was never in the race but gives the impression that there's ability when tried over further in handicaps, possibly next season. (tchd 20-1)
Creevy(IRE) never got into the race, but it might be worth keeping an eye on her in lower-grade nurseries now she's qualified.

5499 E.B.F./FREEBETS.CO.UK FREE BETS MAIDEN STKS (C&G) 1m 14y
2:40 (2:42) (Class 5) 2-Y-0 **£3,885** (£1,156; £577; £288) **Stalls** Centre

Form RPR
4 1 **Averroes (IRE)**[17] 4985 2-9-0 0........................... AdamKirby 6 86+
(C G Cox) *hld up in tch: pushed along to ld over 2f out: sn rdn: edgd rt ins fnl f: eased cl home* **15/8**[1]
0 2 *2 1/4* **Comradeship (IRE)**[17] 5002 2-9-0 0........................... JimmyFortune 17 80+
(J H M Gosden) *a.p: rdn over 1f out: wnt 2nd ins fnl f: nt trble wnr* **5/1**[3]
3 *2 3/4* **Rio Command (IRE)**[18] 4960 2-8-11 0........................... AndreaAtzeni(3) 1 74
(Daniel Mark Loughnane, Ire) *led: hdd over 2f out: rdn over 1f out: no ex and lost 2nd ins fnl f* **9/2**[2]
023 4 *1 1/4* **Sir Bruno (FR)**[13] 5119 2-9-0 75........................... CatherineGannon 13 71
(B Palling) *w ldr tl rdn over 2f out: btn whn n.m.r briefly ins fnl f* **14/1**
5 *nse* **Higgy's Ragazzo (FR)** 2-9-0 0........................... PatDobbs 8 71+
(R Hannon) *hld up in mid-div: hdwy over 2f out: rdn wl over 1f out: one pce* **22/1**
0 6 *nk* **Activate**[24] 4756 2-9-0 0........................... HayleyTurner 7 70
(M L W Bell) *hld up in mid-div: pushed along and sme hdwy 2f out: no imp fnl f* **9/1**
7 *1 1/4* **Cast Of Stars (IRE)** 2-8-11 0........................... JackMitchell(3) 9 68+
(R M Beckett) *hld up in rr: edgd lft and rdn over 1f out: nvr trbld ldrs* **20/1**
8 *3/4* **Natural Law (IRE)** 2-9-0 0........................... DO'Donohoe 14 66
(Saeed Bin Suroor) *s.i.s: sn chsng ldrs: rdn over 3f out: wknd wl over 1f out* **10/1**
9 *1 1/4* **First In The Queue (IRE)** 2-8-9 0........................... SophieDoyle(5) 2 63
(S Kirk) *s.s: hld up in rr: rdn over 1f out: nvr nr ldrs* **66/1**
10 *nk* **Regal Guest** 2-9-0 0........................... EdwardCreighton 10 63+
(M R Channon) *hld up towards rr: pushed along and prog over 3f out: wknd wl over 1f out* **40/1**
0 11 *5* **Almutaham (USA)**[38] 4258 2-9-0 0........................... TPO'Shea 15 52
(J L Dunlop) *s.i.s: a in rr* **7/1**
12 *1* **Mr Maximas** 2-9-0 0........................... NeilChalmers 4 50
(B Palling) *s.i.s: a in rr* **100/1**
0 13 *shd* **Groove Master**[22] 4811 2-9-0 0........................... FergusSweeney 3 50
(A King) *hld up in mid-div: pushed along and wknd over 2f out* **28/1**
40 14 *1 1/4* **Cuts Both Ways (USA)**[11] 5191 2-9-0 0........................... JosedeSouza 16 47
(P F I Cole) *hld up towards rr: pushed along and struggling over 2f out* **66/1**
05 15 *3/4* **Kingsdine (IRE)**[18] 4946 2-9-0 0........................... TGMcLaughlin 11 46
(M S Saunders) *prom tl wknd over 2f out* **66/1**
16 *22* **Sing Of Run** 2-9-0 0........................... RichardSmith 12 —
(J F Panvert) *s.s: sn mid-div: pushed along and struggling over 4f out: lost tch over 3f out: eased over 2f out* **100/1**

1m 36.95s (0.75) **Going Correction** +0.125s/f (Good) **16 Ran SP% 129.3**
Speed ratings (Par 94): **101,98,96,94,94 94,93,92,91,90 85,84,84,83,82 60**
toteswinger: 1&2 £7.10, 1&3 £4.30, 2&3 £5.50. CSF £10.88 TOTE £3.50: £1.50, £2.50, £2.40; EX 17.70.
Owner H E Sheikh Sultan Bin Khalifa Al Nahyan **Bred** G Stimola **Trained** Lambourn, Berks

FOCUS
The time was 1.36.95 compared to 1 38.48 in the opener, all the more impressive considering Averroes won with a deal in hand. The form looks fair, rated around the fourth.

NOTEBOOK

Averroes(IRE) won with a deal in hand. He was heavily backed to confirm the good impression he made on debut at Newbury on August 14th and was never in any danger of failing to complete the mission. He was much more switched on here and travelled easily in behind the leaders. He won with authority and might prove to be one of the better juveniles to grace this venue. He is a Derby entrant and there is no reason to believe he won't stay middle distances next season. His trainer is keen to keep him at 1m this season and the target is the Group 3 Prix des Chenes at Longchamp on September 19th. (op 100-30 tchd 7-2)

Comradeship(IRE) had learned from his Newmarket debut on August 14th and stayed on resolutely without ever looking like troubling the winner. He gave the impression he might appreciate a bit further than 1m this season. (tchd 11-2)

Rio Command(IRE) was rated 81 which set the official template for this race having finished a close second in a 7f maiden at Leopardstown on August 13th. He made it hard for himself by forcing the pace, but time might show he had an impossible task on. (tchd 4-1)

Sir Bruno(FR) was rated 75 and couldn't handle this calibre of contestant. He has a stamina-packed pedigree. (op 16-1)

Higgy's Ragazzo(FR) ran a very respectable debut and considering the improvement his stable's runners usually make for the first run, is one to note next time. (op 33-1 tchd 20-1)

Activate was always in the action and showed more than on debut, but wasn't given a hard time and will repay the consideration. (op 8-1)

Cast Of Stars(IRE) was really getting the hang of things on his debut. He will be much straighter next time and an even stiffer test might help. (op 16-1)

Natural Law(IRE) was always floundering which was disappointing given how well his stable's juveniles are running this season. For that reason he's worth another chance. (op 9-1 tchd 8-1)

First In The Queue(IRE) was very slowly out and was never hurried. In the circumstances this was an acceptable debut. (op 80-1 tchd 50-1)

Almutaham(USA) never got into the race after a poor start. (tchd 13-2)

5500 FREEBETS.CO.UK ONLINE BETTING (S) STKS — 5f 16y

3:15 (3:16) (Class 6) 3-Y-O — **£1,942** (£578; £288; £144) **Stalls** Centre

Form — RPR

0064 **1** **Mamlakati (IRE)**[5] 5345 3-8-7 **69** ... PatDobbs 1 — 56
(R Hannon) *a.p: chalng whn rdn and edgd rt over 1f out: led towards fin: r.o* — **11/10**[1]

00 **2** ½ **Cocktail Party (IRE)**[12] 5145 3-8-7 **47** ...(t) HayleyTurner 9 — 54
(J W Hills) *a.p on stands' rail: led on bit over 2f out: rdn ins fnl f: hdd towards fin* — **14/1**

0304 **3** ¾ **Boundless Applause**[16] 5018 3-8-4 **41** ... AndreaAtzeni(3) 3 — 51
(I A Wood) *in tch: pushed along and sltly outpcd over 3f out: rdn and rallied over 1f out: no ex towards fin* — **12/1**

2000 **4** 2½ **Billy Beetroot (USA)**[3] 5383 3-9-3 **63** ...(t) KevinGhunowa 4 — 52
(R A Harris) *chsd ldrs: rdn wl over 1f out: one pce ins fnl f* — **8/1**

0500 **5** 2¾ **Robin The Till**[7] 5323 3-8-12 **62** ... JimmyFortune 7 — 37
(R Hannon) *prom: rdn and sltly hmpd over 1f out: wknd ins fnl f* — **4/1**[2]

00 **6** 2 **Cheetah Beetah**[17] 4982 3-8-7 **40** ... CatherineGannon 10 — 25
(H S Howe) *led: rdn and hdd over 2f out: wknd jst over 1f out* — **50/1**

000- **7** ¾ **Miss Leona**[422] 3734 3-8-7 **40** ... NeilChalmers 8 — 22
(J M Bradley) *prom tl wknd wl over 1f out* — **33/1**

12-0 **8** nk **Time For Old Time**[16] 5018 3-8-7 **55** ... TPO'Shea 2 — 21
(I A Wood) *s.s: outpcd* — **13/2**[3]

61.02 secs (1.72) **Going Correction** +0.125s/f (Good) — **8** Ran SP% **111.3**

Speed ratings (Par 98): **91,90,89,85,80 77,76,75**

toteswinger: 1&2 £7.50, 1&3 £3.80, 2&3 £9.90. CSF £17.85 TOTE £1.90: £1.10, £3.50, £3.30; EX 16.40.No bid for the winner.

Owner Malih L Al Basti **Bred** Raymond P Doyle **Trained** East Everleigh, Wilts

FOCUS

This was a poor seller in which the winner did not need to improve on her latest form.

Time For Old Time Official explanation: jockey said filly missed the break

5501 BETPASS.CO.UK TELEPHONE BETTING 0800 0112627 H'CAP — 6f 16y

3:50 (3:50) (Class 6) (0-55,55) 3-Y-O+ — **£2,266** (£674; £337; £168) **Stalls** Centre

Form — RPR

5406 **1** **Outer Hebrides**[8] 5283 8-8-10 **54** ...(v) SophieDoyle(5) 6 — 63
(J M Bradley) *hld up in mid-div: squeezed out and lost pl sn after s: hdwy wl over 1f out: rdn to ld cl home* — **12/1**

0030 **2** ½ **The History Man (IRE)**[4] 5374 6-9-2 **55** ...(b) HayleyTurner 11 — 62
(B D Leavy) *a.p: carried hd high and led wl over 1f out: hdd cl home* — **3/1**[1]

5343 **3** 2¼ **Boldinor**[16] 5018 6-8-13 **52** ... NeilChalmers 4 — 52
(M R Bosley) *a.p: rdn wl over 1f out: one pce ins fnl f* — **10/1**

300 **4** ½ **Minnola**[7] 5316 4-9-1 **54** ... AdamKirby 16 — 53
(Rae Guest) *hld up in mid-div: pushed along 3f out: rdn over 1f out: kpt on ins fnl f* — **7/1**[3]

-000 **5** 2¼ **Street Diva (USA)**[11] 5184 4-8-12 **51** ... FergusSweeney 1 — 42
(A B Haynes) *a.p: rdn and wknd ins fnl f* — **33/1**

004 **6** ¾ **Croeso Ynol**[11] 5181 3-8-10 **52** ... TGMcLaughlin 7 — 41
(J L Spearing) *hld up in rr: pushed along over 2f out: rdn wl over 1f out: kpt on ins fnl f: nvr nrr* — **33/1**

0003 **7** hd **Sandy Par**[5] 5345 4-8-5 **49** ...(b) SimonPearce(5) 12 — 37
(J M Bradley) *led: rdn and hdd wl over 1f out: wknd fnl f* — **6/1**[2]

600 **8** nk **Best One**[11] 5184 5-9-1 **54** ...(v) KevinGhunowa 3 — 41
(R A Harris) *s.i.s: sn chsng ldrs: rdn wl over 1f out: wknd ins fnl f* — **12/1**

4001 **9** 1¼ **Cwmni**[31] 4479 3-8-11 **53** ... TPO'Shea 8 — 36
(B Palling) *stdd s: hld up in rr: sn swtchd rt towards stands' side: rdn over 3f out: short-lived effrt over 2f out* — **12/1**

3302 **10** shd **La Belle Joannie**[22] 4812 4-9-2 **55** ... DO'Donohoe 9 — 38
(S Curran) *mid-div: pushed along 3f out: reminder and btn over 1f out* — **12/1**

-000 **11** ½ **Compton Rose**[102] 2202 4-9-1 **54** ... FrankieMcDonald 2 — 35
(H Candy) *mid-div: rdn and btn jst over 1f out* — **20/1**

2000 **12** nk **Gioacchino (IRE)**[10] 5225 4-8-11 **50** ...(t) LPKeniry 13 — 31
(R A Harris) *s.i.s: in rr: rdn over 2f out: n.d* — **20/1**

000- **13** 1 **Oxbridge**[405] 4278 4-8-11 **50** ... RichardThomas 10 — 27
(J M Bradley) *prom: lost pl over 3f out: bhd fnl 2f* — **66/1**

000 **14** 6 **Calypso Girl (IRE)**[4] 5362 3-8-13 **55** ...(v[1]) JimmyFortune 17 — 13
(P D Evans) *hld up in tch: rdn and wknd over 1f out* — **7/1**[3]

1406 **15** 5 **Pintano**[16] 5018 4-8-11 **50** ...(bt) CatherineGannon 5 — —
(J M Bradley) *a towards rr* — **18/1**

1m 12.28s (0.28) **Going Correction** +0.125s/f (Good)

WFA 3 from 4yo+ 3lb — **15** Ran SP% **126.3**

Speed ratings (Par 101): **103,102,99,98,95 94,94,94,92,92 91,91,89,81,75**

toteswinger: 1&2 £23.20, 1&3 £25.80, 2&3 £11.70. CSF £47.20 CT £404.46 TOTE £15.10: £3.60, £1.80, £3.20; EX 46.30.

Owner Asterix Partnership **Bred** St Clare Hall Stud **Trained** Sedbury, Gloucs

FOCUS

Quantity and no quality here. Limited form, rated around the first two.

Pintano Official explanation: jockey said gelding ran too free

5502 BETPASS.CO.UK ONE ACCOUNT MULTIPLE BETTING SERVICE H'CAP — 7f 16y

4:25 (4:29) (Class 6) (0-65,65) 3-Y-O+ — **£2,266** (£674; £337; £168) **Stalls** Centre

Form — RPR

0420 **1** **Cadeaux Fax**[11] 5179 4-8-12 **54** ... JamesMillman(3) 2 — 63
(B R Millman) *a.p: led on bit wl over 2f out: rdn wl over 1f out: drvn out* — **9/1**

6455 **2** ¾ **Stanley Goodspeed**[22] 4816 6-9-11 **64** ...(tp) HayleyTurner 3 — 71
(J W Hills) *hld up towards rr: hdwy 3f out: jinked rt over 1f out: sn rdn: r.o u.p ins fnl f* — **13/2**[2]

6-00 **3** nk **Bidable**[166] 868 5-8-10 **49** ... NeilChalmers 4 — 55
(B Palling) *hld up in mid-div: hdwy over 4f out: rdn 2f out: kpt on ins fnl f* — **25/1**

600 **4** 1 **Charlie Delta**[11] 5184 6-8-13 **52** ...(b) LPKeniry 17 — 55
(R A Harris) *plld hrd in rr: hdwy over 1f out: sn rdn: kpt on ins fnl f* — **25/1**

0006 **5** ¾ **Avoca Dancer (IRE)**[16] 5019 6-9-0 **53** ...(v) CatherineGannon 14 — 54
(Karen George) *hld up towards rr: pushed along and hdwy 3f out: rdn 2f out: hmpd over 1f out: one pce fnl f* — **11/1**

02 **6** hd **Cheap Street**[19] 4905 5-9-5 **58** ... PatDobbs 8 — 59
(J G Portman) *a.p: rdn over 1f out: one pce* — **7/1**[3]

3315 **7** 2½ **Goodbye Cash (IRE)**[4] 5364 5-9-8 **61** 6ex ... JimmyFortune 13 — 55
(P D Evans) *prom: lost pl over 4f out: rdn over 2f out: no real prog fnl f* — **9/2**[1]

1360 **8** hd **Stamford Blue**[11] 5184 8-9-3 **63** ...(b) SPRyan(7) 11 — 57
(R A Harris) *hld up towards rr: rdn over 1f out: kpt on fnl f: n.d* — **14/1**

0001 **9** 1¼ **Stand In Flames**[22] 4812 4-9-9 **62** ... DO'Donohoe 1 — 52
(George Baker) *prom: rdn over 2f out: wknd ins fnl f* — **25/1**

-000 **10** 3¼ **Deo Valente (IRE)**[26] 4648 4-9-9 **62** ... KevinGhunowa 5 — 43
(J M Bradley) *led: hdd wl over 2f out: sn rdn: wknd over 1f out* — **50/1**

0664 **11** 1¾ **Viking Awake (IRE)**[25] 4707 3-8-13 **57** ...(t) FergusSweeney 10 — 34
(J W Unett) *prom tl rdn and wknd jst over 2f out* — **14/1**

0004 **12** 1 **Polar Annie**[18] 4950 4-9-12 **65** ... TGMcLaughlin 16 — 39
(M S Saunders) *bhd fnl 4f* — **8/1**

0243 **13** 2 **Cognac Boy (USA)**[8] 5283 3-8-12 **56** ...(v) RichardThomas 9 — 25
(A B Haynes) *hld up in mid-div: pushed along over 2f out: wknd wl over 1f out* — **16/1**

0305 **14** 1¼ **Jewelled Reef (IRE)**[18] 4937 3-9-0 **58** ... TPO'Shea 15 — 23
(Eve Johnson Houghton) *hld up in mid-div: no hdwy whn hmpd jst over 1f out* — **11/1**

1/30 **15** 13 **Moral Duty (USA)**[33] 4428 4-9-10 **63** ... AdamKirby 7 — —
(J S Moore) *prom: wkng whn bdly hmpd jst over 1f out* — **14/1**

1m 24.35s (1.15) **Going Correction** +0.125s/f (Good)

WFA 3 from 4yo+ 5lb — **15** Ran SP% **121.2**

Speed ratings (Par 101): **98,97,96,95,94 94,91,91,90,86 84,83,80,79,64**

toteswinger: 1&2 £35.40, 1&3 not won, 2&3 £39.50. CSF £63.80 CT £963.91 TOTE £8.70: £3.40, £2.50, £7.30; EX 87.60.Just Spike was withdrawn. Price at time of withdrawal 20/1. Rule 4 does not apply.

Owner Mrs Mette Campbell-Andenaes **Bred** Mrs S Halliwell **Trained** Kentisbeare, Devon

FOCUS

Another poor quality but competitive class six handicap. Sound if limited form for the grade.

Avoca Dancer(IRE) Official explanation: jockey said mare suffered interference in running

Cognac Boy(USA) Official explanation: jockey said gelding was unsuited by the good ground

Jewelled Reef(IRE) Official explanation: jockey said filly suffered interference in running

Moral Duty(USA) Official explanation: jockey said colt suffered interference in running

5503 BETPASS.CO.UK ALL BOOKMAKERS H'CAP — 1m 14y

5:00 (5:02) (Class 5) (0-70,70) 3-Y-O+ — **£4,533** (£1,348; £674; £336) **Stalls** Centre

Form — RPR

0363 **1** **Petomic (IRE)**[11] 5179 4-8-9 **55** ... RossAtkinson(5) 4 — 68
(M Hill) *overall ldr on far side: rdn and hung rt wl over 1f out: c to stands' rail ins fnl f: r.o wl* — **5/1**[2]

3451 **2** 3 **Spring Secret**[3] 5384 3-9-0 **61** 6ex ... CatherineGannon 12 — 66
(B Palling) *chsd wnr on far side: lft 2nd wl over 2f out: sn rdn: kpt on to retake 2nd towards fin: nt trble wnr* — **6/1**

4505 **3** ¾ **Zouk**[55] 3708 3-9-6 **67** ... AdamKirby 9 — 70
(W R Swinburn) *led trio in centre tl they jnd far side gp over 3f out: rdn and chsd wnr over 2f out: no ex and lost 2nd towards fin* — **9/1**

1536 **4** 2¾ **Shared Moment (IRE)**[14] 5101 3-9-1 **62** ...(p) TPO'Shea 8 — 59
(J Gallagher) *hld up in mid-div on far side: hdwy 3f out: rdn over 2f out: carried hd awkwardly fr over 1f out: one pce* — **10/1**

064 **5** 2 **Flying Gazebo (IRE)**[24] 4731 3-8-9 **56** ... TGMcLaughlin 15 — 48
(J S Moore) *chsd ldr in duo on stands' side: rdn to ld that gp over 3f out: edgd lft wl over 1f out: sn btn* — **25/1**

06-5 **6** ¾ **Boo**[163] 693 7-9-5 **60** ...(v) FergusSweeney 14 — 53
(J W Unett) *led stands' side duo tl over 3f out: rdn and wknd wl over 1f out* — **18/1**

0244 **7** ½ **Indian Violet (IRE)**[26] 4655 3-9-7 **68** ... JimmyFortune 6 — 57
(P F I Cole) *prom on far side: rdn over 2f out: wknd ins fnl f* — **9/2**[1]

050 **8** ½ **Weekend Away (IRE)**[26] 4648 3-9-5 **66** ... PatDobbs 10 — 54
(S Kirk) *chsd ldr in trio in centre tl joining far side gp over 3f out: rdn and wknd over 2f out* — **5/1**[2]

4402 **9** hd **Oriental Girl**[19] 4904 4-9-2 **60** ...(v) MarcHalford(3) 5 — 50
(J A Geake) *hld up and bhd on far side: pushed along over 3f out: rdn and edgd rt over 1f out: nvr trbld ldrs* — **11/2**[3]

-050 **10** ¾ **It's Josr**[18] 4938 4-8-12 **53** ...(be) LPKeniry 3 — 41
(I A Wood) *prom on far side: rdn 3f out: sn wknd* — **28/1**

0500 **11** 9 **Nun Today (USA)**[19] 4905 3-7-11 **47** oh2 ...(v) AndreaAtzeni(3) 2 — 12
(Karen George) *racd far side: bhd: pushed along over 2f out: eased whn no ch fnl f* — **25/1**

200- **12** 2¾ **Sir Kyffin's Folly**[345] 6124 4-9-11 **66** ... RichardThomas 7 — 27
(J A Geake) *racd far side: a bhd: eased whn no ch fnl f* — **33/1**

0 **13** 1½ **Halcyon Princess (IRE)**[15] 5063 3-9-6 **67** ... DO'Donohoe 13 — 23
(D G Bridgwater) *stdd s: last of centre trio tl joining far side gp over 3f out: sn struggling: eased whn no ch fnl f* — **33/1**

1m 36.55s (0.35) **Going Correction** +0.125s/f (Good)

WFA 3 from 4yo+ 6lb — **13** Ran SP% **122.6**

Speed ratings (Par 103): **103,100,99,96,94 93,93,92,92,91 82,80,78**

toteswinger: 1&2 £8.60, 1&3 £16.70, 2&3 £6.70. CSF £33.88 CT £275.49 TOTE £6.60: £2.10, £3.10, £3.70; EX 46.10.

Owner EGHQ Partnership **Bred** Neil McGrath **Trained** Littlehempston, Devon

FOCUS
Several participants decided to make an already very difficult race more tricky by choosing different parts of the course to race on. Sound if limited form, with a personal best from the winner.

5504 BETPASS.CO.UK ONLINE BETTING APPRENTICE H'CAP 5f 16y
5:35 (5:35) (Class 6) (0-60,60) 3-Y-0+ **£2,266** (£674; £337; £168) **Stalls** Centre

Form RPR
6614 **1** **Lithaam (IRE)**[11] 5184 5-8-12 **56**....................(p) RyanClark(5) 9 66
(J M Bradley) *s.i.s: hdwy 3f out: rdn wl over 1f out: led ins fnl f: r.o* **9/2**[2]
5333 **2** *1 ½* **Weet A Surprise**[32] 4469 4-9-2 **60**....................(v) AlexEdwards(5) 5 65
(J W Unett) *bhd: hdwy over 1f out: r.o to take 2nd cl home* **11/2**[3]
4134 **3** *1* **Spic 'n Span**[4] 5374 4-9-5 **58**....................(b) SPRyan 8 59
(R A Harris) *led: hung lft jst over 1f out: hdd ins fnl f: no ex* **9/4**[1]
0030 **4** *½* **Fern House (IRE)**[11] 5183 7-8-7 **46** oh1.................... LauraPike 7 46
(Bruce Hellier) *s.i.s: hld up in rr: hdwy over 1f out: sn rdn: kpt on ins fnl f* **28/1**
0020 **5** *½* **Monsieur Reynard**[5] 5345 4-9-1 **54**.................... DavidKenny 2 52
(J M Bradley) *a.p: chsd ldr 3f out tl rdn over 1f out: one pce ins fnl f* **8/1**
0446 **6** *½* **One Way Ticket**[56] 3677 9-8-7 **46** oh1....................(tp) RichardRowe 4 42
(J M Bradley) *hld up in mid-div: rdn and no hdwy fnl f* **25/1**
0566 **7** *hd* **Meikle Barfil**[5] 5345 7-8-7 **46** oh1....................(tp) JosephineBruning 3 41
(J M Bradley) *hld up in mid-div: hdwy 2f out: pushed along whn nt clr run on far rail ins fnl f: nt rcvr* **14/1**
010 **8** *1 ¾* **Bohobe (IRE)**[30] 4536 4-9-0 **58**.................... NoelGarbutt(5) 10 47
(Rae Guest) *hld up in mid-div: lost pl over 3f out: rdn over 1f out: n.d* **7/1**
0563 **9** *6* **Town House**[41] 4182 7-8-0 **46** oh1.................... NoraLooby(7) 6 13
(B P J Baugh) *prom: rdn over 2f out: wknd over 1f out* **16/1**
0505 **10** *4* **Sofinella (IRE)**[20] 4886 6-8-2 **46** oh1.................... JakePayne(5) 1 —
(A W Carroll) *prom tl pushed along and wknd 2f out* **8/1**

60.07 secs (0.77) **Going Correction** +0.125s/f (Good) **10** Ran SP% **118.9**
Speed ratings (Par 101): **98,95,94,93,92 91,91,88,78,72**
toteswinger: 1&2 £5.30, 1&3 £2.50, 2&3 £2.80. CSF £30.20 CT £70.62 TOTE £6.30: £1.60, £2.30, £1.40; EX 42.90 Place 6: £215.60 Place 5: £49.29.
Owner JMB Racing.co.uk **Bred** Shadwell Estate Company Limited **Trained** Sedbury, Gloucs
■ Stewards' Enquiry : S P Ryan one-day ban: careless riding (Sep 14)

FOCUS
The race played into the hands of Lithaam. This was a weak race with half the field out of the weights, but the form looks sound enough.
T/Plt: £450.40 to a £1 stake. Pool: £44,701.10. 72.45 winning tickets. T/Qpdt: £44.40 to a £1 stake. Pool: £2,934.06. 48.80 winning tickets. KH

5185 EPSOM (L-H)
Monday, August 31

OFFICIAL GOING: Good (good to firm in places) (derby course 8.2; 5f course: stands' side 8.1, far side 8.1)
Wind: Breezy, across Weather: Sunny, breezy

5505 TOMPKINS & MAY PARTNERSHIP NEWBUILD EBF MEDIAN AUCTION MAIDEN STKS 7f
2:00 (2:00) (Class 4) 2-Y-0 **£5,180** (£1,541; £770; £384) **Stalls** Low

Form RPR
05 **1** **Constant Contact**[13] 5119 2-9-3 0.................... DavidProbert 1 88+
(A M Balding) *mde all: pushed clr over 2f out: r.o strly* **12/1**
32 **2** *2* **Cash Queen Anna (IRE)**[22] 4817 2-8-12 0.................... RobertWinston 3 78+
(B W Hills) *in tch: hdwy to chse wnr over 3f out: rdn and clr of remainder 2f out: kpt on but no imp on wnr after* **11/8**[1]
3 *5* **Five Cents** 2-9-3 0.................... TedDurcan 10 71+
(Saeed Bin Suroor) *v.s.a: detached in last pl: hdwy on outer jst over 2f out: chsd clr ldng pair over 1f out: kpt on but no imp fnl f* **11/1**
523 **4** *1 ¼* **Interakt**[26] 4638 2-8-12 74.................... PaulHanagan 8 62
(M R Channon) *towards rr: rdn over 3f out: nt clr run and swtchd rt over 2f out: sme hdwy and swtchd lft wl over 1f out: kpt on but nvr nr ldrs* **7/1**[3]
6 **5** *¾* **Buffett**[14] 5109 2-9-3 0.................... DaneO'Neill 9 66
(L M Cumani) *wnt rt s: hld up towards rr: rdn and effrt 3f out: no ch w ldrs fnl 2f* **25/1**
6 **6** *2* **Kerchak (USA)**[19] 4908 2-9-3 0.................... AlanMunro 6 61
(W Jarvis) *stdd after s: t.k.h: hld up in rr: effrt on inner over 2f out: nvr trbld ldrs* **17/2**
60 **7** *2* **Black Daddy**[145] 1188 2-9-0 0.................... PatrickHills(3) 7 56
(R Hannon) *in tch in midfield on outer: racd awkwardly on downhill run 4f out: struggling 3f out and no ch after* **40/1**
032 **8** *2 ½* **Valiant Knight (FR)**[10] 5220 2-9-3 0.................... SteveDrowne 5 49
(R Hannon) *chsd ldrs: rdn over 3f out: outpcd by ldrs over 2f out: bhd fnl f* **10/3**[2]
0 **9** *4* **Until The Man (IRE)**[16] 5017 2-9-3 0.................... KirstyMilczarek 4 39
(R Ingram) *chsd ldrs: losing pl and rdn 4f out: bhd fnl 2f* **150/1**
04 **10** *10* **Bintalaleumydarlin (IRE)**[8] 5290 2-8-12 0.................... J-PGuillambert 2 29+
(M Johnston) *chsd ldrs: rdn and struggling 3f out: wkng whn edgd rt over 2f out: sn bhd* **25/1**

1m 22.17s (-1.13) **Going Correction** -0.10s/f (Good) **10** Ran SP% **115.0**
Speed ratings (Par 96): **102,99,94,92,91 89,87,84,79,68**
toteswinger: 1&2 £6.70, 1&3 £16.60, 2&3 £5.70. CSF £27.97 TOTE £12.70: £2.90, £1.50, £3.30; EX 44.20.
Owner Kingsclere Racing CLub **Bred** Kingsclere Stud **Trained** Kingsclere, Hants

FOCUS
A decent auction maiden. It was run at a fair pace and they finished well strung out. A big step up from the winner.

NOTEBOOK
Constant Contact was a springer in the market and put in an impressive front-running display to run his rivals into submission. He showed ability when close fifth over the similar contours of Brighton on his second outing, but has clearly taken a major step forward to win this in good style. He looks a well-balanced colt with a good attitude and should go on to better things. (op 20-1)
Cash Queen Anna(IRE) set the standard on her placed efforts behind some bright prospects in 6f/7f fillies' maidens at Newbury and Redcar. She tracked the pace against the far rail and moved smoothly into a threatening position, but could not get past the resilient winner. This was a decent enough effort and it gives the form a solid look, but her profile is consistent rather than progressive at this stage. (op 13-8)
Five Cents was the big eyecatcher of the race. He missed the break from an outside draw but did really well to power his way into third from a detached position on debut. He was a 92,000gns breeze-up buy and is a half brother to winners in Australia and Singapore. (op 12-1)
Interakt never looked entirely comfortable on the undulations and was always fighting a losing battle in an effort to grind her way into contention. Her form has stalled in four runs, but she could be the type to do better in strongly run nurseries on more galloping tracks. (op 6-1)
Buffett was never going the pace when 20-1 in a 6f Yarmouth auction maiden on debut, but stuck on quite well over this extra furlong and has improved for the initial experience. He is a first foal of middle-distance winning half-sister to Melbourne Cup second Bauer and should continue to progress with time and distance. (op 33-1)
Kerchak(USA) attracted support in the morning, but struggled to find his rhythm on the turn into the straight and never got involved. A return to a stiffer track will suit and he should be able to confirm the promise of his staying on sixth in a fair Sandown maiden on debut. (op 8-1 tchd 9-1)

5506 CHANTILLY H'CAP 6f
2:35 (2:35) (Class 5) (0-75,74) 3-Y-0 **£3,238** (£963; £481; £240) **Stalls** High

Form RPR
2130 **1** **Theatre Street (IRE)**[139] 1272 3-9-3 **70**.................... TPQueally 1 80
(S Dow) *mde all at fast pce: clr and gng much the best 2f out: rdn and kpt on wl fnl f* **14/1**
0234 **2** *2 ¾* **Merry Diva**[26] 4664 3-9-5 **72**.................... AlanMunro 5 73+
(C F Wall) *chsd ldrs: sltly hmpd over 5f out: sn outpcd by ldng trio: rdn over 2f out: edgd rt fr 2f out: kpt on to go 2nd towards fin: nvr trbld wnr* **7/2**[1]
0344 **3** *nk* **Leadenhall Lass (IRE)**[18] 4952 3-8-13 **66**....................(v[1]) IanMongan 8 66
(P M Phelan) *chsd ldng pair and clr of remainder: rdn to chse clr wnr over 2f out: no imp: lost 2nd towards fin* **15/2**
4201 **4** *1 ½* **Lucy Brown**[18] 4950 3-9-7 **74**.................... SteveDrowne 6 69+
(R Hannon) *stdd s: hld up off the pce in midfield: rdn over 2f out: kpt on u.p fnl f: nvr nr wnr* **6/1**[3]
-400 **5** *1 ¾* **Kingsgate Storm (IRE)**[16] 5031 3-8-9 **62**.................... RobertWinston 3 52
(J R Best) *chsd wnr and clr of remainder: rdn and lost 2nd over 2f out: wknd over 1f out* **25/1**
064 **6** *nse* **Ultimate Respect (USA)**[12] 5163 3-9-3 **70**.................... J-PGuillambert 7 59
(M Johnston) *sn bustled along and off the pce in midfield: rdn and hanging lft fr over 2f out: nvr nr wnr* **17/2**
2332 **7** *½* **Raimond Ridge (IRE)**[3] 5383 3-9-0 **70**.................... MCGeran(3) 9 58
(M R Channon) *s.i.s: a wl bhd in last trio: rdn and effrt on inner 3f out: n.d* **9/2**[2]
6000 **8** *1 ¼* **Wunder Strike (USA)**[25] 4714 3-8-4 **57**....................(p) NickyMackay 10 41
(J R Boyle) *a wl bhd in last trio: nvr a factor* **16/1**
2320 **9** *11* **Cawdor (IRE)**[72] 3163 3-9-7 **74**....................(b[1]) DaneO'Neill 4 23
(H Candy) *s.i.s: nvr gng wl in last trio: wl bhd fr 1/2-way: eased fnl f* **7/2**[1]

68.76 secs (-0.64) **Going Correction** -0.10s/f (Good) **9** Ran SP% **115.6**
Speed ratings (Par 100): **100,96,95,93,91 91,90,89,74**
toteswinger: 1&2 £13.30, 1&3 £22.00, 2&3 £7.60. CSF £62.74 CT £407.75 TOTE £15.30: £2.80, £1.70, £2.40; EX 106.10.
Owner Mark McAllister **Bred** M J Killeen **Trained** Epsom, Surrey

FOCUS
Most of the runners were fairly exposed in this sprint handicap for three-year-olds. There was another blistering front-running display and nothing got into it from behind. The form is rated around the second and third.

5507 TOMPKINS & MAY PARTNERSHIP REACTIVE REPAIRS H'CAP 5f
3:10 (3:10) (Class 2) (0-105,97) 3-Y-0+
£12,462 (£3,732; £1,866; £934; £466; £234) **Stalls** High

Form RPR
0640 **1** **Siren's Gift**[32] 4456 5-9-2 **90**....................(b) DavidProbert 4 98
(A M Balding) *sn led: grad crossed to r on stands' rail: rdn ent fnl f: kpt on wl: all out* **9/2**[3]
2603 **2** *shd* **Jargelle (IRE)**[11] 5203 3-9-5 **95**.................... AlanMunro 7 103
(K A Ryan) *chsd wnr: rdn over 1f out: drvn and ev ch ins fnl f: r.o: jst hld* **7/1**
4043 **3** *1 ¾* **Fol Hollow (IRE)**[13] 5132 4-9-9 **97**.................... AdrianTNicholls 5 99
(D Nicholls) *chsd ldng pair: pushed along jst over 2f out: drvn over 1f out: kpt on but nt pce to chal ldng pair* **11/4**[1]
5400 **4** *½* **Indian Trail**[13] 5132 9-8-13 **87**....................(v) DaneO'Neill 8 87
(D Nicholls) *hld up towards rr: hdwy into midfield 1/2-way: rdn jst over 1f out: kpt on fnl f: unable to rch ldrs* **7/2**[2]
2300 **5** *½* **Kerrys Requiem (IRE)**[9] 5263 3-8-11 **87**.................... PaulHanagan 10 85
(M R Channon) *racd in midfield: rdn and effrt on stands' rail over 1f out: kpt on but nt pce to rch ldrs* **5/1**
5600 **6** *4* **Ginobili (IRE)**[9] 5263 3-8-11 **87**....................(p) RobertWinston 6 71
(Stef Liddiard) *s.i.s: a struggling to go pce in rr: no ch fnl 2f* **33/1**
3P-0 **7** *6* **Starlit Sands**[125] 1582 4-9-8 **96**....................(b[1]) StephenDonohoe 3 58
(Sir Mark Prescott) *chsd ldrs for 2f: sn rdn and struggling fr 1/2-way: wl bhd fnl 2f* **12/1**
0005 **8** *½* **Piscean (USA)**[9] 5263 4-9-0 **88**.................... PaulDoe 2 48
(T Keddy) *v.s.a: a bhd: no ch fr 1/2-way* **9/1**
3000 **9** *2 ¼* **Fault**[11] 5203 3-8-13 **89**....................(vt) TPQueally 1 41
(Stef Liddiard) *s.i.s: a in rr: no ch fr 1/2-way* **20/1**

54.43 secs (-1.27) **Going Correction** -0.025s/f (Good)
WFA 3 from 4yo+ 2lb **9** Ran SP% **121.6**
Speed ratings (Par 109): **109,108,106,105,104 98,88,87,84**
toteswinger: 1&2 £6.90, 1&3 £2.60, 2&3 £4.10. CSF £38.09 CT £104.90 TOTE £5.00: £1.70, £2.30, £1.30; EX 42.40.
Owner J C Smith **Bred** Littleton Stud **Trained** Kingsclere, Hants
■ Stewards' Enquiry : Alan Munro one-day ban: used whip without allowing mount time to respond (Sep 14)

FOCUS
A high-class sprint handicap. The first two had a sustained all-the way duel. The pace was frenetic and seemed likely to set it up for a finisher, but the hold-up runners could not get involved. The time was 0.97 seconds quicker than standard. The winner probably did not have to improve on this year's form.

NOTEBOOK
Siren's Gift cut across the runner-up to grab the near rail in the early stages and set a furious pace. She lost the advantage for a few strides in the last half furlong but showed some fighting qualities to battle back and provide Andrew Balding and David Probert with an early double on the card. She has found a bit less than expected at times but was potentially well treated on numerous pieces of form and cashed in on a sliding mark. (op 11-2 tchd 7-1)
Jargelle(IRE) ran well at York last time and put in another admirable effort, despite getting involved in a speed duel. She will probably receive some punishment for this effort but will remain some way below her peak mark of 102, and should be able to add to her maiden win and Weatherbys Super Sprint success as a juvenile for William Haggas. (op 6-1 tchd 11-2)
Fol Hollow(IRE) raced in third for the whole way. He could not get to grips with the leaders but did well to repel the pursuers and coped with the return to a very sharp track. His mark is edging towards the 100s but he has a feisty attitude and should continue to run well in classy sprint handicaps. (op 3-1 tchd 100-30 in a place)
Indian Trail moved well for a long way, as he often does, but the leaders never really came back to him and he could not land a telling blow in his bid to supplement his valuable course-and-distance win on Derby day. Official explanation: vet said gelding finished distressed (op 9-2 tchd 5-1)

Kerrys Requiem(IRE) was in trouble some way out but kept plugging on and did quite well to latch on to the leading bunch. She is a dependable type but needs to find something extra from somewhere to add to her only previous win in June 2008. (op 6-1 tchd 13-2)

5508 JRA CONDITIONS STKS 1m 2f 18y

3:45 (3:47) (Class 3) 3-Y-O+ £7,477 (£2,239; £1,119; £560) Stalls Low

Form					RPR
1112	1		**Firebet (IRE)**[34] 4405 3-8-8 108 ... PaulHanagan 2 (R A Fahey) *chsd ldr: rdn to ld 3f out: edgd lft to rail 2f out: kpt on wl* 10/11[1]		101
100	2	¾	**Midnight Cruiser (IRE)**[32] 4455 3-8-8 92 ... DaneO'Neill 3 (R Hannon) *led: rdn and hdd 3f out: swtchd lft off rail 2f out: rallied u.p ins fnl f: kpt on* 14/1[3]		99
-130	3	8	**Tranquil Tiger**[23] 4780 5-9-7 114 ... (b) TPQueally 1 (H R A Cecil) *s.i.s and cajoled along early: a 3rd: rdn and effrt over 2f out: no hdwy: wl btn over 1f out* 11/10[2]		88
6-00	4	26	**Maxwil**[18] 4954 4-9-2 82 ... IanMongan 4 (P M Phelan) *s.i.s: hld up in last pl: rdn and lost tch over 2f out: eased fnl f: t.o* 100/1		31

2m 7.04s (-2.66) **Going Correction** -0.10s/f (Good)
WFA 3 from 4yo+ 8lb 4 Ran SP% **107.7**
Speed ratings (Par 107): **106,105,99,78**
CSF £11.56 TOTE £1.90; EX 7.90.

Owner Mrs H Steel **Bred** Derek Veitch And Saleh Ali Hammadi **Trained** Musley Bank, N Yorks

FOCUS

This looked a match and an intriguing tactical duel between the two high-class market leaders, but the race did not develop as expected because Tranquil Tiger had to be rousted along after missing the break and could never adopt his favoured front-running role. Firebet did not need to match his progressive recent form.

NOTEBOOK

Firebet(IRE) went close to landing a four-timer when chasing home Harbinger in Group 3 Gordon Stakes at Goodwood last time. The son of Dubai Destination tracked the leader throughout in this contest, attacked early in the straight and the result was never really in doubt after that, despite the narrow winning margin. This is not his most solid form and he never had to worry about trying to run Tranquil Tiger down, but his rise towards stardom for his current yard has been very impressive. He scored off a mark of 81 last autumn and has found almost 30lb of improvement since. This was only his 11th start and he should be able to win in Group 3 company, and may live up to a higher billing. (tchd Evens)

Midnight Cruiser(IRE) got a very comfortable lead and may be a bit flattered by the form but the 92-rated colt bounced back from a couple of below-par efforts in handicaps and ran a mighty race behind a rival with a 16lb higher official rating. The downside to this performance is that it could sabotage his mark. (op 10-1)

Tranquil Tiger seemed happy enough tracking the leaders during the mid-part of the race but found a disappointing response in the straight and eventually finished well held in what was a slightly unsatisfactory contest. He is a very smart front-runner on fast ground when on song and has a good strike-rate of 7-22, but this was his second tame effort in a row and he will have a bit to prove next time. (op 5-4 tchd Evens)

Maxwil had masses to find on official figures and ran as well as could be expected upped in trip and class on his second run for a new yard. (op 66-1)

5509 TOMPKINS & MAY PARTNERSHIP AMATEUR DERBY (HANDICAP FOR GENTLEMAN AMATEUR RIDERS) 1m 4f 10y

4:20 (4:21) (Class 4) (0-85,83) 4-Y-O+ £6,246 (£1,937; £968; £484) Stalls Centre

Form				RPR
531/	1		**Hibiki (IRE)**[183] 6422 5-11-4 77 ... (p) MrSWalker 1 (P J Hobbs) *trckd ldrs: jnd ldrs gng wl over 2f out: led 2f out: rdn over 1f out: styd on wl and a holding rivals fnl f* 3/1[1]	85
024-	2	¾	**Sleepy Hollow**[311] 6948 4-11-4 82 ... MrStephenHarrison(5) 7 (H Morrison) *stmbld bdly leaving stalls: t.k.h: hld up in tch: n.m.r on inner and lost pl 8f out: effrt and n.m.r ent fnl 2f: sn rdn and edgd lft: chsd wnr ins fnl f: r.o but a hld by wnr* 10/3[2]	89
541	3	¾	**Epsom Salts**[11] 5185 4-10-8 72 ... MrMPrice(5) 4 (P M Phelan) *s.i.s: t.k.h: in tch: chsd ldr 8f out: rdn and ev ch 2f out: one pce fnl 100yds* 3/1[1]	78
4624	4	2¾	**Locum**[10] 5210 4-10-1 65 ... MrDJEustace(5) 8 (M H Tompkins) *stdd s: hld up in tch in rr: effrt on outer over 2f out: styd on fnl f to go 4th fnl 75yds: nt threaten ldrs* 8/1	66
000-	5	¾	**Dani's Girl (IRE)**[31] 3990 6-11-10 83 ... MrSDobson 5 (P M Phelan) *stdd s: t.k.h: hld up in tch in rr: hdwy on outer 4f out: rdn and one pce fr over 1f out* 20/1	83
0006	6	¾	**Goodwood Starlight (IRE)**[59] 3578 4-11-0 76 ... (t) MrJoshuaMoore(3) 9 (G L Moore) *t.k.h: trckd ldrs: rdn and hdwy towards inner over 2f out: chsd ldrs over 1f out: wknd jst ins fnl f* 8/1	75
2411	7	nse	**Penang Cinta**[24] 4735 6-10-9 71 ... MrPCollington(3) 2 (P D Evans) *chsd ldr tl 8f out: styd handy: rdn and unable qck wl over 2f out: no prog fnl 2f* 6/1[3]	70
1246	8	4½	**Dream Of Fortune (IRE)**[18] 3399 5-11-2 80 ... (t) MrJMQuinlan(5) 3 (M G Quinlan) *hld up in tch in last pair: effrt and rdn over 2f out: sn hung lft: wl btn over 1f out* 16/1	72
0500	9	9	**Wicksy Creek**[16] 5018 4-10-0 64 oh19 ... (t) MrMMarris(5) 10 (G C Bravery) *led and sn clr: c bk to field 1/2-way: rdn and hdd 2f out: sn wknd: wl bhd fnl f* 100/1	41

2m 48.51s (9.61) **Going Correction** -0.10s/f (Good) 9 Ran SP% **121.2**
Speed ratings (Par 105): **63,62,62,60,59 59,59,56,50**
toteswinger: 1&2 £5.40, 1&3 £3.30, 2&3 £3.80. CSF £14.01 CT £33.20 TOTE £4.30: £1.80, £2.00, £1.60; EX 19.20.

Owner R A Green **Bred** Albert Conneally **Trained** Withycombe, Somerset

FOCUS

An interesting amateur riders' handicap. It was run at a very sedate pace and the time was over 12 secs above standard, but the form makes a fair bit of sense at face value.

5510 TOMPKINS & MAY PARTNERSHIP PLANNED MAINENANCE H'CAP 1m 2f 18y

4:55 (4:57) (Class 3) (0-90,87) 3-Y-O+ £7,771 (£2,312; £1,155; £577) Stalls Low

Form				RPR
3312	1		**Cill Rialaig**[59] 3578 4-9-8 81 ... SteveDrowne 5 (H Morrison) *hld up in tch: hdwy gng wl to chse ldr jst over 2f out: rdn to ld jst ins fnl f: drvn out* 3/1[2]	91+
3134	2	nk	**Funday**[16] 5028 3-8-12 79 ... PaulHanagan 7 (G L Moore) *dwlt: sn pushed along and hdwy to ld over 8f out: rdn 3f out: hdd jst ins fnl f: kpt on but a hld by wnr* 5/2[1]	88+
0650	3	1	**Ramona Chase**[51] 3840 4-9-9 82 ... GeorgeBaker 3 (M J Attwater) *stdd s: t.k.h: hld up in rr: hdwy on outer wl over 2f out: pressed ldrs and rdn jst over 1f out: unable qck and btn fnl 100yds* 10/1	89
2006	4	3¼	**Admiral Dundas (IRE)**[18] 4957 4-9-3 76 ... AlanMunro 1 (W Jarvis) *led tl over 8f out: chsd ldr tl 5f out: rdn over 2f out: drvn and outpcd over 1f out* 12/1	77
0420	5	¾	**Bold Cross (IRE)**[5] 5349 6-9-8 81 ... PaulFitzsimons 2 (E G Bevan) *stdd after s: t.k.h: hld up in tch in last pair: effrt and n.m.r ent fnl 2f: sn rdn and no prog* 10/1	80
4350	6	11	**The Which Doctor**[9] 5262 4-10-0 87 ... TPQueally 6 (J Noseda) *dwlt: sn in tch on outer: hdwy to chse ldrs and rdn over 3f out: wnt 2nd briefly over 2f out: wknd u.p 2f out: eased ins fnl f* 3/1[2]	64
3240	7	2	**Burns Night**[26] 4641 3-8-11 78 ... J-PGuillambert 4 (M Johnston) *chsd ldrs: pushed along to go 2nd 5f out tl over 2f out: sn wknd: eased ins fnl f* 13/2[3]	51

2m 6.75s (-2.95) **Going Correction** -0.10s/f (Good)
WFA 3 from 4yo+ 8lb 7 Ran SP% **117.8**
Speed ratings (Par 107): **107,106,105,103,102 93,92**
toteswinger: 1&2 £2.40, 1&3 £6.60, 2&3 £5.60. CSF £11.52 CT £66.12 TOTE £3.90: £1.90, £2.00; EX 10.40.

Owner Pangfield Partners **Bred** T J Billington **Trained** East Ilsley, Berks

FOCUS

Not a particularly strong looking 0-90 handicap but two improving fillies fought out an exciting finish, and the first three finished clear of the rest. This is probably godod form for the grade.

NOTEBOOK

Cill Rialaig has been progressing nicely on the Flat and built on her Salisbury win when narrowly beaten at the same track last time. She had a 4lb rise to cope with in a stronger race but showed plenty of tenacity to get the better of an unflinching duel with the runner-up. She has had only eight outings, so could continue to climb the ranks and shapes like worth another try back at 1m4f. (op 100-30 tchd 4-1)

Funday compromised her chance by pulling too hard over 1m4f last time but gave it a brave shot back down in trip, particularly considering she did plenty of work early on under an aggressive ride. She is lightly raced, her form is moving in the right direction and she should be able to add to her Lingfield maiden win over progressive dual subsequent winner Doggerbank in June. (op 9-4 tchd 11-4)

Ramona Chase's headstrong ways have inhibited him from fulfilling his potential but he ran a very promising race behind two improvers here. The handicapper is giving him a chance and on this isolated evidence he should be able to strike in a similar race. (op 11-1 tchd 15-2)

Admiral Dundas(IRE) ran well to a point over a trip possibly on the outer limits of stamina. (op 14-1 tchd 11-1)

Bold Cross(IRE) could not muscle his way into contention after receiving a few bumps when trying to find a run. (op 12-1)

The Which Doctor lost momentum when two rivals on both sides swerved in front of him approaching the 2f pole. (op 100-30 tchd 7-2)

Burns Night, well held with blinkers tried last time, went out very quickly on his first try beyond 8.5f. (op 8-1)

5511 TOMPKINS & MAY PARTNERSHIP VOID MANAGEMENT H'CAP 1m 114y

5:30 (5:31) (Class 4) (0-80,80) 3-Y-O+ £5,180 (£1,541; £770; £384) Stalls Low

Form				RPR
6401	1		**Indy Driver**[37] 4305 4-9-9 72 ... (p) DaneO'Neill 11 (J R Fanshawe) *hld up in rr: swtchd rt and hdwy on outer 3f out: led wl over 1f out: sn hung lft: styd on wl fnl f* 11/1	82+
-316	2	nk	**Addwaitya**[66] 3357 4-9-9 72 ... TedDurcan 10 (C F Wall) *s.i.s and sn niggled along in rr: c wd and hdwy whn sltly hmpd 2f out: chsd wnr ins fnl f: r.o but nvr quite getting to wnr* 10/1	82
0222	3	2½	**Eastern Gift**[11] 5190 4-9-12 75 ... GeorgeBaker 9 (Miss Gay Kelleway) *stdd s: hld up wl bhd: hdwy over 3f out: rdn to ld 2f out: sn hdd and carried lft: kpt on same pce fnl f* 13/2	79
3242	4	hd	**Brooksby**[16] 5016 3-8-9 65 ... (b) SteveDrowne 3 (L A Dace) *chsd ldr: rdn over 3f out: swtchd rt and ev ch 2f out: keeping on same pce and btn whn hmpd ins fnl f* 20/1	68
0144	5	1½	**Northern Spy (USA)**[11] 5190 5-9-11 74 ... TPQueally 2 (S Dow) *racd in midfield: rdn and effrt over 3f out: chsd ldrs 2f out: one pce u.p after* 6/1[3]	74
21	6	2½	**Golden Button (IRE)**[10] 5228 4-9-9 72 ... StephenDonohoe 5 (Sir Mark Prescott) *chsd ldrs: rdn and unable qck over 2f out: lost pl and hung rt 2f out: carried lft over 1f out: plugged on same pce after* 11/4[1]	66
2022	7	1	**Luck Will Come (IRE)**[33] 4441 5-9-7 75 ... Louis-PhilippeBeuzelin(5) 12 (H J Collingridge) *stdd and dropped in bhd after s: rdn and effrt over 3f out: nvr pce to rch ldrs* 7/1	67
3544	8	nse	**Raaeidd (IRE)**[31] 4502 3-9-10 80 ... (p) AlanMunro 1 (M A Jarvis) *racd in midfield: rdn and effrt on inner over 2f out: swtchd rt 2f out: sn wknd* 9/2[2]	71
050	9	9	**Phluke**[40] 4211 8-9-7 70 ... RobertWinston 4 (Eve Johnson Houghton) *chsd ldng pair: drvn over 3f out: wknd qckly 2f out* 33/1	41
0236	10	3¼	**Twilight Star (IRE)**[26] 4641 5-9-13 76 ... (b1) J-PGuillambert 8 (R A Teal) *led and sn clr: hdd 2f out: sn dropped out and bhd* 12/1	40
6600	11	64	**Prince Of Thebes (IRE)**[14] 5095 8-9-8 71 ... KirstyMilczarek 7 (M J Attwater) *racd in midfield tl lost pl 5f out: wl bhd fnl 3f: virtually p.u fnl f: t.o* 25/1	—

1m 43.74s (-2.36) **Going Correction** -0.10s/f (Good)
WFA 3 from 4yo+ 7lb 11 Ran SP% **121.6**
Speed ratings (Par 105): **106,105,103,103,102 99,98,98,90,87 31**
toteswinger: 1&2 £20.70, 1&3 £10.00, 2&3 £14.90. CSF £117.04 CT £575.45 TOTE £10.90: £3.00, £3.20, £1.80; EX 149.30 Place 6 £15.98, Place 5 £8.67.

Owner Mrs C C Regalado-Gonzalez **Bred** Miss K Rausing **Trained** Newmarket, Suffolk

FOCUS

A competitive handicap, involving two last-time-out winners and three others who were runner-up on their previous outing. Twilight Star was revved up in first-time blinkers and ensured the pace was solid. Fair form for the grade, rated around the runner-up.

Golden Button(IRE) Official explanation: jockey said filly was unsuited by the track

Luck Will Come(IRE) Official explanation: jockey said mare was never travelling

Raaeidd(IRE) Official explanation: jockey said colt lost its action on the turn

Prince Of Thebes(IRE) Official explanation: jockey said gelding was never travelling

T/Plt: £35.80 to a £1 stake. Pool: £53,751.13. 1,093.49 winning tickets. T/Qpdt: £3.80 to a £1 stake. Pool: £3,126.70. 602.10 winning tickets. SP

5391 NEWCASTLE (L-H)

Monday, August 31

OFFICIAL GOING: Good to firm (firm in places last 3f; 8.3)

Rail dolled out 4yards on entire straight course up stands'-side rail.

Wind: Fairly strong, half against Weather: Overcast

5512 EUROPEAN BREEDERS' FUND MAIDEN STKS 7f
2:15 (2:17) (Class 4) 2-Y-O

£6,231 (£1,866; £933; £467; £233; £117) **Stalls Low**

Form				RPR
	1		**Cono Zur (FR)** 2-9-3 0 ... JoeFanning 2 (M Johnston) *mde all: rdn over 1f out: styd on strly fnl f* **7/1**	79+
5	2	3	**Unshakable Will (IRE)**[88] 2623 2-9-3 0 ... TomEaves 1 (B Smart) *t.k.h: cl up: outpcd over 2f out: rallied fnl f to go 2nd nr fin: nt rch wnr* **9/2**[2]	72
34	3	nk	**Mr Corby (IRE)**[9] 5251 2-9-3 0 ... TonyCulhane 4 (M R Channon) *t.k.h early: cl up: effrt over 2f out: one pce fnl f: lost 2nd nr fin* **1/1**[1]	71
0	4	4	**Starry Mount**[18] 4933 2-9-3 0 ... RobertHavlin 10 (A B Haynes) *in tch on outside: outpcd over 2f out: no imp fnl f* **16/1**	61
0	5	11	**Vittachi**[21] 4847 2-9-3 0 ... GrahamGibbons 7 (J D Bethell) *dwlt: plld hrd: hld up in tch: outpcd over 2f out: sn wknd* **50/1**	34
0	6	2 1/2	**Generoso (USA)**[25] 4701 2-9-0 0 ... WilliamCarson(3) 11 (S C Williams) *t.k.h: hld up: struggling 3f out: nvr on terms* **18/1**	27
0	7	11	**Drubinca**[35] 4377 2-9-3 0 ... TonyHamilton 8 (S C Williams) *bhd: struggling 1/2-way: nvr on terms* **22/1**	—
	8	1/2	**Caldercruix (USA)** 2-9-3 0 ... MickyFenton 6 (T P Tate) *green in preliminaries and unruly in stalls: dwlt: t.k.h and sn cl up: wknd fr over 2f out* **5/1**[3]	—
66	9	6	**Wing Forward (IRE)**[23] 4774 2-8-5 0 ... BillyCray(7) 5 (A Berry) *plld hrd early: hld up on ins: drvn 1/2-way: sn wknd* **80/1**	—

1m 27.73s (-0.97) **Going Correction** -0.30s/f (Firm) **9 Ran SP% 116.0**

Speed ratings (Par 96): **93,89,89,84,72 69,56,56,49**

toteswinger: 1&2 £4.50, 1&3 £1.80, 2&3 £1.10. CSF £38.21 TOTE £7.50: £2.30, £1.50, £1.10; EX 32.70 Trifecta £46.50 Pool: £260.40 - 4.14 winning units..

Owner T T Bloodstocks **Bred** Jean-Pierre-Joseph Dubois **Trained** Middleham Moor, N Yorks

■ Sixties Rock was withdrawn (14/1, vet's advice). Deduct 5p in the £ under R4. New market formed.

FOCUS

An ordinary maiden run at a steady pace. The form is rated around the placed horses and the averages.

NOTEBOOK

Cono Zur(FR) made a pleasing start, especially considering he looked as though the run would do him good. A 20,000euros half-brother to a 2yo winner in France, a 3yo winner in the US, and Giant Eagle, a bumper and hurdles winner, he knew his job and looked a relentless galloper. There was much to like about his attitude. (old market op 5-1 new market op 5-1)

Unshakable Will(IRE) improved on the form he showed over 6f on his debut back in June. He lacked the speed to threaten the winner, but kept on well to take second near the line and should do better over further. (new market tchd 4-1)

Mr Corby(IRE) has a sprinter's pedigree and, just like at Chester last time, ran like a non-stayer. A drop in trip should suit and, being quite a big horse, he may appreciate a bit of cut. (new market op 6-4, tchd 15-8 in a place)

Starry Mount still looked to be learning and should find his level once handicapped. (new market op 20-1)

Caldercruix(USA) cost $140,000 and is well regarded, judged on his entries in the Champagne Stakes, Royal Lodge, Dewhurst and Racing Post Trophy, but things didn't really go his way and he ran poorly. Green in the preliminaries and upset in the stalls, he started slowly and had to be rushed up to sit handy, but was soon keener than ideal. After receiving a bump or two, his finishing effort was tame. (new market op 7-2 tchd 11-2)

Wing Forward(IRE) Official explanation: jockey said filly was unsuited by the good to firm, firm in places ground

5513 FASHION FOR A GOOD CAUSE CLAIMING STKS 1m 3y(S)
2:50 (2:52) (Class 6) 3-Y-O+ **£2,266** (£674; £337; £168) **Stalls Low**

Form				RPR
0060	1		**Wovoka (IRE)**[5] 5333 6-9-8 77 ... AmyRyan(5) 10 (K A Ryan) *hld up: hdwy to ld over 1f out: drifted lft ins fnl f: kpt on wl* **5/2**[1]	75
6-00	2	1 1/2	**Top Tribute**[130] 1480 4-9-3 61 ... MickyFenton 11 (T P Tate) *plld hrd early: hld up: hdwy over 2f out: edgd lft over 1f out: chsng wnr and keeping on u.p whn n.m.r wl ins fnl f* **9/1**	62
1530	3	nk	**Rowan Lodge (IRE)**[21] 4861 7-9-4 65 ... (b) IJBrennan(7) 12 (Ollie Pears) *stdd s: hld up: hdwy 3f out: edgd lft over 1f out: kpt on u.p fnl f* **3/1**[3]	69
0152	4	4	**Fortunate Bid (IRE)**[22] 4821 3-9-7 72 ... DuranFentiman 13 (Mrs L Stubbs) *led to over 1f out: sn outpcd* **11/4**[2]	61
6-00	5	1 1/4	**Igneous**[36] 4348 3-8-10 45 ow1 ... RobertHavlin 3 (D W Thompson) *hld up: hdwy and in tch over 2f out: no ex over 1f out* **100/1**	47
3004	6	6	**Pianoforte (USA)**[23] 4804 7-9-3 51 ... (b) PaulMulrennan 7 (E J Alston) *hld up in midfield: outpcd over 2f out: n.d after* **16/1**	35
5615	7	1 1/2	**Whaston (IRE)**[33] 4431 4-9-9 55 ... (v) GrahamGibbons 5 (J D Bethell) *chsd ldrs: drvn 3f out: wknd over 1f out* **8/1**	38
0004	8	15	**Reddy Ronnie (IRE)**[24] 4750 5-8-8 43 ... DTDaSilva(7) 8 (D W Thompson) *chsd ldr to 3f out: sn rdn and btn* **50/1**	—
-060	9	1	**Second Reef**[12] 5150 7-9-7 41 ... TomEaves 2 (T A K Cuthbert) *hld up in tch: outpcd 3f out: sn btn* **80/1**	—
0506	10	7	**Chin Wag (IRE)**[23] 4775 5-8-11 50 ... (p) DanielTudhope 4 (J S Goldie) *in tch 3f: sn rdn and wknd* **16/1**	—
00-	11	47	**Another Echo**[386] 4896 3-7-13 0 ... DominicFox(3) 1 (W Storey) *prom 2f: sn lost pl and struggling: virtually p.u fnl 2f* **100/1**	—

1m 41.09s (-2.31) **Going Correction** -0.30s/f (Firm)

WFA 3 from 4yo+ 6lb **11 Ran SP% 118.3**

Speed ratings (Par 101): **99,97,97,93,91 85,84,69,68,61 14**

toteswinger: 1&2 £7.60, 1&3 £2.90, 2&3 £15.60. CSF £26.27 TOTE £3.50: £1.40, £2.70, £1.90; EX 27.00 Trifecta £167.50 Pool: £321.51 - 1.42 winning units..

Owner Dales Homes Ltd **Bred** Rathasker Stud **Trained** Hambleton, N Yorks

Stewards' Enquiry : Amy Ryan three-day ban: careless riding (Sep 14-16)

FOCUS

A modest claimer. They raced up the middle of the track for much of the way, but the front three ended up towards the far side.

5514 S V RUTTER FILLIES' H'CAP 7f
3:25 (3:26) (Class 5) (0-75,73) 3-Y-O+ **£4,415** (£1,321; £660; £330; £164) **Stalls Low**

Form				RPR
201	1		**Poppet's Lovein**[18] 4936 3-9-8 73 ... RobertHavlin 7 (A B Haynes) *unruly bef s: t.k.h: prom: smooth hdwy to ld over 1f out: r.o strly fnl f* **7/1**	83
0354	2	2 3/4	**Leonid Glow**[17] 4996 4-9-12 72 ... PhillipMakin 4 (M Dods) *hld up in tch: effrt over 2f out: styd on to chse wnr wl ins fnl f: r.o* **7/1**	77
6052	3	hd	**Sanvean (IRE)**[18] 4940 3-9-2 67 ... TonyCulhane 5 (M R Channon) *hld up last: rdn and hdwy over 2f out: kpt on u.p fnl f* **9/2**[2]	69
-021	4	1/2	**Dance Club (IRE)**[14] 5112 3-9-0 65 ... JoeFanning 2 (W Jarvis) *chsd ldr: ev ch over 2f tl over 1f out: no ex and lost 2nd wl ins fnl f* **5/1**[3]	66
6512	5	nk	**She's In The Money**[5] 5340 3-9-5 70 ... TonyHamilton 8 (R A Fahey) *swtchd lft and hld up on far rail: nt clr run over 2f and over 1f out: swtchd rt and styd on fnl f: nrst fin* **11/8**[1]	70+
0422	6	2	**Carnival Dream**[7] 5304 4-8-7 53 oh1 ... (b) PJMcDonald 6 (H A McWilliams) *led to over 1f out: sn btn* **28/1**	50
2030	7	2	**Hansomis (IRE)**[15] 5069 5-9-6 66 ... TomEaves 3 (B Mactaggart) *prom: drvn over 2f out: sn outpcd* **12/1**	58
0-03	8	8	**Tina's Best (IRE)**[22] 4821 4-9-6 66 ... PaulMulrennan 1 (E J Alston) *trckd ldrs tl wknd over 1f out* **25/1**	36

1m 26.34s (-2.36) **Going Correction** -0.30s/f (Firm)

WFA 3 from 4yo+ 5lb **8 Ran SP% 116.9**

Speed ratings (Par 100): **101,97,97,97,96 94,92,83**

toteswinger: 1&2 £8.30, 1&3 £12.60, 2&3 £9.50. CSF £55.92 CT £246.94 TOTE £8.80: £2.30, £2.00, £1.90; EX 65.90 Trifecta £288.80 Pool: £765.08 - 1.96 winning units..

Owner Graham Robinson **Bred** G And Mrs Robinson **Trained** Limpley Stoke, Bath

FOCUS

A modest fillies' handicap.

She's In The Money Official explanation: jockey said filly was denied a clear run

5515 BLAYDON RACE (NURSERY) 1m 3y(S)
4:00 (4:01) (Class 2) 2-Y-O

£9,969 (£2,985; £1,492; £747; £372; £187) **Stalls Low**

Form				RPR
21	1		**Layali Al Andalus**[65] 3376 2-9-7 88 ... JoeFanning 2 (M Johnston) *mde all: rdn clr over 1f out: unchal* **1/1**[1]	100+
2310	2	2 3/4	**Bonfire Knight**[11] 5198 2-8-7 74 ... GrahamGibbons 4 (J J Quinn) *prom: hdwy to chse wnr over 1f out: kpt on fnl f: no imp* **8/1**[3]	80
3312	3	2	**Aquarian Spirit**[18] 4931 2-8-12 79 ... TonyHamilton 6 (R A Fahey) *trckd ldrs: effrt and chsd wnr over 2f tl over 1f out: sn one pce* **11/4**[2]	80
1220	4	1	**Tres Coronas (IRE)**[31] 4488 2-8-10 77 ... PhillipMakin 11 (T D Barron) *hld up: hdwy over 1f out: kpt on fnl f: nrst fin* **14/1**	76+
0154	5	1/2	**Jehu**[9] 5265 2-9-0 81 ... (v[1]) TonyCulhane 2 (M R Channon) *awkward s: hld up on ins: effrt over 2f out: sn no imp* **16/1**	79
031	6	1 3/4	**Lethal Combination (USA)**[11] 5191 2-9-0 81 ... MickyFenton 5 (W J Haggas) *chsd wnr to over 2f out: sn rdn and outpcd* **16/1**	75
3014	7	5	**My One Weakness (IRE)**[13] 5136 2-8-3 70 ... DuranFentiman 1 (B Ellison) *t.k.h: chsd ldrs tl rdn and wknd fr 2f out* **14/1**	52
235	8	2 3/4	**Miss Taken (IRE)**[26] 4659 2-7-12 65 oh3 ... PaulQuinn 3 (D Carroll) *dwlt: towards rr: drvn over 2f out: sn btn* **66/1**	41
3134	9	1/2	**Maison Brillet (IRE)**[24] 4739 2-8-9 76 ... PaulMulrennan 10 (J Howard Johnson) *hld up: rdn 3f out: nvr able to chal* **80/1**	51
010	10	3/4	**Rainsborough**[38] 4271 2-7-11 67 ... DominicFox(3) 9 (M R Channon) *midfield: struggling 3f out: sn btn* **100/1**	40
005	11	6	**Moonlight Blaze**[19] 4888 2-7-13 69 ow2 ... KellyHarrison(3) 13 (C W Fairhurst) *sn pushed along in rr: no ch fr 1/2-way* **33/1**	28

1m 39.89s (-3.51) **Going Correction** -0.30s/f (Firm) **11 Ran SP% 119.5**

Speed ratings (Par 100): **105,102,100,99,98 97,92,89,88,88 82**

toteswinger: 1&2 £3.90, 1&3 £1.80, 2&3 £6.10. CSF £10.36 CT £19.19 TOTE £2.00: £1.40, £2.40, £1.10; EX 12.00 Trifecta £62.70 Pool: £398.23 - 4.70 winning units..

Owner Sheikh Hamdan Bin Mohammed Al Maktoum **Bred** Wood Hall Stud Limited **Trained** Middleham Moor, N Yorks

FOCUS

This looks strong form and there was a potentially smart winner, with Layali Al Andalus, who is well regarded by Mark Johnston, recording a time 1.20sec quicker than the 77-rated Wovoka, a 6yo, managed in the earlier claimer. A race to be with.

NOTEBOOK

Layali Al Andalus ◆, sent to the front from the off, travelled well throughout and stayed on strongly for pressure, confirming the good impression he made when winning a Doncaster maiden by seven lengths. He has a number of Group-race entries, but his trainer isn't keen on dropping him back in trip and mentioned the Royal Lodge as a possible target. (op 11-10 tchd 6-5 and 5-4 in a place)

Bonfire Knight ◆, who was unsuited by the drop back to 6f in a sales race last time but still ran well, performed even better on this first attempt at 1m. He simply ran into an above-average rival, but is himself looking nicely handicapped now and may be worth a bet next time. (tchd 17-2)

Aquarian Spirit ran with credit on this first attempt at 1m, a trip he had been shaping as though in need of, but was up against up a couple of well-handicapped rivals. His only win so far came on easy ground. (op 7-2 tchd 4-1)

Tres Coronas(IRE), reported to have run too freely, clipped heels and stumbled last time. She was ridden patiently on this first attempt at 1m but, although keeping on when asked, never looked like mustering the required speed. She managed to win over 5f earlier in the year, but is out of a 1m4f winner and may require a more positive ride next time. (op 12-1 tchd 16-1)

Jehu did not improve for the step up to 1m and fitting of a visor for the first time and is not progressing. Official explanation: jockey said colt stumbled leaving the stalls (tchd 14-1)

Lethal Combination(USA), successful in a 7f maiden on Polytrack last time, got warm beforehand and ran a little disappointingly on this switch to nursery company. (op 14-1)

Moonlight Blaze Official explanation: jockey said colt hung right-handed throughout

5516 PHOENIX SECURITY H'CAP 6f
4:35 (4:35) (Class 4) (0-80,80) 3-Y-O+ **£5,361** (£1,604; £802; £401; £199) **Stalls Low**

Form				RPR
4604	1		**Avontuur (FR)**[3] 5391 7-8-1 62 ow1 ... (b) DeanHeslop(5) 1 (Mrs R A Carr) *led to appr fnl f: rallied to regain ld ins fnl f: kpt on gamely* **7/1**[3]	71
1430	2	1 1/4	**Incomparable**[32] 4461 4-9-5 75 ... (p) TonyHamilton 11 (J A Glover) *t.k.h: cl up: rdn to ld appr fnl f: hdd ins fnl f: one pce* **10/1**	80
0440	3	nk	**John Keats**[3] 5406 6-8-11 67 ... DanielTudhope 9 (J S Goldie) *hld up: hdwy 2f out: kpt on fnl f: nrst fin* **5/1**[2]	71

6010 **4** 2 1/4 **Bravely (IRE)**[26] 4662 5-9-5 **75** .... PaulMulrennan 12 72
(T D Easterby) *hld up: hdwy 2f out: no imp ins fnl f* **8/1**

5006 **5** 1/2 **Wyatt Earp (IRE)**[23] 4784 8-9-5 **75** ....(b) DaleGibson 8 70
(P Salmon) *cl up tl rdn and no ex over 1f out* **9/2**[1]

1012 **6** *hd* **Botham (USA)**[12] 5150 5-8-6 **65** .... KellyHarrison(3) 10 60
(J S Goldie) *hld up: pushed along over 2f out: plugged on fnl f: nvr able to chal* **8/1**

4120 **7** 2 **Sea Salt**[5] 5343 6-8-3 **64** .... LanceBetts(5) 4 52
(R E Barr) *dwlt: sn chsng ldrs: rdn and outpcd fr 2f out* **11/1**

2656 **8** 4 1/2 **Errigal Lad**[31] 4507 4-9-10 **80** .... PJMcDonald 3 54
(J Balding) *prom to 1/2-way: sn lost pl: n.d after* **7/1**[3]

6230 **9** 2 1/4 **Dazzling Bay**[42] 4134 9-9-2 **72** .... DuranFentiman 5 39
(T D Easterby) *t.k.h: hld up: outpcd 1/2-way: sn btn* **16/1**

0621 **10** *nse* **Imperial Sword**[23] 4772 6-8-3 **66** ....(b) JanWilson(7) 7 32
(T D Barron) *s.i.s: a bhd* **7/1**[3]

1m 12.64s (-2.56) **Going Correction** -0.30s/f (Firm) **10** Ran SP% **117.9**
Speed ratings (Par 105): **105,103,102,99,99 99,96,90,87,87**
toteswinger: 1&2 £16.10, 1&3 £11.00, 2&3 £15.90. CSF £75.62 CT £394.42 TOTE £8.60: £2.70, £2.90, £2.60; EX 126.40 Trifecta £124.30 Part won. Pool: £168.08 - 0.50 winning units..
Owner J M Chapman **Bred** Haras D'Etreham **Trained** Huby, N Yorks
■ Stewards' Enquiry : Jan Wilson caution: used whip when out of contention

FOCUS
They seemed to go off quite quickly but, not for the first time on this card, it proved difficult to make up significant ground.
Wyatt Earp(IRE) Official explanation: vet said gelding had been struck into
Errigal Lad Official explanation: jockey said gelding hung right handed throughout

5517 PARKLANDS GOLFCOURSE H'CAP 5f
5:10 (5:10) (Class 5) (0-75,78) 3-Y-O **£3,784** (£1,132; £566; £283; £141) **Stalls** Low

Form RPR

2152 **1** **Noodles Blue Boy**[26] 4653 3-9-4 **72** .... TonyHamilton 3 78
(Ollie Pears) *cl up: rdn over 2f out: led ins fnl f: hld on wl* **5/1**[3]

3620 **2** *nk* **Fasliyanne (IRE)**[18] 4942 3-8-9 **63** ....(b) JoeFanning 4 68
(K A Ryan) *led: rdn 1/2-way: hdd ins fnl f: rallied* **18/1**

1600 **3** 2 1/4 **Piste**[3] 5411 3-9-0 **68** .... TomEaves 8 60
(Miss T Jackson) *hld up in tch: drvn and outpcd 1/2-way: rallied fnl f: fin 4th, nk, 1 1/2l, 2 1/4l: plcd 3rd* **25/1**

-211 **4** 3/4 **Igoyougo**[18] 4942 3-8-10 **71** .... IJBrennan(7) 9 60
(G A Harker) *cl up on outside tl rdn and no ex over 1f out: fin 5th: plcd 4th* **1/1**[1]

2431 **5** 9 **Lucky Art (USA)**[21] 4849 3-9-7 **75** .... PJMcDonald 5 32
(Mrs R A Carr) *cl up tl rdn and wknd fr 2f out: fin 6th: plcd 5th* **7/2**[2]

4040 **6** 8 **Dispol Grand (IRE)**[3] 5405 3-8-13 **67** .... PhillipMakin 6 —
(P T Midgley) *s.i.s: carried lft and hmpd after 1f: sn lost tch: fin 7th: plcd 6th* **12/1**

6036 **D** 1 1/2 **Mazzola**[9] 5264 3-9-0 **68** .... TonyCulhane 7 67
(M R Channon) *stdd s: hld up: swtchd lft over 4f out: smooth hdwy over 2f out: rdn and one pce fnl f: fin 3rd: disq: plcd last* **12/1**

4340 **F** **All Spin (IRE)**[25] 4712 3-8-9 **63** .... PaulMulrennan 2 —
(A P Jarvis) *hld up on far rail: hmpd and fell heavily after 1f: dead* **14/1**

59.15 secs (-1.55) **Going Correction** -0.30s/f (Firm) **8** Ran SP% **120.0**
Speed ratings (Par 100): **100,99,93,92,77 65,97,—**
toteswinger: 1&2 £6.60, 1&3 £19.50, 2&3 £15.90. CSF £90.38 CT £2079.86 TOTE £6.40: £2.20, £3.90, £4.20; EX 65.10 Trifecta £172.60 Part won. Pool: £233.31 - 0.64 winning units..
Owner Ian Bishop **Bred** Fifehead Farms M C Denning **Trained** Norton, N Yorks
■ Stewards' Enquiry : Tony Culhane 14-day ban: dangerous riding (Sep 14-28)

FOCUS
A modest 3yo handicap.

5518 COMPLETE FOOTBALL H'CAP 5f
5:45 (5:49) (Class 6) (0-65,65) 3-Y-O+ **£2,838** (£849; £424; £212; £105) **Stalls** Low

Form RPR

052 **1** **Nomoreblondes**[5] 5345 5-9-2 **65** ....(p) IJBrennan(7) 3 76
(P T Midgley) *prom far side: drvn 1/2-way: led over 1f out: kpt on strly: eased nr fin* **10/1**

0011 **2** 2 1/4 **King Of Swords (IRE)**[15] 5073 5-9-7 **63** ....(p) TonyCulhane 1 66
(N Tinkler) *midfield far side: rdn 1/2-way: hdwy to chse wnr ins fnl f: r.o* **7/1**[2]

0005 **3** *nse* **Milton Of Campsie**[65] 3381 4-9-1 **57** .... MickyFenton 7 60
(J Balding) *in tch centre: outpcd over 2f out: r.o fnl f: no imp* **40/1**

5052 **4** 1 3/4 **Joyeaux**[18] 4929 7-9-6 **62** .... JoeFanning 9 58
(Ollie Pears) *hld up centre: hdwy over 1f out: rdn and one pce fnl f* **15/2**[3]

5123 **5** *nk* **Cayman Fox**[40] 4189 4-9-4 **60** ....(e) PJMcDonald 11 55
(James Moffatt) *led and clr centre: hdd over 1f out: one pce* **11/1**

1440 **6** 1/2 **Rocketball (IRE)**[3] 5411 4-9-3 **64** .... DeanHeslop(5) 6 58
(Mrs L Williamson) *prom towards far side: pushed along 1/2-way: one pce over 1f out* **10/1**

6322 **7** *shd* **Garstang**[11] 5197 6-9-9 **65** ....(b) TomEaves 2 58
(J Balding) *s.i.s: bhd far side tl styd on fnl f: nrst fin* **15/2**[3]

0-05 **8** 3/4 **Glenluji**[3] 5396 4-8-8 **55** .... GaryBartley(5) 12 45
(J S Goldie) *s.i.s: sn wl bhd: gd hdwy centre over 1f out: nrst fin* **11/1**

424 **9** 1/2 **Top Bid**[32] 4469 5-9-6 **62** ....(b) DuranFentiman 10 51
(T D Easterby) *chsd ldr centre: rdn 2f out: sn one pce* **9/1**

5406 **10** 3/4 **Kyzer Chief**[5] 5341 4-9-3 **64** ....(p) LanceBetts(5) 5 50
(R E Barr) *midfield towards centre: effrt over 2f out: btn fnl f* **9/1**

2604 **11** 3/4 **Toy Top (USA)**[3] 5411 6-9-2 **58** ....(b) PhillipMakin 13 41
(M Dods) *racd alone stands' side: rdn and outpcd fr 1/2-way* **9/2**[1]

3005 **12** *hd* **Thunder Bay**[23] 4772 4-9-2 **58** .... TonyHamilton 8 41
(R A Fahey) *sn towards rr centre: drvn 1/2-way: n.d* **14/1**

3550 **13** 5 **Kalhan Sands (IRE)**[11] 5184 4-9-1 **57** .... GrahamGibbons 4 22
(J J Quinn) *bhd and sn outpcd towards far side: no ch fr 1/2-way* **16/1**

59.72 secs (-0.98) **Going Correction** -0.30s/f (Firm) **13** Ran SP% **124.0**
Speed ratings (Par 101): **95,91,91,88,88 87,87,85,85,83 82,82,74**
toteswinger: 1&2 £11.00, 1&3 £56.40, 2&3 £85.30. CSF £81.47 CT £2799.37 TOTE £12.00: £3.30, £1.50, £12.50; EX 59.60 TRIFECTA Not won. Place 6 £88.72, Place 5 £68.87.
Owner Anthony D Copley **Bred** P John And Redmyre Bloodstock **Trained** Westow, N Yorks

FOCUS
A moderate sprint handicap. The main action took place middle to far side.
Kyzer Chief Official explanation: jockey said gelding missed the break
Toy Top(USA) Official explanation: jockey said mare was never travelling
T/Plt: £335.40 to a £1 stake. Pool: £45,699.78. 99.45 winning tickets. T/Qpdt: £97.10 to a £1 stake. Pool: £3,441.34. 26.20 winning tickets. RY

The Form Book, Raceform Ltd, Compton, RG20 6NL

5253 RIPON (R-H)
Monday, August 31

OFFICIAL GOING: Good (7.8)
Rail from back straight to home straight moved out 5m from innermost position but impact on distances not quantified.
Wind: Fresh, behind Weather: Sunny periods

5519 RACING AGAIN TOMORROW (S) STKS 6f
2:25 (2:26) (Class 5) 2-Y-O **£2,729** (£806; £403) **Stalls** Low

Form RPR

4332 **1** **Masked Dance (IRE)**[7] 5303 2-9-2 63 ....(p) DarryllHolland 11 77
(K A Ryan) *mde all: sn swtchd to r far side: clr wl over 1f out: unchal* **9/4**[1]

5534 **2** 9 **Drinking Buddy**[17] 4973 2-9-2 59 .... AndrewElliott 20 50
(D W Thompson) *prom far side: rdn along to chse wnr 2f out: sn drvn and no imp: 2nd of 7 in gp* **11/1**[3]

0020 **3** *nse* **Just The Tonic**[12] 5166 2-8-11 60 .... SamHitchcott 7 45+
(M R Channon) *trckd ldrs stands' side: hdwy over 2f out: rdn to ld that gp over 1f out: sn drvn and kpt on: no ch w far side: 1st of 11 in gp* **5/1**[2]

0543 **4** 1/2 **Cygnet Committee (IRE)**[3] 5393 2-8-4 50 ....(b) JamesPSullivan(7) 18 43
(J S Wainwright) *hld up far side: hdwy over 2f out and sn rdn: drvn and kpt on ins fnl f: 3rd of 7 in gp* **11/1**[3]

5356 **5** *nse* **Gasparilla (IRE)**[10] 5226 2-8-11 50 .... AndrewMullen 15 43
(A J McCabe) *chsd wnr far side: rdn along wl over 2f out: drvn wl over 1f out: kpt on same pce: 4th of 7 in gp* **20/1**

5564 **6** 4 1/2 **Wijikura (IRE)**[19] 4889 2-8-11 61 .... JamieKyne(5) 9 35+
(J J Quinn) *in tch stands' side: hdwy to chse ldrs 2f out: sn rdn and kpt on same pce ins fnl f: 2nd of 11 in gp* **5/1**[2]

05 **7** *hd* **Croft Bridge**[8] 5292 2-9-2 0 .... RoystonFfrench 8 34+
(M Dods) *led stands' side: gp: rdn along over 2f out: sn drvn and grad wknd: 3rd of 11 in gp* **14/1**

0 **8** 3 1/2 **Step To It (IRE)**[80] 2896 2-9-2 0 .... EddieAhern 17 23
(K A Ryan) *hld up far side: hdwy over 2f out: sn rdn and n.d: 5th of 7 in gp* **18/1**

50 **9** 1 1/2 **Kwami Biscuit**[31] 4503 2-9-2 0 .... SilvestreDeSousa 4 19+
(G A Harker) *in tch stands' side: effrt whn nt clr run over 2f out: n.d after: 4th of 11 in gp* **12/1**

00 **10** 2 **Ainthegorgeous**[19] 4888 2-9-2 0 .... PatCosgrave 16 13
(P T Midgley) *chsd ldrs far side: rdn along over 2f out and grad wknd: 6th of 7 in gp* **33/1**

00 **11** 4 **Azzez Life**[13] 5129 2-9-2 0 .... GregFairley 19 —
(R C Guest) *chsd ldrs far side: rdn along 1/2-way: sn wknd: 7th of 7 in gp* **66/1**

30 **12** *hd* **Blue Emirate**[61] 3494 2-8-11 0 ow2 .... SamuelDrury(7) 6 —
(P C Haslam) *a towards rr stands' side: 5th of 11 in gp* **50/1**

006 **13** 4 **Blade Of Glory**[14] 5106 2-8-4 52 ....(v) DeclanCannon(7) 1 —
(A J McCabe) *s.i.s: a in rr stands' side: 6th of 11 in gp* **40/1**

0 **14** 8 **Baze Mac**[21] 4844 2-8-9 0 ow1 .... NeilBrown(3) 13 —
(N Bycroft) *dwlt: sn chsng ldrs on stands' side: rdn along 1/2-way and sn wknd: 7th of 11 in gp* **33/1**

00 **15** *nse* **Al Barq (IRE)**[19] 4915 2-8-11 0 .... JerryO'Dwyer 10 —
(Miss D Mountain) *chsd ldrs stands' side: rdn along 1/2-way: sn wknd: 8th of 11 in gp* **50/1**

0000 **16** *nse* **Daft Lad**[19] 4889 2-9-2 54 ....(v) DNolan 5 —
(L A Mullaney) *chsd ldrs stands' side: rdn along whn hmpd over 2f out and sn wknd: 9th of 11 in gp* **40/1**

0405 **17** 2 **Countrywide Ice (IRE)**[7] 5303 2-9-2 52 ....(b) SaleemGolam 2 —
(K A Ryan) *a bhd stands' side: 10th of 11 in gp* **25/1**

60 **18** 1 **Joel The Mole**[76] 2996 2-8-9 0 .... NSLawes(7) 3 —
(D Nicholls) *a edging rt: bhd stands' side: 11th of 11 in gp* **33/1**

1m 12.2s (-0.80) **Going Correction** -0.275s/f (Firm) **18** Ran SP% **128.1**
Speed ratings (Par 94): **94,82,81,81,81 75,74,70,68,65 60,60,54,44,43 43,41,39**
toteswinger: 1&2 £5.80, 1&3 £2.40, 2&3 £9.90. CSF £26.75 TOTE £3.30: £1.60, £2.60, £2.10; EX 32.80.The winner was bought in for 3,800 gns. Just the Tonic claimed by Mrs Marjorie Fife for £6,000.
Owner J C Fretwell **Bred** Canice Farrell Jnr **Trained** Hambleton, N Yorks

FOCUS
A weak affair and the winner was far too good, producing a clear personal best. Those drawn high seemed at an advantage.

NOTEBOOK
Masked Dance(IRE), tried in first-time cheekpieces, produced an impressive display to win as he liked. Although not drawn particularly well in stall 11, his rider sensibly tracked over to the far rail along with six others and soon had him at the head of affairs. Always travelling well, he had the race won approaching two furlongs out. This would have done his confidence no harm and he was still full of running passing the post. He may well progress for this. (op 7-2)
Drinking Buddy, who had the benefit of a high draw, was well beaten off but was not hard pressed to nab second. He's been running over further in claimers/sellers and this drop back in trip would, ordinarily, have suited him. He has ability and his connections will no doubt place him to good effect. (op 9-1)
Just The Tonic is a good yardstick in this grade. She didn't have a favourable high draw, but emphatically proved the best of those who went up the nearside. She produced another game effort in defeat and she should be up to winning a race of this nature. (op 11-2 tchd 9-2)
Cygnet Committee(IRE) has had plenty of chances and appeared to take a step back on her previous run at Newcastle. The race may have come a shade too quick for her. (op 10-1 tchd 8-1)
Gasparilla(IRE) has shown precious little form in this grade before, but the high draw obviously helped. She ran on stoutly, although she is proving a bit frustrating.
Wijikura(IRE), who came up the nearside, didn't appear to benefit and was well beaten. He is worth another try at this trip, however. (op 7-1 tchd 15-2)

5520 WENDY BENNETT BIRTHDAY CELEBRATION MAIDEN STKS 1m
3:00 (3:00) (Class 5) 3-4-Y-O **£2,914** (£867; £433; £216) **Stalls** High

Form RPR

3- **1** **My Verse**[305] 7097 3-8-12 0 .... WilliamBuick 16 75
(M A Jarvis) *trckd ldrs on inner: effrt over 1f out and sn ev ch: rdn ins fnl f: styd on to ld last 75yds: eased nr fin* **5/2**[1]

55 **2** *nk* **Oneofapear (IRE)**[21] 4838 3-9-0 0 .... NeilBrown(3) 5 79
(G A Swinbank) *led: pushed along 3f out: rdn and jnd 2f out: drvn appr fnl f: hdd and no ex last 75yds* **33/1**

302 **3** 1 1/2 **Mustakmil (IRE)**[17] 5010 3-9-3 72 .... EddieAhern 8 76
(E A L Dunlop) *sn chsng ldrs: hdwy over 3f out: chal wl over 1f out and sn rdn: drvn and ev ch ent fnl f: sn edgd rt and one pce* **5/2**[1]

0 **4** 4 1/2 **Clare Glen (IRE)**[38] 4287 3-8-12 0 .... DavidAllan 15 60
(Lee Smyth, Ire) *chsd ldrs on inner: rdn along 3f out: drvn over 2f out and kpt on same pce* **9/1**

5 **5** ½ **Tobrata**[38] 4277 3-8-10 0.. JohnCavanagh(7) 4 64
(M Brittain) *chsd ldr: rdn along over 3f out: drvn over 2f out and grad wknd* **33/1**

6 7 **Short Supply (USA)** 3-8-12 0.. DNolan 11 43
(T D Walford) *in tch: effrt to chse ldrs over 3f out: rdn along wl over 2f out and sn wknd* **100/1**

7 1½ **Tanfidh** 3-8-12 0.. DarryllHolland 3 39
(M P Tregoning) *hld up towards rr: hdwy on inner wl over 2f out: sn swtchd lft and rdn: no imp* **13/2[3]**

8 ¾ **By Request** 3-8-12 0.. PatCosgrave 12 38
(Sir Mark Prescott) *s.i.s and bhd: hdwy 4f out: rdn along 3f out: sn no imp* **18/1**

9 1¾ **Heavenly Stella (USA)**[29] 4-8-11 0............................ JoshuaCrane(7) 1 34
(G A Swinbank) *stdd s and towards rr: hdwy on outer 3f out: rdn along over 2f out: sn edgd rt and wknd* **66/1**

00 **10** 1 **Emiratesdotcom**[31] 4505 3-9-3 0................................ RoystonFfrench 7 36
(M Johnston) *in tch: effrt 3f out: sn rdn along and wknd over 2f out* **20/1**

0220 **11** 12 **Peaceful Rule (USA)**[21] 4846 3-9-3 70.......................... MichaelHills 14 9
(D Nicholls) *s.i.s: a bhd* **4/1[2]**

6 **12** 1¼ **Convitezza**[15] 5071 3-8-12 0.. PatrickMathers 2 —
(M E Sowersby) *midfield: rdn along over 3f out and sn wknd* **150/1**

1m 40.33s (-1.07) **Going Correction** -0.10s/f (Good)
WFA 3 from 4yo 6lb 12 Ran SP% **119.5**
Speed ratings (Par 103): **101,100,99,94,94 87,85,84,83,82 70,68**
toteswinger: 1&2 £38.00, 1&3 £1.60, 2&3 Not won. CSF £103.09 TOTE £3.30: £1.60, £7.90, £1.60; EX 101.70.
Owner Sheikh Ahmed Al Maktoum **Bred** Darley **Trained** Newmarket, Suffolk

FOCUS
A modest maiden in which the first pair fought it out.
Tanfidh Official explanation: jockey said filly was slow away
Peaceful Rule(USA) Official explanation: jockey said colt was slow away

5521 RIPON CHAMPION TWO YRS OLD TROPHY, 2009 (LISTED RACE) 6f
3:35 (3:36) (Class 1) 2-Y-O

£17,031 (£6,456; £3,231; £1,611; £807; £405) **Stalls** Low

Form RPR

61 **1** **Hold Your Colour (IRE)**[9] 5256 2-9-2 87............................ EddieAhern 2 101+
(B J Meehan) *trckd ldrs: hdwy over 2f out: rdn to chal wl over 1f out: drvn and styd on to ld ins fnl f: kpt on wl* **9/2**

121 **2** 1 **Skylla**[23] 4782 2-8-11 90.. JerryO'Dwyer 7 93
(J R Holt) *cl up: led after 1f: rdn along and jnd 2f out: drvn and hdd ins fnl f: kpt on* **4/1[3]**

1320 **3** ¾ **Di Stefano**[11] 5198 2-9-2 97..(v[1]) SamHitchcott 1 96
(M R Channon) *chsd ldrs on inner: swtchd rt and hdwy 2f out: rdn over 1f out: swtchd lft and drvn ins fnl f: kpt on* **7/1**

2101 **4** 4 **Exotic Beauty**[16] 5038 2-8-11 86.................................... DavidAllan 5 79
(M R Channon) *led 1f: cl up: rdn along over 2f out and grad wknd* **11/4[1]**

2421 **5** 10 **Arabian Pride**[16] 5029 2-9-2 91.................................... DarryllHolland 4 54
(D M Simcock) *chsd ldrs: rdn along over 2f out and sn outpcd* **16/1**

1 **6** 3 **Breathless Kiss (USA)**[53] 3762 2-8-11 0............................ MichaelHills 6 46+
(K A Ryan) *in tch: rdn along and edging rt 1/2-way: sn outpcd* **12/1**

1 **P** **Businessman**[10] 5234 2-9-2 0.. RoystonFfrench 8 —
(M Johnston) *wnt rt s: sn pushed along in rr: rdn and detached whn lost action and stmbld bdly 1/2-way: p.u and dismntd after* **3/1[2]**

1m 12.46s (-0.54) **Going Correction** -0.275s/f (Firm) 7 Ran SP% **115.9**
Speed ratings (Par 102): **92,90,89,84,71 67,—**
toteswinger: 1&2 £3.80, 1&3 £7.10, 2&3 £16.70. CSF £23.39 TOTE £5.10: £2.30, £3.00; EX 25.20.
Owner Sangster Family & Mrs M Findlay **Bred** Trevor Reilly **Trained** Manton, Wilts

FOCUS
An up-to-standard Listed prize for juveniles. The first two were clear and the placed horses help to set the level.

NOTEBOOK
Hold Your Colour(IRE) had won a decent sales race over course and distance on only his second run and he appeared to have come on from that, wearing down the runner-up in good style. His rider gave him ten smacks of the whip to keep him up to his work in the final 2f, but he responded well. (op 11-2)
Skylla came into this in good form, having won a Haydock nursery that had worked out well. Up in class, she made most of the running and was only worn down in the last half-furlong, suggesting that she handled this step up in trip well. She shows plenty of speed and remains progressive and, although she may be worth another try over it in time, a race like the 5f Flying Childers could be within her compass. (op 7-2 tchd 9-2)
Di Stefano, in a first-time visor, seemed to get a bit outpaced approaching a furlong and a half out, before running on resolutely late on. He has done much of his running over the minimum trip, but on this showing looks as though he needs further. He is a horse who tends to find trouble in his races, but there were no real excuses this time. (op 13-2)
Exotic Beauty had a couple of decent animals behind her when landing a Class 3 Conditions race here last time, so this was a bit disappointing. She held every chance but faded late and was well held in the end. The jury is now out. (op 4-1)
Arabian Pride was being pushed along at halfway and was beaten well before the furlong pole. (tchd 14-1)
Breathless Kiss(USA)'s Cheveley Park entry looks lofty to say the least, but she had an excuse here as the rider reported that the filly lost her action. Official explanation: jockey said filly lost its action (op 11-1)
Businessman came out of the stalls awkwardly and broke down approaching the 3f marker. The on-course vet reported that he had a suspected fractured pelvis and, sadly, he had to be put down. (tchd 100-30 and 7-2 in a place)

5522 RIPON ROWELS H'CAP 1m
4:10 (4:11) (Class 2) (0-100,98) 3-Y-0+

£12,462 (£3,732; £1,866; £934; £466; £234) **Stalls** High

Form RPR

4211 **1** **Wannabe King**[11] 5189 3-9-3 94....................................(p) DarryllHolland 6 108
(D R Lanigan) *in tch: gd hdwy 3f out: swtchd lft and effrt to chse ldr wl over 1f out: rdn to ld ent fnl f: kpt on wl* **6/1[1]**

0022 **2** 2¾ **Billy Dane (IRE)**[23] 4779 5-8-11 87................................(p) JamieKyne(5) 17 95
(F P Murtagh) *led: rdn clr 2f out: drvn and hdd ent fnl f: kpt on same pce* **7/1[3]**

2205 **3** 1¾ **Osteopathic Remedy (IRE)**[37] 4310 5-9-1 86.................... DNolan 12 90
(M Dods) *trckd ldrs: hdwy over 2f out: rdn to chse ldng pair over 1f out: drvn and one pce ins fnl f* **12/1**

-022 **4** ¾ **Moynahan (USA)**[23] 4768 4-9-12 97................................ EddieAhern 18 99
(P F I Cole) *hld up: hdwy 3f out: rdn to chse ldrs and n.m.r wl over 1f out: kpt on ins fnl f* **6/1[1]**

3215 **5** nse **Exit Smiling**[16] 5040 7-8-7 83.................................... PaulPickard(5) 8 85
(P T Midgley) *in tch: hdwy over 2f out: n.m.r and swtchd lft over 1f out: sn drvn and kpt on same pce ins fnl f* **25/1**

1304 **6** 2¾ **Flawed Genius**[23] 4801 4-9-1 86..................................(t) SamHitchcott 14 82
(K A Ryan) *s.i.s and in rr: hdwy over 2f out: rdn wl over 1f out: styd on ins fnl f: nrst fin* **16/1**

3106 **7** ½ **Pride Of Kings**[23] 4801 3-8-8 85.................................... GregFairley 19 80
(M Johnston) *prom on inner: rdn along 3f out: drvn 2f out and grad wknd* **13/2[2]**

2240 **8** 1 **Flipando (IRE)**[11] 5200 8-9-7 95.................................... NeilBrown(3) 16 87
(T D Barron) *midfield: hdwy 3f out: swtchd lft and rdn over 2f out: drvn and no imp fr wl over 1f out* **14/1**

1400 **9** 2 **Benandonner (USA)**[31] 4486 6-9-6 96................................ BMcHugh(5) 11 84
(R A Fahey) *chsd ldrs: rdn along over 2f out and grad wknd* **16/1**

0126 **10** nk **One Way Or Another (AUS)**[23] 4779 6-9-6 91........................ PatCosgrave 2 78
(J R Gask) *hld up: a towards rr* **18/1**

3061 **11** 2¾ **Medici Pearl**[19] 4896 5-9-4 89.................................... DavidAllan 15 70
(T D Easterby) *stdd s: hld up: a in rr* **12/1**

460 **12** 1¼ **Jewelled Dagger (IRE)**[28] 4592 5-8-4 80........................ PatrickDonaghy(5) 13 58
(I Semple) *a in rr* **40/1**

-022 **13** ½ **Rattan (USA)**[89] 2597 4-9-6 91.................................... WilliamBuick 5 68
(Rae Guest) *midfield: hdwy on outer over 3f out: rdn along wl over 2f out: sn edgd rt and wknd* **16/1**

0433 **14** 1¾ **Opus Maximus (IRE)**[9] 5249 4-9-2 87................................ RoystonFfrench 3 60
(M Johnston) *hld up: hdwy 3f out: sn rdn along and wknd over 2f out* **12/1**

2110 **15** 1 **City Of The Kings (IRE)**[23] 4768 4-9-10 95........................ SilvestreDeSousa 4 65
(G A Harker) *a towards rr* **25/1**

0400 **16** 6 **Royal Power (IRE)**[34] 4412 6-9-7 92................................ AndrewMullen 9 49
(D Nicholls) *prom: rdn along 1/2-way: sn wknd* **33/1**

1m 38.64s (-2.76) **Going Correction** -0.10s/f (Good)
WFA 3 from 4yo+ 6lb 16 Ran SP% **120.1**
Speed ratings (Par 109): **109,106,104,103,103 100,100,99,97,97 94,93,92,90,89 83**
toteswinger: 1&2 £16.40, 1&3 £14.30, 2&3 £38.30. CSF £43.81 CT £515.40 TOTE £6.80: £1.90, £2.10, £2.80, £2.60; EX 63.00.
Owner Saif Ali & Saeed H Altayer **Bred** Chippenham Lodge Stud Ltd **Trained** Newmarket, Suffolk

FOCUS
A competitive handicap, run at a decent pace. The form should work out.

NOTEBOOK
Wannabe King defied his unfavourable draw in a race that few got in to, completing a hat-trick in the process. Drawn in stall six, his rider soon had him settled and he turned into the straight in sixth with enough to do. Having got a nice tow from Benandonner, he was full of running at the 2f marker where nothing was travelling better. He could be called the winner from some way out, although he took his time to edge past the long-time leader. He is in the Cambridgeshire, but a mile looks at the limit of his stamina and connections could find it hard to place him from here on in. (op 7-1)
Billy Dane(IRE) was given an uncontested lead that he appears to like and it almost paid off. However, just as he had at Haydock, he tired in the closing stages and was collared. He will probably go up again for this effort and he has a progressive, if unlucky, profile. He is another who needs faster ground. (op 9-1)
Osteopathic Remedy(IRE), who won this race last year off a 1lb higher mark, has run some fair races in defeat this summer, but is becoming a bit frustrating. The draw and ground were favourable and the race was run to suit. He ran on late but the cards need to fall his way, although it would be folly to write him off in this type of race. (op 8-1)
Moynahan(USA), fresh from a break, made up eyecatching ground late on. He is proving hard to win with but continues to run with credit in races such as this. He is holding his form and just needs a confidence-booster. His rider subsequently reported that the gelding reared leaving the stalls. Official explanation: jockey said gelding reared leaving the stalls (op 5-1)
Exit Smiling would have welcomed a bit more rain, but he ran a decent race from an unfavourable draw. The handicapper has his measure at present, but he looks set for a positive autumn campaign on this evidence. (op 20-1)
Flawed Genius was never in this after fluffing the start. Official explanation: jockey said gelding missed the break

5523 BILLY NEVETT MEMORIAL H'CAP 6f
4:45 (4:46) (Class 4) (0-85,85) 3-Y-O £4,857 (£1,445; £722; £360) **Stalls** Low

Form RPR

1314 **1** **Medicean Man**[13] 5130 3-9-0 78.................................... LukeMorris 15 87
(J R Gask) *hld up far side: hdwy 2f out: rdn over 1f out: styd on wl to ld ins fnl f* **17/2**

0100 **2** 1¼ **Bajan Tryst (USA)**[11] 5203 3-9-4 82..............................(p) DarryllHolland 12 87
(K A Ryan) *overall ldr far side: rdn along and edgd lft 2f out: drvn and hung lft ent fnl f: sn hdd: kpt on* **20/1**

2026 **3** ½ **Lucky Numbers (IRE)**[11] 5203 3-9-7 85.......................... SilvestreDeSousa 1 88
(Paul Green) *trckd ldrs stands' side: hdwy over 2f out: rdn to ld that gp 2f out and ev ch tl drvn and nt qckn ins fnl f: 1st of 9 in gp* **12/1**

6-40 **4** ¾ **Felday**[120] 1705 3-9-5 83.. TravisBlock 14 84
(H Morrison) *trckd ldrs far side: hdwy over 2f out: rdn over 1f out: kpt on ins fnl f: nrst fin: 3rd of 6 in gp* **8/1[3]**

2340 **5** 3 **Time Medicean**[37] 4326 3-9-3 81.................................... SamHitchcott 7 72
(M R Channon) *hld up stands' side: hdwy over 2f out: rdn to chse ldrs over 1f out: kpt on ins fnl f 2nd of 9 in gp* **12/1**

1603 **6** shd **Mullglen**[21] 4849 3-8-12 76..(b) DavidAllan 13 67
(T D Easterby) *chsd ldr far side: rdn along over 2f out: sn wknd: 4th of 6 in gp* **20/1**

1253 **7** ¾ **Invincible Isle (IRE)**[13] 5130 3-9-0 78.......................... EddieAhern 8 67
(H R A Cecil) *hld up stands' side: hdwy 2f out: sn rdn and kpt on ins fnl f: nt rch ldrs: 3rd of 9 in gp* **3/1[1]**

0205 **8** ½ **Dark Lane**[21] 4849 3-8-12 81.. BMcHugh(5) 16 68
(R A Fahey) *bhd far side: rdn along 2f out: sn no imp: 5th of 6 in gp* **10/1**

4155 **9** 1¼ **Brierty (IRE)**[13] 5130 3-9-3 81.................................... DNolan 10 64
(D Carroll) *hld up stands' side: hdwy 1/2-way: rdn wl over 1f out and n.d: 4th of 9 in gp* **50/1**

1601 **10** 2½ **Ishe Mac**[3] 5405 3-8-11 80 6ex...................................... JamieKyne(5) 2 55
(N Bycroft) *chsd ldrs stands' side: rdn along wl over 2f out: sn wknd: 5th of 9 in gp* **5/1[2]**

-045 **11** 3¾ **Go Go Green (IRE)**[28] 4601 3-9-1 79................................(t) GregFairley 4 42
(D H Brown) *led stands' side gp: rdn along and hdd over 2f out: sn wknd: 6th of 9 in gp* **12/1**

100 **12** 1 **Mabait**[30] 4540 3-9-4 82.. WilliamBuick 11 42
(L M Cumani) *chsd ldrs far side: rdn along wl over 2f out: sn wknd: 6th of 6 in gp* **10/1**

0-40 **13** 1 **Dubai Hills**[114] 1869 3-8-13 77.................................... RoystonFfrench 3 34
(B Smart) *cl up stands' side: rdn along wl over 2f out: sn wknd: 7th of 9 in gp* **40/1**

0103 **14** 1 ¼ **Klynch**[24] 4761 3-9-5 **83** MichaelHills 6 36
(B J Meehan) *dwlt and sltly hmpd s: a in rr stands' side: 8th of 9 in gp* **16/1**

00 **15** 3 ½ **Suzie Quw**[39] 4228 3-9-2 **80** AndrewElliott 5 21
(A P Jarvis) *bhd stands' side fr 1/2-way: last of 9 in gp* **33/1**

1m 10.94s (-2.06) **Going Correction** -0.275s/f (Firm) **15** Ran SP% **127.3**
Speed ratings (Par 102): **102,100,99,98,94 94,93,92,91,87 82,81,80,78,73**
toteswinger: 1&2 £47.20, 1&3 £21.10, 2&3 £68.50. CSF £180.24 CT £2114.80 TOTE £10.70: £3.30, £5.70, £3.60; EX 237.50.
Owner Stuart Dobb & Miss Kate Dobb **Bred** Barry Taylor **Trained** Sutton Veny, Wilts

FOCUS
An ordinary handicap run at a fair pace. The field split into two groups and, as is often the case with big fields over this trip, the far side was the place to be.
Mullglen Official explanation: jockey said gelding hung left-handed throughout
Dark Lane Official explanation: jockey said gelding hung left-handed

5524 PATELEY BRIDGE H'CAP 1m 1f 170y
5:20 (5:20) (Class 5) (0-70,69) 3-Y-O **£2,914** (£867; £433; £216) **Stalls** High

Form RPR

-115 **1** **Upton Seas**[19] 4892 3-9-6 **68** AndrewElliott 2 78
(M W Easterby) *cl up: effrt wl over 2f out: rdn to chal 2f out: led over 1f out: drvn clr ins fnl f* **5/1**

14 **2** 4 **Speed Dating**[14] 5101 3-9-4 **66** PatCosgrave 9 68
(Sir Mark Prescott) *dwlt and sn rdn along to ld after 1 1/2f: pushed along 3f out: rdn and jnd 2f out: drvn and hdd over 1f out: kpt on same pce* **7/4**[1]

6161 **3** 2 **Crystal Feather**[25] 4721 3-9-0 **62** WilliamBuick 11 60
(E F Vaughan) *trckd ldrs: hdwy on outer 3f out and sn cl up: effrt 2f out and ev ch tl drvn and one pce appr fnl f* **4/1**[3]

040- **4** 2 **Madam'X**[261] 7666 3-8-4 **52** SilvestreDeSousa 6 46
(Mrs A Duffield) *towards rr: rdn along over 3f out: styd on appr fnl f: nvr a factor* **33/1**

-555 **5** 1 ½ **Land Hawk (IRE)**[99] 2300 3-9-7 **69** RoystonFfrench 5 60
(J Pearce) *dwlt: sn trcking ldrs: rdn along 3f out: drvn 2f out and sn wknd* **8/1**

4644 **6** nk **Piquante**[18] 4948 3-9-6 **68** EddieAhern 10 58
(M L W Bell) *led 1f: sn stdd and hld up towards rr: smooth hdwy over 3f out: trckd ldrs over 2f out and swtchd rt: sn rdn and btn* **5/2**[2]

0060 **7** 11 **Goswick**[5] 5294 3-7-11 **50** oh2 JamieKyne(5) 7 18
(Micky Hammond) *t.k.h: hld up: a in rr* **50/1**

0020 **8** 5 **Real Desire**[45] 4039 3-8-4 **57** (b[1]) PatrickDonaghy(5) 3 15
(I Semple) *chsd ldrs on inner: rdn along 3f out: sn wknd* **33/1**

2m 5.50s (0.10) **Going Correction** -0.10s/f (Good) **8** Ran SP% **120.6**
Speed ratings (Par 100): **95,91,90,88,87 87,78,74**
toteswinger: 1&2 £2.70, 1&3 £2.60, 2&3 £1.10. CSF £14.94 CT £39.82 TOTE £6.00: £1.60, £1.20, £1.40; EX 12.00 Place 6 £156.03, Place 5 £101.57.
Owner Stephen Curtis & Eric Brook **Bred** S J Curtis - Park Farm Stud **Trained** Sheriff Hutton, N Yorks
■ Steel Trade was withdrawn on vet's advice (10/1, deduct 5p in the £ under R4).

FOCUS
A moderate handicap for three-year-olds.
T/Jkpt: Not won. T/Plt: £76.40 to a £1 stake. Pool: £68,267.48. 652.09 winning tickets. T/Qpdt: £37.10 to a £1 stake. Pool: £4,096.87. 81.50 winning tickets. JR

5344 WARWICK (L-H)
Monday, August 31

OFFICIAL GOING: Good (good to firm in places; 8.6)
Wind: Light, half-behind Weather: Overcast

5525 WARWICK RACECOURSE FOR CONFERENCES H'CAP 6f
1:55 (1:55) (Class 5) (0-70,69) 3-Y-O+ **£2,590** (£770; £385; £192) **Stalls** Low

Form RPR

0424 **1** **Ghost Dancer**[1] 5477 5-9-1 **60** (p) RichardKingscote 8 71+
(J M Bradley) *hld up: pushed along 1/2-way: hdwy over 1f out: rdn to ld wl ins fnl f: r.o* **11/4**[1]

541 **2** nk **Triple Dream**[15] 5065 4-9-2 **64** (p) JackDean(3) 4 74
(J M Bradley) *trckd ldrs: racd keenly: led over 1f out: sn rdn and edgd rt: hdd wl ins fnl f: r.o* **4/1**[3]

-320 **3** 3 **Azure Mist**[11] 5188 4-9-1 **65** AshleyMorgan(5) 3 65
(M H Tompkins) *chsd ldrs: led over 2f out: rdn and hdd over 1f out: no ex ins fnl f* **7/2**[2]

3403 **4** 1 **Peopleton Brook**[16] 5020 7-8-5 **55** (t) RossAtkinson(5) 5 52
(B G Powell) *chsd ldrs: rdn over 1f out: styd on same pce* **16/1**

0006 **5** shd **Blakeshall Diamond**[1] 5480 4-7-12 **50** oh5 DannyBrock(7) 9 47
(A J Chamberlain) *plld hrd: led 5f out: hdd over 2f out: no ex fnl f* **25/1**

1410 **6** ¾ **Chasca (IRE)**[9] 5264 3-9-6 **68** JimCrowley 1 62
(Mrs A J Perrett) *led 1f: trckd ldrs: racd keenly: rdn over 1f out: no ex fnl f* **9/2**

034- **7** 1 ¼ **Sydneysider**[401] 4431 4-9-10 **69** ShaneKelly 2 59
(Eve Johnson Houghton) *s.i.s: sn outpcd: nvr nrr* **9/1**

4045 **8** 1 ½ **Bateleur**[15] 5065 5-9-6 **65** ChrisCatlin 7 51
(M R Channon) *hld up in tch: rdn over 1f out: wknd ins fnl f* **9/1**

1m 11.71s (-0.09) **Going Correction** -0.175s/f (Firm) course record
WFA 3 from 4yo+ 3lb **8** Ran SP% **115.4**
Speed ratings (Par 103): **93,92,88,87,87 86,84,82**
toteswinger: 1&2 £1.90, 1&3 £3.50, 2&3 £2.60. CSF £14.12 CT £38.89 TOTE £3.20: £1.60, £1.30, £1.90; EX 11.80.
Owner E A Hayward **Bred** Floors Farming **Trained** Sedbury, Gloucs

FOCUS
A modest sprint lacking strength in depth with only around half the field coming into the race at or near the top of their form. With the only usual front-runner in the field, Azure Mist, electing not to take on that role, it turned into something of a muddling affair with several of the runners pulling hard early on and all bar one closely bunched turning for home. The form is rated arund the front pair.

5526 TURFTV NURSERY 5f 110y
2:30 (2:31) (Class 5) (0-75,75) 2-Y-O **£2,914** (£867; £433; £216) **Stalls** Low

Form RPR

5006 **1** **Leleyf (IRE)**[10] 5207 2-9-4 **72** ChrisCatlin 3 77
(M R Channon) *mde all: rdn over 1f out: r.o* **8/1**

3343 **2** 1 ½ **Look Whos Next**[20] 4884 2-9-3 **71** RichardMullen 4 71
(E S McMahon) *chsd wnr: rdn and hung lft fr over 1f out: nt run on* **9/2**[2]

2003 **3** nk **Chicita Banana**[12] 5166 2-8-10 **69** MatthewDavies(5) 9 68
(George Baker) *s.i.s: hld up: hdwy over 1f out: rdn and r.o wl ins fnl f: nt rch ldrs* **9/1**

0405 **4** nk **Pherousa**[15] 5060 2-8-8 **62** LiamJones 10 60
(M Blanshard) *hld up in tch: rdn over 1f out: wandered ins fnl f: styd on same pce* **66/1**

1000 **5** 2 ¼ **Itsthursdayalready**[23] 4803 2-9-7 **75** LDettori 6 66
(J G Given) *chsd ldrs: rdn over 1f out: no ex ins fnl f* **15/2**

0535 **6** 1 **Rockabilly Rebel**[16] 5033 2-9-0 **68** RyanMoore 12 55+
(B W Hills) *hld up: styd on u.p fr over 1f out: nt trble ldrs* **6/1**[3]

323 **7** 1 ¼ **Chips O'Toole (IRE)**[11] 5180 2-9-7 **75** MartinDwyer 2 58+
(B J Meehan) *s.i.s: racd keenly and hdwy over 4f out: rdn over 1f out: wknd ins fnl f* **7/2**[1]

663 **8** 1 ¼ **Dixi Heights**[33] 4427 2-8-7 **61** ow1 ShaneKelly 7 40+
(J R Boyle) *dwlt: outpcd: rdn 1/2-way: sme late prog: nvr nrr* **12/1**

2610 **9** 1 ¼ **Velvet Band**[30] 4539 2-9-7 **75** JimCrowley 11 50
(P F I Cole) *prom: rdn over 2f out: wknd fnl f* **14/1**

630 **10** nk **Lairy (IRE)**[20] 4884 2-7-12 **52** oh1 JamieMackay 8 26
(M F Harris) *hld up: racd keenly: rdn over 2f out: n.d* **40/1**

4300 **11** 3 ¼ **Tarrants Way**[21] 4844 2-7-13 **53** (p) AdrianMcCarthy 14 16
(Jennie Candlish) *s.i.s: hld up: rdn over 2f out: sn wknd* **40/1**

0560 **12** 2 ¼ **The Midshipmaid**[7] 5310 2-7-12 **59** ow3 AndrewHeffernan(7) 5 15
(Lucinda Featherstone) *prom: rdn over 2f out: sn wknd* **40/1**

2220 **13** 3 **Listillo (USA)**[30] 4537 2-9-6 **74** (v[1]) JimmyQuinn 1 20
(H J L Dunlop) *dwlt: outpcd* **17/2**

65.66 secs (-0.24) **Going Correction** -0.175s/f (Firm) **13** Ran SP% **121.3**
Speed ratings (Par 94): **94,92,91,91,88 86,85,83,81,81 77,74,70**
toteswinger: 1&2 £15.20, 1&3 £28.80, 2&3 £8.50. CSF £43.82 CT £350.62 TOTE £9.60: £3.30, £2.10, £3.10; EX 60.80.
Owner Box 41 **Bred** Mrs Noelle Walsh **Trained** West Ilsley, Berks

FOCUS
An ordinary nursery with the majority of the runners more exposed than one might ideally like to see in a race like this and most of those that had run in nurseries already having been put in their place.

NOTEBOOK
Leleyf(IRE), with three unplaced efforts in nurseries already to her name, managed to make all which might not say much for the form, but it should be pointed out that the switch to more positive tactics allied to a drop in trip - her most recent run had been at 7f - clearly combined to bring about an improved performance, and earlier in the season she had been considered good enough anyway to contest a couple of Listed races and the Albany Stakes. (op 17-2 tchd 9-1)
Look Whos Next ran his best race to date, but once into the straight and asked for more effort he carried his head badly to one side and looked far from accommodating. He clearly has the ability to win a small race, perhaps in cheekpieces, but needs treating with some caution on this display. (op 5-1)
Chicita Banana ran creditably back in trip while leaving the impression it was plenty sharp enough. She didn't have the best of runs, ending up on the outside having turned for home on the inner, and can probably have this run marked up a little. (op 17-2 tchd 10-1)
Pherousa was never far away, but her head carriage also left something to be desired and, though she was hampered a bit late on, she wouldn't be one to make excuses for. (tchd 80-1)
Itsthursdayalready seemed to have every chance, but couldn't make the frame in a nursery for the second start running and looks high in the handicap. (op 13-2)
Rockabilly Rebel wasn't helped by his outside draw and wide course and never threatened, leaving the impression he needs a step back to 6f. (tchd 11-2)
Chips O'Toole(IRE) seemed to find the trip a bit too far after travelling well behind the leaders into the straight. A return to 5f looks in order. (op 4-1)
Dixi Heights, by Golan and an encouraging eighth on her penultimate run in a race at Windsor that is working out very well, came in for some support but clearly found this test inadequate, soon ridden along but keeping on late. She shouldn't be written off. (op 16-1 tchd 11-1)
Listillo(USA) missed the break and sulked throughout in a change of headgear. He's had plenty of chances and is one to avoid. Official explanation: jockey said colt would not face the visor. (op 8-1)

5527 EUROPEAN BREEDERS' FUND MAIDEN STKS (DIV I) 7f 26y
3:05 (3:06) (Class 5) 2-Y-O **£3,561** (£1,059; £529; £264) **Stalls** Low

Form RPR

4 **1** **Centigrade (IRE)**[44] 4093 2-9-3 0 RyanMoore 2 78+
(W J Haggas) *hld up: hdwy over 2f out: swtchd rt over 1f out: rdn to ld 1f out: r.o* **6/4**[1]

06 **2** ¾ **Start Right**[38] 4286 2-9-3 0 ChrisCatlin 6 76+
(L M Cumani) *chsd ldrs: rdn and ev ch ins fnl f: unable qck nr fin* **20/1**

0 **3** 4 **Spinning Spirit (IRE)**[13] 5129 2-9-3 0 RichardMullen 11 66
(J G Given) *led: rdn and hdd 1f out: no ex ins fnl f* **100/1**

06 **4** nk **Valkov**[18] 4945 2-8-12 0 RichardKingscote 3 60
(Tom Dascombe) *chsd ldr: rdn over 2f out: styd on same pce fnl f* **20/1**

3 **5** 2 ¼ **If I Were A Boy (IRE)**[16] 5026 2-8-12 0 JamesDoyle 1 55
(S Kirk) *prom: rdn over 2f out: wknd ins fnl f* **3/1**[3]

4 **6** ½ **Mufti (IRE)**[17] 5002 2-9-3 0 MartinDwyer 8 59
(B J Meehan) *hld up: effrt over 1f out: nvr trbld ldrs* **9/4**[2]

7 1 ½ **Lisahane Bog** 2-9-3 0 LiamJones 5 55+
(P R Hedger) *s.i.s: in rr: sme hdwy 1/2-way: n.d* **66/1**

0 **8** 1 ¾ **Forgotten Army (IRE)**[35] 4385 2-8-12 0 AshleyMorgan(5) 12 50
(M H Tompkins) *s.i.s: hld up: r.o ins fnl f: nvr nrr* **66/1**

0 **9** 2 ½ **Kilmanseck**[81] 2844 2-9-3 0 ShaneKelly 13 44
(Eve Johnson Houghton) *chsd ldrs tl rdn and wknd over 1f out* **50/1**

60 **10** nk **Meer Und Wind (GER)**[53] 3786 2-8-12 0 JimCrowley 10 38
(P R Webber) *s.i.s: a in rr* **100/1**

06 **11** 1 ½ **Althabea**[46] 4018 2-9-0 0 JackDean(3) 4 40
(Ian Williams) *prom: rdn over 2f out: sn wknd* **100/1**

50 **12** ½ **Themanforacrisis (IRE)**[18] 4945 2-8-10 0 JPFahy(7) 7 38
(R M Beckett) *s.i.s: a in rr* **28/1**

04 **13** ½ **Gabriel's Spirit (IRE)**[16] 5029 2-9-3 0 LDettori 9 37
(Miss Amy Weaver) *hld up: rdn over 2f out: wknd over 1f out* **12/1**

1m 25.59s (0.99) **Going Correction** +0.025s/f (Good) **13** Ran SP% **124.3**
Speed ratings (Par 94): **95,94,89,89,86 86,84,82,79,79 77,76,76**
toteswinger: 1&2 £7.40, 1&3 £25.30, 2&3 £62.00. CSF £40.22 TOTE £2.60: £1.50, £3.80, £12.50; EX 45.00.
Owner Highclere Thoroughbred Racing (Verglas) **Bred** The Irish National Stud **Trained** Newmarket, Suffolk

FOCUS
Few of these had achieved in their short careers so far a performance that would have been good enough in previous years to have won a renewal of this race, but it still looked the stronger division from a form perspective and a few of them had looked open to a fair amount of improvement. The pace wasn't strong, however, and by and large those ridden close up were favoured.

NOTEBOOK
Centigrade(IRE) was one of the leading form fancies and did well in overcoming some more prominently ridden rivals to win with something in hand. He showed a tasty turn of foot early in the straight to get to the front and displayed a good attitude once there and pressed by the runner-up, leaving the impression he was value for a fair bit more than the winning margin. As yet, he holds no fancy entries, but he looks the sort that will develop into a useful sort at least by the end of the season, and is sure to win more races. (op 7-4 tchd 11-8)

Start Right blew what nursery mark he might have had with a much-improved performance, running on strongly to come clear of the rest in the short straight and giving the winner a fright. He is in good hands and looks sure to go one better soon, either at this trip or up at 1m, with this run suggesting maidens as well as nurseries are still an option. (op 16-1)

Spinning Spirit(IRE) looked to have the run of the race out in front but even so stepped up significantly on his recent debut. He is entitled to improve again.

Valkov, who was also prominent throughout, finished close on his heels in fourth having shown limited form in two previous runs, rather confirms that it was an advantage to race close up. (op 22-1)

If I Were A Boy(IRE) appeared to finish a fair third at Newbury on her recent debut when coming home strongly, but was made to look very short of pace on this much quicker track. (op 5-2)

Mufti(IRE) was the only runner of the field holding an entry in one or more of the big juvenile races later this season, but he found himself in a poor position entering the straight and never threatened. Unless he needs further or a more strongly run race, expectations for him will have to be lowered. (op 7-2)

Lisahane Bog, the only newcomer, didn't fare badly after missing the break, and for all the steady pace meant it didn't disadvantage him significantly, he kept on nicely under hands and heels and should improve.

Forgotten Army(IRE) missed the break but ran on and will do better over further in time.

Meer Und Wind(GER) showed enough to suggest that she can be a factor now qualified for low-grade nurseries.

5528 EUROPEAN BREEDERS' FUND MAIDEN STKS (DIV II) 7f 26y

3:40 (3:44) (Class 5) 2-Y-O **£3,561** (£1,059; £529; £264) **Stalls** Low

Form RPR

1 **Sierra Alpha** 2-9-3 0 .... JimCrowley 6 78+
(Mrs A J Perrett) *hld up: swtchd lft and hdwy over 1f out: r.o to ld wl ins fnl f* **28/1**

2 ½ **Dahaam** 2-9-3 0 .... LDettori 7 76+
(Saeed Bin Suroor) *chsd ldrs: rdn to ld over 1f out: edgd lft: hdd wl ins fnl f* **9/2[3]**

2 3 1¾ **King's Parade**[22] 4811 2-9-3 0 .... RyanMoore 4 72
(Sir Michael Stoute) *broke wl and led early: trckd ldr: rdn and ev ch over 1f out: styd on same pce ins fnl f* **11/8[1]**

65 4 ½ **Sounds Of Thunder**[39] 4239 2-8-12 0 .... JimmyQuinn 10 66
(H J L Dunlop) *plld hrd and prom: rdn over 1f out: styd on same pce* **40/1**

0 5 ¾ **Sundream**[18] 4946 2-8-12 0 .... RichardKingscote 3 64
(Tom Dascombe) *sn pushed along to ld: rdn and hdd over 1f out: edgd lft and no ex ins fnl f* **25/1**

55 6 ¾ **Ice Viking (IRE)**[17] 5006 2-9-3 0 .... RichardMullen 2 67
(J G Given) *s.i.s: hld up: racd keenly: shkn up over 2f out: r.o ins fnl f: nt rch ldrs* **16/1**

6 7 2¾ **Ellen Vannin (IRE)**[25] 4701 2-8-12 0 .... ShaneKelly 5 55
(Eve Johnson Houghton) *prom: hung rt 1/2-way: rdn and hung lft over 1f out: sn wknd* **100/1**

8 3¾ **Sefton Park** 2-9-3 0 .... LiamJones 8 51
(C R Egerton) *hld up: bhd fr 1/2-way* **33/1**

0 9 2 **Draco Boy**[19] 4900 2-9-3 0 .... JamesDoyle 1 46
(Andrew Turnell) *trckd ldrs tl rdn over 2f out: sn wknd* **100/1**

4U 10 ½ **New Christmas (USA)**[14] 5109 2-9-3 0 .... MartinDwyer 11 45
(B J Meehan) *nrly fell exiting stalls: a bhd* **15/8[2]**

62 11 5 **Sea Dubai**[26] 4646 2-9-3 0 .... ChrisCatlin 9 32
(R Hannon) *hld up: bhd fr 1/2-way* **9/1**

1m 26.26s (1.66) **Going Correction** +0.025s/f (Good) **11 Ran SP% 125.6**

Speed ratings (Par 94): **91,90,88,87,87 86,83,78,76,75 70**

toteswinger: 1&2 £11.50, 1&3 £7.70, 2&3 £2.70. CSF £154.71 TOTE £35.30: £4.90, £1.50, £1.20; EX 102.00.

Owner K Abdulla **Bred** Millsec Limited **Trained** Pulborough, W Sussex

FOCUS

The slightly weaker of the two divisions judged on achievement so far but arguably the more interesting race, boasting as it did two runners with big-race entries and a couple of newcomers from powerful yards. Interestingly, it was the latter pair that took the first two positions in the end and though both look open to improvement.

NOTEBOOK

Sierra Alpha was unconsidered in the betting but he is related to some top winners in the USA on the female side of his pedigree, and he made a most encouraging debut despite looking very green. On the heels of the leaders turning in, he looked rather unco-ordinated when first asked to pick up but he got the message well inside the last, and passed the post leaving the impression this run will have taught him a lot. He will be suited by a step up to 1m. (tchd 25-1)

Dahaam should also be able to win a similar event kept to this trip at one of the minor tracks. He travelled well into the race and put in a sustained run to lead inside the last, but couldn't fend off the winner's late surge. His Derby entry looks optimistic and his pedigree would suggest he wouldn't want that far anyway. (op 11-2 tchd 6-1)

King's Parade did best of those with previous experience but it's doubtful he improved much if at all on his Leicester debut and probably wants more of a test than he got here to fulfil his potential. He might fall upon a weak maiden next time, but looks one of his stable's lesser lights despite his entries. (op 15-8 tchd 5-4)

Sounds Of Thunder can go into nurseries now with a good run behind her, following a setback last time. She's crying out for a much stiffer test of stamina and might need even further than 1m this year.

Sundream showed up well in front for a long way before inexperience got the better of her late on. She should improve again. (op 22-1)

Ice Viking(IRE) is another stoutly bred and sure to be of more interest in staying nurseries from now on, given the way he caught the eye keeping on nicely. (op 20-1)

New Christmas(USA) looks one to tread very cautiously with. He clearly hadn't learned from his experience last time and nearly went down after falling forwards leaving the stalls. He was allowed time to get back into the race, but made no impression in the straight and was eased. (op 2-1)

Sea Dubai was also disappointing. He was well adrift turning in and, though this clearly wasn't his running, he has something to prove now. (op 8-1)

5529 RICOH ARENA CONDITIONS STKS 7f 26y

4:15 (4:15) (Class 3) 3-Y-O+ **£7,771** (£2,312; £1,155; £577) **Stalls** Low

Form RPR

5260 1 **Taqdeyr**[23] 4796 4-8-11 99 .... PhilipRobinson 7 103+
(M A Jarvis) *mde all: rdn over 1f out: hung lft ins fnl f: styd on* **9/4[2]**

3301 2 1¼ **Khor Dubai (IRE)**[14] 5092 3-8-9 102 .... (v) LDettori 2 101+
(Saeed Bin Suroor) *s.i.s: hld up: hdwy over 1f out: rdn to chse wnr ins fnl f: nt qckn nr fin* **11/8[1]**

1124 3 1½ **Cyflymder (IRE)**[16] 5025 3-8-6 94 .... RyanMoore 5 94
(R Hannon) *chsd ldrs: rdn over 1f out: styd on* **9/2[3]**

1230 4 1 **Barons Spy (IRE)**[10] 5206 8-8-11 87 .... JamesDoyle 1 93
(R J Price) *chsd ldr 2f: wnt 2nd again over 2f out: rdn and ev ch over 1f out: no ex ins fnl f* **25/1**

-035 5 3¾ **Appalachian Trail (IRE)**[36] 4352 8-8-11 100 .... MartinDwyer 3 83
(I Semple) *hld up: rdn over 2f out: eased whn btn ins fnl f* **11/1**

2114 6 15 **Sudden Impact (IRE)**[15] 5069 4-8-6 90 .... (e) ChrisCatlin 6 38
(Paul Green) *s.s: hdwy to chse ldr 5f out: hung rt 3f out: sn rdn and wknd* **10/1**

1m 23.4s (-1.20) **Going Correction** +0.025s/f (Good)

WFA 3 from 4yo+ 5lb **6 Ran SP% 112.3**

Speed ratings (Par 107): **107,105,103,102,98 81**

toteswinger: 1&2 £1.40, 1&3 £2.60, 2&3 £1.90. CSF £5.74 TOTE £3.80: £1.70, £1.40; EX 7.20.

Owner Richie Baines & Stephen Dartnell **Bred** Darley **Trained** Newmarket, Suffolk

FOCUS

A useful conditions event, though only three really had a leading chance at the weights on adjusted official ratings and, with conditions too fast round here for one of them, it not surprisingly developed into a shoot-out between the two market leaders, though they did not finish in the order the market expected after the eventual winner was allowed his own way in front. The form is limited by the fourth and the first two were a little off their recent best.

NOTEBOOK

Taqdeyr had won only on Polytrack up to now but he also had some good form to his name on turf. He was inclined to be keener than his rider would have liked in front but his cause was helped no end by being left alone and, after saving a bit turning for home, he stretched out well in the straight to hold on unchallenged. He was drifting left late on, though, and how much he would have found had his rivals put it to him sooner is open to question. (op 11-4 tchd 7-2)

Khor Dubai(IRE) isn't the easiest to ride or place, being high in the weights and having always come up short in Listed/Group races. For all he had the highest official rating of these, he ran as well as he was allowed to given the amount he was set to do relative to the winner, and didn't seem to do anything wrong. He'll probably go back into handicaps now, but will do well to find one as soft as the one he recent won at Kempton. (tchd Evens)

Cyflymder(IRE) has made great strides this season but was ridden with more restraint than when he was making his way up the weights. He never promised to finish any closer but third place was a creditable effort considering where he was two months back. This run suggests he is only a handicapper, though, albeit a useful one. (tchd 4-1 and 5-1)

Barons Spy(IRE) had little chance at the weights but was given the best possible opportunity of a frame finish by tracking the leader, and duly rewarded his connections with a good effort. (op 20-1)

Appalachian Trail(IRE) is a shadow of his former self, but just hinted at retaining some ability, and might yet be of interest if he gets dropped a fair chunk in the weights for this and has his favoured soft ground next time. (op 10-1)

Sudden Impact(IRE) looked a right madam, missing the break, running wide then carrying her head high and dropping away. She'd been reliable before this and something was clearly troubling her before the trip became an issue. Official explanation: jockey said filly was unsuited by the bottom bend (op 11-1 tchd 8-1)

5530 SYD MERCER MEMORIAL H'CAP 1m 6f 213y

4:50 (4:52) (Class 5) (0-70,69) 3-Y-O+ **£3,238** (£963; £481; £240) **Stalls** Low

Form RPR

0341 1 **Saborido (USA)**[18] 4951 3-8-11 65 .... JimCrowley 6 72
(Mrs A J Perrett) *led 1f: chsd ldrs: rdn to ld over 1f out: edgd lft and hdd ins fnl f: rallied to ld towards fin* **7/2[1]**

6564 2 shd **Pseudonym (IRE)**[5] 5346 7-9-10 65 .... (t) JamieMackay 8 72
(M F Harris) *hld up: racd keenly: hdwy over 2f out: rdn over 1f out: led and hung lft ins fnl f: hdd towards fin* **15/2[3]**

2260 3 ¾ **My Mate Max**[9] 5252 4-9-10 68 .... (p) RussellKennemore[(3)] 9 74
(R Hollinshead) *led after 1f: rdn over 3f out: hdd over 1f out: hmpd wl ins fnl f: styd on* **18/1**

20/0 4 nse **Shore Thing (IRE)**[33] 4417 6-9-12 67 .... (t) MartinDwyer 3 73+
(C R Egerton) *s.s: drvn along early in rr: swtchd lft and hdwy over 1f out: sn rdn: styng on whn hmpd wl ins fnl f* **8/1**

53 5 nse **Zuwaar**[9] 5252 4-9-7 69 .... (tp) JPFahy[(7)] 10 75
(Ian Williams) *hld up: racd keenly: hdwy 2f out: rdn and hung lft fnl f: styd on* **9/2[2]**

2115 6 2 **Rare Ruby (IRE)**[15] 5068 5-9-11 66 .... ShaneKelly 11 69
(Jennie Candlish) *hld up: hdwy 6f out: rdn and hung lft fr over 1f out: no ex wl ins fnl f* **9/2[2]**

43-0 7 6 **Alvee (IRE)**[35] 4388 4-9-7 62 .... RichardMullen 12 57
(J R Fanshawe) *mid-div: hdwy 1/2-way: rdn over 2f out: wknd fnl f* **16/1**

00-2 8 2¾ **Transfered (IRE)**[17] 5011 3-7-12 59 ow5 .... AndrewHeffernan[(7)] 5 50
(Lucinda Featherstone) *hld up: nt clr run over 3f out: sn rdn: wknd over 1f out* **8/1**

4/01 9 3¾ **Mexican Bob**[19] 4893 6-9-10 65 .... RichardKingscote 13 51
(C E Longsdon) *prom: chsd ldr 12f out tl rdn over 2f out: wknd over 1f out* **8/1**

5260 10 7 **Thorny Mandate**[10] 5210 7-8-11 52 .... JimmyQuinn 4 29
(W M Brisbourne) *prom: racd keenly: rdn over 2f out: wknd sn after* **20/1**

000/ 11 15 **Smart John**[18] 4910 9-9-1 56 .... ChrisCatlin 7 13
(S T Lewis) *chsd ldrs: lost pl over 5f out: wknd over 3f out* **50/1**

3m 17.71s (-1.29) **Going Correction** +0.025s/f (Good)

WFA 3 from 4yo+ 13lb **11 Ran SP% 121.6**

Speed ratings (Par 103): **104,103,103,103,103 102,99,97,95,92 84**

toteswinger: 1&2 £6.50, 1&3 £17.70, 2&3 £29.90. CSF £31.31 CT £427.08 TOTE £4.10: £1.60, £2.70, £5.20; EX 33.10.

Owner Tracey, Cotton, James, Slade **Bred** R D Hubbard And R Masterson **Trained** Pulborough, W Sussex

■ Stewards' Enquiry : J P Fahy three-day ban: careless riding (Sep 14-16)

FOCUS

The margin was tight at the end of the day in what was quite a competitive race for all its limitations, with plenty of runners coming here in good form. The pace was generous, and the result makes sense despite the bunch finish.

Rare Ruby(IRE) Official explanation: jockey said mare was unsuited by the good (good to firm in places) ground

5531 WARWICKRACECOURSE.CO.UK MAIDEN STKS 1m 2f 188y

5:25 (5:29) (Class 5) 3-Y-O+ **£2,914** (£867; £433; £216) **Stalls** Low

Form RPR

02 1 **Mathaaq**[17] 4979 3-9-3 0 .... PhilipRobinson 13 75+
(M A Jarvis) *mid-div: hdwy 1/2-way: rdn to ld ins fnl f: styd on* **11/4[2]**

6 2 nk **Duke Of Burgundy (FR)**[28] 4599 6-9-12 0 .... ShaneKelly 2 74
(Jennie Candlish) *hld up: hdwy over 5f out: nt clr run over 3f out and over 1f out: swtchd rt sn after: rdn and ev ch ins fnl f: styd on* **14/1**

0 3 ½ **Country Road (IRE)**[30] 4519 3-9-3 0 .... AdrianMcCarthy 5 74
(P W Chapple-Hyam) *led 3f: chsd ldr tl led again over 4f out: rdn and hung lft fr over 1f out: hdd and unable qck ins fnl f* **11/2**

40 4 1 **Bourne**[88] 2640 3-9-3 0 .... ChrisCatlin 11 72+
(L M Cumani) *a.p: rdn over 2f out: styd on* **16/1**

222- 5 shd **Custody (IRE)**[305] 7098 3-9-3 80 .... (b[1]) RyanMoore 16 72
(Sir Michael Stoute) *hld up: hdwy over 2f out: swtchd rt over 1f out: sn rdn: styd on: nt rch ldrs* **5/2[1]**

5-30 6 10 **Alhaque (USA)**[109] 2002 3-9-3 80 .... JimCrowley 8 54
(W J Haggas) *prom: rdn over 3f out: wknd over 1f out* **7/2[3]**

06 7 *hd* **Laura Land**[10] 5205 3-8-12 0 ... LiamJones 1 48
(W M Brisbourne) *chsd ldrs: rdn over 3f out: wknd over 1f out* **40/1**
8 *6* **Elms School Story** 3-8-12 0 ... MartinDwyer 6 37
(Miss Venetia Williams) *s.i.s: sn pushed along in rr: nvr nrr* **20/1**
9 *hd* **Fairplaytomyself** 4-9-0 0 ... TobyAtkinson(7) 14 37
(P W Hiatt) *s.i.s: hld up: hung rt 8f out: rdn over 2f out: sn wknd* **50/1**
0 10 *3 3/4* **Just Call Me Dave (USA)**[17] 4974 3-9-3 0 ... JamesDoyle 4 35
(Paul Green) *sn pushed along: a in rr: wknd over 2f out* **33/1**
0 11 *shd* **Legend Of Greece (IRE)**[21] 4854 3-8-10 0 ... JPFahy(7) 10 35
(Mrs N Smith) *in rr and rdn 8f out: wknd over 2f out* **100/1**
30 12 *2 1/4* **Iketi (GR)**[136] 1329 3-8-12 0 ... IvaMilickova 3 26
(Jane Chapple-Hyam) *mid-div: hmpd and lost pl after 1f: n.d after: wknd 3f out* **40/1**
0- 13 *9* **Obvious**[343] 6167 3-8-12 0 ... AmirQuinn 17 10
(Miss J Feilden) *prom: led 8f out: hdd over 4f out: rdn whn n.m.r wl over 2f out: sn wknd* **33/1**
14 *9* **Beyonda Dream** 3-8-7 0 ... JPHamblett(5) 15 —
(Lucinda Featherstone) *s.s: a bhd* **100/1**
00- 15 *16* **Ditzy Diva**[327] 6581 3-8-9 0 ... RussellKennemore(3) 9 —
(B G Powell) *chsd ldrs: rdn 5f out: wknd over 3f out* **80/1**

2m 20.17s (-0.93) **Going Correction** +0.025s/f (Good)
WFA 3 from 4yo+ 9lb **15** Ran SP% **126.1**
Speed ratings (Par 103): **104,103,103,102,102 95,95,90,90,87 87,86,79,73,61**
toteswinger: 1&2 £8.90, 1&3 £5.60, 2&3 £17.60. CSF £39.86 TOTE £3.40: £1.40, £4.10, £2.40; EX 48.60.
Owner Hamdan Al Maktoum **Bred** Shadwell Estate Company Limited **Trained** Newmarket, Suffolk

FOCUS
With the pair with the best public form both disappointing again, this race probably doesn't have great strength to it, something probably underlined by the fact the first five finished on top of each other. However, among them a couple of unexposed sorts from some good stables still look to have more to offer and some winners should emerge from it. The pace looked fair.

5532 ENTERTAIN CLIENTS AT WARWICK RACECOURSE H'CAP 1m 2f 188y
5:55 (5:56) (Class 4) (0-80,85) 3-Y-O+ £4,857 (£1,445; £722; £360) Stalls Low

Form RPR
4306 1 **Jawaab (IRE)**[9] 5266 5-9-8 **73** ... RichardMullen 3 83+
(Mark Buckley) *hld up in tch: nt clr run and lost pl over 2f out: hdwy over 1f out: rdn to ld nr fin* **7/2**[2]
3313 2 *1/2* **Souter Point (USA)**[15] 5062 3-8-12 **79** ... JPFahy(7) 13 86
(R Charlton) *hld up in tch: racd keenly: led over 1f out: sn rdn: edgd lft and hdd nr fin* **11/4**[1]
0300 3 *hd* **Holden Eagle**[16] 5034 4-9-5 **73** ... JackDean(3) 10 80
(A G Newcombe) *hld up: plld hrd: hdwy over 1f out: rdn and hung rt ins fnl f: r.o* **33/1**
-540 4 *1 1/4* **Dove Cottage (IRE)**[15] 5062 7-9-1 **66** ... ChrisCatlin 5 70
(W S Kittow) *led: rdn and hdd over 1f out: styd on same pce ins fnl f* **16/1**
0334 5 *1* **Calaloo (IRE)**[63] 3466 3-9-2 **76** ... (b[1]) MartinDwyer 8 79
(C R Egerton) *s.i.s: plld hrd and hdwy to trck ldr after 1f: rdn and ev ch over 1f out: styd on same pce* **14/1**
1311 6 *1/2* **Love In The Park**[24] 4745 4-9-2 **70** ... JackMitchell(3) 11 72
(R Brotherton) *hld up: rdn over 3f out: hdwy over 1f out: styd on same pce ins fnl f* **8/1**
-145 7 *1 1/4* **Latin Scholar (IRE)**[18] 4957 4-9-10 **75** ... JimmyQuinn 7 74
(A King) *chsd ldrs: rdn over 1f out: styd on same pce fnl f* **5/1**[3]
-552 8 *1 1/4* **Lyceana**[18] 4948 4-9-10 **75** ... PhilipRobinson 12 72
(M A Jarvis) *hld up: hdwy 1/2-way: rdn and hung lft over 1f out: no ex* **7/1**
0302 9 *1/2* **Maybe I Wont**[20] 4880 4-8-6 **62** ... JPHamblett(5) 9 58
(Lucinda Featherstone) *trckd ldrs: racd keenly: rdn and hung rt over 1f out: wknd ins fnl f* **14/1**
3013 10 *1 1/4* **Ross Moor**[33] 4437 7-8-13 **64** ... JimCrowley 1 58
(Mike Murphy) *dwlt: a in rr* **12/1**
6050 11 *9* **Flying Squad (UAE)**[10] 5227 5-8-10 **61** ... JamieMackay 4 39
(M F Harris) *stdd s: hld up: a in rr: wknd 3f out* **40/1**

2m 21.22s (0.12) **Going Correction** +0.025s/f (Good)
WFA 3 from 4yo+ 9lb **11** Ran SP% **121.5**
Speed ratings (Par 105): **100,99,99,98,97 97,96,95,95,94 87**
toteswinger: 1&2 £4.00, 1&3 £23.30, 2&3 £21.70. CSF £14.06 CT £279.81 TOTE £4.60: £1.90, £1.60, £5.70; EX 16.40 Place 6: £31.59 Place 5: £23.14.
Owner C C Buckley **Bred** Hascombe And Valiant Studs **Trained** Castle Bytham, Stanford
■ Stewards' Enquiry : J P Fahy five-day ban: used whip with excessive force (Sep 17-20 + 29)

FOCUS
A handicap in which the majority of the field came into the race near or at the top of their game, but it was run at something of a muddling pace for much of the way and for all the market leaders came to the fore. The first two are almost certainly better than the result suggests relative to the remainder and the overall result probably isn't that dependable.
Lyceana Official explanation: jockey said filly was unsuited by the track
T/Plt: £37.40 to a £1 stake. Pool: £35,913.94. 699.48 winning tickets. T/Qpdt: £8.30 to a £1 stake. Pool: £2,234.04. 198.10 winning tickets. CR

5533 - 5538a (Foreign Racing) - See Raceform Interactive

5458 GALWAY (R-H)
Monday, August 31

OFFICIAL GOING: Heavy (last 2 races abandoned due to torrential rain)
last two races abandoned due to waterlogging.

5539a ARDILAUN HOTEL OYSTER STKS (LISTED RACE) 1m 4f
6:55 (7:00) 3-Y-O+ £33,182 (£9,735; £4,638; £1,580)

RPR
1 **Aliyfa (IRE)**[9] 5277 3-8-10 104 ... MJKinane 1 102+
(John M Oxx, Ire) *chsd ldrs in 3rd: racd wd for much: rdn fr 4f out: clsd and chal in 2nd ins fnl f: sn led and styd on best* **11/4**[2]
2 *1/2* **The Bull Hayes (IRE)**[18] 4962 3-8-13 102 ... (b) FMBerry 5 102
(Mrs John Harrington, Ire) *trckd ldr in 2nd: led after 1/2-way: strly pressed and hdd over 2f out: rallied to have ev ch fnl f: kpt on same pce cl home* **9/2**[3]
3 *4 1/2* **Allied Powers (IRE)**[37] 4329 4-9-12 ... DPMcDonogh 4 100+
(M L W Bell) *in tch towards rr in 4th: racd wd for much: 3rd after 1/2-way: 2nd fr 4f out: led over 2f out: sn rdn clr: tired and reduced ld ins fnl f: sn hdd & wknd in 3rd* **1/1**[1]
4 *5 1/2* **Ghimaar**[9] 5277 4-9-9 103 ... (b) PJSmullen 6 86
(D K Weld, Ire) *in tch in rr: racd wd for much: rdn in 4th under 5f out: sn no imp* **11/1**
5 *dist* **Red Rock Canyon (IRE)**[15] 5076 5-9-9 103 ... (p) JMurtagh 2 —
(A P O'Brien, Ire) *led: hdd after 1/2-way: qckly wknd to rr: sn eased: t.o* **12/1**

3m 3.82s (20.72)
WFA 3 from 4yo+ 10lb **5** Ran SP% **110.9**
CSF £15.02 TOTE £3.00: £2.50, £1.50; DF 10.60.
Owner H H Aga Khan **Bred** Hh The Aga Khan's Studs Sc **Trained** Currabeg, Co Kildare

FOCUS
A Listed race run in atrocious conditions which was highlighted by the fact two races still due to be run on the card were abandoned.

NOTEBOOK
Aliyfa(IRE) deserved a change of fortune. Kinane reportedly identified a strip of ground that was less unraceable and he stuck to it. Having been a bit outpaced coming out of the dip, his filly responded really well in the straight and stayed on dourly all the way to the line. At least a near farcical race didn't have a result to match. (op 11/4 tchd 3/1)
The Bull Hayes(IRE) is another dour stayer in the making who appreciates testing conditions, and if he goes hurdling this winter he should make a proper one. He tracked the lead, couldn't go with the favourite when he went for his race off the home bend, but his stamina also really came into play as he rallied strongly inside the last and he might have got there in another few strides. (op 9/2 tchd 5/1)
Allied Powers(IRE) emptied out completely inside the final furlong. He travelled best throughout and McDonogh obviously had no doubts about this horse's stamina as he sent him to the front before the turn into the straight as he opened up a lead. It proved an unwise move as this horse was running on the spot inside the last furlong and in the end finished a well beaten third. (op 4/5)
T/Jkpt: @375.00. Pool of @10,000.00 - 20 winning units. T/Plt: Not won. II

4586 LES LANDES
Monday, August 31

OFFICIAL GOING: Firm

5540a S G HAMBROS H'CAP 1m 100y
3:05 (3:05) 3-Y-O+ £1,460 (£525; £315)

RPR
1 **Grenane (IRE)**[29] 6-8-11 ... JemmaMarshall —
(Mrs A Malzard, Jersey) **4/1**[3]
2 *shd* **Secret Assassin (IRE)**[15] 6-9-11 ... EmmettStack —
(Mrs J L Le Brocq, Jersey) **2/1**[1]
3 *2* **Buckie Massa**[15] 5-10-12 ... AntonyProcter —
(J S O Arthur, Jersey) **7/2**[2]
4 *4* **King Kenny**[29] 4-9-7 ... MattieBatchelor —
(Mrs A Malzard, Jersey) **11/1**
5 *1* **Carr Hall (IRE)**[15] 6-8-12 ow5 ... VinceSlattery —
(Mrs J L Le Brocq, Jersey) **4/1**[3]
6 *1* **La Verte Rue (USA)**[15] 3-8-11 ... MrNCook —
(Mrs A Malzard, Jersey) **4/1**[3]
7 *3* **Wall Street Runner**[15] 8-9-8 ... MrRJKirk —
(Mrs J L Le Brocq, Jersey) **5/1**
8 *3* **Cool Libby (IRE)**[41] 4177 3-8-5 oh6 ... AmyBaker —
(A B Haynes) **6/1**
9 *15* **Blue Savanna**[15] 9-8-8 oh40 ow3 ... PVarley —
(H Le S Vautier, Jersey) **18/1**
10 *1 1/2* **Cronkyvoddy**[15] 8-8-6 oh10 ow1 ... (v) KylieManser —
(Mrs A Malzard, Jersey) **11/2**

1m 51.0s (111.00)
WFA 3 from 4yo+ 6lb **10** Ran SP% **175.5**
Owner Trevor & Mrs Pat Gallienne **Bred** Kilnamoragh Stud **Trained** St Ouen, Jersey

5541a ANIMAL HEALTH TRUST H'CAP 5f
4:50 (4:51) 3-Y-O+ £1,460 (£525; £315)

RPR
1 **Top Level (IRE)**[15] 6-9-10 ... AmyBaker —
(Ms V S Lucas, Jersey) **11/4**[3]
2 *1 1/2* **Toggle**[15] 5-10-4 ... MattieBatchelor —
(Ms V S Lucas, Jersey) **7/2**
3 *hd* **Talamahana**[25] 4690 4-10-10 ... (v) EmmettStack —
(A B Haynes) **9/4**[2]
4 *1* **Majestical (IRE)**[15] 7-10-10 ... (p) AntonyProcter —
(J S O Arthur, Jersey) **11/8**[1]
5 *2 1/2* **Spinning Bailiwick**[98] 3-10-5 ... (b) MrRHodson —
(Ms V S Lucas, Jersey) **8/1**
6 *6* **Fast Freddie**[15] 5-10-12 ... AdamJones —
(Mrs A Malzard, Jersey) **3/1**
7 *3/4* **Rope Bridge (IRE)**[15] 4-10-11 ... MrRJKirk —
(Mrs J L Le Brocq, Jersey) **13/1**
8 *4* **Highland Flight**[15] 11-10-8 ... VinceSlattery —
(J S O Arthur, Jersey) **8/1**

69.00 secs (69.00)
WFA 3 from 4yo+ 2lb **8** Ran SP% **176.1**
Owner The Sterling Partnership **Bred** Kildare Racing Syndicate **Trained** Jersey

4811 LEICESTER (R-H)
Tuesday, September 1

OFFICIAL GOING: Good to firm (good in places; 8.5)
Wind: fresh, behind Weather: Cloudy with sunny spells giving way to a heavy shower prior to the 3-50

5542 EUROPEAN BREEDERS' FUND APOLLO MAIDEN STKS 7f 9y
2:20 (2:21) (Class 4) 2-Y-O £4,857 (£1,445; £722; £360) Stalls Low

Form RPR
2 1 **Markazzi**[18] 4985 2-9-3 0 ... RHills 8 88+
(Sir Michael Stoute) *hld up in tch: led over 1f out: r.o wl: eased toward fin* **4/7**[1]
4 2 *1 3/4* **Sand Skier**[18] 5006 2-9-3 0 ... RoystonFfrench 11 81
(M Johnston) *chsd ldrs: led 2f out: rdn and hdd over 1f out: styd on same pce ins fnl f* **25/1**

3 *4* **Top Spin (IRE)**[51] 3893 2-9-3 0 .... DMGrant 5 71
(John Joseph Murphy, Ire) *a.p: rdn over 2f out: styd on same pce fnl f* **66/1**

00 4 *hd* **Caucus**[18] 4985 2-9-3 0 .... EddieAhern 3 70
(J L Dunlop) *prom: rdn: hung lft and outpcd over 2f out: styd on fr over 1f out* **200/1**

22 5 *1 1/2* **Rjeef (IRE)**[90] 2610 2-9-0 0 .... AhmedAjtebi(3) 7 66
(C E Brittain) *chsd ldr: led over 2f out: sn rdn: hung lft and hdd: no ex fnl f* **20/1**

3 6 *nk* **Cultivar**[18] 4985 2-9-3 0 .... MichaelHills 6 66
(B W Hills) *hld up: hdwy over 2f out: shkn up over 1f out: jinked lft and no ex ins fnl f* **5/1**[2]

7 *nk* **Quick Reaction** 2-9-3 0 .... PatDobbs 10 65
(R Hannon) *prom: outpcd 3f out: n.d after* **50/1**

8 *1/2* **Official Style** 2-9-3 0 .... RyanMoore 14 64+
(Sir Michael Stoute) *s.i.s: hld up: styd on appr fnl f: nvr nrr* **10/1**[3]

9 *3/4* **The Rectifier (USA)** 2-9-3 0 .... TPQueally 1 62
(Stef Liddiard) *s.s: hdwy 1/2-way: outpcd over 2f out: n.d after* **200/1**

10 *3/4* **Mr Irons (USA)** 2-8-12 0 .... Louis-PhilippeBeuzelin(5) 15 60
(Sir Michael Stoute) *hld up: rdn over 1f out: n.d* **50/1**

0 11 *5* **Finest Reserve (IRE)**[20] 4908 2-9-3 0 .... ChrisCatlin 16 47
(M R Channon) *s.i.s: sn pushed along: a in rr* **66/1**

0 12 *1 1/4* **Knowledgeable**[19] 4933 2-9-3 0 .... DavidProbert 4 44
(B Palling) *led: rdn and hdd over 2f out: sn wknd* **300/1**

4 13 *11* **Firefly Mustique**[26] 4717 2-9-3 0 .... DO'Donohoe 9 17
(George Baker) *sn pushed along: a in rr: wknd over 2f out* **200/1**

14 *1* **Futurist** 2-9-3 0 .... LDettori 2 14
(Saeed Bin Suroor) *hld up: sme hdwy 3f out: wknd over 2f out* **12/1**

1m 23.47s (-2.73) **Going Correction** -0.30s/f (Firm) **14** Ran SP% **114.4**
Speed ratings (Par 97): **103,101,96,96,94 94,93,93,92,91 85,84,71,70**
toteswinger: 1&2 £6.30, 1&3 £14.30, 2&3 £49.50. CSF £24.21 TOTE £1.50: £1.10, £3.40, £9.40; EX 17.20.
Owner Hamdan Al Maktoum **Bred** Miss R J Dobson **Trained** Newmarket, Suffolk

FOCUS
Often a good maiden - recent winners include Parthenon, Ibn Khaldun and Dijeerr - and this looked another good edition. That said, a time only 0.63 seconds quicker than the 58-rated Aegean Destiny managed in the following juvenile seller tempers enthusiasm somewhat. They tended to race up the middle of the track.

NOTEBOOK
Markazzi, who holds entries the Champagne Stakes, Royal Lodge, Dewhurst and Racing Post Trophy, confirmed the good impression he made when runner-up on his debut at Newbury. Fitted with a cross-noseband, he settled okay, close up without cover, and found plenty when asked. Richard Hills described the winner as "a very good horse" and this son of Dansili deserves his chance in a decent race. (op 1-2)
Sand Skier ◆ improved significantly on the form he showed on his debut over 6f at Nottingham. Although ultimately no match for the winner, there was much to like about the way he stuck on for pressure and pulled well clear of the remainder. A similar race looks his for the taking. (op 28-1)
Top Spin(IRE) showed ability on his debut on soft ground over this trip at the Curragh. An entry in the Group 2 Beresford Stakes suggests he is well regarded.
Caucus seemed to hit a flat spot when coming under pressure over 2f out and ran on all too late. He's crying out for an increase in distance and will want even further than 1m before long. An interesting horse for nurseries and/or handicaps next year.
Rjeef(IRE), up in trip, wasn't beaten through a lack of stamina. He hung left under pressure and simply wasn't good enough. Nurseries are now an option and he should find easier opportunities. (op 28-1)
Cultivar was only two and a half lengths behind today's winner on his debut at Newbury, so this was disappointing. He was held when momentarily throwing his head up inside the furlong. (op 9-2 tchd 11-2)
Quick Reaction made a respectable debut and is entitled to improve, especially when stepped up in trip. (op 66-1)
Official Style, a stablemate of the winner, was never dangerous but made some late headway. He's likely to do better over a little further. (op 12-1)
Futurist hails from a stable having a good run with their two-year-olds, but he showed nothing. (op 16-1 tchd 20-1)

5543 RANCLIFFE (S) STKS — 7f 9y
2:50 (2:51) (Class 6) 2-Y-O — **£1,942** (£578; £288; £144) **Stalls** Low

Form — RPR

603 1 **Aegean Destiny**[26] 4689 2-8-7 58 .... RyanMoore 4 65+
(R Hannon) *chsd ldrs: rdn to ld over 1f out: styd on wl* **3/1**[1]

10 2 *1 1/4* **Ragsta (IRE)**[48] 3978 2-8-12 64 .... JimCrowley 6 67
(R Hannon) *trckd ldrs: led over 2f out: rdn and hdd over 1f out: hung lft ins fnl f: styd on same pce* **10/3**[2]

3 *7* **Springwell Giant (IRE)** 2-8-5 0 .... DeclanCannon(7) 7 49+
(A J McCabe) *dwlt: outpcd: styd on u.p ins fnl f: nrst fin* **28/1**

00 4 *2 1/4* **The Great Husk (IRE)**[25] 4757 2-8-12 0 .... LPKeniry 12 44
(J S Moore) *prom: edgd lft 6f out: rdn 1/2-way: styd on same pce appr fnl f* **25/1**

6030 5 *nse* **Lady Lefroy (IRE)**[11] 5207 2-8-7 63 .... TonyHamilton 11 39
(R A Fahey) *prom: hmpd and lost pl after 1f: sn pushed along in rr: hdwy u.p over 1f out: n.d* **15/2**

603 6 *1* **Raine Supreme**[18] 4973 2-8-7 56 .... RichardMullen 16 36
(E S McMahon) *chsd ldrs: rdn over 2f out: wknd over 1f out* **7/1**[3]

030 7 *2 3/4* **Dream Of Gerontius (IRE)**[94] 2494 2-8-7 50 .... (b[1]) PatDobbs 15 29
(R Hannon) *sn pushed along in rr: nvr nrr* **22/1**

530 8 *1 3/4* **Dancing Poppy**[56] 3716 2-8-7 63 .... ChrisCatlin 14 25
(M R Channon) *prom: rdn over 2f out: wknd over 1f out* **12/1**

6056 9 *2* **Riffelalp (IRE)**[26] 4699 2-8-7 57 .... EddieAhern 8 20
(Eve Johnson Houghton) *mid-div: hmpd 6f out: in rr and rdn 1/2-way: n.d* **12/1**

40 10 *1/2* **Casey's Rebel (IRE)**[25] 4757 2-8-7 0 .... JerryO'Dwyer 9 19
(M G Quinlan) *sn led: rdn and hdd over 2f out: sn edgd lft: wknd over 1f out* **50/1**

03 11 *1 1/4* **Press To Reset**[8] 5319 2-8-9 0 .... JackDean(3) 3 21
(W G M Turner) *prom: rdn over 4f out: wknd over 2f out* **28/1**

00 12 *6* **Inittowinit**[56] 3716 2-8-7 0 .... (b[1]) DavidProbert 18 —
(W R Muir) *prom tl rdn and wknd over 2f out* **20/1**

00 13 *7* **Sputnik One (IRE)**[20] 4915 2-8-12 0 .... (b[1]) LukeMorris 2 —
(J S Moore) *in rr and drvn along over 4f out: wknd 3f out* **100/1**

606 14 *4 1/2* **Drews Lane**[8] 5319 2-8-7 0 .... (tp) TolleyDean 13 —
(W G M Turner) *stdd s: hld up: a in rr* **40/1**

15 *1 1/4* **City Line (IRE)**[31] 4555 2-8-12 0 .... DMGrant 5 —
(John Joseph Murphy, Ire) *hld up: hdwy 1/2-way: sn rdn: wknd over 2f out* **12/1**

1m 24.1s (-2.10) **Going Correction** -0.30s/f (Firm) **15** Ran SP% **120.7**
Speed ratings (Par 93): **100,98,90,88,87 86,83,81,79,78 77,70,62,57,55**
toteswinger: 1&2 £3.90, 1&3 £28.80, 2&3 £29.00. CSF £11.30 TOTE £3.10: £1.30, £2.60, £8.60; EX 10.30.The winner was bought in for 7,500gns. Ragsta was claimed by G Blum £6,000.
Owner Theobalds Stud **Bred** Theobalds Stud **Trained** East Everleigh, Wilts

FOCUS
A strong race by selling standards and the time was not too bad compared with the earlier good-looking maiden won by Markazzi, being only 0.63 seconds slower. They raced middle to stands' side and the near rail looked a big advantage. The first two finished well clear and showed strong form for the grade.

NOTEBOOK
Aegean Destiny proved well suited by the step up to 7f and looked better than a 58-rated filly, even though she raced against the favoured near rail late on. It wasn't a total surprise connections went to 7,500gns to buy her back. (op 11-2)
Ragsta(IRE) emerges with a deal of credit considering her winning stablemate had the benefit of the rail in the closing stages, whereas she raced slightly wider. Clear of the remainder, she looks a reasonable type for the level and was claimed for £6,000. (op 5-2 tchd 7-2)
Springwell Giant(IRE), an already gelded first foal of a mare who was placed over 5f, struggled to lay up for most of the way and was still well behind 2f out, but he fairly rattled home once switched over to the advantageous stands' rail. He might be flattered, considering where he raced, but he's entitled to be sharper next time. (op 25-1)
The Great Husk(IRE) was having his third start but rather surprisingly still looked a bit green. He might yet do better. (op 16-1)
Lady Lefroy(IRE) seemed happy enough early on, but she was knocked off her stride when squeezed out after about a furlong and immediately came off the bridle. After struggling to recover, she only ran on when the race was as good as over and looks a bit of a lightweight. (tchd 7-1)

5544 SIS H'CAP — 7f 9y
3:20 (3:21) (Class 5) (0-70,70) 3-Y-O+ — **£2,914** (£867; £433; £216) **Stalls** Low

Form — RPR

6405 1 **Balata**[21] 4871 4-9-8 69 .... TGMcLaughlin 1 80
(B R Millman) *hld up: hdwy 3f out: led and hung rt fr over 1f out: rdn out* **15/2**

3624 2 *2 1/4* **Iron Out (USA)**[18] 4984 3-9-2 67 .... JimCrowley 13 70
(R Hollinshead) *chsd ldrs: rdn and ev ch over 1f out: edgd rt and styd on same pce ins fnl f* **4/1**[2]

2336 3 *4* **Monashee Rock (IRE)**[16] 5063 4-9-5 66 .... AdamKirby 10 60
(Matthew Salaman) *mid-div: sn drvn along: hdwy over 2f out: hrd rdn to go 3rd over 1f out: no ex fnl f* **10/3**[1]

5-44 4 *3/4* **Battle Royal (IRE)**[27] 4660 3-8-11 62 .... RichardMullen 6 52
(B Smart) *racd keenly: trckd ldr tl led over 5f out: rdn and hdd over 1f out: no ex fnl f* **13/2**[3]

06-0 5 *1/2* **Indian Tonic (IRE)**[46] 4057 3-9-5 70 .... HayleyTurner 8 59
(W Jarvis) *hld up: rdn 1/2-way: hdwy over 1f out: no imp fnl f* **12/1**

0302 6 *1/2* **Norcroft**[9] 5287 7-8-8 55 oh5 .... (v) AdrianMcCarthy 9 44
(Mrs C A Dunnett) *chsd ldrs: rdn over 2f out: wknd fnl f* **16/1**

4404 7 *hd* **Elusive Warrior (USA)**[22] 4843 6-8-10 57 ow1 .... (p) StephenDonohoe 5 46
(A J McCabe) *led: hdd over 5f out: chsd ldrs: rdn over 2f out: wknd over 1f out* **16/1**

0004 8 *1 1/4* **Richo**[18] 4995 3-9-5 70 .... PAspell 7 53
(S A Harris) *mid-div: hdwy over 2f out: sn rdn: wknd over 1f out* **25/1**

5250 9 *nk* **Party In The Park**[18] 4977 4-8-8 55 oh3 .... (v[1]) ChrisCatlin 4 40
(Miss J A Camacho) *hld up: hdwy over 2f out: sn rdn: wknd wl over 1f out* **16/1**

0201 10 *3/4* **Registrar**[20] 4914 7-8-10 57 .... (p) SaleemGolam 12 40
(Mrs C A Dunnett) *prom: lost pl 1/2-way: hdwy u.p 2f out: wknd fnl f* **11/1**

00 11 *1/2* **Hidden Door (IRE)**[99] 2332 4-9-4 65 .... KirstyMilczarek 3 46
(G Prodromou) *hld up: hdwy over 2f out: rdn and wknd over 1f out* **28/1**

2000 12 *12* **Chinese Profit**[31] 4538 4-8-3 55 oh6 .... (p) Louis-PhilippeBeuzelin(5) 11 —
(G C Bravery) *hld up: rdn 1/2-way: a in rr* **33/1**

13 *4 1/2* **Iron Duke**[13] 5177 3-8-4 55 oh10 .... DMGrant 2 —
(John Joseph Murphy, Ire) *hld up: rdn over 3f out: a in rr* **50/1**

1m 23.54s (-2.66) **Going Correction** -0.30s/f (Firm)
WFA 3 from 4yo+ 4lb **13** Ran SP% **114.0**
Speed ratings (Par 103): **103,100,95,95,94 93,93,92,91,91 90,76,71**
toteswinger: 1&2 £7.70, 1&3 £6.10, 2&3 £4.30. CSF £34.40 CT £123.00 TOTE £6.00: £2.40, £1.70, £1.60; EX 43.00.
Owner The Links Partnership **Bred** Charlock Farm Stud **Trained** Kentisbeare, Devon

FOCUS
A modest handicap and the time was pretty ordinary; 0.07 seconds slower than earlier two-year-old maiden, and only 0.56 seconds quicker the juvenile seller won by a filly rated just 58. They started off towards the stands' side, but nearly all of the runners shunned the rail, which was a surprise, and the front two edged to the middle of the track late on. An improved effort from the winner but not form to be too positive about.
Monashee Rock(IRE) Official explanation: vet said filly bled from the nose

5545 BUY A RACING POST YEARLING BONUS CANDIDATE H'CAP — 1m 3f 183y
3:50 (3:50) (Class 5) (0-70,70) 3-Y-O+ — **£2,914** (£867; £433; £216) **Stalls** High

Form — RPR

502 1 **Fantino**[17] 5035 3-8-7 63 .... DavidProbert 6 70+
(J Mackie) *chsd ldrs: rdn to ld and hung lft over 1f out: styd on* **13/8**[1]

6024 2 *1 1/4* **Princess Flame (GER)**[10] 5244 7-8-11 63 .... KylieManser(5) 5 66
(B G Powell) *hld up: hdwy over 5f out: rdn and ev ch over 1f out: sn hung lft: styd on* **12/1**

1 3 *nk* **Sheila's Castle**[21] 4867 5-9-7 68 .... JamesDoyle 1 71
(S Regan) *hld up: hdwy u.p over 1f out: nt rch ldrs* **10/1**

0210 4 *3* **Crimson Mitre**[22] 4840 4-9-9 70 .... ChrisCatlin 8 68
(J Jay) *led: rdn and hdd over 1f out: no ex ins fnl f* **16/1**

46-5 5 *1/2* **Prince Zafonic**[15] 5113 6-9-4 65 .... JerryO'Dwyer 3 62
(C A Dwyer) *chsd ldr tl rdn over 2f out: edgd rt and no ex fnl f* **14/1**

0601 6 *1 1/4* **Sitwell**[13] 5152 3-8-9 65 .... LPKeniry 2 60
(J R Fanshawe) *hld up: hdwy u.p over 2f out: n.m.r and no ex fnl f* **9/4**[2]

0035 7 *26* **Filun**[11] 5227 4-8-6 56 oh6 .... AndreaAtzeni(3) 7 9
(A Middleton) *s.i.s: hld up: rdn and wknd over 2f out* **20/1**

0-05 8 *14* **Brave Mave**[17] 5034 4-9-9 70 .... HayleyTurner 4 1
(W Jarvis) *prom: pushed along 5f out: rdn and wknd 3f out* **8/1**[3]

2m 33.11s (-0.79) **Going Correction** +0.025s/f (Good)
WFA 3 from 4yo+ 9lb **8** Ran SP% **114.1**
Speed ratings (Par 103): **103,102,101,99,99 98,81,72**
toteswinger: 1&2 £6.50, 1&3 £4.80, 2&3 £8.10. CSF £22.57 CT £149.59 TOTE £2.60: £1.30, £3.30, £1.50; EX 23.70.
Owner Norman A Blyth **Bred** Norman A Blyth **Trained** Church Broughton , Derbys

FOCUS
This race was run in a heavy shower, and there was also lightning about. It was a modest contest and the pace was not strong. The form is rated around the runner-up.
Brave Mave Official explanation: jockey said filly had no more to give

5546 WEATHERBYS PRINTING CONDITIONS STKS 5f 2y
4:20 (4:20) (Class 3) 3-Y-O+ **£7,477** (£2,239; £1,119) **Stalls** Low

Form RPR

0050 **1** **Dandy Man (IRE)**[11] 5233 6-8-9 106 ....(t) LDettori 4 107
(Saeed Bin Suroor) *trckd ldrs: racd keenly: shkn up to ld ins fnl f: r.o wl: readily* **4/6**[1]

0536 **2** *1 1/4* **Peace Offering (IRE)**[31] 4516 9-8-9 104 .... TedDurcan 1 103
(D Nicholls) *trckd ldr: racd keenly: led over 1f out: rdn and hdd ins fnl f: styd on same pce* **9/4**[2]

5403 **3** *2* **Angus Newz**[21] 4885 6-8-4 90 ....(v) HayleyTurner 2 90
(M Quinn) *led: shkn up 2f out: rdn and hdd over 1f out: styd on same pce ins fnl f* **9/2**[3]

59.01 secs (-0.99) **Going Correction** +0.025s/f (Good)
WFA 3 from 6yo+ 1lb 3 Ran SP% **108.9**
Speed ratings (Par 107): **108,106,102**
toteswinger: 1&2 £1.70. CSF £2.49 TOTE £1.60; EX 3.00.
Owner Godolphin **Bred** Mountarmstrong Stud **Trained** Newmarket, Suffolk

FOCUS
It rained heavily prior to this race, which was devalued with three of the declared runners not taking part. The winner is the best guide to this rather muddling race.

NOTEBOOK
Dandy Man(IRE) only had two rivals and was the best off at the weights, having 2lb in hand over Peace Offering, and 11lb over Angus Newz. Rather surprisingly, this was his first success since joining Godolphin, and ended a losing run stretching back to 2007. The ease in grade was the key and, although he was a little keen when held up last of the three runners, he picked up readily without having to be asked for everything. (op 8-11 tchd 4-5 in places)
Peace Offering(IRE) has mainly underperformed this season and it was disappointing he did not give the favourite more to do. (op 2-1)
Angus Newz went off in front but had little chance at these weights. (op 5-1 tchd 4-1)

5547 E B F FILBERT MAIDEN FILLIES' STKS 1m 60y
4:50 (4:51) (Class 4) 2-Y-O **£4,857** (£1,445; £722; £360) **Stalls** High

Form RPR

1 **Quiet** 2-9-0 0 .... SteveDrowne 4 80+
(R Charlton) *a.p: rdn over 1f out: led and hung rt ins fnl f: r.o wl* **14/1**

02 **2** *2 1/2* **Pastello**[26] 4693 2-9-0 0 .... RyanMoore 3 72
(R Hannon) *chsd ldrs: rdn to ld over 1f out: hdd ins fnl f: edgd rt and styd on same pce* **4/1**[3]

6 **3** *1* **La Ville Lumiere (USA)**[21] 4869 2-9-0 0 .... LDettori 8 70
(Saeed Bin Suroor) *led after 1f: pushed along 3f out: rdn and hdd over 1f out: no ex ins fnl f* **10/3**[1]

6 **4** *1/2* **Danehill Intellect (IRE)**[18] 4980 2-9-0 0 .... AdamKirby 12 69
(G A Butler) *chsd ldrs: rdn over 2f out: styd on same pce fnl f* **9/2**

5 *3 1/4* **Danube (IRE)** 2-9-0 0 .... TPQueally 11 62
(H R A Cecil) *prom: rdn over 2f out: wknd over 1f out* **7/2**[2]

6 *4 1/2* **Aalya (IRE)** 2-9-0 0 .... RHills 10 54+
(J L Dunlop) *s.s: hld up: styd on fr over 1f out: nvr nrr* **11/2**

4 **7** *2 1/4* **Romeos Girl**[45] 4075 2-9-0 0 .... TPO'Shea 5 47
(Jennie Candlish) *led 1f: chsd ldr: rdn over 2f out: wknd wl over 1f out* **18/1**

8 *nk* **Zagarock** 2-9-0 0 .... DavidProbert 1 46
(B Palling) *s.i.s: hld up: hdwy over 3f out: wknd 2f out* **80/1**

9 *5* **Seeking Rose** 2-9-0 0 .... KirstyMilczarek 9 35
(E A L Dunlop) *s.s: hld up: hdwy 3f out: wknd 2f out* **25/1**

00 **10** *3/4* **Sarmad (USA)**[35] 4396 2-9-0 0 .... HayleyTurner 6 33
(C E Brittain) *mid-div: rdn and wknd over 2f out* **40/1**

11 *2 1/2* **Suzi's Challenger** 2-9-0 0 .... JimmyQuinn 2 28
(H J Collingridge) *hld up: a in rr: pushed along over 3f out: sn lost tch* **66/1**

12 *6* **Ilkley** 2-8-7 0 .... JamesPSullivan(7) 13 15
(M W Easterby) *hld up: a in rr: pushed along over 4f out: sn wknd* **150/1**

13 *11* **Cornish Baroness** 2-8-11 0 .... PatrickHills(3) 7 —
(R Hannon) *hld up: a in rr: pushed along 5f out: bhd fr 1/2-way* **50/1**

1m 45.52s (0.42) **Going Correction** +0.025s/f (Good) 13 Ran SP% **122.4**
Speed ratings (Par 94): **98,95,94,94,90 86,84,83,78,77 75,69,58**
toteswinger: 1&2 £8.30, 1&3 £10.70, 2&3 £3.70. CSF £69.67 TOTE £15.80: £3.40, £1.40, £2.80; EX 58.10.
Owner K Abdulla **Bred** Juddmonte Farms Ltd **Trained** Beckhampton, Wilts

FOCUS
A fair fillies' maiden.

NOTEBOOK
Quiet, a half-brother to among others smart middle-distance winner Double Crossed, looked quite useful on this racecourse debut. It needs pointing out she carried her head to one side when making her way to the front around a furlong out, but that might have been greenness and she ultimately knuckled down well.
Pastello was a bit keen early on and was forced wide around the first bend, but she kept on quite well in the straight. She looks as though a more galloping track will suit better and she might be capable of more now nurseries are an option. (op 9-2 tchd 7-2)
La Ville Lumiere(USA), ridden from the front, improved on the form she showed on her debut over 6f at Kempton. She is likely to benefit from even further in time. (op 5-2 tchd 4-1)
Danehill Intellect(IRE) ran okay without really improving significantly on the form she showed on her debut at Kempton. (op 13-2)
Danube(IRE), a half-sister to multiple 1m-1m2f winner Doncosaque, showed ability on her debut and should improve. (op 6-1)
Aalya(IRE) started slowly and was never seen with a chance. She is out of a 1m2f winner and should improve with time and distance. Official explanation: jockey said filly moved poorly in the early stages (op 5-1)

5548 LEVY BOARD APPRENTICE H'CAP 1m 1f 218y
5:20 (5:20) (Class 5) (0-70,69) 3-Y-O+ **£3,238** (£963; £481; £240) **Stalls** High

Form RPR

3345 **1** **Bolanderi (USA)**[10] 5244 4-9-5 67 .... AlexEdwards(5) 8 78
(Andrew Turnell) *hld up: hdwy over 2f out: led and edgd rt fr over 1f out: styd on* **10/1**

005 **2** *1 1/4* **Sea Lavender**[29] 4606 3-9-2 66 .... JPFahy 6 75+
(R Charlton) *hld up in tch: rdn to chse wnr ins fnl f: styd on* **5/2**[1]

3230 **3** *2 3/4* **General Tufto**[17] 5035 4-9-6 63 ....(b) DebraEngland 9 66
(C Smith) *hld up: styd on fr over 1f out to go 3rd wl ins fnl f: nt rch ldrs* **8/1**[3]

6340 **4** *1/2* **Kalasam**[27] 4658 5-9-5 62 .... JamesPSullivan 7 64
(M W Easterby) *led: rdn over 2f out: hdd over 1f out: no ex ins fnl f* **5/2**[1]

240 **5** *2 3/4* **Bert's Memory**[28] 4625 5-8-12 55 oh6 .... DeclanCannon 3 52
(Jennie Candlish) *prom: racd keenly: slipped 5f out: rdn over 2f out: styd on same pce appr fnl f* **16/1**

51-0 **6** *2* **Active Asset (IRE)**[27] 4663 7-9-5 69 ....(t) JonathanHinch(7) 4 62
(J A Glover) *hld up: hdwy over 3f out: rdn over 1f out: wknd fnl f* **20/1**

0065 **7** *nse* **Dream On Connie**[20] 4904 3-8-9 62 ....(t) KierenFox(3) 10 54
(W J Knight) *prom: outpcd over 2f out: rallied and swtchd rt wl over 1f out: sn wknd* **5/1**[2]

000- **8** *1 3/4* **Royal Rainbow**[482] 1913 5-8-9 55 oh10 .... JohnCavanagh(3) 5 44
(P W Hiatt) *trckd ldrs: racd keenly: rdn over 3f out: wknd 2f out* **66/1**

0340 **9** *3 3/4* **Mccormack (IRE)**[3] 5423 7-8-9 55 oh10 .... NSLawes(3) 2 36
(Miss T Jackson) *s.i.s: plld hrd and hdwy to trck ldr after 1f: chal 3f out: rdn and wknd wl over 1f out* **40/1**

/000 **10** *5* **Parisian Dream**[27] 4658 5-9-11 68 .... IJBrennan 1 39
(T J Pitt) *hld up: plld hrd: hdwy 3f out: sn rdn and hung rt: wknd 2f out* **25/1**

2m 7.92s (0.02) **Going Correction** +0.025s/f (Good)
WFA 3 from 4yo+ 7lb 10 Ran SP% **112.4**
Speed ratings (Par 103): **100,99,96,96,94 92,92,91,88,84**
toteswinger: 1&2 £7.00, 1&3 £5.20, 2&3 £4.80. CSF £32.87 CT £211.66 TOTE £8.80: £2.70, £1.90, £1.90; EX 40.60 Place 6: £11.03, Place 5: £7.39..
Owner Maori Partnership **Bred** Darley **Trained** Broad Hinton, Wilts

FOCUS
A modest handicap restricted to apprentices who had not ridden more than 20 winners. The first pair appeared to show improved form.
T/Jkpt: £8,138.60 to a £1 stake. Pool: £17,194.31. 1.50 winning tickets. T/Plt: £11.10 to a £1 stake. Pool: £63,878.99. 4,183.26 winning tickets. T/Qpdt: £5.90 to a £1 stake. Pool: £3,583.92. 446.10 winning tickets. CR

5519 RIPON (R-H)
Tuesday, September 1

OFFICIAL GOING: Good changing to good to soft after race 2 (3.00)
Rail from back straight to home straight moved out 5m from innermost position but impact on distances not quantified.
Wind: moderate behind Weather: Sunny periods

5549 CLARO (S) STKS 1m 1f 170y
2:30 (2:30) (Class 5) 3-4-Y-O **£2,590** (£770; £385; £192) **Stalls** High

Form RPR

0206 **1** **Rossini's Dancer**[21] 4876 4-9-11 57 .... PaulHanagan 14 69
(R A Fahey) *midfield: hdwy on inner over 3f out: swtchd lft and effrt over 2f out: rdn to ld over 1f out: sn clr* **13/2**[3]

-500 **2** *7* **Aven Mac (IRE)**[23] 4819 3-8-7 46 .... DavidAllan 10 43
(N Bycroft) *towards rr: rdn along 4f out: hdwy over 2f out: styd on u.p ins fnl f: tk 2nd nr fin* **50/1**

230 **3** *nk* **Whirlijig (IRE)**[40] 4229 4-9-0 71 .... PJMcDonald 12 43
(G A Swinbank) *trckd ldrs: smooth hdwy over 3f out: led on bit over 2f out: sn jnd and shkn up: rdn and hdd over 1f out: sn edgd rt and btn* **1/1**[1]

0000 **4** *2 1/2* **Bestowed**[35] 4402 4-8-12 46 .... AndrewHeffernan(7) 6 42
(M C Chapman) *midfield: hdwy 3f out: rdn to chse ldrs 2f out: sn drvn and no imp* **100/1**

5640 **5** *3/4* **Hey Up Dad**[10] 4004 3-9-4 59 ....(bt) PhillipMakin 2 47
(M Dods) *trckd ldrs: hdwy 3f out: rdn along 2f out: drvn and no hdwy fr wl over 1f out* **11/1**

-030 **6** *7* **Melkatant**[10] 5259 3-8-7 47 .... TomEaves 7 21
(N Bycroft) *bhd tl sme late hdwy* **50/1**

2064 **7** *hd* **Whipma Whopma Gate (IRE)**[9] 5294 4-9-0 50 ....(b[1]) DNolan 11 21
(D Carroll) *mde most tl rdn along and hdd over 2f out: sn drvn and wknd* **9/2**[2]

-060 **8** *9* **La Columbina**[24] 4804 4-9-1 65 .... JamieKyne(5) 5 8
(G A Harker) *a in rr* **14/1**

0350 **9** *1 1/4* **Sirjosh**[2] 5479 3-8-12 55 ....(vt) NickyMackay 9 4
(D Donovan) *prom: rdn along 3f out: drvn over 2f out and sn wknd* **10/1**

0604 **10** *3/4* **Carpe Diem**[22] 4845 4-8-12 51 .... LeeTopliss(7) 8 3
(R A Fahey) *hmpd s: a bhd* **25/1**

3000 **11** *40* **Glamoroso (IRE)**[19] 4927 4-9-5 38 .... AndrewElliott 13 —
(A Kirtley) *a bhd* **100/1**

0330 **12** *1 1/2* **Rowaad**[34] 4435 4-9-5 48 ....(v) GrahamGibbons 4 —
(A E Price) *in tch on inner: rdn along wl over 3f out and wknd qckly* **28/1**

0040 **13** *3/4* **Our Apolonia (IRE)**[8] 5306 3-8-0 43 .... BillyCray(7) 3 —
(A Berry) *a bhd* **125/1**

0 **14** *16* **Sybil's Surprise**[52] 3862 4-9-0 0 .... MickyFenton 1 —
(J Mackie) *chsd ldrs: rapid hdwy and cl up 1/2-way: rdn along 4f out and wknd qckly: sn wl bhd* **80/1**

2m 7.30s (1.90) **Going Correction** +0.275s/f (Good)
WFA 3 from 4yo 7lb 14 Ran SP% **120.8**
Speed ratings (Par 103): **103,97,97,95,94 88,88,81,80,80 48,46,46,33**
toteswinger: 1&2 £43.20, 1&3 £3.10, 2&3 £15.80. CSF £304.58 TOTE £8.00: £2.00, £8.50, £1.30; EX 285.90 Trifecta £201.90 Part won. Pool: £272.94, 0.20 winning units..There was no bid for the winner.
Owner Lets Go Racing 1 **Bred** Heather Raw **Trained** Musley Bank, N Yorks

FOCUS
A weakish seller and it is unlikely that the winner actually improved.
Sirjosh Official explanation: jockey said gelding had no more to give

5550 RIPON LAND ROVER NURSERY 6f
3:00 (3:00) (Class 4) 2-Y-O **£4,533** (£1,348; £674; £336) **Stalls** Low

Form RPR

0102 **1** **Eight Hours**[5] 5358 2-8-2 60 .... PaulHanagan 4 64
(R A Fahey) *trckd ldng pair: hdwy 2f out and sn cl up: rdn to ld ent fnl f: drvn out* **6/1**

2221 **2** *1 1/4* **Gillburg (USA)**[13] 5157 2-9-4 76 ....(p) RobertWinston 3 76
(K A Ryan) *led: hdd over 3f out: rdn to ld again 2f out: drvn and hdd ent fnl f: kpt on u.p* **4/1**[2]

15 **3** *nk* **Novay Essjay (IRE)**[109] 2041 2-8-7 70 .... PatrickDonaghy(5) 9 69
(P C Haslam) *hld up in tch: swtchd outside and hdwy 2f out: rdn to chse ldng pair over 1f out: drvn and kpt on ins fnl f* **18/1**

3100 **4** *2* **Refuse To Wait (IRE)**[11] 5207 2-8-13 71 ....(b[1]) DavidAllan 10 64
(T D Easterby) *towards rr: hdwy over 2f out: rdn wl over 1f out: styd on ins fnl f: nrst fin* **25/1**

4143 **5** *nk* **Kylladdie**[32] 4493 2-9-4 76 .... MickyFenton 11 68
(T P Tate) *wnt rt s and racd alone far side: prom tl rdn along 2f out and sn one pce* **7/1**

0061 **6** *4 ½* **Leleyf (IRE)**[1] 5526 2-9-6 **72** 6ex................................ TonyCulhane 5 57
(M R Channon) *cl up: led over 3f out: rdn and hdd 2f out: drvn over 1f out and sn wknd* **7/1**

6340 **7** *1 ¼* **Silver In The Sand**[18] 4975 2-8-5 **63**........................ GrahamGibbons 6 38
(J D Bethell) *chsd ldrs: rdn along over 2f out and sn wknd* **18/1**

3453 **8** *3 ¼* **Val C**[17] 5033 2-8-7 **65** ow1.. ShaneKelly 8 30
(N P Littmoden) *dwlt: sn chsng ldrs on inner: rdn along 1/2-way and sn wknd* **9/2**[3]

0201 **9** *¾* **Iron Velvet (USA)**[18] 4975 2-9-7 **79**.................................. GregFairley 1 42
(M Johnston) *dwlt and sn rdn along in rr: bhd fr 1/2-way* **3/1**[1]

1m 15.41s (2.41) **Going Correction** +0.10s/f (Good) **9** Ran SP% **116.8**
Speed ratings (Par 97): **87,85,84,82,81 75,74,69,68**
toteswinger: 1&2 £3.50, 1&3 £13.60, 2&3 £14.20. CSF £30.63 CT £413.94 TOTE £7.20: £2.50, £1.40, £4.50; EX 28.50 Trifecta £339.70 Part won. Pool: £459.08, 0.84 winning units..
Owner Aidan J Ryan **Bred** Foxlea Farm And Stud **Trained** Musley Bank, N Yorks

FOCUS
An open nursery, run at a decent pace. The near side was the place to be.

NOTEBOOK
Eight Hours enjoyed the way this was run and made it two wins from five starts this season. He finished second off this mark on soft ground at Ayr five days earlier and his ability to handle this surface was a big help. This looks very much his trip and he is in the right hands to progress further. (op 7-1 tchd 11-2)
Gillburg(USA), with the cheekpieces back on, belatedly opened his account at Hamilton 13 days earlier and proved popular on this return to a nursery. He was put in his place by the winner late on, but deserves credit as he disputed the early running and didn't give up when coming under pressure 2f out. (op 5-1)
Novay Essjay(IRE) was returning from a 109-day break and took a long time to wind up. He stayed on encouragingly from halfway and should benefit nicely for the run, so this lightly-raced gelding should get closer next time out. (tchd 16-1 and 20-1)
Refuse To Wait(IRE) was equipped with first-time blinkers and representing a yard with a decent record in this race. He got going all too late from off the pace and looks a tricky sort, but the return to another furlong may help.
Kylladdie went solo on the far side from his outside draw and gave a fair account of himself, but failed to reverse Haydock form with the runner-up on these much better terms. (op 6-1 tchd 8-1)
Leleyf(IRE) made all at Warwick the previous day and should not be judged harshly on her effort here, as she was not left alone in the lead. The ground was also considerably quicker at Warwick. (op 13-2 tchd 6-1)
Silver In The Sand put in a more encouraging and wasn't given too hard a time of things when her chance was negligible from 2f out. This ground may have been against her. (op 20-1)
Iron Velvet(USA) was a bitter disappointment and his supporters knew their fate after a few furlongs. Something may well have gone amiss. Official explanation: trainer's rep had no explanation for the poor form shown (op 7-2 tchd 4-1 and 9-2 in places)

5551 CITY OF RIPON STKS (H'CAP) 1m 1f 170y
3:30 (3:31) (Class 3) (0-90,90) 3-Y-O+

£8,723 (£2,612; £1,306; £653; £326; £163) **Stalls** High

Form RPR

201 **1** **Distant Memories (IRE)**[45] 4102 3-9-6 **90**.................... MickyFenton 12 108
(T P Tate) *trckd ldng pair on inner: hdwy to ld 3f out: rdn clr wl over 1f out: kpt on strly* **11/4**[1]

0000 **2** *7* **Bolodenka (IRE)**[11] 5206 7-9-8 **90**.................................... BMcHugh(5) 4 93
(R A Fahey) *towards rr: hdwy over 3f out: rdn to chse ldrs 2f out: styd on ins fnl f: no ch w wnr* **20/1**

0546 **3** *1 ¾* **Jeer (IRE)**[56] 3705 5-8-8 **71** oh1..(t) DaleGibson 8 70
(M W Easterby) *hld up towards rr: hdwy 3f out: rdn along wl over 1f out: styd on ins fnl f: nrst fin* **18/1**

1-0 **4** *½* **Ella**[22] 4840 5-9-13 **90**.. PJMcDonald 2 88
(G A Swinbank) *trckd ldrs: hdwy over 3f out: rdn to chse wnr 2f out: sn drvn and kpt on same pce* **22/1**

1426 **5** *3 ½* **Hippolytus**[13] 5160 4-8-13 **76**... TomEaves 11 67
(J J Quinn) *dwlt: hld up in midfield: hdwy on inner over 3f out: swtchd lft and rdn 2f out: sn no imp* **17/2**

1303 **6** *5* **Legislate**[65] 3429 3-9-1 **85**.. DarryllHolland 7 65
(B W Hills) *trckd ldr: effrt over 3f out and sn rdn along: drvn and wknd over 2f out* **4/1**[2]

61 **7** *½* **Knight's Victory (IRE)**[10] 5259 3-8-3 **73**........................... GregFairley 5 52
(M Johnston) *dwlt: a towards rr* **11/2**

1221 **8** *shd* **Wing Play (IRE)**[26] 4716 4-9-4 **81**...................................(p) ShaneKelly 13 60
(H Morrison) *in tch: effrt on inner over 3f out: rdn along over 2f out and sn wknd* **5/1**[3]

1266 **9** *2 ¾* **Society Venue**[29] 4597 4-8-10 **73**...................................... PaulHanagan 9 46
(Jedd O'Keeffe) *led: rdn along and hdd 3f out: drvn wl over 1f out and grad wknd* **18/1**

4-15 **10** *11* **King's Head (IRE)**[195] 584 6-9-4 **86**............................... JamieKyne(5) 1 36
(Miss L A Perratt) *a towards rr* **50/1**

1402 **11** *2 ¼* **Granston (IRE)**[19] 4930 8-9-11 **88**.................................. RobertWinston 10 34
(J D Bethell) *chsd ldrs: rdn along over 3f out: wknd over 2f out* **12/1**

0-00 **12** *46* **Cold Quest (USA)**[14] 5137 5-9-8 **85**................................. PhillipMakin 3 —
(Miss L A Perratt) *in tch: rdn along over 4f out: sn wknd and bhd: eased fnl 2f* **100/1**

2m 7.52s (2.12) **Going Correction** +0.40s/f (Good)
WFA 3 from 4yo+ 7lb **12** Ran SP% **119.5**
Speed ratings (Par 107): **107,101,100,99,96 92,92,92,90,81 79,42**
toteswinger: 1&2 £19.10, 1&3 £18.10, 2&3 £61.90. CSF £66.15 CT £853.74 TOTE £4.20: £1.80, £6.20, £5.00; EX 82.60 Trifecta £291.70 Part won. Pool: £394.27, 0.20 winning units..
Owner Mrs Fitri Hay **Bred** Kildaragh Stud **Trained** Tadcaster, N Yorks

FOCUS
A good and competitive handicap. The winner is most progressive and the placed horses give the form a sound look.

NOTEBOOK
Distant Memories(IRE) found the ground easing in his favour and, very well backed, followed up his course and distance success 45 days previously despite being 7lb higher. He got a copybook ride from Fenton, tracking the early pace from his good draw, before taking it up midway down the home straight. It was clear soon after that his rivals would struggle to reel him in, he is clearly an improving 3yo and deserves to have a crack at something better now. (op 9-2)
Bolodenka(IRE) ◆ finally returned to form. He stayed on well from off the pace back over this longer trip. Coming from near last turning for home is hardly ideal at this venue as well, so he looks a little better than the bare form. (op 16-1)
Jeer(IRE), in a first-time tongue tie, also stayed on stoutly from off the pace and this rates a far more encouraging effort. He was 1lb out of the weights, but his last success came from a 15lb higher mark and he could be coming back to top form. (op 16-1)
Ella showed the benefit of her seasonal bow on Fibresand last month and was another that was suited by the easing ground. She just raced without cover early on and proved somewhat free, which didn't helped. She is entitled to come on again. (op 18-1)
Legislate met support on this first outing for 65 days, but he came unstuck on this surface and is better than he could show. Official explanation: trainer said colt was unsuited by the good to soft

Wing Play(IRE) had been upped 9lb for scoring at Sandown 26 days earlier. He was in trouble around 3f out here though and disappointed, with his rider later reporting he was never travelling. Official explanation: jockey said gelding was never travelling (op 11-2)
Granston(IRE) Official explanation: jockey said gelding was unsuited by the good to soft ground

5552 SAPPER CONDITIONS STKS 5f
4:00 (4:02) (Class 3) 2-Y-O

£6,542 (£1,959; £979; £490; £244; £122) **Stalls** Low

Form RPR

1040 **1** **Absolute Music (USA)**[18] 4989 2-8-11 **97**................ GrahamGibbons 4 83+
(R M H Cowell) *cl up: led over 2f out: rdn over 1f out and kpt on wl fnl f* **11/4**[3]

3025 **2** *1* **Tillys Tale**[21] 4875 2-8-8 **75**... PaulPickard(5) 8 81
(P T Midgley) *cl up: effrt 2f out and ev ch tl rdn along over 1f out and kpt on same pce ins fnl f* **20/1**

00 **3** *2* **Confessional**[59] 3606 2-9-0 0.. DavidAllan 6 77+
(T D Easterby) *stdd s and hld up in rr: hdwy over 2f out: sn rdn and kpt on wl fnl f* **40/1**

135 **4** *1 ¾* **Falasteen (IRE)**[12] 5198 2-9-4 **90**.............................. AdrianTNicholls 1 73
(D Nicholls) *led: rdn along and hdd over 2f out: sn drvn and wknd wl over 1f out* **13/8**[2]

2130 **5** *¾* **Tawaabb**[54] 3779 2-9-4 **98**.. TonyCulhane 7 70
(M R Channon) *trckd ldrs: hdwy 1/2-way: rdn along 2f out: sn drvn and wknd* **11/8**[1]

5006 **6** *6* **Baby Judge (IRE)**[5] 5372 2-8-7 **52**........................ AndrewHeffernan(7) 3 45
(M C Chapman) *prom: rdn along after 2f: sn outpcd and bhd fr 1/2-way* **200/1**

2465 **7** *7* **Goodbye Earl (IRE)**[6] 5337 2-8-2 **70**................................. BillyCray(7) 9 14
(A Berry) *j. awkwardly and wnt rt s: a bhd* **50/1**

61.38 secs (0.68) **Going Correction** +0.10s/f (Good) **7** Ran SP% **116.5**
Speed ratings (Par 99): **98,96,93,90,89 79,68**
toteswinger: 1&2 £3.40, 1&3 £7.30, 2&3 £7.90. CSF £43.83 TOTE £4.10: £1.90, £3.10; EX 37.90 Trifecta £163.70 Pool: £570.82, 2.58 winning units..
Owner Khalifa Dasmal **Bred** Gilbraltar Group Lp **Trained** Six Mile Bottom, Cambs

FOCUS
This concerned three on official ratings, but two failed to run their race so the form is dubious.

NOTEBOOK
Absolute Music(USA) got back to winning ways, but was only workmanlike in shaking off the 75-rated runner-up, from whom she was also getting 2lb. She also had the stands' rail to help late on so, while there was no faulting her attitude, she ran well below her mark of 97. (op 3-1 tchd 5-2 and 100-30 in places)
Tillys Tale was in the firing line throughout and made the winner work hard for her prize. This was also the softest ground she would have encountered yet, so looking strictly at her proximity, connections would do well to find her another nursery before the handicapper can react. (op 14-1)
Confessional took time to pick up from off the pace and still showed signs of experience. He was finished nicely enough and this was much his best effort yet, so he is one to keep an eye on (tchd 33-1)
Falasteen(IRE) was well away and moved well against the stands' rail early on. He came under pressure around halfway, however, and looked uneasy on the track. This was very disappointing, but it is probably wise to give him another chance. (op 11-4)
Tawaabb looked a non stayer over 6f when behind Arcano in the July Stakes 54 days previously. He found next to nothing when push came to shove, racing more towards the centre, and was another that ran miles below his mark. This contrasting surface may have been to blame, but he now has to prove he is not regressing. (op 6-5 tchd 11-10 and 6-4 tchd 13-8 in places)

5553 JADE ANDREWS CELEBRATION FILLIES' MAIDEN AUCTION STKS 5f
4:30 (4:30) (Class 5) 2-Y-O **£2,914** (£867; £433; £216) **Stalls** Low

Form RPR

250 **1** **Bossy Kitty**[14] 5136 2-8-7 66.. JoeFanning 2 66+
(N Tinkler) *trckd ldrs: hdwy and cl up 2f out: rdn to ld 1f out: kpt on* **15/8**[1]

035 **2** *¾* **Silver Linnet (IRE)**[75] 3058 2-8-4 65.............................. DuranFentiman 3 59
(T D Easterby) *sn led: pushed along and jnd 2f out: sn rdn and hdd 1f out: kpt on u.p ins fnl f* **10/3**[2]

0566 **3** *3 ¼* **Kirkby's Gem**[13] 5146 2-7-11 50.. BillyCray(7) 4 48
(A Berry) *cl up: rdn along 2f out: drvn and hung rt over 1f out: sn one pce* **66/1**

405 **4** *¾* **Pepper Lane**[3] 5439 2-8-6 64... BMcHugh(5) 11 52
(J Hetherton) *chsd ldrs: effrt on outer 2f out: sn rdn and kpt on same pce* **8/1**

53 **5** *hd* **Luv U Noo**[24] 4773 2-8-4 0... AndrewElliott 10 44
(A P Jarvis) *in tch: hdwy to chse ldrs wl over 1f out: sn rdn and no imp* **6/1**[3]

560 **6** *nk* **Nabrina (IRE)**[20] 4889 2-7-12 55 ow1.................... AndrewHeffernan(7) 8 44
(M Brittain) *cl up: rdn along 2f out: sn drvn and wknd over 1f out* **25/1**

0 **7** *2 ½* **Lady Compton**[20] 4889 2-8-4 0.. GregFairley 9 34
(R Bastiman) *midfield: rdn along 2f out: nvr nr ldrs* **7/1**

05 **8** *3 ¾* **Daphne Du Maurier (IRE)**[24] 4774 2-8-4 0..................... PaulHanagan 1 21
(I Semple) *s.i.s: sn rdn along: a in rr* **25/1**

9 *20* **Lady Zoe (IRE)** 2-8-4 0... NickyMackay 5 —
(D Donovan) *sn outpcd and bhd fr 1/2-way* **16/1**

00 **10** *8* **Derval (IRE)**[20] 4889 2-8-9 0 ow2................................(t) RobertWinston 6 —
(K A Ryan) *midfield: drvn along 1/2-way and sn bhd* **18/1**

61.77 secs (1.07) **Going Correction** +0.10s/f (Good) **10** Ran SP% **116.1**
Speed ratings (Par 92): **95,93,88,87,87 86,82,76,44,31**
toteswinger: 1&2 £4.00, 1&3 £23.90, 2&3 £19.60. CSF £7.71 TOTE £2.70: £1.40, £1.60, £7.60; EX 8.90 Trifecta £377.00 Part won. Pool: £509.57, 0.10 winning units..
Owner Leeds Plywood And Doors Ltd **Bred** J P Coggan **Trained** Langton, N Yorks

FOCUS
A poor juvenile fillies' maiden. The form makes sense with the two market leaders coming clear.

NOTEBOOK
Bossy Kitty opened her account at the tenth time of asking on this drop back a furlong. Despite being officially rated 66, she did have the best previous form on offer here and would have found this plenty easier than the competitive nursery she contested at York last time. She knuckled down well when pulled out with her challenge and her confidence will be boosted, but she is fully exposed. (op 3-1 tchd 100-30)
Silver Linnet(IRE), returning from a 75-day break, had every chance against the stands' rail and finished a clear second-best. She is just moderate, but has some scope and is entitled to benefit for the run. (op 7-2 tchd 3-1 and 4-1 in places)
Kirkby's Gem helped cut out the early running and kept on resolutely when beaten inside the final furlong. This was better from her, but she is rated 50 and puts the form into perspective.
Pepper Lane, fifth over 6f three days earlier, battled on more towards the centre of the track and left the impression a stiffer test over this trip would be ideal. (tchd 15-2)
Daphne Du Maurier(IRE) Official explanation: jockey said filly reared up as the gates opened
Lady Zoe(IRE) Official explanation: jockey said filly was never travelling

Derval(IRE) Official explanation: jockey said filly had a breathing problem

5554 WAKEMAN STAYERS H'CAP 2m
5:00 (5:00) (Class 6) (0-65,63) 3-Y-O+ **£2,590** (£770; £385; £192) **Stalls** High

Form RPR
2400 **1** **Unawatuna**16 5068 4-9-0 **52** KellyHarrison(3) 7 59
(Mrs K Walton) *a.p: hdwy over 4f out: led 3f out and sn rdn: drvn and hdd wl over 1f out: rallied u.p to ld wl ins fnl f: gamely* **7/1**
4242 **2** ½ **Jackday (IRE)**20 4890 4-9-7 **61** BMcHugh(5) 3 67
(T D Easterby) *hld up towards rr: gd hdwy over 4f out: trckd ldrs wl over 2f out: led on bit wl over 1f out: shkn up appr fnl f and sn drvn: hdd and no ex wl ins fnl f* **5/2**1
-025 **3** 3 **Aleron (IRE)**45 2262 11-9-10 **59** (p) GrahamGibbons 1 62
(J J Quinn) *trckd ldrs: hdwy 3f out: rdn along to chse ldng pair 2f out: drvn and one pce appr fnl f* **7/1**
2220 **4** 5 **Mystified (IRE)**24 4806 6-9-0 **54** (tp) JamieKyne(5) 13 52
(R F Fisher) *trckd ldrs: hdwy over 6f out: led over 4f out: rdn along and hdd 3f out: sn drvn and grad wknd fnl 2f* **8/1**
300 **5** ½ **Rapid Desire (IRE)**22 4838 3-8-7 **55** TomEaves 2 53
(J R Weymes) *prom: rdn along over 3f out: drvn over 2f out: plugged on same pce* **50/1**
5255 **6** 2½ **Lets Roll**21 4873 8-10-0 **63** DanielTudhope 12 58
(C W Thornton) *hld up and bhd: swtchd outside and hdwy over 3f out: rdn along over 2f out: kpt on: nvr rchd ldrs* **13/2**3
4305 **7** 1¾ **Wannarock (IRE)**22 4848 4-8-5 **47** oh2 AndrewHeffernan(7) 14 40
(M C Chapman) *midfield: hdwy on inner 4f out: rdn along to chse ldrs 3f out: sn drvn and n.d* **20/1**
0060 **8** shd **Lady Anne Nevill**29 4593 5-8-12 **47** oh2 (b1) DNolan 8 40
(C W Fairhurst) *hld up in rr: sme hdwy 4f out: rdn along 3f out: nvr a factor* **40/1**
-051 **9** 20 **Leyte Gulf (USA)**25 4742 6-9-8 **57** PhillipMakin 4 30
(C C Bealby) *hld up in midfield: hdwy on outer over 6f out: rdn along to chse ldrs over 3f out: sn wknd* **5/1**2
500 **10** 2¼ **East Of The Sun (IRE)**29 4599 3-7-13 **50** DominicFox(3) 6 21
(T P Tate) *led: rdn along and hdd over 4f out: sn wknd* **11/1**
1003 **11** 7 **Bright Sparky (GER)**24 4806 6-8-13 **48** (vt) DaleGibson 5 12
(M W Easterby) *a towards rr* **14/1**
0/00 **12** 20 **English Archer**13 5162 6-8-12 **47** oh2 AndrewElliott 9 —
(A Kirtley) *a in rr* **80/1**
000 **13** 13 **Skybob**18 4974 3-7-13 **47** oh2 DuranFentiman 11 —
(D W Thompson) *prom: rdn along and wknd 6f out: sn bhd* **80/1**

3m 40.79s (8.99) **Going Correction** +0.40s/f (Good)
WFA 3 from 4yo+ 13lb **13 Ran SP% 121.3**
Speed ratings (Par 101): **93,92,91,88,88 87,86,86,76,75 71,61,55**
toteswinger: 1&2 £6.30, 1&3 £10.60, 2&3 £4.50. CSF £24.46 CT £131.98 TOTE £7.90: £2.80, £1.60, £2.40; EX 33.10 Trifecta £211.10 Part won. Pool: £285.31, 0.44 winning units. Place 6: £194.81, Place 5: £130.87..
Owner Trainers House Enterprises Ltd **Bred** Trainers House Enterprises Limited **Trained** Middleham Moor, N Yorks
■ Stewards' Enquiry : B McHugh caution: excessive use of the whip
D Nolan caution: continued to slap horse down the shoulder in final furlong

FOCUS
A moderate staying handicap. The first three were clear and the winner ran to her recent best.
Unawatuna Official explanation: trainer said, regarding the apparent improvement in form shown, filly seems to run well at Ripon
T/Plt: £524.60 to a £1 stake. Pool: £73,527.30. 102.30 winning tickets. T/Qpdt: £52.20 to a £1 stake. Pool: £4,832.14. 68.50 winning tickets. JR

5555 - 5560a (Foreign Racing) - See Raceform Interactive

3967 LONGCHAMP (R-H)
Tuesday, September 1

OFFICIAL GOING: Good

5561a PRIX DU CONSERVATOIRE (MAIDEN) (C&G) 1m
12:50 (12:49) 2-Y-O **£11,650** (£4,660; £3,495; £2,320; £1,165)

RPR
1 **Stelrock (FR)**65 2-8-13 FPrat(3) —
(P Bary, France)
2 shd **Estimate (FR)**51 2-9-2 ACrastus —
(E Lellouche, France)
3 ¾ **Marine Officer (USA)**25 4807 2-9-2 C-PLemaire —
(J-C Rouget, France) *fin 4th: plcd 3rd*
4 snk **Patriarchal**74 2-9-2 —
(A Fabre, France) *fin 5th: plcd 4th*
5 1 **Philander**25 4807 2-9-2 OPeslier —
(E J O'Neill) *trckd ldrs: 3rd st: sn outpcd and rdn along: cl up whn hmpd appr fnl f: rallied cl home: fin 6th: plcd 5th* **14/5**1
6 nk **Trajectory**25 4807 2-9-2 SPasquier —
(D Smaga, France) *fin 3rd: disqualified and plcd last*

1m 47.4s (9.00) **6 Ran SP% 26.3**
PARI-MUTUEL (including one euro stakes): WIN 12.00; PL 4.60, 2.40; SF65.30.
Owner Ecurie Stella Maris **Bred** Snc Stella Maris **Trained** Chantilly, France

NOTEBOOK
Patriarchal, who showed promise on his debut on soft ground, was hampered by the third before rallying and was not beaten far despite finishing last. He was subsequently promoted a place.
Philander, who showed promise on his debut on soft ground, was hampered by the third before rallying and was not beaten far despite finishing last. He was subsequently promoted a place.

5562a PRIX DE LIANCOURT (LISTED RACE) (FILLIES) 1m 2f 110y
2:30 (2:35) 3-Y-O **£26,699** (£10,680; £8,010; £5,340; £2,670)

RPR
1 **Shalanaya (IRE)**31 4578 3-8-12 CSoumillon 10 107
(M Delzangles, France) **5/2**1
2 3 **Russiana (IRE)**23 3-8-12 OPeslier 3 101
(A Fabre, France)
3 1½ **Jakonda (USA)**19 4969 3-8-12 GMosse 9 98
(A De Royer-Dupre, France)
4 snk **Flash Dance (IRE)**38 4334 3-8-12 MGuyon 4 98
(H-A Pantall, France)
5 2½ **Qertaas (IRE)**19 4969 3-9-2 DBonilla 2 97
(F Head, France)
6 ½ **Sahabah (USA)**78 3-8-12 IMendizabal 5 92
(J E Hammond, France)
7 2½ **Lady Francesca**18 4991 3-8-12 MartinDwyer 11 87
(W R Muir) *prom on outside: disp 4th after 3f: 4th and pushed along st: rdn 2f out: no ex fr 1f out* **28/1**2
8 1½ **You Or No One (IRE)**289 3-8-12 SPasquier 8 84
(Mme B Valenti, Spain)
9 ¾ **Divine Comedy (FR)**19 4969 3-8-12 GBenoist 1 83
(D Smaga, France)
10 6 **Sand River (IRE)**138 3-8-12 ACrastus 7 72
(E Lellouche, France)
11 **Excellent Girl**90 2622 3-9-2 JVictoire 12 76
(Y De Nicolay, France)
12 **Landskia (FR)**49 3968 3-8-12 MBarzalona 6 72
(A Fabre, France)

2m 14.1s (1.10) **12 Ran SP% 32.0**
PARI-MUTUEL: WIN 3.50; PL 1.60, 1.60, 1.80; DF 8.60.
Owner H H Aga Khan **Bred** H H The Aga Khan's Studs S C **Trained** France

NOTEBOOK
Lady Francesca was never closer than the fifth place which she held coming into the straight before gradually falling out of contention. She was finally beaten over ten lengths.

5493 BADEN-BADEN (L-H)
Tuesday, September 1

OFFICIAL GOING: Good

5563a DARLEY OETTINGEN-RENNEN (GROUP 2) 1m
3:45 (3:55) 3-Y-O+ **£38,835** (£14,563; £5,825; £3,883)

RPR
1 **Premio Loco (USA)**66 3404 5-9-2 GeorgeBaker 2 112
(C F Wall) *disp 3rd on ins: wnt 2nd st: led appr fnl f: drvn out* **17/10**1
2 2½ **Konig Concorde (GER)**44 4129 4-9-2 ADeVries 8 106
(C Sprengel, Germany) *hld up in rr but a wl in tch: last st: hdwy 2f out to trck wnr: drvn to take 2nd wl ins fnl f* **104/10**
3 1¼ **Earl Of Fire (GER)**66 3416 4-9-2 DBoeuf 1 103
(W Baltromei, Germany) *led: set gd pce: hdd appr fnl f: one pce* **7/2**2
4 1¼ **Aspectus (IRE)**30 4582 6-9-2 AStarke 6 100
(T Mundry, Germany) *first to show: settled disputing 3rd on outside: 4th st and brought to middle: kpt on same pce u.p fr over 1f out* **17/10**1
5 3 **Caro Jina (FR)**62 3520 3-8-8 ow1 ASuborics 7 90
(A Trybuhl, Germany) *racd in 5th to st: brought wdst: n.d* **6/1**3
6 2½ **Glad Panther**58 3670 3-8-11 DPorcu 3 88
(Uwe Ostmann, Germany) *sn trcking ldr: 3rd st: wknd 1 1/2f out* **81/10**

1m 38.0s (-1.11)
WFA 3 from 4yo+ 5lb **6 Ran SP% 130.3**
(including ten euro stakes): WIN 27; PL 20, 28; SF 343.
Owner Bernard Westley **Bred** Kidder, Cole & Griggs **Trained** Newmarket, Suffolk

NOTEBOOK
Premio Loco(USA) is a really consistent performer who has been running well in Listed company on turf, but took the advantage of a good opportunity to score on his first attempt in this grade. It also gave his rider a first winner at this level. The gelding could be aimed at the Dubai Carnival.

5119 BRIGHTON (L-H)
Wednesday, September 2

OFFICIAL GOING: Firm (good to firm in places; 8.6)
Course dolled out 5m from Wilson Avenue to 3f marker and also as before from after parade ring and across Manor Road.
Wind: Strong, against Weather: Unsettled, late rain

5564 EUROPEAN BREEDERS' FUND MAIDEN STKS 6f 209y
2:30 (2:30) (Class 5) 2-Y-O **£3,784** (£1,132; £566; £283; £141) **Stalls** Low

Form RPR
65 **1** **Kona Coast**19 4986 2-9-3 JimmyFortune 7 73
(J H M Gosden) *chsd ldrs on outer: led 3f out tl wl over 1f out: edgd lft fnl f: led again fnl 75yds: rdn out* **3/1**2
66 **2** ¾ **Walcot Square (IRE)**19 4985 2-9-3 SteveDrowne 3 71
(R Charlton) *led tl 3f out: led wl over 1f out: hrd rdn fnl f: hdd and nt qckn fnl 75yds* **7/4**1
00 **3** 2¾ **Green Earth (IRE)**12 5220 2-9-3 JimCrowley 5 64
(Mrs A J Perrett) *dwlt: hld up in rr: rdn and hdwy 2f out: one pce fnl f* **33/1**
4 2¼ **Landowner** 2-9-3 DaneO'Neill 2 58
(Saeed Bin Suroor) *dwlt: sn chsng ldrs: no ex over 1f out* **9/2**3
0 **5** 1¾ **Light The Way**20 4946 2-9-3 FergusSweeney 1 54
(P J Makin) *bhd: rdn over 2f out: nvr rchd ldrs* **14/1**
0232 **6** ¾ **Bush Master**12 5218 2-9-3 **69** PatDobbs 6 52
(R Hannon) *t.k.h: in tch: outpcd 2f out: sn btn* **17/2**
04 **7** ½ **Nom De La Rosa (IRE)**16 5096 2-8-12 ShaneKelly 4 45
(G L Moore) *prom tl wknd 2f out* **7/1**

1m 24.64s (1.54) **Going Correction** +0.10s/f (Good) **7 Ran SP% 112.2**
Speed ratings (Par 95): **95,94,91,88,86 85,85**
toteswinger: 1&2 £2.10, 1&3 £13.70, 2&3 £17.80. CSF £8.31 TOTE £3.60: £2.10, £1.30; EX 10.40.
Owner H R H Princess Haya Of Jordan **Bred** Stowell Park Stud **Trained** Newmarket, Suffolk

FOCUS
An ordinary juvenile maiden.

NOTEBOOK
Kona Coast, who hung badly right in a stronger 7f Newbury maiden last time, looked the pick of the paddock and didn't have to improve too much to win this, but improve he did. The blinkers, which had been applied for his first two starts, were left off here and he looked much happier as a result. He is entered in some big 6f sales races in the autumn, but on this showing he needs further. (tchd 11-4)
Walcot Square(IRE), who stayed on in promising style over 7f at Newbury in a stronger maiden that has worked out well (the second, a very highly-regarded colt, and fourth there won subsequently) also appeared to improve. He looked the likeliest winner 2f out, but his rider elected to come up the middle of the track and in the end he was worn down by an improving animal. He is bred to be better over further and is sure to win races in due course. (op 9-4 tchd 5-2)
Green Earth(IRE) had made good late headway in a 7f Salisbury maiden on his debut, but didn't seem to build on that last time. He was again a little disappointing, hanging his head a bit awkwardly to the right and he was a little unbalanced. He didn't look an easy ride, but this may not have been his track. (op 28-1)

Landowner, a 280,000euros purchase, and a half-brother to useful handicapper Riggins, does not appear to be one of the stable's leading lights. Fitted with a sheepskin noseband for his debut, he travelled well but failed to respond for pressure and his rider was sympathetic once his chance had gone. He will improve for this. (op 5-1 tchd 4-1)
Light The Way, a bit edgy beforehand and didn't seem to build on the promise shown on her 7f Salisbury debut. She is bred to need further and she ran like it. (op 16-1 tchd 20-1)
Bush Master, the most exposed runner in the field, stayed on well over 5f at Sandown previously, but upped in trip here he was made to look one-paced. The talent is there, but his ideal trip remains open to argument at this point. (op 8-1 tchd 9-1)
Nom De La Rosa(IRE) was also upped in trip here and didn't appear to handle it. She is still learning. (op 9-2)

5565 BRAKES FOOD SERVICE H'CAP — 6f 209y
3:00 (3:00) (Class 5) (0-75,75) 3-Y-O+ **£3,280** (£981; £490; £245; £122) **Stalls** Low

Form | | | | RPR
6065 **1** **Choreography**10 5288 6-9-0 **67**....(b1) SteveDrowne 3 77
(Jim Best) *in tch: effrt and hrd rdn 2f out: styd on to ld ins fnl f* **10/1**
5-56 **2** *1* **Berbice (IRE)**18 5031 4-8-13 **66**....(p) PatDobbs 1 73
(S Donohoe, Ire) *chsd ldrs: led wl over 1f out tl hdd and no ex ins fnl f* **8/1**
2530 **3** *½* **Driven (IRE)**13 5190 4-9-5 **72**.... JimCrowley 2 78
(Mrs A J Perrett) *sn led: hrd rdn and hdd wl over 1f out: kpt on u.p fnl f* **15/8**1
0040 **4** *¾* **Gift Horse**6 5363 9-9-0 **72**....(p) RichardEvans(5) 6 76
(P D Evans) *in rr: outpcd over 2f out: styd on fnl f* **12/1**
2124 **5** *1* **Patavium Prince (IRE)**26 4733 6-9-8 **75**.... DaneO'Neill 4 76
(Miss Jo Crowley) *hld up in 5th: effrt over 2f out: one pce appr fnl f* **9/4**2
0140 **6** *1 ¾* **Lady Florence**15 5124 4-8-12 **65**.... LPKeniry 7 62
(A B Coogan) *pressed ldr: rdn 3f out: wknd wl over 1f out* **5/1**3
1m 23.54s (0.44) **Going Correction** +0.10s/f (Good)
WFA 3 from 4yo+ 4lb **6** Ran SP% **110.1**
Speed ratings (Par 103): **101,99,99,98,97 95**
toteswinger: 1&2 £5.10, 1&3 £2.40, 2&3 £3.00. CSF £78.12 TOTE £10.10: £3.70, £4.10; EX 18.90.
Owner Bill Wallace **Bred** Cheveley Park Stud Ltd **Trained** Lewes, E Sussex
FOCUS
A moderate handicap which was steadily run. The winner was still 9lb off last year's best and the form makes sense.

5566 IAN CARNABY (S) STKS — 5f 213y
3:30 (3:30) (Class 6) 3-Y-O+ **£1,942** (£578; £288; £144) **Stalls** Low

Form | | | | RPR
2060 **1** **Scruffy Skip (IRE)**26 4732 4-9-0 46.... TGMcLaughlin 2 56
(Mrs C A Dunnett) *stmbld sltly s: outpcd and bhd: hdwy and swtchd to stands' rail 2f out: styd on wl on to ld nr fin* **10/1**
3433 **2** *nk* **Boldinor**2 5501 6-9-0 52.... J-PGuillambert 3 55
(M R Bosley) *trckd ldng pair: led 2f out: hrd rdn and kpt on fnl f: hdd nr fin* **11/4**2
4654 **3** *2* **Who's Winning (IRE)**15 5120 8-9-0 49.... JimCrowley 7 49
(B G Powell) *in tch: pressed ldrs 3f out: one pce fnl 2f* **9/2**3
0000 **4** *1 ¼* **Kalligal**9 5323 4-8-9 48.... KirstyMilczarek 1 40
(R Ingram) *led over 1f: styd alone far side st: wl there tl no ex fnl f* **25/1**
0005 **5** *½* **Tightrope (IRE)**55 3775 3-8-12 47....(b) DavidProbert 6 43
(T D McCarthy) *w ldr: led over 3f out tl 2f out: hrd rdn over 1f out: edgd lft and wknd* **33/1**
0260 **6** *¾* **Seneschal**13 5182 8-9-5 76.... SteveDrowne 5 46
(A B Haynes) *hld up in tch: promising effrt to trck ldrs 3f out: hrd rdn and wknd 1f out* **11/10**1
3000 **7** *22* **Hamaasy**33 4479 8-9-0 42....(p) LPKeniry 8 —
(G A Ham) *in tch on outer: wknd over 2f out: sn bhd* **66/1**
1m 11.27s (1.07) **Going Correction** +0.10s/f (Good)
WFA 3 from 4yo+ 2lb **7** Ran SP% **109.8**
Speed ratings (Par 101): **96,95,92,91,90 89,60**
toteswinger: 1&2 £2.90, 1&3 £3.40, 2&3 £1.70. CSF £34.55 TOTE £11.30: £3.20, £1.90; EX 38.10 Trifecta £100.20 Pool: £668.94 - 4.94 winning units..There was no bid for the winner.
Owner C Dunnett, D Cooper, R Clarke & J Power **Bred** Darley **Trained** Hingham, Norfolk
FOCUS
A weak, but competitive seller. The first pair ran to this year's best.

5567 BLAKES BUTCHERS FILLIES' H'CAP — 1m 1f 209y
4:00 (4:00) (Class 5) (0-70,70) 3-Y-O+ **£3,154** (£944; £472; £236; £117) **Stalls** High

Form | | | | RPR
1162 **1** **Caster Sugar (USA)**16 5101 3-9-9 **70**.... PatDobbs 6 79
(R Hannon) *in tch: rdn 3f out: led over 1f out: drvn to get on top: gng away at fin* **6/4**1
3104 **2** *2 ¼* **Evening Sunset (GER)**27 4720 3-9-4 **65**.... MickyFenton 2 69
(M G Quinlan) *hld up in rr: rdn 4f out: hdwy 2f out: drvn to chal 1f out: outpcd fnl 50yds* **9/1**
0123 **3** *1* **Arcola (IRE)**14 5168 3-9-8 **69**.... EddieAhern 3 71
(D M Simcock) *stdd in rr s: sn trcking ldng pair: hrd rdn over 1f out: one pce* **15/8**2
0300 **4** *1 ½* **Bicksta**18 5015 3-8-7 **54**....(b1) LPKeniry 8 53
(E F Vaughan) *sn led: rdn 3f out: hdd and no ex over 1f out* **33/1**
2005 **5** *4 ½* **Oronsay**29 4625 4-8-9 **49** oh3....(t) NickyMackay 5 39
(B R Millman) *mainly chsd ldr tl wknd wl over 1f out* **22/1**
3420 **6** *9* **Sunceleb (IRE)**33 4482 3-9-9 **70**.... SteveDrowne 4 56
(H Morrison) *sn towards rr: rdn 4f out: n.d after* **9/2**3
2m 4.37s (0.77) **Going Correction** +0.10s/f (Good)
WFA 3 from 4yo+ 7lb **6** Ran SP% **110.3**
Speed ratings (Par 100): **100,98,97,96,92 85**
toteswinger: 1&2 £3.80, 1&3 £1.40, 2&3 £2.70. CSF £14.94 CT £23.88 TOTE £2.50: £1.40, £3.10; EX 16.30 Trifecta £41.70 Pool: £464.76 - 8.24 winning units..
Owner Mrs James Wigan **Bred** Mrs James Wigan & London TB Services Ltd **Trained** East Everleigh, Wilts
FOCUS
A modest fillies' handicap. The winner ran to a similar level to Windsor and the fourth limits the form.
Evening Sunset(GER) Official explanation: jockey said filly hung right
Sunceleb(IRE) Official explanation: jockey said filly was never travelling

5568 BRAKES FRESH IDEAS CLAIMING STKS — 1m 1f 209y
4:30 (4:30) (Class 6) 3-4-Y-O **£1,942** (£578; £288; £144) **Stalls** High

Form | | | | RPR
5000 **1** **Buddhist Monk**12 5235 4-9-10 80....(p) EddieAhern 2 79
(Ian Williams) *mde all: sn 4 l clr: pricked ears and idling fr over 1f out: cajoled along and rdn out* **6/4**1
4445 **2** *8* **Kyle Of Bute**3 5482 3-8-9 45....(v1) DaneO'Neill 1 55
(J L Dunlop) *chsd wnr: hrd rdn 2f out: nt pce to trble wnr* **13/2**3
2501 **3** *6* **Fong's Alibi**15 5127 3-8-8 65....(p) LPKeniry 3 42
(J S Moore) *sn last: pushed along over 5f out: hrd rdn and wnt mod 3rd 3f out: n.d* **6/4**1
0550 **4** *17* **Carte D'Oro (IRE)**21 4904 3-8-2 60.... DavidProbert 4 —
(R M Beckett) *racd in 3rd: rdn 4f out: sn hrd drvn in rr and no ch* **9/2**2
2m 3.74s (0.14) **Going Correction** +0.10s/f (Good)
WFA 3 from 4yo 7lb **4** Ran SP% **111.5**
Speed ratings (Par 101): **103,96,91,78**
CSF £11.15 TOTE £2.50; EX 8.10.
Owner Dr Marwan Koukash **Bred** Stanley Estate And Stud Co **Trained** Portway, Worcs
FOCUS
An ideal opportunity for the winner, with the third below par. The runner-up looks the best guide.

5569 ENTREMETTIER APPRENTICE H'CAP — 7f 214y
5:00 (5:00) (Class 6) (0-60,61) 4-Y-O+ **£2,460** (£732; £365; £182) **Stalls** Low

Form | | | | RPR
3060 **1** **Golden Prospect**4 5429 5-8-9 **55**.... NathanAlison(5) 7 63
(J W Hills) *stdd s: restrained in detached last: hdwy fr over 2f out: styd on wl to ld fnl 25yds* **7/2**1
1040 **2** *½* **Hypnotic**18 5019 7-9-0 **60**.... CharlesEddery(5) 8 67
(Jim Best) *led and set gd pce: hrd rdn and edgd rt fr over 1f out: hld on gamely tl hdd fnl 25yds* **9/1**
2144 **3** *1 ¾* **Solo River**16 5108 4-9-2 **60**.... SimonPearce(3) 6 66+
(P J Makin) *chsd ldr: rdn to chal 2f out: one pce fnl f* **13/2**
0060 **4** *1 ½* **Dancer's Legacy**13 5190 4-9-2 **57**.... MCGeran 4 56
(J R Boyle) *in tch: drvn to chse ldrs over 2f out: one pce appr fnl f* **6/1**
3150 **5** *1 ¼* **Goodbye Cash (IRE)**2 5502 5-9-6 **61** 6ex.... RichardEvans 5 57
(P D Evans) *sn chsng ldrs: hrd rdn 2f out: one pce* **11/2**3
-003 **6** *4 ½* **Prince Valentine**27 4697 8-8-2 **50**....(p) HarryBentley(7) 1 35
(G L Moore) *hld up towards rr: sme hdwy over 2f out: wknd over 1f out* **11/1**
0005 **7** *1 ¼* **Silver Hotspur**3 5479 5-9-2 **60**.... AshleyMorgan(3) 9 42
(C R Dore) *stdd s: hld up towards rr: gd hdwy and prom 4f out: wknd 2f out* **5/1**2
006 **8** *5* **Evianne**10 4731 5-8-0 **46** oh1....(b1) KierenFox(5) 2 16
(P W Hiatt) *mid-div on rail: rdn 5f out: wknd 3f out* **80/1**
2001 **9** *24* **Manchestermaverick (USA)**15 5120 4-8-8 **56**(vt) MatthewCosham(7) 3 —
(Dr J R J Naylor) *chsd ldrs tl wknd rapidly 3f out: sn bhd* **6/1**
1m 35.73s (-0.27) **Going Correction** +0.10s/f (Good) **9** Ran SP% **115.7**
Speed ratings (Par 101): **105,104,102,101,100 95,94,89,65**
toteswinger: 1&2 £8.40, 1&3 £7.40, 2&3 £11.50. CSF £36.03 CT £196.65 TOTE £3.90: £1.50, £4.00, £2.10; EX 41.70 Trifecta £269.00 Pool: £618.04 - 1.70 winning units. Place 6: £596.10, Place 5: £427.41..
Owner Michael Wauchope And Partners **Bred** D E And Mrs J Cash **Trained** Upper Lambourn, Berks
■ Stewards' Enquiry : Nathan Alison caution: careless riding
FOCUS
This ordinary handicap for apprentice riders was run at a decent pace, and the form is sound.
Manchestermaverick(USA) Official explanation: vet said gelding bled from the nose
T/Plt: £414.70 to a £1 stake. Pool: £65,824.19. 115.85 winning tickets. T/Qpdt: £45.30 to a £1 stake. Pool: £4,549.46. 74.29 winning tickets. LM

5310 KEMPTON (A.W) (R-H)
Wednesday, September 2

OFFICIAL GOING: Standard
Wind: Light, half behind Weather: Overcast, showers

5570 GROOMED TO PERFECTION, THE KIA SOUL H'CAP — 1m 2f (P)
5:50 (5:52) (Class 5) (0-75,75) 3-Y-O **£2,590** (£770; £385; £192) **Stalls** High

Form | | | | RPR
-020 **1** **Foxtrot Charlie**44 4149 3-8-8 **65**....(b) JimCrowley 3 73
(P Winkworth) *pressed ldr: rdn to ld over 1f out: styd on wl u.p fnl f: all out* **14/1**
53-3 **2** *nk* **Absinthe (IRE)**16 5100 3-9-3 **74**.... AdamKirby 9 81+
(W R Swinburn) *hld up in tch in midfield: swtchd lft and effrt u.p wl over 1f out: no prog tl styd on strly ins fnl f: clsng qckly on wnr at fin* **7/2**2
-223 **3** *1* **Mefraas (IRE)**20 4957 3-9-3 **74**.... TPO'Shea 6 79
(E A L Dunlop) *stdd s: hld up in last pl: hdwy towards inner wl over 1f out: swtchd lft and r.o wl fnl f: wnt 3rd last strides: nt rch ldrs* **5/1**3
3013 **4** *hd* **Assail**28 4649 3-9-4 **75**.... SteveDrowne 4 80
(H Morrison) *sn led: rdn over 2f out: hdd over 1f out: kpt on same pce u.p: lost 2 pls wl ins fnl f* **8/1**
650 **5** *1 ¾* **Supernoverre (IRE)**21 4911 3-8-13 **70**.... IanMongan 10 71
(P Howling) *chsd ldrs: rdn and effrt to chse ldng pair on outer 2f out: one pce u.p fnl f* **20/1**
1014 **6** *¾* **Haafhd Time (IRE)**14 5168 3-8-5 **62**.... RichardKingscote 12 62
(Tom Dascombe) *chsd ldrs: rdn over 2f out: unable qck u.p over 1f out: plugged on same pce fnl f* **5/2**1
0400 **7** *½* **Millway Beach (IRE)**39 4300 3-8-9 **66**....(p) PaulHanagan 8 65
(Pat Eddery) *dwlt: sn pushed along to r in midfield: hmpd bnd over 7f out: rdn over 3f out: plugged on same pce fnl 2f* **33/1**
4365 **8** *½* **Young Dottie**16 5099 3-9-3 **74**.... JimmyQuinn 11 72
(P M Phelan) *stdd s: hld up in last pair: hdwy into midfield over 2f out: no prog u.p fnl 2f* **25/1**
0533 **9** *½* **Peter Grimes (IRE)**31 4563 3-8-9 **66**.... MickyFenton 2 63
(H J L Dunlop) *chsd ldrs on outer: rdn and struggling 3f out: no threat to ldrs after* **12/1**
-302 **10** *nk* **Navajo Nation (IRE)**21 4918 3-9-0 **71**....(b1) MartinDwyer 5 67
(B J Meehan) *s.i.s: hdwy and racd in midfield after 1f: pushed along over 3f out: rdn and lost pl over 2f out: no ch fnl 2f* **8/1**
3423 **11** *7* **Mayolynn (USA)**14 5151 3-9-1 **72**.... TPQueally 1 54
(H R A Cecil) *s.i.s: nvr gng wl and sn pushed along: rdn and toiling over 3f out: wl bhd fnl f* **20/1**
2m 7.11s (-0.89) **Going Correction** +0.05s/f (Slow) **11** Ran SP% **120.4**
Speed ratings (Par 101): **105,104,103,103,102 101,101,101,100,100 94**
toteswinger: 1&2 £20.00, 1&3 £30.00, 2&3 £5.70. CSF £61.16 CT £290.42 TOTE £14.40: £3.30, £1.80, £1.50; EX 118.70.
Owner Foxtrot Racing Partnership **Bred** Capt A L Smith-Maxwell **Trained** Chiddingfold, Surrey
FOCUS
A couple of unexposed performers in just a fair handicap. The time was just over a second above Racing Post standard and the form seems pretty solid. The winner edged towards the centre in the straight.

Peter Grimes(IRE) Official explanation: jockey said gelding hung right-handed

5571 EUROPEAN BREEDERS' FUND MEDIAN AUCTION MAIDEN STKS 6f (P)
6:20 (6:21) (Class 5) 2-Y-O **£3,561** (£1,059; £529; £264) **Stalls** High

Form RPR

02 **1** **Fardyieh**[18] 5026 2-8-12 0 ChrisCatlin 9 81
(C E Brittain) *chsd ldng pair: ev ch wl over 2f out: pushed along to ld 2f out: rdn and pressed jst ins fnl f: edgd lft but styd on strly after* **7/2**[2]

2 **2** ¾ **Lutine Charlie (IRE)**[32] 4515 2-9-3 0 JimCrowley 7 84
(P Winkworth) *chsd ldng trio: clsd 3f out: rdn to chse wnr ent fnl f: pressed wnr fnl 150yds: r.o but no imp after* **2/1**[1]

4 **3** 4 ½ **Barlaman (USA)**[9] 5311 2-9-0 0 AhmedAjtebi(3) 3 70
(Saeed Bin Suroor) *chsd ldr tl led wl over 2f out tl hdd and rdn 2f out: wknd fnl f: jst hld on for 3rd* **2/1**[1]

0 **4** *hd* **Deely Plaza**[9] 5317 2-9-3 0 PatDobbs 5 70
(R Hannon) *chsd ldrs but off the pce: rdn and swtchd lft over 2f out: plugged on to press for 3rd on post but nvr gng pce to threaten ldrs* **50/1**

5 ½ **Pont De Nuit** 2-9-3 0 RyanMoore 10 70+
(R Hannon) *outpcd in midfield: rdn over 2f out: kpt on steadily fnl f: nvr trbld ldrs: bttr for r* **8/1**[3]

06 **6** 1 ¾ **Calm Storm (IRE)**[6] 5368 2-9-3 0 ShaneKelly 1 63
(J Noseda) *sn outpcd in midfield: rdn over 3f out: plugged on same pce and nvr nr ldrs* **25/1**

0 **7** *nse* **Rain On The Wind (IRE)**[9] 5311 2-9-3 0 RichardKingscote 12 63
(S C Williams) *taken down early: led at fast pce: hdd wl over 1f out: wknd qckly jst over 1f out* **12/1**

8 2 ¾ **Sir William Orpen** 2-9-3 0 IanMongan 2 55
(P M Phelan) *wnt rt s and s.i.s: a wl outpcd towards rr: hung lft fr over 2f out: nvr nr ldrs* **66/1**

0 **9** ½ **Rosiliant (IRE)**[30] 4603 2-8-12 0 AdamKirby 8 48
(C G Cox) *s.i.s and sn rdn: a outpcd in rr: sme hdwy u.p fnl f: n.d* **50/1**

10 ¾ **Baralaka** 2-9-3 0 PatCosgrave 4 51
(Sir Mark Prescott) *s.i.s: wl outpcd in rr: wd bnd 3f out: sn swtchd bk to inner: sme modest late hdwy: nvr a factor* **33/1**

11 4 **Professor Bollini (IRE)** 2-9-3 0 DaneO'Neill 11 39
(H J L Dunlop) *alway struggling to go pce in rr* **33/1**

5 **12** 6 **Accountable**[23] 4851 2-9-3 0 SteveDrowne 6 21
(B G Powell) *outpcd in midfield: hmpd and lost pl bnd 4f out: wl bhd fr 1/2-way* **66/1**

1m 13.27s (0.17) **Going Correction** +0.05s/f (Slow) **12** Ran SP% **124.3**
Speed ratings (Par 95): **100,99,93,92,92 89,89,86,85,84 79,71**
toteswinger: 1&2 £3.10, 1&3 £3.70, 2&3 £1.60. CSF £11.06 TOTE £5.10: £1.40, £1.70, £1.40; EX 1.80.
Owner Saeed Manana **Bred** Mrs C R Philipson & Mrs H G Lascelles **Trained** Newmarket, Suffolk

FOCUS
A race lacking much strength in depth but the gallop was soon decent and a race in which two of the market leaders, who had previously shown plenty of promise, pulled clear. The first two ended up towards the centre.

NOTEBOOK
Fardyieh, who was well supported, had shown improved form on her previous start and fully confirmed that promise on this all-weather debut, despite hanging. She may be better than the bare form given she fared the best of the trio that forced a decent gallop, she should stay 7f and may be capable of further progress. (op 9-2)
Lutine Charlie(IRE) ◆ got the perfect tow behind the leading trio on his all-weather debut and fully confirmed the promise shown at Doncaster early last month. He pulled clear of the remainder and is more than capable of picking up a similar event. (op 9-4)
Barlaman(USA), noticeably green on his debut at this track the previous week, failed to build on that against a couple of rivals that had shown fair form on turf. He is capable of winning an ordinary event but is likely to remain vulnerable to the more progressive types in this grade. (op 9-4 tchd 5-2)
Deely Plaza hadn't shown much on his recent debut at Windsor but fared a good deal better on this first run on Polytrack. He shaped as though the step up to 7f would suit and he should be able to pick up a race in due course. (op 66-1)
Pont De Nuit, related to a couple of winners from 5f-1m, attracted support in the day but proved easy to back near the off. He showed ability despite his apparent greenness and is entitled to improve for this experience. (op 5-1)
Calm Storm(IRE) turned in an improved effort and, while likely to remain vulnerable in this type of event, may do better in ordinary handicaps upped to 7f.
Sir William Orpen Official explanation: jockey said gelding hung left-handed

5572 DIGIBET CASINO MAIDEN STKS 7f (P)
6:50 (6:52) (Class 5) 3-Y-O+ **£2,590** (£770; £385; £192) **Stalls** High

Form RPR

04 **1** **Moojeh (IRE)**[77] 3025 3-8-12 0 JerryO'Dwyer 4 74+
(M Botti) *wnt lft s: in tch: rdn to chal jst over 2f out: led ins fnl f: sn drvn clr: eased towards fin* **33/1**

03 **2** 2 ¼ **La Marseillaise (IRE)**[117] 1825 3-8-12 0 MichaelHills 9 68
(B W Hills) *led: rdn and hrd pressed jst over 2f out: hdd ins fnl f: sn outpcd by wnr* **5/1**[2]

3 1 ¾ **Totalitarian** 3-9-3 0 MartinDwyer 11 68
(S A Callaghan) *hld up in tch in midfield: hdwy on inner jst over 2f out: kpt on to go 3rd fnl 100yds: nt gng pce to rch ldrs* **25/1**

23 **4** ½ **Major Lawrence (IRE)**[25] 4786 3-9-3 0 (t) RyanMoore 12 67
(J Noseda) *hld up in bhd ldrs: rdn over 2f out: hrd drvn and nt qckn over 1f out: no imp on ldrs after and lost 3rd fnl 100yds* **4/7**[1]

44 **5** 2 **Dom Polski**[19] 4981 3-9-3 0 (t) AdamKirby 7 62
(W R Swinburn) *chsd ldrs: rdn and unable qck over 2f out: plugged on same pce fnl f* **14/1**

00- **6** 1 ¼ **Spice Run**[351] 5995 6-9-7 0 MickyFenton 6 60
(Stef Liddiard) *chsd ldr: ev ch over 2f out: rdn wl over 1f out: wknd jst ins fnl f* **40/1**

7 2 **Suzi's Dancer** 3-8-12 0 JimmyQuinn 8 48
(H J Collingridge) *s.i.s: bhd: clsd and in tch 1/2-way: rdn and hdwy over 1f out: r.o fnl f: nvr trbld ldrs* **100/1**

8 1 **Sometsuke** 3-9-3 0 (t) JimmyFortune 3 50+
(P J Makin) *hmpd s and v.s.a: wl bhd: clsd and in tch 1/2-way: swtchd ins and hdwy over 1f out: r.o: nvr trbld ldrs* **20/1**

9 2 **Space Station**[93] 3-9-3 0 TonyCulhane 13 45
(S Dow) *hld up towards rr: rdn and sme hdwy over 2f out: wknd u.p over 1f out* **16/1**

04- **10** 2 **Pagan Force (IRE)**[418] 3895 3-9-3 0 JimCrowley 5 39
(Mrs A J Perrett) *t.k.h: hld up wl in tch: rdn and fnd nil over 2f out: sn btn* **9/1**[3]

11 ½ **She Goes Nowhere (IRE)** 3-8-12 0 VinceSlattery 14 33
(M S Tuck) *s.i.s: in tch in rr: rdn and no prog over 2f out* **100/1**

12 ¾ **Barathea's Acclaim** 3-8-12 0 DaneO'Neill 1 31
(P R Hedger) *v.s.a: bhd: hdwy on outer over 3f out: rdn and struggling over 2f out* **100/1**

13 4 ½ **Billy Simmonds** 4-9-7 0 LiamJones 10 26
(Miss J Feilden) *hld up in tch in midfield: rdn over 2f out: edgd rt and wknd 2f out: wl bhd fnl f* **150/1**

0 **14** 7 **Captain Teddo**[25] 4786 3-9-3 0 (t) RobertHavlin 2 5
(R Ingram) *in tch in midfield tl wknd qckly u.p over 2f out: wl bhd fnl f* **150/1**

1m 26.49s (0.49) **Going Correction** +0.05s/f (Slow)
WFA 3 from 4yo+ 4lb **14** Ran SP% **121.2**
Speed ratings (Par 103): **99,96,94,93,91 90,87,86,84,82 81,80,75,67**
toteswinger: 1&2 £29.10, 1&3 £54.50, 2&3 £21.40. CSF £188.20 TOTE £55.90: £7.70, £1.50, £5.60; EX 100.10.
Owner Can Artam **Bred** Shadwell Estate Company Limited **Trained** Newmarket, Suffolk

FOCUS
This looked a good opportunity for the market leader to open his account but, with that one disappointing, this form has an unconvincing look to it. The pace was fair and the winner, who raced in the centre, showed big improvement.

5573 DIGIBET NURSERY 1m (P)
7:20 (7:21) (Class 6) (0-65,65) 2-Y-O **£2,047** (£604; £302) **Stalls** High

Form RPR

040 **1** **Boquito (IRE)**[19] 5006 2-9-2 **60** JerryO'Dwyer 6 69+
(Miss Amy Weaver) *hld up towards rr: hdwy over 3f out: rdn to chal 2f out: led over 1f out: sn in command: eased towards fin* **14/1**

006 **2** 2 ¾ **Rodrigo De Freitas (IRE)**[32] 4534 2-9-2 **60** PatCosgrave 8 60
(J R Boyle) *chsd ldrs: wnt 2nd over 3f out: rdn and ev ch over 2f out: drvn to ld 2f out: hdd over 1f out: kpt on but no ch w wnr fnl f* **25/1**

5653 **3** 1 ½ **Whiepa Snappa (IRE)**[12] 5213 2-9-6 **64** IanMongan 7 61
(P M Phelan) *hld up in midfield: rdn and effrt over 2f out: edging rt u.p fr over 1f out: chsd ldng pair fnl 150yds: r.o but nvr nr enough to chal* **7/1**

1624 **4** 3 **Mary Helen**[20] 4931 2-8-11 **55** LiamJones 1 45
(W M Brisbourne) *s.i.s: bhd: hmpd 6f out: hdwy and rdn on outer over 2f out: styd on to go modest 4th nr fin: nvr trbld ldrs* **20/1**

414 **5** *nk* **Sultan's Choice**[23] 4858 2-9-1 **59** PaulHanagan 9 48
(P D Evans) *bhd: hdwy and ev ch over 2f out: rdn ent fnl 2f: wknd jst over 1f out: no ch w ldng pair fnl f: lost 3rd fnl 150yds* **6/1**[2]

2054 **6** 1 **Yawary**[22] 4868 2-9-4 **62** ChrisCatlin 13 49
(C E Brittain) *chsd ldrs: rdn over 2f out: wknd u.p over 1f out* **13/2**[3]

6364 **7** 2 ½ **Knockenduff**[12] 5213 2-9-2 **60** SamHitchcott 10 42
(M R Channon) *chsd ldr tl led over 3f out: rdn over 2f out: hdd 2f out: wknd u.p over 1f out* **9/1**

005 **8** 1 **Mandarin Express**[18] 5017 2-9-2 **60** MartinDwyer 14 39
(B J Meehan) *led: tl over 3f out: styd chsng ldrs: rdn over 2f out: wknd u.p 2f out* **6/1**[2]

0500 **9** ½ **Golden Pippin**[14] 5166 2-8-12 **56** PatDobbs 12 34
(R Hannon) *in tch on inner: lost pl jst over 3f out: rdn and no prog fr over 2f out* **20/1**

046 **10** *nk* **Execution (IRE)**[37] 4385 2-9-7 **65** JimmyFortune 4 43
(E A L Dunlop) *chsd ldrs on outer tl rdn and btn over 2f out* **10/1**

0036 **11** *nk* **Sixpenny Moon (USA)**[12] 5213 2-9-4 **62** RyanMoore 5 39
(R Hannon) *stdd s: hld up in rr: hamperd 6f out: nvr trbld ldrs* **9/2**[1]

654 **12** 8 **Split The Pot (IRE)**[59] 3658 2-9-4 **62** JimCrowley 11 21
(P R Chamings) *t.k.h: hld up towards rr: lost tch over 2f out: wl bhd fnl 2f* **33/1**

3100 **13** 1 ½ **Highcliffe Bridge (IRE)**[21] 4915 2-8-12 **56** (b[1]) CatherineGannon 2 12
(N P Littmoden) *s.i.s: a bhd* **66/1**

440 **U** **Proper Littlemadam**[41] 4226 2-9-2 **65** Louis-PhilippeBeuzelin(5) 3 —
(M Botti) *stdd after s: t.k.h: hld up towards rr tl stmbld and uns rdr 6f out* **20/1**

1m 41.98s (2.18) **Going Correction** +0.05s/f (Slow) **14** Ran SP% **120.9**
Speed ratings (Par 93): **91,88,86,83,83 82,79,78,78,78 77,69,68,—**
toteswinger: 1&2 £144.90, 1&3 £25.00, 2&3 £92.30. CSF £334.39 CT £2656.65 TOTE £22.00: £6.30, £11.90, £3.70; EX 482.60.
Owner Mrs Melba Bryce **Bred** Darley **Trained** Newmarket, Suffolk

FOCUS
An open event on paper but a reasonable gallop and a race turned into a procession by the winner, who was another to race in the centre in the straight.

NOTEBOOK
Boquito(IRE) had shown promise over 6f on soft on his second start but turned in a much improved effort upped to this trip on his nursery and all-weather debut. He won with plenty in hand and will be interesting if turned out before reassessment. (op 16-1)
Rodrigo De Freitas(IRE), a steadily progressive sort, had the run of the race and turned in his best effort returned to artificial surfaces. He fared the best of those up with the pace, is in good hands and should be able to pick up an ordinary event on this surface.
Whiepa Snappa(IRE)had shown improved form over this trip on his previous start and wasn't far off that level on this all-weather debut. A stiffer overall test of stamina may suit and this relatively unexposed sort may well be capable of better. (op 11-2)
Mary Helen is a fairly reliable type and wasn't disgraced after being hampered by the unseated rider in the early stages and after making her ground on the wide outside in the straight. She's capable of winning a similarly ordinary event on this surface. (op 25-1)
Sultan's Choicehad shaped with promise on her nursery and all-weather debut over 7f on her previous start but failed to improve for the step up to this trip. She has not had much racing and may do better for this yard. (op 11-2 tchd 7-1)
Yawary, who has yet to win a race, has been a fairly consistent sort but she failed to improve for the step up to this trip. The return to shorter is likely to suit but she is vulnerable to the more progressive sorts from her current mark. (op 5-1)
Sixpenny Moon(USA), who failed to improve for the step up to 1m on her previous start, attracted plenty of support back on Polytrack but could never get competitive after being hampered early on. (op 15-2)

5574 DIGIBET.COM CLAIMING STKS 1m (P)
7:50 (7:54) (Class 6) 3-Y-O **£2,047** (£604; £302) **Stalls** High

Form RPR

4224 **1** **Sunshine Always (IRE)**[24] 4814 3-9-7 80 RyanMoore 6 85+
(W J Haggas) *stdd s: hld up in last trio: stl plenty to do 3f out: pushed along and gd hdwy over 2f out: led ins fnl f: sn clr: easily* **4/5**[1]

0-66 **2** 6 **Foxtrot Bravo (IRE)**[190] 662 3-8-13 0 RichardKingscote 4 62
(Miss S L Davison) *chsd ldr after 1f: rdn over 2f out: lost 2nd over 1f out: no ch w wnr fnl f but kpt on to go 2nd again fnl 100yds* **100/1**

0632 **3** 1 **Jiggalong**[24] 4819 3-8-3 61 TPO'Shea 10 50
(Jane Chapple-Hyam) *hld up in last trio: nt clr run on inner and swtchd lft over 2f out: edgd rt fnl f: r.o to go 3rd towards fin: no threat to wnr* **9/1**

The Form Book, Raceform Ltd, Compton, RG20 6NL

3234 **4** 2 **Equipe De Nuit**[3] 5482 3-8-2 70 TobyAtkinson(7) 8 51
(S C Williams) *led: pushed 6 l clr 1/2-way: rdn jst over 2f out: hdd ins fnl f: immediately btn: tired and edgd lft after: lost 2 pls fnl 100yds* **9/1**

550 **5** 2 3/4 **Topcroft**[78] 3009 3-8-11 50 TGMcLaughlin 3 47
(Mrs C A Dunnett) *hld up wl bhd: last and no ch 3f out: hdwy past btn horses on outer 2f out: nvr a factor* **100/1**

-000 **6** 2 1/4 **Portugese Caddy**[37] 4378 3-8-11 71 JimCrowley 5 41
(P Winkworth) *hld up towards rr: nt clr run over 2f out: no ch after* **33/1**

0341 **7** 1 **Head Down**[18] 5016 3-9-4 77 SteveDrowne 7 46
(Mrs L C Jewell) *racd in midfield: drvn and no prog over 2f out: wl btn after* **7/1**[3]

000- **8** 7 **Against The Rules**[272] 7547 3-8-7 47 KirstyMilczarek 12 18
(J A R Toller) *chsd ldr for 1f: struggling u.p over 3f out: wl btn fr over 2f out* **100/1**

0415 **9** 6 **Hold The Bucks (USA)**[123] 1670 3-8-11 67 (p) LukeMorris 9 8
(J S Moore) *racd in midfield: rdn and no hdwy 3f out: sn wl btn: eased ins fnl f* **14/1**

0333 **10** 7 **Statute Book (IRE)**[14] 5169 3-9-1 74 JimmyFortune 2 —
(S Kirk) *styd wd tl 1/2-way: chsd ldrs tl wknd u.p over 2f out: eased fnl f: t.o* **6/1**[2]

6000 **11** 2 **Songful (IRE)**[18] 5018 3-8-1 43 (p) PaulHanagan 11 —
(Pat Eddery) *sn pushed along in midfield: rdn and toiling wl over 2f out: sn wl bhd: t.o* **66/1**

1m 40.38s (0.58) **Going Correction** +0.05s/f (Slow) **11** Ran SP% **116.4**
Speed ratings (Par 99): **99,93,92,90,87 85,84,77,71,64 62**
toteswinger: 1&2 £22.10, 1&3 £4.00, 2&3 £22.60. CSF £150.13 TOTE £1.80: £1.30, £8.10, £1.70; EX 82.30.The winner was claimed by T. D. McCarthy for £20,000. Jiggalong was claimed by P. D. Evans for £7,000.
Owner Cheveley Park Stud **Bred** Moyglare Stud Farm Ltd **Trained** Newmarket, Suffolk

FOCUS
An uncompetitive claimer in which the reasonable gallop increased around halfway. The winner raced in the centre in the straight. It was easy for him with the main dangers not at their best.
Hold The Bucks(USA) Official explanation: jockey said gelding hung left-handed

5575 LEVY BOARD H'CAP 1m (P)
8:20 (8:23) (Class 4) (0-80,80) 3-Y-O **£4,727** (£1,406; £702; £351) **Stalls** High

Form RPR

2162 **1** **The Scorching Wind (IRE)**[39] 4304 3-8-8 70 (t) ChrisCatlin 12 85+
(S C Williams) *t.k.h: hld up in tch: trckd ldrs gng best over 2f out: swtchd lft 2f out: led over 1f out: sn rdn clr: easily* **10/1**

2351 **2** 2 3/4 **Striding Edge (IRE)**[14] 5169 3-8-11 73 MartinDwyer 2 82+
(W R Muir) *hld up wl in bhd: stl plenty to do 2f out: swtchd rt and gd hdwy ent fnl f: r.o wl to go 2nd fnl 75yds: nvr nr wnr* **14/1**

6110 **3** 1 **Cool Hand Jake**[28] 4649 3-9-4 80 (t) FergusSweeney 10 87
(P J Makin) *dwlt: towards rr: hdwy into midfield over 3f out: swtchd to outer and hdwy over 1f out: r.o fnl f to go 3rd fnl 50yds: nvr nr wnr* **7/1**[3]

2002 **4** 1 **Diamond Twister (USA)**[31] 4581 3-8-3 68 MarcHalford(3) 4 72
(J R Best) *chsd ldrs: rdn over 2f out: drvn and kpt on same pce fr wl over 1f out* **33/1**

4122 **5** nk **Play It Sam**[20] 4956 3-8-10 72 (t) ShaneKelly 7 76
(W R Swinburn) *led narrowly on inner: rdn over 2f out: edgd lft u.p and hdd over 1f out: no ch w wnr after: lost 3 pls fnl 100yds* **8/1**

502 **6** 1 1/2 **Respite**[16] 5090 3-9-0 76 MichaelHills 13 76
(W J Haggas) *dwlt: towards rr: rdn and effrt towards inner jst over 2f out: no imp fr over 1f out* **6/1**[2]

0623 **7** nk **Roar Of Applause**[13] 5189 3-9-4 80 (b) EddieAhern 3 80
(B J Meehan) *hld up in tch towards rr: hdwy to chse ldrs over 3f out: rdn and unable qck jst over 2f out: plugged on same pce after* **6/1**[2]

-162 **8** shd **Cut And Thrust (IRE)**[14] 5169 3-8-12 74 (p) PhilipRobinson 6 73
(M A Jarvis) *w ldr: ev ch and rdn over 2f out: drvn wl over 1f out: wknd over 1f out* **8/1**

0212 **9** 3/4 **Indian Art (IRE)**[13] 5182 3-9-3 79 RyanMoore 9 77
(R Hannon) *hld up towards rr: rdn and effrt over 2f out: nvr trbld ldrs* **4/1**[1]

0031 **10** 7 **Kiss A Prince**[22] 4872 3-8-11 73 JimCrowley 5 55
(D K Ivory) *a towards rr: struggling and wd bnd 3f out: no ch after* **16/1**

0614 **11** 1/2 **Best In Class**[14] 5169 3-8-10 72 TedDurcan 8 52
(Tom Dascombe) *in tch in midfield: rdn and struggling 3f out: sn bhd* **16/1**

0241 **12** 3/4 **Arteus**[19] 4981 3-9-0 76 JimmyQuinn 11 55
(Jane Chapple-Hyam) *t.k.h: hld up wl in tch: rdn and wknd over 2f out: wl bhd over 1f out* **20/1**

3105 **13** 1 3/4 **Omnium Duke (IRE)**[16] 5095 3-8-11 73 (b[1]) LiamJones 14 48
(J W Hills) *t.k.h: hld up in rr: rdn and struggling wl over 2f out: no ch after* **40/1**

1m 39.68s (-0.12) **Going Correction** +0.05s/f (Slow) **13** Ran SP% **121.0**
Speed ratings (Par 103): **102,99,98,97,96 95,95,95,94,87 86,86,84**
toteswinger: 1&2 £38.60, 1&3 £26.30, 2&3 £20.60. CSF £141.23 CT £1092.58 TOTE £15.10: £5.00, £3.90, £2.90; EX 268.90.
Owner Chris Watkins And David N Reynolds **Bred** Mark Commins **Trained** Newmarket, Suffolk

FOCUS
A decent handicap for the grade, comprising several winners, and the form could have been rated a length higher. The pace to the straight was only fair at best and the winner continued the theme of racing towards the centre in the straight.

5576 FAREWELL AND HAPPY RETIREMENT DAVE DENNIS H'CAP 6f (P)
8:50 (8:52) (Class 6) (0-65,65) 3-Y-O+ **£2,047** (£604; £302) **Stalls** High

Form RPR

3263 **1** **Cativo Cavallino**[18] 5019 6-9-1 62 NataliaGemelova(3) 4 71
(J E Long) *hmpd sn after s: towards rr on outer: rdn over 2f out: hdwy u.p over 1f out: r.o wl to ld last stride* **7/1**[3]

-403 **2** hd **Rosie Says No**[44] 4154 4-9-1 59 (p) JimCrowley 12 67
(R M H Cowell) *w ldrs on inner: led over 2f out: hung lft u.p over 1f out: kpt on wl tl hdd last stride* **6/1**[2]

0003 **3** 3/4 **Guildenstern (IRE)**[23] 4843 7-9-4 62 JimmyQuinn 3 68+
(P Howling) *stdd and dropped in bhd after s: nt clr run on inner over 2f out: gd hdwy and rdn jst over 1f out: r.o fnl f: nt rch ldrs* **16/1**

1000 **4** 1 1/4 **Hollow Jo**[81] 2920 9-9-6 64 (v) FergusSweeney 9 66
(J R Jenkins) *hld up in tch: hdwy over 2f out: rdn to press ldrs ent fnl f: wknd fnl 75yds* **25/1**

0440 **5** 1 1/4 **Don Pele (IRE)**[17] 5065 7-9-6 64 (p) LukeMorris 2 62
(R A Harris) *chsd ldrs: rdn and unable qck wl over 2f out: plugged on u.p fnl f: nt pce to chal ldrs* **16/1**

0600 **6** nk **Imperial Skylight**[10] 5287 3-9-3 63 ChrisCatlin 7 60
(M R Channon) *sn niggled along towards rr: rdn over 2f out: hdwy u.p over 1f out: kpt on but nt pce to rch ldrs* **33/1**

6052 **7** hd **Rebecca De Winter**[14] 5164 3-9-5 65 EddieAhern 10 61
(David Pinder) *sn in tch: hdwy to chal 2f out: carried lft and rdn over 1f out: wknd ins fnl f* **10/1**

6214 **8** 1 1/4 **Mr Skipiton (IRE)**[32] 4536 4-9-4 62 TGMcLaughlin 8 54
(B J McMath) *towards rr: rdn and hdwy towards inner jst over 2f out: chsd ldrs ent fnl f: btn and eased wl ins fnl f* **2/1**[1]

256 **9** 3/4 **Namu**[10] 5288 6-9-6 64 (p) DaneO'Neill 1 54
(Miss T Spearing) *stdd and dropped in after s: hld up in rr: rdn over 2f out: no real prog* **16/1**

0000 **10** 6 **Cool Sands (IRE)**[23] 4843 7-9-2 60 (v) J-PGuillambert 6 31
(J G Given) *w ldrs tl wknd u.p jst over 2f out: eased ins fnl f* **25/1**

30-0 **11** 3 1/4 **Boho Chic**[25] 4791 3-9-0 65 MatthewDavies(5) 5 25
(George Baker) *w ldrs on outer: ev ch over 2f out: wknd qckly u.p wl over 1f out* **6/1**[2]

0216 **12** 3 1/4 **Green Lagonda (AUS)**[13] 5184 7-9-5 63 PaulDoe 11 13
(P D Evans) *led narrowly tl over 2f out: wknd 2f out: wl bhd fnl f* **8/1**

1m 13.49s (0.39) **Going Correction** +0.05s/f (Slow)
WFA 3 from 4yo+ 2lb **12** Ran SP% **122.9**
Speed ratings (Par 101): **99,98,97,96,94 94,93,92,91,83 78,74**
toteswinger: 1&2 £9.00, 1&3 £16.50, 2&3 £30.40. CSF £49.56 CT £676.99 TOTE £8.30: £2.30, £1.50, £5.20; EX 69.60.
Owner P Saxon **Bred** Miss A M Rees **Trained** Caterham, Surrey
■ Stewards' Enquiry : Luke Morris one-day ban: failed to keep straight from stalls (Aug 16)
Natalia Gemelova four-day ban: excessive use of the whip (Sep 16-19)

FOCUS
An ordinary handicap run at a sound pace throughout. The field fanned across the course but the winner came centre to stands side in the straight. The form is rated around the runner-up.

5577 WEATHERBYS BLOODSTOCK INSURANCE APPRENTICE H'CAP (ROUND 10) 1m 3f (P)
9:20 (9:21) (Class 6) (0-60,60) 3-Y-O+ **£2,047** (£604; £302) **Stalls** High

Form RPR

3000 **1** **Inch Lodge**[18] 5015 7-9-8 59 (t) TobyAtkinson(3) 8 70
(Miss D Mountain) *stdd after s: hld up in rr: gd hdwy ent fnl 2f: led over 1f out: styd on strly to draw clr fnl f* **10/1**

4254 **2** 4 **Piper's Song (IRE)**[28] 4670 6-9-10 58 JamieKyne 14 62
(Patrick Morris) *chsd ldrs: rdn over 2f out: drvn to chse wnr over 1f out: outpcd by wnr fnl f: hld on for 2nd* **6/1**[3]

64 **3** 3/4 **Ocean Of Peace (FR)**[28] 4640 6-9-0 51 IJBrennan(3) 4 54
(M R Bosley) *hld up in rr: stl last and swtchd lft over 2f out: rn fnl f to go 3rd towards fin: no ch w wnr* **16/1**

4632 **4** 1/2 **Transformer (IRE)**[18] 5015 3-9-4 60 SophieDoyle 2 62
(W J Knight) *t.k.h: chsd ldrs: rdn over 3f out: chsd ldr briefly wl over 1f out: outpcd fnl f* **11/4**[1]

6000 **5** 1 3/4 **Sew'N'So Character (IRE)**[6] 5377 8-9-11 59 MCGeran 11 58
(M Blanshard) *in tch: rdn and effrt over 2f out: plugged on same pce u.p fnl 2f* **25/1**

215 **6** 3 1/4 **Medieval Maiden**[14] 5152 6-9-7 55 RossAtkinson 12 49
(Mrs L J Mongan) *stdd s: hld up in rr: hdwy on outer over 3f out: drvn and hung rt over 1f out: kpt on but nvr gng pce to chal ldrs* **20/1**

1260 **7** 2 **Mixing**[41] 4235 7-9-4 57 KierenFox(5) 6 47
(M J Attwater) *hld up in rr: rdn over 3f out: nvr gng pce to rch ldrs* **9/1**

40-6 **8** 3 3/4 **Rising Force (IRE)**[52] 2419 6-9-11 59 (b) RichardEvans 13 43
(J L Spearing) *hld up in midfield: rdn and swtchd lft jst over 2f out: sn wknd* **14/1**

4100 **9** 3/4 **Rosy Dawn**[6] 5365 4-9-2 53 AshleyMorgan(5) 5 36
(J J Bridger) *chsd ldr tl led over 3f out: rdn and hdd over 2f: wknd over 1f out* **14/1**

1005 **10** 1/2 **Sir Haydn**[6] 5377 9-8-13 52 (v) DannyBrock(5) 10 34
(J R Jenkins) *hld up towards rr: nvr trbld ldrs* **25/1**

300- **11** shd **Reel Man**[407] 4278 4-9-2 50 JamesO'Reilly 7 32
(D K Ivory) *t.k.h: hld up in tch in midfield: rdn and struggling over 2f out: sn bhd* **50/1**

5516 **12** 3 1/4 **Inquisitress**[6] 5365 5-8-11 50 RyanClark(5) 3 26
(J J Bridger) *hld up in rr: hdwy on outer 5f out: led wl over 2f out: rdn 2f out: hdd over 1f out: wknd qckly fnl f* **20/1**

34-3 **13** 5 **Compton Falcon**[243] 18 5-9-1 52 RosieJessop(3) 9 19
(H Candy) *led: hdd over 3f out: wknd over 2f out: sn wl bhd* **11/2**[2]

3006 **14** 19 **King's Ransom**[27] 4721 6-9-9 60 MatthewDavies(3) 1 —
(S Gollings) *racd in midfield on outer: hdwy to chse ldrs over 7f out: rdn and wknd over 3f out: t.o and eased fnl f* **12/1**

2m 22.59s (0.69) **Going Correction** +0.05s/f (Slow)
WFA 3 from 4yo+ 8lb **14** Ran SP% **121.5**
Speed ratings (Par 101): **99,96,95,95,93 91,90,87,86,86 86,84,80,66**
toteswinger: 1&2 £22.60, 1&3 £128.60, 2&3 £34.90. CSF £64.74 CT £973.69 TOTE £12.10: £4.00, £2.10, £4.10; EX 93.40 Place 6 £696.41, Place 5 £319.65.
Owner Miss Debbie Mountain **Bred** Gainsborough Stud Management Ltd **Trained** Newmarket, Suffolk

FOCUS
Mainly exposed performers in a moderate handicap. The gallop was only fair and the winner came down the centre. Straightforward form.
T/Plt: £1,157.70 to a £1 stake. Pool: £82,231.92. 51.85 winning tickets. T/Qpdt: £506.60 to a £1 stake. Pool: £7,873.42. 11.50 winning tickets. SP

5365 LINGFIELD (L-H)
Wednesday, September 2

OFFICIAL GOING: Turf course - good to firm; all-weather - standard
Wind: Strong, behind Weather: Fine but cloudy

5578 ASHFORD ENVIRONMENTAL MAIDEN STKS 1m 3f 106y
1:50 (1:50) (Class 5) 3-Y-O+ **£2,729** (£806; £403) **Stalls** High

Form RPR

4024 **1** **Spirit Of Dubai (IRE)**[19] 4991 3-8-12 83 WilliamBuick 3 78
(D M Simcock) *trckd ldng pair: outpcd and 4 l down 4f out: rdn and styd on fr 3f out: wnt 2nd 2f out: led jst ins fnl f: grad asserted* **7/4**[2]

23 **2** 1 1/4 **Samaaha**[24] 4828 3-8-12 0 TedDurcan 4 76
(Saeed Bin Suroor) *trckd ldr: led 3f out: rdn 2f out: hdd and nt qckn jst ins fnl f: eased whn hld nr fin* **11/8**[1]

3002 **3** 7 **Cherish The Moment (IRE)**[9] 5322 3-9-3 70 MichaelHills 7 69
(B W Hills) *led to 3f out: grad wknd fnl 2f* **11/4**[3]

06 **4** 5 **Secret Desert**[19] 4979 3-9-3 0 MartinDwyer 2 60
(D M Simcock) *v s.i.s and needed plenty of rousting early: in tch: outpcd over 4f out: n.d after: eased whn no ch fnl f* **33/1**

05 **5** *9* **Double Whammy**[33] 4480 3-9-3 0 .... LukeMorris 5 45
(Jamie Poulton) *s.i.s: pushed along in last pair after 4f: nvr gng wl after: outpcd over 4f out: eased whn no ch over 1f out* **25/1**

2m 30.12s (-1.38) **Going Correction** -0.05s/f (Good)
WFA 3 from 4yo+ 8lb **5** Ran SP% **111.9**
Speed ratings (Par 103): **103,102,97,93,86**
toteswinger: 1&2 £3.70. CSF £4.65 TOTE £2.60: £1.20, £1.40; EX 5.40.
Owner Ahmad Al Shaikh **Bred** D J Bloodstock, G Roddick & Wrottesley Ltd **Trained** Newmarket, Suffolk

FOCUS
The ground had eased slightly and looked just on the quick side of good if a bit loose on top. This was a modest maiden with the winner running in line with her recent maiden efforts.

5579 BAKER TILLY H'CAP 2m
2:20 (2:21) (Class 6) (0-65,65) 3-Y-0+ **£2,047** (£604; £302) **Stalls** Low

Form RPR
0604 **1** **Trempari**[20] 4935 6-9-9 **47** ....(b) TonyCulhane 8 53
(Mike Murphy) *led after 1f: mde rest: shkn up 3f out: kpt on steadily after: nvr seriously threatened* **16/1**
0221 **2** *2* **Deuce**[15] 5131 3-10-0 **65** ....(b) RobertWinston 4 69
(Eve Johnson Houghton) *settled midfield: rdn 3f out: prog fr over 2f out to take 2nd 1f out: no real imp on wnr* **2/1**[1]
0066 **3** *2 1/2* **Snowberry Hill (USA)**[7] 5339 6-9-12 **50** .... HayleyTurner 12 51
(Lucinda Featherstone) *t.k.h: trckd ldrs: chsd wnr 3f out: drvn and hld fr 2f out: lost 2nd and fdd 1f out* **20/1**
0243 **4** *3/4* **Bari Bay**[26] 4735 3-9-0 **51** .... CatherineGannon 7 51
(J W Mullins) *bmpd s: hld up in last trio: rdn 3f out: sme prog fr 2f out: kpt on: nvr rchd ldrs* **14/1**
5512 **5** *1* **Primera Rossa**[5] 5382 3-8-12 **49** .... LukeMorris 5 48
(J S Moore) *towards rr: rdn over 4f out: plugged on u.p fnl 2f: n.d* **6/1**[3]
5046 **6** *nse* **Lilac Wine**[12] 5217 6-9-9 **47** ....(v[1]) JamesDoyle 10 45
(D J S Ffrench Davis) *led 1f: settled cl up: rdn on inner wl over 3f out: one pce and no prog* **20/1**
0003 **7** *2 1/4* **Alittlemoreflair**[33] 4498 3-8-13 **50** ....(v) DO'Donohoe 6 46
(J Pearce) *wnt rt s: hld up towards rr: dropped to last trio 4f out: shuffled along and sme prog fnl 2f: nvr on terms* **20/1**
0044 **8** *1* **The Composer**[12] 5217 7-9-7 **45** .... PaulHanagan 1 40
(M Blanshard) *hld up: dropped to last trio 1/2-way: nvr on terms after: drvn on outer and plugged on one pce fnl 2f* **13/2**
/465 **9** *10* **Red Army Commander (IRE)**[9] 5322 4-10-0 **52** .... RobertHavlin 2 35
(J A Geake) *wnt rt s: hld up in last trio: prog on outer fr 1/2-way: rdn to chse ldrs 3f out: wknd rapidly over 1f out: eased* **25/1**
3/50 **10** *1 3/4* **Enthusius**[23] 4855 6-9-11 **49** ....(b) RyanMoore 11 29
(G L Moore) *chsd wnr after 2f to 3f out: wknd tamely u.p* **10/3**[2]
6000 **11** *1 1/2* **Royal Arthur**[15] 5131 3-8-8 **45** ....(p) FrankieMcDonald 9 24
(L A Dace) *s.s: t.k.h and hld up in last: nvr a factor* **100/1**
6000 **12** *13* **Silver Surprise**[12] 5217 5-9-4 **45** ....(b) MarcHalford[(3)] 3 8
(J J Bridger) *bmpd s: prom tl wknd rapidly over 3f out: eased over 1f out: t.o* **66/1**

3m 35.76s (0.96) **Going Correction** -0.05s/f (Good)
WFA 3 from 4yo+ 13lb **12** Ran SP% **117.2**
Speed ratings (Par 101): **95,94,92,92,91 91,90,90,85,84 83,77**
toteswinger: 1&2 £9.80, 1&3 £20.60, 2&3 £10.30. CSF £44.27 CT £675.17 TOTE £19.10: £4.90, £1.60, £5.10; EX 77.40.
Owner M Murphy **Bred** Thorsen Feddern And Mike Murphy **Trained** Westoning, Beds

FOCUS
A modest handicap run at a true pace. The form looks sound.
Lilac Wine Official explanation: jockey said mare hung left
The Composer Official explanation: jockey said gelding hung right

5580 TAGWORLDWIDE.COM NOVICE STKS 7f (P)
2:50 (2:50) (Class 5) 2-Y-0 **£3,238** (£963; £481; £240) **Stalls** Low

Form RPR
4 **1** **Zaahy (USA)**[33] 4499 2-8-12 0 .... TPQueally 6 90+
(P W Chapple-Hyam) *hld up: plld out 1/2-way: prog on wd outside over 2f out: swept into ld jst ins fnl f: sn clr: decisively* **9/1**
2 **2** *2 1/2* **Champagne Style (USA)**[21] 4908 2-8-12 0 .... TedDurcan 8 82
(B J Meehan) *hld up on outer: effrt 3f out: rdn to chse ldng pair 2f out: swtchd to inner over 1f out: kpt on to take 2nd nr fin: no ch w wnr* **10/11**[1]
6121 **3** *nk* **Ramamara (IRE)**[4] 5445 2-8-11 78 .... PatCosgrave 3 80
(P D Evans) *trckd ldng pair after 2f: effrt to ld over 2f out: sn hrd pressed: hdd jst ins fnl f: lost 2nd nr fin* **13/2**[3]
1043 **4** *1* **Footstepsofspring (FR)**[11] 5250 2-9-5 88 .... RyanMoore 7 86
(R Hannon) *sn trckd ldr: rdn to chal new ldr over 2f out: nt qckn over 1f out: fdd ins fnl f* **4/1**[2]
13 **5** *3/4* **Dark Eyes (IRE)**[27] 4706 2-8-9 79 .... CatherineGannon 1 74
(D J Coakley) *led to over 2f out: styd cl up on inner: outpcd fnl f* **16/1**
6103 **6** *3/4* **Professor John (IRE)**[12] 5207 2-8-9 82 .... Louis-PhilippeBeuzelin[(5)] 4 77
(M L W Bell) *sn dropped to last trio: rdn and nt qckn over 2f out: plugged on one pce* **10/1**
7 *1* **Kingston Acacia** 2-8-3 0 .... WilliamBuick 5 63
(A M Balding) *s.s: rn green in last: nvr on terms w ldrs: plugged on fnl f* **33/1**
0 **8** *2* **Skyflight**[21] 4900 2-8-8 0 ow1 .... TonyCulhane 2 63+
(Eve Johnson Houghton) *prom 2f: sn dropped to rr: 7th whn hmpd and snatched up over 2f out: nt rcvr* **150/1**

1m 24.43s (-0.37) **Going Correction** -0.05s/f (Stan) **8** Ran SP% **114.3**
Speed ratings (Par 95): **100,97,96,95,94 93,92,90**
toteswinger: 1&2 £3.40, 1&3 £5.60, 2&3 £2.30. CSF £17.64 TOTE £11.40: £2.10, £1.20, £1.60; EX 24.70.
Owner M Al-Qatami & K M Al-Mudhaf **Bred** Grapestock Llc **Trained** Newmarket, Suffolk

FOCUS
Quite an interesting novice event and a winner of some potential.

NOTEBOOK
Zaahy(USA) ♦, last of four on his debut a month earlier, was in no hurry to join issue. He moved up on the outside turning in and scored in most decisive fashion. He will improve again and looks a fair prospect. (op 8-1 tchd 10-1)
Champagne Style(USA) ran a lot better than expected when runner-up first time in a Sandown maiden. Worst drawn, he travelled strongly towards the outer, but under pressure once in line for home he edged left ending up on the inner. No match for the winner, this Racing Post entry should certainly take his maiden. (tchd 5-6 and evens in places)
Ramamara(IRE), attempting to follow up her Windsor success just four days earlier, has made great strides since taking a seller here last month. She is the best guide to the overall value of the form. (op 6-1)
Footstepsofspring(FR), having his eighth start, did not improve for the step up to 7f and will struggle in nurseries from a mark of 88. (op 9-2 tchd 7-2)
Dark Eyes(IRE) had the run of the race and this may be as good as he is. (op 20-1)
Kingston Acacia stayed on late after a slow start and this should have taught her plenty. A maiden should be within her compass.

5581 ARROWS REMOVALS OF LONDON H'CAP (DIV I) 7f (P)
3:20 (3:20) (Class 6) (0-65,65) 3-Y-0 **£1,706** (£503; £252) **Stalls** Low

Form RPR
0000 **1** **La Gifted**[20] 4937 3-8-4 **51** oh3 .... CatherineGannon 8 60
(M R Channon) *chsd clr ldng trio: clsd on them fr over 1f out: cajoled along and styd on fnl f to ld nr fin* **33/1**
0133 **2** *1/2* **Kuanyao (IRE)**[16] 5112 3-8-13 **60** .... PatCosgrave 6 68
(P J Makin) *sn chsd ldng pair: drvn to chal on inner over 1f out: narrow ld 50yds out: sn hdd and outpcd* **11/4**[1]
3202 **3** *nk* **Temperence Hall (USA)**[32] 5118 3-8-4 **54** ....(v) MarcHalford[(3)] 7 61
(J R Best) *led at decent pce: drvn 2f out: edgd rt 1f out: hdd and no ex last 50yds* **13/2**
5044 **4** *2 3/4* **Flamsteed (IRE)**[58] 3676 3-9-4 **65** .... MartinDwyer 10 64
(M Quinn) *pressed ldr: rdn to chal over 1f out: sn nt qckn: wknd ins fnl f* **15/2**
5423 **5** *shd* **Vamos (IRE)**[26] 4749 3-8-11 **58** ....(b) ChrisCatlin 2 57
(J R Gask) *bmpd s: t.k.h early and hld up in last trio: prog to go 6th over 2f out but ldrs already wl clr: r.o fnl f: hopeless task* **3/1**[2]
056 **6** *1/2* **Queen Of Thebes (IRE)**[54] 3803 3-9-4 **65** ....(t) RyanMoore 3 63
(G L Moore) *bmpd s: hld up in last trio and sn wl off the pce: stl last 3f out as ldrs wl clr: r.o fnl f: hopeless task* **6/1**[3]
0330 **7** *1 1/4* **Super Fourteen**[13] 5179 3-8-10 **60** .... PatrickHills[(3)] 4 54
(R Hannon) *chsd ldrs: drvn and lft bhd fr 1/2-way: no ch after* **9/1**
0050 **8** *5* **True Decision**[18] 5016 3-9-3 **64** .... JamesDoyle 1 45
(S Kirk) *hld up towards rr: wl off the pce fr 1/2-way: no prog fnl 2f* **12/1**
0000 **9** *2 3/4* **Allexes (IRE)**[16] 5090 3-8-8 **58** .... JackMitchell[(3)] 11 31
(J R Boyle) *dwlt: a in last trio and nvr gng wl: bhd fr 1/2-way* **33/1**
0004 **10** *1/2* **Quick Single (USA)**[41] 4237 3-9-0 **61** ....(vt) TPQueally 5 33
(P S McEntee) *nvr gng wl and nvr on terms w ldrs: struggling fr 1/2-way* **16/1**

1m 24.48s (-0.32) **Going Correction** -0.05s/f (Stan) **10** Ran SP% **120.5**
Speed ratings (Par 99): **99,98,98,94,94 94,92,87,83,83**
toteswinger: 1&2 £29.50, 1&3 £31.80, 2&3 £6.10. CSF £126.80 CT £695.72 TOTE £44.30: £8.30, £1.30, £2.10; EX 330.80.
Owner Patrick and Simon Trant **Bred** Patrick & Simon Trant **Trained** West Ilsley, Berks

FOCUS
A modest handicap and only four in serious contention turning for home. The form is not too convincing.
Vamos(IRE) Official explanation: jockey said gelding missed the break
Queen Of Thebes(IRE) Official explanation: jockey said filly suffered interference at the start

5582 ARROWS REMOVALS OF LONDON H'CAP (DIV II) 7f (P)
3:50 (3:51) (Class 6) (0-65,65) 3-Y-0 **£1,706** (£503; £252) **Stalls** Low

Form RPR
40 **1** **Whisky Jack**[39] 4304 3-9-4 **65** ....(b) MartinDwyer 3 70
(W R Muir) *dwlt: t.k.h and sn trckd ldr: led wl over 1f out and kicked 2 l clr: a holding on after* **14/1**
5205 **2** *3/4* **Night Lily (IRE)**[21] 4910 3-9-4 **65** ....(t) LukeMorris 9 68
(J Jay) *hld up and racd wd: gng strly 3f out: effrt and drvn over 1f out: r.o to take 2nd last 75yds: too much to do* **8/1**
-030 **3** *hd* **Florentia**[37] 4374 3-9-1 **62** .... PatCosgrave 5 64+
(Sir Mark Prescott) *towards rr: pushed along fr 1/2-way: prog u.p over 1f out on outer: r.o to take 3rd nr fin* **12/1**
0046 **4** *3/4* **Sultans Way (IRE)**[10] 5287 3-8-12 **59** ....(b[1]) PaulHanagan 4 59
(P F I Cole) *t.k.h: led to wl over 1f out: outpcd by wnr: lost 2 pls last 75yds* **7/2**[1]
0666 **5** *1 1/4* **Davids Matador**[16] 5112 3-8-13 **60** .... WilliamBuick 10 57
(Eve Johnson Houghton) *hld up in last pair: stl there over 2f out: drvn and r.o fnl f: nvr nr ldrs* **10/1**
045 **6** *3/4* **Final Drive (IRE)**[19] 4981 3-8-13 **60** .... EdwardCreighton 6 55+
(E J Creighton) *hld up in midfield on inner: gng wl enough whn hmpd over 2f out: drvn and kpt on fr over 1f out: nt rcvr* **10/1**
050 **7** *nk* **Artesium**[26] 4749 3-8-0 **52** .... JamieKyne[(5)] 2 46
(Patrick Morris) *cl up on inner: rdn over 2f out: stl chsng ldrs on inner over 1f out: wknd fnl f* **20/1**
4002 **8** *hd* **Baby Josr**[26] 4749 3-9-0 **61** ....(vt) TomEaves 7 55
(I A Wood) *sn pushed along in last pair: u.p 1/2-way: kpt on fnl f: no ch* **9/2**[3]
0005 **9** *1/2* **Azharia**[26] 4749 3-8-10 **57** .... RyanMoore 8 49
(R Hannon) *chsd ldrs: drvn in 3rd 2f out: wknd fnl f* **4/1**[2]
3505 **10** *50* **Wotasparkler**[12] 5211 3-8-11 **58** ....(v[1]) RobertHavlin 1 —
(W S Kittow) *trckd ldrs: 3rd on inner whn broke down over 2f out and virtually p.u: dead* **10/1**

1m 25.39s (0.59) **Going Correction** -0.05s/f (Stan) **10** Ran SP% **117.9**
Speed ratings (Par 99): **94,93,92,92,90 89,89,89,88,31**
toteswinger: 1&2 £15.10, 1&3 £18.30, 2&3 £8.40. CSF £122.48 CT £1424.80 TOTE £13.60: £3.60, £2.40, £3.70; EX 81.80.
Owner B & Q Partnership **Bred** Peter Onslow **Trained** Lambourn, Berks
■ A hare ran across the track as the runners approached the home turn.

FOCUS
A modest handicap. The time was slow and the form is rated around the placed horses.
Sultans Way(IRE) Official explanation: jockey said gelding hung right throughout

5583 GP LONDON (S) STKS 6f (P)
4:20 (4:21) (Class 6) 2-Y-0 **£2,047** (£604; £302) **Stalls** Low

Form RPR
3634 **1** **Belinsky (IRE)**[8] 5325 2-8-11 72 .... PatCosgrave 5 64
(S A Callaghan) *pressed ldr: led wl over 1f out: hrd pressed fnl f: jst hld on* **4/5**[1]
0000 **2** *shd* **Lochbroom Sunset**[37] 4384 2-8-11 55 .... SaleemGolam 6 64
(S C Williams) *dwlt: sn midfield: effrt 2f out: jnd wnr fnl f: jst hld* **33/1**
0305 **3** *2 1/4* **Avow (USA)**[21] 4915 2-8-11 68 ....(b) LukeMorris 3 57
(J S Moore) *hld up in midfield on inner: nt qckn and lost pl over 2f out: renewed effrt over 1f out: kpt on to take 3rd nr fin* **5/1**[2]
6550 **4** *nk* **Flapjack**[9] 5310 2-8-6 62 .... WilliamBuick 2 51
(R Hannon) *settled in last trio on inner: hdwy over 1f out: pressed for 3rd nr fin: no ch w ldng pair* **10/1**
0300 **5** *nk* **Lofthouse**[7] 5344 2-8-11 62 .... TonyCulhane 11 55+
(M R Channon) *stdd s: hld up in rr: abt 8th 2f out and gng strly: pushed along and kpt on steadily: nvr nr ldrs* **16/1**
0563 **6** *1/2* **Mind The Monarch**[26] 4747 2-8-6 54 .... ChrisCatlin 4 49
(R A Teal) *cl up: rdn and nrly on terms w ldrs over 1f out: fdd ins fnl f* **20/1**

256 **7** *1* **Bazsharani**[10] 5282 2-8-6 67 .... CatherineGannon 1 46
(P D Evans) *led to wl over 1f out: sn wknd* **8/1**[3]
0465 **8** *½* **Steel My Heart (IRE)**[19] 4973 2-8-6 49 .... (v[1]) NeilChalmers 8 44
(Miss D Mountain) *dwlt: a in rr: plugged on fnl f: no ch* **66/1**
604 **9** *¾* **Magneto (IRE)**[62] 3547 2-8-11 54 .... EdwardCreighton 9 47
(E J Creighton) *chsd ldrs and racd wdst of all: cl enough 2f out: sn wknd* **50/1**
0052 **10** *1¾* **New York Lights (IRE)**[26] 4747 2-8-6 54 .... HayleyTurner 7 37
(M D I Usher) *chsd ldrs towards outer: cl enough 2f out: sn wknd* **12/1**
0 **11** *5* **Red Farasi (IRE)**[20] 4945 2-8-6 0 .... GabrielHannon(5) 12 27
(B W Duke) *dwlt: a in last trio: bmpd along and wknd over 1f out* **100/1**
1m 12.83s (0.93) **Going Correction** -0.05s/f (Stan) **11** Ran SP% **118.1**
Speed ratings (Par 93): **91,90,87,87,87 86,85,84,83,81 74**
toteswinger: 1&2 £8.30, 1&3 £2.60, 2&3 £24.90. CSF £45.60 TOTE £1.80: £1.10, £6.40, £1.80; EX 39.30.The winner was bought in for 5,200gns.
Owner Michael Tabor **Bred** Camogue Stud Ltd **Trained** Newmarket, Suffolk
■ Stewards' Enquiry : Saleem Golam caution: excessive use of the whip
Gabriel Hannon one-day ban: used whip when out of contention (Sep 16)

FOCUS
A very ordinary juvenile seller.

NOTEBOOK
Belinsky(IRE), joint-top on official ratings, tended to run with the choke out. After taking charge, in the end it was a very close call. This surface suited his doubtful stamina better than Southwell's Fibresand. (op 5-4 tchd 11-8 in a place)
Lochbroom Sunset, who had 17lb to find with the winner, emerged from the pack after a sluggish start to prove the main danger, and in the end he only just missed out. (op 28-1)
Avow(USA), back in trip and down in class, became outpaced soon after halfway. He stuck on in the closing stages but is proving frustrating. (op 7-1)
Flapjack, already tried over seven, stayed on from the back when it was all over. (op 15-2)
Lofthouse, well beaten in two nurseries, was happy to sit off the pace. He picked up ground in eyecatching fashion late on and is worth bearing in mind. (op 12-1)
Bazsharani, joint best on official figures with the winner, was very weak beforehand. After setting the pace she dropped right away. Official explanation: jockey said filly hung right-handed (op 11-2)

5584 DORMANSLAND H'CAP 6f (P)
4:50 (4:50) (Class 5) (0-70,70) 3-Y-O **£3,238** (£963; £481; £240) **Stalls** Low

Form RPR
0-02 **1** **Timeless Dream**[16] 5110 3-8-12 **67** .... JackMitchell(3) 2 74
(P W Chapple-Hyam) *sn off the pce in midfield: reminders 1/2-way: prog 2f out: drvn and r.o fnl f to ld last 50yds* **6/1**[3]
1364 **2** *¾* **Bold Ring**[16] 5105 3-8-8 **60** .... EdwardCreighton 9 64
(E J Creighton) *chsd ldrs: prog 2f out: clsd over 1f out: jnd ldr last 75yds: sn outpcd by wnr* **25/1**
6251 **3** *¾* **Agnes Love**[14] 5164 3-8-6 **61** .... JackDean(3) 6 64
(J Akehurst) *chsd ldr: clsd u.p over 1f out: led last 150yds: hdd and outpcd last 50yds* **14/1**
-012 **4** *nk* **Desert Streak (FR)**[23] 4859 3-9-2 **68** .... (p) PhilipRobinson 4 69
(C G Cox) *chsd ldrs: effrt on inner 2f out: clsd 1f out: outpcd last 100yds* **5/4**[1]
0031 **5** *2¼* **Hatman Jack (IRE)**[26] 4748 3-8-8 **60** .... HayleyTurner 8 54
(B G Powell) *led: 2 l clr over 2f out: hdd & wknd last 150yds* **11/2**[2]
0500 **6** *2* **Flute Magic**[20] 4937 3-8-5 **57** .... FrankieMcDonald 5 44
(W S Kittow) *reminders after 1f: nvr gng wl in rr: kpt on fr over 1f out* **40/1**
1000 **7** *¾* **Yanza**[90] 2632 3-9-1 **67** .... ChrisCatlin 1 52
(J R Gask) *dwlt: hld up in rr and wl off the pce: pushed along on inner fr 2f out: nvr nr ldrs* **16/1**
4156 **8** *2¾* **Keep Dancing (IRE)**[24] 4829 3-9-2 **68** .... (p) WilliamBuick 11 44
(A M Balding) *trckd ldrs: rdn and no rspnse over 2f out: wknd rapidly over 1f out: eased* **8/1**
0504 **9** *¾* **Pocket's Pick (IRE)**[13] 5197 3-9-4 **70** .... (bt) RyanMoore 7 44
(G L Moore) *rrd s: t.k.h early and hld up in last: wl off the pce 1/2-way: taken to wd outside and drvn over 1f out: no prog* **8/1**
660 **10** *15* **Cool Art (IRE)**[50] 3953 3-8-13 **65** .... (b) JamieMackay 10 —
(Peter Grayson) *racd v wd: in tch over 3f out: wknd over 2f out: t.o* **33/1**
420 **11** *47* **The Cuckoo**[147] 1190 3-8-11 **63** .... CatherineGannon 3 —
(M Quinn) *prom 2f: wknd rapidly and sn t.o* **25/1**
1m 11.16s (-0.74) **Going Correction** -0.05s/f (Stan) **11** Ran SP% **122.0**
Speed ratings (Par 101): **102,101,100,99,96 93,92,89,88,68 5**
toteswinger: 1&2 £17.10, 1&3 £14.00, 2&3 £18.80. CSF £153.21 CT £2060.22 TOTE £6.50: £1.90, £4.40, £3.60; EX 139.50 Place 6: £58.36, Place 5: £46.30..
Owner Times Of Wigan **Bred** Times Of Wigan Ltd **Trained** Newmarket, Suffolk

FOCUS
A competitive handicap but a very short-priced favourite. He disappointed and this is probably ordinary form.
Pocket's Pick(IRE) Official explanation: jockey said gelding hung right
The Cuckoo Official explanation: jockey said gelding bolted to post and stopped quickly
T/Plt: £83.00 to a £1 stake. Pool: £54,919.31. 482.93 winning tickets. T/Qpdt: £40.60 to a £1 stake. Pool: £4,312.20. 78.50 winning tickets. JN

5563 BADEN-BADEN (L-H)
Wednesday, September 2
OFFICIAL GOING: Good

5585a FURSTENBERG-RENNEN (GROUP 3) 1m 2f
3:45 (3:48) 3-Y-O **£29,126** (£12,136; £4,854; £2,427)

RPR
1 **Toughness Danon**[59] 3670 3-9-0 .... JBojko 5 105
(A Wohler, Germany) *prom: 3rd st: r.o fr over 1f out to ld 150yds out: drvn out* **5/2**[2]
2 *1¾* **Palermo (GER)**[81] 3-9-0 .... WMongil 8 101
(C Zschache, Germany) *led: pushed along over 1f out: hdd 150yds out: no ex cl home* **81/10**
3 *½* **Falun (GER)**[37] 4395 3-9-0 .... THellier 1 100
(A Trybuhl, Germany) *mid-div: hdwy towards outside appr st: 4th st: styd on wl fnl f: narrowly missed 2nd* **96/10**
4 *2* **Globus (GER)**[72] 3230 3-9-2 .... FilipMinarik 9 98
(Uwe Ostmann, Germany) *towards rr: drvn ent st: styd on steadily u.p: wnt 4th ins fnl f* **114/10**
5 *nk* **Lady Alida**[38] 4364 3-8-13 .... KKerekes 4 94
(W Figge, Germany) *mid-div: nvr in chalng position* **71/10**
6 *½* **Panyu (GER)**[59] 3670 3-9-0 .... AStarke 3 94
(P Schiergen, Germany) *racd towards rr: effrt ent st: no imp* **4/1**[3]

7 *1* **King Of Sydney (USA)**[31] 4582 3-9-4 .... ASuborics 7 96
(Mario Hofer, Germany) *mid-div towards ins: n.d* **19/10**[1]
8 *9* **Lizzero (GER)**[94] 3-8-11 .... DPorcu 6 71
(R Rohne, Germany) *racd in 2nd to 1 1/2f out: one pce after* **24/1**
9 *6* **Woodlark (IRE)**[458] 2645 3-9-0 ow3 .... (b) MKapusev 2 62
(R Tugusev, Slovakia) *missed break: racd towards rr: n.d* **40/1**
2m 4.48s (-0.51) **9** Ran SP% **130.3**
(Including 10 Euro stake): WIN 35; PL 16, 26, 38; SF 244.
Owner Stall D'Angelo **Bred** Stiftung Gestut Fahrhof **Trained** Germany

VELIEFENDI
Wednesday, September 2
OFFICIAL GOING: Turf course - good; all-weather - standard

5587a ANATOLIA TROPHY (TURKISH GROUP 2) (POLYTRACK) 1m 2f
7:00 (7:07) 3-Y-O+ **£173,611** (£69,444; £34,722; £17,361)

RPR
1 **Balius (IRE)**[108] 2117 6-9-6 .... LDettori 10 120
(Saeed Bin Suroor) *in touch in 5th, 3rd & going well straight, ran on to lead 1 1/2f out, soon clear, comfortably* **27/10**[3]
2 *4½* **Dervis Aga (TUR)** 4-9-6 .... (b) YAkagac 5 111
(S Mutlu, Turkey) *raced towards rear, headway in centre 2f out, finished strongly final f to take 2nd on line* **44/1**
3 *½* **Berathan (TUR)** 3-8-11 .... GKocakaya 7 108
(I Gulbudak, Turkey) *prominent in 3rd, led approaching straight, soon driven, headed 1 1/2f out, kept on under pressure, lost 2nd on line* **39/10**
4 *2* **Beran (TUR)** 6-9-6 .... (t) NSen 3 106
(M H Esin, Turkey) *in touch in 7th early, under pressure half-way & dropped back, stayed on again in straight, never able to challenge* **18/1**
5 *1* **Royal Victory (TUR)** 5-9-3 .... (b) BGokce 11 101
(H Yildiz, Turkey) *towards rear, driven & modest headway from 1 1/2f out, never dangerous* **101/10**
6 *1* **Transacoustic (TUR)** 3-8-11 .... OPeslier 8 100
(S Kulak, Turkey) *held up, headway approaching straight, 6th straight, kept on steadily, never able to challenge* **122/10**
7 *1½* **Led Zeppelin (TUR)** 4-9-6 .... (t) BKurdu 4 99
(G Subasi, Turkey) *prominent in 2nd, close 4th on inside straight, soon driven, stayed on til no extra from over 1f out* **84/10**
8 *2½* **Philatelist (USA)**[11] 5262 5-9-6 .... (b) NCallan 2 94
(M A Jarvis) *raced in 4th on inside, driven & lost place approaching straight, 5th & under pressure straight, one pace* **18/1**
9 *2¾* **Babayigit (TUR)** 5-9-6 .... GYildiz 6 89
(O Yenihayat, Turkey) *raced in 6th til under pressure over 3f out, one pace* **54/1**
10 *¾* **Dogubeyi (TUR)** 4-9-6 .... HKaratas 1 87
(B Akbulut, Turkey) *led,headed approaching straight, with leaders under pressure til no extra from 2f out* **2/5**[1]
11 *3¾* **Fairson (TUR)**[361] 5743 6-9-6 .... SKaya 12 80
(K Ozturk, Turkey) *mid-division, 7th straight, never dangerous* **9/5**[2]
12 *12* **Nusrat (TUR)** 3-8-11 .... SBoyraz 9 54
(I E Dizdar, Turkey) *always towards rear* **16/1**
2m 3.02s (-25.78)
WFA 3 from 4yo+ 7lb **12** Ran SP% **202.3**
(including one lira stakes): WIN 3.70; PL 1.40, 3.25; DF 207.80.
Owner Godolphin **Bred** Stilvi Compania Financiera Sa **Trained** Newmarket, Suffolk
■ Godolphin's first winner in Turkey.

NOTEBOOK
Balius(IRE), who had not been seen since running in Singapore in May, had the usual headgear left off but took well to this surface and ran out an easy winner. He could have Hong Kong at the end of the season and then Dubai next year as the targets.
Philatelist(USA), representing connections that have done well here in the past and having form on this surface, was struggling on the home turn.

5588a FRANCE GALOP-FRBC ISTANBUL TROPHY (TURKISH GROUP 2) (TURF) 1m
9:00 (9:00) 3-Y-O+ **£173,611** (£69,444; £34,722; £17,361)

RPR
1 **Eva's Request (IRE)**[31] 4580 4-9-6 .... AlanMunro 3 111
(M R Channon) *prominent, close 4th on rail straight, pushed along to challenge 1 1/2f out, joined leaders 1f out, led 100yds out, driven out* **1/1**[1]
2 *1* **Damaniyat Girl (USA)**[17] 5064 3-8-12 .... (b) LDettori 10 106
(W J Haggas) *held up, 11th straight, ran on well from 1 1/2f out, finished strongly final f to go 2nd last strides (9.95/1)* **10/1**
3 *½* **Wilside (IRE)**[20] 4971 3-8-12 .... OPeslier 4 105
(M Delzangles, France) *soon close 2nd, ridden & every chance over 1f out, stayed on* **92/10**
4 *nse* **Berraksu (TUR)**[361] 4-9-6 .... SBoyraz 2 107
(H Ergin, Turkey) *led, ran on in straight, headed 100yds out, no extra* **61/10**
5 *1* **Magic Eye (IRE)**[38] 4-9-6 .... APietsch 7 105
(Andreas Lowe, Germany) *towards rear, stayed on from over 1f out, nearest at finish* **92/10**
6 *1* **Chi (TUR)** 3-8-12 .... OYildirim 6 100
(A Ozgen, Turkey) *mid-division, stayed on towards outside from over 1f out, never nearer* **26/5**
7 *½* **The Rising (TUR)** 5-9-6 .... HKaratas 9 102
(C Kurt, Turkey) *towards rear, some late headway but never dangerous* **3/1**[3]
8 *1* **Rokoko (TUR)** 3-8-12 .... (b) SKaya 1 96
(A Basyigit, Turkey) *held up, pushed along straight, unable to quicken* **18/5**
9 *2* **Nihalim (TUR)** 4-9-6 .... GYildiz 5 95
(Y Simsek, Turkey) *in touch, 7th straight, driven over 2f out, no impression* **21/1**
10 *2½* **Orse Gul (TUR)** 3-8-12 .... (b) NCallan 8 86
(M B Oktar, Turkey) *held up, effort entering straight, unable to quicken* **29/1**
11 *7* **Actionmax (TUR)** 4-9-6 .... (t) NSen 13 73
(B Dag, Turkey) *prominent, 3rd on outside straight, weakened from over 1f out* **11/5**[2]

12 7 **Lovely Doyoun (TUR)**^{361} 6-9-6 .... YAkagac 11 57
(A Atci, Turkey) *towards rear, pushed along straight, never dangerous* **143/10**

13 7 **Mayuska (TUR)** 4-9-6 ....(bt) GKocakaya 12 41
(A Atci, Turkey) *always behind* **143/10**

1m 37.88s (2.55)
WFA 3 from 4yo+ 5lb **13** Ran SP% **207.9**
PARI-MUTUEL: WIN 2.00; PL 1.60, 2.90; DF 13.25.
Owner Liam Mulryan **Bred** Ballylinch Stud **Trained** West Ilsley, Berks

NOTEBOOK
Eva's Request(IRE), a Listed and Group 3 winner in Britain earlier in the season, was found a good opportunity and took full advantage to pick up a valuable prize. The Sun Chariot could be on her schedule next.
Damaniyat Girl(USA) has been placed at Group and Listed level at home and seems to have been helped by the fitting of blinkers in recent starts. She finished well to grab second and some very good prizemoney.

5505 EPSOM (L-H)
Thursday, September 3

OFFICIAL GOING: Good to soft (good in places; overall 7.5; home straight - stands' side 8.0, far side 7.4)
Rails dolled out 3yards from mile to winning post increasing advertised distances by circa 5yards.
Wind: Mostly strong, against Weather: Fine but cloudy

5589 ISINGLASS NURSERY 7f
2:20 (2:21) (Class 5) (0-70,70) 2-Y-O **£3,885** (£1,156; £577; £288) **Stalls** Low

Form RPR

2316 **1** **Gold Fix (IRE)**^{13} 5224 2-9-1 **64** .... SamHitchcott 9 66
(M R Channon) *trckd ldrs: 6th st: rdn and prog to ld 2f out: kpt on wl and a holding on* **16/1**

4030 **2** ½ **Timelord (IRE)**^{54} 3842 2-9-3 **66** .... JamesDoyle 14 67
(S Kirk) *hld up and racd on outer: 9th st: rdn 3f out: prog fr 2f out: chsd wnr ent fnl f: styd on but a hld* **12/1**

055 **3** *nk* **Mountrath**^{32} 4564 2-8-7 **59** ....(t) WilliamCarson$^{(3)}$ 5 59
(B R Johnson) *dwlt: t.k.h: hld up in rr: 11th st: sltly hmpd sn after: swtchd to outer 3f out and prog u.p: kpt on wl to take 3rd nr fin* **12/1**

0414 **4** ½ **Keen Bidder**^{27} 4758 2-9-2 **65** .... FergusSweeney 10 64
(D M Simcock) *dwlt: t.k.h: hld up: 10th st: prog over 2f out: clsd on ldrs 1f out: kpt on but nvr quite able to chal* **3/1**^{1}

0344 **5** ½ **Ever So Bold**^{32} 4565 2-8-13 **65** .... RussellKennemore$^{(3)}$ 3 63
(W R Muir) *hld up in midfield: 8th st: rdn to chse ldrs and cl enough 2f out: kpt on all the way to the fin but nvr able to chal* **10/1**

3240 **6** ½ **Cuthbert (IRE)**^{23} 4884 2-9-6 **69** .... J-PGuillambert 7 65
(W Jarvis) *prom: 4th st: effrt to chal 2f out: chsd wnr wl over 1f out tl ent fnl f: fdd* **11/1**

6400 **7** *hd* **Gulf Punch**^{13} 5224 2-8-3 **52** .... JamieMackay 2 48
(M F Harris) *hld up in midfield: lost pl bdly downhill fr 5f out: 13th st: effrt and plld out wd 2f out: styd on but nt rch ldrs* **66/1**

030 **8** 2 **Elizabelle (IRE)**^{20} 4980 2-9-3 **66** .... EddieAhern 8 57
(R Hannon) *dwlt: hld up in rr: 12th st: sn rdn: no prog over 2f out: plugged on: nrst fin* **10/1**

4000 **9** ¾ **Evergreen Dancer (IRE)**^{29} 4647 2-8-11 **60** .... RobertWinston 12 49
(J R Best) *chsd ldr: rdn to chal and upsides over 2f out: edgd lft and fdd fr over 1f out* **40/1**

000 **10** ¾ **Boycott (IRE)**^{12} 5251 2-9-4 **67** ....(b) RobertHavlin 13 54
(J H M Gosden) *prom: 5th whn c across to nr side ent st: nt on terms w ldrs fnl 2f* **14/1**

6535 **11** ¾ **Volatilis (IRE)**^{15} 5166 2-9-1 **64** .... LiamJones 11 49
(J W Hills) *prom: 3rd st: lost pl on inner 2f out: sn wknd* **20/1**

533 **12** 4 **Bandear (IRE)**^{21} 4946 2-9-4 **67** .... ChrisCatlin 1 42
(C E Brittain) *hld up: last st: sn rdn and no prog: bhd fnl 2f* **9/1**^{3}

604 **13** 1 ¾ **Gold Diamond (USA)**^{35} 4451 2-9-7 **70** .... JoeFanning 6 41
(M Johnston) *led to 2f out: sn wknd rapidly* **5/1**^{2}

0060 **14** 4 **Rebecca Romero**^{15} 5166 2-8-1 **50** .... CatherineGannon 4 11
(D J Coakley) *chsd ldr: 7th st: sn wknd* **16/1**

1m 27.54s (4.24) **Going Correction** +0.425s/f (Yiel) **14** Ran SP% **120.7**
Speed ratings (Par 95): **92,91,91,90,89 89,89,86,86,85 84,79,77,73**
toteswingers: 1&2 £40.20, 1&3 £37.20, 2&3 £31.60 CSF £193.62 CT £2460.36 TOTE £21.50: £6.30, £2.30, £4.60; EX 196.80.
Owner Mrs T Burns **Bred** Rathasker Stud **Trained** West Ilsley, Berks

FOCUS
The ground was described as Good to Soft, Good in places following 20mm of overnight rain and there was a headwind in the straight for some of the races on what was a blustery afternoon. This was a really competitive nursery.

NOTEBOOK
Gold Fix(IRE), winner of a seller two starts back, didn't have things go her way when disappointing in a claimer at Wolverhampton last time, but she had earlier run well in defeat off this sort of mark and, having hit the front 2f out, she stayed on well to score. She is taking her racing well and may progress further. (op 14-1)
Timelord(IRE) came with a challenge from two out and seemed to appreciate the step up to 7f, but couldn't get to the winner. He is still a maiden, but should find a race at some stage on this evidence. (op 11-1)
Mountrath, making his handicap debut following three down-the-field runs in maidens, ran a much-improved race in the first-time tongue tie and would have gone even closer to winning but for getting hampered. There should be more to come from him and he can win a small race. (tchd 11-1)
Keen Bidder, slightly below par at Newmarket last time, having been too keen, seemed to appreciate the truer pace in this more competitive contest and kept on right the way to the line, but never looked like getting there. (op 9-2)
Ever So Bold stayed on all too late and could be worth a try at 1m now. He should win a small race at some stage. (op 8-1)
Cuthbert(IRE) isn't really progressing, though this was still better than his latest effort. (op 16-1)
Gulf Punch ran better than her finishing position suggests, staying on well having badly lost her position running down the hill.
Boycott(IRE), the only one to come stands' side, was never on terms. (op 10-1)
Gold Diamond(USA) again faded having made the running. (op 11-2 tchd 6-1)

5590 EUROPEAN BREEDERS' FUND MAIDEN STKS 1m 114y
2:50 (2:51) (Class 4) 2-Y-O **£5,180** (£1,541; £770; £384) **Stalls** Low

Form RPR

3 **1** **Shaayeq (IRE)**^{14} 5191 2-9-3 0.. RobertWinston 1 76+
(M P Tregoning) *hld up in last but wl in tch: prog over 2f out: led wl over 1f out: shkn up and wl in command fnl f* **10/11**^{1}

0 **2** 2 ½ **Shabak Hom (IRE)**^{14} 5191 2-9-3 0.. FergusSweeney 6 70+
(D M Simcock) *hld up in 5th: trckd ldrs gng strly over 2f out: rdn to chse wnr over 1f out: styd on but no imp* **14/1**

05 **3** 3 ¾ **Gordon Flash**^{21} 4953 2-9-3 0.. EddieAhern 7 62
(R Hannon) *trckd ldr tl pressed ldr 3f out: upsides over 2f out: sn outpcd and btn: hung rt fnl f* **14/1**

0 **4** 1 **Whistle Blower**^{27} 4756 2-9-3 0.. RobertHavlin 4 60
(J H M Gosden) *mde most to wl over 1f out: sn outpcd and btn: edgd rt fnl f* **6/1**^{3}

5 1 ½ **Indochina** 2-9-3 0.. JoeFanning 2 57+
(M Johnston) *hld up in 4th: cl enough over 2f out: green and sn btn* **11/4**^{2}

00 **6** 8 **Refuse To Tell**^{29} 4646 2-9-3 0.. ChrisCatlin 3 40
(C E Brittain) *pressed ldr to 3f out: wknd rapidly* **33/1**

1m 50.67s (4.57) **Going Correction** +0.425s/f (Yiel) **6** Ran SP% **109.6**
Speed ratings (Par 97): **96,93,90,89,88 81**
toteswingers: 1&2 £3.10, 1&3 £2.20, 2&3 £8.20 CSF £14.57 TOTE £1.80: £1.10, £5.40; EX 8.90.
Owner Hamdan Al Maktoum **Bred** Shadwell Estate Company Limited **Trained** Lambourn, Berks

FOCUS
Rather a weak maiden.

NOTEBOOK
Shaayeq(IRE) won in good style. A promising third over 7f at Lingfield on debut, he relished the extra distance and quickened nicely despite racing into a headwind. There should be more to come from this Royal Lodge/Dewhurst entrant, though it is doubtful whether he is quite up to mixing it in either of those contests and connections may well go down the nursery route now. (op 8-11 tchd Evens)
Shabak Hom(IRE), behind the winner at Lingfield, was also held up early and chased him best he could having challenged widest of all, but just lacked that bit of acceleration. He is clearly going the right way. (op 20-1 tchd 12-1)
Gordon Flash is now eligible for a mark and should be capable of winning a minor contest once handicapping. (op 12-1)
Whistle Blower didn't get home having made a lot of the running and is another likely to find easier opportunities in nurseries. (tchd 13-2)
Indochina, a son of Sulamani representing a yard that has won this contest twice in the recent past, was too green to really challenge and didn't seem overly keen on racing into the wind in the straight. He should improve markedly on this effort. Official explanation: jockey said colt ran green (op 3-1 tchd 100-30)

5591 STEVE DONOGHUE H'CAP 7f
3:25 (3:25) (Class 4) (0-80,80) 3-Y-O **£5,180** (£1,541; £770; £384) **Stalls** Low

Form RPR

4323 **1** **Hi Shinko**^{15} 5154 3-8-10 **72**.. TGMcLaughlin 5 81
(B R Millman) *pressed ldr: led wl over 1f out: grad c to nr side after: rdn out and wl on top last 150yds* **9/4**^{1}

5101 **2** 1 ¾ **Midnight Fantasy**^{20} 4997 3-8-13 **75**.. SaleemGolam 7 79
(Rae Guest) *hld up in 5th: c towards nr side over 2f out: rdn to chse wnr over 1f out: one pce and readily hld ins fnl f* **13/2**

0150 **3** 3 **Silent Hero**^{51} 3956 3-9-2 **78**.. PhilipRobinson 3 74+
(M A Jarvis) *hld up last: pushed along 3f out: nvr looked happy on trck but kpt on to take 3rd nr fin* **7/2**^{2}

0550 **4** ¾ **Al Sabaheya**^{33} 4540 3-9-4 **80**.. ChrisCatlin 2 74
(C E Brittain) *trckd ldng pair: shkn up and nt qckn 2f out: sn outpcd: lost 3rd nr fin* **5/1**^{3}

4250 **5** 1 ¾ **Aurora Sky (IRE)**^{15} 5169 3-8-10 **72**.. J-PGuillambert 4 61
(J Akehurst) *t.k.h: led to wl over 1f out: wknd* **11/2**

106 **6** ½ **Steel Free (IRE)**^{17} 5090 3-9-0 **76**.. StephenDonohoe 6 64
(M L W Bell) *t.k.h: hld up in 4th: rdn over 2f out: no prog and btn over 1f out* **10/1**

050 **7** 5 **Summers Target (USA)**^{6} 5403 3-7-11 **66** oh1.... AndrewHeffernan$^{(7)}$ 1 41
(R M H Cowell) *hld up in 6th: rdn over 2f out: sn wknd* **20/1**

1m 25.3s (2.00) **Going Correction** +0.425s/f (Yiel) **7** Ran SP% **112.2**
Speed ratings (Par 103): **105,103,99,98,96 96,90**
toteswingers: 1&2 £1.80, 1&3 £15.70, 2&3 £7.10 CSF £16.69 TOTE £3.90: £1.40, £3.50; EX 21.60.
Owner Always Hopeful Partnership **Bred** Mrs Laura Grasby **Trained** Kentisbeare, Devon

FOCUS
The entire field came centre to stands' side in this modest handicap and it was the two who ended up against the rail that pulled clear. The form is best rated around that pair.
Al Sabaheya Official explanation: jockey said filly hung right

5592 MR & MRS WELCH'S WEDDING CELEBRATION H'CAP 6f
4:00 (4:00) (Class 4) (0-85,85) 3-Y-O+ **£6,476** (£1,927; £963; £481) **Stalls** High

Form RPR

0403 **1** **Idle Power (IRE)**^{26} 4791 11-8-6 **71** oh1.. JoeFanning 8 80
(J R Boyle) *trckd ldrs: 4th st: looking for room 2f out: swtchd to nr side rail over 1f out: squeezed through fnl f and r.o wl to ld last stride* **12/1**

0312 **2** *shd* **We Have A Dream**^{15} 5167 4-8-7 **72**.. ChrisCatlin 2 81
(W R Muir) *led: grabbed nr side rail in st: jnd over 1f out: battled on wl but edgd off rail fnl f: hdd post* **11/4**^{2}

0421 **3** ¾ **My Kingdom (IRE)**^{27} 4733 3-9-2 **83**..(t) RobertWinston 5 90+
(H Morrison) *trckd ldng pair: wnt 2nd 2f out but racing three wd of nr side rail: upsides over 1f out to last 100yds: nt qckn* **11/8**^{1}

4104 **4** 3 ¾ **Rocker**^{17} 5098 5-8-13 **78**.. FergusSweeney 4 73
(G L Moore) *hld up in 5th: shkn up and cl enough 2f out: outpcd fr over 1f out* **8/1**

6064 **5** 1 ½ **Gentle Guru**^{13} 5219 5-8-7 **72**.. JamesDoyle 9 62
(R T Phillips) *hld up in 6th: cl enough against nr side rail over 2f out: making no prog whn sltly hmpd over 1f out: wknd* **15/2**^{3}

001 **6** 1 **Wotashirtfull (IRE)**^{14} 5197 4-9-6 **85**..(p) SJCraine 3 72
(J R Boyle) *trckd ldr to 2f out: wknd over 1f out* **14/1**

2030 **7** 1 ½ **Musical Script (USA)**^{15} 5167 6-8-8 **73**..(b) RobertHavlin 1 55
(Mouse Hamilton-Fairley) *s.s: hld up in last: pushed along and in tch over 2f out: sn lft bhd* **16/1**

1m 10.85s (1.45) **Going Correction** +0.425s/f (Yiel)
WFA 3 from 4yo+ 2lb **7** Ran SP% **111.9**
Speed ratings (Par 105): **107,106,105,100,98 97,95**
toteswingers: 1&2 £4.80, 1&3 £4.80, 2&3 £1.50 CSF £43.13 CT £74.48 TOTE £15.50: £5.40, £2.00; EX 58.60.
Owner The Idle B's **Bred** Mountarmstrong Stud **Trained** Epsom, Surrey

■ Stewards' Enquiry : Joe Fanning one-day ban: careless riding (Sep 17)

FOCUS

They went a good gallop from the off and it once again paid to be on the stands' rail in the straight. The form is rated at face value.

5593 AMATO H'CAP — 1m 4f 10y

4:35 (4:40) (Class 5) (0-75,79) 3-Y-0+ **£3,885** (£1,156; £577; £288) **Stalls** Centre

Form RPR

2464 **1** **Spirit Of Adjisa (IRE)**[42] 4229 5-9-10 **75** RobertWinston 11 84
(Pat Eddery) *pressed ldr: grabbed nr side rail in st and led wl over 2f out: rdn clr fr over 1f out: readily* **7/1**[3]

2113 **2** 4 **Air Maze**[32] 4569 3-8-13 **73** StephenDonohoe 10 76
(Sir Mark Prescott) *trckd ldrs: 4th st: rdn over 2f out: chsd wnr over 1f out: sn lft bhd* **11/4**[1]

2040 **3** ¾ **Bramalea**[14] 5195 4-8-10 **61** JamesDoyle 7 62+
(B W Duke) *hld up in midfield: 7th st: effrt over 2f out: taken to outer over 1f out: kpt on wl to take 3rd nr fin* **22/1**

3401 **4** ¾ **Astrolibra**[7] 5377 5-8-5 **61** oh8 SimonPearce(5) 5 61
(M H Tompkins) *trckd ldrs on outer: 5th st: n.m.r against nr side rail over 2f out: rdn and kpt on fr over 1f out: no threat* **12/1**

0452 **5** ½ **Gilded Age**[61] 3635 3-9-1 **75** FergusSweeney 6 74
(A King) *led: failed to grab nr side rail in st and hdd wl over 2f out: lost 2nd over 1f out: fdd fnl f* **6/1**[2]

0612 **6** 1 ¼ **Dice (IRE)**[22] 4911 3-9-1 **75** EddieAhern 1 72+
(L M Cumani) *hld up: 6th st: effrt whn nt clr run 2f out and lost grnd on ldrs: kpt on fnl f: n.d* **11/4**[1]

-034 **7** 1 ¾ **Royal Willy (IRE)**[63] 3551 3-8-10 **70** J-PGuillambert 4 65
(W Jarvis) *s.i.s: hld up: 8th st: nt qckn over 2f out: hanging and nvr on terms w ldrs after* **7/1**[3]

5000 **8** 14 **Admirable Duque (IRE)**[20] 4988 3-8-8 **68** JoeFanning 8 40
(D J S Ffrench Davis) *trckd ldng pair: racd wd in st: hanging and sn lost pl: wknd 2f out: t.o* **14/1**

30 **9** 6 **Bull Market (IRE)**[188] 713 6-9-8 **73** VinceSlattery 9 36
(M S Tuck) *s.i.s: hld up last: wknd 4f out: sn t.o* **40/1**

2m 43.43s (4.53) **Going Correction** +0.425s/f (Yiel)

WFA 3 from 4yo+ 9lb **9** Ran SP% **113.8**

Speed ratings (Par 103): **101,98,97,97,97 96,95,85,81**

toteswingers: 1&2 £10.90, 2&3 £16.50, 1&3 not won CSF £26.16 CT £402.17 TOTE £8.20: £1.80, £1.60, £4.20; EX 31.50.

Owner Darr, Johnson, Weston & Whitaker **Bred** C J Haughey J Flynn And E Mulhern **Trained** Nether Winchendon, Bucks

■ Stewards' Enquiry : Stephen Donohoe one-day ban: careless riding (Sep 17)

FOCUS

The rail once again played a huge part in this moderate handicap. The winner is rated to his best backed up by the fourth to the best of her turf form.

5594 JUDY ALEXANDER 60TH BIRTHDAY CELEBRATION APPRENTICE H'CAP — 1m 2f 18y

5:10 (5:13) (Class 5) (0-75,74) 3-Y-0+ **£3,238** (£963; £481; £240) **Stalls** Low

Form RPR

3110 **1** **Ogre (USA)**[14] 5190 4-9-9 **74** (t) AndrewHeffernan(3) 7 81
(P D Evans) *mde all and sn clr: at least 4 l up ent st: styd on wl: unchal* **4/1**[3]

1010 **2** 2 ½ **Free Tussy (ARG)**[28] 4696 5-9-4 **66** (bt) RossAtkinson 1 68+
(G L Moore) *hld up: pushed along over 4f out: last and detached st: racd wd but prog fr 2f out: styd on wl to take 2nd nr fin* **10/1**

3400 **3** nk **By Command**[25] 4824 4-8-9 **62** KierenFox(5) 8 63
(J W Hills) *hld up in tch: 5th st: effrt over 2f out: disp 2nd fr over 1f out: no imp on wnr* **4/1**[3]

2163 **4** ½ **Drum Dragon**[34] 4495 3-8-12 **70** SimonPearce(3) 3 70
(M H Tompkins) *trckd ldng pair: chsd wnr 3f out: no imp: lost 2nd wl ins fnl f* **7/2**[2]

6435 **5** 2 ¼ **Hucking Hero (IRE)**[111] 2039 4-9-6 **68** MCGeran 4 64
(J R Boyle) *t.k.h: hld up: 6th st: effrt whn sltly hmpd over 2f out: n.d after: plugged on* **15/2**

4110 **6** nk **Penang Cinta**[3] 5509 6-9-9 **71** RichardEvans 6 66
(P D Evans) *chsd wnr to 3f out: nt qckn and sn lost pl: no hdwy fnl 2f* **3/1**[1]

0500 **7** 10 **Paint The Town Red**[20] 5003 4-9-4 **69** KylieManser(3) 2 44
(H J Collingridge) *blindfold on as stalls opened and slowly away: t.k.h and sn in tch: 4th st: struggling whn hmpd over 2f out: wknd* **16/1**

2m 13.09s (3.39) **Going Correction** +0.425s/f (Yiel)

WFA 3 from 4yo+ 7lb **7** Ran SP% **114.0**

Speed ratings (Par 103): **103,101,100,100,98 98,90**

toteswingers: 1&2 £6.70, 1&3 £4.80, 2&3 £8.40 CSF £41.57 CT £168.77 TOTE £4.20: £1.80, £4.20; EX 48.80 Place 6: £872.27 Place 5: £101.12.

Owner Diamond Racing Ltd **Bred** Gulf Coast Farms LLC **Trained** Pandy, Monmouths

■ Stewards' Enquiry : Simon Pearce three-day ban: careless riding (Sep 17-19)

FOCUS

Not much apart from the winner ever got into this and she sets the standard supported by the runner-up to his recent all-weather best.

T/Plt: £1,171.80 to a £1 stake. Pool: £73,037.51. 45.50 winning tickets. T/Qpdt: £88.90 to a £1 stake. Pool: £5,828.23. 48.50 winning tickets. JN

5438 REDCAR (L-H)

Thursday, September 3

OFFICIAL GOING: Good to firm (good in places; 9.9)

Wind: Fresh across Weather: Overcast and showers

5595 BUY YOUR TICKETS ON-LINE @ REDCARRACING.CO.UK NURSERY — 7f

2:00 (2:02) (Class 5) (0-75,70) 2-Y-O **£2,590** (£770; £385; £192) **Stalls** Centre

Form RPR

4362 **1** **William Morgan (IRE)**[29] 4651 2-9-0 **63** TonyHamilton 16 75+
(R A Fahey) *trckd ldrs: smooth hdwy wl over 2f out: led 1 1/2f out: rdn clr ent fnl f: comf* **11/2**[1]

0000 **2** 4 ½ **Edward Whymper**[15] 5166 2-9-0 **63** JimmyQuinn 11 64
(M H Tompkins) *s.i.s and in rr: hdwy 3f out: swtchd rt and rdn along wl over 1f out: kpt on to chse wnr ins fnl f: no imp* **20/1**

0634 **3** nk **High Rolling**[22] 4895 2-9-0 **63** DavidAllan 17 63+
(T D Easterby) *towards rr: hdwy 1/2-way: rdn to chse ldrs wl over 1f out: kpt on same pce ins fnl f* **20/1**

650 **4** 1 ½ **Gold Story**[70] 3310 2-7-10 **52** JamesPSullivan(7) 5 48
(B Ellison) *in tch: hdwy to trck ldrs 3f out: rdn 2f out and ev ch tl drvn and one pce ent fnl f* **28/1**

6523 **5** 2 ½ **Durham Reflection (IRE)**[15] 5157 2-9-4 **70** (p) FrederikTylicki(3) 2 60
(J Howard Johnson) *sn led: rdn along and hdd 2f out: grad wknd appr fnl f* **10/1**

153 **6** shd **Novay Essjay (IRE)**[2] 5550 2-9-2 **70** PatrickDonaghy(5) 13 60
(P C Haslam) *chsd ldrs: effrt and cl up 2f out: sn rdn: wknd over 1f out* **6/1**[2]

3245 **7** hd **Orpen Arms (IRE)**[22] 4889 2-9-1 **64** DanielTudhope 15 53
(R A Fahey) *bhd: hdwy 2f out: sn rdn and kpt on ins fnl f: nt rch ldrs* **9/1**[3]

066 **8** 1 ¾ **Tribal Myth (IRE)**[30] 4618 2-8-11 **60** PJMcDonald 6 45
(K A Ryan) *chsd ldr: cl up 1/2-way: rdn over 2f out and wknd over 1f out* **25/1**

3036 **9** ½ **Flow Chart (IRE)**[20] 4975 2-9-4 **67** PhillipMakin 10 51+
(T D Barron) *dwlt and towards rr: hdwy 1/2-way: in tch and rdn along whn n.m.r over 2f out: sn no imp* **11/1**

505 **10** 2 **Bustard Bay (IRE)**[30] 4618 2-8-12 **61** TomEaves 8 40
(J G Given) *dwlt: sn chsng ldrs: rdn along wl over 2f out and grad wknd* **22/1**

034 **11** ½ **Suzi's A Smartlady (IRE)**[19] 5036 2-9-4 **67** GregFairley 12 44
(M Johnston) *prom: effrt to ld 2f out: sn rdn and hdd 1 1/2f out: edgd lft and wknd appr fnl f* **11/2**[1]

0605 **12** 1 **Kookie**[5] 5440 2-8-4 **53** DuranFentiman 4 28
(R E Barr) *towards rr: hdwy 1/2-way: rdn along over 2f out and sn wknd* **33/1**

3006 **13** ½ **Powerful Pierre**[12] 5256 2-9-2 **65** AndrewElliott 18 39
(Jedd O'Keeffe) *a towards rr* **50/1**

0523 **14** 2 **William Arnold**[21] 4931 2-8-10 **62** KellyHarrison(3) 9 31
(C W Fairhurst) *prom: rdn along wl over 2f out: sn wknd* **12/1**

4215 **15** 5 **Alphacino**[21] 4931 2-8-13 **67** (p) JamieKyne(5) 3 23
(P C Haslam) *bhd fr 1/2-way* **9/1**[3]

4600 **16** 14 **Marchin Star (IRE)**[19] 5036 2-8-1 **50** SilvestreDeSousa 14 —
(M Brittain) *bhd fr 1/2-way* **33/1**

0000 **17** 42 **Woodhouse Mill (IRE)**[19] 5036 2-7-13 **48** oh2 ow1 (v[1]) DaleGibson 7 —
(N Tinkler) *s.i.s: a in rr: wl bhd fr 1/2-way* **100/1**

1m 24.96s (0.46) **Going Correction** +0.05s/f (Good) **17** Ran SP% **120.2**

Speed ratings (Par 95): **99,93,93,91,88 88,88,86,86,83 83,82,81,79,73 57,9**

toteswingers: 1&2 £30.20, 1&3 £19.90, 2&3 £91.50 CSF £117.63 CT £2060.07 TOTE £7.40: £1.50, £4.50, £5.50, £7.70; EX 184.00.

Owner P D Smith Holdings Ltd **Bred** R P Ryan **Trained** Musley Bank, N Yorks

FOCUS

A very competitive nursery in which not many appeared to have excuses. The wind was behind them on all of the races on the straight course.

NOTEBOOK

William Morgan(IRE) took a bit of a grip with his jockey to the start but showed no ill-effects from that by winning very easily after travelling smoothly. He had shaped well on his previous run at Newcastle against a decent sort, and duly built on it. (op 5-1)

Edward Whymper, who came in for support at long prices, was well beaten on the all-weather last time so this run represented a big improvement. He shaped as though another furlong this season would be within his range. (op 28-1)

High Rolling got outpaced at about halfway but stayed on strongly. The step up in trip seemed to suit.

Gold Story did best of those that stayed towards the far side of the track, but he still looked green under pressure in the last half a furlong. (op 33-1)

Durham Reflection(IRE), with cheekpieces on for his nursery debut, was prominent throughout but offered little once joined. (op 12-1)

Novay Essjay(IRE), who returned from a break with a pleasing third in a Ripon nursery two days earlier, sat close to the leaders and had nothing more to give over a furlong out. (tchd 5-1)

Suzi's A Smartlady(IRE), making her handicap debut and stepping up a furlong, was well supported but dropped away tamely after holding every chance. (op 6-1 tchd 13-2)

5596 RACING UK ON CHANNEL 432 MAIDEN AUCTION STKS — 5f

2:30 (2:31) (Class 6) 2-Y-O **£2,047** (£604; £302) **Stalls** Centre

Form RPR

3 **1** **Durham Express (IRE)**[24] 4844 2-9-1 0 PhillipMakin 10 72+
(M Dods) *trckd ldrs: pushed along and sltly outpcd wl over 1f out: swtchd lft and hdwy to chal ent fnl f: sn rdn and kpt on to ld last 100yds: edgd rt nr fin* **9/4**[1]

0523 **2** ½ **Bronze Beau**[8] 5337 2-8-9 72 TomEaves 11 64
(Mrs L Stubbs) *cl up: rdn to ld 1 1/2f out: drvn and edgd lft ent fnl f: hdd and nt qckn last 100yds* **7/2**[3]

5264 **3** ¾ **Clever Molly (IRE)**[24] 4844 2-8-4 57 PaulQuinn 15 57
(E J Alston) *chsd ldrs: hdwy 2f out: rdn along wl over 1f out: styd on wl fnl f* **12/1**

056 **4** ¾ **Hot Rod Mamma (IRE)**[39] 4349 2-7-11 59 BillyCray(7) 14 54
(A Berry) *in tch: hdwy 2f out: sn rdn and kpt on ins fnl f: nrst fin* **66/1**

002 **5** nse **Micky's Knock Off (IRE)**[11] 5292 2-8-9 0 PaulEddery 1 60+
(R C Guest) *led: rdn along 2f out: hdd 1 1/2f out and sn drvn: hld whn n.m.r wl ins fnl f* **16/1**

6 ½ **Cookie Galore** 2-8-0 0 ow1 JamieKyne(5) 6 53
(J A Glover) *dwlt and towards rr: hdwy over 2f out: swtchd rt wl over 1f out: styng on whn n.m.r ent fnl f: nrst fin* **50/1**

000 **7** 2 **Email Exit (IRE)**[25] 4825 2-9-1 53 GeorgeBaker 9 56
(C F Wall) *in tch: rdn along 2f out: edgd lft and one pce fr over 1f out* **22/1**

653 **8** 4 ½ **Amno Dancer (IRE)**[63] 3546 2-8-11 77 JimmyQuinn 8 35
(M H Tompkins) *in tch: effrt over 2f out: sn rdn and wknd* **10/3**[2]

000 **9** 2 ¼ **Burtondale Boy (IRE)**[12] 5253 2-8-11 47 PJMcDonald 5 27
(P T Midgley) *chsd ldrs: rdn along 1/2-way: sn wknd* **66/1**

02 **10** 1 ¼ **Lieu Day Louie (IRE)**[22] 4889 2-8-11 0 DanielTudhope 4 23
(N Wilson) *dwlt and towards rr: hdwy on outer 1/2-way: sn rdn along and wknd* **9/1**

11 nk **Amenable (IRE)** 2-8-11 0 AdrianTNicholls 12 22
(D Nicholls) *s.i.s: a in rr* **16/1**

12 4 ½ **Monsieur Pontaven** 2-8-9 0 GregFairley 13 —
(R Bastiman) *s.i.s and a in rr* **33/1**

58.96 secs (0.36) **Going Correction** +0.05s/f (Good) **12** Ran SP% **117.8**

Speed ratings (Par 93): **99,98,97,95,95 94,91,84,80,78 78,71**

toteswingers: 1&2 £4.10, 1&3 £7.50, 2&3 £6.40 CSF £9.46 TOTE £3.10: £1.30, £1.10, £3.80; EX 13.30.

Owner M J Sedgewick **Bred** Rathbarry Stud **Trained** Denton, Co Durham

FOCUS

None of those with experience had looked anything out of the ordinary, so this was probably only modest stuff.

NOTEBOOK

Durham Express(IRE) shaped well on his debut in a 5f Thirsk maiden and won this in comfortable style after always being prominent. He had little to beat so he will need to improve again to be a factor in handicap company. His trainer believes 6f will be no problem to him and expects him to make a nice three-year-old. (op 4-1)

Bronze Beau, who was in front of Durham Express last time, is exposed but gives the race a marker. He seemed to run up to his usual level. (op 3-1)
Clever Molly(IRE) is another who has had plenty of chances. Her proximity to a horse rated 15lb higher than her, from whom she was getting 5lb, casts doubt on the result. (tchd 11-1)
Hot Rod Mamma(IRE) finished well but never looked dangerous.
Micky's Knock Off(IRE), beaten in a seller last time, showed pace but was beaten when short of room in the latter stages. (op 12-1)
Cookie Galore, whose jockey was putting up a pound overweight, took a little while to work out what was required but caught the eye with her finishing effort. (tchd 66-1)
Amno Dancer(IRE) was eased in trip for this and looked unsuited by that decision, as she was always outpaced. Official explanation: trainer's rep said colt was unsuited by the drop back to five furlongs (op 3-1 tchd 11-4 and 7-2 in places)

5597 WEDDING RECEPTIONS @ REDCAR RACECOURSE H'CAP 6f
3:05 (3:06) (Class 5) (0-75,75) 3-Y-0+ **£2,590** (£770; £385; £192) **Stalls** Centre

Form RPR
1525 **1** **Hotham**[8] 5343 6-8-13 **73** GaryBartley(5) 4 83
(N Wilson) *s.i.s: hdwy to chse ldrs over 3f out: led over 2f out: hld on wl* **9/1**
6041 **2** ¾ **Avontuur (FR)**[3] 5516 7-8-7 **67** 6ex (b) DeanHeslop(5) 5 75
(Mrs R A Carr) *chsd ldr: led 4f out: hdd over 2f out: no ex wl ins fnl f* **6/1**[3]
1443 **3** 1 ¼ **Luminous Gold**[26] 4787 4-9-4 **73** GeorgeBaker 11 77
(C F Wall) *trckd ldrs: effrt 2f out: edgd lft and styd on same pce ins fnl f* **6/1**[3]
6066 **4** ½ **Inter Vision (USA)**[20] 4996 9-9-3 **75** FrederikTylicki(3) 2 77
(A Dickman) *s.i.s: hdwy 2f out: kpt on: nt rch ldrs* **4/1**[1]
2114 **5** 2 ½ **Bid For Gold**[48] 4072 5-9-0 **74** PatrickDonaghy(5) 6 68
(Jedd O'Keeffe) *chsd ldrs: rdn over 2f out: hung lft and sn wknd* **12/1**
4302 **6** 1 ½ **Incomparable**[3] 5516 4-9-6 **75** (b) TonyHamilton 8 64
(J A Glover) *t.k.h in rr: styd on fnl 2f: nvr nr ldrs* **6/1**[3]
2111 **7** ½ **Tangerine Trees**[49] 4015 4-9-4 **73** TomEaves 9 61
(B Smart) *chsd ldrs: wknd jst ins fnl f* **5/1**[2]
5505 **8** 4 **On Offer (IRE)**[8] 5335 3-8-12 **69** (p) DavidAllan 1 44
(T D Easterby) *chsd ldrs: edgd lft and lost pl over 2f out* **20/1**
0110 **9** ½ **Just Sam (IRE)**[6] 5391 4-8-10 **65** PhillipMakin 3 38
(R E Barr) *led tl over 3f out: lost pl over 2f: eased ins fnl f* **8/1**
1m 11.4s (-0.40) **Going Correction** +0.05s/f (Good)
WFA 3 from 4yo+ 2lb **9** Ran SP% **113.1**
Speed ratings (Par 103): **104,103,101,100,97 95,94,89,88**
toteswingers: 1&2 £8.40, 1&3 £12.70, 2&3 £9.70 CSF £60.62 CT £352.14 TOTE £10.70: £1.80, £2.50, £2.00; EX 62.50.
Owner Far 2 Many Sues **Bred** Capt J H Wilson **Trained** Flaxton, N Yorks

FOCUS
Plenty of these seemed to be in good heart, so the form, rated around the first two, should be sound and prove reliable for the grade.

5598 BODDINGTONS REDCAR STRAIGHT-MILE CHAMPIONSHIP (QUALIFIER) (H'CAP) 1m
3:40 (3:40) (Class 4) (0-85,85) 3-Y-0+ **£5,180** (£1,541; £770; £384) **Stalls** Centre

Form RPR
5341 **1** **Collateral Damage (IRE)**[8] 5333 6-8-12 **76** 6ex (t) DavidAllan 1 84
(T D Easterby) *in tch on outer: hdwy over 2f out: rdn over 1f out: styd on to chal ins fnl f: sn drvn and kpt on strly to ld last 100yds* **11/4**[1]
6116 **2** 1 ½ **Celtic Change (IRE)**[19] 5040 5-9-4 **82** (bt) PhillipMakin 12 86
(M Dods) *led: rdn along wl over 1f out: drvn ent fnl f: hdd and no ex last 100yds* **17/2**
610 **3** shd **Reel Buddy Star**[13] 5221 4-9-4 **82** DanielTudhope 5 86
(G M Moore) *prom: rdn along over 2f out: drvn and ev ch over 1f out: kpt on same pce ins fnl f* **14/1**
0/0- **4** ½ **Glenmuir (IRE)**[43] 4218 6-8-1 **72** IJBrennan(7) 3 75
(J J Quinn) *hld up in rr: hdwy over 2f out: rdn wl over 1f out: kpt on ins fnl f: nrst fin* **33/1**
0501 **5** ¾ **Daaweitza**[5] 5438 6-8-11 **80** 6ex (b) LanceBetts(5) 10 81
(B Ellison) *chsd ldr: rdn along 3f out: drvn and outpcd 2f out: swtchd rt over 1f out: rallied ins fnl f: styng on towards fin* **7/1**[3]
4402 **6** 2 ¼ **Kloof**[86] 2795 3-8-8 **77** SilvestreDeSousa 11 72
(K A Ryan) *in tch: hdwy 3f out: rdn to chse ldrs wl over 1f out: sn drvn and wknd ins fnl f* **12/1**
201 **7** 1 **Just Bond (IRE)**[26] 4801 7-9-7 **85** PJMcDonald 7 78
(G R Oldroyd) *hld up in rr: hdwy over 2f out: chsd ldrs and rdn wl over 1f out: no imp* **10/1**
6265 **8** ¾ **Capucci**[7] 5361 4-8-11 **80** (t) JamieKyne(5) 13 71
(J J Quinn) *trckd ldrs: hdwy 3f out: rdn to chse ldng pair 2f out: sn drvn and wknd over 1f out* **14/1**
1461 **9** 2 **Chapter And Verse (IRE)**[19] 5040 3-8-12 **81** PaulEddery 9 67
(B W Hills) *trckd ldrs: rdn along 3f out: drvn over 2f out and sn wknd* **7/2**[2]
000 **10** 2 ¼ **Ansells Pride (IRE)**[26] 4779 6-8-13 **77** TomEaves 6 58
(B Smart) *chsd ldrs: rdn along 3f out: sn wknd* **33/1**
5051 **11** 7 **Lakeman (IRE)**[11] 5295 3-8-4 **73** 6ex DuranFentiman 4 36
(B Ellison) *a towards rr* **18/1**
0000 **12** 18 **Grand Passion (IRE)**[55] 3822 9-9-6 **84** GeorgeBaker 2 5
(C F Wall) *a towards rr* **14/1**
1m 37.27s (-0.73) **Going Correction** +0.05s/f (Good)
WFA 3 from 4yo+ 5lb **12** Ran SP% **119.8**
Speed ratings (Par 105): **105,103,103,102,102 99,98,98,96,93 86,68**
toteswingers: 1&2 £6.10, 1&3 £12.50, 2&3 £37.80 CSF £27.02 CT £284.78 TOTE £3.50: £1.50, £2.00, £3.10; EX 41.10.
Owner Middleham Park Racing Xxv **Bred** Minch Bloodstock And Castletown Stud **Trained** Great Habton, N Yorks

FOCUS
The early gallop looked strong, which resulted in plenty of the horses looking tired at the end. The form looks straightforward rated around those in the frame behind the winner.
Chapter And Verse(IRE) Official explanation: trainer had no explanation for the poor form shown
Grand Passion(IRE) Official explanation: jockey said gelding had no more to give

5599 SUBSCRIBE TO RACING UK MAIDEN STKS 6f
4:15 (4:17) (Class 5) 3-Y-0+ **£2,590** (£770; £385; £192) **Stalls** Centre

Form RPR
3032 **1** **Equinine (IRE)**[20] 4981 3-8-12 66 PaulEddery 11 73
(B W Hills) *trckd ldng pair: hdwy over 2f out: led wl over 1f out: sn rdn and styd on wl fnl f* **11/4**[2]
432 **2** 1 **Miss Frangipane (IRE)**[22] 4913 3-8-9 69 FrederikTylicki(3) 8 70
(J Noseda) *trckd ldrs: hdwy over 2f out: chsd wnr over 1f out and sn rdn: kpt on same pce ins fnl f* **5/4**[1]
4636 **3** 8 **Halcyon Dancer**[20] 4997 3-8-12 56 PhillipMakin 10 44
(M Dods) *led: rdn along over 2f out: hdd wl over 1f out and sn drvn: kpt on one pce* **16/1**
0456 **4** shd **Diamond Blade**[15] 5145 3-9-3 52 (p) DuranFentiman 5 49
(T D Easterby) *cl up: rdn along and ev ch 2f out: sn drvn and kpt on one pce* **33/1**
00 **5** 2 ¾ **Italian Dame**[12] 5254 3-8-12 0 PAspell 12 35
(J R Turner) *towards rr: hdwy over 2f out: sn rdn and kpt on appr fnl f: nvr nr ldrs* **100/1**
3 **6** 1 ½ **Castlecarra (IRE)**[5] 5422 4-8-12 0 JamesPSullivan(7) 9 35
(J Hetherton) *midfield: hdwy over 2f out: sn rdn and no imp* **28/1**
0000 **7** 2 **Town And Gown**[26] 4778 4-8-9 40 GaryBartley(5) 2 24
(J S Goldie) *nvr nr ldrs* **100/1**
000- **8** 1 ¾ **Northgate Lodge (USA)**[269] 7609 4-8-12 43 (b) JohnCavanagh(7) 6 23
(M Brittain) *nvr bttr than midfield* **100/1**
6400 **9** 1 ¼ **Nino Zachetti (IRE)**[20] 4995 3-9-3 45 (b[1]) PaulQuinn 13 19
(E J Alston) *nvr nr ldrs* **100/1**
10 shd **Kilmun** 3-9-3 0 SilvestreDeSousa 4 19
(K A Ryan) *s.i.s: a in rr* **12/1**
0- **11** 3 ¼ **Mayorstone (IRE)**[397] 4647 3-8-12 0 TomEaves 1 —
(B Smart) *outpcd and bhd fr 1/2-way* **12/1**
3332 **12** 10 **Neva A Mull Moment (IRE)**[8] 5338 3-9-3 62 AdrianTNicholls 3 —
(D Nicholls) *chsd ldrs on wd outside: rdn along 1/2-way: sn wknd* **7/1**[3]
13 1 ¾ **Aquapark** 3-9-3 0 TonyHamilton 14 —
(R Craggs) *s.i.s: a outpcd in rr* **100/1**
1m 11.77s (-0.03) **Going Correction** +0.05s/f (Good)
WFA 3 from 4yo 2lb **13** Ran SP% **116.2**
Speed ratings (Par 103): **102,100,90,89,86 84,81,79,77,77 73,59,57**
toteswingers: 1&2 £2.60, 1&3 £8.70, 2&3 £6.90 CSF £6.15 TOTE £4.00: £1.70, £1.10, £3.40; EX 7.10.
Owner South Bank Thoroughbred Racing **Bred** Domenico Fonzo **Trained** Lambourn, Berks

FOCUS
Despite plenty of horses taking their chance, hardly any of them could be given a chance on what they had already shown, so this was a weak contest. The first two are rated close to their marks.

5600 CHRISTMAS PARTIES @ REDCAR RACECOURSE H'CAP 1m 6f 19y
4:50 (4:50) (Class 6) (0-65,65) 3-Y-0+ **£2,047** (£604; £302) **Stalls** Low

Form RPR
0546 **1** **Simple Jim (FR)**[24] 4848 5-8-10 **47** SilvestreDeSousa 10 55
(J Hetherton) *hld up towards rr: hdwy on outer over 3f out: rdn to chse ldrs wl over 1f out: styd on to chal ent fnl f: sn drvn to ld and hld on wl towards fin* **10/1**
0125 **2** hd **Outland (IRE)**[45] 4156 3-8-3 **51** JimmyQuinn 9 59+
(M H Tompkins) *midfield: hdwy and in tch 1/2-way: effrt on outer over 3f out: rdn to chal 2f out: drvn to ld ent fnl f: sn hdd: rallied and kpt on wl towards fin* **10/3**[1]
5543 **3** 1 ¼ **Fenners (USA)**[8] 5339 6-8-5 **49** JamesPSullivan(7) 4 55
(M W Easterby) *trckd ldrs: rdn along and lost pl 1/2-way: hdwy 3f out: rdn 2f out: styd on to chal ent fnl f and ev ch tl no ex last 75yds* **8/1**
1122 **4** 2 ¼ **Zefooha (FR)**[23] 4873 5-10-0 **65** GrahamGibbons 1 68
(T D Walford) *trckd ldrs: hdwy over 3f out: rdn 2f out: sn drvn and led over 1f out: hdd ent fnl f and wknd* **4/1**[2]
-262 **5** 7 **Goldan Jess (IRE)**[9] 4806 5-8-11 **48** LeeVickers 11 41
(P A Kirby) *led: rdn along 4f out: hdd wl over 2f out and grad wknd* **13/2**
4000 **6** 8 **Cripsey Brook**[21] 4927 11-8-11 **48** DavidAllan 5 30
(K G Reveley) *hld up in rr: hdwy over 3f out: rdn along over 2f out: nvr nr ldrs* **22/1**
3200 **7** 1 ½ **Blue Jet (USA)**[7] 5359 5-8-9 **46** oh1 TomEaves 7 26
(R M Whitaker) *prom tl rdn along 4f out and sn wknd* **20/1**
1136 **8** nk **Master Nimbus**[18] 4873 9-9-6 **64** (t) IJBrennan(7) 3 43
(J J Quinn) *trckd ldrs: hdwy 4f out: rdn to ld wl over 2f out: drvn and hdd wl over 1f out: wknd* **9/2**[3]
2003 **9** 4 ½ **Fistral**[24] 4848 5-8-8 **50** JamieKyne(5) 12 23
(P D Niven) *a in rr* **14/1**
4550 **10** 6 **Flora's Pride**[25] 4822 5-8-12 **52** KellyHarrison(3) 8 17
(K G Reveley) *trckd ldrs: hdwy on outer 4f out: rdn along 3f out and sn wknd* **33/1**
3m 4.79s (0.09) **Going Correction** +0.05s/f (Good)
WFA 3 from 5yo+ 11lb **10** Ran SP% **113.5**
Speed ratings (Par 101): **101,100,100,98,94 90,89,89,86,83**
toteswingers: 1&2 £6.90, 1&3 £12.20, 2&3 £5.30 CSF £41.15 CT £282.52 TOTE £14.90: £3.50, £1.70, £2.40; EX 54.50.
Owner R G Fell **Bred** Snc Haras Des Peltrais, Laurent Thibault **Trained** Nawton, N Yorks
■ James Hetherton's first winner since returning to training.
■ Stewards' Enquiry : Jimmy Quinn caution: excessive use of the whip

FOCUS
A modest-looking staying handicap but the form looks sound.

5601 "GO RACING" IN YORKSHIRE APPRENTICE H'CAP 7f
5:20 (5:21) (Class 5) (0-70,70) 3-Y-0+ **£2,590** (£770; £385; £192) **Stalls** Centre

Form RPR
6200 **1** **Carnivore**[71] 3264 7-9-6 **70** DeanHeslop(3) 12 83
(T D Barron) *in tch: smooth hdwy to trck ldrs 1/2-way: led over 2f out: rdn clr over 1f out: hung lft ins fnl f: kpt on* **13/2**[2]
06-2 **2** 2 **Viva Volta**[76] 3105 6-9-4 **70** JamesPSullivan(5) 2 78
(A C Whillans) *midfield: hdwy on wd outside over 2f out: rdn over 1f out: styd on ins fnl f: nrst fin* **11/1**
3043 **3** ¾ **Silly Gilly (IRE)**[6] 5395 5-8-7 **57** LanceBetts(3) 16 63
(R E Barr) *midfield: hdwy to chse ldrs wl over 2f out: rdn wl over 1f out: drvn ent fnl f and kpt on* **6/1**[1]
3660 **4** ½ **Finsbury**[19] 5031 6-8-9 **59** ow1 GaryBartley(3) 19 63
(J S Goldie) *in rr: hdwy on wd outside 3f out: rdn along 2f out: kpt on ins fnl f: nrst fin* **20/1**
5-06 **5** nk **Yorkshire Blue**[6] 5391 10-8-4 **56** oh1 (p) DebraEngland(5) 8 59
(J S Goldie) *midfield: hdwy to chse ldrs 2f out: sn rdn and kpt on ins fnl f: nrst fin* **33/1**
6000 **6** ½ **Mr Lu**[11] 5289 4-8-9 **56** oh3 KellyHarrison 9 58
(J S Goldie) *bhd: hdwy 1/2-way: rdn along 2f out: styd on wl u.p ins fnl f: nrst fin* **50/1**
1061 **7** ½ **Young Gladiator (IRE)**[40] 4312 4-8-12 **59** (b) AndrewMullen 7 60
(Miss J A Camacho) *cl up: effrt over 2f out and ev ch tl rdn and wknd over 1f out* **8/1**
6053 **8** 1 ½ **Another Decree**[20] 4995 4-8-7 **59** (tp) IJBrennan(5) 11 56
(M Dods) *towards rr: rdn along 3f out: kpt on u.p fnl 2f: nvr nr ldrs* **14/1**

0450 **9** *1 ½* **Cigalas**[60] 3656 4-8-13 **63**.. SladeO'Hara(3) 5 56
(Mrs J C McGregor) *s.i.s: hdwy into midfield after 2f: rdn along and styng on whn hmpd over 2f out: sn swtchd lft and kpt on: nvr nr ldrs* **33/1**

0035 **10** *hd* **Kipchak (IRE)**[8] 5349 4-9-7 **70**..................................(p) FrederikTylicki 10 62
(C R Dore) *prom: rdn along 3f out and grad wknd* **9/1**

5350 **11** *nk* **Efidium**[24] 4845 11-8-9 **59**.. JamieKyne(3) 18 50
(N Bycroft) *nvr bttr than midfield* **16/1**

2130 **12** *shd* **King Pin**[36] 4435 4-8-9 **61**.. NSLawes(5) 4 52
(Miss Tracy Waggott) *towards rr tl sme late hdwy* **13/2**[2]

-300 **13** *nk* **Smalljohn**[34] 4504 3-8-10 **68**..................................(v) AdamCarter(7) 17 58
(B Smart) *led 2f: prom tl rdn along wl over 2f out and grad wknd* **20/1**

5105 **14** *¾* **Redwater River**[6] 5391 5-8-4 **56**.........................(b) MatthewLawson(5) 14 44
(Mrs R A Carr) *prom: rdn along wl over 2f out: grad wknd* **14/1**

200 **15** *nk* **Exopuntia**[36] 4436 3-8-5 **56** oh2.. MichaelJStainton 15 43
(R M Whitaker) *a towards rr* **40/1**

-610 **16** *½* **Phantom Serenade (IRE)**[40] 4313 4-8-6 **56** oh2.. PatrickDonaghy(3) 13 42
(M Dods) *a towards rr* **33/1**

3000 **17** *1 ½* **Seldom (IRE)**[70] 3316 3-8-11 **67**.. JohnCavanagh(5) 3 49
(M Brittain) *towards rr fr 1/2-way* **66/1**

36 **18** *1* **Enhancing**[104] 2236 3-8-5 **63**..................................(tp) JonathanHinch(7) 6 42
(J A Glover) *a towards rr* **40/1**

-032 **19** *¾* **Micky Mac (IRE)**[6] 5391 5-8-7 **57**.. PaulPickard(3) 1 34
(C J Teague) *cl up: led after 2f: rdn along and hdd wl over 2f out: sn wknd* **15/2**[3]

1m 25.33s (0.83) **Going Correction** +0.05s/f (Good)
WFA 3 from 4yo+ 4lb **19** Ran SP% **128.1**
Speed ratings (Par 103): **97,94,93,93,92 92,91,90,88,88 87,87,87,86,86 85,83,82,81**
toteswingers: 1&2 £24.00, 1&3 £14.80, 2&3 £10.80 CSF £70.90 CT £478.48 TOTE £9.30: £2.90, £3.10, £1.90, £5.30; EX 142.80 Place 6: £75.25 Place 5: £20.31 .
Owner The Meat Eaters **Bred** Lord Halifax **Trained** Maunby, N Yorks

FOCUS
A modest handicap that looks reasonable form with the third and fourth close to recent marks.
Cigalas Official explanation: jockey said gelding was denied a clear run
Efidium Official explanation: jockey said gelding hung left throughout
T/Jkpt: Not won. T/Plt: £86.90 to a £1 stake. Pool: £59,491.56. 499.70 winning tickets. T/Qpdt: £13.20 to a £1 stake. Pool: £4,770.78. 267.17 winning tickets. JR

5211 SALISBURY (R-H)
Thursday, September 3

OFFICIAL GOING: Good to soft (soft in places) changing to soft (good to soft in places) after race 2 (2.10)
Wind: strong, varying across and head on Weather: sunny spells with occasional heavy showers

5602 AXMINSTER CARPETS APPRENTICE H'CAP (WHIPS SHALL BE CARRIED BUT NOT USED) 1m
1:40 (1:41) (Class 5) (0-70,72) 3-Y-0+ **£3,238** (£963; £481; £240) **Stalls** High

Form RPR

1240 **1** **Miss Mojito (IRE)**[15] 5169 3-8-12 **65**.........................(t) NathanAlison(5) 1 73
(J W Hills) *s.i.s: towards rr: hdwy over 2f out: led over 1f out: edgd lft ent fnl f: jst hld on* **10/1**

0110 **2** *hd* **Gallego**[32] 4563 7-9-6 **66**.. JosephineBruning(3) 2 75
(R J Price) *stdd s: plld hrd towards rr: hdwy fr 3f out: chsd wnr ent fnl f: clsng towards fin: jst failed* **12/1**

2251 **3** *7* **Ailsa Craig (IRE)**[18] 5063 3-9-4 **69**.. CharlesEddery(3) 9 61
(R Hannon) *trckd ldrs: rdn 3f out: one pce fnl 2f* **13/2**

5160 **4** *1 ¼* **Inquisitress**[1] 5577 5-8-6 **52** oh2.. KierenFox(3) 4 42
(J J Bridger) *trckd ldrs after 1f: led wl over 3f out: hung lft and hdd over 1f out: fdd fnl f* **20/1**

033 **5** *1 ¼* **Straight Face (IRE)**[29] 4665 5-8-4 **52**.........................(v) LaurenShea(5) 3 39
(Miss Gay Kelleway) *hld up: rdn over 3f out: sme late prog: nvr trbld ldrs* **12/1**

315 **6** *1* **Flying Silks (IRE)**[15] 5169 3-9-1 **68**.. LukeKilgarriff(5) 11 52
(J R Gask) *mid-div: little imp over 2f out: wknd over 1f out* **15/8**[1]

0341 **7** *2 ¾* **Hallingdal (UAE)**[11] 5285 4-9-10 **72** 6ex.. RyanClark(5) 6 51
(J J Bridger) *trckd ldrs: rdn over 3f out: sn wknd* **6/1**[3]

2341 **8** *nk* **Pretty Officer (USA)**[4] 5484 4-8-11 **59** 6ex.. NoelGarbutt(5) 7 37
(Rae Guest) *awkward leaving stalls: sn trcking ldrs: bmpd over 3f out: grad fdd* **4/1**[2]

450 **9** *3 ½* **Peace Concluded**[40] 4322 3-8-9 **60**.........................(b[1]) DavidKenny(3) 8 29
(B R Millman) *bmpd leaving stalls: sn trcking ldrs: upsides over 3f out tl wl over 2f out: wknd wl over 1f out* **25/1**

6060 **P** **Missrepresentation**[41] 4266 3-8-12 **60**.. RosieJessop 10 —
(J C Fox) *led tl wl over 3f out: wknd rapidly: p.u 2f out: dismntd* **66/1**

1m 49.87s (6.37) **Going Correction** +0.475s/f (Yiel)
WFA 3 from 4yo+ 5lb **10** Ran SP% **117.0**
Speed ratings (Par 103): **87,86,79,78,77 76,73,73,69,—**
toteswingers: 1&2 £12.20, 1&3 £8.20, 2&3 £9.20 CSF £120.06 CT £866.15 TOTE £13.30: £3.10, £3.20, £2.10; EX 92.00.
Owner Gary & Linnet Woodward (2) **Bred** Islanmore Stud **Trained** Upper Lambourn, Berks

FOCUS
The overnight rain meant that the ground was very different from declaration time and was now officially good to soft, soft in places. A strong headwind would have made this even harder hard work for the horses. It's probably significant that the first two home were the slowest to exit the stalls and that meant that they were sheltered from the wind early, whilst the leaders may have gone off too quick in the conditions. The pair ultimately pulled a long way clear of the rest ansd both are rated as having run slight personal bests.

5603 EUROPEAN BREEDERS' FUND NOVICE STKS 1m
2:10 (2:11) (Class 4) 2-Y-0 **£4,695** (£1,397; £698; £348) **Stalls** High

Form RPR

0434 **1** **Raine's Cross**[13] 5214 2-9-0 **95**.. LukeMorris 6 92
(P Winkworth) *trckd ldr early: dropped to last pair after 1f: hdwy over 2f out: led wl over 1f out: 2 l clr ent fnl f: rdn out* **5/4**[1]

2 *½* **Dancing David (IRE)** 2-8-8 0.. MartinDwyer 5 85
(B J Meehan) *hld up: hdwy 3f out: rdn 2f out: chsd wnr ent fnl f: styd on* **13/2**

0061 **3** *5* **First Cat**[13] 5213 2-9-2 **76**.. PatDobbs 2 82
(R Hannon) *trckd ldrs: effrt 3f out: sn tended to lean lft: kpt on same pce* **4/1**[3]

5 **4** *½* **Opera Gal (IRE)**[20] 4985 2-8-7 0.. LPKeniry 1 72
(A M Balding) *led: rdn and hdd wl over 1f out: no ex fnl f* **7/2**[2]

10 **5** *9* **Invincible Prince (IRE)**[40] 4294 2-9-5 **88**.................. RichardKingscote 4 64
(R M Beckett) *trckd ldrs: pushed along 4f out: rdn 3f out: wknd 2f out* **11/1**

0 **6** *3 ¼* **Dutiful**[20] 4986 2-8-12 0.. TonyCulhane 3 50
(M R Channon) *s.i.s: sn trcking ldr: rdn 3f out: wknd 2f out* **16/1**

1m 47.79s (4.29) **Going Correction** +0.475s/f (Yiel) **6** Ran SP% **114.2**
Speed ratings (Par 97): **97,96,91,91,82 78**
toteswingers: 1&2 £2.20, 1&3 £1.90, 2&3 £1.50 CSF £10.44 TOTE £2.00: £1.20, £2.60; EX 10.40.
Owner David Holden **Bred** Richard C J Manning **Trained** Chiddingfold, Surrey

FOCUS
A race won by the high-class Punctilious in 2003 and this year's renewal looked very interesting. The winning time was over two seconds faster than the older handicappers in the opener, suggesting the form is decent, and again the pair that were held up last early eventually pulled well clear of the others.

NOTEBOOK
Raine's Cross, who set the standard having taken on some very decent company in his career so far, including when fourth in a course-and-distance Listed event last time, quickened up well to lead when the gap appeared approaching the last furlong, but had to be kept up to his work in order to hold off the newcomer. He stays this trip well, but he will need to improve if he is to win in higher grade and would struggle to confirm the form with the runner-up were they to meet again. (tchd 6-4 in places)
Dancing David(IRE) ◆, a half-brother to two winners including the 1m4f winner Ordination, ran a blinder on this debut, especially as he faced a stiff task against three previous winners. He travelled very nicely off the pace before looking a little green when first asked to go after the winner, but he kept responding and was closing him down all the way to the line. He is entered for all the biggest 7f and 1m two-year-old contests later in the season, as well as next year's Derby, so is obviously very highly regarded. He seems sure to break his duck before long. (op 5-1)
First Cat, off the mark with a narrow victory in a course-and-distance nursery last time, had it to do with a couple of these on official ratings. Backed beforehand, he saw plenty of daylight on the outside and plugged on to snatch third, but was no match for the first two. A return to nurseries may be in order. (op 13-2 tchd 7-2)
Opera Gal(IRE), a very encouraging fifth behind two subsequent winners on her Newbury debut last month, tried to make all, but this extra furlong in much more testing conditions appeared to find her out. She holds a Fillies' Mile entry and is probably capable of more back on a sounder surface. (op 3-1 tchd 4-1)
Invincible Prince(IRE), very disappointing when a tailed-off last of seven in an Ascot Listed race last time following his successful debut in a hot Kempton maiden, was off the bridle at halfway and dropped tamely away again. He has questions to answer now. (op 14-1)
Dutiful, who only beat one home on his Newbury debut last month, was backed at fancy prices, but having been up there early he eventually found this company far too hot for him. (op 28-1)

5604 EUROPEAN BREEDERS' FUND QUIDHAMPTON MAIDEN FILLIES' STKS (DIV I) 6f 212y
2:40 (2:42) (Class 4) 2-Y-0 **£6,152** (£1,830; £914; £456) **Stalls** High

Form RPR

1 **Kithonia (FR)** 2-9-0 0.. TPQueally 18 73+
(H R A Cecil) *trckd ldrs: rdn over 2f out: squeezed through gap on rails to ld jst ins fnl f: drifted lft: r.o wl* **15/8**[1]

2 *2 ¼* **Lady Slippers (IRE)** 2-9-0 0.. SteveDrowne 7 67
(H J L Dunlop) *trckd ldrs: rdn over 2f out: sltly hmpd jst ins fnl f: kpt on* **33/1**

30 **3** *shd* **Blue Sparkle (IRE)**[17] 5096 2-9-0 0.. LPKeniry 4 67
(Mrs A J Perrett) *prom: led over 2f out: sn rdn: hdd whn sltly hmpd jst ins fnl f: no ex* **28/1**

4 *hd* **Serafina's Flight** 2-9-0 0.. HayleyTurner 13 67
(W R Muir) *hld up towards rr: pushed along and hdwy fr 2f out: swtchd to far side rail ins fnl f: styd on* **28/1**

5 *nk* **Tislimeen** 2-9-0 0.. TonyCulhane 1 66
(M R Channon) *trckd ldrs: rdn over 2f out: kpt on ins fnl f* **16/1**

6 *½* **Free Grain** 2-9-0 0.. TedDurcan 16 67+
(J L Dunlop) *mid-div: rdn whn nt clr run jst over 1f out: kpt on ins fnl f* **16/1**

7 *½* **Fontley** 2-9-0 0.. PaulHanagan 6 63+
(Eve Johnson Houghton) *trckd ldrs tl lost pl over 4f out: nt clr run over 2f out: kpt on fnl f* **40/1**

8 *nk* **Lady Willa (IRE)** 2-9-0 0.. MichaelHills 2 63
(B W Hills) *mid-div: rdn over 2f out: styd on ins fnl f* **14/1**

9 *hd* **Atakora (IRE)** 2-9-0 0.. DaneO'Neill 3 62
(Mrs A J Perrett) *mid-div: effrt over 2f out: sn one pce* **11/1**[3]

10 *¾* **Lost Horizon (IRE)** 2-9-0 0.. PatDobbs 8 61+
(R Hannon) *mid-div: nvr best of runs fr over 2f out: little imp* **16/1**

6 **11** *hd* **Magnificence**[48] 4055 2-9-0 0.. ShaneKelly 15 60
(Sir Michael Stoute) *trckd ldrs: rdn over 2f out: wknd ins fnl f* **7/2**[2]

12 *shd* **Highland Jewel (IRE)** 2-9-0 0.. LukeMorris 11 59
(C G Cox) *a towards rr* **14/1**

0 **13** *3* **Madame Boot (FR)**[31] 4603 2-9-0 0.. RichardSmith 14 52
(P J Makin) *a towards rr* **25/1**

14 *7* **Twilight Memory (USA)** 2-9-0 0.. MartinDwyer 9 34
(B J Meehan) *s.i.s: a towards rr* **12/1**

15 *4 ½* **Seattle Speight (USA)** 2-9-0 0.. RichardKingscote 12 23
(W J Knight) *s.i.s: a towards rr* **20/1**

0 **16** *9* **Dreamy Eyed (IRE)**[13] 5212 2-8-11 0.. JackMitchell(3) 5 1
(Mrs P N Dutfield) *led tl over 2f out: wknd wl over 1f out* **100/1**

1m 34.93s (5.93) **Going Correction** +0.65s/f (Yiel) **16** Ran SP% **125.9**
Speed ratings (Par 94): **92,89,89,89,88 88,87,87,87,86 85,85,82,74,69 58**
toteswingers: 1&2 £15.80, 1&3 £15.90, 2&3 £57.60 CSF £86.86 TOTE £2.60: £1.10, £6.00, £8.00; EX 62.70.
Owner Niarchos Family **Bred** Famille Niarchos **Trained** Newmarket, Suffolk

FOCUS
There was a deluge before this race and the ground was changed to soft, good to soft in places. An interesting first division of this fillies' maiden with only four of the 16 runners having seen the racecourse before, but though they finished in a bit of a heap behind the winner a few of these are likely to make their marks in due course.

NOTEBOOK
Kithonia(FR) ◆, out of a winning half-sister to seven winners including the top-class pair Hernando and Johann Quatz, certainly knew her job. Never far away, she had to be brave to go through the gap between the leader and the inside rail a furlong out, and once through it she tended to hang to her left, but she had the race won by then and did it in style. A Fillies' Mile entry, she is likely to go on to much better things and on breeding the Oaks rather than the 1000 Guineas, for which she was immediately given a 33-1 quote, would appear the more suitable target. (op 5-2)
Lady Slippers(IRE) ◆, a sister to the Coventry Stakes winner CD Europe and a half-sister to three other winners, was never too far off the pace and kept on well to emerge best in the blanket finish for second. This was a promising debut and she shouldn't take long in going one better. (op 40-1)
Blue Sparkle(IRE), who didn't improve from her debut when well beaten at Windsor last time, ran much better here having been handy from the start. She is bred for speed, but appeared to see this trip out well enough in the conditions and will win races. She now qualifies for a mark. (op 20-1)

Serafina's Flight ◆, a half-sister to the stable's dual winner at up to 1m2f Lyra's Daemon, very much caught the eye in finishing strongly from well off the pace. She is bred to stay middle distances and is one to keep a close eye on. (op 33-1)

Tislimeen ◆, a half-sister to a winner over 7f out of the Cherry Hinton winner Torgau, also ran a promising debut especially as she saw plenty of daylight from the outside stall. Improvement can be expected. (op 28-1)

Free Grain ◆, a half-sister to the multiple winner at up to 1m Granary, stayed on pleasingly from the middle of the field late on despite not enjoying the clearest of runs. She is bred to appreciate middle distances in due course and is another to watch. (op 12-1)

Fontley, a half-sister to the multiple winner at up to 1m Muzdaher, also hinted at ability as the race progressed. She is another bred to stay further than this in time. (op 50-1)

Magnificence, who raced keenly when unplaced as favourite for her Newmarket debut, took a strong hold behind the leaders again here before dropping tamely away. She is becoming disappointing. (tchd 9-2)

Seattle Speight(USA) Official explanation: jockey said filly was unsuited by the good, good to soft in places ground

5605 EUROPEAN BREEDERS' FUND QUIDHAMPTON MAIDEN FILLIES' STKS (DIV II) 6f 212y

3:15 (3:16) (Class 4) 2-Y-O **£6,152** (£1,830; £914; £456) **Stalls** High

Form				RPR
	1		**Pipette** 2-9-0 0 ... LPKeniry 8 (A M Balding) *little slowly away: mid-div: hdwy 3f out: rdn to ld wl over 1f out: sn drifted lft: kpt on: drvn out* **7/1**[3]	77
	2	1 ½	**Faithful One (IRE)** 2-9-0 0 ... ShaneKelly 18 (D R Lanigan) *s.i.s: towards rr: hdwy fr over 3f out: rdn 2f out: styd on to chse wnr ent fnl f but a being hld* **25/1**	73+
4	**3**	¾	**Golden Aria (IRE)**[19] 5021 2-9-0 0 ... PatDobbs 2 (R Hannon) *mid-div: hdwy over 3f out: rdn and ev ch over 2f out: kpt on same pce fnl f* **5/2**[1]	71
0	**4**	*shd*	**Wild Rockette**[19] 5026 2-9-0 0 ... MartinDwyer 3 (B J Meehan) *s.i.s: rcvrd wl to trck ldrs after 1f: rdn wl over 2f out: kpt on same pce fnl f* **10/1**	71
65	**5**	½	**Lenkiewicz**[21] 4945 2-8-11 0 ... JamesMillman(3) 4 (B R Millman) *mid-div: rdn over 2f out: styng on whn sltly hmpd over 1f out: kpt on fnl 75yds* **20/1**	70
0	**6**	*nk*	**Miniyamba (IRE)**[26] 4797 2-9-0 0 ... TPQueally 1 (J L Dunlop) *s.i.s: towards rr: stdy prog u.p fr 3f out: styd on ins fnl f* **16/1**	69
	7	1 ¼	**Fame Is The Spur** 2-9-0 0 ... MichaelHills 13 (J W Hills) *prom: rdn 3f out: one pce fnl 2f* **28/1**	66
0	**8**	1 ½	**Mount Juliet (IRE)**[10] 5311 2-9-0 0 ... HayleyTurner 6 (S A Callaghan) *prom: led over 3f out: rdn and hdd wl over 1f out: fdd ins fnl f* **28/1**	62
	9	*hd*	**Red Intrigue (IRE)** 2-9-0 0 ... DaneO'Neill 17 (Mrs A J Perrett) *trckd ldrs: rdn over 3f out: wknd ins fnl f:* **14/1**	62
	10	3	**Cyan Eyed** 2-9-0 0 ... RichardKingscote 14 (Tom Dascombe) *in tch: rdn over 2f out: wknd ent fnl f* **16/1**	54
	11	2	**Plume** 2-9-0 0 ... SteveDrowne 7 (R Hannon) *trckd ldrs: rdn over 3f out: wkng whn squeezed up jst over 2f out* **14/1**	49
0	**12**	3 ¾	**Sirri**[99] 2383 2-8-11 0 ... JackMitchell(3) 5 (C E Brittain) *trckd ldrs for 4f: sn struggling: wknd over 1f out* **40/1**	40
	13	¾	**Lady's Purse** 2-9-0 0 ... TedDurcan 12 (Saeed Bin Suroor) *s.i.s: a towards rr* **8/1**	38
	14	1 ¼	**Lady Christie** 2-9-0 0 ... PaulHanagan 9 (M Blanshard) *mid-div tl 3f out* **50/1**	35
	15	*hd*	**Shelfah (IRE)** 2-9-0 0 ... TPO'Shea 11 (M A Jarvis) *a towards rr* **5/1**[2]	34
	16	9	**Glan Y Mor (IRE)** 2-9-0 0 ... NeilChalmers 15 (F J Brennan) *led tl over 3f out: sn wknd* **25/1**	12
	17	5	**Aimeeskeepingfaith** 2-9-0 0 ... TonyCulhane 16 (M R Channon) *walked out of stalls: a wl bhd* **25/1**	—

1m 33.14s (4.14) **Going Correction** +0.65s/f (Yiel) **17** Ran SP% **130.6**

Speed ratings (Par 94): **102,100,99,99,98 98,96,95,95,91 89,85,84,82,82 72,66**

toteswingers: 1&2 £18.40, 1&3 £73.50, 2&3 £7.40 CSF £184.87 TOTE £9.30: £3.20, £10.90, £1.50; EX 293.00.

Owner George Strawbridge **Bred** George Strawbridge **Trained** Kingsclere, Hants

FOCUS

The second division of this maiden was run in a time 1.79 seconds faster than the first, but they were spread much wider across the track in this heat and it may be that the principals found themselves racing on better ground, rather than the form being stronger. There will still be winners to come out of this.

NOTEBOOK

Pipette ◆, a half-sister to four winners including the smart Day Or Night, was never too far off the pace before taking it up over a furlong out, but once there she hung markedly away to her left. Fortunately she kept on going once straightened and won with some authority. The fact that she managed to win this despite looking green bodes well for the future. (op 9-1 tchd 13-2)

Faithful One(IRE) ◆, out of a winning half-sister to the top-class Favourable Terms, was held up early but made up plenty of late ground to take second and, as the stable's youngsters often improve for a run, it can only be a matter of time before she goes one better. (op 33-1)

Golden Aria(IRE), who showed promise when fourth on her Newbury debut last month, stayed on from the middle of the field over the last couple of furlongs, but lacked the speed to get on terms with the winner. The extra furlong wasn't a problem and she should find a race before too long. (tchd 9-4 and 11-4 in places)

Wild Rockette, who looked in need of the run when well held on her Newbury debut last month, was backed to improve on that and she did so after holding every chance. She may be capable of more on better ground. (op 14-1 tchd 9-1)

Lenkiewicz, unplaced in her first two starts though not disgraced here last time, stayed on late and probably took another step forward. She could be interesting if connections opt for the nursery route. (tchd 18-1 and 25-1)

Miniyamba(IRE) ◆, who pulled hard when well beaten on her Newmarket debut, ran better here, especially as she was given plenty to do and was trapped out wide. Her 230,000gns looks expensive based on what she's achieved so far, but she looks the type to improve with experience and a stiffer test.

Fame Is The Spur, a 30,000gns half-sister to six winners at up to 1m6f including the high-class Battle Of Hastings, ran well for a long way and should come on for the run. (op 33-1 tchd 25-1)

Shelfah(IRE), a sister to the 1m2f winner Bayhirr and a half-sister to four other winners including the top-class Embassy, attracted market support but she never figured at all on this debut and is surely capable of much better than this. (op 8-1 tchd 17-2)

Aimeeskeepingfaith Official explanation: jockey said filly threw her head up in the stalls and missed the break

5606 EUROPEAN BREEDERS' FUND DICK POOLE FILLIES' STKS (LISTED RACE) 6f

3:50 (3:53) (Class 1) 2-Y-O

£20,153 (£7,639; £3,823; £1,906; £954; £479) **Stalls** High

Form				RPR
122	**1**		**Shamandar (FR)**[20] 4989 2-8-12 100 ... MichaelHills 10 (W J Haggas) *stdd bhd ldrs s: shkn up to ld ins fnl f: sn in command: pushed out* **9/4**[2]	99+
10	**2**	¾	**Sweet Sonnet (USA)**[76] 3086 2-8-12 85 ... TedDurcan 7 (Saeed Bin Suroor) *prom: rdn and str chal fr 2f out: kpt on but no ex fnl 75yds* **16/1**	97
01	**3**	¾	**Queen's Grace**[19] 5021 2-8-12 0 ... SteveDrowne 8 (H Morrison) *led: rdn whn hrd pressed fr 2f out: hdd ins fnl f: no ex fnl 75yds* **25/1**	95
0140	**4**	¾	**Jira**[26] 4795 2-9-2 99 ... HayleyTurner 6 (C E Brittain) *s.i.s: hld up: rdn over 2f out: kpt on ins fnl f: nt pce to mount chal* **16/1**	96
1	**5**	½	**Conniption (IRE)**[48] 4047 2-8-12 0 ... MartinDwyer 5 (B J Meehan) *racd keenly: trckd ldrs: rdn to chal whn drifted rt to far side rails fr 2f out: no ex ins fnl f* **15/8**[1]	91+
11	**6**	2 ¼	**Walk On Water**[13] 5208 2-8-12 0 ... TPQueally 1 (H R A Cecil) *racd keenly: trckd ldrs: effrt over 2f out: wknd ins fnl f* **3/1**[3]	84
146	**7**	7	**She's A Character**[36] 4418 2-8-12 97 ... PaulHanagan 9 (R A Fahey) *awkward leaving stalls: trckd ldrs: struggling whn hung rt fr 3f out: wknd over 1f out* **10/1**	63

1m 18.65s (3.85) **Going Correction** +0.65s/f (Yiel) **7** Ran SP% **115.3**

Speed ratings (Par 100): **100,99,98,97,96 93,84**

toteswingers: 1&2 £5.40, 1&3 £5.60, 2&3 £10.30 CSF £36.64 TOTE £2.80: £1.60, £5.90; EX 41.60.

Owner Mr & Mrs R Scott **Bred** Team Hogdala A B **Trained** Newmarket, Suffolk

FOCUS

A race that has been won by some high-class fillies in the past, not least the subsequent Cheveley Park winner Serious Attitude last year. This season's renewal was affected by four non-runners and the deteriorating ground may also have played its part. The jockeys decided to spurn the inside rail this time and raced up the centre.

NOTEBOOK

Shamandar(FR) had been narrowly beaten in the Weatherbys Super Sprint and a Listed race (both over 5f at Newbury) since successful over 6f at Ripon on debut, but the return to this trip did the trick. Well backed, she was held up early but put in a strong finish to hit the front inside the last furlong. She looks a nice sprinter in the making and is now likely to head for the Watership Down Sales race at Ascot later on this month. (op 3-1 tchd 2-1)

Sweet Sonnet(USA), behind both She's A Character and Jira in the Albany last time, turned that form around in no uncertain terms and had every chance having been handy from the start. Her debut win came on fast ground and she can probably go one better back under those conditions. (tchd 20-1)

Queen's Grace, upped in class, made much of the running, and although she couldn't match the front pair from over a furlong out this effort still showed that her 50-1 success in a Newbury fillies' maiden was no fluke. (tchd 22-1)

Jira, back to 6f after not appearing to stay the extra furlong in the Sweet Solera, had to concede 4lb to her rivals as a result of her Listed success at Newmarket in June. Slow to break, she stayed on in the latter stages but was never a threat and may not be the easiest to place from now on. (tchd 14-1)

Conniption(IRE), impressive in a soft-ground Newbury maiden on her debut from which three of those that finished behind her have subsequently won, should have appreciated the rain and she looked a likely winner when making her effort inside the last quarter-mile, but she then drifted right over to the far rail and basically threw it away. Hopefully this was due to her inexperience rather than anything more sinister and her next outing should tell us more. Official explanation: jockey said filly hung right (op 7-4 tchd 13-8)

Walk On Water, up in class following her convincing victories in an Ascot maiden and a Chester conditions event, had her chance but finished weakly and perhaps the softening ground wasn't for her. (tchd 7-2 and 4-1 in a place)

She's A Character, not disgraced in the Albany at Royal Ascot and Vintage Stakes at Goodwood since her impressive Doncaster debut, took a keen hold early and then looked very unhappy as she started to hang. This was far too bad to be true. Official explanation: jockey said filly hung and bit slipped through her mouth (op 9-1 tchd 17-2)

5607 EUROPEAN BREEDERS' FUND LOCHSONG FILLIES' STKS (H'CAP) 6f 212y

4:25 (4:25) (Class 2) (0-100,98) 3-Y-O+

£18,693 (£5,598; £2,799; £1,401; £699; £351) **Stalls** High

Form				RPR
1-42	**1**		**Tropical Paradise (IRE)**[26] 4771 3-8-12 **97** ... AshleyMorgan(5) 9 (P Winkworth) *trckd ldr: rdn to ld over 1f out: hld on wl towards fin: drvn out* **7/1**	104
0051	**2**	*nk*	**Enact**[16] 5130 3-8-11 **91** ... ShaneKelly 11 (Sir Michael Stoute) *hld up: hdwy over 2f out: travelling ok whn swtchd lft over 1f out: rdn to chal wnr jst ins fnl f: kpt on: hld towards fin* **11/4**[1]	98+
2353	**3**	1	**Silver Games (IRE)**[15] 5175 3-8-7 **87** ... TonyCulhane 5 (M R Channon) *stdd in rr s: swtchd rt and bmpd rival over 1f out: gd hdwy to chse ldrs ent fnl f: no ex fnl 100yds* **4/1**[2]	91+
1165	**4**	*nk*	**Romany Princess (IRE)**[13] 5221 4-8-13 **89** ... DaneO'Neill 1 (R Hannon) *hld up: hdwy over 3f out: outpcd 2f out: styd on fnl f* **6/1**[3]	94
2553	**5**	1 ¼	**Pretty Bonnie**[18] 5069 4-8-11 **87** ... KirstyMilczarek 4 (A E Price) *racd keenly: hld up: rdn 3f out: no imp tl styd on fnl f* **8/1**	89
0-40	**6**	½	**Perfect Flight**[36] 4423 4-8-12 **88** ... LukeMorris 6 (M Blanshard) *cl up: effrt 3f out: kpt on same pce fnl 2f* **12/1**	88
15-0	**7**	2	**Nora Mae (IRE)**[138] 1353 3-8-10 **90** ... LPKeniry 8 (S Kirk) *led: drifted rt whn rdn over 2f out: hdd over 1f out: fdd ins fnl f* **28/1**	83
0231	**8**	¾	**Turning Top (IRE)**[5] 5449 3-7-11 **81** 6ex ... RichardRowe(7) 7 (S A Callaghan) *trckd ldr: rdn over 2f out: wknd over 1f out* **7/1**	75
1120	**9**	2 ½	**Mo Mhuirnin (IRE)**[15] 5175 3-8-5 **85** ... PaulHanagan 2 (R A Fahey) *s.i.s: plld way through to sn be in tch: rdn whn bmpd over 1f out: sn wknd* **13/2**	69

1m 32.43s (3.43) **Going Correction** +0.65s/f (Yiel)

WFA 3 from 4yo+ 4lb **9** Ran SP% **121.5**

Speed ratings (Par 96): **106,105,104,104,102 102,99,99,96**

toteswingers: 1&2 £4.80, 1&3 £6.80, 2&3 £3.40 CSF £28.10 CT £91.66 TOTE £9.40: £2.10, £1.50, £2.00; EX 26.40 Trifecta £178.80 Part won. Pool: £241.68 - 0.54 winning units..

Owner S Lovelace & R Muddle **Bred** George E McMahon **Trained** Chiddingfold, Surrey

FOCUS

A decent fillies' handicap and once again the runners raced up the centre early, eventually ending up closer to the stands' rail. The runner-up is on the upgrade with the fourth rated to her mile form.

NOTEBOOK

Tropical Paradise(IRE), back up in trip after her narrow defeat over 6f at Ascot last time, had been raised 5lb for that effort but the result justified the Handicapper's assessment. Never far away, she took over in front more than a furlong from home and battled on well to score. Her connections believe that she is up to winning in Listed company. (op 6-1)

Enact, bumped up 7lb for her recent Nottingham success, had finished unplaced in all four of her previous starts over this trip, so on the face of it could probably have done without the rain. However, after being given a patient ride she quickened up well once switched and pressed the winner hard all the way to the line. Stamina didn't appear to be an issue here. (op 4-1 tchd 9-2 in places)

Silver Games(IRE), dropping to this trip for the first time since April, was very well backed and, having been switched off in last place early, then had to wait in order to see daylight. She was produced to hold every chance in plenty of time, however, but couldn't quicken where it mattered. She has shown her very best form on faster ground. (op 8-1)

Romany Princess(IRE), who had no luck in running in two outings since back-to-back victories at Windsor and Sandown in July, had no such problems this time and was produced to hold every chance against the stands' rail, but she couldn't take advantage. The rain may not have helped her. (op 5-1)

Pretty Bonnie, who had finished unplaced in her two previous tries over this trip on Polytrack, took a keen hold off the pace early, and when asked for her effort the response was limited. (op 15-2)

Perfect Flight, very disappointing on her first attempt at this trip last time following an encouraging return, never posed a threat and, as she has gained her last three wins on soft ground, these conditions shouldn't have been a problem. (tchd 11-1)

Nora Mae(IRE) ◆, not seen since beating only one home in the Fred Darling on her return to action in April, was making her handicap debut. She set the early pace but then gradually started to hang away to her right inside the last 2f as she got tired. She was entitled to need this and remains unexposed, so is worth keeping in mind. (tchd 25-1)

Turning Top(IRE), 3lb wrong and therefore 9lb higher than when winning over a furlong further at Windsor five days earlier, pulled far too hard early and gave herself little chance of seeing her race out. (op 6-1)

5608 SYDENHAMS H'CAP — 5f

5:00 (5:00) (Class 5) (0-70,69) 3-Y-O+ **£3,238** (£963; £481; £240) **Stalls** High

Form — RPR

5412 **1** **Triple Dream**[3] 5525 4-8-11 64 ....(p) JackDean(3) 3 — 76
(J M Bradley) *trckd ldrs: shkn up to ld ent fnl f: on top whn leaned on runner-up towards fin* **9/4**[1]

4045 **2** 1 **Brandywell Boy (IRE)**[10] 5323 6-8-10 60 .... RichardThomas 6 — 68
(D J S Ffrench Davis) *led: rdn and hdd ent fnl f: hld whn leaned on towards fin* **8/1**

020 **3** 1 **Compton Classic**[23] 4886 7-8-13 63 ....(p) TPQueally 10 — 67
(J R Boyle) *hld up: hdwy over 2f out: 1 l 3rd whn rdn ent fnl f: nt qckn* **9/2**[3]

3500 **4** 1 1/4 **Pic Up Sticks**[54] 3845 10-8-13 63 .... MichaelHills 4 — 63
(B G Powell) *rrd leaving stalls: towards rr: stdy prog fr over 1f out: rdn and kpt on fnl f wout rching ldrs* **16/1**

505 **5** 1/2 **Golden Dixie (USA)**[22] 4907 10-9-5 69 .... LukeMorris 2 — 67
(R A Harris) *trckd ldrs: rdn 2f out: kpt on same pce* **10/1**

0632 **6** 1/2 **Matterofact (IRE)**[10] 5323 6-9-3 67 .... DaneO'Neill 9 — 63
(M S Saunders) *trckd ldrs: rdn over 1f out: kpt on same pce* **10/3**[2]

560 **7** 1 **Fromsong (IRE)**[31] 4604 11-8-9 64 .... MarkCoumbe(5) 8 — 57
(D K Ivory) *prom: rdn over 2f out: remained pressing ldr tl fdd ins fnl f* **8/1**

0000 **8** 1/2 **Bold Argument (IRE)**[18] 5065 6-8-13 66 ....(b[1]) JackMitchell(3) 1 — 57
(Mrs P N Dutfield) *s.i.s: bhd: hrd rdn 3f out: no imp* **12/1**

64.36 secs (3.36) **Going Correction** +0.65s/f (Yiel) **8 Ran SP% 116.9**

Speed ratings (Par 103): **99,97,95,93,93 92,90,89**

toteswingers: 1&2 £3.60, 1&3 £3.60, 2&3 £4.70 CSF £21.72 CT £76.39 TOTE £2.90: £1.40, £2.50, £1.70; EX 25.40.

Owner J M Bradley **Bred** Hesmonds Stud Ltd **Trained** Sedbury, Gloucs

■ Stewards' Enquiry : Jack Mitchell caution: used whip on a horse showing no response

Jack Dean one-day ban: careless riding (Sep 17)

FOCUS

An ordinary sprint handicap best rated through the runner-up. They raced more towards the far-side rail this time.

Compton Classic Official explanation: jockey said gelding was unsuited by the good, good to soft in places ground

5609 IRISH THOROUGHBRED MARKETING "PERSIAN PUNCH" CONDITIONS STKS — 1m 6f 21y

5:35 (5:35) (Class 2) 3-Y-O+

£12,462 (£3,732; £1,866; £934; £466; £234) **Stalls** Far side

Form — RPR

5030 **1** **The Betchworth Kid**[15] 5173 4-9-2 104 .... HayleyTurner 4 — 104
(M L W Bell) *hld up: hdwy 3f out: rdn in 3rd 2f out: hung lft bhd front two jst over 1f out: chal between horses ins fnl f: led fnl stride* **4/1**[3]

3604 **2** nse **Basaltico (IRE)**[12] 5248 5-9-5 108 .... DaneO'Neill 5 — 106
(L M Cumani) *led: rdn and hrd pressed fr over 3f out: battled on: ct fnl stride* **10/1**

444 **3** nk **Free Agent**[56] 3778 3-8-5 102 ....(b[1]) RichardKingscote 3 — 103
(R Hannon) *trckd ldrs: rdn 3f out: nvr quite able to chal: fin strly fnl 75yds* **11/1**

0-20 **4** 3/4 **Ajaan**[68] 3390 5-9-2 98 ....(b) TPQueally 2 — 102
(H R A Cecil) *hld up: hdwy to draw upsides over 3f out: rdn over 1f out: no ex and lost two pls towards fin* **11/1**

4424 **5** 1/2 **Tactic**[37] 4405 3-8-7 105 .... TPO'Shea 1 — 103
(J L Dunlop) *trckd ldrs: rdn to chal over 3f out: cl 4th but looked hld whn hmpd by wnr ent fnl f* **9/4**[2]

-122 **6** 16 **Covert Ambition**[47] 4090 4-9-2 109 .... TedDurcan 6 — 87
(Saeed Bin Suroor) *racd in 4th: effrt over 3f out: wknd over 1f out: eased whn btn* **13/8**[1]

3m 14.74s (7.34) **Going Correction** +0.65s/f (Yiel)

WFA 3 from 4yo+ 11lb **6 Ran SP% 114.6**

Speed ratings (Par 109): **105,104,104,104,104 94**

toteswingers: 1&2 £5.30, 1&3 £7.30, 2&3 £6.30 CSF £41.22 TOTE £5.20: £2.80, £3.10; EX 33.30 Place 6: £238.42 Place 5: £35.04.

Owner W H Ponsonby **Bred** R P Williams **Trained** Newmarket, Suffolk

FOCUS

No starting stalls for this race. An interesting conditions event though the early pace was modest and the order didn't change until around half a mile from home, so not form to be too positive about. The field came up the stands' rail in the home straight.

NOTEBOOK

The Betchworth Kid, an unlucky seventh in the Ebor, would have appreciated the easing ground here though not necessarily a tactical race, so the ordinary early gallop wouldn't have been ideal. Switched off out the back as usual, when first moving into contention on the outside entering the last 3f he tended to hang and didn't appear to be finding much, but as soon as he was switched left in order to make his effort between horses he became more interested and put in a sustained effort to snatch the race by a whisker. He will now either go for the Prix du Cadran or the Fenwolf Stakes and then be given a break before joining Alan King for a hurdling campaign. (tchd 9-2)

Basaltico(IRE), who ran his best race since arriving in this country when a close fourth in a Chester Listed handicap last time, had the run of the race out in front for much of the way, but to his credit he battled on gamely when pressured throughout the last half-mile and only went down on the nod. He has winning form on soft ground so the rain would have been welcome and there should be a race in him before the end of the turf campaign. (op 8-1)

Free Agent, a fair way behind Tactic at Newmarket in his most recent outing, had blinkers on for the first time and performed better, but he still didn't look the easiest of rides. He seemed likely to drop right out when getting outpaced around 3f out, but rallied well up the stands' rail and was closing down the front pair at the line. (op 12-1 tchd 10-1)

Ajaan, not seen since finishing seventh in the Northumberland Plate, cruised through to join issue half a mile from home, travelling better than anything, but he couldn't stamp his authority on the race and when it came down to speed in the run to the line, he tended to hang and was found wanting. He was worst in at the weights here, so has at least run his race. (op 10-1)

Tactic, probably not helped by dropping in trip in the Gordon Stakes last time, had chased home Kite Wood at Newmarket before that and was well supported here. He was already hanging even before getting messed about by the winner and the ground had probably gone against him. (op 9-2)

Covert Ambition, runner-up to stable-companions Kirklees and Crime Scene in his last two starts, was attempting beyond 1m2f for the first time but his dam won over 1m4f and an entry for the Irish St Leger suggested connections believed that he would stay. However, he was under pressure and going nowhere 3f from home before dropping right out and it looks a case of back to the drawing board now. (op 11-8 tchd 5-4 and 15-8 in places)

T/Plt: £46.40 to a £1 stake. Pool: £49,766.28. 781.85 winning tickets. T/Qpdt: £14.60 to a £1 stake. Pool: £4,172.84. 210.71 winning tickets. TM

5224 **WOLVERHAMPTON (A.W)** (L-H)

Thursday, September 3

OFFICIAL GOING: Standard

Wind: Fresh half behind Weather: Heavy showers

5610 WILLIAMHILL.COM/BONUS25 - GET £25 FREE BET H'CAP — 5f 20y(P)

5:50 (5:50) (Class 6) (0-60,60) 3-Y-O+ **£2,047** (£604; £302) **Stalls** Low

Form — RPR

-050 **1** **Metal Guru**[21] 4929 5-8-11 55 ....(p) RussellKennemore(3) 5 — 66
(R Hollinshead) *chsd ldrs: rdn jst over 1f out: r.o u.p to ld nr fin* **12/1**

1235 **2** hd **Cayman Fox**[3] 5518 4-9-5 60 ....(e) MickyFenton 8 — 70
(James Moffatt) *led: rdn ins fnl f: hdd nr fin* **3/1**[2]

00 **3** 1 1/2 **Thoughtsofstardom**[20] 5008 6-9-2 57 ....(be) JerryO'Dwyer 1 — 62
(P S McEntee) *hld up towards rr: pushed along over 2f out: swtchd rt ent st: sn rdn: hdwy 1f out: kpt on to take 3rd cl home* **14/1**

6141 **4** 3/4 **Lithaam (IRE)**[3] 5504 5-9-1 56 ....(p) DavidProbert 10 — 58
(J M Bradley) *chsd ldr: ev ch over 2f out: rdn over 1f out: nt qckn ins fnl f* **13/8**[1]

0204 **5** 1 1/2 **Decider (USA)**[38] 4372 6-8-13 54 .... KevinGhunowa 6 — 51
(R A Harris) *a.p: rdn and ev ch over 1f out: fdd towards fin* **12/1**

0063 **6** nse **Welcome Approach**[27] 4750 6-8-13 54 ....(be) DarryllHolland 2 — 51
(J R Weymes) *hld up in mid-div: hdwy over 2f out: sn pushed along: rdn over 1f out: btn whn swtchd lft wl ins fnl f* **12/1**

0000 **7** 3 1/4 **Charlietoo**[21] 4937 3-9-1 57 .... PaulFitzsimons 3 — 42
(E G Bevan) *s.i.s: in rr: pushed along over 3f out: nvr nr ldrs* **33/1**

5250 **8** 1/2 **Admiral Bond (IRE)**[25] 4823 4-8-13 57 ....(p) NataliaGemelova(3) 4 — 40
(G R Oldroyd) *hld up towards rr: c wd st: rdn wl over 1f out: no rspnse* **8/1**[3]

1-00 **9** 1 1/4 **Sir Don (IRE)**[85] 2801 10-8-13 54 ....(p) RoystonFfrench 7 — 33
(E S McMahon) *chsd ldrs: pushed along and lost pl whn nt clr run briefly over 2f out: sn bhd* **20/1**

0000 **10** 15 **Woodcote (IRE)**[20] 4978 7-8-13 54 .... FrankieMcDonald 11 — —
(Peter Grayson) *s.v.s whn rdr late removing blindfold: a wl in rr: eased fnl f* **50/1**

61.46 secs (-0.84) **Going Correction** -0.125s/f (Stan)

WFA 3 from 4yo+ 1lb **10 Ran SP% 113.6**

Speed ratings (Par 101): **101,100,98,97,94 94,89,88,86,62**

toteswingers: 1&2 £4.00, 1&3 £5.30, 2&3 £8.90 CSF £46.01 CT £528.48 TOTE £17.00: £2.60, £1.70, £4.10; EX 45.80.

Owner Moores Metals Ltd **Bred** Reg Hollinshead **Trained** Upper Longdon, Staffs

FOCUS

A weak sprint handicap on paper, but the time was good for the grade and it was probably a better race than it looked. There was a strong early pace and few landed a serious blow from out the back. The winner is the best guide to the level.

Woodcote(IRE) Official explanation: jockey said gelding was slowly away

5611 EBF BUY A RACING POST YEARLING BONUS CANDIDATE MAIDEN STKS — 5f 20y(P)

6:20 (6:21) (Class 5) 2-Y-O **£3,885** (£1,156; £577; £288) **Stalls** Low

Form — RPR

3233 **1** **Waveband**[12] 5253 2-8-12 76 .... RoystonFfrench 2 — 73
(M Johnston) *mde all: rdn over 1f out: drvn out* **10/11**[1]

2200 **2** 1 3/4 **Listillo (USA)**[3] 5526 2-9-3 74 .... DavidProbert 8 — 72
(H J L Dunlop) *hld up in tch: rdn wl over 1f out: kpt on to take 2nd wl ins fnl f: nt trble wnr* **16/1**

0 **3** 1 3/4 **Night Trade (IRE)**[20] 5006 2-8-9 0 .... RussellKennemore(3) 11 — 60
(Mrs D J Sanderson) *chsd ldrs: pushed along and wnt 2nd wl over 1f out: sn rdn: one pce fnl f* **25/1**

65 **4** 1/2 **Ruthie Babe**[12] 5256 2-8-12 0 .... LiamJones 5 — 59
(W J Haggas) *a.p: c wd st: rdn and one pce fnl f* **4/1**[2]

5 6 **Caol Ila (IRE)** 2-8-12 0 .... PatCosgrave 1 — 37
(J G Given) *mid-div: pushed along over 1f out: no hdwy* **33/1**

6 nk **Fear Nothing** 2-9-3 0 .... RichardMullen 12 — 41
(E S McMahon) *mid-div: no hdwy fnl 2f* **11/2**[3]

50 **7** 3 **Turf Time**[78] 3032 2-9-0 0 .... NeilBrown(3) 7 — 30
(J A Glover) *prom: pushed along over 2f out: wkng whn rdn wl over 1f out* **150/1**

400 **8** 1 **Reallymissgreeley (USA)**[36] 4430 2-8-12 0 ....(b[1]) DarryllHolland 4 — 22
(K A Ryan) *mid-div: pushed along over 3f out: sn bhd* **33/1**

0 **9** 1 1/4 **Annia (IRE)**[20] 4989 2-8-12 0 .... JerryO'Dwyer 3 — 17
(N P Littmoden) *t.k.h: w wnr tl wknd wl over 1f out* **11/1**

03 **10** 2 1/4 **Rockweiller**[10] 5318 2-9-3 0 MickyFenton 13 14
(C R Egerton) *s.i.s: outpcd* **33/1**

00 **11** 2 1/2 **Sixbox**[24] 4856 2-8-12 0 JamieMackay 9 —
(D Shaw) *swtchd lft sn after s: outpcd* **200/1**

12 *nk* **Kanace** 2-9-3 0 SaleemGolam 6 4
(Ian Williams) *dwlt: outpcd* **100/1**

13 *nk* **Rightcar Marian** 2-8-12 0 FrankieMcDonald 10 —
(Peter Grayson) *s.i.s: outpcd* **100/1**

61.84 secs (-0.46) **Going Correction** -0.125s/f (Stan) **13** Ran SP% **117.8**
Speed ratings (Par 95): **98,95,92,91,82 81,76,75,73,69 65,65,64**
toteswingers: 1&2 £9.30, 1&3 £11.20, 2&3 £22.40 CSF £18.00 TOTE £1.90: £1.10, £3.10, £5.90; EX 14.90.
Owner Sheikh Hamdan Bin Mohammed Al Maktoum **Bred** Stratford Place Stud **Trained** Middleham Moor, N Yorks

FOCUS
This maiden was run in driving rain which would have made things difficult for these juveniles and unsurprisingly it was another race where making up ground from behind was hard. The first four finished clear.

NOTEBOOK
Waveband, making her all-weather debut, deservedly shed her maiden tag at the sixth attempt and was much too good for her rivals. Dropping back from 6f, she made most and showed a gutsy attitude down the home straight, coming nicely clear. Her previous experience was a big advantage here and it was a case of "job done" as regards to her potential paddock value. She should continue to pay her way, at least. (op Evens tchd 5-4)
Listillo(USA), with the visor abandoned, bounced back to form for the return to this venue and has now finished second on each of his three runs here. He rates a fair benchmark and, while he is fully exposed, should gain reward at some stage this year. (op 14-1)
Night Trade(IRE) came in for a bit of support and she duly stepped up nicely on the level of her Nottingham debut last month. She was a lot more professional this time and requires one more run before qualifying for nurseries. (op 28-1 tchd 22-1)
Ruthie Babe, another all-weather debutante, was well held on this drop back a furlong, but this was a touch better and she now becomes eligible for a nursery. Official explanation: jockey said filly hung right on the bend (op 9-2)
Caol Ila(IRE), a 40,000gns purchase, played up somewhat in the preliminaries and should build on this initial experience.
Fear Nothing was well backed for this racecourse bow, despite having a very tricky draw to overcome. He was never seriously in the hunt after becoming outpaced early on, but still showed some ability as the race went on. This half-brother to the smart Royal Millennium was clearly expected to do better so is one to keep an eye on. (tchd 6-1)
Rockweiller put in an encouraging effort over 6f at Windsor ten days earlier and it was a very strange decision by connections to drop him to the minimum trip He too had a poor draw and was predictably well outpaced, but is no doubt capable of better back over further. He is also now eligible for a mark.

5612 WILLIAMHILL.COM/BONUS25 - QUOTE BONUS25 H'CAP 5f 216y(P)
6:50 (6:51) (Class 5) (0-70,70) 3-Y-O+ **£2,729** (£806; £403) **Stalls** Low

Form RPR

0501 **1** **Bertie Southstreet**[13] 5225 6-8-13 **63** (v) DarryllHolland 2 72
(Karen George) *mde all: clr whn rdn over 1f out: r.o* **6/1**[3]

0566 **2** 1/2 **Royal Envoy (IRE)**[52] 3924 6-9-0 **64** JerryO'Dwyer 12 72
(P Howling) *hld up in rr: pushed along over 3f out: hdwy on ins over 2f out: rdn and wnt 2nd ins fnl f: r.o* **12/1**

144 **3** 1 3/4 **Chief Red Cloud (USA)**[27] 4741 3-8-13 **65** AndrewElliott 13 67+
(A P Jarvis) *hld up in rr: rdn and hdwy over 1f out: swtchd lft ins fnl f: kpt on same pce* **10/1**

1435 **4** 3/4 **Dream Express (IRE)**[17] 5107 4-9-6 **70** RichardMullen 7 70
(P Howling) *hld up towards rr: swtchd rt 2f out: c wd st: hdwy over 1f out: rdn ins fnl f: kpt on towards fin* **5/1**[2]

3050 **5** 1/2 **Fol Liam**[16] 5126 3-8-12 **64** (p) DavidProbert 1 62
(A J McCabe) *a.p: chsd wnr over 3f out: rdn over 2f out: no ex and lost 2nd ins fnl f* **16/1**

5323 **6** 1 1/2 **Yankee Storm**[7] 5374 4-9-4 **68** PatCosgrave 4 61
(M Quinn) *prom: hrd rdn over 2f out: wknd over 1f out* **7/2**[1]

000 **7** 1/2 **Punching**[18] 5073 5-9-5 **69** SimonWhitworth 3 61
(C R Dore) *s.i.s: sn hld up in mid-div: hdwy on ins over 2f out: rdn jst over 1f out: wknd ins fnl f* **40/1**

0040 **8** 3/4 **Kingsmaite**[38] 4375 8-9-1 **65** (b) AmirQuinn 5 54
(S R Bowring) *prom: rdn over 2f out: wknd wl over 1f out* **25/1**

01 **9** 2 **Athaakeel (IRE)**[90] 2683 3-8-13 **65** KevinGhunowa 9 48
(R A Harris) *mid-div: pushed along over 3f out: sme hdwy over 2f out: rdn and wknd over 1f out* **12/1**

1060 **10** 1 3/4 **Just Timmy Marcus**[22] 4914 3-8-13 **65** RoystonFfrench 10 42
(B P J Baugh) *a towards rr* **10/1**

0000 **11** *nk* **A Big Sky Brewing (USA)**[24] 4843 5-9-0 **67** NeilBrown(3) 6 43
(T D Barron) *s.i.s: sn outpcd* **17/2**

3500 **12** 6 **Bahamian Ceilidh**[8] 5345 3-8-12 **67** RussellKennemore(3) 8 24
(B N Pollock) *prom tl wknd wl over 2f out* **66/1**

000 **13** 15 **Westwood**[26] 4787 4-9-6 **70** JamieMackay 11 —
(D Haydn Jones) *towards rr: no ch fnl 3f: eased wl over 1f out* **25/1**

1m 14.35s (-0.65) **Going Correction** -0.125s/f (Stan)
WFA 3 from 4yo+ 2lb **13** Ran SP% **114.8**
Speed ratings (Par 103): **99,98,96,95,94 92,91,90,88,85 85,77,57**
toteswingers: 1&2 £20.80, 1&3 £9.40, 2&3 £21.20 CSF £70.19 CT £730.14 TOTE £8.70: £2.90, £4.10, £4.00; EX 48.10.
Owner Eastington Racing Club **Bred** B Whitehouse **Trained** Higher Eastington, Devon

FOCUS
The weather had cleared up prior to this open sprint handicap. It was yet another race where it paid to race handily and the winner is rated back to his winter form.
Westwood Official explanation: jockey said gelding stopped quickly

5613 WILLIAMHILL.COM/BONUS25 - LIVE CASINO DEALERS CLAIMING STKS 7f 32y(P)
7:20 (7:22) (Class 5) 2-Y-O **£2,729** (£806; £403) **Stalls** High

Form RPR

0030 **1** **Stef And Stelio**[12] 5256 2-9-6 71 (b[1]) LiamJones 1 74
(G A Butler) *mde all: rdn and edgd rt over 1f out: r.o wl* **9/1**

4542 **2** 2 **Zaffature**[13] 5224 2-8-8 62 ow1 (b[1]) DarryllHolland 3 57
(M Botti) *a.p: chsd wnr jst over 2f out: rdn and carried rt jst over 1f out: no imp* **9/4**[1]

0003 **3** 1 1/2 **High Resolution**[13] 5224 2-8-5 58 WilliamCarson(3) 2 53
(S C Williams) *prom: lost pl on ins bnd after 1f: hld up: hdwy on ins 3f out: rdn over 1f out: one pce* **13/2**[3]

1600 **4** 1 3/4 **Underworld Dandy**[22] 4901 2-8-6 63 CatherineGannon 8 47+
(P D Evans) *in rr: pushed along 4f out: hdwy on ins over 1f out: nvr trbld ldrs* **9/1**

4064 **5** 3 1/4 **Bathwick Gino**[13] 5224 2-8-4 54 RoystonFfrench 6 37
(P D Evans) *sn chsng wnr: hrd rdn and lost 2nd jst over 2f out: wknd over 1f out* **25/1**

5665 **6** 2 1/4 **That'Lldonowthen (IRE)**[22] 4912 2-8-1 53 (p) SophieDoyle(5) 10 33
(J S Moore) *hld up towards rr: hmpd over 5f out: swtchd lft to ins 4f out: hdwy on ins wl over 1f out: sn rdn: n.d* **40/1**

2643 **7** 1 1/2 **Saint Sebastian (IRE)**[10] 5303 2-8-7 64 RichardMullen 12 31
(E S McMahon) *sn prom: rdn over 2f out: wknd wl over 1f out* **13/2**[3]

040 **8** 1/2 **Smog (IRE)**[28] 4705 2-8-3 49 (b[1]) FrankieMcDonald 11 25
(B J Meehan) *s.i.s: t.k.h: hdwy on outside over 5f out: pushed along and wknd over 2f out* **16/1**

00 **9** 1 **Teeraha (IRE)**[8] 5337 2-8-1 0 JamieMackay 9 21
(D Shaw) *s.i.s and n.m.r s: a in rr* **150/1**

560 **10** 2 **Kildangan Girl**[7] 5368 2-8-0 0 DavidProbert 5 15
(W R Muir) *prom tl wknd over 3f out* **14/1**

5001 **11** 2 **Dear Mr Fantasy (IRE)**[13] 5224 2-8-12 65 PatCosgrave 4 22
(J W Hills) *s.i.s: short-lived effrt over 3f out* **4/1**[2]

0P **P** **Scintillating (IRE)**[70] 3306 2-8-13 0 MickyFenton 7 —
(R Hollinshead) *mid-div: lost action over 5f out: p.u over 4f out* **66/1**

1m 29.85s (0.25) **Going Correction** -0.125s/f (Stan) **12** Ran SP% **118.4**
Speed ratings (Par 95): **93,90,89,87,83 80,79,78,77,75 72,—**
toteswingers: 1&2 £13.80, 1&3 £6.10, 2&3 £5.20 CSF £29.05 TOTE £11.60: £4.00, £1.02, £3.60; EX 47.50.
Owner Stef Stefanou **Bred** Lady Halifax **Trained** Newmarket, Suffolk

FOCUS
The form of this juvenile seller looks straightforward and, once more, it was another race where those who raced handy were at an advantage.\

NOTEBOOK
Stef And Stelio had the highest official mark (71) of these and was conceding upwards of 7lb all around on this massive drop in class. He also had first-time blinkers applied and they clearly helped him concentrate en route to a first success at the fifth attempt. He obviously had no problems with the trip, has now found his level and could follow up in something similar, providing the headgear continues to hold the desired effect. (op 14-1)
Zaffature looked to have an obvious chance at these weights and was another equipped with first-time blinkers. The headgear ultimately failed to work the oracle with her, however, as she was running around before the winner drifted in front of her late on. She rates the benchmark, but looks one to tread carefully with after this. (tchd 5-2)
High Resolution showed improved form when third in this class over C&D last time out and looked a big player here turning for home. He could only muster the same pace when push came to shove, though, and his ideal trip is still open to some debate. (op 7-1 tchd 9-1)
Underworld Dandy had a chance at the weights and was well backed at big odds for this all-weather bow and return to claiming company. He ran a funny race as he began to race very lazily down the back straight and was near last turning for home. Once the gap opened on the far side, however, he motored home to grab fourth and is evidently talented. Now looks the time to reach for some headgear again. Official explanation: jockey said gelding hung right (op 20-1 tchd 8-1)
Scintillating(IRE) Official explanation: jockey said filly was struck into behind

5614 WILLIAM HILL 0800 444040 - GET £25 FREE BET MEDIAN AUCTION MAIDEN STKS 1m 141y(P)
7:50 (7:51) (Class 6) 3-5-Y-O **£2,047** (£604; £302) **Stalls** Low

Form RPR

2632 **1** **Luc Jordan**[14] 5181 3-9-3 76 DarryllHolland 4 79
(L M Cumani) *a.p: rdn jst over 2f out: r.o u.p to ld wl ins fnl f* **7/2**[3]

0- **2** 3/4 **Aspro Mavro (IRE)**[336] 6425 3-9-3 0 RichardMullen 5 77
(J H M Gosden) *chsd ldr: led 2f out: rdn 1f out: hdd wl ins fnl f* **11/10**[1]

3000 **3** 3 1/2 **Classically (IRE)**[48] 4058 3-9-3 75 SteveDrowne 13 69
(R Charlton) *hld up in mid-div: hdwy over 2f out: hung lft fr over 1f out: one pce* **11/2**

4 7 **At Wits End** 3-9-3 0 KirstyMilczarek 12 53
(J A R Toller) *dwlt: hld up in rr: hdwy over 2f out: rdn and no further prog fnl f* **66/1**

4000 **5** 2 **Susurrayshaan**[21] 4943 3-9-3 47 (p) LiamJones 2 49
(Mrs G S Rees) *led: hdd 2f out: rdn and wknd over 1f out* **66/1**

63 **6** 1 3/4 **Satwa Moon (USA)**[13] 5228 3-9-3 0 StephenDonohoe 7 45+
(E A L Dunlop) *s.i.s: sn mid-div: pushed along 3f out: nt clr run on ins over 2f out: swtchd rt ent st: n.d after* **5/2**[2]

7 1 1/2 **Marina's Ocean**[127] 5-9-4 0 (t) AmirQuinn 1 36
(S R Bowring) *dwlt: a in rr* **150/1**

0-00 **8** 1 **Miss Jodarah (USA)**[14] 5193 3-8-9 32 (b) MarcHalford(3) 10 34
(J R Best) *hld up in tch: pushed along over 3f out: rdn and wknd over 2f out* **200/1**

5 **9** 2 1/4 **Choosy Floosy**[13] 5222 3-8-5 0 TobyAtkinson(7) 9 29
(Pat Eddery) *s.i.s and wnt rt s: a in rr* **50/1**

6000 **10** 3/4 **Cruise Control**[21] 4937 3-9-3 49 DavidProbert 8 32
(R J Price) *s.i.s: a towards rr* **66/1**

-600 **11** 2 **Avonlini**[26] 4805 3-8-5 45 JemmaMarshall(7) 11 22
(B P J Baugh) *prom: rdn over 3f out: wknd over 2f out* **200/1**

0004 **12** 2 1/4 **Smart Tazz**[17] 5102 4-9-9 42 KevinGhunowa 6 22
(S T Lewis) *hld up in mid-div: n.m.r on ins over 3f out: sn bhd* **200/1**

000 **13** 8 **Any Secrets**[40] 4303 3-9-3 40 (p) JamieMackay 3 4
(Karen George) *hld up in mid-div: rdn and short-lived effrt on ins wl over 2f out* **100/1**

1m 49.77s (-0.73) **Going Correction** -0.125s/f (Stan)
WFA 3 from 4yo+ 6lb **13** Ran SP% **123.4**
Speed ratings (Par 101): **98,97,94,88,86 84,83,82,80,79 78,76,68**
toteswingers: 1&2 £1.80, 1&3 £5.50, 2&3 £4.70 CSF £8.17 TOTE £3.90: £1.10, £1.20, £1.50; EX 11.50.
Owner Equibreed S.R.L. **Bred** Equibreed S R L **Trained** Newmarket, Suffolk

FOCUS
The first pair dominated this modest maiden. The winner is rated around the winner.

5615 WILLIAMHILL.COM/BONUS25 - PLAY VEGAS GAMES H'CAP 7f 32y(P)
8:20 (8:21) (Class 3) (0-95,94) 3-Y-O+
£7,477 (£2,239; £1,119; £560; £279; £140) **Stalls** High

Form RPR

0-12 **1** **Leahurst (IRE)**[103] 2270 3-8-11 **89** DarryllHolland 4 109+
(J Noseda) *hld up and bhd: hdwy 2f out: swtchd rt wl over 1f out: shkn up to ld ins fnl f: easily* **5/4**[1]

2010 **2** 2 1/4 **Castles In The Air**[26] 4796 4-9-2 **90** PaulHanagan 5 95
(R A Fahey) *hld up: sn mid-div: hdwy over 2f out: rdn to ld ins fnl f: sn hdd: no ch w wnr* **5/1**[2]

61 **3** 3 1/4 **More Time Tim (IRE)**[52] 3928 4-8-13 **87** PatCosgrave 10 83
(J R Boyle) *a.p: led 2f out: rdn and hdd ins fnl f: one pce* **7/1**[3]

4603 **4** 3/4 **Masai Moon**[19] [5025] 5-9-2 **93**....(p) JamesMillman(3) 8 87
(B R Millman) *hld up: sn bhd: rdn wl over 3f out: nt clr run on ins wl over 1f out: sn swtchd rt and hdwy: nvr trbld ldrs* **12/1**

0200 **5** 1 3/4 **Gallantry**[21] [4954] 7-9-0 **88**.... JerryO'Dwyer 3 77
(P Howling) *s.i.s: hld up in rr: pushed along and kpt on fnl f: n.d* **33/1**

6352 **6** 2 1/2 **Xpres Maite**[7] [5375] 6-8-10 **84**....(b) AmirQuinn 7 67
(S R Bowring) *s.i.s: hld up in rr: pushed along over 3f out: nvr nr ldrs* **20/1**

-010 **7** nk **Brae Hill (IRE)**[35] [4459] 3-9-0 **92**.... StephenDonohoe 11 74
(M L W Bell) *hld up: sn in tch: wknd 2f out* **10/1**

0004 **8** nse **Baby Strange**[17] [5104] 5-9-0 **88**.... JamieMackay 6 70
(D Shaw) *led: hdd 2f out: wknd over 1f out* **20/1**

0330 **9** 2 **Nightjar (USA)**[85] [2814] 4-9-6 **94**.... RoystonFfrench 1 70
(M Johnston) *prom: rdn over 2f out: wknd wl over 1f out* **14/1**

6030 **10** 4 1/2 **Bond City (IRE)**[7] [5363] 7-9-1 **89**....(b) PJMcDonald 2 53
(G R Oldroyd) *prom: chsd ldr over 5f out tl jst over 2f out: rdn and wknd wl over 1f out* **22/1**

1m 27.0s (-2.60) **Going Correction** -0.125s/f (Stan)
WFA 3 from 4yo+ 4lb **10** Ran SP% **113.9**
Speed ratings (Par 107): **109,106,102,101,99 97,96,96,94,89**
toteswingers: 1&2 £2.30, 1&3 £4.70, 2&3 £7.60 CSF £6.50 CT £31.20 TOTE £2.20: £1.10, £1.80, £2.20; EX 9.20.
Owner Mrs Susan Roy **Bred** D And B Egan **Trained** Newmarket, Suffolk
■ Stewards' Enquiry : Jamie Mackay one-day ban: dropped hands and lost sixth place (Sep 17)

FOCUS
This was a decent handicap which was well run. The unexposed winner proved different class and should prove just as effective on turf.

NOTEBOOK
Leahurst(IRE), who won his maiden here, bolted up and made a mockery of his official mark on this return from a 103-day layoff. Taking on his elders for the first time, he was patiently ridden but had to wait for his challenge on the inside coming to the final bend. His response when pulled out for his challenge was immediate, however, and he made up his ground easily coming to the furlong pole. He ultimately came right away without having to be anything like fully extended and simply made mincemeat of this field. Connections have always rated him highly and plan to send him for the Dubai Carnival next year. He certainly looks a pattern performer in the making and ought to have little trouble staying another furlong. (tchd 6-5 and 11-8)
Castles In The Air hit top gear when coming from a similar position as the winner down the home straight, but found that rival in a different league. This was another solid effort, he has now finished runner-up on both his outings on this surface and helps to give the form a decent look. (op 13-2)
More Time Tim(IRE), another 3lb higher, met support and travelled nicely through the race just off the early leaders. He was another who got firmly put in his place by the classy winner, but this was an improved effort in defeat and he can still be found another opening on the all-weather. (op 15-2 tchd 6-1)
Masai Moon was racing in first-time cheekpieces and is rated 4lb higher in this sphere than on turf. He rather went in snatches through the first half, but ran well on down the home straight after meeting some trouble and performed close enough to his recent level. (tchd 11-1 and 14-1)
Brae Hill(IRE) Official explanation: jockey said gelding hung right throughout
Baby Strange Official explanation: one-day ban: in breach of Rule 158 (Sep 17)

5616 WILLIAM HILL 0800 444040 QUOTE BONUS25 H'CAP 1m 1f 103y(P)
8:50 (8:50) (Class 5) (0-75,75) 3-Y-O **£2,729** (£806; £403) **Stalls** Low

Form RPR

50-6 **1** **King's Song (IRE)**[33] [4519] 3-9-0 **68**.... PaulHanagan 4 76+
(Sir Michael Stoute) *t.k.h early: hld up in tch: rdn to ld ins fnl f: drvn out* **11/4**[1]

6214 **2** nk **Veroon (IRE)**[12] [5255] 3-9-3 **71**....(p) J-PGuillambert 1 77
(J G Given) *led: rdn wl over 1f out: hdd ins fnl f: kpt on* **7/2**[2]

-506 **3** nk **Silver Print (USA)**[22] [4910] 3-8-12 **66**.... ShaneKelly 7 71
(W R Swinburn) *a.p: rdn over 2f out: sn hung lft: kpt on towards fin* **9/2**[3]

065 **4** 1 3/4 **Primera Vista**[33] [4519] 3-9-2 **70**.... DarryllHolland 6 72
(L M Cumani) *sn w ldr: ev ch 2f out: rdn and btn over 1f out* **7/2**[2]

1554 **5** 3/4 **Hip Hip Hooray**[28] [4714] 3-9-0 **68**.... DavidProbert 3 68+
(L A Dace) *n.m.r s: hld up and bhd: rdn over 2f out: hung lft over 1f out: nvr able to chal* **12/1**

00 **6** 1 1/2 **Satisfaction Life (IRE)**[15] [5168] 3-9-7 **75**.... JerryO'Dwyer 2 72
(M Botti) *hld up and bhd: pushed along and effrt on ins over 2f out: nvr trbld ldrs* **20/1**

000 **7** 6 **Efficiency**[32] [4569] 3-9-1 **69**.... SteveDrowne 5 53
(M Blanshard) *hld up and bhd: short-lived effrt over 2f out* **25/1**

0620 **8** 11 **Highland Lassie (IRE)**[18] [5063] 3-8-11 **65**.... RichardMullen 8 26
(B J Meehan) *hld up in mid-div: pushed along over 3f out: sn bhd* **25/1**

2m 0.21s (-1.49) **Going Correction** -0.125s/f (Stan) **8** Ran SP% **109.4**
Speed ratings (Par 101): **101,100,100,98,98 96,91,81**
toteswingers: 1&2 £3.70, 1&3 £2.20, 2&3 £3.30 CSF £11.23 CT £36.23 TOTE £3.80: £1.10, £1.40, £3.00; EX 17.60.
Owner Saeed Suhail **Bred** Airlie Stud & Miss K Rausing **Trained** Newmarket, Suffolk

FOCUS
This was a tricky-looking 3yo handicap, but it was run at a sound pace and the form looks fair. The runner-up is the best guide to the form, with the winner rated up 8lb.
King's Song(IRE) Official explanation: trainer's rep said, regarding the apparent improvement in form shown, this was the first time that the colt had raced on a fibre track surface

5617 WILLIAMHILL.COM/BONUS25 - BINGO BONANZAS H'CAP 1m 1f 103y(P)
9:20 (9:21) (Class 6) (0-55,57) 3-Y-O+ **£2,047** (£604; £302) **Stalls** Low

Form RPR

6411 **1** **Valid Point (IRE)**[4] [5470] 3-9-1 **57** 12ex.... StephenDonohoe 5 75+
(Sir Mark Prescott) *chsd ldr: led over 4f out: pushed along over 2f out: clr whn rdn and edgd lft to ins rail wl over 1f out: drvn out* **8/11**[1]

2312 **2** 1 1/2 **King's Icon (IRE)**[4] [5479] 4-8-12 **55**....(p) TobyAtkinson(7) 8 67
(M Wigham) *hld up towards rr: hdwy on outside over 2f out: rdn to chse wnr over 1f out: sn hung lft: no imp towards fin* **9/2**[2]

3535 **3** 2 3/4 **Strike Force**[20] [4972] 5-9-2 **55**....(p) JackMitchell(3) 10 61
(Miss J Feilden) *hld up in rr: stdy prog on outside 4f out: chsd wnr 2f out: sn rdn: lost 2nd over 1f out: one pce* **6/1**[3]

6224 **4** 3 1/4 **Fantasy Ride**[4] [5484] 7-8-9 **50**.... SimonPearce(5) 2 49
(J Pearce) *s.i.s: hld up in rr: pushed along over 2f out: c wd st: sme prog whn rdn and hung lft ins fnl f: n.d* **10/1**

206- **5** nk **Parkview Love (USA)**[19] [7516] 8-9-0 **50**....(b) PatCosgrave 11 49
(J G Given) *hld up in mid-div: pushed along and hdwy on ins over 2f out: wknd wl over 1f out* **66/1**

0260 **6** 2 1/4 **Benitez Bond**[17] [5103] 4-9-0 **50**.... PJMcDonald 3 44
(G R Oldroyd) *led: hdd over 4f out: rdn over 2f out: wknd over 1f out* **22/1**

00/0 **7** 1 3/4 **Bute Street**[18] [5061] 4-8-11 **50**.... WilliamCarson(3) 9 40
(R J Hodges) *s.i.s: hld up towards rr: last and struggling whn hrd rdn over 4f out: c wd st: n.d* **100/1**

0050 **8** 1 3/4 **Desert Hawk**[13] [5210] 8-9-0 **50**....(b) LukeMorris 7 37
(W M Brisbourne) *hld up towards rr: rdn 3f out: no ch whn nt clr run and swtchd rt wl over 1f out* **33/1**

026/ **9** 1 1/2 **View From The Top**[74] [3194] 5-9-5 **55**....(p) DarryllHolland 6 39
(Patrick Allen, Ire) *hld up towards rr: pushed along over 2f out: sn struggling* **12/1**

-600 **10** 7 **The Wily Woodcock**[90] [2686] 5-9-4 **54**....(p) NeilChalmers 4 23
(T Wall) *prom tl wknd wl over 2f out* **100/1**

-566 **11** 1/2 **Noche De Reyes**[28] [4710] 4-9-1 **51**.... ShaneKelly 12 19
(E J Alston) *plld hrd: prom tl rdn and wknd over 2f out* **33/1**

4-00 **12** 1 1/2 **Miskin Flyer**[14] [5179] 3-8-13 **55**.... DavidProbert 1 20
(B Palling) *hld up in tch: wknd over 3f out* **33/1**

0003 **13** 2 1/2 **Kaystar Ridge**[22] [4916] 4-9-1 **51**.... JerryO'Dwyer 13 10
(D K Ivory) *hld up towards rr: stdy prog 5f out: rdn and wknd over 2f out* **40/1**

1m 59.88s (-1.82) **Going Correction** -0.125s/f (Stan)
WFA 3 from 4yo+ 6lb **13** Ran SP% **126.2**
Speed ratings (Par 101): **103,101,99,96,96 94,92,90,89,83 82,81,79**
toteswingers: 1&2 £1.60, 1&3 £1.70, 2&3 £2.80 CSF £4.18 CT £14.04 TOTE £1.90: £1.10, £2.20, £2.00; EX 8.00 Place 6: £44.91 Place 5: £10.52 .
Owner W E Sturt - Osborne House **Bred** Pier House Stud **Trained** Newmarket, Suffolk

FOCUS
This moderate handicap was all about Valid Point, who took another step forward and was value for extra. The form is sound.
T/Plt: £77.60 to a £1 stake. Pool: £79,975.96. 751.95 winning tickets. T/Qpdt: £12.80 to a £1 stake. Pool: £10,332.04. 596.50 winning tickets. KH

5587 VELIEFENDI
Thursday, September 3

OFFICIAL GOING: Good to firm

5618a TOPKAPI TROPHY (TURKISH GROUP 2) (TURF) 1m
7:00 (7:03) 3-Y-O+ **£416,667** (£166,667; £83,333; £41,667)

RPR

1 **Pressing (IRE)**[39] [4364] 6-9-6.... NCallan 6 116
(M A Jarvis) *always prominent, 4th straight on outside, driven to challenge 1 1/2f out, all out to lead last strides* **9/20**[1]

2 hd **Dream Eater (IRE)**[13] [5232] 4-9-6....(t) WilliamBuick 7 116
(A M Balding) *held up, headway & 6th straight, slipped through on rail to challenge 2f out, led 1 1/2f out, 1/2l up inside final f, driven & caught last strides* **58/10**

3 3 **Sabirli (TUR)**[361] [5742] 8-9-6.... ASozen 9 109
(C Kurt, Turkey) *last to straight, switched left 2f out, stayed on to take 3rd inside final 100yds* **53/10**

4 1/2 **Kurtiniadis (IRE)**[361] [5742] 6-9-6.... SKaya 2 107
(S Kulak, Turkey) *tracked leaders, close 5th straight, hard ridden when carried right inside final 2f, disputed 3rd inside final f, one pace* **41/20**[2]

5 1 1/2 **Hatta Fort**[90] [2668] 4-9-6....(bt) LDettori 5 104
(Saeed Bin Suroor) *led 1f, settled pressing leaders, 3rd straight on outside, close up when hampered 2f out, kept on final f to take 5th close home* **77/20**

6 1/2 **Rock Of Rochelle (USA)**[54] [3881] 4-9-6.... GMosse 8 103
(A Kinsella, Ire) *held up, 8th straight, never a factor* **13/2**

7 1/2 **Gladyator (TUR)** 7-9-6.... GKocakaya 1 102
(R Tetik, Turkey) *pressed leaders, 2nd straight on inside, led over 2f out to 1 1/2f out, still 3rd inside final f, weakened in last 100y* **20/1**

8 1/2 **Invincible Son (IRE)** 3-8-12.... HKaratas 3 98
(A Ikier, Turkey) *mid-division, 6th straight, soon beaten* **16/5**[3]

9 12 **Nalin Isyani (TUR)** 5-9-6....(b) NSen 4 73
(H H Basi, Turkey) *led after 1f to over 2f out, hung left & right 2f out, weakened quickly* **137/10**

1m 36.44s (1.11)
WFA 3 from 4yo+ 5lb **9** Ran SP% **201.7**
(including one lira stakes): WIN 1.45; No Place Betting; DF 6.65.
Owner Gary A Tanaka **Bred** Agricola Del Parco **Trained** Newmarket, Suffolk

NOTEBOOK
Pressing(IRE) got up close home to repeat last season's victory in Europe's most valuable mile race. He has never won in Britain but is a highly successful globetrotter, having won in Italy, Germany and now Turkey on his last three starts. The Breeders' Cup Mile is now on his agenda.
Dream Eater(IRE) has been knocking at the door all season and finally scored last time at Listed level. He made a bold bid but was caught almost on the line by his fellow raider.
Hatta Fort had struggled since returning to Europe this season and was fitted with blinkers for the first time. He was hampered at a vital point, otherwise might have finished closer.

5619a BOSPHORUS CUP (TURKISH GROUP 2) (TURF) 1m 4f
8:00 (8:06) 3-Y-O+ **£277,778** (£111,111; £55,556; £27,778)

RPR

1 **Halicarnassus (IRE)**[19] [5023] 5-9-6.... AlanMunro 2 114
(M R Channon) *restrained in 5th on inside, 7th straight, hard ridden over 2f out, moved outside well over 1f out, led well inside final f, ran on well* **2/1**[3]

2 1/2 **Pan River (TUR)** 4-9-6.... NSen 9 113
(R Tetik, Turkey) *mid-division, close 6th on outside straight, led over 1 1/2f out to well inside final f, ran on* **6/4**[2]

3 2 **Sassoaloro (GER)**[27] [4808] 5-9-6.... GMosse 8 110
(H Blume, Germany) *soon close up, 4th straight, not clear run over 2f out, driven over 1f out, stayed on to take 3rd well inside final f* **17/2**

4 1/2 **Annosh (TUR)**[725] [5264] 6-9-3....(t) SKaya 13 106
(Y Simsek, Turkey) *held up in mid-division, 6th straight, got through inside over 2f out, every chance over 1f out, one pace final f* **17/4**

5 2 1/2 **Illustrious Blue**[34] [4484] 6-9-6.... JimCrowley 3 105
(W J Knight) *held up towards rear, 8th on outside straight, kept on under pressure, nearest at finish* **9/4**

6 2 1/2 **Inspector (TUR)**[361] [5741] 5-9-6....(b) HKaratas 4 101
(U Bekmezci, Turkey) *keen early, pressed leader, 2nd straight, led 2f out to over 1 1/2f out, weakened approaching final f* **6/5**[1]

7 nk **Cakilhan (TUR)** 3-8-10.... TAlici 11 100
(G Gungor, Turkey) *last to straight, headway on inside over 2f out, kept on one pace under pressure* **93/10**

8 hd **Genghis Khan (TUR)** 4-9-6....(bt) OYildirim 10 100
(Y Simsek, Turkey) *in rear to straight, kept on one pace on outside* **17/4**

9 *6* **Cardio Dancer (TUR)** 6-9-6 ....(t) GKocakaya 6 91
(Y Simsek, Turkey) *mid-division to half-way, in rear straight, no progress* **17/4**

10 *½* **Oglumemre (TUR)**^{362} 5743 4-9-6 ....(t) MGunduzeli 7 90
(Sab Arslan, Turkey) *pressed leaders, 3rd straight, weakened well over 1f out* **155/10**

11 *nse* **Senatore (TUR)** 4-9-6 .... EYavuz 1 90
(S Aydemir, Turkey) *mid-division on outside til moved up quickly to lead over 5f out, headed 2f out, soon weakened* **14/1**

12 *15* **Out Of Control (TUR)**^{361} 5741 6-9-6 ....(t) FCakar 5 66
(Y Simsek, Turkey) *led to over 5f out, 5th straight, weakened quickly* **17/4**

2m 31.59s (2.79)
WFA 3 from 4yo+ 9lb **12** Ran SP% **258.7**
WIN 3.00; PL 2.50, 2.20; DF 8.80.
Owner Doric Racing **Bred** Yeomanstown Lodge Stud **Trained** West Ilsley, Berks

NOTEBOOK
Halicarnassus(IRE), another seasoned traveller, had shown signs of a revival of late and gave Kite Wood a boost of sorts by taking this valuble prize, finishing strongly to get up inside the last furlong.
Illustrious Blue finished two placed in front of today's winner when scoring at Goodwood in July but could not repeat it, having come from well back to reach his final position.

5337 CATTERICK (L-H)
Friday, September 4

OFFICIAL GOING: Soft
Wind: Moderate across Weather: Raining

5620 CATTERICKBRIDGE.CO.UK MAIDEN STKS 5f
2:30 (2:31) (Class 5) 2-Y-O **£3,412** (£1,007; £504) **Stalls** Low

Form RPR

52 **1** **Comedy Hall (USA)**^{10} 5325 2-9-3 0................................ GregFairley 6 83+
(M Johnston) *sn led towards far side: rdn clr wl over 1f out: styd on* **5/6**^{1}

0 **2** *5* **Magical Macey (USA)**^{108} 2153 2-9-3 0..........................(b^{1}) TomEaves 9 65
(T D Barron) *swtchd rt to r stands' side: sn prom: rdn along 1/2-way: kpt on appr fnl f: no ch w wnr: 1st of 3 in gp* **50/1**

3 *2* **Layla's Lexi** 2-8-12 0.. PaulQuinn 11 53+
(D Nicholls) *s.i.s and towards rr: swtchd rt to stands' side 1/2-way: sn rdn and kpt on fr over 1f out: nrst fin: 2nd of 3 in gp* **33/1**

0 **4** *2½* **Timeless Elegance (IRE)**^{42} 4278 2-8-9 0............... FrederikTylicki(3) 7 44
(J Howard Johnson) *prom towards far side: effrt and cl up 1/2-way: sn rdn and grad wknd fr wl over 1f out: 2nd of 6 in gp* **33/1**

463 **5** *1½* **Jack Luey**^{16} 5146 2-9-3 73.................................... DuranFentiman 4 43
(L A Mullaney) *prom far side: rdn along 2f out: sn drvn and wknd: 3rd of 6 in gp* **12/1**

4203 **6** *¾* **Mercers Row**^{24} 4875 2-9-3 69.. DanielTudhope 2 41
(A Dickman) *prom far side: rdn along 2f out: sn wknd: 4th of 6 in gp* **9/2**^{2}

2300 **7** *4* **Saucy Girl (IRE)**^{13} 5253 2-8-12 67....................................... DavidAllan 5 21
(T D Easterby) *prom: swtchd rt to stands' rail 1/2-way: sn rdn along and wknd wl over 1f out: last of 3 in gp* **16/1**

6430 **8** *½* **Safari Camp (IRE)**^{30} 4639 2-8-12 53.......................... SladeO'Hara(5) 8 25
(A Berry) *prom towards far side: rdn along 2f out: sn hung lft and wknd: 5th of 6 in gp* **100/1**

9 *16* **Redoubtable Grace** 2-9-3 0.. AndrewElliott 3 —
(Mrs R A Carr) *v.s.a: a bhd far side: 6th of 6 in gp* **66/1**

000 **F** **Orpen All Hours (IRE)**^{53} 3925 2-8-7 35............. PatrickDonaghy(5) 12 —
(P C Haslam) *in tch far side: rdn along 1/2-way: hdwy whn clipped heels and fell wl over 1f out* **100/1**

6220 **U** **Mad Millie (IRE)**^{15} 5199 2-8-12 68......................... SilvestreDeSousa 13 —
(J Hetherton) *in tch far side: rdn along 1/2-way: no imp whn hmpd and uns rdr wl over 1f out* **5/1**^{3}

64.37 secs (4.57) **Going Correction** +0.925s/f (Soft) **11** Ran SP% **114.3**
Speed ratings (Par 95): **100,92,88,84,82 81,74,74,48,—,—**
toteswingers: 1&2 £9.40, 1&3 £10.70, 2&3 £67.90 CSF £71.41 TOTE £1.80: £1.10, £8.00, £6.30; EX 52.20.
Owner Sheikh Hamdan Bin Mohammed Al Maktoum **Bred** Stonerside Stable **Trained** Middleham Moor, N Yorks
■ Stewards' Enquiry : David Allan two-day ban: careless riding (Sep 18-19)

FOCUS
Conditions were pretty testing. A dramatic opener with one withdrawn after bursting out of the front of the stalls and a faller after clipping heels, bringing down one other coming to the final furlong.

NOTEBOOK
Comedy Hall(USA), easily the paddock pick, had achieved a RPR of 75 when piped over 6f on the all-weather at Southwell. The drop back in trip was not a problem and despite hanging left, he surged well clear coming to the final furlong. Presumably nurseries now beckon. (op 10-11 tchd Evens)
Magical Macey(USA), absent since making no show on his debut at May, made a beeline for the stands' side, eventually joined by two others. He dominated that side throughout, but the winner was different class. (op 40-1)
Layla's Lexi, quite a tall newcomer, missed the break but showed promise staying on late in the day to finish second best on the stands' side. (op 25-1)
Timeless Elegance(IRE), who made her debut over 7f, improved on that effort to finish second best of those who raced towards the far side.
Jack Luey showed plenty of toe but came up well short in the end. (op 10-1 tchd 14-1)
Mercers Row, tackling soft ground for the first time, showed pace before fading. (op 6-1)
Saucy Girl(IRE) switched to join the other two on the stands' side after 2f, but was never on terms. She seems to be going backwards after finishing runner-up on her debut. (tchd 14-1)

5621 SCORTON CLAIMING STKS 7f
3:00 (3:00) (Class 6) 3-Y-O **£2,388** (£705; £352) **Stalls** Low

Form RPR

4100 **1** **Whispering Spirit (IRE)**^{25} 4845 3-8-0 59..........(v^{1}) SilvestreDeSousa 1 56
(Mrs A Duffield) *chsd ldrs on inner: styd alone on far rails in st: rdn 2f out: drvn ins fnl f: kpt on wl to ld nr fin* **6/1**^{3}

5104 **2** *nk* **Ask Dan (IRE)**^{11} 5306 3-8-11 56...............................(p) TonyHamilton 12 66
(M Dods) *led: rdn along 2f out: drvn over 1f out: hdd and no ex towards fin* **12/1**

0211 **3** *2* **Darcey**^{13} 5254 3-8-6 69.. PaulHanagan 11 56
(R A Fahey) *in tch: hdwy to chse ldrs 1/2-way: rdn to chse ldr over 2f out: drvn over 1f out: no imp ins fnl f* **10/11**^{1}

3224 **4** *6* **Hettie Hubble**^{8} 5362 3-8-6 48.. GregFairley 7 40
(D W Thompson) *towards rr: hdwy 3f out and sn rdn: kpt on u.p fr wl over 1f out: nrst fin* **16/1**

PP03 **5** *shd* **Captain Imperial (IRE)**^{25} 4846 3-8-13 68.......................... MickyFenton 8 46
(T P Tate) *prom: rdn along 3f out: drvn 2f out and sn wknd* **5/2**^{2}

2050 **6** *shd* **Nchike**^{8} 5362 3-8-4 60..(b^{1}) JamieKyne(5) 2 42
(R C Guest) *prom: rdn along over 2f out: sn drvn and wknd wl over 1f out* **33/1**

630 **7** *6* **Sardan Dansar (IRE)**^{26} 4823 3-8-0 46...................... DuranFentiman 5 17
(Mrs A Duffield) *a towards rr* **33/1**

040 **8** *3* **Africa's Star (IRE)**^{32} 4596 3-8-3 52........................... KellyHarrison(3) 6 15
(M Dods) *chsd ldrs: rdn along 3f out: sn wknd* **20/1**

0 **9** *hd* **Taguna (IRE)**^{13} 5254 3-7-9 0.. NoraLooby(7) 13 10
(M Brittain) *a in rr* **250/1**

-030 **10** *4* **Digit**^{44} 4196 3-8-8 54... TomEaves 9 5
(B Smart) *a towards rr* **40/1**

6500 **11** *2¼* **Scotch And Soda (IRE)**^{32} 4594 3-8-0 48.................... AndrewMullen 4 —
(Jedd O'Keeffe) *a in rr* **100/1**

0000 **12** *13* **Ready For Battle (IRE)**^{9} 5342 3-8-7 49.......................(p) PJMcDonald 3 —
(D W Thompson) *stmbld s: a bhd* **100/1**

1m 30.17s (3.17) **Going Correction** +0.625s/f (Yiel) **12** Ran SP% **124.3**
Speed ratings (Par 99): **106,105,103,96,96 96,89,86,85,81 78,63**
toteswingers: 1&2 £8.30, 1&3 £3.40, 2&3 £4.40 CSF £74.71 TOTE £7.60: £2.50, £3.90, £1.10; EX 113.80.
Owner Middleham Park Racing XLII **Bred** David Barry **Trained** Constable Burton, N Yorks
■ Stewards' Enquiry : Nora Looby caution: used whip when out of contention

FOCUS
Plenty of deadwood in this claimer. Trcky form to pin down with the winner racing alone. She ran close to this year's form.

5622 LESLIE PETCH H'CAP 1m 3f 214y
3:30 (3:30) (Class 5) (0-75,75) 3-Y-O+ **£2,914** (£867; £433; £216) **Stalls** High

Form RPR

4561 **1** **Puy D'Arnac (FR)**^{12} 5291 6-9-0 66 6ex.......................... PJMcDonald 6 74+
(G A Swinbank) *in tch: effrt over 3f out and sn pushed along: rdn to chse ldrs 2f out: sn chal and kpt on to ld jst ins fnl f: rdn out* **9/4**^{1}

6534 **2** *1½* **Bavarian Nordic (USA)**^{8} 5375 4-9-6 72................. SilvestreDeSousa 1 78+
(Mrs A Duffield) *trckd ldrs: hdwy over 3f out: rdn to chse ldrs over 2f out: drvn to chse wnr ins fnl f: kpt on* **5/1**^{3}

1210 **3** *nk* **Aureate**^{72} 3266 5-9-4 70... TomEaves 3 75
(B Ellison) *sn led: rdn clr over 2f out: drvn over 1f out: hdd jst ins fnl f and kpt on same pce* **13/2**

215 **4** *1½* **Summer Lodge**^{14} 5210 6-9-3 72............................... FrederikTylicki(3) 4 75
(J A Glover) *trckd ldr: pushed along 3f out: rdn and ev ch 2f out tl wknd appr fnl f* **15/2**

-003 **5** *18* **Highland Love**^{14} 5227 4-8-10 62.................................... MickyFenton 2 36
(J T Stimpson) *prom: rdn to chse ldr over 2f out: drvn wl over 1f out and sn wknd* **25/1**

4222 **6** *8* **Punch Drunk**^{21} 5009 3-8-10 71.. PaulHanagan 8 32
(J G Given) *a in rr: outpcd fnl 3f* **7/2**^{2}

0514 **7** *17* **Harry The Hawk**^{31} 4619 5-9-9 75.............................. GrahamGibbons 7 9
(T D Walford) *trckd ldrs: hdwy to chse ldr over 4f out: rdn along over 3f out: wknd over 2f out and sn eased* **8/1**

0631 **8** *2¼* **Destinys Dream (IRE)**^{33} 4561 4-9-3 72..................... KellyHarrison(3) 5 3
(Miss Tracy Waggott) *a in rr: outpcd fnl 3f* **18/1**

2m 46.22s (7.32) **Going Correction** +0.625s/f (Yiel)
WFA 3 from 4yo+ 9lb **8** Ran SP% **115.0**
Speed ratings (Par 103): **100,99,98,97,85 80,69,67**
toteswingers: 1&2 £3.90, 1&3 £5.60, 2&3 £7.20 CSF £13.89 CT £62.91 TOTE £3.10: £1.50, £1.70, £2.30; EX 17.40.
Owner Barrow Brook Racing **Bred** Mrs Axelle Du Verdier **Trained** Melsonby, N Yorks

FOCUS
A 71-75 handicap run at a sensible pace in the soft ground. Not the most convincing piece of form.
Punch Drunk Official explanation: trainer had no explanation for the poor form shown
Harry The Hawk Official explanation: trainer had no explanation for the poor form shown
Destinys Dream(IRE) Official explanation: jockey said filly was unsuited by the soft ground

5623 RACING UK H'CAP 5f 212y
4:00 (4:01) (Class 4) (0-80,83) 3-Y-O+ **£5,180** (£1,541; £770; £384) **Stalls** Low

Form RPR

2023 **1** **Rio Cobolo (IRE)**^{9} 5340 3-8-4 66..................(v) SilvestreDeSousa 1 74
(Paul Green) *hld up in tch: hdwy 2f out: swtchd rt over 1f out: rdn ins fnl f and styd on strly to ld last 50yds* **9/2**^{1}

1451 **2** *1* **The Nifty Fox**^{12} 5293 5-9-9 83 6ex.................................. DavidAllan 9 88
(T D Easterby) *trckd ldrs: hdwy over 2f out: chal on bit over 1f out: shkn up to ld ins fnl f and sn rdn: hdd and nt qckn last 50yds* **6/1**^{3}

6664 **3** *shd* **Northern Bolt**^{16} 5148 4-9-3 77..(v^{1}) PaulQuinn 6 82
(D Nicholls) *cl up: rdn along wl over 2f out: drvn to ld briefly over 1f out and sn hdd: kpt on wl u.p fnl f* **7/1**

0664 **4** *¾* **Inter Vision (USA)**^{1} 5597 9-8-12 75....................... FrederikTylicki(3) 2 77
(A Dickman) *towards rr: hdwy on inner 2f out: rdn over 1f out: kpt on wl fnl f: nrst fin* **9/1**

0031 **5** *½* **Bonnie Prince Blue**^{9} 5343 6-8-9 76 6ex...........................(b) NSLawes(7) 3 77
(D Nicholls) *in tch: hdwy on outer 2f out: rdn to chse ldrs over 1f out: drvn ent fnl f and sn one pce* **9/2**^{1}

0450 **6** *1½* **Go Go Green (IRE)**^{4} 5523 3-9-3 79.................................. PaulHanagan 5 75
(D H Brown) *led: rdn along over 2f out: drvn and hdd over 1f out: sn wknd* **16/1**

5064 **7** *1* **Misaro (GER)**^{13} 5247 8-9-1 80.............................(v) RichardEvans(5) 4 73
(R A Harris) *chsd ldng pair: rdn along over 2f out: drvn and wknd wl over 1f out* **25/1**

2126 **8** *1¾* **Mandalay King (IRE)**^{16} 5148 4-8-11 71........................... PJMcDonald 7 58
(Mrs Marjorie Fife) *sn pushed along and a in rr* **5/1**^{2}

2016 **9** *1* **Luscivious**^{18} 5104 5-9-4 78.................................(p) GrahamGibbons 8 62
(J A Glover) *a towards rr* **13/2**

1m 16.48s (2.88) **Going Correction** +0.625s/f (Yiel)
WFA 3 from 4yo+ 2lb **9** Ran SP% **112.9**
Speed ratings (Par 105): **105,103,103,102,101 99,98,96,94**
toteswingers: 1&2 £3.30, 1&3 £4.90, 2&3 £6.30 CSF £30.65 CT £184.68 TOTE £3.90: £1.70, £1.40, £2.40; EX 18.90.
Owner The Keely Gang **Bred** Yvonne & Gerard Kennedy **Trained** Lydiate, Merseyside

FOCUS
A tight-knit 66-83 sprint handicap and this time they all stayed on the far side in the home straight. Straightforward form.

5624 ELLERY HILL RATING RELATED MAIDEN STKS — 7f
4:30 (4:30) (Class 6) 3-Y-O+ — **£2,388** (£705; £352) **Stalls** Low

Form — RPR

3406 **1** **Lyric Art (USA)**[26] 4819 3-8-12 58 TomEaves 10 — 58
(B Smart) *in tch: hdwy on outer to chse ldrs 2f out: rdn over 1f out: drvn ins fnl f and styd on wl to ld last 50yds* **12/1**

4042 **2** ½ **Steel Stockholder**[13] 5258 3-8-8 60 JohnCavanagh(7) 8 — 60
(M Brittain) *chsd ldrs: hdwy 3f out: rdn to chse ldr 2f out: drvn to ld briefly wl ins fnl f: hdd and no ex last 50yds* **5/1**[2]

3305 **3** 1 ¼ **Lost In Paris (IRE)**[48] 4105 3-9-1 57 (b) DavidAllan 11 — 56
(T D Easterby) *led: rdn clr over 2f out: drvn over 1f out: hdd & wknd last 100yds* **10/1**

0522 **4** ½ **Silk Gallery (USA)**[16] 5163 4-9-2 55 (t) PJMcDonald 4 — 54
(E J Alston) *in tch: hdwy over 2f out: swtchd lft and rdn to chse ldrs over 1f out: drvn and one pce ins fnl f* **11/2**[3]

5400 **5** hd **Istiqdaam**[31] 4620 4-9-5 60 DaleGibson 7 — 56+
(M W Easterby) *midfield: hdwy over 2f out: rdn to chse ldrs and edgd lft over 1f out: kpt on ins fnl f: nrst fin* **14/1**

3640 **6** 1 **Alacity (IRE)**[7] 5405 3-8-12 53 AndrewElliott 12 — 49
(N Bycroft) *prom: chsd clr ldr over 2f out and sn rdn: drvn over 1f out: wknd ins fnl f* **33/1**

-660 **7** 1 **Elements (IRE)**[11] 5306 3-8-12 55 DuranFentiman 3 — 49+3
(E J Alston) *midfield: hdwy 2f out: rdn and styng on whn n.m.r over 1f out and again wl ins fnl f: kpt on* **80/1**

3004 **8** 1 ¼ **Minnola**[4] 5501 4-8-13 54 FrederikTylicki(3) 2 — 45
(Rae Guest) *dwlt and sn pushed along on inner in midfield: hdwy 2f out: sn rdn and no imp appr fnl f* **10/3**[1]

-535 **9** 5 **Pacific Bay (IRE)**[16] 5158 3-8-12 58 PaulHanagan 1 — 29
(R A Fahey) *in tch: hdwy on inner to chse ldrs 2f out and sn rdn: drvn over 1f out and sn wknd* **9/1**

0-00 **10** 1 **Hardanger (IRE)**[40] 4346 4-9-5 54 TonyHamilton 14 — 31
(T J Fitzgerald) *s.i.s: a towards rr* **50/1**

3430 **11** 16 **Beaux Yeux**[16] 5145 3-8-7 52 PaulPickard(5) 5 — —
(P T Midgley) *a towards rr* **22/1**

-000 **12** ¾ **Ay Tay Tate (IRE)**[14] 5225 3-9-1 55 GrahamGibbons 6 — —
(D Shaw) *a towards rr* **16/1**

003 **13** 3 **Yes Please**[16] 5163 4-9-5 55 SilvestreDeSousa 13 — —
(K A Ryan) *nvr bttr than midfield* **9/1**

0326 **P** **Cindy Incidentally**[30] 4643 3-8-12 47 (b) MickyFenton 15 — —
(Miss Gay Kelleway) *prom: rdn along 3f out: drvn and wknd qckly over 2f out: p.u over 1f out: dismntd* **25/1**

1m 31.5s (4.50) **Going Correction** +0.625s/f (Yiel)
WFA 3 from 4yo 4lb — **14 Ran SP% 118.8**
Speed ratings (Par 101): **99,98,97,96,96 95,93,92,86,85 67,66,63,—**
toteswingers: 1&2 £18.30, 1&3 £26.70, 2&3 £8.90 CSF £66.99 TOTE £18.30: £4.60, £1.60, £3.30; EX 104.50.
Owner H E Sheikh Rashid Bin Mohammed **Bred** Swettenham Stud **Trained** Hambleton, N Yorks

FOCUS
A weak 0-60 rating-related maiden race. Not form to view too positively.
Alacity(IRE) Official explanation: jockey said filly hung right throughout
Cindy Incidentally Official explanation: jockey said filly lost its action

5625 GO RACING AT THIRSK TOMORROW H'CAP — 1m 7f 177y
5:00 (5:00) (Class 5) (0-70,70) 3-Y-O+ — **£3,238** (£963; £481; £240) **Stalls** Low

Form — RPR

2202 **1** **Promise Maker (USA)**[9] 5339 4-9-6 62 GrahamGibbons 3 — 70+
(T D Walford) *trckd ldr: effrt over 2f out: rdn to ld over 1f out: drvn ins fnl f and kpt on wl* **9/2**[2]

3236 **2** 1 ¼ **Princess Rainbow (FR)**[23] 4890 4-10-0 70 PaulHanagan 6 — 76
(Jennie Candlish) *led: rdn along 3f out: drvn 2f out: hdd appr fnl f: kpt on* **10/1**

2521 **3** ¾ **John Forbes**[8] 5359 7-9-7 68 6ex LanceBetts(5) 10 — 73
(B Ellison) *in tch: hdwy to trck ldrs 1/2-way: rdn to chse ldng pair 2f out: sn drvn and ch tl one pce fnl f* **4/1**[1]

5024 **4** 3 ¾ **Sir Sandicliffe (IRE)**[9] 5339 5-9-2 63 DeanHeslop(5) 7 — 64+
(W M Brisbourne) *dwlt: hld up towards rr: hdwy 4f out: rdn to chse ldrs 2f out: sn drvn and kpt on same pce* **16/1**

4314 **5** 10 **Miss Keck**[23] 4890 5-9-12 68 PJMcDonald 9 — 57
(G A Swinbank) *prom: rdn along to chse ldng pair 4f out: drvn over 2f out and grad wknd* **11/2**[3]

0463 **6** ½ **Red Wine**[7] 5410 10-10-0 70 MickyFenton 2 — 58
(J A Glover) *hld up in rr: hdwy 4f out: swtchd wd home turn and racd alone stands' rail: rdn over 2f out and n.d* **12/1**

000 **7** ½ **River Danube**[34] 4551 6-8-9 54 FrederikTylicki(3) 11 — 41
(T J Fitzgerald) *trckd ldrs on outer: effrt 4f out: rdn along 3f out and sn outpcd* **66/1**

2124 **8** ½ **Black Or Red (IRE)**[18] 5094 4-9-9 65 (bt) TonyHamilton 1 — 52
(I A Wood) *chsd ldrs on inner: rdn along 4f out: drvn 3f out and sn wknd* **4/1**[1]

-010 **9** 3 ¾ **Carlton Mac**[22] 4927 4-8-4 51 oh6 (p) JamieKyne(5) 8 — 33
(N Bycroft) *chsd ldrs: rdn along over 6f out: sn lost pl and bhd* **33/1**

0424 **10** 6 **Call Of Duty (IRE)**[21] 4972 4-8-12 59 SladeO'Hara(5) 5 — 34
(Mrs Dianne Sayer) *hld up: a in rr* **8/1**

P05- **11** 4 **Hernando's Boy**[144] 7177 8-9-11 67 TomEaves 4 — 37
(K G Reveley) *chsd ldrs on inner: lost pl 1/2-way and bhd fnl 4f* **28/1**

3m 43.09s (11.09) **Going Correction** +0.625s/f (Yiel) — **11 Ran SP% 115.2**
Speed ratings (Par 103): **97,96,96,94,89 88,88,88,86,83 81**
toteswingers: 1&2 £8.60, 1&3 £3.80, 2&3 £6.20 CSF £47.15 CT £194.34 TOTE £5.30: £2.40, £3.50, £2.10; EX 58.40.
Owner Walford, Hulme & Howarth **Bred** Juddmonte Farms Inc **Trained** Sheriff Hutton, N Yorks

FOCUS
A modest 57-70 stayers' handicap run at just a steady pace. The first two were always 1-2 and the form is rated around the third.

5626 RACING AGAIN ON SATURDAY 19TH SEPTEMBER APPRENTICE H'CAP — 5f
5:30 (5:30) (Class 6) (0-65,65) 3-Y-O — **£2,388** (£705; £352) **Stalls** Low

Form — RPR

211P **1** **Kheley (IRE)**[205] 498 3-9-4 64 DeanHeslop 8 — 72
(W M Brisbourne) *led: hdd briefly 1/2-way: led again 2f out: rdn clr over 1f out: edgd lft ins fnl f: kpt on* **25/1**

2511 **2** 2 **Future Gem**[8] 5362 3-9-4 64 6ex (p) JamieKyne 6 — 64
(A Dickman) *sed awkwardly: swtchd rt and hdwy on outer 1/2-way: rdn to chse wnr and hung bdly lft ins fnl f: kpt on* **15/8**[1]

020 **3** 1 ½ **Red Cell (IRE)**[7] 5396 3-8-8 54 (b) AmyRyan 4 — 49
(I W McInnes) *prom: effrt 2f out: sn rdn and kpt on same pce ins fnl f* **15/2**

6460 **4** ¾ **Zelos Girl (IRE)**[16] 5155 3-8-11 57 JamesO'Reilly 5 — 49
(J G Given) *in tch: effrt 2f out and sn rdn: kpt on ins fnl f* **10/1**

4053 **5** shd **Dispol Kylie (IRE)**[22] 4942 3-9-2 65 PaulPickard(3) 2 — 57
(P T Midgley) *cl up: led briefly 1/2-way: sn rdn and hdd 2f out: sn drvn and grad wknd* **3/1**[2]

00-6 **6** ½ **Faraway Sound (IRE)**[13] 5254 3-9-4 64 (v[1]) PatrickDonaghy 1 — 54
(P C Haslam) *dwlt: swtchd to inner and hdwy 1/2-way: rdn to chse ldrs wl over 1f out: sn drvn and btn* **12/1**

2123 **7** nk **Arriva La Diva**[21] 4999 3-8-1 52 ow1 IJBrennan(5) 9 — 41
(J J Quinn) *prom: rdn along 2f out and sn wknd* **6/1**[3]

0020 **8** 4 **Sleepy Valley (IRE)**[70] 3355 3-8-9 55 (p) LanceBetts 3 — 30
(A Dickman) *chsd ldrs: rdn along over 2f out and sn wknd* **25/1**

64.50 secs (4.70) **Going Correction** +0.925s/f (Soft) — **8 Ran SP% 110.3**
Speed ratings (Par 99): **99,95,93,92,92 91,90,84**
toteswingers: 1&2 £6.60, 1&3 £7.70, 2&3 £4.30 CSF £67.38 CT £380.26 TOTE £12.20: £2.10, £1.30, £2.30; EX 35.80 Place 6: £37.74 Place 5: £21.20.
Owner W M Clare **Bred** Matt Gilsenan **Trained** Great Ness, Shropshire
■ Future Gem turned out to have been the final ride for talented apprentice Jamie Kyne, who tragically died the following night.
■ Stewards' Enquiry : Paul Pickard three-day ban: failed to ride out to the line on a horse that could have been placed (Sep 18-20)

FOCUS
A 51-65 apprentice 5f handicap. They tended to race in one group, neglecting the stands' side. A clear personal best.
Arriva La Diva Official explanation: jockey said filly finished distressed
T/Plt: £24.70 to a £1 stake. Pool: £57,980.04. 1,713.25 winning tickets. T/Qpdt: £21.80 to a £1 stake. Pool: £3,648.28. 123.60 winning tickets. JR

5498 CHEPSTOW (L-H)
Friday, September 4

OFFICIAL GOING: Good to soft (soft in places; 7.5)
All the races were run on the straight course.
Wind: Moderate behind Weather: Mainly sunny

5627 BRISTOL EVENING POST MAIDEN AUCTION STKS — 1m 14y
2:10 (2:12) (Class 6) 2-Y-O — **£2,266** (£674; £337; £168) **Stalls** Centre

Form — RPR

1 **Layline (IRE)** 2-8-9 0 RichardKingscote 10 — 85+
(R M Beckett) *hld up in mid-div: hdwy over 3f out: pushed along to chal over 2f out: rdn and edgd lft over 1f out: led jst ins fnl f: r.o wl* **16/1**

0 **2** 2 **Inside Track (IRE)**[14] 5220 2-8-11 0 DavidProbert 5 — 80
(B J Meehan) *w ldr: rdn to ld over 2f out: edgd lft over 1f out: hdd jst ins fnl f: no ex towards fin* **14/1**

3 **3** 2 ¾ **Venutius**[39] 4385 2-8-9 0 DO'Donohoe 9 — 72+
(E S McMahon) *t.k.h: hld up towards rr: pushed along and prog over 3f out: rdn 2f out: styd on to take 3rd wl ins fnl f: nt trble ldng pair* **9/4**[2]

3 **4** ¾ **Milnagavie**[16] 5165 2-8-6 0 FrancisNorton 2 — 67
(R Hannon) *led: hdd over 2f out: rdn and wknd over 1f out* **11/8**[1]

3033 **5** 4 **Crystal Gale (IRE)**[21] 5002 2-8-11 72 ShaneKelly 6 — 64
(W J Knight) *half-rrd and s.i.s: sn hld up in mid-div: hdwy over 3f out: rdn and wknd wl over 1f out* **5/1**[3]

53 **6** ½ **Cornish Beau (IRE)**[16] 5153 2-8-11 0 SaleemGolam 1 — 62
(M H Tompkins) *t.k.h: sn prom: pushed along 3f out: sn wknd* **11/2**

000 **7** 14 **Captain Blake (IRE)**[22] 4933 2-8-11 0 SamHitchcott 7 — 32
(P D Evans) *towards rr: rdn wl over 2f out: sn struggling* **125/1**

00 **8** nk **Man In The Mirror (IRE)**[8] 5371 2-8-2 0 JosephineBruning(7) 8 — 29
(P L Gilligan) *prom tl rdn and wknd over 3f out* **100/1**

9 4 **Big Talk** 2-9-2 0 TonyCulhane 4 — 27
(S Kirk) *s.i.s: in rr: pushed along 3f out: sn struggling* **25/1**

10 ½ **Tregony Bridge** 2-8-11 0 RobertHavlin 3 — 21
(M Blanshard) *hld up in mid-div: lost pl 4f out: hung lft and struggling fr 3f out* **66/1**

1m 36.6s (0.40) **Going Correction** +0.125s/f (Good) — **10 Ran SP% 124.6**
Speed ratings (Par 93): **103,101,98,97,93 93,79,78,74,74**
toteswingers: 1&2 £27.00, 1&3 £10.00, 2&3 £10.10 CSF £223.54 TOTE £22.30: £5.20, £4.40, £1.10; EX 201.90 TRIFECTA Not won..
Owner Mrs M E Slade **Bred** Mrs M E Slade **Trained** Whitsbury, Hants

FOCUS
This race was hand-timed. Conditions had dried out and riders in the first described the ground as just on the slow side of good. This low-grade maiden was run at just a steady pace, with the field racing down the centre of the track. The market leaders disappointed and the form may not prove too strong.

NOTEBOOK
Layline(IRE) did it well on his debut. A half-brother to a winning 2yo out of a half-sister to good miler Smart Enough, he travelled up nicely and, after challenging going to the two pole, was well on top in the final 50 yards. He should certainly have learned from this introduction and improvement should be forthcoming. (op 14-1 tchd 11-1)
Inside Track(IRE) showed a lot more than he had on his debut at Sandown a fortnight ago, drawing away with the winner who carried him over towards the inside rail, and only giving best inside the last half-furlong. A return to 7f might help. (op 20-1)
Venutius, third at Yarmouth first time, was keen early on and was being niggled along before halfway. He was outpaced by the principals before staying on when it was too late. The longer trip was not a problem, but he might prefer faster ground. (op 4-1 tchd 9-2)
Milnagavie was a promising third on her debut at Kempton and this was disappointing. After making the running, she weakened rather tamely when headed and appeared ill at ease on the track's undulations, holding her head a little high. She is worth another chance back on Polytrack. (tchd 6-4)
Crystal Gale(IRE) again gave problems leaving the stalls and could never really make her presence felt. (op 4-1 tchd 7-2)
Cornish Beau(IRE) is now eligible for nurseries, but needs to settle better if he is to make an impact. (op 8-1)

5628 WESTERN DAILY PRESS (S) STKS — 7f 16y
2:40 (2:43) (Class 6) 3-4-Y-O — **£1,942** (£578; £288; £144) **Stalls** Centre

Form — RPR

3623 **1** **Blue Noodles**[26] 4812 3-8-12 62 AndrewHeffernan(7) 11 — 72
(P D Evans) *a.p: led on bit wl over 2f out: rdn over 1f out: r.o wl* **4/1**[2]

3020 **2** *2* **La Belle Joannie**[4] 5501 4-8-12 55 TolleyDean 14 58
(S Curran) *s.i.s: hld up in rr: hdwy over 3f out: rdn over 1f out: styd on to take 2nd towards fin: nt trble wnr* **20/1**

0010 **3** *1 ½* **Stand In Flames**[4] 5502 4-8-13 62 MatthewDavies(5) 5 60
(George Baker) *a.p: rdn and chsd wnr jst over 2f out: no ex and lost 2nd towards fin* **9/2**[3]

5600 **4** *1 ¾* **Bounty Reef**[30] 4642 3-8-8 46 SamHitchcott 12 47
(P D Evans) *hld up in mid-div: pushed along and lost pl over 4f out: rdn over 3f out: hdwy 2f out: kpt on same pce ins fnl f* **33/1**

5 *3* **Lean Burn (USA)** 3-8-13 0 (t) RichardThomas 10 44
(A G Newcombe) *s.i.s: sn wl in rr: styd on fr over 1f out: nvr nrr* **100/1**

2064 **6** *4 ½* **Breadstick**[20] 5016 3-8-8 67 (b[1]) RobertHavlin 6 27
(H Morrison) *prom: led 3f out: sn rdn and hdd: wknd wl over 1f out* **7/2**[1]

2600 **7** *4* **Rock Art (IRE)**[8] 5367 3-8-9 64 ow1 (b) ShaneKelly 3 17
(B J Meehan) *prom tl rdn and wknd wl over 2f out* **9/2**[3]

0040 **8** *1* **Champion Girl (IRE)**[14] 5228 3-8-8 50 (b[1]) DO'Donohoe 16 13
(D Haydn Jones) *led after 1f to 3f out: wknd over 2f out* **16/1**

00-0 **9** *2 ½* **Spin Sister**[48] 4084 3-8-8 43 LukeMorris 9 6
(J Gallagher) *hld up in tch: lost pl over 4f out: rdn and struggling over 3f out* **80/1**

10 *½* **Berkalani (IRE)** 3-8-8 0 SaleemGolam 1 5
(P D Evans) *s.i.s: a wl in rr* **25/1**

4060 **11** *2 ½* **Pintano**[4] 5501 4-9-9 50 (t) DavidProbert 15 11
(J M Bradley) *led 1f: wknd over 4f out* **50/1**

4200 **12** *nse* **Call Me Courageous (IRE)**[10] 5326 3-8-13 50 (p) KevinGhunowa 4 —
(R A Harris) *hld up in mid-div: hdwy over 3f out: wknd over 2f out* **50/1**

0500 **13** *½* **Dustry (IRE)**[7] 5384 3-8-13 64 (b) FrancisNorton 2 —
(R Hannon) *sn outpcd and wl bhd* **12/1**

0140 **14** *17* **Hillside Lad**[27] 4787 3-9-5 66 (p) RichardKingscote 13 —
(R M Beckett) *swtchd rt after 1f: racd alone on stands' rail: sn prom: rdn and wknd over 2f out* **10/1**

1m 24.69s (1.49) **Going Correction** +0.125s/f (Good)
WFA 3 from 4yo 4lb **14** Ran SP% **118.9**
Speed ratings (Par 101): **96,93,92,90,86 81,76,75,72,72 69,69,68,49**
toteswingers: 1&2 £9.60, 1&3 £6.50, 2&3 £19.70 CSF £86.75 TOTE £5.60: £2.00, £5.90, £2.40; EX 76.30 Trifecta £163.30 Part won. Pool: £220.81 - 0.50 winning units..There was no bid for the winner.
Owner Diamond Racing Ltd **Bred** P And Mrs A G Venner **Trained** Pandy, Monmouths

FOCUS
A reasonable race of its type, run at a good clip. The first three had filled the placings, albeit in a different order, in a heavy-ground seller at Leicester last month. The form is not entirely convincing but the winner rates a small personal best.

5629 SUNSHINE RADIO H'CAP 5f 16y
3:10 (3:12) (Class 6) (0-52,57) 3-Y-O+ **£2,460** (£732; £365; £182) **Stalls** Centre

Form RPR

0051 **1** **Maggie Kate**[28] 4736 4-8-12 52 (b) RobertHavlin 5 57
(R Ingram) *chsd ldrs: rdn to ld jst over 1f out: drvn out* **9/1**

0-00 **2** *nk* **White Ledger (IRE)**[26] 4824 10-8-6 46 oh1 (p) RoystonFfrench 4 50
(R E Peacock) *sn outpcd in rr: rdn over 2f out: hdwy jst over 1f out: r.o u.p to take 2nd post* **33/1**

6000 **3** *shd* **Bookiesindex Boy**[55] 3860 5-8-11 51 FrancisNorton 16 55+
(J R Jenkins) *chsd ldrs: rdn jst over 1f out: ev ch wl ins fnl f: r.o but lost 2nd post* **33/1**

4034 **4** *nk* **Rightcar Lewis**[6] 5422 4-8-6 46 oh1 (b) JamieMackay 7 49
(Peter Grayson) *s.i.s: towards rr: rdn over 3f out: hdwy 2f out: kpt on ins fnl f* **33/1**

3501 **5** *1* **Spirit Of Coniston**[9] 5341 6-9-3 57 6ex TonyCulhane 8 56
(P T Midgley) *led over 1f: rdn and ev ch wl over 1f out: nt qckn ins fnl f* **3/1**[1]

4466 **6** *½* **One Way Ticket**[4] 5504 9-8-6 46 oh1 (tp) SaleemGolam 9 43
(J M Bradley) *mid-div: pushed along over 3f out: lost pl over 1f out: kpt on towards fin* **16/1**

-000 **7** *½* **Rathmolyon**[9] 5345 4-8-6 46 oh1 (b[1]) FrankieMcDonald 13 41
(D Haydn Jones) *prom: led over 3f out: rdn and hdd jst over 1f out: wknd ins fnl f* **66/1**

5050 **8** *½* **Sofinella (IRE)**[4] 5504 6-8-6 46 oh1 LukeMorris 14 40
(A W Carroll) *chsd ldrs: rdn wl over 1f out: wknd ins fnl f* **16/1**

2045 **9** *hd* **Decider (USA)**[1] 5610 6-8-6 46 oh1 (p) KevinGhunowa 1 39
(R A Harris) *prom: ev ch wl over 1f out: rdn and wknd jst ins fnl f* **9/1**

0030 **10** *½* **Sandy Par**[4] 5501 4-8-9 49 (b) DavidProbert 3 40
(J M Bradley) *prom: rdn and ev ch wl over 1f out: wknd jst ins fnl f* **9/2**[2]

002 **11** *nk* **Cocktail Party (IRE)**[4] 5500 3-8-6 47 (t) RichardKingscote 12 37
(J W Hills) *s.i.s: a bhd* **15/2**[3]

5660 **12** *hd* **Meikle Barfil**[4] 5504 7-7-13 46 oh1 (tp) JosephineBruning(7) 15 35
(J M Bradley) *a bhd* **14/1**

2430 **13** *shd* **Miss Pusey Street**[8] 5362 3-8-2 50 AndrewHeffernan(7) 2 39
(P D Evans) *mid-div tl rdn and wknd 2f out* **12/1**

0550 **14** *¾* **Handcuff**[22] 4937 3-8-5 46 SamHitchcott 10 32
(I Semple) *a bhd* **12/1**

60.64 secs (1.34) **Going Correction** +0.125s/f (Good)
WFA 3 from 4yo+ 1lb **14** Ran SP% **119.1**
Speed ratings (Par 101): **94,93,93,92,91 90,89,88,88,87 87,86,86,85**
toteswingers: 1&2 £69.20, 1&3 £40.60, 2&3 £123.50 CSF £285.08 CT £9245.52 TOTE £11.50: £3.20, £8.90, £11.10; EX 406.50 TRIFECTA Not won..
Owner Tommy Tighe **Bred** F L Mallaghan **Trained** Epsom, Surrey

FOCUS
A very moderate sprint in which more than half the runners were out of the handicap. The field spread out across the track and they finished in something of a heap. It is doubtful if the winner had to improve.

5630 FREEBETS.CO.UK H'CAP (DIV I) 1m 14y
3:40 (3:41) (Class 6) (0-65,65) 3-Y-O+ **£2,266** (£674; £337; £168) **Stalls** Centre

Form RPR

4133 **1** **Kargan (IRE)**[15] 5190 4-9-1 64 AndrewHeffernan(7) 7 75+
(R A Farrant) *hld up: sn in tch: led jst over 2f out: rdn ins fnl f: r.o* **5/1**[2]

6210 **2** *1 ¼* **Magroom**[19] 5062 5-9-6 65 MCGeran(3) 4 73
(R J Hodges) *hld up in rr: pushed along and hdwy 2f out: rdn over 1f out: wnt 2nd wl ins fnl f: nt qckn* **6/1**[3]

540- **3** *1* **Mighty Mover (IRE)**[286] 7427 7-8-9 51 oh4 DavidProbert 9 57
(B Palling) *a.p: rdn and ev ch 2f out: edgd lft over 1f out: no ex and lost 2nd wl ins fnl f* **20/1**

060 **4** *nk* **Croeso Cusan**[85] 2859 4-8-11 58 SophieDoyle(5) 1 63
(J L Spearing) *s.i.s: hld up and bhd: hdwy whn swtchd lft wl over 1f out: rdn and one pce ins fnl f* **15/2**

3631 **5** *1 ½* **Petomic (IRE)**[4] 5503 4-9-5 61 6ex TonyCulhane 6 63
(M Hill) *led: pushed along and hdd jst over 2f out: rdn whn carried lft over 1f out: wknd ins fnl f* **13/8**[1]

00 **6** *¾* **D'Artagnans Dream**[42] 4275 3-8-6 58 ow1 GabrielHannon(5) 3 57
(G D Blake) *n.m.r s: hld up: hdwy over 4f out: rdn and btn over 2f out* **14/1**

4000 **7** *14* **Benozzo Gozzoli**[52] 3942 3-8-4 51 oh4 FrancisNorton 5 18
(H Morrison) *prom tl wknd over 3f out* **28/1**

0561 **8** *1 ¾* **Hector Spectre (IRE)**[53] 3929 3-8-8 60 (v) BMcHugh(5) 8 23
(K M Prendergast) *hld up in tch: rdn over 2f out: sn wknd* **6/1**[3]

00/0 **9** *26* **Balfour House**[17] 5124 6-8-9 51 oh6 FrankieMcDonald 2 —
(D Burchell) *hld up in tch: wknd 3f out* **100/1**

1m 37.27s (1.07) **Going Correction** +0.125s/f (Good)
WFA 3 from 4yo+ 5lb **9** Ran SP% **111.0**
Speed ratings (Par 101): **99,97,96,96,94 94,80,78,52**
toteswingers: 1&2 £3.30, 1&3 £25.10, 2&3 £8.80 CSF £32.58 CT £529.18 TOTE £7.10: £2.10, £1.80, £5.40; EX 29.20 Trifecta £270.30 Pool: £405.58 - 1.11 winning units..
Owner M Sawers **Bred** His Highness The Aga Khan's Studs S C **Trained** East Garston, Berks

FOCUS
An ordinary handicap in which the pace was not strong. Modest form with the runner-up the best guide.
Petomic(IRE) Official explanation: jockey said gelding hung right

5631 FREEBETS.CO.UK H'CAP (DIV II) 1m 14y
4:10 (4:10) (Class 6) (0-65,65) 3-Y-O+ **£2,266** (£674; £337; £168) **Stalls** Centre

Form RPR

4512 **1** **Spring Secret**[4] 5503 3-9-0 61 6ex LukeMorris 9 66
(B Palling) *mde all: rdn jst over 2f out: all out* **6/4**[1]

5006 **2** *nk* **Libre**[22] 4938 9-8-9 51 oh1 (p) TolleyDean 3 56
(F Jordan) *s.i.s: hld up towards rr: pushed along and hdwy 2f out: rdn ins fnl f: r.o* **7/1**[3]

50 **3** *½* **Ermine Grey**[89] 2746 8-9-2 58 (b) DO'Donohoe 4 62
(S Gollings) *hld up in tch: rdn over 1f out: kpt on ins fnl f* **15/2**

2650 **4** *2 ¾* **Komreyev Star**[161] 979 7-8-9 51 oh6 RoystonFfrench 1 49
(R E Peacock) *chsd wnr: rdn and ev ch 2f out: fdd fnl f* **16/1**

445- **5** *2 ¼* **Heaven Or Hell (IRE)**[360] 5778 3-8-4 51 SaleemGolam 8 42
(P D Evans) *prom tl rdn and wknd over 1f out* **9/1**

6050 **6** *4* **Inside Story (IRE)**[17] 5126 7-9-9 65 (b) ShaneKelly 5 48
(C R Dore) *hld up and bhd: short-lived effrt over 2f out* **4/1**[2]

502- **7** *9* **Xtravaganza (IRE)**[332] 6558 4-9-1 64 NathanAlison(7) 10 26
(Jamie Snowden) *s.i.s: sn wl in rr* **9/1**

020 **8** *1* **Top Seed (IRE)**[28] 4745 8-9-7 63 VinceSlattery 2 23
(M S Tuck) *hld up in rr: lost tch over 4f out* **33/1**

1m 38.08s (1.88) **Going Correction** +0.125s/f (Good)
WFA 3 from 4yo+ 5lb **8** Ran SP% **113.1**
Speed ratings (Par 101): **95,94,94,91,89 85,76,75**
toteswingers: 1&2 £3.30, 1&3 £5.00, 2&3 £5.30 CSF £12.30 CT £59.34 TOTE £2.10: £1.40, £1.60, £2.20; EX 11.60 Trifecta £48.00 Pool: £389.68 - 6.00 winning units..
Owner Flying Eight Partnership **Bred** Canary Thoroughbreds **Trained** Tredodridge, Vale Of Glamorgan

FOCUS
Division two of this handicap was run in a time the best part of a second slower than the first. This looked a weak race which did not take a great deal of winning. The form is rated around the second and third.
Inside Story(IRE) Official explanation: jockey said gelding moved poorly throughout

5632 LINDLEY CATERING 1ST CHOICE FOR HOSPITALITY H'CAP (DIV I) 6f 16y
4:40 (4:41) (Class 6) (0-60,60) 3-Y-O+ **£2,137** (£635; £317; £158) **Stalls** Centre

Form RPR

330 **1** **Abhainn (IRE)**[30] 4643 3-8-7 48 DavidProbert 2 57
(B Palling) *led: rdn wl over 1f out: hdd ins fnl f: led towards fin: r.o* **8/1**

5205 **2** *½* **Convince (USA)**[41] 4333 8-9-1 59 BMcHugh(5) 13 66
(K M Prendergast) *hld up and bhd: hdwy 3f out: chal 2f out: carried hd high and rdn to ld ins fnl f: hdd towards fin* **7/2**[1]

2336 **3** *2 ¼* **Miss Firefly**[19] 5065 4-8-12 54 WilliamCarson(3) 3 54
(R J Hodges) *hld up in mid-div: hdwy over 2f out: rdn wl over 1f out: swtchd rt ins fnl f: one pce* **7/1**

4061 **4** *nse* **Outer Hebrides**[4] 5501 8-9-2 60 6ex (v) SophieDoyle(5) 14 60
(J M Bradley) *bhd: hdwy over 2f out: rdn wl over 1f out: one pce fnl f* **9/2**[2]

0666 **5** *2 ¼* **Harrison's Flyer (IRE)**[74] 3208 8-8-6 45 (p) KevinGhunowa 7 37
(J M Bradley) *hld up in tch: rdn 2f out: wknd ins fnl f* **16/1**

003 **6** *¾* **Running Flush (USA)**[25] 4860 3-9-3 58 LukeMorris 12 48
(J R Gask) *prom: rdn wl over 1f out: wknd ins fnl f* **11/1**

5030 **7** *2 ½* **Captain Kallis (IRE)**[30] 4664 3-9-4 59 (t) FrankieMcDonald 4 41
(D J S Ffrench Davis) *prom: ev ch 2f out: wknd over 1f out* **16/1**

0022 **8** *½* **Monte Mayor Eagle**[10] 5326 3-8-5 46 JamieMackay 1 26
(D Haydn Jones) *prom: rdn over 2f out: wknd wl over 1f out* **6/1**[3]

0005 **9** *½* **Street Diva (USA)**[4] 5501 4-8-7 51 AmyBaker(5) 9 30
(A B Haynes) *mid-div: pushed along 3f out: sn rdn: bhd fnl 2f* **16/1**

00 **10** *2 ¾* **Merry May**[22] 4950 3-8-4 45 FrancisNorton 10 15
(S Kirk) *a bhd* **66/1**

600 **11** *nk* **Square Of Gold (FR)**[44] 4199 3-8-6 50 MCGeran(3) 11 19
(A W Carroll) *hld up in mid-div: rdn and wknd 2f out* **16/1**

6043 **12** *2* **Clear Hand**[22] 4937 3-8-9 50 (b) RichardSmith 8 13
(B R Millman) *prom tl rdn and wknd over 2f out* **12/1**

0 **13** *5* **Castlefish (IRE)**[13] 5242 5-8-6 45 SamHitchcott 5 —
(D Burchell) *prom tl rdn and wknd 3f out* **33/1**

1m 12.46s (0.46) **Going Correction** +0.125s/f (Good)
WFA 3 from 4yo+ 2lb **13** Ran SP% **122.3**
Speed ratings (Par 101): **101,100,97,97,94 93,89,89,88,84 84,81,75**
toteswingers: 1&2 £12.70, 1&3 £14.90, 2&3 £7.10 CSF £36.88 CT £220.21 TOTE £9.10: £2.30, £1.50, £2.70; EX 72.30 TRIFECTA Not won. .
Owner H Perkins **Bred** Humphrey Okeke **Trained** Tredodridge, Vale Of Glamorgan
■ Stewards' Enquiry : William Carson one-day ban: careless riding (Sep 18)

FOCUS
A moderate handicap, and not a race to be with, although it was run quicker than division two. The winner is rated to his latter 2yo form.

5633 LINDLEY CATERING 1ST CHOICE FOR HOSPITALITY H'CAP (DIV II) 6f 16y
5:10 (5:11) (Class 6) (0-60,60) 3-Y-O+ **£2,137** (£635; £317; £158) **Stalls** Centre

Form RPR

0045 **1** **Bermondsey Bob (IRE)**[30] 4643 3-8-5 47 SamHitchcott 1 55
(J L Spearing) *led: hrd rdn over 1f out: narrowly hdd ins fnl f: led nr fin* **7/1**

6-01 **2** *shd* **Connor's Choice**[20] 5018 4-8-13 **58** SimonPearce(5) 14 66
(Andrew Turnell) *t.k.h: hdwy over 3f out: rdn over 1f out: slt ld ins fnl f: edgd rt and hdd nr fin* **9/2**[3]

0500 **3** *½* **Red Dagger (IRE)**[74] 3215 3-8-4 **46** oh1 FrancisNorton 7 52
(R J Price) *hld up and bhd: hdwy 2f out: hrd rdn over 1f out: ev ch ins fnl f: kpt on* **14/1**

3000 **4** *2 ¼* **Tadlil**[45] 4183 7-8-7 **47** DavidProbert 3 46
(J M Bradley) *hld up in tch: rdn over 1f out: one pce fnl f* **11/1**

0524 **5** *½* **Cardinal**[34] 4533 4-9-3 **57** KevinGhunowa 13 54
(R A Harris) *s.i.s: hld up: pushed along 3f out: rdn 2f out: kpt on same pce fnl f* **11/4**[1]

2000 **6** *½* **Supreme Speedster**[15] 5184 5-8-6 **46** oh1 RichardThomas 2 42
(A G Newcombe) *prom: ev ch over 2f out: rdn and wknd over 1f out* **12/1**

00-0 **7** *shd* **Oxbridge**[4] 5501 4-8-5 **50** BMcHugh(5) 9 45
(J M Bradley) *hld up: pushed along over 2f out: rdn and btn over 1f out* **33/1**

0010 **8** *3 ¼* **Cwmni**[4] 5501 3-8-11 **53** NeilChalmers 12 38
(B Palling) *hld up and bhd: hdwy over 2f out: wknd wl over 1f out* **12/1**

0066 **9** *1 ¼* **Imperial Djay (IRE)**[27] 4787 4-8-8 **48** (p) RobertHavlin 6 29
(J R Holt) *w wnr tl wknd over 2f out* **4/1**[2]

4030 **10** *¾* **Rapanui Belle**[17] 5125 3-8-4 **46** oh1 RoystonFfrench 11 25
(G L Moore) *hld up: pushed along over 2f out: rdn and struggling wl over 1f out* **16/1**

1m 13.21s (1.21) **Going Correction** +0.125s/f (Good)
WFA 3 from 4yo+ 2lb **10** Ran SP% **116.6**
Speed ratings (Par 101): **96,95,95,92,91 90,90,86,84,83**
toteswingers: 1&2 £8.30, 1&3 £20.20, 2&3 £15.60 CSF £38.54 CT £441.13 TOTE £9.30: £2.50, £1.80, £4.40; EX 48.10 Trifecta £290.00 Pool: £517.45 - 1.32 winning units..
Owner A A Campbell **Bred** Pier House Stud **Trained** Kinnersley, Worcs
■ Stewards' Enquiry : Francis Norton two-day ban: excessive use of the whip (Sep 18-19)

FOCUS
A desperate finish to this lowly handicap, which was run in a slightly slower time than the first division. The first pair were well treated on old form.
Cardinal Official explanation: jockey said colt hung left

5634 BETFAIR APPRENTICE TRAINING SERIES H'CAP 7f 16y
5:40 (5:41) (Class 6) (0-60,60) 3-Y-0+ **£2,460** (£732; £365; £182) **Stalls** Centre

Form RPR

6031 **1** **Lordship (IRE)**[8] 5364 5-9-3 **57** 6ex JakePayne(5) 16 69
(A W Carroll) *w ldr: led over 4f out: pushed along over 2f out: r.o wl* **9/2**[2]

004 **2** *2 ½* **Charlie Delta**[4] 5502 6-8-11 **52** (b) SPRyan(6) 14 57
(R A Harris) *hld up in rr: hdwy over 3f out: rdn 2f out: styd on u.p to take 2nd last strides: nt trble wnr* **6/1**

4201 **3** *hd* **Cadeaux Fax**[4] 5502 4-9-11 **60** 6ex SimonPearce 9 64
(B R Millman) *hld up: hdwy to chse wnr 3f out: rdn over 1f out: no ex and lost 2nd last strides* **7/2**[1]

5224 **4** *½* **Dancing Welcome**[16] 5155 3-8-10 **52** (b) JosephineBruning(3) 11 53
(J M Bradley) *hld up: hdwy over 3f out: disp 2nd 2f out: rdn over 1f out: one pce ins fnl f* **16/1**

026 **5** *1 ¾* **Cheap Street**[4] 5502 5-9-9 **58** RosieJessop 12 56
(J G Portman) *hld up in rr: stdy prog 3f out: rdn and wknd 2f out* **8/1**

6000 **6** *2 ¾* **Isabella's Fancy**[73] 3241 4-8-7 **45** (b) DavidKenny(3) 1 36
(A G Newcombe) *hld up in tch: rdn and wknd 2f out* **50/1**

0225 **7** *1 ¼* **Northern Desert (IRE)**[15] 5179 10-9-9 **58** (p) AndrewHeffernan 4 46
(S Curran) *a bhd* **12/1**

0100 **8** *2* **Mocha Java**[39] 4375 6-9-3 **52** LeeNewnes 5 34
(Matthew Salaman) *prom tl wknd over 2f out* **5/1**[3]

2-56 **9** *3 ¼* **The City Kid (IRE)**[14] 5225 6-9-3 **52** JPHamblett 6 25
(G D Blake) *hld up in tch: rdn 3f out: sn wknd* **20/1**

0420 **10** *7* **Just Jimmy (IRE)**[65] 3505 4-9-4 **53** (vt) JamesPSullivan 8 8
(K M Prendergast) *t.k.h: in tch: lost pl over 4f out: bhd fnl 3f* **7/1**

0040 **11** *4* **Dicey Affair**[43] 4240 3-9-6 **59** ByronMoorcroft 2 —
(G L Moore) *hld up in tch: wkng whn n.m.r wl over 2f out* **50/1**

00-5 **12** *½* **Bluebird Chariot**[43] 4238 6-8-10 **45** BillyCray 7 —
(J M Bradley) *led over 2f: pushed along and wknd wl over 2f out* **50/1**

1m 24.74s (1.54) **Going Correction** +0.125s/f (Good)
WFA 3 from 4yo+ 4lb **12** Ran SP% **119.2**
Speed ratings (Par 101): **96,93,92,92,90 87,85,83,79,71 67,66**
toteswingers: 1&2 £8.80, 1&3 £4.20, 2&3 £5.40 CSF £31.01 CT £104.79 TOTE £5.20: £2.00, £2.60, £1.40; EX 42.10 Trifecta £115.10 Pool: £387.61 - 2.49 winning units. Place 6: £615.37 Place 5: £210.84..
Owner Group 1 Racing (1994) Ltd **Bred** John Costello **Trained** Cropthorne, Worcs

FOCUS
A moderate handicap for apprentices who have not ridden more than 20 winners. The winner improved a little on his Ayr win and the form is sound.
T/Jkpt: Not won. T/Plt: £451.20 to a £1 stake. Pool: £72,760.98. 117.70 winning tickets. T/Qpdt: £33.20 to a £1 stake. Pool: £5,715.91. 127.05 winning tickets. KH

5570 KEMPTON (A.W) (R-H)
Friday, September 4

OFFICIAL GOING: Standard
Wind: Brisk against, races 1-5; moderate across, races 6-8 Weather: Fine

5635 CELTIC CONTRACTORS NURSERY (DIV I) 6f (P)
5:45 (5:47) (Class 5) (0-70,70) 2-Y-0 **£2,266** (£674; £337; £168) **Stalls** High

Form RPR

4144 **1** **Wasmi (IRE)**[16] 5166 2-9-0 **63** NCallan 3 66+
(C E Brittain) *hld up bhd ldrs: effrt 2f out: led and edgd lft jst over 1f out: drvn out but a holding rivals* **7/1**

0006 **2** *1* **Precious Coral (IRE)**[11] 5310 2-9-5 **68** HayleyTurner 6 68
(S A Callaghan) *hld up in last trio: rdn jst over 2f out: prog over 1f out: disp 2nd ins fnl f: a hld* **15/8**[1]

0600 **3** *nse* **Bell's Ocean (USA)**[25] 4850 2-9-4 **67** JerryO'Dwyer 2 67
(J Ryan) *prom on outer: lost grnd bnd 3f out and lost pl sn after: effrt over 1f out: prog to dispute 2nd ins fnl f: a hld* **8/1**

065 **4** *½* **Boogie Waltzer**[37] 4427 2-8-3 **52** KirstyMilczarek 10 50
(S C Williams) *trckd ldrs: effrt and nt clr run briefly wl over 1f out: prog to chal 1f out: kpt on same pce* **16/1**

0631 **5** *1 ½* **Candyfloss Girl**[11] 5310 2-9-1 **64** 6ex DaneO'Neill 1 58
(H J L Dunlop) *hld up in rr on outer w usual tail swishing: pushed along and sme prog fr 2f out: nt pce to threaten fnl f* **12/1**

5410 **6** *1 ½* **Rosedale**[24] 4884 2-8-9 **58** JoeFanning 9 47
(J A R Toller) *n.m.r sn after s: hld up: last over 3f out: sme prog on wd outside over 1f out: nvr on terms* **5/1**[2]

0006 **7** *1 ¾* **Campaigner**[25] 4856 2-7-13 **48** JimmyQuinn 7 32
(J W Hills) *hld up in last trio: shuffled along fr 2f out: stuck in bhd main gp 1f out: nvr nr ldrs* **25/1**

006 **8** *nk* **Bookiesindex Girl (IRE)**[59] 3709 2-8-5 **54** AdrianMcCarthy 4 37
(J R Jenkins) *wnt rt s: t.k.h and pressed ldr to 3f out: styd chsng ldrs tl wknd 1f out* **50/1**

015 **9** *nse* **Coolree Star (IRE)**[34] 4525 2-9-7 **70** SteveDrowne 11 53
(J A Glover) *plld hrd and racd awkwardly: hld up in rr on inner: brief effrt 2f out: no prog jst over 1f out* **6/1**[3]

00 **10** *2* **Lairy (IRE)**[4] 5526 2-8-2 **51** NickyMackay 5 28
(M F Harris) *hmpd s: last tl rapid prog rnd wd outside to join ldr 1/2-way: wknd rapidly over 1f out* **20/1**

2602 **11** *2 ¼* **Point To Prove**[18] 5091 2-9-7 **70** PatCosgrave 8 40
(Miss Amy Weaver) *mde most to jst over 1f out: wknd rapidly* **13/2**

1m 14.1s (1.00) **Going Correction** +0.05s/f (Slow) **11** Ran SP% **126.8**
Speed ratings (Par 95): **95,93,93,92,90 88,86,86,86,83 80**
toteswingers: 1&2 £3.70, 1&3 £10.80, 2&3 £7.40 CSF £21.78 CT £116.98 TOTE £7.80: £1.70, £1.40, £3.80; EX 34.40.
Owner Saeed Manana **Bred** Airlie Stud **Trained** Newmarket, Suffolk

FOCUS
An ordinary handicap in which the gallop was only fair. The fillies dominated and the winner raced in the centre in the closing stages.

NOTEBOOK
Wasmi(IRE) was always well placed given the way this race unfolded and again showed a good attitude to notch her second Polytrack win. Equally effective over 7f, she should continue to go well in this type of event. (op 11-2)
Precious Coral(IRE) ◆, who caught the eye over 5f at this course on his previous start, was well supported and ran her best race yet over this extra furlong. She may be a bit better than the bare form, faring the best of those ridden with a degree of patience, and she remains capable of winning a similar event over 6f. (op 9-4 tchd 5-2 in a place early)
Bell's Ocean(USA) has slipped in the weights and ran her best race in nursery company on this all-weather debut. She shaped as though a stiffer test over this trip would have suited and she may do a little better on this surface. (tchd 15-2)
Boogie Waltzer, who hinted at ability on her previous start, confirmed that bit of promise on this all-weather and nursery debut from a decent draw. She is in good hands and is one to keep an eye out for in a similar event.
Candyfloss Girl, who had the run of the race from a good draw when successful over 5f at this course on her previous start, may not be entirely straightforward (again flashed her tail for pressure), but she was better than she was able to show this time having been held up from her wide draw. (op 9-1)
Rosedale, well beaten on her previous run, shaped abetter than the bare facts imply. She was dropped out last in a race run at just an ordinary gallop. Her dam won over middle distances and she is worth a try over 7f. (op 9-1)
Coolree Star(IRE) Official explanation: jockey said colt hung badly right

5636 CELTIC CONTRACTORS NURSERY (DIV II) 6f (P)
6:20 (6:23) (Class 5) (0-70,70) 2-Y-0 **£2,266** (£674; £337; £168) **Stalls** High

Form RPR

500 **1** **Athwaab**[34] 4537 2-9-4 **67** TGMcLaughlin 8 71+
(E A L Dunlop) *hld up in last trio gng wl: prog 2f out: rdn to ld 1f out: styd on wl* **10/1**

6640 **2** *¾* **Wing Of Faith**[14] 5213 2-8-8 **57** SteveDrowne 2 59
(S Kirk) *racd wd: hld up in last trio: last 2f out: rapid prog on wd outside over 1f out: tk 2nd nr fin: too much to do* **12/1**

1004 **3** *hd* **Wigan Lane**[14] 5226 2-8-13 **62** KFallon 10 64+
(P Howling) *trckd ldrs: cl up 2f out: nt clr run over 1f out and swtchd lft: edgd lft u.p: r.o but a hld* **5/1**

2005 **4** *nk* **Do More Business (IRE)**[24] 4868 2-8-13 **65** JackMitchell(3) 4 66
(P M Phelan) *t.k.h early: pressed ldr: rdn and nt qckn 2f out: wnt 2nd again ins fnl f: no imp on wnr: lost 2 pls nr fin* **12/1**

01 **5** *2 ½* **Kapelad Junior (IRE)**[27] 4800 2-9-0 **63** PaulEddery 9 56
(Pat Eddery) *chsd ldrs: rdn to dispute 3rd briefly 2f out: sn nt qckn and outpcd: plugged on* **9/2**[3]

1004 **6** *nk* **Reach For The Sky (IRE)**[25] 4850 2-9-7 **70** DaneO'Neill 6 62
(R Hannon) *led to 1f out: wknd* **4/1**[2]

2306 **7** *1 ¼* **Fasilight**[25] 4858 2-9-6 **69** DarryllHolland 11 57
(M Botti) *t.k.h: hld up in rr: prog on inner 2f out: nt qckn over 1f out: wknd fnl f* **7/2**[1]

0520 **8** *3 ½* **New York Lights (IRE)**[2] 5583 2-7-12 **54** RachelKing(7) 3 32
(M D I Usher) *taken down early: racd wd: prom tl wknd fr 2f out* **25/1**

0000 **9** *hd* **Silvee**[14] 5213 2-7-12 **47** AdrianMcCarthy 1 24
(J J Bridger) *s.s: swtchd to inner fr outside draw: last tl effrt 2f out: sn no prog and btn* **66/1**

3565 **10** *2 ¾* **Gasparilla (IRE)**[4] 5519 2-8-1 **50** NickyMackay 7 19
(A J McCabe) *mounted on crse: nvr beyond midfield: wknd 2f out* **12/1**

230 **11** *nk* **Hachi**[39] 4384 2-8-3 **52** (b[1]) JimmyQuinn 5 20
(J L Spearing) *racd wd in midfield: rdn over 2f out: sn no prog and btn* **10/1**

1m 14.35s (1.25) **Going Correction** +0.05s/f (Slow) **11** Ran SP% **123.7**
Speed ratings (Par 95): **93,92,91,91,88 87,85,81,81,77 76**
toteswingers: 1&2 £26.90, 1&3 £13.30, 2&3 £17.80 CSF £130.20 CT £696.54 TOTE £17.10: £5.10, £4.10, £1.70; EX 159.50.
Owner Hamdan Al Maktoum **Bred** Shadwell Estate Co Ltd **Trained** Newmarket, Suffolk
■ Stewards' Enquiry : K Fallon caution: careless riding

FOCUS
Another open nursery on paper but an improved effort from the winner, who made his ground near the far rail in the straight. The pace was reasonable.

NOTEBOOK
Athwaab ◆ had been disappointing since making an encouraging debut, but she turned in an improved effort back up in trip for this handicap debut. She showed a good turn of foot to win with a bit in hand after travelling strongly and she remains open to further progress. Official explanation: trainer's rep said, regarding the apparent improvement in form shown, filly settled better today than on her two previous runs (op 9-1)
Wing Of Faith did not seem to stay 1m on his previous start but fared better back over this trip on this all-weather debut. He shouldn't have a problem with 7f and is capable of picking up an ordinary event. (op 10-1)
Wigan Lane, having his first run for a new yard, fared the best of those that raced up with the pace and would almost certainly have finished second had he not met trouble at a crucial stage. He should be able to win a race for this yard. (op 9-2)
Do More Business(IRE) proved suited by the return to this trip and, after helping to force a decent gallop, turned in his best effort since his debut run. His yard has winners on sand and he is lightly raced enough to be open to a bit of improvement.
Kapelad Junior(IRE) had shown improved form to win a Redcar seller on his previous start but, although not disgraced, found things much tougher from this mark on this all-weather and nursery debut. (op 5-1 tchd 4-1)

Reach For The Sky(IRE) was not disgraced after racing keenly at the head of affairs on this all-weather debut but was below the form she showed on her nursery debut at Windsor. (tchd 7-2 and 9-2)
Fasilight Official explanation: jockey said filly ran too free

5637 LETCHWORTH COURIERS EBF MAIDEN STKS 1m (P)
6:50 (6:54) (Class 4) 2-Y-O **£5,180** (£1,541; £770; £384) **Stalls** High

Form RPR
1 **Mendip (USA)** 2-9-3 0 TedDurcan 9 84+
(Saeed Bin Suroor) *reluctant to enter stalls: trckd ldng pair: pushed along over 2f out: plld out and swept into ld jst over 1f out: galloped clr: eased nr fin* **5/6**[1]
2 2 ¼ **Musaafer (IRE)** 2-9-3 0 RHills 7 76+
(M A Jarvis) *nt wl away but sn trckd ldr: led jst over 2f out gng strly: shkn up over 1f out: sn hdd: styd on but no ch w wnr* **2/1**[2]
0 3 6 **Miss Wendy**[37] 4427 2-8-7 0 AshleyMorgan(5) 1 58
(M H Tompkins) *chsd ldng trio: rdn and outpcd fr 2f out: plugged on to take modest 3rd ins fnl f* **40/1**
00 4 1 ¾ **Slasl**[51] 3987 2-8-12 0 NCallan 4 54
(C E Brittain) *led to jst over 2f out: sn btn: lost modest 3rd ins fnl f* **20/1**
5 2 **Plato (JPN)** 2-9-3 0 JimmyQuinn 6 55+
(H R A Cecil) *sn pushed along in last and v green: struggling thrght: styd on fnl f: bttr for experience* **11/2**[3]
6 6 **Lord Victor** 2-9-3 0 SebSanders 8 41
(A J McCabe) *a in last trio: struggling wl over 2f out: sn bhd* **20/1**
7 16 **Nurai** 2-8-12 0 (t) DarryllHolland 3 —
(P W D'Arcy) *s.i.s and green in rr: wknd over 2f out: t.o* **20/1**

1m 41.32s (1.52) **Going Correction** +0.05s/f (Slow) **7 Ran SP% 120.0**
Speed ratings (Par 97): **94,91,85,84,82 76,60**
toteswingers: 1&2 £1.10, 1&3 £6.70, 2&3 £7.40 CSF £2.78 TOTE £1.80: £1.50, £1.80; EX 3.40.
Owner Godolphin **Bred** Jayeff B Stables **Trained** Newmarket, Suffolk

FOCUS
Not a race with any strength in depth but the two market leaders pulled clear in the closing stages and look promising colts. The pace was only fair and the winner raced in the centre in the straight.

NOTEBOOK
Mendip(USA) ◆, green and colty in the preliminaries and fitted with a blanket for stalls entry (took a while to load), was much more professional in the race and the $375,000 purchase created a very good impression on this debut. This good-looking sort was well on top at the finish, should be all the better mentally for this experience and is the type to hold his own in stronger company. (tchd 4-6 and 10-11 tchd evens in a place)
Musaafer(IRE) ◆, a 300,000euro first foal of a useful 7f juvenile winner, was well supported on this debut and shaped with a good deal of promise against a potentially smart rival. While he'll have to improve a fair bit to justify entries in several Group 1s in the autumn, he showed more than enough to suggest he can win races for this yard. (op 5-2 tchd 11-4 tchd 3-1 in a place)
Miss Wendy stepped up on her debut form but looks flattered behind a couple of potentially smart types and is better judged on her proximity to the fourth home. Her short-term future lies in ordinary nursery company granted a suitable test of stamina. (op 33-1)
Slasl, upped in trip, had the run of the race but quickly had her limitations exposed when pressure was applied. She is likely to remain vulnerable in this type of event.
Plato(JPN), the first foal of a multiple winner on turf and dirt up to 1m, was relatively easy to back on his racecourse debut and proved a disappointment. However he is in very good hands and is probably worth another chance. (tchd 6-1)

5638 MIDLAND FACILITIES MANAGEMENT EBF MAIDEN FILLIES' STKS 6f (P)
7:20 (7:22) (Class 4) 2-Y-O **£5,180** (£1,541; £770; £384) **Stalls** High

Form RPR
4 1 **Ferris Wheel (IRE)**[14] 5212 2-9-0 0 NCallan 3 78+
(P F I Cole) *trckd ldng trio: pushed along and effrt over 2f out: led over 1f out on outer: styd on wl and drew clr* **11/4**[2]
2 2 ¼ **Alice Alleyne (IRE)** 2-9-0 0 RHills 11 71
(Sir Michael Stoute) *trckd ldng pair: effrt to chal over 1f out: chsd wnr after but sn outpcd: jst hld on for 2nd* **13/8**[1]
3 hd **Thereafter (USA)** 2-9-0 0 SteveDrowne 4 71+
(R Charlton) *chsd ldng quartet: pushed along fr over 2f out: styd on wl fr over 1f out: tk 3rd fnl f and clsd on runner-up fin* **5/1**[3]
4 3 ¼ **Silk Slippers** 2-9-0 0 PatCosgrave 7 61
(John Joseph Murphy, Ire) *pressed ldr gng wl: led over 2f out: sn rdn: hdd over 1f out: wknd fnl f* **8/1**
5 1 ½ **Thoughtful (IRE)** 2-9-0 0 SebSanders 8 56
(J W Hills) *chsd ldng quartet: effrt on inner 2f out and nrly on terms: pushed along and wknd fnl f* **12/1**
6 2 **Catherines Call (IRE)** 2-9-0 0 JimmyQuinn 2 50+
(D Donovan) *slowly away and wnt lft s: rn green in last and nvr on terms: kpt on fr over 1f out* **25/1**
04 7 1 ¼ **Avon Krystal**[31] 4626 2-9-0 0 DaneO'Neill 9 47
(R Hannon) *pushed along in last trio after 2f: nvr on terms: plugged on fr over 1f out* **14/1**
8 5 **Miss Isle Control** 2-8-7 0 DeclanCannon(7) 10 32
(A J McCabe) *s.s: a in last trio: hung rt u.p 2f out: wknd* **33/1**
9 1 **Wild Heather** 2-9-0 0 JerryO'Dwyer 12 29
(J R Holt) *led to over 2f out: wknd rapidly over 1f out* **33/1**

1m 14.21s (1.11) **Going Correction** +0.05s/f (Slow) **9 Ran SP% 116.6**
Speed ratings (Par 94): **94,91,90,86,84 81,80,73,72**
toteswingers: 1&2 £1.70, 1&3 £2.80, 2&3 £2.10 CSF £7.53 TOTE £4.40: £1.20, £1.10, £1.70; EX 8.30.
Owner Fisher,Goldswain,Hunter,Manley,Maynard **Bred** Mrs Sarah Maccann **Trained** Whatcombe, Oxon

FOCUS
This looked an ordinary maiden and one run at a reasonable gallop. The winner raced up the centre in the straight.

NOTEBOOK
Ferris Wheel(IRE), who shaped with a degree of promise on her debut, made her experience tell against several newcomers and bettered the form of that initial run on this all-weather debut. She should stay 7f and may be capable of further progress in ordinary nursery company. (op 3-1 tchd 7-2 tchd 4-1 in a place)
Alice Alleyne(IRE), a half-sister to fairly useful middle distance performer Avalon, attracted support and showed ability - albeit at a modest level - on this racecourse debut. She should stay 7f and is entitled to improve for this experience. (op 6-4 tchd 11-8 tchd 7-4 in a place)
Thereafter(USA), a half-sister to several winners up to middle distances, showed a degree of promise on her racecourse debut. She shaped as though a stiffer test of stamina would have suited and, although this is not strong form, she appeals as the sort to win races. (op 6-1)
Silk Slippers has plenty of winners over a variety of distances (including over hurdles) in her pedigree and she was far from disgraced on this racecourse debut. She too is likely to come on for this run.
Thoughtful(IRE), a half-sister to a 7f-1m winner in France and out of a half-sister to a high-class middle distance filly, showed ability without being knocked about on this debut run. She should do better in ordinary handicaps over further in due course. (tchd 14-1)
Catherines Call(IRE), a half-sister to several winners from 5f-1m6f, was too green to do herself justice on this racecourse debut but is another that should improve for the outing.

5639 CELTIC CONTRACTORS EBF FILLIES' CONDITIONS STKS 7f (P)
7:50 (7:51) (Class 3) 2-Y-O
£7,477 (£2,239; £1,119; £560; £279; £140) **Stalls** High

Form RPR
1 1 **Eolith**[27] 4792 2-9-2 0 JimCrowley 6 83+
(W J Knight) *trckd ldr: rdn jst over 2f out: led over 1f out: sn in command: a holding on nr fin* **11/8**[1]
2 1 **Arte Viva (USA)** 2-8-12 0 KFallon 5 77+
(G A Butler) *trckd ldrs: pushed along over 2f out: prog over 1f out: wnt 2nd ins fnl f: styd on wl but nvr quite able to chal* **9/4**[2]
3 2 **Awaseef (USA)** 2-8-12 0 RHills 3 72+
(J H M Gosden) *trckd ldrs: pushed along 2f out: kpt on to take 3rd ins fnl f: nt pce to chal* **9/2**[3]
4 2 **Art Machine (USA)** 2-8-12 0 SebSanders 4 67+
(Sir Mark Prescott) *pushed along in last pair 1/2-way: no prog tl kpt on fr over 1f out: nrst fin* **14/1**
0 5 1 ½ **Mini Max**[21] 4985 2-8-7 0 GabrielHannon(5) 1 63
(B W Duke) *led: rdn over 2f out: hdd over 1f out: wknd fnl f* **100/1**
6 2 **Eldalil** 2-8-12 0 TPO'Shea 8 63+
(Sir Michael Stoute) *dwlt: trckd ldng pair: pushed along 2f out: wknd jst over 1f out: eased ins fnl f* **7/1**
7 1 **Vanilla Loan (IRE)** 2-8-12 0 DarryllHolland 2 55
(M Botti) *slowly away and awkward s: a in last pair: rdn and no prog over 2f out* **16/1**

1m 27.46s (1.46) **Going Correction** +0.05s/f (Slow) **7 Ran SP% 117.1**
Speed ratings (Par 96): **93,91,89,87,85 83,82**
toteswingers: 1&2 £1.30, 1&3 £1.70, 2&3 £2.20 CSF £4.90 TOTE £2.10: £1.10, £2.20; EX 5.90.
Owner Mrs Alison Ruggles **Bred** Mrs A R Ruggles **Trained** Patching, W Sussex

FOCUS
An interesting conditions event featuring a previous winner and several well-bred newcomers from top yards. The gallop was only a moderate one and the winner raced just off the far rail in the straight.

NOTEBOOK
Eolith, well backed, had created a good impression when beating a subsequent winner (pair clear) at Newmarket on her debut and, although conceding weight all round, she may not have had to improve too much to follow up after enjoying the run of the race. It'll be surprising if there isn't more to come and she will reportedly be aimed at the Group 3 Oh So Sharp Stakes. (op 7-4 tchd 15-8 & tchd 2-1 in places)
Arte Viva(USA) ◆, the first foal of a half-sister to top class Shamardal, attracted support on this debut but failed to settle in a race run at just an ordinary gallop. However she showed more than enough without being unduly knocked about to suggest she can win races, especially when upped to 1m. (op 11-4)
Awaseef(USA), the first foal of an unraced half-sister to top class dirt miler Corinthian, had the run of the race but showed ability on this racecourse debut. She is entitled to improve for this experience and is sure to win a race. (op 3-1)
Art Machine(USA), a half-sister to several winners from 5f-1m, was easy to back on this racecourse debut but shaped with a degree of promise. She left the impression that a much stiffer test of stamina would have suited and she is sure to improve.
Mini Max, soundly beaten on her debut on turf, looks flattered by her proximity after being allowed to dictate an ordinary gallop. Modest handicaps will be the way forward with her in due course. (op 80-1)
Eldalil, the owner's second string, has several winners up to middle distances in her pedigree and she showed ability before getting tired on this racecourse debut. She is likely to fare better given time and longer distances. Official explanation: jockey said filly was denied a clear run (op 6-1)

5640 WEATHERBYS PRINTING APPRENTICE H'CAP (FINAL ROUND) 1m (P)
8:20 (8:20) (Class 4) (0-85,85) 3-Y-O+
£4,984 (£1,492; £746; £373; £186; £93) **Stalls** High

Form RPR
0602 1 **Bomber Command (USA)**[21] 4983 6-9-7 **82** (v) PatrickHills 6 90
(J W Hills) *chsd ldrs: pushed along over 2f out: stdy prog over 1f out: led last 150yds: urged along and a holding on* **7/1**[3]
0004 2 ½ **Stand Guard**[30] 4644 5-9-2 **82** TobyAtkinson(5) 4 89
(P Howling) *hld up in 9th: rapid prog towards inner jst over 2f out to chal over 1f out: upsides ent fnl f: nt qckn* **10/1**
511- 3 1 **Spirit Of A Nation (IRE)**[434] 3442 4-9-5 **85** AshleyMorgan(5) 7 89+
(D H Brown) *s.s: hld up in last pair: effrt on wd outside over 2f out: styd on fr over 1f out: tk 3rd post* **7/1**[3]
3044 4 nse **Laudatory**[21] 4983 3-9-0 **83** MCGeran(3) 3 86
(W R Swinburn) *settled midfield: rdn over 2f out: chsd ldrs over 1f out: styd on but nvr able to chal* **3/1**[1]
1056 5 1 ¼ **Carlitos Spirit (IRE)**[18] 5095 5-8-13 **74** JamesMillman 1 75+
(B R Millman) *trckd ldng trio: effrt to ld wl over 1f out: hdd & wknd last 150yds* **16/1**
-504 6 shd **Quick Release (IRE)**[18] 5095 4-8-8 **74** LauraPike(5) 8 75
(D M Simcock) *hld up in 8th: prog on inner fr over 2f out: nt qckn over 1f out: one pce fnl f* **16/1**
10-5 7 hd **Spate River**[22] 4954 4-9-7 **82** JackMitchell 5 83
(C F Wall) *dwlt: hld up in last pair: nt clr run on inner over 2f out and swtchd to wd outside: sme prog over 1f out: nvr on terms* **3/1**[1]
4511 8 2 ½ **Rock Anthem (IRE)**[14] 5211 5-8-11 **72** DavidProbert 9 67
(Mike Murphy) *prom: led over 2f out to wl over 1f out: wknd fnl f* **13/2**[2]
1406 9 5 **Buddy Holly**[37] 4426 4-9-6 **84** (v) AmyBaker(3) 10 67
(Pat Eddery) *led 2f: chsd ldr: upsides over 2f out: wknd over 1f out* **16/1**
-014 10 hd **Mcconnell (USA)**[206] 490 4-9-2 **80** SophieDoyle(3) 11 62
(G L Moore) *n.m.r on inner after 2f: mostly midfield after: urged along sn after 1/2-way: racd awkwardly fr over 2f out: wknd over 1f out* **20/1**
1616 11 6 **Elusive Fame (USA)**[21] 4984 3-8-5 **76** (b) MatthewLawson(5) 2 43
(M Johnston) *racd freely: led after 2f and sn clr: hdd & wknd rapidly over 2f out* **16/1**

1m 38.59s (-1.21) **Going Correction** +0.05s/f (Slow)
WFA 3 from 4yo+ 5lb **11 Ran SP% 125.7**
Speed ratings (Par 105): **108,107,106,106,105 105,104,102,97,97 91**
toteswingers: 1&2 £19.70, 1&3 £13.70, 2&3 £23.10 CSF £80.52 CT £523.85 TOTE £10.00: £2.30, £3.60, £3.40; EX 103.20.
Owner Gary & Linnet Woodward (2) **Bred** Jeffrey B Feins **Trained** Upper Lambourn, Berks

FOCUS
A competitive handicap run at a decent gallop in which the front runners didn't get home. The winner raced centre to far side in the straight. Fair form for the grade.
Spirit Of A Nation(IRE) ◆ Official explanation: jockey said colt missed the break
Rock Anthem(IRE) Official explanation: jockey said gelding ran flat

Mcconnell(USA) Official explanation: jockey said gelding hung right

5641 CELTIC CONTRACTORS H'CAP 1m 3f (P)
8:50 (8:52) (Class 3) (0-95,94) 3-Y-0+

£7,352 (£2,201; £1,100; £551; £274; £138) **Stalls** High

Form RPR

0045 **1** **Charm School**[91] 2671 4-9-7 **91** .... JimmyFortune 6 99
(J H M Gosden) *hld up in last trio: t.k.h fr 1/2-way on outer: prog 2f out: rdn and rn wl to ld last 100yds* **6/1**

0233 **2** ½ **Safari Sunup (IRE)**[34] 4517 4-9-9 **93** .... JimCrowley 7 100
(P Winkworth) *trckd ldng pair: drvn to go 2nd 2f out: clsd to ld 1f out: r.o but hdd last 100yds* **8/1**

4403 **3** ½ **William Blake**[6] 5437 4-9-1 **85** .... JoeFanning 1 91
(M Johnston) *hld up in last pair: t.k.h 1/2-way: prog on wd outside 2f out: clsd on ldrs 1f out: nt qckn last 150yds* **9/2**[3]

1306 **4** 1 ¾ **Bugaku**[27] 4794 4-9-7 **91** .... KFallon 9 94
(Sir Michael Stoute) *hld up in midfield: pushed along 3f out: sn nt qckn and lost pl: styd on again fnl f* **3/1**[2]

3-26 **5** ½ **Dr Livingstone (IRE)**[84] 2891 4-9-4 **88** .... SteveDrowne 2 90
(C R Egerton) *trckd ldng trio: wnt 3rd wl over 1f out: sn drvn: nt qckn and no imp: one pce fnl f* **33/1**

3204 **6** *shd* **Jabal Tariq**[30] 4661 4-8-12 **82** .... RobertWinston 3 84
(B W Hills) *trckd ldr: led jst over 2f out and kicked on: hdd & wknd 1f out* **10/1**

6-00 **7** *hd* **Pinch Of Salt (IRE)**[13] 5262 6-9-1 **85** .... MartinDwyer 8 87
(A M Balding) *settled midfield: lost pl and pushed along in last trio 1/2-way: struggling over 2f out: kpt on again fnl f* **9/1**

311 **8** 9 **Sounds Of Jupiter (IRE)**[12] 5286 3-8-2 **79** 6ex .... ChrisCatlin 4 65
(D M Simcock) *led to jst over 2f out: wknd rapidly over 1f out* **5/2**[1]

0043 **9** 1 ¼ **Heron Bay**[27] 4770 5-9-10 **94** .... GeorgeBaker 5 77
(C F Wall) *dwlt and rousted along early to stay in tch: a in last trio: wknd over 2f out* **11/2**

2m 18.92s (-2.98) **Going Correction** +0.05s/f (Slow)
WFA 3 from 4yo+ 8lb **9 Ran SP% 134.6**
Speed ratings (Par 107): **112,111,111,110,109 109,109,102,101**
toteswingers: 1&2 £12.90, 1&3 £8.70, 2&3 £6.90 CSF £62.25 CT £250.98 TOTE £9.20: £3.00, £2.50, £1.80; EX 77.50.
Owner H R H Princess Haya Of Jordan **Bred** Highclere Stud **Trained** Newmarket, Suffolk

FOCUS
A valuable and decent quality handicap but mainly exposed types. The gallop only picked up passing the 3f pole and the winner was another to race in the centre. The runner-up looks a sound guide to the form.

NOTEBOOK
Charm School was starting to look disappointing, but stuck on surprisingly well after taking a good hold on only this second all-weather start and on his first run over this longer trip. A stronger gallop and more cover may have suited him and it will be interesting to see if this can be built on. (op 8-1 tchd 9-1)
Safari Sunup(IRE) had the run of the race and extended his run of creditable efforts. He should continue to give a good account on either this surface or on turf, but he's vulnerable to the more progressive or unexposed types from his current rating. (op 15-2)
William Blake, back up in trip and returned to Polytrack, has been running well in some competitive handicaps on turf and, although ridden with more patience from his wide draw than is normally the case, he showed he is equally effective on this surface. He can win again on this surface. (op 7-1)
Bugaku is a tricky ride and, although not beaten far, once again left the impression that a muddling event did not play to his strengths. He hasn't had much racing but will be worth another chance upped to 1m4f plus, especially in races where a decent gallop looks assured. (op 7-2 tchd 4-1)
Dr Livingstone(IRE) has still to show he's as good on Polytrack as on turf and again failed to reproduce his improved reappearance effort over 1m2f. He may be better over slightly shorter.
Jabal Tariq had run well at this course on his all-weather debut in June but, for the third successive time since, was below that level. He has something to prove at present. (op 8-1)
Sounds Of Jupiter(IRE) had been bossing lesser fields from the front on turf but, although he got a relatively easy lead, he proved a disappointment from this 11lb higher mark in this higher grade returned to Polytrack. (op 7-2 tchd 5-1)

5642 EVENTMASTERS.CO.UK BOOK CORPORATE HOSPITALITY AT TWICKENHAM H'CAP 2m (P)
9:20 (9:21) (Class 5) (0-70,70) 4-Y-0+ £2,590 (£770; £385; £192) **Stalls** High

Form RPR

00/5 **1** **Gandalf**[22] 4951 7-9-2 **65** .... HayleyTurner 3 77
(Miss Amy Weaver) *hld up in last pair and wl off the pce: stdy prog fr 4f out but stl plenty to do: wnt 2nd jst over 2f out: sn rdn: stl 4 l down 1f out: styd on relentlessly to ld last strides* **14/1**

4615 **2** *nk* **Jadalee (IRE)**[25] 4840 6-9-7 **70** ....(tp) DarryllHolland 4 82
(G A Butler) *led at gd pce: spreadeagled field fr 4f out: 6 l ahd 2f out: tired fnl f but kpt on gamely: hdd last strides* **7/1**[3]

4213 **3** 12 **Where's Susie**[22] 4948 4-9-2 **65** .... GeorgeBaker 6 63
(M Madgwick) *hld up in rr: plenty to do whn prog fr 4f out: rdn over 2f out: wnt 3rd wl over 1f out: no imp on ldng pair* **10/1**

1160 **4** 8 **Inchpast**[7] 5410 8-9-2 **70** ....(b) AshleyMorgan(5) 2 58
(M H Tompkins) *nvr gng that wl in last trio: reminder after 5f: u.p 4f out and sn lft wl bhd: plugged on past wkng rivals* **25/1**

5003 **5** 2 ¼ **Mista Rossa**[30] 4644 4-9-4 **67** ....(b) SteveDrowne 11 52
(H Morrison) *chsd ldrs: u.p to stay in tch 5f out: lft wl bhd fr over 3f out* **9/1**

-211 **6** ½ **Lady Hestia (USA)**[5] 5483 4-8-12 **61** 6ex .... MartinDwyer 13 46
(M P Tregoning) *chsd ldrs but nvr gng wl and often pushed along: rdn 5f out: sn chsd ldng pair: outpcd 3f out: wknd 2f out* **10/11**[1]

6203 **7** 2 ¾ **Warrior Conquest**[18] 5094 4-9-2 **65** ....(v[1]) JimCrowley 8 46
(W J Knight) *chsd ldr: outpcd over 3f out: lost 2nd and wknd rapidly jst over 2f out* **6/1**[2]

4020 **8** 34 **Colourful Move**[45] 4168 4-8-7 **56** .... RobertHavlin 1 —
(P G Murphy) *chsd ldng pair to 5f out: wknd over 3f out: t.o* **20/1**

00/ **9** 7 **Salt Lake (GER)**[20] 5054 7-8-13 **62** .... PatCosgrave 7 —
(John Joseph Murphy, Ire) *settled in midfield: rdn and struggling 4f out: sn wknd: t.o* **50/1**

-010 **10** 25 **Coda Agency**[58] 3737 6-9-2 **65** .... NCallan 12 —
(D W P Arbuthnot) *prom: rdn and wknd over 6f out: t.o fnl 3f* **8/1**

00-6 **11** 86 **Sir Jake**[30] 4670 5-8-2 **51** oh6 .... KirstyMilczarek 5 —
(T T Clement) *a last: wknd 6f out: sn wl t.o* **50/1**

3m 26.05s (-4.05) **Going Correction** +0.05s/f (Slow) **11 Ran SP% 128.6**
Speed ratings (Par 103): **112,111,105,101,100 100,99,82,78,66 23**
toteswingers: 1&2 £17.70, 1&3 £18.50, 2&3 £10.90 CSF £100.71 CT £1055.67 TOTE £16.10: £4.70, £2.60, £2.20; EX 109.30 Place 6: £59.16 Place 5: £34.53.
Colm White **Bred** Cheveley Park Stud Ltd **Trained** Newmarket, Suffolk

FOCUS
An ordinary handicap and one in which the gallop was soon steadied. The first two pulled well clear and, with the market leader disappointing, this did not take as much winning as seemed likely, with the form rated through the second. The winner edged towards the far rail in the closing stages.
Lady Hestia(USA) Official explanation: jockey said filly ran flat
Sir Jake Official explanation: jockey said horse was never travelling
T/Plt: £62.90 to a £1 stake. Pool: £76,525.33. 886.73 winning tickets. T/Qpdt: £7.90 to a £1 stake. Pool: £8,082.44. 755.06 winning tickets. JN

5578 LINGFIELD (L-H)
Friday, September 4

OFFICIAL GOING: Standard
This meeting featured the return to the saddle of Kieren Fallon, who had been banned from British racing since June 2006 and worldwide since October 2007.
Wind: fresh, half against Weather: overcast

5643 WITHYHAM MEDIAN AUCTION MAIDEN STKS 1m (P)
2:20 (2:21) (Class 6) 2-Y-O £2,729 (£806; £403) **Stalls** High

Form RPR

1 **Mr Mahoganeigh** 2-9-3 0 .... HayleyTurner 6 85+
(M L W Bell) *stdd after s: t.k.h: hld up in tch: hdwy on inner to trck ldrs over 2f out: rdn to ld ent fnl f: sn clr: pushed out: comf* **20/1**

42 **2** 2 ¼ **Rare Malt (IRE)**[16] 5165 2-8-12 0 .... KFallon 2 73
(Miss Amy Weaver) *t.k.h: sn chsng ldr: rdn to ld 2f out: edgd rt over 1f out: hdd ent fnl f: no ch w wnr after* **13/8**[1]

3 ½ **Gifted Apakay (USA)** 2-8-12 0 .... TPQueally 9 72
(E A L Dunlop) *hld up wl in tch: rdn and effrt wl over 1f out: chsd ldng pair 1f out: kpt on same pce fnl f* **20/1**

4 1 **Wajanaat** 2-8-12 0 .... RHills 8 70+
(M P Tregoning) *hld up in last trio on outer: hdwy and edging lft over 1f out: pushed along and kpt on steadily fnl f: nvr trbld ldrs* **13/8**[1]

6 **5** ¾ **Primrose Bankes**[8] 5371 2-8-9 0 .... JackDean(3) 5 68
(W G M Turner) *t.k.h: led at stdy pce: rdn over 2f out: hdd 2f out: wknd ent fnl f* **66/1**

6 3 **Favorite Woods** 2-9-3 0 .... LiamJones 3 67
(W J Haggas) *t.k.h: chsd ldrs: rdn and edgd rt wl over 1f out: sn outpcd and btn* **14/1**[3]

30 **7** 4 ½ **The Cardinal's Hat (FR)**[22] 4933 2-9-3 0 ....(t) JimCrowley 7 57
(P Winkworth) *t.k.h: rdn and struggling over 2f out: bhd fr over 1f out* **33/1**

4 **8** 4 **Taper Jean Girl (IRE)**[21] 4980 2-8-12 0 .... SebSanders 4 43
(M Botti) *plld hrd: hld up in tch in midfield: rdn over 2f out: sn struggling: wl bhd fr over 1f out* **6/1**[2]

9 4 ½ **High On A Hill (IRE)** 2-9-3 0 .... JimmyFortune 11 38
(S Kirk) *s.i.s: hld up in last trio: reminder over 4f out: lost tch over 3f out* **25/1**

10 2 ¾ **Edward Lear** 2-9-3 0 .... LPKeniry 10 32
(E F Vaughan) *stdd and dropped in bhd after s: t.k.h: struggling and rdn over 3f out: no ch fnl 2f* **33/1**

0 **11** 11 **Zeloca (IRE)**[26] 4825 2-8-12 0 ....(t) FergusSweeney 12 —
(Mrs L C Jewell) *t.k.h: hld up in midfield on outer: rdn and dropped to rr wl over 3f out: wl bhd fnl 2f* **150/1**

1m 38.47s (0.27) **Going Correction** -0.10s/f (Stan) **11 Ran SP% 118.5**
Speed ratings (Par 93): **94,91,91,90,89 86,82,78,73,70 59**
toteswingers: 1&2 £5.50, 1&3 £25.70, 2&3 £5.80 CSF £51.15 TOTE £23.00: £5.10, £1.10, £5.70; EX 71.30.
Owner Mrs Lucille Bone **Bred** Mrs Lucille Bone **Trained** Newmarket, Suffolk

FOCUS
A moderate maiden. The winner looks decent.

NOTEBOOK
Mr Mahoganeigh ◆ made a winning debut in the manner of an above-average colt. Having travelled ominously well throughout, he picked up readily in the straight, without coming under maximum pressure. A sizeable individual with loads of scope, this half-brother to Hameildaeme, who was Grade 2-placed over 1m in the US, accounted for a fair yardstick in Rare Malt and looks decent. (tchd 18-1)
Rare Malt(IRE) was the clear form pick but proved easy to back, mainly owing to sustained support for newcomer Wajanaat. Although a little free through the early stages after being rushed up from her inside stall (had been slowly away both previous starts), she had her chance but offered only the one pace for pressure. She edged towards the centre of the track in the straight, which is usually a good move at Lingfield, but quickly looked vulnerable to the winner, who was going the better of the pair turning in and nipped up the inner. She clearly has her limitations, but an ordinary race should come her way. (op Evens tchd 10-11 and 7-4)
Gifted Apakay(USA), a $75,000 half-sister to five winners, including top-class Argentinean 3yo Alexine, showed ability and is open to improvement. (op 16-1)
Wajanaat, out of a smart triple 1m winner, was the subject of a huge gamble but ran as though in need of the experience. After settling quite a way off the pace, she was outpaced turning into the straight and was never dangerous. There ought to be better to come. (op 4-1)
Primrose Bankes was able to set just a steady pace and showed improved form, but she was still comfortably held. (op 100-1)
Favorite Woods lacks size but should be better for this experience. (op 16-1)
Taper Jean Girl(IRE) was too keen and ran below the form she showed first time up over 7f at Kempton. (op 5-1 tchd 9-2 and 13-2)

5644 COLEMANS HATCH H'CAP (DIV I) 7f (P)
2:50 (2:53) (Class 6) (0-55,61) 3-Y-O £2,388 (£705; £352) **Stalls** Low

Form RPR

500 **1** **Artesium**[2] 5582 3-8-11 **52** .... SJCraine 6 59
(Patrick Morris) *hld up towards rr: hdwy over 2f out: rdn wl over 1f out: chal ins fnl f: led fnl 75yds: r.o wl* **16/1**

5205 **2** *nk* **Sermons Mount (USA)**[23] 4905 3-8-12 **53** .... NCallan 4 59
(Mouse Hamilton-Fairley) *chsd ldrs: rdn over 2f out: drvn to ld ent fnl f: edgd rt u.p: hdd and no ex fnl 75yds* **6/1**

651 **3** ¾ **Jonnie Skull (IRE)**[11] 5316 3-9-6 **61** 6ex ....(vt) TPQueally 11 65
(P S McEntee) *chsd ldrs: niggled along over 5f out: rdn to chse ldng pair over 2f out: drvn and kpt on same pce fnl f* **13/2**

0324 **4** 1 ¼ **Short Cut**[22] 4937 3-8-10 **51** ....(t) JamesDoyle 12 52
(S Kirk) *chsd ldrs: wnt 2nd over 3f out: rdn and ev ch 2f out: sn edgd rt u.p: one pce fnl f* **5/1**[3]

0004 **5** *nk* **Ridgeway Silver**[21] 4982 3-8-9 **50** ....(p) FergusSweeney 8 50
(M D I Usher) *in tch: rdn to chse ldng trio over 2f out: one pce u.p fnl f* **25/1**

0000 **6** 1 3/4 **Chasing Amy**[21] 4981 3-8-7 **48** .... JerryO'Dwyer 3 43
(M G Quinlan) *s.i.s: hld up bhd: hdwy 2f out: rdn over 1f out: kpt on but nvr able to chal ldrs* **50/1**
0000 **7** 1/2 **Zim Ho**[28] 4749 3-9-0 **55** .... DaneO'Neill 9 49
(J Akehurst) *led: rdn over 2f out: hdd ent fnl f: wknd fnl 150yds* **10/1**
00-0 **8** 3 1/2 **Yaldas Girl (USA)**[24] 4872 3-9-0 **55** .... SteveDrowne 5 39
(J R Best) *chsd ldr tl over 3f out: sn rdn and struggling: wknd 2f out* **50/1**
00-0 **9** 2 1/4 **Red Horse (IRE)**[17] 5121 3-8-9 **50** .... HayleyTurner 7 28
(M L W Bell) *in tch towards rr: reminder over 4f out: rdn and unable qck over 3f out: wknd wl over 1f out* **9/2**[2]
0000 **10** 3/4 **Iron Man Of Mersey (FR)**[48] 4079 3-8-11 **52** .... SebSanders 10 28
(A W Carroll) *s.i.s: t.k.h: hld up in last trio: rdn on outer over 2f out: n.d* **3/1**[1]
3400 **11** 12 **Elusive Ronnie (IRE)**[30] 4643 3-8-12 **53** .... (p) JimCrowley 1 —
(R A Teal) *s.i.s: a bhd: lost tch 3f out* **33/1**
5610 **12** hd **Eye For The Girls**[22] 4938 3-9-0 **55** .... DarryllHolland 14 —
(M R Channon) *s.i.s: sn in tch in midfield: nt handle bnd and lost pl bnd jst over 2f out: sn wl bhd* **10/1**
-050 **13** 4 1/2 **Sparkling Suzie**[11] 5316 3-9-0 **55** .... (b[1]) LPKeniry 13 —
(J S Moore) *s.i.s: in tch in midfield: rdn and struggling 4f out: wl bhd fnl 2f* **50/1**

1m 24.13s (-0.67) **Going Correction** -0.10s/f (Stan) **13** Ran SP% **124.2**
Speed ratings (Par 99): **99,98,97,96,96 94,93,89,86,86 72,72,66**
toteswingers: 1&2 £18.90, 1&3 £9.30, 2&3 £8.80 CSF £109.95 CT £726.49 TOTE £20.30: £4.70, £2.60, £3.10; EX 112.60.
Owner Rob Lloyd Racing Limited **Bred** Poulton Stud **Trained** Tarporley, Cheshire

FOCUS
A really moderate handicap - between them the front two were 0-23 coming into this. The time was quicker than for division two, though, and the race has been rated slightly on the positive side.
Eye For The Girls Official explanation: jockey said gelding did not face the kickback

5645 HOLTYE MEDIAN AUCTION MAIDEN STKS 5f (P)
3:20 (3:20) (Class 6) 3-5-Y-O **£2,729** (£806; £403) **Stalls** High

Form RPR
2040 **1** **Chantilly Jewel (USA)**[45] 4182 4-8-10 52 .... (b[1]) RichardMullen 2 56
(R M H Cowell) *broke wl but sn rdn along: chsd ldrs: chal over 1f out: rdn to ld 1f out: sn clr: r.o wl* **7/1**[3]
2243 **2** 2 1/4 **Avrilo**[7] 5383 3-8-9 55 .... NickyMackay 3 48
(M S Saunders) *chsd ldrs: rdn and effrt over 1f out: chsd wnr jst ins fnl f: r.o but no ch w wnr* **6/4**[1]
4000 **3** 2 3/4 **Spring Bridge (IRE)**[12] 5283 3-9-0 43 .... (tp) SteveDrowne 8 43
(Mrs L C Jewell) *dwlt: sn bustled along in tch on outer: drvn and edgd lft 1f out: wnt 3rd fnl 75yds: nvr able to threaten ldrs* **66/1**
62 **4** 3/4 **Roodee King**[65] 3498 3-9-0 0 .... KFallon 1 40
(Patrick Morris) *stdd after s: hld up in tch: pushed along over 2f out: swtchd rt and rdn over 1f out: plugged on same pce u.p fnl f* **2/1**[2]
006 **5** 3/4 **Chenin (IRE)**[18] 5105 3-8-9 40 .... LPKeniry 7 33
(Peter Grayson) *sn pressing ldr: led 3f out: rdn 2f out: hdd 1f out: wknd ins fnl f* **66/1**
0- **6** 1/2 **Anfield Star (IRE)**[320] 6846 3-9-0 59 .... SJCraine 4 36
(Patrick Morris) *sn outpcd in last pair: rdn over 2f out: edgd lft u.p wl over 1f out: sme late hdwy but n.d* **10/1**
005 **7** 1 **Little Lost (IRE)**[163] 955 3-8-9 46 .... (p) DarryllHolland 6 27
(Karen George) *led tl 3f out: wknd u.p over 1f out* **9/1**
8 23 **Riggs (IRE)** 3-9-0 0 .... AdamKirby 5 —
(Peter Grayson) *s.i.s: sn rdn and wl outpcd in last pl: t.o* **16/1**

58.53 secs (-0.27) **Going Correction** -0.10s/f (Stan)
WFA 3 from 4yo 1lb **8** Ran SP% **113.8**
Speed ratings (Par 101): **98,94,90,88,87 86,85,48**
toteswingers: 1&2 £3.70, 1&3 £19.10, 2&3 £29.50 CSF £17.77 TOTE £7.90: £1.80, £1.10, £7.40; EX 23.20.
Owner Bottisham Heath Stud **Bred** Two Sisters Stable **Trained** Six Mile Bottom, Cambs

FOCUS
A weak maiden. The winner did not have to improve to take this.

5646 BURSTOW H'CAP 6f (P)
3:50 (3:50) (Class 3) (0-95,92) 3-Y-0+ **£7,771** (£2,312; £1,155; £577) **Stalls** Low

Form RPR
031 **1** **Jaconet (USA)**[18] 5104 4-9-5 **91** .... (b) PhillipMakin 10 110
(T D Barron) *mde all: clr ent fnl 2f: in n.d after: rdn out* **8/1**
4111 **2** 5 **Street Power (USA)**[16] 5167 4-9-2 **88** .... SteveDrowne 2 91
(J R Gask) *s.i.s: sn pushed along and hdwy into midfield: rdn and hdwy wl over 1f out: chsd clr wnr ins fnl f: no imp* **11/10**[1]
5050 **3** nk **Dark Mischief**[36] 4459 3-9-1 **89** .... DaneO'Neill 7 91
(H Candy) *s.i.s: bhd: stl 11th and swtchd rt over 1f out: r.o fnl f to go 3rd nr fin: nvr nr ldrs* **6/1**[2]
3020 **4** nk **Viking Spirit**[25] 4853 7-9-4 **90** .... (t) AdamKirby 11 91
(W R Swinburn) *racd off the pce in midfield: rdn over 2f out: hdwy u.p over 1f out: wnt 3rd ins fnl f tl nr fin: nvr nr wnr* **25/1**
6030 **5** 2 1/4 **Diriculous**[21] 5001 5-9-6 **92** .... (b) KFallon 8 86
(T G Mills) *racd in last trio: pushed along wl over 3f out: rdn over 2f out: kpt on past btn horses fnl f: n.d* **7/1**[3]
66-0 **6** 1/2 **Frognal (IRE)**[20] 5032 3-9-0 **88** .... MartinDwyer 6 80
(B J Meehan) *in tch: rdn and effrt to chse ldrs 2f out: no ch w wnr fr over 1f out: one pce fnl f* **33/1**
2160 **7** nk **Baunagain (IRE)**[18] 5104 4-8-13 **85** .... JimmyFortune 4 76
(P W Chapple-Hyam) *chsd wnr over 4f out: rdn and outpcd jst over 2f out: wknd fnl f* **14/1**
6206 **8** 1 1/2 **Desert Icon (IRE)**[20] 5032 3-8-9 **83** .... JimCrowley 3 69
(W J Knight) *chsd wnr tl over 4f out: styd prom tl rdn and outpcd jst over 2f out: wknd over 1f out* **11/1**
0000 **9** 1/2 **Fault**[4] 5507 3-9-1 **89** .... (tp) TPQueally 9 74
(Stef Liddiard) *chsd ldrs: wd and rdn bnd jst over 2f out: sn wknd* **50/1**
2000 **10** 1 3/4 **Alfresco**[7] 5404 5-8-13 **85** .... (b) RobertWinston 5 64
(J R Best) *a towards rr: rdn and no rspnse over 2f out: nvr on terms* **20/1**
04-6 **11** 6 **Asaint Needs Brass (USA)**[15] 5197 3-8-6 **80** .... HayleyTurner 1 40
(J R Best) *racd off the pce in midfield: rdn and struggling over 2f out: no ch fnl 2f* **66/1**
0-20 **12** 5 **Sir Edwin Landseer (USA)**[20] 5031 9-8-13 **85** .... FergusSweeney 12 29
(G L Moore) *taken down early: awkward leaving stalls and sn dropped in bhd: a last: wl bhd fnl 2f* **40/1**

69.61 secs (-2.29) **Going Correction** -0.10s/f (Stan) course record
WFA 3 from 4yo+ 2lb **12** Ran SP% **118.0**
Speed ratings (Par 107): **111,104,103,103,100 99,99,97,96,94 86,79**
toteswingers: 1&2 £3.60, 1&3 £8.50, 2&3 £3.40 CSF £16.10 CT £60.95 TOTE £10.30: £2.70, £1.10, £2.00; EX 17.10.
Owner R G Toes **Bred** Team Block **Trained** Maunby, N Yorks

FOCUS
A good sprint handicap and the winner blew them away, confirming herself much better on Polytrack. Solid form.

NOTEBOOK
Jaconet(USA) produced a smart performance off a 5lb higher mark than when winning at Wolverhampton last time. After managing to gain a clear lead from stall ten, she set a strong gallop and sustained her run to the line, in the process equalling a track record previously set by Excusez Moi, when carrying 5lb less in a Listed race. She's in the Ayr Gold Cup, but while a 5lb penalty will see her only 1lb higher in that race, it remains to be seen whether she's quite as effective on turf, as well as on a straight course, and in any case she is no sure thing to make the cut. Whatever, though, she now 3-4 on Polytrack and looks an ideal type for decent prizes in the States, or Dubai. (op 7-1)
Street Power(USA) had won his last three starts, but although the last two in that sequence were over this trip, he's never really looked a sprinter. He remains progressive and should do even better in strongly run races over 7f and 1m. A trip to Dubai remains a real possibility. (op 5-4 tchd Evens and 11-8 in places)
Dark Mischief ◆ looked unlucky not to finish quite a bit closer. After starting slowly, he raced well out back for most of the way and was poorly placed, a long way behind the winner and wide, turning into the straight. He ultimately ran on well and could have more to offer. (op 7-1)
Viking Spirit stayed on steadily after being outpaced turning into the straight. He was reported to have bled from the nose last time, so this might have helped his confidence.
Diriculous received a bump approaching the first bend and was always struggling to lay up thereafter. He kept on steadily in the straight, but never threatened. (tchd 8-1)
Frognal(IRE) ran much better than on his belated reappearance and might be capable of more again next time.
Sir Edwin Landseer(USA) Official explanation: jockey said gelding moved poorly throughout

5647 COLEMANS HATCH H'CAP (DIV II) 7f (P)
4:20 (4:20) (Class 6) (0-55,55) 3-Y-0 **£2,388** (£705; £352) **Stalls** Low

Form RPR
-553 **1** **Fitz**[11] 5316 3-9-0 **55** .... LPKeniry 10 62+
(Matthew Salaman) *chsd ldrs: wnt 2nd over 2f out: rdn and clsd on ldr 2f out: led over 1f out: pressed fnl 50yds: hld on* **10/3**[1]
300 **2** nk **Ymir**[16] 5169 3-8-12 **53** .... (p) LiamJones 4 56
(M J Attwater) *sn bustled along: chsd ldrs: rdn and clsd 2f out: chsd wnr fnl 100yds: no ex nr fin* **7/1**
0046 **3** 1 1/2 **Winterfell**[39] 4389 3-8-11 **52** .... TedDurcan 3 51
(C F Wall) *in midfield on inner: rdn and edging rt bnd 2f out: drvn and hdwy ent fnl f: kpt on to go 3rd nr fin* **11/2**[2]
6602 **4** 3/4 **Come On Buckers (IRE)**[11] 5316 3-9-0 **55** .... (b) EdwardCreighton 2 52
(E J Creighton) *led and sn clr: c bk to field 2f out: rdn and hdd over 1f out: lost 3 pls fnl 100yds: fin 5th: plcd 4th* **6/1**[3]
050 **5** nk **Cake Stand**[85] 2863 3-9-0 **55** .... (v[1]) JimmyFortune 14 52
(J A R Toller) *chsd ldrs: clsd on clr ldr 2f out: drvn and chsd ldrs over 1f out: nt qckn and one pce fnl f: fin 6th: plcd 5th* **11/1**
0600 **6** nk **Commandingpresence (USA)**[105] 2220 3-8-2 **50** .... RyanClark[(7)] 11 46
(J J Bridger) *stdd s: hld up wl bhd: swtchd to inner and hdwy over 2f out: chsd ldrs and drvn ent fnl f: no imp fnl 100yds: fin 7th: plcd 6th* **40/1**
040 **7** 1/2 **Countrystyle Lass (IRE)**[25] 4854 3-8-9 **50** .... JimCrowley 12 43
(P Winkworth) *racd in midfield: hdwy to chse ldrs and rdn 2f out: wknd fnl f: fin 8th: plcd 7th* **10/1**
5000 **8** 1/2 **Nun Today (USA)**[4] 5503 3-8-11 **52** .... (v) TPO'Shea 9 45
(Karen George) *s.i.s: wl bhd: hdwy on outer 2f out: styd on fnl f: nvr trbld ldrs: fin 9th: plcd 8th* **18/1**
0000 **9** 1/2 **Love Allowed**[6] 5429 3-8-11 **55** .... MarcHalford[(3)] 8 47
(Jamie Poulton) *racd in midfield: rdn and effrt over 2f out: kpt on but nvr able to threaten ldrs: fin 10th: plcd 9th* **33/1**
0650 **10** 5 **More Tea Vicar (IRE)**[11] 5306 3-8-7 **48** .... (v[1]) RichardMullen 1 26
(Patrick Morris) *s.i.s: a wl bhd: fin 11th: plcd 10th* **40/1**
000 **11** 2 **Cardenio (USA)**[41] 4324 3-8-10 **51** .... SteveDrowne 6 24
(J R Gask) *sn pushed along in midfield: bhd and eased fnl 2f: fin 12th: plcd 11th* **12/1**
000- **12** 1 1/4 **Reel Hope**[380] 5184 3-8-11 **52** .... RobertWinston 7 21
(J R Best) *racd in midfield: rdn and struggling 3f out: wl bhd fnl 2f: fin 13th: plcd 12th* **20/1**
-565 **13** 61 **Lana's Charm**[62] 3625 3-8-11 **52** .... SebSanders 13 —
(P J Makin) *stdd s: t.k.h: hld up in midfield: lost pl and eased fr 2f out: virtually p.u fnl f: t.o: fin 14th: plcd 13th* **9/1**
-300 **D** 1/2 **Well Of Echoes**[14] 5229 3-9-0 **55** .... (t) JamesDoyle 5 53
(J A Glover) *chsd clr ldr tl over 2f out: stl handy and rdn 2f out: chsd ldrs 1f out: one pce fnl 100yds: fin 4th: disqualified - failed to weigh-in* **20/1**

1m 25.02s (0.22) **Going Correction** -0.10s/f (Stan) **14** Ran SP% **123.0**
Speed ratings (Par 99): **94,93,91,90,90 89,89,88,88,82 80,78,8,91**
toteswingers: 1&2 £9.80, 1&3 £5.90, 2&3 £13.10 CSF £24.95 CT £131.15 TOTE £3.20: £1.90, £2.30, £2.30; EX 32.80.
Owner Mrs Victoria Keen **Bred** Bearstone Stud **Trained** Upper Lambourn, Berks
■ A first winner for Matthew Salaman since taking over the licence from his father Taffy.
■ Stewards' Enquiry : James Doyle three-day ban: failed to weigh in (Sep 18-20)
Liam Jones one-day ban: careless riding (Sep 18)

FOCUS
A weak handicap. It was slower than division one and is not a race to be with.
Cardenio(USA) Official explanation: jockey said filly did not face the kickback
Lana's Charm Official explanation: jockey said filly lost its action

5648 FELBRIDGE H'CAP 1m 2f (P)
4:50 (4:50) (Class 3) (0-90,90) 3-Y-0 **£7,771** (£2,312; £1,155; £577) **Stalls** Low

Form RPR
1-1 **1** **Bab Al Salam (USA)**[14] 5221 3-9-0 **86** .... TedDurcan 3 93
(Saeed Bin Suroor) *chsd ldr: rdn to chal over 1f out: drvn to ld ins fnl f: styd on wl* **7/4**[1]
2303 **2** 1/2 **Mutamaashi**[49] 4058 3-9-2 **88** .... RHills 6 94+
(W J Haggas) *hld up in midfield: hdwy on inner 2f out: swtchd rt over 1f out: chsd ldng pair ent fnl f: r.o to go 2nd towards fin: clsng on wnr fin but nvr gng to get there* **85/40**[2]
2130 **3** 1/2 **Almuktahem**[14] 5209 3-8-11 **83** .... (v) TPO'Shea 2 88
(Sir Michael Stoute) *led: rdn over 2f out: drvn over 1f out: hdd ins fnl f: one pce after* **20/1**
2440 **4** 2 3/4 **Fullback (IRE)**[11] 5313 3-9-3 **89** .... LPKeniry 7 89
(J S Moore) *chsd ldng pair: rdn jst over 2f out: drvn ent fnl f: outpcd by ldrs fnl 100yds* **33/1**
0643 **5** 2 1/4 **Everynight (IRE)**[20] 5030 3-8-10 **82** .... DarryllHolland 1 77
(M Botti) *chsd ldng trio: rdn and unable qck jst over 2f out: wknd over 1f out* **8/1**[3]
1215 **6** 4 1/2 **Brett Vale (IRE)**[14] 5223 3-9-4 **90** .... SebSanders 9 76
(Sir Mark Prescott) *stdd and dropped in bhd after s: t.k.h: hld up in last pair: rdn and effrt over 2f out: hung lft and btn over 1f out* **12/1**

1104 **7** *shd* **Norwegian Dancer (UAE)**[14] 5209 3-9-1 **87** ChrisCatlin 5 73
(E S McMahon) *hld up in last pair: rdn and struggling over 2f out: no ch fnl 2f* **16/1**

120 **8** *1 1/2* **Satwa Gold (USA)**[30] 4649 3-8-10 **82** KFallon 4 65
(E A L Dunlop) *racd in midfield: pushed along over 3f out: struggling over 2f out: sn bhd* **12/1**

0313 **9** *nk* **Stan's Cool Cat (IRE)**[21] 5009 3-8-13 **85** MartinDwyer 8 67
(P F I Cole) *racd in last trio: dropped to last pl and rdn 3f out: no ch fnl 2f* **20/1**

2m 3.42s (-3.18) **Going Correction** -0.10s/f (Stan) 9 Ran SP% **113.2**
Speed ratings (Par 105): **108,107,107,105,103 99,99,98,98**
toteswingers: 1&2 £1.90, 1&3 £7.20, 2&3 £9.50 CSF £5.21 CT £48.52 TOTE £2.90: £1.20, £1.70, £4.70; EX 5.90.
Owner Godolphin **Bred** Darley **Trained** Newmarket, Suffolk

FOCUS
A fair handicap which was not strongly run, and in which it paid to race handy. The winner can do better and the runner-up might have won had things gone his way.

NOTEBOOK
Bab Al Salam(USA) was well placed throughout and did enough in the straight to defy a 5lb higher mark than when winning over 1m at Sandown on his reappearance, in the process maintaining his 100% record. He could keep progressing and his connections are no doubt keen to qualify him for Dubai Carnival handicaps - he'll probably need to get up to a rating of about 95 at least. (op 15-8 tchd 11-8 and 2-1 in places)
Mutamaashi ♦, just like at Newmarket last time, was waited with in a race in which it paid to race handy. He stayed on quite well and should find a similar event when things fall kindly. (op 9-4 tchd 11-4 and 3-1 in places)
Almuktahem ran quite well in third, but he was allowed a soft lead and might be flattered. (op 16-1)
Fullback(IRE), back up in trip, was nicely positioned for most of the way but simply wasn't good enough. (op 28-1)
Everynight(IRE) showed little on this first try on Polytrack. (op 15-2)
Brett Vale(IRE) might be worth another chance as he was given a lot to do and tried to make ground out wide. (op 14-1)

5649 HARTFIELD H'CAP — 1m 4f (P)
5:20 (5:20) (Class 4) (0-85,85) 3-Y-O+ **£5,828** (£1,734; £866; £432) **Stalls** Low

Form RPR

221 **1** **Brief Look**[18] 5093 3-8-13 **80** TPQueally 2 88+
(H R A Cecil) *chsd ldr: rdn to chal over 1f out: edging lft ent fnl f: led ins fnl f: rdn out* **4/5**[1]

2102 **2** *1* **Maslak (IRE)**[11] 5308 5-9-7 **79** ChrisCatlin 7 85
(P W Hiatt) *t.k.h: hld up in tch: rdn to chse ldng pair jst over 2f out: chsd wnr fnl 75yds: no imp towards fin* **33/1**

5060 **3** *nk* **Evident Pride (USA)**[15] 5190 6-9-13 **85** AdamKirby 5 91
(B R Johnson) *hld up in last trio: rdn and hdwy 2f out: swtchd rt jst over 1f out: drvn and r.o fnl f: nt pce to chal wnr* **20/1**

-231 **4** *1 1/4* **Putra One (IRE)**[64] 3538 3-9-0 **81** PhilipRobinson 1 85
(M A Jarvis) *led: rdn and pressed ent fnl 2f: hdd ins fnl f: btn fnl 100yds: wknd towards fin* **9/2**[2]

4000 **5** *2 1/4* **Mister New York (USA)**[49] 4060 4-9-8 **80** (b) GeorgeBaker 4 80
(Noel T Chance) *stdd s: hld up in last pair: rdn and unable qck over 2f out: kpt on fnl f: nvr able to threaten ldrs* **40/1**

1116 **6** *1 3/4* **Norman The Great**[20] 5028 5-9-7 **79** FergusSweeney 9 76
(A King) *in tch: rdn and edging lft 3f out: unable qck over 2f out: keeping on same pce and btn whn sltly hmpd over 1f out* **20/1**

122- **7** *3 1/4* **General Ting (IRE)**[386] 5017 4-9-2 **74** SebSanders 3 66
(Sir Mark Prescott) *stdd s: plld hrd: chsd ldrs after 2f out: wknd u.p 2f out* **9/2**[2]

2-33 **8** *31* **Kansai Spirit (IRE)**[32] 4606 3-8-13 **80** JimmyFortune 8 22
(J H M Gosden) *s.i.s: sn pushed along in rr: sme hdwy on outer 3f out: sn struggling: eased fr wl over 1f out: t.o* **9/1**[3]

2m 31.79s (-1.21) **Going Correction** -0.10s/f (Stan)
WFA 3 from 4yo+ 9lb 8 Ran SP% **116.8**
Speed ratings (Par 105): **100,99,99,98,96 95,93,72**
toteswingers: 1&2 £6.00, 1&3 £7.60, 2&3 £28.10 CSF £42.23 CT £336.22 TOTE £1.80: £1.10, £4.90, £4.00; EX 24.90.
Owner K Abdulla **Bred** Juddmonte Farms Ltd **Trained** Newmarket, Suffolk

FOCUS
A fair handicap, run at a steady pace. There is more to come from the winner and the form is rated around the first two.
Norman The Great Official explanation: jockey said gelding hung left
Kansai Spirit(IRE) Official explanation: vet said colt was found to be lame behind

5650 NUTLEY NURSERY — 5f (P)
5:50 (5:50) (Class 4) (0-85,83) 2-Y-O **£5,180** (£1,541; £770; £384) **Stalls** High

Form RPR

314 **1** **Secret Millionaire (IRE)**[5] 5467 2-9-5 **81** SJCraine 5 84
(Patrick Morris) *t.k.h: in tch: hdwy to chse ldng pair 3f out: rdn and edgd lft 1f out: led fnl 75yds: r.o wl* **9/2**[2]

5203 **2** *1/2* **Lucky Mellor**[24] 4868 2-8-9 **71** (b) ChrisCatlin 9 72
(D K Ivory) *sn pushed up to press ldr: ev ch and rdn over 1f out: led fnl 100yds: sn hdd and no ex* **14/1**

1021 **3** *1/2* **Six Diamonds**[15] 5194 2-9-3 **79** RobertWinston 4 78
(H Morrison) *led: rdn and hrd pressed over 1f out: hdd fnl 100yds: one pce after* **5/2**[1]

010 **4** *5* **Excelling (IRE)**[21] 4989 2-9-7 **83** JimmyFortune 8 64
(P J Makin) *s.i.s: pushed along and hdwy into midfield over 3f out: rdn and struggling 2f out: no ch after* **5/2**[1]

0126 **5** *1 1/2* **Six Wives**[5] 5467 2-9-2 **78** JamesDoyle 2 54
(J A Glover) *chsd ldng pair tl 3f out: struggling u.p ent fnl 2f: no ch w ldrs after* **11/1**

5021 **6** *4* **Nepotism**[69] 3385 2-8-11 **73** LPKeniry 6 35
(M S Saunders) *in tch in midfield: rdn whn rn wd and lost pl bnd jst over 2f out: no ch after* **8/1**[3]

604 **7** *1 3/4* **Dusty Spirit**[15] 5180 2-8-4 **66** LiamJones 3 21
(W G M Turner) *in tch in midfield tl dropped out in rr u.p 1/2-way: no ch fnl 2f* **20/1**

4336 **8** *nk* **Super Duplex**[48] 4081 2-8-10 **72** FergusSweeney 7 26
(P M Phelan) *s.i.s: a struggling in rr: no ch fnl 2f* **33/1**

0610 **9** *1 1/4* **Royal Blade (IRE)**[20] 5033 2-8-10 **72** RichardMullen 1 22
(A P Jarvis) *s.i.s: a bhd: no ch fnl 2f: eased ins fnl f* **33/1**

58.40 secs (-0.40) **Going Correction** -0.10s/f (Stan) 2y crse rec 9 Ran SP% **112.1**
Speed ratings (Par 97): **99,98,97,89,87 80,77,77,75**
toteswingers: 1&2 £13.20, 1&3 £3.30, 2&3 £10.10 CSF £60.14 CT £189.78 TOTE £5.20: £1.30, £4.00, £1.60; EX 75.00 Place 6: £33.17 Place 5: £14.79..
Rob Lloyd Racing Limited **Bred** James Delaney **Trained** Tarporley, Cheshire

FOCUS
A modest nursery. The first three came clear.

NOTEBOOK
Secret Millionaire(IRE) is very speedy and his connections felt he was found out by the stiff finish when trying to make all at Beverley five days earlier. Ridden more patiently this time, and switched to a quicker track, he was a little keen early but ultimately stayed on well. He may now be aimed at a Chester nursery on September 26. (tchd 5-1and 11-2 in places)
Lucky Mellor was unable to dominate but still ran an honest race. There should be more to come. (op 16-1)
Six Diamonds was hassled up front by the runner-up and couldn't defy an 8lb rise for her recent course-and-distance victory.
Excelling(IRE), who ran respectably in a Listed race last time, was trying Polytrack for the first time and never really travelled that well after starting slowly. (op 2-1)
Dusty Spirit Official explanation: jockey said colt was denied a clear run
Royal Blade(IRE) Official explanation: jockey said colt lost its action
T/Plt: £19.00 to a £1 stake. Pool: £66,167.46. 2,537.30 winning tickets. T/Qpdt: £3.50 to a £1 stake. Pool: £4,638.15. 957.68 winning tickets. SP

5585 BADEN-BADEN (L-H)
Friday, September 4

OFFICIAL GOING: Soft

5651a COOLMORE STUD - BADEN-BADEN CUP (LISTED RACE) (F&M) — 6f
2:05 (2:09) 3-Y-O+ **£11,650** (£4,854; £1,942; £971)

RPR

1 **La Sylvia (IRE)**[118] 1880 4-8-11 OPeslier 10 98
(E J O'Neill) *trckd ldrs: fnd an opening approaching fnl f: rdn to ld 120yds out: r.o strly* **164/10**

2 *1 3/4* **Bella Platina (GER)**[12] 5-9-2 ADeVries 3 97
(U Stoltefuss, Germany) **21/1**

3 *hd* **Pareia (GER)**[278] 5-8-11 RPiechulek 9 91
(Uwe Ostmann, Germany) **183/10**

4 *1 3/4* **Picobella (GER)**[76] 4-8-11 JBojko 12 86
(A Wohler, Germany) **14/1**

5 *1 3/4* **Maggi Fong**[31] 3-8-9 FVeron 4 80
(H-A Pantall, France) **59/10**[2]

6 *4* **Peace Camp (USA)**[31] 4637 3-9-2 JVictoire 5 74
(A Fabre, France) **9/10**[1]

7 *1/2* **Best Joking (GER)**[31] 4637 4-8-11 AHelfenbein 2 66
(W Hefter, Germany) **11/1**

8 *1 1/2* **Topkapi Diamond (IRE)**[12] 4-9-2 HGrewe 11 66
(E Kurdu, Germany) **92/10**

9 *10* **Airforce (GER)**[76] 3-9-2 ASuborics 1 36
(W Hickst, Germany) **71/10**[3]

10 *1 1/2* **Brass Damask (USA)**[40] 4-8-11 (b) AStarke 8 24
(P Schiergen, Germany) **22/1**

11 *6* **Harquahala (IRE)**[117] 3-8-9 (b) FilipMinarik 7 5
(P Schiergen, Germany) **15/1**

1m 12.2s (1.91)
WFA 3 from 4yo+ 2lb 11 Ran SP% **130.3**
(including ten euro stakes): WIN 174; PL 64, 54, 96; SF 3519.
Owner Frank Cosgrove **Bred** Mrs Brid Cosgrove **Trained** Southwell, Notts

NOTEBOOK
La Sylvia(IRE), formerly trained in Ireland and having her first start since the spring, handled the soft ground well to recod her first Listed success. She could be up to scoring in similar company back in Britain or France, where her trainer has been doing well this season.

5652a ZUKUNFTS-RENNEN (GROUP 3) — 7f
3:10 (3:16) 2-Y-O **£29,126** (£12,136; £4,854; £2,427)

RPR

1 **Hearts Of Fire**[19] 5085 2-9-2 OPeslier 1 112+
(Pat Eddery) *disp 3rd on ins: 4th st: led over 1f out: r.o strly* **7/10**[1]

2 *2* **Noble Alpha (IRE)**[19] 2-9-0 ASuborics 5 102
(Mario Hofer, Germany) *disp 3rd on outside tl moving up to press ldr 3f out: 2nd st: ev ch 1f out: kpt on same pce* **43/10**[2]

3 *1 3/4* **Eternal Power** 2-9-0 APietsch 3 98
(C Von Der Recke, Germany) *led: brought field over to stands' side ent st: hdd over 1f out: one pce fnl f* **115/10**

4 *1* **Zazou (GER)**[19] 2-9-0 AHelfenbein 7 95
(Mario Hofer, Germany) *racd in cl 5th to st: one pce fr over 1f out* **125/10**

5 *2* **Nicea (GER)** 2-8-11 AStarke 6 87
(P Schiergen, Germany) *racd in cl 5th to st: one pce fr wl over 1f out* **22/5**[3]

6 *9* **Shamalgan (FR)**[19] 2-9-0 THellier 2 68
(A Savujev, Czech Republic) *pulling early and restrained in rr: last st: sn btn* **17/1**

7 *3/4* **Paradise Rain**[40] 2-8-13 ADeVries 4 65
(Mario Hofer, Germany) *s.i.s: sn in tch and began pulling: 6th st: wknd wl over 1f out* **58/10**

1m 29.33s (5.43) 7 Ran SP% **131.9**
WIN 17; PL 11, 15, 19; SF 59.
Owner Pat Eddery Racing (Detroit) **Bred** Bearstone Stud **Trained** Nether Winchendon, Bucks

NOTEBOOK
Hearts Of Fire, who has found his stride again of late, followed up his clear-cut Listed success at Deauville by justifying odds-on favouritism in this slightly higher grade. There looks to be more to come in similar company.

5653 - (Foreign Racing) - See Raceform Interactive

4779 HAYDOCK (L-H)

Saturday, September 5

OFFICIAL GOING: 5f & 6f course good to soft; remainder - soft (heavy in places)

Rail realignment increased distances on round course by about 10yards. Inner sprint track in use.

Wind: Fresh, against Weather: Overcast

5654 BETFRED "THE BONUS KING" BE FRIENDLY H'CAP — 5f

1:55 (1:57) (Class 2) (0-100,100) 3-Y-O+

£18,693 (£5,598; £2,799; £1,401; £699; £351) Stalls Centre

Form				RPR
3050	1		**Cheveton**[21] 5039 5-8-9 **91** RobertWinston 1	101
			(R J Price) *in tch: effrt 2f out: r.o ins fnl f to ld towards fin* **16/1**	
1045	2	nk	**Arganil (USA)**[70] 3388 4-9-4 **100** NCallan 6	109
			(K A Ryan) *a.p: effrt over 1f out: led briefly wl ins fnl f: hld fnl strides* **15/2**	
630	3	1 1/4	**Strike Up The Band**[56] 3848 6-9-4 **100** AdrianTNicholls 7	104
			(D Nicholls) *led: rdn over 1f out: hdd wl ins fnl f: nt qckn towards fin* **25/1**	
300	4	1/2	**Tabaret**[18] 5132 6-8-6 **88** SPasquier 3	91
			(R M Whitaker) *in tch: effrt over 1f out to chse ldrs: r.o same pce towards fin* **33/1**	
1060	5	3/4	**Fathom Five (IRE)**[41] 4341 5-8-12 **94** AlanMunro 13	94
			(C F Wall) *prom: rdn and nt qckn over 1f out: kpt on but nt pce of ldrs ins fnl f* **16/1**	
0065	6	3/4	**Captain Dunne (IRE)**[18] 5132 4-9-0 **96** TedDurcan 5	93
			(T D Easterby) *in tch: rdn and nt qckn 2f out: kpt on one pce ins fnl f* **12/1**	
2500	7	nk	**Parisian Pyramid (IRE)**[15] 5206 3-8-11 **94** JoeFanning 16	90+
			(D Nicholls) *stdd s: in rr: rdn over 1f out: styd on ins fnl f: nvr able to rch ldrs* **18/1**	
0106	8	shd	**Sonny Red (IRE)**[18] 5132 5-9-4 **100** KFallon 10	96
			(D Nicholls) *sn pushed along in rr: swtchd lft and hdwy over 1f out: kpt on ins fnl f: nt pce to get competitive* **7/1**[3]	
1224	9	3/4	**Mattamia (IRE)**[16] 5203 3-8-9 **95** ow1 JamesMillman(3) 8	88
			(B R Millman) *midfield: pushed along over 2f out: no hdwy* **12/1**	
3226	10	1 1/2	**Hamish McGonagall**[7] 5420 4-9-4 **100** DavidAllan 4	88
			(T D Easterby) *prom: rdn 2f out: wknd over 1f out* **6/1**[2]	
1011	11	1/2	**Blue Jack**[14] 5263 4-9-3 **99** (b) MartinDwyer 11	85
			(W R Muir) *in rr: rdn over 1f out: styd on ins fnl f: nt pce to chal* **11/2**[1]	
560	12	2 1/2	**Equuleus Pictor**[37] 4461 5-8-4 **86** LiamJones 15	63
			(J L Spearing) *prom: rdn 2f out: hung lft over 1f out: sn wknd* **33/1**	
23	13	shd	**Northern Dare (IRE)**[14] 5263 5-8-11 **93** JimCrowley 12	70
			(D Nicholls) *midfield: pushed along over 2f out: sn outpcd and bhd* **7/1**[3]	
2201	14	3/4	**Bertoliver**[14] 5247 5-8-4 **86** RoystonFfrench 2	60
			(Tom Dascombe) *chsd ldrs: rdn 2f out: wknd over 1f out* **33/1**	
1146	15	nk	**Sudden Impact (IRE)**[5] 5529 4-8-9 **91** ow1 (e) TPQueally 14	64
			(Paul Green) *sn pushed along towards rr: nvr a danger* **18/1**	
400	16	1/2	**Zuzu (IRE)**[50] 4059 3-8-6 **89** (p) ChrisCatlin 17	60
			(M A Jarvis) *midfield: pushed along over 2f out: sn wknd* **20/1**	

61.11 secs (0.01) **Going Correction** +0.25s/f (Good)

WFA 3 from 4yo+ 1lb — **16** Ran SP% **121.5**

Speed ratings (Par 109): **109,108,106,105,104 103,102,102,101,99 98,94,94,92,92 91**

toteswingers: 1&2 £33.60, 1&3 £66.60, 2&3 £45.40 CSF £123.21 CT £2979.45 TOTE £21.00: £3.70, £2.30, £4.20, £7.30; EX 222.90 TRIFECTA Not won..

Owner Mrs K Oseman **Bred** Miss K Rausing **Trained** Ullingswick, H'fords

FOCUS

A typically highly competitive sprint handicap for the grade. Those drawn high struggled to make an impact and the main action developed on the far side. The winner is rated to his turf best, with the second carrying his AW form to here.

NOTEBOOK

Cheveton opened his account on turf this season at the ninth time of asking. He ran no sort of race in the Great St Wilfrid last time, but had won on his only previous start at this course and the ground was in his favour. His attitude under maximum pressure was spot-on and he was nicely on top at the finish, so his confidence ought to be boosted. He won at Southwell from a 2lb higher mark on his return this year and showed last season he can hold his form very well, so a repeat bid in the Portland this week looks on the cards.

Arganil(USA) ◆ looked like justifying market confidence passing the furlong pole. He just ran out of gas, but this was a lot more encouraging on his return to handicap company and he would have decent claims of reversing this form if also heading for the Portland. (op 9-1)

Strike Up The Band set out to make all, as he prefers, and turned in a brave effort. He is entitled to come on for the run and is a likeable sort, but is held by the handicapper. (op 22-1)

Tabaret was helped by his low draw and threw down a promising challenge on the far side, but was done with inside the final furlong. This was another solid display and he ran very close to his mark, so helps to set the level. (op 25-1)

Fathom Five(IRE) had his ground on this return from a 41-day break and his yard is on good form. He was never quite going the pace to mount a serious challenge, but ran well and can be found another winning turn before the season is out. (op 20-1)

Captain Dunne(IRE) was, surprisingly, ridden with more restraint and the change of tactics failed to work, but he was not disgraced. (op 11-1)

Parisian Pyramid(IRE) was doing his best work in the closing stages and ran a much better race, but the 3yo seems to be struggling with the handicapper. (op 25-1)

Sonny Red(IRE), well backed, got markedly outpaced before staying on with purpose in the final stages. He has developed into a tricky sort, but one of these races is within his compass when things fall right. Official explanation: jockey said gelding had no more to give (op 8-1)

Hamish McGonagall showed up well early on, but was cooked before the final furlong and disappointed, as this was the first occasion he had raced with some cut in the ground since he scored at Musselburgh last season. (tchd 7-1)

Blue Jack, 6lb higher, was never in the hunt from off the pace and failed to fire. He was not helped by racing on the near side, however, and is worth another chance. (op 5-1)

5655 BETFRED "SUPPORT THE HARLEY SLACK FUND" SUPERIOR MILE (LISTED RACE) — 1m 30y

2:25 (2:26) (Class 1) 3-Y-O+

£22,708 (£8,608; £4,308; £2,148; £1,076; £540) Stalls Low

Form				RPR
4221	1		**Confront**[15] 5232 4-9-5 116 SPasquier 1	116+
			(Sir Michael Stoute) *mde all: rdn 2f out: edgd lft ins fnl f: r.o wl and a looked in full control: pushed out towards fin* **7/2**[2]	
51	2	1 1/2	**Bushman**[35] 4543 5-9-2 102 JimCrowley 3	110
			(D M Simcock) *in tch: wnt 2nd 2f out: sn rdn whn trying to chal: nt pce of wnr ins fnl f* **11/2**[3]	
-534	3	1 3/4	**Derbaas (USA)**[58] 3783 3-8-11 104 RHills 4	105
			(E A L Dunlop) *chsd wnr tl rdn 2f out: styd on same pce after* **18/1**	
-630	4	hd	**Moyenne Corniche**[39] 4404 4-9-2 101 HayleyTurner 6	106
			(M L W Bell) *racd keenly in midfield: rdn and hdwy over 1f out: styd on ins fnl f: nt pce to chal ldrs* **22/1**	
-21	5	1 3/4	**Rock And Roll Kid (IRE)**[39] 4412 4-9-2 107 DEMullins 5	101
			(Anthony Mullins, Ire) *midfield: effrt and hdwy to chse ldrs 2f out: one pce ins fnl 100yds* **11/2**[3]	
5435	6	1/2	**Charlie Farnsbarns (IRE)**[70] 3404 5-9-2 112 MartinDwyer 8	100
			(B J Meehan) *hld up: pushed along 2f out: sme hdwy ent fnl f: nt pce to chal* **13/2**	
0500	7	nk	**Smokey Oakey (IRE)**[7] 5426 5-9-2 102 JimmyQuinn 9	100
			(M H Tompkins) *in rr: pushed along 2f out: nt clr run over 1f out: sn swtchd lft: kpt on but nvr able to land a blow* **12/1**	
0631	8	2 1/4	**Ordnance Row**[6] 5474 6-9-7 112 DaneO'Neill 10	99
			(R Hannon) *chsd ldrs: rdn over 2f out: wknd over 1f out* **9/1**	
00-0	9	2	**European Dream (IRE)**[140] 1352 6-9-2 93 (p) PAspell 2	90
			(R C Guest) *hld up: pushed along 2f out: nvr on terms* **80/1**	
203-	10	2 1/4	**Rio De La Plata (USA)**[419] 4010 4-9-2 116 TedDurcan 7	85
			(Saeed Bin Suroor) *sn chsd ldrs: rdn and wknd over 1f out: eased whn btn ins fnl f* **11/4**[1]	

1m 47.43s (3.63) **Going Correction** +0.675s/f (Yiel)

WFA 3 from 4yo+ 5lb — **10** Ran SP% **121.5**

Speed ratings (Par 111): **108,106,104,104,102 102,102,99,97,95**

toteswingers: 1&2 £5.40, 1&3 £10.30, 2&3 £16.90 CSF £24.37 TOTE £5.20: £2.30, £1.90, £4.50; EX 33.50 Trifecta £272.90 Pool: £514.33 - 1.40 winning units..

Owner K Abdulla **Bred** Juddmonte Farms Ltd **Trained** Newmarket, Suffolk

FOCUS

The runners in this came over to the stands' side in the home straight before ending up more towards the middle. There was a sound pace on and the form is decent for the class. The first three were always to the fore and winner did not need to match his best.

NOTEBOOK

Confront dead-heated at York 15 days earlier and followed up with a brave display. He set out at a decent enough tempo before getting in a breather turning into the home straight and led the field to the near side. He began to feel the pinch three furlongs out, but kept responding to his rider's urgings and it was clear at the furlong pole he was going to hang on. The winner relished the return to a stiffer test and confirmed his versatility as regards underfoot conditions. He also clearly enjoyed himself in his new front-running role, so a step back up to Group company would be well deserved and there could be more to come from him. Connections will have a look at the Group 1 Prix de la Foret, but also have something in mind for him at Longchamp on Arc weekend. (tchd 4-1)

Bushman ◆, who bounced back to winning ways in good fashion at Newmarket last month, confirmed he is in top form with a solid effort on ground that holds no fears. He rates the benchmark, is up to winning in this company and fully deserves to do so. (op 7-1)

Derbaas(USA), having his first run for 58 days, raced up with the pace and that put him at an advantage. This was a lot more like it from him, he showed no errant traits and is no doubt happier when the mud is flying. (op 20-1)

Moyenne Corniche got no sort of run when last seen at Goodwood 39 days earlier and showed that form to be all wrong with a solid effort. He fared best of those to come from behind and is in the right hands to end his losing sequence. (op 25-1 tchd 20-1)

Rock And Roll Kid(IRE) was making his British debut after running out a comfortable winner of the Galway Mile on his previous start. This was his stiffest task, but he had conditions to suit and came in for good support. He hit a flat spot down the home straight, having to race on the outside of the pack, but was getting back into things late on. The return to a stiffer track can help him find a race of this class. (op 7-1 tchd 9-2)

Charlie Farnsbarns(IRE), gelded since his last outing in June, enjoys this sort of ground and had claims on his best efforts. He was not helped by racing way off the pace, but did some fair late work and left the impression he will get closer next time. (tchd 7-1)

Smokey Oakey(IRE) Official explanation: jockey said gelding was denied a clear run

Ordnance Row was never a serious player after winning a Group 3 on quick ground at Goodwood six days earlier, having finished third in a Group 2 at the same course the previous day. He most likely found this coming too soon. (op 17-2 tchd 10-1)

Rio De La Plata(USA) was returning from a 419-day layoff, but his last six outings had come at the top level, so he had to be of interest in this line-up. The market suggested a big run was expected, but after looking a threat at the three-furlong pole, he went out like a light when push came to shove. It is possible the ground was against him and he is entitled to have needed the run, but he has a lot to prove all the same. Official explanation: jockey said colt had no more to give (op 3-1 tchd 4-1)

5656 BETFRED.COM OLD BOROUGH CUP (HERITAGE H'CAP) — 1m 6f

2:55 (2:55) (Class 2) (0-105,105) 3-Y-O £48,570 (£14,452; £7,222; £3,607) Stalls Low

Form				RPR
0423	1		**Yes Mr President (IRE)**[17] 5170 4-8-9 **90** JoeFanning 12	106+
			(M Johnston) *led for 1f: chsd ldr after: led 2f out: styd on wl to draw clr fnl f* **11/1**	
10	2	6	**Nemo Spirit (IRE)**[42] 4332 4-8-8 **89** MartinDwyer 17	96
			(W R Muir) *bustled along leaving stalls to go prom: led after 1f: racd alone on far side ent st over 4f out: hdd 2f out: kpt on u.p but wl hld by wnr ins fnl f* **11/1**	
1262	3	nk	**Alanbrooke**[15] 5230 3-8-4 **96** (b) RoystonFfrench 6	103
			(M Johnston) *dwlt: racd keenly in midfield: hdwy after 6f: rdn whn chsng ldrs over 2f out: styd on same pce fnl f* **11/2**[2]	
1421	4	3/4	**Kings Destiny**[49] 4103 3-8-6 **98** TedDurcan 2	104
			(M A Jarvis) *in tch: rdn over 2f out: kpt on same pce after* **5/1**[1]	
0250	5	1/2	**Clear Reef**[28] 4793 5-7-13 **80** oh1 ow1 (p) FrankieMcDonald 15	85
			(Jane Chapple-Hyam) *s.i.s: swtchd lft s: hld up: hdwy down centre of trck 2f out: sn chsd ldrs: one pce ins fnl f* **20/1**	
6140	6	1 3/4	**Spring Jim**[41] 4340 8-8-7 **88** HayleyTurner 16	91
			(J R Fanshawe) *hld up: rdn over 2f out: styd on fr 1f out: nvr able to chal ldrs* **14/1**	
00-4	7	nk	**Highland Legacy**[43] 4260 5-8-9 **90** (v[1]) NCallan 18	92
			(M L W Bell) *hld up: rdn and hdwy over 2f out: one pce fnl f* **12/1**	
6500	8	nk	**Hindu Kush (IRE)**[14] 5248 4-9-0 **95** JimCrowley 11	97
			(D Nicholls) *trckd ldrs: effrt on stands' side over 2f out: wknd over 1f out* **18/1**	
-515	9	nse	**Conquisto**[28] 4770 4-8-9 **90** TPQueally 9	92
			(C G Cox) *racd keenly: hld up: hdwy into midfield after 6f: effrt to chse ldrs over 2f out: wknd ins fnl f* **12/1**	
1013	10	3/4	**Hits Only Vic (USA)**[17] 5173 5-9-10 **105** DNolan 5	106
			(D Carroll) *hld up: rdn over 3f out: nvr able to chal* **11/2**[2]	
5230	11	13	**Magicalmysterytour (IRE)**[17] 5173 6-9-3 **98** ChrisCatlin 8	81
			(W J Musson) *midfield: rdn and wknd over 2f out* **8/1**[3]	
1121	12	13	**Lord Theo**[7] 5437 5-8-4 **85** RichardThomas 4	49
			(N P Littmoden) *midfield: lost pl 5f out: sn bhd and struggling* **25/1**	
5100	13	1 1/4	**Som Tala**[17] 5173 6-8-13 **94** KFallon 14	57
			(M R Channon) *in tch: pushed along 4f out: wknd 3f out* **14/1**	

00 **14** *43* **Macorville (USA)**[28] [4769] 6-8-13 **94**................................ DavidAllan 13 —
(G M Moore) *trckd ldrs: pushed along 4f out on stands' rail: wknd over 2f out: t.o* **33/1**

3m 10.36s (6.06) **Going Correction** +0.675s/f (Yiel)
WFA 3 from 4yo+ 11lb **14** Ran SP% **120.7**
Speed ratings (Par 109): **109,105,105,104,104 103,103,103,103,102 95,88,87,62**
toteswingers: 1&2 £17.00, 1&3 £19.50, 2&3 £9.60 CSF £124.16 CT £748.62 TOTE £11.70: £3.10, £3.50, £2.50; EX 112.40 Trifecta £766.80 Pool: £15026.56 -14.50 winning units..
Owner T J Monaghan **Bred** T J Monaghan **Trained** Middleham Moor, N Yorks

FOCUS
Traditionally a strong staying handicap. It was run at an ordinary pace, but it still paid to race handily with the first pair always 1-2. The winner impressed and the runner-up sets the level.

NOTEBOOK
Yes Mr President(IRE) came right away when asked for maximum effort and eventually won pretty much as he pleased. He had looked to be struggling with the handicapper, but this was the first time he had encountered such ground and it evidently proved right up his street. He has been most consistent this season and it was a much-deserved success. Just how he will cope after a likely hike from the handicapper remains to be seen, but he could still have improvement in him on this sort of ground and he fully deserves a shot at the Cesarewitch. He will look well in under a penalty in that. (op 12-1)
Nemo Spirit(IRE) had to be ridden from the gates to get to the lead, but did get pretty much his own way out in front. He found himself alone when keeping to the far side after turning for home and kept on resolutely. It rates a very pleasing effort from this dour stayer, on ground that suits, and he is another for whom the Cesarewitch with surely come into consideration. A return to further should only suit him. (tchd 12-1)
Alanbrooke, 3lb higher, was somewhat surprisingly taken back into midfield and was still taking a keen hold nearing the home turn. He gave his all down the home straight, handling the ground without much fuss and fared best of the 3yos. He has developed into a very likeable stayer and can reach greater heights next year (tchd 7-1)
Kings Destiny had been upped 8lb for his Ripon success 49 days earlier and was well backed for this step up in trip. He was never really a serious threat, but got the trip well enough and remains in good heart. (op 11-2)
Clear Reef, whose best previous effort came when winning earlier in the season on similar ground, was given a very patient ride. He deserves credit, as he was 1lb out of the handicap and stayed on stoutly.
Spring Jim was at a disadvantage in coming from out the back, so he deserves to be rated a touch better than the bare form, as he would also have enjoyed less demanding ground. (op 16-1)
Highland Legacy, equipped with a first-time visor, was making just his second appearance of the season and shaped as though he could come on again for the run. (tchd 10-1)
Conquisto didn't get a great passage through the early parts and was another not at an advantage in being held up right out the back. He again ran keenly under restraint, though, which wouldn't have helped his chance of getting home over the longer trip. Official explanation: jockey said gelding ran too free (op 14-1)
Hits Only Vic(USA) turned in a laboured effort, but was shouldering top weight and given a waiting ride. He still confirmed Ebor form with Magicalmysterytour, despite being 6lb worse off. Official explanation: trainer had no explanation for the poor form shown (tchd 6-1)
Lord Theo Official explanation: jockey said gelding was unsuited by the soft (heavy in places) ground

5657 BETFRED SPRINT CUP (GROUP 1) 6f
3:30 (3:31) (Class 1) 3-Y-O+

£163,809 (£62,095; £31,076; £15,495; £7,762; £3,895) **Stalls** Centre

Form RPR
0132 **1** **Regal Parade**[21] [5024] 5-9-3 109................................ AdrianTNicholls 13 121
(D Nicholls) *hld up: effrt and hdwy whn swtchd lft 2f out: chsd ldr over 1f out: r.o to ld fnl 100yds* **14/1**
4-21 **2** *½* **Fleeting Spirit (IRE)**[57] [3819] 4-9-0 121................................ TPQueally 12 116
(J Noseda) *trckd ldrs gng wl: led over 1f out: hdd fnl 100yds: sn edgd rt: hld fnl strides* **10/3**[1]
1111 **3** *2* **High Standing (USA)**[49] [4087] 4-9-3 113................................ KFallon 8 113
(W J Haggas) *hld up in midfield: hdwy over 1f out: chsd front pair ins fnl f but unable to land a serious blow* **4/1**[2]
-145 **4** *½* **Sayif (IRE)**[27] [4837] 3-9-1 111................................ NCallan 10 111
(P W Chapple-Hyam) *w ldr: rdn and nt qckn over 1f out: edgd lft ins fnl f: styd on but nt pce of ldrs towards fin* **28/1**
0000 **5** *2¼* **Equiano (FR)**[15] [5233] 4-9-3 108................................ OPeslier 5 104
(B W Hills) *led: rdn and hdd over 1f out: wknd ins fnl 150yds* **33/1**
4202 **6** *½* **Asset (IRE)**[6] [5474] 6-9-3 114................................(b) TedDurcan 4 103
(Saeed Bin Suroor) *hld up: edgd rt u.p over 1f out: styd on ins fnl f but nt pce to chal* **20/1**
54-5 **7** *½* **Corrybrough**[16] [5196] 4-9-3 110................................ DaneO'Neill 7 101
(H Candy) *s.i.s: hld up: swtchd lft and hdwy over 2f out: sn rdn to chse ldrs: one pce appr fnl f* **20/1**
3-01 **8** *1¾* **Finjaan**[39] [4406] 3-9-1 116................................ RHills 11 95
(M P Tregoning) *in tch: effrt to chal 2f out: wknd appr fnl f* **7/1**
0-40 **9** *nk* **Bushranger (IRE)**[77] [3140] 3-9-1 114................................ WMLordan 1 94
(David Wachman, Ire) *chsd ldrs: rdn over 2f out: wknd over 1f out* **28/1**
0502 **10** *½* **Judd Street**[16] [5196] 7-9-3 104................................(v) ShaneKelly 9 93
(Eve Johnson Houghton) *racd keenly: hld up: pushed along over 2f out: no imp* **100/1**
3-64 **11** *2* **Al Qasi (IRE)**[56] [3881] 6-9-3 108................................ GMosse 14 86
(P W Chapple-Hyam) *midfield: pushed along over 2f out: wknd over 1f out* **33/1**
0100 **12** *7* **Art Connoisseur (IRE)**[15] [5233] 3-9-1 119................................ HayleyTurner 6 64
(M L W Bell) *chsd ldrs: rdn 2f out: sn wknd* **33/1**
1420 **13** *9* **Main Aim**[39] [4406] 4-9-3 121................................ SPasquier 3 35
(Sir Michael Stoute) *midfield: pushed along and lost pl over 2f out: sn bmpd: eased whn wl btn over 1f out* **9/2**[3]
1430 **14** *7* **J J The Jet Plane (SAF)**[39] [4406] 5-9-3 119................................ JimCrowley 2 13
(R Hannon) *displayed gd spd tl rdn and wknd 3f out: bmpd over 2f out: eased whn wl btn over 1f out* **6/1**

1m 13.74s (-0.76) **Going Correction** +0.25s/f (Good)
WFA 3 from 4yo+ 2lb **14** Ran SP% **120.9**
Speed ratings (Par 117): **115,114,111,111,108 107,106,104,103,103 100,91,79,69**
toteswingers: 1&2 £10.90, 1&3 £10.50, 2&3 £3.90 CSF £55.35 CT £231.37 TOTE £16.90: £3.90, £1.40, £1.70; EX 69.10 Trifecta £589.30 Pool: £7167.61 - 9.00 winning units..
Owner Dab Hand Racing **Bred** Highclere Stud And Harry Herbert **Trained** Sessay, N Yorks
■ The first Group 1 win for Adrian Nicholls.
■ Stewards' Enquiry : Dane O'Neill one-day ban: careless riding (Sep 19)

FOCUS
This year's renewal looked up to par with five previous Group 1 winners in attendance and some improvers lurking. The field came more towards the stands' side and there was no obvious bias with the draw. It was a somewhat surprise result, though, and the form looks a touch suspect, but is best rated through the fourth/fifth. The winner is rated up 8lb.

NOTEBOOK
Regal Parade finished ninth in the Golden Jubilee at Royal Ascot on his only previous outing at this level and had been held in Group 2 events over 7f on his last two outings. He ran out a convincing winner, however, coming from near last to first and his stamina was a decisive tool. He produced a neat turn of foot when asked to pick up coming to two furlongs out and ended up making his challenge down the centre of the track. As the runner-up began to tire, the winner's stamina kicked in and he answered his rider's calls nearing the finish. While this may look a surprise result to some, many high-class handicappers have made the grade in this division and the winner's trainer has for years produced similar sorts to come up trumps in this company. This was also his first run on such ground since winning at Ayr last season and the surface no doubt had a notable bearing on the outcome. Where he goes from here is uncertain, but his consistency will stand him in good stead and a step back up to 7f could be on the cards. The Prix de la Foret at Longchamp next month looks a viable target. (op 16-1)
Fleeting Spirit(IRE) ◆, who missed the Nunthorpe after a setback, was bidding to become the first since Ajdal in 1987 to follow up success in the July Cup in this race. She had questions to answer on the softer ground, but had taken the Temple Stakes on her only previous outing at the course and was well backed. She moved sweetly through the race, tracking the early leaders, and looked to have done enough when quickening clear inside the final two furlongs. Her stride began to shorten in the final 100 yards, however, and she was mugged nearing the finish. It was the ground that most likely cost her, but she suffered an interrupted preparation and still comes out looking the most talented horse in the race. Another crack at the Prix de l'Abbaye back over 5f could well be on her agenda, plus there is another trip to the Breeders' Cup to consider. Wherever she turns up next, she will deserve the utmost respect. (op 4-1 tchd 3-1)
High Standing(USA) ◆ was only the eighth best horse in the field according to official ratings. However, he came into this debut at the top level unbeaten at the trip and, more importantly, unbeaten since joining his connections this year. His success in Group 3 company last time showed his ability to handle a soft surface and it was hard to know just how much improvement he had left in him. He again advertised his quirks at the start, but jumped off adequately and had his chance. He has found his right class, and with the likelihood of a return to better ground sure to suit, the Diadem back at Ascot this month is likely to be next for him. (tchd 9-2)
Sayif(IRE) was representing the Prix Maurice De Gheest form, in which he signalled a return to his best. He got a positive ride, but lacked a gear change when things got serious. He was keeping on inside the final furlong and helps to set the standard. (tchd 33-1)
Equiano(FR) fared best of those who took in the Nunthorpe last time and acquitted himself creditably on ground he had not encountered. He ran close enough to his July Cup form with the runner-up.
Asset(IRE) came from a long way back on this drop in trip and is a talented but tricky performer. (op 25-1)
Corrybrough showed the benefit of his comeback on Polytrack 16 days earlier. He would have enjoyed the ground, looked as though the run would be to his benefit and deserves a confidence booster back at a lower level. (op 16-1)
Finjaan showed his true colours when taking the Lennox Stakes at Goodwood last time and had finished in front of Regal Parade there. He displayed the natural speed required on this drop in trip, but the contrasting surface probably did for him. He is not one to write off in this division just yet.
Bushranger(IRE), with the visor left off, made laboured progress from off the pace, but was returning from a 77-day break and is entitled to come on for the run. The dual Group 1 winner as a juvenile has still to prove he has trained on this year, however. (op 25-1)
Judd Street failed to settle and found it all too hot. (op 80-1)
Al Qasi(IRE) made a sluggish start and was never going the pace, running well below par. (tchd 28-1)
Art Connoisseur(IRE) raced more handily than expected but was done with from halfway and looks a horse who needs plenty of time between his races in order to shine. (op 25-1)
Main Aim had decent claims on the form of his July Cup run behind Fleeting Spirit and had the ground in his favour. He ran no sort of race in the Lennox Stakes on his previous outing, though, and was again very disappointing. This effort leaves him with everything to prove. Official explanation: trainer had no explanation for the poor form shown (op 4-1 tchd 5-1 in places)
J J The Jet Plane(SAF) was having his first start since joining Richard Hannon and attracted support, despite also failing to run his race in the Lennox Stakes in July. He showed his customary early dash, but was cooked before halfway. He had won on soft in his native South Africa, but had probably never seen anything like this and it may well have been to blame. It could also be that he is feeling the effects of a long year, though. Official explanation: jockey said gelding was unsuited by the good to soft ground (op 10-1 tchd 11-1)

5658 BETFREDCASINO.COM NURSERY 6f
4:05 (4:06) (Class 2) 2-Y-O

£15,577 (£4,665; £2,332; £1,167; £582; £292) **Stalls** Centre

Form RPR
1210 **1** **Layla's Hero (IRE)**[16] [5198] 2-8-9 **83**................................ TPQueally 12 101+
(D Nicholls) *midfield: hdwy 3f out: led over 1f out: sn clr: wl in command fnl f* **14/1**
41 **2** *4½* **Yaa Wayl (IRE)**[43] [4282] 2-8-7 **81**................................(t) TedDurcan 9 86
(M A Jarvis) *s.i.s: hld up: hdwy into midfield 3f out: rdn and nt qckn over 2f out: styd on to take 2nd fnl 100yds: nt trble wnr* **6/1**[3]
221 **3** *1¼* **Dubai Set**[21] [5017] 2-8-9 **83** ow1................................ DaneO'Neill 7 84
(R Hannon) *chsd ldrs: rdn over 2f out: kpt on same pce fnl f* **16/1**
3111 **4** *1¼* **Bluie**[24] [4895] 2-8-6 **80**................................ AdrianTNicholls 11 77
(D Nicholls) *led: rdn over 2f out: hdd over 1f out: wknd fnl 100yds* **5/1**[2]
3154 **5** *1* **Pintura**[7] [5433] 2-7-13 **73**................................ CatherineGannon 6 67
(M R Channon) *midfield: pushed along over 2f out: stdy prog to chse ldrs over 1f out: one pce fnl f* **8/1**
111 **6** *½* **Kaptain Kirkup (IRE)**[36] [4493] 2-9-7 **95**................................ KFallon 13 88
(M Dods) *towards rr: hdwy into midfield 3f out: sn pushed along: edgd lft ins fnl f: no imp on ldrs* **9/2**[1]
1413 **7** *1¾* **Fleeting Echo**[35] [4539] 2-8-2 **76**................................ MartinDwyer 10 63
(R Hannon) *prom tl rdn and wknd over 1f out* **12/1**
521 **8** *1¼* **Tasmeem (IRE)**[14] [5253] 2-9-3 **91**................................ RHills 3 75
(B W Hills) *midfield: rdn 2f out: wknd over 1f out* **12/1**
2210 **9** *hd* **She's Ok (IRE)**[18] [5136] 2-8-5 **79**................................ HayleyTurner 4 62
(C E Brittain) *hld up: rdn over 2f out: nvr able to get to ldrs* **22/1**
1020 **10** *3¼* **Raddy 'Ell Pauline (IRE)**[16] [5199] 2-8-12 **86**................................ NCallan 1 63+
(K A Ryan) *chsd ldrs: rdn over 2f out: wknd and eased fnl f* **40/1**
0101 **11** *½* **Ginger Ted (IRE)**[25] [4884] 2-8-3 **77**................................ ChrisCatlin 14 49+
(R C Guest) *in rr: rdn over 2f out: nvr on terms w ldrs* **12/1**
210 **12** *1¼* **Sea Lord (IRE)**[18] [5133] 2-8-10 **84**................................ JoeFanning 15 52
(M Johnston) *in rr: rdn over 2f out: edgd lft over 1f out: nvr on terms* **8/1**
0166 **13** *1¼* **Jack My Boy (IRE)**[18] [5136] 2-8-6 **80**................................ PaulDoe 8 44
(P D Evans) *midfield: pushed along over 3f out: wknd over 1f out* **20/1**
41 **14** *2½* **Marcus Cicero (IRE)**[27] [4825] 2-8-9 **83**................................ JimCrowley 2 40
(P Winkworth) *hld up: rdn over 2f out: sn btn* **20/1**
3422 **15** *13* **Regardless**[29] [4739] 2-7-12 **72** oh4................................(v) JamieMackay 5 —
(Mrs G S Rees) *gd spd tl wknd over 3f out* **66/1**

1m 14.43s (-0.07) **Going Correction** +0.25s/f (Good) **15** Ran SP% **124.8**
Speed ratings (Par 101): **110,104,102,100,99 98,96,94,94,90 89,87,86,82,65**
toteswingers: 1&2 £28.00, 1&3 £40.80, 2&3 £23.70 CSF £92.87 CT £1396.32 TOTE £21.70: £5.20, £2.50, £5.60; EX 189.40.
Owner Dr Marwan Koukash **Bred** Epona Bloodstock Ltd **Trained** Sessay, N Yorks

FOCUS
A good nursery.

NOTEBOOK
Layla's Hero(IRE) bounced right back to form and ran out a clear-cut winner on this return to handicap company. He was 12lb higher than when winning on quick ground at Newcastle on his penultimate outing, but had showed he can go on soft when second to stablemate Bluie at Goodwood. He comprehensively reversed that form, despite making a tardy start and taking time to settle under restraint. The turn of foot he produced when asked for an effort was most taking and there was only going to be one outcome when he hit the front. A likely reaction from the handicapper will make things a lot tougher, but he is the sort his trainer tends to excel with and he could make up into a smart three-year-old. (op 16-1)
Yaa Wayl(IRE) ◆ran green when winning over the minimum at Thirsk when last seen in July and was equipped with a first-time tongue tie for this nursery debut. The step back up a furlong was only expected to suit, but he finished like a horse who is crying out for a stiffer test. This was an improvement and, in very good hands, he looks one to follow. (tchd 13-2)
Dubai Set deservedly opened his account at Lingfield last time, but looked on a stiff mark on this nursery debut and had contrasting ground to deal with. He ran a very solid race, making his effort on the far side, and has developed into a tough performer. He rates the benchmark. (tchd 12-1)
Bluie was another 7lb higher in this quest for the four-timer and, after showing up well through the early parts, the new mark found him out when things got serious. He remains in good form and is another who helps to set the standard. (op 7-1)
Pintura gave his all and most likely ran close to his recent level, but looked to need further. His turn may not be far off again when stepping back up in distance. (op 10-1 tchd 11-1)
Kaptain Kirkup(IRE) was 5lb higher than when winning one of these over course and distance on his previous outing. He lost out by getting outpaced around halfway, but finished with some purpose and looks ready to tackle another furlong. (tchd 4-1)
Sea Lord(IRE) Official explanation: jockey said colt was never travelling

5659 TEXT "BETFRED" TO 83080 FOR MOBILE BETTING STKS (REGISTERED AS THE ASCENDANT STAKES) (LISTED RACE) 1m 30y

4:35 (4:35) (Class 1) 2-Y-O

£19,869 (£7,532; £3,769; £1,879; £941; £472) **Stalls** Low

Form				RPR
412	**1**		**Emerald Commander (IRE)**[18] 5133 2-9-0 109 ... DaneO'Neill 1 (R Hannon) *trckd ldrs: led over 1f out: r.o wl and comf in command fnl f* **1/1**[1]	109+
411	**2**	*2 ½*	**Nideeb**[42] 4294 2-9-3 106 ... NCallan 2 (C E Brittain) *led for 1f: chsd ldr tl regained ld over 4f out: rdn and hdd over 1f out: nt pce of wnr fnl f* **9/2**[3]	104
2113	**3**	*1 ¾*	**Black Snowflake (USA)**[15] 5214 2-9-0 97 ... AhmedAjtebi 7 (Saeed Bin Suroor) *in tch: effrt to chal 2f out: hung lft fr over 1f out: one pce* **6/1**	97
3210	**4**	*1*	**Take It To The Max**[18] 5133 2-9-0 91 ... ChrisCatlin 3 (G M Moore) *hld up: niggled along fr 5f out: really u.p over 2f out: plugged on at one pce wout threatening fnl f* **33/1**	94
1	**5**	*shd*	**Syrian**[47] 4152 2-9-0 0 ... HayleyTurner 8 (M L W Bell) *racd keenly: led after 1f: hdd over 4f out: rdn 2f out: btn over 1f out* **3/1**[2]	94
0431	**6**	*4*	**Universal Circus**[37] 4451 2-8-9 79 ... TedDurcan 5 (M R Channon) *hld up: pushed along over 2f out: lft bhd fnl f* **28/1**	80

1m 48.99s (5.19) **Going Correction** +0.675s/f (Yiel) **6** Ran SP% **113.9**
Speed ratings (Par 103): **101,98,96,95,95 91**
toteswingers: 1&2 £2.20, 1&3 £2.00, 2&3 £2.50 CSF £6.19 TOTE £1.90: £1.40, £2.50; EX 4.10.
Owner W P Drew **Bred** Grangecon Stud **Trained** East Everleigh, Wilts

FOCUS
The form of this Listed event for juveniles looks straightforward.

NOTEBOOK
Emerald Commander(IRE) gained compensation for his narrow defeat in the Acomb Stakes 18 days earlier and did the job readily. The level of his Acomb form made him the one to beat and it is unlikely he had to improve a great deal to score. The step up a furlong proved to his liking, though, and he advertised his versatility as regards underfoot conditions. His dam won up to 1m2f, so he should have little trouble staying further next season and a step into Group company is expected to figure in his plans. The Champagne Stakes back over 7f will probably come a bit too soon, so the Royal Lodge at Ascot this month looks a good target. He would most likely bump into his Acomb conqueror, Elusive Pimpernel, there and it will be fascinating to see who comes out on top if the rematch happens. His connections were also not ruling out the Racing Post Trophy later on. (op 10-11 tchd 5-6 in places)
Nideeb is officially rated 3lb lower than the winner thanks to a last-gasp success at Ascot 42 days previously and was conceding a 3lb penalty, so he gives the form a solid look. Stepping up a furlong, he set out to make all but was unable to dominate as he would have liked. Once getting back in front down the home straight, he made the winner work, but was ultimately outstayed. He remains a nice prospect and could reoppose the winner in the Royal Lodge. Although he would have to improve to reverse this form, he would at least be back on level weights. (tchd 4-1 and 5-1)
Black Snowflake(USA), who won his maiden here, finished third in this class at Salisbury last time and, third best-in here at the weights, also gives the form a straightforward look. He travelled nicely until coming under pressure and could bag one of a similar race reverting to a sounder surface. (op 15-2 tchd 8-1 in places)
Take It To The Max was the first off the bridle, but kept gamely to his task. He finished out the back behind this winner on his previous start, but the softer ground suited much better and he is very useful in his own right. (tchd 25-1)
Syrian arrived for this big step up in class looking totally unexposed, having easily won a Yarmouth maiden 47 days previously. He was well backed, but ultimately spoilt his chances of staying the longer trip by refusing to settle and pulling his way into the lead through the early parts. He had no more to offer from two furlongs out, but it is hard to forget the manner in which he did the job when coming through rivals on his debut and it is unwise to be writing him off on the back of this display. (op 7-2 tchd 4-1)
Universal Circus finished third to Syrian before winning her maiden at Epsom and was always up against it from a mark of 79 in this company. A drop back in trip/class and return to better ground ought to help her find her feet.

5660 "TOP TEN BONUSES" AT BETFRED H'CAP 1m 6f

5:10 (5:10) (Class 3) (0-90,90) 3-Y-O **£9,714** (£2,890; £1,444; £721) **Stalls** Low

Form				RPR
4111	**1**		**Acquisition**[15] 5216 3-8-12 81 ... TPQueally 4 (H R A Cecil) *chsd ldr: rdn to ld over 1f out: styd on wl to draw clr ins fnl f* **2/1**[1]	91+
3212	**2**	*3*	**Omokoroa (IRE)**[44] 4229 3-8-8 77 ... NCallan 3 (M H Tompkins) *racd keenly: hld up: rdn over 2f out: hdwy over 1f out: wnt 2nd ins fnl f: nt trble wnr* **7/2**[3]	83
1214	**3**	*½*	**Sherman McCoy**[24] 4911 3-8-9 81 ow1 ... JamesMillman(3) 2 (B R Millman) *in tch: rdn over 3f out: outpcd over 2f out: sn swtchd lft: kpt on u.p ins fnl f: nvr a serious danger* **8/1**	86
4603	**4**	*½*	**Kudu Country (IRE)**[25] 4882 3-8-2 71 oh1 ... ChrisCatlin 6 (T P Tate) *led: rdn over 2f out: hdd over 1f out: no ex fnl f* **14/1**	75
3121	**5**	*4*	**Red Cadeaux**[35] 4518 3-9-7 90 ... KFallon 5 (E A L Dunlop) *strumbled on bnd after 2f: in rr: nvr travelled after: sme hdwy over 2f out to chse ldrs: wknd 1f out: eased whn btn fnl 75yds* **5/2**[2]	89
2022	**6**	*½*	**Interdiamonds**[13] 5291 3-8-6 75 ... JoeFanning 1 (M Johnston) *trckd ldrs: rdn 3f out: lost pl over 2f out: n.d after* **8/1**	73

3m 8.89s (4.59) **Going Correction** +0.675s/f (Yiel) **6** Ran SP% **113.0**
Speed ratings (Par 105): **113,111,111,110,108 108**
toteswingers: 1&2 £2.40, 1&3 £3.90, 2&3 £5.40 CSF £9.49 TOTE £2.70: £1.70, £2.10; EX 10.60 Place 6: £402.63 Place 5: £75.87.
Owner K Abdulla **Bred** Juddmonte Farms Ltd **Trained** Newmarket, Suffolk

FOCUS
A good 3yo staying handicap. The fourth looks the key to the form and the first three all progressed.

NOTEBOOK
Acquisition made it four wins from her last four outings and completed the task in game fashion. She was 4lb higher than when successful at Salisbury 15 days earlier, but still looked fairly treated and showed she is still very much on an upwards curve. Her pedigree gave hope for this longer trip, but she had yet to race on such a taxing surface. She saw it out stoutly, though, leading around two furlongs out and in no danger from the furlong marker. The handicapper will again have his say and she may benefit for a slight break after looking to endure a hard race. Connections will no doubt be going in search of the all-important black type before long. (op 9-4 tchd 7-4)
Omokoroa(IRE), 3lb higher, again had his chance and gives the form a sound look. He was another for whom the ground was unknown, but he handled it well enough and got the trip. It was more his reluctance to settle early on that hampered his chance and he will probably go up again after this. (op 5-1)
Sherman McCoy didn't help his cause by taking a keen hold through the early parts, but still came through to run his race. He too helps to set the level, having finished third over the trip off 1lb lower at Sandown last time, and should benefit for a return to less demanding ground. (op 7-1)
Kudu Country(IRE) attained a clear lead and set off at a sound pace, enjoying the ground. He was unable to go with the winner when headed, but kept to his task gamely and wasn't disgraced from 1lb out of the handicap. (op 11-1 tchd 16-1)
Red Cadeaux, who was 6lb higher than when winning at Doncaster last month, proved a nightmare for Fallon from the start. He was soon racing lazily and took a false step going into the first bend. He then lost ground and needed plenty of driving to keep tabs with the field. He did respond from the top of the home straight and momentarily looked a danger on the near side, but his stamina eventually gave way. A drop back to 1m4f should suit better again and he has the scope to improve as he matures, but his attitude is now under scrutiny. Official explanation: jockey said colt stumbled on the first bend and was never travelling thereafter (op 11-4)
Interdiamonds, 1lb higher, proved very easy to back and ran below form. That was very likely on account of the even more testing surface and a return to a sound surface should see her back in a much better light. (op 11-2)
T/Jkpt: Not won. T/Plt: £581.20 to a £1 stake. Pool: £156,328.42. 196.32 winning tickets. T/Qpdt: £23.20 to a £1 stake. Pool: £8,485.03. 269.50 winning tickets. DO

5635 KEMPTON (A.W) (R-H)

Saturday, September 5

OFFICIAL GOING: Standard
Wind: Fine Weather: Moderate, half against

5661 TOTEPOOL SIRENIA STKS (GROUP 3) 6f (P)

2:10 (2:11) (Class 1) 2-Y-O

£28,385 (£10,760; £5,385; £2,685; £1,345; £675) **Stalls** High

Form				RPR
163	**1**		**Love Lockdown (IRE)**[17] 5174 2-9-0 0 ... KLatham 7 (G M Lyons, Ire) *sn trckd ldr: shkn up 2f out: clsd to ld jst over 1f out: pushed out last 150yds* **7/2**[2]	109
3110	**2**	*1 ½*	**Iver Bridge Lad**[39] 4407 2-9-0 99 ... MichaelHills 3 (J Ryan) *sn led: rdn 2f out: hdd jst over 1f out: one pce after* **7/1**[3]	104
5113	**3**	*nk*	**Monsieur Chevalier (IRE)**[17] 5172 2-9-3 108 ... PatDobbs 8 (R Hannon) *hld up in 4th: pushed along over 2f out: effrt u.p over 1f out: tk 3rd nr fin: nt pce to chal* **13/8**[1]	106
242	**4**	*nk*	**In Some Respect (IRE)**[14] 5274 2-9-0 0 ... SebSanders 6 (Andrew Oliver, Ire) *s.i.s: t.k.h: hld up in last pair: pushed along over 2f out: sme prog over 1f out: disp 3rd ins fnl f: kpt on* **7/2**[2]	102
0443	**5**	*1*	**Red Avalanche (IRE)**[21] 5057 2-9-0 100 ... (t) GregFairley 5 (P F I Cole) *t.k.h: trckd ldng pair: rdn 2f out: fdd ins fnl f* **16/1**	99
2103	**6**	*1 ½*	**Chaperno (USA)**[27] 4826 2-9-0 94 ... LDettori 2 (Saeed Bin Suroor) *hld up in last: effrt on inner over 2f out: shkn up to dispute 3rd fnl f: hanging and fnd nil* **12/1**	95
3622	**7**	*2 ½*	**Angel's Pursuit (IRE)**[21] 5057 2-9-0 101 ... WilliamBuick 4 (R Hannon) *racd wd: in tch: rdn over 2f out: sn struggling* **16/1**	87

1m 12.96s (-0.14) **Going Correction** +0.025s/f (Slow) **7** Ran SP% **114.5**
Speed ratings (Par 105): **101,99,98,98,96 94,91**
toteswingers: 1&2 £6.60, 1&3 £2.00, 2&3 £1.90 CSF £27.77 TOTE £4.80: £3.10, £2.70; EX 30.80 Trifecta £208.10 Not won. Pool: £281.33 - 0.60 winning units..
Owner Sean Jones **Bred** Moyglare Stud Farm Ltd **Trained** Dunsany, Co. Meath

FOCUS
Probably the strongest running of this race since it was switched from turf, but the early gallop was no more than ordinary and nothing got into it from off the pace.

NOTEBOOK
Love Lockdown(IRE), one of two Irish raiders, had rattled up a hat-trick of wins over this distance earlier in the season before coming unstuck when upped in grade, but his latest effort, when third in a Listed race at York, had been over 5f and the return to his favourite trip was always going to suit. Soon ideally positioned tracking the leader, he was ridden to lead inside the final furlong and stayed on well for pressure, landing quite a gamble in the process. This son of Verglas is a likeable sort, with a long, flowing stride, and connections expect him to stay 7f. (op 15-2)
Iver Bridge Lad, a 5f Listed winner at Sandown earlier in the season, was never travelling behind the favourite at Goodwood in the Molecomb, but he found this less competitive and managed to bag the lead. He briefly looked the winner when kicking 2f out, but in the end couldn't stay on as strongly as Love Lockdown. (op 13-2)
Monsieur Chevalier(IRE), shouldering a 3lb penalty for his Molecomb victory, has already won six times this season and showed he had the stamina for this trip when a running-on third in the Group 2 Gimcrack at York last time. However, the steady early gallop was a problem for him that day, and it was once again his undoing here. A horse who tends to hit a flat spot, he came under the pump early in the straight and, despite sticking on right the way to the line, never looked like winning. He is undoubtedly at his best off a strong early pace, but is beginning to look a little exposed now. (op 5-4 tchd 7-4)
In Some Respect(IRE), though still a maiden, held strong claims on his efforts behind Alfred Nobel and Dick Turpin, but he wasn't the quickest away and had to come from further back than ideal. Like the favourite, he stayed on without threatening to win and connections will surely allow him to break his duck in a maiden sooner rather than later. (op 4-1)
Red Avalanche(IRE), fourth behind the favourite in the Super Sprint, needed to improve for the step back up to 6f and wasn't able to do so. (op 12-1)

Chaperno(USA), who disappointed in a first-time visor at Windsor last time, was going without the headgear on this occasion and he faded having found little when asked. He was reported to have hung right. Official explanation: jockey said colt hung right (tchd 10-1)
Angel's Pursuit(IRE), second in a Listed contest at Deauville last time, once again failed to reproduce his best of this 6f trip. (op 12-1)

5662 TOTESPORT.COM SEPTEMBER STKS (GROUP 3) 1m 4f (P)
2:40 (2:42) (Class 1) 3-Y-0+

£36,900 (£13,988; £7,000; £3,490; £1,748; £877) **Stalls** Centre

Form				RPR
4011	1		**Kirklees (IRE)**[42] 4329 5-9-9 117 LDettori 6 (Saeed Bin Suroor) *hld up towards rr: prog over 2f out: pushed firmly into ld over 1f out: reminder and wl in command fnl f: eased last strides* **7/4**[1]	121+
216	2	3/4	**All The Aces (IRE)**[58] 3781 4-9-4 115 PhilipRobinson 7 (M A Jarvis) *led: kicked on over 3f out: rdn and hdd over 1f out: styd on wl to pull clr of rest but readily hld by wnr* **9/4**[2]	113
0650	3	4 1/2	**Indian Days**[36] 4484 4-9-4 105 SteveDrowne 4 (J G Given) *sn trckd ldrs on outer: rdn to dispute 2nd over 2f out: nt qckn over 1f out: hld on for 3rd but lost further grnd on ldng pair fnl f* **40/1**	105
000/	4	nk	**Sky Crusader**[14] 7-9-4 0 IMendizabal 9 (M Nigge, France) *hld up in last: wdst of all bnd 3f out: prog over 2f out: nt qckn over 1f out: pressed for 3rd nr fin but no threat* **33/1**	105
24-	5	1 1/4	**Inventor (IRE)**[329] 6646 4-9-4 98 TPO'Shea 10 (B J Meehan) *awkward s: sn trckd ldng pair: effrt on inner over 2f out: nt qckn wl over 1f out: fdd* **33/1**	103
6566	6	3/4	**Heliodor (USA)**[39] 4405 3-8-9 104 PatDobbs 2 (R Hannon) *hld up towards rr: rdn 3f out: sn outpcd: n.d after: plugged on* **100/1**	102
-030	7	shd	**King Of Rome (IRE)**[161] 1012 4-9-4 0 PatCosgrave 5 (M F De Kock, South Africa) *hld up towards rr: rdn and nt qckn 2f out: tried to cl over 1f out: fdd ins fnl f* **11/1**	102
0000	8	32	**Kandidate**[18] 5137 7-9-4 106 LPKeniry 1 (C E Brittain) *chsd ldr to 3f out: wknd rapidly: t.o* **22/1**	50
-500	P		**Muhannak (IRE)**[36] 4484 5-9-4 109 SebSanders 3 (R M Beckett) *reluctant to go to post: last whn ref to r bnd after 3f and p.u* **8/1**	—
6442	P		**Curtain Call (FR)**[20] 5076 4-9-7 114 WilliamBuick 8 (L M Cumani) *trckd ldrs: disputing 2nd and poised to chal whn struck into over 2f out: p.u: dead* **9/2**[3]	—

2m 31.19s (-3.31) **Going Correction** +0.025s/f (Slow)
WFA 3 from 4yo+ 9lb **10** Ran SP% **118.4**
Speed ratings (Par 113): **112,111,108,108,107 106,106,85,—,—**
toteswingers: 1&2 £2.10, 1&3 £22.00, 2&3 £19.50 CSF £5.65 TOTE £2.30: £1.10, £1.60, £7.60; EX 7.30 Trifecta £98.90 Pool: £414.66 - 3.10 winning units..
Owner Godolphin **Bred** Darley **Trained** Newmarket, Suffolk

FOCUS
They went just a steady early gallop for this Group 3 contest, which lacked strength-in-depth, and two of the 'big' three drew well clear. Kirkless was value for a bit extra and the form is sound enough.

NOTEBOOK
Kirklees(IRE) emerged victorious in a very decent time. Well beaten in the Dubai Sheema Classic on his one previous try at the distance, this classy sort has been in top form since returning to Britain and supplemented his ready Sandown Listed win with victory in a Group 2 contest at York, for which he acquired a 5lb penalty. Dettori would have been delighted to see them not going a thorough gallop, as he was able to put his superior speed to good use, and the pair quickened into the lead well over 1f out. The runner-up was coming back at him as they crossed the line, suggesting the result may have been different had it been a true test at the distance, but he clearly stays the trip and will now head to Australia, where he is in several races. The Caulfield Cup will be his initial aim, and if all goes well, he may end up taking his chance in the Melbourne Cup, but prospects of him staying the distance of that race are next to zero. (op 13-8 tchd 15-8 ina place)
All The Aces(IRE) ◆ would have pushed the winner even harder if he'd gone stronger early as the pair were really coming strong in the final 100 yards. An out-and-out galloper who could be forgiven his latest effort when hampered in the Princess Of Wales's Stakes at Newmarket, he tried to kick off the final bend, but couldn't match the winner for raw speed. Well clear of the remainder, this lightly-raced 4yo remains capable of better. (op 100-30 tchd 7-2)
Indian Days, ahead of the runner-up at Newmarket last time, hasn't won in well over a year, but he has been contesting decent Group contests virtually all season, running above himself on a few occasions, and he again ran well at long odds. He deserves to find a race again. (op 33-1)
Sky Crusader has developed into something of an AW specialist since leaving Britain and he has progressed again of late since going up to middle distances, winning on numerous occasions at Deauville. He had plenty to find with the best of these, but fared much better than his odds entitled him to, sticking on back in fourth. (tchd 40-1)
Inventor(IRE), a progressive handicapper last year returning from an 11-month absence, ran well to a point and it was understandable that he faded late on. He should improve quite a bit for this and can continue his progression back down in grade.
Heliodor(USA), the sole 3yo in the field, continues to struggle to make an impact at this sort of level and shall remain difficult to place. (op 66-1)
King Of Rome(IRE), a Group 2 winning 3yo when with Aidan O'Brien, isn't really progressing for Mike de Kock, though he was going with the usual tongue tie for this first run since finishing down the field in the Sheema Classic. (op 12-1)
Kandidate was reported to have lost a shoe. Official explanation: jockey said horse lost a front shoe (op 28-1 tchd 20-1)
Muhannak(IRE), who was reluctant to go to post, pulled himself up on the bend passed the stands and is clearly a horse to avoid at present. (tchd 5-1)
Curtain Call(FR), a dual Group winner who was a leading Derby fancy last season, broke down badly with over two to run and sadly had to be put down. (tchd 5-1)

5663 TOTESCOOP6 LONDON MILE H'CAP (SERIES FINAL) 1m (P)
3:10 (3:11) (Class 2) 3-Y-0+

£18,693 (£5,598; £2,799; £1,401; £699; £351) **Stalls** High

Form				RPR
5300	1		**Highly Regal (IRE)**[36] 4501 4-8-6 77 (b) LPKeniry 8 (R A Teal) *hld up bhd ldrs: prog over 2f out: rdn to ld 1f out: styd on wl* **33/1**	86
0040	2	1 1/2	**Tartan Gigha (IRE)**[14] 5249 4-9-5 90 GregFairley 10 (M Johnston) *trckd ldr: rdn to ld 2f out: hdd 1f out: kpt on but outpcd by wnr* **16/1**	96
1122	3	1 1/2	**Sequillo**[24] 4910 3-8-6 82 PatDobbs 5 (R Hannon) *hld up in last trio: rdn and sme prog 2f out: stl only 10th 1f out: styd on wl to take 3rd last strides* **20/1**	85+
0331	4	nk	**Fancy Footsteps (IRE)**[19] 5095 4-8-5 76 DavidProbert 13 (C G Cox) *prom: rdn to dispute 3rd fr over 1f out: kpt on same pce* **13/2**[3]	78
2/00	5	nk	**Apex**[57] 3801 8-7-8 70 AmyBaker(5) 7 (M Hill) *hld up in midfield: rdn and prog 2f out: disp 3rd ins fnl f: one pce last 100yds* **33/1**	71
235	6	shd	**Vainglory (USA)**[28] 4794 5-9-2 87 RichardMullen 11 (D M Simcock) *led: rdn and hdd 2f out: stl disputing 3rd wl ins fnl f: no ex* **9/1**	88
6000	7	nk	**Prince Of Thebes (IRE)**[5] 5511 8-7-13 77 (v[1]) KierenFox(7) 14 (M J Attwater) *a in midfield: rdn whn n.m.r briefly over 2f out: kpt on fr over 1f out: nrst fin* **50/1**	77
1220	8	nk	**Set The Trend**[37] 4455 3-9-10 100 WilliamBuick 15 (A M Balding) *towards rr on inner: rdn and prog against rail 2f out: nt qckn and no imp over 1f out* **11/4**[2]	100
1-11	9	hd	**Musleh (USA)**[22] 4983 3-9-1 91 LDettori 3 (Saeed Bin Suroor) *racd wdst of all in midfield: shkn up over 2f out: nt qckn and no real prog over 1f out: kpt on* **9/4**[1]	90+
0000	10	1 1/4	**Trafalgar Square**[6] 5473 7-8-8 79 KirstyMilczarek 6 (M J Attwater) *s.i.s: wl in rr: last pair on wd outside 2f out: kpt on after: n.d* **66/1**	75+
15-2	11	1	**Multakka (IRE)**[124] 1731 6-9-3 88 TPO'Shea 1 (M P Tregoning) *dropped in fr wdst draw and wl in rr: shkn up over 2f out: no rspnse and btn after* **15/2**	82
0300	12	3/4	**The Snatcher (IRE)**[23] 4954 6-8-11 82 SteveDrowne 12 (R Hannon) *mostly in midfield on inner: pushed along over 3f out: effrt u.p 2f out: wknd fnl f* **33/1**	74
6305	13	nk	**Tourist**[7] 5418 4-8-1 77 MartinLane(5) 4 (D Shaw) *prom: lost pl over 2f out: steadily wknd* **25/1**	69
0020	14	hd	**Green Agenda**[16] 5189 3-8-0 76 AndrewMullen 2 (M Johnston) *a in last trio: rdn and no prog over 2f out* **33/1**	67
010	15	1 3/4	**The Happy Hammer (IRE)**[21] 5030 3-7-12 74 oh11 AdrianMcCarthy 16 (E V Stanford) *chsd ldng pair: stl cl up 2f out: wknd over 1f out* **100/1**	61

1m 38.47s (-1.33) **Going Correction** +0.025s/f (Slow)
WFA 3 from 4yo+ 5lb **15** Ran SP% **123.2**
Speed ratings (Par 109): **107,105,104,103,103 103,103,102,102,101 100,99,99,99,97**
CSF £463.05 CT £10374.32 TOTE £54.90: £9.00, £4.00, £4.40; EX 393.00 TRIFECTA Not won..
Owner J Morton **Bred** Mervyn Stewkesbury **Trained** Ashtead, Surrey

FOCUS
The fourth running of this competitive handicap and for the third time it went to an outsider. They went a decent pace from the off and the front pair had it between them from over 1f out. The winner seemed to show surprise improvement but the form looks sound.

NOTEBOOK
Highly Regal(IRE), who had registered all bar one of his five previous wins over this C&D, scored from a mark of just 46 back in January, so has been most progressive, and following a couple of quiet runs on turf, he came right back to his best to continue that upward curve on the AW. He was always travelling well in behind the speed and picked up really strongly to get on top inside the final furlong. His form figures over the C&D now read - 51113131 - and he remains capable of better at this venue.
Tartan Gigha(IRE) has been a busy horse this year, winning three times, but he has been struggling of late off higher marks than this. Though still 2lb higher than when last winning, he took over early in the straight and kept on right the way to the line having been headed, but was always being held inside the final furlong. He has the Cambridgeshire as an option. (op 20-1)
Sequillo did best of those coming from off the pace and ran really well off his new 4lb higher mark. He has been racing over 1m2f and remains capable of better back at that distance. (op 14-1)
Fancy Footsteps(IRE), who won nicely at the course last time, performed almost as well in this stronger heat off a 7lb higher mark. (op 6-1)
Apex is back on a good mark and ran easily his best race since returning from injury. There is a small race in him on this evidence.
Vainglory(USA) did his best to dig in having been headed, but was swamped inside the final furlong. (op 12-1)
Prince Of Thebes(IRE)was a bit unlucky not to finish close, running on late having been short of room. (tchd 66-1)
Set The Trend was returning to a suitable C&D, having not stayed 1m2f last time, and he tried to close against the inside rail in the straight, but not got close enough to challenge. (op 4-1)
Musleh(USA) could never get a position from his low draw. Bidding to complete a hat-trick of C&D wins, he was up 6lb and found himself trapped widest of all, so perhaps it wasn't a big surprise after all that he didn't get himself involved in the finish. (op 2-1 tchd 11-4)
Multakka(IRE) was another who had his chance severely compromised by a low draw, having to be dropped right in at the back. (op 7-1 tchd 13-2)

5664 TOTESPORT 0800 221 221 CONDITIONS STKS (C&G) 7f (P)
3:45 (3:46) (Class 3) 2-Y-0 **£6,417** (£1,921; £960; £481; £239) **Stalls** High

Form				RPR
1	1		**Quadrille**[34] 4564 2-9-2 0 PatDobbs 3 (R Hannon) *w ldr 2f: trcking after: rdn to chal 2f out: sustained effrt fnl f to ld last strides* **11/10**[1]	95
1	2	hd	**Circumvent**[11] 5325 2-9-2 0 GregFairley 2 (P F I Cole) *mde most: definiate advantage after 2f: rdn and pressed 2f out: kpt on wl fnl f: hdd last strides* **12/1**	95
22	3	4	**Awesome Act (USA)**[8] 5400 2-8-12 0 LDettori 6 (J Noseda) *hld up in 4th: prog over 2f out: clsd on ldng pair over 1f out: effrt petered out fnl f* **11/8**[2]	81
5	4	5	**Gypsy Boy (USA)**[12] 5311 2-8-12 0 TPO'Shea 1 (R Curtis) *trckd ldng pair: rdn over 2f out: wknd over 1f out* **9/1**[3]	68
	5	nk	**On The Cusp (IRE)** 2-8-12 0 PhilipRobinson 5 (M A Jarvis) *stdd s: hld up in last: shkn up over 2f out: sn outpcd and btn* **20/1**	67

1m 26.53s (0.53) **Going Correction** +0.025s/f (Slow) **5** Ran SP% **112.2**
Speed ratings (Par 99): **97,96,92,86,86**
CSF £14.52 TOTE £2.10: £1.20, £4.60; EX 9.40.
Owner The Queen **Bred** The Queen **Trained** East Everleigh, Wilts

FOCUS
A fair conditions race and the front two pulled clear as they fought out a gripping finish.

NOTEBOOK
Quadrille, tidy winner of a 6f Newbury maiden on debut, is certainly bred to appreciate this stiffer test and he just got there, eventually wearing down the game runner-up. Highly regarded by connections, he is likely to have one more run this season before being put away. As for next term, he is fully expected to stay 1m2f. (op 6-4 tchd 13-8 in a place)
Circumvent, narrow winner of a 6f maiden at Southwell on debut, ensured it was a good test at the distance and looked to be repelling the winner for much of the final furlong, but in the end was just run out of it. This was a gallant and much improved effort from a fine, big horse, who his trainer said may have been left a touch short, as he has been hard to get fit on the artificial surface at home. It is reasonable to expect further progress and he may take his chance in the Horris Hill next. (op 10-1 tchd 14-1)
Awesome Act(USA) settled better than when narrowly denied at Newmarket last time, but having started to close inside the final quarter mile, he quickly emptied and ended up well held. (op 6-4 tchd 5-4)
Gypsy Boy(USA), fifth in a 6f maiden at the course on his recent debut, didn't get home over this extra furlong in a stronger contest. (op 15-2 tchd 11-1)

On The Cusp(IRE), who is in several sales races, is out of a mare related to Grandera and George Washington and he very much looked in need of the experience. (op 12-1)

5665 BET IN-PLAY AT TOTESPORT.COM H'CAP 7f (P)
4:20 (4:20) (Class 4) (0-85,85) 3-Y-0+ £4,727 (£1,406; £702; £351) Stalls High

Form RPR

1621 1 **The Scorching Wind (IRE)**[3] 5575 3-8-6 76 6ex.(t) WilliamCarson(3) 10 97+
(S C Williams) *mounted on crse: chsd clr ldr after 3f: clsd tl led over 1f out: sn wl clr* 7/2[2]

1336 2 2 1/4 **Mac's Power (IRE)**[19] 5092 3-8-9 76 (t) RichardMullen 15 88+
(P J O'Gorman) *hld up in rr: gng strly over 2f out: gd prog wl over 1f out: wnt 2nd last 150yds: sn clr of rest but no hope of catching wnr* 16/1

-250 3 3 1/2 **Wigram's Turn (USA)**[78] 3091 4-9-8 85 WilliamBuick 1 90
(A M Balding) *s.s: wl off the pce in last pair: drvn on wd outside wl over 2f out: prog over 1f out: r.o to take 3rd nr fin* 8/1

6410 4 1 **Audemar (IRE)**[7] 5432 3-8-12 79 LPKeniry 9 79+
(E F Vaughan) *settled midfield: effrt on inner over 2f out: prog over 1f out: styd on fnl f to chal for modest 3rd* 16/1

3034 5 nse **Feeling Fab (FR)**[15] 5206 3-9-4 85 J-PGuillambert 11 85
(M Johnston) *dwlt: t.k.h: hld up in rr: rdn over 2f out: hd high but kpt on fr over 1f out: nrst fin* 10/1

6640 6 1/2 **Lindoro**[23] 4954 4-9-8 85 (b[1]) AdamKirby 4 85
(W R Swinburn) *prom in chsng gp: wnt 3rd bhd clr ldrs over 2f out to jst over 1f out: fdd fnl f* 16/1

0500 7 1/2 **Hurricane Spirit (IRE)**[19] 5104 5-9-4 84 MarcHalford(3) 7 83
(J R Best) *sn wl in rr: rdn on outer wl over 2f out: kpt on fr over 1f out: n.d* 25/1

6030 8 1 1/2 **Ocean Legend (IRE)**[11] 5329 4-8-1 71 oh6 (v) TobyAtkinson(7) 6 66
(Miss J Feilden) *led: drew 5 l clr after 3f: hdd over 1f out: stl 3rd wl ins fnl f: wknd* 33/1

1003 9 1 1/2 **Mohtashem (IRE)**[20] 5070 3-9-4 85 (v[1]) TPO'Shea 12 74
(Sir Michael Stoute) *hld up wl in rr: effrt on inner over 2f out: no real prog over 1f out* 15/2[3]

21 10 1/2 **Dhaawiah (USA)**[16] 5193 3-9-1 82 LDettori 5 70
(Saeed Bin Suroor) *hld up in midfield: pushed along over 2f out: no real prog over 1f out: wknd fnl f* 9/4[1]

1600 11 2 1/4 **Aroundthebay**[19] 5104 3-9-3 84 SteveDrowne 14 65
(H J L Dunlop) *chsd ldrs: pushed along 1/2-way: wknd fr 2f out* 33/1

025- 12 29 **Prayer Boat (IRE)**[21] 5049 3-8-12 79 JerryO'Dwyer 8 —
(John Joseph Murphy, Ire) *chsd ldr 3f: wknd rapidly 2f out: eased: t.o* 66/1

35-6 13 7 **Ektimaal**[26] 4852 6-9-8 85 SebSanders 16 —
(E A L Dunlop) *dwlt: sn in midfield on inner: rdn over 2f out: wknd rapidly wl over 1f out: eased: t.o* 16/1

1m 24.5s (-1.50) **Going Correction** +0.025s/f (Slow)
WFA 3 from 4yo+ 4lb 13 Ran SP% 119.7
Speed ratings (Par 105): **109,106,102,101,101 100,100,98,96,96 93,60,52**
toteswingers: 1&2 £6.20, 1&3 £11.90, 2&3 £20.90 CSF £56.77 CT £442.15 TOTE £4.50: £1.90, £3.20, £3.00; EX 46.50.
Owner Chris Watkins And David N Reynolds **Bred** Mark Commins **Trained** Newmarket, Suffolk

FOCUS
A strong handicap run at a decent pace. It was turned into a rout by The Scorching Wind, who impressed and was value for extra.
Dhaawiah(USA) Official explanation: jockey said filly had no more to give

5666 TOTESPORT HOME OF POOL BETTING H'CAP 2m (P)
4:50 (4:50) (Class 4) (0-80,78) 3-Y-0 £4,727 (£1,406; £702; £351) Stalls High

Form RPR

0121 1 **The Last Don (IRE)**[35] 4545 3-9-6 77 TPO'Shea 7 93
(D R Lanigan) *mostly in 5th: pushed along fr 6f out: prog to chse ldng trio over 3f out: drvn to cl over 2f out: sustained effrt to ld jst ins fnl f: kpt on* 5/1[2]

5321 2 3/4 **Ermyn Lodge**[24] 4911 3-8-10 67 (v) FergusSweeney 4 81
(P M Phelan) *led: kicked on over 4f out: drvn and hdd jst ins fnl f: kpt on wl but a hld* 9/1

5321 3 4 **Crocus Rose**[15] 5217 3-8-13 70 SteveDrowne 3 79
(H J L Dunlop) *chsd ldr: rdn to chal over 2f out: stl cl enough over 1f out: wknd fnl f* 13/2

33-2 4 2 **Ascendant**[22] 4974 3-9-7 78 SebSanders 2 85
(Sir Mark Prescott) *trckd ldng trio: wnt 3rd 5f out: drvn to cl on ldng pair over 2f out: cl enough over 1f out: wknd fnl f* 5/2[1]

2012 5 3 1/2 **Teeky**[17] 5168 3-9-7 78 RichardMullen 6 80
(J H M Gosden) *hld up in abt 6th: rdn 4f out: lft bhd by ldrs fr 3f out: nvr on terms after* 6/1[3]

025 6 21 **Lady Rusty (IRE)**[17] 5168 3-8-13 70 LukeMorris 1 47
(P Winkworth) *hld up in last pair: rdn 4f out: wknd over 2f out: t.o* 16/1

002 7 38 **Danse On Wood**[45] 4205 3-9-1 72 LDettori 5 —
(J Noseda) *chsd ldng pair to 5f out: rdn 4f out: wknd over 3f out: virtually p.u over 2f out* 5/1[2]

0316 P **Harlestone Snake**[38] 4442 3-9-4 75 WilliamBuick 8 —
(J L Dunlop) *hmpd after 1f: hld up in last pair: trying to make prog whn broke down and p.u 3f out* 15/2

3m 29.1s (-1.00) **Going Correction** +0.025s/f (Slow) 8 Ran SP% 117.2
Speed ratings (Par 103): **103,102,100,99,97 87,68,—**
toteswingers: 1&2 £8.40, 1&3 £4.30, 2&3 £7.60 CSF £49.87 CT £297.80 TOTE £6.30: £1.90, £2.00, £2.70; EX 48.10.
Owner P Brosnan **Bred** Tally-Ho Stud **Trained** Newmarket, Suffolk
■ Stewards' Enquiry : Fergus Sweeney two-day ban: careless riding (Sep 19-20)

FOCUS
This was a fair staying handicap. The winner progressed again and was value for a little extra.
Danse On Wood Official explanation: jockey said colt did not stay the two miles of today's race

5667 BET TOTEPOOL AT TOTESPORT.COM H'CAP 1m 3f (P)
5:25 (5:25) (Class 4) (0-85,85) 3-Y-0+ £4,727 (£1,406; £702; £351) Stalls High

Form RPR

641 1 **Tinaar (USA)**[27] 4828 3-8-7 76 IMendizabal 10 86+
(G A Butler) *hld up in 6th: prog over 3f out: clsd on ldr fr 2f out: led 1f out: urged along and hld on wl* 4/1[1]

-030 2 3/4 **Overturn (IRE)**[57] 3797 5-9-10 85 AdamKirby 5 94
(W R Swinburn) *led at decent pce: rdn over 2f out: hdd 1f out: rallied wl but a hld* 9/1

/564 3 2 **Sharpazmax (IRE)**[83] 2945 5-9-4 79 SteveDrowne 2 84
(P J Makin) *chsd ldr 1f: sn in 4th: rdn over 3f out: nt qckn over 2f out: styd on again to take 3rd nr fin* 14/1

4043 4 1/2 **Worth A King'S**[15] 5216 3-8-4 73 (v[1]) WilliamBuick 6 78
(Sir Michael Stoute) *chsd ldng pair after 2f: rdn over 3f out: tried to cl on ldr u.p over 2f out: no ex fnl f* 4/1[1]

001 5 nk **Sweet Hollow**[17] 5168 3-8-6 75 (b) LukeMorris 7 79
(C G Cox) *hld up in 7th: rdn on outer over 3f out: no prog tl styd on fr over 1f out: nrst fin* 4/1[1]

3150 6 4 1/2 **King Supreme (IRE)**[31] 4644 4-9-2 77 PatDobbs 3 73
(R Hannon) *a abt same pl: rdn and nt qckn over 2f out: n.d fr over 1f out* 25/1

0021 7 hd **Balnagore**[31] 4644 5-9-2 77 RichardMullen 1 73
(J L Dunlop) *chsd ldr after 1f to over 2f out: wknd over 1f out* 15/2[3]

1160 8 hd **Sir Boss (IRE)**[21] 5034 4-9-5 80 LPKeniry 8 75
(D E Cantillon) *hld up in 8th: sme prog over 2f out but nt on terms: reminders jst over 1f out: wknd fnl f* 12/1

/506 9 1 **Farleigh House (USA)**[7] 5437 5-9-3 78 SebSanders 4 71
(Sir Mark Prescott) *t.k.h: hld up in last pair: shkn up and no prog wl over 2f out: no ch after* 5/1[2]

1145 10 18 **Dubai Storming**[137] 1431 3-8-10 79 DO'Donohoe 9 40
(E A L Dunlop) *dwlt: rousted along early: a last: wknd 3f out: t.o* 20/1

2m 19.29s (-2.61) **Going Correction** +0.025s/f (Slow)
WFA 3 from 4yo+ 8lb 10 Ran SP% 121.4
Speed ratings (Par 105): **110,109,108,107,107 104,104,103,103,90**
toteswingers: 1&2 £10.80, 1&3 £17.60, 2&3 £15.00 CSF £42.78 CT £470.69 TOTE £5.60: £1.90, £3.60, £4.70; EX 46.50 Place 6: £1948.91 Place 5: £592.50.
Owner Fawzi Abdulla Nass **Bred** Robert S Evans **Trained** Newmarket, Suffolk
■ The first winner in Britain for French champion Ioritz Mendizabal.

FOCUS
They went a good gallop throughout and the form is sound.
T/Plt: £2,218.10 to a £1 stake. Pool: £84,321.27. 27.75 winning tickets. T/Qpdt: £149.70 to a £1 stake. Pool: £5,201.84. 25.70 winning tickets. JN

5405 THIRSK (L-H)
Saturday, September 5

OFFICIAL GOING: Soft (8.3)
Wind: Light half behind Weather: Sunny periods

5668 COW HOUSE BANK MAIDEN AUCTION STKS 6f
2:00 (2:03) (Class 4) 2-Y-O £4,274 (£1,271; £635; £317) Stalls High

Form RPR

322 1 **Dance For Julie (IRE)**[39] 4398 2-8-3 77 PatrickDonaghy(5) 12 76+
(P C Haslam) *cl up: led 1/2-way: rdn clr wl over 1f out: styd on strly* 11/4[1]

0 2 1 3/4 **I'm Super Too (IRE)**[33] 4590 2-8-9 0 PJMcDonald 7 71
(G A Swinbank) *bhd: hdwy wl over 1f out: swtchd lft and rdn ent fnl f: styd on: nrst fin* 16/1

6642 3 1 1/2 **Royal Record**[21] 5036 2-7-13 70 ow2 AndrewHeffernan(7) 14 63
(M Brittain) *led: pushed along and hdd 1/2-way: rdn along 2f out: drvn and one pce appr fnl f* 11/4[1]

4 4 4 **Empressofboogie**[31] 4652 2-8-7 0 ow3 TonyHamilton 11 52+
(M Dods) *midfield: hdwy 1/2-way: rdn along to chse ldrs and edgd lft wl over 1f out: sn drvn and kpt on same pce appr fnl f* 12/1[2]

50 5 3/4 **Pavement Games**[9] 5360 2-8-4 0 FrancisNorton 15 47
(R C Guest) *towards rr: hdwy 1/2-way: chsd ldrs and swtchd lft wl over 1f out: sn rdn and no imp appr fnl f* 33/1

6 nk **Maragna (IRE)** 2-8-9 0 SilvestreDeSousa 5 51+
(Paul Green) *dwlt: hdwy and in tch 1/2-way: rdn to chse ldrs over 1f out: drvn and one pce appr fnl f* 22/1

7 3 1/4 **Silvermine Bay (IRE)** 2-8-3 0 ow4 MatthewDavies(5) 8 37+
(A P Jarvis) *chsd ldrs: rdn along wl over 2f out and grad wknd* 66/1

8 4 1/2 **Fourlanends** 2-8-13 0 DanielTudhope 1 32
(N Wilson) *wnt lft s: prom on wd outside: effrt and hanging lft over 2f out: sn rdn and wknd* 28/1

36 9 hd **Opus Dei**[78] 3113 2-8-10 0 FrederikTylicki(3) 10 31
(J A Glover) *sn pushed along in midfield: rdn 1/2-way: sn drvn and wknd* 11/4[1]

10 5 **Kintyre Bay** 2-8-9 0 PhillipMakin 2 12
(T D Barron) *wnt lft s: prom on outer: rdn along and edgd lft over 2f out: sn wknd* 25/1

11 hd **Besty** 2-8-13 0 TomEaves 3 16
(B Smart) *t.k.h: chsd ldrs: rdn along wl over 2f out and sn wknd* 14/1[3]

66 12 nk **Lucy Gliters**[10] 5337 2-8-1 0 DominicFox(3) 6 6
(T P Tate) *in tch: rdn along 1/2-way: sn wknd* 33/1

13 1 1/2 **Naughty Norris** 2-8-10 0 ow1 MickyFenton 9 7
(R Bastiman) *sn outpcd and a bhd* 33/1

0 14 3 3/4 **Thinking**[98] 2467 2-8-13 0 DuranFentiman 4 —
(T D Easterby) *chsd ldrs: rdn along wl over 2f out: sn drvn and wknd* 66/1

1m 14.78s (2.08) **Going Correction** +0.325s/f (Good) 14 Ran SP% 123.7
Speed ratings (Par 97): **99,96,94,89,88 87,83,77,77,70 70,70,68,63**
toteswinger: 1&2 £10.70, 1&3 £2.30, 2&3 £12.60. CSF £54.18 TOTE £3.50: £1.60, £3.30, £1.50; EX 49.10.
Owner Mark James **Bred** Lynn Lodge Stud **Trained** Middleham Moor, N Yorks

FOCUS
After a wet week the going was officially soft and this was confirmed by the riders in the opener. A modest maiden auction race.

NOTEBOOK
Dance For Julie(IRE), whose action suggested she would appreciate soft ground and, after taking charge, she soon put her seal on the race. Value for double the official margin, she might reappear under a penalty in the fillies-only nursery at Doncaster on Thursday. (op 5-2, tchd 3-1 in places)
I'm Super Too(IRE) ◆ is the one to take out of the race. He had shown little on his debut a month earlier but here, after missing a beat at the start, he stayed on in eyecatching fashion to take second spot inside the last furlong. An April foal, he will be suited by a stiffer test and looks a fair long-term prospect. (op 12-1)
Royal Record, having his fifth start, handled the ground and, rated 70, is the best guide to the value of the form. (op 11-2)
Empressofboogie, who wore a rope halter, stepped up on her initial effort and is another who will be suited by a stiffer test. (op 14-1)
Pavement Games, having her third start, was by no means knocked about and is now qualified for a nursery mark. Official explanation: jockey said, regarding the running and riding, his instructions were to do the best he could as the filly had run keenly last time. He added that the filly is small and weak and had no more to give. (op 28-1)
Maragna(IRE), who had two handlers in the paddock and was keen to post, showed ability on his debut from an outside draw. (op 25-1 tchd 20-1)

Opus Dei, disappointing on her second start, was reappearing after an 11-week break. She gave problems in the stalls and, soon struggling, hung right. She looks to be going the wrong way. (op 4-1)

5669 EUROPEAN BREEDERS' FUND MAIDEN STKS (DIV I) 7f
2:30 (2:32) (Class 4) 2-Y-O **£5,342** (£1,589; £794; £396) **Stalls** Low

Form RPR

00 **1** **Cracking Lass (IRE)**[15] 5234 2-8-9 0 FrederikTylicki(3) 12 68
(R A Fahey) *in tch on outer: hdwy to chse ldrs over 2f out: rdn to chal over 1f out: drvn and jinked rt wl ins fnl f: styd on u.p to ld nr fin* **18/1**

6 **2** *nk* **Quite Sparky**[26] 4847 2-9-3 0 MickyFenton 8 72
(T P Tate) *led: rdn along over 2f out: drvn over 1f out: kpt on gamely u.p tl hdd and no ex nr fin* **14/1**

23 **3** *3/4* **Happy Dubai (IRE)**[9] 5360 2-9-3 0 (t) TomEaves 13 70
(B Smart) *chsd ldr: effrt and cl up over 2f out: sn rdn: drvn and ev ch ent fnl f tl no ex fnl 50yds* **5/1**[2]

4 *7* **Antarctic Desert (IRE)** 2-9-3 0 PhillipMakin 3 53
(K A Ryan) *prom: rdn along over 2f out: drvn over 1f out and sn wknd* **12/1**[3]

0 **5** *2* **Lost In The Forest**[27] 4817 2-8-12 0 FrancisNorton 6 43
(A P Jarvis) *chsd ldrs: rdn along 3f out: drvn over 2f out and plugged on same pce* **80/1**

6 **6** *1/2* **North Shadow**[22] 4993 2-9-3 0 GrahamGibbons 5 46
(A D Brown) *t.k.h: in tch: effrt over 3f out: sn rdn along and n.d* **33/1**

2 **7** *1 1/4* **Colepeper**[17] 5157 2-9-3 0 AndrewElliott 9 43
(M Johnston) *dwlt and sn rdn along towards rr: hdwy into midfield over 3f out and sn rdn: drvn over 2f out and nvr nr ldrs* **4/7**[1]

8 *5* **Mr Mohican (IRE)** 2-9-3 0 SilvestreDeSousa 10 31
(Mrs A Duffield) *dwlt: a towards rr* **28/1**

0 **9** *3/4* **Bollin Andrew**[22] 4993 2-9-3 0 PaulHanagan 11 31+
(T D Easterby) *a towards rr* **66/1**

6 **10** *1* **Mr Prize Fighter**[22] 5006 2-9-3 0 DanielTudhope 7 26
(I W McInnes) *s.i.s: a in rr* **100/1**

64 **11** *1/2* **True Loves Kiss**[102] 2360 2-8-12 0 TonyHamilton 2 20
(J A Glover) *a towards rr* **16/1**

12 *17* **Dubara Reef (IRE)** 2-9-3 0 SamHitchcott 4 —
(Paul Green) *dwlt: a in rr* **20/1**

0 **13** *1 3/4* **Irish Eyes**[42] 4308 2-8-12 0 PatrickDonaghy(5) 1 —
(Jedd O'Keeffe) *chsd ldrs on inner: rdn along 1/2-way: sn wknd* **100/1**

1m 30.65s (3.45) **Going Correction** +0.50s/f (Yiel) **13 Ran SP% 121.7**
Speed ratings (Par 97): **100,99,98,90,88 87,86,80,79,78 78,58,56**
toteswinger: 1&2 £24.30, 1&3 £22.00, 2&3 £4.50. CSF £239.32 TOTE £24.20: £3.60, £3.00, £1.70; EX 847.50.
Owner Mel Roberts and Ms Nicola Meese **Bred** Thomas Doherty **Trained** Musley Bank, N Yorks

FOCUS
A modest maiden with very few getting into serious contention.

NOTEBOOK
Cracking Lass(IRE), described by her trainer as a 'timid filly', had lost ground at the start on her two previous runs. Out quickly this time, she travelled strongly but seemed to shy and duck right when asked to go and win her race just inside the last, but straightened, she stayed on to show ahead near the line. With her confidence boosted she seems likely to go down the nursery route. (op 16-1)
Quite Sparky had clearly learnt plenty first time. Soon showing the way, she dug deep only to miss out near the line. She deserves to find a race.
Happy Dubai(IRE), drawn widest of all, went right leaving the stalls. Wearing a tongue tie for the first time, she raced keenly but in the end was only just found wanting. (op 6-1 tchd 9-2)
Antarctic Desert(IRE), who has any amount of size and scope, ran a pleasing first race chasing the leaders until tiring coming to the final furlong. He will probably not be seen to best effect until next year.
Lost In The Forest showed a fraction more than on her debut without threatening.
North Shadow, very keen, took a bump exiting the back straight. (op 50-1 tchd 66-1)
Colepeper, who is not very big, missed a beat at the start and was always struggling. Runner-up on his debut at Hamilton, he must be better than he showed here. Official explanation: trainer had no explanation for the poor form shown (op 4-6)
Mr Mohican(IRE) was very green but showed limited promise staying on down the outside in the final 2f. (op 50-1)
Dubara Reef(IRE) Official explanation: jockey said colt was never travelling

5670 OLD BYLAND H'CAP 1m
3:05 (3:05) (Class 3) (0-95,94) 3-Y-O **£8,159** (£2,428; £1,213; £606) **Stalls** Low

Form RPR

4211 **1** **Tiger Reigns**[30] 4708 3-9-1 88 PhillipMakin 10 97
(M Dods) *trckd ldrs: wnt 2nd over 4f out: led over 3f out: shkn up over 2f out: edgd lft ins fnl f: jst hld on* **15/8**[1]

0430 **2** *nse* **Canwinn (IRE)**[20] 5070 3-8-9 82 (v) TonyCulhane 7 91
(M R Channon) *chsd ldrs: wnt 2nd over 2f out: hung rt over 1f out: swvd rt ins fnl f: hrd rdn and styd on wl towards fin: jst hld* **8/1**[3]

4611 **3** *2* **Off Chance**[14] 5258 3-8-12 85 DuranFentiman 1 89+
(T D Easterby) *hld up in rr: stdy hdwy over 2f out: kpt on same pce fnl f* **14/1**

4011 **4** *2 1/4* **Royal Defence (IRE)**[14] 5255 3-8-11 84 FrancisNorton 8 83
(D Nicholls) *chsd ldr: drvn 4f out: one pce fnl 2f* **14/1**

531 **5** *3 3/4* **Splinter Cell (USA)**[47] 4143 3-8-12 85 DarryllHolland 4 76
(M Botti) *mid-div: drvn 3f out: nvr rchd ldrs* **3/1**[2]

0-50 **6** *8* **Kings Troop**[15] 5221 3-8-6 79 SamHitchcott 9 51
(H R A Cecil) *mid-div: drvn over 3f out: lost pl over 1f out* **20/1**

142 **7** *1/2* **Paquerettza (FR)**[17] 5175 3-8-8 81 TonyHamilton 3 52
(D H Brown) *s.i.s: hdwy on wd outside over 2f out: lost pl over 1f out* **8/1**[3]

41 **8** *12* **Saturn Girl (IRE)**[75] 3221 3-8-5 78 GrahamGibbons 2 21
(S A Callaghan) *chsd ldrs: drvn over 3f out: wknd over 2f out: eased whn bhd* **9/1**

3321 **9** *1 3/4* **Island Chief**[61] 3684 3-8-3 76 (b) PaulHanagan 5 15
(K A Ryan) *led tl over 3f out: wknd over 2f out: eased whn bhd* **10/1**

1m 43.0s (2.90) **Going Correction** +0.50s/f (Yiel) **9 Ran SP% 119.2**
Speed ratings (Par 105): **105,104,102,100,96 88,88,76,74**
toteswinger: 1&2 £6.20, 1&3 £4.10, 2&3 £22.60. CSF £18.58 CT £169.98 TOTE £2.90: £1.20, £3.00, £3.40; EX 23.00.
Owner Joe Buzzeo **Bred** Richard Green And New England Stud **Trained** Denton, Co Durham
■ Stewards' Enquiry : Tony Culhane one-day ban: used whip with excessive frequency and without giving his mount time to respond (Sep 29)

FOCUS
After the withdrawal of Cambridgeshire fancy Invisible Man on account of the ground this turned into a competitive three-year-old handicap. The winner is rated as having run a personal best with the second setting the level.

NOTEBOOK
Tiger Reigns, highly progressive, being 20lb higher than his first handicap success at Newcastle in May and 4lb higher than his latest Haydock win, travelled strongly. Sent to the front once in line for home, he tended to idle and the post came just in time. He will not make the cut in the Cambridgeshire, but that race next year is his long-term target and, meanwhile, he will head to Ayr in two weeks' time. (op 9-4 tchd 7-4 and 5-2 in a place)
Canwinn(IRE), a confirmed soft-ground performer, had the visor back on. He took aim at the winner coming to the final quarter mile, but gave his rider problems coming off a straight line. With everything thrown at him inside the last, he just failed to get there. (op 9-1 tchd 10-1)
Off Chance, 6lb higher than Ripon, travelled strongly as usual. She moved up looking a possible threat to the winner, but on this soft ground she could not raise her game sufficiently. Another opportunity might well come her way. (op 12-1 tchd 11-1)
Royal Defence(IRE), winner of a maiden here and a handicap at Ripon from a 4lb lower mark since being gelded, gave a good account of himself on ground probably softer than he prefers. (tchd 12-1)
Splinter Cell(USA), raised 5lb for his narrow Beverley success, never really threatened. (op 9-2 tchd 5-1)
Kings Troop, on just his third outing this time, continues out of form. (op 16-1)
Saturn Girl(IRE) Official explanation: jockey said filly was unsuited by the soft ground
Island Chief, gelded after his wide-margin Musselburgh success, was back after a two-month break but racing from a 12lb higher mark. After making the running, he dropped right away and was eased. (op 8-1 tchd 11-1)

5671 WIN £100,000 WITH SOCCER SATURDAY SUPER6 STKS (H'CAP) (THE HAMBLETON CUP) 1m 4f
3:40 (3:40) (Class 4) (0-85,85) 3-Y-O+ **£6,864** (£2,042; £1,020; £509) **Stalls** Low

Form RPR

3032 **1** **Rangefinder**[27] 4815 5-9-10 84 DarrylHolland 13 95+
(L M Cumani) *trckd ldr: smooth hdwy to ld 5f out: rdn clr 2f out: drvn ent fnl f: kpt on wl* **7/2**[1]

3214 **2** *3/4* **Sanctuary**[39] 4401 3-8-8 77 TomEaves 14 87+
(B Smart) *hld up in tch: hdwy 3f out: rdn to chse ldrs 2f out: drvn to chse wnr ent fnl f and ch tl no imp towards fin* **7/1**[3]

3534 **3** *2 1/2* **Kingsdale Orion (IRE)**[10] 5334 5-8-9 74 LanceBetts(5) 9 80
(B Ellison) *hld up in rr: hdwy on wd outside wl over 2f out: rdn over 1f out: edgd lft ins fnl f and styd on wl: nrst fin* **8/1**

5123 **4** *3/4* **Demolition**[23] 4930 5-9-10 84 (p) DanielTudhope 12 89
(N Wilson) *in tch: hdwy 3f out: rdn to chse ldrs 2f out: drvn over 1f out: kpt on same pce ins fnl f* **10/1**

2005 **5** *3/4* **King Fingal (IRE)**[34] 4561 4-9-3 77 (t) GrahamGibbons 1 81
(J J Quinn) *prom: effrt to chse wnr over 2f out and sn rdn: drvn wl over 1f out and grad wknd* **7/1**[3]

0046 **6** *1* **Hurlingham**[23] 4930 5-8-7 74 JamesPSullivan(7) 8 76
(M W Easterby) *midfield: hdwy 3f out: rdn to chse ldrs over 2f out: drvn and kpt on same pce fr over 1f out* **14/1**

2252 **7** *1 1/4* **Shaloo Diamond**[10] 5334 4-9-11 85 TonyHamilton 10 85
(R M Whitaker) *hld up in tch: sltly outpcd and rdn along 3f out: drvn and hdwy 2f out: sn no imp* **9/2**[2]

2110 **8** *1 3/4* **Umverti**[31] 4658 4-8-12 72 SilvestreDeSousa 7 69
(N Bycroft) *led: pushed along and hdd 5f out: rdn over 3f out: drvn and rallied 2f out: wknd appr fnl f* **14/1**

5540 **9** *1/2* **Rosbay (IRE)**[10] 5334 5-9-4 78 DuranFentiman 6 74
(T D Easterby) *trckd ldrs: hdwy to chse wnr 3f out and sn rdn: drvn 2f out and sn wknd* **14/1**

330 **10** *1 1/2* **Persian Peril**[10] 5334 5-9-7 81 PJMcDonald 3 75
(G A Swinbank) *hld up: a in rr* **25/1**

0-00 **11** *1 1/2* **Rayhani (USA)**[36] 4510 6-9-11 85 FrancisNorton 11 77
(D Nicholls) *dwlt: hld up: a in rr* **33/1**

130- **12** *8* **Holiday Cocktail**[329] 6113 7-8-8 75 IJBrennan(7) 5 54
(J J Quinn) *a in rr: rdn along 4f out and sn bhd* **40/1**

066 **13** *5* **Spring Goddess (IRE)**[57] 3796 8-9-0 79 MatthewDavies(5) 4 50
(A P Jarvis) *midfield: hdwy on inner 3f out and sn rdn: drvn 2f out and sn wknd* **50/1**

-601 **14** *18* **Coeur De Lionne (IRE)**[35] 4544 5-9-5 79 PaulHanagan 2 21
(E A L Dunlop) *trckd ldrs on inner: hdwy 3f out: rdn over 2f out and sn wknd* **12/1**

2m 43.55s (7.35) **Going Correction** +0.50s/f (Yiel)
WFA 3 from 4yo+ 9lb **14 Ran SP% 124.5**
Speed ratings (Par 105): **95,94,92,92,91 91,90,89,88,87 86,81,78,66**
toteswinger: 1&2 £8.50, 1&3 £10.40, 2&3 £13.00. CSF £27.94 CT £191.78 TOTE £4.70: £2.10, £2.90, £2.90; EX 36.90 Trifecta £262.90 Part won. Pool: £355.40 - 0.30 winning units..
Owner Aston House Stud **Bred** Aston House Stud **Trained** Newmarket, Suffolk

FOCUS
A competitive 77-85 handicap run at a sound pace. The third looks the best guide to the form, rated to his recent best.
Rayhani(USA) Official explanation: jockey said gelding missed the break
Coeur De Lionne(IRE) Official explanation: jockey said gelding lost its action

5672 PERSONAL TOUCHES HAIR SALON H'CAP 1m
4:10 (4:11) (Class 5) (0-70,70) 3-Y-O **£4,274** (£1,271; £635; £317) **Stalls** Low

Form RPR

0055 **1** **Allformary**[31] 4658 3-8-13 65 TomEaves 3 71
(B Smart) *trckd ldrs: t.k.h: hung rt and led over 1f out: hld on towards fin* **12/1**

0020 **2** *1/2* **Sampower Rose (IRE)**[10] 5331 3-8-8 60 DarryllHolland 2 65
(D Carroll) *led: edgd rt and hdd over 1f out: rallied ins fnl f: kpt on wl towards fin: jst hld* **12/1**

2104 **3** *2 3/4* **Swiss Art (IRE)**[26] 4841 3-8-10 62 AndrewElliott 8 61
(Mrs R A Carr) *chsd ldrs: kpt on same pce appr fnl f* **10/1**

2232 **4** *3* **Northern Flyer (GER)**[13] 5295 3-8-6 65 IJBrennan(7) 11 57+
(J J Quinn) *in tch on outer: kpt on fnl 2f: nvr a threat* **3/1**[1]

2341 **5** *1* **Mohawk Ridge**[12] 5306 3-8-13 65 PhillipMakin 12 54+
(M Dods) *in rr: pushed along over 4f out: styd on fnl 2f: nvr nr ldrs* **10/3**[2]

4113 **6** *1 1/4* **Diamond Daisy (IRE)**[22] 4994 3-9-4 70 SilvestreDeSousa 4 56
(Mrs A Duffield) *sn chsng ldrs: effrt 3f out: one pce* **8/1**[3]

-000 **7** *2 1/4* **Mehendi (IRE)**[63] 3636 3-8-8 65 LanceBetts(5) 10 46
(B Ellison) *in rr: drvn over 4f out: sn lost pl: kpt on fnl f* **20/1**

5046 **8** *3/4* **Fernando Torres**[14] 5258 3-8-13 65 FrancisNorton 7 45
(D Nicholls) *trckd ldrs: t.k.h: wknd over 1f out* **14/1**

340 **9** *3 1/4* **Towthorpe**[14] 5259 3-8-8 67 JohnCavanagh(7) 9 39
(M Brittain) *mid-div: lost pl over 2f out* **40/1**

430 **10** *nk* **Dean Iarracht (IRE)**[10] 5331 3-8-10 62 (p) TonyHamilton 15 33
(M Dods) *w ldrs: lost pl over 1f out* **12/1**

-300 **11** *1 3/4* **Mister Fantastic**[10] 5335 3-9-1 67 PJMcDonald 5 34
(M Dods) *in rr: pushed along 4f out: nvr a factor* **33/1**

3025 12 2 3/4 **Red China Blues (USA)**[14] 5255 3-8-5 60 KellyHarrison(3) 1 21
(R E Barr) *s.i.s: sn drvn into midfield: lost pl over 1f out* 16/1
610 13 18 **Imperial House**[36] 4494 3-9-1 67 TonyCulhane 13 —
(M R Channon) *in rr: lost pl over 3f out: sn bhd and eased: t.o* 12/1
1m 44.86s (4.76) **Going Correction** +0.50s/f (Yiel) 13 Ran SP% 121.7
Speed ratings (Par 101): **96,95,92,89,88 87,85,84,81,80 79,76,58**
toteswinger: 1&2 £49.50, 1&3 £17.10, 2&3 £48.90. CSF £148.25 CT £1510.28 TOTE £12.10: £3.70, £4.50, £3.40; EX 133.90.
Owner Alan D Crombie **Bred** Ms R A Myatt **Trained** Hambleton, N Yorks
FOCUS
A modest 60-70 handicap run at a sound pace and it was very difficult to make ground from the back.

5673 WATERHOLMES H'CAP 1m
4:40 (4:40) (Class 5) (0-75,78) 4-Y-O+ **£4,274** (£1,271; £635; £317) **Stalls** Low

Form RPR
5210 1 **Ninth House (USA)**[7] 5441 7-8-8 65 (t) SilvestreDeSousa 8 79+
(Mrs R A Carr) *in tch: hdwy on inner over 3f out: effrt to chse ldr wl over 1f out: rdn to ld ins fnl f: r.o wl* 7/2[1]
3103 2 2 **Tom Tower (IRE)**[10] 5333 5-8-11 68 PJMcDonald 2 77
(A C Whillans) *chsd ldr: hdwy to ld over 2f out: rdn over 1f out: drvn and hdd ins fnl f: one pce* 8/1[3]
1430 3 3 1/2 **Timber Treasure (USA)**[8] 5409 5-8-13 70 FrancisNorton 15 71
(Paul Green) *in tch: hdwy 3f out: rdn to chse ldrs 2f out: drvn over 1f out and no imp* 12/1
0565 4 1/2 **Woodsley House (IRE)**[10] 5333 7-8-9 66 (p) RobertHavlin 10 66
(A G Foster) *in tch: hdwy to chse ldrs 1/2-way: rdn along 3f out: drvn 2f out: kpt on same pce* 20/1
6030 5 1 1/2 **Hartshead**[7] 5441 10-8-6 66 DominicFox(3) 6 63
(W Storey) *s.i.s and in rr: hdwy over 2f out: swtchd rt and rdn over 1f out: kpt on ins fnl f: nrst fin* 16/1
0 6 1/2 **Sarwin (USA)**[8] 5395 6-8-4 68 JoshuaCrane(7) 12 64
(G A Swinbank) *hld up: hdwy on bit over 2f out: shkn up over 1f out: one pce* 18/1
2554 7 1 **Commando Scott (IRE)**[26] 4859 8-8-10 70 NeilBrown(3) 7 63
(I W McInnes) *in tch on outer: rdn along wl over 2f out and sn btn* 12/1
2001 8 7 **Glenridding**[8] 5409 5-9-7 78 (p) MickyFenton 1 55
(J G Given) *led: rdn along 3f out: hdd over 2f out: sn wknd* 9/1
6230 9 3/4 **Very Well Red**[7] 5449 6-8-13 70 DarryllHolland 5 45
(P W Hiatt) *chsd ldrs on outer: rdn along 3f out: sn wknd* 10/1
62-0 10 hd **Desert Vision**[26] 4838 5-8-11 75 (t) JamesPSullivan(7) 3 50
(M W Easterby) *a towards rr* 20/1
006 11 1/2 **Blue Spinnaker (IRE)**[25] 4881 10-8-10 67 DaleGibson 14 41
(M W Easterby) *stdd and swtchd lft s: hld up: a in rr* 12/1
601 12 1 1/2 **Mozayada (USA)**[35] 4548 5-8-9 66 TonyHamilton 4 36
(M Brittain) *in tch: hdwy to chse ldng pair 1/2-way: rdn along wl over 2f out and sn wknd* 10/1
4114 13 20 **Focail Eile**[25] 4881 4-9-4 75 StephenDonohoe 11 —
(J Ryan) *in tch: pushed along 5f out: lost pl and rdn along in rr over 3f out: sn bhd* 4/1[2]
1m 43.01s (2.91) **Going Correction** +0.50s/f (Yiel) 13 Ran SP% 125.3
Speed ratings (Par 103): **105,103,99,99,97 97,96,89,88,88 87,86,66**
toteswinger: 1&2 £17.30, 1&3 £16.30, 2&3 £18.80. CSF £33.31 CT £320.31 TOTE £4.60: £1.90, £3.30, £4.40; EX 49.70.
Owner Michael Hill **Bred** Juddmonte Farms Inc **Trained** Huby, N Yorks
■ Stewards' Enquiry : Joshua Crane ten-day ban: in breach of Rule 158 (Sep 19-28)
FOCUS
A competitive 65-78 handicap run at a very strong pace. The winner is rated to his recent best and the form looks sound around this level.
Tom Tower(IRE) Official explanation: trainer said gelding was subsequently found to be lame
Sarwin(USA) Official explanation: jockey said, regarding the running and riding, that his instructions were to sit in from a wide draw and make a move from 4f out. The trainer stated that the jockey had not ridden to his instructions and he should have been closer turning into the home straight.
Focail Eile Official explanation: jockey said gelding was never travelling

5674 EUROPEAN BREEDERS' FUND MAIDEN STKS (DIV II) 7f
5:15 (5:15) (Class 4) 2-Y-O **£5,342** (£1,589; £794; £396) **Stalls** Low

Form RPR
1 **Layla's Dancer** 2-9-3 0 TonyHamilton 3 79+
(R A Fahey) *trckd ldrs: hdwy over 3f out: chsd ldr over 2f out: rdn to ld 1 1/2f out: kpt on wl u.p ins fnl f* 9/2[3]
6 2 1/2 **Music Maestro (IRE)**[35] 4524 2-9-3 0 DarryllHolland 9 74
(B W Hills) *hld up: hdwy over 3f out: rdn to chse ldrs 2f out: drvn and kpt on ins fnl f* 15/8[1]
3 hd **Scarboro Warning (IRE)** 2-9-3 0 LeeVickers 1 74
(J G Given) *led: pushed along 3f out: rdn and hung lft 2f out: sn hdd and drvn: rallied ins fnl f: kpt on towards fin* 28/1
4 1 3/4 **Ragetti (IRE)** 2-8-12 0 PhillipMakin 7 64+
(J Howard Johnson) *n.m.r sn after s and bhd: hdwy on outer 3f out: rdn to chse ldrs and hung bdly lft wl over 1f out: no ex ins fnl f* 16/1
0 5 8 **Ilkley**[4] 5547 2-8-5 0 JamesPSullivan(7) 10 44+
(M W Easterby) *in tch: hdwy to chse ldrs over 2f out: sn rdn and no imp* 66/1
6 1 1/2 **Pink Flames (IRE)** 2-8-12 0 MickyFenton 5 40
(T P Tate) *prom: rdn along over 3f out: sn drvn and wknd wl over 2f out* 5/1
7 1/2 **Fourth Generation (IRE)** 2-9-3 0 PJMcDonald 2 44
(G A Swinbank) *midfield: hdwy to chse ldrs 3f out: rdn over 2f out and sn wknd* 25/1
005 8 3/4 **Chandrayaan**[19] 5106 2-9-3 0 StephenDonohoe 8 42
(E A L Dunlop) *prom: rdn along over 3f out and sn wknd* 16/1
0 9 5 **Choc'A'Moca (IRE)**[143] 1277 2-9-0 0 NeilBrown(3) 6 30
(I W McInnes) *a towards rr* 66/1
2 10 1 1/4 **Jamarjo (IRE)**[50] 4062 2-9-3 0 PaulHanagan 4 27
(S Gollings) *chsd ldrs: rdn along over 3f out: sn wknd* 7/2[2]
0 11 1 **Nolecce**[98] 2467 2-9-3 0 TomEaves 11 24
(R C Guest) *a in rr* 100/1
00 12 3/4 **Fireflash (IRE)**[31] 4652 2-9-3 0 SilvestreDeSousa 12 22
(Mrs A Duffield) *racd wd: a in rr* 33/1
1m 31.63s (4.43) **Going Correction** +0.50s/f (Yiel) 12 Ran SP% 117.8
Speed ratings (Par 97): **94,93,93,91,82 80,79,78,73,71 70,69**
toteswinger: 1&2 £2.80, 1&3 £35.60, 2&3 £13.20. CSF £12.66 TOTE £7.20: £2.30, £1.10, £5.90; EX 16.20.
Owner Dr Marwan Koukash **Bred** Kevin Buckley **Trained** Musley Bank, N Yorks
FOCUS
Though the time was slower than division one, this was almost certainly the better division. Time may show it to be an above-average maiden.
NOTEBOOK
Layla's Dancer ◆, described by his trainer as a 'big, backward baby,' travelled strongly. He took an age to master the pacesetter Scarboro Warning then had to dig deep to keep the runner-up at bay near the line. His next outing depends on what nursery mark he is given, but he is clearly a youngster with a bright future. (op 4-1)
Music Maestro(IRE), who achieved a RPR of 69 when sixth first time in a Goodwood maiden, is a well-made sort. He didn't look entirely happy on the soft ground but, to his credit, battled away. He deserves to go one better. (op 6-4)
Scarboro Warning(IRE), a rangy newcomer, is bred to need further in time. He showed ahead leaving the back straight and battled back well when headed. He looks sure to find an opening. (op 33-1 tchd 25-1)
Ragetti(IRE), by Hawk Wing out of a winning juvenile hurdler, dropped right out soon after the start. Last of all at halfway, he made ground on the outer but then hung violently left. Sticking on strongly at the finish, this should have taught him plenty. (op 20-1 tchd 14-1)
Pink Flames(IRE), an expensive breeze-up purchase, showed ability and will surely fare much better in less testing conditions. (op 13-2)
Jamarjo(IRE) raced keenly and had already lost his place when badly hampered two and a half furlongs out. (op 9-2)

5675 SEE YOU NEXT YEAR H'CAP 6f
5:45 (5:45) (Class 5) (0-70,70) 4-Y-O+ **£4,274** (£1,271; £635; £317) **Stalls** High

Form RPR
1200 1 **Sea Salt**[5] 5516 6-8-6 63 PaulPickard(5) 14 78
(R E Barr) *in tch: hdwy 2f out: rdn to chal over 1f out: led jst ins fnl f and sn clr* 7/1
2505 2 4 **Tartatartufata**[26] 4842 7-8-13 65 (v) MickyFenton 13 67
(J G Given) *led: rdn along wl over 1f out: sn jnd and drvn: hdd jst ins fnl f and kpt on same pce* 8/1
/0-0 3 1 1/4 **Danum Dancer**[44] 4225 5-8-13 65 LeeVickers 15 63
(N Bycroft) *trckd ldrs: hdwy 2f out: rdn to chse ldng pair over 1f out: sn drvn and no imp ins fnl f* 16/1
0612 4 1/2 **Steel Blue**[8] 5406 9-8-2 59 (p) AmyRyan(5) 1 56
(R M Whitaker) *wnt lft s: swtchd rt in rr after 1f: hdwy 1/2-way: rdn wl over 1f out: kpt on ins fnl f: nrst fin* 11/2[2]
1634 5 1 3/4 **Another Try (IRE)**[16] 5188 4-8-5 62 MatthewDavies(5) 7 53
(A P Jarvis) *trckd ldrs: hdwy 1/2-way: cl up and ev ch 2f out: sn rdn and grad wknd* 8/1
2411 6 1 1/2 **Guto**[9] 5374 6-8-9 64 KellyHarrison(3) 9 50
(W J H Ratcliffe) *stmbld s: sn swtchd to stands' rail and in tch: rdn along and outpcd 1/2-way: kpt on u.p fr over 1f out but nvr a factor* 10/3[1]
240 7 1 1/4 **Top Bid**[5] 5518 5-8-10 62 (b) DuranFentiman 10 44
(T D Easterby) *in tch: rdn along 1/2-way and sn btn* 13/2[3]
0660 8 1 1/2 **Pacific Pride**[8] 5406 6-8-11 63 (b) GrahamGibbons 8 40
(J J Quinn) *cl up: rdn along over 2f out: sn drvn and wknd* 18/1
2440 9 1 **Hits Only Jude (IRE)**[21] 5031 6-8-6 65 (v[1]) NeilFarley(7) 3 39
(D Carroll) *wnt lft s: chsd ldrs on outer: rdn along 1/2-way and sn wknd* 14/1
6013 10 nk **Guest Connections**[119] 1885 6-8-9 68 (v) NSLawes(7) 2 41
(D Nicholls) *s.i.s: a in rr* 9/1
5325 11 1 1/4 **Leading Edge (IRE)**[155] 1091 4-9-2 68 TonyCulhane 5 37
(M R Channon) *in tch: rdn along and outpcd 1/2-way: bhd after* 16/1
1m 14.14s (1.44) **Going Correction** +0.325s/f (Good) 11 Ran SP% 120.2
Speed ratings (Par 103): **103,97,96,95,93 91,89,87,86,85 83**
toteswinger: 1&2 £14.00, 1&3 £24.00, 2&3 £29.50. CSF £63.47 CT £631.44 TOTE £9.00: £2.50, £3.60, £6.60; EX 63.30 Place 6: £275.37 Place 5: £166.38.
Owner Brian Morton **Bred** D R Tucker **Trained** Seamer, N Yorks
FOCUS
A low-grade 58-68 sprint handicap and a runaway winner but not form to take too literally with the first three from the three highest stalls.
T/Plt: £544.30 to a £1 stake. Pool: £53,628.16. 71.92 winning tickets. T/Qpdt: £71.00 to a £1 stake. Pool: £3,859.40. 40.20 winning tickets. JR

5610 WOLVERHAMPTON (A.W) (L-H)
Saturday, September 5

OFFICIAL GOING: Standard
Wind: Light behind Weather: Fine

5676 WILLIAMHILL.COM/BONUS25 - GET £25 FREE BET CLAIMING STKS 7f 32y(P)
5:50 (5:51) (Class 5) 3-Y-O+ **£3,238** (£963; £481; £240) **Stalls** High

Form RPR
0000 1 **Royal Challenge**[6] 5465 8-8-9 63 RoystonFfrench 11 66
(I W McInnes) *broke wl: led early: chsd ldr: led jst over 2f out: hrd rdn fnl f: r.o* 50/1
5035 2 1/2 **Charles Parnell (IRE)**[8] 5406 6-9-1 74 (b) FrederikTylicki(3) 7 74
(M Dods) *s.i.s: sn hld up in mid-div: hdwy on outside 3f out: rdn wl over 1f out: ev ch ins fnl f: kpt on* 5/1[2]
0505 3 1/2 **Fol Liam**[2] 5612 3-8-11 64 (p) RobertWinston 10 67
(A J McCabe) *hld up in rr: pushed along and hdwy over 2f out: c wd st: rdn wl over 1f out: r.o to take 3rd post* 20/1
0206 4 shd **Mutamared (USA)**[8] 5406 9-9-1 80 (t) AlanMunro 3 69
(K A Ryan) *a.p: rdn and ev ch ins fnl f: nt qckn cl home: lost 3rd post* 2/1[1]
1040 5 nk **Sea Land (FR)**[17] 5150 5-8-12 61 DavidAllan 9 66+
(B Ellison) *hld up in rr: hdwy 2f out: rdn over 1f out: n.m.r wl ins fnl f: nvr able to chal* 14/1
6400 6 2 1/4 **Divertimenti (IRE)**[45] 4202 5-8-7 65 SimonPearce(5) 1 59
(C R Dore) *hld up in mid-div: hdwy on ins wl over 1f out: rdn ent fnl f: no imp* 20/1
0630 7 nk **Obe Royal**[10] 5332 5-9-1 70 (b) PaulDoe 8 61+
(P D Evans) *hld up towards rr: sltly hmpd on outside over 2f out: c v wd st: rdn wl over 1f out: nvr trbld ldrs* 15/2
5000 8 1 1/4 **Resplendent Nova**[16] 5188 7-9-1 85 JimmyQuinn 5 58
(P Howling) *chsd ldrs: nt clr run and lost pl bnd after 1f: pushed along over 2f out: c v wd st: rdn and edgd lft 1f out: n.d* 6/1[3]
5000 9 8 **Sammy The Snake (IRE)**[66] 3509 4-9-4 78 JamesDoyle 4 39
(B W Duke) *prom tl n.m.r and wknd 2f out* 25/1
0204 10 5 **King's Sabre**[8] 5403 3-9-6 66 (b[1]) GeorgeBaker 6 30
(W R Muir) *sn led: hdd jst over 2f out: wknd wl over 1f out* 9/1

3141 **11** ½ **Sir Ike (IRE)**[13] 5283 4-9-4 67..(tp) ShaneKelly 12 25
(W S Kittow) *prom tl rdn and wknd wl over 1f out* **17/2**

1m 28.67s (-0.93) **Going Correction** -0.10s/f (Stan)
WFA 3 from 4yo+ 4lb **11** Ran SP% **118.6**
Speed ratings (Par 103): **101,100,99,99,99 96,96,95,85,80 79**
toteswingers: 1&2 not won, 1&3 not won, 2&3 £6.50. CSF £278.63 TOTE £59.20: £18.60, £2.90, £6.20; EX 206.90.Mutamared was claimed by A S Reid for £7,000.
Owner Truck Export **Bred** Capt A L Smith-Maxwell **Trained** Catwick, E Yorks

FOCUS
King's Sabre ensured a decent early gallop in this fair claimer. The form looks sound rated around the first three and fifth.
Fol Liam Official explanation: jockey said gelding hung right-handed
Sammy The Snake(IRE) Official explanation: trainer said gelding had a breathing problem

5677 WILLIAMHILL.COM/BONUS25 POKER TOURNAMENTS H'CAP 7f 32y(P)
6:20 (6:25) (Class 5) (0-75,75) 3-Y-O **£4,209** (£1,252; £625; £312) **Stalls** High

Form RPR
1212 **1** **Regeneration (IRE)**[19] 5112 3-9-1 **72**.......................... HayleyTurner 12 80+
(S A Callaghan) *s.i.s: sn swtchd lft to ins rail: hld up in rr: hdwy on ins wl over 1f out: sn rdn: led jst ins fnl f: drvn out* **11/4**[1]

263 **2** ½ **Espero (IRE)**[22] 4981 3-8-11 **75**.......................... AndrewHeffernan[(7)] 2 82
(R A Farrant) *a.p: led over 1f out: rdn and hdd jst ins fnl f: r.o* **8/1**

5250 **3** 2 ¼ **Doc Jones (IRE)**[16] 5183 3-9-2 **73**.......................... PatCosgrave 5 74+
(P D Evans) *hld up towards rr: c v wd st: hdwy whn hung lft ins fnl f: r.o to take 3rd post* **8/1**

5505 **4** nse **Satwa Star (IRE)**[28] 4791 3-8-12 **69**.......................... TGMcLaughlin 4 70+
(E A L Dunlop) *hld up in mid-div: hdwy wl over 1f out: rdn ent fnl f: no ex and lost 3rd post* **6/1**[2]

2130 **5** hd **Cheap Thrills**[65] 3537 3-9-4 **75**.......................... ShaneKelly 1 75
(J A Osborne) *led: hdd and rdn over 1f out: edgd rt ins fnl f: one pce* **16/1**

2321 **6** 1 **Helieorbea**[17] 5163 3-9-4 **75**.......................... DavidAllan 11 73+
(T D Easterby) *hld up in rr: pushed along over 2f out: kpt on ins fnl f: nvr trbld ldrs* **6/1**[2]

-000 **7** 2 **Amber Sunset**[10] 5349 3-9-1 **72**.......................... GeorgeBaker 9 64
(J Jay) *hld up in tch: lost pl briefly over 3f out: c wd st: rdn over 1f out: wknd ins fnl f* **33/1**

0000 **8** 1 ½ **Versaki (IRE)**[10] 5349 3-8-11 **73**..........................(t) MartinLane[(5)] 8 61
(Ian Williams) *prom: pushed along over 2f out: rdn and wknd over 1f out* **28/1**

2135 **9** nk **All For You (IRE)**[37] 4452 3-8-12 **69**..........................(p) AlanMunro 3 56
(M Botti) *uns rdr and bolted a circ bef s: hld up towards rr: stdy prog on ins over 3f out: wknd ins fnl f* **15/2**[3]

1646 **10** 1 **Kersivay**[33] 4591 3-9-2 **73**.......................... RoystonFfrench 10 58
(Ollie Pears) *t.k.h: hdwy after 1f: ev ch over 2f out: rdn and wknd over 1f out* **16/1**

3300 **11** 4 **Cook's Endeavour (USA)**[10] 5340 3-9-2 **73**..........(p) RobertWinston 7 47
(K A Ryan) *chsd ldr tl rdn over 2f out: wknd wl over 1f out* **12/1**

5400 **12** 3 ½ **Jimwil (IRE)**[10] 5340 3-8-11 **71**..........................(b) FrederikTylicki[(3)] 6 35
(M Dods) *t.k.h: hdwy on outside over 1f out: hung rt and wknd bnd over 2f out* **20/1**

1m 28.3s (-1.30) **Going Correction** -0.10s/f (Stan) **12** Ran SP% **119.8**
Speed ratings (Par 101): **103,102,99,99,99 98,96,94,94,92 88,84**
toteswinger: 1&2 £9.80, 1&3 £6.10, 2&3 not won. CSF £24.49 CT £163.44 TOTE £3.60: £1.40, £2.90, £2.80; EX 29.10.
Owner Tamdown Group Limited **Bred** Tally-Ho Stud **Trained** Newmarket, Suffolk

FOCUS
This fair handicap was delayed by five minutes due to All For You bolting and Cheap Thrills being difficult to load. The form looks straightforward rated around the third and fourth.
Kersivay Official explanation: jockey said gelding ran too free

5678 WILLIAMHILL.COM/BONUS25 - QUOTE BONUS25 H'CAP 5f 216y(P)
6:50 (6:50) (Class 6) (0-65,65) 3-Y-O+ **£2,729** (£806; £403) **Stalls** Low

Form RPR
3332 **1** **Weet A Surprise**[5] 5504 4-8-13 **65**..........................(v) AlexEdwards[(7)] 8 79
(J W Unett) *hld up towards rr: hdwy over 2f out: shkn up to ld ins fnl f: pushed clr* **6/1**[2]

0506 **2** 3 ¾ **Tri Chara (IRE)**[26] 4843 5-8-9 **61**.......................... DavidKenny[(7)] 2 63
(R Hollinshead) *chsd ldr: led 2f out: rdn wl over 1f out: hdd ins fnl f: one pce* **12/1**

2030 **3** 2 ¾ **Pipers Piping (IRE)**[75] 3225 3-9-1 **62**.......................... ShaneKelly 4 55
(J A Osborne) *hld up in tch: pushed along whn briefly n.m.r over 2f out: rdn jst over 1f out: kpt on to take 3rd nr fin* **16/1**

3510 **4** nk **Silvanus (IRE)**[7] 5421 4-9-3 **62**.......................... LiamJones 10 54
(P T Midgley) *hld up in rr: hdwy wl over 1f out: sn edgd lft and rdn: kpt on one pce ins fnl f* **13/2**[3]

3405 **5** ½ **Forever's Girl**[22] 4999 3-8-13 **63**.......................... NataliaGemelova[(3)] 7 54
(G R Oldroyd) *led: hdd 2f out: rdn over 1f out: lost 2nd jst ins fnl f: sn wknd* **25/1**

060 **6** ¾ **Fyodor (IRE)**[16] 5184 8-9-1 **65**..........................(v) RichardEvans[(5)] 1 53
(P D Evans) *s.i.s: hld up towards rr: nt clr run wl over 1f out: rdn ins fnl f: n.d* **13/2**[3]

6302 **7** nk **Loyal Royal (IRE)**[15] 5225 6-8-10 **58**..........................(b) JackDean[(3)] 9 45+
(J M Bradley) *s.i.s: hld up in rr: nt clr run on ins over 2f out: pushed along and nt clr run wl over 1f out: sme hdwy whn n.m.r ent fnl f: n.d after* **4/1**[1]

0535 **8** nk **Ryedane (IRE)**[8] 5411 7-9-3 **62**..........................(b) DavidAllan 12 51+
(T D Easterby) *hdwy over 4f out: rdn and edgd lft over 2f out: wknd wl over 1f out* **6/1**[2]

2100 **9** 1 ½ **Diane's Choice**[9] 5374 6-8-12 **57**..........................(e) DavidProbert 3 39
(Miss Gay Kelleway) *hld up in mid-div: hdwy on ins over 2f out: rdn and wknd over 1f out* **11/1**

50-0 **10** 3 ¼ **Megalo Maniac**[9] 5374 6-8-5 **57**.......................... MarzenaJeziorek[(7)] 6 28
(R A Fahey) *a in rr* **25/1**

140 **11** 9 **Bertbrand**[54] 3926 4-8-11 **59**..........................(p) FrederikTylicki[(3)] 5 1
(I W McInnes) *prom tl wknd wl over 2f out* **17/2**

1m 13.28s (-1.72) **Going Correction** -0.10s/f (Stan)
WFA 3 from 4yo+ 2lb **11** Ran SP% **115.4**
Speed ratings (Par 101): **107,102,98,97,97 96,95,95,93,89 77**
toteswinger: 1&2 £16.30, 1&3 not won, 2&3 not won. CSF £74.31 CT £1095.64 TOTE £6.90: £2.10, £4.30, £4.70; EX 95.90.
Owner J E Price **Bred** Longdon Stud Ltd **Trained** Tedsmore Hall, Shropshire

FOCUS
Less than half of the field ever got meaningfully involved here and the form is not solid.
Ryedane(IRE) Official explanation: jockey said gelding hung left-handed

5679 WILLIAMHILL.COM/BONUS25 - LIVE CASINO DEALERS (S) STKS 1m 4f 50y(P)
7:20 (7:20) (Class 6) 3-5-Y-O **£2,388** (£705; £352) **Stalls** Low

Form RPR
2060 **1** **Ghufa (IRE)**[44] 4220 5-9-4 70.......................... TedDurcan 6 65+
(George Baker) *hld up towards rr: hdwy over 2f out: rdn wl over 1f out: styd on to ld wl ins fnl f* **12/1**

5562 **2** 1 ¾ **Carmela Maria**[6] 5484 4-8-13 57..........................(p) SaleemGolam 8 57
(S C Williams) *sn chsng ldr: lost 2nd 2f out: rdn over 1f out: styd on to retake 2nd nr fin* **5/1**[2]

0000 **3** ½ **Wind Flow**[15] 5227 5-9-9 65..........................(b) CatherineGannon 10 66
(C A Dwyer) *sn led: rdn wl over 1f out: hdd wl ins fnl f: no ex* **8/1**

6640 **4** ½ **Sphere (IRE)**[21] 5015 4-8-13 57..........................(p) HayleyTurner 4 56
(J R Fanshawe) *led early: a.p: shkn up and chsd ldr 2f out: rdn over 1f out: no ex wl ins fnl f* **11/2**[3]

2043 **5** 2 ½ **Lady Valentino**[27] 4818 5-8-8 47..........................(t) PatrickDonaghy[(5)] 3 52
(B D Leavy) *hld up towards rr: pushed along on outside over 2f out: c wd st: rdn and hdwy over 1f out: styd on same pce ins fnl f* **20/1**

2130 **6** nk **Playful Asset (IRE)**[13] 5286 3-8-9 61.......................... RobertWinston 9 56
(P Howling) *hld up in tch: pushed along over 5f out: rdn wl over 2f out: wknd wl over 1f out* **9/2**[1]

4000 **7** 1 ¾ **Am I Blue**[29] 4744 3-8-4 52.......................... JimmyQuinn 1 48
(H J L Dunlop) *hld up in mid-div: pushed along over 2f out: rdn and btn over 1f out* **25/1**

6000 **8** 2 **Flirty (IRE)**[81] 3005 3-8-4 47.......................... ChrisCatlin 11 45
(Rae Guest) *s.i.s: hld up in rr: pushed along wl over 1f out: rdn fnl f: nvr nr ldrs* **40/1**

234/ **9** 1 ¼ **Easterly Breeze (IRE)**[21] 5047 5-9-4 65..........................(b[1]) GeorgeBaker 5 48
(M S Tuck) *hld up in rr: pushed along and swtchd rt wl over 1f out: sn rdn: no rspnse* **9/2**[1]

2420 **10** 3 **Den Maschine**[23] 4944 4-8-13 51.......................... MartinLane[(5)] 12 43
(B N Pollock) *hld up in tch: pushed along and wknd 2f out* **28/1**

5 **11** 4 ½ **Shanghai Star (IRE)**[27] 4818 5-9-2 72.......................... RobbieEgan[(7)] 2 41
(Patrick Allen, Ire) *hld up in tch: rdn and wknd over 2f out* **18/1**

2603 **12** 7 **Canton Road**[11] 5327 3-8-9 62..........................(b) AlanMunro 7 25
(P F I Cole) *hld up in mid-div: rdn and wknd over 2f out* **8/1**

2m 39.41s (-1.69) **Going Correction** -0.10s/f (Stan)
WFA 3 from 4yo+ 9lb **12** Ran SP% **118.1**
Speed ratings (Par 101): **101,99,99,99,97 97,96,94,93,91 88,84**
toteswinger: 1&2 not won, 1&3 £8.20, 2&3 £23.60. CSF £67.78 TOTE £15.30: £4.00, £1.70, £2.60; EX 64.80.There was no bid for the winner. Carmela Maria was claimed by M E Sowersby for £6,000. Sphere was claimed by P T Midgley for £6,000.
Owner Mrs C E S Baker **Bred** Shadwell Estate Company Limited **Trained** Moreton Morrell, Warwicks

FOCUS
Little pace on until past halfway in this seller, after which a sprint finish gave rise to a winning time 3.7 seconds faster than the handicap that followed. Probably not form to take too literally.

5680 WILLIAM HILL 0800 444040 - GET £25 FREE BET H'CAP 1m 4f 50y(P)
7:50 (7:50) (Class 6) (0-60,60) 3-Y-O+ **£2,388** (£705; £352) **Stalls** Low

Form RPR
0024 **1** **Our Kes (IRE)**[19] 5103 7-9-4 **54**.......................... KFallon 2 59
(P Howling) *a.p: pushed along jst over 2f out: led jst over 1f out: rdn out* **7/2**[1]

6043 **2** ¾ **Annambo**[14] 5246 9-9-5 **55**..........................(p) AlanMunro 3 59
(Andrew Reid) *hld up in mid-div: hdwy on ins 2f out: swtchd rt ent st: rdn and r.o to take 2nd nr fin* **4/1**[2]

0200 **3** ½ **Roleplay (IRE)**[19] 5111 4-9-5 **55**..........................(b) TedDurcan 11 58
(J M P Eustace) *a.p: wnt 2nd over 6f out: led and hung lft wl over 1f out: sn hdd: no ex and lost 2nd nr fin* **33/1**

3505 **4** 2 ¼ **Swords**[26] 4862 7-8-11 **52**.......................... MartinLane[(5)] 5 52
(R E Peacock) *led 2f: chsd ldr tl over 6f out: rdn over 1f out: one pce* **9/2**[3]

-002 **5** 1 ¼ **King's Fable (USA)**[7] 5444 6-9-3 **53**..........................(p) TGMcLaughlin 8 51
(Karen George) *s.i.s: hld up in rr: swtchd rt and hdwy over 1f out: sn rdn: no imp fnl f* **5/1**

0153 **6** ¾ **Zalkani (IRE)**[54] 3927 9-9-5 **60**.......................... SimonPearce[(5)] 12 56
(J Pearce) *hld up towards rr: stdd prog on outside over 3f out: c v wd st: hung lft and wknd over 1f out* **8/1**

264 **7** nk **Apache Fort**[33] 4602 6-9-9 **59**..........................(b) PaulDoe 7 55
(T Keddy) *w ldr: led after 2f: rdn and hdd wl over 1f out: wknd ins fnl f* **14/1**

2600 **8** nse **Thorny Mandate**[5] 5530 7-9-2 **52**.......................... JimmyQuinn 10 48
(W M Brisbourne) *hld up towards rr: n.m.r 2f out: hung lft 1f out: n.d* **10/1**

00/0 **9** 1 **Bricks And Porter (IRE)**[23] 4963 9-9-3 **58**..........................(tp) DEMullins[(5)] 1 52
(T G McCourt, Ire) *hld up towards rr: rdn 2f out: no rspnse* **12/1**

0040 **10** 2 **Desert Leader (IRE)**[15] 5210 8-9-4 **54**.......................... DavidProbert 6 45
(W M Brisbourne) *s.i.s: hld up in mid-div: hdwy 5f out: rdn and wknd wl over 1f out* **20/1**

2m 44.14s (3.04) **Going Correction** -0.10s/f (Stan) **10** Ran SP% **119.3**
Speed ratings (Par 101): **85,84,84,82,81 81,81,81,80,79**
toteswinger: 1&2 £6.70, 1&3 £27.00, 2&3 not won. CSF £17.92 CT £401.68 TOTE £2.90: £1.80, £1.60, £7.30; EX 29.40.
Owner S J Hammond **Bred** Yeomanstown Stud **Trained** Newmarket, Suffolk
■ Kieren Fallon's first winner since returning from bans which had prevented him from riding in Britain since June 2006.

FOCUS
Much the slower of the two 1m4f handicaps on the night and muddling with very little solid form on show. Nothing ruined its chances by refusing to settle under the slow pace. Smmoth As Silk (8/1) was withdrawn on vet's advice. R4 applies, deduct 10p in the £.

5681 WILLIAMHILL.COM/BONUS25 - PLAY VEGAS GAMES NOVICE AUCTION STKS 1m 141y(P)
8:20 (8:20) (Class 5) 2-Y-O **£3,412** (£1,007; £504) **Stalls** Low

Form RPR
123 **1** **Pallantes Cross**[7] 5433 2-9-1 93.......................... RobertWinston 3 95+
(M Johnston) *mde all: rdn wl over 1f out: r.o wl* **4/9**[1]

10 **2** 2 ¾ **The Starboard Bow**[15] 5214 2-8-13 88.......................... KFallon 2 86
(S Kirk) *chsd wnr: rdn wl over 1f out: no imp* **11/4**[2]

3 nk **Verity Lane (USA)** 2-8-7 0.......................... HayleyTurner 1 79
(R M H Cowell) *hld up in last: swtchd rt and hdwy to dispute 2nd over 2f out: rdn wl over 1f out: one pce* **9/1**[3]

1m 52.27s (1.77) **Going Correction** -0.10s/f (Stan) **3** Ran SP% **105.9**
Speed ratings (Par 95): **88,85,85**
CSF £1.89 TOTE £1.20; EX 1.30.
Owner Mrs R J Jacobs **Bred** Newsells Park Stud **Trained** Middleham Moor, N Yorks

FOCUS
A numerically thinly-contested novice auction.

NOTEBOOK
Pallantes Cross, for whom this proved little more than an exercise canter, raced with ears pricked, quickly established a 3l lead and needed just a shake of the reins turning in to quicken up and go beyond recall. We learned nothing new about him here, but this will have been a nice fillip for the colt following harder races in defeat the last twice. A third off 91 in a Newmarket nursery most recently marks him out as possibly a touch short of the required standard if he does take up his engagement in the Listed Stardom Stakes at Goodwood. (op 1-2 tchd 2-5)

The Starboard Bow was the first to be urged by its rider, and the response wasn't instantaneous enough to prevent Verity Lane, 2l behind to that point, from joining him turning in. He only managed to secure the runner-up's berth close home, and his Racing Post Trophy entry increasingly looks to be flying high, but his trainer has already asserted that better will follow as a three-year-old. (op 3-1)

Verity Lane(USA), from a yard doing well in the last fortnight, seemed to know her job well enough on this debut and kept the second honest to the line. Dirt-bred to the core, a routine fillies' maiden on Polytrack should be attainable on this evidence. (op 15-2)

5682 WILLIAM HILL 0800 444040 - QUOTE BONUS25 NURSERY 1m 141y(P)
8:50 (8:50) (Class 4) (0-80,79) 2-Y-O **£5,046** (£1,510; £755; £377; £188) **Stalls** Low

Form | | | | RPR
0336 **1** **Llandovery**[12] 5320 2-8-8 **66** .... EdwardCreighton 2 68
(P J McBride) *hld up in tch: hrd rdn jst over 2f out: r.o to ld wl ins fnl f: drvn out* **25/1**

203 **2** *nk* **Pytheas (USA)**[39] 4396 2-9-7 **79** .... JoeFanning 4 80
(M Johnston) *led: rdn wl over 1f out: hdd wl ins fnl f: r.o* **6/5**[1]

5621 **3** *1* **Luminous Star (USA)**[18] 5119 2-9-6 **78** .... SebSanders 5 77+
(R M Beckett) *hld up in last: hdwy on outside over 2f out: c wd st: edgd lft and rdn 1f out: kpt on to take 3rd nr fin* **5/1**[3]

4220 **4** *½* **Layla's Boy**[14] 5251 2-9-2 **77** .... FrederikTylicki(3) 1 75
(R A Fahey) *chsd ldr 2f: prom: wnt 2nd 2f out: hrd rdn and ev ch over 1f out: nt qckn wl ins fnl f* **9/2**[2]

432 **5** *1 ½* **Logos Astra (USA)**[19] 5106 2-9-6 **78** .... TedDurcan 6 73
(D R Lanigan) *prom: chsd ldr over 6f out to 2f out: rdn and hung rt over 1f out: wknd ins fnl f* **9/2**[2]

5424 **6** *3 ½* **Dolphin Rock**[15] 5207 2-8-9 **67** .... LiamJones 3 54
(Mrs G S Rees) *hld up: hdwy 6f out: wkng whn n.m.r briefly ins fnl f* **14/1**

1m 49.43s (-1.07) **Going Correction** -0.10s/f (Stan) **6** Ran SP% **109.0**
Speed ratings (Par 97): **100,99,98,98,97 93**
toteswinger: 1&2 not won, 1&3 £4.10, 2&3 £2.80. CSF £53.10 TOTE £24.10: £5.70, £1.60; EX 60.10.
Owner S A Douch **Bred** S A Douch **Trained** Newmarket, Suffolk

FOCUS
An ordinary-looking nursery produced the second boil-over of the night.

NOTEBOOK
Llandovery looked the least likely winner leaving the back straight, having already been niggled from around halfway and not evidently responding in kind. However, he picked up again with the assistance of the far rail up the straight, and of four horses virtually in a line 100 yards out, he found the most. His mark had looked just fair ahead of his nursery debut at Windsor last time, in which he eventually finished a well-beaten last. Reverting to slightly more patient tactics may have aided his cause this time, but whatever the reason, further improvement must be forthcoming from here on if his defeat of a 13lb higher rated rival is taken literally. (op 28-1 tchd 33-1)

Pytheas(USA), a Royal Lodge Stakes entry, set out to make all for the third time in four career starts, and for the third time was foiled inside the final furlong. This didn't mark the step forward anticipated by a step up in trip, and the fact he was unable to make count a reasonably kindly opening handicap mark was also slightly disappointing. (op 15-8 tchd 11-10 and 2-1 in a place)

Luminous Star(USA) just held on to land a Brighton maiden last time, the only winning form in this line-up. He, too, could have been dealt a worse hand on this nursery bow and, whilst he was on his toes on the way to post, he wasn't as free in this race as when winning. This may be as good as he is. (tchd 13-2)

Layla's Boy loomed large 1f out, but his effort tailed off thereafter. He had excuses last time but hasn't really kicked on from his improved second at Ayr three runs ago. (op 3-1 tchd 11-4)

Logos Astra(USA), runner-up over 7f here last time, did not look like taking a hand from some way out. (op 4-1 tchd 7-2)

5683 WILLIAMHILL.COM/BONUS25 - BINGO BONANZAS H'CAP 1m 141y(P)
9:20 (9:20) (Class 6) (0-60,60) 3-Y-O+ **£2,388** (£705; £352) **Stalls** Low

Form | | | | RPR
3443 **1** **Cheers For Thea (IRE)**[19] 5103 4-9-5 **57** ....(bt) DavidAllan 1 70
(T D Easterby) *hld up towards rr: smooth prog over 3f out: shkn up to ld ins fnl f: sn rdn: r.o* **4/1**[2]

3122 **2** *¾* **King's Icon (IRE)**[2] 5617 4-8-10 **55** ....(p) TobyAtkinson(7) 8 66
(M Wigham) *hld up in mid-div: smooth hdwy over 2f out: rdn and ev ch ins fnl f: nt qckn towards fin* **11/8**[1]

0024 **3** *3 ¾* **The Grey One (IRE)**[15] 5229 6-9-8 **60** ....(p) KevinGhunowa 6 62
(J M Bradley) *hld up in mid-div: hdwy to chse ldr over 3f out: led wl over 1f out: sn rdn: hdd ins fnl f: one pce* **12/1**

04-4 **4** *2 ½* **Follow The Sun (IRE)**[24] 4924 5-9-3 **55** ....(p) DavidProbert 12 52+
(Ronald O'Leary, Ire) *std s: sn swtchd lft: hld up in rr: rdn and hdwy over 1f out: styd on ins fnl f: n.d* **14/1**

1000 **5** *½* **Royal Crest**[42] 4304 3-9-2 **60** .... ShaneKelly 5 54
(J A Osborne) *hld up in tch: pushed along over 3f out: rdn and wknd over 2f out* **10/1**[3]

5-60 **6** *¾* **Highland Starlight (USA)**[44] 4240 3-9-2 **60** .... SebSanders 3 53
(C G Cox) *led 1f: chsd ldr: led wl over 3f out: rdn and hdd wl over 1f out: wknd fnl f* **20/1**

0166 **7** *½* **Hits Only Cash**[9] 5364 7-9-2 **59** ....(p) SimonPearce(5) 4 52+
(J Pearce) *hld up in rr: rdn and styd on fr over 1f out: n.d* **16/1**

0016 **8** *shd* **Zennerman (IRE)**[15] 5229 6-9-3 **58** ....(v) FrederikTylicki(3) 2 50
(W M Brisbourne) *hld up in mid-div: hdwy on ins over 2f out: wknd wl over 1f out* **10/1**[3]

0000 **9** *4 ½* **Ardent Prince**[15] 5229 6-9-3 **55** .... RobertWinston 7 42+
(A J McCabe) *hld up in rr: pushed along and nt clr run on ins over 2f out: swtchd rt ent st: eased whn no ch wl ins fnl f* **25/1**

-000 **10** *25* **Blues Minor (IRE)**[30] 4710 4-9-3 **60** ....(b) RossAtkinson(5) 10 —
(M Mullineaux) *hld up in tch: wknd qckly over 2f out: eased whn no ch fnl f* **40/1**

6 **11** *1 ¾* **Theme Catcher (IRE)**[17] 5152 4-9-3 **60** ....(v[1]) LeeNewnes(5) 13 —
(G Brown) *led after 1f: rdn and hdd wl over 3f out: sn wknd: eased whn no ch over 1f out* **28/1**

26/0 **12** *11* **View From The Top**[2] 5617 5-9-3 **55** ....(p) PatCosgrave 9 —
(Patrick Allen, Ire) *prom: rdn and wknd qckly wl over 2f out: eased wl over 1f out* **20/1**

1m 48.78s (-1.72) **Going Correction** -0.10s/f (Stan)
WFA 3 from 4yo+ 6lb **12** Ran SP% **119.8**
Speed ratings (Par 101): **103,102,99,96,96 95,95,95,91,68 67,57**
toteswinger: 1&2 £1.80, 1&3 £8.80, 2&3 £4.10. CSF £9.16 CT £62.99 TOTE £3.70: £1.70, £1.10, £3.10; EX 13.50 Place 6: £296.45, Place 5: £61.17..
Owner Ron George **Bred** Crone Stud Farms Ltd **Trained** Great Habton, N Yorks

FOCUS
Theme Catcher's early pace helped frame a race which was won in a time 0.65 seconds quicker than the preceding nursery. The form is rated around the first three.
Ardent Prince Official explanation: jockey said gelding lost its action
T/Plt: £280.90 to a £1 stake. Pool: £67,937.03. 176.50 winning tickets. T/Qpdt: £21.80 to a £1 stake. Pool: £8,329.06. 282.20 winning tickets. KH

[4958] LEOPARDSTOWN (L-H)
Saturday, September 5

OFFICIAL GOING: Good to yielding
The 2.40, 3.50, 4.30 and 5.35 were run on the outer track, the rest on the inner.

5685a KILTERNAN STKS (GROUP 3) 1m 2f
2:10 (2:10) 3-Y-O+ **£39,126** (£11,436; £5,417; £1,805)

| | | | RPR
1 **Poet**[6] 5490 4-9-8 113 .... JMurtagh 1 118+
(A P O'Brien, Ire) *mde all: rdn 3f out: styd on strly to go clr over 1f out: comf* **9/4**[1]

2 *4 ½* **Allied Powers (IRE)**[5] 5539 4-9-8 .... JimmyFortune 5 112+
(M L W Bell) *settled bhd ldrs: 5th 1/2-way: rdn 3f out: prog in 4th 1 1/2f out: kpt on to go 2nd ins fnl f: no ch w wnr* **3/1**[2]

3 *3* **Shreyas (IRE)**[23] 4962 4-9-5 109 .... KJManning 7 100
(J S Bolger, Ire) *chsd ldr in 2nd: rdn 3f out: no imp on ldr over 1f out: kpt on same pce: lost 2nd ins fnl f* **9/2**[3]

4 *2* **Johann Zoffany**[70] 3414 3-9-1 108 .... JAHeffernan 3 99
(A P O'Brien, Ire) *chsd ldrs in 3rd: rdn 3f out: no ex 2f out: kpt on same pce* **6/1**

5 *4* **Arch Rebel (USA)**[344] 6261 8-9-8 104 ....(p) FMBerry 6 91+
(Noel Meade, Ire) *v s.i.s: hld up in rr: rdn 3f out: no imp 2f out: mod 6th 1f out: kpt on one pce* **20/1**

6 *1 ½* **Fiery Lad (IRE)**[79] 3082 4-9-8 109 .... EJMcNamara 4 88+
(G M Lyons, Ire) *trckd ldrs: 4th 1/2-way: rdn 2f out: sn no ex* **13/2**

7 *22* **Peter Tchaikovsky**[62] 3665 3-9-1 103 .... CO'Donoghue 2 44+
(A P O'Brien, Ire) *hld up towards rr: rdn and wknd 3f out: t.o* **25/1**

2m 7.02s (-1.18) **Going Correction** +0.20s/f (Good)
WFA 3 from 4yo+ 7lb **7** Ran SP% **110.2**
Speed ratings: **112,108,106,104,101 100,82**
CSF £8.42 TOTE £2.20: £2.00, £1.70; DF 7.30.
Owner Derrick Smith **Bred** Meon Valley Stud **Trained** Ballydoyle, Co Tipperary

FOCUS
A solid Group 3 contest. The winner is rated to his previous best.

NOTEBOOK
Poet has made terrific progress in recent weeks, and won with considerable authority to supplement his victories in a Listed race at Killarney and under top-weight in last Sunday's Irish Cambridgeshire. Clearly a tough sort, and thoroughly suited by plenty of cut in the ground, he established the tone for the race by going straight to the front. Ridden along to maintain the tempo around 3f out, he had his pursuers in trouble early in the straight and stayed on for a commanding win. On this evidence, he could be expected to last out another couple of furlongs, but at the same time there should be no shortage of opportunities for him at between 1m and 1m2f. (op 2/1)
Allied Powers(IRE), who had a hard race when a beaten favourite for a 1m4f Listed race at Galway at the beginning of the week, stayed on towards the outer in the final furlong and a half after looking in trouble early in the straight. He had run a career-best when second to yesterday's Kempton Group 3 winner Kirklees in a Group 2 over a slightly longer trip at York in July, and his win in a competitive handicap at Hamilton earlier in the season proves he stays 1m4f. (op 3/1 tchd 100/30)
Shreyas(IRE), back in trip here after apparently failing to stay 1m4f on her previous visit to this track, ran second behind the winner for most of the way but could not raise her effort on ground that was slower than ideal for her. A dual Listed winner at the venue this season, she won a Group 3 at Gowran last September and has the ability to pick up another Pattern race when conditions are more in her favour. (op 4/1)

5686a COOLMORE FUSAICHI PEGASUS MATRON STKS (GROUP 1) (F&M) 1m
2:40 (2:41) 3-Y-O+ **£135,679** (£39,660; £18,786; £6,262)

| | | | RPR
1 **Rainbow View (USA)**[35] 4522 3-8-12 ....(p) JimmyFortune 4 116+
(J H M Gosden) *trckd ldrs in 4th: rdn into 2nd 1 1/2f out: led over 1f out: kpt on strly fnl f* **5/4**[1]

2 *2* **Heaven Sent**[35] 4522 6-9-3 .... MJKinane 6 112+
(Sir Michael Stoute) *hld up in 6th: rdn into 3rd 1 1/2f out: 2nd 1f out: kpt on same pce fnl f: no imp on wnr* **11/4**[2]

3 *4 ½* **Again (IRE)**[78] 3088 3-8-12 111 .... JMurtagh 7 101+
(David Wachman, Ire) *chsd ldr in 2nd: rdn 2f out: no ex in 4th 1 1/2f out: kpt on same pce to mod 3rd ins fnl f* **3/1**[3]

4 *1 ¼* **Totally Devoted (USA)**[18] 5138 3-8-12 90 .... CO'Donoghue 2 98
(A P O'Brien, Ire) *led: rdn and hdd over 1f out: no ex and kpt on same pce* **33/1**

5 *2 ½* **San Sicharia (IRE)**[36] 4489 4-9-3 104 ....(p) KJManning 1 93
(Ms Joanna Morgan, Ire) *chsd ldrs in 3rd: rdn 2f out: no ex in 5th 1 1/2f out: kpt on same pce* **16/1**

6 *½* **Monivea (IRE)**[41] 4358 3-8-12 93 ....(p) DJMoran 8 91
(Brian Nolan, Ire) *s.i.s: rdn and no imp 2f out: kpt on one pce* **50/1**

7 *6* **Heart Shaped (USA)**[20] 5079 3-8-12 107 .... JAHeffernan 5 77
(A P O'Brien, Ire) *settled in 5th: rdn and no ex 2f out: sn wknd* **10/1**

1m 39.89s (-1.31) **Going Correction** +0.20s/f (Good)
WFA 3 from 4yo+ 5lb **7** Ran SP% **116.0**
Speed ratings: **114,112,107,106,103 103,97**
CSF £5.10 TOTE £1.80: £1.10, £1.80; DF 4.10.
Owner George Strawbridge **Bred** Augustin Stable **Trained** Newmarket, Suffolk

FOCUS
A British one-two. Rainbow View gained a deserved first Group 1 win of the season and became the sixth British-trained winner from the past seven runnings. She is rated to her best mile form this year, with the fourth limiting things.

NOTEBOOK

Rainbow View(USA) gained a deserved first Group 1 of the season. It was her sixth run of the season and she was equipped with cheekpieces for the first time. Well positioned on the approach to the straight, she began to launch her challenge from under 2f down, and got first run as the pacesetter began to run out of steam. For just a stride or so it looked as though the eventual runner-up might get close enough, at least to threaten, but she asserted in good style inside the last. In so doing, she became the sixth British-trained winner of this race from the past seven runnings. The Prix de l'Opera could now be on the agenda, with a possible trip to the Breeders' Cup also on the horizon. (op 7/4)

Heaven Sent had finished in front of Rainbow View when second to Goldikova in the Falmouth Stakes, but the tables were comprehensively turned on soft ground at Goodwood, and once again the going was against the older mare here. Held up in the early stages, she started to improve from under 2f down but failed to find a change of gear in the ground. She is a high-class mare and deserves recognition as such, even though her win-record at Pattern level reveals her in a relatively unflattering light, merely as the winner of the same Newmarket Group 3 event two years in succession. (op 9/4)

Again(IRE) was back in action for the first time since failing to run to form on quick ground in the Coronation Stakes. She came under pressure before the early leader, and it was only inside the last furlong that she managed to overhaul her, by which stage the two British-trained runners had the lion's share of the prize-money in safe keeping. It is hard to be sure whether she can recover her Group 1-winning form. (op 5/2)

5688a TATTERSALLS MILLIONS IRISH CHAMPION STKS (GROUP 1) 1m 2f

3:50 (3:50) 3-Y-0+

£552,427 (£183,495; £86,407; £28,155; £18,446; £8,737)

RPR

1 — **Sea The Stars (IRE)**[18] 5135 3-9-0 133 .... MJKinane 2 138+
(John M Oxx, Ire) *settled bhd ldrs: 5th 1/2-way: hdwy in 3rd 2f out: pushed out to ld over 1f out: kpt on strly fnl f: comf* **4/6**[1]

2 2 1/2 **Fame And Glory**[69] 3438 3-9-0 126 .... JMurtagh 5 131
(A P O'Brien, Ire) *hld up: 7th 1/2-way: hdwy in 3rd 3f out: rdn to chal 2f out: sn led: hdd over 1f out: no ex and kpt on same pce fnl f* **9/4**[2]

3 2 1/2 **Mastercraftsman (IRE)**[18] 5135 3-9-0 127 .... JAHeffernan 7 126
(A P O'Brien, Ire) *chsd ldrs: 3rd 1/2-way: hdwy in 2nd 3f out: rdn to ld briefly over 2f out: hdd under 2f out: no ex in 3rd over 1f out: kpt on same pce* **6/1**[3]

4 9 **Grand Ducal (IRE)**[104] 2306 3-9-0 107 .... CO'Donoghue 1 108
(A P O'Brien, Ire) *chsd ldrs: 4th 1/2-way: rdn in 5th 3f out: no imp in 4th under 2f out: kpt on same pce* **100/1**

5 4 1/2 **Lord Admiral (USA)**[15] 5231 8-9-7 108 ....(b) DPMcDonogh 9 99
(Charles O'Brien, Ire) *hld up towards rr: hdwy to 6th 3f out: rdn and no ex 2f out: kpt on same pce* **150/1**

6 5 **Loch Long (IRE)**[14] 5277 3-9-0 96 .... PShanahan 8 89
(Tracey Collins, Ire) *disp early: sn chsd ldrs: pushed along in 6th 1/2-way: rr 3f out: kpt on one pce* **150/1**

7 1/2 **Casual Conquest (IRE)**[20] 5076 4-9-7 121 ....(bt[1]) PJSmullen 3 88
(D K Weld, Ire) *dwlt: hld up towards rr: rdn in 7th 3f out: no imp 2f out: kpt on one pce* **16/1**

8 19 **Rockhampton (IRE)**[42] 4298 3-9-0 100 .... SMLevey 6 50
(A P O'Brien, Ire) *sn rdn to chse ldrs: disp after 3f: 2nd 1/2-way: rdn and wknd over 3f out* **150/1**

9 4 **Set Sail (IRE)**[18] 5135 3-9-0 102 .... JPO'Brien 4 42
(A P O'Brien, Ire) *sn led: disp after 3f out: rdn and hdd over 2f out: no ex and wknd* **150/1**

2m 3.90s (-4.30) **Going Correction** +0.20s/f (Good)
WFA 3 from 4yo+ 7lb **9** Ran SP% **114.6**
Speed ratings: **125,123,121,113,110 106,105,90,87**
CSF £2.38 TOTE £2.00: £1.10, £1.30, £1.30; DF 2.60.
Owner Christopher Tsui **Bred** Sunderland Holdings **Trained** Currabeg, Co Kildare

FOCUS

The eagerly awaited re-match between Sea The Stars and Fame And Glory was enabled thanks to the drying ground. The Epsom Derby form was confirmed emphatically by the brilliant winner and, in a race run at a frantic pace, it rates his best effort so far. His RPR of 137+ is the highest allotted to a 3yo since the service started more than 20 years ago. The runner-up also posted a clear personal best in defeat.

NOTEBOOK

Sea The Stars(IRE), having his first domestic run of the season, sealed his status as one of the all-time greats of Irish racing with a fifth successive Group 1 victory. Although not the most extravagant in his wins in the 2000 Guineas, the Derby, the Eclipse, and certainly not in the Juddmonte, he could hardly have been more emphatic this time. It is hard to argue with the view of trainer and jockey that this was his best performance yet. Kinane actually took a pull as Fame And Glory made his move and the manner in which he eventually picked up that rival was there for all to see. The continuing drying ground enabled his participation, which had been in some doubt until he day of the race, and it proved him no bother. The ability to handle contrasting types of ground is widely recognised as one of the essential criteria for characterising equine greatness. The prospect of the Arc now beckons, and with it the probability of another ground-related saga. Oxx has not put a foot wrong with the colt yet, and nor he is likely to do so. (op 4/6 tchd 8/13)

Fame And Glory can be expected appreciate the return to 1m4f at Longchamp. He was an honourable second, but with this result confirming Epsom supremacy he will have his work cut out to reverse the form in the event of a rematch taking place. That he won the Irish Derby in such authoritative fashion provides ample proof of the exceptional ability shown by his conqueror. The Breeders' Cup Turf later on really looks the race for him. (op 9/4 tchd 5/2)

Mastercraftsman(IRE) led briefly before Fame And Glory hit the front, but could not sustain the momentum of his challenge after the unforgiving gallop. This rather confirms the view that he is at his very best over 1m and the Queen Elizabeth II Stakes looks likely to be next for him, although Rip Van Winkle would probably be the stable's number one for that should he make it. (op 6/1 tchd 13/2)

Grand Ducal(IRE) emerged with some credit on his first run since winning the Gallinule Stakes at the Curragh in May.

Casual Conquest(IRE) failed to make any impact in first-time blinkers and has to rate very disappointing. Official explanation: trainer said colt scoped dirty post race (op 14/1)

5689a IRISH STALLION FARMS EUROPEAN BREEDERS FUND AUTUMN FILLIES H'CAP 1m 4f

4:30 (4:31) 3-Y-0+ **£56,883** (£16,689; £7,951; £2,708)

RPR

1 — **Les Fazzani (IRE)**[83] 2960 5-9-7 103 .... GFCarroll(5) 6 109
(K A Ryan) *mid-div: hdwy to 5th 2f out: rdn into 2nd 1 1/2f out: led last 200yds: kpt on strly* **12/1**

2 1 1/4 **Cruel Sea (USA)**[14] 5270 4-7-13 83 ....(t) JPO'Brien(7) 12 87
(C F Swan, Ire) *hld up towards rr: hdwy in 9th 2f out: rdn into 4th 1f out: styd on to 2nd ins fnl f: nt rch wnr* **25/1**

3 2 **Elyaadi**[53] 3964 5-8-8 85 .... DPMcDonogh 4 86
(John Queally, Ire) *hld up towards rr: hdwy fr 2f out: rdn into 7th 1f out: kpt on wl fnl f to 3rd on line* **12/1**

4 shd **Adjaliya (IRE)**[77] 3180 3-8-7 93 .... NGMcCullagh 20 94
(John M Oxx, Ire) *chsd ldrs: 7th 1/2-way: rdn into 6th 1 1/2f out: 5th 1f out: kpt on same pce fnl f* **4/1**[1]

5 shd **Taralga (IRE)**[36] 4510 4-8-6 83 .... DJMoran 22 83
(S J Treacy, Ire) *sn chsd ldr in 2nd: led under 4f out: rdn clr over 2f out: chal 1f out: sn hdd: no ex and kpt on same pce* **10/1**

6 3 **Estephe (IRE)**[32] 4635 3-8-4 90 oh4 .... JohnEgan 7 86
(T Stack, Ire) *chsd ldrs: 6th 1/2-way: rdn into 3rd 2f out: no ex over 1f out: kpt on same pce fnl f* **9/1**[3]

7 1 1/4 **Chirkova (USA)**[18] 5143 3-8-7 93 .... CO'Donoghue 9 87
(A P O'Brien, Ire) *mid-div: rdn in 8th 2f out: 5th 1 1/2f out: no ex in 6th 1f out: kpt on same pce* **14/1**

8 nk **Tovaria**[19] 5116 5-8-4 81 .... RPCleary 5 74
(Edward P Harty, Ire) *mid-div: rdn into 8th 1f out: kpt on same pce fnl f* **16/1**

9 7 **Angels Story (IRE)**[76] 3195 4-8-12 89 ....(p) KJManning 19 71
(J S Bolger, Ire) *chsd ldrs: 3rd 1/2-way: rdn into 2nd 2f out: no ex in 4th 1 1/2f out: kpt on one pce* **25/1**

10 3 1/2 **End Of The Affair (IRE)**[44] 4255 5-9-1 92 .... FMBerry 11 68
(V C Ward, Ire) *in rr of mid-div: sme late hdwy in 11th 1f out: no imp fnl f* **14/1**

11 3 **Whispering Wind (IRE)**[53] 3439 6-8-5 82 ....(p) WJSupple 1 54
(Ms Joanna Morgan, Ire) *mid-div: rdn into 9th 1f out: no ex fnl f* **20/1**

12 1 1/4 **Spinning Wings (IRE)**[17] 5178 3-7-13 90 oh9 ....(t) BACurtis(5) 10 60
(T Hogan, Ire) *towards rr: sme late hdwy fr over 1f out* **33/1**

13 1 **Eytarna (IRE)**[27] 4835 3-8-12 98 .... MJKinane 8 66
(John M Oxx, Ire) *chsd ldrs: 4th 1/2-way: rdn in 6th 2f out: no ex and kpt on one pce: eased fnl f* **9/2**[2]

14 5 **Ashka (IRE)**[30] 4729 4-8-5 87 ow3 .... EJMcNamara(5) 21 47
(G M Lyons, Ire) *mid-div best: nvr a factor* **25/1**

15 1 1/4 **Greannmhar (USA)**[53] 3963 3-7-8 90 oh3 .... RPWhelan(10) 16 48
(J S Bolger, Ire) *chsd ldrs: 5th 1/2-way: rdn in 6th 3f out: sn no ex and wknd* **20/1**

16 3/4 **Qeethaara (USA)**[23] 4961 5-8-4 84 .... PBBeggy(3) 2 41
(P A Fahy, Ire) *mid-div: rdn into 7th 2f out: no ex and wknd over 1f out* **20/1**

17 1/2 **Holly Hawk (IRE)**[6] 5492 4-7-9 82 oh9 ow1 .... SBKelly(10) 3 38
(Kevin F O'Donnell, Ire) *towards rr for most: nvr a factor* **20/1**

18 3/4 **Temecula (IRE)**[66] 3517 4-8-1 81 ....(p) ShaneFoley(3) 13 36
(M Halford, Ire) *led: hdd 4f out: rdn in 2nd 3f out: no ex in 4th 2f out: wknd* **33/1**

19 1 3/4 **Chantilly Lace (IRE)**[23] 4961 3-8-4 90 oh2 .... DMGrant 18 42
(Reginald Roberts, Ire) *mid-div: wknd 3f out* **20/1**

20 5 **Lesoto Diamond (IRE)**[30] 4728 7-8-1 81 oh1 .... SMGorey(3) 14 25
(P A Fahy, Ire) *mid-div: wknd 3f out* **20/1**

21 nk **Dance Pass (IRE)**[33] 4609 3-8-12 98 .... PJSmullen 17 42
(D K Weld, Ire) *mid-div: wknd 3f out* **10/1**

22 hd **Lady Songbird (IRE)**[19] 5116 6-8-4 81 oh6 ....(t) MCHussey 23 24
(C F Swan, Ire) *sn towards rr: nvr a factor* **25/1**

2m 33.66s (-1.64) **Going Correction** +0.20s/f (Good)
WFA 3 from 4yo+ 9lb **22** Ran SP% **150.8**
Speed ratings: **113,112,110,110,110 108,107,107,103,100 98,97,97,93,93 92,92,91,90,87 86,86**
CSF £307.72 CT £3747.79 TOTE £19.40: £3.90, £9.20, £3.20, £2.30; DF 752.10.
Owner Dr Marwan Koukash **Bred** J Erhardt And Mrs J Schonwalder **Trained** Hambleton, N Yorks

FOCUS

A useful-looking contest.

NOTEBOOK

Les Fazzani(IRE) has not enjoyed her previous visits to these shores, being found out in Group company, but put up a classy effort and won in the style of a Group performer in a handicap. Held up in mid-division, she always travelled well and, even when the pace increased as they turned into the straight, looked the only one to have matters in hand and powered to the front inside the last to win convincingly. She should be capable of adding to her tally in stakes company, and there's still time. Official explanation: trainer said, regarding the apparent improvement in form, that the filly had benefitted from a complete rest and she had shown good late season form in previous years

5687 - 5691a (Foreign Racing) - See Raceform Interactive

5230 YORK (L-H)

Sunday, September 6

OFFICIAL GOING: Good to soft (good on home bend; 6.7)

Rail realignment reduced distances on round course by 27yards.

Wind: Moderate, half-against. Weather: overcast, light shower race 7

5692 JEN & TONY SMEATON GOLDEN WEDDING ANNIVERSARY STKS (NURSERY) 7f

2:00 (2:00) (Class 4) (0-85,83) 2-Y-O **£5,828** (£1,734; £866; £432) **Stalls** Low

Form RPR

3621 1 — **William Morgan (IRE)**[3] 5595 2-8-9 **71** 6ex .... PaulHanagan 4 76
(R A Fahey) *trckd ldrs: led over 1f out: edgd lft and kpt on wl towards fin* **15/8**[1]

120 2 1/2 **Victoire De Lyphar (IRE)**[8] 5433 2-9-2 **78** ....(v[1]) PhillipMakin 3 82
(P C Haslam) *led tl over 4f out: upsides fnl f: no ex towards fin* **25/1**

2030 3 2 3/4 **We'll Deal Again**[15] 5253 2-7-10 **65** ow1 .... JamesPSullivan(7) 13 62+
(M W Easterby) *hld up: hdwy over 2f out: styd on same pce fnl f* **12/1**

5140 4 2 1/4 **Reeds Bay (IRE)**[15] 5265 2-9-5 **81** ....(b) RobertWinston 2 73
(E S McMahon) *dwlt: effrt over 3f out: upsides over 1f out: kpt on same pce* **40/1**

0040 5 3 3/4 **Uddy Mac**[19] 5136 2-7-12 **60** oh4 .... SilvestreDeSousa 10 42
(N Bycroft) *in rr: hdwy on ins 3f out: sn chsng ldrs: wknd fnl f* **25/1**

521 6 nk **Tominator**[25] 4888 2-9-7 **83** .... GrahamGibbons 5 64
(R Hollinshead) *trckd ldr: led over 4f out: hdd over 1f out: sn wknd* **4/1**[2]

153 7 5 **Leviathan**[44] 4271 2-9-6 **82** .... MickyFenton 14 51
(T P Tate) *chsd ldrs: drvn over 2f out: wknd over 1f out* **20/1**

3213 8 3 1/2 **Bridge Valley**[8] 5445 2-9-5 **81** .... PatDobbs 12 41
(R Hannon) *in rr: lost pl over 2f out* **33/1**

413 9 1 1/4 **Ejaab**[20] 5091 2-9-5 **81** .... TPO'Shea 7 38
(W J Haggas) *in rr: drvn 3f out: nvr a factor* **13/2**[3]

31 10 3 **Abriachan**[18] 5153 2-8-13 **82** .... IJBrennan(7) 9 32
(M G Quinlan) *trckd ldrs: lost pl over 2f out* **7/1**

5610 11 3/4 **Angel Of Fashion (IRE)**[36] 4539 2-8-12 **74** .... MichaelHills 1 22
(B W Hills) *chsd ldrs: lost pl 2f out* **9/1**

643 **12** *hd* **Jimmy The Poacher (IRE)**[15] 5251 2-8-11 **73**.................. DavidAllan 8 20
(T D Easterby) *chsd ldrs: sn drvn along: lost pl 3f out* **16/1**
1m 27.59s (2.29) **Going Correction** +0.325s/f (Good) **12** Ran SP% **122.0**
Speed ratings (Par 97): **99,98,95,92,88 88,82,78,76,73 72,72**
toteswingers: 1&2 £11.90, 1&3 £7.00, 2&3 £51.50. CSF £64.65 CT £481.11 TOTE £2.90: £1.50, £8.40, £4.00; EX 79.30.
Owner P D Smith Holdings Ltd **Bred** R P Ryan **Trained** Musley Bank, N Yorks

FOCUS
A fair and competitive nursery. The time was the best part of five seconds outside standard, suggesting that the ground was riding much as advertised. The runners came over to the stands' side in the home straight.

NOTEBOOK
William Morgan(IRE) was an easy winner of a nursery at Redcar three days earlier and he followed up under the penalty in this more competitive event, handling the easy surface well. After travelling strongly, he battled on willingly to assert despite edging to his left, the front pair pulling away. A mile will not be a problem and he could be the sort for the nursery over that trip at Ayr later in the month. (op 5-2)
Victoire De Lyphar(IRE) had finished last on his previous start but he ran much better here, travelling kindly in the first-time visor and refusing to wilt under pressure. His action suggests the easy ground was in his favour.
We'll Deal Again, whose rider put up a pound overweight, stayed on nicely from the rear of the field and seemed well suited by the return to 7f on this nursery debut. He did carry his head a little high, though. (op 16-1 tchd 9-1)
Reeds Bay(IRE) was away on terms this time and he came through to have his chance, but could not quicken up for pressure. He dealt with the easy ground well enough.
Uddy Mac was out of the weights again and she ran respectably after making her effort widest of all in the straight. (op 28-1 tchd 33-1)
Tominator, a striking winner at Beverley last time, got to the front before the turn but could not hold on. He is probably worth keeping on the right side. (op 5-1)
Leviathan raced nearest the stands' rail and was not disgraced. He may just improve fitness-wise with this first run for six weeks under his belt. Official explanation: jockey said colt had no more to give (op 14-1)
Ejaab struggled to get involved in a race in which it proved difficult to make up ground. (tchd 8-1)
Angel Of Fashion(IRE) was keen through the early stages and she could not sustain her effort in the last 2f. (op 8-1)

5693 EBF BETINTERNET.COM MAIDEN STKS 5f 89y
2:35 (2:37) (Class 3) 2-Y-O **£6,799** (£2,023; £1,011; £505) **Stalls** High

Form RPR
1 **Coolminx (IRE)** 2-8-12 0.................. PaulHanagan 7 81+
(R A Fahey) *sltly hmpd s and sn cl up: effrt to chal 2f out: sn rdn and edgd lft: styd on to ld ent fnl f: drvn and kpt on wl towards fin* **8/1**
2 *1 1/2* **Walvis Bay (IRE)** 2-9-3 0.................. MickyFenton 1 81
(T P Tate) *cl up on wd outside: pushed along and sltly outpcd over 2f out: rdn and hdwy wl over 1f out: chsd wnr ins fnl f: kpt on* **10/1**
2 **3** *1 3/4* **Moorhouse Girl**[24] 4928 2-8-12 0.................. NCallan 10 70
(D H Brown) *cl up on stands' rail: led over 3f out: rdn 2f out: drvn and hdd ent fnl f: sn edgd lft and kpt on same pce* **9/4**[1]
44 **4** *8* **Kalahari Desert (IRE)**[18] 5146 2-9-0 0.................. MichaelJStainton(3) 5 50
(R M Whitaker) *cl up: rdn along 2f out: drvn and one pce fr over 1f out* **11/1**
0 **5** *4 1/2* **Classlin**[29] 4774 2-8-7 0.................. GaryBartley(5) 4 30
(J S Goldie) *towards rr: hdwy to chse ldrs over 2f out: sn rdn and outpcd fr wl over 1f out* **33/1**
0 **6** *nk* **Imjin River (IRE)**[8] 5431 2-8-12 0.................. AshleyMorgan(5) 11 34
(M H Tompkins) *towards rr: hdwy to chse ldrs over 2f out: sn rdn and btn* **12/1**
00 **7** *3 3/4* **Dead Womans Pass (IRE)**[44] 4286 2-8-5 0.................. ShirleyTeasdale(7) 2 17
(N Wilson) *chsd ldrs: rdn along 1/2-way: sn wknd* **100/1**
8 *2 1/4* **Fair Bunny** 2-8-12 0.................. GrahamGibbons 9 10
(A D Brown) *wnt lft s: a towards rr* **25/1**
2 **9** *1 1/2* **Taborcillo**[36] 4546 2-9-3 0.................. PhillipMakin 6 10
(T D Barron) *prom: rdn along 1/2-way: sn wknd* **7/2**[2]
10 *18* **Marius Maximus (IRE)** 2-9-3 0.................. JoeFanning 3 —
(M Johnston) *led: pushed along and hdd over 3f out: sn wknd and bhd* **4/1**[3]
66.09 secs (1.79) **Going Correction** +0.325s/f (Good) **10** Ran SP% **117.0**
Speed ratings (Par 99): **98,95,92,80,72 72,66,62,60,31**
toteswingers: 1&2 £10.30, 1&3 £5.80, 2&3 £7.20. CSF £83.73 TOTE £9.60: £2.40, £3.30, £1.40; EX 85.70.
Owner Mrs H Steel **Bred** D Couper Snr **Trained** Musley Bank, N Yorks

FOCUS
A reasonable maiden. The first three finished well clear.

NOTEBOOK
Coolminx(IRE) was distinctly green on this debut, hanging to her left just past halfway, but she showed fine pace too and ran on strongly once straightened for quite an impressive success. Her half-brother Baycat was an early 2-y-o sprinter but there is stamina on her dam's side and 6f would be no problem at this stage. She is sure to improve with this experience to draw upon. (op 5-1 tchd 9-1 in a place)
Walvis Bay(IRE) ◆ is a half-brother to seven winners including the high-class Pipalong who won the Haydock Sprint Cup nine years ago. Rather isolated on the outside until edging across after halfway, he stuck on willingly for second and looks sure to go one better in the near future. (op 17-2 tchd 8-1)
Moorhouse Girl, a half-sister to classy sprinter Moorhouse Lad, had made a promising debut when green at Beverley. She ran at least as well here and held every chance, but could not quicken up inside the last. The rest were 8l and more behind and she is another who will have no trouble landing a maiden. (tchd 11-4)
Kalahari Desert(IRE) has finished fourth on each of his three starts now and probably did not improve here, although he did turn around Thirsk form with Taborcillo. (op 25-1 tchd 10-1)
Classlin showed slightly more than she had on her debut, despite a tardy start. (op 40-1)
Imjin River(IRE) gave the impression that he will pay his way in time. (op 20-1)
Taborcillo dropped away disappointingly. He had handled similar ground when runner-up in the Thirsk race and this was not his running. (op 100-30 tchd 4-1)
Marius Maximus(IRE), a 120,000gns breeze-ups buy, is a nice type. He showed bright speed before dropping alarmingly back through the field and trailing in last. (op 5-1 tchd 7-2)

5694 BETINTERNET.COM CLAIMING STKS 1m 2f 88y
3:10 (3:10) (Class 4) 3-Y-O+ **£6,540** (£1,946; £972; £485) **Stalls** Low

Form RPR
0050 **1** **Middlemarch (IRE)**[8] 5441 9-8-7 63 ow1.................. (v) GaryBartley(5) 2 77
(J S Goldie) *led: clr 7f out: remained far side and racd alone in home st: 3 l clr over 1f out: unchal* **25/1**
4600 **2** *2 1/2* **Charlie Cool**[17] 5200 6-9-7 94.................. (tp) SilvestreDeSousa 6 81+
(Mrs R A Carr) *hld up towards rr: hdwy over 3f out: styd on wl fnl f: led stands' side gp nr fin: nt rch wnr* **11/4**[1]
3500 **3** *1/2* **Court Masterpiece**[16] 5232 9-9-5 104.................. GrahamGibbons 9 78
(J J Quinn) *hld up in rr: stdy hdwy 3f out: chsng ldrs stands' side over 1f out: kpt on same pce ins fnl f* **4/1**[3]
031 **4** *nse* **Charlie Tokyo (IRE)**[28] 4815 6-9-4 86.................. (v) PaulHanagan 7 77
(R A Fahey) *trckd ldrs: smooth hdwy to ld stands' side over 1f out: no ex ins fnl f* **3/1**[2]
001 **5** *3 1/2* **Malt Or Mash (USA)**[23] 4987 5-9-4 95.................. PatDobbs 5 71
(R Hannon) *chsd ldrs: wnt 2nd over 3f out: fdd ins fnl f* **8/1**
0106 **6** *3 1/2* **Realism (FR)**[44] 4288 9-8-4 63.................. (tp) JamesPSullivan(7) 1 57
(M W Easterby) *hld up in rr: hdwy on ins over 4f out: sn chsng ldrs centre: wknd over 1f out* **16/1**
3003 **7** *1 1/4* **Quince (IRE)**[17] 5186 6-8-12 69.................. (p) SaleemGolam 11 56
(J Pearce) *chsd ldrs: wknd over 1f out* **33/1**
5 **8** *14* **Obara D'Avril (FR)**[8] 1765 7-9-3 0 ow1.................. MHNaughton 10 34
(S G West) *chsd ldrs: drvn over 4f out: lost pl over 2f out* **100/1**
6000 **9** *2 1/4* **Jack Junior (USA)**[37] 4486 5-9-0 90.................. JoeFanning 3 27
(D Nicholls) *hld up towards rr: effrt centre over 3f out: wknd 2f out* **8/1**
4S06 **10** *5* **Neon Blue**[24] 4927 8-8-6 44.................. (p) AmyRyan(5) 8 14
(R M Whitaker) *s.i.s: in rr: drvn 6f out: bhd fnl 3f* **100/1**
6210 **11** *7* **Traphalgar (IRE)**[62] 3695 4-9-7 84.................. NCallan 4 11
(P F I Cole) *trckd ldrs: racd centre home st: wknd 2f out* **8/1**
2m 13.7s (1.20) **Going Correction** +0.325s/f (Good) **11** Ran SP% **119.6**
Speed ratings (Par 105): **108,106,105,105,102 99,98,87,85,81 76**
toteswingers: 1&2 £22.90, 1&3 £21.90, 2&3 £5.60. CSF £93.88 TOTE £34.50: £6.90, £1.40, £1.40; EX 212.10.
Owner W M Johnstone **Bred** Swettenham Stud And Hugo Lascelles **Trained** Uplawmoor, E Renfrews

FOCUS
This was the first race to be run around York's widened bend. A good claimer which was contested by past winners of the Sussex Stakes, John Smith's Cup and November Handicap, although the form may not prove all that solid. The winner, who raced alone in the straight and made all, is the best guide.

5695 BEST ODDS GUARANTEED AT BETINTERNET.COM STKS (H'CAP) 6f
3:45 (3:47) (Class 2) (0-100,96) 3-Y-O+ **£11,656** (£3,468; £1,733; £865) **Stalls** High

Form RPR
2033 **1** **Able Master (IRE)**[22] 5032 3-9-5 **95**.................. RoystonFfrench 16 111+
(B Smart) *chsd ldrs towards stands' side: hdwy 2f out: rdn to ld ent fnl f: edgd rt and kpt on wl* **25/1**
04 **2** *2 1/2* **Kaldoun Kingdom (IRE)**[43] 4330 4-9-1 **89**.................. TonyHamilton 10 97
(R A Fahey) *towards rr: hdwy wl over 2f out: rdn to chse ldrs over 1f out: drvn ent fnl f: kpt on wl towards fin* **9/1**[3]
3132 **3** *nk* **Eton Rifles (IRE)**[43] 4310 4-9-0 **88**.................. PhillipMakin 13 95
(J Howard Johnson) *led: rdn along wl over 2f out: drvn: edgd lft and hdd ent fnl f: kpt on same pce* **7/2**[1]
2304 **4** *1 1/4* **Barons Spy (IRE)**[6] 5529 8-8-13 **87**.................. JamesDoyle 11 90
(R J Price) *hld up: hdwy 2f out: sn rdn and kpt on u.p ins fnl f: nrst fin* **25/1**
2104 **5** *2* **Silver Wind**[9] 5404 4-8-3 **82**.................. (v) SimonPearce(5) 8 79
(P D Evans) *in rr and rdn along 1/2-way: hdwy over 2f out: drvn over 1f out: kpt on ins fnl f: nrst fin* **33/1**
0253 **6** *nk* **Harrison George (IRE)**[7] 5476 4-9-2 **90**.................. PaulHanagan 9 86
(R A Fahey) *towards rr: pushed along and hdwy over 2f out: rdn wl over 1f out: kpt on ins fnl f: nrst fin* **4/1**[2]
0050 **7** *3/4* **Tajneed (IRE)**[35] 4574 6-9-5 **93**.................. TPO'Shea 5 86
(D Nicholls) *prom: rdn along 2f out: sn drvn and wknd appr fnl f* **9/1**[3]
120- **8** *2* **Oratory (IRE)**[372] 5507 3-9-6 **96**.................. PatDobbs 6 83+
(R Hannon) *s.i.s and bhd: hdwy 2f out: kpt on appr fnl f: nvr nr ldrs* **28/1**
3500 **9** *shd* **Ishetoo**[8] 5420 5-9-7 **95**.................. (p) DavidAllan 3 82
(A Dickman) *prom: effrt and ev ch 2f out: sn rdn and wknd over 1f out* **18/1**
0100 **10** *1 3/4* **Horatio Carter**[37] 4486 4-9-4 **92**.................. (p) NCallan 14 73
(K A Ryan) *chsd ldrs: rdn along over 2f out: sn wknd* **33/1**
0010 **11** *1/2* **Baldemar**[71] 3389 4-8-8 **87**.................. BMcHugh(5) 2 66
(R A Fahey) *chsd ldrs on wd outside: rdn 2f out and ev ch tl drvn and wknd appr fnl f* **18/1**
006 **12** *1/2* **Damika (IRE)**[15] 5257 6-9-2 **90**.................. RobertWinston 4 68
(R M Whitaker) *chsd ldrs: rdn along after 2f: drvn and wknd over 2f out: btn whn n.m.r over 1f out* **12/1**
-052 **13** *3/4* **Sea Of Leaves (USA)**[22] 5032 3-8-13 **92**.................. FrederikTylicki(3) 18 67
(J S Goldie) *chsd ldrs towards stands' rail: rdn along wl over 2f out and sn wknd* **12/1**
0000 **14** *1 1/4* **Aldermoor (USA)**[22] 5032 3-8-12 **88**.................. SaleemGolam 7 59
(S C Williams) *dwlt: a towards rr* **33/1**
0000 **15** *nk* **Thebes**[15] 5257 4-9-3 **91**.................. JoeFanning 17 61
(M Johnston) *in midfield: rdn along 1/2-way: sn wknd* **16/1**
241- **16** *3/4* **Master Rooney (IRE)**[314] 7020 3-8-12 **88**.................. TomEaves 1 56
(B Smart) *dwlt and towards rr: swtchd lft and hdwy on wd outside 2f out: sn rdn and wknd* **14/1**
4530 **U** **Excusez Moi (USA)**[22] 5039 7-9-6 **94**.................. (b) SilvestreDeSousa 12 —
(Mrs R A Carr) *swvd rt and uns rdr s* **12/1**
1m 12.42s (0.52) **Going Correction** +0.325s/f (Good)
WFA 3 from 4yo+ 2lb **17** Ran SP% **128.3**
Speed ratings (Par 109): **109,105,105,103,100 100,99,96,96,94 93,93,92,90,90 89,—**
toteswingers: 1&2 £37.70, 1&3 £22.20, 2&3 £10.70. CSF £233.10 CT £1000.77 TOTE £27.20: £4.70, £2.60, £1.60, £6.00; EX 348.10 Trifecta £486.50 Part won. Pool £657.46 - 0.20 winning units..
Owner Ron Hull **Bred** Scuderia Miami Di Sandro Guerra And Co **Trained** Hambleton, N Yorks

FOCUS
A decent and competitive sprint, but not many got into it. The winner produced a clear personal best, with the runner-up a sound guide.

NOTEBOOK
Able Master(IRE), whose yard is back in form, had been running well in handicaps confined to his own age group and ran out a decisive winner against these older rivals. After collaring the long-time leader, he edged across to the stands' rail and the loose Excusez Moi gave him something to chase. He continues on the upgrade and could have more to offer. (op 33-1 tchd 22-1)
Kaldoun Kingdom(IRE), his connections' second string, ran a nice race, running on for second late on. He remains without a win since his juvenile season, but could rectify that granted suitable conditions underfoot like he had here. (op 8-1)
Eton Rifles(IRE) remains progressive and there are more races in him. He had the loose horse to contend with early on, but showed bright pace down the centre and was only reeled in inside the last. (op 5-1 tchd 11-2 in places)
Barons Spy(IRE) faced a more realistic task than at Warwick on Monday, and he ran a sound race. (tchd 33-1 in a place)
Silver Wind ran on well from the back of the field after briefly having to wait for a gap. He has always found a mark above 80 insurmountable. (tchd 40-1)

Harrison George(IRE) was another who was running on from the back. He usually runs well here but really needs a stiffer test. (op 9-2)
Tajneed(IRE) was back at a more suitable trip, but failed to confirm the good impression he had made here two runs back. He is fairly handicapped at present. (op 17-2)
Oratory(IRE) ◆ was a useful 2-y-o but this was his first run for a year. He was taken off his legs by these handicappers, but kept on nicely late on to hint strongly that he retains ability. The return to 7f will very much be in his favour. (op 33-1)
Ishetoo will be suited by the drop back to the minimum, and/or faster ground. (op 25-1 tchd 16-1)
Master Rooney(IRE) bruised a foot last year and was making a belated reappearance. Racing on the outside, he could never make his presence felt, but may be worth affording another chance, as he was not fully wound up here. (op 12-1)

5696 COLLINGWOOD TEAM SERVICE STKS (H'CAP) 2m 88y

4:20 (4:20) (Class 4) (0-80,78) 3-Y-O+ **£5,828** (£1,734; £866; £432) **Stalls** Low

Form RPR

0332 **1** **Dulcie**[10] 5376 3-8-5 **73** ...... AshleyMorgan(5) 1 83
(M H Tompkins) *hld up towards rr: hdwy 6f out: wnt 2nd over 1f out: styd on wl to ld wl ins fnl f* **7/1**[3]

1341 **2** *1* **Deauville Flyer**[37] 4491 3-8-12 **75** ...... RobertWinston 7 83+
(T D Easterby) *hld up: hdwy to trck ldrs 8f out: qcknd to ld 3f out: edgd lft and hdd fnl 75yds* **5/2**[1]

3316 **3** *½* **Simonside**[17] 5185 6-9-6 **70** ...... TomEaves 6 78
(B Ellison) *chsd ldrs: n.m.r over 2f out: styd on wl fnl f* **16/1**

6325 **4** *2 ¾* **Danzatrice**[9] 5410 7-9-3 **67** ...... PaulHanagan 9 71
(C W Thornton) *hld up in rr: effrt over 5f out: nt clr run and swtchd rt over 1f out: kpt on wl* **12/1**

6114 **5** *1* **Baan (USA)**[9] 5410 6-9-3 **67** ......(p) JimmyQuinn 8 70
(H J Collingridge) *chsd ldrs: one pce fnl 3f* **11/1**

5406 **6** *3 ¼* **Amanda Carter**[18] 5170 5-9-11 **78** ...... FrederikTylicki(3) 12 77
(R A Fahey) *hld up in rr: hdwy 7f out: one pce fnl 3f* **16/1**

3014 **7** *5* **Fin Vin De Leu (GER)**[15] 5252 3-8-13 **76** ...... NCallan 4 69
(M Johnston) *led 1f: led after 4f: qcknd over 4f out: hdd 3f out: hung rt and wknd over 1f out* **9/2**[2]

0-06 **8** *nk* **Whenever**[58] 3793 5-9-8 **72** ...... KirstyMilczarek 2 65
(R T Phillips) *s.i.s: hdwy 9f out: outpcd 4f out: wknd 2f out* **16/1**

321 **9** *13* **Spiders Star**[11] 5339 6-8-11 **66** ...... PaulPickard(5) 11 43
(S G West) *hld up in rr: pushed along 6f out: nvr a factor* **7/1**[3]

3153 **10** *1 ½* **Drop The Hammer**[19] 5131 3-7-12 **61** oh2...... SilvestreDeSousa 5 37
(T P Tate) *w ldr: led after 1f: hdd after 4f: drvn 6f out: lost pl over 1f out: eased* **12/1**

1540 **11** *15* **Dazzling Light (UAE)**[18] 5170 4-9-13 **77** ...... PhillipMakin 10 35
(J S Goldie) *trckd ldrs: jnd ldr 7f out: wkng whn sltly hmpd over 2f out: sn bhd and eased* **20/1**

3m 39.22s (4.72) **Going Correction** +0.325s/f (Good)
WFA 3 from 4yo+ 13lb **11** Ran SP% **117.9**
Speed ratings (Par 105): **101,100,100,98,98 96,94,94,87,86 79**
toteswingers: 1&2 £4.70, 1&3 £20.50, 2&3 £13.00. CSF £24.82 CT £276.99 TOTE £8.60: £2.60, £1.60, £5.30; EX 25.50.
Owner Trevor Benton **Bred** Dullingham Park **Trained** Newmarket, Suffolk

FOCUS
A fair handicap for the grade, run at an ordinary pace. The runners stayed on the inside in the home straight. The first pair are progressive and the fourth and fifth are a fair guide to the form.

5697 SIGN UP BONUS AT BETINTERNET.COM STKS (H'CAP) 7f

4:50 (4:52) (Class 4) (0-80,80) 3-Y-O+ **£5,828** (£1,734; £866; £432) **Stalls** Low

Form RPR

3014 **1** **Without Prejudice (USA)**[29] 4802 4-9-2 **79**......(v) FrederikTylicki(3) 14 94+
(J Noseda) *a cl up: led over 2f out: rdn clr wl over 1f out: styd on strly* **6/1**[1]

2110 **2** *3 ¾* **Violent Velocity (IRE)**[9] 5409 6-8-9 **76** ...... IJBrennan(7) 17 81
(J J Quinn) *s.i.s and bhd: swtchd rt and gd hdwy on outer over 2f out: rdn over 1f out: styd on to chse wnr ins fnl f: sn edgd lft and no imp* **12/1**

4326 **3** *¾* **Observatory Star (IRE)**[8] 5441 6-9-5 **79**......(bt) RobertWinston 5 82
(T D Easterby) *hld up in midfield and n.m.r bnd over 4f out: hdwy over 2f out: rdn and n.m.r over 1f out and again ins fnl f: styd on wl nr fin* **7/1**[2]

3643 **4** *shd* **Last Sovereign**[23] 5001 5-9-6 **80** ......(p) JimmyQuinn 2 83
(Jane Chapple-Hyam) *chsd ldrs: rdn along over 2f out: drvn over 1f out: edgd rt and kpt on u.p ins fnl f* **6/1**[1]

0600 **5** *nk* **Cornus**[20] 5107 7-8-13 **73** ......(be) JamesDoyle 13 75
(J A Glover) *in tch: hdwy towards outer 3f out: rdn to chse ldrs 2f out: drvn over 1f out: edgd lft and kpt on same pce ins fnl f* **33/1**

2434 **6** *1 ½* **Misplaced Fortune**[23] 5007 4-8-13 **73** ...... JoeFanning 9 74+
(N Tinkler) *hld up towards rr: hdwy 2f out: nt clr run and swtchd rt wl over 1f out: styd on wl fnl f: nrest at fin* **12/1**

4615 **7** *nse* **Koraleva Tectona (IRE)**[23] 5005 4-9-4 **78** ...... PatDobbs 20 76
(Pat Eddery) *led: rdn along 3f out: hdd over 2f out: sn drvn and grad wknd* **33/1**

1004 **8** *¾* **Dickie Le Davoir**[16] 5225 5-9-0 **74** ......(v) MickyFenton 18 70
(John A Harris) *hld up in rr: hdwy on outer over 2f out: rdn to chse ldrs and edgd lft over 1f out: drvn and edgd lft ins fnl f: no imp* **20/1**

0-00 **9** *1 ¼* **Sadeek**[9] 5409 5-9-2 **76** ...... RoystonFfrench 4 68
(B Smart) *cl up: rdn along over 2f out: drvn wl over 1f out: grad wknd* **33/1**

0205 **10** *½* **Turn Me On (IRE)**[9] 5409 6-9-6 **80** ...... GrahamGibbons 8 71
(T D Walford) *chsd ldrs: rdn along wl over 2f out and grad wknd* **16/1**

-066 **11** *nk* **Oh So Saucy**[41] 4386 5-8-11 **74** ...... JackMitchell(3) 10 70+
(C F Wall) *chsd ldrs: rdn along over 2f out: drvn and hld whn n.m.r over 1f out and again ins fnl f: wknd* **12/1**

00-0 **12** *3 ¼* **Burning Incense (IRE)**[18] 5148 6-9-3 **77** ...... PhillipMakin 7 58
(M Dods) *hld up in rr: stdy hdwy 1/2-way: in tch over 2f out: sn rdn and wknd* **22/1**

-040 **13** *3 ¾* **Game Lad**[71] 3391 7-9-4 **78** ......(t) DavidAllan 15 49
(T D Easterby) *sltly hmpd s: a towards rr* **14/1**

5536 **14** *2 ½* **Celtic Lynn (IRE)**[25] 4896 4-9-1 **75** ...... TonyHamilton 19 39
(M Dods) *in tch: hdwy to chse ldrs 1/2-way: rdn along over 2f out and sn wknd* **11/1**[3]

4000 **15** *¾* **Sir Xaar (IRE)**[73] 3312 6-9-5 **79** ......(v) TomEaves 1 41
(B Smart) *a towards rr* **33/1**

0500 **16** *3 ¼* **Countdown**[79] 3116 7-9-3 **77** ...... PaulHanagan 6 31
(R A Fahey) *in midfield: rdn along wl over 2f out: sn wknd* **7/1**[2]

0000 **17** *1 ¼* **Van Bossed (CAN)**[25] 4891 4-9-6 **80** ...... TPO'Shea 3 30
(D Nicholls) *t.k.h: chsd ldrs: rdn along over 2f out: grad wknd* **20/1**

1m 26.65s (1.35) **Going Correction** +0.325s/f (Good)
WFA 3 from 4yo+ 4lb **17** Ran SP% **123.2**
Speed ratings (Par 105): **105,100,99,99,99 97,97,96,95,94 94,90,86,83,82 79,77**
toteswingers: 1&2 £17.00, 1&3 £4.50, 2&3 £14.00. CSF £70.04 CT £529.23 TOTE £6.40: £1.80, £2.40, £2.00, £2.20; EX 52.30.
Owner C Fox & J Wright **Bred** Castlemartin Stud And Skymarc Farm **Trained** Newmarket, Suffolk

FOCUS
They came down the centre of the home straight in this ordinary handicap. The winner is rated up 6lb on his Newmarket form, with the race rated at face value.
Misplaced Fortune Official explanation: jockey said filly was denied a clear run
Oh So Saucy Official explanation: jockey said mare had a breathing problem

5698 PLAY LIVE CASINO AT BETINTERNET.COM APPRENTICE STKS (H'CAP) 1m 4f

5:20 (5:20) (Class 5) (0-70,70) 4-Y-O+ **£5,051** (£1,503; £751; £375) **Stalls** Centre

Form RPR

2332 **1** **Grandad Bill (IRE)**[14] 5294 6-8-4 **56** oh1...... DebraEngland 5 66+
(J S Goldie) *trckd ldrs: wnt 2nd over 3f out: led appr fnl f: eased nr fin: jst hld on* **9/2**[1]

4036 **2** *hd* **Force Group (IRE)**[22] 5034 5-9-3 **69** ...... AshleyMorgan 2 78
(M H Tompkins) *mid-div: hdwy over 3f out: chsng ldrs and hung lft over 1f out: styd on wl towards fin* **9/2**[1]

-454 **3** *1 ¼* **Elite Land**[99] 2505 6-8-5 **61** ...... AnthonyBetts(4) 1 68
(B Ellison) *mid-div: hdwy to chse ldrs over 3f out: styd on same pce ins fnl f* **17/2**

5-54 **4** *nk* **Leslingtaylor (IRE)**[120] 428 7-9-4 **70** ...... IJBrennan 13 76+
(J J Quinn) *in rr: hdwy 3f out: styd on wl fnl f* **8/1**[3]

0001 **5** *3* **Oddsmaker (IRE)**[14] 5294 8-8-7 **59** ......(t) SimonPearce 12 60
(M A Barnes) *led tl hdd appr fnl f: wknd towards fin* **12/1**

3404 **6** *4* **Kalasam**[5] 5548 5-8-6 **62** ...... AdamCarter(4) 7 57
(M W Easterby) *hld up in rr: kpt on fnl 3f: nvr nr ldrs* **22/1**

2002 **7** *2* **Astronomical (IRE)**[8] 5423 7-8-7 **61** ...... DavidKenny(2) 11 53
(R Hollinshead) *chsd ldrs: wknd over 1f out* **25/1**

0515 **8** *2 ¾* **Sporting Gesture**[30] 4755 12-8-4 **56** oh1...... JamesPSullivan 8 43
(M W Easterby) *in rr: kpt on fnl 3f: nvr nr ldrs* **16/1**

4335 **9** *1* **Resentful Angel**[17] 5195 4-8-10 **62** ...... TobyAtkinson 3 48
(Pat Eddery) *detached in last: hdwy on wd outside over 3f out: edgd lft over 1f out: nvr a factor* **15/2**[2]

-400 **10** *9* **Hannicean**[22] 5035 5-9-1 **67** ...... LeeNewnes 4 38
(R W Price) *s.s: in rr: hdwy over 3f out: sn wknd* **18/1**

0604 **11** *¾* **Dechiper (IRE)**[9] 5395 7-9-0 **68** ...... GarryWhillans(2) 10 38
(R Johnson) *hld up in rr: hdwy on outer over 4f out: lost pl over 1f out* **16/1**

5012 **12** *2 ¼* **Applaude**[12] 5327 4-9-1 **69** ......(p) JohnCavanagh(2) 9 36
(John A Harris) *chsd ldr: lost pl over 3f out* **16/1**

0315 **13** *½* **They All Laughed**[13] 5308 6-8-8 **62** ...... NSLawes(2) 14 28
(Mrs Marjorie Fife) *mid-div: hdwy to chse ldrs over 6f out: lost pl over 2f out* **22/1**

1253 **14** *2 ¼* **Stateside (CAN)**[18] 5160 4-8-6 **62** ...... LeeTopliss(4) 6 24
(R A Fahey) *rrd s: in rr: bhd fnl 3f* **17/2**

600 **15** *17* **Tres Froide (FR)**[12] 5329 4-8-4 **56** oh1...... DeclanCannon 15 —
(N Tinkler) *chsd ldrs: drvn over 6f out: lost pl over 2f out: bhd whn eased* **40/1**

2m 36.48s (3.28) **Going Correction** +0.325s/f (Good) **15** Ran SP% **125.9**
Speed ratings (Par 103): **102,101,101,100,98 96,94,93,92,86 85,84,84,82,71**
toteswingers: 1&2 £3.90, 1&3 £9.80, 2&3 £16.90. CSF £22.10 CT £174.72 TOTE £5.50: £2.20, £2.50, £3.30; EX 24.90 Place 6 £54.10, Place 5 £23.78..
Owner C & B Racing Club **Bred** M Hosokawa **Trained** Uplawmoor, E Renfrews

FOCUS
A modest handicap for apprentices who had not ridden more than 25 winners. The pace was sound and the form should prove solid enough.
Hannicean Official explanation: jockey said gelding missed the break
T/Jkpt: Not won. T/Plt: £27.40 to a £1 stake. Pool: £112,937.18. 3,004.63 winning tickets. T/Qpdt: £12.10 to a £1 stake. Pool: £6,972.31. 424.60 winning tickets. WG

5699 - 5712a (Foreign Racing) - See Raceform Interactive

5651 BADEN-BADEN (L-H)

Sunday, September 6

OFFICIAL GOING: Soft

5707a GROSSER MERCEDES-BENZ PREIS VON BADEN (GROUP 1) 1m 4f

3:45 (3:48) 3-Y-O+ **£145,631** (£58,252; £24,272; £14,563)

RPR

1 **Getaway (GER)**[21] 5082 6-9-6 ...... ADeVries 7 124
(J Hirschberger, Germany) *racd in 3rd to st: led over 1f out: drvn out* **3/1**[2]

2 *3* **Eastern Anthem (IRE)**[21] 5082 5-9-6 ...... LDettori 3 119+
(Saeed Bin Suroor) *hld up in rr but a wl in tch: 5th st: drvn wl over 1f out: kpt on to take 2nd 100yds out: no ch w wnr* **6/1**[3]

3 *½* **Youmzain (IRE)**[70] 3443 6-9-6 ...... KFallon 6 118
(M R Channon) *racd in 4th to st: drvn to go 2nd briefly ins fnl f: one pce* **2/1**[1]

4 *1 ½* **Wiener Walzer (GER)**[21] 5082 3-8-11 ...... FilipMinarik 2 116
(J Hirschberger, Germany) *led to over 1f out: no ex ins fnl f* **3/1**[2]

5 *3* **Kamsin (GER)**[49] 4128 4-9-6 ...... AStarke 5 111
(P Schiergen, Germany) *trckd ldr to st: sn rdn and one pce* **10/1**

6 *1 ¾* **Adelar (GER)**[22] 5059 4-9-6 ...... DBoeuf 4 108
(W Baltromei, Germany) *hld up in 5th: last but wl in tch st: wknd over 1f out* **20/1**

2m 36.06s (2.60)
WFA 3 from 4yo+ 9lb **6** Ran SP% **111.5**
(including 10 euro stake): WIN 30; PL 17, 26; SF 160.
Owner Baron G Von Ullmann **Bred** Baron G Von Ullmann **Trained** Germany

NOTEBOOK
Getaway(GER), narrowly beaten by his stable companion Wiener Walzer in the Rheinland-Pokal last time, was favourite to reverse that form on this softer surface and scored in quite impressive fashion. A third attempt at the Arc is on the agenda now.
Eastern Anthem(IRE), who finished third behind today's fourth and winner at Cologne, ran virtually to the pound with Getaway. There are no definite plans at this stage.
Youmzain(IRE), runner-up in the last two Arcs, with today's winner behind him both times, looked to have a sound chance on form but could not pick up. He would have preferred a stronger gallop and will renew rivalry with the winner at Longchamp.
Wiener Walzer(GER), who beat his stable companion last time, was encountering softer ground and could not respond when challenged.

5561 LONGCHAMP (R-H)

Sunday, September 6

OFFICIAL GOING: Good to soft

5708a PRIX LA ROCHETTE (GROUP 3) 7f

1:15 (1:14) 2-Y-O **£38,835** (£15,534; £11,650; £7,767; £3,883)

RPR

1 **Buzzword**[15] 5261 2-8-11 .... AhmedAjtebi 1 114
(Saeed Bin Suroor) *led 1f: led again 2f out: r.o wl* **11/2**

2 1 1/2 **Siyouni (FR)**[42] 4366 2-8-11 .... CSoumillon 7 110
(A De Royer-Dupre, France) *hld up in 6th to st: gd hdwy 2f out: rdn to take 2nd ins fnl f: no threat to wnr* **9/4**[1]

3 2 **Eightfold Path (USA)**[36] 2-8-11 .... C-PLemaire 6 105
(P Bary, France) *led after 1f to 2f out: kpt on one pce: lost 2nd ins fnl f* **7/2**[2]

4 1 1/2 **Emirates Dream (USA)**[58] 3823 2-8-11 .... OPeslier 5 101
(Saeed Bin Suroor) *racd in 4th to st: 5th on outside 2f out: kpt on same pce* **10/1**

5 3/4 **Barbegal (USA)**[26] 5088 2-8-11 .... MGuyon 2 99
(A Fabre, France) *racd in 3rd tl rdn and btn over 1 1/2f out* **4/1**[3]

6 2 1/2 **Colonial (IRE)**[54] 3967 2-8-11 .... MBarzalona 4 93
(A Fabre, France) *racd in 5th on ins: wnt 4th over 2f out: sn one pce* **6/1**

7 1 **Bertie's Best**[39] 4448 2-8-8 .... TThulliez 3 88
(F Doumen, France) *broke wl: restrained and sn pulling hrd in rr: last st: btn over 2f out* **50/1**

1m 22.83s (2.13) **Going Correction** +0.40s/f (Good) **7 Ran SP% 113.7**
Speed ratings: **104,102,100,98,97 94,93**
PARI-MUTUEL (including 1 Euro stake); WIN 2.00 (coupled with Emirates Dream, Barbegal & Colonial); PL 3.60, 1.90; SF 42.90.
Owner Godolphin **Bred** Darley **Trained** Newmarket, Suffolk

NOTEBOOK
Buzzword produced a stylish victory having always been well up with the pace. He led soon after the start and then settled in second place before taking the advantage halfway up the straight. He drew several lengths clear and never looked likely to be caught. He has now won two of his five races and been runner-up in the other three, and is certainly going the right way. he may well come back for the Prix Jean-Luc Lagardere over the course and distance on Arc day.
Siyouni(FR) was quickly into his stride and then dropped back into sixth place, which he still held coming into the straight. He came with a progressive run one and a half out but never looked like pegging back the winner, having been given an awful lot to do. Connections will think about the Jean-Luc Lagardere or they may wait for the longer Criterium International later in the season.
Eightfold Path(USA) broke well and went to the head of affairs after a furlong. He set a sensible pace and held on to his advantage until the furlong and a half marker. He was very inexperienced compared with the winner and runner-up and this race will have done him good. He may well line up for the Lagardere.
Emirates Dream(USA) settled in fifth place and was brought with a run up the centre of the track. The colt was putting in his best work at the finish and he may well be suited by a longer trip.

5709a PRIX DU PIN (GROUP 3) 7f

2:25 (2:24) 3-Y-O+ **£38,835** (£15,534; £11,650; £7,767; £3,883)

RPR

1 **Proviso**[35] 4580 4-8-11 .... SPasquier 3 112
(A Fabre, France) *squeezed bk s: racd in 5th to st: hdwy on outside over 1f out: drvn to ld 80yds out: r.o* **7/2**[2]

2 nk **Varenar (FR)**[28] 4837 3-8-11 .... CSoumillon 8 113
(A De Royer-Dupre, France) *led: rdn appr fnl f: rdr lost whip ins fnl f: ct 80yds out: r.o* **2/1**[1]

3 shd **Emergency**[24] 4971 3-8-8 .... C-PLemaire 5 110
(D Smaga, France) *disp 6th to st: trckd wnr on outside fr 3f out: rdn over 1f out: kpt on wl* **7/1**

4 3/4 **Entre Deux Eaux (FR)**[24] 4971 3-8-8 .... IMendizabal 6 108
(Robert Collet, France) *trckd ldr: 2nd st: kpt on same pce fr wl over 1f out* **18/1**

5 snk **Gris De Gris (IRE)**[112] 2120 5-9-5 .... GMosse 2 117
(A De Royer-Dupre, France) *prom: 4th on ins: 3rd briefly wl over 1f out: styd on one pce fnl 1 1/2f* **5/1**[3]

6 2 1/2 **Secret Society**[16] 5232 3-8-11 ....(b) HayleyTurner 1 104
(M L W Bell) *disp 6th to st: rdn wl over 1f out: no ex fnl f* **6/1**

7 1/2 **Contest (IRE)**[7] 5495 5-9-1 .... OPeslier 7 104
(C Theodorakis, Greece) *hld up in rr: last st: nvr a factor* **10/1**

8 6 **As De Trebol (USA)**[56] 3908 3-8-11 .... MGuyon 4 86
(G Arizkorreta Elosegui, Spain) *sn racing in 3rd: wknd wl over 1f out* **25/1**

1m 22.13s (1.43) **Going Correction** +0.40s/f (Good)
WFA 3 from 4yo+ 4lb **8 Ran SP% 117.2**
Speed ratings: **108,107,107,106,106 103,103,96**
PARI-MUTUEL: WIN 3.30 (coupled with Emergency); PL 1.70, 1.40, 2.30; SF 4.70.
Owner K Abdulla **Bred** Juddmonte Farms Ltd **Trained** Chantilly, France

NOTEBOOK
Proviso, who since waiting tactics have been used has been showing her best. She was settled in fifth position in the early stages, quickened well from one and a half out to take the lead with just over 50 metres left to run and stayed on gamely to the line. This was her first Group success in over two years and connections will definitely consider the Prix de la Foret next time out.
Varenar(FR) isn't the easiest of horses and soon pulled his way into the lead. He settled down at the beginning of the straight and then quickened a little later, but couldn't hold the winner inside the final furlong and his jockey had lost his whip. There are no plans for this colt at the present moment.
Emergency, held up at the tail of the field in the early stages, was tracking the winner and ran on really well as the race came to an end. She was only beaten just under half a length and has been entered in the Sun Chariot Stakes, although connections might contemplate the Prix de la Foret.
Entre Deux Eaux(FR), well up from the start, settled behind the leader. He stayed on one paced throughout the final furlong and a half.
Secret Society was never much closer and couldn't quicken in the straight, although he was finally beaten under four lengths.

5710a PRIX DU MOULIN DE LONGCHAMP (GROUP 1) 1m

3:05 (3:05) 3-Y-O+ **£221,903** (£88,777; £44,388; £22,175; £11,107)

RPR

1 **Aqlaam**[21] 5086 4-9-2 .... RHills 2 125
(W J Haggas) *trckd ldr: drvn to ld appr fnl f: r.o wl* **7/2**[2]

2 1 1/2 **Famous Name**[21] 5080 4-9-2 .... PJSmullen 7 121+
(D K Weld, Ire) *racd in 3rd: chsd wnr fnl f: r.o same pce u.p* **7/2**[2]

3 2 1/2 **Virtual**[21] 5086 4-9-2 .... JimmyFortune 4 116
(J H M Gosden) *a in tch: 5th st: drvn wl over 1f out: kpt on to take 3rd 100yds out* **7/1**[3]

4 1/2 **Oiseau De Feu (USA)**[63] 3669 3-8-11 .... IMendizabal 3 113?
(J-C Rouget, France) *a in tch: 4th st: rdn wl over 1f out: kpt on to take 4th last strides* **10/1**

5 shd **Gladiatorus (USA)**[21] 5086 4-9-2 .... AhmedAjtebi 9 114?
(Saeed Bin Suroor) *led to appr fnl f: kpt on u.p: no ex ins fnl f* **14/1**

6 1/2 **Calvados Blues (FR)**[63] 3669 3-8-11 .... MGuyon 6 112?
(A Fabre, France) *6th st: nvr a factor* **22/1**

7 8 **Balthazaar's Gift (IRE)**[22] 5024 6-9-2 .... PhilipRobinson 1 95
(C G Cox) *s.i.s: 7th st: wknd 1 1/2f out* **12/1**

8 nk **Summer Fete (IRE)**[37] 4489 3-8-8 .... RichardMullen 5 90
(B Smart) *hld up: last st: rdn and btn over 1 1/2f out* **33/1**

R **Elusive Wave (IRE)**[35] 4580 3-8-8 .... C-PLemaire 8 —
(J-C Rouget, France) *j. and hit nose on side of gate whn stalls opened: then c out: rrd and ref to r* **5/2**[1]

1m 38.87s (0.47) **Going Correction** +0.40s/f (Good)
WFA 3 from 4yo+ 5lb **9 Ran SP% 116.3**
Speed ratings: **115,113,111,110,110 109,101,101,—**
PARI-MUTUEL: WIN 3.30 (coupled with Oiseau De Feu); PL 1.80, 1.70, 2.60; DF 9.50.
Owner Hamdan Al Maktoum **Bred** Granham Farm **Trained** Newmarket, Suffolk

FOCUS
A decent renewal, although it was devalued when Elusive Wave failed to take any part in the race. The form gave a big boost to the absent Goldikova, last year's winner.

NOTEBOOK
Aqlaam, beautifully placed throughout, ran free in the early stages and then settled when another went into the lead. Going well entering the straight, he made a forward move to take control one and a half out and never looked likely to taste defeat. Considering his problems early in his career it was a fine victory, and connections are now looking at the Queen Elizabeth II Stakes at Ascot.
Famous Name was given every possible chance and was third for most of the time but couldn't quicken as well as the winner in the straight. He battled on gamely to the line but never looked like getting on terms, and is another entered in the Queen Elizabeth II.
Virtual, in mid-division from the start, appeared to need time to balance himself in the straight and was putting in his best work at the finish on the far rail. His trainer considered he wasn't suited by the undulations of Longchamp but he did finish closer to the winner than he had at Deauville.
Oiseau De Feu(USA) put up a decent performance and took a little time before finding his stride in the straight and eventually running on. His jockey considered he was unsuited by the soft ground but he may well come back to Longchamp for the Prix Daniel Wildenstein on October 3rd.
Gladiatorus(USA) was soon taken into the lead and set a sensible gallop. His stride began to shorten at the furlong and a half marker but he did battle on well and only lost third place well inside the final furlong. This was a much better effort by this colt, who needs good ground to show his best.
Balthazaar's Gift(IRE) was never seen with a chance and his jockey considered him as totally unsuited by the false ground.
Summer Fete(IRE) was held up and made no show on this occasion.

5711a PRIX DE LUTECE (GROUP 3) 1m 7f

3:35 (3:34) 3-Y-O **£38,835** (£15,534; £11,650; £7,767; £3,883)

RPR

1 **Wajir (FR)**[54] 3970 3-9-4 .... ACrastus 4 115
(E Lellouche, France) *hld up in rr: hdwy and 4th st on outside: led over 1f out: r.o* **5/1**[3]

2 1 **Manighar (FR)**[21] 5087 3-8-9 .... CSoumillon 5 105
(A De Royer-Dupre, France) *racd in 5th: hdwy 6f out: 2nd st: ev ch over 1f out: kpt on one pce u.p fnl f* **5/6**[1]

3 4 **Investissement**[44] 3-8-9 .... OPeslier 2 100
(A Fabre, France) *trckd ldr: disputing 2nd to 5f out: 4th st: rdn wl over 1f out: one pce* **12/1**

4 2 1/2 **Amico Mio (FR)**[84] 2951 3-8-9 ....(p) C-PLemaire 1 97
(J-M Beguigne, France) *led to over 1f out: sn wknd* **10/1**

5 5 **Prankster**[21] 5087 3-8-9 .... SPasquier 6 91
(A Fabre, France) *disp 2nd to 5f out: 5th st: rdn and btn wl over 1f out* **9/2**[2]

6 1 **Mojave Moon**[14] 5297 3-8-11 .... MGuyon 3 92
(A Fabre, France) *racd in 4th to 5f out: last st: sn btn* **7/1**

3m 16.1s (0.10) **Going Correction** +0.40s/f (Good) **6 Ran SP% 118.7**
Speed ratings: **115,114,112,111,108 107**
PARI-MUTUEL: WIN 5.40; PL 2.10, 1.20; SF 14.50.
Owner Ecurie Wildenstein **Bred** Dayton Investments Ltd **Trained** Lamorlaye, France

NOTEBOOK
Wajir(FR), giving weight all round, put up a decent effort. He was brought with a progressive run up the centre of the track to take the lead going in to the final furlong and ran on gamely. It was his second Group success of the season and the target now is the Prix Chaudenay on October 3rd.
Manighar(FR) dropped out last at the beginning of the race, then was moved up towards the leaders rounding the final turn. He went to the head of affairs one and a half out and was immediately joined in the lead by the winner. It wasn't a bad effort by the gelding, who was running in a Group race for the first time.
Investissement, never far from the lead, he was outpaced in the straight and then stayed on to the line.
Amico Mio(FR) went into the lead from the start and was joined by the runner-up rounding the final turn. He fought well but then gradually dropped away inside the final furlong and a half.

5713a PRIX DU ROUVRAY (CLAIMER) 1m

4:45 (4:45) 2-Y-O **£12,136** (£4,854; £3,641; £2,417; £1,214)

RPR

1 **Ayun Tara (FR)**[23] 2-9-5 ....(p) CSoumillon 82
(P Khozian, France)

2 2 **Une Autre Aventure (FR)**[7] 5494 2-9-0 ....(b) IMendizabal 73
(C Boutin, France)

3 snk **Spectacle Du Mars (FR)**[16] 2-9-0 .... SRuis 72
(C Martens, France)

4 2 1/2 **Terradelice (FR)**[79] 2-8-8 .... (6) 67
(Mme L Audon, France)

5 1 **De Viso (IRE)** 2-9-0 65
(R Gibson, France)

6 2 **Akton City (FR)**[9] 2-9-4 64
(J-P Delaporte, France)

7 3/4 **Convocation (IRE)**[26] 2-9-0 ....(b) 59
(Mme M Bollack-Badel, France)

8 3/4 **Style De Lois (FR)**[11] 2-8-10 .... (8) 61
(Robert Collet, France)

9 shd **Freedom Light (FR)**[75] 2-9-0 57
(C Boutin, France)

10 8 **Mythie** 2-8-8 .... JAuge 33
(E J O'Neill) *broke wl: settled towards rr: 11th st: reminders over 2f out: btn over 1f out: eased fnl f* **69/1**[1]

0 **Gooseley Chope (FR)**[7] 5494 2-9-0 .... —
(C Boutin, France)

0 **Benadalid (FR)**[32] 2-8-12 .... (6) —
(C Laffon-Parias, France)

0 **Tadjinne (FR)** 2-8-11 .... —
(J Van Handenhove, France)

1m 42.91s (4.51) **13** Ran SP% **1.4**
PARI-MUTUEL: WIN 3.90; PL 1.80, 3.00, 3.60; DF 17.40.
Owner P Dreux **Bred** Earl Haras Du Camp Benard **Trained** France

NOTEBOOK
Mythie, making her debut, was well beaten and was eased in the closing stages.

5712 - 5713a (Foreign Racing) - See Raceform Interactive

5379 BATH (L-H)

Monday, September 7

OFFICIAL GOING: Good (good to firm in places; 8.6)
Wind: Almost nil Weather: Sunny periods

5714 WESTERN DAILY PRESS MAIDEN AUCTION FILLIES STKS 5f 11y

2:10 (2:10) (Class 6) 2-Y-O **£2,072** (£616; £308; £153) **Stalls** Centre

Form RPR

4054 1 **Pherousa**[7] 5526 2-8-3 62 .... FrancisNorton 7 66
(M Blanshard) *chsd ldrs: nt clr run on ins and swtchd rt over 2f out: pushed along and wnt 2nd over 1f out: led ins fnl f: rdn out* **4/1**[3]

63 2 1 ¾ **Devassa**[10] 5380 2-8-3 0 .... LukeMorris 5 60
(C G Cox) *led: rdn jst over 1f out: hdd ins fnl f: no ex* **7/2**[2]

4403 3 ½ **Little Brazilien**[14] 5310 2-8-5 62 .... (b) WilliamBuick 6 60
(P F I Cole) *towards rr: pushed along and plld out over 2f out: rdn and hdwy on outside over 1f out: kpt on to take 3rd wl ins fnl f* **7/1**

0503 4 1 ¾ **Madam Isshe**[10] 5379 2-8-0 62 .... JakePayne(7) 10 56
(M S Saunders) *wnt rt s: t.k.h: sn prom: pushed along over 2f out: rdn wl over 1f out: one pce fnl f* **20/1**

5 1 ¼ **Dream Number (IRE)** 2-8-3 0 .... MartinDwyer 2 47+
(W R Muir) *dwlt: outpcd and wl in rr: pushed along and hdwy over 1f out: one pce fnl f* **14/1**

6 ½ **Goddess Of Light (IRE)** 2-8-3 0 .... RPCleary 11 45
(Daniel Mark Loughnane, Ire) *carried rt s: sn mid-div: pushed along and hdwy on outside over 2f out: rdn wl over 1f out: wknd ins fnl f* **11/1**

7 1 ¼ **Lucky Diva** 2-8-3 0 .... DavidProbert 1 41
(Rae Guest) *sn outpcd: rdn over 1f out: nvr nrr* **18/1**

002 8 ½ **Gooseberry Bush**[22] 5060 2-8-5 66 .... ChrisCatlin 12 41
(P J Makin) *sn w ldr: rdn and wknd 1f out* **3/1**[1]

05 9 ¾ **L'Isle Joyeuse**[15] 5282 2-8-3 0 .... FrankieMcDonald 8 36
(P Winkworth) *hld up in tch: pushed along and wknd over 1f out* **50/1**

10 ½ **Wee Bobbie** 2-8-4 0 ow1 .... NeilChalmers 3 36
(Mrs P N Dutfield) *sn outpcd* **100/1**

43 11 nse **Peter's Follie**[26] 4889 2-8-9 0 .... RichardSmith 4 40
(Tom Dascombe) *prom tl pushed along and wknd over 2f out* **10/1**

62.26 secs (-0.24) **Going Correction** 0.0s/f (Good) **11** Ran SP% **116.8**
Speed ratings (Par 93): **101,98,97,94,92 91,89,89,87,87 86**
toteswingers: 1&2 £4.60, 1&3 £7.80, 2&3 £3.70 CSF £18.02 TOTE £5.00: £1.60, £1.80, £2.90; EX 23.80.
Owner Messrs Hall, Else & Murray **Bred** Whitsbury Manor Stud & Pigeon House Stud **Trained** Upper Lambourn, Berks

FOCUS
A weak fillies' maiden in which the winner found a little improvement.

NOTEBOOK
Pherousa, officially rated 62, was already thoroughly exposed coming into this, having managed to place in only one of her previous seven starts. However, she came good this time, responding well to pressure to win decisively. She should be competitive in nursery company. (op 7-1)
Devassa showed good speed and had her chance, but the winner was too strong. She's only modest, but nurseries are now an option. (op 100-30 tchd 3-1)
Little Brazilien only ran on when the race was as good as over and never threatened. (op 11-2)
Madam Isshe has improved lately but she still wasn't good enough. She might be better off in low-grade handicaps. (op 18-1 tchd 25-1)
Dream Number(IRE), a half-sister to triple 7f winner Seek N' Destroy, fared best of the newcomers. She made some late headway after a sluggish start and should be better for the experience. (op 16-1 tchd 20-1)
Goddess Of Light(IRE), a half-sister to a 2yo winner in Norway, is another who should come on a good deal for this. (op 14-1)
Gooseberry Bush was very disappointing considering she had today's winner and second-placed finisher behind when runner-up over this course and distance on her return from a break last time. (op 7-2 tchd 11-4)

5715 EVENING POST NURSERY 1m 5y

2:40 (2:43) (Class 5) (0-75,74) 2-Y-O **£2,719** (£809; £404; £202) **Stalls** Low

Form RPR

600 1 **Fantastic Pick**[58] 3865 2-8-2 55 .... MartinDwyer 7 62
(B J Meehan) *a.p: pushed along and lost pl briefly whn n.m.r 3f out: rdn to ld over 1f out: edgd rt ins fnl f: rdn out* **10/1**

054 2 1 ½ **Spanish Duke (IRE)**[32] 4699 2-8-13 66 .... JimmyFortune 5 70
(J L Dunlop) *hld up towards rr: plld out and hdwy over 2f out: rdn over 1f out: chsd wnr jst ins fnl f: kpt on same pce* **9/1**

4315 3 2 ¾ **Diamond Duchess (IRE)**[17] 5213 2-9-7 74 .... TedDurcan 8 72
(D R Lanigan) *hld up in mid-div: pushed along and hdwy whn n.m.r briefly 2f out: sn rdn: no ex ins fnl f:* **8/1**

502 4 2 ¼ **Fantastic Strike (IRE)**[9] 5439 2-9-5 72 .... RoystonFfrench 3 68+
(M Johnston) *hld up towards rr: pushed along over 3f out: hdwy on ins over 2f out: swtchd rt over 1f out: nt clr run and swtchd rt ins fnl f: r.o towards fin* **9/4**[1]

2236 5 nk **Ginger Grey (IRE)**[9] 5433 2-8-11 64 .... (p) JerryO'Dwyer 10 56
(S A Callaghan) *hld up towards rr: hdwy over 2f out: nt clr run and swtchd rt over 1f out: rdn and one pce ins fnl f* **6/1**[2]

0500 6 hd **Queen's Hawk**[31] 4758 2-9-4 71 .... TPQueally 15 63
(D J Coakley) *hld up in mid-div: rn wd bnd over 4f out: hdwy on outside over 3f out: led 2f out: rdn and hdd over 1f out: wknd ins fnl f* **25/1**

4000 7 1 ¾ **Gulf Punch**[4] 5589 2-7-13 52 .... JamieMackay 14 40
(M F Harris) *hld up in rr: pushed along and hdwy on outside over 2f out: rdn and wknd over 1f out* **40/1**

0065 8 ¾ **Captain Cool (IRE)**[14] 5320 2-8-1 54 .... DavidProbert 9 40
(R Hannon) *chsd ldr tl pushed along jst over 2f out: rdn and wknd over 1f out* **25/1**

654 9 ½ **Pebblesonthebeach**[25] 4945 2-9-6 73 .... SebSanders 1 62+
(J W Hills) *prom early: sn stdd into mid-div: hdwy over 3f out: pushed along whn nt clr run on ins 2f out tl jst over 1f out: n.d after* **9/1**

0302 10 2 ¼ **Timelord (IRE)**[4] 5589 2-8-13 66 .... JamesDoyle 12 49+
(S Kirk) *prom: rdn and ev ch wl over 1f out: sn wknd* **7/1**[3]

0000 11 nk **Argyll**[11] 5369 2-8-4 62 .... SimonPearce(5) 13 41
(J Pearce) *led: pushed along and hdd 2f out: rdn and wknd over 1f out* **66/1**

5000 12 2 **Flyinflyout**[11] 5369 2-8-13 66 .... ChrisCatlin 6 41
(M R Channon) *a in rr* **25/1**

040 13 ½ **Musiara**[26] 4915 2-7-12 51 oh1 .... CatherineGannon 4 25
(M R Channon) *s.s: a in rr* **66/1**

050 14 2 ¼ **City Of Rome (IRE)**[25] 4946 2-8-2 55 .... FrancisNorton 11 24
(R Hannon) *a towards rr* **66/1**

006 15 7 **Dancealot Lady (USA)**[19] 5153 2-8-2 55 .... FrankieMcDonald 2 9
(P Winkworth) *hld up in tch: rdn and wknd wl over 2f out* **100/1**

1m 41.41s (0.61) **Going Correction** 0.0s/f (Good) **15** Ran SP% **117.2**
Speed ratings (Par 95): **96,94,91,89,89 89,87,86,86,83 83,81,80,78,71**
toteswingers: 1&2 £17.90, 1&3 £13.90, 2&3 £10.80 CSF £87.96 CT £761.92 TOTE £12.90: £3.40, £3.90, £2.40; EX 101.90.
Owner Raymond Tooth **Bred** Star Pointe Ltd **Trained** Manton, Wilts

FOCUS
An ordinary but competitive nursery. Improved form from the winner with the third helping with the level.

NOTEBOOK
Fantastic Pick ◆, switched from maiden company, proved suited by the step up in trip and showed himself to be well handicapped after a two-month break. A couple of entries in claiming company later in the week suggest his connections were prepared to let him go, but it will be a bit of a surprise if doesn't find another nursery. Official explanation: trainer's rep said, regarding the apparent improvement in form shown, gelding appreciated having a break after its last start and benefitted from today's longer trip (op 8-1)
Spanish Duke(IRE), like the winner, up in trip on his nursery bow, still had plenty to do by the time he was switched out wide early in the straight, but he ran on well for a clear second. He looks handicapped to win in the coming weeks. (op 10-1)
Diamond Duchess(IRE) didn't enjoy the clearest of runs around 2f out but she was in the open for long enough. This was a respectable effort in defeat.
Fantastic Strike(IRE), stepped up 2f in trip on his handicap debut, didn't have much room to play with when trying to stay on in the straight. He couldn't be called unlucky, but can certainly be given another chance. Official explanation: jockey said colt ran in snatches (op 5-2 tchd 11-4)
Ginger Grey(IRE) didn't run badly but he's looking thoroughly exposed. (op 15-2)
Pebblesonthebeach got stuck in behind a tiring horse against the far rail for much of the straight and that cost him any chance. He should be capable of better. (op 10-1 tchd 12-1)
Musiara Official explanation: jockey said filly missed the break

5716 WESTERN DAILY PRESS WEST COUNTRY LIFE (S) STKS 5f 161y

3:10 (3:12) (Class 6) 3-4-Y-O **£1,942** (£578; £288; £144) **Stalls** Centre

Form RPR

0-00 1 **Boho Chic**[5] 5576 3-8-8 65 .... (p) TedDurcan 5 59
(George Baker) *hld up in tch: nt clr run 3f out: rdn over 1f out: led ins fnl f: r.o wl* **11/2**[3]

0005 2 3 ¼ **Helping Hand (IRE)**[9] 5443 4-8-8 49 .... DavidKenny(7) 10 53
(R Hollinshead) *led: rdn over 1f out: hdd ins fnl f: one pce* **7/1**

3P53 3 1 **Talamahana**[7] 5541 4-8-11 47 ow1 .... (v) DaneO'Neill 3 46
(A B Haynes) *hld up in rr: rdn over 2f out: hdwy jst over 1f out: r.o to take 3rd post* **16/1**

1000 4 hd **Kinigi (IRE)**[13] 5326 3-8-10 52 .... (p) AndreaAtzeni(3) 1 49
(R A Harris) *half-rrd s: sn mid-div: pushed along over 2f out: rdn and hdwy on ins over 1f out: one pce ins fnl f* **20/1**

0505 5 ½ **Red Rossini (IRE)**[12] 5345 3-8-13 55 .... JimmyFortune 15 48
(R Hannon) *a.p: chsd ldr over 3f out: rdn over 1f out: lost 2nd jst ins fnl f: one pce* **8/1**

0450 6 1 ¼ **Migliori**[25] 4937 3-8-13 58 .... SaleemGolam 13 43
(Rae Guest) *chsd ldrs: pushed along 3f out: rdn wl over 1f out: wknd fnl f* **9/2**[2]

0010 7 hd **Theta Wave (USA)**[19] 5155 3-9-4 64 .... (p) LukeMorris 9 48
(J R Gask) *mid-div: pushed along over 3f out: rdn wl over 1f out: no hdwy fnl f* **11/4**[1]

0000 8 2 **Calypso Girl (IRE)**[7] 5501 3-8-8 50 .... CatherineGannon 2 31
(P D Evans) *prom: rdn wl over 2f out: wknd wl over 1f out* **20/1**

0000 9 ½ **Bilboa**[38] 4479 4-9-1 41 .... (p) SteveDrowne 4 34
(J M Bradley) *n.m.r s: hld up towards rr: short-lived effrt and carried hd high over 1f out* **50/1**

0260 10 ¾ **Like For Like (IRE)**[10] 5384 3-8-8 53 .... SamHitchcott 17 27
(R J Hodges) *hld up in tch: rdn over 2f out: wknd wl over 1f out* **11/1**

0020 11 9 **Sky High Kid (IRE)**[8] 5468 3-8-13 56 .... ChrisCatlin 8 1
(M R Channon) *dwlt: a in rr* **10/1**

050- 12 9 **Betoula**[278] 7537 3-8-3 0 .... SimonPearce(5) 7 —
(Mrs A L M King) *a bhd* **66/1**

05 13 nk **Rare Bet**[18] 5181 3-8-6 0 ow1 .... JackDean(3) 12 —
(W G M Turner) *w ldr tl pushed along over 3f out: wknd over 2f out* **50/1**

14 1 **Poppy Morris (IRE)** 4-8-7 0 .... JackMitchell(3) 14 —
(A B Haynes) *a towards rr* **40/1**

1m 11.22s (0.02) **Going Correction** 0.0s/f (Good)
WFA 3 from 4yo 2lb **14** Ran SP% **124.5**
Speed ratings (Par 101): **99,94,93,93,92 90,90,87,87,86 74,62,61,60**
toteswingers: 1&2 £8.00, 1&3 £43.20, 2&3 £37.70 CSF £42.63 TOTE £8.10: £2.80, £3.00, £5.80; EX 57.50.There was no bid for the winner.
Owner P K Gardner **Bred** P K Gardner **Trained** Moreton Morrell, Warwicks

FOCUS
A weak seller, contested largely by regressive 3yos. The winner did not need to improve on her reappearance handicap form.
Theta Wave(USA) Official explanation: jockey said gelding hung right

5717 EVENING POST JOBSITE MAIDEN STKS 5f 161y

3:40 (3:42) (Class 5) 3-Y-O+ **£2,590** (£770; £385; £192) **Stalls** Centre

Form RPR

0 1 **Poppanan (USA)**[30] 4786 3-9-3 0 .... TonyCulhane 9 78
(S Dow) *hld up towards rr: hdwy over 2f out: led jst over 1f out: drvn out* **25/1**

0 2 hd **Sometsuke**[5] 5572 3-9-3 0 .... (t) SebSanders 10 77+
(P J Makin) *hld up in rr: pushed along over 2f out: hdwy wl over 1f out: rdn and wnt 2nd wl ins fnl f: r.o* **8/1**[3]

3332 **3** 2 1/4 **Milldown Story**[11] 5373 3-8-12 64 ChrisCatlin 4 64
(B R Millman) *led: hdd over 4f out: chsd ldr: led wl over 1f out: sn hdd and rdn: no ex ins fnl f* **7/2**[2]

4502 **4** 1 **Rainy Night**[9] 5422 3-9-3 60 TPO'Shea 3 66
(R Hollinshead) *chsd ldrs: ev ch wl over 1f out: wknd ent fnl f* **25/1**

23 **5** 2 3/4 **Femme De Fer**[81] 3071 3-8-12 0 AdamKirby 6 52
(C G Cox) *racd keenly: led over 4f out: hdd wl over 1f out: sn rdn and wknd* **4/5**[1]

30-5 **6** 3/4 **Prowl**[26] 4913 3-8-12 70 JimmyFortune 1 49
(E A L Dunlop) *hld up in tch: wandered and pushed along over 2f out: rdn and wknd over 1f out* **8/1**[3]

3/ **7** 2 **Taine (IRE)**[646] 7000 4-9-5 0 SteveDrowne 8 47
(J R Gask) *hld up towards rr: rdn and struggling over 2f out* **20/1**

0-50 **8** 3 1/4 **Bluebird Chariot**[3] 5634 6-9-2 44 JackDean(3) 7 36
(J M Bradley) *mid-div: pushed along over 3f out: sn bhd* **100/1**

9 10 **Anagram** 3-8-12 0 MartinDwyer 2 —
(W R Muir) *s.i.s: outpcd* **33/1**

0000 **10** 2 **Wivny (USA)**[48] 4182 4-9-0 45 (b[1]) TolleyDean 5 —
(H J Evans) *sn outpcd* **100/1**

1m 10.65s (-0.55) **Going Correction** 0.0s/f (Good)
WFA 3 from 4yo+ 2lb **10** Ran SP% **117.4**
Speed ratings (Par 103): **103,102,99,98,94 93,91,86,73,70**
toteswingers: 1&2 £32.10, 1&3 £19.00, 2&3 £3.10 CSF £198.11 TOTE £35.50: £5.80, £2.00, £1.50; EX 161.40.
Owner Joe Cole **Bred** Liberation Farm And Brandywine Farm Llc **Trained** Epsom, Surrey

FOCUS
An ordinary sprint maiden run at an overly strong pace. The favourite disappointed and the race has been rated around the time, with the front pair both big improvers.
Prowl Official explanation: jockey said filly hung left

5718 RITA SIMCOX BIRTHDAY MAIDEN FILLIES' STKS 1m 3f 144y
4:10 (4:12) (Class 5) 3-Y-O+ **£2,719** (£809; £404; £202) **Stalls** Low

Form RPR

3 **1** **Hajmah (IRE)**[24] 4991 3-8-12 0 TedDurcan 7 78+
(Saeed Bin Suroor) *s.i.s: sn prom: wnt 2nd 6f out: led jst over 3f out: rdn clr over 1f out: eased towards fin* **6/4**[1]

222 **2** 2 **Kinetix**[46] 4234 3-8-12 75 JimmyFortune 1 72
(J H M Gosden) *hld up towards rr: hdwy 3f out: sn pushed along: hrd rdn and wnt 2nd 1f out: nt trble wnr* **11/4**[2]

3 3 1/4 **Chincoteague (IRE)** 3-8-12 0 MartinDwyer 5 66+
(B J Meehan) *s.i.s: hld up towards rr: hdwy and swtchd lft wl over 1f out: sn rdn: kpt on to take 3rd wl ins fnl f* **33/1**

4 1 **Ashes Summer (IRE)** 3-8-12 0 TolleyDean 2 65
(P R Webber) *hld up in rr: pushed along 3f out: hdwy on outside 2f out: rdn wl over 1f out: one pce fnl f* **40/1**

62 **5** 2 **Reset City**[38] 4480 3-8-12 0 SteveDrowne 3 61+
(A B Haynes) *hld up in tch: nt clr run on ins and lost pl 3f out: sn swtchd rt: rdn and no hdwy whn hmpd on ins jst over 1f out* **6/1**[3]

0 **6** 3/4 **By Request**[7] 5520 3-8-12 0 SebSanders 10 60+
(Sir Mark Prescott) *s.i.s: hld up: hdwy over 6f out: ev ch 3f out: sn rdn: wknd over 1f out* **14/1**

6542 **7** 1 1/4 **Sana Abel (IRE)**[21] 5093 3-8-12 69 (p) TPO'Shea 8 58
(M A Jarvis) *led 1f: chsd ldr to 6f out: wknd wl over 2f out* **7/1**

00 **8** 3 **Dayanara (USA)**[33] 4648 3-8-12 0 AdamKirby 6 53
(C G Cox) *hld up in mid-div: rdn over 4f out: hdwy over 2f out: wknd over 1f out* **100/1**

04 **9** 2 1/4 **Silk And Satin (USA)**[17] 5205 3-8-12 0 (t) TPQueally 11 49
(H R A Cecil) *hld up in tch: pushed along over 2f out: rdn and wknd over 1f out* **16/1**

10 8 **Court Princess**[249] 6-9-7 0 DaneO'Neill 4 35
(George Baker) *s.s: a in rr* **100/1**

2-00 **11** 51 **Bantu**[68] 3508 4-9-7 70 (bt[1]) NickyMackay 12 —
(J H M Gosden) *led after 1f: hdd jst over 3f out: wknd qckly over 2f out: eased whn no ch wl over 1f out* **28/1**

2m 30.41s (-0.19) **Going Correction** 0.0s/f (Good)
WFA 3 from 4yo+ 9lb **11** Ran SP% **116.8**
Speed ratings (Par 100): **100,98,96,95,94 94,93,91,89,84 50**
toteswingers: 1&2 £2.50, 1&3 £13.60, 2&3 £7.90 CSF £5.29 TOTE £2.60: £1.30, £1.20, £5.70; EX 5.10.
Owner Godolphin **Bred** Darley **Trained** Newmarket, Suffolk

FOCUS
A fair fillies' maiden run at an ordinary pace. The runner-up is the best guide to this form.
Sana Abel(IRE) Official explanation: jockey said filly was denied a clear run
Bantu Official explanation: jockey said filly lost her action; vet said filly lost a front shoe

5719 FREEBETS.CO.UK LAS VEGAS PARTY H'CAP 5f 161y
4:40 (4:43) (Class 5) (0-75,75) 3-Y-O+ **£2,719** (£809; £404; £202) **Stalls** Centre

Form RPR

0-05 **1** **Johnstown Lad (IRE)**[73] 3368 5-9-5 74 (t) ShaneKelly 11 81
(Daniel Mark Loughnane, Ire) *hld up in mid-div: hdwy jst over 1f out: rdn and r.o to ld nr fin: jst hld on* **9/1**

-100 **2** nse **Jordaura**[19] 5167 3-9-4 75 AdamKirby 16 82
(W R Swinburn) *hld up in rr: rdn and hdwy on outside 1f out: r.o u.p towards fin: jst failed* **16/1**

1003 **3** nk **Piazza San Pietro**[8] 5480 3-8-11 68 SebSanders 12 74
(A B Haynes) *hld up in mid-div: hdwy on outside 2f out: sn rdn and edgd lft: led ins fnl f: hdd nr fin* **8/1**

2113 **4** 3 **Solemn**[17] 5219 4-8-12 67 DavidProbert 6 63
(J M Bradley) *chsd ldrs: rdn and sltly outpcd over 2f out: kpt on same pce ins fnl f* **5/1**[1]

2503 **5** nk **Doc Jones (IRE)**[2] 5677 3-8-11 73 RichardEvans(5) 1 68
(P D Evans) *w ldr: led jst over 3f out: rdn over 2f out: hdd ins fnl f: fdd towards fin* **7/1**[3]

4000 **6** 3/4 **Heaven**[14] 5323 4-8-12 67 ChrisCatlin 10 59
(P J Makin) *s.i.s: hld up in rr: pushed along over 2f out: hdwy 1f out: rdn and kpt on one pce ins fnl f* **13/2**[2]

13U **7** nk **Pinball (IRE)**[101] 2454 3-8-1 61 (v) AndreaAtzeni(3) 5 52
(Mrs L Williamson) *s.i.s: towards rr: rdn over 1f out: late hdwy on outside: nvr nrr* **33/1**

5106 **8** nse **Rondeau (GR)**[19] 5167 4-8-12 67 WilliamBuick 3 58
(P R Chamings) *s.s: hld up in rr: hdwy fnl f: nrst fin* **18/1**

5110 **9** 1 1/4 **Realt Na Mara (IRE)**[12] 5343 6-9-1 70 (p) TravisBlock 7 57
(H Morrison) *prom: pushed along over 3f out: hrd rdn over 2f out: wknd ins fnl f* **16/1**

0502 **10** 1/2 **Kyllachy Storm**[22] 5065 5-9-4 73 SamHitchcott 4 58
(R J Hodges) *chsd ldrs: rdn over 2f out: wknd fnl f* **17/2**

2550 **11** hd **Orange Pip**[31] 4761 4-9-6 75 JimmyFortune 8 59
(R Hannon) *racd keenly: led: hdd jst over 3f out: rdn and wknd ins fnl f* **12/1**

0620 **12** nk **Namir (IRE)**[27] 4886 7-9-3 72 (bt) TolleyDean 9 59+
(H J Evans) *hld up in tch: rdn jst over 2f out: wkng whn nt clr run and eased ins fnl f* **14/1**

35 **13** 1 1/4 **Leftontheshelf (IRE)**[55] 3945 3-9-3 74 DaneO'Neill 2 53
(Miss T Spearing) *hld up in mid-div: wknd 1f out* **28/1**

3600 **14** 1 1/4 **Stamford Blue**[7] 5502 8-8-8 63 (b) LukeMorris 14 38
(R A Harris) *dwlt: reminder over 4f out: a in rr* **20/1**

055 **15** 3/4 **Golden Dixie (USA)**[4] 5608 10-9-0 69 CatherineGannon 13 41
(R A Harris) *hld up in tch: rdn and wknd over 2f out* **12/1**

1m 10.28s (-0.92) **Going Correction** 0.0s/f (Good)
WFA 3 from 4yo+ 2lb **15** Ran SP% **124.4**
Speed ratings (Par 103): **106,105,105,101,101 100,99,99,98,97 97,96,95,93,92**
toteswingers: 1&2 £60.10, 1&3 £19.10, 2&3 £46.00 CSF £145.82 CT £817.33 TOTE £13.60: £3.60, £8.20, £2.20; EX 272.10.
Owner Leo Cox **Bred** Mrs J Reilly **Trained** Trim, Co Meath

FOCUS
A modest sprint handicap, but the time was quicker than both the earlier seller and maiden, and the form looks reliable enough. The first three, who came clear, were drawn in double-figure stalls.
Rondeau(GR) Official explanation: jockey said gelding missed the break
Stamford Blue Official explanation: jockey said gelding was never travelling

5720 FREEBETS.CO.UK FREE BETS MAIDEN H'CAP (FOR GENTLEMAN AMATEUR RIDERS) 1m 5f 22y
5:10 (5:10) (Class 5) (0-70,70) 3-Y-O+ **£2,623** (£813; £406; £203) **Stalls** High

Form RPR

2222 **1** **Arab League (IRE)**[25] 4951 4-10-5 56 oh3 MrMPrice(5) 2 57
(R J Price) *led 2f: chsd ldr tl over 7f out: plld out over 2f out: rdn to ld jst ins fnl f: r.o wl* **5/4**[1]

0464 **2** 2 1/4 **Captain Oats (IRE)**[25] 4938 6-10-10 56 oh8 MrSWalker 3 54
(Mrs P Ford) *hld up: hdwy over 3f out: pushed along over 2f out: ev ch wl over 1f out: sn rdn: styd on to take 2nd towards fin* **7/1**

0020 **3** 1/2 **Regal Blush**[26] 4904 3-10-3 64 MrSTwiston-Davies(5) 8 61
(A M Balding) *a.p: chsd ldr over 7f out: rdn and ev ch jst over 1f out: nt qckn fnl f* **5/2**[2]

2340 **4** nk **Regal Angel**[17] 5217 6-10-9 58 MrTRDavid(3) 5 55
(Jean-Rene Auvray) *w ldr: led after 2f: rdn wl over 1f out: hdd jst ins fnl f: no ex and lost 2nd towards fin* **25/1**

63 **5** 3 1/4 **Sushitan (GER)**[34] 4205 4-11-5 70 JosephAkehurst(5) 1 62
(G L Moore) *hld up in tch: lost pl over 6f out: rdn over 2f out: short-lived effrt on outside wl over 1f out* **5/1**[3]

4034 **6** 1 1/4 **Lucy's Perfect**[32] 4687 3-9-9 56 oh11 MrPMillman(5) 7 46
(B R Millman) *hld up: hdwy over 2f out: sn rdn: wknd jst over 1f out* **16/1**

0/00 **7** 34 **Restless Swallow**[25] 3205 4-10-7 56 oh11 MrRMahon(3) 4 —
(R A Harris) *hld up: hdwy over 7f out: pushed along and wknd 3f out: sn rdn and lost tch: eased fnl f* **100/1**

2m 58.14s (6.14) **Going Correction** 0.0s/f (Good)
WFA 3 from 4yo+ 10lb **7** Ran SP% **112.9**
Speed ratings (Par 103): **81,79,79,79,77 76,55**
toteswingers: 1&2 £2.80, 1&3 £1.40, 2&3 £3.20 CSF £10.70 CT £18.93 TOTE £2.20: £1.30, £3.10; EX 10.30 Place 6: £579.36 Place 5: £342.21.
Owner Mrs P A Wallis **Bred** D G Iceton **Trained** Ullingswick, H'fords

FOCUS
A weak maiden handicap - four of the seven runners were out of the weights - and they went a steady pace early on. It is doubtful if the winner had to match his recent form.
T/Jkpt: Not won. T/Plt: £988.80 to a £1 stake. Pool: £68,598.86. 50.64 winning tickets. T/Qpdt: £187.40 to a £1 stake. Pool: £4,711.06. 18.60 winning tickets. KH

5282 FOLKESTONE (R-H)
Monday, September 7

OFFICIAL GOING: Straight course - firm (good to firm in places; 9.6); round course - good to firm (firm in places; 8.0)
Wind: light, across Weather: sunny

5721 BET AFTER THE OFF AT LADBROKES.COM NOVICE STKS 6f
2:20 (2:21) (Class 4) 2-Y-O **£3,885** (£1,156; £577) **Stalls** Low

Form RPR

216 **1** **Danny's Choice**[23] 5057 2-8-11 89 JimCrowley 2 73+
(R M Beckett) *sn pushed up to ld and r on stands' rail: rdn wl over 1f out: styd on wl fnl f* **11/4**[2]

1 **2** 3/4 **Art Scholar (IRE)**[10] 5379 2-9-2 0 PatDobbs 1 76+
(G L Moore) *trckd wnr: effrt and rdn wl over 1f out: kpt on same pce and a hld fnl f* **30/100**[1]

6641 **3** 1 1/4 **Watch Chain (IRE)**[11] 5372 2-8-9 56 AshleyMorgan(5) 3 70?
(M H Tompkins) *stdd and dropped in bhd after s: a 3rd: rdn and effrt wl over 1f out: kpt on same pce after* **40/1**[3]

1m 10.87s (-1.83) **Going Correction** -0.375s/f (Firm) **3** Ran SP% **106.0**
Speed ratings (Par 97): **97,96,94**
CSF £4.14 TOTE £3.40; EX 4.70.
Owner G B Partnership **Bred** R J Cornelius **Trained** Whitsbury, Hants

FOCUS
There was a going change before the opener, the track having dried to Firm, Good to Firm in places. This was slowly run and is not form to trust.

NOTEBOOK
Danny's Choice bagged the lead, and the favoured stands' rail along with it, and would not be passed. She made all when winning her maiden at Nottingham and, having finished sixth in a 5f Listed contest at Deauville last time, she found the step up to 6f to her liking. A quick surface clearly suits best and she will no doubt try her luck at Pattern level again at some stage. (tchd 3-1)
Art Scholar(IRE) got well on top in the end when winning on debut at Bath and was made a short-price favourite to follow up. He came under pressure with 2f to run, though, and never really looked like getting past the filly. His dam was successful at up to 1m5f and he clearly needs another furlong now. (op 1-3 tchd 4-11 in a place)

Watch Chain(IRE) finished so close seems to confirm that the form is worth little, though there is every chance the colt has improved a shade having got his head in front at Southwell last time. (op 50-1)

5722 LADBROKESCASINO.COM MEDIAN AUCTION MAIDEN STKS 7f (S)

2:50 (2:50) (Class 5) 2-Y-0 **£3,238** (£963; £481; £240) **Stalls** Low

Form RPR

1 **Diam Queen (GER)** 2-8-12 0 KFallon 8 69+
(L M Cumani) *chsd ldrs: rdn to chse ldr over 1f out: chal jst ins fnl f: led wl ins fnl f: styd on wl* **9/1**

6 2 ½ **Hooligan Sean**[36] [4564] 2-9-3 0 FergusSweeney 1 73+
(H Candy) *chsd ldr: rdn to ld over 1f out: clr w wnr ins fnl f: hdd and no ex wl ins fnl f* **10/1**

464 3 4 ½ **Gallant Eagle (IRE)**[14] [5317] 2-9-3 75 LPKeniry 11 61+
(S Kirk) *hld up towards rr: hdwy over 3f out: rdn 2f out: kpt on to go 3rd ins fnl f: no ch w ldng pair* **7/2**[2]

0 4 2 **Arnie Guru**[32] [4699] 2-8-10 0 KierenFox(7) 10 56+
(M J Attwater) *in tch in midfield: rdn and edgd rt over 1f out: outpcd by ldrs ent fnl f: kpt on* **100/1**

00 5 nk **D'Urberville**[90] [2793] 2-9-3 0 AdrianMcCarthy 13 55+
(J R Jenkins) *s.i.s: t.k.h: hld up in rr: rdn and hdwy 2f out: hung rt fr over 1f out: styd on fnl f: nvr nr ldrs* **100/1**

6 nk **Avon Lady** 2-8-12 0 HayleyTurner 2 49+
(J R Fanshawe) *in tch on stands' rail: rdn and unable qck ent fnl f: one pce and n.d ins fnl f* **16/1**

0 7 1 ¼ **Stratton Banker (IRE)**[32] [4699] 2-9-0 0 WilliamCarson(3) 7 51
(S C Williams) *led: rdn and hdd over 1f out: wknd qckly fnl f* **33/1**

5 8 3 **Gold Party**[14] [5318] 2-9-3 0 RichardKingscote 9 43
(Tom Dascombe) *hld up in tch: rdn and unable qck ent fnl 2f: wknd over 1f out* **10/1**

0 9 6 **Clayton Flick (IRE)**[14] [5312] 2-9-3 0 RobertHavlin 4 28
(A B Haynes) *s.i.s: t.k.h: hld up in rr: hdwy over 3f out: pushed along and no prog 2f out* **100/1**

00 10 7 **Flotate (USA)**[11] [5368] 2-8-12 0 JimmyQuinn 14 4
(Jane Chapple-Hyam) *chsd ldrs tl 4f out: sn lost pl: wl bhd fnl 2f* **25/1**

11 5 **Kinian (USA)** 2-9-0 0 MarcHalford(3) 3 —
(J R Best) *chsd ldrs: rdn and struggling 1/2-way: wl bhd fnl 2f* **33/1**

03 12 1 ½ **Whipperway (IRE)**[39] [4460] 2-8-12 0 AlanMunro 12 —
(M R Channon) *a bhd: rdn and lost tch 1/2-way: wl bhd fnl 2f* **13/8**[1]

6 P **Best Show (IRE)**[10] [5401] 2-9-3 0 (t) JimCrowley 5 —
(Mrs A J Perrett) *plld hrd: chsd ldrs tl lost action and eased: p.u 5f out: lame* **7/1**[3]

1m 25.9s (-1.40) **Going Correction** -0.375s/f (Firm) **13** Ran SP% **119.6**
Speed ratings (Par 95): **93,92,87,85,84 84,82,79,72,64 58,57,—**
toteswingers: 1&2 £13.50, 1&3 £5.10, 2&3 £8.60 CSF £91.82 TOTE £8.70: £2.60, £3.30, £2.00; EX 125.00 TRIFECTA Not won..
Owner Jaber Abdullah **Bred** The Kingwood Partnership **Trained** Newmarket, Suffolk

FOCUS
This wasn't much of a maiden and it again paid to race near the stands' rail. It was a pleasing start from the winner but the bare form is modest.

NOTEBOOK
Diam Queen(GER) made a winning debut under a vintage Fallon ride. A daughter of Lando whose dam is related to a couple of useful performers, she was cajoled along from some way out, but was responding all the time and the penny dropped plenty soon enough for her to win, getting on top close home once Fallon gave her a couple of slaps with the whip. Described as a slightly lazy and quirky individual, there is undoubtedly more to come and she will improve for the step up to 1m. (op 13-2)
Hooligan Sean, well beaten over 6f on his debut at Newbury, had the advantage of the rail and was soon prominent. He improved for the step up to 7f, keeping on the right the way to the line, but the winner ultimately had a tad too much class. (tchd 9-1)
Gallant Eagle(IRE) fared best of those who raced more towards the centre, staying on for third and giving the form a solid look. He continues to find at least a couple too good in maidens, but it remains to be seen whether he can defy this mark in nurseries. (tchd 4-1)
Arnie Guru, last of nine on last month's C&D debut, has clearly learnt a lot in a short space of time and he stayed on to for fourth.
D'Urberville is now qualified for a handicap mark.
Avon Lady, a daughter of Avonbridge, kept on having been outpaced and should learn from the experience. (op 14-1)
Gold Party was unable to build on his debut effort. (tchd 8-1)
Whipperway(IRE) came under pressure before halfway and was one of the first beaten. The way she dropped out strongly suggests something was amiss. Official explanation: jockey said filly ran flat (op 2-1 tchd 6-4, 9-4 in places and 5-2 in a place)
Best Show(IRE) went wrong after a furlong and was pulled up. It later emerged he had received a serious injury. Official explanation: jockey said colt pulled up lame (op 15-2 tchd 8-1)

5723 WATCH LIVE SPORT AT LADBROKES.COM H'CAP 7f (S)

3:20 (3:22) (Class 5) (0-70,68) 3-Y-0+ **£3,238** (£963; £481; £240) **Stalls** Low

Form RPR

4066 1 **Sham Sheer**[46] [4230] 3-8-11 **61** KFallon 2 69
(L M Cumani) *mde all: rdn wl over 1f out: hrd pressed fnl 100yds: hld on wl* **15/2**

0403 2 hd **Billberry**[23] [5031] 4-9-0 **60** (t) JimCrowley 5 69+
(S C Williams) *stdd and dropped in bhd after s: hld up in last pl: pushed along 2f out: sn swtchd rt and hdwy: drvn to chal wnr ins fnl f: a hld* **3/1**[1]

3203 3 2 ¾ **Azure Mist**[7] [5525] 4-9-5 **65** JimmyQuinn 1 67
(M H Tompkins) *t.k.h: hld up in tch: rdn and hdwy on stands' rail over 1f out: chsd ldng pair and drvn 1f out: wknd fnl 100yds* **7/2**[2]

0-06 4 1 ¼ **Candy Rose**[24] [4992] 4-8-10 **56** PatDobbs 4 54
(M P Tregoning) *trckd ldrs on stands' rail: rdn and hanging rt 2f out: chsd wnr wl over 1f out tl 1f out: wknd ins fnl f* **7/1**

0604 5 2 **Dancer's Legacy**[5] [5569] 4-8-11 **57** PatCosgrave 7 50
(J R Boyle) *chsd ldrs: n.m.r 1/2-way: rdn over 2f out: wknd u.p over 1f out* **15/2**

0024 6 1 ¼ **Diamond Twister (USA)**[5] [5575] 3-9-1 **68** (t) MarcHalford(3) 6 55
(J R Best) *racd in last trio: rdn and edgd rt 2f out: no ch w ldrs fnl f* **4/1**[3]

0-61 7 1 ½ **Miss Bootylishes**[45] [4266] 4-9-8 **68** KevinGhunowa 8 53
(A B Haynes) *chsd ldr tl wl over 1f out: sn wknd u.p* **9/1**

1m 24.56s (-2.74) **Going Correction** -0.375s/f (Firm)
WFA 3 from 4yo+ 4lb **7** Ran SP% **113.3**
Speed ratings (Par 103): **100,99,96,95,92 91,89**
toteswingers: 1&2 £5.20, 1&3 £4.30, 2&3 £2.50 CSF £29.62 CT £92.57 TOTE £9.60: £3.10, £1.90; EX 20.80 Trifecta £56.10 Pool: £482.39 - 6.36 winning units..
Owner Sheikh Mohammed Obaid Al Maktoum **Bred** Brook Stud Bloodstock Ltd **Trained** Newmarket, Suffolk

FOCUS
A moderate handicap and Fallon once again excelled. The winner is rated back to his maiden form.

Miss Bootylishes Official explanation: jockey said filly was unsuited by the ground

5724 LADBROKESPOKER.COM H'CAP 5f

3:50 (3:51) (Class 5) (0-75,74) 3-Y-0+ **£3,885** (£1,156; £577; £288) **Stalls** Low

Form RPR

5113 1 **Corton Charlemagne (IRE)**[16] [5264] 3-8-13 **71** WilliamCarson(3) 2 77
(Rae Guest) *chsd ldrs: rdn and hdwy on stands' rail jst over 1f out: drvn to ld fnl 75yds: styd on wl* **11/8**[1]

3024 2 hd **Magical Speedfit (IRE)**[8] [5480] 4-9-1 **69** KFallon 8 74
(G G Margarson) *bhd: rdn 1/2-way: swtchd rt and hdwy u.p over 1f out: ev ch fnl 100yds: kpt on but hld towards fin* **5/1**[2]

0000 3 1 ½ **Ten Down**[14] [5323] 4-8-6 **60** HayleyTurner 3 60
(M Quinn) *led: rdn 2f out: drvn and hdd fnl 75yds: no ex* **16/1**

4432 4 3 **Simple Rhythm**[16] [5254] 3-8-7 **65** MarcHalford(3) 4 54
(J Ryan) *w ldr: ev ch and rdn over 1f out: wknd jst ins fnl f* **8/1**

1506 5 nse **Chris's Jem**[19] [5164] 3-8-1 **63** DannyBrock(7) 7 52
(J R Jenkins) *chsd ldrs: hdwy and ev ch over 1f out: sn rdn: wknd jst ins fnl f* **25/1**

0060 6 2 ¼ **Lesley's Choice**[31] [4733] 3-9-5 **74** DarryllHolland 1 55
(R Curtis) *bhd: n.m.r on stands' rail 2f out: sn swtchd rt and rdn: no hdwy* **11/1**

3606 7 ½ **Even Bolder**[17] [5219] 6-9-1 **69** LiamJones 5 48
(E A Wheeler) *dwlt: sn rcvrd and in tch: rdn and unable qck 2f out: wknd over 1f out* **11/2**[3]

0040 8 nk **Malapropism**[14] [5323] 9-8-5 **59** oh4 JimmyQuinn 9 37
(M R Channon) *in tch in midfield on outer: rdn and no rspnse 2f out: wl btn fnl f* **14/1**

58.66 secs (-1.34) **Going Correction** -0.375s/f (Firm)
WFA 3 from 4yo+ 1lb **8** Ran SP% **110.0**
Speed ratings (Par 103): **95,94,92,87,87 83,83,82**
toteswingers: 1&2 £2.20, 1&3 £6.60, 2&3 £9.50 CSF £7.42 CT £56.29 TOTE £2.40: £1.10, £1.70, £5.40; EX 8.50 Trifecta £131.70 Pool: £418.55- 2.35 winning units..
Owner Cheval Ct, Alexander, Bottrell & Guest **Bred** Tony Hirschfeld & L K Piggott **Trained** Newmarket, Suffolk
■ Elhamri (9/1) was withdrawn after proving unruly at the start. R4 applies, deduct 10p in the £.

FOCUS
A modest sprint handicap. A slight step up from the winner to beat the frustrating runner-up.

5725 BEST ODDS GUARANTEED AT LADBROKES.COM H'CAP 1m 1f 149y

4:20 (4:20) (Class 4) (0-85,83) 3-Y-0+ **£7,123** (£2,119; £1,059; £529) **Stalls** Centre

Form RPR

213 1 **Ordoney (IRE)**[16] [5266] 4-9-3 **77** KFallon 9 88+
(L M Cumani) *t.k.h: hld up in tch in midfield: rdn over 3f out: drvn to chse ldr over 1f out: ev ch and hung lft ent fnl f: led ins fnl f: r.o wl to assert fnl 75yds* **2/1**[1]

1131 2 ½ **Mick's Dancer**[22] [5062] 4-9-5 **79** DarryllHolland 6 89
(W R Muir) *led: rdn 2f out: hrd pressed and carried lft fr 1f out: hdd ins fnl f: kpt on gamely tl no ex fnl 75yds* **9/4**[2]

-400 3 2 ½ **Watergate (IRE)**[9] [5419] 3-9-0 **81** StephenDonohoe 10 86
(Sir Mark Prescott) *chsd ldr tl over 6f out: rdn to chse ldr again over 2f out tl over 1f out: keeping on same pce whn swtchd rt jst ins fnl f* **11/2**[3]

1510 4 1 **Ethics Girl (IRE)**[9] [5419] 3-8-8 **75** HayleyTurner 3 78
(John Berry) *t.k.h: hld up in tch in midfield: pushed along 4f out: kpt on same pce u.p fnl 2f* **8/1**

0461 5 5 **Master Fong (IRE)**[17] [5223] 3-8-9 **76** MichaelHills 5 68
(B W Hills) *racd in last pair: rdn and no prog 3f out: no ch w ldrs fnl 2f* **13/2**

/06- 6 hd **Shannersburg (IRE)**[69] [2209] 4-9-4 **78** (bt) FergusSweeney 8 70
(A B Haynes) *dwlt: racd in last pair: hdwy on inner wl over 2f out: rdn ent fnl 2f: sn btn* **40/1**

0134 7 37 **Summer Winds**[25] [4957] 4-9-9 **83** (b) RobertHavlin 1 —
(T G Mills) *s.i.s: hdwy to chse ldr over 6f out tl over 2f out: wknd qckly over 1f out: virtually p.u fnl f: t.o* **10/1**

001 8 18 **Saltagioo (ITY)**[40] [4438] 5-9-8 **82** JimCrowley 4 —
(I A Wood) *hld up in tch in midfield: rdn and wknd qckly wl over 2f out: eased fnl 2f: t.o* **25/1**

2m 1.09s (-3.81) **Going Correction** -0.375s/f (Firm)
WFA 3 from 4yo+ 7lb **8** Ran SP% **119.3**
Speed ratings (Par 105): **100,99,97,96,92 92,63,48**
toteswingers: 1&2 £1.90, 1&3 £4.30, 2&3 £3.70 CSF £7.11 CT £21.13 TOTE £3.70: £1.10, £1.10, £2.60; EX 6.50 Trifecta £30.90 Pool: £347.22 - 8.29 winning units..
Owner Sheikh Mohammed Obaid Al Maktoum **Bred** Mrs Mary Coonan **Trained** Newmarket, Suffolk
■ Stewards' Enquiry : K Fallon caution: careless riding

FOCUS
A fair handicap. It was sound run and the form is sound. The winner can rate higher.
Summer Winds Official explanation: jockey said gelding lost its action

5726 BET NOW AT LADBROKES ON 0800 777 888 H'CAP 1m 4f

4:50 (4:51) (Class 5) (0-70,70) 3-Y-0 **£3,238** (£963; £481; £240) **Stalls** High

Form RPR

-426 1 **Qelaan (USA)**[33] [4650] 3-9-4 **70** RHills 1 85
(M P Tregoning) *mde all: pushed along and drew clr over 2f out: rdn wl clr over 1f out: styd on strly* **7/2**[3]

3220 2 12 **Sumani (FR)**[26] [4910] 3-9-1 **67** DarryllHolland 2 63
(S Dow) *chsd wnr thrght: pushed along over 4f out: rdn and nt pce of wnr over 2f out: kpt on for 2nd but no ch w wnr* **10/3**[2]

6040 3 1 ¾ **Wightgold**[100] [2489] 3-7-13 **56** oh6 SophieDoyle(5) 3 49
(H J L Dunlop) *t.k.h: hld up in last pair: rdn and hdwy over 2f out: no ch w wnr fnl 2f: wnt 3rd fnl 100yds* **40/1**

0-34 4 2 ½ **Cluny**[111] [2170] 3-9-0 **66** HayleyTurner 7 55
(J R Fanshawe) *in tch: pushed along and sltly hmpd bnd 4f out: struggling and rdn over 3f out: wl hld fnl 2f* **9/2**

3044 5 3 **Full Of Nature**[15] [5285] 3-9-3 **69** LPKeniry 4 53
(S Kirk) *t.k.h: hld up in last pair: short-lived effrt 3f out: wl btn fnl 2f* **12/1**

5005 6 4 ½ **King's La Mont (IRE)**[21] [5101] 3-8-12 **64** (t) JimCrowley 5 41
(Mrs A J Perrett) *t.k.h: hld up in tch: rdn and struggling 3f out: sn wl btn* **15/2**

0164 7 7 **Fisadara**[23] [5035] 3-8-10 **62** AlanMunro 6 28
(Jane Chapple-Hyam) *in tch in last trio: bhd and rdn 4f out: sn lost tch* **11/4**[1]

2m 35.1s (-5.80) **Going Correction** -0.375s/f (Firm) **7** Ran SP% **112.0**
Speed ratings (Par 101): **104,96,94,93,91 88,83**
toteswingers: 1&2 £2.00, 1&3 £14.40, 2&3 £14.00 CSF £14.91 TOTE £3.90: £2.50, £1.60; EX 19.30 Place 6: £95.07 Place 5: £23.25.
Owner Hamdan Al Maktoum **Bred** Shadwell Farm LLC **Trained** Lambourn, Berks

FOCUS
Nothing got into this as the winner made all for a wide-margin win in this weak handicap. The third was 6lb wrong and the favourite well below par.
Fisadara Official explanation: jockey said filly ran flat
T/Plt: £101.80 to a £1 stake. Pool: £56,967.94. 408.30 winning tickets. T/Qpdt: £12.40 to a £1 stake. Pool: £5,402.75. 320.27 winning tickets. SP

5512 NEWCASTLE (L-H)
Monday, September 7

OFFICIAL GOING: Good to soft (6.9)
Wind: Fresh, half against Weather: Cloudy, bright

5727 PARKLANDS GOLFCOURSE MAIDEN STKS 5f
2:00 (2:00) (Class 5) 3-Y-O+ **£3,154** (£944; £472; £236; £117) **Stalls** High

Form RPR
6030 **1** **Half A Crown (IRE)**[9] 5443 4-9-4 44..........................(v[1]) PhillipMakin 10 64
(M Dods) *s.i.s: hld up: hdwy on stands' rail over 1f out: led ins fnl f: sn clr* **9/1**
0000 **2** 4 1/2 **Town And Gown**[4] 5599 4-8-8 40.................... GaryBartley(5) 8 43
(J S Goldie) *hld up: hdwy whn nt clr run briefly over 1f out: kpt on fnl f on stands' rail to chse wnr wl ins fnl f: r.o* **40/1**
3 **3** 3/4 **Catchpenny**[14] 5304 3-8-12 0.................... PaulHanagan 11 40+
(K A Ryan) *in tch: rdn and edgd lft 2f out: r.o fnl f: no imp* **8/1**
53 **4** nk **Tripbiyah (USA)**[22] 5072 3-9-3 0.................... PJMcDonald 7 44
(G A Swinbank) *cl up: rdn and disp ld fr 2f out to ins fnl f: one pce* **15/8**[1]
000- **5** 2 **Bettys Touch**[404] 4533 4-8-13 45.................... DavidAllan 12 32
(K G Reveley) *midfield: effrt and prom over 1f out: one pce fnl f* **50/1**
443 **6** nk **Fatal Attraction**[93] 2700 4-8-10 59.................... FrederikTylicki(3) 2 31
(Rae Guest) *led to ins fnl f: sn outpcd* **5/1**[3]
36 **7** 3/4 **Castlecarra (IRE)**[4] 5599 4-9-4 0.................... SilvestreDeSousa 1 33
(J Hetherton) *in tch tl rdn and no ex fr over 1f out* **20/1**
6202 **8** 1/2 **Residency (IRE)**[12] 5336 3-9-3 65.................... RichardMullen 6 31
(B Smart) *cl up: rdn over 2f out: btn fnl f* **11/4**[2]
5460 **9** 1 **Tarus (IRE)**[9] 5422 5-8-6 45....................(t) BillyCray(7) 4 23
(A Berry) *chsd ldrs tl wknd wl over 1f out* **66/1**
0 **10** 9 **Old Firm**[37] 4531 3-8-12 0....................(t) PaulPickard(5) 9 —
(D A Nolan) *s.i.s: bhd: no ch fr 1/2-way* **200/1**
500- **11** 36 **Howards Way**[376] 5392 4-9-4 0.................... DuranFentiman 3 —
(D A Nolan) *s.i.s: bhd tl lost tch fr over 2f out: t.o* **66/1**

62.40 secs (1.70) **Going Correction** +0.20s/f (Good)
WFA 3 from 4yo+ 1lb 11 Ran SP% **111.9**
Speed ratings (Par 103): **94,86,85,85,81 81,80,79,77,63 5**
toteswingers: 1&2 £43.80, 1&3 £6.20, 2&3 £38.30 CSF £306.04 TOTE £12.50: £2.50, £8.60, £2.40; EX 232.00.
Owner G N Parker **Bred** Burns Farm Stud **Trained** Denton, Co Durham

FOCUS
Older horse maidens at this time of year are more often than not weak affairs and this one was no exception. With the form par not at their best the winner probably did not have to improve much on his 2yo form.
Residency(IRE) Official explanation: jockey said gelding was never travelling

5728 EUROPEAN BREEDERS' FUND MAIDEN STKS 6f
2:30 (2:30) (Class 5) 2-Y-O **£4,289** (£1,283; £641; £320; £159) **Stalls** High

Form RPR
1 **Fortunes Of Fire** 2-9-3 0.................... PJMcDonald 10 76+
(G A Swinbank) *trckd ldrs: effrt 2f out: led ins fnl f: kpt on wl* **40/1**
322 **2** 1 **Aalsmeer**[84] 2972 2-8-12 93.................... RichardMullen 9 68
(E S McMahon) *led stands' rail to ins fnl f: kpt on same pce* **4/6**[1]
3 1 1/4 **Namecheck (GER)** 2-9-0 0.................... AhmedAjtebi(3) 2 69+
(Saeed Bin Suroor) *wnt lft s: prom: effrt and ev ch 2f out: rdn and wnt lft 1f out: one pce* **6/1**[3]
4 2 1/2 **Kellys Eye (IRE)** 2-9-3 0.................... TomEaves 5 61+
(B Smart) *bhd: rdn and green over 2f out: kpt on fnl f: nrst fin* **28/1**
5 1 1/4 **Silver Socks** 2-9-0 0.................... FrederikTylicki(3) 11 58
(I Semple) *hld up: shkn up and hdwy over 2f out: kpt on fnl f: nvr able to chal* **25/1**
53 **6** 3/4 **Love Delta (USA)**[26] 4888 2-9-3 0.................... JoeFanning 6 55
(M Johnston) *cl up tl rdn and wknd appr fnl f* **7/2**[2]
06 **7** 3/4 **Meetings Man (IRE)**[52] 4067 2-9-3 0.................... DaleGibson 8 53
(Micky Hammond) *midfield: drvn and outpcd over 3f out: kpt on fnl f: n.d* **100/1**
8 nse **Chookie Avon** 2-9-3 0.................... DavidAllan 4 53
(I Semple) *dwlt: rn green in rr: sme late hdwy: nvr rchd ldrs* **50/1**
400 **9** nk **Dazakhee**[16] 5253 2-8-12 0....................(p) TonyHamilton 12 47
(P T Midgley) *dwlt: bhd: struggling over 2f out: edgd lft: nvr on terms* **200/1**
45 **10** 1 3/4 **Cape Kimberley**[13] 5325 2-9-3 0.................... PaulHanagan 7 47
(J G Given) *cl up tl rdn and wknd fr 2f out* **50/1**
566 **11** 3 1/4 **Bonasera (IRE)**[12] 5330 2-8-5 30.................... BillyCray(7) 13 32
(A Berry) *bhd: n.m.r after 2f: nvr on terms* **200/1**
0 **12** 24 **Mark Carmers**[102] 2388 2-9-3 0.................... PhillipMakin 3 —
(T D Barron) *t.k.h in midfield: drvn and wknd qckly over 2f out: eased whn no ch* **80/1**

1m 17.14s (1.94) **Going Correction** +0.20s/f (Good) 12 Ran SP% **113.4**
Speed ratings (Par 95): **95,93,92,88,87 86,85,84,84,82 77,45**
toteswingers: 1&2 £8.90, 1&3 £13.20, 2&3 £3.00 CSF £65.09 TOTE £32.30: £8.30, £1.02, £1.80; EX 128.90.
Owner G H Bell, P Baldwin & Mrs V McGee **Bred** Mrs Zara Campbell-Harris And Adam Barker **Trained** Melsonby, N Yorks

FOCUS
An average juvenile maiden, run at a sound pace. As with the opening maiden the field again came over to the stands' side. A pleasing start from the winner but the bare form is just modest.

NOTEBOOK
Fortunes Of Fire hails from a yard not known for its debut winners and was sent off at 40/1 in the betting ring. He got the job done at the first time of asking in game fashion though, travelling nicely just off the pace before showing a professional attitude when asked to hit the front. This already-gelded son of Avonbridge has an interesting pedigree, as his sire injects a speed influence, but his dam was produced winners over much longer trips. He has scope and, with this experience likely to bring him on a deal, he looks one to follow, so it will be interesting to see how the handicapper rates this.
Aalsmeer's second on her penultimate outing, when narrowly beaten by Misheer in Listed company, made her the clear form pick here. She was bidding to bounce back from a below-par effort at Warwick when last seen in June, however, and stepping up a furlong. The money still came for her and she held every chance against the favoured near rail, but was unable to offer anymore when the winner came at her. A more patient ride first time up over this trip would have probably suited ideally and she is well up to winning a maiden of this class, but it doesn't look like she will be reaching the heights she promised to earlier this season. (op 10-11, tchd 1-1 in places)
Namecheck(GER), whose dam was a high-class middle-distance performer, showed fair ability yet ultimately lost out through greenness. He was not helped by having to race without cover and, while he is no star, should be capable of getting his head in front soon enough. (op 8-1)
Kellys Eye(IRE) took time to get the hang of things, but finished nicely from off the pace and should be all the sharper with this initial experience behind him. Another furlong should also prove ideal. (tchd 33-1)
Silver Socks, bred to make his mark at around this trip, was another that stayed on encouragingly from off the pace and turned in a pleasing debut effort.
Love Delta(USA) settled better than when disappointing at Beverley 26 days earlier, but he was a spent force before the furlong pole and has not built on the promise of his Goodwood debut. His fortunes may improve now he is qualified for nurseries. (op 9-4)
Cape Kimberley Official explanation: jockey said colt became unbalanced in the final two furlongs

5729 PHOENIX SECURITY H'CAP 6f
3:00 (3:00) (Class 6) (0-55,55) 3-Y-O+ **£2,914** (£867; £433; £216) **Stalls** High

Form RPR
4643 **1** **Mayoman (IRE)**[12] 5341 4-9-0 55....................(b[1]) DNolan 14 64
(D Carroll) *prom stands' side: effrt 2f out: led ins fnl f: drvn out: 1st of 9 in gp* **7/1**[3]
6004 **2** 1/2 **Kingsgate Castle**[16] 5254 4-9-0 55....................(b) PaulHanagan 16 62
(Miss Gay Kelleway) *trckd stands' side ldrs: led appr fnl f to ins fnl f: r.o: 2nd of 9 in gp* **14/1**
0230 **3** nk **The Name Is Frank**[9] 5443 4-8-11 55....................(t) MichaelJStainton(3) 7 61
(Mark Gillard) *cl up far side: ev ch and rdn over 1f out: led that gp wl ins fnl f: r.o: 1st of 6 in gp* **14/1**
5202 **4** 1/2 **Elkhorn**[9] 5443 7-8-12 53....................(b) TomEaves 6 57
(Miss J A Camacho) *trckd far side ldrs: led gng wl over 1f out: rdn and hdd wl ins fnl f: one pce: 2nd of 6 in gp* **7/1**[3]
-643 **5** 1/2 **Imperial Echo (USA)**[9] 5443 8-8-8 52.................... NeilBrown(3) 8 55
(T D Barron) *hld up far side: hdwy over 1f out: kpt on ins fnl f: 3rd of 6 in gp* **9/2**[2]
20-4 **6** 1 **Lambrini Lace (IRE)**[12] 5332 4-9-0 55.................... TonyHamilton 10 55
(Mrs L Williamson) *led stands' side gp to appr fnl f: one pce: 3rd of 9 in gp* **11/1**
6406 **7** 1 1/2 **Ursus**[10] 5396 4-8-12 53....................(p) SilvestreDeSousa 13 48+
(C R Wilson) *prom stands' side: rdn over 2f out: no ex over 1f out: 4th of 9 in gp* **7/2**[1]
65-0 **8** nk **Lambency (IRE)**[9] 5443 6-8-7 51.................... KellyHarrison(3) 11 45
(J S Goldie) *bhd stands' side tl gd hdwy fnl f: nrst fin: 5th of 9 in gp* **25/1**
0002 **9** 2 **Head To Head (IRE)**[125] 1781 5-8-10 51....................(bt) GrahamGibbons 17 38
(A D Brown) *hld up stands' side: rdn over 2f out: nvr able to chal: 6th of 9 in gp* **25/1**
0444 **10** 3 1/4 **Strathmore (IRE)**[10] 5396 5-8-10 54.................... FrederikTylicki(3) 1 31
(R A Fahey) *hld up far side: rdn over 2f out: nvr able to chal: 4th of 6 in gp* **14/1**
-050 **11** 6 **Glenluji**[7] 5518 4-8-8 54.................... GaryBartley(5) 15 12
(J S Goldie) *bhd stands' side: drvn over 2f out: nvr on terms: 7th of 9 in gp* **12/1**
4310 **12** 1/2 **Princess Charlmane (IRE)**[24] 5008 6-9-0 55....................(p) DavidAllan 2 11
(C J Teague) *led far side to over 1f out: sn wknd: 5th of 6 in gp* **33/1**
-050 **13** 8 **Danzig Fox**[11] 5364 4-8-11 52.................... GregFairley 3 —
(M Mullineaux) *bhd far side: struggling over 2f out: last of 6 in gp* **33/1**
/00- **14** 2 1/2 **Dowlleh**[25] 5816 5-9-0 55.................... VinceSlattery 9 —
(G Brown) *trckd stands' side ldrs tl wknd fr 2f out: 8th of 9 in gp* **66/1**
0000 **15** 2 1/2 **Prospect Court**[14] 5309 7-8-12 53.................... PJMcDonald 12 —
(A C Whillans) *bhd stands' side: struggling over 2f out: sn btn: last of 9 in gp* **22/1**

1m 16.21s (1.01) **Going Correction** +0.20s/f (Good) 15 Ran SP% **120.8**
Speed ratings (Par 101): **101,100,99,99,98 97,95,94,92,87 79,79,68,65,61**
toteswingers: 1&2 £18.00, 1&3 £24.40, 2&3 £43.20 CSF £92.70 CT £1376.21 TOTE £9.30: £2.30, £5.00, £4.00; EX 149.80.
Owner Tom Tuohy **Bred** James Cosgrove **Trained** Sledmere, E Yorks
■ Stewards' Enquiry : Paul Hanagan caution: excessive use of the whip
Michael J Stainton caution: used whip down the shoulder in the forehand position

FOCUS
Few managed to land a significant blow from off the pace in this wide-open and very tight sprint handicap. Six went to the far side and, with the winner making his challenge more towards the centre late on, there was no real bias with the draw. The second and third are the best guides to the form.

5730 GOSFORTH DECORATING & BUILDING SERVICES (S) STKS 1m (R)
3:30 (3:30) (Class 6) 3-Y-O+ **£1,942** (£578; £288; £144) **Stalls** Centre

Form RPR
0640 **1** **Whipma Whopma Gate (IRE)**[6] 5549 4-8-13 48....................(b) DNolan 5 52
(D Carroll) *chsd ldrs: wnt 2nd over 2f out: led appr fnl f: hld on wl* **16/1**
45 **2** 1 1/2 **Freda's Rose (IRE)**[16] 5259 5-8-10 0.................... RussellKennemore(3) 11 49
(O Brennan) *led tl hdd appr fnl f: kpt on same pce* **16/1**
3524 **3** 1/2 **Ancient Cross**[9] 5423 5-9-1 63....................(t) FrederikTylicki(3) 3 52+
(M W Easterby) *hld up in rr: hdwy on ins and nt clr run over 2f out: styd on over 1f out: no ex ins fnl f* **11/8**[1]
2555 **4** nk **Ingleby Princess**[27] 4876 5-8-13 50.................... SilvestreDeSousa 7 47
(T D Barron) *in tch: effrt over 2f out: chsng ldrs over 1f out: kpt on ins fnl f* **9/1**[3]
0046 **5** 1/2 **Pianoforte (USA)**[7] 5513 7-9-4 51....................(p) GrahamGibbons 6 51
(E J Alston) *t.k.h: trckd ldrs: one pce fnl 2f* **20/1**
0600 **6** 1 1/2 **Goswick**[7] 5524 3-8-8 45.................... PaulHanagan 16 41
(Micky Hammond) *mid-div: effrt over 2f out: kpt on ins fnl f: nt rch ldrs* **80/1**
0540 **7** 3/4 **Ming Vase**[32] 4710 7-9-4 49.................... PJMcDonald 17 45
(P T Midgley) *chsd ldrs: one pce fnl 2f* **25/1**
335 **8** nk **Straight Face (IRE)**[4] 5602 5-9-5 52....................(b) PatrickDonaghy(5) 10 51
(Miss Gay Kelleway) *in rr: styd on fnl 2f: nvr nr ldrs* **14/1**
1606 **9** 1/2 **Not Now Lewis (IRE)**[24] 4977 5-9-5 55.................... SladeO'Hara(5) 14 50
(F P Murtagh) *in rr: kpt on fnl 2f: nvr nr ldrs* **50/1**
3000 **10** nse **Castle Myth (USA)**[12] 5331 3-8-8 48....................(bt[1]) LanceBetts(5) 12 42
(B Ellison) *mid-div: effrt on outer 3f out: nvr a factor* **66/1**
3-52 **11** 1 3/4 **Ulysees (IRE)**[11] 5364 10-9-4 48.................... TonyHamilton 2 39
(I Semple) *t.k.h in mid-div: nvr a threat* **20/1**

6-00 **12** ½ **Zain (IRE)**[81] 3077 5-9-4 46 (t) TomEaves 9 38
(J G Given) *chsd ldrs: effrt 3f out: sn fdd* **66/1**

3300 **13** *nk* **Papa's Princess**[11] 5364 5-8-10 54 KellyHarrison(3) 1 33
(J S Goldie) *trckd ldrs: lost pl over 1f out* **20/1**

2003 **14** 1¾ **Society Music (IRE)**[96] 2590 7-8-13 65 (p) PhillipMakin 15 29
(M Dods) *s.i.s: hld up in last: nvr on terms* **7/2**[2]

0006 **15** 1¼ **Fyodorovich (USA)**[16] 4845 4-9-4 45 PAspell 13 31
(J S Wainwright) *s.s: a in rr* **80/1**

-005 **16** 2 **Igneous**[7] 5513 3-8-10 45 (p) MichaelJStainton(3) 4 25
(D W Thompson) *in rr div: nvr on terms* **66/1**

1m 45.47s (2.07) **Going Correction** +0.20s/f (Good)
WFA 3 from 4yo+ 5lb **16** Ran SP% **119.8**
Speed ratings (Par 101): **97,95,95,94,94 92,91,91,91,91 89,88,88,86,85 83**
toteswingers: 1&2 £24.20, 1&3 £12.20, 2&3 £9.20 CSF £223.52 TOTE £21.30: £4.80, £4.10, £1.80; EX 435.30.There was no bid for the winner. Ancient Cross was subject to a friendly claim.
Owner John Seed & Mrs Angela Seed **Bred** Pat Roche **Trained** Sledmere, E Yorks
■ Freda's Rose was the final runner of Owen Brennan's long training career.

FOCUS
This very weak heat was run at a fair pace and the form is best rated around the winner and second, who were always 1-2.

5731 JOHN SMITH'S MAIDEN STKS 1m (R)
4:00 (4:02) (Class 5) 3-Y-O+ **£3,784** (£1,132; £566; £283; £141) **Stalls** Centre

Form RPR

2022 **1** **Implication**[21] 5102 3-8-12 75 PaulHanagan 5 64
(E A L Dunlop) *hld up in midfield: smooth hdwy to chal over 1f out: rdn to ld last 100yds: r.o* **7/4**[1]

62 **2** ½ **Duke Of Burgundy (FR)**[7] 5531 6-9-8 0 SJCraine 14 69+
(Jennie Candlish) *s.i.s: hld up: hdwy over 2f out: styd on to chse wnr towards fin* **8/1**

4B22 **3** ½ **Northside Prince (IRE)**[12] 5331 3-9-3 65 PJMcDonald 11 67
(G A Swinbank) *cl up: led 4f out: jnd and rdn over 1f out: hdd last 100yds: lost 2nd nr fin* **15/8**[2]

4 ¾ **Cool Baranca (GER)**[44] 3-8-12 0 TonyHamilton 1 60
(P Monteith) *s.i.s: hld up: hdwy over 2f out: r.o fnl f* **40/1**

05 **5** ¾ **Severio (IRE)**[30] 4805 3-8-12 0 AndrewElliott 9 59
(A P Jarvis) *trckd ldrs: rdn over 3f out: rallied 2f out: one pce fnl f* **25/1**

2052 **6** 4 **Barbarian**[73] 3358 3-9-3 70 SilvestreDeSousa 6 54
(A D Brown) *chsd ldrs: effrt 3f out: outpcd fnl 2f* **9/2**[3]

6 **7** ¾ **Short Supply (USA)**[7] 5520 3-8-12 0 GrahamGibbons 3 48
(T D Walford) *hld up: rdn and outpcd over 3f out: kpt on fnl f: no imp* **25/1**

05 **8** 2 **Fabled Dancer (IRE)**[22] 5071 3-9-3 0 DavidAllan 4 48
(E J Alston) *hld up ins: effrt 3f out: outpcd fnl 2f* **50/1**

00 **9** 2½ **Argent Avia**[16] 5259 3-8-12 0 TomEaves 7 37
(M Brittain) *prom: struggling over 2f out: sn btn* **200/1**

10 16 **Spiosra (USA)** 3-8-9 0 KellyHarrison(3) 12 —
(C J Teague) *s.i.s: bhd: rdn over 3f out: nvr on terms* **200/1**

11 20 **Wings Of Kintyre (IRE)** 5-9-3 0 GregFairley 8 —
(A Berry) *led to 4f out: rdn and sn wknd* **200/1**

50 **12** 4½ **Silvertown Boy**[17] 5228 3-9-3 0 PhillipMakin 13 —
(H A McWilliams) *chsd ldrs tl rdn and wknd qckly fr 3f out* **200/1**

1m 45.17s (1.77) **Going Correction** +0.20s/f (Good)
WFA 3 from 4yo+ 5lb **12** Ran SP% **114.5**
Speed ratings (Par 103): **99,98,98,97,96 92,91,89,87,71 51,46**
toteswingers: 1&2 £4.10, 1&3 £2.20, 2&3 £4.00 CSF £15.29 TOTE £2.90: £1.10, £2.10, £1.30; EX 14.70.
Owner Cheveley Park Stud **Bred** Cheveley Park Stud Ltd **Trained** Newmarket, Suffolk

FOCUS
A modest maiden with plenty of inexperienced types and two stood out on official marks. They went 25/1 bar four and three of those filled the places. The bare form is pretty modest.

5732 S.V. RUTTER H'CAP (DIV I) 1m 4f 93y
4:30 (4:31) (Class 6) (0-65,65) 3-Y-O+ **£2,525** (£751; £375; £187) **Stalls** Centre

Form RPR

5301 **1** **Rosewin (IRE)**[12] 5342 3-8-9 60 BMcHugh(5) 8 72+
(A Dickman) *hld up in midfield: drvn over 3f out: styd on to ld jst ins fnl f: sn drew clr: readily* **5/1**[2]

B436 **2** 3 **Hawkit (USA)**[12] 5334 8-9-6 57 TonyHamilton 2 64
(P Monteith) *trckd ldrs: effrt over 2f out: kpt on to take 2nd wl ins fnl f* **7/1**[3]

0516 **3** ½ **Golden Future**[11] 5377 6-9-1 52 PaulHanagan 6 58
(P D Niven) *w ldrs: led 1f out: sn hdd and no ex* **7/1**[3]

1050 **4** 1½ **Piverina (IRE)**[26] 4893 4-8-10 47 TomEaves 9 51
(Miss J A Camacho) *in rr div: hdwy over 3f out: chsng ldrs over 1f out: kpt on same pce* **12/1**

1500 **5** 1½ **World Of Choice (USA)**[35] 4593 4-9-5 56 (b) DaleGibson 7 57
(M W Easterby) *s.i.s: mid-div: effrt and outpcd over 3f out: styd on fnl 2f* **20/1**

6113 **6** 1¾ **Miss Ferney**[9] 5423 5-8-12 54 PaulPickard(5) 10 53
(A Kirtley) *s.i.s: swtchd lft after s: hld up in rr: effrt on wd outside over 2f out: nvr nr ldrs* **10/1**

235 **7** *nk* **Amethyst Dawn (IRE)**[24] 5011 3-8-12 58 DavidAllan 12 56
(T D Easterby) *trckd ldr: pushed along over 4f out: led over 3f out: hdd 1f out: sn wknd* **2/1**[1]

0406 **8** 1½ **Katie Girl**[13] 5328 3-8-0 46 oh1 (p) AndrewMullen 1 42
(Mrs G S Rees) *chsd ldrs: wknd over 1f out* **40/1**

40P6 **9** *hd* **Always Best**[19] 5162 5-8-9 46 oh1 (v) PJMcDonald 4 41
(R Allan) *chsd ldrs: pushed up to chal over 4f out: wknd over 1f out* **33/1**

4500 **10** 1½ **Shanavaz**[8] 5470 3-8-1 50 KellyHarrison(3) 11 43
(C J Teague) *hld up in rr: effrt over 2f out: hung lft and sn wknd* **8/1**

30- **11** 2¼ **Solis (GER)**[110] 7224 6-9-9 65 RyanMania(5) 5 54
(P Monteith) *in rr: nvr a factor* **40/1**

5-06 **12** 8 **Wizard Of Us**[11] 5359 9-8-9 46 oh1 GregFairley 3 23
(M Mullineaux) *led tl hdd over 3f out: sn lost pl and bhd* **20/1**

2m 44.68s (-0.92) **Going Correction** -0.05s/f (Good)
WFA 3 from 4yo+ 9lb **12** Ran SP% **120.2**
Speed ratings (Par 101): **101,99,98,97,96 95,95,94,94,93 91,86**
toteswingers: 1&2 £7.00, 1&3 £8.20, 2&3 £8.80 CSF £37.83 CT £247.81 TOTE £7.10: £1.90, £2.00, £3.00; EX 35.80.
Owner Major P H K Steveney **Bred** E A Bourke M R C V S **Trained** Sandhutton, N Yorks

FOCUS
A poor handicap, run at a sound pace and a bit quicker than the second division. Another improved effort from the winner.

5733 S.V. RUTTER H'CAP (DIV II) 1m 4f 93y
5:00 (5:00) (Class 6) (0-65,64) 3-Y-O+ **£2,525** (£751; £375; £187) **Stalls** Centre

Form RPR

0142 **1** **Shifting Gold (IRE)**[19] 5162 3-9-4 64 (b) AmyRyan(5) 4 72
(K A Ryan) *led to 3f out: sn rdn: swtchd rt and renewed effrt over 1f out: led ins fnl f: gamely* **7/2**[1]

4236 **2** 2½ **Shekan Star**[8] 5469 7-9-7 53 PaulHanagan 5 57
(K G Reveley) *hld up in midfield: effrt over 2f out: chsd wnr ins fnl f: r.o* **8/1**

5050 **3** ½ **The Quiet Genius**[24] 5011 3-9-0 55 TonyHamilton 8 58
(Jedd O'Keeffe) *prom: drvn and outpcd over 3f out: rallied 2f out: kpt on u.p fnl f* **14/1**

-400 **4** 1¼ **Park's Prodigy**[25] 4944 5-9-2 48 PAspell 2 49
(G A Harker) *pressed ldr: led gng wl 3f out: rdn and edgd lft wl over 1f out: hdd ins fnl f: no ex* **12/1**

4062 **5** *hd* **Jenny Soba**[38] 4498 6-9-11 57 DNolan 3 58
(Lucinda Featherstone) *hld up: outpcd over 4f out: rallied over 2f out: kpt on fnl f* **9/2**[2]

4010 **6** 1½ **Hurricane Thomas (IRE)**[24] 4972 5-9-2 51 FrederikTylicki(3) 9 49
(R A Fahey) *hld up: hdwy on ins over 4f out: effrt over 2f out: sn one pce* **5/1**[3]

5060 **7** 2 **Grethel (IRE)**[9] 5423 5-8-6 45 BillyCray(7) 1 40
(A Berry) *t.k.h: chsd ldrs: rdn 3f out: wknd over 1f out* **33/1**

5000 **8** 7 **Ernies Keep**[9] 5442 3-8-1 45 DominicFox(3) 7 29
(W Storey) *midfield: stdy hdwy on outside over 4f out: rdn and wknd over 3f out* **150/1**

0050 **9** *hd* **Sharp Sovereign (USA)**[15] 5294 3-8-9 50 TomEaves 10 34
(I Semple) *hld up: outpcd over 4f out: n.d after* **16/1**

-013 **10** 1 **Jordan's Light (USA)**[9] 5162 6-9-9 60 RyanMania(5) 11 42
(P Monteith) *hld up: struggling over 3f out: sn btn* **15/2**

4206 **11** 3 **King's Counsel (IRE)**[28] 4846 3-9-3 58 SilvestreDeSousa 6 35
(J Hetherton) *cl up tl rdn and wknd over 3f out* **7/1**

2m 45.67s (0.07) **Going Correction** -0.05s/f (Good)
WFA 3 from 5yo+ 9lb **11** Ran SP% **116.3**
Speed ratings (Par 101): **97,95,95,94,94 93,91,87,86,86 84**
toteswingers: 1&2 £7.10, 1&3 £11.50, 2&3 £29.60 CSF £31.55 CT £350.09 TOTE £5.00: £1.90, £2.30, £4.90; EX 36.80.
Owner Hambleton Racing Ltd VIII **Bred** Watership Down Stud **Trained** Hambleton, N Yorks

FOCUS
This second division of the middle-distance handicap was another decidedly moderate affair. It was run at a solid pace, however, and the form looks sound enough with the winner stepping up again.

5734 COMPLETE FOOTBALL H'CAP 2m 19y
5:30 (5:31) (Class 6) (0-65,60) 3-Y-O+ **£2,849** (£847; £423; £211) **Stalls** Low

Form RPR

265- **1** **Sendali (FR)**[161] 6115 5-9-0 46 GrahamGibbons 10 54+
(J D Bethell) *stdd towards rr: smooth hdwy whn n.m.r briefly over 1f out: shkn up to ld ins fnl f: jst hld on* **9/2**[1]

4 **2** *shd* **Whitcombe Spirit**[54] 3986 4-9-3 54 MartinLane(5) 1 60
(Jamie Poulton) *trckd ldrs: rdn over 2f out: effrt whn nt clr run briefly over 1f out: kpt on fnl f: jst hld* **7/1**[2]

0023 **3** 1¾ **Front Rank (IRE)**[9] 5307 9-8-13 50 SladeO'Hara(5) 16 54
(Mrs Dianne Sayer) *cl up: led over 2f out to ins fnl f: kpt on same pce* **15/2**[3]

6026 **4** ½ **Celtic Carisma**[22] 5068 7-8-6 45 IJBrennan(7) 8 48+
(K G Reveley) *hld up: hdwy over 2f out: kpt on ins fnl f* **8/1**

0000 **5** *nk* **King In Waiting (IRE)**[24] 4972 6-9-11 57 (vt) SilvestreDeSousa 9 60
(J Hetherton) *t.k.h: hld up: rdn 3f out: no imp tl styd on wl fnl f* **16/1**

0030 **6** 3¼ **Fistral**[4] 5600 5-9-4 50 TomEaves 11 49
(P D Niven) *led to over 2f out: rallied: wknd ins fnl f* **20/1**

/003 **7** ½ **Uptown Lad (IRE)**[9] 3617 10-8-8 45 DeanHeslop(5) 3 43
(R Johnson) *hld up: rdn over 3f out: kpt on fnl f: n.d* **40/1**

0046 **8** 1½ **Knock Three Times (IRE)**[9] 5442 3-7-11 45 DominicFox(3) 5 42
(W Storey) *hld up: pushed along 4f out: sme late hdwy: nvr on terms* **20/1**

00-2 **9** ½ **Baaher (USA)**[11] 5359 5-9-9 60 GaryBartley(5) 12 56+
(J S Goldie) *bhd tl styd on fr over 1f out: nvr nr ldrs* **9/2**[1]

0040 **10** *nk* **Great Quest (IRE)**[22] 5068 7-9-4 50 (p) PaulHanagan 15 46
(James Moffatt) *towards rr: drvn over 3f out: outpcd fnl 2f* **20/1**

2223 **11** ½ **Border Tale**[9] 4193 9-9-4 50 (v) PJMcDonald 13 45
(James Moffatt) *cl up: ev ch over 2f out: wknd ins fnl f* **16/1**

6600 **12** 4 **Louisa (GER)**[11] 5359 5-8-13 45 TonyHamilton 7 35
(P Monteith) *prom: lost pl over 4f out: n.d after* **33/1**

-500 **13** 1¾ **Prince Rhyddarch**[11] 5359 4-9-10 59 (p) FrederikTylicki(3) 6 47
(I Semple) *trckd ldrs tl wknd fr over 2f out* **8/1**

0-20 **14** *hd* **Transfered (IRE)**[7] 5530 3-8-10 55 ow2 DNolan 2 43
(Lucinda Featherstone) *hld up in midfield: struggling over 2f out: sn btn* **12/1**

/000 **15** 29 **English Archer**[6] 5554 6-8-13 45 AndrewElliott 4 —
(A Kirtley) *cl up: drvn over 5f out: wknd over 3f out: t.o* **66/1**

3m 39.42s (0.02) **Going Correction** -0.05s/f (Good)
WFA 3 from 4yo+ 13lb **15** Ran SP% **123.5**
Speed ratings (Par 101): **97,96,96,95,95 94,93,93,92,92 92,90,89,89,74**
toteswingers: 1&2 £9.20, 1&3 £8.10, 2&3 £8.00 CSF £32.56 CT £239.44 TOTE £6.20: £2.60, £2.90, £3.00; EX 44.90 Place 6: £161.33 Place 5: £23.62 .
Owner Elliott Brothers And Peacock **Bred** Sarl Haras Du Taillis Et Al **Trained** Middleham Moor, N Yorks

FOCUS
A wide-open staying handicap. The second and third are the best guides to this moderate form.

T/Plt: £556.90 to a £1 stake. Pool: £61,068.62. 80.05 winning tickets. T/Qpdt: £30.40 to a £1 stake. Pool: £6,439.73. 156.68 winning tickets. RY

5735 - 5738a (Foreign Racing) - See Raceform Interactive

CRAON (R-H)

Monday, September 7

OFFICIAL GOING: Good to soft

5739a **BAILEYS CRITERIUM DE L'OUEST (LISTED RACE)** **1m 55y**
1:40 (1:39) 2-Y-0 **£26,699** (£10,680; £8,010; £5,340; £2,670)

RPR

1 **Green Rock (FR)**19 2-9-2 .... TThulliez 4 95
(F Doumen, France)
2 nk **Kermiyan (FR)**61 2-9-2 .... CSoumillon 2 94
(J-C Rouget, France)
3 3/4 **Xaarienne**27 2-8-13 .... MGuyon 6 89
(H-A Pantall, France)
4 1 **Que Je T'Aime** 2-8-13 .... SPasquier 3 87
(C Ferland, France)
5 nk **Ceedwell**61 3748 2-8-13 .... OPeslier 5 87
(E Libaud, France)
6 4 **Florio Vincitore (IRE)**13 5324 2-9-2 .... EdwardCreighton 7 81
(E J Creighton) *prom: 2nd 1/2-way: pushed along appr st: sn one pce* **19/1**1
7 nk **Impressioniste (IRE)**8 5494 2-9-2 .... JAuge 1 80
(E J O'Neill) *prom: 3rd 1/2-way: 2nd and drvn st: sn no ex* **25/1**2

1m 46.5s (106.50) **7 Ran** SP% **8.8**
PARI-MUTUEL (including 1 Euro stake): WIN 8.10; PL 2.10, 1.20; SF 9.40.
Owner Saleh Al-Dugish **Bred** Charles Barel **Trained** Bouce, France
■ Stewards' Enquiry : C Soumillon 400euro fine: whip abuse

NOTEBOOK
Florio Vincitore(IRE), whose best previous form was on the all-weather, was found out by this step up in grade.
Impressioniste(IRE), a winner on his debut at Saint Malo before pulling too hard at Deauville, was another to find the rise in grade too much.

5471 GOODWOOD (R-H)

Tuesday, September 8

OFFICIAL GOING: Good to firm (good in places; 8.8)

Lower bend moved out 6 yards to the 2f marker in straight increasing distances by about 10yards.
Wind: Moderate, across, away from stands Weather: Sunny, warm

5740 **BOLLINGER CHAMPAGNE CHALLENGE SERIES H'CAP (FOR GENTLEMAN AMATEUR RIDERS)** **1m 3f**
2:00 (2:00) (Class 5) (0-70,70) 4-Y-0+ **£3,123** (£968; £484; £242) **Stalls** Low

Form RPR

0550 1 **Soundbyte**33 4696 4-10-8 **62** .... MrSTwiston-Davies(5) 6 71
(J Gallagher) *trckd ldrs: pushed along and prog on outer to ld 3f out: drifted lft but clr over 1f out: styd on wl* **6/1**3
1203 2 3 **Sand Repeal (IRE)**10 5444 7-10-3 **57** .... MrRBirkett(5) 8 61
(Miss J Feilden) *led 2f: led again 5f out to 3f out: nt qckn sn after and lost pl: kpt on to regain 2nd over 1f out* **7/1**
5446 3 1/2 **Sinbad The Sailor**26 4951 4-10-2 **56** ....(v) MrJSherwood(5) 5 59
(J W Hills) *dwlt: t.k.h and hld up: prog on inner whn nt clr run over 2f out: kpt on fr over 1f out to take 3rd last 100yds* **9/2**2
1451 4 1 1/4 **Sky Quest (IRE)**10 5444 11-11-2 **68** .... MrJohnEnnis(3) 4 69
(J R Boyle) *hld up in last pair: stdy prog over 3f out: disp 2nd over 1f out: no imp on wnr: wknd last 100yds* **8/1**
5446 5 1 **Bell Island**80 3169 5-11-6 **69** ....(v) MrSWalker 10 68
(Lady Herries) *trckd ldrs: rdn 3f out: nt qckn over 2f out: hld after: one pce fnl f* **5/2**1
6500 6 3 1/4 **Wester Lodge (IRE)**85 2971 7-10-0 **56** oh6........(p) MrDJEustace(7) 3 50
(J M P Eustace) *led after 2f to 5f out: steadily fdd fr 3f out* **20/1**
2303 7 1 3/4 **General Tufto**7 5548 4-10-11 **63** ....(b) MrTRDavid(3) 7 54
(C Smith) *hld up in tch: prog over 3f out: chsd wnr over 2f out to over 1f out: wknd* **11/1**
540- 8 15 **Damascus Gold**480 2153 5-10-3 **57** ....(p) MrAshleePrice(5) 1 22
(Miss Z C Davison) *s.s: nvr gng wl: a in last pair: bhd fr 4f out: t.o* **33/1**
6153 9 7 **Make Amends (IRE)**18 5211 4-10-10 **62** .... MrJoshuaMoore(3) 9 15
(R J Hodges) *prom to 1/2-way: sn wknd: t.o* **8/1**

2m 29.14s (0.84) **Going Correction** +0.025s/f (Good) **9 Ran** SP% **111.8**
Speed ratings (Par 103): **97,94,94,93,92 90,89,78,73**
toteswingers: 1&2 £8.50, 1&3 £6.70, 2&3 £6.80 CSF £45.32 CT £203.04 TOTE £6.80: £2.10, £2.20, £2.20; EX 43.10.
Owner Oliver Parsons **Bred** Mrs R J Gallagher **Trained** Chastleton, Oxon
■ The first Flat winner for Sam Twiston-Davies.

FOCUS
The running rail on the lower bend was dolled out approximately six yards to the 2f marker in the straight, increasing distances by about ten yards. The ground had dried out to an official description of good to firm, good in places. This was a modest handicap. The winner returned to form.
Make Amends(IRE) Official explanation: vet said had lost a left hind shoe post race

5741 **EUROPEAN BREEDERS' FUND SEPTEMBER MAIDEN FILLIES' STKS** **1m**
2:35 (2:36) (Class 5) 2-Y-0 **£3,561** (£1,059; £529; £264) **Stalls** High

Form RPR

1 **Namaskar** 2-9-0 0 .... JimmyFortune 10 80+
(J H M Gosden) *dwlt: hld up in rr: gd prog through rivals fr 2f out: wnt 2nd 150yds out: pushed along firmly and r.o wl to ld last strides* **13/2**
043 2 hd **Silent Secret (IRE)**18 5212 2-9-0 77 .... DaneO'Neill 4 77
(R Hannon) *prom: wnt 2nd 1/2-way: led over 2f out: rdn 2 l clr ins fnl f: collared last strides* **9/2**3
5 3 1 1/4 **Zahoo (IRE)**31 4792 2-9-0 0 .... TPO'Shea 7 74+
(J L Dunlop) *hld up in midfield: prog over 2f out: rdn to press for 2nd 1f out and upsides eventual wnr: sn outpcd* **6/4**1
4 2 **Momtaz** 2-9-0 0 .... NCallan 9 70
(C E Brittain) *hld up in midfield: prog to go cl up over 4f out: disp 2nd fr over 2f out to last 150yds: outpcd* **18/1**
6 5 1 1/2 **Dancing Queen (IRE)**31 4797 2-9-0 0 .... LDettori 14 67
(M A Magnusson) *cl up: shkn up over 2f out: nt qckn and outpcd wl over 1f out: kpt on same pce after* **7/2**2
0 6 1 **Tamtara**11 5397 2-9-0 0 .... JimCrowley 3 64
(Mrs A J Perrett) *prom gng wl: disp 2nd fr over 2f out to jst over 1f out: wknd fnl f* **66/1**
0 7 1 1/2 **Anaya**8 5498 2-9-0 0 .... SamHitchcott 12 61
(M R Channon) *hld up in midfield: rdn 3f out: sn outpcd: no imp on ldrs fnl 2f* **100/1**
8 hd **Treasure Way** 2-9-0 0 .... DavidProbert 13 62+
(P R Chamings) *chsd ldr to 1/2-way: styd cl up: wkng whn hmpd jst ins fnl f* **66/1**
0 9 1 **Forethought**31 4792 2-9-0 0 .... KFallon 8 58
(P Howling) *hld up wl in rr: pushed along on outer over 3f out: no real prog tl kpt on fnl f* **20/1**
0 10 1/2 **Perfect Vision**26 4946 2-9-0 0 .... WilliamBuick 11 57
(C G Cox) *prom 5f: sn lost pl: grad wknd* **33/1**
06 11 nk **Tallawalla (IRE)**16 5284 2-9-0 0 .... TonyCulhane 6 57
(M R Channon) *towards rr: prog on outer and in tch over 2f out: pushed along and steadily wknd over 1f out* **66/1**
12 1 1/4 **Azaday (IRE)** 2-9-0 0 .... AlanMunro 1 54
(C F Wall) *mde most to over 2f out: wknd sn after* **66/1**
13 2 3/4 **Juwireya** 2-9-0 0 .... MartinDwyer 5 48
(M P Tregoning) *dwlt: rn green and detached in last after 3f: nvr on terms after* **25/1**
06 14 1 1/2 **Glamour Profession (IRE)**60 3810 2-9-0 0 .... DarryllHolland 16 45
(R Hannon) *hld up in midfield on inner: n.m.r 5f out and over 4f out: dropped to rr and struggling 3f out* **50/1**
15 3 1/2 **Pilannski** 2-9-0 0 .... JamesDoyle 2 37
(R A Teal) *dwlt: detached in last pair early: in tch at bk of field 5f out: pushed along and wknd over 3f out* **100/1**
0 16 4 **Keleyf Byon Belief (IRE)**15 5312 2-9-0 0 .... PaulFitzsimons 15 28
(Edgar Byrne) *dwlt: a wl in rr: wknd 3f out* **100/1**

1m 41.19s (1.29) **Going Correction** +0.025s/f (Good) **16 Ran** SP% **121.5**
Speed ratings (Par 92): **94,93,92,90,89 88,86,86,85,84 84,83,80,79,75 71**
toteswingers: 1&2 £4.10, 1&3 £4.70, 2&3 £3.20 CSF £33.61 TOTE £7.40: £1.90, £1.60, £1.40; EX 43.60.
Owner K Abdulla **Bred** Juddmonte Farms Ltd **Trained** Newmarket, Suffolk

FOCUS
The runner-up came into this with an official rating of 77 and that one looks the best guide to the strength of the form. The winner should improve considerably. The winning time was 0.99 seconds slower than the following nursery won by the 82-rated Contract Caterer, who carried 7lb more than this lot.

NOTEBOOK
Namaskar overcame greenness to make a winning debut. Having raced well off the pace after a sluggish start, she had to wait for a gap early in the straight and was still three-plus lengths behind the runner-up a furlong out. Despite showing her inexperience under pressure, somewhat climbing on the ground, she was able to make up the requisite ground. She's clearly pretty useful and is entitled to improve. (op 6-1 tchd 7-1)
Silent Secret(IRE), upped in trip, looked the winner when holding a two-length lead a furlong out, but she was pegged back in the final strides. She is obviously up to winning an ordinary maiden, and nurseries are also an option. (op 6-1 tchd 13-2)
Zahoo(IRE) ◆ did well to finish so close considering she was inclined to edge slightly right under pressure and looked both green and uncomfortable on the track. This half-sister to Tactic should continue to improve with time and distance. (op 7-4 tchd 11-8)
Momtaz ◆ emerges with plenty of credit considering she did most of her racing out wide. She has plenty of ability. (op 33-1 tchd 40-1)
Dancing Queen(IRE), a promising sixth on her debut in a July course maiden that's working out quite well, didn't get the run of things this time. Having been tucked away behind the leaders towards the inside rail, she had no room to make her move when trying to pick up early in the straight and couldn't build up sufficient momentum to challenge. She might be worth another chance. (op 3-1 tchd 11-4)
Tamtara stepped up significantly on the form she showed over 7f on her debut and gave the impression she'll continue to improve. (tchd 80-1)
Juwireya might be one to keep in mind for the much longer term. She's considered more of a 3yo prospect by her trainer and was extremely green.

5742 **TOTEEXACTA NURSERY (H'CAP)** **1m**
3:10 (3:11) (Class 4) (0-85,82) 2-Y-0 **£3,885** (£1,156; £577; £288) **Stalls** High

Form RPR

4214 1 **Contract Caterer (IRE)**39 4488 2-9-7 **82** .... LDettori 6 86
(Pat Eddery) *mostly trckd ldr: rdn to chal 2f out: narrow ld jst over 1f out: r.o and jst hld on* **9/4**1
040 2 nk **Flying Destination**18 5220 2-8-10 **71** .... JimCrowley 5 74
(W J Knight) *chsd ldrs: rdn and nt qckn 2f out: renewed effrt 1f out: r.o to take 2nd last 100yds: clsng on wnr fin* **7/1**2
0155 3 3/4 **Cultured Pride (IRE)**32 4758 2-9-0 **75** .... JimmyFortune 8 77
(R Hannon) *trckd ldrs: pushed along fr 3f out: effrt u.p 1f out: styd on fnl f: a hld* **10/1**3
2461 4 1/2 **Cool Valentine**17 5265 2-9-4 **79** .... WilliamBuick 2 82+
(A M Balding) *hld up in 7th: prog to dispute 3rd over 1f out: swtchd rt ins fnl f: r.o but nt pce of ldrs* **9/4**1
3453 5 1/2 **Aattash (IRE)**15 5320 2-8-13 **74** .... TonyCulhane 9 73
(M R Channon) *mde most: pressed 2f out: narrowly hdd jst over 1f out: chsd wnr tl wknd last 100yds* **12/1**
500 6 1 1/4 **Calatrava Cape (IRE)**16 5284 2-8-7 **68** .... TPO'Shea 1 68+
(J L Dunlop) *swtchd fr outside draw to inner and hld up last: effrt and nt clr run on inner wl over 1f out: stl last 1f out: effrt again on inner and nt clr run ins fnl f: nt rcvr* **11/1**
1030 7 3 3/4 **Avon River**17 5265 2-9-7 **82** .... DaneO'Neill 3 70
(R Hannon) *cl up: rdn on outer 2f out: hanging and wknd over 1f out* **22/1**
050 8 3 1/2 **High Holborn (IRE)**26 4945 2-8-12 **73** .... MartinDwyer 4 54
(B J Meehan) *hld up in 6th: hanging bdly rt fr 3f out: wknd and eased over 1f out* **11/1**

1m 40.2s (0.30) **Going Correction** +0.025s/f (Good) **8 Ran** SP% **111.8**
Speed ratings (Par 97): **99,98,97,97,96 95,91,88**
toteswingers: 1&2 £4.50, 1&3 £3.90, 2&3 £6.90 CSF £18.03 CT £126.50 TOTE £3.10: £1.10, £2.70, £3.40; EX 18.90.
Owner ABM Catering Limited **Bred** Tareq Al Mazeedi **Trained** Nether Winchendon, Bucks
■ Stewards' Enquiry : William Buick two-day ban: careless riding (Sep 22-23)

FOCUS
A good nursery run in a time 0.99 seconds faster than Namaskar, who carried 7lb less, managed in the earlier fillies' maiden. Despite the good time, the pace looked only ordinary. The form seems sound despite the bunch finish.

NOTEBOOK

Contract Caterer(IRE), upped in distance, enjoyed a better trip than some of these but only just held on. Although he looked to get the run of the race, he may go on improving, especially over middle distances next year. (tchd 3-1)

Flying Destination, a little keen at about halfway, took a while to pick up for pressure in the straight and ultimately got going too late. He gives the impression there is better to come, and he ought to stay further in time. (op 9-1 tchd 13-2)

Cultured Pride(IRE), up a furlong in trip, was always well enough placed and didn't look to have any excuses. (op 12-1)

Cool Valentine, a convincing nursery winner off a mark of 72 over 7f at Sandown last time, didn't really get the run of things this time. After not having a great deal of room to play with when trying to stay on in the straight, he was never getting there when diving towards the inside rail in search of a clear run late on. (op 5-2 tchd 15-8)

Aattash(IRE) didn't look to go off overly fast and simply wasn't good enough. (op 16-1 tchd 10-1)

Calatrava Cape(IRE) ◆ is significantly better than she showed. Dropped in to last place from the widest stall, she was twice blocked in her run against the far rail in the straight, firstly over a furlong out, and then again inside the distance. She might have gone close with better luck. Official explanation: jockey said filly was denied a clear run (op 8-1)

High Holborn(IRE) ruined any chance he might have had by hanging badly right in the straight, even after he had the far rail to run against. He was duly reported to have hung violently right-handed. Official explanation: jockey said the gelding hung violently right (op 8-1)

5743 PETER WILLETT STKS (REGISTERED AS THE STARDOM STAKES) (LISTED RACE) 7f

3:45 (3:46) (Class 1) 2-Y-O

£17,031 (£6,456; £3,231; £1,611; £807; £405) **Stalls** High

Form RPR

15 **1** **Vale Of York (IRE)**[21] 5133 2-9-0 101 AhmedAjtebi 1 101
(Saeed Bin Suroor) *t.k.h: trckd ldng pair: rdn on outer 2f out: clsd fr 1f out: r.o to ld last strides* **9/2**[3]

326 **2** *1/2* **Mata Keranjang (USA)**[21] 5133 2-9-0 0 MartinDwyer 7 100
(P F I Cole) *trckd ldr: upsides fr 1/2-way: rdn to ld narrowly jst over 1f out: drvn fnl f: hdd last strides* **4/1**[2]

12 **3** *hd* **Atlantis Star**[17] 5250 2-9-0 98 LDettori 9 99
(Saeed Bin Suroor) *t.k.h: hld up bhd ldrs: shkn up 2f out: clsd fnl f: jst outpcd nr fin* **11/2**

0221 **4** *3/4* **Timely Jazz (IRE)**[22] 5106 2-9-0 93 TPO'Shea 8 97
(B J Meehan) *stmbld s but led: rdn over 2f out: narrowly hdd over 1f out: kpt pressing ldr tl no ex last 75yds* **8/1**

1023 **5** *2 1/2* **Silver Grey (IRE)**[17] 5265 2-8-9 79 RobertHavlin 3 86
(R Ingram) *hld up in last trio: wd bnd 5f out: outpcd 2f out and sn rdn: n.d after but styd on ins fnl f* **40/1**

1310 **6** *3/4* **Sir Parky (IRE)**[19] 5198 2-9-0 94 JimmyFortune 5 89
(R Hannon) *sn restrained to last trio: pushed along over 3f out: outpcd fr 2f out: plugged on fnl f* **14/1**

21 **7** *hd* **Mon Cadeaux**[27] 4900 2-9-0 95 WilliamBuick 2 89
(A M Balding) *hld up in 5th: wd bnd 5f out: shkn up over 2f out: nt qckn and lft bhd fr wl over 1f out* **11/4**[1]

8 *8* **Field Of Dream**[98] 2-9-4 0 KFallon 6 73
(L M Cumani) *hld up in last trio: shkn up over 2f out: sn outpcd and btn: lft wl bhd fr over 1f out* **13/2**

1m 26.77s (-0.63) **Going Correction** +0.025s/f (Good) **8** Ran SP% **113.8**
Speed ratings (Par 103): **104,103,103,102,99 98,98,89**
toteswingers: 1&2 £5.40, 1&3 £6.00, 2&3 £5.10 CSF £22.60 TOTE £5.90: £2.10, £1.60, £1.80; EX 29.30.
Owner Godolphin **Bred** Stock Vale Ltd **Trained** Newmarket, Suffolk

FOCUS

An ordinary-looking Listed race and just average form for the grade. The first two advertised the Acomb Stakes form.

NOTEBOOK

Vale Of York(IRE) was a little bit keen early on but he still had plenty left when placed under pressure. He took a while to pick up in the straight, again displaying a knee action that suggests he'll come into his own when there is give underfoot, but still found enough. His connections will apparently now look for a Group race and there are plenty of options at around 7f-1m in the coming weeks. (op 6-1)

Mata Keranjang(USA) wasn't at his best when well behind today's winner in the Acomb Stakes last time, but this was better. He was always well positioned and did absolutely nothing wrong. He is still a maiden, and his connections will have to decide whether to go for a maiden next time or persist in pattern company. (op 5-1)

Atlantis Star, up in trip, did well to finish so close considering he was keen to post, as well as in the race itself, and also got upset in the stalls. On top of that, he also edged left under pressure. He should be capable of better if he can learn to relax. Official explanation: jockey said the colt ran too free and hung left in the straight (op 7-1 tchd 8-1)

Timely Jazz(IRE), off the mark when long odds-on at Wolverhampton last time, recovered from a stumble at the start and had his chance from the front, but he wasn't good enough. (op 7-1)

Silver Grey(IRE), beaten three times in nursery company, holds the form down. (op 50-1 tchd 66-1)

Sir Parky(IRE) had a bit to find but a little better could still have been expected. (tchd 12-1)

Mon Cadeaux, a clear-cut maiden winner over 6f at Salisbury last time, seemed to travel well enough, but he found disappointingly little when asked to make up ground in the straight. He's out of a 1m4f winner, so the step up in trip shouldn't have bothered him. (op 3-1)

Field Of Dream was 2-2 when trained in Italy (both wins over sprint trips), including a Listed race, but his form probably doesn't amount to much in the context of this race. Debuting for Luca Cumani after over three months off, he was too keen early on and found little in the straight. (op 4-1)

5744 BUY A £10,000 RACING POST BONUS YEARLING MAIDEN STKS 1m 1f 192y

4:20 (4:21) (Class 5) 3-Y-O **£3,238** (£963; £481; £240) **Stalls** High

Form RPR

0- **1** **Tahkeem**[298] 7311 3-8-12 0 (p) TPO'Shea 6 72
(M P Tregoning) *hld up in 6th: reminder over 4f out: prog over 3f out to trck ldr 2f out: rdn to ld narrowly 1f out: styd on and jst hld on* **20/1**

3 **2** *shd* **Panto Princess**[85] 2981 3-8-12 0 FrankieMcDonald 9 72+
(H Candy) *s.i.s and rousted along early: mostly in 9th tl tried to cl on ldrs fr 3f out: stl only 6th 1f out: r.o wl to take 2nd last strides: jst failed* **6/1**

3-2 **3** *shd* **Count Of Tuscany (USA)**[31] 4798 3-9-3 0 JimCrowley 1 77
(Mrs A J Perrett) *trckd ldng trio: prog to ld over 2f out and tried to kick on: hdd u.p 1f out: pressed wnr after: jst hld and lost 2nd fnl strides* **9/2**[3]

40 **4** *nk* **Charger**[62] 3751 3-9-3 0 LDettori 5 76
(J Noseda) *t.k.h: hld up in 8th: clsd on ldrs 3f out: rdn and nt qckn on outer 2f out: styd on again fnl f: nrst fin* **5/2**[1]

03 **5** *1 3/4* **Day Of The Eagle (IRE)**[18] 5215 3-9-3 0 KFallon 8 73
(L M Cumani) *trckd ldng quartet: cl up whn n.m.r briefly over 2f out: drvn and effrt on inner over 1f out: one pce fnl f* **11/4**[2]

22-5 **6** *2* **Custody (IRE)**[8] 5531 3-9-3 80 (v) NCallan 10 69
(Sir Michael Stoute) *hld up in 7th: cl enough over 2f out: sn nt qckn: hanging over 1f out: edgd rt fnl f* **9/2**[3]

00- **7** *3* **Kazbow (IRE)**[307] 7200 3-9-3 0 MartinDwyer 2 63
(L M Cumani) *trckd ldr: led over 3f out to over 2f out: stl cl up on inner over 1f out: wknd fnl f* **33/1**

0-0 **8** *16* **Obvious**[8] 5531 3-8-12 0 AmirQuinn 12 26
(Miss J Feilden) *trckd ldng pair to over 3f out: wknd rapidly: t.o* **100/1**

9 *5* **Franco Is My Name** 3-9-3 0 DaneO'Neill 3 21
(P R Hedger) *s.s: mostly in last: lft bhd fr 4f out: t.o* **80/1**

-000 **10** *5* **Miss Jodarah (USA)**[5] 5614 3-8-9 32 (b) MarcHalford(3) 4 6
(J R Best) *led to over 3f out: wknd rapidly: eased over 1f out: t.o* **125/1**

2m 7.76s (-0.24) **Going Correction** +0.025s/f (Good) **10** Ran SP% **116.6**
Speed ratings (Par 101): **101,100,100,100,99 97,95,82,78,74**
toteswingers: 1&2 £11.10, 1&3 £22.50, 2&3 £5.30 CSF £132.29 TOTE £22.50: £5.30, £2.10, £1.70; EX 122.40.
Owner Hamdan Al Maktoum **Bred** Shadwell Estate Company Limited **Trained** Lambourn, Berks

FOCUS

No more than a fair maiden, with a bunch finish. The first two showed improvement.

5745 BOOK UP FOR GOODWOOD REVIVAL STKS (H'CAP) 1m

4:55 (4:55) (Class 4) (0-80,80) 3-Y-O+ **£4,857** (£1,445; £722; £360) **Stalls** High

Form RPR

3361 **1** **Sarah Park (IRE)**[19] 5190 4-9-8 80 LDettori 6 87
(B J Meehan) *trckd ldr to over 4f out: styd cl up on inner: effrt 2f out: led jst over 1f out: rdn out and jst hld on* **9/2**[2]

3332 **2** *hd* **Effigy**[24] 5040 5-9-5 77 DaneO'Neill 9 84
(H Candy) *hld up in midfield: effrt 2f out: rdn and prog over 1f out: wnt 2nd ins fnl f: clsng on wnr fin* **9/4**[1]

310- **3** *1 1/2* **Avertis**[277] 7560 4-9-8 80 (t) MickyFenton 4 84
(Stef Liddiard) *led: rdn and pressed over 2f out: hdd jst over 1f out: one pce fnl f* **25/1**

5000 **4** *nk* **Orchard Supreme**[10] 5448 6-9-7 79 JimmyFortune 7 82
(R Hannon) *stdd s: hld up in last: stdy prog on inner over 2f out: cl up bhd ldrs jst over 1f out: shkn up and kpt on: nvr nr enough to chal* **15/2**

3440 **5** *2 1/2* **Murrin (IRE)**[19] 5190 5-8-10 68 RobertHavlin 8 65
(T G Mills) *hld up: n.m.r 5f out: effrt on outer over 2f out: plugged on but n.d to ldrs* **15/2**

4214 **6** *1 1/2* **Dingaan (IRE)**[17] 5243 6-9-8 80 WilliamBuick 5 74
(A M Balding) *t.k.h early and prom: lost pl and n.m.r 1/2-way: pushed along in last pair 3f out: no real prog* **5/1**[3]

0433 **7** *nk* **Spring Adventure**[41] 4440 3-8-13 76 (v) KFallon 1 69
(E A L Dunlop) *cl up: wnt 2nd over 4f out: chal over 2f out tl wknd over 1f out* **10/1**

5000 **8** *5* **Marmooq**[10] 5429 6-8-6 66 oh1 LiamJones 2 47
(M J Attwater) *racd wd: hld up: prog to go 3rd 1/2-way and racing keenly: rdn over 2f out: wknd rapidly over 1f out* **80/1**

0360 **9** *32* **Thunder Gorge (USA)**[17] 5243 4-9-0 72 NCallan 3 —
(Mouse Hamilton-Fairley) *dwlt: tk v t.k.h and sn cl up: racd awkwardly fr 1/2-way: wknd rapidly over 2f out: virtually p.u* **10/1**

1m 39.04s (-0.86) **Going Correction** +0.025s/f (Good)
WFA 3 from 4yo+ 5lb **9** Ran SP% **112.4**
Speed ratings (Par 105): **105,104,103,103,100 99,98,93,61**
toteswingers: 1&2 £2.90, 1&3 £5.20, 2&3 £10.60 CSF £14.49 CT £221.16 TOTE £5.00: £1.80, £1.40, £6.50; EX 17.10.
Owner Mrs J & D E Cash **Bred** George S O'Malley **Trained** Manton, Wilts

FOCUS

Just a fair handicap and they went a muddling gallop. A personal bdest from the winner, with the third probably limiting the form.

5746 GOODWOOD FREEPHONE 08000 188 191 STKS (H'CAP) 7f

5:30 (5:31) (Class 4) (0-85,85) 3-Y-O+ **£4,857** (£1,445; £722; £360) **Stalls** High

Form RPR

0006 **1** **Mujood**[10] 5424 6-9-5 83 (v) WilliamBuick 8 92
(Eve Johnson Houghton) *sn prom: wnt 4th 4f out: prog to ld narrowly 2f out: edgd lft over 1f out: drvn and hld on wl* **8/1**

0004 **2** *hd* **Satwa Laird**[45] 4326 3-8-13 81 KFallon 1 87
(E A L Dunlop) *t.k.h early: hld up and racd wd: prog over 2f out: hrd rdn to chal ins fnl f: styd on but jst hld* **6/1**

06U0 **3** *1* **South Cape**[26] 4954 6-9-4 82 (p) DaneO'Neill 11 88+
(G L Moore) *dwlt: sn in tch towards rr: prog over 2f out: swtchd to inner sn after: trying to cl whn checked 1f out: kpt on to take 3rd last stride* **9/2**[1]

2231 **4** *shd* **Pegasus Again (USA)**[10] 5448 4-9-3 81 (p) RobertHavlin 12 86
(T G Mills) *led at decent pce: narrowly hdd 2f out: pressed wnr and hung lft over 1f out: lost 2nd and one pce ins fnl f* **5/1**[2]

3245 **5** *shd* **Den's Gift (IRE)**[46] 4262 5-9-5 83 (b) LDettori 5 88
(C G Cox) *chsd ldr to over 2f out: styd cl up: pressing for 3rd ins fnl f: one pce nr fin* **11/2**[3]

0064 **6** *1/2* **Desert Dreamer (IRE)**[13] 5349 8-9-2 80 NCallan 4 84
(P D Evans) *wl in tch: chsd ldrs and cl up fr 2f out: hanging and nt qckn fr over 1f out* **11/1**

6042 **7** *2 1/2* **Cape Hawk (IRE)**[29] 4852 5-9-4 82 JimmyFortune 2 79
(R Hannon) *sn restrained to rr: n.m.r on inner 1/2-way: effrt over 2f out: sn no prog and btn* **9/1**

1300 **8** *1/2* **White Deer (USA)**[25] 4996 5-8-13 77 (v) SilvestreDeSousa 6 73
(G A Harker) *plld hrd in midfield despite decent pce: nt qckn and lost grnd fr 2f out* **12/1**

-606 **9** *shd* **Shamrock Lady (IRE)**[22] 5099 4-8-9 73 TPO'Shea 3 69
(J Gallagher) *chsd ldng pair to wl over 2f out: steadily wknd* **33/1**

0622 **10** *1* **Zowington**[24] 5031 7-9-4 85 WilliamCarson(3) 9 78
(S C Williams) *rel to r and lft many l: a in rr: shkn up and no prog over 2f out* **11/1**

413 **11** *33* **Tuxedo**[39] 4504 4-8-8 72 DarrylHolland 10 —
(P W Hiatt) *prom 3f: sn lost pl on inner: eased and t.o fnl 2f* **12/1**

1m 26.85s (-0.55) **Going Correction** +0.025s/f (Good)
WFA 3 from 4yo+ 4lb **11** Ran SP% **120.6**
Speed ratings (Par 105): **104,103,102,102,102 101,98,98,98,97 59**
toteswingers: 1&2 £13.20, 1&3 £9.70, 2&3 £7.80 CSF £56.95 CT £252.34 TOTE £10.00: £3.30, £2.80, £1.90; EX 72.10 Place 6: £59.05 Place 5: £25.13.
Owner Eden Racing **Bred** Bloomsbury Stud & The Hon Sir David Sieff **Trained** Blewbury, Oxon

FOCUS

A competitive handicap. The form is rated around the winner.

White Deer(USA) Official explanation: jockey said gelding ran too free and did not handle the bend

Tuxedo Official explanation: trainer said the gelding was unsutied by the good to firm, good in places going

T/Jkpt: Not won. T/Plt: £70.70 to a £1 stake. Pool: £79,225.26. 817.59 winning tickets. T/Qpdt: £19.20 to a £1 stake. Pool: £5,163.35. 198.40 winning tickets. JN

5643 **LINGFIELD** (L-H)
Tuesday, September 8

OFFICIAL GOING: Turf course - good to firm (firm in places); all-weather - standard
Wind: fresh, behind Weather: warm and sunny

5747 APRIL THE FIFTH MAIDEN STKS 7f
2:10 (2:14) (Class 5) 3-Y-0+ **£2,729** (£806; £403) **Stalls** High

Form RPR
0220 1 **Orlando's Tale (USA)**[39] 4501 4-9-7 77 LPKeniry 4 83
(J R Fanshawe) *t.k.h: chsd ldrs and grad crossed to stands' rail: led 4f out: mde rest: rdn over 1f out: styd on wl u.p fnl f* **6/1**
2 2 *1* **Wake Up Call**[80] 3168 3-8-9 0 JackMitchell(3) 2 73
(C F Wall) *hld up wl in tch: hdwy to chse wnr over 1f out: r.o u.p for clr 2nd but a hld by wnr* **7/4**[1]
3 *6* **Cappagh Strand (USA)**[33] 4725 3-8-12 0 (t) HayleyTurner 12 57
(David P Myerscough, Ire) *t.k.h: hld up in tch in midfield: swtchd lft over 2f out: shkn up and nt qckn 2f out: nt clr run briefly ent fnl f: chsd ldng pair ins fnl f: no imp* **11/2**[3]
-04 4 *2 1/4* **One Cool Dream**[29] 4854 3-8-12 0 AdamKirby 17 51
(W R Swinburn) *t.k.h: chsd ldrs: rdn and unable qck wl over 1f out: sn outpcd by ldng pair* **9/1**
5 *4* **Fine Art Collector (IRE)** 3-9-3 0 GeorgeBaker 6 45+
(G L Moore) *stdd and dropped in bhd after s: t.k.h: hld up in rr: hdwy over 2f out: styd on past btn horses fnl f: nvr nr ldrs* **20/1**
04 6 *1 1/2* **Keibla Spirit**[19] 5193 3-8-12 0 KirstyMilczarek 3 36
(R Ingram) *t.k.h: hld up in midfield: pushed along and effrt towards outer jst over 2f out: no prog fr wl over 1f out* **66/1**
0-06 7 *nse* **Nativity**[82] 3053 3-8-9 54 JackDean(3) 10 36
(J L Spearing) *stdd s: t.k.h: chsd ldrs after 1f: wnt 2nd 1/2-way: ev ch and rdn 2f out: wknd qckly over 1f out* **66/1**
05 8 *1 1/2* **Red Willow**[26] 4936 3-8-9 0 NataliaGemelova(3) 13 32
(J E Long) *t.k.h: chsd ldrs tl rdn and wknd qckly ent fnl 2f* **125/1**
9 *shd* **Suburbia (USA)** 3-9-3 0 PhilipRobinson 18 37
(M A Jarvis) *hld up in midfield: dropped to rr and struggling 3f out: no ch fnl 2f* **7/2**[2]
6 10 *3/4* **Black Stocking**[120] 1941 4-9-2 0 SebSanders 7 32
(Rae Guest) *stdd s and sn swtchd rt: bhd: edgd lft and plugged on fr over 1f out: n.d* **16/1**
0 11 *hd* **Camilla Knight (IRE)**[25] 4981 3-8-12 0 ChrisCatlin 9 29
(W R Swinburn) *in tch on outer: rdn ent fnl 2f: sn struggling and wl btn after* **33/1**
00 12 *7* **Prince De Fortune**[49] 4180 3-9-3 0 TGMcLaughlin 16 15
(Mrs C A Dunnett) *plld hrd: hld up towards rr: hung lft and wknd over 2f out* **150/1**
0 13 *1/2* **Copper Sovereign**[31] 4786 7-9-7 0 IanMongan 14 16
(Jamie Poulton) *led tl 4f out: chsd ldrs tl wknd qckly over 2f out: wl bhd fnl f* **100/1**
060 14 *30* **A Lot Of Red (IRE)**[48] 4199 3-9-3 51 (t) TedDurcan 11 —
(P J O'Gorman) *a bhd: lost tch 1/2-way: t.o and virtually p.u fnl f* **33/1**
00 15 *6* **Mumtaz Begum**[19] 5193 4-9-2 0 RichardThomas 5 —
(J E Long) *a bhd and nvr gng wl: hung lft and lost tch 1/2-way: t.o* **100/1**

1m 21.35s (-1.95) **Going Correction** -0.575s/f (Hard)
WFA 3 from 4yo+ 4lb **15** Ran SP% **121.2**
Speed ratings (Par 103): **88,86,80,77,72 71,71,69,69,68 68,60,59,25,18**
toteswingers: 1&2 £3.20, 2&3 £6.60 CSF £16.20 TOTE £5.70: £1.90, £1.60, £2.10; EX 14.10 Trifecta £106.50 Pool: £207.34 - 1.44 winning units..
Owner Coriolan Partnership (I) **Bred** Ocala Horses, Llc **Trained** Newmarket, Suffolk

FOCUS
Not a strong maiden despite the size of the field and only a handful could be given a serious chance. The whole field came over to race stands' side and the front pair pulled well clear of the rest. The winner probably did not have to improve.
Keibla Spirit Official explanation: jockey said filly ran too free

5748 TEENOSO NURSERY 7f
2:45 (2:45) (Class 5) (0-75,73) 2-Y-0 **£3,238** (£963; £481; £240) **Stalls** High

Form RPR
6640 1 **Ice Cool Lady (IRE)**[63] 3702 2-9-4 **70** AdamKirby 8 72
(W R Swinburn) *restless stalls: s.i.s: sn in tch: rdn over 1f out: swtchd lft and drvn ins fnl f: qcknd u.p to ld fnl 100yds: sn in command and eased towards fin* **14/1**
000 2 *1 1/4* **Public Service (IRE)**[52] 4075 2-9-7 **73** TedDurcan 9 72
(B J Meehan) *led on stands' rail: rdn 2f out: drvn over 1f out: hdd and nt pce of wnr fnl 100yds* **12/1**
634 3 *1 1/2* **James Barrymore**[15] 5312 2-9-7 **73** PatDobbs 5 68
(R Hannon) *t.k.h: chsd ldrs: rdn and effrt 2f out: drvn to chse ldr over 1f out tl ins fnl f: one pce after* **7/2**[2]
0031 4 *1 1/4* **Shibhan**[18] 5207 2-9-6 **72** ChrisCatlin 6 64
(C E Brittain) *in tch towards rr: hdwy and edging lft looking for run 2f out: hdwy to chse ldrs on outer jst over 1f out: wknd fnl 100yds* **9/4**[1]
040 5 *nk* **Hellenio**[15] 5312 2-8-9 **64** WilliamCarson(3) 4 56+
(S C Williams) *hld up in tch in last pair: rdn and unable qck 2f out: kpt on fnl 100yds: nt pce to threaten ldrs* **12/1**
000 6 *nk* **It's A Deal (IRE)**[55] 3979 2-7-12 **50** CatherineGannon 7 41
(P Winkworth) *chsd ldr: rdn ent fnl 2f: drvn and lost 2nd over 1f out: wknd ins fnl f* **14/1**
5356 7 *1/2* **Oasis Jade**[34] 4639 2-9-3 **69** GeorgeBaker 2 58
(G L Moore) *stdd and dropped in bhd after s: hld up in tch in last pair: rdn and unable qck 2f out: no prog after* **9/1**[3]
006 8 *nk* **Greek Key (IRE)**[19] 5191 2-9-2 **68** HayleyTurner 3 57
(M L W Bell) *t.k.h: hld up in tch on outer: rdn and effrt to chse ldrs over 1f out: drvn ent fnl f: wknd ins fnl f* **7/2**[2]

1m 21.43s (-1.87) **Going Correction** -0.575s/f (Hard) **8** Ran SP% **113.9**
Speed ratings (Par 95): **87,85,83,82,82 81,81,80**
toteswingers: 1&2 £17.80, 1&3 £10.00, 2&3 £8.00 CSF £163.63 CT £729.16 TOTE £15.80: £3.70, £3.70, £1.40; EX 94.40 Trifecta £354.20 Part won. Pool: £478.72 - 0.44 winning units..
Owner London Market Racing Club **Bred** Lodge Park Stud **Trained** Aldbury, Herts

FOCUS
A modest nursery in which only one of these had been successful before, but the winning time was only 0.08 seconds slower than the older horses in the maiden. The winner might be capable of a bit better.

NOTEBOOK
Ice Cool Lady(IRE), disappointing on her nursery debut last time though she did have excuses, was up in trip here and it suited her ideally. Never far off the pace, she didn't respond immediately when first put under pressure but as soon as she was switched around the leader in order to make her effort, she took off and was well on top at the line. She can go on from here. (tchd 12-1)
Public Service(IRE), a very disappointing second favourite on soft ground last time after showing some promise on a quicker surface, hadn't been shaping as though this extra furlong would suit despite his breeding suggesting otherwise, but he made a bold bid to make every yard and only the winner was able to get past him. This was better, but he was probably helped by racing tight against the stands' rail. (tchd 11-1)
James Barrymore, making his turf and nursery debut after showing ability in three Polytrack maidens, travelled well in a handy position and had every chance, but lacked a decisive turn of foot. (op 5-2)
Shibhan, the only previous winner in the field and raised 4lb for last month's Chester success when stepped up to this trip for the first time, was forced to switch to the wide outside in order to make her effort and that probably wasn't ideal. (op 5-2)
Hellenio, making his nursery debut after showing little in three maidens, finished almost 20 lengths behind James Barrymore on the Polytrack here last time and had a 9lb pull. Under the cosh a fair way out, he made a little late progress and may need a return to further. (op 10-1)
It's A Deal(IRE), making her nursery debut after finishing well beaten in three maidens, showed up for a fair way before dropping away. (op 16-1 tchd 20-1)
Oasis Jade, disappointing on her nursery debut at Brighton last time, was up in trip here but she made no impression from the back of the field and never looked happy. She may not have appreciated this fast ground. (op 8-1 tchd 11-1)
Greek Key(IRE), making his nursery debut after showing some ability in three maidens over this trip, dropped away tamely but he did race keenly on the wide outside early and is probably better than this. (op 6-1)

5749 LINGFIELDPARK.CO.UK MEDIAN AUCTION MAIDEN STKS 6f
3:20 (3:21) (Class 5) 2-Y-0 **£2,729** (£806; £403) **Stalls** High

Form RPR
3 1 **Folly Bridge**[27] 4900 2-8-12 0 SteveDrowne 10 82+
(R Charlton) *sn nudged along: chsd ldrs: rdn to chse ldr 2f out: chal over 1f out: led ins fnl f: sn drew clr* **1/2**[1]
5260 2 *2 1/2* **Quaestor (IRE)**[17] 5274 2-9-3 73 RichardKingscote 12 80
(Tom Dascombe) *led: rdn and clr w wnr fr over 1f out: hdd ins fnl f: sn btn* **7/1**[3]
0 3 *8* **Rum King (USA)**[32] 4756 2-9-3 0 PatDobbs 4 56
(R Hannon) *s.i.s: hld up in rr of main gp: edgd lft and hdwy over 2f out: no ch w ldrs fnl 2f: wnt modest 3rd ins fnl f* **6/1**[2]
62 4 *2 1/4* **Freeforaday (USA)**[16] 5282 2-9-3 0 RobertWinston 1 49
(J R Best) *stdd s: hld up in rr of main gp: hdwy over 2f out: no ch w ldrs fnl 2f: wnt modest 4th ins fnl f* **9/1**
5 *4 1/2* **Rose Aurora** 2-8-12 0 TedDurcan 15 39+
(M P Tregoning) *s.i.s: a bhd: no ch fr 1/2-way* **12/1**
60 6 *hd* **Casanova Kid**[12] 5368 2-9-3 0 EdwardCreighton 11 35
(E J Creighton) *sn pushed up to chse ldr tl 2f out: 3rd and wl btn over 1f out: tired rapidly fnl f* **100/1**
0 7 *1/2* **Seeking Stardom**[30] 4825 2-9-3 0 IanMongan 13 33
(P M Phelan) *sn pushed up to chse ldrs: rdn and struggling over 2f out: sn wl btn* **100/1**
0 8 *18* **Mystic Millie (IRE)**[41] 4421 2-8-12 0 PhilipRobinson 9 —
(C G Cox) *racd in midfield: struggling 1/2-way: wl bhd fnl 2f: t.o* **22/1**
000 9 *5* **Restyle**[27] 4915 2-8-12 33 (p) SaleemGolam 2 —
(D K Ivory) *a in rr: struggling bdly fr 1/2-way: t.o* **66/1**
10 *1 1/4* **Pie Poudre** 2-9-3 0 PatCosgrave 8 —
(R Brotherton) *v.s.a: a t.o* **66/1**
11 *1 1/4* **Barafundle Boy** 2-8-10 0 RyanClark(7) 14 —
(J J Bridger) *s.i.s: sn struggling and wl bhd: t.o fnl 4f* **100/1**

68.36 secs (-2.84) **Going Correction** -0.575s/f (Hard) 2y crse rec **11** Ran SP% **121.4**
Speed ratings (Par 95): **95,91,81,78,72 71,71,47,40,38 37**
CSF £4.87 TOTE £1.60: £1.10, £1.90, £2.00; EX 5.50 Trifecta £36.20 Pool: £408.48 - 8.33 winning units..
Owner D J Deer **Bred** The National Stud Never Say Die Club Ltd **Trained** Beckhampton, Wilts

FOCUS
A weak and uncompetitive maiden overall, further devalued by the four non-runners, and the first two came a long way clear of the others. They produced good form which should prove reliable.

NOTEBOOK
Folly Bridge had finished just behind a subsequent winner when a promising third over this trip on her Salisbury debut and didn't need to step up much on that in order to win this. She did have to be put under some strong pressure in order to pick up the leader, but was well on top at the line and although the form is modest, she should be able to win something better. (op 4-7, tchd 4-6 and 8-13 in a place)
Quaestor(IRE), beaten a whisker on the Polytrack here in July, made much of the running in a very valuable sales race at Fairyhouse last time and attempted similar tactics here, having soon bagged the plum position against the stands' rail in front. Keen enough early, he tried his best and pulled right away from the rest, but the filly saw her race out much the better. Currently rated 73, he may be worth a try in a nursery over the minimum trip. (op 15-2)
Rum King(USA), who showed little when beating only one home on his Newmarket debut last month, was well backed earlier in the day and stayed on to take third, but he was never in the same parish as the front pair and may not have achieved that much. (op 7-1)
Freeforaday(USA), runner-up to an easy winner in a modest Folkestone maiden last time, was up a furlong here but he never managed to land a blow. He now qualifies for a mark which will widen his options a little.
Rose Aurora, a half-sister to three winners including one over hurdles, was outpaced from an early stage but her pedigree suggests she will need a much stiffer test in due course.
Casanova Kid, beaten a long way in his first two starts, showed a little bit more here and now qualifies for a mark.

5750 MID-DAY SUN (S) STKS 1m 2f (P)
3:55 (3:56) (Class 6) 3-Y-0+ **£2,047** (£604; £302) **Stalls** Low

Form RPR
3545 1 **Primo Dilettante**[32] 4734 3-9-2 55 ShaneKelly 5 66
(W J Knight) *led tl 5f out: rdn to ld again over 2f out: clr 2f out: styd on u.p fnl f* **8/1**
4414 2 *2 1/2* **Bee Stinger**[162] 1035 7-9-9 75 (b) StephenDonohoe 8 61
(Heather Dalton) *s.i.s: hld up in tch: rdn to chse ldrs 3f out: drvn to chse wnr jst over 1f out: kpt on but nvr gng pce to rch wnr* **9/2**[2]
0/15 3 *1/2* **Guiseppe Verdi (USA)**[25] 4987 5-9-9 75 ChrisCatlin 11 60
(Miss Tor Sturgis) *hld up in last trio: pushed along 4f out: rdn and hdwy on outer over 2f out: kpt on to go 3rd ins fnl f: nvr gng pce to chal wnr* **9/4**[1]
4006 4 *3 1/4* **Divertimenti (IRE)**[3] 5676 5-9-4 65 LPKeniry 13 48
(C R Dore) *t.k.h: hld up in last trio: rdn and effrt jst over 2f out: drvn ent fnl f: no imp* **7/1**

0002 **5** *hd* **Clipperdown (IRE)**8 5367 8-9-2 65 ow1...............(tp) AlanCreighton(3) 4 49
(E J Creighton) *t.k.h: in tch: rdn over 2f out: hrd drvn and nt qckn 2f out: no prog after* **9/1**

-000 **6** *3 1/4* **Dawson Creek (IRE)**24 5019 5-9-4 60.................................. TPQueally 9 41
(B Gubby) *in tch: rdn and struggling over 2f out: no ch fnl 2f* **8/1**

2004 **7** *5* **Gasat (IRE)**12 5367 8-9-6 65.................................. JackMitchell(3) 6 36
(A B Haynes) *s.i.s: hdwy to chse ldr 8f out: led 5f out tl rdn and hdd over 2f out: sn outpcd by wnr: lost 2nd jst over 1f out: wknd fnl f* **11/2**3

0500 **8** *11* **Peal Park**11 5381 3-8-6 47.................................. JamieMackay 7 4
(Karen George) *stdd s: t.k.h: hld up in rr: rdn and lost tch over 3f out: eased fnl f* **50/1**

0060 **9** *1 1/2* **Jacobite Prince (IRE)**9 5482 3-8-11 53......................(b1) SebSanders 3 6
(M H Tompkins) *s.i.s: bhd: hdwy to chse ldrs over 7f out: rdn and wknd over 3f out: wl bhd and eased ins fnl f* **25/1**

2m 5.76s (-0.84) **Going Correction** 0.0s/f (Stan)
WFA 3 from 4yo+ 7lb **9** Ran SP% **114.9**
Speed ratings (Par 101): **103,101,100,98,97 95,91,82,81**
toteswingers: 1&2 £7.30, 1&3 £4.40, 2&3 £2.20 CSF £43.63 TOTE £11.40: £2.60, £1.80, £1.20; EX 65.00 Trifecta £74.10 Pool: £352.70 - 3.52 winning units..The winner was brought in 6,200gns.
Owner O J Williams **Bred** O J Williams **Trained** Patching, W Sussex

FOCUS
An ordinary seller hit by five non-runners and the early pace was very moderate. A clear personal best by the winner at face value.

5751 TULYAR MEDIAN AUCTION MAIDEN STKS 1m (P)
4:30 (4:31) (Class 5) 3-4-Y-O **£2,729** (£806; £403) **Stalls** High

Form RPR

-243 **1** **Woodlark Island (IRE)**24 5027 3-9-3 72.................... RichardMullen 8 81
(M P Tregoning) *led after 1f tl 6f out: chsd ldr after: led 2f out: sn rdn clr: easily* **7/4**1

2 *6* **Crazy Chris**51 4-9-3 0.................................. RichardKingscote 5 62
(Tom Dascombe) *hld up in rr of main gp: hdwy and swtchd rt over 2f out: chsd clr wnr jst ins fnl f: kpt on for clr 2nd but no ch w wnr* **5/2**2

5020 **3** *2 1/2* **Leelu**14 5326 3-8-12 57.................................. HayleyTurner 9 56
(D W P Arbuthnot) *taken down early: chsd ldrs tl led 6f out: rdn and hdd 2f out: sn no ch w wnr: lost 2nd ins fnl f* **20/1**

24 **4** *1 3/4* **Criticize (USA)**26 4936 3-9-3 0.................................. SteveDrowne 7 57
(R Charlton) *in tch in midfield: hung rt fr over 3f out: chsng ldrs and rdn whn hung bdly rt and rn v wd bnd 2f out: no ch after* **3/1**3

-554 **5** *hd* **Orthology (IRE)**20 5151 3-9-3 70..................................(b) SebSanders 1 56
(M H Tompkins) *dwlt: sn pushed along: in tch in midfield: nt clr run on inner and shuffled bk 3f out: swtchd rt and rdn over 2f out: racd awkwardly and no real prog fnl 2f* **12/1**

050 **6** *1 1/4* **Balzarine**13 5348 3-8-12 44.................................. JimmyQuinn 6 48
(M Blanshard) *chsd ldrs: rdn and struggling over 2f out: wl btn over 1f out* **100/1**

00 **7** *3 1/2* **Ryker (IRE)**95 2664 3-9-3 0.................................. RobertWinston 11 45+
(J W Hills) *in tch in midfield: hdwy on outer 3f out: chsng ldrs whn carried v wd and lost any ch bnd 2f out: hung lft over 1f out* **25/1**

6600 **8** *3 3/4* **Yashkur**30 4819 3-8-12 51.................................. ChrisCatlin 10 31
(C E Brittain) *in rr of main gp: rdn and struggling over 4f out: wl btn over 2f out* **66/1**

000 **9** *1 1/2* **Ma Patrice**33 4704 3-8-12 45.................................. KirstyMilczarek 2 27
(T D McCarthy) *t.k.h: chsd ldrs tl wknd qckly u.p 3f out: wl bhd fnl 2f* **100/1**

06 **10** *7* **Jezza**18 5228 3-9-3 0.................................. JamieMackay 3 16
(Karen George) *led for 1f: in tch in midfield after tl wknd u.p 3f out: wl bhd fnl 2f* **100/1**

11 *1* **Silvester** 3-9-3 0.................................. PatCosgrave 12 13
(R M H Cowell) *v.s.a: sn rdn along: a detached in last pair* **66/1**

12 *9* **Stardust Memories (UAE)** 3-8-12 0.................................. TedDurcan 4 —
(John Berry) *s.i.s: sn rdn along: a detached in last pair* **33/1**

1m 37.49s (-0.71) **Going Correction** 0.0s/f (Stan)
WFA 3 from 4yo 5lb **12** Ran SP% **115.1**
Speed ratings (Par 103): **103,97,94,92,92 91,87,84,82,75 74,65**
toteswingers: 1&2 £2.90, 1&3 £5.20, 2&3 £10.60 CSF £5.62 TOTE £2.90: £1.30, £1.40, £2.70; EX 9.40 Trifecta £48.80 Pool: £371.23 - 5.62 winning units..
Owner Lady Tennant **Bred** Stone Ridge Farm **Trained** Lambourn, Berks

FOCUS
Another weak and uncompetitive maiden and only three mattered according to the market. The early pace looked solid enough, though. It probably did not take much winning and the form has been rated at face value.
Criticize(USA) Official explanation: jockey said gelding hung right on final bend
Ryker(IRE) Official explanation: jockey said the gelding hung left in the straight

5752 EUROPEAN BREEDERS' FUND MAIDEN FILLIES' STKS 7f (P)
5:05 (5:07) (Class 5) 2-Y-O **£3,885** (£1,156; £577; £288) **Stalls** Low

Form RPR

1 **Dawnbreak (USA)** 2-9-0 0.................................. TedDurcan 12 77+
(Saeed Bin Suroor) *chsd ldr tl led 2f out: rdn wl over 1f out: styd on wl and a holding runner-up fnl f* **3/1**2

64 **2** *nk* **Texas Queen**11 5398 2-9-0 0.................................. ChrisCatlin 4 76
(M R Channon) *in tch: rdn to chse wnr wl over 1f out: drvn ent fnl f: kpt on but a hld by wnr* **6/1**

3 *2 3/4* **Miss Antonia (IRE)** 2-9-0 0.................................. TPQueally 2 69
(H R A Cecil) *led: rdn and hdd 2f out: outpcd by ldng pair jst over 1f out: kpt on same pce fnl f* **9/4**1

4 *1 1/4* **Shimmering Surf (IRE)** 2-9-0 0.................................. LukeMorris 3 66+
(P Winkworth) *dwlt: sn pushed along in rr of main gp: rdn over 2f out: hdwy u.p fnl f: styd on wl to go 4th towards fin* **40/1**

5 *1/2* **Rahaala (IRE)** 2-9-0 0.................................. RHills 5 65
(Sir Michael Stoute) *chsd ldrs: rdn and unable qck ent fnl 2f: one pce fr over 1f out* **4/1**3

6 *3/4* **Sunrise Lyric (IRE)** 2-9-0 0.................................. HayleyTurner 6 63
(P F I Cole) *t.k.h: hld up in tch in midfield: n.m.r over 2f out: sn pushed along and hdwy: drvn and no prog jst over 1f out* **16/1**

7 *nk* **Sign Of Life** 2-9-0 0.................................. AdamKirby 10 62+
(W R Swinburn) *rn green in rr: pushed along and hdwy: over 1f out: nt clr run and swtchd rt 1f out: styd on steadily ins fnl f: nvr trbld ldrs* **40/1**

8 *2* **Lady Hetherington** 2-9-0 0.................................. IanMongan 1 57
(Jamie Poulton) *taken down early: chsd ldrs: rdn and unable qck ent fnl 2f: wknd over 1f out* **100/1**

9 *1 3/4* **Motrice** 2-9-0 0.................................. SebSanders 9 53
(Sir Mark Prescott) *s.i.s: bhd: clsd and in tch over 4f out: rdn and struggling over 2f out: n.d after* **33/1**

10 *3/4* **Dance With Chance (IRE)** 2-9-0 0.................................. ShaneKelly 8 51
(W R Swinburn) *hld up in tch in rr: rdn and struggling over 2f out: wl hld whn n.m.r 1f out* **50/1**

11 *nk* **Dhan Dhana (IRE)** 2-9-0 0.................................. KirstyMilczarek 7 50
(W J Haggas) *hld up in tch towards rr: nt clr run jst over 2f out: sn rdn and no real hdwy: wl hld whn hmpd 1f out* **25/1**

12 *2 1/2* **Trade Name (IRE)** 2-9-0 0.................................. FergusSweeney 14 44
(H Candy) *v.s.a: t.k.h: styd wd: hdwy to chse ldrs over 4f out: wknd over 2f out* **20/1**

0 **13** *13* **Seattle Speight (USA)**5 5604 2-9-0 0.................. RichardKingscote 11 12
(W J Knight) *bhd: rdn and struggling bdly over 3f out: t.o and eased fnl f* **22/1**

1m 25.68s (0.88) **Going Correction** 0.0s/f (Stan) **13** Ran SP% **119.7**
Speed ratings (Par 92): **94,93,90,89,88 87,87,85,83,82 81,78,64**
toteswingers: 1&2 £5.50, 2&3 £4.90, 1&3 not won. CSF £19.38 TOTE £4.70: £1.70, £2.10, £1.60; EX 28.00 Trifecta £38.50 Pool: £317.72 - 6.10 winning units..
Owner Godolphin **Bred** WinStar Farm LLC **Trained** Newmarket, Suffolk
■ Stewards' Enquiry : Luke Morris two-day ban: careless riding (Sep 22-23)

FOCUS
Not much previous form to go on here with only two having seen the racecourse before, but there were some very interesting debutantes representing top stables, so this was probably an informative maiden and, quite apart from the principals, there were some real eyecatchers further back. The bare form is no better than fairly average.

NOTEBOOK
Dawnbreak(USA), a $270,000 yearling and $560,000 two-year-old, is a half-sister to two multiple dirt winners in the US so there was every chance she would appreciate this surface. Always up with the pace from her wide draw, she went to the front passing the 2f pole and really dug in when it looked as though she might be overhauled by the runner-up. She will have to go some in order to justify her price tag, but this was a good start and she can only improve. (op 7-4)
Texas Queen, who had shown ability in her first two starts, came through to hold every chance starting up the home straight, but as hard as she tried she could never quite get to the winner. A few of those behind are likely to improve past her in time, but she should be able to break her duck before too long. (op 8-1)
Miss Antonia(IRE) ◆, a half-sister to three winners at up to 1m6f on the Flat, one of whom was also successful in bumpers, travelled strongly in the lead, and to her credit didn't fold completely, even after the winner had headed her on the home bend. She will win races. (op 2-1)
Shimmering Surf(IRE) ◆, a 54,000gns yearling whose dam was a smart performer over 1m2f, took a while to realise that was required, but she finished to some effect and will come on for this. She is one to watch out for over a bit further. (op 50-1)
Rahaala(IRE), a 170,000gns foal and a half-sister to a winning juvenile over 6f, was never far away and had every chance turning for home, but lacked a finishing kick. She doesn't look anything special, but should be good enough to winning an ordinary maiden. (op 7-1)
Sunrise Lyric(IRE) ◆, a 68,000gns yearling and 50,000gns two-year-old, took a fierce hold in the middle of the field early but also showed plenty of ability. Out of a half-sister to the high-class Midnight Line, she should have learnt from this and is another to watch out for when stepped up in trip. (op 25-1)
Sign Of Life ◆, a half-sister to four winners at up to 1m4f including the French 2000 Guineas winner Victory Note, made an even bigger impression as she looked clueless early and soon dropped herself out last, but she made some eyecatching late progress once in line for home and is very much one for the notebook.
Motrice ◆ is a half-sister to five winners at up to 2m2f including the stable's smart Foreign Affairs, so she was always likely to find this too sharp. Slowest to break, she did hint at ability late on but the best of her probably won't be seen until faced with a much greater test of stamina. (tchd 40-1)
Trade Name(IRE) ◆, a half-sister to five winners at up to 1m2f, always found herself trapped out wide having started from the outside stall and also ran green, but she did show some ability and can be expected to improve from this debut. Official explanation: jockey said filly hung left (tchd 22-1)
Seattle Speight(USA) Official explanation: jockey said the filly was never travelling

5753 PARTHIA H'CAP 7f (P)
5:40 (5:41) (Class 4) (0-80,80) 3-Y-O+ **£5,180** (£1,541; £770; £384) **Stalls** Low

Form RPR

1233 **1** **Santefisio**45 4326 3-9-3 79.................................. SteveDrowne 1 86+
(P J Makin) *dwlt: sn in tch in midfield: rdn and hdwy jst over 2f out: drvn over 1f out: r.o wl fnl f to ld last stride* **7/2**1

100 **2** *shd* **Secret Witness**38 4540 3-9-1 77.................................. SebSanders 7 81
(J Noseda) *chsd ldrs: rdn jst over 2f out: ev ch ins fnl f: drvn to ld wl ins fnl f: hdd last stride* **8/1**

0525 **3** *nk* **I Confess**17 5243 4-9-3 80..................................(b) RichardEvans(5) 10 85
(P D Evans) *led: rdn wl over 1f out: kpt on wl tl hdd wl ins fnl f: no ex* **4/1**2

000- **4** *1 1/4* **Transfer**321 6911 4-9-2 74.................................. LPKeniry 3 76
(A M Balding) *t.k.h: chsd ldrs: rdn over 2f out: sltly outpcd bnd 2f out: kpt on again fnl f: n.m.r nr fin* **11/1**

0420 **5** *1/2* **Dvinsky (USA)**12 5370 8-9-5 77..................................(b) IanMongan 14 77
(P Howling) *chsd ldr: ev ch and rdn 2f out: wknd jst ins fnl f* **28/1**

000 **6** *2 1/4* **Fiefdom (IRE)**22 5107 7-8-13 71..................................(p) LukeMorris 6 65
(I W McInnes) *in tch towards rr: rdn jst over 2f out: kpt on u.p fnl f but nvr gng pce to chal ldrs* **16/1**

3000 **7** *1/2* **Trade Centre**57 3924 4-8-13 71.................................. RichardMullen 12 64
(W R Muir) *a in rr: rdn over 4f out: nvr gng pce to trble ldrs* **11/1**

0643 **8** *nk* **Buxton**12 5370 5-8-12 70..................................(t) KirstyMilczarek 5 62
(R Ingram) *in tch in midfield: rdn and unable qck jst over 2f out: wl hld fnl f* **9/2**3

1660 **9** *1 3/4* **Halsion Chancer**28 4870 5-9-7 79.................................. RobertWinston 2 66
(J R Best) *chsd ldrs tl wknd u.p over 1f out: eased whn btn wl ins fnl f* **10/1**

5020 **10** *3/4* **Shaded Edge**13 5349 5-8-12 70.................................. AdamKirby 11 55
(D W P Arbuthnot) *a in rr: rdn 4f out: n.d* **12/1**

004 **11** *1 3/4* **Resplendent Alpha**68 3529 5-9-7 79.................................. JimmyQuinn 13 60
(P Howling) *stdd and dropped in bhd after s: n.d* **20/1**

1m 23.84s (-0.96) **Going Correction** 0.0s/f (Stan)
WFA 3 from 4yo+ 4lb **11** Ran SP% **119.1**
Speed ratings (Par 105): **105,104,104,103,102 99,99,99,97,96 94**
toteswingers: 1&2 £7.00, 1&3 £3.10, 2&3 £4.50 CSF £32.34 CT £120.69 TOTE £3.90: £2.00, £4.00, £2.00; EX 38.00 Trifecta £202.00 Pool: £311.21 - 1.14 winning units. Place 6: £10.46 Place 5: £7.08.
Owner Weldspec Glasgow Limited **Bred** D Brocklehurst **Trained** Ogbourne Maisey, Wilts

FOCUS
A fair handicap and they went a decent pace. The majority of the principals were always close up, which makes the winner's effort even more commendable. The third is a pretty sound guide to the form.
T/Plt: £9.90 to a £1 stake. Pool: £56,463.33. 4,141.86 winning tickets. T/Qpdt: £3.00 to a £1 stake. Pool: £3,765.18. 920.78 winning tickets. SP

5759 - 5761a (Foreign Racing) - See Raceform Interactive

4514 DONCASTER (L-H)

Wednesday, September 9

OFFICIAL GOING: Straight course - good to firm (8.9); round course - good (good to firm in places; 8.4)

Rail moved out 4yards from bottom of Rose Hill into the straight increasing distances on round course by 12yards.

Wind: Light across Weather: Warm and sunny

5762 WILKINSON FRENCHGATE NURSERY 7f

2:00 (2:03) (Class 3) (0-95,90) 2-Y-O **£9,714** (£2,890; £1,444; £721) **Stalls** High

Form RPR

3120 **1** **Audacity Of Hope**[18] 5261 2-8-13 **82**......(t) KFallon 7 91+
(P J McBride) *hld up and bhd: hdwy over 2f out: effrt whn n.m.r and swtchd lft over 1f out: sn rdn and styd on to ld ins fnl f: sn edgd rt and kpt on* **3/1**[1]

001 **2** 1 ½ **Pleasant Day (IRE)**[20] 5192 2-8-13 **82**......(b) LDettori 6 85
(B J Meehan) *wnt lft s: trckd ldr: hdwy and cl up over 2f out: rdn to ld over 1f out: drvn and hdd ins fnl f: kpt on towards fin* **10/1**

1040 **3** ½ **Farmer Giles (IRE)**[21] 5174 2-9-2 **85**...... TPQueally 3 87
(M L W Bell) *rrd s and s.i.s: in rr tl hdwy on outer wl over 2f out: rdn and edgd rt over 1f out: drvn to ld briefly ins fnl f: sn hdd and n.m.r: one pce* **25/1**

415 **4** 1 **Miss Smilla**[46] 4306 2-8-8 **77**...... TonyCulhane 4 77
(K A Ryan) *sltly hmpd s: chsd ldrs towards outer: effrt and ev ch 2f out: sn rdn and kpt on same pce* **25/1**

4016 **5** ¾ **Desert Auction (IRE)**[19] 5214 2-9-6 **89**...... SteveDrowne 5 87
(R Hannon) *sltly hmpd s: in tch towards outer: hdwy to chse ldrs 1/2-way: rdn over 2f out: drvn over 1f out: kpt on same pce* **12/1**

01 **6** ½ **Brick Red**[16] 5311 2-8-11 **80**...... WilliamBuick 8 76
(A M Balding) *chsd ldrs: rdn along 2f out: drvn over 1f out: no imp* **5/1**[2]

01 **7** ½ **Ransom Note**[18] 5251 2-8-6 **75**...... MichaelHills 11 70
(B W Hills) *in tch: effrt and nt clr run 2f out: sn swtchd lft and rdn over 1f out: kpt on ins fnl f: nrst fin* **11/2**[3]

11 **8** 2 ¼ **Mr Grinch (IRE)**[12] 5392 2-9-7 **90**...... PhillipMakin 9 81+
(M Dods) *hld up: effrt and pushed along wl over 2f out: rdn and n.m.r 2f out: no imp after* **13/2**

3012 **9** *hd* **Transfixed (IRE)**[19] 5207 2-8-7 **76**...... JohnEgan 2 65
(P D Evans) *led: rdn along over 2f out: drvn and hdd over 1f out: wknd* **16/1**

3120 **10** 4 **Flaneur**[22] 5136 2-8-8 **77**......(b) DavidAllan 10 56
(T D Easterby) *chsd ldrs: rdn along over 2f out: sn wknd* **10/1**

210 **11** 5 **Atacama Crossing (IRE)**[33] 4758 2-9-0 **83**...... TPO'Shea 12 50
(B W Hills) *trckd ldrs on inner: effrt wl over 2f out: sn rdn and wknd* **16/1**

1m 24.51s (-1.79) **Going Correction** -0.325s/f (Firm) **11** Ran SP% **115.7**

Speed ratings (Par 99): **97,95,94,93,92 92,91,89,88,84 78**

toteswinger: 1&2 £6.50, 1&3 £11.60, 2&3 £25.40. CSF £33.41 CT £616.74 TOTE £4.10: £1.50, £3.00, £4.30; EX 43.30 Trifecta £442.80 Part won. Pool: £598.39 - 0.94 winning units..

Owner Four Winds Racing **Bred** Wood Farm Stud (Waresley) **Trained** Newmarket, Suffolk

FOCUS

Typically good and solid nursery form for the meeting and the time was under RP standard, though this is only the third year the track has been up and running so times are still relatively fresh.

NOTEBOOK

Audacity Of Hope, 6lb higher than when finishing second on his nursery debut at Newmarket two starts back, had contested the Group 3 Solario Stakes at Sandown last time and was always going to find this easier. Sporting a first-time tongue tie, he was restrained in last for most of the way and found himself short of room when attempting to close inside the two. He showed a bright change of pace once taken widest of all, though, and ultimately got well on top inside the final furlong. (op 7-2 tchd 4-1)

Pleasant Day(IRE) improved markedly when winning in first-time blinkers at Lingfield last time and he looked reasonably weighted on a mark of 82 for this nursery debut. Soon prominent, he struck the front over 1f out, but the winner proved far too strong in the final furlong.

Farmer Giles(IRE), who had to be replated before the start, was another to be held up in rear on this nursery debut having reared coming out of the gate. He started to close inside the two and stayed on to the line, but was readily swept aside by the winner. All things considering, this was a decent effort. (op 20-1)

Miss Smilla, down 3lb having disappointed on her nursery debut at Newcastle, was seen to better effect over this extra furlong and will find less competitive races elsewhere. (op 28-1)

Desert Auction(IRE), 3lb higher than when winning at Newbury two starts back, found this easier having struggled in a Listed contest at Salisbury last time and ran well without possessing a change of pace. (op 10-1 tchd 9-1 and 14-1)

Brick Red, who dead-heated for a 6f maiden at Kempton, was under pressure over 2f out and could find no extra in the final 100 yards.

Ransom Note, another coming into this having won a maiden, didn't get the best of passages through and crossed the line with plenty left up his sleeve. He can be rated better than the bare form and deserves another chance. Official explanation: jockey said the colt was denied a clear run (op 9-2)

Mr Grinch(IRE) was up to 7f for this nursery debut, but he was under pressure when slightly short of room and could not close afterwards. (op 8-1)

Transfixed(IRE) ran well to a point, but is exposed compared to quite a few of these and she was readily brushed aside in the final furlong. (op 20-1)

5763 SAINSBURY'S FRENCHGATE CONDITIONS STKS 6f

2:35 (2:35) (Class 2) 2-Y-O

£10,904 (£3,265; £1,632; £817; £407; £204) **Stalls** High

Form RPR

6220 **1** **Angel's Pursuit (IRE)**[4] 5661 2-8-13 101...... PatDobbs 2 96
(R Hannon) *trckd ldrs: hdwy wl over 1f out: rdn to ld ent fnl f: edgd rt and kpt on* **11/2**

2165 **2** ¾ **Roodle**[26] 4989 2-8-8 88...... WilliamBuick 3 89
(Eve Johnson Houghton) *hld up: hdwy over 2f out: swtchd outside and rdn to chse ldrs over 1f out: kpt on u.p to chse wnr ins fnl f: no imp towards fin* **7/1**

2134 **3** *nk* **Colonel Mak**[25] 5038 2-8-11 90...... PhillipMakin 5 91+
(D H Brown) *hld up in rr: hdwy over 1f out: swtchd lft and rdn ent fnl f: kpt on wl towards fin* **9/2**[3]

61 **4** *hd* **Transvaal Sky**[29] 4869 2-8-8 86...... RichardKingscote 4 87
(Tom Dascombe) *cl up: rdn along wl over 1f out: ev ch tl drvn and edgd rt ent fnl f: kpt on same pce* **7/2**[2]

512 **5** ¾ **Bond Fastrac**[22] 5136 2-8-13 90...... PJMcDonald 1 90
(G R Oldroyd) *cl up on outer: hdwy to ld 2f out: rdn and hdd ent fnl f: wknd and hld whn n.m.r nr fin* **9/4**[1]

0434 **6** 1 ¼ **Footstepsofspring (FR)**[7] 5580 2-8-13 88...... SteveDrowne 7 86
(R Hannon) *chsd ldrs: rdn along 2f out: n.m.r and swtchd lft over 1f out: sn drvn and one pce* **16/1**

24 **7** 5 **Loveinthesand (IRE)**[46] 4331 2-8-11 0...... GregFairley 8 69
(M Johnston) *led: rdn along 1/2-way: drvn and hdd 2f out: sn wknd* **12/1**

35 **8** ½ **Bilash**[22] 5129 2-8-11 0...... GrahamGibbons 6 68
(R Hollinshead) *chsd ldrs: rdn along 1/2-way: sn wknd* **100/1**

1m 11.43s (-2.17) **Going Correction** -0.325s/f (Firm) **8** Ran SP% **113.6**

Speed ratings (Par 101): **101,100,99,99,98 96,90,89**

toteswinger: 1&2 £8.50, 1&3 £4.70, £6.00. CSF £42.70 TOTE £7.40: £2.00, £2.10, £1.40; EX 50.60 Trifecta £273.00 Pool: £605.09 - 1.64 winning units..

Owner Malih L Al Basti **Bred** Hong Kong Breeders Club **Trained** East Everleigh, Wilts

FOCUS

One or two of these were dropping in grade and taking on some improving sorts, and in the end it was one of the class-droppers that came out on top.

NOTEBOOK

Angel's Pursuit(IRE) ran poorly in the Group 3 Sirenia Stakes last time out, but that race was on Polytrack, and presumably he didn't act on the surface. His previous second in a French Listed race gave him every chance against this lot, he was best in at the weights, and, having travelled well tracking the leaders, he quickened up nicely to assert. He clearly stays 6f without any problems, and his connections now plan to look for a Listed race for him. (op 9-2)

Roodle was another dropping in class having competed in pattern company on her last two starts. Challenging from off the pace out wide, she ran well in defeat against a rival who officially had 8lb in hand of her at the weights, and the return to 6f seemed to suit. (op 8-1)

Colonel Mak, who has done his winning at Hamilton, could have done with a stiffer finish as he was doing all his best work at the end. (op 6-1)

Transvaal Sky, who made all to win her maiden on the Polytrack last time out, had more to do in this company and wasn't allowed her own way in front. It still wasn't a bad effort, though, and there's better to come from her. (op 9-2)

Bond Fastrac likes to be up there and that style of running isn't as effective at this track as it is at places like York and Redcar, where he'd run well on his previous two starts. (op 2-1)

Footstepsofspring(FR), the most experienced runner in the line-up, didn't stay 7f last time and was expected to appreciate the drop back to sprinting. He never really threatened to land a blow, though, and simply looks exposed now. (op 18-1)

5764 DEBENHAMS FRENCHGATE CONDITIONS STKS 1m 2f 60y

3:10 (3:10) (Class 2) 3-5-Y-0 **£15,577** (£4,665; £2,332; £1,167; £582) **Stalls** Low

Form RPR

3340 **1** **Twice Over**[67] 3640 4-9-8 119...... TPQueally 3 119+
(H R A Cecil) *trckd ldr: hdwy on bit and cl up over 2f out: pushed ahd over 1f out: sn clr: easily* **4/6**[1]

10-4 **2** 1 ¾ **Serva Jugum (USA)**[11] 5447 3-8-9 111...... MartinDwyer 4 108
(P F I Cole) *trckd ldng pair: hdwy 3f out: rdn along 2f out: drvn over 1f out: kpt on ins fnl f: edgd lft towards fin* **11/4**[2]

5 **3** ½ **Chock A Block (IRE)**[112] 2176 3-8-9 0...... LDettori 6 107
(Saeed Bin Suroor) *set stdy pce: qcknd 4f out: rdn along and qcknd over 2f out: drvn and hdd over 1f out: edgd rt and one pce ins fnl f* **8/1**[3]

5030 **4** 1 ¼ **Kings Gambit (SAF)**[25] 5023 5-9-8 110...... MickyFenton 2 111
(T P Tate) *trckd ldrs on inner: effrt 3f out and sn rdn along: drvn and one pce fr wl over 1f out* **14/1**

0-36 **5** ½ **Sweet Lilly**[28] 4903 5-8-11 100...... EdwardCreighton 1 99
(M R Channon) *t.k.h: hld up in rr: pushed along 3f out: rdn over 2f out: nvr a factor* **20/1**

2m 10.97s (-0.23) **Going Correction** -0.325s/f (Firm)

WFA 3 from 4yo+ 7lb **5** Ran SP% **109.2**

Speed ratings (Par 109): **87,85,85,84,83**

toteswinger: 1&2 £3.10. CSF £2.65 TOTE £1.60: £1.20, £1.30; EX 2.60.

Owner K Abdulla **Bred** Juddmonte Farms Ltd **Trained** Newmarket, Suffolk

FOCUS

This was quite a weak conditions race, run at a slow pace, and the winner proved a cut above. The form has been taken at face value.

NOTEBOOK

Twice Over has been keeping top company nearly all season, his close-up fourth in the Prince Of Wales's Stakes being the pick of his efforts, and he was always cruising in a race run at a steady gallop. He came home unchallenged and this should act to boost his confidence for a step back up in grade. The Champion Stakes, in which he was second last year, is once again the target. (op 8-11 tchd 4-5 and 8-13)

Serva Jugum(USA), a close fourth in a 1m2f Group 3 at Windsor on his recent reappearance, couldn't match the winner and, having been outpaced, he stayed on to take second close home. He has clearly done well from two to three and should find a race at some stage. (op 5-2 tchd 3-1)

Chock A Block(IRE) was responsible for setting a steady gallop and very much had the run of things, but wasn't good enough to capitalise on it. He had finished a well-beaten last of five on his debut for the yard and may not be seen at his best until next season. (tchd 9-1)

Kings Gambit(SAF) would not have been suited by the way the race was run on this drop in trip and was already booked for fourth when short of room near the line. (tchd 12-1 and 16-1)

Sweet Lilly is not an easy horse to win with, possessing her share of quirks, and she was always likely to struggle to match some of these. (op 16-1)

5765 DFS SCARBROUGH STKS (LISTED RACE) 5f

3:45 (3:45) (Class 1) 2-Y-O+ **£23,704** (£8,964; £4,480; £2,240) **Stalls** High

Form RPR

1056 **1** **Strike The Deal (USA)**[11] 5434 4-9-9 107......(v) KFallon 7 113
(J Noseda) *in rr and rdn along 1/2-way: hdwy 2f out: sn rdn and styd on strly to ld wl ins fnl f: edgd lft nr fin* **9/2**[3]

005 **2** 1 **Spin Cycle (IRE)**[11] 5420 3-9-8 102...... RichardMullen 9 109
(B Smart) *chsd ldrs: hdwy 2f out: rdn to chal and ev ch ent fnl f: sn drvn: edgd rt and no ex fnl 100yds* **12/1**

1603 **3** *nse* **Above Limits (IRE)**[26] 4989 2-7-12 93...... CatherineGannon 3 99
(Tom Dascombe) *led: rdn along and jnd 2f out: drvn over 1f out: hdd ins fnl f: n.m.r and lost 2nd nr line* **16/1**

0501 **4** 1 **Dandy Man (IRE)**[8] 5546 6-9-9 106......(t) LDettori 2 106
(Saeed Bin Suroor) *t.k.h: trckd ldrs: swtchd lft and hdwy to chal on outer over 1f out: sn rdn and ev ch tl edgd rt and wknd wl ins fnl f* **5/2**[1]

1133 **5** ¾ **Inxile (IRE)**[41] 4456 4-9-12 108...... AdrianTNicholls 5 106
(D Nicholls) *prom: chal 2f out: sn rdn and ev ch tl drvn and wkng whn n.m.r ins fnl f* **4/1**[2]

0020 **6** 1 **Captain Gerrard (IRE)**[19] 5233 4-9-9 105...... TomEaves 1 99
(B Smart) *hld up towards rr: swtchd outside and hdwy to chse ldrs over 1f out: sn rdn and no imp ent fnl f* **16/1**

-000 **7** ¾ **Moorhouse Lad**[19] 5233 6-9-9 105...... JimCrowley 8 97
(B Smart) *cl up: rdn along wl over 1f out and grad wknd* **5/1**

3036 **8** *nk* **Hoh Hoh Hoh**[38] 4559 7-9-9 102...... StephenDonohoe 4 96
(R J Price) *chsd ldrs: rdn along wl over 1f out: wknd appr fnl f* **16/1**

6401 **9** *2* **Siren's Gift**[9] 5507 5-9-4 90..........(b) DavidProbert 6 83
(A M Balding) *s.i.s: sn rdn along towards rr: nvr a factor* **16/1**

57.49 secs (-3.01) **Going Correction** -0.325s/f (Firm) **9** Ran SP% **114.6**
Speed ratings: **111,109,109,107,106 104,103,103,100**
toteswinger: 1&2 £11.10, 1&3 £14.10, 2&3 £21.40. CSF £56.28 TOTE £5.60: £2.10, £4.00, £4.30; EX 62.40 TRIFECTA Not won..

Owner M Barber **Bred** Five-D Thoroughbreds, Llc **Trained** Newmarket, Suffolk

FOCUS
There was a good pace on here and eventually that played into the hands of a closer. The winner matched his best, with the second running to his reappearance level and the third up 9lb even allowing for weight-for-age.

NOTEBOOK
Strike The Deal(USA) has struggled somewhat in Group company since his two-year-old days, but this is his grade and he was best in at the weights. Despite sitting down in the stalls, missing the break and struggling to go the early pace - he normally races over 6f - the way this race was run brought his stamina into play. Finding them coming back to him inside the final furlong, he stormed through the pack and eventually won a shade cosily in a course-record time, but his previous efforts suggest he wouldn't be one to bank on back up in class next time - his target is a Group 3 5f race at Newbury later this month. (op 4-1)

Spin Cycle(IRE) ran a sound enough race in second having led the chasing group behind the three leaders for most of the way. He is a difficult horse to place, though, and easier ground will be no help this autumn. Perhaps he can be found an opportunity on the Polytrack as both his siblings were effective on sand. (op 16-1)

Above Limits(IRE) ◆, the only two-year-old in the line-up, ran a cracker against her elders considering she went so fast early on a track that doesn't favour her style of running. On a more speed-favouring track she will be harder to peg back, and is very much one to keep in mind. (op 25-1)

Dandy Man(IRE) had enjoyed a nice confidence-boosting success at Leicester on his previous start, but on this return to pattern company he was keen and, having been brought to have his chance on the outside, could find just the one pace. He's not one for a battle and remains one to oppose. (op 100-30)

Inxile(IRE), who had to give weight all round, often makes the running, but he was denied that role by Above Limits here. The gelding raced keenly in the early stages and didn't see his race out, and will be happier when able to dominate again. (tchd 9-2)

Captain Gerrard(IRE), who has disappointed more often than not this season, could never get competitive. (op 14-1)

Moorhouse Lad, who didn't run too badly in the Nunthorpe last time out and who hit form at around this time last year, was one of those that helped set a strong pace and dropped right out inside the last. (op 4-1 tchd 11-2)

5766 NEW LOOK FRENCHGATE H'CAP — 7f
4:20 (4:20) (Class 2) (0-100,100) 3-Y-O
£12,462 (£3,732; £1,866; £934; £466; £234) **Stalls** High

Form RPR

0033 **1** **Akhenaten**[19] 5206 3-8-10 92.......... TonyCulhane 6 98
(M R Channon) *trckd ldrs: effrt wl over 1f out and sn rdn: drvn ent fnl f and kpt on to ld last 100yds* **13/2**[3]

0026 **2** *3/4* **Vitoria (IRE)**[21] 5175 3-8-5 87.......... RichardMullen 2 91
(B Smart) *cl up: led after 2f: rdn along 2f out and sn hdd: cl up and drvn ent fnl f and ev ch tl no ex towards fin* **10/1**

454 **3** *shd* **Agente Parmigiano (IRE)**[23] 5092 3-8-5 87..........(t) FrancisNorton 10 91
(G A Butler) *hld up in tch: hdwy 2f out: swtchd lft and rdn ent fnl f: sn drvn and ev ch tl nt qckn towards fin* **8/1**

-560 **4** *nk* **Bonnie Charlie**[25] 5032 3-9-4 100.......... PatDobbs 3 103
(R Hannon) *led 2f: cl up tl rdn and slt ld over 1f out: drvn ent fnl f: hdd and no ex last 100yds* **10/1**

122 **5** *1 1/4* **Russian Jar (IRE)**[11] 5432 3-8-4 86.......... WilliamBuick 1 86
(M A Jarvis) *t.k.h: hld up in tch: hdwy on outer 2f out: rdn to chse ldrs over 1f out: ev ch whn drvn and edgd lft ent fnl f: sn one pce* **3/1**[2]

5-03 **6** *3/4* **Wildcat Wizard (USA)**[130] 1677 3-9-1 97.......... KFallon 5 94
(P F I Cole) *dwlt and hld up in rr: hdwy and swtchd wd 2f out: sn rdn and ch over 1f out: drvn ent fnl f and wknd* **9/1**

3516 **7** *nse* **Inheritor (IRE)**[11] 5432 3-8-4 86 oh4.......... RoystonFfrench 8 83
(B Smart) *chsd ldrs: rdn along wl over 2f out and sn wknd* **22/1**

0131 **8** *1 3/4* **Broad Cairn**[14] 5349 3-8-6 88.......... SteveDrowne 9 81
(R Charlton) *trckd ldrs on inner: rdn along 2f out and sn wknd* **5/2**[1]

1-0 **9** *40* **Alkhafif**[76] 3298 3-8-13 95.......... TPO'Shea 4 —
(E A L Dunlop) *dwlt: a towards rr: rdn along and outpcd over 2f out: sn bhd and eased* **33/1**

1m 24.7s (-1.60) **Going Correction** -0.325s/f (Firm) **9** Ran SP% **113.5**
Speed ratings (Par 107): **96,95,95,94,93 92,92,90,44**
toteswinger: 1&2 £11.20, 1&3 £6.80, 2&3 £13.60. CSF £67.82 CT £527.02 TOTE £7.40: £2.30, £3.30, £2.60; EX 75.20 Trifecta £620.00 Part won. Pool: £837.91 - 0.20 winning units..

Owner Box 41 **Bred** Netherfield House Stud **Trained** West Ilsley, Berks

FOCUS
A competitive handicap in which any one of six could still be given a chance with a furlong to run. The first three set the standard.

NOTEBOOK
Akhenaten is a difficult horse to win with, but he has been running well in defeat on turf virtually all season and deserved this. Third off this mark the last twice, he travelled well just in behind the leaders and found plenty under strong pressure to assert close home. He takes his racing well, but things will be tougher now as he is sure to go back up the weights. (op 7-1)

Vitoria(IRE), never involved having been held up at York last time, had earlier finished a good second at Newmarket and she returned to that sort of form here, appreciating the more positive tactics. (op 14-1 tchd 16-1 in a place)

Agente Parmigiano(IRE), like the winner, has been running well in defeat nearly all season and deserves to find a race, but he just couldn't quicken in the final 100 yards. (op 6-1)

Bonnie Charlie has been disappointing this season, but ran well enough having met trouble to suggest he had trained on when seventh at Newmarket last time and this effort seemed to confirm it. He still won't be the easiest to place, though. (tchd 11-1)

Russian Jar(IRE), who has twice finished second in handicaps since winning his maiden, challenged wide and had every chance, but couldn't quicken having been a bit keen early. He looks ready for a return to 1m. (tchd 10-3 tchd 7-2 in a place)

Wildcat Wizard(USA), restrained in rear by Fallon, came to challenge widest of all and could find no extra in the final half a furlong. (tchd 8-1 and 10-1)

Broad Cairn, up 4lb having won at Warwick last time, leaving him on a career-high mark, was tucked away on the rail in behind the leaders, but found very little for pressure and was beaten with 2f to run. This clearly wasn't his true form. (op 3-1 tchd 9-4)

Alkhafif was reported to have lost its action. Official explanation: jockey said that the gelding lost its action (op 25-1)

5767 EVANS FRENCHGATE H'CAP (DIV I) — 5f
4:50 (4:51) (Class 4) (0-85,85) 3-Y-O+ **£6,152** (£1,830; £914; £456) **Stalls** High

Form RPR

4000 **1** **Total Impact**[18] 5247 6-8-13 82.......... FrederikTylicki(3) 8 93
(R A Fahey) *trckd ldrs on inner: swtchd lft and effrt wl over 1f out: sn rdn and styd on to ld ins fnl f: rdn out* **5/2**[1]

0310 **2** *nk* **Rasaman (IRE)**[18] 5247 5-9-1 81..........(v) DanielTudhope 6 91
(J S Goldie) *chsd ldrs towards outer: hdwy 2f out: rdn over 1f out and ev ch tl drvn and nt qckn wl ins fnl f* **15/2**

502 **3** *1 3/4* **Le Toreador**[18] 5247 4-9-5 85..........(t) LDettori 3 89
(K A Ryan) *led 1f: cl up tl led again 2f out and sn rdn: drvn and hdd ins fnl f: kpt on same pce* **5/1**[3]

5100 **4** *1/2* **Earlsmedic**[75] 3347 4-9-3 83.......... SaleemGolam 10 85+
(S C Williams) *dwlt and towards rr: hdwy 2f out and sn rdn: n.m.r ent fnl f: kpt on wl towards fin* **14/1**

5053 **5** *3/4* **Ocean Blaze**[11] 5436 5-8-6 72.......... SteveDrowne 1 71
(B R Millman) *chsd ldrs: rdn along 2f out: drvn appr fnl f and grad wknd* **10/1**

06 **6** *1/2* **Stolt (IRE)**[17] 5293 5-8-7 78.......... GaryBartley(5) 5 75
(N Wilson) *stmbld s: hdwy to ld after 1f: rdn along and hdd 2f out: cl up tl drvn and wknd ent fnl f* **14/1**

6400 **7** *nse* **Kyle (IRE)**[11] 5436 5-8-6 72.......... JohnEgan 2 69
(C R Dore) *stdd s and hld up in rr: effrt and sme hdwy on outer over 2f out: sn rdn and no imp* **33/1**

322 **8** *1* **Haajes**[47] 4285 5-9-2 82..........(t) KFallon 13 85+
(J Balding) *hld up towards rr: effrt 2f out: sn rdn and n.m.r over 1f out: n.d* **9/2**[2]

2110 **9** *hd* **Raccoon (IRE)**[17] 5293 9-8-9 75.......... PJMcDonald 7 68
(Mrs R A Carr) *chsd ldrs: rdn along 1/2-way: sn wknd* **12/1**

510 **10** *nk* **Speedy Senorita (IRE)**[11] 5421 4-8-5 71.......... JimmyQuinn 4 63
(J J Quinn) *prom: rdn along over 2f out: sn drvn and wknd* **25/1**

300 **11** *1/2* **Glasshoughton**[21] 5148 6-8-5 71 oh4.......... RoystonFfrench 11 61
(M Dods) *dwlt: a in rr* **28/1**

58.15 secs (-2.35) **Going Correction** -0.325s/f (Firm) **11** Ran SP% **115.5**
Speed ratings (Par 105): **105,104,101,100,99 98,98,97,96,96 95**
toteswinger: 1&2 £7.80, 1&3 £5.00, 2&3 £8.80. CSF £20.61 CT £88.86 TOTE £3.70: £1.90, £2.50, £2.00; EX 25.30 Trifecta £164.80 Pool: £844.33 -3.79 winning units..

Owner The Wakey Exiles **Bred** C A Cyzer **Trained** Musley Bank, N Yorks

FOCUS
The first division of what was a modest sprint handicap. Straightforward form.

Haajes Official explanation: jockey said the gelding was denied a clear run

5768 EVANS FRENCHGATE H'CAP (DIV II) — 5f
5:25 (5:25) (Class 4) (0-85,84) 3-Y-O+ **£6,152** (£1,830; £914; £456) **Stalls** High

Form RPR

3026 **1** **Incomparable**[6] 5597 4-8-7 75..........(b) FrederikTylicki(3) 9 87
(J A Glover) *cl up: effrt 2f out: rdn to ld over 1f out: drvn and kpt on strly ins fnl f* **6/1**[3]

2203 **2** *2 1/4* **Feelin Foxy**[21] 5149 5-8-13 78.......... TPQueally 11 82
(J G Given) *led: rdn along 2f out: hdd over 1f out: drvn and one pce ins fnl f* **5/1**[2]

1152 **3** *nse* **The Tatling (IRE)**[11] 5436 12-9-0 82.......... JackDean(3) 10 86+
(J M Bradley) *towards rr: hdwy 2f out: sn rdn and styd on ins fnl f* **5/1**[2]

0000 **4** *3/4* **Not My Choice (IRE)**[11] 5421 4-8-5 70 oh6.......... JohnEgan 8 71
(J Balding) *in tch: hdwy 2f out: sn rdn to chse ldrs and kpt on same pce ins fnl f* **33/1**

1330 **5** *1/2* **Efistorm**[11] 5436 8-8-12 82.......... BMcHugh(5) 7 81
(C R Dore) *towards rr: hdwy wl over 1f out: styd on strly ins fnl f: nrst fin* **16/1**

0360 **6** *shd* **Invincible Lad (IRE)**[11] 5420 5-9-5 84.......... KFallon 1 83+
(E J Alston) *wnt lft s: sn rdn along in rr: hdwy on wd outside 2f out: drvn and kpt on ins fnl f: nrst fin* **3/1**[1]

4464 **7** *shd* **Sir Nod**[11] 5421 7-8-7 72.......... TomEaves 13 71
(Miss J A Camacho) *chsd ldrs: rdn along wl over 1f out: drvn appr fnl f and sn wknd* **10/1**

1120 **8** *nk* **Secret Venue**[41] 4464 3-8-5 71.......... AndrewElliott 3 68
(Jedd O'Keeffe) *prom: rdn along 2f out: drvn and wknd over 1f out* **16/1**

6010 **9** *hd* **Rothesay Dancer**[17] 5293 6-9-1 83.......... KellyHarrison(3) 12 80
(J S Goldie) *a towards rr* **11/1**

4506 **10** *1/2* **Go Go Green (IRE)**[5] 5623 3-8-13 79.......... PhillipMakin 4 74
(D H Brown) *chsd ldrs: rdn along over 2f out: wknd over 1f out* **16/1**

0104 **11** *1/2* **Bravely (IRE)**[9] 5516 5-8-10 75.......... DuranFentiman 6 68
(T D Easterby) *s.i.s: a in rr* **22/1**

002 **12** *3 3/4* **Mr Wolf**[14] 5343 8-8-7 72..........(p) GrahamGibbons 2 52
(J J Quinn) *chsd ldrs: rdn along bef 1/2-way: sn lost pl and bhd* **12/1**

57.91 secs (-2.59) **Going Correction** -0.325s/f (Firm)
WFA 3 from 4yo+ 1lb **12** Ran SP% **122.7**
Speed ratings (Par 105): **107,103,103,102,101 101,101,100,100,99 98,92**
toteswinger: 1&2 £7.60, 1&3 £7.60, 2&3 £4.80. CSF £37.44 CT £166.37 TOTE £7.20: £2.80, £1.80, £2.30; EX 44.20 Trifecta £351.70 Pool: £636.99 - 1.34 winning units. Place 6: £130.58, Place 5 £49.31..

Owner Paul J Dixon & Brian Morton **Bred** Mrs Yvette Dixon **Trained** Babworth, Notts

FOCUS
A competitive handicap on paper but not many got into it and the final time was 0.24sec quicker than the first division. The first two were always 1-2 and the winner is rated in line with his AW form.

Invincible Lad(IRE) Official explanation: jockey that the gelding suffered interference at the start

T/Jkpt: £10,166.60 to a £1 stake. Pool: £93,075.35. 6.50 winning tickets. T/Plt: £269.70 to a £1 stake. Pool: £93,690.84. 253.53 winning tickets. T/Qpdt: £36.40 to a £1 stake. Pool: £6,239.68. 126.70 winning tickets. JR

[5589]EPSOM (L-H)

Wednesday, September 9

OFFICIAL GOING: Good to firm (good in places; overall 8.7, home straight: stands' side 8.9 far side 8.3)

Course dolled out 4/5 yards form mile post to winning post adding 5yards to advertised distances.

Wind: Moderate, across Weather: Overcast, drizzle

5769 NIGHTINGALL NURSERY 6f

2:10 (2:11) (Class 4) (0-85,85) 2-Y-O **£5,180** (£1,541; £770; £384) **Stalls** High

Form RPR

6316 **1** **Radio City**[25] 5033 2-8-9 **73** .... SebSanders 7 78+
(R M Beckett) *awkward s: hld up: 6th st: waited bhd ldrs tl asked for effrt over 1f out: led ins fnl f: rdn out: readily* **9/1**

13 **2** 1 1/4 **Bagamoyo**[25] 5038 2-9-7 **85** .... NCallan 5 86
(J R Fanshawe) *awkward s: t.k.h: trckd ldng pair: effrt to ld jst ins fnl f: sn hdd and outpcd* **1/1**[1]

221 **3** 1 1/4 **Bush Tucker (IRE)**[24] 5060 2-9-2 **85** .... AshleyMorgan(5) 3 85+
(P Winkworth) *t.k.h: hld up: awkward downhill over 4f out: 5th st: cl up bhd ldrs looking for room fr 2f out: kpt on one pce fnl f* **9/2**[2]

3150 **4** *nk* **Master Of Dance (IRE)**[47] 4271 2-8-13 **77** .... JimmyFortune 2 73
(R Hannon) *disp ld tl jst ins fnl f: outpcd* **6/1**[3]

0320 **5** 1 1/4 **More Lashes (USA)**[26] 4989 2-8-12 **76** .... AlanMunro 4 69
(M G Quinlan) *disp ld to 1f out: wknd* **12/1**

0406 **6** 1 1/4 **Hill Of Miller (IRE)**[18] 5274 2-9-0 **78** .... ChrisCatlin 6 67
(Rae Guest) *t.k.h: hld up last: no prog 3f out: plugged on fnl f* **20/1**

5100 **7** 1/2 **Slice (IRE)**[18] 5274 2-9-0 **78** .... ShaneKelly 8 65
(Eve Johnson Houghton) *trckd ldrs: 4th st: sn pushed along and lost pl: struggling fnl 2f* **11/1**

1m 11.21s (1.81) **Going Correction** +0.15s/f (Good) **7 Ran SP% 113.3**
Speed ratings (Par 97): **93,91,89,89,87 85,85**
toteswinger: 1&2 £2.30, 1&3 £4.20, 2&3 £1.40. CSF £18.21 CT £47.15 TOTE £8.80: £3.30, £1.60; EX 25.30.
Owner Clipper Logistics **Bred** Baroness Bloodstock & Redmyre Bloodstock **Trained** Whitsbury, Hants

FOCUS
The ground rode as advertised and there was a significant breeze in the horses' faces coming down the hill towards Tattenham Corner. Probably no more than an ordinary nursery and the pace was true from the outset.

NOTEBOOK
Radio City, who hadn't run well over course and distance in July, but had subsequently broken his maiden at Brighton and run well in defeat at Newmarket, scored with authority. Settled in rear, he swept past his rivals to win with a little bit to spare, his rider merely giving him a couple of cursory slaps. Though receiving weight from all the others, he is obviously getting the hang of things. (op 7-1)
Bagamoyo, a heavy-topped nursery debutant, had won on soft ground on his debut and, after another fair effort on faster ground at Ripon, attracted plenty of early money. A colt with plenty of scope, he was on his toes in the paddock and taken down on his own. He looked professional enough in the race, showing a willing attitude and came with a well-timed run, only for Radio City to sweep past. He should be capable of gaining compensation off his current mark and may have simply bumped into a more progressive horse on the day. (op 5-4)
Bush Tucker(IRE) had seen the form of his comfortable Bath maiden victory franked by Pherousa (fifth of six that day), but looked to have plenty on his plate on his nursery debut. He didn't have a great deal of room approaching the last furlong and a half, but stayed on well enough without ever really showing a turn of foot. He could not be considered unlucky, but he may have finished closer if getting the gaps when required. (tchd 4-1 and 5-1)
Master Of Dance(IRE), back down in class, was fractious in the preliminaries and required a second handler. He did much of the donkey work up front, helping set a searching pace, but he could not sustain it. Down 2lb here, this return to sprinting did not seem to help. This display was a little disappointing. (op 8-1)
More Lashes(USA), a filly with plenty of pace and a lovely attitude, had been unlucky at Sandown last month, but was found out in Listed company at Newbury last time. She was given a 13lb hike in the weights subsequently and that was clearly against her here. She helped set the pace, but the writing was on the wall before a furlong out and she dropped away. She has ability and will win a race or two, though connections will find it hard to place her off her present mark. (op 14-1 tchd 16-1)
Hill Of Miller(IRE) stayed on from the back but was beaten a fair way. This was the fastest surface he has encountered but the run could not be considered encouraging. (op 16-1)
Slice(IRE) was taking a significant class drop on ground he would have appreciated, but never looked like getting competitive. He remains relatively unexposed and he may simply have not relished the track. (tchd 12-1)

5770 EUROPEAN BREEDERS' FUND MAIDEN STKS 1m 114y

2:45 (2:46) (Class 4) 2-Y-O **£5,180** (£1,541; £577; £577) **Stalls** Low

Form RPR

33 **1** **Realisation (USA)**[38] 4557 2-9-3 0 .... JoeFanning 3 79+
(M Johnston) *trckd ldr: pushed into ld 2f out: sn in command: dismntd after fin* **1/2**[1]

04 **2** 1 3/4 **Ebony Boom (IRE)**[20] 5192 2-9-3 0 .... IanMongan 5 74
(H R A Cecil) *hld up last but wl in tch: rdn over 2f out: prog to go 2nd over 1f out: hanging and no imp on wnr* **20/1**

0 **3** 1 **Natural Law (IRE)**[9] 5499 2-9-3 0 .... TedDurcan 2 73+
(Saeed Bin Suroor) *trckd ldng pair: shkn up on inner over 2f out: nt qckn and wl hld fr over 1f out* **15/2**[3]

652 **3** *dht* **Sabander Bleue (IRE)**[10] 5466 2-9-3 0 .... ChrisCatlin 4 72
(M R Channon) *led: rdn and hdd 2f out: sn outpcd and btn: plugged on* **7/2**[2]

1m 49.0s (2.90) **Going Correction** +0.15s/f (Good) **4 Ran SP% 105.4**
Speed ratings (Par 97): **93,91,90,90**
toteswinger: 4.90. CSF £9.71 TOTE £1.40; EX 6.90.
Owner Sheikh Hamdan Bin Mohammed Al Maktoum **Bred** Darley **Trained** Middleham Moor, N Yorks

FOCUS
A small and not particularly select field for a maiden run at a modest pace, but some big yards were represented and they looked a nice bunch of colts.

NOTEBOOK
Realisation(USA), who showed promise when third over 7f at Haydock and Chester, had to be just kept up to his work to win with plenty in hand. He certainly appreciated the step up in trip and if he continues to progress, there are better races to be won with him. His rider reported that the colt appeared to lose his backend coming round the bend and he jumped off him immediately after the race. There did not appear to be anything amiss, however. (op 4-7 tchd 8-13 and 4-6 in places)
Ebony Boom(IRE), with whom the penny seems to be dropping, showed modest form when fourth of seven at Lingfield on the all-weather last time. He stayed on in really taking style and finished with a flourish. The ability is there and this was his first try on this surface. He appreciated it. (op 16-1 tchd 14-1)
Natural Law(IRE) looked green on his first start and showed improvement here. He was squeezed for room on the rail, but showed a very willing attitude and he looks a nice horse for next season. (op 4-1 tchd 100-30)
Sabander Bleue(IRE), who had shown improved from when upped to a mile and dropped in class at Beverley last time, ran another solid race. Given another positive ride, he held every chance 2f out, but was tapped for toe before staying on again. (op 4-1 tchd 100-30)

5771 ASHTEAD H'CAP 1m 4f 10y

3:20 (3:22) (Class 4) (0-85,85) 3-Y-O **£6,476** (£1,927; £963; £481) **Stalls** Centre

Form RPR

1342 **1** **Funday**[9] 5510 3-8-12 **79** .... FergusSweeney 6 89
(G L Moore) *trckd ldng trio: pushed along and prog to chse ldr over 2f out: sn drvn: styd on ins fnl f to ld last 50yds* **4/1**[2]

3251 **2** 1/2 **Brilliana**[24] 5061 3-8-13 **80** .... TedDurcan 2 89
(D R Lanigan) *taken down early: trckd ldr after 3f: led 3f out: sn kicked 2 l clr: looked wnr tl wknd and hdd last 50yds* **7/1**

1200 **3** 1/2 **Lively Fling (USA)**[39] 4518 3-9-2 **83** ....(v[1]) JimmyFortune 3 91
(J H M Gosden) *hld up in 5th: effrt 3f out: clsd on ldrs fr 2f out: hanging bdly after: kpt on wl nr fin* **15/2**

1126 **4** 1 3/4 **Halfway House**[19] 5216 3-8-12 **79** .... HayleyTurner 8 84
(M L W Bell) *taken down early: hld up in last pair: effrt 3f out: rdn to cl on ldrs fr 2f out: one pce fnl f* **8/1**

1151 **5** 5 **Upton Seas**[9] 5524 3-8-7 **74** 6ex .... PaulHanagan 1 71
(M W Easterby) *trckd ldr 3f: 3rd and pushed along st: grad outpcd fr over 2f out* **5/2**[1]

-133 **6** 13 **Straits Of Hormuz (USA)**[47] 4274 3-9-0 **81** .... JoeFanning 5 58
(M Johnston) *led: rdn and hdd 3f out: sn wknd: t.o* **10/1**

3133 **7** 11 **Zaaqya**[26] 4988 3-9-4 **85** .... RHills 7 44+
(J L Dunlop) *hld up in last pair: nt gng wl downhill over 4f out: lost tch and eased over 2f out: t.o* **9/2**[3]

2m 39.15s (0.25) **Going Correction** +0.15s/f (Good) **7 Ran SP% 111.2**
Speed ratings (Par 103): **105,104,104,103,99 91,83**
toteswinger: 1&2 £6.60, 1&3 £6.80, 2&3 £9.60. CSF £29.64 CT £193.15 TOTE £4.00: £2.20, £3.70; EX 35.00.
Owner Sir Eric Parker **Bred** Sir Eric Parker **Trained** Lower Beeding, W Sussex

FOCUS
A competitive if ordinary handicap for the money, but for a field with plenty of horses that have shown early pace, they surprisingly went a pedestrian gallop. The winner did not need to improve.
Zaaqya Official explanation: jockey said filly was unsuited by the track

5772 GOLFER'S PUTT TO WIN BIRTHDAY H'CAP 1m 2f 18y

3:55 (3:58) (Class 4) (0-85,83) 3-Y-O+ **£5,180** (£1,541; £770; £384) **Stalls** Low

Form RPR

3331 **1** **Potentiale (IRE)**[10] 5473 5-8-13 **77** 6ex ....(p) RHills 2 87
(J W Hills) *hld up in last: smooth prog fr 3f out to trck ldrs 2f out: stuck in bhd them tl plld out 1f out: shkn up and r.o to ld last 75yds* **4/1**[2]

130/ **2** 1/2 **Prince Picasso**[88] 3464 6-8-9 **73** .... PaulHanagan 8 82
(R A Fahey) *hld up: rousted along and reminders over 5f out: prog to go 3rd 4f out: drvn up to ld narrowly over 1f out: hdd and hld last 75yds* **7/1**

251 **3** 2 3/4 **Kaleo**[20] 5186 5-8-11 **75** ow1 .... DarryllHolland 7 79
(S Dow) *led at decent pce: tried to kick on 3f out: hdd and no ex over 1f out* **15/8**[1]

4515 **4** 3 **Constant Cheers (IRE)**[24] 5062 6-9-0 **78** .... AdamKirby 6 76
(W R Swinburn) *chsd ldng pair to 4f out: rdn and nt qckn wl over 2f out: tried to cl on ldrs again over 1f out: fdd* **9/2**[3]

5143 **5** 2 3/4 **Emperor Court (IRE)**[16] 5321 5-9-5 **83** .... NCallan 4 75
(P J Makin) *chsd ldr: chal over 2f out to over 1f out: wknd* **5/1**

1002 **6** 23 **Mohathab (IRE)**[23] 5095 4-9-2 **80** ....(b) PatCosgrave 3 26
(J R Boyle) *hld up: 5th and rdn st: sn wknd: t.o* **16/1**

2m 9.78s (0.08) **Going Correction** +0.15s/f (Good) **6 Ran SP% 108.0**
Speed ratings (Par 105): **105,104,102,100,97 79**
toteswinger: 1&2 £4.10, 1&3 £1.90, 2&3 £3.90. CSF £28.22 CT £58.75 TOTE £5.10: £1.60, £4.00; EX 30.30.
Owner J W Hills **Bred** Copperhead Stable **Trained** Upper Lambourn, Berks

FOCUS
A fair handicap, run at a sensible pace. The winner was not obviously well treated (2lb wrong) under his penalty and this is unconvincing form.

5773 WALTON DOWNS MAIDEN STKS 1m 2f 18y

4:30 (4:33) (Class 5) 3-Y-O+ **£3,238** (£963; £481; £240) **Stalls** Low

Form RPR

5532 **1** **Monetary Fund (USA)**[18] 5259 3-9-3 72 ....(t) NCallan 3 83
(G A Butler) *trckd ldng pair: wnt 2nd ent st: pushed into ld over 1f out: sn drew away* **15/8**[2]

2332 **2** 6 **Alqaffay (IRE)**[19] 5215 4-9-10 73 .... RHills 1 71
(J H M Gosden) *led: shkn up over 2f out: hdd over 1f out: sn no ch w wnr* **11/10**[1]

2452 **3** 13 **Kessraa (IRE)**[24] 5072 3-9-3 67 .... ChrisCatlin 2 45
(M R Channon) *nvr gng wl: lost tch w ldrs fr 1/2-way: poor 4th st: tk remote 3rd ins fnl f* **10/1**

06 **4** 8 **Pellinore (USA)**[27] 4955 3-8-12 0 ....(v[1]) LPKeniry 5 24
(E F Vaughan) *chsd ldr tl ent st: sn rdn and wknd: lost remote 3rd ins fnl f* **40/1**

05 **5** 48 **Ettrick Mill**[214] 440 3-9-3 0 .... JoeFanning 4 —
(M Johnston) *nvr gng wl: lost tch by 1/2-way: poor last st: t.o whn virtually p.u fnl f* **6/1**[3]

2m 10.22s (0.52) **Going Correction** +0.15s/f (Good)
WFA 3 from 4yo 7lb **5 Ran SP% 108.2**
Speed ratings (Par 103): **103,98,87,81,43**
CSF £4.14 TOTE £2.40: £1.50, £1.10; EX 4.50.
Owner A D Spence **Bred** Stonestreet Thoroughbred Holdings Llc **Trained** Newmarket, Suffolk

FOCUS
A weakish and poorly-contested maiden, but run at a true pace and the two principals had it to themselves. The winner is rated to his best turf form.

5774 CROYDON H'CAP 7f

5:00 (5:00) (Class 4) (0-85,85) 3-Y-O **£6,476** (£1,927; £963; £481) **Stalls** Low

Form RPR

2253 **1** **Belle Des Airs (IRE)**[26] 5005 3-8-12 **82** .... JackMitchell(3) 9 89
(R M Beckett) *mde all: pushed along firmly and in command fr 2f out: unchal* **11/2**[3]

3231 **2** 1 1/4 **Hi Shinko**[6] 5591 3-8-11 **78** 6ex........ TGMcLaughlin 4 82
(B R Millman) *chsd wnr after 2f: rdn and no imp fr 2f out: kpt on* **7/4**[1]

4361 **3** 3 **Fajita**[12] 5403 3-8-3 **75**........(p) JemmaMarshall(5) 1 71+
(G L Moore) *hld up: lost grnd downhill: 6th and detached st: rdn over 2f out: plld out wd over 1f out: kpt on to take 3rd last strides* **12/1**

0-1 **4** nk **Conry (IRE)**[14] 5340 3-8-4 **78**........ TobyAtkinson(7) 8 73+
(Patrick Morris) *n.m.r s: t.k.h: cl up on outer: 3rd st: hanging lft fr over 2f out: nt qckn* **13/2**

0350 **5** 4 **Daddy's Gift (IRE)**[75] 3347 3-9-0 **81**........ JimmyFortune 2 65+
(R Hannon) *chsd wnr 2f: bdly hmpd sn after: 5th st: tried to cl 2f out: wknd fnl f* **12/1**

1500 **6** 4 1/2 **The Winged Assasin (USA)**[11] 5448 3-8-6 **73**........ SimonWhitworth 7 45
(J Akehurst) *nvr on terms: last and wl bhd st: no ch* **14/1**

5032 **7** 1/2 **Desert Falls**[11] 5418 3-8-11 **78**........ J-PGuillambert 6 56+
(R M Whitaker) *t.k.h: chsd ldrs: 4th st: wknd wl over 1f out: eased fnl f* **7/2**[2]

1m 24.3s (1.00) **Going Correction** +0.15s/f (Good) **7 Ran SP% 109.4**
Speed ratings (Par 103): **100,98,95,94,90 85,84**
toteswinger: 1&2 £3.30, 1&3 £9.90, 2&3 £4.90. CSF £14.19 CT £97.89 TOTE £6.10: £2.80, £1.60; EX 20.80 Place 6: £36.83, Place: £20.30..
Owner Mrs M E Slade **Bred** Mrs M E Slade **Trained** Whitsbury, Hants

FOCUS
An ordinary handicap run at a steady pace, and a rough race which was not without incident. The front pair were 1-2 almost throughout and the form is rated around the runner-up.
The Winged Assasin(USA) Official explanation: jockey said gelding was hampered at the start
T/Plt: £34.90 to a £1 stake. Pool: £50,514.24. 1,054.22 winning tickets. T/Qpdt: £12.50 to a £1 stake. Pool: £3,384.10. 199.70 winning tickets. JN

5661
KEMPTON (A.W) (R-H)
Wednesday, September 9

OFFICIAL GOING: Standard
Wind: Virtually nil until strong behind after Race 3 (6.50) Weather: Bright getting dark

5775 DAY TIME, NIGHT TIME, GREAT TIME CLASSIFIED STKS — 1m 2f (P)
5:50 (5:50) (Class 6) 3-Y-0+ **£2,047** (£604; £302) **Stalls** High

Form RPR

000- **1** **Arty Crafty (USA)**[301] 7289 3-8-11 52........ SebSanders 4 54+
(Sir Mark Prescott) *drvn to chse ldrs: chal 7f out: rdn and carried wd bnd over 2f out: styd on u.p to ld cl home* **7/4**[1]

-000 **2** hd **Sircozy (IRE)**[39] 4545 3-8-8 52........ WilliamCarson(3) 11 54+
(S C Williams) *chsd ldrs tl outpcd over 4f out: rdn and wd into st over 2f out: rallied and styd on strly fr over 1f out: fin wl to take 2nd nr fin* **13/2**[3]

2-50 **3** 1/2 **Sestet**[210] 494 4-9-4 52........ NickyMackay 6 53
(S Dow) *chsd ldrs: styd on inner as ldr wnt wd bnd over 2f out and led wl over 1f out: sn rdn: hdd and no ex cl home* **14/1**

000 **4** 1/2 **Through The Forest (USA)**[31] 4828 3-8-11 54........(p) AdamKirby 2 54+
(W R Swinburn) *chsd ldrs: rdn over 3f out carried wd: hmpd and stmbld bnd over 2f out: rallied to chse ldrs again over 1f out: styd on ins fnl f but nvr quite gng pce to chal* **33/1**

-665 **5** 1 1/2 **Chateauneuf (IRE)**[41] 4472 3-8-11 55........ DarryllHolland 12 49
(B W Hills) *in rr: hdwy on ins fr 3f out: rdn to chse ldrs over 1f out: one pce ins fnl f* **8/1**

-060 **6** 3/4 **Miss Perfectionist**[44] 4375 3-8-11 54........ KirstyMilczarek 5 47
(P Howling) *in rr: rdn over 2f out: styd on fr over 1f out and kpt on ins fnl f: nvr gng pce to get to ldrs* **40/1**

000- **7** nk **Marjury Daw (IRE)**[308] 7200 3-8-11 55........ PatCosgrave 9 47
(J G Given) *chsd ldrs: rdn and one pce 3f out: styd on again fnl f* **20/1**

0450 **8** hd **Final Son**[64] 3710 4-9-4 53........ NCallan 3 46
(A P Jarvis) *sn led: rn wd bnd over 2f out: hdd wl over 1f out but styd on terms tl wknd ins fnl f* **16/1**

4600 **9** 1 **Majd Aljazeera**[29] 4872 3-8-8 55........(t) AndreaAtzeni(3) 8 44
(D M Simcock) *sn chsng ldrs: rdn over 3f out: wknd fnl f* **20/1**

0004 **10** 1 1/2 **Haling Park (UAE)**[34] 4704 3-8-11 55........ FergusSweeney 13 41
(G L Moore) *in rr: pushed along 3f out: styd on fnl f but nvr in contention* **4/1**[2]

-600 **11** 3 1/4 **Law And Order**[63] 3741 3-8-6 52........(p) RossAtkinson(5) 14 35
(Miss J R Tooth) *a in rr* **50/1**

0050 **12** nk **Whiterocks**[11] 5430 3-8-11 52........ AlanMunro 10 34
(M R Channon) *a in rr* **25/1**

5606 **13** 3 3/4 **Warrants Attention (IRE)**[27] 4934 3-8-11 55........ LPKeniry 1 27
(A M Balding) *rdn on outside 4f out: a in rr* **16/1**

2m 9.00s (1.00) **Going Correction** -0.10s/f (Stan)
WFA 3 from 4yo 7lb **13 Ran SP% 120.0**
Speed ratings (Par 101): **92,91,91,91,89 89,89,88,88,86 84,84,81**
toteswinger: 1&2 £5.30, 1&3 £7.70, 2&3 £11.70. CSF £11.81 TOTE £3.00: £1.10, £2.70, £4.30; EX 30.00.
Owner Mrs Sonia Rogers **Bred** Airlie Stud **Trained** Newmarket, Suffolk
■ Stewards' Enquiry : William Carson two-day ban: excessive use of the whip (Sep 23-24)
Seb Sanders seven-day ban: excessive use of the whip, using whip in the incorrect place and causing wealing (Sep 23-29)

FOCUS
A typically tight classified event. The first four were closely covered at the finish and the form is rated around the fourth.
Arty Crafty(USA) Official explanation: trainer's rep said, regarding the apparent improvement in form shown, that the filly has matured and strengthened over the past eight months
Final Son Official explanation: jockey said gelding hung left throughout

5776 RELOADERS NURSERY — 5f (P)
6:20 (6:20) (Class 5) (0-70,70) 2-Y-0 **£2,590** (£770; £385; £192) **Stalls** High

Form RPR

5162 **1** **Italian Tom (IRE)**[28] 4912 2-9-4 **67**........ LukeMorris 12 73
(R A Harris) *mde all: shkn up over 1f out: asserted ins fnl f: readily* **2/1**[1]

0240 **2** 1 1/2 **I'Malwaysright (IRE)**[85] 3006 2-9-7 **70**........ DaneO'Neill 3 71
(D R C Elsworth) *t.k.h: rn wd bnd over 3f out: stl wd bnd over 2f out: styd on wl fr over 1f out and fin strly to take 2nd last strides but no ch w wnr* **8/1**[3]

106 **3** hd **Duke Of Rainford**[32] 4782 2-8-4 **53**........ PaulHanagan 1 53
(D Nicholls) *awkward s: in rr and sn outpcd: hdwy towards ins fr 2f out and chsd wnr ins fnl f but no imp: lost 2nd last strides* **9/1**

5402 **4** 1/2 **Papageno**[16] 5310 2-9-1 **64**........ NCallan 6 62
(J R Jenkins) *chsd ldrs: wnt 2nd and rdn 2f out: outpcd by wnr 1f out: lost 2nd and one pce ins fnl f* **10/1**

2440 **5** 1 1/2 **Vilnius**[10] 5467 2-8-9 **61**........ MCGeran(3) 8 54
(M R Channon) *broke wl: awkward: t.k.h and lost pl over 3f out: styd on to chse ldrs 2f out: outpcd fnl f* **11/1**

6546 **6** 3/4 **Tucker's Law**[23] 5091 2-9-4 **67**........ FergusSweeney 9 57
(B R Millman) *chsd ldrs: rdn 2f out: wknd fnl f* **10/1**

1305 **7** hd **Annia Galeria (IRE)**[16] 5310 2-8-4 **56**........ AndreaAtzeni(3) 4 45
(C A Dwyer) *chsd ldrs: rdn over 2f out: wknd 1f out* **12/1**

0003 **8** 1/2 **Tulip Explosion**[19] 5226 2-8-3 **52**........ PaulEddery 5 39
(D Shaw) *in rr: rdn over 2f out: nvr gng pce to get into contention* **20/1**

0504 **9** hd **Exceed Power**[16] 5310 2-8-7 **56**........(t) JoeFanning 7 43
(D M Simcock) *t.k.h and v wd bnd over 3f out: nvr any ch after but mod prog fnl f* **13/2**[2]

0062 **10** hd **Angie's Nap (USA)**[13] 5372 2-8-5 **54**........(p) ChrisCatlin 10 40
(P S McEntee) *chsd wnr 3f: sn btn* **10/1**

060 **11** 3/4 **Speedyfix**[50] 4176 2-8-1 **50**........(t) AdrianMcCarthy 11 33
(Mrs C A Dunnett) *t.k.h and v wd bnd over 3f out: nt rcvr and a bhd* **40/1**

60.25 secs (-0.25) **Going Correction** -0.10s/f (Stan) **11 Ran SP% 118.3**
Speed ratings (Par 95): **98,95,95,94,92 90,90,89,89,89 87**
toteswinger: 1&2 £3.90, 1&3 £8.40, 2&3 £12.90. CSF £18.25 CT £123.03 TOTE £2.70: £1.10, £3.10, £3.80; EX 19.80.
Owner S Mares **Bred** Tom Radley **Trained** Earlswood, Monmouths

FOCUS
A moderate nursery run at a strong early pace.

NOTEBOOK
Italian Tom(IRE) was very well backed and got off the mark for current connections at the first time of asking. He had the best of the draw, but deserves a lot of credit for knuckling down to stretch clear in the home straight considering he helped cut out the early running. This was his second win, a first outside of plating company and he is a likeable sprinter. (tchd 7-4 & 9-4 in places)
I'Malwaysright(IRE) was returning from an 85-day break and conceding upwards of 3lb all around. Keen early on, he got a patient ride from his modest draw and ultimately stayed on too late in the day. Now looks the time to try him over 6f again. (tchd 9-1)
Duke Of Rainford, with the tongue-tie left off, was housed in stall 1 so this rates a solid effort. He is now back on a fair mark and can find another one of these before the season is out. (op 8-1 tchd 10-1)
Papageno raced off a 1lb higher mark than when finishing second over C&D 16 days earlier. He held every chance and ran right up to form, so rates the benchmark. (op 8-1 tchd 11-1)
Vilnius has had plenty of chances and is another who helps set the standard.
Speedyfix Official explanation: jockey said gelding hung left

5777 LEVY BOARD H'CAP — 5f (P)
6:50 (6:51) (Class 4) (0-85,84) 3-Y-0 **£4,727** (£1,406; £702; £351) **Stalls** High

Form RPR

3066 **1** **Evelyn May (IRE)**[10] 5471 3-8-1 **72**........ AshleyMorgan(5) 10 81
(B W Hills) *in rr: hdwy 2f out: styd on to ld appr fnl f: kpt on wl* **6/1**[3]

40 **2** 1 3/4 **Brenin Taran**[25] 5032 3-9-1 **84**........(p) AndreaAtzeni(3) 9 87
(D M Simcock) *in rr: hdwy over 2f out: styd on fr over 1f out and chsd wnr wl ins fnl f but nvr any ch* **6/4**[1]

500 **3** 1 1/2 **Love You Louis**[31] 4829 3-8-7 **73**........(b) PaulHanagan 6 70
(J R Jenkins) *chsd ldrs on outside thrght: rdn over 2f out: one pce fnl f* **11/1**

3010 **4** 3/4 **Island Legend (IRE)**[12] 5405 3-8-9 **75**........ RichardKingscote 11 70
(J M Bradley) *led: rdn 1/2-way: hdd appr fnl f: wknd ins fnl f* **6/1**[3]

1-40 **5** 1 1/2 **Sharp Bullet (IRE)**[23] 5098 3-9-0 **80**........ AdamKirby 3 69
(W R Swinburn) *broke wl: sn rdn and outpcd: mod prog ins fnl f* **10/1**

134 **6** 1 1/4 **Angel Song**[14] 5340 3-8-10 **76**........ SebSanders 7 61
(Sir Mark Prescott) *chsd ldrs: rdn 1/2-way: wknd appr fnl f* **4/1**[2]

-P55 **7** 2 **The Magic Of Rio**[20] 5197 3-8-9 **75**........ FrankieMcDonald 8 53
(Peter Grayson) *chsd ldrs: rdn 1/2-way: wknd appr fnl f* **50/1**

0200 **8** 6 **Lucky Leigh**[20] 5203 3-8-13 **79**........ AlanMunro 1 35
(M R Channon) *sn wl bhd* **16/1**

59.52 secs (-0.98) **Going Correction** -0.10s/f (Stan) **8 Ran SP% 113.8**
Speed ratings (Par 103): **103,100,97,96,94 92,89,79**
toteswinger: 1&2 £2.60, 1&3 £15.20, 2&3 £10.80. CSF £15.28 CT £96.81 TOTE £7.50: £2.40, £1.10, £3.60; EX 17.80.
Owner Mrs B W Hills **Bred** Mrs S Dutfield **Trained** Lambourn, Berks

FOCUS
A modest 3yo sprint. It was another race run at a strong early pace and the winning time was almost half a second quicker than the preceding nursery. The winner is rated back to something like her best.
Island Legend(IRE) Official explanation: jockey said gelding hung left
Lucky Leigh Official explanation: jockey said filly did not face the kickback

5778 DIGIBET.COM MAIDEN AUCTION STKS — 6f (P)
7:20 (7:22) (Class 5) 2-Y-0 **£2,590** (£770; £385; £192) **Stalls** High

Form RPR

1 **San Cassiano (IRE)** 2-8-9 0........ SebSanders 12 75+
(R M Beckett) *chsd ldrs: drvn to ld 2f out: kpt on strly fnl f* **7/2**[2]

2 1 **Locksley Hall (USA)** 2-9-1 0........ JimmyFortune 10 78+
(E F Vaughan) *in tch: hdwy on ins over 2f out: styd on to chse wnr ins fnl f: kpt on but a hld* **8/1**

0 **3** 1 1/4 **Ongoodform (IRE)**[53] 4093 2-9-0 0........ NCallan 6 73
(P W D'Arcy) *t.k.h: chsd ldrs: rdn: green and hung bdly lft thrght fnl f but kpt on* **20/1**

22 **4** 1/2 **Lutine Charlie (IRE)**[7] 5571 2-9-0 0........ LukeMorris 7 72
(P Winkworth) *chsd ldrs: rdn over 2f out: styd on same pce fnl f* **1/1**[1]

0 **5** 2 **Baralaka**[7] 5571 2-8-8 0........ RosieJessop(7) 4 67
(Sir Mark Prescott) *in rr: styd on wl fr over 1f out: gng on cl home* **66/1**

3 **6** hd **Search For The Key (USA)**[40] 4492 2-9-1 0........ AlanMunro 8 66
(P F I Cole) *chsd ldrs: rdn and outpcd 3f out: styd on again fnl f* **15/2**[3]

4 **7** 1/2 **Phoenix Rose (IRE)**[63] 3744 2-8-4 0........ AdrianTNicholls 9 54
(J R Best) *led tl hdd 2f out: wknd over 1f out* **20/1**

5 **8** 3 1/4 **Caldermud (IRE)**[31] 4825 2-8-9 0........ JackMitchell(3) 3 52
(J R Best) *chsd ldrs on outside: rdn and wknd over 2f out* **12/1**

9 2 1/2 **Addictive Dream (IRE)** 2-9-1 0........ AdamKirby 5 47+
(W R Swinburn) *s.i.s: a towards rr* **50/1**

40 **10** 6 **Ballyvonane (USA)**[107] 2328 2-8-10 0........ TGMcLaughlin 11 24
(L A Dace) *a towards rr* **100/1**

11 12 **Banged Up Abroad (IRE)** 2-8-9 0........ JerryO'Dwyer 1 —
(M G Quinlan) *wnt bdly lft s and slowly away: a wl bhd* **66/1**

1m 12.85s (-0.25) **Going Correction** -0.10s/f (Stan) **11 Ran SP% 118.3**
Speed ratings (Par 95): **97,95,94,93,90 90,89,85,82,74 58**
toteswinger: 1&2 £4.80, 1&3 £3.50, 2&3 £16.20. CSF £29.48 TOTE £3.70: £1.40, £2.60, £5.00; EX 21.80.
Owner P D Savill **Bred** Peter Savill **Trained** Whitsbury, Hants

FOCUS
This could turn out to be a fair juvenile maiden as they looked a good bunch in the paddock and several hold fancy entries. There was an average pace on and two newcomers fought it out.

NOTEBOOK
San Cassiano(IRE), already gelded, was the subject of a gamble for this debut and he got off to a perfect start. He knew his job as he broke well from his decent draw to lie up early on and showed a willing attitude to fend off the runner-up inside the final furlong. It is surprising that as a half-brother to the former smart juvenile Celtic Silence he made only £600 at the breeze-ups, but he is clearly a useful prospect and now looks a very good purchase. Stepping up another furlong should also suit and, with improvement likely for this experience, he rates one to follow. (op 9-2 tchd 3-1)
Locksley Hall(USA), entered in the Mill Reef, travelled nicely off the pace on the inside and put his best foot forward when getting the split two furlongs out. He found the winner too resolute thereafter, but this was a very nice introduction and he should soon be winning. (op 15-2)
Ongoodform(IRE) did very well to bag third considering he hung right over to the stands' rail in the final furlong. He is clearly still very much learning his trade, but looks likely to go forward again for this outing. (op 16-1)
Lutine Charlie(IRE) was the clear form pick on the level of his two previous outings. He was produced with his chance, but lacked the gear change required to close on the first pair and can have no excuses. He helps to give the form a sound look and does now have the option of nurseries. (op 11-10 tchd 10-11 tchd 5-4 and 6-5 in a place)
Baralaka ◆, who finished well behind the fourth over C&D on his debut a week ago, prodiced a much improved effort. He again looked green in the preliminaries and through the first half of the race. There was a fair bit to like about the manner in which he stayed on after straightening for home, however, and this good-looking colt is one to keep an eye on.
Search For The Key(USA) has a US pedigree and it looked a good move switching him to this surface. He proved one-paced when asked for his effort, though, and his Group-race entries are clearly far too ambitious as he looks just modest. The step up a furlong ought to help his cause, however. (op 13-2 tchd 8-1)
Banged Up Abroad(IRE) Official explanation: jockey said colt jumped left from stalls

5779 DIGIBET CLAIMING STKS — 1m (P)
7:50 (7:50) (Class 6) 3-Y-0+ — £2,047 (£604; £302) Stalls High

Form			Horse	Jockey	RPR
0035	1		**Millfield (IRE)**[22] 5124 6-9-8 66 (P R Chamings) *hld up in rr: stdy hdwy over 2f out: str run between horses wl ins fnl f to ld cl home* **15/2**	GeorgeBaker 12	74
2005	2	½	**Dichoh**[33] 4731 6-9-4 70 (v) (M Madgwick) *in tch: hdwy over 2f out: styd on u.p to chal wl ins fnl f and upsides tl no ex cl home* **25/1**	AdamKirby 2	69
1135	3	shd	**Diggeratt (USA)**[10] 5465 3-8-6 72 (p) (R A Fahey) *chsd ldrs: rdn over 2f out: styd on to chal ins fnl f: slt advantage fnl 25yds: hdd and no ex cl home* **3/1**[2]	PaulHanagan 11	62
1251	4	½	**Royal Dignitary (USA)**[10] 5465 9-9-12 85 (D Nicholls) *led: rdn and kpt on whn strly chal fr over 1f out: narrowly hdd fnl 25yds and no ex cl home* **5/2**[1]	AdrianTNicholls 9	76
3100	5	2½	**Captain Jacksparra (IRE)**[23] 5107 5-9-4 78 (K A Ryan) *chsd ldrs: rdn and hung lft wl over 1f out: styd on same pce fnl f* **4/1**[3]	DarryllHolland 3	62
0040	6	2½	**Shake On It**[20] 4305 5-8-5 54 (M R Hoad) *in rr: rdn along towards outside 3f out: mod prog fnl f* **66/1**	AndreaAtzeni(3) 6	46
0	7	1	**Mississippian (IRE)**[44] 4378 5-8-8 70 (C J Mann) *in tch: rdn 3f out: effrt to chse ldrs over 2f out: nvr in contention: wknd sn after* **8/1**	HayleyTurner 10	44
0056	8	1¼	**Double Valentine**[128] 1728 6-8-7 52 (R Ingram) *in rr: rdn 3f out: mod prog fnl f* **25/1**	KirstyMilczarek 8	40
5630	9	nk	**Takitwo**[35] 4645 6-8-8 57 (P D Cundell) *in rr tl styd on fnl 2f* **20/1**	ChrisCatlin 7	40
000	10	½	**Whispered Lands (IRE)**[51] 4145 3-8-2 47 (J R Boyle) *chsd ldrs: rdn 3f out: sn btn* **100/1**	NickyMackay 4	38
1003	11	5	**Pressing Matters (IRE)**[12] 5403 3-9-3 72 (p) (M Botti) *chsd ldrs tl hung rt and nt run on over 2f out* **10/1**	TedDurcan 5	42

1m 38.86s (-0.94) **Going Correction** -0.10s/f (Stan)
WFA 3 from 5yo+ 5lb — **11** Ran SP% **120.5**
Speed ratings (Par 101): **100,99,99,98,96 93,92,91,91,90 85**
toteswinger: 1&2 £32.00, 1&3 £8.00, 2&3 £14.90. CSF £184.04 TOTE £9.70: £2.10, £4.60, £1.50; EX 146.10.
Owner Inhurst Players **Bred** Limestone Stud **Trained** Baughurst, Hants

FOCUS
An ordinary claimer, run at a solid pace. Probably not form to take too positively.

5780 DIGIBET H'CAP — 1m (P)
8:20 (8:20) (Class 5) (0-75,82) 3-Y-0+ — £2,590 (£770; £385; £192) Stalls High

Form			Horse	Jockey	RPR
	1		**Miss Minnies (IRE)**[25] 5047 3-9-0 73 (David P Myerscough, Ire) *trckd ldrs: gng wl whn nt clr run appr fnl 2f: drvn and qckned to ld appr fnl f: sn clr: comf* **10/1**[3]	JoeFanning 8	84+
6211	2	2½	**The Scorching Wind (IRE)**[4] 5665 3-9-6 82 12ex (t) (S C Williams) *stdd into mid-div: stdy hdwy on outside over 2f out and styd on wl fr over 1f out to chse wnr ins fnl f but a comf hld* **8/13**[1]	WilliamCarson(3) 6	85
0006	3	2½	**Fiefdom (IRE)**[1] 5753 7-9-3 71 (I W McInnes) *in tch: rdn over 2f out: styd on wl fnl f but nvr gng pce to trble ldng duo* **25/1**	PaulHanagan 11	68
1022	4	shd	**Forbidden (IRE)**[34] 4724 6-9-3 71 (t) (Daniel Mark Loughnane, Ire) *in rr: pushed along and hung rt over 2f out: styd on wl fr over 1f out to take 4th cl home but nvr a threat* **25/1**	ShaneKelly 2	68
00-4	5	½	**Penchesco (IRE)**[182] 807 4-9-4 72 (Pat Eddery) *chsd ldrs: rdn to ld 2f out: hdd appr fnl f: sn btn* **20/1**	PaulEddery 1	68+
-600	6	hd	**Regional Counsel**[83] 3055 5-8-13 72 (A M Hales) *towards rr: rdn over 2f out: styd on fnl f but nvr in contention* **33/1**	MartinLane(5) 14	67
3602	7	½	**Gazboolou**[23] 5107 5-9-7 75 (David Pinder) *chsd ldrs: rdn over 2f out: wknd fnl f* **20/1**	FergusSweeney 4	69
2223	8	½	**Eastern Gift**[9] 5511 4-9-7 75 (Miss Gay Kelleway) *chsd ldrs: rdn over 2f out: wknd over 1f out* **15/2**[2]	GeorgeBaker 9	68
1264	9	½	**Chief Exec**[23] 5107 7-9-5 73 (b) (J R Gask) *in rr: rdn over 2f out: sme prog fnl f* **10/1**[3]	LukeMorris 10	64
4600	10	1¼	**Minority Report**[43] 4400 9-8-10 69 (K A Ryan) *s.i.s: a towards rr* **33/1**	AmyRyan(5) 3	57
1600	11	3¾	**April Fool**[35] 4641 5-9-1 69 (v) (J A Geake) *chsd ldrs over 5f* **25/1**	RichardThomas 7	48
2300	12	1	**Toolentidhaar (USA)**[11] 5449 5-9-3 71 (Andrew Turnell) *sn led: hdd & wknd 2f out* **50/1**	HayleyTurner 5	48
5130	13	½	**My Shadow**[49] 4211 4-9-6 74 (S Dow) *in rr: sme hdwy on ins 2f out: sn btn* **20/1**	DarryllHolland 12	50

1m 37.95s (-1.85) **Going Correction** -0.10s/f (Stan)
WFA 3 from 4yo+ 5lb — **13** Ran SP% **125.5**
Speed ratings (Par 103): **105,102,100,99,99 99,98,98,97,96 92,91,91**
toteswinger: 1&2 £2.20, 1&3 £41.00, 2&3 £6.20. CSF £15.39 CT £186.06 TOTE £6.80: £2.10, £1.10, £5.80; EX 22.00.
Owner David Kelly **Bred** Sean O'Gorman **Trained** Newbridge, Co Kildare

FOCUS
A fair handicap. The winner appears progressive but the well-in favourite disappointed. The form is rated around the third.
Chief Exec Official explanation: jockey said gelding was never travelling
My Shadow Official explanation: jockey said gelding hung right

5781 KIA SOUL, SAFE BET H'CAP — 1m 4f (P)
8:50 (8:50) (Class 4) (0-85,85) 3-Y-0+ — £4,727 (£1,406; £702; £351) Stalls Centre

Form			Horse	Jockey	RPR
251	1		**Ottoman Empire (FR)**[30] 4838 3-9-3 85 (D R Lanigan) *hld up trcking ldrs: led 2f out: edgd rt to far rail and styd on u.p fnl f* **5/4**[1]	TedDurcan 4	92+
4333	2	hd	**Phoenix Flight (IRE)**[23] 5097 4-9-7 80 (p) (H J Evans) *in rr: hdwy 2f out: sn hung rt and swtchd lft: str run appr fnl f and fin wl to take 2nd cl home but nt rch wnr* **8/1**	SebSanders 5	87
5342	3	1	**Can Can Star**[11] 5448 6-9-1 81 (A W Carroll) *chsd ldrs: rdn: swtchd lft and hdwy 2f out: chsd wnr fnl f: kpt on but no imp: lost 2nd cl home* **10/1**	DebraEngland(7) 9	86
5601	4	6	**Herrera (IRE)**[21] 5162 4-8-10 69 (R A Fahey) *in rr: rdn 3f out: styd on fr 2f out to take mod 4th fnl f* **25/1**	PaulHanagan 1	64
5/50	5	1½	**Alessano**[32] 4793 7-9-7 80 (b) (G L Moore) *chsd ldr: chal over 2f out tl jst ins fnl 2f: wknd qckly fnl f* **25/1**	GeorgeBaker 3	73
5050	6	1	**Capable Guest (IRE)**[18] 5252 7-8-10 69 (M R Channon) *a towards rr* **20/1**	ChrisCatlin 2	60
24-2	7	3	**Sleepy Hollow**[9] 5509 4-9-9 82 (H Morrison) *chsd ldrs: rdn 3f out: wknd qckly over 2f out* **7/1**[3]	SteveDrowne 8	69
30/0	8	1	**Actodos (IRE)**[23] 5094 5-8-13 75 (B R Millman) *sn led: hdd & wknd qckly 2f out* **50/1**	JamesMillman(3) 7	60
51	9	3½	**Amazing Tiger (GER)**[83] 3061 3-8-11 79 (M Johnston) *plld hrd: chsd ldrs tl stdd to mid-div after 3f: rdn and effrt over 3f out: nvr rchd ldrs and wknd qckly* **4/1**[2]	JoeFanning 6	58

2m 31.77s (-2.73) **Going Correction** -0.10s/f (Stan)
WFA 3 from 4yo+ 9lb — **9** Ran SP% **111.6**
Speed ratings (Par 105): **105,104,104,100,99 98,96,95,93**
toteswinger: 1&2 £2.80, 1&3 £5.60, 2&3 £11.20. CSF £10.69 CT £66.48 TOTE £2.20: £1.10, £2.20, £2.70; EX 11.30.
Owner Plantation Stud **Bred** S C E A Haras De La Perelle **Trained** Newmarket, Suffolk
■ Stewards' Enquiry : Ted Durcan caution: excessive use of the whip

FOCUS
A fair handicap, run at a decent pace. The first three pulled clear and the form is sound, although the winner's task was eased by his market rivals disappointing.
Amazing Tiger(GER) Official explanation: jockey said colt ran too freely

5782 BOOK KEMPTON TICKETS ON 0844 579 3008 H'CAP — 1m 3f (P)
9:20 (9:21) (Class 6) (0-65,65) 3-Y-O — £2,047 (£604; £302) Stalls High

Form			Horse	Jockey	RPR
6356	1		**Ebony Eyes**[20] 5195 3-9-4 65 (W J Knight) *in tch: hdwy 2f out: styd on u.p to ld fnl 110yds: rdn out* **7/1**	JimCrowley 2	68+
	2	1	**Ghent (IRE)**[25] 5046 3-9-0 61 (p) (David P Myerscough, Ire) *in tch: hdwy over 2f out: rdn and styd on strly fnl f to chse wnr nr fin but nvr any ch* **4/1**[1]	SebSanders 7	62
0502	3	1¼	**Abulharith**[12] 5381 3-8-13 60 (R A Harris) *chsd ldr: rdn over 2f out: led wl over 1f out: hdd fnl 110yds: sn btn and lost 2nd wl ins fnl f* **16/1**	LukeMorris 1	59
0-40	4	½	**Tuppenny Piece**[34] 4722 3-8-10 60 (W R Swinburn) *towards rr: rdn and hdwy whn swtchd sharply lft 2f out: hdwy appr fnl f: fin wl but nvr a danger* **25/1**	AndreaAtzeni(3) 11	59+
605	5	hd	**Chanrossa (IRE)**[40] 4498 3-8-13 60 (E A L Dunlop) *in rr: hdwy on ins over 2f out: styd on same pce fnl f* **33/1**	TGMcLaughlin 14	57
0350	6	½	**M'Lady Rousseur (IRE)**[54] 4054 3-9-1 62 (D R C Elsworth) *in rr: hdwy whn hmpd 2f out: rcvrd and styd on again fnl f* **22/1**	DaneO'Neill 12	61+
6323	7	1½	**Jiggalong**[7] 5574 3-9-0 61 (R Ingram) *in rr: rdn over 2f out: sme prog fnl f* **6/1**[3]	ChrisCatlin 6	55
004	8	nk	**Mediterranean Sea (IRE)**[31] 4828 3-8-11 58 (J R Jenkins) *in tch: rdn and hdwy to chse ldrs over 3f out: one pce fnl 2f* **12/1**	PaulHanagan 8	51
6200	9	½	**Red Reef**[13] 5366 3-9-0 61 (D J Coakley) *sn led: hdd & wknd wl over 1f out* **14/1**	DarryllHolland 3	53
0415	10	3¼	**Bubses Boy**[22] 5131 3-8-7 59 (P Howling) *in rr: sme hdwy whn hmpd 2f out: nt rcvr* **10/1**	AshleyMorgan(5) 5	46
-006	11	½	**Refuse Toulouse (IRE)**[111] 2211 3-8-13 60 (C G Cox) *chsd ldrs: rdn over 3f out: wknd over 2f out* **10/1**	AdamKirby 10	46
	12	½	**Mallorey**[35] 4676 3-9-1 62 (t) (A M Hales) *in rr: sme hdwy on ins over 3f out: wknd 2f out* **14/1**	HayleyTurner 13	47
5506	13	1¼	**Adnams**[33] 4744 3-9-3 64 (C F Wall) *chsd ldrs: rdn 3f out: wknd over 2f out: eased whn no ch fnl f* **5/1**[2]	TedDurcan 4	47

2m 22.15s (0.25) **Going Correction** -0.10s/f (Stan) — **13** Ran SP% **119.7**
Speed ratings (Par 99): **95,94,93,93,92 92,91,91,90,88 88,87,86**
toteswinger: 1&2 £4.00, 1&3 £79.20, 2&3 £22.10. CSF £34.30 CT £442.80 TOTE £6.70: £2.60, £2.50, £4.40; EX 30.60 Place 6: £46.06, Place 5: £28.36..
Owner D G Hardisty Bloodstock **Bred** D G Hardisty Bloodstock **Trained** Patching, W Sussex

FOCUS
This weak handicap was a race in which it paid to race handily and the form is sound but limited, rated around the placed horses.

T/Plt: £85.40 to a £1 stake. Pool: £62,954.16. 537.90 winning tickets. T/Qpdt: £51.40 to a £1 stake. Pool: £6,110.88. 87.90 winning tickets. ST

NANCY

Wednesday, September 9

OFFICIAL GOING: Good

5783a PRIX RENAULT NANCY (MAIDEN) 1m 1f 165y

2:10 (2:16) 3-Y-O **£9,223** (£3,689; £2,767; £1,845; £922)

RPR

1 **Happy Wedding (IRE)**[113] 3-8-13 .... FVeron 85
(H-A Pantall, France)

2 *1* **Double Handful (GER)**[31] 3-9-2 .... KKerekes 86
(M Figge, Germany)

3 *1 1/2* **Silver Lady (FR)**[43] 3-8-13 .... CSoumillon 80
(J-P Carvalho, Germany)

4 *1 1/2* **Al Batal (FR)**[21] 3-9-2 80
(W Baltromei, Germany)

5 *2* **Dame Anouska (IRE)**[32] 4810 3-8-13 .... JAuge 73
(E J O'Neill) *cl up on ins: pushed along and dropped bk to 5th 2f out: kpt on same pce fnl 1 1/2f* **13/2**[1]

6 *1 1/2* **Limurn (IRE)**[33] 3-8-13 ....(b) 70
(D Sepulchre, France)

7 *3/4* **Unavita (GER)**[41] 3-8-13 68
(H Blume, Germany)

8 *1 1/2* **Luciole (FR)**[186] 3-8-13 65
(Mme G Matter, France)

9 *1/2* **Biarritz (FR)** 3-8-13 64
(H Steinmetz, Germany)

10 *hd* **Everyday (FR)** 3-9-2 67
(F Wintz, France)

0 **Sagawest (FR)**[127] 3-9-2 .... —
(Ecurie Saint Simeon, Belgium)

0 **Salza Du Moulin (FR)** 3-8-13 .... —
(F Meckes, France)

0 **Antara Rose (GER)** 3-8-13 .... —
(W Hefter, Germany)

2m 2.53s (122.53) **13** Ran SP% **13.3**
PARI-MUTUEL (including 1 Euro stake): WIN 4.30; PL 1.50, 1.40, 2.00; DF 5.00.
Owner Mlle I Pantall **Bred** Newsells Park Stud Ltd **Trained** France

NOTEBOOK
Dame Anouska(IRE), who ran well on softer ground at Saint-Malo last time, could not build on this and looks a little short of gears.

5784a PRIX DE LA COMMUNAUTE URBAINE DU GRAND NANCY (CLAIMER) 1m 4f

3:40 (3:45) 3-Y-O **£6,796** (£2,718; £2,039; £1,359; £680)

RPR

1 **Black Law (FR)** 3-9-4 .... DBonilla 70
(R Rohne, Germany)

2 *1/2* **Shingara (IRE)** 3-8-8 .... GMasure 59
(W Hefter, Germany)

3 *1 1/2* **Bryman (FR)** 3-9-4 ....(b) FBlondel 67
(C Aubert, France)

4 *2* **Lilly Gold (FR)**[67] 3-9-1 ....(b) 61
(Mlle S-V Tarrou, France)

5 *3/4* **Golden Chance (FR)** 3-8-8 52
(P Lefevre, France)

6 *1* **Victorian Tycoon (IRE)**[18] 5278 3-9-1 .... JAuge 58
(E J O'Neill) *midfield: pushed along 2f out: plugged on at same pce* **7/2**[1]

7 *1 1/2* **Finja (GER)**[29] 3-9-1 55
(T Clout, France)

8 *nk* **A Votre Sante (GER)**[96] 3-8-8 48
(W Baltromei, Germany)

9 *2* **Rousseau (FR)** 3-9-4 ....(p) 55
(Frau C Bocskai, Switzerland)

10 *1* **Amneris (FR)** 3-8-11 46
(A Blanpin, France)

0 **King Goldenfort (IRE)**[35] 3-8-11 ....(b) —
(J Van Handenhove, France)

0 **Stormy Blues (FR)**[43] 3-9-1 ....(b) —
(P Munsch, France)

0 **Amuseur (FR)** 3-8-11 ....(p) —
(P Lefevre, France)

R **Burlada**[66] 3-8-11 .... —
(C Laffon-Parias, France)

U **Takounba (FR)** 3-8-11 .... —
(J Schiestel Fils, France)

2m 36.79s (156.79) **15** Ran SP% **22.2**
PARI-MUTUEL: WIN 8.90; PL 2.80, 2.40, 3.20; DF 29.50.
Owner C Thiriet **Bred** C Thiriet **Trained** Germany

NOTEBOOK
Victorian Tycoon(IRE), who handles a sound surface and ran well enough on Polytrack at Deauville last time, could not quicken up this time on ground he should handle.

5627 CHEPSTOW (L-H)

Thursday, September 10

OFFICIAL GOING: Good (good to firm in places; 8.7)

Wind: Light behind Weather: Sunny

5785 E.B.F./BETPASS.CO.UK ONE ACCOUNT, MULTIPLE BETTING SERVICE MAIDEN STKS (DIV I) 7f 16y

1:50 (1:51) (Class 5) 2-Y-O **£3,561** (£1,059; £529; £264) **Stalls** High

Form RPR

1 **Hunting Tartan** 2-9-3 0 .... RobertHavlin 4 87+
(J H M Gosden) *sn hld up in tch: led jst over 2f out: pushed clr ins fnl f: readily* **11/4**[2]

2 *3 1/4* **Forest Runner** 2-9-3 0 .... DO'Donohoe 9 75+
(Saeed Bin Suroor) *s.i.s: hdwy over 5f out: ev ch over 2f out: one pce appr fnl f* **9/1**

3 *4* **Yabtree (IRE)** 2-9-3 0 .... JimCrowley 10 64
(R Charlton) *racd sltly detached on stands' rail: w ldr: led over 3f out tl jst over 2f out: wknd over 1f out* **12/1**

62 4 *1/2* **Lava Lamp (GER)**[23] 5129 2-9-3 0 .... J-PGuillambert 8 63
(M Johnston) *hdwy over 5f out: pushed along 3f out: sn wknd* **7/4**[1]

0 5 *1* **Seaside Sizzler**[13] 5400 2-9-3 0 .... RichardKingscote 7 62+
(R M Beckett) *prom: lost pl over 4f out: pushed along and no hdwy fnl 2f* **7/2**[3]

00 6 *hd* **Red Eddie**[20] 5220 2-9-3 0 .... DaneO'Neill 2 60
(B J Meehan) *hld up in mid-div: rdn and wknd over 2f out* **50/1**

7 *1* **Goodison Goal (IRE)** 2-8-5 0 .... JamesPSullivan(7) 5 52+
(Patrick Morris) *dwlt: nvr nr ldrs* **50/1**

8 *hd* **Apache Kid (IRE)** 2-9-0 0 .... JamesMillman(3) 11 57
(B R Millman) *bhd fnl 5f* **22/1**

0 9 *3* **Dauntsey Park (IRE)**[45] 4377 2-9-3 0 .... JamesDoyle 6 49
(Miss Tor Sturgis) *led: hdd over 3f out: wknd over 2f out* **100/1**

10 *7* **Wavertree Bounty** 2-8-12 0 .... LiamJones 1 27
(C F Wall) *a in rr* **50/1**

0 11 *1 3/4* **Mr Maximas**[10] 5499 2-9-3 0 ....(p) NeilChalmers 3 27
(B Palling) *bhd: rdn wl over 2f out: sn struggling* **100/1**

1m 22.78s (-0.42) **Going Correction** -0.275s/f (Firm) **11** Ran SP% **115.2**
Speed ratings (Par 95): **91,87,82,82,81 80,79,79,75,67 65**
toteswinger: 1&2 £4.90, 1&3 £7.50, 2&3 £7.70. CSF £25.53 TOTE £3.50: £1.50, £2.50, £3.40; EX 19.10.
Owner K Abdulla **Bred** Juddmonte Farms Ltd **Trained** Newmarket, Suffolk

FOCUS
A good maiden for the track, made more interesting by a clutch of well-bred newcomers. The winner was impressive and the first two were clear.

NOTEBOOK
Hunting Tartan is well-related, being by Oasis Dream out of mare successful twice over 1m and, as this is the time of year when his trainer usually starts to unveil his better two-year-olds, he had to be worth a look in the market. He was well-supported and, as the betting suggested would be the case, he was thoroughly professional in the race, taking a prominent position from the start and then quickening up impressively at the 2f pole before going on to a decisive success. (op 9-2)
Forest Runner, a choicely-bred debutant who cost 240,000gns, represented a yard with a strong team of juveniles and, given that many of those to have run this season were sharp enough to collect first time out, he had to be respected. He performed creditably, chasing the pace from the start before keeping the winner honest in the closing stages, and it does not take a great deal of imagination to picture him breaking his duck before too long. (op 15-2)
Yabtree(IRE), another newcomer, raced virtually alone up the stands' rail, but that did not seem to inhibit his effort, as he was always in the vanguard and stayed on well enough in the closing stages to suggest he can find a suitable opening at some stage. (op 10-1)
Lava Lamp(GER) set to the standard, based on his third over 6f at Nottingham just over three weeks previously, but the level he had reached there suggested he might well be vulnerable to an unraced or less-exposed rival. So it proved and, although he did nothing obviously wrong, he simply did not have sufficient speed to cope with the first three. (op 5-4)
Seaside Sizzler had shown some promise on his debut, finishing in mid-division in a Newmarket maiden over this trip, and, with his stable enjoying a good run in recent days, following a quieter spell, there were reasons for expecting improvement. Some was forthcoming, too, and he was staying on well enough in the closing stages to suggest a longer trip will suit him, but he will almost certainly need to progress again in order to score in an event of this type. (op 9-2)
Red Eddie appeared to have taken a step forward from his first to second starts, despite finishing last of 11, and, although that run seemed to leave him with a bit to find against some of these, more progression could not be discounted. He probably did take another step forward, even if it was nothing like enough for him to trouble those ahead of him, and he should be able to make some sort of mark now that he is qualified for nurseries. (op 66-1 tchd 40-1)

5786 E.B.F./BETPASS.CO.UK ONE ACCOUNT, MULTIPLE BETTING SERVICE MAIDEN STKS (DIV II) 7f 16y

2:20 (2:20) (Class 5) 2-Y-O **£3,561** (£1,059; £529; £264) **Stalls** High

Form RPR

6 1 **Guest Book (IRE)**[12] 5431 2-9-3 0 .... J-PGuillambert 8 81+
(M Johnston) *a.p: led over 2f out: rdn over 1f out: rn green wl ins fnl f: kpt on* **15/8**[1]

05 2 *1/2* **Viking Dancer**[20] 5220 2-9-3 0 .... NeilChalmers 10 80
(A M Balding) *hld up: hdwy over 3f out: ev ch over 2f out: rdn and kpt on ins fnl f* **14/1**

0 3 *2 1/2* **Old Money**[24] 5096 2-8-12 0 .... JamesDoyle 2 69
(H J L Dunlop) *w ldr: led over 3f out: rdn and hdd over 2f out: kpt on same pce fnl f* **40/1**

52 4 *hd* **Onyx Of Arabia (IRE)**[35] 4699 2-9-3 0 .... DaneO'Neill 3 73
(B J Meehan) *a.p: rdn jst over 2f out: one pce fnl f* **11/4**[2]

5 5 *1* **Kajima**[74] 3420 2-9-3 0 .... JimCrowley 1 71
(R Hannon) *hld up in tch: rdn over 2f out: one pce fnl f* **7/2**[3]

6 *2 3/4* **Graymalkin (IRE)** 2-9-3 0 .... DO'Donohoe 4 69+
(Saeed Bin Suroor) *hld up and bhd: rdn over 3f out: nvr trbld ldrs* **8/1**

00 7 *20* **Knowledgeable**[9] 5542 2-9-3 0 .... LukeMorris 9 14
(B Palling) *hld up in mid-div: rdn and struggling over 3f out* **100/1**

3 8 *2 1/2* **Saint Thomas (IRE)**[35] 4693 2-9-3 0 .... SamHitchcott 6 7
(J A Osborne) *bhd: pushed along over 3f out: no ch fnl 2f* **11/1**

0 9 *3* **Typical Female**[36] 4646 2-8-12 0 .... RobertHavlin 7 —
(A B Haynes) *led: hdd over 3f out: wknd wl over 2f out* **100/1**

063 10 *23* **Tiger Hawk (USA)**[29] 4915 2-9-3 51 .... StephenDonohoe 5 —
(K M Prendergast) *s.i.s: a struggling in rr* **100/1**

1m 21.5s (-1.70) **Going Correction** -0.275s/f (Firm) **10** Ran SP% **115.2**
Speed ratings (Par 95): **98,97,94,94,93 90,67,64,60,34**
toteswinger: 1&2 £13.00, 1&3 £47.80, 2&3 £47.80. CSF £30.29 TOTE £2.50: £1.10, £3.20, £8.30; EX 39.90.
Owner Sheikh Hamdan Bin Mohammed Al Maktoum **Bred** Darley **Trained** Middleham Moor, N Yorks

FOCUS
There was more strength in depth in this second division, at least among those with experience, and a handful of runners had shown enough to suggest they possessed what it takes to notch a maiden-race victory. The winner built on his debut, with the sixth capable of better.

NOTEBOOK
Guest Book(IRE) had shown promise first time out, staying on nicely for sixth after finding himself outpaced in a decent 6f Newmarket maiden, and his pedigree indicated the step up in distance should be no problem. He certainly did stay the trip well enough, grinding his rivals down rather than beating them for speed, but he still looked green in the closing stages, wandering slightly under pressure and needing plenty of encouragement to cope with the track's undulations. (op 5-2 tchd 7-4)
Viking Dancer had established a fair level of form on his two previous starts, improving second time out to take fifth of 11 at Sandown, and he appeared to progress again here, battling on well without seriously threatening the winner. (op 12-1 tchd 11-1 and 20-1)
Old Money lost any chance she might have had on her debut by forfeiting ground at the start, but she broke markedly better this time, actually leading in mid-race and, not surprisingly, she showed significantly better form here. (op 50-1)

Onyx Of Arabia(IRE), whose dam was a prolific winner at this sort of distance, came here with solid form, having made a sound debut and then filled second spot in a fair maiden over this trip at Folkestone five weeks previously. He was never too far away, although unable to muster sufficient pace in the closing stages to promise a first victory, although he is probably the best guide to the form. (tchd 5-2 and 7-2)
Kajima fluffed the start on his debut in a Salisbury maiden in June, eventually finishing fifth of seven after attracting support, but runners from his stable have frequently shown improved form after their introduction and a smart pedigree made him of further interest. He ran a fair race, if not necessarily taking a giant leap forward, and he should eventually make an impact in handicaps. (op 11-4 tchd 5-2 and 4-1)
Graymalkin(IRE), by Singspiel out of a mare who was Listed placed over 7f as a three-year-old, is bred to appreciate longer distances in time but, with his stable going so well at present, his appeal in this event was obvious. He was outpaced when the pace quickened 2f out though and, while he came home in pleasing style, he will almost certainly need further, or perhaps a winter's maturity, before fulfilling any potential he possesses. (op 12-1)
Saint Thomas(IRE) Official explanation: jockey said colt lost its action

5787 BETPASS.CO.UK ALL BOOKMAKERS MEDIAN AUCTION MAIDEN STKS — 1m 14y

2:55 (2:56) (Class 5) 2-Y-O — **£2,590** (£770; £385; £192) **Stalls** High

Form				RPR
5	**1**		**Higgy's Ragazzo (FR)**[10] 5499 2-9-3 0 .... JimCrowley 11	77+
			(R Hannon) *dwlt: hdwy over 5f out: edgd lft and rdn 2f out: led 1f out: r.o* **15/8**[1]	
0	**2**	*1*	**First In The Queue (IRE)**[10] 5499 2-9-3 0 .... JamesDoyle 10	73
			(S Kirk) *s.i.s: sn hld up in mid-div: pushed along and hdwy 3f out: rdn and hung lft 2f out: r.o ins fnl f: tk 2nd towards fin* **16/1**	
5234	**3**	*1*	**Interakt**[10] 5505 2-8-12 74 .... SamHitchcott 1	66
			(M R Channon) *led: hdd over 5f out: a.p: rdn and ev ch over 1f out: nt qckn ins fnl f* **4/1**[2]	
0432	**4**	*1 ½*	**Edgewater (IRE)**[14] 5369 2-9-3 77 .... DaneO'Neill 13	71+
			(B J Meehan) *a.p: led on stands' rail over 5f out: rdn 2f out: hdd 1f out: hld whn faltered towards fin* **9/2**[3]	
	5	*nk*	**Ipswich Lad** 2-9-3 0 .... NeilChalmers 14	69+
			(A M Balding) *s.s: in rr: pushed along and sme hdwy 3f out: sn outpcd: rdn over 1f out: styd on fnl f* **16/1**	
0	**6**	*7*	**Mr Harmoosh (IRE)**[13] 5400 2-8-12 0 .... JPHamblett(5) 6	52
			(E F Vaughan) *t.k.h: prom: rdn and wknd 2f out* **20/1**	
0	**7**	*2*	**Lauberhorn**[45] 4385 2-9-3 0 .... LukeMorris 7	48
			(Eve Johnson Houghton) *prom tl pushed along and wknd wl over 2f out* **100/1**	
	8	*nk*	**Architrave** 2-9-3 0 .... StephenDonohoe 5	52+
			(Sir Mark Prescott) *dwlt: in rr: sme prog over 2f out: nvr nr ldrs* **14/1**	
	9	*3 ½*	**Katchmore (IRE)** 2-8-12 0 .... SophieDoyle(5) 8	40
			(Jean-Rene Auvray) *dwlt: t.k.h in mid-div: pushed along 3f out: sn wknd* **66/1**	
	10	*4 ½*	**Persian Poet** 2-9-3 0 .... J-PGuillambert 2	31
			(M Johnston) *prom: pushed along over 4f out: wknd over 3f out* **7/1**	
	11	*½*	**Dubai Phantom (USA)** 2-9-3 0 .... (b[1]) RobertHavlin 4	30
			(D M Simcock) *dwlt: a in rr* **25/1**	
0	**12**	*3*	**Cuckoo Rock (IRE)**[50] 4209 2-9-3 0 .... SaleemGolam 3	23
			(J G Portman) *a towards rr* **100/1**	
0	**13**	*35*	**Bahamian Sun (IRE)**[40] 4515 2-9-3 0 .... (t) RichardKingscote 9	—
			(Tom Dascombe) *prom tl rdn and wknd over 2f out: eased whn no ch over 1f out* **40/1**	

1m 35.26s (-0.94) **Going Correction** -0.275s/f (Firm) **13 Ran SP% 118.4**
Speed ratings (Par 95): **93,92,91,89,89 82,80,79,76,71 71,68,33**
toteswinger: 1&2 £15.10, 1&3 £4.90, 2&3 £19.00. CSF £34.58 TOTE £3.00: £1.40, £5.50, £1.40; EX 34.90.
Owner I Higginson **Bred** Thierry Grandsir & Patrick Bruneau **Trained** East Everleigh, Wilts

FOCUS
None of those with previous form set an especially exacting standard, but a small of group of newcomers added spice to what, on paper, looked no more than a run-of-the-mill maiden. The form is fair, rated around the third and fourth.

NOTEBOOK
Higgy's Ragazzo(FR) had not fared too badly on his only previous outing, finishing fifth over this course and distance and, given the methods employed by his trainer, improvement seemed highly likely. He was well backed, suggesting progress was confidently expected, and he duly found it, running out a decisive winner after taking a prominent position from the outset. (op 5-2 tchd 11-4 in places)
First In The Queue(IRE) ◆, behind the winner of this race when a slow-starting 66-1 shot on his debut, got a great deal closer this time, staying on in eye-catching style in the closing stages and, while the form of this event is nothing out of the ordinary, he looks capable of going one better in the near future.
Interakt had already had four attempts at breaking her duck, doing best when second over 7f at Epsom in July and, as her profile did not suggest she was making progress, her supporters had to hope the extra distance would make a difference. It probably did too, as, after leading for much of the race, she stayed on well and, despite her lengthening sequence of losing runs, she seems to have a sound-enough attitude. (tchd 9-2)
Edgewater(IRE) lined up with an official rating of 77, but that appeared to flatter him, as he had been beaten five lengths when second off 75 in an all-weather nursery on his latest outing. He ran a solid race, figuring prominently from the start, but he is beginning to look exposed and is likely to remain vulnerable to more progressive rivals. Official explanation: jockey said gelding ducked sharply right inside the final furlong. (op 4-1 tchd 7-2)
Ipswich Lad, a previously-unraced son of Halling out of a mare who stayed 1m1f, was outpaced in the early stages, but stayed on encouragingly in the second half of the contest and should do better next season, when able to race over markedly longer trips.
Architrave was another debutant to make late progress, in his case after a running green in the first couple of furlongs and, given his trainer's patient approach, this gelded son of Hernando seems likely to improve with time. (op 16-1)
Dubai Phantom(USA) Official explanation: jockey said colt stumbled after a furlong and a half
Bahamian Sun(IRE) Official explanation: jockey said gelding had a breathing problem

5788 BETPASS.CO.UK TELEPHONE BETTING CLAIMING STKS — 6f 16y

3:30 (3:31) (Class 6) 3-Y-O+ — **£1,942** (£578; £288; £144) **Stalls** High

Form				RPR
543	**1**		**Who's Winning (IRE)**[8] 5566 8-8-5 49 .... (t) KirstyMilczarek 5	59
			(B G Powell) *broke wl: led 1f: a.p: pushed along over 2f out: rdn to ld ins fnl f: drvn out* **16/1**	
3420	**2**	*¾*	**Dressed To Dance (IRE)**[23] 5120 5-8-10 72 .... (v) LukeMorris 11	62
			(R A Harris) *s.i.s: hld up and bhd: hdwy on stands' rail over 2f out: rdn and ev ch 1f out: kpt on* **2/1**[1]	
2260	**3**	*¾*	**Interactive (IRE)**[130] 1710 6-8-9 57 .... RichardKingscote 1	58
			(Andrew Turnell) *led after 1f: hrd rdn over 1f out: hdd ins fnl f: nt qckn* **11/2**[2]	
40	**4**	*nk*	**Castano**[43] 4428 5-8-7 57 .... (p) RichardSmith 10	55
			(B R Millman) *hld up and bhd: rdn and hdwy whn nt clr run over 1f out: swtchd lft ins fnl f: nvr able to chal* **14/1**	
0614	**5**	*½*	**Outer Hebrides**[6] 5632 8-8-4 54 .... (v) SophieDoyle(5) 4	56
			(J M Bradley) *a.p: rdn over 1f out: one pce ins fnl f* **7/1**[3]	
6665	**6**	*½*	**Harrison's Flyer (IRE)**[6] 5632 8-8-5 45 .... (p) KevinGhunowa 2	50
			(J M Bradley) *hld up in tch: rdn over 1f out: one pce ins fnl f* **20/1**	
0404	**7**	*1 ¼*	**Gift Horse**[8] 5565 9-8-5 70 .... (p) SamHitchcott 3	46
			(P D Evans) *bhd: pushed along 3f out: hrd rdn 2f out: nvr trbld ldrs* **2/1**[1]	
0006	**8**	*hd*	**Supreme Speedster**[6] 5633 5-8-5 45 .... RichardThomas 7	45
			(A G Newcombe) *s.i.s: hld up: pushed along and no hdwy fnl 2f* **33/1**	
/60-	**9**	*3*	**Lord Orpen (IRE)**[585] 415 5-7-12 38 .... (v) JamesPSullivan(7) 6	36
			(Patrick Morris) *bhd fnl 3f* **66/1**	
0500	**10**	*nse*	**Nordic Light (USA)**[15] 5345 5-8-5 40 .... (bt) SaleemGolam 8	36
			(J M Bradley) *w ldrs tl rdn and wknd wl over 1f out* **66/1**	

1m 10.68s (-1.32) **Going Correction** -0.275s/f (Firm) **10 Ran SP% 117.8**
Speed ratings (Par 101): **97,96,95,94,93 93,91,91,87,87**
toteswinger: 1&2 £3.50, 1&3 £32.10, 2&3 £3.40. CSF £47.94 TOTE £11.40: £7.70, £4.00, £5.90; EX 69.00.Gift Horse was claimed by David Nicholls for £5,000
Owner Miss Anna Bucknall **Bred** Colin Kennedy **Trained** Upper Lambourn, Berks

FOCUS
As is often the case in claimers, a handful of runners appeared to have obvious chances of getting involved, while the remainder looked out of their depth. The winner ran to his form of last winter and the form appears fairly sound for the grade.
Gift Horse Official explanation: jockey said gelding was never travelling.

5789 BETPASS.CO.UK FREE MEMBERSHIP MAIDEN FILLIES' STKS — 7f 16y

4:05 (4:06) (Class 5) 3-Y-O — **£2,590** (£770; £385; £192) **Stalls** High

Form				RPR
6	**1**		**Diktat Queen**[109] 2298 3-9-0 0 .... SaleemGolam 9	75
			(Rae Guest) *s.i.s: sn hld up in mid-div: hdwy and pushed along over 3f out: rdn over 1f out: led cl home: r.o* **10/1**	
2	**2**	*nk*	**Bended Knee**[19] 5242 3-9-0 0 .... DaneO'Neill 8	74
			(H Candy) *sn led: rdn over 1f out: hdd cl home* **8/11**[1]	
4020	**3**	*4 ½*	**Izzi Mill (USA)**[88] 2949 3-9-0 72 .... PaulEddery 2	62
			(D R C Elsworth) *led early: chsd ldr: rdn and lost 2nd jst over 1f out: wknd ins fnl f* **17/2**[3]	
050	**4**	*4*	**Jewelled Reef (IRE)**[10] 5502 3-9-0 58 .... LukeMorris 7	51
			(Eve Johnson Houghton) *n.m.r s: hld up towards rr: stdy hdwy over 3f out: rdn and wknd over 1f out* **16/1**	
0-0	**5**	*6*	**Rumramah (USA)**[21] 5193 3-9-0 0 .... KirstyMilczarek 11	35
			(D M Simcock) *s.i.s: hld up in rr: short-lived effrt on stands' rail over 2f out* **20/1**	
00	**6**	*2*	**Rebel Woman**[51] 4164 3-9-0 0 .... SamHitchcott 6	25
			(J A Osborne) *prom tl wknd wl over 2f out: fin 7th: plcd 6th* **33/1**	
00-5	**7**	*7*	**Lady Meg (IRE)**[15] 5348 3-9-0 40 .... NeilChalmers 10	7
			(B Palling) *prom tl wknd 3f out: fin 8th: plcd 7th* **100/1**	
-403	**8**	*¾*	**Casting Couch (IRE)**[21] 5181 3-9-0 68 .... JimCrowley 5	5
			(B W Hills) *sn bhd: fin 9th: plcd 8th* **11/2**[2]	
6-0	**9**	*3 ¾*	**Anasy (USA)**[21] 5193 3-9-0 0 .... LiamJones 3	—
			(T Keddy) *hld up in tch: rdn and wknd 3f out: fin 10th: plcd 9th* **80/1**	
5	**10**	*½*	**Bahamian Mouse (IRE)**[28] 4947 3-9-0 0 .... RichardKingscote 13	—
			(Andrew Turnell) *a bhd: fin 11th: plcd 10th* **50/1**	
00-0	**11**	*3 ½*	**Welsh Passion**[31] 4854 3-9-0 25 .... FrankieMcDonald 4	—
			(D Haydn Jones) *sn bhd: fin 12th: plcd 11th* **100/1**	
U55	**D**	*1 ¼*	**Louise Sauvage**[21] 5193 3-9-0 0 .... RichardThomas 12	31
			(M D I Usher) *hld up in mid-div: lost pl over 4f out: rdn and short-lived effrt 2f out: fin 6th: disq: rdr carried wrong weight* **25/1**	

1m 21.53s (-1.67) **Going Correction** -0.275s/f (Firm) **12 Ran SP% 115.5**
Speed ratings (Par 98): **98,97,92,87,81 77,69,68,64,63 59,79**
toteswinger: 1&2 £3.50, 1&3 £14.30, 2&3 £3.70. CSF £16.56 TOTE £8.30: £2.10, £1.10, £2.00; EX 25.10.
Owner Barry Stewart **Bred** Brook Stud Bloodstock Ltd And B Stewart **Trained** Newmarket, Suffolk

FOCUS
Not the most competitive of fillies' maidens, at least on paper, and plenty in the line-up appeared to have severely limited ability. The form is a bit fluid and is best rated at face value through the runner-up.
Casting Couch(IRE) Official explanation: jockey said filly was never travelling

5790 BETPASS.CO.UK BETTING H'CAP — 1m 2f 36y

4:40 (4:43) (Class 6) (0-55,55) 3-Y-O+ — **£2,072** (£616; £308; £153) **Stalls** Low

Form				RPR
6121	**1**		**Recalcitrant**[14] 5365 6-9-6 **55** .... SaleemGolam 13	64
			(S Dow) *a.p: wnt 2nd and pushed along 3f out: led over 2f out: rdn over 1f out: all out* **9/2**[2]	
	2	*hd*	**Coolnaharan (IRE)**[35] 1687 9-8-8 **50** .... JamesPSullivan(7) 7	58+
			(Lee Smyth, Ire) *led early: hld up in tch: lost pl on ins bnd over 5f out: hdwy on ins 3f out: rdn 2f out: r.o ins fnl f* **22/1**	
5300	**3**	*2 ½*	**Uig**[34] 4744 8-9-1 **50** .... KirstyMilczarek 14	53
			(H S Howe) *sn prom: led over 3f out: rdn and hdd over 2f out: no ex ins fnl f* **16/1**	
035	**4**	*1*	**Precious Citizen (USA)**[19] 5246 4-9-1 **50** .... LiamJones 16	51
			(J R Gask) *hld up in tch: rdn wl over 1f out: one pce fnl f* **13/2**[3]	
6004	**5**	*½*	**Blazing Buck**[28] 4934 3-8-10 **55** .... MCGeran(3) 2	57+
			(A W Carroll) *hld up towards rr: pushed along and hdwy on ins over 2f out: sn nt clr run and swtchd rt: rdn wl over 1f out: styd on ins fnl f* **20/1**	
6-00	**6**	*nk*	**Berrynarbor**[13] 5381 4-9-1 **50** .... SimonWhitworth 11	50
			(A G Newcombe) *s.i.s: hld up in rr: pushed along over 3f out: rdn and hdwy over 1f out: one pce ins fnl f* **33/1**	
4000	**7**	*2 ½*	**Rockabout (IRE)**[13] 5384 3-8-13 **55** .... DaneO'Neill 12	50
			(B J Meehan) *hld up towards rr: hdwy over 2f out: rdn wl over 1f out: eased whn no imp towards fin* **20/1**	
0536	**8**	*¾*	**Seventh Hill**[74] 3421 4-9-6 **55** .... RichardKingscote 1	48
			(M Blanshard) *hld up in tch: n.m.r briefly 3f out: sn wknd* **12/1**	
0/31	**9**	*1 ½*	**Picot De Say**[37] 4625 7-9-2 **51** .... RichardThomas 15	41+
			(C Roberts) *hld up in rr: pushed along over 2f out: n.d* **3/1**[1]	
0500	**10**	*¾*	**It's Josr**[10] 5503 4-9-4 **53** .... (be) KevinGhunowa 6	42
			(I A Wood) *sn led: rn sltly wd ent st over 4f out: sn hdd: rdn and wknd 2f out* **33/1**	
-000	**11**	*½*	**Heavenly Saint**[21] 5179 4-9-0 **54** .... SimonPearce(5) 8	42
			(C Roberts) *s.i.s: a in rr* **25/1**	
4640	**12**	*½*	**Boffin**[13] 5381 4-8-11 **49** .... RussellKennemore(3) 9	36
			(Eve Johnson Houghton) *hld up in mid-div: rdn and wknd 3f out* **16/1**	
/5-0	**13**	*1 ¾*	**No Supper (IRE)**[56] 4021 5-9-0 **49** .... TravisBlock 10	32
			(Tim Vaughan) *t.k.h: sn mid-div: rdn and hdwy 3f out: wknd wl over 1f out* **7/1**	

5460 **14** *1 1/4* **Imperium**[12] 5429 8-9-1 **55**....(p) SophieDoyle(5) 5 36
(Jean-Rene Auvray) *a towards rr* **33/1**

6035 **15** *shd* **Touch Of Style (IRE)**[26] 5015 5-9-1 **50**.... J-PGuillambert 4 30
(T D McCarthy) *prom: led over 4f out tl over 3f out: wknd wl over 2f out* **14/1**

-503 **16** *98* **Major Value**[32] 4813 3-8-13 **55**....(b[1]) LukeMorris 3 —
(C G Cox) *a bhd: rdn over 5f out: lost tch over 3f out: sn eased* **16/1**

2m 7.55s (-3.05) **Going Correction** -0.275s/f (Firm)
WFA 3 from 4yo+ 7lb **16** Ran SP% **127.6**
Speed ratings (Par 101): **101,100,98,98,97 97,95,94,93,93 92,92,90,89,89 11**
toteswinger: 1&2 £27.80, 1&3 £15.20, 2&3 £63.90. CSF £109.40 CT £1480.20 TOTE £4.70: £1.90, £5.40, £3.80, £2.40; EX 246.80.
Owner T Staplehurst **Bred** T Staplehurst **Trained** Epsom, Surrey

FOCUS
A poor handicap, with none in the line-up rated higher than 55, but it looked fairly competitive all the same. Not form to be too positive about, though.
Picot De Say Official explanation: jockey said gelding was unsuited by the good, good to firm in places ground.
Heavenly Saint Official explanation: jockey said filly jumped awkwardly from the stalls
Touch Of Style(IRE) Official explanation: trainer said gelding was unsuited by the track

5791 FREEBETS.CO.UK H'CAP — 1m 14y
5:10 (5:12) (Class 6) (0-65,66) 3-Y-O+ **£2,072** (£616; £308; £153) **Stalls** High

Form RPR

2102 **1** **Magroom**[6] 5630 5-9-6 **65**.... MCGeran(3) 4 73
(R J Hodges) *hld up in mid-div: rdn over 3f out: hdwy 2f out: led ins fnl f: edgd lft: r.o* **4/1**[1]

5121 **2** *nk* **Spring Secret**[6] 5631 3-9-5 **66** 6ex.... LukeMorris 12 72
(B Palling) *a.p: pushed along over 3f out: rdn wl over 1f out: sn edgd lft: r.o ins fnl f* **5/1**[2]

0400 **3** *1/2* **Binfield (IRE)**[64] 3736 4-9-1 **60**.... RussellKennemore(3) 15 66
(B G Powell) *a.p: rdn wl over 2f out: ev ch ins fnl f: carried lft towards fin: kpt on* **10/1**

6-56 **4** *1 3/4* **Bosamcliff (IRE)**[12] 5449 4-9-0 **61**.... RichardEvans(5) 9 63
(P D Evans) *hld up in tch: rdn over 3f out: edgd lft jst over 1f out: one pce* **8/1**[3]

0334 **5** *3/4* **Russian Angel**[27] 5013 5-8-4 **51** oh1.... SophieDoyle(5) 10 51
(Jean-Rene Auvray) *led over 6f out: hrd rdn jst over 1f out: hdd ins fnl f: fdd towards fin* **10/1**

1004 **6** *3* **Clippity Clop (IRE)**[57] 3985 3-8-13 **60**.... TravisBlock 16 52
(J A Osborne) *hld up wl in rr: pushed along over 3f out: rdn and hdwy 2f out: nvr trbld ldrs* **16/1**

4060 **7** *3/4* **Wavertree Warrior (IRE)**[40] 4533 7-8-11 **53**....(b) RichardThomas 6 45
(N P Littmoden) *towards rr: rdn wl over 2f out: nvr nr ldrs* **16/1**

06-0 **8** *1 1/4* **Dado Mush**[16] 5329 6-8-11 **53**....(p) KirstyMilczarek 14 42
(T T Clement) *hld up in mid-div: pushed along 3f out: no hdwy fnl 2f* **16/1**

0020 **9** *1/2* **Baby Josr**[8] 5582 3-8-10 **57**....(v) RichardKingscote 5 44
(I A Wood) *w ldrs: rdn over 3f out: wknd 2f out* **16/1**

-003 **10** *2 3/4* **Bidable**[10] 5502 5-8-9 **51** oh2.... NeilChalmers 3 32
(B Palling) *led over 1f: rdn and wknd wl over 2f out* **10/1**

4205 **11** *11* **Silca Meydan**[31] 4860 3-8-10 **57**.... SamHitchcott 8 12
(M R Channon) *s.i.s: a in rr* **12/1**

123 **12** *15* **Atacama Sunrise**[11] 5479 3-9-2 **63**.... DO'Donohoe 13 —
(J Pearce) *s.i.s: in rr: rdn on stands' rail over 3f out: short-lived effrt over 2f out* **5/1**[2]

1m 33.95s (-2.25) **Going Correction** -0.275s/f (Firm)
WFA 3 from 4yo+ 5lb **12** Ran SP% **122.9**
Speed ratings (Par 101): **100,99,99,97,96 93,92,91,91,88 77,62**
toteswinger: 1&2 £3.90, 1&3 £13.00, 2&3 £10.80. CSF £24.20 CT £196.41 TOTE £5.20: £2.20, £1.60, £3.70; EX 20.10.
Owner Mrs A Hart Mrs A Hodges Mrs C Penny **Bred** Mrs M Chaworth-Musters **Trained** Charlton Mackrell, Somerset

FOCUS
This looked quite a poser for punters, seemingly made all the tougher when two withdrawals reduced the field to fewer than 16 runners, thereby restricting each-way opportunities. At least half the field seemed to have place claims, but the market got it right as far as the winner was concerned and the form looks sound, with the fourth the best guide.
Dado Mush Official explanation: jockey said gelding was unsuited by the track.
Atacama Sunrise Official explanation: jockey said filly was never travelling

5792 FREEBETS.CO.UK FREE BETS H'CAP — 5f 16y
5:45 (5:46) (Class 6) (0-65,63) 3-Y-O+ **£2,072** (£616; £308; £153) **Stalls** High

Form RPR

1414 **1** **Lithaam (IRE)**[7] 5610 5-8-5 **56**....(p) RyanClark(7) 7 73
(J M Bradley) *mde all: clr over 1f out: r.o wl* **11/4**[1]

1356 **2** *4 1/2* **Bluebok**[13] 5411 8-8-12 **59**....(bt) JackDean(3) 13 60
(J M Bradley) *a.p: chsd wnr 3f out: rdn over 1f out: no imp* **12/1**

0205 **3** *1/2* **Monsieur Reynard**[10] 5504 4-8-7 **54**.... MCGeran(3) 5 53
(J M Bradley) *a.p: rdn and one pce ins fnl f* **12/1**

3200 **4** *nk* **Shakespeare's Son**[14] 5374 4-8-11 **60**....(b) SimonPearce(5) 3 58
(H J Evans) *hld up towards rr: hdwy wl over 1f out: sn rdn: one pce fnl f* **9/1**

4U23 **5** *3/4* **Towy Boy (IRE)**[17] 5323 4-8-11 **55**....(vt) RichardKingscote 4 50
(I A Wood) *hld up in mid-div: rdn and hdwy jst over 1f out: one pce fnl f* **6/1**[3]

6600 **6** *1 1/2* **Meikle Barfil**[6] 5629 7-8-1 **50**....(tp) SophieDoyle(5) 9 40
(J M Bradley) *hld up and bhd: sme hdwy jst over 1f out: rdn and no imp ins fnl f* **33/1**

3363 **7** *nk* **Miss Firefly**[6] 5632 4-8-10 **54**.... KirstyMilczarek 12 43
(R J Hodges) *s.i.s: hld up in rr: pushed along 2f out: rdn and sme hdwy over 1f out: no further prog fnl f* **9/2**[2]

5004 **8** *nk* **Pic Up Sticks**[7] 5608 10-9-2 **63**.... RussellKennemore(3) 10 51
(B G Powell) *prom tl wknd 1f out* **16/1**

0300 **9** *1 1/4* **Sandy Par**[6] 5629 4-8-7 **51**....(b) KevinGhunowa 1 34
(J M Bradley) *hld up in tch: rdn 2f out: wknd 1f out* **33/1**

0000 **10** *2 1/4* **Compton Rose**[10] 5501 4-8-10 **54**.... FrankieMcDonald 6 29
(H Candy) *mid-div: rdn over 2f out: no rspnse* **40/1**

0400 **11** *hd* **Malapropism**[3] 5724 9-8-11 **55**.... SamHitchcott 2 29
(M R Channon) *prom tl rdn and wknd jst over 2f out* **16/1**

00-0 **12** *1 3/4* **Wavertree Princess (IRE)**[30] 4886 4-8-13 **57**.... LiamJones 8 25
(C F Wall) *prom tl wknd over 2f out* **8/1**

4666 **13** *1 3/4* **One Way Ticket**[6] 5629 9-8-5 **49** oh4....(tp) SaleemGolam 11 11
(J M Bradley) *s.i.s: outpcd* **33/1**

57.84 secs (-1.46) **Going Correction** -0.275s/f (Firm)
WFA 3 from 4yo+ 1lb **13** Ran SP% **118.7**
Speed ratings (Par 101): **100,92,92,91,90 87,87,86,84,81 81,78,75**
toteswinger: 1&2 £10.80, 1&3 £9.00, 2&3 £23.70. CSF £36.17 CT £361.04 TOTE £3.00: £3.30, £6.20, £6.50; EX 23.00 Place 6: £61.34, Place 5: £16.00..
Owner JMB Racing.co.uk **Bred** Shadwell Estate Company Limited **Trained** Sedbury, Gloucs
■ A 1-2-3 at his local track for Milton Bradley.

FOCUS
Another difficult riddle to complete the card and this time, with a race distance of 5f, the draw was seemingly an even bigger factor for punters to consider. Once again though, the favourite proved best and the form appears sound enough.
T/Plt: £107.40 to a £1 stake. Pool: £50,316.81. 341.73 winning tickets. T/Qpdt: £11.80 to a £1 stake. Pool: £4,127.01. 257.30 winning tickets. KH

5762 DONCASTER (L-H)
Thursday, September 10

OFFICIAL GOING: Straight course - good to firm (8.8); round course - good (good to firm in places; 8.8)
Rail moved out 4yards from Rose Hill into the straight increasing distances on round course by 12yards.
Wind: Light, half behind Weather: fine and sunny

5793 CROWNHOTEL-BAWTRY.COM EBF MAIDEN STKS — 1m (S)
2:00 (2:00) (Class 3) 2-Y-O **£6,799** (£2,023; £1,011; £505) **Stalls** High

Form RPR

1 **Coordinated Cut (IRE)** 2-9-3 0.... KFallon 3 85+
(P W Chapple-Hyam) *w'like: scope: tall: dwlt: sn chsng ldrs: pushed along over 3f out: led over 1f out: edgd lft and rn green ins fnl f: styd on wl towards fin* **10/11**[1]

2 *1 1/4* **Tactician** 2-9-3 0.... HayleyTurner 10 82+
(M L W Bell) *unf: t.k.h in rr: hdwy: swtchd lft and nt clr run over 2f out: chsng ldrs whn nt clr run over 1f out: styng on whn hmpd ins fnl f* **12/1**

40 **3** *1* **Muwalla**[15] 5347 2-9-3 0.... NCallan 1 80
(C E Brittain) *lw: w ldrs: led over 2f out: hdd over 1f out: styd on same pce* **16/1**

3 **4** *hd* **Munsarim (IRE)**[34] 4756 2-9-3 0.... RHills 5 80
(J L Dunlop) *w'like: hmpd s: hld up: hdwy on outer to chal over 1f out: hung rt: kpt on same pce* **4/1**[2]

0 **5** *1* **Quick Reaction**[9] 5542 2-9-3 0.... MJKinane 6 77+
(R Hannon) *str: hmpd s: mid-div: hdwy over 2f out: edgd lft: styd on fnl f* **14/1**

5 **6** *2 1/2* **Karamojo Bell**[27] 5002 2-9-3 0.... MickyFenton 7 72
(T P Tate) *w'like: str: chsd ldrs: outpcd over 1f out* **50/1**

0 **7** *hd* **Arlequin**[31] 4847 2-9-3 0.... AlanMunro 9 71
(J D Bethell) *leggy: chsd ldrs: lost pl over 1f out* **100/1**

3 **8** *nk* **Chain Of Events**[55] 4048 2-9-3 0.... MichaelHills 4 71
(B W Hills) *lw: swvd rt s: led: qcknd over 3f out: hung rt and hdd over 2f out: lost pl over 1f out* **9/2**[3]

00 **9** *9* **Beyond The City (USA)**[36] 4638 2-9-3 0.... PatDobbs 8 51
(R Hannon) *chsd ldrs: lost pl 2f out: sn bhd* **80/1**

1m 37.99s (-1.31) **Going Correction** -0.30s/f (Firm) **9** Ran SP% **115.0**
Speed ratings (Par 99): **94,92,91,91,90 88,87,87,78**
toteswinger: 1&2 £3.30, 1&3 £5.40, 2&3 £10.10. CSF £14.03 TOTE £2.00: £1.10, £2.30, £3.60; EX 14.20 Trifecta £104.10 Pool: £594.21 - 4.22 winning units..
Owner Lawrie Inman **Bred** Hascombe And Valiant Studs **Trained** Newmarket, Suffolk

FOCUS
This is often a good maiden and, with five of these juveniles holding Group 1 entries, they looked a promising bunch. There was no real pace on early, however, and the overall form looks worth treating with a degree of caution, with the third the best guide.

NOTEBOOK
Coordinated Cut(IRE) cost 325,000gns and arrived at the track with a tall reputation after being well backed in ante-post lists for next year's Derby in the days leading up to this. After that he was already co-favourite with most firms for that event without even having set foot on a racecourse, so he was obviously going to need to win this to give any justification to the support. Sent off a very warm favourite, he duly got his head in front at the first time of asking and did it well enough, without being visually that impressive. He ran green pretty much throughout and first became outpaced with around 4f to run. He responded to his rider's urgings, though, and ultimately looked better the further he went. He has a pronounced knee action too, so this lively surface was probably not ideal and it was his raw ability that saw him home. He has the scope to progress as he matures and, although his dam got no further than 1m1f at three, she has already produced a winner over 2m so stamina should not be a problem next year. There should be a deal of improvement to come from this initial experience and, while he is well entered up, remembering his trainer's handling of Authorized, it will very likely be the Racing Post Trophy for him. The likelihood of easier ground in that should be more to his liking and it will be very interesting to see how he gets on in such company. He was later trimmed into 16/1 for the Epsom showpiece and therefore made clear favourite with many firms, but one cannot back him seriously for that until he has been tested in Group company. (op Evens tchd 11-10 in places)
Tactician is bred to make his mark over middle distances next season and did not go unbacked for this debut outing. He showed plenty of promise and would have given the winner more to think about had he got a clear passage, as he found plenty of trouble when attempting to challenge. Like the winner he is also well entered and should soon be going one better, before thinking about a step up in class.
Muwalla came into this with the benefit of two previous outings and wasn't disgraced in a conditions event on his previous outing, considering he still looked green. The step up to this trip enabled him to post an improved display, indeed he shaped as though a stronger pace would've been more in his favour, and he looks the obvious benchmark for the race. He now qualifies for nurseries and is well up to finding an opening. (tchd 14-1)
Munsarim(IRE) finished third to the promising Al Zir on his debut at Newmarket last month, when slowly away and proving distinctly green. He was not helped when hampered somewhat at the start and was held up for his effort. A stronger pace may have likely helped him and he had to come wide with his challenge, but he just left the impression this extra furlong stretched his stamina to the limit. He also hung right again here and perhaps an easier surface would be more in his favour. (tchd 9-2)
Quick Reaction stepped up on the level of his Leicester debut nine days earlier and enjoyed the step up to this trip, but would've been seen to even better effect in a more truly-run race. He should not remain a maiden for long. (op 16-1 tchd 12-1)

Chain Of Events was a disappointment on this return from a 55-day break. He got himself a little warm beforehand, but had pretty much the run of the race and dropped out tamely when things got serious. Perhaps a return to softer ground is what he wants. Official explanation: jockey said colt hung right

5794 ROBINSONS DESIGNER FASHION AT BAWTRY H'CAP 1m 2f 60y

2:35 (2:36) (Class 2) (0-110,109) 3-Y-O+**£16,190** (£4,817; £2,407; £1,202) **Stalls** Low

Form RPR

16-0 **1** **Mawatheeq (USA)**[145] 1352 4-9-4 **102**.............................. RHills 8 111+
(M P Tregoning) *stdd s: hld up in rr: smooth hdwy on outer 3f out: rdn to ld over 1f out: edgd lft ins fnl f: comf* **7/2[1]**

0141 **2** 1 1/4 **Eastern Aria (UAE)**[12] 5419 3-8-10 **101**.............................. JoeFanning 9 104
(M Johnston) *lw: chsd ldr: hdwy 3f out: led over 2f out and sn rdn: drvn and hdd over 1f out: kpt on u.p ins fnl f* **7/2[1]**

0111 **3** 1 1/2 **Fanjura (IRE)**[19] 5262 4-9-9 **107**.............................. LDettori 6 107
(B W Hills) *lw: trckd ldng pair: effrt and hdwy 3f out: rdn 2f out: sn drvn and kpt on same pce ent fnl f* **7/2[1]**

5130 **4** *hd* **Australia Day (IRE)**[4] 4404 6-8-13 **97**.............................. MartinDwyer 2 97
(P R Webber) *led: rdn along 3f out: sn drvn and hdd over 2f out: kpt on same pce* **11/2[2]**

5316 **5** 1/2 **Bazergan (IRE)**[19] 5262 4-8-11 **95** oh6..............................(tp) NCallan 3 94
(C E Brittain) *hld up: hdwy over 3f out: swtchd rt and rdn 2f out: no imp appr fnl f* **12/1[3]**

5556 **6** 1/2 **Alfathaa**[21] 5200 4-9-3 **101**.............................. KFallon 1 99
(W J Haggas) *trckd ldng pair on inner: rdn along 3f out: drvn wl over 1f out and sn btn* **7/2[1]**

2m 6.14s (-5.06) **Going Correction** -0.30s/f (Firm)
WFA 3 from 4yo+ 7lb **6** Ran SP% **112.0**
Speed ratings (Par 109): **108,107,105,105,105 104**
toteswinger: 1&2 £3.40, 1&3 £2.90, 2&3 £1.60. CSF £15.73 CT £44.00 TOTE £4.70: £2.10, £2.20; EX 18.80 Trifecta £56.00 Pool: £552.82 - 7.30 winning units..
Owner Hamdan Al Maktoum **Bred** Shadwell Farm LLC **Trained** Lambourn, Berks

FOCUS
A decent handicap, but hit by three non-runners. Despite the small field, it was still wide open according to the market with four of the six runners sent off as 7-2 co-favourites. The early pace looked solid enough and the winning time was almost five seconds faster than Twice Over took to win the conditions event over the same trip the previous day. None of the past ten winners of the contest had been officially rated above 99, whilst three-year-olds enjoyed a 50% strike-rate within the same period. The form is a bit muddling but best rated through the runner-up to her Beverley form.

NOTEBOOK
Mawatheeq(USA), a progressive sort in a light campaign at three, hadn't been seen since a modest effort in soft ground on his reappearance in the Newbury Spring Cup back in April, but his stable is in much better form now. Switched off last early by Richard Hills, he produced a smart turn of foot when delivered with his effort widest of all, and despite hanging away to the inside rail under pressure after hitting the front over a furlong out he saw his race out well. The Cambridgeshire is a possibility, but his rider raised concerns over the Dip on the Rowley Mile after his performance in a Group 3 there last October, and as his trainer thinks he will get further they may look at the Cumberland Lodge Stakes at the end of this month. (op 4-1 tchd 100-30)
Eastern Aria(UAE), the only three-year-old in the field and the only filly, winner of six of her 13 previous outings this season, was 6lb higher than when scoring at Beverley last month and had a 4lb pull with Fanjura for a four-length beating at Sandown prior to that. In the slipstream of the leader from the start, she ranged alongside him inside the last 3f before edging to the front, but had no answer to the winner's turn of foot. She is very tough and a glance at her form figures show that she tends to win on every other start, so many will want to be on her to go one better next time. (op 4-1)
Fanjura(IRE), 9lb higher in his bid for a four-timer, had Dettori back on who had been aboard for his last two victories. He had every chance when coming under pressure passing the 2f pole, but couldn't quicken up and perhaps the Handicapper has his measure now. (op 3-1)
Australia Day(IRE), reappearing just four days after bolting up in a maiden hurdle at Worcester, would have found these conditions ideal and he soon established his usual position out in front. He very much had the run of the race, but came under pressure soon after being joined by the runner-up inside the last 3f and he couldn't find much more. He remains 7lb above his last winning mark on the Flat. (op 9-2 tchd 6-1)
Bazergan(IRE), behind both Fanjura and Eastern Aria at Sandown last time, was held up at the back of the field and seemed to get outpaced when asked for an effort 2f from home, and by the time he got into gear it was far too late. He had it to do from 6lb wrong, but may prefer a stiffer track in any case. (op 14-1)
Alfathaa, without a win since his second start at two, had finished unplaced in all four of his starts this term but had been far from disgraced and was back over a more suitable trip. Rejected by Richard Hills in favour of the winner, he was very keen in the early stages and, when eventually asked for more effort, didn't find an awful lot. (op 4-1)

5795 WEATHERBYS INSURANCE £300,000 2-Y-O STKS 6f 110y

3:10 (3:11) (Class 2) 2-Y-O

£183,517 (£73,421; £36,710; £18,336; £9,168; £9,168) **Stalls** High

Form RPR

0334 **1** **Swilly Ferry (USA)**[21] 5198 2-8-3 86.............................. WilliamBuick 21 96
(B W Hills) *hld up in mid-div: gd hdwy towards stands' side over 2f out: hung lft over 1f out: r.o to ld last 75yds* **16/1**

212 **2** 1 **Taajub (IRE)**[22] 5172 2-8-9 108.............................. RHills 4 99
(W J Haggas) *lw: trckd overall ldr on far side: edgd lft and hdwy to ld appr fnl f: hdd and no ex wl ins fnl f* **15/8[1]**

4014 **3** 1 1/2 **Lucky General (IRE)**[26] 5022 2-8-6 94.............................. SteveDrowne 1 92+
(R Hannon) *in rr far side: hdwy over 2f out: hmpd over 1f out: kpt on wl fnl f* **33/1**

10 **4** *nk* **Fremont (IRE)**[86] 2993 2-9-2 91.............................. JimmyFortune 19 101
(R Hannon) *dwlt: hdwy over 2f out: kpt on wl fnl f* **25/1**

5211 **5** 1 1/2 **Take Ten**[15] 5344 2-8-9 88.............................. JoeFanning 15 91+
(M Johnston) *chsd ldrs: hmpd over 1f out: kpt on same pce* **8/1[3]**

1143 **6** *nk* **Lamh Albasser (USA)**[15] 5347 2-9-2 94..............................(p) LDettori 9 96+
(Saeed Bin Suroor) *hld up in midfield: hdwy over 2f out: nt clr run over 1f out: kpt on ins fnl f* **20/1**

1213 **7** 1 **Perfect Ch'l (IRE)**[13] 5392 2-8-2 81 ow1.............................. MartinDwyer 2 79
(I A Wood) *chsd ldrs far side: one pce appr fnl f* **50/1**

31 **8** 3/4 **Sunraider (IRE)**[17] 5317 2-8-3 86.............................. FrancisNorton 11 83+
(B W Hills) *str: in rr: hdwy over 2f out: styng on whn hmpd over 1f out* **16/1**

0202 **9** 1 **Carnaby Street (IRE)**[21] 5198 2-8-6 88.............................. PatDobbs 12 79
(R Hannon) *mid-div: hdwy over 2f out: nvr nr ldrs* **16/1**

1030 **10** 2 1/4 **Eternal Instinct**[23] 5136 2-8-4 79.............................. KellyHarrison 8 70
(J S Goldie) *in rr: kpt on fnl 2f: nvr on terms* **100/1**

3203 **11** *hd* **Di Stefano**[10] 5521 2-8-9 97..............................(v) AlanMunro 10 78+
(M R Channon) *chsd ldrs: hung lft over 2f out: one pce whn hmpd over 1f out* **16/1**

11 **12** 1/2 **Spying**[28] 4939 2-8-3 94.............................. SilvestreDeSousa 16 68
(Mrs A Duffield) *t.k.h in rr: rdn and hung lft 3f out: nvr a factor* **9/2[2]**

1020 **13** 1 3/4 **Step In Time (IRE)**[23] 5136 2-9-2 81.............................. RoystonFfrench 14 76
(M Johnston) *swtg: mid-div: nvr a factor* **100/1**

521 **14** 1/2 **Lowdown (IRE)**[44] 4410 2-9-2 92.............................. GregFairley 13 74
(M Johnston) *chsd ldrs: wknd over 2f out* **10/1**

1550 **15** *nse* **Ghostwing**[21] 5198 2-8-9 97.............................. TonyHamilton 17 67
(R A Fahey) *in rr-div: nvr on terms* **50/1**

6211 **16** 4 1/2 **William Morgan (IRE)**[4] 5692 2-8-3 65.............................. PaulHanagan 3 49
(R A Fahey) *in rr far side: nvr a factor* **20/1**

3022 **17** 2 1/2 **Rakaan (IRE)**[14] 5368 2-8-9 95..............................(b) KFallon 6 48+
(B J Meehan) *led overall on far side: clr over 3f out: hung lft over 2f out: hdd & wknd qckly appr fnl f: eased fnl 75yds* **16/1**

536 **18** 3 3/4 **On The Bounty**[30] 4884 2-8-9 72.............................. FrederikTylicki 18 38
(R A Fahey) *swtg: racd stands' side: in rr fnl 2f* **150/1**

621 **19** 10 **Trailblazing**[62] 3792 2-9-2 85.............................. NCallan 7 17+
(M Johnston) *lw: chsd ldrs towards far side: lost pl over 2f out: bhd whn eased ins fnl f* **20/1**

1m 17.22s (-2.68) **Going Correction** -0.30s/f (Firm) 2y crse rec **19** Ran SP% **129.2**
Speed ratings (Par 101): **103,101,100,99,98 97,96,95,94,92 91,91,89,88,88 83,80,76,64**
toteswinger: 1&2 £12.80, 1&3 not won, 2&3 £12.90. CSF £44.30 TOTE £19.60: £4.70, £1.30, £11.30; EX 57.50 Trifecta £868.50 Part won. Pool: £1,173.69 - 0.60 winning units..
Owner John C Grant **Bred** Kilboy Estate, Inc **Trained** Lambourn, Berks

FOCUS
This was a very valuable contest so it was unsurprising to see such a competitive line-up. Only two of the runners had yet to get on the score sheet. The pace was strong and the field elected to shun the near-side rail, with the main action developing on the far side late on. The form is best rated around the fifth, sixth and seventh.

NOTEBOOK
Swilly Ferry(USA) overcame his high draw to score in a race where the pace was on the opposite flank. He picked up strongly when asked for an effort and mastered the runner-up inside the final furlong, after hanging right over to the far side. He ran with credit twice in quick succession at York's Ebor meeting last month and finished with purpose on both occasions, so it cannot be considered surprising he relished this extra half furlong. He came into this officially rated 22lb lower than the runner-up and was getting just 6lb from that rival, so it is fair to assume that one ran below par. This son of Wiseman's Ferry has developed into a very tough customer and his previous experience of running in big fields was a definite advantage in this. He is also value for further as he covered so much ground. Just how he will now cope after a likely reaction from the Handicapper remains to be seen, though, and he holds no big-race engagements.
Taajub(IRE) was the clear form pick on his second to Showcasing in the Gimcrack last time out, for which he had been officially reassessed on a mark of 108. That gave him an obvious chance at these weights, but he went into that Group race with a rating of 87 and now has to prove it was no fluke as, looking at his performance here, he has probably run to a mark in the 90s. It may be that things could have been different had he been held onto for longer this time, but his rider was not totally to blame as Rakaan had opened up a clear advantage at that stage. He is not going to prove easy to place now. (op 6-4 tchd 2-1 after 11-8 in a place early)
Lucky General(IRE) is a tough cookie and again advertised that with a solid effort in defeat. He was helped by being housed in stall 1, but rates a good benchmark for the race as he looks handicapped to his best. (tchd 40-1)
Fremont(IRE) caught the eye staying on late in the day on first outing since finishing eighth in the Coventry. He was not well in at the weights and drawn on the far side, so deserves credit. He has the scope to build on this, just the third start of his career. (op 16-1)
Take Ten fared best of the four Mark Johnston inmates and was done no favours when the winner came across him, so must be rated better than the bare form. He was ridden more patiently over this stiffer test and there could be a decent pot in him before the season's end. (op 12-1)
Lamh Albasser(USA) was equipped with first-time cheekpieces and was never going the pace to land a serious blow, but was keeping on for pressure. A return to further is what he needs, but he is another who is not straightforward to place now.
Perfect Ch'l(IRE), whose rider put up 1lb overweight, was facing her stiffest task to date and ran a brave race considering she came under pressure from an early stage. This ground was probably fast enough for her and she wouldn't look out of place if heading to the Watership Down Stud Sales Stakes over this trip at Ascot later this month.
Sunraider(IRE), the winner's stablemate, wasn't disgraced on this step out of maiden company, considering it was just his third outing. He should be placed to advantage when switching to a nursery and now looks ready to tackle 7f.
Carnaby Street(IRE) finished in front of the winner at York last time, but never looked like confirming that form on 3lb worse terms. (op 18-1 tchd 20-1)
Spying hails from a yard in form and appeared to have a decent chance at the weights. He was dropping back from 7f, but never looked happy and was beaten before his draw came into play. This was not his true running. Official explanation: trainer had no explanation for the poor form shown. (op 13-2)
Rakaan(IRE), one of only two maidens in the line-up and disappointing since his third to Canford Cliffs and Xtension in the Coventry, was responsible for the strong pace before weakening. (op 20-1)

5796 DFS PARK HILL STKS (GROUP 2) (F&M) 1m 6f 132y

3:45 (3:48) (Class 1) 3-Y-O+

£56,770 (£21,520; £10,770; £5,370; £2,690; £1,350) **Stalls** Low

Form RPR

4425 **1** **The Miniver Rose (IRE)**[97] 2672 3-8-6 96.............................. PatDobbs 11 106
(R Hannon) *hld up in rr: hdwy and nt clr run 4f out and again 3f out: swtchd rt and effrt 2f out: sn rdn and styd on to ld ent fnl f: sn drvn and hld on gamely towards fin* **28/1**

4300 **2** *shd* **Starfala**[21] 5202 4-9-4 100.............................. NCallan 10 106
(P F I Cole) *trckd ldrs on inner: swtchd rt and effrt 3f out: rdn to ld and hung rt wl over 1f out: drvn and hdd ent fnl f: kpt on wl u.p and ev ch tl no ex nr fin* **33/1**

3-21 **3** 2 1/2 **Tanoura (IRE)**[21] 5202 3-8-6 107.............................. MJKinane 6 103
(John M Oxx, Ire) *lw: dwlt: hld up and bhd: hdwy on outer 3f out: rdn to chse ldrs 2f out: drvn ent fnl f: sn no imp: lame* **6/5[1]**

1432 **4** *shd* **Shemima**[26] 5058 4-9-4 111.............................. TPQueally 3 103
(A De Royer-Dupre, France) *lengthy: hld up in tch: hdwy whn sltly hmpd 3f out: rdn to chse ldrs over 2f out: sn drvn and kpt on same pce appr fnl f* **3/1[2]**

2245 **5** 3 **Princess Taylor**[21] 5202 5-9-4 98.............................. AlanMunro 5 99
(M Botti) *trckd ldng pair: hdwy to ld over 3f out and sn edgd lft: rdn over 2f out: drvn and hdd wl over 1f out: grad wknd* **33/1**

1201 **6** 6 **Sesenta (IRE)**[22] 5173 5-9-4 100.............................. KFallon 8 91
(W P Mullins, Ire) *hld up: pushed along and outpcd 1/2-way: sn lost pl and bhd: hdwy 4f out: drvn to chse ldrs wl over 2f out: wknd 2f out* **8/1**

2232 **7** *nk* **Victoria Montoya**[12] 5425 4-9-4 97.............................. WilliamBuick 1 91
(A M Balding) *lw: led to 1/2-way: prom tl rdn along and hung rt over 3f out: sn wknd* **16/1**

0312 **8** 17 **Cassique Lady (IRE)**[42] 4458 4-9-4 101.............................. JimmyFortune 9 68
(Mrs L Wadham) *swtg: in tch: pushed along 4f out: rdn over 3f out and sn wknd* **25/1**

-102 **9** *13* **Perfect Truth (IRE)**[38] 4609 3-8-6 104........................ RHills 4 52
(A P O'Brien, Ire) *swtg: cl up: led and qcknd pce 1/2-way: rdn along and hdd over 3f out: drvn and wknd over 2f out: eased* **15/2**[3]

3m 2.81s (-3.89) **Going Correction** -0.30s/f (Firm)
WFA 3 from 4yo+ 12lb **9** Ran SP% **112.4**
Speed ratings (Par 115): **98,97,96,96,94 91,91,82,75**
toteswinger: 1&2 £45.30, 1&3 £7.90, 2&3 £14.20. CSF £665.15 TOTE £31.20: £5.10, £7.30, £1.20; EX 624.40 Trifecta £938.10 Part won. Pool: £1,237.78 - 0.50 winning units..
Owner Mrs J Wood **Bred** Tullamaine Castle & Robert Clay **Trained** East Everleigh, Wilts
■ Stewards' Enquiry : N Callan four-day ban: used whip with excessive frequency without giving mount time to respond (Sep 24-25, 27-28)

FOCUS
An interesting Park Hill and many of these fillies and mares had been taking each other on for much of the season. The early gallop was very modest and didn't quicken up until Richard Hills injected some pace aboard Perfect Truth around 1m from home. Three-year-olds had taken seven of the last ten runnings and the classic generation struck again. This doesn't look strong form for the grade.

NOTEBOOK
The Miniver Rose(IRE) hadn't been seen since finishing a well-beaten fifth in the Oaks, but the three-month break had obviously done her good. Having been held up at the back early, she weaved her way through between horses up the home straight before hitting the front over a furlong from home and the proved very game in a driving finish. She stays very well and will probably return next year.
Starfala, without a win in a year and yet to score on turf, had plenty to find with a few of these on recent form and her stamina for this sort of trip wasn't yet proven, so this was a blinding effort. Never far off the pace, she briefly hit the front coming to the last furlong and rallied in splendid style even after the winner had headed her. She deserves to win a Pattern race on this evidence. (op 28-1)
Tanoura(IRE), a progressive filly who had two of today's rivals behind when winning the Galtres Stakes at the Ebor meeting, was taking another step up in trip and probably with that in mind was soon switched off in last place. She stayed on gradually all the way up the home straight, but was never quite getting there quickly enough and only just managed to snatch third. Many will consider that she was given too much to do, but it's worth noting that she was side by side with the winner passing the 3f pole and, in any case, she was subsequently found to be lame. Official explanation: trainer's rep said filly finished lame (op 13-8 tchd 11-10 & 7-4 in a place)
Shemima, whose stamina wasn't in doubt, was the highest rated in the field. The stable's runners over here always have to be respected, especially its fillies, and she travelled very nicely just off the pace for most of the way. She had every chance coming to the last 2f, but then put her head up and looked to be feeling the ground. These were probably the fastest conditions she had encountered so far and so is worth another chance back on an easier surface. (op 100-30 tchd 7-2 and 11-4)
Princess Taylor, without a win in nearly a year, had work to do to reverse recent form with a few of these. Always close to the pace, she took over passing the 3f pole but had no more to give once headed coming to the last furlong. (op 28-1 tchd 25-1)
Sesenta(IRE), upped in grade following her game victory in the Ebor, hadn't gone quite as well in her last piece of work as before her York victory according to connections. Held up early, she seemed to get outpaced when the tempo quickened inside the final mile and, though she managed to get back within hailing distance of the leaders once into the home straight, she never looked like playing a part in the finish. (op 11-2)
Victoria Montoya, who had to be walked to post, set a very modest early pace and remained handy after losing the advantage a mile from home. However, she was made to look very pedestrian over the last 3f and even this looked an inadequate test. (op 11-1)
Cassique Lady(IRE), runner-up when stepped up to this sort of trip at Glorious Goodwood, had three of today's rivals behind her that day but she was unable to confirm the form with any of them and never looked like getting involved. (op 20-1)
Perfect Truth(IRE), who had possible excuses for her two defeats since winning the Cheshire Oaks, was trying this sort of trip for the first time but she is bred to get it. Handy from the off, she was set alight to lead entering the final mile and increased the tempo, but once headed 3f from home she emptied completely and, rather like in the Oaks, this was far too bad to be true. (op 8-1)

5797 EUROPEAN BREEDERS' FUND CARRIE RED FILLIES' NURSERY STKS (H'CAP) 6f 110y

4:20 (4:22) (Class 2) 2-Y-O **£25,904** (£7,708; £3,852; £1,924) **Stalls** High

Form RPR

003 **1** **In The Slips (USA)**[24] 5096 2-8-7 **74**........................ GregFairley 15 84+
(P F I Cole) *str: mid-div: hdwy over 1f out: r.o to ld last 75yds: rdn clr* **28/1**

4401 **2** *2 1/4* **Yurituni**[23] 5136 2-8-6 **73**........................ SilvestreDeSousa 2 77+
(Eve Johnson Houghton) *led tl hdd and no ex ins fnl f* **6/1**[1]

001 **3** *shd* **Paleo (IRE)**[13] 5398 2-8-11 **78**........................ MJKinane 16 82+
(R Hannon) *lw: in rr stands' side: hdwy over 2f out: styd on strly ins fnl f* **6/1**[1]

311 **4** *shd* **Bahamian Music (IRE)**[31] 4858 2-8-11 **78**........................ PaulHanagan 13 81
(R A Fahey) *dwlt: in rr: hdwy 2f out: styd on strly ins fnl f* **9/1**

5221 **5** *1/2* **Hasty (IRE)**[49] 4239 2-9-3 **84**........................ MichaelHills 10 86
(B W Hills) *lw: chsd ldrs: kpt on same pce fnl f* **15/2**[3]

104 **6** *1 1/4* **Bahati (IRE)**[40] 4539 2-9-2 **83**........................ TPQueally 4 82
(J G Portman) *swtg: s.s: hdwy far side over 3f out: hung lft 2f out: kpt on same pce* **7/1**[2]

501 **7** *1/2* **Emirates Hills**[24] 5096 2-8-9 **76**........................ NCallan 12 73
(E F Vaughan) *dwlt: hld up towards rr: effrt over 2f out: kpt on fnl f* **28/1**

2101 **8** *1* **Yer Woman (IRE)**[50] 4208 2-9-1 **82**........................ JimmyFortune 14 77
(R Hannon) *hld up in rr: edgd rt and hdwy towards stands' side 2f out: nvr nr ldrs* **14/1**

2216 **9** *hd* **Water Biscuit**[12] 5427 2-8-13 **80**........................ MartinDwyer 11 74
(B J Meehan) *mid-div: effrt over 2f out: nvr nr ldrs* **8/1**

0352 **10** *1 1/4* **Silver Linnet (IRE)**[9] 5553 2-7-12 **65**........................ DuranFentiman 8 56
(T D Easterby) *t.k.h: sn w ldr: wknd appr fnl f* **20/1**

5262 **11** *nk* **Avonrose**[15] 5347 2-9-7 **88**........................ JoeFanning 6 78
(M Johnston) *swtg: mid-div: effrt over 2f out: nvr a factor* **20/1**

045 **12** *1 1/4* **My Sister**[20] 5212 2-8-1 **68**........................ JamieMackay 7 54
(M D I Usher) *hld up in mid-div: swtchd lft to r far side over 2f out: hung lft and wknd over 1f out* **66/1**

310 **13** *6* **Damietta (USA)**[12] 5433 2-9-2 **83**........................ LDettori 1 53
(Saeed Bin Suroor) *chsd ldrs towards far side: wknd over 1f out: eased ins fnl f* **12/1**

1213 **14** *7* **Ramamara (IRE)**[8] 5580 2-9-2 **83**........................ JohnEgan 5 34
(P D Evans) *stmbld s: sn chsng ldrs far side: rdn 3f out: sn lost pl* **25/1**

4213 **15** *2 1/2* **Silver Symphony (IRE)**[31] 4858 2-9-1 **82**........................ KFallon 9 26
(P F I Cole) *mid-div: rdn over 2f out: sn btn* **16/1**

441 **16** *1 1/4* **Tarita (IRE)**[28] 4928 2-8-10 **77**........................ FrancisNorton 3 17
(R Hannon) *trckd ldrs: effrt over 2f out: lost pl over 1f out* **28/1**

1m 17.92s (-1.98) **Going Correction** -0.30s/f (Firm) 2y crse rec **16** Ran SP% **119.4**
Speed ratings (Par 98): **99,96,96,96,95 94,93,92,92,90 90,89,82,74,71 69**
toteswinger: 1&2 £39.60, 1&3 £29.70, 2&3 £8.60. CSF £173.68 CT £1213.17 TOTE £39.40: £6.70, £2.30, £2.20, £2.20; EX 341.50 TRIFECTA Not won..
Owner Mr & Mrs C Wright & P F I Cole **Bred** Stratford Place Stud **Trained** Whatcombe, Oxon

FOCUS
A very competitive fillies' nursery with seven last-time-out winners lining up. As with the earlier sales race over C&D the near side was again ignored and this time the far rail as well. Once more the real action came down the centre of the course, though, and the form looks sound enough despite there being just an average pace on, and should work out.

NOTEBOOK
In The Slips(USA) showed her best form when third to Emirate Hills in a Windsor maiden 24 days earlier and readily reversed that form, opening her account at the fourth attempt. This stiffer test was always likely suit according to her pedigree and she saw the trip out best of all, looking better the further she went. She has clearly begun life in this sphere at the right end of the weights and should only appreciate stepping up in trip as she matures, so there ought to be more to come. (op 25-1)
Yurituni's success at York 23 days previously looked much better after Swilly Ferry, who finished third that day, landed the sales race earlier on this card. Racing off a mark 6lb higher, she did most of the donkey work and only got picked off by the winner late on. She did get pretty much the run of things here, but remains progressive and can go in again when reverting to 6f. (tchd 11-2 and 13-2)
Paleo(IRE), well backed for this nursery bow, lacked the natural pace to land a serious blow but was running on stoutly at the end and this rates an improved display. She is in the right hands to win again and could prove happier when back on an easier surface. (op 8-1 tchd 11-2)
Bahamian Music(IRE) was 3lb higher for this return to turf. She was doing her best work towards the finish on this slight drop in trip and did very little wrong. She is not weighted out of winning yet and a return to 7f should see her back in the winner's enclosure. (op 8-1 tchd 15-2)
Hasty(IRE), whose yard has a good record in this race, was last seen getting off the mark at Kempton 49 days earlier. She came through with her chance, but failed to see it out like the principals and, on this showing, is held by the Handicapper. (op 6-1)
Bahati(IRE) was not the best away, but still emerged with a chance more towards the far side and helps to set the standard of this contest. (tchd 15-2)
Damietta(USA) Official explanation: jockey said filly had no more to give
Ramamara(IRE) Official explanation: jockey said filly stumbled leaving the stalls

5798 JAPAN RACING ASSOCIATION SCEPTRE STKS (LISTED RACE) (F&M) 7f

4:50 (4:52) (Class 1) 3-Y-O+ **£23,704** (£8,964; £4,480; £2,240) **Stalls** High

Form RPR

-130 **1** **Fantasia**[88] 2952 3-9-1 113........................ KFallon 5 115+
(L M Cumani) *lw: trckd ldrs: hdwy wl over 1f out: rdn to ld ent fnl f: sn drvn and kpt on wl* **5/6**[1]

2021 **2** *2* **Shamwari Lodge (IRE)**[22] 5175 3-8-10 101........................ MJKinane 1 105+
(R Hannon) *lw: prom centre: hdwy 2f out: sn rdn and ev ch over 1f out: drvn and kpt on same pce ins fnl f* **3/1**[2]

3025 **3** *1/2* **Say No Now (IRE)**[19] 5260 3-8-10 100........................ MartinDwyer 6 104
(D R Lanigan) *prom: hdwy to ld 2f out: drvn and hdd ent fnl f: kpt on* **20/1**

0640 **4** *1* **Red Dune (IRE)**[25] 5069 4-9-0 99........................ LDettori 12 103
(M A Jarvis) *lw: chsd ldrs on stands' rail: effrt 2f out: sn rdn and kpt on same pce* **16/1**

6003 **5** *1* **Royal Confidence**[20] 5232 4-9-0 102........................ MichaelHills 3 100
(B W Hills) *prom centre: rdn along 2f out: drvn and wknd over 1f out* **7/1**[3]

0102 **6** *nk* **Iasia (GR)**[27] 5005 3-8-10 82........................ TPQueally 9 97
(Jane Chapple-Hyam) *hld up: hdwy 2f out: sn rdn and kpt on ins fnl f: n.d* **66/1**

0406 **7** *4 1/2* **King's Starlet**[19] 5260 3-8-10 96........................ SteveDrowne 10 85
(H Morrison) *swtg: led: rdn along and hdd 2f out: sn wknd* **28/1**

5 **8** *1/2* **Cilium (IRE)**[11] 5487 3-8-10 0........................ JoeFanning 11 84
(Andrew Oliver, Ire) *chsd ldrs: rdn along over 2f out: sn drvn and wknd* **66/1**

3320 **9** *3 1/2* **Please Sing**[19] 5260 3-8-10 99........................ TonyCulhane 13 75
(M R Channon) *lw: a in rr* **16/1**

4610 **10** *4* **Carcinetto (IRE)**[11] 5474 7-9-0 98........................ JohnEgan 7 66
(P D Evans) *chsd ldrs: rdn along over 2f out and sn wknd* **66/1**

1m 22.69s (-3.61) **Going Correction** -0.30s/f (Firm)
WFA 3 from 4yo+ 4lb **10** Ran SP% **116.5**
Speed ratings (Par 111): **108,105,105,104,102 102,97,96,92,88**
toteswinger: 1&2 £1.80, 1&3 £6.10, 2&3 £9.90. CSF £3.16 TOTE £1.80: £1.10, £1.40, £3.90; EX 3.50 Trifecta £27.10 Pool: £690.91 - 18.83 winning units..
Owner George Strawbridge **Bred** Ronchalon Racing Uk Ltd **Trained** Newmarket, Suffolk

FOCUS
The field split into two early with the main group racing up the stands' rail, whilst Royal Confidence gave a lead to Shamwari Lodge up the centre of the track. Three-year-olds had been successful six times in the past seven years and Fantasia extended the sequence. The form looks sound rated around the three in the frame behind the winner.

NOTEBOOK
Fantasia seemed to have the world at her feet when bolting up in the Nell Gwyn on her reappearance and carried a 5lb penalty for that success here, but she still had upwards of 6lb in hand of her rivals on adjusted official ratings. Given a break since a modest effort in the Prix de Diane in June, she was back over a more suitable trip here and travelled powerfully just behind the leaders for most of the way. Once asked the question by Fallon, she quickened up smartly to put these rivals well and truly in their place and is now likely to step back up in class for the Sun Chariot. (op 4-5 tchd 4-6)
Shamwari Lodge(IRE), up in grade after comfortably winning a York handicap off a mark of 95 last month, had every chance and was probably unfortunate to come up against such a talented rival in a race like this. Racing away from the main bunch up the centre didn't seem to do her any harm, except that she took a keen grip early, and this effort shows that she is well up to this grade, but she may appreciate stepping back up to 1m. (op 7-2 tchd 4-1)
Say No Now(IRE), who hasn't quite been getting home over further since winning a Nottingham maiden on her reappearance, was always to the fore in the nearside group and ran a fine race in defeat. She has run right up to form judged on official ratings.
Red Dune(IRE), fourth behind Royal Confidence in this race last year, reversed that form and had her chance in the nearside group, but she didn't look entirely happy on this quick ground. She has bled in two of her previous four starts this season and that always has to be a concern. (tchd 12-1)
Royal Confidence, representing a stable that had taken three of the last seven runnings of this, had been successful at this meeting for the past two seasons but had nothing of the calibre of Fantasia in opposition when winning this contest last year. She showed bright speed to lead the runner-up down the centre of the track in the early stages, but had run her race on reaching the 2f pole. (tchd 8-1)
Iasia(GR), clear of a subsequent winner when runner-up in a Newmarket handicap off a mark of 80 last time, travelled well off the pace but when asked for her effort the response was limited. She had a mountain to climb on these terms, so wasn't disgraced. (tchd 80-1)
King's Starlet, running creditably at a similar level since easily winning a Polytrack maiden on her reappearance, led the main group against the stands' rail but had little left once headed entering the last quarter-mile. (op 33-1)
Cilium(IRE), down in trip after failing to see out an extra 2f in a Curragh Group 3 last time, took a keen grip at the back of the field early and once switched left for her effort she didn't find much. (op 100-1 tchd 50-1)
Please Sing, placed at a similar level on four occasions already this season, ran below form when behind a couple of these at Sandown last time and ran moderately again. (op 20-1)

Carcinetto(IRE), having her 20th start of the year, fluffed the start and, although she soon took a handy position, she dropped right out inside the last 2f.

5799 MEADOWHALL FABULOUS FASHIONISTA H'CAP 6f

5:25 (5:27) (Class 3) (0-90,90) 3-Y-0+ **£9,714** (£2,890; £1,444; £721) **Stalls** High

Form				RPR
1045	**1**		**Silver Wind**[4] 5695 4-8-12 **82**................................(v) SilvestreDeSousa 18 (P D Evans) *w ldrs: led last 150yds: hld on towards fin* **12/1**	89
5251	**2**	*hd*	**Hotham**[7] 5597 6-8-4 **79** 6ex.. PaulPickard(5) 17 (N Wilson) *w ldrs stands' side: kpt on wl ins fnl f: jst hld* **20/1**	85
6453	**3**	*½*	**Atlantic Story (USA)**[19] 5257 7-9-3 **87**..................(bt) GrahamGibbons 20 (M W Easterby) *mde most against stands' side rail: hdd ins fnl f: no ex* **9/1**[3]	92
5105	**4**	*¾*	**Sunrise Safari (IRE)**[19] 5257 6-9-3 **87**............................ PaulHanagan 8 (R A Fahey) *t.k.h: sn towards rr: hdwy over 1f out: styd on strly ins fnl f* **14/1**	89+
0200	**5**	*nk*	**Servoca (CAN)**[12] 5424 3-9-1 **87**....................................(t) MichaelHills 9 (B W Hills) *mid-div: hdwy in centre over 1f out: hung lft: kpt on same pce ins fnl f* **33/1**	88
3102	**6**	*shd*	**Rasaman (IRE)**[1] 5767 5-8-11 **81**..............................(v) DanielTudhope 19 (J S Goldie) *chsd ldrs stands' side: nt clr run over 1f out and ins fnl f: styd on* **15/2**[1]	86+
4400	**7**	*1 ¼*	**Vhujon (IRE)**[12] 5424 4-8-13 **83**... TPQueally 15 (P D Evans) *mid-div: hdwy over 1f out: styd on: nt rch ldrs* **14/1**	80+
6000	**8**	*hd*	**Methaaly (IRE)**[41] 4485 6-8-7 **77**...................................(be) AlanMunro 13 (M Mullineaux) *in rr-div: hdwy over 2f out: kpt on fnl f* **33/1**	73+
2-11	**9**	*½*	**Tagula Night (IRE)**[14] 5370 3-8-12 **84**.........................(vt) ShaneKelly 14 (W R Swinburn) *mid-div: kpt on fnl 2f: nvr nr ldrs* **8/1**[2]	79
2122	**10**	*1 ¼*	**Red Cape (FR)**[19] 5257 6-9-5 **89**................................ AndrewElliott 12 (Mrs R A Carr) *chsd ldrs: wknd appr fnl f* **9/1**[3]	80
000	**11**	*shd*	**Maxwell Hawke (IRE)**[13] 5404 3-8-4 **76** oh1................(t) WilliamBuick 3 (P W Chapple-Hyam) *swtchd rt after 1f: in rr on outer: hdwy and swtchd lft over 1f: nvr nr ldrs* **33/1**	67+
4131	**12**	*nk*	**Ingleby Lady**[32] 4820 3-9-3 **89**.. PhillipMakin 16 (T D Barron) *lw: dwlt: sn in tch: wknd jst ins fnl f* **12/1**	79
1002	**13**	*nk*	**Bajan Tryst (USA)**[10] 5523 3-8-10 **82**..................................(p) NCallan 10 (K A Ryan) *w ldrs towards centre: wknd appr fnl f* **33/1**	71
/052	**14**	*¾*	**Hamoody (USA)**[12] 5424 5-9-4 **88**................................. JimmyFortune 5 (P W Chapple-Hyam) *lw: in rr: sme hdwy whn nt clr run over 1f out: nvr on terms* **8/1**[2]	74+
3050	**15**	*shd*	**Internationaldebut (IRE)**[55] 4037 4-9-6 **90**......................... JohnEgan 2 (J Balding) *trckd ldrs towards far side: wknd over 1f out* **33/1**	76
0041	**16**	*nse*	**Seamus Shindig**[27] 5001 7-8-11 **88**................................ AmyScott(7) 11 (H Candy) *in rr: sme hdwy whn nt clr run over 1f out: eased* **18/1**	74+
5123	**17**	*1 ¼*	**Summer Dancer (IRE)**[15] 5349 5-8-12 **82**...................... TonyCulhane 6 (P T Midgley) *lw: mid-div: outpcd over 2f out* **16/1**	64
0002	**18**	*½*	**Fishforcompliments**[17] 5305 5-9-2 **89**...................(p) FrederikTylicki(3) 4 (R A Fahey) *lw: mid-div: sme hdwy on outside whn bmpd over 1f out: wknd ins fnl f: eased* **14/1**	69
0050	**19**	*3 ¾*	**Piscean (USA)**[10] 5507 4-9-4 **88**................................. RoystonFfrench 7 (T Keddy) *hood removed v late: s.s: a in rr* **28/1**	56
4140	**20**	*¾*	**Dancing Maite**[33] 4784 4-8-13 **83**.. KFallon 1 (S R Bowring) *racd wd towards far side: chsd ldrs: lost pl over 1f out* **16/1**	49

1m 10.65s (-2.95) **Going Correction** -0.30s/f (Firm)
WFA 3 from 4yo+ 2lb **20** Ran SP% **129.3**
Speed ratings (Par 107): **107,106,106,105,104 104,102,102,101,100 100,99,99,98,98 98,96,95,90,89**
toteswinger: 1&2 £70.00, 1&3 £30.20, 2&3 £55.10. CSF £245.72 CT £1358.49 TOTE £13.70: £3.60, £6.80, £3.20, £4.20; EX 258.90 Trifecta £421.80 Part won. Pool: £570.06 - 0.60 winning units. Place 6: £26.40, Place 5: £16.30..
Owner Silver Wind Partnership **Bred** W H R John And Partners **Trained** Pandy, Monmouths
■ Stewards' Enquiry : William Buick one-day ban: careless riding (Sep 24)

FOCUS

It doesn't come much more open than this good sprint handicap. It was a race in which it paid to race handily and this time those draw high held a distinct advantage. The form looks pretty sound rated around the first three.

NOTEBOOK

Silver Wind finished strongly at York four days earlier and, ridden much more positively here, bounced back to winning ways. He showed a most resolute attitude when challenged throughout the final furlong and recorded his third success of the year. This was also his highest winning mark he had defied to date so it must rate a career-best display. (op 16-1)

Hotham gamely registered a first win over the trip at Redcar a week previously and ran a blinder in defeat off a 6lb higher mark. He remains in top form and gives the form a sound look.

Atlantic Story(USA), fifth in this last season, was never far away on the stands' rail and ran right up to his best, also giving the form a good look. He remains winless on turf since 2004, however, and really needs a stiffer test over this distance. He is also not going to get any respite from the Handicapper with his continued consistency. (op 10-1 tchd 11-1)

Sunrise Safari(IRE) ran his usual sort of race, but deserves credit as he was drawn towards the far side and is another who helps to set the standard. (op 16-1)

Servoca(CAN), who has just a maiden success to his name, did best of those to be held up and this was a lot better from him. He is an in-and-out performer, but is certainly weighted to win at present and his turn could be near again.

Rasaman(IRE), second at the track 24 hours earlier, lasted out the extra furlong without fuss and would have gone close with a clear passage inside the last 100yards. The recent addition of a visor looks to have made all the difference to him and he certainly deserves to find another opening, but the Handicapper will have his say now. Official explanation: jockey said gelding was denied a clear run (op 9-1 tchd 7-1)

Tagula Night(IRE) was 6lb higher in a better race and was in trouble shortly after passing the 2f marker. This was the first time he had raced in a field larger than ten runners and so it well could be that the experience helps him in the future. (op 7-1)

Hamoody(USA) Official explanation: jockey said horse was denied a clear run.

Seamus Shindig was never a serious threat, but should be forgiven this effort as it didn't suit a hold-up horse and he also got no sort of run nearing the final furlong. (op 16-1)

Piscean(USA) Official explanation: jockey said colt was slow away

T/Jkpt: Not won. T/Plt: £35.10 to a £1 stake. Pool: £124,523.18. 2,584.89 winning tickets. T/Qpdt: £4.70 to a £1 stake. Pool: £7,226.01. 1,125.45 winning tickets. WG

[5769]EPSOM (L-H)

Thursday, September 10

OFFICIAL GOING: Good to firm (good in places; overall 8.8, home straight: stands' side 9.1 far side 8.4)
Wind: Moderate, across Weather: Fine, warm

5800 DAVID SMITH MEDIAN AUCTION MAIDEN FILLIES' STKS 6f

2:10 (2:10) (Class 5) 2-Y-0 **£3,238** (£963; £481; £240) **Stalls** High

Form				RPR
03	**1**		**Fenella Rose**[77] 3317 2-8-11 72..........................(v1) WilliamCarson(3) 1 (S C Williams) *mde all: 2 l clr and gng best 2f out: shkn up over 1f out: drvn out to hold on fin* **11/2**	73
323	**2**	*½*	**L'Enchanteresse (IRE)**[37] 4626 2-8-11 77.................. JackMitchell(3) 7 (M L W Bell) *hld up in tch: 4th st: effrt over 2f out: rdn to chse wnr over 1f out: styd on wl and gaining at fin* **15/8**[1]	71+
432	**3**	*2 ¼*	**Art Summer**[13] 5380 2-9-0 71...................................... EdwardCreighton 5 (D M Simcock) *t.k.h: hld up in tch: 5th and pushed along st: prog to dispute 2nd over 1f out: nt qckn fnl f* **7/2**[3]	64
0	**4**	*2 ¾*	**Aldorable**[71] 3507 2-8-11 0.. MarcHalford(3) 4 (R A Teal) *prom: chsd wnr ent st: no imp over 2f out: wknd over 1f out* **33/1**	56
	5	*1 ¾*	**Aqua Vitae (IRE)** 2-8-11 0.. AhmedAjtebi(3) 8 (Saeed Bin Suroor) *s.s and also s.i.s: nvr on terms w ldrs: 6th st: plugged on fnl f* **11/4**[2]	51+
04	**6**	*½*	**Recette**[18] 5282 2-9-0 0.. TPO'Shea 3 (R Ingram) *chsd wnr tl ent st: steadily wknd* **25/1**	49
0	**7**	*¾*	**Aimeeskeepingfaith**[7] 5605 2-9-0 0.................................. ChrisCatlin 6 (M R Channon) *n.m.r s: t.k.h early and hld up: last and struggling st: nvr on terms after* **28/1**	50+
	8	*5*	**Universal Pride** 2-9-0 0.. FergusSweeney 2 (J Gallagher) *s.s: a in last trio: 7th st: bhd over 2f out* **20/1**	32

1m 10.64s (1.24) **Going Correction** -0.05s/f (Good) **8** Ran SP% **114.1**
Speed ratings (Par 92): **89,88,85,81,79 78,77,71**
toteswinger: 1&2 £3.70, 1&3 £2.70, 2&3 £2.10. CSF £15.55 TOTE £6.20: £1.50, £1.10, £1.50; EX 17.30.
Owner Tweenhills Racing XV **Bred** Waney Racing Group Inc **Trained** Newmarket, Suffolk

FOCUS

This was nothing more than a modest maiden and the runners headed down the middle in the straight. The form is rated around the placed horses.

NOTEBOOK

Fenella Rose, sporting a first-time visor, was also stepping up to 6f on this return from a break. She had everything in trouble with 2f to run and stayed on well to hold the closing runner-up. The headgear clearly made a difference and she should prove just as effective back at 5f. (op 5-1 tchd 4-1)

L'Enchanteresse(IRE), off since being beaten at short odds in heavy ground early last month, was helped by the faster surface and kept on right the way to the line on this return to 6f, but never quite looked like getting to the winner. (tchd 5-2)

Art Summer has been on the premises in similarly modest events but it was no surprise she again came up short. (op 3-1 tchd 11-4)

Aldorable improved markedly on her debut effort and will be one to watch out for in low-grade handicaps. (tchd 28-1)

Aqua Vitae(IRE), whose price increased significantly when sold as a 2yo, holds no major entries and any chance she had was ended with a very slow start. She showed distinct signs of greenness and didn't look overly happy on the track, keeping on late into fifth. She should fare a lot better next time. (op 7-2 tchd 4-1)

Recette was beaten well over 2f out. She should do better in nurseries. (op 33-1 tchd 20-1)

5801 EUROPEAN BREEDERS' FUND MEDIAN AUCTION MAIDEN STKS 7f

2:45 (2:46) (Class 4) 2-Y-0 **£5,180** (£1,541; £770; £384) **Stalls** Low

Form				RPR
3	**1**		**Five Cents**[10] 5505 2-9-0 0.. AhmedAjtebi(3) 5 (Saeed Bin Suroor) *trckd ldrs: 4th st: prog to ld 2f out: edgd lft and bmpd rival over 1f out: urged along and hld on* **1/1**[1]	75+
034	**2**	*hd*	**White Devil**[29] 4908 2-9-3 77.. DavidProbert 6 (A M Balding) *reluctant to enter stalls: t.k.h early: led: rdn and hdd 2f out: bmpd over 1f out: kpt on but a jst hld* **9/4**[2]	75
0	**3**	*4*	**Sir William Orpen**[8] 5571 2-9-0 0.................................. JackMitchell(3) 1 (P M Phelan) *chsd ldng pair: awkward bnd ent st and sn dropped to 4th: wnt 3rd again jst over 2f out: no imp* **33/1**	66+
	4	*1 ¾*	**Rawnaq (IRE)** 2-9-3 0.. TPO'Shea 3 (M Johnston) *dwlt: last and nt on terms: shkn up over 2f out: sme late prog* **7/1**[3]	61+
0230	**5**	*1 ½*	**Fantastic Prince**[62] 3792 2-9-3 79..............................(b1) GeorgeBaker 2 (P F I Cole) *hld up: 5th st: shkn up and no prog 3f out* **8/1**	56
06	**6**	*4 ½*	**Dinkie Short**[12] 5428 2-9-3 0.. JimmyQuinn 4 (W R Muir) *chsd ldr to over 2f out: wknd* **33/1**	45

1m 24.84s (1.54) **Going Correction** -0.05s/f (Good) **6** Ran SP% **110.3**
Speed ratings (Par 97): **89,88,84,82,80 75**
toteswinger: 1&2 £1.60, 1&3 £5.90, 2&3 £7.40. CSF £3.27 TOTE £1.90: £1.30, £1.30; EX 2.80.
Owner Godolphin **Bred** Brook Stud Bloodstock Ltd **Trained** Newmarket, Suffolk

FOCUS

The front two in the market came clear in what was a relatively weak maiden. All the runners stayed on the far rail this time.

NOTEBOOK

Five Cents, a well-beaten third having been very slowly away and green over the course and distance on his debut, knew more this time and, despite again showing signs of inexperience, giving the second a bump over 1f out, he just did enough to hold on. He was the best horse on the day and could progress further in nurseries, with a drop to 6f unlikely to be a problem in time. (op 5-6, tchd 11-10 in a place)

White Devil came in for good support beforehand and led after about a furlong. He made the winner dig deep, rallying having been headed and received a bump, but couldn't quite get back up. He should find a small race eventually and will be helped by racing on a more conventional track. (op 3-1)

Sir William Orpen improved on his initial effort and was helped by the step up to 7f. He is the type to fare better in low-grade handicaps.

Rawnaq(IRE), who is bred for middle distances, was slow to start and trailed for most of the race. He stayed on late for fourth, having looked uncomfortable on the track, and should post a much-improved showing next time. (tchd 10-1)

Fantastic Prince, officially rated 79, didn't improve for the blinkers, failing to come down the hill and weakening in the straight. (op 7-1)

Dinkie Short faded having been up there early. He is now qualified for a handicap mark. (op 20-1)

5802 JUMP JOCKEYS DERBY H'CAP (TO BE RIDDEN BY NATIONAL HUNT JOCKEYS) 1m 4f 10y

3:20 (3:21) (Class 4) (0-80,79) 4-Y-O+ £6,476 (£1,927; £963; £481) Stalls Centre

Form RPR

5413 1 **Epsom Salts**[10] 5509 4-11-5 74 SamThomas 7 84
(P M Phelan) *dwlt: hld up: 7th and prog st: clsd over 2f out: rdn to ld over 1f out: hld on wl fnl f* 3/1[1]

2324 2 3/4 **Seventh Cavalry (IRE)**[19] 5266 4-10-10 65 RobertThornton 13 74
(A King) *dwlt: hld up in rr: prog on outer and 5th st: smooth effrt over 2f out: jnd wnr over 1f out: hung lft sn after: fnd nil and outbattled* 11/2[2]

0102 3 1 1/4 **Free Tussy (ARG)**[7] 5594 5-10-11 66 (bt) PhilipHide 3 73
(G L Moore) *hld up in rr: 10th st: stdy prog over 2f out: edgd lft over 1f out: wnt 3rd ent fnl f: one pce* 16/1

51R4 4 3 3/4 **Inspirina (IRE)**[39] 4561 5-11-2 71 SJCraine 5 72
(R Ford) *prom: led 4f out: drew at least 2 l clr 3f out: sn rdn: hdd and fdd over 1f out* 11/1

000 5 2 1/4 **Sufad**[24] 5094 4-10-10 65 LiamTreadwell 10 62
(T D McCarthy) *settled in rr: 9th st: rdn and prog on inner over 2f out: cl enough over 1f out: fdd fnl f* 33/1

0051 6 4 **Merrymadcap (IRE)**[19] 5244 7-11-4 73 WayneHutchinson 11 64
(Matthew Salaman) *trckd ldrs: 4th st: no prog over 2f out: steadily wknd* 12/1

1355 7 3 1/4 **Kidlat**[19] 5266 4-11-8 77 (t) WilsonRenwick 12 63
(B G Powell) *hld up in midfield: 6th and wl in tch st: steadily wknd over 2f out* 10/1

1100 8 nk **Yonder**[28] 4948 5-10-11 66 TomScudamore 1 51
(H Morrison) *mounted on crse: mde most to over 4f out: 2nd st but u.p: sn btn* 8/1[3]

2-20 9 2 1/4 **Yossi (IRE)**[10] 4007 5-11-10 79 (vt[1]) DaveCrosse 2 61
(Jim Best) *dwlt: sn prom: rdn 5f out: 8th and losing pl st: sn no ch* 33/1

00 10 25 **Sri Kuantan (IRE)**[21] 5185 5-11-8 77 (t) PAspell 6 19
(R C Guest) *trckd ldr: led briefly over 4f out: 3rd st: sn wknd rapidly: t.o* 33/1

12-6 11 dist **Alsadaa (USA)**[138] 585 6-11-8 77 ColinBolger 9 —
(Mrs L J Mongan) *dropped to last and rdn 7f out: sn wl t.o: virtually p.u fnl 2f* 3/1[1]

2m 40.36s (1.46) **Going Correction** -0.05s/f (Good) 11 Ran SP% 116.3

Speed ratings (Par 105): **93,92,91,89,87 85,82,82,81,64** —

toteswinger: 1&2 £2.90, 1&3 £5.50, 2&3 £9.30. CSF £18.70 CT £219.38 TOTE £3.10: £1.60, £2.00, £3.70; EX 17.60.

Owner The Epsom Racegoers **Bred** Heatherwold Stud **Trained** Epsom, Surrey

FOCUS

A novelty event for jump jockeys but sound-enough form rated around the first three.

Merrymadcap(IRE) Official explanation: jockey said gelding was unsuited by the track.

Alsadaa(USA) Official explanation: jockey said gelding was never travelling; vet said gelding had an irregular heartbeat post race.

5803 HEADLEY H'CAP 1m 114y

3:55 (3:55) (Class 4) (0-80,80) 3-Y-O £5,180 (£1,541; £770; £384) Stalls Low

Form RPR

6160 1 **Chadwell Spring (IRE)**[21] 5195 3-8-4 66 oh3 JimmyQuinn 6 74
(Miss J Feilden) *hld up in last: gd prog on inner over 2f out: plld out over 1f out: drvn ahd last 150yds: sn clr* 33/1

5450 2 2 1/2 **Fazbee (IRE)**[12] 5432 3-8-13 75 FergusSweeney 1 77
(P W D'Arcy) *trckd ldng pair tl wnt 2nd ent st: rdn to ld 2f out: edgd rt over 1f out: hdd and outpcd last 150yds* 8/1

0113 3 1 1/4 **Cheam Forever (USA)**[19] 5243 3-8-10 72 ChrisCatlin 4 71
(R Charlton) *led: rdn and hdd 2f out: edgd rt over 1f out: one pce* 2/1[1]

4120 4 2 **Royal Superlative**[39] 4569 3-8-7 72 JackMitchell(3) 3 67
(R M Beckett) *chsd ldr tl ent st: sn rdn: nt qckn over 2f out: one pce after* 3/1[2]

0631 5 1 **Sahaal (USA)**[19] 5242 3-9-4 80 (tp) TPO'Shea 2 72
(M P Tregoning) *hld up: 4th st: hanging and nt qckn over 2f out: no imp on ldrs after* 3/1[2]

0236 6 5 **Pegasus Lad (USA)**[18] 5295 3-8-5 67 DavidProbert 5 48
(M Johnston) *hld up: 5th st: awkward on trck fr 3f out and sn struggling* 13/2[3]

1m 44.88s (-1.22) **Going Correction** -0.05s/f (Good) 6 Ran SP% 110.7

Speed ratings (Par 103): **103,100,99,97,97 92**

toteswinger: 1&2 £12.20, 1&3 £5.50, 2&3 £3.80. CSF £248.24 TOTE £26.70: £26.70, £17.40; EX 117.80.

Owner R J Creese **Bred** William P Fogarty **Trained** Exning, Suffolk

FOCUS

This was an open if ordinary handicap and the winner is rated as having run a personal best.

5804 RICHMOND H'CAP 7f

4:30 (4:31) (Class 5) (0-75,75) 3-Y-O+ £3,238 (£963; £481; £240) Stalls Low

Form RPR

6441 1 **King's Colour**[12] 5429 4-8-13 73 JackMitchell(3) 3 85+
(B R Johnson) *bmpd s: hld up in 7th: stdy prog fr 3f out: shkn up to ld jst over 1f out: drvn and kpt on wl* 7/4[1]

1101 2 3/4 **Ogre (USA)**[7] 5594 4-9-3 74 (t) CatherineGannon 9 81
(P D Evans) *stdd s: hld up in last: rdn and prog on wd outside fr over 2f out: wnt 2nd last 100yds: styd on but a hld* 11/4[2]

0003 3 1/2 **Lodi (IRE)**[13] 5404 4-9-4 75 (t) AdamKirby 2 81
(J Akehurst) *hld up in tch: 4th st: chal over 1f out: chsd wnr to last 100yds: kpt on* 15/2

-652 4 1 1/4 **Advertise**[63] 3790 3-8-8 69 DavidProbert 4 69
(A M Balding) *bmpd s: hld up in tch: 5th st: effrt over 2f out: cl enough over 1f out: hanging and nt qckn* 6/1[3]

6124 5 2 1/4 **Steel Blue**[5] 5675 9-8-4 61 oh2 (p) JimmyQuinn 1 57
(R M Whitaker) *chsd ldr: upsides 2f out to over 1f out: sn fdd* 16/1

2220 6 1 3/4 **Ken's Girl**[21] 5182 5-8-13 70 FergusSweeney 7 61
(W S Kittow) *hld up in tch: pushed along 3f out: nvr on terms* 11/1

0206 7 1 **Compton's Eleven**[12] 5429 8-8-11 68 EdwardCreighton 8 57
(M R Channon) *hld up: 8th st: rdn and no rspnse wl over 2f out* 20/1

0006 8 3 1/4 **Purus (IRE)**[21] 5188 7-9-3 74 ChrisCatlin 6 54
(R A Teal) *trckd ldng pair to over 2f out: sn wknd* 14/1

1m 22.41s (-0.89) **Going Correction** -0.05s/f (Good)

WFA 3 from 4yo+ 4lb 8 Ran SP% 114.7

Speed ratings (Par 103): **103,102,101,100,97 95,94,90**

toteswinger: 1&2 £2.70, 1&3 £4.30, 2&3 £5.40. CSF £6.61 CT £27.13 TOTE £2.60: £1.40, £1.60, £2.00; EX 7.70.

Owner Tann Racing **Bred** Cheveley Park Stud Ltd **Trained** Ashtead, Surrey

FOCUS

This was a fairly modest handicap but the winner steppped up again and the form looks sound rated around those in the frame behind him.

5805 ST HELIER H'CAP 6f

5:00 (5:01) (Class 4) (0-80,78) 3-Y-O+ £5,180 (£1,541; £770; £384) Stalls High

Form RPR

3443 1 **Leadenhall Lass (IRE)**[10] 5506 3-8-6 67 ow1 (v) JackMitchell(3) 1 73
(P M Phelan) *chsd ldr 2f: styd cl up: led 2f out: hanging lft but styd on wl fnl f* 7/2[3]

326 2 2 **Louphole**[21] 5196 7-8-8 64 AdrianMcCarthy 4 64
(J R Jenkins) *hld up in 4th: clsd on ldrs over 2f out: wnt 2nd over 1f out and looked dangerous: fnd nil fnl f* 8/1

6060 3 6 **Peter Island (FR)**[12] 5424 6-9-8 78 (v) ChrisCatlin 2 58
(J Gallagher) *fast away: led to 2f out: sn wknd* 3/1[2]

0000 4 3 **Silver Guest**[12] 5424 4-9-5 75 EdwardCreighton 6 46
(M R Channon) *s.i.s: bdly outpcd in 5th: nvr on terms: tk remote 4th fnl f* 16/1

0531 5 3 1/4 **Diddums**[11] 5477 3-8-0 65 NathanAlison(7) 3 25
(J W Hills) *stdd s: hld up in last and immediately t.o: r.o fnl f: nvr in the r* 3/1[2]

1301 6 2 **Theatre Street (IRE)**[10] 5506 3-9-4 76 6ex PatCosgrave 5 30
(S Dow) *in tch: chsd ldr 4f out to over 2f out: wknd rapidly over 1f out* 2/1[1]

68.86 secs (-0.54) **Going Correction** -0.05s/f (Good)

WFA 3 from 4yo+ 2lb 6 Ran SP% 122.5

Speed ratings (Par 105): **101,98,90,86,82 79**

toteswinger: 1&2 £5.00, 1&3 £2.60, 2&3 £4.70. CSF £32.96 TOTE £5.40: £2.30, £3.90; EX 34.20 Place 6: £666.37, Place 5: £464.08..

Owner The Lime Street Syndicate **Bred** R N Auld **Trained** Epsom, Surrey

■ Stewards' Enquiry : Nathan Alison 21-day ban: insufficient effort (Sep 24-Oct 3, Oct 5-15)

FOCUS

This was run at a very fast pace thanks to Peter Island and the field came home well strung out. The form looks weak.

Diddums Official explanation: jockey said, regarding riding, that his instructions were to drop the gelding out and come through horses as late as possible, adding that he thought the leaders had gone too quick and they would come back to him, but with hindsight he had sat too far off the pace; trainer said, regarding running and riding, that in his opinion the jockey should have sat closer to the pace and made his effort sooner

Theatre Street(IRE) Official explanation: jockey said filly was never travelling.

T/Plt: £198.40 to a £1 stake. Pool: £49,872.27. 183.50 winning tickets. T/Qpdt: £75.30 to a £1 stake. Pool: £3,064.27. 30.10 winning tickets. JN

5775 KEMPTON (A.W) (R-H)

Thursday, September 10

OFFICIAL GOING: Standard

Wind: Moderate, across. Weather: Starting bright, getting dark

5806 KEMPTON FOR CONFERENCES APPRENTICE H'CAP 1m (P)

5:35 (5:36) (Class 5) (0-70,69) 3-Y-O £2,590 (£770; £385; £192) Stalls High

Form RPR

5503 1 **Captain Flasheart (IRE)**[18] 5295 3-8-10 63 ow3 AshleyMorgan(3) 12 73+
(S C Williams) *stdd in mid-div: stdy hdwy fr 3f out: qcknd to ld ins fnl 2f: pushed clr ins fnl f: comf* 3/1[1]

2053 2 2 **Layer Cake**[15] 5348 3-8-10 65 KierenFox(5) 8 70
(J W Hills) *in rr tl gd hdwy over 2f out: drvn and qcknd to chse wnr appr fnl f: kpt on but nvr any ch* 9/1

-030 3 4 1/2 **Markhesa**[48] 4275 3-8-13 66 JPHamblett(3) 9 60
(C F Wall) *trckd ldrs on outside and rn wd bnd 3f out: rdn and kpt on to dispute 2nd over 1f out: sn outpcd* 20/1

6242 4 4 **Iron Out (USA)**[9] 5544 3-8-12 67 DavidKenny(5) 2 52
(R Hollinshead) *in rr tl hdwy over 2f out: styd on same pce fr over 1f out* 5/1[2]

2424 5 2 1/2 **Brooksby**[10] 5511 3-9-5 69 (b) MartinLane 5 48
(L A Dace) *chsd ldr tl over 2f out: wknd over 1f out* 7/1[3]

0503 6 nk **Waahej**[23] 5126 3-8-9 62 ByronMoorcroft(3) 11 40
(P W Hiatt) *in rr: rdn 3f out: mod prog fnl 2f* 9/1

1 7 1/2 **Aegean Shadow**[50] 4199 3-8-13 66 TobyAtkinson(3) 10 43
(M Wigham) *in rr tl mod prog fnl 2f* 15/2

1404 8 8 **Uncle Brit**[30] 4872 3-8-12 65 (b[1]) RosieJessop(3) 7 22
(Sir Mark Prescott) *sn drvn 4l clr: kpt that advantage tl hdd & wknd ins fnl 2f* 12/1

-665 9 hd **Mitra Jaan (IRE)**[66] 3693 3-8-13 66 (t) LeeNewnes(3) 4 23
(W R Swinburn) *chsd ldrs: rdn 3f out: sn wknd* 8/1

000 10 6 **Viva La Vida**[18] 5295 3-8-7 62 RyanPowell(5) 13 5
(J Ryan) *chsd ldrs over 5f* 50/1

-554 11 22 **Eyes Like A Hawk (IRE)**[26] 5019 3-8-9 59 (t) RossAtkinson 6 —
(Tom Dascombe) *a in rr* 8/1

1m 38.83s (-0.97) **Going Correction** -0.075s/f (Stan) 11 Ran SP% 122.6

Speed ratings (Par 101): **101,99,94,90,88 87,87,79,79,73 51**

toteswinger: 1&2 £11.10, 1&3 £40.20, 2&3 £42.70. CSF £32.44 CT £476.78 TOTE £4.00: £1.30, £2.60, £8.00; EX 40.20.

Owner Paul W Stevens **Bred** Mrs Marion Daly **Trained** Newmarket, Suffolk

FOCUS

With Uncle Brit tearing off like a scalded cat, the race was run at a furious tempo and that set the race up for the gambled-on winner. The form is rated through the runner-up to his three-year-old best.

Aegean Shadow Official explanation: jockey said filly suffered interference in running

Eyes Like A Hawk(IRE) Official explanation: jockey said filly bled from the nose.

5807 PANORAMIC BAR & RESTAURANT MAIDEN STKS 7f (P)

6:05 (6:07) (Class 5) 2-Y-O £2,590 (£770; £385; £192) Stalls High

Form RPR

1 **Fallen Idol** 2-9-3 0 RobertHavlin 10 81+
(J H M Gosden) *trckd ldrs: drvn 2f out: str run fnl f to ld cl home* 4/1[3]

2 2 1/2 **Golden Shaheen (IRE)**[15] 5330 2-9-3 0 TedDurcan 5 80
(Saeed Bin Suroor) *trckd ldr: chal 2f out: rdn to take narrow advantage over 1f out: hdd and no ex cl home* 15/8[1]

4 3 hd **Saboteur**[12] 5431 2-9-0 0 AhmedAjtebi(3) 1 79
(Saeed Bin Suroor) *chsd ldrs: rdn 2f out: kpt on wl thrght fnl f: gng on cl home* 10/3[2]

2 4 4 **Resuscitator (USA)**[21] 5191 2-9-3 0 FergusSweeney 13 69
(Mrs H S Main) *led: rdn whn strly chal fr 2f out: narrowly hdd over 1f out: wknd fnl 110yds* 13/2

	5	1	**Louisiana Gift (IRE)** 2-9-3 0.. GeorgeBaker 4	67
			(J W Hills) *chsd ldrs: rdn over 2f out: styd on same pce fr over 1f out* **66/1**	
0	6	5	**Kingston Acacia**[8] 5580 2-8-12 0..................................... DavidProbert 9	49+
			(A M Balding) *chsd ldrs: rdn over 3f out: wknd 2f out* **25/1**	
	7	1	**Luck Of The Draw (IRE)** 2-9-3 0........................... StephenDonohoe 12	52
			(Sir Mark Prescott) *in rr: rdn along over 3f out: styd on fr over 1f out* **40/1**	
	8	hd	**Passionate Cry (USA)** 2-9-3 0.................................. HayleyTurner 11	51
			(W J Knight) *in tch: rdn 3f out: wknd over 2f out* **20/1**	
0	9	2 ½	**Lisahane Bog**[10] 5527 2-9-3 0... TGMcLaughlin 7	45
			(P R Hedger) *in rr and rdn over 4f out: mod prog fnl f* **66/1**	
	10	1	**Invincible Hero (IRE)** 2-9-3 0.......................................(t) AdamKirby 8	43+
			(J Noseda) *wnt lft s and s.i.s: rdn: rn green and hung rt over 2f out: mod prog ins fnl f* **16/1**	
	11	1 ¼	**During The War (USA)** 2-9-3 0... ChrisCatlin 6	39
			(L M Cumani) *s.i.s: rdn 4f out: a towards rr* **20/1**	
	12	½	**Hannah Greeley (USA)** 2-8-12 0.................................. PatCosgrave 14	33
			(J R Boyle) *sn bhd* **66/1**	
	13	5	**Robust Wish (USA)** 2-9-3 0.. TPO'Shea 3	26
			(B J Meehan) *rn green and sn rdn: a bhd* **66/1**	
	14	¾	**Carnacki (USA)** 2-9-3 0... DarryllHolland 2	24
			(J Noseda) *s.i.s: a in rr* **12/1**	

1m 25.76s (-0.24) **Going Correction** -0.075s/f (Stan) **14** Ran SP% **126.5**
Speed ratings (Par 95): **98,97,97,92,91 85,84,84,81,80 78,78,72,71**
toteswinger: 1&2 £3.20, 1&3 £3.10, 2&3 £2.00. CSF £11.69 TOTE £5.50: £1.60, £1.30, £1.20; EX 15.90.
Owner Normandie Stud Ltd **Bred** Normandie Stud Ltd **Trained** Newmarket, Suffolk

FOCUS
An above-average field on looks, and the first three were clear and appear useful.

NOTEBOOK
Fallen Idol, a good-looking Pivotal half-brother to two smart performers around 1m4f, only got there just in time but he should be more effective at 1m, and over even further next season. Havlin reported than he had become a bit unbalanced when switching out, and had taken a while to pick up, but that is understandable. He can be followed with interest. (op 7-2 tchd 100-30 and 9-2 in a place)
Golden Shaheen(IRE) improved mentally for his debut and looked the winner when taking the lead. Though just run out of it, he is well up to winning a typical maiden. (op 2-1 tchd 5-2 and 11-4 in places)
Saboteur looked more effective here stepped up to 7f, and on this evidence 1m should be within his range. There are maidens for the taking. (op 5-1 tchd 3-1)
Resuscitator(USA) travelled well with the pace, but he was comfortably left behind by better horses in the final furlong. He can win a maiden, albeit at a slightly lower level than the second and third. (op 5-1)
Louisiana Gift(IRE) cost 62,000euros as a foal but changed hands for just 10,000gns earlier this year, which is not an encouraging sign, but this first appearance was a promising one. A Cadeaux Genereux half-brother to a 1m1f winner, he also has other winners in the family and he can make up into a fair handicapper.
Kingston Acacia, who comes from a good Australian family, was sharper than on her debut. She is another who will be at home in handicaps when qualified.

5808 EUROPEAN BREEDERS' FUND MAIDEN FILLIES' STKS 6f (P)
6:35 (6:44) (Class 5) 2-Y-O **£3,561** (£1,059; £529; £264) **Stalls** High

Form				RPR
0	1		**Interlace**[11] 5478 2-9-0 0.. StephenDonohoe 11	78+
			(Sir Mark Prescott) *trckd ldrs tl rdn and outpcd over 2f out: styd on strly fr over 1f out: qcknd ins fnl f and edgd lft: led fnl 30yds: pushed out* **10/1**	
642	2	1 ¼	**Battlemaiden (IRE)**[11] 5478 2-8-11 0.......................... AhmedAjtebi(3) 10	74
			(Saeed Bin Suroor) *led: rdn 2f out: styd on fr over 1f out: hdd and no ex fnl 30yds* **10/11**[1]	
35	3	1	**If I Were A Boy (IRE)**[10] 5527 2-9-0 0................................. JamesDoyle 7	71
			(S Kirk) *in tch: rdn over 2f out: str run fr over 1f out and styd on wl fnl f but nt pce of ldng duo* **3/1**[2]	
20	4	1 ¾	**Memory And Magic (USA)**[35] 4711 2-9-0 0.............. PhilipRobinson 2	66
			(C G Cox) *reluctant to enter stalls: sn chsng ldr: rdn and one pce whn carried lft ins fnl f: wknd nr fin* **16/1**	
	5	¾	**Nurture (IRE)** 2-8-11 0.. PatrickHills(3) 12	66+
			(R Hannon) *in rr: pushed along and str run fr over 1f out: fin fast: nvr nrr* **16/1**	
	6	2	**Desert Poppy (IRE)** 2-9-0 0... AdamKirby 6	58
			(W R Swinburn) *chsd ldrs: rdn 2f out: wknd fnl f* **9/1**[3]	
	7	shd	**Elsie's Orphan** 2-9-0 0.. DavidProbert 4	57
			(P R Chamings) *in tch: rdn and styd on fr 2f out: no imp ins fnl f and sn wknd* **66/1**	
	8	1	**Pont D'Avignon** 2-9-0 0.. ChrisCatlin 9	54
			(P Winkworth) *s.i.s: in rr on outside: hung bdly lft and rn green 2f out: styd on fnl f* **20/1**	
	9	5	**May Chorus (IRE)** 2-9-0 0... PatCosgrave 8	41+
			(J R Boyle) *reluctant to enter stalls: slowly away: a in rr* **66/1**	
	10	4 ½	**Akubra (IRE)** 2-9-0 0.. FergusSweeney 5	26
			(Norma Twomey) *sn bhd* **66/1**	
	11	8	**Wannabee (IRE)** 2-8-11 0.. MarcHalford(3) 3	2
			(J J Bridger) *s.i.s: a in rr* **66/1**	

1m 12.82s (-0.28) **Going Correction** -0.075s/f (Stan) **11** Ran SP% **119.0**
Speed ratings (Par 92): **98,96,95,92,91 89,88,87,80,74 64**
toteswinger: 1&2 £4.70, 1&3 £5.90, 2&3 £1.30. CSF £19.43 TOTE £13.00: £2.90, £1.10, £1.60; EX 37.10.
Owner Cheveley Park Stud **Bred** Cheveley Park Stud Ltd **Trained** Newmarket, Suffolk

FOCUS
In general, an average bunch on looks but an improved effort from the winner.

NOTEBOOK
Interlace stepped up hugely from her debut to rattle home and the way she stretched clear near the finish was quite taking. A sister to Feet So Fast, she is from a good family up to 7f and an extra furlong should not be a problem. She looks progressive. (op 16-1)
Battlemaiden(IRE) tried to make all for the third time in succession, only to be run out of it late on. She is good enough to win a routine maiden but can de re-directed to nurseries if necessary. (op Evens tchd 11-10 in a place)
If I Were A Boy(IRE), expected by her trainer to be suited by the return to 6f, actually got going a shade too late and it is hard to know which trip suits her best at present. She can get off the mark when everything falls into place. (op 4-1)
Memory And Magic(USA), who did reasonably well from a wide stall, continues to show ability in maidens. She shows signs of temperament but cannot be ruled out in this company, with nurseries another an option now. (op 12-1 tchd 11-1)
Nurture(IRE), a 50,000gns purchase earlier this year, is by Bachelor Duke and from a decent family either side of 1m, so slightly longer trips will suit her as she matures. (op 12-1)
Desert Poppy(IRE), a 32,000gns daughter of Oasis Dream and out of a dam who was a very speedy juvenile, should improve for this first experience. (op 8-1 tchd 10-1)
Elsie's Orphan, a Pastoral Pursuits debutante out of a speedy family, is bred to be quick. However, she probably needs a bit more time.
Pont D'Avignon has plenty of pace in her pedigree and can be expected to show more as she gains experience. (op 16-1)

5809 KEMPTON.CO.UK H'CAP 6f (P)
7:05 (7:14) (Class 6) (0-60,60) 3-Y-O **£2,047** (£604; £302) **Stalls** High

Form				RPR
6025	1		**Come On Buckers (IRE)**[6] 5647 3-9-1 **57**............(b) EdwardCreighton 9	62
			(E J Creighton) *mde all: rdn 2f out: hld on wl fnl f* **3/1**[1]	
5456	2	nk	**If Only**[34] 4749 3-8-12 **57**.. WilliamCarson(3) 1	61+
			(J Jay) *in rr tl rdn and hdwy fr 2f out: styd on wl fnl f and clsng on wnr nr fin but a hld* **14/1**	
4560	3	1 ¼	**One Cool Kitty**[51] 4179 3-9-0 **59**................................. JackMitchell(3) 4	59+
			(M G Quinlan) *chsd ldrs: rdn to go 2nd appr fnl f: no imp on wnr and outpcd for 2nd cl home* **16/1**	
3055	4	1	**Clerical (USA)**[11] 5480 3-8-12 **57**........................(p) AndreaAtzeni(3) 10	54
			(R M H Cowell) *in rr tl hdwy 3f out: rdn over 2f out: styd on ins fnl f: gng on cl home* **9/2**[2]	
6665	5	nk	**Davids Matador**[8] 5582 3-9-4 **60**.................................. DarryllHolland 12	56
			(Eve Johnson Houghton) *bmpd s: chsd ldrs: rdn over 2f out: one pce fnl f* **9/2**[2]	
0004	6	nk	**Billy Beetroot (USA)**[10] 5500 3-8-11 **60**..........................(t) SPRyan(7) 5	55
			(R A Harris) *reluctant to enter stalls: in rr: rdn over 2f out: styd on ins fnl f: kpt on cl home* **12/1**	
3642	7	nk	**Bold Ring**[8] 5584 3-9-1 **60**... AlanCreighton(3) 7	54
			(E J Creighton) *chsd ldrs: rdn over 2f out: wknd ins fnl f* **6/1**[3]	
6606	8	2	**Blushing Maid**[28] 4950 3-8-11 **58**...................................... AmyBaker(5) 6	46
			(H S Howe) *sn chsng wnr: rdn 3f out: wknd over 1f out* **25/1**	
4044	9	1	**Abu Derby (IRE)**[14] 5373 3-9-4 **60**................................(t) PatCosgrave 3	44
			(J G Given) *bhd fr 1/2-way* **20/1**	
-420	10	¾	**Officer Mor (USA)**[85] 3031 3-9-1 **57**.................................... JimCrowley 8	39
			(A P Jarvis) *outpcd* **14/1**	
0200	11	2 ¼	**Sky High Kid (IRE)**[3] 5716 3-9-4 **60**.................................... ChrisCatlin 2	35
			(M R Channon) *in tch tl rn wd bnd 3f out: no ch whn hung bdly lft sn after* **25/1**	
0-00	12	6	**Django Reinhardt**[50] 4199 3-8-9 **58**............................. LukeKilgarriff(7) 11	14
			(J R Gask) *bmpd s: a in rr* **25/1**	

1m 12.87s (-0.23) **Going Correction** -0.075s/f (Stan) **12** Ran SP% **118.9**
Speed ratings (Par 99): **98,97,95,94,94 93,93,90,89,88 85,77**
toteswinger: 1&2 £15.40, 1&3 £14.60, 2&3 £42.90. CSF £45.22 CT £574.15 TOTE £4.30: £1.40, £4.30, £6.70; EX 53.20.
Owner The Vixens **Bred** D Houlihan **Trained** Mill Hill, London NW7

FOCUS
A good pace set by the winner in this moderate handicap but not form to be too positive about.

5810 LEVY BOARD FILLIES' H'CAP 7f (P)
7:35 (7:40) (Class 4) (0-80,80) 3-Y-O+ **£4,727** (£1,406; £702; £351) **Stalls** High

Form				RPR
3310	1		**Perfect Silence**[27] 5005 4-9-7 **75**..............................(b[1]) AdamKirby 9	83
			(C G Cox) *mde virtually all: hrd rdn and styd on gamely whn strly chal thrght fnl f: all out* **3/1**[1]	
5314	2	hd	**My Best Bet**[22] 5154 3-9-4 **76**.. TedDurcan 7	81+
			(M R Channon) *in rr: rdn 3f out: hdwy on ins over 2f out: str chal u.p and upsides thrght fnl f: no ex last strides* **9/1**	
	3	1	**Bibury**[129] 1757 3-9-0 **72**.. HayleyTurner 11	75
			(David P Myerscough, Ire) *hmpd sn after s: chsd ldrs and t.k.h: rdn 2f out: kpt on same pce ins fnl f* **11/2**[3]	
0203	4	1 ½	**Beautiful Filly**[24] 5090 3-8-6 **69**..................................(b) MartinLane(5) 10	68
			(D M Simcock) *s.i.s: in rr: rdn and hdwy over 2f out: chsd ldrs over 1f out: kpt on same pce ins fnl f* **11/1**	
62	5	nk	**Sweet Gale (IRE)**[13] 5404 5-9-2 **73**................................ AndreaAtzeni(3) 8	73
			(Mike Murphy) *in rr: hdwy over 2f out: rdn and styd on over 1f out but nvr gng pce to get into contention* **4/1**[2]	
5504	6	1 ¼	**Al Sabaheya**[7] 5591 3-9-8 **80**.. ChrisCatlin 4	75
			(C E Brittain) *chsd ldrs: hung rt and outpcd over 2f out: sme prog fnl f* **14/1**	
1004	7	1	**To Be Or Not To Be**[13] 5409 4-9-7 **75**................................... LukeMorris 12	69
			(John Berry) *hmpd sn after s: chsd ldrs: rdn 3f out: wknd ins fnl f* **4/1**[2]	
1200	8	2 ½	**Perfect Friend**[43] 4422 3-9-6 **78**.. JamesDoyle 3	63
			(S Kirk) *outpcd tl sme prog whn nt clr run over 2f out: nvr a factor after* **25/1**	
2006	9	1 ¾	**Song Of Praise**[57] 3989 3-9-1 **73**.. JimmyQuinn 13	53
			(M Blanshard) *hmpd sn after s: t.k.h: chsd ldrs tl wknd qckly appr fnl f* **33/1**	
1556	10	7	**Miss Mujanna**[35] 4714 4-9-2 **70**.................................... J-PGuillambert 6	33
			(J Akehurst) *s.i.s: sn chsng ldrs: wkng whn n.m.r over 2f out* **16/1**	

1m 25.51s (-0.49) **Going Correction** -0.075s/f (Stan)
WFA 3 from 4yo+ 4lb **10** Ran SP% **118.1**
Speed ratings (Par 102): **99,98,97,95,95 94,93,90,88,80**
toteswinger: 1&2 £4.50, 1&3 £4.20, 2&3 £5.90. CSF £31.54 CT £144.11 TOTE £4.50: £2.10, £2.10, £1.80; EX 38.70.
Owner Wild Beef Racing (Mr & Mrs R J Vines) **Bred** R J Vines **Trained** Lambourn, Berks

FOCUS
The winner made nearly all, having dictated a modest tempo. The form is ordinary for the grade, rated around the third and fourth.
Perfect Friend Official explanation: jockey said filly was denied a clear run.

5811 DAY TIME, NIGHT TIME, GREAT TIME CLAIMING STKS 7f (P)
8:05 (8:07) (Class 6) 2-Y-O **£2,047** (£604; £302) **Stalls** High

Form				RPR
3005	1		**Newton Circus**[14] 5369 2-8-13 71.................................... DaneO'Neill 4	65+
			(R Hannon) *in tch: hdwy and swtchd lft over 2f out: str run to ld over 1f out: drvn out* **7/1**	
0100	2	½	**Rainsborough**[10] 5515 2-9-0 67... ChrisCatlin 5	65
			(M R Channon) *in rr: hdwy on outside whn hmpd over 2f out: str run fr over 1f out and kpt on to press wnr cl home but a hld* **14/1**	
0344	3	1 ¼	**Chocolate Cookie (IRE)**[13] 5379 2-8-8 66............................. JimCrowley 2	56
			(R Hannon) *hld up in rr: hdwy whn n.m.r fr 2f out tl qcknd and hdwy appr fnl f: kpt on but nvr gng pce to rch wnr* **9/2**[3]	
040	4	½	**Magneto (IRE)**[8] 5583 2-9-0 54................................. EdwardCreighton 3	60
			(E J Creighton) *bmpd s: in rr: hdwy on outside over 2f out: styd on wl u.p fnl f but nt trble ldrs* **50/1**	
3003	5	1 ¼	**George Baker (IRE)**[24] 5109 2-9-0 78.....................(p) MatthewDavies(5) 9	62
			(George Baker) *chsd ldrs: rdn and styd on to chal over 1f out: wknd ins fnl f* **7/1**	
440U	6	shd	**Proper Littlemadam**[8] 5573 2-9-1 65.................................... JerryO'Dwyer 8	58
			(M Botti) *chsd ldrs: rdn to chal over 1f out: wknd ins fnl f* **16/1**	

0312 **7** 4 1/2 **Ibmab**[13] 5393 2-9-1 68 .... TGMcLaughlin 10 47
(Mrs L Stubbs) *in rr: hdwy on ins to chse ldrs over 2f out: wknd fnl f* **4/1**[2]

0060 **8** *nk* **Blade Of Glory**[10] 5519 2-8-8 52 ow1 ....(p) JamesDoyle 6 39
(A J McCabe) *led 1f: led again 3f out: hdd & wknd qckly over 1f out* **100/1**

0002 **9** 1 1/4 **Lochbroom Sunset**[8] 5583 2-8-10 55 .... WilliamCarson(3) 11 41
(S C Williams) *plld hrd: chsd ldrs: wknd ins fnl 2f* **9/4**[1]

0005 **10** 6 **Double Rollover**[20] 5224 2-8-12 48 ....(p) DarryllHolland 1 25
(W R Muir) *chsd ldrs tl wknd 2f out* **50/1**

05 **11** 1/2 **Ridgeway Sapphire**[28] 4933 2-8-9 0 .... LeeNewnes(5) 7 26
(M D I Usher) *sn bhd* **25/1**

0P **12** 11 **Rock Of Behistun (IRE)**[20] 5224 2-8-6 0 .... JosephineBruning(7) 13 —
(P L Gilligan) *bmpd s: plld hrd and led after 1f: hdd 3f out: sn btn* **66/1**

0000 **13** *dist* **Restyle**[2] 5749 2-8-8 33 ....(p) SaleemGolam 14 —
(D K Ivory) *veered lft s: hmpd and dropped to rr after 2f: t.o* **50/1**

1m 26.92s (0.92) **Going Correction** -0.075s/f (Stan) **13** Ran SP% **118.7**
Speed ratings (Par 93): **91,90,89,88,87 86,81,81,79,73 72,59,—**
toteswinger: 1&2 £29.70, 1&3 £5.60, 2&3 £13.50. CSF £95.16 TOTE £8.90: £2.00, £3.70, £1.60; EX 42.70.Newton Circus was claimed by Ollie Pears for £6,000. Rainsborough was claimed by Sean Curran for £7,000.
Owner D Boocock **Bred** Overbury Stallions Ltd And D Boocock **Trained** East Everleigh, Wilts
■ Stewards' Enquiry : Dane O'Neill caution: careless riding

FOCUS
A routine gallop, but those near the front were either short-runners or lacking in ability, leaving the finish to a number of hold-up performers. The winner is rated 2lb below his previous best.

NOTEBOOK
Newton Circus had run respectably in his first nursery last time, and this drop to claimers did the trick. Whether he will be able to repeat this back in handicap company is open to debate, but he showed a decent turn of foot to take the lead and is a fair sort for this grade. (op 9-2)
Rainsborough's only win was in a seller, but he had been quite highly tried in two recent nurseries and, like the winner, is above average for this sort of race. This was a good Polytrack debut and he looks capable of winning on the surface. (op 16-1)
Chocolate Cookie(IRE) has not progressed since her early races and this may well be her right level now. She did not get the best of runs through the pack but found a smart turn of foot when the gaps appeared, suggesting that she is capable of winning when she gets the breaks. (op 3-1)
Magneto(IRE) was stepping up from sprints and shaped as if he will be even better at 1m. (op 66-1)
George Baker(IRE) was fading late on and should be suited by a return to 6f. (op 10-1)
Lochbroom Sunset looks more like a sprinter. (op 5-1)

5812 KEMPTON FOR TEAM BUILDING EVENTS H'CAP — 2m (P)
8:35 (8:36) (Class 5) (0-70,66) 3-Y-0+ **£2,590** (£770; £385; £192) **Stalls** High

Form RPR

001 **1** **Rose Row**[20] 5227 5-10-0 66 .... GeorgeBaker 5 76+
(Mrs Mary Hambro) *hld up in rr: hdwy on outside fr 3f out: rdn to ld ins fnl 2f: clr fnl f and eased fnl 110yds* **13/2**[3]

00-3 **2** 5 **Bathwick Man**[18] 4625 4-8-12 50 ....(tp) StephenDonohoe 7 52
(D E Pipe) *chsd ldrs: rdn 6f out: styd on u.p to chse easy wnr fr over 1f out* **4/1**[2]

0021 **3** 1 3/4 **Aaman (IRE)**[12] 5430 3-8-6 57 .... HayleyTurner 3 57
(E F Vaughan) *led: pushed along 3f out: hdd ins fnl 2f: wknd into 3rd fnl f* **11/10**[1]

0515 **4** *nk* **The Saucy Snipe**[24] 5097 3-8-5 56 .... DavidProbert 2 56
(P Winkworth) *in tch: rdn and styd on to chse ldrs 3f out: no ch w wnr ins fnl 2f and styd on same pce* **25/1**

2434 **5** 3 1/2 **Bari Bay**[8] 5579 3-8-0 51 .... NickyMackay 6 46
(J W Mullins) *in tch: rdn 4f out and nvr in contention* **20/1**

5001 **6** 7 **Eloise**[16] 5328 3-8-2 53 ....(b) JimmyQuinn 1 40
(Sir Mark Prescott) *chsd ldr: rdn 3f out: wknd over 2f out* **7/1**

156 **7** 4 **Medieval Maiden**[8] 5577 6-8-10 55 .... KierenFox(7) 8 37
(Mrs L J Mongan) *in tch tl rdn and wknd 4f out* **25/1**

401 **8** 25 **Eightdaysaweek**[16] 5327 3-9-1 66 .... ChrisCatlin 4 18
(A J McCabe) *hung lft thrght and racd on outside tl hung lft off trck 4f out: eased: t.o* **20/1**

3m 28.97s (-1.13) **Going Correction** -0.075s/f (Stan)
WFA 3 from 4yo+ 13lb **8** Ran SP% **110.7**
Speed ratings (Par 103): **99,96,95,95,93 90,88,75**
toteswinger: 1&2 £5.50, 1&3 £1.20, 2&3 £1.90. CSF £29.32 CT £46.69 TOTE £8.10: £1.80, £1.10, £1.10; EX 33.90.
Owner Mrs Richard Hambro **Bred** Cotswold Stud **Trained** Bourton-on-the-Hill, Gloucs

FOCUS
The pace was a humdrum one, but the winner had no problem arriving from the rear. The form looks sound rated around those in the frame behind the winner.
Eightdaysaweek Official explanation: jockey said filly hung left throughout

5813 MIX BUSINESS WITH PLEASURE H'CAP — 7f (P)
9:05 (9:07) (Class 6) (0-65,65) 3-Y-0+ **£2,047** (£604; £302) **Stalls** High

Form RPR

2430 **1** **Tamasou (IRE)**[41] 4496 4-9-8 64 .... DavidProbert 14 78
(A J McCabe) *trckd ldrs: drvn to ld jst ins fnl f: drvn out* **3/1**[1]

2164 **2** 1 1/2 **Ugenius**[16] 5329 5-9-6 62 .... TGMcLaughlin 6 72
(Mrs C A Dunnett) *in tch: hdwy over 2f out: drvn to take slt ld 1f out: hdd sn after: styd on same pce* **10/1**

4552 **3** 1 **Stanley Goodspeed**[10] 5502 6-9-8 64 ....(tp) HayleyTurner 11 71
(J W Hills) *in rr: rdn and hdwy on ins over 2f out: chsd ldrs u.p 1f out: styd on same pce ins fnl f* **9/2**[2]

-000 **4** 1 **Chosen Son (IRE)**[22] 5164 3-9-2 62 .... DarryllHolland 13 65
(P J O'Gorman) *stdd s and plld hrd: in tch 1/2-way: hdwy 2f out: sn rdn: styd on fnl f but no imp on ldrs* **16/1**

1150 **5** 1 **Sovereignty (JPN)**[16] 5329 7-9-1 62 .... SophieDoyle(5) 9 64
(D K Ivory) *chsd ldr: led over 2f out: hdd & wknd 1f out* **8/1**

-022 **6** 2 **Art Market (CAN)**[33] 4791 6-9-4 60 .... FergusSweeney 12 56
(Miss Jo Crowley) *chsd ldrs: rdn and ev ch 2f out: wknd fnl f* **5/1**[3]

6260 **7** 1 1/2 **Fine Ruler (IRE)**[139] 1495 5-9-7 63 .... GeorgeBaker 3 55
(M R Bosley) *in rr: nvr gng pce to get into contention* **16/1**

0506 **8** 3 **Sam's Cross (IRE)**[11] 5477 4-9-1 60 .... MarcHalford(3) 8 44
(J J Bridger) *chsd ldrs over 4f* **33/1**

566 **9** 1 **Queen Of Thebes (IRE)**[8] 5581 3-9-5 65 ....(t) JimCrowley 4 45
(G L Moore) *in rr: sme hdwy on outside 3f out: nvr in contention and sn wknd* **12/1**

6-0 **10** *nk* **Clearing House**[140] 1478 4-9-2 58 .... SaleemGolam 2 39
(R W Price) *swtchd rt s: bhd most of way* **66/1**

005 **11** 3/4 **Fortina's Boy (USA)**[19] 5242 3-9-4 64 ....(t) AdamKirby 7 41
(W R Swinburn) *sn led: hdd & wknd over 2f out* **25/1**

1000 **12** 4 **Romantic Verse**[12] 5449 4-9-3 62 ....(b) MichaelJStainton(3) 10 30
(S Curran) *wd and a in rr* **40/1**

0021 **13** 4 **Lytton**[140] 1475 4-9-4 60 ....(v) LiamJones 1 17
(R Ford) *rrd bdly s and lost 6l: nt rcvr and a in rr* **14/1**

1m 25.26s (-0.74) **Going Correction** -0.075s/f (Stan)
WFA 3 from 4yo+ 4lb **13** Ran SP% **116.9**
Speed ratings (Par 101): **101,99,98,97,95 93,91,88,87,86 86,81,76**
toteswinger: 1&2 £12.80, 1&3 £4.00, 2&3 £7.40. CSF £32.09 CT £138.70 TOTE £3.40: £1.70, £2.80, £1.70; EX 40.50 Place 6 £44.06, Place 5 £15.80..
Owner Brooklands Racing **Bred** Garry Gleeson **Trained** Averham Park, Notts

FOCUS
A deccent gallop set the race up for the winner, who normally runs over further. The form looks good for the grade, rated around the first three.
Lytton Official explanation: jockey said gelding reared at the start and was slowly away
T/Plt: £67.10 to a £1 stake. Pool: £62,624.73. 680.98 winning tickets. T/Qpdt: £22.60 to a £1 stake. Pool: £7,167.77. 234.10 winning tickets. ST

5814 - 5821a (Foreign Racing) - See Raceform Interactive

5793 DONCASTER (L-H)
Friday, September 11

OFFICIAL GOING: Good to firm (good in places on round course; str 8.7 rnd 8.8)
All dolling removed and all distances as advertised.
Wind: Light across Weather: Sunny and dry

5822 POLYPIPE FLYING CHILDERS STKS (GROUP 2) — 5f
1:35 (1:36) (Class 1) 2-Y-O
£45,416 (£17,216; £8,616; £4,296; £2,152; £1,080) **Stalls** High

Form RPR

5131 **1** **Sand Vixen**[28] 4989 2-8-11 100 .... LDettori 9 108+
(Saeed Bin Suroor) *lw: trckd ldrs gng wl: hdwy 2f out: swtchd lft and effrt over 1f out: rdn and qcknd to ld ins fnl f* **9/2**[3]

150 **2** 1 **Bould Mover**[42] 4487 2-9-0 99 .... GrahamGibbons 2 105
(R Curtis) *cl up: led 2f out: and sn rdn: drvn ent fnl f: sn hdd and kpt on* **50/1**

1022 **3** *hd* **Mister Manannan (IRE)**[23] 5174 2-9-0 104 .... AdrianTNicholls 4 104
(D Nicholls) *lw: dwlt: hdwy and cl up after 1f: effrt 2f out: sn rdn to chal and ev ch tl drvn and no ex ins fnl f* **10/1**

1010 **4** 1 1/4 **Rose Blossom**[22] 5199 2-8-11 91 .... PaulHanagan 5 97
(R A Fahey) *trckd ldrs: effrt 2f out: sn rdn and carried sltly lft over 1f out: sn drvn and one pce* **20/1**

3336 **5** 1 **Archers Road (IRE)**[23] 5174 2-9-0 99 .... RyanMoore 7 96
(M R Channon) *sn outpcd in rr: rdn along 1/2-way: drvn and hung lft wl over 1f out: styd on ins fnl f: nrst fin* **14/1**

0211 **6** *nse* **Piccadilly Filly (IRE)**[27] 5057 2-8-11 98 .... EdwardCreighton 8 93
(E J Creighton) *towards rr: rdn along 1/2-way: hdwy over 1f out: kpt on u.p ins fnl f: nrst fin* **16/1**

0641 **7** *nk* **Star Rover (IRE)**[23] 5174 2-9-0 105 .... JohnEgan 3 95
(P D Evans) *chsd ldrs: rdn along 2f out: sn drvn and edgd lft and wknd* **14/1**

311 **8** *hd* **Our Jonathan**[13] 5452 2-9-0 93 .... JamieSpencer 6 102+
(K A Ryan) *lost many l s and bhd: hdwy wl over 1f out: styd on u.p ins fnl f: nrst fin* **4/1**[2]

1121 **9** *shd* **Misheer**[65] 3748 2-9-0 109 .... NCallan 10 94
(C E Brittain) *lw: t.k.h to s: led: rdn along and hdd 2f out: sn wknd* **6/4**[1]

1004 **10** 3 1/4 **Swan Wings**[28] 4989 2-8-11 91 .... WilliamBuick 1 79
(A M Balding) *dwlt: in tch on outer: rdn along over 2f out: sn wknd* **66/1**

58.10 secs (-2.40) **Going Correction** -0.225s/f (Firm) 2y crse rec **10** Ran SP% **114.7**
Speed ratings (Par 107): **110,108,108,106,104 104,103,103,103,98**
toteswinger: 1&2 £37.50, 1&3 £5.40, 2&3 £49.30. CSF £207.50 TOTE £4.90: £1.60, £10.20, £2.20; EX 333.10 TRIFECTA Not won..
Owner Godolphin **Bred** Mrs M Campbell-Andenaes **Trained** Newmarket, Suffolk
■ Stewards' Enquiry : John Egan one-day ban: excessive use of the whip (Sep 25)

FOCUS
This Group 2 is usually won by a fast juvenile but very few of the recent winners have gone on to make the grade as top-class sprinters; the exception in recent years being Fleeting Spirit. They went pretty fast and it was no surprise that the juvenile track record was broken. Fillies had a good recent record, having won half of the previous ten renewals, and that record was improved. The form is solid and the winner has more to offer.

NOTEBOOK
Sand Vixen ◆, a daughter of Dubawi, had been progressive since winning her maiden on Polytrack, finishing third in the Princess Margaret and winning a Listed race back at 5f on fast ground (runner-up won since). She travelled well behind the leaders and, once pulled out to challenge, the result was never in doubt. She looks to have more to offer and will be aimed at the Cheveley Park Stakes now. (op 4-1)
Bould Mover, a dual winner at 5f on fast ground but held in Group company since, reversed previous form with a couple of these, having been at the head of affairs for most of the way. He kept on gamely when headed to secure second, and the Harry Rosebery at Ayr or Cornwallis at Ascot could be on the agenda, providing he gets his ground.
Mister Manannan(IRE) is a pretty consistent performer, having finished runner-up in the Molecomb and Roses Stakes, and seemed to run his race but could not produce the extra late on. He is probably the best guide to the level of the form. (op 11-1)
Rose Blossom, a 5f and 6f winner on fast ground but held in Group company on her other two starts, ran a better race at this level having got a good lead into the race, and she may be able to win in Listed company. (op 25-1)
Archers Road(IRE), a consistent, tough sort, was unable to go the pace but was noted staying on well in the closing stages and still looks to have something to offer. (op 18-1 tchd 20-1)
Piccadilly Filly(IRE), whose first three runs were at 6f, had improved since being dropped to 5f, winning on Polytrack and taking a Listed race at Deauville on good ground. Although she is improving, she found this step up in grade taking her off her feet early before she too stayed on late.
Star Rover(IRE), another tough and consistent sort, had beaten today's third and fifth in the Roses Stakes but he had to race on the outside of the field and weakened in the closing stages. His rider reported the colt hung left. Official explanation: jockey said colt hung left throughout
Our Jonathan ◆, a clear winner at Pontefract and then successful in a Listed race over 5f on Polytrack in Ireland, was stepping up in grade but lost all chance by standing still as the stalls opened. It looked to cost him at least six lengths and he did well to finish as close as he did. With a level break compensation awaits. (op 5-1 tchd 11-2)
Misheer, whose only defeat in four previous starts was by Jealous Again in the Queen Mary; was dropping back in trip having won the Cherry Hinton over 6f. She was given a positive ride from her rail draw but was the first of the leading trio to weaken and maybe the positive tactics did not suit. (op 11-8)

Swan Wings had been held by today's winner on her two previous starts and again proved that she is not up to this level.

5823 LADBROKES MALLARD STKS (H'CAP) 1m 6f 132y

2:05 (2:05) (Class 2) (0-110,102) 3-Y-O+**£32,380** (£9,635; £4,815; £2,405) **Stalls** Low

Form				RPR
0024	**1**		**Nanton (USA)**[23] 5173 7-9-10 **98** ... DanielTudhope 11	109
			(J S Goldie) *hld up and bhd: swtchd outside and hdwy over 2f out: str run fr over 1f out to ld ins fnl f: sn clr* **12/1**	
0216	**2**	*3*	**Manyriverstocross (IRE)**[23] 5173 4-9-9 **97** ... JamieSpencer 9	104
			(A King) *hld up towards rr: hdwy over 3f out: rdn to chse ldrs 2f out: drvn and kpt on ins fnl f: tk 2nd nr line* **11/2**[3]	
3144	**3**	*¾*	**Cosmic Sun**[21] 5230 3-8-8 **94** ... PaulHanagan 7	100
			(R A Fahey) *lw: chsd ldng pair: pushed along and sltly outpcd over 4f out: hdwy to chse ldr 3f out: drvn and ev ch over 1f out tl one pce ins fnl f* **7/2**[1]	
2050	**4**	*2½*	**Record Breaker (IRE)**[23] 5173 5-9-9 **97** ... (b) RoystonFfrench 5	100+
			(M Johnston) *swtg: chsd ldr: hdwy to ld 3f out: rdn wl over 1f out: drvn ent fnl f: sn hdd & wknd* **12/1**	
2124	**5**	*½*	**Hawk Mountain (UAE)**[21] 5235 4-8-10 **84** ... GrahamGibbons 10	86
			(J J Quinn) *lw: hld up in midfield: hdwy over 4f out: rdn along to chse ldrs wl over 2f out: sn drvn and no imp fr over 1f out* **9/2**[2]	
1066	**6**	*½*	**Dolly Penrose**[14] 5410 4-8-10 **84** oh1 ... (v[1]) ChrisCatlin 6	86
			(M R Channon) *dwlt: hld up towards rr: hdwy over 3f out: rdn to chse ldrs 2f out: sn drvn and no imp* **50/1**	
0321	**7**	*3¼*	**Just Lille (IRE)**[16] 5346 6-9-5 **93** ... (p) SilvestreDeSousa 8	90
			(Mrs A Duffield) *midfield: effrt on inner over 3f out: rdn along whn nt clr run and outpcd over 2f out: sn swtchd rt and drvn: nt rch ldrs* **12/1**	
3064	**8**	*9*	**Bugaku**[7] 5641 4-8-13 **87** ... RyanMoore 3	73
			(Sir Michael Stoute) *in tch: rdn along 4f out: wknd 3f out* **13/2**	
-600	**9**	*14*	**Waldvogel (IRE)**[23] 5173 5-9-13 **101** ... KFallon 1	68
			(L M Cumani) *chsd ldrs: rdn along 4f out: drvn 3f out and sn wknd* **11/1**	
1556	**10**	*2¾*	**Fiulin**[27] 5023 4-10-0 **102** ... (p) JerryO'Dwyer 2	66
			(M Botti) *led: rdn along 4f out: hdd 3f out and sn wknd* **16/1**	
1410	**11**	*38*	**Desert Sea (IRE)**[23] 5173 6-9-8 **96** ... SebSanders 4	10
			(D W P Arbuthnot) *lw: in tch on inner: effrt to chse ldrs 5f out: rdn along 3f out: wkng whn n.m.r over 2f out: sn bhd and eased* **12/1**	

3m 2.64s (-4.06) **Going Correction** -0.225s/f (Firm)
WFA 3 from 4yo+ 12lb **11** Ran SP% **116.1**
Speed ratings (Par 109): **101,99,99,97,97 97,95,90,83,81 61**
toteswinger: 1&2 £6.90, 1&3 £6.80, 2&3 £3.80. CSF £75.71 CT £284.17 TOTE £12.30: £2.70, £2.30, £1.80; EX 38.90 Trifecta £341.90 Pool: £831.66 - 1.80 winning units..
Owner J S Morrison **Bred** Samuel H And Mrs Rogers, Jr **Trained** Uplawmoor, E Renfrews

FOCUS
This high-class stayers' handicap is often won by an improver and 3yos have a very good record but on this occasion it was won by the oldest runner in the field. The form of the Ebor had taken a few knocks in recent days with defeats for the winner, third and fifth but, in a race with similar conditions and over a similar trip, it was upheld by the fourth and sixth. Solid form, with clear personal bests from both the first two.

NOTEBOOK
Nanton(USA) ◆, who is best known for his form at around 1m2f, ran well when a somewhat unlucky fourth in the Ebor on his first attempt at the trip. Settled out the back, he was going notably well early in the straight before sweeping down the outside to lead going into the final furlong and won in comfortable fashion. He is entered in both the Cambridgeshire and Cesarewitch and could go for both, although the Doonside Cup at Ayr next week is a possibility if the ground is not soft. (op 10-1)

Manyriverstocross(IRE) ran well when sixth in the Ebor having scored over 1m6f at Goodwood on his previous start and, although 7lb higher, was 2lb better off with Nanton. He ran his race but could not match the pace of his old rival late on, and may soon go hurdling. Official explanation: jockey said gelding missed the break (tchd 6-1)

Cosmic Sun, a dual 1m4f winner and not beaten far on his only previous try at this trip, came to have every chance but lacked an extra gear in the final furlong. He is 6lb above his last winning mark and looks held by the Handicapper now. However, he can be expected to improve again over the winter and should make up into a decent stayer. (tchd 4-1)

Record Breaker(IRE), a tough stayer who is effective at 1m4f plus, appreciates fast ground and made a bold bid under a positive ride before being outstayed in the closing stages. He is another who looks high enough in the handicap, being 9lb above his last winning mark. (op 14-1)

Hawk Mountain(UAE), a dual course and distance winner this year, all of whose wins had been gained at this trip, stayed on pretty well having been one of the first under pressure. (op 13-2)

Dolly Penrose, a dual winner at 1m6f but both times on testing ground, did not perform badly in the first-time visor, doing her best work late on. (tchd 40-1)

Just Lille(IRE), who was up 3lb for her last win, never got involved, although she finished well ahead of the remainder. (op 14-1)

5824 DFS DONCASTER CUP (GROUP 2) 2m 2f

2:40 (2:41) (Class 1) 3-Y-O+ **£56,770** (£21,520; £10,770; £5,370; £2,690) **Stalls** Low

Form				RPR
4-01	**1**		**Askar Tau (FR)**[23] 5171 4-9-4 110 ... (v) RyanMoore 3	115+
			(M P Tregoning) *lw: trckd ldng pair: hdwy 3f out: nt clr run 2f out: swtchd ins and rdn over 1f out: drvn and kpt on wl to ld last 75yds* **5/2**[2]	
4121	**2**	*nk*	**Darley Sun (IRE)**[49] 4260 3-8-2 94 ow1 ... ChrisCatlin 4	111
			(D M Simcock) *trckd ldrs: hdwy over 3f out: led over 2f out: rdn over 1f out: drvn and edgd lft ent fnl f: hung rt and hdd last 75yds: no ex towards fin* **6/1**[3]	
5-13	**3**	*3*	**Geordieland (FR)**[85] 3048 8-9-4 117 ... MJKinane 2	110
			(J A Osborne) *hld up in rr: smooth hdwy on outer 3f out: chal 2f out: rdn wl over 1f out and ev ch tl wknd ins fnl f* **13/8**[1]	
5632	**4**	*11*	**Drill Sergeant**[23] 5171 4-9-1 108 ... JoeFanning 6	95
			(M Johnston) *lw: led: rdn along 3f out: drvn and hdd over 2f out: grad wknd* **6/1**[3]	
31/0	**5**	*2¾*	**Deutschland (USA)**[23] 5173 6-9-1 0 ... KFallon 5	92
			(W P Mullins, Ire) *cl up: rdn along 4f out: drvn 3f out: sn wknd and eased* **15/2**	

3m 54.15s (-4.05) **Going Correction** -0.225s/f (Firm)
WFA 3 from 4yo+ 14lb **5** Ran SP% **107.0**
Speed ratings (Par 115): **100,99,98,93,92**
toteswinger: 1&2 £7.30 CSF £15.75 TOTE £3.40: £1.80, £2.00; EX 14.80.
Owner Nurlan Bizakov **Bred** Gestut Zoppenbroich & Aerial Bloodstock **Trained** Lambourn, Berks

FOCUS
A disappointing turnout numerically and the overall quality was pretty ordinary for the level, with the race weaker for the absence of a Ballydoyle representative (Aidan O'Brien had won the race for the last two years), just like the Goodwood Cup and Lonsdale Cup earlier in the season. The pace seemed sound enough. The form is a bit guessy but Askar Tau has been rated close to his York effort.

NOTEBOOK
Askar Tau(FR) is a progressive stayer and produced a career best. His Lonsdale Cup success didn't amount to much in the grand scheme of things, with Drill Sergeant only 1 1/4l away in second that day, but this was significantly better, and he made light of a 3lb penalty. This step back up in trip was obviously very much in his favour and he overcame trouble in running to get on top near the line, taking his record to 2-2 in a visor, as well as when ridden by Ryan Moore. He was hemmed in by the Jamie Osborne-trained runner when first looking to make a move in the straight, with that one travelling much the better of the pair, and he was forced to switch inside. Even then he didn't have that much room to play with, but a suitable gap appeared when Darley Sun drifted off the rail and he picked up well inside the final furlong to take full advantage. A scopey gelding who seems to thrive on his racing, the winner promises to make an even better 5yo, and the Ascot Gold Cup will be his big aim next year. In the shorter term, a race like the Prix du Cadran could be a suitable end of season target, but it remains to be seen whether he'll be effective on soft ground. (op 9-4)

Darley Sun(IRE) impressed when winning a 3yo handicap at Ascot by ten lengths on his previous start, but that was gained off a mark of just 83, and this was much tougher. He was open to further improvement, however, especially over this longer trip, and ran a good race in defeat. He was only pegged back in the final few strides, after edging right, and the 1lb overweight he carried cannot have helped, although it's worth remembering that Askar Tau had been denied a clear run, and looked value for slightly more than the winning margin. It's fair to say that he is now looking ridiculously well handicapped for the Cesarewitch as the weights came out when he was rated just 94, and he has only 7st 11lb. The downside, however, is that he'll currently struggle to make the cut and, while his connections may want to turn him out in the hope he can pick up a penalty for the Newmarket race, doing that without having too hard a race will be no easy task. (tchd 5-1)

Geordieland(FR) looked set for a good season when winning the Group 2 Henry II Stakes at Sandown on his reappearance, but he underperformed when beaten a long way in the Ascot Gold Cup, and this was another tame effort. He had upwards of 6lb in hand on official figures, and looked set to overwhelm this lot when looming up towards outside in the straight, seemingly full of running. However, despite finding enough to keep the winner hemmed in around two furlongs from the finish, he soon flattened out. The jockey change from regular rider Shane Kelly to Mick Kinane, who was getting to know the horse ahead of a possible tilt at the Breeders' Cup Marathon, made no difference. Jamie Osborne is still keen on a trip to the States with this 8yo, reasoning that the likely strong pace at Santa Anita will suit, and the Prix du Cadran is another possible target. However, it has to be said, this horse needs to prove he retains his ability for such tasks. (tchd 7-4)

Drill Sergeant couldn't repeat the form he showed when runner-up behind today's winner in the Lonsdale Cup. He was hassled up front and looked a non-stayer over this longer trip. (op 13-2 tchd 7-1)

Deutschland(USA) ran well in the Ebor and looked worth a try over this longer trip, but he ran poorly. (op 9-1 tchd 7-1)

5825 DFS MAY HILL STKS (GROUP 2) (FILLIES) 1m (S)

3:15 (3:16) (Class 1) 2-Y-O
£45,416 (£17,216; £8,616; £4,296; £2,152; £1,080) **Stalls** High

Form				RPR
6221	**1**		**Pollenator (IRE)**[14] 5397 2-8-12 83 ... RyanMoore 5	107
			(R Hannon) *hld up towards rr: hdwy 2f out: rdn and edgd lft ent fnl f: sn drvn and kpt on wl to ld last 75yds* **14/1**	
32	**2**	*½*	**Hibaayeb**[19] 5284 2-8-12 0 ... NCallan 6	106
			(C E Brittain) *str: cl up: rdn 2f out: styd on to chal and ev ch ins fnl f tl nt qckn last 75yds* **40/1**	
1	**3**	*1*	**Seta**[41] 4542 2-8-12 0 ... KFallon 1	104
			(L M Cumani) *w'like: str: scope: tall: lw: trckd ldrs: hdwy on outer to ld 2f out: rdn and edgd rt ent fnl f: sn drvn and edgd lft: hdd and no ex last 75yds* **4/7**[1]	
0145	**4**	*2¼*	**Gallic Star (IRE)**[34] 4795 2-8-12 98 ... ChrisCatlin 2	99
			(M R Channon) *chsd ldrs: hdwy over 2f out: rdn wl over 1f out: kpt on same pce appr fnl f* **20/1**	
011	**5**	*½*	**Clarietta**[35] 4758 2-8-12 85 ... TedDurcan 4	98
			(J L Dunlop) *chsd ldrs: rdn along over 2f out: kpt on same pce* **9/1**[3]	
2122	**6**	*1¾*	**Virginia Hall**[20] 5279 2-8-12 105 ... SebSanders 7	94
			(Sir Mark Prescott) *hld up: a in rr* **11/2**[2]	
1	**7**	*shd*	**Quiet**[10] 5547 2-8-12 0 ... SteveDrowne 3	94
			(R Charlton) *w'like: str: lw: led: rdn along over 2f out: sn hdd & wknd* **11/1**	

1m 37.93s (-1.37) **Going Correction** -0.225s/f (Firm) **7** Ran SP% **111.2**
Speed ratings (Par 104): **97,96,95,93,92 91,90**
toteswinger: 1&2 £13.40, 1&3 £2.90, 2&3 £8.00. CSF £348.14 TOTE £12.30: £3.30, £6.10; EX 224.90.
Owner The Royal Ascot Racing Club **Bred** Tullamaine Castle Stud **Trained** East Everleigh, Wilts
■ Stewards' Enquiry : N Callan caution: used whip without giving filly time to respond

FOCUS
This Group 2 has thrown up its share of good fillies, if no real superstars, but has proved to be a good pointer to the Meon Valley Stud Fillies' Mile at the end of the month, with four of the last ten winners of this having gone on to follow up at Ascot, including three of the last four. There was a turn-up though, with the odds-on favourite apparently having every chance and being well held. This looked one of the lesser renewals with the first two showing big improvement. Seta was up 7lb on her debut win.

NOTEBOOK
Pollenator(IRE), the winner of maiden over 7f last time, had beaten Hibaayeb into third when second the time before. Although clearly on the upgrade, she was taking a big rise in grade and stepping up in trip. Held up out the back, she made good headway entering the final furlong and put her previous experience to good use to settle matters. She was a first pattern winner for her sire and is likely to be aimed for the Oaks now, for which she is quoted at around 20/1. (op 16-1)

Hibaayeb, third to two subsequently successful fillies, including Pollenator, on her debut and runner-up at Folkestone next time, was up in trip and taking a big step up in grade. She ran a fine race and battled on well in the closing stages, so should not be too long in getting off the mark.

Seta was sent off a hot favourite having been an impressive winner of a Newmarket maiden on debut from which the placed horses had subsequently been successful. A little keen early, everything appeared to be going to plan when she moved to the front at around the quarter-mile pole, but she did not pick up as well as expected when the challenges came inside the last. The bookmakers doubled her price for the 1000 Guineas to 16/1 but her trainer was not too disappointed as this half-sister to five winners has done some growing and is still on the weak side. She may have one more run this season and is in the Fillies' Mile, but something like the Rockfel looks more likely at this point. Official explanation: trainer had no explanation for the poor form shown (tchd 8-13)

Gallic Star(IRE), a 6f winner on fast ground and held in Listed and Group 3 company, appeared to run her race and, rated 98, is probably a fair guide to the level. (op 14-1)

Clarietta, a dual winner over 7f on easy ground, including on this track, beat two subsequent winners in a nursery last time but was found out by the big step up in grade. (op 10-1)

Virginia Hall had the highest mark of those with official ratings, having been placed in Listed and Group 3 company in France, but she never got involved having been held up off the pace. Official explanation: trainer had no explanation for the poor form shown (op 7-1)

Quiet, a half-sister to the smart middle-distance winner Double Crossed, was the winner of 1m Leicester maiden on her debut. She raced up with the pace but faded right out of things in the closing stages, finding the step up in grade too much at this early stage of her career. (op 10-1 tchd 12-1)

5826 FRANK WHITTLE PARTNERSHIP H'CAP 6f 110y
3:50 (3:53) (Class 2) (0-105,102) 3-Y-0+ **£12,952** (£3,854; £1,926; £962) **Stalls** High

Form RPR

-000 **1** **Brave Prospector**[24] 5132 4-9-3 **97**....(t) JamieSpencer 2 107
(P W Chapple-Hyam) *trckd ldrs: hdwy 2f out: rdn to ld over 1f out: drvn and edgd rt ins fnl f: kpt on* **16/1**

0102 **2** 1 1/4 **Castles In The Air**[8] 5615 4-8-10 **90**.... PaulHanagan 3 97
(R A Fahey) *lw: hld up in tch nr stands' rail: hdwy 2f out: rdn to chse ldrs over 1f out: drvn and edgd lft ins fnl f: kpt on* **5/1**[2]

5043 **3** hd **Jimmy Styles**[13] 5434 5-9-8 **102**.... RyanMoore 10 109
(C G Cox) *lw: chsd ldrs: rdn and hdwy over 1f out: drvn and kpt on ins fnl f* **5/2**[1]

5010 **4** shd **Musaalem (USA)**[34] 4796 5-9-4 **98**.... RHills 8 104
(W J Haggas) *swtg: hld up towards rr: swtchd rt and smooth hdwy 2f out: rdn to chse ldrs over 1f out: one pce ins fnl f: n.m.r and eased nr fin* **5/1**[2]

0-15 **5** 1 3/4 **Big Noise**[34] 4796 5-8-13 **93**.... TedDurcan 4 95
(Dr J D Scargill) *towards rr: hdwy 2f out: swtchd lft and rdn to chse ldrs ent fnl f: kpt on* **8/1**

0005 **6** hd **Pearly Wey**[13] 5424 6-8-8 **88**.... WilliamBuick 5 89
(C G Cox) *lw: chsd ldrs: rdn along wl over 1f out: drvn ent fnl f and kpt on same pce* **11/1**

2000 **7** 3/4 **Celtic Sultan (IRE)**[20] 5249 5-8-10 **90**.... MickyFenton 11 90
(T P Tate) *led on stands' rail: rdn along 2f out: sn drvn and hdd: grad wknd* **12/1**

530U **8** 2 **Excusez Moi (USA)**[5] 5695 7-9-0 **94**....(b) PJMcDonald 9 89
(Mrs R A Carr) *s.i.s and in rr: hdwy 2f out: sn rdn and n.d* **16/1**

4060 **9** 3/4 **Drawnfromthepast (IRE)**[84] 3091 4-8-12 **92**.... MJKinane 7 85
(J A Osborne) *chsd ldrs: rdn along over 2f out: sn drvn and wknd* **20/1**

1602 **10** 1 1/2 **Lowther**[20] 5249 4-8-12 **92**....(e) KFallon 6 81
(A Bailey) *unruly in stalls and blind removed late: s.i.s and in rr: hdwy on wd outside over 2f out: rdn to chse ldrs over 1f out: wknd ent fnl f* **13/2**[3]

3040 **11** 2 1/4 **Spanish Bounty**[12] 5476 4-9-1 **95**.... PatCosgrave 1 78
(J G Portman) *prom: rdn along 2f out: sn drvn and wknd* **40/1**

1m 16.98s (-2.92) **Going Correction** -0.225s/f (Firm) **11 Ran SP% 121.3**
Speed ratings (Par 109): **107,105,105,105,103 103,102,99,99,97 94**
toteswinger: 1&2 £10.30, 1&3 £8.80, 2&3 £3.30. CSF £97.20 CT £280.47 TOTE £20.70: £4.20, £2.00, £1.40; EX 99.70 Trifecta £737.40 Pool: £1036.37 - 1.04 winning units.
Owner Saleh Al Homaizi & Imad Al Sagar **Bred** Times Of Wigan Ltd **Trained** Newmarket, Suffolk

FOCUS
A good sprint handicap run at a furious pace and the form looks strong, rated around the placed horses.

NOTEBOOK
Brave Prospector had become a difficult horse to predict, but his Stewards' Cup run two starts back, when he made up a huge amount of ground to take fourth on his side, proved his ability remained. He was certainly in the mood this time, as he didn't lose much ground at the start and travelled supremely well. His response to pressure was also pleasing and he was a clear-cut winner. He's obviously pretty smart off a strong pace at around this trip, and his confidence may have been boosted, but it remains to be seen whether he can repeat this sort of form. If he can, he'll be a contender in the Ayr Gold Cup under a 5lb penalty, although his connections said he wants quick ground. Official explanation: trainer's rep said, regarding apparent improvement in form, that the colt missed the break last time and was suited by the trip of 6 1/2f and the good to firm ground, adding that the colt had been disappointing previously because the yard had been out of form (tchd 20-1)
Castles In The Air was 4lb lower than in future following his recent second placing over 7f at Wolverhampton. One of only two runners to race against the near-side rail early on, he stayed on well for strong pressure to get the best of the bunch for second. He should be suited by a return to slightly further. (op 9-1)
Jimmy Styles, fourth in the Great St Wilfrid, before running third in a Listed race at the July course, ran up to his mark on this return to handicap company. He didn't help his chance by edging right under pressure late on, however. (op 3-1)
Musaalem(USA), too keen when disappointing over 7f at the July course on his previous start, appreciated the strong pace and ran much better, despite his jockey having to stop riding in the final few strides. (tchd 11-2)
Big Noise didn't build on his recent encouraging fifth placing at the Newmarket July course. He might appreciate a return to 7f.
Pearly Wey is attractively handicapped and offered some encouragement. (op 17-2)
Celtic Sultan(IRE) went off too fast against the stands' rail and was swamped late on.
Lowther seemed unsuited by this drop in trip, although he did get upset in the stalls and his jockey also had a bit of bother removing the blindfold. The colt ended up stuck out very wide and can probably be given another chance. (op 7-1 tchd 15-2)

5827 SANDS VENUE AND STATE CLUB GAINSBOROUGH CONDITIONS STKS 7f
4:25 (4:26) (Class 2) 2-Y-0 **£10,904** (£3,265; £1,632) **Stalls** High

Form RPR

1 **1** **Al Zir (USA)**[35] 4756 2-9-2 0.... LDettori 3 107
(Saeed Bin Suroor) *unf: scope: tall: mde all: shkn up wl over 1f out: pushed clr ent fnl f* **30/100**[1]

15 **2** 5 **Treadwell (IRE)**[87] 2993 2-9-0 98.... MJKinane 2 92
(J A Osborne) *trckd wnr: hdwy over 2f out: rdn wl over 1f out: one pce appr fnl f* **4/1**[2]

1322 **3** 2 1/2 **Practitioner**[27] 5022 2-9-0 94....(b) SteveDrowne 4 86
(H J L Dunlop) *lw: dwlt: hld up: effrt over 2f out: sn rdn and outpcd* **8/1**[3]

1m 25.27s (-1.03) **Going Correction** -0.225s/f (Firm) **3 Ran SP% 108.0**
Speed ratings (Par 101): **96,90,87**
CSF £1.88 TOTE £1.30; EX 1.70.
Owner Godolphin **Bred** Jacks Or Better Farm Inc **Trained** Newmarket, Suffolk

FOCUS
A disappointing turnout for this good conditions race which in recent seasons has been won by promising types, although only Librettist developed into a top-notch performer, winning the Jacques le Marois and the Moulin as a 4yo. This year's renewal fell to a colt from the same stable, the impressive Al Zir. The form could have been rated higher.

NOTEBOOK
Al Zir(USA), a half-brother to high-class winners in the US and a $1.6m sales topper in the spring, had scored on his debut over 7f on easy ground and built on that with an all-the way success. He travelled well throughout and picked up when asked to beat two horses rated in the 90s by a wide margin, which suggests he ran to a mark of around 110, and on that basis is a worthy contender for either the Dewhurst or the Racing Post Trophy, his two big-race entries. (op 1-3)
Treadwell(IRE) had improved on his debut success when fifth in the Coventry in June but had been absent since. He is bred to stay this trip and held off the third well enough, but was no match for the winner. (tchd 9-2)
Practitioner, a winner over 6f on fast and runner-up in Listed company over 7f, was always at the rear and could never land a blow, but seemed to run close to his official mark with the runner-up.

5828 AGRIARGO UK (MCCORMICK) CLASSIFIED STKS 1m 2f 60y
4:55 (4:55) (Class 3) 3-Y-0+
£9,346 (£2,799; £1,399; £700; £349; £175) **Stalls** Low

Form RPR

013 **1** **Dangerous Midge (USA)**[42] 4481 3-8-11 79.... MartinDwyer 4 91
(B J Meehan) *midfield: hdwy and in tch on outer over 3f out: rdn wl over 1f out: str run appr fnl f: led last 100yds* **14/1**

2125 **2** 1 1/4 **Lady Artemisia (IRE)**[43] 4458 3-8-8 85.... WilliamBuick 1 90+
(M L W Bell) *lw: trckd ldrs on inner: effrt and nt clr run over 2f out and again wl over 1f out: sn swtchd rt and rdn: styd on strly on outer ins fnl f: nt rch wnr* **6/1**[3]

1000 **3** 1 1/4 **Full Speed (GER)**[24] 5137 4-9-4 84.... PJMcDonald 3 86
(G A Swinbank) *trckd ldrs: hdwy 3f out: rdn to ld briefly over 1f out: hdd jst ins fnl f: rallied towards fin* **33/1**

1520 **4** shd **Dark Prospect**[45] 4404 4-9-4 84....(p) NCallan 2 86
(M A Jarvis) *lw: trckd ldng pair: swtchd rt and hdwy 2f out: rdn to ld jst ins fnl f: sn drvn: hdd & wknd last 100yds* **20/1**

-145 **5** 1/2 **Muraweg (IRE)**[121] 1992 3-8-11 85.... RHills 7 85
(J H M Gosden) *dwlt: hld up in rr: hdwy on outer over 2f out: rdn to chse ldrs over 1f out: sn drvn and no imp ins fnl f* **4/1**[2]

3604 **6** 1/2 **Presbyterian Nun (IRE)**[23] 5170 4-9-1 85.... LDettori 6 81
(J L Dunlop) *midfield: hdwy 3f out: n.m.r 2f out: swtchd lft and hdwy over 1f out: rdn and ch ent fnl f: sn drvn and wknd* **15/2**

111 **7** 3/4 **Prince Of Johanne (IRE)**[20] 5266 3-8-11 85.... RyanMoore 8 83
(J Noseda) *hld up and bhd: hdwy wl over 2f out: rdn and edgd lft wl over 1f out: styd on ins fnl f: nrst fin* **11/4**[1]

0120 **8** 2 1/4 **Thin Red Line (IRE)**[41] 4520 3-8-11 84.... PaulHanagan 10 78
(E A L Dunlop) *lw: chsd ldrs: rdn along 3f out: grad wknd* **6/1**[3]

4210 **9** 3/4 **Summer Gold (IRE)**[34] 4781 5-9-1 82.... DavidAllan 5 74
(E J Alston) *hld up: effrt 3f out: sn rdn along and nvr nr ldrs* **16/1**

-020 **10** 1 **Alcalde**[21] 5230 3-8-11 85.... JoeFanning 9 75
(M Johnston) *trckd ldr: hdwy to chal wl over 3f out: rdn and slt ld 2f out: sn drvn and hdd over 1f out: wknd* **20/1**

3102 **11** 1/2 **Geneva Geyser (GER)**[27] 5027 3-8-11 85.... MickyFenton 12 74
(J M P Eustace) *wnt rt s: sn led: jnd and rdn along over 3f out: drvn and hdd 2f out: cl up tl wknd ent fnl f* **16/1**

2m 7.07s (-4.13) **Going Correction** -0.225s/f (Firm)
WFA 3 from 4yo+ 7lb **11 Ran SP% 117.9**
Speed ratings (Par 107): **107,106,105,104,104 104,103,101,101,100 99**
toteswinger: 1&2 £17.50, 1&3 £30.20, 2&3 £45.90. CSF £93.54 TOTE £18.20: £3.80, £2.30, £9.30; EX 113.40 Place 6: £1112.41 Place 5: £264.87.
Owner Iraj Parvizi **Bred** Tony Holmes & Dr Walter Zent **Trained** Manton, Wilts

FOCUS
A fair, competitive classified contest. It was well run and the form is sound with the winner progressing again.

NOTEBOOK
Dangerous Midge(USA) ◆ appreciated the switch to this galloping track and gained his second win from four starts. He came under pressure over three furlongs out, but gradually responded and was a decisive winner, albeit the runner-up enjoyed a luckless trip. He will almost certainly continue to improve as he goes up in distance and must be kept onside. (tchd 12-1)
Lady Artemisia(IRE) looked desperately unlucky not to give the winner more of a race. She continually had her path blocked from around three furlongs out until inside the final quarter mile, and had too much ground to make up when finally in the clear. (op 15-2)
Full Speed(GER) was always well positioned and seemed to have his chance. This was a respectable effort in defeat. (op 25-1)
Dark Prospect ran a little better than of late without suggesting he'll be worth a bet next time. (op 18-1 tchd 16-1)
Muraweg(IRE) had been off since shaping well at York back in May, so he's entitled to come on for this. (op 5-1)
Presbyterian Nun(IRE) couldn't sustain her challenge when in the clear and was a little disappointing. (op 7-1 tchd 13-2)
Prince Of Johanne(IRE) had won his last three starts, and the two latest victories in that sequence were gained under hold-up rides from Ryan Moore, but this time his jockey looked overconfident. The colt was left with it all to do at the top of the straight, having been held up last of all, and after being taken inside with his challenge, was slightly checked on more than one occasion. (op 7-2)
T/Plt: £2,026.20 to a £1 stake. Pool: £107,698.13. 38.80 winning tickets. T/Qpdt: £128.90 to a £1 stake. Pool: £6,977.73. 40.05 winning tickets. JR

5260 SANDOWN (R-H)
Friday, September 11

OFFICIAL GOING: Good to firm (good in places; 8.8)
Home bend at mid configuration adding about 4yards to advertised distances on round course.
Wind: Moderate behind Weather: Bright with cloud

5829 MILWARD PRINT GROUP EBF MAIDEN STKS 5f 6y
2:15 (2:18) (Class 4) 2-Y-0 **£5,180** (£1,541; £770; £384) **Stalls** High

Form RPR

5U5 **1** **Wellington Fair**[22] 5180 2-9-3 0....(v[1]) AdamKirby 6 80
(C G Cox) *sn led: drvn appr fnl f: styd on strly ins fnl f* **17/2**

2 1 1/4 **Racy** 2-9-3 0.... JimmyFortune 8 76+
(Sir Michael Stoute) *w'like: scope: in tch: hdwy 2f out: chsd wnr wl over 1f out: sn rdn and edgd rt: styd on but a readily hld* **5/4**[1]

5 **3** 3 **Swiss Cross**[92] 2853 2-9-3 0.... JimCrowley 7 65
(G A Butler) *unf: scope: lw: in tch: rdn 2f out: hdwy over 1f out: styd on to take 3rd ins fnl f but no imp on ldng duo* **10/3**[2]

03 **4** 1 1/2 **Machine Gun Kelly (IRE)**[27] 5017 2-9-3 0.... GeorgeBaker 9 59
(G L Moore) *chsd ldr tl over 3f out: sn rdn: wknd appr fnl f* **11/2**[3]

5 1 **Be Grateful (IRE)** 2-8-12 0.... TravisBlock 2 51+
(H Morrison) *w'like: bit bkwd: pushed along and outpcd after 2f: styd on fr over 1f out but nvr in contention* **33/1**

0 **6** 6 **Blue Neptune**[79] 3263 2-9-3 0.... DarryllHolland 5 34
(W R Muir) *w'like: chsd ldr over 3f out: sn rdn: wknd wl over 1f out* **16/1**

7 3 1/4 **Finch Flyer (IRE)** 2-9-3 0.... RichardMullen 3 22
(G L Moore) *w'like: outpcd and rdn in rr: wl bhd tl sme hdwy fnl f* **40/1**

00 **8** hd **Satin Princess (IRE)**[48] 4302 2-8-12 0.... GregFairley 1 17
(A M Hales) *leggy: s.i.s: sn chsng ldrs: rdn and hung lft 2f out: sn wknd* **100/1**

9 3 1/2 **Cereal Killer (IRE)** 2-9-3 0 .... PatDobbs 4 9
(R Hannon) *lengthy: unf: s.i.s: sn rdn and a bdly outpcd* **10/1**

60.94 secs (-0.66) **Going Correction** -0.10s/f (Good) 9 Ran SP% **114.8**
Speed ratings (Par 97): **101,99,94,91,90 80,75,75,69**
toteswinger: 1&2 £5.00, 1&3 £6.80, 2&3 £3.30. CSF £19.35 TOTE £10.90: £2.50, £1.10, £1.50; EX 27.40.
Owner Ken Lock Racing **Bred** Ken Lock Racing Ltd **Trained** Lambourn, Berks
■ Stewards' Enquiry : Jimmy Fortune £140 fine: late arrival into parade ring

FOCUS
Those with form did not set too high a standard but this shaped as though it could well be a better than the average 5f maiden staged on this track. Pleasing debuts by second and fifth.

NOTEBOOK
Wellington Fair, who was visored for the first time, had shown ability on his debut but had not been on his best behaviour when unseating his rider here on his second start, and suffered problems again in the stalls last time, though that wasn't entirely his fault. He had a behaviour expert down at the start with him this time and, although still breaking to his left, was soon at the head of affairs, never looking like being caught after quickening the pace over a furlong out. He is a speedy individual who looks capable of better, especially if he can continue to behave at the start. (op 9-1 tchd 15-2)
Racy ◆ looked a promising type on pedigree and in the paddock, being by Medicean and out of Soar, a dual Group winner as a two-year-old, and this was an encouraging display on his debut. He was always sat in a position ready to strike after breaking well, but could not find the gears to mount a serious challenge when entering the marker. A burly type, connections felt this 5f, though stiff, was sharp enough, as his dam improved for the step up to 6f, and he shaped as though that would also be the case for him. (op 10-11 tchd 11-8)
Swiss Cross was not unfancied on debut when not getting the best of runs and once again came in for some support. He did not get the best of breaks but travelled well enough behind the leaders and, although lacking the pace to get on terms, showed he has ability. He should not be long in getting off the mark. (op 7-1)
Machine Gun Kelly(IRE) had the advantage of being drawn against the far-side rail and got a handy break to sit behind the leader, but this drop back to 5f seemed to be his undoing as he could not match strides with the principals in the final half of the race. He looks capable of landing a nursery when stepped back up. (op 5-1 tchd 9-2)
Be Grateful(IRE) ◆ fared better than her finishing position suggested as she ran green and was always struggling to go the pace until finding her feet and doing her best work in the latter part of the race. (tchd 40-1)

5830 LONDON STOCK EXCHANGE H'CAP 5f 6y
2:50 (2:50) (Class 4) (0-80,79) 3-Y-O+ **£4,857** (£1,445; £722; £360) **Stalls** High

Form RPR
0305 **1** **Make My Dream**[34] 4787 6-8-6 **66** .... TPO'Shea 5 74
(J Gallagher) *chsd ldrs: rdn over 2f out: kpt on u.p fnl f to ld last strides* **6/1**[3]
2051 **2** *hd* **Cape Royal**[18] 5323 9-9-0 **74** ....(bt) KevinGhunowa 1 81
(J M Bradley) *lw: disp ld tl slt advantage fr 2f out: kpt on wl u.p fnl f: ct last strides* **12/1**
4115 **3** 3/4 **Royal Intruder**[28] 5001 4-9-3 **77** .... JimmyFortune 3 81+
(S Donohoe, Ire) *hld up in tch: hdwy fr 2f out: n.m.r 1f out: drvn and qcknd ins fnl f: nt rch ldng duo* **6/4**[1]
4005 **4** *nk* **Dazed And Amazed**[40] 4567 5-9-5 **79** .... PatDobbs 2 82
(R Hannon) *chsd ldrs: rdn and qcknd to chal 1f out: styd on same pce* **10/1**
2200 **5** 1 3/4 **Ivory Silk**[40] 4567 4-9-1 **75** ....(b) StephenDonohoe 6 72+
(J R Gask) *hld up in rr: nt much daylight fr over 1f out but styd on strly: gng on cl home* **7/2**[2]
0000 **6** *hd* **Commander Wish**[13] 5420 6-8-5 **65** oh8 ....(p) GregFairley 8 61
(Lucinda Featherstone) *chsd ldrs: rdn 2f out: wknd ins fnl f* **16/1**
0521 **7** *hd* **Nomoreblondes**[11] 5518 5-8-11 **71** 6ex ....(p) TonyCulhane 7 66
(P T Midgley) *disp ld 3f: wknd 1f out* **13/2**
0060 **8** 2 3/4 **Blades Princess**[23] 5149 3-9-1 **76** ....(b[1]) AlanMunro 4 62
(E S McMahon) *rdn 2f out: a outpcd* **20/1**

60.45 secs (-1.15) **Going Correction** -0.10s/f (Good)
WFA 3 from 4yo+ 1lb 8 Ran SP% **117.3**
Speed ratings (Par 105): **105,104,103,103,100 99,99,95**
toteswinger: 1&2 £4.90, 1&3 £7.60, 2&3 £3.20. CSF £75.27 CT £163.03 TOTE £7.70: £1.90, £2.90, £1.10; EX 60.40.
Owner Mrs Irene Clifford **Bred** The Valentines **Trained** Chastleton, Oxon

FOCUS
An open sprint with some coming back to form and others looking for a resurgence in form. It was run at a decent pace. The form is rated around the front pair.

5831 HOEKSTRA FRUIT EXPORTERS EBF MAIDEN STKS 1m 14y
3:25 (3:26) (Class 4) 2-Y-O **£5,180** (£1,541; £770; £384) **Stalls** High

Form RPR
2 **1** **Hot Prospect**[49] 4286 2-9-3 0 .... PhilipRobinson 1 91+
(M A Jarvis) *w'like: scope: lw: mde all: reminder over 1f out: sn lengthened and in command: readily* **8/15**[1]
2 2 **Morana (IRE)** 2-9-3 0 .... AlanMunro 4 87+
(P W Chapple-Hyam) *unf: tall: lw: chsd ldrs: drvn and styd on to chse wnr appr fnl f: no imp but styd on strly for clr 2nd* **11/2**[2]
46 **3** 4 1/2 **Philander**[10] 5561 2-9-3 0 .... DaneO'Neill 2 77+
(E J O'Neill) *w'like: chsd wnr over 5f out: rdn and no imp over 2f out: lost 2nd over 1f out: wknd ins fnl f* **16/1**
4 1/2 **Spoken** 2-9-3 0 .... RichardKingscote 3 76+
(R Charlton) *w'like: scope: lw: s.i.s: in rr: pushed along and hdwy fr 3f out: styd on fnl f but nvr gng pce to trble ldrs* **16/1**
25 **5** 2 1/4 **Corsica (IRE)**[14] 5407 2-9-3 0 .... GregFairley 7 71
(M Johnston) *chsd wnr tl over 5f out: rdn over 3f out: sn one pce: wknd over 1f out* **9/1**[3]
0 **6** 9 **Lyric Poet (USA)**[14] 5401 2-9-0 0 .... AhmedAjtebi(3) 6 51
(Saeed Bin Suroor) *w'like: scope: lengthy: chsd ldrs: rdn over 3f out and nvr any ch after* **18/1**
7 5 **Monterey (IRE)** 2-9-3 0 .... TPQueally 10 40+
(T G Mills) *unf: s.i.s: rdn and green fr over 3f out: a bhd* **14/1**
8 3/4 **Lajidaal (USA)** 2-9-3 0 .... TPO'Shea 9 38
(M P Tregoning) *w'like: scope: bit bkwd: sn rdn: green and a bhd* **25/1**
9 57 **Bravo Bravo** 2-9-3 0 .... TonyCulhane 8 —
(Eve Johnson Houghton) *w'like: bit bkwd: slowly away: sn t.o* **66/1**

1m 42.31s (-0.99) **Going Correction** +0.075s/f (Good) 9 Ran SP% **119.6**
Speed ratings (Par 97): **107,105,100,100,97 88,83,83,26**
toteswinger: 1&2 £2.20, 1&3 £3.90, 2&3 £6.30. CSF £4.13 TOTE £1.60: £1.20, £1.50, £1.50; EX 5.40.
Owner A D Spence **Bred** Highclere Stud & Hmh Management **Trained** Newmarket, Suffolk

FOCUS
A quality maiden, contested by five runners with Group 1 entries and several others with the pedigrees to be well above average. Most, however, are the type to be seen to much better advantage over further next year.

NOTEBOOK
Hot Prospect ◆ took them along at a decent clip and record a time just outside a second slower than the juvenile record over a mile, held by no other than Reference Point. It was also just under a half a second quicker than the three-year-old handicap which was to follow. He had the whole field in trouble from the three-furlong marker before running on to score in quite taking fashion. He had made a very encouraging debut when chasing home subsequent Listed winner Vale Of York, and looks one to follow for next season. He is likely to be put away after one more run in about a month's time, and there are no solid commitments. (op 8-11)
Morana(IRE) ◆ is related to the smart miler Blythe Knight and this was a most pleasing debut. He did not handle the home bend particularly well, although that would have had little bearing on the outcome as the winner just held too many guns for him to mount a serious challenge. A similar race oiught to be a formality, but connections are toying with stepping him straight up in class for the Royal Lodge. However he fares there, he has the makings of a smart middle-distance three-year-old. (op 9-2 tchd 6-1)
Philander had twice not been beaten far in France and this was again an encouraging display on his British debut. After chasing the winner for most of the way he could not maintain the effort, but he kept on well enough to suggest he should find an opportunity if continuing this progression.
Spoken ◆ is a half-brother to three useful middle-distance winners, out of his stable's classy middle-distance filly Spout. He reared leaving the stalls but performed pleasingly without ever getting on terms and looks capable of much better in time. (op 12-1)
Corsica(IRE) has failed to build upon an encouraging debut and, after running keenly, was a spent force form two furlongs out. This was a shade disappointing again. (op 12-1)
Lyric Poet(USA) was close enough if good enough when entering the straight but looked very one-paced. (op 20-1)
Monterey(IRE) is a well regarded colt who cost 230,000 guineas and is from a highly successful family, his dam, who won the Musidora, having already produced several classy middle-distance types, including Playful Act, Percussionist, Echoes In Eternioty and this colt's stablemate Petara Bay. There was little immediate promise here, but he was far too green to do himself justice and should be a different proposition next year. (op 12-1 tchd 16-1)
Bravo Bravo, a 110,000gns purchase, ran very green and was always detached.

5832 AIM H'CAP 1m 14y
4:00 (4:01) (Class 3) (0-90,89) 3-Y-O **£7,771** (£2,312; £1,155; £577) **Stalls** High

Form RPR
5-21 **1** **Stoic (IRE)**[13] 5435 3-8-13 **84** .... TPQueally 3 98+
(J Noseda) *hld up in tch: hdwy 3f out: sn drvn: styd on to ld appr fnl f: rdn out* **15/8**[1]
01 **2** 1/2 **Fanunalter**[37] 4648 3-9-4 **89** .... DarryllHolland 8 102+
(M Botti) *lw: s.i.s: hld up in rr: stdy hdwy on outside fr 3f out: drvn and qcknd over 1f out: chsd wnr ins fnl f but a jst hld* **11/4**[2]
351 **3** 1 3/4 **Bravo Echo**[55] 4095 3-9-0 **85** .... JimmyFortune 1 94
(J H M Gosden) *lw: chsd ldr after 1f: drvn to ld 2f out: hdd over 1f out: hung rt u.p ins fnl f and readily outpcd* **6/1**[3]
1440 **4** 3 1/4 **Glowing Praise**[13] 5432 3-8-9 **80** .... RichardMullen 7 81
(E S McMahon) *plld hrd and led 1f: stdd to trck ldrs: rdn 3f out and no imp: one pce fnl 2f* **16/1**
1000 **5** *nk* **Yorgunnabelucky (USA)**[13] 5419 3-9-0 **85** .... GregFairley 6 85
(M Johnston) *sn chsng ldrs: rdn 3f out: one pce fnl 2f* **16/1**
-000 **6** *hd* **Full Toss**[28] 4983 3-9-3 **88** .... DaneO'Neill 5 88
(R Hannon) *in rr: pushed along and stl last over 2f out: kpt on fr over 1f out: fin wl but nt a threat* **18/1**
3264 **7** 3/4 **Star Links (USA)**[22] 5189 3-8-12 **83** .... PatDobbs 9 81
(R Hannon) *chsd ldrs: rdn over 3f out: one pce: sme prog again fnl f* **14/1**
4610 **8** 1 **Chapter And Verse (IRE)**[8] 5598 3-8-10 **81** .... MichaelHills 2 77
(B W Hills) *led after 1f: hdd 2f out: wknd appr fnl f* **10/1**
0005 **9** 6 **Archie Rice (USA)**[13] 5432 3-9-1 **86** .... AlanMunro 4 67
(W Jarvis) *s.i.s: rdn 3f out: a bhd* **20/1**
1-4 **10** 1 1/2 **Albaher**[140] 1487 3-8-9 **80** .... TPO'Shea 10 58
(J L Dunlop) *swtg: rdn over 3f out: a in rr* **25/1**

1m 42.74s (-0.56) **Going Correction** +0.075s/f (Good) 10 Ran SP% **117.1**
Speed ratings (Par 105): **105,104,102,99,99 99,98,97,91,89**
toteswinger: 1&2 £3.20, 1&3 £2.40, 2&3 £4.30. CSF £6.90 CT £25.68 TOTE £3.10: £1.40, £1.60, £2.00; EX 9.90.
Owner Highclere Thoroughbred Racing (Gimcrack) **Bred** Darley **Trained** Newmarket, Suffolk

FOCUS
A decent 3-y-o handicap which was run at an ordinary pace. It is worth being positive about the form and the race looks set to yield its fair share of winners.

NOTEBOOK
Stoic(IRE) ◆ had been progressing nicely since his debut last season and ran out a ready winner to follow up his recent Newmarket success. Connections were very pleased with the way he stuck to his task when challeneged by the runner-up, especially after getting a bit of a rough ride on the way through. He remains on an upward curve and looks well capable of defying a 4 or 5lb rise in the weights. (op 2-1 tchd 9-4)
Fanunalter ◆ is a big, imposing individual and this was a decent effort under top weight. Impressive when scoring at Kempton, after which he was given a mark of 89, he might just have been a shade unlucky not to follow up. His action was a bit high coming up the straight and once again he didn't handle the home bend particularly well, but he moved up menacingly in the straight and looked the likely winner until the similarly unexposed Stoic pulled out more. This was a most pleasing effort against a well handicapped rival and he remains a decent prospect. (op 100-30 tchd 7-2)
Bravo Echo had been raised 2lb after returning to winning ways when landing a valuable prize at Newmarket in July and this was another solid effort. Always up with the pace, he had his chance and kept on well enough in the final furlong, but he had no answers to the front pair towards the finish. (op 5-1)
Glowing Praise ran with plenty of credit and did not help his cause by pulling hard. He stuck to his task gamely and, if settling better, should be found an opening before long.
Yorgunnabelucky(USA), dropped back to a mile after some disappointing efforts since scoring at Redcar in June, shaped better.
Full Toss ◆ caught the eye somewhat when staying on strongly in the final furlong from the rear. He has had a disappointing time of it since a successful two-year-old campaign and might just be returning to form. (op 16-1 tchd 14-1)

5833 MAIN MARKET H'CAP 1m 14y
4:35 (4:35) (Class 4) (0-80,80) 3-Y-O+ **£4,857** (£1,445; £722; £360) **Stalls** High

Form RPR
5110 **1** 1 **Rock Anthem (IRE)**[7] 5640 5-8-12 **72** .... AndreaAtzeni(3) 7 79
(Mike Murphy) *lw: hld up in rr: stdy hdwy on outside over 2f out to chse ldr appr fnl f: kpt on but a hld: fin 2nd, 1l: awrdd r* **4/1**[2]
4321 **2** 1 3/4 **Poyle Meg**[28] 5010 3-9-1 **77** ....(p) JimCrowley 1 78
(R M Beckett) *chsd ldrs: rdn 3f out: styd on same pce fr over 1f out: fin 3rd: plcd 2nd* **17/2**
3222 **3** *hd* **Truly Asia (IRE)**[23] 5151 3-8-13 **75** .... JimmyFortune 3 76
(R Charlton) *chsd ldrs: rdn over 3f out: one pce fnl 2f: fin 4th: plcd 3rd* **9/2**[3]

4430 **4** 2 ½ **El Libertador (USA)**[12] 5475 3-8-11 73 StephenCarson 9 68
(E A Wheeler) *led 2f: styd pressing ldr and ev ch 2f out: wknd sn after: fin 5th: plcd 4th* **10/1**

2154 **5** 9 **Palacefield (IRE)**[13] 5448 3-9-2 78 AlanMunro 5 51
(P W Chapple-Hyam) *in tch whn pushed along after 2f: dropped to rr and rdn 3f out: sn wknd: fin 6th: plcd 5th* **7/2**[1]

1102 **6** 2 **Gallego**[8] 5602 7-8-2 66 JosephineBruning(7) 6 35
(R J Price) *s.i.s: rdn over 3f out: a in rr: fin 7th: plcd 6th* **6/1**

1124 **D** **Desert Kiss**[25] 5099 4-9-9 80 AdamKirby 4 88
(W R Swinburn) *lw: trckd ldr: led after 2f: hrd drvn whn chal 2f out: styd on wl u.p thrght fnl f: fin 1st: disq: jockey weighed in light* **4/1**[2]

1m 43.19s (-0.11) **Going Correction** +0.075s/f (Good)
WFA 3 from 4yo+ 5lb **7 Ran SP% 114.3**
Speed ratings (Par 105): **102,100,100,97,88 86,103**
toteswinger: 1&2 £8.10, 1&3 £4.60, 2&3 £4.30. CSF £36.70 CT £157.90 TOTE £5.40: £2.70, £3.90; EX 43.60.
Owner Ronald Bright **Bred** Mervyn Stewkesbury **Trained** Westoning, Beds
■ Stewards' Enquiry : Adam Kirby three-day ban: weighed in 1lb light (Sep 25, 27-28)

FOCUS
A small but competitive handicap which had a controversial outcome when the winner was disqualified because her rider weighed in at 9st 7.5lb, as opposed to the 9st 9lb she was allotted. Sound but ordinary form.
Palacefield(IRE) Official explanation: jockey said colt ran flat

5834 PKF H'CAP 1m 2f 7y
5:05 (5:08) (Class 4) (0-85,82) 3-Y-O **£4,857** (£1,445; £722; £360) **Stalls High**

Form RPR

2145 **1** **Senses (USA)**[48] 4299 3-8-13 77 DarryllHolland 3 82
(J Noseda) *lw: hld up in rr: hdwy on outside over 2f out: sn rdn: hd high and hung rt ins fnl f: led fnl 100yds: in command cl home* **8/1**

3345 **2** ½ **Calaloo (IRE)**[11] 5532 3-8-12 76 (b) JimCrowley 1 80
(C R Egerton) *in tch: rdn 3f out: hdwy over 2f out: led 1f out: hdd and no ex u.p fnl 100yds* **12/1**

1 **3** 2 ¼ **Life's Challenge (USA)**[26] 5071 3-9-4 82 GregFairley 2 82+
(M Johnston) *w'like: leggy: chsd ldrs: rdn over 3f out: led 2f out: hdd 1f out: outpcd ins fnl f* **7/2**[1]

1223 **4** 1 **Sequillo**[6] 5663 3-9-4 82 JimmyFortune 5 80
(R Hannon) *stdd s and hld up in rr: drvn and hdwy fr 2f out: styd on appr fnl f: sn one pce* **9/2**[2]

0402 **5** ¾ **Nawaadi (USA)**[21] 5223 3-8-12 76 (v¹) TPO'Shea 6 72
(J H M Gosden) *lw: chsd ldrs: rdn to ld 3f out: hdd 2f out: wknd fnl f* **7/1**[3]

-016 **6** 1 ½ **Directorship**[30] 4902 3-9-4 82 RichardKingscote 7 75
(P R Chamings) *swtg: t.k.h towards rr: pushed along and styd on fnl 2f: nvr in contention* **12/1**

3223 **7** ¾ **Nbhan (USA)**[25] 5102 3-8-13 77 DaneO'Neill 8 69
(L M Cumani) *lw: chsd ldrs: rdn over 3f out: wknd over 1f out* **15/2**

0530 **8** 1 ¼ **Swift Chap**[15] 5366 3-8-6 73 AndreaAtzeni(3) 11 62
(B R Millman) *t.k.h: chsd ldrs: rdn 3f out: wknd wl over 1f out* **14/1**

2042 **9** 1 ¼ **Russian George (IRE)**[20] 5255 3-9-2 80 GeorgeBaker 12 67
(S Gollings) *in tch: rdn and effrt 3f out: nvr nr ldrs and sn wknd: lame* **16/1**

4230 **10** 12 **Decision**[21] 5209 3-9-0 78 AdamKirby 9 41
(C G Cox) *lw: led tl hdd 3f out: sn btn* **7/1**[3]

2m 10.41s (-0.09) **Going Correction** +0.075s/f (Good) **10 Ran SP% 116.2**
Speed ratings (Par 103): **103,102,100,100,99 98,97,96,95,86**
toteswinger: 1&2 £18.60, 1&3 £8.40, 2&3 £11.10. CSF £99.01 CT £398.52 TOTE £9.00: £2.30, £3.40, £2.10; EX 125.00 Place 6: £18.47 Place 5: £14.31.
Owner Sir Robert Ogden **Bred** Dr K K Jayaraman Et Al **Trained** Newmarket, Suffolk

FOCUS
A competitive handicap, but run at just a fair pace. The form is a bit muddling, with a few of these becoming disappointing.
Russian George(IRE) Official explanation: jockey said gelding finished lame
T/Jkpt: Not won. T/Plt: £36.60 to a £1 stake. Pool: £66,813.37. 1,330.73 winning tickets. T/Qpdt: £28.60 to a £1 stake. Pool: £4,261.45. 109.90 winning tickets. ST

5676 WOLVERHAMPTON (A.W) (L-H)
Friday, September 11

OFFICIAL GOING: Standard
Wind: Almost nil Weather: Fine

5835 WILLIAMHILL.COM/BONUS25 - GET £25 FREE BET CLAIMING STKS 5f 216y(P)
5:40 (5:43) (Class 5) 2-Y-O **£3,885** (£1,156; £577; £288) **Stalls Low**

Form RPR

3005 **1** **Existentialist**[20] 5241 2-8-6 75 HayleyTurner 2 61+
(J G Portman) *hld up and bhd: pushed along over 2f out: hdwy wl over 1f out: rdn to ld towards fin: edgd lft: r.o* **10/1**

1123 **2** ½ **Diamond Laura**[21] 5208 2-8-12 86 SilvestreDeSousa 7 66+
(Mrs R A Carr) *chsd ldrs: pushed along over 2f out: rdn wl over 1f out: kpt on towards fin* **10/11**[1]

1065 **3** nk **Lady Pattern (IRE)**[20] 5265 2-8-12 80 ShaneKelly 8 65+
(P W D'Arcy) *sn led: rdn over 1f out: hdd towards fin* **5/2**[2]

3224 **4** ½ **Yeadon**[34] 4774 2-8-9 74 FrederikTylicki(3) 10 63+
(R A Fahey) *a.p: chsd ldr 3f out: rdn over 1f out: lost 2nd wl ins fnl f: hld whn n.m.r nr fin* **11/2**[3]

0645 **5** 1 **Bathwick Gino**[8] 5613 2-8-2 54 (v¹) MartinLane(5) 9 55
(P D Evans) *a.p: rdn wl over 1f out: no ex ins fnl f* **33/1**

000 **6** 3 ¾ **Teeraha (IRE)**[8] 5613 2-8-3 0 JamieMackay 1 40
(D Shaw) *broke wl: stdd to rr sn after s: pushed along over 2f out: nvr nr ldrs* **100/1**

7 hd **Magenta Strait** 2-8-4 0 PaulQuinn 6 40
(R Hollinshead) *s.i.s: hld up and bhd: hdwy over 2f out: wknd wl over 1f out* **40/1**

0660 **8** 21 **London Girl (IRE)**[21] 5226 2-8-0 46 ow5 (p) JamesPSullivan(7) 5 —
(A J McCabe) *led early: prom tl wknd wl over 2f out: eased fnl f* **66/1**

9 156 **Calle Vistamar** 2-8-6 0 ow9 AlexEdwards(7) 4 —
(S Wynne) *s.s: rel to r: a t.o* **100/1**

1m 15.11s (0.11) **Going Correction** -0.10s/f (Stan) **9 Ran SP% 114.3**
Speed ratings (Par 95): **95,94,93,93,91 86,86,58,—**
toteswinger: 1&2 £1.10, 1&3 £14.70, 2&3 £1.90. CSF £19.52 TOTE £10.20: £2.00, £1.02, £1.40; EX 26.20.Existentialist was claimed by A. E. Price for £13,000.
Owner Paul Moulton **Bred** R F And S D Knipe **Trained** Compton, Berks

FOCUS
A fairly wide range of ability on show. The pace was sound and the principals, who finished in a heap, raced centre to far side in the straight. The proximity of the fifth holds the form down to an extent.

NOTEBOOK
Existentialist, who had a good chance at the weights on this all-weather debut, had faced some stiff tasks since winning her maiden but appreciated the drop in grade and showed a good attitude. She should be able to win again in this type of event. (op 8-1 tchd 11-1)
Diamond Laura, a consistent type, was the pick of the weights dropped in grade and ran another solid race - despite getting tapped for toe at a crucial stage. She is a gutsy sort but, although vulnerable to the more progressive types from her current mark in nurseries, she should continue to give a good account. (op 8-11 tchd 4-6 and Evens)
Lady Pattern(IRE) had an obvious chance on these terms and turned in a creditable effort down in grade on this all-weather debut. She may struggle to win a handicap from her 80 mark but she should be able to pick up a similar event on either turf or on all-weather. (op 4-1)
Yeadon was far from disgraced on this Polytrack debut given he had a few pounds to find strictly on official ratings. This trip seems to suit better than 5f and, although he has had a few chances, he should be able to pick up an ordinary event. (op 13-2)
Bathwick Gino had plenty to find at the weights and raced keenly in the first time visor so deserves plenty of credit in the circumstances. The drop back to this trip proved no inconvenience but he will be of more interest in ordinary handicaps unless the handicapper overreacts. (op 28-1)
Magenta Strait, the first foal of a multiple 1m-1m2f winner, hinted at ability after a tardy start on this racecourse debut and is entitled to improve for the experience. (op 33-1)

5836 WILLIAMHILL.COM/BONUS25 - POKER TOURNAMENTS H'CAP 5f 216y(P)
6:10 (6:11) (Class 5) (0-70,71) 3-Y-O+ **£3,238** (£963; £481; £240) **Stalls Low**

Form RPR

3000 **1** **Charles Darwin (IRE)**[27] 5020 6-8-7 57 FrancisNorton 2 68
(M Blanshard) *hld up: stdy prog over 3f out: pushed along to ld wl ins fnl f: drvn out* **16/1**

0042 **2** 1 **Lucky Dan (IRE)**[14] 5405 3-9-3 69 SilvestreDeSousa 1 77
(Paul Green) *hld up and sn bhd: nt clr run on ins over 2f out: hdwy wl over 1f out: sn rdn: swtchd rt ins fnl f: fin wl* **11/2**[3]

0420 **3** ½ **Espy**[18] 5323 4-9-3 67 JamesDoyle 4 73
(S Kirk) *a.p: chsd ldr over 3f out: rdn over 1f out: kpt on same pce fnl f* **9/2**[2]

1260 **4** nk **Billy Red**[15] 5374 5-9-1 65 (b) FergusSweeney 8 70
(J R Jenkins) *led: rdn 1f out: hdd and no ex wl ins fnl f* **16/1**

3321 **5** 3 ½ **Weet A Surprise**[6] 5678 4-9-0 71 6ex (v) AlexEdwards(7) 11 65
(J W Unett) *hld up towards rr: hdwy on outside over 2f out: c wd st: rdn wl over 1f out: no further prog* **4/1**[1]

4405 **6** ¾ **Don Pele (IRE)**[9] 5576 7-8-9 64 (p) MartinLane(5) 7 56
(R A Harris) *hld up in rr: pushed along over 2f out: kpt on fr jst over 1f out: n.d* **8/1**

4354 **7** ¾ **Dream Express (IRE)**[8] 5612 4-9-6 70 IanMongan 6 59
(P Howling) *hld up: sn mid-div: pushed along and short-lived effrt over 1f out* **6/1**

-046 **8** 2 **Wotatomboy**[37] 4664 3-8-5 60 MichaelJStainton(3) 12 43
(R M Whitaker) *in rr: pushed along over 3f out: short-lived effrt on ins wl over 1f out* **50/1**

0625 **9** ¾ **Miss Daawe**[35] 4754 5-8-11 61 TomEaves 5 41
(B Ellison) *prom: pushed along over 2f out: wkng whn n.m.r wl over 1f out* **22/1**

1130 **10** hd **Fyelehk (IRE)**[26] 5065 3-8-12 64 DavidProbert 3 44
(B R Millman) *chsd ldrs on ins: pushed along over 2f out: rdn and wknd over 1f out* **11/2**[3]

2600 **11** 7 **Green Onions**[46] 4374 3-8-11 63 NeilChalmers 13 20
(A J Lidderdale) *a in rr: rdn and no ch wl over 1f out* **66/1**

1306 **12** 1 **Grand Palace (IRE)**[181] 843 6-9-6 70 (v) VinceSlattery 9 24
(H J Evans) *chsd ldrs tl pushed along and wknd wl over 1f out* **40/1**

1m 13.46s (-1.54) **Going Correction** -0.10s/f (Stan)
WFA 3 from 4yo+ 2lb **12 Ran SP% 116.4**
Speed ratings (Par 103): **106,104,104,103,98 97,96,94,93,93 83,82**
toteswinger: 1&2 £9.30, 1&3 £13.00, 2&3 £2.80. CSF £97.55 CT £379.77 TOTE £13.90: £4.20, £2.10, £2.40; EX 142.10.
Owner The Breeze-In Partnership **Bred** M And P Associates **Trained** Upper Lambourn, Berks

FOCUS
Mainly exposed performers in an ordinary handicap, but sound form. The pace was sound and the first four pulled clear. The winner raced centre to far side in the straight.
Fyelehk(IRE) Official explanation: jockey said gelding never travelled

5837 WILLIAMHILL.COM/BONUS25 - QUOTE BONUS25 H'CAP 1m 5f 194y(P)
6:40 (6:40) (Class 4) (0-80,80) 3-Y-O+ **£5,046** (£1,510; £755; £377; £188) **Stalls Low**

Form RPR

6152 **1** **Jadalee (IRE)**[7] 5642 6-9-4 70 (tp) KFallon 9 81
(G A Butler) *prom: led over 12f out: pushed along over 2f out: edgd rt and rdn over 1f out: drvn out* **7/4**[1]

5164 **2** 1 **Murcar**[29] 4951 4-9-4 70 (b) IanMongan 1 79
(C G Cox) *hld up in mid-div: hdwy over 3f out: sn pushed along: rdn jst over 2f out: swtchd lft and styd on to take 2nd cl home* **11/2**[3]

2124 **3** nk **Trip The Light**[14] 5402 4-9-8 77 (v) FrederikTylicki(3) 3 86
(R A Fahey) *hld up in mid-div: hdwy on ins over 3f out: sn pushed along: chsd wnr and rdn 2f out: no ex and lost 2nd cl home* **15/2**

1022 **4** 6 **Maslak (IRE)**[7] 5649 5-10-0 80 PhillipMakin 7 81
(P W Hiatt) *led early: a.p: chsd wnr over 3f out tl rdn 2f out: wknd ins fnl f* **12/1**

1035 **5** 9 **Pelham Crescent (IRE)**[69] 3635 6-9-10 76 DavidProbert 2 64
(B Palling) *s.i.s: hld up in rr: pushed along over 4f out: rdn over 2f out: nvr nr ldrs* **33/1**

5606 **6** 2 **Dunaskin (IRE)**[13] 4840 9-9-11 77 TomEaves 6 62
(B Ellison) *sn led: hdd over 12f out: rdn and wknd over 4f out* **16/1**

6315 **7** ½ **Galilean Moon**[29] 4948 3-8-12 75 SebSanders 10 60
(Sir Michael Stoute) *prom: chsd wnr after 3f tl pushed along over 3f out: wknd wl over 2f out* **4/1**[2]

1250 **8** 4 ½ **Chookie Hamilton**[16] 5334 5-9-4 75 PatrickDonaghy(5) 5 53
(I Semple) *hld up in tch: lost pl and pushed along wl over 3f out: no ch fnl 2f* **20/1**

0056 **9** 2 **Salute (IRE)**[65] 3737 10-9-5 71 RobertHavlin 8 46
(P G Murphy) *hld up in mid-div: pushed along 7f out: bhd fnl 5f* **16/1**

1/0- **10** dist **City Well**[419] 4200 6-9-7 73 FergusSweeney 4 —
(Mrs L J Young) *s.i.s: a in rr: t.o fnl 4f* **66/1**

3m 0.75s (-5.25) **Going Correction** -0.10s/f (Stan)
WFA 3 from 4yo+ 11lb **10 Ran SP% 112.2**
Speed ratings (Par 105): **111,110,110,106,101 100,100,97,96,—**
toteswinger: 1&2 £7.90, 1&3 £7.20, 2&3 £7.70. CSF £10.56 CT £55.30 TOTE £3.00: £1.50, £2.40, £2.80; EX 12.90.
Owner Brian Shrubsall & Stef Stefanou **Bred** Hawthorn Villa Stud **Trained** Newmarket, Suffolk

FOCUS
A fair handicap run at an ordinary gallop. The first four pulled clear and the winner raced in the centre in the straight. He did not need to match his Kempton latest.

City Well Official explanation: jockey said gelding was reluctant to race

5838 WILLIAMHILL.COM/BONUS25 LIVE CASINO DEALERS H'CAP 1m 4f 50y(P)
7:10 (7:10) (Class 6) (0-55,55) 3-Y-O £2,729 (£806; £403) Stalls Low

Form RPR

0-05 **1** **Largem**[18] 5314 3-8-11 **53** SimonWhitworth 8 59+
(J R Jenkins) *hld up in rr: hdwy on outside wl over 1f out: sn rdn: led ins fnl f: edgd lft: styd on* **16/1**

0233 **2** 1 1/2 **Jachol (IRE)**[16] 5331 3-8-13 **55** (p) SebSanders 12 59
(W J Haggas) *hld up in rr: stdy prog 8f out: pushed along over 2f out: carried hd high and ev ch 1f out: styd on same pce* **7/2**[2]

-000 **3** 1/2 **Saute**[52] 4171 3-8-13 **55** ShaneKelly 1 58
(W R Swinburn) *sn led: hdd over 8f out: prom: rdn over 2f out: ev ch fr wl over 1f out tl no ex wl ins fnl f* **33/1**

2330 **4** 3/4 **Tinkerbelle (IRE)**[19] 5286 3-8-11 **53** TedDurcan 6 55
(J L Dunlop) *hld up in mid-div: stdy prog 3f out: rdn and ev ch over 1f out: nt qckn ins fnl f* **12/1**

0622 **5** 3/4 **Galiotto (IRE)**[36] 4722 3-8-8 **53** JackMitchell(3) 9 54
(C F Wall) *a.p: rdn and ev ch wl over 1f out: one pce ins fnl f* **9/4**[1]

6462 **6** *hd* **Screaming Brave**[12] 5470 3-8-13 **55** TonyCulhane 2 55
(M R Channon) *t.k.h: led early: led over 8f out tl over 4f out: led 3f out: rdn over 1f out: hdd ins fnl f: one pce whn n.m.r towards fin* **6/1**[3]

5036 **7** 1/2 **Shadows Lengthen**[16] 5331 3-8-12 **54** KFallon 3 54
(M W Easterby) *prom: lost pl on ins 6f out: pushed along over 3f out: nt clr run briefly over 2f out: rdn and rallied wl over 1f out: sn swtchd lft: one pce fnl f* **8/1**

5300 **8** 1/2 **One Scoop Or Two**[70] 3575 3-8-13 **55** (t) SJCraine 11 54
(F Sheridan) *swtchd lft to ins sn after s: hld up in rr: hdwy on ins wl over 1f out: sn rdn: no imp fnl f* **66/1**

4000 **9** 1/2 **Brad's Luck (IRE)**[35] 4744 3-8-12 **54** FrancisNorton 5 54+
(M Blanshard) *hld up in mid-div: pushed along 3f out: nt clr run fr jst over 1f out: eased wl ins fnl f* **25/1**

0403 **10** 2 1/2 **Black River Falls (USA)**[12] 5470 3-8-12 **54** (b) TomEaves 7 48
(I Semple) *hld up in mid-div: short-lived effrt on outside 3f out* **10/1**

-000 **11** 7 **Sampower Quin (IRE)**[73] 3474 3-8-13 **55** DNolan 10 38
(D Carroll) *hld up in mid-div: pushed along over 3f out: bhd fnl 2f* **33/1**

1025 **12** 6 **Kochanski (IRE)**[16] 5342 3-8-13 **55** PhillipMakin 4 28
(J R Weymes) *prom: wnt 2nd over 6f out: led over 4f out to 3f out: sn pushed along and wknd* **25/1**

2m 42.12s (1.02) **Going Correction** -0.10s/f (Stan) **12** Ran SP% **116.1**
Speed ratings (Par 99): **92,91,90,90,89 89,89,88,88,86 82,78**
toteswinger: 1&2 not won, 1&3 not won, 2&3 not won. CSF £66.84 CT £1856.83 TOTE £14.10: £7.30, £1.40, £12.30; EX 87.10.
Owner D Bryans **Bred** Mrs P J Rowland **Trained** Royston, Herts

FOCUS
A moderate handicap run at just an ordinary gallop. The winner raced in the centre in the straight. The form is a bit muddling and not that solid.
Largem Official explanation: trainer said, regarding apparent improvement in form, that the gelding appears to be strengthening and maturing.
Shadows Lengthen Official explanation: jockey said gelding was denied a clear run
Brad's Luck(IRE) Official explanation: jockey said gelding was denied a clear run

5839 WILLIAM HILL 0800 444040 - GET £25 FREE BET MEDIAN AUCTION MAIDEN STKS 1m 141y(P)
7:40 (7:42) (Class 5) 2-Y-O £2,914 (£867; £433; £216) Stalls Low

Form RPR

5420 **1** **Sejanus**[29] 4931 2-9-3 73 PhillipMakin 1 74
(K A Ryan) *mde all: rdn wl over 1f out: drvn out and hld on wl ins fnl f* **3/1**[2]

33 **2** *nk* **Venutius**[7] 5627 2-9-3 0 GrahamGibbons 3 73
(E S McMahon) *a.p: chsd ldr jst over 3f out: rdn and sustained chal fr over 1f out: nt qckn nr fin* **5/4**[1]

06 **3** 1 1/4 **Masterful Act (USA)**[22] 5192 2-9-3 0 TonyCulhane 6 71
(J R Best) *hld up in tch: hdwy 2f out: sn rdn along: styd on towards fin* **50/1**

0 **4** 1 1/2 **Perceptive**[28] 5000 2-8-12 0 HayleyTurner 9 63+
(J R Fanshawe) *hld up towards rr: pushed along over 2f out: styd on over 1f out: nrst fin* **16/1**

53 **5** 1 1/4 **Gracelightening**[14] 5407 2-8-12 0 SilvestreDeSousa 2 60
(Paul Green) *chsd wnr tl jst over 3f out: rdn over 2f out: wknd over 1f out* **8/1**[3]

6 1 1/4 **Hold Me** 2-8-12 0 IanMongan 8 57
(H R A Cecil) *hld up towards rr: pushed along over 3f out: nvr trbld ldrs* **8/1**[3]

7 8 **Albacocca** 2-8-12 0 SebSanders 7 47+
(Sir Mark Prescott) *s.s: in rr: pushed along over 3f out: no rspnse* **10/1**

00 **8** 1 **Winston's Lad**[81] 3218 2-9-3 0 JimmyQuinn 5 43
(P Howling) *hld up in tch: wknd wl over 1f out* **50/1**

9 10 **Reve De Mardi** 2-8-12 0 MatthewDavies(5) 4 22
(George Baker) *s.i.s: hld up in mid-div: rdn and bhd fnl 2f* **40/1**

000 **10** 26 **Ellies Image**[33] 4817 2-8-12 50 J-PGuillambert 10 —
(B P J Baugh) *a towards rr: rdn over 4f out: eased whn no ch over 2f out* **100/1**

1m 50.97s (0.47) **Going Correction** -0.10s/f (Stan) **10** Ran SP% **114.0**
Speed ratings (Par 95): **93,92,91,90,89 88,80,80,71,48**
toteswinger: 1&2 £3.90, 1&3 £14.50, 2&3 £14.50. CSF £6.82 TOTE £4.20: £1.10, £1.30, £10.70; EX 9.20.
Owner Mrs Margaret Forsyth **Bred** Mrs F S Williams **Trained** Hambleton, N Yorks

FOCUS
An uncompetitive event run at a reasonable gallop. The winner raced centre to far side in the straight and got the run of the race in front. He and the second basically ran to form.

NOTEBOOK
Sejanus looked to have decent claims if his previous run could be forgiven and he showed a gutsy attitude to beat his main market rival on this Polytrack debut. His two best efforts have been on artificial surfaces and he may be capable of a little better in this sphere. (op 100-30 tchd 7-2)
Venutius, who attracted plenty of support, looked to have solid claims on this company on his all-weather debut and he seemed to give it his best shot under a forceful ride. This confirmed he is capable of winning in ordinary nursery company or away from progressive types in this grade. (op 13-8)
Masterful Act(USA) gave trouble at the start but turned in easily his best effort upped in trip against a couple of fair sorts on this third, and qualifying run for a handicap mark. He has physical scope and may be capable of further progress. (op 66-1)
Perceptive had been soundly beaten on her debut but turned in a better showing on this first run on Polytrack. She should have no problems staying 1m2f and will be of more interest once qualified for a handicap mark. (op 14-1)
Gracelightening confirmed the improvement shown on turf on her previous start and again left the impression that a stiffer test of stamina and the switch to ordinary handicap company would see her in a better light. (op 13-2)
Hold Me, a 15,000gns half-sister to several winners in the US, hails from a yard that has been going really well but was very easy to back and did not show enough on this racecourse debut to suggest she would be of much short term interest. (op 6-1)

5840 WILLIAMHILL.COM/BONUS25 - PLAY VEGAS GAMES MAIDEN STKS 1m 141y(P)
8:10 (8:11) (Class 5) 3-Y-O+ £2,729 (£806; £403) Stalls Low

Form RPR

423 **1** **Awesome Surprise (USA)**[14] 5394 3-8-10 74 ShaneKelly 11 72+
(J Noseda) *chsd ldr: led over 2f out: hdd 1f out: sn rdn: led cl home* **13/8**[1]

2 1/2 **Monaco (GER)** 3-9-1 0 KFallon 2 76+
(L M Cumani) *prom: jinked rt bnd over 7f out: pushed along over 2f out: rdn to ld 1f out: hdd cl home* **4/1**[3]

3 3 **Ulzana (IRE)** 3-9-1 0 SebSanders 3 69+
(Sir Mark Prescott) *s.i.s: hld up towards rr: pushed along and hdwy on ins over 3f out: one pce ins fnl f* **10/1**

542 **4** 5 **Landofthefourones (USA)**[26] 5071 3-9-1 70 TedDurcan 4 57
(D R Lanigan) *a.p: hmpd bnd over 7f out: rdn 3f out: wknd 2f out* **11/4**[2]

0 **5** 2 1/2 **Luisa Tetrazzini (IRE)**[51] 4199 3-8-10 0 PhillipMakin 1 47
(K A Ryan) *led: pushed along and hdd over 2f out: rdn and wknd jst over 1f out* **20/1**

0 **6** *hd* **Fairplaytomyself**[11] 5531 4-8-9 0 TobyAtkinson(7) 5 46
(P W Hiatt) *s.s: hld up in rr: swtchd rt and pushed along over 2f out: rdn wl over 1f out: nvr nr ldrs* **50/1**

6600 **7** *nk* **Elements (IRE)**[7] 5624 3-8-10 52 GrahamGibbons 6 46
(E J Alston) *hld up towards rr: pushed along and short-lived effrt over 3f out* **33/1**

8 15 **Denices Desert** 3-8-10 0 JimmyQuinn 10 11
(M Botti) *s.i.s: sme prog over 6f out: pushed along and wknd over 3f out* **12/1**

0000 **9** 3 1/2 **Vin De Rose**[12] 5482 3-8-10 40 MarkCoumbe(5) 12 8
(John A Harris) *prom tl pushed along and wknd over 3f out* **100/1**

0 **10** 27 **Elevate Bobbob**[178] 855 3-8-8 0 BillyCray(7) 9 —
(A Berry) *a in rr: pushed along and lost tch 3f out: t.o* **100/1**

1m 49.77s (-0.73) **Going Correction** -0.10s/f (Stan)
WFA 3 from 4yo 6lb **10** Ran SP% **113.2**
Speed ratings (Par 103): **99,98,95,91,89 89,88,75,72,48**
toteswinger: 1&2 £1.30, 1&3 £8.50, 2&3 £2.00. CSF £7.74 TOTE £2.80: £1.30, £3.00, £2.50; EX 13.70.
Owner D Brennan **Bred** W S Farish & Skara Glen Stables **Trained** Newmarket, Suffolk

FOCUS
A race lacking strength in depth but the first three pulled clear. The winner did not need to improve but the first three can all do better. The gallop was an ordinary one and the winner raced centre to far side in the straight.
Fairplaytomyself Official explanation: jockey said filly missed the break and ran green
Denices Desert Official explanation: jockey said filly ran green

5841 WILLIAM HILL 0800 444040 - QUOTE BONUS25 NURSERY 7f 32y(P)
8:40 (8:40) (Class 4) (0-80,76) 2-Y-O £5,046 (£1,510; £755; £377; £188) Stalls High

Form RPR

0356 **1** **Thomas Baines (USA)**[30] 4901 2-8-10 **65** HayleyTurner 3 70+
(M L W Bell) *hld up in rr: pushed along and hdwy over 1f out: led ins fnl f: r.o wl* **8/1**

6652 **2** 1 1/4 **Saxby (IRE)**[22] 5187 2-8-12 **67** TonyCulhane 4 69
(M R Channon) *a.p: chsd ldr over 4f out: rdn over 1f out: ev ch ins fnl f: nt qckn cl home* **9/2**[3]

0461 **3** 1 1/2 **Russian Davis (IRE)**[23] 5166 2-8-13 **68** KFallon 2 68+
(R M H Cowell) *hld up: pushed along whn n.m.r briefly jst over 1f out: r.o to take 3rd cl home* **6/4**[1]

0236 **4** *nse* **Al Khimiya (IRE)**[64] 3786 2-9-1 **70** TedDurcan 6 68
(S A Callaghan) *hld up: pushed along and hdwy wl over 1f out: kpt on one pce fnl f* **4/1**[2]

240 **5** 3/4 **Cafe Greco**[34] 4790 2-9-5 **74** SebSanders 5 70
(P J Makin) *sn led: pushed along and edgd rt over 1f out: rdn and hdd ins fnl f: one pce* **11/2**

034 **6** 4 **Electric City (IRE)**[15] 5360 2-9-7 **76** AlanMunro 1 63
(M G Quinlan) *led early: chsd ldr tl over 4f out: wknd over 1f out* **16/1**

1m 29.63s (0.03) **Going Correction** -0.10s/f (Stan) **6** Ran SP% **110.6**
Speed ratings (Par 97): **95,93,91,91,90 86**
toteswinger: 1&2 £3.40, 1&3 £3.40, 2&3 £1.60. CSF £41.41 TOTE £5.30: £5.10, £4.20; EX 45.30.
Owner R A Green **Bred** Joseph Joyce **Trained** Newmarket, Suffolk

FOCUS
Not the strongest of nurseries and one in which an ordinary gallop picked up approaching the home turn. The winner raced centre to far side in the straight and the second helps with the level.

NOTEBOOK
Thomas Baines(USA) has been disappointing since a luckless run at Windsor in April but he finally came good on this all-weather debut and on this second run since being gelded. A stronger overall gallop would have suited and he may well be able to progress further on Polytrack.
Saxby(IRE) is a reliable yardstick who had the run of the race and looks the best guide to the worth of this form on only this second all-weather start. His consistency means he'll get little respite from the handicapper but he should continue to give a good account. (op 13-2 tchd 7-1 and 4-1)
Russian Davis(IRE), 9lb higher than when showing improved form at Kempton on his previous start, looks a bit better than the bare form after racing far too keenly in a race run at just an ordinary gallop. He'll be suited by more of an end-to-end gallop and will be worth another chance. (op 5-4)
Al Khimiya(IRE), who came from a race that threw up several winners last time, was not disgraced on only this second start on Polytrack. She too may have been better suited by a stronger overall gallop. (op 7-2 tchd 5-1)
Cafe Greco, dropped in distance for this nursery debut, fared better than at Lingfield on his previous start. He is fairly unexposed but is going to have to settle better if he is going to progress. (op 7-1 tchd 5-1)
Electric City(IRE), who proved easy to back, had the run of the race but folded tamely on this nursery debut back up in trip. Her mark looks a stiff one and she is going to have to show a bit more before she is worth a bet. (op 14-1)

5842 WILLIAMHILL.COM/BONUS25 - BINGO BONANZAS H'CAP 7f 32y(P)
9:10 (9:12) (Class 6) (0-55,55) 3-Y-O+ £2,729 (£806; £403) Stalls High

Form RPR

-005 **1** **Obe Brave**[19] 5287 6-8-12 **55** (p) SebSanders 9 65
(Lee Smyth, Ire) *sn chsng ldr: led over 2f out: hrd rdn over 1f out: all out* **18/1**

1222 **2** *shd* **King's Icon (IRE)**[6] 5683 4-8-5 55........................(b[1]) TobyAtkinson(7) 10 65
(M Wigham) *hld up in mid-div: hdwy 2f out: rdn over 1f out: r.o ins fnl f* **5/2[1]**
0601 **3** *nse* **Golden Prospect**[9] 5569 5-8-11 54........................ LiamJones 5 64
(J W Hills) *s.i.s: hld up in rr: hdwy over 1f out: r.o wl towards fin* **6/1[3]**
0042 **4** *1* **Kingsgate Castle**[4] 5729 4-8-12 55........................(b) KFallon 3 62
(Miss Gay Kelleway) *hld up towards rr: hdwy on ins wl over 1f out: rdn and nt qckn ins fnl f* **7/2[2]**
6200 **5** *1 3/4* **Vanadium**[27] 5019 7-8-12 55........................ FergusSweeney 12 57
(G L Moore) *sn prom: rdn jst over 1f out: one pce* **8/1**
6000 **6** *3/4* **Danish Art (IRE)**[83] 3174 4-8-5 55........................ JamesPSullivan(7) 7 55
(M W Easterby) *hld up towards rr: hdwy over 1f out: one pce fnl f* **33/1**
0002 **7** *2* **Annes Rocket (IRE)**[13] 5429 4-8-7 55........................ GabrielHannon(5) 8 50
(J C Fox) *hld up in rr: c wd st: pushed along and hung lft over 1f out: nvr trbld ldrs* **9/1**
0030 **8** *3* **Yes Please**[7] 5624 4-8-12 55........................(v[1]) PhillipMakin 6 42
(K A Ryan) *prom: pushed along over 2f out: wknd over 1f out* **50/1**
0000 **9** *3 1/2* **Ardent Prince**[6] 5683 6-8-12 55........................ DavidProbert 11 32
(A J McCabe) *s.i.s: hld up towards rr: rdn wl over 1f out: no rspnse* **20/1**
6000 **10** *1 1/4* **The Wily Woodcock**[8] 5617 5-8-11 54........................(p) NeilChalmers 4 28
(T Wall) *hld up in rr: rdn over 2f out: no rspnse* **80/1**
4060 **11** *2* **Lady Amberlini**[79] 3272 4-8-11 54........................ TravisBlock 1 22
(C R Dore) *hld up in mid-div: pushed along over 2f out: wknd wl over 1f out* **40/1**
0300 **12** *4 1/2* **Dhhamaan (IRE)**[21] 5225 4-8-12 55........................(bt) SilvestreDeSousa 2 11
(Mrs R A Carr) *led: rdn and hdd over 2f out: wknd qckly over 1f out* **8/1**

1m 27.93s (-1.67) **Going Correction** -0.10s/f (Stan) **12** Ran SP% **115.9**
Speed ratings (Par 101): **105,104,104,103,101 100,98,95,91,89 87,82**
toteswinger: 1&2 £20.70, 1&3 £20.70, 2&3 £20.70. CSF £59.48 CT £318.17 TOTE £11.90: £5.20, £1.50, £1.80; EX 97.30 Place 6: £27.70 Place 5: £23.48.
Owner Mark Devlin **Bred** Helshaw Grange Stud, E Kent & Mrs E Co **Trained** Dungannon, Co Tyrone

FOCUS
A moderate handicap run at a strong gallop throughout. Sound form. The principals raced centre to far side in the straight.
Ardent Prince Official explanation: jockey said gelding lost its action
T/Plt: £21.60 to a £1 stake. Pool: £72,225.28. 2,433.84 winning tickets. T/Qpdt: £10.10 to a £1 stake. Pool: £7,401.38. 541.40 winning tickets. KH

5843 - 5849a (Foreign Racing) - See Raceform Interactive

MARSEILLE BORELY (L-H)
Friday, September 11

OFFICIAL GOING: Good to soft

5850a PRIX TWIG (MAIDEN) (C&G) 1m 1f
12:55 (12:58) 2-Y-O **£6,796** (£2,718; £2,039; £1,359; £680)

RPR
1 **Laristan (FR)** 2-8-12 .... IMendizabal —
(J-C Rouget, France)
2 *hd* **Ridge City (IRE)** 2-8-12 .... SRichardot —
(P Khozian, France)
3 *hd* **Bahamian Box** 2-8-12 .... GMillet —
(T Larriviere, France)
4 *2* **Quillin** 2-8-12 .... DBonilla —
(E J O'Neill) *led after 1f: set slow pce: rdn 2f out: hdd 100yds out: one pce* **17/2[1]**
5 *3* **Franklino (FR)** 2-8-12 .... —
(K Borgel, France)
6 *3/4* **Bakoulele (FR)** 2-9-2 ....(p) —
(C Scandella, France)
7 *2* **Peace And Liberty (FR)** 2-9-2 .... —
(M Pimbonnet, France)
8 *3/4* **Les Yeux Noirs (FR)** 2-8-12 .... —
(F Rossi, France)
9 *10* **Parisis (FR)** 2-8-12 .... —
(J-M Capitte, France)

1m 51.2s (111.20) **9** Ran SP% **10.5**
PARI-MUTUEL (including 1 Euro stake): WIN 2.30; PL 1.30, 2.60, 2.00;DF 10.70.
Owner H H Aga Khan **Bred** H H Aga Khan **Trained** Pau, France

5247 CHESTER (L-H)
Saturday, September 12

OFFICIAL GOING: Good to firm (good in places; 8.2)
Wind: Light, half-against Weather: Warm and sunny

5852 HEATHCOTES OUTSIDE E B F MAIDEN STKS 7f 2y
2:15 (2:15) (Class 4) 2-Y-O **£5,828** (£1,734; £866; £432) **Stalls** Low

Form RPR
06 **1** **Kumbeshwar**[21] 5251 2-8-12 0........................ RichardEvans(5) 1 80
(P D Evans) *mde all: pushed along whn pressed 3f out: rdn over 1f out: plld out ex towards fin* **14/1**
3 **2** *1/2* **Medicinal Compound**[15] 5408 2-9-3 0........................ JohnEgan 2 79
(K A Ryan) *sn rdn along bhd front quartet: swtchd lft to chal on rail over 1f out: r.o u.p: hld towards fin* **10/3[2]**
24 **3** *1 1/2* **Laureldean Spirit (IRE)**[44] 4460 2-8-12 0........................ TonyHamilton 5 70
(R A Fahey) *racd keenly: chsd ldrs: effrt to chal over 1f out: no ex fnl 75yds* **5/6[1]**
04 **4** *1 1/2* **Deely Plaza**[10] 5571 2-9-3 0........................ MartinDwyer 6 71
(R Hannon) *trckd ldrs: rdn over 1f out: styd on same pce ins fnl f* **17/2[3]**
03 **5** *4 1/2* **Spinning Spirit (IRE)**[12] 5527 2-9-3 0........................ TPQueally 8 60
(J G Given) *pressed wnr: rdn over 1f out: wknd ins fnl f* **16/1**
002 **6** *32* **Lilyannabanana**[16] 5360 2-8-12 70........................ CatherineGannon 3 —
(P D Evans) *s.i.s: a struggling and sn wl bhd* **9/1**
7 *19* **Peace And Glory (IRE)** 2-8-12 0........................ RichardKingscote 7 —
(J W Unett) *missed break: a stuggling and sn wl bhd: eased over 1f out* **33/1**

1m 26.63s (0.13) **Going Correction** -0.125s/f (Firm) **7** Ran SP% **113.7**
Speed ratings (Par 97): **94,93,91,90,84 48,26**
toteswingers: 1&2 £5.00, 1&3 £4.40, 2&3 £1.20. CSF £59.32 TOTE £16.50: £6.30, £2.30; EX 66.50.
Owner G E Amey **Bred** G E Amey **Trained** Pandy, Monmouths
■ Stewards' Enquiry : Richard Evans caution: excessive use of the whip
T P Queally one-day ban: careless riding (Sep 27)

FOCUS
The going had firmed up slightly overnight, and the official description was changed to good to firm, good in places, with the GoingStick reading 8.2. No more than a fair maiden, rated around the fourth. Improvement from the winner.

NOTEBOOK
Kumbeshwar stepped up greatly on his debut effort when sixth in a stronger heat here last time, and this was another big step forward. Drawn in the best stall, he bounced out well to again make the running and was able to take the field along at a sensible gallop. He came under pressure before the turn into the straight, but his pedigree suggests he is not short of stamina, and he kept finding, holding his rivals at bay slightly cosily. A step up to a mile won't hurt him in nurseries and he should get a lot further next year. (op 11-1 tchd 16-1)
Medicinal Compound was never travelling from an early stage but his rider didn't stop shoving, stayed on the rail, and, when the split came in the straight, kept on well for second. He'll improve further as he gathers experience. (op 4-1 tchd 9-2)
Laureldean Spirit(IRE) was all the rage beforehand, but she proved a bit disappointing. Always towards the outer, she swung widest into the straight and her effort petered out close home. She hadn't run on ground this quick before and perhaps it didn't suit her. (op Evens tchd 11-10 in places)
Deely Plaza, stepping up to 7f for the first time, enjoyed a good lead through the race and couldn't have too many excuses. Handicaps are now an option for him, though. (op 15-2 tchd 9-1)
Spinning Spirit(IRE) travelled well to the turn in on the winner's shoulder but was one-paced once let down, and a drop back to sprinting looks in order now that he's eligible to run in nursery company. (op 14-1 tchd 11-1)
Lilyannabanana Official explanation: jockey said filly never travelled
Peace And Glory(IRE) Official explanation: jockey said filly ran very green

5853 CHESHIRE LIFE NURSERY (H'CAP) 7f 2y
2:45 (2:45) (Class 3) (0-95,84) 2-Y-O **£9,146** (£2,737; £1,368; £684; £340) **Stalls** Low

Form RPR
310 **1** **Bab At The Bowster (IRE)**[21] 5265 2-9-0 77........................ LiamJones 3 79+
(W J Haggas) *in rr: hdwy 3f out: r.o ins fnl f to ld towards fin* **4/1[1]**
0120 **2** *nk* **Transfixed (IRE)**[3] 5762 2-8-13 76........................ CatherineGannon 1 77
(P D Evans) *racd keenly: trckd ldrs: led wl over 2f out: rdn over 1f out: hdd towards fin* **9/2[2]**
032 **3** *3/4* **Demonstrative (USA)**[21] 5251 2-8-9 72........................ SilvestreDeSousa 6 71+
(M Johnston) *chsd ldrs: rdn and outpcd 3f out: rallied over 1f out: styd on ins fnl f: nt quite pce to get to front pair* **4/1[1]**
0320 **4** *3/4* **Antonius Moris (IRE)**[42] 4525 2-9-7 84........................ RichardKingscote 7 82+
(Tom Dascombe) *hld up: hdwy 3f out: chsd ldrs 2f out: trying to chal whn n.m.r and checked ins fnl f: styd on u.ptowards fin* **10/1**
2212 **5** *1/2* **Gillburg (USA)**[11] 5550 2-9-0 77........................(p) JohnEgan 4 73
(K A Ryan) *led: hdd wl over 2f out: rdn over 1f out: no ex fnl 75yds* **4/1[1]**
014 **6** *13* **Royal Box**[26] 5091 2-8-12 75........................ MartinDwyer 2 38+
(R Hannon) *chsd ldrs: lost pl over 4f out: struggling after* **9/2[2]**
2425 **7** *1 3/4* **Il Forno**[61] 3925 2-8-11 74........................ AndrewMullen 5 33
(D Nicholls) *racd keenly w ldr tl hung rt fr 3f out: sn wknd* **9/1[3]**

1m 26.84s (0.34) **Going Correction** -0.125s/f (Firm) **7** Ran SP% **115.5**
Speed ratings (Par 99): **93,92,91,90,90 75,73**
toteswinger: 1&2 £8.10, 1&3 £6.50, 2&3 £3.40. CSF £22.57 CT £76.07 TOTE £5.40: £2.50, £2.40; EX 21.30.
Owner Findlay & Bloom **Bred** Raymond P Doyle **Trained** Newmarket, Suffolk

FOCUS
Not as good a nursery as the rating band would have one believe, as the top weight weighed in at 11lb below the ceiling for the race. There was something of a blanket finish as well. The second and fourth help with the level.

NOTEBOOK
Bab At The Bowster(IRE) was disappointing at Sandown on her handicap debut but she was too keen that day and settled better here. Pushed along entering the straight, she found the ones in front getting tired and stayed on best to take the race close home, suggesting there is more to come from her in similar races run at a strong gallop. Official explanation: trainer said, regarding apparent improvement in form, that the filly was better suited by the stronger pace. (op 5-1)
Transfixed(IRE) takes her racing extremely well and, turned out just three days after having too much use made of her at Doncaster, returned to form with a sound effort in defeat. She was ridden more patiently this time and it suited her. (op 4-1)
Demonstrative(USA) was stuck out wide all the way to the turn into the straight and didn't run at all badly in the circumstances. He should remain of interest of his current sort of mark. (op 5-1 tchd 6-1 in places)
Antonius Moris(IRE), who had the worst of the draw, got the longer trip well and would have finished a bit closer had he not been hampered late on. (op 8-1)
Gillburg(USA), who was not left alone in front, was running over 7f for the first time and found his stamina running out inside the last. (op 5-1)
Royal Box sweated up beforehand and disappointed. His maiden win came on soft ground and perhaps conditions were too quick for him. (op 4-1)
Il Forno raced much too keenly and didn't get home. Official explanation: jockey said gelding hung right-handed throughout (op 8-1)

5854 SPORTINGBET.COM STAND CUP (LISTED RACE) 1m 4f 66y
3:15 (3:15) (Class 1) 3-Y-O+ **£23,704** (£8,964; £4,480; £2,240) **Stalls** Low

Form RPR
6054 **1** **Snoqualmie Girl (IRE)**[23] 5202 3-8-1 98........................ SilvestreDeSousa 3 103
(D R C Elsworth) *trckd ldrs: pushed along over 3f out: wnt 2nd 2f out: swtchd rt over 1f out: r.o to chal ins fnl f: led cl home* **9/1**
6341 **2** *hd* **Traffic Guard (USA)**[14] 5446 5-9-6 114........................ MartinDwyer 5 113
(P F I Cole) *prom: led after 2f: rdn over 1f out: pressed ins fnl f: hdd cl home* **15/8[1]**
6503 **3** *6* **Indian Days**[7] 5662 4-9-1 105........................ TPQueally 1 98
(J G Given) *led for 2f: chsd ldr tl rdn 2f out: wknd ins fnl f* **11/2**
30/2 **4** *1* **Blue Bajan (IRE)**[120] 2056 7-9-1 111........................ JohnEgan 2 96
(Andrew Turnell) *hld up: hdwy over 5f out: pushed along over 3f out: no imp on ldrs fr over 1f out* **11/4[2]**
11U0 **5** *8* **Hatton Flight**[70] 3620 5-9-1 99........................(b) WilliamBuick 4 84
(A M Balding) *hld up: pushed along 6f out: struggling after: lost tch 3f out* **10/1**
136 **6** *21* **Urban Poet (USA)**[14] 5425 3-8-6 108........................ AhmedAjtebi 6 50
(Saeed Bin Suroor) *prom: chsd ldrs after 2f: rdn and wknd over 4f out: lost tch 3f out: t.o* **5/1[3]**

2m 34.93s (-4.97) **Going Correction** -0.125s/f (Firm)
WFA 3 from 4yo+ 9lb **6** Ran SP% **112.6**
Speed ratings (Par 111): **111,110,106,106,100 86**
toteswinger: 1&2 £4.90, 1&3 £19.10, 2&3 £3.80. CSF £26.54 TOTE £10.10: £3.40, £1.70; EX 31.90.
Owner J C Smith **Bred** Littleton Stud **Trained** Newmarket, Suffolk

FOCUS
Only two of these had won at Listed level before, and they fought out the finish. The early pace wasn't that strong. Ordinary form for the grade, with the winner the best guide.

NOTEBOOK

Snoqualmie Girl(IRE), one of two three-year-olds in the field and the only filly, had shaped well in the Galtres Stakes on her return from a ten-week break last time, and coped well enough with the ground to run down the leader close home. Softer conditions will undoubtedly suit her better and she could be in for a good autumn granted a bit of rain as she hasn't been over-raced this season. (tchd 8-1)

Traffic Guard(USA) pulled his way to the front turning into the straight for the first time. He proceeded to pull out a bit of a gap on the rest, but used up plenty of energy in doing so and, although he still looked likely to take some catching when kicking off the final bend, he was eventually worn down. He'd have been happier tracking a strong pace, as at Windsor last time. (op 2-1 tchd 9-4)

Indian Days, third in a Group 3 on the Polytrack last time, doesn't have much of a strike-rate but he's consistent enough. This was another sound effort. (tchd 5-1 and 6-1)

Blue Bajan(IRE) was expected to need this having had a break since May, and the way he ran confirmed that view. His connections are preparing him for a tilt at the Cesarewitch before another hurdling campaign over the winter. (op 3-1 tchd 100-30 in places)

Hatton Flight, who ran poorly when last seen, was returning from a 70-day break. He had a task on at the weights and never threatened to land a blow. (tchd 15-2)

Urban Poet(USA) never looked at home on the track and ran another poor race in Godolphin blue. He looks to need a flat, galloping track. (op 9-2 tchd 11-2)

5855 CARLSBERG CONDITIONS STKS 7f 122y

3:55 (3:57) (Class 3) 3-Y-O+ £9,066 (£2,697; £1,348; £673) Stalls Low

Form				RPR
0105	1		**Dijeerr (USA)**[124] 1929 5-9-4 109 (vt) AhmedAjtebi(3) 4 (Saeed Bin Suroor) *w ldr: led over 2f out: rdn over 1f out: kpt on wl and a doing enough towards fin* **4/1**[2]	106
1243	2	¾	**Cyflymder (IRE)**[12] 5529 3-8-12 96 MartinDwyer 2 (R Hannon) *in rr: wnt 3rd 3f out: rdn over 1f out: wnt 2nd ins fnl f: styd on u.p but a looked hld by wnr* **6/1**[3]	99
6100	3	1 ¾	**Carcinetto (IRE)**[2] 5798 7-8-11 98 RichardEvans(5) 1 (P D Evans) *chsd ldrs: pushed along and dropped to last 3f out: kpt on u.p ins fnl f: tk 3rd cl home: nt pce to chal* **7/1**	95
1120	4	nk	**Cloudy Start**[43] 4486 3-9-0 106 TPQueally 3 (H R A Cecil) *led: hdd over 2f out: u.p over 1f out: kpt on same pce fnl f* **8/13**[1]	96

1m 32.07s (-1.73) **Going Correction** -0.125s/f (Firm)
WFA 3 from 5yo+ 5lb 4 Ran SP% **108.7**
Speed ratings (Par 107): **103,102,100,100**
CSF £22.99 TOTE £4.20; EX 20.30.
Owner Godolphin **Bred** Monticule **Trained** Newmarket, Suffolk

FOCUS

This was something of a tactical affair. The early pace was ordinary and they sprinted from the turn in. With the favourite disappointing the runner-up is the best guide to the form.

NOTEBOOK

Dijeerr(USA) was best in at the weights and has won fresh before, so a 124-day layoff wasn't a concern. Sitting on the shoulder of his main market rival through the early stages, he quickened up nicely enough to take the advantage entering the straight, but he didn't stretch clear as he'd threatened to. The bare form of this race doesn't look that much, and he carried his head a little high, so perhaps he wouldn't be one to totally trust in better company. (op 100-30 tchd 3-1)

Cyflymder(IRE) would have been 9lb better off at the weights with the winner had this been a handicap, so he performed with great credit to take second. However, any rise in the weights on the back of this is likely to make his tough to place in the near future. (op 5-1)

Carcinetto(IRE), who won a handicap over the C&D last month, was making a quick reappearance having finished down the field behind Fantasia at Doncaster two days earlier. She never threatened really, but her best chance of success will come in similar events restricted to fillies. (op 6-1)

Cloudy Start made the early running but, once passed by the winner entering the straight, struggled to stay in contact. He had run a great race considering how much use was made of him in the Totesport Mile at Goodwood last time, but surprisingly that competitive handicap has yet to produce a winner. Official explanation: trainer had no explanation for the poor form shown (op 5-6 tchd 10-11 in places)

5856 HEATHCOTES OUTSIDE H'CAP 5f 16y

4:30 (4:31) (Class 4) (0-85,84) 3-Y-O+ £5,504 (£1,637; £818; £408) Stalls Low

Form				RPR
066	1		**Stolt (IRE)**[3] 5767 5-8-8 78 GaryBartley(5) 1 (N Wilson) *mde all: kicked clr over 1f out: r.o wl and in command fnl f* **7/2**[1]	93
2000	2	3 ¼	**Bel Cantor**[15] 5404 6-8-12 77 (p) J-PGuillambert 2 (W J H Ratcliffe) *chsd ldrs: wnt 2nd 2f out: rdn over 1f out: nt pce of wnr after* **9/2**[3]	80
353	3	½	**Excellent Show**[40] 4601 3-8-13 79 TomEaves 6 (B Smart) *hld up: nt clr run 3f out: hdwy over 1f out: kpt on u.p ins fnl f* **9/1**	80
0005	4	1 ½	**Supermassive Muse (IRE)**[21] 5247 4-8-10 75 (p) GrahamGibbons 3 (E S McMahon) *chsd ldrs: racd in 2nd pl fr 3f out to 2f out: styd on same pce fnl f* **4/1**[2]	71
0315	5	½	**Miss Chamanda (IRE)**[14] 5436 3-9-3 83 JohnEgan 8 (P D Evans) *s.i.s: bhd: rdn and hdwy over 1f out: no imp on ldrs* **12/1**	77+
5023	6	nk	**Le Toreador**[3] 5767 4-9-5 84 (tp) TPQueally 9 (K A Ryan) *racd on outside: chsd ldrs: lost pl 3f out: rdn over 1f out: kpt on ins fnl f but unable to chal* **6/1**	77+
5100	7	hd	**Colorus (IRE)**[19] 5323 6-8-0 70 oh4 (p) PaulPickard(5) 4 (W J H Ratcliffe) *chsd ldrs: rdn over 2f out: outpcd over 1f out: n.d after* **9/1**	62
1200	8	1 ½	**Secret Venue**[3] 5768 3-8-0 71 PatrickDonaghy(5) 10 (Jedd O'Keeffe) *towards rr: hdwy into midfield 3f out: wknd ins fnl 100yds* **20/1**	58
0231	9	1	**Rio Cobolo (IRE)**[8] 5623 3-8-4 70 oh1 (v) SilvestreDeSousa 11 (Paul Green) *in rr: outpcd over 2f out* **9/1**	53
3630	10	9	**Sir Geoffrey (IRE)**[94] 2826 3-8-9 75 (t) MartinDwyer 5 (J A Glover) *w wnr for 1f: rdn on outside over 2f out: wknd wl over 1f out* **14/1**	26

59.72 secs (-1.28) **Going Correction** -0.125s/f (Firm)
WFA 3 from 4yo+ 1lb 10 Ran SP% **123.8**
Speed ratings (Par 105): **105,99,99,96,95 95,95,92,91,76**
toteswinger: 1&2 £4.70, 1&3 £10.80, 2&3 £11.50. CSF £20.66 CT £139.18 TOTE £4.40: £1.70, £1.90, £3.50; EX 21.40.
Owner Darron McIntyre Frank Tobin **Bred** Seamus Phelan **Trained** Flaxton, N Yorks

FOCUS

A typical Chester sprint in which the draw proved all important. Nothing got into it from the rear and there is some doubt over the form.

Le Toreador Official explanation: jockey said gelding hung right

5857 HEATHCOTES ACC LIVERPOOL CATERING PARTNERS H'CAP 1m 7f 195y

5:05 (5:07) (Class 4) (0-80,80) 3-Y-O+ £5,504 (£1,637; £818; £408) Stalls Low

Form				RPR
330-	1		**Mith Hill**[36] 6861 8-9-2 68 (vt) TPO'Shea 3 (Ian Williams) *mde all: rdn whn hrd pressed over 2f out: fnd ex ins fnl f: styd on* **17/2**	77
0066	2	2	**Double Banded (IRE)**[84] 3146 5-10-0 80 JohnEgan 8 (K A Ryan) *in tch: effrt over 3f out: wnt 2nd over 2f out: sn upsides and rdn: nt qckn ins fnl f* **7/2**[2]	86
3206	3	2 ¾	**Relative Strength (IRE)**[26] 5094 4-9-8 74 (v) WilliamBuick 4 (A M Balding) *chsd ldrs: lost pl after 5f: pushed along and outpcd over 2f out: kpt on to take 3rd fnl 100yds: nt trble front 2* **7/2**[2]	77
6244	4	1 ¾	**Nawamees (IRE)**[23] 5185 11-8-11 63 (p) CatherineGannon 6 (P D Evans) *chsd ldr: pushed along over 3f out: lost 2nd over 2f out: plugged on at one pce after* **16/1**	64
60-4	5	1 ¼	**Abstract Folly (IRE)**[33] 4848 7-8-11 63 GrahamGibbons 2 (J D Bethell) *hld up: tk clsr order 1/2-way: pushed along over 2f out: u.p on wd outside ent st wl over 1f out: chal for 3rd pl tl no ex fnl 100yds* **9/1**	63
1/32	6	1 ¾	**Doubly Guest**[49] 4301 5-9-4 70 MartinDwyer 1 (Tim Vaughan) *in tch: rdn over 2f out: wknd over 1f out: eased whn btn ins fnl 100yds* **11/4**[1]	69
21-1	7	5	**Don't Stop Me Now (IRE)**[65] 3837 4-9-0 66 DJMoran 7 (John Joseph Hanlon, Ire) *hld up: pushed along over 2f out: nvr on terms w ldrs* **7/1**[3]	57
1	8	12	**Drussell (IRE)**[176] 902 3-8-12 77 TPQueally 5 (S Donohoe, Ire) *hld up: pushed along over 2f out: wl bhd fnl f* **9/1**	54

3m 25.47s (-2.53) **Going Correction** -0.125s/f (Firm)
WFA 3 from 4yo+ 13lb 8 Ran SP% **120.0**
Speed ratings (Par 105): **101,100,98,97,97 96,93,87**
toteswinger: 1&2 £8.80, 1&3 £7.40, 2&3 £3.10. CSF £40.35 CT £127.56 TOTE £10.60: £3.00, £1.90, £1.80; EX 55.90.
Owner P J Vogt **Bred** Floors Farming, Hmh Management Ltd & John Warren **Trained** Portway, Worcs

■ Stewards' Enquiry : John Egan caution: careless riding.

FOCUS

On a day when those making the running were proving hard to peg back the winner was allowed to dictate his own pace from the start. He is rated to last year's Flat form.

5858 HEATHCOTES H'CAP 1m 2f 75y

5:40 (5:40) (Class 5) (0-75,74) 3-Y-O £4,047 (£1,204; £601; £300) Stalls High

Form				RPR
2142	1		**Veroon (IRE)**[9] 5616 3-9-3 73 (p) J-PGuillambert 6 (J G Given) *broke wl: led early: sn trckd ldrs: effrt over 1f out: sn chal: led narrowly fnl 100yds: pushed out cl home* **7/1**	78
6013	2	½	**Wilbury Star (IRE)**[16] 5366 3-9-4 74 (b) MartinDwyer 3 (R Hannon) *broke wl: chsd ldrs: effrt over 1f out: str chal ins fnl f: nt qckn cl home* **9/2**[2]	78
-253	3	nse	**Oriental Cavalier**[95] 2779 3-8-13 69 (p) GrahamGibbons 9 (R Hollinshead) *a.p: rdn to ld over 1f out: hdd narrowly fnl 100yds: hld cl home* **7/1**	73
3023	4	1 ¼	**Mustakmil (IRE)**[12] 5520 3-9-4 74 TPO'Shea 1 (E A L Dunlop) *midfield: hdwy over 1f out: sn rdn to chse ldrs: hung lft u.p ins fnl f: styd on but nt pce to chal front trio* **7/2**[1]	76
2226	5	3	**Punch Drunk**[8] 5622 3-9-1 71 (p) TPQueally 4 (J G Given) *hld up: rdn and sme prog 1f out: nvr able to chal* **13/2**	67
0530	6	1 ¼	**Trumpstoo (USA)**[20] 5295 3-8-11 67 TonyHamilton 5 (R A Fahey) *hld up: pushed along 2f out: rdn over 1f out: no imp on ldrs* **16/1**	61
164	7	1 ½	**Vita Mia**[15] 5382 3-8-9 65 CatherineGannon 7 (P D Evans) *sn led: rdn over 2f out: hdd over 1f out: wknd ins fnl f* **6/1**[3]	56
2600	8	2	**Bessie Lou (IRE)**[20] 5295 3-8-11 67 JohnEgan 2 (K A Ryan) *racd keenly: hld up: rdn over 1f out: no imp whn eased fnl 100yds* **12/1**	54
-315	9	1 ¼	**Dr Jameson (IRE)**[107] 2406 3-8-10 73 FrazerWilliams(7) 8 (R A Fahey) *hld up: effrt on outside ent st wl over 1f out: no imp on ldrs: wknd fnl f* **8/1**	58

2m 10.98s (-1.22) **Going Correction** -0.125s/f (Firm) 9 Ran SP% **117.7**
Speed ratings (Par 101): **99,98,98,97,95 94,92,91,90**
toteswinger: 1&2 £6.20, 1&3 £6.90, 2&3 £4.20. CSF £39.31 CT £232.41 TOTE £8.90: £2.30, £2.30, £2.70; EX 46.50 Place 6 £357.45, Place 5 £96.88.
Owner Danethorpe Racing Partnership **Bred** C M Farrell **Trained** Willoughton, Lincs

FOCUS

Not too many got into this. Ordinary but sound form.

Punch Drunk Official explanation: jockey said filly hung left

T/Plt: £640.50 to a £1 stake. Pool: £67,841.19. 77.31 winning tickets. T/Qpdt: £46.10 to a £1 stake. Pool: £3,258.60. 52.30 winning tickets. DO

5822 DONCASTER (L-H)

Saturday, September 12

OFFICIAL GOING: Good to firm (good in places on round course; str 8.7 rnd 8.6)

Wind: Light, across Weather: Sunny and dry

5859 DFS CHAMPAGNE STKS (GROUP 2) (C&G) 7f

1:55 (1:56) (Class 1) 2-Y-O

£56,770 (£21,520; £10,770; £5,370; £2,690; £1,350) Stalls High

Form				RPR
313	1		**Poet's Voice**[25] 5133 2-8-12 108 LDettori 2 (Saeed Bin Suroor) *lw: mde all: edgd lft 2f out: shkn up and qcknd over 1f out: rdn ins fnl f and kpt on wl* **11/8**[1]	114+
	2	¾	**Viscount Nelson (USA)**[34] 4833 2-8-12 0 JMurtagh 1 (A P O'Brien, Ire) *w'like: athletic: trckd ldng pair: swtchd rt and effrt to chse wnr 2f out: rdn over 1f out: kpt on u.p ins fnl f* **11/2**[3]	112
111	3	hd	**Silver Grecian**[64] 3817 2-9-1 102 MichaelHills 4 (J Ryan) *lw: hld up in tch: hdwy over 2f out: n.m.r wl over 1f out: rdn to chse ldng pair over 1f out: kpt on ins fnl f: nrst fin* **9/2**[2]	114
3254	4	4 ½	**Roi De Vitesse (IRE)**[15] 5416 2-8-12 99 JamesMillman 5 (B R Millman) *chsd ldrs: hdwy over 2f out: sn rdn and one pce appr fnl f* **40/1**	100

211 **5** 3 3/4 **Layali Al Andalus**[12] 5515 2-8-12 98.................................. JoeFanning 6 91
(M Johnston) *w'like: scope: tall: chsd ldrs: rdn along over 2f out: sn hung lft and wknd wl over 1f out* **9/2**[2]

26 **6** 1 1/2 **Emperor Claudius (USA)**[64] 3817 2-8-12 0......................... SMLevey 3 87
(A P O'Brien, Ire) *chsd wnr: rdn along wl over 2f out: sn drvn and wknd* **16/1**

7 4 1/2 **Await The Dawn (USA)**[52] 4215 2-8-12 0....................... CO'Donoghue 7 76
(A P O'Brien, Ire) *w'like: scope: tall: chsd ldrs: rdn along over 2f out: sn edgd lft and wknd* **11/1**

1m 24.91s (-1.39) **Going Correction** -0.05s/f (Good) **7** Ran SP% **110.5**
Speed ratings (Par 107): **105,104,103,98,94 92,87**
toteswinger: 1&2 £2.50, 1&3 £2.50, 2&3 £3.10. CSF £8.65 TOTE £2.20: £1.40, £2.70; EX 9.60.
Owner Godolphin **Bred** Darley **Trained** Newmarket, Suffolk
■ Stewards' Enquiry : S M Levey one-day ban: failed to keep colt straight leaving stalls (Sep 27)

FOCUS
This race has gone to some talented juveniles in the past, who have sometimes gone on to run respectably as three-year-olds. However, since Dubai Destination in 2001, only one winner has scored again. Possibly more interesting is a list of those who were beaten in the race but went on to achieve Group-race triumphs the next season. The form is about average in comparison with recent winners of this race with the fourth setting the level.

NOTEBOOK
Poet's Voice ◆, a fine-looker, every inch the type to develop into a strong three-year-old, has lots of natural pace, which is sure to be an asset in races at around a mile. It was interesting to hear from the jockey that the plan was to try to drop him in, but because he broke so well there was no chance of doing that. He also reported that although the winner is headstrong, he is sensible and a passing reference to him being like the awesome Dubai Millennium (as a juvenile) will not put his supporters off him for the big races ahead. The bookmakers predictably shortened him for the 2000 Guineas, for which he is a top-priced 20-1. Official explanation: jockey said he failed to keep straight from the stalls as he was unable to control the colt (op 6-4)
Viscount Nelson(USA), the mount of Murtagh, was one of a couple chasing a third straight win. He sat behind the winner for much of the way and looked a big danger about a furlong out, but his run flattened out and he only just held on for second. It is impossible to know where he features in the pecking order at Ballydoyle, but he shaped like a horse who will probably appreciate at least 1m2f next season. (op 9-2)
Silver Grecian ◆ came into the race unbeaten, with his three victories including the Group 2 Superlative Stakes, in which he beat subsequent Solario winner Shakespearean. Carrying a 3lb penalty, he did not have a lot of room in the chasing pack but his run looked uninterrupted and he possibly did not get going early enough. All things considered, it was a great effort and he will head for the Dewhurst if remaining in good heart. No doubt connections have an eye on the Guineas with him and some will argue that he emerges the best horse from the race. (op 4-1)
Roi De Vitesse(IRE) has proved to be a decent juvenile during a busy campaign. His connections should be proud of his achievements.
Layali Al Andalus, chasing a hat-trick, is well regarded but this was a step up in class after winning a nursery and he did not look up to it. (op 5-1)
Emperor Claudius(USA) ran Silver Grecian close at Newmarket last time but could get nowhere near on this occasion. (op 18-1)
Await The Dawn(USA) won easily over 1m on soft ground under Murtagh on his debut but failed to get involved in this, looking green under pressure in the closing stages. Official explanation: jockey said colt never travelled (op 14-1 tchd 10-1)

5860 LADBROKES PORTLAND (HERITAGE H'CAP) 5f 140y
2:25 (2:29) (Class 2) 3-Y-O+

£46,732 (£13,995; £6,997; £3,502; £1,747; £877) **Stalls** High

Form RPR

5 **1** **Santo Padre (IRE)**[15] 5412 5-9-1 95............................ CO'Donoghue 16 107+
(David Marnane, Ire) *dwlt and bhd stands' side: hdwy 2f out: effrt and nt clr run wl over 1f out: rdn and squeezed through jst ins fnl f: sn led and kpt on strly* **14/1**

2010 **2** 1 1/4 **Everymanforhimself (IRE)**[28] 5039 5-9-3 97.........(v) JamieSpencer 22 105
(K A Ryan) *hld up towards rr stands' side: swtchd lft and hdwy wl over 1f out: rdn and ev ch ent fnl f: sn drvn and kpt on same pce: 2nd of 10 in gp* **16/1**

0656 **3** 1/2 **Captain Dunne (IRE)**[7] 5654 4-9-1 95........................ DavidAllan 2 101
(T D Easterby) *prom far side: hdwy to ld that gp 2f out and sn overall ldr: rdn over 1f out: hdd and no ex ins fnl f: 1st of 12 in gp* **33/1**

0000 **4** 1/2 **Green Manalishi**[25] 5132 8-8-8 88..............................(p) DO'Donohoe 17 93
(K A Ryan) *hld up stands' side: swtchd lft and hdwy wl over 1f out: sn rdn and styd on wl fnl f: nrst fin: 3rd of 10 in gp* **50/1**

5000 **5** 1/2 **Ishetoo**[6] 5695 5-8-12 95...(p) FrederikTylicki(3) 1 98
(A Dickman) *lw: in tch far side: hdwy to chse ldrs over 2f out: rdn and ch over 1f out: drvn and one pce ins fnl f: 2nd of 12 in gp* **20/1**

0406 **6** 1/2 **Oldjoesaid**[21] 5263 5-9-3 97... DaneO'Neill 19 98+
(H Candy) *dwlt and in rr stands' side: hdwy and nt clr run wl over 1f out: sn rdn and kpt on ins fnl f: nrst fin: 4th of 10 in gp* **14/1**

0311 **7** 1/2 **Jaconet (USA)**[8] 5646 4-9-1 95..(b) KFallon 20 95
(T D Barron) *overall ldr stands' side: rdn along 2f out: sn hdd and grad wknd: 5th of 10 in gp* **10/1**[3]

230 **8** 1/2 **Northern Dare (IRE)**[7] 5654 5-8-12 92............................ PaulQuinn 23 90
(D Nicholls) *chsd ldrs stands' side: rdn along 2f out: drvn over 1f out: grad wknd: 6th of 10 in gp* **25/1**

1000 **9** nk **Striking Spirit**[28] 5039 4-9-4 98... TedDurcan 7 95
(D Nicholls) *dwlt: in tch far side: switrchd to far rail and rdn 2f out: kpt on ins fnl f: 3rd of 12 in gp* **25/1**

000 **10** shd **Fullandby (IRE)**[14] 5420 7-9-0 94..................................(b) JoeFanning 15 90
(T J Etherington) *towards rr stands' side: hdwy wl over 1f out: sn rdn and kpt on ins fnl f: 7th of 10 in gp* **28/1**

1011 **11** nk **Johannes (IRE)**[21] 5257 6-9-2 96.................................... PaulHanagan 9 91
(R A Fahey) *hld up far side: hdwy over 2f out: sn rdn and no imp appr fnl f: 4th of 12 in gp* **8/1**[2]

2020 **12** 1 **Buachaill Dona (IRE)**[25] 5132 6-9-8 102.................... AdrianTNicholls 3 94
(D Nicholls) *in tch far side: hdwy 2f out: sn rdn and kpt on same pce: 5th of 12 in gp* **33/1**

0000 **13** 3/4 **Peak District (IRE)**[14] 5420 5-8-4 89.............................. AmyRyan(5) 24 78
(K A Ryan) *swtg: chsd ldr stands' side: rdn along 2f out: sn drvn and edgd rt over 1f out: wknd: 8th of 10 in gp* **33/1**

1302 **14** nk **Judge 'n Jury**[13] 5491 5-9-7 101.................................(t) KevinGhunowa 8 89
(R A Harris) *cl up far side: rdn along over 2f out and grad wknd: 6th of 12 in gp* **20/1**

0201 **15** 1/2 **Barney McGrew (IRE)**[25] 5132 6-9-9 103........................ PhillipMakin 21 90
(M Dods) *chsd ldrs stands' side: hdwy over 2f out: sn rdn and wknd wl over 1f out: 9th of 10 in gp* **12/1**

6441 **16** 1/2 **Markab**[28] 5039 6-9-10 104.. PatCosgrave 4 89
(H Candy) *lw: prom far side: rdn along over 2f out: sn wknd: 7th of 12 in gp* **7/1**[1]

5012 **17** nk **Tony The Tap**[21] 5263 8-8-12 92..................................... DarryllHolland 12 76
(W R Muir) *a in rr far side: 8th of 12 in gp* **18/1**

4064 **18** 1/2 **Intrepid Jack**[25] 5132 7-9-8 102.................................(b) JimmyFortune 18 84
(H Morrison) *lw: chsd ldrs stands' side: rdn along over 2f out: sn drvn and wknd: 10th of 10 in gp* **10/1**[3]

0300 **19** 2 **River Falcon**[25] 5132 9-9-0 94...................................... DanielTudhope 14 70
(J S Goldie) *lw: a towards rr far side: 9th of 12 in gp* **25/1**

0000 **20** 2 1/2 **Orpsie Boy (IRE)**[21] 5263 6-8-8 88.........................(p) KirstyMilczarek 10 55
(N P Littmoden) *dwlt: a in rr far side: 10th of 12 in gp* **22/1**

2010 **21** 1 1/4 **Group Therapy**[14] 5420 4-9-9 103.. NCallan 13 66
(N P Littmoden) *chsd ldrs far side: rdn along over 2f out: sn wknd: 11th of 12 in gp* **33/1**

1121 **22** 2 3/4 **Pavershooz**[54] 4135 4-9-0 94... DuranFentiman 6 47
(N Wilson) *led far side gp: rdn along 1/2-way: sn hdd & wknd: last of 12 in gp* **7/1**[1]

66.72 secs (-1.78) **Going Correction** -0.05s/f (Good)
WFA 3 from 4yo+ 2lb **22** Ran SP% **129.0**
Speed ratings (Par 109): **109,107,106,106,105 104,104,103,102,102 102,101,100,99,99 98,97,97,94,91 89,85**
toteswinger: 1&2 £121.20, 1&3 £472.90, 2&3 £181.90. CSF £189.42 CT £7219.35 TOTE £20.20: £5.10, £3.70, £10.80, £14.20; EX 328.90 Trifecta £27778.10 Part won. Pool: £37,538.03 - 0.80 winning units..
Owner Victor Partnership **Bred** Victor Stud Bloodstock & Brend **Trained** Bansha, Co Tipperary

FOCUS
This long-established and highly competitive handicap again attracted a capacity field. The majority of recent runnings had been won by horses drawn high but a low stall was not necessarily a disadvantage, as two of the last four winners had come from box five. The form is solid with the winner progressing from his Irish form.

NOTEBOOK
Santo Padre(IRE), a useful Irish-trained sprinter whose form suggested he was best at 5f on soft ground or Polytrack, was settled off the pace on the stands' side and picked up well to hit the front inside the final furlong and win going away. This was only the five-year-old's ninth appearance and, having completed a hat-trick here, he certainly appears to be going the right way. There are no immediate plans but he could make up into a Pattern-class sprinter next season. (op 16-1)
Everymanforhimself(IRE) ran a fine race considering he missed a beat at the start, but came through to have his chance entering the last furlong, only to have no answer to the winner's finishing pace. He takes his racing well and may go for the Ayr Gold Cup next week. (op 20-1)
Captain Dunne(IRE) had not won for a year and had looked best at 5f, but he ran a fine race, having tracked the pace on the far side, and did best of those drawn low. He may have gone for home a little too soon and was just unable to find any extra when the challengers appeared closer to the stands' side. He is likely to go for a 5f race at York next month.
Green Manalishi showed signs of a return to form last time and was 17lb below his highest winning mark. Fitted with first-time cheekpieces, he had to race on the outside of the stands' side group but travelled well and came to have his chance entering the last furlong. He is well handicapped if able to build on this.
Ishetoo, another whose best form had been at 5f on fast ground, was 2lb above his last winning mark but ran well, having been under pressure from some way out, sticking on to finish second best of those drawn on the far side. (op 28-1)
Oldjoesaid ◆ had a bit to find with several of these and his best form was at 5f with cut in the ground. However, the stable jockey preferred him to Markab and the decision was justified, as his mount kept on well in the latter stages and looks the sort who could make his mark in a similar contest before the end of the season, especially given an easier surface. Official explanation: jockey said gelding was denied a clear run (op 16-1)
Jaconet(USA), a five-time winner this season including the last two on Polytrack, made a good start and soon got to the nearside rail at the head of her group. She maintained the lead until entering the last furlong but had nothing in reserve. (op 8-1)
Northern Dare(IRE), another who is best on soft ground, was 5lb above his latest winning mark but ran on in a manner which suggests he could figure if sent to Ayr. (op 22-1)
Striking Spirit, who had conditions to suit, had beaten Pavershooz in July but had a bit to find with several of these on more recent form. He performed creditably racing nearest the far-side rail. (op 28-1)
Fullandby(IRE), winner of this race in 2007 and eighth last year, had not won for a year but was 8lb below his latest winning mark. He was staying on and, having won most of his races in late summer and early autumn, might just be running back into form.
Johannes(IRE) ◆ has won four of his six starts this season, including the last two, and was 7lb higher than for his latest success. He tracked the leaders, but got stuck behind tiring rivals when trying to make ground and did not get clear until inside the last furlong. He finished well and would have been a few places closer with a clear passage. (op 9-1)
Markab had a tough task off a mark of 104, as nothing had won this rated higher than 100 in recent seasons. (op 8-1)
Orpsie Boy(IRE) Official explanation: jockey said gelding never travelled
Pavershooz is arguably best at 5f but faded out of contention before stamina became an issue. (op 8-1)

5861 LADBROKES ST LEGER STKS (GROUP 1) (ENTIRE COLTS & FILLIES) 1m 6f 132y
3:00 (3:03) (Class 1) 3-Y-O

£306,586 (£116,218; £58,163; £29,000; £14,527; £7,290) **Stalls** Low

Form RPR

1332 **1** **Mastery**[25] 5134 3-9-0 111.. TedDurcan 7 119
(Saeed Bin Suroor) *trckd ldng pair: hdwy 3f out: cl up over 1f out and sn rdn to chal: drvn ins fnl f and styd on gamely to ld nr fin* **14/1**

5011 **2** 3/4 **Kite Wood (IRE)**[28] 5023 3-9-0 115.. LDettori 4 118
(Saeed Bin Suroor) *swtg: chsd clr ldr: hdwy 3f out: led over 2f out: jnd and rdn over 1f out: drvn ins fnl f and kpt on gamely tl hdd and no ex nr fin* **9/4**[1]

4351 **3** 1 3/4 **Monitor Closely (IRE)**[25] 5134 3-9-0 116...................... JimmyFortune 2 116+
(P W Chapple-Hyam) *lw: hld up: smooth hdwy on outer 3f out: trckd ldrs on bit wl over 1f out: rdn and hung bdly lft ins fnl f: one pce* **7/2**[3]

3213 **4** 1 **Father Time**[25] 5134 3-9-0 115.. JamieSpencer 5 114
(H R A Cecil) *hld up in rr: hdwy 3f out: chsd ldrs 2f out and sn rdn: drvn over 1f out: btn whn edgd rt and bmpd ins fnl f* **7/1**

3232 **5** shd **Mourayan (IRE)**[30] 4962 3-9-0 116..................................(b) FMBerry 8 117+
(John M Oxx, Ire) *hld up and bhd: hdwy over 2f out: rdn along wl over 1f out: styng on whn hmpd ins fnl f: nt rcvr* **6/1**

22 **6** 2 1/4 **Changingoftheguard (IRE)**[24] 5173 3-9-0 114............... JMurtagh 3 111
(A P O'Brien, Ire) *lw: trckd ldrs on inner: hdwy 3f out: chsd ldng pair over 2f out: sn rdn and btn wl over 1f out* **3/1**[2]

0035 **7** 4 1/2 **Above Average (IRE)**[25] 5134 3-9-0 101......................... MichaelHills 6 106
(B W Hills) *chsd ldrs: rdn along 3f out: sn drvn and wknd* **50/1**

26 **8** 39 **Von Jawlensky (IRE)**[58] 4033 3-9-0 104....................... CO'Donoghue 1 55
(A P O'Brien, Ire) *w'like: led and clr at gd pce: rdn along over 3f out: hdd over 2f out: wknd qckly and eased* **80/1**

3m 4.81s (-1.89) **Going Correction** -0.05s/f (Good) **8** Ran SP% **114.6**
Speed ratings (Par 115): **103,102,101,101,101 99,97,76**
toteswinger: 1&2 £4.70, 1&3 £8.10, 2&3 £2.60. CSF £46.00 CT £139.09 TOTE £16.10: £2.80, £1.10, £1.60; EX 42.20 Trifecta £213.50 Pool: £20,294.28 - 70.32 winning units..

Owner Godolphin **Bred** Darley **Trained** Newmarket, Suffolk

■ A 1-2 for Godolphin, their fifth St Leger in all and their first British Classic since Rule Of Law in the 2004 Leger.

■ Stewards' Enquiry : Ted Durcan one-day ban:excessive use of whip (Sep 27)
Jimmy Fortune three-day ban: careless riding (Sep 27-29)

FOCUS

On paper, this was only a six-runner affair considering the best these horses had achieved on the racecourse. Possibly the most disappointing fact about this season's final Classic was the lack of Group 1 form. For instance, last year, both the English Oaks and Irish Derby winners tried their luck, but the best pieces of Group 1 form on offer in 2009 were thirds in the Irish Derby and the Grand Prix de Paris. The pace looked acceptable after a fairly slow start, and the finish was fought out by the Godolphin pair. The form looks below-par for the race with the third rated to his Voltigeur form.

NOTEBOOK

Mastery was the second string for Godolphin but had shown more than enough to be respected in a race of this nature. The winner of the Derby Italiano in May, his win has to be considered something of a surprise, but he has looked a top-class colt, and he showed great tenacity in beating his better-fancied stablemate. His ability to handle the quicker ground may have counted in the final stages but he still emerges a deserved winner. He may run again this season and will stay in training at four. (tchd 16-1)

Kite Wood(IRE) ◆ did not start 2009 really well but had improved in the second half of the season. Wins at Newmarket and Newbury catapulted him to the head of the ante-post lists for the St Leger, and it seems unfortunate that at this time of the year he could not run on some easier ground, a surface that would have suited him better. In the perfect position throughout, he attempted to kick at a crucial stage and stuck to his guns when challenged, making the winner work hard. This was by far his best performance for Godolphin and he is another one they can look forward to this season and beyond. (op 5-2 tchd 2-1)

Monitor Closely(IRE) ◆ was supplemented for this historic race after taking the Great Voltigeur on his first attempt at 1m4f, were he comfortably beat Mastery, who was carrying a penalty. Jimmy Fortune tried to settle him towards the rear early, but his mount refused to drop his head, which was always going to make his task difficult. The impression one got is that he did not see out the trip as well as the first two (he was upsides if not in front of the pushed-along winner a furlong and a half out) but he remains an exciting prospect over slightly shorter distances. The trainer may send him for a race in Hong Kong, where the ground is usually fast. (op 4-1)

Father Time, the popular trainer's first runner in the race since Ramruma's second in 1999, was well placed but lost his winning chance by appearing to hang from over two out. He probably found the going too quick but his jockey reported that he did not feel his mount stayed the trip. The St Simon Stakes could be on the agenda for him. (op 13-2)

Mourayan(IRE) was arguably the horse with the best form in the race, as four and of the five horses to have beaten him since his maiden success included Sea The Stars, Fame And Glory, Golden Sword and Profound Beauty. Not a bad list by anyone's standards. After being held up, he was at the back of the pack as everything closed up and encountered all sorts of problems when the jockey tried to get through the bunch. His next move was then hampered by Monitor Closely and his run of bad fortune was complete. It is not difficult to argue that he may have won with a clear passage and it will be interesting to see what connections decide to do with him now. He could go for the Prix Chaudenay on Arc weekend. (tchd 7-1)

Changingoftheguard(IRE), who had never contested a Group race, probably ran as well as he was entitled to and did little wrong after taking a hold in midfield. His connections must wish Age Of Aquarius had made the line-up (he was a high-profile absentee at the final entry stage due to being stiff behind after a routine canter), as he finished in front of the winner in the Grand Prix de Paris. Changingoftheguard has been sold and now joins Australian trainer David Hayes. (op 7-2)

5862 DFS PARK STKS (GROUP 2) 7f

3:35 (3:35) (Class 1) 3-Y-0+

£90,832 (£34,432; £17,232; £8,592; £4,304; £2,160) **Stalls** High

Form RPR

0100 **1** **Duff (IRE)**[70] 3638 6-9-4 109 .... FMBerry 6 117
(Edward Lynam, Ire) *led and racd alone stands' rail: rdn and qcknd clr over 2f out: drvn ent fnl f: jst hld on* **7/1**

-033 **2** *nk* **Cat Junior (USA)**[13] 5474 4-9-4 114 .... (t) JamieSpencer 3 116+
(B J Meehan) *hld up centre: effrt 2f out and sn rdn: drvn over 1f out: styd on u.p ins fnl f: jst failed* **5/1**[3]

1-30 **3** *hd* **Arabian Gleam**[88] 2990 5-9-4 115 .... (p) JMurtagh 1 116
(J Noseda) *trckd ldrs centre: effrt 2f out and sn rdn: drvn ent fnl f and styd on to have ev ch tl nt qckn nr fin* **11/2**

1016 **4** *nk* **Ouqba**[46] 4406 3-9-0 114 .... RHills 4 113
(B W Hills) *lw: trckd ldrs centre: hdwy 2f out: rdn over 1f out: styd on and ev ch ins fnl f: drvn and no ex towards fin* **4/1**[2]

231- **5** *1 3/4* **Stimulation (IRE)**[329] 6814 4-9-4 118 .... DarryllHolland 5 110
(H Morrison) *trckd ldr centre: effrt 2f out: sn rdn and wknd over 1f out* **7/4**[1]

14- **6** *42* **Himalya (IRE)**[452] 3103 3-9-0 110 .... LDettori 2 —
(J Noseda) *s.i.s: t.k.h and sn swtchd to centre: led that gp tl rdn along 2f out and sn wknd: eased over 1f out* **10/1**

1m 24.38s (-1.92) **Going Correction** -0.05s/f (Good)

WFA 3 from 4yo+ 4lb **6** Ran SP% **110.0**

Speed ratings (Par 115): **108,107,107,107,105 57**

toteswinger: 1&2 £7.60, 1&3 £5.20, 2&3 £2.90. CSF £38.92 TOTE £8.20: £3.50, £2.20; EX 45.10.

Owner Kilboy Estate **Bred** Kilboy Estate **Trained** Dunshaughlin, Co Meath

■ Stewards' Enquiry : F M Berry one-day ban: excessive use of whip (Sep 27)
Jamie Spencer two-day ban: excessive use of whip (Sep 27-28)

FOCUS

This good Group 2 again attracted a single-figure field. The winner is rated to his form in this race two years ago with the runner-up close to his three-year-old best.

NOTEBOOK

Duff(IRE) had not previously won above Group 3 level but finished a neck second to Arabian Gleam in this race in 2007. Making a return to his optimum trip, he set the pace nearest the stands' rail until the hard-pulling Himalya went on and took the rest to the centre of the track, leaving him isolated. That may have helped him, though, as his rider was able to kick on soon after halfway and steal a two or three-length advantage, which proved vital in the closing stages. He is a thoroughly likeable sort and it would be no surprise if he goes for the Foret and Challenge Stakes again. (op 9-1)

Cat Junior(USA) had not won since his racecourse debut, but had been runner-up to Stimulation in the Challenge Stakes last season. He had been running well since his return but found trouble, despite the small field, before being galvanised by Spencer, although the winner had enough in reserve. (op 9-2 tchd 11-2)

Arabian Gleam, successful in the two previous renewals, could not complete the hat-trick. He was friendless in the market but made a bold bid, only coming off third-best in a close finish. His only two wins on turf had been the last two renewals of this race and he goes well for Johnny Murtagh. The Challenge Stakes looks a reasonable target depending how he comes out of this. (op 4-1)

Ouqba was held up off the pace but his rider was first to react when the winner kicked clear and did his best to close the gap, but ultimately he was edged out and the manoeuvre probably cost him in the end. (op 7-2)

Stimulation(IRE) ◆ was sent off favourite despite not having run since beating Cat Junior in the Challenge Stakes last October, having had a setback in spring. He was never far away but was one of the first under pressure and faded as if the outing was needed. He was not given a hard time once beaten and the run should bring him on with a repeat win in the Challenge Stakes in mind, and possibly the Foret beforehand. (op 5-2)

Himalya(IRE), not seen since finishing fourth in 2008 Coventry, missed the break before taking a strong hold, which resulted in Frankie Dettori having to take him off heels and wide of the others. Once seeing daylight, he raced to the front and, apart from the winner, all the others followed him. Not surprisingly, he faded soon after Duff went for home and will have to settle better if he is to realise his early potential. (op 8-1 tchd 7-1)

5863 DONCASTER PREMIER INN & TABLE TABLE H'CAP 1m (S)

4:05 (4:12) (Class 2) (0-110,109) 3-Y-0+£16,190 (£4,817; £2,407; £1,202) **Stalls** High

Form RPR

1000 **1** **Manassas (IRE)**[87] 3014 4-8-9 97 ow1 .... DaneO'Neill 7 104
(B J Meehan) *trckd ldrs: hdwy to ld over 2f out: rdn over 1f out: jnd and drvn ins fnl f: kpt on gamely towards fin* **10/1**

0415 **2** *1/2* **Balcarce Nov (ARG)**[22] 5232 4-9-2 104 .... RobertWinston 6 110
(T P Tate) *swtg: hld up towards rr: hdwy 3f out: rdn to chse ldrs and n.m.r over 1f out: kpt on u.p ins fnl f* **14/1**

12- **3** *shd* **Secrecy**[349] 6305 3-8-8 101 .... LDettori 13 106+
(Saeed Bin Suroor) *lw: hld up towards rr: gd hdwy on outer 2f out: rdn to chal ent fnl f: sn drvn and ev ch tl no ex last 50yds* **13/2**[2]

1002 **4** *3/4* **Alazeyab (USA)**[23] 5200 3-8-10 103 .... RHills 9 106
(M A Jarvis) *cl up: led over 3f out: rdn and hdd over 2f out: drvn ent fnl f and kpt on same pce* **7/1**[3]

0162 **5** *hd* **Brief Encounter (IRE)**[19] 5313 3-8-7 100 .... LPKeniry 8 103+
(A M Balding) *midfield: hdwy 2f out: swtchd rt and rdn over 1f out: drvn and kpt on ins fnl f: nrst fin* **10/1**

3520 **6** *nk* **Kay Gee Be (IRE)**[23] 5200 5-8-4 95 oh3 .... AndreaAtzeni(3) 3 98
(W Jarvis) *t.k.h: chsd ldrs: effrt 2f out and sn rdn: drvn and kpt on same pce ins fnl f* **20/1**

0101 **7** *hd* **We'll Come**[35] 4768 5-9-6 108 .... (b) DarryllHolland 4 110
(M A Jarvis) *s.i.s and towards rr: hdwy over 2f out: swtchd lft and rdn over 1f out: kpt on ins fnl f: nrst fin* **10/1**

4106 **8** *nk* **Swop (IRE)**[13] 5476 6-9-2 104 .... KFallon 11 106
(L M Cumani) *hld up towards rr: hdwy over 2f out: rdn over 1f out: kpt on ins fnl f: nrst fin* **13/2**[2]

0244 **9** *2 3/4* **Webbow (IRE)**[23] 5200 7-8-7 95 oh2 .... DavidAllan 10 90
(N Tinkler) *chsd ldrs: rdn along over 2f out: sn drvn and wknd* **8/1**

1403 **10** *nk* **Espiritu (FR)**[49] 4296 3-8-6 99 .... (v) JamieSpencer 12 92
(J Noseda) *lw: dwlt: a in rr* **9/2**[1]

0402 **11** *5* **Tartan Gigha (IRE)**[7] 5663 4-8-7 95 oh2 .... JoeFanning 5 77
(M Johnston) *chsd ldrs: rdn along over 2f out: sn edgd lft and wknd over 1f out* **20/1**

1300 **12** *1 1/2* **Mahadee (IRE)**[35] 4768 4-8-8 96 ow1 .... (b) NCallan 2 75
(C E Brittain) *swtg: trckd ldrs: effrt over 2f out: sn rdn and wknd over 1f out* **28/1**

-120 **13** *19* **Suits Me**[175] 913 6-9-7 109 .... PaulHanagan 1 42
(T P Tate) *lw: led: rdn along and hdd over 3f out: sn wknd* **22/1**

1m 37.09s (-2.21) **Going Correction** -0.05s/f (Good)

WFA 3 from 4yo+ 5lb **13** Ran SP% **119.7**

Speed ratings (Par 109): **109,108,108,107,107 107,106,106,103,103 98,97,78**

toteswinger: 1&2 £33.60, 1&3 £17.90, 2&3 £20.70. CSF £134.11 CT £1019.11 TOTE £12.60: £3.60, £4.70, £2.40; EX 191.40 Trifecta £1052.90 Part won. Pool: £1,422.87 - 0.60 winning units..

Owner Mrs R Philipps **Bred** Mrs Rebecca Philipps **Trained** Manton, Wilts

FOCUS

An interesting mix of three-year-olds and older handicappers in this solid-looking event. The pace looked fair and the winning time was good, but that may have been deceiving, as plenty took a grip and finished well after being outpaced. The form is slightly muddling although the runner-up to sixth were close to their marks.

NOTEBOOK

Manassas(IRE), absent since finishing midfield in the Royal Hunt Cup, looked keen towards the head of affairs but that did not stop him pulling out plenty to prove a brave winner. Unbeaten at this course, he is not in the Cambridgeshire, so it remains to be seen where he is aimed. (op 12-1 tchd 14-1)

Balcarce Nov(ARG) has been running nicely and his previous run was a good effort over 7f. Stepped back up to 1m, he finished well and was gaining with every stride. Interestingly, he has been given an entry for a Listed race next week.

Secrecy ◆, stepping up to 1m on his debut for Godolphin, looked to have plenty to do against some seasoned handicappers but emerges as the horse to take from the race. This was a great effort after such a lengthy absence and the loss of a shoe during the race. (op 8-1 tchd 6-1)

Alazeyab(USA) returned to form on at York last time and had every opportunity here before weakening inside the final half-furlong. (op 8-1 tchd 9-1)

Brief Encounter(IRE), returning to turf after a good run on the Polytrack at Kempton last time, was pushed along at halfway and never got on terms. (op 8-1)

Kay Gee Be(IRE) pulled hard and did not have a great deal left for the finish. A stronger-run contest will suit him. (op 22-1 tchd 25-1)

We'll Come does not always look straightforward and tends to need things to fall in place for him. Given a quiet ride, he was held up behind horses for as long as the jockey dared, and although he stayed on well, he never reached the leaders. (op 15-2)

Swop(IRE) ◆ didn't show much under an apprentice last time on his reappearance after a break but ran better than his finishing position suggests here. He was not given a hard time from a furlong out but stayed on nicely. (op 6-1 tchd 5-1)

Espiritu(FR), gelded since his last run, was ridden patiently but could not quicken significantly when asked to make ground under pressure. Official explanation: jockey said gelding ran flat (op 5-1 tchd 6-1)

5864 MOSSPM.CO.UK NURSERY (H'CAP) 1m (S)

4:40 (4:43) (Class 2) 2-Y-0 £12,952 (£3,854; £1,926; £962) **Stalls** High

Form RPR

4112 **1** **Azizi**[14] 5433 2-9-7 89 .... RHills 3 99+
(W J Haggas) *lw: dwlt and hld up in rr: gd hdwy 2f out: rdn to chal and edgd lft over 1f out: led and hung lft ins fnl f: styd on wl* **13/8**[1]

622 **2** *2 1/4* **Baltimore Clipper (USA)**[14] 5428 2-8-6 74 .... PaulHanagan 7 79+
(P F I Cole) *lw: cl up: led after 3f: rdn along over 2f out: drvn over 1f out: hdd and n.m.r ent fnl f: kpt on same pce* **10/1**

062 **3** *1/2* **Start Right**[12] 5527 2-8-11 79 .... KFallon 8 83+
(L M Cumani) *lw: hld up in tch: hdwy 3f out: chsd ldrs 2f out: rdn and ev ch over 1f out: drvn and n.m.r ent fnl f: kpt on same pce* **6/1**[3]

2311 **4** *3 3/4* **Whippers Love (IRE)**[15] 5399 2-8-12 80 .... JoeFanning 5 76
(M Johnston) *led 3f: cl up: rdn along 2f out: ev ch tl drvn over 1f out and wknd ent fnl f* **4/1**[2]

1310 **5** *4* **Toga Tiger (IRE)**[22] 5214 2-9-7 **89** DarryllHolland 1 76
(M R Channon) *in tch: hdwy on wd outside 3f out: rdn along over 2f out and n.d* **25/1**

006 **6** *4 ½* **Azlak (USA)**[30] 4953 2-7-12 **66** oh2 NickyMackay 6 43
(C E Brittain) *chsd ldrs: rdn along over 2f out and sn wknd* **50/1**

2111 **7** *5* **Mister Angry (IRE)**[42] 4527 2-9-6 **88** NCallan 2 54
(M Johnston) *lw: chsd ldrs: rdn along over 2f out: sn wknd* **7/1**

2125 **8** *1 ½* **Gunner Lindley (IRE)**[22] 5207 2-9-6 **88** MichaelHills 4 51
(B W Hills) *in tch: rdn along wl over 2f out and sn wknd* **10/1**

01 **9** *6* **Dromore (IRE)**[30] 4945 2-8-12 **80** LPKeniry 9 30
(A M Balding) *chsd ldrs on outer: rdn along 3f out: sn wknd* **18/1**

1m 37.89s (-1.41) **Going Correction** -0.05s/f (Good) **9** Ran SP% **114.1**
Speed ratings (Par 101): **105,102,102,98,94 90,85,83,77**
toteswinger: 1&2 £4.80, 1&3 £3.70, 2&3 £9.10. CSF £19.21 CT £79.37 TOTE £2.50: £1.40, £2.70, £1.80; EX 21.00 Trifecta £174.20 Pool: £1,592.14 - 6.76 winning units..

Owner Hamdan Al Maktoum **Bred** Shadwell Estate Company Limited **Trained** Newmarket, Suffolk

FOCUS
A smaller field than usual for this decent nursery and none of the trainers represented had been responsible for a recent winner of the race.

NOTEBOOK
Azizi ◆, who is bred to win a Guineas, was a well-backed favourite, having been a dual winner at 7f on fast ground and Polytrack. He travelled well under restraint on this step up in trip but hung persistently left as he moved through to challenge. However, once in front he straightened up and scored comfortably. He is on the upgrade and can make up into a Pattern performer if the progress continues, with a Listed race likely to be next on the agenda. (tchd 5-4)

Baltimore Clipper(USA), runner-up over 7f and 1m on Polytrack and good ground, was making his handicap debut and ran another creditable race, taking over 3f out and responding to pressure to hold all bar the winner. He deserves to pick up a similar contest. (tchd 12-1)

Start Right, runner-up over 7f on good ground last time, was making his handicap debut and was well supported. He came through to challenge just ahead of the winner but could not match that rival's pace and his effort flattened out inside the last furlong. (op 13-2 tchd 7-1)

Whippers Love(IRE), a dual winner at around this trip in nurseries, made the running on this bid for the hat-trick but was taken on for the lead three furlongs out and could not respond. To be fair, he did not give way until entering the final furlong and was clear of the rest. (op 5-1 tchd 11-2)

Toga Tiger(IRE), a winner over 7f on fast ground but well beaten in Listed company last time, was down in grade but never got involved, having been held up. (op 16-1)

Azlak(USA), another making his handicap debut but racing from 2lb out of the handicap, was close up early but failed to trouble the leaders in the closing stages. (op 40-1)

Mister Angry(IRE), bidding for a four-timer, raced prominently early but was one of the first in trouble and dropped away. His wins had been on easy ground and Polytrack and this surface may not have suited. (tchd 15-2)

5865 UNIVERSALRECYCLINGCOMPANY.CO.UK H'CAP — 1m 4f
5:15 (5:15) (Class 2) (0-105,95) 3-Y-O+ **£12,952** (£3,854; £1,926; £962) **Stalls** Low

Form RPR

-020 **1** **Precision Break (USA)**[24] 5173 4-9-10 **94** KFallon 6 103
(P F I Cole) *trckd ldrs: hdwy 3f out: rdn to ld over 1f out: drvn ins fnl f and hld on wl* **4/1**[3]

2122 **2** *½* **Falcon Rock (IRE)**[14] 5437 4-9-3 **87** (p) JamieSpencer 8 95
(S A Callaghan) *dwlt: hld up in rr: hdwy 3f out: swtchd rt and rdn to chal over 1f out: drvn and ev ch ins fnl f tl edgd lft and nt qckn towards fin* **2/1**[1]

0620 **3** *2 ¾* **Night Crescendo (USA)**[21] 5262 6-9-5 **89** (p) DarryllHolland 3 93
(Mrs A J Perrett) *trckd ldrs: hdwy 2f out: effrt over 1f out: rdn and ch whn n.m.r ent fnl f: sn one pce* **8/1**

0620 **4** *4 ½* **Snoqualmie Boy**[22] 5235 6-9-1 **85** RobertWinston 5 81
(T P Tate) *hld up: hdwy on outer 3f out: rdn along 2f out: sn drvn and wknd over 1f out* **17/2**

1505 **5** *¾* **Quai D'Orsay**[35] 4767 3-9-1 **94** JoeFanning 2 89
(M Johnston) *chsd ldr: hdwy over 3f out: led over 2f out: rdn and edgd lft wl over 1f out: sn hdd & wknd fnl f* **3/1**[2]

1100 **6** *10* **Matraash (USA)**[25] 5137 3-8-13 **92** RHills 1 71
(M Johnston) *led: rdn along 3f out: hdd over 2f out and sn wknd* **7/1**

2m 30.26s (-4.84) **Going Correction** -0.05s/f (Good)
WFA 3 from 4yo+ 9lb **6** Ran SP% **112.5**
Speed ratings (Par 109): **114,113,111,108,108 101**
toteswinger: 1&2 £1.50, 1&3 £4.30, 2&3 £3.30. CSF £12.51 CT £58.35 TOTE £3.40: £2.00, £1.90; EX 9.00 Trifecta £30.80 Pool: £967.62 - 23.20 winning units. Place 6 £625.76, Place 5 £347.28.

Owner Mrs Fitri Hay **Bred** Gainesway Thoroughbreds Ltd **Trained** Whatcombe, Oxon

FOCUS
This was depleted by a couple of non-runners, which inevitably made it a tactical affair. It remains to be seen whether the form proves to be reliable, although the winner is generally progressive.

NOTEBOOK
Precision Break(USA) was disappointing in the Ebor after a good effort at Glorious Goodwood but came back with a gusty display. This success came off a career-high mark, so he will obviously need to improve to win again. He has an entry in the Cesarewitch. (op 11-4)

Falcon Rock(IRE), who has been a model of consistency, was fitted with cheekpieces for the first time but again took second spot. He came there to have every chance but looked paceless under pressure. (op 3-1)

Night Crescendo(USA) did not perform too well 1m2f at Sandown on his previous run and was raised back up to 1m4f. His rider held on to him for as long as he could but his change of pace was not instant, and he could not catch the first two. (op 7-1)

Snoqualmie Boy has not won since 2006 and was dropped in distance after running over 2m. He was the first to be outpaced but ran on again once finding his stride. (op 10-1 tchd 8-1)

Quai D'Orsay has looked a tough handicapper but he had no answer to the chasing pack once he was joined. (tchd 11-4)

Matraash(USA), who had run poorly since two victories earlier in the season, dropped away quickly after having the run of the race. Official explanation: jockey said colt lost its action (op 8-1 tchd 17-2)

T/Jkpt: Not won. T/Plt: £1,392.40 to a £1 stake. Pool: £171,659.00. 89.99 winning tickets. T/Qpdt: £54.40 to a £1 stake. Pool: £9,196.34. 125.00 winning tickets. JR

4163 FFOS LAS (L-H)
Saturday, September 12

OFFICIAL GOING: Good (good to firm in places; 8.2)
Insufficient data available to compile standard times and consequently no speed ratings. The two-day meeting was originally scheduled for Great Leighs.
Wind: Almost nil Weather: Sunny

5866 TOTESPORTBINGO.COM MAIDEN AUCTION STKS — 5f
2:05 (2:07) (Class 4) 2-Y-O **£3,885** (£1,156; £577; £288) **Stalls** High

Form RPR

023 **1** **Morgans Choice**[27] 5060 2-8-11 73 FrancisNorton 3 70
(J L Spearing) *sn led: rdn fnl f: r.o* **3/1**[2]

006 **2** *shd* **Dimaire**[37] 4688 2-8-5 49 JamieMackay 1 64
(D Haydn Jones) *led early: chsd wnr: rdn over 1f out: chal ins fnl f: r.o* **28/1**

5 **3** *1 ¾* **Dream Number (IRE)**[5] 5714 2-8-4 0 DavidProbert 6 56
(W R Muir) *a.p: rdn and ev ch over 1f out: nt qckn fnl f* **3/1**[2]

4 *1 ½* **Hounds Ditch** 2-8-11 0 JimmyQuinn 5 58+
(Eve Johnson Houghton) *s.i.s: outpcd and sn wl in rr: rdn and wnt 4th over 1f out: kpt on towards fin: n.d* **12/1**[3]

0 **5** *2* **The Mighty Atom (USA)**[14] 5452 2-8-7 0 HayleyTurner 4 47
(P J Prendergast, Ire) *sn bhd: pushed along over 3f out: rdn and struggling over 2f out* **1/1**[1]

57.79 secs (57.79) **5** Ran SP% **111.1**
toteswinger: 1&2 £24.50. CSF £53.53 TOTE £2.80: £1.30, £9.50; EX 52.80.
Owner G M Eales **Bred** T E Pocock **Trained** Kinnersley, Worcs

FOCUS
A very weak and uncompetitive maiden auction and the order hardly changed during the course of the race. Tricky form to pin down with the runner-up a puzzle.

NOTEBOOK
Morgans Choice set the standard here having been placed in a couple of weak maiden auction events in his last two starts, and his replacement rider made sure that experience was put to good use by bouncing him out of the stalls in front. He faced determined challenges on both sides over the last two furlongs, but he responded gamely and despite hanging away to his left under pressure late on, saw his race out in determined style. He was 18lb well in with the runner-up on adjusted official ratings, though, so wouldn't appear that well handicapped off a mark of 73 with nurseries in mind. (op 11-4 tchd 5-2)
Dimaire, well beaten in her first three starts over further and officially rated just 49, has shown some early speed in her previous outings and she tracked the winner from the start. She was almost upsides him entering the last quarter-mile and tried her hardest, but just lost out. This was an improvement and this trip seemed to suit her better, but it may not be wise to make too much of how well she appeared to perform at these weights. (op 20-1)
Dream Number(IRE), who looked green before showing a little promise on her Bath debut, made progress to hold every chance against the nearside rail over a furlong out, but then couldn't quicken with the front pair. She may need a bit more time and might be one for nurseries after one more run. (op 4-1)
Hounds Ditch, from a yard that doesn't produce many winning debutants, is a half-brother to the stable's smart sprinter Judd Street, but he could never get into the race after missing the break. (op 10-1)
The Mighty Atom(USA) had finished eighth of ten on her debut in a Dundalk Listed race a fortnight earlier. She was soon off the bridle and going nowhere, however, and looked far from happy. It may be that she needs easier ground and must have been showing something at home to have made her debut at such a high level. (op 6-5)

5867 E.B.F/TOTESPORTGAMES.COM MAIDEN STKS — 6f
2:35 (2:37) (Class 4) 2-Y-O **£5,180** (£1,541; £770; £384) **Stalls** High

Form RPR

62 **1** **Glen Shiel (USA)**[17] 5337 2-9-3 0 RoystonFfrench 9 76+
(M Johnston) *w ldrs: rdn to ld and edgd lft over 1f out: drvn out* **7/1**[3]

2 *½* **Stefanki (IRE)** 2-9-3 0 TonyCulhane 6 75+
(R Curtis) *dwlt: sn hld up in tch: rdn over 1f out: chal ins fnl f: nt qckn towards fin* **11/4**[2]

3 *2 ¾* **Exceedthewildman** 2-9-3 0 LukeMorris 7 67
(J S Moore) *bhd: pushed along over 4f out: rdn and hdwy over 1f out: kpt on same pce ins fnl f* **50/1**

222 **4** *½* **Lean Machine**[14] 5431 2-9-3 79 PatDobbs 5 65
(R Hannon) *led over 1f: w ldr: led over 2f out: rdn and hdd over 1f out: wknd ins fnl f* **4/6**[1]

65 **5** *nse* **Buffett**[12] 5505 2-9-3 0 HayleyTurner 3 65
(L M Cumani) *s.i.s: hld up in rr: pushed along and effrt 2f out: rdn 1f out: kpt on towards fin* **12/1**

0 **6** *1 ¼* **Robens Rock (IRE)**[31] 4888 2-9-3 0 JamesDoyle 4 61
(A B Haynes) *hld up in tch: rdn over 1f out: wknd ins fnl f* **16/1**

00 **7** *7* **Kilmanseck**[12] 5527 2-9-3 0 JimmyQuinn 8 40
(Eve Johnson Houghton) *w ldr: led over 4f out: hdd and rdn over 2f out: wknd wl over 1f out* **50/1**

69.97 secs (69.97) **7** Ran SP% **116.7**
toteswinger: 1&2 £1.10, 1&3 £33.20, 2&3 £31.90. CSF £27.51 TOTE £7.70: £2.10, £1.80; EX 58.50.
Owner Sheikh Hamdan Bin Mohammed Al Maktoum **Bred** Marablue Farm Llc **Trained** Middleham Moor, N Yorks

FOCUS
A fair little maiden, but not that competitive according to the market. Not an easy race to assign figures to and the first two should be capable of better.
NOTEBOOK
Glen Shiel(USA) had looked in need of this return to 6f after finishing runner-up over the minimum trip at Catterick last time, and so it proved. He did have to be niggled along to take a handy position early and hung away to his left under pressure late on, but always kept on finding and ran out a ready winner. Nurseries now beckon. (op 11-2 tchd 8-1)
Stefanki(IRE) ◆, a half-brother to two winners at up to 1m including the quite useful Akua-Ba, had obviously shown something at home to be sent off second favourite and he justified that position. He even looked like winning when brought with his effort over a furlong out and pulled clear of the rest, but the winner proved too determined. He will win races. (op 3-1 tchd 9-4)
Exceedthewildman ◆, a half-brother to a winner at up to 1m5f and also a winner over jumps in France, was perhaps not surprisingly taken off his feet early, but he stayed on well as the race progressed and can be expected to build on this given time and distance. (op 66-1)
Lean Machine, runner-up in his first three starts, was very disappointing as he held a decent position up with the pace early, but found little when put under pressure passing the two-furlong pole. This was a step backwards. Official explanation: jockey said colt hung left-handed (op 8-11 tchd 5-6)
Buffett probably wouldn't have been suited by this drop back in trip and made little impact from the back of the field under pressure, but he does now qualify for a mark and may show a bit more in that sphere back over further. (op 16-1 tchd 8-1)

Robens Rock(IRE), who showed plenty of early pace before lack of a previous run told on his debut over an extra furlong and a half at Beverley, pulled hard on the wide outside early and eventually paid the penalty. (op 20-1)

5868 TOTESPORTCASINO.COM CLAIMING STKS 1m (R)
3:05 (3:10) (Class 5) 2-Y-O **£3,238** (£963; £481; £240) **Stalls** Low

Form RPR

0 **1** **Dr Mathias**[14] 5428 2-8-13 0 .... DavidProbert 8 70
(W R Muir) *t.k.h: early in tch: rdn over 2f out: edgd lft over 1f out and ins fnl f: r.o to ld last stride* **9/1**[3]

6031 **2** *shd* **Aegean Destiny**[11] 5543 2-8-7 64 ow1 .... PatDobbs 2 64
(R Hannon) *led: rdn and narrowly hdd over 1f out: led ins fnl f: hdd last stride* **7/4**[2]

1545 **3** *1 ¼* **Jehu**[12] 5515 2-9-2 80 .... (v) TonyCulhane 1 70
(M R Channon) *a.p: slt ld on bit over 1f out: sn pushed along: hdd and rdn ins fnl f: fnd little* **1/1**[1]

0 **4** *3 ¾* **Pearl Of Kent (IRE)**[41] 4564 2-8-4 0 .... LukeMorris 6 50
(P D Evans) *t.k.h early: pressed ldr: rdn and wknd over 1f out* **12/1**

00 **5** *hd* **Pollan Bay (IRE)**[19] 5319 2-8-9 0 .... JamesDoyle 7 54
(S Kirk) *s.i.s: sn swtchd lft to ins: hld up in rr: stdy prog 3f out: rdn and wknd wl over 1f out* **40/1**

0000 **6** *6* **Captain Blake (IRE)**[8] 5627 2-8-6 45 .... JimmyQuinn 3 38
(P D Evans) *hld up in mid-div: hrd rdn over 2f out: sn wknd* **40/1**

040 **7** *5* **Avon Krystal**[8] 5638 2-8-2 0 .... FrancisNorton 4 23
(R Hannon) *a towards rr: no ch wl over 1f out* **20/1**

000 **8** *1 ¼* **Book Of Truth (USA)**[38] 4646 2-8-4 58 .... MartinLane(5) 5 27
(D M Simcock) *hld up towards rr: pushed along over 4f out: struggling wl over 2f out* **25/1**

00 **9** *4* **Superhoops**[19] 5319 2-8-6 0 .... RoystonFfrench 9 15
(H S Howe) *hld up in mid-div: hdwy over 4f out: ev ch 3f out: rdn and wknd wl over 1f out* **100/1**

1m 42.5s (102.50) **9** Ran SP% **118.5**
toteswinger: 1&2 £4.00, 1&3 £7.30, 2&3 £1.02. CSF £25.08 TOTE £7.80: £2.10, £1.10, £1.10; EX 26.80.The winner was claimed by P. D. Evans for £12,000.

Owner Dulverton Equine **Bred** Herminoe Partnership **Trained** Lambourn, Berks

FOCUS
A modest claimer in which less than half the field could be given a realistic chance and the market suggested it was a two-horse race, but neither came out on top. The placed horses ran to form.

NOTEBOOK
Dr Mathias, who only beat one home on his Goodwood debut having met trouble in running, showed just what he was capable of here. Never far off the pace, he was delivered with his effort at the last possible moment and flew down the wide outside to snatch the race on the post. He still has improvement left and can probably win something a bit better. He was claimed by David Evans. (tchd 15-2)

Aegean Destiny, up a furlong having been bought back by connections after comfortably winning a Leicester seller last time, tried to make just about all the running and was a bit unfortunate, especially as some will believe that the 1lb overweight might have made the difference. She managed to beat off the challenge of her main market rival, but no sooner had she done so than the winner mugged her on the line. (op 15-8 tchd 13-8)

Jehu, by far the most exposed in the field, was still the one to beat with an official mark of 80 and having been contesting much better races than this lately. Everything seemed to go perfectly for him too, as he travelled sweetly behind the leaders and looked sure to win when looming alongside the leader a furlong out, but once there he found very little and finished weakly. He has questions to answer after this. (op 5-4)

Pearl Of Kent(IRE), seventh of eight on her debut in a 6f Newbury maiden from which the only horse to finish behind her plus the winner have scored since, was rather keen in a handy position early but she managed to stay in touch until coming to the last furlong. She appeared to be hanging late on, so may need easier ground and might also be capable of a bit more when she learns to settle. (op 14-1 tchd 16-1)

Pollan Bay(IRE), well beaten in his first two starts including in a seller last time, made modest late progress and now qualifies for a mark. (tchd 33-1)

5869 TOTESPORT HOME OF POOL BETTING H'CAP 1m (R)
3:40 (3:41) (Class 5) (0-70,72) 3-Y-0+ **£4,857** (£1,445; £722; £360) **Stalls** Low

Form RPR

51 **1** **Ela Gorrie Mou**[13] 5479 3-8-12 64 .... EdwardCreighton 1 73+
(T T Clement) *hld up in tch on ins: pushed along over 2f out: rdn to ld ins fnl f: r.o* **7/2**[1]

3451 **2** *¾* **Bolanderi (USA)**[11] 5548 4-9-4 72 .... AlexEdwards(7) 8 80
(Andrew Turnell) *hld up: hdwy over 1f out: rdn and chal ins fnl f: kpt on* **14/1**

1211 **3** *1* **Morocchius (USA)**[15] 5395 4-8-12 64 .... (p) BMcHugh(5) 10 70
(Miss J A Camacho) *a.p: wnt 2nd over 3f out: led on bit over 1f out: rdn and hdd ins fnl f: nt qckn* **7/2**[1]

0040 **4** *2* **Richo**[11] 5544 3-8-11 68 .... MarkCoumbe(5) 9 68
(S A Harris) *s.i.s: hld up: stdy hdwy on outside over 3f out: rdn and ev ch over 1f out: wknd wl ins fnl f* **25/1**

5452 **5** *1* **Jewelled**[15] 5384 3-9-1 67 .... HayleyTurner 6 64
(J W Hills) *hld up and bhd: swtchd rt to outside over 2f out: rdn and sme prog over 1f out: kpt on one pce fnl f* **4/1**[2]

425 **6** *1* **Tanforan**[24] 5160 7-8-13 67 .... BillyCray(7) 5 63
(B P J Baugh) *prom: pushed along over 3f out: rdn and wknd over 2f out* **12/1**

000/ **7** *1* **Sir Orpen (IRE)**[701] 6148 6-8-4 56 oh1 .... AmyBaker(5) 7 50
(J F Panvert) *led: rdn and hdd over 1f out: sn wknd* **33/1**

4131 **8** *nk* **Cavendish Road (IRE)**[25] 5121 3-9-2 68 .... DavidProbert 3 60
(W R Muir) *prom tl wknd over 3f out* **7/1**

62-5 **9** *3 ¾* **Ibbetson (USA)**[145] 1401 4-9-8 69 .... PatDobbs 2 53
(W R Swinburn) *chsd ldr tl over 3f out: rdn and wknd over 2f out* **5/1**[3]

66-0 **10** *nk* **Ros Cuire (IRE)**[47] 4375 4-8-4 56 oh4 .... MartinLane(5) 4 39
(W A Murphy, Ire) *s.i.s: hld up and bhd: pushed along over 3f out: no rspnse* **25/1**

1m 39.33s (99.33)
WFA 3 from 4yo+ 5lb **10** Ran SP% **118.6**
toteswinger: 1&2 £6.20, 1&3 £5.00, 2&3 £12.70. CSF £53.32 CT £190.95 TOTE £5.60: £2.00, £3.80, £1.70; EX 75.90.

Owner P Charalambous **Bred** Peter Charles **Trained** Newmarket, Suffolk

FOCUS
Not a bad handicap for the grade, run at a solid pace. The winner may do better again.

5870 TOTESPORT.COM H'CAP 1m 6f (R)
4:15 (4:17) (Class 2) (0-100,99) 3-Y-O **£15,577** (£4,665; £2,332; £1,167; £582; £292) **Stalls** Low

Form RPR

0211 **1** **Royal Diamond (IRE)**[38] 4670 3-8-2 80 oh1 .... KoseiMiura 7 90
(Sir Mark Prescott) *hld up: stdy hdwy over 3f out: rdn to ld jst over 1f out: styd on wl* **5/1**[3]

1202 **2** *1 ½* **Chiberta King**[35] 4767 3-8-11 89 .... DavidProbert 6 97
(A M Balding) *led 3f: chsd ldr: led 3f out tl rdn and hdd over 1f out: nt qckn ins fnl f* **9/2**[2]

3151 **3** *hd* **Times Up**[28] 5034 3-8-13 91 .... JimmyQuinn 5 98
(J L Dunlop) *a.p: rdn and ev ch over 1f out: nt qckn ins fnl f* **4/1**[1]

3432 **4** *1 ¾* **Non Dom (IRE)**[22] 5216 3-8-2 80 oh1 .... FrancisNorton 1 85
(H Morrison) *hld up: sme hdwy over 3f out: rdn over 2f out: styd on same pce fnl f* **7/1**

1121 **5** *3* **Recession Proof (FR)**[15] 5402 3-8-13 91 .... HayleyTurner 3 92
(S A Callaghan) *hld up in rr: hrd rdn over 2f out: no imp whn edgd lft over 1f out* **4/1**[1]

1303 **6** *½* **Clowance House**[51] 4248 3-8-9 87 .... TonyCulhane 8 87
(R Charlton) *w ldr: led after 3f: hdd 3f out: wknd 2f out* **12/1**

-160 **7** *hd* **Kimberley Downs (USA)**[86] 3051 3-8-4 82 .... RoystonFfrench 2 82
(M Johnston) *prom tl pushed along and wknd over 3f out* **8/1**

511 **8** *2 ¼* **Lethal Glaze (IRE)**[19] 5315 3-9-7 99 .... PatDobbs 4 96
(R Hannon) *a bhd* **11/1**

3m 1.42s (181.42) **8** Ran SP% **116.8**
toteswinger: 1&2 £6.30, 1&3 £7.40, 2&3 £5.90. CSF £28.37 CT £99.22 TOTE £5.30: £2.20, £1.50, £2.00; EX 37.20.

Owner E B Rimmer-Osborne House **Bred** Moyglare Stud Farm Ltd **Trained** Newmarket, Suffolk

■ A winner on his first ride in Britain for 19-year-old Japanese riding sensation Kosei Miura.

FOCUS
A decent and valuable staying handicap contested by some progressive and in-form three-year-olds, but the early pace seemed ordinary. Another step forward from the winner and the next two are on the upgrade too.

NOTEBOOK
Royal Diamond(IRE) ♦, whose 19-year-old jockey was having his first ride in this country, is proven over the trip and was 8lb higher in his bid for a hat-trick. He was only 1lb better off with Lethal Glaze for a six-length beating at Haydock in July, but the ground was very different there and he has undoubtedly improved in the meantime. Travelling well off the pace on the outside of the field, he gradually moved into contention up the home straight, and though he came off the bridle a fair way out, kept on finding enough to hit the front a furlong from home and win going away. He can probably keep on improving and his young rider did look very tidy here. (op 11-2 tchd 6-1)

Chiberta King, now 16lb higher than for his most recent success at Newmarket in May, has run well a couple of times off only slightly lower marks than this in the meantime and had been shaping as though this longer trip would suit. In and out of the lead throughout the contest, he kept on galloping, and though the winner proved too strong, he saw this trip out well enough. (tchd 4-1)

Times Up, put up 7lb for last month's Newmarket victory, was another trying this trip for the first time. Always in a handy position, he had every chance inside the last couple of furlongs and was just found wanting for a bit of finishing speed. He is another with a future as a staying handicapper. (op 9-2)

Non Dom(IRE), mostly consistent this season but now off a career-high mark, didn't seem to stay in his only previous try over this trip, but he ran on fairly well in the latter stages here, and though the pace they went didn't test his stamina thoroughly, it's probably worth giving him the benefit of the doubt. (op 13-2)

Recession Proof(FR), in fine form lately having won three of his last five starts and finishing runner-up in the other two, was 3lb higher than when dead-heating over a similar trip to this at Newmarket last time, but he never made much impact from off the pace and this was a bit disappointing. (op 9-2)

Clowance House, less than two lengths behind Chiberta King at Newmarket in May and 8lb better off, hadn't shown much in two starts over staying trips since, though he was out of his depth in the Queen's Vase at Royal Ascot. After having made much of the running, he didn't appear to get home here either. (op 8-1)

5871 TOTESPORT 0800 221 221 H'CAP 5f
4:50 (4:54) (Class 3) (0-95,94) 3-Y-0+ **£9,714** (£2,890; £1,444; £721) **Stalls** High

Form RPR

220 **1** **Haajes**[3] 5767 5-8-8 83 ow1 .... (t) TonyCulhane 1 92+
(J Balding) *chsd ldrs: rdn over 1f out: led ins fnl f: r.o* **4/1**[2]

3040 **2** *1* **The Jobber (IRE)**[26] 5098 8-8-7 82 .... FrancisNorton 6 87
(M Blanshard) *hld up in tch: pushed along to ld jst over 1f out: rdn and hdd ins fnl f: nt qckn* **10/1**

3634 **3** *nse* **Sharpened Edge**[21] 5264 3-8-4 80 oh2 .... DavidProbert 9 85
(B Palling) *a.p: hrd rdn and edgd lft over 1f out: ev ch ins fnl f: r.o* **8/1**

2034 **4** *½* **First In Command (IRE)**[23] 5183 4-8-7 82 ow1 ....(t) EdwardCreighton 8 88+
(Daniel Mark Loughnane, Ire) *hld up in mid-div: hdwy whn n.m.r over 1f out: rdn fnl f: kpt on towards fin* **6/1**

1010 **5** *1 ¾* **Impressible**[23] 5203 3-8-13 89 .... RoystonFfrench 2 86
(E J Alston) *led: rdn and hdd jst over 1f out: wknd ins fnl f* **9/1**

35-0 **6** *1 ¼* **Toms Laughter**[14] 5420 5-9-5 94 .... (b) LukeMorris 7 86
(R A Harris) *s.i.s: hld up: hdwy 2f out: rdn over 1f out: wknd fnl f* **9/2**[3]

0500 **7** *nk* **Cake (IRE)**[25] 5132 4-9-1 90 .... PatDobbs 4 81
(R Hannon) *hld up and bhd: pushed along and effrt over 1f out: sn rdn and btn* **14/1**

1214 **8** *¾* **Rocket Rob (IRE)**[14] 5436 3-8-8 84 .... HayleyTurner 5 72
(S A Callaghan) *hld up and bhd: pushed along 2f out: no rspnse* **7/2**[1]

043 **9** *3* **Kay Two (IRE)**[23] 5183 7-8-10 85 .... (p) JimmyQuinn 3 63
(R J Price) *w ldr tl pushed along and wknd over 1f out* **8/1**

56.35 secs (56.35)
WFA 3 from 4yo+ 1lb **9** Ran SP% **122.7**
toteswinger: 1&2 £13.50, 1&3 £5.10, 2&3 £16.40. CSF £46.44 CT £317.14 TOTE £4.80: £1.90, £3.60, £3.30; EX 59.00.

Owner Willie McKay **Bred** Irish National Stud **Trained** Scrooby, Notts

FOCUS
A decent sprint handicap run at a strong pace and the main action unfolded up the centre of the track. Sound form.

NOTEBOOK
Haajes ♦ was without a win since February, but has nonetheless been running well in defeat this summer and met all sorts of trouble when only eighth of 11 at Doncaster three days earlier. He had no such problems here, having raced on the wide outside throughout from his low draw, and responded well to vigorous driving to lead inside the last furlong. He is even better on softer ground, so could be in for a productive autumn.

The Jobber(IRE), back on the same mark as for his last success at Salisbury in June, tracked the pace early and never stopped trying. He can win off his current rating if able to reproduce this. (op 8-1)

Sharpened Edge, 2lb wrong, was therefore only 6lb better off with Rocket Rob for a near three-length beating at Sandown last month. She normally likes to do it from the front, but wasn't able to do that here, so this was a good effort, though she was inclined to hang away to her left in the second half of the contest. Official explanation: jockey said filly hung left-handed

First In Command(IRE) ◆, 6lb above his last winning mark including the overweight and just behind Kay Two at Chepstow last time, was meeting that rival on the same terms here and was unlucky not to go very close. He was right there with every chance over a furlong from home when squeezed out between the weakening Kay Two and the hanging Sharpened Edge, but he ran on again once in the clear and wasn't beaten at all far. He deserves compensation. Official explanation: jockey said gelding suffered interference in running (op 7-1 tchd 11-2)

Impressible, who needs to dominate and wasn't able to do that at York last time, ran fast for half a mile but was given no peace by Kay Two and that may have counted against her. She is much better when able to lead on her own, but still looks on a very stiff mark in any case. (tchd 10-1)

Toms Laughter ◆, who ran well for a long way on his belated return in a Beverley Listed event last month, attracted market support beforehand, but the race didn't really go his way. Firstly he missed the break, and then as the race unfolded he found himself isolated against the stands' rail which may not have been ideal. He remains 5lb above his last winning mark, but he may still just have needed it and shouldn't be written off. (op 7-1 tchd 8-1)

Rocket Rob(IRE), extremely consistent in recent months, is still 7lb higher than for his last success. Dropped out as usual, he was making heavy weather of it from some way out and the handicapper may have hold of him now. (tchd 4-1)

Kay Two(IRE) Official explanation: jockey said gelding bled from the nose

5872 BET WITH TOTESPORT AT FFOS LAS H'CAP (DIV I) 1m 2f (R)

5:25 (5:26) (Class 6) (0-55,58) 3-Y-0+ **£2,266** (£674; £337; £168) **Stalls** Low

Form / RPR

5302 **1** **Chichen Daawe**[30] 4943 3-8-6 **48** RoystonFfrench 10 55+
(B Ellison) *hld up and bhd: swtchd rt over 2f out: rdn and hdwy over 1f out: r.o u.p to ld towards fin* **3/1**[1]

4626 **2** *nk* **Screaming Brave**[1] 5838 3-9-2 **58** TonyCulhane 7 64
(M R Channon) *hld up in mid-div: smooth prog over 3f out: led on bit wl over 1f out: sn rdn: hdd towards fin* **3/1**[1]

443 **3** *1* **Corrib (IRE)**[60] 3949 6-8-12 **47** DavidProbert 2 51
(B Palling) *hld up in mid-div: smooth hdwy over 3f out: rdn 1f out: nt qckn* **3/1**[1]

0000 **4** *4* **Benozzo Gozzoli**[8] 5630 3-8-4 **46** oh1 FrancisNorton 4 42
(H Morrison) *led: hdd over 2f out: rdn wl over 1f out: wknd fnl f* **12/1**

0000 **5** *5* **Heavenly Saint**[2] 5790 4-9-5 **54** RichardThomas 8 40
(C Roberts) *chsd ldr: led over 2f out: hrd rdn and hdd wl over 1f out: sn wknd* **16/1**

45-5 **6** *5* **Heaven Or Hell (IRE)**[8] 5631 3-8-7 **49** LukeMorris 1 25
(P D Evans) *prom tl rdn and wknd over 2f out* **17/2**[2]

5360 **7** *2* **Generous Lad (IRE)**[13] 5484 6-8-11 **46** oh1 (p) JamesDoyle 12 18
(A B Haynes) *prom: rdn over 4f out tl wknd over 3f out* **10/1**[3]

000 **8** *nse* **Shosolosa (IRE)**[14] 5438 7-8-7 **47** oh1 ow1 MarkCoumbe(5) 11 19
(S A Harris) *hld up in rr: rdn and struggling over 2f out* **33/1**

/6-0 **9** *1 ½* **Toberogan (IRE)**[13] 5489 8-9-6 **55** PatDobbs 6 24
(W A Murphy, Ire) *a in rr* **16/1**

0000 **10** *nk* **Annes Sound (IRE)**[30] 4944 3-7-11 **46** RichardRowe(7) 5 14
(Patrick Morris) *s.i.s: a in rr* **20/1**

640- **11** *20* **Who Art Thou (USA)**[359] 6058 3-8-10 **52** ow2 VinceSlattery 3 —
(D R Gandolfo) *hld up in mid-div: pushed along over 4f out: sn struggling: lost tch fnl 3f* **25/1**

2m 9.13s (129.13)
WFA 3 from 4yo+ 7lb **11** Ran SP% **125.6**
toteswinger: 1&2 £4.20, 1&3 £3.40, 2&3 £4.20. CSF £11.68 CT £30.86 TOTE £5.10: £2.30, £1.40, £1.60; EX 14.80.
Owner Mrs Andrea M Mallinson **Bred** C Mallinson **Trained** Norton, N Yorks

FOCUS
A moderate handicap in which late market support resulted in three horses going off as co-favourites, and they dominated the closing stages. Sound form to this weak race, which was the better of the two divisions.

Corrib(IRE) Official explanation: jockey said mare was denied a clear run
Generous Lad(IRE) Official explanation: jockey said gelding hung left

5873 BET WITH TOTESPORT AT FFOS LAS H'CAP (DIV II) 1m 2f (R)

6:00 (6:03) (Class 6) (0-55,61) 3-Y-0+ **£2,266** (£674; £337; £168) **Stalls** Low

Form / RPR

3400 **1** **Arlene Phillips**[29] 5011 3-8-7 **45** PatDobbs 9 50
(R Hannon) *hld up towards rr: stdy prog 3f out: led 2f out: drvn out ins fnl f* **8/1**

00 **2** *nk* **Arabian Silk (IRE)**[58] 4004 3-8-7 **50** MartinLane(5) 3 54
(D M Simcock) *hld up in mid-div: rdn and hdwy over 2f out: chsd wnr wl over 1f out: r.o ins fnl f* **22/1**

00-0 **3** *nk* **Mr Plod**[19] 5314 4-9-4 **49** (v[1]) StephenCarson 8 53
(Andrew Reid) *hld up in rr: hdwy 2f out: rdn over 1f out: kpt on same pce ins fnl f* **33/1**

000- **4** *1 ¾* **Feeling (IRE)**[27] 6753 5-9-0 **45** DavidProbert 2 45
(D Burchell) *prom early: hld up in tch on ins: rdn over 1f out: one pce ins fnl f* **9/2**[3]

0056 **5** *1 ¾* **Ba Dreamflight**[28] 5015 4-9-0 **45** TravisBlock 7 42
(H Morrison) *led after 2f to 7f out: pushed along 4f out: rdn wl over 1f out: wknd ins fnl f* **4/1**[2]

0400 **6** *shd* **Mystic Touch**[42] 4533 3-9-1 **53** JamesDoyle 4 49
(A B Haynes) *hld up in mid-div: hdwy over 5f out: led on bit over 3f out: pushed along and hdd 2f out: rdn and wknd fnl f* **20/1**

0400 **7** *¾* **Billy Smart (IRE)**[58] 4010 3-8-11 **49** (t) LukeMorris 1 44
(A J Lidderdale) *plld hrd towards rr: nt clr run on ins over 2f out: sn swtchd rt: rdn over 1f out: n.d* **16/1**

0404 **8** *¾* **Bolton Hall (IRE)**[14] 5444 7-9-0 **45** (tp) VinceSlattery 5 38
(W K Goldsworthy) *s.i.s: hld up towards rr: rdn over 3f out: no rspnse* **6/1**

0- **9** *½* **Indian Haze (IRE)**[43] 4511 3-8-9 **47** FrancisNorton 10 39
(Daniel Mark Loughnane, Ire) *prom: wkng whn n.m.r over 2f out* **12/1**

5451 **10** *4 ½* **Primo Dilettante**[4] 5750 3-9-9 **61** 6ex JimmyQuinn 12 44
(W J Knight) *w ldr: led 7f out tl over 3f out: rdn over 2f out: wkng whn n.m.r on ins wl over 1f out* **9/4**[1]

2m 9.60s (129.60)
WFA 3 from 4yo+ 7lb **10** Ran SP% **120.0**
toteswinger: 1&2 £42.60, 1&3 £27.40, 2&3 £41.30. CSF £172.74 CT £5410.44 TOTE £11.20: £2.70, £7.80, £5.20; EX 204.40 Place 6 £108.78, Place 5 £27.15.
Owner Theakston Stud Syndicate **Bred** Theakston Stud **Trained** East Everleigh, Wilts

FOCUS
Another weak handicap and only three of these had tasted success before. The winning time was nearly half a second slower than the first division.

Feeling(IRE) Official explanation: jockey said gelding was denied a clear run

T/Plt: £182.30 to a £1 stake. Pool: £48,024.77. 192.28 winning tickets. T/Qpdt: £11.30 to a £1 stake. Pool: £3,591.10. 233.50 winning tickets. KH

[5740] GOODWOOD (R-H)

Saturday, September 12

OFFICIAL GOING: Good to firm (good in places)
Unlike for the meeting earlier in the week, the rails were at their normal configuration and all distances were as advertised.
Wind: Brisk, half behind Weather: Fine

5874 WHITELEY CLINIC STKS (H'CAP) 7f

2:10 (2:10) (Class 2) (0-100,100) 3-Y-0+
£11,215 (£3,358; £1,679; £840; £419; £210) **Stalls** High

Form / RPR

0221 **1** **Golden Desert (IRE)**[14] 5424 5-9-8 **100** AlanMunro 9 109
(T G Mills) *s.i.s: sn chsd ldng quartet: plld out wl over 1f out: clsd on ldng pair fnl f: drvn ahd last 75yds: r.o wl* **4/1**[2]

020 **2** *1* **Noble Citizen (USA)**[35] 4796 4-8-11 **89** StephenDonohoe 5 95
(D M Simcock) *trckd ldr: rdn to chal over 1f out: edgd ahd 150yds out: hdd and outpcd last 75yds* **8/1**

1060 **3** *1 ¾* **Dunn'o (IRE)**[21] 5249 4-9-2 **94** JimCrowley 10 95
(C G Cox) *taken down early: led at gd pce: hrd pressed over 1f out: hdd & wknd last 150yds* **7/1**[3]

0605 **4** *2* **Vitznau (IRE)**[19] 5313 5-9-6 **98** RyanMoore 3 94+
(R Hannon) *hld up in last pair and wl off the pce: tried to cl fr over 2f out: rdn over 1f out: styd on but no ch* **16/1**

0542 **5** *¾* **Isphahan**[22] 5221 6-8-8 **86** oh2 (v) ChrisCatlin 8 80
(A M Balding) *wl off the pce in last trio: rdn 3f out: kpt on fr 2f out: nvr gng pce to threaten ldrs* **9/1**

1005 **6** *¾* **King's Wonder**[13] 5476 4-8-11 **89** RichardMullen 1 81
(W R Muir) *taken down early: t.k.h early in 4th: cl enough 2f out: nt qckn and hd high over 1f out: wknd fnl f* **18/1**

0-11 **7** *1 ½* **Crown Choice**[136] 1607 4-8-12 **90** AdamKirby 6 78
(W R Swinburn) *swtg: trckd ldng pair: cl enough 2f out: rdn and nt qckn over 1f out: wknd fnl f* **4/1**[2]

1021 **8** *2* **Suruor (IRE)**[44] 4459 3-9-2 **98** SebSanders 4 78+
(D M Simcock) *dwlt: pushed along in last pair and wl off the pce: sme prog u.p fr 3f out: rchd 6th over 1f out: sn wknd* **7/2**[1]

0000 **9** *¾* **Beaver Patrol (IRE)**[28] 5039 7-9-0 **92** ShaneKelly 7 72
(Eve Johnson Houghton) *hld up in 6th: rdn 3f out: wknd over 2f out* **28/1**

5-55 **10** *4* **Jet D'Eau (FR)**[13] 5474 3-9-3 **99** (b) GeorgeBaker 2 67
(G L Moore) *dismntd twice at post: off the pce in 7th: pushed along 3f out: no prog: hanging and wknd over 1f out: eased* **12/1**

1m 24.84s (-2.56) **Going Correction** -0.175s/f (Firm)
WFA 3 from 4yo+ 4lb **10** Ran SP% **118.1**
Speed ratings (Par 109): **107,105,103,101,100 99,98,95,95,90**
toteswinger: 1&2 £11.30 1&3 £12.40, 2&3 £16.50. CSF £36.64 CT £225.52 TOTE £5.20: £2.10, £3.10, £2.40; EX 82.20 TRIFECTA Not won..
Owner S Parker **Bred** Mervyn Stewkesbury **Trained** Headley, Surrey

FOCUS
A tight handicap, guaranteed to be run at a strong pace with at least four confirmed pacesetters in the field. Surprisingly not much got involved from off the pace, but it was another personal best from the winner.

NOTEBOOK

Golden Desert(IRE) was suited by the strong pace. He had enough pace to win over 6f here last time off a career high 92 and was off 100 now. Handling the fast ground well, he was always travelling well within his capabilities and quickened smartly to settle the race in a matter of strides and won with plenty in hand. This was his first success at class 2 level and it won't be the last. Connections are looking at the 7f heritage handicap at Ascot on September 26, in which he was a close fifth last year. (op 9-2)

Noble Citizen(USA) hasn't won for nearly a year and had been struggling since running well in Dubai during the winter, but he was nicely backed here despite his stable saddling the favourite too. He couldn't get to the front but took a tow and showed a good attitude when asked to quicken inside the last. He was unfortunate to meet a horse in such good form. Rated 98 in May, he was off 89 here. However all three wins have been over this distance and suitable races won't be easy to find. (op 10-1 tchd 11-1)

Dunn'o(IRE) won the race for pace to lead but his best form has been over a stiffer test of a mile at Sandown and he didn't have any finishing kick over this sharper circuit. He was also 4lb higher than when winning last time in May. (op 8-1)

Vitznau(IRE) is still a pound higher than when last successful in April 2008 but has been as high as 104 and there was some encouragment to be taken from this. He's never won beyond 7f but he did finish well enough to think that another try at a mile might be worthwhile. (op 14-1)

Isphahan was 2lb out of the handicap and therefore 6lb higher than when a narrow second at Sandown last time over a more suitable mile. He clearly needs further than this. (op 12-1)

King's Wonder couldn't lead but still looked to be doing too much and paid the penalty. He's still 5lb higher than when winning his last race here in May. (op 16-1 tchd 20-1)

Crown Choice ◆ hadn't run since winning twice at Kempton in April. He got tired in the end but was right on the pace much of the way and will be of interest with this run under his belt.

Suruor(IRE) blew this at the start. The strong pace meant that he had to be used to get into position up the straight and never got time to get balanced and find momentum. It was hardly surprising he weakened and there will be others days when things fall better for him. (op 3-1)

Jet D'Eau(FR) Official explanation: jockey said filly never travelled

5875 SELECT RACING UK ON SKY 432 STKS (GROUP 3) 1m 1f 192y

2:40 (2:40) (Class 1) 3-Y-0+ **£36,900** (£13,988; £7,000; £3,490; £1,748) **Stalls** High

Form / RPR

1015 **1** **Mac Love**[14] 5426 8-9-3 117 MickyFenton 3 97
(Stef Liddiard) *stdd s: t.k.h and hld up in last: stdy prog on outer fr 3f out: led gng strly over 1f out: sn in command: rdn out* **15/2**

4313 **2** *1* **Stotsfold**[35] 4809 6-9-3 116 AdamKirby 5 95
(W R Swinburn) *lw: hld up in 4th: t.k.h downhill 5f out: clsd on ldrs 3f out: led 2f out to over 1f out: hrd rdn and nt qckn* **6/4**[1]

2613 **3** *½* **Perfect Stride**[22] 5231 4-9-0 113 RyanMoore 4 91
(Sir Michael Stoute) *lw: t.k.h: trckd ldr 4f: dropped to last and shkn up over 2f out: sn outpcd: drvn and styd on fnl f to press for 2nd nr fin* **3/1**[3]

2101 **4** *1 ½* **Palavicini (USA)**[22] 5231 3-8-10 113 JimCrowley 2 91
(J L Dunlop) *lw: t.k.h: trckd ldr after 4f: led briefly jst over 2f out: nt qckn wl over 1f out: fdd* **2/1**[2]

5154 5 2 1/4 **Constant Cheers (IRE)**[3] 5772 6-9-0 78 ShaneKelly 1 83?
(W R Swinburn) *led: stdy pce to 1/2-way: hdd and outpcd jst over 2f out* 100/1

2m 6.81s (-1.19) **Going Correction** -0.175s/f (Firm)
WFA 3 from 4yo+ 7lb 5 Ran SP% **111.1**
Speed ratings (Par 113): **97,96,95,94,92**
CSF £19.54 TOTE £8.20: £2.60, £1.60; EX 16.70.
Owner Vimal Khosla **Bred** Kingwood Bloodstock **Trained** Great Shefford, Berks

FOCUS
This was always going to be a tactical race with no obvious pace and the fact that the designated pacemaker Constant Cheers seemed to set only a modest one for the first four furlongs was always going to put the three runners who truly got 1m2f at a distinct disadvantage. Questionable form.

NOTEBOOK
Mac Love found the modest pace playing straight into his hands, as he has never won beyond an extended mile in his lengthy career and was able to use his unquestioned pace inside the last furlong. Just as when he won his latest race, a Group 3 at Salisbury in August, he was ridden with complete confidence and was never in any danger once coaxed ahead under another inspired ride from Micky Fenton. A mile surely remains his optimum and connections may now call it quits for the season with this willing gelding, who at the age of eight has never been better. (tchd 6-1)
Stotsfold, who needs every yard of 1m2f to produce his best, didn't appear best served by his stablemate Constant Cheers. He clearly showed no ill effects from his hard race in the Arlington Million in Chicago but had to take the initiative with two furlongs to run and didn't have the required kick when Mac Love came at him. He still showed a fine attitude and he still has no Group 2 penalties. He also handes some give in the ground so his season looks far from over. (op 5-4 tchd 13-8)
Perfect Stride, who was marginally inferior at official ratings with the first two, had enough pace to win over a mile at Ascot in April but was always doing too much off the modest early pace. When the pace quickened two out he was in big trouble but nothing finished better. He had finished five and a half lengths behind Palavacini in a nine-furlong Group 3 at York but was able to comfortably reverse that on only 3lb better terms, a creditable effort under the circumstances. (op 7-2)
Palavicini(USA) was first to sense things were wrong but his dash for glory over two out was short lived. This was slightly disappointing, even under these circumstances. (tchd 3-1 in a place)
Constant Cheers(IRE) finished last but was only beaten just over five lengths and certainly didn't have a hard race. If this run is taken unwisely at face value, then he's a snip off his current mark of 78, especially as he needs this trip and more. However, he was almost certainly flattered, having set a far weaker pace than had been anticipated for his stablemate.

5876 HOLT'S AUCTIONEERS STKS (H'CAP) 1m 4f
3:10 (3:12) (Class 4) (0-80,79) 3-Y-O **£5,180** (£1,541; £770; £384) **Stalls** High

Form RPR
3551 1 **Rockfella**[54] 4150 3-8-7 **68** AlanMunro 2 74
(D J Coakley) *led and sn 5 l clr: c bk to field 4f out: jnd and pushed along firmly over 2f out: fought on wl to regain advantage 1f out: hrd pressed again nr fin: plld out more to hold on* 12/1
2414 2 hd **Mykingdomforahorse**[28] 5027 3-8-9 **70** ChrisCatlin 1 76
(M R Channon) *hld up in last pair: stdy prog on outer fr 3f out: wnt 3rd 2f out: hrd rdn to take 2nd last 100yds: sn threatened wnr: jst hld* 10/1
2103 3 1 **Andhaar**[21] 5255 3-9-2 **77** TGMcLaughlin 8 81
(E A L Dunlop) *swtg: dwlt: hld up in last: pushed along and prog on outer wl over 2f out: trying to cl but edgd rt 1f out: r.o to take 3rd nr fin* 10/1
-313 4 1 **Going For Gold**[37] 4709 3-9-4 **79** RyanMoore 5 83+
(R Charlton) *dwlt: hld up towards rr: dropped to last pair over 3f out: looking for room over 2f out: nt qckn sn after: styng on whn hmpd 1f out: r.o again last 75yds* 3/1[1]
0606 5 nk **Sam Sharp (USA)**[22] 5209 3-9-0 **75** IanMongan 7 77+
(H R A Cecil) *swtg: in tch: prog to go 2nd over 3f out: jnd wnr over 2f out to 1f out: hld after: wknd last 100yds* 4/1[2]
3340 6 hd **Cry For The Moon (USA)**[22] 5216 3-9-3 **78** JimCrowley 9 80
(Mrs A J Perrett) *hld up in midfield: rdn and prog to dispute 3rd 2f out: nt pce to cl on ldng pair: edgd lft 1f out: kpt on after* 13/2
1-6 7 16 **Hazy Dancer**[129] 1789 3-9-2 **77** RichardMullen 10 53
(M P Tregoning) *swtg: trckd ldrs: rdn 3f out: wknd rapidly over 2f out: t.o* 8/1
13 8 7 **Ladies Dancing**[192] 755 3-9-1 **76** ShaneKelly 11 41
(J A Osborne) *swtg: chsd ldr to 4f out: wknd rapidly wl over 2f out: t.o* 14/1
0-1 9 12 **Brooklyn Spirit**[91] 2930 3-9-2 **77** AdamKirby 4 23
(C G Cox) *lw: chsd ldng pair: disp 2nd 4f out: sn rdn: wknd rapidly over 2f out: t.o* 11/2[3]

2m 37.19s (-1.21) **Going Correction** -0.175s/f (Firm) 9 Ran SP% **117.4**
Speed ratings (Par 103): **97,96,96,95,95 95,84,79,71**
toteswinger: 1&2 £14.90, 1&3 £30.60, 2&3 £11.40. CSF £126.61 CT £1252.50 TOTE £18.00: £3.50, £2.60, £3.60; EX 146.50.
Owner L M A Hurley **Bred** Ascagnano S P A **Trained** West Ilsley, Berks
■ Stewards' Enquiry : Jim Crowley caution: careless riding.

FOCUS
An extremely tight handicap with some unexposed horses, some of which didn't perform but won by one who did. Muddling form on balance.
Ladies Dancing Official explanation: jockey said gelding hung right

5877 PAUL KELLY STKS (H'CAP) 5f
3:45 (3:48) (Class 5) (0-75,75) 3-Y-O **£3,238** (£963; £481; £240) **Stalls** Low

Form RPR
3151 1 **Mythical Blue (IRE)**[17] 5345 3-9-1 **72** RyanMoore 3 80
(J M Bradley) *mde virtually all: rdn over 1f out: kpt on wl* 7/4[1]
2435 2 3/4 **Edith's Boy (IRE)**[15] 5383 3-8-4 **61** ChrisCatlin 11 66
(S Dow) *prom on outer: w wnr 1/2-way: persistent chal after: a jst hld ins fnl f* 10/1
3320 3 1 1/4 **Raimond Ridge (IRE)**[12] 5506 3-8-12 **72** MCGeran(3) 9 73
(M R Channon) *towards rr on outer: rdn and prog fr 2f out: styd on to take 3rd nr fin* 12/1
220 4 3/4 **Night Affair**[21] 5264 3-9-4 **75** AdamKirby 6 73
(D W P Arbuthnot) *lw: pressed wnr to 1/2-way: sn u.p: nt qckn over 1f out: one pce after* 11/2[2]
2150 5 nk **Under Review (IRE)**[140] 1505 3-8-10 **72** DeanHeslop(5) 7 69
(T D Barron) *lw: s.i.s: sn rcvrd and swtchd to nr side: cl up 2f out: nt qckn over 1f out: grad fdd fnl f* 7/1[3]
13U0 6 1/2 **Pinball (IRE)**[5] 5719 3-8-4 **61** (v) NeilChalmers 2 56
(Mrs L Williamson) *s.i.s: last trio: rdn 1/2-way: trying to make prog whn n.m.r 1f out: kpt on* 16/1
-165 7 hd **Silky Way (GR)**[51] 4223 3-8-8 **65** JimCrowley 4 59
(P R Chamings) *cl up: nt qckn 2f out: fdd over 1f out* 11/1
0363 8 1 1/2 **Mazzola**[12] 5517 3-8-11 **68** AlanMunro 5 57
(M R Channon) *cl up bhd ldrs: rdn 2f out: fdd over 1f out* 7/1[3]
0641 9 hd **Mamlakati (IRE)**[12] 5500 3-8-5 **62** RichardMullen 8 50
(R Hannon) *sn in last trio: outpcd after 2f: nvr on terms after* 11/1
0400 10 5 **Louie's Lad**[13] 5477 3-7-12 **62** oh14 ow1 (p) KierenFox(7) 1 32
(J J Bridger) *outpcd after 2f: bhd rest of way* 66/1

57.20 secs (-1.20) **Going Correction** -0.175s/f (Firm) 10 Ran SP% **117.6**
Speed ratings (Par 101): **102,100,98,97,97 96,96,93,93,85**
toteswinger: 1&2 £3.00, 1&3 £6.40, 2&3 £20.80. CSF £20.88 CT £170.47 TOTE £2.50: £1.50, £2.10, £3.70; EX 16.80.
Owner Clifton Hunt **Bred** John O'Dowd **Trained** Sedbury, Gloucs

FOCUS
A typically tricky three-year-old sprint handicap. The first three were all close to their recent best, but not a race to rate too positively.
Pinball(IRE) Official explanation: jockey said filly was slow into stride
Louie's Lad Official explanation: jockey said gelding hung right out of stalls and never travelled

5878 STARLIT STKS (LISTED RACE) 6f
4:20 (4:20) (Class 1) 3-Y-O+
£22,708 (£8,608; £4,308; £2,148; £1,076; £540) **Stalls** Low

Form RPR
2024 1 **Tamagin (USA)**[14] 5434 6-9-0 **109** (p) StephenDonohoe 3 113
(J Pearce) *lw: led and sn 3l clr: c bk to runner-up over 2f out: hdd jst over 1f out: n.m.r but rallied to ld nr fin* 9/2[2]
2415 2 hd **Mac Gille Eoin**[42] 4523 5-9-0 **96** JimCrowley 7 112
(J Gallagher) *chsd wnr: clsd over 2f out: drvn to ld jst over 1f out and edgd lft: hdd nr fin* 5/1[3]
0301 3 2 1/4 **Mullein**[27] 5069 4-8-13 **99** SebSanders 10 104+
(R M Beckett) *settled in last pair and wl off the pce: shkn up and prog 2f out: styd on wl fnl f to take 3rd nr fin* 11/2
4300 4 nk **J J The Jet Plane (SAF)**[7] 5657 5-9-4 **118** RyanMoore 9 108
(R Hannon) *w.w off the pce: prog to chse ldng pair 2f out: nt qckn over 1f out: fdd and lost 3rd nr fin* 9/4[1]
0504 5 1 **Express Wish**[13] 5474 5-9-0 **105** ShaneKelly 5 101
(J Noseda) *lw: w.w off the pce: rdn to cl on ldrs 2f out: no imp 1f out: one pce* 6/1
100- 6 2 3/4 **Galpin Junior (USA)**[329] 6815 3-8-12 **108** (t) AlanMunro 6 92
(B J Meehan) *bit bkwd: dwlt: outpcd in last pair: brief effrt on outer over 2f out: sn btn* 33/1
1666 7 1/2 **Rowe Park**[44] 4456 6-9-0 **104** SteveDrowne 1 90
(Mrs L C Jewell) *swtg: chsd clr ldng pair: rdn over 2f out: sn lost 3rd: wknd over 1f out* 14/1
0500 8 1/2 **Beckermet (IRE)**[14] 5434 7-9-0 **98** ChrisCatlin 2 89
(R F Fisher) *lw: chsd ldng trio but nt on terms: no imp over 2f out: sn wknd* 16/1

69.10 secs (-3.10) **Going Correction** -0.175s/f (Firm) course record
WFA 3 from 4yo+ 2lb 8 Ran SP% **110.8**
Speed ratings (Par 111): **113,112,109,109,108 104,103,103**
toteswinger: 1&2 £4.20, 1&3 £3.30, 2&3 £5.70. CSF £25.41 TOTE £5.70: £1.60, £1.80, £1.30; EX 28.40.
Owner Killarney Glen **Bred** Stonehaven Farm LLC **Trained** Newmarket, Suffolk

FOCUS
A Listed race in which some tarnished stars were attempting to recapture former glories, but it was won in the gamest style by Tamagin, who set a new course record. The first pair were always 1-2 and the second looks the key to the form.

NOTEBOOK
Tamagin(USA) won in the gamest style and set a new course record. The last of ten career wins came off a mark of 100 in a 6f Windsor handicap in June, but his four runs in defeat since have been the best of his lengthy career, which has been rejuvenated since joining Jeff Pearce. He had moved to 109 for his most recent when a length fourth to Palace Moon in Listed class at Newmarket last month, which left him 5lb short on adjusted figures with J J The Jet Plane. Relishing the very quick ground and showing fine pace, he looked in trouble when Mac Gille Eoin edged ahead of him inside the last, a situation made worse by the leader edging to the left, making things tight, but this was enough to re-charge him. He is a possible for the Ayr Gold Cup, for which he is already top weight and would incurr a small penalty, but his trainer says he is extremely ground dependent and it must be fast going. There is also the Diadem over six at Ascot on September 26th. If the ground stays to his liking, he is worth a shot at either. (op 7-2)
Mac Gille Eoin, 13lb inferior to the winner on official ratings, lost nothing in defeat, producing a career-best effort.Connections are considering blinkers to curb the tendency to hang, and with 8st 11lb he would have a big chance in the Ayr Gold Cup if conditions were suitable. (op 7-1)
Mullein had won a Listed fillies' race over this distance at Pontefract last time. The early pace caught her out, but she stayed on well enough and any chance to get back among her own sex would be a big advantage. (op 5-1 tchd 6-1)
J J The Jet Plane(SAF) was officially best of these, but while he was much better back on this firmer surface after disappointing at Haydock at Group 1 level on soft last time, it was still disappointing given his close third to Fleeting Spirit in the July Cup. He never looked likely to play a serious hand. (op 2-1 tchd 5-2)
Express Wish was dropping back from seven furlongs and that was a major disadvantage under such fast conditions. (op 15-2 tchd 8-1)
Galpin Junior(USA), despite an official mark of 108, was always struggling on his belated reappearance. (op 25-1)
Rowe Park is better over a furlong shorter, but still wouldn't have bothered the first two at that trip. (op 10-1)
Beckermet(IRE) hasn't won for two years and it's hard to see where a win is likely to come from, even though he has slipped down the ratings from his peak of 110 and would now get into plenty of handicaps. (op 20-1)

5879 E B F BUY A £10,000 RACING POST BONUS YEARLING MAIDEN STKS 1m
4:55 (4:55) (Class 4) 2-Y-O **£4,857** (£1,445; £722; £360) **Stalls** High

Form RPR
02 1 **Manhattan Fox (USA)**[15] 5407 2-9-3 0 AlanMunro 5 77+
(B J Meehan) *lw: sn led: clr whn hung lft fr over 5f out: hung across to nr side rail in st but stl wl clr: rdn fnl 2f: hld on* 11/10[1]
00 2 1 1/4 **Finest Reserve (IRE)**[11] 5542 2-9-3 0 ChrisCatlin 6 74
(M R Channon) *stdd s: hld up last: shkn up 2f out: prog over 1f out: r.o to ld far side gp nr fin* 16/1
6 3 1/2 **Magnetic Force (IRE)**[22] 5220 2-9-3 0 RyanMoore 1 73
(Sir Michael Stoute) *w'like: chsd ldr: lft in ld of far side gp over 3f out: hdd 2f out: led again over 1f out but nt on terms w wnr: hdd nr fin* 3/1[2]
35 4 3/4 **Banks And Braes**[21] 5251 2-9-3 0 SteveDrowne 2 72
(R Hannon) *leggy: in tch: rdn over 2f out: edgd lft and nt qckn: kpt on same pce fnl f* 4/1[3]
6 5 2 **Berling (IRE)**[29] 5002 2-9-3 0 JimCrowley 4 67
(J L Dunlop) *w'like: scope: tall: chsd ldrs: lft in 2nd of quartet styng far side over 3f out: drvn to ld gp 2f out to over 1f out: wknd* 7/1

1m 39.49s (-0.41) **Going Correction** -0.175s/f (Firm) 5 Ran SP% **111.0**
Speed ratings (Par 97): **95,93,93,92,90**
toteswinger: 1&2 £14.00. CSF £18.73 TOTE £2.00: £1.40, £3.50; EX 21.80.

Owner Catesby W Clay **Bred** Runnymede Farm Inc Et Al **Trained** Manton, Wilts

FOCUS

Tricky form to pin down. The fact that the winner was able to chart an extremely wayward and disadvantageous course and still win this race means either he is out of the ordinary or his opponents are average, and the latter might be the safest assumption until future form proves otherwise.

NOTEBOOK

Manhattan Fox(USA) had the benefit of two previous races, so why he tried to run off the track a furlong after the start, then veered left again, virtually unridable, off the home turn is a mystery. Alan Munro decided not to fight the colt, who finally stopped when he got to the stands rail but still kept running and despite having no company he readily held the far side players at bay. He won't get away with this again but he does have an engine – all he needs is the steering to match. (op 6-4)

Finest Reserve(IRE), whose two previous runs had been over seven, needed this trip and gave the impression that there might be more to come in nurseries. (tchd 20-1)

Magnetic Force(IRE) was more awake than on debut at Sandown and was able to take advantage of the winner's deviations but looked very one paced and needs all of a mile on this evidence. (op 2-1)

Banks And Braes was another stepping up in trip as his pedigree suggested. He is now qualified for nurseries, where a mile looks the minimum requirement. (op 9-2 tchd 7-2)

5880 COUNTRYSIDE ALLIANCE STKS (H'CAP) 1m 1f

5:30 (5:31) (Class 2) (0-100,95) 3-Y-O+

£11,215 (£3,358; £1,679; £840; £419; £210) **Stalls** High

Form RPR

5505 **1** **Tartan Gunna**[16] 5375 3-8-10 **88**................................ GregFairley 3 95
(M Johnston) *dwlt: sn rcvrd: led after 2f: urged along to up the pce 3f out: edgd lft 2f out: hdd 1f out: rallied to ld again last 75yds* **16/1**

0031 **2** *nk* **Resort**[26] 5099 3-8-10 **88**................................ RyanMoore 4 94
(Sir Michael Stoute) *led 2f: trckd ldr: chal and slt bump 2f out: drvn to ld narrowly 1f out: hdd and no ex last 75yds* **6/1**

0203 **3** *1* **Greylami (IRE)**[21] 5262 4-9-4 **90**................................ ChrisCatlin 2 94+
(T G Mills) *heavily restrained s: hld up in last: prog and wdst of all over 2f out: wnt 3rd 1f out: styd on but nvr able to chal* **5/1[3]**

0050 **4** *1 3/4* **Bound By Honour (SAF)**[25] 5137 6-9-8 **94**................(b) GeorgeBaker 1 94
(G L Moore) *hld up in 6th: effrt on inner over 2f out: rn into trble wl over 1f out: kpt on fnl f to take 4th* **25/1**

5000 **5** *1 1/4* **Bon Spiel**[35] 4781 5-9-7 **93**................................ AdamKirby 10 90
(L M Cumani) *mostly trckd ldng pair: hrd rdn and nt qckn 2f out: lost 3rd 1f out: fdd* **25/1**

4320 **6** *nk* **Proponent (IRE)**[21] 5262 5-9-8 **94**................................ AlanMunro 8 91
(R Charlton) *lw: t.k.h: hld up in last trio: effrt and cl enough 2f out: nt qckn over 1f out: no prog after* **9/2[2]**

0- **7** *2* **Time 'N' Talent**[77] 3409 3-8-2 **83** ow1................................ MarcHalford(3) 9 75
(James Leavy, Ire) *cl up: rdn 3f out: stl chsng ldrs 2f out: wknd over 1f out* **12/1**

1250 **8** *1 1/4* **Resurge (IRE)**[22] 5221 4-9-0 **86**................................ IanMongan 5 75
(W S Kittow) *racd on outer: in tch: prog to join ldrs 4f out: rdn over 2f out: wknd over 1f out* **14/1**

0411 **9** *23* **Invisible Man**[27] 5070 3-9-3 **95**................................ RobertHavlin 6 34
(J H M Gosden) *lw: hld up in last trio: shkn up over 2f out: no rspnse and sn wknd: eased: t.o: lame* **13/8[1]**

1m 55.01s (-1.29) **Going Correction** -0.175s/f (Firm)

WFA 3 from 4yo+ 6lb **9** Ran SP% **115.2**

Speed ratings (Par 109): **98,97,96,95,94 93,92,91,70**

toteswinger: 1&2 £8.00, 1&3 £11.80, 2&3 £3.30. CSF £108.27 CT £553.53 TOTE £19.60: £3.50, £1.60, £1.70; EX 121.90 Place 6 £292.50, Place 5 £118.69.

Owner Mrs I Bird **Bred** Cheveley Park Stud Ltd **Trained** Middleham Moor, N Yorks

FOCUS

The race lost a signficant edge with the disappointing run of leading Cambridgeshire contender Invisible Man, who dropped away quickly over two furlongs out. Slight personal bests from the first two, who were always up there, but not the most convincing of form.

NOTEBOOK

Tartan Gunna came back to his better early season form when twice successful on Polytrack and once on turf, the final one off 83 over 7f at Beverley in April. This first attempt at nine furlongs suited his forcing tactics and although thrice beaten off 89, was very effective off a 1lb lower mark. (op 14-1)

Resort, racing off a 5lb higher mark than when winning at Windsor, looked likely to prevail inside the last but didn't get home quite so well as the winner. This was the furthest she has yet tried and this was signficantly harder than her Windsor task. (tchd 11-2 and 13-2)

Greylami(IRE) needs at least another furlong and came wide and from off the pace. He has only once been higher than this mark of 90 so this was a fine effort under the circumstances. (op 13-2)

Bound By Honour(SAF) was unlucky not to have finished closer, this being his best run of the season with blinkers reapplied. He was stopped for a run and switched to the rail a furlong out and was gaining at the line. If the blinkers work next time he'll be interesting, especially over another furlong, or possibly two. (op 20-1)

Bon Spiel had been sharpened by a run at Haydock in early August and showed his first worthwhile form since December. He has dropped from 103 to 93.

Proponent(IRE) couldn't sustain his run from the rear and the handicapper gives him hardly any respite. He won off 90 in May 2008 and was off 94 here. (op 6-1 tchd 4-1)

Invisible Man was bidding to pick up a penalty in order to ensure he makes the cut in the Cambridgeshire, for which he was ante-post favourite, but something went amiss and he returned lame. Official explanation: vet said colt returned lame (op 11-8 tchd 15-8)

T/Plt: £354.20 to a £1 stake. Pool: £68,500.66. 141.15 winning tickets. T/Qpdt: £33.70 to a £1 stake. Pool: £3,693.10. 81.00 winning tickets. JN

5835 WOLVERHAMPTON (A.W) (L-H)

Saturday, September 12

OFFICIAL GOING: Standard

Wind: Light half-against Weather: Fine and sunny

5881 WILLIAMHILL.COM/BONUS25 - GET £25 FREE BET H'CAP 5f 20y(P)

5:50 (5:50) (Class 6) (0-60,60) 3-Y-O **£2,388** (£705; £352) **Stalls** Low

Form RPR

5024 **1** **Rainy Night**[5] 5717 3-9-1 **60**................................ RussellKennemore(3) 5 66
(R Hollinshead) *mde all: rdn over 1f out: jst hld on* **11/4[1]**

6003 **2** *hd* **Jolly Ranch**[26] 5105 3-8-6 **51**................................ KellyHarrison(3) 4 56
(A G Newcombe) *chsd ldrs: rdn over 1f out: r.o: jst failed* **8/1**

0300 **3** *1* **Rapanui Belle**[8] 5633 3-8-7 **49** ow1................................(b[1]) FergusSweeney 10 50+
(G L Moore) *hld up in mid-div: hdwy over 1f out: sn rdn: r.o: nt rch ldrs* **22/1**

3335 **4** *1 3/4* **Imaginary Diva**[34] 4829 3-9-1 **60**................................ FrederikTylicki(3) 7 55
(G G Margarson) *chsd wnr: rdn over 1f out: styd on same pce fnl f* **5/1[3]**

6050 **5** *1* **Lady Vivien**[16] 5374 3-9-4 **60**................................ PhillipMakin 1 52+
(D H Brown) *hmpd sn after s: in rr: swtchd rt and hdwy over 1f out: r.o: nvr rchd ldrs* **3/1[2]**

3462 **6** *2 1/4* **You'relikemefrank**[26] 5105 3-8-6 **48**................................(b[1]) PJMcDonald 8 31
(J Balding) *chsd ldrs: rdn and hung lft over 1f out: styd on same pce* **9/1**

5646 **7** *3/4* **Moneysupermarket (IRE)**[24] 5158 3-8-1 **50**................ TobyAtkinson(7) 2 31
(Patrick Morris) *edgd lft sn after s: in rr: drvn along 1/2-way: styng on whn hung lft ins fnl f: nvr nrr* **16/1**

0203 **8** *1 1/4* **Red Cell (IRE)**[8] 5626 3-8-6 **53**................................(b) AmyRyan(5) 11 29
(I W McInnes) *in rr: drvn along 1/2-way: no rspnse* **16/1**

00-0 **9** *5* **Chatterszaha**[18] 5326 3-8-10 **55**................................ WilliamCarson(3) 3 13
(C Drew) *mid-div: rdn 1/2-way: wknd over 1f out* **33/1**

4604 **10** *3/4* **Zelos Girl (IRE)**[8] 5626 3-8-13 **55**................................ PatCosgrave 9 11
(J G Given) *chsd ldrs: rn wd turning for home: sn wknd* **16/1**

62.05 secs (-0.25) **Going Correction** -0.10s/f (Stan) **10** Ran SP% **114.4**

Speed ratings (Par 99): **98,97,96,93,91 88,86,84,76,75**

toteswinger: 1&2 £7.20, 1&3 £12.79, 2&3 not won. CSF £24.81 CT £410.04 TOTE £3.50: £1.90, £3.30, £7.10; EX 25.50.

Owner N Chapman **Bred** Broughton Bloodstock **Trained** Upper Longdon, Staffs

■ Stewards' Enquiry : Fergus Sweeney one-day ban: careless riding (Sep 27)

FOCUS

A modest three year-old sprint handicap to open the card. It was run at a furious pace and the form looks solid rated around the first three.

Lady Vivien ◆ Official explanation: jockey said filly suffered interference and saddle slipped

5882 WILLIAMHILL.COM/BONUS25 - POKER TOURNAMENTS MAIDEN FILLIES' STKS 5f 216y(P)

6:20 (6:21) (Class 5) 3-Y-O+ **£2,729** (£806; £403) **Stalls** Low

Form RPR

3230 **1** **Gurteen Diamond**[201] 655 3-8-5 61................................ AndrewHeffernan(7) 4 71
(P D Evans) *trckd ldrs: shkn up over 1f out: rdn to ld and hung lft wl ins fnl f: r.o* **7/1**

2 **2** *2* **South African (USA)**[33] 4860 3-8-12 0................................ FergusSweeney 9 65
(M A Magnusson) *led: rdn and hdd wl ins fnl f: no ex* **11/4[2]**

0 **3** *hd* **Anagram**[5] 5717 3-8-12 0................................(b[1]) TomEaves 1 64
(W R Muir) *in tch: lost pl and pushed along 1/2-way: hdwy u.str.p over 1f out: r.o wl ins fnl f: nrst fin* **25/1**

0 **4** *2 1/2* **Tongalooma**[15] 5394 3-8-12 0................................ PJMcDonald 2 56
(James Moffatt) *chsd ldr over 2f: remained handy: rdn over 1f out: wknd ins fnl f* **66/1**

5 *nse* **Fiamma D'Oro (IRE)**[21] 5269 3-8-12 0................................ RMBurke 12 56
(David P Myerscough, Ire) *hld up: hdwy u.p hung lft over 1f out: styd on: nt rch ldrs* **5/2[1]**

64 **6** *hd* **Eliza Doolittle**[31] 4913 3-8-12 0................................ PatCosgrave 8 55
(J R Fanshawe) *mid-div: drvn along 1/2-way: styd on fnl f: nvr trbld ldrs* **15/2**

0 **7** *5* **Lhashan**[56] 4097 3-8-12 0................................ LiamJones 13 39
(M A Jarvis) *in rr: hdwy to chse ldr over 3f out: rdn wl over 1f out: wknd fnl f* **16/1**

5224 **8** *1/2* **Silk Gallery (USA)**[8] 5624 4-9-0 54................................(t) DuranFentiman 10 38
(E J Alston) *prom: lost pl over 4f out: drvn along 1/2-way: sme hdwy over 2f out: wknd wl over 1f out* **13/2[3]**

6-00 **9** *nk* **Hekaaya (IRE)**[13] 5479 3-8-9 53................................(v[1]) FrederikTylicki(3) 7 37
(M P Tregoning) *mid-div: rdn over 2f out: wknd over 1f out* **20/1**

0 **10** *6* **Jeannie (IRE)**[127] 1825 3-8-5 0................................ NatashaEaton(7) 6 17
(A Bailey) *mid-div: hmpd over 3f out: wknd over 2f out* **40/1**

11 *1 3/4* **Deportista** 3-8-10 0 ow1................................ RussellKennemore(3) 3 13
(J A Pickering) *s.s: outpcd: t.o 1/2-way: mod late prog* **66/1**

6 **12** *hd* **Almatlaie (USA)**[33] 4860 3-8-12 0................................ RichardKingscote 5 11
(J W Unett) *hld up in tch: hmpd over 3f out: wknd over 2f out* **33/1**

0 **13** *15* **Mrs Medley**[113] 2250 3-8-12 0................................ JamieMackay 11 —
(D Shaw) *s.s: a outpcd: t.o fr 1/2-way* **100/1**

1m 15.05s (0.05) **Going Correction** -0.10s/f (Stan)

WFA 3 from 4yo 2lb **13** Ran SP% **116.7**

Speed ratings (Par 100): **95,92,92,88,88 88,81,81,80,72 70,70,50**

toteswinger: 1&2 £6.80, 1&3 £17.80, 2&3 £17.80. CSF £24.54 TOTE £8.80: £2.70, £1.40, £5.50; EX 31.60.

Owner William Slattery **Bred** Cheveley Park Stud Ltd **Trained** Pandy, Monmouths

FOCUS

A moderate maiden fillies' stakes, run at an even gallop and very few landed any sort of blow. The winner is rated as having run a personal best but the form is not convincing.

Deportista Official explanation: jockey said filly was slowly away and ran green

Mrs Medley Official explanation: jockey said filly was slowly away

5883 WILLIAMHILL.COM/BONUS25 - QUOTE BONUS25 H'CAP 7f 32y(P)

6:50 (6:53) (Class 7) (0-50,54) 3-Y-O+ **£2,183** (£644; £322) **Stalls** High

Form RPR

0001 **1** **La Gifted**[10] 5581 3-9-1 **54**................................ SamHitchcott 12 60
(M R Channon) *a.p: led wl over 1f out: sn rdn and hung lft: styd on u.p* **7/1[3]**

0430 **2** *1* **Mansii**[15] 5391 4-8-12 **50**................................(t) AndreaAtzeni(3) 7 55
(P J McBride) *chsd ldr tl led 2f out: sn rdn and hdd: styd on u.p* **9/2[2]**

3 *nse* **Read The Script (IRE)**[462] 2852 4-9-1 **50**................ RichardKingscote 5 55+
(Tom Dascombe) *hld up: racd keenly: hdwy and hung lft over 1f out: sn rdn: styd on* **11/4[1]**

0000 **4** *hd* **Herbert Crescent**[22] 5229 4-8-12 **50**................................ FrederikTylicki(3) 3 54
(Ollie Pears) *mid-div: rdn and hdwy over 2f out: edgd lft and styd on fnl f* **9/2[2]**

000 **5** *2 1/2* **Star Acclaim**[47] 4376 4-8-8 **50**................................ TobyAtkinson(7) 4 48
(E V Stanford) *hld up: hdwy and hung lft fr over 1f out: nt rch ldrs* **14/1**

436 **6** *hd* **Colombard (IRE)**[14] 5443 4-9-1 **50**................................ SJCraine 10 47
(Patrick Morris) *hld up: hdwy over 2f out: rdn and hung lft over 1f out: styd on* **11/1**

-500 **7** *2 3/4* **Kannon**[178] 867 4-9-1 **50**................................ TomEaves 9 40
(I W McInnes) *s.i.s: sn pushed along in rr: rdn over 1f out: styd on but nvr trbld ldrs* **20/1**

6000 **8** *2* **Yahwudhee (FR)**[52] 4192 4-8-8 **50**................................ JamesPSullivan(7) 6 34
(M W Easterby) *trckd ldrs: plld hrd: rdn over 1f out: wknd fnl f* **25/1**

/0-0 **9** *1/2* **My Jeanie (IRE)**[86] 3077 5-9-1 **50**................................ RichardSmith 2 33
(J C Fox) *chsd ldrs: rdn over 2f out: wkng whn n.m.r over 1f out* **20/1**

0-06 **10** *1 3/4* **Minwir (IRE)**[211] 540 4-9-1 **50**................................ LiamJones 8 28
(W M Brisbourne) *hld up: hdwy 1/2-way: wknd over 1f out* **16/1**

6000 **11** *1 1/2* **Tamino (IRE)**[91] 2921 6-9-1 **50**................................(t) AmirQuinn 1 24
(P Howling) *sn drvn to ld: rdn and hdd 2f out: wknd fnl f* **16/1**

34-0 12 15 **Mugeba**[38] 4665 8-9-1 **50** JerryO'Dwyer 11 —
(C A Dwyer) *sn pushed along towards rr: bhd fr 1/2-way* **40/1**

1m 29.27s (-0.33) **Going Correction** -0.10s/f (Stan)
WFA 3 from 4yo+ 4lb 12 Ran SP% **118.1**
Speed ratings (Par 97): **97,95,95,95,92 92,89,87,86,84 82,65**
toteswinger: 1&2 £7.10, 1&3 £5.30, 2&3 £7.60. CSF £36.41 CT £110.94 TOTE £6.00: £2.50, £1.80, £1.70; EX 23.90.
Owner Patrick and Simon Trant **Bred** Patrick & Simon Trant **Trained** West Ilsley, Berks

FOCUS
A run-of-the-mill handicap run at an even pace but the form is not solid with the runner-up to his recent best the guide.

5884 WILLIAMHILL.COM/BONUS25 - LIVE CASINO DEALERS H'CAP 7f 32y(P)
7:20 (7:21) (Class 4) (0-80,80) 3-Y-O+ **£5,046** (£1,510; £755; £377; £188) **Stalls** High

Form RPR
0512 1 **Captain Macarry (IRE)**[29] 4996 4-9-6 **80** (v) TomEaves 5 90
(B Smart) *chsd ldrs: rdn to ld ins fnl f: r.o* **11/4**[2]
1003 2 nk **Mark Of Meydan**[26] 5107 4-8-12 **72** PhillipMakin 8 81
(M Dods) *hld up: hdwy over 2f out: rdn and ev ch ins fnl f: r.o* **14/1**
4026 3 2 **Kloof**[9] 5598 3-8-11 **75** FergusSweeney 3 77
(K A Ryan) *s.i.s: hld up: hdwy over 1f out: rdn and r.o wl: nt rch ldrs* **16/1**
0002 4 ¾ **Malcheek (IRE)**[15] 5409 7-8-13 **73** DavidAllan 6 75
(T D Easterby) *led: rdn and edgd rt over 1f out: hdd and unable qck ins fnl f* **10/1**
1 5 shd **Miss Minnies (IRE)**[3] 5780 3-9-1 **79** 6ex RMBurke 1 78
(David P Myerscough, Ire) *a.p: rdn to chse ldr and swtchd lft over 1f out: ev ch ins fnl f: no ex* **5/2**[1]
4051 6 shd **Balata**[11] 5544 4-9-1 **75** TGMcLaughlin 2 76+
(B R Millman) *hld up: pushed along 4f out: hdwy on outside wl over 1f out: sn rdn: styd on: nt pce to chal* **11/1**
0006 7 nk **This Ones For Eddy**[14] 5418 4-8-11 **71** PJMcDonald 4 71
(J Balding) *prom: lost pl 4f out: last ent st: r.o ins fnl f* **50/1**
0646 8 1 ¼ **Desert Dreamer (IRE)**[4] 5746 8-9-1 **80** RichardEvans(5) 7 77
(P D Evans) *hld up: pushed along 1/2-way: rdn over 1f out: n.d* **16/1**
1305 9 ½ **Arthur's Edge**[23] 5182 5-8-12 **72** RichardKingscote 10 68
(B Palling) *trckd ldrs: wnt 2nd over 4f out: rdn over 2f out: wknd ins fnl f* **9/1**[3]
3245 10 12 **Leonaldo (USA)**[170] 974 4-9-3 **77** LiamJones 9 40
(J R Gask) *hld up: hdwy over 2f out: rdn and wknd over 1f out* **14/1**
6160 11 2 ¼ **Elusive Fame (USA)**[8] 5640 3-8-11 **75** (b) JoeFanning 11 30
(M Johnston) *prom: rdn over 2f out: sn wknd* **16/1**

1m 27.38s (-2.22) **Going Correction** -0.10s/f (Stan)
WFA 3 from 4yo+ 4lb 11 Ran SP% **115.6**
Speed ratings (Par 105): **108,107,105,104,104 104,103,102,101,88 85**
toteswinger: 1&2 £14.10, 1&3 not won, 2&3 not won. CSF £40.63 CT £532.93 TOTE £4.20: £1.70, £2.80, £5.00; EX 33.70.
Owner Anthony D Gee **Bred** Humphrey Okeke **Trained** Hambleton, N Yorks

FOCUS
A competitive handicap which was run at an even pace and produced a cracking finish. The time was good for the grade and the form looks pretty solid, rated around the third and fourth.
Kloof ♦ Official explanation: jockey said colt hung right
Desert Dreamer(IRE) Official explanation: jockey said gelding ran flat

5885 WILLIAM HILL 0800 444040 - GET £25 FREE BET H'CAP 2m 119y(P)
7:50 (7:50) (Class 6) (0-60,57) 3-Y-O+ £2,388 (£705; £352) **Stalls** Low

Form RPR
0663 1 **Snowberry Hill (USA)**[10] 5579 6-9-6 **49** KFallon 3 58
(Lucinda Featherstone) *a.p: led 3f out: sn pushed clr: hung rt fr over 1f out: rdn out* **7/2**[2]
5631 2 1 ¼ **Follow The Dream**[30] 4935 6-9-12 **55** TGMcLaughlin 12 67+
(Karen George) *dwlt: hld up and bhd: 10th and stl gng wl 3f out: hdwy on outer over 2f out: rdn and swtchd lft over 1f out: r.o to go 2nd ins fnl f: too much to do* **4/1**[3]
1450 3 2 ¼ **Dazzling Begum**[16] 5359 4-9-2 **50** (p) SimonPearce(5) 4 55
(J Pearce) *prom: rdn to chse wnr over 2f out: styd on* **8/1**
1060 4 5 **Squirtle (IRE)**[33] 4848 6-9-13 **56** LiamJones 5 55
(W M Brisbourne) *hld up: hdwy over 6f out: rdn over 3f out: styd on same pce fnl 2f* **16/1**
640 5 2 **Apache Fort**[7] 5680 6-9-13 **56** (b) SilvestreDeSousa 8 53
(T Keddy) *hld up in tch: rdn over 3f out: wknd over 1f out* **16/1**
3/2- 6 2 ¼ **Bluecrop Boy**[298] 7376 5-9-5 **51** JackMitchell(3) 11 45
(D J S Ffrench Davis) *hld up: rdn over 3f out: mod late prog* **16/1**
6030 7 4 **Adage**[30] 3927 6-9-2 **45** (tp) FrankieMcDonald 9 34
(David Pinder) *s.i.s: hld up: pushed along at several stages: nvr on terms* **33/1**
500/ 8 2 ¾ **Pekan One**[62] 6221 7-9-2 **45** (bt) PatCosgrave 7 31
(John G Carr, Ire) *hld up: rdn over 3f out: wknd over 2f out* **66/1**
0-32 9 12 **Bathwick Man**[2] 5812 4-9-7 **50** (tp) StephenDonohoe 1 21
(D E Pipe) *drvn along to ld: stdd pce over 10f out: hdd over 8f out: chsd ldr whn nt clr run and swtchd rt over 7f out: led again 5f out: rdn and hdd 3f out: wknd and eased over 1f out* **11/4**[1]
101 10 8 **Looks The Business (IRE)**[21] 5246 8-10-0 **57** FergusSweeney 13 19
(A B Haynes) *chsd ldr tl led over 8f out: sn edgd lft: hdd 5f out: rdn and wknd over 2f out* **8/1**
0005 11 17 **Susurrayshaan**[9] 5614 3-8-8 **50** (p) DaleGibson 10 —
(Mrs G S Rees) *chsd ldrs: rdn over 4f out: wknd sn after* **40/1**

3m 39.8s (-2.00) **Going Correction** -0.10s/f (Stan)
WFA 3 from 4yo+ 13lb 11 Ran SP% **115.6**
Speed ratings (Par 101): **100,99,98,96,95 94,92,90,85,81 73**
toteswinger: 1&2 £3.30, 1&3 £18.10, 2&3 £11.90. CSF £17.40 CT £103.82 TOTE £5.50: £1.90, £2.20, £2.10; EX 24.10.
Owner J Roundtree **Bred** Russell S Fisher And Joe Sagginario **Trained** Atlow, Derbyshire

FOCUS
An ordinary handicap, which was run at an even pace. The winner is back to something like his winter form.

5886 WILLIAMHILL.COM/BONUS25 - PLAY VEGAS GAMES H'CAP 1m 141y(P)
8:20 (8:20) (Class 5) (0-70,69) 3-Y-O+ **£4,209** (£1,252; £625; £312) **Stalls** Low

Form RPR
0030 1 **Lujano**[20] 5289 4-8-13 **63** FrederikTylicki(3) 10 71
(Ollie Pears) *mde all: rdn over 1f out: edgd rt towards fin: styd on* **16/1**
060 2 1 ¼ **Bid For Glory**[23] 5190 5-9-4 **65** (v) JerryO'Dwyer 5 70+
(H J Collingridge) *hld up: swtchd rt and hdwy over 1f out: r.o wl: nt rch wnr* **9/1**
0646 3 ½ **Ultimate Respect (USA)**[12] 5506 3-9-1 **68** JoeFanning 2 72
(M Johnston) *a.p: chsd wnr over 6f out: rdn over 2f out: hung lft and nt run on fnl f* **7/2**[1]
5400 4 1 ¾ **Ergo (FR)**[15] 5395 5-9-6 **67** (v) PJMcDonald 9 67
(James Moffatt) *hld up: hdwy u.p over 2f out: styd on: nt trbld ldrs* **8/1**
0243 5 1 ¼ **The Grey One (IRE)**[7] 5683 6-8-13 **60** (p) KevinGhunowa 8 57
(J M Bradley) *mid-div: racd keenly: rdn over 2f out: styd on same pce appr fnl f* **10/1**
-503 6 1 **Margarita (IRE)**[14] 5449 3-9-1 **68** (t) KFallon 12 63
(J R Fanshawe) *prom: rdn over 3f out: edgd lft and no ex fnl f* **4/1**[2]
3061 7 2 ¾ **Pha Mai Blue**[32] 4871 4-9-5 **66** PatCosgrave 11 55
(J R Boyle) *hld up in tch: rdn over 3f out: wknd over 1f out* **8/1**
2462 8 nk **Lunar River (FR)**[23] 5195 6-9-7 **68** (t) FergusSweeney 4 56
(David Pinder) *hld up in tch: lost pl over 4f out: n.d after* **6/1**[3]
0023 9 ½ **Follow The Flag (IRE)**[18] 5329 5-9-8 **69** (p) RobertWinston 13 56
(A J McCabe) *swtchd lft sn after s: hld up: pushed along over 3f out: n.d* **8/1**
35-0 10 6 **Mandarin Spirit (IRE)**[15] 5395 9-9-5 **66** (b) TomEaves 7 39
(Miss L A Perratt) *trckd ldrs: plld hrd: rdn and wknd over 1f out* **33/1**
000 11 3 ¾ **Hidden Door (IRE)**[11] 5544 4-8-13 **60** KirstyMilczarek 1 24
(G Prodromou) *trckd ldrs: racd keenly: rdn over 2f out: wknd over 1f out* **20/1**
130 12 1 ¾ **Provost**[18] 5329 5-9-4 **65** DaleGibson 6 25
(M W Easterby) *hld up: rdn over 3f out: wknd over 2f out* **20/1**

1m 49.48s (-1.02) **Going Correction** -0.10s/f (Stan)
WFA 3 from 4yo+ 6lb 12 Ran SP% **127.3**
Speed ratings (Par 103): **100,98,98,96,95 94,92,92,91,86 83,81**
toteswinger: 1&2 £20.60, 1&3 not won, 2&3 not won. CSF £159.95 CT £643.26 TOTE £20.50: £5.70, £3.40, £2.00; EX 306.00.
Owner David Scott and Co (Pattern Makers) Ltd **Bred** D Scott **Trained** Norton, N Yorks

FOCUS
A 56-70 handicap run at a modest gallop and half of the field had already been successful at the track. The winner is rated back to last winter's form.
The Grey One(IRE) Official explanation: jockey said gelding ran too free

5887 WILLIAM HILL 0800 444040 - QUOTE BONUS25 H'CAP 1m 141y(P)
8:50 (8:50) (Class 4) (0-85,85) 3-Y-O+ **£5,046** (£1,510; £755; £377; £188) **Stalls** Low

Form RPR
1152 1 **Mountain Cat (IRE)**[24] 5160 5-9-1 **78** RobertWinston 2 91
(G A Swinbank) *trckd ldrs: led wl over 1f out: sn rdn and edgd lft: hung rt nr fin: jst hld on* **5/2**[1]
5060 2 ½ **Farleigh House (USA)**[7] 5667 5-8-12 **75** StephenDonohoe 5 87+
(Sir Mark Prescott) *hld up: hdwy over 2f out: n.m.r wl over 1f out: rdn and r.o wl ins fnl f* **12/1**
5253 3 3 **I Confess**[4] 5753 4-8-12 **80** (b) RichardEvans(5) 9 85
(P D Evans) *chsd ldr tl led over 2f out: rdn and hdd wl over 1f out: no ex ins fnl f* **10/1**[3]
4102 4 nk **Clientele (USA)**[17] 5349 3-9-0 **83** JoeFanning 1 87
(M Johnston) *chsd ldrs: rdn over 1f out: swtchd lft: styd on same pce fnl f* **4/1**[2]
010 5 ½ **Just Bond (IRE)**[9] 5598 7-9-8 **85** PJMcDonald 8 88
(G R Oldroyd) *s.s: hld up: r.o ins fnl f: nt rch ldrs* **16/1**
3530 6 1 ¾ **Brasingaman Hifive**[14] 5441 4-8-12 **75** DaleGibson 10 74
(Mrs G S Rees) *hld up: effrt over 2f out: no ex ins fnl f* **33/1**
4205 7 1 ¾ **Bold Cross (IRE)**[12] 5510 6-9-3 **80** PaulFitzsimons 13 75
(E G Bevan) *hld up: rdn over 2f out: n.d* **20/1**
4106 8 nk **Beauchamp Viceroy**[16] 5375 5-9-5 **82** (tp) KFallon 12 76
(G A Butler) *prom: rdn and hung lft over 1f out: no ex* **14/1**
-130 9 ½ **Tanto Faz (IRE)**[70] 3639 4-9-8 **85** LiamJones 3 78
(W J Haggas) *led: rdn and hdd over 2f out: wknd fnl f* **4/1**[2]
5000 10 hd **Spinning**[14] 5441 6-8-11 **79** (b) DeanHeslop(5) 6 72
(T D Barron) *s.i.s: hld up: rdn over 2f out: a in rr* **12/1**
2000 11 nk **Hyde Lea Flyer**[14] 5441 4-8-12 **75** GrahamGibbons 11 67
(E S McMahon) *hld up: hdwy u.p over 2f out: wknd over 1f out* **33/1**

1m 47.66s (-2.84) **Going Correction** -0.10s/f (Stan)
WFA 3 from 4yo+ 6lb 11 Ran SP% **116.2**
Speed ratings (Par 105): **108,107,104,104,104 102,101,100,100,100 99**
toteswinger: 1&2 £10.20, 1&3 £5.70, 2&3 £10.20. CSF £33.36 CT £258.35 TOTE £3.90: £1.60, £4.20, £3.40; EX 46.60.
Owner S Rudolf **Bred** Mrs Mary Gallagher **Trained** Melsonby, N Yorks

FOCUS
Five course and distance winners in the line up, for this 71-85 handicap which was run at an even gallop. The third is a pretty sound guide to the form.
Just Bond(IRE) ♦ Official explanation: jockey said gelding was slowly away

5888 WILLIAMHILL.COM/BONUS25 - BINGO BONANZAS H'CAP 1m 1f 103y(P)
9:20 (9:20) (Class 6) (0-52,52) 3-Y-O+ £2,388 (£705; £352) **Stalls** Low

Form RPR
40 1 **Eagle Nebula**[94] 2830 5-8-11 **50** JackMitchell(3) 13 61
(B R Johnson) *hld up: hdwy to ld over 1f out: rdn and r.o wl* **8/1**
0465 2 2 ½ **Pianoforte (USA)**[5] 5730 7-8-13 **49** (b) GrahamGibbons 11 55
(E J Alston) *chsd ldrs: rdn and ev ch over 1f out: styd on same pce ins fnl f* **8/1**
226 3 nk **Gifted Heir (IRE)**[13] 5484 5-9-0 **50** (p) NeilChalmers 7 55
(A Bailey) *hld up: hdwy u.p over 1f out: edgd lft: r.o* **12/1**
0000 4 shd **Wednesdays Boy (IRE)**[40] 4588 6-8-10 **49** (p) FrederikTylicki(3) 10 54
(P D Niven) *mid-div: hdwy 1/2-way: rdn and hung lft fr over 1f out: r.o* **16/1**
0062 5 nk **Libre**[8] 5631 9-9-2 **52** (p) TolleyDean 6 56
(F Jordan) *hld up: rdn over 1f out: r.o ins fnl f: nt rch ldrs* **12/1**
1005 6 1 ½ **Mick Is Back**[37] 4721 5-9-2 **52** (v) KFallon 3 53
(G G Margarson) *prom: racd keenly: pushed along over 3f out: sn lost pl: hmpd over 1f out: swtchd lft: n.m.r ins fnl f: eased whn btn towards fin* **7/2**[1]
06-5 7 1 ¼ **Parkview Love (USA)**[9] 5617 8-8-13 **49** (b) PatCosgrave 12 47
(J G Given) *chsd ldr tl led over 5f out: rdn and hdd over 1f out: wknd ins fnl f* **20/1**
0435 8 nk **Lady Valentino**[7] 5679 5-9-0 **50** (t) RobertWinston 1 48
(B D Leavy) *chsd ldrs: rdn over 2f out: wknd fnl f* **6/1**[2]
5040 9 3 ¾ **Lytham (IRE)**[16] 5377 8-8-11 **52** AmyBaker(5) 2 42
(A W Carroll) *hld up in tch: rdn and wknd over 2f out* **15/2**[3]
-233 10 1 **Kassuta**[26] 5111 5-8-10 **49** AndreaAtzeni(3) 8 37
(R M H Cowell) *led: hdd over 5f out: rdn over 2f out: wknd over 1f out* **6/1**[2]

300 11 *8* **Paul's Pet**[31] 4904 4-9-2 **52** .... TGMcLaughlin 4 23
(Karen George) *hld up: rdn over 2f out: sn wknd* **22/1**

2m 0.17s (-1.53) **Going Correction** -0.10s/f (Stan) **11** Ran SP% **115.2**
Speed ratings (Par 101): **102,99,99,99,99 97,96,96,93,92 85**
toteswinger: 1&2 not won, 1&3 not won, 2&3 £14.20. CSF £69.04 CT £765.30 TOTE £11.30: £3.40, £2.30, £2.50; EX 101.30 Place 6: £136.39, Place 5: £52.81..
Owner Tann Racing **Bred** Juddmonte Farms Ltd **Trained** Ashtead, Surrey

FOCUS
Lots of out-of-form horses in the line-up but the form looks soudn enough rated around the placed horses and fifth.
Gifted Heir(IRE) Official explanation: jockey said gelding hung right
Wednesdays Boy(IRE) Official explanation: jockey said gelding hung left
Mick Is Back Official explanation: jockey said gelding was denied a clear run
Lady Valentino Official explanation: jockey said mare had a breathing problem
T/Plt: £250.30 to a £1 stake. Pool: £71,684.75. 209.05 winning tickets. T/Qpdt: £42.30 to a £1 stake. Pool: £7,160.64. 125.10 winning tickets. CR

5889 - (Foreign Racing) - See Raceform Interactive

5485 CURRAGH (R-H)
Saturday, September 12
OFFICIAL GOING: Round course - soft; straight course - soft to heavy

5890a IRISH NATIONAL STUD BLANDFORD STKS (GROUP 2) (F&M) 1m 2f
2:45 (2:46) 3-Y-O+ **£72,572** (£21,213; £10,048; £3,349)

RPR
1 **Chinese White (IRE)**[13] 5487 4-9-5 112 .... PJSmullen 3 116
(D K Weld, Ire) *trckd ldr in 2nd: clsr order travelling wl fr over 3f out: chal and led 1 1/2f out on stands' side: rdn clr ins fnl f* **11/10**[1]
2 *2* **Roman Empress (IRE)**[23] 5201 3-8-12 112 .... JAHeffernan 1 112
(A P O'Brien, Ire) *led: strly pressed and hdd 1 1/2f out on stands' side: no imp whn briefly short of room and swtchd ins fnl f: kpt on wout matching wnr* **8/1**[3]
3 *1 3/4* **She's Our Mark**[31] 4923 5-9-5 106 .... DMGrant 4 109
(Patrick J Flynn, Ire) *racd last of the 5: rdn to be clsr in 4th over 2f out on stands' side: sn no imp and kpt on wout threatening in 3rd* **10/1**
4 *11* **Lady Marian (GER)**[20] 5300 4-9-5 .... MJKinane 5 87
(Saeed Bin Suroor) *t.k.h early: sn racd in 3rd: rdn over 2f out on stands' side: sn no ex in 4th* **11/8**[2]
5 *7* **Festival Princess (IRE)**[13] 5487 4-9-5 99 ....(b[1]) DPMcDonogh 2 73
(Mrs John Harrington, Ire) *racd mainly towards rr in 4th: rdn 3f out: sn last on stands' side and dropped bhd* **25/1**

2m 17.35s (7.85) **Going Correction** +1.10s/f (Soft)
WFA 3 from 4yo+ 7lb **5** Ran SP% **113.8**
Speed ratings: **112,110,109,100,94**
CSF £10.81 TOTE £1.70: £1.20, £2.70; DF 8.50.
Owner Lady O'Reilly **Bred** Skymarc Farm & Castlemartin St **Trained** The Curragh, Co Kildare
■ Stewards' Enquiry : P J Smullen caution: careless riding

FOCUS
A small but select field for this Group 2. It has been rated around the runner-up to her recent form.

NOTEBOOK
Chinese White(IRE) continued her progression with a comprehensive victory in this Group 2 event. The outcome was never in doubt once the daughter of Dalakhani closed on the runner-up and, not for the first time this term, she saw out this trip in good style. She had previously stepped up on her couple of Listed wins by taking a Group 3 event here last time, and the Group 1 Prix de l'Opera on Arc day is next. (op 5/4 tchd 1/1)
Roman Empress(IRE) had finished a length and a half behind Chinese White when they clashed at Gowran Park last month. She stepped up on that effort in the Yorkshire Oaks when a creditable third behind Dar Re Mi and dual Oaks heroine Sariska but, after making the running, was outclassed here. (op 13/2)
She's Our Mark plugged on for a share of the spoils but never looked like playing a leading role. She has proved a tremendous money-spinner for connections, given she has won three of her seven starts this term, including a victory over Chinese White when the latter made her seasonal bow at Gowran in atrocious ground. (op 12/1)
Lady Marian(GER) was easy to back and failed to run her race. She had previously hinted at a return to her best when she suffered a narrow defeat in the Group 1 Prix Jean Romanet at Deauville just under three weeks ago, but the former German-trained four-year-old, who rounded off last term with victory in the Group 1 Prix de l'Opera at the expense of the Irish-trained pair Lush Lashes and Katiyra, found little when asked a serious question. This certainly wasn't the filly we saw at Longchamp last year. Official explanation: vet said filly was blowing hard post race, but was otherwise normal (op 5/4 tchd 6/4)
Festival Princess(IRE) was blinkered for the first time but struggled to make an impact after the field tacked over to the stands' rail turning for home.

5891a THE IRISH FIELD ST.LEGER (GROUP 1) 1m 6f
3:20 (3:20) 3-Y-O+ **£155,388** (£51,262; £24,563; £8,543; £5,873; £3,203)

RPR
1 **Alandi (IRE)**[21] 5277 4-9-11 116 .... MJKinane 8 118+
(John M Oxx, Ire) *trckd ldrs: 3rd fr 1/2-way: 2nd bef st: sn rdn: led ins fnl f: sn jnd: styd on best to ld again cl home* **3/1**[2]
2 *1/2* **Clowance**[463] 2792 4-9-8 .... KJManning 1 114
(R Charlton) *towards rr: clsd fr over 4f out: rdn in mod 3rd fr over 2f out: clsd fr over 1f out: chal and on terms ins fnl f: hdd and kpt wout matching wnr cl home* **25/1**
3 *5* **Schiaparelli (GER)**[20] 5297 6-9-11 .... OPeslier 6 111
(Saeed Bin Suroor) *led: travelling wl st: strly pressed fr under 2f out: hdd ins fnl f: sn dropped to 3rd and no ex* **2/1**[1]
4 *18* **Profound Beauty (IRE)**[30] 4962 5-9-8 113 .... PJSmullen 4 82
(D K Weld, Ire) *towards rr: clsd fr over 5f out: sn trckd ldrs: dropped to mod 3rd over 3f out: sn 4th and no ex u.p* **7/2**[3]
5 *2 1/2* **All The Aces (IRE)**[7] 5662 4-9-11 .... PhilipRobinson 2 82
(M A Jarvis) *sn mid-div: mod 5th and no ex u.p fr over 3f out* **8/1**
6 *19* **Moon Indigo**[51] 4255 3-9-0 96 .... JPO'Brien 5 55
(A P O'Brien, Ire) *sn cl up: rdn in 3rd after 6f: lost pl fr over 5f out: sn no ex* **33/1**
7 *12* **Bashkirov**[21] 5277 4-9-11 95 .... RPWalsh 7 38
(Luke Comer, Ire) *sn towards rr: no ex u.p fr over 4f out* **100/1**
8 *3* **Yeats (IRE)**[86] 3048 8-9-11 122 .... JAHeffernan 3 34
(A P O'Brien, Ire) *prom: pushed along over 5f out: sn rdn: 4th bef st: wknd and eased fr 2f out* **4/1**

3m 14.82s (10.12) **Going Correction** +1.10s/f (Soft)
WFA 3 from 4yo+ 11lb **8** Ran SP% **119.4**
Speed ratings: **115,114,111,101,100 89,82,80**
CSF £71.64 TOTE £5.50: £2.10, £5.90, £1.10; DF 122.50.
Owner H H Aga Khan **Bred** Hh The Aga Khan's Studs Sc **Trained** Currabeg, Co Kildare
■ Stewards' Enquiry : M J Kinane caution: excessive use of the whip

FOCUS
The runner-up has been rated as recording a personal best, along with the progressive winner.

NOTEBOOK
Alandi(IRE), whose jockey decided to ride in this St Leger rather than the Doncaster version, eventually got his head in front inside the final furlong. He had first come to prominence when he recorded an impressive Listed success at Navan, when Yeats had trailed home a long way adrift in sixth place in atrocious conditions last April. The Prix Du Cadran over Arc weekend is a likely target for this colt now, who underlined his honestly and toughness with this gritty display. (op 11/4)
Clowance had been declared for the Park Hill Stakes at Doncaster, but connections elected to travel here. The underfoot conditions had swung the decision and she ran a cracker. She had reportedly had a series of niggly injuries and, considering this was her first run since June 2008, when she ran fourth to Look Here in the Epsom Oaks, she should be open to some improvement, and will apparently tackle some nice staying races this autumn.
Schiaparelli(GER) looked to be travelling like a winner early in the straight, but this triple Group 1 winner couldn't sustain the gallop and, once headed, soon had no more to offer in this ground. (op 5/2)
Profound Beauty(IRE) did not handle the ground and finished a long way back as a result. Melbourne is the next stop for the Danehill mare, who is vying for favouritism with most firms for the Flemington showpiece. She finished fifth in it last year and faster ground should play to her strengths. (op 4/1)
All The Aces(IRE), a Group 3 performer in Britain, had conditions in his favour but never got in a blow.
Moon Indigo didn't have to perform front-running duties, but was one of the first beaten after leaving the back straight.
Yeats(IRE) was bidding for a second win in the race, but the four-time Gold Cup winner ran below-par on ground far from ideal. Seeking his eighth Group 1 victory, he raced close to the pace, but, once his rider began to niggle over half a mile from home, the writing was on the wall. He had atoned for two previous defeats in this race with his 2007 triumph, but the ground didn't dry out enough for the multiple winner this time. (op 7/2)

5892a LADBROKES.COM VINCENT O'BRIEN NATIONAL STKS (GROUP 1) (ENTIRE COLTS & FILLIES) 7f
3:50 (3:50) 2-Y-O
£145,728 (£46,213; £21,941; £7,378; £4,951; £2,524)

RPR
1 **Kingsfort (USA)**[78] 3363 2-9-1 .... DPMcDonogh 4 117+
(Kevin Prendergast, Ire) *trckd ldrs in 3rd: clsr in 2nd fr under 2f out: led under 1f out: styd on wl u.p fnl f: reducing ld cl home* **9/4**[2]
2 *nk* **Chabal (IRE)**[7] 5690 2-9-1 .... KJManning 1 116+
(J S Bolger, Ire) *t.k.h and sn settled in rr: rdn under 2f out: styd on wl in 2nd ins fnl f: nt quite rch wnr* **9/2**[3]
3 *1 3/4* **Beethoven (IRE)**[37] 4723 2-9-1 103 .... MJKinane 3 112
(A P O'Brien, Ire) *trckd ldr in 2nd: led fr 2f out: hdd under 1f out: sn no imp u.p and kpt on same pce* **25/1**
4 *3/4* **Air Chief Marshal (IRE)**[13] 5486 2-9-1 110 .... JPO'Brien 2 110
(A P O'Brien, Ire) *led: hdd fr 2f out: 3rd over 1f out: sn no imp: kpt on same pce u.p* **20/1**
5 *3/4* **Senior**[62] 3893 2-9-1 .... PJSmullen 6 108
(Edward Lynam, Ire) *trckd ldrs in 4th: no imp u.p and kpt on same pce fr over 1f out* **28/1**
6 *hd* **Alfred Nobel (IRE)**[48] 4359 2-9-1 112 .... JAHeffernan 5 108
(A P O'Brien, Ire) *racd towards rr in 5th: rdn to cl over 1f out: no ex ins fnl f* **1/1**[1]

1m 33.63s (6.53) **Going Correction** +0.90s/f (Soft) **6** Ran SP% **111.0**
Speed ratings: **98,97,95,94,93 93**
CSF £11.96 TOTE £3.30: £1.40, £2.50; DF 12.30.
Owner Norman Ormiston **Bred** Airlie Stud **Trained** Friarstown, Co Kildare
■ Stewards' Enquiry : D P McDonogh caution: improper use of the whip

FOCUS
While the finish of this Group 1 event was fought out by two maiden winners, both having their second starts, there is every chance they are very smart colts with bright futures ahead of them. The race is tricky to rate but the third and fourth are the best guides.

NOTEBOOK
Kingsfort(USA) ◆ had carried a big reputation into his debut here in June, and after holding the runner-up's last furlong charge here he was cut for the 2000 Guineas. Close up in a race in which the early pace was only moderate, he warmed to his task after the tempo increased and, after hitting the front early in the final furlong, kept on well to win driven out. Trainer Kevin Prendergast said of the winner: "We were going to give him a break after his win, with today's race in mind, and when he picked up a virus we were forced to give him that break. He's done his bit for the season and won't run again this year. He's a tall, lanky colt and you'd think he will improve over the winter." (op 7/4)
Chabal(IRE) ◆ had won at Leopardstown only a week previously and there was plenty to like about his performance here. He failed to settle out the back and had to wait for a gap entering the final furlong before running on well under pressure in the closing stages. He is likely to have another run this season, according to trainer Jim Bolger. (op 6/1)
Beethoven(IRE), having his seventh race, had won a 6f maiden at Leopardstown on his previous start. He ran second here until edging ahead under 2f out and, although no match for the first two in the closing stages, kept on to the line.
Air Chief Marshal(IRE), runner-up to Alfred Nobel in the Group 1 Phoenix Stakes here in July before finishing second in a 6f Group 3 event last time, made the running and raised the tempo before halfway. Headed under 2f out, he kept on under pressure.
Senior, third over course and distance on his only previous start, tracked the leaders and, although unable to raise his effort one and a half furlongs out, kept on well enough.
Alfred Nobel(IRE), on a four-timer and seeking a second Group 1 win following his Phoenix Stakes victory over 6f here in July, was the disappointment of the race. Held up in rear, he was angled right to try and challenge from 2f out but he never really posed much of a threat and could make no impression in the closing stages. It is possible that he might have gone over the top for the season, although trainer Aidan O'Brien had expressed reservations about how he would cope with testing ground at this distance. (op 11/10)

5895a LADBROKES.COM BLENHEIM STKS (LISTED RACE) 6f
5:20 (5:21) 2-Y-O **£27,493** (£8,066; £3,843; £1,309)

RPR
1 **Song Of My Heart (IRE)**[13] 5485 2-8-12 84 .... MJKinane 2 102+
(David Wachman, Ire) *mid-div: clsr in 5th fr under 2f out: 4th over 1f out: squeezed way between horses to chal and ld ins fnl f: styd on wl to draw clr cl home* **5/1**[3]
2 *1 1/2* **Wrong Answer**[13] 5488 2-9-1 96 .... CDHayes 6 100
(Kevin Prendergast, Ire) *chsd ldrs: hdwy to ld under 2f out: hdd and kpt on same pce ins fnl f* **13/2**
3 *1* **Mister Tee**[4] 5754 2-9-1 103 .... KLatham 3 97
(G M Lyons, Ire) *cl up: led after 1/2-way: hdd under 2f out: remained prom: kpt on same pce u.p ins fnl f* **7/4**[1]

4 nk **Rahya Cass (IRE)**[14] 5452 2-8-12 91 (t) WMLordan 7 93
(T Stack, Ire) *mid-div: rdn to go 5th over 1f out: no imp in 4th whn swished tail ins fnl f: kpt on same pce* **7/1**

5 4 **Atasari (IRE)**[112] 2286 2-8-12 82 KJManning 5 81
(J S Bolger, Ire) *prom: 2nd under 2f out: 3rd over 1f out: no ex in 5th fnl f* **12/1**

6 3 1/2 **Queen Of Troy (IRE)**[14] 5450 2-8-12 JAHeffernan 9 71
(A P O'Brien, Ire) *mid-div: 6th under 2f out: no ex fr over 1f out* **10/1**

7 1 **Captains Dilemma (IRE)**[15] 5414 2-9-1 74 WJSupple 11 71
(P D Deegan, Ire) *led briefly early: lost pl fr 1/2-way: no imp and kpt on same pce fr 2f out* **33/1**

8 1/2 **Intapeace (IRE)**[14] 5452 2-8-12 88 DPMcDonogh 4 66
(Francis Ennis, Ire) *prom: sn led: hdd after 1/2-way: 3rd under 2f out: no ex fr over 1f out* **10/1**

9 1 1/4 **Motto Bello (IRE)**[14] 5453 2-8-12 PJSmullen 8 62
(Andrew Oliver, Ire) *towards rr for most: nvr a factor* **25/1**

10 14 **Rock Jock (IRE)**[1] 5843 2-9-1 96 MCHussey 1 23
(Tracey Collins, Ire) *sn trckd ldrs: 4th after 1/2-way: lost pl and wknd fr under 2f out* **4/1**[2]

11 20 **Tamara Who (IRE)**[21] 5267 2-8-12 DMGrant 10 —
(John E Kiely, Ire) *towards rr: dropped bhd fr 2f out* **66/1**

1m 17.44s (2.74) **Going Correction** +0.475s/f (Yiel) **11 Ran SP% 133.0**
Speed ratings: **100,98,96,96,90 86,84,84,82,63 37**
CSF £42.49 TOTE £4.90: £1.50, £3.20, £1.60; DF 25.10.
Owner Mrs Ciaran Conroy **Bred** Michael Collins **Trained** Goolds Cross, Co Tipperary

FOCUS
The race has been rated on the balance of the form of the second, third, fourth and fifth.

NOTEBOOK
Song Of My Heart(IRE) ◆ followed up her debut win over 6f here last month by again showing her ability to handle testing ground. Held up, she began to close 2f out and came through between horses to lead well inside the final furlong. She ran on well and was extending her advantage near the finish. Well regarded by her trainer, she has the Cheveley Park Stakes as a possible target.
Wrong Answer, a winner at this level over 5f on similar ground back in May, was back in trip here after making little impact over 7f on her previous start. She went to the front under 2f out but had no answer when the winner arrived. (op 5/1)
Mister Tee, placed five times, including at Group 2 level, before getting off the mark at Dundalk four days previously, raced prominently and had every chance before finding no extra under pressure inside the final furlong. (op 7/4 tchd 15/8)
Rahya Cass(IRE), a maiden winner over the course and trip on yielding ground, had run fourth over 5f at Dundalk on her previous start. She made headway for pressure over a furlong out but failed to make much impression.
Atasari(IRE), a course and distance winner on heavy ground in May, was back from a long break here. She raced prominently and had every chance from 2f out before weakening over the final furlong.
T/Jkpt: @241.80. Pool of @10,000.00 - 31 winning units. T/Plt: @35.10. Pool of @14,973.51 - 319 winning units. II

5714 BATH (L-H)
Sunday, September 13

OFFICIAL GOING: Firm (good to firm in places; 9.8)
Wind: Moderate across Weather: Broken cloud

5899 MELKSHAM MOTOR SPARES FILLIES' NURSERY (H'CAP) 5f 161y
2:25 (2:27) (Class 4) (0-85,78) 2-Y-O **£4,415** (£1,321; £660; £330; £164) **Stalls** Centre

Form RPR

4012 1 **Yurituni**[3] 5797 2-9-2 73 SilvestreDeSousa 7 83+
(Eve Johnson Houghton) *sn led: pushed along 2f out: shkn up and styd on strly ins fnl f* **11/8**[1]

6310 2 3/4 **Quaker Parrot**[43] 4539 2-9-4 75 RichardKingscote 5 83
(Tom Dascombe) *trckd ldrs: chsd wnr fr over 1f out: styd on u.p ins fnl f but a readily hld* **10/1**

6133 3 3 3/4 **Any Day (IRE)**[34] 4850 2-8-7 71 JPFahy(7) 6 66
(R M Beckett) *in tch: hdwy towards outside over 2f out: styd on u.p to go 3rd fnl f but nvr any ch w ldng duo* **7/2**[2]

0330 4 3 1/2 **Mrs Boss**[62] 3918 2-9-4 78 JamesMillman(3) 10 62
(B R Millman) *chsd wnr tl over 2f out: wknd appr fnl f* **33/1**

534 5 3/4 **Admirable Duchess**[38] 4711 2-9-0 71 NCallan 1 52
(D J S Ffrench Davis) *t.k.h: chsd ldrs tl hmpd wl over 1f out: nt rcvr but styd on again cl home* **11/1**

01 6 3/4 **Katehari (IRE)**[20] 5318 2-9-1 72 MartinDwyer 2 51
(A M Balding) *s.i.s: in rr: rdn over 2f out and no imp* **5/1**[3]

560 7 8 **Bazsharani**[11] 5583 2-8-5 62 SimonWhitworth 3 14
(P D Evans) *a in rr* **40/1**

561 8 1 3/4 **Wanchai Whisper**[23] 5226 2-8-12 69 CatherineGannon 9 15
(P D Evans) *chsd ldrs: rdn to go 2nd over 2f out: edgd rt u.p wl over 1f out and sn wknd* **9/1**

1m 10.29s (-0.91) **Going Correction** -0.225s/f (Firm) **8 Ran SP% 113.8**
Speed ratings (Par 94): **97,96,91,86,85 84,73,71**
toteswingers: 1&2 £3.20, 1&3 £2.40, 2&3 £6.10. CSF £16.63 CT £40.74 TOTE £2.30: £1.10, £2.20, £1.40; EX 9.90 Trifecta £54.90 Pool: £337.31 - 4.54 winning units..
Owner Mrs M Findlay **Bred** Jeremy Green And Sons **Trained** Blewbury, Oxon

FOCUS
A couple of fair types ran in this, but it seemed a mainly ordinary nursery. Another step forward from the winner, and solid form.

NOTEBOOK
Yurituni had every chance on her recent efforts and duly collected another win after making most of the running. She appears to be a very quick horse and is due to have a break now. (op 10-11)
Quaker Parrot tried to go with the winner early, but could not live with her. She got outpaced before staying on again inside the final furlong. (tchd 9-1 and 12-1)
Any Day(IRE), who was really well backed, lacked the pace to stay in touch but kept on for pressure, without looking that dangerous. (op 11-2)
Mrs Boss, without a visor this time, sat close to the leader but had nothing left for the business end of the race. (op 25-1)
Admirable Duchess ◆ was making some progress when squeezed out by a couple of rivals over a furlong out. Her rider eased off from that point. Official explanation: jockey said filly suffered interference in running (op 12-1 tchd 16-1 and 10-1)
Katehari(IRE), another to attract market confidence, was slowly away and never recovered. She is better than she showed. (op 17-2)
Bazsharani took a strong hold early and failed to make any impact. (op 50-1)
Wanchai Whisper, claimed for 11,500gns when winning a seller for William Haggas last time, raced prominently but could not keep going at the same pace under pressure. Official explanation: trainer said filly was unsuited by the firm (good to firm in places) ground (op 8-1)

5900 FSPDISTRIBUTION.COM CLAIMING STKS 5f 11y
3:00 (3:01) (Class 6) 3-Y-O+ **£2,266** (£674; £337; £168) **Stalls** Centre

Form RPR

160 1 **Green Lagonda (AUS)**[11] 5576 7-8-10 62 PaulHanagan 9 71
(P D Evans) *trckd ldrs: rdn 2f out: led jst ins fnl f: styd on wl u.p* **11/1**

0000 2 1 **Fault**[9] 5646 3-9-1 85 (t) MickyFenton 4 73
(Stef Liddiard) *w ld tl slt ld appr fnl 2f: narrowly hdd 1f out: styd on u.p to hold 2nd but a hld by wnr* **5/1**[3]

0640 3 3/4 **Misaro (GER)**[9] 5623 8-8-10 77 ow3 (b) SPRyan(7) 5 72
(R A Harris) *chsd ldrs: rdn 2f out: styd on ins fnl f but nvr gng pce to chal* **11/4**[1]

1202 4 hd **Caribbean Coral**[26] 5125 10-8-13 64 NCallan 10 67
(A B Haynes) *in tch: hdwy to chse ldrs 2f out: styd on same pce u.p fnl f* **8/1**

1130 5 nse **Swinbrook (USA)**[15] 5421 8-8-8 74 (b[1]) WilliamCarson(3) 8 65
(R A Harris) *chsd ldrs: rdn and one pce 1/2-way: hdwy on outside over 1f out: styd on ins fnl f* **6/1**

-001 6 shd **Boho Chic**[6] 5716 3-8-4 60 (p) DO'Donohoe 6 58
(George Baker) *chsd ldrs: rdn over 2f out: slt ld 1f out: sn hdd: wknd nr fin* **10/1**

-060 7 3 3/4 **Galeota (IRE)**[43] 4516 7-8-3 94 CharlesEddery(7) 7 50
(R Hannon) *s.i.s: in rr: styd on fnl f* **7/2**[2]

5000 8 2 1/4 **Bahamian Ceilidh**[10] 5612 3-8-2 60 CatherineGannon 1 35
(B N Pollock) *sn led: hdd appr fnl 2f: wknd qckly fnl f* **33/1**

4000 9 1 3/4 **Triskaidekaphobia**[18] 5345 6-8-13 44 (t) PaulFitzsimons 3 39
(Miss J R Tooth) *in tch: rdn 1/2-way: sn wknd* **66/1**

0060 10 2 **Fizzlephut (IRE)**[18] 5345 7-8-12 48 (b) FrankieMcDonald 2 30
(Miss J R Tooth) *reluctant to post: sn outpcd* **66/1**

00 11 10 **Captain Teddo**[11] 5572 3-8-11 0 (t) FrancisNorton 11 —
(R Ingram) *a outpcd* **100/1**

61.14 secs (-1.36) **Going Correction** -0.225s/f (Firm)
WFA 3 from 6yo+ 1lb **11 Ran SP% 115.3**
Speed ratings (Par 101): **101,99,98,97,97 97,91,88,85,82 66**
toteswingers: 1&2 £11.40, 1&3 £10.10, 2&3 £4.60. CSF £63.36 TOTE £14.60: £2.70, £1.90, £1.60; EX 96.40 Trifecta £211.30 Part won. Pool: £285.56 - 0.44 winning units..
Owner M D Jones **Bred** P Brain **Trained** Pandy, Monmouths

FOCUS
Plenty of well-known names took part in this claimer, so the form should be sound for the grade, especially as the leaders went a good gallop. The fourth looks the best guide.

5901 MOTOR FACTOR SINCE 1968 H'CAP 5f 161y
3:35 (3:35) (Class 4) (0-85,89) 3-Y-O+ **£6,476** (£1,927; £963; £481) **Stalls** Centre

Form RPR

04 1 **Filligree (IRE)**[22] 5257 4-9-3 85 WilliamCarson(3) 4 93
(Rae Guest) *in rr and pushed along 1/2-way: hdwy over 1f oit: styd on u.p to ld fnl 75yds* **7/2**[1]

001 2 1 **Artistic License (IRE)**[14] 5471 4-9-10 89 NCallan 1 94
(M R Channon) *chsd ldrs tl rdn and one pce 3f out: styd on again fr 2f out and drvn to chal fnl 75yds: kpt on same pce* **11/2**[3]

1523 3 3/4 **The Tatling (IRE)**[4] 5768 12-9-0 82 JackDean(3) 2 84
(J M Bradley) *trckd ldrs: led travelling wl appr fnl f: hdd and no ex fnl 75yds* **7/2**[1]

4002 4 2 **Bobbie Soxer (IRE)**[26] 5130 3-8-12 79 TedDurcan 7 74
(J L Dunlop) *outpcd and pushed along 3f out: swtchd rt and hdwy 1f out: hung lft and fnd little ins fnl f* **11/2**[3]

5035 5 2 3/4 **Doc Jones (IRE)**[6] 5719 3-8-6 73 (p) PaulHanagan 3 59
(P D Evans) *led: rdn fr 3f out: hdd over 1f out and sn wknd* **9/2**[2]

5020 6 1 3/4 **Kyllachy Storm**[6] 5719 5-8-8 73 MickyFenton 5 53
(R J Hodges) *stmbld s: sn rcvrd to press ldr 2f: wknd ins fnl 2f* **8/1**

1350 7 1 3/4 **Desperate Dan**[15] 5424 8-8-11 76 (v) PatCosgrave 6 50
(A B Haynes) *chsd ldrs to 1/2-way* **10/1**

69.78 secs (-1.42) **Going Correction** -0.225s/f (Firm)
WFA 3 from 4yo+ 2lb **7 Ran SP% 113.6**
Speed ratings (Par 105): **100,98,97,95,91 89,86**
toteswingers: 1&2 £3.80, 1&3 £4.60, 2&3 £3.10. CSF £22.58 TOTE £4.00: £2.40, £1.80; EX 12.50.
Owner The Filligree Partnership **Bred** T Hirschfeld **Trained** Newmarket, Suffolk

FOCUS
Not many runners but a decent sprint. The pace was strong which suited those held up. A clear personal best from the winner.

5902 FIRST LINE ALL MAKES SPECIALIST H'CAP 5f 161y
4:10 (4:10) (Class 3) (0-95,95) 3-Y-O
£8,723 (£2,612; £1,306; £653; £326; £163) **Stalls** Centre

Form RPR

3111 1 **Golden Destiny (IRE)**[22] 5245 3-9-4 95 (p) NCallan 8 105
(P J Makin) *w ldr: led 3f out: drvn and styd on gamely thrght fnl f* **5/2**[1]

02 2 nk **Brenin Taran**[4] 5777 3-8-4 84 (p) AndreaAtzeni(3) 6 93
(D M Simcock) *rdn: hung lft and styd on to chse wnr jst ins fnl f: str burst fnl 50yds but a jst hld* **4/1**[2]

3202 3 5 **Strictly**[22] 5264 3-8-5 82 PaulHanagan 4 74
(Sir Michael Stoute) *in tch: rdn fr 3f out: styd on to take wl hld 3rd fnl f* **4/1**[2]

-000 4 1/2 **Thunderous Mood (USA)**[92] 2934 3-8-13 90 MartinDwyer 10 80
(P F I Cole) *in rr: rdn 1/2-way: kpt on towards outside fr over 1f out to take 4th ins fnl f but nvr gng pce to get into contention* **8/1**

6042 5 1 **White Shift (IRE)**[22] 5245 3-8-4 81 oh2 SilvestreDeSousa 2 68
(P Howling) *led tl hdd 3f out: styd chsng wnr tl wknd fnl f* **16/1**

3005 6 1 **Kerrys Requiem (IRE)**[13] 5507 3-8-8 85 TedDurcan 5 69
(M R Channon) *stdd s: in rr: sme hdwy on ins over 1f out: nt clr run ins fnl f: nvr a threat* **6/1**[3]

6006 7 nk **Ginobili (IRE)**[13] 5507 3-8-8 85 ow1 (p) MickyFenton 1 67
(Stef Liddiard) *chsd ldrs: rdn 3f out: wknd 2f out* **22/1**

2210 8 1 1/4 **Super Academy (USA)**[27] 5090 3-8-4 81 oh3 CatherineGannon 9 59
(J A Osborne) *a outpcd* **16/1**

-010 9 2 1/4 **Raggle Taggle (IRE)**[57] 4096 3-8-5 89 JPFahy(7) 3 60
(R M Beckett) *sn rdn along and outpcd* **9/1**

68.99 secs (-2.21) **Going Correction** -0.225s/f (Firm) **9 Ran SP% 120.1**
Speed ratings (Par 105): **105,104,97,97,95 94,94,92,89**
toteswingers: 1&2 £3.50, 1&3 £3.40, 2&3 £3.90. CSF £13.05 CT £39.70 TOTE £3.50: £1.30, £2.00, £1.50; EX 12.50 Trifecta £27.70 Pool: £363.69 - 9.69 winning units..
Owner H J W Davies P Spencer-Jones M H Holland **Bred** Yeomanstown Stud **Trained** Ogbourne Maisey, Wilts

FOCUS
An interesting little contest, that featured a couple of very in-form horses and a few that could be given every chance if returning to their best. The winner's time was by far the best of the three races run over the distance and the first two came clear. Another step up from Golden Desert.

NOTEBOOK
Golden Destiny(IRE), chasing a four-timer, has improved since the cheekpieces were fitted and is a brave sort, as she fought on really well to keep her sequence going after racing at the head of affairs. Connections hope to try and find a fillies' handicap or a Listed event for her next. (op 11-4 tchd 3-1)
Brenin Taran, making a fairly quick reappearance, attracted market support and was the only one to give the winner any problems. He travelled strongly and was only just denied. (op 11-2)
Strictly looked in the handicapper's grip on her previous outing, but was still unexposed. Held up in midfield, she had her chance but could not get on terms. (op 100-30 tchd 3-1)
Thunderous Mood(USA) was dropping in class after running in some better races this season. Keen early, he kept on and is gradually improving. (op 16-1)
White Shift(IRE) did not see which way Golden Destiny went when they clashed last time over course and distance, and endured a similar fate again. (tchd 14-1)
Kerrys Requiem(IRE) always usually runs her race but has gone a long time without success. Another to be held up, she made her way through horses and may have finished third with a clear run. Official explanation: jockey said filly was denied a clear run (op 9-2)
Ginobili(IRE) was prominent for a while, but faded. (op 25-1 tchd 20-1)
Super Academy(USA) was very keen at the rear and had nothing left at the end.
Raggle Taggle(IRE) disappointed last time in her first handicap and did so again. She was under pressure a long way out and may need easier ground. (op 12-1 tchd 14-1)

5903 MELKSHAMMOTORSPARES.CO.UK H'CAP — 2m 1f 34y
4:45 (4:45) (Class 2) (0-100,94) 3-Y-O+
£17,446 (£5,224; £2,612; £1,307; £652; £327) **Stalls** Centre

Form — RPR
1151 **1** **Callisto Moon**[53] 4212 5-9-2 **82**....(p) NCallan 3 — 88
(R Curtis) *mde all: rdn 4l clr 3f out: styd on wl fr over 1f out* **9/2**[3]
-164 **2** *1* **Woolfall Treasure**[46] 4417 4-9-8 **88**.... PatCosgrave 5 — 93+
(G L Moore) *chsd ldrs: drvn along fr 4f out: outpcd by wnr 3f out: styd on to go 2nd 1f out and kpt on wl but a hld* **5/2**[1]
100/ **3** *1* **Raslan**[21] 6335 6-9-3 **83**....(vt) PaulHanagan 1 — 87
(D E Pipe) *chsd wnr: rdn and outpcd 3f out: styd on fr 2f out but lost 2nd 1f out: styd on ins fnl f* **7/2**[2]
0045 **4** *3/4* **Keenes Day (FR)**[22] 5248 4-9-12 **92**.... J-PGuillambert 2 — 95
(M Johnston) *chsd ldrs: rdn over 3f out: sn outpcd: styd on again fnl f* **5/2**[1]
-140 **5** *nk* **Right Option (IRE)**[42] 1356 5-8-3 **76**.... BillyCray(7) 7 — 79
(J L Flint) *in rr: hrd rdn over 3f out in last pl: kpt on fr over 1f out: fin wl* **20/1**
040- **6** *5* **Enjoy The Moment**[400] 4843 6-10-0 **94**.... MartinDwyer 6 — 91
(J A Osborne) *rdn and hung lft 3f out: a in rr* **20/1**
5642 **P** **Pseudonym (IRE)**[13] 5530 7-8-2 **75** oh9....(t) JPFahy(7) 4 — —
(M F Harris) *p.u lame after 5f* **16/1**

3m 52.37s (0.47) **Going Correction** -0.125s/f (Firm) **7** Ran SP% **113.0**
Speed ratings (Par 109): **93,92,92,91,91 89,—**
toteswingers: 1&2 £2.70, 1&3 £4.00, 2&3 £3.00. CSF £15.77 TOTE £6.00: £2.40, £1.90; EX 17.60.
Owner B Bedford & Mrs Gill White **Bred** Barton Stud **Trained** Lambourn, Berks
■ Stewards' Enquiry : Pat Cosgrave one-day ban: used whip with excessive frequency (Sep 27)

FOCUS
A valuable stayers' handicap. All of these had claims when showing their best form, but the winner's jockey deserves praise for a good front-running ride, which effectively stole the contest. Ordinary form for the grade.

NOTEBOOK
Callisto Moon, given a break since winning at Sandown in late July, and 16lb higher than his first victory this season, was allowed an easy lead before battling on really well to collect another success. While he has clearly improved, this success had a lot to do with the jockey poaching a lead off the home bend. He holds an entry in the Cesarewitch but will need this sort of ground to take his place in the line-up. (op 6-1 tchd 4-1)
Woolfall Treasure had run in a couple of marathons, so this was a drop in trip for him. He moved nicely in midfield but was never going to catch the winner once that horse had gained an advantage over him. (tchd 3-1)
Raslan ◆, having his first run on the Flat since taking part in the 2007 Cesarewitch, bolted up by 16 lengths at Newton Abbot when last seen and did not shape too badly in this. He can be found something whilst the ground suits. (tchd 4-1)
Keenes Day(FR) ran a similar race to the runner-up, but was even more outpaced at a crucial stage. (op 11-4 tchd 9-4)
Right Option(IRE), who has been running well over hurdles during the summer, was keen and failed to handle the home bend. He did keep on quite well but was easily held. (tchd 18-1)
Enjoy The Moment, absent since finishing last in the 2008 Shergar Cup Stayers, showed more than enough to suggest he will be winning again, as he closed right up going strongly when the field bunched, and was not given a hard time once his chance was gone. (op 18-1 tchd 16-1)
Pseudonym(IRE), running from 9lb out of the handicap, was pulled up very early. (op 12-1)

5904 UNITED AFTERMARKET NETWORK (UAN) H'CAP — 1m 2f 46y
5:20 (5:20) (Class 3) (0-95,91) 3-Y-O **£8,723** (£2,612; £1,306; £653; £326) **Stalls** Low

Form — RPR
1-11 **1** **Bab Al Salam (USA)**[9] 5648 3-9-4 **91**.... TedDurcan 7 — 99
(Saeed Bin Suroor) *trckd ldrs: wnt 2nd over 5f out: slt ld fr ins fnl 2f: hrd drvn whn chal fnl f: hld on all out* **5/6**[1]
-110 **2** *hd* **Rosika**[71] 3618 3-8-10 **83**.... PaulHanagan 1 — 91
(Sir Michael Stoute) *sn led: rdn over 3f out: narrowly hdd ins fnl 2f: rallied u.p and str chal thrght fnl f: no ex cl home* **7/1**
3132 **3** *1* **Souter Point (USA)**[13] 5532 3-8-2 **82**.... JPFahy(7) 2 — 88
(R Charlton) *in tch: rdn and hdwy fr 3f out: chsd ldng duo over 1f out: kpt on thrght fnl f but a hld* **4/1**[2]
0016 **4** *4* **Dubai Crest**[15] 5419 3-9-0 **87**.... NCallan 3 — 85
(Mrs A J Perrett) *towards rr but in tch: rdn and styd on to cl fr 3f out: nvr gng pce to trble ldrs and wknd over 1f out* **9/2**[3]
1040 **5** *15* **Norwegian Dancer (UAE)**[9] 5648 3-8-13 **86**.... FrancisNorton 6 — 54
(E S McMahon) *plld hrd: sn chsng ldr tl over 5f out: wknd fr 3f out* **14/1**

2m 8.30s (-2.70) **Going Correction** -0.125s/f (Firm) **5** Ran SP% **111.9**
Speed ratings (Par 105): **105,104,104,100,88**
toteswingers: 1&2 £5.70. CSF £7.49 TOTE £1.50: £1.40, £3.10; EX 5.30.
Owner Godolphin **Bred** Darley **Trained** Newmarket, Suffolk

FOCUS
This looked the most interesting race on the card, as it contained some useful handicappers and a couple of unexposed types representing big stables. It was a shame that two major players were taken out in the morning. The third is the best guide to the form.

NOTEBOOK
Bab Al Salam(USA), raised 5lb for winning just over a week previously, was trying to win his fourth consecutive race to remain unbeaten, and he did so by a small margin. However, one would suspect that he could have found a little bit more had things got desperate. On the positive side, the handicapper cannot be too hard on him. (op Evens)
Rosika, the only filly in the line-up, had been absent since running in a decent handicap at Haydock at the start of July. She gained her maiden success over course and distance and ran really well at the same venue again, rallying for pressure to reclaim second after looking held. Punters were clearly not expecting a good effort when considering the way she drifted, so she should build on the run. (op 4-1)
Souter Point(USA) has been running consistently throughout this year but was raised 3lb for finishing an unlucky second on his last outing. He came through to appear dangerous about two furlongs out, but he could not quicken again. (tchd 7-2)
Dubai Crest ran with the choke out and did not have much left for the finish. He was not beaten far, but never looked dangerous. (op 7-1 tchd 15-2)
Norwegian Dancer(UAE), over ten lengths behind the winner last time, has shown his best form at Chester but had no chance here after pulling very hard early.

5905 MAKING MOTORPARTS SIMPLE H'CAP — 1m 5y
5:50 (5:51) (Class 6) (0-60,60) 3-Y-O+ **£2,266** (£674; £337; £168) **Stalls** Low

Form — RPR
320 **1** **Seasonal Cross**[15] 5429 4-9-7 **58**.... NCallan 4 — 67+
(S Dow) *in rr tl rapid hdwy fr 3f out: drvn to ld wl over 1f out: hld on all out cl home* **4/1**[1]
0033 **2** *nk* **Rose Cheval (USA)**[17] 5367 3-8-12 **54**.... FrancisNorton 5 — 60
(M R Channon) *chsd ldrs: rdn 3f out: styd on u.p fnl 2f: chsd wnr ins fnl f and kpt on but a jst hld* **20/1**
504 **3** *3/4* **Jewelled Reef (IRE)**[3] 5789 3-9-2 **58**.... MickyFenton 12 — 62
(Eve Johnson Houghton) *in rr: hdwy on outside over 2f out: styd on u.p thrght fnl f: gng on cl home* **17/2**
3214 **4** *1 1/4* **Dr Wintringham (IRE)**[15] 5449 3-9-4 **60**.... TedDurcan 13 — 61
(Karen George) *stdd s and dropped out rr: hdwy on outside over 2f out: styd on u.p fnl f but nvr gng pce to rch ldrs* **9/2**[2]
0500 **5** *1 1/4* **Second To Nun (IRE)**[16] 5384 3-8-13 **55**.... SilvestreDeSousa 11 — 53
(Jean-Rene Auvray) *chsd ldrs: rdn 3f out: one pce fr over 1f out* **11/1**
0063 **6** *1 1/4* **Lennie Briscoe (IRE)**[21] 5287 3-9-3 **59**.... JamesDoyle 14 — 54
(S Kirk) *in rr: pushed along and sme hdwy fr 2f out: kpt on ins fnl f but nvr a danger* **14/1**
042 **7** *3/4* **Charlie Delta**[9] 5634 6-8-12 **52**....(b) WilliamCarson(3) 1 — 46+
(R A Harris) *pressed ldrs: led over 4f out: hdd & wknd wl over 1f out* **15/2**[3]
2220 **8** *5* **Feasible**[35] 4824 4-9-7 **58**.... PatCosgrave 7 — 40
(J G Portman) *chsd ldrs: wd bnd 5f out: styd prom tl wknd 2f out* **9/1**
4100 **9** *3/4* **Montmartre (USA)**[16] 5384 3-8-11 **60**.... JPFahy(7) 2 — 40
(David Pinder) *chsd ldrs: rdn over 3f out: wknd fr 2f out* **16/1**
050- **10** *1 1/4* **Tattercoats (FR)**[268] 7734 3-8-2 **47**.... AndreaAtzeni(3) 9 — 24
(M Botti) *a towards rr* **20/1**
560 **11** *13* **Tignello (IRE)**[43] 4533 4-9-6 **57**.... PaulHanagan 8 — 3
(G L Moore) *t.k.h: chsd ldrs 5f: eased whn no ch fnl f* **8/1**
0000 **12** *6* **Iron Man Of Mersey (FR)**[9] 5644 3-8-7 **49**.... MartinDwyer 3 — —
(A W Carroll) *led 1f: styd pressing ldrs tl over 3f out: eased whn no ch fnl f* **16/1**
300 **13** *27* **Lancaster Lad (IRE)**[75] 3473 4-8-9 **46**....(b) CatherineGannon 10 — —
(A B Haynes) *led after 1f tl over 4f out: sn wknd: eased whn no ch fnl f* **50/1**

1m 40.05s (-0.75) **Going Correction** -0.125s/f (Firm)
WFA 3 from 4yo+ 5lb **13** Ran SP% **119.8**
Speed ratings (Par 101): **98,97,96,95,94 93,92,87,86,85 72,66,39**
toteswingers: 1&2 £18.70, 1&3 £11.30, 2&3 £24.50. CSF £88.76 CT £677.96 TOTE £4.80: £1.80, £4.60, £4.00; EX 80.10 Trifecta £465.80 Part won. Pool: £629.56 - 0.64 winning units..
Owner Mrs Alicia Aldis **Bred** Adrienne And Michael Barnett **Trained** Epsom, Surrey

FOCUS
A very moderate handicap, in which fillies dominated the finish. It was strong run and the form is ordinary.
Lancaster Lad(IRE) Official explanation: jockey said colt ran too free
T/Plt: £25.20 to a £1 stake. Pool: £58,371.45. 1,686.36 winning tickets. T/Qpdt: £5.40 to a £1 stake. Pool: £4,464.13. 610.10 winning tickets. ST

5866 FFOS LAS (L-H)
Sunday, September 13

OFFICIAL GOING: Good to firm (good in places; 8.6)
Wind: Almost nil Weather: Mainly sunny

5906 E.B.F./TOTEPLACEPOT MAIDEN FILLIES' STKS — 1m (R)
2:10 (2:11) (Class 4) 2-Y-O **£5,180** (£1,541; £770; £384) **Stalls** Low

Form — RPR
6 **1** **Chain Of Office**[16] 5397 2-9-0 0.... LiamJones 7 — 72
(W J Haggas) *t.k.h: sn led: rn green bnd over 4f out: clr over 3f out: rdn over 1f out: r.o wl* **15/8**[1]
2 *1* **Cheetah** 2-9-0 0.... KFallon 8 — 70+
(L M Cumani) *led early: hld up in tch: chsd wnr over 2f out: rdn and nt qckn ins fnl f* **4/1**[3]
00 **3** *1/2* **Sandy Shaw**[15] 5428 2-9-0 0.... JimmyQuinn 1 — 69
(J W Hills) *hld up towards rr: pushed along over 2f out: hdwy wl over 1f out: sn rdn: r.o ins fnl f* **16/1**
4 *3 1/2* **Lovely Eyes (IRE)** 2-9-0 0.... RoystonFfrench 3 — 61+
(D M Simcock) *prom: outpcd over 3f out: kpt on to take 4th nr fin* **7/1**
63 **5** *nk* **La Ville Lumiere (USA)**[12] 5547 2-8-11 0.... AhmedAjtebi(3) 4 — 60
(Saeed Bin Suroor) *sn chsng wnr: pushed along and lost 2nd over 2f out: rdn and wknd over 1f out* **2/1**[2]
6 *3/4* **Nefyn** 2-9-0 0.... RichardMullen 6 — 59
(W R Muir) *hld up towards rr: pushed along and prog over 3f out: wknd over 2f out* **16/1**
7 *3 1/4* **Jasmeno** 2-9-0 0.... TravisBlock 2 — 52
(H Morrison) *s.i.s: hld up in rr: pushed along 3f out: sn struggling* **22/1**

1m 41.07s (101.07) **7** Ran SP% **116.7**
toteswingers: 1&2 £2.40, 1&3 £7.10, 2&3 £10.80. CSF £10.30 TOTE £3.30: £1.30, £2.60; EX 13.20.
Owner J M Greetham **Bred** J M Greetham **Trained** Newmarket, Suffolk

FOCUS
A modest pace allowed the winner to dictate affairs from the front. Not easy to assess but the race has been rated in line with the following event for colts.

NOTEBOOK

Chain Of Office pulled hard in the lead and she was generally an awkward conveyance, but by the home turn she had established a four-length lead and, given a breather, surged again to keep on well near the finish. This built on the promise she showed when making late headway on her debut at Newmarket late last month, and once she learns to settle better there could still be more to come. (op 5-2)

Cheetah ◆, who was easy to back, moved up to the heels of the leader in the straight but although she looked a threat two furlongs from home she could never quite peg back the winner. This was still a thoroughly likeable debut and, from the same family as Derby winner Kahyasi, she is bred to improve for middle distances next year. (op 3-1)

Sandy Shaw was ridden patiently and began to make progress in the straight. However, she still had several lengths to make up on the winner with only a furlong left to run, and although she could not bridge the gap she was doing her best work at the finish. She now qualifies for a mark and looks up to winning a race. (op 20-1)

Lovely Eyes(IRE) could not get going as well as her 55,000gns price tag might have suggested, though she did make up some ground in the last half furlong. (op 8-1)

La Ville Lumiere(USA) had the winner in her sights but began to labour three furlongs out and was well beaten. (op 15-8 tchd 9-4)

Jasmeno Official explanation: jockey said filly missed the break

5907 TOTESWINGER MAIDEN STKS — 1m (R)

2:45 (2:47) (Class 4) 2-Y-O — £5,180 (£1,541; £770; £384) Stalls Low

Form — RPR

5 **1** **Sharaayeen**[20] 5312 2-9-0 0 ... TPO'Shea 4 77
(B W Hills) *sn chsng ldr: hit rails over 5f out: led over 2f out: rdn over 1f out: r.o* **5/2[2]**

35 **2** *1* **Royal Etiquette (IRE)**[46] 4424 2-9-0 0 ... JamesDoyle 5 75
(H J L Dunlop) *hld up in mid-div: hdwy over 3f out: swtchd rt 2f out: sn rdn: r.o to take 2nd wl ins fnl f* **7/1[3]**

04 **3** *1 1/4* **Harlestone Times (IRE)**[30] 5000 2-9-0 0 ... JimmyQuinn 11 72
(J L Dunlop) *hld up in mid-div: stdy hdwy over 4f out: chsd wnr wl over 1f out: sn rdn: no ex and lost 2nd wl ins fnl f* **11/1**

0 **4** *2 3/4* **Loden**[16] 5401 2-9-0 0 ... KFallon 12 66
(L M Cumani) *hld up: hdwy over 5f out: pushed along 2f out: swtchd rt over 1f out: one pce fnl f* **8/1**

60 **5** *nk* **Ilston Lord (IRE)**[15] 5428 2-9-0 0 ... KirstyMilczarek 8 66+
(M P Tregoning) *hld up in rr: pushed along and sme hdwy over 2f out: hmpd over 1f out: kpt on ins fnl f* **16/1**

02 **6** *2 1/4* **Comradeship (IRE)**[13] 5499 2-9-0 0 ... RichardMullen 6 61
(J H M Gosden) *sn led: hdd over 2f out: sn rdn: wknd fnl f* **13/8[1]**

0 **7** *hd* **Round Won (USA)**[30] 5000 2-9-0 0 ... LiamJones 9 61+
(W J Knight) *hld up in mid-div: sme prog over 3f out: rdn over 2f out: sltly hmpd over 1f out: wknd ins fnl f* **80/1**

8 *1/2* **State Visit** 2-8-11 0 ... FrederikTylicki(3) 3 59
(W R Muir) *s.i.s: hld up in rr: pushed along and reminder over 2f out: shkn up 1f out: n.d* **33/1**

0 **9** *2 1/2* **The Mighty Mod (USA)**[87] 3052 2-9-0 0 ... AdrianTNicholls 13 54
(M Johnston) *in rr: pushed along over 4f out: rdn over 2f out: nvr nr ldrs* **18/1**

06 **10** *3* **Il Portico**[31] 4933 2-9-0 0 ... SamHitchcott 7 47
(M R Channon) *t.k.h towards rr: pushed along over 3f out: no rspnse* **100/1**

11 *7* **Lovers Causeway (USA)** 2-9-0 0 ... RoystonFfrench 14 32+
(M Johnston) *prom: pushed along and wknd over 3f out* **10/1**

0 **12** *8* **Taliesin**[24] 5180 2-9-0 0 ... KevinGhunowa 10 14+
(Mrs A M Thorpe) *led early: hld up in tch: n.m.r and lost pl 6f out: bhd fnl 4f* **33/1**

13 *1 1/4* **Kingspark Boy (IRE)** 2-8-11 0 ... JackMitchell(3) 2 11+
(W K Goldsworthy) *s.i.s: hld up in rr: pushed along 3f out: sn struggling* **33/1**

1m 40.61s (100.61) — **13** Ran SP% **129.9**
toteswingers: 1&2 £7.20, 1&3 £9.70, 2&3 £19.70. CSF £22.27 TOTE £4.10: £1.40, £3.20, £4.70; EX 29.00.

Owner Hamdan Al Maktoum **Bred** D D And Mrs Jean P Clee **Trained** Lambourn, Berks

FOCUS

A decent maiden run at a reasonable pace, but only those able to go with it early on were involved at the finish. The runner-up sets the level.

NOTEBOOK

Sharaayeen briefly lost momentum as he jinked against the rail on the first turn, but that might have been in his favour as he then settled to track the early leader before striking for home two furlongs out and he kept up the gallop all the way to the line. A stronger pace and being ridden prominently suited better here, and he looks on course to take up his entry in the Racing Post Trophy. Connections suggested he would not want ground conditions any quicker than he got today. (op 7-2)

Royal Etiquette(IRE) was feeling the pace two furlongs out, but when moved out wider to find some space he showed some finishing speed to make good late progress, and he improved for this step up in trip. (op 15-2 tchd 8-1)

Harlestone Times(IRE) made steady progress but he lacked the pace of the winner and his run just flattened out near the line. He is bred to appreciate longer distances later in his career and that looked the case here. (op 12-1)

Loden tracked the early leaders until he began to struggle three furlongs from home, and although he holds a Derby entry his performance on the course will need to improve considerably to justify connections' hopes.

Ilston Lord(IRE), another holding a Derby entry, still looked green but made up some ground late on when moved out wide for a clear run. (op 12-1)

Comradeship(IRE) fought for the early lead but he had set too fast a pace and began to struggle three furlongs from home. Official explanation: jockey said colt was unsuited by the good to firm (good in places) ground (op 7-4 tchd 6-4)

5908 TOTEQUADPOT NURSERY — 5f

3:20 (3:21) (Class 4) (0-85,85) 2-Y-O — £4,857 (£1,445; £722; £360) Stalls High

Form — RPR

654 **1** **Ruthie Babe**[10] 5611 2-7-13 63 ... KirstyMilczarek 5 67
(W J Haggas) *t.k.h: hld up: hdwy over 2f out: swtchd lft wl over 1f out: rdn to ld ins fnl f: r.o* **10/3[2]**

141 **2** *1* **Secret Millionaire (IRE)**[9] 5650 2-9-7 85 ... SJCraine 8 85
(Patrick Morris) *hld up: stdy prog over 3f out: led on bit jst over 1f out: rdn and hdd ins fnl f: nt qckn* **6/4[1]**

6040 **3** *1/2* **Dusty Spirit**[9] 5650 2-8-2 66 ow2 ... RichardThomas 3 64
(W G M Turner) *s.i.s: in rr: rdn over 1f out: r.o ins fnl f: tk 3rd nr fin* **14/1**

0616 **4** *1* **Leleyf (IRE)**[12] 5550 2-8-13 77 ... KFallon 6 72
(M R Channon) *prom: led over 2f out: pushed along and hdd jst over 1f out: rdn and no ex ins fnl f* **9/2[3]**

0100 **5** *1 1/2* **Mijas Playa**[29] 5033 2-8-12 79 ... JackMitchell(3) 2 68
(C A Dwyer) *prom: rdn over 1f out: wknd ins fnl f* **9/1**

0500 **6** *7* **King's Approach (IRE)**[18] 5344 2-9-0 78 ... TPO'Shea 1 42
(R Hannon) *led: hdd over 2f out: wknd wl over 1f out* **14/1**

2523 **7** *4 1/2* **True Red (IRE)**[23] 5218 2-7-13 63 ow1 ... JimmyQuinn 9 11
(Mrs N S Evans) *spd over 2f* **7/1**

58.04 secs (58.04) — **7** Ran SP% **117.1**
toteswingers: 1&2 £1.50, 1&3 £9.70, 2&3 £19.70. CSF £9.13 CT £60.18 TOTE £4.60: £1.80, £2.20; EX 9.80.

Owner Exors of the Late F C T Wilson **Bred** Lord Huntingdon **Trained** Newmarket, Suffolk

FOCUS

Plenty of early pace in this reasonable nursery and those that played their cards late held the advantage. Straightforward form.

NOTEBOOK

Ruthie Babe set off freely but was restrained behind the leaders until driven up in the final furlong where she had enough in reserve to find more when challenged. The least experienced runner in the field, she was relatively unexposed and got in on what looked a lenient mark for her handicap debut. She had nevertheless been steadily improving in her three previous runs, and although her best run was last time at Wolverhampton, she reportedly did not handle the bend there. This straight course suited her much better. (op 11-4 tchd 7-2 and 4-1 in a place)

Secret Millionaire(IRE), a dual winner at this trip, moved up travelling by far the best, but though he readily got the better of Leleyf directly on his inside, he found disappointingly little against the challenge of the doughty winner. He might just be in the grip of the handicapper now. (op 9-4, tchd 5-2 in places)

Dusty Spirit was slowly away but made up a good ground in the final furlong and was closing at the finish. On this evidence he should be up to winning a race if dropped in grade. (op 20-1 tchd 12-1)

Leleyf(IRE) raced prominently but was unable to get an easy lead and did too much too early. In any case, she looked to have a tough enough task off a 5lb higher rating than her last win. (op 4-1 tchd 7-2)

Mijas Playa showed early speed but was feeling the pace with a furlong still to go and this former course and distance winner looks to have gone off the boil. (op 8-1)

King's Approach(IRE) led early but, unable to get an easy lead, the pace was too strong and he began to struggle from halfway.

5909 TOTEPOOL H'CAP — 1m 4f (R)

3:55 (3:56) (Class 3) (0-95,93) 3-Y-O- £7,569 (£2,265; £1,132; £566; £282) Stalls Low

Form — RPR

-112 **1** **Petrovsky**[120] 2084 3-8-13 90 ... AdrianTNicholls 2 100+
(M Johnston) *mde all: edgd rt over 2f out: rdn wl over 1f out: r.o wl* **3/1[1]**

2044 **2** *2* **Sehoy (USA)**[23] 5216 3-8-6 83 ... RichardMullen 8 90
(J H M Gosden) *hld up: hdwy over 3f out: rdn and chsd wnr wl over 1f out: no imp fnl f* **8/1**

4320 **3** *1 1/4* **Resplendent Light**[25] 5170 4-9-1 86 ... FrederikTylicki(3) 1 91
(W R Muir) *a.p: nt clr run and swtchd lft over 2f out: rdn wl over 1f out: one pce fnl f* **4/1[2]**

6042 **4** *3/4* **Dance The Star (USA)**[39] 4644 4-9-1 88 ... MartinLane(5) 6 92
(D M Simcock) *s.i.s: hld up in rr: prog on outside over 3f out: rdn 2f out: one pce fnl f* **7/1**

2046 **5** *2 1/2* **Jabal Tariq**[9] 5641 4-8-13 81 ... TPO'Shea 7 81
(B W Hills) *hld up: sn in tch: chsd wnr over 3f out tl tl wl over 1f out: sn wknd* **10/1**

5121 **6** *shd* **Act Of Kalanisi (IRE)**[64] 3850 3-8-8 85 ... RoystonFfrench 3 85
(M Johnston) *hld up towards rr: pushed along 4f out: rdn over 2f out: sn struggling* **5/1**

-400 **7** *hd* **Camps Bay (USA)**[25] 5173 5-9-11 93 ... KirstyMilczarek 9 92
(Mrs A J Perrett) *hld up towards rr: effrt 3f out: hung lft fr over 2f out: btn over 1f out* **10/1**

0- **8** *14* **William Hogarth**[24] 6459 4-8-11 79 oh4 ... LiamJones 5 56
(W K Goldsworthy) *chsd wnr: rdn over 4f out: lost 2nd over 3f out: sn wknd* **33/1**

5 **9** *11* **South Wing (IRE)**[44] 4510 5-9-0 82 ... KFallon 4 41
(Eoin Griffin, Ire) *broke wl: sn stdd into mid-div: bhd fnl 4f: eased whn no ch over 1f out* **9/2[3]**

2m 33.92s (153.92)
WFA 3 from 4yo+ 9lb — **9** Ran SP% **124.6**
toteswingers: 1&2 £3.70, 1&3 £7.20, 2&3 £19.60. CSF £30.51 CT £102.14 TOTE £4.80: £2.00, £2.80, £1.90; EX 51.30.

Owner Sheikh Hamdan Bin Mohammed Al Maktoum **Bred** Gainsborough Stud Management Ltd **Trained** Middleham Moor, N Yorks

FOCUS

A good handicap for the grade but, when the market leader allowed to dictate a steady pace, the rest of the field were at a disadvantage. The winner did not need to improve on his Newmarket form.

NOTEBOOK

Petrovsky enjoyed himself in the lead and, typical of a Mark Johnston runner, found enough in reserve to repel the challengers when they loomed up two furlongs out. Despite running up a hat-trick of wins over the winter, this was his first success on turf. However, he had run second over this trip at Newmarket on his last start back in May and the 4lb rise in the weights did not look prohibitive, so as the market suggested, he was not winning out of turn. (tchd 100-30 and 4-1 in a place)

Sehoy(USA) might not have helped his cause by racing wide of the pack early on, but he looked a serious danger when challenging the winner two furlongs out until running out of steam in the final furlong. After several below-par efforts this was a step in the right direction, and he might improve again on a less testing track. (op 13-2)

Resplendent Light was in the process of making a challenge when getting squeezed out as a gap between the winner and Jabal Tariq closed, and he had to switch to the inside rail to continue his move. He was somewhat unlucky, losing around three lengths at a crucial stage, though it might not have been enough to overhaul the winner. (op 8-1)

Dance The Star(USA) missed the break but made some late progress. He ran his best race for some time on the all-weather at Kempton last month and once again hinted at a return to form. (op 8-1 tchd 13-2)

Jabal Tariq moved up around the final turn but his challenge petered out with two furlongs still to go. He may have gone for home too early, but ultimately was not favoured by the fast ground. (op 14-1)

Act Of Kalanisi(IRE) was held up against the inside rail and was caught out as the pace lifted two furlongs out, suggesting that the two miles over which he was successful at Chester last time might be more suitable. (op 9-2)

South Wing(IRE) Official explanation: jockey said gelding stopped very quickly

5910 TOTEEXACTA FILLIES' H'CAP — 1m 2f (R)

4:30 (4:30) (Class 4) (0-80,78) 3-Y-O+ £5,046 (£1,510; £755; £377; £188) Stalls Low

Form — RPR

2421 **1** **Some Sunny Day**[24] 5195 3-9-3 72 ... TravisBlock 6 79
(H Morrison) *chsd ldr after 2f: rdn over 2f out: led wl over 1f out: hld on wl ins fnl f* **6/1[2]**

0330 **2** *nk* **In Secret**[29] 5035 3-8-13 **68** .... JimmyQuinn 1 74
(J L Dunlop) *s.i.s: hld up in mid-div: rdn jst over 2f out: hdwy over 1f out: r.o u.p ins fnl f* **15/2**[3]
2045 **3** *1* **Rio Guru (IRE)**[44] 4495 4-9-4 **69** .... MCGeran(3) 9 73
(M R Channon) *s.i.s: hld up in rr: rdn wl over 2f out: hdwy on ins fnl f: tk 3rd post* **10/1**
51 **4** *nse* **Paisley**[23] 5215 3-9-4 **73** .... KFallon 3 77
(L M Cumani) *hld up in tch: pushed along over 3f out: rdn and ev ch jst ins fnl f: nt qckn* **8/11**[1]
-443 **5** *hd* **Nesayem (IRE)**[78] 3384 3-8-7 **67** .... MartinLane(5) 4 71
(D M Simcock) *hld up in mid-div: rdn 2f out: hdwy 1f out: nt qckn wl ins fnl f* **25/1**
2306 **6** *nk* **La Rosa Nostra**[22] 5243 4-9-8 **70** .... TPO'Shea 8 73
(W R Swinburn) *led: rdn over 2f out: hdd wl over 1f out: no ex ins fnl f* **14/1**
5310 **7** *2* **Bavarica**[39] 4658 7-9-2 **67** .... JackMitchell(3) 7 66
(Miss J Feilden) *s.i.s: hld up in rr: rdn over 2f out: nvr trbld ldrs* **18/1**
1553 **8** *3 1/4* **Sparkling Crystal (IRE)**[29] 5037 3-9-3 **75** .... PatrickHills(3) 2 67
(B W Hills) *chsd ldr 2f: prom: rdn over 2f out: wknd wl over 1f out* **10/1**

2m 8.41s (128.41)
WFA 3 from 4yo+ 7lb **8** Ran SP% **117.9**
toteswingers: 1&2 £6.00, 1&3 £7.00, 2&3 £9.40. CSF £51.44 CT £447.28 TOTE £5.90: £1.40, £2.10, £2.40; EX 81.10.
Owner Miss B Swire **Bred** Miss B Swire **Trained** East Ilsley, Berks

FOCUS
A tight handicap with six horses charging for the line from a furlong out and they were separated by less than two lengths at the finish. The winner was up 5lb on her previous AW form but this form is not entirely solid.

5911 PAT JACOBS AND NIGEL JONES H'CAP 5f
5:05 (5:07) (Class 6) (0-60,62) 3-Y-O+ **£2,590** (£770; £385; £192) **Stalls** High

Form RPR
0053 **1** **Milton Of Campsie**[13] 5518 4-9-2 **57** .... KFallon 10 67+
(J Balding) *hld up: sn in tch: led jst over 1f out: rdn ins fnl f: r.o wl* **13/8**[1]
0452 **2** *1 1/2* **Brandywell Boy (IRE)**[10] 5608 6-9-7 **62** .... RichardThomas 1 67
(D J S Ffrench Davis) *hld up: hdwy over 2f out: rdn and ev ch 1f out: nt qckn* **10/3**[2]
0450 **3** *nk* **Decider (USA)**[9] 5629 6-8-5 **46** oh1 .... (p) KirstyMilczarek 2 50
(R A Harris) *w ldrs: led wl over 1f out: sn rdn and hdd: no ex ins fnl f* **12/1**
020 **4** *shd* **Cocktail Party (IRE)**[9] 5629 3-8-5 **47** .... (t) LiamJones 6 51
(J W Hills) *hld up: stdy hdwy over 2f out: ev ch over 1f out: rdn and nt qckn ins fnl f* **14/1**
000 **5** *1 1/4* **Best One**[13] 5501 5-8-11 **52** .... (v) KevinGhunowa 4 51
(R A Harris) *hld up: hdwy over 2f out: rdn jst over 1f out: one pce* **8/1**[3]
5155 **6** *1* **Andrasta**[20] 5309 4-8-11 **52** .... RoystonFfrench 8 47
(S A Harris) *w ldr tl rdn wl over 1f out: wknd ins fnl f* **12/1**
0065 **7** *3/4* **Blakeshall Diamond**[13] 5525 4-7-12 **46** oh1 .... DannyBrock(7) 11 39
(A J Chamberlain) *led: hung lft over 2f out: hdd wl over 1f out: sn wknd* **20/1**
2560 **8** *2 1/4* **Namu**[11] 5576 6-8-13 **59** .... (p) SophieDoyle(5) 7 44
(Miss T Spearing) *played up in stalls: s.s: a in rr* **10/1**
00-0 **9** *3 1/4* **Bahama Baileys**[54] 4183 4-8-6 **50** .... (b) JackMitchell(3) 5 23
(C A Dwyer) *hld up in tch: pushed along 3f out: rdn and wknd wl over 1f out: eased wl ins fnl f* **14/1**
10 *2 3/4* **Papa Power (IRE)**[710] 5961 6-8-5 **46** oh1 .... (t) JimmyQuinn 3 9
(K M Prendergast) *stdd s: t.k.h in rr: rdn wl over 1f out: no rspnse: eased whn no ch ins fnl f* **8/1**[3]

57.43 secs (57.43)
WFA 3 from 4yo+ 1lb **10** Ran SP% **126.0**
toteswingers: 1&2 £2.70, 1&3 £9.60, 2&3 £10.50. CSF £7.55 CT £53.90 TOTE £2.50: £1.20, £1.70, £4.50; EX 7.70 Place 6: £42.34 Place 5: £9.21.
Owner Willie McKay **Bred** Slatch Farm Stud **Trained** Scrooby, Notts

FOCUS
A moderate sprint handicap.
Namu Official explanation: jockey said mare missed the break
T/Plt: £115.30 to a £1 stake. Pool: £49,696.67. 314.54 winning tickets. T/Qpdt: £21.60 to a £1 stake. Pool: £4,046.67. 138.30 winning tickets. KH

5874 GOODWOOD (R-H)
Sunday, September 13

OFFICIAL GOING: Good to firm (8.9)
Wind: Brisk, half-behind. Weather: Cloudy

5912 TOTESWINGER STKS (H'CAP) 1m 4f
1:30 (1:30) (Class 4) (0-85,82) 3-Y-O+ **£5,180** (£1,541; £770; £384) **Stalls** High

Form RPR
3065 **1** **Trachonitis (IRE)**[39] 4670 5-8-13 **67** .... AdrianMcCarthy 8 76
(J R Jenkins) *stdd s: hld up last: plld wd 3f out: rapid prog and swept by field fr over 2f out to ld over 1f out: rdn out* **16/1**
5404 **2** *1 1/4* **Dove Cottage (IRE)**[13] 5532 7-8-12 **66** .... FergusSweeney 3 73
(W S Kittow) *taken down early: led at mod pce: drew 4 l clr 4f out: rdn and hdd over 1f out: styd on same pce* **11/2**[3]
-140 **3** *1* **Cosmea**[32] 4903 4-9-13 **81** .... DaneO'Neill 2 86
(A King) *s.i.s: hld up in 4th: clsd on ldrs fr 3f out: rdn and nt qckn 2f out: styd on again fr over 1f out* **8/1**
4 *nk* **Nampour (FR)**[232] 4-10-0 **82** .... PhilipRobinson 7 87
(P J Hobbs) *chsd ldr: pushed along to cl fr 3f out: nt qckn and lost 2nd 2f out: styd on again fnl f* **7/2**[1]
4113 **5** *1 3/4* **Turjuman (USA)**[29] 5034 4-8-13 **67** .... ChrisCatlin 4 69
(W J Musson) *trckd ldng pair: clsd over 2f out: jst pushed along and stl disputing 3rd over 1f out: fdd fnl f* **9/2**[2]
110 **6** *1 3/4* **Alicante**[44] 4506 3-8-9 **72** .... SebSanders 6 71
(Sir Mark Prescott) *in tch in midfield: drvn 3f out: sn outpcd: nvr on terms after* **7/2**[1]
3141 **7** *3/4* **Wee Charlie Castle (IRE)**[14] 5469 6-9-10 **78** .... TomEaves 5 76
(I Semple) *taken down early: s.i.s: in tch in rr: rdn 3f out: outpcd fr over 2f out: nvr on terms after* **13/2**
00-5 **8** *20* **Dani's Girl (IRE)**[13] 5509 6-9-13 **81** .... IanMongan 1 47
(P M Phelan) *s.v.s: sn in tch: wnt 5th 5f out: rdn over 3f out: wknd rapidly over 1f out: eased: t.o* **14/1**

2m 38.5s (0.10) **Going Correction** -0.075s/f (Good)
WFA 3 from 4yo+ 9lb **8** Ran SP% **115.0**
Speed ratings (Par 105): **96,95,94,94,93 91,91,78**
toteswingers: 1&2 £19.90, 1&3 £19.30, 2&3 £9.00. CSF £101.28 CT £766.70 TOTE £20.80: £4.20, £2.40, £2.80; EX 119.40.
Owner Mr & Mrs C Schwick **Bred** D H W Dobson **Trained** Royston, Herts

FOCUS
Drying conditions, including a strong wind blowing across the track into the stands, resulted in a change in the going to good to firm all round. The winner only had to run somewhere near this year's form to take this somewhat muddling event.

5913 GG CLUB PARTY JUVENILE STKS (NURSERY H'CAP) 7f
2:00 (2:02) (Class 4) (0-85,85) 2-Y-O **£4,857** (£1,445; £722; £360) **Stalls** High

Form RPR
4212 **1** **Astonishment (IRE)**[22] 5265 2-9-2 **80** .... AdamKirby 6 84+
(S Kirk) *chsd ldr: hrd rdn 2f out: clsd u.p to ld last 150yds: sn in command* **3/1**[2]
245 **2** *1 1/4* **Cansili Star**[32] 4900 2-9-2 **80** .... PhilipRobinson 1 81
(M A Jarvis) *led: gng best 2f out: shkn up over 1f out: hdd and nt qckn last 150yds* **4/1**[3]
0304 **3** *1* **Sheer Force (IRE)**[24] 5191 2-8-8 **72** .... HayleyTurner 7 70
(W J Knight) *s.v.s: sn in tch in last: plld wd over 2f out: hrd rdn and prog after: styd on to take 3rd ins fnl f* **12/1**
U013 **4** *1 3/4* **Kurtanella**[24] 5187 2-9-7 **85** .... DaneO'Neill 9 79
(R Hannon) *chsd ldng pair: rdn and no imp over 1f out: fdd ins fnl f and lost 3rd* **7/1**
1545 **5** *1 1/2* **Pintura**[8] 5658 2-8-8 **72** .... ChrisCatlin 2 62
(M R Channon) *trckd ldng trio: rdn to dispute 3rd over 1f out: nt qckn and no imp after: wknd fnl f* **9/4**[1]
5250 **6** *shd* **Chairman Pat (USA)**[23] 5213 2-8-4 **73** .... RossAtkinson(5) 5 63
(Tom Dascombe) *hld up in last trio but wl in tch: rdn over 2f out: hanging rt after and no imp on ldrs* **16/1**
0060 **7** *3* **Campaigner**[9] 5635 2-7-12 **69** oh16 ow7 .... KierenFox(7) 4 52
(J W Hills) *hld up in 8th: rdn over 2f out: no prog* **100/1**
6443 **8** *3/4* **Orsett Lad (USA)**[38] 4699 2-8-9 **73** .... RobertHavlin 3 54
(J R Best) *wl in tch in abt 5th: effrt to dispute 3rd 2f out: shkn up and nt qckn over 1f out: sn wknd* **20/1**
13 **9** *30* **Gobama**[15] 5440 2-8-12 **76** .... SebSanders 8 —
(J W Hills) *dwlt: hld up in 6th: lost pl 2f out and sn heavily eased: t.o* **8/1**

1m 27.05s (-0.35) **Going Correction** -0.075s/f (Good) **9** Ran SP% **118.7**
Speed ratings (Par 97): **99,97,96,94,92 92,89,88,54**
toteswingers: 1&2 £4.70, 1&3 £7.70, 2&3 £9.20. CSF £16.03 CT £127.96 TOTE £3.90: £1.50, £2.00, £2.50; EX 19.70.
Owner Mrs Barbara Facchino **Bred** Barouche Stud (ire) Ltd **Trained** Upper Lambourn, Berks

FOCUS
A fair nursery, but the pace was ordinary and the race was dominated by those that raced prominently.

NOTEBOOK
Astonishment(IRE), proven at the trip and raised 1lb for his solid effort on his nursery debut at Sandown last time, was always on the shoulder of the leader and quickened up well to seize the initiative inside the last furlong. He was one of the more exposed runners in the race, but he remains at the top of his game and should find other opportunities. (op 4-1)
Cansili Star had been rather disappointing in two starts since chasing home the smart Showcasing on his Yarmouth debut and had not seemed to stay this trip in his only previous try, though that was on easier ground than this. Making his nursery debut, he had the run of the race out in front and kept on well, but couldn't cope with the winner's turn of foot. Stamina didn't seem to be an issue on this sounder surface. (op 7-2 tchd 5-1 and 11-2 in a place)
Sheer Force(IRE), who had pulled hard in his last couple of starts after showing ability in his first two outings, was another making his nursery debut and he deserves extra credit for finishing as close as he did. Firstly, he was very awkward exiting the stalls and gave his rivals a start, and then once in line for home was forced to circle the entire field in order to get a run. He fared much the best of those that tried to come from off the pace and can win a similar event if building on this.
Official explanation: jockey said colt missed the break (op 11-1 tchd 10-1)
Kurtanella, third of four in a moderately run contest on her first try over this trip at Epsom last time, raced handily and had every chance but her stamina for the distance still remains unproven. (op 6-1 tchd 8-1)
Pintura, back over a more suitable trip, was close enough if good enough, but failed to pick up as well as might have been expected. Although forced to race a little wide from a low draw, this was still rather disappointing. (op 3-1)
Chairman Pat(USA), who failed to see out 1m at Salisbury last time, made a brief effort on the outside once into the straight, but was hanging inside the last furlong and did not look comfortable. (op 20-1)
Orsett Lad(USA) didn't help his chances by taking a grip early but still ran moderately. (op 22-1)
Gobama never got into it and was eased right off inside the last 2f, as though something were amiss. Official explanation: jockey said filly hung badly left (tchd 15-2 and 9-1)

5914 VINTAGEATGOODWOOD.COM STKS (H'CAP) 1m
2:35 (2:35) (Class 4) (0-85,92) 3-Y-O+ **£5,180** (£1,541; £770; £384) **Stalls** High

Form RPR
2121 **1** **Kaolak (USA)**[14] 5475 3-10-0 **92** .... (v) ChrisCatlin 10 100
(J Ryan) *trckd ldr: rdn over 2f out: clsd and upsides over 1f out: drvn ahd ins fnl f: jst hld on* **9/2**[2]
1-52 **2** *nse* **Truism**[15] 5448 3-9-7 **85** .... PhilipRobinson 1 93
(Mrs A J Perrett) *racd wd early: hld up in 7th: prog over 2f out: urged along to cl over 1f out: wnt 2nd last 75yds and clsd on wnr: jst failed* **6/1**[3]
4254 **3** *3/4* **Barliffey (IRE)**[30] 5003 4-8-12 **71** .... (v) SebSanders 3 78
(D J Coakley) *v s.i.s and reminders to get in tch in last: u.p again fr 1/2-way: prog on outer over 2f out: styd on wl to take 3rd nr fin* **8/1**
-221 **4** *1/2* **Jesse James (IRE)**[27] 5100 3-9-9 **87** .... RobertHavlin 8 92
(J H M Gosden) *trckd ldrs: poised in bhd 3f out gng wl: rdn and nt qckn 2f out: styd on fnl f but unable to chal* **3/1**[1]
0420 **5** *hd* **Cape Hawk (IRE)**[5] 5746 5-9-9 **82** .... DaneO'Neill 5 87
(R Hannon) *sn trckd ldng trio: rdn over 2f out: nt qckn wl over 1f out: styd on but nvr able to mount a chal* **9/1**
2212 **6** *1/2* **Carbon Hoofprint**[22] 5243 3-9-3 **81** .... FergusSweeney 11 84
(P J Makin) *mde most: rdn 2f out: jnd over 1f out: hdd ins fnl f: lost several pls nr fin* **9/2**[2]
6U03 **7** *6* **South Cape**[5] 5746 6-9-4 **82** .... (p) MatthewDavies(5) 2 72
(G L Moore) *wl in tch: rdn over 2f out: wknd wl over 1f out* **9/1**
0000 **8** *1 1/2* **Prince Of Thebes (IRE)**[8] 5663 8-8-1 **67** .... (v) KierenFox(7) 9 53
(M J Attwater) *trckd ldng pair to over 2f out: sn wknd* **16/1**
0000 **9** *10* **Alfresco**[9] 5646 5-9-2 **75** .... (b) GregFairley 4 37
(J R Best) *plld hrd: hld up in 8th: rdn over 3f out: sn wknd: t.o* **33/1**

1m 37.28s (-2.62) **Going Correction** -0.075s/f (Good)
WFA 3 from 4yo+ 5lb **9** Ran SP% **115.6**
Speed ratings (Par 105): **110,109,109,108,108 108,102,100,90**
toteswingers: 1&2 £5.00, 1&3 £5.90, 2&3 £10.00. CSF £31.67 CT £211.02 TOTE £4.90: £1.80, £1.90, £2.60; EX 25.90.
Owner Simon Kerr **Bred** Mr And Mrs Robert Courtney Sr Et Al **Trained** Newmarket, Suffolk

FOCUS
This race threatened to be run at a good pace with a number in the line-up who like to force the issue, but as it turned out they didn't go mad up front and there was something of a bunch finish. A decent race for the grade, and the form looks sound.
Carbon Hoofprint Official explanation: jockey said he lost an iron leaving stalls

5915 TURFTV STKS (H'CAP) 1m 1f 192y
3:10 (3:11) (Class 4) (0-85,82) 3-Y-0+ **£5,180** (£1,541; £770; £384) **Stalls** High

Form RPR

1603 **1** **Featherweight (IRE)**[27] 5101 3-9-1 **76**............................ MichaelHills 3 85
(B W Hills) *mde all: set mod pce to 4f out but untrbld by rivals: shkn up and drew 2 l clr 2f out: unchal after* **10/3**[1]

4020 **2** *2* **Oriental Girl**[13] 5503 4-8-9 **63** oh4..............................(v) RobertHavlin 6 68
(J A Geake) *t.k.h: prom: prog over 2f out: rdn to chse wnr wl over 1f out: styd on but no imp* **25/1**

0605 **3** *1* **Humble Opinion**[20] 5321 7-9-8 **76**.........................(b[1]) FergusSweeney 7 79
(A King) *t.k.h: hld up in last trio: gng strly 3f out: prog over 2f out: styd on fr over 1f out to take 3rd ins fnl f: too much to do* **9/1**

003 **4** *nk* **Royal Amnesty**[64] 3847 6-9-9 **77**...................................(b) TomEaves 5 79+
(I Semple) *hld up last in modly run r: stl last and bhd wall of rivals 2f out: swtchd outside and prog over 1f out: r.o fnl f: hopeless task* **7/1**[3]

3410 **5** *¾* **Hallingdal (UAE)**[10] 5602 4-8-9 **70**............................ RyanClark[(7)] 9 71
(J J Bridger) *dwlt: sn in midfield: prog on inner 1/2-way: chsd wnr 3f out to wl over 1f out: wknd ins fnl f* **16/1**

0066 **6** *hd* **Goodwood Starlight (IRE)**[13] 5509 4-9-8 **76**..............(t) DaneO'Neill 11 77
(G L Moore) *hld up in abt 8th in modly run r: wl in rr 2f out: prog on outer over 1f out: styd on: too much to do* **11/1**

6503 **7** *nk* **Ramona Chase**[13] 5510 4-10-0 **82**...................................... AdamKirby 8 82
(M J Attwater) *stdd s: hld up in last quartet in modly run r: effrt on inner over 2f out: drvn and styd on fnl f: too much to do* **6/1**[2]

0442 **8** *hd* **Dreamwalk (IRE)**[22] 5244 3-9-5 **80**...............................(v) SebSanders 1 80
(R M Beckett) *t.k.h: hld up in last trio: prog on outer wl over 2f out: drvn to try to cl over 1f out: wknd fnl f* **7/1**[3]

3210 **9** *2* **Voortrekker**[44] 4481 3-8-12 **73**................................ HayleyTurner 13 69
(D J Coakley) *s.i.s: pushed up and sn prom: disp 2nd 3f out to over 2f out: fdd over 1f out* **11/1**

4410 **10** *nk* **Supercast (IRE)**[71] 3635 6-9-3 **76**............................ AshleyMorgan[(5)] 4 71
(F Sheridan) *snatched up in midfield after 1f: effrt on outer over 2f out: drvn to try to cl over 1f out: sn wknd* **12/1**

5545 **11** *4 ½* **Hip Hip Hooray**[10] 5616 3-8-6 **67**...................................... ChrisCatlin 12 53
(L A Dace) *prom tl wknd wl over 2f out* **14/1**

3-0 **12** *1 ¾* **Colangnik (USA)**[42] 4569 3-8-6 **70**.............................. MarcHalford[(3)] 2 52
(J R Best) *sn chsd wnr: rdn and wknd 3f out* **33/1**

2m 8.27s (0.27) **Going Correction** -0.075s/f (Good)
WFA 3 from 4yo+ 7lb 12 Ran SP% **116.1**
Speed ratings (Par 105): **95,93,92,92,91 91,91,91,89,89 85,84**
toteswingers: 1&2 £17.70, 1&3 £7.30, 2&3 £62.10. CSF £94.98 CT £691.35 TOTE £3.70: £1.70, £7.00, £3.90; EX 123.80.
Owner Jeremy Gompertz & Patrick Milmo **Bred** Jeremy Gompertz **Trained** Lambourn, Berks
■ Stewards' Enquiry : Ashley Morgan two-day ban: careless riding (Sep 27-28)

FOCUS
This looked a fairly competitive affair on paper, but the winner was given an easy time of things in front. The sets the standard and the form is less than solid.

5916 GOODWOOD REVIVAL 18-20 SEPTEMBER STKS (H'CAP) 6f
3:45 (3:45) (Class 4) (0-85,83) 3-Y-0+
£4,984 (£1,492; £746; £373; £186; £93) **Stalls** Low

Form RPR

2064 **1** **Mutamared (USA)**[8] 5676 9-9-3 **75**...........................(t) StephenCarson 9 82
(Andrew Reid) *mde virtually all in middle of crse: modest pce to 1/2-way: jnd over 2f out: drvn over 1f out: battled on wl fnl f* **20/1**

0321 **2** *hd* **Equinine (IRE)**[10] 5599 3-8-10 **70**.............................. MichaelHills 4 76
(B W Hills) *w ldrs: jnd wnr over 1f out: upsides ent fnl f: nt qckn and a jst hld last 100yds* **5/1**

1516 **3** *1 ¾* **Shangani**[26] 5130 3-9-0 **81**.. AmyScott[(7)] 8 82
(H Candy) *pressed wnr and racd middle: upsides and rdn over 2f out to over 1f out: one pce fnl f* **11/2**

625 **4** *1 ¼* **Sweet Gale (IRE)**[3] 5810 5-9-1 **73**...................................... SebSanders 7 70
(Mike Murphy) *s.s: no trble in rcvring and cl up after 2f: w ldrs over 1f out towards far rail: fdd fnl f* **9/2**[3]

5030 **5** *1* **Bahamian Lad**[44] 4507 4-9-0 **72**...................................... DaneO'Neill 5 66
(R Hollinshead) *cl up: easily outpcd fr 2f out: n.d after* **12/1**

0541 **6** *nk* **Indian Skipper (IRE)**[21] 5288 4-8-13 **76**................(p) AshleyMorgan[(5)] 3 69
(M H Tompkins) *dwlt: hld up in last: outpcd 2f out: rdn over 1f out: plugged on: no ch* **4/1**[2]

4213 **7** *1 ¼* **My Kingdom (IRE)**[10] 5592 3-9-9 **83**............................(t) HayleyTurner 1 72
(H Morrison) *racd clst of field to nr side rail: in tch: rdn and nt qckn wl over 1f out: sn outpcd* **10/3**[1]

1020 **8** *2* **Highland Harvest**[30] 5001 5-9-1 **73**.............................. RobertHavlin 2 55
(Jamie Poulton) *hld up bhd ldrs: rdn and outpcd fr 2f out: fdd* **10/1**

1m 11.5s (-0.70) **Going Correction** -0.075s/f (Good)
WFA 3 from 4yo+ 2lb 8 Ran SP% **114.9**
Speed ratings (Par 105): **101,100,98,96,95 95,93,90**
toteswingers: 1&2 £10.20, 1&3 £13.20, 2&3 £4.70. CSF £116.81 CT £641.03 TOTE £22.30: £4.00, £1.70, £2.40; EX 57.50.
Owner A S Reid **Bred** E J Hudson Jr, Irrevocable Trust & Kilroy T'Bred **Trained** Mill Hill, London NW7

FOCUS
They came up the centre of the track in this sprint handicap and the early pace wasn't breakneck. Prominent racers were favoured again and the form is ordinary.

5917 RACING UK ON SKY 432 STKS (H'CAP) 2m
4:20 (4:20) (Class 4) (0-85,85) 3-Y-0+ **£5,180** (£1,541; £770; £384) **Stalls** Low

Form RPR

1021 **1** **Rotative**[33] 4882 4-10-0 **85**.. AdamKirby 5 96+
(W R Swinburn) *cl up in 3rd: pushed along and effrt over 3f out: led wl over 2f out: hrd rdn and styd on wl whn pressed fnl 2f* **9/2**[3]

6045 **2** *½* **Wicked Daze (IRE)**[22] 5252 6-9-7 **78**..........................(v) HayleyTurner 4 88
(K A Ryan) *t.k.h early: hld up in 4th: effrt to chse wnr over 2f out: hrd rdn and styd on: nvr quite able to chal* **3/1**[1]

1604 **3** *5* **Inchpast**[9] 5642 8-8-6 **68**...(b) AshleyMorgan[(5)] 3 72
(M H Tompkins) *hld up in 6th: rdn over 3f out: sn outpcd: kpt on fnl 2f to take 3rd nr fin* **8/1**

-046 **4** *¾* **Absolut Power (GER)**[46] 4417 8-9-2 **73**........................ RobertHavlin 6 76
(J A Geake) *led to wl over 2f out: steadily outpcd: lost 3rd nr fin* **7/1**

5142 **5** *9* **Hawridge King**[22] 5252 7-9-7 **78**................................ FergusSweeney 7 70
(W S Kittow) *hld up in 5th: reminder wl over 4f out: effrt to chse ldrs over 2f out: sn rdn and wknd* **4/1**[2]

6040 **6** *1 ¾* **Casual Garcia**[18] 5339 4-8-9 **66** oh1.................................(b) SebSanders 2 56
(Sir Mark Prescott) *s.s: hld up last: effrt on inner and in tch wl over 2f out: sn rdn and wknd* **12/1**

2513 **7** *4* **Alnwick**[18] 5346 5-9-8 **79**.. DaneO'Neill 1 64
(P D Cundell) *chsd ldr to over 3f out: wknd rapidly* **4/1**[2]

3m 26.97s (-2.03) **Going Correction** -0.075s/f (Good) 7 Ran SP% **114.5**
Speed ratings (Par 105): **102,101,99,98,94 93,91**
toteswingers: 1&2 £4.00, 1&3 £9.20, 2&3 £5.60. CSF £18.44 TOTE £5.90: £3.20, £2.10; EX 17.60.
Owner Pendley Farm **Bred** Pendley Farm **Trained** Aldbury, Herts
■ Stewards' Enquiry : Adam Kirby one-day ban: used whip in incorrect place (Sep 29)

FOCUS
A fair staying handicap. It was steadily run and the form is tricky to pin down, but there are positives to be taken from the front pair.

5918 TURFTV FOR BETTING SHOPS STKS (H'CAP) 7f
4:55 (4:57) (Class 4) (0-85,89) 3-Y-0+ **£5,180** (£1,541; £770; £384) **Stalls** High

Form RPR

0061 **1** **Mujood**[5] 5746 6-9-9 **89** 6ex..................................(v) AndrewHeffernan[(7)] 6 96
(Eve Johnson Houghton) *hld up bhd ldrs: smooth prog over 2f out: led wl over 1f out: rdn out and a doing enough fnl f* **4/1**[2]

2531 **2** *1* **Belle Des Airs (IRE)**[4] 5774 3-9-11 **88** 6ex...................... SebSanders 4 90
(R M Beckett) *led at decent pce: shkn up over 2f out: hdd wl over 1f out and sn nt qckn in 3rd: kpt on to regain 2nd ins fnl f* **3/1**[1]

4464 **3** *½* **Salient**[14] 5476 5-9-4 **84**.. KierenFox[(7)] 7 87
(M J Attwater) *trckd ldrs: shkn up over 2f out: effrt to chal and w wnr wl over 1f out: sn hld: lost 2nd ins fnl f* **3/1**[1]

3541 **4** *1 ½* **Ivory Lace**[26] 5124 8-9-2 **75**.. HayleyTurner 3 74
(S Woodman) *stdd s: hld up in last pair: effrt on outer over 2f out: hanging rt after: kpt on to take 4th ins fnl f* **9/1**[3]

-104 **5** *1 ½* **Perfect Pride (USA)**[14] 5471 3-9-7 **84**.............................. AdamKirby 5 77
(C G Cox) *stdd s: hld up in last pair: rdn over 2f out: one pce and no real prog* **4/1**[2]

3505 **6** *nse* **Daddy's Gift (IRE)**[4] 5774 3-9-4 **81**................................(v[1]) DaneO'Neill 1 74
(R Hannon) *t.k.h: trckd ldr to jst over 2f out: grad wknd* **11/1**

5060 **7** *3 ¼* **Sam's Cross (IRE)**[3] 5813 4-8-0 **66** oh5 ow1............ RyanClark[(7)] 8 52
(J J Bridger) *t.k.h: trckd ldr to over 2f out: wknd* **16/1**

1m 25.84s (-1.56) **Going Correction** -0.075s/f (Good)
WFA 3 from 4yo+ 4lb 7 Ran SP% **114.2**
Speed ratings (Par 105): **105,103,103,101,99 99,96**
toteswingers: 1&2 £3.50, 1&3 £3.40, 2&3 £2.60. CSF £16.38 CT £39.99 TOTE £5.90: £2.90, £1.70; EX 21.20.
Owner Eden Racing **Bred** Bloomsbury Stud & The Hon Sir David Sieff **Trained** Blewbury, Oxon

FOCUS
An ordinary handicap but five of these had won at this track before. Straightforward form.

5919 TOTEEXACTA STKS (H'CAP) 5f
5:30 (5:31) (Class 4) (0-85,85) 3-Y-0+ **£5,180** (£1,541; £770; £384) **Stalls** Low

Form RPR

0535 **1** **Ocean Blaze**[4] 5767 5-8-9 **72**.. ChrisCatlin 5 78
(B R Millman) *mde all: hrd rdn and drifted rt fr 2f out: jnd fnl f: hld on u.p* **9/2**[3]

0512 **2** *hd* **Cape Royal**[2] 5830 9-8-4 **74**...(bt) RyanClark[(7)] 9 79
(J M Bradley) *racd alone in centre: on terms w ldrs: pushed along fr 2f out: upsides whn wnr drifted across to join him ins fnl f: kpt on wl: jst hld* **4/1**[2]

6341 **3** *nk* **Lenny Bee**[15] 5436 3-9-7 **85**.. PhillipMakin 3 89
(D H Brown) *chsd ldrs: rdn 2f out: nt on terms 1f out: styd on against nr side rail to take 3rd nr fin* **11/4**[1]

0306 **4** *½* **Our Piccadilly (IRE)**[24] 5183 4-9-0 **77**.......................... FergusSweeney 4 79
(W S Kittow) *hld up in last trio: effrt 2f out: chsd ldng pair ins fnl f: kpt on but lost 3rd nr fin* **13/2**

034 **5** *¾* **Peopleton Brook**[13] 5525 7-8-3 **66** oh13........................(t) HayleyTurner 6 65
(B G Powell) *chsd ldrs: rdn 1/2-way: tried to cl over 1f out: kpt on one pce* **16/1**

4406 **6** *½* **Rocketball (IRE)**[13] 5518 4-8-1 **71** oh4 ow5.......... AndrewHeffernan[(7)] 2 69
(Mrs L Williamson) *pressed wnr to over 1f out: fdd ins fnl f* **28/1**

3305 **7** *nk* **Efistorm**[4] 5768 8-9-5 **82**.. SebSanders 8 79
(C R Dore) *sn in last trio: rdn over 2f out: plugged on fr over 1f out but nvr gng pce to threaten* **13/2**

3204 **8** *¾* **Requisite**[25] 5149 4-8-1 **71**..(v) AmyScott[(7)] 1 65
(I A Wood) *a struggling to keep up w the pce in last trio: plugged on fnl f: n.d* **16/1**

12/0 **9** *5* **Jimmy Ryan (IRE)**[22] 5263 8-9-8 **85**................................ AdamKirby 7 61
(T D McCarthy) *taken down early and walked to post: chsd ldrs: rdn and hung rt over 1f out: wknd rapidly fnl f* **16/1**

57.57 secs (-0.83) **Going Correction** -0.075s/f (Good)
WFA 3 from 4yo+ 1lb 9 Ran SP% **112.6**
Speed ratings (Par 105): **103,102,102,101,100 99,98,97,89**
toteswingers: 1&2 £5.30, 1&3 £4.40, 2&3 £3.60. CSF £22.15 CT £57.49 TOTE £5.80: £2.20, £1.70, £1.50; EX 23.70 Place 6 £600.56, Place 5 £114.59..
Owner Gary Hancock (Staffs) **Bred** Longdon Stud And Robin Lawson **Trained** Kentisbeare, Devon

FOCUS
Apart from Cape Royal, who came up the centre of the track, the rest of the field tended to race more towards the stands' rail. The performance of the Milton Bradley-trained gelding showed that there was little bias, though. All four sprints over the two-day meeting were won by the pacesetter. This is slightly suspect form with the fifth and sixth out of the weights.
T/Jkpt: Not won. T/Plt: £400.30 to a £1 stake. Pool: £62,220.15. 113.45 winning tickets. T/Qpdt: £38.70 to a £1 stake. Pool: £5,474.21. 104.46 winning tickets. JN

5920 - (Foreign Racing) - See Raceform Interactive

5889 CURRAGH (R-H)
Sunday, September 13

OFFICIAL GOING: Soft

5921a IRISH DAILY MIRROR RENAISSANCE STKS (GROUP 3) 6f
2:45 (2:45) 3-Y-0+ **£40,407** (£11,825; £5,611; £1,883)

RPR

1 **Snaefell (IRE)**[14] 5491 5-9-3 **106**...(b[1]) FMBerry 6 111
(M Halford, Ire) *hld up in rr: pushed along 2f out: rdn into 3rd 1f out: styd on to ld last 100yds: kpt on wl* **8/1**

2 2 1/2 **Girouette (IRE)**[28] 5079 4-9-3 105 .... MCHussey 5 103
(Tracey Collins, Ire) *chsd ldrs in 3rd: rdn to ld 2f out: kpt on fr over 1f out: hdd last 100yds and no ex* **10/3**[3]

3 2 **Alexander Youth (IRE)**[74] 3516 3-8-12 86 .... WMLordan 2 94
(David Wachman, Ire) *settled bhd ldrs: 5th 1/2-way: rdn in 6th 2f out: in rr over 1f out: kpt on to go 3rd ins fnl f: no imp on ldrs* **20/1**

4 3/4 **Royal Rock**[106] 2481 5-9-3 .... GeorgeBaker 1 94
(C F Wall) *chsd ldrs in 4th: rdn into 2nd over 1f out: no ex fnl f and kpt on same pce* **5/2**[1]

5 1/2 **Vocalised (USA)**[28] 5079 3-9-6 111 .... (t) KJManning 8 98
(J S Bolger, Ire) *hld up towards rr: pushed along 1/2-way: 5th 2f out: no ex fr 1f out: kpt on same pce fnl f* **5/1**

6 4 1/2 **Danehill Destiny**[65] 3824 3-8-12 .... (t) JMurtagh 4 75
(W J Haggas) *led: hdd 2f out: rdn in 2nd 1 1/2f out: no ex in 4th 1f out: wknd fnl f* **3/1**[2]

7 3 1/2 **Undaunted Affair (IRE)**[126] 1918 3-8-12 .... PJSmullen 3 64
(K A Ryan) *chsd ldr in 2nd: rdn in 3rd 1 1/2f out: no ex over 1f out: wknd fnl f* **14/1**

1m 15.91s (1.21) **Going Correction** +0.55s/f (Yiel)
WFA 3 from 4yo+ 2lb 7 Ran SP% **115.9**
Speed ratings: **113,109,107,106,105 99,94**
CSF £35.65 TOTE £7.30: £2.80, £2.20; DF 15.30.
Owner Lady Clague **Bred** Newberry Stud Farm **Trained** the Curragh, Co Kildare

FOCUS
A race run at a good pace thanks to Danehill Destiny. It has been rated at face value for now, with the runner-up the best guide.

NOTEBOOK
Snaefell(IRE), fitted with blinkers for the first time, came from behind and ran on well to get on top and go clear in the closing stages. It was his seventh win and the blinkers seemed to do the trick. (op 9/1)
Girouette(IRE) handles testing ground well and, after going to the front over 2f out, looked as if she might steal a march on her rivals. However, the winner proved too strong for her well inside the final furlong. (op 7/2 tchd 3/1)
Alexander Youth(IRE), back from a break and dropping down in trip, chased the leaders and kept on inside the final furlong without ever holding a winning chance having had only one rival behind her 2f out.
Royal Rock, having his first run since May, went second under pressure over 1f out before finding no extra inside the last. He might have found the ground too testing following his long break. (op 5/2 tchd 2/1)
Vocalised(USA), whose four wins over 7f included the Greenham Stakes and the Tetrarch Stakes early this season, was dropped to this trip here last month having had a three-month break. Held up in rear, he was driven along at halfway and gave the impression that a return to 7f will suit. (op 9/2)

5924a SOLONAWAY STKS (GROUP 3) 1m
4:15 (4:15) 3-Y-0+ £39,126 (£11,436; £5,417; £1,805)

RPR

1 **Border Patrol**[108] 2411 3-9-1 .... KJManning 2 115
(R Charlton) *settled bhd ldrs: hdwy in 4th 3f out: travelled wl in 3rd 2f out: rdn to take narrow ld 1f out: kpt on wl u.p fnl f* **3/1**[3]

2 nk **Poet**[8] 5685 4-9-9 116 .... JMurtagh 6 118
(A P O'Brien, Ire) *led: rdn over 2f out: narrowly hdd 1f out: kpt on: no ex cl home* **2/1**[1]

3 3 1/2 **Zafisio (IRE)**[98] 2756 3-9-1 .... GrahamGibbons 1 106+
(R Curtis) *chsd ldrs in 3rd: rdn in 5th 2f out: u.p in 6th 1f out: kpt on same pce fnl f* **16/1**

4 1 **Rayeni (IRE)**[113] 2288 3-9-1 113 .... MJKinane 4 104+
(John M Oxx, Ire) *chsd ldr in 2nd: rdn 2f out: no ex in 3rd over 1f out: kpt on same pce fnl f* **9/4**[2]

5 shd **Lahaleeb (IRE)**[42] 4580 3-9-1 .... DarryllHolland 5 103
(M R Channon) *hld up towards rr: nt clr run fr under 2f out: swtchd ins fnl f and kpt on wl wout threatening* **13/2**

6 1 1/2 **Libano (IRE)**[147] 1393 3-9-4 .... PJSmullen 8 103
(D K Weld, Ire) *hld up towards rr: clsr in 6th 2f out: rdn and no ex in 5th over 1f out: kpt on one pce* **14/1**

7 3/4 **Chintz (IRE)**[14] 5487 3-8-12 96 .... (p) WMLordan 7 95
(David Wachman, Ire) *chsd ldrs: 4th 1/2-way: rdn 2f out: no ex over 1f out* **33/1**

8 3 1/2 **King Jock (USA)**[22] 5249 8-9-6 100 .... (b[1]) MCHussey 3 91
(R J Osborne, Ire) *chsd ldrs: 5th 1/2-way: rdn and dropped to rr over 2f out: no imp* **33/1**

1m 48.08s (6.18) **Going Correction** +0.825s/f (Soft)
WFA 3 from 4yo+ 5lb 8 Ran SP% **120.9**
Speed ratings: **102,101,98,97,97 95,94,91**
CSF £10.09 TOTE £4.20: £1.10, £1.50, £4.10; DF 11.40.
Owner Elite Racing Club **Bred** Elite Racing Club **Trained** Beckhampton, Wilts

FOCUS
A very good Group 3 contest. The in-form runner-up sets the standard, while the fifth looked very unlucky.

NOTEBOOK
Border Patrol was fancied by connections to land this Group 3 event and he obliged at the expense of the Ballydoyle favourite. This was his first start for 108 days and, always travelling, he got the better of front-running Poet inside the final furlong. Despite tiring in this ground and idling in the closing stages according to his jockey, he stuck to his task well to record his fourth consecutive victory for Roger Charlton. The son of Selkirk should be open to some improvement and better ground should help his cause. Charlton will consider a trip to Longchamp over Arc weekend, as he feels the colt could make a Group 1 horse. The Lockinge is a target next year. (op 11/4)
Poet was also seeking his fourth consecutive win. He soon established his authority at the head of affairs and, turning in, had several of his rivals in trouble, with the exception of the winner. Winner of the Irish Cambridgeshire over this course and distance and successful in a Group 3 at Leopardstown last weekend, he made the winner battle hard once headed. (op 3/1 tchd 100/30)
Zafisio(IRE), winner of the Group 1 Criterium International in heavy ground last November, was one of three British raiders in the field. Having his first run in Ireland, he travelled well but, once asked a serious question, was unable to raise his game enough to make his presence felt.
Rayeni(IRE) was returning from a break since chasing home Mastercraftsman in the Boylesports Irish 2,000 Guineas last May. The unbeaten juvenile had ground conditions in his favour but the lack of a recent run told in the end. He should be open to some improvement. (op 2/1 tchd 5/2)
Lahaleeb(IRE) endured a nightmare passage and could never get in a blow (she was full of running passing the winning post). The run is best forgotten. (op 7/1)
Libano(IRE), winner of four consecutive races in contrasting ground, including a Group 3, shaped reasonably well on his first outing for Dermot Weld. Considering this was his first start since last April, he looks another who should benefit from the run. (op 12/1)

5925 - 5926a (Foreign Racing) - See Raceform Interactive

5708
LONGCHAMP (R-H)
Sunday, September 13

OFFICIAL GOING: Good

5927a PRIX AL KHOR 7f
1:05 (1:06) 2-Y-0 £16,505 (£6,602; £4,951; £3,301; £1,650)

RPR

1 **Lope De Vega (IRE)**[18] 2-9-0 .... MGuyon 100
(A Fabre, France) **9/10**[1]

2 2 1/2 **Heaven's Heart (IRE)**[22] 5279 2-8-11 .... GMosse 91
(Y De Nicolay, France)

3 2 **Irish Cat (IRE)**[13] 2-8-11 .... OPeslier 86
(Robert Collet, France)

4 3/4 **Menelas**[43] 2-8-11 84
(P Bary, France)

5 2 **Where's The Soap (FR)**[23] 5240 2-8-11 .... DBonilla 79
(Tom Dascombe) *led to 1/2-way: 3rd on ins st: one pce fr wl over 1f out* **31/1**[2]

6 1/2 **Tall Chief (IRE)**[39] 2-9-0 81
(R Pritchard-Gordon, France)

7 2 1/2 **Cherie Bibie (FR)**[63] 2-8-11 72
(C Lerner, France)

1m 22.1s (1.40) 7 Ran SP% **55.8**
PARI-MUTUEL (including 1 Euro stake): WIN 1.90; PL 1.40, 1.60; SF 4.60.
Owner Gestut Ammerland **Bred** Gestut Ammerland **Trained** Chantilly, France

NOTEBOOK
Where's The Soap(FR) was smartly out of the stalls but was checked by her rider and tucked in behind the leader. She found nothing in the straight and just stayed on one pace.

5928a QATAR PRIX DU PETIT COUVERT (GROUP 3) 5f (S)
1:35 (1:37) 3-Y-0+ £38,835 (£15,534; £11,650; £7,767; £3,883)

RPR

1 **War Artist (AUS)**[14] 5493 6-9-4 .... OPeslier 4 119
(J M P Eustace) *disp 3rd on outside: hdwy wl over 1f out: drvn to ld cl home* **2/1**[2]

2 snk **Stern Opinion (USA)**[40] 4637 4-8-12 .... SPasquier 2 112
(P Bary, France) *led after 2f: drvn 1f out: ct cl home* **9/2**[3]

3 2 **Bluster (FR)**[25] 3-8-11 .... C-PLemaire 1 105
(Robert Collet, France) *racd in 3rd on rail: 4th 1 1/2f out: kpt on steadily u.p* **16/1**

4 1 1/2 **Benbaun (IRE)**[23] 5233 8-9-2 .... (v) JamieSpencer 6 103
(K A Ryan) *led 2f: pressed ldr tl over 1f out: one pce* **5/4**[1]

5 3 **Delvita (FR)**[35] 4837 5-8-9 .... MGuyon 3 86
(J-V Toux, France) *disp 5th: rdn and btn 2f out* **11/1**

6 3 **Manzila (FR)**[14] 5495 6-8-9 .... (p) FBlondel 5 75
(Mme C Barande-Barbe, France) *disp 5th: outpcd 1/2-way* **40/1**

56.50 secs (0.20) **Going Correction** +0.30s/f (Good)
WFA 3 from 4yo+ 1lb 6 Ran SP% **112.6**
Speed ratings: **113,112,109,107,102 97**
PARI-MUTUEL: WIN 3.40; PL 1.90, 2.10; SF 12.80.
Owner R Plersch **Bred** S Kirkham **Trained** Newmarket, Suffolk

NOTEBOOK
War Artist(AUS) was tucked in behind the leaders in the early stages, came with his run on the outside from the furlong marker and ran on bravely to take the lead in the last 50 yards. It was his first win over 5f for two and a half years and he certainly looks effective over the minimum distance. All being well he will be back over the course and distance for the Prix de l'Abbaye.
Stern Opinion(USA), quickly out of the stalls, tried to go from pillar to post and looked the likely winner at the furlong marker. Hard ridden inside the final furlong, he just failed to hold off the winner. This was just his second race after a long layoff and he has now earned a tilt at the Abbaye.
Bluster(FR) was always well placed on the rail next to the winner but was outpaced at the furlong marker and then ran on well as the race came to a close.
Benbaun(IRE) ran below expectations. He was well away and had every chance at the furlong marker but just kept on one-paced. The eight-year-old had an off day but is still likely to come back and attempt to win the Abbaye for a second time.

5929a QATAR PRIX VERMEILLE (GROUP 1) (F&M) 1m 4f
2:40 (2:46) 3-Y-0+ £166,427 (£66,583; £33,291; £16,631; £8,330)

RPR

1 snk **Stacelita (FR)**[91] 2952 3-8-8 .... C-PLemaire 9 114
(J-C Rouget, France) *trckd pcemaker: 3rd on ins st: led on rails 1 1/2f out: drvn fnl f: ct last strides: fin 2nd, snk: awrdd r* **4/5**[1]

2 1 1/2 **Plumania**[43] 4578 3-8-8 .... OPeslier 5 112
(A Fabre, France) *hld up: hdwy and 7th on outside st: styd on u.p fnl f: nrst fin: fin 3rd: plcd 2nd* **20/1**

3 shd **Board Meeting (IRE)**[43] 4578 3-8-8 .... ACrastus 11 111
(E Lellouche, France) *hld up towards rr: swtchd outside over 2f out: stdy prog to be nrst at fin: fin 4th: plcd 3rd* **12/1**

4 snk **Soberania (GER)**[42] 4583 3-8-8 .... JVictoire 2 111
(A Wohler, Germany) *a in tch: 8th st: hdwy on ins wl over 1f out: 3rd whn hmpd 1f out: r.o: fin 5th: plcd 4th* **28/1**

5 **Dar Re Mi**[24] 5201 4-9-3 0 .... JimmyFortune 3 115
(J H M Gosden) *prom: 5th st: hdwy over 1 1/2f out: sn swtchd rt: r.o wl to ld last strides: fin 1st: disq: plcd 5th* **11/4**[2]

6 1/2 **Becqu Adoree (FR)**[51] 3-8-8 .... FBlondel 4 110
(Mme G Lecomte, France) *a.p: 4th st: disp 3rd on ins fnl f: one pce* **33/1**

7 1 1/2 **Armure**[29] 5058 4-9-3 .... GMosse 7 108
(A De Royer-Dupre, France) *in midfield: hdwy on outside over 2f out: kpt on at one pce* **10/1**[3]

8 1 **Tres Rapide (IRE)**[29] 5058 4-9-3 .... DBoeuf 6 106
(H-A Pantall, France) *towards rr: sme prog fnl 2f: nvr a factor* **33/1**

9 hd **Tangaspeed (FR)**[94] 4-9-3 .... LDettori 13 106
(R Laplanche, France) *s.i.s: styd on fr over 1f out: nvr a factor* **40/1**

10 6 **Volver (IRE)**[30] 5012 3-8-8 .... IMendizabal 1 96
(J-C Rouget, France) *led to over 1 1/2f out* **100/1**

11 2 **Kalla**[31] 4969 3-8-8 .... MGuyon 8 93
(A Fabre, France) *prom: 2nd st on outside: rdn and ev ch 2f out: wknd over 1f out* **12/1**

12 *3* **Umirage**[29] 5058 4-9-3 .... TThulliez 10 88
(H Blume, Germany) *hdwy on outside and 7th st: weakeend over 2f out*
50/1

2m 29.1s (-1.30) **Going Correction** +0.175s/f (Good)
WFA 3 from 4yo+ 9lb **12** Ran SP% **126.2**
Speed ratings: **113,112,112,112,114 112,111,110,110,106 105,103**
PARI-MUTUEL: WIN 1.90 (coupled with Volver); PL 1.50, 4.50, 3.60;DF 17.10.
Owner M Schwartz & Ecurie Monastic **Bred** J -P Dubois **Trained** Pau, France
■ Stewards' Enquiry : Jimmy Fortune two-day ban: careless riding (Sep 27-28)

FOCUS
A controversial outcome to this Group 1 event. The performance of the fifth is a slight concern but the form looks solid rated around the fourth, seventh, eighth and ninth.

NOTEBOOK
Stacelita(FR) maintained her unbeaten run thanks to help from the Longchamp stewards. She had been hailed as the next Zarkava as she looked to become the first filly since Pistol Packer to complete the Prix Saint-Alary, Prix de Diane and Vermeille treble, but the brilliance of her last victory at Chantilly in June was not evident on her first run since. She had taken her unbeaten record to five when beating Tamazirte by four lengths in that race and could be expected to need the run, with the Arc in connections' thoughts, but she will have to come on for the race, as she initially finished second entirely on merit.The race appeared to be going exactly to plan as her pacemaker settled into her duties and Christophe Lemaire was able to sit in just behind. When that stablemate shifted left to let Stacelita through over 2f out she was soon through the gap. However, she was headed close home by the older filly and connections can count themselves lucky to get the race in the stewards' room. Nevertheless, she looks sure to improve for this first outing in three months and is clearly high class.
Plumania reversed form with Board Meeting from Deauville at the beginning of last month. She kept on quite well but this looks as good as she is. It paid to be close to the pace for the principals were never too far away. She can win more races in lesser company. She has now been marked down for the Prix de Royallieu on October 3.
Board Meeting(IRE) took a little time to balance in the straight but finished really well. Her connections have decided to bring her back in distance next time out and she will line up for the Prix de l'Opera on Arc day.
Soberania(GER) had finished second in the German Oaks on her last start and was another who attempted to make her run on the inside. She was slightly hampered by Dar Re Mi but it was an incident that would been passed over quickly in Britain. She wouldn't have been involved in the fight for the major spoils in this race but the stewards considered she was stopped from obtaining the best possible prize money by Dar Re Mi. She is relatively lightly raced, and this was a solid enough effort.
Dar Re Mi had finished runner-up to Zarkava in this event 12 months ago and looked most unfortunate not to land her third Group 1 race in succession. She had bounced back to winning form in the Pretty Polly at the Curragh before flooring dual Oaks heroine Sariska in the Yorkshire Oaks. She entered the race in the form of her life and was always handily placed towards the inside rail before making her move in the final 2f. She followed through the gap left by Volver and readily wore down Stacelita near the finish but was adjudged to have caused a slight infringement to Soberania. Connections are lodging an appeal against the change in the order.
Becqu Adoree(FR) had won a Listed event at Vichy on her latest start and was another who ran well, taking a major step up in class. She was held up in mid-division in the early stages and could keep on only at the same pace at the business end, but she is another who can win again in the right grade.
Armure was held up off the pace, which appears not quite the right tactics for a filly who had won over further. She did stay on in the closing stages and will do better when given a stiffer test or ridden a little more handily.

5930a QATAR PRIX NIEL (GROUP 2) (C&F) 1m 4f
3:10 (3:17) 3-Y-O **£71,942** (£27,767; £13,252; £8,835; £4,417)

RPR

1 **Cavalryman**[61] 3970 3-9-2 .... LDettori 3 115
(A Fabre, France) *racd in 3rd to st: drvn 1 1/2f out: led ins fnl f: r.o* **4/7**[1]

2 *1/2* **Beheshtam (FR)**[61] 3970 3-9-2 .... C-PLemaire 4 115
(A De Royer-Dupre, France) *racd in 4th: clsd up over 3f out but jst last ent st: hdwy over 1f out: styd on steadily* **10/3**[2]

3 *3/4* **Aizavoski (IRE)**[48] 4395 3-9-2 .... ACrastus 5 113
(E Lellouche, France) *led after 1 1/2f out tl hdd ins fnl f: lost 2nd cl home* **14/1**

4 *nk* **Claremont (IRE)**[91] 2951 3-9-2 .... MGuyon 1 113
(A Fabre, France) *led 1 1/2f: 2nd st: rdn over 1f out: kpt on at one pce* **13/2**[3]

5 *3* **Topclas (FR)**[15] 5463 3-9-2 .... SPasquier 6 108
(P Demercastel, France) *hld up in rr: hdwy over 3f out: 4th on ins st: rdn and btn wl over 1f out* **20/1**

2m 30.1s (-0.30) **Going Correction** +0.175s/f (Good) **5** Ran SP% **111.5**
Speed ratings: **110,109,109,108,106**
PARI-MUTUEL: WIN 1.40 (coupled with Claremont); PL 1.10, 1.30; SF 4.20.
Owner Godolphin S N C **Bred** Darley **Trained** Chantilly, France

FOCUS
The Prix Niel has proved to be one of the most influential trials for the Prix de l'Arc de Triomphe in recent years, with five of the last ten winners going on to complete the double.

NOTEBOOK
Cavalryman, who had St Leger winner Mastery behind him when winning the Grand Prix de Paris, looked the most likely candidate for Arc glory in this year's race, and was given a confident ride by Frankie Dettori, asserting close home after not being suited by the modest gallop set by Aizavoski. His victory was a tenth in the race for trainer Andre Fabre, who has completed the Niel/Arc double twice before, with Hurricane Run and Rail Link, as well as saddling Peintre Celebre to finish second in this race before winning the Arc. He will have to be supplemented for the Arc but is expected to take his chance with Frankie Dettori in the saddle.
Beheshtam(FR) had finished well behind the winner when they had met in the Grand Prix de Pari and this was much better. Fourth for much of the race, he came with his run up the centre of the track and looked extremely dangerous inside the final furlong, but could never peg back the winner. His connections still have to decide on his next race; it could be the Arc but is more likely to be the Prix du Conseil de Paris.
Aizavoski(IRE) went into the lead as there were no other takers for that job early on. After setting a sensible pace, he was still at the head of affairs at the furlong marker and then couldn't quite quicken like the winner and runner-up. He's unlikely to contest the Arc this year but it has been marked down as a target for 2010.
Claremont(IRE) was given every chance in the straight and stayed on well, but he was one-paced and was only beaten a total of a length and a half.

5931a QATAR PRIX FOY (GROUP 2) (C&F) 1m 4f
3:40 (3:45) 4-Y-O+ **£71,942** (£27,767; £13,252; £8,835)

RPR

1 **Spanish Moon (USA)**[77] 3443 5-9-2 .... RyanMoore 6 121
(Sir Michael Stoute) *led after 2f: rdn and r.o wl fnl f* **9/4**[2]

2 *3/4* **Vision D'Etat (FR)**[88] 3013 4-9-2 .... OPeslier 5 120+
(E Libaud, France) *hld up in rr: stl last and rdn appr fnl f: r.o under hand ride to take 2nd clsng stages* **4/5**[1]

3 *1/2* **Crossharbour**[29] 5059 5-9-2 .... SPasquier 2 119
(A Fabre, France) *racd in 3rd: disputing 2nd on outside st: hdwy wl over 1f out: hung rt and bmpd wnr's quarters appr fnl f: one pce* **13/2**[3]

4 *2 1/2* **Buccellati**[100] 2670 5-9-2 ....(v) WilliamBuick 4 115
(A M Balding) *led 2f: racd keenly and began pulling hrd over 4f out: disp 2nd on ins tl rdn and one pce fr over 1f out* **8/1**

2m 28.7s (-1.70) **Going Correction** +0.175s/f (Good) **4** Ran SP% **110.8**
Speed ratings: **115,114,114,112**
PARI-MUTUEL: WIN 1.90 (coupled with Crossharbour); PL 1.10, 1.10;SF 3.90.
Owner K Abdulla **Bred** Juddmonte Farms Inc **Trained** Newmarket, Suffolk

NOTEBOOK
Spanish Moon(USA) followed up his success in the Grand Prix de Saint-Cloud in June. The Sir Michael Stoute-trained colt has limited opportunities as a result of a ban in Britain due to misbehaviour at the stalls, but he went in smoothly enough here and Moore soon had him dictating the pace. He gradually wound it up in the straight and had the race won just inside the final furlong, as he galloped on strongly. Connections have yet to decide whether he will turn out for the Arc de Triomphe.
Vision D'Etat(FR) was having his first run since winning the Prince of Wales's Stakes at Royal Ascot in June and his connections had made no secret of the fact that the outing was needed beforehand. The four-year-old had battled on courageously when beating Tartan Bearer half a length at Ascot when encountering fast ground for the first time, and conditions were more suitable on this return. As usual, he was held up in the early stages but didn't look to be travelling as well as the winner when his rider pushed him along in the final 4f. However, he got his second wind inside the final furlong and was really keeping on in the closing stages, without his rider giving him a punishing race. It was a typical French effort by a horse involved in a trial, and last year's Arc fifth could well improve past the winner in three weeks time.
Crossharbour, settled in third place, ran a little free in the early stages. He moved up to challenge the winner at the furlong marker and was only run out of second place with 100 yards left to run. This was just his second race in 11 months and it will certainly have done him good.
Buccellati wasn't really up to the task. Second for much of the race, he couldn't go the pace when things warmed up in the straight and gradually dropped out of contention. He is now being aimed at the Canadian International.

5932a QATAR PRIX GLADIATEUR (GROUP 3) 1m 7f 110y
4:10 (4:13) 4-Y-O+ **£38,835** (£15,534; £11,650; £7,767; £3,883)

RPR

1 **Kasbah Bliss (FR)**[14] 5497 7-9-2 .... TThulliez 1 112
(F Doumen, France) *hld up in 7th: nt clr run 2f out to appr fnl f: rdn and r.o strly to ld cl home* **5/2**[1]

2 *3/4* **Pointilliste (USA)**[61] 3969 6-9-2 .... ACrastus 8 111
(E Lellouche, France) *wnt 2nd after 3f: led over 2f out: drvn fnl f: ct cl home* **4/1**[3]

3 *nk* **Incanto Dream**[344] 6497 5-9-0 ....(p) YLerner 9 109
(C Lerner, France) *hld up in rr: 9th st: hdwy on outside wl over 1f out: kpt on steadily fnl f: nrest at fin* **11/1**

4 *3* **Winkle (IRE)**[29] 5058 4-8-11 .... C-PLemaire 6 102
(M Delzangles, France) *cl up early: settled racing in 8th to st: hdwy on outside 2f out: 2nd appr fnl f: one pce* **3/1**[2]

5 *nk* **Candy Gift (ARG)**[21] 5297 6-9-0 .... TJarnet 4 105
(T Clout, France) *a cl up: 4th st: 2nd wl over 1f out: rdn and no ex fnl f* **20/1**

6 *2* **Bassel (FR)**[46] 4-8-12 .... DBoeuf 2 100
(H-A Pantall, France) *led 1f: 4th on ins st: rdn and one pce fr over 1f out* **11/1**

7 *3/4* **Bluefields (FR)**[31] 8-8-12 .... DBonilla 5 99
(E Leray, France) *racd in 5th to st: brushed by wnr 1 1/2f out: one pce* **25/1**

8 *3* **Barongo (IRE)**[37] 4808 4-8-12 .... MGuyon 7 96
(U Suter, France) *a in tch: wnt 3rd 4f out: disp 2nd over 1 1/2f out: sn wknd* **16/1**

9 *2* **Quartz Jem (IRE)**[68] 5-8-12 .... IMendizabal 10 93
(Mme Pia Brandt, France) *last st: a in rr* **25/1**

10 *2* **Centennial (IRE)**[45] 4457 4-9-0 ....(b) JimmyFortune 3 93
(J H M Gosden) *led to over 2f out: wknd 1 1/2f out* **7/1**

3m 18.4s (-3.10) **Going Correction** +0.175s/f (Good) **10** Ran SP% **121.1**
Speed ratings: **114,113,113,111,111 110,110,108,107,106**
PARI-MUTUEL: WIN 4.50; PL 1.80, 1.50, 2.70; DF 6.90.
Owner Henri De Pracomtal **Bred** Haras D'Ecouves Et H De Pracomtal **Trained** Bouce, France

NOTEBOOK
Kasbah Bliss(FR) had no chance of ending up in the winner's enclosure at the 2f marker as he was completely shut in and had nowhere to go until the furlong pole. He then quickened like a class act to take the lead close home. He was landing back-to-back victories in this race and now goes on to the Prix du Cadran on Arc day, providing the ground isn't testing.
Pointilliste(USA), always well up as usual, went into the lead a furlong and a half out but could do nothing when the winner came bustling on as the race came to a close. He hadn't been out for two months and no doubt there is something to work on for the Cadran in three weeks time.
Incanto Dream put up an excellent performance considering he was making his seasonal debut after a break of nearly a year. Held up early on, he started his run before the final furlong up the centre of the track and was putting in his best work at the finish. He was runner-up in the Cadran a year ago and goes for the same race again.
Winkle(IRE), who was towards the tail of the field in the early stages, ran up the far rail as the race came to a close. This was her first attempt over this longer distance.
Centennial(IRE) was asked to make all the running but dropped out quickly when things warmed up in the straight. He finished a well-beaten last and clearly doesn't get the distance.

2587 TABY (R-H)
Sunday, September 13
OFFICIAL GOING: Turf course - good; all-weather - standard

5933a STOCKHOLM CUP INTERNATIONAL (GROUP 3) (TURF) 1m 4f
4:00 (4:05) 3-Y-O+ **£52,770** (£21,988; £10,554; £7,036; £4,398)

RPR

1 **Touch Of Hawk (FR)**[35] 3-8-9 .... LennartHammer-Hansen 8 108
(Wido Neuroth, Norway) *mid-div: prog to chal 1f out: led ins fnl 100yds: r.o wl* **83/10**[3]

2 *1/2* **Munsef**[22] 5248 7-9-4 .... JimCrowley 5 107
(Ian Williams) *mid-div: hdwy to go 3rd 4f out: tk 2nd 100yds out: r.o* **12/5**[2]

3 *1 1/2* **Appel Au Maitre (FR)**[21] 5302 5-9-4 .... FJohansson 6 105
(Wido Neuroth, Norway) *mid-div: wnt 2nd 4f out: led briefly ins fnl f: styd on at one pce* **7/10**[1]

4 2 **Volo Cat (FR)**[21] 5302 5-9-4 .... JacobJohansen 1 101
(B Olsen, Denmark) *towards rr tl 4f out: styd on fr over 1f out: nvr nrr* **38/1**

5 2 1/2 **Luca Brasi (FR)**[21] 5302 5-9-4 .... ManuelMartinez 10 97
(F Castro, Sweden) *mid-div: hdwy 1/2-way: led 4f out tl hdd & wknd ins fnl f* **13/1**

6 1/2 **Alnitak (USA)**[21] 5302 8-9-4 ....(b) KAndersen 2 97
(B Olsen, Denmark) *last to 1/2-way: nvr nr to chal* **37/1**

7 2 1/2 **Shade Of Pale (GER)**[119] 4-9-4 ....(b) CarlosLopez 3 93
(Yvonne Durant, Sweden) *a towards rr: nvr a factor* **35/1**

8 1 1/2 **Quilboquet (BRZ)**[21] 5302 6-9-4 .... P-AGraberg 7 90
(L Reuterskiold Jr, Sweden) *nvr nrr than mid-div* **31/1**

9 2 **Django (SWE)**[42] 4585 6-9-4 .... MLarsen 9 87
(Jessica Long, Denmark) *racd in 2nd to 4f out: grad wknd* **20/1**

10 8 **Just Nu (SWE)** 4-9-4 .... DinaDanekilde 4 74
(H I Larsen, Sweden) *led: 4 l clr at 1/2-way: wknd 4f out: t.o* **28/1**

2m 31.9s (2.70)
WFA 3 from 4yo+ 9lb **10** Ran SP% **125.4**
TOTE: WIN 9.31; PL 1.33, 1.15, 1.02; DF 46.80.
Owner Stall E & F **Bred** Dieter Burkle **Trained** Norway

5542 LEICESTER (R-H)

Monday, September 14

OFFICIAL GOING: Good to firm (8.4)

Wind: Light against Weather: Cloudy with sunny spells

5934 LADBROKES.COM MAIDEN AUCTION STKS 5f 218y

2:30 (2:33) (Class 5) 2-Y-O **£3,399** (£1,011; £505; £252) **Stalls** Low

Form RPR

0 **1** **Bathwick Gold (IRE)**[33] 4900 2-9-3 0 .... CatherineGannon 12 73
(P D Evans) *chsd ldrs: pushed along 1/2-way: rdn to ld and hung lft fr over 1f out: r.o* **66/1**

3 **2** 1/2 **Merchant Of Medici**[108] 2430 2-8-13 0 .... MartinDwyer 8 68
(W R Muir) *led 5f out: hdd over 3f out: rdn: ev ch and hung lft fr over 1f out: r.o* **2/1**[2]

3 nk **Kenyan Cat** 2-8-9 0 .... DO'Donohoe 11 63
(George Baker) *s.i.s: sn pushed along in rr: hdwy over 1f out: r.o wl* **100/1**

4 1/2 **Sidney Melbourne (USA)** 2-8-13 0 .... NCallan 6 65
(J R Best) *prom: rdn 1/2-way: sn outpcd: rallied over 1f out: r.o wl* **20/1**

40 **5** 1 1/2 **Romeos Girl**[13] 5547 2-8-5 0 .... AdrianMcCarthy 13 53
(Jennie Candlish) *hld up in tch: rdn over 2f out: styd on same pce fnl f* **50/1**

0546 **6** hd **Yawary**[12] 5573 2-8-6 60 .... ChrisCatlin 5 56+
(C E Brittain) *chsd ldrs: led over 3f out: rdn and hdd whn bmpd over 1f out: nt clr run ins fnl f: one pce* **12/1**

00 **7** shd **Rosiliant (IRE)**[12] 5571 2-8-12 0 .... AdamKirby 10 59
(C G Cox) *led 1f: chsd ldrs: rdn over 2f out: no ex ins fnl f* **66/1**

6 **8** 1 1/4 **Cookie Galore**[11] 5596 2-8-4 0 .... SilvestreDeSousa 4 47
(J A Glover) *plld hrd: trckd ldrs: rdn over 2f out: edgd rt over 1f out: styd on same pce* **13/2**[3]

64 **9** 1/2 **Admiral Cochrane (IRE)**[33] 4906 2-8-12 0 .... RichardMullen 1 53+
(W Jarvis) *s.i.s: hdwy over 3f out: rdn over 2f out: sn outpcd* **15/2**

10 1 1/4 **Rakhapura (IRE)** 2-8-12 0 .... DaneO'Neill 9 50+
(P R Webber) *s.i.s: sn pushed along in rr: effrt over 2f out: nvr on terms* **50/1**

11 2 **Fazza** 2-8-11 0 .... JimCrowley 7 43
(D W P Arbuthnot) *sn pushed along in rr: n.d* **20/1**

522 **12** 3 1/2 **Filwa (IRE)**[17] 5379 2-8-10 75 .... JamieSpencer 2 46+
(B J Meehan) *trckd ldrs: rdn over 2f out: wknd over 1f out* **7/4**[1]

13 10 **Sue And Sue** 2-8-1 0 .... AndreaAtzeni(3) 3 —
(G Woodward) *s.i.s: sn pushed along in rr: lost tch over 2f out* **100/1**

1m 14.43s (1.43) **Going Correction** -0.025s/f (Good) **13** Ran SP% **120.9**
Speed ratings (Par 95): **89,88,87,87,85 85,84,83,82,80 78,73,60**
toteswinger: 1&2 £35.10, 1&3 £50.80, 2&3 £30.10. CSF £194.49 TOTE £44.10: £11.40, £1.10, £8.00; EX 258.90 TRIFECTA Not won..
Owner Bathwick Gold Partnership **Bred** Johnston King **Trained** Pandy, Monmouths

FOCUS
A modest but competitive maiden, rateda round the principals. They were spread out across the track in the closing stages.

NOTEBOOK
Bathwick Gold(IRE) showed very little on his debut at Salisbury but this represented significant improvement. After showing plenty of speed, he didn't help his chance by edging left, impeding the runner-up at the same time, but he still did enough. This was not a bad effort conceding weight all round and he should be competitive in handicaps.
Merchant Of Medici showed ability behind subsequent Vintage Stakes winner Xtension on his debut back in May, but he was reported by the vet to have returned lame on his right-fore that day and had been off since. His chance was not helped when he was carried left by the winner in the closing stages, but whatever, he looks a fair sort in the making. (op 5-2 tchd 7-4, 11-4 in places)
Kenyan Cat, a 16,000gns purchase, raced more towards the far side than the front two late on but still finished well.
Sidney Melbourne(USA), a $27,000 half-brother to four winners, looked set to finish well back when outpaced at halfway, but he ran on strongly when finally getting the idea. He looks to have a fair amount of ability and is open to improvement. (op 40-1)
Romeos Girl was getting weight from most of these and looks pretty limited, but she does at least now have the option of nurseries.
Cookie Galore pulled much too hard early on. (op 9-1 tchd 11-2)
Filwa(IRE), who was the clear form pick, did not impress with her action under pressure and was soon floundering when the pace increased. Official explanation: jockey said filly was unsuited by the good to firm ground (tchd 13-8 and 9-4)

5935 LADBROKES.COM DESFORD NURSERY (DIV I) 7f 9y

3:00 (3:04) (Class 4) (0-70,70) 2-Y-O **£4,209** (£1,252; £625; £312) **Stalls** Low

Form RPR

0006 **1** **Truly Magic**[17] 5379 2-8-6 55 .... ChrisCatlin 7 60+
(H J L Dunlop) *hld up: hdwy over 1f out: led ins fnl f: readily* **40/1**

0040 **2** 2 1/2 **Looks Like Slim**[26] 5166 2-8-7 56 .... MartinDwyer 2 55
(P F I Cole) *led: hdd 1/2-way: rdn to ld over 1f out: hdd and unable qck ins fnl f* **16/1**

0062 **3** nse **Precious Coral (IRE)**[10] 5635 2-9-6 69 .... JamieSpencer 8 68
(S A Callaghan) *hld up: rdn over 2f out: hdwy over 1f out: r.o* **7/2**[1]

003 **4** hd **Mighty Clarets (IRE)**[76] 3487 2-9-4 67 .... RichardMullen 3 65
(R A Fahey) *prom: rdn over 2f out: hung rt over 1f out: styd on* **7/1**[3]

4020 **5** 1 **Folletta (IRE)**[35] 4850 2-9-5 68 .... WilliamBuick 14 64
(R Hannon) *a.p: rdn and ev ch over 1f out: no ex ins fnl f* **8/1**

443 **6** 1 **Green Community (USA)**[14] 5498 2-9-3 66 .... DaneO'Neill 5 59
(E F Vaughan) *s.i.s: hld up: hdwy 1/2-way: rdn and hung rt over 1f out: no ex ins fnl f* **7/2**[1]

3053 **7** 2 3/4 **Avow (USA)**[12] 5583 2-9-1 64 ....(b) LPKeniry 11 50
(J S Moore) *chsd ldrs: led 1/2-way: rdn and hdd over 1f out: wknd ins fnl f* **14/1**

5320 **8** 3/4 **Storm Hawk (IRE)**[32] 4931 2-9-4 70 ....(v[1]) AndreaAtzeni(3) 6 54
(Pat Eddery) *chsd ldrs: rdn over 2f out: wandered and wknd fnl f* **6/1**[2]

050 **9** 2 1/2 **Creevy (IRE)**[14] 5498 2-8-10 59 .... JamesDoyle 4 37
(S Kirk) *hld up: rdn over 2f out: n.d* **16/1**

3000 **10** 3 1/4 **Tarrants Way**[14] 5526 2-8-1 50 .... AdrianMcCarthy 13 20
(Jennie Candlish) *hld up: hdwy u.p over 2f out: wknd over 1f out* **50/1**

064 **11** 1 1/2 **Valkov**[14] 5527 2-9-2 65 .... RichardKingscote 1 31
(Tom Dascombe) *prom: rdn 1/2-way: wknd 2f out* **8/1**

3540 **12** 1 1/2 **Acting Elegant**[24] 5226 2-8-3 52 .... CatherineGannon 9 15
(P D Evans) *in rr and pushed along: wknd over 2f out* **28/1**

1000 **13** 57 **Highcliffe Bridge (IRE)**[12] 5573 2-8-5 54 ....(b) KirstyMilczarek 10 —
(N P Littmoden) *prom: rdn 1/2-way: sn hung rt and wknd: t.o* **40/1**

1m 26.94s (0.74) **Going Correction** -0.025s/f (Good) **13** Ran SP% **122.2**
Speed ratings (Par 97): **94,91,91,90,89 88,85,84,81,78 76,74,9**
toteswinger: 1&2 £63.80, 1&3 £15.30, 2&3 £11.60. CSF £583.67 CT £2924.44 TOTE £58.10: £10.00, £4.90, £1.20; EX 286.70 TRIFECTA Not won..
Owner The Ex Pats **Bred** Burwell Bloodstock **Trained** Lambourn, Berks

FOCUS
A weak nursery and not a race to dwell on, but pretty solid form.

NOTEBOOK
Truly Magic was possibly at an advantage in making her move against the stands'-side rail, with most of her rivals racing a few horse widths away from the fence. She raced well off the pace early on, but picked up in good style once switched to the rail and was ultimately a clear-cut winner. She's obviously a fair bit better than her current rating of 55 suggests, but it would not be a surprise if she proves flattered by the bare form. Official explanation: trainer's rep said, regarding apparent improvement in form, that the filly was better suited by the firmer ground and step up in trip. (op 66-1)
Looks Like Slim ran an improved race to take second. He was always well placed and had his chance but proved no match for the winner, who may have been racing on quicker ground.
Precious Coral(IRE) played up before the start, proving reluctant to go behind the stalls. In the race itself, she was given a hold-up ride, with Spencer perhaps keen to preserve her questionable stamina, and she kept on for pressure after having to switch into the clear, but was never mustering the required speed. (op 9-2)
Mighty Clarets(IRE), up in trip on his nursery debut, after over two months off, briefly looked a big danger when keeping on inside the final furlong, but he displayed an exaggerated knee action and his run soon flattened out. He needs easy ground on this evidence. (op 11-2 tchd 5-1)
Folletta(IRE) had to be niggled along early, before coming back on the bridle, and was then back under pressure well over 2f out. Her rather choppy action suggests a return to easy ground will suit. (op 13-2)
Green Community(USA) was inclined to hang right and might not have enjoyed the ground, which was the quickest she has encountered to date. (tchd 9-2)
Storm Hawk(IRE), visored for the first time, showed up well for much of the way, but his response to pressure was tame. (op 10-1 tchd 11-1)
Highcliffe Bridge(IRE) Official explanation: jockey said filly hung badly right

5936 LADBROKES.COM CLAIMING STKS 1m 1f 218y

3:30 (3:30) (Class 5) 3-Y-O+ **£2,590** (£770; £385; £192) **Stalls** High

Form RPR

0001 **1** **Buddhist Monk**[12] 5568 4-9-11 80 ....(v[1]) JamieSpencer 7 82+
(Ian Williams) *chsd ldr tl led after 1f: qcknd clr 4f out: rdn 3f out: stl clr ent fnl f: hld on: all out* **6/4**[1]

0030 **2** 1/2 **Quince (IRE)**[8] 5694 6-9-5 69 ....(p) KFallon 2 75+
(J Pearce) *hld up and wl off the pce: pushed along over 3f out: hdwy over 1f out: rdn and r.o wl ins fnl f: nt quite get to wnr: edge rt towards fin* **9/2**[3]

2100 **3** nk **Traphalgar (IRE)**[8] 5694 4-9-13 84 .... NCallan 6 82+
(P F I Cole) *hld up and wl off the pce: rdn and hdwy to chse wnr who was clr over 2f out: r.o: nt quite get there: n.m.r towards fin* **10/3**[2]

0425 **4** 10 **Location**[12] 5381 3-8-4 52 .... CatherineGannon 5 46
(P D Evans) *hld up wl off the pce: sme hdwy over 3f out: rdn and hung rt over 2f out: nvr on terms* **6/1**

165- **5** 6 **World Time**[12] 6678 4-9-0 70 ....(v[1]) FergusSweeney 8 37
(Tim Vaughan) *s.i.s: hld up and bhd: rdn over 4f out: nvr any ch* **8/1**

000- **6** nk **Finnegans Rainbow**[30] 3589 7-9-1 35 .... LeeVickers 1 38
(M C Chapman) *chsd ldng pair: rdn over 3f out: sn wknd* **40/1**

00-0 **7** 6 **A One (IRE)**[51] 4321 10-8-9 45 .... SophieDoyle(5) 9 25
(H J Manners) *led 1f: chsd wnr: rdn and wknd 3f out: lost 2nd sn after* **50/1**

2m 6.31s (-1.59) **Going Correction** -0.025s/f (Good)
WFA 3 from 4yo+ 7lb **7** Ran SP% **111.1**
Speed ratings (Par 103): **105,104,104,96,91 91,86**
toteswinger: 1&2 £1.90, 1&3 £2.20, 2&3 £1.90. CSF £8.06 TOTE £2.10: £1.90, £3.30; EX 9.50 Trifecta £16.50 Pool: £367.49 - 16.42 winning units..
Owner Dr Marwan Koukash **Bred** Stanley Estate And Stud Co **Trained** Portway, Worcs
■ Stewards' Enquiry : K Fallon caution: careless riding.

FOCUS
A fair claimer in which the first three finished clear.

5937 LADBROKESCASINO.COM H'CAP 5f 218y

4:00 (4:00) (Class 4) (0-85,77) 3-Y-O **£5,180** (£1,541; £770; £384) **Stalls** Low

Form RPR

0050 **1** **Fesko**[17] 5409 3-9-1 74 .... RHills 7 85
(M Johnston) *hld up: swtchd lft and hdwy 2f: rdn to ld over 1f out: edgd rt and r.o wl* **17/2**

2321 **2** 3 **Hightime Heroine (IRE)**[28] 5110 3-9-4 77 .... JamieSpencer 5 80+
(J Noseda) *trckd ldrs: led over 2f out: rdn and hdd over 1f out: swished tail and no ex ins fnl f* **9/4**[1]

0422 **3** 3/4 **Lucky Dan (IRE)**[3] 5836 3-8-10 69 .... SilvestreDeSousa 4 69
(Paul Green) *plld hrd and prom: rdn over 1f out: styd on same pce ins fnl f* **6/1**

1002 **4** 1/2 **Jordaura**[7] 5719 3-9-2 75 .... AdamKirby 2 75+
(W R Swinburn) *s.i.s: hdwy over 3f out: rdn and hmpd over 1f out: styd on* **4/1**[2]

1221 **5** 2 1/2 **Hand Painted**[26] 5154 3-9-3 76 .... TravisBlock 9 67
(P J Makin) *hld up: hdwy over 1f out: styd on same pce fnl f* **9/2**[3]

0-53 **6** hd **Golden Rosie (IRE)**[39] 4700 3-8-11 70 .... WilliamBuick 1 60
(B W Hills) *hld up in tch: racd keenly: rdn over 1f out: no ex* **12/1**

2350 **7** 1 **Hellbender (IRE)**[44] 4535 3-8-8 67 .... LPKeniry 6 54
(S Kirk) *prom: rdn over 1f out: wknd fnl f* **33/1**

0410 **8** 1/2 **Sutton Veny (IRE)**[23] 5264 3-8-11 70 .... MartinDwyer 8 56
(J R Gask) *chsd ldrs: rdn over 2f out: wknd over 1f out* **20/1**

1456 9 7 **Red Kyte**[17] 5405 3-8-13 **72**....................(p) NCallan 3 46+
(K A Ryan) *led: rdn and hdd over 2f out: hmpd and wknd sn after* **25/1**
1m 12.37s (-0.63) **Going Correction** -0.025s/f (Good) **9** Ran SP% **113.0**
Speed ratings (Par 103): **103,99,98,97,94 93,92,91,82**
toteswinger: 1&2 £4.50, 1&3 £7.50, 2&3 £2.50. CSF £26.75 CT £124.33 TOTE £12.40: £3.20, £1.60, £1.50; EX 34.80 Trifecta £204.00 Pool: £397.13 - 1.44 winning units..
Owner C H Greensit & W A Greensit **Bred** C H And W A Greensit **Trained** Middleham Moor, N Yorks

FOCUS
A weak 3yo sprint handicap for the grade. The winner was another to race up the near rail and has been rated back to her best AW form.

5938 LADBROKES.COM DESFORD NURSERY (DIV II) 7f 9y
4:30 (4:31) (Class 4) (0-70,70) 2-Y-O £4,209 (£1,252; £625; £312) Stalls Low

Form RPR
5560 1 **Pullyourfingerout (IRE)**[33] 4901 2-9-0 **63**.................... KFallon 5 71
(B G Powell) *a.p: rdn to ld 1f out: r.o* **11/1**
006 2 ½ **White Dart**[17] 5400 2-9-3 **66**.................... ChrisCatlin 10 73
(M R Channon) *hld up: hung rt over 2f out: hdwy over 1f out: r.o: nt rch wnr* **5/1**[2]
0066 3 ¾ **Baby Judge (IRE)**[13] 5552 2-7-13 **51** ow1.......... AndreaAtzeni(3) 13 56
(M C Chapman) *led: rdn and hdd 1f out: styd on same pce ins fnl f* **40/1**
4144 4 1¼ **Keen Bidder**[11] 5589 2-9-2 **65**.................... FergusSweeney 3 67
(D M Simcock) *mid-div: hdwy over 2f out: rdn over 1f out: one pce fnl f* **9/2**[1]
654 5 1½ **Sounds Of Thunder**[14] 5528 2-9-5 **68**.................... DaneO'Neill 9 66+
(H J L Dunlop) *hld up: hdwy over 2f out: hung rt over 1f out: styd on: nt rch ldrs* **14/1**
003 6 ¾ **Green Earth (IRE)**[12] 5564 2-9-5 **68**.................... JimCrowley 2 64
(Mrs A J Perrett) *hld up: hdwy 1/2-way: rdn and edgd rt over 1f out: styd on same pce* **8/1**
600 7 nk **Black Daddy**[14] 5505 2-8-6 **55**.................... WilliamBuick 14 50
(R Hannon) *mid-div: hdwy over 2f out: sn rdn: no ex fnl f* **11/2**[3]
02 8 2½ **Ragsta (IRE)**[13] 5543 2-8-10 **66**.................... RichardRowe(7) 1 55
(C A Dwyer) *s.i.s: sn wl adrift: n.d* **17/2**
2334 9 nk **Nina Rose**[33] 4901 2-9-7 **70**.................... AdamKirby 11 58
(C G Cox) *chsd ldrs: rdn over 2f out: sn wknd* **5/1**[2]
4600 10 1½ **Pepi Royal (IRE)**[34] 4884 2-8-12 **61**.................... PaulEddery 7 46
(Pat Eddery) *chsd ldr: rdn over 2f out: sn wknd* **18/1**
0000 11 1 **Gulf Punch**[7] 5715 2-8-1 **50**.................... JamieMackay 8 32
(M F Harris) *hld up: hdwy over 2f out: rdn and wknd wl over 1f out* **40/1**
600 12 2¾ **Verona Lad**[35] 4847 2-8-6 **55**.................... AdrianMcCarthy 4 30
(Jennie Candlish) *s.i.s: sn drvn along: a in rr* **125/1**
602 13 1½ **Blue Avon**[40] 4652 2-8-10 **59**.................... RichardMullen 12 31
(R A Fahey) *mid-div: rdn 1/2-way: wknd over 2f out* **20/1**
054 14 11 **Bury St Edmunds**[21] 5319 2-8-4 **53**.................... CatherineGannon 6 —
(A G Newcombe) *prom: racd keenly: rdn over 2f out: sn wknd* **50/1**
1m 26.74s (0.54) **Going Correction** -0.025s/f (Good) **14** Ran SP% **121.2**
Speed ratings (Par 97): **95,94,93,92,90 89,89,86,86,84 83,80,78,65**
toteswinger: 1&2 £13.70, 1&3 £59.20, 2&3 £31.50. CSF £63.55 CT £2205.63 TOTE £14.60: £4.20, £1.80, £9.50; EX 74.10 TRIFECTA Not won..
Owner K Rhatigan **Bred** T Quayle **Trained** Upper Lambourn, Berks

FOCUS
A modest nursery run in a time 0.20 seconds quicker than the first division won by the 55-rated Truly Magic. The form should work out.

NOTEBOOK
Pullyourfingerout(IRE) ran an improved race with Fallon taking over in the saddle. He was held by a couple of these rivals on recent form, but was always well placed and stayed on best. A rise in the weights might find him out, but it's possible he'll be given a break now and his connections believe he could improve over further in time. (op 16-1)
White Dart travelled enthusiastically but still responded to pressure and showed improved form on this nursery debut. He looks up to winning a similar race. (op 3-1 tchd 11-4)
Baby Judge(IRE), trying 7f for the first time, was given a positive ride and kept on to post a respectable effort. However, he's now gone 11 races without winning. (op 50-1)
Keen Bidder gained his only win so far on easy ground and these conditions were probably plenty fast enough. Official explanation: jockey said colt hung left (op 11-2 tchd 7-1)
Sounds Of Thunder again ran as though she needs further than 7f. There might be a handicap in her over 1m-plus. (op 16-1)
Black Daddy didn't improve on this switch to nursery company. (op 8-1 tchd 17-2)
Nina Rose looked a little unlucky when ahead of today's winner at Salisbury last time, so this has to be considered very disappointing. (op 6-1 tchd 9-2)

5939 LADBROKESCASINO.COM MAIDEN STKS 1m 3f 183y
5:00 (5:01) (Class 5) 3-Y-O+ £3,238 (£963; £481; £240) Stalls High

Form RPR
P 1 **Spirit Is Needed (IRE)**[105] 2538 3-8-12 0.................... J-PGuillambert 3 74+
(M Johnston) *led after 1f: hdd 9f out: chsd ldr: led again 3f out: rdn clr fr over 1f out* **11/1**
0 2 3¼ **Tanfidh**[14] 5520 3-8-8 0 ow1.................... RHills 10 69+
(M P Tregoning) *led 1f: chsd ldrs and rn green and sn pushed along: reminder 4f out: nt clr run wl over 1f out: styd on to go 2nd ins fnl f: no ch w wnr* **15/8**[1]
2-24 3 shd **Moonbeam Dancer (USA)**[28] 5093 3-8-7 70.................... ChrisCatlin 4 59+
(D M Simcock) *s.s: hld up: hdwy over 3f out: rdn whn hmpd over 1f out: no ex: fin 4th: plcd 3rd* **11/4**[2]
0 4 4 **Amroth**[121] 2074 3-8-7 0.................... CatherineGannon 8 56
(P D Evans) *hld up: hdwy u.p over 2f out: sn hung rt: 3rd whn hung lft over 1f out: no ex: fin 3rd, 3 ¼l, 4l: disq: plcd 4th* **4/1**[3]
5 7 **Bluegrass Lion (USA)** 3-8-12 0.................... SilvestreDeSousa 5 50
(Paul Green) *s.s: bhd: rdn over 3f out: n.d* **14/1**
00-0 6 3½ **Royal Rainbow**[13] 5548 5-9-2 44.................... ByronMoorcroft(5) 6 45
(P W Hiatt) *chsd ldrs: led 9f out: rdn and hdd 3f out: wknd over 1f out* **80/1**
00 7 nse **Sula Dream**[42] 4606 3-8-12 0.................... FergusSweeney 2 45
(J Pearce) *hld up: effrt 3f out: sn wknd* **66/1**
00 8 shd **Just Call Me Dave (USA)**[14] 5531 3-8-12 0.................... JamesDoyle 7 45
(Paul Green) *prom: rdn over 3f out: wknd over 1f out* **40/1**
9 hd **Isintshelovely (IRE)**[8] 6-9-2 0.................... KFallon 9 39
(B G Powell) *s.i.s: sn prom: rdn and wknd over 1f out: eased* **14/1**
06 10 21 **Katya Kabanova**[28] 5093 3-8-7 0.................... HayleyTurner 1 7
(J R Fanshawe) *hld up: rdn 6f out: hung rt and wknd over 3f out* **25/1**
2m 33.27s (-0.63) **Going Correction** -0.025s/f (Good)
WFA 3 from 5yo+ 9lb **10** Ran SP% **112.1**
Speed ratings (Par 103): **101,98,96,96,91 89,89,89,88,74**
toteswinger: 1&2 £6.60, 1&3 £7.10, 2&3 £1.30. CSF £30.31 TOTE £13.00: £3.70, £1.50, £1.40; EX 34.80 Trifecta £285.60 Part won. Pool: £386.01 - 0.44 winning units..
Owner Mrs Joan Keaney **Bred** Mrs Joan Keaney **Trained** Middleham Moor, N Yorks

FOCUS
An uncompetitive maiden run at just an ordinary pace. The time, and the likes of the seventh hold down the form.
Isintshelovely(IRE) Official explanation: trainer said mare was unsuited by the good to firm ground

5940 LADBROKES.COM H'CAP 1m 60y
5:30 (5:30) (Class 5) (0-75,74) 3-Y-O £3,885 (£1,156; £577; £288) Stalls High

Form RPR
1156 1 **Edgeworth (IRE)**[52] 4275 3-9-1 **71**.................... KFallon 14 79+
(B G Powell) *chsd ldrs: led over 6f out: rdn and hung lft fr over 1f out: styd on wl: eased nr fin* **4/1**[1]
5364 2 2 **Shared Moment (IRE)**[14] 5503 3-8-4 **60**..........(p) DO'Donohoe 13 63
(J Gallagher) *s.i.s: hld up: hdwy over 2f out: rdn over 1f out: styd on to go 2nd wl ins fnl f: no ch w wnr* **12/1**
6210 3 ½ **Harriet's Girl**[26] 5175 3-9-4 **74**.................... AndrewElliott 11 76
(A P Jarvis) *s.i.s: hld up: plld hrd: hdwy over 1f out: r.o: nt rch ldrs* **7/1**[3]
1000 4 1¼ **Saa'Ida (IRE)**[34] 4881 3-9-1 **71**....................(b[1]) ChrisCatlin 8 70+
(C E Brittain) *hld up: rdn over 2f out: r.o wl ins fnl f: neaerst fin* **22/1**
2503 5 ½ **Kheskianto (IRE)**[23] 5258 3-7-12 **61**.................... RachelKing(7) 7 59
(M C Chapman) *hld up in tch: racd keenly: rdn over 1f out: wknd wl ins fnl f* **16/1**
6-05 6 hd **Indian Tonic (IRE)**[13] 5544 3-8-11 **67**.................... HayleyTurner 9 64
(W Jarvis) *led: hdd over 6f out: rdn over 1f out: no ex ins fnl f* **20/1**
504 7 1 **Stellar Cause (USA)**[84] 3207 3-8-12 **68**.................... MartinDwyer 12 63
(P F I Cole) *prom: hmpd over 6f out: rdn 3f out: no ex fnl f* **9/1**
3100 8 hd **Diapason (IRE)**[44] 4540 3-9-0 **70**.................... RichardKingscote 4 65
(Tom Dascombe) *plld hrd and prom: rdn 3f out: outpcd wl over 1f out: styd on ins fnl f* **14/1**
6245 9 ¾ **Hel's Angel (IRE)**[32] 4940 3-9-3 **73**.................... SilvestreDeSousa 5 66
(Mrs A Duffield) *hld up: rdn over 2f out: styd on but nt pce to mount a chal* **12/1**
4210 10 ½ **Petsas Pleasure**[26] 5160 3-8-13 **69**.................... DaneO'Neill 6 61
(Ollie Pears) *hld up: rdn over 2f out: nt trble ldrs* **16/1**
1503 11 4 **Burza**[15] 5475 3-9-1 **71**.................... NCallan 1 54+
(J Mackie) *chsd ldrs: rdn and hung rt over 2f out: wknd and eased fnl f* **9/2**[2]
0020 12 1½ **Jazacosta (USA)**[31] 5003 3-9-0 **70**.................... JimCrowley 3 49
(Mrs A J Perrett) *hld up: rdn over 2f out: a in rr* **14/1**
13 21 **Vain Boteli (GER)**[79] 3-9-2 **72**.................... WilliamBuick 2 3
(R Ford) *plld hrd and prom: rdn over 2f out: sn wknd* **14/1**
1m 44.7s (-0.40) **Going Correction** -0.025s/f (Good) **13** Ran SP% **118.6**
Speed ratings (Par 101): **101,99,98,97,96 96,95,95,94,94 90,88,67**
toteswinger: 1&2 £17.20, 1&3 £6.70, 2&3 £21.30. CSF £51.97 CT £268.02 TOTE £4.40: £2.60, £4.90, £2.90; EX 70.90 Trifecta £245.00 Part won. Pool: £331.20 - 0.20 winning units. Place 6: £140.01, Place 5: £35.36..
Owner K Rhatigan **Bred** Yvonne & Gerard Kennedy **Trained** Upper Lambourn, Berks

FOCUS
Hand-timed. A modest handicap in which the winner showed significantly improved form.
Vain Boteli(GER) Official explanation: jockey said gelding was unsuited by the good to firm ground
T/Plt: £121.60 to a £1 stake. Pool: £65,894.38. 395.50 winning tickets. T/Qpdt: £14.10 to a £1 stake. Pool: £5,441.93. 284.44 winning tickets. CR

5289 MUSSELBURGH (R-H)
Monday, September 14

OFFICIAL GOING: Good (good to firm in places; 7.6)
Both bends and rails moved in 3m from last fixture but impact on distances not quantified.
Wind: Virtually nil Weather: Overcast

5941 TOTEPLACEPOT H'CAP (DIV I) 7f 30y
2:20 (2:20) (Class 6) (0-65,65) 3-Y-O+ £2,266 (£674; £337; £168) Stalls High

Form RPR
6060 1 **Clumber Place**[22] 5295 3-8-4 **53**.................... FrancisNorton 5 59
(R C Guest) *chsd ldr: hdwy over 2f out: rdn and edgd lft over 1f out: drvn ins fnl f and kpt on to ld nr line* **50/1**
1401 2 hd **Nufoudh (IRE)**[31] 4977 5-8-8 **56**.................... KellyHarrison(3) 4 63
(Miss Tracy Waggott) *led: pushed clr 1/2-way: rdn along 2f out: drvn ent fnl f: hdd nr line* **11/2**[3]
0423 3 ½ **Grand Diamond (IRE)**[34] 4876 5-9-6 **65**..........(p) DanielTudhope 9 71
(J S Goldie) *trckd ldrs on inner: hdwy over 2f out: rdn over 1f out: drvn and ev ch whn n.m.r ins fnl f: kpt on* **9/4**[1]
0103 4 ½ **Optical Illusion (USA)**[34] 4878 5-8-12 **57**.................... PaulHanagan 7 62
(R A Fahey) *trckd ldrs: hdwy over 2f out: rdn over 1f out: drvn and kpt on ins fnl f: no ex towards fin* **11/2**[3]
1440 5 4½ **Maison Dieu**[45] 4504 6-9-1 **60**.................... DuranFentiman 8 53+
(E J Alston) *hld up towards rr: hdwy over 3f out: rdn along over 2f out and no imp appr fnl f* **11/1**
4506 6 ¾ **Darfour**[33] 4897 5-8-4 **54**....................(v) PaulPickard(5) 2 45
(J S Goldie) *chsd ldrs on outer: rdn along 3f out: drvn over 2f out and sn one pce* **11/1**
7 1¾ **Ambitious Choice (IRE)**[28] 5115 3-8-2 **51** oh4..........(tp) DaleGibson 10 36
(Muredach Kelly, Ire) *s.i.s: a towards rr* **100/1**
4030 8 nk **Devinius (IRE)**[31] 5003 4-8-13 **58**.................... RobertWinston 3 44
(G A Swinbank) *midfield: pushed along 1/2-way: sn rdn and wknd 3f out* **8/1**
012 9 1½ **Ms Sophie Eleanor (USA)**[34] 4879 3-9-2 **65**.................... PhillipMakin 6 48
(T D Barron) *t.k.h: chsd ldrs: rdn along wl over 2f out and sn wknd* **4/1**[2]
2250 10 2¾ **Jamieson Gold (IRE)**[18] 5364 6-8-10 **55**..........(p) RoystonFfrench 1 31
(Miss L A Perratt) *s.i.s: a bhd* **14/1**
1m 27.6s (-2.70) **Going Correction** -0.35s/f (Firm)
WFA 3 from 4yo+ 4lb **10** Ran SP% **118.9**
Speed ratings (Par 101): **101,100,100,99,94 93,91,91,89,86**
toteswinger: 1&2 £28.40, 1&3 £23.80, 2&3 £3.60. CSF £313.22 CT £921.38 TOTE £72.50: £12.20, £1.80, £1.20; EX 315.60.
Owner The Clumber Park Syndicate **Bred** Worksop Manor Stud **Trained** Stainforth, S Yorks

FOCUS
After a dry night the going was good, good to firm in places. The opening contest was an ordinary handicap run at a blazing pace and there was a shock winner. The first four finished compressed but the form seems sound enough.

Clumber Place Official explanation: trainer had no explanation for the apparent improvement in form

5942 CMYK (S) STKS 7f 30y

2:50 (2:51) (Class 6) 2-Y-O **£1,942** (£578; £288; £144) **Stalls High**

Form RPR

5235 **1** **Durham Reflection (IRE)**[11] 5595 2-8-8 70............ FrederikTylicki(3) 12 75
(J Howard Johnson) *mde all: rdn clr over 2f out: drvn over 1f out and styd on strly* **2/1**[1]

2450 **2** 4 ½ **Orpen Arms (IRE)**[11] 5595 2-8-6 62.............................. PaulHanagan 6 59
(R A Fahey) *trckd ldrs: hdwy 3f out: rdn to chse wnr 2f out: drvn and edgd rt and appr fnl f: sn no imp* **3/1**[2]

465 **3** 5 **Ya Boy Sir (IRE)**[22] 5290 2-8-11 54.............................. RobertWinston 10 51+
(I Semple) *s.i.s and bhd: hdwy 1/2-way: rdn along over 2f out: kpt on appr fnl f* **33/1**

3500 **4** 2 ¼ **Gentle Beat (IRE)**[15] 5467 2-8-11 65......................(p) DuranFentiman 11 46
(T D Easterby) *prom: rdn along 3f out: drvn over 2f out and sn wknd* **9/1**

44 **5** 9 **Empressofboogie**[9] 5668 2-8-3 0.............................. KellyHarrison(3) 4 18
(M Dods) *midfield: effrt on outer 3f out: nvr a factor* **4/1**[3]

3005 **6** 4 ½ **Lofthouse**[12] 5583 2-8-11 59.............................. FrancisNorton 9 12
(M R Channon) *chsd ldrs: rdn along 3f out: sn wknd* **9/1**

000 **7** 2 ¼ **Howdoyalikemenow (IRE)**[49] 4384 2-8-6 0....................(b) JohnEgan 8 —
(K A Ryan) *a towards rr* **100/1**

00 **8** 2 ½ **Land Of Plenty (IRE)**[19] 5330 2-8-6 0.............................. RoystonFfrench 5 —
(M Johnston) *a towards rr* **16/1**

00 **9** 3 **Step To It (IRE)**[14] 5519 2-8-11 0.............................. PhillipMakin 3 —
(K A Ryan) *bhd fr 1/2-way* **25/1**

050 **10** 13 **Daphne Du Maurier (IRE)**[13] 5553 2-8-1 0.................. PaulPickard(5) 7 —
(I Semple) *chsd wnr: rdn along over 3f out and sn wknd* **66/1**

11 12 **Stolen Affection** 2-8-6 0.............................. MartinLane(5) 2 —
(J R Weymes) *dwlt: green and a in rr* **40/1**

1m 27.46s (-2.84) **Going Correction** -0.35s/f (Firm) 2y crse rec **11** Ran SP% **115.9**
Speed ratings (Par 93): **102,96,91,88,78 73,70,67,64,49 35**
toteswinger: 1&2 £2.80, 1&3 £9.30, 2&3 £9.90. CSF £7.48 TOTE £2.90: £1.10, £1.60, £3.90; EX 8.80.The winner was bought in for 14,500gns.
Owner Transcend Bloodstock LLP **Bred** Zubieta Ltd **Trained** Billy Row, Co Durham

FOCUS
A modest seller for juveniles in which all of the 11 runners were chasing a first win. The winner produced a good performance for the grade and the form looks sound. The pace was strong and not many got into it. They finished well strung out and the time was slightly quicker than in the opening handicap for older horses.

NOTEBOOK
Durham Reflection(IRE) set a scorching early pace, was given a breather approaching the 3f pole and then opened up again to land a gamble and run his rivals into submission. There was quite a bit to like about this determined display but the form does not amount to much and the balance of his six previous runs suggest he is going to find life tough again when sent back into nurseries off a current mark of 70. (op 11-4 tchd 3-1)
Orpen Arms(IRE) was the only runner to pose any kind of threat to the winner. She deserves a bit of credit for chasing home a rival with an 8lb higher official rating but her form seems to have stalled and she could be tough to place unless she finds a bit of improvement. (tchd 5-2 and 7-2)
Ya Boy Sir(IRE) had plenty to prove on these terms and ran as well as can be expected but he has been generally disappointing since showing some promise in a Hamilton maiden on debut. (tchd 40-1)
Gentle Beat(IRE) got a bit warm and could only plug on after being under pressure a long way out. He has been found wanting off tough marks in nurseries and the step up from 5f and switch to selling company has not helped turn things around. (op 7-1)
Empressofboogie never got anywhere near the leader up in trip and down in grade on her third start. It is hard to know what her optimum distance is, but she is a half-sister to multiple 5f winner Empress Jain, and could do better when switched back to sprint trips in nurseries. (op 9-2)

5943 RACING POST H'CAP 1m 6f

3:20 (3:20) (Class 5) (0-75,71) 3-Y-O+ **£3,885** (£1,156; £577; £288) **Stalls High**

Form RPR

566 **1** **Ifatfirst (IRE)**[22] 5291 6-9-2 59.............................. DanielTudhope 6 68
(J S Goldie) *trckd ldrs on inner: hdwy 3f out: swtchd lft and rdn to chal 2f out: sn led and clr over 1f out: drvn ins fnl f and kpt on* **13/2**[3]

0352 **2** 1 **Grand Art (IRE)**[15] 5469 5-10-0 71.............................. PhillipMakin 7 79
(P T Midgley) *hld up in rr: hdwy on inner 3f out: rdn to chse ldng pair over 2f out: swtchd lft and drvn to chse wnr over 1f out: kpt on wl fnl f* **11/4**[1]

3513 **3** 7 **Dramatic Solo**[25] 5185 4-9-5 67..............................(b) MartinLane(5) 2 66
(A P Jarvis) *set gd pce: stdd 1/2-way: rdn and qcknd over 3f out: drvn 2f out: sn hdd and kpt on same pce* **11/4**[1]

1523 **4** 4 ½ **Terminate (GER)**[26] 5161 7-9-1 58.............................. FrancisNorton 4 51
(A Berry) *trckd ldrs: effrt over 3f out: sn rdn along and nvr nr ldrs* **12/1**

2401 **5** 1 ½ **Birkside**[34] 4874 6-9-13 70.............................. RoystonFfrench 1 61
(Miss L A Perratt) *trckd ldng pair: hdwy over 3f out: rdn along 4f out: drvn 3f out and sn wknd* **8/1**

001 **6** 12 **Harcas (IRE)**[37] 4806 7-9-0 57..............................(v) PaulHanagan 3 32
(M Todhunter) *chsd ldr: hdwy and cl up 1/2-way: rdn along over 3f out: wknd wl over 2f out* **7/2**[2]

000 **7** 16 **Santiago Atitlan**[19] 5333 7-9-8 68.............................. FrederikTylicki(3) 5 22
(P Monteith) *hld up: a in rr* **28/1**

3m 0.45s (-4.85) **Going Correction** -0.35s/f (Firm) **7** Ran SP% **111.1**
Speed ratings (Par 103): **99,98,94,91,91 84,75**
toteswinger: 1&2 £5.40, 1&3 £3.00, 2&3 £1.90. CSF £23.30 TOTE £6.90: £3.60, £1.70; EX 33.30.
Owner Mrs Janis Macpherson **Bred** Mrs Belinda Strudwick **Trained** Uplawmoor, E Renfrews

FOCUS
A fair handicap. It was run at a stop-start gallop and the first two pulled a long way clear of the rest. Unturbed but reliable form.
Ifatfirst(IRE) Official explanation: trainer said, regarding apparent improvement in form, that the gelding was better suited by the good ground
Harcas(IRE) Official explanation: jockey said gelding hung right-handed throughout

5944 SUBSCRIBE ONLINE AT RACINGUK.COM CLAIMING STKS 1m 1f

3:50 (3:51) (Class 5) 3-Y-O+ **£3,885** (£1,156; £577; £288) **Stalls High**

Form RPR

0003 **1** **King Of The Moors (USA)**[22] 5289 6-9-2 56............(b) FrancisNorton 8 67
(R C Guest) *t.k.h: mde all: rdn along over 2f out: styd on strly appr fnl f* **16/1**

0535 **2** 3 ½ **Bed Fellow (IRE)**[22] 5294 5-8-13 41.............................. PhillipMakin 5 57
(P Monteith) *sn chsng wnr: rdn along wl over 2f out: drvn over 1f out and no imp fnl f* **80/1**

6211 **3** 1 ½ **Fremen (USA)**[33] 4897 9-9-12 82.............................. AdrianTNicholls 7 69+
(D Nicholls) *dwlt and hld up towards rr: hdwy over 4f out: trckd ldrs 3f out: swtchd lft and rdn 2f out: sn no imp* **5/4**[1]

0000 **4** 6 **Kings Point (IRE)**[24] 5206 8-10-0 83.............................. PaulHanagan 4 57
(D Nicholls) *trckd ldng pair: effrt over 3f out: sn rdn: drvn along over 2f out and sn btn* **9/4**[2]

3000 **5** 2 ¾ **Papa's Princess**[7] 5730 5-8-4 54.............................. KellyHarrison(3) 2 31+
(J S Goldie) *hld up: a towards rr* **20/1**

0131 **6** 6 **Dabbers Ridge (IRE)**[74] 3539 7-8-13 80.................. FrederikTylicki(3) 1 28+
(I W McInnes) *hld up: a towards rr* **9/2**[3]

0200 **7** 7 **Willyn (IRE)**[16] 5438 4-8-5 52..............................(p) DuranFentiman 3 —
(J S Goldie) *trckd ldrs: pushed along 1/2-way: sn rdn and wknd over 3f out* **20/1**

1m 51.32s (-3.38) **Going Correction** -0.35s/f (Firm) **7** Ran SP% **110.0**
Speed ratings (Par 103): **101,97,96,91,88 83,77**
toteswinger: 1&2 £9.60, 1&3 £2.90, 2&3 £6.30. CSF £763.18 TOTE £11.50: £3.10, £5.20; EX 119.90.Papa's Princess was claimed by D J Moffatt for £4,000.
Owner Shaun Taylor **Bred** Frank Brown, Hedberg Hall & K Hernandez **Trained** Stainforth, S Yorks

FOCUS
A decent claimer. The first three in the betting held official ratings between 80 and 83, but there was a major surprise. The form is best viewed through the front pair.

5945 GREGGS OF SCOTLAND LONG SERVICE NURSERY 5f

4:20 (4:22) (Class 3) (0-90,88) 2-Y-O
£7,477 (£2,239; £1,119; £560; £279; £140) **Stalls Low**

Form RPR

0025 **1** **Micky's Knock Off (IRE)**[11] 5596 2-8-1 68 ow3............ FrancisNorton 4 78+
(R C Guest) *trckd ldrs: hdwy 2f out: rdn to ld over 1f out: drvn ins fnl f and kpt on strly* **11/2**[3]

3511 **2** 2 **Mister Hughie (IRE)**[30] 5033 2-8-12 79.............................. PaulHanagan 6 82
(M R Channon) *swtchd lft after 1f and sn trcking ldrs: effrt 2f out: rdn and hdwy on inner to chal over 1f out and ev ch tl drvn and one pce ins fnl f* **9/4**[1]

1050 **3** 2 ½ **Here Now And Why (IRE)**[48] 4407 2-9-7 88.................... PhillipMakin 2 82+
(K A Ryan) *cl up: effrt 2f out: sn rdn and ev ch tl drvn and one pce appr fnl f* **7/1**

0213 **4** 4 ½ **Six Diamonds**[10] 5650 2-8-13 80.............................. RobertWinston 1 58
(H Morrison) *led: rdn along 2f out: drvn and hdd over 1f out: sn wknd* **7/2**[2]

3011 **5** ½ **Ignatieff (IRE)**[34] 4875 2-9-2 83.............................. DuranFentiman 3 59
(Mrs L Stubbs) *cl up: rdn along 2f out: drvn and wknd over 1f out* **13/2**

400 **6** 1 **Kristen Jane (USA)**[18] 5360 2-8-0 74 oh12 ow9.. AndrewHeffernan(7) 8 46
(Miss L A Perratt) *wnt rt s and bhd tl sme late hdwy* **66/1**

0451 **7** 7 **Camacho Flyer (IRE)**[19] 5337 2-8-1 73 ow1.............(v) PaulPickard(5) 7 20
(P T Midgley) *a towards rr* **6/1**

4650 **8** 16 **Goodbye Earl (IRE)**[13] 5552 2-7-12 65 oh1.............................. PaulQuinn 5 —
(A Berry) *awkward s: trckd ldrs whn hmpd after 1f: sn bhd and eased fnl 2f* **20/1**

59.46 secs (-0.94) **Going Correction** -0.15s/f (Firm) **8** Ran SP% **114.7**
Speed ratings (Par 99): **101,97,93,86,85 84,73,47**
toteswinger: 1&2 £4.50, 1&3 £6.50, 2&3 £2.60. CSF £18.38 CT £87.94 TOTE £7.90: £2.30, £1.40, £2.00; EX 19.90.
Owner Miss Alison Ibbotson **Bred** J Cullinan **Trained** Stainforth, S Yorks
■ Stewards' Enquiry : Paul Hanagan two-day ban: careless riding (Sep 28-29)

FOCUS
A hot nursery, four of the runners having won on their previous start. There was a suspicion that the leaders may have gone off a bit fast, but the winner did the job in good style and the second and third give the form a very solid look.

NOTEBOOK
Micky's Knock Off(IRE), tucked in just behind the furious pace, hit the front at the furlong pole and surged to victory to give Richard Guest and Francis Norton a treble on the card. He displayed a good cruising speed and showed a decent turn of foot faced with a serious examination in a warm event on his nursery debut. He should be capable of further progress and could have quite a bit of room to successfully operate in nurseries. (op 12-1)
Mister Hughie(IRE) gave it a good shot in his bid for a hat-trick after wins in a Bath seller and Newmarket nursery, but a 9lb rise for his last success has just anchored him. (op 2-1 tchd 5-2)
Here Now And Why(IRE), winner of a Ripon maiden and Thirsk novice stakes, also finished fifth behind Monsieur Chevalier in the Super Sprint at Newbury. He was out of his depth on level terms behind the same rival in a Group 3 last time, but has rebounded with a decent effort faced with a much more realistic assignment. He deserves some extra credit because he kept grinding away after the other two trailblazers faded. (op 5-1)
Six Diamonds, along with Ignatieff, attacked in the early stages but could not sustain her effort and was in serious trouble before entering the final furlong. She could bounce back if avoiding a destructive battle for the lead next time. (op 4-1 tchd 9-2)
Ignatieff(IRE) chased the early speed, but coudn't maintain his effort. (op 5-1)

5946 WATCH RACING UK ONLINE AT RACINGUK.COM H'CAP 5f

4:50 (4:51) (Class 5) (0-70,70) 3-Y-O+ **£3,238** (£963; £481; £240) **Stalls Low**

Form RPR

6563 **1** **Wicked Wilma (IRE)**[17] 5411 5-8-11 58.............................. FrancisNorton 8 67
(A Berry) *cl up: effrt to ld wl over 1f out: rdn and edgd lft ent fnl f: kpt on wl* **11/4**[1]

3506 **2** 1 **Dalarossie**[29] 5073 4-8-6 53.............................. DaleGibson 11 58
(E J Alston) *hld up towards rr: hdwy 2f out: rdn over 1f out: styd on wl to chse wnr ins fnl f: sn drvn and no imp* **12/1**

420 **3** 1 **Steelcut**[16] 5436 5-9-6 70.............................. FrederikTylicki(3) 14 72
(R A Fahey) *chsd ldrs on outer: rdn and hdwy wl over 1f out: ev ch appr fnl f: sn drvn and one pce* **4/1**[3]

4 ½ **San Diego Prince**[17] 5415 5-8-8 55..............................(tp) JohnEgan 5 55
(Muredach Kelly, Ire) *trckd ldrs: effrt and nt clr run over 1f out: swtchd rt and rdn ent fnl f: kpt on* **12/1**

0002 **5** ¾ **Town And Gown**[7] 5727 4-8-1 51 oh6.............................. KellyHarrison(3) 6 48
(J S Goldie) *hld up: hdwy 2f out: sn rdn and styd on to chse ldrs ent fnl f: sn drvn and one pce* **22/1**

5015 **6** nk **Spirit Of Coniston**[10] 5629 6-8-11 58.............................. PhillipMakin 3 54+
(P T Midgley) *led: rdn along over 2f out: drvn and hdd wl over 1f out: wkng whn n.m.r ent fnl f* **7/2**[2]

-000 **7** 1 ¼ **Distant Sun (USA)**[19] 5343 5-9-4 65.............................. RobertWinston 4 59+
(Miss L A Perratt) *dwlt and towards rr: hdwy 2f out: swtchd rt and effrt whn nt clr run over 1f out: nt rcvr* **9/1**

0430 **8** nk **Blazing Heights**[17] 5411 6-8-10 57..............................(v) DanielTudhope 7 48+
(J S Goldie) *dwlt and in rr: hdwy wl over 1f out: sn rdn and n.m.r appr fnl f: n.d* **9/1**

0060 **9** ½ **Hosanna**[17] 5396 3-8-3 51 oh1.............................. PaulHanagan 13 40
(J Barclay) *towards rr: hdwy 2f out: sn rdn and n.d* **33/1**

000 **10** ¾ **Clanachy**[17] 5394 3-8-3 51 oh4.............................. AndrewMullen 2 37
(A G Foster) *cl up on inner: rdn along 2f out: sn drvn and wkng whn edgd rt over 1f out* **28/1**

5500 11 *1* **Handcuff**[10] 5629 3-8-3 **51** oh6..............................(v) RoystonFfrench 1 36+
(I Semple) *midfield on inner: effrt whn hmpd over 2f out: nvr a factor* **25/1**
000- 12 *8* **Ourbelle**[380] 5501 4-8-1 **53** oh6 ow2.............................. PaulPickard(5) 10 7
(Miss Tracy Waggott) *s.i.s: a in rr* **80/1**
-000 13 *6* **Adab (IRE)**[89] 3031 4-8-0 **54** oh6 ow3................(p) AndrewHeffernan(7) 9 —
(Miss Tracy Waggott) *cl up on outer: rdn along over 2f out and sn wknd* **50/1**

59.49 secs (-0.91) **Going Correction** -0.15s/f (Firm)
WFA 3 from 4yo+ 1lb **13** Ran SP% **122.1**
Speed ratings (Par 103): **101,99,97,97,95 95,93,92,92,90 89,76,66**
toteswinger: 1&2 £8.20, 1&3 £3.50, 2&3 £9.70. CSF £35.81 CT £136.80 TOTE £4.00: £1.70, £4.00, £1.70; EX 43.80.
Owner Mrs Thelma White **Bred** Gerry O'Sullivan **Trained** Cockerham, Lancs

FOCUS
A moderate handicap. The majority of runners were struggling for form and six were out of the weights. Solid but limited form.
Spirit Of Coniston ◆ Official explanation: jockey said gelding hung left
Blazing Heights Official explanation: jockey said gelding was denied a clear run

5947 SCOTTISH RACING YOUR BETTER BET H'CAP 1m 4f 100y
5:20 (5:22) (Class 6) (0-65,63) 3-Y-0+ **£2,590** (£770; £385; £192) **Stalls** High

Form RPR
0015 1 **Oddsmaker (IRE)**[8] 5698 8-9-2 **59**......................(t) AndrewHeffernan(7) 2 71
(M A Barnes) *mde all: rdn and qcknd clr wl over 2f out: drvn ins fnl f and styd on strly* **8/1**
3321 2 *1 ¼* **Grandad Bill (IRE)**[8] 5698 6-9-2 **55**.......................... KellyHarrison(3) 8 65
(J S Goldie) *in tch: hdwy 3f out: rdn to chse 2f out: drvn and hung rt over 1f out: kpt on u.p ins fnl f: nt rch wnr* **5/2**[1]
6404 3 *5* **Sphere (IRE)**[9] 5679 4-9-7 **57**..................................(p) PhillipMakin 9 59
(P T Midgley) *trckd wnr 3f: styd prom on inner: effrt and rdn along 3f out: drvn 2f out and kpt on same pce* **12/1**
4151 4 *6* **Patavium (IRE)**[16] 5423 6-9-8 **58**............................... RoystonFfrench 3 50
(E W Tuer) *t.k.h: trckd ldrs: hdwy to chse wnr after 3f: rdn along 3f out: drvn over 2f out and grad wknd* **7/1**
000 5 *2* **Angels And Demons (IRE)**[50] 4354 3-8-1 **46** ow1..... FrancisNorton 10 35
(R C Guest) *midfield: hdwy on inner and in tch over 3f out: sn rdn and hung bdly lft 2f out: sn wknd* **5/1**[2]
4550 6 *¾* **Bourse (IRE)**[22] 5294 4-8-12 **48**................................(p) AndrewMullen 5 36
(A G Foster) *midfield: effrt 3f out: sn rdn and n.d* **16/1**
4324 7 *1* **Regent's Secret (USA)**[26] 5162 9-9-4 **54**..................(p) DanielTudhope 1 40+
(J S Goldie) *hld up: a in rr* **14/1**
-434 8 *1* **Hard Luck Story**[134] 1691 3-9-1 **63**............................ FrederikTylicki(3) 7 48
(I Semple) *in tch: rdn along over 3f out and sn wknd* **22/1**
1253 9 *1 ¾* **Love In The West (IRE)**[19] 5342 3-9-1 **60**.................... RobertWinston 12 42+
(G A Swinbank) *hld up: a towards rr* **6/1**[3]
2542 10 *3 ½* **Piper's Song (IRE)**[12] 5577 6-9-7 **57**................................ SJCraine 4 33+
(Patrick Morris) *hld up in rr: sme hdwy on outer 3f out: sn rdn and nvr a factor* **10/1**
0600 11 *10* **Grethel (IRE)**[7] 5733 5-8-9 **45**..................................... PaulHanagan 11 5+
(A Berry) *chsd ldrs: rdn along over 4f out and sn wknd* **40/1**
0300 12 *6* **Wilmington**[71] 3653 5-8-7 **48**..................................... LanceBetts(5) 6 —+
(Mrs J C McGregor) *hld up: a in rr* **50/1**

2m 40.93s (-1.07) **Going Correction** -0.35s/f (Firm)
WFA 3 from 4yo+ 9lb **12** Ran SP% **121.2**
Speed ratings (Par 101): **89,88,84,80,79 79,78,77,76,74 67,63**
toteswinger: 1&2 £5.40, 1&3 £23.10, 2&3 £9.90. CSF £28.47 CT £249.96 TOTE £11.90: £3.80, £1.50, £4.10; EX 31.60.
Owner D Maloney **Bred** Margaret Conlon **Trained** Farlam, Cumbria

FOCUS
A minor middle-distance handicap. It looked reasonably competitive but again it was a major advantage to race prominently and hardly anything got into it. They finished at long intervals behind the first two and this is probably form to treat with caution.
Love In The West(IRE) Official explanation: jockey said filly suffered interference in running

5948 TOTEPLACEPOT H'CAP (DIV II) 7f 30y
5:50 (5:53) (Class 6) (0-65,65) 3-Y-0+ **£2,266** (£674; £337; £168) **Stalls** High

Form RPR
5243 1 **Ancient Cross**[7] 5730 5-9-6 **63**..................................(t) PhillipMakin 6 75+
(M W Easterby) *hld up towards rr: smooth hdwy 3f out: swtchd ins wl over 1f out: qcknd to ld ent fnl f and sn rdn clr* **2/1**[1]
2060 2 *3 ½* **No Grouse**[51] 4312 9-9-1 **58**.. DuranFentiman 7 61
(E J Alston) *hld up in tch: hdwy 3f out: rdn to chse ldrs 2f out: sn drvn and ev ch tl kpt on same pce fnl f* **20/1**
0060 3 *1 ¼* **Shunkawakhan (IRE)**[22] 5289 6-8-12 **55**.....................(p) RobertWinston 5 55
(Miss L A Perratt) *hld up and bhd: stdy hdwy 3f out: trckd ldrs and n.m.r 2f out: sn swtchd lft and rdn to have ev ch appr lfnl f: sn drvn and kpt on same pce* **16/1**
2000 4 *½* **Fathey (IRE)**[18] 5363 3-9-1 **65**.................................... FrederikTylicki(3) 3 62
(R A Fahey) *prom: rdn along 3f out: drvn 2f out and grad wknd* **8/1**
0606 5 *2* **Ace Of Spies (IRE)**[31] 4998 4-8-13 **56**.........................(p) PaulHanagan 8 50
(G A Harker) *dwlt and sn rdn along to go cl up after 1f: rdn to ld wl over 2f out: drvn over 1f out: hdd ent fnl f and wknd* **11/2**[3]
5000 6 *2 ¼* **Slip Star**[31] 4977 6-8-1 **49** oh4.................................... MartinLane(5) 10 37
(T J Etherington) *in tch on inner: hdwy to chse ldrs 1/2-way: rdn along wl over 2f out and sn wknd* **25/1**
7 *1 ½* **Four Kicks (IRE)**[17] 5413 3-8-6 **53**................................ JohnEgan 4 36
(Muredach Kelly, Ire) *chsd ldrs: rdn along over 3f out and sn wknd* **9/1**
200 8 *2 ½* **H Harrison (IRE)**[31] 4977 9-9-0 **57**............................... RoystonFfrench 9 35
(I W McInnes) *led: rdn along 3f out: hdd wl over 2f out: sn drvn and wknd wl over 1f out* **10/1**
050 9 *hd* **Needy McCredie**[29] 5071 3-8-2 **49** oh4.......................... FrancisNorton 2 25
(J R Turner) *a in rr* **8/1**
6604 10 *6* **Finsbury**[11] 5601 6-9-1 **58**... DanielTudhope 1 21
(J S Goldie) *chsd ldrs on outer: rdn along 4f out: drvn 3f out and sn wknd* **5/1**[2]

1m 27.59s (-2.71) **Going Correction** -0.35s/f (Firm)
WFA 3 from 4yo+ 4lb **10** Ran SP% **121.2**
Speed ratings (Par 101): **101,97,95,95,92 90,88,85,85,78**
toteswinger: 1&2 £12.80, 1&3 £20.10, 2&3 £32.40. CSF £51.66 CT £531.26 TOTE £2.90: £1.50, £3.00, £4.00; EX 59.20 Place 6: £390.11, Place 5: £186.95..
Owner P J Bown **Bred** Darley **Trained** Sheriff Hutton, N Yorks

FOCUS
A modest handicap run at a frenetic pace. The second and third help set the level.
T/Jkpt: Not won. T/Plt: £1,407.70 to a £1 stake. Pool: £58,044.57. 30.10 winning tickets. T/Qpdt: £530.40 to a £1 stake. Pool: £3,512.64. 4.90 winning tickets. JR

5595 REDCAR (L-H)
Monday, September 14

OFFICIAL GOING: Good to firm (8.9)
Wind: Moderate, half against Weather: overcast

5949 EUROPEAN BREEDERS' FUND MAIDEN FILLIES' STKS 6f
2:10 (2:11) (Class 5) 2-Y-0 **£3,561** (£1,059; £529; £264) **Stalls** Centre

Form RPR
3224 1 **Secret Queen**[26] 5165 2-9-0 **85**..................................... TPO'Shea 5 85+
(B J Meehan) *w ldrs: led over 3f out: rdn over 1f out: sn drew clr* **6/4**[1]
00 2 *7* **Mooinooi**[47] 4427 2-9-0 0..........................(p) GrahamGibbons 12 64
(T D Walford) *chsd ldrs: edgd rt over 1f out: kpt on: no ch w wnr* **40/1**
3 *hd* **Chardonnay** 2-9-0 0..................................... PJMcDonald 9 63+
(G A Swinbank) *s.i.s: hdwy 2f out: styd on wl ins fnl f: will improve* **20/1**
4 4 *2 ¼* **Chushka**[47] 4430 2-9-0 0.. TomEaves 10 57
(B Smart) *s.i.s: hdwy 2f out: kpt on ins fnl f* **7/2**[3]
2 5 *hd* **Melundy**[16] 5439 2-9-0 0.. TGMcLaughlin 13 56
(Mrs L Stubbs) *s.i.s: hld up stands' side: hdwy over 2f out: chsng ldrs over 1f out: hung lft: wknd towards fin* **3/1**[2]
6 *½* **Tobougie On Down** 2-8-7 0..............................(e[1]) JonathanHinch(7) 3 55
(J A Glover) *problems in stalls: s.s: hdwy outer 2f out: hung lft: nvr nr ldrs* **100/1**
7 *shd* **Alhena (IRE)** 2-9-0 0...................................... StephenDonohoe 7 54+
(K A Ryan) *in rr-div: hdwy 2f out: styd on ins fnl f: will improve* **22/1**
8 *shd* **Interest Free** 2-9-0 0.. DavidAllan 4 54
(T D Easterby) *chsd ldrs: edgd lft over 1f out: one pce* **50/1**
5 9 *¾* **Caol Ila (IRE)**[11] 5611 2-9-0 0.................................... SebSanders 2 52
(J G Given) *wnt lft s: sn w ldrs on outside: wknd over 1f out* **14/1**
6 10 *2* **Laureldean Desert**[32] 4928 2-9-0 0.............................. TonyHamilton 8 46
(R A Fahey) *mid-div: outpcd over 2f out: grad wknd* **16/1**
0 11 *nk* **Fair Bunny**[8] 5693 2-9-0 0... JimmyQuinn 1 45
(A D Brown) *w ldrs: lost pl over 1f out* **80/1**
05 12 *1* **Scooby Dee**[32] 4928 2-8-11 0.............................. MichaelJStainton(3) 6 42
(R M Whitaker) *chsd ldrs: sn drvn along: lost pl over 2f out* **50/1**
00 13 *16* **Wedding Dream**[49] 4370 2-9-0 0...........................(b[1]) MickyFenton 11 —
(K A Ryan) *sn rdn: led over 2f: lost pl 2f out: sn bhd and heavily eased* **100/1**

1m 12.97s (1.17) **Going Correction** +0.15s/f (Good) **13** Ran SP% **118.5**
Speed ratings (Par 92): **98,88,88,85,85 84,84,84,83,80 80,78,57**
toteswinger: 1&2 £17.80, 1&3 £8.40, 2&3 £77.80. CSF £87.01 TOTE £2.40: £1.10, £9.80, £3.90; EX 64.50.
Owner Jaber Abdullah **Bred** Rabbah Bloodstock Limited **Trained** Manton, Wilts

FOCUS
This was a moderate fillies' maiden with the winner proving in a different league.

NOTEBOOK
Secret Queen ran out an easy winner. Below her best over 1m at Kempton last time, she had earlier shown fair form in a couple of 7f maidens and took the race by the scruff of the neck 3f out. She sprinted clear to win with any amount in hand, despite swishing her tail, and it wouldn't surprise to see her take her chance in the Redcar Two-Year-old Trophy next time over the C&D. (op 13-8)
Mooinooi is from a good sprinting family and she showed plenty of ability in the first-time cheekpieces. Now qualified for a handicap mark, she should pick up a race in that sphere. (op 50-1)
Chardonnay, a daughter of Piccolo who was slowly away, came through late for third and this has to go down as a promising start. She will stay an extra furlong and should find a small race at some stage. (op 22-1)
Chushka, a promising fourth on debut, was again slowly away and soon outpaced on ground quicker than ideal. She never looked like winning, making a little late headway, and will probably fare better in nurseries. (op 4-1)
Melundy, runner-up over C&D on debut, failed to improve on that and proved most disappointing. (op 5-2 tchd 7-2)
Tobougie On Down, very much bred to be a juvenile, was wearing an eyeshield for this racecourse debut and, despite giving trouble in the stalls and being slowly away, she actually shaped with a fair amount of promise.
Alhena(IRE), a half-sister to the Moyglare Stud Stakes winner Mail The Desert, got going late and should improve. (tchd 20-1)

5950 WEDDING RECEPTIONS @ REDCAR RACECOURSE NURSERY 5f
2:40 (2:42) (Class 6) (0-65,65) 2-Y-0 **£2,104** (£626; £312; £156) **Stalls** Centre

Form RPR
1510 1 **On The Piste (IRE)**[18] 5372 2-8-11 **60**......................... GaryBartley(5) 14 64
(L A Mullaney) *mid-div: hdwy u.p 2f out: styd on to ld ins fnl f: r.o* **33/1**
034 2 *1* **Lewyn**[108] 2435 2-9-7 **65**..................................(b[1]) StephenDonohoe 17 65
(K A Ryan) *overall ldr towards stands' side: hung bdly lft and hdd ins fnl f: no ex* **9/1**
5606 3 *nk* **Nabrina (IRE)**[13] 5553 2-8-2 **53**.............................. JohnCavanagh(7) 3 52
(M Brittain) *chsd ldrs: keeing on same pce whn hmpd ins fnl f* **33/1**
3505 4 *½* **Oondiri (IRE)**[15] 5467 2-9-2 **60**................................... DavidAllan 4 58
(T D Easterby) *w ldrs: kpt on same pce ins fnl f* **4/1**[2]
4530 5 *shd* **Val C**[13] 5550 2-9-6 **64**.. SebSanders 1 61
(N P Littmoden) *racd alone far side: w ldrs: kpt on same pce ins fnl f* **8/1**[3]
6413 6 *1* **Watch Chain (IRE)**[7] 5721 2-8-7 **56**.......................... AshleyMorgan(5) 2 50
(M H Tompkins) *mid-div: hdwy 2f out: styd on wl ins fnl f: n.m.r towards fin* **5/2**[1]
0600 7 *shd* **Speedyfix**[5] 5776 2-8-6 **50**....................................(tp) JimmyQuinn 7 43
(Mrs C A Dunnett) *in rr: hdwy 2f out: edgd lft ins fnl f nt rch ldrs* **33/1**
5663 8 *nk* **Kirkby's Gem**[13] 5553 2-8-2 **53**................................... BillyCray(7) 11 45
(A Berry) *in rr: styd on fnl 2f: nt rch ldrs* **40/1**
0000 9 *nk* **Social Grace**[15] 5467 2-9-7 **65**................................... TonyHamilton 13 56
(D H Brown) *chsd ldrs: one pce fnl 2f* **16/1**
1063 10 *½* **Duke Of Rainford**[5] 5776 2-8-9 **53**............................ GrahamGibbons 16 42
(D Nicholls) *chsd ldrs: wknd appr fnl f* **8/1**[3]
5004 11 *½* **Avec Moi**[33] 4912 2-8-4 **48**... TPO'Shea 15 35
(Mrs C A Dunnett) *in rr: sme hdwy 2f out: nvr a factor* **28/1**
060 12 *1 ¾* **Jigajig**[19] 5337 2-7-8 **45**...................................(v[1]) ShirleyTeasdale(7) 18 26
(N Wilson) *chsd ldrs: wknd over 1f out* **100/1**
3050 13 *2 ¼* **Annia Galeria (IRE)**[5] 5776 2-8-7 **56**......................... BMcHugh(5) 6 29
(C A Dwyer) *chsd ldrs: wknd over 1f out* **20/1**
2465 14 *1 ¾* **Reel Credit Crunch**[24] 5226 2-9-4 **62**............................(b) TomEaves 5 29
(I W McInnes) *chsd ldrs: wkng whn hmpd jst ins fnl f* **28/1**
000 15 *2 ¾* **Azzez Life**[14] 5519 2-8-1 **45**...................................(b[1]) KoseiMiura 9 —
(R C Guest) *chsd ldrs: lost pl 2f out* **50/1**

4305 **16** *1* **Southwark Newshawk**[18] 5372 2-8-9 **56**.............. WilliamCarson(3) 10 9
(Mrs C A Dunnett) *a in rr* **25/1**

500 **17** *1 1/2* **Turf Time**[1] 5611 2-7-11 **48**.............................. JamesPSullivan(7) 12 —
(J A Glover) *rrd s: a in rr* **16/1**

0000 **18** *1/2* **Minnie Rocket**[22] 5292 2-7-8 **45**.............................. MatthewLawson(7) 8 —
(R C Guest) *mid-div: reminders after 1f: sn lost pl* **100/1**

60.20 secs (1.60) **Going Correction** +0.15s/f (Good) **18** Ran SP% **123.3**
Speed ratings (Par 93): **93,91,90,90,89 88,88,87,87,86 85,82,79,76,72 70,68,67**
toteswinger: 1&2 £34.40, 1&3 £157.60, 2&3 £67.30. CSF £284.57 CT £9796.19 TOTE £29.60: £3.70, £2.60, £6.60, £1.90; EX 311.80.
Owner K Humphries & Sons Roofing Contractors **Bred** C Kelly **Trained** Great Habton, North Yorkshire

FOCUS
This was a weak if competitive nursery. The form is rated around the placed horses.

NOTEBOOK
On The Piste(IRE) sprang a 33/1 surprise. Twice a selling winner this term, she was soon struggling having been hampered at the start on her recent handicap debut at Southwell and appreciated the return to turf. She came through to challenge over 1f out and stayed on well to score, suggesting she will get another furlong or so in time. (op 40-1)
Lewyn, off since May and sporting first-time blinkers for this nursery debut, was soon on the pace more towards the stands' side and saw her race out well, despite hanging left, but was unable to repel the winner. (op 13-2 tchd 6-1)
Nabrina(IRE), racing from a mark of just 53, improved on her form in maidens, keeping on despite getting slightly hampered, and should be suited by 6f before long.
Oondiri(IRE) has been sliding in the weights since going handicapping and it was no surprise to see a better effort returned to a track she goes well at. (op 5-1 tchd 3-1)
Val C showed good speed against the far rail, but wasn't quite on terms with those centre-track at the business end. (op 7-1)
Watch Chain(IRE), 4lb higher than when winning a nursery at Southwell last month, ran well when last of three in a fair contest at Folkestone last time, and he wasn't disgraced on this drop back in trip. (op 3-1 tchd 100-30)
Speedyfix kept on inside the final 2f to register an improved effort. (op 50-1)

5951 EUROPEAN BREEDERS' FUND - DOUBLE TRIGGER MAIDEN STKS (FOR THE DOUBLE TRIGGER TROPHY) 1m 1f
3:10 (3:13) (Class 5) 2-Y-O **£3,561** (£1,059; £529; £264) **Stalls** Low

Form RPR

022 **1** **Navy List (FR)**[21] 5312 2-9-0 81.............................. AhmedAjtebi(3) 8 85+
(Saeed Bin Suroor) *led 1f: trckd ldrs: shkn up to ld over 2f out: rdn wl clr over 1f out: eased fnl 75yds* **11/10**[1]

054 **2** *11* **Storm Command (IRE)**[15] 5466 2-9-3 57.......................... TomEaves 2 59
(B Smart) *chsd ldrs: drvn over 2f out: edgd rt and wnt modest 2nd over 1f out* **40/1**

3 **3** *3/4* **Ting Ting (USA)**[15] 5466 2-8-12 0.............................. MickyFenton 5 53
(T P Tate) *s.i.s: drvn to ld after 1f: hdd over 2f out: kpt on same pce* **13/2**[3]

5 **4** *nse* **Indochina**[11] 5590 2-9-3 0.............................. GregFairley 9 57
(M Johnston) *chsd ldrs: effrt over 2f out: kpt on same pce* **3/1**[2]

0 **5** *2* **Architrave**[4] 5787 2-9-3 0.............................. SebSanders 7 53+
(Sir Mark Prescott) *drvn to chse ldrs: drvn and outpcd over 3f out: hung lft: kpt on same pce fnl 2f* **15/2**

6 *2 1/4* **Claddagh** 2-9-3 0.............................. TPO'Shea 11 49
(M Johnston) *in rr: hdwy over 2f out: sn outpcd* **16/1**

66 **7** *shd* **North Shadow**[9] 5669 2-9-3 0.............................. JimmyQuinn 10 49
(A D Brown) *in rr: hdwy on wd outside over 2f out: wknd over 1f out* **33/1**

00 **8** *1 1/2* **Bollin Andrew**[9] 5669 2-9-3 0.............................. DavidAllan 1 46+
(T D Easterby) *s.i.s: a towards rr* **100/1**

0 **9** *3/4* **Edward Longshanks (USA)**[31] 4993 2-9-3 0.............................. DNolan 4 44
(T P Tate) *in rr: drvn over 4f out: nvr a factor* **40/1**

0 **10** *3/4* **Check The Anchor (IRE)**[16] 5439 2-9-0 0........... MichaelJStainton(3) 6 43
(N Tinkler) *s.i.s: mid-div: drvn over 4f out: sn wknd* **100/1**

1m 53.67s (0.67) **Going Correction** 0.0s/f (Good) **10** Ran SP% **113.4**
Speed ratings (Par 95): **97,87,86,86,84 82,82,81,80,79**
toteswinger: 1&2 £7.60, 1&3 £2.60, 2&3 £8.30. CSF £63.26 TOTE £1.80: £1.10, £3.80, £1.60; EX 37.70.
Owner Godolphin **Bred** Berend Van Dalfsen **Trained** Newmarket, Suffolk

FOCUS
This was turned into a procession by Navy List but the form is very weak behind him.

NOTEBOOK
Navy List(FR) eased to the front inside the final 3f and came home to win eased down. Runner-up on each of his last two starts and officially rated 81, he looks to be getting better all the time and will obviously have no trouble staying further. (op 7-4)
Storm Command(IRE), with an official rating of 57, was well and truly put in his place by the winner, but this still represented improved form as he proved too good for the remainder. He may do better still in nurseries. (op 50-1)
Ting Ting(USA), ahead of the second at Beverley last time, was made plenty of use of on this rise in trip and didn't get home. This was a bit disappointing. (op 7-1 tchd 6-1)
Indochina, expected to improve markedly on his recent debut effort at Epsom when very green, was made to look very slow back in fourth and is unlikely to be seen at his best until contesting 1m4f-plus handicaps next term. (op 2-1)
Architrave ◆, eighth on his debut only four days earlier, again hinted at ability and is another sure to do better in middle-distance handicaps next season. (op 9-1 tchd 7-1)
Claddagh, an already-gelded son of Dubai Destination with plenty of speed in the pedigree, never got into it and will do better in time. (op 10-1)

5952 MARKET CROSS JEWELLERS H'CAP 1m 6f 19y
3:40 (3:40) (Class 5) (0-70,70) 3-Y-O **£2,752** (£818; £409; £204) **Stalls** Low

Form RPR

-313 **1** **Veiled**[18] 5376 3-9-7 **70**.............................. SebSanders 6 83+
(Sir Mark Prescott) *hld up: effrt on outside over 3f out: led 2f out: styd on wl* **4/1**[2]

1336 **2** *3* **Bollin Judith**[27] 5131 3-8-7 **56**.............................. DavidAllan 3 62
(T D Easterby) *chsd ldrs: drvn over 5f out: wandered and hung lft: styd on same pce fnl 2f* **7/1**

4212 **3** *1/2* **Addison De Witt**[19] 5342 3-8-7 **61**.....................(v) PatrickDonaghy(5) 5 66
(Micky Hammond) *t.k.h: trckd ldrs: effrt over 3f out: nt clr run over 2f out: swtchd outside: styd on ins fnl f* **9/1**

3434 **4** *1/2* **Classic Contours (USA)**[22] 5291 3-9-2 **70**..................... BMcHugh(5) 2 75
(J J Quinn) *led: qcknd over 4f out: hdd over 2f out: kpt on same pce* **11/2**

600 **5** *hd* **Beat The Shower**[35] 4838 3-8-2 **51** oh3.............................. KoseiMiura 4 56
(P D Niven) *chsd ldrs: drvn 4f out: led over 2f out: sn hdd: one pce* **16/1**

3311 **6** *1 1/2* **Twist Again (IRE)**[16] 5442 3-9-7 **70**.............................. JimmyQuinn 8 73
(P Howling) *hld up in midfield: hdwy to chse ldrs 6f out: nt clr run over 2f out: wknd ins fnl f* **10/3**[1]

4032 **7** *1* **Khayar (IRE)**[16] 5442 3-8-7 **61**.............................. AshleyMorgan(5) 7 62
(M H Tompkins) *t.k.h in rr: hdwy to trck ldrs 9f out: pushed along over 5f out: one pce fnl 3f* **9/2**[3]

4006 **8** *3/4* **Tae Kwon Do (USA)**[19] 5342 3-8-4 **53** oh1 ow2.................. TPO'Shea 1 55+
(Miss J A Camacho) *hld up in rr: hdwy on ins over 3f out: n.m.r: wknd and eased ins fnl f* **14/1**

3m 5.91s (1.21) **Going Correction** 0.0s/f (Good) **8** Ran SP% **111.7**
Speed ratings (Par 101): **96,94,94,93,93 92,92,91**
toteswinger: 1&2 £4.10, 1&3 £3.80, 2&3 £7.30. CSF £30.31 CT £230.73 TOTE £3.60: £1.70, £2.00, £2.20; EX 22.20.
Owner Cheveley Park Stud **Bred** Cheveley Park Stud Ltd **Trained** Newmarket, Suffolk

FOCUS
A good little race of its type. The winner was value for extra and the placed horses help with the standard.
Tae Kwon Do(USA) Official explanation: jockey said gelding was denied a clear run

5953 SUBSCRIBE TO RACING UK (S) STKS 1m 2f
4:10 (4:11) (Class 6) 3-5-Y-O **£2,047** (£604; £302) **Stalls** Low

Form RPR

-434 **1** **Kind Heart**[20] 5327 3-8-5 73.............................. KoseiMiura 12 57+
(Sir Mark Prescott) *t.k.h towards rr: hdwy on outside over 3f out: rdn to ld 2f out: hld on wl towards fin* **10/11**[1]

3523 **2** *1* **Bold Indian (IRE)**[15] 5465 5-9-3 55.............................. DavidAllan 1 60
(M E Sowersby) *hood removed v late: s.i.s: hld up in rr: hld up in rr: stdy hdwy over 3f out: nt clr run and swtchd outside over 1f out: chsng wnr and no ex last 75yds* **12/1**

0306 **3** *2 1/4* **Melkatant**[13] 5549 3-8-5 45.............................. JimmyQuinn 11 51
(N Bycroft) *in rr: hdwy on outer over 2f out: kpt on same pce fnl f* **33/1**

5554 **4** *2* **Ingleby Princess**[7] 5730 5-8-9 50.............................. NeilBrown(3) 8 47
(T D Barron) *trckd ldrs: led over 2f out: sn hdd and no ex* **8/1**[3]

5500 **5** *shd* **Flora's Pride**[11] 5600 5-8-7 50.............................. BMcHugh(5) 7 46
(K G Reveley) *in rr-div: hdwy on outer over 3f out: one pce fnl f* **25/1**

6100 **6** *1 1/4* **Phantom Serenade (IRE)**[11] 5601 4-9-3 54.............................. TomEaves 3 49
(M Dods) *trckd ldrs: nt clr run on ins over 2f out: wknd over 1f out* **25/1**

6401 **7** *hd* **Whipma Whopma Gate (IRE)**[7] 5730 4-8-12 47.................(b) DNolan 6 43
(D Carroll) *chsd ldrs: one pce whn n.m.r over 1f out* **7/1**[2]

0040 **8** *1/2* **Blastie**[16] 5423 4-9-3 50.............................. GrahamGibbons 5 47
(T D Walford) *chsd ldrs: hung rt bnd over 5f out: one pce appr fnl f: eased towards fin* **33/1**

0630 **9** *2 1/4* **Run Free**[14] 5294 5-8-12 46.............................. GaryBartley(5) 2 43
(N Wilson) *led: hdd over 2f out: lost pl over 1f out* **66/1**

0460 **10** *shd* **Bivouac (UAE)**[18] 5364 5-9-3 56.............................. PJMcDonald 10 43
(G A Swinbank) *trckd ldrs: chal 2f out: hung lft and sn wknd* **7/1**[2]

2m 6.25s (-0.85) **Going Correction** 0.0s/f (Good)
WFA 3 from 4yo+ 7lb **10** Ran SP% **111.3**
Speed ratings (Par 101): **103,102,100,98,98 97,97,97,95,95**
toteswinger: 1&2 £4.40, 1&3 £4.80, 2&3 £15.80. CSF £11.14 TOTE £1.90: £1.30, £2.00, £6.00; EX 12.10.The winner was sold to Paul Howling for 13,000gns.
Owner B Haggas **Bred** J B Haggas **Trained** Newmarket, Suffolk

FOCUS
This was a weak contest and the likes of the third hold down the form.
Whipma Whopma Gate(IRE) Official explanation: jockey said filly was denied a clear run

5954 CHRISTMAS PARTIES @ REDCAR RACECOURSE MAIDEN STKS 7f
4:40 (4:41) (Class 5) 3-Y-O+ **£2,752** (£818; £409; £204) **Stalls** Centre

Form RPR

-335 **1** **Justonefortheroad**[95] 2845 3-9-3 70.............................. TonyHamilton 9 75+
(R A Fahey) *wnt lft s: t.k.h: trckd ldrs: stmbld after 1f: hdwy over 2f out: styd on to ld jst ins fnl f: r.o* **5/2**[2]

332 **2** *1* **El Ameen**[17] 5394 3-9-3 75.............................. TPO'Shea 12 73
(M Johnston) *chsd ldrs: rdn to chal over 2f out: kpt on same pce ins fnl f* **1/1**[1]

3 **3** *1 1/2* **Totalitarian**[12] 5572 3-9-3 0.............................. JerryO'Dwyer 5 69
(S A Callaghan) *wnt rt s: w ldrs: led over 2f out: carried hd high: hdd jst ins fnl f: kpt on same pce* **5/1**[3]

0-0 **4** *8* **See That Girl**[80] 3352 3-8-5 0.............................. AdamCarter(7) 7 44+
(B Smart) *mid-div: hdwy to chse ldrs over 2f out: sn lost pl* **66/1**

0563 **5** *1/2* **Port Ronan (USA)**[15] 5468 3-9-3 45..............................(p) PAspell 10 48
(J S Wainwright) *t.k.h: led: hdd over 2f out: sn wknd* **80/1**

0-20 **6** *nse* **Safari Song (IRE)**[35] 4846 3-9-3 70.............................. TomEaves 2 47
(B Smart) *shld up: hdwy to chse ldrs over 2f out: sn wknd* **8/1**

3400 **7** *3/4* **Towthorpe**[9] 5672 3-8-10 64.............................. JohnCavanagh(7) 3 46
(M Brittain) *dwlt: hdwy to chse ldrs over 3f out: sn lost pl* **33/1**

4300 **8** *3/4* **Beaux Yeux**[10] 5624 3-8-12 50..............................(p) MickyFenton 4 39
(P T Midgley) *chsd ldrs: lost pl over 2f out* **50/1**

0 **9** *3 3/4* **Spiosra (USA)**[7] 5731 3-8-12 0..............................(t) DNolan 6 29
(C J Teague) *chsd ldrs: lost pl over 2f out: sn bhd* **125/1**

0- **10** *6* **Freddie Bolt**[348] 6383 3-9-3 0.............................. DavidAllan 8 19
(F Watson) *dwlt and hmpd s: a in rr* **100/1**

0000 **11** *2 3/4* **Tump Mac**[15] 5465 5-9-7 39..............................(t) JimmyQuinn 11 14
(N Bycroft) *hld up in rr: hdwy over 3f out: lost pl over 2f out* **100/1**

1m 25.1s (0.60) **Going Correction** +0.15s/f (Good)
WFA 3 from 5yo 4lb **11** Ran SP% **116.8**
Speed ratings (Par 103): **102,100,99,90,89 89,88,87,83,76 73**
toteswinger: 1&2 £2.60, 1&3 £3.20, 2&3 £2.40. CSF £5.24 TOTE £3.70: £1.20, £1.10, £2.00; EX 11.00.
Owner The Pontoon Partnership **Bred** Wellsummers Farm & Hammarsfield B'Stock **Trained** Musley Bank, N Yorks

FOCUS
Three came a long way clear in what was a weak maiden. The fifth holds down the form.

5955 REDCAR RACECOURSE CONFERENCE & EVENTS VENUE APPRENTICE H'CAP 6f
5:10 (5:10) (Class 5) (0-70,69) 3-Y-O+ **£2,752** (£818; £409; £204) **Stalls** Centre

Form RPR

-065 **1** **Yorkshire Blue**[11] 5601 10-8-7 **54**..............................(p) DebraEngland 12 62
(J S Goldie) *hld up in rr: hdwy over 1f out: styd on to ld last strides* **14/1**

1100 **2** *shd* **Just Sam (IRE)**[11] 5597 4-9-3 **64**.............................. BillyCray 1 72
(R E Barr) *swtchd rt s: led: kpt on gamely: jst ct fnl strides* **20/1**

403 **3** *hd* **John Keats**[14] 5516 6-9-5 **66**..............................(p) JamesPSullivan 6 73
(J S Goldie) *hld up towards rr: hdwy stands' side over 1f out: styd on strly ins fnl f* **4/1**[1]

105 **4** *1/2* **Minturno (USA)**[19] 5340 3-9-2 **68**..............................(p) NSLawes(3) 11 74
(Mrs A Duffield) *chsd ldrs: effrt 2f out: w ldrs ins fnl f: no ex* **18/1**

0221 **5** *nk* **Who's Shirl**[17] 5391 3-9-6 **69**.............................. MatthewDavies 3 74
(C W Fairhurst) *mid-div: hdwy 2f out: upsides ins fnl f: no ex* **11/2**[3]

2024 **6** *2 1/4* **Elkhorn**[7] 5729 7-8-7 **54** oh1..............................(b) SimonPearce 9 52
(Miss J A Camacho) *w ldrs: t.k.h: rdn over 1f out: sn wknd* **9/2**[2]

0050 **7** *nk* **Thunder Bay**[14] 5518 4-8-3 **55**.....(p) FrazerWilliams(5) 5 52
(R A Fahey) *trckd ldrs: effrt 2f out: fdd appr fnl f* **20/1**

4000 **8** *2* **Jimwil (IRE)**[9] 5677 3-9-2 **68**.....(b) DavidKenny(3) 8 59
(M Dods) *hld up towards rr: hdwy stands' side 2f out: sn hmpd: no ch after* **25/1**

0021 **9** *½* **Darcy's Pride (IRE)**[17] 5396 5-8-10 **57**.....(t) TobyAtkinson 4 47
(P T Midgley) *in rr-div: hdwy over 1f out: nvr nr ldrs* **12/1**

0000 **10** *hd* **Sea Rover (IRE)**[37] 4783 5-9-4 **68**..... JohnCavanagh(3) 2 57
(M Brittain) *chsd ldrs on outer: wknd over 1f out* **20/1**

5530 **11** *3* **Elijah Pepper (USA)**[17] 5409 4-9-6 **67**..... RosieJessop 10 47
(T D Barron) *restless in stalls: s.s: hdwy stands' side whn wnt rt over 1f out: wknd* **13/2**

0004 **12** *hd* **Angaric (IRE)**[19] 5343 6-8-10 **62**..... AdamCarter(5) 14 41
(B Smart) *w ldrs towards stands' side: lost pl over 1f out* **14/1**

0604 **13** *2½* **Foreign Rhythm (IRE)**[16] 5443 4-8-4 **54** oh7..... MatthewLawson(3) 7 26
(N Tinkler) *chsd ldrs far side: wknd over 1f out* **33/1**

0450 **14** *10* **Bateleur**[14] 5525 5-8-12 **64**.....(v) RyanClark(5) 13 6
(M R Channon) *s.s: hdwy stands' side 3f out: lost pl 2f out: sn bhd* **18/1**

1m 12.23s (0.43) **Going Correction** +0.15s/f (Good)
WFA 3 from 4yo+ 2lb **14** Ran SP% **119.5**
Speed ratings (Par 103): **103,102,102,101,101 98,98,95,94,94 90,90,86,73**
toteswinger: 1&2 £34.80, 1&3 £9.60, 2&3 £5.30. CSF £273.04 CT £1374.39 TOTE £18.40: £5.00, £4.00, £2.00; EX 235.70 Place 6: £46.71, Place 5: £19.96..
Owner John Murphy **Bred** R T And Mrs Watson **Trained** Uplawmoor, E Renfrews
■ Stewards' Enquiry : Rosie Jessop two-day ban: careless riding (Sep 28-29)
Billy Cray one-day ban: failed to keep straight from stalls (Sep 28)

FOCUS
This was a low-grade sprint handicap and the form is solid but limited.
Elkhorn Official explanation: trainer's rep said gelding ran too free
T/Plt: £27.60 to a £1 stake. Pool: £50,780.84. 1,340.03 winning tickets. T/Qpdt: £3.10 to a £1 stake. Pool: £3,628.82. 857.30 winning tickets. WG

3442 SAINT-CLOUD (L-H)
Monday, September 14

OFFICIAL GOING: Good to soft

5956a PRIX HERMIERES (MAIDEN FILLIES) 7f
1:25 (1:30) 2-Y-O **£11,650** (£4,660; £3,495; £2,330; £1,165)

RPR

1 **Late Romance (USA)**[42] 2-8-9..... MBarzalona(5) 89
(A Fabre, France)

2 *1* **Green Dandy (IRE)**[29] 2-9-0..... OPeslier 87
(E J O'Neill) *racd in 2nd: disp ld gng wl 2f out: hdd and no ex fnl 150yds* **11/2**[1]

3 *2* **Wadowice (FR)**[35] 2-9-0..... JVictoire 82
(Mme Pia Brandt, France)

4 *snk* **Gotlandia (FR)**[29] 2-9-0..... 81
(Y De Nicolay, France)

5 *2* **Mark Of Brazil (FR)**[23] 5279 2-9-0..... 76
(F Chappet, France)

6 *2* **Bhaylana (USA)**[29] 2-9-0..... 71
(N Clement, France)

7 *2½* **Dikta Melody (FR)**[40] 2-9-0..... 65
(P Demercastel, France)

8 *1* **Greensleeves (FR)**[35] 2-9-0..... 62
(J E Pease, France)

9 *1½* **Insouciance (FR)**[102] 2-9-0..... 59
(D Prod'Homme, France)

10 *2½* **Timpanist (USA)** 2-9-0..... 52
(Mme C Head-Maarek, France)

0 **Night Of Idaho (FR)** 2-9-0..... —
(M Houdoin, France)

0 **Ma Gypsy Dancer (FR)** 2-9-0..... —
(F Cohen, France)

0 **Vertana (IRE)** 2-9-0..... —
(H-A Pantall, France)

0 **Kimberlais (FR)** 2-9-0..... —
(Rod Collet, France)

0 **Trofee Dore (FR)** 2-9-0..... —
(Mme R-W Allen, France)

1m 25.7s (-6.50) **15** Ran SP% **15.4**
PARI-MUTUEL: WIN 10.30; PL 3.70, 2.50, 2.80; DF 29.00.
Owner Sheikh Mohammed **Bred** Darley **Trained** Chantilly, France

5654 HAYDOCK (L-H)
Tuesday, September 15

OFFICIAL GOING: 5f & 6f - good to firm (good in places; 9.2); 1m 4f & 1m 6f - good to soft (good in places; 7.9)
Rail realignment increased distances on round course by about 16yds.
Wind: Light to moderate, half-behind Weather: Sunny intervals

5957 E B F TAYLORMADE BETTING MAIDEN STKS 5f
2:30 (2:32) (Class 5) 2-Y-O **£3,885** (£1,156; £577; £288) **Stalls** Centre

Form RPR

02 **1** **Magical Macey (USA)**[11] 5620 2-9-3 0.....(b) PhillipMakin 10 80
(T D Barron) *mde all: rdn over 1f out: edgd lft ent fnl f: r.o and wl on top at fin* **7/1**[3]

003 **2** *1½* **Confessional**[14] 5552 2-9-3 82..... DavidAllan 2 75
(T D Easterby) *in tch: clsd 2f out: chsd wnr over 1f out: tried to chal ins fnl f: jinked lft abt 100yds out: nt qckn* **4/1**[2]

6 **3** *1¼* **Fear Nothing**[12] 5611 2-9-3 0..... RichardMullen 1 71
(E S McMahon) *chsd ldrs: effrt and edgd lft fr 2f out: racd alone on far rail 1f out: styd on same pce wl ins fnl f* **4/1**[2]

024 **4** *3* **Fawley Green**[24] 5256 2-9-3 78..... FrancisNorton 7 60
(W R Muir) *w wnr tl rdn 2f out: nt qckn over 1f out: one pce afer* **15/8**[1]

0340 **5** *½* **Olympic Ceremony**[24] 5256 2-9-3 70..... PaulHanagan 3 58
(R A Fahey) *chsd ldrs: rdn over 2f out: sn no imp and outpcd* **15/2**

0 **6** *13* **Royal Cheer**[48] 4430 2-8-12 0..... SilvestreDeSousa 9 6
(Mrs A Duffield) *towards rr: pushed along 3f out: nvr on terms* **33/1**

0300 **7** *3* **Lees Anthem**[110] 2408 2-9-3 0.....(v) DNolan 5 —
(C J Teague) *w ldrs tl rdn over 2f out: wknd wl over 1f out* **14/1**

8 *7* **Ancient Oak** 2-9-3 0..... PJMcDonald 6 —
(H A McWilliams) *missed break: green: a outpcd and bhd* **50/1**

59.67 secs (-1.43) **Going Correction** -0.50s/f (Hard) **8** Ran SP% **110.6**
Speed ratings (Par 95): **91,88,86,81,81 60,55,44**
toteswingers: 1&2 £4.80, 1&3 £6.00, 2&3 £4.10 CSF £32.74 TOTE £7.90: £1.80, £1.70, £1.60; EX 22.20.
Owner K J Alderson **Bred** Silver Springs Stud Farm Inc & Mrs J Costelloe **Trained** Maunby, N Yorks

FOCUS
The ground on the new sprint track was very quick and they broke the one minute barrier. Quite an interesting 5f maiden and a highly progressive winner. The runner-up helps with the level.

NOTEBOOK
Magical Macey(USA), blinkered for the first time when runner-up in a weaker race run on soft ground on his second start, showed bags of toe racing towards the stands' side. He came home as straight as a gun barrel - unlike the placed horses. He has improved with each outing and nurseries presumably now beckon. (tchd 13-2 and 8-1)
Confessional, rated 82 after finishing third in a Class 3 event at Ripon on his first start after being gelded, was outpaced for a few strides at halfway. He posed a big threat to the winner but threw away his chance by diving first left, then coming right inside the last. He is not straightforward but has the ability to find a 6f maiden, but he might struggle in nurseries from this inflated mark. (op 5-2)
Fear Nothing, on his toes beforehand, had shown little when badly drawn on his debut on the Polytrack at Wolverhampton. He showed bags of pace but went left and ended up racing against the far-side rail. All speed, there ought to be a race to be won with him. (tchd 5-1)
Fawley Green, who had shown speed on his three previous starts, seemed likely to be suited by the drop back to five but he couldn't lead and dropped away tamely. (op 11-4 tchd 7-4)
Olympic Ceremony, rated 70, was having his seventh start and already looks fully exposed. (op 8-1 tchd 6-1)
Lees Anthem\n\x\x , a wayward type, was back after an absence of 110-days, during which he was gelded. He showed plenty of speed before dropping right away. He has a fair level of ability but has plenty to prove now. (op 12-1)

5958 E B F CHESS TELECOM MAIDEN STKS 6f
3:00 (3:05) (Class 5) 2-Y-O **£3,885** (£1,156; £577; £288) **Stalls** Centre

Form RPR

0220 **1** **Elusive Sue (USA)**[28] 5136 2-8-12 72..... PaulHanagan 10 76
(R A Fahey) *trckd ldrs: wnt 2nd wl over 2f out: rdn whn edgd lft and led 1f out: continued to edge lft ins fnl f: r.o wl* **5/2**[1]

23 **2** *2¼* **Call To Arms (IRE)**[39] 4738 2-9-3 0..... JoeFanning 5 74
(M Johnston) *led: rdn and eged lft over 1f out: sn hdd: nt qckn ins fnl f* **4/1**[3]

06 **3** *3½* **Frontline Boy (IRE)**[25] 5234 2-9-3 0..... AndrewElliott 2 70+
(A P Jarvis) *a.p: rdn 2f out: u.p but stl cl 3rd whn n.m.r and hmpd ins fnl f: unable to get on terms w front 2 after* **14/1**

4 **4** *7* **Via Aurelia (IRE)**[29] 5109 2-8-12 0..... RichardMullen 3 38
(J R Fanshawe) *trckd ldrs: pushed along and wknd over 1f out* **15/2**

6 **5** *2½* **Maragna (IRE)**[10] 5668 2-9-3 0..... SilvestreDeSousa 9 35
(Paul Green) *midfield: pushed along 3f out: wl outpcd fr 2f out* **5/1**

6 *10* **Redden** 2-9-3 0..... KFallon 6 14+
(W J Haggas) *got upset whn loading: sn pushed along towards rr: wl outpcd fr 2f out* **11/4**[2]

46 **7** *3¾* **Ed's A Red**[25] 5208 2-8-5 0..... BillyCray(7) 7 —
(A Berry) *missed break: wnt rt s: in rr: pushed along and edgd lft 4f out: nvr on terms* **100/1**

8 *59* **Starlight Boy** 2-8-12 0..... DeanHeslop(5) 4 —
(S Wynne) *rrd coming out of stalls: slowly away: sn wl bhd: t.o* **66/1**

1m 12.51s (-1.99) **Going Correction** -0.50s/f (Hard) **8** Ran SP% **112.8**
Speed ratings (Par 95): **93,90,85,76,72 59,54,—**
toteswingers: 1&2 £2.90, 1&3 £4.70, 2&3 £5.00 CSF £12.52 TOTE £3.70: £1.60, £1.40, £3.10; EX 14.90.
Owner P D Smith Holdings Ltd **Bred** Mike G Rutherford **Trained** Musley Bank, N Yorks

FOCUS
There were problems loading these and the race was off over five minutes after the advertised time. The winner is rated to her best.

NOTEBOOK
Elusive Sue(USA), runner-up twice before disappointing in a York nursery, has an official rating of 72. She was loaded last and dived left as she took the lead inside the last. Another try in nursery company seems likely but it may be from an increased mark. (op 11-4 tchd 3-1)
Call To Arms(IRE), only third at 4/11 here after a fine debut when runner-up at Thirsk, took them along but he hung left and ended up on the far-side rail. The winner swept by him inside the last and he may be more straightforward on less-firm ground. (op 7-2 tchd 100-30)
Frontline Boy(IRE), who improved on his debut when sixth in a maiden company at York, was coming to the end of his tether when the runner-up left him with no room against the far-side rail just inside the last. This at least opens up the nursery route for him. (op 16-1 tchd 12-1)
Via Aurelia(IRE), fourth first time in a weak event at Yarmouth, was left behind in the final 2f and may need a step up to 7f or even 1m. (op 11-2)
Maragna(IRE) was run off his feet by the halfway mark. Official explanation: jockey said colt hung left-handed (op 8-1)
Redden, a well-made, good-bodied son of Pivotal, went to post very gingerly. Kept away from the others behind the stalls, he proved awkward to load and reared over, unseating his rider. After missing the break he could never go the pace, but hopefully this will have taught him what the game is about and he can be expected to do much better, especially on less-firm ground. (op 7-2 tchd 9-4)

5959 E B F HALLIWELLS LLP CLASSIFIED STKS 6f
3:30 (3:33) (Class 3) 3-Y-O+ **£10,361** (£3,083; £1,540; £769) **Stalls** Centre

Form RPR

0503 **1** **Dark Mischief**[11] 5646 3-8-11 89..... DaneO'Neill 10 102+
(H Candy) *racd nr side: mde all: rdn over 1f out: r.o: comf on top at fin* **9/4**[1]

6212 **2** *1* **Silaah**[32] 5001 5-8-13 87..... AdrianTNicholls 8 99
(D Nicholls) *racd nr side: hld up bhd wnr: hdwy 2f out: wnt 2nd and hung lft fr over 1f out: sn chalng: nt qckn towards fin* **4/1**[2]

6034 **3** *7* **Masai Moon**[12] 5615 5-8-11 89 ow1..... JamesMillman(3) 3 79
(B R Millman) *in tch in centre of trck: effrt over 2f out: outpcd by front pair fnl f* **7/1**

44-5 **4** *2* **Beat The Bell**[250] 86 4-8-13 89..... KFallon 6 72
(J A Osborne) *hld up: pushed along to chse ldrs 3f out: wknd 1f out* **9/1**

0263 **5** *1½* **Lucky Numbers (IRE)**[15] 5523 3-8-11 85..... SilvestreDeSousa 2 68
(Paul Green) *chsd ldrs: rdn 2f out: wknd 1f out* **13/2**

3044 **6** *¾* **Barons Spy (IRE)**[9] 5695 8-8-13 87..... JamesDoyle 7 65
(R J Price) *hld up: rdn over 2f out: sn wknd* **5/1**[3]

0000 **7** 1 1/4 **Favourite Girl (IRE)**[26] 5203 3-8-8 90 .... DavidAllan 1 59
(T D Easterby) *racd in centre of trck: showed gd spd: rdn over 2f out: wknd over 1f out* **12/1**

402- **8** 3/4 **Guertino (IRE)**[416] 4416 4-8-13 87 .... DNolan 4 59
(C J Teague) *prom: rdn over 2f out: sn wknd* **33/1**

1m 10.41s (-4.09) **Going Correction** -0.50s/f (Hard)
WFA 3 from 4yo+ 2lb 8 Ran SP% **113.9**
Speed ratings (Par 107): **107,105,96,93,91 90,89,88**
toteswingers: 1&2 £2.40, 1&3 £4.90, 2&3 £5.90 CSF £11.12 TOTE £3.50: £1.60, £2.00, £2.40; EX 9.40.
Owner First Of Many Partnership **Bred** Jeremy Green And Sons And P Bickmore **Trained** Kingston Warren, Oxon

FOCUS
A tight knit 0-90 classified stakes with just 8lb between them on official ratings, but in the end the first two pulled a long way clear. They raced nearest the fence and may be flattered.

NOTEBOOK
Dark Mischief, a third winner in a row to race from stall ten, is now rated 89 having been as high as 95 after his success on his reappearance at Newmarket in April. He went the wrong way mentally afterwards and had to be gelded, but he ran a race full of promise when third on his return at Lingfield. One of only two horses to race against the stands'-side rail, he ran out a decisive winner in the end. The gelding operation has put him back on the right tracks and, likely to face a stiff hike in the ratings after the first two finished well clear, this unexposed sprinter will be of real interest if turning out under a penalty at Ascot on Friday week. (op 5-2)
Silaah, weak in the betting beforehand, was having his second start since joining David Nicholls. He sat on the winner's tail down the stands' side but, after looking a major threat, he tended to drift left and was very much second best at the line. He went into this rated 87 but after finishing well clear his mark will shoot up. (op 100-30)
Masai Moon, runner-up on his return at Kempton, has largely disappointed since. He raced towards the far side and, like the remainder, was left for dead by the first two. (tchd 8-1)
Beat The Bell, whose last three wins at three were on Polytrack, was having his first outing since January and his first for this yard. He set off towards the centre but came stands' side at halfway before drifting back to the centre. This will have put an edge on him but the stable is going through a lengthy drought. (tchd 17-2 and 10-1)
Lucky Numbers(IRE) raced towards the centre and ended up well beaten. (op 7-1)

5960 AINSCOUGH VANGUARD H'CAP 6f
4:00 (4:03) (Class 4) (0-85,85) 3-Y-O+ £5,504 (£1,637; £818; £408) Stalls Centre

Form RPR

5212 **1** **Cape Vale (IRE)**[46] 4507 4-9-6 85 .... AdrianTNicholls 6 93
(D Nicholls) *mde all: rdn and edgd lft fr over 1f out: jst doing enough towards fin* **5/2**[1]

1055 **2** 1/2 **Novellen Lad (IRE)**[25] 5206 4-9-6 85 .... DavidAllan 3 92
(E J Alston) *chsd wnr thrght: effrt to chal fr 2f out: edgd lft fr over 1f out: nt qckn and hld fnl strides* **7/2**[2]

2050 **3** hd **Dark Lane**[15] 5523 3-8-13 80 .... PaulHanagan 7 86
(R A Fahey) *chsd ldrs: rdn and nt qckn over 1f out: r.o wl at fin* **7/1**

2310 **4** shd **Rio Cobolo (IRE)**[3] 5856 3-8-4 71 oh2 .... (v) SilvestreDeSousa 10 77
(Paul Green) *hld up in rr: pushed along 3f out: outpcd over 1f out: prog wl ins fnl f: fin wl* **5/1**[3]

0000 **5** 1/2 **Methaaly (IRE)**[5] 5799 6-8-12 77 .... (be) RichardMullen 2 81
(M Mullineaux) *s.i.s: chsd ldrs: rdn and edgd lft whn outpcd by front pair over 1f out: kpt on towards fin* **9/1**

6005 **6** nk **Cornus**[9] 5697 7-8-8 73 .... (be) JamesDoyle 4 76
(J A Glover) *hld up: rdn and outpcd over 1f out: styd on deep ins fnl f: run flattened out fnl strides* **10/1**

0412 **7** 3 1/2 **Avontuur (FR)**[12] 5597 7-8-1 71 oh2 .... (b) DeanHeslop(5) 9 64
(Mrs R A Carr) *s.i.s: hld up: effrt over 2f out: wknd fnl f* **6/1**

1m 11.59s (-2.91) **Going Correction** -0.50s/f (Hard)
WFA 3 from 4yo+ 2lb 7 Ran SP% **113.3**
Speed ratings (Par 105): **99,98,98,97,97 96,92**
toteswingers: 1&2 £3.30, 1&3 £3.90, 2&3 £5.00 CSF £11.14 CT £52.00 TOTE £3.30: £2.20, £2.40; EX 13.00.
Owner Lady O'Reilly **Bred** Derek Veitch **Trained** Sessay, N Yorks
■ Miss Chamanda (6/1) was withdrawn on vet's advice. R4 applies, deduct 10p in the £.
■ Stewards' Enquiry : David Allan one-day ban: used whip with excessive frequency (Sep 29)

FOCUS
A 71-85 sprint handicap and with the stands' side seemingly favoured they raced in one group on that side. The rail proved an advantage again and the compressed finish limits the form.

5961 PRINCE'S TRUST/PAVER SMITH H'CAP 1m 6f
4:30 (4:30) (Class 4) (0-85,81) 3-Y-O+ £5,504 (£1,637; £818; £408) Stalls Low

Form RPR

3-24 **1** **Ascendant**[10] 5666 3-8-13 77 .... StephenDonohoe 6 86+
(Sir Mark Prescott) *sn led: rdn and hdd over 2f out: continued to chal for press: rallied to regain ld ins fnl f: plld out ex towards fin* **3/1**[1]

-401 **2** 1 1/4 **Bajan Parkes**[22] 5308 6-9-12 79 .... DavidAllan 5 86
(E J Alston) *led early: chsd wnr: rdn to ld over 2f out: hdd ins fnl f: no ex cl home* **18/1**

1156 **3** 1/2 **Rare Ruby (IRE)**[15] 5530 5-8-13 66 .... JoeFanning 8 73
(Jennie Candlish) *hld up: sme hdwy 7f out: pushed along 4f out: effrt to chse ldrs over 2f out: styd on u.p ins fnl f* **15/2**

0362 **4** hd **Force Group (IRE)**[9] 5698 5-9-2 69 .... RichardMullen 10 75
(M H Tompkins) *chsd ldrs: rdn and hung lft over 2f out: styd on ins fnl f: nt quite pce to chal* **7/2**[2]

1243 **5** hd **Trip The Light**[4] 5837 4-9-7 79 .... (v) BMcHugh(5) 3 85
(R A Fahey) *hld up: pushed along over 3f out: styd on ins fnl f: nt quite get to ldrs* **5/1**

1025 **6** 3 1/2 **Haarth Sovereign (IRE)**[29] 5094 5-9-12 79 .... (t) TomEaves 9 81
(W R Swinburn) *hld up: pushed along over 4f out: kpt on ins fnl f: nvr able to chal* **16/1**

1320 **7** 15 **Hada Men (USA)**[25] 5235 4-9-10 77 .... KFallon 1 59+
(L M Cumani) *hld up: pushed along over 4f out: toiling fnl 3f: eased whn wl btn fnl f* **4/1**[3]

2-15 **8** 8 **Scarab (IRE)**[213] 549 4-10-0 81 .... GrahamGibbons 4 53+
(T D Walford) *broke wl: chsd ldrs: rdn and wknd over 2f out: eased whn wl btn fnl f* **11/1**

3m 3.16s (-1.14) **Going Correction** +0.05s/f (Good)
WFA 3 from 4yo+ 11lb 8 Ran SP% **115.1**
Speed ratings (Par 105): **105,104,104,103,103 101,93,88**
toteswingers: 1&2 £7.00, 1&3 £4.50, 2&3 £16.00 CSF £56.97 CT £372.29 TOTE £3.90: £1.30, £4.00, £2.30; EX 57.20.
Owner Cheveley Park Stud **Bred** Cheveley Park Stud Ltd **Trained** Newmarket, Suffolk

FOCUS
The going on the traditional outside course was on the easy side of good. A competitive 66-81 handicap and the first five finished in a bunch. The winner should progress.

5962 HALLIWELLS LLP H'CAP (FOR GENTLEMAN AMATEUR RIDERS) 1m 3f 200y
5:00 (5:00) (Class 5) (0-70,70) 4-Y-O+ £3,123 (£968; £484; £242) Stalls Centre

Form RPR

42-3 **1** **No Wonga**[19] 5359 4-10-3 55 .... MrTRDavid(3) 8 66+
(P D Evans) *hld up in midfield: hdwy to ld 3f out: drew clr over 1f out: styd on wl* **15/2**

064 **2** 3 **Randama Bay (IRE)**[39] 4740 4-10-11 65 .... MrCMartin(5) 11 70
(I A Wood) *hld up: plld to wd outside over 3f out: edgd lft and hdwy to chse wnr over 2f out: no imp fnl f* **18/1**

2221 **3** 1/2 **Arab League (IRE)**[8] 5720 4-10-6 60 6ex .... MrMPrice(5) 14 64
(R J Price) *hld up: hdwy to chse ldrs over 2f out: sn rdn: nt qckn over 1f out: kpt on ins fnl f* **4/1**[1]

5150 **4** 1 3/4 **Sporting Gesture**[9] 5698 12-10-6 55 .... MrOGreenall 1 57+
(M W Easterby) *prom: rdn over 2f out: keeping on u.p whn n.m.r and hmpd ins fnl f: no imp on ldrs after* **12/1**

5501 **5** 1 1/4 **Soundbyte**[7] 5740 4-11-2 68 6ex .... MrSTwiston-Davies(3) 12 67
(J Gallagher) *prom: rdn over 2f out: styd on same pce fr over 1f out* **9/2**[2]

4014 **6** 3 1/2 **Astrolibra**[12] 5593 5-10-4 60 .... MrDJEustace(7) 4 54
(M H Tompkins) *midfield: lost pl 6f out: pushed along 3f out: kpt on one pce fr 2f out* **14/1**

0430 **7** 4 1/2 **Channel Crossing**[61] 4021 7-10-2 54 .... MrBenBrisbourne(3) 10 40
(S Wynne) *led: rdn and hdd 3f out: wknd over 2f out* **33/1**

1224 **8** 3 1/2 **Zefooha (FR)**[12] 5600 5-10-7 63 .... MrLStrong(7) 3 44
(T D Walford) *prom tl rdn and wknd over 4f out* **6/1**[3]

1034 **9** 3 **Ibrox (IRE)**[22] 5308 4-11-5 68 .... MrSWalker 7 44
(A D Brown) *midfield: rdn and wknd over 3f out* **9/1**

5503 **10** 2 1/2 **Shady Gloom (IRE)**[22] 5308 4-11-4 70 .... MrJoshuaMoore(3) 2 42
(K A Ryan) *prom: chal 3f out: rdn and wknd over 2f out* **20/1**

6000 **11** 1 **Grethel (IRE)**[1] 5947 5-9-9 51 oh6 .... MrATBrook(7) 5 21
(A Berry) *racd keenly: hld up: hdwy on wd outside 5f out: sn handy: wknd 3f out* **40/1**

-065 **12** 11 **Still Dreaming**[17] 5444 5-9-11 51 oh6 .... (b) MrJSherwood(5) 9 4
(R J Price) *s.i.s: hld up: hdwy after 4f: rdn and wknd 4f out* **40/1**

-000 **13** 3 1/4 **Thunderstruck**[105] 2569 4-10-11 60 .... MrSDobson 13 8
(J A Glover) *hld up: hdwy after 2f: sn prom: rdn and wknd over 2f out* **40/1**

4046 **P** **Kalasam**[9] 5698 5-10-6 60 .... MrJakeGreenall(5) 6 —
(M W Easterby) *hld up: racd wd and p.u after 4f* **8/1**

2m 34.81s (1.61) **Going Correction** +0.05s/f (Good) 14 Ran SP% **120.0**
Speed ratings (Par 103): **96,94,93,92,91 89,86,84,82,80 79,72,70,—**
toteswingers: 1&2 £33.70, 1&3 £7.20, 2&3 £16.40 CSF £126.75 CT £616.24 TOTE £9.20: £3.40, £6.20, £1.90; EX 206.30 Place 6: £34.42 Place 5: £12.86.
Owner B J Mould **Bred** Exors Of The Late Lord Crawshaw **Trained** Pandy, Monmouths
■ Stewards' Enquiry : Mr C Martin two-day ban: careless riding (Sept 29-30)

FOCUS
A modest 51-70 amateur riders' handicap run at a sound pace. The winner showed improved form.
Kalasam Official explanation: jockey said bridle broke
T/Jkpt: £23,076.00 to a £1 stake. Pool: £97,504.45. 3.00 winning tickets. T/Plt: £46.70 to a £1 stake. Pool: £77,957.57. 1,216.82 winning tickets. T/Qpdt: £14.60 to a £1 stake. Pool: £4,989.34. 251.20 winning tickets. DO

5747 LINGFIELD (L-H)
Tuesday, September 15

OFFICIAL GOING: Good (good to soft in places on round course) changing to good to soft after race 1 (2.20)
Meeting switched to turf to allow rmaintenance work on the Polytrack.
Wind: Moderate, against Weather: Overcast, occasional rain from race 3 onwards

5963 ASHURST WOOD CLAIMING STKS 1m 2f
2:20 (2:22) (Class 6) 3-Y-O+ £2,047 (£604; £302) Stalls Low

Form RPR

2513 **1** **Kaleo**[6] 5772 5-9-12 74 .... DarryllHolland 1 78+
(S Dow) *mde all: clr over 3f out: rdn over 1f out: unchal* **5/4**[2]

4452 **2** 7 **Kyle Of Bute**[13] 5568 3-8-11 53 .... (v) WilliamBuick 3 56
(J L Dunlop) *dwlt: pushed up to chse wnr after 2f: rdn and no imp over 2f out: plugged on* **12/1**

0112 **3** 1 1/4 **Theocritus (USA)**[16] 5473 4-9-8 77 .... JamieSpencer 4 57
(D M Simcock) *dwlt: nvr gng sweetly and cajoled along to stay in tch: wnt 3rd over 3f out and disp 2nd over 1f out tl ins fnl f: no ch w wnr* **6/5**[1]

4001 **4** 22 **Simpsons Gamble (IRE)**[19] 5367 6-9-2 58 .... (p) LPKeniry 2 —+
(R A Teal) *trckd wnr 2f: styd in 3rd tl wknd over 3f out: sn bhd* **9/1**[3]

000- **5** 16 **Leaf Hollow**[451] 3267 3-8-8 36 .... FrankieMcDonald 5 —
(M Madgwick) *reminders in last trio after 3f: a struggling: t.o over 2f out* **100/1**

000- **6** nk **Newcastle Sam**[363] 6018 4-9-1 30 .... JerryO'Dwyer 8 —
(J J Bridger) *struggling in last trio after 4f: t.o over 2f out* **100/1**

0-00 **7** 1 1/4 **Rindless**[14] 1958 4-8-10 40 .... RichardSmith 7 —
(J F Panvert) *hld up in rr: nvr on terms: wknd over 4f out: t.o over 2f out* **100/1**

2m 10.48s (-0.02) **Going Correction** +0.10s/f (Good)
WFA 3 from 4yo+ 7lb 7 Ran SP% **110.6**
Speed ratings (Par 101): **104,98,97,79,67 66,65**
toteswingers: 1&2 £3.10, 1&3 £1.30, 2&3 £4.30 CSF £15.00 TOTE £2.50: £1.60, £2.30; EX 12.70.
Owner John Robinson and Derek Stubbs **Bred** Gestut Hof Ittlingen **Trained** Epsom, Surrey

FOCUS
Following around 4mm of rain, the ground was changed from good to firm to good, good to soft in places on the round course. A very moderate claimer in which few could be given a realistic chance and the betting made it between two of these, though ultimately it became a one-horse race. The winner is capable of better than this bare form.
Theocritus(USA) Official explanation: trainer said gelding was unsuited by the good (good to soft in places) ground

5964 COWDEN H'CAP 1m 3f 106y
2:50 (2:50) (Class 5) (0-75,76) 3-Y-O+ £3,070 (£906; £453) Stalls High

Form RPR

4261 **1** **Qelaan (USA)**[8] 5726 3-9-7 76 6ex .... RHills 5 92+
(M P Tregoning) *mounted on crse: mde all: rdn wl over 2f out: kpt on wl and safely holding runner-up fnl 2f* **5/6**[1]

5312 **2** *3* **Squad**[19] 5366 3-8-10 **65** ... PaulDoe 3 74
(S Dow) *dwlt: hld up tl prog after 4f: chsd wnr 3f out: sn rdn: styd on but no imp fnl 2f* **6/1**[3]

0403 **3** *5* **Bramalea**[12] 5593 4-8-13 **60** ... AdamKirby 8 62
(B W Duke) *taken down early: trckd ldrs after 4f: outpcd fr 3f out: n.d after: wnt modest 3rd 1f out* **12/1**

0516 **4** *2 1/4* **Merrymadcap (IRE)**[5] 5802 7-9-12 **73** ... LPKeniry 6 71
(Matthew Salaman) *trckd ldng pair to over 4f out: rdn to chse ldng duo again 3f out: sn lft bhd: lost 3rd 1f out* **14/1**

-603 **5** *1* **Yvonne Evelyn (USA)**[26] 5195 4-9-1 **62** ... NCallan 1 59
(J R Gask) *chsd wnr to 3f out: lost pl rapidly and sn wl btn: plugged on fnl f* **14/1**

3116 **6** *nk* **Love In The Park**[15] 5532 4-9-7 **68** ... JimCrowley 7 64
(R Brotherton) *in tch: dropped in rr and pushed along 6f out: nvr on terms after: struggling fr 3f out* **4/1**[2]

1240 **7** *20* **Cossack Prince**[75] 3521 4-9-7 **68** ... IanMongan 2 41+
(Mrs L J Mongan) *chsd ldrs: dropped inrr and rdn 6f out: struggling after: eased whn no ch 2f out* **16/1**

0- **8** *32* **Warrior Nation (FR)**[69] 3759 3-9-2 **71** ... NeilChalmers 4 —
(A J Chamberlain) *dropped to last 8f out: sn wknd: hopelessly t.o* **66/1**

2m 31.62s (0.12) **Going Correction** +0.10s/f (Good)
WFA 3 from 4yo+ 8lb **8** Ran SP% **117.2**
Speed ratings (Par 103): **103,100,97,95,94 94,80,56**
toteswingers: 1&2 £1.20, 1&3 £4.60, 2&3 £4.00 CSF £6.68 CT £36.83 TOTE £1.90: £1.10, £1.30, £2.10; EX 5.80.
Owner Hamdan Al Maktoum **Bred** Shadwell Farm LLC **Trained** Lambourn, Berks

FOCUS
An ordinary handicap and another all-the-way winner, who can rate a fair bit higher.
Cossack Prince Official explanation: trainer said gelding was unsuited by the good to soft ground

5965 FOREST ROW MAIDEN STKS 7f
3:20 (3:21) (Class 5) 3-Y-0+ **£2,729** (£806; £403) **Stalls** High

Form RPR

2- **1** **Bawaardi (IRE)**[415] 4446 3-9-1 0 ... RHills 4 69+
(J H M Gosden) *stdd s: hld up in rr: stdy prog fr 3f out: wnt 2nd 1f out: shkn up ins fnl f: led last strides* **11/8**[1]

0 **2** *nse* **Space Station**[13] 5572 3-9-1 0 ... PaulDoe 8 66
(S Dow) *led: rdn 2f out: hrd pressed and edgd lft fnl f: hdd last strides* **9/1**

6000 **3** *2 3/4* **Commandingpresence (USA)**[11] 5647 3-8-3 48 ... RyanClark(7) 7 54
(J J Bridger) *t.k.h early: prom: pressed ldr 1/2-way: upsides 2f out to jst over 1f out: fdd ins fnl f* **33/1**

00- **4** *3/4* **In The Mood (IRE)**[352] 6319 3-8-10 0 ... J-PGuillambert 1 52
(W Jarvis) *dwlt: tried to switch fr wdst draw but a racing towards outer: effrt fr rr over 2f out: rdn and plugged on: n.d* **4/1**[2]

60 **5** *1 1/4* **Black Stocking**[7] 5747 4-9-0 0 ... MickyFenton 6 56+
(Rae Guest) *dwlt: detached in last after 3f and racd on outer: occasional reminder and styd on steadily fr over 2f out: nrst fin: improve* **16/1**

04-0 **6** *1 1/4* **Pagan Force (IRE)**[13] 5572 3-9-1 70 ... JimCrowley 9 51
(Mrs A J Perrett) *racd against rail: trckd ldr to 1/2-way: rdn and nt qckn over 2f out: fdd* **5/1**[3]

00- **7** *2* **Ausonius**[343] 6552 3-9-1 0 ... WilliamBuick 3 46
(L M Cumani) *trckd ldrs: pushed along over 2f out: grad wknd fnl 2f* **8/1**

0000 **8** *2 3/4* **Cross Reef**[53] 4266 4-9-0 48 ...(v[1]) LPKeniry 2 36
(R A Harris) *cl up bhd ldrs tl wknd rapidly 2f out* **40/1**

05 **9** *9* **Distant Dreamer (USA)**[29] 5110 3-8-10 0 ... TGMcLaughlin 10 12+
(Rae Guest) *racd against rail: chsd ldrs tl wknd rapidly fr 3f out* **20/1**

000 **10** *3/4* **Day In Dubai**[33] 4950 3-8-10 47 ... RichardThomas 5 10
(J J Bridger) *a in rr: struggling by 1/2-way: sn bhd* **50/1**

1m 24.46s (1.16) **Going Correction** +0.10s/f (Good)
WFA 3 from 4yo 4lb **10** Ran SP% **117.9**
Speed ratings (Par 103): **97,96,93,92,91 90,87,84,74,73**
toteswingers: 1&2 £5.90, 1&3 £34.70, 2&3 £3.70 CSF £14.74 TOTE £2.00: £1.10, £2.50, £7.10; EX 13.30.
Owner Hamdan Al Maktoum **Bred** Millsec Limited **Trained** Newmarket, Suffolk

FOCUS
A weak and uncompetitive maiden and only a handful of these could be given much of a chance. Three of the market leaders were returning from long layoffs including the winner, who is much better than the bare form.
Day In Dubai Official explanation: trainer said filly was unsuited by the good to soft ground

5966 EUROPEAN BREEDERS' FUND MAIDEN STKS 7f
3:50 (3:51) (Class 5) 2-Y-0 **£3,561** (£1,059; £529; £264) **Stalls** High

Form RPR

1 **Magician's Cape (IRE)** 2-9-3 0 ... NCallan 11 79+
(Sir Michael Stoute) *racd against nr side rail: trckd ldng pair: plld out jst over 1f out: pushed along and r.o to ld ins fnl f: comf* **9/1**[3]

5 **2** *3/4* **Swift Return**[22] 5317 2-9-0 0 ... WilliamCarson(3) 10 73
(S C Williams) *racd against nr side rail: led: rdn over 1f out: hdd ins fnl f: styd on but no match for wnr* **4/1**[2]

05 **3** *1* **Another Magic Man (USA)**[26] 5191 2-9-0 0 ... MarcHalford(3) 9 71
(J R Best) *trckd ldr and racd one off nr side rail: chal 2f out: nt qckn ent fnl f: sn lost 2nd: kpt on* **25/1**

4 *1 1/2* **Santa Margherita** 2-8-12 0 ... MickyFenton 8 62+
(H J L Dunlop) *s.s: racd against nr side: in rr of gp: outpcd and pushed along over 2f out: styd on wl fr over 1f out to take 4th ins fnl f* **66/1**

0 **5** *3* **Halyard (IRE)**[74] 3584 2-9-3 0 ... AdamKirby 6 59+
(W R Swinburn) *racd towards outer: prom: chsd ldng trio 2f out but nt on terms: pushed along and lost 4th ins fnl f* **4/1**[2]

6 *1 1/4* **Agent Archie (USA)** 2-9-3 0 ... RobertWinston 4 56
(J R Best) *trckd ldrs on outer: nvr on terms fr over 2f out: shuffled along and kpt on* **25/1**

4 **7** *hd* **Al Dafa (USA)**[31] 5017 2-9-3 0 ... LDettori 5 56+
(Saeed Bin Suroor) *sn led gp that racd wd: shkn up over 2f out: nt on terms after: fdd over 1f out* **10/11**[1]

0 **8** *3/4* **Eltheeb**[18] 5401 2-9-3 0 ... RHills 2 54+
(J L Dunlop) *hld up in rr of gp racing wd: nursed along fr over 2f out: nvr on terms* **16/1**

9 *1/2* **Spring Heather (IRE)** 2-8-12 0 ... WilliamBuick 7 48
(J L Dunlop) *racd towards nr side: cl up tl wknd over 2f out* **16/1**

0 **10** *2* **Grand Mary (IRE)**[18] 5380 2-8-12 0 ... JamieSpencer 1 43+
(P F I Cole) *dwlt: hld up last of gp racing wd: nursed along and sme prog over 2f out: light reminder whn no ch over 1f out: sn eased* **25/1**

0 **11** *7* **Sefton Park**[15] 5528 2-9-3 0 ... JimCrowley 3 30+
(C R Egerton) *w ldrs out wd: rdn over 2f out: sn wknd* **66/1**

1m 24.98s (1.68) **Going Correction** +0.10s/f (Good) **11** Ran SP% **128.7**
Speed ratings (Par 95): **94,93,92,90,86 85,85,84,83,81 73**
toteswingers: 1&2 £8.10, 1&3 £11.40, 2&3 £19.60 CSF £47.44 TOTE £10.60: £2.30, £1.60, £6.60; EX 20.40.
Owner Niarchos Family **Bred** The Niarchos Family **Trained** Newmarket, Suffolk

FOCUS
An interesting maiden with a few of these having caught the eye on their debuts, but it went to a newcomer. Those that raced closest to the nearside rail dominated but there is more to come from the winner.

NOTEBOOK
Magician's Cape(IRE) ◆ raced strongly behind the leaders towards the nearside and, after being switched left for his effort, produced a nice turn of foot to score. Out of a winner over 1m2f who is a half-sister to the very smart Ocean Silk, he can be expected to improve for further. (op 8-1 tchd 13-2)
Swift Return ◆, a major eye-catcher on his Windsor debut, is bred to have appreciated this extra furlong and was ridden much more positively this time from his good draw. He never stopped trying and it shouldn't be long before he goes one better. (op 5-1)
Another Magic Man(USA), who ran a bit better when switched to Polytrack here last time, looked the stable's second string on jockey bookings but he was always handy and ran well having held every chance. He needed this for a mark, which will open up a few more opportunities.
Santa Margherita ◆, out of a half-sister to three winners at up to 1m2f, very much caught the eye as she missed the break and raced out the back, but was noted making good late progress without being by any means knocked about. She is one to watch.
Halyard(IRE), an eye-catcher when looking in need of the experience on his Sandown debut, was ridden much more prominently this time but didn't pick up when asked. He may be one for handicaps in due course. (op 5-1 tchd 7-2)
Agent Archie(USA), a $180,000 half-brother to two winners in Germany at up to 1m2f, showed a hint of ability on this debut and should improve.
Al Dafa(USA), very green when fourth of nine over 6f on debut here in August, raced prominently on the outside which may not have been the best position, but it was still disappointing that he found so little when ridden passing the 2f pole. (op 11-10 tchd 6-5 and 5-4 in places)
Grand Mary(IRE) had been well beaten over 5f on debut, but as a half-sister to the high-class Rajeem this extra 2f should have been within her compass. However, she was in the wrong position on the wide outside from her low draw and a mid-race move came to nothing. (op 40-1)

5967 FELBRIDGE NURSERY 6f
4:20 (4:23) (Class 5) (0-70,68) 2-Y-O **£3,238** (£963; £481; £240) **Stalls** High

Form RPR

000 **1** **Dragonessa (IRE)**[62] 3979 2-8-5 **52** ... NeilChalmers 10 57
(B Palling) *racd jst off nr side rail: mostly pressed ldr: led 2f out: drvn and kpt on wl* **10/1**

000 **2** *3/4* **Lairy (IRE)**[11] 5635 2-7-12 **45** ... JamieMackay 12 48
(M F Harris) *racd against nr side rail: mde most: drifted lft and hdd 2f out: kpt on but a hld* **9/1**

6003 **3** *1/2* **Bell's Ocean (USA)**[11] 5635 2-9-7 **68** ... JerryO'Dwyer 2 70+
(J Ryan) *dwlt: racd wdst of all thrght: wl on terms: rdn 2f out: kpt on wl but a hld* **6/1**[3]

0050 **4** *1/2* **Chandrayaan**[10] 5674 2-9-1 **62** ...(v[1]) TGMcLaughlin 11 62+
(E A L Dunlop) *racd towards nr side: chsd ldrs: sltly hmpd after 1f: plld out and effrt 2f out: styd on: a hld* **5/1**[2]

0000 **5** *1 3/4* **Silvee**[11] 5636 2-7-8 **46** ow1 ... AmyBaker(5) 13 41
(J J Bridger) *racd against nr side rail: cl up bhd ldr: effrt 2f out: sn nt qckn: wknd fnl f* **20/1**

0054 **6** *1 3/4* **Do More Business (IRE)**[11] 5636 2-9-5 **66** ... IanMongan 5 58+
(P M Phelan) *racd towards outer: wl in rr: pushed along and sme prog 2f out: nt rch ldrs: no hdwy fnl f* **15/2**

015 **7** *nk* **Kapelad Junior (IRE)**[11] 5636 2-9-2 **63** ... PaulEddery 6 52+
(Pat Eddery) *racd towards outer: chsd ldrs: sltly hmpd after 1f: urged along 2f out: grad fdd over 1f out* **13/2**

6402 **8** *1 1/2* **Wing Of Faith**[11] 5636 2-8-12 **59** ... LPKeniry 7 45+
(S Kirk) *racd off nr side rail in midfield: sltly hmpd after 1f: effrt and n.m.r wl over 1f out: sn wknd* **4/1**[1]

0000 **9** *nse* **Mrs Puff (IRE)**[23] 5284 2-8-5 **52** ... CatherineGannon 8 36
(P D Evans) *racd towards outer: nvr on terms w ldrs: n.d fnl 2f* **16/1**

3360 **10** *5* **Super Duplex**[11] 5650 2-9-7 **68** ... FrankieMcDonald 9 37
(P M Phelan) *stdd s: racd against nr side rail: hld up in last: rdn and wknd 2f out* **20/1**

0000 **11** *4 1/2* **Evergreen Dancer (IRE)**[12] 5589 2-8-10 **57** ...(v[1]) RobertWinston 4 12+
(J R Best) *reluctant to enter stalls: prom towards outer: wkng rapidly whn hmpd over 1f out* **12/1**

050 **12** *12* **Arkellion**[33] 4946 2-8-9 **56** ow1 ... NCallan 3 —
(P D Evans) *free to post: dwlt: racd on outer: nvr on terms: t.o* **16/1**

1m 12.46s (1.26) **Going Correction** +0.10s/f (Good) **12** Ran SP% **124.1**
Speed ratings (Par 95): **95,94,93,92,90 88,87,85,85,78 72,56**
toteswingers: 1&2 £34.30, 1&3 £18.90, 2&3 £21.00 CSF £101.66 CT £604.04 TOTE £11.50: £3.20, £3.80, £2.40; EX 85.00.
Owner Derek And Jean Clee **Bred** D D & Mrs J P Clee **Trained** Tredodridge, Vale Of Glamorgan

FOCUS
A reasonably competitive low-grade nursery, but a couple of these ran about on reaching the path after a furlong and a few suffered in the resulting concertina effect. The draw played its part too, with four of the first five starting from double-figure stalls, but the market also proved significant with the first two well backed.

NOTEBOOK
Dragonessa(IRE), making her nursery debut after finishing well beaten in three maidens, was keen enough early but despite that found enough to battle on well and come out on top. This looks to be her trip and she still has plenty of scope. Official explanation: trainer's rep said, regarding apparent improvement in form, that the filly was better suited by the return to turf and softer ground. (op 16-1 tchd 8-1)
Lairy(IRE), who has become very disappointing, was well backed to perform better here though much of that may have been down to his draw and he has run well on easy ground before now. Despite appearing to shy at the path after a furlong, he was always up there against the nearside rail and kept on going, but whether he can do any better next time is debatable. (op 25-1)
Bell's Ocean(USA) ◆, 1lb higher than when showing a return to form to finish third on his sand debut at Kempton last time, raced up with the pace throughout and emerges with plenty of credit as he was forced to race wide throughout from his low draw. (op 4-1 tchd 7-1)
Chandrayaan, unplaced in four maidens and tackling his shortest trip to date, had a first-time visor on for this nursery debut and he was a significant market mover earlier in the day. Not done any favours in the early stages, he didn't get going until it was too late. (tchd 4-1)
Silvee, already exposed as extremely moderate, appeared to run much better here but she had the rails draw so may have been flattered.
Do More Business(IRE), closely matched with a few of these on recent Kempton Polytrack running, met trouble after a furlong and soon had plenty to do but he did stay on late and can be rated a bit better than his final position. (op 6-1 tchd 8-1)

Wing Of Faith, in front of three of these when runner-up on his sand debut at Kempton last time, got interfered with after a furlong and then briefly came off the bridle. He was travelling better behind the leaders halfway though the contest, but then found very little under pressure. He looks worth another try back on Polytrack. (op 6-1)

5968 BETFAIR APPRENTICE TRAINING SERIES H'CAP — 6f

4:50 (4:50) (Class 5) (0-75,75) 3-Y-O — **£3,070** (£906; £453) **Stalls** High

Form — RPR

324 **1** — **Simple Rhythm**[8] 5724 3-8-0 **64** ... RyanPowell(8) 2 — 70+
(J Ryan) *mde virtually all and racd wd: drew clr over 2f out: abt 4 l clr ins fnl f: nudged along and nrly ct* **25/1**

1406 **2** *hd* **Reject**[27] 5154 3-9-0 **70** ... DebraEngland 5 — 76+
(W J Haggas) *hld up against nr side rail: last wl over 1f out: rapid prog and squeezed through to take 2nd jst ins fnl f: r.o wl and nrly ct wnr napping* **5/1**[3]

2342 **3** *¾* **Merry Diva**[15] 5506 3-9-2 **72** ... SimonPearce 9 — 76+
(C F Wall) *racd against nr side rail: hld up: tried for run and checked over 1f out: r.o wl fnl f: gaining fin* **11/4**[1]

1625 **4** *2 ¼* **Cape Melody**[24] 5264 3-8-10 **74** ... RyanClark(8) 1 — 70
(H Morrison) *racd wd: chsd ldrs: no ch w wnr whn wnt 2nd briefly 1f out: one pce after* **5/1**[3]

3142 **5** *hd* **My Best Bet**[5] 5810 3-9-5 **75** ... MatthewDavies 4 — 71
(M R Channon) *hld up in rr: effrt 2f out: sme prog over 1f out: nvr rchd ldrs* **7/2**[2]

3203 **6** *1 ¼* **Raimond Ridge (IRE)**[3] 5877 3-9-2 **72** ... AshleyMorgan 7 — 64
(M R Channon) *v awkward s: hld up in last pair: effrt 2f out: hanging lft but kpt on: no ch* **7/1**

0344 **7** *2* **Riflessione**[18] 5383 3-8-8 **69** ... (p) JakePayne(5) 6 — 55
(R A Harris) *chsd ldrs: swtchd to r against nr side rail 1/2-way: wknd jst over 1f out* **10/1**

5040 **8** *nse* **Pocket's Pick (IRE)**[13] 5584 3-8-6 **65** ... (tp) RichardRowe(3) 8 — 51
(G L Moore) *racd towards nr side but nt against rail: w wnr to 1/2-way: sn outpcd: hanging lft and lost 2nd 1f out: wknd* **22/1**

4045 **9** *1 ½* **Rio Royale (IRE)**[18] 5403 3-9-2 **72** ... AmyScott 3 — 53
(Mrs A J Perrett) *racd wd: chsd ldrs: wknd fr 2f out* **16/1**

1m 11.68s (0.48) **Going Correction** +0.10s/f (Good) — **9** Ran SP% **117.9**
Speed ratings (Par 101): **100,99,98,95,95 93,91,91,89**
toteswingers: 1&2 £11.40, 1&3 £8.10, 2&3 £4.20 CSF £148.26 CT £469.84 TOTE £18.30: £4.20, £1.60, £1.50; EX 66.20 Place 6: £143.21 £63.05 .
Owner J Ryan **Bred** P Quinlan **Trained** Newmarket, Suffolk

FOCUS
An ordinary apprentice handicap and a messy contest. The form is sound.
Riflessione Official explanation: jockey said colt hung right
T/Plt: £383.10 to a £1 stake. Pool: £51,826.41. 98.75 winning tickets. T/Qpdt: £195.90 to a £1 stake. Pool: £3,547.87. 13.40 winning tickets. JN

5478 YARMOUTH (L-H)

Tuesday, September 15

OFFICIAL GOING: Good to firm (7.9)
Wind: fresh, half behind Weather: overcast, breezy

5969 E B F / BUY A RACING POST YEARLING BONUS CANDIDATE MAIDEN FILLIES' STKS — 6f 3y

2:10 (2:12) (Class 4) 2-Y-O — **£5,046** (£1,510; £755; £377; £188) **Stalls** High

Form — RPR

0 **1** — **Dylanesque**[31] 5021 2-9-0 0 ... PhilipRobinson 7 — 77+
(M A Jarvis) *chsd ldng trio: rdn to press ldr over 1f out: r.o u.p to ld wl ins fnl f* **10/3**[2]

2 **2** *shd* **Alice Alleyne (IRE)**[11] 5638 2-9-0 0 ... RyanMoore 8 — 77+
(Sir Michael Stoute) *chsd ldng pair tl wnt 2nd over 2f out: rdn to ld narowly over 1f out: kpt on u.p tl hdd and no ex wl ins fnl f* **1/1**[1]

0 **3** *½* **Chaussini**[16] 5478 2-9-0 0 ... RobertHavlin 9 — 75+
(J A R Toller) *hld up in midfield: hdwy over 2f out: shkn up to chse ldng pair over 1f out: kpt on u.p ins fnl f* **40/1**

44 **4** *5* **Tia Juana (IRE)**[18] 5380 2-8-11 0 ... AhmedAjtebi(3) 6 — 60
(Saeed Bin Suroor) *led tl rdn and hdd over 1f out: wknd ent fnl f* **9/1**

5 **5** *¾* **Caramelita**[37] 4826 2-8-7 0 ... DannyBrock(7) 4 — 58
(J R Jenkins) *in tch in midfield: rdn and hung rt over 1f out: sn outpcd by ldrs: plugged on same pce fnl f* **100/1**

6 *½* **Cojo (IRE)** 2-9-0 0 ... MartinDwyer 2 — 59+
(B J Meehan) *towards rr: rdn 1/2-way: hdwy ent fnl 2f: keeping on but no ch w ldrs whn hmpd and swtchd lft over 1f out: kpt on same pce fnl f* **8/1**[3]

7 *1 ½* **Tudor Princess** 2-9-0 0 ... SebSanders 5 — 52
(W R Muir) *s.i.s: towards rr: pushed along and sme hdwy wl over 1f out: edgd lft and no imp ent fnl f* **20/1**

8 *2 ¾* **Sparkling Smile (IRE)** 2-9-0 0 ... TedDurcan 1 — 44
(D R Lanigan) *s.i.s: a bhd: no ch fnl 2f* **18/1**

0 **9** *2 ½* **Rosetta Hill**[78] 3458 2-9-0 0 ... SimonWhitworth 11 — 36
(J R Jenkins) *chsd ldr tl over 2f out: wknd qckly over 1f out: wl btn fnl f* **25/1**

10 *½* **Scarcity (IRE)** 2-9-0 0 ... HayleyTurner 3 — 35
(E A L Dunlop) *s.i.s: rn green and a bhd: no ch fnl 2f* **22/1**

0 **11** *3* **Evening Glow**[32] 4980 2-9-0 0 ... ChrisCatlin 10 — 26
(C E Brittain) *sn pushed along in midfield: struggling 1/2-way: bhd fnl 2f* **66/1**

1m 12.42s (-1.98) **Going Correction** -0.275s/f (Firm) — **11** Ran SP% **117.3**
Speed ratings (Par 94): **102,101,101,94,93 92,90,87,83,83 79**
toteswingers: 1&2 £2.20, 1&3 £30.20, 2&3 £12.80 CSF £6.50 TOTE £3.60: £1.10, £1.20, £8.70; EX 7.70 Trifecta £363.50 Pool: £677.99 - 1.38 winning units..
Owner Helena Springfield Ltd **Bred** Meon Valley Stud **Trained** Newmarket, Suffolk

FOCUS
Three drew well clear in what was just an ordinary maiden, and the form looks sound.

NOTEBOOK
Dylanesque ran well for a long way over 6f at Newbury on debut and she was always likely to improve for that initial experience. Soon tracking the speed, she stayed on too strongly for the favourite inside the final furlong and looks likely to stay 7f before long. (op 4-1)
Alice Alleyne(IRE), runner-up at Kempton on debut, was driven to lead over 1f out and held every chance, but was unable to pull out extra in the finish. She will want further than this, but is clearly no star. (tchd 5-4)
Chaussini improved markedly on her debut effort, closing inside the final 2f before being unable to quicken in the last 100 yards. She should improve again and has a future. (op 50-1)
Tia Juana(IRE) quickly backed out of it having been headed and may find easier opportunities in nurseries. (op 7-1 tchd 13-2 and 10-1)
Caramelita, last of five in a conditions race at Windsor on debut, was again well held and she too should find life easier once handicapping. (op 80-1)
Cojo(IRE), from a good family and entered in the Cheveley Park, is going to need further than this and she was unable to get into the race, trying to stay on when hampered inside the final 2f. She should improve markedly. (tchd 9-1)

5970 FIRSTBET.COM £50 MATCHED BET 0800 230 0800 NURSERY (FOR THE JACK LEADER CHALLENGE TROPHY) — 1m 3y

2:40 (2:40) (Class 4) (0-85,82) 2-Y-O — **£4,415** (£1,321; £660; £330; £164) **Stalls** High

Form — RPR

41 **1** — **Sulwaan (IRE)**[16] 5466 2-8-12 **73** ... TPO'Shea 4 — 85+
(M Johnston) *awkward leaving stalls and s.i.s: sn rcvrd and ld after 1f: mde rest: rdn ent fnl 2f: styd on wl and a holding rival fnl f* **9/2**[3]

41 **2** *½* **Togiak (IRE)**[22] 5312 2-9-7 **82** ... SebSanders 7 — 93+
(E A L Dunlop) *trckd ldrs: wnt 2nd 4f out: rdn to chal over 1f out: clr w wnr fr over 1f out: kpt on but a hld fnl f* **6/4**[1]

635 **3** *7* **Branderburgo (IRE)**[61] 4006 2-8-11 **75** ... (p) AndreaAtzeni(3) 2 — 71
(M Botti) *chsd ldrs: rdn and effrt jst over 2f out: drvn and outpcd by ldng pair over 1f out: no ch w ldrs fnl f* **8/1**

4431 **4** *2 ¼* **Dashing Doc (IRE)**[32] 5002 2-9-3 **78** ... RyanMoore 1 — 69
(D R C Elsworth) *t.k.h: led for 1f: chsd wnr tl 4f out: rdn over 2f out: wknd u.p wl over 1f out* **7/2**[2]

2343 **5** *½* **Interakt**[5] 5787 2-8-9 **70** ... ChrisCatlin 5 — 59
(M R Channon) *in tch towards rr: hdwy 1/2-way: chsd ldrs and rdn ent fnl 2f: wknd u.p over 1f out* **11/1**

1036 **6** *1* **Professor John (IRE)**[13] 5580 2-9-7 **82** ... HayleyTurner 3 — 69
(M L W Bell) *hld up in last pair: rdn and effrt ent fnl 2f: no prog and wl btn over 1f out* **14/1**

0050 **7** *¾* **Shark Man (IRE)**[24] 5265 2-8-8 **72** ... JackMitchell(3) 6 — 58
(P J McBride) *hld up in tch in rr: rdn and effrt on outer over 2f out: wknd wl over 1f out: wl bhd fnl f* **25/1**

1m 38.06s (-2.54) **Going Correction** -0.275s/f (Firm) — **7** Ran SP% **110.4**
Speed ratings (Par 97): **101,100,93,91,90 89,89**
toteswingers: 1&2 £2.20, 1&3 £7.10, 2&3 £3.60 CSF £10.84 TOTE £5.70: £2.10, £1.70; EX 11.30.
Owner Hamdan Al Maktoum **Bred** Martin Francis **Trained** Middleham Moor, N Yorks

FOCUS
A fair nursery and the front pair drew right away. They both improved and produced good efforts.

NOTEBOOK
Sulwaan(IRE), workmanlike winner of a modest maiden at Beverley last time, was soon bowling along in front and kept finding when challenged by the favourite. He always looked to be doing enough inside the final furlong and this scopey son of King's Best remains open to further improvement. (op 11-2)
Togiak(IRE), whose Kempton maiden win received a boost when runner-up Navy List won easily at Redcar the previous day, looked to be on a reasonable mark for this nursery debut and he threw down a strong challenge inside the final quarter mile, but was unable to get past the determined winner. He was clear of the remainder and should relish a step up to 1m2f later in the season. (tchd 5-4 and 7-4)
Branderburgo(IRE) looked ready for this step up to 1m, having contested three maidens at shorter, and he ran well to a point, but couldn't race on with the front pair. The first-time cheekpieces didn't have much of an effect. (op 7-1)
Dashing Doc(IRE) appreciated the step up to 1m when winning at Newmarket last time, but he needed to have improved for this return to handicaps and he ended up well held back in fourth, having raced keen early. (op 4-1)
Interakt travelled well in behind the pace, but failed to quicken when asked and she faded from over 1f out. (tchd 12-1)

5971 THOMAS PRIOR MEMORIAL MAIDEN STKS — 6f 3y

3:10 (3:12) (Class 5) 3-Y-O+ — **£3,406** (£1,019; £509; £254; £126) **Stalls** High

Form — RPR

4322 **1** — **Miss Frangipane (IRE)**[12] 5599 3-8-12 67 ... RyanMoore 2 — 57
(J Noseda) *cl up: shkn up to ld 2f out: sn edgd rt and hrd pressed: drvn ins fnl f: a jst doing enough* **1/4**[1]

060 **2** *hd* **Nativity**[7] 5747 3-8-9 54 ... JackDean(3) 5 — 56
(J L Spearing) *stdd s: hld up in tch in rr: rdn and hdwy jst over 2f out: ev ch over 1f out: unable qck fnl 100yds* **20/1**[3]

0-6 **3** *3 ½* **Freeing**[34] 4913 3-8-12 0 ... KirstyMilczarek 3 — 48+
(J A R Toller) *in tch: hung lft: lost pl and hmpd 2f out: styd on u.p to go 3rd fnl 100yds: no ch w ldng pair* **13/2**[2]

0000 **4** *1 ¼* **Divine White**[34] 4905 6-8-7 45 ... (v[1]) DTDaSilva(7) 6 — 42
(G P Enright) *led: rdn and hdd 2f out: sn sltly hmpd and swtchd lft: outpcd ent fnl f* **66/1**

0006 **5** *1* **Sorrel Point**[40] 4718 6-9-5 43 ... (t) JimmyQuinn 1 — 44
(H J Collingridge) *hld up in last pair: shkn up and effrt 2f out: rdn and no prog over 1f out* **33/1**

6 *6* **Donny Bowl** 4-9-2 0 ... FrederikTylicki(3) 4 — 26
(I W McInnes) *chsd ldr tl 2f out: sn wandered and lost pl: bhd fnl f* **20/1**[3]

1m 12.96s (-1.44) **Going Correction** -0.275s/f (Firm)
WFA 3 from 4yo+ 2lb — **6** Ran SP% **107.3**
Speed ratings (Par 103): **98,97,93,91,90 82**
toteswingers: 1&2 £2.40, 1&3 £1.20, 2&3 £2.00 CSF £7.81 TOTE £1.20: £1.10, £5.30; EX 4.40.
Owner Netherfield House Stud **Bred** John Foley & Miss A Foley **Trained** Newmarket, Suffolk

FOCUS
A typically weak 3yo-plus sprint maiden and red-hot favourite Miss Frangipane made really hard work of winning.

5972 TED BURMAN MEMORIAL (S) STKS — 7f 3y

3:40 (3:40) (Class 6) 3-Y-O — **£1,942** (£578; £288; £144) **Stalls** High

Form — RPR

0000 **1** — **Sairaam (IRE)**[29] 5108 3-8-7 52 ... KirstyMilczarek 12 — 56+
(C Smith) *chsd ldrs: hdwy to ld 2f out: rdn clr ent fnl f: r.o wl and in command fnl f* **16/1**

-000 **2** *2 ½* **Musigny (USA)**[23] 5283 3-8-12 53 ... AlanMunro 2 — 55+
(W Jarvis) *stdd after s: bhd: rdn 1/2-way: hdwy u.p and swtchd rt over 1f out: styd on wl to chse wnr fnl 75yds: nvr nr enough to chal* **14/1**

0000 **3** *1 ¾* **Versaki (IRE)**[10] 5677 3-8-7 68 ... (t) MartinLane(5) 6 — 50
(Ian Williams) *w ldr: rdn over 2f out: drvn and chsd wnr over 1f out: btn ent fnl f: lost 2nd fnl 75yds* **5/1**[2]

0006 **4** *½* **Portugese Caddy**[13] 5574 3-8-12 66 ... LukeMorris 4 — 49
(P Winkworth) *s.i.s: pushed along and hdwy into midfield over 4f out: chsd ldrs and edgd lft over 1f out: sn drvn and one pce fnl f* **9/2**[1]

4000 **5** *½* **Jack's House (IRE)**[27] 5158 3-8-9 49 ... (t) FrederikTylicki(3) 5 — 48
(Miss J A Camacho) *racd off the pce in midfield: rdn and effrt over 2f out: hdwy and chsd ldrs over 1f out: no imp u.p ent fnl f* **10/1**

0040 **6** *1* **Wicklewood**[21] 5326 3-8-12 42 ... (v) PaulQuinn 1 — 45
(Mrs C A Dunnett) *stdd after s: bhd: rdn 4f out: hdwy u.p over 1f out: plugged on fnl f: nvr trbld ldrs* **20/1**

5400 **7** 1 **Tilerium's Dream (IRE)**[37] 4819 3-8-12 50........................(p) TPO'Shea 8 43
(K A Ryan) *led: rdn over 2f out: hdd 2f out: wknd u.p over 1f out: wl btn fnl f* **20/1**

0500 **8** 2 **Bromhead (USA)**[16] 5479 3-9-3 57..........................(t) SaleemGolam 9 43
(Mrs C A Dunnett) *chsd ldrs: rdn wl over 2f out: no hdwy u.p 2f out and wl btn after* **8/1**

200 **9** 9 **Count On Guest**[18] 5403 3-8-12 56...........................(t) JimmyQuinn 3 15
(G G Margarson) *chsd ldrs: rdn and struggling over 3f out: wl btn fnl 2f* **6/1**[3]

0600 **10** ½ **Fantasy Land (IRE)**[29] 5112 3-8-7 60.........................(bt) MartinDwyer 10 9
(B J Meehan) *prom and clr in ldng trio: ev ch over 2f out: rdn and hung lft 2f out: sn wl btn* **8/1**

-005 **11** 3½ **Soldier Soldier**[68] 3773 3-8-12 0............................(t) SimonWhitworth 11 5
(J R Jenkins) *s.i.s: a towards rr: reminder over 5f out: lost tch wl over 2f out* **66/1**

406 **12** 2 **Pure Heir (USA)**[18] 5394 3-8-7 53.......................................ChrisCatlin 13 —
(T D Barron) *s.i.s: a towards rr: nvr on terms* **8/1**

0400 **13** 11 **Hopeful Lady**[16] 5470 3-8-4 39.......................................KellyHarrison(3) 7 —
(I W McInnes) *a in rr: t.o fr over 2f out* **66/1**

1m 24.82s (-1.78) **Going Correction** -0.275s/f (Firm) **13** Ran SP% **116.6**
Speed ratings (Par 99): **99,96,94,93,93 91,90,88,78,77 73,71,58**
toteswingers: 1&2 £50.20, 1&3 £18.50, 2&3 £20.30 CSF £209.59 TOTE £16.90: £5.10, £4.70, £2.10; EX 377.50 Trifecta £247.60 Part won. Pool: £334.68 - 0.10 winning units..There was no bid for the winner.
Owner Phil Martin & Trev Sleath **Bred** Shadwell Estate Company Limited **Trained** Temple Bruer, Lincs
■ Stewards' Enquiry : Kelly Harrison £140 fine: failed to mount after signal had been given

FOCUS
A very weak seller which has been rated negatively.
Count On Guest Official explanation: jockey said gelding never travelled

5973 AT THE RACES CONDITIONS STKS 6f 3y
4:10 (4:10) (Class 3) 3-Y-O+ **£7,477** (£2,239; £1,119; £560) **Stalls** High

Form RPR

2350 **1** **Awinnersgame (IRE)**[90] 3011 3-8-7 105.............................RyanMoore 5 104
(J Noseda) *trckd ldng pair: rdn and hdwy between horses 1f out: rdn to ld ins fnl f: r.o wl* **6/5**[1]

5100 **2** 1¼ **Global City (IRE)**[45] 4523 3-8-7 100..............................(t) TedDurcan 2 100
(Saeed Bin Suroor) *chsd ldr: rdn to chal over 1f out: one pce u.p ins fnl f: wnt 2nd towards fin* **5/2**[2]

4033 **3** nk **Angus Newz**[14] 5546 6-8-4 90.......................................MartinDwyer 1 94
(M Quinn) *led: rdn 2f out: hdd and one pce ins fnl f: lost 2nd towards fin* **9/2**[3]

4344 **4** 3 **Five Star Junior (USA)**[31] 5032 3-8-7 93............................ShaneKelly 4 90
(Mrs L Stubbs) *stdd after s: hld up in last pl: rdn and effrt over 1f out: outpcd 1f out* **6/1**

1m 12.8s (-1.60) **Going Correction** -0.275s/f (Firm)
WFA 3 from 6yo 2lb **4** Ran SP% **106.5**
Speed ratings (Par 107): **99,97,96,92**
CSF £4.29 TOTE £2.00; EX 3.20.
Owner Saeed Suhail **Bred** J Joyce **Trained** Newmarket, Suffolk

FOCUS
This was a decent little conditions race but the time was poor. The form makes sense but should not be trusted implicitly.

NOTEBOOK
Awinnersgame(IRE), runner-up in the Free Handicap earlier in the season, had been off since finishing ninth in a first-time visor in the Jersey Stakes at Royal Ascot and this looked a nice opportunity for him to get off the mark for the season. He picked up well when switched off the rail and ran on to win with a bit in hand. He won't be easy to place for the remainder of the season, however. (op 5-4 tchd 11-10 and 11-8 in a place)
Global City(IRE), unable to cope with soft ground in the Stewards' Cup, returned to form, keeping on to just take second, but was no match for the winner. He could pick up small conditions race at some point. (op 11-4 tchd 3-1)
Angus Newz is always dangerous in small-field contests, but she ideally needs some cut in the ground and was readily brushed aside by the winner inside the final furlong. (op 5-1 tchd 11-2)
Five Star Junior(USA), who has been running consistently well in handicaps, was the only one not to feature. (op 9-2)

5974 PETER DUNNETT MEMORIAL SPRINT H'CAP 5f 43y
4:40 (4:40) (Class 4) (0-85,88) 3-Y-O+ **£5,046** (£1,510; £755; £377; £188) **Stalls** High

Form RPR

1000 **1** **Colorus (IRE)**[3] 5856 6-8-0 68 oh2..........................(p) PaulPickard(5) 10 77
(W J H Ratcliffe) *chsd ldr tl led 2f out: hanging lft after: pushed along and a holding rivals fnl f* **8/1**[3]

115 **2** ¾ **Whiskey Junction**[19] 5370 5-9-1 78.....................................SebSanders 7 84
(M Quinn) *led tl 2f out: sn rdn: carried lft fnl f: kpt on same pce u.p* **6/1**[2]

0001 **3** nk **Total Impact**[6] 5767 6-9-8 88 6ex...............................FrederikTylicki(3) 1 93
(R A Fahey) *chsd ldng: rdn and pressed ldrs over 1f out: carried lft and unable qck u.p fnl f* **7/4**[1]

2400 **4** 2¾ **Devil You Know (IRE)**[32] 5001 3-9-3 81.........................(t) RyanMoore 9 76
(D R C Elsworth) *stdd s: hld up in tch in rr: hdwy 2f out: chsd ldng trio and hung lft 1f out: no prog after* **6/1**[2]

2000 **5** ½ **Lucky Leigh**[6] 5777 3-9-1 79.......................................SamHitchcott 5 73
(M R Channon) *in tch: rdn and unable qck wl over 1f out: wknd u.p 1f out* **22/1**

0242 **6** 1¾ **Magical Speedfit (IRE)**[8] 5724 4-8-6 69..............................ChrisCatlin 2 56
(G G Margarson) *sn niggled along in midfield: rdn ent fnl 2f: kpt on same pce u.p* **8/1**[3]

2330 **7** 1¼ **Onceaponatime (IRE)**[19] 5370 4-8-2 68 oh1.............KellyHarrison(3) 4 51
(M D Squance) *broke wl: sn stdd and hld up in tch: rdn and unable qck 2f out: wl btn 1f out: swtchd rt ins fnl f* **9/1**

1360 **8** ¾ **Russian Rocket (IRE)**[19] 5374 7-8-5 68 oh6.................SaleemGolam 3 48
(Mrs C A Dunnett) *t.k.h: hld up in tch in last pair: rdn and no prog ent fnl 2f: n.d* **9/1**

0000 **9** 4½ **Thumberlina**[16] 5480 3-8-4 68 oh23..............................(b[1]) JimmyQuinn 6 32+
(Mrs C A Dunnett) *a bhd: no ch fr over 1f out: eaesd wl ins fnl f* **66/1**

61.14 secs (-1.06) **Going Correction** -0.275s/f (Firm)
WFA 3 from 4yo+ 1lb **9** Ran SP% **113.0**
Speed ratings (Par 105): **97,95,95,90,90 87,85,84,76**
toteswingers: 1&2 £7.90, 1&3 £4.60, 2&3 £2.60 CSF £53.99 CT £121.44 TOTE £10.10: £2.20, £2.00, £1.70; EX 63.90 Trifecta £353.00 Part won. Pool: £477.12 - 0.64 winning units..
Owner J Sheard & W J S Ratcliffe **Bred** M Ervine **Trained** Newmarket, Suffolk

FOCUS
This was a modest sprint handicap. The near rail was favoured and the form is pretty solid.
Thumberlina Official explanation: jockey said filly missed the break

5975 LOWESTOFT JOURNAL H'CAP 1m 3f 101y
5:10 (5:10) (Class 5) (0-70,70) 3-Y-O+ **£3,238** (£963; £481; £240) **Stalls** Low

Form RPR

1000 **1** **Chalice Welcome**[19] 5365 6-9-0 61.........................JackMitchell(3) 1 72
(N B King) *hld up in midfield: hdwy 3f out: swtchd rt and rdn wl over 1f out: led over 1f out: r.o wl fnl f* **20/1**

6245 **2** 1 **Incendo**[31] 5035 3-9-0 66..(t) HayleyTurner 11 75
(J R Fanshawe) *hld up in tch towards rr: hdwy gng wl over 2f out: ev ch and rdn wl over 1f out: chsd wnr clr of remainder fnl f: one pce* **7/2**[2]

4602 **3** 5 **Watson's Bay**[25] 5227 4-9-7 65...AlanMunro 9 69+
(P Howling) *stdd s: t.k.h: hld up in rr: hdwy over 2f out: nt clr run ent fnl 2f: swtchd rt wl over 1f out: r.o to go 3rd wl ins fnl f: nvr threatened ldrs* **7/1**

3020 **4** 3½ **Navajo Nation (IRE)**[13] 5570 3-9-2 68.............................MartinDwyer 4 64
(B J Meehan) *led at stdy pce tl qckng 4f out: rdn and hdd over 1f out: sn btn* **6/1**[3]

-100 **5** ¾ **Madam President**[26] 5195 4-9-10 68...............................ShaneKelly 10 64+
(W R Swinburn) *hld up in tch in midfield: hdwy to chse ldrs over 3f out: n.m.r ent fnl 2f: sn rdn and nt qckning whn hmpd over 1f out: no ch w ldrs after: plugged on* **25/1**

4020 **6** 4 **Royal Premier (IRE)**[16] 5483 6-8-12 56..........................(v) JimmyQuinn 5 45
(H J Collingridge) *hld up along leaving stalls: sn chsng ldr: rdn and effrt 4f out: ev ch and drvn wl over 2f out: wknd wl over 1f out* **14/1**

1526 **7** ½ **Graylyn Ruby (FR)**[25] 5227 4-9-12 70.................................LukeMorris 8 58+
(J Jay) *hld up wl in tch: rdn and effrt wl over 2f out: wknd wl over 1f out: wl btn whn nt clr run and swtchd rt ins fnl f* **14/1**

021 **8** 3 **Fantino**[14] 5545 3-9-2 68..TedDurcan 6 51+
(J Mackie) *t.k.h: chsd ldrs: rdn and pressed ldrs over 3f out: btn 2f out: eased wl ins fnl f* **9/4**[1]

1550 **9** ½ **La Diosa (IRE)**[29] 5095 3-8-6 58.......................................ChrisCatlin 2 41
(Mrs S Lamyman) *hld up in tch in rr: rdn and no hdwy 3f out: nvr on terms* **33/1**

/040 **10** ½ **Homebred Star**[19] 5365 8-8-5 56 oh11............................DTDaSilva(7) 7 38
(G P Enright) *stdd s: hld up in rr: swtchd to outer and hdwy 4f out: rdn and btn over 2f out* **100/1**

/6-0 **11** 1¼ **Present**[168] 378 5-8-9 56 oh9.......................................FrederikTylicki(3) 12 36
(Miss Diana Weeden) *chsd ldrs on outer: rdn 4f out: wl bhd fr over 2f out* **50/1**

015 **12** ¾ **Rough Sketch (USA)**[16] 5483 4-8-13 57............................SebSanders 3 36+
(Sir Mark Prescott) *t.k.h: chsd ldrs: rdn over 3f out: btn 2f out: eased wl ins fnl f* **7/1**

2m 27.21s (-1.49) **Going Correction** -0.15s/f (Firm)
WFA 3 from 4yo+ 8lb **12** Ran SP% **120.1**
Speed ratings (Par 103): **99,98,94,92,91 88,88,86,85,85 84,83**
toteswingers: 1&2 £20.60, 1&3 £23.00, 2&3 £6.90 CSF £87.35 CT £561.64 TOTE £25.30: £6.30, £2.00, £2.10; EX 182.00 Trifecta £237.30 Pool £320.68 - 1.00 winning units. Place 6: £143.21 Place 5: £63.05 .
Owner The Dyball Partnership **Bred** The Dyball Partnership **Trained** Newmarket, Suffolk

FOCUS
This was a moderate handicap. The winner ran to his best and the form is solid.
Fantino Official explanation: jockey said gelding stopped quickly
T/Plt: £18.30 to a £1 stake. Pool: £57,279.24. 2,277.71 winning tickets. T/Qpdt: £12.20 to a £1 stake. Pool: £3,006.77. 181.60 winning tickets. SP

5465 BEVERLEY (R-H)
Wednesday, September 16

OFFICIAL GOING: Good to firm (9.3)
Wind: Fresh across Weather: Overcast

5976 BEVERLEY ANNUAL BADGEHOLDERS (S) NURSERY 5f
2:00 (2:06) (Class 6) (0-65,63) 2-Y-O **£2,729** (£806; £403) **Stalls** High

Form RPR

5224 **1** **Zelos Dream (IRE)**[31] 5060 2-9-4 63.........................FrederikTylicki(3) 14 64
(Rae Guest) *hld up towards rr: smooth hdwy wl over 1f out: nt clr run and swtchd rt enterng fnl f: rdn and squeezed through to ld last 50yds: drvn and kpt on nr fin* **11/4**[1]

0060 **2** shd **Powerful Pierre**[13] 5595 2-9-2 63..........................(v[1]) PatrickDonaghy(5) 8 64
(Jedd O'Keeffe) *dwlt: sn cl up: rdn over 1f out: drvn and hung rt ent fnl f: kpt on to ld ins fnl f: hdd and edgd lft last 50yds: kpt on wl towards line* **25/1**

660 **3** nk **Lucy Gliters**[11] 5668 2-8-0 45....................................DominicFox(3) 9 45+
(T P Tate) *towards rr: hdwy wl over 1f out: sn rdn and n.m.r ent fnl f: styd on strly towards fin* **16/1**

0203 **4** 1¼ **Just The Tonic**[16] 5519 2-9-1 57.....................................PJMcDonald 7 52+
(Mrs Marjorie Fife) *hld up in tch: hdwy wl over 1f out: nt clr run and swtchd rt ent fnl f: sn rdn and styd on wl towards fin* **15/2**[3]

6430 **5** ¾ **Saint Sebastian (IRE)**[13] 5613 2-8-13 55....................(p) PaulHanagan 5 47
(E S McMahon) *prom: rdn along wl over 1f out: drvn and one pce ent fnl f* **7/1**[2]

0246 **6** ½ **Daisy Brown**[35] 4889 2-9-1 57..JimmyQuinn 4 48
(N Tinkler) *s.i.s and bhd: swtchd lft and hdwy 2f out: rdn and kpt on ins fnl f: nrst fin* **20/1**

0500 **7** shd **Summa Cum Laude**[18] 5439 2-8-11 53.............(v[1]) SilvestreDeSousa 16 43+
(Mrs A Duffield) *wnt lft s: sn in rr and rdn along: swtchd lft and drvn 2f out: hdwy over 1f out: kpt on strly ins fnl f: nrst fin* **12/1**

0052 **8** 1 **Prettiest Star (IRE)**[26] 5226 2-8-11 53.....................(p) DavidAllan 11 40+
(K A Ryan) *led: rdn along 2f out: drvn over 1f out: hdd ins fnl f: wkng whn n.m.r last 100yds* **8/1**

5650 **9** 1 **Gasparilla (IRE)**[12] 5636 2-7-13 48..............................DeclanCannon(7) 12 31
(A J McCabe) *cl up: rdn along wl over 1f out: drvn and wknd appr fnl f* **14/1**

4405 **10** nk **Vilnius**[7] 5776 2-9-5 61...SamHitchcott 1 43
(M R Channon) *midfield: hdwy on wd outside over 1f out: sn rdn and chsd ldrs ent fnl f: sn drvn and btn* **18/1**

5346 **11** 2 **Dower Glen**[24] 5292 2-9-2 58...TomEaves 10 33
(I Semple) *dwlt: a towards rr* **20/1**

6406 **12** nk **Dispol Kabira**[23] 5303 2-8-8 50.......................................FrancisNorton 13 24+
(D W Thompson) *midfield: rdn along 2f out: no hdwy whn n.m.r ins fnl f* **16/1**

5434 **13** 4 **Cygnet Committee (IRE)**[16] 5519 2-9-1 57.......................(b) PAspell 2 16
(J S Wainwright) *chsd ldrs: rdn along 1/2-way: sn wknd* **50/1**

4650 **14** 3/4 **Reel Credit Crunch**[2] 5950 2-8-13 62..........(b) IJBrennan(7) 15 19+
(I W McInnes) *bmpd s: chsd ldrs on inner: rdn along and wknd over 1f out: n.m.r and hmpd ins fnl f* **12/1**

63.94 secs (0.44) **Going Correction** -0.20s/f (Firm) **14** Ran SP% **116.5**
Speed ratings (Par 93): **88,87,87,85,84 83,83,81,80,79 76,75,69,68**
toteswingers: 1&2 £20.00, 1&3 £18.50, 2&3 £88.80. CSF £80.61 CT £844.11 TOTE £3.20: £1.60, £7.00, £6.70; EX 83.10.There was no bid for the winner.
Owner Beadle Booth Bloodstock Limited **Bred** John Malone **Trained** Newmarket, Suffolk
■ Pepper Lane was withdrawn (14/1, bolted bef s). R4 applies, deduct 5p in the £.
■ Stewards' Enquiry : Patrick Donaghy two-day ban: careless riding (Sept 30 -1st Oct)
Frederik Tylicki caution: used whip with excessive frequency

FOCUS
Moderate form, as is to be expected for the grade. It has been rated around the runner-up.

NOTEBOOK
Zelos Dream(IRE) benefited from the drop in class to gain her first success at the sixth attempt. She had to work hard for a gap, only getting in the clear about a furlong out, but she responded gamely to pressure. She's only small, but her attitude might see her win more races at a low level. (op 100-30 tchd 7-2)
Powerful Pierre is struggling to justify his £32,000 price tag but he ran well in a first-time visor on this drop in grade, losing out only on the nod. (op 28-1)
Lucy Gliters had to be niggled along pretty much throughout but she gradually responded to pressure and was not beaten far. This effort came off a mark of just 45, however, and she's clearly pretty moderate. (op 14-1 tchd 18-1)
Just The Tonic held a few of today's rivals on her recent Ripon running, but she still wasn't good enough. Although she had to wait for a clear run over a furlong out, she could not be described as unlucky. Official explanation: jockey said filly was denied a clear run (op 8-1 tchd 9-1)
Saint Sebastian(IRE) was far from ideally drawn but that's no real excuse. He was held when bumped slightly near the line. (op 11-1)
Summa Cum Laude, reported to have hung left-handed throughout last time, didn't go a yard early on in a first-time visor before finally consenting to run on when the race was as good as over. (tchd 10-1 and 14-1)
Dispol Kabira is considerably better than she showed as she was keeping towards the far-side rail in about fourth when losing all momentum after being stopped in her run around a furlong out. (op 14-1)

5977 WATCH RACING UK ON SKY CHANNEL 432 MAIDEN STKS 5f
2:35 (2:36) (Class 5) 2-Y-O £3,238 (£963; £481; £240) Stalls High

Form RPR
23 **1** **Elusive Trader (USA)**[23] 5311 2-9-3 0.......... SebSanders 12 72
(R Hannon) *cl up: rdn to ld over 1f out: drvn ins fnl f and kpt on* **10/11**[1]
2004 **2** 3/4 **Final Ovation (IRE)**[24] 5292 2-9-3 68.......... GrahamGibbons 9 69
(J J Quinn) *led: rdn along 2f out: drvn and hdd over 1f out: kpt on gamely u.p ins fnl f* **11/1**
2036 **3** shd **Mercers Row**[12] 5620 2-9-3 68.......... DanielTudhope 13 69
(A Dickman) *chsd ldrs on inner: rdn and hdwy over 1f out: swtchd lft and drvn ent fnl f: styd on* **5/1**[2]
0 **4** 3/4 **Besty**[11] 5668 2-9-3 0.......... TomEaves 3 66
(B Smart) *chsd ldrs on outer: hdwy 1/2-way: rdn and ch over 1f out: sn drvn and kpt on same pce ins fnl f* **40/1**
00 **5** 1 1/4 **Thinking**[11] 5668 2-9-3 0.......... DavidAllan 2 62+
(T D Easterby) *in tch: hdwy 2f out: sn rdn and kpt on ins fnl f: nrst fin* **100/1**
6 3/4 **Ravenfield (IRE)** 2-9-3 0.......... PaulHanagan 5 59
(D H Brown) *in rr: hdwy 2f out: sn rdn and kpt on ent fnl f: nrst fin* **33/1**
444 **7** 1 1/2 **Kalahari Desert (IRE)**[10] 5693 2-9-0 0.......... MichaelJStainton(3) 10 54
(R M Whitaker) *chsd ldrs: rdn along wl over 1f out: grad wknd* **12/1**
8 hd **Woldgate** 2-8-12 0.......... LanceBetts(5) 7 53
(G R Oldroyd) *midfield: rdn along 1/2-way: nvr a factor* **66/1**
20 **9** 2 **Taborcillo**[10] 5693 2-9-3 0.......... PhillipMakin 6 46
(T D Barron) *chsd ldrs: rdn along 1/2-way: sn wknd* **14/1**
0 **10** 1/2 **Redoubtable Grace**[12] 5620 2-9-3 0.......... SilvestreDeSousa 4 44
(Mrs R A Carr) *dwlt: a in rr* **100/1**
11 1/2 **Media Jury** 2-9-3 0.......... PAspell 14 42
(J S Wainwright) *a towards rr* **66/1**
3 **12** 3 3/4 **Layla's Lexi**[12] 5620 2-8-12 0.......... AdrianTNicholls 8 30+
(D Nicholls) *dwlt: sn outpcd and rdn along: a bhd* **6/1**[3]
00 **13** 25 **Remember Dougie (IRE)**[24] 5292 2-8-12 0.......... FrancisNorton 11 —
(A Berry) *in tch: rdn along and wknd 1/2-way: sn bhd* **100/1**

62.90 secs (-0.60) **Going Correction** -0.20s/f (Firm) **13** Ran SP% **117.4**
Speed ratings (Par 95): **96,94,94,93,91 90,87,87,84,83 82,76,36**
toteswingers: 1&2 £4.60, 1&3 £2.80, 2&3 £7.30 CSF £11.99 TOTE £1.90: £1.10, £2.90, £1.70; EX 14.70.
Owner Trevor C Stewart **Bred** Overbrook Farm **Trained** East Everleigh, Wilts

FOCUS
A modest sprint maiden. The winning time was 1.04 seconds quicker than the earlier selling nursery won the 63-rated Zelos Dream. The placed horses anchor the level.

NOTEBOOK
Elusive Trader(USA) failed to improve on his debut effort when beaten at odds on over 6f on Polytrack last time, but this drop in trip suited and he handled the turf just fine at the first attempt. He needed to be strongly ridden to assert, however, and looks just a fair type who is probably worthy of an official rating in the low-70s. (op Evens tchd 11-10 in a place)
Final Ovation(IRE) had run well below form on his last three starts, and two of those efforts came in selling company, but this was better. He showed plenty of speed but was hassled by the winner pretty much throughout, and ultimately only just held on to second. A less-demanding 5f is likely to suit better. (tchd 14-1)
Mercers Row showed pace before fading last time, but he got going too late on this occasion. (tchd 9-2 and 11-2)
Besty stepped up significantly on his debut effort and looks the type to progress again. (tchd 33-1)
Thinking had shown next to nothing on his first two starts, but this was a little better and nurseries are now an option.
Ravenfield(IRE) gave the impression he'll be better for the run. (tchd 28-1)
Layla's Lexi had today's third-placed finisher behind when making a promising debut on soft ground at Catterick, so this has to be considered a very disappointing performance. She was never travelling and, while a step up in trip will probably help, she now has something to prove. (op 11-2 tchd 9-2)

5978 ORIGINAL BARROWBOYS H'CAP 5f
3:10 (3:10) (Class 5) (0-75,75) 3-Y-O+ £4,209 (£1,252; £625; £312) Stalls High

Form RPR
0112 **1** **King Of Swords (IRE)**[16] 5518 5-8-8 63..........(p) AndrewElliott 2 69
(N Tinkler) *chsd ldrs on outer: styd on fnl f: led last strides: jst hld on* **25/1**
0035 **2** nse **Caranbola**[19] 5405 3-8-2 65.......... JohnCavanagh(7) 5 71
(M Brittain) *hmpd s: detached in last: gd hdwy on wd outside over 1f out: fin wl: jst failed* **33/1**
2133 **3** hd **La Capriosa**[19] 5405 3-8-9 68.......... FrederikTylicki(3) 13 73
(J A Glover) *led on far side: hdd fnl strides* **9/2**[1]
4060 **4** shd **Kyzer Chief**[16] 5518 4-8-4 62.......... KellyHarrison(3) 9 67
(R E Barr) *w ldrs: kpt on wl fnl f* **25/1**
3164 **5** shd **Hysterical Lady**[37] 4849 3-9-1 71.......... AdrianTNicholls 4 75
(D Nicholls) *wnt rt s: sn w ldrs: edgd lft fnl f: r.o* **20/1**
2403 **6** hd **Artsu**[35] 4899 4-9-4 73.......... PhillipMakin 11 78+
(M Dods) *hld up towards rr: hdwy whn nt clr run over 1f out: styd on wl ins fnl f* **13/2**[3]
1051 **7** shd **Select Committee**[18] 5421 4-8-13 68..........(v) GrahamGibbons 3 71
(J J Quinn) *trckd ldrs: kpt on wl fnl f* **16/1**
4410 **8** 1 1/4 **Angelo Poliziano**[35] 4899 3-9-1 71..........(v[1]) SilvestreDeSousa 10 70
(Mrs A Duffield) *restless in stalls: wnt lft s: chsd ldrs: kpt on same pce fnl f* **12/1**
5350 **9** shd **Ryedane (IRE)**[11] 5678 7-8-5 60..........(b) DuranFentiman 6 58
(T D Easterby) *wnt lft and hmpd s: bhd: hdwy over 1f out: kpt on: nt rch ldrs* **25/1**
1521 **10** shd **Noodles Blue Boy**[16] 5517 3-9-5 75.......... FrancisNorton 7 73
(Ollie Pears) *mid-div: drvn and outpcd over 2f out: kpt on fnl f* **6/1**[2]
4516 **11** hd **Captain Scooby**[21] 5335 3-8-12 71.......... MichaelJStainton(3) 16 68
(R M Whitaker) *rr-div: hdwy whn n.m.r appr fnl f: nvr trbld ldrs* **8/1**
6004 **12** 1 **Piste**[16] 5517 3-8-11 67.......... TomEaves 8 61
(Miss T Jackson) *chsd ldrs: wknd appr fnl f* **33/1**
5462 **13** 3/4 **Peninsular War**[50] 4399 3-9-3 73.......... PaulHanagan 1 67+
(R A Fahey) *hld up: swtchd rt over 3f out: styng on whn nt clr run jst ins fnl f* **18/1**
3000 **14** 1 1/2 **Spiritofthewest (IRE)**[55] 4227 3-9-5 75.......... SebSanders 15 61
(D H Brown) *reminders after s: a towards rr* **11/1**
1-00 **15** nk **Embra (IRE)**[114] 2312 4-8-7 62.......... JoeFanning 14 47+
(T J Etherington) *chsd ldrs on inner: wknd and eased last 150yds* **16/1**
0-00 **16** 11 **Loch Jipp (USA)**[35] 4891 4-9-1 70..........(v) PAspell 17 15
(J S Wainwright) *chsd ldrs on ins: lost pl over 1f out: eased ins fnl f: t.o* **12/1**

62.47 secs (-1.03) **Going Correction** -0.20s/f (Firm)
WFA 3 from 4yo+ 1lb **16** Ran SP% **119.8**
Speed ratings (Par 103): **100,99,99,99,99 98,98,96,96,96 96,94,93,90,90 72**
toteswingers: 1&2 £66.80, 1&3 £14.50, 2&3 £33.40 CSF £645.10 CT £4509.72 TOTE £23.30: £4.60, £6.20, £2.10, £7.90; EX 858.00.
Owner P Alderson & J Raybould **Bred** Maurice G McAuley **Trained** Langton, N Yorks
■ Stewards' Enquiry : Frederik Tylicki three-day ban: weighed in heavier than he weighed out (Sep 30, Oct 1 & 5)

FOCUS
There was a remarkably close finish to this modest sprint handicap, and it was obviously a seriously competitive contest. The form is limited, though.

5979 WATCH RACING UK ON VIRGIN MEDIA 536 H'CAP 1m 4f 16y
3:45 (3:46) (Class 4) (0-85,81) 3-Y-O £5,180 (£1,541; £770; £384) Stalls High

Form RPR
1111 **1** **Point Of Light**[35] 4917 3-9-3 80.......... SebSanders 3 90+
(Sir Mark Prescott) *mde all: pushed along over 3f out: rdn over 2f out: clr over 1f out: rdn out* **4/5**[1]
3011 **2** 2 1/2 **Rosewin (IRE)**[9] 5732 3-8-4 66 6ex.......... PaulHanagan 4 72+
(A Dickman) *bolted rdrless to s: dwlt: sn trcking ldng pair: hdwy to chse wnr 7f out: effrt and cl up 3f out: rdn over 2f out: kpt on u.p ins fnl f* **10/3**[2]
-520 **3** 1 1/4 **Battle Planner (USA)**[21] 5334 3-9-4 81..........(p) TomEaves 2 84
(I Semple) *trckd wnr 5f: pushed along and outpcd 3f out: rdn over 2f out: styd on ins fnl f: tk 3rd nr line* **9/1**
4524 **4** hd **Maybeme**[18] 5419 3-8-5 68.......... DuranFentiman 1 71
(N Bycroft) *s.i.s: hld up: hdwy to chse ldng pair over 4f out: rdn 3f out: drvn over 2f out and kpt on same pce* **4/1**[3]

2m 38.7s (-2.20) **Going Correction** -0.20s/f (Firm) **4** Ran SP% **108.6**
Speed ratings (Par 103): **99,97,96,96**
CSF £3.76 TOTE £1.60; EX 3.70.
Owner Syndicate 2007 **Bred** Watership Down Stud **Trained** Newmarket, Suffolk

FOCUS
Not a strong handicap for the grade, but a good in-form winner who can rate higher.

5980 EUROPEAN BREEDERS' FUND MAIDEN FILLIES' STKS 7f 100y
4:20 (4:23) (Class 5) 2-Y-O £3,885 (£1,156; £577; £288) Stalls High

Form RPR
432 **1** **Silent Secret (IRE)**[8] 5741 2-9-0 77.......... FrancisNorton 5 72
(R Hannon) *t.k.h: trckd ldrs: hrd rdn 1f out: styd on to ld last 50yds: all out* **6/5**[1]
02 **2** 1/2 **Whirly Dancer**[18] 5417 2-9-0 0.......... JimmyQuinn 14 71
(H R A Cecil) *dwlt: sn chsng ldrs: led 3f out: hrd rdn 1f out: styd on: hdd and no ex towards fin* **5/1**[2]
3 1/2 **Tashzara (IRE)** 2-8-11 0.......... FrederikTylicki(3) 11 70
(Christopher Phillips, Ire) *in tch: effrt over 2f out: sn chsng ldng pair: hrd rdn and styd on strly ins fnl f* **12/1**
0405 **4** 3 1/2 **Uddy Mac**[10] 5692 2-9-0 56..........(b[1]) DuranFentiman 12 61
(N Bycroft) *chsd ldrs: one pce fnl 2f* **25/1**
600 **5** 3 **Emerald Glade (IRE)**[18] 5439 2-9-0 52.......... DavidAllan 9 54
(T D Easterby) *towards rr: hdwy on outer over 2f out: kpt on: nvr nr ldrs* **25/1**
6 1/2 **China Lily (USA)** 2-9-0 0.......... PaulHanagan 8 53
(Saeed Bin Suroor) *s.s: towards rr: hdwy over 2f out: swtchd lft jst ins fnl f: kpt on: nvr nr ldrs* **9/1**
50 **7** 2 3/4 **Nafura**[19] 5397 2-9-0 0.......... DO'Donohoe 4 47
(Saeed Bin Suroor) *in tch: drvn 4f out: no threat* **8/1**[3]
220U **8** nse **Mad Millie (IRE)**[12] 5620 2-9-0 65.......... AdrianTNicholls 13 47
(J Hetherton) *led tl hdd 3f out: wknd over 1f out* **20/1**
9 2 1/4 **Fashionable Gal (IRE)** 2-9-0 0.......... SebSanders 2 52+
(Sir Mark Prescott) *s.s: in rr: hdwy over 1f out: nvr on terms* **25/1**
10 7 **Always De One** 2-9-0 0.......... JoeFanning 7 25
(M Johnston) *in rr and sn drvn along: nvr on terms* **16/1**
0 **11** shd **Gadobout Dancer**[35] 4888 2-9-0 0.......... TomEaves 6 25
(I W McInnes) *swvd lft s: a in rr* **100/1**
0006 **12** 6 **Maiwand**[19] 5393 2-9-0 34.......... SilvestreDeSousa 3 11+
(Mrs R A Carr) *chsd ldrs: lost pl over 2f out: eased whn bhd ins fnl f* **150/1**
0 **13** 3 1/2 **Rain In The Course**[16] 5498 2-9-0 0.......... SamHitchcott 10 —
(M R Channon) *mid-div: sn drvn along: lost pl 2f out: eased whn bhd ins fnl f* **100/1**

1m 32.48s (-1.32) **Going Correction** -0.20s/f (Firm) **13** Ran SP% **115.7**
Speed ratings (Par 92): **99,98,97,93,90 89,86,86,84,76 75,69,65**
toteswingers: 1&2 £2.90, 1&3 £6.20, 2&3 £10.70 CSF £5.95 TOTE £2.20: £1.20, £2.00, £3.00; EX 8.20.
Owner Noel O'Callaghan **Bred** Roland H Alder **Trained** East Everleigh, Wilts

FOCUS
Just a fair fillies' maiden. The winning time was 0.41 seconds quicker than the following maiden auction contest won by Epic. The fourth and fifth limit the form.
NOTEBOOK
Silent Secret(IRE) coped with this slight drop back in trip on a stiff track but she was made to work hard, only getting on top well inside the final furlong. Things are likely to be tougher from now on, but she's likely to benefit from further. (op 5-4 tchd 13-8)
Whirly Dancer, runner-up over course and distance on her previous start, looked to run her best race so far. She ensured the 77-rated winner had to work hard and looks a fair enough type. (op 11-2 tchd 4-1)
Tashzara(IRE), a half-sister to dual 7f-1m winner Mull Of Killough, made a pleasing debut in third. She took a while to get the idea when first coming under pressure but finished well. (tchd 10-1 after early 18-1 in a place)
Uddy Mac ran quite well, but she came into this with an official rating of only 56 and will be probably be better off in low-grade handicaps. (op 22-1)
Emerald Glade(IRE) will be better in low-grade handicaps. (op 66-1 tchd 20-1)
China Lily(USA), a 75,000gns first foal of a 3yo winner in the US, missed the break and ran very green, never looking likely to get involved, but she seemed to finally be getting the idea late on. (op 11-1 tchd 8-1)
Fashionable Gal(IRE) failed to ever get in a blow after starting slowly and looking inexperienced. She's likely to appreciate quite a bit further in time. (op 28-1)

5981 BEVERLEY RACECOURSE MAIDEN AUCTION STKS 7f 100y
4:50 (4:51) (Class 6) 2-Y-O **£2,914** (£867; £433; £216) **Stalls** High

Form RPR
65 **1** **Epic (IRE)**[42] 4646 2-8-11 0 .... JoeFanning 1 76
(M Johnston) *qckly away and mde all: rdn along 2f out: drvn ins fnl f and styd on wl* **9/1**
2 *1 1/4* **Indian Valley (USA)** 2-8-8 0 .... SilvestreDeSousa 4 70+
(Rae Guest) *chsd ldrs: hdwy over 2f out: rdn over 1f out: kpt on ins fnl f: nrst fin* **9/1**
54 **3** *shd* **Crunched**[18] 5428 2-8-11 0 .... SebSanders 6 73
(M L W Bell) *trckd ldng pair: chsd wnr over 4f out: rdn along over 2f out: drvn over 1f out: kpt on same pce ins fnl f* **3/1**[3]
4022 **4** *1 1/4* **Keyta Bonita (IRE)**[19] 5392 2-8-4 73 .... PaulHanagan 2 63
(M G Quinlan) *chsd ldrs: hdwy over 2f out and sn rdn: drvn over 1f out and kpt on same pce fnl f* **5/2**[2]
02 **5** *1 1/4* **I'm Super Too (IRE)**[11] 5668 2-8-9 0 .... PJMcDonald 7 65
(G A Swinbank) *prom: effrt over 2f out and sn rdn along: drvn over 1f out but hung badly rt: wknd ent fnl f* **9/4**[1]
05 **6** *8* **Vittachi**[16] 5512 2-8-9 0 .... (p) JimmyQuinn 5 46
(J D Bethell) *midfield: hdwy 4f out: rdn along 3f out: sn no imp* **50/1**
0 **7** *9* **Master Leon**[53] 4308 2-8-9 0 .... TomEaves 10 25
(B Smart) *s.i.s: a bhd* **14/1**
0P5 **8** *2* **Ochilview Warrior (IRE)**[21] 5330 2-8-10 0 ow1 .... DanielTudhope 8 21
(R Bastiman) *t.k.h: midfield: effrt on inner 3f out: sn rdn along and nvr a factor* **66/1**
000 **9** *10* **Magic Millie (IRE)**[38] 4817 2-8-5 54 ow1 .... AdrianTNicholls 9 —
(J Hetherton) *s.i.s: a in rr* **50/1**
0000 **10** *dist* **Woodhouse Mill (IRE)**[13] 5595 2-8-8 38 .... AndrewElliott 3 —
(N Tinkler) *in rr whn j. path after 2f and lost action: sn bhd: t.o 1/2-way and virtually p.u fnl 2f* **150/1**
1m 32.89s (-0.91) **Going Correction** -0.20s/f (Firm) **10** Ran SP% **117.1**
Speed ratings (Par 93): **97,95,95,94,92 83,73,70,59,—**
toteswingers: 1&2 £13.70, 1&3 £5.90, 2&3 £7.20 CSF £85.70 TOTE £8.40: £1.90, £2.80, £1.20; EX 58.00.
Owner Racegoers Club Owners Group **Bred** P D Savill **Trained** Middleham Moor, N Yorks
FOCUS
A weak maiden run in a time 0.41 seconds slower than earlier fillies' contest won by the 77-rated Silent Secret. The seventh and eighth govern the merit of the form.
NOTEBOOK
Epic(IRE) managed to get to the front, despite being drawn out widest, and he stuck on gamely pressure in the straight. Things are likely to be tougher from now on, but he shouldn't get too harsh a mark and has the scope to progress into a fair 3yo. (op 7-1)
Indian Valley(USA), a $72,000 half-sister to, among others, very useful US dirt filly Chayya Dance, a triple winner at around 6f-1m, made a satisfactory debut. The only newcomer in the line, she kept on well enough in the closing stages and should be better for the experience, but this wasn't much of a race. (op 14-1)
Crunched had his chance and ran okay, but this was probably just a modest effort on the figures. Handicaps are now an option. (op 5-1)
Keyta Bonita(IRE) ran below the form she had shown on three of her first four starts. She's had a few chances now and is looking exposed. (tchd 11-4)
I'm Super Too(IRE) may well have threatened the winner had he not ruined his chance by hanging badly right against the far rail all the way up the straight. His recent second placing at Thirsk came on soft ground and on this evidence he'll benefit from a return to that sort of going. (op 2-1 tchd 15-8 and 11-4 in places)
Woodhouse Mill(IRE) Official explanation: jockey said filly lost its action

5982 STARS OF THE FUTURE APPRENTICE CLASSIFIED STKS (DIV I) 1m 100y
5:20 (5:21) (Class 6) 3-Y-O+ **£1,876** (£554; £277) **Stalls** High

Form RPR
0000 **1** **Why Nee Amy**[54] 4279 3-8-5 48 .... LauraPike(5) 6 59
(T Keddy) *trckd ldrs: hdwy 2f out: rdn over 1f out: chal ins fnl furlong: styd on to ld last 100yds* **16/1**
0122 **2** *1/2* **Zaplamation (IRE)**[24] 5289 4-8-11 55 .... IJBrennan(3) 14 59+
(J J Quinn) *trckd ldrs: smooth hdwy over 3f out: led on bit over 1f out: shkn up ent fnl f and sn rdn: hdd and nt qckn last 100yds* **11/10**[1]
0000 **3** *4* **Western Art (USA)**[90] 3066 4-8-11 53 .... JamesPSullivan(3) 8 49
(M W Easterby) *in tch: effrt 3f out: hdwy on outer 2f out: rdn to chse ldrs and hung rt ent fnl f: sn one pce* **15/2**[2]
0056 **4** *1 1/2* **Boss Hog**[17] 5465 4-9-0 50 .... PaulPickard 3 46+
(P T Midgley) *hld up and bhd: pushed along and hdwy 3f out: rdn over 2f out: drvn over 1f out: styd on ins fnl f: nrst fin* **16/1**
0006 **5** *1* **Danish Art (IRE)**[5] 5842 4-9-0 55 .... MartinLane 5 44
(M W Easterby) *chsd ldrs: hdwy over 2f out and sn rdn: drvn over 1f out and one pce* **9/1**[3]
000- **6** *1 1/2* **Govenor Eliott (IRE)**[350] 6374 4-9-0 52 .... LanceBetts 7 41
(A J Lockwood) *chsd ldr: rdn over 2f out: drvn over 1f out and grad wknd* **40/1**
3004 **7** *nk* **Well Of Echoes**[12] 5647 3-8-4 55 ow1 .... (t) JonathanHinch(7) 2 41
(J A Glover) *chsd ldng pair on outer: rdn along wl over 2f out: wknd over 1f out* **20/1**
6040 **8** *2 1/2* **Carpe Diem**[15] 5549 4-8-9 49 .... (v) LeeTopliss(5) 9 35
(R A Fahey) *hld up in tch: hdwy on inner 3f out: rdn to chse ldrs 2f out: sn drvn and btn over 1f out* **11/1**
0- **9** *3 3/4* **Riverside**[492] 2041 4-8-9 55 .... JohnCavanagh(5) 1 27
(M Brittain) *a in rr* **100/1**
000- **10** *nk* **Mojeerr**[338] 6702 3-8-7 53 .... DeclanCannon(3) 11 26
(A J McCabe) *a towards rr* **25/1**
5060 **11** *2 3/4* **I See Nice Sea**[21] 5342 3-8-10 52 .... (b[1]) JamesO'Reilly 10 20
(Ollie Pears) *set str pce: rdn along over 2f out: drvn and hdd over 1f out: wknd* **25/1**
-360 **12** *2* **Rascal In The Mix (USA)**[52] 4354 3-8-10 55 .... SladeO'Hara 13 16+
(R M Whitaker) *dwlt: in rr whn bdly hmpd after 1f: a bhd* **14/1**
640- **13** *7* **Tumbleweed Di**[439] 3665 5-8-11 44 .... TobyAtkinson(5) 12 1
(John A Harris) *dwlt: a bhd* **18/1**
1m 45.67s (-1.93) **Going Correction** -0.20s/f (Firm)
WFA 3 from 4yo+ 4lb **13** Ran SP% **117.3**
Speed ratings (Par 101): **101,100,96,95,94 92,92,89,85,85 82,80,73**
toteswingers: 1&2 £8.90, 1&3 £27.20, 2&3 £3.70 CSF £31.66 TOTE £21.50: £4.90, £1.20, £1.50; EX 65.90.
Owner B Neaves **Bred** D E Jenkins **Trained** Newmarket, Suffolk
■ Stewards' Enquiry : Toby Atkinson caution: use of whip
Declan Cannon five-day ban: careless riding (Oct 1-5)
FOCUS
Moderate form, although the winning time was 0.96 seconds quicker than the second division won the 55-rated Pacific Bay.
I See Nice Sea Official explanation: jockey said filly had no more to give

5983 STARS OF THE FUTURE APPRENTICE CLASSIFIED STKS (DIV II) 1m 100y
5:55 (5:55) (Class 6) 3-Y-O+ **£1,876** (£554; £277) **Stalls** High

Form RPR
5350 **1** **Pacific Bay (IRE)**[12] 5624 3-8-5 55 .... LeeTopliss(5) 10 60+
(R A Fahey) *chsd ldng pair: hdwy and cl up over 3f out: chal over 2f out: led wl over 1f out: rdn clr appr fnl f: drvn out* **5/1**[2]
635 **2** *1* **Carragold**[42] 4656 3-8-5 54 .... JohnCavanagh(5) 11 58
(M Brittain) *bhd: hdwy on outer 2f out: sn rdn: str run ins fnl f: styd on to take 2nd nr fin* **10/1**
001 **3** *1/2* **Tropical Duke (IRE)**[38] 4819 3-8-10 55 .... PaulPickard 3 57
(R E Barr) *in tch: hdwy to chse ldrs 2f out: drvn and edgd rt over 1f out: kpt on u.p ins fnl f* **3/1**[1]
3004 **4** *2 1/4* **Bicksta**[14] 5567 3-8-10 51 .... (v[1]) MartinLane 6 52
(E F Vaughan) *chsd ldrs: hdwy 3f out: rdn over 2f out: drvn and one pce appr fnl f* **7/1**[3]
0020 **5** *3/4* **Russian Music (USA)**[21] 5332 4-8-11 49 .... (b) JamesPSullivan(3) 1 51
(M W Easterby) *towards rr: hdwy on outer wl over 2f out: rdn along wl over 1f out: kpt on ins fnl f: nrst fin* **12/1**
3400 **6** *11* **Mccormack (IRE)**[15] 5548 7-8-9 42 .... NSLawes(5) 9 27
(Miss T Jackson) *in tch: hdwy 3f out: rdn along over 2f out and sn no imp* **25/1**
0606 **7** *4 1/2* **Unconsoled**[17] 5468 3-8-5 44 .... DavidKenny(5) 5 18
(J Hetherton) *led: rdn along 3f out: drvn 2f out: sn hdd & wknd over 1f out* **100/1**
0000 **8** *1 3/4* **Adozen Dreams**[17] 5468 3-8-3 47 .... TerenceFury(7) 13 14
(N Bycroft) *a in rr* **66/1**
0000 **9** *2 1/2* **Grey Gurkha**[35] 4887 8-8-11 42 .... IJBrennan(3) 12 9
(I W McInnes) *hld up: a towards rr* **14/1**
2345 **10** *1* **Paint Splash**[38] 4819 3-8-10 50 .... DeanHeslop 7 7
(T D Barron) *midfield: hdwy to chse ldrs 1/2-way: rdn along wl over 2f out and sn wknd* **3/1**[1]
0040 **11** *1/2* **Reddy Ronnie (IRE)**[16] 5513 5-9-0 43 .... (v[1]) LanceBetts 14 6
(D W Thompson) *chsd ldr: cl up 1/2-way: rdn along 3f out and sn wknd* **22/1**
-000 **12** *21* **Pinewood Lulu**[24] 5283 4-8-11 43 ow2 .... (b[1]) AndrewYoxall(5) 8 —
(S A Harris) *towards rr: wd st: sn bhd and eased fnl 2f* **66/1**
1m 46.63s (-0.97) **Going Correction** -0.20s/f (Firm)
WFA 3 from 4yo+ 4lb **12** Ran SP% **114.8**
Speed ratings (Par 101): **96,95,94,92,91 80,76,74,71,70 70,49**
toteswingers: 1&2 £7.00, 1&3 £3.90, 2&3 £7.20 CSF £49.97 TOTE £5.40: £1.60, £2.60, £1.90; EX 48.60 Place 6: £55.85, Place 5: £23.04..
Owner Mrs H Steel **Bred** Ms N Clarke **Trained** Musley Bank, N Yorks
FOCUS
The winning time was 0.96 seconds slower than the first division won by the 48-rated Why Nee Amy. It has been rated around the principals.
T/Plt: £55.20 to a £1 stake. Pool: £51,542.09. 681.07 winning tickets. T/Qpdt: £32.40 to a £1 stake. Pool: £3,229.45. 73.75 winning tickets. JR

5806 KEMPTON (A.W) (R-H)
Wednesday, September 16
OFFICIAL GOING: Standard
Wind: Moderate ahead Weather: Bright spells early

5984 DAY TIME, NIGHT TIME, GREAT TIME MEDIAN AUCTION MAIDEN FILLIES' STKS 1m (P)
5:45 (5:46) (Class 6) 2-Y-O **£2,047** (£604; £302) **Stalls** High

Form RPR
5 **1** **Wild Rose**[16] 5498 2-9-0 0 .... HayleyTurner 12 74+
(M L W Bell) *chsd ldrs: rdn to chal appr fnl f: led ins fnl f: sn drvn to repel chalr: styd on strly and in command cl home* **13/2**[2]
3 **2** *3/4* **Awaseef (USA)**[12] 5639 2-9-0 0 .... RHills 6 72
(J H M Gosden) *chsd ldrs: slt ld appr fnl f: hdd jst ins fnl f: styd chalng tl outpcd cl home* **4/6**[1]
4 **3** *1 3/4* **Serafina's Flight**[13] 5604 2-9-0 0 .... MartinDwyer 2 68
(W R Muir) *in tch: rdn: hdwy and continually flashed tail fr 3f out: styd on wl fnl f but nvr gng pce to trble ldng duo* **8/1**[3]
0 **4** *2 1/4* **Million Dollars (USA)**[24] 5284 2-9-0 0 .... JimmyFortune 9 63
(Saeed Bin Suroor) *disp ld tl slt advantage ins fnl 3f: rdn over 2f out: hdd appr fnl f: wknd ins fnl f* **9/1**
5 *nk* **Temple Queen** 2-9-0 0 .... JamesDoyle 3 65+
(S Kirk) *in rr whn hmpd and pushed lft after 2f: styd on outer and hdwy fr 2f out: fin wl but nt rch ldrs* **100/1**
0 **6** *1/2* **Charpoy Cobra**[19] 5398 2-9-0 0 .... KirstyMilczarek 11 61
(J A R Toller) *s.i.s: in rr whn hmpd after 2f: stl plenty to do over 2f out: hdwy on outside over 1f out: fin wl* **16/1**
65 **7** *8* **Primrose Bankes**[12] 5643 2-8-11 0 .... JackDean(3) 4 44
(W G M Turner) *towards rr and rdn along fr 1/2-way: nvr in contention* **50/1**
0 **8** *2 1/4* **Albacocca**[5] 5839 2-9-0 0 .... StephenDonohoe 10 39
(Sir Mark Prescott) *mid-div and rdn 1/2-way: sn bhd* **40/1**

0 **9** 1 1/2 **Seeking Rose**[15] 5547 2-9-0 0 .... TGMcLaughlin 5 36
(E A L Dunlop) *in rr: sme hdwy on ins over 2f out: sn wknd* **66/1**
0 **10** hd **Silk Runner (IRE)**[46] 4542 2-9-0 0 .... ChrisCatlin 1 35
(J W Hills) *disp ld tl 3f out: wknd over 2f out* **80/1**
11 nk **Belle Zorro** 2-9-0 0 .... J-PGuillambert 8 34
(M L W Bell) *slt ld tl hdd ins fnl 3f: sn btn* **40/1**
12 1/2 **Philippa Jane** 2-9-0 0 .... FrankieMcDonald 7 33
(P Winkworth) *t.k.h: chsd ldrs and hmpd after 2f: styd wl there tl wknd qckly over 2f out* **100/1**
13 22 **Khazara** 2-9-0 0 .... FergusSweeney 14 —
(A King) *mid-div whn bdly hmpd after 2f: nt rcvr* **33/1**
14 10 **Scarlet Ridge** 2-9-0 0 .... PatCosgrave 13 —
(D K Ivory) *extremely slowly away: v green and sn t.o* **33/1**

1m 39.26s (-0.54) **Going Correction** -0.10s/f (Stan) **14** Ran SP% **117.7**
Speed ratings (Par 90): **98,97,95,93,92 92,84,82,80,80 80,79,57,47**
toteswingers: 1&2 £2.10, 1&3 £6.30, 2&3 £2.20. CSF £10.47 TOTE £6.70: £1.60, £1.10, £2.40; EX 14.90.
Owner Saif Ali & Saeed H Altayer **Bred** Biddestone Stud **Trained** Newmarket, Suffolk

FOCUS
This was just an ordinary maiden. The second and third are the best guide.

NOTEBOOK
Wild Rose, a promising fifth at Chepstow on debut, was always nicely placed in behind the speed and, having come to challenge the favourite, she stayed on the stronger of the pair. This trip looks about right for her and it will be interesting to see what mark she is given for nurseries. (op 6-1 tchd 5-1)
Awaseef(USA) looked to be crying out for this trip when third over 7f here on debut and she was understandably made a short-price favourite. She had every chance, leading a furlong out, but couldn't quicken on and the winner was always doing too much for her in the final 100 yards. (tchd 8-11)
Serafina's Flight confirmed the promise of her debut effort, sticking on in third despite flashing her tail under pressure. She will require 1m2f before long and looks capable of landing a small maiden. (op 10-1)
Million Dollars(USA) blew all chance at the start on debut, being very slowly away and running green, but she had clearly learnt from that and showed up well for a long way. She is the type to find a small race in handicaps. (op 7-1)
Temple Queen ◆, whose pedigree is a blend of speed and stamina, ran a race full of promise, running on late having been hampered early and got well behind. This was an eyecatching debut and she is one to watch out for in a similar contest. Official explanation: jockey said filly suffered interference in running (op 66-1)
Charpoy Cobra was another to come home well having been interfered with after a couple of furlongs, making rapid headway in the straight. She will be qualified for a mark after one more run and should fare better in that sphere. Official explanation: jockey said filly reared in stalls (op 20-1 tchd 25-1)
Belle Zorro Official explanation: jockey said filly was slowly away

5985 NORMAN ANDERTON MEMORIAL NURSERY — 1m (P)
6:20 (6:21) (Class 6) (0-65,65) 2-Y-O — £2,047 (£604; £302) Stalls High

Form — RPR
6004 **1** **Underworld Dandy**[13] 5613 2-9-2 **60** .... GeorgeBaker 5 65+
(P D Evans) *in rr tl hdwy fr 3f out: drvn and qcknd to ld ins fnl f: kpt on strly* **16/1**
0165 **2** nk **Right Rave (IRE)**[18] 5433 2-9-4 **65** .... AndreaAtzeni(3) 9 69
(P J McBride) *in tch: hdwy on outer fr 3f out: str run to chal appr fnl f: kpt on u.p ins fnl f but a hld by wnr* **4/1**[1]
3640 **3** 2 1/2 **Knockenduff**[14] 5573 2-9-2 **60** .... TedDurcan 1 59
(M R Channon) *in rr: rdn and hdwy on outside fr 2f out: styd on wl fnl f but nvr any threat to ldng duo* **25/1**
0000 **4** nk **Boycott (IRE)**[13] 5589 2-9-6 **64** ....(b) JimmyFortune 12 62
(J H M Gosden) *plld hrd: led: rdn over 2f out: kpt advantage tl hdd & wknd ins fnl f* **9/1**[3]
0062 **5** 1 1/2 **Rodrigo De Freitas (IRE)**[14] 5573 2-9-5 **63** .... PatCosgrave 7 58
(J R Boyle) *chsd ldrs: drvn to chal fr 3f out: edgd rt u.p and stl ev ch over 1f out: wknd ins fnl f* **6/1**[2]
0460 **6** 1 **Execution (IRE)**[14] 5573 2-9-4 **62** .... TGMcLaughlin 4 55
(E A L Dunlop) *towards rr tl hdwy over 2f out: drvn to chse ldrs over 1f out: eased whn hld wl ins fnl f* **33/1**
0405 **7** 1 **Hellenio**[8] 5748 2-9-6 **64** .... ChrisCatlin 14 54
(S C Williams) *chsd ldrs: rdn over 2f out: wknd ins fnl f* **11/1**
0010 **8** hd **Dear Mr Fantasy (IRE)**[13] 5613 2-9-0 **65** .... AmyScott(7) 8 55
(J W Hills) *hld up in rr and on outside thrght: styd on fr over 1f out but nvr any threat* **25/1**
040 **9** hd **Carnaval Court (IRE)**[16] 5498 2-9-6 **64** ....(v[1]) MartinDwyer 6 54
(A M Balding) *chsd ldrs: rdn 3f out: wknd ins fnl f* **9/1**[3]
004 **10** 1 **Thewinnatakesitall**[38] 4811 2-9-3 **61** .... KevinGhunowa 2 48
(H J Evans) *in rr: rdn and sme prog into mid-div over 2f out: sn wknd* **33/1**
0000 **11** 2 **Open Glory (FR)**[20] 5369 2-9-5 **63** .... RichardKingscote 3 46
(Tom Dascombe) *pressed ldrs: ev ch fr 3f out tl wknd wl over 1f out* **28/1**
066 **12** 1/2 **Calm Storm (IRE)**[14] 5571 2-9-6 **64** .... ShaneKelly 11 46
(J Noseda) *in tch: rdn and sme hdwy 3f out: nvr in contention and sn wknd* **4/1**[1]
003 **13** nk **Mary Celest (IRE)**[85] 3232 2-9-2 **60** .... RobertWinston 10 41
(K A Ryan) *chsd ldrs: rdn 3f out: wknd qckly 2f out* **16/1**
054 **14** 1 **Chat De Soie (IRE)**[18] 5417 2-9-2 **60** .... LPKeniry 13 39
(J S Moore) *a towards rr* **16/1**

1m 40.13s (0.33) **Going Correction** -0.10s/f (Stan) **14** Ran SP% **117.3**
Speed ratings (Par 93): **94,93,91,90,89 88,87,87,87,86 84,83,83,82**
toteswingers: 1&2 £7.20, 1&3 £63.90, 2&3 £12.40. CSF £72.54 CT £1657.71 TOTE £28.00: £8.30, £3.40, £8.70; EX 87.70.
Owner David Mort **Bred** S & Mrs M Bayless **Trained** Pandy, Monmouths

FOCUS
A competitive nursery. It has been rated around the balance of the principals.

NOTEBOOK
Underworld Dandy, well beaten in two previous runs in nurseries, had finished a running-on fourth in a 7f claimer at Wolverhampton last time and this first try at 1m brought about marked improvement. Racing off a mark of 60, he started to close before they hit the straight and stayed on well having quickened to lead inside the final furlong. There may be more to come at this distance. (tchd 14-1)
Right Rave(IRE), another who had failed to shine in two previous nursery outings, is bred to be suited this trip and she came with a strong challenge from a furlong out, but was always being held by the winner. (op 5-1, tchd 11-2 in a place)
Knockenduff, disappointing off this mark over C&D last time, had to be dropped in from her poor draw in stall one and, though she ran on well down the straight, she never looked like winning. This was a good effort and she may have gone close to winning had she been able to obtain a better early position. (op 16-1)
Boycott(IRE) refused to settle on this step up to 1m, but toughed it out as best he could and was still in contention a furlong out, though it was clear he was going to fade eventually. (op 8-1)
Rodrigo De Freitas(IRE), up 3lb having finished second over C&D on his nursery debut, came to hold every chance but couldn't see it out as strongly as those around him. (op 15-2)
Execution(IRE) ran a lot better than he had on his recent nursery debut, though still doesn't quite look up to winning off this mark. (op 25-1)
Dear Mr Fantasy(IRE) shaped with a bit of promise on this nursery debut. (op 16-1)
Calm Storm(IRE), upped in trip, never really threatened to land a blow. (tchd 7-2)

5986 LEVY BOARD H'CAP — 1m (P)
6:50 (6:51) (Class 4) (0-85,85) 3-Y-O — £4,727 (£1,406; £702; £351) Stalls High

Form — RPR
3362 **1** **Mac's Power (IRE)**[11] 5665 3-8-12 **79** ....(t) WilliamBuick 7 93+
(P J O'Gorman) *hld up in rr: smooth hdwy on ins fr 3f out: led on bit 1f out: shkn up to assert ins fnl f: easily* **15/2**[3]
0444 **2** 1 1/4 **Laudatory**[12] 5640 3-9-2 **83** .... AdamKirby 9 92
(W R Swinburn) *chsd ldrs: drvn along 3f out: styd on to take slt ld 2f out: hdd 1f out: kpt on but nt pce of wnr* **13/2**[2]
2241 **3** 2 3/4 **Sunshine Always (IRE)**[14] 5574 3-9-0 **81** .... KirstyMilczarek 14 84
(T D McCarthy) *chsd ldrs: rdn to take slt ld ins fnl 3f: hdd 2f out: outpcd by ldng duo fnl f* **8/1**
22 **4** nk **Shakalaka (IRE)**[63] 3984 3-8-11 **78** .... FergusSweeney 6 81
(G L Moore) *in rr: pushed along and hdwy over 2f out: styd on u.p to take 4th ins fnl f but nvr gng pce to get into contention* **25/1**
2341 **5** hd **Formula (USA)**[30] 5102 3-8-12 **79** .... RyanMoore 3 81
(R Hannon) *in rr: pushed along fr 3f out: styd on fnl 2f but nvr gng pce to get into contention* **16/1**
3512 **6** 2 **Striding Edge (IRE)**[14] 5575 3-8-8 **75** .... ShaneKelly 4 73
(W R Muir) *hld up in rr: hdwy over 2f out: chsd ldrs on far rail over 1f out: wknd ins fnl f* **16/1**
-506 **7** 1 **Kings Troop**[11] 5670 3-8-7 **74** ....(b[1]) RobertWinston 5 70
(H R A Cecil) *hld up in rr and racd towards outside: rdn 3f out: styd on same pce fnl 2f* **33/1**
1230 **8** 1/2 **Charlotte Point (USA)**[28] 5175 3-9-3 **84** .... MartinDwyer 8 78
(P F I Cole) *chsd ldrs: rdn over 3f out: wknd appr fnl f* **25/1**
0600 **9** 1/2 **Mishrif (USA)**[20] 5375 3-9-2 **83** .... JimCrowley 11 76
(J R Jenkins) *chsd ldrs tl grad wknd fr over 2f out* **28/1**
3215 **10** 1 **Park Lane**[18] 5437 3-9-0 **81** .... MichaelHills 10 72
(B W Hills) *chsd ldrs: rdn 3f out: wknd over 1f out* **10/1**
414 **11** 1 **Mutawarath (IRE)**[20] 5363 3-9-2 **83** .... RHills 12 72
(W J Haggas) *led 1f: chsd ldrs tl wknd ins fnl 2f* **11/4**[1]
2654 **12** 5 **Militarist (USA)**[35] 4909 3-9-4 **85** ....(b[1]) JimmyFortune 2 63
(J H M Gosden) *chsd ldrs: rdn and wknd over 2f out* **11/1**
4003 **13** 6 **Watergate (IRE)**[9] 5725 3-9-0 **81** .... StephenDonohoe 13 46
(Sir Mark Prescott) *drvn to ld after 1f: hdd ins fnl 3f: sn wknd* **8/1**

1m 37.89s (-1.91) **Going Correction** -0.10s/f (Stan) **13** Ran SP% **117.3**
Speed ratings (Par 103): **105,103,101,100,100 98,97,97,96,95 94,89,83**
toteswingers: 1&2 £41.90, 1&3 £15.60, 2&3 £12.00. CSF £52.16 CT £418.33 TOTE £9.20: £4.00, £3.00, £4.80; EX 41.70.
Owner Michael McDonnell **Bred** Ballyhane Stud **Trained** Newmarket, Suffolk

FOCUS
This was a fair handicap run at a decent gallop. The form looks strong rated around the third, fourth and fifth.
Mutawarath(IRE) Official explanation: jockey said colt hung left

5987 DIGIBET MEDIAN AUCTION MAIDEN STKS — 1m 4f (P)
7:20 (7:21) (Class 6) 3-4-Y-O — £2,047 (£604; £302) Stalls Centre

Form — RPR
062 **1** **Bengal Tiger**[23] 5314 3-9-3 70 .... DavidProbert 7 85+
(A M Balding) *trckd ldrs: drvn to ld over 2f out: c clr fr over 1f out: easily* **11/8**[1]
2435 **2** 7 **Buckie Boy (IRE)**[39] 4789 3-9-3 70 .... IanMongan 9 72
(H R A Cecil) *pressed ldr tl slt advantage 6f out: def ldr over 3f out: hdd over 2f out: sn no ch w wnr but styd on for clr 2nd* **5/1**[3]
004 **3** 10 **Felicia**[60] 4084 4-9-6 45 .... KirstyMilczarek 13 51
(J E Long) *chsd ldrs: rdn over 3f out: styd on for wl btn 3rd fr over 2f out* **50/1**
2333 **4** 1 3/4 **Astrodiva**[26] 5205 3-8-7 70 .... AshleyMorgan(5) 1 48
(M H Tompkins) *in rr tl styd on fr 3f out to take modd 4th fnl 2f* **8/1**
4 **5** 1 1/2 **Xtra Special**[125] 2002 3-8-12 0 .... RyanMoore 3 46
(Sir Michael Stoute) *in tch: rdn over 5f out: no imp on ldrs and styd on same pce fnl 3f* **3/1**[2]
0 **6** 1 **Mistoffelees**[23] 5322 3-9-3 0 .... ChrisCatlin 2 49
(L M Cumani) *in rr: pushed along over 3f out: modest prog fnl 2f* **33/1**
00-0 **7** hd **Reel Man**[14] 5577 4-9-6 47 .... MarkCoumbe(5) 10 49
(D K Ivory) *nvr in contention* **50/1**
0- **8** 10 **Six Of Clubs**[357] 6199 3-9-0 0 ....(p) JackDean(3) 11 33
(W G M Turner) *chsd ldrs 9f* **80/1**
9 8 **Dance Gdansk (IRE)** 3-9-3 0 .... SteveDrowne 5 20
(M Blanshard) *a in rr* **66/1**
0 **10** 1 3/4 **Franco Is My Name**[8] 5744 3-9-3 0 .... TGMcLaughlin 8 17
(P R Hedger) *a in rr: no ch whn hung bdly lft fr 3f out* **66/1**
11 nk **Prince Pippin (IRE)** 3-9-3 0 .... JamesDoyle 6 17
(S Curran) *a in rr* **80/1**
0- **12** 1/2 **Saint Chapelle (IRE)**[326] 6978 3-8-12 0 .... JimCrowley 12 11
(Mrs A J Perrett) *slt ld tl narrowly hdd 6f out: wknd 3f out* **13/2**
00-0 **13** 108 **Mister Wilberforce**[77] 3498 3-9-3 30 ....(b[1]) LiamJones 4 —
(M Mullineaux) *chsd ldrs 7f: sn wknd: t.o* **100/1**

2m 32.74s (-1.76) **Going Correction** -0.10s/f (Stan)
WFA 3 from 4yo 8lb **13** Ran SP% **121.5**
Speed ratings (Par 101): **101,96,89,88,87 86,86,80,74,73 73,73,—**
toteswingers: 1&2 £3.10, 1&3 £17.80, 2&3 £23.60. CSF £8.72 TOTE £2.20: £1.02, £3.30, £13.30; EX 10.30.
Owner Kingsclere Racing CLub **Bred** Kingsclere Stud **Trained** Kingsclere, Hants

FOCUS
A moderate maiden in which they finished well spread out. The third and seventh underline the weakness of the form.

5988 DIGIBET.COM H'CAP — 1m 4f (P)
7:50 (7:52) (Class 6) (0-60,60) 3-Y-O — £2,047 (£604; £302) Stalls Centre

Form — RPR
-056 **1** **Rowan Tiger**[97] 2865 3-9-2 **58** .... PatCosgrave 12 68+
(J R Boyle) *t.k.h: chsd ldrs: rdn and hdwy fr 2f out: styd on u.p to ld ins fnl f: drvn out and in command cl home* **10/1**
010 **2** 1 1/4 **Cape Marien (IRE)**[57] 4178 3-9-4 **60** .... TedDurcan 5 68
(D R Lanigan) *chsd ldrs: rdn over 2f out: drvn to chal ins fnl f: outpcd by wnr fnl 100yds* **8/1**[3]

5204 **3** *1* **Silent Act (USA)**[35] 4904 3-9-2 **58** JimCrowley 11 66+
(Mrs A J Perrett) *hld up in tch: n.m.r over 2f out: drvn and hdwy over 1f out: styd on strly fnl f and gng on cl home but nt rch ldng duo* **5/1**[2]
0402 **4** *1 1/4* **Salybia Bay**[24] 5286 3-9-3 **59** RyanMoore 7 63
(R Hannon) *in rr tl rapid hdwy to ld 7f out: rdn 3f out: hdd ins fnl f: sn wknd* **9/2**[1]
0600 **5** *2 1/2* **Mellow Mixture**[30] 5101 3-9-4 **60** (t) JimmyFortune 13 60
(S Kirk) *sn led: hdd 7f out: styd chsng ldrs: rdn over 3f out: wknd over 1f out* **20/1**
4150 **6** *1/2* **Bubses Boy**[7] 5782 3-9-3 **59** IanMongan 2 58
(P Howling) *swtchd rt after s: hld up in rr: hdwy on outside fr 2f out: kpt on but nvr gng pce to get into contention* **16/1**
0040 **7** *2 1/2* **Mediterranean Sea (IRE)**[7] 5782 3-9-2 **58** AdrianMcCarthy 8 53
(J R Jenkins) *in rr: drvn and styd on fnl 2f but nvr in contention* **20/1**
6055 **8** *3/4* **Chanrossa (IRE)**[7] 5782 3-9-4 **60** TGMcLaughlin 6 54
(E A L Dunlop) *chsd ldrs: rdn 3f out: wknd fr 2f out* **14/1**
0406 **9** *1 1/2* **Mac Wolf**[53] 4320 3-9-0 **56** PatDobbs 3 48
(M G Quinlan) *chsd ldrs tl grad wknd fnl 2f* **25/1**
6324 **10** *1* **Transformer (IRE)**[14] 5577 3-9-3 **59** ShaneKelly 9 49
(W J Knight) *in rr: rdn and sme hdwy over 2f out: nvr rchd ldrs and sn wknd* **9/2**[1]
450 **11** *3* **Anessia**[46] 4519 3-9-1 **57** RichardKingscote 14 42
(Tom Dascombe) *chsd ldrs tl wknd qckly 3f out* **20/1**
5506 **12** *nk* **Suhailah**[55] 4234 3-9-4 **60** (p) LiamJones 4 45
(M J Attwater) *nvr bttr than mid-div* **50/1**
3230 **13** *3 1/4* **Jiggalong**[7] 5782 3-9-4 **60** ChrisCatlin 1 40
(R Ingram) *in rr: sme hdwy on outside over 3f out: sn wknd* **12/1**
440 **14** *3 3/4* **Park Melody (IRE)**[44] 4606 3-9-4 **60** MartinDwyer 10 34
(B J Meehan) *chsd ldrs tl wknd 4f out* **16/1**

2m 36.09s (1.59) **Going Correction** -0.10s/f (Stan) **14 Ran SP% 119.4**
Speed ratings (Par 99): **90,89,88,87,86 85,84,83,82,81 79,79,77,74**
toteswingers: 1&2 £22.10, 1&3 £17.40, 2&3 £6.50. CSF £80.35 CT £455.12 TOTE £12.20: £3.90, £2.90, £1.50; EX 102.20.
Owner Rowan Stud Partnership 1 **Bred** Rowan Farm Stud **Trained** Epsom, Surrey

FOCUS
A moderate handicap but fairly good form for the grade, with the runner-up the best guide.
Rowan Tiger Official explanation: trainer said, regarding the apparent improvement of form, that he gelding had matured and strenghened since its last run
Park Melody(IRE) Official explanation: vet said filly was struck into behind

5989 DIGIBET CASINO CLASSIFIED CLAIMING STKS 6f (P)
8:20 (8:22) (Class 5) 3-Y-0+ **£2,590** (£770; £385; £192) **Stalls** High

Form RPR
4203 **1** **Steelcut**[2] 5946 5-8-10 70 ow1 TedDurcan 2 76+
(R A Fahey) *in rr: hdwy over 2f out: styd on wl to ld fnl 100yds: c clr: comf* **4/1**[1]
600 **2** *2 1/2* **Fromsong (IRE)**[13] 5608 11-8-10 69 MarkCoumbe(5) 9 73
(D K Ivory) *chsd ldrs: drvn to ld wl over 1f out: hdd and outpcd fnl 100yds* **12/1**
6460 **3** *1/2* **Perfect Act**[18] 5429 4-9-5 68 AdamKirby 7 76+
(C G Cox) *hmpd s and bhd: rdn and hdwy ins fnl 2f: styd on u.p fnl f but nvr a threat to wnr* **7/1**[3]
0004 **4** *1 3/4* **Hollow Jo**[14] 5576 9-9-1 62 (v) FergusSweeney 11 66
(J R Jenkins) *in rr: pushed along and styd on fnl 2f: one pce ins fnl f* **11/1**
0303 **5** *1/2* **Pipers Piping (IRE)**[11] 5678 3-8-5 61 ChrisCatlin 3 57
(J A Osborne) *bmpd after s and bhd: stl towards rr and rdn 2f out: styd on fnl f but nvr in contention* **11/1**
-050 **6** *shd* **Wreningham**[27] 5184 4-9-1 57 ShaneKelly 12 64
(M D Squance) *slt ld tl hdd wl over 1f out: wknd ins fnl f* **14/1**
0203 **7** *nk* **Compton Classic**[13] 5608 7-8-10 69 (p) PatCosgrave 8 59
(J R Boyle) *rdr lost iron and veered lft s: bhd: rdn and hdwy over 1f out: styng on cl home* **6/1**[2]
5230 **8** *nk* **High Curragh**[19] 5409 6-9-1 70 (p) RobertWinston 1 63
(K A Ryan) *t.k.h: chsd ldrs tl hung bdly rt fr over 2f out: continued to hang and nvr a factor after* **8/1**
0642 **9** *1 1/4* **Dove Mews**[19] 5403 3-8-13 68 HayleyTurner 4 59
(M L W Bell) *chsd ldrs: rdn over 2f out: wknd over 1f out* **8/1**
241 **10** *6* **Simple Rhythm**[1] 5968 3-8-4 64 RyanPowell(7) 5 39
(J Ryan) *w ldr tl ins fnl 3f: rdn 2f out: wknd qckly over 1f out* **14/1**
6002 **11** *1 1/4* **Joss Stick**[17] 5477 4-8-2 57 DebraEngland(7) 10 31
(J J Bridger) *in tch over 3f* **16/1**
4600 **12** *15* **Trip Switch**[77] 3502 3-8-5 67 (b) MartinDwyer 6 —
(W R Muir) *late removing hood: v.s.a and a in rr* **20/1**

1m 11.96s (-1.14) **Going Correction** -0.10s/f (Stan) **12 Ran SP% 117.3**
WFA 3 from 4yo+ 2lb
Speed ratings (Par 103): **103,99,99,96,96 95,95,95,93,85 83,63**
toteswingers: 1&2 £15.40, 1&3 £8.10, 2&3 £22.80. CSF £52.51 TOTE £5.00: £1.90, £4.00, £2.50; EX 57.20.Steelcut was claimed by Andrew Reid for £7,000.
Owner A Rhodes Haulage And P Timmins **Bred** Mrs B Skinner **Trained** Musley Bank, N Yorks

FOCUS
A low-grade sprint. The fourth limits the level.
High Curragh Official explanation: jockey said gelding hung right
Trip Switch Official explanation: jockey said gelding missed the break

5990 GROOMED TO PERFECTION, KIA SOUL H'CAP 2m (P)
8:50 (8:50) (Class 6) (0-65,65) 3-Y-O **£2,047** (£604; £302) **Stalls** High

Form RPR
0664 **1** **Perception (IRE)**[41] 4703 3-9-4 **62** SteveDrowne 9 69
(R Charlton) *led 4f: styd chsng ldrs tl rdn to ld appr fnl f: hld on all out* **9/1**[3]
0420 **2** *1/2* **Honorable Endeavor**[33] 5011 3-8-13 **57** (p) LPKeniry 5 63
(E F Vaughan) *in rr tl hdwy over 3f out: styd on u.p fr over 2f out to chse wnr ins fnl f: kpt on but a hld* **20/1**
5204 **3** *3 1/4* **Mymateeric**[35] 4917 3-8-6 **50** (b) LiamJones 12 53+
(J Pearce) *in rr: rdn and styd on fr over 2f out: kpt on ins fnl f but nvr gng pce to rch ldng duo* **20/1**
0333 **4** *3 1/2* **Soul Singer**[19] 5381 3-8-8 **52** RichardKingscote 8 50
(J G Portman) *chsd ldrs: hrd rdn fr over 2f out: wknd appr fnl f* **20/1**
5154 **5** *3* **The Saucy Snipe**[6] 5812 3-8-12 **56** DavidProbert 4 51
(P Winkworth) *chsd ldrs: led 4f out: rdn 3f out: hdd & wknd over 1f out* **9/1**[3]
235 **6** *shd* **Spinning Waters**[69] 3776 3-9-4 **62** ShaneKelly 7 57
(Eve Johnson Houghton) *mid-div: rdn 5f out: sme prog over 2f out: one pce fnl f* **12/1**
2235 **7** *1 3/4* **Persian Memories (IRE)**[19] 5382 3-9-6 **64** TedDurcan 6 56
(J L Dunlop) *in rr: rdn and sme hdwy 3f out: styd on same pce fr over 1f out* **10/1**
0401 **8** *4 1/2* **Stormy Morning**[19] 5382 3-9-7 **65** AdamKirby 14 52
(W R Swinburn) *chsd ldrs fr 1/2-way: rdn over 3f out: wknd qckly appr fnl f* **6/1**[2]
00-0 **9** *3 1/4* **Coeur Brule (FR)**[26] 5215 3-8-7 **51** PaulFitzsimons 2 34
(Edgar Byrne) *chsd ldrs: rdn 3f out: sn btn* **80/1**
653 **10** *1 1/2* **Any Given Moment (IRE)**[19] 5382 3-8-10 **54** ChrisCatlin 13 35
(D M Simcock) *nvr travelling in rr fr 1/2-way: rdn and no prog fnl 4f* **10/3**[1]
5454 **11** *20* **Strategic Princess (IRE)**[18] 5430 3-8-9 **53** MartinDwyer 10 10
(P F I Cole) *a towards rr* **9/1**[3]
3103 **12** *6* **Astroleo**[17] 5483 3-8-7 **51** NickyMackay 1 1
(M H Tompkins) *chsd ldrs: hung lft and wknd qckly 3f out* **14/1**
0203 **13** *32* **Regal Blush**[9] 5720 3-9-6 **64** WilliamBuick 3 —
(A M Balding) *led after 4f: hdd 4f out and wknd rapidly: eased: t.o* **12/1**
3050 **14** *5* **Windpfeil (IRE)**[33] 5011 3-8-11 **55** (b) JimmyFortune 11 —
(J H M Gosden) *chsd ldrs tl weakemed qckly over 3f out: eased: t.o* **12/1**

3m 29.22s (-0.88) **Going Correction** -0.10s/f (Stan) **14 Ran SP% 121.7**
Speed ratings (Par 99): **98,97,96,94,92 92,91,89,88,87 77,74,—,—**
toteswingers: 1&2 £41.30, 1&3 £68.20, 2&3 £39.60. CSF £183.99 CT £3493.29 TOTE £9.80: £2.50, £5.40, £8.70; EX 155.80.
Owner De La Warr Racing **Bred** Zanim Ralphy Meahjohn **Trained** Beckhampton, Wilts

FOCUS
Quite a competitive staying handicap. The second and third help set the level.
Mymateeric Official explanation: jockey said gelding suffered interference in runing
Spinning Waters Official explanation: jockey said gelding suffered interference in running
Regal Blush Official explanation: jockey said filly stopped quickly
Windpfeil(IRE) Official explanation: jockey said gelding suffered interference in running

5991 LONDON LITE SINGLE FILE H'CAP 7f (P)
9:20 (9:21) (Class 5) (0-75,75) 3-Y-O+ **£2,590** (£770; £385; £192) **Stalls** High

Form RPR
2040 **1** **Defector (IRE)**[20] 5370 3-8-11 **68** MartinDwyer 4 76
(W R Muir) *in tch: rdn and styd on to chse wnr over 1f out: kpt on u.p to ld fnl 25yds* **16/1**
532 **2** *3/4* **Milne Bay (IRE)**[123] 2088 4-8-10 **71** (t) RyanPowell(7) 2 78
(D M Simcock) *sn led: 4l clr and rdn over 2f out: tiring ins fnl f: hdd and no ex fnl 25yds* **13/2**[3]
2160 **3** *1* **Support Fund (IRE)**[42] 4641 5-9-1 **69** ShaneKelly 9 73
(Eve Johnson Houghton) *in rr: wd bnd 3f out: str run appr fnl f: fin wl* **8/1**
5100 **4** *hd* **Carmenero (GER)**[18] 5418 6-9-0 **68** LPKeniry 8 72+
(C R Dore) *in rr: hdwy on ins fr 2f out: hrd drvn and styd on fnl f: gng on cl home* **20/1**
6430 **5** *shd* **Buxton**[8] 5753 5-9-2 **70** (t) PatDobbs 10 73
(R Ingram) *chsd ldrs: rdn and outpcd 3f out: styd on again fnl f: kpt on cl home* **7/1**
0300 **6** *1/2* **Musical Script (USA)**[13] 5592 6-9-4 **72** (b) ChrisCatlin 7 74
(Mouse Hamilton-Fairley) *s.i.s: bhd: hdwy fr 2f out: kpt on fnl f* **10/1**
0124 **7** *1* **Desert Streak (FR)**[14] 5584 3-8-11 **68** (p) AdamKirby 5 66+
(C G Cox) *in rr: rdn over 2f out: styd on on fnl f: nt rch ldrs* **7/2**[1]
0500 **8** *2* **Greystoke Prince**[24] 5287 4-8-4 **63** Louis-PhilippeBeuzelin(5) 3 57
(W R Swinburn) *chsd ldr tl over 1f out: sn wknd* **33/1**
0-36 **9** *3/4* **Queen Sally (IRE)**[33] 5007 3-8-8 **65** RichardKingscote 13 56
(Tom Dascombe) *chsd ldrs: rdn 3f out: wknd 2f out* **9/1**
5303 **10** *nk* **Driven (IRE)**[14] 5565 4-9-7 **75** JimCrowley 6 66
(Mrs A J Perrett) *in tch: rdn 3f out: sme prog over 2f out: nvr rchd ldrs: sn btn* **9/2**[2]
6300 **11** *hd* **Obe Royal**[11] 5676 5-8-10 **69** (b) RichardEvans(5) 11 60
(P D Evans) *in tch: rdn 3f out: wknd 2f out* **7/1**

1m 25.21s (-0.79) **Going Correction** -0.10s/f (Stan)
WFA 3 from 4yo+ 3lb **11 Ran SP% 122.5**
Speed ratings (Par 103): **100,99,98,97,97 97,95,93,92,92 92**
toteswingers: 1&2 £23.10, 1&3 £32.40, 2&3 £13.70. CSF £121.32 CT £931.98 TOTE £19.80: £4.80, £3.20, £2.10; EX 175.80 Place 6: £74.96, Place 5: £67.12..
Owner David Knox & Partners **Bred** Grenane House Stud, Steve Hillen & Sean Graham **Trained** Lambourn, Berks

FOCUS
This had looked an open handicap but hardly anything got into it. The runner-up is the best guide to the form.
Queen Sally(IRE) Official explanation: jockey said filly hung left on bend
T/Plt: £107.80 to a £1 stake. Pool: £60,046.17. 406.31 winning tickets. T/Qpdt: £43.10 to a £1 stake. Pool: £6,207.12. 106.40 winning tickets. ST

5829 SANDOWN (R-H)
Wednesday, September 16

OFFICIAL GOING: Sprint course - soft; round course good to soft (soft in places)
Round courswe dolled out about 4yds from &f to 3f pole, adding circa 6yds to advertised distances.
Wind: Strong, behind Weather: Fine

5992 BUY A RACING POST YEARLING BONUS CANDIDATE NURSERY 5f 6y
2:20 (2:21) (Class 5) (0-75,73) 2-Y-O **£3,238** (£963; £481; £240) **Stalls** High

Form RPR
1621 **1** **Italian Tom (IRE)**[7] 5776 2-9-10 **73** 6ex RobertWinston 8 80
(R A Harris) *mde all: drifted off rail fr 1/2-way: rdn 2f out: kpt on wl fnl f* **4/1**[3]
152 **2** *1* **Drift And Dream**[56] 4208 2-9-5 **68** TedDurcan 6 71
(C F Wall) *lw: hld up but sn cl up on rail: rdn to chse wnr over 1f out: looked dangerous ent fnl f: kpt on same pce after* **4/1**[3]
2501 **3** *2 1/4* **Bossy Kitty**[15] 5553 2-9-5 **68** JimmyFortune 7 63
(N Tinkler) *prom: chsd wnr 1/2-way to over 1f out: one pce fnl f* **10/3**[2]
042 **4** *6* **Pose (IRE)**[27] 5180 2-9-7 **70** RyanMoore 5 44
(R Hannon) *lw: settled in rr: pushed along after 2f: sn struggling: wnt modest 4th over 1f out: no imp on ldrs* **3/1**[1]
130 **5** *2* **Waltz Around (IRE)**[18] 5433 2-9-7 **70** ChrisCatlin 3 37
(C E Brittain) *settled in last trio: pushed along 1/2-way: sn struggling: wknd and bhd over 1f out* **9/1**
440 **6** *1/2* **Guesswork**[86] 3210 2-9-2 **68** (p) AndreaAtzeni(3) 1 33
(W Jarvis) *racd wd in rr: pushed along 1/2-way: wknd and bhd over 1f out* **16/1**

560 **7** *8* **Softly Spoken**[53] 4302 2-7-11 **53** ow1 .... AmyScott(7) 4 —
(A W Carroll) *racd wd: chsd wnr to 1/2-way: sn wknd: bhd whn eased fnl f* **16/1**

63.90 secs (2.30) **Going Correction** +0.35s/f (Good) **7** Ran SP% **109.8**
Speed ratings (Par 95): **95,93,89,80,77 76,63**
toteswingers: 1&2 £2.60, 1&3 £3.20, 2&3 £3.60 CSF £18.61 CT £53.14 TOTE £4.50: £2.80, £2.70; EX 18.70.
Owner S Mares **Bred** Tom Radley **Trained** Earlswood, Monmouths

FOCUS
The rail was four yards in on the sprint course. The time suggested that the ground was riding soft, as advertised. The first three raced closest to the rail in this fair nursery and finished clear. The pace was only ordinary and nothing got into the race from the rear.

NOTEBOOK
Italian Tom(IRE) had made a winning debut for the Harris yard at Kempton a week earlier and he followed up under the penalty, making all again and holding on well enough after drifting away from the fence. He was bought out of a seller (having been successful in that grade earlier in the year) but is better than that level and he has a bit of scope for further improvement. He is versatile as far as ground conditions are concerned and should have no problem with 6f. (op 3-1 tchd 9-2)
Drift And Dream, runner-up over C&D when last seen almost two months ago, went early to post. Remaining closest to the rail, she went after the winner going to the final furlong but could not get to him. She handled the soft ground well enough. (tchd 9-2)
Bossy Kitty, successful in a Ripon maiden auction last time, ran respectably but has now been beaten three times from this mark in nurseries. (op 4-1 tchd 3-1)
Pose(IRE)'s Chepstow second has been boosted by the winner Secret Millionaire but she was a little disappointing on this nursery bow, coming under a drive at halfway and only plugging on for a modest fourth. It is fair to assume she did not handle the soft conditions. (op 11-4 tchd 100-30)
Waltz Around(IRE) found this trip too sharp and played little part. She is not progressing. (op 12-1 tchd 17-2)
Guesswork, tried in cheekpieces for the first time and keen to post on this first run in nearly three months, was always in rear, albeit from the worst draw. (op 14-1 tchd 12-1)
Softly Spoken, who was getting a lot of weight from her rivals, did show up prominently before drifting left into the centre of the track and trailing in soundly beaten. (op 22-1)

5993 EUROPEAN BREEDERS' FUND MAIDEN STKS 1m 14y
2:55 (2:55) (Class 4) 2-Y-O **£5,180** (£1,541; £770; £384) **Stalls** High

Form RPR
1 **Zeitoper** 2-9-3 0 .... LDettori 3 80+
(Saeed Bin Suroor) *w'like: athletic: dwlt: hld up in tch: prog 3f out: shkn up to go 2nd wl over 1f out: clsd on ldr fnl f: r.o to ld last stride* **3/1**[2]
0 **2** *nse* **Botanist**[33] 4986 2-9-3 0 .... RyanMoore 9 80+
(Sir Michael Stoute) *led: shkn up to draw 2 l clr wl over 1f out: drvn fnl f: hdd last stride* **10/11**[1]
3 *3 1/4* **Centurio** 2-9-3 0 .... RichardKingscote 6 73+
(R Charlton) *unf: dwlt: hld up in tch: effrt over 2f out: wnt 3rd over 1f out but outpcd: no imp after* **10/1**
5 **4** *3/4* **Henry San (IRE)**[35] 4908 2-9-3 0 .... FergusSweeney 8 71
(A King) *str: mostly chsd ldr to wl over 1f out: one pce* **8/1**[3]
0 **5** *shd* **First Instance**[90] 3064 2-9-3 0 .... GregFairley 7 71
(M Johnston) *str: disp 2nd tl shkn up 3f out: tried to keep w ldrs fr over 2f out: outpcd over 1f out* **16/1**
0 **6** *2 3/4* **Mawaddah (IRE)**[53] 4323 2-9-3 0 .... PatDobbs 1 65
(R Hannon) *w'like: trckd ldrs on outer: shkn up and in tch over 2f out: wknd jst over 1f out* **25/1**
7 *3/4* **Lis Pendens** 2-9-3 0 .... MartinDwyer 2 63+
(W R Muir) *str: dwlt: a last: shkn up over 2f out: wknd over 1f out* **33/1**

1m 47.1s (3.80) **Going Correction** +0.20s/f (Good) **7** Ran SP% **110.3**
Speed ratings (Par 97): **89,88,85,84,84 82,81**
toteswingers: 1&2 1.10 1&3 £3.60, 2&3 £4.10 CSF £5.60 TOTE £2.70: £1.70, £1.30; EX 5.20.
Owner Godolphin **Bred** Darley **Trained** Newmarket, Suffolk

FOCUS
The round course was dolled out up to four yards from 7f out to the 3f pole, adding up to six yards to all race distances. The winning jockey in this race described the ground as good to soft. The form is not easy to pin down but this was probably a fair maiden. The runners kept away from the inside rail down the back and then came over to race centre-to stands' side in the home straight.

NOTEBOOK
Zeitoper, who had been held up and raced a little lazily early on, had two lengths to make up entering the final furlong but really found his stride in the final 50 yards to snatch the race. A son of Godolphin's 1000 Guineas and Oaks winner Kazzia, he is a brother to Eastern Anthem who won this year's Dubai Sheema Classic. Sure to learn from what was a relatively sympathetic introduction, he looks a decent prospect for next year, when he should get 1m2f. (op 5-2 tchd 100-30)
Botanist disappointed on his debut at Newbury but knew more here and was well supported. Attempting to make all, the race looked his when he went for home approaching the last, but he hung to his left a little up the final hill and that gave the winner something to aim at. His Racing Post Trophy entry looks overly optimistic but he should have no problem making amends for this defeat. (tchd 5-6)
Centurio ◆ was notably green in rear through the early stages but, racing on the outside in the home straight, he ran on nicely to show plenty of promise for the future. He comes from a fine middle-distance family on the dam's side and there are races to be won with him. (op 14-1)
Henry San(IRE), fifth over 7f on his debut here, ran a satisfactory race upped to 1m and is the type to make his mark in handicaps in due course. (tchd 13-2)
First Instance, who showed little on his debut over 6f at Ripon back in June, was just about the first in trouble and may need more time, although he seemed to get the longer trip.
Mawaddah(IRE), who raced closest to the stands' rail in the straight, could never get into the picture and did not really build on his debut effort.
Lis Pendens, an already gelded son of a dam who won over 1m, was in rear throughout but should improve for the experience.

5994 INKERMAN LONDON NOVICE STKS 7f 16y
3:30 (3:31) (Class 3) 2-Y-O
£6,854 (£2,052; £1,026; £513; £256; £128) **Stalls** High

Form RPR
0 **1** **Fontley**[13] 5604 2-8-7 0 .... WilliamBuick 5 81+
(Eve Johnson Houghton) *trckd ldng pair: wnt 2nd over 2f out: sn chalng: drvn to ld ins fnl f: battled on wl* **5/1**
40 **2** *hd* **Spa's Dancer (IRE)**[33] 4986 2-8-12 0 .... MichaelHills 6 85
(J W Hills) *led: rdn and pressed 2f out: hdd ins fnl f: kpt on wl u.p: jst hld* **4/1**[3]
120 **3** *2 1/2* **Cumulus Nimbus**[25] 5261 2-9-4 88 .... RyanMoore 4 85
(R Hannon) *t.k.h early: hld up in 4th: rdn over 2f out: chsd ldng pair over 1f out: no imp ins fnl f* **11/4**[2]
01 **4** *2* **Fairy Promises (USA)**[48] 4468 2-8-13 0 .... RobertWinston 2 75
(Pat Eddery) *lw: chsd ldr to over 2f out: sn rdn and nt qckn: wl hld over 1f out* **7/1**
152 **5** *3/4* **Treadwell (IRE)**[5] 5827 2-9-2 98 .... ShaneKelly 3 76
(J A Osborne) *lw: t.k.h early: hld up in last: effrt over 2f out: sn rdn and nt qckn: wl hld over 1f out* **5/2**[1]
02 **6** *6* **Starwatch**[38] 4826 2-8-9 0 .... MarcHalford(3) 1 57
(J J Bridger) *t.k.h early: hld up in 5th: rdn 3f out: sn struggling* **14/1**

1m 34.86s (5.36) **Going Correction** +0.20s/f (Good) **6** Ran SP% **111.1**
Speed ratings (Par 99): **77,76,73,71,70 63**
toteswingers: 1&2 £4.00, 1&3 £3.30, 2&3 £2.70 CSF £24.32 TOTE £5.70: £2.70, £2.60; EX 31.30.
Owner Mrs Virginia Neale **Bred** Sarah J Leigh And Robin S Leigh **Trained** Blewbury, Oxon

FOCUS
A reasonable novice stakes, but it was very steadily run and the time was over seven seconds outside standard. With the two market leaders below par the form may not be too solid. The first two showed improvement. As in the previous race the field came down the centre of the track in the home straight.

NOTEBOOK
Fontley, the only filly in the line-up, as well as the least experienced runner, came here after finishing seventh on her debut in a Salisbury maiden. Straightening for home in third place, she soon came through to become the leader's main challenger and she showed a commendably tough attitude to score. Connections may try to earn some black type with her if she comes out of this well. Her dam was a smart middle-distance filly for Luca Cumani and she should get 1m2f plus in time. (op 6-1 tchd 9-2)
Spa's Dancer(IRE) settled better allowed to lead and he stuck on well enough when tackled, just having to give best to the filly inside the last. Much will depend on how the handicapper assesses him. (op 5-1 tchd 11-2 in places)
Cumulus Nimbus, out of his depth behind Shakespearean in the Solario over C&D last time, was conceding weight all round. A little keen as they dawdled early on, he momentarily looked a threat in the straight but could never quite get to the first two. (op 7-2)
Fairy Promises(USA), whose maiden win came in heavy ground, tracked the pace before weakening. She might not have stayed the extra furlong but looks the type who may not be easy to place. Official explanation: caution: careless riding (op 15-2 tchd 8-1)
Treadwell(IRE) had made a satisfactory return to the track when second of three to the smart Al Zir at Doncaster last week. Another who took time to settle, he failed to pick up in the straight and this was disappointing. He looks one to be a little wary of. (op 13-8)
Starwatch divided a very useful pair at Windsor last time but looks to have been flattered by that. He pulled in rear in the early stages here and was the first beaten. (tchd 12-1, 16-1 in a place)

5995 FORTUNE STKS (LISTED RACE) 1m 14y
4:05 (4:06) (Class 1) 3-Y-O+ **£22,708** (£8,608; £4,308; £2,148; £1,076) **Stalls** High

Form RPR
1532 **1** **Bankable (IRE)**[18] 5447 5-9-3 114 .... (t) RyanMoore 6 109+
(G L Moore) *b: lw: hld up: trckd ldng pair after 3f: clsd over 2f out: shkn up to ld over 1f out and sn in command: drvn out last 100yds* **4/7**[1]
20-2 **2** *1* **Ada River**[25] 5260 4-8-12 100 .... WilliamBuick 5 102
(A M Balding) *lw: led: rdn and pressed 2f out: hdd and outpcd over 1f out: styd on fnl f* **15/2**[3]
1604 **3** *1 1/4* **Cadre (IRE)**[46] 4543 4-9-3 94 .... JimmyFortune 2 104+
(J H M Gosden) *trckd ldng pair 3f: shkn up and nt qckn over 2f out: sn outpcd: styd on again to take 3rd ins fnl f* **14/1**
0130 **4** *2* **Laa Rayb (USA)**[17] 5496 5-9-3 111 .... (b) RoystonFfrench 3 100
(M Johnston) *pressed ldr: rdn to chal and upsides 2f out: sn nt qckn and btn: wknd fnl f* **5/1**[2]
340- **5** *6* **Zulu Chief (USA)**[355] 6261 4-9-3 100 .... PatCosgrave 1 87
(M F De Kock, South Africa) *stdd s: hld up in last: rdn over 2f out: sn wknd* **8/1**

1m 45.28s (1.98) **Going Correction** +0.20s/f (Good) **5** Ran SP% **109.9**
Speed ratings (Par 111): **98,97,95,93,87**
toteswingers: 1&2 £4.10. CSF £5.46 TOTE £1.50: £1.10, £2.60; EX 5.00.
Owner Ramzan Kadyrov **Bred** Barronstown Stud And Cobra **Trained** Lower Beeding, W Sussex

FOCUS
This event used to be run over 7f at the previous Sandown meeting. This was not a strong Listed race, and the pace was just steady. The winner stood out at these weights. They raced nearer to the stands' rail up the straight than in the previous two races on the round course.

NOTEBOOK
Bankable(IRE), having his second start for the Moore stable, converted a straightforward chance comfortably enough. Refitted with a tongue tie, he had come on for his second at Windsor and the ground suited him on this drop back in trip. A consistent performer, although his strike rate has not been great over the last couple of seasons, he is now set to miss the Cambridgeshire, in which he has top weight, and head down under for a valuable race at Flemington at the end of October before a likely spell in Dubai. (op 8-13 tchd 4-6)
Ada River, runner-up to Strawberrydaiquiri on her reappearance over C&D last time, when she had raced keenly under restraint, was able to make her own running this time. She could not counter when headed by the winner but stuck on well for second. This was a solid run on these terms and she could enjoy success back against her own sex. (op 9-1)
Cadre(IRE) had a lot to find at these weights. He was outpaced by the principals a quarter-mile out but, sticking closest to the fence, he was running on inside the last. (op 16-1 tchd 12-1)
Laa Rayb(USA) has been found wanting in small fields since his win in the totesport Mile at Goodwood and that was again the case here. He was close enough with 2f to run, but did not find anything when the pressure was on. (tchd 9-2)
Zulu Chief(USA), formerly with Aidan O'Brien, has been gelded since his last appearance a year ago. He had a stiff task on these terms and was always at the back of the field. (op 7-1 tchd 6-1)

5996 MARBANK CONSTRUCTION FILLIES' H'CAP 1m 14y
4:40 (4:41) (Class 4) (0-85,85) 3-Y-O **£4,857** (£1,445; £722; £360) **Stalls** High

Form RPR
3-1 **1** **My Verse**[16] 5520 3-8-8 **75** .... WilliamBuick 12 83+
(M A Jarvis) *lw: hld up in last trio: stdy prog over 2f out: rdn to ld over 1f out: flashed tail u.p but in command fnl f* **9/2**[2]
0110 **2** *1 1/2* **Flapper (IRE)**[28] 5175 3-7-11 **71** .... AmyScott(7) 7 76
(J W Hills) *trckd ldr: chal over 2f out: upsides wl over 1f out: chsd wnr after: kpt on but no imp last 150yds* **10/1**
6400 **3** *nk* **Fanditha (IRE)**[17] 5475 3-8-12 **79** .... RyanMoore 5 83
(R Hannon) *trckd ldrs: lost pl sltly over 3f out: rdn and prog 2f out: styd on wl fnl f: nrly snatched 2nd* **15/2**
1150 **4** *3 3/4* **Aromatic**[53] 4328 3-9-2 **83** .... (b1) JimmyFortune 1 79
(J H M Gosden) *led: pressed over 2f out: hdd over 1f out: wknd fnl f* **11/2**[3]
022 **5** *1/2* **Tinshu (IRE)**[44] 4605 3-8-11 **78** .... HayleyTurner 3 73
(D Haydn Jones) *hld up in last: urged along 3f out: reminder and passed wkng rivals to take 5th 1f out: nvr on terms* **6/1**
5-00 **6** *4* **Nora Mae (IRE)**[13] 5607 3-9-4 **85** .... GeorgeBaker 2 72
(S Kirk) *lw:hld up in last trio: cl enough over 2f out: sn rdn and wknd* **9/1**
3332 **7** *3* **Something Perfect (USA)**[80] 3429 3-8-13 **80** .... (v1) IanMongan 9 61
(H R A Cecil) *sltly bmpd s: trckd ldrs: cl up over 2f out: rdn and wknd rapidly sn after* **6/1**

0-41 **8** 1 1/4 **Netta (IRE)**[34] 4947 3-8-13 **80**........ SteveDrowne 8 58
(P J Makin) *wnt rt s: trckd ldrs: shkn up over 2f out: wknd rapidly wl over 1f out* **4/1**[1]

1m 44.8s (1.50) **Going Correction** +0.20s/f (Good) 8 Ran SP% **113.0**
Speed ratings (Par 100): **100,98,98,94,93 89,86,85**
toteswingers: 1&2 £6.50, 1&3 £8.80, 2&3 £12.30 CSF £46.76 CT £328.91 TOTE £4.90: £2.00, £3.00, £2.40; EX 31.10.
Owner Sheikh Ahmed Al Maktoum **Bred** Darley **Trained** Newmarket, Suffolk

FOCUS
A fair handicap for fillies. The pace was ordinary and they raced down the centre of the home straight again. Improved form from the winner.
Netta(IRE) Official explanation: jockey said filly never travelled

5997 WATCH RACING UK ON SKY CHANNEL 432 H'CAP 1m 2f 7y
5:10 (5:12) (Class 4) (0-80,80) 3-Y-O+ **£4,857** (£1,445; £722; £360) **Stalls** High

Form RPR
040 **1** **Hanoverian Baron**[64] 3956 4-9-3 **72**........ SteveDrowne 6 80
(A G Newcombe) *hld up in last trio: stdy prog over 2f out: rdn to cl on ldrs over 1f out: styd on wl to ld last 50yds* **16/1**

3-32 **2** 1/2 **Absinthe (IRE)**[14] 5570 3-9-1 **76**........ AdamKirby 3 83
(W R Swinburn) *lw: trckd ldr: racd against nr side rail in st: led 2f out: hung rt briefly 1f out: kpt on wl: hdd last 50yds* **11/4**[1]

3531 **3** 1 1/2 **Entreat**[28] 5151 3-9-5 **80**........(v) RyanMoore 9 84
(Sir Michael Stoute) *hld up in last trio: stdy prog in centre 3f out: rdn to chal over 1f out: no ex ins fnl f* **5/1**[2]

3631 **4** 2 **African Cheetah**[135] 1739 3-9-1 **76**........ GregFairley 5 77
(M Johnston) *hld up in midfield: dropped to rr 4f out: nt clr run 3f out to over 2f out and last briefly: pushed along and styd on steadily fnl 2f to take 4th nr fin* **6/1**

1331 **5** nk **Kargan (IRE)**[12] 5630 4-8-8 **68**........ AndrewHeffernan(5) 1 68
(R A Farrant) *hld up in last trio: gng strly over 2f out: effrt to chse ldng trio over 1f out: nt pce to threaten u.p: lost 4th nr fin* **11/2**[3]

431 **6** 1 3/4 **Critical Path (IRE)**[55] 4234 3-9-2 **77**........ WilliamBuick 2 74
(A M Balding) *sn trckd ldrs: racd against nr side rail in st: outpcd over 2f out: nvr on terms after* **13/2**

0140 **7** 1 **Mcconnell (USA)**[12] 5640 4-9-9 **78**........ GeorgeBaker 4 73
(G L Moore) *led to 2f out: wknd over 1f out* **20/1**

5520 **8** 3/4 **Lyceana**[16] 5532 4-9-6 **75**........ TedDurcan 10 69
(M A Jarvis) *chsd ldrs: cl enough over 2f out: wknd over 1f out* **12/1**

1-60 **9** 12 **Shooting Party (IRE)**[42] 4649 3-9-1 **76**........ PatDobbs 8 48
(R Hannon) *mostly chsd ldng pair to over 2f out: wknd rapidly: t.o* **13/2**

2m 14.0s (3.50) **Going Correction** +0.20s/f (Good)
WFA 3 from 4yo 6lb 9 Ran SP% **118.0**
Speed ratings (Par 105): **94,93,92,90,90 89,88,87,78**
toteswingers: 1&2 £12.00, 1&3 £14.20, 2&3 £3.80 CSF £61.33 CT £262.95 TOTE £23.00: £5.70, £1.20, £2.20; EX 103.80 Place 6: £76.04, Place 5: £28.14..
Owner Paul Moulton **Bred** S Coughlan **Trained** Yarnscombe, Devon

FOCUS
Fair handicap form. They spread from the centre of the track across to the hedge on the stands' side in the latter stages. The form is pretty solid but limited.
T/Plt: £170.60 to a £1 stake. Pool: £57,217.30. 244.80 winning tickets. T/Qpdt: £48.60 to a £1 stake. Pool: £3,987.60. 60.60 winning tickets. JN

5969 YARMOUTH (L-H)
Wednesday, September 16

OFFICIAL GOING: Good to firm (8.2)
Wind: Fresh, half behind Weather: Bright and breezy

5998 LYNN BRENNAN 60TH BIRTHDAY H'CAP (DIV I) 7f 3y
1:40 (1:41) (Class 6) (0-60,60) 3-Y-O+ **£2,007** (£597; £298; £149) **Stalls** High

Form RPR
5031 **1** **Captain Flasheart (IRE)**[6] 5806 3-9-1 **60**........ WilliamCarson(3) 4 81+
(S C Williams) *t.k.h: chsd ldr tl rdn to ld wl over 1f out: sn drew wl clr: eased and rdr dropped reins towards fin* **11/8**[1]

U120 **2** 6 **Many Welcomes**[32] 5019 4-8-13 **57**........ JemmaMarshall(5) 7 62
(B P J Baugh) *hld up in rr: hdwy over 2f out: rdn and styd on fr over 1f out: wnt 2nd fnl 100yds: no ch w wnr* **9/1**[3]

6100 **3** 1/2 **Eye For The Girls**[12] 5644 3-8-13 **55**........ DarryllHolland 9 58
(M R Channon) *led: rdn ent fnl 2f: hdd wl over 1f out: no ch w wnr after: lost 2nd fnl 100yds* **25/1**

1050 **4** 1/2 **Rough Rock (IRE)**[33] 5008 4-8-12 **51**........ JerryO'Dwyer 16 54
(C A Dwyer) *chsd ldng pair: rdn and unable qck over 2f out: plugged on same pce u.p fnl 2f* **33/1**

0054 **5** 2 3/4 **Cheery Cat (USA)**[33] 4998 5-8-10 **49**........(p) AlanMunro 2 45
(J Balding) *in tch in midfield on outer: rdn and effrt over 2f out: one pce and no ch w wnr fnl 2f* **6/1**[2]

-004 **6** 3/4 **Westport**[28] 5150 6-9-5 **58**........ NCallan 1 52
(R Bastiman) *stdd after s: hld up bhd: rdn and plugged on past btn horses fr over 1f out: n.d* **12/1**

0026 **7** 1/2 **Ocean Countess (IRE)**[17] 5479 3-9-0 **56**........(v) TPQueally 8 48
(Miss J Feilden) *s.i.s: bhd: sme modest hdwy u.p fnl f: n.d* **12/1**

3026 **8** 1/2 **Norcroft**[15] 5544 7-8-13 **52**........(v) VinceSlattery 12 43
(Mrs C A Dunnett) *a towards rr: rdn and no hdwy over 2f out: sme modest hdwy ins fnl f: n.d* **18/1**

0-0 **9** nse **Hayley's Girl**[56] 4199 3-7-13 **46**........ AmyBaker(5) 5 36
(S W James) *chsd ldrs: rdn over 2f out: wl btn over 1f out* **100/1**

5003 **10** 1/2 **Red Dagger (IRE)**[12] 5633 3-8-5 **47**........ LiamJones 13 36
(R J Price) *in tch in midfield: pushed along and unable qck over 2f out: rdn and btn wl over 1f out* **20/1**

0-60 **11** 2 3/4 **Contemplate**[155] 1269 3-8-4 **46** oh1........ KoseiMiura 11 28
(Dr J D Scargill) *hld up in tch in midfield: rdn and wknd over 2f out: wl bhd fnl f* **20/1**

0/06 **12** 3/4 **Memphis Marie**[30] 5111 5-8-7 **46** oh1........ EdwardCreighton 14 27
(P J McBride) *chsd ldrs: struggling u.p over 2f out: wl btn fnl 2f* **50/1**

0600 **13** 1 1/2 **Count Ceprano (IRE)**[22] 5329 5-9-2 **60**........(p) SimonPearce(5) 15 37
(C R Dore) *dwlt: a bhd: pushed along and no rspnse 1/2-way: nvr a factor* **14/1**

0405 **14** 1 3/4 **Djalalabad (FR)**[79] 3470 5-8-8 **47**........(tp) CatherineGannon 10 20
(Mrs C A Dunnett) *taken down early: a in rr: rdn and no hdwy over 2f out: wl bhd fnl 2f* **25/1**

0506 **15** 2 1/2 **Cake Stand**[12] 5647 3-8-11 **53**........(v) RobertHavlin 3 20
(J A R Toller) *in tch: rdn and wknd qckly jst over 2f out: eased whn wl bhd ins fnl f* **33/1**

1m 22.84s (-3.76) **Going Correction** -0.45s/f (Firm)
WFA 3 from 4yo+ 3lb 15 Ran SP% **119.8**
Speed ratings (Par 101): **103,96,95,95,91 91,90,89,89,89 86,85,83,81,78**
toteswingers: 1&2 £5.90, 1&3 £8.10, 2&3 £24.60 CSF £11.72 CT £226.02 TOTE £2.30: £1.30, £3.20, £4.40; EX 13.40 TRIFECTA Not won..
Owner Paul W Stevens **Bred** Mrs Marion Daly **Trained** Newmarket, Suffolk

FOCUS
The runners came up the centre of the track in this very weak handicap. The winner proved a class apart and was value for a little more.
Bicksta Official explanation: £650 fine: double declaration

5999 FIRSTBET.COM £50 MATCHED BET 0800 230 0800 CLAIMING STKS 1m 3y
2:10 (2:12) (Class 5) 3-Y-O **£3,238** (£963; £481; £240) **Stalls** High

Form RPR
2113 **1** **Darcey**[12] 5621 3-7-12 **65**........ CatherineGannon 3 78+
(R A Fahey) *chsd clr ldng pair: wnt 2nd 2f out: rdn to ld ent fnl f: r.o strly u.p to draw wl clr fnl f* **4/1**[3]

3000 **2** 6 **Cook's Endeavour (USA)**[11] 5677 3-8-9 **70**........ TonyHamilton 7 75
(K A Ryan) *led and clr w rival: hdd 5f out: rdn and lost 2nd 2f out: no ch w wnr fnl 150yds: plugged on to regain modest 2nd fnl 50yds* **20/1**

6230 **3** 1 1/4 **Roar Of Applause**[14] 5575 3-9-0 **79**........ JamieSpencer 6 77
(B J Meehan) *stdd s: hld up in rr: rdn and hdwy over 2f out: drvn to chse ldng trio 2f out: edgd lft u.p over 1f out: wnt 2nd but no ch w wnr ins fnl f: lost 2nd fnl 50yds* **9/4**[1]

3613 **4** 1 1/2 **Fajita**[7] 5774 3-8-6 **75**........(p) RichardMullen 1 66
(G L Moore) *stdd after s: hld up off the pce in midfield: hdwy over 2f out: rdn and nt qckn 2f out: one pce fnl f* **4/1**[3]

2344 **5** 1 **Equipe De Nuit**[14] 5574 3-8-3 **65**........ SaleemGolam 8 60
(S C Williams) *clr w ldr tl led 5f out: reminder and kicked clr 4f out: rdn and hdd over 1f out: wknd fnl f* **12/1**

6- **6** 11 **Private Equity (IRE)**[279] 7640 3-8-4 **0**........ LiamJones 4 36
(W Jarvis) *stdd s: t.k.h: hld up in last trio: rdn and lost tch wl over 2f out* **50/1**

3610 **7** 1/2 **Cruikadyke**[42] 4649 3-8-11 **83**........ NCallan 2 42
(P F I Cole) *stdd s: hld up in last trio: rdn and no rspnse over 2f out: no ch after: eased ins fnl f* **11/4**[2]

1m 35.81s (-4.79) **Going Correction** -0.45s/f (Firm) 7 Ran SP% **111.9**
Speed ratings (Par 101): **105,99,97,96,95 84,83**
toteswingers: 1&2 £14.90, 1&3 £2.30, 2&3 £10.30 CSF £69.33 TOTE £3.60: £2.40, £3.30; EX 91.30 Trifecta £212.90 Pool: £382.75 - 1.33 winning units..Darcey was claimed by Miss A Weaver for £9,000.
Owner R Cowie **Bred** Raymond Cowie **Trained** Musley Bank, N Yorks

FOCUS
An ordinary claimer and this time the runners raced closer to the stands' rail. The early pace looked modest. Darcey was rated to her best.
Cruikadyke Official explanation: jockey said colt never travelled

6000 EUROPEAN BREEDERS' FUND MAIDEN STKS 7f 3y
2:45 (2:45) (Class 4) 2-Y-O **£5,046** (£1,510; £755; £377; £188) **Stalls** High

Form RPR
1 **Business As Usual** 2-9-3 **0**........ PhilipRobinson 8 80+
(M A Jarvis) *mde all: rdn and qcknd clr w rival wl over 1f out: forged ahd fnl 75yds: styd on wl* **9/4**[1]

2 2 1/4 **Govern** 2-9-3 **0**........ TPQueally 6 74
(H R A Cecil) *chsd wnr: rdn and qcknd clr w wnr wl over 1f out: ev ch tl btn fnl 75yds: wknd towards fin* **4/1**[2]

3 1 1/2 **Mont Agel** 2-9-3 **0**........ JamieSpencer 10 71+
(M L W Bell) *stdd s: hld up in last pl: pushed along 4f out: hdwy and edging lft fr over 1f out: kpt on to go 3rd nr fin: nvr gng pce to threaten ldng pair* **9/2**[3]

0 **4** nk **Sternlight (IRE)**[23] 5317 2-9-3 **0**........ RichardMullen 1 70
(E S McMahon) *s.i.s: hld up in last trio: hdwy wl over 2f out: rdn and racd awkwardly wl over 1f out: chsd ldng pair ins fnl f: kpt on same pce* **16/1**

5 2 **The Only Boss (IRE)** 2-9-3 **0**........ LiamJones 2 65
(W J Haggas) *broke wl: sn stdd and plld hrd: chsd ldrs: rdn and outpcd by ldng pair wl over 1f out: wknd ins fnl f* **10/1**

6 nk **Readymade (IRE)** 2-9-3 **0**........ NCallan 9 64
(Sir Michael Stoute) *hld up in midfield: pushed along 3f out: rdn and outpcd 2f out: edgd lft and plugged on same pce after* **11/2**

7 1 1/4 **Liberty Square (USA)** 2-9-0 **0**........(t) AhmedAjtebi(3) 4 63+
(Saeed Bin Suroor) *s.i.s: hld up in last trio: shkn up over 3f out: rdn no real porgress over 2f out: keeping on same pce and no ch w ldrs whn carried lft ent fnl f: eased towards fin* **15/2**

8 18 **Spirit Land (IRE)** 2-9-3 **0**........ SaleemGolam 7 16
(M H Tompkins) *s.i.s: sn rcvrd to chse ldrs: lost pl qckly wl over 2f out: t.o fnl 2f* **50/1**

1m 25.03s (-1.57) **Going Correction** -0.45s/f (Firm) 8 Ran SP% **113.0**
Speed ratings (Par 97): **90,87,85,85,83 82,81,60**
toteswingers: 1&2 £3.40, 1&3 £3.80, 2&3 £6.50 CSF £10.98 TOTE £3.10: £1.50, £1.80, £1.70; EX 13.10 Trifecta £48.50 Pool: £367.47 - 5.60 winning units..
Owner P Makin **Bred** Paulyn Limited **Trained** Newmarket, Suffolk

FOCUS
This time the runners raced centre-to-far side. This was probably a decent maiden featuring some interesting debutants from big yards. The winner looks sure to do plenty better.

NOTEBOOK
Business As Usual ◆, representing the stable that had taken this race in 2006 and 2007, was very well backed beforehand and the market was proved right. Always up with the pace, it looked as though the runner-up would give him a race a furlong from home, but one crack with the whip was enough to make him change gear and he stretched right out to win with a lot of authority. A half-brother to two winners at up to 1m2f including the useful Guilia, he looks a very nice prospect indeed and is likely to be given one more run this season. (op 15-8 tchd 5-2)
Govern ◆, a half-brother to two winners at up to 1m2f including the useful Posteritas, kept the favourite company the whole way and may even have hit the front for a few strides entering the last furlong, but he was then completely left for dead. This was a pleasing enough debut, though, and he will win races. (op 5-1)
Mont Agel ◆, a half-brother to three winners at up to 1m4f including the useful Hotel Du Cap, took plenty of time to find his stride and raced green out the back in the early stages, but he eventually realised what was required and stayed on to snatch third. His breeding suggests that he will need a greater test of stamina and he should improve with experience. (tchd 4-1 and 5-1)
Sternlight(IRE), the only one of these to have raced before when down the field on his Windsor debut, still looked green despite that but this was an improvement and there is a race in him. (op 12-1)

The Only Boss(IRE), a 42,000gns colt out of a half-sister to the high-class US miler Sohgol and the winning sprinter Sherjawy, took a grip in the early stages but showed up for a long way and should have benefited from the run. (op 18-1 tchd 20-1)
Readymade(IRE), from the stable that had won this race four times in the past six years including both divisions last year, is out of a winner in Listed company who was herself out of the champion filly Northern Trick. He never got into this, but is probably capable of a lot better. (op 6-1 tchd 13-2 and 5-1)
Liberty Square(USA), who cost $280,000 as a yearling, was tongue-tied for this debut but never got into the race after missing the break. His breeding could make him of real interest if tried on sand at some point. (op 13-2 tchd 6-1 and 8-1 in places)

6001 DANNY WRIGHT MEMORIAL (S) STKS 1m 2f 21y
3:20 (3:21) (Class 6) 3-4-Y-O **£1,942** (£578; £288; £144) **Stalls** Low

Form RPR
1000 **1** **Night Knight (IRE)**[35] 4916 3-9-3 63..........................(v) JamieSpencer 1 63
(M L W Bell) *stdd after s: hld up in midfield: hdwy to trck ldrs 4f out: rdn to ld over 1f out: edgd lft ent fnl f: hrd drvn and pressed fnl 75yds: hld on: all out* **11/4**[2]
0000 **2** *hd* **Hidden Door (IRE)**[4] 5886 4-8-13 60.............................. SaleemGolam 6 53
(G Prodromou) *stdd s: hld up towards rr: hdwy over 4f out: plld out and rdn over 1f out: str chal ins fnl f: unable qck and hld nr fin* **7/1**
650 **3** *2 ¾* **Dream On Connie**[15] 5548 3-8-12 60..............................(t) TPQueally 11 52
(W J Knight) *chsd clr ldr: clsd 3f out: rdn to ld over 2f out: drvn and hdd over 1f out: carried lft ent fnl f: no ex fnl 100yds* **9/4**[1]
0000 **4** *½* **Yeoman Of England (IRE)**[41] 4719 3-8-12 52................. AlanMunro 5 51
(C F Wall) *t.k.h: hld up in midfield: pushed along wl over 2f out: swtchd rt and hdwy 1f out: kpt on u.p ins fnl f: nvr gng pce to threaten ldrs* **8/1**
5416 **5** *½* **Chantilly Dancer (IRE)**[35] 4918 3-8-9 51............... WilliamCarson(3) 4 50
(M Quinn) *chsd ldrs: rdn and effrt on inner over 3f out: n.m.r fr 2f out: keeping on same pce and btn whn swtchd rt ins fnl f* **13/2**[3]
0030 **6** *2 ¼* **Kaystar Ridge**[13] 5617 4-9-4 44.. JerryO'Dwyer 9 46
(D K Ivory) *led: clr after 1f: rdn over 3f out: hdd over 2f out: edgd rt and wknd ent fnl f* **22/1**
0506 **7** *5* **Nchike**[12] 5621 3-8-12 51..(b) DarryllHolland 2 36
(R C Guest) *stdd s: t.k.h: hld up in last pair: rdn and no prog over 2f out* **17/2**
0-00 **8** *7* **Duchess Of Doom (IRE)**[121] 2143 3-8-7 49................ JamieMackay 10 17
(C Gordon) *stdd s: a last pl: lost tch wl over 2f out* **40/1**

2m 9.10s (-1.40) **Going Correction** -0.325s/f (Firm)
WFA 3 from 4yo 6lb **8** Ran SP% **111.7**
Speed ratings (Par 101): **92,91,89,89,88 87,83,77**
toteswingers: 1&2 £4.70, 1&3 £1.50, 2&3 £4.10 CSF £21.19 TOTE £3.90: £1.70, £1.90, £1.50; EX 26.90 Trifecta £89.20 Pool: £507.53 - 4.21winning units..The winner was bought in for 6,600gns.
Owner Scotney,Asplin,Symonds,Ball,Chelingworth **Bred** John Lyons **Trained** Newmarket, Suffolk

FOCUS
A typical seller, though the early pace was reasonable enough. The winner is rated back to his best.

6002 VAUXHALL HOLIDAY PARK H'CAP (FOR THE GOLDEN JUBILEE TROPHY) 1m 2f 21y
3:55 (3:55) (Class 3) (0-90,88) 3-Y-0+ **£7,477** (£2,239; £1,119; £560; £279; £140) **Stalls** Low

Form RPR
1130 **1** **Agilete**[25] 5266 7-8-10 **79**.. SimonPearce(5) 6 87
(J Pearce) *hld up wl in tch in last trio: jostled bnd over 5f out: hdwy 3f out: ev ch 2f out: rdn to ld 1f out: kpt on gamely and jst lasted* **20/1**
01- **2** *hd* **Cygnet**[335] 6760 3-8-12 **82**.. KFallon 3 90+
(L M Cumani) *s.i.s: sn niggled along in last trio: pushed along and looking for run fr 3f out: swtchd rt and reminder over 1f out: hdwy ins fnl f: chsd wnr fnl 75yds: clsng fin but nvr quite getting to wnr* **9/2**[2]
463 **3** *½* **Red Jade**[21] 5334 4-9-3 **81**.. TonyHamilton 7 88
(R A Fahey) *t.k.h: hld up in tch towards rr: rdn and effrt jst over 2f out: hdwy u.p over 1f out: edgd lft u.p but kpt on ins fnl f* **9/2**[2]
3102 **4** *1 ¼* **Clerk's Choice (IRE)**[26] 5209 3-9-1 **85**.......................... AlanMunro 9 90
(W Jarvis) *s.i.s: hld up in tch in last: pushed along over 3f out: rdn and hdwy 2f out: nt clr run over 1f out tl ins fnl f: r.o cl home: nvr able to chal ldrs* **4/1**[1]
1001 **5** *shd* **Mount Hadley (USA)**[18] 5418 5-9-10 **88**.............................. NCallan 4 92
(G A Butler) *in tch: rdn and hdwy over 2f out: ev ch 2f out tl ins fnl f: wknd fnl 75yds* **12/1**
1103 **6** *2 ¾* **Fastnet Storm (IRE)**[26] 5209 3-9-3 **87**........................ MickyFenton 2 86
(T P Tate) *led: hrd pressed and rdn over 2f out: hdd 1f out: wknd fnl 150yds* **4/1**[1]
1210 **7** *3 ¾* **Lord Theo**[11] 5656 5-9-7 **85**.. RobertHavlin 1 76
(N P Littmoden) *stmbld leaving stalls: chsd ldrs tl drvn and wknd ent fnl 2f* **8/1**[3]
00 **8** *¾* **Sri Kuantan (IRE)**[6] 5802 5-8-13 **77**..........................(t) PhilipRobinson 8 67
(R C Guest) *chsd ldr: ev ch and rdn over 2f out: wknd u.p over 1f out* **22/1**
9 *6* **El Presidente (IRE)**[178] 929 4-9-0 **81**........................ JackMitchell(3) 10 59
(N B King) *hld up wl in tch: rdn and btn over 2f out: wl bhd fnl f* **50/1**
55 **10** *8* **Angel Rock (IRE)**[39] 4779 4-9-7 **85**.............................. DarryllHolland 5 47+
(M Botti) *t.k.h: chsd ldrs: rdn and struggling over 2f out: towards rr whn nt clr run and hmpd 2f out: bhd after* **8/1**[3]

2m 5.77s (-4.73) **Going Correction** -0.325s/f (Firm)
WFA 3 from 4yo+ 6lb **10** Ran SP% **117.3**
Speed ratings (Par 107): **105,104,104,103,103 101,98,97,92,86**
toteswingers: 1&2 £78.60, 1&3 £13.10, 2&3 £4.70 CSF £106.67 CT £489.40 TOTE £21.10: £3.60, £1.70, £2.10; EX 187.10 TRIFECTA Not won..
Owner S & M Supplies (Aylsham) Ltd **Bred** J W Parker And Lavington Stud **Trained** Newmarket, Suffolk

FOCUS
A decent handicap run at a good pace and the winning time was 3.33 seconds faster than the seller. Perhaps the leaders went of too quick, however, as the last four horses on the bend into the straight were the first four home. A personal best from the winner.

NOTEBOOK
Agilete, a five-time winner over similar trips this year and 10lb higher than for the last of those, finished last of eight off 1lb higher last time but bounced right back here. Given a patient ride, he made his move down the outside to hit the front over a furlong out and kept on finding enough to just hold on with nothing to spare. (tchd 18-1)
Cygnet, not seen since scraping home in a Nottingham maiden on his second start last October, was also held up way off the pace but unlike the winner made his move through the field rather than around it. He finished well and would have got there with a little further to go, but it was noticeable that his rider was very sparing with the whip, giving him just one crack but otherwise using just hands and heels. He remains unexposed compared with his rivals and not being beaten up here may pay dividends in the longer term. (tchd 7-2)
Red Jade, who signalled a return to form on his debut for the yard at Ayr last month, finished well from off the pace down the wide outside and was still gaining at the line. He was unproven on ground as fast as this and, though he seemed to handle it, will be of more interest back on an easier surface. (op 7-1)
Clerk's Choice(IRE), just ahead of Fastnet Storm at Chester last time and 1lb worse off, was another to finish well from the back of the field but he didn't look the easiest of rides, firstly missing the break and then needing to be urged along on occasions. (tchd 9-2)
Mount Hadley(USA), put up 8lb for last month's Beverley success, raced in midfield early but moved into a challenging position entering the last 2f and had every chance. He was still second half a furlong from home, but was then run right out of the frame by stronger finishers. (op 10-1)
Fastnet Storm(IRE), up 1lb after only just being beaten into third at Chester last time, set the pace but may have done too much and had nothing left once headed over a furlong from home. (op 5-1 tchd 6-1)
Angel Rock(IRE) Official explanation: trainer said colt was unsuited by the good to firm ground

6003 E B F ATTHERACES.COM JOHN MUSKER FILLIES' STKS (LISTED RACE) 1m 2f 21y
4:30 (4:36) (Class 1) 3-Y-O+
£22,432 (£8,540; £4,276; £2,136; £1,068; £536) **Stalls** Low

Form RPR
5031 **1** **Nashmiah (IRE)**[17] 5472 3-8-13 107.. NCallan 10 102+
(C E Brittain) *hld up in tch in midfield: hdwy 3f out: rdn and ev ch ent fnl 2f: led jst over 1f out: edgd lft u.p but styd on wl fnl f* **9/2**[3]
-400 **2** *¾* **Mooakada (IRE)**[60] 4094 3-8-9 92.. TPO'Shea 2 97+
(J H M Gosden) *hld up in tch in midfield: pushed along jst over 3f out: rdn and nt qckn on outer 2f out: hdwy ent fnl f: edgd lft but wnt 2nd fnl 75yds: kpt on* **20/1**
4152 **3** *1 ½* **Splashdown**[35] 4903 3-8-13 102... KFallon 3 98
(L M Cumani) *t.k.h: hld up in tch in midfield: hdwy 3f out: ev ch 2f out: drvn over 1f out: edgd lft u.p and one pce ins fnl f* **7/4**[1]
414 **4** *1 ¼* **Queen Of Pentacles (IRE)**[45] 4566 3-8-9 88................... DaneO'Neill 4 92
(J Noseda) *hld up towards rr: rdn and effrt on outer 3f out: hdwy u.p ent fnl f: edgd lft but styd on wl to go 4th wl ins fnl f* **11/1**
1243 **5** *1* **Flame Of Gibraltar (IRE)**[27] 5202 3-8-9 102..................... TPQueally 11 90
(H R A Cecil) *chsd ldr after 2f: ev ch 3f out: rdn 3f out: led over 2f out: hdd jst over 1f out: keeping on same pce and btn whn short of room and eased wl ins fnl f* **11/4**[2]
5005 **6** *1* **Badiat Alzaman (IRE)**[17] 5472 3-8-9 86....................... JamieSpencer 6 90+
(D M Simcock) *stdd s: hld up in last pl: hdwy whn nt clr run: clipped heels and stmbld over 2f out: rdn 2f out: no prog over 1f out* **20/1**
3141 **7** *shd* **Kaloni (IRE)**[32] 5037 3-8-9 82.. MickyFenton 9 89+
(Mrs P Sly) *led for 1f: chsd ldr tl 8f out: chsd ldrs after: rdn wl over 2f out: wknd over 1f out: btn whn nt clr run and snatched up ins fnl f* **28/1**
-365 **8** *3 ¼* **Sweet Lilly**[7] 5764 5-9-1 100.. AlanMunro 7 82
(M R Channon) *stdd after s: hld up towards rr: hdwy towards inner over 2f out: no prog and btn over 1f out* **12/1**
1-65 **9** *½* **Amanjena**[82] 3333 4-9-1 87.. DarryllHolland 8 81
(A M Balding) *t.k.h: hld up wl in tch: rdn 3f out: wknd u.p ent fnl 2f* **33/1**
31 **10** *1* **Crimson Ribbon (USA)**[124] 2051 3-8-9 0.................... NickyMackay 12 79
(J H M Gosden) *dwlt: hdwy to ld after 1f: rdn and hdd over 2f out: wknd wl over 1f out* **20/1**
1415 **11** *18* **Cwm Rhondda (USA)**[32] 5037 4-9-1 74......................... JackMitchell 13 47
(P W Chapple-Hyam) *hld up towards rr: rdn and lost tch wl over 2f out: wl bhd fnl f* **50/1**

2m 5.20s (-5.30) **Going Correction** -0.325s/f (Firm)
WFA 3 from 4yo+ 6lb **11** Ran SP% **119.9**
Speed ratings (Par 108): **108,107,106,105,104 103,103,100,100,99 85**
toteswingers: 1&2 £17.20, 1&3 £4.00, 2&3 £13.10 CSF £95.50 TOTE £5.60: £1.70, £5.00, £1.30; EX 114.30 Trifecta £248.40 Pool: £701.76 - 2.09 winning units..
Owner Saeed Manana **Bred** Deerpark Stud **Trained** Newmarket, Suffolk
■ Stewards' Enquiry : K Fallon one-day ban: careless riding (Sep 30)

FOCUS
Quite a competitive renewal of this fillies' Listed contest. The early pace didn't appear to be that strong, but even so the winning time was 0.57 seconds faster than the preceding Class 3 handicap. The winner did not need to match her best.

NOTEBOOK
Nashmiah(IRE), already a three-time winner in Listed company this year and narrowly best in here on adjusted official ratings, was never too far off the pace and travelled strongly into contention down the outside once in line for home. Taking over a furlong out, she saw her race out well despite edging towards the inside rail and she is now likely to take her chance in the Sun Chariot. (tchd 4-1 and 5-1)
Mooakada(IRE), very disappointing in her last two starts including when miles behind Flame Of Gibraltar in the Ribblesdale, reportedly had a breathing problem last time but she bounced back to form here. Finishing well from off the pace, she was still gaining at the line but the winner had poached too much of a lead. If she can reproduce this then she can win a Listed race, as she still doesn't have that many miles on the clock.
Splashdown, successful in Listed company over this trip at Newbury in June, was well backed earlier in the day but she didn't look very happy beforehand and proved awkward to load. Once under way, she raced prominently and had every chance passing the 2f pole, but then couldn't quicken further. (op 2-1, tchd 21-10 in a place)
Queen Of Pentacles(IRE) ◆, a fair fourth when stepped up to this level over an extra 2f at Newbury last time, stayed on well down the wide outside and looks in need of a return to further. She didn't see the racecourse until May and still has a bit of scope. (op 9-1 tchd 17-2)
Flame Of Gibraltar(IRE), whose best effort so far was when runner-up in the Ribblesdale, was down to this trip for the first time since easily winning her maiden over it at Lingfield in June. Always up with the pace, she was in front passing the 2f pole, but had nothing more to offer after being headed a furlong later and perhaps she does need a longer trip now. (op 7-2 tchd 4-1)
Badiat Alzaman(IRE) faced a huge task here as she had finished behind Nashmiah at Goodwood last time and was 12lb worse off, but having been held up last early she ran into traffic when trying to get closer in the straight and would have finished a bit closer otherwise, though she would never have won. (op 28-1)
Kaloni(IRE), winner of a couple of fair handicaps this summer, was up against it at this level but she ran with plenty of credit here having been handy throughout, and she was still fighting for a place when pinched against the inside rail by Flame Of Gibraltar half a furlong from home. (tchd 33-1)

6004 SEA-DEER H'CAP 1m 3y
5:00 (5:04) (Class 4) (0-85,82) 3-Y-0+ **£6,308** (£1,888; £944; £472; £235) **Stalls** High

Form RPR
1331 **1** **Arizona John (IRE)**[18] 5441 4-9-4 **74**.................................. SJCraine 2 81
(J Mackie) *hld up in midfield: hdwy to trck ldrs gng wl over 1f out: rdn to chal ins fnl f: led on post* **7/2**[1]
1450 **2** *nse* **King Columbo (IRE)**[33] 5003 4-8-12 **68**.................... CatherineGannon 7 75
(Miss J Feilden) *chsd ldr: rdn jst over 2f out: led over 1f out: kpt on wl u.p tl hdd on post* **8/1**

4426 **3** 2 ¼ **Dear Maurice**[44] 4605 5-9-5 **75**...(p) TPQueally 4 77
(E A L Dunlop) *stdd s: hld up wl off the pce: shkn up and no hdwy over 2f out: hdwy u.p over 1f out: kpt on to go 3rd towards fin: nt pce to trble ldng pair* **13/2**[3]

0655 **4** *nk* **Hustle (IRE)**[28] 5167 4-9-7 **77**... DarryllHolland 1 78
(Miss Gay Kelleway) *led: rdn 2f out: hdd over 1f out: wknd ins fnl f* **15/2**

4011 **5** ½ **Indy Driver**[16] 5511 4-9-7 **77**...(p) DaneO'Neill 8 77
(J R Fanshawe) *hld up in midfield: hdwy over 2f out: chsd ldrs and drvn over 1f out: one pce ent fnl f: wknd fnl 75yds* **12/1**

P600 **6** *9* **Sonny Parkin**[33] 5003 7-8-9 **70**...(v) SimonPearce(5) 3 50
(J Pearce) *awkward leaving stalls and s.i.s: a wl bhd* **25/1**

-135 **7** *15* **Pearl Of Manacor (IRE)**[167] 1082 3-9-3 **77**... AlanMunro 6 24
(M R Channon) *stdd s: a bhd: struggling and rdn 1/2-way: t.o* **12/1**

6435 **U** **Everynight (IRE)**[12] 5648 3-9-8 **82**...(p) KFallon 5 —
(M Botti) *tried to get under stalls and uns rdr s* **4/1**[2]

1m 35.85s (-4.75) **Going Correction** -0.45s/f (Firm)
WFA 3 from 4yo+ 4lb **8** Ran SP% **112.2**
Speed ratings (Par 105): **105,104,102,102,101 92,77,—**
toteswingers: 1&2 £5.90, 1&3 £6.00, 2&3 £6.60 CSF £30.51 CT £172.63 TOTE £4.80: £1.70, £2.50, £2.20; EX 27.30 Trifecta £397.50 Pool: £590.88 - 1.10 winning units..
Owner Derbyshire Racing **Bred** Abergwaun Farms **Trained** Church Broughton , Derbys

FOCUS
A tight-looking handicap, rated around the principals.
Sonny Parkin Official explanation: jockey said gelding missed the break

6005 LYNN BRENNAN 60TH BIRTHDAY H'CAP (DIV II) 7f 3y
5:30 (5:36) (Class 6) (0-60,60) 3-Y-0+ **£2,007** (£597; £298; £149) **Stalls** High

Form RPR

1 **Vertigo On Course (IRE)**[320] 7124 4-8-12 **51**... TonyHamilton 6 66+
(R A Fahey) *chsd ldrs: wnt 2nd gng wl over 2f out: shkn up to join ldr 2f out: rdn to ld over 1f out: r.o strly fnl f* **7/2**[1]

513 **2** 2 ½ **Jonnie Skull (IRE)**[12] 5644 3-8-11 **53**...(vt) KFallon 10 60+
(P S McEntee) *led: rdn over 2f out: hdd over 1f out: nt pce of wnr ins fnl f but styd on for clr 2nd* **5/1**[3]

2010 **3** 4 ½ **Registrar**[15] 5544 7-9-4 **57**...(p) SaleemGolam 8 53
(Mrs C A Dunnett) *chsd ldr: rdn over 2f out: hrd drvn and nt pce of ldng pair over 1f out: hld on for 3rd fnl f* **10/1**

6006 **4** *1* **Imperial Skylight**[14] 5576 3-8-6 **51**... MCGeran(3) 3 43
(M R Channon) *in tch in midfield: effrt u.p on outer over 2f out: no ch w ldng pair over 1f out: plugged on* **20/1**

5065 **5** ½ **Confide In Me**[26] 5229 5-9-4 **57**...(bt) NCallan 5 49
(G A Butler) *in tch in midfield: rdn and effrt 3f out: sme hdwy u.p to press for 3rd over 1f out: one pce fnl f* **4/1**[2]

0046 **6** *1* **Croeso Ynol**[16] 5501 3-8-8 **50**... RobertHavlin 14 38
(J L Spearing) *stdd s: hld up in rr: rdn and hdwy over 2f out: hung lft fr over 1f out: kpt on steadily but nvr gng pce to threaten ldrs* **22/1**

000- **7** 1 ½ **Miss Jabba (IRE)**[331] 6858 3-8-5 **47**... CatherineGannon 1 31
(Miss J Feilden) *hld up in tch in midfield: rdn and hdwy over 2f out: no prog u.p fr over 1f out* **40/1**

4300 **8** ½ **Athboy Auction**[36] 4880 4-8-7 **46**...(t) JerryO'Dwyer 9 30
(H J Collingridge) *s.i.s: sn in tch in midfield: rdn and unable qck 3f out: no ch w ldrs fr wl over 1f out* **22/1**

6435 **9** *nk* **Imperial Echo (USA)**[9] 5729 8-8-13 **52**... JamieSpencer 4 35+
(T D Barron) *stdd after s: t.k.h and hld up in rr: hdwy but stl plenty to do whn nt clr run ent fnl f: swtchd rt ins fnl f: n.d* **4/1**[2]

0400 **10** 1 ½ **Dicey Affair**[12] 5634 3-8-13 **55**...(p) RichardMullen 2 33
(G L Moore) *stdd after s: hld up towards rr: rdn and no rspnse 3f out: n.d* **33/1**

0/06 **11** ½ **So Glamorous**[39] 4786 4-9-3 **56**... AlanMunro 13 34
(C F Wall) *chsd ldrs tl edgd rt and wknd ent fnl 2f* **14/1**

0010 **12** *nse* **Bright Falcon**[33] 4998 4-8-10 **49**...(p) MickyFenton 16 27
(J Balding) *chsd ldrs tl wknd qckly u.p over 2f out* **22/1**

00- **13** ¾ **Querido (GER)**[359] 6177 5-9-7 **60**... VinceSlattery 7 35
(M Bradstock) *stdd s: hld up in rr: pushed along and no rspnse 1/2-way: n.d* **25/1**

0000 **14** *nse* **Warners Bay (IRE)**[25] 5254 4-8-9 **48** oh1 ow2... TPQueally 15 23
(R Bastiman) *s.i.s: hld up in rr: struggling over 3f out: no ch whn hung lft ins fnl f* **50/1**

1m 23.25s (-3.35) **Going Correction** -0.45s/f (Firm)
WFA 3 from 4yo+ 3lb **14** Ran SP% **123.6**
Speed ratings (Par 101): **101,98,93,91,91 90,88,87,87,85 85,85,84,84**
toteswingers: 1&2 £7.10, 1&3 £10.20, 2&3 £6.90 CSF £19.03 CT £166.89 TOTE £6.20: £2.30, £1.80, £2.60; EX 41.40 Trifecta £158.70 Pool: £472.10 - 2.20 winning units. Place 6: £57.61, Place 5: £36.86.
Owner G Devlin **Bred** Gainsborough Stud Management Ltd **Trained** Musley Bank, N Yorks

FOCUS
Another moderate handicap in which they raced centre-to-stands' side and the winning time was 0.41 seconds slower than the first division. Big improvement from the winner.
T/Jkpt: Not won. T/Plt: £54.50 to a £1 stake. Pool: £61,137.54. 818.29 winning tickets. T/Qpdt: £8.10 to a £1 stake. Pool: £4,667.40. 421.25 winning tickets. SP

6006 - 6008a (Foreign Racing) - See Raceform Interactive

5358 AYR (L-H)
Thursday, September 17

OFFICIAL GOING: Good to soft (good in places) changing to good after race 5 (4.20)
Wind: Fresh, half against Weather: Overcast

6009 MILLAR CALLAGHAN 10TH ANNIVERSARY MAIDEN AUCTION STKS 6f
2:20 (2:22) (Class 5) 2-Y-0 **£4,015** (£1,194; £597; £298) **Stalls** High

Form RPR

623 **1** **Jeannie Galloway (IRE)**[34] 4993 2-8-4 73... PaulHanagan 9 71
(R A Fahey) *trckd ldrs: rdn to ld ins fnl f: kpt on wl* **7/1**

2 ½ **Horseradish** 2-8-11 0... HayleyTurner 11 77+
(M L W Bell) *s.i.s: sn in midfield: effrt over 1f out: styd on wl fnl f: tk 2nd last stride* **14/1**

2 **3** *nse* **Antoniola (IRE)**[84] 3310 2-8-9 0... DavidAllan 17 75
(T D Easterby) *dwlt: sn in midfield: effrt and hdwy over 1f out: ev ch ins fnl f: kpt on: lost 2nd last stride* **4/1**[1]

5360 **4** 1 ¼ **Brinscall**[35] 4931 2-8-8 60... TonyHamilton 20 70
(R A Fahey) *cl up: led 2f out to ins fnl f: kpt on same pce* **20/1**

2 **5** ½ **Walvis Bay (IRE)**[11] 5693 2-9-2 0... MickyFenton 6 77
(T P Tate) *towards rr: rdn 1/2-way: hdwy over 1f out: kpt on fnl f: no imp* **11/2**[3]

2420 **6** ¾ **Angelena Ballerina (IRE)**[82] 3396 2-8-1 82...(p) KellyHarrison(3) 15 62
(A Bailey) *trckd ldrs: effrt over 2f out: one pce over 1f out* **5/1**[2]

65 **7** *3* **Sydney Bridge**[59] 4132 2-8-11 0...(p) TomEaves 18 60
(I Semple) *in midfield: pushed along over 2f out: outpcd over 1f out* **100/1**

25 **8** 1 ¼ **Catbells (IRE)**[27] 5208 2-8-3 0... AshleyMorgan(5) 12 54+
(A Bailey) *slowly away: bhd tl hdwy over 1f out: nvr rchd ldrs* **10/1**

0 **9** *nk* **All Moving Parts (USA)**[19] 5439 2-8-13 0... PAspell 8 58
(J S Wainwright) *missed break: bhd tl hdwy over 1f out: n.d* **100/1**

0 **10** 2 ¼ **Sumay Buoy (IRE)**[21] 5360 2-8-5 0 ow1... LanceBetts(5) 19 48
(Mrs J C McGregor) *hung lft thrght: in midfield: effrt over 2f outk: wknd over 1f out* **100/1**

0 **11** 2 ¾ **Silvermine Bay (IRE)**[12] 5668 2-8-4 0... DaleGibson 7 34
(A P Jarvis) *bhd and sn struggling: kpt on fnl f: nvr on terms* **100/1**

2643 **12** *shd* **Clever Molly (IRE)**[14] 5596 2-8-4 61... PaulQuinn 16 33
(E J Alston) *led to 2f out: sn rdn and btn* **20/1**

0 **13** 1 ¼ **Amenable (IRE)**[14] 5596 2-8-9 0... AdrianTNicholls 3 35
(D Nicholls) *cl up on outside tl wknd over 2f out* **20/1**

4 **14** *shd* **Antarctic Desert (IRE)**[12] 5669 2-8-11 0... PhillipMakin 10 36
(K A Ryan) *prom tl rdn and wknd over 2f out* **17/2**

3525 **15** 1 ¼ **Tislaam (IRE)**[33] 5036 2-8-13 79...(v[1]) SamHitchcott 5 35
(M R Channon) *racd wd in rr: drvn 1/2-way: nvr on terms* **20/1**

16 1 ¼ **Show Willing (IRE)** 2-8-4 0... AndrewElliott 14 22
(A P Jarvis) *cl up tl rdn and wknd over 2f out* **40/1**

00 **17** 4 ½ **Nolecce**[12] 5674 2-8-9 0... FrancisNorton 13 13
(R C Guest) *chsd ldrs: rdn and wkng whn n.m.r over 2f out* **100/1**

33 **18** ½ **Lord Raglan (IRE)**[59] 4132 2-8-6 0... MartinLane(5) 1 14
(A P Jarvis) *bhd and sn drvn along: no ch fr 1/2-way* **40/1**

19 ½ **Chichina (USA)** 2-8-6 0... GregFairley 2 —
(M Johnston) *s.i.s: bhd on outside: nvr on terms* **25/1**

1m 12.6s (-1.00) **Going Correction** -0.30s/f (Firm) **19** Ran SP% **123.6**
Speed ratings (Par 95): **94,93,93,91,90 89,85,84,83,80 77,77,75,75,73 71,65,65,64**
toteswingers: 1&2 £21.30, 1&3 £5.90, 2&3 £14.70 CSF £88.02 TOTE £6.20: £2.50, £5.70, £2.00; EX 110.30.
Owner David Renwick **Bred** G And J Bloodstock **Trained** Musley Bank, N Yorks

FOCUS
Following a dry night the ground was officially good to soft, good in places. The jockeys agreed with the official assessment and winning time for this opener was 2.5 seconds outside standard. Quantity as opposed to quality in this fair maiden auction event and with the stalls against the stands' rail, the whole field wanted to come up the nearside of the track. Those drawn low were at a major disadvantage.

NOTEBOOK
Jeannie Galloway(IRE), making her debut for the yard, was back in trip after running well over 7f in her last two starts. She was never far off the pace from her middle draw and, once hitting the front over a furlong out, saw it out well. Currently rated 73, her new yard should be able to find more opportunities for her and she is likely to step back up in trip.
Horseradish, a 12,000gns colt out of a winning juvenile sprinter and one of just three newcomers in the field, gave himself a bit to do following a tardy start but he finished strongly and came through to snatch second close to the line. He should come on from this and find a race or two. (tchd 16-1)
Antoniola(IRE), well backed when an encouraging second on debut at Newcastle in June after having not enjoyed the clearest of runs, had no such problems here and was bang there with every chance towards the outside a furlong out, but couldn't quicken sufficiently. He might just have needed it and an opportunity should be found. (op 3-1)
Brinscall, like the winner making her debut for the Fahey yard, was back down to a more suitable trip and showed good speed from the stands'-rail draw, but couldn't hold on after losing the advantage over a furlong from home.
Walvis Bay(IRE), who looked as though this longer trip would suit when runner-up on his York debut, was again doing his best work late and may need to step up again. This was still a good effort from his low draw, however. (op 9-2)
Angelena Ballerina(IRE), already placed a few times and not beaten far in a couple of Listed races, was returning from a short break. She was never far away and had her chance, but she is more exposed than most and is not going to be easy to place. (op 6-1)
Sydney Bridge was taking a drop in class on this third outing, but she could never get into it after missing the break.
Tislaam(IRE), placed a couple of times in five previous outings, had a visor on for the first time but he never figured and, though he was badly drawn, he looks to be going the wrong way. (op 22-1)

6010 BREWIN DOLPHIN INVESTMENT MANAGEMENT H'CAP 5f
2:50 (2:52) (Class 5) (0-70,70) 3-Y-0+ **£5,051** (£1,503; £751; £375) **Stalls** High

Form RPR

3210 **1** **Medici Time**[33] 5031 4-9-5 **69**...(v) RichardMullen 6 77
(T D Easterby) *racd far side: in rr and pushed along: hdwy over 2f out: swtchd rt 1f out: styd on to ld towards fin: 1st of 10 that gp* **22/1**

1520 **2** ¾ **Taurus Twins**[76] 3592 3-9-0 **70**...(b) MartinLane(5) 7 75
(R J Price) *racd far side: chsd ldrs: led that side over 1f out: hdd towards fin: 2nd of 10 that gp* **14/1**

0000 **3** ½ **Chosen One (IRE)**[44] 4620 4-8-8 **58**... TomEaves 24 62
(B Smart) *racd stands' side: trckd ldrs: led that gp jst ins fnl f: r.o towards fin* **14/1**

0025 **4** ¾ **Town And Gown**[3] 5946 4-8-2 **55** oh10... KellyHarrison(3) 15 56
(J S Goldie) *racd stands' side: in rr: hdwy 2f out: styd on wl ins fnl f* **40/1**

-000 **5** *nk* **Killer Class**[29] 5148 4-8-10 **63**... FrederikTylicki(3) 19 63
(J S Goldie) *racd stands' side: chsd ldrs: styd on same pce fnl f* **14/1**

2422 **6** *nk* **Sunley Sovereign**[20] 5396 5-8-0 **57**...(b) JamesPSullivan(7) 3 56
(Mrs R A Carr) *racd far side: mid-div: hdwy to chse ldrs over 2f out: kpt on fnl f: 3rd of 10 that gp* **16/1**

0524 **7** *nk* **Joyeaux**[17] 5518 7-8-11 **61**... PaulHanagan 18 59
(Ollie Pears) *racd stands' side: mid-div: hdwy over 2f out: kpt on same pce fnl f* **12/1**

6000 **8** *nk* **Divine Spirit**[36] 4891 8-9-5 **69**... PhillipMakin 4 65
(M Dods) *racd far side: towards rr: hdwy over 2f out: kpt on fnl f: 4th of 10 that gp* **25/1**

1050 **9** *nk* **Highland Warrior**[37] 4886 10-9-4 **68**... MickyFenton 17 63
(P T Midgley) *racd stands' side: mid-div on outer: hdwy 2f out: kpt on ins fnl f* **28/1**

U606 **9** *dht* **Buy On The Red**[36] 4899 8-9-5 **69**...(b) PaulQuinn 21 64
(D Nicholls) *racd stands' side: led that side tl jst ins fnl f: kpt on same pce* **25/1**

0500 **11** *nk* **Glenluji**[10] 5729 4-8-5 **55** oh2... HayleyTurner 23 49
(J S Goldie) *racd stands' side: in rr and pushed along: styd on fnl 2f: nvr nr ldrs* **33/1**

5062 **12** *1* **Dalarossie**[3] 5946 4-8-5 **55** oh2...(b[1]) DaleGibson 8 46
(E J Alston) *racd far side: chsd ldrs: one pce over 1f out: 5th of 10 that gp* **25/1**

0130 **13** *shd* **Guest Connections**[12] [5675] 6-9-3 **67**....................(v) AdrianTNicholls 22 57+
(D Nicholls) *racd stands' side: in rr: hdwy then nt clr run over 1f: nvr a factor* **14/1**

3052 **14** *shd* **Sweet Applause (IRE)**[104] [2651] 3-9-3 **68**.............................. AndrewElliott 5 58
(A P Jarvis) *racd far side: in rr div: kpt on fnl 2f: nvr a factor: 6th of 10 that gp* **50/1**

2352 **15** *1 1/4* **Cayman Fox**[14] [5610] 4-8-10 **60**..(e) PJMcDonald 9 46
(James Moffatt) *swtchd lft s: led far side: hdd that gp and wknd over 1f out: 7th of 10 that gp* **20/1**

4300 **16** *nse* **Blazing Heights**[3] [5946] 6-8-9 **59** ow2.......................(b[1]) DanielTudhope 1 44
(J S Goldie) *racd far side: towards rr: nvr a factor: 8th of 10 that gp* **20/1**

1600 **17** *1* **Grimes Faith**[20] [5411] 6-8-5 **60**..(p) AmyRyan(5) 14 42
(K A Ryan) *racd stands' side: mid-div on outer: lost pl over 1f out* **25/1**

5000 **18** *nk* **Handcuff**[3] [5946] 3-8-4 **55** oh10.......................................(p) AndrewMullen 2 36
(I Semple) *racd far side: chsd ldrs: wknd over 1f out: 9th of 10 that gp* **100/1**

1556 **19** *1/2* **Andrasta**[4] [5911] 4-8-2 **57** oh3 ow2.................................. DeanHeslop(5) 20 36
(S A Harris) *racd stands' side: chsd ldrs: lost pl over 1f out* **28/1**

5302 **20** *hd* **Imprimis Tagula (IRE)**[21] [5370] 5-8-13 **68**................(v) GaryBartley(5) 10 46
(A Bailey) *swtchd lft and racd far side: a towards rr: last of 10 that gp* **10/1[2]**

5631 **21** *nk* **Wicked Wilma (IRE)**[3] [5946] 5-9-0 **64** 6ex.................... FrancisNorton 16 41
(A Berry) *racd stands' side: w ldr: hung lft and wknd qckly jst ins fnl f* **11/1[3]**

3402 **22** *1 3/4* **Grudge**[20] [5411] 4-9-1 **65**... TonyHamilton 13 36
(Ollie Pears) *racd stands' side: chsd ldrs: sn drvn along: lost pl over 1f out* **14/1**

6250 **23** *hd* **Miss Daawe**[6] [5836] 5-8-6 **61**... LanceBetts(5) 11 31
(B Ellison) *racd stands' side: mid-div on outer: wknd 2f out* **20/1**

3611 **24** *1/2* **The Bear**[24] [5309] 6-8-9 **64**.. AndrewHeffernan(5) 12 32+
(Miss L A Perratt) *restless in stalls: hood removed v late: s.s: racd stands' side: sn chsng ldrs: wknd 2f out* **8/1[1]**

59.32 secs (-0.78) **Going Correction** -0.30s/f (Firm)
WFA 3 from 4yo+ 1lb **24** Ran SP% **124.7**
Speed ratings (Par 103): **94,92,92,90,90 89,89,88,88,88 87,86,86,86,84 83,82,81,81,80 80,77,77,76**
Tote Swingers: 1&2 £46.00, 1&3 not won, 2&3 not won. CSF £249.87 CT £4496.14 TOTE £28.60: £6.50, £4.20, £4.80, £15.60; EX 195.40.

Owner Mrs C A Hodgetts **Bred** Mrs Fiona Denniff **Trained** Great Habton, N Yorks

FOCUS
A very competitive sprint handicap and the field predictably split, with the larger group of 14 coming stands' side whilst the smaller group of ten stayed far side. Although the first two came from the far-side group, there were several on the nearside not beaten far, so any advantage was minimal. The third and fourth limit the level.

Guest Connections Official explanation: jockey said gelding was denied a clear run

Wicked Wilma(IRE) Official explanation: jockey said mare hung left

The Bear Official explanation: trainer said gelding missed the break

6011 EUROPEAN BREEDERS' FUND NOVICE STKS 1m
3:20 (3:21) (Class 4) 2-Y-O **£5,828** (£1,734; £866; £432) **Stalls** Low

Form RPR

315 **1** **Simenon (IRE)**[26] [5261] 2-9-5 **98**... LPKeniry 5 95+
(A M Balding) *trckd ldrs gng wl: led over 2f out: sn rdn: edgd lft ins fnl f: r.o* **13/8[1]**

1 **2** *1 1/4* **Notorize**[19] [5428] 2-9-2 **0**....................................... RichardKingscote 2 88
(R M Beckett) *trckd ldrs: effrt and wnt 2nd over 1f out: kpt on same pce ins fnl f* **7/2[3]**

15 **3** *1* **Syrian**[12] [5659] 2-9-0 **97**... HayleyTurner 1 84
(M L W Bell) *dwlt: hld up last: hdwy over 2f out: edgd lft and kpt on u.p fnl f* **9/4[2]**

0145 **4** *2 1/4* **Haltela (IRE)**[40] [4803] 2-9-5 **77**...(p) PhillipMakin 3 84
(K A Ryan) *led tl rdn and hdd over 2f out: edgd lft and one pce over 1f out* **20/1**

31 **5** *4* **Right Step**[34] [4993] 2-9-5 **85**... AndrewElliott 8 75
(A P Jarvis) *wnt rt s: sn chsng ldrs: outpcd over 2f out: btn over 1f out* **8/1**

1045 **6** *hd* **Ananda Kanda (USA)**[23] [5324] 2-9-0 **79**............................ TomEaves 6 70
(B Ellison) *checked s: hld up in tch: outpcd over 2f out: sn no imp* **50/1**

06 **7** *8* **Alotago (IRE)**[19] [5417] 2-8-7 **0**... AdrianTNicholls 4 45
(D Nicholls) *t.k.h: hld up in tch: struggling over 2f out: sn btn* **100/1**

6 **8** *2 3/4* **Hotgrove Boy**[25] [5290] 2-8-12 **0**...................................... AndrewMullen 7 44
(A G Foster) *prom: reminders 1/2-way: sn rdn and wknd fr 2f out* **200/1**

1m 41.79s (-2.01) **Going Correction** -0.30s/f (Firm) **8** Ran SP% **110.4**
Speed ratings (Par 97): **98,96,95,93,89 89,81,78**
toteswingers: 1&2 £1.80, 1&3 £1.80, 2&3 £2.90 CSF £7.03 TOTE £2.40: £1.10, £1.60, £1.40; EX 6.80.

Owner Mr Greenwood, Ms James & Mr Cockburn **Bred** Max Morris **Trained** Kingsclere, Hants

FOCUS
A strong novice event, though only half the field mattered as far as the market was concerned. The pace looked solid enough. A pleasing effort fom the winner, who is potentially smart.

NOTEBOOK
Simenon(IRE), dropping in class after finishing fifth in the Solario where the stop-start gallop probably didn't suit him, travelled like a dream here and he cruised to the front over 2f from home. Although he didn't exactly pull away, he was always doing more than enough and he is likely to step back up in class for a 1m Listed event at Pontefract next month. (op 6-4 tchd 15-8 and 2-1 in places)

Notorize, who overcame a poor draw to make a winning debut over this trip at Goodwood, put in a strong challenge up the inside rail entering the last 2f and stayed on well, though he could never get on terms with the winner. He still has scope and there will be another day. (op 4-1)

Syrian, the form of whose Yarmouth debut victory has worked out well, pulled too hard when unplaced in a soft-ground Listed race over this trip at Haydock last time and he was inclined to race freely at the back of the field here. He did stay on over the last couple of furlongs, but was also looking about him and he still looked green despite this being his third start. Perhaps he is more one for next year. (tchd 5-2)

Haltela(IRE), in cheekpieces rather than blinkers on this occasion and, racing beyond 6f for the first time, made much of the running but didn't exactly fall in a heap once headed. He faced a stiff task on these terms and this looked more a case of better quality opposition beating him rather than lack of stamina. (op 28-1)

Right Step, who shaped as though this extra furlong would suit when winning at Newcastle last time, was well supported earlier in the day but proved very disappointing. Diving out to his right exiting the stalls, he raced very keenly on the wide outside early, didn't take the home bend too well, and eventually dropped right out. (op 11-2)

6012 JOHN SMITH'S (S) STKS 1m 2f
3:50 (3:51) (Class 4) 3-Y-O+ **£6,476** (£1,927; £963; £481) **Stalls** Low

Form RPR

0120 **1** **Applaude**[11] [5698] 4-9-5 **69**..(b) PhillipMakin 14 73+
(John A Harris) *hld up: nt clr run fr 3f out tl swtchd rt and hdwy over 1f out: edgd rt and led wl ins fnl f: r.o* **22/1**

3121 **2** *1 1/4* **Boundless Prospect (USA)**[198] [744] 10-9-0 **68**. AndrewHeffernan(5) 6 71
(P D Evans) *hld up: hdwy on outside over 2f out: edgd lft and chsd wnr over 1f out: ev ch wl ins fnl f: r.o* **10/1**

0031 **3** *3/4* **King Of The Moors (USA)**[3] [5944] 6-9-5 **56**............(b) FrancisNorton 12 69
(R C Guest) *chsd clr ldr: led over 2f out: 3 l clr over 1f out: hdd and no ex wl ins fnl f* **9/1[3]**

2404 **4** *1/2* **Red Skipper (IRE)**[21] [5364] 4-9-2 **55**........................... AndrewMullen 10 65
(N Wilson) *prom: nt clr run briefly over 2f out: effrt and edgd lft over 1f out: r.o ins fnl f* **12/1**

2061 **5** *nk* **Rossini's Dancer**[16] [5549] 4-9-5 **66**...................................... PaulHanagan 3 67
(R A Fahey) *trckd ldrs: outpcd over 2f out: rallied fnl f: no imp* **4/1[1]**

660 **6** *1 1/2* **Spring Goddess (IRE)**[12] [5671] 8-9-0 **75**........................ AndrewElliott 13 59
(A P Jarvis) *bhd: rdn over 2f out: kpt on fnl f: nvr rchd ldrs* **14/1**

0501 **7** *shd* **Middlemarch (IRE)**[11] [5694] 9-9-0 **63**.........................(v) GaryBartley(5) 8 64
(J S Goldie) *hld up on ins: rdn over 2f out: styd on fnl f: n.d* **4/1[1]**

3110 **8** *nk* **Tufton**[35] [4930] 6-9-5 **74**... TonyHamilton 11 64+
(R A Fahey) *midfield on ins: nt clr run over 2f out to over 1f out: rdn and one pce* **15/2[2]**

0-04 **9** *hd* **Jim Martin**[24] [5305] 4-8-9 **60**....................................... JamesPSullivan(7) 4 60
(Miss L A Perratt) *unruly bef s: chsd ldrs tl rdn and wknd over 1f out* **25/1**

246 **10** *6* **Clear Sailing**[154] [1314] 6-9-2 **68**...............................(p) FrederikTylicki(3) 2 51
(Ollie Pears) *set decent gallop: clr after 3f: hdd over 2f out: wknd over 1f out* **9/1[3]**

3226 **11** *nk* **Lucayan Dancer**[19] [5438] 9-9-5 **62**................................. AdrianTNicholls 9 51
(D Nicholls) *hld up: hdwy on outside 3f out: rdn and wknd fr 2f out* **12/1**

2603 **12** *hd* **My Mate Mal**[21] [5361] 5-9-5 **63**... TomEaves 7 50
(B Ellison) *in tch: drvn 3f out: wknd wl over 1f out* **16/1**

30-0 **13** *8* **Solis (GER)**[10] [5732] 6-9-2 **65**... MickyFenton 5 31
(P Monteith) *s.i.s and sn outpcd: nvr on terms* **20/1**

006 **14** *8* **Kingsholm**[8] [4139] 7-8-11 **56**...(p) AmyRyan(5) 1 15
(N Wilson) *s.s: bhd: drvn over 3f out: sn btn* **66/1**

2m 8.10s (-3.90) **Going Correction** -0.30s/f (Firm) **14** Ran SP% **123.2**
Speed ratings (Par 105): **103,102,101,101,100 99,99,99,99,94 94,93,87,81**
toteswingers: 1&2 £22.10, 1&3 £42.60, 2&3 £10.80 CSF £225.48 TOTE £29.60: £7.20, £4.70, £3.10; EX 76.90.The winner bought in for 7,500gns.

Owner Stan Wright **Bred** G Reed **Trained** Eastwell, Leics

FOCUS
A decent prize resulted in a competitive race for this seller and there was a good pace on thanks to the front-running Clear Sailing. The third to fifth limit the level of the form.

6013 WILLIAMHILL.COM/BONUS25 H'CAP (FOR THE KILKERRAN CUP) 1m 2f
4:20 (4:21) (Class 2) (0-100,94) 3-Y-O+ **£12,952** (£3,854; £1,926; £962) **Stalls** Low

Form RPR

1234 **1** **Demolition**[12] [5671] 5-8-6 **83**...(p) GaryBartley(5) 2 96
(N Wilson) *chsd ldr: led over 2f out: clr over 1f out: hld on wl fnl f* **9/1**

5121 **2** *1 1/4* **Plaisterer**[63] [4003] 4-9-1 **90**... JackMitchell(3) 5 101+
(C F Wall) *dwlt: hld up: hdwy 2f out: shkn up to chse wnr ins fnl f: flashed tail: r.o* **4/1[1]**

3010 **3** *2 1/2* **Hillview Boy (IRE)**[26] [5262] 5-9-1 **87**.......................... DanielTudhope 14 93
(J S Goldie) *in tch on outside: effrt over 2f out: kpt on same pce ins fnl f* **9/2[2]**

6450 **4** *nk* **Bucked Off (SAF)**[29] [5170] 5-9-2 **88**................................ MickyFenton 6 93
(T P Tate) *led to over 2f out: rdn and edgd rt over 1f out: nt qckn* **33/1**

5402 **5** *1/2* **Stevie Thunder**[30] [5137] 4-8-12 **89**.................................. MartinLane(5) 1 93
(Ian Williams) *in tch: drvn 3f out: kpt on u.p fnl f* **8/1[3]**

4020 **6** *shd* **Granston (IRE)**[16] [5551] 8-9-1 **87**...................................... PhillipMakin 4 91
(J D Bethell) *chsd ldrs: drvn 3f out: plugged on u.p fnl 2f* **25/1**

4450 **7** *3/4* **Ladies Best**[29] [5173] 5-9-6 **92**.. TomEaves 11 94
(B Ellison) *in tch: rdn 3f out: one pce fnl 2f* **11/1**

0314 **8** *nk* **Charlie Tokyo (IRE)**[11] [5694] 6-9-0 **86**......................(v) TonyHamilton 13 88
(R A Fahey) *hld up on outside: effrt over 2f out: no imp over 1f out* **14/1**

5600 **9** *1/2* **Unbreak My Heart (IRE)**[51] [4404] 4-9-5 **91**..................... PaulHanagan 3 92
(R A Fahey) *hld up: effrt u.p over 2f out: no ex fnl f* **9/1**

1500 **10** *hd* **King Charles**[19] [5437] 5-9-8 **94**... HayleyTurner 10 94+
(E A L Dunlop) *hld up last: nt clr run briefly over 2f out: sn rdn and no imp* **16/1**

1030 **11** *4* **Moheebb (IRE)**[19] [5437] 5-9-4 **93**.........................(b) FrederikTylicki(3) 12 85
(Mrs R A Carr) *bhd: drvn over 3f out: nvr able to chal* **14/1**

1401 **12** *5* **Marvo**[29] [5160] 5-8-6 **83**... AshleyMorgan(5) 9 65
(M H Tompkins) *hld up: effrt on outside 3f out: wknd 2f out* **9/1**

4000 **13** *shd* **Wise Dennis**[28] [5200] 7-9-8 **94**... AndrewElliott 8 76
(A P Jarvis) *hld up: drvn over 3f out: btn fnl 2f* **28/1**

2m 6.31s (-5.69) **Going Correction** -0.30s/f (Firm) **13** Ran SP% **117.1**
Speed ratings (Par 109): **110,109,107,106,106 106,105,105,105,104 101,97,97**
toteswingers: 1&2 £7.90, 1&3 £12.20, 2&3 £5.30 CSF £42.99 CT £186.94 TOTE £10.80: £3.10, £2.00, £1.90; EX 47.70.

Owner M Wormald **Bred** P D And Mrs Player **Trained** Flaxton, N Yorks

FOCUS
A competitive handicap and, thanks to a generous pace, the winning time was 1.19 seconds faster than standard and 1.79 seconds quicker than the seller, suggesting the ground was drying out. Strong form.

NOTEBOOK
Demolition, whose last two wins have come over 1m4f, was well backed beforehand. Always up with the pace, he was sent for home over 2f out and soon established a significant advantage and, with proven stamina on his side, was never going to be caught. He may turn out again over 1m5f back here on Saturday. (op 11-1 tchd 8-1)

Plaisterer, a renowned tail-swisher who has been in good form during the summer, was 7lb higher than for her latest win at Doncaster on this return from a short break. Given plenty to do, she took a while to pick up and had to weave her way through the field, but finished strongly only to find the winner had gone beyond recall. The drying ground may not have been ideal, so this was still a good effort and she doesn't have that many miles on the clock. (tchd 9-2)

Hillview Boy(IRE), whose latest effort at Sandown could be ignored, was forced to race a bit wider than was probably ideal throughout, but he kept on going to finish a very respectable third. Now 7lb higher than when winning in decent style on soft ground at Doncaster last month, he remains unexposed on the level and is one to keep on-side. (op 11-2 tchd 6-1)

Bucked Off(SAF), formerly trained in South Africa, was beaten a very long way on his British debut at York last month and has looked very awkward in the past. He raced keenly out in front here too and set a very decent pace, so it is to his great credit that he kept on going even after being headed and there are races in him over here if he can be straightened out. (op 40-1)
Stevie Thunder, 3lb higher than when narrowly beaten on his first attempt at this trip at York last time, had every chance against the inside rail and looks worth persevering with over this sort of distance. (tchd 15-2)
Granston(IRE) showed up for a long way and ran with credit, but he has been proving very inconsistent recently. (op 20-1)
Ladies Best, well beaten in the Ebor last time but off the same mark as when making a winning reappearance at Pontefract in April, plugged on late but lacked the pace to put in a challenge. His rider reported that he had hung left. Official explanation: jockey said gelding hung left-handed in the straight (tchd 12-1)

6014 JOHN SMITH'S H'CAP (DIV I) 1m
4:50 (4:53) (Class 4) (0-85,85) 3-Y-0+ £6,152 (£1,830; £914; £456) Stalls Low

Form RPR
1032 1 **Faithful Ruler (USA)**^{21} 5361 5-9-4 81 .... PaulHanagan 3 95+
(R A Fahey) hld up: gd hdwy over 2f out: led on bit appr fnl f: rdn and sn clr 8/1
11-3 2 3 **Spirit Of A Nation (IRE)**^{13} 5640 4-9-3 85 .... AndrewHeffernan(5) 4 92
(D H Brown) unruly bef s: hld up: effrt over 2f out: hdwy over 1f out: chsd wnr wl ins fnl f: r.o: no imp 4/1^{1}
0054 3 1 3/4 **Doric Echo**^{22} 5333 3-8-5 72 .... GregFairley 10 76
(B Smart) cl up: led 2f out to appr fnl f: one pce 14/1
2155 4 1/2 **Exit Smiling**^{17} 5522 7-9-6 83 .... MickyFenton 7 85
(P T Midgley) prom: effrt over 2f out: edgd rt over 1f out: kpt on same pce 11/1
6560 5 1/2 **Veiled Applause**^{19} 5441 6-8-9 75 .... FrederikTylicki(3) 1 76
(J J Quinn) midfield on ins: drvn and outpcd over 2f out: kpt on fnl f: no imp 5/1^{2}
1305 6 1/2 **Ezdeyaad (USA)**^{74} 3656 5-9-4 81 .... PJMcDonald 8 81
(G A Swinbank) hld up: effrt on outside over 2f out: one pce fr over 1f out 9/1
5535 7 hd **Thousand Miles (IRE)**^{36} 4909 3-9-1 82 .... RichardMullen 2 82
(P W Chapple-Hyam) prom tl rdn and no ex over 1f out 13/2^{3}
1162 8 1 1/2 **Celtic Change (IRE)**^{14} 5598 5-9-5 82 ....(bt) PhillipMakin 11 79
(M Dods) wnt rt s: led after 1f to 2f out: sn no ex 9/1
0200 9 hd **Kinsya**^{21} 5375 6-8-12 80 .... AshleyMorgan(5) 9 76
(M H Tompkins) hld up on outside: effrt and rdn 2f out: sn btn 13/2^{3}
3210 10 5 **Island Chief**^{12} 5670 3-8-4 76 ....(b) AmyRyan(5) 5 61
(K A Ryan) chsd ldrs tl wknd over 2f out 16/1
0000 11 14 **Moves Goodenough**^{19} 5441 6-8-12 75 ....(p) HayleyTurner 6 29+
(A G Foster) hld up: struggling 3f out: sn btn and eased 28/1

1m 40.39s (-3.41) **Going Correction** -0.30s/f (Firm)
WFA 3 from 4yo+ 4lb 11 Ran SP% 118.8
Speed ratings (Par 105): **105,102,100,99,99 98,98,97,96,91 77**
toteswingers: 1&2 £5.20, 1&3 £9.20, 2&3 £7.50 CSF £40.43 CT £456.92 TOTE £6.40: £2.30, £2.00, £4.10; EX 24.00.
Owner George Murray **Bred** WinStar Farm LLC **Trained** Musley Bank, N Yorks

FOCUS
The ground was changed to good before this race. This was a fair handicap run at a decent pace, and the form looks solid.
Moves Goodenough Official explanation: jockey said gelding never travelled

6015 RACINGPOST.COM H'CAP 7f 50y
5:20 (5:22) (Class 5) (0-75,75) 3-Y-0+ £4,533 (£1,348; £674; £336) Stalls Low

Form RPR
5125 1 **She's In The Money**^{17} 5514 3-9-3 74 .... PaulHanagan 4 84+
(R A Fahey) prom: drvn to ld over 1f out: edgd lft: kpt on strly fnl f 6/1^{2}
3542 2 2 1/4 **Leonid Glow**^{17} 5514 4-9-4 72 .... PhillipMakin 10 77
(M Dods) hld up: smooth hdwy 2f out: chsd wnr ins fnl f: r.o 10/1
0000 3 1 3/4 **Rising Shadow (IRE)**^{65} 3941 8-9-7 75 .... FrancisNorton 8 76+
(A D Brown) hld up: hdwy on ins whn nt clr run over 1f out: swtchd rt and styd on ins fnl f 25/1
1066 4 hd **Steel Free (IRE)**^{14} 5591 3-9-3 74 .... HayleyTurner 3 74
(M L W Bell) prom: rdn over 2f out: edgd lft over 1f out: r.o 12/1
004 5 1 3/4 **Izzibizzi**^{40} 4799 4-9-5 73 ....(p) KirstyMilczarek 2 69
(E A L Dunlop) hld up on ins: rdn over 2f out: kpt on fnl f: nrst fin 20/1
0-1 6 1/2 **Brushing**^{36} 4913 3-8-10 72 .... AshleyMorgan(5) 6 66
(M H Tompkins) hld up in midfield: effrt on outside over 2f out: no imp over 1f out 11/1
0-41 7 shd **Dance Card**^{20} 5394 4-9-3 74 ....(t) FrederikTylicki(3) 1 69+
(A G Foster) cl up: led over 2f out to over 1f out: sn no ex 4/1^{1}
3006 8 3/4 **Eastern Hills**^{20} 5404 4-8-11 70 .... LanceBetts(5) 5 63
(J S Wainwright) midfield: drvn 3f out: no imp fnl 2f 11/1
0016 9 1 1/4 **Mujaadel (USA)**^{20} 5409 4-9-6 74 ....(p) AndrewMullen 9 64
(D Nicholls) chsd ldrs tl rdn and wknd over 1f out 12/1
6003 10 1/2 **Bere Davis (FR)**^{20} 5409 4-8-13 72 .... AndrewHeffernan(5) 7 61
(P D Evans) set decent gallop: hdd over 2f out: wknd over 1f out 8/1^{3}
000 11 4 **Charging Indian (IRE)**^{76} 3592 3-9-2 73 .... MickyFenton 14 51
(P T Midgley) stdd in rr: rdn 3f out: sn btn 20/1
145 12 1 1/2 **Rising Kheleyf (IRE)**^{45} 4591 3-9-1 72 .... PJMcDonald 11 46
(G A Swinbank) hld up: rdn and edgd lft over 2f out: sn btn 12/1
2422 13 34 **Stellite**^{22} 5333 9-8-11 70 .... GaryBartley(5) 12 —
(J S Goldie) upset in stalls: hld up on outside: pushed along 3f out: wknd and eased fr 2f out 10/1

1m 31.05s (-2.35) **Going Correction** -0.30s/f (Firm)
WFA 3 from 4yo+ 3lb 13 Ran SP% 116.7
Speed ratings (Par 103): **101,98,96,96,94 93,93,92,91,90 86,84,45**
CSF £61.24 CT £1439.92 TOTE £4.60: £1.90, £3.90, £7.30; EX 50.10.
Owner Cavan Pickering & Stewart Whitehead **Bred** Hermes Services Ltd **Trained** Musley Bank, N Yorks

FOCUS
Thanks to Bere Davis going off very fast, this was run at a scorching early pace but he never had a hope of maintaining the gallop. A fair handicap, with the runner-up a decent guide.
Stellite Official explanation: jockey said gelding became upset in stalls

6016 JOHN SMITH'S H'CAP (DIV II) 1m
5:50 (5:53) (Class 4) (0-85,84) 3-Y-0+ £6,152 (£1,830; £914; £456) Stalls Low

Form RPR
3411 1 **Collateral Damage (IRE)**^{14} 5598 6-9-4 80 ....(t) DavidAllan 5 89
(T D Easterby) trckd ldrs: smooth hdwy to dispute ld over 1f out: led ins fnl f: gamely 7/4^{1}
4230 2 hd **Gala Casino Star (IRE)**^{30} 5137 4-9-8 84 .... PaulHanagan 7 93
(R A Fahey) prom: rdn to ld over 1f out: hdd ins fnl f: rallied 6/1^{2}
5-00 3 nk **Silver Rime (FR)**^{21} 5363 4-9-6 82 .... PhillipMakin 3 90
(Miss L A Perratt) hld up: stdy hdwy to trck ldrs whn n.m.r briefly 2f out: sn rdn: kpt on u.p fnl f 11/1
0100 4 2 3/4 **Keys Of Cyprus**^{20} 5409 7-9-1 77 .... AdrianTNicholls 8 79
(D Nicholls) cl up: led over 2f out to over 1f out: nt qckn 11/1
4065 5 1 1/2 **Magic Echo**^{21} 5363 5-9-5 81 .... TomEaves 2 80
(M Dods) dwlt: hld up: rdn over 2f out: kpt on fnl f: nrst fin 12/1
0404 6 hd **Richo**^{5} 5869 3-8-1 70 oh2 .... KellyHarrison(3) 9 69
(S A Harris) s.i.s: hld up: hdwy over 2f out: kpt on fnl f: no imp 33/1
3144 7 3 1/2 **Casino Night**^{21} 5361 4-8-8 75 .... DeanHeslop(5) 4 66
(F P Murtagh) hld up: effrt over 2f out: sn rdn and no imp 12/1
2114 8 nk **Moody Tunes**^{36} 4897 6-9-0 81 .... MartinLane(5) 10 71
(A P Jarvis) led to over 2f out: wknd over 1f out 20/1
2101 9 3/4 **Ninth House (USA)**^{12} 5673 7-8-9 71 ....(t) PJMcDonald 6 60
(Mrs R A Carr) midfield: drvn and outpcd over 2f out: n.d after 7/1^{3}
6100 10 19 **Golden Penny**^{74} 3656 4-8-10 75 .... FrederikTylicki(3) 11 22
(A G Foster) in tch: rdn 3f out: sn wknd 25/1
220 P **Ocean Transit (IRE)**^{50} 4422 4-9-5 81 .... HayleyTurner 1 —
(R J Price) sn bhd: p.u and dismntd after 2f 9/1

1m 40.84s (-2.96) **Going Correction** -0.30s/f (Firm)
WFA 3 from 4yo+ 4lb 11 Ran SP% 116.7
Speed ratings (Par 105): **102,101,101,98,97 97,93,93,92,73** —
toteswingers: 1&2 £3.80, 1&3 £6.00, 2&3 £10.10 CSF £11.37 CT £90.03 TOTE £2.40: £1.30, £2.30, £3.20; EX 12.60 Place 6: £414.20 Place 5: £163.34 .
Owner Middleham Park Racing Xxv **Bred** Minch Bloodstock And Castletown Stud **Trained** Great Habton, N Yorks

FOCUS
The early pace seemed fair enough in this, though the winning time was nearly half a second slower than the first division. Good, solid handicap form.
Golden Penny Official explanation: jockey said gelding was unsuited by the good ground
Ocean Transit(IRE) Official explanation: jockey said saddle slipped
T/Jkpt: Not won. T/Plt: £287.90 to a £1 stake. Pool: £75,432.08. 191.20 winning tickets. T/Qpdt: £17.10 to a £1 stake. Pool: £5,105.77. 220.20 winning tickets. RY

5066 PONTEFRACT (L-H)
Thursday, September 17

OFFICIAL GOING: Last 6f - good to firm; remainder - good to firm (firm in places; 8.8)
Wind: Virtually nil Weather: Overcast

6017 PONTEFRACT APPRENTICE H'CAP 1m 2f 6y
2:30 (2:30) (Class 5) (0-70,69) 3-Y-0+ £3,238 (£963; £481; £240) Stalls Low

Form RPR
0513 1 **Baltimore Jack (IRE)**^{19} 5438 5-9-4 62 .... NSLawes 6 74
(T D Walford) mde all: rdn clr over 1f out: styd on wl u.p 11/4^{1}
0020 2 2 3/4 **Astronomical (IRE)**^{11} 5698 7-9-3 61 ....(p) DavidKenny 8 67
(R Hollinshead) sn trcking wnr: cl up 1/2-way: effrt 3f out: rdn over 2f out and ev ch tl drvn and one pce fr over 1f out 4/1^{2}
0003 3 nk **Dinner Date**^{18} 5484 7-8-6 57 .... TraceyAddey(7) 7 62
(T Keddy) hld up towards rr: hdwy 2f out: rdn to chse ldng pair ent fnl f kpt on 6/1
440 4 2 1/4 **Bogula (IRE)**^{90} 3120 3-8-8 58 .... LauraPike 5 59
(Mrs A Duffield) t.k.h: chsd ldrs: rdn along 3f out: drvn wl over 1f out: plugged on same pce 9/1
0466 5 1 1/2 **Grey Command (USA)**^{19} 5423 4-8-12 56 .... JohnCavanagh 1 54
(M Brittain) trckd ldrs on inner: pushed along over 3f out: rdn over 2f out and sn btn 5/1^{3}
0450 6 2 **Royal Fantasy (IRE)**^{19} 5438 6-9-0 58 ....(p) RichardRowe 4 52
(N Tinkler) sn trcking ldng pair: pushed along on inner 3f out: rdn over 2f out and sn wknd 10/1
4303 7 2 **Timber Treasure (USA)**^{12} 5673 5-9-4 69 .... JordanLDodd(7) 9 59
(Paul Green) hld up: a towards rr 13/2
000 8 2 1/4 **Treetops Hotel (IRE)**^{22} 5339 10-8-4 55 oh10 .... MatthewCosham(7) 2 40
(L R James) a in rr 80/1

2m 11.96s (-1.74) **Going Correction** -0.20s/f (Firm)
WFA 3 from 4yo+ 6lb 8 Ran SP% 111.3
Speed ratings (Par 103): **98,95,95,93,92 90,89,87**
toteswingers: 1&2 £3.80, 1&3 £2.80, 2&3 £4.50 CSF £12.95 CT £56.82 TOTE £2.80: £1.30, £1.80, £2.00; EX 16.00.
Owner D Swales **Bred** P Monagnan And J Collins And G Dillon **Trained** Sheriff Hutton, N Yorks

FOCUS
A modest 58-69 apprentice handicap run at a sound pace and significantly the first two were one-two throughout. The form could have been rated a bit higher.

6018 TOTESWINGER MEDIAN AUCTION MAIDEN STKS 5f
3:00 (3:02) (Class 5) 2-Y-0 £3,238 (£963; £481; £240) Stalls Low

Form RPR
2 1 **Citrus Star (USA)**^{30} 5129 2-9-3 0 .... AlanMunro 2 84+
(C F Wall) mde all: rdn clr over 1f out: styd on strly 6/4^{1}
4252 2 4 1/2 **Key Art (IRE)**^{36} 4906 2-9-3 73 .... DarryllHolland 10 68
(J Noseda) cl up: effrt 2f out: sn rdn and ev ch: drvn appr fnl f and kpt on same pce 11/4^{2}
6 3 nse **Flaxen Lake**^{115} 2335 2-9-0 0 .... RussellKennemore(3) 4 68
(R Hollinshead) trckd ldrs: hdwy 2f out: nt clr run and swtchd rt over 1f out: sn rdn and kpt on ins fnl f 66/1
0350 4 nk **Kakapuka**^{43} 4647 2-9-3 68 .... JimmyQuinn 7 67
(Mrs A L M King) trckd ldrs: hdwy over 2f out: rdn wl over 1f out: kpt on u.p ins fnl f 10/1
34 5 1 **My Mandy (IRE)**^{22} 5337 2-8-7 67 .... Louis-PhilippeBeuzelin(5) 1 58
(Ian Williams) chsd ldrs on inner: rdn along 2f out: sn drvn and btn over 1f out 6/1^{3}
6 nk **Suranam** 2-9-3 0 .... LiamJones 3 66+
(W J Haggas) s.i.s and in rr: hdwy 2f out: nt clr run and hmpd over 1f out: sn swtchd rt and kpt on ins fnl f: bttr for r 9/1
350 7 3/4 **Bilash**^{8} 5763 2-9-3 0 .... GrahamGibbons 5 59
(R Hollinshead) cl up: rdn along over 2f out: drvn wl over 1f out: wknd ent fnl f 12/1
0 8 8 **Loss Leader (IRE)**^{140} 1623 2-9-3 0 .... DuranFentiman 8 30
(T D Easterby) chsd ldrs: rdn along over 2f out and sn wknd 80/1

0400 **9** 6 **Lady Bucket**[22] 5337 2-8-12 40........ TolleyDean 11 —
(Paul Green) *sn outpcd and a bhd* **100/1**

62.93 secs (-0.37) **Going Correction** -0.20s/f (Firm) **9** Ran SP% **111.5**
Speed ratings (Par 95): **94,86,86,86,84 84,82,70,60**
toteswingers: 1&2 £1.60, 1&3 £12.80, 2&3 £17.10 CSF £5.25 TOTE £2.30: £1.20, £1.30, £7.30; EX 4.60.
Owner Induna Racing Partners Two **Bred** Stephen McDonald **Trained** Newmarket, Suffolk
■ Stewards' Enquiry : Russell Kennemore one-day ban: careless riding (Oct 1)

FOCUS
This maiden has produced several subsequently decent sprinters in the recent past but this year's line-up looked just fair at best, judged on official ratings. The winner did it well but the runner-up is not progressing.

NOTEBOOK
Citrus Star(USA) had shown plenty of promise on his debut at Nottingham and built on that in emphatic fashion in the end. He made the most of his low draw and disputed the lead from the start but, after a brief hesitation when asked to go about his business, soon went clear and looks capable of further improvement with this behind him. (op 11-8 tchd 7-4 in places)
Key Art(IRE) had shown enough in four starts to suggest he could win a race like this and had every chance. He was no match for the winner but ran his race and, rated 73, helps set the standard, along with the fourth and fifth. (tchd 3-1)
Flaxen Lake, who had been absent since finishing well beaten on his debut in May, ran much better, keeping on nicely having tracked the leaders throughout. He should come on again for this and is one to watch for in handicaps once qualified.
Kakapuka ran pretty well considering he raced wide for most of the trip. He is probably worth another try in handicaps. (op 12-1)
My Mandy(IRE) has had plenty of experience and is consistent but does not appear to be improving. She is another who may be suited by going handicapping. (op 13-2)
Suranam showed a measure of ability despite running green.
Bilash ran close to previous form with the winner but does not appear to be getting home in his races and may need more time to develop. (op 14-1)

6019 SUBSCRIBE TO RACING UK ONLINE AT RACINGUK.TV H'CAP 1m 4y
3:30 (3:30) (Class 4) (0-80,80) 3-Y-0+ **£5,180** (£1,541; £770; £384) **Stalls** Low

Form RPR
5024 **1** **Kiwi Bay**[19] 5441 4-9-6 **78**........ DarryllHolland 9 87+
(M Dods) *dwlt: hld up and bhd: hdwy over 2f out: effrt and n.m.r over 1f out: squeezed through and rdn: styd on strly ins fnl f to ld nr fin* **9/1**
2050 **2** nk **Turn Me On (IRE)**[11] 5697 6-9-8 **80**........ GrahamGibbons 7 88
(T D Walford) *hld up: stdy hdwy 3f out qcknd to ld over 1f out: and sn rdn: drvn ins fnl f: hdd and no ex nr fin:* **14/1**
3 **3** 1 **Bibury**[7] 5810 3-8-10 **72**........ JimmyQuinn 5 78
(David P Myerscough, Ire) *in tch on inner: hdwy 3f out: swtchd rt and effrt to chse ldrs over 1f out: sn rdn and kpt on wl fnl f* **11/1**
6305 **4** 1 ¼ **Shadowtime**[20] 5395 4-8-4 **67**........ PaulPickard(5) 1 70
(Miss Tracy Waggott) *trckd ldrs on inner: effrt 2f out: rdn and squeezed through on rail to ld briefly 1 1/2f out: sn hdd and drvn: kpt on one pce* **11/4**[1]
06 **5** 1 ½ **Sarwin (USA)**[12] 5673 6-8-10 **68**........ RobertWinston 2 68+
(G A Swinbank) *led: pushed along and hdd 3f out: drvn wl over 1f out and grad wknd* **13/2**[3]
0454 **6** ½ **Tarzan (IRE)**[26] 5258 3-9-1 **77**........(b[1]) J-PGuillambert 3 76
(M Johnston) *chsd ldrs: rdn along over 2f out: sn drvn and no imp appr last* **5/1**[2]
0460 **7** ¾ **Samarinda (USA)**[141] 1603 6-9-8 **80**........ PaulEddery 4 77+
(Mrs P Sly) *hld up in rr: hdwy over 2f out: swtchd rt to chse ldrs whn n.m.r over 1f out: sn drvn and one pce* **16/1**
2020 **8** 4 ½ **Motafarred (IRE)**[40] 4801 7-9-8 **80**........ PhilipRobinson 8 67
(Micky Hammond) *chsd ldrs: rdn along 3f out: sn drvn and wknd* **8/1**
5330 **9** 1 ½ **Intersky Charm (USA)**[19] 5441 5-8-7 **68** oh2 ow2 RussellKennemore(3) 10 52
(R M Whitaker) *nvr bttr than midfield* **20/1**
400 **10** nse **Addikt (IRE)**[22] 5333 4-8-11 **74**........ PatrickDonaghy(5) 14 58
(G A Harker) *s.i.s: a in rr* **40/1**
3216 **11** 2 **Helieorbea**[12] 5677 3-8-13 **75**........ DuranFentiman 6 54
(T D Easterby) *a towards rr* **14/1**
2032 **12** 1 ¾ **Thunderball**[90] 3116 3-9-3 **79**........(b) TPO'Shea 12 54
(J A Glover) *t.k.h: cl up: led 3f out: rdn and hdd wl over 1f out: wknd qckly* **14/1**

1m 43.13s (-2.77) **Going Correction** -0.20s/f (Firm)
WFA 3 from 4yo+ 4lb **12** Ran SP% **119.2**
Speed ratings (Par 105): **105,104,103,102,100 100,99,95,93,93 91,89**
toteswingers: 1&2 £20.50, 1&3 £15.00, 2&3 £35.50 CSF £129.15 CT £1409.00 TOTE £9.70: £2.50, £4.10, £3.70; EX 108.40.
Owner Kiwi Racing **Bred** Templeton Stud **Trained** Denton, Co Durham

FOCUS
A competitive 67-87 handicap run at a very strong gallop and those who raced up with the pace didn't figure at the finish. Sound form, with a personal best from the winner.
Addikt(IRE) Official explanation: jockey said colt was unsuiited by the good to firm ground
Helieorbea Official explanation: jockey said gelding never travelled

6020 PONTEFRACT PARK FILLIES' H'CAP 6f
4:00 (4:00) (Class 3) (0-90,90) 3-Y-0+
£9,346 (£2,799; £1,399; £700; £349; £175) **Stalls** Low

Form RPR
2530 **1** **Invincible Isle (IRE)**[17] 5523 3-8-5 **77**........ JimmyQuinn 2 85+
(H R A Cecil) *trckd ldng pair on inner: hdwy 2f out: swtchd rt over 1f out: rdn and qcknd to ld ins fnl f: kpt on wl* **4/1**[3]
4346 **2** 1 ¾ **Misplaced Fortune**[11] 5697 4-8-1 **76** oh3..(v) Louis-PhilippeBeuzelin(5) 3 79
(N Tinkler) *trckd ldrs: hdwy wl over 1f out: sn rdn and kpt on ins fnl f* **6/1**
-212 **3** ½ **Russian Spirit**[56] 4227 3-8-9 **81**........ PhilipRobinson 6 83
(M A Jarvis) *led: rdn along 2f out: drvn over 1f out: hdd & wknd last 100yds* **3/1**[1]
0012 **4** 1 **Artistic License (IRE)**[4] 5901 4-9-5 **89**........ AlanMunro 4 88
(M R Channon) *sn pushed along and outpcd towards rr: hdwy 2f out: rdn wl over 1f out: kpt on ins fnl f: nrst fin* **7/2**[2]
0333 **5** 7 **Angus Newz**[2] 5973 6-9-6 **90**........ RobertWinston 5 68
(M Quinn) *chsd ldr: rdn along 2f out: sn drvn and wknd over 1f out* **5/1**
054 **6** 9 **Catalan Bay (AUS)**[28] 5182 5-8-6 **76** oh3........(bt[1]) TPO'Shea 1 27+
(J R Gask) *v.s.a: rdr lost iron and bhd: hdwy 1/2-way: rdn to chse ldrs on outer 2f out: sn wknd* **6/1**

1m 15.48s (-1.42) **Going Correction** -0.20s/f (Firm)
WFA 3 from 4yo+ 2lb **6** Ran SP% **112.5**
Speed ratings (Par 104): **101,98,98,96,87 75**
toteswingers: 1&2 £4.90, 1&3 £2.70, 2&3 £3.60 CSF £27.27 TOTE £4.60: £2.90, £3.30; EX 29.00.
Owner H E Sheikh Sultan Bin Khalifa Al Nahyan **Bred** Ascagnano S P A **Trained** Newmarket, Suffolk

FOCUS
An open-looking 72-90 fillies-only sprint handicap run at a very strong pace. A personal best from the winner in a pretty weak race for the grade.

NOTEBOOK
Invincible Isle(IRE), who took her maiden over 7f at Doncaster in June, was given a perfect lead in. She went in pursuit of the leader once in line for home and sealed victory in a matter of strides. This trip looks her best. Official explanation: trainer's rep said, regarding the apparent improvement in form shown, filly was better suited by today's stiffer track (op 15-2)
Misplaced Fortune, out of luck when the headgear was left off at York, made her effort towards the centre on straightening up had to run from 3lb out of the weights. She stuck to her guns to claim second spot near the line. Right at the top of her game, she deserves another success. (op 13-2 tchd 7-1)
Russian Spirit, raised 4lb after finishing runner-up on her handicap debut, was keen at the head of affairs. She hung right in the home straight and readily swept aside by the winner, she lost second near the line. She is all speed and worth a try over five. (op 9-4)
Artistic License(IRE), having her second outing in four days, as usual struggled to go the pace. She stuck on from halfway but might continue to struggle after being raised 6lb after her Goodwood success. (op 11-4)
Angus Newz, having her second outing in three days, was unable to dominate and ran poorly dropping right away in the home straight. (op 9-2 tchd 4-1)
Catalan Bay(AUS), in blinkers for the first time, blew the start and her rider seemed to have problems with his off-side iron. She ran much too keenly and, after getting on terms turning in, was soon on the retreat. She looks far from straightforward. Official explanation: jockey said mare jinked at start and he lost an iron (op 10-1 tchd 11-1)

6021 PONTEFRACT STAYERS CHAMPIONSHIP H'CAP (ROUND 6) 2m 1f 22y
4:30 (4:30) (Class 5) (0-75,75) 3-Y-0+ **£3,238** (£963; £481; £240) **Stalls** Low

Form RPR
3322 **1** **Theola (IRE)**[19] 5430 3-8-12 **71**........ JimmyQuinn 5 80
(M H Tompkins) *hld up: smooth hdwy 4f out: trckd ldrs over 2f out: rdn to chal over 1f out: led jst ins fnl f: sn drvn and edgd rt: kpt on wl* **4/1**[1]
35 **2** 1 ½ **Zuwaar**[17] 5530 4-9-3 **69**........(tp) Louis-PhilippeBeuzelin(5) 4 76
(Ian Williams) *hld up and bhd: stdy hdwy over 4f out: chsd ldrs on outer over 2f out: rdnto chal over 1f out and ev ch tl drvn and no ex wl ins fnl f* **5/1**[3]
2204 **3** 4 ½ **Mystified (IRE)**[16] 5554 6-8-9 **59** oh5 ow2........(tp) NeilBrown(3) 7 61
(R F Fisher) *led: rdn along 3f out: drvn over 1f out: hdd jst ins fnl f and wknd* **16/1**
2422 **4** 2 ¾ **Jackday (IRE)**[16] 5554 4-8-10 **62**........ BMcHugh(5) 11 60+
(T D Easterby) *hld up: hdwy over 4f out: rdn over 2f out: plugged on: nvr nr ldrs* **4/1**[1]
2021 **5** 6 **Promise Maker (USA)**[13] 5625 4-9-6 **67**........ GrahamGibbons 8 58
(T D Walford) *trckd ldrs: effrt and hdwy 3f out: rdn to chse ldr 2f out: sn drvn and wknd* **9/2**[2]
/050 **6** 10 **Secret Ploy**[32] 5068 9-9-4 **65**........ TravisBlock 1 44
(H Morrison) *in tch: rdn along 1/2-way: drvn and outpcd fnl 4f* **14/1**
/20- **7** nk **Kanpai (IRE)**[343] 6606 7-8-11 **58**........ SJCraine 3 37
(J G M O'Shea) *trckd ldrs on inner: effrt 4f out: rdn along 3f out and sn btn* **15/2**
6230 **8** 29 **Haldibari (IRE)**[32] 5068 5-8-10 **57** oh2........ TPO'Shea 10 1
(S Lycett) *prom: rdn along 5f out: sn wknd* **14/1**
43/0 **9** 11 **Brads House (IRE)**[33] 5028 7-9-9 **75**........ ByronMoorcroft(5) 2 6
(J G M O'Shea) *a in rr: bhd fnl 4f* **33/1**
6041 **10** 15 **Trempari**[15] 5579 6-8-10 **57** oh5........(b) RobertWinston 9 —
(Mike Murphy) *cl up: rdn along 5f out: drvn 3f out: sn wknd and bhd* **9/1**

3m 43.38s (-6.62) **Going Correction** -0.20s/f (Firm)
WFA 3 from 4yo+ 12lb **10** Ran SP% **118.8**
Speed ratings (Par 103): **107,106,104,102,100 95,95,81,76,69**
toteswingers: 1&2 £6.40, 1&3 £17.90, 2&3 £18.70 CSF £24.52 CT £292.86 TOTE £4.20: £1.60, £2.40, £5.20; EX 27.40.
Owner Robert M Jones **Bred** Richard Klay And Dr M Klay **Trained** Newmarket, Suffolk

FOCUS
A modest 57-75 stayers' handicap and the pace was very sound. The form makes sense.
Trempari Official explanation: trainer's rep said gelding boiled over in the preliminaries

6022 BOOK YOUR CHRISTMAS PARTY HERE ON 0113 2876387 MAIDEN STKS 1m 2f 6y
5:00 (5:00) (Class 5) 3-Y-0+ **£3,238** (£963; £481; £240) **Stalls** Low

Form RPR
2 **1** **Alainmaar (FR)**[19] 5435 3-9-3 0........ TPO'Shea 10 99+
(M A Jarvis) *cl up: led after 3f: rdn clr over 1f out: kpt on strly* **1/2**[1]
2 12 **Feathered Crown (FR)**[252] 3-9-3 0........ IanMongan 3 76+
(H R A Cecil) *trckd ldrs: cl up fr 1/2-way: rdn along over 2f out: drvn wl over 1f out: kpt on: no ch w wnr* **9/1**[3]
50 **3** 9 **Obara D'Avril (FR)**[11] 5694 7-9-4 0........ MHNaughton 4 52+
(S G West) *in tch: hdwy on outer to chse ldrs 1/2-way: rdn over 3f out: drvn over 2f out: plugged on same pce* **50/1**
452 **4** 1 ¾ **Freda's Rose (IRE)**[10] 5730 5-9-1 0........ RussellKennemore(3) 7 46
(O Brennan) *prom 2f: pushed along and lost pl 1/2-way: rdn and sme hdwy over 2f out: plugged on: nvr a factor* **33/1**
60 **5** 10 **Convitezza**[17] 5520 3-8-9 0........ NeilBrown(3) 2 26
(M E Sowersby) *s.i.s: a bhd: t.o fnl 3f* **100/1**
-226 **6** 2 **Capeability (IRE)**[155] 1291 3-9-3 90........ AlanMunro 9 27
(M R Channon) *prom: rdn along 3f out: drvn over 2f out and sn wknd* **5/2**[2]
06 **7** 1 **Mistic Academy (IRE)**[34] 4974 4-9-4 0........ DuranFentiman 8 20
(Miss J E Foster) *led 3f: chsd ldrs: rdn along over 3f out: sn wknd* **100/1**
8 12 **Falcon's Tribute (IRE)**[17] 7-8-13 0........ PaulPickard(5) 5 —
(P Salmon) *s.i.s: t.k.h and sn in tch: rdn along over 3f out and sn wknd* **100/1**
0 **9** 39 **Billy Simmonds**[15] 5572 4-9-9 0........ JimmyQuinn 6 —
(Miss J Feilden) *a bhd: t.o fnl 3f* **100/1**

2m 9.81s (-3.89) **Going Correction** -0.20s/f (Firm)
WFA 3 from 4yo+ 6lb **9** Ran SP% **114.1**
Speed ratings (Par 103): **107,97,90,88,80 79,78,68,37**
toteswingers: 1&2 £2.20, 1&3 £5.60, 2&3 £11.50 CSF £6.15 TOTE £1.40: £1.02, £1.80, £5.10; EX 5.40.
Owner Hamdan Al Maktoum **Bred** Fares Stables Ltd **Trained** Newmarket, Suffolk

FOCUS
Just three to consider seriously in this maiden. The winner certainly impressed but beat little.

6023 SUPPORT THE MALTON FIRE DISASTER APPEAL H'CAP 1m 4y
5:30 (5:30) (Class 5) (0-70,70) 3-Y-0+ **£3,238** (£963; £481; £240) **Stalls** Low

Form RPR
2110 **1** **Wiseman's Diamond (USA)**[20] 5395 4-9-3 **65**........ GrahamGibbons 6 73
(P T Midgley) *hld up in rr: stdy hdwy 3f out: rdn to chse ldrs over 1f out: drvn to ld last 100yds: styd on wl* **4/1**[1]

1136 **2** *nk* **Diamond Daisy (IRE)**[12] 5672 3-9-2 **68**.............................. SJCraine 11 76+
(Mrs A Duffield) *hld up: hdwy 3f out: effrt and nt clr run wl over 1f out: sn swtchd lft and hmpd: swtchd rt and styd on u.p to chal ins fnl f: nt qckn nr fin* **18/1**

0642 **3** *2 1/4* **Aussie Blue (IRE)**[19] 5441 5-8-13 **64**.................. RussellKennemore(3) 7 66
(R M Whitaker) *trckd ldrs: hdwy over 2f out: rdn over 1f out: led ent fnl f and sn drvn: hdd and no ex last 100yds* **5/1**[2]

1601 **4** *3/4* **Chadwell Spring (IRE)**[7] 5803 3-9-3 **69** 6ex.................... JimmyQuinn 8 72+
(Miss J Feilden) *hld up in rr: stdy hdwy 3f out: chsd ldrs and n.m.r whn swtchd ins wl over 1f out: sn rdn and nt clr run ent fnl f: kpt on towards fin* **15/2**[3]

4600 **5** *hd* **Black Dahlia**[44] 4619 4-9-2 **64**.. TPO'Shea 16 64
(J A Glover) *sn led: rdn along over 2f out: drvn and hdd ent fnl f: grad wknd* **14/1**

6305 **6** *2* **Mutually Mine (USA)**[19] 5449 3-9-0 **66**............................. PaulEddery 3 62
(Mrs P Sly) *dwlt and towards rr: hdwy over 3f out: rdn to chse ldrs over 1f out: n.m.r ent fnl f: sn drvn and wknd* **11/1**

4431 **7** *1/2* **Cheers For Thea (IRE)**[12] 5683 4-9-1 **63**.............(bt) DuranFentiman 17 58
(T D Easterby) *towards rr: hdwy over 2f out: rdn over 1f out: kpt on ins fnl f: nrst fin* **9/1**

1010 **8** *nk* **Betteras Bertie**[43] 4663 6-9-6 **68**............................... AlanMunro 13 62
(M Brittain) *s.i.s and bhd tl styd on fnl 2f: nrst fin* **18/1**

0520 **9** *2 1/4* **Diamond Lass (IRE)**[39] 4822 4-8-7 **60**............................ BMcHugh(5) 9 49
(R A Fahey) *a in midfield* **12/1**

5530 **10** *1 3/4* **Mister Jingles**[59] 4140 6-8-9 **57**.................................... J-PGuillambert 10 42
(R M Whitaker) *chsd ldrs: rdn along 3f out: grad wknd* **16/1**

6150 **11** *7* **Natural Rhythm (IRE)**[25] 5289 4-8-8 **56** oh3...........(b) RobertWinston 2 26
(Mrs R A Carr) *cl up: rdn along over 2f out: sn edgd rt and grad wknd* **20/1**

0400 **12** *2* **Know By Now**[26] 5258 3-8-5 **60**...............................(b[1]) DominicFox(3) 5 26
(T P Tate) *chsd ldrs on inner: rdn along over 2f out: drvn wl over 1f out and sn wknd* **25/1**

5305 **13** *14* **Border Owl (IRE)**[78] 3496 4-9-3 **70**............................. PaulPickard(5) 14 5
(P Salmon) *dwlt: a in rr* **10/1**

0-30 **14** *2 1/4* **Ella Woodcock (IRE)**[22] 5333 5-9-8 **70**............................ IanMongan 12 —
(E J Alston) *chsd ldrs on outer: rdn along 3f out: sn wknd* **14/1**

0010 **15** *11* **Barataria**[19] 5441 7-9-5 **70**.. NeilBrown(3) 4 —
(R Bastiman) *rrd and lost many l s: a bhd* **16/1**

1m 43.85s (-2.05) **Going Correction** -0.20s/f (Firm) **15** Ran SP% **127.8**
WFA 3 from 4yo+ 4lb
Speed ratings (Par 103): **102,101,99,98,98 96,96,95,93,91 84,82,68,66,55**
toteswingers: 1&2 £18.00, 1&3 £7.30, 2&3 £22.10 CSF £83.44 CT £385.09 TOTE £5.50: £2.10, £5.70, £2.30; EX 76.10 Place 6: £155.91 Place 5: £100.07.
Owner D I Perry **Bred** Hatta Bloodstock International **Trained** Westow, N Yorks

FOCUS
A modest 56-70 handicap run at a sound pace and plenty of traffic problems early in the home straight. Another solid effort from the winner.
Barataria Official explanation: jockey said gelding missed the break
T/Plt: £139.70 to a £1 stake. Pool: £42,517.19. 222.15 winning tickets. T/Qpdt: £91.30 to a £1 stake. Pool: £2,938.69. 23.80 winning tickets. JR

5881 WOLVERHAMPTON (A.W) (L-H)
Thursday, September 17

OFFICIAL GOING: Standard
Wind: Almost nil Weather: Cloudy

6024 WILLIAMHILL.COM/BONUS25 - GET £25 FREE BET CLAIMING STKS 7f 32y(P)
5:40 (5:42) (Class 5) 3-Y-O+ **£2,914** (£867; £433; £216) **Stalls** High

Form RPR

3360 **1** **Aeroplane**[131] 1861 6-9-10 **101**.. JamieSpencer 7 102+
(S A Callaghan) *hld up in mid-div: smooth prog 2f out: rdn to ld wl ins fnl f: cleverly* **4/5**[1]

2630 **2** *3/4* **Orpenindeed (IRE)**[69] 3795 6-9-2 **87**................................ SebSanders 2 92
(M Botti) *w ldr: led jst over 2f out: rdn jst over 1f out: hdd wl ins fnl f: nt qckn* **13/2**[2]

3430 **3** *2 1/4* **Autumn Blades (IRE)**[20] 5404 4-8-12 **75**......................... DavidProbert 6 82
(A Bailey) *a.p: edgd lft and rdn wl over 1f out: one pce ins fnl f* **20/1**

1060 **4** *2* **Beauchamp Viceroy**[5] 5887 5-9-8 **82**.....................(tp) DaneO'Neill 1 86
(G A Butler) *led: hdd jst over 2f out: rdn over 1f out: wknd ins fnl f* **8/1**[3]

2005 **5** *3/4* **Gallantry**[14] 5615 7-9-8 **87**... JerryO'Dwyer 5 84
(P Howling) *hld up in tch: pushed along over 2f out: rdn wl over 1f out: wknd fnl f* **12/1**

3330 **6** *1 1/2* **Statute Book (IRE)**[15] 5574 3-8-9 **72**............................. JamesDoyle 10 69
(S Kirk) *hld up in rr: hdwy wl over 1f out: rdn and one pce fnl f* **40/1**

3000 **7** *1/2* **Obe Royal**[1] 5991 5-8-9 **69**...(b) PatCosgrave 11 66
(P D Evans) *s.i.s: hld up towards rr: rdn and sme prog wl over 1f out: no hdwy fnl f* **40/1**

5662 **8** *3/4* **Royal Envoy (IRE)**[14] 5612 6-8-11 **66**......................... TobyAtkinson(7) 3 73
(P Howling) *hld up in tch: pushed along over 2f out: rdn and wknd wl over 1f out* **40/1**

3046 **9** *1 3/4* **Flawed Genius**[17] 5522 4-9-6 **86**..(t) KFallon 12 72+
(K A Ryan) *s.s: pushed along 3f out: rdn 1f out: a in rr* **8/1**[3]

0405 **10** *6* **Sea Land (FR)**[12] 5676 5-8-8 **60**.................................... SteveDrowne 8 44+
(B Ellison) *hld up in mid-div: pushed along 3f out: bhd fnl 2f* **40/1**

0160 **11** *4* **Zennerman (IRE)**[12] 5683 6-8-5 **55**......................(v) AhmedAjtebi(3) 9 31
(W M Brisbourne) *hld up in mid-div: pushed along over 2f out: c wd bnd wl over 1f out: sn bhd* **100/1**

0000 **12** *60* **Alan Devonshire**[47] 4526 4-9-4 **69**................................ GeorgeBaker 4 —
(M H Tompkins) *plld hrd: hdwy over 5f out: sddle slipped and rn wd bnd 3f out: sn eased* **33/1**

1m 27.21s (-2.39) **Going Correction** -0.125s/f (Stan) **12** Ran SP% **117.3**
WFA 3 from 4yo+ 3lb
Speed ratings (Par 103): **108,107,104,102,101 99,99,98,96,89 84,16**
toteswingers: 1&2 £1.70, 1&3 £6.70, 2&3 £15.70 CSF £5.55 TOTE £1.60: £1.10, £2.60, £4.10; EX 9.20.Aeroplane was subject to a friendly claim.
Owner Saleh Al Homaizi & Imad Al Sagar **Bred** C R Mason **Trained** Newmarket, Suffolk

FOCUS
An above-average claimer run at just a fair gallop, with three of the first four (but not the winner) racing with the pace.
Statute Book(IRE) Official explanation: jockey said colt was hampered soon after start
Flawed Genius Official explanation: jockey said gelding hung left

Alan Devonshire Official explanation: jockey said gelding ran too freely and saddle slipped

6025 WILLIAMHILL.COM/BONUS25 - POKER TOURNAMENTS H'CAP 1m 5f 194y(P)
6:10 (6:12) (Class 6) (0-60,60) 3-Y-O+ **£2,047** (£604; £302) **Stalls** Low

Form RPR

0510 **1** **Leyte Gulf (USA)**[16] 5554 6-9-6 **56**.. DaneO'Neill 5 66+
(C C Bealby) *hld up towards rr: stdy prog over 3f out: swtchd lft to ins rail wl over 1f out: led 1f out: drvn out* **16/1**

2023 **2** *1* **Debdene Bank (IRE)**[27] 5229 6-9-8 **58**......................... GeorgeBaker 13 67
(Mrs Mary Hambro) *hld up in mid-div: stdy hdwy over 5f out: rdn 2f out: ev ch 1f out: edgd lft and nt qckn ins fnl f* **16/1**

0/00 **3** *3* **Bute Street**[14] 5617 4-8-9 **48**... MCGeran(3) 2 53
(R J Hodges) *led early: chsd ldr over 5f: prom: pushed along over 3f out: rdn wl over 1f out: one pce fnl f* **50/1**

6631 **4** *shd* **Snowberry Hill (USA)**[5] 5885 6-9-5 **55** 6ex............................ KFallon 9 60
(Lucinda Featherstone) *t.k.h in tch: jnd ldrs over 2f out: ev ch 1f out: one pce* **5/2**[1]

445 **5** *1* **Bernabeu (IRE)**[38] 4857 7-9-5 **55**.. JamesDoyle 6 58
(S Curran) *sn led: rdn over 2f out: hdd 1f out: wknd ins fnl f* **25/1**

4-40 **6** *1/2* **Dark Energy**[8] 4862 5-9-10 **60**....................................(t) PatCosgrave 3 63
(M J Scudamore) *s.s: hld up in rr: pushed along wl over 2f out: rdn wl over 1f out: styd on fnl f: n.d* **40/1**

3-00 **7** *1 1/2* **Alvee (IRE)**[17] 5530 4-9-10 **60**.....................................(v[1]) JamieSpencer 7 60
(J R Fanshawe) *a.p: rdn and ev ch over 2f out: wknd over 1f out* **10/1**

5662 **8** *shd* **Little Carmela**[18] 5483 5-9-3 **60**...................................... TobyAtkinson(7) 8 60
(S C Williams) *hld up towards rr: rdn wl over 2f out: nvr nr ldrs* **6/1**[2]

6000 **9** *shd* **Thorny Mandate**[12] 5680 7-8-13 **49**................................. LiamJones 11 49
(W M Brisbourne) *t.k.h in rr: pushed along and short-lived effrt on ins over 2f out* **25/1**

0432 **10** *3/4* **Annambo**[12] 5680 9-9-7 **57**...(p) StephenCarson 1 56
(Andrew Reid) *prom: pushed along over 2f out: rdn and wknd fnl f* **11/1**

3333 **11** *1 1/2* **Dontpaytheferryman (USA)**[25] 5294 4-8-11 **50** MichaelJStainton(3) 10 47+
(R A Fahey) *plld hrd: sddle sn slipped: a in rr* **6/1**[2]

5054 **12** *nse* **Swords**[12] 5680 7-9-0 **50**.. SebSanders 4 47
(R E Peacock) *s.i.s: sn hld up in mid-div: pushed along over 3f out: wknd over 2f out* **8/1**

0004 **13** *1* **Good Effect (USA)**[23] 3348 5-8-13 **49**................................(t) ShaneKelly 12 45
(Tim Vaughan) *s.s: a in rr* **15/2**[3]

3m 9.68s (3.68) **Going Correction** -0.125s/f (Stan) **13** Ran SP% **121.3**
Speed ratings (Par 101): **84,83,81,81,81 80,79,79,79,79 78,78,77**
toteswingers: 1&2 not won, 1&3 not won, 2&3 not won. CSF £244.19 CT £11856.43 TOTE £21.00: £6.50, £6.60, £24.40; EX 304.70.
Owner Robert Jenkinson **Bred** Paradigm Thoroughbred Inc **Trained** Barrowby, Lincs

FOCUS
The pace was weak, even for 1m6f, and only quickened three furlongs out.
Leyte Gulf(USA) Official explanation: trainer's rep said, regarding the apparent improvement in form shown, gelding was better suited by the drop in trip
Dontpaytheferryman(USA) Official explanation: jockey said saddle slipped

6026 EUROPEAN BREEDERS' FUND MEDIAN AUCTION MAIDEN STKS 5f 216y(P)
6:40 (6:41) (Class 5) 2-Y-O **£3,561** (£1,059; £529; £264) **Stalls** Low

Form RPR

1 **Armour**[12] 5690 2-9-3 0.. JamieSpencer 7 77+
(M J Grassick, Ire) *led early: a.p: pushed along whn n.m.r over 1f out: led wl ins fnl f: r.o* **11/10**[1]

43 **2** *3/4* **Barlaman (USA)**[15] 5571 2-9-0 0................................(t) AhmedAjtebi(3) 8 74
(Saeed Bin Suroor) *sn led: rdn and hdd wl ins fnl f: nt qckn* **4/1**[3]

6 **3** *nk* **Blue Lyric**[18] 5478 2-8-12 0.. KFallon 9 68
(L M Cumani) *sn w ldr: rdn and ev ch ins fnl f: sn edgd rt: nt qckn* **3/1**[2]

4 *7* **Servetius (USA)** 2-9-3 0.. DaneO'Neill 3 52+
(G A Butler) *s.i.s: hld up in rr: rdn wl over 1f out: kpt on to take 4th nr fin* **10/1**

50 **5** *shd* **Holkham**[34] 5000 2-9-3 0.. ChrisCatlin 6 52
(N P Littmoden) *s.i.s: hld up towards rr: pushed along over 1f out: kpt on ins fnl f: n.d* **66/1**

0 **6** *nse* **Luck Of The Draw (IRE)**[7] 5807 2-9-3 0............................ SebSanders 2 51
(Sir Mark Prescott) *hld up towards rr: pushed along over 2f out: nvr nr ldrs* **20/1**

00 **7** *3/4* **R Woody**[21] 5368 2-9-3 0.. SteveDrowne 5 49
(Mrs L C Jewell) *hld up in tch: pushed along over 2f out: wknd over 1f out* **100/1**

0 **8** *1* **Kanace**[14] 5611 2-9-3 0.. ShaneKelly 1 46
(Ian Williams) *hld up in mid-div: short-lived effrt on ins 2f out* **66/1**

9 *3/4* **Atherton (IRE)** 2-9-3 0.. PatCosgrave 4 44
(J G Given) *s.i.s: sn hld up in mid-div: hdwy over 2f out: rdn and wknd over 1f out* **33/1**

1m 15.82s (0.82) **Going Correction** -0.125s/f (Stan) **9** Ran SP% **113.4**
Speed ratings (Par 95): **89,88,87,78,78 78,77,75,74**
toteswingers: 1&2 £1.10, 1&3 £1.70, 2&3 £2.40 CSF £5.43 TOTE £1.90: £1.10, £1.80, £1.10; EX 5.20.
Owner Mrs S Grassick **Bred** The National Stud **Trained** Pollardstown, Co Kildare

FOCUS
The first three, who finished clear, all set a reasonable standard for the track.

NOTEBOOK
Armour, an Irish challenger, ran respectably in a valuable Leopardstown maiden first time out. Though he took the drop from 7f to 6f in his stride, this Azamour half-brother to a winner at around 1m should stay further as he matures, and the way he quickened through a narrow gap to win showed plenty of courage considering his lack of experience. (op 6-5 tchd 5-4 in places)
Barlaman(USA), wearing a tongue-tie for the first time, controlled it in front but he did not corner that sharply into the straight and was done for finishing speed. He is capable of winning a run-of-the-mill maiden but is now qualified for nurseries. (op 100-30 tchd 3-1 and 9-2)
Blue Lyric's only previous race was on turf, but this was an encouraging switch to Polytrack. She finished close to the first two, but well clear of the rest, suggesting she can win an all-weather maiden. (tchd 7-2)
Servetius(USA), who changed hands for £30,000 earlier this year, is a half-brother to six winners up to 1m1f, and his sire Eurosilver was a good performer in the US either side of 1m. This good-looking sort made a satisfactory debut and should do better with racing. (tchd 12-1)
Holkham is now qualified for nurseries, and they should be more suitable than maidens.

Luck Of The Draw(IRE), a 60,000euros yearling brother of no fewer than four winners from 6f to 1m6f, including one over hurdles, runs as if he needs 7f already. However, he looks a potential improver and should be monitored. (op 16-1)

6027 WILLIAMHILL.COM/BONUS25 - QUOTE BONUS25 H'CAP 1m 5f 194y(P)
7:10 (7:11) (Class 5) (0-75,75) 3-Y-O **£2,914** (£867; £433; £216) **Stalls** Low

Form RPR
0434 1 **Worth A King'S**[12] 5667 3-9-7 **73**.....(v) RyanMoore 2 82
(Sir Michael Stoute) *led early: chsd ldr: led 2f out: hrd rdn and wnt clr jst over 1f out: styd on wl* **11/4**[2]
6126 2 4 ½ **Dice (IRE)**[14] 5593 3-9-9 **75**..... KFallon 4 79+
(L M Cumani) *hld up: pushed along over 3f out: hdwy over 1f out: wnt 2nd wl ins fnl f: no ch w wnr* **5/2**[1]
1132 3 1 **Air Maze**[14] 5593 3-9-8 **74**..... SebSanders 5 75
(Sir Mark Prescott) *hld up: hdwy on ins over 3f out: rdn wl over 1f out: sn chsng wnr: no imp: lost 2nd: wl ins fnl f* **7/2**[3]
654 4 1 **Westlin' Winds (IRE)**[32] 5061 3-9-5 **71**..... SteveDrowne 3 71
(C R Egerton) *prom: rdn wl over 1f out: sn btn* **14/1**
5035 5 7 **Merchant Man**[19] 5442 3-8-4 **56** oh1.....(p) MartinDwyer 1 46
(J D Bethell) *sn led: pushed along and hdd 2f out: wknd over 1f out* **14/1**
-511 6 ¾ **Sparkaway**[65] 3962 3-8-8 **60**..... ChrisCatlin 6 49
(W J Musson) *hld up in rr: pushed along over 3f out: sn struggling* **4/1**

3m 4.41s (-1.59) **Going Correction** -0.125s/f (Stan) **6** Ran SP% **110.8**
Speed ratings (Par 101): **99,96,95,95,91 90**
toteswingers: 1&2 £5.20, 1&3 £4.80, 2&3 £1.02 CSF £9.77 TOTE £3.20: £2.20, £1.80; EX 9.80.
Owner Mrs Denis Haynes **Bred** Wretham Stud **Trained** Newmarket, Suffolk

FOCUS
There was a modest gallop until halfway in this ordinary handicap.

6028 WILLIAMHILL.COM/BONUS25 - LIVE CASINO DEALERS H'CAP 5f 216y(P)
7:40 (7:40) (Class 5) (0-70,70) 3-Y-O+ **£2,914** (£867; £433; £216) **Stalls** Low

Form RPR
2604 1 **Billy Red**[6] 5836 5-9-1 **65**.....(b) FergusSweeney 6 75
(J R Jenkins) *mde all: rdn ins fnl f: r.o wl* **13/2**[3]
400 2 1 ¼ **Tudor Prince (IRE)**[34] 5001 5-9-2 **66**..... ShaneKelly 5 72+
(A W Carroll) *s.i.s: sn hld up in mid-div: rdn and r.o wl ins fnl f: tk 2nd post* **11/1**
2301 3 shd **Gurteen Diamond**[5] 5882 3-8-10 **67** 6ex..... RichardEvans(5) 7 73+
(P D Evans) *hld up in mid-div: stdy hdwy over 3f out: rdn and r.o ins fnl f: tk 3rd post* **13/2**[3]
4203 4 hd **Espy**[6] 5836 4-9-3 **67**..... GeorgeBaker 2 72+
(S Kirk) *s.i.s: sn hld up in mid-div: hdwy on ins wl over 1f out: r.o ins fnl f* **10/3**[1]
4106 5 ½ **Chasca (IRE)**[17] 5525 3-9-0 **66**..... KFallon 1 69
(Mrs A J Perrett) *chsd wnr over 1f: prom: wnt 2nd again wl over 1f out: rdn ins fnl f: no ex and lost 2nd cl home* **15/2**
2052 6 1 ½ **Convince (USA)**[13] 5632 8-8-10 **60**..... ChrisCatlin 4 59+
(K M Prendergast) *s.i.s: hld up towards rr: sme hdwy on ins wl over 1f out: rdn and no further prog fnl f* **6/1**[2]
2234 7 hd **Halaak (USA)**[29] 5164 3-8-9 **64**.....(b) AhmedAjtebi(3) 8 62
(D M Simcock) *hld up in tch: fdd ins fnl f* **14/1**
606 8 1 ½ **Fyodor (IRE)**[12] 5678 8-9-0 **64**.....(v) PatCosgrave 13 57
(P D Evans) *hld up in rr: pushed along over 1f out: nvr nrr* **16/1**
0600 9 ½ **Bahamian Bliss**[27] 5225 4-8-7 **57**..... SteveDrowne 12 49
(J A R Toller) *towards rr: pushed along over 3f out: rdn jst over 1f out: n.d* **50/1**
11P1 10 ¾ **Kheley (IRE)**[13] 5626 3-9-4 **70**..... LiamJones 3 59
(W M Brisbourne) *prom: chsd wnr over 4f out tl pushed along wl over 1f out: wknd ins fnl f* **9/1**
6004 11 2 ¼ **Stormburst (IRE)**[108] 2534 5-8-6 **56** oh11..... DavidProbert 10 38
(A J Chamberlain) *hld up towards rr: pushed along over 2f out: no rspnse* **50/1**
4515 12 1 ¼ **Steel City Boy (IRE)**[175] 971 6-9-6 **70**..... DaneO'Neill 9 48
(D Shaw) *hld up in mid-div: pushed along and wknd over 1f out* **14/1**
000 13 ¾ **Punching**[14] 5612 5-9-3 **67**..... SimonWhitworth 11 43
(C R Dore) *a towards rr* **33/1**

1m 13.65s (-1.35) **Going Correction** -0.125s/f (Stan)
WFA 3 from 4yo+ 2lb **13** Ran SP% **120.2**
Speed ratings (Par 103): **104,102,102,101,101 99,99,97,96,95 92,90,89**
toteswingers: 1&2 £45.30, 1&3 £13.80, 2&3 £15.60 CSF £75.89 CT £488.16 TOTE £7.50: £3.70, £2.90, £2.50; EX 72.30.
Owner Mrs Irene Hampson **Bred** D R Tucker **Trained** Royston, Herts

FOCUS
Races in which Billy Red makes it are invariably run at a good tempo, and this was no exception.
Tudor Prince(IRE) Official explanation: jockey said gelding missed the break
Convince(USA) Official explanation: jockey said gelding reared up in stalls

6029 WILLIAM HILL 0800 444040 - GET £25 FREE BET MAIDEN FILLIES' STKS 1m 141y(P)
8:10 (8:13) (Class 5) 3-Y-O+ **£2,729** (£806; £403) **Stalls** Low

Form RPR
2620 1 **Lady Francesca**[16] 5562 3-8-12 94..... MartinDwyer 2 80+
(W R Muir) *chsd ldr: led jst over 2f out: pushed along over 5f out: readily* **2/5**[1]
232 2 1 ¾ **Expressive**[27] 5228 3-8-12 69..... RyanMoore 8 74
(Sir Michael Stoute) *hld up in mid-div: hdwy on ins over 2f out: rdn and chsd wnr over 5f out: nt qckn ins fnl f* **3/1**[2]
3 3 3 **Cappagh Strand (USA)**[9] 5747 3-8-12 0.....(t) KFallon 3 67
(David P Myerscough, Ire) *a.p: chsd wnr 2f out tl over 1f out: sn rdn: one pce* **7/1**[3]
0- 4 8 **Bonnie Bea**[274] 7708 3-8-12 0..... ShaneKelly 6 49+
(B I Case) *hld up in mid-div: pushed along over 3f out: rdn wl over 1f out: tk modest 4th cl home* **33/1**
0 5 nk **Barathea's Acclaim**[15] 5572 3-8-12 0..... DaneO'Neill 5 48
(P R Hedger) *s.i.s: hld up towards rr: hdwy on ins 2f out: sn rdn: wknd over 1f out* **33/1**
64 6 1 ½ **Herecomethegirls**[22] 5348 3-8-5 0..... MalinHolmberg(7) 9 45
(M L W Bell) *a towards rr* **20/1**
6 7 ¾ **Broughtons Point**[18] 5482 3-8-12 0..... ChrisCatlin 10 43
(W J Musson) *stdd s: hld up in rr: nvr nr ldrs* **50/1**
0-00 8 3 **Spin Sister**[13] 5628 3-8-12 40..... JerryO'Dwyer 11 36
(J Gallagher) *prom: pushed along 3f out: wknd wl over 1f out* **33/1**
0000 9 17 **Pinewood Lulu**[1] 5983 4-8-12 43.....(b) MarkCoumbe(5) 1 —
(S A Harris) *led: rdn and hdd jst over 2f out: wknd qckly wl over 1f out* **40/1**

1m 49.42s (-1.08) **Going Correction** -0.125s/f (Stan)
WFA 3 from 4yo 5lb **9** Ran SP% **126.9**
Speed ratings (Par 100): **99,97,94,87,87 86,85,82,67**
toteswingers: 1&2 £1.20, 1&3 £1.20, 2&3 £2.40 CSF £2.09 TOTE £1.40: £1.02, £1.20, £1.50; EX 2.30.
Owner David & Gwyn Joseph **Bred** The Duke Of Devonshire & Floors Farming **Trained** Lambourn, Berks

FOCUS
There was a decent gallop, which sorted out the better runners from the rest, and the first three finished clear.
Herecomethegirls Official explanation: jockey said, regarding the running and riding, her orders wer e to keep the filly balanced , not run too wide and push her out with hands and heels in the home straight; trainer's rep confirmed this adding that the filly appeared to be outclassed and that the jockey was having just her fifth ride.

6030 WILLIAMHILL.COM/BONUS25 - PLAY VEGAS GAMES CONDITIONS STKS 1m 141y(P)
8:40 (8:40) (Class 3) 3-Y-O+ **£7,569** (£2,265; £1,132; £566; £282) **Stalls** Low

Form RPR
1-12 1 **Gitano Hernando**[132] 1822 3-8-9 104..... KFallon 7 114+
(M Botti) *a.p: pushed along and wnt 2nd 2f out: led over 1f out: rdn out* **3/1**[2]
2300 2 2 **Mia's Boy**[28] 5200 5-9-0 104..... RyanMoore 5 110
(C A Dwyer) *hld up towards rr: hdwy 2f out: rdn and chsd wnr jst over 2f out: no imp* **6/1**
3012 3 nk **Khor Dubai (IRE)**[17] 5529 3-8-9 102.....(v) TedDurcan 3 109
(Saeed Bin Suroor) *hld up in tch: rdn over 1f out: nt qckn ins fnl f* **9/1**
2536 4 4 ½ **Cesare**[19] 5426 8-9-0 114..... JamieSpencer 4 99
(J R Fanshawe) *hld up towards rr: pushed along over 2f out: hdwy wl over 1f out: sn rdn: nvr trbld ldrs* **2/1**[1]
14- 5 nk **Acclaimed (IRE)**[362] 6123 4-9-0 103..... ShaneKelly 6 99
(J Noseda) *hld up: stdy hdwy 6f out: pushed along wl over 2f out: wknd wl over 1f out* **16/1**
21 6 2 ¼ **Foolin Myself**[21] 5375 4-9-0 100.....(b) TPQueally 2 94
(M L W Bell) *w ldr: led on bit over 3f out: shkn up and hdd over 1f out: fnd nil: rdn and wknd fnl f* **9/2**[3]
330- 7 1 ½ **Metropolitan Man**[468] 2788 6-9-0 104..... FergusSweeney 9 91
(D M Simcock) *hld up towards rr: stdy prog over 2f out: wknd wl over 1f out* **40/1**
500P 8 4 ½ **Muhannak (IRE)**[12] 5662 5-9-0 109.....(b) GeorgeBaker 11 81
(R M Beckett) *swtchd lft to ins sn after s: hld up in rr: pushed along over 3f out: sn struggling* **20/1**
9 1 ¼ **Salden Licht**[360] 5-9-0 98..... LukeMorris 10 78
(J M P Eustace) *hld up: sn towards rr: pushed along over 3f out: rdn and struggling wl over 1f out* **66/1**
0 10 10 **Wymering File (IRE)**[36] 4903 4-9-3 0..... SebSanders 1 59
(M J Grassick, Ire) *led: hdd over 3f out: wknd over 2f out* **20/1**
0-01 11 9 **Scartozz**[155] 1283 7-9-0 84.....(p) JerryO'Dwyer 8 36+
(M Botti) *prom: ev ch wl over 2f out: sn pushed along: wknd qckly wl over 1f out: sn eased* **100/1**

1m 46.48s (-4.02) **Going Correction** -0.125s/f (Stan)
WFA 3 from 4yo+ 5lb **11** Ran SP% **121.1**
Speed ratings (Par 107): **112,110,109,105,105 103,102,98,97,88 80**
toteswingers: 1&2 £7.00, 1&3 £3.70, 2&3 £13.30 CSF £21.05 TOTE £5.60: £1.20, £1.80, £3.50; EX 23.10.
Owner Team Valor **Bred** Newsells Park Stud Limited **Trained** Newmarket, Suffolk

FOCUS
A quality turnout for the track, run at a fair if unspectacular gallop, and producing a winner who is going places.

NOTEBOOK
Gitano Hernando ◆ has looked progressive this season and the way he picked up in the home straight marks him down as one to follow. Connections say he is best suited by a fast pace and, given that there was some concern about the drop in trip here, a return to 1m2f would not be a problem. However, he looks high-class from 1m upwards. (op 11-4 tchd 100-30)
Mia's Boy ran a fine race in defeat. He is a very smart miler but is hard to place off a mark of 104 and usually has to be content with some place money. (op 7-1)
Khor Dubai(IRE) , who has been running over 7f, was not guaranteed to appreciate the extra distance but he performed with credit in this competitive company. He has done well on turf but his two efforts on Polytrack suggest he is just as effective on this surface. (tchd 8-1)
Cesare, only just short of winning a Group 1 at his peak, was outstandingly the star of the race on his best form. However, he has looked out of touch since Royal Ascot (a track where he has always excelled) and on this occasion he was never happy. Although he stayed on past beaten rivals, the overall response was disappointing and he needs to show much more before he can be considered to be anything like the horse he was. (op 5-2 tchd 11-4, 3-1 in a place)
Acclaimed(IRE), having only her third race, had been absent for a year. This was a satisfactory return to action and this Cambridgeshire entry can step up if all is well. (op 14-1)
Foolin Myself's all-weather win was on Fibresand, but in any case this was a better race. (tchd 5-1)

6031 WILLIAM HILL 0800 444040 - QUOTE BONUS25 H'CAP 1m 1f 103y(P)
9:10 (9:10) (Class 5) (0-70,70) 3-Y-O **£2,914** (£867; £433; £216) **Stalls** Low

Form RPR
-000 1 **Inconspicuous Miss (USA)**[77] 3548 3-8-8 **65**..... MatthewDavies(5) 4 71
(George Baker) *hld up in rr: hdwy on outside over 3f out: rdn to ld over 1f out: drvn out* **20/1**
3434 2 hd **Demeanour (USA)**[43] 4650 3-9-4 **70**.....(p) SebSanders 7 76
(E A L Dunlop) *a.p: wnt 2nd 7f out: led wl over 2f out: rdn and hdd over 1f out: r.o* **3/1**[1]
6240 3 nk **Arashi**[21] 5366 3-8-10 **62**.....(p) SteveDrowne 11 67
(Lucinda Featherstone) *hld up in tch: ev ch over 2f out: rdn and edgd lft whn n.m.r over 1f out: swtchd rt ins fnl f: r.o* **20/1**
1000 4 2 ¼ **Sullenberger (IRE)**[78] 3511 3-8-10 **62**..... TPQueally 9 62
(J A Osborne) *hld up in tch: rdn wl over 1f out: one pce fnl f* **12/1**
5610 5 ½ **Hector Spectre (IRE)**[13] 5630 3-9-1 **67**.....(v) DaneO'Neill 1 66
(K M Prendergast) *hld up towards rr: pushed along over 2f out: rdn and hdwy over 1f out: nt rch ldrs* **4/1**[2]
2100 6 1 **Brer Rabbit**[154] 1315 3-9-0 **66**..... DavidProbert 8 63
(B W Hills) *half-rrd s: sn hld up in mid-div: hdwy over 2f out: rdn jst over 1f out: no imp* **8/1**[3]
0046 7 nk **Clippity Clop (IRE)**[7] 5791 3-9-1 **67**..... ChrisCatlin 6 63
(J A Osborne) *led early: sn hld up in mid-div: nt clr run on ins jst over 2f out: rdn over 1f out: nvr trbld ldrs* **12/1**

5300 **8** *4* **Kimberley Rocks (IRE)**[20] 5384 3-8-8 **60**........................ MartinDwyer 5 48
(R M Beckett) *hld up towards rr: nt clr run on ins briefly jst over 2f out: nvr nr ldrs* **20/1**

0-34 **9** *1 1/2* **Group Leader (IRE)**[34] 5010 3-9-1 **67**........................ FergusSweeney 13 52
(J R Jenkins) *hld up towards rr: squeezed through and short-lived effrt jst over 2f out* **8/1**[3]

00 **10** *6* **Halcyon Princess (IRE)**[17] 5503 3-8-8 **60**....................(p) LiamJones 12 32
(D G Bridgwater) *s.i.s: hld up towards rr: pushed along over 4f out: no rspnse* **50/1**

11 *12* **Heavens Peak**[45] 4615 3-9-1 **67**........................ ShaneKelly 10 14
(M J Grassick, Ire) *prom tl pushed along and wknd over 2f out* **10/1**

445 **12** *5* **Eurotanz (IRE)**[36] 4916 3-8-10 **62**........................ TravisBlock 3 —
(H Morrison) *sn led: hdd wl over 2f out: sn wknd* **8/1**[3]

1m 59.83s (-1.87) **Going Correction** -0.125s/f (Stan) **12** Ran SP% **119.1**
Speed ratings (Par 101): **103,102,102,100,100 99,98,95,94,88 78,73**
toteswingers: 1&2 £19.30, 1&3 not won, 2&3 not won CSF £76.64 CT £1263.33 TOTE £32.50: £8.40, £2.30, £9.10; EX 170.90 Place 6: £108.83 Place 5: £79.29 .
Owner Jerry Jamgotchian **Bred** Jerry Jamgotchian **Trained** Moreton Morrell, Warwicks

FOCUS
A modest handicap, but a close three-way finish.
T/Plt: £313.90 to a £1 stake. Pool: £55,157.94. 128.24 winning tickets. T/Qpdt: £5.90 to a £1 stake. Pool: £8,721.19. 1,081.60 winning tickets. KH

5998 YARMOUTH (L-H)
Thursday, September 17

OFFICIAL GOING: Good to firm (firm in places 8.4)
Wind: medium, half behind Weather: overcast, breezy

6032 EUROPEAN BREEDERS' FUND SPRINT MAIDEN STKS 6f 3y
2:10 (2:13) (Class 5) 2-Y-O **£4,037** (£1,208; £604; £302; £150) **Stalls** Centre

Form RPR

03 **1** **Ongoodform (IRE)**[8] 5778 2-9-3 0........................ NCallan 10 85+
(P W D'Arcy) *a gng wl: trckd ldrs tl led jst over 2f out: shkn up and wnt clr over 1f out: edgd lft after: easily* **5/2**[1]

00 **2** *5* **Notice Given**[20] 5401 2-9-3 0........................ TPQueally 8 70
(H R A Cecil) *stdd s: hld up in tch in rr: hdwy to chse wnr wl over 1f out: nt pce of wnr over 1f out: edgd lft and one pce fnl f* **4/1**[3]

0 **3** *2 1/4* **Pirate's Song**[19] 5431 2-9-3 0........................ RobertHavlin 5 63
(J A R Toller) *plld hrd: chsd ldrs: wnt 2nd briefly and shkn up 2f out: sn unable qck: rdn and wknd over 1f out* **11/4**[2]

4 *1/2* **Sir Frank Wappat** 2-9-3 0........................ RoystonFfrench 4 62
(M Johnston) *chsd ldr tl shkn up and rn green fr over 2f out: wknd over 1f out* **8/1**

60 **5** *1 1/4* **Magnificence**[14] 5604 2-8-12 0........................ WilliamBuick 7 53
(Sir Michael Stoute) *led tl rdn and hdd jst over 2f out: sn lost pl: wl btn over 1f out* **5/1**

6 *6* **Marjolly (IRE)** 2-9-0 0........................ AndreaAtzeni(3) 6 40
(M Botti) *s.i.s: in tch in rr: rdn and struggling over 2f out: bhd fnl 2f* **20/1**

7 *9* **Lady Brickhouse** 2-8-12 0........................ SilvestreDeSousa 1 —
(M D Squance) *s.i.s: in tch in rr: rdn and struggling over 2f out: wl bhd fnl 2f* **40/1**

1m 12.29s (-2.11) **Going Correction** -0.35s/f (Firm) **7** Ran SP% **110.2**
Speed ratings (Par 95): **100,93,90,89,88 80,68**
toteswingers: 1&2 £3.30, 1&3 £2.10, 2&3 £3.40 CSF £11.86 TOTE £3.20: £1.80, £2.80; EX 14.50 Trifecta £54.60 Pool: £398.28 - 5.39 winning units..
Owner Dr J S Kinnear **Bred** Stephanie Hanly **Trained** Newmarket, Suffolk

FOCUS
An ordinary-looking maiden.

NOTEBOOK
Ongoodform(IRE) ran well at Kempton last time at long odds, and proved that effort was no fluke by taking this by a wide and impressive margin. He probably did not beat a great deal, and one would imagine his future lies in handicaps. (op 11-4)
Notice Given had been well beaten in a couple of maidens, one at this course, and was dropped to 6f for the first time. Held up, he got closest to the winner passing the post but was easily held. (op 9-2)
Pirate's Song, who was very keen early, gave the impression that he was still inexperienced, considering the way he wandered inside the final furlong. (op 100-30 tchd 5-2)
Sir Frank Wappat, related to winners, showed plenty of pace but spoilt his first start by edging left in the latter stages, and raising his head over a furlong out. However, as this was his first run, he was possibly green and can easily be given another chance. (op 15-2 tchd 7-1)
Magnificence was not beaten very far at Salisbury last time, despite finishing 11th but, fitted with a noseband for the first time, she rarely looked dangerous here after losing her position 2f from home. (op 4-1 tchd 11-2)

6033 E B F / FIRSTBET.COM £50 MATCHED BET 0800 230 0800 MAIDEN STKS 1m 3y
2:40 (2:43) (Class 4) 2-Y-O **£5,046** (£1,510; £755; £377; £188) **Stalls** Centre

Form RPR

2 **1** **Rigidity**[34] 5002 2-9-3 0........................ TPQueally 5 81+
(H R A Cecil) *trckd ldr: pushed into ld 2f out: hrd pressed and edgd lft ent fnl f: rdn and asserted ins fnl f: r.o wl* **8/13**[1]

2 *2* **Bab Al Shams (IRE)** 2-9-3 0........................ LDettori 4 76+
(Saeed Bin Suroor) *stdd s: t.k.h: hld up in tch in rr: trckd wnr through 2f out: rdn to chal jst over 1f out: btn fnl 100yds: eased wl ins fnl f* **15/8**[2]

06 **3** *8* **Green For Luck (IRE)**[82] 3376 2-9-3 0........................ NCallan 2 58
(S Gollings) *hld up in tch in rr: swtchd lft and hdwy over 2f out: outpcd u.p over 1f out: wl btn fnl f* **25/1**

0 **4** *1 1/4* **Temple Fair (USA)**[31] 5106 2-9-3 0........................ RoystonFfrench 1 55
(M Johnston) *led tl rdn and hdd 2f out: outpcd u.p over 1f out: wl hld fnl f* **14/1**[3]

000 **5** *2 1/4* **Carlcol Girl**[31] 5106 2-8-12 0........................ AdrianMcCarthy 3 45
(Mrs C A Dunnett) *chsd ldrs: rdn over 2f out: outpcd by ldng pair over 1f out: wknd ins fnl f* **200/1**

6 *9* **Light The City (IRE)** 2-9-3 0........................ KoseiMiura 7 29
(C E Brittain) *hld up in tch in rr: rdn and losing tch whn hung lft ent fnl 2f: sn wl bhd* **33/1**

1m 38.5s (-2.10) **Going Correction** -0.35s/f (Firm) **6** Ran SP% **110.7**
Speed ratings (Par 97): **96,94,86,84,82 73**
toteswingers: 1&2 £1.02, 1&3 £3.30, 2&3 £2.70 CSF £1.89 TOTE £1.70: £1.10, £1.50; EX 2.20.
Owner Thomas Barr **Bred** Miss K Rausing **Trained** Newmarket, Suffolk

FOCUS
Going back in history, some nice horses have taken this prize. In 1999 Beat Hollow was successful, a year later Mot Juste won on her debut and Alwaary landed the spoils last season.

NOTEBOOK
Rigidity caught the eye on his debut and showed normal progression, plus a decent turn of foot, to get off the mark. A horse with a few nice entries, he should be capable of holding his own at a higher grade. (tchd 4-7 and 4-6)
Bab Al Shams(IRE), a 200,000gns half-brother to winners, including the once smart Hazeymm, shaped with promise on his debut after being ridden with restraint, especially as he looked in need of the run. He came clear of the third, which should augur well. (op 9-4 tchd 5-2 in places)
Green For Luck(IRE) had a small chance just over a furlong out, but was readily outpaced when the two principals shot clear. (op 20-1 tchd 16-1)
Temple Fair(USA) looked green at Wolverhampton but put in a more professional effort this time. A galloping sort, he might stay 1m2f as a juvenile. (op 16-1 tchd 20-1)
Carlcol Girl, without the visor after showing very little in three starts, was not disgraced. (tchd 250-1)
Light The City(IRE), a half-brother to a filly that has yet to win, was very disappointing and showed little. (op 28-1)

6034 EASTERN POWER SYSTEMS (S) NURSERY 1m 3y
3:10 (3:11) (Class 6) (0-65,64) 2-Y-O **£1,942** (£578; £288; £144) **Stalls** Centre

Form RPR

5406 **1** **Rakhine (IRE)**[77] 3547 2-9-2 **59**........................ TPQueally 4 60
(P F I Cole) *in tch: hdwy and rdn over 2f out: drvn to chal jst ins fnl f: led fnl 75yds: drvn out* **10/1**

0033 **2** *1* **High Resolution**[14] 5613 2-8-12 **58**........................ WilliamCarson(3) 8 57
(S C Williams) *chsd ldr tl rdn to ld 2f out: hrd drvn over 1f out: hdd and no ex fnl 75yds* **7/2**[1]

0632 **3** *nse* **Glen Lass**[41] 4757 2-9-3 **60**........................(p) LukeMorris 10 59
(J S Moore) *sn towards rr and niggled along: rdn fr 1/2-way: stl last over 2f out: hdwy and swtchd rt over 1f out: hung lft u.p but styd on strly fnl f: nrly snatched 2nd on post* **7/1**

0305 **4** *2* **Lady Lefroy (IRE)**[16] 5543 2-9-1 **58**........................ RoystonFfrench 11 52
(R A Fahey) *chsd ldrs: rdn and ev ch ent fnl 2f: unable qck ent fnl f: hung lft and one pce fnl f* **9/1**

000 **5** *nk* **Noverre Over There (IRE)**[20] 5400 2-8-13 **56**........ EdwardCreighton 1 52+
(M E Rimmer) *towards rr: niggled along 1/2-way: rdn and in tch whn nt clr run over 1f out tl ins fnl f: styd on fnl 75yds: nvr able to chal* **12/1**

2106 **6** *nse* **Kate Skate**[72] 3719 2-9-7 **64**........................ AdrianMcCarthy 3 58
(Miss Gay Kelleway) *stdd and dropped in bhd after s: t.k.h: hld up towards rr: hdwy 3f out: chsng ldrs whn nt clr run 1f out tl ins fnl f: kpt on fnl 75yds: nt able to chal* **10/1**

5200 **7** *1* **New York Lights (IRE)**[13] 5636 2-8-2 **52**........................ RachelKing(7) 7 43
(M D I Usher) *t.k.h: led tl rdn and hdd 2f out: plugging on same pce whn n.m.r and carried lft ins fnl f* **20/1**

600 **8** *1 1/4* **Blinka Me**[52] 4385 2-8-12 **55**........................ NCallan 9 44
(M H Tompkins) *in tch midfield: effrt to chse ldrs and drvn ent fnl 2f: no prog over 1f out: hld whn carried lft ins fnl f* **11/2**[2]

000F **9** *3 1/4* **Orpen All Hours (IRE)**[13] 5620 2-8-2 **45**..............(p) SilvestreDeSousa 5 26
(P C Haslam) *t.k.h: trckd ldrs: rdn and unable qck 2f out: wknd u.p over 1f out* **9/1**

0050 **10** *3/4* **Mandarin Express**[15] 5573 2-9-1 **58**........................ LDettori 12 38
(B J Meehan) *stdd s: hld up in rr: rdn and short-lived effrt jst over 2f out: wl btn ent fnl f* **6/1**[3]

0050 **11** *13* **Double Rollover**[7] 5811 2-8-5 **48**........................(v[1]) WilliamBuick 13 —
(W R Muir) *hld up towards rr: rdn and no real prog ent fnl 2f: btn whn sltly hmpd 1f out: eased after* **16/1**

000 **12** *3/4* **Fast Elaine (IRE)**[24] 5319 2-8-2 **45**........................ RichardThomas 6 —
(Mrs L C Jewell) *in tch in midfield tl lost pl u.p over 2f out: wl bhd and eased ins fnl f* **40/1**

1m 39.91s (-0.69) **Going Correction** -0.35s/f (Firm) **12** Ran SP% **123.3**
Speed ratings (Par 93): **89,88,87,85,85 85,84,83,80,79 66,65**
toteswingers: 1&2 £16.50, 1&3 £12.90, 2&3 £2.90 CSF £46.77 CT £277.14 TOTE £12.00: £2.50, £2.00, £2.80; EX 72.00 Trifecta £208.60 Part won. Pool: £281.95 - 0.89 winning units..The winner was brought in 5,800gns. Glen Lass was claimed by J Pearce for £5,000. High Resolution was claimed by L A Perratt for £5,000.
Owner Meyrick & Dunnington-Jefferson **Bred** Ballyhane Stud **Trained** Whatcombe, Oxon

FOCUS
A very moderate seller.

NOTEBOOK
Rakhine(IRE), without blinkers after disappointing in them last time, travelled nicely towards the inside of the course and showed a fair change of gear to gain his first win. This was his first run since being gelded.
High Resolution was keen towards the head of affairs and appeared to run his race. He was claimed by Linda Perratt for £5,000. (op 9-2)
Glen Lass flew home after coming under strong pressure very early on. She might have won in a few more strides and was claimed by Jeff Pearce for £5,000. (op 6-1)
Lady Lefroy(IRE) was always thereabouts and had no obvious excuses. (op 10-1)
Noverre Over There(IRE) looked the unluckiest participant, as he was staying on well when met by a wall of horses over a furlong out. He came home strongly once pulled into the clear, but it was all too late.
Kate Skate finished well after looking to get outpaced and stopped in her effort. Official explanation: jockey said filly was denied a clear run (op 8-1)
Blinka Me, stepped up in trip and eased in class, looks like a horse who may still need a bit of time. It seems unlikely that he will take up his Derby entry next year. (op 13-2)
Mandarin Express, dropped into a seller for the first time, did not get into the contest after being held up. Official explanation: jockey said gelding hung left (op 15-2)
Fast Elaine(IRE) Official explanation: jockey said filly lost its action

6035 MOULTON NURSERIES NURSERY 7f 3y
3:40 (3:40) (Class 4) (0-80,78) 2-Y-O **£5,046** (£1,510; £755; £377; £188) **Stalls** Centre

Form RPR

0663 **1** **Baby Judge (IRE)**[3] 5938 2-7-9 **55** oh5........................ AndreaAtzeni(3) 4 57
(M C Chapman) *mde all: rdn and edgd lft over 1f out: drvn and hrd pressed ins fnl f: hld on wl nr fin* **7/1**

343 **2** *hd* **Newbury Street**[32] 5066 2-8-3 **60**........................ CatherineGannon 6 62
(R A Fahey) *t.k.h: chsd wnr: rdn and effrt 2f out: str chal ins fnl f: unable qck and hld nr fin* **11/4**[2]

5330 **3** *3/4* **Bandear (IRE)**[14] 5589 2-8-6 **63**........................ KoseiMiura 7 63
(C E Brittain) *hld up in tch: rdn and hdwy over 2f out: chsd ldng pair over 1f out: kpt on same pce ins fnl f* **17/2**

6401 **4** *2 1/2* **Ice Cool Lady (IRE)**[9] 5748 2-9-5 **76** 6ex........................ AdamKirby 5 69
(W R Swinburn) *hld up wl in tch: shkn up and nt qckn ent fnl 2f: drvn and one pce fr over 1f out* **7/2**[3]

2040 **5** *2 1/4* **Baileys Vision**[21] 5369 2-8-10 **67**........................ RoystonFrench 2 55
(M Johnston) *a in rr: rdn over 5f out: hung rt and no prog 2f out* **20/1**

202 **6** *8* **Victoire De Lyphar (IRE)**[11] 5692 2-9-7 **78**........................(b[1]) NCallan 3 46
(P C Haslam) *t.k.h: chsd ldrs: rdn and nt qckn wl over 2f out: drvn and btn ent fnl 2f: eased whn wl bhd ins fnl f* **15/8**[1]

1m 24.42s (-2.18) **Going Correction** -0.35s/f (Firm) **6** Ran SP% **111.5**
Speed ratings (Par 97): **98,97,96,94,91 82**
toteswingers: 1&2 £5.60, 1&3 £11.90, 2&3 £4.50 CSF £26.06 TOTE £9.00: £3.10, £2.00; EX 32.80.
Owner Roy Gowans **Bred** James Hampton Jones **Trained** Market Rasen, Lincs

FOCUS
All of these had managed to finish in the frame at least once, so this should be reliable, if unspectacular, form for the level.

NOTEBOOK
Baby Judge(IRE), running from 5lb out of the handicap and making a fairly quick reappearance, was having his 12th start of the year and had hardly looked a candidate for victory despite a fair effort last time. However, he certainly showed plenty of resolution and just kept his head in front. (op 17-2)
Newbury Street, up in trip on his handicap debut, was keen whilst tracking the winner and took a while to fully get going. If building on this effort, he can win something similar over this trip of slightly further. (op 5-2 tchd 9-4)
Bandear(IRE) didn't make much of an impression on her handicap debut at Epsom (she may not have liked the course) but ran much better here under another tidy ride from her Japanese jockey. (op 8-1 tchd 9-1)
Ice Cool Lady(IRE) got off the mark on the all-weather earlier this month but never looked like repeating that victory. (op 4-1 tchd 9-2 in a place)
Baileys Vision had been running deplorably in similar races, and only shaped marginally better here after getting outpaced. Official explanation: jockey said filly never travelled (op 16-1)
Victoire De Lyphar(IRE), wearing blinkers for the first time, had run really well in a first-time visor on his previous outing but this time found little once in a challenging position. Official explanation: trainer's rep said gelding was unsuited by the good to firm (firm in places) ground (op 2-1 tchd 7-4, 9-4 in places)

6036 AT THE RACES "VICTORY VASE" H'CAP (FOR THE VICTORY VASE) 1m 6f 17y
4:10 (4:10) (Class 2) (0-100,98) 3-Y-0+
£12,462 (£3,732; £1,866; £934; £466; £234) **Stalls** High

Form RPR
2151 **1** **Akmal**[27] 5230 3-9-4 **98**.. RHills 5 106+
(J L Dunlop) *son led: mde rest: rdn ent fnl 2f: styd on wl and a holding rivals fnl f* **5/4**[1]

1406 **2** *½* **Spring Jim**[12] 5656 8-9-2 **86**.................................... WilliamBuick 4 93
(J R Fanshawe) *hld up in last pair: hdwy over 3f out: chsd wnr jst over 2f out: rdn wl over 1f out: drvn and kpt on same pce fr over 1f out* **13/2**

0262 **3** *½* **Mystery Star (IRE)**[26] 5248 4-10-0 **98**..........................(p) TedDurcan 1 104
(M H Tompkins) *hld up in last pair: rdn and effrt over 2f out: swtchd rt 2f out: chsd ldng pair ent fnl f: kpt on* **6/1**[3]

0410 **4** *shd* **Valmari (IRE)**[27] 5235 6-9-1 **85**......................................(b) NCallan 2 91
(C E Brittain) *t.k.h: chsd wnr tl 12f out: in tch after: rdn and dropped to last over 3f out: rallied u.p ent fnl f: styd on but nvr had pce to threaten ldrs* **16/1**

1145 **5** *3 ¼* **Hendersyde (USA)**[55] 4260 4-9-5 **89**.............................(t) AdamKirby 3 91
(W R Swinburn) *t.k.h early: chsd ldng pair: rdn and unable qck wl over 2f out: wknd u.p over 1f out* **9/2**[2]

453 **6** *hd* **Rugell (ARG)**[20] 5402 4-9-0 **88**.................................... TPQueally 6 86
(H R A Cecil) *chsd wnr 12f out tl rdn and unable qck over 2f out: sonn struggling and wl btn after* **13/2**

3m 2.05s (-5.55) **Going Correction** -0.225s/f (Firm)
WFA 3 from 4yo+ 10lb **6** Ran SP% **109.5**
Speed ratings (Par 109): **106,105,105,105,103 103**
toteswingers: 1&2 £2.70, 1&3 £2.70, 2&3 £5.20 CSF £9.31 TOTE £1.90: £1.20, £2.50; EX 9.90.
Owner Hamdan Al Maktoum **Bred** Shadwell Estate Company Limited **Trained** Arundel, W Sussex

FOCUS
All of these are capable of a decent level of form when at their best, but this is probably not a result to not take too seriously, as it appeared to end up being a sprint over the last 3f.

NOTEBOOK
Akmal has been in fabulous form during 2009. Chasing his fifth victory of the campaign, and 5lb higher than for his last run, he dictated matters under Richard Hills and pulled out plenty for pressure while quickening. An enthusiastic type, who looks to really try, he is always one to fear at this sort of level. (op 13-8 tchd 7-4 in places)
Spring Jim has gone well for this rider before and loomed up to look a danger 2f from home, but he did not possess the same gears the winner and was outpaced. A stronger gallop would have suited him better, but that was never likely to happen in a small field. (op 6-1 tchd 7-1)
Mystery Star(IRE), wearing cheekpieces for the first time, stayed on well but could not get to the leader. (tchd 13-2)
Valmari(IRE) dropped out for a short time as the pace increased but finished well once finding her stride.
Hendersyde(USA) disappointed at Ascot last time after a good run in the Northumberland Plate, and arguably did so again. (op 4-1)
Rugell(ARG) seemed to improve when stepped up in trip on his previous outing, but offered little once off the bridle about 3f out. (op 11-2)

6037 FIRSTBET.COM £50 MATCHED BET 0800 230 0800 H'CAP 2m
4:40 (4:40) (Class 5) (0-70,76) 3-Y-0+ **£3,238** (£963; £481; £240) **Stalls** High

Form RPR
3131 **1** **Veiled**[3] 5952 3-9-5 **76** 6ex.. RosieJessop[(7)] 5 89+
(Sir Mark Prescott) *t.k.h: hld up in tch in last pl: smooth hdwy to ld on bit over 2f out and sn clr: v easily* **5/4**[1]

3411 **2** *9* **Saborido (USA)**[17] 5530 3-9-3 **67**.................................. JimCrowley 1 66
(Mrs A J Perrett) *chsd ldng pair: pushed along and effrt to join ldr 4f out: chsd wnr and drvn over 2f out: sn no ch w wnr* **5/4**[1]

3050 **3** *1 ½* **Wannarock (IRE)**[16] 5554 4-8-3 **48** oh3.......................... RachelKing[(7)] 2 45
(M C Chapman) *t.k.h: hld up in last pair: swtchd rt and effrt 3f out: no ch w wnr but pressing for 2nd over 1f out tl no ex fnl 100yds* **14/1**[3]

6-00 **4** *hd* **Present**[2] 5975 5-8-10 **48** oh1.. RoystonFfrench 4 45
(Miss Diana Weeden) *chsd wnr tl drvn over 2f out: sn no ch w wnr: stl ev ch of being 2nd tl no ex ins fnl f* **25/1**

0030 **5** *4 ½* **Alittlemoreflair**[15] 5579 3-7-12 **48** oh1..................(v) SilvestreDeSousa 6 40
(J Pearce) *led: rdn 4f out: hdd over 2f out: no ch w wnr after: wknd and dropped to last ent fnl f* **8/1**[2]

3m 34.59s (-0.01) **Going Correction** -0.225s/f (Firm)
WFA 3 from 4yo+ 12lb **5** Ran SP% **110.5**
Speed ratings (Par 103): **91,86,85,85,83**
CSF £2.97 TOTE £2.10: £1.10, £1.20; EX 2.90.
Owner Cheveley Park Stud **Bred** Cheveley Park Stud Ltd **Trained** Newmarket, Suffolk

FOCUS
This otherwise very modest staying handicap featured a pair of progressive 3yos and they dominated the pre-race betting.

6038 REEVE PROPERTY RESTORATION H'CAP (DIV I) 6f 3y
5:10 (5:11) (Class 6) (0-60,60) 3-Y-0+ **£2,007** (£597; £298; £149) **Stalls** Centre

Form RPR
3043 **1** **Boundless Applause**[17] 5500 3-8-4 **46**.................... SilvestreDeSousa 4 54
(I A Wood) *in tch in midfield: hdwy u.p over 2f out: led over 1f out: hrd pressed ins fnl f: kpt on wl towards fin* **12/1**

4035 **2** *½* **Comptonspirit**[24] 5323 5-9-5 **59**.. NCallan 5 65
(B P J Baugh) *in tch in midfield: hdwy and bmpd rival 2f out: rdn to chse wnr over 1f out: hrd drvn and ev ch ins fnl f: unable qck towards fin* **10/3**[1]

1000 **3** *¾* **Diane's Choice**[12] 5678 6-9-2 **56**................................(e) AdamKirby 7 60
(Miss Gay Kelleway) *taken down early: hld up towards rr: swtchd lft and hdwy u.p over 1f out: chsd ldng pair ins fnl f: kpt on* **9/1**

600 **4** *1 ½* **Stylish Mover**[54] 4303 4-8-6 **46**.........................(t) CatherineGannon 6 45
(R Ingram) *v.s.a: bhd: swtchd lft and hdwy u.p ent fnl f: r.o wl to go 4th ins fnl f: nvr trbld ldrs* **20/1**

2004 **5** *¾* **Shakespeare's Son**[7] 5792 4-9-6 **60**................................ JimCrowley 8 57
(H J Evans) *s.i.s: in tch towards rr: hdwy u.p to chse ldrs 2f out: wknd ins fnl f* **9/2**[2]

4332 **6** *hd* **Boldinor**[15] 5566 6-8-12 **52**.. NeilChalmers 9 48
(M R Bosley) *towards rr: effrt u.p on stands' side ent fnl 2f: styd on ins fnl f: nvr trbld ldrs* **11/2**[3]

0601 **7** *nk* **Scruffy Skip (IRE)**[15] 5566 4-9-0 **54**.......................... TGMcLaughlin 2 51+
(Mrs C A Dunnett) *bhd and sn pushed along: drvn 4f out: hdwy u.p on outer over 1f out: no imp ins fnl f: eased towards fin* **9/1**

0654 **8** *½* **Louisiade (IRE)**[44] 4621 8-7-13 **46** oh1......................(p) RachelKing[(7)] 11 40
(M C Chapman) *chsd ldrs: shkn up 1/2-way: rdn 2f out: wknd jst over 1f out* **16/1**

0400 **9** *2 ½* **Dynamo Dave (USA)**[18] 5477 4-8-8 **48**...................(b) RobertHavlin 10 35
(M D I Usher) *chsd ldr: rdn ent fnl 2f: wknd u.p over 1f out* **14/1**

5006 **10** *¾* **Bollin Franny**[33] 5020 5-8-6 **46** oh1............................ RichardThomas 3 30
(J E Long) *led: rdn and bmpd 2f out: hdd over 1f out: edgd lft and sn wknd* **14/1**

0401 **11** *3* **Equinity**[29] 5155 3-8-9 **51**..(t) SaleemGolam 12 26
(J Pearce) *plld hrd: chsd ldr tl 2f out: sn wknd* **9/1**

1m 12.81s (-1.59) **Going Correction** -0.35s/f (Firm)
WFA 3 from 4yo+ 2lb **11** Ran SP% **118.3**
Speed ratings: **96,95,94,92,91 91,90,90,86,85 81**
CSF £52.16 CT £389.14 TOTE £14.00: £3.80, £1.70, £3.40; EX 72.80 TRIFECTA Not won..
Owner M I Forbes **Bred** D R Tucker **Trained** Upper Lambourn, Berks

FOCUS
A very weak-looking sprint for moderate horses.\n
Stylish Mover Official explanation: jockey said gelding stumbled at the start and was slowly away
Bollin Franny Official explanation: vet said gelding returned lame

6039 REEVE PROPERTY RESTORATION H'CAP (DIV II) 6f 3y
5:45 (5:45) (Class 6) (0-60,59) 3-Y-0+ **£2,007** (£597; £298; £149) **Stalls** Centre

Form RPR
1005 **1** **Welsh Opera**[34] 5008 4-8-12 **54**............................ WilliamCarson[(3)] 5 64+
(S C Williams) *t.k.h: chsd ldrs: rdn to ld over 1f out: styd on wl u.p fnl f* **6/1**[3]

21 **2** *1 ¼* **Averoo**[19] 5443 4-9-5 **58**......................................(p) SilvestreDeSousa 7 63
(M D Squance) *in tch towards rr: niggled along 4f out: hdwy and edgd rt u.p jst over 1f out: kpt on to go 2nd last stride: nvr had pce to threaten wnr* **7/4**[1]

3244 **3** *shd* **Short Cut**[13] 5644 3-8-9 **50**..(t) WilliamBuick 1 55
(S Kirk) *stdd s: t.k.h and hld up in tch on outer: rdn and effrt 2f out: kpt on u.p fnl f to snatch 2nd on post* **8/1**

6533 **4** *shd* **Dualagi**[35] 4950 5-9-3 **56**.. JimCrowley 6 61
(M R Bosley) *led: rdn and hdd over 1f out: drvn and btn ins fnl f: lost 2 pls cl home* **8/1**

006 **5** *3 ¼* **Avoncreek**[29] 5150 5-8-1 **45**.................................. JemmaMarshall[(5)] 11 40
(B P J Baugh) *chsd ldr tl wl over 1f out: wknd u.p over 1f out* **25/1**

215 **6** *2* **Titus Gent**[39] 4823 4-9-6 **59**.. AdamKirby 10 48
(J Ryan) *s.i.s: in tch towards rr: hdwy to chse ldrs and rdn ent fnl 2f: wknd over 1f out* **7/2**[2]

3524 **7** *nk* **Briannsta (IRE)**[25] 5283 7-9-0 **53**.............................. RichardThomas 9 41
(J E Long) *in tch towards rr: rdn and unable qck jst over 2f out: n.d fr over 1f out* **22/1**

0540 **8** *1 ¼* **Rhapsilian**[18] 5480 5-8-13 **52**.................................(b) AdrianMcCarthy 4 36
(J R Jenkins) *stdd s: hld up in tch in rr: rdn and no rspnse 2f out* **16/1**

2-00 **9** *11* **Time For Old Time**[17] 5500 3-8-9 **50**..................(p) CatherineGannon 12 1
(I A Wood) *stdd after s: t.k.h: hld up in tch: rdn and wknd qckly over 2f out: wl bhd fnl f* **18/1**

1m 12.13s (-2.27) **Going Correction** -0.35s/f (Firm)
WFA 3 from 4yo+ 2lb **9** Ran SP% **114.4**
Speed ratings (Par 101): **101,99,99,99,94 92,91,90,75**
toteswingers: 1&2 £3.30, 1&3 £7.60, 2&3 £3.60 CSF £16.71 CT £85.15 TOTE £7.90: £2.10, £1.30, £1.50; EX 20.70 TRIFECTA Not won. Place 6: £13.36 Place 5: £7.14.
Owner Paul W Stevens **Bred** Usk Valley Stud **Trained** Newmarket, Suffolk

FOCUS
Much like the first division, there were no equine stars on show in this, but most of the them were capable of going close on their best day.
Time For Old Time Official explanation: trainer's rep said filly was unsuited by the good to firm (firm in places) ground
T/Plt: £28.10 to a £1 stake. Pool: £53,600.09. 1,390.52 winning tickets. T/Qpdt: £25.20 to a £1 stake. Pool: £3,130.28. 91.60 winning tickets. SP

6040 - 6043a (Foreign Racing) - See Raceform Interactive

5653 CHANTILLY (R-H)
Thursday, September 17

OFFICIAL GOING: Good

6044a PRIX D'ARENBERG (GROUP 3) 5f 110y
12:20 (12:21) 2-Y-0 **£38,835** (£15,534; £11,650; £7,767; £3,883)

RPR
1 **Sorciere (IRE)**[46] 4579 2-8-8 .... GMosse 1 106
(C Lerner, France) *mde all: comf* **6/5**[2]

2 *1 ½* **Dolled Up (IRE)**[25] 5299 2-8-11 .... OPeslier 2 104
(Robert Collet, France) *racd in 2nd: rdn to chse wnr over 1f out: kpt on: nt rch wnr* **9/10**[1]

3	hd	**Kelty In Love (FR)**[57] 2-8-8 FBlondel 4	100
		(T Larriviere, France) *racd in 4th: rdn 1 1/2f out: wnt 3rd fnl f: styd on u.p* **13/1**	
4	3/4	**Irish Cat (IRE)**[4] 5927 2-8-8 IMendizabal 3	98
		(Robert Collet, France) *racd in 3rd: pushed along over 1 1/2f out: unable qck* **9/10**[1]	
5	3/4	**Nosedive**[29] 5174 2-8-11 C-PLemaire 5	98
		(W J Haggas) *racd in last: pushed along over 1f out: no imp* **32/5**[3]	

65.80 secs (1.30) **5** Ran SP% **171.4**
PARI-MUTUEL: WIN 2.20; PL 1.10, 1.10; SF 3.60.
Owner Lady O'Reilly **Bred** Petra Bloodstock Agency Ltd **Trained** France

NOTEBOOK
Sorciere(IRE) showed her true form on this occasion. Smartly into her stride, she made virtually every yard of the running and quickened when shaken up from a furlong and a half out. She is certainly an individual with plenty of speed, and she'll be tried over 6f again when she lines up for the Criterium de Maisons-Laffitte next month. She's a filly worth following.
Dolled Up(IRE), who never runs a bad race, followed the winner for much of the five and a half furlongs. Unsuited by a lack of early pace, she couldn't quicken when things got serious a furlong and a half out but stayed on well and bravely took second place. The intention now is to run her in the Cheveley Park Stakes at Newmarket at the end of the month.
Kelty In Love(FR), a provincially trained filly, put up a decent performance. Fourth in the early stages, she quickened from two out and just failed to capture second place.
Irish Cat(IRE), third in the early stages, stayed on one-paced and wasn't beaten far for third place.
Nosedive was completely unsuited by lack of early pace and remained in last position throughout. He just couldn't quicken when things warmed up and, only beaten just over three lengths, is better than this form suggests.

6045a PRIX D'AUMALE (GROUP 3) (FILLIES) 1m
12:55 (12:56) 2-Y-O **£38,835** (£15,534; £11,650; £7,767; £3,883)

			RPR
1		**Middle Club**[56] 4245 2-8-9 IMendizabal 6	103
		(R Hannon) *a cl up: 3rd and pushed along st: rdn to ld 1 1/2f out: drvn out* **33/10**[3]	
2	hd	**Baahama (IRE)**[43] 2-8-9 OPeslier 1	103
		(A Fabre, France) *a cl up: 4th on ins st: edgd out and drvn wl over 1f out: chsd wnr fnl 150yds: kpt on steadily* **27/10**[1]	
3	2	**On Verra (IRE)**[29] 2-8-9 TThulliez 8	98
		(F Doumen, France) *hld up: last to 1 1/2f out: r.o down outside to take 3rd last strides* **24/1**	
4	snk	**American Nizzy (FR)**[26] 5279 2-8-9 GMosse 7	98
		(Y De Nicolay, France) *7th st: effrt on outside fr wl over 1f out: tk 4th on line* **5/1**	
5	nse	**Poppet's Treasure**[32] 2-8-9 SPasquier 3	98
		(R Pritchard-Gordon, France) *disp 5th: 6th on ins st: hdwy 2f out: wnt 2nd on rail 1 1/2f out: one pce fnl f and lost 3rd last strides* **19/1**	
6	snk	**Lixirova (FR)**[26] 5279 2-8-9 DBoeuf 4	97
		(D Smaga, France) *taken down early: led to 1 1/2f out: no ex fnl f* **12/1**	
7	2 1/2	**Beta Leo (USA)**[32] 5085 2-8-9 C-PLemaire 5	92
		(P Bary, France) *racd in 5th to st: rdn over 2f out: btn over 1f out* **12/1**	
8	1/2	**Ruler Of My Heart (IRE)**[26] 5280 2-8-9 DBonilla 2	91
		(Tom Dascombe) *trckd ldr: 2nd st: wknd wl over 1f out* **29/10**[2]	

1m 37.5s (-0.50) **8** Ran SP% **117.0**
PARI-MUTUEL: WIN 4.30; PL 1.80, 1.90, 4.60; DF 7.50.
Owner R J McCreery **Bred** Stowell Hill Ltd **Trained** East Everleigh, Wilts

NOTEBOOK
Middle Club, well up from the start, took control of the race a furlong and a half out and stayed on bravely to the line. This was a game performance and the filly is unlikely to race again this season, but her connections are already thinking about the Prix de Diane as she acted so well at the track. She will definitely stay a longer trip.
Baahama(IRE) looked dangerous running into the final furlong and just failed to peg back the winner. Connections are now likely to have a serious look at the Prix Marcel Boussac.
On Verra(IRE), dropped in last early on, was still in the same position rounding the final turn. Brought with a run up the centre of the track, she never looked like threatening the winner and runner-up.
American Nizzy(FR) was another who was given a waiting race. She made her challenge up the centre of the track and finished well without quite getting to the third.
Ruler Of My Heart(IRE) broke well and settled in second position, but she couldn't go the pace when things quickened up two out and just stayed on one-paced.

6009 AYR (L-H)
Friday, September 18

OFFICIAL GOING: Good (7.2)
Wind: Breezy, half behind Weather: Overcast

6046 BE PERSONNEL EBF MAIDEN STKS (DIV I) 7f 50y
1:50 (1:52) (Class 4) 2-Y-O **£4,857** (£1,445; £722; £360) **Stalls** Low

Form				RPR
4	1		**Hanson'D (IRE)**[28] 5234 2-9-3 0 NCallan 5	85+
			(K A Ryan) *trckd ldrs: rdn to ld over 1f out: edgd rt: drew clr fnl f* **4/7**[1]	
2332	2	6	**George Benjamin**[39] 4847 2-9-3 68 AdrianTNicholls 9	70
			(D Nicholls) *led to over 1f out: kpt on fnl f: nt pce of wnr* **8/1**[3]	
	3	2	**Monkton Vale (IRE)** 2-9-3 0 DanielTudhope 2	65
			(N Wilson) *hld up: hdwy over 1f out: kpt on u.p fnl f: no imp* **50/1**	
2	4	hd	**Gritstone**[37] 4888 2-9-3 0 PaulHanagan 10	65
			(R A Fahey) *midfield on ins: rdn over 2f out: hdwy over 1f out: no imp fnl f* **9/2**[2]	
5	5	2 1/2	**Silver Socks**[11] 5728 2-9-0 0 FrederikTylicki(3) 4	58
			(I Semple) *pressed ldr: rdn and ev ch over 2f out: sn one pce: wknd ins fnl f* **20/1**	
	6	6	**Green Lightning (IRE)** 2-9-3 0 GregFairley 3	44
			(M Johnston) *rn green and sn bhd: drvn 3f out: nvr able to chal* **14/1**	
64	7	shd	**Big Wave Bay (IRE)**[21] 5407 2-9-3 0 RichardMullen 8	44
			(A P Jarvis) *hld up: drvn 3f out: btn fnl 2f* **33/1**	
	8	1 3/4	**Sixties Rock** 2-9-3 0 TonyHamilton 11	39
			(J A Glover) *wnt rt s: sn cl up on outside: edgd lft and wknd fr 2f out* **66/1**	
	9	4 1/2	**Acol** 2-9-3 0 AndrewMullen 6	28
			(A G Foster) *walked to s: missed break: bhd: rdn 1/2-way: sn wknd* **125/1**	
065	10	28	**Dinkys Diamond (IRE)**[46] 4595 2-9-3 57 TomEaves 1	—
			(B Ellison) *prom: struggling 1/2-way: lost tch fnl 2f* **66/1**	

1m 30.97s (-2.43) **Going Correction** -0.325s/f (Firm) **10** Ran SP% **113.1**
Speed ratings (Par 97): **100,93,90,90,87 80,80,78,73,41**
toteswingers: 1&2 £1.80, 1&3 £15.00, 2&3 £65.00 CSF £5.11 TOTE £1.60: £1.02, £1.90, £13.90; EX 5.80.
Owner Joseph Ogden, J Hanson, John Ogden **Bred** Swordlestown Stud **Trained** Hambleton, N Yorks

FOCUS
Just a fair maiden overall, run at an ordinary pace. Hanson'D did it well in the end from the consistent if limited runner-up.

NOTEBOOK
Hanson'D(IRE), fourth to the ill-fated Businessman in the Convivial maiden at York first time out, confirmed that promise with a useful performance. A flashy chestnut, he was a little edgy in the paddock and did not settle particularly well in the race, but was always well placed before striking the front. He edged to his right for a time but that did not stop him from drawing well clear of some toiling opposition. Likely to take a big step up in grade in the the Racing Post Trophy at Doncaster, a race his yard won with Palace Episode four years ago, he would need to improve considerably on the bare form of this win but is a nice prospect. (op 8-13 tchd 4-6 in places)
George Benjamin, officially rated 68 having been placed in each of his four maidens, is the one to hang the form on. He was put in his place by the favourite in the final furlong but did nothing wrong and his turn will come round. (op 9-1)
Monkton Vale(IRE) ◆ is modestly bred and already gelded, but he made a very pleasing debut, staying on for third. He will stay further than this and could well appreciate easier ground too. (op 40-1)
Gritstone did not really build on his Beverley debut second and perhaps lacks a little scope for improvement. (op 5-1)
Silver Socks was still third a furlong out, but his stamina for this longer trip began to run out from that point. (op 16-1)
Green Lightning(IRE) was green both in the preliminaries and the race but did make a little modest progress when it was all over. He has a decent middle-distance pedigre and will come into his own over further. (op 10-1 tchd 9-1)

6047 BE PERSONNEL EBF MAIDEN STKS (DIV II) 7f 50y
2:20 (2:20) (Class 4) 2-Y-O **£4,857** (£1,445; £722; £360) **Stalls** Low

Form				RPR
52	1		**Unshakable Will (IRE)**[18] 5512 2-9-3 0 TomEaves 9	77
			(B Smart) *mde all: rdn over 2f out: hld on wl fnl f* **5/2**[1]	
	2	3/4	**Huntingfortreasure** 2-9-3 0 PhillipMakin 8	75+
			(M Dods) *hld up: hdwy on outside over 2f out: chsd wnr 1f out: kpt on u.p* **12/1**	
	3	4	**Thistlestar (USA)** 2-8-12 0 PaulHanagan 3	60+
			(R A Fahey) *plld hrd early: cl up: effrt over 2f out: lost 2nd and no ex fr 1f out* **4/1**[3]	
265	4	3 1/4	**Count Bertoni (IRE)**[75] 3652 2-9-3 75 NCallan 7	57
			(S Gollings) *trckd ldrs tl edgd lft and wknd over 1f out* **11/2**	
	5	3/4	**Dies Solis** 2-9-3 0 TonyHamilton 4	56
			(I Semple) *s.i.s: hld up: hdwy over 2f out: no ex over 1f out* **14/1**	
	6	7	**Tres Amigos** 2-9-3 0 AdrianTNicholls 5	38
			(D Nicholls) *hld up: hdwy over 2f out: wknd over 1f out* **7/1**	
0	7	2	**Original Dancer (IRE)**[127] 2017 2-9-3 0 GregFairley 10	34
			(M Johnston) *chsd ldrs tl rdn and wknd fr 3f out* **10/3**[2]	
00	8	10	**Musical Delight**[47] 4568 2-9-3 0 AndrewElliott 2	9+
			(A P Jarvis) *prom tl rdn and wknd fr 1/2-way: eased whn no ch ins fnl f* **80/1**	

1m 32.48s (-0.92) **Going Correction** -0.325s/f (Firm) **8** Ran SP% **115.1**
Speed ratings (Par 97): **92,91,86,82,82 74,71,60**
toteswingers: 1&2 £4.40, 1&3 £2.30, 2&3 £13.30 CSF £34.16 TOTE £3.40: £1.20, £2.40, £1.50; EX 38.50.
Owner Richard Page **Bred** Dominic O'Neill And Julie White **Trained** Hambleton, N Yorks

FOCUS
A weaker race than division one, and the time was a little slower. The first two finished clear.

NOTEBOOK
Unshakable Will(IRE)'s connections wanted more use made of him than had been on the case when he was second at Newcastle last time, and he was soon in front. Quickening up on the crown of the bend, he was kept right up to his work to hold off his pursuers. A willing sort, he will get 1m and may go for a nursery next. (tchd 7-2)
Huntingfortreasure was slow to find his stride and raced in rear, but he stayed on well down the outside in the straight and was closing on the winner at the line. A half-brother to several winners, including the yard's fair handicapper Zhitomir and Toylsome, who won the Prix de la Foret, he should not let the family down. This trip looks about right for him. (tchd 11-1)
Thistlestar(USA), a half-sister to a number of winners, took a keen tug early on and was soon restrained behind the winner. She kept trying up the straight but could never bridge the gap and was caught for second spot entering the last as she tired. Provided she settles better she should have no problem winning a maiden. (op 11-4)
Count Bertoni(IRE) seemed to run his race on his first start since leaving Tom Tate, but he is not really progressing. It may be that he needed this, though. (tchd 5-1 and 13-2)
Dies Solis ◆, whose dam won at 7f-1m, ran an encouraging race on this debut, keeping on without being knocked about after a slow start. There is definitely ability there and he is one to keep an eye on. (tchd 12-1 in places)
Tres Amigos could never make his presence felt and this trip might be further than he wants at this stage. He is likely to need time. (op 10-1 tchd 13-2)
Original Dancer(IRE), off the track since his debut back in May, was pushed along to hold a prominent early position before being steadily left behind up the straight. A big colt, he is still green and a long way from the finished product. (op 5-1)

6048 WEST SOUND & WEST FM NURSERY H'CAP 6f
2:55 (2:56) (Class 3) (0-95,87) 2-Y-O **£9,066** (£2,697; £1,348; £673) **Stalls** High

Form				RPR
0140	1		**My One Weakness (IRE)**[18] 5515 2-7-13 70 MartinLane(5) 1	75
			(B Ellison) *chsd ldr: drvn over 2f out: led ins fnl f: sn hrd pressed: hld on gamely* **9/1**	
5112	2	hd	**Mister Hughie (IRE)**[4] 5945 2-8-13 79 SamHitchcott 8	83
			(M R Channon) *prom: effrt whn n.m.r briefly over 1f out: disp ld ins fnl f: jst hld* **6/1**[3]	
1002	3	nk	**Gertmegalush (IRE)**[19] 5467 2-9-0 80 (b) GrahamGibbons 9	83
			(J D Bethell) *trckd ldrs: effrt over 2f out: kpt on wl last 100yds* **10/1**	
1114	4	1 1/4	**Bluie**[13] 5658 2-9-0 80 AdrianTNicholls 4	79
			(D Nicholls) *led: rdn 2f out: hdd ins fnl f: kpt on same pce* **9/2**[1]	
021	5	1 3/4	**Hold On Tiger (IRE)**[22] 5360 2-8-11 77 TomEaves 7	71+
			(I Semple) *t.k.h: hld up: nt clr run over 2f out: hdwy over 1f out: no imp fnl f* **14/1**	
1340	6	1 1/4	**Maison Brillet (IRE)**[18] 5515 2-7-11 70 JamesPSullivan(7) 12	62+
			(J Howard Johnson) *dwlt: bhd: rdn whn blkd and hit rail wl over 2f out: kpt on fnl f: n.d* **10/1**	
521	7	1	**Comedy Hall (USA)**[14] 5620 2-9-7 87 GregFairley 10	74
			(M Johnston) *dwlt: towards rr: drvn 1/2-way: no imp fnl 2f* **5/1**[2]	
1021	8	nse	**Eight Hours**[17] 5550 2-7-12 64 (b[1]) PaulHanagan 6	51
			(R A Fahey) *hld up: drvn and hdwy 2f out: no imp appr fnl f* **5/1**[2]	
003	9	4 1/2	**Sovereign Secure (IRE)**[27] 5256 2-8-8 77 ow4 FrederikTylicki(3) 5	51
			(Lee Smyth, Ire) *trckd ldrs tl rdn and wknd fr 2f out* **25/1**	

1202 **10** *1* **Transfixed (IRE)**[6] 5853 2-8-10 **76**.......................... SilvestreDeSousa 3 47
(P D Evans) *dwlt: bhd and drvn over 2f out: nvr on terms* **10/1**

6640 **11** *9* **Little Perisher**[31] 5136 2-9-2 **82**.................................... AndrewElliott 2 26
(A P Jarvis) *hld up on outside: rdn and edgd rt over 2f out: sn wknd* **40/1**

1m 11.15s (-2.45) **Going Correction** -0.325s/f (Firm) **11** Ran SP% **116.0**
Speed ratings (Par 99): **103,102,102,100,98 96,95,95,89,87 75**
toteswingers: 1&2 £11.30, 1&3 £21.60, 2&3 £12.10 CSF £61.32 CT £564.24 TOTE £10.10: £2.80, £2.60, £4.10; EX 84.80.
Owner Koo's Racing Club **Bred** Epona Bloodstock Ltd **Trained** Norton, N Yorks

FOCUS

A fair nursery which was strongly run. Sound form.

NOTEBOOK

My One Weakness(IRE), who raced too keenly when stepped up to 1m last time, following a sound run at York, was a pound well in on this drop back in trip. Getting over from his low draw to chase the pace, he nosed ahead inside the last and got the verdict on the nod. He showed a willing attitude under pressure that will help him in future engagements. (op 10-1 tchd 11-1 in a place)
Mister Hughie(IRE) came here in good heart, posting back-to-back wins before a second at Musselburgh in Monday. He ran another fine race and just missed out, after being stopped in his run for a stride approaching the last furlong and having to switch left. He appears to be just as effective at this trip as the minimum. (tchd 11-2)
Gertmegalush(IRE), racing off a 4lb higher mark, finished well against the rail. This was only his second run over 6f and he is well worth continuing with at this trip. (op 15-2)
Bluie, whose winning streak was halted at Haydock, set the pace nearest the fence and was still in front inside the last before being swamped. This was a sound effort but the handicapper just has his measure. (op 11-2)
Hold On Tiger(IRE) gained his maiden win over C&D and ran respectably on this nursery debut. He would have been closer with a clear run. (op 11-1)
Maison Brillet(IRE), behind today's winner over 1m last time, was already under pressure when he was hampered against the rail just past halfway. (op 16-1)
Comedy Hall(USA)'s Catterick maiden win has been franked by the runner-up, but that race was on soft ground and the drying conditions here were against him. He was slowly away for the third time in four starts and could never get into it. (op 4-1 tchd 11-2)
Sovereign Secure(IRE), who has yet to run in her home country of Ireland, showed up well for half a mile. (op 28-1)
Transfixed(IRE) Official explanation: jockey said filly hung right-handed; trainer said filly lost a right-fore shoe

6049 MAC ASPHALT HARRY ROSEBERY STKS (FOR THE SOUTH AYRSHIRE CUP) (LISTED RACE) 5f

3:30 (3:32) (Class 1) 2-Y-O

£19,869 (£7,532; £3,769; £1,879; £941; £472) **Stalls** High

Form RPR

0223 **1** **Mister Manannan (IRE)**[7] 5822 2-9-3 104................. AdrianTNicholls 8 110+
(D Nicholls) *pressed ldr: led 2f out: drvn clr* **15/8**[1]

14 **2** *3 1/2* **Puff (IRE)**[29] 5199 2-8-12 93.. PhillipMakin 6 92
(R M Beckett) *hld up: hdwy and swtchd lft over 1f out: styd on to chse wnr wl ins fnl f: nt rch wnr* **6/1**[3]

3222 **3** *nk* **Aalsmeer**[11] 5728 2-8-12 93.. RichardMullen 5 91
(E S McMahon) *prom: effrt over 2f out: chsd wnr briefly ins fnl f: kpt on* **16/1**

3365 **4** *nse* **Archers Road (IRE)**[7] 5822 2-9-3 99............................. SamHitchcott 1 96
(M R Channon) *bhd: drvn 1/2-way: hdwy over 1f out: kpt on u.p fnl f* **18/1**

1211 **5** *2* **Duchess Dora (IRE)**[19] 5467 2-8-12 93..................... GrahamGibbons 4 84
(J J Quinn) *trckd ldrs: rdn over 2f out: no ex ins fnl f* **8/1**

1212 **6** *hd* **Skylla**[18] 5521 2-8-12 94.. JerryO'Dwyer 10 83
(J R Holt) *led to 2f out: sn rdn: no ex ins fnl f* **7/2**[2]

631 **7** *1 3/4* **Vanishing Grey (IRE)**[21] 5380 2-8-12 87..................... RobertWinston 7 77
(B J Meehan) *dwlt: bhd: hdwy u.p over 2f out: no further imp appr fnl f* **9/1**

0503 **8** *4* **Here Now And Why (IRE)**[4] 5945 2-9-3 88.......................... NCallan 3 68
(K A Ryan) *midfield: effrt over 2f out: edgd rt and wknd over 1f out* **25/1**

1014 **9** *13* **Exotic Beauty**[18] 5521 2-8-12 86.................................. PaulHanagan 12 31+
(M R Channon) *prom 2f: qckly lost pl: eased fr 2f out* **11/1**

00 **10** *3* **Lady Laurem**[26] 5292 2-8-12 0.. RossSmith 2 —
(D A Nolan) *dwlt: a outpcd* **250/1**

57.40 secs (-2.70) **Going Correction** -0.325s/f (Firm) **10** Ran SP% **116.1**
Speed ratings (Par 103): **108,102,101,101,98 98,95,89,68,63**
toteswingers: 1&2 £5.50, 1&3 £10.00, 2&3 £20.90 CSF £13.39 TOTE £2.80: £1.40, £2.20, £3.70; EX 14.00.
Owner Mrs Maureen Quayle **Bred** Mull Enterprises Ltd **Trained** Sessay, N Yorks

FOCUS

An up-to-scratch edition of this Listed event and a cracking effort for the grade from Mister Manannan. It was run at a fast pace and the form should hold up.

NOTEBOOK

Mister Manannan(IRE) had only won one of his six previous starts, but he had been placed in the Molecomb, the Roses and the Flying Childers Stakes on his last three starts and thoroughly deserved this win. Tracking the leader, he eased to the front over a furlong out and came away for a comprehensive victory. This professional colt has a nice attitude and he looks sure to make a smart sprinter next season, with the Cornwallis Stakes at Ascot the obvious race for the rest of this season. (op 7-4 tchd 2-1 tchd 9-4 in places)
Puff(IRE), fourth in the Lowther over 6f last time, ran well on her first try against the colts, running on nicely once switched out. She will not mind a return to further but is clearly a smart filly at this trip too. (op 9-2)
Aalsmeer is still a maiden and has been turned over at odds-on on three of her four starts, finishing a head second to Misheer at this level on the other occasion. After chasing the pacesetters she got into second place briefly inside the last but was caught for that position late on. This looks her trip.
Archers Road(IRE) had work to do with Mister Manannan on last week's meeting at Doncaster. He was outpaced in rear for the first part of the race but was running on strongly late on and would have been third with a bit further to run. (op 20-1)
Duchess Dora(IRE), who had today's nursery third Gertmegalush back in second when winning at Beverley, showed pace behind the leaders and ran her race with no excuses. (op 10-1)
Skylla, who grabbed the rail and the lead but could do nothing when the winner passed her and lost another four places inside the last. This was her first defeat at 5f. (tchd 4-1)
Vanishing Grey(IRE) was on her toes in the preliminaries and a bit slowly away in the race. She was found wanting in this company but was not disgraced. (op 16-1)
Exotic Beauty was eased off by her rider not long after halfway. Official explanation: jockey said filly hung right-handed throughout (op 16-1)

6050 WILLIAM HILL (AYR) BRONZE CUP H'CAP 6f

4:05 (4:08) (Class 2) 3-Y-O+

£18,693 (£5,598; £2,799; £1,401; £699; £351) **Stalls** Centre

Form RPR

0100 **1** **Baldemar**[12] 5695 4-9-5 **87**.. BMcHugh(5) 4 95
(R A Fahey) *sn in tch far side: effrt over 1f out: styd on to ld towards fin: 1st of 11 in gp* **18/1**

1310 **2** *nk* **Ingleby Lady**[8] 5799 3-9-10 **89**... PhillipMakin 2 96
(T D Barron) *trckd far side ldr: ev ch fnl f: kpt on u.p: jst hld: 2nd of 11 in gp* **28/1**

0000 **3** *hd* **Burnwynd Boy**[35] 5001 4-9-0 **77**...................................... GregFairley 1 83
(D Nicholls) *led far side: rdn 2f out: kpt on u.p: hdd towards fin: 3rd of 11 in gp* **40/1**

0056 **4** *1/2* **Esoterica (IRE)**[22] 5363 6-9-4 **86**.............................. GaryBartley(5) 7 91
(J S Goldie) *bhd far side: rdn 1/2-way: effrt and hdwy over 1f out: kpt on fnl f: nrst fin: 4th of 11 in gp* **33/1**

6643 **5** *1/2* **Northern Bolt**[14] 5623 4-9-0 **77**.......................................(v) PaulQuinn 8 80
(D Nicholls) *dwlt: sn in tch far side: drvn over 2f out: kpt on u.p fnl f: 5th of 11 in gp* **28/1**

2122 **6** *nk* **Silaah**[3] 5959 5-9-10 **87**.. AdrianTNicholls 3 89
(D Nicholls) *midfield far side: effrt and cl up appr fnl f: one pce ins fnl f: 6th of 11 in gp* **6/1**[1]

1054 **7** *shd* **Sunrise Safari (IRE)**[8] 5799 6-9-7 **87**....................(v) FrederikTylicki(3) 5 89
(R A Fahey) *trckd far side ldrs: drvn over 2f out: one pce fnl f: 7th of 11 in gp* **12/1**

1004 **8** *shd* **Earlsmedic**[9] 5767 4-9-6 **83**....................................... SaleemGolam 12 85+
(S C Williams) *swtchd to r far side gp s: hld up: drvn and hdwy over 1f out: kpt on u.p: 8th of 11 in gp* **16/1**

-404 **9** *hd* **Felday**[18] 5523 3-9-4 **83**... RobertWinston 22 86+
(H Morrison) *prom stands' side: hdwy to ld that gp ins fnl f: kpt on: nt rch far side: 1st of 13 in gp* **8/1**[2]

2201 **10** *1* **Haajes**[6] 5871 5-9-10 **87** 5ex..(t) JohnEgan 13 87+
(J Balding) *midfield on outer of stands' side gp: effrt and cl up over 1f out: kpt on fnl f: 2nd of 13 in gp* **22/1**

0300 **11** *nk* **Bond City (IRE)**[15] 5615 7-9-8 **85**................................ PJMcDonald 19 86+
(G R Oldroyd) *hld up stands' side: nt clr run over 2f out: swtchd lft and hdwy over 1f out: r.o fnl f: 3rd of 13 in gp* **50/1**

1026 **12** *nk* **Rasaman (IRE)**[8] 5799 5-9-4 **81**................................(v) DanielTudhope 18 79+
(J S Goldie) *cl up stands' side: drvn over 2f out: kpt on u.p fnl f: 4th of 13 in gp* **8/1**[2]

5311 **13** *hd* **Turnkey**[30] 5147 7-9-5 **82**... AndrewMullen 11 78
(D Nicholls) *bhd far side: reminders after 2f: drvn 1/2-way: plugged on fnl f: n.d: 9th of 11 in gp* **20/1**

0552 **14** *nk* **Novellen Lad (IRE)**[3] 5960 4-9-8 **85**.......................... DuranFentiman 26 82+
(E J Alston) *cl up stands' side: led 2f out to ins fnl f: one pce: 5th of 13 in gp* **14/1**

2512 **15** *1/2* **Hotham**[8] 5799 6-8-10 **78** 5ex.. MartinLane(5) 17 73+
(N Wilson) *dwlt: bhd stands' side: hdwy whn nt clr run over 2f out: kpt on fnl f: nrst fin: 6th of 13 in gp* **11/1**[3]

0000 **16** *nk* **Princess Valerina**[32] 5104 5-8-12 **80**......................... AshleyMorgan(5) 9 72
(D Haydn Jones) *towards rr far side: drvn and outpcd over 2f out: n.d after: 10th of 11 in gp* **66/1**

1230 **17** *1/2* **Rash Judgement**[20] 5424 4-9-10 **87**............................. RichardMullen 21 80+
(W S Kittow) *dwlt: towards rr stands' side: hdwy whn nt clr run over 2f out: kpt on same pce fnl f: 7th of 13 in gp* **22/1**

0503 **18** *1* **Dark Lane**[3] 5960 3-9-2 **81**.. PaulHanagan 15 71+
(R A Fahey) *prom stands' side tl rdn and wknd over 1f out: 8th of 13 in gp* **14/1**

0030 **19** *1 1/4* **Quiet Elegance**[54] 4353 4-9-0 **77**.............................. TonyHamilton 25 63+
(E J Alston) *hld up stands' side: n.m.r over 2f out: no imp fnl f: 9th of 13 in gp* **33/1**

0451 **20** *1/2* **Silver Wind**[8] 5799 4-9-11 **88** 5ex...(v) NCallan 6 73+
(P D Evans) *in tch far side tl wknd over 2f out: last of 11 in gp* **20/1**

0002 **21** *1 3/4* **Bel Cantor**[6] 5856 6-8-13 **79**...................................(p) KellyHarrison(3) 14 58+
(W J H Ratcliffe) *led stands' side to 2f out: sn btn: 10th of 13 in gp* **25/1**

4000 **22** *1* **Vhujon (IRE)**[8] 5799 4-9-8 **85**................................(v1) SilvestreDeSousa 16 61+
(P D Evans) *hld up stands' side: drvn over 2f out: sn btn: 11th of 13 in gp* **18/1**

0535 **23** *4* **Solar Spirit (IRE)**[49] 4507 4-9-5 **82**........................(p) GrahamGibbons 27 46+
(J J Quinn) *bhd stands' side: drvn 1/2-way: btn fnl 2f: 12th of 13 in gp* **12/1**

050- **24** *3 3/4* **Geojimali**[210] 7239 7-8-7 **77**.................................. JamesPSullivan(7) 23 30+
(J S Goldie) *beihnd stands' side: drvn 1/2-way: nvr on terms: last of 13 in gp* **33/1**

1m 10.49s (-3.11) **Going Correction** -0.325s/f (Firm)
WFA 3 from 4yo+ 2lb **24** Ran SP% **133.6**
Speed ratings (Par 109): **107,106,106,105,105 104,104,104,104,102 102,101,101,101,100 100,99,98,96,95 93,92,86,81**
toteswingers: 1&2 £83.20, 1&3 £99.90, 2&3 £43.40 CSF £467.34 CT £8701.06 TOTE £23.30: £5.30, £9.50, £11.30, £6.80; EX 592.10 Trifecta £1224.10 Part won. Pool: £1654.20 - 0.20 winning units..
Owner A Rhodes Haulage And P Timmins **Bred** Hellwood Stud Farm **Trained** Musley Bank, N Yorks

■ Stewards' Enquiry : B McHugh one-day ban: used whip with excessive frequency (5th Oct)

FOCUS

The inaugural Bronze Cup was in essence a consolation race for those who failed to get into the consolation race, but it was no less competitive for that. There was a spread of 11lb between the 24 runners, with topweight Silver Wind running off 88, which translated to 8st 4lb in the long handicap. As expected the field split into two, but what was not anticipated was the huge advantage those who raced on the far side enjoyed, with the first eight home all coming from that group of 11. Straightforward form amongst the principals.

NOTEBOOK

Baldemar is a pretty useful sprinter when on song as he showed when successful for Karl Burke at Epsom on Derby day. Having his second run for Fahey, he was always getting a tow on the far side and came through to show ahead in the last 50 yards. He could go for the Coral Sprint at York next month if he gets in. (op 20-1)
Ingleby Lady, who was running well prior to a lesser effort at Doncaster, was always up with the pace from her favourable draw and stuck on for second, just held by the winner. This was a commendable effort. (op 33-1)
Burnwynd Boy, drawn in stall one, provided the pace was only collared inside the last. He finished last off 105 in the Gold Cup here a year ago for another yard, and was a full two stone lower this time after a string of lacklustre efforts since joining the Nicholls stable. This was certainly a step back in the right direction.
Esoterica(IRE) was without the regular headgear and having his first run over a trip this short for more than three years. He finished well against the inside rail to grab fourth.
Northern Bolt ran on late for fifth, and while his losing run continues this was an encouraging effort. (op 25-1)
Silaah, another of the Nicholls team, momentarily looked like completing a clean sweep for the four lowest stalls but weakened out of fourth late on. He remains in good form but his run at Haydock earlier in the week might just have taken the edge off him. (op 7-1)
Sunrise Safari(IRE), a stablemate of the winner, ran respectably with the visor back on.
Earlsmedic finished eighth overall but only had three behind him in the favoured far-side group.

Felday ♦'s supporters can count themselves unlucky in that he was beaten by the draw. Having his second run back after a break, he was a fairly comfortable 'winner' among the 13 who raced down the stands' side and should be kept on the right side. There could be a nice handicap in him, providing he is more favourably drawn. (op 9-1 tchd 10-1)
Haajes, 1lb badly in under his Ffos Las penalty, raced on the outer of the stands'-side bunch and stuck on for second in his group. He remains in good heart and has the option of reverting to 5f. (tchd 28-1 in places)
Bond City(IRE) ran a better race without the blinkers, finishing only eleventh overall but third on his side. He is due to go be dropped 3lb now.
Rasaman(IRE), who was 1lb well in, was another to run respectably on the 'wrong' side of the track. (op 9-1)
Novellen Lad(IRE), who sweated up, ran reasonably enough on this quick reappearance. (op 16-1)
Hotham could not take advantage of being 3lb well in under his penalty.
Rash Judgement ran better than the bare form indicates as he encountered an interrupted passage. Official explanation: jockey said gelding was denied a clear run (op 20-1)
Bel Cantor, fourth in the Silver Cup last year, was responsible for the pace on the near side before weakening.

6051 BAM PROPERTIES H'CAP — 5f
4:40 (4:42) (Class 4) (0-85,84) 3-Y-O+ £6,476 (£1,927; £963; £481) **Stalls** Centre

Form RPR

4116 **1** **Guto**[13] 5675 6-8-0 **70** oh6 .... MartinLane(5) 3 78
(W J H Ratcliffe) *racd far side: chsd ldrs: sn drvn along: styd on wl fnl f: led nr fin: 1st of 8 that gp* **16/1**

3541 **2** ¾ **Grissom (IRE)**[23] 5335 3-8-4 **77** .... BillyCray(7) 8 82
(A Berry) *swtchd rt s: racd stands' side: w ldr: that that side 1f out: kpt on wl towards fin: 1st of 6 that gp* **20/1**

320 **3** *nk* **Hypnosis**[20] 5436 6-8-13 **78** .... TonyHamilton 11 82
(N Wilson) *swtchd lft s: led far side: hdd towards fin: 2nd of 8 that gp* **20/1**

1064 **4** *hd* **Spring Green**[22] 5370 3-8-11 **77** .... RobertWinston 6 81
(H Morrison) *racd far side: w ldr: styd on same pce fnl 150yds: 3rd of 8 that gp* **7/1**

4512 **5** ½ **The Nifty Fox**[14] 5623 5-9-5 **84** .... TomEaves 1 86
(T D Easterby) *racd far side: chsd ldrs: kpt on same pce fnl f: 4th of 8 that gp* **11/2**[3]

0606 **6** ¾ **Flash McGahon (IRE)**[55] 4311 5-9-3 **82** ....(b) AdrianTNicholls 5 81
(D Nicholls) *dwlt: racd far side: in rr: hdwy over 1f out: kpt on: nt rch ldrs: 5th of 8 that gp* **5/1**[2]

0100 **7** *hd* **Rothesay Dancer**[9] 5768 6-9-1 **83** .... KellyHarrison(3) 13 82+
(J S Goldie) *racd stands' side: hld up in rr: nt clr run over 1f out: swtchd ins: fin wl: 2nd of 6 that gp* **16/1**

2140 **8** 1 **Blue Tomato**[42] 4753 8-8-10 **75** .... PaulHanagan 4 70
(Miss L A Perratt) *racd far side: dwlt: hld up towards rr: effrt over 1f out: kpt on: nvr trbld ldrs: 6th of 8 that gp* **20/1**

0160 **9** *shd* **Luscivious**[14] 5623 5-8-9 **77** ....(p) FrederikTylicki(3) 2 71
(J A Glover) *racing far side: sn trcking ldrs: one pce appr fnl f: 7th of 8 that gp* **16/1**

0200 **10** ¾ **Sandwith**[50] 4464 6-8-8 **73** .... AndrewMullen 12 65
(A G Foster) *rrd s: racd stands' side: in rr: sme hdwy over 1f out: nvr a threat: 3rd of 6 that gp* **25/1**

0000 **11** *hd* **Northern Fling**[50] 4461 5-9-3 **82** .... PaulQuinn 7 73
(D Nicholls) *racd far side: a towards rr: nvr a factor: last of 8 that gp* **11/1**

6624 **12** *nse* **Fivefootnumberone (IRE)**[26] 5293 3-8-7 **73** ......(b[1]) GrahamGibbons 10 64
(J J Quinn) *racd stands' side: chsd ldrs: fdd 1f out: 4th of 6 that gp* **14/1**

661 **13** *nk* **Stolt (IRE)**[6] 5856 5-9-0 **84** 6ex .... GaryBartley(5) 15 74
(N Wilson) *racd stands' side: led that gp: edgd lft: hdd & wknd qckly 1f out: 5th of 6 that gp* **9/2**[1]

1503 **14** 3 **La Zamora**[26] 5293 3-8-13 **79** .... PhillipMakin 9 58
(T D Barron) *racd stands' side: chsd ldrs: rdn over 2f out: lost pl over 1f out: last of 6 that gp* **10/1**

58.47 secs (-1.63) **Going Correction** -0.325s/f (Firm)
WFA 3 from 5yo+ 1lb **14 Ran SP% 122.6**
Speed ratings (Par 105): **100,98,98,98,97 96,95,94,93,92 92,92,91,87**
toteswingers: 1&2 £36.60, 1&3 £41.00, 2&3 £57.80 CSF £311.50 CT £6454.86 TOTE £25.10: £6.30, £4.40, £7.70; EX 314.40.
Owner W J H Ratcliffe **Bred** H B Hughes **Trained** Newmarket, Suffolk

FOCUS
A fair sprint handicap. They split into two groups and again the far side came out on top, but the bias was not as pronounced over 5f and the overall runner-up was one of the half-dozen to race on the stands' side. The form seems sound.
The Nifty Fox Official explanation: jockey said gelding hung right-handed final 2f

6052 INVESTEC STRUCTURED PRODUCTS H'CAP — 1m
5:15 (5:15) (Class 5) (0-70,70) 3-Y-O £4,533 (£1,348; £674; £336) **Stalls** Low

Form RPR

5430 **1** **Pokfulham (IRE)**[22] 5362 3-8-1 **56** ....(v) KellyHarrison(3) 1 64
(J S Goldie) *led 1f: chsd ldrs: chal on ins 1f out: edgd rt: kpt on to ld towards fin* **10/1**

0551 **2** *hd* **Allformary**[13] 5672 3-9-4 **70** .... TomEaves 6 78
(B Smart) *chsd ldrs: drvn 3f out: slt ld jst ins fnl f: hdd and no ex cl home* **9/1**

3415 **3** 2½ **Mohawk Ridge**[13] 5672 3-8-13 **65** ....(p) PhillipMakin 4 67
(M Dods) *hld up towards rr: gd hdwy on outside over 2f out: edgd lft over 1f out: styd on same pce ins fnl f* **9/2**[1]

3604 **4** *nk* **Digger Derek (IRE)**[10] 5331 3-8-8 **60** .... PaulHanagan 14 61
(R A Fahey) *awkward s: hld up in rr: hdwy on inner over 2f out: kpt on wl ins fnl f* **13/2**[2]

4300 **5** ¾ **Dean Iarracht (IRE)**[13] 5672 3-8-8 **60** ....(p) TonyHamilton 5 60
(M Dods) *dwlt: hld up towards rr: hdwy on inner over 3f out: hung lft: one pce ins fnl f* **20/1**

2120 **6** *hd* **Whotsit (IRE)**[19] 5473 3-8-9 **61** ....(b) JerryO'Dwyer 12 60
(Miss Amy Weaver) *chsd ldrs: led 3f out: hdd jst ins fnl f: fdd* **16/1**

0534 **7** 3 **Moon Lightning (IRE)**[47] 4562 3-8-10 **67** .... AshleyMorgan(5) 9 62+
(M H Tompkins) *swtchd lft after s: hld up in rr: hdwy 3f out: one pce whn hmpd over 1f out* **7/1**[3]

6000 **8** 1¼ **Bessie Lou (IRE)**[6] 5858 3-9-1 **67** .... RobertWinston 3 57+
(K A Ryan) *chsd ldrs: sn pushed along: one pce whn n.m.r 1f out* **18/1**

6405 **9** 1½ **Hey Up Dad**[17] 5549 3-8-5 **57** ow1 ....(bt) PJMcDonald 11 44
(M Dods) *hld up in midfield: hdwy 3f out: hung lft and wknd over 1f out* **11/1**

6105 **10** ¾ **Athania (IRE)**[44] 4642 3-9-2 **68** ....(v) RichardMullen 2 53
(A P Jarvis) *chsd ldrs: effrt on outer 3f out: wknd over 1f out* **7/1**[3]

0526 **11** *nk* **Barbarian**[11] 5731 3-9-4 **70** .... SilvestreDeSousa 7 54
(A D Brown) *mid-div: sn drvn along: wknd over 1f out* **16/1**

3006 **12** 3¼ **Avoir Choisi (IRE)**[72] 3734 3-9-0 **69** .... FrederikTylicki(3) 13 46
(I Semple) *in rr: hdwy on outside over 3f out: lost pl over 1f out* **16/1**

1524 **13** 16 **Fortunate Bid (IRE)**[18] 5513 3-9-4 **70** .... GrahamGibbons 10 12
(Mrs L Stubbs) *swtchd lft after s: hdwy to ld after 1f: hdd 3f out: lost pl over 1f out: eased whn bhd ins fnl f* **12/1**

6-40 **14** 1½ **Northern Acres**[135] 1793 3-9-3 **69** .... AdrianTNicholls 8 8
(D Nicholls) *in rr: drvn over 3f out: bhd and eased 2f out* **8/1**

1m 40.83s (-2.97) **Going Correction** -0.325s/f (Firm) **14 Ran SP% 122.7**
Speed ratings (Par 101): **101,100,98,98,97 97,94,92,91,90 90,87,71,69**
toteswingers: 1&2 £12.60, 1&3 £11.50, 2&3 £8.80 CSF £99.03 CT £467.07 TOTE £12.70: £3.60, £2.50, £2.50; EX 148.60.
Owner Ambrose Turnbull **Bred** Killian Farm **Trained** Uplawmoor, E Renfrews
■ Stewards' Enquiry : P J McDonald one-day ban: careless riding (Oct 5)
Phillip Makin one-day ban: careless riding (Oct 5)

FOCUS
A modest handicap which was run at a strong pace. Sound but limited form, rated through the third.

6053 M & M FABRICATIONS H'CAP (FOR THE EGLINTON & WINTON CHALLENGE CUP) — 2m 1f 105y
5:45 (5:47) (Class 4) (0-80,76) 4-Y-O+ £6,476 (£1,927; £963; £481) **Stalls** Low

Form RPR

00/ **1** **Ecole D'Art (USA)**[34] 3183 8-8-13 **68** .... JohnEgan 14 76
(J J Lambe, Ire) *s.i.s: hld up: gd hdwy on outside over 2f out: led over 1f out: styd on wl* **25/1**

3254 **2** 1¼ **Danzatrice**[12] 5696 7-8-12 **67** .... PaulHanagan 4 74
(C W Thornton) *hld up and bhd: hdwy over 2f out: chsd wnr ins fnl f: r.o* **8/1**

3163 **3** *nk* **Simonside**[12] 5696 6-8-10 **70** .... MartinLane(5) 12 76
(B Ellison) *cl up: led over 3f out: sn rdn: hdd over 1f out: kpt on u.p* **5/1**[1]

-133 **4** 3½ **Summer Soul (IRE)**[26] 5291 7-9-2 **71** ....(p) RobertWinston 13 73
(Miss Lucinda V Russell) *cl up: led after 4f to over 3f out: kpt on same pce fr over 1f out* **14/1**

2556 **5** 1¼ **Lets Roll**[17] 5554 8-8-5 **60** .... PJMcDonald 6 60
(C W Thornton) *hld up: hdwy over 2f out: kpt on fnl f: no imp* **12/1**

1/42 **6** 1¼ **Pagan Starprincess**[118] 2262 5-7-13 **57** oh1 .... KellyHarrison(3) 9 56
(G M Moore) *hld up: hdwy 3f out: rdn and one pce over 1f out* **11/2**[2]

6312 **7** ¾ **No Rules**[53] 4388 4-8-6 **66** .... AshleyMorgan(5) 16 64
(M H Tompkins) *hld up: effrt 3f out: kpt on same pce fr 2f out* **6/1**[3]

0-20 **8** 2¼ **Baaher (USA)**[11] 5734 5-8-5 **60** .... RichardMullen 1 55
(J S Goldie) *midfield on ins: rdn and effrt over 3f out: outpcd fnl 2f* **12/1**

1605 **9** 8 **Forrest Flyer (IRE)**[26] 5291 5-8-11 **66** ow1 .... PhillipMakin 10 52
(I Semple) *bhd: outpcd over 4f out: n.d after* **22/1**

5000 **10** 4½ **Prince Rhyddarch**[11] 5734 4-7-11 **59** ....(p) JamesPSullivan(7) 5 39
(I Semple) *midfield: effrt over 3f out: wknd fr 2f out* **28/1**

14-5 **11** 1¾ **Woody Waller**[132] 1886 4-9-0 **72** .... FrederikTylicki(3) 3 50
(J Howard Johnson) *in tch: effrt over 3f out: wknd fr 2f out* **6/1**[3]

04-0 **12** 1½ **Sphinx (FR)**[21] 5410 11-9-7 **76** ....(b) TonyHamilton 8 52
(E W Tuer) *cl up tl rdn and wknd fr 2f out* **20/1**

/54- **13** *nk* **According To Pete**[237] 5993 8-8-13 **68** .... TomEaves 17 44
(J M Jefferson) *led 4f: chsd ldrs: rdn 4f out: wknd fnl 2f* **8/1**

3400 **14** 30 **Merrion Tiger (IRE)**[50] 4462 4-8-4 **59** .... GregFairley 2 —
(A G Foster) *in tch on ins tl rdn and wknd 4f out: t.o* **40/1**

3m 51.53s (-8.97) **Going Correction** -0.325s/f (Firm) **14 Ran SP% 123.7**
Speed ratings (Par 105): **108,107,107,105,105 104,104,103,99,97 96,95,95,81**
toteswingers: 1&2 £50.30, 1&3 £45.90, 2&3 £14.60 CSF £208.43 CT £1189.37 TOTE £36.70: £10.80, £3.40, £2.90; EX 447.40 Place 6: £3941.52 Place 5: £2957.48 .
Owner Mighty Macs Syndicate **Bred** Darley Stud **Trained** Dungannon, Co. Tyrone

FOCUS
An ordinary staying handicap. The pace was not strong and the first two both came from the back of the field. Sound but limited form, the winner rated in line with his best recent hurdles efforts.
Woody Waller Official explanation: jockey said gelding lost its action but returned sound
T/Jkpt: Not won. T/Plt: £1,707.80 to a £1 stake. Pool: £78,492.40. 33.55 winning tickets. T/Qpdt: £298.80 to a £1 stake. Pool: £5,209.88. 12.90 winning tickets. RY

5021 NEWBURY (L-H)
Friday, September 18

OFFICIAL GOING: Good to firm (8.0)
Rail from 1mto 5f on round course moved out 6m increasing advertised distances by 12m.
Wind: Moderate behind Weather: Cloudy

6054 DUBAI DUTY FREE GOLF WORLD CUP E B F MAIDEN STKS — 6f 8y
1:40 (1:43) (Class 4) 2-Y-O £5,504 (£1,637; £818; £408) **Stalls** Centre

Form RPR

1 **Pastoral Player** 2-9-3 0 .... SteveDrowne 9 92+
(H Morrison) *s.i.s: hld up in rr tl gd hdwy over 2f out: qckd to chse ldr ins fnl f: drvn to ld last strides whn carried lft but won gng away* **12/1**

2 **2** *nk* **Locksley Hall (USA)**[9] 5778 2-9-3 0 .... JimmyFortune 12 91+
(E F Vaughan) *led: rdn over 1f out: edgd lft u.p cl home and hdd last strides* **9/4**[1]

3 **3** 4 **Kalypso King (USA)**[25] 5317 2-9-3 0 .... RyanMoore 3 79
(R Hannon) *chsd ldrs: rdn over 2f out: outpcd by ldng duo fnl f* **5/2**[2]

4 ½ **London Gold** 2-9-3 0 .... FergusSweeney 6 78+
(H Candy) *chsd ldr: rdn over 2f out: styd on same pce appr fnl f* **50/1**

5 3 **Strictly Dancing (IRE)** 2-8-12 0 .... WilliamBuick 7 64+
(A M Balding) *sn towards rr: drvn along over 2f out: kpt on fnl f but nvr anywhere nr ldrs* **20/1**

6 ½ **Midwestern (USA)** 2-9-3 0 .... TedDurcan 13 67
(M L W Bell) *chsd ldrs: rdn over 2f out: wknd appr fnl f* **33/1**

7 2 **Darshonin** 2-9-3 0 .... ShaneKelly 10 61
(J Noseda) *in tch: rdn 3f out: outpcd 2f out: kpt on again ins fnl f* **14/1**

8 ¾ **Scottish Boogie (IRE)** 2-9-3 0 .... DavidProbert 8 59
(S Kirk) *chsd ldrs: rdn 3f out: wknd ins fnl 2f* **66/1**

00 **9** *nk* **Seeking Stardom**[10] 5749 2-9-3 0 .... IanMongan 15 58
(P M Phelan) *chsd ldrs: rdn 3f out: wknd 2f out* **100/1**

06 **10** 1¼ **Dutiful**[15] 5603 2-9-3 0 .... AlanMunro 4 54
(M R Channon) *chsd ldrs: rdn ins fnl 3f: wknd 2f out* **66/1**

11 2¼ **Avon Rock** 2-9-3 0 ....(t) SimonWhitworth 14 47+
(J W Hills) *s.i.s: a towards rr* **100/1**

12 ½ **Monograph** 2-9-3 0 .... MichaelHills 2 46
(J W Hills) *a in rr* **66/1**

13 *1* **Alkhataaf (USA)** 2-9-3 0 .... TPO'Shea 1 43
(J L Dunlop) *a in rr* **4/1[3]**

14 *hd* **Tamarind Hill (IRE)** 2-9-3 0 .... JimCrowley 11 42
(C R Egerton) *s.i.s: a towards rr* **50/1**

1m 12.66s (-0.34) **Going Correction** +0.025s/f (Good) **14** Ran SP% **111.8**
Speed ratings (Par 97): **103,102,97,96,92 91,89,88,87,86 83,82,81,80**
toteswingers: 1&2 £5.20, 1&3 £8.00, 2&3 £1.50 CSF £33.27 TOTE £13.00: £3.40, £1.40, £1.20; EX 52.10.

Owner The Pursuits Partnership **Bred** Whitsbury Manor Stud & Pigeon House Stud **Trained** East Ilsley, Berks

■ Imperial Delight was withdrawn (12/1, unruly in the stalls). R4 applies, deduct 5p in the £.

FOCUS
There was a fair breeze behind the runners up the straight in this maiden, which featured some interesting newcomers taking on rivals with form in the book.

NOTEBOOK
Pastoral Player, a half-brother to four other juvenile winners, was on his toes beforehand but settled well in the pack and produced an impressive turn of foot to close down Locksley Hall, who had got first run on him, inside the final furlong and a half. His stable won a division of this race two years ago with Stimulation, and like him one suspects that this colt will never want further than 7f. He looks to have a bright future, though. (op 9-1)
Locksley Hall(USA), runner-up on his debut at Kempton, was towards the fore throughout and did nothing wrong in defeat, finishing well clear of the rest. A reproduction of this form should see him off the mark soon enough. (op 7-2)
Kalypso King(USA), another with the benefit of a previous run under his belt, rallied to take third late on and shapes as though he wants 7f, which makes sense given that he's out of a mare who finished second in the Oaks. (op 9-4 tchd 11-4)
London Gold, who did not look the stable's number one going by jockey bookings, outran his odds and shaped encouragingly. A half-brother to a dual winner over 5f, an ordinary maiden should come his way before too long.
Strictly Dancing(IRE), a half-sister to two winners, and out of the Nunthorpe winner Lochangel, was the only filly in the field. She showed signs of greenness but ran on well at the business end and is entitled to improve for her debut effort.
Midwestern(USA) looks the type to benefit from more time, but it was an encouraging debut from this American-bred colt.
Darshonin, a 200,000gns purchase, was another who ran green. He's by Pivotal and some ease in the ground might help him in the coming weeks. (op 12-1)
Alkhataaf(USA), a half-brother to Dewhurst winner Mujahid, was the disappointment of the race, struggling to get involved at any point. The market suggested better was expected. (op 7-2 tchd 9-2)

6055 DUBAI DUTY FREE FULL OF SURPRISES E B F FILLIES' CONDITIONS STKS 7f (S)
2:10 (2:15) (Class 2) 2-Y-O

£11,215 (£3,358; £1,679; £840; £419; £210) **Stalls** Centre

Form RPR

1 **Silver Rock (IRE)** 2-8-12 0 .... JimmyFortune 6 84+
(M A Magnusson) *trckd ldrs: drvn to ld jst ins fnl f: styd on strly fnl 100yds* **9/1**

0 2 *3/4* **Lost Horizon (IRE)**[15] 5604 2-8-12 0 .... DaneO'Neill 2 82
(R Hannon) *towards rr: hdwy fr 3f out: chsd ldrs fr 2f out: wnt 2nd ins fnl f and kpt on but a readily hld by wnr* **9/1**

3 *2* **Maristar (USA)** 2-8-12 0 .... SteveDrowne 3 77
(G A Butler) *towards rr: hdwy over 2f out: kpt on wl fnl f but nvr quite gng pce of ldng duo* **16/1**

4 *1* **Red Fantasy (IRE)** 2-8-12 0 .... MichaelHills 8 77+
(B W Hills) *in rr: pushed along 3f out: hdwy fr 2f out: shkn up and styd on wl thrght fnl f: fin wl* **20/1**

31 5 *nk* **Moonline Dancer (FR)**[34] 5026 2-9-2 81 .... RyanMoore 1 78
(R Hannon) *chsd ldrs: rdn to ld over 2f out: hdd jst ins fnl f: wknd fnl 100yds* **7/1[3]**

1 6 *1/2* **Dawnbreak (USA)**[10] 5752 2-9-2 0 .... LDettori 12 77
(Saeed Bin Suroor) *t.k.h: chsd ldrs: rdn 2f out: wknd ins fnl f* **5/2[2]**

32 7 *1 1/4* **Boogie Diva**[21] 5397 2-8-12 0 .... TedDurcan 4 72+
(M Botti) *in tch: pushed along over 2f out: stl green u.p fnl f: sme prog fnl 100yds* **15/8[1]**

41 8 *1 3/4* **Ferris Wheel (IRE)**[14] 5638 2-9-2 0 .... JimCrowley 7 71+
(P F I Cole) *chsd ldrs: rdn 3f out: no imp on ldrs 2f out: wknd over 1f out* **14/1**

003 9 *5* **Ashkalara**[36] 4945 2-8-12 66 .... KirstyMilczarek 9 53
(H S Howe) *slowly away: sn rcvrd to chse ldrs: rdn 3f out: wknd 2f out* **50/1**

10 *6* **Ramayana (IRE)** 2-8-12 0 .... AlanMunro 10 38
(M R Channon) *plld hrd: led tl hdd over 2f out: wknd qckly* **66/1**

11 *shd* **Mavalenta (IRE)** 2-8-12 0 .... WilliamBuick 11 38
(J W Hills) *chsd ldrs: rdn and green 3f out: sn wknd* **66/1**

12 *3/4* **Rosie's Magic** 2-8-12 0 .... FrankieMcDonald 5 36
(W De Best-Turner) *chsd ldrs: rdn 3f out: sn wknd* **150/1**

1m 26.01s (0.31) **Going Correction** +0.025s/f (Good) **12** Ran SP% **118.8**
Speed ratings (Par 98): **99,98,95,94,94 93,92,90,84,77 77,76**
toteswingers: 1&2 £12.60, 1&3 £27.90, 2&3 £32.70 CSF £84.95 TOTE £11.40: £2.70, £3.60, £4.20; EX 104.20.

Owner Eastwind Racing Ltd and Martha Trussell **Bred** Soc Finanza Locale Consulting Srl **Trained** Upper Lambourn, Berks

FOCUS
An interesting conditions race for fillies won by a quietly backed newcomer.

NOTEBOOK
Silver Rock(IRE), a daughter of Rock Of Gibraltar out of a mare who won over 1m2f, knew her job first time up, travelled well up with the pace and, when asked to go on, picked up for her rider. It's difficult to know what the form is worth but we'll learn more if she's stepped up into Listed company next time. (op 8-1 tchd 10-1)
Lost Horizon(IRE), despite having finished down the field on her debut, was well backed beforehand. A daughter of Elusive City, she clearly appreciated these quicker conditions compared to the soft ground she encountered at Salisbury, and on this evidence winning a maiden should be a formality. (tchd 15-2)
Maristar(USA) ◆, who's by Giant's Causeway out of a mare who won the Breeders' Cup Distaff, wasn't knocked about to achieve a staying-on third. She looked one of the nicer long-term prospects in the race and should soon get off the mark, either on turf or on Polytrack, which, given her pedigree, should suit her just as well. (op 40-1 tchd 50-1)
Red Fantasy(IRE), who was one of the first off the bridle, showed signs of inexperience when asked to make up ground from the rear, but she stayed on well and this daughter of High Chaparral should come into her own next season. (op 25-1)
Moonline Dancer(FR), who holds a Cheveley Park entry, was one of the first to kick for home but weakened quite badly inside the last. The return to 7f didn't suit her and a drop back to sprinting looks in order. (op 9-2)
Dawnbreak(USA), a winner on the Polytrack first time up, was drawn highest of all and raced on the stands' side of the bunch. She could have done with getting cover, though, as she raced far too keenly through the early stages and didn't have anything in reserve for the finish. Official explanation: jockey said filly ran too freely (op 11-4)
Boogie Diva was denied a clear run for some time, but she failed to make much progress once she saw daylight and it would be stretching things to suggest she was unlucky. (op 3-1)
Ashkalara Official explanation: trainer said filly was in season

6056 DUBAI DUTY FREE ARC TRIAL (GROUP 3) 1m 3f 5y
2:45 (2:45) (Class 1) 3-Y-O+

£36,900 (£13,988; £7,000; £3,490; £1,748; £877) **Stalls** Low

Form RPR

-101 1 **Doctor Fremantle**[71] 3781 4-9-8 113 .... RyanMoore 6 120+
(Sir Michael Stoute) *stdd s: hld up in rr tl hdwy 3f out: nt clr run and swtchd rt over 2f out: styd on wl u.p fnl f: led last stride* **3/1[3]**

-336 2 *nse* **Look Here**[55] 4298 4-9-0 116 .... JimCrowley 4 112
(R M Beckett) *sn trcking ldr: rdn into slt ld ins fnl 2f: kpt advantage u.p fnl f tl ct last stride* **7/4[1]**

2021 3 *1* **Campanologist (USA)**[20] 5447 4-9-6 114 .... LDettori 3 116
(Saeed Bin Suroor) *sn led: narrowly hdd ins fnl 2f: styd pressing ldr and ev ch ins fnl f: outpcd fnl 100yds* **9/4[2]**

340- 4 *3* **City Leader (IRE)**[335] 6816 4-9-3 114 .... TedDurcan 5 109
(B J Meehan) *t.k.h in rr: swtchd rt and shkn up over 2f out: no imp on ldrs: and styd on same pce fr over 1f out* **14/1**

0321 5 *1 3/4* **Halicarnassus (IRE)**[15] 5619 5-9-8 110 .... AlanMunro 2 111
(M R Channon) *chsd ldrs: rdn 3f out: wknd 2f out* **14/1**

0300 6 *4 1/2* **King Of Rome (IRE)**[13] 5662 4-9-3 110 .... PatCosgrave 1 99
(M F De Kock, South Africa) *chsd ldrs: rdn 3f out: wknd qckly 2f out* **22/1**

2m 19.97s (-1.23) **Going Correction** +0.025s/f (Good) **6** Ran SP% **109.8**
Speed ratings (Par 113): **105,104,104,102,100 97**
toteswingers: 1&2 £1.50, 1&3 £1.50, 2&3 £1.60 CSF £8.27 TOTE £3.80: £2.00, £1.50; EX 8.30.

Owner K Abdulla **Bred** Juddmonte Farms Ltd **Trained** Newmarket, Suffolk

FOCUS
The rail from the 1m start on the Round course to the 5f point was 6m out, increasing race distances by 12m. The race title is a misnomer, but nevertheless this looked a good race for a Group 3 contest, and it produced a thrilling finish. A personal best from Doctor Fremantle, but Look Here continues below her best.

NOTEBOOK
Doctor Fremantle did well to pick the front two up having allowed them to get first run on him. He has the look of a classic Sir Michael Stoute-trained older horse, improving with racing and tough to boot - the largest winning distance he's recorded in his last three successes has been by a neck - and the next step has to be another crack at a Group 1 contest. He wouldn't look up to winning an Arc, but there are other plenty of other valuable Group 1 contests on the continent that he could go for, with races like the Canadian International and Hong Kong Vase appealing most at this stage. (op 11-4 tchd 100-30)
Look Here was favoured by the weights but was again below her very best form. Well placed throughout, she responded well to pressure to get the better of Campanologist, but succumbed to the winner's turn of foot on the line. A stronger all-round pace would have suited her better, as perhaps would have softer ground. (op 5-2 tchd 11-4)
Campanologist(USA) reverted to front-running tactics and was able to dictate a pace to suit himself. He's probably a little flattered by the bare form but he's a solid performer at this level. (op 2-1 tchd 15-8)
City Leader(IRE) had been off the track since finishing down the field in last year's Champion Stakes. Not knocked about on this reappearance, he should come on plenty for the run, and connections will presumably have been more than happy with his comeback. He holds the Champion Stakes entry again this year. (tchd 12-1 and 16-1 in a place)
Halicarnassus(IRE), who won a valuable Group 2 in Turkey last time out, took this race two years ago. Worst in at the weights under his 5lb penalty, he wasn't quite at his best, and perhaps his recent travels had taken their toll. (op 12-1 tchd 11-1)
King Of Rome(IRE) has struggled for form since finishing down the field in the Sheema Classic back in March. (op 16-1)

6057 HAYNES, HANSON & CLARK CONDITIONS STKS 1m (S)
3:20 (3:21) (Class 2) 2-Y-O

£11,215 (£3,358; £1,679; £840; £419; £210) **Stalls** Low

Form RPR

1 1 **Ameer (IRE)**[21] 5400 2-9-2 0 .... LDettori 7 88+
(Saeed Bin Suroor) *mde all: drvn over 2f out: styd on resolutely thrght fnl f and wl in command clsng stages* **6/5[1]**

1 2 *3/4* **Private Story (USA)**[28] 5220 2-9-2 0 .... RyanMoore 5 86
(R Hannon) *chsd ldrs: niggled along fr 4f out: styd on u.p fnl 2f and chsd wnr ins fnl f but a hld* **9/2[3]**

3 *1* **Lunar Victory (USA)** 2-8-12 0 .... JimmyFortune 3 80+
(J H M Gosden) *hld up towards rr: stdy hdwy over 2f out: drvn and effrt between horses appr fnl f and briefly chsd wnr ins fnl f and swtchd lft: nvr gng pce to chal and one pce fnl 100yds* **3/1[2]**

31 4 *1* **Shaayeq (IRE)**[15] 5590 2-9-2 77 ....(v[1]) TPO'Shea 1 82
(M P Tregoning) *chsd ldrs: rdn to chse wnr appr fnl 2f: nvr gng pce to chal: kpt on same pce fnl f* **8/1**

5 *10* **Tahseen** 2-8-12 0 .... TedDurcan 2 56+
(M P Tregoning) *s.i.s: in rr: sn pushed along and v green: a bhd* **11/1**

026 6 *1* **Starwatch**[2] 5994 2-8-12 0 .... MarcHalford 4 54
(J J Bridger) *chsd wnr tl rdn over 2f out and sn wknd* **80/1**

1m 38.68s (-1.02) **Going Correction** +0.025s/f (Good) **6** Ran SP% **109.3**
Speed ratings (Par 101): **106,105,104,103,93 92**
toteswingers: 1&2 £2.00, 1&3 £1.20, 2&3 £2.10 CSF £6.58 TOTE £1.90: £1.40, £2.20; EX 5.80.

Owner Godolphin **Bred** E Puerari, Oceanic Blds & Charleton Blds **Trained** Newmarket, Suffolk

FOCUS
A race with a rich history, having been won by the likes of Nayef, King's Theatre, Unfuwain, Rainbow Quest, Shergar and Henbit in the past. Other future top-class performers have been beaten in the race, too (Authorized was third in 2006 for example), so it's always worth looking further down the field for future stars as well.

NOTEBOOK
Ameer(IRE), who made a good impression on his debut, dictated throughout and found plenty for pressure. The race very much went his way, but there's plenty of stamina in his pedigree and he looks a promising middle-distance prospect for next season. He's in the Timeform Million sales race at Newmarket next month, but dropping back to 7f isn't likely to be in his favour. Softer ground might be, though. (op 11-10 tchd Evens)
Private Story(USA), who has the Goffs Million Mile as his big autumn target, is a lazy type but he kept responding to pressure and kept on well up the rail to take second. This should have set him up nicely for his trip to Ireland. (op 7-2)

Lunar Victory(USA) ◆, one of only two newcomers in the line-up, looks the one to take from the race. Having travelled well under a patient ride, he kept on well under considerate handling and shaped like the type to benefit greatly from the experience. His pedigree is a mix of speed and stamina as his sire Speightstown won the Breeders' Cup Sprint while his dam won over 1m2f, so it's difficult to know what his ideal distance will be next season. He'll look a certainty to win his maiden next time out, before returning to better company. (op 11-2 tchd 6-1 in places)
Shaayeq(IRE), representing a yard that had won this race four times in the previous ten years, hadn't achieved a great deal when successful at Epsom on his previous start, but a Dewhurst entry suggested connections believed he was capable of better. The fitting of a visor for the first time was off-putting, though, and his response under pressure in the race itself was limited. His sights will have to be lowered now. (op 11-2 tchd 5-1 in places)
Tahseen, whose rider carried the owner's second colours, was too green to do himself justice on his debut. Bred to stay much further than this in time (his dam won over 1m6f), he won't come into his own until next season. (op 12-1)

6058 DUBAI DUTY FREE CUP (LISTED RACE) 7f (S)
3:55 (3:55) (Class 1) 3-Y-0+
£22,708 (£8,608; £4,308; £2,148; £1,076; £540) **Stalls** Centre

Form RPR

3201 **1** **Ashram (IRE)**[25] 5313 3-8-13 110 (v) TedDurcan 6 113
(Saeed Bin Suroor) *mde all: rdn along 2f out: styd on strly fnl f* **6/1**

0-25 **2** *2 ½* **Huntdown (USA)**[28] 5232 3-8-13 111 LDettori 5 108+
(Saeed Bin Suroor) *chsd ldrs: rdn to go 2nd over 1f out: no imp on wnr ins fnl f* **3/1[2]**

65 **3** *1 ¾* **Festoso (IRE)**[62] 4087 4-8-11 101 (b[1]) RyanMoore 3 98
(H J L Dunlop) *in rr: drvn along 3f out: styd on u.p to take 3rd ins fnl f but nvr any ch w ldng duo* **20/1**

31-5 **4** *nk* **Stimulation (IRE)**[6] 5862 4-9-2 118 DarryllHolland 4 103
(H Morrison) *chsd ldrs: rdn and wnt narrow 2nd 2f out but nvr nr wnr: wknd fnl f* **6/4[1]**

0020 **5** *2 ¼* **Prime Defender**[34] 5024 5-9-2 108 MichaelHills 1 97
(B W Hills) *chsd wnr: rdn 3f out: lost 2nd 2f out: sn btn* **8/1**

5-60 **6** *3 ½* **Tariq**[111] 2483 5-9-2 110 JimmyFortune 2 88
(P W Chapple-Hyam) *bmpd and stmbld s: bhd: rdn: hung lft and no rspnse 2f out* **11/2[3]**

1m 23.72s (-1.98) **Going Correction** +0.025s/f (Good)
WFA 3 from 4yo+ 3lb 6 Ran SP% **110.5**
Speed ratings (Par 111): **112,109,107,106,104 100**
toteswingers: 1&2 £2.50, 1&3 £8.40, 2&3 £8.60 CSF £23.40 TOTE £7.20: £2.90, £1.80; EX 16.10.
Owner Godolphin **Bred** Waterford Hall Stud **Trained** Newmarket, Suffolk

FOCUS
Like in the previous race a Godolphin colt was allowed an uncontested lead and proceeded to make every yard. The winner is rated back to his juvenile best.

NOTEBOOK
Ashram(IRE) was the only runner in the race arriving here off the back of a win and this former Guineas hopeful, who is probably at his best over this trip, settled well in front and was never really threatened. He would have to take another step up to play a major part in the Group 2 Challenge Stakes at Newmarket on Champions Day, but at least we know the C&D suits, as he recorded his best efforts as a juvenile there when winning the Group 3 Somerville Tattersall Stakes and finishing sixth in the Dewhurst. (op 15-2)
Huntdown(USA), stablemate of the winner and the choice of Frankie Dettori, looked to hold strong claims in this company, but with Ashram dictating a pace to suit himself, he was always playing catch-up once that rival got first run. (tchd 100-30 and 7-2 in places)
Festoso(IRE), who wouldn't ideally want the ground this quick, ran a sound race in first-time blinkers on her return from a two-month break. She ought to find conditions turning in her favour in the coming weeks and will be interesting back in fillies'-only Listed company.
Stimulation(IRE), who won the Challenge Stakes last term, was favoured by the weights here but he looked a candidate to bounce following his return from an 11-month absence at Doncaster just six days earlier, and perhaps the race did come too soon for him. (op 11-8 tchd 13-8)
Prime Defender, who had a job on at the weights, is more effective over 6f. (op 10-1)
Tariq, who'd been off the track since May, could make little impression from well off the pace. He was entitled to need the run but this was still a very tame effort. Official explanation: jockey said horse had stumbled leaving teh stalls, lost a shoe, and got struck into. (op 5-1 tchd 9-2)

6059 DUBAI DUTY FREE FINEST SURPRISE STKS (H'CAP) 1m 2f 6y
4:30 (4:30) (Class 4) (0-85,85) 3-Y-0+ **£4,857** (£1,445; £722; £360) **Stalls** Low

Form RPR

3506 **1** **The Which Doctor**[18] 5510 4-9-8 85 RyanMoore 1 93
(J Noseda) *t.k.h: stdd in tch: hdwy and n.m.r over 2f out: swtchd rt and qcknd over 1f out: led ins fnl f: drvn out* **7/2[2]**

2402 **2** *½* **Brouhaha**[36] 4957 5-9-1 78 RichardKingscote 7 85
(Tom Dascombe) *trckd ldr: chal fr 3f out: led over 2f out: kpt on u.p tl hdd ins fnl f and styd on same pce* **8/1**

2210 **3** *1 ¼* **Wing Play (IRE)**[17] 5551 4-9-4 81 (p) ShaneKelly 3 85+
(H Morrison) *hld up towards rr: hdwy on ins fr 4f out: nt clr run fr 2f out tl swtchd rt jst ins fnl f: carried hd awkwardly but styd on cl home* **8/1**

0-61 **4** *1* **King's Song (IRE)**[15] 5616 3-8-3 72 WilliamBuick 11 74
(Sir Michael Stoute) *chsd ldrs: rdn and effrt 2f out: nvr quite on terms: wknd ins fnl f* **3/1[1]**

3452 **5** *¾* **Calaloo (IRE)**[7] 5834 3-8-6 75 (b) SteveDrowne 4 76
(C R Egerton) *hld up in tch: hdwy over 2f out: sn rdn and no imp: styd on u.p ins fnl f but nvr a threat* **7/1[3]**

3550 **6** *1 ¼* **Kidlat**[8] 5802 4-9-0 77 (t) JimCrowley 2 75
(B G Powell) *chsd ldrs: rdn over 3f out: styd wl there tl wknd fnl f* **12/1**

-004 **7** *hd* **Maxwil**[18] 5508 4-8-12 75 IanMongan 6 73+
(P M Phelan) *hld up in rr: hdwy 2f out: rdn and edgd lft over 1f out: kpt on ins fnl f but nvr a threat* **33/1**

3326 **8** *1 ¾* **Princely Hero (IRE)**[52] 1894 5-9-5 82 LDettori 8 76
(C Gordon) *sn led: hdd appr fnl 2f: wknd appr fnl f* **16/1**

6053 **9** *6* **Humble Opinion**[5] 5915 7-8-13 76 (b) FergusSweeney 9 58
(A King) *t.k.h: chsd ldrs: rdn over 2f out: sn btn* **7/1[3]**

1600 **10** *¾* **Sir Boss (IRE)**[13] 5667 4-8-10 80 RosieJessop[(7)] 10 61
(D E Cantillon) *in rr: sme prog towards outside 3f out: nvr rchd ldrs and bhd fnl 2f* **16/1**

2m 7.66s (-1.14) **Going Correction** +0.025s/f (Good)
WFA 3 from 4yo+ 6lb 10 Ran SP% **116.8**
Speed ratings (Par 105): **105,104,103,102,102 101,101,99,94,94**
toteswingers: 1&2 £8.60, 1&3 £4.30, 2&3 £10.20 CSF £31.87 CT £210.81 TOTE £4.40: £2.00, £2.20, £2.60; EX 37.90.
Owner G C Stevens **Bred** Limestone And Tara Studs **Trained** Newmarket, Suffolk

FOCUS
There was a fairly steady early pace to this handicap and it developed into a bit of a sprint.
The Which Doctor Official explanation: trainer's representative had no explanation for the apparent improvement of form
Wing Play(IRE) Official explanation: jockey said gelding had been denied a clear run

6060 DUBAI DUTY FREE FOUNDATION H'CAP 1m 4f 5y
5:05 (5:05) (Class 4) (0-85,81) 3-Y-0+ **£4,857** (£1,445; £722; £360) **Stalls** Low

Form RPR

0015 **1** **Sweet Hollow**[13] 5667 3-8-12 75 (b) LukeMorris 6 83
(C G Cox) *chsd ldrs tl rdn 3f out and outpcd: rallied u.p over 1f out and styd on to ld fnl 50yds: hung rt cl home* **13/2**

002- **2** *1 ¾* **Benfleet Boy**[168] 6983 5-9-3 72 MichaelHills 2 77
(B G Powell) *led at modest pce tl qcknd fr 4f out: styd on u.p fr 2f out: hdd and outpcd fnl 50yds* **11/2**

1030 **3** *nk* **Tilos Gem (IRE)**[36] 4957 3-8-13 76 TPO'Shea 4 81
(M Johnston) *chsd ldr: rdn to chal 1f out: styd on same pce ins fnl f* **8/1**

1403 **4** *1 ½* **Cosmea**[5] 5912 4-9-12 81 DaneO'Neill 1 83
(A King) *s.i.s: hld up in rr: drvn and hdwy on outside fr 2f out: one pce ins fnl f* **5/1[3]**

5233 **5** *nk* **Colonel Flay**[28] 5217 5-9-3 72 TedDurcan 8 74
(Mrs P N Dutfield) *hld up in rr: rdn and no prog fr 3f out: styd on ins fnl f but nvr gng pce to get into contention* **3/1[1]**

5643 **6** *1 ¼* **Sharpazmax (IRE)**[13] 5667 5-9-10 79 SteveDrowne 5 79
(P J Makin) *t.k.h: hld up in tch: hrd dtievn and sme prog over 2f out: nvr rchd ldrs: wknd ins fnl f* **13/2**

6010 **7** *½* **Coeur De Lionne (IRE)**[13] 5671 5-9-10 79 RyanMoore 7 78
(E A L Dunlop) *chsd ldrs: rdn over 2f out: little rspnse: wknd ins fnl f* **9/2[2]**

2m 37.09s (1.59) **Going Correction** +0.025s/f (Good)
WFA 3 from 4yo+ 8lb 7 Ran SP% **113.0**
Speed ratings (Par 105): **95,93,93,92,92 91,91**
toteswingers: 1&2 £6.40, 1&3 £8.20, 2&3 £7.10 CSF £40.40 CT £288.34 TOTE £7.70: £3.70, £2.80; EX 48.50 Place 6: £135.65 Place 5: £97.46.
Owner The City & Provincial Partnership **Bred** Genesis Green Stud Ltd **Trained** Lambourn, Berks

FOCUS
An ordinary handicap run at a modest pace.
T/Plt: £476.70 to a £1 stake. Pool: £53,229.09. 81.50 winning tickets. T/Qpdt: £17.70 to a £1 stake. Pool: £4,761.07. 198.30 winning tickets. ST

5431 NEWMARKET (R-H)
Friday, September 18

OFFICIAL GOING: Good to firm (8.8)
A card confined to 2-y-os and the far-side course was used.
Wind: Light across Weather: Cloudy with sunny spells

6061 EXPRESS COFFEE CARS MEDIAN AUCTION MAIDEN STKS 6f
2:00 (2:00) (Class 4) 2-Y-0 **£3,885** (£1,156; £577; £288) **Stalls** Low

Form RPR

1 **Side Glance** 2-9-3 0 LPKeniry 4 83+
(A M Balding) *bit bkwd: w'like: lengthy: hld up: hdwy over 1f out: sn rdn: r.o to ld wl ins fnl f: readily* **50/1**

5 **2** *½* **Sophie's Beau (USA)**[35] 5000 2-9-3 0 MartinDwyer 11 79
(B J Meehan) *leggy: chsd ldr tl led over 4f out: rdn over 1f out: hdd wl ins fnl f* **6/1[3]**

66 **3** *½* **Kerchak (USA)**[18] 5505 2-9-3 0 JoeFanning 12 77
(W Jarvis) *lengthy: hld up: hdwy over 1f out: r.o: nt rch ldrs* **28/1**

042 **4** *¾* **Suited And Booted (IRE)**[21] 5401 2-9-3 80 PatDobbs 1 75
(R Hannon) *lw: led: hdd over 4f out: chsd ldr: rdn over 1f out: styd on same pce ins fnl f* **11/4[2]**

5 *¾* **Dever Dream** 2-8-12 0 KoseiMiura 6 68
(W J Haggas) *bit bkwd: lengthy: unf: chsd ldrs: rdn over 1f out: no ex ins fnl f* **33/1**

6 *1 ½* **Free For All (IRE)** 2-9-3 0 GeorgeBaker 9 71+
(S Kirk) *w'like: scope: str: bit bkwd: s.s and lost many l: nt clr run and hung lft over 1f out: r.o wl ins fnl f: nrst fin* **50/1**

3 **7** *1* **Dherghaam (IRE)**[28] 5234 2-9-3 0 RHills 2 67+
(E A L Dunlop) *chsd ldrs: rdn over 1f out: styd on same pce* **5/6[1]**

8 *½* **Little Garcon (USA)** 2-9-0 0 AndreaAtzeni[(3)] 8 64
(M Botti) *unf: scope: tall: angular: lean: hld up in tch: racd keenly: rdn over 1f out: wknd ins fnl f* **33/1**

9 *1 ¼* **Water Gipsy** 2-8-12 0 TPQueally 5 55
(G L Moore) *str: bit bkwd: prom: pushed along 2f out: wknd over 1f out* **66/1**

0060 **10** *3 ¼* **Bookiesindex Girl (IRE)**[14] 5635 2-8-12 51 AdrianMcCarthy 7 45
(J R Jenkins) *prom: rdn and hung rt over 2f out: wknd over 1f out* **150/1**

11 *nk* **Tuscan Gold** 2-9-3 0 SebSanders 10 49+
(Sir Mark Prescott) *unf: tall: lw: s.s: sn pushed along: a in rr* **25/1**

0 **12** *3 ½* **Hayek**[42] 4756 2-9-3 0 KFallon 3 48+
(W Jarvis) *st: bit bkwd: hld up: pushed along 1/2-way: wknd 2f out* **20/1**

1m 13.26s (1.06) **Going Correction** +0.125s/f (Good) 12 Ran SP% **119.5**
Speed ratings (Par 97): **97,96,95,94,93 91,90,89,88,83 83,78**
toteswingers: 1&2 £24.90, 1&3 £47.30, 2&3 £47.30 CSF £308.07 TOTE £46.80: £9.10, £2.00, £8.00; EX 271.10.
Owner Kingsclere Racing CLub **Bred** Kingsclere Stud **Trained** Kingsclere, Hants

FOCUS
An average maiden judged on the form on offer with half the field making their debuts.

NOTEBOOK
Side Glance, by the useful miler Passing Glance, was friendless in the market beforehand but made a very encouraging debut. Travelling well just off the pace until loosing his footing when nudged along over the furlong marker, he tended to carry his head to the right but still quickened up well to take the advantage towards the finish. He's an unfurnished gelding who is bred to get further in time but did his job well. (op 40-1)
Sophie's Beau(USA) had shaped with promise at the July course on his debut and this was another step in the right direction. Always up with the pace, he briefly looked set to score after seeing off most of the dangers, but he was eventually collared. He can go one better before long. (op 9-2)
Kerchak(USA) ◆, dropped back in trip after a couple efforts over 7f, ran a promising race, doing all his best work in the final furlong. A step back up in trip could see him find a similar opportunity now he's qualified for a mark. (op 25-1)
Suited And Booted(IRE) looked to have strong claims dropping back to 6f but, after being up with the pace for most of the way, his effort flattened out. (tchd 3-1)
Dever Dream was another who ran with credit after being up with the pace most of the way but had no more to give inside the distance. (tchd 40-1)
Free For All(IRE) should come on a bundle for this race as he completely missed the break and was not given too hard a time when keeping on from an impossible position. Official explanation: jockey said colt hung left (op 40-1)
Dherghaam(IRE) was disappointing as he held a decent position before being a little squeezed up over two furlongs out, and then failing to find anything when asked. (op 5-4)
Little Garcon(USA) was coltish beforehand. (tchd 25-1)

Tuscan Gold Official explanation: jockey said colt lost its action early

6062 E B F TRADITIONAL PASTY & PIE COMPANY MAIDEN FILLIES' STKS 1m

2:30 (2:33) (Class 4) 2-Y-O £5,180 (£1,541; £770; £384) Stalls Low

Form RPR

43 **1** **Golden Aria (IRE)**[15] 5605 2-9-0 0 PatDobbs 12 79
(R Hannon) *lw: hld up in tch: plld hrd: rdn to ld ins fnl f: styd on* **5/1**[3]

2 *½* **Timepiece** 2-9-0 0 TPQueally 11 78+
(H R A Cecil) *w'like: scope: chsd ldrs: pushed along 3f out: led wl over 1f out: rdn and hdd ins fnl f: styd on* **11/8**[1]

3 *shd* **Gertrude Bell** 2-9-0 0 RobertHavlin 8 78+
(J H M Gosden) *leggy: hld up: nt clr run over 2f out: hdwy and nt clr run over 1f out: sn rdn: r.o* **14/1**

4 *2¾* **Woodford Belle (USA)** 2-9-0 0 MartinDwyer 15 72
(B J Meehan) *w'like: scope: hld up: outpcd 1/2-way: swtchd rt and hdwy on outside over 1f out: rdn and hung lft ins fnl f: styd on same pce* **25/1**

4 **5** *1½* **Miss Miracle**[21] 5397 2-9-0 0 AdamKirby 7 68
(C G Cox) *leggy: lean: chsd ldr tl led 2f out: sn rdn and hdd: no ex fnl f* **4/1**[2]

6 *nse* **Little Oz (IRE)** 2-9-0 0 DO'Donohoe 10 68
(E A L Dunlop) *unf: bit bkwd: dwlt: hld up: effrt whn hmpd over 1f out: swtchd lft and r.o ins fnl f: nvr able to chal* **100/1**

0 **7** *2* **Consider Yourself (USA)**[21] 5398 2-9-0 0 JamieSpencer 6 64
(M L W Bell) *w'like: bit bkwd: hld up: swtchd rt 5f out: hdwy over 2f out: rdn over 1f out: wknd fnl f* **33/1**

4 **8** *1¼* **Al Joza**[72] 3733 2-9-0 0 ChrisCatlin 1 61
(C E Brittain) *w'like: leggy: b: led 6f: sn rdn: wknd fnl f* **12/1**

06 **9** *nk* **Miniyamba (IRE)**[15] 5605 2-9-0 0 JoeFanning 13 60
(J L Dunlop) *lw: prom: rdn over 2f out: hung lft over 1f out: sn wknd* **14/1**

00 **10** *1¾* **Forethought**[10] 5741 2-9-0 0 HayleyTurner 9 57
(P Howling) *chsd ldrs: pushed along 3f out: rdn and wknd over 1f out* **40/1**

11 *nk* **Astromoon** 2-9-0 0 JimmyQuinn 4 59+
(M H Tompkins) *w'like: scope: s.i.s: hld up: shkn up over 3f out: nvr on terms* **100/1**

12 *1½* **Saggiatore** 2-9-0 0 TGMcLaughlin 5 53
(E A L Dunlop) *lengthy: scope: bit bkwd: hld up in tch: rdn and wknd over 2f out* **40/1**

13 *hd* **Balsha (USA)** 2-9-0 0 RHills 2 52
(E A L Dunlop) *w'like: scope: bit bkwd: dwlt: sn prom: rdn over 2f out: wknd over 1f out* **14/1**

1m 40.94s (2.34) **Going Correction** +0.125s/f (Good) **13 Ran SP% 120.1**
Speed ratings (Par 94): **93,92,92,89,88 88,86,84,84,82 82,81,80**
toteswingers: 1&2 £2.20, 1&3 £11.90, 2&3 £5.50 CSF £11.79 TOTE £5.80: £2.00, £1.10, £5.00; EX 16.90.

Owner Thurloe Thoroughbreds XX **Bred** Mrs Mary Coonan **Trained** East Everleigh, Wilts

FOCUS
Often a decent fillies' maiden and this renewal should throw up plenty of future winners.

NOTEBOOK
Golden Aria(IRE) proved too good. The winner has progressed steadily as she has been upped in trip and once again this was another step forward. She was keen enough early on before finding cover but she saw this trip out well after hitting the front inside the final furlong. She is a good-actioned filly who will now be put away for the season. (op 11-2 tchd 4-1)
Timepiece ◆, a half-sister to Passage Of Time and Father Time, ran with plenty of credit in defeat and was just beaten by a race hardened individual. After racing up with the pace, she had to be ridden along from three furlongs out but stuck to her task well when headed inside the distance. She has plenty of scope for improvement, especially with the ground thought to be plenty lively enough for her. (op 5-4 tchd 6-4)
Gertrude Bell ◆ was a little slowly away but stayed on well from the rear after being switched to the centre and looks to have a promising future, especially when upped in trip as her breeding would suggest. (op 16-1 tchd 12-1)
Woodford Belle(USA) was another who showed promise and, though never troubling the principals, stayed on well enough from the rear. (op 33-1)
Miss Miracle, a half sister to champion hurdle winner Katchit and Lingfield Oaks Trial winner Miracle Seeker, confirmed initial promise with another sound effort and should be capable of finding an opening before long. (op 5-1 tchd 11-2)
Little Oz(IRE) missed the break slightly and was also far too keen early on but this was an encouraging debut. Official explanation: jockey said filly was denied a clear run
Astromoon Official explanation: jockey said filly lost its action

6063 EXPRESS CAFES NURSERY H'CAP 7f

3:05 (3:05) (Class 3) (0-95,88) 2-Y-O £7,771 (£2,312; £1,155; £577) Stalls Low

Form RPR

1201 **1** **Audacity Of Hope**[9] 5762 2-9-9 88 6ex (t) KFallon 4 93
(P J McBride) *lw: hld up: hdwy to chse ldr over 1f out: rdn to ld wl ins fnl f: r.o* **4/6**[1]

2100 **2** *hd* **Sea Lord (IRE)**[13] 5658 2-9-3 82 JoeFanning 6 87
(M Johnston) *lw: led: rdn over 1f out: edgd rt and hdd wl ins fnl f: r.o* **7/2**[2]

4316 **3** *3¾* **Universal Circus**[13] 5659 2-9-2 81 ChrisCatlin 3 76
(M R Channon) *prom: rdn to chse ldr 2f out: sn edgd lft: no ex fnl f* **12/1**

3345 **4** *3½* **Zinjbar (USA)**[44] 4647 2-8-8 73 KoseiMiura 5 59
(C E Brittain) *chsd ldr tl rdn 2f out: n.m.r sn after: hung lft over 1f out: sn wknd* **14/1**

4215 **5** *2½* **Arabian Pride**[18] 5521 2-9-7 86 JamieSpencer 2 66
(D M Simcock) *sn chsng ldrs: effrt and nt clr run over 1f out: sn wknd* **10/1**[3]

2626 **6** *2* **Florio Vincitore (IRE)**[11] 5739 2-8-13 78 EdwardCreighton 1 53
(E J Creighton) *hld up: racd keenly: wknd over 1f out* **20/1**

1m 26.98s (1.58) **Going Correction** +0.125s/f (Good) **6 Ran SP% 110.4**
Speed ratings (Par 99): **95,94,90,86,83 81**
toteswingers: 1&2 £1.30, 1&3 £2.30, 2&3 £3.10 CSF £3.07 TOTE £1.60: £1.10, £2.40; EX 3.00.

Owner Four Winds Racing **Bred** Wood Farm Stud (Waresley) **Trained** Newmarket, Suffolk

FOCUS
There was a sound pace on here despite the small field and the first pair came clear.

NOTEBOOK
Audacity Of Hope moved up to challenge entering the furlong marker but had to be quite seriously shaken up to gain control. He failed to make the step up to Group class but has since been fitted with a tongue-tie and commands plenty of respect at this level. (tchd 8-13 and 8-11)
Sea Lord(IRE) ◆ had to bounce back to form after a couple of disappointing efforts, including when upped to Group level, but he did so. He was soon taking them along and made the winner dig deep to gain the upper hand towards the finish, although he didn't help his chance by hanging off the rails. The form of his all-the-way debut success at Ascot has worked out well and he obviously has a fair amount of ability, so it should not be too long before he goes one better if repeating this performance. (op 11-2 tchd 100-30)
Universal Circus didn't seem to handle softer conditions when tested in Listed company, but he had his chance here and was simply unable to match the pace of the front pair entering the final furlong. (op 9-1 tchd 14-1)
Zinjbar(USA) chased the runner-up for much of the way but lacked the pace to mount any serious threat. Still, this was a better effort returned to turf after being a little disappointing on two attempts on Polytrack. (tchd 12-1)
Arabian Pride was well held when tried in a Listed race last time and he had his chance here, but was beaten when hampered at the furlong marker. (op 9-1 tchd 11-1)
Florio Vincitore(IRE) Official explanation: jockey said gelding hung right

6064 £250000 TATTERSALLS TIMEFORM MILLIONS SPRINT 6f

3:40 (3:41) (Class 2) 2-Y-O
£135,425 (£55,400; £24,650; £12,300; £6,150; £2,450) Stalls Low

Form RPR

51 **1** **Society Rock (IRE)**[35] 5006 2-9-3 81 GeorgeBaker 9 94+
(J R Fanshawe) *str: lw: hld up: hdwy over 2f out: rdn to ld and hung lft wl ins fnl f: r.o* **7/1**

2115 **2** *hd* **Take Ten**[8] 5795 2-9-3 88 JoeFanning 4 93
(M Johnston) *lw: chsd ldr: led 2f out: sn rdn: hdd and carried lft wl ins fnl f: r.o* **4/1**[2]

1404 **3** *½* **Jira**[15] 5606 2-8-12 100 KoseiMiura 3 87
(C E Brittain) *lw: hld up: hdwy over 2f out: rdn over 1f out: r.o* **6/1**

43 **4** *2½* **Saboteur**[8] 5807 2-9-3 0 AhmedAjtebi 12 84
(Saeed Bin Suroor) *s.i.s: hdwy over 3f out: rdn and ev ch over 1f out: no ex ins fnl f* **10/1**

001 **5** *¾* **Cracking Lass (IRE)**[13] 5669 2-8-12 72 MartinDwyer 8 77+
(R A Fahey) *sn pushed along and prom: lost pl over 4f out: last and rdn over 2f out: r.o ins fnl f* **66/1**

2 **6** *hd* **Robinson Cruso**[25] 5317 2-9-3 0 PhilipRobinson 11 81
(M A Jarvis) *w'like: lengthy: chsd ldrs: rdn and ev ch over 1f out: no ex ins fnl f* **7/2**[1]

34 **7** *1¼* **Iptkaar (USA)**[40] 4817 2-8-12 0 ChrisCatlin 10 72
(C E Brittain) *leggy: bit bkwd: chsd ldrs: outpcd over 3f out: styd on fnl f* **66/1**

2331 **8** *4* **Waveband**[15] 5611 2-8-12 76 RoystonFfrench 7 60
(M Johnston) *lw: sn led: rdn and hdd 2f out: wknd fnl f* **25/1**

5210 **9** *nk* **Lowdown (IRE)**[8] 5795 2-9-3 92 RHills 1 65
(M Johnston) *prom: rdn over 2f out: sn wknd* **15/2**

01 **10** *shd* **Magnus Thrax (USA)**[36] 4933 2-9-3 81 PatDobbs 5 64
(R Hannon) *str: lw: hld up: hdwy 1/2-way: rdn and wknd over 1f out* **9/2**[3]

651 **11** *¾* **Kona Coast**[16] 5564 2-9-3 77 RobertHavlin 2 62
(J H M Gosden) *s.i.s: hdwy over 3f out: rdn and wknd over 1f out* **25/1**

1m 12.55s (0.35) **Going Correction** +0.125s/f (Good) **11 Ran SP% 118.7**
Speed ratings (Par 101): **102,101,101,97,96 96,94,89,89,88 87**
toteswingers: 1&2 £9.00, 1&3 £11.10, 2&3 £3.40 CSF £34.60 TOTE £8.10: £2.60, £1.80, £1.50; EX 41.50 Trifecta £239.10 Pool: £420.20 - 1.30 winning units..

Owner Simon Gibson **Bred** San Gabriel Investments **Trained** Newmarket, Suffolk

■ Stewards' Enquiry : George Baker one-day ban: careless riding (Oct 5)

FOCUS
A modest turnout in field size for such a valuable prize and the overall quality looked average for the level, but at least they went a decent pace. The third sets the level. The winner had to survive a stewards' enquiry.

NOTEBOOK
Society Rock(IRE) failed to see out 7f on his debut but ran out a comfortable winner when dropped back to this trip at Nottingham. He travelled well restrained in the rear and moved smoothly through the field to lay down his challenge entering the final furlong. He had to dig deep to get the upper hand but ran out a game winner. He is related to some smart sprinters and he himself seems to have plenty of pace, but with another year on his back he will probably cope with being stepped up to 1m. (op 10-1 tchd 12-1)
Take Ten ◆ didn't get the run of things when fifth in a valuable event last time but he was always at the head of proceedings here and the winner had to pull out all the stops to gain the initiative. This was a very genuine effort from a likeable colt, who can gain some compensation soon. (op 5-1 tchd 7-2)
Jira had won a Listed fillies' race, albeit probably not one of the toughest contests in that division, and set the standard. She came through with a steady run doing all her best work in the final furlong and looked as though she might even land this before her run flattened out in the final 75 yards. (op 4-1 tchd 13-2)
Saboteur missed the break but soon recovered. He could only keep on at the same pace without ever getting on terms and is likely to benefit from a step back up in trip. (op 12-1)
Cracking Lass(IRE) won a soft-ground maiden but had struggled in the past with 6f and that once again proved the case as she was struggling from half way. She stayed on again when it was all too late and will appreciate being stepped back up in trip.
Robinson Cruso held every chance entering the final furlong only for his effort to falter. This was a sound enough effort on only his second start and looks capable progressing further. (tchd 4-1 and 9-2 in places)

6065 E B F W.O.W. MAIDEN STKS 7f

4:15 (4:16) (Class 4) 2-Y-O £5,180 (£1,541; £770; £384) Stalls Low

Form RPR

00 **1** **Forgotten Army (IRE)**[18] 5527 2-9-3 0 JimmyQuinn 3 70
(M H Tompkins) *lengthy: led 1f: chsd ldr: rdn to ld over 1f out: edgd lft ins fnl f: styd on gamely* **16/1**

2 *nk* **Verdant** 2-8-12 0 Louis-PhilippeBeuzelin(5) 4 70+
(Sir Michael Stoute) *w'like: str: swtg: chsd ldrs: rn green: rdn over 2f out: r.o* **1/2**[1]

0 **3** *½* **Invincible Hero (IRE)**[8] 5807 2-9-3 0 (t) TPQueally 1 68
(J Noseda) *w'like: led 6f out: rdn and hdd over 1f out: r.o* **5/1**[2]

4 *½* **Essexbridge** 2-9-3 0 PatDobbs 2 67+
(R Hannon) *unf: chsd ldrs: outpcd over 1f out: r.o wl towards fin* **15/2**[3]

04 **5** *1¾* **Sassanian (IRE)**[58] 4188 2-9-3 0 IvaMilickova 5 62
(Jane Chapple-Hyam) *leggy: hld up in tch: rdn over 2f out: outpcd sn after: styd on ins fnl f* **14/1**

30 **6** *3* **Rock Of Eire**[25] 5312 2-9-3 0 EdwardCreighton 6 55
(E J Creighton) *leggy: hld up: racd keenly: rdn over 2f out: no imp fr over 1f out* **25/1**

1m 29.64s (4.24) **Going Correction** +0.125s/f (Good) **6 Ran SP% 111.5**
Speed ratings (Par 97): **80,79,79,78,76 73**
toteswingers: 1&2 £3.50, 1&3 £5.40, 2&3 £1.60 CSF £24.73 TOTE £16.30: £4.40, £1.10; EX 35.40.

Owner Miss Clare Hollest **Bred** J Hutchinson **Trained** Newmarket, Suffolk

FOCUS
A weak 2yo maiden run at just a fair pace. There was a blanket finish.

NOTEBOOK

Forgotten Army(IRE) disputed the lead throughout until gaining the initiative inside the final furlong under some heavy driving. He had failed to figure on his two previous starts after some untidy starts but, nonetheless, he was making inroads all too late on his latest appearance at Warwick after failing to handle the bend. He got his act together at the start this time and looks an honest type with no immediate plans. (tchd 12-1)

Verdant was very green in the preliminaries and got upset at the start, but he travelled well enough just behind the leaders when the race got under way. There was no immediate response when asked for an effort but he eventually started to wear down the winner and was closing at the finish. He will have benefited from the experience and should be able to build upon this effort. (op 4-7 tchd 8-11)

Invincible Hero(IRE) raced too freely disputing the lead and probably could have done with a bigger field to get some cover. He kept on well enough in the closing stages but displayed a high action and would probably be better suited with some ease underfoot. (op 11-2 tchd 9-2)

Essexbridge found the pace a bit too hot entering the final two furlongs but was running on at the death. (op 5-1)

6066 MC SEAFOOD MEDIAN AUCTION MAIDEN STKS 1m
4:50 (4:51) (Class 4) 2-Y-O **£3,885** (£1,156; £577; £288) **Stalls Low**

Form RPR

0 **1** **Wigmore Hall (IRE)**^{35} 5000 2-9-3 0 JamieSpencer 5 90+
(M L W Bell) *w'like: leggy: lw: hld up: hdwy over 2f out: rdn to ld and hung lft over 1f out: sn clr: eased towards fin* **9/4^{1}**

0553 **2** 4 1/2 **Mountrath**^{15} 5589 2-9-0 60 (t) AndreaAtzeni$^{(3)}$ 1 73
(B R Johnson) *prom: rdn and ev ch 2f out: styd on same pce fr over 1f out* **20/1**

0 **3** hd **Phonic (IRE)**^{58} 4209 2-9-3 0 TPQueally 6 73+
(J L Dunlop) *leggy: lw: hld up: hdwy 3f out: sn rdn: styd on: nt trble ldrs* **33/1**

5 **4** 1 3/4 **Ipswich Lad**^{8} 5787 2-9-3 0 LPKeniry 11 69
(A M Balding) *str: lw: chsd ldrs: rdn over 2f out: hung lft over 1f out: no ex* **4/1^{2}**

022 **5** 3/4 **Pastello**^{17} 5547 2-8-12 73 PatDobbs 7 62
(R Hannon) *chsd clr ldr: rdn and ev ch over 1f out: wknd ins fnl f* **5/1^{3}**

6 1 1/4 **Widezain (IRE)** 2-9-3 0 EdwardCreighton 4 64+
(M R Channon) *unf: lean: angular: tall: s.s: bhd: hdwy u.p over 1f out: nvr nrr* **50/1**

04 **7** 1 3/4 **Whistle Blower**^{15} 5590 2-9-3 0 (b^{1}) RobertHavlin 14 61
(J H M Gosden) *led and sn clr: rdn and hdd over 1f out: wknd fnl f* **16/1**

8 1 3/4 **Wulfrida (IRE)** 2-8-12 0 KoseiMiura 2 52
(J R Fanshawe) *w'like: scope: tall: hld up: hdwy over 2f out: wknd fnl f* **25/1**

9 hd **Varachi** 2-9-3 0 TGMcLaughlin 10 56
(E A L Dunlop) *w'like: bit bkwd: in rr and pushed along: rdn over 2f out: n.d* **66/1**

10 nk **Asterrlini (IRE)** 2-8-12 0 PhilipRobinson 3 51
(C E Brittain) *w'like: leggy: mid-div: rdn and lost pl 1/2-way: n.d after* **25/1**

11 1 **Helaku (IRE)** 2-9-3 0 MartinDwyer 13 53
(R Hannon) *w'like: scope: tall: bit bkwd: s.s: hdwy 1/2-way: rdn: edgd lft and wknd over 1f out* **7/1**

12 nk **Kahfre** 2-9-3 0 RHills 8 53
(E A L Dunlop) *str: s.i.s: in rr and given reminders over 4f out: nvr on terms* **10/1**

30 **13** 2 **Akula (IRE)**^{48} 4524 2-9-3 0 JimmyQuinn 12 48+
(M H Tompkins) *mid-div: hdwy 1/2-way: wknd over 2f out* **14/1**

005 **14** 1/2 **D'Urberville**^{11} 5722 2-9-3 0 AdrianMcCarthy 9 47
(J R Jenkins) *w'like: hld up: hdwy 4f out: wknd over 2f out* **66/1**

1m 39.68s (1.08) **Going Correction** +0.125s/f (Good) **14** Ran SP% **121.9**
Speed ratings (Par 97): **99,94,94,92,91 90,88,87,86,86 85,85,83,82**
toteswingers: 1&2 £19.00, 1&3 £22.00, 2&3 £33.00 CSF £56.33 TOTE £3.90: £1.50, £5.20, £7.60; EX 80.70.
Owner M B Hawtin **Bred** K And Mrs Cullen **Trained** Newmarket, Suffolk

FOCUS

A modest maiden.

NOTEBOOK

Wigmore Hall(IRE) was disappointing on debut when rather coltish and being eased off when his chance had gone, but this was a much more professional performance. Once again he was rather coltish in the preliminaries, but he settled down when the race began and moved through the field from the rear quite smoothly, although showing a little greenness when asked to go between two horses over the furlong marker. After getting through, he displayed a good turn of foot to kick clear and put the race to bed, winning with any amount in hand and in a quicker time than the fillies' maiden earlier on the card. He is held in some regard by connections and looks a promising individual, provided he goes the right way, but what he beat here is clearly questionable. (op 4-1, tchd 9-2 in places)

Mountrath had benefited from a first-time tongue-tie when third at Epsom last time and this was another step forward. Always at the fore and holding every chance at the furlong marker, he was ultimately no match for the winner but held on well for second. (op 16-1 tchd 14-1)

Phonic(IRE) put in an improved display after failing to figure over 7f back in July. He clearly appreciated the step up to 1m, as he made little impression from the midfield until staying on stoutly in the final furlong. (op 40-1)

Ipswich Lad confirmed the promise of his debut with a sound effort. He chased the clear leader for most of the way but could only muster the same pace in the latter stages. (tchd 7-2)

Pastello set the standard after a couple of placed efforts in modest affairs. She held her chance but was another who could only keep on at the same pace. (op 7-2)

Widezain(IRE) ran with a degree of promise and had a nice introduction without ever threatening. (op 66-1)

Helaku(IRE) Official explanation: jockey said colt was unsuited by the good to firm ground

6067 THAI STREET CAFE & NORFOLK ICE CREAM NURSERY H'CAP 1m 1f
5:25 (5:26) (Class 4) (0-85,81) 2-Y-O **£5,180** (£1,541; £770; £384) **Stalls Low**

Form RPR

0316 **1** **Lethal Combination (USA)**^{18} 5515 2-9-7 81 JamieSpencer 5 84
(W J Haggas) *stdd s: hld up: hdwy u.p over 1f out: r.o to ld post* **13/2**

0613 **2** nk **First Cat**^{15} 5603 2-9-6 80 PatDobbs 2 82
(R Hannon) *racd alone 2f: hld up in tch: rdn to ld ins fnl f: hdd post* **11/2^{3}**

0562 **3** 3/4 **Rezwaan**^{21} 5399 2-8-7 67 RHills 6 68
(E A L Dunlop) *chsd ldr: led over 3f out: rdn and hdd ins fnl f: unable qck towards fin* **13/8^{1}**

061 **4** 1 3/4 **Leitzu (IRE)**^{18} 5498 2-8-11 71 EdwardCreighton 4 68+
(M R Channon) *lw: hld up: rdn over 2f out: hdwy over 1f out: r.o: nt rch ldrs* **9/2^{2}**

053 **5** 3 3/4 **Gordon Flash**^{15} 5590 2-8-5 65 MartinDwyer 7 55
(R Hannon) *led: hdd over 3f out: rdn over 1f out: wknd fnl f* **16/1**

656 **6** 3 **Number One Guy**^{47} 4557 2-8-12 72 TPQueally 10 56
(M H Tompkins) *lw: hld up: hdwy 3f out: rdn over 1f out: sn wknd* **14/1**

2240 **7** 4 1/2 **Brunette (IRE)**^{28} 5213 2-8-10 70 JoeFanning 9 45
(R Hannon) *prom: rdn over 2f out: wknd over 1f out* **25/1**

006 **8** 6 **Refuse To Tell**^{15} 5590 2-7-12 58 oh8 KoseiMiura 8 21
(C E Brittain) *prom: rdn over 4f out: wknd 3f out* **50/1**

002 **9** 1 1/2 **Rose Alba (IRE)**^{18} 5498 2-8-7 67 JimmyQuinn 1 27
(J L Dunlop) *chsd ldrs tl rdn over 2f out: sn wknd* **11/2^{3}**

1m 53.28s (1.58) **Going Correction** +0.125s/f (Good) **9** Ran SP% **118.7**
Speed ratings (Par 97): **97,96,96,94,91 88,84,79,77**
toteswingers: 1&2 £5.40, 1&3 £3.70, 2&3 £4.30 CSF £43.33 CT £86.10 TOTE £10.00: £2.50, £2.50, £1.10; EX 29.90 Place 6: £71.23 Place 5: £8.18.
Owner Findlay & Bloom **Bred** Indian Creek **Trained** Newmarket, Suffolk
■ Stewards' Enquiry : Kosei Miura two-day ban: used whip when out of contention (Oct 5-6)

FOCUS

A competitive nursery, run at an ordinary pace and the form looks sound enough.

NOTEBOOK

Lethal Combination(USA) paid the price for mixing it with a well-treated rival last time off same mark but had previously been progressing well. Different tactics were employed this time, as he was held up off the pace, but he steadily closed under pressure to get up in the dying strides. (op 8-1 tchd 6-1)

First Cat raced alone on the stands' side before joining the main group after a furlong. He closed on the leaders steadily from the three-furlong marker to take the lead inside the distance, only to get mugged on the line. He has a progressive profile and there seems no reason why he cannot add to his sole success after this effort. (op 6-1 tchd 7-1)

Rezwaan raced prominently throughout before taking the lead over two furlongs from the finish. He stuck to his task well when headed inside the final furlong but could not find any extra. This step up in trip didn't bother him and he should be found an opportunity to lose his maiden status before long. (op 7-4)

Leitzu(IRE), a winner against her own sex over 1m last time, ran a strange race as she looked likely to finish well beaten at halfway but stayed on again towards the latter stages. (op 11-2)

Gordon Flash led until over two furlongs out but could only muster the same pace from there on.
T/Plt: £206.40 to a £1 stake. Pool: £43,166.21. 152.60 winning tickets. T/Qpdt: £10.30 to a £1 stake. Pool: £4,776.98. 340.94 winning tickets. CR

6024 WOLVERHAMPTON (A.W) (L-H)
Friday, September 18

OFFICIAL GOING: Standard

Wind: Nil Weather: Fine

6068 WILLIAMHILL.COM/BONUS25 - GET £25 FREE BET NURSERY H'CAP 5f 20y(P)
5:50 (5:51) (Class 4) (0-85,82) 2-Y-O **£5,046** (£1,510; £755; £377; £188) **Stalls Low**

Form RPR

231 **1** **Monsieur Joe (IRE)**^{26} 5282 2-9-3 78 AdamKirby 7 83+
(W R Swinburn) *a.p: hung lft fr over 1f out: led ins fnl f: r.o* **5/2^{1}**

6164 **2** 1 1/4 **Leleyf (IRE)**^{5} 5908 2-9-2 77 CatherineGannon 5 78
(M R Channon) *led after 1f: rdn jst over 1f out: sltly bmpd ins fnl f: sn hdd: nt qckn* **12/1**

0204 **3** shd **High Spice (USA)**^{42} 4752 2-9-5 80 StephenDonohoe 2 80
(R M H Cowell) *hld up: hdwy on ins over 1f out: sn rdn: kpt on ins fnl f* **8/1**

2032 **4** 1 1/4 **Lucky Mellor**^{14} 5650 2-8-12 73 (b) TolleyDean 4 69
(D K Ivory) *led 1f: chsd ldr: rdn over 1f out: lost 2nd ins fnl f: one pce* **13/2^{3}**

3060 **5** 1/2 **Dancing Freddy (IRE)**^{55} 4327 2-9-4 82 JackMitchell$^{(3)}$ 1 76
(J G Given) *hld up in tch: pushed along 2f out: rdn jst over 1f out: one pce* **8/1**

3161 **6** shd **Radio City**^{9} 5769 2-9-4 79 6ex SebSanders 6 72
(R M Beckett) *s.i.s: hld up in rr: rdn jst over 1f out: kpt on fnl f: nt trble ldrs* **4/1^{2}**

4450 **7** 3/4 **Senate Majority**^{38} 4884 2-8-1 62 (b^{1}) DaleGibson 8 53
(T D Easterby) *hld up: hrd rdn jst over 1f out: n.d* **22/1**

3205 **8** 3 1/4 **More Lashes (USA)**^{9} 5769 2-9-1 76 HayleyTurner 3 55
(M G Quinlan) *hld up in rr: pushed along wl over 1f out: no rspnse* **9/1**

5610 **9** 1 **Wanchai Whisper**^{5} 5899 2-8-3 69 AndrewHeffernan$^{(5)}$ 9 44
(P D Evans) *hld up: short-lived effrt on outside wl over 1f out* **20/1**

61.29 secs (-1.01) **Going Correction** -0.125s/f (Stan) **9** Ran SP% **110.9**
Speed ratings (Par 97): **103,101,100,98,98 97,96,91,89**
toteswingers: 1&2 £3.60, 1&3 £3.50, 2&3 not won. CSF £31.91 CT £200.05 TOTE £3.40: £1.30, £3.40, £2.60; EX 33.40.
Owner Mrs Helen Checkley **Bred** Nicola And Eleanor Kent **Trained** Aldbury, Herts
■ Stewards' Enquiry : Stephen Donohoe one-day ban: excessive use of the whip (Oct 5)

FOCUS

A modest nursery.

NOTEBOOK

Monsieur Joe(IRE), easy winner of a Folkestone maiden, looked to be making his handicap debut off a fair mark and, despite hanging left under pressure, he got well on top inside the final furlong. There is more to come from this progressive sprinter. (op 7-2)

Leleyf(IRE), already having her 14th start of the season, remains 5lb higher than when last winning, but had run well off this mark at Ffos Las last time and she again gave her all in defeat. She received a bump, but it made no difference to the result. (op 10-1)

High Spice(USA) has been keeping some decent company and she appreciated the drop in grade, staying on to just miss second. (op 7-1 tchd 9-1)

Lucky Mellor has been running well without winning in similar contests, but he had gone up another 2lb and wasn't good enough having held every chance. (op 11-2)

Dancing Freddy(IRE) is coming down the weights but still doesn't look up to winning. (op 9-1 tchd 10-1)

Radio City, shouldering a 6lb penalty for his recent Epsom victory, lacked the speed to get into this having been slowly away and the drop to 5f was clearly against him. (op 3-1 tchd 11-4)

6069 WILLIAMHILL.COM/BONUS25 - POKER TOURNAMENTS MEDIAN AUCTION MAIDEN FILLIES' STKS 5f 216y(P)
6:20 (6:21) (Class 5) 2-Y-O **£3,238** (£963; £481; £240) **Stalls Low**

Form RPR

1 **Gouray Girl (IRE)** 2-9-0 0 AdamKirby 1 73+
(W R Swinburn) *s.i.s: sn hld up in mid-div: pushed along and hdwy over 1f out: rdn to ld cl home* **16/1**

5 **2** nk **Nurture (IRE)**^{8} 5808 2-8-11 0 PatrickHills$^{(3)}$ 10 72
(R Hannon) *led early: w ldr: pushed along and carried rt jst over 1f out: led ins fnl f: rdn and hdd cl home* **5/1^{3}**

2 **3** 3/4 **Pictures (IRE)**^{31} 5119 2-9-0 0 KFallon 6 70
(L M Cumani) *sn led: rdn and edgd rt jst over 1f out: hdd ins fnl f: nt qckn* **6/4^{1}**

4 **4** 1/2 **Tartufo Dolce (IRE)**^{133} 1841 2-9-0 0 PatCosgrave 12 69
(J G Given) *hld up in mid-div: hdwy on outside over 2f out: c wd st: swtchd lft jst over 1f out: rdn and kpt on ins fnl f* **14/1**

5 1 ½ **City Gossip (IRE)** 2-8-11 0 .... JackMitchell(3) 5 64
(M G Quinlan) *hld up in mid-div: hmpd and lost pl after 1f: hdwy on ins wl over 1f out: one pce fnl f* **50/1**

4 6 1 **Art Machine (USA)**[14] 5639 2-9-0 0 .... SebSanders 3 61
(Sir Mark Prescott) *prom: pushed along wl over 1f out: rdn and fdd ins fnl f* **9/4**[2]

7 2 ½ **Bird On The Wire** 2-8-11 0 .... JackDean(3) 2 54
(W G M Turner) *prom: rdn over 1f out: wknd ins fnl f* **80/1**

04 8 ¾ **Faithful Duchess (IRE)**[19] 5478 2-9-0 0 .... HayleyTurner 11 51
(E A L Dunlop) *prom: pushed along and wknd over 1f out* **9/1**

30 9 ¾ **Gypsy Jazz (IRE)**[69] 3858 2-9-0 0 .... SJCraine 8 49
(Jennie Candlish) *mid-div: pushed along over 3f out: rdn over 2f out: wknd wl over 1f out* **66/1**

00 10 ¾ **Aimeeskeepingfaith**[8] 5800 2-9-0 0 .... CatherineGannon 13 49+
(M R Channon) *sn bhd* **80/1**

11 8 **Feel The Magic (IRE)** 2-8-9 0 .... SophieDoyle(5) 7 23
(S Kirk) *a in rr* **66/1**

12 nk **Fareham Town** 2-9-0 0 .... StephenDonohoe 4 22
(S Kirk) *s.s: a in rr* **33/1**

1m 15.13s (0.13) **Going Correction** -0.125s/f (Stan) **12 Ran SP% 120.3**
Speed ratings (Par 92): **94,93,92,91,89 88,85,84,83,82 71,71**
toteswingers: 1&2 not won, 1&3 £6.20, 2&3 £6.20. CSF £94.00 TOTE £16.10: £4.10, £2.10, £1.10; EX 170.00.
Owner Alan Le Herissier **Bred** George S O'Malley **Trained** Aldbury, Herts
■ Stewards' Enquiry : K Fallon caution: used whip down the shoulder in the forehand position

FOCUS
Nothing more than an ordinary maiden.

NOTEBOOK
Gouray Girl(IRE), sister to a multiple 1m winner, was ridden under restraint following a sluggish start, but started to stay on well once asked for an effort and she showed a nice attitude to get up close home. She will benefit from an extra furlong and looks a filly of obvious potential. (op 14-1)
Nurture(IRE), backed beforehand, shaped with a ton of promise when finishing fast following a slow start on debut at Kempton and she certainly knew more this time, but couldn't repel the winner's late run. A small race should come her way on this evidence. (op 11-2 tchd 7-2)
Pictures(IRE), a promising second at Brighton on debut, soon led under Fallon and had her chance, but didn't really respond to strong pressure and could only keep on at the one pace. (op 5-4 tchd 7-4)
Tartufo Dolce(IRE) stepped up on her debut effort at Nottingham, staying on well having been carried wide into the straight. (op 25-1)
City Gossip(IRE), a daughter of Shinko Forest, shaped with a good deal of promise considering she was hampered and lost her position early. She was going on at the finish and should improve. (tchd 40-1)
Art Machine(USA) was the main disappointment of the race, failing to build on her debut effort and not looking suited by the drop in trip. She probably deserves another chance, but may be more of a handicap prospect now. (op 4-1)

6070 WILLIAMHILL.COM/BONUS25 - QUOTE BONUS25 H'CAP 7f 32y(P)
6:50 (6:51) (Class 6) (0-65,65) 3-Y-O **£2,729** (£806; £403) **Stalls High**

Form RPR

6231 1 **Blue Noodles**[14] 5628 3-8-10 62 .... AndrewHeffernan(5) 5 72
(P D Evans) *t.k.h: mde all: rdn over 1f out: drvn out* **6/1**

1610 2 1 ¼ **Peper Harow (IRE)**[21] 5404 3-9-3 64 .... DavidProbert 3 71
(M D I Usher) *hld up towards rr: stdy prog over 2f out: rdn and r.o ins fnl f: tk 2nd cl home* **18/1**

0303 3 nk **Florentia**[16] 5582 3-9-2 63 .... SebSanders 7 69+
(Sir Mark Prescott) *hld up in mid-div: hdwy over 2f out: rdn wl over 1f out: kpt on ins fnl f* **10/1**

2151 4 ¾ **First Blade**[32] 5105 3-9-1 62 .... (b) AmirQuinn 12 66
(S R Bowring) *sn hld up in tch: chsd wnr over 2f out: rdn and lost 2nd ins fnl f: no ex* **25/1**

443 5 shd **Chief Red Cloud (USA)**[15] 5612 3-9-4 65 .... HayleyTurner 1 72+
(A P Jarvis) *hld up towards rr: nt clr run and swtchd rt wl over 1f out: gd late hdwy: nrst fin* **7/2**[1]

0600 6 nk **Just Timmy Marcus**[15] 5612 3-9-2 63 .... CatherineGannon 11 66
(B P J Baugh) *s.i.s: hld up in rr: pushed along over 2f out: rdn and hdwy on ins over 1f out: nt rch ldrs* **25/1**

5061 7 ½ **Bermondsey Girl**[55] 4304 3-9-1 65 .... JackMitchell(3) 9 67
(C F Wall) *hld up towards rr: hdwy on outside over 2f out: c wd st: rdn over 1f out: kpt on same pce ins fnl f* **4/1**[2]

132 8 ¾ **Jonnie Skull (IRE)**[2] 6005 3-9-0 61 .... (vt) TolleyDean 6 61
(P S McEntee) *hld up in tch: rdn and wknd over 1f out* **6/1**

0214 9 ½ **Dance Club (IRE)**[18] 5514 3-9-4 65 .... KFallon 2 63
(W Jarvis) *prom: lost pl on ins over 3f out: sn pushed along: short-lived effrt wl over 1f out* **11/2**[3]

606 10 ¾ **You've Been Mowed**[21] 5403 3-8-12 62 .... MCGeran(3) 8 58
(R J Price) *prom: rdn wl over 1f out: wknd fnl f* **22/1**

360 11 6 **Enhancing**[15] 5601 3-8-13 60 .... StephenDonohoe 10 40
(J A Glover) *prom: rdn 3f out: wknd wl over 1f out* **50/1**

-600 12 hd **Thurston (IRE)**[53] 4375 3-8-13 60 .... AdamKirby 4 40
(D J S Ffrench Davis) *s.i.s: in rr: pushed along over 3f out: rdn over 2f out: sn struggling* **50/1**

1m 28.03s (-1.57) **Going Correction** -0.125s/f (Stan) **12 Ran SP% 116.5**
Speed ratings (Par 99): **103,101,101,100,100 99,99,98,97,97 90,89**
toteswingers: 1&2 not won, 1&3 £5.60, 2&3 not won. CSF £97.78 CT £1057.14 TOTE £7.30: £2.20, £7.50, £4.10; EX 111.90.
Owner Diamond Racing Ltd **Bred** P And Mrs A G Venner **Trained** Pandy, Monmouths

FOCUS
A moderate handicap.
Thurston(IRE) Official explanation: jockey said gelding never travelled

6071 WILLIAMHILL.COM/BONUS25 - LIVE CASINO DEALERS NURSERY H'CAP 7f 32y(P)
7:20 (7:21) (Class 5) (0-75,75) 2-Y-O **£3,561** (£1,059; £529; £264) **Stalls High**

Form RPR

4643 1 **Gallant Eagle (IRE)**[11] 5722 2-9-7 75 .... DavidProbert 12 79+
(S Kirk) *hld up in rr: hdwy on outside over 5f out: wnt 2nd 4f out: led over 1f out: sn rdn: drvn out* **16/1**

045 2 ½ **Kinky Afro (IRE)**[20] 5428 2-8-13 67 .... CatherineGannon 6 70
(J S Moore) *hld up: pushed along over 2f out: hdwy on ins over 1f out: swtchd rt ins fnl f: r.o to take 2nd towards fin* **12/1**

3561 3 nse **Thomas Baines (USA)**[7] 5841 2-9-3 71 6ex .... HayleyTurner 10 74+
(M L W Bell) *sn swtchd lft to ins: t.k.h in rr: pushed along and hdwy over 1f out: rdn and r.o ins fnl f* **5/1**[2]

060 4 1 ¼ **Pat Seamur**[92] 3064 2-8-12 66 .... DO'Donohoe 3 66
(E A L Dunlop) *a.p: rdn and ev ch over 1f out: no ex towards fin* **6/5**[1]

556 5 1 ¼ **Ice Viking (IRE)**[18] 5528 2-9-3 71 .... PatCosgrave 2 68
(J G Given) *hld up in tch: rdn over 1f out: one pce fnl f* **22/1**

445 6 hd **Mellifera**[26] 5284 2-9-4 72 .... AdamKirby 5 68
(W R Swinburn) *led early: chsd ldr to 4f out: rdn over 2f out: btn over 1f out* **6/1**[3]

3445 7 ¾ **Ever So Bold**[15] 5589 2-8-10 64 .... KirstyMilczarek 8 58
(W R Muir) *hld up towards rr: pushed along over 2f out: n.d* **25/1**

0330 8 hd **Motivational (IRE)**[35] 4975 2-9-6 74 .... ChrisCatlin 1 68
(D R Lanigan) *hld up: sn bhd: pushed along over 2f out: nvr nr ldrs* **20/1**

0002 9 6 **Public Service (IRE)**[10] 5748 2-9-5 73 .... KFallon 4 52
(B J Meehan) *sn led: rdn and hdd over 1f out: wknd fnl f* **9/1**

003 10 8 **Killusty Fancy (IRE)**[40] 4811 2-9-0 68 .... StephenDonohoe 9 28
(D J S Ffrench Davis) *hld up: n.m.r bnd after 1f: bhd fnl 3f* **66/1**

4021 11 23 **Sands Of Dee (USA)**[25] 5303 2-8-10 64 .... SebSanders 7 —
(J A Glover) *prom tl pushed along and wknd over 3f out: eased whn no ch wl over 1f out* **16/1**

1m 29.97s (0.37) **Going Correction** -0.125s/f (Stan) **11 Ran SP% 120.3**
Speed ratings (Par 95): **92,91,91,89,88 88,87,87,80,71 44**
toteswingers: 1&2 £20.90, 1&3 not won, 2&3 £20.90. CSF £188.10 CT £1130.72 TOTE £15.50: £4.60, £3.90, £1.70; EX 161.00.
Owner J C Smith **Bred** Peter Reynolds And Robert Dore **Trained** Upper Lambourn, Berks

FOCUS
A modest nursery.

NOTEBOOK
Gallant Eagle(IRE) ran better than his finishing position suggested at Folkestone last time and looked fairly treated for this handicap debut. He made a quick forward move down the back and, having got the front in the straight, stayed on well and was always doing enough. The step up to 7f has definitely seen him improve. (op 12-1)
Kinky Afro(IRE), back down to 7f for this nursery debut, was staying on against the rail when forced to switch 1f out. She ran on right the way to the line, looking a shade unlucky, and looks capable of winning something similar. (op 10-1)
Thomas Baines(USA), shouldering a 6lb penalty for his recent C&D success, was given a bit too much to do and by the time he got going, the winner had already flown. He can be rated a bit better than the bare form. (op 4-1)
Pat Seamur, well fancied to make a winning handicap debut from a mark of 66, was always nicely placed in behind the leader and held every chance having straightened for home, but didn't see it out as well as those around him. (op 2-1 tchd 9-4)
Ice Viking(IRE) looked a likely improver for this move into handicaps and ran well, but the best of him won't be seen until he tackles trips at 1m and further. (op 20-1 tchd 25-1)
Mellifera ran well to a point, but stopped quickly from 1f out. (tchd 9-1)
Public Service(IRE) failed to build on his recent Lingfield second. Official explanation: vet said gelding had a breathing problem (op 8-1 tchd 7-1)
Sands Of Dee(USA) Official explanation: vet said gelding was lame near-fore

6072 WILLIAM HILL 0800 444040 - GET £25 FREE BET H'CAP 7f 32y(P)
7:50 (7:50) (Class 4) (0-85,80) 3-Y-O+ **£5,046** (£1,510; £755; £377; £188) **Stalls High**

Form RPR

000 1 **Mabait**[18] 5523 3-9-1 80 .... KFallon 5 88+
(L M Cumani) *hld up in tch: pushed along over 2f out: rdn to ld ins fnl f: r.o* **6/1**[2]

2640 2 1 ¼ **Chief Exec**[9] 5780 7-8-13 75 ow2 .... (b) AdamKirby 9 81
(J R Gask) *s.i.s: sn swtchd lft: hld up in rr: pushed along and hdwy over 1f out: rdn and ev ch ins fnl f: nt qckn* **10/1**

0 3 1 ¼ **Sanjay's Choice (IRE)**[23] 5335 3-8-7 72 .... CatherineGannon 4 74
(T G McCourt, Ire) *sn chsng ldr: led 2f out: rdn over 1f out: hdd ins fnl f: no ex* **33/1**

2533 4 ½ **I Confess**[6] 5887 4-8-13 80 .... (b) RichardEvans(5) 1 81
(P D Evans) *a.p: pushed along 4f out: rdn wl over 1f out: one pce* **7/4**[1]

0230 5 nk **Follow The Flag (IRE)**[6] 5886 5-8-0 69 .... (p) DeclanCannon(7) 6 69
(A J McCabe) *hld up towards rr: pushed along 3f out: rdn over 1f out: r.o ins fnl f: nvr nrr* **12/1**

25 6 1 **Ravi River (IRE)**[38] 4870 5-9-2 78 .... PatCosgrave 10 76
(J R Boyle) *hld up in rr: pushed along and hdwy on ins over 1f out: rdn and one pce ins fnl f* **9/1**

4655 7 ¾ **Justcallmehandsome**[29] 5190 7-8-6 73 .... (v) SophieDoyle(5) 8 69
(D J S Ffrench Davis) *hld up towards rr: pushed along over 2f out: rdn ins fnl f: n.d* **28/1**

0010 8 5 **Dig Deep (IRE)**[20] 5418 7-9-4 80 .... (t) HayleyTurner 3 62
(J J Quinn) *hld up in mid-div: pushed along 3f out: wknd 1f out* **16/1**

0010 9 4 **Glenridding**[13] 5673 5-9-2 78 .... (p) J-PGuillambert 2 49
(J G Given) *led: pushed along and hdd 2f out: rdn over 1f out: wknd fnl f* **8/1**

15-0 10 10 **Richelieu**[17] 5559 7-8-13 78 .... EJMcNamara(3) 7 22
(J J Lambe, Ire) *hld up: sn in tch: pushed along and wknd 2f out: eased whn no ch ins fnl f* **7/1**[3]

1m 27.4s (-2.20) **Going Correction** -0.125s/f (Stan)
WFA 3 from 4yo+ 3lb **10 Ran SP% 113.3**
Speed ratings (Par 105): **107,105,104,103,103 102,101,95,90,79**
toteswingers: 1&2 not won, 1&3 £10.60, 2&3 £17.00. CSF £62.53 CT £1843.47 TOTE £9.50: £2.30, £2.60, £6.60; EX 61.50.
Owner Sheikh Mohammed Obaid Al Maktoum **Bred** L A C Ashby Newhall Estate Farm **Trained** Newmarket, Suffolk

FOCUS
A fair handicap.

6073 WILLIAMHILL.COM/BONUS25 - PLAY VEGAS GAMES MEDIAN AUCTION MAIDEN STKS 1m 141y(P)
8:20 (8:20) (Class 6) 3-5-Y-O **£2,388** (£705; £352) **Stalls Low**

Form RPR

2632 1 **Espero (IRE)**[13] 5677 3-8-12 79 .... AndrewHeffernan(5) 1 72+
(R A Farrant) *hld up: hdwy wl over 1f out: rdn fnl f: led towards fin* **5/6**[1]

2 ½ **Illuminative (USA)** 3-9-3 0 .... JimmyFortune 6 71+
(J H M Gosden) *s.i.s: hld up towards rr: hdwy on outside 4f out: pushed along over 2f out: rdn over 1f out: carried hd high: r.o wl towards fin: tk 2nd post* **13/2**[3]

3022 3 shd **Mr Udagawa**[43] 4691 3-9-3 70 .... SebSanders 7 70
(R M Beckett) *led: pushed along over 1f out: rdn and hdd towards fin: lost 2nd post* **11/4**[2]

4 4 3 **At Wits End**[15] 5614 3-9-3 0 .... KirstyMilczarek 3 63
(J A R Toller) *chsd ldr 2f: prom: wnt 2nd again wl over 1f out: rdn and one pce ins fnl f* **12/1**

0 5 1 ¾ **Suzi's Dancer**[16] 5572 3-8-12 0 .... JimmyQuinn 9 54
(H J Collingridge) *prom: chsd ldr over 6f out tl rdn wl over 1f out: sn wknd* **16/1**

006 **6** *hd* **D'Artagnans Dream**[14] 5630 3-8-12 54..............(b[1]) GabrielHannon[(5)] 12 59
(G D Blake) *s.s: hld up towards rr: pushed along over 2f out: rdn and short-lived effrt over 1f out* **33/1**

0 **7** *2 1/2* **Fulfilment (IRE)**[63] 4057 3-8-12 0..................... ChrisCatlin 8 48
(W J Musson) *a in rr* **20/1**

0 **8** *1* **Marina's Ocean**[15] 5614 5-9-3 0.......................(t) AmirQuinn 5 46
(S R Bowring) *s.i.s: sn hld up in tch: pushed along and wknd over 2f out* **66/1**

P0 **9** *29* **The Coach**[28] 5228 3-9-3 0.......................... NeilChalmers 10 —
(T Wall) *a in rr: pushed along over 3f out: sn lost tch* **100/1**

1m 51.34s (0.84) **Going Correction** -0.125s/f (Stan)
WFA 3 from 4yo+ 5lb **9** Ran SP% **118.3**
Speed ratings (Par 101): **91,90,90,87,86 86,83,82,57**
toteswingers: 1&2 £3.80, 1&3 £1.40, 2&3 £1.70 CSF £7.16 TOTE £1.60: £1.10, £2.20, £1.20; EX 9.90.
Owner M Sawers **Bred** Derek Christopher Shields **Trained** East Garston, Berks

FOCUS
A moderate maiden.
The Coach Official explanation: jockey said gelding never travelled

6074 WILLIAM HILL 0800 444040 - QUOTE BONUS25 H'CAP 1m 1f 103y(P)
8:50 (8:50) (Class 6) (0-65,65) 3-Y-O+ £2,729 (£806; £403) Stalls Low

Form RPR

1660 **1** **Hits Only Cash**[13] 5683 7-9-2 58.....................(p) StephenDonohoe 5 67
(J Pearce) *hld up towards rr: pushed along over 3f out: hdwy over 2f out: swtchd lft over 1f out: rdn fnl f: r.o to ld cl home* **20/1**

0461 **2** *hd* **Resplendent Ace (IRE)**[67] 3923 5-9-6 62.................. IanMongan 1 71
(P Howling) *hld up towards rr: pushed along over 3f out: hdwy on ins wl over 1f out: sn rdn: ev ch wl ins fnl f: r.o* **5/1[2]**

602 **3** *nk* **Bid For Glory**[6] 5886 5-9-9 65.....................(v) JimmyQuinn 3 73
(H J Collingridge) *hld up in mid-div: hdwy on ins over 2f out: led over 1f out: hrd rdn ins fnl f: hdd cl home* **5/2[1]**

3023 **4** *2 3/4* **Streets Apart (USA)**[37] 4904 4-9-8 64.....................(p) AdamKirby 13 66
(W R Swinburn) *sn led: hdd 7f out: chsd ldr: rdn and ev ch wl over 1f out: no ex ins fnl f* **10/1[3]**

2435 **5** *nse* **The Grey One (IRE)**[6] 5886 6-9-4 60..................(p) KevinGhunowa 12 62
(J M Bradley) *hld up in mid-div: stdy prog over 3f out: swtchd rt to outside over 2f out: rdn over 1f out: kpt on towards fin* **14/1**

0650 **6** *1/2* **Dubburg (USA)**[42] 4759 4-9-5 61.......................... ChrisCatlin 6 62
(W J Musson) *stdd s: hld up in rr: r.o fr over 1f out: nvr nrr* **20/1**

4003 **7** *1/2* **By Command**[15] 5594 4-9-6 62.............................. KFallon 4 62
(J W Hills) *prom: pushed along over 2f out: rdn and one pce ins fnl f* **5/1[2]**

4002 **8** *2 3/4* **Lush (IRE)**[22] 5365 4-9-5 64....................... PatrickHills[(3)] 8 58
(R Hannon) *hld up in mid-div: reminder 5f out: lost pl over 3f out: n.d after* **16/1**

00-0 **9** *hd* **Nesno (USA)**[21] 5395 6-9-7 63.....................(p) SebSanders 2 60+
(J D Bethell) *led early: led 7f out: rdn and hdd over 1f out: eased whn btn ins fnl f* **5/1[2]**

6-00 **10** *4* **Dado Mush**[8] 5791 6-9-2 65.......................(p) LauraPike[(7)] 11 50
(T T Clement) *prom: lost pl over 3f out: bhd fnl 2f* **50/1**

5510 **11** *4* **Appelouse**[22] 5364 4-8-9 58........................ DTDaSilva[(7)] 7 35
(D W Thompson) *hld up towards rr: rdn over 3f out: no ch whn hung lft and rdn jst over 1f out* **28/1**

2010 **12** *17* **High Five Society**[56] 4269 5-9-3 59...................(bt) AmirQuinn 9 —
(S R Bowring) *s.i.s: sn hld up in tch: rdn over 3f out: wknd 2f out: eased whn no ch ins fnl f* **33/1**

1m 59.88s (-1.82) **Going Correction** -0.125s/f (Stan) **12** Ran SP% **118.1**
Speed ratings (Par 101): **103,102,102,100,100 99,99,96,96,93 89,74**
toteswingers: 1&2 not won, 1&3 not won, 2&3 £2.00. CSF £111.30 CT £346.01 TOTE £24.50: £4.80, £2.50, £1.30; EX 96.50.
Owner Oceana racing **Bred** G S Shropshire **Trained** Newmarket, Suffolk

FOCUS
A competitive handicap.
Nesno(USA) Official explanation: jockey said gelding lost its action

6075 WILLIAMHILL.COM/BONUS25 - BINGO BONANZA'S H'CAP 1m 4f 50y(P)
9:20 (9:20) (Class 5) (0-75,72) 3-Y-O £3,561 (£1,059; £529; £264) Stalls Low

Form RPR

0030 **1** **Blue Tango (IRE)**[51] 4442 3-8-8 62.....................(b) JimmyQuinn 9 66
(Mrs A J Perrett) *led after 2f to 8f out: chsd ldr: led wl over 1f out: sn rdn: jst hld on* **20/1**

4402 **2** *shd* **Madamlily (IRE)**[49] 4506 3-8-13 67..................... HayleyTurner 5 71
(J J Quinn) *hld up and bhd: rdn wl over 1f out: str run ins fnl f: edgd lft towards fin: jst failed* **8/1**

3023 **3** *1 1/4* **Tiger Flash**[19] 5482 3-8-13 67............................... KFallon 1 69
(W J Haggas) *hld up in rr: hdwy on ins over 2f out: rdn jst over 1f out: kpt on ins fnl f* **4/1[3]**

1500 **4** *nk* **Royal Trooper (IRE)**[21] 5402 3-9-4 72.................... PatCosgrave 7 74
(J G Given) *swtchd lft sn after s: hld up in rr: stdy prog on outside 3f out: rdn over 1f out: kpt on ins fnl f* **12/1**

2 **5** *1 1/4* **Ghent (IRE)**[9] 5782 3-8-7 61.....................(p) DavidProbert 4 61
(David P Myerscough, Ire) *set slow pce: hdd after 2f: prom: rdn jst over 2f out: one pce ins fnl f* **5/2[1]**

2321 **6** *1 1/4* **Broughtons Paradis (IRE)**[43] 4722 3-8-9 63............. ChrisCatlin 2 61
(W J Musson) *t.k.h: prom: led after 4f: rdn and hdd over 1f out: wknd wl ins fnl f* **11/4[2]**

6505 **7** *12* **Supernoverre (IRE)**[16] 5570 3-9-1 69..................... IanMongan 6 49
(P Howling) *hld up: hdwy over 5f out: pushed along over 2f out: wknd wl over 1f out* **8/1**

8 *2 3/4* **Black Rock Lake (IRE)**[20] 5459 3-8-11 65.......... CatherineGannon 3 41
(T G McCourt, Ire) *wnt rt s: t.k.h early in tch: pushed along over 3f out: wknd over 2f out* **25/1**

2m 41.47s (0.37) **Going Correction** -0.125s/f (Stan) **8** Ran SP% **113.8**
Speed ratings (Par 101): **93,92,92,91,91 90,82,80**
toteswingers: 1&2 not won, 1&3 not won, 2&3 £12.10 CSF £166.32 CT £776.75 TOTE £18.50: £3.30, £2.20, £1.90; EX 76.00 Place 6: £361.34, Place 5: £161.98..
Owner The Green Dot Partnership **Bred** Paul Ennis **Trained** Pulborough, W Sussex

FOCUS
A low-grade middle-distance handicap.
Black Rock Lake(IRE) Official explanation: jockey said filly hung right
T/Plt: £102.00 to a £1 stake. Pool: £69,539.74. 497.30 winning tickets. T/Qpdt: £38.20 to a £1 stake. Pool: £7,481.28. 144.89 winning tickets. KH

6081 - 6087a (Foreign Racing) - See Raceform Interactive

6046 AYR (L-H)
Saturday, September 19

OFFICIAL GOING: Good (good to firm in places; 7.4)
Wind: Fresh, half against Weather: Overcast

6088 NIGEL ANGUS MEMORIAL NURSERY H'CAP 1m
1:35 (1:37) (Class 2) 2-Y-O
£12,462 (£3,732; £1,866; £934; £466; £234) Stalls High

Form RPR

41 **1** **Centigrade (IRE)**[19] 5527 2-8-12 81..................... HayleyTurner 8 89+
(W J Haggas) *hld up: swtchd rt and hdwy over 2f out: edgd lft and led wl ins fnl f: styd on* **3/1[1]**

3123 **2** *3/4* **Aquarian Spirit**[19] 5515 2-8-10 79..................... TonyHamilton 10 83
(R A Fahey) *led: rdn whn hrd pressed over 1f out: hdd wl ins fnl f: r.o* **5/1[2]**

1620 **3** *1* **Butch And Sundance**[30] 5198 2-9-3 86....................... NCallan 2 88
(B J Meehan) *trckd ldrs: effrt and ev ch over 1f out to ins fnl f: kpt on same pce* **17/2**

1303 **4** *1* **Ingleby Spirit**[25] 5324 2-8-11 83.................. FrederikTylicki[(3)] 14 83
(R A Fahey) *prom: effrt over 2f out: kpt on same pce fnl f* **25/1**

31 **5** *1/2* **Our Joe Mac (IRE)**[40] 4847 2-9-5 88..................... PaulHanagan 7 88+
(R A Fahey) *hld up in tch: hdwy whn nt clr run over 1f out: styd on fnl f* **3/1[1]**

6522 **6** *4 1/2* **Flaming Miracle**[26] 5320 2-8-7 76........................ LPKeniry 12 65
(A M Balding) *trckd ldr: rdn over 2f out: wknd appr fnl f* **8/1[3]**

2204 **7** *3 3/4* **Tres Coronas (IRE)**[19] 5515 2-8-7 76 ow1................ TomEaves 9 57
(T D Barron) *t.k.h early: prom tl wknd 2f out* **11/1**

31 **8** *4 1/2* **Tut (IRE)**[24] 5330 2-8-5 79........................... MartinLane[(5)] 13 50+
(A P Jarvis) *dwlt: sn in tch: hdwy over 2f out: wkng whn hmpd over 1f out* **16/1**

621 **9** *12* **Tanto Quanto (IRE)**[23] 5371 2-8-10 79..................(b) SebSanders 6 23
(W R Muir) *bhd: struggling 1/2-way: sn btn: t.o* **22/1**

1m 42.68s (-1.12) **Going Correction** -0.175s/f (Firm) **9** Ran SP% **110.7**
Speed ratings (Par 101): **98,97,96,95,94 90,86,82,70**
toteswingers: 1&2 £3.20, 1&3 £6.20, 2&3 £8.90. CSF £16.40 CT £97.97 TOTE £4.00: £1.40, £2.00, £2.70; EX 19.30.
Owner Highclere Thoroughbred Racing (Verglas) **Bred** The Irish National Stud **Trained** Newmarket, Suffolk
■ Aattash was withdrawn (12/1, ref to ent stalls). R4 applies, deduct 5p in the £.
■ Stewards' Enquiry : Paul Hanagan two-day ban: careless riding (Oct 5-6)

FOCUS
This looked a strong nursery, with four last-time-out maiden winners lining up. There was just an ordinary early pace on, however, which limits the form.

NOTEBOOK
Centigrade(IRE) ◆ did very well to defy the pace bias and follow up his Warwick maiden success 19 days earlier. He travelled sweetly out the back and, although taking time to hit top gear when pulled to the outside with his effort, he was always going to get there. Value for further than the bare margin, the extra furlong suited and he could turn out to be a good deal better than this class in due course. Next year 1m2f should also pose him few problems. (op 7-2 tchd 4-1)
Aquarian Spirit set the moderate early pace and got very much the run of things. With that in mind, he has to rate as somewhat flattered, but there was still plenty to like about his attitude in the final two furlongs and he is a most genuine performer. (op 6-1 tchd 9-2)
Butch And Sundance, with the blinkers abandoned, was suited by racing up with the early pace and also rates as a little flattered. It was still a lot better from him on this step up in distance, though, and he has evidently found his level. (op 16-1)
Ingleby Spirit was forced to race on the outer of the pack from his outside stall. He threw down a serious challenge in the home straight, but his effort flattened out inside the last furlong. He is another likeable performer and should strike again this season. (op 20-1)
Our Joe Mac(IRE), up in trip, was the stable's first choice on jockey bookings and he got a confident ride on this nursery debut. He didn't get the best of passages inside the final two furlongs, but it was the lack of pace that did for him, as he was unable to land a serious blow. This gelding is well worth another chance. (op 11-4 tchd 7-2)
Flaming Miracle broke adequately this time and raced handily before weakening from the two-furlong pole. He must prove the handicapper hasn't got his measure. (tchd 15-2)
Tanto Quanto(IRE) Official explanation: jockey said colt ran too free

6089 WILLIAM HILL (AYR) SILVER CUP H'CAP 6f
2:05 (2:08) (Class 2) 3-Y-O+
£31,155 (£9,330; £4,665; £2,335; £1,165; £585) Stalls Centre

Form RPR

042 **1** **Kaldoun Kingdom (IRE)**[13] 5695 4-8-12 89............... BMcHugh[(5)] 2 99
(R A Fahey) *dwlt: sn in tch far side: led that gp over 1f out: drvn and styd on wl fnl f: 1st of 12 in gp* **8/1[1]**

6020 **2** *nk* **Lowther**[8] 5826 4-9-1 92........................(be[1]) GaryBartley[(5)] 3 101
(A Bailey) *cl up far side: effrt and ev ch over 1f out: kpt on u.p towards fin: 2nd of 12 in gp* **28/1**

0004 **3** *1/2* **Green Manalishi**[7] 5860 8-9-2 88.................(p) CO'Donoghue 11 97+
(K A Ryan) *in tch far side: effrt whn nt clr run briefly over 1f out: kpt on wl fnl f: 3rd of 12 in gp* **16/1**

1600 **4** *1 1/4* **Mastership (IRE)**[23] 5375 5-9-4 90...............(p) GrahamGibbons 5 94
(J J Quinn) *hld up far side: hdwy over 1f out: r.o ins fnl f: 4th of 12 in gp* **22/1**

000 **5** *hd* **Fullandby (IRE)**[7] 5860 7-9-9 95......................... AlanMunro 8 98
(T J Etherington) *bhd and sn pushed along far side: hdwy over 1f out: kpt on fnl f: nrst fin: 5th of 12 in gp* **33/1**

0021 **6** *hd* **Quest For Success (IRE)**[64] 4037 4-9-9 95............... PaulHanagan 9 98
(R A Fahey) *in tch far side: drvn over 2f out: kpt on same pce fnl f: 6th of 12 in gp* **11/1**

3000 **7** *1 1/4* **River Falcon**[7] 5860 9-9-8 94......................... DanielTudhope 4 93
(J S Goldie) *hld up far side: rdn and hdwy over 1f out: kpt on fnl f: no imp: 7th of 12 in gp* **40/1**

0500 **8** *1 1/4* **Tajneed (IRE)**[13] 5695 6-9-7 93..................... AdrianTNicholls 12 88
(D Nicholls) *dwlt: hld up on outside of far side gp: effrt over 2f out: no ex over 1f out: 8th of 12 in gp* **18/1**

-104 **9** *3/4* **Master Of Disguise**[50] 4490 3-9-7 95......................... LDettori 7 88
(C G Cox) *hld up far side: effrt on outside of that gp over 2f out: nvr able to chal: 9th of 12 in gp* **10/1[3]**

0520 **10** *nk* **Sea Of Leaves (USA)**[13] 5695 3-9-4 92.................... HayleyTurner 6 84
(J S Goldie) *bhd far side: pushed along 2f out: nvr able to chal: 10th of 12 in gp* **16/1**

0-00 **11** *nk* **Protector (SAF)**[56] 4310 8-9-4 90...................(t) RobertHavlin 16 88+
(A G Foster) *hld up stands' side: rdn and hdwy whn no room over 1f out: styd on wl to ld that gp nr fin: no ch w far side: 1st of 13 in gp* **66/1**

0000 **12** *nk* **Thebes**[13] 5695 4-9-5 **91** JoeFanning 10 81
(M Johnston) *cl up far side tl rdn and wknd over 1f out: 11th of 12 in gp* **33/1**
1006 **13** *½* **Mister Hardy**[52] 4423 4-9-5 **94** FrederikTylicki(3) 27 85+
(R A Fahey) *chsd stands' side ldrs: rdn over 2f out: led that gp 1f out to nr fin: 2nd of 13 in gp* **18/1**
1111 **14** *1* **My Gacho (IRE)**[29] 5206 7-9-6 **92** (v) J-PGuillambert 20 80+
(M Johnston) *wnt lft s: bhd stands' side tl gd hdwy over 1f out: nrst fin: 3rd of 13 in gp* **18/1**
3505 **15** *nk* **Pusey Street Lady**[34] 5069 5-9-9 **95** TPO'Shea 1 80
(J Gallagher) *led far side to over 1f out: sn wknd: last of 12 in gp* **25/1**
6400 **16** *nk* **Joseph Henry**[35] 5039 7-9-7 **93** LPKeniry 24 79+
(D Nicholls) *midfield stands' side: effrt over 2f out: edgd lft and kpt on fnl f: 4th of 13 in gp* **25/1**
011 **17** *2 ¼* **Invincible Force (IRE)**[48] 4560 5-9-8 **94** (b) PhillipMakin 15 73+
(Paul Green) *bhd stands' side: drvn over 2f out: kpt on fnl f: no imp: 5th of 13 in gp* **20/1**
3-00 **18** *½* **Six Of Hearts**[7] 5889 5-9-2 **93** (p) MHarley(5) 19 74+
(Cecil Ross, Ire) *blkd s: sn prom stands' side: ev ch that gp over 1f out: no ex ins fnl f: 6th of 13 in gp* **18/1**
0110 **19** *nk* **Johannes (IRE)**[7] 5860 6-9-10 **96** TonyHamilton 25 76+
(R A Fahey) *in tch stands' side: drvn over 2f out: one pce over 1f out: 7th of 13 in gp* **11/1**
1303 **19** *dht* **Roker Park (IRE)**[21] 5420 4-9-9 **95** (p) NCallan 13 75+
(K A Ryan) *hld up in tch stands' side: rdn over 1f out: no imp: 8th of 13 in gp* **9/1**[2]
2121 **21** *shd* **Cape Vale (IRE)**[4] 5960 4-9-4 **90** 5ex CDHayes 26 69+
(D Nicholls) *led stands' side gp to 1f out: sn rdn and btn: 9th of 13 in gp* **11/1**
1220 **22** *nse* **Red Cape (FR)**[9] 5799 6-9-3 **89** AndrewElliott 22 68+
(Mrs R A Carr) *chsd stands' side ldrs tl wknd over 1f out: 10th of 13 in gp* **28/1**
1460 **23** *1 ¼* **Sudden Impact (IRE)**[14] 5654 4-9-4 **90** (e) TomEaves 14 66+
(Paul Green) *bhd: rdn along 1/2-way: nvr on terms: 11th of 13 in gp* **66/1**
1000 **24** *shd* **Horatio Carter**[13] 5695 4-9-1 **92** (p) AmyRyan(5) 23 67+
(K A Ryan) *cl up stands' side gp tl wknd over 1f out: 12th of 13 in gp* **40/1**
6144 **25** *18* **Aye Aye Digby (IRE)**[21] 5424 4-9-6 **92** RobertWinston 18 13+
(H Candy) *dwlt: sn in tch on outside of stands' side gp: wknd 2f out: eased fnl f: last of 13 in gp* **20/1**

1m 11.12s (-2.48) **Going Correction** -0.175s/f (Firm)
WFA 3 from 4yo+ 2lb **25 Ran SP% 130.2**
Speed ratings (Par 109): **109,108,107,106,106 105,104,102,101,101 100,100,99,98,97 97,94,93,93,93 93,93,91,91,67**
toteswingers: 1&2 £53.50, 1&3 £9.10, 2&3 £155.70 CSF £228.42 CT £3560.09 TOTE £10.10: £2.60, £7.30, £3.30, £7.40; EX 156.10 Trifecta £1475.10 Part won. Pool: £1,993.40 - 0.10 winning units..
Owner P D Smith Holdings Ltd **Bred** Gainsborough Stud Management Ltd **Trained** Musley Bank, N Yorks
■ Stewards' Enquiry : Robert Havlin one-day ban: careless riding (Oct 5)

FOCUS
A strong and tight handicap, with the field covered by 8lb. The far-side group dominated from the furlong pole and those on the stands' side have been allowed 3lb as a result.

NOTEBOOK
Kaldoun Kingdom(IRE) was representing the trainer/jockey combination successful in the Bronze Cup and gave them another win in straightforward style. He was obviously well drawn in stall two, but he moved nicely and knuckled down when asked to master the runner-up. He has been most consistent and has plenty of experience of big-field sprints, but had gone without success since scoring over course and distance in 2007 and the handicapper appeared to have him where he wanted him. However, this was his first run of the season away from York, and he had shaped as though he would appreciate a change of scenery. It was a much-deserved success on ground faster than he likes. (op 15-2 tchd 9-1 in places)
Lowther had excuses for his below-par run at Doncaster last time and was equipped with first-time blinkers in addition to his usual eyeshield. He was awash with sweat, but that didn't stop him running a blinder. He had a cracking draw in stall three, but he lacked the resolution of the winner late on, although this proved his effectiveness for the distance and it was just his seventh career start. (op 33-1)
Green Manalishi ◆, fourth in the Portland a week previously, got a patient ride on the far side. He had to wait for his challenge inside the final furlong, so rates better than the bare form, and is no doubt back in top form. His turn is surely not far off again. (tchd 18-1)
Mastership(IRE) usually runs over further these days and came here with plenty to prove. He had a great draw and bounced back to his best, but he is just tricky to win with. (op 33-1)
Fullandby(IRE), who has a good record at this venue, looked to be struggling two furlongs out but he finished very strongly. The blinkers were abandoned and, although he is clearly weighted to win, he has developed into a tricky customer. (op 40-1)
Quest For Success(IRE) had been left for this meeting after scoring at Hamilton in July. His 5lb rise looked to find him out. (tchd 12-1)
River Falcon ran a much-improved race from a decent draw, but didn't show enough to suggest his losing run will end anytime soon.
Master Of Disguise Official explanation: jockey said colt ran flat
Protector(SAF) ◆ was the big eyecatcher on the near side. The eight-year-old was returning from a 56-day break and the ground was quick enough for him, but he ran a lot better than the bare form suggests. He was held up on the near side but endured a nightmare passage inside the final furlong and would have been a decisive winner on that side with a clear run. It was just his third outing of the season and he looks well worth supporting next time.
Mister Hardy was returning from a 52-day break and ran an honest race over a trip plenty sharp enough. (op 25-1)
My Gacho(IRE) again gave trouble at the start and then broke awkwardly. He was finishing with purpose before being tight for room on the near rail, however, and he does not look weighted out of winning again when reverting to another furlong. (op 16-1)
Aye Aye Digby(IRE) Official explanation: jockey said gelding hung left-handed from halfway

6090 LAUNDRY COTTAGE STUD FIRTH OF CLYDE STKS (GROUP 3) (FILLIES) 6f
2:35 (2:39) (Class 1) 2-Y-O
£39,739 (£15,064; £7,539; £3,759; £1,883; £945) **Stalls** Centre

Form RPR
31 **1** **Distinctive**[21] 5439 2-8-12 80 TomEaves 3 101+
(B Smart) *racd far side: hld up: hdwy and swtchd rt over 1f out: str run to ld last 75yds: sn clr: 1st of 7 that gp* **33/1**
4111 **2** *3 ¾* **Midnight Martini**[30] 5198 2-8-12 84 RobertWinston 7 90
(T D Easterby) *racd far side: led that gp tl over 1f out: kpt on wl ins fnl f: 2nd of 7 that gp* **12/1**
1 **3** *nk* **Astrophysical Jet**[32] 5129 2-8-12 0 GrahamGibbons 1 89
(E S McMahon) *swvd lft s: racd far side: w ldr: led that side over 1f out: hdd and no ex ins fnl f: 3rd of 7 that gp* **10/1**
12 **4** *shd* **Beyond Desire**[30] 5199 2-8-12 105 NCallan 14 97+
(M A Jarvis) *led stands' side: edgd rt and kpt on fnl f: no ch w wnr far side: 1st of 6 that gp* **1/1**[1]
15 **5** *¾* **Conniption (IRE)**[16] 5606 2-8-12 95 LDettori 13 94+
(B J Meehan) *racd stands' side: trckd ldr: wnt 2nd over 2f out: edgd rt and styd on same pce: 2nd of 6 that gp* **7/1**[3]
250 **6** *3 ¾* **Catbells (IRE)**[2] 6009 2-8-12 0 HayleyTurner 5 75
(A Bailey) *racd far side: in rr: rdn and outpcd over 2f out: 4th of 7 that gp* **40/1**
0300 **7** *shd* **Eternal Instinct**[9] 5795 2-8-12 78 GaryBartley 4 75
(J S Goldie) *racd far side: trckd ldrs: lost pl over 1f out: 5th of 7 that gp* **100/1**
2125 **8** *nk* **Jeanie Johnston (IRE)**[56] 4295 2-8-12 95 CO'Donoghue 11 82+
(A P Jarvis) *racd stands' side: w ldrs: wknd over 1f out: 3rd of 6 that gp* **20/1**
1460 **9** *1* **She's A Character**[16] 5606 2-8-12 94 PaulHanagan 2 71
(R A Fahey) *racd far side: chsd ldrs: lost pl over 1f out: 6th of 7 that gp* **33/1**
11 **10** *3 ½* **Music Show (IRE)**[28] 5241 2-8-12 89 AlanMunro 10 68+
(M R Channon) *racd stands' side: chsd ldrs: lost pl over 1f out: 4th of 6 that gp* **5/1**[2]
05 **11** *3 ¾* **Classlin**[13] 5693 2-8-12 0 DanielTudhope 8 49
(J S Goldie) *racd far side: in rr: nvr on terms: last of 7 that gp* **200/1**
12 **12** *3 ½* **Amary (IRE)**[72] 3782 2-8-12 90 SebSanders 9 47+
(C E Brittain) *racd stands' side: sn wl outpcd and in rr: 5th of 6 that gp* **22/1**
5016 **13** *6* **Hairspray**[36] 4989 2-8-12 94 JoeFanning 12 29+
(M R Channon) *racd stands' side: chsd ldrs: hung lft and lost pl 2f out: sn bhd and eased: last of 6 that gp* **28/1**

1m 11.98s (-1.62) **Going Correction** -0.175s/f (Firm) **13 Ran SP% 118.3**
Speed ratings (Par 102): **103,98,97,97,96 91,91,90,89,84 79,75,67**
toteswingers: 1&2 £19.60, 1&3 £19.20, 2&3 £28.10 CSF £359.52 TOTE £40.10: £6.90, £2.40, £3.60; EX 190.40 TRIFECTA Not won..
Owner Mr & Mrs G Middlebrook **Bred** Mr & Mrs G Middlebrook **Trained** Hambleton, N Yorks
■ Stewards' Enquiry : Graham Gibbons one-day ban: failed to keep straight from the stall (Oct 5)

FOCUS
This Group 3 for juvenile fillies was another contest in which a low draw proved crucial, with the first three coming from stalls three, seven and one. It paid to race handily and the form has to be treated with some caution, but it was hard not to be impressed with the winner.

NOTEBOOK
Distinctive had plenty to find with the leading form contenders, having taken just an average Redcar maiden last time out, but that came on just her second outing. She duly improved a bundle, drawing clear of those on the far side and looking better the further she went. That confirmed her trainer's belief that she will relish 7f, but she evidently has natural pace too. Previous victors of this event have a mixed history, although Airwave's win in 2002 gives the list a big boost. The stable's winner of this race two years ago, Unilateral, took in the Cheveley Park Stakes on her next outing and that would be a viable target for this daughter of Tobougg. However, her trainer said she may be put away for the year as he sees her as a Guineas filly.
Midnight Martini came into this debut in Group company in search of a four-timer, having taken the valuable sales race at York's Ebor meeting 30 days earlier. Well backed, she was ridden aggressively on the far side and held every chance. She was firmly put in her place by the winner, but this rates another improved run and she has developed into a tough sprinter. This also significantly enhances her potential paddock value. (op 16-1 tchd 11-1)
Astrophysical Jet won at Nottingham on her debut last time out. Along with the runner-up, she cut out most of the running on the near side and refused to go down lightly when put under maximum pressure. Considering she is bred to enjoy longer trips as she matures, this was a very promising display. (op 12-1 tchd 14-1)
Beyond Desire had little chance from the outside stall, but she was only just denied a place and still ran a big race to come out on top of the near-side group. Whether she would have beaten the winner if she had raced on the far side is debatable, but she deserves another chance and it wouldn't be surprising to see her head for the Cheveley Park. (op 10-11 tchd 11-10)
Conniption(IRE) was somewhat disappointing at Salisbury last time and was taking another step up in grade. She did well, running out a clear second-best on the near side, and handled the quicker ground without much fuss. (op 15-2 tchd 8-1)
Jeanie Johnston(IRE) was held by Beyond Desire on the form of her run behind Lady Of The Desert in the Princess Margaret Stakes in July. She ran her race, but was left behind by the first pair on the stands' side inside the final furlong. (op 18-1 tchd 16-1)

6091 WILLIAM HILL (AYR) GOLD CUP (HERITAGE H'CAP) 6f
3:10 (3:14) (Class 2) 3-Y-O+
£93,465 (£27,990; £13,995; £7,005; £3,495; £1,755) **Stalls** Centre

Form RPR
0433 **1** **Jimmy Styles**[8] 5826 5-9-2 **100** (p) LDettori 15 110
(C G Cox) *hld up far side gp: on outer 2f out: drvn to ld ins fnl f: hld on wl: 1st of 18 in gp* **14/1**
2010 **2** *hd* **Barney McGrew (IRE)**[7] 5860 6-9-5 **103** TomEaves 6 112
(M Dods) *hld up far side: pushed along 1/2-way: hdwy to dispute ld ins fnl f: kpt on: jst hld: 2nd of 18 in gp* **20/1**
1413 **3** *¾* **Knot In Wood (IRE)**[49] 4523 7-9-5 **108** BMcHugh(5) 9 115
(R A Fahey) *trckd far side ldrs: led that gp over 1f out to ins fnl f: r.o: 3rd of 18 in gp* **11/1**
1002 **4** *½* **Evens And Odds (IRE)**[49] 4523 5-9-4 **102** AdrianTNicholls 3 108
(D Nicholls) *prom far side: effrt and ev ch that gp over 1f out: one pce fnl f: 4th of 18 in gp* **7/1**[1]
1060 **5** *½* **Sonny Red (IRE)**[14] 5654 5-9-2 **100** JoeFanning 11 105+
(D Nicholls) *dwlt: bhd far side: hdwy over 1f out: keeping on whn n.m.r towards fin: 5th of 18 in gp* **28/1**
4660 **6** *hd* **Tombi (USA)**[29] 5232 5-9-2 **103** FrederikTylicki(3) 27 112+
(J Howard Johnson) *prom stands' side: rdn 1/2-way: styd on to ld that gp wl ins fnl f: nt rch far side: 1st of 8 in gp* **33/1**
0600 **7** *½* **Hogmaneigh (IRE)**[84] 3405 6-9-2 **100** DanielTudhope 2 102
(J S Goldie) *hld up far side: hdwy over 1f out: kpt on ins fnl f: 6th of 18 in gp* **16/1**
6043 **8** *hd* **Advanced**[35] 5039 6-8-10 **99** AmyRyan(5) 4 100
(K A Ryan) *cl up far side: effrt and ev ch over 1f out: kpt on same pce fnl f: 7th of 18 in gp* **8/1**[2]
0433 **9** *nk* **Fol Hollow (IRE)**[19] 5507 4-8-10 **97** KellyHarrison(3) 25 103+
(D Nicholls) *led stands' side: drvn over 2f out: hdd wl ins fnl f: kpt on: 2nd of 8 in gp* **40/1**
4363 **10** *nk* **Redford (IRE)**[56] 4297 4-9-4 **102** HayleyTurner 26 107+
(M L W Bell) *hld up stands' side: hdwy over 2f out: rdn and kpt on u.p fnl f: 3rd of 8 in gp* **12/1**
0241 **11** *½* **Genki (IRE)**[49] 4523 5-9-5 **103** SteveDrowne 17 101
(R Charlton) *midfield far side: rdn over 2f out: kpt on fnl f: nt pce to chal: 8th of 18 in gp* **12/1**

0640 **12** 1/2 **Intrepid Jack**[7] 5860 7-9-4 **102**.. RobertHavlin 13 99
(H Morrison) *hld up far side: hdwy over 1f out: no imp fnl f: 9th of 18 in gp* **25/1**

0452 **13** *hd* **Arganil (USA)**[14] 5654 4-9-2 **100**.. NCallan 24 101+
(K A Ryan) *cl up stands' side: disp ld ent fnl f: edgd lft and no ex last 100yds: 4th of 8 in gp* **33/1**

0522 **14** 1/2 **Signor Peltro**[20] 5476 6-9-2 **100**.. SebSanders 8 95
(H Candy) *midfield far side: drvn over 2f out: kpt on same pce fnl f: 10th of 18 in gp* **10/1**[3]

0006 **15** 1 3/4 **Hitchens (IRE)**[35] 5039 4-8-13 **97**.................................... PhillipMakin 23 88+
(T D Barron) *trckd stands' side ldrs tl rdn and no ex over 1f out: 5th of 8 in gp* **22/1**

0102 **16** *shd* **Everymanforhimself (IRE)**[7] 5860 5-8-13 **97**........(v) RobertWinston 22 88+
(K A Ryan) *hld up stands' side: drvn over 2f out: nvr able to chal: 6th of 8 in gp* **25/1**

0000 **17** 1/2 **Striking Spirit**[7] 5860 4-8-7 **98**.. NSLawes(7) 7 86
(D Nicholls) *led far side to over 1f out: sn btn: 11th of 18 in gp* **20/1**

0110 **18** 3/4 **Blue Jack**[14] 5654 4-9-1 **99**.......................................(b) PaulHanagan 16 84
(W R Muir) *dwlt: bhd far side: rdn 1/2-way: sme late hdwy: nt pce to chal: 12th of 18 in gp* **33/1**

3015 **19** 3 **Zidane**[21] 5434 7-9-4 **102**...(t) LPKeniry 1 78
(J R Fanshawe) *hld up far side: drvn over 2f out: sn no imp: 13th of 18 in gp* **12/1**

5060 **20** *shd* **Valery Borzov (IRE)**[35] 5039 5-9-3 **101**.................(v) GrahamGibbons 21 79+
(D Nicholls) *cl up stands' side tl edgd lft and wknd over 1f out: 7th of 8 in gp* **33/1**

0020 **21** 2 1/2 **Wi Dud**[32] 5132 5-8-12 **101**........................... Louis-PhilippeBeuzelin(5) 10 69
(K A Ryan) *cl up far side tl rdn and wknd over 1f out: 14th of 18 in gp* **40/1**

4152 **22** 2 3/4 **Mac Gille Eoin**[7] 5878 5-8-12 **96**....................................(b[1]) TPO'Shea 12 56
(J Gallagher) *trckd far side ldrs tl wknd over 2f out: 15th of 18 in gp* **14/1**

0600 **23** 1/2 **Madame Trop Vite (IRE)**[63] 4087 3-9-2 **102**..............(b[1]) AlanMunro 19 61
(K A Ryan) *prom far side tl rdn and wknd 2f out: 16th of 18 in gp* **80/1**

0-00 **24** 3/4 **Magic Cat**[112] 2485 3-9-0 **100**..(p) AndrewElliott 18 56
(A P Jarvis) *prom far side tl rdn and wknd over 2f out: 17th of 18 in gp* **100/1**

0001 **25** 2 1/2 **Brave Prospector**[8] 5826 4-9-1 **102** 5ex...................(t) JackMitchell(3) 20 56+
(P W Chapple-Hyam) *hld up in tch on outside of stands' side gp: rdn and wknd fr 2f out: last of 8 in gp* **16/1**

1406 **26** 3 1/2 **Abbondanza (IRE)**[20] 5474 6-9-6 **104**.......................(p) TonyHamilton 14 42
(I Semple) *chsd far side ldrs tl rdn and wknd over 2f out: last of 18 in gp* **66/1**

1m 11.35s (-2.25) **Going Correction** -0.175s/f (Firm)
WFA 3 from 4yo+ 2lb **26** Ran SP% **133.6**
Speed ratings (Par 109): **108,107,106,106,105 105,104,104,103,103 102,102,101,101,98 98,98,97,93,92 89,85,85,84,80 76**
toteswingers: 1&2 £120.80, 1&3 £84.80, 2&3 £34.60 CSF £279.88 CT £3249.26 TOTE £16.00: £3.60, £5.80, £3.20, £2.70; EX 927.40 Trifecta £9887.60 Pool: £35,954.24 - 3.70 winning units..
Owner Gwyn Powell and Peter Ridgers **Bred** Barry Minty **Trained** Lambourn, Berks

■ Stewards' Enquiry : L Dettori caution: used whip with excessive frequency
Adrian T Nicholls two-day ban: used whip down the shoulder in the forehand positon (Oct 5-6)
Frederik Tylicki four-day ban: used whip with excessive frequency (Oct 5-8)
Kelly Harrison four-day ban: used whip with excessive frequency (Oct 5-8)

FOCUS
One of the top sprint handicaps of the season. Unsurprisingly, given the results of the Bronze and Silver Cups, the far side was the place to be and only eight elected to stay on the stands' side. The draw wasn't quite as crucial this time, though, with the winner coming out of 15. It was a fractionally slower winning time than the Silver Cup, but the form still looks straightforward enough. Again, those on the satnds' side have been allowed 3lb to counter the bias.

NOTEBOOK
Jimmy Styles had the cheekpieces back on and was also 2lb lower for this slight drop back in trip. Buried away on the far side soon after the start, he was pulled wide with his challenge and picked up strongly for pressure. He took a little time to get on top close home, but was always going to get up and finally won the big pot connections had been searching for. This must rate as a career-best effort and the re-application of the headgear looked to play its part. A likely rise back up the weights may mean he will need to go back into Listed company and, looking at his run in such company on his penultimate start, success in that grade is entirely possible. (tchd 16-1 in a place)
Barney McGrew(IRE) wasn't on a going day in the Portland a week previously, but he showed his true colours again and was only narrowly held. He got a patient ride early on, but came under heavy pressure nearing the two-furlong marker. He responded gamely and came through with every chance, but the concession of 3lb to Jimmy Styles was just beyond him. He registered a career-best in defeat. (tchd 18-1)
Knot In Wood(IRE) momentarily looked like defying top weight when hitting the front inside the final furlong. His talented rider's claim helped on that front, but this was still a tough ask and he deserves plenty of credit. He is a rock-solid benchmark, as he finished third last time out off 2lb lower in the Stewards' Cup, and the Diadem at Ascot is his next intended target. (op 12-1)
Evens And Odds(IRE) fared best of the David Nicholls team. He just failed to confirm Goodwood form with the top weight, on 2lb worse terms, but did nothing wrong and is another who helps to give the form a decent look. (op 13-2 tchd 15-2)
Sonny Red(IRE) stayed on late and ran close enough to his York form with the runner-up. However, his temperament still fails to convince.
Tombi(USA), who ran well in Listed company last time, came out on top of those on the near side. He remains in good heart and deserves extra credit.
Hogmaneigh(IRE) was returning from an 84-day break and having his first run for Jim Goldie. He posted a solid effort on ground plenty quick enough for him and performed close enough to his last-time-out form with the winner on identical terms. (tchd 20-1 in a place)
Advanced was 10lb lower than when successful in this race in 2007 and ran very well in the Great St Wilfrid last time. That meant he was closely matched with the winner, who was one place behind him there. He had his chance, but ultimately paid for being so positively ridden early on. (tchd 9-1 and 10-1 in a place)
Fol Hollow(IRE) is another to emerge with credit, finishing second of those on the near side. He is just held by the handicapper and seems to find this trip stretching his stamina.
Redford(IRE) looked very interesting back at 6f, but wasn't helped at all by being drawn in stall 26. He would have found the ground quicker than he cares for, so this was no disgrace, but his optimum trip remains open to debate.
Genki(IRE) wasn't disgraced from stall 17 on this return to a quicker surface, but he never looked like confirming the form of his Stewards' Cup success with Knot In Wood and Evens And Odds off a 7lb higher mark. (tchd 11-1)
Mac Gille Eoin Official explanation: jockey said filly hung left-handed throughout
Brave Prospector Official explanation: jockey said colt lost a right front shoe

6092 WILSONS AUCTIONS H'CAP 7f 50y
3:50 (3:50) (Class 3) (0-95,93) 3-Y-0+

£11,091 (£3,321; £1,660; £831; £414; £208) **Stalls** High

Form RPR

2536 **1** **Harrison George (IRE)**[13] 5695 4-9-4 **90**..................... PaulHanagan 14 101
(R A Fahey) *sn w ldr: led over 2f out: styd on strly fnl f* **8/1**[3]

2053 **2** 2 **Osteopathic Remedy (IRE)**[19] 5522 5-9-0 **86**.............. PhillipMakin 12 93+
(M Dods) *hld up towards rr: hdwy and nt clr run over 1f out: styd on strly ins fnl f: tk 2nd nr fin* **8/1**[3]

4-41 **3** *hd* **Prime Exhibit**[37] 4954 4-9-2 **88**.. SteveDrowne 2 94+
(R Charlton) *trckd ldrs: quite keen: effrt over 2f out: styd on wl ins fnl f* **2/1**[1]

060 **4** 3/4 **Damika (IRE)**[13] 5695 6-9-2 **88**..(p) LDettori 3 92
(R M Whitaker) *led tl over 2f out: rallied over 1f out: kpt on same pce* **7/1**[2]

6630 **5** 1/2 **Kyllachy Star**[20] 5490 3-9-0 **89**...................................... TonyHamilton 10 91
(R A Fahey) *t.k.h in rr: effrt on outer over 2f out: styd on fnl f: nvr trbld ldrs* **16/1**

5151 **6** 3/4 **Zomerlust**[23] 5363 7-9-1 **87**.......................................(b[1]) GrahamGibbons 1 88
(J J Quinn) *trckd ldrs: t.k.h: one pce fnl f* **7/1**[2]

5050 **7** 1 **Something (IRE)**[33] 5104 7-9-7 **93**.............................. AdrianTNicholls 8 91+
(D Nicholls) *hld up in rr: hmpd after 1 1/2f: hdwy and nt clr run 2f out: wknd ins fnl f* **14/1**

0050 **8** 3 **Arabian Spirit**[56] 4310 4-9-0 **86**.. HayleyTurner 7 77
(E A L Dunlop) *hld up in rr: edgd lft after 1 1/2f: hdwy on ins over 2f out: chsng ldrs over 1f out: sn wknd* **20/1**

4024 **9** 1 1/4 **Dixey**[26] 5313 4-9-4 **90**.. NCallan 5 78
(M A Jarvis) *chsd ldrs: wknd fnl f* **11/1**

1024 **10** 9 **Clientele (USA)**[7] 5887 3-8-8 **83**.. JoeFanning 9 48
(M Johnston) *chsd ldrs: drvn over 3f out: lost pl over 2f out: sn bhd* **10/1**

1m 31.18s (-2.22) **Going Correction** -0.175s/f (Firm)
WFA 3 from 4yo+ 3lb **10** Ran SP% **115.3**
Speed ratings (Par 107): **105,102,102,101,101 100,99,95,94,83**
toteswingers: 1&2 £10.00, 1&3 £4.60, 2&3 £5.50 CSF £69.57 CT £180.52 TOTE £7.10: £2.10, £1.80, £1.40; EX 33.90.
Owner P D Smith Holdings Ltd **Bred** R P Ryan **Trained** Musley Bank, N Yorks

FOCUS
A decent handicap, but run at an uneven pace.

NOTEBOOK
Harrison George(IRE) got a shrewd ride from Hanagan, who had him well positioned early on, despite being drawn widest of all, and then perfectly placed to strike two furlongs out. The decision to kick on soon afterwards proved decisive, and although the form may be somewhat muddling, he has been threatening to do this for a while. It was his first victory since last year and this is his trip, but a likely reaction from the handicapper will probably scupper him next time. It may be different if connections are able to find him a suitable race under a penalty, however, as his confidence will be high after this. (op 5-1 tchd 9-1 in a place)
Osteopathic Remedy(IRE) stayed on best of those from off the pace and ran right up to his previous level on ground he would have found quick enough. He deserves to win again. (op 12-1)
Prime Exhibit was racing off 6lb higher than when winning at Sandown 37 days previously. The form has not worked out well, but he was another who would have been seen to better effect off a stronger early pace. He is not one to abandon. (op 3-1 tchd 7-2 in a place)
Damika(IRE) was sent into the early lead by one of the best front-running jockeys around. He had very much the run of things, but kept on gamely enough when headed and this was much better from him in first-time cheekpieces. He is well treated at present and a return to 6f on easier ground should only help his cause. (op 6-1)
Kyllachy Star caught the eye staying on from way off the pace on the outside down the home straight. On this showing he may well pop up again this season. (op 12-1)
Zomerlust proved too free in first-time blinkers, but a more even pace would have helped him. (op 8-1)
Something(IRE), with the tongue tie left off, was another not suited by the way the race unfolded, but is not proving simple to predict. (op 10-1)
Clientele(USA) Official explanation: trainer had no explanation for the poor form shown

6093 WILLIAMHILL.COM DOONSIDE CUP STKS (LISTED RACE) 1m 2f
4:25 (4:25) (Class 1) 3-Y-0+

£34,062 (£12,912; £6,462; £3,222; £1,614; £810) **Stalls** High

Form RPR

331 **1** **Prince Siegfried (FR)**[43] 4760 3-8-8 111........................ LDettori 7 116+
(Saeed Bin Suroor) *mde all: c centre 3f out: shkn up over 1f out: styd on strly: v comf* **11/8**[1]

301- **2** 3 1/4 **Baila Me (GER)**[356] 6324 4-8-9 111.. AlanMunro 8 105+
(Saeed Bin Suroor) *trckd ldrs: effrt to chse wnr 2f out: kpt on: no imp* **7/1**

66-5 **3** 1 1/2 **Arch Rebel (USA)**[14] 5685 8-9-0 104..............(p) CO'Donoghue 5 107
(Noel Meade, Ire) *in rr and sn drvn along: hdwy over 4f out: sn chsng ldrs: kpt on same pce fnl 2f* **12/1**

0241 **4** 1/2 **Nanton (USA)**[8] 5823 7-9-0 105........................ DanielTudhope 11 106
(J S Goldie) *stdd and swtchd lft s: hld up in rr: hdwy over 2f out: styd on same pce* **11/2**[3]

1442 **5** *nk* **Dream Lodge (IRE)**[29] 5231 5-9-0 109........................... PaulHanagan 3 105
(R A Fahey) *chsd wnr: effrt over 2f out: kpt on same pce* **7/2**[2]

-320 **6** 6 **Casilda (IRE)**[21] 5447 4-8-9 99.. LPKeniry 6 88
(A M Balding) *chsd ldrs: wknd appr fnl f* **11/1**

6000 **7** 16 **Unbreak My Heart (IRE)**[2] 6013 4-9-0 91..................... TonyHamilton 4 61
(R A Fahey) *mid-div: lost pl over 2f out: eased ins fnl f* **16/1**

3430 **8** 15 **Primo Way**[31] 5160 8-9-0 54.. DuranFentiman 1 31
(D A Nolan) *in rr: bhd fnl 3f: t.o* **100/1**

2m 6.00s (-6.00) **Going Correction** -0.175s/f (Firm)
WFA 3 from 4yo+ 6lb **8** Ran SP% **115.1**
Speed ratings (Par 111): **117,114,113,112,112 107,94,82**
toteswingers: 1&2 £3.40, 1&3 £5.90, 2&3 £5.80 CSF £11.98 TOTE £2.20: £1.20, £2.20, £3.00; EX 5.90.
Owner Godolphin **Bred** Haras Saint Pair Du Mont **Trained** Newmarket, Suffolk

FOCUS
A standard Listed event.

NOTEBOOK
Prince Siegfried(FR), the sole three-year-old in the field, was taken wide from the start and then pointed towards the centre of the track after turning for home. He had his rivals in trouble when asserting two furlongs out and there was only going to be one winner from the furlong marker. This was his first success in Pattern company, although he was placed in Group 2 company in July, and Group races are where his future lies. His two wins this year have come from the front and that will be a slight concern as he steps back up in grade, but he also appeals as the type to come into his own as a four-year-old. (tchd 13-8 and 5-4 in places)

Baila Me(GER) ◆ kept on stoutly to give her connections a one-two. This was her first outing for since being purchased after winning at the top level in Germany last season and she left the impression she would come on a bundle for the run. A return to easier ground and a longer trip should also help, so she looks one to side with next time. (op 15-2)
Arch Rebel(USA) ran in snatches and proved hard work. It is testament to his talent that he bagged third place on ground quicker than he cares for, but at the age of eight he looks to have his own ideas. (op 14-1 tchd 16-1 in a place)
Nanton(USA), a winner over 1m6f in handicap company eight days earlier, made a tardy start and was soon restrained. He was always getting there too late, but given the way the race was run it was a decent effort and he remains in top form. He is versatile as regards distance, as his entries in the Cambridgeshire and Cesarewitch imply, but a more positive ride over this sort of trip is required. (op 5-1 tchd 9-2)
Dream Lodge(IRE) kept on resolutely under maximum pressure, but he still looked to find this too hot despite it being a drop in class. (op 4-1 tchd 100-30)

6094 WILLIAMHILL.COM AYRSHIRE H'CAP — 1m

5:00 (5:00) (Class 2) (0-100,98) 3-Y-O+

£24,924 (£7,464; £3,732; £1,868; £932; £468) **Stalls** High

Form — RPR

0000 **1** **Extraterrestrial**[30] 5200 5-9-2 **95** FrederikTylicki(3) 6 — 106
(R A Fahey) *hld up: gd hdwy 2f out: led ent fnl f: drvn out* **15/2**

0222 **2** *1 3/4* **Billy Dane (IRE)**[19] 5522 5-8-8 **89** (p) MartinLane(5) 14 — 96
(F P Murtagh) *led: rdn over 2f out: hdd appr fnl f: rallied: kpt on fin* **10/1**

0355 **3** *nk* **Appalachian Trail (IRE)**[19] 5529 8-9-8 **98** (b) TomEaves 9 — 104
(I Semple) *prom gng wl: smooth hdwy to ld appr fnl f to ent fnl f: sn rdn: one pce last 100yds* **25/1**

2111 **4** *1 1/4* **Tiger Reigns**[14] 5670 3-8-13 **93** PhillipMakin 1 — 97
(M Dods) *prom on ins: effrt whn nt clr run over 1f out: swtchd rt and styd on fnl f* **6/1**[3]

3645 **5** *shd* **Scuffle**[30] 5200 4-9-6 **96** SteveDrowne 12 — 100
(R Charlton) *trckd ldr: ev ch over 1f out: one pce ins fnl f* **9/2**[2]

4000 **6** *3/4* **Royal Power (IRE)**[19] 5522 6-8-13 **89** AdrianTNicholls 7 — 91
(D Nicholls) *trckd ldrs: effrt whn nt clr run briefly over 1f out: one pce fnl f* **33/1**

0460 **7** *1 1/4* **Lang Shining (IRE)**[28] 5262 5-9-2 **97** Louis-PhilippeBeuzelin(5) 8 — 96
(Sir Michael Stoute) *hld up: hdwy on outside over 1f out: edgd lft: no imp fnl f* **7/1**

0002 **8** *nse* **Bolodenka (IRE)**[18] 5551 7-9-1 **91** PaulHanagan 13 — 90
(R A Fahey) *hld up: rdn over 2f out: styd on fnl f: no imp* **8/1**

2140 **9** *2 1/4* **Wigwam Willie (IRE)**[20] 5490 7-8-9 **90** (tp) AmyRyan(5) 2 — 84
(K A Ryan) *hld up: drvn over 2f out: nvr able to chal* **16/1**

0110 **10** *1 1/4* **The Osteopath (IRE)**[42] 4779 6-9-4 **94** TonyHamilton 5 — 85
(M Dods) *midfield: rdn over 2f out: btn over 1f out* **18/1**

2400 **11** *1 1/4* **Flipando (IRE)**[19] 5522 8-9-0 **93** NeilBrown(3) 4 — 82
(T D Barron) *hld up on ins: outpcd over 2f out: sn n.d* **12/1**

12 *13* **Authentic**[69] 4-8-13 **89** LDettori 11 — 49
(L M Cumani) *midfield: effrt over 2f out: wknd wl over 1f out: eased whn btn fnl f* **7/2**[1]

1m 40.51s (-3.29) **Going Correction** -0.175s/f (Firm)
WFA 3 from 4yo+ 4lb — **12** Ran SP% **124.8**
Speed ratings (Par 109): **109,107,106,105,105 104,103,103,101,100 98,85**
toteswingers: 1&2 £24.20, 1&3 £52.60, 2&3 £22.00 CSF £84.85 CT £1837.34 TOTE £10.30: £2.80, £3.80, £5.90; EX 138.80.
Owner G J Paver **Bred** Lostford Manor Stud **Trained** Musley Bank, N Yorks

FOCUS
A very competitive handicap, run at a fair pace.

NOTEBOOK
Extraterrestrial bounced right back to form after some below-par efforts and gained a second success of the campaign. He had dropped to the same mark as when taking the Spring Cup at Newbury in April and completed the task readily. He picked up strongly when a gap opened for him nearing the furlong marker and this was the quickest ground he has scored on. His confidence will be boosted, but his profile dictates he is one to take on again next time. Official explanation: trainer had no explanation for the apparent improvement in form shown (op 8-1)
Billy Dane(IRE), 2lb higher, got to the front early on from his outside stall and set a sound enough pace. He fought off every challenge bar the winner, and for all that he is genuine, the handicapper clearly has him in his grip. (op 12-1 tchd 14-1)
Appalachian Trail(IRE) was going easily two furlongs out and looked set to go close, but his reluctance to settle early on probably cost him. This as far as he wants to go, however, and he is one to look out for when dropping back to 7f on easier ground. (op 22-1)
Tiger Reigns had his chance, but was another 5lb higher in much better company. Given that the ground would have been lively enough for him, it wasn't a bad effort by any means. (op 11-2)
Scuffle, well backed, had been dropped another pound despite running well in a hot handicap at York on her previous start. She was unable to land a significant blow, but ran close to her recent level and wasn't disgraced. (op 7-1)
Royal Power(IRE) has been out of sorts mainly this term, but has dropped to an attractive mark and this was a lot more encouraging.
Lang Shining(IRE) had his chance and, coming wide with his effort down the home straight, can have no excuses. (op 11-2 tchd 15-2)
Flipando(IRE) Official explanation: jockey said gelding hung badly right in the straight
Authentic has been patiently handled since joining his connections this year. Having a first run for them after 69 days, he began to feel the pinch after three furlongs out and ultimately ran miles below expectations, shaping as though something went amiss. (op 11-2 tchd 3-1 in places)

6095 SKED CONSTRUCTION - CONCRETE'S WHAT WE DO - H'CAP — 1m 5f 13y

5:35 (5:36) (Class 3) (0-90,90) 3-Y-O+ **£11,527** (£3,430; £1,714; £856) **Stalls** Low

Form — RPR

4066 **1** **Amanda Carter**[13] 5696 5-8-10 **75** FrederikTylicki(3) 6 — 92+
(R A Fahey) *hld up: hdwy 3f out: led 2f out: rdn clr fnl f* **6/1**

2341 **2** *8* **Demolition**[2] 6013 5-9-8 **89** 6ex (p) GaryBartley(5) 12 — 95
(N Wilson) *cl up: led after 3f: rdn 3f out: hdd 2f out: kpt on same pce fnl f* **9/2**[2]

5400 **3** *nk* **Dazzling Light (UAE)**[13] 5696 4-8-13 **75** DanielTudhope 16 — 80
(J S Goldie) *hld up: hdwy on outside over 2f out: edgd lft: kpt on fnl f: nrst fin* **18/1**

5150 **4** *2* **Conquisto**[14] 5656 4-9-13 **89** SteveDrowne 11 — 92
(C G Cox) *hld up: rdn and effrt 3f out: hung lft: one pce fnl 2f* **11/2**[3]

056/ **5** *2* **Hunting Tower**[8] 5847 5-9-6 **82** CO'Donoghue 4 — 82
(J J Lambe, Ire) *led 4f: cl up: drvn over 4f out: rallied over 3f out: outpcd fnl 2f* **7/1**

111 **6** *1 1/4* **Stanstill (IRE)**[42] 4785 3-9-5 **90** RobertWinston 8 — 88
(G A Swinbank) *t.k.h: prom: rdn 3f out: outpcd fr 2f out* **3/1**[1]

0-00 **7** *8* **Bogside Theatre (IRE)**[127] 2031 5-10-0 **90** AndrewElliott 14 — 77
(G M Moore) *hld up: hdwy and prom after 4f: rdn and wknd fr 2f out* **33/1**

2103 **8** *9* **Aureate**[15] 5622 5-8-4 **71** oh1 MartinLane(5) 7 — 45
(B Ellison) *prom: drvn over 4f out: wknd over 3f out* **9/1**

6/6 **9** *7* **Folk Tune (IRE)**[11] 5067 6-9-9 **85** GrahamGibbons 9 — 49
(J J Quinn) *bhd: drvn over 3f out: sn btn* **25/1**

-150 **10** *6* **King's Head (IRE)**[18] 5551 6-9-3 **79** TonyHamilton 2 — 35
(Miss L A Perratt) *cl up: lost pl over 4f out: sn rdn and btn* **25/1**

-000 **11** *19* **Rayhani (USA)**[14] 5671 6-9-5 **81** AdrianTNicholls 17 — 10
(D Nicholls) *t.k.h: hld up: hdwy and prom 1/2-way: wknd qckly over 3f out: eased whn btn* **11/1**

2m 49.41s (-4.59) **Going Correction** -0.175s/f (Firm)
WFA 3 from 4yo+ 9lb — **11** Ran SP% **119.6**
Speed ratings (Par 107): **107,102,101,100,99 98,93,88,83,80 68**
toteswingers: 1&2 £11.30, 1&3 £26.90, 2&3 £19.30 CSF £33.07 CT £468.33 TOTE £8.80: £2.70, £2.20, £3.50; EX 47.40 Place 6: £358.54, Place 5: £199.78..
Owner Mrs Janis Macpherson **Bred** James G Thom **Trained** Musley Bank, N Yorks
■ An eighth winner at the meeting for the Fahey stable.

FOCUS
A fair handicap, run at a sound pace.

NOTEBOOK
Amanda Carter finally ended her losing run and did it in emphatic fashion. Patiently ridden early on, she made her move after turning for home and hit top gear coming to two furlongs out. She was soon in front and stayed on strongly, rating full value for her wide-winning margin. She was dropping back from 2m and was 3lb higher than when previously successful last term. She could be in trouble after a probable reaction from the handicapper, for all that she is in the right hands. (op 7-1 tchd 8-1)
Demolition was penalised for resuming winning ways here two days earlier and was given another positive ride despite this being a step back up three furlongs in trip. He ran his heart out, doing very well to hold on for second, and has been a credit to connections. (op 7-2)
Dazzling Light(UAE) was given a lot to do from off the pace, but stayed on stoutly without seriously threatening and registered her best effort for some time. She stays very well and is on a fair mark, so may be able to build on this in the coming weeks. (op 20-1 tchd 25-1 in places)
Conquisto appreciated the sounder surface and moved nicely into contention from off the pace, but failed to find an extra gear when asked for maximum effort. Perhaps dropping back yet another furlong is what he ideally requires. (op 8-1)
Hunting Tower, best known these days for his hurdling exploits, cut out a lot of the early running but lost his position when coming under pressure exiting the back straight. He kept on for pressure, though, and ran close to his previous level. (op 9-2)
Stanstill(IRE), returning from a 42-day break, was seeking a four-timer off a 3lb higher mark. He wasn't disgraced, but found this different to the small-field handicaps he's been winning. (op 9-2 tchd 11-4 and 5-1 in places)
Folk Tune(IRE) Official explanation: jockey said horse was unsuited by the good (good to firm places) ground
Rayhani(USA) Official explanation: jockey said gelding had no more to give
T/Jkpt: Not won. T/Plt: £650.20 to a £1 stake. Pool: £131,339.83. 147.45 winning tickets. T/Qpdt: £101.60 to a £1 stake. Pool: £8,022.60. 58.40 winning tickets. RY

5620 CATTERICK (L-H)

Saturday, September 19

OFFICIAL GOING: Good to firm (good in places; 8.9)
Wind: Light hal behind Weather: Sunny periods

6096 E.B.F./BLUE SQUARE POKER MAIDEN STKS — 5f 212y

1:25 (1:26) (Class 5) 2-Y-O **£3,885** (£1,156; £577; £288) **Stalls** Low

Form — RPR

20 **1** **Colepeper**[14] 5669 2-9-3 0 GregFairley 2 — 87+
(M Johnston) *mde all: rdn clr over 1f out: kpt on strly* **7/4**[1]

2 *5* **Johannesgray (IRE)** 2-9-3 0 DO'Donohoe 12 — 70+
(D Nicholls) *dwlt: sn prom: chsd wnr 4f out: rdn along 2f out: drvn over 1f out and kpt on: no ch w wnr* **8/1**

642 **3** *4 1/2* **Texas Queen**[11] 5752 2-8-12 73 SamHitchcott 8 — 52+
(M R Channon) *outpcd and pushed along towards rr: rdn along 3f out: hdwy 2f out: sn drvn and no imp* **2/1**[2]

2244 **4** *1 1/4* **Yeadon**[8] 5835 2-9-3 77 SilvestreDeSousa 9 — 53
(R A Fahey) *chsd ldrs: rdn along 2f out: sn edgd lft and drvn: no imp* **7/1**[3]

355 **5** *1 1/4* **So Bazaar (IRE)**[40] 4844 2-9-3 64 PJMcDonald 5 — 49
(G A Swinbank) *chsd ldrs: hdwy 1/2-way: rdn along 2f out: sn drvn and one pce* **15/2**

5342 **6** *1 1/2* **Drinking Buddy**[19] 5519 2-8-10 57 JamesPSullivan(7) 7 — 45
(D W Thompson) *towards rr: swtchd outside and rdn over 2f out: styd on appr fnl f: nvr nr ldrs* **66/1**

0040 **7** *2 1/4* **No Quarter (IRE)**[27] 5290 2-8-10 60 IJBrennan(7) 10 — 38
(A Dickman) *in tch: rdn along 3f out: sn drvn and wknd* **66/1**

5400 **8** *6* **Clear Ice (IRE)**[42] 4803 2-9-3 55 AndrewMullen 6 — 20
(D Nicholls) *in tch: rdn along 1/2-way: sn wknd* **50/1**

0 **9** *2 3/4* **Tai Hang (IRE)**[57] 4257 2-8-12 0 RichardThomas 1 — 7
(A P Jarvis) *chsd ldrs: rdn along 1/2-way: sn wknd* **50/1**

1m 12.56s (-1.04) **Going Correction** -0.05s/f (Good) — **9** Ran SP% **112.0**
Speed ratings (Par 95): **104,97,91,89,88 86,83,75,71**
toteswingers: 1&2 £2.90, 1&3 £1.80, 2&3 £5.00 CSF £15.64 TOTE £2.60: £1.30, £1.60, £1.10; EX 16.50.
Owner Sheikh Hamdan Bin Mohammed Al Maktoum **Bred** Whitley Stud **Trained** Middleham Moor, N Yorks

FOCUS
An ordinary maiden on paper but it was run at a sound pace.

NOTEBOOK
Colepeper ◆ ran out a decisive winner. Having only his third start, the imposing son of Cape Cross always looked in command. He is clearly progressing and should have no problem following up. He looks the type to keep progressing as a three-year-old. (op 7-2)
Johannesgray(IRE) was well backed beforehand and showed a decent level of ability. He was probably unlucky to run into an above-average winner, and a similar race should be well within his compass in the coming weeks. (op 9-2 tchd 17-2)
Texas Queen was soon outpaced, before staying on all too late. She might do better stepped up in trip, but is starting to look exposed. (op 6-4)
Yeadon looks flattered by his mark of 77 and also doesn't convince with his head carriage. Official explanation: jockey said colt hung left-handed throughout (tchd 6-1)
Drinking Buddy, placed in sellers of late, was always outpaced and could never land a blow. He is clearly limited but might be seen in a better light in modest handicaps over slightly further. (tchd 50-1)

6097 BLUE SQUARE SP GUARANTEE H'CAP (DIV I) — 1m 5f 175y

2:00 (2:00) (Class 6) (0-65,65) 3-Y-O+ **£2,047** (£604; £302) **Stalls** Low

Form — RPR

5461 **1** **Simple Jim (FR)**[16] 5600 5-9-0 **51** SilvestreDeSousa 3 — 56
(J Hetherton) *in tch: hdwy 4f out: rdn to chse ldr wl over 1f out: drvn to chal ent fnl f: styd on to ld last 100yds* **9/4**[1]

1450 **2** *nk* **Diktalina**[22] 5382 3-8-4 **51**.................... KoseiMiura 2 56
(W R Muir) *set even pce: rdn and qcknd over 2f out: drvn over 1f out: hdd and no ex last 100yds* **15/2**
0244 **3** *1 1/4* **Sir Sandicliffe (IRE)**[15] 5625 5-9-5 **61**.................... DeanHeslop(5) 5 64
(W M Brisbourne) *dwlt: hld up in rr: hdwy on inner over 3f out: swtchd rt and rdn 2f out: drvn to chse ldng pair ent fnl f: edgd lft and no ex last 100yds* **5/1**[2]
5433 **4** *3/4* **Fenners (USA)**[16] 5600 6-8-13 **50**....................(p) DaleGibson 6 52
(M W Easterby) *chsd ldng pair: pushed along 1/2-way: rdn along on inner 5f out: drvn wl over2f out: kpt on wl u.p fnl f* **6/1**[3]
5000 **5** *2 1/4* **Shanavaz**[12] 5732 3-8-0 **47**....................(p) JamieMackay 7 46
(C J Teague) *t.k.h: hld up towards rr: swtchd lft and hdwy 2f out: sn rdn and kpt on appr fnl f: nrst fin* **16/1**
5622 **6** *hd* **Carmela Maria**[14] 5679 4-9-1 **59**....................(p) IJBrennan(7) 9 58
(M E Sowersby) *trckd ldrs: effrt 3f out and sn rdn along: drvn wl over 1f out and grad wknd* **8/1**
05-0 **7** *2 1/2* **Hernando's Boy**[15] 5625 8-9-11 **65**.................... MichaelJStainton(3) 4 60
(K G Reveley) *in tch: effrt 4f out: rdn along 3f out: drvn and no imp fnl 2f* **14/1**
00-0 **8** *1 1/4* **Firestorm (IRE)**[108] 2592 5-8-9 **46** oh1....................(b) PJMcDonald 8 40
(C W Fairhurst) *cl up: rdn along 3f out: drvn 2f out and grad wknd* **80/1**
2405 **9** *10* **Bert's Memory**[18] 5548 5-8-12 **49**.................... AdrianMcCarthy 10 29
(Jennie Candlish) *hld up towards rr: hdwy to chse ldrs on outer 5f out: rdn along wl over 2f out and sn wknd* **9/1**
0060 **10** *10* **Bridgewater Boys**[23] 5377 8-9-7 **58**....................(b) CatherineGannon 1 24
(T J Pitt) *dwlt: a in rr* **25/1**
3m 5.43s (1.83) **Going Correction** -0.05s/f (Good)
WFA 3 from 4yo+ 10lb **10** Ran SP% **112.2**
Speed ratings (Par 101): **92,91,91,90,89 89,87,87,81,75**
toteswingers: 1&2 £6.50, 1&3 £3.70, 2&3 £6.80 CSF £18.57 CT £74.70 TOTE £2.80: £1.10, £2.40, £1.80; EX 20.60.
Owner R G Fell **Bred** Snc Haras Des Peltrais, Laurent Thibault **Trained** Nawton, N Yorks

FOCUS
A 46-65 handicap run at an even pace.
Bert's Memory Official explanation: jockey said mare failed to get the trip

6098 BLUE SQUARE GAMES (S) STKS 1m 5f 175y
2:30 (2:30) (Class 6) 3-Y-O **£2,047** (£604; £302) **Stalls** Low

Form RPR
4344 **1** **Saffron's Son (IRE)**[24] 5342 3-8-10 50....................(b) PJMcDonald 12 56
(P T Midgley) *hld up: stdy hdwy 5f out: chsd ldrs over 2f out: rdn to chal over 1f out: led jst ins fnl f: drvn out* **7/1**
0250 **2** *1 1/2* **Tropical Bachelor (IRE)**[34] 5068 3-8-10 64........(b[1]) CatherineGannon 6 54
(T J Pitt) *led: rdn along over 2f out: drvn and jnd over 1f out: hdd jst ins fnl f: kpt on u.p* **85/40**[1]
0000 **3** *2 1/2* **Flirty (IRE)**[14] 5679 3-8-5 47.................... AdrianMcCarthy 1 46
(Rae Guest) *trckd ldng pair: effrt 3f out: rdn 2f out: sn swtchd rt and drvn whn n.m.r over 1f out: sn one pce* **9/1**
0220 **4** *7* **Moggy (IRE)**[37] 4943 3-8-5 54.................... DO'Donohoe 4 36
(G A Harker) *hld up in tch: hdwy to trck ldrs 1/2-way: effrt 3f out: rdn 2f out: sn drvn and plugged on one pce* **9/2**[3]
0036 **5** *1 1/2* **Nouailhas**[77] 3629 3-8-8 52 ow1.................... RussellKennemore(3) 8 40
(R Hollinshead) *chsd ldr: rdn along over 3f out: drvn 2f out and sn wknd* **18/1**
0-36 **6** *14* **Game Roseanna**[48] 4562 3-8-3 58 ow3.................... DeanHeslop(5) 9 18
(W M Brisbourne) *hld up in rr: effrt and sme hdwy over 4f out: sn rdn and nvr a factor* **4/1**[2]
64-0 **7** *3 3/4* **Bigalo's Star (IRE)**[127] 2060 3-8-10 75.................... GregFairley 5 15
(L A Mullaney) *hld up: a in rr* **7/1**
4540 **8** *1 1/4* **Gold Maha**[17] 4434 3-8-4 46 ow6.................... IJBrennan(7) 7 15
(M E Sowersby) *a in rr* **25/1**
4400 **9** *12* **Just Dan**[25] 5328 3-8-10 42....................(p) DaleGibson 11 —
(R Hollinshead) *a in rr* **28/1**
0000 **10** *93* **Rose Avelina**[20] 5470 3-7-12 35.................... JamesPSullivan(7) 10 —
(I W McInnes) *chsd ldrs: rdn along and lost pl 1/2-way: sn bhd* **66/1**
0000 **P** **Skybob**[18] 5554 3-8-10 20....................(v[1]) SamHitchcott 2 —
(D W Thompson) *in tch tl lost action and p.u over 7f out* **66/1**
3m 4.07s (0.47) **Going Correction** -0.05s/f (Good) **11** Ran SP% **120.7**
Speed ratings (Par 99): **96,95,93,89,88 80,78,78,71,18** —
toteswingers: 1&2 £5.60, 1&3 £29.00, 2&3 £11.70 CSF £22.38 TOTE £9.40: £2.30, £1.40, £2.00; EX 20.60.There was no bid for the winner.
Owner M E Elsworthy **Bred** Premier Enterprises **Trained** Westow, N Yorks

FOCUS
A very moderate seller run at an even gallop.

6099 BLUE SQUARE NURSERY H'CAP 7f
3:05 (3:06) (Class 4) (0-85,81) 2-Y-O **£4,533** (£1,348; £674; £336) **Stalls** Low

Form RPR
5216 **1** **Tominator**[13] 5692 2-9-4 **81**.................... RussellKennemore(3) 8 86
(R Hollinshead) *trckd ldrs: hdwy on inner 2f out: rdn to ld ent fnl f: edgd rt and kpt on wl* **4/1**[1]
3161 **2** *1 3/4* **Gold Fix (IRE)**[16] 5589 2-8-7 **67**.................... CatherineGannon 3 68
(M R Channon) *towards rr: hdwy over 2f out and sn rdn: drvn over 1f out: styd on strly ins fnl f: tk 2nd nr line* **7/1**
5453 **3** *hd* **Jehu**[7] 5868 2-9-3 **77**....................(v) SamHitchcott 2 77
(M R Channon) *in tch: n.m.r over 4f out: hdwy on outer over 2f out: rdn to chal over 1f out and ev ch: drvn and edgd lft ins fnl f: kpt on* **11/2**[3]
236 **4** *nk* **Izuizorizuain't (IRE)**[41] 4817 2-7-12 **58** oh1.......... SilvestreDeSousa 4 57+
(K A Ryan) *in tch and niggled along after 2f: hdwy on outer 1/2-way: rdn 2f out: drvn over 1f out and kpt on same pce* **4/1**[1]
1536 **5** *3/4* **Novay Essjay (IRE)**[16] 5595 2-8-4 **69**....................(p) PatrickDonaghy(5) 5 67
(P C Haslam) *a.p: rdn to ld 2f out: drvn over 1f out: hdd ent fnl f: wknd* **9/2**[2]
2010 **6** *1 1/2* **Iron Velvet (USA)**[18] 5550 2-9-2 **76**.................... GregFairley 6 70
(M Johnston) *cl up: led after 1f: rdn along and hdd 2f out: sn drvn and wkng whn n.m.r over 1f out* **4/1**[1]
5230 **7** *1 1/2* **William Arnold**[16] 5595 2-7-12 **58** oh2.................... JamieMackay 1 48
(C W Fairhurst) *led 1f: chsd ldrs on inner tl rdn along 3f out and sn wknd* **14/1**
0603 **8** *9* **Charity Fair**[23] 5358 2-7-12 **58** oh9.................... KoseiMiura 7 26
(A Berry) *s.i.s: a in rr* **40/1**
1m 27.36s (0.36) **Going Correction** -0.05s/f (Good) **8** Ran SP% **115.2**
Speed ratings (Par 97): **95,93,92,92,91 89,88,77**
toteswingers: 1&2 £6.70, 1&3 £2.50, 2&3 £2.70 CSF £32.51 CT £155.57 TOTE £5.90: £1.90, £2.60, £3.10; EX 20.20.
Owner Mrs Susy Haslehurst **Bred** Mrs S L Brimble **Trained** Upper Longdon, Staffs

FOCUS
A wide-open nursery which was run at a sound pace. Three in the line-up had already been successful at this track, and although the first seven home were within six lengths of each other, it should throw up a few winners.

NOTEBOOK
Tominator ◆, a winner on his penultimate start at Beverley, followed up here in good style. He doesn't lack for size and should make into a smart three year-old. (op 9-2 tchd 7-2)
Gold Fix(IRE), running off a 3lb higher mark for his latest Epsom success, kept on well to snatch second place and should stay further. (op 15-2 tchd 13-2)
Jehu ran another sound race and should be able to score again before the season is finished. (op 5-1)
Izuizorizuain't(IRE) lacked a bit of experience compared to some of these. She didn't look entirely happy on this sharp track but did do some good late work and it shouldn't be too long before she loses her maiden tag. Official explanation: jockey said filly hung right-handed (op 5-1)
Novay Essjay(IRE), a winner on his debut at Ripon, was wearing cheekpieces for the first time and had every chance before weakening close home. (op 5-1 tchd 11-2)

6100 BLUE SQUARE SEPTEMBER H'CAP 1m 3f 214y
3:35 (3:36) (Class 3) (0-90,90) 3-Y-O+ **£7,771** (£2,312; £1,155; £577) **Stalls** High

Form RPR
0600 **1** **Pevensey (IRE)**[105] 2706 7-8-13 **86**....................(p) IJBrennan(7) 1 98+
(J J Quinn) *hld up and bhd: hdwy out over 2f out: rdn over 1f out: styd on strly ins fnl f to ld last 75yds* **13/2**[3]
0452 **2** *1 1/4* **Wicked Daze (IRE)**[6] 5917 6-8-12 **78**....................(v) SilvestreDeSousa 10 88
(K A Ryan) *cl up: led 1/2-way: rdn over 2f out: drvn 2f out: rdn to ld and hung lft over 1f out: drvn ins fnl f: hdd and no ex last 75yds* **15/8**[1]
0440 **3** *2 1/4* **Lost Soldier Three (IRE)**[28] 5252 8-9-1 **81**.................... AndrewMullen 4 87
(D Nicholls) *trckd ldng pair: effrt over 3f out: rdn over 2f out: drvn and edgd lft over 1f out: drvn and hung lft ins fnl f: kpt on* **17/2**
5241 **4** *nk* **Embsay Crag**[29] 5209 3-7-12 **79**.................... JamesPSullivan(7) 9 85
(Mrs K Walton) *cl up: led after 3f and rn wd paddock bnd: rdn along and hdd 2f out: swtchd rt and rallied ent fnl f: sn drvn and wknd* **17/2**
0003 **5** *1 3/4* **Full Speed (GER)**[8] 5828 4-9-4 **84**.................... PJMcDonald 11 87+
(G A Swinbank) *in tch on inner: lost pl and towards rr home turn: hdwy whn n.m.r over 1f out: hmpd jst ins fnl f: kpt on towards fin* **10/1**
0- **6** *1/2* **Royal Entourage**[13] 5706 4-9-4 **84**.................... DO'Donohoe 2 86
(C A Mulhall) *hld up towards rr: hdwy over 3f out: rdn along 2f out: sn drvn and no imp appr fnl f* **16/1**
2060 **7** *hd* **Cheshire Prince**[21] 5437 5-9-5 **90**.................... DeanHeslop(5) 6 92
(W M Brisbourne) *in tch: effrt 3f out: rdn along over 2f out: sn drvn and no imp* **16/1**
/0- **8** *1* **Stellino (GER)**[124] 1947 6-8-13 **79**.................... KoseiMiura 5 79
(James Moffatt) *hld up: a towards rr* **20/1**
0000 **9** *1/2* **Takaatuf (IRE)**[29] 5209 3-8-7 **81**.................... GregFairley 7 81
(M Johnston) *led 3f: cl up tl rdn to ld again 2f out: sn drvn: hdd over 1f out and wknd qckly* **7/2**[2]
2m 36.05s (-2.85) **Going Correction** -0.05s/f (Good)
WFA 3 from 4yo+ 8lb **9** Ran SP% **117.0**
Speed ratings (Par 107): **107,106,104,104,103 102,102,102,101**
toteswingers: 1&2 £5.10, 1&3 £4.70, 2&3 £5.70 CSF £19.35 CT £106.83 TOTE £9.30: £2.70, £1.20, £1.80; EX 26.40.
Owner Dum Spiro Spero **Bred** Barronstown Stud And Orpendale **Trained** Settrington, N Yorks

FOCUS
An interesting 76-90 handicap run at a sound pace.

NOTEBOOK
Pevensey(IRE), who was well supported beforehand, flew home to run out an easy winner. The seven-year-old was 4lb lower than his last winning mark and his useful apprentice was able to claim a further 7lb off his back. He can score again. (op 11-2 tchd 8-1)
Wicked Daze(IRE) has had only a few starts for Kevin Ryan, and he is also well handicapped on old form. He should be able to go one better in the coming weeks. (op 5-2 tchd 7-4)
Lost Soldier Three(IRE) has won off a 23lb higher mark. His rider had to briefly snatch up at a crucial stage. (op 8-1 tchd 9-1)
Embsay Crag, up 3lb for his latest Chester success, ran with credit, up in class, and he should continue to pay his way for the rest of the year. He lacks nothing in determination. (op 9-1)
Royal Entourage, making his debut for his current trainer after winning his last two for Ger Lyons, was slowly into stride and never really looked happy. (op 12-1 tchd 11-1)
Cheshire Prince Official explanation: jockey said gelding stumbled on the bend and lost its action

6101 BLUE SQUARE CASINO MAIDEN STKS 7f
4:10 (4:11) (Class 5) 3-4-Y-O **£3,238** (£963; £481; £240) **Stalls** Low

Form RPR
2-4 **1** **Great Art (IRE)**[63] 4097 3-9-3 0.................... AdrianMcCarthy 2 71+
(P W Chapple-Hyam) *trckd ldrs: hdwy over 2f out: rdn to chse ldr wl over 1f out: styd on ent fnl f to ld last 100yds* **2/5**[1]
0422 **2** *1/2* **Steel Stockholder**[15] 5624 3-8-10 60.................... JohnCavanagh(7) 7 70
(M Brittain) *cl up: led 1/2-way: rdn clr 2f out: drvn ent fnl f: hdd and no ex last 100yds* **11/2**[2]
3000 **3** *6* **Business Class (BRZ)**[52] 4435 4-9-6 60.................... SamHitchcott 6 56
(D Nicholls) *led: rdn along and hdd 1/2-way: drvn 2f out and kpt on same pce* **16/1**
340 **4** *1 3/4* **Miss Kittyhawk (IRE)**[63] 4097 3-8-12 65.................... SilvestreDeSousa 3 45
(Rae Guest) *chsd ldrs: hdwy wl over 2f out: sn rdn and plugged on same pce* **6/1**[3]
5 *2 1/2* **Magic Queen (IRE)** 3-8-12 0.................... RichardThomas 8 39
(A P Jarvis) *chsd ldrs: rdn along 3f out: sn wknd* **20/1**
5635 **6** *8* **Port Ronan (USA)**[5] 5954 3-9-3 45....................(p) PAspell 4 24
(J S Wainwright) *dwlt: a in rr* **50/1**
1m 27.04s (0.04) **Going Correction** -0.05s/f (Good)
WFA 3 from 4yo 3lb **6** Ran SP% **113.7**
Speed ratings (Par 103): **97,96,89,87,84 75**
toteswingers: 1&2 £1.10, 1&3 £1.80, 2&3 £3.70 CSF £3.27 TOTE £1.30: £1.30, £1.60; EX 2.50.
Owner Matthew Green **Bred** Hascombe And Valiant Studs **Trained** Newmarket, Suffolk

FOCUS
A maiden lacking strength in depth, run at an even pace.

6102 BLUE SQUARE SP GUARANTEE H'CAP (DIV II) 1m 5f 175y
4:45 (4:47) (Class 6) (0-65,61) 3-Y-O+ **£2,047** (£604; £302) **Stalls** Low

Form RPR
4543 **1** **Elite Land**[13] 5698 6-9-9 **61**.................... LanceBetts(5) 5 71
(B Ellison) *hld up in rr: stdy hdwy 1/2-way: led 3f out: rdn clr wl over 1f out: drvn ins fnl f: kpt on* **2/1**[1]
4004 **2** *1 1/4* **Park's Prodigy**[12] 5733 5-8-13 **46**.................... SilvestreDeSousa 9 54
(G A Harker) *hld up towards rr: hdwy 5f out: rdn to chse ldrs over 2f out: drvn and edgd lft over 1f out: kpt on u.p ins fnl f: hung lft and tk 2nd towards fin* **7/2**[2]

2000 **3** 1 3/4 **Blue Jet (USA)**[16] 5600 5-8-12 **45** PaulQuinn 2 50
(R M Whitaker) *hld up towards rr: hdwy 5f out: chsd wnr wl over 2f out and sn rdn: drvn and wandered over 1f out: hld whn n.m.r and lost 2nd towards fin* **16/1**

0405 **4** 12 **Fell Pack**[24] 5339 5-8-10 **50** IJBrennan(7) 4 38
(J J Quinn) *in tch: hdwy to chse ldrs over 4f out: rdn along 3f out: drvn over 2f out and sn outpcd* **11/2**[3]

3150 **5** 3 1/4 **They All Laughed**[13] 5698 6-9-8 **60** (p) PatrickDonaghy(5) 1 43
(Mrs Marjorie Fife) *chsd ldrs: rdn along over 4f out: drvn 3f out and sn wknd* **16/1**

5060 **6** 3/4 **Royal Keva (IRE)**[55] 4348 3-8-3 **51** DeanHeslop(5) 6 33
(A D Brown) *chsd ldrs: rdn along 4f out: drvn wl over 2f out and sn wknd* **40/1**

016 **7** 18 **Harcas (IRE)**[5] 5943 7-9-10 **57** (b) PJMcDonald 3 13
(M Todhunter) *led: rdn along 4f out: hdd 3f out and sn drvn: wknd 2f out* **10/1**

5234 **8** 34 **Terminate (GER)**[5] 5943 7-9-6 **58** SladeO'Hara(5) 8 —
(A Berry) *midfield: rdn along and lost pl 1/2-way: sn bhd* **20/1**

4464 **9** 1 1/4 **Lady Sorcerer**[23] 5359 4-9-3 **50** RichardThomas 10 —
(A P Jarvis) *prom: rdn along 1/2-way: wknd over 4f out* **16/1**

000 **10** 1 3/4 **Ingenue**[22] 5381 3-8-2 **45** (b[1]) KoseiMiura 7 —
(Sir Mark Prescott) *chsd ldrs: rdn along after 3f: lost pl 7f out and sn bhd* **11/2**[3]

3m 2.29s (-1.31) **Going Correction** -0.05s/f (Good)
WFA 3 from 4yo+ 10lb **10** Ran SP% **120.3**
Speed ratings (Par 101): **101,100,99,92,90 90,79,60,59,58**
toteswingers: 1&2 £4.10, 1&3 £8.10, 2&3 £16.20 CSF £9.13 CT £89.23 TOTE £2.80: £1.40, £1.80, £5.50; EX 12.50.
Owner Dan Gilbert **Bred** T Umpleby **Trained** Norton, N Yorks
■ Stewards' Enquiry : Silvestre De Sousa one-day ban: careless riding (Oct 5)

FOCUS
This was run at a sound pace.
Lady Sorcerer Official explanation: jockey said filly ran too free

6103 BLUE SQUARE H'CAP 7f
5:20 (5:23) (Class 6) (0-60,60) 3-Y-O+ **£2,388** (£705; £352) **Stalls** Low

Form RPR
0011 **1** **La Gifted**[7] 5883 3-9-1 **57** CatherineGannon 12 64
(M R Channon) *chsd ldrs: hdwy 2f out: rdn to chse wnr over 1f out: drvn ins fnl f: styd on wl to ld nr fin* **11/1**

4012 **2** 1/2 **Nufoudh (IRE)**[5] 5941 5-8-12 **56** PatrickDonaghy(5) 2 63
(Miss Tracy Waggott) *qckly away and led: rdn clr wl over 1f out: drvn ins fnl f: hdd and no ex nr fin* **10/3**[1]

0530 **3** 3/4 **Another Decree**[16] 5601 4-9-4 **57** (tp) PJMcDonald 14 62
(M Dods) *dwlt and towards rr: hdwy wl over 1f out: rdn ent fnl f and styd on strly towards fin* **20/1**

4435 **4** 1 1/4 **Soto**[31] 5150 6-8-11 **57** JamesPSullivan(7) 6 59
(M W Easterby) *stmbld s and s.i.s: bhd tl hdwy wl over 1f out: sn rdn and styd on: nrst fin* **7/1**

0510 **5** 1/2 **Secret City (IRE)**[22] 5405 3-9-3 **59** (b) KoseiMiura 7 59
(R Bastiman) *chsd ldr: rdn along 2f out: drvn over 1f out: kpt on same pce ins fnl f* **25/1**

6431 **6** shd **Mayoman (IRE)**[12] 5729 4-9-5 **58** (b) DNolan 8 58
(D Carroll) *trckd ldrs: hdwy on inner over 2f out: rdn wl over 1f out: drvn over 1f out and no imp* **9/2**[2]

5145 **7** shd **Royal Premium**[27] 5295 3-8-9 **58** (v) BillyCray(7) 9 57
(Mrs G S Rees) *midfield: hdwy on outer over 2f out: rdn to chse ldrs whn edgd lft wl over 1f out: sn drvn and kpt on same pce* **14/1**

4000 **8** 1 **Only A Game (IRE)**[55] 4355 4-8-13 **57** (t) LanceBetts(5) 13 55
(I W McInnes) *towards rr: hdwy on outer 1/2-way: rdn to chse ldrs: drvn and ch over 1f out: wknd ins fnl f* **25/1**

0602 **9** 3/4 **No Grouse**[5] 5948 9-9-5 **58** DaleGibson 15 54
(E J Alston) *in tch: hdwy to chse ldrs 3f out: rdn along 2f out: drvn over 1f out and wknd ent fnl f* **16/1**

000 **10** 4 1/2 **H Harrison (IRE)**[5] 5948 9-8-11 **57** IJBrennan(7) 10 43+
(I W McInnes) *a towards rr* **14/1**

6065 **11** 5 **Ace Of Spies (IRE)**[5] 5948 4-9-3 **56** (p) DO'Donohoe 3 28
(G A Harker) *a outpcd in rr* **14/1**

0210 **12** 5 **Lytton**[9] 5813 4-9-7 **60** (v) SamHitchcott 1 19
(R Ford) *dwlt: sn chsng ldrs on inner: rdn along 4f out and sn wknd* **12/1**

4521 **13** dist **Arjemis**[24] 5338 3-9-2 **58** PAspell 4 —
(C R Wilson) *chsd ldrs on inner: rdn along over 3f out and sn wknd: b.b.v* **6/1**[3]

1m 27.63s (0.63) **Going Correction** -0.05s/f (Good)
WFA 3 from 4yo+ 3lb **13** Ran SP% **122.4**
Speed ratings (Par 101): **94,93,92,91,90 90,90,89,88,83 77,71,—**
toteswingers: 1&2 £3.60, 1&3 £40.60, 2&3 £18.20 CSF £47.47 CT £767.23 TOTE £9.30: £2.80, £1.70, £6.20; EX 35.90 Place 6: £7.63, Place 5: £6.13..
Owner Patrick and Simon Trant **Bred** Patrick & Simon Trant **Trained** West Ilsley, Berks
■ Stewards' Enquiry : D Nolan caution: used whip down the shoulder in the forehand position

FOCUS
With five previous course winners and two last-time-out winners in the line-up, this looked a very competitive 46-60 handicap. It was run at a furious pace.
Ace Of Spies(IRE) Official explanation: jockey said gelding hung right
Arjemis Official explanation: jockey said filly bled from the nose
T/Plt: £5.80 to a £1 stake. Pool: £36,302.57. 4,526.40 winning tickets. T/Qpdt: £3.30 to a £1 stake. Pool: £2,366.30. 516.90 winning tickets. JR

6054 NEWBURY (L-H)
Saturday, September 19

OFFICIAL GOING: Good to firm (8.7)
Rail from 1mto 5f on round course moved out 6m increasing advertised distances by 12m.
Wind: Nil Weather: Sunny

6104 TOTESCOOP6 NURSERY H'CAP 6f 8y
1:50 (1:50) (Class 3) 2-Y-O
£9,346 (£2,799; £1,399; £700; £349; £175) **Stalls** Centre

Form RPR
410 **1** **Marcus Cicero (IRE)**[14] 5658 2-8-12 **83** JimCrowley 7 86+
(P Winkworth) *lw: trckd ldrs: n.m.r over 1f out: swtchd lft and str run ins fnl f to take slt ld fnl 110yds: all out* **16/1**

1 **2** shd **Haadeeth**[26] 5311 2-8-8 **79** RHills 6 82
(M P Tregoning) *str: trckd ldr: slt ld jst ins fnl 2f: rdn appr fnl f: narrowly hdd fnl 110yds: rallied and kpt on but a jst hld* **9/4**[1]

1630 **3** 1/2 **Craicattack (IRE)**[28] 5274 2-8-4 **75** WilliamBuick 1 76
(J S Moore) *chsd ldrs: rdn 2f out: styd on to chal ins fnl f: no ex fnl 50yds* **16/1**

1504 **4** nse **Master Of Dance (IRE)**[10] 5769 2-8-6 **77** RichardMullen 2 78
(R Hannon) *lw: towards rr: pushed along 3f out: hdwy fr 2f out: styd on to chal jst ins fnl f: no ex cl home* **16/1**

5242 **5** 1 1/2 **Joe Packet**[37] 4945 2-8-6 **77** MartinDwyer 9 74
(J G Portman) *swtg: t.k.h early: chsd ldrs: rdn and ev ch over 1f out tl ins fnl f: wknd fnl 75yds* **17/2**

2150 **6** 3 **Deloria**[21] 5433 2-7-13 **75** AndrewHeffernan(5) 8 63
(Eve Johnson Houghton) *chsd ldrs: rdn over 2f out: wknd fnl f* **12/1**

2602 **7** nse **Quaestor (IRE)**[11] 5749 2-8-8 **79** RichardKingscote 10 66
(Tom Dascombe) *led tl hdd jst ins fnl 2f: wknd fnl f* **15/2**

31 **8** 1/2 **La Pantera**[122] 2175 2-8-11 **82** RichardHughes 5 68
(R Hannon) *lw: stdd s: hld up towards rr: rdn over 2f out: a outpcd* **9/2**[2]

12 **9** 5 **Art Scholar (IRE)**[12] 5721 2-9-7 **92** (p) RyanMoore 11 63
(G L Moore) *broke wl: stdd rr after 1f: rdn over 2f out and no rspnse* **5/1**[3]

0600 **10** 7 **Kirsty's Boy (IRE)**[30] 5198 2-8-12 **83** TedDurcan 4 33
(J S Moore) *lw: rdn over 2f out: a in rr* **33/1**

1m 12.56s (-0.44) **Going Correction** -0.075s/f (Good) **10** Ran SP% **116.2**
Speed ratings (Par 99): **99,98,98,98,96 92,92,91,84,75**
toteswingers: 1&2 £9.10, 1&3 £20.40, 2&3 £9.10 CSF £51.99 CT £625.58 TOTE £21.60: £4.80, £1.60, £4.10; EX 75.30 TRIFECTA Not won..
Owner Kennet Valley Thoroughbreds VIII **Bred** Knockainey Stud **Trained** Chiddingfold, Surrey

FOCUS
This didn't look that strong a race for the class beforehand, and a bunch finish would seem to confirm that impression, but a time only 0.16 seconds slower than the Mill Reef might suggest otherwise. They tended to race up the middle of the track.

NOTEBOOK
Marcus Cicero(IRE) didn't look particularly well treated beforehand considering he was racing off the same mark as when beaten 20l in a Haydock nursery on his previous start, but that run was a mystery to his connections, who didn't know whether a poor draw and/or the easy going was to blame. He was therefore better judged on his earlier Windsor maiden success, although in fairness the bare form of that race hardly suggested he was favourably handicapped off a mark of 83, and this easily rates as a career best. He had to wait for a gap over a furlong out before being switched, but responded in the desired manner once under maximum pressure. He's lightly raced, so there may yet be more to come. Official explanation: trainer said, regarding the apparent improvement in form shown, gelding had an unfavourable draw at Haydock last time and appeared to be better suited by today's faster ground (op 20-1)

Haadeeth had dead-heated in just an ordinary affair on his debut, and this was an improved performance. The fact he was entered in the Mill Reef suggests his connections think a bit of him and he did little wrong, battling on well after showing speed from the start, although he was possibly still a little green. He ought to continue to progress. (op 5-2 tchd 11-4 in places)

Craicattack(IRE) appreciated the return to better ground and ran respectably. Although only fair, he's just the type who might nick a half-decent nursery off a light weight, or he should at least continue to pick up prize-money. (op 20-1)

Master Of Dance(IRE) is already looking pretty exposed but this was a respectable effort. (op 20-1)

Joe Packet got warm beforehand and was keen, so it was no surprise he folded late on after briefly looking a big threat a furlong out. He has more ability than his finishing position suggests, but he must learn to relax. (op 11-1 tchd 8-1)

La Pantera looked a nice enough prospect when winning a Goodwood maiden in May, but she had been off since and never really travelled that fluently on her return. This performance leaves her with plenty to prove. (op 11-4)

Art Scholar(IRE), already fitted with cheekpieces, sweated up and ran poorly. Official explanation: jockey said colt ran flat (op 11-2)

6105 DUBAI DUTY FREE MILL REEF STKS (GROUP 2) 6f 8y
2:20 (2:20) (Class 1) 2-Y-O
£45,416 (£17,216; £8,616; £4,296; £2,152; £1,080) **Stalls** Centre

Form RPR
11 **1** **Awzaan**[72] 3782 2-9-1 108 RHills 5 113+
(M Johnston) *lw: hld up in rr: stdy hdwy over 2f out to ld appr fnl f: sn drvn and hung lft ins fnl f: kpt on strly* **11/4**[2]

2201 **2** 1 1/4 **Angel's Pursuit (IRE)**[10] 5763 2-9-1 101 RichardHughes 7 106
(R Hannon) *lw: hld up towards rr: hdwy over 1f out: drvn and styd on wl to go 2nd fnl 100yds but no imp on wnr* **14/1**

11 **3** 1 **Quarrel (USA)**[28] 5250 2-9-1 95 MichaelHills 2 103
(W J Haggas) *lw: led: rdn along 2f out: hdd appr fnl f: one pce u.p whn hung rt fnl 110yds* **13/2**[3]

2113 **4** 3/4 **Radiohead**[29] 5233 2-9-4 113 (t) JamieSpencer 6 104
(B J Meehan) *ponied to s: heavily restrained sn after s and 2 l off penultimate horse: rapid hdwy over 2f out and qcknd to chal over 1f out: sn one pce: wknd fnl 110yds* **5/4**[1]

4113 **5** 1 **Stargaze (IRE)**[50] 4487 2-9-1 103 WilliamBuick 3 98
(A M Balding) *lw: trckd ldr: rdn 2f out: wknd ins fnl f and no ch w ldrs whn hmpd fnl 110yds* **10/1**

1343 **6** 3 **Colonel Mak**[10] 5763 2-9-1 92 KFallon 4 89
(D H Brown) *chsd ldrs: rdn 2f out: wknd qckly over 1f out* **14/1**

14 **7** 1 1/2 **Wisecraic**[28] 5274 2-9-1 86 RichardKingscote 1 84
(Tom Dascombe) *chsd ldrs: rdn over 2f out: wknd qckly over 1f out* **25/1**

1m 12.4s (-0.60) **Going Correction** -0.075s/f (Good) **7** Ran SP% **110.7**
Speed ratings (Par 107): **101,99,98,97,95 91,89**
toteswingers: 1&2 £7.30, 1&3 £2.40, 2&3 £7.80 CSF £36.21 TOTE £3.30: £2.00, £5.40; EX 49.20.
Owner Hamdan Al Maktoum **Bred** Shadwell Estate Company Limited **Trained** Middleham Moor, N Yorks

FOCUS
Despite not always attracting a particularly big field, the form of the Mill Reef has tended to work out at the top level in recent years - six of the last ten winners were subsequently successful in Group 1 company, including the last three. Although there was only one previous Group winner in the line up, it's worth pointing out there were none at all last year and that didn't stop the winner, Lord Shanakill, going on to prove himself to be high class. This season's race looked limited for the level, with the winning time disappointing, only 0.16 seconds quicker than the earlier nursery won by the 83-rated Marcus Cicero, which can probably be explained by a steady pace through the first furlong or so.

NOTEBOOK

Awzaan ◆ looked a quality prospect when successful on his first two starts, particularly when a 5l winner of a conditions event on the July course, and he confirmed that impression here. His 72-day break since that success was apparently at the instructions of his owner, and it has clearly benefited the colt greatly, although if anything he was considered by connections to be a bit heavy today. Upped in grade, this son of Alhaarth was given a waiting ride and travelled strongly throughout. Once asked to pick up, he displayed a neat turn of foot and quickly saw off Radiohead's challenge, before appearing to idle once clear. The runner-up briefly looked a threat when staying on strongly inside the final furlong, but Awzaan soon pulled up out more, not allowing that rival to land any sort of blow. Despite the relatively slow final time, the winner does look a high-class prospect, particularly considering he's entitled to come on for this run, and he must have a strong chance in the Middle Park, which is apparently his intended target. He's also got a Dewhurst entry, and his breeding suggests he'll get at least 7f, but that said, there always has to be a question mark when a horse has the sort of natural speed this one possess. Straight afterwards he was a best-price 20-1 shot for the Guineas with Skybet and Ladbrokes. (op 5-2 tchd 3-1)

Angel's Pursuit(IRE) ◆ was having his ninth start but this looked a career-best performance by some way, and he's obviously thriving right now, having reportedly had shin issues through the summer. A conditions race success at Doncaster last time, his first win since his debut, was a step in the right direction, and he extended his superiority over Colonel Mak significantly here. He's in the Redcar Two-Year-Old Trophy. (tchd 16-1)

Quarrel(USA) was something of an unknown coming into this, as his narrow success on debut at Ascot was followed by victory at Chester, a track that doesn't really lend itself to big performances. Whatever, though, he showed himself to be a pretty smart colt. He lacked the natural speed of the front two, but kept on well for third, giving the impression he might benefit from a step up to 7f. (op 15-2 tchd 6-1)

Radiohead, carrying a 3lb penalty for his Norfolk success, was trying 6f for the first time after a fine run against older horses in the Nunthorpe. Heavily restrained as the stalls opened, he made a big move towards the outer after halfway, and he made rapid progress to join the pacesetters. The winner was going every bit as well, however, and Brian Meehan's colt soon began to flounder when placed under maximum pressure. He looked a non-stayer, but Jamie Spencer felt the race was totally unsatisfactory, reasoning that slow early pace, followed by a dash from about halfway, did not suit this colt, who is considered at his best off an end-to-end gallop. (op 11-10 tchd 11-8 in places)

Stargaze(IRE) looked to be hanging a little before coming under pressure, but to his credit he stuck on as well as he could. He just wasn't good enough, although perhaps he's now ready for a step up in distance. (op 12-1)

Colonel Mak was outclassed. (op 16-1 tchd 18-1)

Wisecraic didn't appear to be totally letting himself down on the quick ground. (op 28-1)

6106 JOHN SMITH'S STKS (HERITAGE H'CAP) 1m 2f 6y

2:50 (2:53) (Class 2) (0-105,104) 3-Y-O+

£62,310 (£18,660; £9,330; £4,670; £2,330; £1,170) **Stalls** Low

Form RPR

5-50 **1** **Almiqdaad**[28] 5262 3-8-12 **93** RHills 17 105
(M A Jarvis) *sn trcking ldrs: drvn to ld 2f out: hld on wl thrght fnl f* **14/1**

20-1 **2** 1 1/4 **Drunken Sailor (IRE)**[6] 5923 4-9-2 **94** (b) PBBeggy(3) 10 104
(Paul W Flynn, Ire) *chsd ldrs: drvn to chal over 2f out: kpt on u.p fnl f but a hld by wnr* **18/1**

6620 **3** 1/2 **Sweet Lightning**[42] 4781 4-8-13 **88** MartinDwyer 8 97
(W R Muir) *lw: in rr tl styd on fr 3f out: wnt 3rd u.p 1f out: styd on wl but no imp on ldng duo* **7/1**

-132 **4** hd **Class Is Class (IRE)**[31] 5170 3-9-0 **95** RyanMoore 16 103+
(Sir Michael Stoute) *prom: rdn and hmpd 3f out: sn rcvr and drvn along: styd on wl fr over 1f out but nvr gng pce to rch ldrs* **7/2**[1]

0451 **5** hd **Charm School**[15] 5641 4-9-7 **96** 5ex JimmyFortune 5 104
(J H M Gosden) *lw: in rr: drvn: edgd to rt and hdwy fr 3f out: styd on strly fr over 1f out: fin wl* **16/1**

3121 **6** 1 1/4 **Cill Rialaig**[19] 5510 4-8-11 **86** 5ex DarryllHolland 9 92+
(H Morrison) *lw: sn mid-div: hdwy on outside fr 3f out: styd on fr over 1f out but nvr gng pce to rch ldrs* **12/1**

0210 **7** 1 1/2 **Press The Button (GER)**[19] 5248 6-9-2 **91** SJCraine 12 94
(J R Boyle) *chsd ldrs: wnt 2nd over 3f out: sn rdn: wknd fnl f* **33/1**

3132 **8** 1/2 **Antinori (IRE)**[28] 5262 3-9-2 **97** (p) AdamKirby 14 99
(W R Swinburn) *lw: sn in tch: hdwy to chse ldrs 3f out: hrd drvn over 2f out: wknd ins fnl f* **7/1**

0030 **9** 1 1/4 **Laterly (IRE)**[32] 5137 4-9-1 **90** MickyFenton 1 90
(T P Tate) *sn led and 4 l clr: rdn 3f out: hdd 2 f out: wknd over 1f out* **25/1**

0504 **9** dht **Bound By Honour (SAF)**[7] 5880 6-9-5 **94** (b) GeorgeBaker 18 94
(G L Moore) *towards rr: hdwy fr 3f out: kpt on fr over 1f out but nvr a threat* **40/1**

41/1 **11** 1/2 **Broomielaw**[49] 4541 5-9-6 **95** MJKinane 11 94
(E A L Dunlop) *lw: in rr: rdn and sme prog on outside over 2f out but nvr in contention* **13/2**[3]

3165 **12** 1/2 **Bazergan (IRE)**[9] 5794 4-9-0 **89** (bt[1]) RichardMullen 19 87
(C E Brittain) *s.i.s: in rr: rdn over 3f out: styd on fnl 2f: nvr a threat* **25/1**

0052 **13** 2 **Montaff**[43] 4760 3-9-9 **104** (v) ChrisCatlin 4 99+
(M R Channon) *swtg: in tch on ins sme hdwy 3f out: rdn and nt clr run ins fnl 2f: n.d after* **25/1**

1131 **14** 1/2 **Royal Destination (IRE)**[32] 5137 4-9-10 **99** KFallon 2 93
(J Noseda) *chsd ldrs: rdn 3f out: wknd qckly 2f out* **9/2**[2]

0-56 **15** nk **My Aunt Fanny**[20] 5472 4-8-11 **86** WilliamBuick 7 79
(A M Balding) *lw: a towards rr* **25/1**

500 **16** 2 3/4 **Logic Way (USA)**[127] 2055 5-9-9 **98** (vt[1]) NJeanpierre 6 86
(Miss D Mountain) *sn chsng ldr tl over 3f out: wknd wl over 2f out* **100/1**

332- **17** 4 1/2 **Howdigo**[365] 6079 4-8-8 **86** MarcHalford(3) 3 66+
(J R Best) *swtg: s.i.s: in rr tl sme prog 3f out: nvr a threat and sn wknd* **33/1**

0000 **18** 4 **Kandidate**[14] 5662 7-9-2 **98** DebraEngland(7) 20 71
(C E Brittain) *bhd fr 1/2-way* **40/1**

3100 **19** 7 **Kavachi (IRE)**[50] 4486 6-9-1 **90** RichardHughes 15 50
(G L Moore) *bit bkwd: swtchd lft s: in rr sme prog over 3f out bhd* **22/1**

6-00 **20** 11 **Talking Hands**[20] 5476 3-8-13 **94** TedDurcan 13 35
(S Kirk) *a in rr* **100/1**

2m 4.29s (-4.51) **Going Correction** -0.075s/f (Good)

WFA 3 from 4yo+ 6lb **20** Ran SP% **135.8**

Speed ratings (Par 109): **115,114,113,113,113 112,111,110,109,109 109,108,107,106,106 104,100,97,92,83**

toteswingers: 1&2 £70.30, 1&3 £36.40, 2&3 £59.20 CSF £240.97 CT £1954.17 TOTE £23.60: £4.20, £2.80, £2.90, £1.70; EX 459.90 TRIFECTA Not won..

Owner Hamdan Al Maktoum **Bred** Shadwell Estate Company Limited **Trained** Newmarket, Suffolk

FOCUS

This is usually a red-hot handicap - subsequent Group 1 scorer Presvis bolted up in last year's race - and it's been a good Cambridgeshire trial in recent seasons. For example, four of the last five winners of that aforementioned Newmarket handicap were beaten in this race: Tazeez (unplaced last year), Formal Decree (3rd 2006), Blue Monday (2nd 2005), and Spanish Don (unplaced before 100-1 success at HQ in 2004). This year's race looked very competitive and they went a good gallop. Perhaps not a vintage renewal but strong form all the same.

NOTEBOOK

Almiqdaad ◆ didn't make his reappearance until August after suffering a hairline crack to his pelvis, and he had been well held on both his starts, but there was more encouragement last time and he had been eased 3lb. He built on that effort with a very useful performance, and he deserves extra credit considering he was drawn out wide. Although he looked in danger of getting to the front too soon after the early pace began to collapse in the straight, and had his tongue hanging out for much of the way, credit to him, he ran on well. Michael Jarvis apparently thought he could be his best 3yo at the start of the year, and there could be more to come. However, he's said to be unlikely to take up his engagement in the Cambridgeshire, and that's understandable. The drop in trip probably wouldn't suit and also, being quite a heavy-topped colt, it's questionable whether he would act on the Rowley Mile. (op 16-1)

Drunken Sailor(IRE), an Irish-trained challenger, had gained his last two wins at 1m4f, but he was never too far away on this drop in trip and the good gallop suited. He kept on well, but was always being held by the winner. (op 20-1)

Sweet Lightning, unlucky in running at Goodwood, before being reported to have run flat at Haydock, can have no real excuses this time. He stayed on well for pressure from well off the pace but simply found a couple too good. He's in the Cambridgeshire but the shorter trip at Newmarket might not be ideal. (op 9-1)

Class Is Class(IRE) ◆ had more use made of him this time, but he basically seemed to find this trip on the short side. He kept on, but couldn't muster the pace to pose a serious threat and is likely to benefit from a return to 1m4f. A colt who still has scope, he should make a nice 4yo. (op 5-1 tchd 11-2)

Charm School ◆, 1lb well in under the penalty he picked up for his recent win over 1m3f on Polytrack, was set plenty to do (can be keen) and could never quite get there. He's always been quite well regarded and could be the one to take from the race for the Cambridgeshire as the likely strong pace at Newmarket will suit and he gives the impression we've yet to see the best of him. The slight drop in trip shouldn't be too much of an inconvenience, and he goes on most types of ground. (op 14-1)

Cill Rialaig ◆ was 1lb wrong under the penalty she incurred for winning at Epsom, but this was a good run in defeat. This was only her seventh start on the Flat and she has a progressive profile. She'll struggle to make the cut for the Cambridgeshire, however. (op 10-1)

Press The Button(GER) probably paid for chasing the decent pace, but he still ran well. (op 50-1)

Antinori(IRE) had been progressing nicely, and a 5lb rise for his recent second at Sandown, when he made up a lot of late ground and finished well ahead of today's winner, didn't seem excessive, but he seemed to run a bit flat. He was produced with his chance in the straight but found only the one pace.

Laterly(IRE) proved relucant to enter the stalls, before going on to set a good gallop. (op 33-1)

Bound By Honour(SAF), 2lb wrong, continues to struggle to rediscover his South African form and lacks scope. (op 33-1)

Broomielaw created a good impression on his belated return to the track when winning at Newmarket in August, but he couldn't defy a 7lb rise. He probably raced further back was ideal, but that's no real excuse. (tchd 6-1 and 7-1 in places)

Royal Destination(IRE), up 7lb for his York win, didn't travel all that fluently and made only a brief effort in the straight before being eased. Official explanation: jockey said gelding hung right (op 7-1)

Kavachi(IRE) Official explanation: jockey said gelding lost its action

6107 DUBAI DUTY FREE WORLD TROPHY (GROUP 3) 5f 34y

3:25 (3:25) (Class 1) 3-Y-O+

£36,900 (£13,988; £7,000; £3,490; £1,748; £877) **Stalls** Centre

Form RPR

0561 **1** **Strike The Deal (USA)**[10] 5765 4-9-0 109 (v) KFallon 5 116
(J Noseda) *in rr: pushed along over 3f out: str run appr fnl f: qcknd ins fnl f to ld clsng stages* **9/2**[2]

0012 **2** nk **Total Gallery (IRE)**[51] 4456 3-8-13 111 RichardHughes 3 115
(J S Moore) *led and kpt narrow advantage: styd on wl fnl f: hdd and no ex clsng stages* **5/1**[3]

3004 **3** 1/2 **J J The Jet Plane (SAF)**[7] 5878 5-9-0 118 JimmyFortune 8 113
(R Hannon) *lw: chsd ldrs: rdn to chal appr fnl f: nt qcknd fnl 110yds* **8/1**

-212 **4** 1 1/2 **Triple Aspect (IRE)**[77] 3638 3-8-13 112 RyanMoore 4 108
(W J Haggas) *trckd ldrs: rdn and n.m.r 1f out: styd on to take 4th cl home but nvr gng pce of ldng trio* **5/4**[1]

3600 **5** nk **Look Busy (IRE)**[20] 5491 4-9-2 102 TedDurcan 1 109
(A Berry) *chsd ldrs: rdn 2f out: wknd ins fnl f* **25/1**

052 **6** 1 3/4 **Spin Cycle (IRE)**[10] 5765 3-8-13 105 (v[1]) RichardMullen 6 100
(B Smart) *chsd ldrs: rdn 2f out: wknd fnl f* **14/1**

0206 **7** 2 1/4 **Captain Gerrard (IRE)**[10] 5765 4-9-0 102 JimCrowley 9 92
(B Smart) *lw: t.k.h early: chsd ldrs: rdn 2f out: wknd appr fnl f* **16/1**

0422 **8** shd **Sohraab**[21] 5420 5-9-0 102 DarryllHolland 7 92
(H Morrison) *rdn 1/2-way: a outpcd* **14/1**

5-06 **9** 2 **Toms Laughter**[7] 5871 5-9-0 91 (b) KevinGhunowa 2 85
(R A Harris) *chsd ldrs tl wknd qckly over 1f out* **33/1**

60.04 secs (-1.36) **Going Correction** -0.075s/f (Good)

WFA 3 from 4yo+ 1lb **9** Ran SP% **116.4**

Speed ratings (Par 113): **107,106,105,103,102 100,96,96,93**

toteswingers: 1&2 £5.10, 1&3 £3.60, 2&3 £5.10 CSF £27.53 TOTE £5.40: £2.00, £1.80, £1.80; EX 29.70 Trifecta £241.70 Pool: £473.67 - 1.45 winning units..

Owner M Barber **Bred** Five-D Thoroughbreds, Llc **Trained** Newmarket, Suffolk

FOCUS

The form looks solid enough for Group 3 level, without being spectacular. They raced middle to stands' side.

NOTEBOOK

Strike The Deal(USA) was soon outpaced and pushed along in the rear, but just as when winning a Listed race over this trip at Doncaster last time, he responded well to a strong Fallon drive in the second half of the contest. He'll be just as effective back over 6f, provided they go quick, and he might just need the extra furlong when stepping up in class. He's in the Diadem, but if connections want to stick to the minimum distance perhaps the Prix de l'Abbaye will be considered. A fast surface is considered essential. (tchd 4-1 and 5-1 in places)

Total Gallery(IRE) produced another smart effort, despite getting warm and racing a little freely. He should continue to progress, and the Group 2 Diadem Stakes at Ascot is apparently the plan, although he'll have to switch off better there considering he'll be going back up to 6f. (op 9-2)

J J The Jet Plane(SAF) seemed to lose his way a little mid-season, but there was encouragement in this effort considering he's probably better over 6f. (op 15-2 tchd 7-1)

Triple Aspect(IRE) wasn't at his best and being short of room around a furlong out was no real excuse. He's so far shown his best form over Sandown's stiff 5f, and on flatter tracks perhaps he needs 6f. Official explanation: jockey said colt suffered interference in running (op 15-8)

Look Busy(IRE) had no easy task under her 5lb penalty and had something to find with the four who finished ahead of her, including 9lb with the winner. (op 20-1)

Spin Cycle(IRE) was another who had something to find with the principals at the weights and was well held. (tchd 16-1)

6108 E B F DUBAI TENNIS CHAMPIONSHIPS MAIDEN STKS (DIV I) 7f (S)

4:00 (4:01) (Class 4) 2-Y-O **£5,180** (£1,541; £770; £384) **Stalls** Centre

Form RPR

1 **Beauchamp Yorker** 2-9-3 0 JimmyFortune 3 85+
(H Candy) *w'like: sn led: narrowly hdd 2f out: styd chalng and led again jst ins fnl f: styd on gamely* **20/1**

3 2 *hd* **Mufarrh (IRE)**[29] 5220 2-9-3 0 RHills 10 84+
(J L Dunlop) *str: swtg: trckd ldrs: slt ld 2f out: rdn and hdd jst ins fnl f: styd pressing wnr but no ex cl home* **6/4**[1]

0 3 *4 ½* **Official Style**[18] 5542 2-9-3 0 RyanMoore 7 75+
(Sir Michael Stoute) *w'like: scope: in tch: pushed along 2f out: styd on wl under hand riding fnl f and fin strly to take 3rd cl home* **5/2**[2]

0 4 *hd* **The Rectifier (USA)**[18] 5542 2-9-3 0 MickyFenton 15 71+
(Stef Liddiard) *t.k.h: hld up in rr tl rapid hdwy 3f out to press ldrs over 2f out: no ex and wknd ins fnl f* **33/1**

5 *nse* **Christmas Carnival** 2-9-3 0 MartinDwyer 11 71
(B J Meehan) *w'like: athletic: lw: chsd ldrs: drvn to chal 2f out: one pce ins fnl f: wknd nr fin* **12/1**

60 6 *2* **Fireback**[57] 4258 2-9-3 0 WilliamBuick 12 66
(A M Balding) *mid-div: pushed along and hdwy over 2f out: nvr in contention and one pce fr over 1f out* **25/1**

7 *6* **Trovare (USA)** 2-9-3 0 JimCrowley 8 51+
(Mrs A J Perrett) *w'like: scope: bit bkwd: s.i.s: in rr: pushed along over 2f out: styd on fnl f but nvr a threat* **25/1**

8 *shd* **Contredanse (IRE)** 2-8-12 0 JamieSpencer 6 46+
(B J Meehan) *w'like: scope: s.i.s: in rr: pushed along and green over 2f out: sme mod prog fnl f* **10/1**

9 *1 ¼* **Galatian** 2-9-0 0 JamesMillman(3) 5 48
(B R Millman) *chsd ldrs: rdn ins fnl 3f: wknd ins fnl 2f* **40/1**

10 *nk* **Yes Maggie (IRE)** 2-8-12 0 ChrisCatlin 4 42+
(M R Channon) *w'like: leggy: in tch: early outpcd after 2f: sme mod prog nr fin* **18/1**

5 11 *½* **Pont De Nuit**[17] 5571 2-9-3 0 RichardHughes 2 46
(R Hannon) *s.i.s: towards rr tl sme prog into midfield ins fnl 3f: sn dropped away* **9/1**[3]

12 *nse* **Pomeroy** 2-9-3 0 RichardKingscote 13 46+
(Tom Dascombe) *w'like: leggy: in rr: pushed along and n.m.r over 2f out: mod prog clsng stages* **25/1**

0 13 *nk* **Cereal Killer (IRE)**[8] 5829 2-9-3 0 RichardMullen 14 45
(R Hannon) *rdn and green 3f out: a in rr* **28/1**

0 14 *1* **Novillero**[29] 5212 2-8-12 0 GabrielHannon(5) 9 42
(J C Fox) *pressed ldr over 4f: wknd over 2f out* **150/1**

0 15 *1* **Barafundle Boy**[11] 5749 2-8-10 0 RyanClark(7) 1 40
(J J Bridger) *leggy: chsd ldrs: rdn 3f out: sn wknd* **150/1**

1m 27.26s (1.56) **Going Correction** -0.075s/f (Good) **15** Ran SP% **127.1**
Speed ratings (Par 97): **88,87,82,82,82 80,73,73,71,71 70,70,70,69,68**
toteswingers: 1&2 £10.70, 1&3 £16.00, 2&3 £2.00 CSF £49.46 TOTE £32.20: £6.50, £1.40, £1.40; EX 95.00.

Owner Erik Penser **Bred** E Penser **Trained** Kingston Warren, Oxon

FOCUS

Traditionally this hasn't been the strongest of juvenile maidens by Newbury's standards, although last year's winner Alazeyab has reached a handicap mark in the 100s. The winning time was 0.27 seconds slower than the second division won by Critical Moment.

NOTEBOOK

Beauchamp Yorker, a brother to 6f-1m winner Beauchamp Viceroy, 7f scorer Beauchamp Wizard, and Beauchamp Xerxes, who won over 1m, displayed a pleasing attitude to make a winning debut. Given a positive ride, he responded well to strong pressure to get the better of the race-experienced favourite, and the pair were well clear. He doesn't hold any big-race entries but is now likely to be aimed at a conditions race over 1m. (tchd 18-1)

Mufarrh(IRE) was a beaten favourite but this still confirmed the promise he showed on his debut over this trip at Sandown as he pulled well clear of the remainder in second. He probably needed to win this to justify his Group-race entries this year, but he's still pretty useful. (op Evens tchd 13-8)

Official Style ◆ improved on the form he showed when running green on his debut at Leicester. This Dewhurst entry was not given a hard time to take third and should continue to progress, especially when stepped up in trip. Official explanation: jockey said colt suffered interference in running (op 9-2)

The Rectifier(USA) couldn't reverse Leicester form from his debut with Official Style, but he still ran well. After racing keenly, he made a big move after halfway and briefly looked a threat, before his exertions told. He looks a nice enough type in the making.

Christmas Carnival, a 70,000gns purchase, showed up well before getting tired and should be better for the run. (tchd 10-1 and 14-1)

Fireback ran okay after almost two months off and could step up on this now that handicaps are an option. (op 33-1)

Contredanse(IRE), a 200,000gns purchase, was one of only two fillies in the line up. She missed the break and ran green, but made some late headway and ought to be all the better for this. (tchd 9-1 and 11-1)

Galatian Official explanation: jockey said gelding ran green

6109 E B F DUBAI TENNIS CHAMPIONSHIPS MAIDEN STKS (DIV II) 7f (S)

4:35 (4:37) (Class 4) 2-Y-O **£5,180** (£1,541; £770; £384) **Stalls** Centre

Form RPR

3 1 **Critical Moment (USA)**[22] 5400 2-9-3 0 MichaelHills 4 84+
(B W Hills) *w'like: scope: str: lw: sn w ldr: slt ld 4f out: but strly pressed fr over 2f out tl narrowly hdd appr fnl f: rdn: rallied and styd upsides tl led last stride* **1/1**[1]

2 *nse* **Lay Claim (USA)** 2-9-3 0 RyanMoore 6 85+
(Sir Michael Stoute) *unf: scope: slt ld tl narrowly hdd 4f out: styd upsides and slt ld appr fnl f: jnd ins fnl f and kpt on under hand driving: hdd last stride* **13/2**[2]

3 *1 ½* **Colonel Carter (IRE)** 2-9-3 0 MartinDwyer 3 80+
(B J Meehan) *tall: scope: in rr tl pushed along and hdwy 3f out: chsd ldrs over 1f out: kpt on but a hld* **20/1**

4 *1 ½* **Vimiero (USA)** 2-9-3 0 AdamKirby 14 76+
(W R Swinburn) *rangy: bit bkwd: hld up towards rr: stdy hdwy fr 2f out: kpt on wl fnl f but nvr gng pce of ldrs* **25/1**

5 *nk* **Rasmy** 2-9-3 0 RHills 7 76+
(M P Tregoning) *tall: leggy: scope: chsd ldrs: rdn 2f out: wknd ins fnl f* **8/1**[3]

6 *3 ½* **Beaumont's Party (IRE)** 2-9-3 0 RichardHughes 8 68+
(R Hannon) *w'like: scope: t.k.h in rr: hdwy to cl on ldrs 2f out: sn no imp and fdd fnl f* **8/1**[3]

7 *½* **Shamir** 2-9-3 0 MickyFenton 10 66+
(Miss Jo Crowley) *w'like: hld hold: broke wl: stdd towards rr: hdwy ins fnl 2f: styd on fnl f but nvr a threat* **66/1**

06 8 *2* **Take My Hand**[85] 3344 2-8-12 0 ChrisCatlin 13 56
(M R Channon) *t.k.h: towards rr on outside: rdn and sme hdwy 2f out: nvr rchd ldrs* **33/1**

0 9 *hd* **Baoli**[122] 2175 2-8-12 0 JimmyFortune 9 55
(R Hannon) *chsd ldrs: rdn over 2f out: sn wknd* **40/1**

10 *1* **Celtic Ransom** 2-9-3 0 KFallon 11 58
(J W Hills) *w'like: scope: bit bkwd: trckd ldrs: rdn over 2f out: sn wknd* **20/1**

11 *8* **Viviani (IRE)** 2-9-3 0 JimCrowley 1 38
(Mrs A J Perrett) *w'like: scope: str: bit bkwd: in tch whn rdn 3f out: sn towards rr* **8/1**[3]

0 12 *4 ½* **Painswick (USA)**[22] 5401 2-9-3 0 TedDurcan 5 39+
(J L Dunlop) *athletic: unf: t.k.h early: chsd ldrs: rdn and wknd wl over 2f out* **16/1**

13 *15* **Daryainur (IRE)** 2-8-9 0 MarcHalford(3) 12 —
(W De Best-Turner) *scope: slowly away: rcvrd to tack on to main gp d after 2f: rdn: green and wknd 3f out: sn wl bhd* **100/1**

1m 26.99s (1.29) **Going Correction** -0.075s/f (Good) **13** Ran SP% **123.8**
Speed ratings (Par 97): **89,88,87,85,85 81,80,78,78,76 67,62,45**
toteswingers: 1&2 £3.50, 1&3 £10.50, 2&3 £14.30 CSF £7.31 TOTE £1.90: £1.20, £2.40, £3.80; EX 10.00.

Owner K Abdulla **Bred** Juddmonte Farms Inc **Trained** Lambourn, Berks

FOCUS

The winning time was 0.27 seconds quicker than debutant Beauchamp Yorker recorded in the first division. They looked a good bunch in the paddock and this race should produce a few winners.

NOTEBOOK

Critical Moment(USA) built on the promise he showed when clear of the remainder in third on his debut over this trip at the July course and was a game winner. This one-time Royal Lodge entrant is evidently pretty useful and deserves his chance in something decent now. (op 11-8 tchd 6-4)

Lay Claim(USA) ◆, a half-brother to numerous winners, including smart 7f/1m winner Fantastic View, only just failed against a colt with the benefit of a run on this racecourse debut. He was ridden out with mainly hands-and-heels late on and looks almost sure to go on from this, although he holds no Group-race entries. (op 15-2 tchd 8-1)

Colonel Carter(IRE), a 50,000gns purchase, out of a 5f-7.5f winner, including at Stakes level, showed plenty of ability. He should go on from this and looks a useful prospect.

Vimiero(USA) ◆, a $155,000 purchase, never posed a threat but was noted doing some good late work. A big colt, he should be all the better for this experience and is likely to go close next time. (op 20-1)

Rasmy, a 68,000gns half-brother to a 1m winner, showed up well to a point before getting tired. Like a lot of these, he's open to improvement. (tchd 15-2 and 11-1)

Beaumont's Party(IRE), an 85,000euros purchase, was a bit keen early and struggled to land a blow. (op 5-1)

Shamir ran as though he'll improve a good deal on this form in time. (op 80-1)

Painswick(USA) Official explanation: jockey said colt stopped quickly

6110 JOHN SMITH'S CONCORDE CLUB CONDITIONS STKS 1m 1f

5:10 (5:11) (Class 3) 3-Y-O+

£7,477 (£2,239; £1,119; £560; £279; £140) **Stalls** Low

Form RPR

4356 1 **Charlie Farnsbarns (IRE)**[14] 5655 5-8-11 110 MartinDwyer 6 104
(B J Meehan) *chsd ldrs: pushed along 3f out: styd on u.p to ld jst ins fnl f: kpt on wl* **4/1**[2]

2001 2 *1* **Beauchamp Xerxes**[40] 4854 3-8-8 95 WilliamBuick 5 104
(G A Butler) *lw: t.k.h early: in tch: hdwy 3f out: hdwy and swtchd rt 2f out: sn hanging continually lft u.p but kpt on fnl f to take 2nd last stride* **20/1**

1-26 3 *nse* **Peligroso (FR)**[97] 2954 3-8-6 106 TedDurcan 2 102
(Saeed Bin Suroor) *lw: trckd ldr: led over 3f out: rdn 2f out: hdd jst ins fnl f: styd on same pce and lost 2nd last stride* **13/2**

-561 4 *shd* **Glass Harmonium (IRE)**[93] 3050 3-9-1 112 RyanMoore 4 111+
(Sir Michael Stoute) *hld up in tch: pushed along and sme prog 2f out: hanging rt and rdn ins fnl f: styd on clsng stages to press for 2nd but nvr gng to get to wnr* **10/11**[1]

0-10 5 *3 ¼* **General Eliott (IRE)**[106] 2668 4-8-11 109 KFallon 1 95
(P F I Cole) *hld up in rr: drvn along 3f out: no imp and readily hld whn hmpd jst ins fnl f* **11/2**[3]

1200 6 *nk* **Suits Me**[7] 5863 6-9-6 103 MickyFenton 7 103
(T P Tate) *led: hdd over 3f out: styd trcking ldrs tl fdd fnl f* **18/1**

1m 52.78s (-2.72) **Going Correction** -0.075s/f (Good)
WFA 3 from 4yo+ 5lb **6** Ran SP% **111.1**
Speed ratings (Par 107): **109,108,108,107,105 104**
toteswingers: 1&2 £7.20, 1&3 £2.70, 2&3 £11.00 CSF £65.14 TOTE £4.60: £2.10, £4.30; EX 48.20.

Owner The English Girls **Bred** Tinnakill Partnership I **Trained** Manton, Wilts

FOCUS

A decent conditions contest.

NOTEBOOK

Charlie Farnsbarns(IRE) was entitled to need the run last time considering he had been off for over two months after being gelded. The slight step back up in trip and drop in grade were also in his favour and he was a decisive enough winner, taking advantage of being best off at the weights. He's now likely to try and follow up last year's shock win in the Group 3 Darley Stakes at Newmarket next month. (op 11-2)

Beauchamp Xerxes had been struggling to reproduce the form he showed when second in a 1m3f Listed race at Goodwood earlier in the year, and was even below his best when winning a maiden last time, but this was more like it. He had plenty to find at the weights, but clearly ran well above his official mark, despite continually hanging left. He is pretty smart on a going day. (op 16-1)

Peligroso(FR), a Group 3 winner for a different stable in Germany last year, was well below form in that country when last seen in June, but this was more encouraging. He travelled quite well, but couldn't sustain his run to the line and is entitled to come on a little for this. (op 5-1)

Glass Harmonium(IRE) ◆ had been off since winning the Hampton Court at Royal Ascot and he was poorly in the at the weights for this return, particularly considering he was conceding 4lb to a couple of smart older horses. The trip also looked shorter than ideal and he didn't run at all badly all things considered, even though he did hang right a little. He can do better when returned to further. (tchd Evens and 11-10 in places)

General Eliott(IRE), returning from over three months off with the headgear removed, has a tremendous record when fresh but was unproven over this trip. Ridden patiently, possibly to conserve his stamina, he failed to pick up in the straight and, in truth, this was a little disappointing, even allowing for the stamina doubts. (op 6-1 tchd 13-2)

Suits Me had plenty to find at the weights and looks better on Polytrack. He'll surely be considered for a trip to Dubai early next year, as the artificial surface at Meydan ought to suit. (op 16-1 tchd 14-1)

6111 ROY BOULTER RETIREMENT H'CAP 7f (S)
5:45 (5:47) (Class 4) (0-80,81) 3-Y-O **£4,857** (£1,445; £722; £360) **Stalls** Centre

Form RPR

2331 **1** **Santefisio**[11] 5753 3-9-5 **81** JimmyFortune 3 85
(P J Makin) *s.i.s: towards rr tl gd hdwy over 2f out: styd on u.p fnl f to take slt advantage fnl 50yds: hld on all out* **9/2**[2]

6234 **2** *nse* **Wilfred Pickles (IRE)**[21] 5435 3-8-13 **75** JimCrowley 1 79
(Mrs A J Perrett) *in tch: stdy hdwy over 2f out: led wl over 1f out: hrd rdn ins fnl f and narrowly hdd fnl 50yds: edgd lft and styd upsides: jst failed* **14/1**

3-1 **3** *½* **Zero Money (IRE)**[123] 2151 3-8-13 **75** RichardKingscote 17 79+
(R Charlton) *in rr: pushed along over 2f out: hdwy over 1f out and kpt on wl fnl f to take 3rd cl home* **8/1**

0450 **4** *nse* **All About You (IRE)**[24] 5333 3-9-2 **78** (b) MichaelHills 10 81
(W J Haggas) *sn led: pushed along and hdd wl over 1f out: styd pressing ldrs ins fnl f: one pce whn tight for room cl home* **12/1**

20 **5** *hd* **Dance And Dance (IRE)**[21] 5418 3-9-3 **79** TedDurcan 15 81
(E F Vaughan) *chsd ldrs: rdn and one pce over 2f out: kpt on again ins fnl f* **12/1**

3212 **6** *½* **George Thisby**[36] 4990 3-8-10 **75** JamesMillman[(3)] 13 76
(B R Millman) *lw: chsd ldrs: rdn and one pce over 2f out: styd on ins fnl f* **12/1**

4213 **7** *½* **Block Party**[38] 4902 3-9-4 **80** (v[1]) RyanMoore 4 79
(R Charlton) *mid-div tl gd hdwy over 2f out: chsd ldrs ins fnl f: wknd cl home* **3/1**[1]

0000 **8** *¾* **Maxwell Hawke (IRE)**[9] 5799 3-8-11 **73** (t) JamieSpencer 5 70
(P W Chapple-Hyam) *stdd s and hld up in rr: gd hdwy over 2f out: drvn to chse ldrs and no imp appr fnl f: wknd ins fnl f* **15/2**[3]

2-04 **9** *2½* **Hay Fever (IRE)**[33] 5110 3-8-11 **73** MickyFenton 14 64
(Eve Johnson Houghton) *pushed along 3f out: a outpcd* **40/1**

6524 **10** *1* **Advertise**[9] 5804 3-8-6 **68** WilliamBuick 16 56
(A M Balding) *nvr gng pce to get into contention* **11/1**

-605 **11** *½* **Spiritual Art**[20] 5477 3-8-7 **69** (p) PaulDoe 12 55
(L A Dace) *lw: chsd ldrs 5f* **33/1**

1521 **12** *7* **Secret Hero**[49] 4535 3-8-7 **69** (b) RichardMullen 8 37
(R Hannon) *in tch: rdn 3f out: sn btn* **8/1**

4305 **13** *nk* **El Libertador (USA)**[8] 5833 3-8-8 **70** (t) StephenCarson 2 37
(E A Wheeler) *pressed ldrs to 1/2-way: wknd over 2f out* **20/1**

14 *20* **Simla Sunset (IRE)**[59] 4214 3-8-9 **71** MartinDwyer 11 —
(J R Gask) *chsd ldrs tl wknd rapidly over 2f out* **25/1**

1m 25.91s (0.21) **Going Correction** -0.075s/f (Good) **14** Ran SP% **129.2**
Speed ratings (Par 103): **95,94,94,94,94 93,92,92,89,88 87,79,79,56**
toteswingers: 1&2 £14.00, 1&3 £7.90, 2&3 £15.00 CSF £68.80 CT £525.16 TOTE £6.00: £2.20, £4.10, £2.40; EX 93.60 Place 6: £64.11, Place 5: £28.16..
Owner Weldspec Glasgow Limited **Bred** D Brocklehurst **Trained** Ogbourne Maisey, Wilts
■ Stewards' Enquiry : Jim Crowley one-day ban: careless riding (Oct 5)

FOCUS
A competitive handicap, and they were spread out all over the track in the closing stages.
El Libertador(USA) Official explanation: jockey said colt ran flat
T/Plt: £76.70 to a £1 stake. Pool: £85,869.82. 816.81 winning tickets. T/Qpdt: £8.80 to a £1 stake. Pool: £5,560.50. 465.40 winning tickets. ST

6061 NEWMARKET (R-H)
Saturday, September 19

OFFICIAL GOING: Good to firm (8.4)
Far side course used.
Wind: Virtually nil Weather: Dry and bright, quite warm

6112 RACING SOUTH AFRICA H'CAP 6f
1:45 (1:47) (Class 4) (0-85,85) 3-Y-O+ **£5,180** (£1,541; £770; £384) **Stalls** High

Form RPR

4000 **1** **Good Gorsoon (USA)**[28] 5257 4-8-7 **77** AshleyMorgan[(5)] 10 90+
(B W Hills) *mde all: shkn up and drew clr 2f out: styd on wl fnl f: easily* **6/1**[3]

2014 **2** *3¾* **Lucy Brown**[19] 5506 3-8-8 **75** ow1 PatDobbs 8 77
(R Hannon) *hld up in midfield: rdn and effrt ent fnl 2f: kpt on u.p to go modest 2nd fnl 100yds: no ch w wnr* **12/1**

6110 **3** *1* **Getcarter**[22] 5404 3-8-2 **76** CharlesEddery[(7)] 11 75
(R Hannon) *s.i.s: sn rcvrd and chsd wnr over 5f out: rdn and unable qck 2f out: no ch w wnr fr over 1f out: lost 2nd fnl 100yds* **9/1**

6-06 **4** *1¼* **Frognal (IRE)**[15] 5646 3-9-4 **85** NickyMackay 6 80
(B J Meehan) *t.k.h: hld up in midfield: swtchd lft and effrt u.p wl over 1f out: plugged on fnl f: no ch w wnr* **12/1**

0201 **5** *nk* **Brunelleschi**[22] 5404 6-8-8 **80** (b) JosephineBruning[(7)] 3 74
(P L Gilligan) *chsd wnr early: styd handy: rdn along and nt qckn ent fnl 2f: one pce and wl hld fr over 1f out* **15/2**

3540 **6** *1¾* **Dream Express (IRE)**[8] 5836 4-8-6 **71** oh3 KirstyMilczarek 2 60
(P Howling) *restless and burst out of stalls sltly early: stdd and hld up in rr: effrt and hung rt wl over 1f out: nvr trbld ldrs* **16/1**

2100 **7** *1¼* **Esteem Machine (USA)**[21] 5424 5-9-6 **85** LukeMorris 7 70
(R A Teal) *taken down early: stdd s: hld up in rr: swtchd rt and hdwy over 1f out: nvr trbld ldrs* **11/1**

040 **8** *2½* **Resplendent Alpha**[11] 5753 5-8-6 **71** oh4 JimmyQuinn 9 49+
(P Howling) *s.i.s: hld up in rr: rdn and no prog over 1f out: n.m.r ent fnl f* **9/1**

5416 **9** *2¼* **Indian Skipper (IRE)**[6] 5916 4-8-11 **76** (p) SaleemGolam 5 47
(M H Tompkins) *chsd ldrs: rdn and struggling ent fnl 2f: wl btn over 1f out* **5/1**[2]

0600 **10** *2¾* **A Lot Of Red (IRE)**[11] 5747 3-8-5 **72** oh24 ow1 (t) JohnEgan 1 35+
(P J O'Gorman) *racd in midfield: rdn and struggling 1/2-way: bhd and no ch whn hmpd wl over 1f out* **100/1**

6021 **11** *1¾* **Fleeting Star (USA)**[44] 4695 3-8-11 **78** (v) TPQueally 4 35+
(J Noseda) *chsd ldrs tl wknd qckly wl over 1f out: wl bhd and eased wl ins fnl f* **10/3**[1]

1m 11.19s (-1.01) **Going Correction** -0.05s/f (Good)
WFA 3 from 4yo+ 2lb **11** Ran SP% **116.4**
Speed ratings (Par 105): **104,99,97,96,95 93,91,88,85,81 79**
toteswingers: 1&2 £28.60, 1&3 £13.30, 2&3 £3.40 CSF £75.01 CT £479.30 TOTE £6.90: £2.30, £4.50, £2.60; EX 94.40.
Owner Triermore Stud & Partner **Bred** Jayeff 'B' Stables **Trained** Lambourn, Berks

FOCUS
6mm of water had been applied to the final 6f the previous night, but the going remained good to firm, with the GoingStick reading 8.4. This looked a fairly open race beforehand but the winner was never in any danger.
Dream Express(IRE) Official explanation: jockey said gelding hung right
Fleeting Star(USA) Official explanation: jockey said filly lost its action

6113 BLOODSTOCK SOUTH AFRICA E B F FILLIES' H'CAP 1m 4f
2:25 (2:26) (Class 3) (0-95,88) 3-Y-O+ **£9,066** (£2,697; £1,348; £673) **Stalls** High

Form RPR

-502 **1** **Anice Stellato (IRE)**[26] 5321 3-9-2 **86** PatCosgrave 5 93
(R M Beckett) *chsd ldng pair: rdn and effrt over 2f out: drvn to press ldr over 1f out: led fnl 150yds: styd on gamely: all out* **9/1**

4560 **2** *nk* **Storyland (USA)**[30] 5202 4-9-12 **88** KirstyMilczarek 1 95
(W J Haggas) *hld up wl in tch in midfield: hdwy to press ldrs wl over 2f out: led narrowly 2f out: drvn over 1f out: hdd fnl 150yds: kpt on gamely but a jst hld* **5/1**[3]

2211 **3** *hd* **Brief Look**[15] 5649 3-8-13 **83** TPQueally 4 90
(H R A Cecil) *chsd ldr tl pushed along to ld wl over 2f out: edgd lft and narrowly hdd 2f out: kpt on gamely and stl ev ch tl unable qck ins fnl f* **5/4**[1]

-462 **4** *2½* **Cascata (IRE)**[35] 5037 3-8-10 **80** ShaneKelly 2 83
(L M Cumani) *hld up wl in tch in midfield: hdwy to chse ldrs wl over 2f out: sn rdn and unable qck: drvn and one pce fr over 1f out* **4/1**[2]

4104 **5** *hd* **Valmari (IRE)**[2] 6036 6-9-9 **85** (b) LiamJones 7 88
(C E Brittain) *hld up in pair: rdn and outpcd over 3f out: styd on steadily u.p fnl f: nvr gng pce to threaten ldrs* **8/1**

1233 **6** *½* **Arcola (IRE)**[17] 5567 3-7-10 **69** AndreaAtzeni[(3)] 8 71
(D M Simcock) *stdd and dropped in bhd after s: rdn and unable qck 3f out: plugged on same pce fnl 2f* **10/1**

0010 **7** *15* **It's Dubai Dolly**[31] 5168 3-8-7 **77** DavidProbert 6 56
(A J Lidderdale) *led tl wl over 2f out: rdn and btn ent fnl 2f: eased whn wl bhd ins fnl f* **20/1**

2m 31.68s (-1.82) **Going Correction** -0.05s/f (Good)
WFA 3 from 4yo+ 8lb **7** Ran SP% **116.1**
Speed ratings (Par 104): **104,103,103,102,101 101,91**
toteswingers: 1&2 £3.70, 1&3 £4.50, 2&3 £2.70 CSF £54.23 CT £95.01 TOTE £10.00: £2.60, £2.80; EX 43.90.
Owner Clipper Logistics **Bred** Irish National Stud **Trained** Whitsbury, Hants

FOCUS
A decent fillies' handicap, although the top weight was rated 7lb below the ceiling for the race.

NOTEBOOK
Anice Stellato(IRE)'s connections had hopes that she might turn out to be Oaks class earlier in the season, but she was much too keen and didn't make the grade. She showed in defeat at Windsor last month that she had a race in her off her current mark though, and, having settled well here, she showed admirable resolution in a three-way finish. This was only her fifth start, she clearly gets 1m4f well, and there should be plenty more to come from her, especially as a four-year-old. (op 8-1 tchd 10-1)
Storyland(USA), who won this race last year off a 12lb lower mark, has not had much of a season but she bounced back to form at a track which clearly suits. She won twice last autumn and perhaps she can build on this. (tchd 6-1)
Brief Look, chasing a hat-trick following success on the Polytrack of late, had every chance but just came up a little short back on turf. By Sadler's Wells, she won't mind easier ground, and there's every chance she'll get it now. (op 11-8 tchd 13-8)
Cascata(IRE) travelled kindly into contention but was seen off by the first three from the Dip. She didn't quite stay the extra two furlongs and will be suited by a drop back to 1m2f. (op 5-1 tchd 6-1)
Valmari(IRE), making a quick reappearance after turning out at Yarmouth two days earlier, didn't run too badly but probably found the race coming a bit soon. (op 17-2 tchd 15-2)
Arcola(IRE) was up in class and needs some respite from the handicapper. (op 12-1)

6114 PHUMELELA GOLD ENTERPRISES H'CAP 1m 2f
3:00 (3:01) (Class 2) (0-100,95) 3-Y-O **£12,952** (£3,854; £1,926; £962) **Stalls** High

Form RPR

1142 **1** **Honimiere (IRE)**[21] 5419 3-8-11 **88** JimmyQuinn 7 97+
(G A Swinbank) *mde all: gng best and pushed clr 2f out: in command after: comf* **9/4**[1]

4-55 **2** *2½* **Pachattack (USA)**[129] 1988 3-9-4 **95** ShaneKelly 8 99
(G A Butler) *taken down early: chsd ldng pair: rdn to chse wnr ent fnl 2f: sn outpcd by wnr and wl hld after: edgd lft u.p but hld on gamely for 2nd fnl f* **9/1**

0006 **3** *nse* **Full Toss**[8] 5832 3-8-8 **85** PatDobbs 3 88
(R Hannon) *hld up wl in tch: hdwy over 3f out: rdn and unable qck ent fnl 2f: kpt on same pce u.p fr over 1f out* **13/2**

4560 **4** *hd* **Too Much Trouble**[29] 5230 3-9-3 **94** JohnEgan 5 97
(M R Channon) *hld up wl in tch: rdn and unable qck over 2f out: hrd drvn and hdwy to press for 2nd 1f out: kpt on* **7/1**

110 **5** *1¼* **Prince Of Johanne (IRE)**[8] 5828 3-8-8 **85** TPQueally 4 86
(J Noseda) *s.i.s: in tch in rr: rdn and unable qck 3f out: n.m.r on far rail 2f out: sn hung lft u.p: swtchd rt 1f out: hung lft again fnl f: nvr trbld wnr* **3/1**[2]

3532 **6** *7* **Call It On (IRE)**[41] 4827 3-8-10 **87** SaleemGolam 6 75
(M H Tompkins) *t.k.h: chsd wnr tl ent fnl 2f: sn wknd u.p* **4/1**[3]

2m 6.05s (0.25) **Going Correction** -0.05s/f (Good) **6** Ran SP% **111.6**
Speed ratings (Par 107): **97,95,94,94,93 88**
toteswingers: 1&2 £2.40, 1&3 £3.70, 2&3 £12.80 CSF £22.15 CT £110.83 TOTE £3.10: £1.90, £3.60; EX 13.40.
Owner Mrs J Porter & Mrs David Parkinson **Bred** Peter Collier **Trained** Melsonby, N Yorks

FOCUS
This looked quite an interesting handicap on paper but it proved a one-horse race.

NOTEBOOK
Honimiere(IRE) was allowed to set a modest gallop out in front and, on a day when it was also proving hard to come from off the pace, she was handed the race on a plate. She won without having a hard race and continues to look progressive, but the bare form probably flatters her, and if the handicapper wallops her for this she could be vulnerable. (op 5-2)
Pachattack(USA) was dropping in class having contested Pattern races in her four starts since winning her maiden. She looked to have plenty on at the weights on her handicap debut, but she ran all right on her first start since May and is entitled to come on for the run. Official explanation: jockey said filly was unsuited by the good to firm ground (op 8-1 tchd 10-1)
Full Toss, who was just done in the photo for second, was arguably assisted into posting an improved effort by the steady early gallop, as the majority of his form is over shorter so he had the advantage of pace at the finish. (op 6-1 tchd 5-1)
Too Much Trouble, another whose stable had high hopes for him earlier in the season, still looks too high in the handicap. (op 12-1)
Prince Of Johanne(IRE), representing a stable in form, is a confirmed hold-up performer and the way this race was run wouldn't have suited him one bit. (op 11-4)

Call It On(IRE) simply would not settle off the pedestrian early gallop and is another who will appreciate a stronger pace in future. (op 9-2)

6115 INVESTEC CESAREWITCH TRIAL HERITAGE H'CAP 2m 2f

3:40 (3:41) (Class 2) (0-105,100) 3-Y-O+£25,904 (£7,708; £3,852; £1,924) Stalls High

Form				RPR
3313	1		**Bernie The Bolt (IRE)**[29] 5230 3-7-12 **87** oh4................ DavidProbert 7 (A M Balding) *stdd s: hld up in rr: hdwy 5f out: chsd ldr and clr of remainder over 2f out: rdn to ld ins fnl f: styd on strly and sn clr* **9/2**[3]	102+
2623	2	4 ½	**Alanbrooke**[14] 5656 3-8-7 **96**.................(b) RoystonFfrench 2 (M Johnston) *s.i.s: bhd early: stdy hdwy to chse ldrs after 2f: effrt to ld over 4f out: rdn and clr w wnr over 2f out: hdd ins fnl f: no ex* **5/2**[1]	106+
4131	3	13	**Epsom Salts**[9] 5802 4-8-3 **79**....................................... LukeMorris 5 (P M Phelan) *stdd s: hld up in rr: rdn and effrt on outer over 4f out: no ch w ldng pair fnl 2f: wnt poor 3rd jst ins fnl f* **20/1**	72
0662	4	1 ¼	**Double Banded (IRE)**[7] 5857 5-8-5 **81**................................ JohnEgan 1 (K A Ryan) *hld up in midfield: hdwy over 4f out: rdn to chse ldr 3f out tl over 2f out: sn no ch w ldng pair: lost poor 3rd jst ins fnl f* **14/1**	73+
3-42	5	½	**Ragamuffin Man (IRE)**[22] 5410 4-7-10 **75**..............(v) AndreaAtzeni(3) 4 (W J Knight) *t.k.h: led tl rdn and hdd over 4f out: wknd over 2f out: sn wl btn* **13/2**	66
6043	6	1 ½	**Inchpast**[6] 5917 8-7-12 **74** oh6.................................(b) NickyMackay 6 (M H Tompkins) *chsd ldng pair tl over 4f out: sn rdn: wknd u.p over 2f out and wl btn after* **33/1**	64
0042	7	5	**Baddam**[13] 5346 7-8-9 **85**....................................... SaleemGolam 9 (Ian Williams) *chsd ldr: shkn up 7f out: rdn and ev ch 5f: sn struggling: no ch fnl 2f* **20/1**	69
2121	8	2	**Saga De Tercey (FR)**[22] 5410 4-8-11 **87**...................... JimmyQuinn 11 (G A Swinbank) *t.k.h: hld up towards rr: pushed along and effrt 5f out: rdn and btn 3f out: sn wl bhd* **10/3**[2]	68
2143	9	2 ½	**Aleatricis**[70] 3850 4-8-8 **84** ow1.. PatCosgrave 3 (J J Quinn) *fly-jmpd leaving stalls: hld up in rr: rdn and short-lived effrt over 4f out: wl bhd fr over 2f out* **25/1**	62
0530	10	13	**Inchnadamph**[29] 5235 9-8-4 **80**...(t) LiamJones 8 (T J Fitzgerald) *t.k.h: hld up towards rr: rdn and struggling 5f out: wl bhd fnl 3f: t.o* **14/1**	43

3m 47.8s (-7.00) **Going Correction** -0.05s/f (Good)
WFA 3 from 4yo+ 13lb **10** Ran SP% **112.8**
Speed ratings (Par 109): **113,111,105,104,104 103,101,100,99,93**
toteswingers: 1&2 £4.30, 1&3 £3.40, 2&3 £3.70 CSF £14.66 CT £198.44 TOTE £5.60: £2.20, £1.50, £3.30; EX 16.30 Trifecta £82.70 Pool: £403.72 - 3.61 winning units..
Owner B P McGuire **Bred** John Munnelly **Trained** Kingsclere, Hants

FOCUS
A trial for the Cesarewitch but quite a valuable prize in its own right. The early pace was strong, the final time smart, and this proved a real test at the trip.

NOTEBOOK
Bernie The Bolt(IRE), one of only two in the race not entered in the Cesarewitch, was 4lb out of the handicap but was well supported. He finished a place behind Alanbrooke at York last time, but in a race run at a good gallop, sitting further back in the pack helped him conserve energy for the finish here and reverse the form in no uncertain manner. The two three-year-olds in the field, they are clearly both progressive stayers ahead of the handicapper, and can win again. (op 4-1)
Alanbrooke, who sweated up beforehand, sat closer to the strong early gallop than the winner and kicked for home plenty soon enough. He was a sitting duck inside the final two furlongs, but still held off the older horses easily, and he probably didn't do his Cesarewitch chances any harm with this defeat. (op 4-1)
Epsom Salts, along with the winner not entered in the Cesarewitch, was held up towards the rear and came with a good late run to take the minor placing. He's been doing all his winning at around 1m4f but he's just a galloper and the step up in trip proved no bother to him at all. This opens up some new opportunities. (op 16-1)
Double Banded(IRE) travelled up threateningly but from the three-furlong pole he began to struggle. His stamina appeared to give out over this extended trip and 2m is probably his limit. (op 17-2)
Ragamuffin Man(IRE) was largely responsible for the strong gallop and, having raced freely in front, unsurprisingly dropped out of contention in the closing stages. (op 8-1 tchd 6-1)
Inchpast didn't run too badly considering he was 6lb out of the handicap and raced close enough to the strong pace. (op 22-1)
Saga De Tercey(FR) was the disappointment of the race. Despite having conditions to suit, he never picked up for pressure and was well below his best. A tilt at the Cesarewitch must be in doubt now. (op 4-1)

6116 BETTING WORLD CLAIMING STKS 1m 4f

4:15 (4:17) (Class 4) 3-5-Y-O £6,476 (£1,927; £963; £481) Stalls High

Form				RPR
2156	1		**Brett Vale (IRE)**[15] 5648 3-9-1 88................................ StephenDonohoe 6 (Sir Mark Prescott) *stdd s: t.k.h: hld up in rr: hdwy over 3f out: rdn to chal 2f out: led narrowly ent fnl f: styd on wl to assert fnl 75yds* **11/4**[2]	80+
0	2	1 ½	**Everaard (USA)**[43] 4759 3-8-5 62... JohnEgan 5 (D R C Elsworth) *t.k.h: trckd ldng pair: hdwy to join ldr over 4f out: led over 2f out: hdd narrowly ent fnl f: edgd lft and btn fnl 75yds* **12/1**	68
1300	3	1 ¾	**Tanto Faz (IRE)**[7] 5887 4-9-0 83.. LiamJones 1 (W J Haggas) *t.k.h: hld up in tch: hdwy to trck ldrs but nt clr run over 3f out tl swtchd lft over 1f out: plugged on same pce fnl f: wnt 3rd last stride* **10/3**[3]	66+
015	4	shd	**Malt Or Mash (USA)**[13] 5694 5-8-13 85................................ PatDobbs 2 (R Hannon) *sn led at stdy gallop: jnd and qcknd 4f out: rdn and hdd over 2f out: keeping on same pce u.p whn n.m.r and hmpd over 1f out: one pce after: lost 3rd last stride* **2/1**[1]	65+
1402	5	5	**Urban Space**[33] 5097 3-8-3 65... DavidProbert 3 (D Burchell) *chsd ldr tl over 4f out: rdn 3f out: drvn and btn ent fnl f lft u.p wl over 2f out: wknd over 1f out* **9/2**	55
6060	6	1 ½	**Zelos Diktator**[49] 4519 3-8-0 44.................................(p) AndreaAtzeni(3) 4 (Rae Guest) *hld up in last pl: rdn and outpcd over 4f out: plugged on fnl f but n.d* **40/1**	52

2m 35.61s (2.11) **Going Correction** -0.05s/f (Good)
WFA 3 from 4yo+ 8lb **6** Ran SP% **111.4**
Speed ratings (Par 105): **90,89,87,87,84 83**
toteswingers: 1&2 £2.90, 1&3 £2.00, 2&3 £5.20 CSF £32.07 TOTE £3.70: £2.00, £3.40; EX 29.20.Brett Vale was claimed by Mr P. R. Hedger for £40,000. Malt Or Mash was subject of a friendly claim.
Owner G D Waters **Bred** Mrs O Murtagh **Trained** Newmarket, Suffolk

FOCUS
Not a bad claimer on paper, as it featured three horses rated in the mid- to high 80s, but the proximity of the 62-rated Everaard in second, even allowing for weight-for-age, suggests the winner didn't have to run to anything like his rating to score.

Urban Space Official explanation: jockey said gelding hung left

6117 SPORTSWORLD SOUTH AFRICA 2010 H'CAP 1m

4:50 (4:50) (Class 3) (0-90,89) 3-Y-O+ £7,771 (£2,312; £1,155; £577) Stalls High

Form				RPR
210-	1		**Intense**[351] 6439 3-9-0 **85**.. PatDobbs 4 (B W Hills) *swtg: chsd ldr: pushed into ld 2f out: edgd rt but rdn and forged 2 l clr 1f out: styd on wl* **15/2**	95
5111	2	1 ¼	**Credit Swap**[50] 4502 4-9-1 **89**................................ TobyAtkinson(7) 8 (M Wigham) *hld up in tch towards rr: rdn over 2f out: hdwy on far rail ent fnl f: r.o to snatch 2nd nr fin: nt pce to threaten wnr* **7/2**[1]	96
1521	3	nk	**Mountain Cat (IRE)**[7] 5887 5-9-3 **84**.................................. ShaneKelly 2 (G A Swinbank) *stmbld leaving stalls: sn rcvrd and led at stdy gallop: rdn and qcknd 3f out: hdd 2f out: edgd rt over 1f out: kpt on same pce fnl f* **6/1**[3]	91
1030	4	¾	**Spirit Of Sharjah (IRE)**[29] 5221 4-9-7 **88**.......................... JimmyQuinn 6 (Miss J Feilden) *t.k.h: hld up in tch towards rr: rdn and effrt over 2f out: hdwy over 1f out: chsd ldng pair ins fnl f: kpt on same pce fnl 100yds* **12/1**	93
0004	5	1	**Ellemujie**[21] 5437 4-9-1 **87**.. JamesO'Reilly(5) 10 (D K Ivory) *hld up in last pair: rdn and outpcd 3f out: hdwy and swtchd lft over 1f out: styd on u.p fnl f: nvr trbld ldrs* **8/1**	90
1000	6	shd	**Tudor Key (IRE)**[29] 5221 3-9-0 **85**..................................... TPQueally 9 (Mrs A J Perrett) *t.k.h: chsd ldrs: rdn wl over 2f out: unable qck whn nt clr run and swtchd lft over 1f out: plugging on same pce and hld whn nt clr run ins fnl f* **20/1**	88
2054	7	1	**Thief Of Time (IRE)**[37] 4954 3-9-1 **86**.............................. PatCosgrave 1 (P W Chapple-Hyam) *t.k.h: sn chsng ldrs: rdn and unable qck over 2f out: lost pl over 1f out and n.d after* **15/2**	86
2543	8	¾	**Barliffey (IRE)**[6] 5914 4-8-8 **75** oh4...................................(v) JohnEgan 5 (D J Coakley) *stdd s: t.k.h: hld up in last pl: rdn and unable qck over 3f out: nvr trbld ldrs* **6/1**[3]	74
5425	9	1 ¼	**Isphahan**[7] 5874 6-9-3 **84**...(v) DavidProbert 7 (A M Balding) *t.k.h: hld up in midfield: swtchd to outer after 2f out: rdn and unable qck wl over 2f out: wknd 2f out* **11/2**[2]	80

1m 37.76s (-0.84) **Going Correction** -0.05s/f (Good)
WFA 3 from 4yo+ 4lb **9** Ran SP% **113.3**
Speed ratings (Par 107): **102,100,100,99,98 98,97,96,95**
toteswingers: 1&2 £6.00, 1&3 £8.00, 2&3 £4.30 CSF £33.25 CT £168.86 TOTE £9.30: £2.50, £2.00, £1.80; EX 30.80.
Owner K Abdulla **Bred** Juddmonte Farms Ltd **Trained** Lambourn, Berks
■ Stewards' Enquiry : Shane Kelly two-day ban: careless riding (Oct 5-6)

NOTEBOOK
Intense, despite being awash with sweat beforehand, took this race apart with a smart turn of foot on her belated seasonal return. She's clearly had her problems, but was thought good enough to contest a Group 3 on her final start at two and, in hindsight, a mark of 85 underestimated her ability. The form looks solid with two in-form older horses filling the places, and her ability to quicken should see her progress quickly up the ranks. Her pedigree suggests she'll get a bit further, but she's clearly very effective over a mile, and getting her some black type is likely to be the priority now. (op 9-1)
Credit Swap, given a break after completing a three-timer in July, resumed off a 3lb higher mark and did best of those held up for a run, finding a gap alongside the far rail in the closing stages. He can soon regain the winning thread on this evidence. (op 3-1)
Mountain Cat(IRE) has been in great form over the summer but a 6lb rise for his latest success found him out against a well-handicapped, unexposed rival. He ran right up to his mark. (op 9-2 tchd 13-2)
Spirit Of Sharjah(IRE) needs to be held up and that often means he finds trouble in running. He proved his stamina for a mile here, which gives him more options, but he remains difficult to win with. (tchd 14-1)
Ellemujie was back over a mile and down to the mark he last won off, but he got going far too late and could never land a blow. A stronger all-round gallop would have aided his cause. (op 17-2 tchd 9-1)
Tudor Key(IRE), who has struggled since winning on the Polytrack in July, might be suited by a return to the sand as he's recorded two of his three best RPRs on the surface. (op 16-1)

6118 KENILWORTH QUARANTINE STATION H'CAP 5f

5:25 (5:27) (Class 5) (0-75,77) 3-Y-O+ £3,885 (£1,156; £577; £288) Stalls High

Form				RPR
5351	1		**Ocean Blaze**[6] 5919 5-9-8 **77** 6ex.................................... TPQueally 9 (B R Millman) *chsd ldr tl pushed into ld over 1f out: rdn and clr ent fnl f: drvn out and a holding on towards fin* **5/1**[2]	87
2110	2	¾	**Step It Up (IRE)**[20] 5477 5-9-1 **70**.................................. PatCosgrave 2 (J R Boyle) *towards rr: rdn and effrt jst over 2f out: r.o wl fnl f: wnt 2nd towards fin: clsng on wnr but nvr gng to get there* **10/1**	77
4433	3	nk	**Luminous Gold**[16] 5597 4-9-3 **72**...................................... IanMongan 12 (C F Wall) *hld up towards rr: hdwy on far rail 1/2-way: rdn to chse ldrs and swtchd lft over 1f out: chsd clr wnr fnl 100yds tl towards fin: kpt on* **9/2**[1]	78
0214	4	1 ¼	**Multahab**[32] 5125 10-8-2 **64** ow1...........................(tp) TobyAtkinson(7) 5 (M Wigham) *chsd ldrs after 1f: rdn and effrt wl over 1f out: edgd rt over 1f out: one pce fnl f* **16/1**	66
1131	5	1 ¾	**Corton Charlemagne (IRE)**[12] 5724 3-9-0 **73**............ AndreaAtzeni(3) 3 (Rae Guest) *towards rr: pushed along 1/2-way: hdwy u.p on outer fnl f: nt rch ldrs* **6/1**[3]	68
6200	6	hd	**Namir (IRE)**[12] 5719 7-9-2 **71**......................................(bt) JohnEgan 6 (H J Evans) *led to s: hld up in last trio: rdn and hdwy towards far rail enterring fnl f: kpt on fnl f but nvr trbld ldrs* **7/1**	66
0661	7	nk	**Evelyn May (IRE)**[10] 5777 3-8-12 **73**........................ AshleyMorgan(5) 11 (B W Hills) *stdd s: hld up in midfield: hdwy 1/2-way: rdn and unable qck whn n.m.r over 1f out: no ch fnl f* **13/2**	67
1012	8	hd	**Silver Prelude**[20] 5480 8-8-6 **64**..............................(t) WilliamCarson(3) 10 (S C Williams) *led at fast gallop: rdn and hdd over 1f out: lost 2nd fnl 100yds: fdd towards fin* **9/1**	57
1000	9	1 ¼	**Mango Music**[21] 5436 6-9-6 **75**................................... StephenDonohoe 7 (M Quinn) *sn niggled along in midfield: rdn and no prog fnl 2f* **20/1**	63
5404	10	¾	**Cosmic Destiny (IRE)**[26] 5323 7-8-7 **62**.............................. DavidProbert 8 (E F Vaughan) *a towards rr: rdn and no prog fr wl over 1f out* **11/1**	48
-430	11	¾	**Handsome Cross (IRE)**[29] 5219 8-9-3 **72**.............................. PatDobbs 1 (W J Musson) *a bhd: nvr a factor* **16/1**	55
200	12	17	**The Cuckoo**[17] 5584 3-7-12 **61** oh2................................ NathanAlison(7) 4 (M Quinn) *a towards rr: lost tch rapidly 1/2-way: t.o fnl f* **50/1**	—

58.15 secs (-0.95) **Going Correction** -0.05s/f (Good)
WFA 3 from 4yo+ 1lb **12** Ran SP% **120.9**
Speed ratings (Par 103): **105,103,103,101,98 98,97,97,95,94 93,65**
toteswingers: 1&2 £8.60, 1&3 £4.70, 2&3 £12.60 CSF £55.64 CT £248.95 TOTE £6.30: £1.90, £4.10, £2.20; EX 57.10 Place 6: £636.12, Place 5: £159.85..

Owner Gary Hancock (Staffs) **Bred** Longdon Stud And Robin Lawson **Trained** Kentisbeare, Devon
■ Stewards' Enquiry : Nathan Alison one-day ban: used whip when out of contention

FOCUS
They went a good pace here.
The Cuckoo Official explanation: jockey said gelding was unsuited by the good to firm ground
T/Plt: £590.80 to a £1 stake. Pool: £55,567.85. 68.65 winning tickets. T/Qpdt: £24.30 to a £1 stake. Pool: £4,332.80. 131.70 winning tickets. SP

6068 WOLVERHAMPTON (A.W) (L-H)
Saturday, September 19

OFFICIAL GOING: Standard
Wind: Light across Weather: Overcast

6119 WILLIAMHILL.COM/BONUS25 - GET £25 FREE BET H'CAP 5f 20y(P)
5:50 (5:51) (Class 6) (0-55,55) 3-Y-O+ £2,388 (£705; £352) Stalls Low

Form RPR
4503 **1** **Decider (USA)**[6] 5911 6-9-0 **52**..........(p) KirstyMilczarek 2 61
(R A Harris) *trckd ldrs: edgd lft 4f out: stmbld over 3f out: led over 1f out: sn hung rt: rdn out* **4/1**[2]
2053 **2** ½ **Monsieur Reynard**[9] 5792 4-8-12 **53**.......... MCGeran(3) 6 60
(J M Bradley) *s.i.s: hdwy 1/2-way: swtchd lft 1f out: rdn and r.o* **5/1**[3]
0302 **3** 1¾ **The History Man (IRE)**[19] 5501 6-8-11 **54**.......(b) AndrewHeffernan(5) 1 55+
(B D Leavy) *sn pushed along and prom: hmpd and lost pl 4f out: sn drvn along: hdwy over 1f out: r.o: nt rch ldrs* **3/1**[1]
03 **4** 1¾ **Thoughtsofstardom**[16] 5610 6-9-3 **55**..........(be) JerryO'Dwyer 5 50
(P S McEntee) *chsd ldrs: rdn over 1f out: edgd lft and no ex ins fnl f* **5/1**[3]
2500 **5** ½ **Admiral Bond (IRE)**[16] 5610 4-8-10 **55**..........(p) AnthonyBetts(7) 13 48
(G R Oldroyd) *hld up: swtchd lft sn after s: hdwy over 1f out: nt rch ldrs* **16/1**
0050 **6** nk **Sir Loin**[26] 5323 8-8-3 **46** oh1..........(v) SophieDoyle(5) 11 38
(P Burgoyne) *chsd ldr tl led 1/2-way: rdn: edgd rt and hdd over 1f out: no ex ins fnl f* **50/1**
0000 **7** ¾ **Triskaidekaphobia**[6] 5900 6-8-10 **48**..........(bt) PaulFitzsimons 3 39+
(Miss J R Tooth) *led to 1/2-way: sn rdn: ev ch over 1f out: no ex fnl f: eased nr fin* **16/1**
56-0 **8** 1¼ **Our Wee Girl (IRE)**[50] 4479 3-9-1 **54**..........(p) GeorgeBaker 7 39
(Miss Tor Sturgis) *trckd ldrs: rdn over 1f out: wknd fnl f* **8/1**
6006 **9** ¾ **Meikle Barfil**[9] 5792 7-8-8 **46**..........(tp) EdwardCreighton 9 28
(J M Bradley) *s.i.s: sn outpcd: hdwy over 1f out: wknd ins fnl f* **20/1**
0052 **10** nk **Helping Hand (IRE)**[12] 5716 4-8-7 **52**.......... DavidKenny(7) 8 33
(R Hollinshead) *prom: rdn 1/2-way: hung lft and wknd over 1f out* **9/1**
0003 **11** 4 **Spring Bridge (IRE)**[15] 5645 3-8-11 **50**..........(t) FrankieMcDonald 10 16
(Mrs L C Jewell) *sn outpcd: bhd fr 1/2-way* **66/1**
61.26 secs (-1.04) **Going Correction** -0.20s/f (Stan)
WFA 3 from 4yo+ 1lb 11 Ran SP% **119.4**
Speed ratings (Par 101): **100,99,96,93,92 92,91,89,87,87 81**
toteswingers: 1&2 £10.90, 1&3 £4.80, 2&3 £4.00 CSF £24.46 CT £69.22 TOTE £5.40: £1.80, £2.10, £1.60; EX 25.20.
Owner Robert Bailey **Bred** Green Willow Farms **Trained** Earlswood, Monmouths
■ Stewards' Enquiry : Sophie Doyle six-day ban: careless riding (Oct 5-9)

FOCUS
Half the field had placed last time out, and the market leaders filled the first four finishing positions. Triskaidekaphobia and Sir Loin additionally ensured a decent early gallop, but the form is limited with the winner rated to his best recent form.

6120 WILLIAMHILL.COM/BONUS25 - POKER TOURNAMENTS H'CAP 5f 216y(P)
6:20 (6:21) (Class 5) (0-75,74) 3-Y-O+ £3,238 (£963; £481; £240) Stalls Low

Form RPR
0305 **1** **Bahamian Lad**[6] 5916 4-9-6 **74**.......... JerryO'Dwyer 2 81+
(R Hollinshead) *trckd ldrs: a gng wl: shkn up to ld over 1f out: r.o wl: hung lft towards fin* **7/2**[2]
3500 **2** 2 **Hellbender (IRE)**[5] 5937 3-9-4 **74**.......... GeorgeBaker 8 75
(S Kirk) *hld up: hdwy over 1f out: sn rdn: r.o* **15/2**
0051 **3** 1 **Obe Brave**[8] 5842 6-8-6 **60** oh1..........(p) SaleemGolam 7 58+
(Lee Smyth, Ire) *chsd ldr tl led over 2f out: rdn and hdd over 1f out: styd on same pce ins fnl f* **7/1**[3]
6420 **4** 1 **Bold Ring**[9] 5809 3-8-7 **63** ow1.......... EdwardCreighton 11 58
(E J Creighton) *sn outpcd: hdwy over 2f out: rdn and hung lft over 1f out: styd on* **33/1**
00- **5** 1¼ **Boule Masquee**[18] 5557 5-9-4 **72**.......... LukeMorris 4 63
(David P Myerscough, Ire) *s.s: bhd: r.o u.p ins fnl f: nvr nrr* **12/1**
322 **6** hd **Milne Bay (IRE)**[3] 5991 4-8-10 **71**..........(t) LauraPike(7) 1 62
(D M Simcock) *chsd ldrs: rdn over 1f out: no ex fnl f* **2/1**[1]
-021 **7** 2 **Timeless Dream**[17] 5584 3-9-2 **72**.......... DarryllHolland 10 57
(P W Chapple-Hyam) *chsd ldrs: rdn 1/2-way: wknd fnl f* **7/1**[3]
0350 **8** nk **Kipchak (IRE)**[16] 5601 4-9-1 **69**..........(p) TravisBlock 6 53
(C R Dore) *trckd ldrs: racd keenly tl pushed along over 3f out: outpcd fnl 2f* **16/1**
3060 **9** 1 **Grand Palace (IRE)**[8] 5836 6-8-13 **67**..........(v) VinceSlattery 12 48
(H J Evans) *sn pushed along in rr: sme hdwy whn nt clr run 2f out: n.d* **50/1**
2-60 **10** ½ **Solitary**[36] 5007 3-9-2 **72**.......... FrankieMcDonald 3 51
(H Candy) *sn pushed along towards rr: rdn and wknd over 2f out* **16/1**
0104 **11** 24 **Island Legend (IRE)**[10] 5777 3-9-1 **74**.......... JackDean(3) 5 —
(J M Bradley) *sn led: rdn and hdd over 2f out: wknd over 1f out* **33/1**
1m 13.41s (-1.59) **Going Correction** -0.20s/f (Stan)
WFA 3 from 4yo+ 2lb 11 Ran SP% **119.6**
Speed ratings (Par 103): **102,99,98,96,95 94,92,91,90,89 57**
toteswingers: 1&2 £3.20, 1&3 £6.70, 2&3 £11.80 CSF £30.27 CT £180.86 TOTE £5.10: £1.50, £3.30, £2.60; EX 29.80.
Owner Graham Brothers Racing Partnership **Bred** J D Graham **Trained** Upper Longdon, Staffs

FOCUS
All bar Irish raider Boule Masquee managed to break on terms, but by the turn in only one horse was still travelling with purpose. The strong pace suited the winner who is rated back to his best.
Island Legend(IRE) Official explanation: jockey said gelding lost its action

6121 WILLIAMHILL.COM/BONUS25 - QUOTE BONUS25 H'CAP 1m 5f 194y(P)
6:50 (6:51) (Class 4) (0-85,83) 3-Y-O £6,308 (£1,888; £944; £472) Stalls Low

Form RPR
1211 **1** **The Last Don (IRE)**[14] 5666 3-9-7 **83**.......... DarryllHolland 3 95+
(D R Lanigan) *a.p: pushed along for a couple of strides after 2f: chsd ldr over 9f out: led over 4f out: pushed clr fnl 3f: hung rt 2f out: readily* **11/10**[1]
0140 **2** 7 **Fin Vin De Leu (GER)**[13] 5696 3-8-13 **75**.......... GregFairley 2 76
(M Johnston) *led: hdd over 4f out: sn rdn: outpcd fr over 2f out* **9/4**[2]
2212 **3** 32 **Deuce**[17] 5579 3-8-5 **67**..........(b) LukeMorris 1 32+
(Eve Johnson Houghton) *in tch but sn pushed along: rdn 7f out: wknd 4f out: clr 3rd and no ch w front pair whn eased fr over 2f out: t.o* **7/2**[3]
4010 **4** 21 **Eightdaysaweek**[9] 5812 3-8-4 **66** ow1.......... RoystonFfrench 4 —
(A J McCabe) *chsd ldrs: rdn 7f out: wknd over 4f out: t.o* **16/1**
3m 1.28s (-4.72) **Going Correction** -0.20s/f (Stan) 4 Ran SP% **106.5**
Speed ratings (Par 103): **105,101,82,70**
CSF £3.71 TOTE £2.20.
Owner P Brosnan **Bred** Tally-Ho Stud **Trained** Newmarket, Suffolk

FOCUS
The best race of the evening attracted a numerically disappointing turnout, but the winner continues to shape like a progressive horse. An improved effort from him, although the runner-up was below par.

6122 WILLIAMHILL.COM/BONUS25 - LIVE CASINO DEALERS (S) STKS 7f 32y(P)
7:20 (7:27) (Class 6) 2-Y-O £2,047 (£604; £302) Stalls High

Form RPR
1 **Push Me (IRE)** 2-8-6 0.......... LiamJones 9 58+
(M S Tuck) *hld up: hdwy 3f out: sn jnd ldr: shkn up to ld ins fnl f: styd on* **12/1**
0530 **2** 1¾ **Avow (USA)**[5] 5935 2-8-11 64..........(b) LukeMorris 5 59
(J S Moore) *chsd ldr tl led 1/2-way: rdn and hung lft over 1f out: hdd and unable qck ins fnl f* **4/1**[2]
3 **3** 1¾ **Springwell Giant (IRE)**[18] 5543 2-8-4 0.......... DeclanCannon(7) 6 55+
(A J McCabe) *s.i.s: hld up: hdwy over 2f out: rdn and hung rt over 1f out: r.o: nt rch ldrs* **6/1**[3]
0020 **4** ½ **Lochbroom Sunset**[9] 5811 2-8-11 65.......... SaleemGolam 1 53
(S C Williams) *chsd ldrs: rdn over 2f out: sn outpcd: styd on again fr over 1f out* **4/1**[2]
42 **5** 6 **Dontbugthebunny (USA)**[26] 5319 2-8-1 0.......... MatthewDavies(5) 7 34
(George Baker) *hld up: pushed along on outer over 2f out: hung lft over 1f out: nvr trbld ldrs* **7/2**[1]
0 **6** 4 **Bellaharry (IRE)**[19] 5498 2-8-6 0.......... KirstyMilczarek 12 24
(Matthew Salaman) *s.i.s: hdwy 6f out: rdn 1/2-way: wknd 2f out* **25/1**
00 **7** 14 **Zeloca (IRE)**[15] 5643 2-7-13 0..........(t) RyanPowell(7) 2 —
(Mrs L C Jewell) *led to 1/2-way: sn rdn: wknd 2f out* **66/1**
0 **P** **Calle Vistamar**[8] 5835 2-8-6 0.......... FrankieMcDonald 3 —
(S Wynne) *sn drvn along and reluctant in rr: bhd whn p.u fnl 4f* **100/1**
1m 29.63s (0.03) **Going Correction** -0.20s/f (Stan) 8 Ran SP% **90.5**
Speed ratings (Par 93): **91,89,87,86,79 75,59,—**
toteswingers: 1&2 £6.70, 1&3 not won, 2&3 not won. CSF £35.69 TOTE £5.20: £2.10, £2.10, £1.30; EX 26.00.Winner bought in for 5,500gns.
Owner G S Tuck **Bred** Mrs Dolores Gleeson **Trained** Oldbury on the Hill, Gloucs
■ The first winner for Matthew Tuck since taking over the licence from his uncle John Tuck.

FOCUS
This race was delayed after original favourite Pearl Of Kent (3/1F, deduct 25p in the £), the last to load, got her nose under the gate and broke loose, but the market was not reformed. A weakish seller but there could be more to come from the winner.

NOTEBOOK
Push Me(IRE) was the only debutant in the line-up, but the protracted hold-up didn't faze her. Held up early, she looked to be travelling all over the more experienced Avow as the two joined battle turning in and finally broke that one's resolve inside the last 50 yards in receipt of just a couple of light taps. There was a little interest in the post-race auction following this resolute effort, before connections bought her back in for 5,500 guineas. (op 16-1 tchd 11-1)
Avow(USA), friendless before the off, probably travelled a touch too wastefully in trying to keep tabs on pacesetter Zeloca, and his rider was getting urgent far further out than the winner's. He has placed in both starts at this grade, both on Polytrack, without fully convincing as a winner in waiting. (op 11-4)
Springwell Giant(IRE), already gelded, has gifted his rivals a start on both his outings now, and he additionally looked a touch awkward under pressure late on. (op 5-1 tchd 4-1)
Lochbroom Sunset lost his pitch at a vital moment turning in and posted his second lesser performance since just failing over 6f at Lingfield two runs ago. A drop back to that trip needs considering. (op 7-2 tchd 11-2)
Dontbugthebunny(USA) had shaped as if a drop in trip would do the trick over a mile at Windsor last time, but it all happened a bit quickly for her here and she is already in a little danger of becoming tripless. (op 5-1 tchd 100-30)

6123 WILLIAM HILL 0800 444040 - GET £25 FREE BET H'CAP 7f 32y(P)
7:50 (7:50) (Class 6) (0-65,65) 3-Y-O+ £2,388 (£705; £352) Stalls High

Form RPR
1642 **1** **Ugenius**[9] 5813 5-9-5 **63**.......... TGMcLaughlin 5 71
(Mrs C A Dunnett) *hld up: hdwy on ins over 1f out: rdn to ld ins fnl f: jst hld on* **5/1**[2]
4050 **2** hd **Sea Land (FR)**[2] 6024 5-9-2 **60**.......... GeorgeBaker 1 67
(B Ellison) *hld up: hdwy over 1f out: sn rdn and hung lft: r.o wl: jst failed* **13/2**
1000 **3** nk **Diego Rivera**[74] 3722 4-9-3 **61**.......... TravisBlock 4 68
(P J Makin) *a.p: rdn and ev ch ins fnl f: r.o* **7/1**
0033 **4** 1¾ **Guildenstern (IRE)**[17] 5576 7-9-4 **62**.......... JimmyQuinn 2 64+
(P Howling) *hld up: hdwy on ins over 1f out: sn rdn: nt rch ldrs* **6/1**[3]
5 nse **Kalypso (IRE)**[11] 5758 3-9-4 **65**.......... DarryllHolland 9 66
(David P Myerscough, Ire) *led: rdn over 1f out: hdd and no ex ins fnl f* **7/2**[1]
/00- **6** 2½ **Giant Slalom**[8] 5846 5-9-4 **62**.......... PatCosgrave 11 57
(T G McCourt, Ire) *s.i.s: hdwy over 5f out: rdn to chse ldr wl over 1f out: no ex fnl f* **12/1**
0500 **7** ½ **Sign Of The Cross**[25] 5329 5-9-2 **60**.......... LiamJones 8 54
(C R Dore) *s.i.s: hld up: hdwy over 2f out: rdn over 1f out: edgd lft and no ex ins fnl f* **25/1**
0001 **8** ½ **Royal Challenge**[14] 5676 8-9-4 **62**.......... RoystonFfrench 6 54
(I W McInnes) *chsd ldrs: rdn over 2f out: no ex fnl f* **12/1**
0260 **9** 1½ **Norcroft**[3] 5998 7-9-3 **61**..........(p) VinceSlattery 7 49
(Mrs C A Dunnett) *hld up: hdwy over 2f out: rdn and hung lft over 1f out: sn wknd* **25/1**
00-0 **10** 1¼ **Roman Maze**[40] 4859 9-9-2 **60**.......... LukeMorris 3 45
(W M Brisbourne) *hld up: rdn 3f out: nvr on terms* **16/1**
3506 **11** 3¾ **Fortunate Flame**[41] 4816 3-9-3 **64**.......... GregFairley 10 38
(K A Ryan) *chsd ldr: rdn and ev ch over 2f out: hung lft and wknd over 1f out* **9/1**

510 **12** *23* **Rabbit Fighter (IRE)**[138] 1737 5-9-6 **64**............................ AdamKirby 12 —
(D Shaw) *s.i.s: hdwy to chse ldrs 6f out: rdn over 2f out: sn wknd* **16/1**
1m 28.64s (-0.96) **Going Correction** -0.20s/f (Stan)
WFA 3 from 4yo+ 3lb **12** Ran SP% **123.8**
Speed ratings (Par 101): **97,96,96,94,94 91,90,90,88,87 82,56**
toteswingers: 1&2 £12.80, 1&3 £4.30, 2&3 £27.50 CSF £39.46 CT £232.29 TOTE £7.40: £2.40, £3.20, £3.00; EX 30.80.
Owner Mrs Christine Dunnett **Bred** Three Acres Stud **Trained** Hingham, Norfolk

FOCUS
They didn't appear to go off very hard in this handicap, but the winning time was still one second faster than that of the preceding seller. The form looks solid enough.

6124 WILLIAMHILL.COM/BONUS25 - PLAY VEGAS GAMES H'CAP 1m 141y(P)
8:20 (8:21) (Class 5) (0-70,70) 3-Y-O **£3,885** (£1,156; £577; £288) **Stalls** Low

Form RPR
0661 **1** **Sham Sheer**[12] 5723 3-9-4 **70**............................ KFallon 1 76+
(L M Cumani) *chsd ldr to over 6f out: remained handy: wnt 2nd again over 3f out: led over 2f out: sn rdn: hung rt ins fnl f: styd on wl* **2/1**[1]
1050 **2** *1 ¾* **Omnium Duke (IRE)**[17] 5575 3-9-4 **70**............................ JimmyQuinn 7 72
(J W Hills) *hld up: hdwy over 2f out: rdn over 1f out: r.o* **12/1**
5555 **3** *nk* **Land Hawk (IRE)**[19] 5524 3-9-1 **67**............................ LiamJones 2 69
(J Pearce) *hld up in tch: pushed along over 2f out: rdn over 1f out: r.o* **10/3**[2]
4625 **4** *2 ¼* **Chantilly Pearl (USA)**[28] 5258 3-9-0 **66**............................ PatCosgrave 5 63
(J G Given) *a.p: rdn over 3f out: styd on same pce fnl f* **8/1**[3]
0100 **5** *1 ¼* **The Happy Hammer (IRE)**[14] 5663 3-8-11 **63**............................ MickyFenton 4 57
(E V Stanford) *prom: rdn over 2f out: no ex fnl f* **9/1**
4044 **6** *1* **Millharbour (IRE)**[26] 5322 3-8-12 **64**............................ DarryllHolland 6 56
(B W Hills) *led: rdn and hdd over 2f out: no ex fnl f* **11/1**
41-0 **7** *5* **Dream Huntress**[245] 205 3-8-2 **61**............................ AmyScott(7) 11 43
(J W Hills) *s.s: hld up and bhd: hdwy on outer over 2f out: sn hung rt and wknd* **33/1**
445 **8** *2 ¾* **Dom Polski**[17] 5572 3-9-3 **69**............................(t) AdamKirby 13 45
(W R Swinburn) *hld up: hdwy u.p 2f out: wknd over 1f out* **10/1**
0-01 **9** *1 ½* **Molly The Witch (IRE)**[44] 4719 3-8-8 **60**............................ ChrisCatlin 8 33
(W J Musson) *hld up: rdn over 2f out: sn wknd* **14/1**
4000 **10** *14* **Duke Of Normandy (IRE)**[8] 4918 3-8-8 **60**............................ GregFairley 9 3
(B P J Baugh) *prom: chsd ldr over 6f out to over 3f out: wknd over 2f out* **50/1**
04 **11** *7* **Clare Glen (IRE)**[13] 5703 3-9-3 **69**............................(p) SaleemGolam 3 —
(Lee Smyth, Ire) *s.i.s: sn pushed into mid-div: rdn over 3f out: wknd over 2f out* **20/1**
1m 48.18s (-2.32) **Going Correction** -0.20s/f (Stan) **11** Ran SP% **119.0**
Speed ratings (Par 101): **102,100,100,98,97 96,91,89,87,75 69**
toteswingers: 1&2 £5.50, 1&3 £17.30, 2&3 £9.00 CSF £27.93 CT £80.99 TOTE £3.60: £1.80, £3.90, £1.50; EX 37.90.
Owner Sheikh Mohammed Obaid Al Maktoum **Bred** Brook Stud Bloodstock Ltd **Trained** Newmarket, Suffolk

FOCUS
A modest handicap, rated around the placed horses.

6125 EUROPEAN BREEDERS' FUND MAIDEN STKS 1m 141y(P)
8:50 (8:51) (Class 5) 2-Y-O **£3,885** (£1,156; £577; £288) **Stalls** Low

Form RPR
6 **1** **Miss Starlight**[22] 5398 2-8-12 0............................ EdwardCreighton 2 78+
(P J McBride) *hld up: hdwy over 2f out: rdn to chse clr ldr and hung lft over 1f out: r.o wl to ld towards fin* **6/1**
0 **2** *1* **Krymian**[38] 4908 2-9-3 0............................ KFallon 3 81+
(Sir Michael Stoute) *chsd ldr: led over 2f out: sn pushed clr: rdn and stl a healthy advantage fnl f: rdr looked over both shoulders: hdd towards fin* **7/2**[3]
4 **3** *5* **Exemplary**[25] 5324 2-9-3 0............................ GregFairley 5 70
(M Johnston) *hld up: hmpd after 1f: hdwy and hung lft fr over 1f out: nvr any ch* **2/1**[1]
30 **4** *6* **Saint Thomas (IRE)**[9] 5786 2-9-3 0............................ LiamJones 6 58
(J A Osborne) *chsd ldrs: rdn 1/2-way: wknd over 2f out* **14/1**
02 **5** *1 ½* **Shabak Hom (IRE)**[16] 5590 2-9-3 0............................ ChrisCatlin 8 55
(D M Simcock) *hld up: racd keenly: rdn over 2f out: sn wknd* **9/4**[2]
0360 **6** *2 ½* **Coolella (IRE)**[23] 5358 2-8-12 55............................ DarryllHolland 1 44
(J R Weymes) *chsd ldrs tl rdn and wknd over 2f out* **33/1**
6 **7** *5* **Lord Victor**[15] 5637 2-9-3 0............................ AdamKirby 4 39
(A J McCabe) *sn led: rdn and hdd over 2f out: wknd wl over 1f out* **33/1**
8 *11* **Sharakti (IRE)** 2-9-3 0............................ PatCosgrave 7 16
(A J McCabe) *s.i.s: a in rr: rdn 1/2-way: sn wknd* **40/1**
1m 50.19s (-0.31) **Going Correction** -0.20s/f (Stan) **8** Ran SP% **115.6**
Speed ratings (Par 95): **93,92,87,82,81 78,74,64**
toteswingers: 1&2 £3.30, 1&3 £2.40, 2&3 £2.60 CSF £27.20 TOTE £6.70: £1.80, £1.60, £1.30; EX 25.70.
Owner Maelor Racing **Bred** T J Cooper **Trained** Newmarket, Suffolk

FOCUS
This was the slower of the two races over the extended mile by two seconds, and also the most dramatic. Fair form for the track.

NOTEBOOK
Miss Starlight got going too late on debut at Newmarket, but despite hanging a little to the left under pressure, she knew exactly what to do when set alight this time. The win adds yet further to her yard's 25 per cent strike-rate with juveniles this term, and she will consequently warrant a close look whether sent the nursery or novice stakes route next time. (tchd 13-2)
Krymian looked home for all money 1f out but was caught late on. He had been one of the best-backed runners of the evening and was taken to improve markedly on a grass-green debut at Sandown last month. All was going to plan as Fallon kicked on the colt turning in and quickly opened up a 4l lead, but anxious looks over both shoulders at the furlong pole were quickly followed by a shortening of stride from his partner. Some punters might have appreciated greater recourse to the whip from the former champion at that point, but in all fairness the far greater momentum had lain with Miss Starlight from halfway up the straight and it's doubtful she would have been for catching whatever had been tried. (op 9-4)
Exemplary could have done without receiving a shove after the first furlong, but that alone can't explain away an effort which never ignited and didn't represent much of a step up on his Southwell debut. (tchd 9-4, 5-2 in places)
Shabak Hom(IRE) briefly joined Exemplary at the top of the market, but proved too keen under restraint early on and subsided quite disappointingly. (op 3-1 tchd 100-30)

6126 WILLIAM HILL 0800 444040 - QUOTE BONUS25 H'CAP 1m 4f 50y(P)
9:20 (9:20) (Class 6) (0-60,60) 3-Y-O+ **£2,388** (£705; £352) **Stalls** Low

Form RPR
4033 **1** **Bramalea**[4] 5964 4-9-8 **60**............................ AdamKirby 5 69
(B W Duke) *hmpd s: hld up: hdwy 2f out: rdn to ld ins fnl f: r.o* **7/1**
5360 **2** *½* **Seventh Hill**[9] 5790 4-9-3 **55**............................ JimmyQuinn 4 63
(M Blanshard) *wnt rt s: hld up in tch: racd keenly: rdn and ev ch ins fnl f: r.o* **14/1**
0241 **3** *2 ¾* **Our Kes (IRE)**[14] 5680 7-9-5 **57**............................ KFallon 9 61
(P Howling) *prom: n.m.r wl over 6f out: rdn to ld over 1f out: hdd and unable qck ins fnl f* **3/1**[1]
0404 **4** *nk* **Smooth As Silk (IRE)**[29] 5227 4-9-7 **59**............................(b) MickyFenton 1 62
(C R Egerton) *hld up: hdwy over 1f out: r.o: nrst fin* **7/1**
5353 **5** *nk* **Strike Force**[16] 5617 5-9-3 **55**............................(p) GeorgeBaker 2 58
(Miss J Feilden) *hld up: hdwy over 1f out: r.o: nt rch ldrs* **4/1**[3]
2 **6** *3* **Coolnaharan (IRE)**[9] 5790 9-9-2 **54**............................ SaleemGolam 8 52
(Lee Smyth, Ire) *chsd ldrs: rdn over 2f out: wknd ins fnl f* **14/1**
0035 **7** *2 ¼* **Highland Love**[15] 5622 4-9-8 **60**............................ ChrisCatlin 12 55
(J T Stimpson) *chsd ldrs: led over 2f out: rdn and hdd over 1f out: wknd ins fnl f* **12/1**
2003 **8** *2 ½* **Roleplay (IRE)**[14] 5680 4-9-3 **55**............................(b) LukeMorris 6 46
(J M P Eustace) *hmpd s: hld up: hdwy over 3f out: rdn: hung lft and wknd over 1f out* **16/1**
9 *1 ½* **Lugato (GER)**[65] 3837 7-9-2 **54**............................(p) LiamJones 10 42
(Lee Smyth, Ire) *chsd ldr: rdn and ev ch over 2f out: wknd fnl f* **40/1**
0/00 **10** *1 ¾* **Bricks And Porter (IRE)**[14] 5680 9-9-5 **57**............................(vt[1]) PatCosgrave 7 42
(T G McCourt, Ire) *hmpd s: hld up: hdwy over 9f out: edgd lft wl over 6f out: rdn over 4f out: wknd over 2f out* **28/1**
/464 **11** *8* **Emerald Rock (CAN)**[215] 571 4-9-8 **60**............................(p) RichardKingscote 11 33
(Tom Dascombe) *led: rdn and hdd over 2f out: wknd over 1f out* **7/2**[2]
200 **12** *15* **Top Seed (IRE)**[15] 5631 8-9-8 **60**............................ VinceSlattery 3 9
(M S Tuck) *hld up: a in rr: wknd 4f out* **40/1**
2m 39.0s (-2.10) **Going Correction** -0.20s/f (Stan) **12** Ran SP% **127.5**
Speed ratings (Par 101): **99,98,96,96,96 94,92,91,90,89 83,73**
toteswingers: 1&2 £10.10, 1&3 £9.00, 2&3 £9.10 CSF £106.97 CT £365.23 TOTE £8.30: £2.00, £3.70, £1.70; EX 159.70.
Owner P J Cave **Bred** P J Cave **Trained** Lambourn, Berks
■ Stewards' Enquiry : Jimmy Quinn one-day ban: used whip with excessive frequency

FOCUS
They didn't go off too hard in this finale, and the winning time was 2.7 seconds slower than standard. Sound but limited form.
Bricks And Porter(IRE) Official explanation: jockey said gelding hung left
T/Plt: £157.50 to a £1 stake. Pool: £56,726.70. 262.80 winning tickets. T/Qpdt: £30.10 to a £1 stake. Pool: £6,283.70. 154.30 winning tickets. CR

6127 - 6130a (Foreign Racing) - See Raceform Interactive

5927 LONGCHAMP (R-H)
Saturday, September 19

OFFICIAL GOING: Good

6131a PRIX DE FONTENOY (UNRACED COLTS & GELDINGS) 1m
1:05 (1:02) 2-Y-O **£11,650** (£4,660; £3,495; £2,330; £1,165)

RPR
1 **Royal Revival** 2-9-2............................ MGuyon 85+
(A Fabre, France)
2 *2 ½* **Meer Royal (FR)** 2-9-2............................ SPasquier 80
(P Demercastel, France)
3 *¾* **Royal Bench (IRE)** 2-9-2............................ FBlondel 78
(Robert Collet, France)
4 *hd* **Sir Ector (USA)** 2-9-2............................ 77
(J E Pease, France)
5 *3* **Caunton Beck (FR)** 2-9-2............................ IMendizabal 71
(E J O'Neill) *racd in 2nd: pushed along appr st: drvn 1 1/2f out: styd on tl no ex clsng stages* **39/1**[1]
6 *1 ½* **Saristan (FR)** 2-9-2............................ 68
(A De Royer-Dupre, France)
7 *1* **Chapi Chapo (FR)** 2-9-2............................ 65
(B De Montzey, France)
8 *6* **Vivre Libre** 2-9-2............................ 52
(E Lellouche, France)
1m 43.7s (5.30) **8** Ran SP% **2.5**
PARI-MUTUEL (Including 1 Euro stake): WIN 1.80; PL 1.20, 4.30, 4.30;DF 18.90.
Owner Sheikh Mohammed **Bred** Newsells Park Stud Limited **Trained** Chantilly, France

6132a PRIX DU PRINCE DU ORANGE (GROUP 3) 1m 2f
2:45 (2:45) 3-Y-O **£38,835** (£15,534; £11,650; £7,767; £3,883)

RPR
1 **Cirrus Des Aigles (FR)**[21] 5463 3-9-2............................ FBlondel 4 114
(Mme C Barande-Barbe, France) *in tch: disputing 3rd st: rdn to chal appr fnl f: r.o to ld cl home: drvn out* **186/10**
2 *¾* **World Heritage**[55] 4367 3-9-2............................ SPasquier 7 112
(P Bary, France) *racd in 2nd: rdn to ld 1 1/2f out: fnd more whn pressed fnl f tl hdd cl home* **4/5**[1]
3 *1* **Allybar (IRE)**[34] 5084 3-9-2............................ OPeslier 6 110
(C Laffon-Parias, France) *led: pushed along st: rdn and hdd 1 1/2f out: styd on steadily after* **83/10**[3]
4 *hd* **Byword**[34] 5084 3-9-2............................ MGuyon 1 110
(A Fabre, France) *mid-div: disputing 5th on ins st: pushed along over 1 1/2f out: wnt 4th over 1f out: nvr in chalng position* **4/5**[1]
5 *2 ½* **Sri Putra**[34] 5084 3-9-2............................ PhilipRobinson 5 105
(M A Jarvis) *hld up in 7th: pushed along st: no imp on ldrs* **31/10**[2]
6 *hd* **Vesuve (IRE)**[34] 5084 3-9-2............................(b) ACrastus 2 104
(E Lellouche, France) *racd in last: pushed along st: n.d* **44/5**
7 *1 ½* **Almoradi (IRE)**[21] 3-9-2............................ C-PLemaire 3 101
(A De Royer-Dupre, France) *mid-div: disputing 5th st: drvn 1 1/2f out: unable qck* **11/1**
8 *6* **Guest Ville (FR)**[89] 3230 3-9-2............................ TJarnet 8 89
(Mlle S-V Tarrou, France) *in tch: disputing 3rd st: wknd fr 1 1/2f out* **25/1**
2m 6.30s (2.30) **Going Correction** +0.225s/f (Good) **8** Ran SP% **173.7**
Speed ratings: **111,110,109,109,107 107,106,101**
PARI-MUTUEL: WIN 19.60; PL 3.20, 1.60, 2.30; DF 23.80.
Owner J-C A Dupouy **Bred** Yvon Lelimouzin & Benoit Deschamps **Trained** France

NOTEBOOK
Cirrus Des Aigles(FR), one of the most consistent and genuine horses trained in France, was running for the 19th time this season and thoroughly deserved his Group 3 success. Tucked in behind the leader early on, he was brought with a well-timed challenge halfway up the straight and took the advantage with 50 yards left to run. There are no plans for the moment.

World Heritage settled in second place early on and looked the likely winner when taking over the lead halfway up the straight. He wasn't able to fend off the late challenge of the winner, though.
Allybar(IRE) tried to make all the running but had nothing in reserve when tackled with a furlong and a half left to run. He stayed on gamely to take third place off the favourite by a narrow margin.
Byword was once again a disappointing favourite. Sixth turning into the straight, he looked dangerous but was one-paced throughout the final furlong. He is a better horse than he is showing for the moment.
Sri Putra put up a disappointing effort as he had finished ahead of several of these when winning a Group 2 at Deauville. Held up in the early stages, he was ridden along before the straight and found nothing during the final two furlongs. His jockey felt that he had no horse under him on this occasion and he may well be better suited now by 1m4f.

6133a PRIX DES CHENES (GROUP 3) (C&G) 1m

3:15 (3:16) 2-Y-O **£38,835** (£15,534; £11,650; £7,767; £3,883)

RPR

1 **Behkabad (FR)**[45] 2-9-2 .... C-PLemaire 1 108
(J-C Rouget, France) *in tch: disputing last st: rdn and 3rd over 1f out: qckn fnl f to chal cl home: led on line* **7/5**[1]

2 3/4 **Arasin (IRE)**[17] 2-9-2 .... GMosse 4 106
(P Bary, France) *racd in 2nd: rdn and chalng 1 1/2f out: led briefly cl home tl hdd on line* **16/5**[3]

3 3/4 **Emirates Dream (USA)**[13] 5708 2-9-2 .... OPeslier 2 105
(Saeed Bin Suroor) *led: pushed along 2f out: rdn 1 1/2f out: r.o tl hdd cl home: kpt on* **17/10**[2]

4 6 **Black Snowflake (USA)**[14] 5659 2-9-2 .... AhmedAjtebi 3 92
(Saeed Bin Suroor) *racd in last: disputing last st: sn pushed along: unable qck fr over 1 1/2f out* **17/10**[2]

5 4 **Averroes (IRE)**[19] 5499 2-9-2 .... PhilipRobinson 5 83
(C G Cox) *in tch: disputing last st: pushed along 2f out: sn one pce* **31/5**

1m 39.3s (0.90) **Going Correction** +0.225s/f (Good) **5 Ran SP% 153.4**
Speed ratings: **106,105,104,98,94**
PARI-MUTUEL: WIN 2.40; PL 1.40, 1.70; SF 5.20.
Owner H H Aga Khan **Bred** H H The Aga Khan's Studs S C **Trained** Pau, France

NOTEBOOK
Behkabad(FR), who was given a fine ride by his jockey, looks a real classic prospect for next year. Held up in the early stages, he was a little outpaced early in the straight before coming with a late challenge. He took the advantage in the dying stages of the mile, will definitely stay further and may not be seen out again this year. If he does reappear it will be in the Criterium International at Saint-Cloud, and he is already been talked about as a horse for the Prix du Jockey-Club next year.
Arasin(IRE), beaten by Behkabad at Deauville in August, again found the winner too strong. Always well up, he started to challenge for the lead early in the straight and took it up running into the final furlong. He was then run out of things in the final strides.
Emirates Dream(USA) tried to make all the running and set a decent pace. Still going well halfway up the straight, he looked the likely winner at the furlong marker, but he didn't quite get home. It was a genuine performance and there is surely more improvement in this lightly raced colt.
Black Snowflake(USA) was always in fourth position and played no hand at all in the finish.
Averroes(IRE) hung a lot during the race. He was still there coming out of the final turn but a beaten force soon after. He certainly didn't show his best here, and connections felt he is better suited to a straight track.

5303 HAMILTON (R-H)

Sunday, September 20

OFFICIAL GOING: Good (good to firm in places on straight; good to soft in places on the loop; 8.2)
Races over a mile plus were approximately 70 yards shorter than the official distances due to rail realignment to provide fresh ground.
Wind: Fresh, across Weather: Sunny

6134 TOTEPLACEPOT NURSERY H'CAP 6f 5y

2:10 (2:10) (Class 4) (0-85,83) 2-Y-O **£6,476** (£1,927; £963; £481) **Stalls** Low

Form RPR

2135 1 **Emerald Girl (IRE)**[37] 4975 2-8-7 **69** .... PaulHanagan 3 73
(R A Fahey) *trckd ldrs: rdn and edgd rt fr over 2f out: led ins fnl f: styd on wl* **7/2**[2]

2116 2 1 **Farmers Wish (IRE)**[36] 5022 2-9-3 **79** .... FrancisNorton 9 80
(J L Spearing) *led: rdn 2f out: hdd ins fnl f: kpt on fin* **5/1**

1404 3 1/2 **Reeds Bay (IRE)**[14] 5692 2-9-3 **79** .... (b) AdrianTNicholls 4 79
(E S McMahon) *hld up: rdn over 2f out: hdwy over 1f out: kpt on wl fnl f* **9/1**

4006 4 4 **Kristen Jane (USA)**[6] 5945 2-7-5 **60** oh7 .... MatthewLawson(7) 7 48
(Miss L A Perratt) *trckd ldrs: drvn 1/2-way: rallied and ch appr fnl f: wknd ins fnl f* **40/1**

6400 5 3/4 **Little Perisher**[2] 6048 2-9-6 **82** .... AlanMunro 5 67
(A P Jarvis) *bhd and sn outpcd: swtchd lft and hdwy 2f out: kpt on fnl f: no imp* **25/1**

221 6 3 1/4 **Dance For Julie (IRE)**[15] 5668 2-8-13 **80** .... PatrickDonaghy(5) 2 56
(P C Haslam) *dwlt: hld up: hdwy and cl up 1/2-way: wknd over 1f out* **3/1**[1]

12 7 2 3/4 **Bow Beaver (USA)**[38] 4939 2-9-4 **83** .... FrederikTylicki(3) 6 50
(J Howard Johnson) *cl up untl rdn and wknd over 1f out* **4/1**[3]

6040 8 3 1/2 **Gold Diamond (USA)**[17] 5589 2-8-5 **67** .... JoeFanning 8 24
(M Johnston) *dwlt: bhd: drvn 1/2-way: nvr on terms* **7/1**

3300 9 2 **Cambuslang (IRE)**[39] 4895 2-7-13 **61** oh1 ow1 .... (p) DuranFentiman 1 12
(I Semple) *prom: ev ch over 2f out: rdn and wknd wl over 1f out* **66/1**

1m 12.2s **Going Correction** +0.025s/f (Good) **9 Ran SP% 114.2**
Speed ratings (Par 97): **101,99,99,93,92 88,84,80,77**
toteswingers: 1&2 £5.50, 1&3 £7.90, 2&3 £8.60 CSF £20.79 CT £144.08 TOTE £5.30: £1.60, £2.00, £2.30; EX 25.80.
Owner M Wynne **Bred** Tally-Ho Stud **Trained** Musley Bank, N Yorks

FOCUS
A fair nursery and the form is sound.

NOTEBOOK
Emerald Girl(IRE), who was towards the top of the betting, carried over her stable's good run of form from Ayr. She hadn't been suited to the demands of Catterick last time out but proved far more at home on this more conventional track. The stiffer finish helped a great deal and she saw her race out particularly well. (op 100-30 tchd 4-1)
Farmers Wish(IRE), who was highly tried last time out, was back over the right trip in the right grade and returned to her best. She looked very fit beforehand, travelled well on the front end and found plenty for pressure, just getting outbattled in the finish. (tchd 11-2)
Reeds Bay(IRE) was staying on really well at the finish, as one might expect of a colt who stays 7f. He clearly needs a stiff track to be effective over this distance. (op 8-1)
Kristen Jane(USA) was racing from 7lb out of the handicap, ran her best race to date. She didn't quiet see the 6f trip out but should be able to go close off her current mark on an easier track.
Little Perisher, making a quick reappearance after finishing down the field at Ayr two days earlier, hasn't progressed since the spring and is fully exposed. (op 33-1)
Dance For Julie(IRE), a winner in soft ground at Thirsk last time, had run well enough on a quicker surface before that, so it's difficult to say that the conditions were to blame for this disappointing effort. However, she did race nearest the stands' rail, which might have been a disadvantage.
Official explanation: jockey said filly ran flat (tchd 100-30 in places)
Bow Beaver(USA) didn't see it out and was another who failed to run his race. (op 6-1)

6135 TOTEPOOL SUPPORTS VARIETY CLUB CONDITIONS STKS 6f 5y

2:40 (2:40) (Class 2) 3-Y-O+

£12,462 (£3,732; £1,866; £934; £466; £234) **Stalls** Low

Form RPR

1323 1 **Eton Rifles (IRE)**[14] 5695 4-8-9 88 .... FrederikTylicki 7 96+
(J Howard Johnson) *w ldr: led wl over 1f out: drvn out fnl f* **6/4**[1]

5000 2 1 **Beckermet (IRE)**[8] 5878 7-8-9 96 .... RoystonFfrench 5 93+
(R F Fisher) *trckd ldrs: rdn over 2f out: chsd wnr ins fnl f: r.o* **10/1**

00-5 3 1 1/4 **Major Cadeaux**[127] 2076 5-9-2 114 .... PaulHanagan 9 96+
(R A Fahey) *slt ld to wl over 1f out: sn rdn: lost 2nd and kpt on same pce fnl f* **7/4**[2]

2001 4 3/4 **Sea Salt**[15] 5675 6-8-9 70 .... KellyHarrison 4 87?
(R E Barr) *bhd tl hdwy over 1f out: kpt on fnl f: nrst fin* **50/1**

6045 5 5 **Pawan (IRE)**[40] 4885 9-8-10 83 ow1 .... (b) AnnStokell 1 73
(Miss A Stokell) *outpcd and bhd: sme hdwy over 1f out: nvr able to chal* **50/1**

300 6 2 3/4 **City Dancer (IRE)**[22] 5420 3-8-2 93 .... FrancisNorton 6 59
(A Berry) *trckd ldrs: effrt 2f out: wknd over 1f out* **7/1**[3]

7 2 1/4 **Fourtowns Flyer (IRE)**[49] 4573 5-8-9 0 .... TonyHamilton 2 57
(Lee Smyth, Ire) *prom: hung rt thrght: wknd wl over 1f out* **100/1**

0003 8 8 **Burnwynd Boy**[2] 6050 4-8-9 77 .... RobertHavlin 8 33
(D Nicholls) *w ldrs: rdn and lost pl over 2f out: sn n.d* **20/1**

6-40 9 5 **Garnica (FR)**[113] 2483 6-9-2 107 .... AdrianTNicholls 3 25
(D Nicholls) *dwlt: hld up: pushed along over 2f out: sn wknd* **14/1**

1m 11.85s (-0.35) **Going Correction** +0.025s/f (Good)
WFA 3 from 4yo+ 2lb **9 Ran SP% 114.3**
Speed ratings (Par 109): **103,101,100,99,92 88,85,75,68**
toteswingers: 1&2 £4.90, 1&3 £1.90, 2&3 £4.70 CSF £16.84 TOTE £2.80: £1.20, £2.40, £1.30; EX 25.30.
Owner Transcend Bloodstock LLP **Bred** Grangecon Stud **Trained** Billy Row, Co Durham

FOCUS
An interesting conditions event. The time, and the prominenece of the fourth, undermine the form.

NOTEBOOK
Eton Rifles(IRE) looked to have plenty to do strictly on the ratings but with one or two below their best, he probably didn't need to improve to come out on top. He arrived here at the top of his game, having finished third last time out in a handicap at York that is working out particularly well, and, always towards the fore, he saw the trip out strongly. The handicapper ought not to put him much at all, as Sea Salt, who is rated just 70, finished pretty close in fourth, and there should be more to come from him, especially on softer ground. (op 2-1 tchd 9-4 in places)
Beckermet(IRE), who is on a two-year-long losing run, appreciated the drop in class and ran a better race than of late. He remains too high in the handicap on this evidence, though, as Eton Rifles, who is rated 8lb inferior, beat him off levels. (op 14-1)
Major Cadeaux has moved stables and was having his first start since finishing fifth in the Lockinge. Racing over a trip short of his best, this looked like a prep race for bigger prizes later this autumn, and as such it wasn't a terrible effort, as he was well up there until getting tired in the closing stages. He should come on plenty for the outing. (op 13-8 tchd 15-8 in places)
Sea Salt performance doesn't do much for the value of the form but it was fine effort from the gelding, who not too long ago was contesting sellers. (op 40-1)
Garnica(FR), running for the first time since finishing last in a Group 3 at Haydock back in May, had a leading chance on the ratings, but he was desperately weak in the market beforehand and ran accordingly. He needs soft ground to be seen at his best. (op 10-1)

6136 E B F SCOTTISH BUILDING SOCIETY MAIDEN STKS 1m 65y

3:10 (3:10) (Class 5) 2-Y-O **£3,885** (£1,156; £577; £288) **Stalls** High

Form RPR

4 1 **Think Its All Over (USA)**[38] 4939 2-9-3 0 .... MickyFenton 9 75+
(T P Tate) *trckd ldrs: rdn over 3f out: led over 1f out: styd on strly* **3/1**[2]

5 2 1 1/4 **Pena Dorada (IRE)**[23] 5408 2-9-3 0 .... AndrewElliott 6 72+
(A P Jarvis) *in tch: rdn over 2f out: swtchd lft and hdwy over 1f out: styd on strly fnl f: tk 2nd cl home* **40/1**

6523 3 hd **Sabander Bleue (IRE)**[11] 5770 2-9-3 72 .... AlanMunro 1 72
(M R Channon) *trckd ldrs: rdn and hung rt over 2f out: chsd wnr ins fnl f: lost 2nd cl home* **4/1**[3]

2204 4 1 3/4 **Layla's Boy**[15] 5682 2-9-3 76 .... PaulHanagan 7 68
(R A Fahey) *pressed ldr: disp ld and edgd rt over 2f out: one pce appr fnl f* **9/4**[1]

04 5 3 1/4 **Starry Mount**[20] 5512 2-9-3 0 .... RobertHavlin 3 61
(A B Haynes) *hld up: rdn and outpcd over 3f out: rallied over 1f out: no imp* **25/1**

5 6 1 **Danceintothelight**[21] 5466 2-9-3 0 .... PhillipMakin 2 59
(K A Ryan) *s.i.s: hld up: rdn 3f out: edgd lft and outpcd fnl 2f* **14/1**

0 7 1 **Moonbalej**[23] 5401 2-9-3 0 .... JoeFanning 8 57
(M Johnston) *led: rdn over 2f out: edgd lft and hdd over 1f out: sn btn* **6/1**

30 8 nk **Decimus Meridius (IRE)**[23] 5407 2-9-0 0 .... FrederikTylicki(3) 4 56
(J Howard Johnson) *in tch: rdn 3f out: swtchd lft 2f out: sn btn* **12/1**

5 9 3 1/4 **Elie Shore**[23] 5393 2-8-12 0 .... RoystonFfrench 5 44
(P C Haslam) *towards rr: drvn over 3f out: sn wknd* **50/1**

1m 48.11s (-0.29) **Going Correction** -0.175s/f (Firm) **9 Ran SP% 112.7**
Speed ratings (Par 95): **94,92,92,90,87 86,85,85,82**
toteswingers: 1&2 £21.60, 1&3 £3.20, 2&3 £20.60 CSF £113.82 TOTE £3.80: £1.30, £7.60, £1.60; EX 114.20.
Owner Mrs Fitri Hay **Bred** B Wayne Hughes **Trained** Tadcaster, N Yorks

FOCUS
An ordinary maiden rated primarily round the third.

NOTEBOOK
Think Its All Over(USA) didn't shape badly on his debut and Derby and Racing Post Trophy entries suggested he was well thought of, so it shouldn't have come as a surprise that he found the required improvement to win second time up. A US-bred son of Tiznow, the winner ground this out in determined style, seeing the trip out strongly, but he has a way to go to justify his Group race entries. (op 4-1 tchd 11-4)
Pena Dorada(IRE), who had been well held on his debut at Thirsk, responded well to pressure here and flew home once switched to the outside to challenge. Stamina looks to be his forte. (op 33-1 tchd 50-1)
Sabander Bleue(IRE) ran another solid race in defeat, but he won't come into his own until he tackles a trip next year. (op 7-2)
Layla's Boy didn't see the trip out as well as the first three and perhaps he doesn't really want to go much further than 7f at this stage of his career. (op 6-4)

Moonbalej, who was stepping up in trip, looked interesting on paper. However, having been given a positive ride, he hung badly under pressure, looking far from straightforward. Official explanation: jockey said colt hung left-handed in straight (op 8-1)

6137 TOTEEXACTA PREMIER CLAIMING STKS 1m 1f 36y

3:40 (3:40) (Class 4) 3-5-Y-O **£5,180** (£1,541; £770; £384) **Stalls** High

Form				RPR
0064	1		**Admiral Dundas (IRE)**[20] 5510 4-9-5 75 JoeFanning 6	84
			(W Jarvis) *trckd ldrs: effrt over 2f out: led ins fnl f: kpt on* **7/2**[2]	
1201	2	*hd*	**Sunnyside Tom (IRE)**[27] 5305 5-9-4 84 PaulHanagan 4	83
			(R A Fahey) *trckd ldr: led over 2f out: rdn and edgd lft: hdd ins fnl f: rallied* **11/10**[1]	
33	3	*2*	**First Bay (IRE)**[27] 5305 3-8-13 0 FrederikTylicki(3) 3	83
			(J Howard Johnson) *hld up: rdn and outpcd over 3f out: rallied over 1f out: kpt on: nt pce of first two* **7/2**[2]	
5245	4	*12*	**Gaily Noble (IRE)**[29] 4649 3-9-4 82 SebSanders 1	61
			(A B Haynes) *trckd ldrs tl rdn and wknd over 2f out* **17/2**[3]	
0000	5	*2*	**Jack Junior (USA)**[14] 5694 5-8-13 84 AdrianTNicholls 2	46
			(D Nicholls) *led to over 2f out: hung rt and wknd over 1f out* **12/1**	
-000	6	*2*	**Cold Quest (USA)**[19] 5551 5-9-6 76 PhillipMakin 5	50
			(Miss L A Perratt) *hld up: outpcd over 3f out: rallied over 2f out: wknd over 1f out* **40/1**	

1m 56.68s (-3.02) **Going Correction** -0.175s/f (Firm)
WFA 3 from 4yo+ 5lb **6** Ran SP% **112.7**
Speed ratings (Par 105): **106,105,104,93,91 89**
toteswingers: 1&2 £1.70, 1&3 £2.20, 2&3 £1.80 CSF £7.85 TOTE £5.30: £2.10, £1.40; EX 9.60.
Owner Dr J Walker **Bred** John Hussey And Stephen Hillen **Trained** Newmarket, Suffolk

FOCUS
A fair claimer in which the winner is rated to his best form of the past year or so.

6138 TOTESUPER7 BUTTONHOOK H'CAP 1m 5f 9y

4:10 (4:10) (Class 3) (0-95,96) 3-Y-0+
£10,592 (£3,172; £1,586; £793; £396; £198) **Stalls** High

Form				RPR
1010	1		**Braveheart Move (IRE)**[30] 5230 3-9-1 91 SebSanders 5	98+
			(Sir Mark Prescott) *hld up in tch: drvn over 2f out: led ins fnl f: hld on wl* **5/1**[3]	
5-31	2	*nk*	**Merchant Of Dubai**[23] 5402 4-10-0 95 KFallon 9	102+
			(G A Swinbank) *prom: stdy hdwy over 4f out: drvn to ld over 2f out: hdd ins fnl f: kpt on: hld nr fin* **9/2**[2]	
1435	3	*1*	**Gordonsville**[30] 5235 6-9-1 82 DanielTudhope 2	87
			(J S Goldie) *hld up: rdn over 3f out: hdwy 2f out: kpt on fnl f: nrst fin* **15/2**	
3210	4	*½*	**Just Lille (IRE)**[9] 5823 6-9-8 92 (p) JackMitchell(3) 8	96
			(Mrs A Duffield) *prom: drvn over 2f out: kpt on u.p ins fnl f* **11/1**	
1121	5	*1*	**Petrovsky**[7] 5909 3-9-6 96 6ex JoeFanning 7	99
			(M Johnston) *led: rdn and hdd over 2f out: outpcd ins fnl f* **5/2**[1]	
2500	6	*shd*	**Chookie Hamilton**[9] 5837 5-8-4 76 oh4 PatrickDonaghy(5) 3	79
			(I Semple) *hld up: hdwy and prom over 2f out: sn rdn: swtchd lft ent fnl f: kpt on* **40/1**	
1534	7	*1½*	**Antigua Sunrise (IRE)**[36] 5037 3-8-1 77 PaulHanagan 10	78
			(R A Fahey) *trckd ldrs: drvn 3f out: no ex fnl f* **9/1**	
2142	8	*hd*	**Sanctuary**[15] 5671 3-8-5 81 RoystonFfrench 6	81
			(B Smart) *chsd ldr: rdn and ev ch over 2f out: wknd ins fnl f* **13/2**	
5000	9	*1¾*	**Hindu Kush (IRE)**[15] 5656 4-9-9 90 AdrianTNicholls 4	88
			(D Nicholls) *hld up: rdn 3f out: sn outpcd: nvr a factor* **10/1**	

2m 50.51s (-3.39) **Going Correction** -0.175s/f (Firm)
WFA 3 from 4yo+ 9lb **9** Ran SP% **118.4**
Speed ratings (Par 107): **103,102,102,101,101 101,100,100,99**
toteswingers: 1&2 £6.20, 1&3 £8.80, 2&3 £6.40 CSF £28.56 CT £169.96 TOTE £7.50: £2.20, £1.70, £2.30; EX 43.00.
Owner Moyglare Stud Farm Ltd **Bred** Moyglare Stud Farm Ltd **Trained** Newmarket, Suffolk
■ Stewards' Enquiry : Seb Sanders two-day ban: used whip with excessive frequency (Oct 5-6)

FOCUS
A good handicap and the form looks fairly sound. The front pair progressed.

NOTEBOOK
Braveheart Move(IRE), representing a stable with a fine record at this track, returning to form on this drop back in distance. A difficult ride, he tends to be keen in the early stages and then takes plenty of driving at the business end, but as a result Seb Sanders is a good partner for him, and under a strong ride (which resulted in a whip ban) the colt got up in the closing stages to win ever so slightly cosily. A gutsy sort, he remains lightly raced and open to further improvement, especially as a four-year-old. Official explanation: two-day ban: used whip with excessive frequency and down the shoulder in the forehand position (Oct 5-6) (op 7-1)
Merchant Of Dubai ◆, unlucky in running when a beaten favourite in this race last year, lost little in defeat on his return visit. He ideally likes plenty of cut in the ground and, having had only three starts this season, he'll be fresher than most for an autumn campaign. It wouldn't be a surprise to see him return to the winner's enclosure soon. (op 13-2)
Gordonsville can usually be relied upon to run his race, and even though the ground wasn't as fast as he would like it over the whole track, he again posted a sound effort from off the pace. (op 7-1)
Just Lille(IRE), a winner three times and runner-up twice in her previous five visits to this track, couldn't keep that record going, but she still ran a fine race to finish fourth as she didn't get the clearest of runs. (tchd 12-1)
Petrovsky was able to set a sensible pace. However, he was tackled from two furlongs out and, despite battling away, didn't quite see his race out, and perhaps the combination of a longer trip and easier ground found him out. (op 9-4)
Chookie Hamilton finished well once switched to the outside to challenge. He didn't run badly considering he was 4lb out of the handicap. (op 50-1)

6139 TOTESWINGER H'CAP 1m 3f 16y

4:40 (4:41) (Class 5) (0-70,69) 3-Y-O **£3,238** (£963; £481; £240) **Stalls** High

Form				RPR
4111	1		**Valid Point (IRE)**[17] 5617 3-9-2 67 SebSanders 1	80+
			(Sir Mark Prescott) *cl up: led over 3f out: edgd rt and drew clr fr 2f out: eased nr fin* **6/5**[1]	
0024	2	*3¾*	**Regal Lyric (IRE)**[21] 5469 3-8-11 62 MickyFenton 4	65
			(T P Tate) *hld up: hdwy and prom over 4f out: chsd wnr over 2f out: kpt on fnl f: no imp* **8/1**[3]	
3305	3	*2½*	**Acquavella**[30] 5205 3-9-2 67 PaulHanagan 6	66
			(R A Fahey) *set modest pce: rdn and hdd over 3f out: kpt on same pce fnl 2f* **11/1**	
4304	4	*nk*	**Bow To No One (IRE)**[37] 4994 3-8-13 64 AndrewElliott 8	62
			(A P Jarvis) *in tch: outpcd over 2f out: kpt on ins fnl f: no imp* **14/1**	
0512	5	*½*	**My Girl Jode**[59] 4230 3-8-12 63 KFallon 2	61
			(M H Tompkins) *t.k.h early: trckd ldrs: effrt over 2f out: one pce over 1f out* **9/4**[2]	
4105	6	*½*	**Carter**[25] 5331 3-8-9 60 TonyHamilton 3	57
			(W M Brisbourne) *t.k.h: hld up on outside: rdn over 3f out: no imp fnl 2f* **16/1**	
4030	7	*1½*	**Black River Falls (USA)**[9] 5838 3-8-4 55 oh3 (b) RoystonFfrench 5	49
			(I Semple) *dwlt: sn in tch: rdn and outpcd fnl 2f* **16/1**	
0200	8	*8*	**Real Desire**[20] 5524 3-8-7 58 oh1 ow3 (b) TomEaves 9	39
			(I Semple) *bhd: struggling over 3f out: sn btn* **50/1**	

2m 23.95s (-1.65) **Going Correction** -0.175s/f (Firm) **8** Ran SP% **116.1**
Speed ratings (Par 101): **99,96,94,94,93 93,92,86**
toteswingers: 1&2 £6.20, 1&3 £8.80, 2&3 £6.40 CSF £12.27 CT £74.08 TOTE £2.20: £1.10, £1.60, £2.00; EX 11.80.
Owner W E Sturt - Osborne House **Bred** Pier House Stud **Trained** Newmarket, Suffolk

FOCUS
A moderate handicap, run at a steady pace. The progressive Valid Point was value for extra and there is more to come from him.

6140 TOTETRIFECTA H'CAP 6f 5y

5:10 (5:10) (Class 5) (0-70,68) 3-Y-O **£3,238** (£963; £481; £240) **Stalls** Low

Form				RPR
2134	1		**Cheyenne Red (IRE)**[25] 5335 3-9-1 65 PhillipMakin 1	71
			(M Dods) *hld up: effrt and hdwy over 1f out: led wl ins fnl f: r.o wl* **9/2**[1]	
5112	2	*1¼*	**Future Gem**[16] 5626 3-8-12 65 (p) FrederikTylicki(3) 4	67
			(A Dickman) *prom: rdn over 2f out: styd on fnl f: tk 2nd cl home* **6/1**[3]	
3053	3	*nk*	**Lost In Paris (IRE)**[16] 5624 3-8-7 57 (b) DuranFentiman 8	58
			(T D Easterby) *t.k.h: led: clr over 1f out: hdd and no ex wl ins fnl f: lost 2nd cl home* **7/1**	
6202	4	*½*	**Two Turtle Doves (IRE)**[32] 5158 3-8-8 58 RobertHavlin 3	58
			(M Mullineaux) *in tch: rdn over 2f out: kpt on u.p ins fnl f* **8/1**	
0224	5	*5*	**Unbelievable Jeff**[86] 3342 3-8-4 54 oh6 PaulHanagan 6	39
			(J Balding) *in tch: rdn over 2f out: hdwy over 1f out: sn no imp* **5/1**[2]	
3021	6	*3¼*	**Liberty Trail (IRE)**[27] 5304 3-9-4 68 TomEaves 9	43
			(I Semple) *wnt rt s: cl up tl rdn and wknd wl over 1f out* **10/1**	
1144	7	*2¼*	**Crystallize**[89] 3243 3-9-3 67 SebSanders 2	35
			(A B Haynes) *hld up: effrt and swtchd rt 2f out: sn rdn and btn* **12/1**	
0302	8	*hd*	**Kings Ace (IRE)**[24] 5362 3-8-10 60 (v) AndrewElliott 7	28
			(A P Jarvis) *trckd ldrs tl wknd over 2f out* **5/1**[2]	
01	9	*9*	**Sleepy Blue Ocean**[102] 2820 3-9-1 65 KFallon 5	6
			(J Balding) *bhd: edgd rt thrght: no ch fr 1/2-way* **8/1**	

1m 12.2s **Going Correction** +0.025s/f (Good) **9** Ran SP% **117.3**
Speed ratings (Par 101): **101,99,98,98,91 87,84,84,72**
toteswingers: 1&2 £7.80, 1&3 £7.70, 2&3 £11.20 CSF £32.02 CT £189.24 TOTE £5.40: £1.80, £2.30, £2.80; EX 30.50 Trifecta £198.70 Part won. Pool: £268.60 - 0.90 winning units. Place 6: £25.71, Place 5: £9.82..
Owner The Westerners **Bred** Crandon Park Stud **Trained** Denton, Co Durham

FOCUS
Another moderate handicap, run at a good pace. The form should prove reliable.
Unbelievable Jeff Official explanation: jockey said gelding hung left throughout
Sleepy Blue Ocean Official explanation: trainer said colt had a breathing problem
T/Plt: £22.30 to a £1 stake. Pool: £56,547.74. 1,847.31 winning tickets. T/Qpdt: £7.50 to a £1 stake. Pool: £3,457.80. 337.50 winning tickets. RY

6141 - 6147a (Foreign Racing) - See Raceform Interactive

CARPENTRAS
Sunday, September 20

OFFICIAL GOING: Very soft

6148a PRIX DE VELLERON (CLAIMER) 7f 110y

1:30 (1:30) 2-Y-O **£3,883** (£1,553; £1,165; £777; £388)

			RPR
1		**Mythie**[14] 5713 2-8-8 J-MSanchez	60
		(E J O'Neill) *hdwy 3f out: led dist: edgd rt: r.o: claimed by K Borgel for Ecurie Winning 10:252 euros* **77/10**[1]	
2	*2*	**J'Assume (FR)**[44] 2-9-7 (b) JCaldero	68
		(K Borgel, France)	
3	*4*	**L'Inconscient (FR)** 2-9-4 (b) RCampos	56
		(K Borgel, France)	
4	*6*	**Destination Finale**[65] 2-9-1 (p)	39
		(C Boutin, France)	
5	*¾*	**Ficogrande (FR)**[71] 2-8-8 (b)	30
		(C Boutin, France)	
6	*nse*	**Dear Cat (FR)** 2-8-8	30
		(R Martens, France)	
7	*8*	**Sea Country (FR)**[71] 2-9-1	18
		(J Rossi, France)	
8	*¾*	**Swanee River (FR)** 2-9-1 (b)	16
		(M Pimbonnet, France)	

8 Ran SP% **11.5**
PARI-MUTUEL (including one euro stakes): WIN 8.70; PL 2.30, 1.80,2.00; DF 13.90.
Owner Ballygallon Stud Ltd **Bred** Ballygallon Stud Ltd **Trained** Southwell, Notts

6149a PRIX DE MONTEUX (CLAIMER) 1m 5f 165y

3:00 (3:00) 3-Y-O **£3,883** (£1,553; £1,165; £777; £388)

			RPR
1		**Girl Of Star (FR)** 3-8-12 FPardon	59
		(F Pardon, France)	
2	*2*	**Victorian Tycoon (IRE)**[11] 5784 3-9-2 (b) J-MSanchez	60
		(E J O'Neill)	
3	*7*	**Majoran (FR)** 3-9-2 (b) GMillet	50
		(T Larriviere, France)	
4	*shd*	**La Tride (FR)** 3-8-12	45
		(S Labate, France)	
5	*2*	**Metal Princess** 3-8-8	38
		(K Borgel, France)	
6	*10*	**Wild Demon (FR)**[382] 3-9-3	32
		(C Boutin, France)	
7	*½*	**River Of Glory (ITY)** 3-8-11	26
		(J Heloury, Italy)	
8	*4*	**Jacopin (FR)** 3-9-2 (b)	25
		(T Larriviere, France)	
9	*5*	**Take The Race (FR)** 3-8-11	12
		(W J Cargeeg, France)	
10	*dist*	**Teenie Girl (FR)** 3-8-8	—
		(W J Cargeeg, France)	

11 **Impression Sunrise (FR)**[115] 3-8-11 ... —
(F Vermeulen, France)
2m 59.99s (179.99) **11** Ran
PARI-MUTUEL: WIN 4.10; PL 1.80, 2.10, 1.60; DF 8.30.
Owner F Pardon **Bred** Earl De La Vastine & Mme Colette Dibatista **Trained** France

5739 CRAON (R-H)
Sunday, September 20

OFFICIAL GOING: Good to soft

6150a PRIX ONDE AMERE 1m 4f
1:50 (1:50) 3-Y-O **£12,621** (£5,049; £3,786; £2,524; £1,262)

RPR
1 **Voodoo's Son (FR)**[85] 3418 3-9-4 ... ACrastus 94
(D Sepulchre, France)
2 *1* **Sagarian (FR)**[23] 3-9-4 ... MickaelForest 92
(J-C Rouget, France)
3 *2* **Gold And Song (FR)** 3-9-4 ... THuet 89
(A Couetil, France)
4 *½* **Malavita** 3-9-1 ... 85
(H-A Pantall, France)
5 *3* **Gifted Icon (IRE)** 3-9-1 ... 81
(N Clement, France)
6 *3* **Lord Des Evees (FR)**[190] 845 3-9-4 ... 79
(J Boisnard, France)
7 *3* **Emitard (FR)**[178] 3-9-4 ... 74
(Mme M Verdu-Estrabol, France)
8 *8* **Riotista (IRE)**[22] 5462 3-8-8 ... JAuge 51
(E J O'Neill) *pressed ldr early: settled on ins disputing 2nd: pushed along over 2f out: 3rd st: sn rdn and wknd* **64/1**[1]
9 *15* **Holiday Maker** 3-8-8 ... 27
(H-A Pantall, France)
10 *dist* **Kabira (FR)** 3-8-11 ...(b) —
(A Couetil, France)
2m 34.37s (154.37) **10** Ran SP% **1.5**
PARI-MUTUEL (including one euro stakes): WIN 4.30; PL 1.40, 1.20,2.10; DF 7.10.
Owner J Le Helloco **Bred** Mme D Sepulchre & J Le Helloco **Trained** France

4582 DUSSELDORF (R-H)
Sunday, September 20

OFFICIAL GOING: Good

6151a WETTENLEIP-JUNIOREN PREIS (LISTED RACE) 1m
3:20 (3:30) 2-Y-O **£11,650** (£4,272; £2,330; £1,165)

RPR
1 **Go Country (FR)** 2-9-0 ... FilipMinarik 3 99
(P Schiergen, Germany) **73/10**
2 *¾* **Barzini (GER)** 2-9-0 ... RPiechulek 5 97
(Uwe Ostmann, Germany) **8/1**
3 *1 ¼* **Prakasa (FR)** 2-8-13 ... ASuborics 2 94
(W Hickst, Germany) **19/5**[3]
4 *½* **Pallantes Cross**[15] 5681 2-9-0 ... RobertWinston 7 94
(M Johnston) *racd in 4th: clsd up on outside and 3rd st: rdn wl over 1f out: lost 3rd last strides* **29/10**[2]
5 *hd* **Kite Hunter (IRE)** 2-9-2 ... AHelfenbein 6 95
(Mario Hofer, Germany) **47/10**
6 *1 ½* **Port Cros (GER)** 2-8-12 ... JBojko 1 88
(J Hirschberger, Germany) **8/5**[1]
7 *8* **Mlle Lando (GER)** 2-8-13 ... APietsch 8 71
(M Rulec, Germany) **12/1**
1m 36.94s (-4.22) **7** Ran SP% **133.3**
TOTE: WIN 83; PL 25, 25, 18; SF 755.
Owner M Jaber **Bred** R Ernst & J Ince **Trained** Germany

4129 FRANKFURT (L-H)
Sunday, September 20

OFFICIAL GOING: Soft

6152a EURO-CUP (GROUP 3) 1m 2f
3:40 (3:45) 3-Y-O+ **£31,068** (£9,709; £4,854; £2,913)

RPR
1 **Querari (GER)**[21] 3-8-10 ... JVictoire 1 109
(A Wohler, Germany) *mde all: clr 1f out: r.o wl* **9/5**[2]
2 *2 ½* **Adolfina (GER)**[22] 5461 4-8-12 ... KKerekes 8 100
(W Figge, Germany) *hld up in rr: last tl hdwy 3f out: 4th on wd outside st: rdn over 1f out: chsd wnr fnl f: no imp* **138/10**
3 *½* **Norderney (GER)**[50] 4578 3-8-7 ... JiriPalik 5 100
(P Schiergen, Germany) *disp 4th early: dropped bk to 6th on far side: last st: r.o fr over 1f out: nvr nr to chal* **9/2**[3]
4 *nk* **Walzertraum (USA)**[22] 5461 4-9-2 ... AGoritz 7 102
(J Hirschberger, Germany) *disp 4th: 5th st: one pce fr over 1f out* **6/4**[1]
5 *3* **Ephigenie (GER)**[42] 3-8-7 ... ABest 4 93
(T Mundry, Germany) *disp 2nd: 2nd st: rdn and btn wl over 1f out* **58/10**
6 *½* **Daveron (GER)**[28] 5296 4-8-12 ... IMendizabal 6 91
(A Trybuhl, Germany) *dwlt s: sn disputing 2nd: lost pl on fnl turn: 6th st: sn btn* **17/2**
7 *3 ½* **Glad Panther**[19] 5563 3-8-12 ... DPorcu 3 90
(Uwe Ostmann, Germany) *disp 4th: 5th st: sn btn* **123/10**
2m 14.07s (5.50)
WFA 3 from 4yo 6lb **7** Ran SP% **133.4**
TOTE: WIN 28; PL 13, 26, 20; SF 334.
Owner Stiftung Gestut Fahrhof **Bred** Stiftung Gestut Fahrhof **Trained** Germany

3185 SAN SIRO (R-H)
Sunday, September 20

OFFICIAL GOING: Good

6153a PREMIO FEDERICO TESIO (GROUP 3) 1m 3f
3:50 (4:12) 3-Y-O+ **£42,136** (£19,563; £10,971; £5,485)

RPR
1 **Voila Ici (IRE)**[68] 3969 4-9-1 ... MDemuro 8 114
(V Caruso, Italy) *hld up in 7th tl hdwy on outside 1/2-way: 3rd st: narrow ldr 3f out: 2 l clr 1 1/2f out: pushed out and r.o wl* **94/100**[1]
2 *hd* **Ashalanda (FR)**[84] 3442 3-8-5 ... C-PLemaire 2 111
(A De Royer-Dupre, France) *hld up: last st: swtchd outside to follow wnr over 2f out: rdn over 1f out: tk 2nd 1f out: r.o but too late to worry wnr* **7/5**[2]
3 *2 ½* **Themelie Island (IRE)**[28] 5296 4-8-8 ... OPeslier 1 102
(A Trybuhl, Germany) *a cl up: 3rd st: wnt 2nd wl over 2f out: rdn 2f out: one pce fr over 1f out* **13/1**
4 *4* **Camill (IRE)**[21] 5-8-12 ... GHind 4 100
(S Sokol, Czech Republic) *5th st: hrd rdn 2f out: one pce* **34/1**
5 *½* **Apprimus (IRE)**[98] 3-8-5 ... URispoli 5 99
(S Botti, Italy) *trckd ldr to st: stl cl 2nd 3f out: sn wknd* **48/10**[3]
6 *3 ½* **Storm Mountain (IRE)**[126] 2115 6-8-12 ... DVargiu 7 93
(B Grizzetti, Italy) *hld up: last to appr st: n.d* **12/1**
7 *5 ½* **Proud Boris (GER)**[330] 6992 5-8-12 ... JRatislav 6 83
(J Hanacek, Slovakia) *6th st: rdn and btn over 2f out* **76/1**
8 *9* **Pedra Pompas**[56] 5-8-12 ... GMarcelli 3 68
(M Gasparini, Italy) *led to 3f out: sn bhd* **22/1**
2m 17.9s (-0.70)
WFA 3 from 4yo+ 7lb **8** Ran SP% **133.8**
TOTE: WIN 1.94; PL 1.13, 1.28, 1.77; DF 2.19.
Owner Scuderia Incolinx **Bred** Soc Finanza Locale Consulting Srl **Trained** Italy

6134 HAMILTON (R-H)
Monday, September 21

OFFICIAL GOING: Good (good to firm in places; 8.9)
Races over a mile plus were approximately 70 yards shorter than the official distances due to rail realignment to provide fresh ground.
Wind: Fresh, half behind Weather: Overcast, raining

6154 EUROPEAN BREEDERS' FUND MAIDEN STKS 6f 5y
2:10 (2:12) (Class 5) 2-Y-O **£3,885** (£1,156; £577; £288) **Stalls** Low

Form RPR
42 1 **Sand Skier**[20] 5542 2-9-3 0 ... JoeFanning 4 85+
(M Johnston) *mde all: rdn clr fnl f: readily* **8/11**[1]
2 *4* **Tatiana Romanova (USA)** 2-8-12 0 ... PaulHanagan 9 68+
(R A Fahey) *prom: effrt and edgd rt 2f out: kpt on fnl f: nt rch wnr* **12/1**[3]
2 3 *½* **Exceedingly Bold**[30] 5256 2-9-3 0 ... AdrianMcCarthy 2 72
(Miss Gay Kelleway) *cl up: effrt 2f out: kpt on same pce fnl f* **9/4**[2]
4 *1 ¾* **Excellent Vision** 2-9-3 0 ... RichardMullen 8 66
(B Smart) *trckd ldrs: rdn over 2f out: edgd lft over 1f out: one pce* **14/1**
5 *1 ¼* **Shayla** 2-8-12 0 ... PJMcDonald 1 58
(G A Swinbank) *s.s: bhd and outpcd: hdwy over 1f out: kpt on fnl f: nrst fin* **40/1**
0 6 *hd* **Chookie Avon**[14] 5728 2-9-3 0 ... TomEaves 3 62
(I Semple) *hld up: pushed along over 2f out: no imp* **66/1**
7 *¾* **Celendine** 2-8-12 0 ... KFallon 6 58+
(G A Swinbank) *dwlt: bhd and sn niggled along: hdwy and edgd rt over 2f out: sn outpcd* **20/1**
00 8 *5* **Clayton Flick (IRE)**[14] 5722 2-9-3 0 ... RobertHavlin 7 45
(A B Haynes) *cl up tl rdn and wknd over 1f out* **50/1**
1m 12.46s (0.26) **Going Correction** -0.075s/f (Good) **8** Ran SP% **113.7**
Speed ratings (Par 95): **95,89,89,86,85 84,83,77**
toteswinger: 1&2 £2.90, 1&3 £1.20, 2&3 £2.20. CSF £10.87 TOTE £2.00: £1.02, £2.60, £1.10; EX 11.60.
Owner Sheikh Hamdan Bin Mohammed Al Maktoum **Bred** Rabbah Bloodstock Limited **Trained** Middleham Moor, N Yorks

FOCUS
This was probably a decent maiden for the track.

NOTEBOOK
Sand Skier didn't have to improve that much on the level of his previous Leicester second to win this, but he still did the business in great style. He made most of the running and came right away when asked for his effort, despite still showing a little inexperience. The drop back in trip was a slight worry beforehand, but he clearly has plenty of pace and looks a very nice performer in the making. He certainly has the scope to rate higher as he matures and appeals as one to follow. (tchd 5-6 in places)
Tatiana Romanova(USA), from a stable in red-hot form, is bred to enjoy a stiffer test in due course and she ran accordingly. There was more than enough in this initial effort to think this late foal can be placed to strike in the coming weeks. (tchd 14-1)
Exceedingly Bold was the main market rival to the winner on the strength of his highly encouraging debut display at Ripon behind a subsequent Listed winner. He ran with the choke out through the early stages, however, and paid the price when the race got really serious around 2f out. This was somewhat disappointing, but he is a horse of fair ability and will last longer again when consenting to settle. (op 3-1)
Excellent Vision, who cost 190,000gns this year, was beginning his career over a suitable trip on breeding and proved very easy to back. He ran green when asked for an effort, but was keeping on nicely in the closing stages and should be a lot sharper for the run. (tchd 16-1)
Shayla caught the eye running on when the race was effectively over. She proved clueless after a tardy start and got well behind, so the fact she finished fifth bodes well with the future in mind.
Official explanation: jockey said that the filly was slowly away (op 33-1)

6155 TOTESPORT.COM EBF FLOWER OF SCOTLAND FILLIES' H'CAP 6f 5y
2:40 (2:42) (Class 3) (0-95,94) 3-Y-O+ **£11,009** (£3,275; £1,637; £817) **Stalls** Centre

Form RPR
0262 1 **Vitoria (IRE)**[12] 5766 3-9-1 88 ... RichardMullen 5 102+
(B Smart) *mde all: qcknd over 1f out: kpt on strly* **11/4**[1]
0056 2 *2 ¾* **Kerrys Requiem (IRE)**[8] 5902 3-8-12 85 ... AlanMunro 3 90
(M R Channon) *hld up in tch: rdn over 2f out: hdwy over 1f out: chsd wnr ins fnl f: r.o* **6/1**[3]

0501 **3** ¾ **Fesko**[7] 5937 3-8-7 **80** 6ex.. JoeFanning 2 82
(M Johnston) *chsd wnr tl rdn and one pce fr over 1f out* **11/4**[1]

0025 **4** shd **Crystal Moments**[22] 5471 3-8-12 **85**.. KFallon 6 87
(E A L Dunlop) *t.k.h: prom: effrt over 2f out: one pce over 1f out* **15/2**

1000 **5** 1½ **Rothesay Dancer**[3] 6051 6-8-8 **82**........................ KellyHarrison(3) 9 79
(J S Goldie) *hld up: effrt over 2f out: nvr able to chal* **9/1**

2-14 **6** ½ **Sakhee's Pearl**[60] 4228 3-8-12 **85**............................ AdrianMcCarthy 10 81
(Miss Gay Kelleway) *cl up: rdn over 2f out: wknd fnl f* **7/2**[2]

1m 11.44s (-0.76) **Going Correction** -0.075s/f (Good)
WFA 3 from 4yo+ 2lb **6** Ran SP% **111.6**
Speed ratings (Par 104): **102,98,97,97,95 94**
toteswinger: 1&2 £3.60, 1&3 £1.80, 2&3 £3.60. CSF £19.11 CT £46.92 TOTE £3.10: £2.00, £2.50; EX 18.50.
Owner H E Sheikh Rashid Bin Mohammed **Bred** Tom Deane **Trained** Hambleton, N Yorks

FOCUS
The feature handicap, and it was decimated by non-runners. There was just an average pace on early. The winner impressed and has more to offer.

NOTEBOOK
Vitoria(IRE) ◆ has taken time to come good this term, but her latest second at Doncaster was good form and the decision to drop her back in trip here worked the oracle. She travelled best throughout and went nicely clear as her rivals began to feel the pinch after 2f out. It was clear at the furlong marker she had the race in safe keeping and she had something left in the tank passing the post. Her stable's runners are now back in decent form and her confidence will be sky high after this, so she could have more to offer as a sprinter. Trainer Brian Smart also believes she will rate higher as a 4yo. (op 4-1)
Kerrys Requiem(IRE) hit a flat spot 3f out before running on with purpose again inside the final furlong and continues to prove very hard to catch right. She still helps to set the standard. (op 11-2 tchd 5-1)
Fesko won nicely at Leicester when dropping back to this trip a week earlier and proved popular under her penalty. She lacked the natural pace of the winner and a more galloping track over this trip is what she really needs, as she was staying on again when meeting the rising finish here. (tchd 4-1)
Crystal Moments was a little free early on and could only keep on at the same pace when push came to shove. She ran close to her recent level so is another who sets the standard and will need some respite from the handicapper before getting her head back in front. (tchd 7-1)
Rothesay Dancer is a five-time winner at this venue and was stepping back up a furlong for this quick reappearance. She also proved free through the early parts and got going too late from off the pace, having been restrained out the back. (op 10-1)
Sakhee's Pearl was disappointing on her return from a 60-day break. It was her first outing as a sprinter, but she was beaten before the trip became an issue. Official explanation: trainer said that the filly was unsuited by the good, good to firm in places, going (op 3-1 tchd 4-1)

6156 TOTESPORTCASINO.COM APPRENTICE H'CAP (FINAL OF THE HAMILTON PARK APPRENTICE SERIES) 1m 3f 16y
3:10 (3:10) (Class 6) (0-65,65) 3-Y-O+ **£2,266** (£674; £337; £168) **Stalls** High

Form RPR
00-1 **1** **Arty Crafty (USA)**[12] 5775 3-8-11 **57**................................ RosieJessop 4 68+
(Sir Mark Prescott) *trckd ldrs: rdn and outpcd over 4f out: rallied over 2f out: led over 1f out: drew clr fnl f* **9/4**[1]

-520 **2** 4½ **Ulysees (IRE)**[14] 5730 10-8-5 **51** oh3.................................. SFeeney(7) 5 53
(I Semple) *t.k.h: prom: smooth hdwy to ld over 3f out: hdd over 1f out: nt pce of wnr* **16/1**

0151 **3** 1 **Oddsmaker (IRE)**[7] 5947 8-9-10 **63** 6ex.................(t) AndrewHeffernan 8 63
(M A Barnes) *led 2f: cl up: led 6f out to over 3f out: styd upsides: one pce appr fnl f* **5/2**[2]

0500 **4** 3¾ **Sharp Sovereign (USA)**[14] 5733 3-8-5 **51** oh5..............(p) LanceBetts 1 45
(I Semple) *prom: effrt over 3f out: edgd rt and no imp fr 2f out* **14/1**

4362 **5** ¾ **Hawkit (USA)**[14] 5732 8-9-4 **57**....................................... MartinLane 7 50
(P Monteith) *hld up in tch: rdn over 3f out: sn outpcd: n.d after* **4/1**[3]

405- **6** ½ **Circus Clown (IRE)**[355] 6386 4-8-9 **51** oh1...................... NSLawes(3) 6 43
(P Monteith) *bhd: drvn over 3f out: nvr able to chal* **22/1**

0-00 **7** 4 **Solis (GER)**[4] 6012 6-9-9 **62**..................................(v) IJBrennan 3 47
(P Monteith) *bhd and nt keen: sn drvn along: nvr on terms* **16/1**

0504 **8** 21 **Naomh Geileis (USA)**[34] 5128 4-9-12 **65**.....................(b[1]) PaulPickard 2 15
(M Johnston) *t.k.h: led after 2f to 6f out: rdn and wknd over 3f out: t.o* **10/1**

2m 23.62s (-1.98) **Going Correction** -0.30s/f (Firm)
WFA 3 from 4yo+ 7lb **8** Ran SP% **111.2**
Speed ratings (Par 101): **95,91,91,88,87 87,84,69**
toteswinger: 1&2 £8.40, 1&3 £2.30, 2&3 £9.40. CSF £36.42 CT £91.79 TOTE £2.30: £1.10, £4.00, £1.80; EX 39.70.
Owner Mrs Sonia Rogers **Bred** Airlie Stud **Trained** Newmarket, Suffolk
■ Stewards' Enquiry : Andrew Heffernan one-day ban: used whip with excessive frequency (Oct 5th)
Rosie Jessop six-day ban: excessive use of the whip (Oct 5-10)

FOCUS
This moderate handicap for apprentice riders was run at a strong early pace. The winner is progressive and the form is solid if limited in behind.
Hawkit(USA) Official explanation: jockey said that the gelding was never travelling

6157 TOTESPORTGAMES.COM H'CAP 1m 1f 36y
3:40 (3:40) (Class 5) (0-70,70) 3-Y-O+ **£3,238** (£963; £481; £240) **Stalls** High

Form RPR
1000 **1** **Shy Glance (USA)**[26] 5334 7-9-6 **69**................................ TonyHamilton 5 77
(P Monteith) *hld up: hdwy over 2f out: rdn to ld ins fnl f: r.o wl* **33/1**

460 **2** ¾ **Nisaal (IRE)**[23] 5438 4-8-9 **65**......................................(p) IJBrennan(7) 12 71
(J J Quinn) *prom: effrt over 2f out: chsd wnr ins fnl f: kpt on u.p* **7/1**[3]

2660 **3** 1¼ **Society Venue**[20] 5551 4-9-6 **69**.. PaulHanagan 4 72
(Jedd O'Keeffe) *led: rdn over 2f out: hdd ins fnl f: kpt on same pce* **9/1**

0104 **4** 1¾ **Moonage Daydream (IRE)**[23] 5418 4-8-13 **62**....................(b) DNolan 3 62
(T D Easterby) *hld up: hdwy over 2f out: kpt on ins fnl f: nrst fin* **16/1**

4-16 **5** 2¼ **Social Rhythm**[29] 5289 5-8-2 **56** oh2.................... PatrickDonaghy(5) 6 51
(A C Whillans) *missed break: bhd: hdwy on outside over 3f out: edgd rt and kpt on fr 2f out: no imp* **20/1**

0501 **6** 1½ **Funky Munky**[42] 4845 4-9-0 **63**...................................... PJMcDonald 8 55
(G A Swinbank) *trckd ldrs: rdn over 2f out: sn one pce* **11/2**[2]

3054 **7** nk **Shadowtime**[4] 6019 4-8-13 **67**........................... AndrewHeffernan(5) 1 58
(Miss Tracy Waggott) *t.k.h: in tch: outpcd over 2f out: r.o ins fnl f* **11/2**[2]

4500 **8** ½ **Cigalas**[18] 5601 4-8-9 **63**.. LanceBetts(5) 10 53
(Mrs J C McGregor) *hld up in tch: rdn over 2f out: sn one pce* **33/1**

4300 **9** hd **Primo Way**[2] 6093 8-8-4 **56** oh2.................................. KellyHarrison(3) 14 46
(D A Nolan) *hld up: hdwy over 2f out: wknd fnl f* **28/1**

0126 **10** 1 **Botham (USA)**[21] 5516 5-9-1 **64**.................................. DanielTudhope 16 52
(J S Goldie) *hld up: rdn over 2f out: nvr able to chal* **12/1**

-300 **11** ¾ **Ella Woodcock (IRE)**[4] 6023 5-9-7 **70**..............................(b) DavidAllan 2 56
(E J Alston) *trckd ldr: drvn over 2f out: wknd over 1f out* **18/1**

0020 **12** 1 **Kool Katie**[23] 5423 4-8-8 **57**.. AndrewElliott 7 41
(Mrs G S Rees) *midfield: rdn 3f out: hung rt and wknd 2f out* **33/1**

5340 **13** 9 **Moon Lightning (IRE)**[3] 6052 3-8-13 **67**..........................(b[1]) KFallon 15 32+
(M H Tompkins) *plld hrd: hld up: rdn over 3f out: wknd over 2f out: eased whn no ch fnl f* **5/1**[1]

0002 **14** ½ **Transmission (IRE)**[39] 4932 4-9-1 **64**.............................. TomEaves 11 28
(B Smart) *trckd ldrs tl rdn and wknd over 2f out* **12/1**

5654 **15** ¾ **Woodsley House (IRE)**[16] 5673 7-9-2 **65**.....................(p) RobertHavlin 9 27
(A G Foster) *s.v.s: bhd: struggling over 3f out: sn btn* **16/1**

1m 57.6s (-2.10) **Going Correction** -0.30s/f (Firm)
WFA 3 from 4yo+ 5lb **15** Ran SP% **119.4**
Speed ratings (Par 103): **97,96,95,93,91 90,90,89,89,88 87,87,79,78,77**
toteswinger: 1&2 £53.50, 1&3 £40.70, 2&3 £29.00. CSF £237.18 CT £2266.22 TOTE £44.60: £10.20, £4.10, £3.00; EX 386.10.
Owner Walcal Property Development Ltd **Bred** R D Hubbard And Constance Sczesny **Trained** Rosewell, Midlothian

FOCUS
A moderate handicap. The winner is among those to limit the form.
Shy Glance(USA) Official explanation: trainer was unable to offer any explanation for the apparent improvement of form
Moon Lightning(IRE) Official explanation: jockey said that the colt lost its action, although the horse returned sound
Woodsley House(IRE) Official explanation: jockey said that the gelding was slowly away

6158 RACINGPOST.COM MAIDEN STKS 1m 1f 36y
4:10 (4:10) (Class 5) 3-4-Y-O **£2,590** (£770; £385; £192) **Stalls** High

Form RPR
552 **1** **Oneofapear (IRE)**[21] 5520 3-9-3 78................................ PJMcDonald 5 80+
(G A Swinbank) *mde all: rdn whn pressed 2f out: kpt on strly fnl f* **9/4**[2]

32 **2** 5 **Passkey**[32] 5193 3-8-12 0.. SebSanders 7 68+
(Sir Mark Prescott) *trckd ldrs: effrt and ev ch 2f out: hung rt and no ex ins fnl f: sn eased* **1/2**[1]

4 **3** 2¾ **Cool Baranca (GER)**[14] 5731 3-8-12 63........................ TonyHamilton 4 60
(P Monteith) *hld up in tch: hdwy over 2f out: edgd rt and outpcd fnl 2f* **14/1**[3]

055 **4** 22 **Ettrick Mill**[12] 5773 3-9-3 0.. JoeFanning 2 23
(M Johnston) *trckd wnr: rdn 4f out: wknd over 2f out* **25/1**

3050 **5** ½ **Trade Price (GR)**[29] 5295 3-9-3 47..................................(b[1]) TomEaves 6 23
(I Semple) *in tch: effrt over 3f out: wknd over 2f out* **100/1**

000 **6** 9 **Mister Biscuit (USA)**[33] 5163 3-8-10 30.......................... IJBrennan(7) 1 5
(Miss L A Perratt) *hld up: struggling over 3f out: sn btn* **100/1**

7 nse **Lion Road (USA)** 3-9-3 0.. RobertHavlin 8 5
(A B Haynes) *missed break: hld up: struggling over 3f out: sn btn* **40/1**

1m 57.16s (-2.54) **Going Correction** -0.30s/f (Firm) **7** Ran SP% **112.4**
Speed ratings (Par 103): **99,94,92,72,72 64,64**
toteswinger: 1&2 £1.30, 1&3 £2.00, 2&3 £2.00. CSF £3.57 TOTE £3.20: £1.80, £1.10; EX 3.90.
Owner Mrs I Gibson & Dr C Emmerson **Bred** Tyrone Molloy **Trained** Melsonby, N Yorks

FOCUS
A moderate maiden, run at a fair pace. The first three came well clear. The decisive winner's task was eased by the runner-up appearing to either go wrong or become unbalanced.

6159 TOTESPORTBINGO.COM H'CAP 5f 4y
4:40 (4:41) (Class 4) (0-80,73) 3-Y-O+ **£5,180** (£1,541; £770; £384) **Stalls** Centre

Form RPR
5-00 **1** **Mandarin Spirit (IRE)**[9] 5886 9-8-12 **63**....................(b) TonyHamilton 7 73
(Miss L A Perratt) *mde all: sn clr: kpt on wl fnl f: unchal* **14/1**

0510 **2** 1½ **Select Committee**[5] 5978 4-9-3 **68**.................................(v) TomEaves 4 73
(J J Quinn) *chsd wnr: rdn 2f out: kpt on ins fnl f* **9/2**[3]

35-0 **3** hd **Hazelrigg (IRE)**[33] 5148 4-9-8 **73**..................................... DavidAllan 2 77
(T D Easterby) *rrd in stalls: dwlt: bhd: rdn and edgd rt 2f out: hdwy ent fnl f: kpt on wl: nrst fin* **8/1**

0000 **4** ¾ **Distant Sun (USA)**[7] 5946 5-9-0 **65**................................ PJMcDonald 6 66
(Miss L A Perratt) *in tch: effrt over 2f out: kpt on same pce ins fnl f* **12/1**

0500 **5** ½ **Highland Warrior**[4] 6010 10-9-3 **68**.. KFallon 8 67
(P T Midgley) *dwlt: hld up: hdwy 2f out: no ex ins fnl f* **9/1**

5240 **6** ¾ **Joyeaux**[4] 6010 7-8-10 **61**.. PaulHanagan 1 58
(Ollie Pears) *hld up in tch: rdn and outpcd 2f out: kpt on ins fnl f: no imp* **4/1**[2]

0352 **7** hd **Caranbola**[5] 5978 3-8-13 **65**.. AlanMunro 3 61
(M Brittain) *chsd ldrs: rdn over 2f out: no ex over 1f out* **10/3**[1]

0000 **8** 1¼ **First Order**[45] 4733 8-9-2 **72**..................................(v) AnnStokell(5) 10 63
(Miss A Stokell) *t.k.h: prom: rdn over 2f out: btn fnl f* **20/1**

0005 **9** nk **Killer Class**[4] 6010 4-8-9 **63**.................................... KellyHarrison(3) 9 53
(J S Goldie) *in tch: effrt over 1f out: btn ins fnl f* **13/2**

59.68 secs (-0.32) **Going Correction** -0.075s/f (Good)
WFA 3 from 4yo+ 1lb **9** Ran SP% **114.8**
Speed ratings (Par 105): **99,96,96,95,94 93,92,90,90**
toteswinger: 1&2 £13.00, 1&3 £19.00, 2&3 £7.10. CSF £75.47 CT £549.65 TOTE £16.60: £3.20, £1.90, £2.50; EX 140.10.
Owner Peter Tsim **Bred** W Haggas And W Jarvis **Trained** East Kilbride, South Lanarks

FOCUS
An ordinary sprint handicap and the form seems sound.
First Order Official explanation: jockey said that the gelding ran too free

6160 BET IN PLAY AT TOTESPORT.COM H'CAP (DIV I) 5f 4y
5:10 (5:11) (Class 6) (0-65,64) 3-Y-O+ **£1,942** (£578; £288; £144) **Stalls** Centre

Form RPR
0531 **1** **Milton Of Campsie**[8] 5911 4-9-4 **63** 6ex................................ KFallon 5 75+
(J Balding) *hld up in tch: effrt over 1f out: led ins fnl f: r.o wl* **13/8**[1]

0620 **2** 1 **Dalarossie**[4] 6010 4-8-8 **53**.. DavidAllan 4 60
(E J Alston) *led or disp ld to ins fnl f: kpt on wl* **10/3**[2]

2024 **3** 2½ **Caribbean Coral**[8] 5900 10-9-5 **64**................................ RobertHavlin 3 62+
(A B Haynes) *dwlt: hld up: hdwy over 1f out: r.o ins fnl f* **9/1**

0254 **4** nse **Town And Gown**[4] 6010 4-8-2 **50** oh2......................... KellyHarrison(3) 1 48
(J S Goldie) *dwlt: sn in tch: rdn and edgd rt 2f out: kpt on ins fnl f* **7/1**[3]

0000 **5** ½ **Kheylide (IRE)**[24] 5391 3-8-10 **59**.............................(p) DominicFox(3) 6 55
(Mrs D J Sanderson) *cl up: rdn over 2f out: one pce over 1f out* **16/1**

405 **6** 1½ **Berrymead**[45] 4736 4-8-10 **60** ow5................................ AnnStokell(5) 2 51+
(Miss A Stokell) *missed break: bhd tl hdwy over 1f out: nrst fin* **22/1**

0404 **7** ½ **Coconut Moon**[44] 4772 7-7-12 **50** oh5................................ BillyCray(7) 13 39
(A Berry) *disp ld on outside to ent fnl f: kpt on same pce* **33/1**

0004 **8** ½ **Howards Tipple**[28] 5309 5-8-7 **52** oh3 ow2........................(p) TomEaves 8 39
(I Semple) *prom tl rdn and no ex over 1f out* **14/1**

0055 **9** ½ **Rainbow Bay**[61] 4191 6-8-1 **51** oh5 ow1........................(v) PaulPickard(5) 9 37+
(Miss Tracy Waggott) *dwlt: bhd: effrt on outside over 1f out: nvr rchd ldrs* **20/1**

5-00 **10** *nk* **Lambency (IRE)**[14] 5729 6-8-0 **50**....(p) MartinLane(5) 7 35
(J S Goldie) *cl up tl rdn and wknd appr fnl f* **12/1**
010 **11** *½* **Nabra**[24] 5391 5-8-7 **52**.... AlanMunro 12 35
(M Brittain) *trckd ldrs tl rdn and wknd over 1f out* **25/1**
59.90 secs (-0.10) **Going Correction** -0.075s/f (Good)
WFA 3 from 4yo+ 1lb **11** Ran SP% **119.8**
Speed ratings (Par 101): **97,95,91,91,90 88,87,86,85,85 84**
toteswinger: 1&2 £2.80, 1&3 £3.00, 2&3 £5.20. CSF £6.42 CT £37.97 TOTE £2.60: £1.40, £1.20, £2.10; EX 10.60.
Owner Willie McKay **Bred** Slatch Farm Stud **Trained** Scrooby, Notts

FOCUS
A weak sprint handicap in which four raced from out of the weights. The winner did it well and could have more to offer.
Berrymead Official explanation: jockey said that the filly was slowly away

6161 BET IN PLAY AT TOTESPORT.COM H'CAP (DIV II) 5f 4y
5:40 (5:42) (Class 6) (0-65,64) 3-Y-O+ **£1,942** (£578; £288; £144) **Stalls** Centre

Form RPR
5462 **1** **Captain Royale (IRE)**[33] 5159 4-8-1 **51** ow1....(p) AndrewHeffernan(5) 1 60
(Miss Tracy Waggott) *in tch gng wl: hdwy to ld over 1f out: kpt on wl fnl f* **11/2**[3]
4226 **2** *1* **Sunley Sovereign**[4] 6010 5-8-12 **57**....(b) AndrewElliott 11 62
(Mrs R A Carr) *mde most to over 1f out: kpt on u.p ins fnl f* **11/4**[2]
0060 **3** *nk* **Revue Princess (IRE)**[63] 4141 4-9-1 **60**....(b) DavidAllan 9 64
(T D Easterby) *cl up: effrt and ev ch over 1f out: r.o ins fnl f* **11/1**
6110 **4** *4 ½* **The Bear**[4] 6010 6-9-5 **64**.... KFallon 3 52+
(Miss L A Perratt) *walked to post: dwlt and rdr lost iron briefly sn after s: hld up: hdwy over 1f out: nrst fin* **9/4**[1]
0020 **5** *1* **Tenancy (IRE)**[38] 5008 5-8-1 **51**.... DeanHeslop(5) 6 36
(S A Harris) *cl up tl rdn and no ex fr over 1f out* **20/1**
-060 **6** *½* **Blow Your Mind**[24] 5396 3-8-7 **53**....(b[1]) PaulHanagan 4 36+
(Karen McLintock) *midfield: drvn over 2f out: no imp fnl f* **16/1**
0204 **7** *1 ¾* **What A Fella**[22] 5468 3-8-4 **50** oh3....(p) PaulQuinn 5 26+
(Mrs A Duffield) *bhd and rdn along: hdwy over 1f out: nrst fin* **25/1**
0603 **8** *½* **Lucky Buddha**[49] 4594 3-8-8 **54**.... TonyHamilton 8 29
(Jedd O'Keeffe) *cl up tl rdn and no ex fr 2f out* **9/1**
5000 **9** *3 ¼* **Glenluji**[4] 6010 4-8-4 **52**.... KellyHarrison(3) 13 15+
(J S Goldie) *walked to post: bhd and outpcd: no imp fr 2f out* **8/1**
0600 **10** *nk* **Mr Rooney (IRE)**[33] 5159 6-7-12 **50** oh5.... BillyCray(7) 2 12+
(A Berry) *bhd and outpcd: edgd rt 1/2-way: nvr able to chal* **50/1**
6600 **11** *1 ¾* **Badtanman**[26] 5336 3-8-2 **53** oh5 ow3....(v[1]) PatrickDonaghy(5) 7 9+
(Peter Grayson) *wnt rt s: sn outpcd: no ch fr 1/2-way* **80/1**
0060 **12** *1* **Howards Prince**[33] 5159 6-8-1 **51** oh5 ow1....(b) PaulPickard(5) 12 3
(D A Nolan) *prom tl wandered and wknd fr 2f out* **80/1**
59.36 secs (-0.64) **Going Correction** -0.075s/f (Good)
WFA 3 from 4yo+ 1lb **12** Ran SP% **121.2**
Speed ratings (Par 101): **102,100,99,92,91 90,87,86,81,81 78,76**
toteswinger: 1&2 £4.40, 1&3 £12.00, 2&3 £6.10. CSF £20.71 CT £167.13 TOTE £7.20: £2.50, £1.70, £3.40; EX 30.50 Place 6: £55.73, Place 5: £45.96..
Owner H Conlon **Bred** Skymarc Farm Inc **Trained** Spennymoor, Co Durham

FOCUS
This second division of the sprint handicap was another poor affair and again there were four competing from out of the weights. It paid to race handily. The form is limited.
Mr Rooney(IRE) Official explanation: jockey said that the gelding hung right handed throughout
T/Plt: £115.90 to a £1 stake. Pool: £54,281.36. 341.81 winning tickets. T/Qpdt: £122.90 to a £1 stake. Pool: £3,189.61. 19.20 winning tickets. RY

5984 KEMPTON (A.W) (R-H)
Monday, September 21

OFFICIAL GOING: Standard
Wind: Medium, across Weather: bright and sunny

6162 GEORGE'S APPEAL - TO SAVE TINY LIVES EBF MAIDEN STKS 1m (P)
2:30 (2:33) (Class 4) 2-Y-O **£5,342** (£1,589; £794; £396) **Stalls** High

Form RPR
2 **1** **Get A Grip (IRE)**[38] 5000 2-9-3 0.... GeorgeBaker 8 81
(J A R Toller) *trckd ldng pair tl wnt 2nd gng wl over 2f out: led 2f out: sn rdn: asserted ins fnl f: rdn out* **3/1**[2]
2 **2** *2 ½* **Dahaam**[21] 5528 2-9-3 0.... LDettori 9 77+
(Saeed Bin Suroor) *led: rdn over 2f out: hdd 2f out: hanging rt u.p after: stl ev ch tl btn ins fnl f: eased towards fin* **8/11**[1]
3 *2 ¼* **Argaum (IRE)** 2-9-3 0.... AdamKirby 7 71+
(W R Swinburn) *niggled along early: racd in midfield: effrt and rdn over 2f out: chsd clr ldng pair wl over 1f out: kpt on same pce* **12/1**
4 *2 ¾* **Persona Non Grata (IRE)** 2-9-3 0....(b[1]) RichardKingscote 6 65+
(R Charlton) *sn niggled along in midfield: rdn and struggling wl over 2f out: styd on and edgd rt u.p ent fnl f: snatched 4th on post: nvr trbld ldrs* **20/1**
5 *shd* **Tom Wade (IRE)** 2-9-3 0.... PhilipRobinson 11 64
(M A Jarvis) *sn bustled along to chse ldrs: rdn and unable qck over 2f out: plugged on same pce and wl hld after: lost 4th on post* **8/1**[3]
6 *1* **Highland Quaich** 2-9-3 0.... DaneO'Neill 5 62
(D R C Elsworth) *racd off the pce in midfield: rdn and effrt on outer over 2f out: no imp but kpt on steadily fnl f* **33/1**
0 **7** *12* **High On A Hill (IRE)**[17] 5643 2-9-3 0.... JamesDoyle 4 36
(S Kirk) *a in rr: struggling bdly fr 1/2-way* **66/1**
0 **8** *hd* **Foxtrot Foxtrot**[123] 2187 2-9-3 0.... JimCrowley 3 35
(P Winkworth) *chsd ldr tl over 2f out: wknd qckly 2f out and wl bhd fnl f* **50/1**
9 *½* **King's Realm (IRE)** 2-9-3 0.... StephenDonohoe 10 34
(Sir Mark Prescott) *s.i.s: rn green and a bhd: lost tch over 3f out* **33/1**
10 *13* **The Love Guru** 2-9-0 0.... JackMitchell(3) 1 6
(J R Boyle) *v.s.a: rn green in detached last thrght: t.o* **66/1**
1m 40.23s (0.43) **Going Correction** +0.025s/f (Slow) **10** Ran SP% **117.3**
Speed ratings (Par 97): **98,95,93,90,90 89,77,77,76,63**
toteswinger: 1&2 £1.40, 1&3 £4.20, 2&3 £2.70. CSF £5.29 TOTE £4.10: £1.40, £1.02, £3.00; EX 6.20.
Owner M Barber **Bred** Eimear Mulhern J Flynn & Abbeville Stud **Trained** Newmarket, Suffolk

FOCUS
From a form persepective the right two horses filled the first two places. From a form persepective the right two horses filled the first two places.

NOTEBOOK
Get A Grip(IRE) was runner-up first time in a 7f Newmarket maiden won by Destination Aim which had already produced an easy winner in Wigmore Hall, who was eighth. There is stamina on his dam's side but pace to go with it from Royal Applause so this mile suited him admirably. He had been withdrawn due to getting upset before his previous attempt to run here, and for that reason he'd been at the stables from 6am this time, and the pre-planning paid dividends with no hitches. (op 5-2 tchd 9-4)
Dahaam, who was beaten half a length by Sierra Alpha over 7f at Warwick in what looked a weaker race than one the winner came from, was suited by the step up trip and is another whose bottom line holds stamina. He was set a tough task trying to make all, and was unfortunate to come up against a horse who might be a touch above average. (op 5-6 tchd 10-11)
Argaum(IRE) showed more than enough to win races. From the good mare Poppy Carew and a half-brother to Cutting Crew and Mad Carew, he will stay further than this next year and is one to look out for. (op 20-1)
Persona Non Grata(IRE), worryingly, was gelded and blinkered on debut but didn't do much wrong for a horse with a strong stamina influence. He kept on well and if he stays sound of mind he might be of interest when he gets a trip. (op 33-1)
Tom Wade(IRE), a 90,000gns two-year-old, showed signs of immaturity but a decent attitude. He'll be wiser next time. (op 15-2)
Highland Quaich, despite having a pedigree that didn't scream a mile, kept on well enough without ever looking a threat. (op 40-1)

6163 AVANTA E B F MAIDEN FILLIES' STKS (DIV I) 7f (P)
3:00 (3:01) (Class 4) 2-Y-O **£4,695** (£1,397; £698; £348) **Stalls** High

Form RPR
1 **Muwakaba (USA)** 2-9-0 0.... RHills 10 82+
(Sir Michael Stoute) *t.k.h: hld up towards rr: stdd and swtchd lft over 2f out: rdn and gd hdwy on outer over 1f out: qcknd to ld fnl 100yds: r.o wl* **7/2**[1]
2 *1* **Sing Sweetly** 2-9-0 0.... NCallan 3 77
(G A Butler) *t.k.h: hld up in tch in midfield: swtchd lft and hdwy 2f out: pressed ldrs u.p ins fnl f: nt pce of wnr fnl 75yds* **12/1**
3 *¾* **Flouncing (IRE)** 2-9-0 0.... LiamJones 5 77+
(W J Haggas) *t.k.h: hld up towards rr: sltly hmpd over 2f out: sn rdn and hdwy: chsd ldrs and edging rt whn nt clr run over 1f out: swtchd lft 1f out: r.o wl fnl f: nt rch ldng pair* **25/1**
4 *nk* **Mirabella (IRE)** 2-9-0 0.... RichardHughes 14 75+
(R Hannon) *led: rdn jst over 2f out: drvn ent fnl f: hdd fnl 100yds: no ex and lost 2 pls wl ins fnl f* **7/2**[1]
5 *1 ¼* **Deirdre** 2-9-0 0.... JimmyFortune 4 71+
(J H M Gosden) *chsd ldrs: effrt u.p over 2f out: kpt on same pce fnl f* **6/1**[2]
0 **6** *1 ¾* **Lady Willa (IRE)**[18] 5604 2-9-0 0.... MichaelHills 2 67
(B W Hills) *chsd ldrs: rdn over 2f out: pressed ldr and ev ch 2f out tl jst ins fnl f: wknd fnl 150yds* **10/1**
7 *2 ¾* **Vert Chapeau** 2-9-0 0.... LPKeniry 11 60
(E F Vaughan) *t.k.h: hld up wl in tch: rdn and unable qck over 2f out: wknd u.p over 1f out* **33/1**
0 **8** *½* **Atakora (IRE)**[18] 5604 2-9-0 0.... JimCrowley 6 59
(Mrs A J Perrett) *racd keenly: pressed ldr tl rdn and wknd ent fnl 2f: no ch fnl f* **8/1**
9 *1 ¾* **Baggsy (IRE)** 2-9-0 0.... AmirQuinn 12 55
(Miss J Feilden) *in tch in midfield: pushed along 1/2-way: rdn and styd on same pce fr wl over 2f out* **66/1**
10 *nk* **Jennerous Blue** 2-8-11 0.... JackMitchell(3) 1 54
(D K Ivory) *s.i.s: a towards rr: rn green and hung lft bnd 3f out: plugged on same pce u.p after* **100/1**
11 *shd* **Morning Drive** 2-9-0 0.... AdamKirby 7 54+
(W R Swinburn) *in tch towards rr: n.m.r 1/2-way: rdn and unable qck over 2f out: n.d after* **20/1**
11 *dht* **Miss Mittagong (USA)** 2-9-0 0.... RichardKingscote 8 54+
(R M Beckett) *awkward leaving stalls and s.i.s: rn green in rr: n.d whn hung rt over 1f out* **15/2**[3]
0 **13** *2 ¼* **Motrice**[13] 5752 2-9-0 0.... StephenDonohoe 13 48+
(Sir Mark Prescott) *s.i.s rn green and a bhd* **20/1**
14 *1 ¼* **Olney Lass** 2-9-0 0.... DaneO'Neill 9 45
(W J H Ratcliffe) *s.i.s: a bhd* **66/1**
1m 27.75s (1.75) **Going Correction** +0.025s/f (Slow) **14** Ran SP% **118.7**
Speed ratings (Par 94): **91,89,89,88,87 85,82,81,79,79 79,79,76,75**
toteswinger: 1&2 £7.80, 1&3 £14.70, 2&3 £46.90. CSF £44.58 TOTE £3.80: £2.00, £3.50, £7.90; EX 54.30.
Owner Hamdan Al Maktoum **Bred** Shadwell Farm LLC **Trained** Newmarket, Suffolk

FOCUS
An interesting maiden. The single outings of the three runners with experience didn't seem to amount to much so it is encouraging that the first five home were debutants. All could be worth keeping an eye on.

NOTEBOOK
Muwakaba(USA) is a filly that clearly has plenty of pace. She didn't seem to get a great passage towards the rear at halfway but showed a dash of class up the home straight to win with some authority. There is stamina in her dam line where Urban Sea, the dam of Sea The Stars, crops up, so we might see her in a better grade next time when she could have the class to cope with it. (op 5-2)
Sing Sweetly is bred to want much further so this was a very pleasing debut. Her sire Singspiel was best at around 1m2f and her dam, Sweetness Herself was good from 1m3f to nearly 2m. This filly's relations wanted 1m4f to get warm but she still showed a good kick inside the last furlong having been on the pace. Her stable is in good form but we won't see the best of her until next year. (op 16-1)
Flouncing(IRE) ◆ was stopped in her run over two out but still showed a decent turn of pace and will be a different proposition next time, when she will possibly be suited by another furlong. This was a good debut. (op 28-1)
Mirabella(IRE) had it tough on her debut, racing on the pace and only getting tired near the finish. Like all her stable's runners, she'll be more tuned up next time and will certainly stay a mile. (tchd 3-1)
Deirdre is from the good Normandie Stud family that produced Duncan and Samuel, who were both late developers and needed much further than this. The same is likely to be true of this daughter of Dubawi, who is likely to add to the family's winning tally. (op 5-1 tchd 7-1)
Lady Willa(IRE) did best of those that had run before, and it may have suited her to be ridden slightly more forcefully than on her debut. She'll stay further. (op 12-1)
Vert Chapeau might be best at this trip for the time being. (op 66-1)
Atakora(IRE) finished further behind Lady Willa than on her debut but this was purely due to pressing the pace. (op 10-1)

Miss Mittagong(USA) was nibbled at in the market but, when asked to come from the rear, was soon hanging badly to her right and couldn't be ridden. (op 14-1)

6164 AVANTA E B F MAIDEN FILLIES' STKS (DIV II) 7f (P)
3:30 (3:32) (Class 4) 2-Y-O **£4,695** (£1,397; £698; £348) **Stalls** High

Form | | | | RPR
3 **1** **Magic Doll (USA)**[24] 5398 2-9-0 0 ... LDettori 11 78+
(Saeed Bin Suroor) *wnt sltly lft s: chsd ldr: rdn to chal over 2f out: led 2f out: styd on wl u.p: eased nr fin* **9/4**[1]
2 **2** *1 ½* **Faithful One (IRE)**[18] 5605 2-9-0 0 ... TedDurcan 10 73
(D R Lanigan) *sltly hmpd s: hld up wl in tch: swtchd rt and rdn over 2f out: chsd wnr ins fnl f: kpt on* **7/2**[2]
3 *nk* **Thrill** 2-9-0 0 ... NickyMackay 4 72+
(J H M Gosden) *in tch: rdn and sltly outpcd over 2f out: rallied ins fnl f: styd on to go 3rd last stride: nt pce to threaten wnr* **16/1**
2 **4** *shd* **Flip Flop (IRE)**[28] 5318 2-9-0 0 ... MichaelHills 12 72
(B W Hills) *led: rdn and hrd pressed over 2f out: hdd 2f out: one pce and lost 2 pls ins fnl f* **11/2**[3]
5 *1 ½* **Sheila Toss (IRE)** 2-9-0 0 ... RichardHughes 6 68
(R Hannon) *hld up in tch in midfield: effrt and edgd rt over 2f out: sn swtchd lft and rdn: styd on steadily fnl f: nvr gng pce to threaten ldrs* **25/1**
6 *nse* **Eleanora Duse (IRE)** 2-9-0 0 ... RyanMoore 5 68
(Sir Michael Stoute) *towards rr: pushed along over 3f out: rdn over 2f out: hdwy towards inner over 1f out: kpt on same pce fnl f* **12/1**
04 **7** *2 ¼* **Wild Rockette**[18] 5605 2-9-0 0 ... MartinDwyer 1 63
(B J Meehan) *hld up in rr: rdn and effrt jst over 2f out: no prog tl kpt on steadily ins fnl f: nvr trbld ldrs* **20/1**
3 **8** *2 ½* **Thereafter (USA)**[17] 5638 2-9-0 0 ... SteveDrowne 14 56
(R Charlton) *s.i.s: sn pushed up into midfield: pushed along and struggling over 3f out: outpcd wl over 2f out and n.d after* **8/1**
9 *1 ½* **Contrary (IRE)** 2-9-0 0 ... TGMcLaughlin 7 53
(E A L Dunlop) *s.i.s: t.k.h and hld up in rr: nudged along ent fnl 2f: kpt on: n.d* **100/1**
10 *1* **Tap Dance Way (IRE)** 2-9-0 0 ... JimCrowley 2 50+
(P R Chamings) *s.i.s: hld up in rr: rdn and no real prog over 2f out* **100/1**
4 **11** *2 ½* **Momtaz**[13] 5741 2-9-0 0 ... NCallan 13 44
(C E Brittain) *chsd ldng pair tl jst over 2f out: wknd qckly u.p over 1f out* **7/1**
12 *1 ¼* **Allannah Abu** 2-9-0 0 ... StephenDonohoe 9 41+
(Sir Mark Prescott) *s.i.s and sltly hmpd s: rn green and a bhd: rdn and no prog over 3f out* **66/1**
13 *shd* **Ocean Rosie (IRE)** 2-9-0 0 ... JerryO'Dwyer 8 40
(Miss J Feilden) *rn green and sn pushed along in midfield: lost pl and rdn jst over 3f out: n.d* **100/1**
14 *11* **Banco Busto (IRE)** 2-9-0 0 ... MickyFenton 3 13
(H S Howe) *s.i.s: hung lft and rn green thrght: t.o fnl 2f* **100/1**

1m 26.77s (0.77) **Going Correction** +0.025s/f (Slow) **14** Ran SP% **119.6**
Speed ratings (Par 94): **96,94,93,93,92 92,89,86,84,83 80,79,79,66**
toteswinger: 1&2 £3.80, 1&3 £9.40, 2&3 £12.90. CSF £9.26 TOTE £3.10: £1.30, £1.80, £4.40; EX 13.60.
Owner Godolphin **Bred** Gainsborough Farm Llc **Trained** Newmarket, Suffolk

FOCUS
Much better public form had been shown by the experienced runners here and it was reflected in a time 0.98 faster than the first division. Straightforward maiden form.

NOTEBOOK
Magic Doll(USA)'s Newmarket debut third over this distance had been boosted by the sixth-placed Miss Starlight landing a touch at Wolverhampton next time. She knew exactly what was required here, unlike on her debut when slowly away and immature, and won with a bit in hand. With Lammtarra and Kammtarra in the bottom line, a mile should be readily accessible. (op 100-30 tchd 7-2 in a place)
Faithful One(IRE) again found one too good as on her debut at Salisbury over this trip. Once again she showed a good attitude but gives the impression she will be even better with a winter behind her. (op 11-4 tchd 4-1)
Thrill ◆ did best of the newcomers and, despite her dam showing plenty of pace, she has the reserves of her sire Pivotal, and stayed on resolutely enough to indicate that this is the right trip at present. She'll be harder to contain next time.
Flip Flop(IRE) has stamina in her pedigree so did well to go so close at Windsor over six on her debut, but this was a grade higher and she lost nothing in defeat. Another furlong won't be a bother. (op 9-2 tchd 4-1)
Sheila Toss(IRE), a 155,000gns yearling, showed enough on her debut to indicate that she has the ability to repay some of that purchase price. She kept on well without having a hard time and, like all her stable's better runners, will step up several gears next time. (op 33-1)
Eleanora Duse(IRE) comes from a Ballymacoll Stud family with a stamina influence and showed enough potential without ever looking likely to get involved. We won't see the best of her until next season. (op 11-1)
Wild Rockette finished about the same distance behind Faithful One as on her debut but will be interesting in nurseries around this trip or a bit further. (tchd 25-1)
Thereafter(USA) failed to build on her debut third but, even though that was six and this was a furlong further, we won't see her at her best until she races beyond a mile. (tchd 7-1)
Tap Dance Way(IRE) was never in the race but gave the impression she has ability. Official explanation: jockey said the filly hung left in the straight
Banco Busto(IRE) Official explanation: jockey said the filly hung left throughout

6165 ROOKS RIDER H'CAP 1m 4f (P)
4:00 (4:00) (Class 3) (0-95,89) 3-Y-O **£7,352** (£2,201; £1,100; £551; £274) **Stalls** Centre

Form | | | | RPR
166 **1** **Highland Glen**[95] 3051 3-9-4 **89** ... RyanMoore 4 101
(Sir Michael Stoute) *awkward leaving stalls and v.s.a: hdwy to ld over 10f out: mde rest: qcknd 3f out: hrd pressed and drvn ins fnl f: r.o wl* **2/1**[1]
511 **2** *1* **Ottoman Empire (FR)**[12] 5781 3-9-4 **89** ... TedDurcan 2 99
(D R Lanigan) *chsd ldrs: wnt 2nd over 7f out: rdn 3f out: hung rt u.p jst over 2f out: rallied u.str.p to press wnr ins fnl f: no ex fnl 75yds* **9/4**[2]
6411 **3** *hd* **Tinaar (USA)**[16] 5667 3-8-11 **82** ... WilliamBuick 3 92
(G A Butler) *t.k.h early: hld up in tch in last pair: rdn 3f out: chsd ldng pair over 1f out: kpt on u.p ins fnl f: nt rch ldrs* **9/4**[2]
3040 **4** *3 ¾* **Barwell Bridge**[31] 5230 3-9-3 **88** ... JamesDoyle 1 92
(S Kirk) *t.k.h: led tl over 10f out: chsd wnr tl over 7f out: rdn and unable qck 3f out: wknd over 1f out* **8/1**[3]
-505 **5** *11* **Simple Solution (USA)**[89] 3280 3-8-10 **81** ... MichaelHills 5 67
(B W Hills) *in tch in last pair: pushed along over 4f out: lost tch over 2f out* **16/1**

2m 31.19s (-3.31) **Going Correction** +0.025s/f (Slow) **5** Ran SP% **111.9**
Speed ratings (Par 105): **112,111,111,108,101**
toteswinger: 1&2 £4.00. CSF £6.99 TOTE £2.80: £1.60, £1.30; EX 6.70.
Owner The Queen **Bred** The Queen **Trained** Newmarket, Suffolk

FOCUS
Despite there being only five runners, it was an extremely tight handicap with some seriously in-form contenders. Decent form.

NOTEBOOK
Highland Glen was having his first run since being gelded after failing to load at Goodwood. Before that he had faced an impossible task from the rear when sixth in the King George V Handicap at Royal Ascot (three places behind Barwell Bridge) and before that he couldn't operate in the Haydock mud. His sole previous success had come when an easy winner of a modest 1m2f maiden at Lingfield in May, but this performance told us a whole lot more as he served it up to them the hard way and showed fine battling qualities. He was tardy leaving the stalls but Ryan Moore wanted him in front and, when the fight began in earnest up the home straight, the gelding was equal to it. The surface suits him and, while he was no doubt fit, he might be a bit sharper next time as this was his first run for 95 days. There is no reason why he shouldn't stay a little further. (op 3-1)
Ottoman Empire(FR) was on a hat-trick having won his latest start off 85 over course and distance and was 4lb higher for a head win. He tended to idle that night but, despite the rail to help here, couldn't get past the winner. Time might show this was his best performance to date at level weights. (op 15-8)
Tinaar(USA) was another on a hat-trick, having moved from a winning mark of 76 over a furlong less here last time to 82, which was probably enough for a three-quarter length win. She needs to be ridden with restraint and took a while to get rolling up the straight, but she finished to good enough effect to think that 1m4f round here is the right distance. There will be easier handicaps with bigger fields than this. (tchd 15-8 and 5-2 in places)
Barwell Bridge is still 1lb higher than when a career best third to Cosmic Sun at Royal Ascot and there didn't seem an excuse. (op 9-1 tchd 10-1)
Simple Solution(USA) was having her first run for 89 days and was left behind. (op 20-1)

6166 SPARKS CHARITY MAIDEN FILLIES' STKS 1m 4f (P)
4:30 (4:30) (Class 4) 3-4-Y-O **£4,727** (£1,406; £702; £351) **Stalls** Centre

Form | | | | RPR
232 **1** **Samaaha**[19] 5578 3-8-12 79 ... LDettori 6 75+
(Saeed Bin Suroor) *mde all: pushed along and drew clr over 2f out: easily* **6/4**[1]
0-4 **2** *3 ¾* **Beauchamp Xiara**[130] 2006 3-8-12 0 ... DaneO'Neill 9 69+
(H Candy) *chsd ldrs: rdn to chse clr wnr 2f out: no imp u.p after* **3/1**[2]
2222 **3** *4 ½* **Kinetix**[14] 5718 3-8-12 75 ... JimmyFortune 1 59
(J H M Gosden) *chsd ldr: hung bdly lft and btn wl over 2f out: lost 2nd and wl btn 2f out* **3/1**[2]
6403 **4** *½* **Chatanoogachoochoo**[22] 5473 4-9-6 64 ... JimmyQuinn 8 59
(M Hill) *t.k.h: chsd ldrs: rdn and outpcd jst over 2f out: wl btn but pressing for modest 3rd ins fnl f* **11/1**
4 **5** *½* **Ashes Summer (IRE)**[14] 5718 3-8-12 0 ... TolleyDean 10 58
(P R Webber) *t.k.h: rdn and effrt on inner over 2f out: plugged on same pce* **15/2**[3]
6 *2* **Slick Mover (IRE)**[163] 4-9-6 0 ... MichaelHills 5 55
(B G Powell) *s.i.s: in tch: hdwy to chse ldrs over 6f out: rdn and wknd over 2f out* **33/1**
0000 **7** *5* **Miss Jodarah (USA)**[13] 5744 3-8-9 38 ... (b) MarcHalford(3) 2 47?
(J R Best) *t.k.h: hld up in tch towards rr: rdn and struggling over 3f out: wl bhd fnl 2f* **100/1**
00-0 **8** *3 ½* **Reel Hope**[17] 5647 3-8-12 47 ... SteveDrowne 7 41
(J R Best) *stdd after s: t.k.h and hld up in last pair: pushed along over 6f out: lost tch over 3f out* **100/1**
00 **9** *33* **Duchess Of Alba**[23] 5435 4-9-6 0 ... (t) AdamKirby 4 —
(G C Bravery) *stdd s: hld up in last pair: rdn and lost tch 3f out: t.o and virtually p.u fnl f* **100/1**

2m 36.48s (1.98) **Going Correction** +0.025s/f (Slow)
WFA 3 from 4yo 8lb **9** Ran SP% **116.0**
Speed ratings (Par 102): **94,91,88,88,87 86,83,80,58**
toteswinger: 1&2 £2.60, 1&3 £2.10, 2&3 £4.80. CSF £6.22 TOTE £2.10: £1.10, £1.40, £1.40; EX 9.50.
Owner Godolphin **Bred** Darley **Trained** Newmarket, Suffolk

FOCUS
Some frustrating fillies were on show. The time was poor and the front pair are better than the facts.
Kinetix Official explanation: jockey said that the filly hung left throughout

6167 ENTREPRENEUR COUNTRY H'CAP 6f (P)
5:00 (5:00) (Class 4) (0-85,85) 3-Y-O **£4,727** (£1,406; £702; £351) **Stalls** High

Form | | | | RPR
1103 **1** **Getcarter**[2] 6112 3-8-9 **76** ... RichardHughes 11 83+
(R Hannon) *stdd s: hld up towards rr: pushed along and hdwy 2f out: rdn to chse clr ldr ins fnl f: qcknd to ld towards fin* **2/1**[1]
0360 **2** *½* **Ray Of Joy**[41] 4870 3-9-1 **82** ... JimmyQuinn 12 88
(J R Jenkins) *t.k.h: gd hdwy 2f out: rdn and qcknd to ld jst over 1f out: clr whn wnt rt u.p ins fnl f: hdd and no ex towards fin* **6/1**[3]
1146 **3** *1 ¼* **Victoria Sponge (IRE)**[58] 4317 3-9-3 **84** ... DaneO'Neill 3 86
(R Hannon) *stdd s: hld up in rr: swtchd ins and hdwy wl over 1f out: r.o wl to chse ldng pair ins fnl f: gng on fin* **10/1**
1126 **4** *¾* **Dametime (IRE)**[6] 6086 3-8-11 **78** ... (t) ShaneKelly 5 78
(Daniel Mark Loughnane, Ire) *wnt lft s: chsd ldrs: ev ch u.p 2f out: one pce fnl f* **25/1**
6042 **5** *2 ¼* **Cut The Cackle (IRE)**[22] 5471 3-8-6 **78** ... AshleyMorgan(5) 4 71
(P Winkworth) *restless in stalls: t.k.h: chsd ldrs on outer: rdn ent fnl 2f: wknd jst over 1f out* **12/1**
6510 **6** *2* **Comadoir (IRE)**[25] 5370 3-8-13 **80** ... IanMongan 6 67
(Miss Jo Crowley) *led: rdn and jnd 2f out: hdd jst over 1f out: wknd ins fnl f* **16/1**
2023 **7** *nk* **Strictly**[8] 5902 3-9-1 **82** ... RyanMoore 8 68
(Sir Michael Stoute) *s.i.s: a towards rr: rdn and hanging rt wl over 2f out: plld out ent fnl 2f: nvr trbld ldrs* **9/2**[2]
0002 **8** *½* **Bobs Dreamflight**[87] 3342 3-8-11 **78** ... TPQueally 9 62
(D K Ivory) *restless in stalls: in tch in midfield: rdn and unable qck over 2f out: wknd u.p over 1f out* **11/1**
24-0 **9** *1* **Moscow Eight (IRE)**[137] 1803 3-9-1 **82** ... RichardKingscote 10 63
(Tom Dascombe) *in tch: effrt to chse ldrs u.p wl over 1f out: drvn and wknd over 1f out* **6/1**[3]
1030 **10** *4* **Klynch**[21] 5523 3-9-1 **82** ... (b) MartinDwyer 2 51
(B J Meehan) *s.i.s: a bhd: rn wd bnd 3f out: no ch and hung rt fnl 3f* **20/1**
4-60 **11** *1 ¼* **Asaint Needs Brass (USA)**[17] 5646 3-8-8 **75** ... SteveDrowne 7 41
(J R Best) *chsd ldrs: swtchd lft and rdn over 2f out: sn struggling: bhd fnl f* **50/1**

1m 12.08s (-1.02) **Going Correction** +0.025s/f (Slow) **11** Ran SP% **121.7**
Speed ratings (Par 103): **107,106,104,103,100 98,97,96,95,90 88**
toteswinger: 1&2 £4.20, 1&3 £7.20, 2&3 £10.00. CSF £14.28 CT £103.57 TOTE £3.00: £1.30, £2.00, £3.20; EX 15.50.
Owner Mrs J K Powell **Bred** C R Mason **Trained** East Everleigh, Wilts

FOCUS
A fair handicap. The form looks solid enough.

6168 AVANTA H'CAP 1m (P)
5:30 (5:30) (Class 4) (0-85,85) 3-Y-O+ £4,727 (£1,406; £702; £351) Stalls High

Form RPR
5000 1 **Hurricane Spirit (IRE)**[16] 5665 5-9-3 **80**........................ SteveDrowne 9 88
(J R Best) *t.k.h: hld up towards rr: rdn and gd hdwy towards inner wl over 1f out: chal ent fnl f: led ins fnl f: r.o wl* **20/1**
1445 2 1 **Northern Spy (USA)**[21] 5511 5-8-9 **72**.............................. TPQueally 1 78
(S Dow) *chsd ldrs: rdn and effrt over 2f out: kpt on same pce u.p ins fnl f* **10/1**
1435 3 nk **Emperor Court (IRE)**[12] 5772 5-9-6 **83**................................ NCallan 2 88
(P J Makin) *t.k.h: chsd ldrs on outer: led over 4f out: rdn and hrd pressed 2f out: hdd and no ex ins fnl f* **16/1**
4104 4 shd **Audemar (IRE)**[16] 5665 3-8-11 **78**.............................. RichardHughes 5 83+
(E F Vaughan) *t.k.h: hld up towards rr: hdwy and edging rt looking for run wl over 1f out: chsd ldrs ins fnl f: one pce fnl 100yds* **5/1**[2]
0224 5 1 1/2 **Forbidden (IRE)**[3] 6078 6-8-8 **71**..............................(bt[1]) ShaneKelly 10 76+
(Daniel Mark Loughnane, Ire) *hmpd sn after s: bhd: stl bhd but in tch whn nt clr run over 1f out: hmpd jst ins fnl f: r.o wl fnl 100yds: nvr able to chal* **20/1**
0221 6 hd **Implication**[14] 5731 3-8-8 **75**... RyanMoore 14 80+
(E A L Dunlop) *towards rr: effrt towards inner ent fnl 2f: in tch whn bdly hmpd and lost any ch jst ins fnl f: pushed along and kpt on after but nt rcvr* **6/4**[1]
/005 7 hd **Apex**[16] 5663 8-8-3 **71** oh1.. AmyBaker(5) 11 72
(M Hill) *dwlt: towards rr: hdwy into midfield: rdn ent fnl 2f: kpt on same pce fnl f* **14/1**
1600 8 nk **Elusive Fame (USA)**[9] 5884 3-8-7 **74**............................(v[1]) GregFairley 4 74
(M Johnston) *chsd ldr tl over 4f out: rdn over 2f out: wknd u.p over 1f out* **33/1**
060 9 3 **Jaser**[51] 4517 4-9-6 **83**.. JimmyFortune 7 76
(P W Chapple-Hyam) *hld up in tch towards rr: rdn and hanging rt over 2f out: nvr trbld ldrs* **12/1**
6021 10 1 3/4 **Bomber Command (USA)**[17] 5640 6-9-5 **85**.............(v) PatrickHills(3) 6 74
(J W Hills) *in tch in midfield on outer: rdn and unable qck ent fnl 2f: wknd over 1f out* **8/1**
004 11 1 1/2 **L'Hirondelle (IRE)**[89] 3282 5-9-8 **85**............................ EddieAhern 3 73+
(M J Attwater) *chsd ldrs tl led over 6f out: hdd over 4f out: chsd ldr tl wknd u.p wl over 1f out: eased whn losing pl over 1f out* **10/1**
3314 12 14 **Fancy Footsteps (IRE)**[16] 5663 4-8-10 **76**...................... JackMitchell(3) 8 57+
(C G Cox) *in tch: effrt and rdn on inner ent fnl 2f: one pce and struggling to hold pl whn bdly hmpd and almost b.d jst ins fnl f: nt rcvr* **13/2**[3]
0000 13 dist **Mangham (IRE)**[25] 5375 4-9-7 **84**................................ JimCrowley 12 —
(D H Brown) *led tl over 6f out: lost pl qckly 4f out: t.o and virtually p.u fnl 3f: b.b.v* **20/1**

1m 38.63s (-1.17) **Going Correction** +0.025s/f (Slow)
WFA 3 from 4yo+ 4lb **13 Ran SP% 136.8**
Speed ratings (Par 105): **106,105,104,104,103 102,102,102,99,97 96,82,—**
toteswinger: 1&2 £48.90, 1&3 £62.70, 2&3 £19.50. CSF £225.65 CT £3433.38 TOTE £31.70: £7.10, £4.20, £5.80; EX 378.10 Place 6: £7.72, Place 5: £6.74..
Owner The Little House Partnership **Bred** Knocktoran Stud **Trained** Hucking, Kent

FOCUS
An extremely rough race going to the last furlong where Fancy Footsteps was smashed into the rail following a domino effect and was extremely lucky not to come down. Ordinary form for the grade.
Implication Official explanation: jockey said filly suffered interference in running
Jaser Official explanation: jockeys said the colt hung right
Fancy Footsteps(IRE) Official explanation: jockey said the filly suffered interference in running
Mangham(IRE) Official explanation: vet said the gelding bled from the nose
T/Plt: £13.50 to a £1 stake. Pool: £44,777.69. 2,410.70 winning tickets. T/Qpdt: £4.50 to a £1 stake. Pool: £3,145.80. 514.00 winning tickets. SP

5934 LEICESTER (R-H)
Monday, September 21

OFFICIAL GOING: Good to firm (8.3)
Wind: Light behind Weather: Overcast

6169 TODAY'S THE BIG DAY FILLIES' NURSERY 5f 218y
2:20 (2:23) (Class 5) (0-75,75) 2-Y-O £3,238 (£963; £481; £240) Stalls Low

Form RPR
6100 1 **Angel Of Fashion (IRE)**[15] 5692 2-9-4 **72**................. RobertWinston 11 77+
(B W Hills) *chsd ldrs: rdn over 1f out: edgd rt ins fnl f: styd on to ld towards fin* **3/1**[1]
3102 2 nk **Quaker Parrot**[8] 5899 2-9-2 **75**.............................. RossAtkinson(5) 9 80+
(Tom Dascombe) *chsd ldr: led over 4f out: rdn over 2f out: edgd rt ins fnl f: hdd towards fin* **3/1**[1]
4106 3 1 3/4 **Rosedale**[17] 5635 2-8-3 **57** ow1.................................... RoystonFfrench 1 56
(J A R Toller) *hld up: rdn over 2f out: hung rt and r.o ins fnl f: nt rch ldrs* **8/1**[3]
1560 4 2 3/4 **Bubbelas**[38] 4975 2-9-0 **68**.. GrahamGibbons 6 59
(J J Quinn) *led: hdd over 4f out: chsd ldrs: rdn over 2f out: styd on* **16/1**
0000 5 3/4 **Mrs Puff (IRE)**[6] 5967 2-7-12 **52**.............................. SilvestreDeSousa 7 41
(P D Evans) *hld up: pushed along 4f out: rdn over 2f out: edgd rt and r.o wl towards fin: nvr nrr* **16/1**
4306 6 nse **Bathwick Xaara**[33] 5166 2-8-13 **67**................................. PatCosgrave 3 56
(J G Portman) *chsd ldrs: rdn over 2f out: styd on same pce fnl f* **12/1**
5010 7 1/2 **Emirates Hills**[11] 5797 2-9-7 **75**.................................(v[1]) ChrisCatlin 10 62
(E F Vaughan) *s.i.s: sn chsng ldrs: rdn over 2f out: no ex fnl f* **7/1**[2]
1044 8 1 **White Daffodil (IRE)**[26] 5344 2-8-13 **67**.............................. PatDobbs 12 53+
(R Hannon) *hld up: rdn over 2f out: hdwy over 1f out: no imp whn nt clr run and eased ins fnl f* **8/1**[3]
6654 9 1 1/2 **Venture Girl (IRE)**[25] 5372 2-8-3 **57**.............................. DuranFentiman 13 37
(T D Easterby) *hld up: rdn over 3f out: n.d* **12/1**
4464 10 1 3/4 **Abbi Jicaro**[25] 5358 2-7-12 **52** oh3.................................. DavidProbert 2 26
(Mrs L Williamson) *s.i.s: hld up: rdn 1/2-way: a in rr* **40/1**
0040 11 3 3/4 **Avec Moi**[7] 5950 2-8-1 **55** oh4 ow3................................ FrancisNorton 5 18
(Mrs C A Dunnett) *hld up: hdwy over 3f out: sn rdn: wknd over 2f out* **40/1**
0564 12 3/4 **Hot Rod Mamma (IRE)**[18] 5596 2-8-5 **59**................ FrankieMcDonald 4 20
(A Berry) *hld up: rdn and wknd over 2f out* **25/1**
0006 13 2 1/4 **Teeraha (IRE)**[10] 5835 2-7-12 **52** oh3................................ JamieMackay 8 6
(D Shaw) *plld hrd and prom: rdn and wknd over 2f out* **100/1**

1m 12.07s (-0.93) **Going Correction** -0.25s/f (Firm) **13 Ran SP% 121.6**
Speed ratings (Par 92): **96,95,93,89,88 88,87,86,84,82 77,76,73**
toteswinger: 1&2 £4.30, 1&3 £9.80, 2&3 £6.70. CSF £10.29 CT £69.15 TOTE £3.90: £1.40, £1.10, £3.70; EX 15.40 Trifecta £105.50 Pool: £202.52 - 1.42 winning units..
Owner John Sillett **Bred** Grangemore Stud **Trained** Lambourn, Berks

FOCUS
A decent fillies' nursery in which the main action took place towards the centre of the track. Solid form.

NOTEBOOK
Angel Of Fashion(IRE), dropped in trip and grade, justified good market support and gained her second course-and-distance win. Having travelled well towards the outer, she was made to work hard by the runner-up, and changed her legs under strong pressure, but still just did enough. She won't appeal if a short price to follow up. (op 6-1)
Quaker Parrot showed good speed throughout and kept on well after coming under pressure before the winner, although she didn't help herself by edging right. A rise in the weights will force her up in class. (op 5-2 tchd 15-8 and 7-2)
Rosedale, carrying 1lb overweight, raced away from the front two and never looked like winning, before running around a little when keeping on into third. (tchd 9-1)
Bubbelas hasn't progressed since winning a maiden on his second start and was comfortably held in second. (op 20-1)
Mrs Puff(IRE) lacked the pace of some of these and didn't offer much. (op 25-1)

6170 CLEAN 'N FRESH (S) STKS 7f 9y
2:50 (2:52) (Class 6) 3-Y-O £1,942 (£578; £288; £144) Stalls Low

Form RPR
3445 1 **Equipe De Nuit**[5] 5999 3-8-8 **65**.............................. WilliamCarson(3) 2 73+
(S C Williams) *mde all against nr side rail: rdn clr fr over 1f out: styd on wl: hung rt nr fin* **3/1**[1]
2040 2 6 **King's Sabre**[16] 5676 3-8-8 **65**.............................. RussellKennemore(3) 8 58
(W R Muir) *a.p: rdn to chse wnr over 3f out: no ex whn hung lft ins fnl f* **9/1**
0003 3 1 3/4 **Versaki (IRE)**[6] 5972 3-9-2 **68**......................................(t) JamieSpencer 6 60+
(Ian Williams) *hld up: hrd rdn fr over 2f out: hdwy and hung rt fr over 1f out: wnt 3rd ins fnl f: nvr trbld ldrs* **5/1**[2]
0004 4 3 **Kinigi (IRE)**[14] 5716 3-8-11 **51**...................................... KirstyMilczarek 11 46
(R A Harris) *mid-div: drvn along and hdwy over 2f out: no imp fr over 1f out* **28/1**
5004 5 1/2 **Deckchair**[29] 5287 3-8-11 **49**......................................(v) RobertWinston 12 45
(S Curran) *chsd ldrs: rdn over 2f out: wknd fnl f* **16/1**
0000 6 nk **Jimwil (IRE)**[7] 5955 3-9-2 **68**......................................(b) PhillipMakin 10 49
(M Dods) *s.i.s: in rr: rdn over 2f out: sme hdwy and hung rt over 1f out: n.d* **7/1**
5606 7 6 **Rosie Two**[28] 5316 3-8-7 **50** ow1................................ FergusSweeney 4 25
(W S Kittow) *hld up: rdn over 2f out: nvr on terms* **33/1**
0506 8 5 **Balzarine**[13] 5751 3-8-6 **47**... FrancisNorton 13 12
(M Blanshard) *prom: rdn 1/2-way: wknd over 2f out* **33/1**
010 9 2 1/4 **Athaakeel (IRE)**[18] 5612 3-8-6 **63**.................................. KevinGhunowa 3 6
(R A Harris) *chsd ldrs: rdn over 3f out: wknd over 2f out* **16/1**
0430 10 6 **Clear Hand**[17] 5632 3-8-11 **49**......................................(b) DarryllHolland 5 —
(B R Millman) *chsd ldrs tl rdn and wknd 1/2-way* **20/1**
16 11 3 **Jenny's Pride (IRE)**[28] 5306 3-8-6 **56**................................ ChrisCatlin 14 —
(John A Harris) *chsd ldrs: drvn along over 3f out: wknd sn after* **13/2**[3]
0-50 12 12 **Lady Meg (IRE)**[11] 5789 3-8-6 **40**.................................... DavidProbert 15 —
(B Palling) *prom: rdn 1/2-way: sn wknd* **50/1**
0064 13 6 **Portugese Caddy**[6] 5972 3-9-2 **66**..............................(b[1]) LukeMorris 1 —
(P Winkworth) *s.s and looked reluctant in rr: a bhd* **10/1**
0000 14 1/2 **Vin De Rose**[10] 5840 3-8-8 **35**.................................. FrederikTylicki(3) 9 —
(John A Harris) *sn pushed along in rr: lost tch 1/2-way* **100/1**

1m 24.06s (-2.14) **Going Correction** -0.25s/f (Firm) **14 Ran SP% 115.4**
Speed ratings (Par 99): **102,95,93,89,89 88,81,76,73,66 63,49,42,42**
toteswinger: 1&2 £10.10, 1&3 £7.50, 2&3 £9.70. CSF £26.77 TOTE £4.90: £1.40, £2.90, £2.00; EX 35.00 Trifecta £292.20 Part won. Pool: £394.87 - 0.65 winning units..The winner was bought in for 5,000gns.
Owner Hamill, Ostlere & George **Bred** A B Phipps **Trained** Newmarket, Suffolk

FOCUS
A standard seller in which the winner was one of the best off at the weights, but shrewd tactics also played a big part. The winner is rated just above the best of this year's form.
Lady Meg(IRE) Official explanation: vet said the filly lost a shoe
Portugese Caddy Official explanation: jockey said that the gelding was slowly away

6171 ENLIVEN H'CAP 5f 2y
3:20 (3:21) (Class 4) (0-85,85) 3-Y-O+ £4,857 (£1,445; £722; £360) Stalls Low

Form RPR
0236 1 **Le Toreador**[9] 5856 4-9-4 **84**......................................(tp) JamieSpencer 7 97
(K A Ryan) *mde all: rdn and edgd rt over 1f out: r.o* **5/1**[3]
0013 2 1 1/2 **Total Impact**[6] 5974 6-9-2 **85**.............................. FrederikTylicki(3) 10 93
(R A Fahey) *hld up in tch: pushed along 1/2-way: rdn over 1f out: r.o to go 2nd wl ins fnl f: nt trble wnr* **4/1**[1]
2000 3 1 **Legal Eagle (IRE)**[33] 5148 4-8-10 **76**.......................... SilvestreDeSousa 1 80
(Paul Green) *chsd ldrs: rdn over 1f out: styd on* **6/1**
0261 4 nse **Incomparable**[12] 5768 4-9-2 **82**....................................(b) GrahamGibbons 4 86
(J A Glover) *trckd ldrs: rdn over 1f out: edgd rt and unable qck nr fin* **8/1**
3534 5 1/2 **Nickel Silver**[37] 5031 4-8-10 **76**................................(b) RoystonFfrench 9 78
(B Smart) *chsd ldrs: rdn over 1f out: sn edgd lft: styd on same pce ins fnl f* **9/2**[2]
3051 6 nk **Make My Dream**[10] 5830 6-8-5 **71** oh3.................................... TPO'Shea 3 74+
(J Gallagher) *s.i.s: hld up: hdwy and nt clr run ins fnl f: nvr able to chal* **16/1**
00 7 3 1/2 **Doric Lady**[30] 5263 4-8-13 **79**.. KirstyMilczarek 8 67
(J A R Toller) *s.i.s: sn pushed along in rr: hdwy 1f out: eased wl ins fnl f* **10/1**
0402 8 2 1/2 **The Jobber (IRE)**[9] 5871 8-9-2 **82**................................ FrancisNorton 5 61
(M Blanshard) *s.i.s: sn prom: rdn 1/2-way: wknd over 1f out* **15/2**
5233 9 7 **The Tatling (IRE)**[8] 5901 12-8-13 **82**................................ JackDean(3) 6 36
(J M Bradley) *s.i.s: sn pushed along and nvr gng wl: a in rr: lost tch fnl 2f* **12/1**

58.12 secs (-1.88) **Going Correction** -0.25s/f (Firm) **9 Ran SP% 114.7**
Speed ratings (Par 105): **105,102,101,100,100 99,94,90,78**
toteswinger: 1&2 £3.60, 1&3 £8.10, 2&3 £8.70. CSF £25.13 CT £122.73 TOTE £6.10: £1.70, £2.00, £2.50; EX 31.00 Trifecta £223.00 Part won. Pool: £301.36 - 0.50 winning units..
Owner Guy Reed **Bred** G Reed **Trained** Hambleton, N Yorks

FOCUS
A fair sprint handicap and very few got into it. They raced towards the stands' side. The winner remains largely progressive.
Make My Dream Official explanation: jockey said the gelding was denied a clear run

The Jobber(IRE) Official explanation: jockey said the gelding was never travelling

6172 TRIPLE VELVET CLAIMING STKS 1m 1f 218y
3:50 (3:50) (Class 6) 3-4-Y-O **£1,942** (£578; £288; £144) **Stalls** High

Form RPR
1003 **1** **Traphalgar (IRE)**[7] 5936 4-9-3 83 RobertWinston 10 69+
(P F I Cole) *hld up: hdwy 1/2-way: swtchd lft over 2f out: rdn to ld 1f out: edgd rt: styd on* **5/4**[1]
0011 **2** *1 1/2* **Buddhist Monk**[7] 5936 4-9-11 80 (tp) JamieSpencer 1 74+
(Ian Williams) *set stdy pce: tried to qckn over 4f out: sn rdn and looked reluctant: hdd 1f out: kpt on but nvr looked likely to get bk up* **2/1**[2]
0004 **3** *1 3/4* **Bestowed**[20] 5549 4-8-6 45 RachelKing(7) 6 58
(M C Chapman) *chsd ldr: rdn over 1f out: styd on same pce fnl f* **50/1**
2-00 **4** *nk* **Moscow Oznick**[102] 2859 4-8-12 58 RossAtkinson(5) 7 61
(Tom Dascombe) *hld up: rdn and hung rt fr over 1f out: nt rch ldrs* **8/1**[3]
4410 **5** *nk* **Fleur De'Lion (IRE)**[34] 5123 3-8-4 55 DavidProbert 3 54
(S Kirk) *chsd ldrs: rdn over 2f out: ev ch over 1f out: no ex ins fnl f* **14/1**
000 **6** *4 1/2* **Cherry Belle (IRE)**[80] 3588 3-8-2 49 (v) SilvestreDeSousa 8 43
(P D Evans) *hld up: rdn over 4f out: sme hdwy over 1f out: hung rt and no ex fnl f* **33/1**
5023 **7** *18* **Abulharith**[12] 5782 3-8-13 60 LukeMorris 5 18
(R A Harris) *mid-div: hdwy u.p over 2f out: wknd over 1f out: eased fnl f* **10/1**
0-00 **8** *25* **Lily Of The Nile (UAE)**[43] 4828 3-8-2 42 (p) FrankieMcDonald 2 —
(J G Portman) *prom: pushed along 1/2-way: wknd 4f out: t.o* **66/1**
/000 **9** *20* **Days Of Thunder (IRE)**[43] 4812 4-9-3 35 KevinGhunowa 4 —
(B R Summers) *plld hrd and prom: wknd 4f out: t.o* **150/1**
10 *hd* **Spiders Tern** 4-9-2 0 JackDean(3) 9 —
(J M Bradley) *s.s and unruly during early stages: sn t.o* **100/1**

2m 5.46s (-2.44) **Going Correction** -0.25s/f (Firm)
WFA 3 from 4yo 6lb **10** Ran SP% **112.7**
Speed ratings (Par 101): **99,97,96,96,95 92,77,57,41,41**
toteswinger: 1&2 £1.20, 1&3 £8.40, 2&3 £10.30. CSF £3.58 TOTE £1.60: £1.10, £1.40, £8.70; EX 3.60 Trifecta £72.70 Pool: £698.37 - 7.10 winning units..Bestowed was claimed by David Evans for £4,000. Traphalgar was claimed by Ollie Pears for £8,000.
Owner The Fairy Story Partnership **Bred** Deepwood Farm Stud **Trained** Whatcombe, Oxon

FOCUS
An ordinary claimer in which the close proximity of the 45-rated Bestowed does little for the form.
Days Of Thunder(IRE) Official explanation: jockey said that the gelding ran too free

6173 EBF MENTOS NOVICE STKS 7f 9y
4:20 (4:21) (Class 4) 2-Y-O **£5,180** (£1,541; £770; £384) **Stalls** Low

Form RPR
12 **1** **Circumvent**[16] 5664 2-9-5 93 TPO'Shea 5 95+
(P F I Cole) *awkward leaving stalls: sn led: shkn up over 1f out: styd on wl: hung rt nr fin: comf* **4/9**[1]
403 **2** *2* **Muwalla**[11] 5793 2-8-12 84 ChrisCatlin 6 80
(C E Brittain) *chsd wnr: pushed along 1/2-way: rdn over 1f out: styd on same pce fnl f* **3/1**[2]
1002 **3** *9* **Rainsborough**[11] 5811 2-8-12 70 (t) RobertWinston 1 58
(S Curran) *prom: rdn 1/2-way: wknd fnl f* **33/1**
014 **4** *2* **Flipping**[41] 4883 2-9-5 84 FergusSweeney 2 60
(W S Kittow) *chsd ldrs: rdn over 2f out: hung rt and wknd over 1f out* **11/1**[3]

1m 24.13s (-2.07) **Going Correction** -0.25s/f (Firm) **4** Ran SP% **105.5**
Speed ratings (Par 97): **101,98,88,86**
toteswinger: 1&2 £2.10. CSF £1.88 TOTE £1.40; EX 1.80 TRIFECTA Not won..
Owner The Fairy Story Partnership **Bred** Deepwood Farm Stud **Trained** Whatcombe, Oxon

FOCUS
A disappointing turnout numerically, but still quite a useful effort from the winner, who did not need to improve but has more to offer.

NOTEBOOK
Circumvent ◆ had shown himself to be potentially decent on a couple of starts on artificial surfaces and confirmed that impression on his first turf outing. It's true he was allowed an easy enough lead, but he only had to be pushed out with mainly hands and heels and was much the best. A big, scopey gelding, he should do well next year. (op 8-11)
Muwalla, dropped in trip, proved no match for the above-average winner but he was well clear of the remainder and this still rates as a decent effort in defeat. (op 2-1)
Rainsborough was out of his depth and offered little on his debut for this yard, with a tongue-tie fitted for the first time. (op 25-1)
Flipping had previously shown a liking for soft ground and this quick going was no use to him. (op 15-2 tchd 7-1)

6174 JOHN WEST H'CAP 1m 60y
4:50 (4:50) (Class 5) (0-75,75) 3-Y-O+ **£2,914** (£867; £433; £216) **Stalls** High

Form RPR
6005 **1** **Black Dahlia**[4] 6023 4-8-9 64 FrederikTylicki(3) 9 75
(J A Glover) *chsd ldrs: swtchd lft 2f out: squeezed through to ld over 1f out: sn rdn: r.o* **8/1**
2305 **2** *3/4* **Follow The Flag (IRE)**[3] 6072 5-9-2 68 (p) RobertWinston 8 77
(A J McCabe) *hld up: pushed along 1/2-way: hdwy over 3f out: swtchd lft over 2f out: rdn and hung rt ins fnl f: r.o* **7/1**
2442 **3** *3* **Ours (IRE)**[27] 5329 6-9-3 69 (p) ChrisCatlin 4 72
(John A Harris) *hld up: pushed along over 2f out: hdwy over 1f out: nt rch ldrs* **6/1**[2]
6056 **4** *1 1/2* **Hypnotist (UAE)**[22] 5475 3-8-8 64 KoseiMiura 1 63
(C E Brittain) *chsd ldrs: led over 1f out: sn hdd: no ex ins fnl f* **14/1**
3050 **5** *3* **Tourist**[16] 5663 4-9-8 74 GrahamGibbons 5 67
(D Shaw) *s.s: hld up: hdwy over 1f out: no ex fnl f* **16/1**
2300 **6** *1 1/2* **Very Well Red**[16] 5673 6-8-13 68 WilliamCarson(3) 10 58
(P W Hiatt) *led: rdn and hdd over 1f out: wknd ins fnl f* **16/1**
000 **7** *1* **Black Rain**[23] 5448 4-9-3 69 FrancisNorton 3 56
(M Wigham) *hld up in tch: rdn over 2f out: edgd rt: wknd fnl f* **16/1**
410 **8** *nk* **Saturn Girl (IRE)**[16] 5670 3-9-5 75 JamieSpencer 11 62
(S A Callaghan) *hld up: rdn over 2f out: no ch whn hung rt fnl f* **4/1**[1]
2300 **9** *1/2* **Kildare Sun (IRE)**[51] 4548 7-8-12 64 (p) DavidProbert 2 50
(J Mackie) *hld up: rdn over 3f out: edgd rt and wknd fnl f* **12/1**
3642 **10** *3/4* **Shared Moment (IRE)**[7] 5940 3-8-4 60 (p) TPO'Shea 6 44
(J Gallagher) *chsd ldr: rdn over 2f out: ev ch over 1f out: wknd fnl f* **13/2**[3]
4030 **11** *hd* **Royal Composer (IRE)**[23] 5443 6-8-8 60 oh7 RoystonFfrench 7 44
(T D Easterby) *s.s: a in rr: bhd fr 1/2-way* **33/1**
1250 **12** *3 1/4* **Dancing Jest (IRE)**[23] 5441 5-8-10 62 DarryllHolland 12 38
(Rae Guest) *prom tl rdn and wknd over 2f out* **11/1**

1m 42.17s (-2.93) **Going Correction** -0.25s/f (Firm)
WFA 3 from 4yo+ 4lb **12** Ran SP% **114.5**
Speed ratings (Par 103): **104,103,100,98,95 94,93,92,92,91 91,88**
toteswinger: 1&2 £8.60, 1&3 £5.40, 2&3 £8.20. CSF £60.81 CT £365.61 TOTE £8.10: £2.60, £2.80, £2.20; EX 55.50.
Owner Paul J Dixon & Brian Morton **Bred** Worksop Manor Stud **Trained** Babworth, Notts

FOCUS
A modest handicap but solid form, rated through the second.
Saturn Girl(IRE) Official explanation: trainer's representative said that the filly was unsuited by the good to firm ground

6175 CADBURY "HANDS AND HEELS" APPRENTICE SERIES H'CAP 7f 9y
5:20 (5:20) (Class 5) (0-70,69) 3-Y-O+ **£3,238** (£963; £481; £240) **Stalls** Low

Form RPR
2555 **1** **Hobson**[23] 5429 4-9-5 67 AmyScott 2 76
(Eve Johnson Houghton) *s.i.s: hld up: swtchd rt and hdwy over 2f out: led over 1f out: pushed out: eased fnl strides* **8/1**[3]
2431 **2** *3/4* **Ancient Cross**[7] 5948 5-9-5 67 6ex (t) JamesPSullivan 1 74
(M W Easterby) *hld up: hdwy over 2f out: pushed along and ev ch ins fnl f: unable qck towards fin* **13/8**[1]
0-20 **3** *4* **Witchry**[37] 5031 7-9-1 63 DavidKenny 10 59
(A G Newcombe) *hld up in tch: led 2f out: hdd over 1f out: styd on same pce* **10/1**
0342 **4** *1/2* **Mudhish (IRE)**[40] 4914 4-9-7 69 (b) DebraEngland 7 64
(C E Brittain) *chsd ldrs: gng wl enough over 1f out: shkn up and fnd nil* **9/2**[2]
000 **5** *3 1/2* **Royal Adelaide (IRE)**[136] 1837 3-8-1 55 oh10 NathanAlison(3) 6 40
(J A Osborne) *chsd ldrs: pushed along 1/2-way: wknd over 1f out* **50/1**
2360 **6** *1 3/4* **Sion Hill (IRE)**[22] 5479 8-8-8 56 (p) TobyAtkinson 8 37
(John A Harris) *led: hdd 2f out: wknd over 1f out* **16/1**
0420 **7** *1 1/2* **Charlie Delta**[8] 5905 6-8-4 55 oh3 (b) JakePayne(3) 5 32
(R A Harris) *hld up: pushed along over 2f out: sn outpcd* **11/1**
2244 **8** *3 1/2* **Dancing Welcome**[17] 5634 3-8-1 55 oh4 (b) RyanClark(3) 9 22
(J M Bradley) *chsd ldr: pushed along over 2f out: wknd over 1f out* **14/1**
6640 **9** *1* **Viking Awake (IRE)**[21] 5502 3-8-2 56 oh1 ow1 (t) AlexEdwards(3) 3 20
(J W Unett) *hld up: a towards rr* **12/1**
1640 **10** *5* **Jilly Why (IRE)**[24] 5411 8-9-2 64 (b) JohnCavanagh 12 15
(Paul Green) *prom: pushed along over 2f out: wknd over 1f out* **22/1**
11 *27* **Polar Gold**[1044] 7-8-7 55 oh6 RichardRowe 11 —
(A J Chamberlain) *hld up: wknd 1/2-way: t.o* **100/1**
6020 **12** *8* **Rockson (IRE)**[28] 5316 3-8-4 55 oh2 (t) CharlesEddery 4 —
(Ian Williams) *s.i.s: hld up: wknd over 2f out: t.o* **28/1**

1m 23.54s (-2.66) **Going Correction** -0.25s/f (Firm)
WFA 3 from 4yo+ 3lb **12** Ran SP% **115.8**
Speed ratings (Par 103): **105,104,99,99,95 93,91,87,86,80 49,40**
toteswinger: 1&2 £4.40, 1&3 £14.80, 2&3 £6.30. CSF £20.21 CT £136.84 TOTE £9.30: £2.80, £1.50, £3.20; EX 25.10 Trifecta £212.90 Part won. Pool: £287.71 - 0.95 winning units. Place 6: £13.29, Place 5: £8.60..
Owner Anthony Pye-Jeary And Mel Smith **Bred** Hunscote House Farm Stud **Trained** Blewbury, Oxon
■ Stewards' Enquiry : Charles Eddery seven-day ban: use of whip (Oct 11 - 15)

FOCUS
A modest handicap, and these apprentice riders had not ridden more than ten winners prior to April 6 this year. They went a strong pace and the main action took place up the centre of the track late on. The form looks solid.
Jilly Why(IRE) Official explanation: trainer's representative said the mare was unsuited by the good to firm ground
Rockson(IRE) Official explanation: jockey said the filly lost its action
T/Jkpt: £7,100.00 to a £1 stake. Pool: £10,000.00. 1.00 winning ticket. T/Plt: £16.00 to a £1 stake. Pool: £61,602.15. 2,796.48 winning tickets. T/Qpdt: £7.90 to a £1 stake. Pool: £3,895.63. 363.90 winning tickets. CR

5976 BEVERLEY (R-H)
Tuesday, September 22
OFFICIAL GOING: Good to firm (firm in places; 9.0)
Wind: Moderate against Weather: Sunny periods

6177 SEASON FINALE (S) STKS 1m 4f 16y
2:00 (2:00) (Class 5) 3-4-Y-O **£2,590** (£770; £385; £192) **Stalls** High

Form RPR
4043 **1** **Sphere (IRE)**[8] 5947 4-8-11 57 (p) NCallan 4 59+
(P T Midgley) *trckd ldr: hdwy over 3f out and sn cl up: rdn 2f out and sn led: clr appr fnl f: rdn out* **5/2**[1]
2502 **2** *3 1/2* **Tropical Bachelor (IRE)**[3] 6098 3-8-8 64 (b) PaulHanagan 3 59
(T J Pitt) *led: rdn along 3f out and sn jnd: drvn 2f out and sn hdd: kpt on same pce* **5/2**[1]
0504 **3** *2* **Flying Phoebe**[23] 5470 3-8-3 51 GregFairley 5 51
(Mrs L Stubbs) *hld up in rr: hdwy on outer 3f out: rdn along 2f out: styd on to chse ldng pair over 1f out: nrst fin* **5/1**[3]
40-4 **4** *3 1/4* **Madam'X**[22] 5524 3-8-3 51 SilvestreDeSousa 8 46
(Mrs A Duffield) *in tch: effrt over 4f out: rdn along 3f out: plugged on same pce fnl 2f* **4/1**[2]
5002 **5** *3* **Aven Mac (IRE)**[21] 5549 3-8-0 48 ow2 PaulPickard(5) 6 44
(N Bycroft) *hld up in rr: hdwy to chse ldrs 2f out and sn rdn: drvn wl over 1f out and sn wknd* **10/1**
0100 **6** *7* **Carlton Mac**[18] 5625 4-9-7 41 (b) FrancisNorton 7 41
(N Bycroft) *hld up: hdwy on inner to chse ldrs 3f out: rdn over 2f out and sn wknd* **22/1**
-500 **7** *19* **First Hand**[28] 5328 3-8-3 43 (b[1]) DaleGibson 2 —
(M W Easterby) *chsd ldrs: rdn along 1/2-way: drvn and wknd 4f out* **40/1**
0000 **8** *17* **Glamoroso (IRE)**[14] 5549 4-9-2 37 AndrewElliott 9 —
(A Kirtley) *chsd ldng pair: hdwy 4f out: rdn along 3f out: sn wknd* **100/1**

2m 40.81s (-0.09) **Going Correction** +0.10s/f (Good)
WFA 3 from 4yo 8lb **8** Ran SP% **110.7**
Speed ratings (Par 103): **104,101,100,98,96 91,78,67**
toteswinger: 1&2 £2.20, 1&3 £4.20, 2&3 £3.60 CSF £8.08 TOTE £2.90: £1.10, £1.30, £1.90; EX 7.40.Winner bought by D. Penman for 8.000gns.
Owner David Mann **Bred** St Clare Hall Stud **Trained** Westow, N Yorks

FOCUS
After a sustained dry spell the ground was on the quick side and on a very breezy day it was getting faster all the time. A dire opener on the final day's racing this year and a tactical affair with the first two in that position throughout. Weak form.

6178 CERUTTIS 50 YEARS IN EAST YORKSHIRE H'CAP 7f 100y
2:30 (2:32) (Class 5) (0-75,75) 3-Y-O+ **£3,238** (£963; £481; £240) **Stalls** High

Form RPR
3104 **1** **Rio Cobolo (IRE)**[7] 5960 3-8-12 **69**...(v) PhillipMakin 6 79
(Paul Green) *t.k.h: hld up towards rr and sltly hmpd after 1f: in rr tl hdwy 2f out: nt clr run and swtchd lft over 1f out: sn rdn and styd on to ld last 100yds* **15/2**[2]

6644 **2** *nk* **Inter Vision (USA)**[18] 5623 9-9-5 **73**... DanielTudhope 5 83
(A Dickman) *s.i.s and hld up in rr: hdwy on wd outside over 2f out: str run over 1f out: rdn to ld briefly ins fnl f: sn drvn and hdd last 100yds: nt qckn* **11/1**

3030 **3** *4* **Salerosa (IRE)**[40] 4932 4-8-10 **64**... DuranFentiman 2 65
(Mrs A Duffield) *hld up: hdwy 3f out: rdn to chse ldrs 2f out: drvn and ev ch appr fnl f: sn one pce* **22/1**

2650 **4** *1* **Capucci**[19] 5598 4-9-7 **75**... GrahamGibbons 8 74
(J J Quinn) *dwlt and sn pushed along into midfield: hdwy and in tch 4f out: chsd ldrs over 2f out and sn rdn: drvn and ch ent fnl f: kpt on same pce* **11/2**[1]

0032 **5** *½* **Tiger Dream**[25] 5395 4-8-10 **69**... AmyRyan(5) 3 67+
(K A Ryan) *towards rr: hdwy 2f out: nt clr run and swtchd lft over 1f out: rdn and styd on wl fnl f: nrst fin* **8/1**[3]

1660 **6** *shd* **West End Lad**[24] 5418 6-9-1 **72**...(b) RussellKennemore(3) 11 70+
(S R Bowring) *in tch whn n.m.r 3f out: sn pushed along and hdwy 2f out: rdn and one pce appr fnl f* **14/1**

1406 **7** *nk* **Lady Florence**[20] 5565 4-8-5 **64**... Louis-PhilippeBeuzelin(5) 13 60
(A B Coogan) *chsd ldrs: rdn along over 2f out: drvn over 1f out and sn one pce* **14/1**

010 **8** *nk* **Mozayada (USA)**[17] 5673 5-8-12 **66**... FrancisNorton 15 62
(M Brittain) *chsd ldrs: hdwy 3f out: led 2f out and sn rdn: drvn and hdd jst ins fnl f: wknd* **12/1**

0063 **9** *2* **Fiefdom (IRE)**[13] 5780 7-9-2 **70**... PaulHanagan 1 62+
(I W McInnes) *midfield: hdwy 2f out: sn rdn along and n.m.r wl over 1f out: no imp* **20/1**

1054 **10** *½* **Minturno (USA)**[8] 5955 3-8-11 **68**...(p) SilvestreDeSousa 7 60+
(Mrs A Duffield) *in tch whn awkward bnd at 1/2-way: sn rdn along and towards rr after* **15/2**[2]

6463 **11** *7* **Ultimate Respect (USA)**[10] 5886 3-8-12 **69**... JoeFanning 4 41+
(M Johnston) *dwlt: racd wd in midfield: rdn along over 2f out: n.d and wl hld whn n.m.r over 1f out* **11/1**

410 **12** *¾* **Arteus**[20] 5575 3-9-3 **74**...(p) DarryllHolland 9 45
(Jane Chapple-Hyam) *cl up: led briefly over 2f out: sn rdn and hdd: drvn and wknd wl over 1f out* **12/1**

2300 **13** *¾* **Andean Margin (IRE)**[24] 5418 3-8-6 **70**...(b) JamesPSullivan(7) 14 39
(M W Easterby) *prom: effrt 3f out: sn rdn and wknd wl over 1f out* **22/1**

0003 **14** *21* **Nuit Sombre (IRE)**[24] 5418 9-9-0 **68**...(v) TonyHamilton 10 —
(G A Harker) *led: rdn along 3f out: hdd over 2f out and wknd: bhd and eased over 1f out* **15/2**[2]

1m 33.93s (0.13) **Going Correction** +0.10s/f (Good)
WFA 3 from 4yo+ 3lb **14** Ran SP% **120.6**
Speed ratings (Par 103): **103,102,98,96,96 96,95,95,93,92 84,83,83,59**
toteswinger: 1&2 £20.60, 1&3 £38.10, 2&3 £53.00 CSF £85.12 CT £1730.34 TOTE £8.30: £2.80, £5.80, £6.00; EX 102.40.
Owner The Keely Gang **Bred** Yvonne & Gerard Kennedy **Trained** Lydiate, Merseyside

FOCUS
A wide-open 64-75 handicap run at a furious pace which suited those held up.

6179 VICKY'S BIG ANNIVERSARY DAY NOVICE STKS 5f
3:00 (3:00) (Class 4) 2-Y-O **£3,885** (£1,156; £577; £288) **Stalls** High

Form RPR
1 **1** **Coolminx (IRE)**[16] 5693 2-9-0 0... PaulHanagan 3 83+
(R A Fahey) *mde all: rdn over 1f out: drvn ins fnl f and kpt on wl* **1/1**[1]

16 **2** *hd* **Dorback**[42] 4883 2-9-5 0... DaneO'Neill 5 87+
(H Candy) *trckd wnr on inner: hdwy 2f out: swtchd lft and rdn to chal over 1f out: drvn and ev ch ins fnl f: kpt on: jst hld* **7/4**[2]

00 **3** *3* **Fair Bunny**[8] 5949 2-8-7 0... GrahamGibbons 6 64
(A D Brown) *hld up: pushed along bef 1/2-way: hdwy 2f out: rdn over 1f out: kpt on ins fnl f: nrst fin* **100/1**

4 **4** *½* **Burnt Cream**[129] 2089 2-8-7 0... TomEaves 4 62
(B Smart) *dwlt: trckd ldrs: hdwy over 2f out: rdn wl over 1f out: drvn and wknd appr fnl f* **15/2**[3]

0515 **5** *3½* **Brambleberry**[33] 5194 2-9-5 83... RichardKingscote 1 62
(Tom Dascombe) *cl up: rdn along 2f out: sn drvn and grad wknd* **14/1**

4510 **6** *22* **Camacho Flyer (IRE)**[8] 5945 2-9-0 72...(v) NCallan 2 —
(P T Midgley) *dwlt: sn chsng ldrs: rdn along 2f out and sn wknd* **20/1**

65.50 secs (2.00) **Going Correction** +0.225s/f (Good) **6** Ran SP% **110.5**
Speed ratings (Par 97): **93,92,87,87,81 46**
toteswinger: 1&2 £1.10, 1&3 £12.60, 2&3 £19.60 CSF £2.83 TOTE £1.50: £1.20, £1.60; EX 2.90.

Owner Mrs H Steel **Bred** D Couper Snr **Trained** Musley Bank, N Yorks

FOCUS
A match on paper turned out to be just that in this interesting novice event. The blustery headwind almost certainly accounted for the slow time and the first two can rate higher.

NOTEBOOK
Coolminx(IRE), who is not that big, won despite looking inexperienced first time at York. Here she took a keen hold in front but answered her rider's every call in the gamest possible fashion and just clung on. She will probably go searching for some black type now. (op 10-11 tchd 11-10)
Dorback, who created such a big impression when scoring at Windsor on his debut, flopped at Nottingham next time after which he scoped badly. An imposing individual, he looks to have grown a fair bit in his six weeks' absence. Happy to accept a lead when pulled off the fence, he threw down a determined challenge and was only just denied. Six furlongs on less quick ground will suit him even better. (op 13-8 tchd 11-8)
Fair Bunny, 22 lengths behind Coolminx on her debut at York, showed little next time. Struggling to keep up in last, she stayed on late to snatch third spot. She was sheltered from the wind much of the race and she was almost certainly flattered. This will have blown a likely low nursery mark out of the water.
Burnt Cream, fourth on her debut in an ordinary maiden at Thirsk, was much too keen and tired late on. Quite a big filly, she will make a better three-year-old but will need to learn to settle better. (op 11-1 tchd 12-1)
Brambleberry matched strides with the winner but was put in her place in the end. Her two wins have come over the sharp five on the Polytrack at Lingfield.
Camacho Flyer(IRE) was out of his depth and, dropping right away, was eventually eased right off. (op 33-1)

6180 VIOLET AND EDDIE SMITH MEMORIAL CONDITIONS STKS 5f
3:30 (3:30) (Class 3) 3-Y-O+
£7,477 (£2,239; £1,119; £560; £279; £140) **Stalls** High

Form RPR
6563 **1** **Captain Dunne (IRE)**[10] 5860 4-8-9 96... DavidAllan 8 105+
(T D Easterby) *trckd ldng pair: swtchd lft and effrt wl over 1f out: qcknd to ld appr fnl f and sn clr* **10/11**[1]

0455 **2** *4½* **Pawan (IRE)**[2] 6135 9-8-10 83 ow6...(b) AnnStokell(5) 4 91
(Miss A Stokell) *towards rr: hdwy on outer 2f out and sn rdn: styd on ins fnl f to take 2nd nr line* **40/1**

0005 **3** *½* **Ishetoo**[10] 5860 5-8-6 94...(p) FrederikTylicki(3) 2 83
(A Dickman) *chsd ldrs on outer: hdwy 2f out: rdn to chse wnr ent fnl f: sn drvn and kpt on same pce* **3/1**[2]

0000 **4** *1¾* **Matsunosuke**[33] 5196 7-9-8 99... DarryllHolland 5 91+
(A B Coogan) *hld up: hdwy wl over 1f out: rdn whn n.m.r and swtchd rt ins fnl f: nrst fin* **18/1**

02-0 **5** *2* **Guertino (IRE)**[7] 5959 4-8-11 87 ow2... DNolan 7 72
(C J Teague) *dwlt: chsd ldrs tl rdn along and outpcd fr wl over 1f out* **66/1**

0200 **6** *¾* **Buachaill Dona (IRE)**[10] 5860 6-9-3 101... AdrianTNicholls 3 75
(D Nicholls) *cl up: rdn to ld 2f out: drvn and hdd appr fnl f: sn wknd* **6/1**[3]

0-00 **7** *7* **Percolator**[94] 3145 3-8-3 95... JoeFanning 9 37
(P F I Cole) *led: rdn along and hdd 2f out: sn wknd* **10/1**

63.69 secs (0.19) **Going Correction** +0.225s/f (Good)
WFA 3 from 4yo+ 1lb **7** Ran SP% **110.0**
Speed ratings (Par 107): **107,99,99,96,93 91,80**
toteswinger: 1&2 £3.90, 1&3 £1.40, 2&3 £7.10 CSF £39.71 TOTE £1.90: £1.40, £4.50; EX 25.20.

Owner Middleham Park Racing Xv **Bred** Ballybrennan Stud Ltd **Trained** Great Habton, N Yorks

FOCUS
A wide rangy of ability on show in this 5f Class 3 sprint. The winner is rated to his best.

NOTEBOOK
Captain Dunne(IRE), third in the Portland at Doncaster, enjoyed being given a nice lead, taking cover from the headwind. Pulled out coming to the final furlong, he quickened clear in a matter of strides, value for six or seven lengths. Though best suited by the minimum trip, he will take his chance in the 6f Sprint Trophy at York's final meeting next month. (op 11-10 tchd 5-6)
Pawan(IRE), carrying 6lb overweight, is a regular in this race and went one better than his third in 2005. He stayed on from the back to replicate his form and placing behind the winner at Southwell in 2008. (op 33-1)
Ishetoo, a length behind the winner when they were third and fifth respectively in the Portland, ran respectably but he is much happier on flatter tracks. He will probably meet the winner again at York. (op 7-2)
Matsunosuke, saddled with a 5lb penalty, was dropped in at the start and never threatened. He looks off the boil at present. Official explanation: jockey said gelding ran too free (op 16-1 tchd 20-1)
Guertino(IRE), who like Pawan had plenty to find, stayed on to snatch fifth spot on just his second start for this stable after over a year on the sidelines.
Buachaill Dona(IRE) showed ahead briefly coming to the final furlong but the way he stopped suggests he has a problem. Official explanation: jcokey said that he eased donw on the gelding on the run to the line, as when he hit the front the horse lost its action and hung right, whereupon he felt it prudent to hold the horse together in the closing stages. (op 11-2 tchd 13-2)
Percolator, 4lb ahead of the winner on official ratings, took a Group 3 at two but then suffered a knee chip. On her third start this time she looked very lean and, after taking them along, fell in a heap and dropped right away. This might well prove to have been her swansong. (op 11-2)

6181 EUROPEAN BREEDERS' FUND MAIDEN STKS 7f 100y
4:00 (4:03) (Class 5) 2-Y-O **£3,753** (£1,108; £554) **Stalls** High

Form RPR
3 **1** **Namecheck (GER)**[15] 5728 2-9-3 0... DaneO'Neill 5 84+
(Saeed Bin Suroor) *trckd ldr: hdwy 3f out: led over 2f out: pushed clr over 1f out: easily* **2/5**[1]

4 **2** *6* **Battle Study (IRE)**[25] 5408 2-9-3 0... GrahamGibbons 7 66+
(A J McCabe) *chsd ldrs on inner: hdwy over 2f out: rdn to chse wnr over 1f out: sn drvn and no imp on wnr* **33/1**

3 *2½* **Princess Emma** 2-8-12 0... PaulHanagan 6 55+
(R A Fahey) *dwlt and towards rr: hdwy 1/2-way: chsd ldrs wl over 1f out: swtchd lft ent fnl f and kpt on to take 3rd nr line: bttr for r* **16/1**

032 **4** *¾* **Amtaar**[42] 4869 2-8-12 69... NCallan 1 53
(C E Brittain) *wnt lft s: sn led: rdn along and hdd over 2f out: drvn over 1f out and grad wknd* **8/1**[3]

5 *1½* **Ostentation** 2-9-3 0... JoeFanning 8 60+
(M Johnston) *s.i.s and green in rr: hdwy wl over 2f out: kpt on ins fnl f: nrst fin: bttr for r* **5/1**[2]

6 *11* **Henry Havelock** 2-9-3 0... TonyHamilton 4 29
(C Grant) *a bhd* **100/1**

05 **7** *hd* **Ilkley**[17] 5674 2-8-5 0... JamesPSullivan(7) 2 24
(M W Easterby) *chsd ldrs: pushed along 1/2-way: sn lost pl and bhd* **100/1**

0 **8** *10* **Miss Isle Control**[18] 5638 2-8-5 0... DeclanCannon(7) 3 —
(A J McCabe) *dwlt: sn chsng ldrs: rdn along 3f out: sn wknd* **100/1**

1m 36.1s (2.30) **Going Correction** +0.10s/f (Good) **8** Ran SP% **111.0**
Speed ratings (Par 95): **90,83,80,79,77 65,64,53**
toteswinger: 1&2 £3.80, 1&3 £2.70, 2&3 £9.40 CSF £21.34 TOTE £1.40: £1.02, £5.00, £3.00; EX 16.30.
Owner Godolphin **Bred** Darley **Trained** Newmarket, Suffolk

FOCUS
A weak maiden and the Godolphin colt was backed as if defeat was out of the question. He won easily and can do better.

NOTEBOOK
Namecheck(GER) had shown plenty of promise when third first time at Newcastle, and the runner-up had boosted the form considerably since. He had the leader covered and strode well clear when pushed along for a few strides, value for double the official margin. He had clearly learnt plenty first time and should be up to making his mark in much stronger company. He looks to have plenty of natural speed and a slight drop back in trip will not be a problem. (op 4-6)
Battle Study(IRE), a well-beaten fourth on his debut at Thirsk three weeks earlier, stayed on to claim second spot. He has plenty of size and scope and should make a fair handicapper at three. (op 25-1)
Princess Emma, who looks as though she may need more time, kept on to secure a modest third spot. (op 11-1 tchd 10-1)
Amtaar, a weak-looking, narrow filly, went left from her outside draw. She took them along but hung left coming off the final turn and tired in the end. She earned a rating of 69 when placed in two all-weather maidens and that type of surface probably suits her better at this stage. (op 6-1)

Ostentation, a rangy newcomer, was clueless. He walked out of the stalls and was never in contention. The penny was starting to drop late on and this half-brother to smart Hatta Fort will hopefully have learnt plenty from this first day at school. (op 9-2 tchd 11-2)

6182 MKM BUILDING SUPPLIES H'CAP — 1m 100y

4:30 (4:30) (Class 5) (0-75,75) 3-Y-O — **£3,238** (£963; £481; £240) **Stalls** High

Form — RPR

2101 **1** **Just Five (IRE)**[70] 3936 3-9-1 **72** .... PhillipMakin 5 77
(M Dods) *trckd ldrs: hdwy 3f out: rdn to chse wnr over 1f out: drvn ins fnl f and styd on gamely to ld nr line* **9/2**[3]

2350 **2** *hd* **Amethyst Dawn (IRE)**[15] 5732 3-8-4 **61** oh5 .... DuranFentiman 8 66
(T D Easterby) *led: clr wl over 2f out: rdn over 1f out: drvn ins fnl f: wknd and hdd nr line* **8/1**

2450 **3** *3/4* **Hel's Angel (IRE)**[8] 5940 3-9-2 **73** .... SilvestreDeSousa 1 76
(Mrs A Duffield) *hld up and bhd: hdwy on outer 3f out: rdn wl over 1f out: styd on strly ins fnl f: nrst fin* **15/2**

0363 **4** *1 1/2* **Steel Trade**[31] 5259 3-8-11 **68** .... DavidAllan 7 68
(M Brittain) *dwlt: hld up: hdwy 1/2-way: rdn to chse ldrs wl over 1f out: drvn and one pce ent fnl f* **8/1**

2324 **5** *1/2* **Northern Flyer (GER)**[17] 5672 3-8-2 **66** ow1 .... IJBrennan(7) 3 65
(J J Quinn) *trckd ldrs: effrt over 2f out and sn rdn: drvn over 1f out and kpt on same pce* **3/1**[1]

0200 **6** *1* **Green Agenda**[17] 5663 3-9-4 **75** .... JoeFanning 6 72
(M Johnston) *dwlt: midfield: hdwy on inner 3f out: sn rdn and no imp* **6/1**

0202 **7** *1 1/2* **Sampower Rose (IRE)**[17] 5672 3-8-8 **65** ow1 .... DarryllHolland 4 58
(D Carroll) *chsd ldr: rdn along wl over 2f out: drvn wl over 1f out and sn wknd* **4/1**[2]

0460 **8** *7* **Wotatomboy**[11] 5836 3-8-4 **61** oh6 .... PaulQuinn 2 39+
(R M Whitaker) *s.i.s: a in rr* **40/1**

1m 47.45s (-0.15) **Going Correction** +0.10s/f (Good) — **8** Ran SP% **113.9**
Speed ratings (Par 101): **104,103,103,101,101 100,98,91**
toteswinger: 1&2 £8.00, 1&3 £4.80, 2&3 £12.30 CSF £39.50 CT £264.89 TOTE £3.40: £1.60, £2.50, £2.80; EX 44.80.
Owner Just Five Racing Partners **Bred** Rathbarry Stud **Trained** Denton, Co Durham

FOCUS
A modest 61-75 three-year-olds' only handicap run at a sound pace. The winner is rated to his mark.
Sampower Rose(IRE) Official explanation: trainer's rep said filly was unsuited by the good to firm, firm in places ground
Wotatomboy Official explanation: jockey said filly was slow away

6183 BRIAN AND JASON MERRINGTON MEMORIAL AMATEUR RIDERS' H'CAP (DIV I) — 1m 1f 207y

5:00 (5:00) (Class 6) (0-60,64) 3-Y-0+ — **£2,186** (£677; £338; £169) **Stalls** High

Form — RPR

0106 **1** **Hurricane Thomas (IRE)**[15] 5733 5-9-13 **50** .... MissPhillipaTutty(5) 10 58
(R A Fahey) *trckd ldr: hdwy to ld 3f out: rdn clr 2f out: kpt on wl u.p fnl f* **8/1**

3225 **2** *1 1/2* **Tivers Song (USA)**[24] 5423 5-9-11 **48** ow2 .... (b) MissABevan(5) 16 53
(John A Harris) *hld up and bhd: hdwy on outer wl over 2f out: rdn over 1f out: kpt on ins fnl f* **11/2**[2]

3500 **3** *shd* **Efidium**[19] 5601 11-10-11 **64** ow6 .... MrSebSpencer(7) 8 69
(N Bycroft) *hld up towards rr: hdwy 4f out: effrt on wd outside 2f out: rdn over 1f out: kpt on ins fnl f* **25/1**

0000 **4** *2 1/2* **Thunderstruck**[7] 5962 4-11-2 **62** ow2 .... MrMSeston 6 62
(J A Glover) *towards rr: hdwy 1/2-way: chsd ldrs 3f out: rdn 2f out: drvn and kpt on same pce appr fnl f* **40/1**

3021 **5** *2 1/4* **Chichen Daawe**[10] 5872 3-9-8 **51** .... DaleSwift(5) 12 47
(B Ellison) *in tch: hdwy over 3f out: rdn to chse ldrs over 2f out: drvn over 1f out and sn one pce* **4/1**[1]

3153 **6** *1/2* **Fossgate**[23] 5469 8-10-9 **55** .... (b) MissSBrotherton 2 50
(J D Bethell) *trckd ldrs: hdwy over 3f out: rdn to chse wnr over 2f out: drvn along over 1f out and sn one pce* **7/1**[3]

4460 **7** *2* **Wellesley**[36] 5103 3-10-3 **55** .... (p) MissGAndrews 11 46+
(W R Swinburn) *trckd ldrs on inner: hdwy over 2f out: rdn and nt clr run over 1f out: swtchd lft to outer and kpt on u.p ins fnl f* **11/1**

3002 **8** *2* **Cecina Marina**[34] 5161 6-9-7 **46** oh1 .... MrJHBrooke(7) 7 33
(Mrs K Walton) *in tch: rdn along 3f out and sn no imp* **33/1**

0400 **9** *1* **Bernix**[40] 4932 7-9-8 **47** .... (p) MissLWilson(7) 1 32
(N Tinkler) *nvr bttr than midfield* **100/1**

0433 **10** *3 1/2* **Silly Gilly (IRE)**[19] 5601 5-10-6 **57** .... MrMWall(5) 14 35+
(R E Barr) *led: rdn along and hdd 3f out: grad wknd* **7/1**[3]

0040 **11** *1/2* **Bold Bomber**[34] 5145 3-9-1 **46** oh1 .... MissACraven(7) 4 23
(Paul Green) *racd wd: prom: rdn along 3f out and sn wknd* **40/1**

0000 **12** *6* **English Archer**[15] 5734 6-9-7 **46** oh1 .... (tp) MrATBrook(7) 13 11
(A Kirtley) *a in rr* **100/1**

4404 **13** *1 3/4* **Bogula (IRE)**[5] 6017 3-10-6 **58** .... MrSWalker 15 19+
(Mrs A Duffield) *a towards in rr* **8/1**

65 **14** *2 1/2* **Persian Tomcat (IRE)**[28] 5328 3-9-5 **46** .... MrPCollington(3) 5 2
(Miss J Feilden) *in tch: hdwy to chse ldrs over 3f out: rdn along over 2f out and sn wknd* **9/1**

06-0 **15** *5* **Smart Pick**[54] 4465 6-9-7 **46** oh1 .... (p) MrMMcGhee(7) 3 —
(Mrs L Williamson) *a towards rr* **100/1**

2m 8.14s (1.14) **Going Correction** +0.10s/f (Good)
WFA 3 from 4yo+ 6lb — **15** Ran SP% **115.6**
Speed ratings (Par 101): **99,97,97,95,93 93,91,90,89,86 86,81,80,78,74**
toteswinger: 1&2 £11.90, 1&3 £27.70, 2&3 £29.50 CSF £47.28 CT £1047.57 TOTE £9.90: £2.40, £2.30, £8.30; EX 70.90.
Owner N D Tutty **Bred** P D Savill **Trained** Musley Bank, N Yorks
■ Stewards' Enquiry : Miss G Andrews three-day ban: two for careless riding (Oct 6 - 13), one-day ban: used whip when out of contention (Oct 6)

FOCUS
A 46-60 amateur riders' handicap run at a sound pace. Limited but sound form.

6184 BRIAN AND JASON MERRINGTON MEMORIAL AMATEUR RIDERS' H'CAP (DIV II) — 1m 1f 207y

5:30 (5:31) (Class 6) (0-60,58) 3-Y-0+ — **£2,186** (£677; £338; £169) **Stalls** High

Form — RPR

013 **1** **Tropical Duke (IRE)**[6] 5983 3-10-0 **55** .... MissVBarr(5) 3 65
(R E Barr) *in rr: hdwy wl over 2f out: rdn to chse ldrs wl over 1f out: styd on to ld ent fnl f: sn clr* **7/1**[3]

0000 **2** *3* **Fitzwarren**[55] 4436 8-9-10 **45** .... (tp) DaleSwift(5) 8 49
(A D Brown) *chsd ldrs: hdwy 3f out: rdn along 2f out: drvn and kpt on ins fnl f* **80/1**

00-0 **3** *1 3/4* **Mojeerr**[6] 5982 3-10-0 **53** .... MrPCollington(3) 12 54
(A J McCabe) *bhd: hdwy over 2f out: nt clr run and swtchd lft over 1f out: sn rdn and kpt on wl fnl f: nrst fin* **40/1**

4-44 **4** *1 1/2* **Follow The Sun (IRE)**[17] 5683 5-10-9 **53** .... (p) MrSWalker 10 51
(Ronald O'Leary, Ire) *hld up in tch: hdwy 1/2-way: rdn to chse ldr wl over 2f out: drvn over 1f out: kpt on same pce* **5/1**[1]

0024 **5** *3/4* **Emperor's Well**[40] 4932 10-10-1 **50** .... (b) MissJoannaMason(5) 15 46+
(M W Easterby) *led: rdn clr 3f out: hdd ent fnl f: wknd* **7/1**[3]

3410 **6** *2 1/4* **Pretty Officer (USA)**[19] 5602 4-10-5 **56** .... MrSamDavis(7) 14 48
(Rae Guest) *trckd ldrs: hdwy 3f out: rdn over 2f out: drvn and kpt on same pce fr over 1f out* **8/1**

4506 **7** *nse* **Royal Fantasy (IRE)**[5] 6017 6-11-0 **58** .... (v[1]) MissEJJones 7 49
(N Tinkler) *midfield: hdwy over 3f out: rdn to chse ldrs over 2f out: sn no imp* **14/1**

6260 **8** *1* **Moon Money (IRE)**[55] 4432 3-10-3 **56** .... MrJoshuaMoore(3) 4 45
(K A Ryan) *towards rr: hdwy on wd outside over 2f out: sn rdn and edgd rt over 1f out: kpt on same pce appr fnl f* **16/1**

4240 **9** *1 1/4* **Call Of Duty (IRE)**[18] 5625 4-10-9 **58** .... MissECSayer(5) 11 45
(Mrs Dianne Sayer) *towards rr: swtchd outside and hdwy over 2f out: sn rdn and n.d* **13/2**[2]

0-00 **10** *2 1/2* **Mycenean Prince (USA)**[16] 4972 6-9-10 **45** .... MrCAHarris(5) 5 27
(S A Harris) *a midfield* **33/1**

2444 **11** *2 3/4* **Rain Stops Play (IRE)**[24] 5438 7-10-2 **51** .... MissJRRichards(5) 9 27
(N G Richards) *towards rr: sme hdwy over 3f out: sn rdn and nvr a factor* **5/1**[1]

000- **12** *5* **College Land Boy**[14] 5637 5-9-8 **45** .... MrATBrook(7) 13 11
(A Kirtley) *prom: rdn along 1/2-way: sn wknd* **80/1**

060 **13** *1 1/2* **Doctor Of Music (IRE)**[39] 5010 3-9-10 **53** ow2 .... MrJNewman(7) 6 16
(B Smart) *dwlt and reminders s: a in rr* **9/1**

4006 **14** *15* **Mccormack (IRE)**[6] 5983 7-10-1 **45** .... (p) MissTJackson 1 —
(Miss T Jackson) *racd wd: trckd ldrs: hdwy and prom 4f out: rdn along 3f out and sn wknd* **40/1**

0600 **15** *3 1/4* **Antipodean (UAE)**[23] 5465 3-9-4 **45** .... (b) MissWGibson(5) 2 —
(P T Midgley) *chsd ldrs: effrt over 3f out: rdn wl over 2f out and sn wknd* **50/1**

2m 8.69s (1.69) **Going Correction** +0.10s/f (Good)
WFA 3 from 4yo+ 6lb — **15** Ran SP% **117.6**
Speed ratings (Par 101): **97,94,93,92,91 89,89,88,87,85 83,79,78,66,63**
toteswinger: 1&2 £125.50, 1&3 £40.80, 2&3 £165.40 CSF £507.46 CT £18931.04 TOTE £8.10: £2.70, £21.10, £11.30; EX 512.40 Place 6: £40.54, Place 5: £29.37..
Owner Brian Morton **Bred** George Ward **Trained** Seamer, N Yorks
■ Stewards' Enquiry : Mr J Newman six-day ban: used whip when out of contention (Oct 6, 13, 28, Nov 18, 24, 30)

FOCUS
Division two and a 45-58 weight range this time. The winner and fourth were in the last three turning in, suggesting the pace was strong. The runner-up limits the form.
T/Plt: £36.50 to a £1 stake. Pool: £52,308.97. 1,044.73 winning tickets. T/Qpdt: £5.80 to a £1 stake. Pool: £3,054.70. 386.20 winning tickets. JR

5721 FOLKESTONE (R-H)

Tuesday, September 22

OFFICIAL GOING: Good to firm (9.7)
Wind: Medium, behind Weather: Bright and sunny

6185 LIPSCOMB.CO.UK NURSERY — 5f

2:20 (2:21) (Class 5) (0-75,72) 2-Y-O — **£2,729** (£806; £403) **Stalls** Low

Form — RPR

624 **1** **Freeforaday (USA)**[14] 5749 2-9-2 **67** .... SteveDrowne 3 73
(J R Best) *hld up towards rr: hdwy 1/2-way: led ent fnl f: r.o wl u.p* **4/1**[2]

0403 **2** *1* **Dusty Spirit**[9] 5908 2-8-10 **64** .... JackDean(3) 1 66
(W G M Turner) *chsd ldrs: ev ch and rdn over 1f out: kpt on same pce u.p fnl 150yds* **6/1**[3]

6541 **3** *3 1/2* **Ruthie Babe**[9] 5908 2-9-4 **69** 6ex .... MichaelHills 2 59
(W J Haggas) *hld up in tch: nt clr run and shuffled bk 2f out: swtchd rt over 1f out: rdn and edgd rt fnl f: wnt 3rd towards fin but nt pce to threaten ldng pair* **11/10**[1]

632 **4** *1/2* **Devassa**[15] 5714 2-8-13 **64** .... AdamKirby 7 52
(C G Cox) *chsd ldr tl rdn to ld ent fnl 2f: hdd ent fnl f: sn outpcd* **10/1**

5055 **5** *4* **Grace Jicaro**[48] 4639 2-7-11 **51** oh1 ow2 .... AndreaAtzeni(3) 5 25
(Mrs L Williamson) *led tl rdn and hdd 2f out: wknd u.p over 1f out* **28/1**

0541 **6** *3/4* **Pherousa**[15] 5714 2-9-3 **68** .... JimmyQuinn 8 39
(M Blanshard) *hld up towards rr on outer: pushed along and effrt ent fnl 2f: rdn and no hdwy over 1f out* **10/1**

4000 **7** *nk* **Diamond Affair (IRE)**[26] 5372 2-8-6 **57** .... (t) ChrisCatlin 4 31+
(M G Quinlan) *awkward leaving stalls and slowly away: rdn and no real prog whn hmpd over 1f out: n.d* **25/1**

0005 **8** *2 3/4* **Azif**[24] 5445 2-9-7 **72** .... DavidProbert 6 32
(Miss Gay Kelleway) *in tch: rdn and struggling whn edgd lft over 1f out: wl bhd fnl f* **16/1**

58.99 secs (-1.01) **Going Correction** -0.125s/f (Firm) — **8** Ran SP% **113.3**
Speed ratings (Par 95): **103,101,95,95,88 87,86,82**
toteswinger: 1&2 £3.40, 1&3 £2.40, 2&3 £2.60 CSF £27.53 CT £42.20 TOTE £5.10: £1.50, £1.50, £1.10; EX 28.00 Trifecta £76.50 Pool: £523.12 - 5.06 winning units..
Owner John Best **Bred** Susan Mauer **Trained** Hucking, Kent

FOCUS
A modest nursery. They raced stands' side and the first pair finished clear.

NOTEBOOK
Freeforaday(USA) had shown ability in maiden company and was clearly on a good mark on this nursery debut. Dropped back a furlong in trip, he travelled well and picked up in good style when getting a gap inside the final two furlongs. The John Best horses seem to be in better form now following a quiet spell and this one must have a big chance of following up. (op 5-1)
Dusty Spirit showed good speed against the stands' rail throughout and readily reversed recent Ffos Las form with the disappointing Ruthie Babe. The winner was simply too good, however. (op 11-2 tchd 5-1)
Ruthie Babe, just as when winning a similar event at Ffos Las on her previous start, raced keenly under restraint, and she didn't make she use of stall two. Her response under pressure was disappointing, even allowing for her initially being a little short of room, and she needs to learn to settle better if she's to fulfil her potential. (op 13-8 tchd 7-4)
Devassa had been contesting some pretty modest nurseries and she looked poorly handicapped on this switch to nursery company. (op 7-1)

Pherousa was very disappointing considering she had Devassa behind her when winning a Bath maiden on her previous start. (op 8-1 tchd 11-1)

6186 EASTWELL MANOR H'CAP 5f
2:50 (2:51) (Class 6) (0-60,60) 3-Y-O+ £2,047 (£604; £302) Stalls Low

Form RPR
034 1 **Thoughtsofstardom**[3] 6119 6-8-5 49 (be) KellyHarrison(3) 4 56
(P S McEntee) *stdd after s and swtchd to trck ldrs on stands' rail: t.k.h: effrt and rdn to chal jst over 1f out: led ins fnl f: r.o wl* 13/2

2303 2 nk **The Name Is Frank**[15] 5729 4-9-0 55 (t) EddieAhern 5 61
(Mark Gillard) *chsd ldr: rdn to chal wl over 1f out: ev ch tl unable qck u.str.p fnl 100yds* 3/1[1]

0051 3 ½ **Welsh Opera**[5] 6039 4-9-2 60 6ex (v) WilliamCarson(3) 8 64
(S C Williams) *in tch: swtchd rt and effrt over 1f out: ev ch u.p ins fnl f: unable qck fnl 150yds* 7/2[2]

3354 4 1 **Imaginary Diva**[10] 5881 3-9-3 59 ChrisCatlin 3 60
(G G Margarson) *hld up in tch on stands' rail: nt clr run and edging rt looking for run over 1f out: swtchd lft and kpt on fnl 100yds: nt rch ldrs* 14/1

0040 5 ½ **Pic Up Sticks**[12] 5792 10-9-5 60 KFallon 11 59
(B G Powell) *sn bhd and niggled along: hdwy and swtchd rt ins fnl f: r.o but nvr able to rch ldrs* 13/2

5326 6 hd **Chandika**[25] 5383 3-9-4 60 AdamKirby 1 58
(C G Cox) *led: rdn and hrd pressed wl over 1f out: hdd ins fnl f: wknd fnl 100yds* 9/2[3]

0003 7 2 ¾ **Ten Down**[15] 5724 4-9-3 58 MartinDwyer 7 46+
(M Quinn) *hmpd sn after s: bhd: effrt and rdn over 1f out: no prog and btn whn carried rt ins fnl f* 8/1

4000 8 2 ¼ **Dynamo Dave (USA)**[5] 6038 4-8-7 48 (b) RobertHavlin 9 28
(M D I Usher) *towards rr: rdn and no rspnse over 1f out: wknd fnl f* 28/1

59.03 secs (-0.97) **Going Correction** -0.125s/f (Firm)
WFA 3 from 4yo+ 1lb 8 Ran SP% 113.3
Speed ratings (Par 101): **102,101,100,99,98 98,93,90**
toteswinger: 1&2 £5.10, 1&3 £6.80, 2&3 £2.50 CSF £25.84 CT £78.80 TOTE £8.50: £2.20, £1.90, £1.30; EX 33.20 Trifecta £180.50 Pool: £353.80 - 1.45 winning units..
Owner Eventmaker Racehorses **Bred** B Bargh **Trained** Newmarket, Suffolk
■ Stewards' Enquiry : Eddie Ahern two-day ban: used whip with excessive frequency (Oct 6-7)

FOCUS
A moderate but competitive sprint handicap. Limited form.

Chandika Official explanation: jockey said filly hung right throughout

6187 TOTEQUADPOT H'CAP 7f (S)
3:20 (3:22) (Class 4) (0-85,82) 3-Y-O+ £5,180 (£1,541; £770; £384) Stalls Low

Form RPR
0516 1 **Balata**[10] 5884 4-9-0 75 TGMcLaughlin 4 81
(B R Millman) *taken down early: hld up in last pair: pushed along and hdwy over 2f out: n.m.r 2f out: sn rdn to press ldrs: led fnl 50yds: all out* 6/1

0500 2 shd **Kaabari (USA)**[37] 5064 3-9-2 80 ChrisCatlin 5 85
(C E Brittain) *chsd ldr: pushed along over 2f out: ev ch and drvn over 1f out: led fnl 100yds: hdd and no ex fnl 50yds* 14/1

1240 3 nk **Maswerte (IRE)**[41] 4909 3-9-3 81 KFallon 3 85
(L M Cumani) *led: pushed along 3f out: rdn and hrd pressed over 1f out: hdd and no ex fnl 100yds* 5/2[1]

0033 4 ¾ **Lodi (IRE)**[12] 5804 4-9-0 75 (t) AdamKirby 2 81+
(J Akehurst) *chsd ldrs: pushed along over 2f out: rdn wl over 2f out: nt enough room fnl f: eased whn nt clr run 100yds out* 4/1[2]

0000 5 ½ **Vhujon (IRE)**[4] 6050 4-9-7 82 TPQueally 6 84
(P D Evans) *stdd and swtchd lft after s: hld up in last pair: swtchd rt and hdwy over 1f out: chsng ldrs whn nt clr run and swtchd rt again ins fnl f: kpt on: nt rch ldrs* 11/2

0403 6 ½ **The Galloping Shoe**[43] 4853 4-9-3 78 SebSanders 1 81+
(J Noseda) *pushed along early: trckd ldrs on stands' rail: nt clr run fnl 2f: nvr able to chal* 9/2[3]

5414 7 2 ½ **Ivory Lace**[9] 5918 8-8-11 75 JackMitchell(3) 7 69
(S Woodman) *hld up towards rr: pushed along 3f out: hdwy u.p and edgd lft 2f out: wknd fnl f* 10/1

1m 25.4s (-1.90) **Going Correction** -0.125s/f (Firm)
WFA 3 from 4yo+ 3lb 7 Ran SP% 112.2
Speed ratings (Par 105): **105,104,104,103,103 102,99**
toteswinger: 1&2 £13.10, 1&3 £4.70, 2&3 £8.80 CSF £77.21 TOTE £8.00: £3.40, £6.10; EX 84.40.
Owner The Links Partnership **Bred** Charlock Farm Stud **Trained** Kentisbeare, Devon

FOCUS
Hand-timed. A fair handicap run at just a modest pace through the early stages. Things became rather messy late on and they finished in a heap.

6188 TOTESUPER7 H'CAP 1m 7f 92y
3:50 (3:50) (Class 6) (0-60,57) 3-Y-O+ £2,047 (£604; £302) Stalls High

Form RPR
4503 1 **Dazzling Begum**[10] 5885 4-8-13 47 (p) SimonPearce(5) 11 54+
(J Pearce) *stdd after s: hld up wl in rr: stl plenty to do over 2f out: smooth hdwy on inner to ld over 1f out: in command and pushed out fnl f* 6/1[3]

0000 2 3 ¼ **Am I Blue**[17] 5679 3-9-1 55 JimmyQuinn 9 58
(H J L Dunlop) *stdd s: t.k.h: hld up wl in rr: rdn and hdwy over 2f out: chsd wnr 1f out: no imp* 22/1

6300 3 1 ¾ **Bedarra Boy**[30] 5286 3-8-10 50 MartinDwyer 4 51
(D W P Arbuthnot) *chsd ldrs: rdn to chse ldr over 2f out: led wl over 1f out: hdd over 1f out: edgd rt and one pce fnl f* 16/1

0403 4 ½ **Wightgold**[15] 5726 3-8-3 48 SophieDoyle(5) 12 48
(H J L Dunlop) *t.k.h: hld up in midfield early: steadily dropped towards rr 9f out: hdwy and n.m.r over 2f out: chsd ldrs over 1f out: hung rt and plugged on same pce fnl f* 14/1

4030 5 4 **Googoobarabajagal (IRE)**[24] 5430 3-8-8 48 (b[1]) FergusSweeney 6 44
(W S Kittow) *t.k.h: hld up in tch in midfield: rdn and effrt over 2f out: no prog and btn over 1f out* 7/1

2032 6 ½ **Sand Repeal (IRE)**[14] 5740 7-10-0 57 TPO'Shea 10 52
(Miss J Feilden) *stdd after s: hld up towards rr: rdn and hdwy on outer jst over 2f out: no prog over 1f out* 8/1

0000 7 4 ½ **Ingenue**[3] 6102 3-8-8 48 ow3 (b) SebSanders 8 38
(Sir Mark Prescott) *early reminders and sn led: 3 l clr and rdn wl over 2f out: wandered u.p and hdd wl over 1f out: sn wknd* 12/1

6003 8 4 ½ **Double Spectre (IRE)**[31] 4168 7-10-0 57 RobertHavlin 3 41
(Jean-Rene Auvray) *hld up in midfield: reminders over 5f out: wknd u.p jst over 2f out* 16/1

000 9 nk **Emiratesdotcom**[22] 5520 3-8-10 50 RoystonFfrench 13 34
(M Johnston) *nvr gng wl: sn pushed along in midfield: rdn over 8f out: drvn and dropped to rr 2f out: wl btn after* 14/1

-424 10 7 **Lady Pilot**[114] 2519 7-10-0 57 KFallon 2 32
(Jim Best) *t.k.h: hld up in tch in midfield on outer: rdn and no hdwy over 2f out: eaesd whn no ch over 1f out* 5/2[1]

0-00 11 11 **Shape Shifter (USA)**[23] 5483 3-8-5 45 RichardThomas 14 7
(J R Best) *chsd ldrs: rdn 4f out: wknd u.p over 2f out: eased whn wl bhd fnl f* 66/1

213 12 1 **Aaman (IRE)**[12] 5812 3-9-2 56 LPKeniry 7 17
(E F Vaughan) *chsd ldr: rdn and unable qck over 2f out: wknd qckly ent fnl 2f: wl bhd and eased ins fnl f* 7/2[2]

006- 13 48 **Amouretta**[140] 7149 4-9-2 45 (p) KirstyMilczarek 5 —
(T T Clement) *awkward leaving stalls and s.i.s: a bhd and nvr gng wl: lost tch 4f out: wl t.o fnl 3f* 66/1

3m 24.0s (-5.70) **Going Correction** -0.35s/f (Firm)
WFA 3 from 4yo+ 11lb 13 Ran SP% 128.8
Speed ratings (Par 101): **101,99,98,98,95 95,93,90,90,86 81,80,54**
toteswinger: 1&2 £31.60, 1&3 £29.30, 2&3 £37.40 CSF £140.82 CT £2052.40 TOTE £8.70: £2.10, £6.50, £5.70; EX 116.50 TRIFECTA Not won..
Owner Macniler Racing Partnership **Bred** Ian Bryant **Trained** Newmarket, Suffolk

FOCUS
Hand-timed. A really moderate staying handicap dominated by hold-up horses. The winner ran to her turf best.

Emiratesdotcom Official explanation: jockey said gelding was never travelling

Lady Pilot Official explanation: jockey said mare hung left throughout

Aaman(IRE) Official explanation: jockey said colt ran flat

6189 TOTEEXACTA MAIDEN STKS 1m 1f 149y
4:20 (4:20) (Class 5) 3-Y-O+ £2,729 (£806; £403) Stalls Centre

Form RPR
4 1 **Game Stalker (USA)**[140] 1771 3-9-3 0 LDettori 7 79+
(Saeed Bin Suroor) *mde virtually all: 3 l clr whn j. path and stmbld over 2f out: rdn and in command over 1f out: eased wl ins fnl f* 30/100[1]

3-60 2 2 ¾ **Naheell**[26] 5366 3-9-3 65 SaleemGolam 9 68
(G Prodromou) *chsd ldrs: rdn to chse wnr over 2f out: drvn and btn over 1f out: no ch w wnr after* 12/1[3]

040 3 10 **Silk And Satin (USA)**[15] 5718 3-8-12 60 (t) TPQueally 5 42
(H R A Cecil) *chsd wnr tl over 2f out: sn btn and no ch fnl 2f* 4/1[2]

00 4 1 ¾ **Legend Of Greece (IRE)**[22] 5531 3-9-3 46 DavidProbert 10 43
(Mrs N Smith) *sn pushed along in last pl: wnt 4th over 3f out: lost tch u.p 3f out* 40/1

0005 5 19 **Free Falling**[36] 5100 3-8-12 52 (b[1]) WandersonD'Avila 3 —
(A J Lidderdale) *chsd ldrs tl dropped to last over 3f out: sn lost tch: t.o* 22/1

2m 3.07s (-1.83) **Going Correction** -0.35s/f (Firm) 5 Ran SP% 111.4
Speed ratings (Par 103): **93,90,82,81,66**
toteswinger: 1&2 £5.00 CSF £5.36 TOTE £1.30: £1.02, £5.60; EX 5.70 Trifecta £7.70 Pool: £404.69 - 38.41 winning units..
Owner Godolphin **Bred** Darley **Trained** Newmarket, Suffolk

FOCUS
A very weak, uncompetitive maiden in which half the declared runners were absentees. Not form to be with.

6190 TOTETRIFECTA H'CAP 1m 1f 149y
4:50 (4:50) (Class 4) (0-80,79) 3-Y-O+ £5,180 (£1,541; £770; £384) Stalls Centre

Form RPR
-352 1 **Silverglas (IRE)**[23] 5475 3-8-12 73 PatDobbs 8 79
(M P Tregoning) *trckd ldng pair: wnt 2nd over 2f out: swtchd lft and jnd ldr wl over 1f out: sn rdn: led ins fnl f: rdn out* 13/8[1]

2233 2 ½ **Mefraas (IRE)**[20] 5570 3-8-13 74 TPO'Shea 7 79
(E A L Dunlop) *led: rdn ent fnl 2f: kpt on tl hdd and unable qck ins fnl f* 5/1[3]

0602 3 nk **Farleigh House (USA)**[10] 5887 5-9-10 79 SebSanders 5 84
(Sir Mark Prescott) *stdd s: t.k.h: hld up in last trio: rdn and hdwy wl over 1f out: wnt 3rd ins fnl f: kpt on wl* 9/2[2]

6314 4 ½ **African Cheetah**[6] 5997 3-9-1 76 RoystonFfrench 9 80
(M Johnston) *in tch in midfield: effrt on inner and rdn ent fnl 2f: chsng ldrs and keeping on whn nt clr run ins fnl f: swtchd lft fnl 100yds: kpt on but nt able to chal* 11/2

3162 5 ¾ **Addwaitya**[22] 5511 4-9-6 75 TedDurcan 3 77
(C F Wall) *s.i.s: sn pushed up and racd in midfield: rdn and effrt on outer wl over 1f out: edgd rt u.p but kpt on fnl f: nt pce to rch ldrs* 17/2

0666 6 1 ¼ **Goodwood Starlight (IRE)**[9] 5915 4-9-7 76 (t) EddieAhern 2 76
(G L Moore) *chsd ldrs: rdn and unable qck wl over 1f out: kpt on same pce u.p fnl f* 16/1

2245 7 4 ½ **Forbidden (IRE)**[1] 6168 6-8-13 71 (bt) AndreaAtzeni(3) 6 63+
(Daniel Mark Loughnane, Ire) *stdd s: hld up in last: rdn and no rspnse wl over 2f out: nvr on terms* 16/1

5046 8 nk **Al Sabaheya**[12] 5810 3-9-3 78 (b) ChrisCatlin 1 69
(C E Brittain) *chsd ldr tl over 2f out: wknd u.p over 1f out* 33/1

5006 9 10 **The Winged Assasin (USA)**[13] 5774 3-8-9 70 SimonWhitworth 4 43
(J Akehurst) *t.k.h: hld up in last trio: rdn and lost tch over 2f out* 66/1

2m 3.08s (-1.82) **Going Correction** -0.35s/f (Firm)
WFA 3 from 4yo+ 6lb 9 Ran SP% 115.1
Speed ratings (Par 105): **93,92,92,91,91 90,86,86,78**
toteswinger: 1&2 £2.90, 1&3 £3.20, 2&3 £4.60 CSF £9.81 CT £30.36 TOTE £2.90: £1.30, £1.80, £1.90; EX 13.80 Trifecta £32.80 Pool: £378.11 - 8.51 winning units. Place 6 £214.49, Place 5 £165.93.
Owner Mrs B Sumner **Bred** Mrs Mary Coonan **Trained** Lambourn, Berks

FOCUS
They went a modest pace through the early stages and it paid to race handy. There was something of a bunch finish and the form looks ordinary for the level, if solid enough.

T/Plt: £187.10 to a £1 stake. Pool: £59,911.33. 233.75 winning tickets. T/Qpdt: £154.70 to a £1 stake. Pool: £3,785.20. 18.10 winning tickets. SP

6191 - 6197a (Foreign Racing) - See Raceform Interactive

6044 CHANTILLY (R-H)

Tuesday, September 22

OFFICIAL GOING: Good

6198a PRIX TURENNE (LISTED RACE) (C&G) 1m 4f

2:50 (2:51) 3-Y-O **£26,699** (£10,680; £8,010; £5,340; £2,670)

RPR

1 **Shahwardi (FR)**[35] 3-8-11 .... C-PLemaire 8 103
(A De Royer-Dupre, France)

2 *hd* **Makt (FR)**[24] 5463 3-8-11 .... (p) OPeslier 3 102
(T Doumen, France)

3 *1 1/2* **Marinous (FR)**[32] 3-8-11 .... DBonilla 1 100
(F Head, France)

4 *2* **Ile De Re (FR)**[41] 4926 3-8-11 .... ALemaitre 7 97
(F Head, France)

5 *1* **Gallilei (FR)**[100] 2951 3-8-11 .... GMosse 4 95
(A De Royer-Dupre, France)

6 *1 1/2* **Acteur Celebre**[119] 2369 3-8-11 .... ACrastus 6 93
(E Lellouche, France)

7 *10* **Strike Ballot (USA)**[57] 4395 3-8-11 .... (b) SPasquier 5 77
(Mme C Head-Maarek, France)

8 *dist* **Serva Jugum (USA)**[13] 5764 3-8-11 .... IMendizabal 2 —
(P F I Cole) *hld up: pushed along 1/2-way: last and rdn st: t.o* **15/2**[1]

2m 27.1s (-3.90) **8** Ran SP% **11.8**

PARI-MUTUEL: WIN 2.30; PL 1.30, 3.10, 2.50; DF 16.00.

Owner H H Aga Khan **Bred** H H The Aga Khan's Studs S C **Trained** Chantilly, France

■ Stewards' Enquiry : O Peslier 100euro fine: whip abuse

NOTEBOOK

Serva Jugum(USA), who had run well in a conditions stakes at Doncaster on his previous outing, ran no sort of race here and something must have been amiss. Official explanation: jockey had no explanation for the poor form shown

5912 GOODWOOD (R-H)

Wednesday, September 23

OFFICIAL GOING: Good (good to firm in places; 8.5)

Lower bend dolled out about 7yds from 6f to winning post adding about 12yds to advertised distances on round course.

Wind: Virtually nil Weather: Light drizzle early, otherwise overcast

6199 ELECTROLUX PROFESSIONAL EBF MAIDEN STKS 7f

2:00 (2:01) (Class 5) 2-Y-O **£3,561** (£1,059; £529; £264) **Stalls** High

Form RPR

1 **Workforce** 2-9-3 0........ RyanMoore 1 93+
(Sir Michael Stoute) *s.i.s: in rr: pushed along and hdwy over 2f out: swtchd rt to ins and qcknd to ld 1f out: sn clr: impressive* **3/1**[1]

0 2 *6* **Oasis Dancer**[33] 5220 2-9-3 0........ GeorgeBaker 11 73
(R M Beckett) *trckd ldr: upsides 4f out: led 3f out: rdn and styd on fr 2f out: hdd 1f out and sn no ch w wnr bur kpt on wl for 2nd* **9/2**[2]

3 3 *3/4* **Exceedthewildman**[11] 5867 2-9-3 0........ JimmyFortune 2 71+
(J S Moore) *towards rr: pushed along and hdwy on outside over 2f out: styd on wl fnl f to cl on 2nd ins fnl f but nvr any ch w impressive wnr* **6/1**[3]

030 4 *2 1/2* **Whipperway (IRE)**[16] 5722 2-8-12 76........ ChrisCatlin 12 60
(M R Channon) *chsd ldrs: rdn 3f out: styd on same pce u.p fnl 2f* **12/1**

00 5 *1/2* **Haatheq (USA)**[26] 5400 2-9-3 0........ RHills 5 64
(J L Dunlop) *chsd ldrs on outside: rdn and hung rt 2f out: no imp: wknd fnl f* **8/1**

5 6 *1* **Suntrap**[26] 5401 2-9-3 0........ ShaneKelly 4 61
(W J Knight) *in rr: sme prog on outside fr 2f out but nvr in contention* **20/1**

00 7 *1/2* **Until The Man (IRE)**[23] 5505 2-9-3 0........ KirstyMilczarek 10 60+
(R Ingram) *slt ld tl hdd 3f out: wknd fr 2f out and hld whn n.m.r over 1f out* **150/1**

0320 8 *2* **Valiant Knight (FR)**[23] 5505 2-9-3 75........ RichardHughes 3 55
(R Hannon) *chsd ldrs towards outside: rdn 2f out: no imp: wknd fnl f and eased: no ch whn hung lft cl home* **6/1**[3]

9 *3/4* **Life And Soul (IRE)** 2-9-3 0........ JimCrowley 6 53
(Mrs A J Perrett) *in tch: rdn to chse ldrs ins fnl 3f: nvr in contention and wknd 2f out* **8/1**

0 10 *4 1/2* **Old Devil Moon (IRE)**[62] 4243 2-9-3 0........ (t) JamesDoyle 8 42
(T G Mills) *chsd ldrs: rdn 3f out: wknd qckly 2f out* **50/1**

11 *3* **River Landing** 2-8-10 0........ JPFahy(7) 7 34
(R M Beckett) *s.i.s: green and a in rr* **33/1**

12 *12* **Roybuoy** 2-9-3 0........ DavidProbert 9 4
(H J L Dunlop) *in rr: rdn and sme prog to get in tch w main gp 3f out: sn wknd* **22/1**

1m 27.4s **Going Correction** +0.025s/f (Good) **12** Ran SP% **116.3**

Speed ratings (Par 95): **101,94,93,90,89 88,88,85,85,79 76,62**

toteswingers: 1&2 £4.70, 1&3 £2.90, 2&3 £5.60 CSF £14.80 TOTE £3.30: £1.60, £2.00, £2.10; EX 19.20.

Owner K Abdulla **Bred** Juddmonte Farms Ltd **Trained** Newmarket, Suffolk

FOCUS

Clerk of the course Seamus Buckley reported that the track had been watered extensively since the last meeting and the official going was described as good, good to firm in places, with the GoingStick reading 8.5. A fair maiden won in impressive style by Workforce, who looks a potential Group horse.

NOTEBOOK

Workforce wasn't best away and was towards the rear early, but he made ground up quickly through the pack in the straight and drew right away inside the last to score by a wide margin. He took a good while to pull up after the line, suggesting he had plenty left in the tank, and a mile is sure to suit him if he runs again this year. He was given a 33-1 quote for the 2000 Guineas afterwards, but although he's by King's Best, his dam is a sister to St Leger winner Brian Boru, and he looks a middle-distance prospect for next season. A big, strong colt, it'll be interesting to see how he develops over the winter. (tchd 7-2)

Oasis Dancer, prominent throughout from his good draw, improved on his debut effort at Sandown, reversing form with the increasingly disappointing Valiant Knight in the process. The latter had perhaps too much use made of him early from his wide draw and, having looked a threat two furlongs out, dropped out tamely in the closing stages. (op 11-2)

Exceedthewildman was well backed to improve on his debut third at Ffos Las, and having been dropped in from his low draw, he finished well down the outside in the straight. Although by a sprinter, there's plenty of stamina on the dam's side of his pedigree, and he'll appreciate a longer trip than this in time. (op 14-1)

Whipperway(IRE) ran poorly at Folkestone last time but her previous effort at this track suggested there was a race to be won with her. She might just need easier ground to be seen at her best, though. (op 8-1)

Haatheq(USA), who was a bit keen early, travelled strongly to two furlongs out but found little under pressure. He is now eligible for handicaps and will be of far more interest in that sphere. (op 7-1)

Suntrap tended to hang in the straight and didn't look entirely happy on the track.

Until The Man(IRE) Official explanation: jockey said colt hung left

6200 EBF GOODWOOD FOOD MAIDEN STKS 1m 1f

2:35 (2:36) (Class 4) 2-Y-O **£4,695** (£1,397; £698; £348) **Stalls** High

Form RPR

6 1 **Agent Archie (USA)**[8] 5966 2-9-3 0........ RobertWinston 9 70+
(J R Best) *mde virtually all: drvn along fr 2f out: styd on strly fnl f* **7/2**[2]

0 2 *1 1/2* **Regal Guest**[23] 5499 2-9-3 0........ ChrisCatlin 8 67
(M R Channon) *hmpd and dropped to rr after 1f: drvn and hdwy on outside fr over 2f out: str run fnl f to take 2nd cl home but no ch w wnr* **5/1**

3 *1/2* **Loyaliste (FR)** 2-9-3 0........ RichardHughes 7 66
(R Hannon) *sluggish fr stalls and towards rr: drvn and styd on fr over 2f out: kpt on thrght fnl f and clsng nr fin to take 3rd* **3/1**[1]

0540 4 *hd* **Chat De Soie (IRE)**[7] 5985 2-8-12 60........ RyanMoore 2 61
(J S Moore) *chsd wnr sn after s: rdn and no imp over 2f out: one pce ins fnl f and dropped bk to 4th cl home* **6/1**

0 5 *7* **Apache Kid (IRE)**[13] 5785 2-9-3 0........ DarryllHolland 6 52
(B R Millman) *chsd ldrs: rdn along 3f out: wknd fr 2f out* **8/1**

6 *2 1/2* **Stormglass** 2-9-3 0........ MartinDwyer 4 50+
(W R Muir) *in rr whn hmpd after 1f: sn rdn along and v green: sme prog fnl 2f* **4/1**[3]

0 7 *1* **Harry Paget (IRE)**[53] 4534 2-9-3 0........ SteveDrowne 5 45
(J R Best) *chsd ldrs: rdn 4f out: hung rt and wknd ins fnl 3f* **25/1**

0000 8 *3 1/2* **Vadition (IRE)**[33] 5213 2-8-5 45........ RyanClark(7) 3 33
(J J Bridger) *sn in tch: chsd ldrs and rdn over 3f out: sn btn* **100/1**

600 9 *6* **Polebrook**[65] 4152 2-9-3 30........ HayleyTurner 10 26
(J R Jenkins) *chsd ldrs to 1/2-way* **100/1**

2m 0.67s (4.37) **Going Correction** +0.025s/f (Good) **9** Ran SP% **115.1**

Speed ratings (Par 97): **81,79,79,79,72 70,69,66,61**

toteswingers: 1&2 £3.80, 1&3 £3.50, 2&3 £3.90 CSF £21.15 TOTE £5.10: £1.50, £1.80, £1.40; EX 25.20.

Owner D Gorton **Bred** Earle I Mack **Trained** Hucking, Kent

FOCUS

An ordinary maiden and weak form for the track, although it could work out better than rated.

NOTEBOOK

Agent Archie(USA) sweated up beforehand and was a little keen early, but he settled better once joined by Chat De Soie up front, and proceeded to set a fairly sedate early gallop. As a result he was best placed when the sprint for home began. He galloped on well enough to hold his pursuers at bay, and clearly appreciated the step up in trip from 7f, but the fourth is only rated 57 and it's doubtful the form is worth that much. He's seen as a middle-distance prospect for next year. (op 9-2 tchd 100-30)

Regal Guest stayed on from the back of the field to take second but was never a real danger to the winner. Modest handicaps will be his game after one more run. (op 7-1)

Loyaliste(FR) had been due to contest a class 2 conditions event at Newbury the previous week, but was a late withdrawal. This looked much easier pickings, but he wasn't up to it on his debut. He's entitled to come on for the run, though. (op 13-8)

Chat De Soie(IRE), who boasts a moderate-looking mark of 57, was always well placed towards the fore in a race not run at a great early gallop. She looks flattered by the bare form. (op 7-1 tchd 8-1)

Apache Kid(IRE), who didn't show a great deal on his debut at Chepstow, was another who wasn't far off the gallop early, and that was no bad thing given the way the race played out. (op 10-1)

Stormglass, a 110,00gns son of Galileo, ran very green towards the rear of the field and only made some late headway past beaten horses. He hails from a stable not known for winning with juveniles first time up and is entitled to come on plenty for this experience. (op 13-2)

6201 AGGORA KITCHEN STKS (H'CAP) 6f

3:10 (3:10) (Class 4) (0-80,76) 3-Y-O+ **£4,857** (£1,445; £722; £360) **Stalls** Low

Form RPR

3122 1 **We Have A Dream**[20] 5592 4-9-4 74........ MartinDwyer 6 89
(W R Muir) *mde virtually all: hrd rdn: strly chal and hung rt ins fnl f: hld on all out* **3/1**[1]

3050 2 *hd* **Arthur's Edge**[11] 5884 5-8-9 70........ AshleyMorgan(5) 9 84
(B Palling) *trckd ldrs: rdn to chal 1f out: jojned wnr thrght fnl f and carried rt: no ex last strides* **9/2**[2]

-051 3 *2* **Johnstown Lad (IRE)**[16] 5719 5-9-6 76........ (t) ShaneKelly 10 84
(Daniel Mark Loughnane, Ire) *trckd ldrs: rdn to chal appr fnl f: outpcd by ldng duo ins fnl f* **5/1**[3]

4062 4 *1 1/2* **Reject**[8] 5968 3-8-12 70........ LiamJones 3 73
(W J Haggas) *s.i.s: in rr: hdwy 2f out: chsd ldrs over 1f out and no imp* **5/1**[3]

1134 5 *1/2* **Solemn**[16] 5719 4-8-10 66........ (b) DavidProbert 1 67
(J M Bradley) *chsd ldrs: rdn 3f out: wknd ins fnl f* **8/1**

0243 6 *hd* **Forest Dane**[31] 5288 9-8-3 64........ SophieDoyle(5) 8 65
(Mrs N Smith) *s.i.s: rdn 1/2-way and chsd ldrs over 2f out: wknd fnl f* **9/1**

3000 7 *6* **Mogok Ruby**[39] 5031 5-9-2 72........ RobertWinston 4 53+
(L Montague Hall) *in tch whn rdn and hmpd 2f out: sn btn* **28/1**

5315 8 *nse* **Diddums**[13] 5805 3-8-3 68........ AmyScott(7) 7 49
(J W Hills) *in rr: swtchd to outside and pushed along over 2f out: nvr in contention* **14/1**

0004 9 *1/2* **Silver Guest**[13] 5805 4-9-0 70........ ChrisCatlin 2 50
(M R Channon) *outpcd* **33/1**

0664 10 *12* **Finnegan McCool**[38] 5065 3-8-11 69........ (p) JimCrowley 5 10
(R M Beckett) *chsd ldrs: rdn 1/2-way: sn wknd* **16/1**

1m 11.67s (-0.53) **Going Correction** +0.025s/f (Good)

WFA 3 from 4yo+ 2lb **10** Ran SP% **116.6**

Speed ratings (Par 105): **104,103,101,99,98 98,90,90,89,73**

toteswingers: 1&2 £4.50, 1&3 £4.70, 2&3 £7.80 CSF £16.20 CT £65.27 TOTE £3.60: £1.30, £1.80, £2.60; EX 19.10 Trifecta £41.30 Pool: £380.40 - 6.80 winning units..

Owner The Dreaming Squires **Bred** Whitsbury Manor Stud **Trained** Lambourn, Berks

FOCUS
The pace held up well in this sprint and very few got into it. Straightforward and sound form.

6202 FIRST DRINKS BRANDS FOUNDATION STKS (LISTED RACE) 1m 1f 192y
3:45 (3:46) (Class 1) 3-Y-O+ **£22,708** (£8,608; £4,308; £2,148) **Stalls** High

Form RPR
3401 **1** **Twice Over**[14] 5764 4-9-0 119 TPQueally 1 119+
(H R A Cecil) *disp 2nd tl trckd ldr over 6f out: shkn up to ld appr fnl 2f: c readily clr fr over 1f out: easily* **2/5**[1]
6133 **2** 2 1/2 **Perfect Stride**[11] 5875 4-9-0 112 RyanMoore 3 113
(Sir Michael Stoute) *sn led: rdn and hdd appr fnl 2f: sn no ch w wnr but easily 2nd best* **4/1**[2]
1113 **3** 4 1/2 **Fanjura (IRE)**[13] 5794 4-9-0 106 RHills 5 104
(B W Hills) *trckd ldr tl over 6f out: styd in 3rd: rdn 3f out: no imp on ldng duo over 2f out: no ch whn hung lft appr fnl f* **15/2**[3]
0520 **4** 7 **Montaff**[4] 6106 3-8-8 104 (v) ChrisCatlin 4 91
(M R Channon) *a in last: rdn and sme prog 3f out: little rspnse u.p and wknd over 2f out* **25/1**

2m 5.47s (-2.53) **Going Correction** +0.025s/f (Good)
WFA 3 from 4yo+ 6lb **4** Ran SP% **107.0**
Speed ratings (Par 111): **111,109,105,99**
CSF £2.25 TOTE £1.30; EX 2.10.
Owner K Abdulla **Bred** Juddmonte Farms Ltd **Trained** Newmarket, Suffolk

FOCUS
A small turnout for this Listed contest and a straightforward success for the winner, who was a class above.

NOTEBOOK
Twice Over has now had a couple of confidence-boosting successes in preparation for another tilt at the Champion Stakes. Although not beaten far in the Lockinge, this looks his best trip nowadays, and, while perhaps not top class, he may not have to be to go one better in the Champion Stakes this year, with the likes of Sea The Stars and one or two of the top Aidan O'Brien-trained three-year-olds appearing to have more pressing engagements at this stage. Easier ground won't bother him. (op 4-9 tchd 1-2 in places)
Perfect Stride was given a good ride from the front and simply bumped into a high-class rival, too good for him at the weights. Nevertheless, it's slightly puzzling why he keeps running at this track, where he has rarely shown, while his record of three wins from three starts and top three career RPRs have come at Ascot. Clearly that is his venue. (op 9-2 tchd 7-2 and 5-1 in places)
Fanjura(IRE), who sweated up beforehand, hung under pressure from over a furlong out and looked far from comfortable on the track. He faced a stiff task at the weights and promises to continue to be difficult to place off his current mark. (op 13-2)
Montaff, making a quick reappearance for the prize money, picked up his share without ever threatening the first two. He's another who looks impossible to place off his current mark. (op 20-1)

6203 PIPER CHAMPAGNE STKS (H'CAP) 1m 3f
4:20 (4:20) (Class 4) (0-85,85) 3-Y-O **£4,857** (£1,445; £722; £360) **Stalls** Low

Form RPR
4003 **1** **Fanditha (IRE)**[7] 5996 3-8-12 79 RichardHughes 5 87
(R Hannon) *hld up in rr: hrd rdn 2f out: drvn to ld jst ins fnl f: forged clr fnl 110yds: comf* **11/1**
13 **2** 2 1/4 **Plymouth Rock (IRE)**[72] 3922 3-9-1 82 RyanMoore 4 86
(J Noseda) *trckd ldrs in 4th: rdn and n.m.r over 2f out: drvn and qcknd between horses to chal 1f out: edgd rt to rail: styd chsng wnr but a wl hld* **5/2**[1]
1200 **3** 3 **Mabuya (UAE)**[24] 5475 3-9-1 82 JimmyFortune 3 82
(P J Makin) *hld up in last pl: t.k.h and stdd ins fnl 4f: rdn over 2f out: styd on u.p fr over 1f out to take n.d 3rd nr fin* **7/2**[3]
4525 **4** hd **Gilded Age**[20] 5593 3-8-8 75 HayleyTurner 2 74
(A King) *chsd ldrs: drvn along over 3f out: styd wl there tl wknd fnl f* **14/1**
1455 **5** hd **Muraweg (IRE)**[12] 5828 3-9-3 84 (b[1]) RHills 1 83
(J H M Gosden) *sn chsng ldr: rdn to chal 2f out: slt ld over 1f out: hdd jst ins fnl f and sn wknd* **4/1**
2325 **6** 3 1/4 **State Banquet (USA)**[30] 5315 3-9-4 85 (p) SteveDrowne 6 79
(H Morrison) *led: pushed along and idled 6f out: rdn over 3f out: hdd & wknd over 1f out: no ch whn crossed and hit rail ins fnl f* **11/4**[2]

2m 26.5s (-1.80) **Going Correction** +0.025s/f (Good) **6** Ran SP% **112.5**
Speed ratings (Par 103): **107,105,103,103,102 100**
CSF £38.74 TOTE £14.50: £4.60, £1.40; EX 28.10.
Owner A P Patey **Bred** Lynch Bages Ltd & Samac Ltd **Trained** East Everleigh, Wilts

FOCUS
The early pace was strong and unsurprisingly those who raced up with the gallop didn't get home. It was set up for a finisher and Manditha produced a minor personal best.

6204 MERBURY CATERING CONSULTANTS STKS (H'CAP) 1m 4f
4:55 (4:55) (Class 4) (0-80,86) 3-Y-O+ **£4,857** (£1,445; £722; £360) **Stalls** Low

Form RPR
0355 **1** **Pelham Crescent (IRE)**[12] 5837 6-9-12 75 DavidProbert 6 85
(B Palling) *in tch: rdn along fr 3f out: styd on u.p to press ldr ins fnl f: sn str chal: led last strides* **14/1**
4060 **2** hd **Buddy Holly**[19] 5640 4-9-10 73 PatDobbs 5 83
(Pat Eddery) *chsd ldrs: drvn and qcknd to ld jst ins fnl f: edgd rt u.p and strly chal ins fnl f: hdd last strides* **16/1**
0506 **3** 1 1/4 **Capable Guest (IRE)**[14] 5781 7-8-13 65 MCGeran[(3)] 7 73
(M R Channon) *mid-div: hdwy and rdn over 2f out: sn n.m.r: swtchd to lft over 1f out: styd on ins fnl f but nt rch ldng duo* **9/1**
0651 **4** 2 1/2 **Trachonitis (IRE)**[10] 5912 5-9-10 73 6ex AdrianMcCarthy 4 77
(J R Jenkins) *towards rr: hdwy on outside over 3f out: drvn to chal 2f out: led sn after: hdd jst ins fnl f: sn wknd* **15/2**[3]
3003 **5** hd **Holden Eagle**[23] 5532 4-9-9 75 JackDean[(3)] 1 79
(A G Newcombe) *in rr: hdwy on outside fr 3f out: rdn and styng on one pce whn hung rt over 1f out: sn btn* **12/1**
1111 **6** 2 **Point Of Light**[7] 5979 3-10-1 86 6ex StephenDonohoe 10 86
(Sir Mark Prescott) *led: rdn appr fnl 3f: hdd jst ins fnl 2f: btn whn edgd rt u.p ins fnl f* **6/4**[1]
0224 **7** shd **Maslak (IRE)**[12] 5837 5-9-12 75 ChrisCatlin 9 75
(P W Hiatt) *chsd ldrs: rdn along 4f out: styng on same pced whn hmpd ins fnl f* **9/1**
3425 **8** 2 1/4 **Gross Prophet**[70] 3977 4-9-11 74 MartinDwyer 8 71
(A J Lidderdale) *t.k.h: chsd ldr: rdn 3f out: wknd ins fnl 2f* **7/1**[2]
0 **9** 1 1/4 **Weststern (GER)**[123] 549 6-9-8 71 (t) GeorgeBaker 11 66
(G L Moore) *chsd ldrs: rdn over 2f out: no imp and sn btn* **25/1**
1/ **10** 2 **Come April**[837] 2455 5-9-12 75 JimmyFortune 3 67
(P R Webber) *in rr: pushed along and sme prog fr 3f out: nvr in contention and sn wknd* **10/1**

5450 **11** 1 3/4 **Amwell Brave**[32] 5246 8-8-12 61 oh16 HayleyTurner 2 50
(J R Jenkins) *in rr: rdn and tried to improve 3f out but nt much daylight: nvr any threat and sn bhd again* **100/1**
0050 **12** 7 **Zaif (IRE)**[39] 5028 6-8-6 62 (b[1]) TobyAtkinson[(7)] 12 40
(D J S Ffrench Davis) *s.i.s: t.k.h early: a towards rr* **33/1**

2m 39.38s (0.98) **Going Correction** +0.025s/f (Good)
WFA 3 from 4yo+ 8lb **12** Ran SP% **121.4**
Speed ratings (Par 105): **97,96,96,94,94 92,92,91,90,89 88,83**
toteswingers: 1&2 £43.50, 1&3 £30.80, 2&3 £23.30 CSF £220.78 CT £2137.94 TOTE £19.50: £4.70, £3.70, £2.60; EX 287.30.
Owner Wayne Devine **Bred** Cathal M Ryan **Trained** Tredodridge, Vale Of Glamorgan

FOCUS
Fair handicap form and a personal best from the winner.

6205 MERBURY 19TH ANNIVERSARY APPRENTICE STKS (H'CAP) 5f
5:30 (5:30) (Class 5) (0-70,71) 3-Y-O+ **£3,238** (£963; £481; £240) **Stalls** Low

Form RPR
4522 **1** **Brandywell Boy (IRE)**[10] 5911 6-8-11 62 TobyAtkinson[(5)] 11 70
(D J S Ffrench Davis) *chsd ldrs: rdn 2f out: str run to chal ins fnl f: led fnl 50yds: hld on all out* **9/2**[2]
0040 **2** hd **Tiger Trail (GER)**[92] 3252 5-8-3 54 JPFahy[(5)] 6 61
(Mrs N Smith) *in rr: rdn and hdwy over 1f out: str run ins fnl f: pressed wnr last strides but a jst hld* **18/1**
4141 **3** nse **Lithaam (IRE)**[13] 5792 5-8-13 66 (p) RyanClark[(7)] 9 73
(J M Bradley) *led: rdn over 1f out: hdd fnl 50yds: kpt pressing wnr: no ex last strides and narrowly lost 2nd* **11/4**[1]
3630 **4** 2 1/4 **Mazzola**[11] 5877 3-9-4 65 MCGeran 4 64
(M R Channon) *chsd ldrs: rdn 2f out: styd on same pce ins fnl f* **12/1**
3562 **5** 1/2 **Bluebok**[13] 5792 8-8-13 59 (bt) DavidProbert 8 56
(J M Bradley) *chsd ldrs: rdn 1/2-way: styd on same pce fr over 1f out* **8/1**[3]
6060 **6** nk **Even Bolder**[16] 5724 6-9-0 65 LeeNewnes[(5)] 5 61
(E A Wheeler) *s.i.s: in rr but in tch: pushed along and hdwy fr over 1f out but nvr gng pce to be competitive* **14/1**
0345 **7** 2 1/4 **Peopleton Brook**[10] 5919 7-8-4 53 (t) Louis-PhilippeBeuzelin[(3)] 2 41
(B G Powell) *in tch whn slt hmpd 3f out: sn pushed along: kpt on fnl f but nvr in contention* **9/2**[2]
6335 **8** hd **Cheshire Rose**[27] 5374 4-8-7 58 (tp) AndrewHeffernan[(5)] 10 45
(A M Hales) *chsd ldrs: rdn 1/2-way: wknd ins fnl f* **8/1**[3]
4005 **9** 2 1/4 **Kingsgate Storm (IRE)**[23] 5506 3-8-11 58 MarcHalford 7 37
(J R Best) *chsd ldrs: rdn and one pce 1/2-way: swtchd rt u.p over 1f out but no ch* **16/1**
0001 **10** nk **Colorus (IRE)**[8] 5974 6-9-4 71 6ex (p) LeonnaMayor[(7)] 1 49
(W J H Ratcliffe) *chsd ldrs: sddle slipped and hung rt 3f out: nt rcvr* **12/1**
0020 **11** 7 **Joss Stick**[7] 5989 4-8-8 57 AshleyMorgan[(3)] 3 10
(J J Bridger) *outpcd* **33/1**

59.03 secs (0.63) **Going Correction** +0.025s/f (Good)
WFA 3 from 4yo+ 1lb **11** Ran SP% **121.4**
Speed ratings (Par 103): **95,94,94,91,90 89,86,85,82,81 70**
toteswingers: 1&2 £21.60, 1&3 £3.30, 2&3 £16.60 CSF £85.21 CT £272.09 TOTE £5.00: £1.60, £6.30, £1.50; EX 119.70 Place 6: £56.94 Place 5: £43.45.
Owner P B Gallagher **Bred** Mountarmstrong Stud **Trained** Lambourn, Berks

FOCUS
An ordinary sprint handicap in which the principals raced more towards the centre of the track and most were fairly prominent, too. Sound but limited form.
Colorus(IRE) Official explanation: jockey said saddle slipped
T/Plt: £160.60 to a £1 stake. Pool: £57,861.92. 262.87 winning tickets. T/Qpdt: £111.40 to a £1 stake. Pool: £3,871.30. 25.70 winning tickets. ST

6162 KEMPTON (A.W) (R-H)
Wednesday, September 23

OFFICIAL GOING: Standard
Wind: Light, across Weather: Dull

6206 KEMPTON.CO.UK MEDIAN AUCTION MAIDEN STKS 5f (P)
5:50 (5:52) (Class 6) 3-4-Y-O **£2,047** (£604; £302) **Stalls** High

Form RPR
4352 **1** **Edith's Boy (IRE)**[11] 5877 3-9-3 62 NCallan 3 62
(S Dow) *mde all: drvn 3 l clr ins fnl f: styd on but only jst hld on* **8/13**[1]
2 hd **Looby Loo** 3-8-12 0 AlanMunro 8 56+
(P W Chapple-Hyam) *sn in 5th: effrt 2f out: r.o to take 2nd last 100yds: gaining fast on wnr at fin* **3/1**[2]
4626 **3** 3 1/4 **You'relikemefrank**[11] 5881 3-9-3 47 (p) IanMongan 6 50
(J Balding) *chsd wnr: no imp u.p over 1f out: lost 2nd last 100yds* **20/1**
3003 **4** 1 1/2 **Rapanui Belle**[11] 5881 3-8-12 49 (b) FergusSweeney 7 39
(G L Moore) *t.k.h early: chsd ldrs: nt qckn over 1f out: fdd fnl f* **14/1**[3]
624 **5** 2 1/4 **Roodee King**[19] 5645 3-9-3 50 SJCraine 4 36
(Patrick Morris) *dwlt: outpcd and sn in trble in last: plugged on fnl f* **14/1**[3]
5000 **6** 3 1/2 **Noverre To Hide (USA)**[39] 5018 3-9-3 45 (b[1]) RobertWinston 2 28+
(J R Best) *sn chsd ldrs on outer: lost grnd bnd 2f out: hanging over 1f out: wknd and eased* **20/1**
0030 **7** 1 1/4 **Spring Bridge (IRE)**[4] 6119 3-9-3 50 (tp) RobertHavlin 5 19
(Mrs L C Jewell) *racd v wd thrght: lost plenty of grnd bnd fr over 3f out to 2f out: wknd* **33/1**

59.83 secs (-0.67) **Going Correction** -0.075s/f (Stan) **7** Ran SP% **112.7**
Speed ratings (Par 101): **102,101,96,94,90 84,82**
toteswingers: 1&2 £1.60, 1&3 £2.40, 2&3 £6.30 CSF £2.47 TOTE £1.70: £1.40, £1.60; EX 3.40.
Owner A Lindsay **Bred** C Grehan **Trained** Epsom, Surrey
■ Stewards' Enquiry : Alan Munro caution: used whip without giving filly time to respond

FOCUS
A desperately weak maiden. The winner is rated to form.
Noverre To Hide(USA) Official explanation: jockey said gelding hung right-handed

6207 COUNSEL AND CARE CHARITY MAIDEN STKS 5f (P)
6:20 (6:21) (Class 5) 2-Y-O **£2,590** (£770; £385; £192) **Stalls** High

Form RPR
3 **1** **Felsham**[42] 4906 2-9-3 0 DaneO'Neill 4 68+
(H Candy) *pressed ldr: rdn to ld narrowly 1f out: fnd enough to hold off chalrs last 100yds* **8/11**[1]
2 nk **Liberty Lady (IRE)** 2-8-12 0 JerryO'Dwyer 10 62
(D Donovan) *wnt lft s: sn pressed ldrs on inner: pushed along after 2f: effrt over 1f out: 2nd and tried to chal ins fnl f: a jst hld* **33/1**
03 **3** hd **Night Trade (IRE)**[20] 5611 2-8-9 0 RussellKennemore[(3)] 9 62
(Mrs D J Sanderson) *sn chsd ldng pair and a cl up: rdn over 1f out: kpt on wl enough but a hld* **11/4**[2]

00 **4** *1* **Rain On The Wind (IRE)**[21] 5571 2-9-3 0 .... SaleemGolam 6 63
(S C Williams) *taken down early: cl up: pressed ldrs over 1f out: sn nt qckn: kpt on but no imp after* **9/2**[3]

00 **5** *1 3/4* **The Two G'S**[114] 2533 2-8-12 0 .... PatCosgrave 11 56+
(P D Evans) *narrow ldr to 1f out: sing to weaken whn n.m.r and spooked last 75yds* **16/1**

6 *1 1/2* **Winifred Jo** 2-8-12 0 .... SteveDrowne 7 46+
(J R Gask) *dwlt: nvr on terms w ldrs: wnt 7th 1/2-way: pushed along and kpt on* **14/1**

7 *1 3/4* **Kai Mook** 2-8-12 0 .... CatherineGannon 2 40+
(R Ingram) *dwlt: last and wl outpcd: pushed along and styd on quite wl fr over 1f out: nrst fin* **33/1**

00 **8** *2 1/4* **Polish Steps (IRE)**[48] 4688 2-8-12 0 .... ShaneKelly 3 32
(J A Osborne) *dwlt: rcvrd to chse ldrs: cl up tl wknd jst over 1f out* **25/1**

9 *3/4* **Belle Park** 2-8-12 0 .... NickyMackay 5 29
(Karen George) *dwlt: outpcd in last trio: nvr on terms* **66/1**

0 **10** *2* **Rightcar Marian**[20] 5611 2-8-12 0 .... JamieMackay 12 22
(Peter Grayson) *reminder sn after s: a towards rr: wknd over 1f out* **66/1**

0 **11** *11* **Lady Zoe (IRE)**[22] 5553 2-8-9 0 .... AndreaAtzeni(3) 8 —
(D Donovan) *n.m.r s: lost pl bdly after 1f: moving poorly in rr after: t.o* **50/1**

60.85 secs (0.35) **Going Correction** -0.075s/f (Stan) **11** Ran SP% **130.0**
Speed ratings (Par 95): **94,93,93,91,88 86,83,80,78,75 58**
toteswingers: 1&2 £1.40, 1&3 £14.20, 2&3 £11.20 CSF £47.66 TOTE £2.10: £1.20, £7.60, £1.10; EX 51.80.
Owner Six Too Many **Bred** Mrs R D Peacock **Trained** Kingston Warren, Oxon

FOCUS
A moderate maiden that produced a tight finish. There may be better to come from the winner.

NOTEBOOK
Felsham confirmed the promise of his debut third at Sandown, just doing enough to get off the mark. As on debut, his trainer went down to the start to help in the loading of this colt, but it worked as he broke well and soon bagged a good position. It's hard to know whether he had to show improved form to win, but he'll need to step up on this if he is to make an impact in nurseries. (op 5-6 tchd Evens)
Liberty Lady(IRE) ◆ finished strongly up the inside and nearly made a winning debut. She is the one to take from this race.
Night Trade(IRE) is showing improved form with each start and this was her best effort, despite being slightly short of room in the final furlong. (op 7-2)
Rain On The Wind(IRE) couldn't get to the front having broken a touch slowly from the stalls. Still, he kept on well and can do better if getting on the lead. (op 6-1)
Kai Mook Official explanation: jockey said filly was slowly away

6208 DIGIBET H'CAP — 1m 2f (P)
6:50 (6:50) (Class 6) (0-55,55) 3-Y-O+ **£1,942** (£578; £288; £144) **Stalls High**

Form RPR

006 **1** **New World Order (IRE)**[56] 4437 5-9-5 55 .... (t) KFallon 4 65+
(Edgar Byrne) *mde all: set stdy pce tl wound it up fr 3f out: booted on over 1f out: hld on nr fin: text book ride* **9/2**[3]

01 **2** *1/2* **Eagle Nebula**[11] 5888 5-9-2 55 .... JackMitchell(3) 11 64+
(B R Johnson) *hld up in 7th: prog jst over 2f out: wnt 2nd jst ins fnl f: clsd on wnr fin but nvr gng to get there* **4/1**[2]

6045 **3** *3* **Dancer's Legacy**[16] 5723 4-9-5 55 .... PatCosgrave 14 58
(J R Boyle) *trckd ldng pair: pushed along 3f out: wnt 2nd over 1f out to jst ins fnl f: one pce* **8/1**

4463 **4** *1* **Sinbad The Sailor**[15] 5740 4-9-5 55 .... (v) EddieAhern 9 56
(J W Hills) *chsd wnr: pushed along 3f out: nt qckn and hld over 1f out: sn lost 2nd and fdd* **11/4**[1]

-503 **5** *1* **Sestet**[14] 5775 4-9-4 54 .... NickyMackay 5 54
(S Dow) *mounted on crse: trckd ldng trio: effrt over 2f out: no imp over 1f out* **16/1**

3200 **6** *3/4* **Onenightinlisbon (IRE)**[25] 5449 5-9-5 55 .... SJCraine 13 53
(J R Boyle) *hld up in 5th: pushed along 3f out: one pce and mde no prog* **20/1**

0202 **7** *nk* **La Belle Joannie**[19] 5628 4-9-5 55 .... JamesDoyle 6 53
(S Curran) *hld up in 8th: pushed along 3f out: outpcd sn after: no real prog* **16/1**

0056 **8** *1 1/4* **Mick Is Back**[11] 5888 5-9-1 51 .... (p) DaneO'Neill 1 46
(G G Margarson) *hld up in 10th: no ch after pce lifted 3f out: wd bnd 2f out: modest late prog* **16/1**

/30- **9** *nse* **Take It There**[55] 356 7-9-2 52 .... (t) TPQueally 10 47
(A J Lidderdale) *t.k.h: hld up in 11th: no ch after pce lifted 3f out: modest late prog* **25/1**

2350 **10** *3/4* **Gracechurch (IRE)**[22] 4150 6-9-3 53 .... DarryllHolland 8 47
(R J Hodges) *hld up in 12th: nvr any ch after pce lifted 3f out* **14/1**

0005 **11** *4 1/2* **Sew'N'So Character (IRE)**[21] 5577 8-9-4 54 .... SteveDrowne 7 39
(M Blanshard) *hld up in 6th: pushed along 3f out: outpcd over 2f out: wknd over 1f out* **16/1**

-600 **12** *2 1/2* **James Pollard (IRE)**[137] 1890 4-9-5 55 .... NCallan 3 35
(B J Llewellyn) *plld hrd: hld up in 9th: no prog over 2f out: wknd over 1f out* **20/1**

0625 **13** *6* **Libre**[11] 5888 9-9-2 52 .... (p) RichardHughes 2 21
(F Jordan) *hld up in last: wknd 2f out: eased* **12/1**

2m 6.89s (-1.11) **Going Correction** -0.075s/f (Stan) **13** Ran SP% **127.2**
Speed ratings (Par 101): **101,100,98,97,96 96,95,94,94,94 90,88,83**
toteswingers: 1&2 £4.30, 1&3 £11.40, 2&3 £15.30 CSF £23.79 CT £148.38 TOTE £5.80: £2.40, £2.30, £3.30; EX 35.60.
Owner R P Behan **Bred** Tullamaine Castle Stud **Trained** Upper Lambourn, Berks

FOCUS
A weak handicap in which it paid to race handily. Reliable form.
La Belle Joannie Official explanation: jockey said filly ran too free
James Pollard(IRE) Official explanation: jockey said gelding ran too free
Libre Official explanation: jockey said gelding hung left-handed

6209 DIGIBET.COM H'CAP — 1m 2f (P)
7:20 (7:21) (Class 4) (0-85,82) 3-Y-O **£4,727** (£1,406; £702; £351) **Stalls High**

Form RPR

6321 **1** **Luc Jordan**[20] 5614 3-8-13 77 .... KFallon 5 84+
(L M Cumani) *hld up in 10th: wound up arnd outer 2f out: prog wl over 1f out: r.o to ld ins fnl f: rdn out* **5/1**[3]

1421 **2** *nk* **Veroon (IRE)**[11] 5858 3-8-12 76 .... (p) J-PGuillambert 10 82
(J G Given) *hld up in 5th: shkn up and effrt wl over 1f out: prog to chal ent fnl f: pressed wnr after: a hld* **10/1**

3415 **3** *1 1/4* **Formula (USA)**[7] 5986 3-9-1 79 .... RichardHughes 2 82
(R Hannon) *pressed ldr: chal fr over 2f out: drvn to ld briefly jst ins fnl f: sn outpcd* **8/1**

224 **4** *nk* **Shakalaka (IRE)**[7] 5986 3-9-0 78 .... PatDobbs 9 81
(G L Moore) *hld up in 6th: shkn up over 1f out: n.m.r after: r.o wl last 75yds but no ch then* **5/1**[3]

4213 **5** *3/4* **Bomber Brown (IRE)**[48] 4716 3-8-10 77 .... JackMitchell(3) 7 78
(P W Chapple-Hyam) *hld up in 8th: nt qckn wl over 1f out: styd on ins fnl f: nrst fin but no ch* **10/1**

1-44 **6** *nse* **Trueblue Wizard (IRE)**[209] 689 3-8-8 72 .... (b[1]) MartinDwyer 6 73
(W R Muir) *led: rdn 3f out: hdd and fdd jst ins fnl f* **16/1**

510 **7** *3/4* **Al Qeddaaf (IRE)**[96] 3115 3-8-13 77 .... TPO'Shea 8 76+
(W J Haggas) *hld up in 9th: trapped bhd wall of rivals wl over 1f out: styd on ins fnl f: no ch* **4/1**[2]

210 **8** *1/2* **Dome Rocket**[55] 4455 3-9-2 80 .... (p) JimCrowley 11 78
(W J Knight) *mostly trckd ldng pair: nt qckn and lost 3rd over 1f out: fdd and lost more pls fnl f* **8/1**

-506 **9** *2 1/2* **Latin Tinge (USA)**[125] 2189 3-9-2 80 .... ChrisCatlin 1 73
(P F I Cole) *hld up in last and racd wd: no prog 2f out: nvr on terms after* **33/1**

1103 **10** *1/2* **Cool Hand Jake**[21] 5575 3-9-2 80 .... (t) FergusSweeney 4 72
(P J Makin) *dwlt: racd wd: sn chsd ldng trio: stl wl in tch over 1f out: wknd fnl f* **7/2**[1]

2050 **11** *3* **Union Island (IRE)**[33] 5209 3-9-4 82 .... (v[1]) NCallan 3 68
(K A Ryan) *nudged s then stmbld: hld up in 7th: rdn and losing pl whn hmpd wl over 1f out: no ch after and eased* **14/1**

2m 6.42s (-1.58) **Going Correction** -0.075s/f (Stan) **11** Ran SP% **131.4**
Speed ratings (Par 103): **103,102,101,101,100 100,100,99,97,97 95**
toteswingers: 1&2 £5.20, 1&3 £13.90, 2&3 £17.50 CSF £61.36 CT £416.23 TOTE £5.50: £2.10, £3.90, £3.00; EX 24.50.
Owner Equibreed S.R.L. **Bred** Equibreed S R L **Trained** Newmarket, Suffolk
■ A double for Kieren Fallon, his first winners on the Kempton Polytrack.

FOCUS
A fair 3yo handicap. The winner is progressing now.

6210 DIGIBET CASINO CLAIMING STKS — 1m 4f (P)
7:50 (7:51) (Class 6) 3-Y-O+ **£2,047** (£604; £302) **Stalls Centre**

Form RPR

0035 **1** **Mista Rossa**[19] 5642 4-9-8 66 .... TravisBlock 1 72+
(H Morrison) *mde all: rdn and edgd lft fr over 2f out: drvn clr over 1f out: styd on wl* **5/1**[2]

1066 **2** *3 1/2* **Majehar**[49] 4644 7-9-4 66 .... NCallan 7 63
(A G Newcombe) *hld up in midfield: hrd rdn wl over 2f out: prog over 1f out: styd on wl to take 2nd nr fin* **10/1**

4200 **3** *1/2* **Cayman Sky**[47] 4744 3-8-12 62 .... (b) RichardHughes 12 64
(R Hannon) *hld up in midfield: effrt over 2f out: prog to dispute 2nd over 1f out: no ch w wnr: kpt on* **7/1**

0330 **4** *1/2* **Ballinteni**[87] 3431 7-9-11 84 .... JerryO'Dwyer 4 68
(M G Quinlan) *trckd ldng trio: effrt over 2f out: drvn to chse wnr over 1f out but hanging and nt qckn: lost 2 pls nr fin* **9/2**[1]

0601 **5** *3/4* **Ghufa (IRE)**[18] 5679 5-9-4 70 .... TedDurcan 6 60
(George Baker) *hld up in last quartet: gng strly 3f out: prog on inner over 2f out to dispute 2nd over 1f out: fdd fnl f* **11/2**[3]

2601 **6** *hd* **Clovis**[26] 5381 4-9-2 65 .... (p) EddieAhern 10 59+
(Andrew Turnell) *hld up in last pair: effrt whn nt clr run wl over 2f out: swtchd ins and nt clr run wl over 1f out: kpt on fnl f* **7/1**

6300 **7** *2 1/4* **Little Sark (IRE)**[50] 4625 4-9-2 50 .... PatCosgrave 14 54
(P D Evans) *mostly chsd ldng pair to wl over 1f out: sn fdd* **33/1**

/153 **8** *1* **Guiseppe Verdi (USA)**[15] 5750 5-9-4 70 .... ChrisCatlin 8 55
(Miss Tor Sturgis) *mostly chsd wnr: rdn over 3f out: lost 2nd over 1f out: wknd rapidly fnl f* **9/2**[1]

0001 **9** *nk* **Inch Lodge**[21] 5577 7-9-1 66 .... (t) TobyAtkinson(7) 9 59
(Miss D Mountain) *s.s: mostly in last: outpcd and wd over 2f out: plugged on: no ch* **10/1**

3000 **10** *5* **Imperial Harry**[22] 4378 6-9-0 67 .... (p) JimCrowley 13 43
(Jean-Rene Auvray) *t.k.h: trckd ldrs: nt qckn over 2f out: wknd rapidly over 1f out* **25/1**

00/5 **11** *6* **Iffy**[27] 5367 8-9-1 63 .... SteveDrowne 3 35
(A B Haynes) *dwlt: hld up in last quartet: taken to r wd 1/2-way: rdn and effrt 4f out: wknd wl over 2f out* **20/1**

00- **12** *6* **Axinit (GER)**[288] 6606 9-9-2 54 .... (t) EdwardCreighton 2 27
(E J Creighton) *wl in rr: drvn and effrt on outer 4f out: wknd 3f out: t.o* **66/1**

2m 33.85s (-0.65) **Going Correction** -0.075s/f (Stan)
WFA 3 from 4yo+ 8lb **12** Ran SP% **124.6**
Speed ratings (Par 101): **99,96,96,96,95 95,93,93,93,89 85,81**
toteswingers: 1&2 £13.10, 1&3 £12.30, 2&3 £16.00 CSF £55.10 TOTE £6.80: £2.60, £5.00, £3.40; EX 79.50.Clovis was claimed by R Venn for £6000.
Owner Wood Street Syndicate IV **Bred** The National Stud **Trained** East Ilsley, Berks

FOCUS
A modest claimer where the winner dicated. The form is sound but limited.

6211 KIA SOUL, SAFE BET NURSERY — 1m (P)
8:20 (8:23) (Class 6) (0-75,75) 2-Y-O **£2,047** (£604; £302) **Stalls High**

Form RPR

0401 **1** **Boquito (IRE)**[21] 5573 2-9-0 68 .... JerryO'Dwyer 2 77+
(Miss Amy Weaver) *t.k.h early: hld up in rr: prog on outer fr over 2f out: swept into ld jst over 1f out: sn pushed clr: eased last 75yds* **6/1**

0062 **2** *1 1/4* **White Dart**[9] 5938 2-8-12 66 .... ChrisCatlin 6 72+
(M R Channon) *t.k.h early: hld up wl in rr: plenty to do whn nt clr run over 2f out: swtchd out wd and rapid prog over 1f out: only 7th ent fnl f: r.o wl to take 2nd: no ch w wnr* **7/2**[2]

3153 **3** *1 1/4* **Diamond Duchess (IRE)**[16] 5715 2-9-5 73 .... TedDurcan 11 73
(D R Lanigan) *trckd ldng trio: rdn to press ldr wl over 1f out: no ch w wnr fnl f: kpt on* **5/1**[3]

655 **4** *1/2* **Buffett**[11] 5867 2-8-13 67 .... KFallon 12 66
(L M Cumani) *trckd ldng pair: rdn and nt qckn over 2f out: styd chsng ldrs but outpcd fnl f* **13/8**[1]

651 **5** *nse* **Agony And Ecstasy**[53] 4534 2-9-0 75 .... JPFahy(7) 14 74
(R M Beckett) *led at decent pce: drvn and hdd jst over 1f out: grad fdd* **11/1**

4540 **6** *1 1/4* **Dream Spinner**[33] 5213 2-9-2 70 .... EddieAhern 9 66
(J L Dunlop) *trckd ldrs: cl up jst over 2f out: nt qckn wl over 1f out: plugged on* **16/1**

0205 **7** *shd* **Folletta (IRE)**[9] 5935 2-9-0 68 .... RichardHughes 8 64
(R Hannon) *rn in snatches in midfield: urged along and effrt over 2f out: in the hunt for a pl over 1f out: no rspnse after* **20/1**

5160 **8** *6* **Emma Dora (IRE)**[26] 5399 2-9-3 **71** .... DaneO'Neill 7 54
(D R C Elsworth) *wl in tch on outer in midfield: rdn over 2f out: no prog: wknd over 1f out* **66/1**

063 **9** *hd* **Masterful Act (USA)**[12] 5839 2-9-2 **73** .... MarcHalford(3) 5 55
(J R Best) *s.i.s: hld up in last pair: rdn 3f out: no real prog* **20/1**

1000 **10** *3/4* **Slice (IRE)**[14] 5769 2-9-7 **75** .... (b[1]) NCallan 4 56
(Eve Johnson Houghton) *hld up in midfield: rdn and no prog over 2f out: wknd over 1f out* **33/1**

2405 **11** *8* **Cafe Greco**[12] 5841 2-9-3 **71** .... FergusSweeney 3 34
(P J Makin) *s.i.s: t.k.h early: hld up in last pair: gng wl enough 3f out: rdn and no prog over 2f out* **16/1**

4430 **12** *8* **Orsett Lad (USA)**[10] 5913 2-9-5 **73** .... RobertWinston 13 19
(J R Best) *pressed ldr to wl over 1f out: heavily eased sn after: t.o* **16/1**

300 **13** *hd* **The Cardinal's Hat (FR)**[19] 5643 2-8-12 **66** .... (t) JimCrowley 10 11
(P Winkworth) *t.k.h early: a wl in rr: struggling over 2f out: sn wknd: t.o* **40/1**

1m 39.57s (-0.23) **Going Correction** -0.075s/f (Stan) **13 Ran SP% 133.6**
Speed ratings (Par 93): **98,96,95,95,94 93,93,87,87,86 78,70,70**
toteswingers: 1&2 £2.70, 1&3 £7.20, 2&3 £4.40 CSF £29.32 CT £125.48 TOTE £7.60: £2.50, £2.10, £2.00; EX 32.50.
Owner Mrs Melba Bryce **Bred** Darley **Trained** Newmarket, Suffolk

FOCUS
A moderate nursery, but the form looks good for the class and should work out.

NOTEBOOK
Boquito(IRE) ◆ put the race to bed with a telling turn of foot between the two and the one pole to sweep down the outside and go clear. He had been hiked up 8lb for his course-and-distance win last time, but he is firmly on the upgrade for he was just as impressive here and he looks a useful colt in-the-making. (op 7-1)
White Dart ◆ finished like a train from a mile back but the winner had already gone. Still, this was a very taking effort and he should not be long in winning a similar event. (op 5-1)
Diamond Duchess(IRE) helps to give the form further solidity and she again ran her race, sticking on well having raced close to the pace throughout. On the downside, she is vulnerable to improvers so is going to be vulnerable in this sort of company. (op 7-1)
Buffett, upped in trip for his handicap debut, was a bit free in the early stages and although he kept on well enough at the business end, he lacked the instant gear change of the winner. (op 7-4 tchd 9-4)
Agony And Ecstasy was too free on the lead and couldn't see her race out. (op 9-1 tchd 12-1)
Orsett Lad(USA) Official explanation: trainer said jockey heavily eased gelding as it felt wrong

6212 BOOK KEMPTON TICKETS ON 0844 579 3008 H'CAP 7f (P)
8:50 (8:52) (Class 4) (0-80,80) 3-Y-O+ **£4,727** (£1,406; £702; £351) **Stalls High**

Form RPR

0165 **1** **Arachnophobia (IRE)**[40] 4984 3-9-1 **77** .... RobertWinston 8 86
(Pat Eddery) *trckd ldr after 2f: rdn over 2f out: sustained chal and drvn into narrow ld ins fnl f: all out* **12/1**

4301 **2** *nk* **Tamasou (IRE)**[13] 5813 4-8-10 **69** .... DavidProbert 3 77
(A J McCabe) *prom: chsd ldng pair over 2f out: drvn to chal fnl f: styd on: jst hld* **7/1**

6554 **3** *shd* **Hustle (IRE)**[7] 6004 4-9-4 **77** .... GeorgeBaker 2 85
(Miss Gay Kelleway) *c across fr wd draw to ld after 1f: drvn over 2f out: narrowly hdd ins fnl f: kpt on wl* **17/2**

0-14 **4** *1 3/4* **Conry (IRE)**[14] 5774 3-9-2 **78** .... EddieAhern 6 80
(Patrick Morris) *hld up towards rr: rdn on outer over 2f out: prog over 1f out: styd on to take 4th nr fin* **20/1**

3006 **5** *nk* **Musical Script (USA)**[7] 5991 6-8-13 **72** .... (b) NCallan 13 74
(Mouse Hamilton-Fairley) *t.k.h early: hld up in midfield: rdn over 2f out: kpt on fr over 1f out: nt pce to threaten ldrs* **14/1**

3000 **6** *1 1/4* **The Snatcher (IRE)**[18] 5663 6-9-6 **79** .... RichardHughes 12 78
(R Hannon) *chsd ldrs: pushed along on inner bef 1/2-way: stl chsng 2f out: no imp after but kpt on* **8/1**

0565 **7** *hd* **Carlitos Spirit (IRE)**[19] 5640 5-8-10 **72** .... JamesMillman(3) 4 70
(B R Millman) *racd wd: wl in tch bhd ldrs: rdn and nt qckn 2f out: no imp after* **25/1**

6460 **8** *hd* **Desert Dreamer (IRE)**[11] 5884 8-9-1 **79** .... RichardEvans(5) 5 77
(P D Evans) *hmpd s: hld up wl in rr: shkn up on outer over 2f out: kpt on: nvr rchd ldrs* **25/1**

305 **9** *1/2* **Cheap Thrills**[18] 5677 3-8-13 **75** .... ShaneKelly 11 70
(J A Osborne) *led 1f: chsd ldng pair after 2f to over 2f out: fdd over 1f out* **50/1**

1002 **10** *shd* **Secret Witness**[15] 5753 3-9-2 **78** .... TPQueally 10 73
(J Noseda) *dwlt: t.k.h and sn cl up: rdn to chse ldrs over 2f out: no imp over 1f out: fdd and lost pls wl ins fnl f* **10/3[1]**

6434 **11** *1 1/4* **Last Sovereign**[17] 5697 5-9-2 **80** .... (p) Louis-PhilippeBeuzelin(5) 14 73
(Jane Chapple-Hyam) *mostly in midfield on inner: drvn over 2f out: no prog wl over 1f out: fdd* **9/2[2]**

0000 **12** *1/2* **Trafalgar Square**[18] 5663 7-9-4 **77** .... JimCrowley 1 68
(M J Attwater) *hld up in last fr wd draw and keen early: swtchd to inner and effrt over 2f out: racd awkwardly over 1f out: sn btn* **50/1**

00-4 **13** *3 1/2* **Transfer**[15] 5753 4-9-1 **74** .... LPKeniry 9 56
(A M Balding) *t.k.h early: hld up: rdn over 3f out: sn struggling in rr* **9/1**

1-5 **14** *1/2* **Beauchamp Wizard**[24] 5473 4-9-1 **74** .... (t) KFallon 7 55
(G A Butler) *hld up wl in rr and racd wd: rdn over 2f out: no prog and btn after* **6/1[3]**

1m 24.76s (-1.24) **Going Correction** -0.075s/f (Stan)
WFA 3 from 4yo+ 3lb **14 Ran SP% 130.4**
Speed ratings (Par 105): **104,103,103,101,101 99,99,99,98,98 97,96,92,92**
toteswingers: 1&2 £24.90, 1&3 £21.00, 2&3 £4.00 CSF £96.65 CT £798.31 TOTE £16.40: £3.50, £2.90, £5.90; EX 116.40.
Owner Pat Eddery Racing (Sharpo) **Bred** Michael Staunton **Trained** Nether Winchendon, Bucks

FOCUS
A fair handicap. The first three were clear and the form is rated around them.
Trafalgar Square Official explanation: jockey said gelding was denied a clear run

6213 PANORAMIC BAR & RESTAURANT H'CAP 7f (P)
9:20 (9:22) (Class 6) (0-55,55) 3-Y-O+ **£2,047** (£604; £302) **Stalls High**

Form RPR

350 **1** **Straight Face (IRE)**[16] 5730 5-9-2 **52** .... (b) GeorgeBaker 13 61
(Miss Gay Kelleway) *hld up in midfield on inner: prog 3f out to chse ldng pair over 2f out: plld out and effrt over 1f out: r.o to ld nr fin* **15/2**

2052 **2** *nk* **Sermons Mount (USA)**[19] 5644 3-9-2 **55** .... (p) NCallan 14 62
(Mouse Hamilton-Fairley) *t.k.h: prom on inner: chsd ldr 3f out: drvn to cl and ld over 1f out: over a l ahd ins fnl f: worn down nr fin* **11/2[2]**

0406 **3** *2 1/4* **Shake On It**[14] 5779 5-9-0 **53** .... AndreaAtzeni(3) 2 55
(M R Hoad) *dropped in fr wd draw and hld up in last pair: swtchd to inner over 2f out and prog: drvn and styd on to take 3rd nr fin* **20/1**

460 **4** *1 1/4* **Dilli Dancer**[25] 5429 4-9-0 **55** .... GabrielHannon(5) 9 54
(G D Blake) *led: rdn over 2f out: hdd over 1f out: wknd ins fnl f* **20/1**

0065 **5** *1/2* **Avoca Dancer (IRE)**[23] 5502 6-9-3 **53** .... (v) RichardHughes 3 53+
(Karen George) *hld up in rr: pushed along and no prog over 2f out: shkn up and styd on steadily fr over 1f out: nvr nr ldrs* **7/1**

4050 **6** *1/2* **Djalalabad (FR)**[7] 5998 5-9-3 **53** .... (tp) RobertWinston 10 49
(Mrs C A Dunnett) *t.k.h: hld up in midfield: effrt over 2f out: sme prog and tried to cl on ldrs over 1f out: fdd ins fnl f* **16/1**

0040 **7** *1/2* **Minnola**[19] 5624 4-9-2 **52** .... (b[1]) SaleemGolam 6 47
(Rae Guest) *prom: disp 3rd over 2f out: nt qckn after: fdd fnl f* **14/1**

6300 **8** *1* **Takitwo**[14] 5779 6-9-5 **55** .... (v) DaneO'Neill 12 47
(P D Cundell) *nvr bttr than midfield: outpcd over 2f out: plugged on fnl f* **7/1**

-064 **9** *3/4* **Candy Rose**[16] 5723 4-9-4 **54** .... (tp) PatDobbs 7 44
(M P Tregoning) *trckd ldrs: rdn and nt qckn over 2f out: grad wknd fr over 1f out* **4/1[1]**

0020 **10** *2 3/4* **Annes Rocket (IRE)**[12] 5842 4-9-5 **55** .... SamHitchcott 11 38
(J C Fox) *plld hrd: hld up in last pair: no real prog over 2f out: eased* **9/1**

5001 **11** *1 1/4* **Artesium**[19] 5644 3-9-2 **55** .... SJCraine 8 33
(Patrick Morris) *cl up: n.m.r 3f out: sn lost pl: wknd 2f out* **13/2[3]**

3600 **12** *3* **Bobble Rock (IRE)**[24] 5479 3-9-2 **55** .... (b[1]) JimCrowley 4 25
(J R Best) *t.k.h: chsd ldr to 3f out: sn wknd* **33/1**

0-6 **13** *hd* **Anfield Star (IRE)**[19] 5645 3-9-2 **55** .... EddieAhern 5 25
(Patrick Morris) *prom on outer: wknd wl over 2f out* **25/1**

1m 25.85s (-0.15) **Going Correction** -0.075s/f (Stan)
WFA 3 from 4yo+ 3lb **13 Ran SP% 124.3**
Speed ratings (Par 101): **97,96,94,92,92 91,90,89,88,85 84,80,80**
toteswingers: 1&2 £6.10, 1&3 £29.20, 2&3 £32.10 Place 6: £60.20 Place 5: £55.26 CSF £48.03 CT £845.35 TOTE £7.00: £2.60, £2.30, £6.80; EX 18.90.
Owner KingsClubSyndicate I **Bred** P J Towell **Trained** Exning, Suffolk

FOCUS
Competitive enough for the grade and the form looks fairly reliable.
Annes Rocket(IRE) Official explanation: jockey said saddle slipped
T/Plt: £100.50 to a £1 stake. Pool: £60,423.34. 438.70 winning tickets. T/Qpdt: £79.50 to a £1 stake. Pool: £5,437.30. 50.60 winning tickets. JN

5949 REDCAR (L-H)
Wednesday, September 23

OFFICIAL GOING: Good to firm (9.0)
Wind: fresh 1/2 behind Weather: fine but breezy

6214 EUROPEAN BREEDERS' FUND MAIDEN STKS 7f
1:45 (1:48) (Class 5) 2-Y-O **£3,885** (£1,156; £577; £288) **Stalls Centre**

Form RPR

322 **1** **Cash Queen Anna (IRE)**[23] 5505 2-8-12 75 .... MichaelHills 3 71
(B W Hills) *mde most: rdn along wl over 1f out: drvn ent fnl f and kpt on* **5/6[1]**

2 *1/2* **Much Acclaimed (IRE)** 2-9-3 0 .... MickyFenton 8 75+
(T P Tate) *trckd ldrs: pushed along and outpcd over 3f out: hdwy 2f out: rdn and edgd rt over 1f out: kpt on wl fnl f* **20/1**

233 **3** *3/4* **Happy Dubai (IRE)**[18] 5669 2-9-3 73 .... (v[1]) TomEaves 2 73
(B Smart) *trckd ldrs: hdwy wl over 2f out: rdn to chal and edgd rt over 1f out and ev ch tl drvn and one pce ins fnl f* **8/1[3]**

33 **4** *2* **Weekend Millionair (IRE)**[28] 5330 2-9-3 0 .... PhillipMakin 7 68
(P D Evans) *cl up: rdn along wl over 2f out: hung lft wl over 1f out: sn drvn and one pce* **20/1**

5 *1/2* **Baraconti (IRE)** 2-9-3 0 .... PaulHanagan 10 67
(R A Fahey) *trckd ldrs: hdwy over 2f out: pushed along whn n.m.r and swtchd lft over 1f out: sn rdn and no imp* **14/1**

6 *hd* **Art Excellence** 2-9-3 0 .... JamieSpencer 9 66
(S A Callaghan) *dwlt and in rr: hdwy and in tch 1/2-way: chsd ldrs over 2f out: sn rdn and kpt on same pce* **9/2[2]**

7 *8* **Fighting Talk (IRE)** 2-9-3 0 .... RoystonFfrench 5 56+
(M Johnston) *cl up: rdn along over 2f out: wkng whn n.m.r and hmpd over 1f out* **9/1**

0 **8** *9* **Naughty Norris**[18] 5668 2-9-3 0 .... DanielTudhope 11 24
(R Bastiman) *in tch: rdn along 3f out and sn wknd* **200/1**

0 **9** *1 1/4* **Avon Grounds**[84] 3500 2-9-3 0 .... RichardKingscote 4 21
(J M Bradley) *chsd ldrs: rdn along 1/2-way and sn wknd* **80/1**

00 **10** *8* **Check The Anchor (IRE)**[9] 5951 2-9-3 0 .... PJMcDonald 1 —
(N Tinkler) *bmpd s: sn outpcd and a in rr* **150/1**

11 *16* **Bollin Jasmine** 2-8-12 0 .... DavidAllan 6 —
(T D Easterby) *s.i.s: a outpcd and bhd* **80/1**

1m 23.6s (-0.90) **Going Correction** -0.15s/f (Firm) **11 Ran SP% 113.7**
Speed ratings (Par 95): **99,98,97,95,94 94,85,75,73,64 46**
toteswingers: 1&2 £7.00, 1&3 £2.10, 2&3 £13.90 CSF £25.96 TOTE £1.60: £1.02, £4.30, £2.20; EX 23.20.
Owner South Bank Thoroughbred Racing **Bred** Ballylinch Stud **Trained** Lambourn, Berks

FOCUS
A blustery day and the going was good to firm on a watered track. A fair maiden, in which the pace was decent, and the first six finished a long way clear of the rest. The winner did not need to match her previous form.

NOTEBOOK
Cash Queen Anna(IRE) set a clear standard on her placed efforts behind some bright prospects in 6f/7f maidens, including a clear second ahead of subsequent winner Five Cents at Epsom last time. She was strong in the market but had to work quite hard under a positive ride to get off the mark on the fourth attempt. She looks a nice type but her profile is consistent rather than progressive, and she will need to find something extra when switched to nurseries. (op Evens tchd 4-5 and 11-10 in a place)
Much Acclaimed(IRE) took a while to get the hang of things but stayed on strongly, and almost gave the winner a scare in the closing stages. He is a gelded brother to Few Are Chosen, a dual 1m winner at three, and a half-brother to Dabbers Ridge, a useful multiple 6f-1m winner. He is the one to take out of the race. (tchd 25-1)
Happy Dubai(IRE), rated 73, gives the form a solid look. He plugged on well and put in another respectable effort, but he has not really progressed in four starts and a first-time visor has failed encourage improvement. (tchd 17-2)
Weekend Millionair(IRE) had something to find on figures but stuck to his task quite well after coming under pressure some way out. He has scope for mental and physical progress and should do better in time. (op 16-1)
Baraconti(IRE) stayed on steadily after getting a bit tapped for speed. He is a gelded half-brother to several winners, including 1m2f-1m4f winner Cosmic String. This trip is likely to be a bare minimum for him this year and he should do better with time and stiffer test.

Art Excellence was not given a hard time on debut and should have learned quite a bit from the experience. He is a 32,000gns half-brother to Dignify, a dual 7f-1m winner at two, who was later fourth in the Italian Oaks. (tchd 5-1)

6215 HOLD YOUR CHRISTMAS PARTY HERE NURSERY 1m

2:15 (2:17) (Class 6) (0-65,65) 2-Y-O **£1,942** (£578; £288; £144) **Stalls** Centre

Form RPR

6001 **1** **Fantastic Pick**^{16} 5715 2-9-5 **63** ... PaulHanagan 11 76+
(B J Meehan) *w ldrs: led over 3f out: styd on str to draw clr fnl f: readily* **11/4^{1}**

400 **2** *3* **Ella Grace (USA)**^{39} 5036 2-8-11 **58** ... FrederikTylicki$^{(3)}$ 13 65
(R A Fahey) *swvd lft s: w ldrs: styd on same pce fnl f* **12/1**

1652 **3** *1 3/4* **Right Rave (IRE)**^{7} 5985 2-9-7 **65** ... JamieSpencer 1 68+
(P J McBride) *in rr far side: hdwy towards far side over 2f out: kpt on same pce fnl f* **9/2^{2}**

060 **4** *2 3/4* **Mason Hindmarsh**^{40} 4993 2-8-7 **56** ... BMcHugh$^{(5)}$ 8 53
(Karen McLintock) *chsd ldrs: kpt on same pce fnl 2f* **20/1**

6343 **5** *3/4* **High Rolling**^{20} 5595 2-9-6 **64** ... DavidAllan 18 59
(T D Easterby) *led tl over 3f out: fdd fnl f* **7/1^{3}**

2034 **6** *1 1/2* **Just The Tonic**^{7} 5976 2-8-13 **57** ... PJMcDonald 15 49
(Mrs Marjorie Fife) *chsd ldrs: wandered 2f out: kpt on one pce* **14/1**

0000 **7** *1 1/2* **Gulf Punch**^{9} 5938 2-8-6 **50** ... (p) AndrewMullen 10 39
(M F Harris) *chsd ldrs: one pce fnl 2f* **40/1**

5646 **8** *hd* **Wijikura (IRE)**^{23} 5519 2-9-2 **60** ... TomEaves 5 48
(J J Quinn) *mid-div: hdwy and swtchd rt 2f out: kpt on: nvr nr ldrs* **16/1**

060 **9** *1 1/2* **Wood Fair**^{94} 3187 2-9-7 **65** ... AndrewElliott 16 50
(A P Jarvis) *mid-div: rdn over 2f out: nvr nr ldrs* **22/1**

400 **10** *3* **Musiara**^{16} 5715 2-8-6 **50** ... JoeFanning 3 28
(M R Channon) *s.i.s: t.k.h in rr: nvr on terms* **40/1**

0000 **11** *3/4* **Argyll**^{16} 5715 2-9-1 **59** ... DO'Donohoe 12 36
(J Pearce) *hmpd s: in rr and sn drvn along on stands' side: nvr on terms* **50/1**

6030 **12** *1 1/2* **Charity Fair**^{4} 6099 2-7-12 **49** ... BillyCray$^{(7)}$ 2 22
(A Berry) *s.s: racd towards far side: nvr on terms* **33/1**

6403 **13** *nk* **Knockenduff**^{7} 5985 2-9-2 **60** ... FrancisNorton 9 33
(M R Channon) *in rr: nvr on terms* **10/1**

0500 **14** *7* **Countrymans Dream**^{41} 4931 2-8-2 **46** ... JimmyQuinn 6 3
(J R Weymes) *chsd ldrs towards far side: lost pl 3f out: sn bhd* **80/1**

3400 **15** *1 3/4* **Silver In The Sand**^{22} 5550 2-9-1 **59** ... GrahamGibbons 4 13
(J D Bethell) *in rr div towards far side: bhd fnl 2f* **16/1**

000 **16** *2 1/2* **Buzz Bird**^{32} 5253 2-8-10 **54** ow1 ... PhillipMakin 20 —
(T D Barron) *chsd ldrs stands' side: hung lft and lost pl 3f out* **14/1**

0006 **17** *2 3/4* **Captain Blake (IRE)**^{11} 5868 2-8-1 **45** ... SilvestreDeSousa 14 —
(P D Evans) *mid-div: sn drvn along: lost pl 3f out: rdr dropped whip* **25/1**

1m 37.26s (-0.74) **Going Correction** -0.15s/f (Firm) **17** Ran SP% **123.2**

Speed ratings (Par 93): **97,94,92,89,88 87,85,85,84,81 80,78,78,71,69 67,64**

toteswingers: 1&2 £11.20, 1&3 £4.20, 2&3 £13.20 CSF £33.52 CT £156.56 TOTE £3.60: £1.30, £1.60, £1.90, £4.20; EX 37.60.

Owner Raymond Tooth **Bred** Star Pointe Ltd **Trained** Manton, Wilts

FOCUS

An ordinary-looking nursery, but the two market leaders finished first and third, and an unexposed type, who attracted some support, was second, so the form could be solid. The time was decent for the grade.

NOTEBOOK

Fantastic Pick looked an improved performer when a decisive winner upped to this trip and back from a break at Bath this month. He had an 8lb rise to deal with but kept winding things up under a prominent ride, and eventually forged clear for an authoritative success. He looks a resolute galloper rather than a horse with sharp weapons, but is clearly progressing and should appreciate a further move up in trip. He may attempt to defy a penalty in a 1m2f Nottingham nursery next Wednesday. (op 4-1)

Ella Grace(USA), making her nursery debut, did very little in her last two maiden runs, but travelled much more fluently in this and stayed on in determined fashion. Up 2f in trip, she is unexposed at the distance and has started her handicap career on a modest rating, one that she could be capable of quite a bit of progress off. (op 14-1)

Right Rave(IRE) deserves credit for coming from some way back in a race where the first two were always prominent. She has gone the right way with an ever-increasing emphasis on stamina in nurseries since winning a 5f Yarmouth maiden. (op 7-2)

Mason Hindmarsh ran respectably faced with a much more realistic target up in trip on his nursery debut. (op 33-1)

High Rolling's keeping-on third over 7f here this month had been boosted by the winner and the fifth. The son of Fantastic Light had an interesting chance stepped up to 1m, and was given an aggressive ride, but he was caught a bit flat-footed when the pace quickened and could only plug on after that. (op 6-1 tchd 5-1)

Just The Tonic was not disgraced stepped up from 5f on her second run since leaving Mick Channon, but was comfortably shaken off by the principals, and has now had 11 chances without success.

Charity Fair n Official explanation: jockey said filly was unsuited by the good to firm ground (tchd 40-1)

Buzz Bird Official explanation: jockey said filly moved poorly and hung left-handed (tchd 12-1)

6216 SUBSCRIBE TO RACING UK H'CAP (DIV I) 6f

2:50 (2:50) (Class 6) (0-65,65) 3-Y-O+ **£1,706** (£503; £252) **Stalls** Centre

Form RPR

1002 **1** **Just Sam (IRE)**^{9} 5955 4-9-0 **64** ... PaulPickard$^{(5)}$ 7 73
(R E Barr) *mde all: rdn clr over 1f out: kpt on strly ins fnl f* **9/2^{1}**

4241 **2** *nk* **Ghost Dancer**^{23} 5525 5-9-6 **65** ... (p) JamieSpencer 11 73+
(J M Bradley) *stdd s and hld up in rr: hdwy 2f out: swtchd rt and rdn over 1f out: styd on strly ins fnl f: jst hld* **9/2^{1}**

0246 **3** *1 1/2* **Elkhorn**^{9} 5955 7-8-8 **53** ... (b) TomEaves 9 57
(Miss J A Camacho) *in tch: hdwy over 2f out: sn rdn: drvn to chse wnr and edgd lft ent fnl f: kpt on* **6/1^{3}**

0550 **4** *2* **Rainbow Bay**^{2} 6160 6-8-3 **53** oh6 ow2 ... (p) PatrickDonaghy$^{(5)}$ 10 51
(Miss Tracy Waggott) *prom: chsd wnr 2f out and sn rdn: drvn over 1f out and grad wknd* **20/1**

3013 **5** *1 3/4* **Gurteen Diamond**^{6} 6028 3-9-4 **65** ... PhillipMakin 3 57
(P D Evans) *chsd ldrs: rdn along 2f out: sn drvn and kpt on same pce* **8/1**

6040 **6** *1 3/4* **Foreign Rhythm (IRE)**^{9} 5955 4-8-6 **51** oh4 ... DO'Donohoe 2 38
(N Tinkler) *midfield and sn rdn along: drvn over 2f out: sn no imp* **40/1**

065 **7** *3/4* **Avoncreek**^{6} 6039 5-8-1 **51** oh6 ... JemmaMarshall$^{(5)}$ 1 36
(B P J Baugh) *chsd ldrs: rdn along over 2f out: grad wknd* **40/1**

0424 **8** *3/4* **Kingsgate Castle**^{12} 5842 4-8-11 **56** ... (v) PaulHanagan 5 39
(Miss Gay Kelleway) *chsd ldrs: rdn along over 2f out: grad wknd* **9/1**

-603 **9** *1/2* **Maryolini**^{205} 738 4-9-0 **59** ... RichardKingscote 8 40
(Tom Dascombe) *prom: rdn along over 2f out: sn edgd lft and wknd* **11/2^{2}**

-000 **10** *1 3/4* **Lambency (IRE)**^{2} 6160 6-8-3 **51** oh1 ... (p) KellyHarrison$^{(3)}$ 4 27
(J S Goldie) *a towards rr* **20/1**

3500 **11** *nk* **Ryedane (IRE)**^{7} 5978 7-9-1 **60** ... (b) DavidAllan 6 35
(T D Easterby) *in tch: rdn along 1/2-way: drvn and wknd 2f out* **7/1**

000- **12** *5* **Kunte Kinteh**^{426} 4327 5-8-10 **55** ... AdrianTNicholls 12 15
(D Nicholls) *s.i.s: a towards rr* **14/1**

69.88 secs (-1.92) **Going Correction** -0.15s/f (Firm)

WFA 3 from 4yo+ 2lb **12** Ran SP% **120.7**

Speed ratings (Par 101): **106,105,103,100,98 96,95,94,93,91 90,84**

toteswingers: 1&2 £3.10, 1&3 £6.30, 2&3 £6.40 CSF £23.49 CT £124.05 TOTE £4.80: £1.80, £1.90, £2.40; EX 11.70.

Owner P Cartmell **Bred** John J Carroll **Trained** Seamer, N Yorks

FOCUS

An ordinary sprint handicap, and sound form. The two market leaders adopted different tactics but filled the first two places.

6217 BODDINGTONS REDCAR STRAIGHT-MILE CHAMPIONSHIP (QUALIFIER) (PREMIER CLAIMING STKS) 1m

3:25 (3:27) (Class 4) 3-Y-O+ **£5,180** (£1,541; £770; £384) **Stalls** Centre

Form RPR

3000 **1** **White Deer (USA)**^{15} 5746 5-9-3 77 ... (p) SilvestreDeSousa 1 86
(G A Harker) *hld up towards rr: effrt 3f out: sn chsng ldrs: edgd rt and led 1f out: forged clr* **11/1**

4330 **2** *4* **Opus Maximus (IRE)**^{23} 5522 4-9-9 86 ... BMcHugh$^{(5)}$ 4 88
(M Johnston) *chsd ldrs: hung lft and upsides over 1f out: styd on same pce ins fnl f* **7/2^{2}**

4000 **3** *1/2* **Benandonner (USA)**^{23} 5522 6-10-0 94 ... PaulHanagan 11 87
(R A Fahey) *chsd ldrs: rdn and outpcd 2f out: styd on wl ins fnl f: snatched 3rd nr line: lame* **11/4^{1}**

0004 **4** *1/2* **Kings Point (IRE)**^{9} 5944 8-9-7 83 ... (b) FrancisNorton 6 79
(D Nicholls) *racd wd towards far side: led tl hdd and no ex 1f out* **14/1**

-002 **5** *3 1/2* **Top Tribute**^{23} 5513 4-8-11 60 ... MickyFenton 2 61
(T P Tate) *hld up in rr: effrt over 2f out: kpt on: nvr nr ldrs* **9/1**

4256 **6** *2 1/4* **Tanforan**^{11} 5869 7-8-6 65 ... BillyCray$^{(7)}$ 8 58
(B P J Baugh) *s.i.s: hdwy over 2f out: kpt on: nvr nr ldrs* **33/1**

2514 **7** *shd* **Royal Dignitary (USA)**^{14} 5779 9-9-6 82 ... AdrianTNicholls 10 65
(D Nicholls) *chsd ldrs: wknd over 1f out* **9/1**

4652 **8** *6* **Pianoforte (USA)**^{11} 5888 7-8-11 51 ... (b) GrahamGibbons 5 45+
(E J Alston) *chsd ldrs: wknd 2f out* **33/1**

2000 **9** *3 1/2* **Exopuntia**^{20} 5601 3-8-6 52 ow1 ... (p) MichaelJStainton$^{(3)}$ 9 37
(R M Whitaker) *sn towards rr and drvn along* **80/1**

4-60 **10** *9* **Magic Haze**^{42} 4892 3-8-13 57 ... JimmyQuinn 7 21+
(Miss S E Hall) *chsd ldrs: wknd over 2f out: bhd whn eased ins fnl f* **50/1**

1316 **11** *14* **Dabbers Ridge (IRE)**^{9} 5944 7-8-8 80 ... GaryBartley$^{(5)}$ 3 —
(I W McInnes) *in rr: drvn over 2f out: sn bhd: virtually p.u* **14/1**

0460 **R** **Flawed Genius**^{6} 6024 4-9-4 86 ... (t) AmyRyan$^{(5)}$ 12 —
(K A Ryan) *ref to r: lft in stalls: tk no part* **5/1^{3}**

1m 35.67s (-2.33) **Going Correction** -0.15s/f (Firm)

WFA 3 from 4yo+ 4lb **12** Ran SP% **116.3**

Speed ratings (Par 105): **105,101,100,100,96 94,94,88,84,75 61,—**

toteswingers: 1&2 £12.90, 1&3 £12.30, 2&3 £3.40 CSF £47.56 TOTE £12.90: £4.00, £1.80, £1.60; EX 69.20.

Owner Ian Bellamy **Bred** Fleetwood Bloodstock Et Al **Trained** Thirkleby, N Yorks

FOCUS

A hot claimer. Six of the runners held an official rating between 80 and 94 and the winner is rated back to his best.

Benandonner(USA) Official explanation: vet said gelding returned lame

Magic Haze Official explanation: trainer's rep said gelding lost a shoe

6218 WIN A VIP DAY OUT @ REDCARRACING.CO.UK H'CAP 1m 2f

4:00 (4:00) (Class 5) (0-70,67) 3-Y-O+ **£2,590** (£770; £385; £192) **Stalls** Low

Form RPR

5131 **1** **Baltimore Jack (IRE)**^{6} 6017 5-9-5 **62** ... GrahamGibbons 6 76+
(T D Walford) *trckd ldr: hdwy to ld 3f out: rdn clr wl over 1f out: styd on wl* **6/4^{1}**

1136 **2** *1 1/4* **Miss Ferney**^{16} 5732 5-8-5 **53** ... PaulPickard$^{(5)}$ 2 62
(A Kirtley) *midfield: hdwy on inner to trck ldrs over 4f out: rdn to chal wl over 2f out: n.m.r and swtchd rt wl over 1f out: sn drvn and kpt on wl fnl f* **15/2^{2}**

6206 **3** *2 3/4* **Eijaaz (IRE)**^{50} 4619 8-9-8 **65** ... SilvestreDeSousa 8 68
(G A Harker) *hld up in rr: hdwy on outer 3f out: rdn 2f out: styd on ins fnl f: nrst fin* **16/1**

006 **4** *1/2* **French Art**^{26} 5395 4-9-4 **61** ... JamieSpencer 5 63
(N Tinkler) *stdd s: hld up and bhd: hdwy over 3f out: chsd ldrs 2f out: sn swtchd rt and rdn: one pce* **17/2^{3}**

100 **5** *shd* **Wood Fairy**^{26} 5395 3-9-4 **67** ... PaulHanagan 4 69
(R A Fahey) *trckd ldrs: hdwy 3f out: rdn along over 2f out: drvn wl over 1f out and kpt on same pce* **17/2^{3}**

0001 **6** *3* **Chalice Welcome**^{8} 5975 6-9-3 **67** 6ex ... DavidKenny$^{(7)}$ 10 63
(N B King) *trckd ldrs: hdwy 4f out: chsd ldng pair over 2f out: sn rdn and one pce fr wl over 1f out* **18/1**

-564 **7** *2 1/4* **Bosamcliff (IRE)**^{13} 5791 4-9-3 **60** ... TomEaves 11 52
(P D Evans) *chsd ldrs: rdn along 3f out: sn drvn and btn* **14/1**

6526 **8** *3* **Island Music (IRE)**^{39} 5037 4-9-2 **62** ... (p) FrederikTylicki$^{(3)}$ 9 48
(J J Quinn) *nvr bttr than midfield* **22/1**

-060 **9** *1 3/4* **West With The Wind**^{25} 5438 4-9-8 **65** ... (b^{1}) MickyFenton 7 47
(T P Tate) *sn led: rdn along and hdd 3f out: sn wknd* **16/1**

0302 **10** *1* **Quince (IRE)**^{9} 5936 6-9-6 **63** ... (v) DO'Donohoe 3 43
(J Pearce) *hld up in rr: sme hdwy over 3f out: sn rdn along and nvr a factor* **9/1**

4665 **11** *1 1/4* **Grey Command (USA)**^{6} 6017 4-8-6 **56** ... JohnCavanagh$^{(7)}$ 15 34
(M Brittain) *chsd ldrs: hdwy over 4f out: rdn along over 3f out and sn wknd* **33/1**

0305 **12** *1 1/2* **Hartshead**^{18} 5673 10-9-4 **64** ... DominicFox$^{(3)}$ 13 39
(W Storey) *hld up: a in rr* **20/1**

0006 **13** *17* **Slip Star**^{9} 5948 6-8-5 **53** oh8 ... MartinLane$^{(5)}$ 14 —
(T J Etherington) *a towards rr* **100/1**

2m 4.76s (-2.34) **Going Correction** -0.15s/f (Firm)

WFA 3 from 4yo+ 6lb **13** Ran SP% **119.6**

Speed ratings (Par 103): **103,102,99,99,99 96,95,92,91,90 89,88,74**

toteswingers: 1&2 £3.70, 1&3 £9.10, 2&3 £18.40 CSF £11.87 CT £136.24 TOTE £2.40: £1.30, £2.10, £3.50; EX 15.90.

Owner D Swales **Bred** P Monagnan And J Collins And G Dillon **Trained** Sheriff Hutton, N Yorks

FOCUS
A modest handicap run at a steady pace. Straightforward form.

6219 WEDDING RECEPTIONS AT REDCAR RACECOURSE (S) STKS 1m 2f
4:35 (4:38) (Class 6) 3-5-Y-0 £2,047 (£604; £302) Stalls Low

Form RPR
1006 1 **Phantom Serenade (IRE)**[9] 5953 4-9-1 54 PhillipMakin 4 65
(M Dods) *trckd ldrs: led 3f out: edgd rt and drew clr over 1f out* 7/1
5232 2 3¾ **Bold Indian (IRE)**[9] 5953 5-9-1 55 TomEaves 5 58
(M E Sowersby) *s.i.s: hld up in midfield: hdwy on ins over 3f out: chsd wnr appr fnl f: no imp* 4/1[3]
2204 3 2½ **Moggy (IRE)**[4] 6098 3-8-4 54 SilvestreDeSousa 1 49
(G A Harker) *led tl 3f out: kpt on one pce* 13/2
3063 4 1 **Melkatant**[9] 5953 3-8-4 45 JimmyQuinn 7 47
(N Bycroft) *chsd ldrs: drvn over 4f out: sn outpcd: styd on wl fnl f* 9/1
5005 5 nk **Flora's Pride**[9] 5953 5-8-5 50 BMcHugh(5) 6 46
(K G Reveley) *hld up in rr: hdwy over 3f out: sn chsng ldrs: one pce* 14/1
0000 6 2 **Grethel (IRE)**[8] 5962 5-8-10 40 JoeFanning 2 43
(A Berry) *dwlt: sn chsng ldrs: one pce fnl 3f* 25/1
332 7 12 **Rose Cheval (USA)**[10] 5905 3-8-4 54 FrancisNorton 11 21
(M R Channon) *chsd ldrs: effrt over 3f out: lost pl over 1f out* 5/2[1]
500 8 ½ **Aquarian Dancer**[68] 4034 4-8-3 40 EleanorMcGowan(7) 14 20
(Jedd O'Keeffe) *racd wd: t.k.h in rr: sme hdwy 3f out: sn wknd* 66/1
-006 9 2¾ **Home Before Dark**[40] 4995 3-8-6 40 MichaelJStainton(3) 8 20
(R M Whitaker) *chsd ldrs: drvn over 4f out: lost pl 3f out: sn bhd* 100/1
0030 10 14 **Elusive Style (IRE)**[30] 5306 3-8-4 44 AdrianTNicholls 9 —
(S P Griffiths) *s.i.s: in rr: bhd fnl 3f* 100/1
05-P 11 100 **Longspur**[61] 4288 5-9-1 70 JamieSpencer 10 —
(M W Easterby) *tubed: in rr: bhd and drvn 4f out: virtually p.u over 2f out: eventually completed* 7/2[2]

2m 5.64s (-1.46) **Going Correction** -0.15s/f (Firm)
WFA 3 from 4yo+ 6lb 11 Ran SP% 120.6
Speed ratings (Par 101): **99,96,94,93,92 91,81,81,79,67** —
toteswingers: 1&2 £8.10, 1&3 £8.10, 2&3 £12.00 CSF £35.79 TOTE £9.50: £2.20, £1.70, £2.30; EX 46.20.The winner was bought in 6,500gns.
Owner North Briton Racing **Bred** Redpender Stud Ltd **Trained** Denton, Co Durham

FOCUS
A weak seller, run at a solid pace and rated around the second and fourth.
Rose Cheval(USA) Official explanation: trainer had no explanation for the poor form shown
Longspur Official explanation: jockey said gelding lost its action

6220 BUY YOUR TICKETS ONLINE @ REDCARRACING.CO.UK H'CAP 5f
5:10 (5:10) (Class 5) (0-70,70) 3-Y-0+ £2,590 (£770; £385; £192) Stalls Centre

Form RPR
4121 1 **Triple Dream**[20] 5608 4-9-5 69 (p) RichardKingscote 9 86+
(J M Bradley) *trckd ldrs: hdwy 2f out: rdn to ld over 1f out: edgd rt ins fnl f and sn clr* 9/2[2]
1423 2 3¾ **Bedloe's Island (IRE)**[35] 5148 4-9-3 67 FrancisNorton 2 68
(N Bycroft) *towards rr: rdn along 1/2-way: hdwy wl over 1f out: swtchd lft and drvn to chse wnr ent fnl f: sn edgd rt and no imp* 11/4[1]
0500 3 ½ **Thunder Bay**[9] 5955 4-7-12 55 FrazerWilliams(7) 4 54
(R A Fahey) *bhd: swtchd lft to wd outside and hdwy 1/2-way: sn rdn and kpt on wl fnl f: nrst fin* 16/1
0210 4 1¼ **Darcy's Pride (IRE)**[9] 5955 5-8-7 57 (t) TonyHamilton 7 51
(P T Midgley) *prom: rdn along and sltly outpcd 2f out: sn drvn and edgd lft over 1f out: kpt on u.p ins fnl f* 16/1
4000 5 ½ **Kyle (IRE)**[14] 5767 5-9-0 69 BMcHugh(5) 1 61
(C R Dore) *midfield: swtchd rt and rdn along 1/2-way: hdwy wl over 1f out: kpt on u.p ins fnl f* 12/1
0005 6 hd **Kheylide (IRE)**[2] 6160 3-8-8 59 (p) SilvestreDeSousa 3 51
(Mrs D J Sanderson) *towards rr: swtchd lft and hdwy 2f out: sn rdn and kpt on ins fnl f* 10/1
1505 7 ¾ **Under Review (IRE)**[11] 5877 3-9-5 70 PhillipMakin 10 59
(T D Barron) *cl up: led 1/2-way: rdn and hdd over 1f out: sn drvn and wknd* 12/1
0604 8 nk **Kyzer Chief**[7] 5978 4-8-9 62 KellyHarrison(3) 16 50
(R E Barr) *chsd ldrs on outer: hdwy 2f out and sn rdn: drvn over 1f out and sn one pce* 8/1[3]
5053 9 nk **Rio Sands**[32] 5254 4-8-6 56 DO'Donohoe 14 43
(R M Whitaker) *nvr bttr than midfield* 33/1
5630 10 nse **Town House**[23] 5504 7-7-12 55 oh10 BillyCray(7) 13 42
(B P J Baugh) *in tch: hdwy to chse ldrs 1/2-way: rdn along wl over 1f out: drvn and wknd appr fnl f* 100/1
6040 11 1¼ **Toy Top (USA)**[23] 5518 6-8-7 57 (b) TomEaves 8 39
(M Dods) *led: pushed along and hdd 1/2-way: sn rdn and wknd wl over 1f out* 20/1
0002 12 hd **Francis Albert**[24] 5468 3-8-4 55 oh2 AdrianTNicholls 15 36
(M Mullineaux) *a towards rr* 25/1
-605 13 ½ **Green Poppy**[79] 3672 3-8-4 55 oh1 RoystonFfrench 6 35
(B Smart) *chsd ldrs on outer: rdn along over 2f out: drvn and hld whn hmpd over 1f out* 16/1
4440 14 ½ **Strathmore (IRE)**[16] 5729 5-8-5 55 oh2 (b[1]) PaulHanagan 5 33
(R A Fahey) *s.i.s: a bhd* 12/1

57.24 secs (-1.36) **Going Correction** -0.15s/f (Firm)
WFA 3 from 4yo+ 1lb 14 Ran SP% 118.3
Speed ratings (Par 103): **104,98,97,95,94 94,92,92,91,91 89,89,88,87**
toteswingers: 1&2 £2.70, 1&3 £28.30, 2&3 £16.00 CSF £16.16 CT £188.92 TOTE £5.40: £1.90, £1.40, £6.30; EX 15.80.
Owner J M Bradley **Bred** Hesmonds Stud Ltd **Trained** Sedbury, Gloucs

FOCUS
They went a blistering pace in this fair sprint handicap. The winner is improving fast now.

6221 SUBSCRIBE TO RACING UK H'CAP (DIV II) 6f
5:40 (5:41) (Class 6) (0-65,65) 3-Y-0+ £1,706 (£503; £252) Stalls Centre

Form RPR
4564 1 **Diamond Blade**[20] 5599 3-8-5 52 (p) DuranFentiman 3 59
(T D Easterby) *mde all: kpt on u.p: hld on towards fin* 16/1
4405 2 ¾ **Maison Dieu**[9] 5941 6-9-1 60 DavidAllan 6 65
(E J Alston) *chsd ldrs: styd on fnl f: no ex last 75yds* 11/2
6-34 3 hd **Verinco**[28] 5338 3-8-11 65 (p) AdamCarter(7) 4 69
(B Smart) *chsd ldrs: kpt on same pce ins fnl f* 10/1
0300 4 1 **Hansomis (IRE)**[23] 5514 5-9-3 65 NeilBrown(3) 10 66
(B Mactaggart) *s.s: hdwy and swtchd towards far side over 1f out: styd on: nt rch ldrs* 5/1[3]
0650 5 ¾ **Ace Of Spies (IRE)**[4] 6103 4-8-11 56 SilvestreDeSousa 1 55
(G A Harker) *s.i.s: hdwy 2f out: nvr nr ldrs* 9/2[2]
0651 6 1¼ **Yorkshire Blue**[9] 5955 10-8-6 54 (p) KellyHarrison(3) 8 49
(J S Goldie) *in rr: effrt 2f out: kpt on: nvr nr ldrs* 3/1[1]
0000 7 1¾ **Ronnie Howe**[69] 3999 5-8-6 51 oh1 (b) FrancisNorton 9 41
(S R Bowring) *chsd ldrs: wknd over 1f out* 18/1
06 8 nk **Navajo Joe (IRE)**[28] 5343 4-9-5 64 GrahamGibbons 2 53
(R Johnson) *in rr: kpt on fnl 2f: nvr on terms* 16/1
3000 9 ½ **Dhhamaan (IRE)**[12] 5842 4-8-6 51 oh6 (bt) AndrewElliott 13 39
(Mrs R A Carr) *racd stands' side: mid-div: nvr nr ldrs* 14/1
0000 10 2¾ **Mission Impossible**[15] 4894 4-8-12 57 RoystonFfrench 7 36
(Miss Tracy Waggott) *mid-div: effrt over 2f out: wknd over 1f out* 33/1
100 11 4 **Nabra**[2] 6160 5-8-2 54 ow2 JohnCavanagh(7) 12 21
(M Brittain) *racd towards stands' side: sn outpcd: nvr a factor* 25/1
4040 12 4½ **Coconut Moon**[2] 6160 7-7-13 51 oh6 BillyCray(7) 5 5
(A Berry) *racd towards stands' side: chsd ldrs: wknd and eased over 1f out* 22/1
000- 13 22 **Valentine Bay**[278] 7734 3-8-4 51 oh3 (b[1]) PaulHanagan 11 —
(M Mullineaux) *chsd ldrs: lost pl 3f out: bhd whn virtually p.u ins fnl f: t.o* 40/1

1m 10.49s (-1.31) **Going Correction** -0.15s/f (Firm)
WFA 3 from 4yo+ 2lb 13 Ran SP% 121.6
Speed ratings (Par 101): **102,101,100,99,98 96,94,94,93,89 84,78,49**
toteswingers: 1&2 £13.30, 1&3 £11.30, 2&3 £8.80 CSF £99.84 CT £950.25 TOTE £22.10: £4.80, £2.60, £2.70; EX 108.50 Place 6: £21.72 Place 5: £15.12.
Owner D A West **Bred** Bumble Bloodstock **Trained** Great Habton, N Yorks

FOCUS
A minor handicap. The runners who raced prominently on the centre to far side of the track dominated. The form is rated around the principals.
T/Jkpt: Not won. T/Plt: £16.00 to a £1 stake. Pool: £59,497.47. 2,712.44 winning tickets. T/Qpdt: £9.50 to a £1 stake. Pool: £3,087.00. 238.60 winning tickets. WG

4416 MAISONS-LAFFITTE (R-H)
Wednesday, September 23

OFFICIAL GOING: Good

6222a PRIX HULA DANCER (WOMEN PROFESSIONALS) (LEFT-HANDED) 1m (S)
4:55 (4:56) 3-Y-0 £11,650 (£4,660; £3,495; £2,330; £1,165)

RPR
1 **Chakacha (FR)**[25] 5462 3-9-3 PaulineProd'homme 86
(D Prod'Homme, France)
2 snk **Darbaza (FR)**[339] 3-8-8 BrigitteRenk 77
(A De Royer-Dupre, France)
3 ½ **Shampagne**[40] 5012 3-9-3 CelineLaunay(6) 91
(P F I Cole) *midfield: 5th st: pushed along 2f out: drvn and disputing 2nd 1f out: kpt on* 9/10[1]
4 nse **Prime Spirit (IRE)**[55] 4459 3-8-11 78
(X-Thomas Demeaulte, France)
5 2 **Polyegos (IRE)**[25] 5462 3-9-1 78
(C Laffon-Parias, France)
6 2½ **Kinouzeme (FR)**[192] 3-8-8 65
(P Costes, France)
7 2½ **Western Isle (USA)**[156] 3-9-1 66
(H-A Pantall, France)
8 3 **Danseur Russe (FR)**[70] 3-9-0 58
(J E Pease, France)
9 dist **Wiwurgh (USA)**[21] 3-9-2 —
(C Boutin, France)

1m 41.2s (-1.10) 9 Ran SP% 52.6
PARI-MUTUEL: WIN 21.40; PL 2.50, 1.50, 1.20; DF 36.50.
Owner B Giraudon **Bred** Mme Aliette & Gilles Forien **Trained** France
■ Stewards' Enquiry : Brigitte Renk four-day ban: careless riding (Oct 7-10)

NOTEBOOK
Shampagne was always on the outside and fifth in the early stages. Beautifully placed to challenge in the straight, he made some late progress but never looked like getting on terms with the winner and runner-up.

6206 KEMPTON (A.W) (R-H)
Thursday, September 24

OFFICIAL GOING: Standard
Wind: Virtually nil Weather: Starting sunny

6223 PANORAMIC BAR & RESTAURANT MEDIAN AUCTION MAIDEN STKS 1m (P)
5:30 (5:33) (Class 6) 3-5-Y-0 £2,047 (£604; £302) Stalls High

Form RPR
2052 1 **Night Lily (IRE)**[22] 5582 3-8-12 66 (t) LukeMorris 2 67
(J Jay) *trckd ldr after 2f: chal 3f out: sn led gng wl: rdn 2f out: hld on wl* 14/1
2236 2 ½ **Cloudesley (IRE)**[92] 3279 3-9-3 70 LPKeniry 11 71
(A M Balding) *in tch: rdn along 4f out: styd on fr 2f out: str run ins fnl f to take 2nd cl home and clsng on wnr but jst hld* 4/1[2]
0532 3 nk **Layer Cake**[14] 5806 3-8-10 68 KierenFox(7) 6 70
(J W Hills) *mid-div: hdwy fr 3f out: chsd wnr over 1f out: styng on whn edgd rt ins fnl f: no imp and lost 2nd cl home* 10/1
20 4 1¾ **Miss Sophisticat**[26] 5449 3-8-12 69 (v) EddieAhern 10 61
(W J Knight) *sn led: hdd after 2f: styd chsng ldrs: rdn over 2f out: styd on same pce fr over 1f out* 7/1[3]
34-0 5 5 **Sydneysider**[24] 5525 4-9-7 65 ShaneKelly 3 55
(Eve Johnson Houghton) *chsd ldrs: rdn 3f out: styd on same pce u.p fnl 2f* 33/1
0000 6 1 **Very Distinguished**[65] 4178 3-8-12 48 JamesDoyle 7 48
(S Kirk) *s.i.s: in rr: rdn over 2f out: styd on fnl f: nvr in contention* 50/1
0-2 7 1¾ **Aspro Mavro (IRE)**[21] 5614 3-9-3 0 RichardMullen 1 49
(J H M Gosden) *led after 2f: rdn whn jnd 3f out: sn hdd: wknd over 1f out* 1/2[1]
8 nse **Blues Jazz** 3-9-3 0 MartinDwyer 9 49
(Miss Gay Kelleway) *s.i.s: in rr: pushed along 3f out: sme prog fnl 2f* 33/1
3054 9 1¾ **Gun For Sale (USA)**[38] 5111 4-9-7 48 (t[1]) TravisBlock 4 45
(P J Makin) *s.i.s: t.k.h: sme prog towards outside 3f out: nvr in contention* 25/1

00-0 **10** *1 ¼* **Julie Mill (IRE)**[44] 4867 3-8-12 30 .... DaneO'Neill 12 38
(R A Teal) *a in rr* **66/1**

5 **11** *3 ½* **Fine Art Collector (IRE)**[16] 5747 3-9-3 0 .... PatDobbs 5 35
(G L Moore) *t.k.h: chsd ldrs: rdn over 2f out: wknd qckly over 1f out* **12/1**

00 **12** *6* **Set Em Up Mo**[31] 5316 3-8-12 50 .... (p) LiamJones 14 17
(M J Attwater) *mid-div: rdn 3f out: sn wknd* **66/1**

6000 **13** *3 ½* **Yashkur**[16] 5751 3-8-12 48 .... ChrisCatlin 8 9
(C E Brittain) *reluctant to load: a in rr* **66/1**

14 *8* **Swirl Tango** 3-8-12 0 .... JimmyQuinn 13 —
(F Jordan) *s.i.s: a towards rr* **66/1**

1m 38.95s (-0.85) **Going Correction** -0.10s/f (Stan)
WFA 3 from 4yo 4lb **14** Ran SP% **140.3**
Speed ratings (Par 101): **100,99,99,97,92 91,89,89,87,86 83,77,73,65**
toteswingers: 1&2 £10.50, 1&3 £10.90, 2&3 £7.80 CSF £78.50 TOTE £23.30: £3.50, £1.10, £2.80; EX 107.00.
Owner White & Mrs D Snell **Bred** Keith Wills **Trained** Newmarket, Suffolk

FOCUS
A weak maiden. Straightforward enough form, rated around the principals.
Very Distinguished Official explanation: jockey said filly missed the break
Aspro Mavro(IRE) Official explanation: trainer's rep had no explanation for the poor form shown

6224 BOOK KEMPTON TICKETS ON 0844 579 3008 H'CAP 1m (P)
6:00 (6:01) (Class 6) (0-65,71) 3-Y-0+ **£2,047** (£604; £302) **Stalls** High

Form RPR

0035 **1** **Integria**[65] 4181 3-9-4 65 .... (b) LukeMorris 4 74+
(J M P Eustace) *towards rr: gd prog over 2f out: rdn and qcknd to ld appr fnl f: sn clr: readily* **12/1**

66-6 **2** *1 ¼* **Rosco Flyer (IRE)**[44] 4872 3-9-4 65 .... PatCosgrave 8 71
(J R Boyle) *s.i.s: in rr: rdn over 2f out and styd on wl fr over 1f out: kpt on ins fnl f to take 2nd fnl 50yds but no imp on wnr* **6/1**[2]

1505 **3** *1 ¾* **Sovereignty (JPN)**[14] 5813 7-8-12 60 .... SophieDoyle(5) 14 62
(D K Ivory) *t.k.h: sn led: rdn and kpt slt advantage tl hdd over 1f out: outpcd ins fnl f* **15/2**

500 **4** *nk* **Phluke**[24] 5511 8-9-4 61 .... StephenCarson 13 63
(Eve Johnson Houghton) *sn pressing ldr: upsides and rdn ins fnl 3f: one pce fnl f* **25/1**

-510 **5** *¾* **Having A Ball**[154] 1479 5-9-8 65 .... ChrisCatlin 9 65
(P D Cundell) *in rr tl hdwy towards outside over 2f out: styd on fnl f but nvr gng pce to trble ldrs* **20/1**

1131 **6** *hd* **Darcey**[8] 5999 3-9-10 71 6ex .... HayleyTurner 3 75+
(Miss Amy Weaver) *chsd ldrs: rdn over 2f out: wknd ins fnl f* **13/2**[3]

0200 **7** *½* **Baby Josr**[14] 5791 3-9-0 61 .... (v) MartinDwyer 10 60
(I A Wood) *n.m.r sn after s and in rr: pushed along 3f out: mod prog fnl f* **20/1**

5024 **8** *nk* **Fire King**[27] 5384 3-9-1 62 .... RobertHavlin 12 60
(J A Geake) *chsd ldrs: rdn to chal wl over 1f out: wknd qckly ins fnl f* **12/1**

5-55 **9** *shd* **Four Tel**[90] 3331 5-9-8 65 .... RichardKingscote 6 63
(Tom Dascombe) *s.i.s: in rr: sme hdwy on outside over 2f out: sn rdn and no imp* **11/4**[1]

200- **10** *1 ¾* **Under Fire (IRE)**[291] 7591 6-9-1 58 .... KirstyMilczarek 2 52
(A W Carroll) *t.k.h: chsd ldrs: rdn over 2f out: wknd fnl f* **33/1**

506 **11** *nk* **Valfurva (IRE)**[41] 4981 3-9-4 65 .... KFallon 5 63+
(L M Cumani) *in tch: pushed along to chse ldrs over 2f out: n.m.r ins fnl f and eased whn hld* **13/2**[3]

0000 **12** *1 ½* **Marmooq**[16] 5745 6-9-8 65 .... IanMongan 7 55
(M J Attwater) *a towards rr* **16/1**

00- **13** *½* **Dealmaker Frank (USA)**[37] 5144 4-9-7 64 .... (p) ShaneKelly 11 53
(Daniel Mark Loughnane, Ire) *mid-div towards ins: rdn over 2f out and sn bhd* **14/1**

2600 **14** *¾* **Fine Ruler (IRE)**[14] 5813 5-9-4 61 .... VinceSlattery 1 48
(M R Bosley) *plld hrd towards rr on outside: rdn: hung lft and no rspnse ins fnl 3f* **33/1**

1m 39.2s (-0.60) **Going Correction** -0.10s/f (Stan)
WFA 3 from 4yo+ 4lb **14** Ran SP% **126.6**
Speed ratings (Par 101): **99,97,96,95,94 94,94,93,93,92 91,90,89,89**
toteswingers: 1&2 £11.50, 1&3 £33.60, 2&3 £19.20 CSF £81.08 CT £611.39 TOTE £17.20: £4.80, £2.50, £3.90; EX 138.60.
Owner J C Smith **Bred** Littleton Stud **Trained** Newmarket, Suffolk

FOCUS
A moderate handicap which was a slightly messy race. There might be better to come from the winner.
Four Tel Official explanation: jockey said gelding hung left throughout

6225 KEMPTON.CO.UK MAIDEN STKS 1m 4f (P)
6:30 (6:31) (Class 5) 3-Y-0+ **£2,590** (£770; £385; £192) **Stalls** High

Form RPR

222 **1** **Blue Nymph**[49] 4687 3-8-11 78 .... JimCrowley 4 78+
(R M Beckett) *s.i.s: chsd ldr after 2f: drvn to ld 2f out: sn clr: easily* **4/7**[1]

-306 **2** *5* **Alhaque (USA)**[24] 5531 3-9-2 77 .... JamieSpencer 11 70
(W J Haggas) *chsd ldrs: rdn and styd on fr over 2f out: chsd wnr 1f out but nvr any ch* **8/1**[3]

2-56 **3** *3 ¾* **Custody (IRE)**[16] 5744 3-9-2 72 .... (p) RichardHughes 3 64
(Sir Michael Stoute) *trckd ldrs: pushed along and hdwy 3f out: styd on u.p fnl 2f to take a wl hld 3rd wl ins fnl f* **5/1**[2]

42 **4** *nk* **Rougham**[39] 5061 3-9-2 0 .... LPKeniry 1 63
(A M Balding) *led: rdn 3f out: hdd 2f out: sn no ch w wnr: lost 2nd 1f out and sn wknd* **5/1**[2]

0 **5** *4* **Court Princess**[17] 5718 6-9-5 0 .... DaneO'Neill 8 52
(George Baker) *in rr: rdn and hdwy 3f out: styd on fnl 2f but nvr anywhere nr ldrs* **50/1**

/04- **6** *1 ¼* **Edgefour (IRE)**[78] 1638 5-9-5 45 .... ShaneKelly 7 50
(B I Case) *chsd ldrs but nvr on terms: pushed along 3f out: wknd 2f out* **25/1**

0 **7** *14* **Walls Way**[31] 5322 5-9-7 0 .... MCGeran(3) 9 33
(A W Carroll) *a in rr* **66/1**

06 **8** *shd* **Be Kind**[31] 5314 3-8-11 0 .... DarryllHolland 6 27
(Karen George) *chsd ldrs: rdn along 6f out: wknd over 3f out* **33/1**

000- **9** *1* **The Beat Is On**[447] 3674 3-8-11 23 .... KirstyMilczarek 5 26
(A W Carroll) *a in rr* **66/1**

00 **10** *2 ¼* **Hilltop Alchemy**[66] 4151 3-8-9 0 .... DannyBrock(7) 10 27
(J R Jenkins) *a in rr* **100/1**

11 *5* **Bristol Delauriere (FR)**[474] 5-9-10 0 .... RichardKingscote 2 19
(Miss N A Lloyd-Beavis) *a in rr* **100/1**

2m 33.38s (-1.12) **Going Correction** -0.10s/f (Stan)
WFA 3 from 5yo+ 8lb **11** Ran SP% **121.8**
Speed ratings (Par 103): **99,95,93,92,90 89,80,80,79,77 74**
toteswingers: 1&2 £2.10, 1&3 £1.90, 2&3 £3.60 CSF £6.40 TOTE £1.70: £1.02, £2.00, £1.80; EX 7.60.
Owner J H Richmond-Watson **Bred** Lawn Stud **Trained** Whitsbury, Hants

FOCUS
A poor maiden. The winner did not have to run to her mark to collect in this race.

6226 KEMPTON FOR CONFERENCES H'CAP 1m 4f (P)
7:00 (7:03) (Class 6) (0-60,59) 3-Y-0+ **£2,047** (£604; £302) **Stalls** High

Form RPR

4320 **1** **Annambo**[7] 6025 9-9-6 57 .... (v) StephenCarson 8 66
(Andrew Reid) *hld up towards rr: hdwy on ins 4f out: drvn to ld 2f out: rdn out* **9/1**

4024 **2** *3 ½* **Salybia Bay**[8] 5988 3-9-0 59 .... RichardHughes 9 64+
(R Hannon) *chsd ldrs: rdn 3f out: styd on to chse wnr ins fnl f but a wl hld* **9/2**[2]

4634 **3** *nk* **Sinbad The Sailor**[1] 6208 4-9-4 55 .... (v) LiamJones 3 58
(J W Hills) *led 3f: styd trcking ldr tl led again 4f out: rdn and hdd 2f out: sn no ex and lost 2nd ins fnl f* **7/2**[1]

-404 **4** *2 ¼* **Tuppenny Piece**[15] 5782 3-8-11 59 .... AndreaAtzeni(3) 5 59
(W R Swinburn) *mid-div and hrd drvn 5f out: styd on u.p fnl 3f but nvr gng pce to get into contention* **8/1**

1536 **5** *½* **Zalkani (IRE)**[19] 5680 9-9-3 59 .... RichardEvans(5) 4 58
(J Pearce) *in rr tl shkn up and hdwy over 2f out: styd on fnl f but nvr a threat* **16/1**

0025 **6** *1 ½* **King's Fable (USA)**[19] 5680 6-9-1 52 .... (p) DarryllHolland 13 49
(Karen George) *in rr: awkward into st over 3f out: rdn and wandered over 2f out: sn rdn: mod prog fr over 1f out* **9/1**

643 **7** *1 ¼* **Ocean Of Peace (FR)**[22] 5577 6-8-13 50 .... JimCrowley 14 45+
(M R Bosley) *chsd ldrs: rdn over 2f out: wknd appr fnl f* **13/2**[3]

3300 **8** *hd* **Ede's Dot Com (IRE)**[183] 959 5-9-6 57 .... IanMongan 7 52
(P M Phelan) *in rr: rdn over 3f out: mod prog fnl 2f* **33/1**

560 **9** *¾* **Medieval Maiden**[14] 5812 6-9-1 52 .... PaulDoe 6 46
(Mrs L J Mongan) *in rr: rdn and hdwy on outside over 3f out: chsd ldrs over 2f out: sn wknd* **25/1**

4600 **10** *16* **Imperium**[14] 5790 8-9-6 57 .... (b) DaneO'Neill 1 27
(Jean-Rene Auvray) *a in rr* **33/1**

2000 **11** *16* **Red Reef**[15] 5782 3-9-0 59 .... EddieAhern 11 5
(D J Coakley) *led after 3f: hdd 4f out: hung rt and wknd qckly ins fnl 3f* **16/1**

0-00 **12** *1 ¾* **Fantastic Morning**[88] 3421 5-9-4 55 .... (p) JimmyQuinn 10 —
(F Jordan) *chsd ldrs 1m* **66/1**

0350 **13** *5* **Filun**[23] 5545 4-9-7 58 .... (b) LPKeniry 12 —
(A Middleton) *chsd ldrs: rdn and wknd 4f out* **10/1**

2600 **P** **Mixing**[22] 5577 7-9-3 54 .... KirstyMilczarek 2 —
(M J Attwater) *chsd ldrs: rdn 4f out: wknd: lost action and p.u 2f out: dismntd* **12/1**

2m 32.96s (-1.54) **Going Correction** -0.10s/f (Stan)
WFA 3 from 4yo+ 8lb **14** Ran SP% **124.6**
Speed ratings (Par 101): **101,98,98,96,96 95,94,94,94,83 72,71,68,—**
toteswingers: 1&2 £22.10, 1&3 £24.10, 2&3 £4.60 CSF £49.64 CT £176.04 TOTE £15.20: £4.30, £1.90, £1.40; EX 95.20.
Owner A S Reid **Bred** Sheikh Mohammed Bin Rashid Al Maktoum **Trained** Mill Hill, London NW7

FOCUS
A tight handicap, run at a proper pace. The winner is rated back to his best form of recent years.
Zalkani(IRE) Official explanation: jockey said gelding was denied a clear run
Mixing Official explanation: jockey said gelding suffered interference on bend and was pulled up

6227 "BUY A £10,000 RACING POST BONUS YEARLING" NURSERY 6f (P)
7:30 (7:31) (Class 5) (0-70,73) 2-Y-0 **£2,590** (£770; £385; £192) **Stalls** High

Form RPR

1441 **1** **Wasmi (IRE)**[20] 5635 2-9-4 67 .... ChrisCatlin 12 79+
(C E Brittain) *mde all: rdn 2 l clr over 1f out: styd on strly: unchal* **10/3**[1]

343 **2** *2 ¾* **Mr Corby (IRE)**[24] 5512 2-9-5 68 .... AlanMunro 10 69
(M R Channon) *chsd ldrs: wnt 2nd ins fnl 3f: sn rdn: no ch w wnr fr over 1f out but hld on wl for 2nd* **9/2**[2]

6315 **3** *shd* **Candyfloss Girl**[20] 5635 2-9-1 64 .... DavidProbert 6 65
(H J L Dunlop) *chsd ldrs tl rdn and outpcd on outside fr 3f out: rallied and styd on wl fnl f to press for 2nd cl home but nvr any ch w wnr* **14/1**

3560 **4** *½* **Oasis Jade**[16] 5748 2-9-2 65 .... PatDobbs 4 64+
(G L Moore) *hld up in rr: stl plenty to do on outside over 2f out: str run fnl f: gng on cl home* **33/1**

0033 **5** *½* **Bell's Ocean (USA)**[9] 5967 2-9-5 68 .... JerryO'Dwyer 9 66
(J Ryan) *chsd wnr tl ins fnl 3f: styd chsng ldrs and rdn over 2f out: wknd cl home* **9/2**[2]

6020 **6** *1 ¾* **Point To Prove**[20] 5635 2-9-6 69 .... HayleyTurner 7 61
(Miss Amy Weaver) *in tch: n.m.r 2f out: edgd rt u.p and hdwy over 1f out: wknd ins fnl f* **20/1**

0033 **7** *1 ¼* **Chicita Banana**[24] 5526 2-9-1 69 .... MatthewDavies(5) 8 58
(George Baker) *in tch: rdn over 2f out: no imp on ldrs and styd on same pce* **15/2**

553 **8** *1 ½* **Love Match**[49] 4701 2-9-5 68 .... SteveDrowne 3 52+
(R Charlton) *in rr: sme hdwy on ins whn hmpd over 1f out: nvr in contention after* **5/1**[3]

1500 **9** *4 ½* **Dixie Bright (USA)**[28] 5369 2-9-4 67 .... (v[1]) JimCrowley 11 38
(J G Given) *chsd ldrs: rdn 3f out: wkng whn hmpd over 1f out* **14/1**

0046 **10** *1 ½* **Reach For The Sky (IRE)**[20] 5636 2-9-7 70 .... RichardHughes 5 40+
(R Hannon) *stdd s: hld up in rr: hdwy on ins 2f out: styng on same pce whn hmpd and wknd over 1f out* **14/1**

1m 12.94s (-0.16) **Going Correction** -0.10s/f (Stan) **10** Ran SP% **115.6**
Speed ratings (Par 95): **97,93,93,92,91 89,87,85,79,77**
toteswingers: 1&2 £2.70, 1&3 £5.70, 2&3 £10.30 CSF £17.88 CT £187.65 TOTE £4.90: £1.50, £1.70, £4.60; EX 18.40.
Owner Saeed Manana **Bred** Airlie Stud **Trained** Newmarket, Suffolk

FOCUS
A moderate nursery, but the winner impressed. The form seems solid.

NOTEBOOK
Wasmi(IRE) ◆ had already scored twice on Polytrack, including over this course and distance 20 days before this contest, but she needed to up her game to add to that record after being raised 4lb by the handicapper. She is a big, powerful filly, though, apparently strengthening up all the time, and she showed improved form again here, making virtually all the running and staying on far too strongly for the rest. (op 9-2 tchd 3-1)

Mr Corby(IRE) performed right up to his best on this handicap bow, but he was readily outpointed by the winner and does not looked blessed with a scintillating finishing kick. (op 4-1 tchd 7-2 and 5-1 in places)

Candyfloss Girl, fifth behind Wasmi on her latest outing, posted another solid effort but is clearly not progressing at anything like the rate of her old rival. (op 16-1)

Oasis Jade she appears to need a little help from the handicapper to take an event of this type. (op 40-1)

Bell's Ocean(USA) is another whose rating is beginning to look beyond her and, although she has now made the first five on each of her last three starts, her overall profile does not suggest she is especially progressive. (op 7-2)

6228 DAY TIME, NIGHT TIME, GREAT TIME CLAIMING STKS 7f (P)

8:00 (8:02) (Class 6) 2-Y-O £2,047 (£604; £302) Stalls High

Form RPR

2364 1 **Al Khimiya (IRE)**[13] 5841 2-9-0 69 JamieSpencer 5 68
(S A Callaghan) *led after 1f: hrd rdn fr over 1f out: in command cl home* **15/2**

4533 2 1 1/4 **Jehu**[5] 6099 2-9-9 77 ChrisCatlin 12 74
(M R Channon) *chsd ldrs: rdn over 2f out: chsd wnr fnl f but a hld* **3/1**[2]

006 3 1/2 **Catchanova (IRE)**[34] 5212 2-9-1 64 (t) EddieAhern 1 65
(Eve Johnson Houghton) *in rr: rdn fr 3f out: stl plenty to do 2f out: styd on wl fr over 1f out to take 3rd cl home* **33/1**

0 4 shd **Pont D'Avignon**[14] 5808 2-8-0 0 LukeMorris 13 49
(P Winkworth) *led 1f: styd chsng ldrs: rdn over 2f out: no imp on wnr over 1f out: kpt on same pce ins fnl f* **8/1**

1066 5 shd **Kate Skate**[7] 6034 2-8-6 64 MartinDwyer 6 55
(Miss Gay Kelleway) *bmpd s: t.k.h: sn chsng ldrs and wnt 2nd 3f out: rdn and no imp fr 2f out: one pce ins fnl f* **20/1**

20 6 3/4 **Ragsta (IRE)**[10] 5938 2-8-7 66 RichardRowe(7) 4 61+
(C A Dwyer) *chsd ldrs on outside tl outpcd fr 3f out: sn rdn: rallied fr over 1f out: gng on cl home* **25/1**

40 7 hd **Taper Jean Girl (IRE)**[20] 5643 2-9-1 0 AndreaAtzeni(3) 14 65
(M Botti) *chsd ldrs: rdn 3f out: n.m.r on ins fnl f: swtchd lft and one pce fnl 100yds* **25/1**

3020 8 1/2 **Timelord (IRE)**[17] 5715 2-8-13 68 LDettori 7 59
(S Kirk) *bmpd s: sn chsng ldrs: rdn over 2f out: wknd ins fnl f* **6/1**[3]

0 9 1 **Theladyisatramp**[38] 5096 2-9-0 0 HayleyTurner 11 57
(M L W Bell) *plld hrd: hung rt after 1f: mid-div: rdn and hung rt 2f out: sn wknd* **14/1**

0312 10 shd **Aegean Destiny**[12] 5868 2-9-0 65 RichardHughes 8 60+
(R Hannon) *wnt rt s: hmpd after 1f: in rr: hdwy on outside over 2f out and sn hung lft to stands' side: nvr in contention* **5/2**[1]

0 11 nk **Rose Bed (IRE)**[143] 1719 2-8-10 0 AlanMunro 10 52
(M G Quinlan) *hmpd in rr after 1f: rdn and sme prog into mid-div over 2f out: sn wknd* **50/1**

0023 12 1 3/4 **Rainsborough**[3] 6173 2-9-6 70 (t) JackMitchell(3) 2 61
(S Curran) *slowly away: a in rr* **20/1**

13 3 1/2 **High Trail (IRE)** 2-8-0 0 DavidProbert 9 29
(Rae Guest) *bhd fr 1/2-way* **50/1**

0 14 1 **Naseby (USA)**[64] 4201 2-9-9 0 SteveDrowne 3 49
(R Charlton) *nvr bttr than mid-div: bhd fnl 3f* **33/1**

1m 26.75s (0.75) **Going Correction** -0.10s/f (Stan) 14 Ran SP% **124.4**
Speed ratings (Par 93): **91,89,89,88,88 87,87,87,85,85 85,83,79,78**
toteswingers: 1&2 £7.70, 1&3 £28.50, 2&3 £43.60 CSF £28.34 TOTE £9.60: £3.00, £1.80, £7.40; EX 37.60.Catchanova was the subject of a friendly claim. Pont D'Avignon was claimed by F J Brennan for £3,000.

Owner David F O'Rourke **Bred** Plantation Stud **Trained** Newmarket, Suffolk

FOCUS
A typically modest juvenile claimer.

NOTEBOOK

Al Khimiya(IRE), fourth off a mark of 70 when held up in a Wolverhampton nursery on her latest start, had solid claims going into this race, but seemed to show improved form nonetheless for more forcing tactics. She led shortly after the stalls opened and, setting a decent gallop, was never headed. (op 9-2)

Jehu seemed to run right up his best, being among the leading group from the outset, and he looks the marker for those assessing the standard of this race. (op 5-1)

Catchanova(IRE), who had not shown a great deal in three turf maidens, improved on this Polytrack debut and can be placed to win a similar event. (tchd 40-1)

Pont D'Avignon did not improve as much as might have been expected following her encouraging first appearance and, after chasing the speed for much of the contest, was tiring in the closing stages. (op 6-1)

Kate Skate was another to lose ground in the closing stages and there remains a doubt as to whether she truly stays further than 6f. (op 16-1)

Aegean Destiny, making her Polytrack debut after a series of solid efforts on turf, represented a stable still banging in two-year-old winners at a tremendous rate. Not surprisingly, she was well supported, but, after appearing to be hampered shortly after the stalls opened, she could never get into a challenging position and, somewhat eccentrically, finished the race under the stands' rail. (op 3-1)

6229 LEVY BOARD H'CAP 1m (P)

8:30 (8:30) (Class 3) (0-95,91) 3-Y-O
£4,777 (£4,777; £1,100; £551; £274; £138) Stalls High

Form RPR

212 1 **Penitent**[38] 5092 3-8-13 86 JamieSpencer 7 99+
(W J Haggas) *broke wl: stdd in rr tl gd hdwy on ins fr 2f out: wnt 2nd 1f out and 1 l down: styd on strly u.p ins fnl f to force dead heat on line* **7/2**[2]

-211 1 dht **Stoic (IRE)**[13] 5832 3-9-3 90 ShaneKelly 2 103+
(J Noseda) *plld hrd early: trckd ldrs: wnt 2nd over 4f out: drvn and qcknd to ld appr fnl f and 1 l clr ins fnl f: hrd drvn and styd on fnl 100yds: jnd on line* **7/2**[2]

-110 3 3 1/4 **Musleh (USA)**[19] 5663 3-9-4 91 LDettori 3 97
(Saeed Bin Suroor) *sn led and set mod pce for over 3f: drvn and qcknd over 2f out: hdd appr fnl f: sn no ex u.p ins fnl f and wknd fnl 100yds* **3/1**[1]

3621 4 1/2 **Mac's Power (IRE)**[8] 5986 3-8-12 85 6ex (t) RichardMullen 4 90+
(P J O'Gorman) *plld hrd 2f: chsd ldrs: rdn and effrt 2f out: nt pce of ldng duo appr fnl f: no ex ins fnl f and wknd fnl 100yds* **5/1**[3]

1466 5 1 1/4 **Hunterview**[61] 4316 3-9-3 90 (b[1]) PhilipRobinson 1 92+
(M A Jarvis) *v.s.a: sn plld hrd and chsd ldrs after 3f: rdn over 2f out and sn wknd* **14/1**

13 6 2 **Elliptical (USA)**[26] 5432 3-9-0 87 KFallon 6 84
(G A Butler) *rdn along 3f out: a towards rr* **5/1**[3]

00 7 4 **Wajaha (IRE)**[99] 3016 3-9-3 90 TPO'Shea 5 78
(J H M Gosden) *chsd ldr tl over 4f out: rdn over 2f out and sn btn* **12/1**

1m 37.93s (-1.87) **Going Correction** -0.10s/f (Stan) 7 Ran SP% **117.1**
Speed ratings (Par 105): **105,105,101,101,100 98,94**Win: Stoic £4.40, Penitent £4.40. Places: Stoic £2.50, Penitent £2.00 CSF: Stoic, Penitent £8.42, Penitent, Stoic £8.42. Exacta Stoic, Penitent £10.90, Penitent, Stoic £10.60; toteswingers: Stoic & Penitent £3.30, Stoic&3 £1.10, Penitent&3 £2.10 TOTE £0.027: £Owner, £Cheveley Park Stud, £Bred, £Cheveley Park Stud LtdTrained Newmarket, Suffolk.

Owner Highclere Thoroughbred Racing (Gimcrack) **Bred** Darley **Trained** Newmarket, Suffolk

FOCUS
A decent little race that resulted in a deat heat. The first pair can go in again.

NOTEBOOK

Penitent ◆ led two furlongs from home and looked to have the prize in the bag before being caught - and deprived of an outright victory - in the dying strides. He is on an upwards curve and remains one to follow as he should settle better with more experience. (tchd 3-1 and 9-2)

Stoic(IRE) ◆ was stepping up in distance for this and it promised to suit him. He needed every yard of the 1m trip to snatch a share of the spoils, making his finishing thrust after squeezing through close to the inside rail, and may well handle a little further given the opportunity. (tchd 3-1 and 9-2)

Musleh(USA), who is bred for this surface, had completed an all-weather hat-trick when scoring here in mid-August. He had run below par on his only subsequent outing, but he had been trapped out wide in a bigger field that day and was unable to dominate, as he had when previously looking progressive. A good benchmark. (tchd 5-2 and 7-2 in places)

Mac's Power(IRE) needed to post a career-best to beat some of these under his penalty and, although he tried hard, the task proved too much for him. The should still be more to come from him. (op 13-2)

Hunterview, successful in a Southwell handicap in March, has not found winning easy since then and seems to need some help from the handicapper. Tried in blinkers, he spoilt his chance from the gates here. (tchd 12-1)

Elliptical(USA) was having his first run on Polytrack this season, though, and, while he had fared well when trying the surface as a juvenile, he ran below his best on this occasion. (op 4-1)

Wajaha(IRE) was returning from a layoff and down in class. She performed well below her mark, though. (tchd 11-1)

6230 SUBSCRIBE TO RACING UK H'CAP 6f (P)

9:00 (9:02) (Class 5) (0-75,75) 3-Y-O+ £2,590 (£770; £385; £192) Stalls High

Form RPR

5321 1 **Fantasy Gladiator**[28] 5373 3-8-13 70 DO'Donohoe 8 81+
(R M H Cowell) *trckd ldrs: drvn to ld 1f out: styd on wl u.p* **9/2**[2]

4205 2 1 1/2 **Dvinsky (USA)**[16] 5753 8-9-6 75 (b) IanMongan 11 82
(P Howling) *chsd ldrs: drvn to chal appr fnl f: chsd wnr ins fnl f but a hld* **5/2**[1]

4603 3 1 1/2 **Perfect Act**[8] 5989 4-8-13 68 AdamKirby 1 70
(C G Cox) *hld up in rr: hdwy fr 2f out: swtchd lft and styd on wl appr fnl f: tk 3rd ins fnl f but no imp on ldng duo* **8/1**

622 4 3 **Quasi Congaree (GER)**[99] 3036 3-8-13 70 (t) MartinDwyer 10 63
(I A Wood) *led: rdn over 2f out: hdd 1f out: wknd ins fnl f* **5/1**[3]

0060 5 hd **Song Of Praise**[14] 5810 3-8-13 70 JimmyQuinn 3 62
(M Blanshard) *in tch: swtchd rt to ins and hdwy over 2f out: sn hrd drvn: wknd fnl f* **33/1**

3300 6 1 1/4 **Onceaponatime (IRE)**[9] 5974 4-9-1 70 AlanMunro 2 59
(M D Squance) *towards rr: sme hdwy towards outside and rdn over 2f out: nvr gng pce to get into contention* **20/1**

4444 7 1 3/4 **Top Town Girl**[47] 4788 3-8-6 70 (p) JPFahy(7) 4 53
(R M Beckett) *chsd ldrs: rdn 3f out: wknd fr 2f out* **16/1**

250 8 hd **Leading Edge (IRE)**[19] 5675 4-8-12 67 ChrisCatlin 9 50
(M R Channon) *rdn 3f out: a outpcd* **20/1**

1060 9 hd **Rondeau (GR)**[17] 5719 4-9-4 73 JimCrowley 6 55
(P R Chamings) *bmpd s: a outpcd* **8/1**

4140 10 2 1/4 **Ben's Dream (IRE)**[55] 4494 3-8-12 69 (t) DavidProbert 5 44
(A M Balding) *wnt rt s: chsd ldrs: rdn 3f out: sn wknd* **14/1**

3-00 11 2 3/4 **Retro (IRE)**[105] 2849 3-9-0 71 RichardHughes 7 38
(R Hannon) *outpcd most of way* **9/1**

2124 12 1 1/4 **My Sweet Georgia (IRE)**[196] 819 3-8-12 69 MickyFenton 12 32
(Stef Liddiard) *in rr: sme prog on ins whn hmpd 2f out: n.d after* **14/1**

1m 11.68s (-1.42) **Going Correction** -0.10s/f (Stan)
WFA 3 from 4yo+ 2lb 12 Ran SP% **127.3**
Speed ratings (Par 103): **105,103,101,97,96 95,92,92,92,89 85,83**
toteswingers: 1&2 £2.70, 1&3 £11.90, 2&3 £8.30 CSF £17.00 CT £95.19 TOTE £6.00: £2.10, £1.50, £3.60; EX 23.40 Place 6: £124.80, Place 5: £32.60..

Owner The Fantasy Fellowship **Bred** R S A Urquhart **Trained** Six Mile Bottom, Cambs

FOCUS
A modest handicap, run at a solid pace. The winner has more to offer on this surface.
T/Plt: £210.80 to a £1 stake. Pool: £71,256.83. 246.73 winning tickets. T/Qpdt: £7.60 to a £1 stake. Pool: £10,399.60. 1,007.70 winning tickets. ST

6017 PONTEFRACT (L-H)

Thursday, September 24

OFFICIAL GOING: Last 6f - good to firm; remainder - good to firm (firm in places; 9.0)

Wind: Light behind Weather: Fine and dry

6231 EUROPEAN BREEDERS' FUND POPPIN LANE MAIDEN STKS 6f

2:30 (2:30) (Class 4) 2-Y-O £5,180 (£1,541; £770; £384) Stalls Low

Form RPR

2 1 **Racy**[13] 5829 2-9-3 0 RyanMoore 6 86+
(Sir Michael Stoute) *mde virtually all: pushed clr wl over 1f out: styd on strly* **4/11**[1]

40 2 5 **Antarctic Desert (IRE)**[7] 6009 2-9-3 0 PhillipMakin 4 71
(K A Ryan) *chsd ldrs: rdn along and hdwy 2f out: styd on ins fnl f: no ch w wnr* **66/1**

04 3 1 3/4 **Besty**[8] 5977 2-9-3 0 TomEaves 1 66
(B Smart) *chsd ldng pair: hdwy to chse wnr wl over 1f out: sn rdn and kpt on same pce* **22/1**

4 3 **Karaka Jack** 2-9-3 0 RoystonFfrench 5 60+
(M Johnston) *s.i.s and green in rr: rdn and sme hdwy whn hung lft and rn green 2f out: kpt on ins fnl f* **12/1**[3]

423 5 2 1/2 **Ghost (IRE)**[59] 4377 2-9-3 85 MichaelHills 2 49
(B W Hills) *cl up: rdn along 2f out: sn drvn and wknd: eased fnl f* **7/2**[2]

0 6 4 1/2 **Ajara Boy**[83] 3571 2-9-3 0 RichardSmith 3 36
(Tom Dascombe) *dwlt: a outpcd in rr* **100/1**

1m 15.61s (-1.29) **Going Correction** -0.175s/f (Firm) 6 Ran SP% **110.1**
Speed ratings (Par 97): **101,94,92,88,84 78**
toteswingers: 1&2 £5.30, 1&3 £2.40, 2&3 £14.10 CSF £38.31 TOTE £1.40: £1.10, £14.50; EX 24.60.

Owner Cheveley Park Stud **Bred** Cheveley Park Stud Ltd **Trained** Newmarket, Suffolk
FOCUS
An uncompetitive maiden. Racy did not have much to beat but was a decent winner.
NOTEBOOK
Racy ◆, a most promising runner-up over 5f at Sandown on his debut, was very solid in the market. A strong, sturdily-made Medicean colt, he laid it down to his market rival and quickened right away once in line for home. Value for double the official margin, he looks a very nice prospect and can win again in a much higher grade. (tchd 2-5)
Antarctic Desert(IRE), a big, well-made Green Desert colt, had shown ability on his debut over 7f at Thirsk before disappointing on easy ground at Ayr just a week ago. He stayed on to secure second spot but will not be seen at his best until handicapping at three over 7f or a mile.
Besty, keen to post, chased the two market leaders but was no match for the winner and lost second place in the end. This at least opens up the nursery route. (op 20-1)
Karaka Jack, half asleep in the paddock, was very green and was soon pushed along in the rear. He stayed on in his own time in the home straight and will have learnt plenty from this introduction. (op 16-1 tchd 11-1)
Ghost(IRE), rated 90, finished runner-up in a decent Newmarket maiden before finishing a well-beaten third at Windsor. Very green, he sat upsides and was allowed to take the lead for a few strides going into the home turn. He was soon left for dead by the winner, though, and faded badly. He has a lot to prove after this. Official explanation: jockey said colt ran too free early (tchd 4-1)
Ajara Boy, now trained by Tom Dascombe, showed little on his debut and it was the same story here. (tchd 66-1)

6232 BEST HORSE RACING SKY CHANNEL 432 FILLIES' NURSERY 1m 4y
3:00 (3:00) (Class 4) (0-85,82) 2-Y-O **£4,533** (£1,348; £674; £336) **Stalls** Low

Form				RPR
0031	**1**		**In The Slips (USA)**[14] 5797 2-9-7 **82** .... RyanMoore 5 (P F I Cole) *hld up in rr: gd hdwy on outer over 2f out: str run to appr fnl f: rdn ins fnl f and styd on strly* **1/1**[1]	92+
5006	**2**	2 ½	**Calatrava Cape (IRE)**[16] 5742 2-8-7 **68** .... TedDurcan 1 (J L Dunlop) *dwlt: hld up in rr: hdwy over 2f out: effrt and nt clr run over 1f out: swtchd ins and rdn ent fnl f: styd on* **9/4**[2]	73+
41	**3**	2 ½	**Miss Whippy**[31] 5319 2-7-12 **59** .... DavidProbert 2 (M L W Bell) *trckd ldrs: effrt over 2f out: sn rdn and flashed tail: drvn over 1f out: kpt on u.p ins fnl f: tk 3rd nr fin* **13/2**[3]	58
4154	**4**	shd	**Miss Smilla**[15] 5762 2-8-10 **76** .... Louis-PhilippeBeuzelin(5) 7 (K A Ryan) *trckd ldng pair: cl up 1/2-way: rdn to ld wl over 1f out: drvn: edgd rt and hdd appr fnl f: grad wknd* **9/1**	75
6066	**5**	7	**Emeralds Spirit (IRE)**[44] 4875 2-7-12 **59** oh5 .... SilvestreDeSousa 8 (J R Weymes) *led: rdn along 3f out: hdd wl over 1f out and sn wknd* **66/1**	42
2350	**6**	2 ½	**Miss Taken (IRE)**[24] 5515 2-7-12 **59** oh1 .... (b[1]) AndrewMullen 3 (D Carroll) *chsd ldr on inner: rdn along over 3f out: wknd 2f out* **28/1**	37

1m 43.55s (-2.35) **Going Correction** -0.175s/f (Firm) **6** Ran SP% **109.0**
Speed ratings (Par 94): **104,101,99,98,91 89**
toteswingers: 1&2 £1.70, 1&3 £2.10, 2&3 £2.40 CSF £3.18 CT £6.32 TOTE £2.10: £1.30, £1.70; EX 4.10.
Owner Mr & Mrs C Wright & P F I Cole **Bred** Stratford Place Stud **Trained** Whatcombe, Oxon
FOCUS
A 59-82 fillies' nursery. The market suggested a match and it turned out that way, although it was very much a one-sided contest. The first two finished clear of the third and the form looks solid.
NOTEBOOK
In The Slips(USA), raised 8lb for her decisive Doncaster success, made her effort on the outer turning in. She came clear in the final furlong and would have a live chance if turning out under a penalty. (op 6-5 tchd 5-4)
Calatrava Cape(IRE), badly hampered twice when sixth off the same mark at Goodwood, was settled in last. She was short of room for a few strides when attempting to come between horses once in line for home but in the end was very much second best. (op 2-1 tchd 5-2)
Miss Whippy, a Windsor selling-race winner, is a habitual tail swisher and in the end proved no match for the first two. (op 7-1 tchd 11-2)
Miss Smilla, fourth over seven from a 1lb lower mark at Doncaster, went on once in line for home but was soon swallowed up and lost third place in the end. This trip on an uphill track looks to stretch her stamina. (op 8-1)
Emeralds Spirit(IRE), 5lb out of the handicap, raced keenly in front but stopped to nothing when headed. She is very modest but looks more of a sprinter. (op 100-1 tchd 50-1)
Miss Taken(IRE), in first-time blinkers, had finished well beaten on her nursery debut and it was the same story here. (tchd 25-1)

6233 TRINIDAD & TOBAGO DAY ON 5TH OCTOBER H'CAP 5f
3:30 (3:31) (Class 5) (0-75,75) 3-Y-O+ **£3,238** (£963; £481; £240) **Stalls** Low

Form				RPR
5060	**1**		**Go Go Green (IRE)**[15] 5768 3-9-0 **74** .... FrederikTylicki(3) 11 (D H Brown) *cl up: led 2f out: rdn appr fnl f: sn drvn and styd on wl towards fin* **9/1**	85
1121	**2**	½	**King Of Swords (IRE)**[8] 5978 5-8-13 **69** 6ex .... (p) AndrewElliott 4 (N Tinkler) *trckd ldng pair: effrt 2f out: rdn to chse wnr ent fnl f: sn drvn and kpt on* **7/1**	78
020	**3**	5	**Mr Wolf**[15] 5768 8-9-0 **70** .... (p) TonyHamilton 2 (J J Quinn) *led: rdn along and hdd 2f out: sn drvn and wknd appr fnl f* **9/2**[3]	61
4620	**4**	3	**Peninsular War**[8] 5978 3-9-2 **73** .... PaulHanagan 1 (R A Fahey) *chsd ldrs on inner: rdn along 2f out: sn drvn and wknd* **7/2**[1]	53
0000	**5**	nk	**Spiritofthewest (IRE)**[8] 5978 3-9-4 **75** .... PhillipMakin 6 (D H Brown) *in tch: hdwy 2f out: sn rdn and no imp appr fnl f* **33/1**	54
6600	**6**	½	**Pacific Pride**[19] 5675 6-8-6 **62** oh1 ow1 .... (b) GrahamGibbons 5 (J J Quinn) *swtchd lft to inner s: in tch: effrt and hdwy 1/2-way: rdn along 2f out and n.d* **18/1**	40
5102	**7**	2 ¾	**Select Committee**[3] 6159 4-8-5 **68** .... (v) IJBrennan(7) 7 (J J Quinn) *towards rr: effrt and rdn 2f out: sn edgd lft and nvr a factor* **4/1**[2]	36+
0006	**8**	nse	**Commander Wish**[13] 5830 6-8-7 **63** oh4 ow2 .... KevinGhunowa 9 (Lucinda Featherstone) *stmbld s: a in rr* **12/1**	30+
1214	**9**	1	**Ingleby Star (IRE)**[44] 4877 4-9-0 **75** .... (p) GaryBartley(5) 12 (N Wilson) *dwlt: sn chsng ldrs on outer: rdn along over 2f out and sn wknd* **14/1**	39+
1110	**10**	½	**Tangerine Trees**[21] 5597 4-9-3 **73** .... TomEaves 10 (B Smart) *in rr: effrt and rdn along 2f out: sn edgd lft and nvr a factor* **12/1**	35+
0040	**11**	nk	**Dickie Le Davoir**[18] 5697 5-8-11 **72** .... MarkCoumbe(5) 8 (John A Harris) *s.i.s: a in rr* **18/1**	33+
4244	**12**	2 ¾	**Oriental Rose**[41] 4997 3-8-7 **64** .... PJMcDonald 3 (G M Moore) *a towards rr* **25/1**	15+

61.96 secs (-1.34) **Going Correction** -0.175s/f (Firm)
WFA 3 from 4yo+ 1lb **12** Ran SP% **122.3**
Speed ratings (Par 103): **103,102,94,89,88 88,83,83,82,81 80,76**
toteswingers: 1&2 £16.50, 1&3 £12.80, 2&3 £6.00 CSF £73.04 CT £333.16 TOTE £10.20: £3.30, £2.20, £2.50; EX 141.10.
Owner S Bolland P Holling **Bred** Edmond And Richard Kent **Trained** Maltby, S Yorks
FOCUS
A competitive 62-75 5f handicap run at a breakneck pace. It was almost impossible to make up ground from the rear and the first three occupied those positions throughout. The first two finished clear.

6234 DALBY SCREW-DRIVER H'CAP 1m 2f 6y
4:00 (4:00) (Class 2) (0-100,94) 3-Y-O **£12,462** (£3,732; £1,866; £934; £466) **Stalls** Low

Form				RPR
0112	**1**		**Laaheb**[54] 4541 3-9-10 **94** .... RHills 6 (M A Jarvis) *sn led: qcknd 1/2-way: qcknd 3f out: clr over 1f out: easily* **11/10**[1]	109+
4033	**2**	4	**William Blake**[20] 5641 4-9-10 **88** .... GregFairley 1 (M Johnston) *t.k.h: trckd wnr on inner: hdwy over 2f out: swtchd rt and rdn to chse wnr wl over 1f out: sn drvn and kpt on same pce* **5/1**[3]	91
0200	**3**	4	**Motafarred (IRE)**[7] 6019 7-8-13 **80** .... FrederikTylicki(3) 2 (Micky Hammond) *hld up in rr: hdwy on inner 2f out: sn rdn and kpt on u.p ins fnl f* **20/1**	76
1131	**4**	hd	**Larkham (USA)**[40] 5027 3-9-2 **86** .... GeorgeBaker 5 (R M Beckett) *sn cl up: effrt over 2f out and sn rdn along: drvn and edgd lft over 1f out: sn one pce* **5/2**[2]	81
1140	**5**	¾	**Shavansky**[54] 4526 5-9-5 **86** .... JamesMillman(3) 4 (B R Millman) *hld up in rr: effrt and hdwy 3f out: rdn 2f out: sn drvn and one pce* **8/1**	80

2m 9.48s (-4.22) **Going Correction** -0.175s/f (Firm)
WFA 3 from 4yo+ 6lb **5** Ran SP% **108.7**
Speed ratings (Par 109): **109,105,102,102,101**
toteswingers: 1&2 £4.90 CSF £6.82 TOTE £1.90: £1.40, £1.80; EX 6.00.
Owner Hamdan Al Maktoum **Bred** Darley **Trained** Newmarket, Suffolk
FOCUS
An 86-94 handicap and an easy winner of real potential. The runner-up is a consistent sort.
NOTEBOOK
Laaheb ◆, having just his fifth start after being unraced at two, was 6lb higher than when second at Newmarket seven weeks earlier. A grand, robust type, he dictated things from the front. Winding up the gallop in the final half-mile, he surged clear once in line for home and was value for double the official margin. Bred to improve with age, he looks sure to make a smart four-year-old. (op Evens tchd 11-8)
William Blake, winner of his first three races, has now gone 19 starts since without adding to his score. He finished clear second best and the handicapper has him to a tee. (op 4-1 tchd 7-2)
Motafarred(IRE) came out just third best but he is 11lb higher than for his last success and is arguably better over a mile. (tchd 18-1)
Larkham(USA), 3lb higher than for his hard-fought Newbury success, found this too tough. (op 100-30 tchd 7-2)
Shavansky, unsuited by the give at Godwood, was back after a seven-week break and never threatened. (op 7-1)

6235 EUROPEAN BREEDERS' FUND FRIER WOOD MAIDEN STKS 1m 4y
4:30 (4:30) (Class 4) 2-Y-O **£5,180** (£1,541; £770; £384) **Stalls** Low

Form				RPR
2	**1**		**Musaafer (IRE)**[20] 5637 2-9-3 0 .... RHills 2 (M A Jarvis) *mde all: pushed clr wl over 1f out: easily* **4/11**[1]	92+
002	**2**	6	**Finest Reserve (IRE)**[12] 5879 2-9-3 76 .... PaulHanagan 6 (M R Channon) *chsd wnr: rdn along 2f out: drvn and edgd lft over 1f out: kpt on: no ch w wnr* **9/1**[3]	74
05	**3**	2 ¾	**Architrave**[10] 5951 2-9-3 0 .... StephenDonohoe 4 (Sir Mark Prescott) *chsd ldng pair: rdn along over 2f out: n.m.r and swtchd rt over 1f out: kpt on same pce* **25/1**	68+
	4	8	**Florensky (IRE)** 2-9-0 0 .... AhmedAjtebi(3) 5 (Saeed Bin Suroor) *s.i.s and green in rr: pushed along after 2f: hdwy to chse ldrs 1/2-way: rdn along over 2f out and sn wknd* **4/1**[2]	49+
0	**5**	1 ½	**Spirit Land (IRE)**[8] 6000 2-9-3 0 .... SaleemGolam 1 (M H Tompkins) *in tch: hdwy and in tch 3f out: sn rdn and wknd 2f out* **100/1**	46+
060	**6**	1	**Meetings Man (IRE)**[17] 5728 2-9-3 65 .... DaleGibson 7 (Micky Hammond) *chsd ldrs: rdn along 3f out: wknd 2f out* **66/1**	44
00	**7**	shd	**Red Barcelona (IRE)**[26] 5428 2-9-3 0 .... TedDurcan 9 (M H Tompkins) *a in rr* **28/1**	43

1m 44.45s (-1.45) **Going Correction** -0.175s/f (Firm) **7** Ran SP% **113.1**
Speed ratings (Par 97): **100,94,91,83,81 80,80**
toteswingers: 1&2 £1.70, 1&3 £2.70, 2&3 £4.00 CSF £4.37 TOTE £1.40: £1.10, £2.30; EX 3.20.
Owner Hamdan Al Maktoum **Bred** Mountarmstrong Stud **Trained** Newmarket, Suffolk
FOCUS
A one-sided maiden race and an effortless winner, another to make all on the day. He looks a useful prospect.
NOTEBOOK
Musaafer(IRE) ◆, a Dewhurst and Racing Post entry who was runner-up to a Godolphin newcomer on the Polytrack at Kempton on his debut, is an attractive, athletic-looking colt. Keen to get on with it in front, he quickened right away once in line for home for an effortless success, value for a dozen lengths. He is clearly well regarded. (tchd 2-5)
Finest Reserve(IRE), rated 76 after his second of five in a maiden at Goodwood, finished clear second best but is likely to struggle from that sort of mark in nursery company. (tchd 17-2 and 10-1)
Architrave, already gelded, wore a blanket for stalls entry. He had shown little on his first two starts but finished clear third best here. A handicap mark in the low 70s will leave little room for error, however. (op 20-1)
Florensky(IRE), who has a middle-distance pedigree, is a rangy, good-bodied colt. He lost ground at the start and then looked very inexperienced. Soon driven along, he took closer order at halfway but tired turning in and was eased near the line. He will not be able to show his true mettle until next year. (op 9-2)

6236 PONTEFRACT APPRENTICE H'CAP 1m 2f 6y
5:00 (5:00) (Class 5) (0-75,73) 3-Y-O+ **£3,238** (£963; £481; £240) **Stalls** Low

Form				RPR
1111	**1**		**Valid Point (IRE)**[4] 6139 3-9-8 **73** 6ex .... RosieJessop 4 (Sir Mark Prescott) *mde all: rdn clr wl over 1f out: easily* **4/6**[1]	87+
3200	**2**	4	**Avitus**[87] 3454 3-8-1 **57** .... AdamCarter(5) 1 (Micky Hammond) *hld up in rr: hdwy over 2f out: rdn wl over 1f out: swtchd ins and squeezed through ent fnl f: drvn and kpt on to take 2nd nr fin* **14/1**	61
5463	**3**	hd	**Jeer (IRE)**[23] 5551 5-9-11 **70** .... (t) JamesPSullivan 7 (M W Easterby) *hld up in rr: hdwy over 3f out: swtchd lft over 2f out: sn rdn to chse wnr over 1f out: drvn and one pce ent fnl f: lost 2nd nr fin* **4/1**[2]	74
6200	**4**	5	**Nice Time (IRE)**[36] 5168 3-9-4 **69** .... SimonPearce 2 (M H Tompkins) *trckd ldrs on inner: pushed along whn n.m.r and hmpd over 2f out: sn lost pl and bhd: hdwy over 1f out: kpt on ins fnl f* **17/2**[3]	66+

1260 **5** 2 ¾ **Mister Fizzbomb (IRE)**[25] 5469 6-9-6 **65**........................(v) IJBrennan 8 55
(T D Walford) *sn trcking wnr: rdn along 3f out: drvn 2f out and sn wknd* **18/1**

0242 **6** 12 **Princess Flame (GER)**[23] 5545 7-9-6 **65**........................ KylieManser 5 33
(B G Powell) *in tch: hdwy to join ldrs 1/2-way: rdn along over 3f out and sn wknd* **9/1**

0100 **7** 1 ¼ **Betteras Bertie**[7] 6023 6-9-6 **68**.............................. JohnCavanagh(3) 3 34
(M Brittain) *s.i.s: sn in tch: hdwy on wd outside to chse ldrs 4f out: rdn 3f out and sn wknd* **40/1**

2m 12.12s (-1.58) **Going Correction** -0.175s/f (Firm)
WFA 3 from 5yo+ 6lb **7** Ran SP% **114.9**
Speed ratings (Par 103): **99,95,95,91,89 79,78**
toteswingers: 1&2 £4.40, 1&3 £1.90, 2&3 £7.30 CSF £12.41 CT £25.07 TOTE £1.70: £1.10, £5.30; EX 13.90 Place 6: £7.26, Place 5: £5.22..
Owner W E Sturt - Osborne House **Bred** Pier House Stud **Trained** Newmarket, Suffolk
■ Stewards' Enquiry : James P Sullivan two-day ban: careless riding (Oct 8-9)

FOCUS
A modest 57-70 apprentices' handicap and another all-the-way winner in Valid Point, who may not have stopped improving yet.
Betteras Bertie Official explanation: trainer said gelding did not appear to act on the good to firm ground
T/Plt: £5.80 to a £1 stake. Pool: £60,039.02. 7,523.91 winning tickets. T/Qpdt: £5.40 to a £1 stake. Pool: £3,417.90. 467.90 winning tickets. JR

6237 - (Foreign Racing) - See Raceform Interactive

5956 SAINT-CLOUD (L-H)
Thursday, September 24
OFFICIAL GOING: Good to soft

6238a PRIX JOUBERT (LISTED RACE) (FILLIES) 1m 4f
2:40 (2:40) 3-Y-O **£26,699** (£10,680; £8,010; £5,340; £2,670)

RPR
1 **Eastern Aria (UAE)**[14] 5794 3-8-12 .... JoeFanning 4 102
(M Johnston) *trckd ldr to st: led wl over 1f out: drvn clr: r.o wl* **16/5**[1]

2 2 **Superstition (FR)**[61] 4334 3-8-12 .... SPasquier 1 98
(W Hefter, Germany)

3 4 **Black Rose (FR)**[32] 5298 3-8-12 .... IMendizabal 7 92
(F Chappet, France)

4 ½ **Verenitsa (FR)**[198] 3-8-12 .... ACrastus 6 91
(E Lellouche, France)

5 2 ½ **Serasana**[97] 3-8-12 .... C-PLemaire 2 87
(A De Royer-Dupre, France)

6 4 **Terre Du Vent (FR)**[88] 3442 3-9-2 .... GMosse 3 85
(Y De Nicolay, France)

2m 33.8s (-6.60) **6** Ran SP% **23.8**
PARI-MUTUEL: WIN 4.20; PL 2.60, 5.90; SF 40.70.
Owner Sheikh Hamdan Bin Mohammed Al Maktoum **Bred** Darley **Trained** Middleham Moor, N Yorks

NOTEBOOK
Eastern Aria(UAE), always up with the leader, she quickened again one and a half out and finally won with something in hand. This was her 15th run and seventh victory of the season and she is an exceptionally game filly. Connections are now looking for a Group race for her.

4766 ASCOT (R-H)
Friday, September 25
OFFICIAL GOING: Good (good to firm in places; straight course: stands' side: 8.4, centre 8.4, far side 8.7; round course 9.1)
Wind: virtually nil Weather: bright and sunny

6239 EBF RATCLIFFES SYNDICATION CLASSIFIED STKS 1m 2f
2:00 (2:00) (Class 3) 3-Y-O+
£11,215 (£3,358; £1,679; £840; £419; £210) **Stalls** High

Form RPR
1 **1** **Rainbow Peak (IRE)**[144] 1729 3-8-10 90.............................. KFallon 7 99+
(M A Jarvis) *stdd s: t.k.h and hld up in last trio: still 10th over 2f out: nt clr run 2f out: swtchd ins and hdwy over 1f out: nt clr run and swtchd lft 1f out: rdn and qcknd to chal fnl 50yds: led nr fin* **9/2**[2]

2033 **2** hd **Greylami (IRE)**[13] 5880 4-9-2 90.............................. JimmyFortune 4 97
(T G Mills) *stdd after s: hld up towards rr: effrt and nt clr run 2f out: hdwy between horses over 1f out: drvn to ld fnl 100yds: hdd and no ex nr fin* **13/2**[3]

2-12 **3** 1 **Tryst**[126] 2241 4-9-2 90.. RyanMoore 8 95+
(Sir Michael Stoute) *hld up wl in tch: chsng ldrs and swtchd lft ent fnl 2f: rdn to ld over 1f out: drvn ent fnl f: hdd and one pce fnl 100yds* **11/8**[1]

-325 **4** 1 ½ **Rafiqa (IRE)**[40] 5070 3-8-7 90.................................... AlanMunro 2 89
(C F Wall) *chsd ldrs: rdn 3f out: drvn and pressed ldr ent fnl 2f tl no ex fnl 150yds* **15/2**

3304 **5** ¾ **Ballinteni**[2] 6210 7-9-2 84.. JerryO'Dwyer 1 91+
(M G Quinlan) *stdd after s: hld up in last trio: hdwy and nt clr run 2f out: swtchd lft and hdwy to chse ldrs ent fnl f: kpt on same pce fnl 150yds* **100/1**

0164 **6** ¾ **Dubai Crest**[12] 5904 3-8-10 87.................................... JimCrowley 9 89
(Mrs A J Perrett) *in tch in midfield: effrt and n.m.r fr 2f out tl 1f out: kpt on same pce u.p fnl f* **16/1**

6002 **7** 1 ¼ **Charlie Cool**[19] 5694 6-9-2 90..........................(tp) SilvestreDeSousa 6 87
(Mrs R A Carr) *stdd after s: hld up in last trio: rdn and effrt over 2f out: nvr gng pce to trble ldrs* **12/1**

14 **8** hd **Bawadi (USA)**[32] 5315 3-8-10 90.................................... LDettori 3 87
(Saeed Bin Suroor) *chsd ldr: rdn to chal over 2f out: led narrowly wl over 1f out: sn hdd: wknd fnl f* **11/1**

-650 **9** 1 ¾ **Amanjena**[9] 6003 4-8-13 87.. WilliamBuick 5 81
(A M Balding) *hld up in tch in midfield: plld wd and effrt on outer 2f out: drvn and kpt on same pce fr over 1f out* **20/1**

0405 **10** ½ **Norwegian Dancer (UAE)**[12] 5904 3-8-10 86.................. TedDurcan 10 83
(E S McMahon) *chsd ldrs on inner: rdn and unable qck over 2f out: keeping on same pce and btn whn nt clr run and eased 1f out: no ch after* **66/1**

0465 **11** 9 **Jabal Tariq**[12] 5909 4-9-2 81.................................... MichaelHills 11 69+
(B W Hills) *sn bustled along to ld: rdn over 2f out: hdd wl over 1f out: wknd ent fnl f* **33/1**

2m 5.72s (-1.28) **Going Correction** +0.05s/f (Good)
WFA 3 from 4yo+ 6lb **11** Ran SP% **117.5**
Speed ratings (Par 107): **107,106,106,104,104 103,102,102,101,100 93**
toteswingers: 1&2 £4.70, 1&3 £1.30, 2&3 £4.40 CSF £32.91 TOTE £4.90: £1.70, £1.90, £1.30; EX 41.30 Trifecta £52.20 Pool: £1168.74 - 16.55 winning units..
Owner P D Savill **Bred** P D Savill **Trained** Newmarket, Suffolk

FOCUS
A decent classified event and, as ever in such events, there was little between the runners on official ratings, with 6lb covering the majority of the field. There appeared to be just an average pace on, but the first pair were both given patient rides and the form looks sound enough rated around the placed horses.

NOTEBOOK
Rainbow Peak(IRE) came into this under the "could be anything" category having won on his debut in a decent Kempton maiden back in May, after which he was sidelined with a hairline fracture of his pelvis. He came in for support on track and was ridden right out the back on this step up 2f in trip. He initially tried to make his effort on the inside nearing the 2f marker, but found nowhere to go and had to be switched wide with his challenge. That move gave him plenty to do, but he quickened up smartly when in the clear and was always going to get up nearing the business end. His rider deserves a lot of credit, but it was a most taking display from this gelded half-brother to the smart Celtic Heroine and he looks a pattern performer in the making. Easier ground may also prove more to his liking as well as he has plenty of size about him. (op 6-1)
Greylami(IRE) brought some decent handicap form to the table and was stepping back up to his optimum trip. He too was well backed late on and settled in mid-field through the early parts. Like the winner he also had to wait for his challenge around 2f out, though he met nothing like as much trouble as that one, and soon after finding the gap he powered to the lead. He proved unable to cope with the late surge of Rainbow Peak and doesn't have the strike-rate perhaps one should for his ability, but he certainly deserves to find another opening after this. (op 9-1 tchd 6-1)
Tryst proved all the rage on this first run since finishing second to Roaring Forte over 7f at Newmarket 144 days earlier, where he was actually made a short-priced favourite. Making only his fourth career start, he raced just off the early pace and was produced with every chance but ultimately got outstayed by the first pair. He is evidently highly regarded and it isn't hard to see why he was being aimed at the Cambridgeshire as a stiff 1m1f is probably his optimum trip. However, he re idally needed to collect a penalty here in order to ensure a run in that, so it is probably back to the drawing board for connections now. (op 10-11 tchd 6-4)
Rafiqa(IRE) was best in at the weights on official figures and had run right up to her mark in a handicap on her latest outing 40 days previously. She was forced to race on the outer from her low draw and didn't travel with much fluency. She still showed a gutsy attitude to throw down a challenge from 2f out, though, and performed very close to her previous level. This longer trip appeared to find out her stamina, however. (op 9-1 tchd 10-1)
Ballinteni, fourth in a claimer at Kempton two days earlier, stayed on stoutly from way off the pace and registered a greatly improved display. His proximity doesn't obviously do much for the form at first glance, but he was back over his optimum trip here and showed some smart form last year, so shouldn't be used to hold it down too much.
Dubai Crest wasn't at all disgraced and performed right up to his best, helping to set the level. (op 20-1)
Charlie Cool, second in a claimer at York last time, made his effort widest of all in the home straight and turned in one of his better efforts, but he remains below his previous best. (op 14-1)
Bawadi(USA) disputed the early running and had his chance, but ultimately failed to see it out, despite this being a drop back in trip on his turf bow. It was just his third outing, but he looks to have been assessed too high after his debut in win August. (op 12-1)
Norwegian Dancer(UAE) came here with plenty to prove, but he should be rated better than the bare form as he endured a troubled passage in the home straight and is clearly very useful on his day. Official explanation: jockey said colt was denied a clear run

6240 JEAN BRYANT MEMORIAL H'CAP 6f
2:35 (2:36) (Class 2) (0-100,100) 3-Y-O
£12,462 (£3,732; £1,866; £934; £466; £234) **Stalls** Centre

Form RPR
011- **1** **Rulesn'regulations**[297] 7523 3-8-6 **88**.............................. WilliamBuick 5 96+
(Matthew Salaman) *w ldrs tl led 1/2-way: rdn and edgd rt u.p fr wl over 1f out: styd on gamely fnl f* **20/1**

0512 **2** nk **Enact**[22] 5607 3-8-11 **93**.. RyanMoore 6 100+
(Sir Michael Stoute) *s.i.s and sltly hmpd s: bhd: hdwy and edging rt fr over 1f out: squeezed between horses to chse wnr wl ins fnl f: r.o wl but nt quite rch wnr* **2/1**[1]

6415 **3** ½ **Son Of The Cat (USA)**[39] 5092 3-8-9 **91**..........................(t) KFallon 12 97
(B Gubby) *hld up towards rr: hdwy towards far side over 2f out: ev ch and drvn 1f out: unable qck fnl 100yds* **12/1**

5604 **4** hd **Bonnie Charlie**[16] 5766 3-9-4 **100**............................ RichardHughes 4 105
(R Hannon) *w ldrs: pressed wnr and rdn 2f out: kpt on same pce u.p fnl f* **7/1**[2]

2113 **5** ½ **Gilt Edge Girl**[119] 2443 3-8-4 **86** oh1.............................. LukeMorris 10 90
(C G Cox) *stdd s: hld up towards rr: hdwy on far side over 2f out: pressed ldrs and drvn over 1f out: no ex fnl 100yds* **7/1**[2]

2005 **6** hd **Servoca (CAN)**[15] 5799 3-8-5 **87**............................(t) MichaelHills 2 90
(B W Hills) *hld up in midfield: hdwy jst over 2f out: rdn to chse ldrs over 1f out: one pce ins fnl f* **16/1**

022 **7** 2 ¼ **Brenin Taran**[12] 5902 3-8-1 **86** oh1..........................(p) AndreaAtzeni(3) 7 82
(D M Simcock) *chsd ldrs: rdn and struggling to hold pl over 2f out: btn whn sltly hmpd over 1f out* **17/2**

0310 **8** ½ **Noverre To Go (IRE)**[41] 5032 3-8-12 **94**................(t) RichardKingscote 9 88
(Tom Dascombe) *in tch in midfield: rdn and nt qckn 2f out: one pce and n.d ins fnl f* **8/1**[3]

0004 **9** 2 ½ **Thunderous Mood (USA)**[12] 5902 3-8-8 **90**................ MartinDwyer 13 76
(P F I Cole) *stdd and dropped in bhd after s: effrt and hanging rt 2f out: no imp* **50/1**

-204 **10** nk **Macdillon**[34] 5263 3-8-10 **92**.. FergusSweeney 11 77
(W S Kittow) *chsd ldrs: rdn and struggling over 2f out: no ch fnl f* **12/1**

2060 **11** 2 ½ **Desert Icon (IRE)**[21] 5646 3-7-13 **86** oh4............ AndrewHeffernan(5) 1 63
(W J Knight) *led narrowly tl 1/2-way: wknd rapidly over 1f out: no ch fnl f* **33/1**

0-10 **12** 6 **Aakef (IRE)**[141] 1803 3-8-4 **86**.. TPO'Shea 8 44
(M A Jarvis) *in tch in midfield: lost pl and dropped to rr jst over 2f out: wl bhd fnl f* **12/1**

1m 13.61s (-0.79) **Going Correction** +0.05s/f (Good) **12** Ran SP% **118.6**
Speed ratings (Par 107): **107,106,105,105,105 104,101,101,97,97 94,86**
toteswingers: 1&2 £3.40, 1&3 £11.90, 2&3 £35.40 CSF £59.17 CT £541.86 TOTE £23.80: £5.20, £1.50, £3.00; EX 71.20 Trifecta £493.60 Part won. Pool: £667.11 - 0.10 winning units..
Owner M Salaman & J H Widdows **Bred** Marshalla Salaman **Trained** Upper Lambourn, Berks

FOCUS
A decent 3yo sprint handicap in which three raced from out of the weights. The runners raced down the centre of the track before ending up more towards the far side and there was a tight finish, largely due to the lack of real early pace. The fourth, fifth and sixth help set the level.

NOTEBOOK

Rulesn'regulations, who looked fit, was making a belated return to action after winning twice on the all-weather late last year, having had a chip on his knee removed, and this was a tremendous effort. Contesting a handicap for the first time and upped significantly in grade, he helped cut out the early running. As the race began to hot up he knuckled down gamely and was always doing enough to hold off the fast-finishing runner-up. While this proves he can do it on turf, this track often suits a horse effective on Polytrack. Considering he looked much in need of the run beforehand there should really be more to come from him. His connections also believe he will come into his own next year, with a trip to Dubai a possibility, and there could be a decent pot in him as a 4yo. (old market op 20-1, new market op 20-1)

Enact, another 2lb higher, was very well backed back on a quicker surface. She wasn't the best away, but had come from behind when just missing out on her previous outing. She really lost out by meeting a troubled passage just as the race got serious 2f out and, while she was motoring inside the closing stages, the winner was beyond recall. This filly remains progressive and really needs more use made of her over this distance, so any losses should only be lent. (old market op 11-4 tchd 3-1 in places, new market op 2-1)

Son Of The Cat(USA), who got warm beforehand, came there with every chance and ran right up to his previous level on this drop back a furlong. He has developed into a very useful handicapper and sets the level. (old market op 14-1 new market op 12-1)

Bonnie Charlie came in for some support and he ran another solid race, but is just struggling to find his optimum trip this season. (old market op 17-2 tchd 9-1, new market op 8-1 tchd 7-1)

Gilt Edge Girl, 1lb out of the weights, progressed nicely earlier in the season but was reappearing after a 119-day break so has presumably had a problem. Stepping back up a furlong, she did enough to suggest she would be sharper for the run and will not mind a return to easier ground. (old market op 10-1 tchd 8-1, new market op 8-1)

Servoca(CAN) posted a return to form at Doncaster 15 days earlier and was back against his own age group here. He came there with every chance and turned in a decent effort considering he would have enjoyed a more truly run race. (old market op 14-1, new market op 16-1)

Brenin Taran arrived in decent form having finished runner-up on his two previous starts, but was found out in this company by the step back up a furlong. He is now due to race from a 3lb higher mark. (old market op 11-1 tchd 10-1, new market op 9-1)

Aakef(IRE) Official explanation: jockey said gelding lost its action

6241 WATERSHIP DOWN STUD SALES RACE (FILLIES) 6f 110y

3:10 (3:12) (Class 2) 2-Y-O

£123,100 (£49,250; £24,625; £12,300; £6,150; £6,150) **Stalls** Centre

Form RPR

1221 **1** **Shamandar (FR)**[22] 5606 2-8-5 104 MichaelHills 7 87+
(W J Haggas) *racd stands' side: grad swtchd rt to r on far side: hld up in midfield: hdwy and rdn over 2f out: led ent fnl f: styd on wl* **8/11**[1]

053 **2** ½ **Dubawi Heights**[36] 5199 2-8-12 99 LDettori 16 93+
(S A Callaghan) *racd far side: a.p: led overall over 1f out tl ent fnl f: kpt on gamely but a hld fnl f: 2nd of 21 in gp* **13/2**[2]

655 **3** 2¼ **Lenkiewicz**[22] 5605 2-8-2 72 AndreaAtzeni 17 76
(B R Millman) *racd far side: in tch tl outpcd and lost pl over 2f out: rallied u.p over 1f out: styd on wl to go 3rd last stride: nt pce to rch ldrs: 3rd of 21 in gp* **40/1**

2100 **4** shd **She's Ok (IRE)**[20] 5658 2-8-2 78 KoseiMiura 19 76
(C E Brittain) *racd far side: chsd ldrs: rdn wl over 1f out: chsd ldng pair ins fnl f: kpt on same pce: lost 3rd last stride: 4th of 21 in gp* **28/1**

0424 **5** ¾ **Pose (IRE)**[9] 5992 2-8-10 70 RyanMoore 4 82+
(R Hannon) *racd stands' side: chsd ldrs: lft in ld stands' side gp 2f out: r.o wl to fin clr of that gp but no ch w far side ldrs: 1st of 6 in gp* **33/1**

22 **6** ½ **Baby Dottie**[47] 4825 2-7-12 0 CatherineGannon 14 69
(P M Phelan) *racd far side: led that gp: ev ch and rdn over 2f out: wknd u.p ent fnl f: 5th of 21 in gp* **33/1**

3304 **7** hd **Mrs Boss**[12] 5899 2-7-12 78 DavidProbert 18 68
(B R Millman) *racd far side: rdn and effrt u.p 2f out: edgd rt and no imp fnl f: 6th of 21 in gp* **80/1**

0020 **8** 1 **Gooseberry Bush**[18] 5714 2-7-12 66 KellyHarrison 23 65
(P J Makin) *racd far side: in tch: rdn and unable qck 2f out: edgd rt and plugged on same pce fnl f: 7th of 21 in gp* **125/1**

021 **9** shd **Fardyieh**[23] 5571 2-8-6 78 ChrisCatlin 13 73
(C E Brittain) *racd far side: prom: rdn and stuggling 2f out: wknd u.p over 1f out: 8th of 21 in gp* **20/1**

0104 **10** ½ **Excelling (IRE)**[21] 5650 2-8-0 83 JimmyQuinn 9 66
(P J Makin) *racd far side: hld up towards rr: effrt u.p 2f out: no real prog: n.d: 9th of 21 in gp* **16/1**

3426 **11** ½ **Poppy N'Penny (IRE)**[29] 5369 2-8-0 69 KirstyMilczarek 3 64
(W J Haggas) *overall ldr on stands' side tl hung bdly rt fr 1/2-way: jnd far side gp 2f out: sn hdd: wknd fnl f:10th of 21 in gp* **66/1**

51 **12** ½ **Theladyinquestion**[35] 5212 2-8-6 83 WilliamBuick 11 69
(A M Balding) *racd on far side: in tch in midfield: rdn and effrt 2f out: sn edgd rt and no prog: 11th of 21 in gp* **10/1**[3]

6300 **13** ½ **So Surreal (IRE)**[46] 4850 2-8-6 71 (b[1]) FergusSweeney 6 68
(G L Moore) *racd stands' side: chsd ldrs: rdn over 2f out: no ch w far side fr wl over 1f out: 2nd of 6 in gp* **150/1**

2161 **14** 2½ **Danny's Choice**[18] 5721 2-8-13 89 JimCrowley 10 68
(R M Beckett) *racd far side: hld up in midfield: rdn and no hdwy ent fnl 2f: no ch fnl f: 12th of 21 in gp* **25/1**

2130 **15** 1¼ **Perfect Ch'I (IRE)**[15] 5795 2-8-1 81 SilvestreDeSousa 1 52
(I A Wood) *racd stands' side: a towards rr: 3rd of 6 in gp* **16/1**

0 **16** shd **Fame Is The Spur**[22] 5605 2-8-8 0 HayleyTurner 12 59
(J W Hills) *racd far side: in tch tl wknd u.p jst over 2f out: 13th of 21 in gp* **66/1**

0220 **17** 1¾ **Magic Lantern**[27] 5428 2-8-6 74 PatDobbs 2 52
(R Hannon) *racd stands' side: in tch: rdn 1/2-way: no ch w far side fnl 2f: 4th of 6 in gp* **50/1**

0 **18** 1¼ **Cyan Eyed**[22] 5605 2-8-8 0 RichardKingscote 22 51
(Tom Dascombe) *racd far side: in tch tl wknd u.p over 2f out: 14th of 21 in gp* **100/1**

6423 **19** ½ **Royal Record**[20] 5668 2-8-0 69 AndrewHeffernan 20 41
(M Brittain) *racd far side: in tch: rdn and struggling over 2f out: no ch fr wl over 1f out: 15th of 21 in gp* **100/1**

5 **20** 2 **Thoughtful (IRE)**[21] 5638 2-8-6 0 LiamJones 15 42
(J W Hills) *racd far side: in tch in midfield: rdn and struggling over 2f out: wl btn fnl 2f: 16th of 21 in gp* **150/1**

4 **21** shd **One Cool Poppy (IRE)**[43] 4946 2-8-2 0 LukeMorris 27 38
(H J L Dunlop) *racd far side: a bhd: rdn and no hdwy over 2f out:17th of 21 in gp* **66/1**

0 **22** 2¾ **Born A Dancer (IRE)**[41] 5026 2-7-12 0 AmyScott 21 26
(J W Hills) *racd far side: a bhd: 18th of 21 in gp* **150/1**

022 **23** 2 **Jozafeen**[33] 5290 2-7-12 63 DuranFentiman 8 21
(R Bastiman) *racd stands' side: wnt rt s: sn swtchd lft to stands' side: sn rdn: no ch fnl 2f: 5th of 6 in gp* **100/1**

0020 **24** 4½ **Micky's Bird**[33] 5290 2-8-2 54 ow4 PaulEddery 25 12
(R C Guest) *racd far side: a bhd: 19th of 21 in gp* **200/1**

505 **25** 1 **Pavement Games**[20] 5668 2-8-1 0 ow3 FrancisNorton 26 8
(R C Guest) *racd far side: a bhd: 20th of 21 in gp* **66/1**

0005 **26** 1 **Ellmolell**[60] 4379 2-8-4 54 ow2 MartinDwyer 5 9
(S Kirk) *racd stands' side: a bhd: 6th of 6 in gp* **200/1**

1553 **27** 10 **Cultured Pride (IRE)**[17] 5742 2-8-8 76 ow1 RichardHughes 24 —
(R Hannon) *racd far side: a bhd: lost tch 2f out: 21st of 21 in gp* **33/1**

1m 21.39s (-0.45) **Going Correction** +0.05s/f (Good) **27** Ran SP% **131.3**

Speed ratings (Par 98): **104,103,100,100,99 99,99,97,97,97 96,96,95,92,91 91,89,87,87,84 84,81,79,74,73 71,60**

toteswingers: 1&2 £2.80, 1&3 £87.10, 2&3 £159.40 CSF £4.43 TOTE £1.80: £1.20, £2.30, £19.10; EX 6.90 Trifecta £415.70 Pool: £1550.61 - 2.76 winning units..

Owner Mr & Mrs R Scott **Bred** Team Hogdala A B **Trained** Newmarket, Suffolk

■ This was likely to have been the final running of this valuable event.

FOCUS

An event with a very valuable prize on offer for juvenile fillies', but there was a disappointing turnout this season with only eight of the 27-strong field having managed to shed their maiden tags. The majority of runners raced far side and the smaller group towards the stands' side looked to be at a disadvantage. The proximity of several rated in the 60s and 70s limits the form.

NOTEBOOK

Shamandar(FR) had an exceptional chance at the weights on this return to suitably quicker ground and was backed accordingly. She duly followed up her Listed win at Salisbury 22 days earlier, but had to work very hard in order to land the spoils and ran below her official rating. She deserves extra credit though, as she had to go across to the main group towards the far side from her single-figure stall and covered much more ground than Dubawi Heights, who pushed her all the way to the line. This was also the furthest distance she had tackled to date and, despite her dam being placed over 1m4f, her effort suggested the trip stretched her stamina to the limit. She has had a cracking season and her two defeats to date saw her only beaten very narrowly, so she is a credit to her yard. She is in the Group 1 Cheveley Park and, although that will come soon enough, she is an intended runner there providing she comes out of this sufficiently well. Her connections are rightly striking while the iron is hot and she is entitled to take her chance in that, but will obviously need to step up plenty to take a hand. (op 10-11 tchd Evens)

Dubawi Heights was the chief threat to the winner on paper having run a massive race for a maiden when third in the Lowther Stakes on her previous outing. She is rated 5lb inferior to the winner, but was conceding her 7lb so it was a tough ask. Having raced prominently in the far-side group she refused to give in without a fight and proved her Lowther run to be no fluke. A maiden would be hers for the taking in the coming weeks and she proved well suited by this extra distance. (op 11-2)

Lenkiewicz showed her best form over slightly further at Salisbury last time out and was given a mark of 72. That left her with plenty to find coming here, but she ran above herself and is evidently a useful filly in the making. She should not be long in scoring. (op 50-1)

She's Ok(IRE) showed her true colours again aided by this return to suitably quicker ground, and this experienced filly seems a sensible guide to the form. (op 25-1)

Pose(IRE), whose stable won this last year, ran out a clear-cut winner of the small group that raced more towards the unfavoured near side and emerges from the race with plenty of credit as she also had plenty on at the weights. This showed her flop on easy ground last time to be all wrong, she saw out the longer trip without a fuss and looks a winner waiting to happen.

Baby Dottie, a runner-up on her two previous outings, was on her toes returning from a 47-day break and gave a decent account of herself. She should hit the net when returning to lesser company.

Theladyinquestion was the potential big improver in the race, but she was disappointing. She won nicely at Salisbury in August and seemed sure to enjoy the extra distance. After racing handily she felt the pinch soon after the 2f pole and had no more to give. This was just her third outing, though, and it is too soon to be writing her off. (op 12-1)

6242 PRINCESS ROYAL E B F PRICEWATERHOUSECOOPERS STKS (LISTED RACE) (F&M) 1m 4f

3:45 (3:47) (Class 1) 3-Y-O+

£25,546 (£9,684; £4,846; £2,416; £1,210; £607) **Stalls** High

Form RPR

0241 **1** **Spirit Of Dubai (IRE)**[23] 5578 3-8-9 83 WilliamBuick 1 101
(D M Simcock) *hld up in last trio: rdn and effrt 2f out: n.m.r over 1f out tl ins fnl f: drvn and qcknd between horses ins fnl f: r.o wl to ld on post* **20/1**

0311 **2** shd **Polly's Mark (IRE)**[48] 4767 3-8-12 103 RichardHughes 5 104
(C G Cox) *hld up in tch in midfield: hdwy over 2f out: rdn to ld over 1f out: hrd pressed 1f out: battled on gamely tl hdd on post* **2/1**[1]

-200 **3** ½ **Mischief Making (USA)**[90] 3390 4-9-3 98 TGMcLaughlin 6 100
(E A L Dunlop) *s.i.s and pushed along early: racd in last trio: hdwy on inner over 1f out: ev ch ins fnl f: unable qck fnl 50yds* **16/1**

2455 **4** nk **Princess Taylor**[15] 5796 5-9-3 98 (t) TedDurcan 7 100
(M Botti) *chsd ldr: rdn and clsd over 2f out: ev ch fr wl over 1f out: no ex fnl 75yds* **5/1**[3]

3330 **5** ½ **Uvinza**[36] 5202 3-8-9 100 JimCrowley 4 99
(W J Knight) *hld up in tch in midfield: hdwy on outer over 2f out: ev ch over 1f out tl one pce fnl 100yds* **9/1**

0541 **6** ¾ **Snoqualmie Girl (IRE)**[13] 5854 3-8-12 105 SilvestreDeSousa 3 101
(D R C Elsworth) *hld up in last trio: effrt on outer 2f out: chsd ldrs ent fnl f: one pce and no imp after* **3/1**[2]

2610 **7** 6 **Phillipina**[54] 4566 3-8-9 103 RyanMoore 2 91+
(Sir Michael Stoute) *chsd ldng pair: rdn and effrt over 2f out: wknd over 1f out:* **11/2**

0-14 **8** 15 **Multiplication**[116] 2535 3-8-9 76 ShaneKelly 8 70+
(W J Knight) *led: clr 7f out: rdn and hrd pressed ent fnl 2f: hdd & wknd qckly over 1f out: eased ins fnl f* **40/1**

2m 30.26s (-2.24) **Going Correction** +0.05s/f (Good)

WFA 3 from 4yo+ 8lb **8** Ran SP% **113.5**

Speed ratings (Par 111): **109,108,108,108,108 107,103,93**

toteswingers: 1&2 £2.80, 1&3 £87.10, 2&3 £159.40 CSF £59.51 TOTE £14.70: £2.30, £1.30, £3.80; EX 38.00 Trifecta £1282.20 Part won. Pool: £1732.78 - 0.46 winning units..

Owner Ahmad Al Shaikh **Bred** D J Bloodstock, G Roddick & Wrottesley Ltd **Trained** Newmarket, Suffolk

FOCUS

Despite Multiplication attaining a clear lead and eventually dropping right out, the early pace in this Listed event looked no more than average and the first six were very closely covered at the finish. Therefore the form, which is limited for the grade, should be treated with some caution.

NOTEBOOK

Spirit Of Dubai(IRE) stuck her head out where it really mattered and just prevailed. She arrived here on the back of a maiden success at Lingfield, where she ran below her mark of 83 in winning and had taken seven outings to come good. That makes her a surprise winner on this big step up in class, but she did show on her seasonal reappearance, when beaten seven lengths in the Lingfield Oaks Trial, that she was a talented filly. Things went to pieces on her next three starts, but her maiden win had clearly done her confidence a power of good and the manner in which she went through runners to get up here shows she is a genuine filly. She is to be kept in training as a 4yo and her trainer believes she can reach greater heights next season as she comes from a late-maturing family. (tchd 25-1)

Polly's Mark(IRE), who was well in when landing a handicap at the Shergar meeting over C&D on her previous start, was penalised for her success in this grade on her penultimate outing. She took it up between the final 2f and only got reeled in by the winner at the line, but she would have surely landed the hat-trick had she consented to settle better through the early parts. Her previous best efforts have been on easier ground and her supporters shouldn't abandon her, as there should be another one of these in her when she gets a stronger early pace. Ground permitting she could head to the Pride Stakes at Newmarket next month and will stay in training next year. (tchd 9-4, 5-2 in places)

Mischief Making(USA) was returning from a 90-day layoff and appeared to have a stiff task at the weights, over a trip short of her best. She ran a blinder, however, making her effort against the far rail and not being beaten at all far. Considering she too would have enjoyed more of a test this has to rate as a promising return and a step back up in trip should only help. (tchd 14-1)

Princess Taylor again gave her all in defeat on this drop down in trip and class. She helps to set the level and deserves another winning turn, but always seems to find a few too good. (op 6-1 tchd 9-2)

Uvinza showed her York flop to be all wrong and enjoyed this return to a track where she finished third in the Ribblesdale at the Royal Meeting in June. She came under pressure from the home turn, but kept battling away and a return to slightly more positive tactics should suit ideally. (op 12-1)

Snoqualmie Girl(IRE), in front of Princess Taylor and Uvinza at York two runs back, had resumed winning ways at Chester since. She was allowed to get behind down the far side and was nearer last than first turning in. She still picked up and looked a big player when switched to the outside 2f out, but her effort flattened out inside the final furlong. (op 7-2)

Phillipina, behind Polly's Mark at Newbury on her previous start, was in trouble shortly after turning into the home straight and failed to raise her game for the return to quicker ground. She has now run of out excuses. (op 4-1)

6243 DJP INTERNATIONAL H'CAP 1m (S)
4:20 (4:25) (Class 4) (0-85,83) 3-Y-O **£7,123** (£2,119; £1,059; £529) **Stalls** Centre

Form RPR

4404 **1** **Glowing Praise**[14] 5832 3-8-13 **78** LDettori 12 88
(E S McMahon) *hld up in tch in midfield: hdwy over 2f out: rdn to chse ldr 2f out: led over 1f out: hung rt ins fnl f: styd on wl* **9/1**

0042 **2** ½ **Satwa Laird**[17] 5746 3-9-4 **83** RyanMoore 10 92
(E A L Dunlop) *stdd s: hld up towards rr: hdwy over 2f out: chsd ldng pair jst over 1f out: swtchd lft ins fnl f: pressed wnr wl ins fnl f: kpt on* **7/1**[3]

2303 **3** 1¾ **Roar Of Applause**[9] 5999 3-9-0 **79** (b) MartinDwyer 14 84
(B J Meehan) *hld up trcking ldrs: hdwy to ld gng wl jst over 2f out: rdn and hdd over 1f out: carried rt and n.m.r ins fnl f: wknd towards fin* **25/1**

-240 **4** 2 **Laurie Grove (IRE)**[163] 1291 3-9-4 **83** JimmyFortune 16 83
(T G Mills) *hld up towards rr: hdwy over 2f out: rdn to chse ldrs over 1f out: one pce and no imp ins fnl f* **14/1**

2431 **5** 1½ **Woodlark Island (IRE)**[17] 5751 3-8-10 **75** TedDurcan 9 72
(M P Tregoning) *chsd ldrs: rdn and unable qck ent fnl 2f: drvn and plugged on same pce fr over 1f out* **7/1**[3]

121 **6** ½ **Regeneration (IRE)**[20] 5677 3-8-13 **78** HayleyTurner 2 74+
(S A Callaghan) *stdd s: hld up in rr: effrt and rdn jst over 2f out: kpt on steadily u.p ins fnl f: nvr gng pce to threaten ldrs* **11/1**

1561 **7** *hd* **Edgeworth (IRE)**[11] 5940 3-8-12 77 6ex WilliamBuick 1 72
(B G Powell) *in tch: rdn and effrt to press ldrs ent fnl 2f: wknd u.p over 1f out* **16/1**

420 **8** 1¾ **Paquerettza (FR)**[20] 5670 3-9-2 **81** JimCrowley 13 72
(D H Brown) *led: rdn over 2f out: sn hdd: wknd over 1f out and no ch fnl f* **16/1**

2401 **9** 1½ **Miss Mojito (IRE)**[22] 5602 3-7-12 **70** (t) KierenFox[(7)] 17 58
(J W Hills) *v.s.a: bhd: sme modest hdwy and edging rt over 1f out: n.d* **33/1**

6100 **10** 3¼ **Compton Blue**[27] 5429 3-8-4 **69** oh2 CatherineGannon 11 49
(R Hannon) *chsd ldrs: struggling u.p over 2f out: wknd qckly wl over 1f out* **40/1**

2640 **11** 2½ **Star Links (USA)**[14] 5832 3-9-2 **81** RichardHughes 3 56+
(R Hannon) *swtchd rt sn after s: hld up in rr: short-lived effrt over 2f out: n.d: eased ins fnl f* **16/1**

1-40 **12** ¾ **Albaher**[14] 5832 3-8-10 **75** TPO'Shea 8 48
(J L Dunlop) *in tch in midfield: rdn and hanging rt over 2f out: sn wl btn* **33/1**

5040 **13** 3¼ **Global**[26] 5475 3-9-2 **81** PatDobbs 5 46
(R Hannon) *chsd ldr tl over 2f out: sn wknd u.p: wl bhd fnl f* **33/1**

2112 **14** *hd* **The Scorching Wind (IRE)**[16] 5780 3-9-0 **79** (t) ChrisCatlin 15 44
(S C Williams) *chsd ldrs tl wknd qckly u.p wl over 1f out* **5/1**[2]

4423 **15** 1 **Laughing Boy (IRE)**[32] 5322 3-8-13 **78** KFallon 6 41+
(L M Cumani) *chsd ldrs: pushed along over 3f out: drvn and edging rt wl over 1f out: sn btn: eased whn no ch fnl f* **4/1**[1]

-505 **16** *hd* **Brief Candle**[27] 5448 3-9-2 **81** (t) ShaneKelly 4 43
(W R Swinburn) *in tch in midfield: rdn and struggling over 2f out: wl btn fnl 2f* **16/1**

055 **17** 4 **Capo Regime**[43] 4956 3-8-4 **69** oh4 SilvestreDeSousa 7 22
(P Howling) *plld hrd: hld up towards rr: pushed along and struggling over 3f out: wl bhd whn hung rt 2f out* **50/1**

1m 41.0s (0.40) **Going Correction** +0.05s/f (Good) **17** Ran SP% **127.3**
Speed ratings (Par 103): **100,99,97,95,94 93,93,91,90,87 84,83,80,80,79 79,75**
toteswingers: 1&2 £11.80, 1&3 £48.40, 2&3 £30.30 CSF £69.17 CT £1565.26 TOTE £10.20: £2.90, £1.90, £4.40, £4.30; EX 112.00 Trifecta £924.60 Part won. Pool: £1249.55 - 0.40 winning units..
Owner J C Fretwell **Bred** Wyck Hall Stud Ltd **Trained** Lichfield, Staffs

FOCUS
This has often been won in the past by a progressive 3yo with pretensions to bigger and better things. However, there wasn't an obvious candidate on paper with such credentials this year and the form looks only fair rated through the third horse. The field raced in two groups early on, avoiding the near side, before merging towards the far rail coming to the two-furlong pole. The form looks pretty strong for the grade, rated through the runner-up and backed up by the third and fourth.
Miss Mojito(IRE) Official explanation: jockey said filly missed the break
The Scorching Wind(IRE) Official explanation: trainer had no explanation for the poor form shown
Laughing Boy(IRE) Official explanation: trainer's rep had no explanation for the poor form shown
Capo Regime Official explanation: jockey said gelding ran too free and hung right

6244 BOLLINGER CHAMPAGNE CHALLENGE SERIES FINAL H'CAP (FOR GENTLEMAN AMATEUR RIDERS) 1m 4f
4:55 (4:55) (Class 4) (0-80,77) 4-Y-O+
£6,002 (£1,875; £937; £469; £234; £118) **Stalls** High

Form RPR

6005 **1** **Crossbow Creek**[53] 4602 11-11-6 **73** MrMRimell 5 81
(M G Rimell) *stdd s: hld up in last trio: hdwy and in tch whn nt clr run over 2f out tl swtchd lft over 1f out: edgd rt but r.o to ld ins fnl f: rdn out* **25/1**

3321 **2** 1½ **Safebreaker**[35] 5210 4-10-13 **69** (p) MrJoshuaMoore[(3)] 10 75
(K A Ryan) *hld up wl in tch: rdn and effrt over 2f out: swtchd lft ent fnl f: chsd wnr ins fnl f: one pce* **7/2**[1]

0210 **3** 1½ **Balnagore**[20] 5667 5-11-3 **70** MrSWalker 1 74
(J L Dunlop) *led tl over 7f out: led again over 3f out: rdn over 2f out: hdd ins fnl f: btn fnl 100yds* **5/1**[3]

6244 **4** *nk* **Locum**[25] 5509 4-10-4 **64** MrDJEustace[(7)] 11 67
(M H Tompkins) *dwlt: in tch towards rr: hdwy 4f out: swtchd lft and effrt 2f out: pressed ldrs over 1f out: one pce after* **9/1**

4514 **5** 1¾ **Sky Quest (IRE)**[17] 5740 11-10-10 **66** MrJohnEnnis[(3)] 9 66
(J R Boyle) *hld up in last trio: swtchd lft and hdwy on outer 2f out: no imp fnl f* **14/1**

0326 **6** 5 **Sand Repeal (IRE)**[3] 6188 7-10-5 **63** oh6 MrRBirkett[(5)] 6 56
(Miss J Feilden) *t.k.h: mostly chsd ldr tl over 2f out: wknd over 1f out: wl btn fnl f* **14/1**

6023 **7** 1¼ **Watson's Bay**[10] 5975 4-10-9 **65** MrPCollington[(3)] 8 56
(P Howling) *stdd s: t.k.h: hld up in last pl: swtchd lft and hdwy 2f out: sn no imp: wl btn whn stmbld towards fin* **9/2**[2]

1364 **8** *hd* **Gloucester**[28] 4988 6-11-7 **77** MrSTwiston-Davies[(3)] 4 68+
(M J Scudamore) *t.k.h: hld up in tch: hdwy to trck ldrs wl over 2f out: rdn and fnd nil wl over 1f out: btn and n.m.r sn after* **5/1**[3]

1423 **9** 3 **Drawn Gold**[35] 5210 5-10-5 **63** oh1 MrStephenHarrison[(5)] 3 49+
(R Hollinshead) *dwlt: racd wd: in tch tl lost pl and rdn bnd 3f out: sn wl btn* **11/2**

-030 **10** 12 **Sagarich (FR)**[5] 4893 5-10-3 **63** oh13 MrJMQuinlan[(7)] 2 31
(M G Quinlan) *t.k.h: chsd ldr tl led over 7f out: hdd over 3f out: sn lost pl u.p: wl bhd fnl 2f* **40/1**

2m 35.23s (2.73) **Going Correction** +0.05s/f (Good) **10** Ran SP% **118.7**
Speed ratings (Par 105): **92,91,90,89,88 85,84,84,82,74**
toteswingers: 1&2 £24.10, 1&3 £35.70, 2&3 £7.10 CSF £113.06 CT £529.07 TOTE £47.50: £7.00, £1.60, £2.10; EX 113.40 Trifecta £619.30 Pool: £1355.94 - 1.62 winning units. Place 6:£40.82 Place 5: £33.44.
Owner Mark Rimell **Bred** Mrs M R T Rimell **Trained** Leafield, Oxon

FOCUS
An open and competitive handicap for gentleman amateur riders. There was no real pace on early but the form is pretty straightforward.
Watson's Bay Official explanation: vet said colt returned lame on its near-fore
T/Jkpt: Not won. T/Plt: £52.20 to a £1 stake. Pool: £129,723.08. 1,813.33 winning tickets. T/Qpdt: £39.70 to a £1 stake. Pool: £6,297.48. 117.22 winning tickets. SP

5957 HAYDOCK (L-H)
Friday, September 25

OFFICIAL GOING: Good to firm (good in places 1m & further; 6f 8.4, 1m & 1m 2f 8.3)
Rail realignment increased advertised distancs on round course by 16yds.
Wind: Light, half- against Weather: Cloudy

6245 VALE UK MAIDEN FILLIES' STKS 6f
2:10 (2:13) (Class 5) 2-Y-O **£3,238** (£963; £481; £240) **Stalls** Centre

Form RPR

0 **1** **Plume**[22] 5605 2-9-0 0 DaneO'Neill 11 77+
(R Hannon) *w ldr: led over 3f out: rdn and hung lft over 1f out: r.o wl to draw clr ins fnl f: eased cl home* **7/4**[1]

0 **2** 4½ **Posy Fossil (USA)**[33] 5284 2-9-0 0 SaleemGolam 13 63
(S C Williams) *s.i.s: sn trckd ldrs: effrt over 2f out: kpt on to take 2nd wl ins fnl f: no ch w wnr* **9/2**[2]

3 1¼ **Coin From Heaven (IRE)** 2-8-10 0 PaulHanagan 10 55
(R A Fahey) *chsd ldrs: wnt 2nd over 2f out: rdn over 1f out: no imp on wnr ent fnl f: lost 2nd and no ex wl ins fnl f* **6/1**[3]

0 **4** *hd* **Shelfah (IRE)**[22] 5605 2-9-0 0 PhilipRobinson 5 58
(M A Jarvis) *in tch: rdn and nt qckn 2f out: styd on u.p wl ins fnl f: nt pce of ldrs* **13/2**

5 *hd* **Princess Lexi (IRE)** 2-8-10 0 TonyHamilton 7 54+
(K A Ryan) *bhd: rn green: hdwy 2f out: kpt on steadily ins fnl f: should improve* **25/1**

5 **6** 3 **Hathaway (IRE)**[132] 2089 2-9-0 0 EddieAhern 12 49
(W M Brisbourne) *midfield: pushed along 3f out: plugged on at one pce fnl 2f* **11/1**

002 **7** 6 **Mooinooi**[11] 5949 2-9-0 0 (p) GrahamGibbons 8 31
(T D Walford) *chsd ldrs: rdn over 2f out: wknd over 1f out* **9/1**

0 **8** 4 **Ramayana (IRE)**[7] 6055 2-9-0 0 SamHitchcott 9 19
(M R Channon) *in rr div: pused along 2f out: nvr able to get on terms w ldrs* **25/1**

9 6 **Bravo Blue (IRE)** 2-8-10 0 LPKeniry 4 —
(T H Caldwell) *a bhd: nvr on terms* **50/1**

00 **10** 1¼ **Titoli Di Coda (IRE)**[62] 4302 2-8-7 0 JPFahy[(7)] 6 —
(L M Cumani) *midfield: rdn over 2f out: wknd over 1f out* **33/1**

11 ¾ **Bullet Duck (IRE)** 2-8-10 0 RichardSmith 3 —
(Tom Dascombe) *missed break: rn green: a bhd* **66/1**

00 **12** ¾ **Lady Compton**[24] 5553 2-9-0 0 GregFairley 1 —
(R Bastiman) *wnt lft s: in tch: wknd over 2f out* **66/1**

00 **13** ¾ **Princess Neenee (IRE)**[28] 5408 2-8-9 0 (t) PaulPickard[(5)] 2 —
(Paul Green) *midfield: pushed along over 4f out: wknd over 2f out* **80/1**

6356 **14** 1½ **Sweet Mirasol (IRE)**[31] 5325 2-9-0 63 JamieSpencer 14 —
(K A Ryan) *led: hdd over 3f out: wknd over 2f out* **12/1**

1m 15.24s (0.74) **Going Correction** +0.10s/f (Good) **14** Ran SP% **125.0**
Speed ratings (Par 92): **99,93,91,91,90 86,78,73,65,63 62,61,60,58**
toteswingers: 1&2 £4.00, 1&3 £3.90, 2&3 £7.30 CSF £9.06 TOTE £2.80: £1.60, £2.20, £2.10; EX 14.20.
Owner Highclere Thoroughbred Racing Touchstone **Bred** James Robert Mitchell **Trained** East Everleigh, Wilts

FOCUS
This opening event was an ordinary maiden for fillies which seemed to lack strength in depth and is not easy to pin down, but the winner did the job in great style.

NOTEBOOK
Plume ◆ was a massive mover throughout the day. She was backed at 14-1 on the exchanges in the morning and sent off as 7-4 favourite. She travelled smoothly up with the pace, forged clear inside the final 2f and ran out an easy winner. It is hard to say what the form amounts to and there did seem to be an advantage to race towards the stands' rail, but the style of victory was impressive and represents a major leap forward from her debut 11th over 7f on soft ground at Salisbury. She has plenty of scope for physical progression and could go on to better things. (op 9-4 tchd 11-4)

Posy Fossil(USA) did not show a great deal when 33-1 on debut over 7f at Folkestone but she attracted some support this time and stuck to her task well in the vain pursuit of the winner. She is related to several winners and was bought back for 56,000gns at the sales in April. Open to improvement, she should be able to win a similar event. (op 13-2 tchd 7-1)

Coin From Heaven(IRE) was always prominent and shaped with plenty of promise on debut behind two experienced rivals. She is the third foal of a dam still waiting for a first winner but is by a stallion who gets plenty of two-year-old winners. (op 5-1 tchd 9-2)

Shelfah(IRE) had a tricky draw from stall five and was forced to race up the centre of the track, but she plugged on quite well and put a debut disappointment on soft ground behind her. (op 7-1 tchd 8-1)

Princess Lexi(IRE) weaved her way into a never-nearer fifth from a long way back. This was a promising debut effort by the daughter of Rock Of Gibraltar, particularly as this trip is likely to prove a bare minimum this season. (op 22-1)

Hathaway(IRE) kept responding after being scrubbed along some way stepped up in trip on her second start after four months off. She should be sharper next time but needs to develop a bit more tactical speed to make a big impact in a similar event. (op 12-1 tchd 10-1)

Mooinooi was second at 40-1 behind an 85-rated runaway winner at Redcar last week but put in a very tame effort with first-time cheekpieces applied. (op 10-1 tchd 8-1)

6246 VALE UK MAIDEN STKS (C&G) 6f

2:45 (2:45) (Class 5) 2-Y-O **£3,238** (£963; £481; £240) **Stalls** Centre

Form				RPR
24	1		**Atlaal (USA)**[38] 5129 2-9-0 0 ... RHills 3	72+
			(M A Jarvis) *a little fractious in stalls: chsd ldr: eased into ld over 2f out: shkn up to draw clr over 1f out: wl in command after* **1/5**[1]	
05	2	6	**Sharp Shoes**[40] 5066 2-9-0 0 ... PhillipMakin 5	52+
			(Mrs A Duffield) *chsd ldrs: rdn and outpcd over 2f out: kpt on to take 2nd wl ins fnl f: no ch w wnr* **33/1**	
0	3	2 1/4	**Marius Maximus (IRE)**[19] 5693 2-9-0 0 ... GregFairley 6	41
			(M Johnston) *led: rdn and hdd over 2f out: outpcd and no ch w wnr over 1f out: wknd and lost 2nd wl ins fnl f* **7/1**[2]	
65	4	17	**Maragna (IRE)**[10] 5958 2-9-0 0 ... RobertWinston 4	—
			(Paul Green) *in tch: rdn and outpcd over 3f out: wl btn over 2f out* **12/1**[3]	
60	5	4	**Mr Prize Fighter**[20] 5669 2-9-0 0 ... DNolan 2	—
			(I W McInnes) *in tch: lost pl after 2f: struggling and bhd after* **33/1**	
0	6	2	**Ancient Oak**[10] 5957 2-9-0 0 ... TomEaves 1	—
			(H A McWilliams) *sn bhd: toiling after 2f: nvr on terms* **100/1**	

1m 15.72s (1.22) **Going Correction** +0.10s/f (Good) **6** Ran SP% **110.4**

Speed ratings (Par 95): **95,87,84,61,56 53**

toteswingers: 1&2 £3.30, 1&3 £1.10, 2&3 £3.90 CSF £12.24 TOTE £1.10: £1.02, £9.30; EX 9.40.

Owner Hamdan Al Maktoum **Bred** Jaime S Carrion, Trustee **Trained** Newmarket, Suffolk

FOCUS

An uncompetitive maiden and a straightforward success for the favourite against weak opposition.

NOTEBOOK

Atlaal(USA) was turned over at 1-4 at Nottingham last time but, taking on a much lower calibre of opposition, still set the standard. He travelled well for most of the way, hit the front approaching the 2f pole and powered clear for a comfortable success. This win told us anything new about the $410,000 colt but it should have boosted his confidence. He ought to be capable of much better and it will be interesting to see what opening mark he receives from the Handicapper. (op 2-9)

Sharp Shoes had beaten just one horse in two 5f maidens at Pontefract and Thirsk. Upped in trip, he settled better off the decent pace and stayed on quite well. He is flattered by his proximity to the eased down winner but this was a definite step in the right direction from a colt who is out of a prolific sprint winner.

Marius Maximus(IRE) went out like a light after leading early on his debut at York early this month and it was a similar story this time. He cost plenty at the breeze-up sales and seems to have a lot of natural pace, but he is one to watch until he starts lasting longer in races. (op 6-1)

Maragna(IRE) was in serious trouble at halfway.

Mr Prize Fighter was not seen to any better effect faced with his sharpest test so far.

6247 VALE UK NURSERY 6f

3:20 (3:22) (Class 4) (0-80,80) 2-Y-O **£4,857** (£1,445; £722; £360) **Stalls** Centre

Form				RPR
1122	1		**Mister Hughie (IRE)**[7] 6048 2-9-6 **79** ... SamHitchcott 14	86
			(M R Channon) *hld up: hdwy 2f out: rdn 1f out: sn led: r.o wl and plld away towards fin* **7/2**[2]	
0150	2	2 1/4	**Coolree Star (IRE)**[21] 5635 2-8-9 **68** ... TonyHamilton 5	68
			(J A Glover) *rrd s: sn prom: led over 2f out: rdn over 1f out: hdd jst ins fnl f: nt qckn towards fin* **20/1**	
624	3	1/2	**Lava Lamp (GER)**[15] 5785 2-9-0 **73** ... GregFairley 13	72
			(M Johnston) *in rr: swtchd lft and pushed along over 2f out: hdwy over 1f out: styd on ins fnl f: clsng at fin: nt pce to mount a serious chal* **8/1**	
2326	4	nk	**Bush Master**[23] 5564 2-8-10 **69** ... DaneO'Neill 2	67
			(R Hannon) *awkward s: hld up: hdwy over 2f out: rdn whn chsd ldrs over 1f out: styd on same pce fnl 100yds* **33/1**	
31	5	1	**Five Cents**[15] 5801 2-9-3 **79** ... AhmedAjtebi(3) 11	74
			(Saeed Bin Suroor) *a.p: rdn to chal over 2f out: no ex fnl 100yds* **5/2**[1]	
15	6	2 1/4	**Petougg**[45] 4883 2-9-1 **77** ... FrederikTylicki(3) 3	65
			(W Jarvis) *chsd ldrs: chal 2f out: rdn over 1f out: wknd fnl 100yds* **16/1**	
426	7	1/2	**Crushing (IRE)**[83] 3606 2-8-8 **67** ... TomEaves 12	54
			(T D Barron) *in tch: rdn and swtchd lft over 1f out: one pce fnl f* **8/1**	
1200	8	4	**Ballodair (IRE)**[38] 5136 2-9-6 **79** ... PaulHanagan 8	54
			(R A Fahey) *midfield: pushed along 3f out: wknd wl over 1f out* **7/1**[3]	
2125	9	1/2	**Gillburg (USA)**[13] 5853 2-9-3 **76** ... (b) JamieSpencer 10	49
			(K A Ryan) *led: hdd over 2f out: wknd over 1f out* **9/1**	
405	10	2 1/4	**Almuntaser (IRE)**[69] 4075 2-7-13 **63** ow4 ... MartinLane(5) 7	29
			(Ian Williams) *missed break: towards rr: rdn 3f out: wl btn 2f out* **66/1**	
001	11	1/2	**Avongate**[54] 4568 2-9-7 **80** ... EddieAhern 1	45
			(R Hannon) *in tch: wknd ent fnl 2f* **22/1**	

1m 14.95s (0.45) **Going Correction** +0.10s/f (Good) **11** Ran SP% **114.9**

Speed ratings (Par 97): **101,98,97,96,95 92,91,86,85,82 82**

toteswingers: 1&2 £24.00, 1&3 £5.90, 2&3 £40.90 CSF £74.98 CT £532.49 TOTE £4.50: £1.60, £6.40, £2.80; EX 115.40.

Owner Liam Mulryan **Bred** Mcmac Syndicate **Trained** West Ilsley, Berks

FOCUS

A decent nursery run at a strong pace. The first five finished clear of the rest and the time was quicker than both previous maiden contests. The form looks solid but somewhat limited.

NOTEBOOK

Mister Hughie(IRE) scythed his way through some potential traffic problems against the near rail and quickened up well to register his third win of the season. He is due to go up 3lb from tomorrow and may receive some additional punishment for this success, but he is a tough and genuine performer who is tactically versatile and should be able to win more races. (tchd 3-1)

Coolree Star(IRE) had hung and raced awkwardly in two runs for his current yard since getting the better of a sustained tussle in a Yarmouth seller in July. The return to a straight track on fast turf seems to have suited him and he deserves plenty of credit for hanging in there after dictating the decent pace up the centre of the track. (op 25-1 tchd 28-1)

Lava Lamp(GER) ◆ flashed home after being switched from the near rail to the middle of the track. He may not have handled the undulations at Chepstow last time but bounced back with a promising effort. He is a half-brother to top-class Lady Marian, a 1m3f-1m4f winner at three, and to useful German miler Lucidor. He should be capable of further progress and both his style of racing and pedigree suggest he is worth another try at 7f. (tchd 17-2)

Bush Master tracked the speed down the centre of the track but could not find the gears needed to pose a big threat. He was too keen over 7f last time and this could prove to be his optimum trip, but he has a bit to find on the balance of his form to live up to this mark. (tchd 28-1)

Five Cents ran respectably on his nursery debut but looked a bit short of tactical pace in his bid to add to his 7f Epsom maiden win over a 77-rated rival last month. A return to 7f should suit and remains capable of better off a fair mark of 79. (op 9-4, tchd 11-4 in a place)

6248 VALE UK (S) STKS 1m 2f 95y

3:55 (3:56) (Class 4) 3-4-Y-O **£6,476** (£1,927; £963; £481) **Stalls** Centre

Form				RPR
0112	1		**Buddhist Monk**[4] 6172 4-9-10 80 ... (t) JamieSpencer 3	77+
			(Ian Williams) *in tch gng wl: led wl over 1f out: sn rdn and hung lft: kpt on wl and on top at fin* **6/4**[1]	
3346	2	1 1/4	**Pyrus Time (IRE)**[29] 5366 3-9-0 71 ... JamesDoyle 6	71
			(J S Moore) *stdd s: hld up: hdwy 2f out: rdn to chal over 1f out: edgd lft ins fnl f: nt qckn* **10/1**	
5665	3	1 1/4	**Quinsman**[50] 4691 3-9-0 64 ... LPKeniry 1	69+
			(J S Moore) *in tch: rdn to chse ldrs 2f out: styd on same pce fnl f* **20/1**	
2533	4	1/2	**Oriental Cavalier**[13] 5858 3-9-0 70 ... (p) GrahamGibbons 4	69+
			(R Hollinshead) *chsd ldr: nosed ahd 3f out: rdn and hdd wl over 1f out: stl cl 3rd whn n.m.r and hmpd 1f out: eased whn no further imp fnl 100yds* **15/8**[2]	
1201	5	8	**Applaude**[8] 6012 4-9-10 68 ... (b) PhillipMakin 2	56
			(John A Harris) *s.i.s: hld up: pushed along and outpcd 3f out: edgd rt whn struggling 2f out: n.d after* **11/2**[3]	
5040	6	2	**Stellar Cause (USA)**[11] 5940 3-9-0 68 ... EddieAhern 5	48
			(P F I Cole) *led: hdd 3f out: wknd over 2f out* **10/1**	
6	7	32	**Kinetic Art (IRE)**[79] 3731 4-9-3 0 ... MichaelJStainton(3) 7	—
			(R M Whitaker) *chsd ldrs: pushed along 5f out: wknd 4f out: t.o* **100/1**	

2m 13.77s (0.77) **Going Correction** +0.10s/f (Good)

WFA 3 from 4yo 6lb **7** Ran SP% **114.1**

Speed ratings (Par 105): **100,99,98,97,91 89,64**

toteswingers: 1&2 £3.40, 1&3 £6.10, 2&3 £17.30 CSF £17.55 TOTE £2.40: £1.30, £4.80; EX 16.90.The winner was bought in for £16,000.

Owner Dr Marwan Koukash **Bred** Stanley Estate And Stud Co **Trained** Portway, Worcs

FOCUS

Not a bad seller in which all seven runners had official ratings between 64 and 80. The pace was steady and it got messy in the closing stages.

Applaude Official explanation: jockey said gelding hung right

6249 GRIFFITHS & ARMOUR H'CAP 1m 30y

4:30 (4:31) (Class 3) (0-95,94) 3-Y-O+

£8,723 (£2,612; £1,306; £653; £326; £163) **Stalls** Low

Form				RPR
30	1		**Mull Of Killough (IRE)**[27] 5419 3-9-1 **91** ... JamieSpencer 6	102
			(J L Spearing) *trckd ldrs: rdn to chal 2f out: led over 1f out: kpt on wl towards fin* **4/1**[3]	
0033	2	1/2	**Light From Mars**[35] 5221 4-9-2 **91** ... FrederikTylicki(3) 5	101
			(B R Millman) *midfield: hdwy 3f out: rdn to chal fr over 1f out: kpt on but looked hld fnl 100yds* **7/2**[2]	
3056	3	2	**Ezdeyaad (USA)**[8] 6014 5-8-9 **81** ... RobertWinston 8	86
			(G A Swinbank) *racd keenly: chsd ldrs: led 4f out: rdn and hdd over 1f out: styd on same pce ins fnl f* **12/1**	
6103	4	nk	**Reel Buddy Star**[22] 5598 4-8-10 **82** ... DanielTudhope 11	86
			(G M Moore) *a.p: rdn over 2f out: nt qckn over 1f out: styd on same pce ins fnl f* **25/1**	
0005	5	1	**Yorgunnabelucky (USA)**[14] 5832 3-8-7 **83** ... JoeFanning 1	85
			(M Johnston) *midfield: rdn over 2f out: styd on ins fnl f: nt pce to chal ldrs* **16/1**	
1114	6	1 1/4	**The Cayterers**[61] 4339 7-9-2 **91** ... MCGeran(3) 4	90
			(A W Carroll) *hld up: rdn 2f out: kpt on ins fnl f: nvr able to chal* **14/1**	
0321	7	nse	**Faithful Ruler (USA)**[8] 6014 5-9-1 **87** 6ex ... PaulHanagan 7	85
			(R A Fahey) *s.i.s: in rr: checked 2f out: nvr able to get on terms* **5/2**[1]	
1100	8	1	**City Of The Kings (IRE)**[25] 5522 4-9-3 **94** ... PatrickDonaghy(5) 2	90
			(G A Harker) *hld up: pushed along 2f out: nvr on terms* **25/1**	
0603	9	1 1/4	**Dunn'o (IRE)**[13] 5874 4-9-8 **94** ... PhilipRobinson 9	87
			(C G Cox) *led: hdd 4f out: rdn over 2f out: wknd over 1f out* **9/2**	
105	10	3	**Just Bond (IRE)**[13] 5887 7-8-13 **85** ... PJMcDonald 10	71
			(G R Oldroyd) *bhd: pushed along over 2f out: lost tch fnl f* **16/1**	

1m 43.46s (-0.34) **Going Correction** +0.10s/f (Good)

WFA 3 from 4yo+ 4lb **10** Ran SP% **122.8**

Speed ratings (Par 107): **105,104,102,102,101 99,99,98,97,94**

toteswingers: 1&2 £4.60, 1&3 £10.50, 2&3 £11.00 CSF £19.57 CT £156.86 TOTE £5.20: £1.70, £1.80, £3.50; EX 15.40.

Owner Noel B Lawless **Bred** Owenstown Stud **Trained** Kinnersley, Worcs

FOCUS

A decent handicap run at a fair pace. The first three home came across to the middle to near side in the straight, and for the fifth year in a row the race was won by a fairly unexposed 3yo. The form looks reasonable rated around those in the frame behind the winner.

NOTEBOOK

Mull Of Killough(IRE) missed several engagements during the summer and had a bit to prove after running well below his best over 1m2f last time, but he bounced back in good style dropped back to 1m and has added to his wins at Thirsk and Warwick on his first two starts. He seems to have a good attitude, should not go up much for this win and remains capable of further improvement. (op 9-2)

Light From Mars fought hard but could not wear down the winner in the closing stages. He does not have much margin for error off this mark but is a likeable type who has finished in the money more often than not since making a winning reappearance over 8.5f at Windsor in April. (op 5-1 tchd 11-2)

Ezdeyaad(USA) was brushed aside after making an enterprising move down the middle of the track early in the straight but he did quite well to hang on for third after it looked like he might drop away.

Reel Buddy Star did best of those who stayed towards the far side and emerges with some credit, but he has found life difficult since getting hit hard for a clear-cut all-the-way win at Newcastle last month. (op 28-1 tchd 22-1)

Yorgunnabelucky(USA) was never a factor. He looked promising when running away with a weak 1m2f Redcar maiden in June but has not gone on in handicaps since.

The Cayterers has made dramatic progress since joining his current yard and is competing at a much higher level than ever looked likely. He could not into the main action off the steady gallop here and should do better off a stronger pace next time, but the Handicapper may have caught up with him. Official explanation: jockey said gelding hung right in straight (op 12-1)

Faithful Ruler(USA) was a devastating winner at Ayr last week but put in a lacklustre effort under a penalty and may not have acted on this faster ground. Official explanation: jockey said gelding never travelled (op 9-4 tchd 3-1)

6250 BET ONLINE AT CORBETTSPORTS.COM P.J.A. APPRENTICE SERIES H'CAP 1m 30y

5:05 (5:05) (Class 4) (0-80,80) 3-Y-O+ **£5,504** (£1,637; £818; £408) **Stalls** Low

Form RPR

0325 **1** **Tiger Dream**[3] 6178 4-8-8 **69**...(p) AmyRyan(3) 7 78
(K A Ryan) *towards rr: hdwy over 3f out: rdn to ld over 1f out: sn edgd rt: kpt on wl towards fin* **11/2**[3]

4220 **2** ½ **Handsome Falcon**[30] 5333 5-9-3 **75**... FrederikTylicki 10 83
(R A Fahey) *stmbld s: hld up: hdwy 3f out: rdn over 2f out: chsd wnr ins fnl f: kpt on but nvr gng to get there* **7/2**[2]

30/2 **3** 1 ½ **Prince Picasso**[16] 5772 6-8-11 **76**... LeeTopliss(7) 5 81
(R A Fahey) *led: hrd pressed 3f out: bmpd over 2f out: hdd over 1f out: styd on same pce ins fnl f* **11/1**

-345 **4** 1 ¾ **Burma Rock (IRE)**[30] 5349 3-8-9 **76**... JPFahy(5) 2 77
(L M Cumani) *hld up: hdwy over 1f out: styd on ins fnl f: nt pce to get competitive* **13/2**

3150 **5** ¾ **Dr Jameson (IRE)**[13] 5858 3-8-1 **70**... MarzenaJeziorek(7) 8 69+
(R A Fahey) *midfield: hdwy 4f out: chal fr 3f out: bmpd over 2f out: fdd ins fnl f* **25/1**

0206 **6** nk **Johnmanderville**[36] 5189 3-8-12 **77**...(p) MartinLane(3) 3 76+
(A P Jarvis) *trckd ldrs: chal 3f out: nt qckning whn n.m.r and hmpd over 2f out: sn lost grnd: kpt on ins fnl f but no imp on ldrs* **8/1**

6660 **7** 1 ½ **Nevada Desert (IRE)**[51] 4663 9-8-8 **66**... MichaelJStainton 9 61
(R M Whitaker) *midfield: lost pl and bmpd over 2f out: n.d after* **20/1**

2203 **8** 1 ½ **Snow Dancer (IRE)**[27] 5441 5-8-5 **66**...(b) PatrickDonaghy(3) 14 58
(H A McWilliams) *slow into stride: racd keenly: prom after 1f: rdn over 3f out: wknd over 2f out* **12/1**

5313 **9** 1 ¼ **Entreat**[9] 5997 3-9-1 **80**...(v) Louis-PhilippeBeuzelin(3) 12 69
(Sir Michael Stoute) *trckd ldrs: chal 3f out: hung lft over 2f out: wknd over 1f out* **11/4**[1]

3030 **10** 3 ¼ **Timber Treasure (USA)**[8] 6017 5-8-8 **69**...(b) PaulPickard(3) 13 51
(Paul Green) *midfield: effrt 3f out: wknd over 1f out* **16/1**

0106 **11** 3 **Bahamian Kid**[71] 4019 4-8-13 **71**...(p) RussellKennemore 11 46
(R Hollinshead) *in rr: hdwy 3f out: no imp on ldrs: wknd over 1f out* **50/1**

1m 44.44s (0.64) **Going Correction** +0.10s/f (Good)
WFA 3 from 4yo+ 4lb **11 Ran SP% 121.2**
Speed ratings (Par 105): **100,99,98,96,95 95,93,92,90,87 84**
toteswingers: 1&2 £4.70, 1&3 £11.00, 2&3 £9.70 CSF £25.38 CT £211.19 TOTE £7.30: £2.10, £1.70, £3.00; EX 30.40 Place 6: £34.30 Place 5: £27.05.
Owner Mrs Angie Bailey & Mrs T Marnane **Bred** Grundy Bloodstock Srl **Trained** Hambleton, N Yorks
■ Stewards' Enquiry : Frederik Tylicki caution: used whip without giving gelding time to respond
Amy Ryan caution: careless riding
Louis-Philippe Beuzelin four-day ban: careless riding (Oct 9-12)

FOCUS
A reasonable apprentice handicap run at a good pace and the winner is rated back to the best of this year's form. Things got a bit rough in the straight.
T/Plt: £75.90 to a £1 stake. Pool: £54,486.23. 523.94 winning tickets. T/Qpdt: £43.40 to a £1 stake. Pool: £3,461.13. 59.00 winning tickets. DO

6119 WOLVERHAMPTON (A.W) (L-H)

Friday, September 25

OFFICIAL GOING: Standard
Wind: Almost nil Weather: Fine

6251 WILLIAMHILL.COM/BONUS25 - GET £25 FREE BET H'CAP 5f 216y(P)

5:45 (5:45) (Class 6) (0-55,58) 3-Y-O+ **£2,729** (£806; £403) **Stalls** Low

Form RPR

404 **1** **Castano**[15] 5788 5-9-1 **54**... JamesMillman(3) 6 61
(B R Millman) *hld up: c wd st: rdn and hdwy 1f out: r.o wl to ld last strides* **4/1**[2]

3630 **2** hd **Miss Firefly**[15] 5792 4-9-0 **53**... WilliamCarson(3) 13 60+
(R J Hodges) *broke wl: sn hld up in rr: swtchd lft and str run ins fnl f: r.o to take 2nd last strides* **14/1**

5031 **3** nk **Decider (USA)**[6] 6119 6-9-1 **58** 6ex...(p) SPRyan(7) 1 64
(R A Harris) *sn chsng ldr: led over 3f out: rdn over 1f out: hdd last strides* **3/1**[1]

U235 **4** hd **Towy Boy (IRE)**[15] 5792 4-8-13 **54**...(vt) RossAtkinson(5) 11 59
(I A Wood) *t.k.h: sn in tch: rdn over 1f out: edgd lft ins fnl f: r.o* **8/1**

3023 **5** ½ **The History Man (IRE)**[6] 6119 6-8-11 **54**...(b) DavidKenny(7) 9 57
(B D Leavy) *sn prom: ev ch over 2f out: rdn wl over 1f out: nt qckn wl ins fnl f* **7/1**

6436 **6** 1 **Bahkov (IRE)**[28] 5384 3-8-11 **54**... SimonPearce(5) 5 54
(Andrew Turnell) *chsd ldr early: a.p: rdn over 1f out: no ex ins fnl f* **6/1**[3]

0040 **7** ¾ **Well Of Echoes**[9] 5982 3-9-3 **55**...(t) RoystonFfrench 10 53
(J A Glover) *led: hdd over 3f out: rdn wl over 2f out: wknd over 1f out* **25/1**

030- **8** 1 ½ **Gracie's Games**[280] 7734 3-9-3 **55**... StephenDonohoe 2 48
(R J Price) *s.i.s: in rr: pushed along over 3f out: rdn wl over 1f out: nvr trbld ldrs* **33/1**

5005 **9** 1 ½ **Admiral Bond (IRE)**[6] 6119 4-8-12 **55**...(p) AnthonyBetts(7) 3 43
(G R Oldroyd) *hld up: rdn over 1f out: no rspnse* **11/1**

5650 **10** 2 ½ **Rydal (USA)**[104] 2921 8-9-2 **52**...(v) IanMongan 8 32
(Miss Jo Crowley) *prom tl wknd 2f out* **9/1**

1m 14.79s (-0.21) **Going Correction** -0.125s/f (Stan)
WFA 3 from 4yo+ 2lb **10 Ran SP% 114.7**
Speed ratings (Par 101): **96,95,95,95,94 93,92,90,88,84**
toteswingers: 1&2 £10.30, 1&3 £3.40, 2&3 £9.50 CSF £57.52 CT £194.81 TOTE £3.90: £2.00, £3.50, £1.20; EX 62.40.
Owner H G Gooding & Mrs A A Gooding **Bred** Mrs V J Bjerke & Mrs E K Tope-Ottesen **Trained** Kentisbeare, Devon
■ Stewards' Enquiry : William Carson one-day ban: careless riding (Oct 9)

FOCUS
Exposed performers in a moderate handicap, where the gallop was decent and the principals finished in a heap. The winner raced in the centre in the straight and the form is sound enough.

6252 WILLIAMHILL.COM/BONUS25 - POKER TOURNAMENTS (S) STKS 5f 216y(P)

6:20 (6:22) (Class 6) 3-4-Y-O **£2,047** (£604; £302) **Stalls** Low

Form RPR

436F **1** **Romantic Queen**[53] 4604 3-8-8 **68**...(t) MatthewDavies(5) 3 67+
(George Baker) *hld up towards rr: hdwy on ins wl over 1f out: rdn to ld ins fnl f: r.o wl* **13/2**[3]

4240 **2** 1 ½ **Kingsgate Castle**[2] 6216 4-9-0 **56**...(v) StephenDonohoe 10 61
(Miss Gay Kelleway) *chsd ldr: led wl over 1f out: sn rdn and edgd lft: hdd ins fnl f: no ex* **11/4**[1]

0044 **3** 1 ½ **Kinigi (IRE)**[4] 6170 3-8-8 **56**...(p) RossAtkinson(5) 2 57
(R A Harris) *hld up in tch: nt clr run and swtchd lft over 1f out: swtchd rt ins fnl f: r.o one pce* **8/1**

0000 **4** nse **Yanza**[23] 5584 3-8-13 **64**... SteveDrowne 12 57
(J R Gask) *hld up in mid-div: rdn wl over 1f out: r.o ins fnl f* **8/1**

100 **5** ½ **Athaakeel (IRE)**[4] 6170 3-8-13 **63**... KevinGhunowa 8 55
(R A Harris) *hld up and bhd: c wd st: rdn and hdwy over 1f out: kpt on same pce ins fnl f* **12/1**

6363 **6** ½ **Halcyon Dancer**[22] 5599 3-8-7 **55**... TomEaves 4 48
(M Dods) *s.i.s: t.k.h in rr: pushed along over 2f out: rdn wl over 1f out: kpt on ins fnl f: nvr trbld ldrs* **11/2**[2]

0100 **7** hd **Theta Wave (USA)**[18] 5716 3-9-4 **62**...(p) RobertHavlin 9 58
(J R Gask) *hld up in tch: rdn over 1f out: one pce* **12/1**

0000 **8** 1 ¾ **Deo Valente (IRE)**[25] 5502 4-9-0 **58**...(p) LPKeniry 1 47
(J M Bradley) *led: rdn and hdd wl over 1f out: swtchd rt jst ins fnl f: sn wknd* **12/1**

5 **9** ½ **Fast Living**[80] 3712 4-9-0 **0**... RoystonFfrench 6 46
(A M Hales) *prom: rdn jst over 1f out: wknd ins fnl f* **33/1**

6000 **10** ½ **Fantasy Land (IRE)**[10] 5972 3-8-7 **60**...(bt) EddieAhern 5 39
(B J Meehan) *hld up in mid-div: rdn and no imp whn nt clr run jst ins fnl f* **14/1**

6000 **11** ½ **Trip Switch**[9] 5989 3-9-4 **67**...(b) DarryllHolland 11 49
(W R Muir) *a in rr* **18/1**

1m 14.84s (-0.16) **Going Correction** -0.125s/f (Stan)
WFA 3 from 4yo 2lb **11 Ran SP% 115.6**
Speed ratings (Par 101): **96,94,92,91,91 90,90,88,87,86 86**
toteswingers: 1&2 £4.50, 1&3 £13.30, 2&3 £6.20 CSF £24.17 TOTE £7.90: £2.30, £1.60, £2.20; EX 23.40.There was no bid for the winner.
Owner The Betfair Radioheads **Bred** G B Turnbull Ltd **Trained** Moreton Morrell, Warwicks

FOCUS
Not too many reliable or in-form types in an ordinary seller. The pace was sound and the winner raced against the inside rail in the straight. She matched her previous best.
Trip Switch Official explanation: jockey said gelding moved poorly throughout

6253 WILLIAMHILL.COM/BONUS25 - QUOTE BONUS25 H'CAP 5f 20y(P)

6:50 (6:51) (Class 4) (0-85,85) 3-Y-O+ **£5,046** (£1,510; £755; £377; £188) **Stalls** Low

Form RPR

605- **1** **Mondovi**[385] 5681 5-9-0 **85**... RossAtkinson(5) 3 96+
(Tom Dascombe) *hld up in mid-div: hdwy on ins wl over 1f out: led jst ins fnl f: sn hung rt: r.o* **8/1**

2032 **2** 1 **Feelin Foxy**[16] 5768 5-8-12 **78**... TPQueally 8 85
(J G Given) *led: rdn and hdd jst ins fnl f: kpt on* **15/2**[3]

2005 **3** hd **Ivory Silk**[14] 5830 4-9-4 **84**...(b) SteveDrowne 9 91
(J R Gask) *hld up and bhd: pushed along over 3f out: c wd st: rdn and hdwy whn edgd lft ins fnl f: r.o* **9/1**

3220 **4** 1 ¼ **Garstang**[25] 5518 6-8-12 **78**...(b) IanMongan 2 80
(J Balding) *a.p: rdn whn sltly bmpd 1f out: kpt on same pce* **6/1**[2]

0500 **5** ¾ **Little Pete (IRE)**[56] 4485 4-9-5 **85**...(t) LPKeniry 6 84
(A M Balding) *hld up and bhd: pushed along over 3f out: rdn over 2f out: kpt on ins fnl f: nvr nrr* **8/1**

0603 **6** nse **Chjimes (IRE)**[36] 5197 5-9-2 **82**... TravisBlock 4 81
(C R Dore) *s.i.s: outpcd in rr: hdwy on ins wl over 1f out: rdn ins fnl f: one pce* **16/1**

5122 **7** 1 ¾ **Cape Royal**[12] 5919 9-8-9 **75**...(bt) KevinGhunowa 11 68
(J M Bradley) *prom: w ldr whn hung rt bnd over 2f out: wknd ins fnl f* **20/1**

6300 **8** ¾ **Sir Geoffrey (IRE)**[13] 5856 3-8-5 **72**...(t) RoystonFfrench 7 62
(J A Glover) *bhd: pushed along over 3f out: rdn and struggling over 1f out* **33/1**

0000 **9** ¾ **Almaty Express**[73] 3938 7-8-9 **75**...(b) DarryllHolland 5 63
(J R Weymes) *hld up in mid-div: hdwy over 2f out: wknd wl over 1f out* **20/1**

2-22 **10** 1 ¾ **Sirenuse (IRE)**[37] 5149 3-9-0 **81**... TomEaves 1 62
(B Smart) *racd keenly: prom: rdn and bmpd sltly 1f out: wknd ins fnl f* **7/4**[1]

61.09 secs (-1.21) **Going Correction** -0.125s/f (Stan)
WFA 3 from 4yo+ 1lb **10 Ran SP% 113.0**
Speed ratings (Par 105): **104,102,102,100,98 98,96,94,93,90**
toteswingers: 1&2 £11.10, 1&3 £15.20, 2&3 £11.40 CSF £62.51 CT £560.66 TOTE £10.60: £3.20, £1.70, £2.60; EX 85.90.
Owner K Dyer & C Bellamy **Bred** Branston Stud Ltd **Trained** Lambourn, Berks
■ Tom Dascombe's first winner sent out from Michael Owen's Cheshire yard.
■ Stewards' Enquiry : Ross Atkinson one-day ban: careless riding (Oct 9)

FOCUS
A fair handicap and one run at a strong pace throughout. The first three ended up in the centre in the straight and the winner returned towards her best form.
Garstang Official explanation: jockey said gelding lost a front shoe prior to race
Sirenuse(IRE) Official explanation: vet said filly finished distressed

6254 WILLIAMHILL.COM/BONUS25 - LIVE CASINO DEALERS MAIDEN STKS 7f 32y(P)

7:20 (7:24) (Class 4) 2-Y-O **£3,885** (£1,156; £577; £288) **Stalls** High

Form RPR

20 **1** **Kings Bayonet**[36] 5198 2-9-3 **0**... TPQueally 1 76
(H R A Cecil) *a.p: swtchd rt 2f out: edgd rt over 1f out: led jst ins fnl f: drvn out* **9/4**[1]

0 **2** 1 **Robust Wish (USA)**[15] 5807 2-9-3 **0**... EddieAhern 5 74
(B J Meehan) *hld up in rr: pushed along over 2f out: rdn and hdwy wl over 1f out: r.o u.p to take 2nd wl ins fnl f* **16/1**

3 3 **Major Maximus** 2-8-12 **0**... MatthewDavies(5) 12 66
(George Baker) *hld up in rr: swtchd rt to outside 3f out: hdwy over 2f out: c wd st: rdn and edgd lft over 1f out: one pce ins fnl f* **33/1**

32 **4** *2* **Al Naouwee (USA)**[27] 5440 2-9-3 0.......................... RoystonFfrench 6 61+
(B Smart) *led: rdn and hdd jst ins fnl f: wknd towards fin* **3/1**[2]
06 **5** *3/4* **Be A Devil**[95] 3226 2-9-0 0.......................... RussellKennemore(3) 10 59
(W R Muir) *hld up in mid-div: hdwy on ins wl over 1f out: sn rdn: wknd ins fnl f* **50/1**
5 **6** *1* **Louisiana Gift (IRE)**[15] 5807 2-9-3 0.......................... GeorgeBaker 2 57
(J W Hills) *chsd ldrs: pushed along over 2f out: swtchd lft and rdn over 1f out: wknd ins fnl f* **7/2**[3]
7 *2 1/2* **Bona Fortuna** 2-9-3 0.......................... StephenDonohoe 7 51+
(Sir Mark Prescott) *s.i.s: sn wl in rr: nvr nr ldrs* **20/1**
0 **8** *4 1/2* **Liebelei (USA)**[64] 4226 2-8-12 0.......................... DaneO'Neill 8 35
(H J L Dunlop) *hld up in mid-div: rdn over 2f out: wknd wl over 1f out* **17/2**
3 **9** *4* **Scarboro Warning (IRE)**[20] 5674 2-9-3 0.......................... LeeVickers 9 30+
(J G Given) *sn w ldr: ev ch over 2f out: wknd wl over 1f out* **13/2**
0 **10** *7* **Nurai**[21] 5637 2-8-12 0..........................(t) DarryllHolland 3 8
(P W D'Arcy) *prom tl wknd 2f out* **33/1**
11 *6* **Joury** 2-8-12 0.......................... MickyFenton 4 —
(S A Callaghan) *s.i.s: a wl in rr* **20/1**

1m 28.89s (-0.71) **Going Correction** -0.125s/f (Stan) **11** Ran SP% **125.1**
Speed ratings (Par 97): **99,97,94,92,91 90,87,82,77,69 62**
toteswingers: 1&2 £12.60, 1&3 £19.80, 2&3 £44.70 CSF £41.08 TOTE £3.60: £1.20, £6.20, £7.00; EX 63.70.
Owner W H Ponsonby **Bred** Mickley Stud & C J Whiston **Trained** Newmarket, Suffolk

FOCUS
Not the strongest of maidens and the market leader failed to reproduce his turf form, but there were a couple of interesting performances. The gallop was reasonable and the winner raced centre to stands' side in the straight. He stepped forward slightly on his previous best.

NOTEBOOK
Kings Bayonet, out of his depth in a valuable sales race at York, appreciated the return to this company and, although getting loose in the paddock, did enough to get off the mark after enjoying the run of the race on his all-weather debut and first run over 7f. He should appreciate the step up to 1m and will be interesting in ordinary handicaps. (op 2-1 tchd 11-4)
Robust Wish(USA) had been well beaten on his debut at Kempton but was nibbled at in the market and turned in a much better effort. He should stay 1m and looks capable of picking up an ordinary event on this surface. (op 33-1 tchd 40-1)
Major Maximus ◆, a half-brother to 1m winner Hasty Retreat, shaped well from the widest draw on this racecourse debut. He was forced to make his ground widest of all, was green under pressure and left the impression he would be able to pick up a similar event with this experience behind him. (op 66-1)
Al Naouwee(USA), who looked to have strong claims in this company on his all-weather debut, failed to settle, was harried for the lead throughout and failed to match his previous turf run. However, he's not a bad sort on looks and will be worth another chance in ordinary company.
Official explanation: jockey said colt ran too keenly (op 11-4 tchd 5-2)
Be A Devil again had his limitations exposed in this company but was far from disgraced on his first run for over three months. Modest handicaps will be the way forward with him.
Louisiana Gift(IRE) failed to build on the promise shown at Kempton earlier in the month but the step up to 1m should suit in due course and he will be one to keep an eye on when qualified for a handicap mark.. (op 9-2)
Bona Fortuna ◆, a Derby entry, gave trouble at the start (loaded with a blanket) and was very green in the race. However, he caught the eye in the closing stages without being knocked about. This son of a 1m4f winner will be of more interest over middle distances next year. (op 16-1)

6255 WILLIAM HILL 0800 444040 - GET £25 FREE BET MEDIAN AUCTION MAIDEN STKS 7f 32y(P)
7:50 (7:51) (Class 6) 3-5-Y-O **£2,388** (£705; £352) **Stalls** High

Form RPR
44 **1** **Tiddliwinks**[28] 5394 3-9-3 0.......................... PhillipMakin 5 78+
(K A Ryan) *chsd ldr: led wl over 2f out: pushed clr wl over 1f out: rdn fnl f: eased nr fin* **5/2**[2]
2244 **2** *5* **Global Conquest (IRE)**[55] 4550 3-8-12 75.......................... DarryllHolland 9 60
(Pat Eddery) *hld up in mid-div: pushed along over 3f out: hdwy wl over 1f out: rdn and chsd wnr fnl f: no imp* **6/4**[1]
0- **3** *1/2* **Lord Of The Dance (IRE)**[323] 7204 3-9-3 0.......................... LukeMorris 6 64
(J M P Eustace) *hld up in tch: rdn over 2f out: one pce fnl f* **6/1**[3]
4 *1 3/4* **Abbashinko** 3-8-12 0.......................... RichardSmith 12 55
(Tom Dascombe) *chsd ldrs: wnt 2nd over 2f out: rdn jst over 1f out: wknd ins fnl f* **40/1**
5500 **5** *nk* **Dark Camellia**[49] 4748 4-9-1 55..........................(t) DaneO'Neill 10 56+
(H J L Dunlop) *s.i.s: hld up and bhd: sme hdwy over 1f out: rdn and kpt on ins fnl f: n.d* **14/1**
6 *4 1/2* **Cheers Big Ears (IRE)** 3-9-3 0.......................... RobertWinston 11 48
(J R Best) *hld up and bhd: pushed along and hung lft bnd over 2f out: nvr nr ldrs* **14/1**
000 **7** *3 1/4* **Paul's Pet**[13] 5888 4-9-6 48.......................... ChrisCatlin 7 41
(Karen George) *a in rr* **40/1**
5000 **8** *3 3/4* **Venetian Lady**[63] 4281 3-8-9 44..........................(p) JackMitchell(3) 1 26
(Mrs A Duffield) *chsd ldrs: sltly hmpd on ins bnd after 1f: pushed along over 3f out: rdn and wknd wl over 1f out* **50/1**
326P **9** *5* **Cindy Incidentally**[21] 5624 3-8-9 47..........................(b) KellyHarrison(3) 3 14
(Miss Gay Kelleway) *led: hdd wl over 2f out: sn wknd* **25/1**
10 *4* **Lady Picola** 3-8-12 0.......................... RichardKingscote 4 4
(Tom Dascombe) *hld up in mid-div: pushed along over 3f out: sn bhd* **16/1**
0000 **11** *nse* **Cruise Control**[22] 5614 3-9-3 46.......................... StephenDonohoe 8 9
(R J Price) *a in rr* **50/1**
6004 **12** *6* **Stylish Mover**[8] 6038 4-9-6 46..........................(t) RobertHavlin 2 —
(R Ingram) *s.s: a in rr* **20/1**

1m 28.17s (-1.43) **Going Correction** -0.125s/f (Stan)
WFA 3 from 4yo 3lb **12** Ran SP% **119.5**
Speed ratings (Par 101): **103,97,96,94,94 89,85,81,75,70 70,64**
toteswingers: 1&2 £2.20, 1&3 £5.10, 2&3 £3.50 CSF £6.17 TOTE £3.70: £1.80, £1.10, £2.30; EX 8.50.
Owner Guy Reed **Bred** Guy Reed **Trained** Hambleton, N Yorks

FOCUS
An uncompetitive maiden run at a fair gallop. Limited form. The winner raced in the centre in the straight.
Cheers Big Ears(IRE) Official explanation: jockey said colt had no more to give
Cruise Control Official explanation: jockey said gelding hung left throughout
Stylish Mover Official explanation: jockey said gelding possibly resented tongue strap

6256 WILLIAMHILL.COM/BONUS25 - PLAY VEGAS GAMES H'CAP 1m 141y(P)
8:20 (8:23) (Class 6) (0-55,61) 3-Y-O+ **£2,729** (£806; £403) **Stalls** Low

Form RPR
6520 **1** **Pianoforte (USA)**[2] 6217 7-9-0 51..........................(b) GrahamGibbons 6 60
(E J Alston) *hld up in tch: nt clr run jst over 2f out: rdn to ld jst ins fnl f: drvn out* **10/1**
0000 **2** *1/2* **Royal Island (IRE)**[27] 5443 7-9-1 52.......................... VinceSlattery 12 60
(M G Quinlan) *hld up towards rr: hdwy wl over 1f out: ev ch ent fnl f: sn rdn: nt qckn* **2/1**[1]
2005 **3** *1 1/4* **Vanadium**[14] 5842 7-9-4 55.......................... GeorgeBaker 1 60
(G L Moore) *a.p: led wl over 1f out: rdn and hdd jst ins fnl f: nt qckn* **8/1**[3]
5303 **4** *3 1/4* **Rowan Lodge (IRE)**[25] 5513 7-9-3 54..........................(b) KFallon 8 53
(Ollie Pears) *hld up towards rr: hdwy 2f out: c wd st: hung lft over 1f out: no imp fnl f* **8/1**[3]
5-04 **5** *2* **Headache**[60] 4376 4-9-1 52..........................(t) DaneO'Neill 9 46
(B W Duke) *hld up in mid-div: pushed along and hdwy over 2f out: rdn over 1f out: wknd fnl f* **16/1**
0165 **6** *1/2* **Broughtons Silk**[26] 5484 4-9-2 53.......................... ChrisCatlin 11 46
(W J Musson) *hld up in rr: pushed along wl over 1f out: nvr nr ldrs* **16/1**
200 **7** *1 1/4* **Kirstys Lad**[102] 2971 7-9-1 52.......................... AlanMunro 5 43
(M Mullineaux) *hld up towards rr: hdwy on ins over 2f out: wknd fnl f* **40/1**
2330 **8** *nk* **Aggbag**[35] 5229 5-9-3 54.......................... PhillipMakin 13 44
(Miss M E Rowland) *hld up in rr: rdn over 1f out: n.d* **25/1**
0061 **9** *4* **New World Order (IRE)**[2] 6208 5-9-10 61 6ex..........................(t) TPQueally 2 43
(Edgar Byrne) *led after 1f: hdd wl over 1f out: sn rdn and wknd* **5/2**[2]
50-6 **10** *8* **State Function (IRE)**[136] 1956 4-9-4 55..........................(t) SaleemGolam 7 20
(G Prodromou) *prom tl pushed along and wknd wl over 1f out* **25/1**
6060 **11** *11* **Not Now Lewis (IRE)**[18] 5730 5-9-2 53.......................... PJMcDonald 3 —
(F P Murtagh) *led 1f: w ldr tl pushed along jst over 2f out: wknd qckly* **22/1**
0000 **12** *47* **Hamaasy**[23] 5566 8-9-0 51.......................... LPKeniry 4 —
(G A Ham) *w ldrs tl wknd qckly wl over 3f out: eased whn no ch over 2f out* **100/1**

1m 48.71s (-1.79) **Going Correction** -0.125s/f (Stan) **12** Ran SP% **120.5**
Speed ratings (Par 101): **102,101,100,97,95 95,94,93,90,83 73,31**
toteswingers: 1&2 £8.10, 1&3 £13.60, 2&3 £7.00 CSF £29.39 CT £179.74 TOTE £9.90: £2.60, £1.80, £3.00; EX 39.90.
Owner Nigel & Val Leadbeater **Bred** Cashmark Farm **Trained** Longton, Lancs

FOCUS
A moderate handicap run at an ordinary gallop. The first three pulled clear and principals ended up towards the inside rail in the straight. The form is rated around them.
New World Order(IRE) Official explanation: trainer said gelding was unsuited by the drop in trip

6257 WILLIAM HILL 0800 444040 - QUOTE BONUS25 H'CAP 1m 1f 103y(P)
8:50 (8:50) (Class 5) (0-75,75) 3-Y-O **£3,885** (£1,156; £577; £288) **Stalls** Low

Form RPR
5036 **1** **Waahej**[15] 5806 3-8-4 61 oh1.......................... ChrisCatlin 2 67
(P W Hiatt) *prom: lost pl 6f out: hdwy on ins over 2f out: swtchd rt ent st: led ins fnl f: drvn out* **22/1**
5343 **2** *hd* **Insolence (USA)**[38] 5128 3-8-13 70.......................... WilliamBuick 5 76
(Sir Michael Stoute) *prom: pushed along and lost pl over 3f out: c wd st: rdn wl over 1f out: rallied u.str.p ins fnl f: r.o* **9/2**[2]
0552 **3** *3/4* **Too Tall**[38] 5124 3-8-11 68.......................... KFallon 6 72
(L M Cumani) *hdwy over 6f out: hdwy to join ldr 6f out: rdn 2f out: nt qckn ins fnl f* **4/1**[1]
4224 **4** *hd* **Starla Dancer (GER)**[34] 5259 3-8-13 70.......................... PaulHanagan 3 74
(R A Fahey) *led: rdn wl over 1f out: hdd ins fnl f: nt qckn* **6/1**[3]
2400 **5** *3/4* **Burns Night**[25] 5510 3-9-4 75.......................... RoystonFfrench 7 77
(M Johnston) *s.i.s: hdwy over 6f out: pushed along over 3f out: outpcd over 2f out: styd on ins fnl f* **13/2**
0204 **6** *1* **Navajo Nation (IRE)**[10] 5975 3-8-11 68.......................... EddieAhern 8 68
(B J Meehan) *prom: rdn over 2f out: swtchd rt 1f out: one pce* **13/2**
0246 **7** *1 1/2* **Diamond Twister (USA)**[18] 5723 3-8-9 66..........................(t) RobertWinston 4 63+
(J R Best) *t.k.h: sn bhd: nt clr run over 2f out: rdn over 1f out: no rspnse* **9/2**[2]
2412 **8** *7* **West With The Wind (USA)**[27] 5449 3-9-1 72.......................... AlanMunro 9 54
(P W Chapple-Hyam) *hld up in tch: pushed along wl over 2f out: wknd wl over 1f out* **13/2**

2m 0.90s (-0.80) **Going Correction** -0.125s/f (Stan) **8** Ran SP% **115.0**
Speed ratings (Par 101): **98,97,97,96,96 95,94,87**
toteswingers: 1&2 £19.50, 1&3 £14.80, 2&3 £3.30 CSF £118.44 CT £488.49 TOTE £20.30: £4.20, £1.60, £1.90; EX 147.90.
Owner P W Hiatt **Bred** David John Brown **Trained** Hook Norton, Oxon

FOCUS
A fair handicap, but a tactical race off a slow pace, and the bare form may not be entirely reliable. The pace only picked up rounding the home turn and the first two raced in the centre.
Burns Night Official explanation: jockey said colt hung right throughout

6258 WILLIAMHILL.COM/BONUS25 - BINGO BONANZA'S H'CAP 1m 5f 194y(P)
9:20 (9:20) (Class 4) (0-80,85) 3-Y-O+ **£5,046** (£1,510; £755; £377; £188) **Stalls** Low

Form RPR
5505 **1** **Bushy Dell (IRE)**[27] 5446 4-8-8 65.......................... AmyBaker(5) 7 75
(Miss J Feilden) *a.p: pushed along over 2f out: led ent fnl f: sn rdn: jst hld on* **14/1**
0011 **2** *nse* **Rose Row**[15] 5812 5-9-9 75.......................... HayleyTurner 10 85+
(Mrs Mary Hambro) *stdd s: hld up in rr: smooth hdwy on ins wl over 1f out: hrd rdn and r.o ins fnl f: jst failed* **8/1**
0/00 **3** *4 1/2* **Actodos (IRE)**[16] 5781 5-9-1 70.......................... JamesMillman(3) 1 74
(B R Millman) *chsd ldr: led wl over 1f out: sn rdn: hdd ent fnl f: wknd towards fin* **25/1**
1311 **4** *nk* **Veiled**[8] 6037 3-8-13 82 12ex.......................... RosieJessop(7) 6 85
(Sir Mark Prescott) *hld up towards rr: smooth prog on outside over 3f out: c wd st: rdn wl over 1f out: hung lft wl ins fnl f: one pce* **2/1**[1]
635 **5** *3/4* **Sushitan (GER)**[18] 5720 4-9-4 70.......................... GeorgeBaker 3 72
(G L Moore) *hld up in mid-div: hdwy 2f out: sn pushed along: rdn and no imp fnl f* **10/1**
1521 **6** *2 1/2* **Jadalee (IRE)**[14] 5837 6-9-9 75..........................(tp) KFallon 4 74
(G A Butler) *t.k.h: sn in tch: pushed along over 2f out: wknd ins fnl f* **5/2**[2]
2-31 **7** *1 1/2* **No Wonga**[10] 5962 4-8-4 61 6ex.......................... AndrewHeffernan(5) 9 58
(P D Evans) *hld up in mid-div: pushed along and edgd lft jst over 1f out: sn btn* **15/2**[3]
10 **8** *3 1/2* **Remember Ramon (USA)**[48] 4770 6-10-5 85.......... StephenDonohoe 8 77
(J R Gask) *led: pushed along and hdd wl over 1f out: sn rdn and wknd* **14/1**
00 **9** *1 3/4* **Bull Market (IRE)**[22] 5593 6-9-4 70.......................... VinceSlattery 5 59
(M S Tuck) *hld up towards rr: pushed along over 2f out: sn struggling* **66/1**

330- **10** 4 **Cavendish**[422] 4516 5-9-0 66...........(b) LukeMorris 2 50
(J M P Eustace) *hld up in mid-div: pushed along over 5f out: wknd wl over 1f out: eased fnl f* **20/1**

3m 1.75s (-4.25) **Going Correction** -0.125s/f (Stan)
WFA 3 from 4yo+ 10lb **10** Ran SP% **117.3**
Speed ratings (Par 105): **107,106,104,104,103 102,101,99,98,96**
toteswingers: 1&2 £18.60, 1&3 £16.50, 2&3 £36.60 CSF £119.12 CT £2771.56 TOTE £18.30: £3.80, £2.30, £6.90; EX 146.10 Place 6: £ 39.68 Place 5: £22.70.
Owner R J Creese **Bred** Don Commins **Trained** Exning, Suffolk

FOCUS
A fair handicap run at a reasonable gallop. The first two, who raced centre to far side in the straight, pulled clear of the remainder.
T/Plt: £55.90 to a £1 stake. Pool: £80,623.39. 1,052.65 winning tickets. T/Qpdt: £47.50 to a £1 stake. Pool: £7,828.93. 121.90 winning tickets. KH

6239 ASCOT (R-H)

Saturday, September 26

OFFICIAL GOING: Good (good to firm in places) changing to good to firm after race 4 (3.40)
Wind: virtually nil Weather: sunny and warm

6267 DELOITTE ROSEMARY STKS (H'CAP) (LISTED RACE) (F&M) 1m (R)
1:55 (1:56) (Class 1) (0-110,107) 3-Y-0+

£22,708 (£8,608; £4,308; £2,148; £1,076; £540) **Stalls** High

Form RPR

2504 **1** **Ahla Wasahl**[35] 5260 3-8-11 97........... AhmedAjtebi 2 101
(D M Simcock) *mid-div: hdwy 2f out: sn rdn: led ent fnl f: kpt on wl: drvn out* **33/1**

1214 **2** ½ **Alsace Lorraine (IRE)**[27] 5472 4-8-7 89 oh1........... JamieSpencer 3 96+
(J R Fanshawe) *t.k.h in midfield: stl travelling wl whn sltly hmpd and nt clr run 2f out tl jst over 1f out: shkn up and r.o wl whn clr run but unable to rch wnr* **15/2**

6-00 **3** ½ **Headford View (IRE)**[27] 5490 5-8-13 95...........(p) CO'Donoghue 14 97
(James Halpin, Ire) *hld up towards rr: rdn and stdy prog fr over 2f out: kpt on wl fnl f* **33/1**

3611 **4** *nk* **Sarah Park (IRE)**[18] 5745 4-8-7 89 oh5........... EddieAhern 11 90
(B J Meehan) *t.k.h in mid-div: hdwy over 2f out: rdn to chse wnr briefly ins fnl f: kpt on* **25/1**

0212 **5** *nk* **Shamwari Lodge (IRE)**[16] 5798 3-9-1 101........... RichardHughes 16 106+
(R Hannon) *swtg: mid-div: travelling ok whn nt clr run 2f out: sn swtchd off rails: rdn and r.o whn nt clr run ent fnl f* **9/2**[1]

2-11 **6** *nk* **Applause (IRE)**[59] 4433 3-8-6 92........... ShaneKelly 13 92+
(J Noseda) *lw: s.i.s: bhd: rdn over 2f out: 15th and plenty to do u.p ent fnl f: r.o wl: nrst fin* **11/2**[2]

6201 **7** ½ **Lady Francesca**[9] 6029 3-8-8 94........... MartinDwyer 10 93
(W R Muir) *sn led: rdn and hrd pressed fr over 2f out: kpt on gamely tl hdd ent fnl f: no ex* **22/1**

2002 **8** 2 ¼ **Ermine And Velvet**[44] 4947 3-8-3 89 oh4........... KoseiMiura 12 83
(C E Brittain) *trckd ldrs: rdn 3f out: kpt on same pce fnl 2f* **66/1**

0312 **9** *shd* **Resort**[14] 5880 3-8-4 90........... PaulHanagan 9 84+
(Sir Michael Stoute) *trckd ldrs: rdn over 2f out: one pce fr over 1f out* **11/1**

10 ¾ **Aspectoflove (IRE)**[21] 5691 3-8-8 94........... RyanMoore 1 86+
(John M Oxx, Ire) *on toes: swtg: restrained and sn swtchd rt s: bhd: swtchd lft and hdwy 2f out: swtchd to far side rails ent fnl f but running on whn nowhere to go: eased* **7/1**[3]

0242 **11** 1 ¼ **Damaniyat Girl (USA)**[24] 5588 3-9-7 107...........(b) LDettori 15 96
(W J Haggas) *hld up towards rr of midfield: rdn over 2f out: no imp* **14/1**

-550 **12** 1 ¾ **Jet D'Eau (FR)**[14] 5874 3-8-12 98...........(b) PatCosgrave 18 83
(G L Moore) *s.i.s: a towards rr* **40/1**

1241 **13** *nse* **Annabelle's Charm (IRE)**[41] 5064 4-9-3 99........... KFallon 4 84+
(L M Cumani) *t.k.h: prom: rdn over 2f out: wkng whn sltly hmpd jst over 1f out* **12/1**

0-22 **14** ¾ **Ada River**[10] 5995 4-9-4 100........... WilliamBuick 6 84
(A M Balding) *lw: trckd ldr: rdn 3f out: wknd over 1f out* **12/1**

1010 **15** 2 ¼ **Cosmopolitan**[57] 4489 4-8-9 91........... NickyMackay 5 70
(J H M Gosden) *lw: cl up: rdn 3f out: sn one pce: wknd over 1f out* **20/1**

3533 **16** 4 ½ **Silver Games (IRE)**[23] 5607 3-8-3 89 oh2........... ChrisCatlin 8 58
(M R Channon) *s.i.s: a towards rr* **20/1**

2226 **U** **Balaagha (USA)**[41] 5064 3-9-0 100........... RHills 17 —
(M A Jarvis) *v unruly in stalls and uns rdr bef stalls opened* **12/1**

1m 39.82s (-0.88) **Going Correction** +0.10s/f (Good)
WFA 3 from 4yo+ 4lb **17** Ran SP% **123.4**
Speed ratings (Par 111): **108,107,107,106,106 106,105,103,103,102 101,99,99,98,96 91,—**
toteswinger: 1&2 £48.10, 1&3 £111.30, 2&3 £65.50. CSF £247.38 CT £8324.47 TOTE £33.80: £6.50, £2.30, £6.40, £5.10; EX 411.30 TRIFECTA Not won..
Owner Sultan Ali **Bred** Dachel Stud **Trained** Newmarket, Suffolk

FOCUS
A highly competitive distaff handicap. The pace was not overly strong and there were several notable hard-luck stories, as is often the case here in big fields on the round course. The form is limited as a result. Three-year-olds have now won the last nine runnings.

NOTEBOOK
Ahla Wasahl was a surprise winner. Racing wide from her low draw, and settling in mid-division, she obtained an uninterrupted run down the outer in the straight to strike the front a furlong out. She had been held in this grade previously this season but underwent a minor breathing operation after her penultimate run and her trainer had been hopeful. She may go to the Dubai carnival in the new year. (op 40-1)
Alsace Lorraine(IRE), another drawn low, Alsace Lorraine, was arguably the unluckiest loser, as she had nowhere to go from the two pole until entering the last. The filly closed when there was clear daylight in front of her, but the winner had taken first run. A return to 1m2f will suit her. (op 9-1)
Headford View(IRE) Irish-trained mare, missed the trouble and ran on stoutly down the outer for third. She had been held off this mark in the Bunbury Cup on her one previous appearance in this country. (op 50-1)
Sarah Park(IRE), racing from 5lb out of the handicap, ran a solid race from what was effectively a 9lb higher mark than when winning at Goodwood. She is an admirably tough filly.
Shamwari Lodge(IRE) ◆, runner-up to Fantasia over 7f at Doncaster last time, was another who met trouble and she passed the line with plenty of running still in her. She is well worth another chance. Official explanation: jockey said filly was denied a clear run (op 11-2)
Applause(IRE), off the track since a winning handicap debut at Redcar two months ago, missed the break and was held up in rear. She ran on steadily in the straight but was never within striking distance of the leaders. Official explanation: jockey said filly was slowly away (op 7-2)
Lady Francesca, back in this grade after a belated maiden win on the all-weather last time, soon took over in front and was only collared a furlong or so out. (op 25-1)
Resort, back down to a mile, showed up prominently until fading in the final furlong. (op 9-1)
Aspectoflove(IRE) was another to suffer from traffic problems, and would have been closer otherwise. Official explanation: jockey said filly was denied a clear run (tchd 13-2 and 15-2)
Annabelle's Charm(IRE), in the same ownership as the runner-up, took a keen grip early on and her exertions told in the latter stages. (op 11-1)
Ada River, runner-up at Sandown when able to lead, did not have things her way this time and faded after racing close behind the pace. (op 14-1)

6268 JUDDMONTE ROYAL LODGE STKS (GROUP 2) (C&G) 1m (R)
2:30 (2:31) (Class 1) 2-Y-0

£86,188 (£32,671; £16,351; £8,152; £4,083; £2,049) **Stalls** High

Form RPR

1 **Joshua Tree (IRE)**[11] 6082 2-8-12 0........... CO'Donoghue 5 112
(A P O'Brien, Ire) *w'like: attr: athletic: hld up: c wd ent st: gd hdwy over 2f out: led over 1f out: sn drifted rt: kpt on wl: rdn out* **12/1**

31 **2** 1 ¼ **Waseet**[44] 4953 2-8-12 0........... RHills 2 109
(J L Dunlop) *hld up: swtchd lft and hdwy fr 2f out: rdn over 1f out: kpt on to chse wnr jst ins fnl f: a being hld* **6/1**[3]

151 **3** *hd* **Vale Of York (IRE)**[18] 5743 2-8-12 104........... AhmedAjtebi 4 110+
(Saeed Bin Suroor) *lw: racd keenly trcking ldrs: rdn to chal 2f out: drifted rt and ev ch over 1f out: sn hmpd by wnr: kpt on but no ex* **5/1**[2]

21 **4** 2 ¾ **High Twelve (IRE)**[51] 4713 2-8-12 0........... JimmyFortune 7 103+
(J H M Gosden) *s.i.s: last of gp: nt clr run briefly over 2f out: sn rdn: styd on fnl f: nvr trbld ldrs* **7/2**[1]

105 **5** 4 **Dreamspeed (IRE)**[36] 5214 2-8-12 98........... WilliamBuick 3 94
(A M Balding) *lw: prom tl rdn wl over 2f out: wknd jst over 1f out* **25/1**

6 *nse* **Mikhail Glinka (IRE)**[39] 5140 2-8-12 0........... JMurtagh 8 94
(A P O'Brien, Ire) *tall: lengthy: mid-div: rdn over 2f out: little prog whn sltly hmpd jst over 1f out: nt pce to chal* **9/1**

4111 **7** 4 **Frozen Power (IRE)**[29] 5416 2-8-12 109........... LDettori 1 91+
(Saeed Bin Suroor) *trckd ldr: rdn and ev ch 2f out: cl 3rd but hld whn bdly hmpd jst over 1f out* **7/2**[1]

2214 **8** 6 **Timely Jazz (IRE)**[18] 5743 2-8-12 101........... MartinDwyer 10 84+
(B J Meehan) *lw: racd keenly: led: rdn over 2f out: hdd over 1f out: cl 4th but hld whn bdly hmpd on rails ent fnl f: eased* **16/1**

14 **9** *shd* **Black Spirit (USA)**[35] 5261 2-8-12 100...........(t) AdamKirby 9 72
(C G Cox) *cl up: rdn wl over 2f out: wknd wl over 1f out* **7/1**

4312 **10** 1 ½ **Dubai Miracle (USA)**[36] 5214 2-8-12 99........... JamieSpencer 11 68+
(D M Simcock) *w'like: str: on toes: trckd ldrs: rdn 3f out: wknd 2f out* **20/1**

1m 39.55s (-1.15) **Going Correction** +0.10s/f (Good) 2y crse rec **10** Ran SP% **120.1**
Speed ratings (Par 107): **109,107,107,104,100 100,96,90,90,89**
toteswinger: 1&2 £10.80, 1&3 £14.10, 2&3 £6.90. CSF £84.75 TOTE £18.00: £5.40, £3.20, £2.90; EX 123.60 Trifecta £3029.70 Pool: £8,311.28 - 2.03 winning units..
Owner D Smith, Mrs J Magnier, M Tabor **Bred** Castlemartin Stud & Skymarc Farm **Trained** Ballydoyle, Co Tipperary
■ Stewards' Enquiry : C O'Donoghue five-day ban: careless riding (Oct 10-14)

FOCUS
The Royal Lodge has had very little bearing on the following season's Classics for a number of years and this far from vintage version looks unlikely to buck that trend. It was steadily run and the winner had to survive a stewards' inquiry after causing trouble for those in behind, but he won on merit. The first four came clear and all showed improved form.

NOTEBOOK
Joshua Tree(IRE), successful in a Gowran maiden on debut before finishing runner-up in a Listowel nursery, was the O'Brien second string on jockey bookings. He came with a sweeping run down the outside to lead and ran on very well, but he edged to his right as he did so, despite his rider having the whip in the correct hand, and caused a chain reaction. A nice prospect, he was having his first run on a sound surface and he will have learned a lot from the experience gained here. If he runs again this term it is likely to be in the Racing Post Trophy at Doncaster. Bookmakers were not particularly impressed and quotes of 25-1 for the Guineas and 33-1 for the Derby were issued after the race. (op 16-1)
Waseet, a Sandown maiden winner and supplemented for £20,000, briefly had to wait for a run early in the home straight as the winner picked up on his outer from just behind him, but that cannot be used as an excuse. He ran on well enough for second and his rider was not too hard on him when he was held. (op 8-1)
Vale Of York(IRE), another supplementary entry, raced keenly up with the pace. The winner drifted across him without causing him any major problems and he stuck on well enough for third. He saw out the trip well and looks a decent middle-distance prospect. (op 11-2 tchd 6-1)
High Twelve(IRE), taking a big step up in grade after winning a Sandwon maiden, required two handlers in the paddock and became warm down at the start. Last into the straight, he stayed on steadily in the final two furlongs without troubling the principals. He has further improvement in him. (op 9-4)
Dreamspeed(IRE) found himself in trouble when the pace lifted in the straight. He was not up to this standard, but did turn around Salisbury running with Dubai Miracle. (op 33-1)
Mikhail Glinka(IRE) is a stablemate of the winner and arrived here with a similar profile, a maiden victory preceding a nursery second. He ran on from the back without ever getting into the race but at least kept a straight course this time. (op 10-1 tchd 11-1)
Frozen Power(IRE), the choice of Dettori and another supplemented, was under pressure in third when he was hampered as a result of the winner leaning in on Vale Of York. He would have been closer without the interference but his sights will have to be lowered. Official explanation: jockey said colt suffered interference in running (tchd 9-2 and 5-1 in places)
Timely Jazz(IRE) was the worst affected in the trouble. He was keen in front through the early parts but had been headed and was held when he was tightened up badly on the rail. Official explanation: jockey said colt suffered interference in running (op 22-1)
Black Spirit(USA), the Solario fourth, was well enough placed in fifth turning into the straight but soon faded. (op 10-1 tchd 12-1 in places)

6269 MEON VALLEY STUD FILLIES' MILE (GROUP 1) 1m (R)
3:05 (3:06) (Class 1) 2-Y-0

£123,758 (£46,913; £23,478; £11,706; £5,864; £2,943) **Stalls** High

Form RPR

322 **1** **Hibaayeb**[15] 5825 2-8-12 104........... NCallan 6 110
(C E Brittain) *swtg: trckd ldrs: rdn whn squeezed through to ld on rails ent fnl f: hung lft: kpt on: drvn out* **8/1**

313 **2** ¾ **Lady Darshaan (IRE)**[80] 3748 2-8-12 100........... RichardHughes 3 108+
(J S Moore) *trckd ldr: rdn and ev ch ent fnl f: ¾ l down whn hit on nose by winning rdr's whip fnl 125yds: carried lft: kpt on* **9/1**

3 1 ½ **You'll Be Mine (USA)**[21] 5684 2-8-12 0........... JMurtagh 4 105
(A P O'Brien, Ire) *w'like: scope: mid-div: rdn whn swtchd lft jst ins fnl f: styd on: wnt 3rd towards fin* **7/2**[2]

131 **4** ½ **Sent From Heaven (IRE)**[28] 5427 2-8-12 103........... MichaelHills 8 105+
(B W Hills) *unf: scope: swtg: led: rdn and hdd ent fnl f: cl 3rd but hld whn squeezed out and snatched up fnl 150yds: lost 3rd towards fin* **8/1**

321 **5** ½ **Dyna Waltz**[38] 5165 2-8-12 79........... JimmyFortune 1 103
(J H M Gosden) *mid-div on outside: effrt over 2f out: kpt on same pce* **20/1**

1204 **6** *1* **Blue Angel (IRE)**[28] [5427] 2-8-12 102................................ RyanMoore 5 101
(R Hannon) *lw: sn struggling to go pce: last 4f out: styd on fnl f: nvr a threat* **14/1**

5210 **7** *hd* **Chantilly Creme (USA)**[35] [5279] 2-8-12 0........................ SPasquier 9 100
(R Gibson, France) *edgy: swtg: hld up: effrt over 2f out: fdd fnl f* **18/1**

14 **8** *1* **Long Lashes (USA)**[27] [5488] 2-8-12 108...............................(t) LDettori 7 98
(Saeed Bin Suroor) *lengthy: str: hld up: effrt to dispute 4th over 1f out: fdd ent fnl f* **5/2**[1]

1012 **9** *2 3/4* **Mudaaraah**[28] [5427] 2-8-12 102.. RHills 2 95
(J L Dunlop) *hld up: hdwy over 2f out u.p: wknd over 1f out* **11/2**[3]

1m 39.78s (-0.92) **Going Correction** +0.10s/f (Good) 2y crse rec **9** Ran SP% **115.1**
Speed ratings (Par 106): **108,107,105,105,104 103,103,102,99**
toteswinger: 1&2 £12.10, 1&3 £5.80, 2&3 £7.50. CSF £76.95 TOTE £7.90: £1.80, £4.00, £2.10; EX 77.70 Trifecta £625.20 Pool: £19,028.42 - 22.52 winning units..
Owner Mohammed Al Nabouda **Bred** Rabbah Bloodstock Limited **Trained** Newmarket, Suffolk
■ Stewards' Enquiry : N Callan three-day ban: careless riding (Oct 10-12)

FOCUS
This was not a strong renewal of this Group 1. Recent May Hill winner Pollenator was not supplemented, and Seta, third at Doncaster, was another absentee, as were the principals from the Moyglare Stud Stakes. The pace was only ordinary and nothing got into it from the rear. The time was similar to that for the Royal Lodge and, as in that race, the stewards had a look at the winner before the placings were confirmed. Hibaayeb is rated up 5lb on her Doncaster form, with improvment from the placed fillies too.

NOTEBOOK
Hibaayeb, the sole maiden in the line-up, was supplemented for this after splitting Pollenator and Seta in the May Hill. Turning for home in third, she squeezed through against the rail to lead but then drifted to her left, inconveniencing both the second and third. She is a tough and progressive filly but she could struggle at the top level next year, when her trainer sees her more as an Oaks prospect than a Guineas filly. She is around 25-1 for both Classics. Don't confuse her, incidentally, with the Ed Dunlop-trained Habaayib, who goes for the Cheveley Park Stakes next week. (op 9-1 tchd 7-1)
Lady Darshaan(IRE), a progressive filly, ran a big race on this rise in grade on her return from a break. After holding every chance, she was a close second and probably just held when she was struck across the nose by the winning rider's whip. The step up in trip was not a problem and there is a nice prize to be won with her.
You'll Be Mine(USA) ◆, whose dam Quarter Moon was runner-up in three Classics, was the chosen Ballydoyle participant. She stayed on late on this first try at the trip and, sure to have learned from this, looks a smart middle-distance prospect. (op 3-1)
Sent From Heaven(IRE), successful in Group 3 company at Goodwood last time, attempted to make all again but was headed inside the last. Almost immediately she was hampered by the winner, which probably cost her third place. (tchd 15-2 tchd 10-1 in a place and 9-1 in places)
Dyna Waltz represented the same connections as last year's winner Rainbow View. She ran respectably but was not up to this big rise in grade, having only landed a Polytrack maiden last time. (op 16-1)
Blue Angel(IRE), fourth to Sent From Heaven at Goodwood, ran on late from the back but was never a factor.
Chantilly Creme(USA), who reportedly strained back muscles when virtually pulled up last time, did not fully see out this longer trip. (op 20-1)
Long Lashes(USA), who became bogged down in the Curragh mud behind Termagant in the Moyglare, was fitted with a tongue-tie for the first time. She was never really able to pick up from the rear and was below par. Official explanation: jockey said filly ran free and hung left in straight (op 3-1 tchd 100-30 and 7-2 in places)
Mudaaraah, who had failed by a nose to reel in Sent From Heaven at Goodwood, could not get involved from the back of the field. (op 5-1 tchd 6-1)

6270 TOTESPORT.COM CHALLENGE CUP (HERITAGE H'CAP) 7f
3:40 (3:40) (Class 2) 3-Y-0+
£93,465 (£27,990; £10,500; £10,500; £3,495; £1,755) **Stalls** Centre

Form RPR

0430 **1** **Advanced**[7] [6091] 6-8-12 **99**.............................. AmyRyan(5) 20 109
(K A Ryan) *a.p: tk narrow advantage wl over 1f out: hld on gamely ins fnl f: drvn out* **33/1**

2614 **2** *nk* **Axiom**[35] [5249] 5-9-4 **100**................................ LDettori 19 109
(L M Cumani) *lw: trckd ldrs: rdn to mount serious chal ent fnl f: kpt on but no ex nr fin* **12/1**

0500 **3** *1* **Something (IRE)**[7] [6092] 7-8-9 **91**..............................(p) PaulQuinn 29 98
(D Nicholls) *hld up towards rr: weaved way through fr 2f out: swtchd lft ins fnl f: kpt on wl: nrst fin* **33/1**

3003 **3** *dht* **Proclaim**[28] [5424] 3-8-7 **92**..............................(v) JoeFanning 21 99
(M Johnston) *chsd ldrs: rdn to ld briefly 2f out: kpt on gamely: no ex towards fin* **25/1**

4100 **5** *1/2* **Giganticus (USA)**[63] [4297] 6-9-1 **97**.............................. RHills 24 103
(B W Hills) *mid-div: hdwy 2f out: nt clr run briefly ent fnl f: kpt on: clsng at fin* **16/1**

0060 **6** *1* **Mister Hardy**[7] [6089] 4-8-11 **93**.............................. TedDurcan 27 96
(R A Fahey) *lw: in tch: cl up and travelling ok over 1f out: rdn ent fnl f: nt qckn* **16/1**

-101 **7** *nse* **Swift Gift**[42] [5025] 4-9-2 **98**.............................. MartinDwyer 26 103+
(B J Meehan) *hld up towards rr: rdn and hdwy 2f out: nt clr run over 1f out: kpt on ins fnl f: clsng at fin* **14/1**

1022 **8** *nse* **Castles In The Air**[15] [5826] 4-8-7 **94**.............................. BMcHugh(5) 13 97
(R A Fahey) *prom: rdn over 2f out: kpt on same pce fnl f* **11/1**

3030 **9** *hd* **Roker Park (IRE)**[7] [6089] 4-8-13 **95**..............................(p) NCallan 16 97
(K A Ryan) *mid-div: rdn over 2f out: kpt on ins fnl f* **33/1**

2211 **10** *1/2* **Golden Desert (IRE)**[14] [5874] 5-9-9 **105**.............................. AlanMunro 12 106
(T G Mills) *chsd ldrs: rdn over 2f out: kpt on same pce fnl f* **16/1**

0141 **11** *nk* **Without Prejudice (USA)**[20] [5697] 4-8-6 **88**..............(v) WilliamBuick 25 88+
(J Noseda) *mid-div: rdn over 2f out: kpt on ins fnl f* **14/1**

-155 **12** *1/2* **Big Noise**[15] [5826] 5-8-5 **92**.............. Louis-PhilippeBeuzelin(5) 7 91+
(Dr J D Scargill) *hld up towards rr: rdn 2f out: kpt on fnl f* **18/1**

6200 **13** *shd* **Capricorn Run (USA)**[112] [2707] 6-8-13 **95**..................(v) JamesDoyle 22 94
(A J McCabe) *led tl 2f out: fdd ins fnl f* **50/1**

5121 **14** *nse* **Captain Macarry (IRE)**[14] [5884] 4-8-7 **89** ow1..............(v) TomEaves 15 88
(B Smart) *chsd ldrs: rdn over 2f out: fdd ins fnl f* **33/1**

5220 **15** *nk* **Signor Peltro**[7] [6091] 6-9-5 **101**.............................. DaneO'Neill 2 99+
(H Candy) *lw: hld up: swtchd lft and rdn 2f out: sme late hdwy: nvr trbld ldrs* **20/1**

4152 **16** *1* **Balcarce Nov (ARG)**[14] [5863] 4-9-9 **105**.............................. MickyFenton 28 100
(T P Tate) *swtg: mid-div: wknd ins fnl f* **20/1**

1001 **17** *hd* **Baldemar**[8] [6050] 4-8-9 **91**.............................. PaulHanagan 4 86+
(R A Fahey) *nvr bttr than mid-div* **33/1**

0500 **18** *1/2* **Glow Star (SAF)**[27] [5476] 5-8-8 **90**.............................. ShaneKelly 23 84
(G L Moore) *sme late hdwy but mainly towards rr* **100/1**

6054 **19** *3/4* **Vitznau (IRE)**[14] [5874] 5-9-1 **97**.............................. RichardHughes 17 89
(R Hannon) *nvr bttr than mid-div* **40/1**

0060 **20** *nk* **Dhaular Dhar (IRE)**[35] [5249] 7-8-13 **95**.............................. JamieSpencer 8 86+
(J S Goldie) *nt clr run ent fnl f: a towards rr* **20/1**

3630 **21** *3/4* **Redford (IRE)**[7] [6091] 4-9-6 **102**..............................(v[1]) HayleyTurner 3 98+
(M L W Bell) *t.k.h early: a towards rr* **10/1**[3]

0202 **22** *1/2* **Noble Citizen (USA)**[14] [5874] 4-8-9 **91**..............(be) StephenDonohoe 11 79+
(D M Simcock) *in tch: rdn over 2f out: sn btn* **28/1**

1431 **23** *1 1/4* **Seek N' Destroy (IRE)**[28] [5432] 3-8-7 **92**.............................. MichaelHills 14 84+
(B W Hills) *mid-div tl wknd over 1f out* **9/1**[2]

0605 **24** *shd* **Sonny Red (IRE)**[7] [6091] 5-9-4 **100**.............................. JimCrowley 10 85+
(D Nicholls) *mid-div tl wknd over 1f out* **25/1**

0331 **25** *1* **Akhenaten**[17] [5766] 3-8-10 **95**.............................. ChrisCatlin 9 77
(M R Channon) *chsd ldrs: rdn over 2f out: wknd over 1f out* **33/1**

6043 **26** *nse* **Cadre (IRE)**[10] [5995] 4-9-1 **97**.............................. JimmyFortune 18 79
(J H M Gosden) *swtg: pushed along fr 1/2-way in mid-div: btn 2f out* **28/1**

2010 **27** *4* **Al Muheer (IRE)**[42] [5024] 4-9-10 **106**..............................(b) EddieAhern 6 78+
(C E Brittain) *mid-div tl wknd over 1f out* **33/1**

5411 **28** *1 1/4* **Marching Time**[27] [5476] 3-8-11 **96**.............................. RyanMoore 5 65+
(Sir Michael Stoute) *rdn 2f out: a towards rr* **7/1**[1]

1m 25.89s (-2.11) **Going Correction** -0.025s/f (Good)
WFA 3 from 4yo+ 3lb **28** Ran SP% **138.7**
Speed ratings (Par 109): **111,110,109,109,108 107,107,107,107,106 106,105,105,105,105 104,104,103,102,102 101,100,99,99,**WIN: £52.10; PL: Advanced £11.00, Axiom £2.70, Something £9.10, Proclaim £9.80; EX: £620.50; CSF: £351.41; TRICAST: Adv-Ax-S £6,297.47, Adv-Ax-P £4,878.30. toteswinger: Adv & Ax £107.80, Adv & S £261.10, Adv & P £163.10, Ax & S £135.90, Ax & P £53.00. TOTE £027: £Owner, £T Doherty and McHeen, £Bred, £Gestut GorlsdorfTrained Hambleton, N Yorks.

FOCUS
A very valuable and competitive handicap, and fairly solid form. Leading ante-post fancy Leahurst was an absentee because of the ground. The whole field converged on the far side and high numbers were markedly favoured, with the first seven all drawn 19 or higher. The field finished in a heap.

NOTEBOOK
Advanced, eighth in last Saturday's Ayr Gold Cup, was always prominent. He went for home just after the furlong pole and held on well under his promising apprentice. This was only his second win since he took the 2007 version of the big Ayr race.
Axiom, on whom Dettori substituted for Fallon, chased the winner through inside the last and was just held. This was a second solid run in succession off this career-high mark. (tchd 14-1)
Something(IRE), who was fitted with cheekpieces for the first time, weaved his way through and finished well for a share of third place. He has not won on turf since May 2005 but could rectify that if things go his way. (tchd 28-1)
Proclaim, back up in trip and with the visor retained, did best of the three-year-olds, but was another well served by a high draw. (tchd 28-1)
Giganticus(USA) had won the Buckingham Palace Stakes off 6lb lower at the Royal meeting and put in another solid effort in one of these big-field handicaps. (op 20-1)
Mister Hardy, in midfield behind a stablemate in the Ayr Silver Cup last week, ran creditably, albeit from a favourable draw. (tchd 18-1)
Swift Gift, the Victoria Cup and was 7lb higher than when winning at Newbury last time, was putting in some sterling late work. (op 16-1)
Castles In The Air had a big-field course-and-distance success under his belt, having taken the Ladies' race on King George day. Another 4lb higher, he was right up with the pace until fading inside the last. (tchd 14-1)
Roker Park(IRE), the winner's stablemate, was keeping on and could be worth another try over 7f.
Golden Desert(IRE) was on a hat-trick, but he was 13lb higher than for the first of his two Goodwood wins. Not particularly well drawn, and a little slowly away, he probably ran as well as could be expected. (op 14-1)
Without Prejudice(USA), who was hoisted 9lb for his York win, was one who would have finished a bit closer with a clearer run. (op 16-1)
Big Noise ◆ did best of those drawn in single figures. He is relatively lightly raced and is one to keep an eye on. (op 16-1)
Balcarce Nov(ARG) Official explanation: jockey said colt was denied a clear run
Dhaular Dhar(IRE) was fifth and fourth in the last two runnings of this, but he was badly drawn this time and got no run. This can be written off. Official explanation: jockey said horse was denied a clear run (op 16-1)
Redford(IRE), visored for the first time, could never get out of rear-division but is another who could be worth persevering with. (op 14-1)
Seek N' Destroy(IRE), who was raised 9lb for his Newmarket win, could never get into it from a middle draw. He is worth another chance. (tchd 17-2)
Marching Time, on a hat-trick but a further 5lb higher, finished last of all and his draw must have had something to do with this lacklustre effort. Official explanation: trainer's rep had no explanation for the poor form shown (op 13-2 tchd 15-2 in a place)

6271 QUEEN ELIZABETH II STKS (SPONSORED BY SONY) (GROUP 1) 1m (R)
4:15 (4:15) (Class 1) 3-Y-0+ **£141,925** (£53,800; £26,925; £13,425) **Stalls** High

Form RPR

4421 **1** **Rip Van Winkle (IRE)**[59] [4419] 3-8-13 130.............................. JMurtagh 1 128+
(A P O'Brien, Ire) *lw: trckd ldr: shkn up to ld wl over 2f out: r.o strly: rdn out* **8/13**[1]

2-12 **2** *1 1/4* **Zacinto**[28] [5426] 3-8-13 113.............................. RyanMoore 5 125
(Sir Michael Stoute) *lw: hld up in 4th: tk clsr order 2f out: sn rdn: chsd wnr ent fnl f: kpt on but no ex towards fin* **18/1**

2021 **3** *3 1/4* **Delegator**[28] [5426] 3-8-13 121.............................. LDettori 2 118
(Saeed Bin Suroor) *lw: trckd ldng pair: moved smoothly through to trck wnr 2f out: sn rdn: unable to mount serious chal: lost 2nd ent fnl f* **5/2**[2]

3121 **4** *10* **Aqlaam**[20] [5710] 4-9-3 120.............................. RHills 3 96+
(W J Haggas) *led: varied pce early: qcknd ent st: rdn and hdd wl over 2f out: sn hung lft and hld: eased* **15/2**[3]

1m 38.82s (-1.88) **Going Correction** +0.10s/f (Good)
WFA 3 from 4yo 4lb **4** Ran SP% **107.5**
Speed ratings (Par 117): **113,111,108,98**
CSF £10.96 TOTE £1.50; EX 9.90.
Owner Mrs John Magnier, M Tabor & D Smith **Bred** Roberto Brogi **Trained** Ballydoyle, Co Tipperary

FOCUS
Despite the small field, this was a fascinating renewal of one of the season's top mile events. There was no Goldikova, and Classic winners Ghanaati and Mastercraftsman were absent, the latter having been declared as a precaution in case something happened to Rip Van Winkle. Lockinge winner Virtual missed the race because of the fastish ground. With just four runners a tactical race was on the cards, especially with no pacemakers in the line-up, but as it turned out they went a decent gallop and the time was over a second inside the standard. They raced some way off the inside rail in the back straight. Rip Van Winkle is rated a couple of lengths off his best, with big improvement from Zacinto.

NOTEBOOK

Rip Van Winkle(IRE) had made his own running when an impressive winner of the Sussex Stakes, but did not need to here as Aqlaam did the job for him. Not permitting that rival his own way in front, the favourite was always in close attendance before leading in the straight and kicking away. Zacinto drew alongside inside the last, but the winner had more left in the tank and was well on top in the end. He will step up in trip for the Breeders' Cup Classic now, provided his foot problems allow him to be trained for the race. The return to 1m2f will not trouble this admirable colt, who bustled up Sea The Stars in the Eclipse. (tchd 4-6 in places)

Zacinto was a couple of lengths adrift of the others in fourth entering the straight but he improved to challenge inside the final furlong. He stuck his neck out gamely, but could not prevent the winner asserting late on. This was a fine effort from a colt having only his fifth start and he reversed Goodwood form with Delegator. There is more to come from him and he has several options, including the Champion Stakes over an extra two furlongs and both the turf and dirt versions of the Breeders' Cup Mile. (op 16-1)

Delegator, impressive in beating Zacinto in the Celebration Mile on his Godolphin debut, raced in third place. He closed in the straight as Rip Van Winkle pressed on but could not quite get in a challenge. There were no real excuses but he does not seem to quite get home over a stiff mile, and he has now been found wanting at the top level four times now this year. The Breeders' Cup Mile could be next for him. (tchd 11-4)

Aqlaam was beaten six lengths by Goldikova in the Jacques le Marois before winning the Moulin. Making the running, but with Rip Van Winkle breathing down his neck, he was headed by that horse early in the straight and soon dropped away. Richard Hills reported that he had hung left. The colt has had more than his share of training problems and returned sore, so retirement is reportedly being considered. Official explanation: jockey said colt hung left (op 8-1 tchd 7-1)

6272 MILES & MORRISON OCTOBER STKS (LISTED RACE) (F&M) 7f

4:50 (4:50) (Class 1) 3-Y-O+

£22,708 (£8,608; £4,308; £2,148; £1,076; £540) **Stalls** Centre

Form RPR

2103 **1** **Golden Stream (IRE)**[41] 5064 3-8-13 101 RyanMoore 5 106
(Sir Michael Stoute) *swtg: hld up: swtchd rt and hdwy over 2f out: rdn to ld jst ins fnl f: kpt on: drvn out* **5/1**[2]

6404 **2** 1 **Red Dune (IRE)**[16] 5798 4-8-13 98 LDettori 4 100
(M A Jarvis) *lw: mid-div: swtchd lft and hdwy over 1f out: sn rdn: r.o fnl f: wnt 2nd towards fin* **10/1**

1300 **3** nk **Greenisland (IRE)**[41] 5069 3-8-10 96 SteveDrowne 7 99
(H Morrison) *led: rdn whn hdd jst ins fnl f: no ex* **16/1**

0403 **4** ¾ **Chantilly Tiffany**[33] 5313 5-8-13 103 JimmyFortune 3 97
(E A L Dunlop) *lw: hld up: hdwy over 1f out: sn rdn: kpt on: nt rch ldrs* **14/1**

0500 **5** ¾ **First City**[64] 4259 3-8-10 92 WilliamBuick 2 96
(D M Simcock) *squeezed up leaving stalls: hld up: rdn 2f out: styd on wout troubling ldrs* **20/1**

0035 **6** 1 ½ **Royal Confidence**[16] 5798 4-8-13 102 MichaelHills 10 92
(B W Hills) *mid-div: hdwy whn nt clr run 2f out: sn rdn: kpt on same pce fnl f* **7/1**[3]

3200 **7** ¾ **Please Sing**[16] 5798 3-8-10 97 ChrisCatlin 6 90
(M R Channon) *mid-div: nt clr run whn swtchd rt 2f out: sn rdn: no imp* **20/1**

6150 **8** nk **Penny's Gift**[57] 4489 3-9-2 106 RichardHughes 1 95
(R Hannon) *trckd ldrs: effrt over 1f out: wknd ins fnl f* **8/1**

-421 **9** 1 ¼ **Tropical Paradise (IRE)**[23] 5607 3-8-10 100 JimCrowley 11 86
(P Winkworth) *t.k.h: trckd ldrs: rdn 2f out: wknd ent fnl f* **4/1**[1]

0004 **10** 2 ¾ **Totally Devoted (USA)**[16] 5815 3-8-11 0 ow1 JMurtagh 12 80
(A P O'Brien, Ire) *prom: rdn over 2f out: wknd over 1f out* **8/1**

-506 **11** ½ **Medicea Sidera**[119] 2500 5-8-13 95 JamieSpencer 8 78
(E F Vaughan) *cl up: rdn over 2f out: wknd over 1f out* **16/1**

00-1 **12** 3 ½ **Glowing (IRE)**[87] 3516 4-9-5 103 NCallan 9 75+
(L M Cumani) *w'like: attr: mid-div: hdwy 3f out: sn rdn: wknd over 1f out* **8/1**

1m 26.36s (-1.64) **Going Correction** -0.025s/f (Good)

WFA 3 from 4yo+ 3lb 12 Ran SP% **119.5**

Speed ratings (Par 111): **108,106,106,105,104 103,102,101,100,97 96,92**

toteswinger: 1&2 £10.40, 1&3 £16.20, 2&3 £27.60. CSF £54.96 TOTE £6.20: £2.40, £2.90, £4.40; EX 67.80 Trifecta £1160.40 Pool: £1,725.02 - 1.10 winning units..

Owner The Queen **Bred** The Queen **Trained** Newmarket, Suffolk

FOCUS

A competitive fillies' Listed event. The field raced in the centre of the track before edging over towards the far rail in the last quarter-mile.

NOTEBOOK

Golden Stream(IRE) was switched over to the far side to deliver her run and raced closest to the rail in the end. She showed ahead entering the last and saw it out well. Fifth in the Fillies' Mile a year ago, she has gained both her wins this term at Listed level. (op 6-1 tchd 13-2)

Red Dune(IRE), who has broken blood vessels twice this season, travelled well towards the stands' side and ran on inside the last when let down. This was the first time she has made the first three in a stakes race. (op 9-1)

Greenisland(IRE), back at a more suitable trip after a try over 6f, made the running until the winner went on, and stuck on willingly. She is proving largely consistent. (tchd 14-1 and 20-1 in a place)

Chantilly Tiffany ran on well from the rear to post her best effort since the Royal meeting here. She would have ideally preferred a bit of cut. (op 10-1)

First City, whose stablemate won the earlier fillies' Listed race, had a lot to find on these terms but stayed on down the near side for a respectable fifth. (op 33-1)

Royal Confidence suffered a little trouble in running, although she was in the clear in time had she been good enough. (op 8-1)

Tropical Paradise(IRE) failed to cope with this step up in grade. Not for the first time, she raced rather keenly. (op 9-2)

Glowing(IRE), well beaten on her debut for Luca Cumani, was reported to have lost a front shoe. Official explanation: vet said filly lost a front shoe (op 13-2 tchd 6-1)

6273 TABAC GORDON CARTER STKS (H'CAP) 2m

5:25 (5:25) (Class 3) (0-95,95) 3-Y-O+ **£7,771** (£2,312; £1,155; £577) **Stalls** High

Form RPR

1600 **1** **Kimberley Downs (USA)**[14] 5870 3-7-10 80(v[1]) Louis-PhilippeBeuzelin(5) 4 89+
(M Johnston) *mde all: shkn up to forge clr over 2f out: styd on strly: readily* **15/2**

1642 **2** 4 ½ **Woolfall Treasure**[13] 5903 4-9-8 89 (b) RyanMoore 6 93+
(G L Moore) *mid-div: hdwy over 3f out: sn rdn: styd on to chse wnr over 1f out but nvr any ch* **3/1**[1]

30-1 **3** shd **Mith Hill**[14] 5857 8-8-6 76 oh3 (tp) AndreaAtzeni(3) 1 79+
(Ian Williams) *trckd wnr: rdn 3f out: sn outpcd by wnr: lost 2nd narrowly over 1f out: styd on same pce* **9/1**

1421 **4** 2 ¾ **Sweetheart**[59] 4417 5-8-13 80 NCallan 2 80+
(Jamie Poulton) *lw: mid-div: hdwy to trck ldrs 7f out: rdn wl over 2f out: styd on same pce* **4/1**[2]

2063 **5** ¾ **Relative Strength (IRE)**[14] 5857 4-8-9 76 oh3 (v) WilliamBuick 8 75
(A M Balding) *trckd ldrs: rdn 4f out: wl hld fr over 2f out* **15/2**

1214 **6** nk **Perfect Shot (IRE)**[27] 5481 3-8-7 86 TedDurcan 3 85
(J L Dunlop) *hld up: swtchd lft and rdn 2f out: no imp and hung rt fr over 1f out* **9/2**[3]

1455 **7** 1 **Hendersyde (USA)**[9] 6036 4-9-7 88 AdamKirby 9 86
(W R Swinburn) *hld up: hdwy on outer 3f out: sn rdn: styd on same pce* **11/1**

4006 **8** 22 **Tungsten Strike (USA)**[29] 5402 8-9-4 85 MartinDwyer 5 56
(Mrs A J Perrett) *missed break and could nt get into prom position after being short of room: rn in snatches: a in rr* **16/1**

006/ **9** 3 ½ **Sagredo (USA)**[34] 6400 5-10-0 95 LDettori 10 62
(Jonjo O'Neill) *trckd ldrs: rdn 3f out: wknd 2f out: eased fnl f* **12/1**

3m 31.06s (2.06) **Going Correction** +0.10s/f (Good)

WFA 3 from 4yo+ 12lb **9** Ran SP% **118.6**

Speed ratings (Par 107): **98,95,95,94,93 93,93,82,80**

toteswinger: 1&2 £6.40, 1&3 £13.30, 2&3 £8.20. CSF £31.17 CT £211.19 TOTE £8.80: £2.70, £1.60, £3.30; EX 39.00 Trifecta £292.10 Pool: £1,591.17 - 4.03 winning units. Place 6: £3,443.87, Place 5: £416.55..

Owner Favourites Racing XIX **Bred** Gaines-Gentry Thoroughbreds **Trained** Middleham Moor, N Yorks

FOCUS

A decent staying handicap, if not the strongest turnout for the grade. The winner enjoyed the run of the race but the form seems sound.

NOTEBOOK

Kimberley Downs(USA) made all the running in a first-time visor and, after kicking away in the entrance to the home straight, he was never going to be caught. This longer trip was fine for him and his rider got the tactics spot on. This was the colt's first win on turf. (op 9-1)

Woolfall Treasure, back in the blinkers, could not go with the winner when that one kicked, but he stuck on for second and remains in fine form. He just lacks a change of gear. (op 7-2 tchd 4-1 and 9-2 in a place)

Mith Hill, with cheekpieces instead of a visor, was 3lb wrong at the weights so, in effect, 8lb above his winning mark at Chester. He ran a solid race again but, like the runner-up, could not counter when the winner went for home. (tchd 10-1)

Sweetheart, not seen since since taking the Goodwood Stakes from an 8lb lower mark, travelled quite well, but was unable to quicken when let down over this 5f shorter trip. (op 100-30 tchd 3-1)

Relative Strength(IRE), who was 3lb out of the handicap, was one of the first in trouble but plugged on for fifth. (op 10-1 tchd 7-1)

Perfect Shot(IRE) hung under pressure, not for the first time, and could never get into the race. (op 11-2 tchd 6-1)

Sagredo(USA) Official explanation: jockey said gelding had no more to give

T/Jkpt: Not won. T/Plt: £8,069.50 to a £1 stake. Pool: £189,578.23. 17.15 winning tickets. T/Qpdt: £156.80 to a £1 stake. Pool: £11,512.53. 54.32 winning tickets. TM

5852 CHESTER (L-H)

Saturday, September 26

OFFICIAL GOING: Good to firm (8.2)

Rumnning rail out 5yds from 6f to top of home straight increasing distances by about 10yds per circuit.

Wind: Light, against Weather: Overcast turning fine

6274 SPORTINGBET.COM MAIDEN FILLIES' STKS 7f 2y

2:15 (2:16) (Class 4) 2-Y-O **£5,180** (£1,541; £770; £384) **Stalls** Low

Form RPR

2 **1** **Jacqueline Quest (IRE)**[42] 5021 2-9-0 0 TPQueally 2 90+
(H R A Cecil) *led for 1f: chsd ldr tl regained ld over 2f out: wnt clr over 1f out: easily* **2/7**[1]

5 **2** 9 **A Pocketful Of Rye (IRE)**[80] 3733 2-9-0 0 FrancisNorton 9 66
(J A Osborne) *chsd ldrs: niggled along and outpcd by front pair 3f out: kpt on to take mod 2nd ins fnl f: no ch w wnr* **14/1**

3 1 ¼ **Marie Cuddy (IRE)** 2-9-0 0 SamHitchcott 1 63+
(M R Channon) *racd keenly: led after 1f: pushed along and hdd over 2f out: sn checked whn n.m.r: wl outpcd by wnr over 1f out: lost 2nd ins fnl f: no ex* **7/1**[2]

0 **4** 1 **Sparkling Smile (IRE)**[11] 5969 2-9-0 0 J-PGuillambert 10 60+
(D R Lanigan) *hld up: pushed along and outpcd 3f out: kpt on steadily fnl f: nvr a danger* **33/1**

5 7 **Madame Excelerate** 2-9-0 0 LiamJones 6 43
(W M Brisbourne) *missed break: towards rr: pushed along 4f out: lost tch 2f out* **50/1**

6 6 **Let Them Eat Cake** 2-9-0 0 TonyHamilton 7 29
(R A Fahey) *missed break: bhd: pushed along over 3f out: lost tch 2f out* **10/1**[3]

06 **7** 18 **Lady Pacha**[27] 5466 2-9-0 0 CatherineGannon 4 —
(T J Pitt) *chsd ldrs: rn wd and lost pl after 2f: sn bhd: lost tch 2f out: t.o* **50/1**

1m 27.71s (1.21) **Going Correction** +0.275s/f (Good) 7 Ran SP% **112.9**

Speed ratings (Par 94): **104,93,92,91,83 76,55**

toteswinger: 1&2 £2.50, 1&3 £2.20, 2&3 £4.60. CSF £5.59 TOTE £1.30: £1.10, £4.20; EX 6.20.

Owner N Martin **Bred** Roundhill Stud & C & M Murphy **Trained** Newmarket, Suffolk

FOCUS

An uncompetitive fillies' maiden but an above-average winner.

NOTEBOOK

Jacqueline Quest(IRE) ◆ didn't have to be hard ridden to pull many lengths clear in the straight before being eased near the line. She got a good lead into the race from Marie Cuddy and travelled well, never giving her supporters any worries, and she looks an uncomplicated type. This performance confirmed the potential she showed when runner-up on her debut over 6f at Newbury and a rise in class surely awaits. She doesn't hold any Group 1 entries this year, but is in next season's Irish Guineas and is clearly well regarded. (op 1-3 tchd 4-11 in places)

A Pocketful Of Rye(IRE) ran okay without looking to improve a great deal on the form she showed on her debut over 6f at Kempton.

Marie Cuddy(IRE), a 130,000euros purchase, was too keen on this racecourse debut. She's bred to want further - sister to 1m-1m6f winner Liszt, out of a smart multiple 1m-1m4f scorer in Norway - but will need to learn to settle. (op 15-2 tchd 8-1)

Sparkling Smile(IRE) showed little on her debut at Yarmouth but this was a little better. She should come into her own over further next year. (op 25-1)

6275 I-PAYE LTD NURSERY H'CAP 5f 16y

2:50 (2:50) (Class 3) 2-Y-O **£9,714** (£2,890; £1,444; £721) **Stalls** Low

Form RPR

1354 **1** **Falasteen (IRE)**[25] 5552 2-8-10 86 FrancisNorton 4 91
(D Nicholls) *mde most: rdn whn pressed and jnd by runner-up over 1f out: def advantage fnl 150yds: r.o gamely* **9/4**[1]

0121 **2** ½ **Yurituni**[13] 5899 2-8-3 **79** .... SilvestreDeSousa 7 82
(Eve Johnson Houghton) *w wnr: rdn and disputing ld over 1f out: c off 2nd best fnl 150yds: nt qckn cl home* **3/1**[3]

2130 **3** 3 **Ramamara (IRE)**[16] 5797 2-8-2 **83** .... AndrewHeffernan(5) 2 75
(P D Evans) *in rr: rdn over 1f out: styd on u.p ins fnl f: nt pce to trble front pair* **6/1**

4542 **4** ½ **Fratellino**[102] 2995 2-9-8 **98** .... RobertWinston 5 89
(A J McCabe) *chsd ldrs: rdn and nt qckn over 1f out: kpt on same pce ins fnl f* **11/4**[2]

2020 **5** hd **Transfixed (IRE)**[8] 6048 2-8-1 **77** .... CatherineGannon 8 67
(P D Evans) *chsd ldrs: rdn over 1f out: nt qckn over 1f out: kpt on same pce fnl f* **14/1**

1102 **6** 1¾ **Iver Bridge Lad**[21] 5661 2-9-11 **104** .... MarcHalford(3) 10 88
(J Ryan) *in tch: pushed along 2f out: rn wd and lost pl ent st wl over 1f out: no imp after* **12/1**

1642 **7** 1 **Leleyf (IRE)**[8] 6068 2-8-2 **78** .... LiamJones 9 58
(M R Channon) *hld up: effrt whn nt clr run briefly over 1f out: nvr able to find pce to chal* **16/1**

61.87 secs (0.87) **Going Correction** +0.275s/f (Good) **7 Ran SP% 117.0**
Speed ratings (Par 99): **104,103,98,97,97 94,92**
toteswinger: 1&2 £2.50, 1&3 £3.50, 2&3 £4.10. CSF £9.70 CT £35.08 TOTE £3.10: £2.10, £2.10; EX 10.10.
Owner Dr Marwan Koukash **Bred** Mrs Anne Marie Burns **Trained** Sessay, N Yorks
■ Stewards' Enquiry : Francis Norton caution: used whip with excessive frequency

FOCUS
Just a fair nursery for the grade.

NOTEBOOK
Falasteen(IRE) showed himself to be well treated on this first handicap start. Getting to the lead was obviously a big advantage and, although a little keen, he responded gamely to pressure when strongly challenged in the straight. His attitude should see him win more races. (op 3-1)
Yurituni was given a good ride to sit handy from stall seven and she looked the likeliest winner at the top of the straight, but she could not get by the game winner. She's holding her form well. (tchd 7-2)
Ramamara(IRE) wasn't sharp enough to take advantage of the inside stall (horse drawn one a non-runner) and by the time she got going in the straight the front two were long gone. (op 7-1 tchd 11-2)
Fratellino had been off since finishing second in a sub-standard Windsor Castle in June and a mark of 98 looked plenty high enough for this first handicap start. As it turned out, he ran creditably and is entitled to be sharper next time. (op 3-1 tchd 7-2)
Transfixed(IRE) wasn't helped by a wide draw on this drop in trip (op 12-1)
Iver Bridge Lad covered a lot of ground from stall ten, even allowing for the non runners.
Leleyf(IRE) Official explanation: jockey said filly was denied a clear run

6276 CRABBIES ALCOHOLIC GINGER BEER MAIDEN FILLIES' STKS 1m 2f 75y
3:20 (3:22) (Class 4) 3-Y-0+ **£5,828** (£1,734; £866; £432) **Stalls** High

Form RPR

6 **1** **Benedicte (IRE)**[43] 4991 3-8-12 0 .... JerryO'Dwyer 7 67
(M Botti) *chsd ldr: pushed along over 2f out: rdn to ld over 1f out: styd on dourly towards fin* **7/2**[3]

4435 **2** 1 **Nesayem (IRE)**[13] 5910 3-8-9 67 .... JackMitchell(3) 2 65
(D M Simcock) *hld up: effrt and hdwy to chse ldrs 3f out: styd on to take 2nd fnl 100yds: nvr able to get to wnr* **11/4**[2]

6360 **3** 1¼ **Triple Cee (IRE)**[29] 5382 3-8-12 56 .... SamHitchcott 1 62
(M R Channon) *chsd ldrs: outpcd 3f out: proged u.p ins fnl f: styd on to go 3rd towards fin but unable to get to front 2* **10/1**

2 **4** nk **Crazy Chris**[18] 5751 4-9-4 0 .... RichardKingscote 5 61
(Tom Dascombe) *led: pushed along over 2f out: rdn and hdd over 1f out: no ex fnl 100yds* **6/4**[1]

03 **5** 4 **Amroth**[12] 5939 3-8-12 0 .... TPQueally 6 53
(P D Evans) *chsd ldrs on and off the bridle: rdn over 3f out: wknd ent fnl 2f* **8/1**

P **Amber Glow**[35] 5-8-11 0 .... BillyCray(7) 3 —
(A Berry) *s.i.s: bhd: pushed along wl over 7f out: hung rt 6f out: lost tch over 5f out: t.o whn p.u 2f out* **25/1**

2m 13.9s (1.70) **Going Correction** +0.275s/f (Good)
WFA 3 from 4yo+ 6lb **6 Ran SP% 112.9**
Speed ratings (Par 102): **104,103,102,101,98** —
toteswinger: 1&2 £1.50, 1&3 £5.70, 2&3 £5.20. CSF £13.70 TOTE £4.90: £1.80, £2.00; EX 11.20.
Owner The Great Partnership **Bred** Ascagnano S P A **Trained** Newmarket, Suffolk

FOCUS
They looked a moderate bunch on both form and the way they raced.
Amber Glow Official explanation: jockey said bit slipped through mare's mouth and it hung left

6277 SPORTINGBET.COM STKS (HERITAGE H'CAP) 1m 2f 75y
3:50 (3:50) (Class 2) (0-105,100) **£28,195** (£8,443; £4,221; £2,113; £1,054) **Stalls** High

Form RPR

3032 **1** **Mutamaashi**[22] 5648 3-8-12 **91** .... TPO'Shea 3 94+
(W J Haggas) *dwlt: hld up: hdwy over 1f out: rdr dropped whip whn chalng ins fnl f: led fnl 150yds: r.o and a doing enough under hand riding towards fin* **2/1**[1]

0025 **2** ½ **Goliaths Boy (IRE)**[36] 5209 3-8-3 **82** .... SilvestreDeSousa 5 84
(R A Fahey) *racd keenly: chsd ldr: led over 2f out: rdn whn pressed over 1f out: hdd fnl 150yds: r.o u.p but looked hld after* **8/1**

1161 **3** shd **Hollow Green (IRE)**[31] 5334 3-8-4 **83** .... CatherineGannon 4 85
(P D Evans) *racd keenly: hld up: effrt to chal fnl f: r.o u.p but a looked hld* **11/1**

3330 **4** 1 **Mirrored**[37] 5200 3-9-7 **100** .... TPQueally 1 100
(Sir Michael Stoute) *trckd ldrs: effrt to chal over 1f out: no ex fnl 100yds* **10/3**[3]

1211 **5** 9 **Kaolak (USA)**[13] 5914 3-9-2 **95** .... FrancisNorton 2 79
(J Ryan) *led: pushed along and hdd over 2f out: wknd ent fnl f* **85/40**[2]

2m 13.73s (1.53) **Going Correction** +0.275s/f (Good) **5 Ran SP% 107.9**
Speed ratings (Par 107): **104,103,103,102,95**
CSF £16.32 TOTE £2.80: £1.70, £2.80; EX 14.70.
Owner Hamdan Al Maktoum **Bred** Shadwell Estate Company **Trained** Newmarket, Suffolk

FOCUS
A most disappointing turnout numerically for this valuable 3yo handicap, and the pace was muddling, resulting in a time only 0.17 seconds quicker than the earlier moderate-looking maiden.

NOTEBOOK
Mutamaashi had not had things go his way the last twice, but he made no mistake this time, despite O'Shea dropping his whip in the closing stages. He gives the impression he'll do even better in a strongly run race, but he'll probably need to in order to defy a weight rise. (op 9-4)
Goliaths Boy(IRE) has only a maiden win to his name but he wasn't beaten far over this course and distance last time and this was another solid effort in defeat.
Hollow Green(IRE), 5lb higher than when winning at Ayr on her previous start, was the first off the bridle and needed reminders a fair way out. She got going too late and probably would have preferred a stronger-run race, as well as slightly easier ground. (op 17-2 tchd 8-1)
Mirrored ran better than at York on his previous start, but he was still well held after racing a little keener than ideal and seems to have lost his way. (op 11-4 tchd 7-2)
Kaolak(USA) surprisingly went without the visor he had fitted for his last three wins. Back up in trip for what was a hat-trick bid, and 3lb higher, he was again allowed to dominate, but he is a very sizeable individual with a huge stride and this tight, turning track did not play to his strengths. He can be given another chance, especially if the headgear is re-fitted. Official explanation: vet said colt finished lame (op 9-4 tchd 5-2)

6278 INNOSPEC H'CAP 7f 2y
4:25 (4:26) (Class 3) (0-95,95) 3-Y-0+ **£11,009** (£3,275; £1,637; £817) **Stalls** Low

Form RPR

4600 **1** **Desert Dreamer (IRE)**[3] 6212 8-8-5 **81** oh2 .... CatherineGannon 7 88
(P D Evans) *s.i.s: in rr: hdwy on outer over 2f out: led jst ins fnl f: r.o: edgd lft towards fin* **20/1**

0100 **2** 1 **Brae Hill (IRE)**[23] 5615 3-8-13 **92** .... TPQueally 5 97
(M L W Bell) *chsd ldrs: effrt to chal on inner 1f out: r.o u.p but looked hld fnl 75yds* **13/2**[2]

0604 **3** 1¼ **Damika (IRE)**[7] 6092 6-8-8 **87** .... MichaelJStainton(3) 10 88
(R M Whitaker) *bhd: sn pushed along: prog u.p ins fnl f: gng on at fin but nt rch front 2* **16/1**

0000 **4** 1¾ **Celtic Sultan (IRE)**[15] 5826 5-8-12 **88** .... RobertWinston 8 85
(T P Tate) *chsd ldrs: rdn and tried to chal over 1f out: styd on same pce fnl 100yds* **17/2**

0202 **5** 1 **Lowther**[7] 6089 4-9-0 **95** .... (be) GaryBartley(5) 13 93+
(A Bailey) *s.i.s: midfield: pushed along over 2f out: snatched up whn n.m.r over 1f out: kpt on ins fnl f: unable to get to ldrs* **7/1**[3]

110 **6** 1 **Invincible Force (IRE)**[7] 6089 5-9-3 **93** .... (b) SilvestreDeSousa 3 85
(Paul Green) *led: rdn over 1f out: hdd jst ins fnl f: wknd fnl 100yds* **7/2**[1]

4220 **7** ¾ **Guilded Warrior**[27] 5476 6-8-12 **88** .... LiamJones 6 78
(W S Kittow) *pushed along to chse ldrs: outpcd over 1f out: n.d afrer* **11/1**

0564 **8** nse **Esoterica (IRE)**[8] 6050 6-8-11 **87** .... (v) DanielTudhope 9 77+
(J S Goldie) *midfield: snatched up whn nt clr run over 1f out: no imp after* **14/1**

1230 **9** 2¼ **Summer Dancer (IRE)**[16] 5799 5-8-6 **82** .... PJMcDonald 2 66
(P T Midgley) *hld up: pushed along over 2f out: nvr on terms* **17/2**

0611 **10** ½ **Mujood**[13] 5918 6-8-10 **91** .... (v) AndrewHeffernan(5) 4 72
(Eve Johnson Houghton) *midfield tl lost pl 3f out: bhd after* **7/1**[3]

4-54 **11** 1 **Beat The Bell**[11] 5959 4-8-9 **85** .... FrancisNorton 1 63
(J A Osborne) *pressed ldr: rdn over 1f out: wknd ent fnl f* **8/1**

1110 **12** 4 **My Gacho (IRE)**[7] 6089 7-9-3 **93** .... (v) J-PGuillambert 14 61+
(M Johnston) *s.i.s: bhd: pushed along 2f out: eased whn n.d ins fnl f* **14/1**

1m 27.18s (0.68) **Going Correction** +0.275s/f (Good)
WFA 3 from 4yo+ 3lb **12 Ran SP% 125.0**
Speed ratings (Par 107): **107,105,104,102,101 100,99,99,96,94 93,89**
toteswinger: 1&2 £43.50, 1&3 £49.50, 2&3 £27.60. CSF £152.68 CT £2204.83 TOTE £30.60: £6.20, £2.80, £5.90; EX 248.00.
Owner R Piff **Bred** Gainsborough Stud Management Ltd **Trained** Pandy, Monmouths

FOCUS
A good handicap run at a very strong pace.

NOTEBOOK
Desert Dreamer(IRE), a confirmed hold-up performer who is more often than not reliant on the leaders coming back to him, had the race run to suit. He made his move out very wide, but had sufficient momentum and was a decisive winner from 2lb out of the weights. This win flatters him and it remains to be seen whether he'll follow up.
Brae Hill(IRE) had to wait for a gap and only got in the clear at the cutaway at the top of the straight. He kept on well against the far rail but had no answer to the winner's late burst. (op 11-2)
Damika(IRE), without the cheekpieces this time, stayed on past beaten horses from well off the fast gallop. (op 12-1 tchd 18-1)
Celtic Sultan(IRE) ◆ was unable to dominate, confirming the pace was hot, but he kept on well in the straight and emerges with credit. He's not had things go his way lately and could find a race when things fall kindly. (op 11-1)
Lowther looked unlucky not to go close. He looked to be getting into full stride when blocked in his run around a furlong out and couldn't recover. (op 8-1)
Invincible Force(IRE) had to work hard to lead and was hassled throughout his stay in front by Beat The Bell. (op 9-2 tchd 3-1)
Esoterica(IRE) Official explanation: jockey said gelding was denied a clear run

6279 ADVANCED INSULATION PLC H'CAP 6f 18y
5:00 (5:01) (Class 4) (0-85,85) 3-Y-0+ **£7,123** (£2,119; £1,059; £529) **Stalls** Low

Form RPR

0260 **1** **Rasaman (IRE)**[8] 6050 5-9-2 **81** .... (v) DanielTudhope 3 90
(J S Goldie) *a.p: rdn over 1f out: r.o ins fnl f: led towards fin* **7/2**[1]

0020 **2** ½ **Bel Cantor**[8] 6050 6-8-9 **77** .... (p) KellyHarrison(3) 2 84
(W J H Ratcliffe) *led: pushed along and tried to slip field over 2f out: rdn over 1f out: hdd towards fin* **8/1**[3]

2222 **3** hd **Kingswinford (IRE)**[30] 5363 3-8-4 **76** .... AndrewHeffernan(5) 1 82+
(P D Evans) *prom: pushed along whn nt qckn and n.m.r over 2f out: r.o ins fnl f: gaining fnl strides* **11/2**[2]

2130 **4** 1 **My Kingdom (IRE)**[13] 5916 3-9-2 **83** .... (t) RobertWinston 10 86+
(H Morrison) *hld up: hmpd whn nt clr run over 2f out: plld wd ent st wl over 1f out: hdwy and edgd lft ins fnl f: r.o towards fin: nt rch ldrs* **14/1**

5334 **5** ¾ **I Confess**[8] 6072 4-8-9 **79** .... (v[1]) RichardEvans(5) 7 80
(P D Evans) *prom: rdn 1/2-way: nt qckn over 1f out: kpt on ins fnl f: one pce cl home* **10/1**

5350 **6** ¾ **Solar Spirit (IRE)**[8] 6050 4-8-8 **80** .... IJBrennan(7) 14 78
(J J Quinn) *bhd: plld wd ent st wl over 1f out: hung lft ins fnl f: styd on but nt pce to get to ldrs* **33/1**

5412 **7** shd **Grissom (IRE)**[8] 6051 3-8-4 **78** .... BillyCray(7) 6 76+
(A Berry) *in tch: hmpd whn n.m.r over 2f out: u.p after: styd on ins fnl f: one pce fnl 75yds* **12/1**

0000 **8** 1 **Orpsie Boy (IRE)**[14] 5860 6-9-6 **85** .... J-PGuillambert 8 80
(N P Littmoden) *midfield: pushed along 1/2-way: rdn over 1f out: plugged on at one pce ins fnl f* **12/1**

5210 **9** ½ **Noodles Blue Boy**[10] 5978 3-8-8 **75** .... FrancisNorton 12 68+
(Ollie Pears) *s.i.s: in rr: pushed along over 1f out: kpt on ent fnl f: eased whn no imp towards fin* **16/1**

3523 **10** ¾ **Memphis Man**[30] 5363 6-8-9 **74** .... CatherineGannon 5 65+
(P D Evans) *midfield: outpcd over 1f out: eased whn btn ins fnl f* **11/1**

3050 **11** ¾ **Efistorm**[13] 5919 8-8-12 **80** .... JackMitchell(3) 9 68
(C R Dore) *lost pl after 1f: pushed along towards rr 4f out: hdwy 2f out: no imp on ldrs over 1f out: wknd ins fnl f* **33/1**

0003 **12** *¾* **Legal Eagle (IRE)**[5] 6171 4-8-11 **76**..................(b[1]) SilvestreDeSousa 11 62
(Paul Green) *in tch: n.m.r 2f out: rdn and hung lft over 1f out: wknd fnl f* **12/1**

0040 **13** *hd* **Earlsmedic**[8] 6050 4-9-0 **82**..................................(v) WilliamCarson(3) 13 67
(S C Williams) *midfield: hdwy 1/2-way: rdn and outpcd over 1f out: wknd ins fnl f* **16/1**

0005 **14** *1 ¼* **Methaaly (IRE)**[11] 5960 6-8-10 **75**..................................(b) LiamJones 4 56+
(M Mullineaux) *missed break: bhd: nvr on terms: eased whn btn over 1f out* **8/1**[3]

1m 15.43s (1.63) **Going Correction** +0.275s/f (Good)
WFA 3 from 4yo+ 2lb **14** Ran SP% **124.6**
Speed ratings (Par 105): **100,99,99,97,96 95,95,94,93,92 91,90,90,88**
toteswinger: 1&2 £8.00, 1&3 £6.70, 2&3 £11.50. CSF £31.94 CT £138.89 TOTE £4.80: £1.90, £3.20, £2.60; EX 32.50.
Owner Paul Moulton **Bred** Rasana Partnership **Trained** Uplawmoor, E Renfrews
■ Stewards' Enquiry : J-P Guillambert two-day ban: careless riding (Oct 10-11)
Robert Winston caution: careless riding.

FOCUS
A fair, competitive sprint handicap run at a strong pace. The first three finishers emerged from the bottom three stalls.
Grissom(IRE) Official explanation: jockey said gelding was denied a clear run
Memphis Man Official explanation: jockey said gelding was denied a clear run
Efistorm Official explanation: vet said gelding bled from the nose
Methaaly(IRE) Official explanation: jockey said gelding hit its head on the stalls and was slowly away

6280 CRUISE NIGHTCLUB H'CAP 1m 5f 89y
5:35 (5:35) (Class 4) (0-80,81) 3-Y-O+ **£7,123** (£2,119; £1,059; £529) **Stalls** Low

Form RPR

4641 **1** **Spirit Of Adjisa (IRE)**[23] 5593 5-10-1 **81**...................... RobertWinston 2 90
(Pat Eddery) *in tch: pushed along to cl 3f out: chal 2f out: led over 1f out: sn edgd lft: r.o gamely ins fnl f: plld out ex towards fin* **4/1**[3]

4003 **2** *1 ¼* **Dazzling Light (UAE)**[7] 6095 4-9-9 **75**......................... DanielTudhope 4 82
(J S Goldie) *hld up: hdwy 3f out: chsd wnr over 1f out: r.o and tried to chal ins fnl f: no further imp cl home* **3/1**[2]

1640 **3** *8* **Vita Mia**[14] 5858 3-8-1 **62**... CatherineGannon 8 58
(P D Evans) *chsd ldrs: wnt 2nd over 3f out: led over 2f out: hdd over 1f out: wknd and lost tch w front pair ins fnl f* **9/1**

352 **4** *1 ½* **Zuwaar**[9] 6021 4-8-11 **70**..(tp) JPFahy(7) 1 64
(Ian Williams) *s.i.s: midfield: hdwy to chse ldrs 3f out: wknd over 1f out* **9/4**[1]

6310 **5** *1 ½* **Destinys Dream (IRE)**[22] 5622 4-9-3 **72**.................... KellyHarrison(3) 7 64
(Miss Tracy Waggott) *missed break: hld up: sme hdwy over 2f out: outpcd over 1f out* **8/1**

3000 **6** *9* **Ella Woodcock (IRE)**[5] 6157 5-8-13 **65**....................(b) FrancisNorton 3 44
(E J Alston) *led after 1f: clr over 4f out to over 3f out: hdd over 2f out: sn wknd* **12/1**

2501 **7** *9* **Inspector Clouseau (IRE)**[43] 4972 4-9-1 **70**............... DominicFox(3) 6 37
(T P Tate) *led for 1f: chsd ldr tl pushed along over 3f out: sn wknd* **10/1**

0000 **8** *1 ½* **Thorny Mandate**[9] 6025 7-8-9 **61** oh14........................... LiamJones 9 26
(W M Brisbourne) *missed break: hld up in rr: pushed along over 2f out: sn outpcd* **20/1**

2m 55.98s (2.78) **Going Correction** +0.275s/f (Good)
WFA 3 from 4yo+ 9lb **8** Ran SP% **118.4**
Speed ratings (Par 105): **102,101,96,95,94 88,83,82**
toteswinger: 1&2 £4.00, 1&3 £7.10, 2&3 £7.00. CSF £17.13 CT £103.03 TOTE £5.60: £2.00, £1.60, £2.60; EX 20.40 Place 6: £78.07, Place 5: £64.36..
Owner Darr, Johnson, Weston & Whitaker **Bred** C J Haughey J Flynn And E Mulhern **Trained** Nether Winchendon, Bucks

FOCUS
A fair handicap run at a decent pace.
T/Plt: £77.40 to a £1 stake. Pool: £63,565.80. 599.14 winning tickets. T/Qpdt: £44.30 to a £1 stake. Pool: £2,612.30. 43.60 winning tickets. DO

6245 HAYDOCK (L-H)
Saturday, September 26

OFFICIAL GOING: Good to firm (8.3)
Rail realignment increased advertised distances on round course by 21yds.
Wind: light, half against Weather: overcast

6281 GORDON PLANT MEMORIAL TROPHY H'CAP 1m 6f
2:25 (2:25) (Class 3) (0-90,88) 3-Y-O+
£11,215 (£3,358; £1,679; £840; £419; £210) **Stalls** Low

Form RPR

2U0 **1** **Lochiel**[47] 4840 5-9-12 **86**.. PJMcDonald 8 93
(G A Swinbank) *trckd ldrs: effrt over 3f out: hung lft: led over 1f out: hld on towards fin* **13/2**

0302 **2** *½* **Overturn (IRE)**[21] 5667 5-9-11 **88**......................... FrederikTylicki(3) 4 94
(W R Swinburn) *led: qckd over 3f out: hdd appr fnl f: rallied: no ex towards fin* **3/1**[2]

1642 **3** *nk* **Murcar**[15] 5837 4-8-13 **73**...(b) IanMongan 2 79
(C G Cox) *s.i.s: sn midfield: effrt over 3f out: hung lft and kpt on fnl f* **9/2**[3]

4353 **4** *shd* **Gordonsville**[6] 6138 6-9-8 **82**... DanielTudhope 10 88
(J S Goldie) *hld up in rr: hdwy over 2f out: styd on fnl f: nt quite rch ldrs* **11/4**[1]

4403 **5** *3 ½* **Lost Soldier Three (IRE)**[7] 6100 8-9-7 **81**.................. AdrianTNicholls 7 83+
(D Nicholls) *chsd ldrs: drvn over 3f out: one pce fnl 2f: eased towards fin* **8/1**

064 **6** *5* **Red Kestrel (USA)**[46] 4882 4-9-9 **83**.................................. PhillipMakin 1 78
(K A Ryan) *hld up in midfield: effrt over 2f out: sn rdn: lost pl over 2f out* **12/1**

4012 **7** *1 ½* **Bajan Parkes**[11] 5961 6-9-8 **82**.. DavidAllan 3 75
(E J Alston) *chsd ldrs: drvn over 3f out: lost pl over 2f out* **9/1**

115/ **8** *46* **Indian Pipe Dream (IRE)**[165] 6250 7-9-13 **87**................ DO'Donohoe 5 20
(S Gollings) *s.i.s: sn pushed along detached in last: t.o 4f out* **25/1**

3m 3.12s (-1.18) **Going Correction** +0.075s/f (Good) **8** Ran SP% **115.8**
Speed ratings (Par 107): **106,105,105,105,103 100,99,73**
toteswinger: 1&2 £4.90, 1&3 £5.80, 2&3 £5.80. CSF £26.72 CT £97.66 TOTE £7.70: £2.20, £1.50, £2.20; EX 32.00 Trifecta £114.00 Pool: £187.96 - 1.22 winning units..
Owner G Hawkes & Partner **Bred** D W Barker **Trained** Melsonby, N Yorks

FOCUS
Most of those who ran in this race did not look to have much in hand of the handicapper, so the form is probably just ordinary.

NOTEBOOK
Lochiel was thrashed at Southwell last time, but, after travelling well into the race, he got to the front and held on gamely under pressure despite hanging a little. He wins in his turn but this success came off a career-high mark, so he will need to improve to be competitive next time. (op 6-1)
Overturn(IRE) ◆, trying this sort of trip for the first time, was a little less exposed than most and attracted plenty of market support. Sent straight into the lead, he got all of his rivals off the bridle at some stage of the contest and battled on bravely to get placed. He should win something similar. (op 13-2)
Murcar, another to be held up, kept on without really looking like winning. (op 7-2)
Gordonsville ran well at Hamilton just under a week previously and was strong in the betting here. Held up, he could never get to the first two home, after his rider bided his time up the home straight. (op 3-1)
Lost Soldier Three(IRE) has been coming down the weights and stayed on again after being outpaced. (op 7-1)
Red Kestrel(USA) had held his form fairly well but this was a disappointing effort. (op 10-1 tchd 9-1)
Bajan Parkes, a course winner, was beaten shortly after the home bend. Official explanation: jockey said, regarding running and riding, gelding had tired in the home straight and would have not produced more or achieved a better placing for more vigorous riding in the final half-furlong (op 8-1)
Indian Pipe Dream(IRE), having his first run since being pulled up over hurdles at Market Rasen in April, never got competitive and was soon behind. (tchd 22-1)

6282 MANCHESTER EVENING NEWS H'CAP 6f
3:00 (3:01) (Class 2) (0-100,99) 3-Y-O+ **£12,952** (£3,854; £1,926; £962) **Stalls** Centre

Form RPR

0060 **1** **Hitchens (IRE)**[7] 6091 4-9-2 **95**... PhillipMakin 5 105
(T D Barron) *hld up in rr: hdwy 2f out: styd on wl ins fnl f: led post* **7/1**[3]

6050 **2** *shd* **Prohibit**[56] 4523 4-9-4 **97**.. RobertHavlin 13 107
(J H M Gosden) *racd keenly: hdwy over 2f out: led over 1f out: edgd lft: jst ct* **3/1**[1]

2200 **3** *¾* **Red Cape (FR)**[7] 6089 6-8-9 **88**....................................... AndrewElliott 2 95
(Mrs R A Carr) *chsd ldrs on outer: kpt on wl fnl f* **20/1**

5520 **4** *½* **Novellen Lad (IRE)**[8] 6050 4-8-6 **85**.................................... DavidAllan 1 91
(E J Alston) *chsd ldrs on wd outside: kpt on same pce ins fnl f* **14/1**

0056 **5** *hd* **Pearly Wey**[15] 5826 6-8-7 **86**.. PhilipRobinson 3 91
(C G Cox) *dwlt: hdwy on outside 2f out: kpt on ins fnl f* **8/1**

1020 **6** *nse* **Everymanforhimself (IRE)**[7] 6091 5-9-6 **99**.............(v) DarryllHolland 7 104+
(K A Ryan) *hmpd s: hld up in rr: hdwy and nt clr run over 1f out: styd on strly: nt rch ldrs* **7/1**[3]

5000 **7** *1* **Tajneed (IRE)**[7] 6089 6-8-11 **90**................................(b) AdrianTNicholls 11 92
(D Nicholls) *swvd lft s: sn w ldrs: fdd fnl 150yds* **6/1**[2]

41 **8** *nk* **Filligree (IRE)**[13] 5901 4-8-6 **88**.............................. WilliamCarson(3) 8 89
(Rae Guest) *carried lft s: mid-div: effrt over 2f out: kpt on: nvr rchd ldrs* **9/1**

5535 **9** *1* **Pretty Bonnie**[23] 5607 4-8-8 **87**...................................... KirstyMilczarek 6 85
(A E Price) *chsd ldrs on outer: wknd over 1f out* **22/1**

4510 **10** *nk* **Silver Wind**[8] 6050 4-8-1 **85**..(v) MartinLane(5) 4 82
(P D Evans) *chsd ldrs: drvn and outpcd over 2f out: lost pl over 1f out* **20/1**

0656 **11** *3 ¼* **Confuchias (IRE)**[212] 696 5-9-4 **97**...................................... PaulEddery 9 83
(Pat Eddery) *swvd lft s: sn chsng ldrs: drvn over 2f out: lost pl over 1f out: eased ins fnl f* **14/1**

0600 **12** *7* **Drawnfromthepast (IRE)**[15] 5826 4-8-6 **88**........... FrederikTylicki(3) 12 52
(J A Osborne) *led tl hdd & wknd over 1f out: eased ins fnl f* **12/1**

1m 13.62s (-0.88) **Going Correction** +0.075s/f (Good)
WFA 3 from 4yo+ 2lb **12** Ran SP% **120.3**
Speed ratings (Par 109): **108,107,106,106,105 105,104,104,102,102 98,88**
toteswinger: 1&2 £10.20, 1&3 £23.60, 2&3 £14.80. CSF £27.77 CT £419.27 TOTE £8.10: £2.80, £1.70, £5.10; EX 35.50 TRIFECTA Not won..
Owner Laurence O'Kane **Bred** Curragh Bloodstock Agency Ltd **Trained** Maunby, N Yorks

FOCUS
A competitive sprint that provided a tight finish.

NOTEBOOK
Hitchens(IRE) did not disgrace himself in the Ayr Gold Cup the previous weekend and returned to his best after picking up in game style once the gaps had opened. He is just the sort to fear in big-field sprints for years to come, but there are no immediate plans for him.
Prohibit hit the front after travelling strongly, and the race looked over. However, once in the lead he tended to doss, and was collared in virtually the last stride. (op 4-1 tchd 11-4)
Red Cape(FR) also returned to form after a slightly below-par performance in the Ayr Silver Cup. His connections have enjoyed a fantastic summer with him. (op 16-1)
Novellen Lad(IRE) did well after racing prominently and his turn should not be far away, although a drop of a few pounds in the handicap would help.
Pearly Wey ◆ took a long time to get going from the rear of the pack, and only stayed on rather than quickened. He is handicapped to win again. (op 7-1 tchd 13-2)
Everymanforhimself(IRE) did not get going very quickly after leaving the stalls and never looked like getting involved in the fight for first place after meeting a little trouble. (op 8-1)
Tajneed(IRE) helped to set a decent pace but could not sustain it inside the final two furlongs. (op 13-2 tchd 7-1)
Filligree(IRE) got pushed along at halfway and could make no impact. (tchd 8-1)

6283 BETFRED LESTER PIGGOTT "START TO FINISH" H'CAP 5f
3:35 (3:36) (Class 2) (0-100,100) 3-Y-O+**£16,190** (£4,817; £2,407; £1,202) **Stalls** Centre

Form RPR

0043 **1** **Green Manalishi**[7] 6089 8-8-9 **90**...............................(p) DarryllHolland 12 102
(K A Ryan) *trckd ldrs: effrt appr fnl f: r.o wl to ld last 50yds: readily* **4/1**[1]

0105 **2** *1* **Impressible**[14] 5871 3-8-5 **87**... DavidProbert 1 95
(E J Alston) *racd wd: w overall ldr: led jst ins fnl f: hdd and no ex towards fin* **25/1**

4533 **3** *hd* **Atlantic Story (USA)**[16] 5799 7-8-7 **88**..................(bt) GrahamGibbons 5 96
(M W Easterby) *rrd s: in rr out wd: hdwy over 1f out: styd on wl ins fnl f* **10/1**

4330 **4** *nk* **Fol Hollow (IRE)**[7] 6091 4-9-1 **96**................................ AdrianTNicholls 2 103
(D Nicholls) *racd wd: overall ldr: hdd jst ins fnl f: no ex* **12/1**

1000 **5** *1 ¼* **Mandurah (IRE)**[49] 4766 5-8-6 **87**.. GregFairley 4 89
(B P J Baugh) *racd wd: chsd ldrs: kpt on same pce fnl f* **33/1**

3413 **6** *nk* **Lenny Bee**[13] 5919 3-8-4 **86** oh1.................................... RoystonFfrench 9 87
(D H Brown) *led stands' side gp: edgd lft and one pce fnl f* **12/1**

3110 **7** *½* **Jaconet (USA)**[14] 5860 4-8-12 **93**.....................................(b) PhillipMakin 7 92
(T D Barron) *racd wd: chsd ldrs: styd on same pce appr fnl f* **8/1**

0-00 **8** *nk* **Copper Dock (IRE)**[20] 5699 5-8-2 **88**.................................(t) BACurtis(5) 10 86
(T G McCourt, Ire) *stdd s: hld up towards rr: kpt on fnl 2f: nvr nr ldrs* **28/1**

0000 **9** *¾* **River Falcon**[7] 6089 9-8-6 **90**.................................. KellyHarrison(3) 15 85
(J S Goldie) *in rr: hung lft over 1f out: nvr nr ldrs* **16/1**

2260 **10** 1 1/4 **Hamish McGonagall**[21] 5654 4-9-4 **99** DavidAllan 6 90
(T D Easterby) *racd wd: hld up: hdwy 2f out: nvr nr ldrs* **7/1**[3]
1041 **11** shd **Doctor Parkes**[54] 4601 3-8-4 **86** DaleGibson 14 77
(E J Alston) *chsd ldrs: hung lft and wknd over 1f out* **14/1**
4066 **12** 3/4 **Oldjoesaid**[14] 5860 5-9-1 **96** FergusSweeney 13 86+
(H Candy) *rrd s: a towards rr: hmpd ins fnl f* **5/1**[2]
0500 **13** 2 3/4 **Piscean (USA)**[16] 5799 4-8-5 **86** (b) KirstyMilczarek 11 64
(T Keddy) *s.i.s: t.k.h in rr: sme hdwy over 2f out: lost pl over 1f out* **20/1**
0360 **14** 2 1/4 **Hoh Hoh Hoh**[17] 5765 7-9-0 **100** MartinLane(5) 8 77+
(R J Price) *chsd ldrs: lost pl over 1f out: hmpd ins fnl f: eased* **12/1**

60.24 secs (-0.86) **Going Correction** +0.075s/f (Good)
WFA 3 from 4yo+ 1lb **14** Ran SP% **123.4**
Speed ratings (Par 109): **109,107,107,106,104 104,103,102,101,99 99,98,93,90**
toteswinger: 1&2 £32.20, 1&3 £6.40, 2&3 £44.90. CSF £116.44 CT £985.35 TOTE £4.20: £2.00, £8.60, £3.90; EX 130.20 Trifecta £637.50 Part won. Pool: £861.60 - 0.30 winning units..
Owner Mrs S McCarthy, J Brennan & J Smith **Bred** E Aldridge **Trained** Hambleton, N Yorks

FOCUS
Loads of familiar names in this cracking sprint, and much depended on who was feeling their best on the day. The field split and it paid to finish towards the centre of the course.

NOTEBOOK
Green Manalishi, who won this race as a four-year-old, had been more than hinting at a return to form in recent starts and duly built on them with a commanding display once asked to get to the front. He is worth keeping onside if turned out again soon, but connections plan to give him a break for a couple of weeks.
Impressible helped to set the gallop towards the middle and battled on very well to claim second. She has had a good season and continues to show improvement. (op 33-1)
Atlantic Story(USA) got behind but stayed on very well to grab third. All of his winning form is over much further. (op 16-1)
Fol Hollow(IRE), back to 5f, showed his usual speed and ran up to his best.
Mandurah(IRE) was always somewhere near the leading bunch and kept going to the line. He needs to be eased a few pounds in the handicap.
Lenny Bee, who raced near the stands' side early, was another three-year-old to run well but was ultimately held under pressure. (op 14-1 tchd 16-1)
Jaconet(USA) could not lead this time but was running on a little at the end. (op 7-1 tchd 9-1)
Doctor Parkes Official explanation: jockey said gelding hung left throughout
Oldjoesaid, another winner of this race, had been showing glimpses of a return to form, so this was disappointing even allowing for being on what looked the wrong side. Official explanation: jockey said gelding missed the break (op 6-1 tchd 13-2)

6284 E B F THE MILLSTONE PUB REOPENS FOR BUSINESS MAIDEN FILLIES' STKS 1m 30y
4:05 (4:05) (Class 5) 2-Y-O **£3,885** (£1,156; £577; £288) **Stalls** Low

Form RPR
53 **1** **Zahoo (IRE)**[18] 5741 2-9-0 0 DO'Donohoe 2 74
(J L Dunlop) *trckd ldrs: drvn over 2f out: styd on to ld jst ins fnl f: hld on wl* **11/8**[1]
65 **2** 1 **Dancing Queen (IRE)**[18] 5741 2-9-0 0 PhillipMakin 4 72
(M A Magnusson) *led: hdd and no ex jst ins fnl f* **4/1**[3]
00 **3** nk **Anaya**[18] 5741 2-8-11 0 MCGeran(3) 8 71
(M R Channon) *trckd ldrs: t.k.h: effrt over 2f out: kpt on ins fnl f* **50/1**
3 **4** nk **Miss Antonia (IRE)**[18] 5752 2-9-0 0 IanMongan 3 70
(H R A Cecil) *trckd ldrs: styd on same pce fnl f* **3/1**[2]
5 3/4 **Yankee Bright (USA)** 2-8-11 0 FrederikTylicki(3) 10 69+
(J G Given) *s.i.s: effrt over 3f out: kpt on fnl f* **25/1**
6 hd **Aktia (IRE)** 2-9-0 0 KirstyMilczarek 1 68
(L M Cumani) *s.i.s: hdwy on ins over 4f out: styd on steadily fnl f: will improve* **16/1**
00 **7** 11 **Fine Lace (IRE)**[38] 5165 2-9-0 0 TolleyDean 9 44
(D J S Ffrench Davis) *mid-div: rdn over 3f out: lost pl 2f out* **66/1**
8 2 1/2 **Mrs E** 2-8-7 0 JamesPSullivan(7) 7 39
(M W Easterby) *s.s: sme hdwy over 3f out: sn wknd* **40/1**
00 **9** 1 3/4 **Albacocca**[10] 5984 2-8-7 0 RosieJessop(7) 6 35+
(Sir Mark Prescott) *s.s: in rr: bhd fnl 2f* **66/1**
10 2 1/2 **Lily Rio (IRE)** 2-9-0 0 DavidProbert 5 29
(W R Muir) *hld up in rr: bhd fnl 2f* **16/1**
0 **11** 8 **Alhena (IRE)**[12] 5949 2-9-0 0 DarryllHolland 12 12
(K A Ryan) *s.i.s: bhd fnl 2f: eased* **10/1**

1m 46.38s (2.58) **Going Correction** +0.075s/f (Good) **11** Ran SP% **119.2**
Speed ratings (Par 92): **90,89,88,88,87 87,76,73,72,69 61**
toteswinger: 1&2 £2.60, 1&3 £12.10, 2&3 £24.70. CSF £6.92 TOTE £2.20: £1.20, £1.60, £7.30; EX 9.60.
Owner Hamdan Al Maktoum **Bred** Shadwell Estate Company Limited **Trained** Arundel, W Sussex

FOCUS
An ordinary-looking event, in which the early pace was not strong.

NOTEBOOK
Zahoo(IRE) shaped well at Goodwood last time and gained a deserved success by running all the way to the line under a strong ride. There was a brief scare for her jockey passing the post as his mount jinked, but the job was already done by then and she remains progressive. (op 7-4)
Dancing Queen(IRE) ◆ was not quite good enough to reverse form with the winner on their meeting last time. That said, there are clear signs to show she is progressing.
Anaya is going the right way with experience, keeping on strongly inside the final furlong after getting a little outpaced.
Miss Antonia(IRE), who caught the eye on her debut, was not given a hard time by her rider in the final 100 yards after holding every chance at one stage. (op 5-2)
Yankee Bright(USA) ◆ got the idea up the home straight and should have a future. (op 33-1)
Aktia(IRE) ◆, closely related to the very useful two-year-old 6f winner Fashion Rocks, was given a good ride on her debut and should show the benefit next time. (op 12-1)
Lily Rio(IRE) Official explanation: jockey said filly ran green

6285 E B F JULIE FITZPATRICK MAIDEN STKS (C&G) 1m 30y
4:40 (4:40) (Class 5) 2-Y-O **£3,885** (£1,156; £577; £288) **Stalls** Low

Form RPR
6 **1** **Graymalkin (IRE)**[16] 5786 2-9-0 0 DO'Donohoe 1 83
(Saeed Bin Suroor) *s.i.s: sn chsng ldrs: drvn on inner over 3f out: edgd rt over 2f out: edgd lft and styd on to ld wl ins fnl f* **7/1**[3]
0623 **2** 1/2 **Start Right**[14] 5864 2-9-0 80 KirstyMilczarek 4 82
(L M Cumani) *w ldr: t.k.h: rdn to ld over 1f out: jnd whn jinked rt and hdd wl ins fnl f: no ex* **13/8**[2]
62 **3** 3 1/4 **Super Collider**[29] 5408 2-9-0 0 PhilipRobinson 2 75
(M A Jarvis) *led: qcknd over 3f out: hdd over 1f out: one pce* **5/4**[1]
0 **4** 6 **Isdaar (IRE)**[140] 1866 2-9-0 0 RobertHavlin 7 62+
(J H M Gosden) *s.i.s: in rr: hdwy on inner 4f out: kpt on fnl 2f: will improve* **16/1**
4420 **5** 1 1/4 **Music Of The Moor (IRE)**[29] 5407 2-9-0 78 (b[1]) DNolan 6 59
(T P Tate) *trckd ldrs: drvn over 2f out: hung lft and sn lost pl* **10/1**
0 **6** 3 **King's Realm (IRE)**[5] 6162 2-8-7 0 RosieJessop(7) 5 52+
(Sir Mark Prescott) *trckd ldrs: effrt on outside over 3f out: lost pl over 2f out* **33/1**
0 **7** shd **State Visit**[13] 5907 2-9-0 0 DavidProbert 8 52+
(W R Muir) *w ldrs: rdn over 2f out: wknd over 1f out* **25/1**
0 **8** 36 **Dubara Reef (IRE)**[21] 5669 2-9-0 0 TolleyDean 3 —
(Paul Green) *chsd ldrs: lost pl after 2f: sn wl bhd: hopelessly t.o* **66/1**

1m 44.51s (0.71) **Going Correction** +0.075s/f (Good) **8** Ran SP% **118.3**
Speed ratings (Par 95): **99,98,95,89,88 85,84,48**
toteswinger: 1&2 £3.10, 1&3 £2.50, 2&3 £2.00. CSF £19.38 TOTE £8.20: £1.90, £1.20, £1.20; EX 28.50.
Owner Godolphin **Bred** Darley **Trained** Newmarket, Suffolk
■ Stewards' Enquiry : D O'Donohoe one-day ban: careless riding (Oct 10)

FOCUS
A couple of nice types have won this maiden in the past, and the top-rated runner in this had a mark of 80, so the race should prove to be fairly good.

NOTEBOOK
Graymalkin(IRE) did not show much on his debut (he was reported after this win to have not handled the undulating track at Chepstow) and looked to have a bit to do halfway up the home straight, but he responded well to pressure and got up close to the winning line. He adds yet another winner to Godolphin's already impressive haul this season. (tchd 13-2)
Start Right did not run too badly in a decent nursery last time and again ran his race here. He looked set to score coming to the final furlong, but the winner proved just that bit too strong in the dying strides. (op 11-8)
Super Collider had been progressing nicely, so this was a little disappointing. He was far from disgraced but did not see out the trip as strongly as the first two. (op 13-8 tchd 7-4)
Music Of The Moor(IRE) had not been out since running disappointingly in May. He was never close enough to get involved. (op 12-1)

6286 EUROPEAN BREEDERS' FUND "REPROCOLOR" FILLIES' H'CAP 1m 2f 95y
5:15 (5:19) (Class 3) (0-90,89) 3-Y-O+ **£12,952** (£3,854; £1,926; £962) **Stalls** Centre

Form RPR
14 **1** **Gripsholm Castle (USA)**[93] 3315 3-9-8 **89** IanMongan 7 105+
(H R A Cecil) *led 3f: c wd st and led over 2f out: drew clr appr fnl f* **10/3**[1]
6046 **2** 7 **Presbyterian Nun (IRE)**[15] 5828 4-9-8 **83** (p) PhilipRobinson 8 86
(J L Dunlop) *trckd ldrs: t.k.h: wd st: hung lft and tk 2nd over 1f out: no ch w wnr* **9/2**[2]
2100 **3** 3 1/2 **Summer Gold (IRE)**[15] 5828 5-9-6 **81** DavidAllan 2 78
(E J Alston) *trckd ldrs: t.k.h: c wd over 3f out: one pce* **12/1**
3130 **4** 1 1/2 **Stan's Cool Cat (IRE)**[22] 5648 3-9-4 **85** (b[1]) GregFairley 4 79
(P F I Cole) *in rr: pushed along 6f out: outpcd over 3f out: wandered: nvr a factor* **8/1**
0453 **5** 4 **Rio Guru (IRE)**[13] 5910 4-8-6 **70** ow1 MCGeran(3) 1 57
(M R Channon) *in rr: pushed along over 5f out: nvr on terms: hung lft and collided w running rail ins fnl f* **15/2**
12 **6** 23 **Assabiyya (IRE)**[34] 5285 3-9-5 **86** DO'Donohoe 5 50+
(Saeed Bin Suroor) *w ldr: led after 3f: remained far side and hdd over 2f out: sn wknd: bhd whn eased over 1f out: t.o* **11/2**[3]

2m 12.02s (-0.98) **Going Correction** +0.075s/f (Good)
WFA 3 from 4yo+ 6lb **6** Ran SP% **87.2**
Speed ratings (Par 104): **106,100,97,96,93 74**
toteswinger: 1&2 £2.20, 1&3 £4.60, 2&3 £4.40. CSF £10.69 CT £57.88 TOTE £3.50: £1.80, £2.20; EX 9.90.
Owner Gestut Ammerland **Bred** Aleyrion Bloodstock **Trained** Newmarket, Suffolk

FOCUS
A decent handicap for fillies and mares, with only 8lb separating seven of the runners. However, there was trouble before the off, as \Sterling Sound and Grantsville decided to be proper madams and refuse to go in the stalls.

NOTEBOOK
Gripsholm Castle(USA), having her first run since the end of June, was dropping in class after an outing in Listed company and showed the benefit by striding clear once asked to quicken. It is worth noting that she was brought up the centre of the course once turning in, a route others decided to shun. (op 7-2 tchd 4-1)
Presbyterian Nun(IRE), wearing cheekpieces for the first time, followed the winner towards the middle of the course but never had a hope of catching her. She hung a little when making her bid. (op 5-1 tchd 7-2)
Summer Gold(IRE) kept plugging away to capture third. (op 11-1 tchd 14-1)
Stan's Cool Cat(IRE), fitted with blinkers for the first time, did not find a great deal when asked to chase the leading pair and could not bridge the gap to the third either. (op 9-1 tchd 7-1)
Rio Guru(IRE) started to hang under pressure, which negated her chance of being placed. Official explanation: jockey said filly hung left (op 9-1 tchd 10-1)
Assabiyya(IRE) got turned over at 4-9 last time and put up another lacklustre performance after having an easy lead. Official explanation: jockey said filly ran flat (op 5-1 tchd 9-2)
T/Plt: £38.00 to a £1 stake. Pool: £83,474.81. 1,603.23 winning tickets. T/Qpdt: £4.90 to a £1 stake. Pool: £4,396.06. 652.10 winning tickets. WG

6223 KEMPTON (A.W) (R-H)
Saturday, September 26

OFFICIAL GOING: Standard
Wind: virtually nil Weather: bright and sunny

6287 PANORAMIC BAR & RESTAURANT MAIDEN STKS 1m 2f (P)
5:45 (5:49) (Class 5) 3-Y-O+ **£2,590** (£770; £385; £192) **Stalls** High

Form RPR
1 **Mutamayez** 3-9-3 0 AlanMunro 9 77+
(M A Jarvis) *in tch: effrt between horses wl over 1f out: qcknd to ld over 1f out: clr fnl f: comf* **6/5**[1]
323 **2** 3 **Ramora (USA)**[41] 5061 3-8-12 75 JimmyQuinn 3 63
(H R A Cecil) *chsd ldng trio: pushed along and hdwy to chse ldr over 5f out: rdn over 3f out: ev ch 2f out: nt pce of wnr over 1f out: kpt on to go 2nd nr fin* **3/1**[2]
3-3 **3** hd **Meyyal (USA)**[43] 4979 3-9-3 0 EddieAhern 7 68
(B W Hills) *chsd ldng pair: rdn to ld on inner 2f out: hdd over 1f out: sn outpcd by wnr and wl hld fnl f: lost 2nd nr fin* **4/1**[3]
060 **4** 1 1/2 **Dramatic Jewel (USA)**[46] 4867 3-9-3 46 GeorgeBaker 13 65
(J W Hills) *in tch in midfield: n.m.r on inner 3f out: rdn and hdwy 2f out: chsd ldrs and n.m.r wl over 1f out: one pce fnl f* **66/1**
06 **5** 3/4 **Mistoffelees**[10] 5987 3-9-3 0 PatCosgrave 2 64+
(L M Cumani) *hld up towards rr: hdwy and wl in tch over 2f out: nudged along and no prog wl over 1f out: rdn and styd on steadily ins fnl f: nvr rchd ldrs* **33/1**
00 **6** 1 1/2 **Catchmeifyoucan (FR)**[80] 3751 3-9-3 0 DaneO'Neill 5 61
(C G Cox) *dwlt: sn in tch: hdwy on outer to chse ldrs 5f out: rdn over 2f out: outpcd wl over 1f out and wl hld fnl f* **25/1**

7 2 3/4 **Northern Genes (AUS)** 3-8-5 0 ow2 NeilChalmers 12 44
(M R Bosley) *s.i.s: hld up in last trio: hdwy into midfield wl over 2f out: no imp fnl 2f* **66/1**

8 5 **Father Figure (USA)**[94] 3-9-3 0 StephenCarson 6 47
(Heather Dalton) *chsd ldr tl over 5f out: wknd qckly u.p over 2f out* **25/1**

9 3 1/4 **Bengers Lass (USA)** 3-8-12 0 StephenDonohoe 8 36
(R Curtis) *s.i.s: hld up in last trio: rdn and struggling over 3f out: no ch fnl 2f* **50/1**

66 10 1 1/2 **Tribal Rule**[110] 2763 3-9-3 0 (t) JimCrowley 10 38
(Mrs A J Perrett) *led: hdd and rdn 2f out: wknd rapidly* **8/1**

11 1 3/4 **Dovedon Earl** 3-9-3 0 LPKeniry 1 35
(T Keddy) *s.i.s: hld up in last trio: rdn and struggling over 3f out: sn wl bhd* **100/1**

2m 6.76s (-1.24) **Going Correction** -0.10s/f (Stan)
WFA 3 from 4yo 6lb **11** Ran SP% **118.1**
Speed ratings (Par 103): **100,97,97,96,95 94,92,88,85,84 83**
toteswinger: 1&2 £1.50, 1&3 £2.60, 2&3 £2.80. CSF £4.60 TOTE £2.00: £1.10, £1.20, £1.30; EX 5.20.
Owner Hamdan Al Maktoum **Bred** Ptarmigan Bloodstock Ltd **Trained** Newmarket, Suffolk

FOCUS
No more than a run of the mill maiden.

6288 BOOK KEMPTON TICKETS ON 0844 579 3008 H'CAP 1m 2f (P)
6:15 (6:22) (Class 6) (0-65,65) 3-Y-0+ **£2,047** (£604; £302) **Stalls** High

Form RPR

20 1 **Blue Turk**[45] 4916 4-8-13 **56** PatCosgrave 6 64
(J R Boyle) *hld up in tch in midfield: hdwy over 2f out: rdn to chse ldr over 1f out: led ins fnl f: r.o wl: eased nr fin* **16/1**

0033 2 1 **Dinner Date**[9] 6017 7-9-6 **63** LPKeniry 2 69
(T Keddy) *stdd and dropped in after s: towards rr: stdy hdwy 7f out: rdn to ld and edgd rt over 1f out: drvn and hdd ins fnl f: kpt on same pce* **14/1**

2036 3 1/2 **Apotheosis**[42] 5035 4-9-7 **64** EddieAhern 12 69
(W R Swinburn) *chsd ldrs: swtchd lft and rdn wl over 1f out: kpt on u.p to go 3rd wl ins fnl f* **5/1**[1]

6315 4 3/4 **Petomic (IRE)**[22] 5630 4-9-0 **62** RossAtkinson(5) 11 66
(M Hill) *t.k.h: chsd ldr tl led ent fnl 2f: edgd rt u.p and hdd over 1f out: one pce after* **8/1**[3]

2602 5 3/4 **Noah Jameel**[30] 5377 7-8-13 **56** DaneO'Neill 10 58
(A G Newcombe) *towards rr: stl plenty to do 2f out: swtchd lft and hdwy on outer over 1f out: r.o fnl f: nt rch ldrs* **11/1**

642 6 1/2 **Randama Bay (IRE)**[11] 5962 4-9-8 **65** RichardHughes 8 67
(I A Wood) *chsd ldrs: rdn and outpcd 2f out: rallied u.p fnl f: nt pce to chal ldrs* **5/1**[1]

00 7 1 1/2 **Mississippian (IRE)**[17] 5779 5-9-7 **64** HayleyTurner 7 63
(C J Mann) *v.s.a: t.k.h: hld up in rr: rdn and hdwy wl over 1f out: drvn and no prog over 1f out* **33/1**

0500 8 hd **Zaif (IRE)**[3] 6204 6-9-5 **62** ChrisCatlin 9 60
(D J S Ffrench Davis) *hld up in last pair: hdwy on outer and pushed along 3f out: c wd bnd 2f out: r.o fnl f: nvr trbld ldrs* **22/1**

4612 9 hd **Resplendent Ace (IRE)**[8] 6074 5-9-8 **65** JimmyQuinn 5 66+
(P Howling) *hld up in rr: last over 2f out: nt clr run and swtchd lft wl over 1f out: r.o fnl f: nvr trbld ldrs* **15/2**[2]

6601 10 1 1/2 **Hits Only Cash**[8] 6074 7-9-5 **62** (p) StephenDonohoe 4 57
(J Pearce) *dwlt: bustled along early: towards rr: pushed along 3f out: hdwy over 1f out: nvr trbld ldrs* **14/1**

024 11 4 1/2 **Almahaza (IRE)**[61] 4373 5-9-4 **61** NeilChalmers 13 52+
(A J Chamberlain) *in tch: rdn and unable qck whn hmpd and dropped to rr wl over 1f out: no ch after* **9/1**

300- 12 1 **Josr's Magic (IRE)**[289] 7642 5-9-1 **58** JimCrowley 1 43
(T E Powell) *t.k.h: hld up towards rr: sme hdwy on outer 3f out: wknd 2f out* **25/1**

3340 13 1 1/4 **National Monument (IRE)**[39] 5123 3-9-2 **65** ShaneKelly 3 48
(J A Osborne) *chsd ldrs: rdn whn hmpd and lost pl qckly wl over 1f out: sn bhd* **40/1**

4323 14 7 **Prince Charlemagne (IRE)**[150] 1609 6-9-4 **61** GeorgeBaker 14 32
(G L Moore) *led tl rdn and hdd 2f out: wknd qckly wl over 1f out: eased ins fnl f* **8/1**[3]

2m 8.23s (0.23) **Going Correction** -0.10s/f (Stan)
WFA 3 from 4yo+ 6lb **14** Ran SP% **118.4**
Speed ratings (Par 101): **95,94,93,93,92 92,91,90,90,89 85,85,84,78**
toteswinger: 1&2 £48.10, 1&3 £17.80, 2&3 £12.10. CSF £211.30 CT £1292.47 TOTE £18.80: £5.30, £3.50, £2.00; EX 363.90.
Owner Byerley Thoroughbred Racing **Bred** Manor Farm Packers Ltd **Trained** Epsom, Surrey

Almahaza(IRE) Official explanation: jockey said gelding was denied a clear run
National Monument(IRE) Official explanation: jockey said gelding hung right throughout

6289 MIX BUSINESS WITH PLEASURE H'CAP 1m 2f (P)
6:45 (6:51) (Class 5) (0-70,70) 3-Y-0 **£2,590** (£770; £385; £192) **Stalls** High

Form RPR

0-11 1 **Arty Crafty (USA)**[5] 6156 3-8-6 **58** ow1 StephenDonohoe 5 66+
(Sir Mark Prescott) *chsd ldrs on outer: rdn 3f out: hdwy u.p to ld 1f out: edgd rt and hrd pressed ins fnl f: fnd ex and hld off rivals towards fin* **4/5**[1]

000 2 1/2 **Noble Dictator**[30] 5366 3-8-8 **60** JimmyQuinn 9 67
(E F Vaughan) *hld up towards rr: hdwy over 2f out: rdn and in tch whn nt clr run jst over 1f out: sn swtchd lft: str run to press wnr ins fnl f: no ex and hld towards fin* **10/1**

-500 3 shd **The Dial House**[40] 5101 3-9-4 **70** ShaneKelly 1 77
(J A Osborne) *v.s.a: hld up in rr: hdwy jst over 2f out: hanging rt and no hdwy over 1f out: hdwy on outer 1f out: pressed wnr ins fnl f: no ex and hld nr fin* **33/1**

-444 4 2 3/4 **Freedom Fire (IRE)**[67] 4178 3-8-12 **64** MickyFenton 8 65
(J M P Eustace) *chsd ldr: ev ch 2f out: drvn over 1f out: keeping on same pce and btn whn bmpd and nt clr run wl ins fnl f* **14/1**

6446 5 1 1/2 **Piquante**[26] 5524 3-9-0 **66** HayleyTurner 12 64
(M L W Bell) *hld up wl in tch: trckd ldrs 2f out: rdn to chal over 1f out: wknd fnl 100yds* **9/1**[3]

00 6 1/2 **Colangnik (USA)**[13] 5915 3-9-3 **69** NCallan 11 66
(J R Best) *hld up in tch in midfield: hdwy to chse ldrs and rdn wl over 1f out: one pce and no imp ent fnl f* **20/1**

5450 7 hd **Hip Hip Hooray**[13] 5915 3-9-0 **66** (p) SteveDrowne 13 64+
(L A Dace) *dwlt: sn rcvrd to chse ldrs: rdn and effrt 2f out: n.m.r ent fnl f: sn swtchd lft and bmpd rival: nt clr run and no hdwy after* **33/1**

0201 8 1 1/4 **Foxtrot Charlie**[24] 5570 3-9-2 **68** (b) JimCrowley 14 62
(P Winkworth) *led: rdn ent fnl 2f: hdd 1f out: wknd fnl f* **5/2**[2]

0234 9 21 **Fine Tolerance**[42] 5015 3-8-4 **56** oh3 NickyMackay 4 8+
(J R Boyle) *in tch in midfield: rdn and hdwy over 5f out: wknd u.p wl over 1f out: eased fnl f* **25/1**

0000 10 2 1/2 **Allexes (IRE)**[24] 5581 3-8-4 **56** oh3 (p) LukeMorris 3 3+
(J R Boyle) *hld up in rr: lost tch over 2f out: eased over 1f out: t.o* **66/1**

0060 11 1 **Refuse Toulouse (IRE)**[17] 5782 3-8-4 **56** WilliamBuick 10 1+
(C G Cox) *in tch tl lost pl and rdn over 3f out: wl bhd and eased over 1f out* **25/1**

0000 12 9 **Ma Patrice**[18] 5751 3-8-4 **56** oh11 ChrisCatlin 7 —
(T D McCarthy) *s.i.s: a bhd: hmpd and lost tch 4f out: sn t.o: eased fr wl over 1f out* **66/1**

0000 P **Whispered Lands (IRE)**[17] 5779 3-8-1 **56** oh10 AndreaAtzeni(3) 2 —
(J R Boyle) *a towards rr: pushed along over 7f out: rdn and no rspnse over 5f out: lost action and eased 4f out: p.u and dismntd 2f out: lame* **66/1**

2m 5.63s (-2.37) **Going Correction** -0.10s/f (Stan) **13** Ran SP% **132.7**
Speed ratings (Par 101): **105,104,104,102,101 100,100,99,82,80 79,72,—**
toteswinger: 1&2 £5.30, 1&3 £17.40, 2&3 £40.50. CSF £11.78 CT £192.94 TOTE £2.10: £1.50, £2.10, £11.10; EX 18.80.
Owner Mrs Sonia Rogers **Bred** Airlie Stud **Trained** Newmarket, Suffolk

FOCUS
Just an ordinary handicap.
Refuse Toulouse(IRE) Official explanation: jockey said colt never travelled
Ma Patrice Official explanation: trainer said filly had a breathing problem

6290 LEVY BOARD CONDITIONS STKS 1m 2f (P)
7:15 (7:19) (Class 3) 3-Y-0+
£7,352 (£2,201; £1,100; £551; £274; £138) **Stalls** High

Form RPR

5666 1 **Heliodor (USA)**[21] 5662 3-8-10 103 RichardHughes 2 107
(R Hannon) *sn led: mde rest: rdn wl over 1f out: looked vulnerable ins fnl f: fnd ex and styd on wl fnl 75yds: wnt lft nr fin* **14/1**

012 2 nk **Wasan**[91] 3397 4-9-4 110 MartinDwyer 8 109
(E A L Dunlop) *in tch: pushed along 6f out: rdn and hdwy to chse wnr over 1f out: str chal jst ins fnl f: no ex: hld and wnt lft nr fin* **2/1**[1]

3-6 3 1 **Copperbeech (IRE)**[128] 2190 3-8-5 107 TedDurcan 3 101+
(Saeed Bin Suroor) *chsd ldr over 8f out tl 4f out: lost pl bnd 2f out: rallied u.p to chse ldng pair ins fnl f: keeping on but hld whn hmpd and eased nr fin* **8/1**

0012 4 2 **Beauchamp Xerxes**[7] 6110 3-8-10 95 EddieAhern 6 101
(G A Butler) *stdd s: hld up towards rr: hdwy on outer over 2f out: kpt on u.p fnl f: nvr had pce to rch ldrs* **13/2**[3]

1000 5 3/4 **Philatelist (USA)**[24] 5587 5-9-2 103 (v[1]) NCallan 7 99
(M A Jarvis) *t.k.h: hld up in tch in midfield: rdn and effrt on inner 2f out: chsd ldng pair over 1f out: swtchd lft jst ins fnl f: no imp after and lost 2 pls fnl 150yds* **8/1**

14-5 6 2 **Acclaimed (IRE)**[9] 6030 4-9-2 103 ShaneKelly 10 95
(J Noseda) *chsd wnr tl over 8f out: chsd wnr again 4f out: rdn and nt qckn wl over 1f out: wknd over 1f out* **11/2**[2]

-000 7 2 3/4 **Rock Ascot (URU)**[60] 4408 5-9-2 90 GeorgeBaker 9 90
(G L Moore) *hld up in last trio: rdn and no prog over 2f out* **100/1**

3006 8 3 **King Of Rome (IRE)**[8] 6056 4-9-2 110 PatCosgrave 5 84
(M F De Kock, South Africa) *chsd ldrs: rdn and struggling over 2f out: no ch fr wl over 1f out* **8/1**

023 9 6 **Perks (IRE)**[62] 4352 4-9-2 104 JimmyQuinn 4 72
(J L Dunlop) *s.i.s: a in rr: struggling u.p over 2f out* **8/1**

32-0 10 5 **Doubnov (FR)**[134] 2055 6-9-2 95 StephenDonohoe 1 62
(Ian Williams) *v.s.a: a last: lost tch over 2f out* **66/1**

2m 3.81s (-4.19) **Going Correction** -0.10s/f (Stan)
WFA 3 from 4yo+ 6lb **10** Ran SP% **115.6**
Speed ratings (Par 107): **112,111,110,109,108 107,104,102,97,93**
toteswinger: 1&2 £9.00, 1&3 £22.30, 2&3 £2.90. CSF £41.92 TOTE £15.10: £3.60, £1.50, £2.80; EX 72.70.
Owner Mrs J Wood **Bred** Kim Nardelli Et Al **Trained** East Everleigh, Wilts
■ Stewards' Enquiry : Richard Hughes two-day ban: careless riding (+ four days deferred) (Oct 10-15)

FOCUS
Quite a decent conditions event and the pace looked very honest. The winning time was very fast.

NOTEBOOK
Heliodor(USA) put up a terrific effort. He thrived for more positive tactics, having been held up in all his previous races this season. He appeared to love being allowed to bowl along in a rhythm and responded well when the challengers came to his quarters approaching the final furlong. This was a drop in grade so it wasn't a complete surprise, but he has definitely posted an improved performance. (tchd 16-1)
Wasan had every chance when getting into the clear early in the straight, but the concession of 8lb to the winner proved beyond him. Still, this was a very decent effort in defeat and he is still going to be a threat when stepped back up in class. (op 13-8)
Copperbeech(IRE) found a second wind late in the day, having dropped away early in the straight, and this was a much more encouraging effort than her debut for Godolphin in the spring. She isn't bred to want any further, but she shapes like she's worth a try at it. (op 13-2 tchd 9-1)
Beauchamp Xerxes stayed on well from off the pace and this keen-going sort appreciated the decent gallop. He had a very stiff task on these terms so connections will be very pleased with this. (op 8-1)
Philatelist(USA) raced too freely in the first-time visor, but he kept on well up the inside and this was a real step in the right direction after some quiet runs. (op 10-1 tchd 15-2)
Acclaimed(IRE) dropped away in the final furlong and shaped like a non-stayer. (op 15-2 tchd 8-1)
Doubnov(FR) Official explanation: jockey said gelding lost its action final 2f

6291 "BUY A £10,000 RACING POST BONUS YEARLING" MEDIAN AUCTION MAIDEN STKS 1m (P)
7:45 (7:50) (Class 6) 2-Y-0 **£2,047** (£604; £302) **Stalls** High

Form RPR

03 1 **Natural Law (IRE)**[17] 5770 2-9-3 0 (p) TedDurcan 6 80+
(Saeed Bin Suroor) *led after 1f: mde rest: hrd pressed and rdn ent fnl 2f: styd on strly fnl f* **7/1**[3]

02 2 1 1/4 **Inside Track (IRE)**[22] 5627 2-9-3 0 MartinDwyer 8 77
(B J Meehan) *led briefly after s: sn stdd bk to trck ldrs: effrt u.p to chse ldng pair 2f out: kpt on same pce u.p: wnt 2nd fnl 100yds* **11/4**[1]

52 3 1 **Swift Return**[11] 5966 2-9-3 0 NCallan 10 75
(S C Williams) *led sn after s tl hdd after 1f: trckd ldrs after: effrt to chal ent fnl 2f: hung lft and nt qckn over 1f out: continued to hang lft and btn ins fnl f: lost 2nd fnl 100yds* **4/1**[2]

5 4 4 **Temple Queen**[10] 5984 2-8-12 0 JamesDoyle 3 61
(S Kirk) *chsd ldrs: wnt 2nd 6f out: rdn and unable qck jst over 2f out: no ch w ldng trio fnl f* **7/1**[3]

0 **5** *1 ½* **Dubai Phantom (USA)**[16] 5787 2-9-3 0...............(b) StephenDonohoe 4 63
(D M Simcock) *t.k.h: chsd ldrs: rdn and unable qck over 2f out: wl outpcd by ldrs 2f out: wl hld after* **50/1**

0 **6** *hd* **Foxtrot Delta (IRE)**[30] 5368 2-9-3 0.......................... JimCrowley 12 62
(P Winkworth) *in tch in midfield: rdn and effrt on inner jst over 2f out: drvn and wknd over 1f out* **16/1**

0 **7** *2 ½* **Belle Zorro**[10] 5984 2-8-12 0.......................... HayleyTurner 9 52
(M L W Bell) *hld up in tch in midfield: rdn and outpcd over 2f out: no ch w ldrs fnl 2f* **25/1**

8 *shd* **Tammela** 2-8-12 0.......................... AlanMunro 7 52+
(A P Jarvis) *s.i.s: rn green and sn pushed along in rr: sme modest late hdwy: nvr trbld ldrs* **66/1**

0 **9** *½* **Heligoland**[29] 5379 2-8-12 0.......................... ChrisCatlin 2 50
(A G Newcombe) *s.i.s: t.k.h: hld up towards rr on outer: outpcd wl over 2f out: plugged on fnl f: n.d* **100/1**

10 *1* **Cordiality** 2-9-3 0.......................... GeorgeBaker 13 53+
(J R Fanshawe) *s.i.s: rn green and sn nudged along in rr: nvr on terms* **10/1**

04 **11** *2 ¼* **Loden**[13] 5907 2-9-3 0.......................... WilliamBuick 11 48
(L M Cumani) *s.i.s: in tch in rr: rdn and no prog over 2f out* **4/1**[2]

12 *3 ¼* **Set To Go** 2-9-3 0.......................... DaneO'Neill 1 41
(H J L Dunlop) *s.i.s: sn in midfield: rdn and struggling 3f out: sn bhd* **66/1**

13 *10* **Roar Talent (USA)** 2-9-3 0.......................... SteveDrowne 5 19
(J R Best) *s.i.s: rn green in rr: lost tch over 3f out* **50/1**

1m 39.96s (0.16) **Going Correction** -0.10s/f (Stan) **13** Ran SP% **118.4**
Speed ratings (Par 93): **95,93,92,88,87 87,84,84,83,82 80,77,67**
toteswinger: 1&2 £5.70, 1&3 £6.10, 2&3 £3.80. CSF £25.60 TOTE £6.90: £3.00, £1.60, £1.90; EX 29.20.
Owner Godolphin **Bred** Mount Coote Stud **Trained** Newmarket, Suffolk

FOCUS
No more than a fair maiden.

NOTEBOOK
Natural Law(IRE) wore cheekpieces the first time and the headgear had a positive effect on the Lomitas colt who posted an improved effort to get off the mark. Having bounced out to lead and make all the running, he looked like getting swamped at the cutaway but to his credit he knuckled down well and was well in charge in the final half furlong. His sire's progeny have a better record on turf than Polytrack, so it's likely this colt has more to offer on grass and he still has a couple of big sales race entries. (op 9-2 tchd 15-2)
Inside Track(IRE) stayed on well without having the change of gear to bustle up the winner in the straight. He is improving, though, and can be expected to find a maiden soon. (op 5-2 tchd 7-2)
Swift Return darted up the inside at the cutaway and looked a big threat, but his run flattened out and he was caught for second by the stronger-finishing Inside Track. He clearly has ability and backend nurseries look the way forward now. (op 7-2 tchd 3-1)
Temple Queen did well to get across smartly from her low draw and she tracked the pace throughout before finding the going too tough at the business end. She remains open to improvement and clearly has ability. (op 8-1 tchd 9-1)
Dubai Phantom(USA) stepped up plenty on his poor debut run. Official explanation: jockey said colt ran too free
Foxtrot Delta(IRE) also stepped up on his first start without screaming out that he's a certain future winner. (op 20-1)

6292 SUBSCRIBE TO RACING UK CLAIMING STKS 6f (P)
8:15 (8:17) (Class 6) 2-Y-O **£2,047** (£604; £302) **Stalls** High

Form RPR

6522 **1** **Saxby (IRE)**[15] 5841 2-8-13 69.......................... ChrisCatlin 10 70
(M R Channon) *mde all: edgd lft u.p fr over 1f out: a holding runner-up thrght fnl f* **6/1**[3]

5302 **2** *hd* **Avow (USA)**[7] 6122 2-8-5 61..........................(b) SophieDoyle(5) 6 66
(J S Moore) *t.k.h: sn w wnr: rdn and ev ch fr 2f out: nt qckn and a jst hld fnl f* **25/1**

0653 **3** *1* **Lady Pattern (IRE)**[15] 5835 2-9-0 78.......................... EddieAhern 9 67
(P W D'Arcy) *wnt lft s: in tch: hdwy u.p to chse ldng pair over 1f out: one pce fnl f* **7/2**[2]

0060 **4** *1 ½* **French Connexion (IRE)**[30] 5369 2-8-5 60.......................... LukeMorris 8 54
(J S Moore) *hmpd s: hld up towards rr: hdwy and rdn on inner jst over 2f out: edgd lft and drvn over 1f out: kpt on but nvr had pce to rch ldrs* **50/1**

5 *½* **Fire Raiser** 2-9-0 0.......................... LPKeniry 11 61
(A M Balding) *v.s.a: racd in last pair: hdwy towards inner jst over 2f out: rdn and edging out lft ent fnl f: kpt on: nvr trbld ldrs* **16/1**

0035 **6** *1 ½* **George Baker (IRE)**[16] 5811 2-8-5 72..........................(p) MatthewDavies(5) 7 53
(George Baker) *hld up in rr: swtchd to outer and rdn over 2f out: sn hung lft and no prog: nvr trbld ldrs* **12/1**

1232 **7** *½* **Diamond Laura**[15] 5835 2-8-9 80.......................... NCallan 12 51
(Mrs R A Carr) *chsd ldrs: effrt on inner and rdn jst over 2f out: wknd u.p ent fnl f* **4/5**[1]

5504 **8** *½* **Flapjack**[24] 5583 2-7-11 58.......................... CharlesEddery(7) 5 44
(R Hannon) *s.i.s: a towards rr: rdn wl over 2f out: plugged on but nvr trbld ldrs* **33/1**

0 **9** *1 ½* **Show Willing (IRE)**[9] 6009 2-8-8 0.......................... AndrewElliott 4 43
(A P Jarvis) *t.k.h: in tch tl wknd u.p over 2f out* **66/1**

0204 **10** *4* **Lochbroom Sunset**[7] 6122 2-8-9 60.......................... SaleemGolam 2 32
(S C Williams) *in tch in midfield: rdn and struggling over 2f out: wl bhd fnl f* **33/1**

1m 12.95s (-0.15) **Going Correction** -0.10s/f (Stan) **10** Ran SP% **118.8**
Speed ratings (Par 93): **97,96,95,93,92 90,90,89,87,82**
toteswinger: 1&2 £12.60, 1&3 £3.60, 2&3 £13.40. CSF £143.13 TOTE £8.20: £1.80, £4.30, £1.70; EX 90.00.Saxby was claimed by G A Harker for £13,000.
Owner Mrs M Findlay **Bred** R N Auld **Trained** West Ilsley, Berks
■ Stewards' Enquiry : Chris Catlin one-day ban: excessive use of the whip (Oct 10)
Sophie Doyle one-day ban: used whip with excessive frequency (Oct 10)

FOCUS
A modest claimer.

NOTEBOOK
Saxby(IRE) made all the running and proved thoroughly resolute in the closing stages to hold off Avow. The 69-rated winner is what he is, but he is commendably genuine and that proved enough against these rivals. He can continue to pay his way at this level. (op 7-1 tchd 8-1)
Avow(USA) had a bit to find on these terms and he was quite keen early so he did well to push the winner all the way; this is one of his best efforts so far. (op 20-1)
Lady Pattern(IRE) continues to run with credit. Official explanation: jockey said filly hung left (op 100-30 tchd 4-1)
French Connexion(IRE) wasn't disgraced. (op 66-1)
Fire Raiser is much more interesting from a long-term perspective and he didn't shape at all badly in fifth. He can be expected to do better in time. (op 12-1)

Show Willing(IRE) Official explanation: jockey said filly ran too free

6293 DAY TIME, NIGHT TIME, GREAT TIME CLAIMING STKS 6f (P)
8:45 (8:45) (Class 6) 3-Y-O+ **£2,047** (£604; £302) **Stalls** High

Form RPR

0060 **1** **Ginobili (IRE)**[13] 5902 3-9-1 80..........................(b) MickyFenton 3 65
(Stef Liddiard) *hld up bhd: rdn and hdwy on outer 2f out: ev ch 1f out: led fnl 150yds: hld on wl* **8/1**

431 **2** *hd* **Who's Winning (IRE)**[16] 5788 8-9-2 52..........................(t) KirstyMilczarek 5 63
(B G Powell) *bhd: rdn and outpcd 4f out: hdwy u.p 2f out: ev ch 1f out: pressed wnr fnl f: a jst hld* **14/1**

000 **3** *2* **Sweet Kiss (USA)**[42] 5020 4-8-10 49.......................... JimCrowley 10 51
(M J Attwater) *dwlt: sn rcvrd to chse ldng trio: hdwy u.p over 2f out: ev ch 1f out: one pce after* **33/1**

1000 **4** *½* **Esteem Machine (USA)**[7] 6112 5-9-7 86.......................... LukeMorris 4 61
(R A Teal) *stdd and swtchd rt to rail after s: hdwy over 2f out: rdn to ld jst over 1f out: hdd fnl 150yds: one pce after* **2/1**[2]

60 **5** *hd* **Shadow Bay (IRE)**[93] 3299 3-9-3 67.......................... SamHitchcott 11 58
(Miss Z C Davison) *sn outpcd in rr: rdn over 3f out: hdwy on inner jst over 2f out: ev ch 1f out: no ex fnl f* **33/1**

0641 **6** *2 ¼* **Mutamared (USA)**[13] 5916 9-9-7 79.......................... StephenCarson 12 54
(Andrew Reid) *w ldrs: ev ch and rdn over 2f out: wknd jst ins fnl f: btn whn n.m.r and eased ins fnl f* **6/4**[1]

0004 **7** *1 ¼* **Tadlil**[22] 5633 7-9-3 47.......................... SteveDrowne 8 46
(J M Bradley) *led narrowly tl 3f out: struggling whn squeezed and hmpd wl over 1f out: wl hld after* **25/1**

002 **8** *hd* **Fromsong (IRE)**[10] 5989 11-9-2 65.......................... MarkCoumbe(5) 7 49
(D K Ivory) *sn pressing ldrs on outer: led 3f out: rdn 2f out: hdd jst over 1f out: wkng whn n.m.r ins fnl f* **7/1**[3]

1m 13.0s (-0.10) **Going Correction** -0.10s/f (Stan)
WFA 3 from 4yo+ 2lb **8** Ran SP% **113.3**
Speed ratings (Par 101): **96,95,93,92,92 89,87,87**
toteswinger: 1&2 £13.00, 1&3 £30.10, 2&3 £35.40. CSF £103.12 TOTE £10.50: £2.10, £2.60, £5.50; EX 125.70.Ginobili was claimed by Andrew Reid for £6,000.
Owner David Gilbert **Bred** Victor Stud Bloodstock Ltd **Trained** Great Shefford, Berks

FOCUS
A strong pace to this claimer and the speed folded in the closing stages allowing the hold-up horses to burst onto the scene.

6294 KEMPTON.CO.UK H'CAP 7f (P)
9:15 (9:15) (Class 5) (0-70,73) 3-Y-O+ **£2,590** (£770; £385; £192) **Stalls** High

Form RPR

0000 **1** **Trade Centre**[18] 5753 4-9-5 **69**.......................... MartinDwyer 2 77
(W R Muir) *sn prom: w ldr over 3f out: ev ch and rdn jst over 2f out: led fnl 75yds: jst lasted* **10/1**

0351 **2** *hd* **Millfield (IRE)**[17] 5779 6-9-6 **70**.......................... GeorgeBaker 4 77
(P R Chamings) *stdd and dropped in bhd after s: plld hrd: hld up in last trio: hdwy over 1f out: squeezed between horses ins fnl f: r.o wl: nt quite rch wnr* **8/1**

-066 **3** *nse* **Muftarres (IRE)**[30] 5370 4-9-4 **68**..........................(t) NCallan 7 75
(G A Butler) *wnt lft s: t.k.h: hld up in tch: rdn and effrt 2f out: swtchd lft 1f out: str run fnl f: nt quite rch ldrs* **11/2**[3]

3100 **4** *hd* **Bold Marc (IRE)**[55] 4560 7-9-5 **69**.......................... AndrewElliott 5 76
(A P Jarvis) *t.k.h: chsd ldrs tl led 4f out: hrd pressed and rdn jst over 2f out: hdd fnl 75yds: lost 2 pls last strides* **10/1**

1603 **5** *1* **Support Fund (IRE)**[10] 5991 5-9-5 **69**.......................... ShaneKelly 9 73
(Eve Johnson Houghton) *hld up in last trio: rdn and hdwy over 1f out: r.o ins fnl f: nt pce to rch ldrs* **12/1**

4032 **6** *hd* **Billberry**[19] 5723 4-9-4 **68**..........................(t) JimCrowley 8 71
(S C Williams) *t.k.h: hld up in tch in rr: rdn and effrt on outer 2f out: kpt on but no imp fnl f* **5/1**[2]

5054 **7** *½* **Satwa Star (IRE)**[21] 5677 3-9-2 **69**.......................... TGMcLaughlin 10 70
(E A L Dunlop) *plld hrd: chsd ldr tl 4f out: styd handy: rdn to press ldrs over 1f out: one pce ins fnl f* **13/2**

3212 **8** *nse* **Equinine (IRE)**[13] 5916 3-9-6 **73**.......................... WilliamBuick 12 74
(B W Hills) *led tl 4f out: chsd ldrs after: rdn and effrt on inner 2f out: kpt on same pce ins fnl f* **4/1**[1]

100 **9** *1 ¾* **Sendreni (FR)**[129] 2185 5-9-6 **70**..........................(t) DaneO'Neill 14 67
(M Wigham) *t.k.h: hld up in tch: rdn and effrt over 1f out: no imp fnl f* **6/1**

0645 **10** *½* **Gentle Guru**[23] 5592 5-9-5 **69**.......................... SteveDrowne 6 65
(R T Phillips) *sltly hmpd s: t.k.h: in tch: rdn and effrt over 2f out: wknd jst ins fnl f* **20/1**

1m 26.04s (0.04) **Going Correction** -0.10s/f (Stan)
WFA 3 from 4yo+ 3lb **10** Ran SP% **121.4**
Speed ratings (Par 103): **95,94,94,94,93 93,92,92,90,89**
toteswinger: 1&2 £10.20, 1&3 £9.70, 2&3 £11.10. CSF £91.05 CT £495.21 TOTE £11.50: £3.60, £4.00, £2.50; EX 174.30 Place 6: £35.90, Place 5: £32.85..
Owner K Mercer,C Edginton,S Jones,M Dawson **Bred** Usk Valley Stud **Trained** Lambourn, Berks

FOCUS
A tight handicap with just 4lb separating the whole field so no surprise to see a bunch finish.
Billberry Official explanation: trainer said gelding lost a hind shoe
T/Plt: £33.50 to a £1 stake. Pool: £61,076.08. 1,327.46 winning tickets. T/Qpdt: £12.70 to a £1 stake. Pool: £5,872.92. 341.50 winning tickets. SP

6295 - 6297a (Foreign Racing) - See Raceform Interactive

4919 GOWRAN PARK (R-H)
Saturday, September 26

OFFICIAL GOING: Good to firm

6298a DENNY CORDELL LAVARACK & LANWADES STUD FILLIES STKS (GROUP 3) 1m 1f 100y
4:00 (4:02) 3-Y-O+ **£50,485** (£14,757; £6,990; £2,330)

RPR

1 **Ave**[45] 4903 3-8-11 .... RichardMullen 9 106+
(Sir Michael Stoute) *trckd ldrs: 5th travelling best st: qcknd to ld 1 1/2f out: sn rdn clr: easily* **11/4**[2]

2 *1 ½* **Choose Me (IRE)**[16] 5815 3-8-11 102.......................... DPMcDonogh 1 102
(Kevin Prendergast, Ire) *hld up towards rr: 10th into st: 7th and hdwy under 2f out: 3rd 1f out: r.o* **12/1**

3 *1 ½* **Rose Hip (IRE)**[8] 6078 5-9-2 96.......................... WMLordan 2 99
(Joseph G Murphy, Ire) *mid-div: 7th 1/2-way: 6th on outer ent st: chal under 2f out: 2nd and no imp 1f out: kpt on* **14/1**

4 *3* **Beach Bunny (IRE)**[54] 4609 4-9-2 113 .... CDHayes 4 93
(Kevin Prendergast, Ire) *hld up towards rr: 9th 1/2-way: 7th under 2f out: kpt on* **12/1**

5 *hd* **Shreyas (IRE)**[21] 5685 4-9-2 108 ....(p) DJMoran 8 92
(J S Bolger, Ire) *prom: 3rd and drvn along 1/2-way: 2nd and chal 2f out: no ex fr over 1f out* **7/1**

6 *shd* **Timabiyra (IRE)**[45] 4923 3-8-11 96 ....(b[1]) MJKinane 5 92
(John M Oxx, Ire) *hld up: 8th 1/2-way: rdn and no imp st: kpt on same pce fr over 1f out* **14/1**

7 *2 1/2* **She's Our Mark**[14] 5890 5-9-5 106 .... DMGrant 10 90
(Patrick J Flynn, Ire) *2nd early: dropped to 6th and drvn along 1/2-way: no imp u.p st* **11/2**[3]

8 *3 1/2* **Rare Ransom**[83] 3-8-11 99 .... PJSmullen 7 80
(D K Weld, Ire) *trckd ldrs on outer: cl 4th 1/2-way: chal st: no ex fr over 1 1/2f out* **12/1**

9 *4* **Chirkova (USA)**[21] 5689 3-8-11 92 .... JPO'Brien 6 72
(A P O'Brien, Ire) *towards rr: no imp st* **25/1**

10 *1 1/4* **Roman Empress (IRE)**[14] 5890 3-8-11 112 .... JAHeffernan 3 69
(A P O'Brien, Ire) *prom: 2nd 1/2-way: led 2f out: hdd 1 1/2f out: sn wknd* **5/2**[1]

11 *10* **Forest Storm**[16] 5815 3-8-11 97 .... MHarley 11 49
(J S Bolger, Ire) *led: rdn and hdd 2f out: sn wknd: eased ins fnl f* **25/1**

1m 58.05s (-8.95)
WFA 3 from 4yo+ 5lb **11** Ran SP% **127.2**
CSF £39.81 TOTE £3.80: £2.00, £2.70, £3.00; DF 90.20.
Owner Plantation Stud **Bred** Plantation Stud **Trained** Newmarket, Suffolk
■ Stewards' Enquiry : D J Moran caution: ride with more care

FOCUS
The gradually progressive third has been rated as running a personal best, with the winner and runner-up performing to their previous marks.

NOTEBOOK
Ave followed up her Listed race win at Salisbury with a smoothly achieved win on ground which jockey Richard Mullen reported as being probably a bit quick for her. After tracking the leaders, she moved up to avail herself of an opening and went to the front well over 1f out. Once she led, there was always going to be one outcome. The Group 2 Pride Stakes at Newmarket is a race that will be considered. (op 7/2)
Choose Me(IRE), a Listed winner over just short of 1m on very testing ground at Tipperary on her previous start, had won on good ground last season and, although she never really troubled the winner, she made good headway in the straight and kept on well.
Rose Hip(IRE), a consistent performer in handicaps this year and with three wins to her credit, had it to do at the weights, but she produced her best run to date, securing valuable black type in the process. She made headway into sixth on the final bend and kept on after being asked to raise her effort under 2f out.
Beach Bunny(IRE), only touched off by Dar Re Mi in the Group 1 Pretty Polly Stakes in June, had run below par over 1m4f in a Group 3 on soft ground at Cork on her previous start and, while she never held a winning chance, she made headway from behind inside the last 4f and kept on to be nearest at the finish. (op 14/1)
Shreyas(IRE), winner of this race last year and twice a Listed winner at Leopardstown this season, was dropping back to a more suitable trip. She raced prominently and after being ridden along in third at halfway, she went second early in the straight before finding no extra from over 1f out.
Roman Empress(IRE) had the form to go close, but she disappointed, leading early in the straight only to weaken quickly when headed by the winner. (op 2/1)

6299 - 6301a (Foreign Racing) - See Raceform Interactive

6267
ASCOT (R-H)
Sunday, September 27

OFFICIAL GOING: Good to firm (straight: stands' side: 9.0, centre 9.0, far side 9.5; round 9.7)
Wind: Virtually nil Weather: Sunny and warm

6302 123RACING LAUNCHES IN USA H'CAP — 1m 4f
2:05 (2:05) (Class 2) (0-105,100) 3-Y-O+
£11,215 (£3,358; £1,679; £840; £419; £210) **Stalls High**

Form / RPR

0504 **1** **Record Breaker (IRE)**[16] 5823 5-9-6 **96** ....(b) RHills 3 107+
(M Johnston) *swtg: hld up last: c wd ent st: rdn and rapid hdwy fr 2f out to ld ins fnl f: r.o strly* **11/4**[1]

1304 **2** *3 3/4* **Australia Day (IRE)**[17] 5794 6-9-6 **96** .... MartinDwyer 2 101
(P R Webber) *lw: led after 1f: rdn over 2f out: hdd ins fnl f: kpt on but nt pce of wnr* **10/1**

4350 **3** *1/2* **Unleashed (IRE)**[36] 5248 4-9-10 **100** ....(b[1]) EddieAhern 10 105
(H R A Cecil) *in tch: wnt 2nd over 2f out: sn rdn: kpt on same pce fnl f* **9/1**

1600 **4** *hd* **Dansili Dancer**[39] 5173 7-9-10 **100** .... PhilipRobinson 8 104
(C G Cox) *mid-div: rdn and hdwy over 2f out: chal for 2nd wl over 1f out: kpt on same pce fnl f* **14/1**

5602 **5** *3/4* **Storyland (USA)**[8] 6113 4-9-0 **90** .... KirstyMilczarek 4 93
(W J Haggas) *hld up towards rr: pushed along 5f out: stdy prog fr over 2f out: styng on in 4 l 6th whn nt clr run ins fnl f: swtchd lft: kpt on* **15/2**[3]

6000 **6** *1 3/4* **Waldvogel (IRE)**[16] 5823 5-9-8 **98** .... KFallon 9 99
(L M Cumani) *hld up: shkn up and hdwy on rails to chse ldrs on bnd 3f out: nt best of runs fr 2f out: fdd fnl 100yds* **16/1**

0404 **7** *1 1/2* **Barwell Bridge**[6] 6165 3-8-4 **88** .... DavidProbert 5 86
(S Kirk) *on toes: trckd ldr: rdn over 3f out: wknd over 1f out* **10/1**

0/0- **8** *14* **Misty Dancer**[477] 2830 10-8-11 **87** .... PaulHanagan 11 64
(Miss Venetia Williams) *mid-div: rdn over 3f out: wknd over 2f out* **33/1**

2022 **9** *4 1/2* **Chiberta King**[15] 5870 3-8-6 **90** .... WilliamBuick 6 61
(A M Balding) *trckd ldrs: bmpd after 3f: hung lft and lost pl on bnd over 7f out: rdn over 3f out: wknd over 2f out* **3/1**[2]

6203 **10** *21* **Night Crescendo (USA)**[15] 5865 6-8-12 **88** ....(p) JimCrowley 1 27
(Mrs A J Perrett) *lw: mid-div: rdn 3f out: wknd over 2f out: eased* **8/1**

11 *8* **Body Gold (ARG)**[713] 6-9-2 **92** .... SteveDrowne 12 19
(P J Makin) *bit bkwd: led for 1f: prom tl bit slipped through mouth after 3f: nt rcvr and bhd fnl 7f* **66/1**

2m 28.16s (-4.34) **Going Correction** -0.125s/f (Firm)
WFA 3 from 4yo+ 8lb **11** Ran SP% **119.7**
Speed ratings (Par 109): **109,106,106,106,105 104,103,94,91,77 71**
toteswinger: 1&2 £8.00, 1&3 £7.00, 2&3 £20.70 CSF £31.89 CT £224.65 TOTE £3.80: £1.50, £2.80, £3.50; EX 35.30 Trifecta £395.40 Pool: £951.22 - 1.78 winning units..
Owner Triplin Racing **Bred** Sir E J Loder **Trained** Middleham Moor, N Yorks

FOCUS
A really strong-looking handicap full of tough and consistent types. Solid form, with a personal best from Record Breaker.

NOTEBOOK
Record Breaker(IRE) got a really good ride from off the gallop and won in impressive style, once his jockey asked him to make his way to the front. The horse clearly loves his trips to the Berkshire course and is one to respect when asked to return, but he will find things difficult now after scoring off a career-high mark. (op 7-2 tchd 4-1 in places)
Australia Day(IRE) is a proven front-runner but had never been tried over this distance on the Flat. He had a fairly easy time out in front, but kept going all the way to the line under pressure, suggesting he gets the trip. He has a Listed novices' hurdle at Kempton in about three weeks as his next aim.
Unleashed(IRE) was fitted with blinkers for the first time after running in Listed and Group 3 contests since June last year. He travelled well on the inside rail and looked a potential winner turning in, but he hit a flat spot before running on bravely to retake third place. (op 11-1)
Dansili Dancer, who performed poorly in the Ebor last time, was another to move into contention sweetly but did not get home as well as those in front of him. He ran like a horse that needs a little help from the handicapper. (op 12-1)
Storyland(USA) looked a shade high in the weights due to her consistency but was unlucky not to have finished even closer here, as she was staying on well when running into the back ends of the third and fourth. Once switched after being halted in her run, she kept on well. (op 13-2 tchd 8-1)
Waldvogel(IRE) ◆, dropping in trip, is shaping like a horse gradually getting better. The gaps did not open when his rider needed them inside the final two furlongs, and he was not that hard on his mount once his chance was gone. (op 14-1)
Barwell Bridge was always thereabouts and put up another solid display. (op 12-1 tchd 9-1)
Misty Dancer made a satisfactory return after along layoff and should be straighter next time
Chiberta King has enjoyed a good season and put up another fine effort last time over 1m6f at Ffos Las. However, he pulled a bit early on and had nothing left when needing some reserves. (op 4-1)
Night Crescendo(USA), who won this race last season, was extremely disappointing and is not one to trust. (op 7-1 tchd 9-1 in a place)
Body Gold(ARG), having his first run since October 2007, was a decent sort in Argentina, winning a Group 2 on dirt in 2006, but he had trouble handling a bend when the bit slipped through his mouth and was manoeuvred wide at that point to get out of the way of his rivals. Official explanation: jockey said bit slipped through going into Swinley Bottom (tchd 100-1 in places)

6303 GROSVENOR CASINOS CUMBERLAND LODGE STKS (GROUP 3) — 1m 4f
2:40 (2:41) (Class 1) 3-Y-O+
£36,900 (£13,988; £7,000; £3,490; £1,748; £877) **Stalls High**

Form / RPR

6-01 **1** **Mawatheeq (USA)**[17] 5794 4-9-0 106 .... RHills 6 119+
(M P Tregoning) *lw: hld up towards rr: c wd ent st: rdn and gd hdwy fr over 2f out: edgd rt over 1f out: led ent fnl f: styd on wl* **7/2**[1]

0213 **2** *2 1/4* **Campanologist (USA)**[9] 6056 4-9-3 114 .... DaneO'Neill 11 116
(Saeed Bin Suroor) *trckd ldrs: led wl over 2f out: sn rdn: hdd ent fnl f: kpt on but nt pce of wnr* **9/2**[2]

2123 **3** *nk* **Kingdom Of Fife**[29] 5447 4-9-0 112 .... RyanMoore 5 113
(Sir Michael Stoute) *hld up towards rr: rdn and stdy prog fr over 2f out: styd on fnl f* **9/2**[2]

10-0 **4** *1/2* **Red Rocks (IRE)**[183] 1012 6-9-0 0 .... MartinDwyer 12 112
(B J Meehan) *lw: bit bkwd: mid-div: hdwy on inner 3f out: sn rdn: chsd ldr wl over 1f out tl fnl f: styd on same pce* **11/1**

00P0 **5** *3/4* **Muhannak (IRE)**[10] 6030 5-9-0 107 .... RichardKingscote 13 111
(R M Beckett) *hld up towards rr: rdn over 2f out: styd on fr over 1f out: nvr trbld ldrs* **50/1**

1014 **6** *3/4* **Palavicini (USA)**[15] 5875 3-8-9 113 .... EddieAhern 3 112
(J L Dunlop) *lw: mid-div: rdn and hdwy over 2f out: kpt on same pce fnl f* **10/1**

3615 **7** *1 3/4* **Illustrious Blue**[24] 5619 6-9-3 110 .... JimCrowley 10 110
(W J Knight) *hld up towards rr: rdn and styd on past btn horses fr 2f out: nvr a danger* **16/1**

6324 **8** *4 1/2* **Drill Sergeant**[16] 5824 4-9-0 108 .... GregFairley 8 99
(M Johnston) *lw: led: rdn and hdd wl over 2f out: wknd over 1f out* **10/1**

2340 **9** *hd* **Masterofthehorse (IRE)**[61] 4405 3-8-6 119 .... KFallon 2 99
(Miss D Mountain) *mid-div: rdn over 2f out: wknd over 1f out* **7/1**[3]

5033 **10** *2 1/4* **Indian Days**[15] 5854 4-9-0 104 .... SteveDrowne 9 95
(J G Given) *lw: trckd ldrs: rdn over 3f out: wknd over 1f out* **33/1**

-000 **11** *26* **Macarthur**[183] 1012 5-9-0 0 .... C-PLemaire 7 54
(M F De Kock, South Africa) *w ldr tl over 3f out: wknd qckly: eased over 1f out* **10/1**

0010 **12** *26* **Inch Lodge**[4] 6210 7-9-0 55 ....(t) KirstyMilczarek 1 12
(Miss D Mountain) *bit bkwd: s.i.s: racd wd: sn drvn to be prom: wknd qckly over 3f out: virtually p.u* **150/1**

2m 27.33s (-5.17) **Going Correction** -0.125s/f (Firm)
WFA 3 from 4yo+ 8lb **12** Ran SP% **118.1**
Speed ratings (Par 113): **112,110,110,109,109 108,107,104,104,103 85,68**
toteswinger: 1&2 £4.40, 1&3 £5.50, 2&3 £3.10 CSF £18.55 TOTE £5.00: £1.80, £1.60, £2.60; EX 17.00 Trifecta £41.60 Pool: £1,284.55 - 19.26 winning units..
Owner Hamdan Al Maktoum **Bred** Shadwell Farm LLC **Trained** Lambourn, Berks

FOCUS
A really good field for a classy contest, and decent form for the grade with the winner up 5lb.

NOTEBOOK
Mawatheeq(USA) ◆ put up an awesome performance after being given a fine waiting ride. He flew past most of his rivals from the two-furlong marker, despite edging right, and was in a different class. Evidently well thought of, he has plenty of scope to hold his own at Group 2 level at least, when considering this visually impressive effort. Connections will now consider supplementing him for the Champion Stakes, a plan that worked in the past for the trainer/owner's Nayef, who took this Ascot race before being added to the Group 1 at Newmarket in October, which he went on to win. (op 4-1)
Campanologist(USA), who reportedly got upset at Newbury last time, which made him run too freely, moved into the lead looking the winner, but he had no answer to the winner as he swept past (the 3lb he gave away made no difference to the result). He has become a fine servant to the Godolphin stable. (op 4-1 tchd 5-1 in places)
Kingdom Of Fife, running over 1m4f for the first time this season, kept staying on but lacked pace at a crucial stage. (tchd 5-1)
Red Rocks(IRE), back at Brian Meehan's stable after a spell in America, had not set foot on a course since Dubai in the spring, but showed his undoubted class with a battling display. Connections will be delighted with his run. (op 12-1)
Muhannak(IRE) is a quirky sort now, but ran on really well after making his jockey work hard from an early stage.
Palavicini(USA), trying 1m4f for the first time, shaped well but looked like a horse that did not get home. (op 12-1)
Illustrious Blue had lots to do from the final bend and had no chance of catching the leading bunch. (op 20-1)
Masterofthehorse(IRE), given a break since making his debut for the Debbie Mountain stable at Goodwood, disappointed once again. Official explanation: trainer said colt was found to be lame near-fore following day (op 8-1)

Macarthur, returning from a lengthy absence and without the tongue tie, dropped out alarmingly. (op 11-1 tchd 9-1)

6304 JOHN GUEST DIADEM STKS (GROUP 2) 6f
3:15 (3:15) (Class 1) 3-Y-0+

£56,770 (£21,520; £10,770; £5,370; £2,690; £1,350) **Stalls** Centre

Form RPR
1454 **1** **Sayif (IRE)**[22] 5657 3-8-12 111 RHills 7 119
(P W Chapple-Hyam) *racd centre: chsd ldrs: rdn to ld jst over 1f out: r.o strly* **11/1**
0241 **2** *2 ½* **Tamagin (USA)**[15] 5878 6-9-0 109 (p) StephenDonohoe 13 112
(J Pearce) *lw: broke v sharply: overall ldr: racd alone far side: rdn and hdd jst over 1f out: kpt on but no ex* **12/1**
3013 **3** *nk* **Mullein**[15] 5878 4-8-11 99 JimCrowley 12 108
(R M Beckett) *hld up last of centre gp: rdn and hdwy over 1f out: r.o wl fnl f: wnt 3rd line: nrst fin* **33/1**
1113 **4** *nse* **High Standing (USA)**[22] 5657 4-9-0 113 RyanMoore 6 110+
(W J Haggas) *squeezed out leaving stalls: racd centre: hld up: hdwy wl over 1f out: sn rdn: r.o ins fnl f* **5/2**[1]
0205 **5** *nk* **Prime Defender**[9] 6058 5-9-0 107 (b[1]) MichaelHills 11 110
(B W Hills) *lw: hld up: hdwy over 2f out: sn rdn: r.o ins fnl f* **28/1**
2026 **6** *½* **Asset (IRE)**[22] 5657 6-9-0 112 (b) MartinDwyer 5 108
(Saeed Bin Suroor) *racd centre: chsd ldrs: rdn and ev ch ent fnl f: kpt on same pce* **9/1**
6421 **7** *hd* **Mariol (FR)**[28] 5495 6-9-0 112 C-PLemaire 2 107
(Robert Collet, France) *racd stands' side: hld up: jnd main centre gp over 2f out: sn rdn: r.o ins fnl f* **17/2**
4412 **8** *nse* **Dream Eater (IRE)**[24] 5618 4-9-0 114 (t) WilliamBuick 14 107
(A M Balding) *racd in centre gp: hld up: hdwy 2f out: sn rdn: kpt on same pce fnl f* **8/1**[3]
0043 **9** *2* **J J The Jet Plane (SAF)**[8] 6107 5-9-0 118 (b[1]) DaneO'Neill 4 101
(R Hannon) *led centre gp tl over 1f out: one pce fnl f* **12/1**
4133 **10** *hd* **Knot In Wood (IRE)**[8] 6091 7-9-0 110 PaulHanagan 9 101
(R A Fahey) *lw: racd centre: mid-div: effrt over 1f out: wknd ins fnl f* **12/1**
1000 **11** *3* **Art Connoisseur (IRE)**[22] 5657 3-9-4 119 EddieAhern 15 98
(M L W Bell) *hld up: rdn 2f out: no imp: wknd fnl f* **16/1**
1241 **12** *3 ¼* **Palace Moon**[29] 5434 4-9-0 107 SteveDrowne 8 82
(H Morrison) *chsd ldrs in centre tl 2f out* **13/2**[2]
0002 **13** *1* **Beckermet (IRE)**[7] 6135 7-9-0 96 ChrisCatlin 1 79
(R F Fisher) *prom in centre: rdn over 2f out: sn btn* **66/1**
00-6 **14** *13* **Galpin Junior (USA)**[15] 5878 3-8-12 104 (t) TPO'Shea 3 40
(B J Meehan) *racd stands' side: chsd ldrs tl over 2f out* **100/1**

1m 12.57s (-1.83) **Going Correction** +0.075s/f (Good)
WFA 3 from 4yo+ 2lb **14** Ran SP% **119.7**
Speed ratings (Par 115): **115,111,111,111,110 110,109,109,107,106 102,98,97,79**
toteswinger: 1&2 £33.90, 1&3 £74.00, 2&3 £94.50 CSF £133.23 TOTE £13.90: £4.20, £4.30, £10.10; EX 182.40 TRIFECTA Not won..
Owner Saleh Al Homaizi & Imad Al Sagar **Bred** Crandon Park Stud **Trained** Newmarket, Suffolk

FOCUS
A competitive Group 2 sprint. The runners spread into two groups early but soon became one, apart from the runner-up who stuck to the far side. Improved form from the winner.

NOTEBOOK
Sayif(IRE) has been doing really well this season and came into this race off the back of a huge run in the Sprint Cup. He was hardly taking a big prize out of turn and was an impressive winner on his side of the track. (op 12-1)
Tamagin(USA) shows terrific pace and displayed his customary early speed towards the far-side of the track. He has to emerge with almost as much credit as the winner after doing things on his own, and underlines the fact there is not much of a gap between very good handicappers and Group-class sprinters. Connections may bring him back for a race at Ascot in a few weeks time but, long term, he could go to Dubai and Hong Kong. (op 14-1)
Mullein travelled very well at the rear of the pack that stayed stands' side and finished strongly.
High Standing(USA) has showed enormous progression this year and earned his place at this level as a result. Unbeaten under Moore in three previous attempts, he eventually found his stride but was already held when losing third late on. (tchd 9-4)
Prime Defender ◆, wearing blinkers for the first time, was running on inside the final furlong and might be returning to his best. (tchd 33-1)
Asset(IRE) is rarely disgraced, as his effort in the Sprint Cup proved, and he did well again. However, he could not quicken when looking a big threat over a furlong out. (op 10-1)
Mariol(FR) ran a blinder in the Prix Maurice De Gheest two starts ago and duly landed a Group 3 on his most recent outing. He got outpaced for a few strides when the tempo lifted but finished well. (op 10-1)
Dream Eater(IRE), sporting blinkers after Jimmy Fortune suggested having them fitted, showed good pace on his side but weakened. (op 9-1 tchd 10-1)
J J The Jet Plane(SAF), sporting blinkers for the first time, showed good pace on his side but weakened. (op 10-1)
Art Connoisseur(IRE) was returning to the place of his greatest successes and defended an unbeaten record at the course. Carrying a 6lb penalty, he was disappointing and made very little impact. (op 12-1)
Palace Moon came with a promising move at one stage, but dropped away quickly from just over a furlong out. (op 6-1 tchd 7-1)

6305 BRIGHTWELLS ASCOT SALES NURSERY H'CAP 7f
3:50 (3:51) (Class 3) 2-Y-O

£6,854 (£2,052; £1,026; £513; £256; £128) **Stalls** Centre

Form RPR
0012 **1** **Pleasant Day (IRE)**[18] 5762 2-9-2 84 (b) MartinDwyer 4 92
(B J Meehan) *lw: trckd ldrs: rdn to ld and hung rt over 1f out: drifted to far rail: r.o* **15/2**
61 **2** *2* **Guest Book (IRE)**[17] 5786 2-8-11 79 RHills 8 82
(M Johnston) *w'like: str: swtg: w ldr: rdn and ev ch fr 2f out: bmpd over 1f out: carried rt: kpt on but no ex towards fin* **15/8**[1]
1444 **3** *½* **Keen Bidder**[13] 5938 2-7-12 66 oh1 NickyMackay 5 68
(D M Simcock) *lw: hld up: hdwy 2f out: sn rdn to chse ldrs: carried rt ins fnl f: kpt on* **16/1**
0403 **4** *1 ¼* **Farmer Giles (IRE)**[18] 5762 2-9-4 86 HayleyTurner 2 86+
(M L W Bell) *restrained s: last: swtchd rt and nt clr run over 2f out: swtchd lft over 1f out: rdn and hdwy ent fnl f: kpt on* **11/1**
2121 **5** *¾* **Astonishment (IRE)**[14] 5913 2-9-3 85 JamesDoyle 3 85+
(S Kirk) *led: rdn and hdd whn bmpd by wnr over 1f out: disputing cl 2nd whn squeezed out and stmbld ins fnl f: nt rcvr* **6/1**[3]
0165 **6** *1* **Desert Auction (IRE)**[18] 5762 2-9-7 89 RyanMoore 7 84
(R Hannon) *in tch: rdn over 2f out: sn one pce* **10/1**
034 **7** *4* **Machine Gun Kelly (IRE)**[16] 5829 2-8-1 69 ow1 RichardThomas 1 54
(G L Moore) *swtg: in tch: rdn 1/2-way: btn 2f out* **16/1**
040 **8** *½* **Nom De La Rosa (IRE)**[25] 5564 2-7-10 69 ow1 Louis-PhilippeBeuzelin(5) 11 52
(G L Moore) *in tch: rdn 2f out: sn wknd* **33/1**
102 **9** *2* **The Starboard Bow**[22] 5681 2-9-4 86 KFallon 6 64
(S Kirk) *lw: hld up: nudged along 1/2-way: hdwy over 2f out: wknd over 1f out* **12/1**
114 **10** *2* **Bahamian Music (IRE)**[17] 5797 2-8-13 81 PaulHanagan 10 54
(R A Fahey) *lw: trckd ldrs: rdn wl over 2f out: wknd wl over 1f out* **5/1**[2]

1m 27.42s (-0.58) **Going Correction** +0.075s/f (Good) **10** Ran SP% **117.3**
Speed ratings (Par 99): **106,103,103,101,100 99,95,94,92,90**
toteswinger: 1&2 £3.70, 1&3 £24.50, 2&3 £11.40 CSF £22.04 CT £225.32 TOTE £7.80: £2.20, £1.50, £4.10; EX 26.50 Trifecta £639.30 Pool: £1,114.51 - 1.29 winning units..
Owner Jaber Abdullah **Bred** Patrick J Gleeson **Trained** Manton, Wilts
■ Stewards' Enquiry : Martin Dwyer four-day ban: careless riding (+ three days deferred) (Oct 11-17)

FOCUS
A good and competitive nursery, and solid form.

NOTEBOOK
Pleasant Day(IRE) had improved since blinkers were fitted and gained another win, but not before hampering one of his main rivals in the process. He gives the impression that he is far from straightforward (the jockey got a 4-day ban for his efforts), but talented. (op 9-1)
Guest Book(IRE) ◆ was the least exposed in the line-up and is a bull of a horse. He sweated up before the off and performed well again, but gave the impression he was still green, as he jinked towards the centre of the course yards from the line. (op 5-2 tchd 11-4 in a place)
Keen Bidder came from a stable that was in great form and ran on strongly after being hard ridden over a furlong out. (op 12-1)
Farmer Giles(IRE) did not get going early enough to make an impact after being switched a couple of times. He was finishing very quickly, however. (op 10-1)
Astonishment(IRE), raised 5lb for winning at Goodwood, is consistent but had his chance of a place taken away when the winner hung across him. In fact, the horse looked lucky to stay upright when hampered. (op 15-2)
Desert Auction(IRE) finished behind a couple of these rivals last time, and did so again (tchd 11-1)
The Starboard Bow Official explanation: jockey said colt hung right under pressure
Bahamian Music(IRE) failed to run up to her recent level and something was presumably amiss. (op 7-2 tchd 11-2 in a place)

6306 SIS LIVE FENWOLF STKS (LISTED RACE) 2m
4:25 (4:25) (Class 1) 3-Y-O+

£22,708 (£8,608; £4,308; £2,148; £1,076; £540) **Stalls** High

Form RPR
0-45 **1** **Electrolyser (IRE)**[92] 3390 4-9-3 95 PhilipRobinson 4 102
(C G Cox) *lw: mde all: hrd pressed fr over 1f out: styd on wl ins fnl f: rdn out* **4/1**[3]
-013 **2** *¾* **Oasis Knight (IRE)**[29] 5425 3-8-5 100 (v) KFallon 3 101
(M P Tregoning) *lw: trckd ldrs: rdn whn swtchd lft 2f out: styd on to take 2nd nr fin* **7/2**[2]
2131 **3** *hd* **Swingkeel (IRE)**[37] 5235 4-9-3 97 RyanMoore 6 101
(J L Dunlop) *lw: hld up in last pair: hdwy over 2f out: sn rdn: chal for 2nd ent fnl f: styd on* **6/4**[1]
0454 **4** *½* **Keenes Day (FR)**[14] 5903 4-9-3 91 RHills 5 100
(M Johnston) *a little slow away: in tch: chsd wnr over 2f out: ev ch ent fnl f: no ex: lost 2 pls nr fin* **8/1**
0301 **5** *1 ¼* **The Betchworth Kid**[24] 5609 4-9-3 104 HayleyTurner 2 99
(M L W Bell) *hld up in last: swtchd out for effrt ent st: nt pce to mount chal* **4/1**[3]
302- **6** *22* **Peppertree Lane (IRE)**[253] 6517 6-9-3 106 JimCrowley 1 72
(A P Boxhall) *trckd wnr: rdn over 3f out: wknd 2f out* **20/1**

3m 31.71s (2.71) **Going Correction** -0.125s/f (Firm)
WFA 3 from 4yo+ 12lb **6** Ran SP% **118.1**
Speed ratings (Par 111): **88,87,87,87,86 75**
toteswinger: 1&2 £3.30, 1&3 £1.80, 2&3 £2.10 CSF £19.40 TOTE £4.50: £2.50, £2.10; EX 23.70.

Owner Mr And Mrs P Hargreaves **Bred** Darley **Trained** Lambourn, Berks

FOCUS
A decent staying event in which they finished rather compressed. The form has been rated at something like face value.

NOTEBOOK
Electrolyser(IRE), absent since a good run in the Northumberland Plate, where he was in front of The Betchworth Kid and Keenes Day, was allowed an easy lead and duly held on after dictating. However, the grey did show battling qualities when asked to pull out a little bit more towards the finish. He is around an 8-1 shot for the Totesport Cesarewitch next month and trainer Clive Cox confirmed it is his intended target. He gets a 4lb penalty for this win. (op 5-1)
Oasis Knight(IRE) seemed to run quite well in the March Stakes and has improved since a visor was fitted. A little keen early, he responded well to his rider's urgings and claimed second. It is worth giving him another chance. (op 3-1 tchd 4-1)
Swingkeel(IRE) won a hot-looking race at York on his previous start and ran well without getting to the winner. (op 5-2)
Keenes Day(FR) seemed to lack gears after being a big danger to the winner a furlong out. He lost two places in the final 100 yards. (op 15-2)
The Betchworth Kid has been in great heart all year and can be given another chance, as he will be better chasing a stronger pace. (op 9-2 tchd 11-2 and 6-1 in places)
Peppertree Lane(IRE), absent since a moderate time of it over hurdles, was prominent before dropping away quickly. (op 16-1 tchd 14-1)

6307 BRUNSWICK H'CAP 1m (S)
5:00 (5:00) (Class 2) (0-100,99) 3-Y-O+

£12,462 (£3,732; £1,866; £934; £466; £234) **Stalls** Centre

Form RPR
2032 **1** **Elna Bright**[53] 4641 4-8-6 84 JackMitchell(3) 5 93
(B R Johnson) *hld up: hdwy over 2f out: rdn to ld over 1f out: edgd lft ins fnl f: drvn out* **14/1**
5566 **2** *½* **Alfathaa**[17] 5794 4-9-8 97 (p) RHills 4 105
(W J Haggas) *chsd ldrs tl lost pl over 2f out: rdn over 1f out: r.o ins fnl f: wnt 2nd towards fin* **9/2**[2]
1112 **3** *¾* **Credit Swap**[8] 6117 4-8-8 90 TobyAtkinson(7) 3 96
(M Wigham) *hld up: rdn over 1f out: styd on wl ins fnl f: nrst fin* **5/1**[3]
4504 **4** *shd* **Bucked Off (SAF)**[10] 6013 5-8-13 88 MickyFenton 11 94
(T P Tate) *led: sn clr: rdn and hdd over 1f out: awkward hd carriage but kpt on* **20/1**
5051 **5** *nk* **Tartan Gunna**[15] 5880 3-8-12 91 GregFairley 1 96
(M Johnston) *chsd clr ldr tl rdn 2f out: kpt on ins fnl f* **12/1**
1654 **6** *2 ½* **Romany Princess (IRE)**[24] 5607 4-9-0 89 RyanMoore 8 89
(R Hannon) *lw: hld up: sme late prog u.p: nvr a factor* **7/1**

2400 **7** ½ **Huzzah (IRE)**[38] 5200 4-9-8 **97** MichaelHills 7 96
(B W Hills) *hld up: rdn 2f out: little imp* **9/1**

4030 **8** 1¼ **Espiritu (FR)**[15] 5863 3-9-6 **99** (v) WilliamBuick 10 95
(J Noseda) *mid-div: tk clsr order over 2f out: sn rdn: kpt on same pce* **12/1**

012 **9** 7 **Fanunalter**[16] 5832 3-9-1 **94** KFallon 2 75
(M Botti) *lw: mid-div: smooth hdwy to trck ldrs over 2f out: rdn over 1f out: wknd tamely* **9/4**[1]

4643 **10** 7 **Salient**[14] 5918 5-8-8 **83** KirstyMilczarek 9 48
(M J Attwater) *trckd ldrs: rdn over 2f out: sn wknd* **33/1**

1m 39.73s (-0.87) **Going Correction** +0.075s/f (Good)
WFA 3 from 4yo+ 4lb **10** Ran SP% **117.9**
Speed ratings (Par 109): **107,106,105,105,105 102,102,101,94,87**
toteswinger: 1&2 £13.50, 1&3 £10.80, 2&3 £6.80 CSF £76.85 CT £368.04 TOTE £19.00: £4.20, £2.20, £2.10; EX 123.40 Trifecta £1574.30 Part won. Pool: £2,127.48 - 0.60 winning units.Place 6 £339.30, Place 5 £156.38.
Owner Peter Crate **Bred** D R Tucker **Trained** Ashtead, Surrey

FOCUS
A decent handicap. The first five came nicely clear and the form is pretty straightforward.

NOTEBOOK
Elna Bright only lost out in a narrow fashion at Brighton on his previous outing (he reportedly lost two shoes there) and went one better after finishing strongly. His stable is in good form. (op 10-1 tchd 9-1)
Alfathaa, tried in cheekpieces for the first time, was well supported both in this race and for the Cambridgeshire during the morning, but he failed to deliver again. He is frustrating but could still head to Newmarket. (op 6-1)
Credit Swap had his winning run halted by a narrow margin at Newmarket, albeit after a decent break, and did not get going early enough to get to the winner here. He will not be without a chance in the Cambridgeshire if lining up. (op 6-1)
Bucked Off(SAF) was unlucky not to finish placed after being given an enterprising ride. The only negative was that his head came up late on. (op 16-1)
Tartan Gunna was a brave winner at Goodwood (the form had been enhanced by the third since) and he appeared to run up to his best, which helps to set the level. (op 10-1 tchd 9-1)
Fanunalter moved nicely and looked a player until finding nothing when put under pressure. Official explanation: jockey said colt stopped quickly (tchd 2-1 and 5-2)
Salient Official explanation: jockey said gelding lost its left front plate
T/Jkpt: Not won. T/Plt: £1,124.70 to a £1 stake. Pool: £137,437.70. 89.20 winning tickets. T/Qpdt: £354.60 to a £1 stake. Pool: £7,716.36. 16.10 winning tickets. TM

5941 MUSSELBURGH (R-H)
Sunday, September 27

OFFICIAL GOING: Good to firm (firm in places on straight course; 7.9)
Wind: Fresh, half-against. Weather: Overcast

6308 ROYAL SCOTS CUP H'CAP 5f
1:55 (1:55) (Class 6) (0-65,64) 3-Y-O **£2,590** (£770; £385; £192) **Stalls** Low

Form RPR
1063 **1** **Hawkeyethenoo (IRE)**[39] 5158 3-8-8 **54** (v) GaryBartley(5) 3 72+
(J S Goldie) *stdd s: hld up: stdy hdwy over 1f out: shkn up to ld ins fnl f: comf* **7/2**[3]

0533 **2** 1¼ **Lost In Paris (IRE)**[7] 6140 3-9-2 **57** (b) DavidAllan 1 71
(T D Easterby) *led: rdn over 1f out: hdd ins fnl f: kpt on same pce* **7/4**[1]

6040 **3** 6 **Zelos Girl (IRE)**[15] 5881 3-8-8 **52** FrederikTylicki(3) 2 44
(J G Given) *pressed ldr: rdn and edgd rt 2f out: sn outpcd* **12/1**

0000 **4** ¾ **Clanachy**[13] 5946 3-8-6 **47** AndrewMullen 4 36
(A G Foster) *chsd ldrs tl rdn and no ex over 1f out* **33/1**

6202 **5** 1¾ **Fasliyanne (IRE)**[27] 5517 3-9-4 **64** (v[1]) AmyRyan(5) 8 47
(K A Ryan) *chsd ldrs: effrt 2f out: btn fnl f* **3/1**[2]

5260 **6** shd **Inthawain**[39] 5158 3-8-11 **52** DuranFentiman 7 35
(N Wilson) *s.i.s: sn rdn in rr: no imp fnl 2f* **16/1**

0200 **7** 2½ **Sleepy Valley (IRE)**[23] 5626 3-8-10 **51** (p) DanielTudhope 6 25
(A Dickman) *hld up: rdn 1/2-way: btn over 1f out* **16/1**

-000 **8** hd **Shining Times (IRE)**[30] 5396 3-8-8 **49** ow1 (b[1]) TomEaves 5 22
(P T Midgley) *hld up in tch: drvn 1/2-way: sn wknd* **20/1**

59.01 secs (-1.39) **Going Correction** -0.275s/f (Firm) **8** Ran SP% **110.7**
Speed ratings (Par 99): **100,98,88,87,84 84,80,79**
toteswinger: 1&2 £2.00, 1&3 £4.80, 2&3 £3.60. CSF £9.34 CT £58.55 TOTE £5.20: £1.40, £1.10, £2.30; EX 10.40.
Owner J S Goldie, F Connor, G Brown **Bred** S Leigh & R Leigh & Islandmore Stud **Trained** Uplawmoor, E Renfrews

FOCUS
A modest sprint to open proceedings, run at a scorching pace on very fast ground. The first pair finished clear and the form is rated at face value.

6309 SCOTTISH RACING YOUR BETTER BET H'CAP 7f 30y
2:30 (2:30) (Class 4) (0-80,77) 3-Y-O+ **£5,180** (£1,541; £770; £384) **Stalls** High

Form RPR
0024 **1** **Malcheek (IRE)**[15] 5884 7-9-2 **72** DavidAllan 2 87
(T D Easterby) *trckd ldr: led over 1f out: styd on strly to go clr fnl f* **15/2**

0014 **2** 5 **Sea Salt**[7] 6135 6-8-9 **70** PaulPickard(5) 10 72
(R E Barr) *hld up in tch: hdwy on outside over 2f out: edgd rt and chsd wnr ins fnl f: r.o* **5/1**[3]

033 **3** nk **John Keats**[13] 5955 6-8-4 **67** JamesPSullivan(7) 5 68
(J S Goldie) *hld up: rdn and hdwy over 1f out: kpt on fnl f: no imp* **10/1**

4220 **4** ½ **Stellite**[10] 6015 9-8-9 **70** GaryBartley(5) 8 69
(J S Goldie) *hld up: effrt over 1f out: no imp fnl f* **14/1**

2640 **5** 1½ **Zabeel Tower**[39] 5160 6-8-11 **67** TonyHamilton 9 62
(R Allan) *trckd ldrs tl rdn and no ex appr fnl f* **8/1**

20- **6** shd **He's Got Rhythm (IRE)**[8] 6129 4-9-3 **73** (b) LPKeniry 6 68
(David Marnane, Ire) *trckd ldrs: drvn over 2f out: no ex over 1f out* **14/1**

1102 **7** 1¼ **Violent Velocity (IRE)**[21] 5697 6-9-0 **77** IJBrennan(7) 7 69
(J J Quinn) *dwlt: hld up: effrt over 2f out: no ex appr fnl f* **9/2**[2]

4111 **8** nse **Dark Moment**[39] 5158 3-8-12 **74** (p) FrederikTylicki(3) 3 66
(A Dickman) *hld up in tch: drvn over 2f out: sn outpcd: n.d after* **4/1**[1]

2215 **9** 2¼ **Who's Shirl**[13] 5955 3-8-7 **69** KellyHarrison(3) 4 54+
(C W Fairhurst) *hld up: rdn over 2f out: gd hdwy on ins whn nt clr run appr fnl f to last 100yds: nt rcvr* **12/1**

-001 **10** 1 **Mandarin Spirit (IRE)**[6] 6159 9-8-13 **69** 6ex (b) PhillipMakin 1 52
(Miss L A Perratt) *led tl rdn and hdd over 1f out: wknd ent fnl f* **12/1**

1m 26.42s (-3.88) **Going Correction** -0.325s/f (Firm)
WFA 3 from 4yo+ 3lb **10** Ran SP% **115.5**
Speed ratings (Par 105): **109,103,102,102,100 100,99,99,96,95**
toteswinger: 1&2 £8.70, 1&3 £11.30, 2&3 £8.30. CSF £44.42 CT £387.02 TOTE £8.40: £2.60, £2.50, £2.80; EX 42.20.
Owner Mrs Susie Dicker **Bred** Carrigbeg Stud **Trained** Great Habton, N Yorks

FOCUS
A fair handicap largely contested by in-form horses, and again a race run at a cracking pace. The very fast conditions meant it was very difficult to get into the race from behind. The winner posted his best effort for some time.
Who's Shirl Official explanation: jockey said filly was denied a clear run

6310 RACING UK (S) STKS 1m 4f 100y
3:05 (3:05) (Class 6) 3-Y-O+ **£2,590** (£770; £385; £192) **Stalls** High

Form RPR
0356 **1** **Andorn (GER)**[19] 4600 5-9-4 60 LeeVickers 7 62
(P A Kirby) *dwlt: t.k.h and led after 1f: hdd 9f out: rdn to ld over 2f out: edgd rt over 1f out: hld on wl fnl f* **9/1**

2221 **2** 1½ **Graceful Descent (FR)**[39] 5161 4-9-5 68 DanielTudhope 8 61
(J S Goldie) *hld up: stdy hdwy over 4f out: effrt and chsd wnr over 1f out: kpt on fnl f: no imp last 50yds* **6/5**[1]

015 **3** ½ **Birkside**[13] 5943 6-9-10 65 PhillipMakin 3 67+
(Miss L A Perratt) *hld up: hdwy and prom whn n.m.r and swtchd lft over 1f out: kpt on u.p fnl f* **3/1**[2]

6332 **4** 2½ **Tesserae**[45] 4934 3-8-8 55 ow3 RobertHavlin 1 53
(A B Haynes) *led 1f: chsd ldrs: effrt over 2f out: one pce over 1f out* **12/1**

2362 **5** nk **Shekan Star**[20] 5733 7-9-5 53 TonyHamilton 9 56
(K G Reveley) *hld up: drvn over 3f out: plugged on fnl f: no imp* **15/2**[3]

0006 **6** 1¼ **Grethel (IRE)**[4] 6219 5-8-6 37 BillyCray(7) 4 48
(A Berry) *t.k.h: cl up: led 9f out: rdn and hdd over 2f out: btn fnl f* **50/1**

5043 **7** 7 **Flying Phoebe**[5] 6177 3-8-7 51 ow2 TomEaves 2 39
(Mrs L Stubbs) *dwlt: t.k.h: in tch: rdn over 2f out: sn wknd* **12/1**

0005 **8** 9 **Angels And Demons (IRE)**[13] 5947 3-8-5 40 FrancisNorton 5 24
(R C Guest) *prom: lost pl after 4f: rdn and struggling fr 3f out* **22/1**

2m 41.49s (-0.51) **Going Correction** -0.325s/f (Firm)
WFA 3 from 4yo+ 8lb **8** Ran SP% **113.9**
Speed ratings (Par 101): **88,87,86,85,84 83,79,73**
toteswinger: 1&2 £3.50, 1&3 £5.30, 2&3 £1.80. CSF £20.13 TOTE £8.60: £2.00, £1.10, £1.40; EX 25.00.The winner was bought in for £8,500.
Owner Preesall Garage **Bred** Gestut Schlenderhan **Trained** Castleton, N Yorks

FOCUS
A weak seller run at something of a stop-start gallop and a result that looks to flatter one or two. Again, it was an advantage to race close up. A race to be negative about.

6311 EUROPEAN BREEDERS' FUND FILLIES' H'CAP 1m
3:40 (3:43) (Class 3) (0-90,83) 3-Y-O+
£10,592 (£3,172; £1,586; £793; £396; £198) **Stalls** High

Form RPR
0345 **1** **Feeling Fab (FR)**[22] 5665 3-9-10 **82** J-PGuillambert 5 87
(M Johnston) *t.k.h: led to over 1f out: carried hd high u.p: styd on wl fnl f to regain ld cl home* **6/1**[3]

1251 **2** nk **She's In The Money**[10] 6015 3-9-5 **80** FrederikTylicki(3) 1 84
(R A Fahey) *stdd in tch: hdwy over 2f out: rdn to ld ins fnl f: kpt on: hdd cl home* **5/2**[1]

0-20 **3** shd **Burgundy Ice (USA)**[39] 5175 3-9-11 **83** DO'Donohoe 2 87
(Saeed Bin Suroor) *hld up in tch: effrt on outside 2f out: kpt on u.p fnl f* **9/2**[2]

0040 **4** hd **To Be Or Not To Be**[17] 5810 4-9-3 **74** WilliamCarson(3) 3 78
(John Berry) *t.k.h: trckd wnr: led over 1f out to ins fnl f: kpt on fin* **10/1**

2011 **5** 1½ **Poppet's Lovein**[27] 5514 3-9-7 **79** RobertHavlin 6 79+
(A B Haynes) *t.k.h: hld up: hdwy and prom over 1f out: sn rdn: kpt on fnl f: no imp whn n.m.r towards fin* **9/2**[2]

0- **6** 2¾ **July Days (IRE)**[19] 5760 3-9-9 **81** LPKeniry 8 75
(David Marnane, Ire) *t.k.h: trckd ldrs tl rdn and wknd over 1f out* **14/1**

1102 **7** 8 **Flapper (IRE)**[11] 5996 3-8-8 **73** AmyScott(7) 7 50
(J W Hills) *bhd: detached after 3f: shortlived effrt over 2f out: sn btn* **7/1**

040- **8** 2½ **Lock 'N' Load (IRE)**[351] 6655 3-8-10 **68** TomEaves 4 39
(B Smart) *trckd ldrs: lost pl over 2f out: sn wknd* **16/1**

1m 39.74s (-1.46) **Going Correction** -0.325s/f (Firm)
WFA 3 from 4yo 4lb **8** Ran SP% **113.4**
Speed ratings (Par 104): **94,93,93,93,91 89,81,78**
toteswinger: 1&2 £4.20, 1&3 £5.70, 2&3 £3.10. CSF £21.02 CT £73.65 TOTE £7.90: £2.20, £1.10, £1.50; EX 26.00.
Owner A D Spence **Bred** Alain Decrion & Sunland Holdings Ltd **Trained** Middleham Moor, N Yorks
■ Stewards' Enquiry : William Carson caution: careless riding.
Frederik Tylicki caution: used whip with excessive frequency.

FOCUS
A valuable prize but a weak field with just eight going to post and the top weight having an official rating of just 83, 7lb below the ceiling. The gallop wasn't as strong as a couple of the earlier races on the card, but once again a prominent pitch was an advantage. There was a bunch finish and the form is limited but sound.

NOTEBOOK
Feeling Fab(FR) put up an extraordinary performance. Soon at the head of affairs, she looked beaten when she was headed and then sandwiched between the eventual third and fourth, but despite carrying her head high in unattractive fashion, she rallied in commendable style to snatch the lead back almost on the line. She seemed suited by the longer trip, having raced mostly at 7f this year, and if anything left the impression a bit further won't come amiss. (op 5-1 tchd 13-2)
She's In The Money can be counted a little unlucky. The subject of a late jockey change, she unseated her rider before the start and once racing didn't take up her usual position near the head of affairs and got too far back as a result. She made steady progress all the way in the straight to get her head in front narrowly only to be mugged on the line. She can win before the season is out. (op 3-1)
Burgundy Ice(USA) needs no excuses. Off a career high mark, she had her chance against the far rail but wasn't quite good enough while putting any reservations about her stamina to bed.
To Be Or Not To Be ran a cracker but still left the impression that she may benefit from dropping back to 7f. She looked the likely winner when hitting the front going well, but she wasn't quite able to maintain her run late on and won't get the chance to run over an easier 1m than this.
Poppet's Lovein gave no trouble beforehand and settled better than she has been. She seemed to have her chance. (op 7-2)
July Days(IRE) has been raced over all sorts of trips in Ireland but left the impression she would have preferred a sharper test. (op 16-1)
Flapper(IRE) is another that has often gone for the front but she seemed to get squeezed leaving the stalls and, on ground possibly faster than ideal, lost touch going down the far side having been taken very wide. This effort is best forgotten. (op 9-1)
Lock 'N' Load(IRE) showed little on her handicap debut and first run in nearly a year. (op 22-1 tchd 25-1)

6312 TOTEEXACTA CLAIMING STKS 1m 1f
4:15 (4:15) (Class 4) 4-Y-O+ **£5,180** (£1,541; £770; £384) **Stalls** High

Form RPR
0313 **1** **King Of The Moors (USA)**[10] 6012 6-8-8 64 (b) FrancisNorton 8 73
(R C Guest) *mde all: rdn 2f out: kpt on wl fnl f* **13/2**

2012 **2** ½ **Sunnyside Tom (IRE)**[7] 6137 5-9-8 84 FrederikTylicki(3) 4 89
(R A Fahey) *trckd ldrs on ins: n.m.r over 1f out: squeezed through to chse wnr ins fnl f: r.o* **11/4**[2]
0006 **3** 2¾ **Royal Power (IRE)**[8] 6094 6-9-11 87 AdrianTNicholls 3 84
(D Nicholls) *trckd wnr: effrt 2f out: edgd rt 1f out: one pce ins fnl f* **5/1**[3]
5003 **4** 5 **Court Masterpiece**[21] 5694 9-9-13 98 GrahamGibbons 5 76
(J J Quinn) *hld up in tch: effrt over 2f out: edgd rt and wknd over 1f out* **2/1**[1]
0601 **5** nk **Wovoka (IRE)**[27] 5513 6-8-10 75 AmyRyan(5) 6 63
(K A Ryan) *hld up: drvn over 2f out: sn no imp* **11/1**
0006 **6** 7 **Cold Quest (USA)**[7] 6137 5-9-13 76 (p) TomEaves 2 61
(Miss L A Perratt) *hld up: drvn over 2f out: sn btn* **50/1**
5352 **7** 8 **Bed Fellow (IRE)**[13] 5944 5-8-10 50 TonyHamilton 1 28
(P Monteith) *prom tl rdn and wknd over 2f out* **33/1**
460R **L** **Flawed Genius**[4] 6217 4-9-4 85 (tp) PhillipMakin 7 —
(K A Ryan) *lft at s* **13/2**

1m 50.6s (-4.10) **Going Correction** -0.325s/f (Firm) course record **8** Ran SP% **116.6**
Speed ratings (Par 105): **105,104,102,97,97 91,84,—**
toteswinger: 1&2 £4.30, 1&3 £4.90, 2&3 £3.40. CSF £25.29 TOTE £9.90: £2.10, £1.20, £1.90; EX 32.20.
Owner Shaun Taylor **Bred** Frank Brown, Hedberg Hall & K Hernandez **Trained** Stainforth, S Yorks

FOCUS
A Sussex Stakes winner and a German 2,000 Guineas winner in opposition in this claimer but neither could manage better than third in a race won by one readily held in an Ayr seller last time. As in the earlier races, out in front was a good place to be. The form is sound but limited.

6313 SCOTTISH RACING H'CAP 1m 6f
4:50 (4:50) (Class 4) (0-80,85) 3-Y-0+ **£6,476** (£1,927; £963; £481) **Stalls** High

Form RPR
-241 **1** **Ascendant**[12] 5961 3-9-12 85 PhillipMakin 4 96+
(Sir Mark Prescott) *mde all: rdn 2f out: hld on wl fnl f* **5/6**[1]
P1 **2** hd **Spirit Is Needed (IRE)**[13] 5939 3-9-4 77 J-PGuillambert 6 88+
(M Johnston) *trckd wnr: drvn fr 3f out: kpt on u.p fnl f: jst hld* **4/1**[2]
5661 **3** 6 **Ifatfirst (IRE)**[13] 5943 6-9-2 65 DanielTudhope 3 68
(J S Goldie) *prom: effrt over 2f out: no imp wl over 1f out* **9/1**
0-45 **4** 2¼ **Abstract Folly (IRE)**[15] 5857 7-8-9 61 FrederikTylicki(3) 2 61
(J D Bethell) *hld up: rdn over 2f out: edgd rt: no imp* **8/1**[3]
1410 **5** 2¾ **Wee Charlie Castle (IRE)**[14] 5912 6-10-0 77 TomEaves 5 73
(I Semple) *hld up: drvn over 2f out: btn over 1f out* **12/1**
4022 **6** 2 **Madamlily (IRE)**[9] 6075 3-8-10 69 GrahamGibbons 1 63
(J J Quinn) *chsd ldrs tl rdn and wknd fr 2f out* **8/1**[3]
1500 **7** 7 **King's Head (IRE)**[8] 6095 6-9-13 76 (p) TonyHamilton 7 61
(Miss L A Perratt) *hld up: n.m.r briefly over 2f out: sn rdn and btn* **33/1**

3m 0.91s (-4.39) **Going Correction** -0.325s/f (Firm)
WFA 3 from 6yo+ 10lb **7** Ran SP% **117.4**
Speed ratings (Par 105): **99,98,95,94,92 91,87**
toteswinger: 1&2 £1.80, 1&3 £2.50, 2&3 £3.80. CSF £4.71 TOTE £2.00: £1.40, £2.10; EX 5.30.
Owner Cheveley Park Stud **Bred** Cheveley Park Stud Ltd **Trained** Newmarket, Suffolk

FOCUS
Three-year-olds had won both previous runnings of this race and they provided the first two from three runners, the pair pulling well clear of some modest and exposed opposition in a race run at no more than a fair pace. The winner was another to make all. The first two could be worth following.

6314 ROYAL SCOTS H'CAP 5f
5:20 (5:20) (Class 6) (0-65,65) 4-Y-0+ **£2,590** (£770; £385; £192) **Stalls** Low

Form RPR
0004 **1** **Distant Sun (USA)**[6] 6159 5-9-1 65 FrederikTylicki(3) 6 74
(Miss L A Perratt) *prom: rdn to ld over 1f out: kpt on strly fnl f* **11/2**
6310 **2** 2 **Wicked Wilma (IRE)**[10] 6010 5-9-2 63 FrancisNorton 2 65
(A Berry) *prom: effrt and chsd wnr over 1f out: kpt on fnl f: nt rch wnr* **7/2**[1]
0050 **3** nk **Killer Class**[6] 6159 4-8-11 63 GaryBartley(5) 8 64
(J S Goldie) *hld up: hdwy and prom appr fnl f: kpt on ins fnl f* **11/1**
4066 **4** ¾ **Rocketball (IRE)**[14] 5919 4-8-10 62 DeanHeslop(5) 11 60
(Mrs L Williamson) *cl up: led briefly over 1f out: one pce ins fnl f* **5/1**[3]
5104 **5** ¾ **Silvanus (IRE)**[22] 5678 4-9-0 61 PhillipMakin 7 57+
(P T Midgley) *s.i.s: hld up: n.m.r 1/2-way: swtchd rt and effrt over 1f out: no imp fnl f* **4/1**[2]
42 **6** nk **Strensall**[44] 4976 12-8-4 51 DuranFentiman 3 45
(R E Barr) *in tch: rdn and outpcd 2f out: kpt on ins fnl f: no imp* **10/1**
0000 **7** 1¼ **Molly Two**[32] 5341 4-8-8 55 TomEaves 4 45
(L A Mullaney) *led to over 1f out: sn rdn and btn* **20/1**
0304 **8** nk **Fern House (IRE)**[27] 5504 7-8-4 51 oh6 AndrewMullen 10 40
(Bruce Hellier) *bhd: effrt on outside 1/2-way: btn fnl f* **25/1**
3000 **9** 1 **Blazing Heights**[10] 6010 6-8-5 55 KellyHarrison(3) 1 40
(J S Goldie) *t.k.h: hld up on stands' rail: pushed along 2f out: n.d* **10/1**
-002 **10** 1¾ **Windjammer**[32] 5341 5-8-6 53 (v) DavidAllan 9 32
(L A Mullaney) *cl up: ev ch over 2f out to over 1f out: sn wknd* **9/1**

58.78 secs (-1.62) **Going Correction** -0.275s/f (Firm) **10** Ran SP% **119.4**
Speed ratings (Par 101): **101,97,97,96,94 94,92,91,90,87**
toteswinger: 1&2 £5.50, 1&3 £10.10, 2&3 £9.10. CSF £25.75 CT £214.67 TOTE £6.60: £2.30, £1.60, £4.20; EX 35.80 Place 6 £16.61, Place 5 £11.05.
Owner Ken McGarrity **Bred** Forging Oaks Llc **Trained** East Kilbride, South Lanarks

FOCUS
A low-grade event to end proceedings, but it provided a decisive winner. The pace was a good one with three front-runners taking each other on. The form seems sound.
T/Plt: £14.50 to a £1 stake. Pool: £50,425.77. 2,533.76 winning tickets. T/Qpdt: £3.50 to a £1 stake. Pool: £3,731.50. 780.00 winning tickets. RY

6315 - 6321a (Foreign Racing) - See Raceform Interactive

5920 CURRAGH (R-H)
Sunday, September 27

OFFICIAL GOING: Good

6316a C.L. WELD PARK STKS (GROUP 3) (FILLIES) 7f
2:45 (2:49) 2-Y-0 **£45,506** (£13,351; £6,361; £2,166)

RPR
1 **Lady Springbank (IRE)**[66] 4245 2-8-12 WJSupple 1 99
(P D Deegan, Ire) *towards rr on outer: hdwy into 6th fr 2f out: rdn to chal and dispute ld 1f out: led and styd on wl ins fnl f* **25/1**
2 ½ **Bikini Babe (IRE)**[50] 4795 2-8-12 JoeFanning 4 98
(M Johnston) *cl up: led fr 3f out: strly pressed and jnd 1f out: sn hdd and kpt on wout matching wnr* **9/2**[2]
3 1¼ **Corcovada (IRE)**[14] 5922 2-8-12 90 FMBerry 2 95
(Edward P Harty, Ire) *towards rr on inner: 8th and hdwy fr 2f out: 4th and kpt on wout threatening u.p fr 1f out* **7/1**
4 1 **Queen Of Troy (IRE)**[15] 5895 2-8-12 84 JAHeffernan 12 93
(A P O'Brien, Ire) *trckd ldrs: sn 4th: 3rd and no imp u.p fr 1f out: kpt on same pce* **12/1**
5 1¼ **Lady Lupus (IRE)**[14] 5922 2-8-12 CO'Donoghue 6 89
(A P O'Brien, Ire) *sn in rr: rdn into 9th 1f out: r.o wl wout threatening fnl f* **16/1**
6 hd **Picture Perfect (IRE)**[14] 5922 2-8-12 JMurtagh 3 89
(David Wachman, Ire) *trckd ldrs: sn 3rd: dropped to 5th and no imp u.p 1f out: kpt on same pce* **7/4**[1]
7 shd **Dazzling Day**[14] 5922 2-8-12 85 CDHayes 5 89
(Kevin Prendergast, Ire) *sn trckd ldrs: 7th 2f out: u.p in 6th and no imp fr 1f out* **16/1**
8 nk **Roan Inish (CAN)**[66] 4251 2-8-12 KJManning 7 89+
(J S Bolger, Ire) *prom: short of room and hmpd fr 2f out: sn no imp* **13/2**[3]
9 ½ **Cornakill (USA)**[14] 5922 2-8-12 85 DPMcDonogh 10 87
(Kevin Prendergast, Ire) *mid-div on inner: short of room and no imp u.p fr under 2f out* **10/1**
10 2 **Dainty Steps (IRE)**[39] 5176 2-8-12 82 DMGrant 9 82
(John Joseph Murphy, Ire) *sn chsd ldrs: 10th 2f out: sn no imp u.p* **33/1**
11 2½ **Anaverna (IRE)**[22] 5684 2-8-12 81 PJSmullen 11 75
(D K Weld, Ire) *sn towards rr: 11th 2f out: sn no imp* **8/1**
12 15 **Rosa Muscosa (USA)**[46] 4920 2-8-12 73 MHarley 8 38
(J S Bolger, Ire) *sn led: rdn after 3f: hdd fr 3f out: 2nd 2f out: sn wknd* **33/1**

1m 24.02s (-3.08) **Going Correction** -0.30s/f (Firm) **12** Ran SP% **129.8**
Speed ratings: **105,104,103,101,100 100,100,99,99,96 94,76**
CSF £144.73 TOTE £41.60: £7.70, £2.30, £2.40; DF 399.30.
Owner Mark Gittins **Bred** Mrs M Gittins **Trained** The Curragh, Co Kildare

FOCUS
This did not look a particularly strong renewal of this Group 3 event and it produced an upset.

NOTEBOOK
Lady Springbank(IRE) scored on her Irish debut. She came from off the pace to deliver her challenge over a furlong out before getting on top and running on well in the closing stages.
Bikini Babe(IRE) went to the front well over 2f out and kept on well although the winner had her measure well inside the final furlong. (op 4/1)
Corcovada(IRE) was unproven on this type of ground but she handled it quite well and made headway on the inside from 2f out, running on well from fifth place over a furlong out. (op 6/1)
Queen Of Troy(IRE) tracked the leaders and kept on after failing to raise her effort over a furlong out.
Picture Perfect(IRE) appeared to have no excuses and she was getting nowhere from over a furlong out. (op 9/4 tchd 6/4)

6317a GOFFS MILLION SPRINT 6f
3:20 (3:26) 2-Y-0
£956,310 (£276,699; £131,067; £63,106; £30,097; £8,737)

RPR
1 **Lucky General (IRE)**[17] 5795 2-9-3 RichardHughes 2 108+
(R Hannon) *sn settled in rr of mid-div: hdwy into 6th travelling wl over 1f out: chal u.p and led ins fnl f: styd on wl* **11/2**[3]
2 1¾ **Full Mandate (IRE)**[29] 5427 2-8-12 MJKinane 10 98
(R Hannon) *a.p: led under 2f out: rdn over 1f out: strly pressed and hdd ins fnl f: kpt on same pce* **9/1**
3 ¾ **King Ledley (USA)**[36] 5275 2-9-3 101 (b) DPMcDonogh 1 101
(Kevin Prendergast, Ire) *towards rr: prog travelling wl into 9th over 1f out: rdn and r.o wl wout threatening fnl f: swtchd and 3rd cl home* **8/1**
4 hd **Beethoven (IRE)**[15] 5892 2-9-3 111 JMurtagh 16 100
(A P O'Brien, Ire) *chsd ldrs: rdn in 4th over 1f out: no imp and kpt on same pce ins fnl f* **9/2**[1]
5 ¾ **Air Chief Marshal (IRE)**[15] 5892 2-9-3 110 JAHeffernan 14 98
(A P O'Brien, Ire) *sn chsd ldrs: rdn in 8th over 1f out: sn no imp and kpt on wout threatening* **10/1**
6 nk **Walk On Bye (IRE)**[63] 4359 2-8-12 102 WMLordan 19 92
(T Stack, Ire) *trckd ldrs: travelling wl 2f out: 3rd over 1f out: sn no imp u.p and kpt on same pce* **5/1**[2]
7 hd **Gibraltar Blue (IRE)**[36] 5273 2-8-12 CO'Donoghue 5 91
(T Stack, Ire) *sn trckd ldrs travelling wl: 2nd over 1f out: sn no imp: kpt on same pce u.p* **6/1**
8 ½ **Velvet Flicker (IRE)**[21] 5701 2-8-12 93 CDHayes 17 90
(Kevin Prendergast, Ire) *towards rr: prog travelling wl 2f out: 5th over 1f out: sn no imp u.p: kpt on same pce* **16/1**
9 1¼ **Moran Gra (USA)**[36] 5275 2-9-3 98 (b[1]) FMBerry 12 91
(Ms Joanna Morgan, Ire) *chsd ldrs: u.p in 7th over 1f out: sn no imp* **12/1**
10 ½ **Bethrah (IRE)** 2-8-12 PJSmullen 9 84
(D K Weld, Ire) *loaded wout rdr: dwlt: towards rr: rdn to go 10th over 1f out: sn no imp and kpt on* **20/1**
11 5 **Moonlight Cass (IRE)**[28] 5485 2-8-12 KLatham 18 69
(David P Myerscough, Ire) *towards rr: n.d and kpt on same pce fr 2f out* **66/1**
12 1 **Miss Cueta (IRE)**[12] 6085 2-8-12 68 (b[1]) RPCleary 11 66
(M Halford, Ire) *prom: no ex u.p fr under 2f out* **66/1**
13 shd **Rigid Rock (IRE)**[16] 5844 2-9-3 84 PShanahan 3 71
(J T Gorman, Ire) *sn trckd ldrs: no ex u.p fr under 2f out* **50/1**
14 1¼ **Historic Occasion (IRE)**[15] 5893 2-9-3 (b[1]) NGMcCullagh 20 67
(D K Weld, Ire) *sn mid-div: no imp fr under 2f out* **50/1**
15 2½ **Reggae Dancer (IRE)**[16] 5843 2-9-3 75 SMLevey 15 60
(A P O'Brien, Ire) *rdn to sn ld: hdd fr under 2f out: sn wknd* **50/1**
16 nk **Free Judgement (USA)**[15] 5893 2-9-3 KJManning 4 59
(J S Bolger, Ire) *sn mid-div: no imp fr under 2f out* **9/1**
17 ¾ **Capulet Monteque (IRE)**[29] 5452 2-8-12 88 WJLee 13 52
(T Stack, Ire) *prom: wknd fr under 2f out* **40/1**
18 ¾ **Tamara Who (IRE)**[15] 5895 2-8-12 GFCarroll 6 49
(John E Kiely, Ire) *sn towards rr: nvr a factor* **100/1**
19 1¼ **Step In Time (IRE)**[17] 5795 2-9-3 JoeFanning 7 51
(M Johnston) *sn prom: wknd fr 2f out* **33/1**
20 5 **Silk Slippers**[23] 5638 2-8-12 DMGrant 8 31
(John Joseph Murphy, Ire) *sn towards rr: nvr a factor* **33/1**

1m 12.31s (-2.39) **Going Correction** -0.30s/f (Firm) **20** Ran SP% **141.2**
Speed ratings: **103,100,99,99,98 98,97,97,95,94 88,86,86,84,81 81,80,79,77,70**
CSF £58.79 TOTE £7.30: £2.00, £3.70, £2.90, £1.70; DF 63.90.
Owner Mrs J Wood **Bred** K Molloy **Trained** East Everleigh, Wilts
■ This valuable event is to be discontinued.

FOCUS
A rock-solid sales race.

NOTEBOOK

Lucky General(IRE), twice a winner over the trip at Windsor, came from well off the pace to land this huge prize for Richard Hannon, who also sent out the runner-up. Trapped on the inside from his low draw early on, he travelled well in midfield when switched. When asked to close under 2f out, he picked up well and ran on to hit the front inside the final furlong. According to Richard Hannon jnr, the colt is unlikely to run again this season, but he is expected to get 7f and perhaps a mile next year, with the Greenham a likely early-season target. (op 8/1)

Full Mandate(IRE), winner of a 6f maiden at Newbury and runner-up in a Group 3 over the trip at Ascot in July, was soon in the front line on the stands' rail and was the overall leader from 2f out. She came under pressure over a furlong out and could find no extra when taken on by the winner. (op 8/1)

King Ledley(USA) had been placed at Group 3 and Group 2 level and was dropping back in trip here. Drawn next to the stands' rail, he was in rear until starting to run on 2f out and finished best of all. He is to continue his career in the US.

Beethoven(IRE) took time to win his maiden, something he achieved when scoring over this trip at Leopardstown early last month. Subsequently third in the Group 1 National Stakes, he tracked the leaders and kept on after coming under pressure in fourth place over a furlong out. (op 5/1)

Air Chief Marshal(IRE), like stablemate Beethoven, has had a busy season. Fourth in the National Stakes on his previous start, he chased the leaders and, after closing under 2f out, kept on under pressure.

Walk On Bye(IRE) was done no favours by the draw. She was soon tracking the leaders and looked a possibility when going third over a furlong out, only to weaken inside the final furlong. (op 4/1)

Step In Time(IRE) has been struggling in competitive races of late and seems to have regressed.

6318a JUDDMONTE BERESFORD STKS (GROUP 2) 1m

3:55 (3:57) 2-Y-O **£72,572** (£21,213; £10,048; £3,349)

RPR

1 **St Nicholas Abbey (IRE)**[42] 5081 2-9-1 .... JMurtagh 6 112+
(A P O'Brien, Ire) *sn racd towards rr in 7th: prog fr bef st: 3rd over 2f out: sn chal u.p in 2nd: led ins fnl f: styd on wl: comf* **2/5**[1]

2 ¾ **Layali Al Andalus**[15] 5859 2-9-1 .... JoeFanning 8 105
(M Johnston) *trckd ldr in 2nd: rdn to ld over 2f out: sn strly pressed and hdd ins fnl f: kpt on wl wout matching wnr* **10/1**

3 1 ½ **Passion For Gold (USA)**[30] 5408 2-9-1 .... AlanMunro 9 102
(Saeed Bin Suroor) *trckd ldrs: 4th over 2f out: sn rdn: no imp u.p and kpt on wout threatening fr over 1f out* **7/1**[2]

4 nk **Montecchio (IRE)**[98] 3197 2-9-1 96 .... DPMcDonogh 7 101
(Kevin Prendergast, Ire) *towards rr: prog in 5th fr over 2f out: 3rd and kpt on same pce u.p fr 1f out* **14/1**

5 4 ½ **Bobbyscot (IRE)**[49] 4833 2-9-1 103 .... WJSupple 5 91
(P D Deegan, Ire) *sn mid-div: 6th over 2f out: sn no imp u.p and kpt on* **20/1**

6 2 ½ **Lastofthemohicans (FR)**[45] 4960 2-9-1 .... JAHeffernan 2 86
(A P O'Brien, Ire) *sn led: strly pressed and hdd over 2f out: no ex fr over 1f out* **50/1**

7 nk **Top Spin (IRE)**[26] 5542 2-9-1 .... DMGrant 3 85
(John Joseph Murphy, Ire) *sn chsd ldrs: rdn early st: no imp fr 2f out* **100/1**

8 nk **Reiteration (USA)**[77] 3893 2-9-1 .... (t) KJManning 1 84
(J S Bolger, Ire) *trckd ldrs: dropped to 7th 2f out: sn no imp u.p* **8/1**[3]

9 nk **Senior**[15] 5892 2-9-1 .... PJSmullen 4 84
(Edward Lynam, Ire) *dwlt: in rr: no imp u.p fr 2f out* **14/1**

1m 41.6s (-0.30) **Going Correction** -0.30s/f (Firm) **9** Ran SP% **125.2**
Speed ratings: **89,88,86,86,81 79,79,78,78**
CSF £6.70 TOTE £1.40: £1.10, £3.30, £2.10; DF 9.80.
Owner Derrick Smith **Bred** Barton Bloodstock & Villiers S **Trained** Ballydoyle, Co Tipperary

FOCUS

This race has produced many talented performers, notably Sea The Stars last season. However, at face value the form looks ordinary considering the previous efforts of the runner-up.

NOTEBOOK

St Nicholas Abbey(IRE) ◆ supplied Ballydoyle with their tenth winner of the Beresford and he won in the style of a very promising classic contender for next term. Always travelling, Johnny Murtagh was happy to settle the impressive course-and-distance winner off the pace as stablemate Lastofthemohicans set a decent clip up front. The favourite was pushed along to close but the response was impressive when asked to go about his business. He was far superior to what the winning margin suggested and on this evidence he'll certainly appreciate going further next season. The Racing Post Trophy could be pencilled in for him and he could well emerge as the number one Ballydoyle Derby hope next year. (op 1/2)

Layali Al Andalus, winner of two of his previous four starts, showed more here on this favourable ground. He had failed to take the step forward in the Champagne Stakes but he appreciated this easier surface. His trainer expressed his satisfaction afterwards and he was beaten by a very good horse. (op 8/1)

Passion For Gold(USA), winner of a decent Thirsk maiden over this trip a month ago, was expected to play a leading role. He held every chance at halfway but when the tempo increased he was found wanting. (op 8/1)

Montecchio(IRE) was held up before creeping closer passing the 3f pole but was another who struggled to raise his game. (op 14/1 tchd 16/1)

Bobbyscot(IRE) struggled over this longer journey, but may have needed this outing considering it was his first run since June. (op 25/1)

6319a GOFFS MILLION MILE 1m

4:30 (4:32) 2-Y-O

£956,310 (£276,699; £131,067; £63,106; £30,097; £8,737)

RPR

1 **Shakespearean (IRE)**[36] 5261 2-9-3 .... JoeFanning 14 99
(M Johnston) *sn led: strly pressed fr over 2f out: styd on wl fnl f: all out* **3/1**[2]

2 shd **Marfach (USA)**[36] 5275 2-9-3 98 .... (p) KJManning 19 99
(J S Bolger, Ire) *a.p: 3rd 2f out: sn chal u.p: styd on wl fnl f: jst failed* **25/1**

3 hd **Nurture (IRE)**[9] 6069 2-8-12 .... FMBerry 10 94+
(R Hannon) *sn mid-div: 8th 2f out: rdn into 6th fr 1f out: styd on wl: nt quite rch 1st 2* **33/1**

4 ½ **Famous (IRE)**[28] 5488 2-8-12 105 .... JAHeffernan 17 92
(A P O'Brien, Ire) *a.p: 4th 2f out: kpt on same pce u.p fnl f* **11/1**

5 shd **Is Feidir Linn (IRE)**[55] 4612 2-9-3 .... DJMoran 12 97
(J T Gorman, Ire) *cl up: 2nd 2f out: kpt on same pce u.p fnl f* **100/1**

6 1 **Cadley Road (IRE)**[42] 5085 2-9-3 .... RichardHughes 2 95
(R Hannon) *prom: dropped to 7th 2f out: styd on u.p wout threatening fr over 1f out* **8/1**

7 ½ **Crystal Gal (IRE)**[15] 5893 2-8-12 .... DPMcDonogh 8 89
(Kevin Prendergast, Ire) *sn mid-div: prog 3f out: 5th 2f out: kpt on same pce u.p fr over 1f out* **6/1**[3]

8 2 **Lord High Admiral (IRE)**[136] 2019 2-9-3 .... JMurtagh 11 90
(A P O'Brien, Ire) *sn trckd ldrs: dropped to 9th 2f out: sn no imp u.p* **8/1**

9 1 ¼ **Utrillo (IRE)**[36] 5275 2-9-3 .... CO'Donoghue 13 87
(A P O'Brien, Ire) *towards rr: no imp and kpt on same pce fr over 2f out* **50/1**

10 nk **Private Story (USA)**[9] 6057 2-9-3 .... PatDobbs 15 86
(R Hannon) *towards rr: kpt on same pce u.p fr 2f out* **14/1**

11 1 **Stunning View (IRE)**[62] 4390 2-9-3 .... PJSmullen 1 84
(D K Weld, Ire) *sn chsd ldrs: 6th 2f out: sn no imp u.p* **8/1**

12 ¾ **Azmeel**[43] 5022 2-9-3 .... MJKinane 5 82
(J H M Gosden) *towards rr: effrt on outer in mid-div fr 3f out: 11th and no imp fr 2f out* **2/1**[1]

13 ¾ **Style Queen (IRE)**[45] 4959 2-8-12 .... MHarley 9 76
(J S Bolger, Ire) *towards rr: n.d fr over 2f out* **50/1**

14 4 ½ **A Mind Of Her Own (IRE)**[118] 2557 2-8-12 .... WMLordan 16 66
(David Wachman, Ire) *sn chsd ldrs: no ex fr 2f out* **25/1**

15 nk **Rockin N Reelin (USA)**[14] 5920 2-9-3 64 .... CDHayes 3 70
(J T Gorman, Ire) *mid-div: dropped towards rr fr over 3f out: sn no imp* **100/1**

16 6 **On The Cusp (IRE)**[22] 5664 2-9-3 .... AlanMunro 7 57
(M A Jarvis) *mid-div: no ex fr over 2f out* **50/1**

17 ¾ **Legendary Lad (IRE)**[22] 5690 2-9-3 .... PShanahan 18 55
(D K Weld, Ire) *mid-div: 10th and wknd fr 2f out* **33/1**

18 2 **Diamondgeezer Luke (IRE)**[5] 6194 2-9-3 65 .... WJLee 6 51
(F Costello, Ire) *prom: wknd fr over 2f out* **100/1**

19 ¾ **Bintalaleumydarlin (IRE)**[27] 5505 2-8-12 .... WJSupple 4 44
(M Johnston) *mid-div best: no ex fr 3f out* **66/1**

1m 38.92s (-2.98) **Going Correction** -0.30s/f (Firm) **19** Ran SP% **144.9**
Speed ratings: **102,101,101,101,101 100,99,97,96,96 95,94,93,89,88 82,82,80,79**
CSF £94.94 TOTE £5.10: £1.60, £4.40, £3.70, £3.00; DF 155.10.
Owner Sheikh Hamdan Bin Mohammed Al Maktoum **Bred** Mrs H Owen **Trained** Middleham Moor, N Yorks

■ The final running of this valuable event.
■ Stewards' Enquiry : Joe Fanning one-day ban: used whip with excessive frequency (Oct 11)
D J Moran one-day ban: used whip with excessive frequency (Oct 11)

FOCUS

A very valuable contest in which the form looks solid but limited.

NOTEBOOK

Shakespearean(IRE), a Group 3 winner at Sandown on his previous start, had to do it the hard way here. He made virtually all and kept on gamely under pressure in the closing stages, repelling all challengers to win all out in a photo finish. Mark Johnston will wait to see how he comes out of the race before deciding if he will run again this season. (op 5/1)

Marfach(USA) had finished in the frame in a Group 3 and a Group 2 on his two previous starts and he only just failed to get up having raced prominently throughout. He had every chance having started his challenge under pressure over a furlong out.

Nurture(IRE), runner-up in a 6f maiden at Wolverhampton on the second of her two previous starts, began to creep into the race from 2f out and finished well.

Famous(IRE), runner-up in the Group 1 Moyglare Stakes on her previous start, was stepping up in trip. She was always in the leading group and kept on under pressure having had every chance from 2f out. (op 12/1)

Is Feidir Linn(IRE), sixth of nine over 7f at Naas on his only previous start, showed up well, racing prominently and appearing to head the winner briefly before halfway. He remained in contention and kept on under pressure.

Cadley Road(IRE), runner-up in a Listed race on his previous start, performed creditably without troubling the principals, having hit a flat spot. (op 9/1 tchd 7/1)

Private Story(USA), who ran well in a good conditions race last time, was settled out the back and never got involved.

Azmeel, winner of both his previous starts, made some progress over 3f out but was done with fully 2f out. (op 7/4 tchd 9/4)

On The Cusp(IRE) is well bred but probably found this coming too quickly after his debut earlier in the month.

Bintalaleumydarlin(IRE), had shown only moderate form previously and was out of her depth in this grade.

ARGENTAN (R-H)

Sunday, September 27

OFFICIAL GOING: Good to firm

6322a PRIX DE JUVIGNY SUR ORNE (MAIDEN COLTS & GELDINGS) 1m 1f 165y

1:00 (12:00) 2-Y-O **£6,311** (£2,524; £1,893; £1,262; £631)

RPR

1 **Fylarchos (FR)** 2-8-6 .... JClaudic(6) 72
(C Laffon-Parias, France)

2 2 **Spectacle Du Mars (FR)**[13] 2-9-2 .... MSautjeau 72
(C Martens, France)

3 1 ½ **Quillin**[16] 5850 2-9-2 .... JAuge 69
(E J O'Neill) *trckd ldr: 2nd st: one pce fr over 1f out*

4 3 **Daniel's Victory (FR)** 2-8-13 .... (3) 63
(G Botti, Italy)

5 1 **Saga Hill (FR)** 2-8-13 .... (3) 62
(W Menuet, France)

6 snk **Franz Quercus (FR)** 2-8-9 .... (3) 57
(Y De Nicolay, France)

7 1 **Celebrity Choice (IRE)** 2-8-12 55
(E Libaud, France)

7 dht **Maitre Pierre (FR)** 2-8-12 55
(C Diard, France)

9 3 **Novy Nick (FR)** 2-8-12 50
(C Diard, France)

9 Ran

PARI-MUTUEL (including one euro stakes): WIN 10.30; PL 3.30, 2.20,2.50: DF 12.00.
Owner L Marinopoulos **Bred** Stilvi Compania **Trained** Chantilly, France

NOTEBOOK

Quillin was encountering very different conditions to his debut run but performed creditably, if not having the speed to trouble the winner.

5082 COLOGNE (R-H)
Sunday, September 27

OFFICIAL GOING: Good

6323a GROSSE EUROPA MEILE (GROUP 2) 1m
3:40 (3:50) 3-Y-O+ £38,835 (£14,563; £5,825; £3,883)

RPR
1 **Premio Loco (USA)**26 5563 5-9-4 GeorgeBaker 1 113
(C F Wall) *disputed 3rd, 3rd straight, driven to lead inside final 100y, ran on* **11/10**1
2 3/4 **Earl Of Fire (GER)**26 5563 4-9-1 DBoeuf 3 108
(W Baltromei, Germany) *led to inside final 100y, ran on one pace* **6/1**
3 3 **Konig Concorde (GER)**26 5563 4-9-1 SPasquier 7 101
(C Sprengel, Germany) *disputed 3rd to half-way, 4th straight, disputed 3rd over 1f out, kept on one pace* **9/2**3
4 2 1/2 **Runaway**42 5086 7-9-1 TJarnet 5 95
(R Pritchard-Gordon, France) *held up, 5th straight, headway to dispute 3rd over 1f out, hung left under pressure, one pace* **7/2**2
5 3 **Magic Eye (IRE)**25 5588 4-8-11 THellier 6 84
(Andreas Lowe, Germany) *held up, 6th straight, never a factor* **12/1**
6 6 **Globus (GER)**25 5585 3-8-10 ASuborics 2 74
(Uwe Ostmann, Germany) *tracked leader, 2nd straight, soon weakened* **9/1**
7 1/2 **Four Dancers (GER)**56 4582 4-9-1 HGrewe 4 74
(Frau E Mader, Germany) *disputed 3rd to half-way, last & beaten straight* **25/1**

1m 35.21s (-3.18)
WFA 3 from 4yo+ 4lb **7** Ran SP% **123.8**
TOTE: WIN 16; PL 11, 14, 13; SF 77.
Owner Bernard Westley **Bred** Kidder, Cole & Griggs **Trained** Newmarket, Suffolk

NOTEBOOK
Premio Loco(USA), who improved on Polytrack last winter, has raised his game again of late and two trips to Germany have now produced two Group 2 wins. He confied his superiority over the placed horses here and connections are hoping to get an invitation to Hong Kong at the end of the year. If that doesn't materialise, he will be aimed at the Dubai Carnival.

6324a PREIS VON EUROPA (GROUP 1) 1m 4f
4:15 (4:26) 3-Y-O+ £97,087 (£32,039; £14,563; £6,796)

RPR
1 **Jukebox Jury (IRE)**28 5497 3-8-13 RoystonFfrench 1 120
(M Johnston) *jumped start, led 1 1/2f, tracked leader til led again over 2f out, ridden well over 1f out, all out* **5/2**1
2 nse **Eastern Anthem (IRE)**21 5707 5-9-6 LDettori 3 119
(Saeed Bin Suroor) *held up, 9th straight, headway 3f out, close 5th 2f out, driven over 1f out, 2nd 1f out, ran on well, just failed* **5/2**1
3 2 1/2 **Eliot (GER)**84 3670 3-8-13 THellier 2 116
(T Mundry, Germany) *close up, went 3rd on inside straight, outpaced 2f out, 5th 1f out, rallied to regain 3rd close home* **12/1**
4 nk **Poseidon Adventure (IRE)**14 6-9-6 (b) KKerekes 6 115
(W Figge, Germany) *held up in rear, last straight, good headway on rails over 2f out, driven to go 3rd at distance, no extra closing stages* **16/1**
5 2 **Schiller Danon (GER)**42 5082 3-8-13 ASuborics 4 112
(W Hickst, Germany) *mid-division, 6th straight, driven to dispute 3rd well over 1f out, one pace* **14/1**
6 hd **Enroller (IRE)**39 5171 4-9-6 DarryllHolland 5 111
(W R Muir) *led after 1 1/2f, headed over 2f out, driven & 4th 1f out, one pace* **12/1**
7 1 1/2 **Bronze Cannon (USA)**71 4369 4-9-6 RichardMullen 10 109
(J H M Gosden) *mid-division, 5th & pushed along straight, ridden 2f out, never able to challenge* **9/2**2
8 2 1/2 **Ambassador (GER)**29 5461 5-9-6 AStarke 9 105
(T Mundry, Germany) *disputed 3rd, 4th straight, ridden 2f out, soon weakened* **33/1**
9 hd **Guantana (GER)**35 5296 4-9-3 SPasquier 8 101
(J Hirschberger, Germany) *held up in rear, 8th straight, never a factor* **14/1**
10 18 **Toughness Danon**25 5585 3-8-13 (b) JBojko 7 76
(A Wohler, Germany) *pulling & headway after 3f on outside, 7th straight, soon beaten* **10/1**3

2m 29.56s (-3.34)
WFA 3 from 4yo+ 8lb **10** Ran SP% **122.0**
TOTE: WIN 42; PL 15, 14, 18; SF 77.
Owner A D Spence **Bred** Paul Nataf **Trained** Middleham Moor, N Yorks

NOTEBOOK
Jukebox Jury(IRE) was always well placed and sprinted clear at the right time to just do enough for victory. He is developing into a top-class perfomer after a quietish start to the season and the Canadian International could be his next race.
Eastern Anthem(IRE) always takes a little while to get going and could never quite poke his nose in front. He needs a strong gallop and possibly a long straight to be most effective.
Enroller(IRE) soon took the early lead off the winner but was readily left behind when the principals made their bid. He probably wants easier ground.
Bronze Cannon(USA) has become a little disappointing since his success at Royal Ascot.

MONT-DE-MARSAN (R-H)
Sunday, September 27

OFFICIAL GOING: Good

6325a PRIX DES SOPHORAS (CLAIMER) 7f
2:30 (12:00) 2-Y-O £4,854 (£1,942; £1,456; £971; £485)

RPR
1 **Joukov (FR)** 2-9-1 J-BHamel —
(F Seguin, France)
2 1 1/2 **Piuside (IRE)** 2-8-11 (b) CBrechon —
(F Sanchez, France)
3 3/4 **Affaire De Famille (FR)** 2-9-1 PSogorb —
(Mme C Dufreche, France)
4 nk **Miss Reel (FR)** 2-8-11 —
(F Rohaut, France)
5 1 1/2 **Keltina (FR)** 2-8-11 —
(M Roussel, France)
6 2 **Nova San (IRE)** 2-9-4 (b) —
(F Sanchez, France)
7 3 **Belle Eponine**62 4371 2-9-4 IMendizabal —
(E J O'Neill)
8 snk **Pazko (FR)** 2-9-4 —
(L A Urbano-Grajales, France)
9 snk **Corola (FR)** 2-8-8 —
(W Walton, France)
10 1 1/2 **British Luck (SPA)** 2-9-1 (b) —
(Y Durepaire, Spain)
0 **Twin Deficit** 2-8-11 (b) —
(R Litt, France)
0 **Tumeritespius (IRE)** 2-8-8 —
(F Sanchez, France)
0 **Lavirca Nath (FR)**-8-11 —
(D Barone, France)
0 **Mantadia (FR)** 2-8-8 —
(B De Montzey, France)
0 **Iron Prince** 2-8-11 (b) —
(Mlle A Imaz-Ceca, France)

1m 28.1s (88.10) **15** Ran
PARI-MUTUEL: WIN 8.60; PL 2.80, 12.50, 3.60; DF 97.10.
Owner Diego Alfonso Sarabia Rodriguez **Bred** Sarl Ecurie Jarlan **Trained** France

NOTEBOOK
Belle Eponine, the winner of a Redcar seller earlier in the summer, failed to figure on her first trip to France.

5899 BATH (L-H)
Monday, September 28

OFFICIAL GOING: Firm (10.0)
Wind: Virtually nil Weather: Cloudy

6328 FREEBETS.CO.UK LEAGUE FOOTBALL FREE BETS MAIDEN STKS 5f 161y
2:10 (2:11) (Class 5) 2-Y-O £2,719 (£809; £404; £202) Stalls Centre

Form RPR
0220 1 **Rakaan (IRE)**18 5795 2-9-3 90 MartinDwyer 3 82
(B J Meehan) *trckd ldr: led 2f out: sn hung lft: rdn and veered bdly lft jst ins fnl f: styd on on strly* **8/11**1
6 2 2 1/4 **Desert Poppy (IRE)**18 5808 2-8-12 0 ShaneKelly 2 73+
(W R Swinburn) *sn led: rdn and hdd 2f out: styng on same pce whn bdly hmpd jst ins fnl f: rcvrd to comf hold 2nd* **8/1**3
53 3 1 3/4 **Dream Number (IRE)**16 5866 2-8-9 0 RussellKennemore(3) 4 64
(W R Muir) *chsd ldrs: rdn over 2f out: styd on same pce fr over 1f out* **25/1**
2200 4 2 **Reddy To Star (IRE)**48 4868 2-9-3 76 TPO'Shea 6 63
(C G Cox) *in rr: rdn over 2f out: styd on fr over 1f out but nvr gng pce to get into contention* **11/1**
5 5 1 1/4 **Memorandum** 2-8-12 0 SteveDrowne 8 54
(R Charlton) *broke wl: green and towards rr tl mproved to trck ldrs over 3f out: rdn and one pce fr over 1f out* **9/2**2
4066 6 2 3/4 **Hill Of Miller (IRE)**19 5769 2-9-3 74 (e1) RichardMullen 9 49
(Rae Guest) *s.i.s: bhd: rdn 3f out: nt clr run and swtchd lft to ins over 2f out: styd on u.p but nvr in contention* **20/1**
5600 7 3 1/2 **Ballachulish**37 5256 2-9-3 62 DaneO'Neill 5 41
(H Candy) *chsd ldrs: rdn over 2f out: sn btn* **33/1**
0604 8 4 1/2 **Miss Roma (IRE)**53 4689 2-8-12 45 (p) JoeFanning 7 24
(R A Harris) *chsd ldrs on outside: rdn over 3f out: wknd over 2f out* **100/1**
00 9 2 3/4 **Annia (IRE)**25 5611 2-8-12 0 MickyFenton 1 9
(N P Littmoden) *plunged s and in rr: a outpcd* **33/1**

1m 10.8s (-0.40) **Going Correction** -0.125s/f (Firm) **9** Ran SP% **113.9**
Speed ratings (Par 95): **97,94,91,89,87 83,79,73,69**
toteswingers: 1&2 £3.00, 1&3 £4.40, 2&3 £7.10 CSF £6.84 TOTE £1.80: £1.02, £2.30, £4.10; EX 8.80 Trifecta £39.90 Pool: £509.13 - 9.43 winning units..
Owner Saleh Al Homaizi & Imad Al Sagar **Bred** L Mulryan & M Fahy **Trained** Manton, Wilts

FOCUS
An ordinary juvenile maiden won in unconvincing style by Rakaan. The form makes sense.

NOTEBOOK
Rakaan(IRE) hung badly left under pressure and didn't look totally keen. Without the blinkers this time and ridden less aggressively than has been the case lately, he picked up for pressure but badly hampered the runner-up when wandering. He's useful but is not sure to progress. (op 10-11)
Desert Poppy(IRE) is better than she showed considering she was squeezed up against the rail a furlong out, but that said, she probably wouldn't have won, as she still looked very green. This was an improvement on her first effort and there ought to be more to come. Official explanation: jockey said filly suffered interference in running (op 7-1 tchd 13-2)
Dream Number(IRE) travelled strongly but found only the one pace. She should be able to make her mark in low-grade handicap company. (op 33-1 tchd 22-1)
Reddy To Star(IRE) has a regressive profile but he's better than this run implies as he seemed to stumble early on and lost his place, before making some late headway. (tchd 9-1)
Memorandum is bred to want further, being a half-sister to 1m2f winner Atlas Silk, out of a smart dual 1m1f-1m4f scorer. (op 7-2)
Annia(IRE) Official explanation: jockey said filly stumbled on leaving stalls

6329 JOHN SISK 150TH ANNIVERSARY CLAIMING STKS 5f 11y
2:40 (2:40) (Class 6) 3-Y-O+ £2,072 (£616; £308; £153) Stalls Centre

Form RPR
3500 1 **Desperate Dan**15 5901 8-8-6 73 (v) AmyBaker(5) 9 75
(A B Haynes) *in rr: rdn along over 3f out: str run fr 2f out: chal fnl 110yds: led cl home: hld on gamely* **14/1**
601 2 nse **Green Lagonda (AUS)**15 5900 7-8-6 67 AndrewHeffernan(5) 4 75
(P D Evans) *trckd ldrs: drvn and styd on to chal 1f out: led jst ins fnl f: kpt slt advantage tl hdd cl home: rallied: jst failed* **9/1**
6326 3 1 3/4 **Matterofact (IRE)**25 5608 6-9-0 68 DaneO'Neill 8 72
(M S Saunders) *s.i.s: in rr: rdn and hdwy fr 2f out: nt clr run 1f out: swtchd rt and kpt on but no imp on ldng duo* **12/1**
0132 4 1 **Total Impact**7 6171 6-9-4 86 BMcHugh(5) 6 77
(R A Fahey) *chsd ldrs: rdn over 2f out: styd on u.p fr over 1f out but nvr gng pce to chal* **1/1**1
0002 5 hd **Fault**15 5900 3-8-12 80 MickyFenton 3 66
(Stef Liddiard) *sn led: rdn to keep slt advantage whn chal fr over 2f out: hdd jst ins fnl f: wknd fnl 50yds* **13/2**2

403 **6** *nk* **Misaro (GER)**[15] 5900 8-8-8 75.....(b) RossAtkinson(5) 11 65
(R A Harris) *rdn towards rr: hdwy u.p on outside fr 2f out: styd on fnl f but nvr a threat* **7/1**[3]

1343 **7** *3/4* **Spic 'n Span**[28] 5504 4-8-9 58.....(b) JoeFanning 10 59
(R A Harris) *pressed ldr: chal gng wl fr over 2f out: rdn and ev ch 1f out: fnd little u.p and wknd ins fnl f* **15/2**

P533 **8** *3* **Talamahana**[21] 5716 4-8-4 47..... DO'Donohoe 7 43
(A B Haynes) *in rr: rdn along 3f out: a outpcd* **66/1**

0000 **9** *7* **Rathmolyon**[24] 5629 4-8-1 41.....(b) JamieMackay 5 15
(D Haydn Jones) *chsd ldrs to 1/2-way: sn btn* **100/1**

0 **10** *21* **Poppy Morris (IRE)**[21] 5716 4-8-3 0..... FrankieMcDonald 1 —
(A B Haynes) *earlty spd: wknd qckly bef 1/2-way* **150/1**

61.85 secs (-0.65) **Going Correction** -0.125s/f (Firm)
WFA 3 from 4yo+ 1lb **10** Ran SP% **115.1**
Speed ratings (Par 101): **100,99,97,95,95 94,93,88,77,43**
toteswingers: 1&2 £21.20, 1&3 £13.80, 2&3 £12.10 CSF £131.42 TOTE £14.70: £3.20, £2.60, £3.00; EX 85.80 Trifecta £344.20 Part won. Pool: £465.20 - 0.50 winning units..

Owner Joe McCarthy **Bred** Sheikh Amin Dahlawi **Trained** Limpley Stoke, Bath

■ Stewards' Enquiry : Andrew Heffernan three-day ban: used whip with excessive frequency (Oct 12-14)

FOCUS
The leaders went off a bit too fast, with Fault and Spic 'N Span taking each other on. This was a fair claimer, with the winner not needing to match his summer form.
Matterofact(IRE) Official explanation: jockey said mare had been denied a clear run

6330 VINCI CONSTRUCTION H'CAP — 2m 1f 34y
3:10 (3:10) (Class 5) (0-75,73) 3-Y-0+ **£2,719** (£809; £404; £202) **Stalls** Centre

Form RPR
2116 **1** **Lady Hestia (USA)**[24] 5642 4-10-0 **62**..... MartinDwyer 4 73+
(M P Tregoning) *racd in 2nd: 5 l bhd ldr: clsd to 2 l 4f out: shkn up to ld 2 out: sn in command and pushed along: readily* **6/4**[1]

1402 **2** *2 1/4* **Fin Vin De Leu (GER)**[9] 6121 3-9-13 **73**..... JoeFanning 3 78
(M Johnston) *led: sn 5 ll clr: stl 2 l ahd 4f out: rdn 3f out: hdd 2f out: sn no ch w wnr but clr 2nd best* **7/4**[2]

0440 **3** *7* **The Composer**[26] 5579 7-8-11 **45**..... SteveDrowne 2 42
(M Blanshard) *racd in 4th: impr to cl on ldng pair 7f out but nvr on terms: rdn over 3f out and tk modest 3rd sn after: kpt that position but no further prog* **12/1**

2356 **4** *1* **Spinning Waters**[12] 5990 3-9-0 **60**..... ShaneKelly 1 55
(Eve Johnson Houghton) *racd in 3rd and clsd on ldng pair 7f out: nvr on terms and rdn over 3f out whn dropped bk to 4th: and styd there at same pce* **3/1**[3]

3m 46.01s (-5.89) **Going Correction** -0.125s/f (Firm)
WFA 3 from 4yo+ 12lb **4** Ran SP% **109.1**
Speed ratings (Par 103): **108,106,103,103**
CSF £4.48 TOTE £2.00; EX 3.00.

Owner Mr And Mrs A E Pakenham **Bred** Shadwell Farm LLC **Trained** Lambourn, Berks

FOCUS
They were soon well strung out, but a time over five seconds above standard suggests they went a modest gallop, and that was the visual impression. A pretty weak race but the winner was value for extra.

6331 YOUR LAND WINS WITH LINDEN HOMES MAIDEN STKS — 1m 2f 46y
3:40 (3:40) (Class 5) 2-Y-0 **£2,590** (£770; £385; £192) **Stalls** Low

Form RPR
43 **1** **Exemplary**[9] 6125 2-9-3 0..... JoeFanning 2 79+
(M Johnston) *trckd ldr 7f out: drvn to ld 2f out: hung bdly lft wl over 1f out and wnt lft again ins fnl f: readily* **13/8**[1]

44 **2** *2* **Duty And Destiny (IRE)**[51] 4797 2-8-12 0..... MartinDwyer 1 71
(B J Meehan) *led: rdn and hdd 2f out: hmpd and snatched up wl over 1f out: styd on u.p to hold 2nd but no ch w wnr* **7/4**[2]

0 **3** *hd* **Futurist**[27] 5542 2-9-3 0..... DO'Donohoe 6 75
(Saeed Bin Suroor) *s.i.s: sn chsng ldrs: rdn over 2f out: styd on to dispute 2nd ins fnl f but nvr any ch w wnr* **12/1**

4 **4** *1 1/2* **Lovely Eyes (IRE)**[15] 5906 2-8-12 0..... RichardMullen 3 67
(D M Simcock) *chsd ldrs: rdn and styd on fr 2f out: crossed and swtchd rt over 1f out: styd on same pce ins fnl f* **7/2**[3]

00 **5** *12* **Groove Master**[28] 5499 2-9-3 0..... DaneO'Neill 5 50
(A King) *in rr: styd to take mod 5th ins fnl f* **25/1**

00 **6** *hd* **Mr Maximas**[18] 5785 2-9-3 0..... SteveDrowne 8 50
(B Palling) *chsd ldrs tl rn wd bnd over 5f out: sn bhd* **66/1**

00 **7** *11* **Radsky**[35] 5319 2-9-3 0..... TPO'Shea 4 32
(J G Portman) *s.i.s: sn chsng ldrs: wknd qckly 3f out* **66/1**

00 **8** *25* **Taliesin**[15] 5907 2-9-3 0..... KevinGhunowa 7 —
(Mrs A M Thorpe) *plld hrd in rr: lost tch 1/2-way* **100/1**

2m 11.15s (0.15) **Going Correction** -0.125s/f (Firm) **8** Ran SP% **112.2**
Speed ratings (Par 95): **94,92,92,91,81 81,72,52**
toteswingers: 1&2 £1.60, 1&3 £4.20, 2&3 £4.00 CSF £4.52 TOTE £2.40: £1.10, £1.20, £2.40; EX 5.00 Trifecta £37.30 Pool: £507.14 - 10.04 winning units..

Owner Sheikh Hamdan Bin Mohammed Al Maktoum **Bred** Darley **Trained** Middleham Moor, N Yorks

■ Stewards' Enquiry : Joe Fanning two-day ban: careless riding (Oct 12-13)

FOCUS
A fair maiden, but with 1m2f representing quite a test for juveniles the pace was unsurprisingly modest early. The front pair and the sixth help with the level.

NOTEBOOK
Exemplary ◆ was a bit disappointing when a beaten favourite over an extended 1m at Wolverhampton last time, but there was a lot of money for him on this step up in distance and switch to turf, and he won readily. The race was in safe keeping when he hung left over a furlong out, possibly feeling the ground a little. He's likely to stay really well next year and should progress, but before then he could be up to winning a decent nursery over this sort of trip. (tchd 7-4)

Duty And Destiny(IRE) didn't improve for this significant step up in distance. She seemed to enjoy herself in an easy lead early on, racing with her ears pricked, but she changed her legs turning into the straight, not looking comfortable on the track and/or ground. Quickly in trouble when challenged, she was held when hampered by the winner over a furlong out. (tchd 6-4)

Futurist showed nothing on his debut at Leicester but this was obviously much better. Although seemingly limited, he does give the impression he'll come on again for this. (op 11-1)

Lovely Eyes(IRE) has some stamina in her pedigree and ran respectably, but she never posed a serious threat. (op 4-1 tchd 9-2)

6332 EBF / THERMOLAST ROOFING MAIDEN FILLIES' STKS — 1m 2f 46y
4:10 (4:12) (Class 5) 3-Y-0+ **£3,885** (£1,156; £577; £288) **Stalls** Low

Form RPR
02 **1** **Tanfidh**[14] 5939 3-8-12 0..... TPO'Shea 5 79+
(M P Tregoning) *led after 2f: hdd 6f out: trcking ldr whn carried v wd and lost pl bnd over 4f out: drvn and rallied to ld again over 2f out: sn in command: comf* **8/11**[1]

3 **2** *2* **Chincoteague (IRE)**[21] 5718 3-8-12 0..... MartinDwyer 6 66
(B J Meehan) *led 2f: t.k.h: styd trcking ldrs: rdn and one pce over 2f out: styd on fnl f to take wl-hld 2nd nr fin* **5/2**[2]

-244 **3** *1/2* **Moonbeam Dancer (USA)**[14] 5939 3-8-12 65..... RichardMullen 3 65
(D M Simcock) *chsd ldrs: lft w slt advange bnd over 4f out: rdn 3f out: hdd over 2f out: sn no ch w wnr: styd on same pce and lost wl hld 2nd cl home* **4/1**[3]

0 **4** *10* **Denices Desert**[17] 5840 3-8-12 0..... SteveDrowne 2 45
(M Botti) *t.k.h: in tch: chsd ldrs and rdn over 3f out: wknd qckly 2f out* **25/1**

06 **5** *11* **Fairplaytomyself**[17] 5840 4-8-13 0..... AndrewHeffernan(5) 1 23
(P W Hiatt) *plld hrd: led 6f out: rn v wd bnd over 4f out: styd chsng ldrs and upside over 3f out: rdn over 2f out: sn wknd* **66/1**

0-0 **6** *25* **Saint Chapelle (IRE)**[12] 5987 3-8-12 0..... DaneO'Neill 4 —
(Mrs A J Perrett) *in tch tl wknd qckly 4f out: eased whn no ch fnl 3f: t.o* **33/1**

2m 9.06s (-1.94) **Going Correction** -0.125s/f (Firm)
WFA 3 from 4yo 6lb **6** Ran SP% **114.8**
Speed ratings (Par 100): **102,100,100,92,83 63**
toteswingers: 1&2 £30.10, 1&3 £22.10, 2&3 £11.00 CSF £2.91 TOTE £1.90: £1.10, £1.20; EX 3.10.

Owner Hamdan Al Maktoum **Bred** Shadwell Estate Company Limited **Trained** Lambourn, Berks

FOCUS
A weak fillies' maiden. The winner is capable of better.
Fairplaytomyself Official explanation: jockey said filly hung badly right-handed on bend
Saint Chapelle(IRE) Official explanation: jockey said filly hung badly left-handed

6333 NASH PARTNERSHIP & GL HEARN "HANDS AND HEELS" APPRENTICE SERIES H'CAP — 1m 5y
4:40 (4:40) (Class 5) (0-70,68) 3-Y-0 **£2,590** (£770; £385; £192) **Stalls** Low

Form RPR
3033 **1** **Florentia**[10] 6070 3-9-0 **63**..... PaulPickard 6 68
(Sir Mark Prescott) *in tch: pushed along and hdwy over 2f out: styd on to chal ins fnl f: led last strides* **7/2**[1]

4525 **2** *shd* **Jewelled**[16] 5869 3-9-4 **67**..... KierenFox 3 72
(J W Hills) *led 1f: styd chsng ldrs: led again 2f out: pushed along and kpt slt advantage fnl f: hdd last strides* **13/2**

5043 **3** *2* **Jewelled Reef (IRE)**[15] 5905 3-8-10 **59**..... JosephineBruning 9 59
(Eve Johnson Houghton) *in rr: hdwy on outside over 2f out: pushed along to chal 1f out: wknd ins fnl f* **7/1**

4254 **4** *1/2* **Location**[14] 5936 3-8-5 **54** oh3..... DebraEngland 5 53+
(P D Evans) *in rr: hdwy over 3f out: chsd ldrs and rdn 2f out: one pce ins fnl f* **12/1**

2440 **5** *1/2* **Indian Violet (IRE)**[28] 5503 3-9-3 **66**..... AndrewHeffernan 1 64
(P F I Cole) *chsd ldrs: drvn along over 2f out: one pce appr fnl f* **9/2**[2]

3501 **6** *3/4* **Pacific Bay (IRE)**[12] 5983 3-8-6 **58**..... LeeTopliss(3) 2 54
(R A Fahey) *t.k.h: led after 1f: hdd 2f out: sn wknd* **6/1**[3]

2034 **7** *1 1/4* **Beautiful Filly**[18] 5810 3-9-5 **68**..... LauraPike 8 62
(D M Simcock) *dropped in rr after 3f: styd on fr over 1f out but nvr in contention* **8/1**

0200 **8** *3 1/4* **Jazacosta (USA)**[14] 5940 3-9-5 **68**..... DavidKenny 7 54
(Mrs A J Perrett) *in rr: wd bnd over 4f out: drvn along 3f out: styd on fr over 1f out but nvr in contention* **12/1**

6000 **9** *1/2* **Motor Home**[35] 5316 3-8-6 **60** ow5..... FJHayes(5) 4 45
(A M Balding) *chsd ldrs: pushed along and wknd 3f out* **11/1**

1m 41.04s (0.24) **Going Correction** -0.125s/f (Firm) **9** Ran SP% **115.4**
Speed ratings (Par 101): **93,92,90,90,89 89,87,84,84**
toteswingers: 1&2 £4.70, 1&3 £7.40, 2&3 £6.00 CSF £26.34 CT £151.59 TOTE £4.40: £1.20, £2.10, £2.90; EX 30.90 Trifecta £143.80 Pool: £561.83 - 2.89 winning units. Place 6: £50.83 Place 5: £36.38 .

Owner Neil Greig **Bred** W N Greig **Trained** Newmarket, Suffolk

■ Stewards' Enquiry : F J Hayes seven-day ban: used whip in contravention of race conditions (Oct 15-17, 21-24)

FOCUS
A very modest handicap in which these apprentice riders were not allowed to use their whips. The winner ran to her AW latest.
Jewelled Official explanation: jockey said filly hung right-handed
T/Plt: £65.10 to a £1 stake. Pool: £48,056.07. 538.16 winning tickets. T/Qpdt: £4.30 to a £1 stake. Pool: £4,055.56. 684.40 winning tickets. ST

5564 BRIGHTON (L-H)
Monday, September 28

OFFICIAL GOING: Good to firm (7.9)
Wind: virtually nil Weather: overcast

6334 EUROPEAN BREEDERS' FUND MEDIAN AUCTION MAIDEN STKS — 6f 209y
2:20 (2:21) (Class 6) 2-Y-0 **£2,775** (£830; £415; £207; £103) **Stalls** Low

Form RPR
0542 **1** **Spanish Duke (IRE)**[21] 5715 2-9-3 70..... EddieAhern 4 77+
(J L Dunlop) *chsd ldrs: swtchd rt and effrt on outer ent fnl 2f: drvn to ld jst over 1f out: clr ins fnl f: eased towards fin* **9/4**[2]

6343 **2** *3 1/2* **James Barrymore**[20] 5748 2-9-3 73..... RichardHughes 2 68+
(R Hannon) *stdd s: t.k.h early: hld up in tch in midfield: switching rt ent fnl 2f: hdwy to chse wnr over 1f out: no imp whn rdr dropped whip ins fnl f: eased towards fin* **15/8**[1]

2406 **3** *2* **Cuthbert (IRE)**[25] 5589 2-9-3 67..... KirstyMilczarek 5 61
(W Jarvis) *t.k.h early: hld up in tch: rdn and effrt on outer over 2f out: chsd ldrs over 1f out: wl outpcd by ldng pair fnl f* **6/1**[3]

06 **4** *3/4* **Mr Harmoosh (IRE)**[18] 5787 2-9-3 0..... RichardKingscote 6 59
(E F Vaughan) *stdd s: t.k.h: hld up in last pair: stl 8th and swtchd rt jst over 1f out: styd on steadily fnl f: nvr trbld ldrs* **20/1**

5 *nk* **Notte Di Note (IRE)** 2-8-12 0..... DarryllHolland 8 53
(L M Cumani) *restless stalls: in tch in midfield: hdwy over 3f out: rdn to ld ent fnl 2f: hdd over 1f out: wknd fnl f* **16/1**

46 **6** 2 ½ **Art Machine (USA)**[10] 6069 2-8-12 0 .... PatCosgrave 7 49+
(Sir Mark Prescott) *prom: pushed along over 3f out: rdn and wknd ent fnl 2f: btn whn hung lft and hmpd 1f out* **17/2**

0 **7** ¾ **Scottish Boogie (IRE)**[10] 6054 2-9-3 0 .... GeorgeBaker 1 50+
(S Kirk) *bustled along after s: led over 5f out tl rdn and hdd ent fnl 2f: wkng whn n.m.r over 1f out* **11/1**

006 **8** 1 ¼ **Alfalevva**[41] 5119 2-9-3 25 .... SamHitchcott 3 46
(M R Channon) *led tl over 5f out: chsd ldr tl over 2f out: wknd u.p wl over 1f out* **100/1**

05 **9** 2 **Light The Way**[26] 5564 2-9-3 0 .... FergusSweeney 9 44+
(P J Makin) *stdd s: t.k.h: hld up in last pair: rdn and no rspnse over 2f out* **25/1**

1m 22.66s (-0.44) **Going Correction** -0.10s/f (Good) **9** Ran SP% **114.2**
Speed ratings (Par 93): **98,94,91,90,90 87,86,85,83**
toteswingers: 1&2 £1.50, 2&3 £3.90, 1&3 not won. CSF £6.61 TOTE £3.00: £1.10, £1.40, £1.90; EX 6.40.
Owner Windflower Overseas Holdings Inc **Bred** Windflower Overseas Holdings Inc **Trained** Arundel, W Sussex

FOCUS
A modest juvenile maiden. A slight personal best from the winner, and the runner-up is pretty consistent.

NOTEBOOK
Spanish Duke(IRE) took time to hit top gear on this drop back a furlong, but the further he went the better he looked and he came home a comfortable winner. He has improved with each of his five outings to date, is well suited by a sound surface and there should be more to come after this confidence boost when he steps back up in trip. He also has the scope to keep progressing as a 3yo when middle-distances should be much more to his liking. (op 15-8 tchd 7-4 and 5-2)
James Barrymore was representing last year's winning stable and had solid market support. Having been waited with through the first half of the race, he met some trouble when trying to improve yet ultimately found the winner far too strong. He probably wants more use made of him over this trip and he helps to set the level, but looks in need of respite from the handicapper. (op 5-2 tchd 11-4)
Cuthbert(IRE), having his sixth outing, hit a flat spot after turning for home. He kept on gamely enough for pressure, though, and is another who helps to set the standard. He was later reported to have lost a right shoe. Official explanation: jockey said colt lost a right-hind shoe (op 13-2 tchd 8-1)
Mr Harmoosh(IRE), back down in trip, settled better under restraint. He was never a serious threat from out the back, but kept on steadily under a fairly considerate ride and now has the option of nurseries. (op 22-1)
Notte Di Note(IRE), a cheap purchase whose dam won as a 3yo in Italy, has a pedigree that suggests she will come into her own next year over further. She turned in a fair debut display and is entitled to improve for the experience, as she was distinctly green in the preliminaries. (op 14-1 tchd 18-1)
Art Machine(USA) had been well backed when disappointing over 6f last time. Making her turf debut and easy to back here, she proved just one paced when it mattered. She now qualifies for a mark and it will be interesting to see how she fares in that sphere. (op 7-1 tchd 13-2)

6335 CRABBIES ALCOHOLIC GINGER BEER H'CAP (DIV I) 5f 213y
2:50 (2:51) (Class 6) (0-58,58) 3-Y-0+ **£2,137** (£635; £317; £158) **Stalls** Low

Form RPR

6410 **1** **Mamlakati (IRE)**[16] 5877 3-9-2 **58** .... RichardHughes 11 71
(R Hannon) *sn chsng ldr: shkn up to ld ent 2f out: rdn clr over 1f out: drvn and kpt on wl ins fnl f* **8/1**

4312 **2** 2 ¼ **Who's Winning (IRE)**[2] 6293 8-8-12 **52** ....(t) KirstyMilczarek 1 58
(B G Powell) *broke wl: chsd ldrs: rdn to chse clr ldr over 1f out: kpt on but no imp ins fnl f* **11/4**[1]

0513 **3** 3 **Welsh Opera**[6] 6186 4-9-1 **58** .... WilliamCarson(3) 9 54
(S C Williams) *hld up towards rr: edgd rt u.p wl over 1f out: styd on u.p fnl f to go 3rd fnl 50yds: nvr trbld ldrs* **7/2**[2]

0003 **4** ½ **Diane's Choice**[11] 6038 6-9-2 **56** ....(e) GeorgeBaker 6 51
(Miss Gay Kelleway) *racd in midfield: rdn and unable qck ent fnl 2f: hung lft over 1f out: plugged on fnl 100yds* **9/1**

0055 **5** ½ **Tightrope (IRE)**[26] 5566 3-8-4 **46** ....(b) DavidProbert 3 39
(T D McCarthy) *sn led: hdd and rdn ent fnl 2f: sn outpcd by wnr: lost 2nd over 1f out: wknd ins fnl f* **16/1**

2603 **6** ½ **Interactive (IRE)**[18] 5788 6-9-2 **56** .... RichardKingscote 7 47
(Andrew Turnell) *t.k.h early: hld up in rr: rdn and effrt on outer over 2f out: styd on ins fnl f: nvr trbld ldrs* **7/1**[3]

3326 **7** 1 ¾ **Boldinor**[11] 6038 6-8-10 **50** .... JimCrowley 2 36
(M R Bosley) *t.k.h: hld up towards rr: rdn and effrt on inner over 2f out: no real prog* **15/2**

400 **8** 2 ¼ **Bertbrand**[23] 5678 4-8-12 **55** ....(b) AndreaAtzeni(3) 5 34
(I W McInnes) *chsd ldrs: rdn and struggling over 2f out: wknd wl over 1f out* **16/1**

0505 **9** 1 ¾ **Freepressionist**[45] 4982 3-8-3 **52** .... JPFahy(7) 8 25
(R A Teal) *hld up in rr: rdn and no prog over 2f out: wl hld whn sltly hmpd wl over 1f out* **12/1**

0-00 **10** nk **Bahama Baileys**[15] 5911 4-8-8 **48** .... JerryO'Dwyer 12 20
(C A Dwyer) *chsd ldrs: rdn and struggling over 2f out: no ch fr wl over 1f out* **33/1**

0000 **11** 1 ½ **Thumberlina**[13] 5974 3-8-4 **46** oh1 ....(b) AdrianMcCarthy 10 13
(Mrs C A Dunnett) *s.i.s: a bhd* **100/1**

69.50 secs (-0.70) **Going Correction** -0.10s/f (Good) **11** Ran SP% **117.7**
WFA 3 from 4yo+ 2lb
Speed ratings (Par 101): **100,97,93,92,91 91,88,85,83,82 80**
toteswingers: 1&2 £6.10, 1&3 £6.70, 2&3 £3.10 CSF £30.21 CT £94.92 TOTE £8.60: £3.30, £1.50, £1.50; EX 37.30.
Owner Malih L Al Basti **Bred** Raymond P Doyle **Trained** East Everleigh, Wilts

FOCUS
A moderate handicap run slightly quicker than division II. The placed horses set the level and the form looks sound.

6336 CRABBIES ALCOHOLIC GINGER BEER CLAIMING STKS 6f 209y
3:20 (3:20) (Class 6) 4-Y-0+ **£1,942** (£578; £288; £144) **Stalls** Low

Form RPR

4303 **1** **Autumn Blades (IRE)**[11] 6024 4-9-3 75 ....(p) DavidProbert 3 79
(A Bailey) *chsd ldrs: upsides ldrs and travelling much the best over 2f out: rdn to ld 1f out: immediately hung lft: pushed out hands and heels and kpt narrow advantage after* **11/8**[2]

0010 **2** hd **Royal Challenge**[9] 6123 8-8-5 55 .... SilvestreDeSousa 1 66
(I W McInnes) *chsd ldr tl over 2f out: sn drvn: rallied to ld over 1f out: hdd 1f out: kpt on gamely but a hld* **8/1**[3]

2360 **3** 4 **Twilight Star (IRE)**[28] 5511 5-9-7 75 .... DarrylHolland 2 71
(R A Teal) *led tl drvn and hdd over 1f out: wkng whn hmpd jst ins fnl f* **1/1**[1]

2600 **4** 3 **Norcroft**[9] 6123 7-8-7 50 ....(p) AdrianMcCarthy 5 49
(Mrs C A Dunnett) *chsd ldng trio: rdn over 2f out: wknd u.p wl over 1f out* **16/1**

000 **5** 1 ½ **Lancaster Lad (IRE)**[15] 5905 4-7-13 44 ow1 ....(p) JPFahy(7) 4 44
(A B Haynes) *v.s.a: a detached in last pl: nvr on terms* **33/1**

1m 22.62s (-0.48) **Going Correction** -0.10s/f (Good) **5** Ran SP% **112.0**
Speed ratings (Par 101): **98,97,93,89,88**
CSF £12.40 TOTE £2.10: £1.10, £1.90; EX 8.10.
Owner John Stocker **Bred** Dr D Crone & P Lafarge & P Johnston **Trained** Newmarket, Suffolk
■ Stewards' Enquiry : Silvestre De Sousa two-day ban: used whip with excessive frequency (Oct 12-13)

FOCUS
A tricky claimer. The first pair came clear and the form is rated around the runner-up. The enigmatic winner was 4lb off his best.
Twilight Star(IRE) Official explanation: jockey said gelding had a breathing problem

6337 TRY CRABBIES ALCOHOLIC GINGER BEER H'CAP 7f 214y
3:50 (3:51) (Class 5) (0-70,70) 3-Y-0+ **£3,027** (£906; £453; £226; £112) **Stalls** Low

Form RPR

060 **1** **You've Been Mowed**[10] 6070 3-8-4 **59** .... KellyHarrison(3) 5 67
(R J Price) *mde all: rdn ent fnl 2f: clr wl over 1f out: kpt on gamely fnl f: all out* **25/1**

1021 **2** 1 ¼ **Magroom**[18] 5791 5-9-3 **68** .... WilliamCarson(3) 8 73+
(R J Hodges) *hld up towards rr: rdn over 2f out: styd on u.p fnl f to go 2nd wl ins fnl f: nt rch wnr* **7/1**

1310 **3** nk **Cavendish Road (IRE)**[16] 5869 3-9-2 **68** .... DavidProbert 4 72
(W R Muir) *chsd ldng pair: rdn and unable qck over 2f out: edgd rt u.p over 1f out: kpt on to chse clr wnr fnl 100yds: lost 2nd wl ins fnl f* **7/1**

4405 **4** 1 ¼ **Murrin (IRE)**[20] 5745 5-8-11 **66** .... JPFahy(7) 7 67
(T G Mills) *pushed along briefly leaving stalls: t.k.h after 1f: hld up in midfield: rdn and hdwy 2f out: edgd lft u.p and chsd ldng pair 1f out: kpt on but nvr gng to rch wnr* **6/1**[3]

5551 **5** nk **Hobson**[7] 6175 4-8-12 **67** .... AmyScott(7) 6 67
(Eve Johnson Houghton) *v.s.a: bhd: c towards centre and hdwy wl over 2f out: kpt on steadily ins fnl f: nvr gng to rch wnr* **4/1**[1]

0023 **6** nse **Napoletano (GER)**[39] 5188 8-9-3 **65** ....(p) DarryllHolland 3 65
(S Dow) *plld hrd: chsd wnr: rdn and unable qck jst over 2f out: no imp after: lost 4 pls fnl 100yds* **8/1**

0651 **7** ¾ **Choreography**[26] 5565 6-9-8 **70** ....(b) SilvestreDeSousa 9 69
(Jim Best) *t.k.h: hld up in tch in midfield: rdn and unable qck over 2f out: swtchd lft over 1f out: plugged on fnl f: nvr gng pce to rch wnr* **9/2**[2]

3030 **8** 1 ½ **Driven (IRE)**[12] 5991 4-9-8 **70** .... JimCrowley 10 65
(Mrs A J Perrett) *stdd s: hld up in rr: nt clr run 2f out: rdn and no real prog over 1f out* **8/1**

2513 **9** 6 **Ailsa Craig (IRE)**[25] 5602 3-9-3 **69** .... RichardHughes 1 50
(R Hannon) *t.k.h: hld up in tch in midfield: rdn and hdwy on inner jst over 2f out: no prog and btn whn nt clr run 1f out: no ch and nt pushed after* **8/1**

0030 **10** 8 **Danzadil (IRE)**[51] 4791 3-8-1 **56** oh4 .... AndreaAtzeni(3) 2 19
(R A Teal) *hld up in last trio: rdn 4f out: wl bhd and eased fr over 1f out* **50/1**

1m 35.13s (-0.87) **Going Correction** -0.10s/f (Good)
WFA 3 from 4yo+ 4lb **10** Ran SP% **116.6**
Speed ratings (Par 103): **100,98,98,97,96 96,96,94,88,80**
toteswingers: 1&2 £2.10, 1&3 £3.60, 2&3 £9.20 CSF £190.54 CT £1375.20 TOTE £27.60: £7.00, £2.80, £2.20; EX 324.40.
Owner Mrs K Oseman **Bred** T E Pocock **Trained** Ullingswick, H'fords

FOCUS
A very competitive handicap for the class. The winner was allowed to dictate and not many got into it. The winner and third are the best guide to the form.
Ailsa Craig(IRE) Official explanation: jockey said filly stopped quickly

6338 BRAND NEW CRABBIES ALCOHOLIC GINGER BEER APPRENTICE H'CAP 1m 1f 209y
4:20 (4:20) (Class 6) (0-65,65) 3-Y-O **£2,590** (£770; £385; £192) **Stalls** High

Form RPR

3122 **1** **Squad**[13] 5964 3-9-5 **65** .... Louis-PhilippeBeuzelin 2 72
(S Dow) *stdd s: hld up in rr: rdn and effrt on outer 2f out: r.o wl u.p fnl f to ld towards fin* **2/1**[1]

3603 **2** nk **Triple Cee (IRE)**[2] 6276 3-8-7 **56** .... MatthewDavies(3) 6 62
(M R Channon) *chsd ldng pair tl 7f out: rdn over 2f out: sltly hmpd wl over 1f out: drvn to chse ldr over 1f out: led fnl 75yds: hdd and no ex towards fin* **13/2**

6403 **3** 2 **Vita Mia**[2] 6280 3-9-2 **62** .... RichardEvans 1 64
(P D Evans) *led for 2f: chsd ldr after: rdn over 2f out: edgd rt u.p wl over 1f out: led over 1f out: hdd fnl 75yds: one pce* **4/1**[2]

64U0 **4** 5 **Granny McPhee**[42] 5112 3-8-9 **60** .... NatashaEaton(5) 7 52+
(A Bailey) *v.s.a: bhd: clsd and in tch 1/2-way: hdwy u.p but hanging lft over 1f out: hmpd and lost pl over 1f out: n.d after* **40/1**

4522 **5** hd **Kyle Of Bute**[13] 5963 3-8-7 **53** ....(v) MartinLane 4 45
(J L Dunlop) *racd keenly: chsd ldr tl led 8f out: clr 7f out: rdn over 2f out: hdd over 1f out: wknd fnl f* **6/1**[3]

0040 **6** 1 ½ **Haling Park (UAE)**[19] 5775 3-8-4 **53** ....(p) JPFahy(3) 5 42
(G L Moore) *stdd s: hld up in tch in rr: rdn and effrt on outer over 2f out: no real prog* **11/1**

0056 **7** 1 ¼ **King's La Mont (IRE)**[21] 5726 3-8-12 **61** ....(tp) AmyScott(3) 8 47
(Mrs A J Perrett) *racd in midfield tl chsd ldng pair 7f out tl over 2f out: sn hung lft: wknd 2f out* **12/1**

05-4 **8** 1 ½ **Lava Steps (USA)**[84] 3674 3-9-2 **65** .... DTDaSilva(3) 3 48
(P F I Cole) *t.k.h early: hld up in midfield: rdn over 3f out: wknd u.p wl over 1f out* **8/1**

2m 1.94s (-1.66) **Going Correction** -0.10s/f (Good) **8** Ran SP% **110.5**
Speed ratings (Par 99): **102,101,100,96,96 94,93,92**
toteswingers: 1&2 £3.10, 1&3 £2.90, 2&3 £4.30 CSF £14.29 CT £43.63 TOTE £2.50: £1.10, £2.10, £1.80; EX 17.30.
Owner Classics P'ship, Devine, Snell & Chua **Bred** Juddmonte Farms Ltd **Trained** Epsom, Surrey

FOCUS
A moderate but well run handicap in which the first pair fought it out.

6339 HARDINGS BAR & CATERING SERVICES H'CAP 6f 209y
4:50 (4:50) (Class 6) (0-60,60) 3-Y-0+ **£2,460** (£732; £365; £182) **Stalls** Low

Form RPR

0260 **1** **Ocean Countess (IRE)**[12] 5998 3-8-12 **54** .... CatherineGannon 13 63
(Miss J Feilden) *in tch: rdn and effrt jst over 2f out: led ins fnl f: r.o strly and sn clr* **14/1**

2013 **2** 1 3/4 **Cadeaux Fax**[24] 5634 4-9-4 **60** JamesMillman(3) 16 65
(B R Millman) *racd on outer: towards rr: rdn ent fnl 2f: hdwy over 1f out: wanting to hang lft but r.o fnl f to go 2nd last stride: nvr gng to rch wnr* **9/2**[1]

0000 **3** shd **Only A Game (IRE)**[9] 6103 4-9-2 **55** (t) SilvestreDeSousa 9 60
(I W McInnes) *hld up wl in tch: rdn and hdwy jst over 2f out: led over 1f out: hdd and edgd rt ins fnl f: no ex: lost 2nd last stride* **20/1**

1505 **4** nk **Goodbye Cash (IRE)**[26] 5569 5-9-0 **58** RichardEvans(5) 10 66+
(P D Evans) *s.i.s: bhd: switching rt and rdn jst over 2f out: r.o strly ins fnl f: nt rch ldrs* **12/1**

6013 **5** 1 **Golden Prospect**[17] 5842 5-9-7 **60** EddieAhern 5 61
(J W Hills) *hld up in tch in midfield: hdwy on inner and squeezed through over 1f out: kpt on same pce ins fnl f* **6/1**[2]

2500 **6** 1/2 **Party In The Park**[27] 5544 4-8-13 **52** PatCosgrave 4 52
(J R Boyle) *s.i.s: towards rr: swtchd rt and hdwy 2f out: chsd ldrs ins fnl f: kpt on same pce* **10/1**

0064 **7** 1 3/4 **Imperial Skylight**[12] 6005 3-8-8 **50** SamHitchcott 15 44
(M R Channon) *s.i.s and bustled along early: racd in midfield: rdn and bmpd 2f out: hdwy over 1f out: no imp ins fnl f* **25/1**

0464 **8** 1 3/4 **Sultans Way (IRE)**[26] 5582 3-9-1 **57** RichardHughes 14 46
(P F I Cole) *in tch: effrt u.p over 2f out: drvn and ev ch 2f out: wknd jst over 1f out* **6/1**[2]

0000 **9** 3/4 **H Harrison (IRE)**[9] 6103 9-8-11 **53** KellyHarrison(3) 7 41
(I W McInnes) *chsd ldrs: rdn over 2f out: wknd over 1f out: wl hld fnl f* **25/1**

5305 **10** 1 **Charismatic Lady**[54] 4669 3-9-4 **60** JimCrowley 6 45
(Jane Chapple-Hyam) *bhd: pushed along 4f out: sme hdwy on inner 2f out: sn nt clr run and no ch after* **16/1**

5000 **11** nk **Kannon**[16] 5883 4-9-5 **58** GeorgeBaker 2 43
(I W McInnes) *chsd ldrs: edgd out rt and rdn over 2f out: wknd over 1f out: wl btn fnl f* **20/1**

1320 **12** 1/2 **Jonnie Skull (IRE)**[10] 6070 3-8-13 **55** (vt) SaleemGolam 8 38
(P S McEntee) *chsd ldrs: rdn and wknd ent fnl 2f: no ch fnl f* **8/1**[3]

6655 **13** 1/2 **Davids Matador**[18] 5809 3-9-2 **58** (p) FergusSweeney 3 39
(Eve Johnson Houghton) *led: rdn over 2f out: edgd lft u.p and hdd over 1f out: sn wknd* **14/1**

00-0 **14** 2 1/4 **Ausonius**[13] 5965 3-9-2 **58** DarrylHolland 1 33
(L M Cumani) *s.i.s: a bhd* **14/1**

0400 **15** 3 1/4 **Countrystyle Lass (IRE)**[24] 5647 3-8-6 **48** DavidProbert 12 14
(P Winkworth) *sn chsng ldr tl over 2f out: sn lost pl: wl bhd fnl f* **25/1**

1m 22.3s (-0.80) **Going Correction** -0.10s/f (Good)
WFA 3 from 4yo+ 3lb **15 Ran SP% 121.6**
Speed ratings (Par 101): **100,98,97,97,96 95,93,91,90,89 89,88,88,85,82**
toteswingers: 1&2 £18.10, 1&3 £29.10, 2&3 £24.10 CSF £70.18 CT £1293.08 TOTE £16.40: £3.80, £2.40, £7.90; EX 126.30.
Owner Ocean Trailers Ltd **Bred** Don Commins **Trained** Exning, Suffolk
■ Stewards' Enquiry : Fergus Sweeney one-day ban: careless riding (Oct 12)

FOCUS
A weak handicap. The form makes some sense and the first two recorded minor personal bests.
Cadeaux Fax Official explanation: jockey said gelding stumbled at start
Goodbye Cash(IRE) Official explanation: jockey said mare was denied a clear run
Charismatic Lady Official explanation: jockey said filly was denied a clear run

6340 CRABBIES ALCOHOLIC GINGER BEER H'CAP (DIV II) 5f 213y
5:20 (5:20) (Class 6) (0-58,58) 3-Y-0+ **£2,137** (£635; £317; £158) **Stalls** Low

Form RPR

0016 **1** **Boho Chic**[15] 5900 3-8-10 **56** (p) MatthewDavies(5) 1 69+
(George Baker) *w ldrs: led 4f out: mde rest: pushed clr and hung lft over 1f out: in command fnl f: eased fnl 50yds* **6/1**[2]

3032 **2** 3/4 **The Name Is Frank**[6] 6186 4-9-2 **55** (t) EddieAhern 6 61
(Mark Gillard) *led for 1f: disp ld after: rdn over 2f out: nt pce of wnr over 1f out: plugged on ins fnl f* **2/1**[1]

5600 **3** 1 **Namu**[15] 5911 6-9-4 **57** (p) JimCrowley 8 60
(Miss T Spearing) *stdd s: hld up in rr: rdn and effrt on outer wl over 1f out: kpt on u.p fnl f: nvr trbld wnr* **10/1**

4562 **4** nk **If Only**[18] 5809 3-9-0 **58** WilliamCarson(3) 11 60
(J Jay) *racd in midfield: hdwy to chse ldrs over 2f out: outpcd by wnr over 1f out: hanging lft and kpt on same pce ins fnl f* **6/1**[2]

0451 **5** 2 3/4 **Bermondsey Bob (IRE)**[24] 5633 3-8-9 **50** SamHitchcott 9 43
(J L Spearing) *in tch in midfield: effrt and rdn 2f out: sn chsng ldrs: hung lft u.p and nt pce of wnr over 1f out: wknd ins fnl f* **11/1**

5240 **6** 3/4 **Briannsta (IRE)**[11] 6039 7-8-11 **50** (b) RichardThomas 10 41
(J E Long) *in tch in midfield: rdn and effrt to chse ldrs over 2f out: struggling wl over 1f out: wl hld after* **16/1**

6010 **7** nk **Scruffy Skip (IRE)**[11] 6038 4-8-13 **52** JerryO'Dwyer 2 42
(Mrs C A Dunnett) *dwlt: sn rcvrd and in tch: rdn over 2f out: outpcd by wnr over 1f out but stl ch of 2nd 1f out: wknd fnl f* **7/1**[3]

0-50 **8** 9 **Queens Flight**[35] 5316 3-8-9 **50** RichardKingscote 4 11
(Tom Dascombe) *in tch: rdn and effrt on inner and hung lft over 1f out: sn wknd: no ch and eased ins fnl f* **16/1**

0050 **9** 5 **Kingsgate Storm (IRE)**[5] 6205 3-9-3 **58** GeorgeBaker 3 3
(J R Best) *a towards rr: rdn and no prog 3f out: wl bhd and eased ins fnl f* **9/1**

2000 **10** 1 3/4 **Lily Jicaro (IRE)**[40] 5145 3-8-9 **50** CatherineGannon 5 —
(Mrs L Williamson) *wnt freely to post: prom: led after 1f tl 4f out: rdn over 2f out: edgd lft and wknd qckly wl over 1f out: eased ins fnl f* **25/1**

0000 **11** 8 **Yellow River (USA)**[46] 4937 3-8-4 **45** (bt[1]) DavidProbert 7 —
(E J Creighton) *s.i.s: towards rr: pushed along 4f out: rdn and wknd 2f out: wl bhd and eased ins fnl f* **100/1**

69.72 secs (-0.48) **Going Correction** -0.10s/f (Good)
WFA 3 from 4yo+ 2lb **11 Ran SP% 118.4**
Speed ratings (Par 101): **99,98,96,96,92 91,91,79,72,70 59**
toteswingers: 1&2 £4.90, 1&3 £15.50, 2&3 £5.70 CSF £18.43 CT £123.66 TOTE £6.00: £2.00, £1.20, £3.40; EX 26.60.
Owner P K Gardner **Bred** P K Gardner **Trained** Moreton Morrell, Warwicks

FOCUS
A poor handicap. The form is straightforward and the winner was value 2l.

6341 HARDINGS H'CAP 5f 59y
5:50 (5:50) (Class 6) (0-65,65) 3-Y-0+ **£2,590** (£770; £385; £192) **Stalls** Low

Form RPR

410 **1** **Simple Rhythm**[12] 5989 3-9-0 **65** Louis-PhilippeBeuzelin(5) 5 74
(J Ryan) *mde all: rdn clr wl over 1f out: styd on wl fnl f* **8/1**

2340 **2** 1 1/2 **Halaak (USA)**[11] 6028 3-8-13 **62** (b) AndreaAtzeni(3) 8 66
(D M Simcock) *in tch in midfield: pushed along 4f out: lost pl and rdn wl over 2f out: hdwy over 1f out: chsd clr wnr jst ins fnl f: kpt on* **13/2**

0060 **3** 3/4 **Style Award**[66] 4281 4-8-13 **61** (p) KellyHarrison(3) 3 62
(W J H Ratcliffe) *s.i.s: bhd: hdwy on inner jst over 2f out: rdn over 1f out: kpt on fnl f: nvr gng pce to rch wnr* **14/1**

2144 **4** 3/4 **Multahab**[9] 6118 10-8-10 **62** (tp) TobyAtkinson(7) 4 61
(M Wigham) *chsd rt and chsd wnr over 2f out: edgd rt after: kpt on same pce: lost 2 pls fnl f* **3/1**[1]

6304 **5** nse **Mazzola**[5] 6205 3-9-5 **65** SamHitchcott 7 63
(M R Channon) *chsd wnr tl over 2f out: sn carried rt and unable qck: one pce after* **5/1**[2]

0243 **6** 4 **Caribbean Coral**[7] 6160 10-9-5 **64** GeorgeBaker 2 48
(A B Haynes) *hld up in rr: switching out rt but hanging lft fr 2f out: no prog: n.d* **11/2**[3]

056 **7** shd **Berrymead**[7] 6160 4-8-10 **60** ow5 AnnStokell(5) 6 44
(Miss A Stokell) *s.i.s: a towards rr: c centre over 3f out: n.d* **20/1**

4040 **8** 1 1/2 **Cosmic Destiny (IRE)**[9] 6118 7-8-10 **60** MartinLane(5) 1 38
(E F Vaughan) *in tch in midfield: rdn wl over 2f out: keeping on same pce and no hdwy whn hmpd 2f out: n.d after* **8/1**

2030 **9** 3 **Red Cell (IRE)**[16] 5881 3-8-7 **53** (b) SilvestreDeSousa 10 20
(I W McInnes) *chsd ldrs: rdn wl over 2f out: wknd 2f out* **33/1**

341 **10** hd **Thoughtsofstardom**[6] 6186 6-8-3 **55** 6ex (be) CarolineKelly(7) 9 22
(P S McEntee) *in tch: lost pl over 2f out: no ch after* **10/1**

61.56 secs (-0.74) **Going Correction** -0.10s/f (Good)
WFA 3 from 4yo+ 1lb **10 Ran SP% 116.1**
Speed ratings (Par 101): **101,98,97,96,96 89,89,87,82,82**
CSF £58.90 CT £735.08 TOTE £11.30: £2.70, £2.00, £5.20; EX 67.20 Place 6: £ 69.72 Place 5: £59.30.
Owner J Ryan **Bred** P Quinlan **Trained** Newmarket, Suffolk
■ Stewards' Enquiry : Andrea Atzeni one-day ban plus four deferred: careless riding (Oct 12-16)

FOCUS
An ordinary sprint and another winner from the front. The runner-up is a pretty sound guide.
Caribbean Coral Official explanation: jockey said gelding hung left
Berrymead Official explanation: jockey said filly hung right from 2f out
T/Plt: £43.00 to a £1 stake. Pool: £62,417.45. 1,058.81 winning tickets. T/Qpdt: £22.40 to a £1 stake. Pool: £3,744.66. 123.35 winning tickets. SP

6251 WOLVERHAMPTON (A.W) (L-H)
Monday, September 28

OFFICIAL GOING: Standard
Wind: Light half behind Weather: Fine

6342 WILLIAMHILL.COM/BONUS25 - GET £25 FREE BET APPRENTICE H'CAP 1m 4f 50y(P)
2:00 (2:00) (Class 6) (0-65,65) 3-Y-0+ **£2,388** (£705; £352) **Stalls** Low

Form RPR

136- **1** **Red Expresso (IRE)**[222] 7775 4-9-4 **61** RyanPowell(5) 5 68
(Ollie Pears) *hld up and bhd: hdwy wl over 1f out: sn edgd lft: edgd lft and led cl home* **12/1**

6030 **2** nk **My Mate Mal**[11] 6012 5-9-8 **63** AdamCarter(3) 12 70
(B Ellison) *led: rdn wl over 1f out: hdd cl home* **12/1**

0000 **3** 1 1/4 **Mehendi (IRE)**[23] 5672 3-8-11 **62** AnthonyBetts(5) 1 67
(B Ellison) *hld up: sn wl in rr: c wd st: rdn and hdwy over 1f out: styd on towards fin* **3/1**[1]

34/0 **4** nk **Easterly Breeze (IRE)**[23] 5679 5-9-7 **62** (bt) AlexEdwards(3) 3 67
(Mrs L J Young) *hld up in mid-div: stdy prog over 3f out: chsd ldr wl over 1f out: sn rdn: lost 2nd ins fnl f: no ex whn n.m.r towards fin* **14/1**

/660 **5** 3 1/2 **King's Revenge**[114] 2040 6-9-11 **63** NSLawes 6 62
(S Lycett) *hld up and bhd: pushed along and hdwy over 2f out: rdn over 1f out: no imp* **8/1**

2060 **6** 7 **King's Counsel (IRE)**[21] 5733 3-8-10 **56** MatthewLawson 11 44
(J Hetherton) *chsd ldr: rdn over 3f out: lost 2nd wl over 1f out: sn wknd* **25/1**

0400 **7** 3 **Desert Leader (IRE)**[23] 5680 8-8-13 **51** RichardRowe 4 34
(W M Brisbourne) *hld up in mid-div: rdn wl over 2f out: sn struggling* **20/1**

5365 **8** 2 3/4 **Zalkani (IRE)**[4] 6226 9-9-0 **59** SophieSilvester(7) 7 38
(J Pearce) *hld up: sn wl in rr: c wd st: sn struggling* **5/1**[3]

03-0 **9** 1 **Sir Billy Nick**[19] 63 4-9-3 **55** (p) SPRyan 10 32
(S Wynne) *prom: rdn over 3f out: wknd 2f out* **66/1**

001- **10** 7 **Yab Adee**[276] 7379 5-9-8 **65** KatiaScallan(5) 2 31
(M P Tregoning) *hld up in tch: pushed along and wknd wl over 3f out* **11/2**

0301 **11** 6 **Blue Tango (IRE)**[10] 6075 3-9-5 **65** (b) CharlesEddery 9 21
(Mrs A J Perrett) *t.k.h in tch: rdn over 2f out: wknd wl over 1f out* **9/2**[2]

2m 38.26s (-2.84) **Going Correction** -0.225s/f (Stan)
WFA 3 from 4yo+ 8lb **11 Ran SP% 118.5**
Speed ratings (Par 101): **100,99,98,98,96 91,89,87,87,82 78**
toteswingers: 1&2 £24.10, 1&3 £8.20, 2&3 £6.90 CSF £145.15 CT £548.87 TOTE £16.80: £4.20, £2.20, £1.50; EX 195.00.
Owner We-Know Partnership **Bred** Lodge Park Stud **Trained** Norton, N Yorks
■ Stewards' Enquiry : Charles Eddery one-day ban: failed to ride to draw (Oct 12)

FOCUS
This apprentices' handicap was run at a decent gallop and produced a good finish. The form is not entirely solid and the winner is the best guide.

6343 NEAL WOOD MEMORIAL NURSERY H'CAP (DIV I) 5f 216y(P)
2:30 (2:30) (Class 6) (0-65,65) 2-Y-O **£2,388** (£705; £352) **Stalls** Low

Form RPR

0504 **1** **Chandrayaan**[13] 5967 2-9-4 **62** (v) TGMcLaughlin 12 66
(E A L Dunlop) *broke wl: hld up in mid-div: pushed along over 2f out: swtchd rt and hdwy over 1f out: r.o to ld cl home* **15/2**[3]

040 **2** 3/4 **Gower Sophia**[32] 5372 2-9-5 **63** (v[1]) DavidAllan 2 65
(M Brittain) *led: rdn wl over 1f out: hdd cl home* **33/1**

060 **3** 2 **Take My Hand**[9] 6109 2-9-2 **60** ChrisCatlin 8 56
(M R Channon) *hld up and bhd: hdwy over 2f out: rdn ins fnl f: kpt on same pce: tk 3rd cl home* **10/1**

065 **4** 3/4 **Cane Cat (IRE)**[33] 5344 2-8-10 **54** JimmyQuinn 6 48
(A W Carroll) *hld up in tch: pushed along and ev ch and edgd lft over 1f out: hrd rdn and no ex ins fnl f* **10/1**

0450 **5** 1 1/2 **My Sister**[18] 5797 2-9-0 **63** LeeNewnes(5) 3 52
(M D I Usher) *hld up towards rr: rdn and hdwy over 1f out: one pce fnl f* **5/1**[2]

033 **6** 3/4 **Mexican Milly (IRE)**[44] 5036 2-9-2 **60** MichaelHills 11 47
(B W Hills) *prom on outside: pushed along over 2f out: c wd st: swtchd lft over 1f out: sn rdn: no imp* **5/1**[2]

0043 **7** ½ **Wigan Lane**[24] 5636 2-9-7 **65**................................ KFallon 5 51
(P Howling) *chsd ldr tl wl over 1f out: sn swtchd lft: rdn and one pce whn swtchd lft ins fnl f* **3/1**[1]

001 **8** *nk* **Dragonessa (IRE)**[13] 5967 2-8-13 **57**.............................. NeilChalmers 7 41
(B Palling) *prom: pushed along over 2f out: wknd over 1f out* **12/1**

2234 **9** 2½ **Out The Ring (IRE)**[110] 2800 2-9-6 **64**.................... StephenDonohoe 10 41
(Miss Gay Kelleway) *s.i.s: pushed along whn swtchd lft wl over 1f out: nvr nr ldrs* **8/1**

5000 **10** *1* **Cariad Coch**[38] 5226 2-8-6 **50**................................ DuranFentiman 13 24
(Mrs L Stubbs) *bhd: c wd st: rdn wl over 1f out: no rspnse* **66/1**

6300 **11** *7* **Quinner (IRE)**[32] 5358 2-9-6 **64**................................. TPQueally 4 17
(P D Evans) *chsd ldrs tl rdn and wknd over 3f out* **20/1**

5000 **12** *4* **Summa Cum Laude**[12] 5976 2-8-6 **53**..................(v) JackMitchell(3) 1 —
(Mrs A Duffield) *pushed along over 3f out: a in rr* **14/1**

1m 14.71s (-0.29) **Going Correction** -0.225s/f (Stan) **12** Ran SP% **122.9**
Speed ratings (Par 93): **92,91,88,87,85 84,83,83,79,78 69,63**
toteswingers: 1&2 £23.70, 1&3 £13.70, 2&3 £39.60 CSF £241.78 CT £2536.47 TOTE £6.40: £2.80, £8.90, £3.90; EX 140.30.
Owner Mohammed Jaber **Bred** Whatton Manor Stud **Trained** Newmarket, Suffolk

FOCUS
A competitive-looking nursery that produced another close finish. The form is modest and limited, with the runner-up the best guide.

NOTEBOOK
Chandrayaan got up to catch the long-time leader Gower Sophia near the line. Having looked slightly unlucky when well backed on his previous start, he found plenty when asked to pick up from off the pace and may have more to offer. (op 11-2)
Gower Sophia, making her Polytrack debut, had the visor replacing blinkers and made a bold bid from the front, despite her rider reporting that she hung right, only to have the prize snatched away from her. She can win one of these if the headgear works as well next time. Official explanation: jockey said filly hung right (op 40-1)
Take My Hand, making her handicap and Polytrack debuts, wasn't the quickest away but picked her way through the field to get to the heels of the leaders turning in. She was unable to change gear in the latter stages, but this was an improved effort nonetheless. (op 9-1)
Cane Cat(IRE) was backed at long odds and looked a big threat turning for home, but her effort flattened out. (op 16-1)
My Sister was down in grade and had been dropped in the weights, but did not arrive on the scene until too late having been unable to go the early pace. She looks worth a try over further. (op 15-2)
Mexican Milly(IRE), making her Polytrack debut, had her chance turning in but couldn't pick up and a return to turf seems likely. (tchd 6-1)
Wigan Lane, off top weight and sent off favourite, showed up early but faded once in line for home. (op 7-2 tchd 9-2)

6344 WILLIAMHILL.COM/BONUS25 - POKER TOURNAMENTS MEDIAN AUCTION MAIDEN STKS 5f 216y(P)
3:00 (3:02) (Class 5) 3-5-Y-O **£2,729** (£806; £403) **Stalls** Low

Form RPR
3323 **1** **Milldown Story**[21] 5717 3-8-12 64................................ ChrisCatlin 1 62+
(B R Millman) *chsd ldrs: pushed along over 3f out: rdn wl over 1f out: led ins fnl f: r.o wl* **4/5**[1]

040 **2** 2¼ **Hay Fever (IRE)**[9] 6111 3-9-3 70..............................(b[1]) WilliamBuick 4 60
(Eve Johnson Houghton) *hld up towards rr: hdwy on ins over 2f out: pushed along and edgd rt over 1f out: sn rdn: r.o to take 2nd nr fin* **6/1**[3]

0035 **3** ½ **Turkish Lokum**[69] 4179 3-8-12 60................................ LukeMorris 11 53
(J M P Eustace) *a.p: led wl over 1f out: sn edgd lft and rdn: hdd ins fnl f: no ex* **12/1**

0003 **4** 1½ **Commandingpresence (USA)**[13] 5965 3-8-12 50............. LPKeniry 8 48
(J J Bridger) *a.p: rdn over 1f out: one pce* **20/1**

33 **5** ½ **Catchpenny**[21] 5727 3-8-12 0.................................... PhillipMakin 2 50+
(K A Ryan) *hld up and bhd: rdn and sme hdwy whn carried rt over 1f out: n.d after* **9/2**[2]

60-0 **6** *hd* **Place The Duchess**[97] 3242 3-8-12 42..........................(t) JimmyQuinn 3 46?
(A J Lidderdale) *s.i.s: hld up in rr: c wd st: rdn jst over 1f out: nvr trbld ldrs* **66/1**

0 **6** *dht* **She Goes Nowhere (IRE)**[26] 5572 3-8-12 0..................... LiamJones 9 46
(M S Tuck) *bhd: pushed along and hdwy over 2f out: rdn and wknd over 1f out* **9/1**

00-0 **8** *2* **Professor Malone**[74] 3994 4-9-5 42........................(p) StephenDonohoe 5 45
(M S Tuck) *hld up in rr: pushed along over 2f out: rdn jst over 1f out: nvr nr ldrs* **100/1**

0006 **9** 2¼ **Chasing Amy**[24] 5644 3-8-12 46.................................... TPQueally 7 32
(M G Quinlan) *w ldr: led over 4f out: rdn and hdd wl over 1f out: wknd fnl f* **50/1**

00-0 **10** *11* **Valentine Bay**[5] 6221 3-8-12 48.................................(be) RobertHavlin 10 —
(M Mullineaux) *chsd ldrs: pushed along over 3f out: rdn and wknd over 2f out: c v wd st: eased whn no ch ins fnl f* **80/1**

00 **11** 3¾ **Mrs Medley**[16] 5882 3-8-12 0.................................... GrahamGibbons 6 —
(D Shaw) *led over 1f: w ldr tl rdn 2f out: sn wknd: eased whn no ch ins fnl f* **66/1**

1m 14.58s (-0.42) **Going Correction** -0.225s/f (Stan)
WFA 3 from 4yo 2lb **11** Ran SP% **117.6**
Speed ratings (Par 103): **93,90,89,87,86 86,86,83,80,66 61**
toteswingers: 1&2 £2.80, 1&3 £4.60, 2&3 £7.30 CSF £5.81 TOTE £1.70: £1.02, £2.60, £3.50; EX 6.60.
Owner Mrs J E & J F S Laws **Bred** W V Poole And L And A Loake **Trained** Kentisbeare, Devon
■ Stewards' Enquiry : T P Queally one-day ban: failed to ride to draw (Oct 12)
Graham Gibbons one-day ban: failed to ride to draw (Oct 12)

FOCUS
A weak-looking older-horse maiden that ultimately was dominated by the favourite.

6345 NEAL WOOD MEMORIAL NURSERY H'CAP (DIV II) 5f 216y(P)
3:30 (3:32) (Class 6) (0-65,65) 2-Y-O **£2,388** (£705; £352) **Stalls** Low

Form RPR
3432 **1** **Newbury Street**[11] 6035 2-9-1 **62**.............................. FrederikTylicki(3) 1 65+
(R A Fahey) *a.p: n.m.r on ins jst over 2f out: led wl over 1f out: sn rdn: drvn out* **7/4**[1]

600 **2** ½ **Kilt Rock (IRE)**[35] 5317 2-9-5 **63**................................ JamesDoyle 4 68+
(T G Mills) *hld up in tch: chsd wnr over 1f out: sn rdn: r.o towards fin* **11/4**[2]

054 **3** *nk* **Pepper Lane**[27] 5553 2-8-6 **57**.................................. IJBrennan(7) 7 58
(J Hetherton) *a.p: rdn over 2f out: r.o towards fin* **10/1**

6000 **4** 2¼ **Speedyfix**[14] 5950 2-8-3 **47**..(tp) JimmyQuinn 3 43+
(Mrs C A Dunnett) *s.i.s: hld up in rr: nt clr run on ins over 2f out: hdwy wl over 1f out: rdn ins fnl f: one pce* **22/1**

5230 **5** 3½ **True Red (IRE)**[15] 5908 2-9-2 **60**............................ StephenDonohoe 11 44
(Mrs N S Evans) *led: rdn over 2f out: hdd wl over 1f out: wknd fnl f* **25/1**

6301 **6** *nse* **Agent Boo**[32] 5358 2-9-7 **65**..............................(b) GrahamGibbons 8 49
(E S McMahon) *chsd ldr: ev ch 2f out: lost 2nd wl over 1f out: sn rdn: wknd fnl f* **11/2**[3]

3000 **7** ½ **Saucy Girl (IRE)**[24] 5620 2-9-2 **60**................................ DavidAllan 2 42
(T D Easterby) *bhd: pushed along over 3f out: short-lived effrt on ins over 2f out* **25/1**

0405 **8** ½ **Zaskia (IRE)**[83] 3709 2-8-10 **54**................................ PhillipMakin 9 35
(K A Ryan) *hld up in mid-div: rdn over 2f out: wknd wl over 1f out* **33/1**

6455 **9** *shd* **Bathwick Gino**[17] 5835 2-9-5 **63**..................................(v) TPQueally 6 43
(P D Evans) *s.i.s: rdn wl over 1f out: a bhd* **20/1**

0000 **10** *2* **Flyinflyout**[21] 5715 2-9-5 **63**...................................... ChrisCatlin 5 37
(M R Channon) *s.i.s: outpcd* **12/1**

00 **11** 1¼ **Rightcar**[32] 5372 2-8-7 **51**... LPKeniry 12 23
(Peter Grayson) *hld up towards rr: pushed along over 2f out: struggling whn rdn wl over 1f out* **50/1**

0350 **12** *7* **Mr Smithson (IRE)**[29] 5467 2-9-6 **64**............................ TomEaves 10 14
(B Ellison) *prom: lost pl over 3f out: bhd fnl 2f* **16/1**

1m 14.63s (-0.37) **Going Correction** -0.225s/f (Stan) **12** Ran SP% **122.8**
Speed ratings (Par 93): **93,92,91,88,84 84,83,82,82,80 78,69**
toteswingers: 1&2 £2.10, 1&3 £3.60, 2&3 £9.20 CSF £5.97 CT £39.37 TOTE £3.30: £1.30, £1.80, £2.40; EX 8.50.
Owner J J Staunton **Bred** R A Fahey **Trained** Musley Bank, N Yorks
■ Stewards' Enquiry : Stephen Donohoe one-day ban: failed to ride to draw (Oct 12)

FOCUS
This second division of the nursery was run in a similar time to that of the first and the firsdt two may be capable of better.

NOTEBOOK
Newbury Street had been beaten only narrowly on his handicap debut, and a 2lb higher mark didn't look a problem, especially as he had a good draw in stall one. Always well placed chasing the pace on the inside, he got first run on the second and the drop back to 6f didn't cause him any bother. (op 6-4 tchd 2-1)
Kilt Rock(IRE), for whom there was a big market move, found one too good for him on this handicap debut. Short of room on the inside turning into the straight, the winner got first run and he could never quite peg him back. He has the ability to win a similar race even off a slightly higher mark, but the bookmakers will be more wary next time. (op 7-2)
Pepper Lane, another running in a handicap for the first time, finished well, putting any stamina doubts to rest. (op 8-1)
Speedyfix, who showed a bit more in the cheekpieces last time, again had the headgear on, and this was another sound effort, albeit from a good draw. (op 28-1 tchd 33-1)
True Red(IRE) used up plenty of energy getting over from her wide draw to take them along. Considering 5f is more her trip, she didn't run too badly in the circumstances. (op 22-1)
Agent Boo, who won in soft ground last time out when blinkers were fitted for the first time, had the headgear on again. He was a little disappointing and perhaps give in the ground is the key to him rather than the blinds. (op 7-1)

6346 WILLIAMHILL.COM/BONUS25 - LIVE CASINO DEALERS FILLIES' H'CAP 1m 1f 103y(P)
4:00 (4:00) (Class 4) (0-80,80) 3-Y-O+ **£5,046** (£1,510; £755; £377; £188) **Stalls** Low

Form RPR
322 **1** **Expressive**[11] 6029 3-8-8 **72** ow2.................................. RyanMoore 1 78
(Sir Michael Stoute) *broke wl: hld up in tch: pushed along over 2f out: rdn over 1f out: r.o to ld nr fin* **5/1**[2]

4105 **2** *hd* **Hallingdal (UAE)**[15] 5915 4-9-0 **73**............................... LPKeniry 4 79+
(J J Bridger) *hld up towards rr: c wd st: hdwy and rdn over 1f out: r.o ins fnl f: tk 2nd last strides* **20/1**

216 **3** *nk* **Golden Button (IRE)**[28] 5511 4-8-13 **72**.................. StephenDonohoe 7 77
(Sir Mark Prescott) *sn led: rdn over 1f out: hdd nr fin* **5/1**[2]

54 **4** ¾ **Suba (USA)**[29] 5475 3-9-1 **79**...................................... KFallon 2 83
(L M Cumani) *hld up in tch: pushed along and wnt 2nd jst over 2f out: rdn over 1f out: no ex towards fin* **7/4**[1]

5304 **5** *5* **Suzi Spends (IRE)**[50] 4815 4-9-7 **80**.............................. JimmyQuinn 10 73
(H J Collingridge) *hld up towards rr: stdy prog on ins 2f out: rdn over 1f out: wknd ins fnl f* **8/1**[3]

4620 **6** 2¼ **Lunar River (FR)**[16] 5886 6-8-9 **68**...............................(t) ChrisCatlin 11 57
(David Pinder) *hld up in rr: pushed along wl over 1f out: nvr nr ldrs* **28/1**

0010 **7** *nk* **Becuille (IRE)**[45] 4992 4-8-11 **70**..............................(b) NickyMackay 8 58
(B J Meehan) *hld up in mid-div: rdn and wknd wl over 1f out* **16/1**

1204 **8** 1¼ **Royal Superlative**[18] 5803 3-8-4 **71** ow1.................. JackMitchell(3) 5 56
(R M Beckett) *led early: prom: rdn over 2f out: wknd wl over 1f out* **12/1**

20-0 **9** ¾ **Fantasy Princess (USA)**[61] 4422 4-9-4 **77**..................(t) WilliamBuick 6 61
(G A Butler) *hld up in rr: pushed along over 1f out: no rspnse* **11/1**

5205 **10** 3¼ **Bookiebasher Babe (IRE)**[52] 4759 4-8-13 **72**............. FrancisNorton 9 49
(M Quinn) *sn chsng ldr: pushed along and lost 2nd jst over 2f out: rdn and wknd wl over 1f out* **28/1**

1m 58.93s (-2.77) **Going Correction** -0.225s/f (Stan)
WFA 3 from 4yo+ 5lb **10** Ran SP% **114.4**
Speed ratings (Par 102): **103,102,102,101,97 95,95,94,93,90**
toteswingers: 1&2 £13.20, 1&3 £3.20, 2&3 £18.00 CSF £99.53 CT £519.38 TOTE £6.50: £1.10, £5.50, £2.30; EX 98.70.
Owner Cheveley Park Stud **Bred** Cheveley Park Stud Ltd **Trained** Newmarket, Suffolk
■ Stewards' Enquiry : Jimmy Quinn two-day ban: careless riding (Oct 12-13)

FOCUS
A fair fillies' handicap that resulted in another close finish but the form seems sound enough rated around the third and fourth.

6347 WILLIAM HILL 0800 444040 - GET £25 FREE BET MAIDEN STKS 5f 20y(P)
4:30 (4:31) (Class 4) 2-Y-O **£3,885** (£1,156; £577; £288) **Stalls** Low

Form RPR
3432 **1** **Look Whos Next**[28] 5526 2-9-3 72.............................. GrahamGibbons 8 75
(E S McMahon) *mde all: rdn 1f out: r.o wl* **3/1**[2]

00 **2** 1½ **Mount Juliet (IRE)**[25] 5605 2-8-12 0............................. HayleyTurner 2 65
(S A Callaghan, U.S.A) *a.p: chsd wnr wl over 1f out: sn rdn: nt qckn ins fnl f* **11/2**[3]

432 **3** *2* **Barlaman (USA)**[11] 6026 2-9-0 74..............................(t) AhmedAjtebi(3) 7 62
(Saeed Bin Suroor) *hld up towards rr: c v wd st: hdwy over 1f out: sn rdn: hung lft wl ins fnl f: nvr nrr* **15/8**[1]

63 **4** ¾ **Flaxen Lake**[11] 6018 2-9-0 0.............................. RussellKennemore(3) 4 60
(R Hollinshead) *hld up in mid-div: hdwy wl over 1f out: sn rdn: one pce fnl f* **8/1**

5 **5** 1½ **Be Grateful (IRE)**[17] 5829 2-8-12 0................................ TravisBlock 3 49
(H Morrison) *a.p: pushed along over 1f out: one pce* **11/2**[3]

50 **6** ¾ **Caol Ila (IRE)**[14] 5949 2-8-12 0.................................. J-PGuillambert 1 47
(J G Given) *mid-div: pushed along over 3f out: rdn over 1f out: no hdwy* **25/1**

06 **7** *nk* **Blue Neptune**[17] 5829 2-9-3 0.................................... WilliamBuick 10 51
(W R Muir) *hld up in tch: c wd st: rdn jst over 1f out: wknd ins fnl f* **33/1**

6324 **8** 2 1/2 **Pinnacle Lad (IRE)**[107] 2906 2-9-3 74 FrancisNorton 5 43
(J L Spearing) *chsd wnr tl pushed along wl over 1f out: rdn and wknd ins fnl f* **10/1**

9 hd **Future Regime (IRE)** 2-8-12 0 SJCraine 9 36
(Patrick Morris) *s.i.s and wnt lft: hld up towards rr: rdn wl over 1f out: no rspnse* **33/1**

00 **10** 5 **Kanace**[11] 6026 2-9-3 0 StephenDonohoe 12 23
(Ian Williams) *s.i.s: a in rr* **100/1**

11 3/4 **Bom Boms (IRE)** 2-9-3 0 RichardSmith 11 20
(Tom Dascombe) *s.i.s: a in rr* **40/1**

61.26 secs (-1.04) **Going Correction** -0.225s/f (Stan) **11** Ran SP% **123.9**
Speed ratings (Par 97): **99,96,93,92,89 88,88,84,83,75 74**
toteswingers: 1&2 £4.10, 1&3 £2.80, 2&3 £4.40 CSF £20.38 TOTE £4.70: £1.90, £2.40, £1.10; EX 24.90.
Owner S L Edwards **Bred** S L Edwards **Trained** Lichfield, Staffs

FOCUS
A modest sprint maiden and not that many ever got into it. The winner produced a slight personal best.

NOTEBOOK
Look Whos Next didn't impress everyone with his attitude when runner-up off 71 in a Warwick nursery last month, but his rider made sure there was no messing around on this sand debut back over the minimum trip and soon had him bowling along in front. He never really looked like being caught and may be able to find a nursery off this mark under similar tactics. (op 7-2 tchd 11-4)
Mount Juliet(IRE), who didn't get home over 7f at Salisbury last time, fared much better on this first try over the minimum trip. Having been handy from the start, she had every chance turning in but went for a run up the inside rail, which isn't always ideal here, and the winner was always holding her. She now qualifies for a mark. (tchd 6-1)
Barlaman(USA), another trying the minimum trip for the first time after showing ability in three Polytrack maidens over 6f, was always playing catch-up after slightly missing the break but his biggest problem was that he was taken seven-wide on the turn into the home straight and, though he stayed on, was never going to make up the ground he lost as a result. (op 9-4 tchd 5-2 and 11-4 in places)
Flaxen Lake had a chance turning for home, but lacked a turn of foot in the straight. He will have more opportunities now that he can be handicapped, but may need a stiffer track or an extra furlong. (op 9-1 tchd 10-1)
Be Grateful(IRE) showed up for a long way, but still looked as though she was learning the game and may be one for handicaps further down the line. (op 8-1 tchd 9-1)
Caol Ila(IRE) didn't improve much for the return to the minimum trip, but is another for whom nurseries now become an option. (tchd 28-1)

6348 WILLIAMHILL.COM/BONUS25 - PLAY VEGAS GAMES H'CAP 7f 32y(P)
5:00 (5:00) (Class 4) (0-85,83) 3-Y-O **£5,046** (£1,510; £755; £377; £188) **Stalls High**

Form RPR

0001 **1** **Mabait**[10] 6072 3-9-4 83 KFallon 5 91
(L M Cumani) *chsd ldr 1f: a.p: rdn jst over 1f out: r.o to ld last strides* **4/1**[3]

3212 **2** nse **Hightime Heroine (IRE)**[14] 5937 3-8-12 77 RyanMoore 1 84
(J Noseda) *hld up in tch: rdn to ld wl ins fnl f: hdd last strides* **7/2**[2]

1503 **3** 3/4 **Silent Hero**[25] 5591 3-9-2 81 (p) PhilipRobinson 6 86+
(M A Jarvis) *hld up in mid-div: pushed along over 2f out: c wd st: rdn and edgd lft over 1f out: r.o to take 3rd last strides* **17/2**

5301 **4** 1/2 **Invincible Isle (IRE)**[11] 6020 3-9-2 81 TPQueally 9 85
(H R A Cecil) *chsd ldr after 1f: ev ch over 2f out: lost 2nd wl over 1f out: rdn ins fnl f: kpt on* **11/4**[1]

4106 **5** shd **Snow Bay**[33] 5340 3-8-13 78 TomEaves 4 82
(B Smart) *led: rdn over 1f out: hdd and no ex wl ins fnl f* **20/1**

1425 **6** 2 **My Best Bet**[13] 5968 3-8-10 78 MCGeran(3) 3 76
(M R Channon) *hld up towards rr: rdn wl over 1f out: nvr trbld ldrs* **12/1**

0263 **7** 2 3/4 **Kloof**[16] 5884 3-8-10 75 PhillipMakin 8 66
(K A Ryan) *hld up towards rr: rdn and sme hdwy wl over 1f out: wknd ins fnl f* **8/1**

-000 **8** 3 1/4 **Baariq**[63] 4386 3-8-12 77 WilliamBuick 2 59
(P W Chapple-Hyam) *hld up towards rr: pushed along and hdwy on ins over 2f out: rdn wl over 1f out: wknd ins fnl f* **20/1**

5350 **9** 4 1/2 **Peter's Gift (IRE)**[66] 4284 3-8-7 72 ChrisCatlin 7 42
(K A Ryan) *hld up in mid-div: pushed wd over 2f out: sn bhd* **40/1**

032 **10** 17 **La Marseillaise (IRE)**[26] 5572 3-8-7 72 MichaelHills 10 —
(B W Hills) *a in rr: eased whn no ch wl over 1f out* **14/1**

1m 27.39s (-2.21) **Going Correction** -0.225s/f (Stan) **10** Ran SP% **116.8**
Speed ratings (Par 103): **103,102,102,101,101 99,95,92,87,67**
toteswingers: 1&2 £5.60, 2&3 £6.40, 1&3 not won. CSF £17.97 CT £115.92 TOTE £4.90: £2.00, £1.50, £2.60; EX 15.90.
Owner Sheikh Mohammed Obaid Al Maktoum **Bred** L A C Ashby Newhall Estate Farm **Trained** Newmarket, Suffolk

FOCUS
A decent and quite competitive 3yo handicap in which it proved difficult to come from off the pace and produced another close finish.
La Marseillaise(IRE) Official explanation: jockey said filly was outpaced throughout

6349 WILLIAM HILL 0800 444040 - QUOTE BONUS25 H'CAP 1m 141y(P)
5:30 (5:30) (Class 6) (0-65,64) 3-Y-O+ **£2,388** (£705; £352) **Stalls Low**

Form RPR

4310 **1** **Cheers For Thea (IRE)**[11] 6023 4-9-8 63 (bt) DavidAllan 9 77+
(T D Easterby) *hld up towards rr: c wd st: hdwy to ld over 1f out: shkn up ins fnl f: readily* **11/2**[2]

2403 **2** 1 3/4 **Arashi**[11] 6031 3-9-4 64 (p) KFallon 5 72
(Lucinda Featherstone) *plld hrd: sn mid-div: hdwy over 3f out: pushed along over 2f out: c wd st: ev ch over 1f out: rdn and nt qckn ins fnl f* **11/2**[2]

1 **3** 4 1/2 **Vertigo On Course (IRE)**[12] 6005 4-9-1 59 FrederikTylicki(3) 6 57
(R A Fahey) *a.p: shkn up to ld wl over 1f out: sn rdn and hdd: wknd ins fnl f* **5/4**[1]

06-5 **4** nse **Womaniser (IRE)**[61] 4438 5-9-2 57 (p) J-PGuillambert 3 55
(T Keddy) *hld up in tch: nt clr run briefly wl over 1f out: sn rdn: one pce fnl f* **8/1**[3]

0500 **5** 2 **True Decision**[26] 5581 3-9-0 60 JamesDoyle 1 53
(S Kirk) *sn chsng ldr: lost 2nd over 6f out: prom: rdn and wknd ins fnl f* **50/1**

0200 **6** nk **Hold The Star**[41] 5121 3-9-3 63 TPQueally 12 55
(E F Vaughan) *hld up towards rr: nt clr run wl over 1f out: sn swtchd rt: kpt on ins fnl f: n.d* **50/1**

5303 **7** 2 **Another Decree**[9] 6103 4-9-2 57 (tp) PhillipMakin 11 45
(M Dods) *hld up towards rr: nt clr run after 1f: rdn over 2f out: nvr nr ldrs* **33/1**

0506 **8** 1/2 **Inside Story (IRE)**[24] 5631 7-9-9 64 (b) LPKeniry 13 50
(C R Dore) *hld up in rr: rdn over 3f out: hdwy on ins over 2f out: wknd ins fnl f* **33/1**

5000 **9** 1 1/4 **Sign Of The Cross**[9] 6123 5-9-3 58 LiamJones 4 42
(C R Dore) *hld up in tch: pushed along and ev ch wl over 1f out: sn wknd* **33/1**

040 **10** 3/4 **Lyrical Intent**[180] 1075 3-9-0 60 JimmyQuinn 10 42
(P Howling) *s.i.s: hld up in rr: pushed along over 3f out: no rspnse* **100/1**

1460 **11** 2 **King Of Legend (IRE)**[60] 4465 5-8-13 61 (t) IJBrennan(7) 2 38
(A G Foster) *prom: chsd ldr over 6f out tl pushed along over 2f out: wknd over 1f out* **16/1**

5016 **12** 1 1/4 **Funky Munky**[7] 6157 4-9-8 63 PJMcDonald 7 37
(G A Swinbank) *hld up in tch: pushed along and lost pl over 3f out: c wd st: sn bhd* **14/1**

0402 **13** 9 **Hypnotic**[26] 5569 7-9-5 60 (b[1]) WilliamBuick 8 14
(Jim Best) *sn led: clr over 6f out: rdn and hdd wl over 1f out: sn wknd: eased fnl f* **18/1**

1m 48.42s (-2.08) **Going Correction** -0.225s/f (Stan)
WFA 3 from 4yo+ 5lb **13** Ran SP% **117.9**
Speed ratings (Par 101): **100,98,94,94,92 92,90,90,89,88 86,85,77**
CSF £33.76 CT £61.07 TOTE £6.20: £1.90, £1.90, £1.30; EX 42.10 Place 6: £89.63 Place 5: £36.70 .
Owner Ron George **Bred** Crone Stud Farms Ltd **Trained** Great Habton, N Yorks
■ Stewards' Enquiry : William Buick three-day ban: careless riding (Oct 12-14)

FOCUS
A moderate handicap run at a decent gallop. The winner recorded another personal best.
T/Jkpt: £97,342.30 to a £1 stake. Pool: £137,101.94. 1.00 winning ticket. T/Plt: £49.10 to a £1 stake. Pool: £70,865.78. 1,052.27 winning tickets. T/Qpdt: £4.10 to a £1 stake. Pool: £5,221.64. 929.12 winning tickets. KH

6350 - 6353a (Foreign Racing) - See Raceform Interactive

5371 SOUTHWELL (L-H)
Tuesday, September 29

OFFICIAL GOING: Standard
Wind: fresh 1/2 behind Weather: fine but blustery

6354 BET AFTER THE OFF AT LADBROKES.COM NURSERY (DIV I) 5f (F)
1:50 (1:50) (Class 5) (0-70,70) 2-Y-O **£3,412** (£1,007; £504) **Stalls High**

Form RPR

0620 **1** **Angie's Nap (USA)**[20] 5776 2-8-5 54 (p) ChrisCatlin 3 58
(P S McEntee) *mde all: rdn and hung lft 2f out: hld on wl* **10/1**

0062 **2** 1 1/4 **Dimaire**[17] 5866 2-9-1 64 JamieMackay 12 64
(D Haydn Jones) *dwlt: sn chsng ldrs: edgd lft and styd on same pce fnl f* **22/1**

345 **3** 1 1/2 **My Mandy (IRE)**[12] 6018 2-9-2 65 (p) EddieAhern 9 59
(Ian Williams) *hld up stands' side: effrt over 2f out: edgd lft: styd on to take 3rd nr line* **12/1**

3000 **4** 1/2 **Lees Anthem**[14] 5957 2-8-12 61 DNolan 1 53
(C J Teague) *chsd ldrs far side: edgd lft over 1f out: kpt on same pce* **12/1**

6550 **5** 1 1/4 **Princess Shamal**[33] 5372 2-8-10 59 FergusSweeney 8 47
(J R Jenkins) *in rr: sn drvn along: hdwy over 1f out: nvr nr ldrs* **14/1**

5365 **6** hd **Novay Essjay (IRE)**[10] 6099 2-8-13 67 PatrickDonaghy(5) 4 54
(P C Haslam) *chsd ldrs: rdn over 1f out: one pce* **7/2**[2]

20U0 **7** 1/2 **Mad Millie (IRE)**[13] 5980 2-8-13 62 SilvestreDeSousa 2 47
(J Hetherton) *chsd ldrs: wknd over 1f out* **8/1**[3]

0210 **8** 5 **Koo And The Gang (IRE)**[115] 2714 2-9-7 70 TomEaves 6 37
(B Ellison) *stmbld s: sn drvn along in rr: sme hdwy over 2f out: sn wknd* **15/8**[1]

6500 **9** 1 1/4 **Gasparilla (IRE)**[13] 5976 2-7-9 47 oh2 NataliaGemelova(3) 7 10
(A J McCabe) *sn outpcd and in rr* **33/1**

0000 **10** 2 3/4 **Burtondale Boy (IRE)**[26] 5596 2-7-13 48 oh2 ow1 FrankieMcDonald 5 —
(P T Midgley) *rrd s: t.k.h in rr: bhd fnl 2f* **20/1**

0000 **11** 3 3/4 **Nidamar**[39] 5226 2-8-1 50 oh2 ow3 FrancisNorton 10 —
(Mrs R A Carr) *chsd ldrs: edgd lft and lost pl over 2f out* **66/1**

59.69 secs (-0.01) **Going Correction** -0.175s/f (Stan) **11** Ran SP% **112.8**
Speed ratings (Par 95): **93,91,88,87,85 85,84,76,74,70 64**
toteswingers: 1&2 £13.50, 1&3 £4.90, 2&3 £10.20 CSF £206.99 CT £2686.28 TOTE £11.60: £3.30, £3.30, £2.50; EX 122.00 TRIFECTA Not won..
Owner Eventmaker Racehorses **Bred** James Millar & Janice Millar **Trained** Newmarket, Suffolk

FOCUS
There had been no significant rainfall here for at least a month and, despite plenty of watering, the kickback in this opener looked severe. Perhaps it wasn't a surprise that this modest sprint nursery was dominated by those that raced handily from the start and, in view of the kickback, those that made no impression from off the pace can be forgiven. Limited form, with the winner back to her best.

NOTEBOOK
Angie's Nap(USA) had been disappointing on Polytrack since going close off 2lb lower from a bad draw over course and distance last month, but she was well berthed this time and she made just about every yard. The form may not amount to much, but she seemed to win with a bit in hand and she does seem to like it here. (tchd 9-1)
Dimaire, bumped up 15lb after going down narrowly to a 73-rated rival in a five-runner Ffos Las maiden last time, was a big drifter in the market throughout the day, but she belied that with a decent effort and she did well to get across and take a handy position having started from an unfavourably high draw. This performance suggests that the handicapper was justified in raising her and she still has a bit of scope for further improvement. (op 18-1)
My Mandy(IRE), often placed but still a maiden after nine attempts coming into this, had cheekpieces on for the first time and she also ran well from a high draw, especially as she raced closest to the stands' rail for most of the way, though that did mean that she raced out of the kickback. (op 9-1)
Lees Anthem, who had gone the wrong way since throwing away a winning opportunity on his Newcastle debut, was trying sand for the first time and he was always handy against the far rail. This was encouraging enough to make him worth another try here. (op 14-1 tchd 11-1)
Princess Shamal, yet to make the frame in six previous outings but far from disgraced in her last two including over this course and distance, can be given some credit as she was getting all the kickback at the back of the field early, so she probably did well to finish where she did. (op 12-1)
Novay Essjay(IRE), having his first try on sand and racing over the minimum trip for the first time since his successful racecourse debut, seemed to have every chance with few excuses. (op 4-1 tchd 3-1)
Koo And The Gang(IRE), successful and then only narrowly beaten in two outings over course and distance in May, was having his first start since June but he could never get into the race after slightly missing the break. His rider reported that he stumbled at the start and the vet reported that he had lost a shoe. Official explanation: jockey said gelding stumbled on leaving stalls; vet said gelding lost a shoe (op 2-1)

Burtondale Boy(IRE), making his sand and nursery debuts having shown nothing in four previous starts, was backed at big prices earlier in the day but he jumped in the air as the stalls opened and basically lost his chance there and then. (tchd 22-1)

6355 BET AFTER THE OFF AT LADBROKES.COM NURSERY (DIV II) 5f (F)
2:20 (2:20) (Class 5) (0-70,70) 2-Y-O £3,412 (£1,007; £504) Stalls High

Form RPR
052 **1** **Heslington**[167] 1275 2-9-7 **70**........ RobertWinston 3 73
(M Brittain) *w ldrs: led 1f out: hld on towards fin* **9/2**[2]
4000 **2** ½ **Clear Ice (IRE)**[10] 6096 2-8-6 **55**........ AdrianTNicholls 8 56
(D Nicholls) *led 1f: w ldrs: styd on wl ins fnl f: tk 2nd nr fin* **20/1**
0342 **3** ¾ **Lewyn**[15] 5950 2-9-4 **67**........(b) NCallan 6 65
(K A Ryan) *dwlt and wnt lft s: t.k.h: led after 1f: hdd 1f out: no ex* **7/2**[1]
0400 **4** ½ **Avec Moi**[8] 6169 2-7-13 **48** oh2 ow1........ JimmyQuinn 1 44
(Mrs C A Dunnett) *wnt lft s: sn chsng ldrs: kpt on same pce fnl f* **17/2**[3]
4440 **5** ¾ **Kalahari Desert (IRE)**[13] 5977 2-8-8 **60**........ MichaelJStainton(3) 4 54
(R M Whitaker) *chsd ldrs: kpt on one pce fnl 2f* **9/1**
450 **6** 2 **Cape Kimberley**[22] 5728 2-9-2 **65**........ J-PGuillambert 10 51
(J G Given) *sn outpcd and in rr: kpt on fnl 2f: nvr nr ldrs* **9/1**
6430 **7** nk **Clever Molly (IRE)**[12] 6009 2-8-12 **61**........ PaulQuinn 11 46+
(E J Alston) *hld up stands' side: in rr: kpt on fnl 2f: nvr nr ldrs* **14/1**
005 **8** nk **Thinking**[13] 5977 2-9-0 **63**........ DuranFentiman 5 47
(T D Easterby) *hmpd s: sn chsng ldrs: lost pl over 1f out* **9/2**[2]
050 **9** 3¾ **Ridgeway Sapphire**[19] 5811 2-7-11 **53**........ RachelKing(7) 12 24+
(M D I Usher) *sn wl outpcd and in rr* **25/1**
00F0 **10** hd **Orpen All Hours (IRE)**[12] 6034 2-7-12 **47** oh2........(p) SilvestreDeSousa 2 17
(P C Haslam) *chsd ldrs: lost pl over 1f out* **14/1**
000 **11** 4 **Gessabelle**[45] 5029 2-7-10 **48** oh1 ow1........(t) AndreaAtzeni(3) 9 4
(P S McEntee) *sn outpcd and bhd* **28/1**
005 **12** ½ **Somewhere Else**[52] 4773 2-8-1 **50** oh2 ow3........ FrancisNorton 7 4
(A Berry) *dwlt: sn outpcd and bhd* **100/1**

59.39 secs (-0.31) **Going Correction** -0.175s/f (Stan) **12 Ran SP% 115.5**
Speed ratings (Par 95): **95,94,93,92,91 87,87,86,80,80 74,73**
toteswingers: 1&2 £24.60, 1&3 £3.40, 2&3 £18.00 CSF £94.66 CT £355.83 TOTE £4.40: £1.80, £7.80, £1.70; EX 124.50 Trifecta £209.50 Part won. Pool: £283.12 - 0.56 winning units..
Owner Mel Brittain **Bred** Lucy Lawson And Partners **Trained** Warthill, N Yorks

FOCUS
This looked even weaker than the first division, with all 12 runners maidens coming into it, but the winning time was 0.3 seconds quicker. Again the race was dominated by the pacesetters and the action all took place centre to far side. Straightforward form.

NOTEBOOK
Heslington ♦, who split a couple of subsequent winners when runner-up in his most recent outing at Beverley in April, was making his sand and nursery debuts. He was soon able to take a handy position from his good draw and having hit the front a furlong out, was then always doing enough. He is entitled to come on for this and can progress further. (op 5-1 tchd 11-2 and 7-2)
Clear Ice(IRE), making his sand debut after becoming disappointing on turf, ran much better here having been up with the pace from the off and was still going forward at the line. (op 18-1)
Lewyn, who seemed to improve for the fitting of blinkers when runner-up in a Redcar nursery last time, was another making her sand debut but not much went right for her here. She swerved away to her left exiting the stalls, barging into Thinking in the process, and then had to expend plenty of energy in order to get to the front within the first 2f. It was little surprise that she was unable to respond when the winner collared her a furlong from home and she can win a small race like this granted a trouble-free passage. (tchd 100-30 and 4-1)
Avec Moi, an exposed maiden and 3lb wrong, was well backed beforehand and she did run creditably, but she did have the plum draw. (op 16-1)
Kalahari Desert(IRE), making his sand debut and closely matched with Thinking on recent Beverley running, is by a sire who boasts a decent level-stake profit on this surface and he was another to run with credit having been handy throughout. (op 8-1)
Thinking can be forgiven this performance in view of the buffeting he took from Lewyn early on and he is worth another chance. (op 5-1)

6356 BET WITH LADBROKES ON 0800 777888 MAIDEN AUCTION STKS 6f (F)
2:50 (2:53) (Class 5) 2-Y-O £4,094 (£1,209; £604) Stalls Low

Form RPR
00 **1** **Amenable (IRE)**[12] 6009 2-8-10 0........ AndrewMullen 1 77
(D Nicholls) *mde all: hld on wl* **100/1**
2 **2** ¾ **Horseradish**[12] 6009 2-8-11 0........ HayleyTurner 9 76
(M L W Bell) *trckd ldrs: chal on bit over 1f out: sn rdn: no ex last 75yds* **4/11**[1]
6 **3** 8 **Marjolly (IRE)**[12] 6032 2-8-10 0........ AndreaAtzeni(3) 4 54
(M Botti) *chsd ldrs: sn drvn along: one pce fnl 2f* **40/1**
60 **4** 1 **Cookie Galore**[15] 5934 2-8-4 0........ RoystonFfrench 10 42
(J A Glover) *sn chsng ldrs: wknd fnl f* **25/1**
40 **5** 1¼ **Phoenix Rose (IRE)**[20] 5778 2-8-4 0........ AdrianTNicholls 2 38
(J R Best) *chsd ldrs: wknd over 1f out* **16/1**
0 **6** shd **Hambleton**[153] 1610 2-8-12 0........ TomEaves 12 46
(B Smart) *chsd ldrs: drvn 3f out: hung lft: wknd over 1f out* **12/1**[3]
7 5 **True To Form (IRE)** 2-8-10 0........ StephenDonohoe 6 32
(Sir Mark Prescott) *s.s: bhd tl sme hdwy fnl 2f: nvr on terms* **20/1**
6 **8** 1¼ **House Of Rules**[31] 5439 2-8-9 0........ TonyHamilton 8 24
(Miss J A Camacho) *sn outpcd and bhd: sme hdwy 2f out: nvr on terms* **14/1**
4 **9** nk **Hounds Ditch**[17] 5866 2-8-10 0........ JimmyQuinn 7 30
(Eve Johnson Houghton) *dwlt: mid-div and reminders over 2f out: nvr on terms* **10/1**[2]
0 **10** 19 **Atherton (IRE)**[12] 6026 2-8-13 0........ J-PGuillambert 5 —
(J G Given) *sn drvn along: lost pl over 4f out: sn bhd: t.o* **80/1**
3603 **11** ½ **Usquaebach**[33] 5372 2-8-4 55........(b) ChrisCatlin 11 —
(S Curran) *mid-div: lost pl over 4f out: sn wl bhd: t.o* **20/1**

1m 16.51s (0.01) **Going Correction** -0.05s/f (Stan) **11 Ran SP% 120.7**
Speed ratings (Par 95): **97,96,85,84,82 82,75,73,73,48 47**
toteswingers: 1&2 £21.10, 1&3 £91.80, 2&3 £10.20 CSF £138.85 TOTE £74.70: £19.90, £1.02, £11.50; EX 197.00 TRIFECTA Not won..
Owner Turton Brown Williams Lindley **Bred** Michael Downey & Roalso Ltd **Trained** Sessay, N Yorks

FOCUS
A very uncompetitive maiden and again very few ever got into it, but the result was a massive surprise to most people. There was no fluke and the first two came a long way clear.

NOTEBOOK
Amenable(IRE) had been well beaten in two turf maidens and was a long way behind Horseradish at Ayr last time, but this was a totally different ballgame. Soon given his head from the inside stall, he looked to be a sitting duck for the favourite coming to the last furlong, but he responded splendidly to pressure and ran out a deserved winner at a huge price. It will be interesting to see how the handicapper assesses this, but he certainly seemed to relish the switch to this surface and looks well worth bringing back here. Official explanation: trainer's rep said she had no explanation for the apparent improvement in form
Horseradish had shown plenty of ability when second of 19 on his Ayr debut earlier in the month and this looked a straightforward opportunity to go one better, despite the different surface. Having broken much better from the stalls than he did at Ayr, he travelled very sweetly just behind the leaders and his rider was still sitting motionless over a furlong from home. However, he didn't find as much off the bridle as had looked likely, and the also the winner found a bit more than might have been expected. This effort is difficult to gauge as he did pull a mile clear of the rest and he obviously has the ability to win his maiden before too long. He may be happier back on turf. (op 8-15, tchd 4-7 in places)
Marjolly(IRE), beaten a long way when sixth of seven on his Yarmouth debut, came off the bridle rounding the home bend but plugged on to finish a remote third. He may do better once handicapped.
Cookie Galore, not disgraced in a couple of turf maidens, raced prominently on the wide outside until the furlong pole and is likely to do better in handicaps for which she now qualifies. Official explanation: jockey said filly missed the break (op 20-1)
Phoenix Rose(IRE), who showed a hint of ability in a couple of Polytrack maidens, showed up for a fair way and will also have more options now that she qualifies for a mark. (op 12-1)
Hambleton, not seen since finishing well beaten in a decent Pontefract maiden in April, didn't run too badly and is entitled to strip fitter for the outing. (op 14-1 tchd 16-1)

6357 GET THE VIP TREATMENT AT LADBROKESCASINO.COM H'CAP 1m (F)
3:20 (3:20) (Class 4) (0-85,83) 3-Y-O+ £5,828 (£1,734; £866; £432) Stalls Low

Form RPR
1400 **1** **Mcconnell (USA)**[13] 5997 4-9-1 **76**........ GeorgeBaker 12 87+
(G L Moore) *hld up: smooth hdwy on outer over 3f out: shkn up over 2f out: led over 1f out: wl in command whn eased towards fin* **5/1**[2]
4423 **2** 1¼ **Ours (IRE)**[8] 6174 6-8-13 **74**........(p) ChrisCatlin 4 80
(John A Harris) *dwlt: in rr: swtchd outside after 2f: hdwy and hung lft over 2f out: styd on to take flattered 2nd nr fin* **6/1**[3]
10-3 **3** nk **Avertis**[21] 5745 4-9-5 **80**........(t) MickyFenton 5 85
(Stef Liddiard) *w ldrs: led over 4f out: hdd over 1f out: kpt on same pce* **9/2**[1]
1043 **4** ½ **Swiss Art (IRE)**[24] 5672 3-8-8 **73**........ SilvestreDeSousa 2 77
(Mrs R A Carr) *chsd ldrs: one pce fnl 2f* **9/2**[1]
0300 **5** 4½ **Celtic Step**[59] 4548 5-8-13 **74**........ PhillipMakin 9 68
(P D Niven) *led tl over 4f out: hung lft over 1f out: sn fdd* **22/1**
2160 **6** 4 **Helieorbea**[12] 6019 3-8-8 **73**........ DuranFentiman 6 58
(T D Easterby) *in rr: reminders after s: rn in snatches: lost pl 2f out* **18/1**
0340 **7** 4½ **Boy Blue**[34] 5333 4-9-3 **78**........ DaleGibson 8 52
(P Salmon) *s.i.s: in rr and drvn over 3f out: nvr on terms* **14/1**
100 **8** nk **Mozayada (USA)**[7] 6178 5-9-2 **77**........ FrancisNorton 1 51
(M Brittain) *trckd ldrs: effrt on ins 3f out: lost pl over 1f out* **9/1**
5512 **9** shd **Allformary**[11] 6052 3-8-9 **74**........ TomEaves 13 47
(B Smart) *chsd ldrs: lost pl over 1f out* **17/2**
0310 **10** ½ **Marning Star**[31] 5448 4-8-10 **71**........(t) SaleemGolam 7 43
(Ian Williams) *chsd ldrs: wknd 2f out* **16/1**
6-50 **11** 27 **Decameron (USA)**[122] 2470 4-9-6 **81**........ JoeFanning 11 —
(R A Harris) *chsd ldrs: drvn over 3f out: sn lost pl and bhd: virtually p.u: t.o* **12/1**

1m 43.89s (0.19) **Going Correction** -0.05s/f (Stan)
WFA 3 from 4yo+ 4lb **11 Ran SP% 117.7**
Speed ratings (Par 105): **97,95,95,94,90 86,81,81,81,81 54**
toteswingers: 1&2 £5.40, 1&3 £5.80, 2&3 £7.00 CSF £35.17 CT £148.10 TOTE £5.40: £2.50, £1.60, £1.50; EX 32.70 Trifecta £229.40 Part won. Pool: £310.08 - 0.86 winning units..
Owner Joe McCarthy **Bred** Hall Et Al Farm **Trained** Lower Beeding, W Sussex

FOCUS
A fair handicap run at a good pace and the front four pulled nicely clear. Straightforward form.

6358 GOLF AND RACING AT SOUTHWELL H'CAP 1m (F)
3:50 (3:50) (Class 6) (0-60,60) 3-Y-O+ £2,388 (£705; £352) Stalls Low

Form RPR
0003 **1** **Business Class (BRZ)**[10] 6101 4-9-5 **57**........ AdrianTNicholls 12 73
(D Nicholls) *w ldrs: led over 2f out: kpt on strly fnl f* **8/1**[3]
0564 **2** 2¼ **Boss Hog**[13] 5982 4-9-3 **55**........ NCallan 6 66
(P T Midgley) *trckd ldrs: chal over 2f out: styd on same pce appr fnl f* **8/1**[3]
0050 **3** 6 **Prince Golan (IRE)**[99] 3224 5-8-13 **58**........(p) AlexEdwards(7) 7 55+
(J W Unett) *s.s: bhd: hdwy on outside over 2f out: kpt on wl ins fnl f to take modest 3rd towards fin* **33/1**
4061 **4** 1¼ **Lyric Art (USA)**[25] 5624 3-9-3 **59**........ TomEaves 9 53
(B Smart) *in rr div: hdwy over 3f out: kpt on: nvr nr ldrs* **8/1**[3]
0234 **5** hd **Byron Bay**[31] 4656 7-9-6 **58**........(p) GrahamGibbons 3 52
(R Johnson) *led: hdd over 2f out: wknd over 1f out* **4/1**[1]
0033 **6** ½ **Versaki (IRE)**[8] 6170 3-8-11 **58**........(t) MartinLane(5) 4 51
(Ian Williams) *chsd ldrs: wknd over 1f out* **14/1**
03 **7** ½ **Tar (IRE)**[33] 5377 5-8-12 **55**........(v) MarkCoumbe(5) 14 46
(John A Harris) *in rr: hdwy over 2f out: nvr on terms* **14/1**
5531 **8** nk **Fitz**[25] 5647 3-9-2 **58**........ LPKeniry 13 49
(Matthew Salaman) *trckd ldrs: drvn over 2f out: wknd over 1f out* **8/1**[3]
-000 **9** 7 **Dado Mush**[11] 6074 6-9-1 **60**........ LauraPike(7) 8 35
(T T Clement) *s.i.s: in rr and swtchd wd after 2f: sn bhd* **10/1**
633 **10** 10 **Coole Dodger (IRE)**[47] 4932 4-9-3 **55**........ RoystonFfrench 11 —
(B Ellison) *mid-div: lost pl over 4f out: sn bhd* **7/1**[2]
0-42 **11** 1½ **Michael Collins (IRE)**[29] 5536 3-9-2 **58**........(p) ChrisCatlin 5 —
(Ms Maria Kelly, Ire) *mid-div: lost pl 3f out* **22/1**
0636 **12** 6 **Lennie Briscoe (IRE)**[16] 5905 3-9-2 **58**........ GeorgeBaker 1 —
(S Kirk) *chsd ldrs: sn pushed along: lost pl 3f out: bhd whn eased ins fnl f* **12/1**
5035 **13** 60 **Kheskianto (IRE)**[15] 5940 3-9-4 **60**........ RobertWinston 2 —
(M C Chapman) *w ldrs: lost pl 3f out: sn bhd and eased: virtually p.u: hopelessly t.o* **10/1**

1m 43.65s (-0.05) **Going Correction** -0.05s/f (Stan)
WFA 3 from 4yo+ 4lb **13 Ran SP% 123.4**
Speed ratings (Par 101): **98,95,89,88,88 87,87,87,80,70 68,62,2**
toteswingers: 1&2 £17.70, 1&3 £63.20, 2&3 £40.60 CSF £73.14 CT £2034.41 TOTE £10.70: £3.50, £3.00, £8.40; EX 87.30 TRIFECTA Not won..
Owner Michael Reay **Bred** Haras Valente **Trained** Sessay, N Yorks

FOCUS
A moderate handicap but a wide open betting race; however, it concerned only the first two in the final quarter-mile. The form is rated around the runner-up.
Coole Dodger(IRE) Official explanation: jockey said gelding never travelled
Kheskianto(IRE) Official explanation: trainer said filly had a breathing problem

6359 DAVE MORGAN MEMORIAL H'CAP 5f (F)
4:20 (4:26) (Class 3) (0-90,90) 3-Y-O+ £9,714 (£2,890; £1,444; £721) Stalls High

Form RPR
3606 **1** **Invincible Lad (IRE)**[20] 5768 5-8-12 **83**........ PatCosgrave 2 98+
(E J Alston) *w ldrs: led 2f out: styd on strly: eased towards fin* **7/2**[1]

0606 2 1 3/4 **Lesley's Choice**[22] 5724 3-8-5 **77**........................(b[1]) FrankieMcDonald 14 83
(R Curtis) *led after 1f: hdd 2f out: kpt on same pce* **50/1**
1324 3 1 1/2 **Rebel Duke (IRE)**[160] 1457 5-9-3 **88**.......................... TonyHamilton 6 88
(Ollie Pears) *chsd ldrs: kpt on same pce appr fnl f* **11/2[2]**
5125 4 1 **The Nifty Fox**[11] 6051 5-8-12 **83**.. TedDurcan 4 80
(T D Easterby) *chsd ldrs: one pce fnl 2f* **8/1[3]**
4552 5 1/2 **Pawan (IRE)**[7] 6180 9-8-10 **86** ow3..............................(b) AnnStokell(5) 3 81
(Miss A Stokell) *dwlt: in rr: reminders after 1f: hdwy and edgd lft 2f out: kpt on: nt rch ldrs* **9/1**
3511 6 1 1/2 **Ocean Blaze**[10] 6118 5-8-10 **81**.. ChrisCatlin 13 71
(B R Millman) *led 1f: w ldr: one pce appr fnl f* **14/1**
1600 7 3/4 **Luscivious**[11] 6051 5-9-4 **89**......................................(p) GrahamGibbons 5 76
(J A Glover) *mid-div: kpt on fnl 2f: nvr trbld ldrs* **10/1**
1161 8 3/4 **Guto**[11] 6051 6-8-2 **76** oh2.. KellyHarrison(3) 9 60
(W J H Ratcliffe) *chsd ldrs: fdd over 1f out* **12/1**
004 9 1 1/4 **Tabaret**[24] 5654 6-9-2 **87**.. EddieAhern 11 67
(R M Whitaker) *in rr stands' side: nvr on terms* **12/1**
020 10 1/2 **Imprimis Tagula (IRE)**[12] 6010 5-8-8 **79** ow1...........(v) RobertWinston 7 57
(A Bailey) *mid-div: drvn over 2f out: nvr a factor* **10/1**
0040 11 3 **Baby Strange**[26] 5615 5-8-11 **87**.. MartinLane(5) 8 54
(D Shaw) *dwlt: in rr and sn drvn along* **18/1**
203 12 1 1/2 **Hypnosis**[11] 6051 6-8-7 **78**.. DuranFentiman 12 40
(N Wilson) *sn outpcd and in rr* **28/1**

57.84 secs (-1.86) **Going Correction** -0.175s/f (Stan)
WFA 3 from 5yo+ 1lb **12** Ran SP% **109.6**
Speed ratings (Par 107): **107,104,101,100,99 97,95,94,92,91 87,84**
toteswingers: 1&2 £41.30, 1&3 £4.80, 2&3 £48.40 CSF £165.62 CT £717.33 TOTE £4.70: £2.00, £13.20, £2.20; EX 138.30 Trifecta £352.70 Part won. Pool: £476.68 - 0.30 winning units..
Owner Con Harrington **Bred** Mrs Chris Harrington **Trained** Longton, Lancs
■ Flash McGahon was withdrawn (17/2, burst out of stalls). R4 applies, deduct 10p in the £.

FOCUS
Fast and furious stuff in this decent sprint handicap for the grade. There looks more to come from the winner.

NOTEBOOK
Invincible Lad(IRE) ◆, who had been far from disgraced though unplaced in his recent starts, was a stone higher than when successful over this trip in his only previous try on Fibresand last October. He was very well backed earlier in the day and the withdrawal of Flash McGahon meant that he inherited the lowest stall. He made full use of it too, and once he had hit the front over a furlong from home the result was never in doubt. The way he won this would make him of obvious interest if turned out quickly under a penalty. (tchd 100-30 and 4-1)
Lesley's Choice, on the decline since winning off 3lb higher at Kempton in March, had the worst of the draw but he showed blinding speed in the first-time blinkers towards the nearside of the track and kept on going to finish clear second best. Much will now depend on whether the headgear works again.
Rebel Duke(IRE) was making his debut for the yard after five months off, but he has won after longer layoffs in the past and has a good record over this course and distance. He travelled well just behind the leaders and kept on well, but the winner was always running all over him. There will be another day. (op 13-2)
The Nifty Fox, making his sand debut, likes to get his toe in on turf so this surface might have been expected to suit him and he ran well having been handy from the start.
Pawan(IRE), a good second on disadvantageous terms in a Beverley conditions event last time, had to carry 3lb overweight but was still 5lb lower than when scoring over course and distance at the start of the year. Backed beforehand, he stayed on having hung over to the far rail but never offered a threat and is very hard to win with these days. (op 14-1)
Ocean Blaze ◆, up another 4lb in her bid for a hat-trick, was making her sand debut but she is best suited by a sound surface on turf so this surface may not have been ideal. Nevertheless she ran really well considering she soon found herself racing tight against the stands' rail, and she may well be able to defy this mark back on turf given suitable conditions. (op 10-1)
Luscivious didn't come into this in the best of form, but he had been successful in his last two visits here, the most recent over this trip off 4lb lower last month. However, with so much pace on here he could never get to the front and was always being held. (op 14-1)

6360 WATCH LIVE SERIE A AT LADBROKES.COM H'CAP 1m 4f (F)
4:50 (4:50) (Class 4) (0-85,82) 3-Y-O **£5,828** (£1,734; £866; £432) **Stalls** Low

Form RPR
4110 1 **Lucky Punt**[79] 3069 3-8-13 **77**.. FergusSweeney 1 84
(B G Powell) *mde all: qcknd over 2f out: edgd rt fnl f: hld on gamely: all out* **16/1**
0226 2 hd **Interdiamonds**[24] 5660 3-8-10 **74**.. JoeFanning 2 81
(M Johnston) *trckd wnr: drvn over 3f out: upsides over 1f out: crowded: no ex wl ins fnl f: jst hld* **8/1[3]**
5321 3 3/4 **Monetary Fund (USA)**[20] 5773 3-9-0 **78**................................(t) NCallan 6 83
(G A Butler) *trckd ldrs: keen: effrt 3f out: upsides over 1f out: no ex ins fnl f* **11/4[2]**
5004 4 1 1/4 **Royal Trooper (IRE)**[11] 6075 3-8-8 **72**.............................. TomEaves 5 75
(J G Given) *hld up in last: effrt 3f out: kpt on ins fnl f: nvr able to chal* **20/1**
1111 5 1 1/2 **Valid Point (IRE)**[5] 6236 3-8-9 **73** 6ex.......................... StephenDonohoe 3 74
(Sir Mark Prescott) *trckd ldrs: drvn over 3f out: upsides over 1f out: wknd fnl 75yds* **4/6[1]**

2m 38.9s (-2.10) **Going Correction** -0.05s/f (Stan) **5** Ran SP% **108.4**
Speed ratings (Par 103): **105,104,104,103,102**
CSF £114.47 TOTE £11.50: £3.70, £2.70; EX 36.40.
Owner I S Smith **Bred** S A Douch **Trained** Upper Lambourn, Berks

FOCUS
A decent handicap despite the small field and though the pace looked solid enough, the field remained tightly packed throughout and the result was in doubt until the last few strides. It is hard to rate the form any higher than this.
Valid Point(IRE) Official explanation: trainer's rep had no explanation for the poor form shown

6361 MEMBERSHIP OF SOUTHWELL GOLF CLUB H'CAP 7f (F)
5:20 (5:21) (Class 5) (0-75,75) 3-Y-O+ **£3,753** (£1,108; £554) **Stalls** Low

Form RPR
0303 1 **Salerosa (IRE)**[7] 6178 4-8-10 **64**.............................. SilvestreDeSousa 14 78
(Mrs A Duffield) *sn trcking ldrs: styd on to ld appr fnl f: hld on wl* **5/1[1]**
4400 2 1 **Hits Only Jude (IRE)**[24] 5675 6-9-6 **74**.............................. DNolan 1 85
(D Carroll) *w ldrs: led 2f out: hdd appr fnl f: no ex ins fnl f* **16/1**
4-12 3 3 1/2 **Ishiadancer**[34] 5332 4-8-13 **67**.. PhillipMakin 12 69
(E J Alston) *chsd ldrs: led over 2f out: sn hdd: kpt on same pce* **7/1[3]**
1445 4 1 3/4 **Restless Genius (IRE)**[97] 3268 4-8-8 **67**.......................... LanceBetts(5) 2 64
(B Ellison) *in tch: kpt on fnl 2f: nvr trbld ldrs* **14/1**
0401 5 1 1/2 **Defector (IRE)**[13] 5991 3-9-0 **71**.. GeorgeBaker 13 64
(W R Muir) *s.i.s: hdwy on outer to chse ldrs over 3f out: one pce fnl 2f* **13/2[2]**
4040 6 1 1/2 **Elusive Warrior (USA)**[28] 5544 6-8-8 **62** oh2 ow1...(p) RobertWinston 4 51
(A J McCabe) *rdn to ld: hdd 3f out: one pce* **8/1**
6346 7 1 1/2 **Jonny Lesters Hair (IRE)**[43] 5107 4-9-0 **68**.................. DuranFentiman 6 53
(T D Easterby) *chsd ldrs: one pce fnl 2f* **11/1**
2400 8 1/2 **Luckier (IRE)**[122] 2498 3-9-3 **74**.. EddieAhern 9 57
(S Kirk) *chsd ldrs: one pce fnl 2f* **28/1**
6421 9 5 **Ugenius**[10] 6123 5-8-12 **66**.. TGMcLaughlin 7 36
(Mrs C A Dunnett) *in rr and sn drvn along: nvr on terms* **7/1[3]**
0543 10 3 1/4 **Doric Echo**[12] 6014 3-9-0 **71**..(p) TomEaves 11 32
(B Smart) *s.i.s: a bhd* **12/1**
0300 11 1/2 **Ocean Legend (IRE)**[24] 5665 4-8-4 **65**..................(v) TobyAtkinson(7) 8 25
(Miss J Feilden) *s.i.s: a bhd* **8/1**
006 12 3/4 **Caledonia Princess**[111] 2826 3-9-1 **72**.................. GrahamGibbons 10 30
(R Curtis) *w ldrs: led 3f out: sn hdd & wknd* **16/1**
0400 13 1 3/4 **Game Lad**[23] 5697 7-9-7 **75**..(t) TedDurcan 5 28
(T D Easterby) *a in rr: bhd fnl 4f* **16/1**
1300 14 5 **Provost**[17] 5886 5-8-9 **63**.. DaleGibson 3 —
(M W Easterby) *s.s: a bhd* **50/1**

1m 29.41s (-0.89) **Going Correction** -0.05s/f (Stan)
WFA 3 from 4yo+ 3lb **14** Ran SP% **123.0**
Speed ratings (Par 103): **103,101,97,95,94 92,90,90,84,80 80,79,77,71**
toteswingers: 1&2 £22.00, 1&3 £6.10, 2&3 £20.90 CSF £89.44 CT £588.99 TOTE £6.00: £3.10, £3.50, £2.70; EX 97.50 TRIFECTA Not won. Place 6: £252.60 Place 5: £25.75 .
Owner David K Barker & Phil White **Bred** Pedro Rosas **Trained** Constable Burton, N Yorks

FOCUS
An ordinary handicap, but competitive nonetheless and the pace looked sound. The front pair came nicely clear with a clear personal best from the winner.
Caledonia Princess Official explanation: jockey said filly had no more to give
T/Jkpt: Not won. T/Plt: £365.40 to a £1 stake. Pool: £71,212.46. 142.26 winning tickets. T/Qpdt: £16.30 to a £1 stake. Pool: £5,719.06. 259.30 winning tickets. WG

5525 WARWICK (L-H)
Tuesday, September 29

OFFICIAL GOING: Good to firm (8.7)
Wind: Light half behind Weather: Fine

6362 BLUE SQUARE CASINO H'CAP 6f
2:10 (2:10) (Class 6) (0-65,69) 3-Y-O+ **£1,942** (£578; £288; £144) **Stalls** Low

Form RPR
301 1 **Abhainn (IRE)**[25] 5632 3-8-4 **51**.. DavidProbert 1 65
(B Palling) *mde all: rdn and edgd rt over 1f out: drvn out* **11/2[2]**
2412 2 1/2 **Ghost Dancer**[6] 6216 5-9-6 **65**..(p) RyanMoore 5 77
(J M Bradley) *t.k.h: trckd wnr: chalng whn rdn and edgd rt ins fnl f: nt qckn cl home* **8/13[1]**
4204 3 5 **Bold Ring**[10] 6120 3-8-13 **60**.. EdwardCreighton 7 56
(E J Creighton) *hld up in mid-div: pushed along and hdwy over 1f out: rdn and one pce fnl f* **20/1**
550 4 3 1/4 **Golden Dixie (USA)**[22] 5719 10-9-6 **65**.............................. LukeMorris 8 51
(R A Harris) *hld up in mid-div: rdn wl over 1f out: no imp fnl f* **20/1**
1042 5 1/2 **Green Velvet**[47] 4950 4-9-2 **61**.. TravisBlock 4 45
(P J Makin) *hld up in tch: rdn over 1f out: wknd ins fnl f* **16/1**
06-6 6 1 **Royal Manor**[270] 15 4-9-4 **63**.. RichardKingscote 10 44
(Tom Dascombe) *n.m.r s: hld up in rr: pushed along and effrt over 1f out: rdn and no prog fnl f* **11/1**
602 7 shd **Nativity**[14] 5971 3-8-10 **60**.. JackDean(3) 12 41
(J L Spearing) *hld up towards rr: pushed along over 2f out: no rspnse* **33/1**
0000 8 2 **Bahamian Ceilidh**[16] 5900 3-8-6 **53**.............................. WilliamBuick 9 27
(B N Pollock) *hld up towards rr: rdn over 1f out: no rspnse* **33/1**
4451 9 1 **Equipe De Nuit**[8] 6170 3-9-5 **69** 6ex.......................... WilliamCarson(3) 11 40
(S C Williams) *prom tl rdn and wknd wl over 1f out* **8/1[3]**
6060 10 8 **Blushing Maid**[19] 5809 3-8-9 **56**.. SteveDrowne 6 —
(H S Howe) *hld up in tch: rdn and wknd wl over 1f out* **40/1**

1m 10.19s (-1.61) **Going Correction** -0.225s/f (Firm) course record
WFA 3 from 4yo+ 2lb **10** Ran SP% **120.5**
Speed ratings (Par 101): **101,100,93,89,88 87,87,84,83,72**
toteswingers: 1&2 £2.70, 1&3 £12.70, 2&3 £5.80 CSF £9.04 CT £68.92 TOTE £6.00: £2.10, £1.02, £4.60; EX 14.20.
Owner H Perkins **Bred** Humphrey Okeke **Trained** Tredodridge, Vale Of Glamorgan

FOCUS
A surprise result, with the winner outbattling the odds-on favourite after the latter had looked the more likely winner entering the last furlong. The front pair were always 1-2 and the winner is rated back to his 2yo form.

6363 BLUE SQUARE E. B. F. MAIDEN FILLIES' STKS 7f 26y
2:40 (2:43) (Class 5) 2-Y-O **£4,094** (£1,209; £604) **Stalls** Low

Form RPR
25 1 **Subtefuge**[30] 5478 2-9-0 0.. TPQueally 7 80+
(H R A Cecil) *mde all: pushed along over 1f out: hung rt and rdn ins fnl f: r.o wl* **10/1**
2 3 **Rule Of Nature** 2-9-0 0.. RyanMoore 8 73+
(Sir Michael Stoute) *a.p: chsd wnr jst over 1f out: no imp* **5/2[2]**
3 1 3/4 **Cotton Top (IRE)** 2-8-11 0.. MCGeran(3) 2 68
(M R Channon) *chsd wnr: pushed along 2f out: rdn and lost 2nd jst over 1f out: one pce* **33/1**
2 4 2 1/2 **Lady Slippers (IRE)**[26] 5604 2-9-0 0.............................. SteveDrowne 4 62
(H J L Dunlop) *a.p: pushed along wl over 1f out: one pce* **11/2[3]**
4 5 2 **Red Fantasy (IRE)**[11] 6055 2-9-0 0.............................. MichaelHills 13 59+
(B W Hills) *s.i.s: sn hld up in mid-div: pushed along jst over 2f out: no hdwy* **7/4[1]**
0 6 3/4 **Antoella (IRE)**[42] 5129 2-9-0 0.. ShaneKelly 5 55+
(Ian Williams) *s.i.s: sn hld up in tch: rdn and wknd over 1f out* **100/1**
7 1 1/4 **Extreme Green** 2-9-0 0.. DavidProbert 9 54+
(A M Balding) *s.i.s: hld up towards rr: swtchd rt over 2f out: pushed along wl over 1f out: nvr nr ldrs* **22/1**
0 8 2 **Red Intrigue (IRE)**[26] 5605 2-9-0 0.............................. JimCrowley 3 52+
(Mrs A J Perrett) *s.i.s: sn hld up in mid-div: sme hdwy on ins over 2f out: rdn whn lost action over 1f out: eased ins fnl f* **8/1**
0 9 hd **Albeed**[59] 4542 2-9-0 0.. TPO'Shea 11 50+
(J L Dunlop) *hld up in rr: pushed along 2f out: nvr nr ldrs* **28/1**
0 10 nk **Spring Heather (IRE)**[14] 5966 2-9-0 0.......................(t) RichardMullen 12 46
(J L Dunlop) *pushed along over 2f out: a in rr* **50/1**
0 11 2 1/2 **Areeg (IRE)**[37] 5284 2-9-0 0.. AlanMunro 14 40
(W Jarvis) *rdn over 2f out: a in rr* **100/1**

12 *13* **Zazy's Gift** 2-9-0 0 DO'Donohoe 1 7
(George Baker) *s.i.s: a in rr* **100/1**
1m 24.72s (0.12) **Going Correction** -0.075s/f (Good) **12** Ran SP% **116.2**
Speed ratings (Par 92): **96,92,90,87,85 84,83,80,80,80 77,62**
toteswingers: 1&2 £22.10, 1&3 £5.30, 2&3 £30.60 CSF £33.40 TOTE £10.00: £2.00, £1.50, £4.70; EX 44.80.
Owner Dr Catherine Wills **Bred** St Clare Hall Stud **Trained** Newmarket, Suffolk

FOCUS
The pace was ordinary, and there were few position changes. Consequently, the first four were prominent throughout and nothing got into it from behind. Much-improved form from the winner.

NOTEBOOK
Subtefuge had learnt from her two previous races, and the switch to front-running suited her. Her earlier form was nothing special, but she looks well suited by fast ground and is improving. (op 8-1)
Rule Of Nature, a white-faced Oasis Dream newcomer out of a well-related maiden, has winners in the family up to 1m. Although no match for the winner, she briefly threatened and will be a major contender in maiden company next time out. (op 3-1 tchd 7-2)
Cotton Top(IRE), a half-sister to three winners up to 1m1f on the Flat, including the hurdler Letham Island, made a promising debut. Her dam stayed 1m3f and it is likely that she will come into her own at 1m and just beyond as she matures. (op 66-1)
Lady Slippers(IRE) did not appear to improve on her debut, which had been on soft ground. However, she still ran well enough to suggest that her turn will come. (op 9-2 tchd 7-2)
Red Fantasy(IRE) did not live up to her first performance but she was poorly drawn and can do better. (op 2-1 tchd 9-4 and 5-2 in a place)
Antoella(IRE) was suited by the step up to 7f and ran much better than on her debut. She will be more at home in nurseries after one more run.
Red Intrigue(IRE) was in the process of running a decent race when hanging badly right in the straight, with Jim Crowley reporting that the bit had slipped. She should be good enough to win when handicapped. Official explanation: jockey said bit slipped through filly's mouth (op 17-2 tchd 9-1)

6364 BLUE SQUARE POKER E. B. F. MAIDEN STKS (C&G) 7f 26y
3:10 (3:11) (Class 5) 2-Y-O £3,561 (£1,059; £529; £264) Stalls Low

Form				RPR
4	1		**Landowner**[27] 5564 2-8-11 0 AhmedAjtebi(3) 9 (Saeed Bin Suroor) *mde all: pushed along over 1f out: edgd rt ins fnl f: r.o* **7/1**[3]	68
000	2	*1*	**Kilmanseck**[17] 5867 2-9-0 59 WilliamBuick 6 (Eve Johnson Houghton) *w wnr: rdn over 1f out: ev ch ins fnl f: nt qckn* **66/1**	65
04	3	*½*	**Sternlight (IRE)**[13] 6000 2-9-0 0 RichardMullen 1 (E S McMahon) *hld up in tch: edgd rt over 1f out: rdn and kpt on same pce fnl f* **2/1**[2]	64+
052	4	*½*	**Viking Dancer**[19] 5786 2-9-0 77 DavidProbert 5 (A M Balding) *a.p: rdn whn carried rt over 1f out: kpt on one pce ins fnl f* **4/6**[1]	63+
00	5	*11*	**Drubinca**[29] 5512 2-8-11 0 WilliamCarson(3) 4 (S C Williams) *hld up in last: rdn wl over 1f out: sn struggling* **100/1**	43+
00	6	*9*	**Avon Grounds**[6] 6214 2-8-11 0 (p) JackDean(3) 8 (J M Bradley) *s.i.s: hld up: pushed along over 3f out: struggling fnl 2f* **66/1**	13

1m 26.06s (1.46) **Going Correction** -0.075s/f (Good) **6** Ran SP% **109.8**
Speed ratings (Par 95): **88,86,86,85,73 62**
toteswingers: 1&2 £4.50, 1&3 £4.60, 2&3 £1.70 CSF £178.05 TOTE £4.60: £2.30, £6.40; EX 47.10.
Owner Godolphin **Bred** Compagnia Generale S R L **Trained** Newmarket, Suffolk

FOCUS
From a form point of view, the proximity of the runner-up, who had been beaten around a dozen lengths in three previous maidens, is worrying. However, the pace was slack and that undoubtedly contributed to the bunched finish. Probably not form to take at face value.

NOTEBOOK
Landowner broke well and was in the right position to kick off the home turn. While he has some way to go to reach the standard normally expected of his stable's juveniles, he deserves credit for his battling attitude. (op 9-2)
Kilmanseck appeared to step up hugely on previous efforts. However, the initial delight of his connections will be tempered to some extent by the fact that his opening mark of 59 looks likely to rise significantly following this. (op 40-1)
Sternlight(IRE) broke better than in his first two races and is gradually improving with experience. In theory he could probably win a weak maiden but nurseries look the safer option now he is handicapped. (op 11-4)
Viking Dancer's trainer was hopeful of a big run, so failing to reach the first three will have come as a disappointment. In previous races he has looked likely to be suited by a good gallop, so the pedestrian tempo here was against him. He should not be written off yet. (tchd 4-7 and 8-11)

6365 BLUE SQUARE GAMES H'CAP 1m 22y
3:40 (3:40) (Class 5) (0-75,74) 3-Y-O+ £2,914 (£867; £433; £216) Stalls Low

Form				RPR
1133	1		**Cheam Forever (USA)**[19] 5803 3-9-1 72 (v1) RichardKingscote 2 (R Charlton) *mde all: rdn wl over 1f out: r.o wl* **3/1**[2]	80
0051	2	*1 ½*	**Black Dahlia**[8] 6174 4-8-13 69 6ex FrederikTylicki(3) 1 (J A Glover) *chsd wnr: rdn and ev ch over 1f out: nt qckn ins fnl f* **9/4**[1]	74
5553	3	*2*	**Land Hawk (IRE)**[10] 6124 3-8-5 67 SimonPearce(5) 7 (J Pearce) *hld up in mid-div: pushed along and hdwy wl over 1f out: rdn and one pce ins fnl f* **13/2**	67
0030	4	*nk*	**Bere Davis (FR)**[12] 6015 4-8-13 71 AndrewHeffernan(5) 9 (P D Evans) *racd keenly: a.p: rdn wl over 1f out: one pce fnl f* **8/1**	70
6000	5	*4 ½*	**A Lot Of Red (IRE)**[10] 6112 3-8-3 60 oh13 (bt1) DavidProbert 3 (P J O'Gorman) *hld up towards rr: pushed along and effrt 3f out: rdn and wknd over 1f out* **33/1**	49
1362	6	*½*	**Diamond Daisy (IRE)**[12] 6023 3-9-1 72 SJCraine 4 (Mrs A Duffield) *hld up in tch: rdn wl over 1f out: wknd ent fnl f* **9/2**[3]	60
0050	7	*1 ¾*	**Apex**[8] 6168 8-8-12 70 RossAtkinson(5) 6 (M Hill) *hld up towards rr: sme prog on outside bnd 3f out: rdn and wknd wl over 1f out* **14/1**	54
20-0	8	*¾*	**Daniel Thomas (IRE)**[69] 4211 7-9-6 73 JimCrowley 8 (Mrs A L M King) *hld up in last: rdn wl over 1f out: no rspnse* **20/1**	55

1m 39.68s (-1.32) **Going Correction** -0.075s/f (Good)
WFA 3 from 4yo+ 4lb **8** Ran SP% **112.8**
Speed ratings (Par 103): **103,101,99,99,94 94,92,91**
toteswingers: 1&2 £2.40, 1&3 £3.30, 2&3 £3.90 CSF £9.87 CT £38.62 TOTE £3.80: £1.50, £1.60, £2.40; EX 11.70.
Owner H R H Sultan Ahmad Shah **Bred** Robert W McCann Et Al **Trained** Beckhampton, Wilts

FOCUS
For the fourth consecutive race, the money went to a front-runner. The race was not strong run but the form makes sense at face value.

Apex Official explanation: trainer said gelding finished sore behind

6366 BLUE SQUARE NURSERY (DIV I) 7f 26y
4:10 (4:10) (Class 5) (0-75,75) 2-Y-O £2,590 (£770; £385; £192) Stalls Low

Form				RPR
0036	1		**Green Earth (IRE)**[15] 5938 2-9-0 68 JimCrowley 6 (Mrs A J Perrett) *hld up in tch: rdn to ld jst ins fnl f: drvn out* **9/1**	74
2365	2	*1 ½*	**Ginger Grey (IRE)**[22] 5715 2-8-7 61 AlanMunro 3 (S A Callaghan, U.S.A) *hld up in mid-div: hdwy over 1f out: sn rdn: wnt 2nd wl ins fnl f: kpt on* **13/8**[1]	63
0234	3	*1 ½*	**Sir Bruno (FR)**[29] 5499 2-9-5 73 DavidProbert 9 (B Palling) *a.p: rdn to ld over 1f out: edgd rt and hdd jst ins fnl f: nt qckn* **6/1**[3]	72
204	4	*1 ¾*	**Memory And Magic (USA)**[19] 5808 2-9-1 69 PhilipRobinson 2 (C G Cox) *a.p: rdn over 1f out: one pce fnl f* **9/2**[2]	63
1400	5	*1 ¼*	**Danzoe (IRE)**[45] 5033 2-9-2 75 AndrewHeffernan(5) 8 (D Donovan) *hld up in mid-div: pushed along over 2f out: carried rt over 1f out: one pce fnl f* **11/1**	66
000	6	*¾*	**Expensive Legacy**[47] 4945 2-8-4 58 LukeMorris 1 (H J L Dunlop) *in rr: pushed along over 3f out: hrd rdn over 1f out: nvr trbld ldrs* **22/1**	47
000	7	*¾*	**Dead Womans Pass (IRE)**[23] 5693 2-7-5 52 oh4.. ShirleyTeasdale(7) 5 (N Wilson) *chsd ldr tl over 2f out: wkng whn edgd rt over 1f out* **66/1**	39
0400	8	*1 ¼*	**Carnaval Court (IRE)**[13] 5985 2-8-8 62 WilliamBuick 4 (A M Balding) *bhd: pushed along over 3f out: rdn and struggling 2f out* **15/2**	46
4033	9	*¾*	**Little Brazilien**[22] 5714 2-8-10 64 MartinDwyer 7 (P F I Cole) *reminders after 1f: pushed along over 3f out: a in rr* **14/1**	48
0002	10	*½*	**Lairy (IRE)**[14] 5967 2-7-12 52 oh5 JamieMackay 10 (M F Harris) *led: hdd over 1f out: sn rdn: eased whn btn ins fnl f* **40/1**	38+

1m 24.08s (-0.52) **Going Correction** -0.075s/f (Good) **10** Ran SP% **115.6**
Speed ratings (Par 95): **99,97,95,93,92 91,90,89,88,87**
toteswingers: 1&2 £6.20, 1&3 £6.60, 2&3 £3.90 CSF £23.50 CT £99.94 TOTE £12.00: £3.80, £1.40, £2.00; EX 29.70.
Owner The Green Dot Partnership **Bred** Woodcote Stud Ltd **Trained** Pulborough, W Sussex
■ Stewards' Enquiry : William Buick two-day ban: used whip when out of contention (Oct 15-16)

FOCUS
By far the strongest gallop on the round course to date, with the winner not making all this time. The form looks straightforward with a step forward from the winner.

NOTEBOOK
Green Earth(IRE) had shaped well in four previous races and he gets this trip well, with the testing tempo suiting him ideally. He should stay further as he matures. (op 17-2 tchd 8-1)
Ginger Grey(IRE) has now raced 11 times without success and the funds of his regular supporters will be getting dangerously low by now. However, he continues to run well and it is hard to believe that his trainer will be unable to find the right race for him. (op 11-4)
Sir Bruno(FR) made an encouraging nursery debut, and this sort of mark should be about right with a bit more experience. His maiden form showed he has what it takes to win races. (op 7-1 tchd 15-2)
Memory And Magic(USA), stepping up a furlong for this first try in handicap company, ran well enough to suggest that the right opportunity will come along. (op 7-2 tchd 5-1)
Danzoe(IRE) was trying a longer trip and seemed to stay it well enough, if remaining short of his best. (tchd 13-2)
Expensive Legacy had achieved nothing in maidens, but this was a little more promising, and she may do even better at 1m. (op 18-1)
Lairy(IRE) went off plenty quick enough and ran himself into the ground. Official explanation: jockey said gelding was unsuited by the good to firm ground (tchd 33-1)

6367 BLUE SQUARE NURSERY (DIV II) 7f 26y
4:40 (4:41) (Class 5) (0-75,73) 2-Y-O £2,590 (£770; £385; £192) Stalls Low

Form				RPR
5455	1		**Pintura**[16] 5913 2-9-5 71 SamHitchcott 2 (M R Channon) *hld up in tch: rdn over 1f out: r.o u.p to ld cl home* **13/8**[1]	73
0500	2	*shd*	**Creevy (IRE)**[15] 5935 2-8-2 54 DavidProbert 7 (S Kirk) *a.p: wnt 2nd 3f out: rdn to ld jst over 1f out: hdd cl home* **25/1**	56
4050	3	*1 ¼*	**Hellenio**[13] 5985 2-8-8 60 WilliamBuick 8 (S C Williams) *led: rdn and hdd jst over 1f out: no ex towards fin* **12/1**	59
0061	4	*nse*	**Truly Magic**[15] 5935 2-8-9 61 RichardMullen 6 (H J L Dunlop) *hld up towards rr: hdwy wl over 1f out: pushed along whn nt clr run and swtchd rt wl ins fnl f: kpt on* **15/2**	60
0060	5	*2 ¾*	**Greek Key (IRE)**[21] 5748 2-9-2 68 JamieSpencer 3 (M L W Bell) *s.i.s: t.k.h: sn mid-div: hdwy over 1f out: hung rt n.m.r ins fnl f: eased whn hld towards fin* **11/2**[3]	62+
5006	6	*¾*	**Queen's Hawk**[22] 5715 2-9-1 67 TPQueally 5 (D J Coakley) *hld up towards rr: pushed along and sme prog over 1f out: rdn and no imp ins fnl f* **9/2**[2]	57
000	7	*3 ½*	**Rosiliant (IRE)**[15] 5934 2-9-0 66 PhilipRobinson 1 (C G Cox) *chsd ldr to 3f out: sn pushed along: wknd over 1f out* **10/1**	47
0000	8	*3*	**Gulf Punch**[6] 6215 2-7-12 50 oh2 (p) JamieMackay 9 (M F Harris) *hld up towards rr: pushed along 2f out: no rspnse* **50/1**	24
006	9	*nse*	**Red Eddie**[19] 5785 2-8-11 63 MartinDwyer 10 (B J Meehan) *hld up in mid-div: pushed along 3f out: wkng whn hmpd wl over 1f out* **16/1**	36
120	10	*5*	**Decree Absolute (USA)**[58] 4565 2-9-7 73 PaulFitzsimons 4 (Miss J R Tooth) *s.i.s: pushed along over 2f out: a in rr* **20/1**	34

1m 25.59s (0.99) **Going Correction** -0.075s/f (Good) **10** Ran SP% **116.7**
Speed ratings (Par 95): **91,90,89,89,86 85,81,77,77,72**
toteswingers: 1&2 £10.10, 1&3 £6.50, 2&3 £26.80 CSF £53.87 CT £391.78 TOTE £2.30: £1.40, £6.70, £3.30; EX 50.70.
Owner R Bastian **Bred** Dulverton Equine **Trained** West Ilsley, Berks
■ Stewards' Enquiry : Jamie Spencer three-day ban + five deferred: careless riding (Oct 13-20)

FOCUS
Not as strong a pace as division one, and a significantly slower time. Straightforward and modest nursery form.

NOTEBOOK
Pintura has been running with credit all season, and he was good enough to a beat a largely modest-looking line-up, though a rise of more than 1-2lb for winning this would make things difficult. Connections felt the drop in grade helped following some good efforts in better company. (op 15-8 tchd 2-1)
Creevy(IRE)'s previous form had been uninspiring, and this was a big improvement. She is much more comfortable in handicaps, but there was not a great deal behind. (op 22-1)
Hellenio tried to pull off the front-running trick employed to such good effect earlier in the day, setting a less frenetic tempo than seen in the previous race. Though he was run out of it in the end, this trip suits him best at present. (tchd 14-1)
Truly Magic ◆ was unlucky in failing to get a run between the three ahead of her and would have made her presence felt had she found one. Much improved when stepped up to this trip on her nursery debut, she is one to note next time. (op 6-1 tchd 5-1)

Greek Key(IRE) did not have the best of fortune late on, with Spencer easing him down when out of the places, but he was not seriously unlucky. However, he did show some minor ability in maidens and is worth monitoring. Official explanation: jockey said colt hung right in closing stages (op 7-1 tchd 15-2)
Queen's Hawk is well exposed, and has yet to win a nursery. (tchd 4-1)
Red Eddie was hampered on this nursery debut, but he looked well beaten at the time.

6368 BLUE SQUARE H'CAP — 1m 6f 213y
5:10 (5:11) (Class 4) (0-85,84) 3-Y-0+ £5,180 (£1,541; £770; £384) Stalls Low

Form RPR
2603 1 **My Mate Max**[29] 5530 4-8-12 **68**..........(p) TPQueally 8 76
(R Hollinshead) *led: rdn and hdd over 2f out: rallied to ld wl ins fnl f: styd on* **9/2[3]**
124- 2 ½ **Spanish Conquest**[157] 6838 5-8-13 **69**..........(t) JamieSpencer 7 76
(P J Hobbs) *chsd ldr: led over 2f out: sn c to stands' rail: rdn over 1f out: hdd wl ins fnl f: nt qckn* **2/1[1]**
32-0 3 hd **Howdigo**[10] 6106 4-10-0 **84**.......... SteveDrowne 2 91+
(J R Best) *hld up: hdwy over 1f out: rdn and styd on same pce fnl f* **5/1**
1425 4 1¼ **Hawridge King**[16] 5917 7-9-4 **77**.......... JamesMillman(3) 3 82
(W S Kittow) *hld up in tch: rdn wl over 1f out: one pce ins fnl f* **4/1[2]**
3406 5 2 **Cry For The Moon (USA)**[17] 5876 3-8-10 **77**.......... JimCrowley 1 80
(Mrs A J Perrett) *stdd s: hld up in last: stdy prog over 4f out: rdn and btn over 1f out* **4/1[2]**
3m 22.63s (3.63) **Going Correction** -0.075s/f (Good)
WFA 3 from 4yo+ 11lb 5 Ran SP% **108.2**
Speed ratings (Par 105): **87,86,86,85,84**
CSF £13.40 TOTE £5.20: £2.20, £1.40; EX 12.60.
Owner Tim Leadbeater **Bred** Tim Leadbeater **Trained** Upper Longdon, Staffs

FOCUS
The field was soon racing in single file at two length intervals until stacking up half a mile from home. Following a modest tempo, the dash began off the home turn. It is doubtful the winner had to improve on this year's modest form.

6369 BLUE SQUARE AMATEUR RIDERS' H'CAP — 1m 2f 188y
5:40 (5:40) (Class 6) (0-60,61) 3-Y-0+ £1,873 (£581; £290; £145) Stalls Low

Form RPR
121 1 **Sceilin (IRE)**[42] 5122 5-11-0 **60**..........(t) MrSWalker 4 66+
(J Mackie) *hld up in tch: rdn wl over 1f out: r.o u.p to ld last strides* **5/2[1]**
1061 2 shd **Hurricane Thomas (IRE)**[7] 6183 5-10-5 **56** 6ex... MissPhillipaTutty(5) 2 62
(R A Fahey) *led: edgd rt over 1f out: sn rdn: hdd last strides* **5/1[2]**
2252 3 nk **Tivers Song (USA)**[7] 6183 5-9-10 **47** ow1..........(b) MissABevan(5) 14 52+
(John A Harris) *hld up towards rr: rdn and hdwy over 1f out: r.o u.p ins fnl f* **9/1**
2544 4 ½ **Location**[1] 6333 3-9-9 **51**.......... MissIsabelTompsett(3) 6 56
(P D Evans) *hld up towards rr: prog over 3f out: pushed along over 1f out: kpt on u.p ins fnl f* **12/1**
0/-0 5 1¼ **Akram (IRE)**[66] 4321 7-11-0 **60**..........(p) MrAJBerry 7 63
(Jonjo O'Neill) *hld up in tch: c to stands' rail wl over 1f out: sn rdn: one pce ins fnl f* **20/1**
1205 6 ½ **Gala Sunday (USA)**[31] 5438 9-10-11 **57**..........(bt) MissSBrotherton 3 59
(M W Easterby) *a.p: ev ch wl over 1f out: fdd ins fnl f* **10/1**
3535 7 ¾ **Strike Force**[10] 6126 5-10-4 **55**..........(p) MissALHutchinson(5) 15 55+
(Miss J Feilden) *hld up in rr: c v wd to stands' rail st: pushed along over 1f out: styd on ins fnl f: n.d* **14/1**
0020 8 ¾ **Cecina Marina**[7] 6183 6-9-7 **46** oh1.......... MrJHBrooke(7) 10 45
(Mrs K Walton) *prom: rdn over 1f out: wknd ins fnl f* **50/1**
0044 9 1 **Rehabilitation**[33] 5365 4-10-11 **57**..........(tp) MissGAndrews 1 54
(W R Swinburn) *s.i.s: sn hld up in mid-div: rdn jst over 1f out: no hdwy* **6/1[3]**
0044 10 ½ **Artreju (GER)**[39] 5211 6-9-13 **52**.......... MissKLoftus(7) 11 49
(P Butler) *hld up in rr: hdwy and rdn over 1f out: fdd ins fnl f* **33/1**
5003 11 ½ **Efidium**[7] 6183 11-10-8 **61** ow3.......... MrSebSpencer(7) 8 57
(N Bycroft) *hld up in rr: hdwy over 1f out: wknd ins fnl f* **16/1**
6000 12 hd **Corlough Mountain**[54] 4698 5-9-11 **48**.......... MissMBryant(5) 17 43
(P Butler) *hld up in mid-div: pushed along and btn over 1f out* **50/1**
0350 13 2¾ **Touch Of Style (IRE)**[19] 5790 5-10-1 **50**.......... MrJoshuaMoore(3) 5 41
(T D McCarthy) *hld up in mid-div: hdwy over 3f out: rdn and wknd wl over 1f out* **25/1**
004 14 6 **Bounty Reef**[25] 5628 3-9-0 **46**.......... MissHJones(7) 9 27
(P D Evans) *plld hrd: prom tl wknd 3f out* **50/1**
2m 21.35s (0.25) **Going Correction** -0.075s/f (Good)
WFA 3 from 4yo+ 7lb 14 Ran SP% **116.3**
Speed ratings (Par 101): **96,95,95,95,94 94,93,92,92,91 91,91,89,85**
toteswingers: 1&2 £4.10, 1&3 £5.00, 2&3 £6.70 CSF £12.27 CT £93.53 TOTE £2.70: £1.60, £1.80, £2.60; EX 16.50 Place 6: £203.68 Place 5: £160.54.
Owner W I Bloomfield **Bred** J S Bolger **Trained** Church Broughton , Derbys

FOCUS
The pace was just a medium one for an amateur riders' race. The form seems sound, if limited.
T/Plt: £162.10 to a £1 stake. Pool: £68,367.51. 307.86 winning tickets. T/Qpdt: £46.50 to a £1 stake. Pool: £3,378.92. 53.70 winning tickets. KH

6287 KEMPTON (A.W) (R-H)
Wednesday, September 30

OFFICIAL GOING: Standard
Wind: Light, across Weather: Fine

6370 KEMPTON.CO.UK CLASSIFIED CLAIMING STKS — 1m (P)
5:50 (5:50) (Class 6) 3-4-Y-0 £2,047 (£604; £302) Stalls High

Form RPR
5640 1 **King's Masque**[55] 4719 3-9-4 66.......... DarryllHolland 5 74
(W R Muir) *hld up in last quartet: taken to wd outside over 2f out: gd prog to ld and edgd rt jst over 1f out: sn jnd: r.o wl* **20/1**
562 2 nk **Berbice (IRE)**[22] 5758 4-9-12 67..........(b¹) RichardHughes 6 77
(S Donohoe, Ire) *hld up in midfield: cruising bhd ldrs over 2f out: prog to chal over 1f out: w wnr fnl f and sn clr of rest: nt qckn last 50yds* **9/2[1]**
3300 3 3 **Super Fourteen**[28] 5581 3-8-9 59 ow1.......... DaneO'Neill 8 57
(R Hannon) *trckd ldr: rdn to ld narrowly 2f out: hdd jst over 1f out: tightened up sn after but already outpcd: clung on to 3rd* **20/1**
3363 4 shd **Monashee Rock (IRE)**[29] 5544 4-9-4 66.......... AdamKirby 4 62
(Matthew Salaman) *mounted on crse: hld up in last pair: taken to wd outside 2f out: styd on fr over 1f out: nrly snatched 3rd* **12/1**
4434 5 1 **Red Suede Shoes**[40] 5223 3-9-8 67.......... TGMcLaughlin 7 68
(B R Millman) *dwlt and pushed up into midfield: plld out and hanging over 2f out: drvn and sme prog fr over 1f out: nvr gng pce to threaten* **9/1[3]**
0614 6 ½ **Jeremiah (IRE)**[32] 5429 3-9-6 67..........(p) JamesDoyle 9 65
(J G Portman) *trckd ldng trio: drvn 2f out: trying to cl whn n.m.r briefly over 1f out: wnt 3rd ins fnl f: btn and eased nr fin* **14/1**
3306 7 1¼ **Statute Book (IRE)**[13] 6024 3-8-13 70.......... EddieAhern 13 55
(S Kirk) *trckd ldng pair: mde dart for inner and looked dangerous 2f out: nt qckn over 1f out: fdd ins fnl f* **9/2[1]**
1353 8 nk **Diggeratt (USA)**[21] 5779 3-8-12 68..........(p) PaulHanagan 2 53
(R A Fahey) *trckd ldrs: hrd rdn and cl up 2f out: stl chsng 1f out: wknd* **9/2[1]**
6105 9 shd **Hector Spectre (IRE)**[13] 6031 3-9-0 67..........(v) TPQueally 10 55
(K M Prendergast) *hld up towards rr: pushed along over 2f out: chsd ldng gp and nt clr run briefly over 1f out: shuffled along and kpt on* **8/1[2]**
000 10 1½ **Charging Indian (IRE)**[13] 6015 3-8-8 69.......... FrankieMcDonald 12 45
(P T Midgley) *wl in tch in abt 6th: pushed along to cl on ldrs over 2f out: no imp over 1f out: fdd* **8/1[2]**
1300 11 3½ **Sapphire Rose**[69] 4224 3-8-8 59.......... RichardMullen 11 37
(J G Portman) *a in rr: rdn and struggling over 2f out* **40/1**
0060 12 2¾ **Solent Ridge (IRE)**[40] 5211 4-9-4 70.......... LPKeniry 14 37
(J S Moore) *led to 2f out: wknd jst over 1f out: eased* **14/1**
1240 13 4 **My Sweet Georgia (IRE)**[6] 6230 3-8-12 69.......... JackMitchell(3) 1 29
(Stef Liddiard) *dropped in fr wd draw and hld up last: rdn 3f out: no prog* **25/1**
1m 38.06s (-1.74) **Going Correction** -0.10s/f (Stan)
WFA 3 from 4yo 4lb 13 Ran SP% **123.6**
Speed ratings (Par 101): **104,103,100,100,99 99,97,97,97,95 92,89,85**
toteswingers: 1&2 £15.70, 1&3 £49.50, 2&3 £11.50 CSF £107.38 TOTE £23.80: £10.20, £2.00, £5.50; EX 136.20.Super Fourteen was claimed by Fred Carnis for £5,000.
Owner A Patrick, C Edginton & M Caddy **Bred** Deerfield Farm **Trained** Lambourn, Berks

FOCUS
This was an open contest and it was run at a sound pace, which produced a good winning time for the class. Not form to rate too positively with the runner-up probably the best guide.

6371 GROOMED TO PERFECTION, THE KIA SOUL CLASSIFIED STKS — 1m 3f (P)
6:20 (6:23) (Class 6) 3-Y-0+ £2,047 (£604; £302) Stalls High

Form RPR
0060 1 **Giant Sequoia (USA)**[57] 4625 5-9-7 55..........(t) EddieAhern 10 62+
(Jane Chapple-Hyam) *trckd ldrs: gng easily over 2f out: effrt to ld over 1f out and stl gng wl: rdn out fnl f* **7/2[1]**
0002 2 1½ **Sircozy (IRE)**[21] 5775 3-8-11 55.......... WilliamCarson(3) 11 59
(S C Williams) *settled in last quartet: rdn and prog fr 2f out: r.o to take 2nd last 150yds: no real imp on wnr* **5/1[3]**
0004 3 1¾ **Through The Forest (USA)**[21] 5775 3-9-0 54..........(p) AdamKirby 9 56
(W R Swinburn) *prom: trckd ldr 1/2-way: led wl over 2f out: drvn and hdd over 1f out: one pce and lost 2nd last 150yds* **9/2[2]**
0-03 4 ½ **Mr Plod**[18] 5873 4-9-7 51..........(v) StephenCarson 7 56
(Andrew Reid) *hld up in last quartet: effrt on outer over 2f out: styd on fr over 1f out: nvr gng pce to threaten* **16/1**
0024 5 nk **Royal Bet (IRE)**[44] 5113 3-9-0 52.......... HayleyTurner 4 55
(M L W Bell) *plld hrd: hld up in last pair: hanging whn asked for effrt over 2f out: prog over 1f out: styd on: no ch* **7/2[1]**
0-03 6 1¾ **Mojeerr**[8] 6184 3-9-0 50.......... RobertWinston 12 52
(A J McCabe) *trckd ldrs: effrt on inner to dispute 3rd 2f out: sn rdn and fnd nil: wknd fnl f* **12/1**
050 7 ½ **Head First**[32] 5435 3-9-0 50.......... RichardMullen 8 51
(W Jarvis) *hld up in 8th: prog 3f out: disp 3rd 2f out: sn outpcd u.p: wknd fnl f* **25/1**
0400 8 3¾ **Mediterranean Sea (IRE)**[14] 5988 3-9-0 54.......... PaulHanagan 3 45
(J R Jenkins) *awkward s: trckd ldrs: pushed along over 3f out: no real prog after: wknd over 1f out* **14/1**
0-60 9 1¾ **Pezula**[48] 4955 3-9-0 53.......... RobertHavlin 13 42
(R T Phillips) *trckd ldrs on inner: n.m.r over 2f out and then hmpd: no prog over 1f out* **33/1**
0060 10 6 **Luthien (IRE)**[47] 5011 3-9-0 55..........(p) RichardHughes 1 32
(A M Hales) *chsd ldr to 1/2-way: styd cl up: drvn over 2f out: lost pl wl over 1f out: wknd rapidly and eased* **12/1**
6000 11 3¾ **Bobble Rock (IRE)**[7] 6213 3-9-0 55.......... SebSanders 2 25
(J R Best) *hld up in last pair: pushed along on outer 4f out: no prog over 2f out: sn bhd* **33/1**
000 12 31 **Halcyon Princess (IRE)**[13] 6031 3-9-0 55..........(p) JerryO'Dwyer 14 —
(D G Bridgwater) *led to wl over 2f out: sn wknd and eased: t.o* **33/1**
2m 21.5s (-0.40) **Going Correction** -0.10s/f (Stan)
WFA 3 from 4yo+ 7lb 12 Ran SP% **119.9**
Speed ratings (Par 101): **97,95,94,94,94 92,92,89,88,84 81,58**
toteswingers: 1&2 £6.00, 1&3 £2.40, 2&3 £4.20 CSF £20.28 TOTE £4.10: £2.00, £1.80, £2.40; EX 31.50.
Owner Mrs Jane Chapple-Hyam **Bred** Strategy Bloodstock **Trained** Newmarket, Suffolk

FOCUS
This tight classified stakes was run at a fair pace and the form looks sound enough for the class, with the placed horses setting the standard.
Giant Sequoia(USA) ◆ Official explanation: trainer said, regarding apparent improvement in form, that this was the first time the gelding had run from her yard, and had shown improvement since having physiotherapy for a back problem.
Luthien(IRE) Official explanation: jockey said filly stopped quickly

6372 "BUY A £10,000 RACING POST BONUS YEARLING" MAIDEN AUCTION STKS — 7f (P)
6:50 (6:53) (Class 5) 2-Y-O £2,590 (£770; £385; £192) Stalls High

Form RPR
0 1 **Confucius Fortune (IRE)**[65] 4377 2-8-13 0.......... PatCosgrave 10 80+
(J R Boyle) *bmpd s: sn trckd ldrs: gd prog fr 2f out to ld over 1f out: rdn and r.o wl* **16/1**
2 2 1¼ **Indian Valley (USA)**[14] 5981 2-8-9 0.......... EddieAhern 8 73+
(Rae Guest) *cl up: trckd ldr over 2f out: poised to chal but wnr already scooted clr on inner: rdn and r.o to go 2nd ins fnl f: no ch to chal* **5/2[2]**
53 3 2½ **One Good Emperor (IRE)**[34] 5368 2-9-2 0.......... RobertWinston 11 74
(J R Best) *pressed ldr: led over 2f out and tried to kick on: hdd over 1f out: easily outpcd* **2/1[1]**
4 ¾ **Christmas Coming** 2-9-0 0.......... DaneO'Neill 2 70+
(D R C Elsworth) *s.s: rn green in last pair: taken to outer and effrt over 2f out: styd on steadily fnl 2f: nrst fin* **20/1**

5 ¾ **Soul Station (FR)** 2-8-11 0 RichardKingscote 14 65
(R Charlton) *trckd ldng pair on inner: effrt over 2f out: outpcd over 1f out: plugged on* **14/1**

03 6 ½ **Sir William Orpen**[20] 5801 2-8-7 0 ow1 JackMitchell(3) 13 63
(P M Phelan) *led to over 2f out: styd chsng ldrs: wknd fnl f* **7/1**[3]

0 7 1 **Tuscan Gold**[12] 6061 2-8-12 0 SebSanders 5 63
(Sir Mark Prescott) *late into paddock: wl in rr: pushed along fr over 2f out: kpt on steadily fnl 2f: nvr nr ldrs* **20/1**

8 ¾ **St Ignatius** 2-9-2 0 TPQueally 1 65
(R M Beckett) *trckd ldng pair on outer: rdn and hanging over 2f out: wknd over 1f out* **25/1**

9 1 ½ **Hot Chilli** 2-8-10 0 LPKeniry 4 55
(J R Fanshawe) *hld up in 8th: effrt on inner over 2f out: no prog over 1f out: sn wknd* **33/1**

0 10 2 ¾ **Saladin's Vow (USA)**[46] 5029 2-9-2 0 (b[1]) HayleyTurner 3 54
(G A Butler) *wl in rr: rdn and brief effrt on inner over 2f out: wknd over 1f out* **20/1**

11 1 ½ **Classical Piece (USA)** 2-8-13 0 EdwardCreighton 9 48+
(Mrs D J Sanderson) *tended to run green in midfield: shkn up over 2f out: wknd over 1f out* **40/1**

12 7 **Dormer Fleet** 2-8-11 0 RichardMullen 12 28
(J H M Gosden) *dwlt: sn pushed along in last: rn green and nvr a factor* **8/1**

13 17 **Treadingtheboards** 2-8-5 0 FrankieMcDonald 7 —
(Mouse Hamilton-Fairley) *dwlt: in tch 4f: wknd rapidly over 2f out: t.o* **66/1**

1m 26.42s (0.42) **Going Correction** -0.10s/f (Stan) **13 Ran SP% 123.1**
Speed ratings (Par 95): **93,91,88,87,87 86,85,84,82,79 77,69,50**
toteswingers: 1&2 £15.60, 1&3 £10.50, 2&3 £1.50 CSF £53.41 TOTE £27.40: £3.20, £1.40, £1.20; EX 123.90.

Owner Albert Kwok **Bred** M Ervine **Trained** Epsom, Surrey

FOCUS
A fair juvenile maiden, run at an ordinary pace. The placed horses set the level, which is fairly fluid.

NOTEBOOK
Confucius Fortune(IRE) showed the benefit of his debut experience at Windsor in July and shed his maiden tag on this first run since. He got squeezed at the start and had to come from a midfield position, but as the race got serious he hit top gear and was well on top at the finish. The extra furlong proved right up his street and he rates a useful prospect.

Indian Valley(USA) was perfectly positioned to strike when asked for maximum effort, but lacked the resolution of the winner. This sharper test may not have been totally in her favour, however, and she ought to learn again for the experience so can soon go one better. (op 9-4 tchd 2-1 and 11-4 in a place)

One Good Emperor(IRE)'s stable has been back among the winners of late and he was well backed. He was given every chance and got the longer trip well enough, but lacked the tactical speed of the first pair. A stronger pace would have helped, though, as he was keen early on. He now has the option of nurseries and certainly isn't one to give up on. (op 9-4 tchd 5-2)

Christmas Coming ◆, whose dam was a 7f 2yo winner and has already produced a triple winner at the distance, made a pleasing debut. He was clueless through the early parts, but stayed on very nicely from off the pace late in the day and looks one to be with next time out.

Soul Station(FR) raced handily from his decent draw and had his chance, but ultimately lost out through greenness. His stable's debutants are most often a lot sharper after their initial outings and he should get closer next time.

Sir William Orpen, another well drawn, did little to help his chances of lasting home by again refusing to settle. He is capable of making his mark as he becomes more streetwise. (op 15-2 tchd 6-1)

Tuscan Gold lacked the pace to land a telling blow, but this was far more encouraging and he will relish being sent over further in due course. He needs one more run for a mark. (op 25-1)

6373 DIGIBET NURSERY 1m (P)
7:20 (7:24) (Class 4) (0-85,82) 2-Y-O **£3,885** (£1,156; £577; £288) **Stalls High**

Form RPR

0622 1 **White Dart**[7] 6211 2-8-8 **69** CatherineGannon 7 79+
(M R Channon) *chsd ldr: rdn to cl and ld over 1f out: sn clr: 4 l up ins fnl f: in n.d after* **3/1**[2]

1364 2 2 **Jairzihno**[37] 5320 2-9-0 **78** MarcHalford(3) 10 82
(J R Best) *sn last: urged along and struggling 3f out: prog on outer 2f out: styd on wl to take 2nd last 100yds* **8/1**

4011 3 1 ¾ **Boquito (IRE)**[7] 6211 2-8-13 **74** 6ex JerryO'Dwyer 4 74
(Miss Amy Weaver) *hld up in 6th: drvn over 2f out and no prog: kpt on fnl f to take 3rd nr fin* **7/4**[1]

4614 4 ½ **Cool Valentine**[22] 5742 2-9-4 **79** WilliamBuick 8 78
(A M Balding) *cl up whn snatched up after 1f and dropped to 5th: rdn and effrt 2f out: disp 3rd ent fnl f but no ch: one pce* **7/2**[3]

0402 5 ½ **Flying Destination**[22] 5742 2-8-13 **74** ShaneKelly 9 72
(W J Knight) *chsd ldng pair: rdn over 2f out: no imp over 1f out: plugged on* **7/1**

000 6 1 **Beyond The City (USA)**[20] 5793 2-7-12 **59** DavidProbert 6 54
(R Hannon) *led at str pce: tried to kick on over 2f out: hdd & wknd over 1f out: lost 4 pls last 100yds* **16/1**

0413 7 7 **Arken Lad**[54] 4757 2-8-6 **67** (e[1]) JimmyQuinn 3 47
(D Donovan) *t.k.h on outer: chsd ldng trio: wknd over 2f out* **25/1**

1m 38.81s (-0.99) **Going Correction** -0.10s/f (Stan) **7 Ran SP% 116.9**
Speed ratings (Par 97): **100,98,96,95,95 94,87**
toteswingers: 1&2 £3.40, 1&3 £2.50, 2&3 £2.70 CSF £27.74 CT £53.79 TOTE £3.90: £2.30, £5.20; EX 26.10.

Owner Leon Crouch **Bred** Jeremy Gompertz **Trained** West Ilsley, Berks

■ Stewards' Enquiry : David Probert two-day ban: careless riding (Oct 14-15)

FOCUS
A competitive nursery in which the winner impressed.

NOTEBOOK
White Dart had finished second on his two previous outings and deservedly went one better in good style. He left it too late over C&D last time, but the more positive tactics did the trick and he reversed that form with Boquito. Indeed, if anything he really hit the front too soon here and also ran freely early on, so should really rate better than the bare margin. It wouldn't be surprising to see him follow up. (tchd 7-2)

Jairzihno posted an improved effort proving he gets the trip, but again looked a tricky ride. (op 9-1 tchd 10-1)

Boquito(IRE) was 6lb worse off with the winner under his penalty. He turned in a somewhat laboured display, however, and it looked a case of the outing coming too soon. (op 15-8 tchd 2-1)

Cool Valentine could only muster the same pace when it mattered in the home straight, but wasn't helped by being shuffled back early on and really wants more of an end-to-end gallop. (tchd 4-1)

Flying Destination was 3lb higher for this all-weather bow. He again hit a flat spot when asked for maximum effort and is another who likely wants more of a test over this trip. (op 6-1)

6374 DIGIBET.COM H'CAP 7f (P)
7:50 (7:51) (Class 4) (0-85,85) 3-Y-O+ **£4,727** (£1,406; £702; £351) **Stalls High**

Form RPR

2503 1 **Wigram's Turn (USA)**[25] 5665 4-9-7 **85** WilliamBuick 9 94
(A M Balding) *s.s: hld up in last: plenty to do whn plld out wd over 2f out: gd prog wl over 1f out: swept into ld last 75yds: decisively* **4/1**[1]

2413 2 1 **Sunshine Always (IRE)**[14] 5986 3-9-0 **81** KirstyMilczarek 6 87
(T D McCarthy) *t.k.h: hld up in 8th: stdy prog over 2f out: pushed into ld ins fnl f: hdd and outpcd last 75yds* **13/2**[3]

6020 3 1 ¼ **Gazboolou**[21] 5780 5-8-11 **75** EddieAhern 4 78
(David Pinder) *pressed ldr: narrow advantage 2f out: hdd and outpcd ins fnl f* **12/1**

3101 4 nk **Perfect Silence**[20] 5810 4-9-0 **78** (b) AdamKirby 12 80
(C G Cox) *trckd ldrs: effrt on inner over 2f out: drvn to try to chal over 1f out: outpcd fnl f* **9/2**[2]

254 5 nk **Sweet Gale (IRE)**[17] 5916 5-8-8 **72** JimCrowley 5 73
(Mike Murphy) *hld up in last pair: stdy prog over 2f out: rdn to cl on ldrs over 1f out: sn outpcd* **14/1**

0500 6 shd **Arabian Spirit**[11] 6092 4-9-5 **83** TGMcLaughlin 10 84
(E A L Dunlop) *chsd ldng pair: rdn over 2f out: kpt on same pce fr over 1f out: outpcd fnl f* **15/2**

3351 7 1 **Justonefortheroad**[16] 5954 3-8-8 **75** PaulHanagan 2 73
(R A Fahey) *wl in tch: effrt to chse ldrs 2f out: one pce after: outpcd fnl f* **13/2**[3]

2124 8 2 **Arabian Pearl (IRE)**[90] 3537 3-8-10 **77** AlanMunro 13 70
(P W Chapple-Hyam) *led: narrowly hdd 2f out: pressed ldr to jst over 1f out: wknd rapidly fnl f* **9/1**

50-6 9 1 ¼ **Carved Emerald**[170] 1268 4-9-7 **85** RobertHavlin 8 75
(D R C Elsworth) *wl in tch: effrt on inner over 2f out: no prog over 1f out: wknd fnl f* **33/1**

2040 10 1 ¾ **Makaam (USA)**[56] 4648 3-9-0 **81** TPO'Shea 7 66
(M P Tregoning) *chsd ldng pair: u.p over 2f out: sn lost pl and wknd* **7/1**

0050 11 shd **Silver Hotspur**[28] 5569 5-8-7 **76** SimonPearce(5) 14 61
(C R Dore) *awkward s: mostly in last trio: u.p wl over 2f out: no real prog* **25/1**

1m 25.46s (-0.54) **Going Correction** -0.10s/f (Stan)
WFA 3 from 4yo+ 3lb **11 Ran SP% 120.3**
Speed ratings (Par 105): **99,97,96,96,95 95,94,92,90,88 88**
toteswingers: 1&2 £3.40, 1&3 £30.00, 2&3 £13.80 CSF £30.77 CT £298.55 TOTE £5.70: £1.50, £2.30, £4.20; EX 32.50.

Owner David Brownlow **Bred** Lone Cedar Thoroughbred Holdings, Llc **Trained** Kingsclere, Hants

FOCUS
Not a bad handicap for the grade, run at a fair pace and the form looks sound with the third a pretty sound guide.

6375 DIGIBET MEDIAN AUCTION MAIDEN STKS 1m 4f (P)
8:20 (8:20) (Class 5) 3-5-Y-O **£2,590** (£770; £385; £192) **Stalls Centre**

Form RPR

4352 1 **Buckie Boy (IRE)**[14] 5987 3-9-3 68 TPQueally 8 86
(H R A Cecil) *dwlt and pushed along early to chse ldrs: effrt 3f out: led over 2f out and kicked on: styd on wl and in command fr over 1f out* **11/4**[2]

-044 2 2 ½ **Mubrook (USA)**[60] 4544 4-9-11 81 RichardHughes 13 82
(L M Cumani) *trckd ldrs on inner: pushed up to chal over 2f out: chsd wnr after: nt qckn and a hld fr over 1f out* **4/6**[1]

-220 3 10 **Storming Sioux**[56] 4655 3-8-12 67 LiamJones 11 61
(W J Haggas) *trckd ldrs: prog to go 2nd 3f out: upsides over 2f out: sn lft wl bhd by ldng pair* **7/1**[3]

4 6 **Summer Affair (IRE)**[298] 4-9-11 0 ShaneKelly 9 59+
(B I Case) *hld up in midfield: hmpd bhd wkng rival jst over 3f out whn trying to make prog: outpcd in 6th over 2f out: plugged on slowly* **66/1**

060 5 4 **Brandy Butter**[70] 4205 3-9-3 57 (v) WilliamBuick 12 49
(A M Balding) *sn last: detached and rdn 1/2-way: looked reluctant after: styd on u.p to pass toiling rivals fnl 2f* **20/1**

30 6 nk **Awani**[36] 5328 3-8-12 49 RichardKingscote 1 44
(E F Vaughan) *trckd ldng pair: prog to ld over 3f out: hdd & wknd rapidly over 2f out* **40/1**

0 7 1 ¼ **Dance Gdansk (IRE)**[14] 5987 3-9-3 0 SteveDrowne 7 46
(M Blanshard) *dwlt: nvr beyond midfield: outpcd fr over 3f out: no ch over 2f out* **66/1**

8 7 **Keepholdin (IRE)**[155] 4-9-11 0 EddieAhern 5 35
(N P Mulholland) *s.s: mostly in last trio: lft bhd fr over 3f out: no ch after* **66/1**

-664 9 ½ **Superior Duchess**[89] 3568 4-9-6 49 IvaMilickova 2 29
(Jane Chapple-Hyam) *wd bnd after 3f: a towards rr: outpcd fr over 3f out: sn bhd* **33/1**

10 8 **Grand Exit** 3-8-12 0 RobertWinston 4 16
(A J McCabe) *racd wd: chsd ldrs: wknd 3f out: sn wl bhd* **50/1**

6030 11 4 ½ **Sadaska**[43] 5131 3-8-9 44 WilliamCarson(3) 10 —
(S C Williams) *led to over 3f out: wknd rapidly: wl bhd over 1f out* **25/1**

000 12 29 **Hilltop Alchemy**[6] 6225 3-8-10 0 (v[1]) DannyBrock(7) 6 —
(J R Jenkins) *chsd ldr to 4f out: wknd rapidly: t.o* **66/1**

2m 31.54s (-2.96) **Going Correction** -0.10s/f (Stan)
WFA 3 from 4yo 8lb **12 Ran SP% 121.1**
Speed ratings (Par 103): **105,103,96,92,90 89,88,84,83,78 75,56**
toteswingers: 1&2 £1.30, 1&3 £2.70, 2&3 £2.30 CSF £4.69 TOTE £3.70: £1.10, £1.02, £2.50; EX 7.60.

Owner North South Partnership **Bred** John Kirby **Trained** Newmarket, Suffolk

■ Stewards' Enquiry : Danny Brock three-day ban: used whip when out of contention (Oct 14-16)

FOCUS
No strength in depth here and the two market leaders dominated and finished clear. The winner is the best guide to the form.

Mubrook(USA) Official explanation: jockey said gelding suffered interference in running

6376 BOOK KEMPTON TICKETS ON 0844 579 3008 H'CAP 1m 4f (P)
8:50 (8:51) (Class 5) (0-70,69) 3-Y-O **£2,590** (£770; £385; £192) **Stalls Centre**

Form RPR

0561 1 **Rowan Tiger**[14] 5988 3-8-12 **63** PatCosgrave 11 74+
(J R Boyle) *settled midfield: tightened up off bnd sn after 3f out: gd prog sn after: led over 1f out: drvn and styd on wl* **9/1**[3]

-111 2 1 ¼ **Arty Crafty (USA)**[4] 6289 3-8-12 **63** 6ex SebSanders 8 70
(Sir Mark Prescott) *trckd ldrs: pushed along over 3f out: hrd rdn to try to cl fr over 2f out: kpt on to take 2nd ins fnl f* **4/5**[1]

3561 **3** *1* **Ebony Eyes**[21] 5782 3-9-4 **69** JimCrowley 10 74+
(W J Knight) *hld up in last pair: c wd bnd over 3f out: prog on outer over 2f out: styd on wl fnl f to snatch 3rd last stride* **10/1**
2202 **4** *1/2* **Sumani (FR)**[23] 5726 3-9-0 **65** DarryllHolland 13 70
(S Dow) *led: hrd rdn 2f out: hdd over 1f out: rdr dropped whip sn after: one pce* **11/1**
5063 **5** *3/4* **Silver Print (USA)**[27] 5616 3-9-3 **68** AdamKirby 5 71
(W R Swinburn) *mostly pressed ldr: chal fr 3f out: nt qckn 2f out: one pce fr over 1f out* **8/1**[2]
5050 **6** *6* **Supernoverre (IRE)**[12] 6075 3-9-2 **67** IanMongan 7 61
(P Howling) *hld up towards rr: lost pl and in last pair wl over 2f out: sme prog wl over 1f out: fdd fnl f* **25/1**
4000 **7** *2* **Millway Beach (IRE)**[28] 5570 3-8-13 **64** (p) RobertWinston 2 55
(Pat Eddery) *towards rr: rdn and hanging over 2f out: no real prog and n.d after* **25/1**
0001 **8** *3* **Inconspicuous Miss (USA)**[13] 6031 3-8-13 **69** MatthewDavies(5) 6 55
(George Baker) *dwlt: hld up in last: brought v wd bnd over 3f out: sn no prog and btn* **25/1**
6636 **9** *1 3/4* **Lake Kalamalka (IRE)**[48] 4948 3-9-4 **69** EddieAhern 9 52
(J L Dunlop) *chsd ldrs: rdn in 5th over 3f out: wknd rapidly over 2f out: eased fnl f* **25/1**
006 **10** *3 1/4* **Colangnik (USA)**[4] 6289 3-9-4 **69** SteveDrowne 14 47
(J R Best) *cl up on inner: lost pl over 3f out: wknd tamely over 2f out* **25/1**
0146 **11** *1/2* **Haafhd Time (IRE)**[28] 5570 3-8-10 **61** RichardKingscote 12 38
(Tom Dascombe) *prom on inner: rdn and lost pl over 3f out: wknd rapidly over 2f out* **12/1**

2m 32.13s (-2.37) **Going Correction** -0.10s/f (Stan) **11** Ran SP% **121.0**
Speed ratings (Par 101): **103,102,101,101,100 96,95,93,92,90 89**
toteswingers: 1&2 £4.00, 1&3 £21.70, 2&3 £5.40 CSF £16.01 CT £74.77 TOTE £12.80: £2.70, £1.30, £2.50; EX 28.50.
Owner Rowan Stud Partnership 1 **Bred** Rowan Farm Stud **Trained** Epsom, Surrey

FOCUS
This moderate handicap was run at an ordinary pace. The first five came clear though and the form appears sound.
Lake Kalamalka(IRE) Official explanation: trainer's rep said, regarding running, that the filly had had a long season

6377 SPONSOR AT KEMPTON H'CAP 6f (P)
9:20 (9:21) (Class 6) (0-60,60) 3-Y-O+ £2,047 (£604; £302) Stalls High

Form RPR
0600 **1** **Sam's Cross (IRE)**[17] 5918 4-9-0 **59** MCGeran(3) 12 67
(J J Bridger) *in tch in midfield: prog wl over 1f out: sustained effrt to ld last 150yds: hung lft but hld on* **10/1**
3450 **2** *nk* **Peopleton Brook**[7] 6205 7-9-4 **60** (t) SteveDrowne 2 67
(B G Powell) *hld up in rr fr wd draw: prog and threaded through fr over 1f out: wnt 2nd wl ins fnl f: clsd on wnr fin* **12/1**
-000 **3** *1 3/4* **Embra (IRE)**[14] 5978 4-9-3 **59** GregFairley 5 60
(T J Etherington) *stdd s: t.k.h and hld up: effrt on outer 2f out: styd on fnl f to snatch 3rd on post* **16/1**
4032 **4** *shd* **Rosie Says No**[28] 5576 4-9-4 **60** (p) JimCrowley 6 61
(R M H Cowell) *chsd ldr to 1/2-way: sn rdn: styd pressing to 1f out: kpt on* **11/4**[1]
6003 **5** *nk* **Namu**[2] 6340 6-9-3 **59** (p) DaneO'Neill 11 59
(Miss T Spearing) *dwlt: hld up in rr: effrt on inner 2f out: nvr quite on terms w ldrs but styng on at fin* **6/1**
354 **6** *hd* **Desert Pride**[76] 4023 4-9-3 **59** (v) IanMongan 9 58
(W S Kittow) *prom: chsd ldr 1/2-way: chal on inner fr 2f out: nt qckn 1f out: one pce* **11/2**[3]
000 **7** *nk* **Kelamon**[53] 4787 5-9-2 **58** AdamKirby 10 57
(S C Williams) *led at str pce: kpt on whn pressed 2f out: hdd last 150yds: lost several pls after* **7/1**
5065 **8** *hd* **Chris's Jem**[23] 5724 3-9-2 **60** EddieAhern 4 58
(J R Jenkins) *chsd ldng trio: rdn 2f out: one pce and no imp ent fnl f: lost pls nr fin* **25/1**
0334 **9** *hd* **Guildenstern (IRE)**[11] 6123 7-9-4 **60** JimmyQuinn 7 57
(P Howling) *hld up in last pair: effrt on outer 2f out: styd on fnl f to join main bunch nr fin* **9/2**[2]
3U06 **10** *shd* **Pinball (IRE)**[18] 5877 3-8-13 **60** (v) AndreaAtzeni(3) 3 57
(Mrs L Williamson) *hld up in tch and keen early: tried to cl on ldrs fr 2f out: nt qckn over 1f out: one pce* **25/1**
-012 **11** *nk* **Connor's Choice**[26] 5633 4-8-13 **60** SimonPearce(5) 1 56
(Andrew Turnell) *racd wd to 1/2-way and t.k.h early: wnt prom over 3f out: nt qckn wl over 1f out: fading nr fin* **10/1**
046 **12** *7* **Keibla Spirit**[22] 5747 3-9-2 **60** RobertHavlin 8 34
(R Ingram) *stdd s: plld hrd and hld up: wknd over 2f out: b.b.v* **40/1**

1m 12.74s (-0.36) **Going Correction** -0.10s/f (Stan) **12** Ran SP% **128.9**
WFA 3 from 4yo+ 2lb
Speed ratings (Par 101): **98,97,95,95,94 94,94,93,93,93 93,83**
toteswingers: 1&2 £47.00, 1&3 £38.50, 2&3 £51.90 CSF £132.43 CT £1972.58 TOTE £14.60: £4.60, £4.30, £7.50; EX 248.50 Place 6: £42.66, Place 5: £11.00.
Owner J J Bridger **Bred** Gainsborough Stud Management Ltd **Trained** Liphook, Hants

FOCUS
With merely 2lb covering the entire field this was more like a classified event. Not that surprisingly there was a bunched finish behind the first pair, and they look the best guides.
Keibla Spirit Official explanation: jockey said filly had bled from the nose
T/Plt: £59.00 to a £1 stake. Pool: £67,563.28. 835.33 winning tickets. T/Qpdt: £8.60 to a £1 stake. Pool: £8,048.46. 685.44 winning tickets. JN

5727 NEWCASTLE (L-H)
Wednesday, September 30

OFFICIAL GOING: Good to firm (7.6)
Wind: Fairly strong, across Weather: Cloudy

6378 E.B.F./CAPE HADDIE MAIDEN FILLIES' STKS 6f
1:40 (1:46) (Class 5) 2-Y-O £3,784 (£1,132; £566; £283; £141) Stalls High

Form RPR
63 **1** **Wishbone (IRE)**[31] 5478 2-9-0 0 JamieSpencer 4 78+
(M G Quinlan) *trckd ldrs gng wl: smooth hdwy over 1f out: shkn up and led ins fnl f: comf* **4/9**[1]
3604 **2** *1 1/2* **Brinscall**[13] 6009 2-9-0 72 TonyHamilton 2 70
(R A Fahey) *cl up: drvn over 2f out: led over 1f out to ins fnl f: no ch w wnr* **9/2**[2]
04 **3** *6* **Timeless Elegance (IRE)**[26] 5620 2-9-0 0 PhillipMakin 1 52
(J Howard Johnson) *t.k.h: led to over 1f out: wknd ins fnl f* **66/1**
50 **4** *1* **Hedgerow (IRE)**[52] 4817 2-9-0 0 DanielTudhope 6 49
(A Dickman) *bhd: rdn 1/2-way: sme hdwy over 1f out: nvr on terms* **16/1**
506 **5** *1 3/4* **Love And Devotion**[33] 5380 2-8-11 67 AhmedAjtebi(3) 5 44
(Saeed Bin Suroor) *cl up tl rdn and wknd over 1f out* **8/1**[3]
6 *8* **Path Of Peace** 2-9-0 0 JoeFanning 7 20
(J D Bethell) *hld up in tch: shkn up over 2f out: wknd wl over 1f out* **28/1**

1m 17.03s (1.83) **Going Correction** +0.225s/f (Good) **6** Ran SP% **109.4**
Speed ratings (Par 92): **96,94,86,84,82 71**
toteswingers: 1&2 £1.02, 1&3 £9.20, 2&3 £11.00 CSF £2.58 TOTE £1.50: £1.10, £1.90; EX 2.90 Trifecta £17.70 Pool: £454.18 - 18.89 winning units..
Owner G Morrin **Bred** Anthony Kirwan **Trained** Newmarket, Suffolk

FOCUS
A maiden lacking strength in depth and the pace was ordinary. Straightforward form.

NOTEBOOK
Wishbone(IRE) ◆ had shown ability in both starts before this and didn't have to improve to get off the mark. She should continue to progress in nurseries and this strong traveller can win again. (op 4-6)
Brinscall, having her second start for Richard Fahey, showed a similar contest should be within her grasp. She looks straightforward and might improve when upped to 7f. (op 4-1 tchd 5-1)
Timeless Elegance(IRE) took a hold in front and didn't get home. She might do better in modest handicaps next year. (op 50-1)
Hedgerow(IRE) did some good late work and is another who might do better in modest handicaps next year. (tchd 14-1)
Love And Devotion was disappointing. She is clearly going the wrong way and looks one to have reservations about. (op 15-2)

6379 NUA PURE IRISH DRIPPING H'CAP (DIV I) 5f
2:10 (2:10) (Class 6) (0-60,60) 3-Y-O+ £1,748 (£520; £260; £129) Stalls High

Form RPR
0530 **1** **Rio Sands**[7] 6220 4-9-1 **56** DO'Donohoe 10 66
(R M Whitaker) *prom: nt clr run over 2f out to over 1f out: led 1f out: drvn out* **9/1**
4060 **2** *1/2* **Ursus**[23] 5729 4-8-12 **53** ow1 (p) PhillipMakin 7 61
(C R Wilson) *hld up in tch: hdwy over 1f out: chsd wnr ins fnl f: r.o* **5/1**[3]
6000 **3** *1 1/4* **Star Addition**[46] 5041 3-8-4 **46** oh1 DuranFentiman 2 50
(E J Alston) *hld up: hdwy over 1f out: kpt on fnl f: nrst fin* **80/1**
0352 **4** *1/2* **Comptonspirit**[13] 6038 5-9-5 **60** J-PGuillambert 9 62
(B P J Baugh) *cl up: rdn to ld briefly appr fnl f: one pce ins fnl f* **7/2**[2]
0056 **5** *1 1/2* **Kheylide (IRE)**[7] 6220 3-9-0 **59** (p) DominicFox(3) 4 55
(Mrs D J Sanderson) *prom on outside: drvn over 2f out: one pce over 1f out* **11/1**
5504 **6** *4* **Rainbow Bay**[7] 6216 6-8-0 **46** oh1 (p) AndrewHeffernan(5) 5 28
(Miss Tracy Waggott) *cl up: drvn and outpcd 2f out: no imp fnl f* **7/1**
3100 **7** *2 1/2* **Princess Charlmane (IRE)**[23] 5729 6-8-13 **54** (p) DNolan 8 27
(C J Teague) *led tl rdn and hdd appr fnl f: wknd ins fnl f* **11/1**
0304 **8** *1* **Bees River (IRE)**[35] 5341 3-8-1 **48** MartinLane(5) 1 17
(A P Jarvis) *prom on outside: rdn over 2f out: wknd over 1f out* **12/1**
5003 **9** *4* **Thunder Bay**[7] 6220 4-8-7 **53** (b[1]) BMcHugh(5) 6 8
(R A Fahey) *cl up: rdn over 2f out: wknd wl over 1f out* **10/3**[1]
0-00 **10** *11* **Take That**[37] 5309 4-8-5 **46** oh1 AdrianTNicholls 3 —
(S P Griffiths) *t.k.h: hld up: rdn over 2f out: wknd wl over 1f out: t.o* **66/1**

63.10 secs (2.40) **Going Correction** +0.225s/f (Good)
WFA 3 from 4yo+ 1lb **10** Ran SP% **111.6**
Speed ratings (Par 101): **89,88,86,85,83 76,72,71,64,47**
toteswingers: 1&2 £7.40, 1&3 £12.50, 2&3 £62.30 CSF £51.16 CT £3373.83 TOTE £10.20: £3.10, £1.90, £9.60; EX 70.60 TRIFECTA Not won..
Owner Barry & The Barflys **Bred** Hellwood Farm And J B Pemberton **Trained** Scarcroft, W Yorks

FOCUS
A modest sprint handicap, which was run at a sound pace on the stands' side, and very few got into it from behind. The form is not that solid and the fourth looks the best guide.
Rio Sands Official explanation: trainer had no explanation for the apparent improvement in form shown
Thunder Bay Official explanation: trainer had no explanation for the poor form shown

6380 NUA PURE IRISH DRIPPING H'CAP (DIV II) 5f
2:40 (2:40) (Class 6) (0-60,60) 3-Y-O+ £1,748 (£520; £260; £129) Stalls High

Form RPR
0603 **1** **Revue Princess (IRE)**[9] 6161 4-9-5 **60** (b) DavidAllan 10 70
(T D Easterby) *cl up: effrt over 1f out: led ins fnl f: rdn and flashed tail: r.o wl* **3/1**[1]
300- **2** *2* **Tanley**[295] 7618 4-8-11 **52** MickyFenton 2 55
(J F Coupland) *led: crossed to stands' rail after 1f: rdn over 1f out: hdd ins fnl f: kpt on same pce* **12/1**
6050 **3** *1* **Green Poppy**[7] 6220 3-8-12 **54** PhillipMakin 9 59+
(B Smart) *hld up: no room fr 1/2-way: hdwy and squeezed through ins fnl f: r.o strly* **15/2**
6202 **4** *hd* **Dalarossie**[9] 6160 4-9-0 **55** DuranFentiman 8 53
(E J Alston) *hld up in tch: hdwy over 1f out: no imp fnl f* **10/3**[2]
6300 **5** *1/2* **Town House**[7] 6220 7-7-12 **46** oh1 BillyCray(7) 6 42
(B P J Baugh) *hld up: hdwy over 1f out: kpt on same pce fnl f* **20/1**
0406 **6** *2* **Foreign Rhythm (IRE)**[7] 6216 4-8-5 **46** (p) DO'Donohoe 1 35
(N Tinkler) *s.i.s: hld up: hdwy whn nt clr run over 1f out: rdn and no imp fnl f* **20/1**
2104 **7** *2* **Darcy's Pride (IRE)**[7] 6220 5-9-2 **57** (t) TonyHamilton 4 39
(P T Midgley) *chsd ldrs: rdn over 2f out: wknd over 1f out* **5/1**[3]
00-5 **8** *1/2* **Bettys Touch**[23] 5727 4-8-0 **46** oh1 PaulPickard(5) 7 26
(K G Reveley) *s.i.s: hld up: effrt on outside over 2f out: no imp over 1f out* **8/1**
0040 **9** *1/2* **Bahamian Ballad**[33] 5396 4-8-7 **48** (v) JoeFanning 3 26
(J D Bethell) *chsd ldrs tl rdn and wknd over 1f out* **12/1**
0000 **10** *2 1/2* **Handcuff**[13] 6010 3-7-11 **46** oh1 (b[1]) JamesPSullivan(7) 5 15
(I Semple) *prom: rdn over 2f out: edgd lft and wknd over 1f out* **33/1**

61.70 secs (1.00) **Going Correction** +0.225s/f (Good)
WFA 3 from 4yo+ 1lb **10** Ran SP% **115.5**
Speed ratings (Par 101): **101,97,96,95,95 91,88,87,87,83**
toteswingers: 1&2 £24.90, 1&3 £4.30, 2&3 £26.00 CSF £38.10 CT £252.41 TOTE £3.20: £1.70, £4.90, £2.50; EX 45.50 Trifecta £254.10 Part won. Pool: £343.39 - 0.46 winning units..
Owner S A Heley **Bred** Raymond Shanahan **Trained** Great Habton, N Yorks

FOCUS
The second division of the sprint handicap was run well over a second quicker than the first and the form has been rated at face value.

Foreign Rhythm(IRE) ◆ Official explanation: jockey said filly was denied a clear run

6381 E.B.F./BIOBOX MAIDEN STKS (C&G) 6f
3:15 (3:15) (Class 4) 2-Y-O £5,051 (£1,503; £751; £375) Stalls High

Form RPR
5 1 **The Only Boss (IRE)**[14] 6000 2-9-0 0 JamieSpencer 1 74+
(W J Haggas) *set stdy pce: mde all: drew clr on bit appr fnl f: v easily* 4/11[1]
0 2 3 3/4 **Sixties Rock**[12] 6046 2-9-0 0 TonyHamilton 4 51
(J A Glover) *plld hrd: chsd ldrs: effrt and wnt 2nd over 1f out: no ch w wnr* 9/1[3]
06 3 3 **Anna's Boy**[42] 5157 2-9-0 0 PhillipMakin 5 42
(A Berry) *hld up: rdn over 2f out: plugged on fnl f: n.d* 33/1
4 9 **Honest Broker (IRE)** 2-9-0 0 JoeFanning 2 15
(M Johnston) *trckd wnr: rdn over 2f out: wknd over 1f out* 9/2[2]
5 6 **Billionaire Boy (IRE)** 2-9-0 0 SJCraine 3 —
(Patrick Morris) *trckd ldrs tl rdn and wknd fr 2f out* 12/1

1m 17.18s (1.98) **Going Correction** +0.225s/f (Good) 5 Ran SP% **112.1**
Speed ratings (Par 97): **95,90,86,74,66**
CSF £4.76 TOTE £1.50: £1.02, £3.90; EX 4.50.
Owner Mohammed Jaber **Bred** Ms Natalie Cleary **Trained** Newmarket, Suffolk

FOCUS
A poor maiden run at an ordinary gallop. The winner scored very easily.

NOTEBOOK
The Only Boss(IRE) ◆ didn't have to improve from his debut run to land this contest, but he appears a likeable sort and he holds a couple of entries in valuable sales races. He can progress. (op 8-15)
Sixties Rock, a keen-going sort, is flattered by his proximity to the winner, but this was an improved effort and he might find a small maiden at this time of year if able to build on this and learns to settle better. (op 11-1 tchd 12-1)
Anna's Boy showed marked improvement as he had shown very little on easier ground. However, another step forward is required to get off the mark. (op 28-1 tchd 25-1)
Honest Broker(IRE), a half-brother to Avoca Dancer, showed nothing and a watching brief is advised for the time being. (op 7-2 tchd 3-1 in places)
Billionaire Boy(IRE), a £100,000 half-brother to a winning juvenile sprinter, also showed little on this debut. (op 9-1 tchd 14-1)

6382 E.B.F./GOLDENSHEAF/DINAAIDEN STKS 1m (R)
3:50 (3:51) (Class 4) 2-Y-O £5,051 (£1,503; £751; £375) Stalls Low

Form RPR
00 1 **Arlequin**[20] 5793 2-9-3 0 JamieSpencer 4 77+
(J D Bethell) *t.k.h: prom: effrt and ev ch whn n.m.r briefly over 1f out: squeezed through to ld ins fnl f: r.o wl* 10/1
2 3/4 **Judiciary (IRE)** 2-9-0 0 AhmedAjtebi(3) 1 74+
(Saeed Bin Suroor) *led: rdn and edgd lft over 1f out: hdd ins fnl f: kpt on u.p* 4/1[2]
3 1 1/2 **Pentominium** 2-9-3 0 JoeFanning 9 71+
(M Johnston) *hld up: pushed along and rn green over 3f out: hdwy 2f out: r.o ins fnl f* 11/2[3]
335 4 3 **City Vaults Girl (IRE)**[69] 4226 2-8-12 73 TonyHamilton 7 59
(R A Fahey) *hld up in tch: effrt over 2f out: no imp over 1f out* 10/3[1]
0 5 4 **Ginger Jack**[34] 5371 2-9-3 0 DO'Donohoe 8 56
(Saeed Bin Suroor) *prom: effrt over 2f out: wknd over 1f out* 7/1
5233 6 1 1/4 **Sabander Bleue (IRE)**[10] 6136 2-9-3 72 TonyCulhane 3 53
(M R Channon) *cl up: rdn over 2f out: wknd over 1f out* 4/1[2]
7 1/2 **Across The Sea (USA)** 2-9-3 0 MickyFenton 5 52+
(T P Tate) *s.i.s: sn in tch: drvn after 3f: wknd fr 3f out* 8/1
0 8 2 **Mr Mohican (IRE)**[25] 5669 2-9-3 0 SJCraine 6 47
(Mrs A Duffield) *hld up on ins: shortlived effrt over 2f out: sn btn* 80/1

1m 45.78s (2.38) **Going Correction** +0.075s/f (Good) 8 Ran SP% **112.4**
Speed ratings (Par 97): **91,90,88,85,81 80,80,78**
toteswingers: 1&2 £8.10, 1&3 £13.30, 2&3 £4.00 CSF £48.00 TOTE £14.40: £3.10, £1.80, £2.40; EX 71.90 Trifecta £280.10 Part won. Pool: £378.63 - 0.46 winning units..
Owner Dr Anne J F Gillespie **Bred** Dr A J F Gillespie **Trained** Middleham Moor, N Yorks
■ Stewards' Enquiry : Ahmed Ajtebi caution: careless riding

FOCUS
An interesting if limited maiden with some nicely bred newcomers. The winner found minor improvement.

NOTEBOOK
Arlequin ◆ had the benefit of a couple of starts. The son of Rock Of Gibraltar had shown distinct promise last time out at Doncaster behind Coordinated Cut and clearly he has a future. He should stay further and make a nice 3yo. (op 12-1)
Judiciary(IRE) ◆, a 95,000gns brother to a multiple winner in Italy and a half-brother to a winner in Spain, did best of the newcomers. His stable remains in good form and he should have little trouble going one better in similar company next time. (op 7-2 tchd 9-2)
Pentominium ◆, a 75,000gns half-brother to three winners at up to 1m4f including the smart Epatha, was held up off an ordinary gallop and, despite looking green, did some good late work. He also should have no trouble losing his maiden tag. (op 6-1)
City Vaults Girl(IRE), back from a two-month break, has now been beaten favourite the last three times. However, this could work out to be stronger form than first thought and she is in the right hands to be placed to good effect. (op 3-1 tchd 7-2)
Sabander Bleue(IRE) was disappointing as he appeared to have the run of the race. He needs to bounce back after this. (op 5-1)
Across The Sea(USA), an expensive purchase, was too green to do himself justice. (tchd 15-2)

6383 42ND STREET H'CAP 1m (R)
4:25 (4:25) (Class 5) (0-70,68) 3-Y-O+ £2,978 (£886; £442; £221) Stalls Low

Form RPR
0301 1 **Lujano**[18] 5886 4-8-11 62 BMcHugh(5) 7 74
(Ollie Pears) *mde all: rdn 2f out: kpt on wl fnl f* 8/1
3502 2 1 1/2 **Amethyst Dawn (IRE)**[8] 6182 3-8-6 56 DavidAllan 2 65
(T D Easterby) *trckd wnr thrght: effrt and ev ch over 2f out: kpt on same pce ins fnl f* 7/2[1]
0006 3 4 **Ella Woodcock (IRE)**[4] 6280 5-9-5 65 (b) DuranFentiman 11 64+
(E J Alston) *hld up: plenty to do ent st: hdwy over 1f out: kpt on fnl f: nt pce of first two* 16/1
0540 4 1/2 **Shadowtime**[9] 6157 4-9-1 66 AndrewHeffernan(5) 10 64
(Miss Tracy Waggott) *in tch: effrt over 2f out: kpt on same pce ins fnl f* 9/2[3]
3050 5 2 3/4 **Border Owl (IRE)**[13] 6023 4-9-7 67 (v[1]) DanielTudhope 9 59
(P Salmon) *s.i.s: hld up: effrt and hdwy over 2f out: no ex appr fnl f* 16/1
0004 6 3/4 **Fathey (IRE)**[16] 5948 3-8-13 63 TonyHamilton 8 53
(R A Fahey) *t.k.h: cl up: rdn over 2f out: no ex over 1f out* 10/1
6423 7 hd **Aussie Blue (IRE)**[13] 6023 5-9-4 64 JamieSpencer 4 54
(R M Whitaker) *hld up: drvn and outpcd 3f out: short-lived effrt over 1f out: sn no imp* 4/1[2]
1044 8 3/4 **Cause For Applause (IRE)**[188] 964 3-8-4 54 oh1 ow1 AdrianTNicholls 1 42
(R Craggs) *trckd ldrs: drvn over 2f out: wknd over 1f out* 66/1
2100 9 hd **Petsas Pleasure**[16] 5940 3-9-4 68 JoeFanning 12 56
(Ollie Pears) *in tch: rdn over 2f out: wknd over 1f out* 9/1
060 10 1 **Navajo Joe (IRE)**[7] 6221 4-9-4 64 PJMcDonald 6 49
(R Johnson) *bhd: drvn over 3f out: nvr on terms* 25/1
0030 11 9 **Society Music (IRE)**[23] 5730 7-9-3 63 (p) PhillipMakin 3 28
(M Dods) *in tch tl rdn and wknd fr 2f out* 14/1
0160 12 11 **Media Stars**[156] 1556 4-8-8 54 FrancisNorton 5 —
(R Johnson) *bhd: lost tch 1/2-way: t.o* 33/1

1m 44.97s (1.57) **Going Correction** +0.075s/f (Good)
WFA 3 from 4yo+ 4lb 12 Ran SP% **117.3**
Speed ratings (Par 103): **95,93,89,89,86 85,85,84,84,83 74,63**
toteswingers: 1&2 £6.00, 1&3 £26.30, 2&3 £17.30 CSF £35.18 CT £450.63 TOTE £10.80: £2.60, £1.50, £6.40; EX 33.00 TRIFECTA Not won..
Owner David Scott and Co (Pattern Makers) Ltd **Bred** D Scott **Trained** Norton, N Yorks

FOCUS
A 56-70 handicap with the top weight 3lb below the ceiling rating. An ordinary gallop ensured those who raced up with the pace held a distinctive advantage. The winner posted another personal best.

6384 HENRY COLBECK FISH & CHIPS H'CAP 2m 19y
5:00 (5:00) (Class 5) (0-70,69) 3-Y-O £2,978 (£886; £442; £221) Stalls Low

Form RPR
3116 1 **Twist Again (IRE)**[16] 5952 3-9-7 69 JoeFanning 4 77+
(P Howling) *trckd ldrs: effrt over 2f out: led ins fnl f: kpt on wl* 10/3[1]
400 2 1/2 **Orsippus (USA)**[22] 3005 3-8-12 60 DavidAllan 6 66
(Michael Smith) *trckd ldrs: led over 2f out to ins fnl f: hld towards fin* 20/1
0320 3 1 3/4 **Khayar (IRE)**[16] 5952 3-8-12 60 SaleemGolam 3 64
(M H Tompkins) *hld up in tch: effrt on ins over 2f out: sn rdn: kpt on same pce fnl f* 7/2[2]
0005 4 8 **Shanavaz**[11] 6097 3-8-2 50 oh5 (p) JamieMackay 1 45
(C J Teague) *s.i.s: hld up: outpcd over 2f out: plugged on fnl f: nt rch ldrs* 16/1
5306 5 1/2 **Trumpstoo (USA)**[18] 5858 3-9-1 63 TonyHamilton 5 57
(R A Fahey) *t.k.h: hld up: effrt 3f out: wknd over 1f out* 5/1[3]
44 6 3 1/4 **Madam'X**[8] 6177 3-8-3 51 DuranFentiman 7 41
(Mrs A Duffield) *cl up: led over 3f out to over 2f out: wknd wl over 1f out* 16/1
4502 7 39 **Diktalina**[11] 6097 3-8-5 53 FrancisNorton 2 —
(W R Muir) *set stdy pce: rdn and hdd over 3f out: wkng whn n.m.r over 2f out* 10/3[1]
1530 8 1 **Drop The Hammer**[24] 5696 3-8-9 57 MickyFenton 8 —
(T P Tate) *hld up: rdn and hdwy on outside over 4f out: wknd over 2f out* 8/1

3m 39.41s (0.01) **Going Correction** +0.075s/f (Good) 8 Ran SP% **112.7**
Speed ratings (Par 101): **102,101,100,96,96 95,75,75**
toteswingers: 1&2 £10.20, 1&3 £3.30, 2&3 £13.80 CSF £64.57 CT £245.00 TOTE £3.20: £1.30, £4.70, £1.70; EX 67.50 Trifecta £249.40 Part won. Pool: £337.09 - 0.91 winning units..
Owner Liam Sheridan **Bred** Michael Dalton **Trained** Newmarket, Suffolk
■ Stewards' Enquiry : David Allan two-day ban: used whip with excessive freaquency down the shoulder in the forehand (Oct 14-15)

FOCUS
An ordinary gallop to this staying handicap and the form is not entirely convincing.
Drop The Hammer Official explanation: jockey said filly had no more to give

6385 Q GOLD GREEN PALM H'CAP 1m 4f 93y
5:30 (5:30) (Class 5) (0-75,75) 3-Y-O+ £3,139 (£926; £463) Stalls Low

Form RPR
5063 1 **Capable Guest (IRE)**[7] 6204 7-9-1 65 TonyCulhane 6 72
(M R Channon) *hld up in tch: lost pl over 2f out: rallied over 1f out: styd on u.p to ld towards fin* 11/2[2]
2154 2 nk **Summer Lodge**[26] 5622 6-9-3 72 BMcHugh(5) 4 79
(J A Glover) *t.k.h: trckd ldrs: effrt over 2f out: ev ch wl ins fnl f: jst hld* 7/1[3]
3144 3 3/4 **African Cheetah**[8] 6190 3-9-3 75 JoeFanning 8 80+
(M Johnston) *cl up: led over 2f out: edgd lft over 1f out: kpt on tl hdd and no ex towards fin* 11/8[1]
6040 4 2 **Dechiper (IRE)**[24] 5698 7-9-3 67 DavidAllan 5 69
(R Johnson) *hld up: hdwy over 2f out: sn rdn: kpt on same pce fnl f* 8/1
2240 5 1/2 **Zefooha (FR)**[15] 5962 5-8-12 62 (p) DuranFentiman 2 63
(T D Walford) *led: rdn and hdd over 2f out: sn one pce* 16/1
1440 6 2 **Casino Night**[13] 6016 4-9-5 74 DeanHeslop(5) 3 72
(F P Murtagh) *dwlt: hld up: rdn and hdwy over 2f out: styng on whn nt clr run ins fnl f: sn btn* 16/1
4400 7 2 1/2 **That'll Do Nicely (IRE)**[38] 5294 6-8-11 61 PhillipMakin 7 55
(N G Richards) *hld up on outside: effrt 3f out: wknd over 1f out* 10/1
5260 8 6 **Graylyn Ruby (FR)**[15] 5975 4-9-4 68 SJCraine 9 53
(J Jay) *trckd ldrs tl rdn and wknd fr 2f out* 8/1
2000 9 16 **Real Desire**[10] 6139 3-7-10 61 oh6 ow1 JamesPSullivan(7) 1 20
(I Semple) *hld up: struggling over 2f out: sn btn: t.o* 100/1

2m 45.39s (-0.21) **Going Correction** +0.075s/f (Good)
WFA 3 from 4yo+ 8lb 9 Ran SP% **114.1**
Speed ratings (Par 103): **103,102,102,100,100 99,97,93,82**
toteswingers: 1&2 £4.40, 1&3 £2.80, 2&3 £3.50 CSF £43.02 CT £80.71 TOTE £4.40: £1.50, £2.40, £1.10; EX 24.30 Trifecta £63.00 Pool: £574.02 - 6.42 winning units. Place 6: £69.53, Place 5: £63.79..
Owner M Channon **Bred** Mountarmstrong Stud **Trained** West Ilsley, Berks
■ Stewards' Enquiry : B McHugh caution: used whip down the shoulder in the forehand.

FOCUS
A steady gallop for this 61-75 handicap and ordinary form for the grade, with the third to his best.
T/Jkpt: Not won. T/Plt: £245.00 to a £1 stake. Pool: £58,777.70. 175.10 winning tickets. T/Qpdt: £27.10 to a £1 stake. Pool: £4,323.50. 117.92 winning tickets. RY

5126 **NOTTINGHAM** (L-H)

Wednesday, September 30

OFFICIAL GOING: Good to firm (good in places; 8.4)

Rail moved out 4.5m from 1m start to 4f marker adding circa 8 yds to advertised distances on round course.

Wind: Light 1/2 against Weather: Fine

6386 E B F UK HYGIENE MAIDEN STKS 6f 15y

2:20 (2:20) (Class 5) 2-Y-O **£3,885** (£1,156; £577; £288) **Stalls** High

Form RPR

00 **1** **Skyflight**[28] 5580 2-8-12 0 SilvestreDeSousa 6 68
(Eve Johnson Houghton) *led tl narowly hdd over 2f out: hung lft: kpt on to ld towards fin* **11/2**[3]

0 **2** ½ **Fazza**[16] 5934 2-9-3 0 MartinDwyer 5 72
(D W P Arbuthnot) *led: narrow ld over 2f out: hdd and no ex wl ins fnl f* **12/1**

3 *hd* **Cloud's End** 2-8-12 0 LiamJones 4 68+
(W J Haggas) *chsd ldrs: sn drvn along: wl outpcd and lost pl over 2f out: swtchd outside over 1f out: fin strly: will improve* **6/4**[2]

60 **4** 3 **Macroy**[41] 5180 2-9-0 0 JamesMillman(3) 1 62
(B R Millman) *w ldrs: rdn 2f out: wknd jst ins fnl f* **25/1**

4 **5** 2¼ **Sir Frank Wappat**[13] 6032 2-9-3 0 RoystonFfrench 3 55
(M Johnston) *w ldrs: rdn over 2f out: carried hd high and hung lft: lost pl over 1f out* **11/8**[1]

0 **6** 2 **Pie Poudre**[22] 5749 2-9-3 0 TomEaves 2 49+
(R Brotherton) *s.s: a outpcd in rr* **100/1**

00 **7** 27 **Little Buddy**[83] 3786 2-9-3 0 StephenDonohoe 7 —
(R J Price) *s.s: a detached in rr and hung lft: virtually p.u ins fnl f* **100/1**

1m 17.23s (2.33) **Going Correction** -0.025s/f (Good) 7 Ran SP% **111.0**

Speed ratings (Par 95): **83,82,82,78,75 72,36**

toteswingers: 1&2 £5.00, 1&3 £1.70, 2&3 £2.70 CSF £58.46 TOTE £7.30: £2.40, £4.90; EX 66.40.

Owner Mrs P Robeson **Bred** Southcourt Stud **Trained** Blewbury, Oxon

FOCUS

An ordinary looking maiden with little depth. It is hard to rate the form much higher.

NOTEBOOK

Skyflight put her experience to good use to get home narrowly. She had shown only a glimmer of ability at long odds in two previous starts and looked in trouble when coming under pressure at halfway. However, she rallied to lead inside the last and managed to hold on. She should not be unduly burdened by the handicapper after this. (op 100-30)

Fazza made considerable improvement on his debut, showing in front over 2f out and only losing out narrowly to his more experienced rival. He should make his mark in due course. (op 11-1 tchd 14-1)

Cloud's End ◆, a half-sister to Airwave, opened up as favourite but drifted and her inexperience told in the race, as she was unable to go the pace and looked well held before staying on in good style late on. It would be no surprise to see her improve past the two that beat her next time and she looks the one to take from the race. (op 15-8 tchd 11-8)

Macroy had shown limited ability on two previous outings and improved on those performances, showing plenty of pace on the outside of his field until weakening in the closing stages. He also now qualifies for handicaps. (op 16-1)

Sir Frank Wappat never looked happy, always hanging left and then carrying his head high from around halfway. He did the same on similar ground on his debut and it may be that he needs some give to enable him to stretch out fully but, until he has proven that is true, he looks one to treat with caution. Official explanation: jockey said colt hung left (op 15-8 tchd 9-4)

6387 UK HYGIENE WASHROOM SERVICES H'CAP 5f 13y

2:50 (2:50) (Class 5) (0-75,74) 3-Y-O **£2,590** (£770; £385; £192) **Stalls** High

Form RPR

2000 **1** **Secret Venue**[18] 5856 3-8-13 69 TomEaves 8 77
(Jedd O'Keeffe) *mde all: hld on gamely* **13/2**

2115 **2** ¾ **Igoyougo**[30] 5517 3-9-1 71 SilvestreDeSousa 1 76
(G A Harker) *w ldrs: rdr dropped whip 1f out: no ex wl ins fnl f* **9/2**[1]

1514 **3** *hd* **First Blade**[12] 6070 3-8-6 62 (b) JimmyQuinn 9 66+
(S R Bowring) *stmbld s: hld up in rr stands' side: hdwy and nt clr run 1f out: swtchd lft and styd on wl ins fnl f* **11/2**[3]

4031 **4** 1 **Battle**[33] 5383 3-9-3 73 TravisBlock 3 74
(H Morrison) *mid-div: effrt over 2f out: upsides 1f out: kpt on same pce* **5/1**[2]

1315 **5** 1¼ **Corton Charlemagne (IRE)**[11] 6118 3-8-13 72 WilliamCarson(3) 7 68
(Rae Guest) *stmbld s: sn chsng ldrs: one pce fnl 2f* **9/2**[1]

2036 **6** ¾ **Raimond Ridge (IRE)**[15] 5968 3-8-10 69 MCGeran(3) 4 62
(M R Channon) *dwlt: in rr: hdwy and swtchd outside over 1f out: one pce* **9/1**

2025 **7** 7 **Fasliyanne (IRE)**[3] 6308 3-8-8 64 (b) TedDurcan 2 32
(K A Ryan) *w ldrs: lost pl over 1f out* **12/1**

4316 **8** 1¼ **Lucky Art (USA)**[30] 5517 3-9-4 74 AndrewElliott 5 38
(Mrs R A Carr) *stmbld s: w ldrs: lost pl over 1f out* **12/1**

5325 **9** 3¾ **Desert Strike**[104] 3053 3-9-4 74 NCallan 6 24
(P F I Cole) *trckd ldrs: toko t.k.h: wknd over 1f out* **12/1**

60.75 secs (-0.25) **Going Correction** -0.025s/f (Good) 9 Ran SP% **114.8**

Speed ratings (Par 101): **101,99,99,97,95 94,83,81,75**

toteswingers: 1&2 £6.10, 1&3 £7.50, 2&3 £5.90 CSF £35.61 CT £172.56 TOTE £7.70: £2.10, £1.50, £2.40; EX 35.80.

Owner Ken And Delia Shaw-KGS Consulting LLP **Bred** Sherwoods Transport Ltd **Trained** Middleham Moor, N Yorks

FOCUS

An ordinary sprint handicap but quite competitive and the form looks sound enough.

First Blade Official explanation: jockey said gelding stumbled on leaving stalls

Lucky Art(USA) Official explanation: jockey said gelding stumbled on leaving stalls and felt wrong thereafter

6388 UKHYGIENE.COM H'CAP 2m 9y

3:25 (3:25) (Class 4) (0-85,85) 3-Y-O **£6,476** (£1,927; £963; £481) **Stalls** Low

Form RPR

2313 **1** **Dazinski**[31] 5481 3-9-2 80 TedDurcan 1 91
(M H Tompkins) *trckd ldrs: smooth hdwy to chal 3f out: styd on under pressture to take def advantage last 75yds* **7/2**[3]

3212 **2** 2 **Ermyn Lodge**[25] 5666 3-8-8 72 (v) FergusSweeney 6 81
(P M Phelan) *led: jnd 3f out: hdd and no ex wl ins fnl f* **11/4**[1]

1134 **3** 6 **Curacao**[34] 5376 3-9-0 78 NCallan 2 81
(Mrs A J Perrett) *trckd ldrs: t.k.h: effrt over 3f out: rallying whn rdr dropped whip over a f out: one pce after: eased clsng stages* **4/1**

2143 **4** 11 **Sherman McCoy**[25] 5660 3-8-13 80 JamesMillman(3) 5 68
(B R Millman) *trckd ldrs: drvn 5f out: lost pl over 3f out* **3/1**[2]

6231 **5** 1 **Sally Forth**[34] 5376 3-9-4 82 ChrisCatlin 3 69
(R Charlton) *dwlt: hdwy to chse ldrs after 3f: jnd ldr 10f out: drvn over 4f out: lost pl over 3f out* **9/2**

3m 32.36s (2.06) **Going Correction** +0.225s/f (Good) 5 Ran SP% **112.1**

Speed ratings (Par 103): **103,102,99,93,93**

toteswinger: 1&2 £6.90 CSF £13.63 TOTE £4.30: £2.00, £1.70; EX 10.00.

Owner Mrs Beryl Lockey **Bred** Darley **Trained** Newmarket, Suffolk

FOCUS

This staying handicap has thrown up a couple of useful performers in recent seasons in Bulwark and Juniper Girl and it looked a competitive contest despite the small field. The runner-up us rated to previous Kempton form.

6389 E B F UK HYGIENE ENVIRO-DRY MAIDEN FILLIES' STKS 1m 75y

4:00 (4:01) (Class 5) 2-Y-O **£3,885** (£1,156; £577; £288) **Stalls** Low

Form RPR

1 **Bint Almatar (USA)** 2-9-0 0 TedDurcan 8 71
(Saeed Bin Suroor) *trckd ldrs: effrt over 2f out: styd on wl ins fnl f: led nr fin* **2/1**[1]

5 **2** ½ **Michevious Spirit (IRE)**[32] 5417 2-9-0 0 NCallan 2 70
(K A Ryan) *trckd ldrs: chal over 2f out: narrow ld ins fnl f: hdd towards fin* **4/1**[3]

3 ½ **Shaluca** 2-9-0 0 GrahamGibbons 4 69
(E S McMahon) *w ldr: led over 5f out: jnd over 2f out: hdd and no ex last 75yds* **10/3**[2]

4 8 **Mausin (IRE)** 2-9-0 0 TravisBlock 6 51
(H Morrison) *in rr: hdwy 4f out: sn outpcd: kpt on fnl 2f* **16/1**

0 **5** 1½ **Twilight Memory (USA)**[27] 5604 2-9-0 0 MartinDwyer 9 48
(B J Meehan) *w ldrs: upsides over 2f out: wknd over 1f out* **7/1**

6 1¾ **Napoleons Mistress (IRE)** 2-9-0 0 GregFairley 5 44+
(P F I Cole) *trckd ldrs: t.k.h: drvn over 3f out: wknd over 1f out* **10/1**

0 **7** 3¾ **Suzi's Challenger**[29] 5547 2-9-0 0 JimmyQuinn 7 36
(H J Collingridge) *in rr: hdwy over 4f out: sn chsng ldrs: lost pl over 1f out* **33/1**

000 **8** 4½ **Antique Diamond (IRE)**[96] 3337 2-9-0 31 NeilChalmers 1 26
(Lucinda Featherstone) *s.s: t.k.h in rr: hdwy over 4f out: lost pl over 2f out* **150/1**

9 *nk* **Mme De Stael** 2-9-0 0 StephenDonohoe 3 25+
(Sir Mark Prescott) *s.s: green and sn detached in last: nvr on terms* **16/1**

00 **10** *nk* **Gadobout Dancer**[14] 5980 2-9-0 0 (p) TomEaves 10 25
(I W McInnes) *sn chsng ldrs: drvn 4f out: sn lost pl* **100/1**

1m 49.53s (3.93) **Going Correction** +0.225s/f (Good) 10 Ran SP% **114.4**

Speed ratings (Par 92): **89,88,88,80,78 76,73,68,68,67**

toteswingers: 1&2 £2.20, 1&3 £2.60, 2&3 £3.50 CSF £9.77 TOTE £2.80: £1.10, £1.80, £1.60; EX 10.20.

Owner Godolphin **Bred** Darley **Trained** Newmarket, Suffolk

FOCUS

Debutantes have a good recent record in this fillies' maiden and there were a couple of well-bred types making their debut for good yards. The first three pulled well clear but this is not a race to go overboard about.

NOTEBOOK

Bint Almatar(USA) ◆ is a daughter of a Listed winner who was runner-up in the Poule d'Essai des Pouliches. She was never far away but looked held when coming under pressure before running on in the final furlong to lead near the line. She has a fair amount of size about her and should come on considerably for the experience. (op 5-2 tchd 11-4)

Michevious Spirit(IRE) improved from her debut effort and had a good battle with the third before getting the upper hand, only to have the winner pounce late on her outside. She should be up to winning a maiden on this evidence. (tchd 7-2)

Shaluca, a daughter of the Oaks runner-up Noushkey and half-sister to a couple of 1m2f winners, was given a positive ride on this debut and showed plenty of tenacity under pressure. Connections will look for another race for her providing the ground stays good, but she has some filling out to do and looks to have a future. (op 7-2 tchd 5-2)

Mausin(IRE) ran on late having been in the rear turning for home. Out of a mile winner from the family of Authorized, she is the type to do better next season. (op 12-1)

Twilight Memory(USA) had been well beaten on soft ground on her debut and showed up until left behind in the last quarter-mile. She might find her niche in handicaps in due course. (op 8-1 tchd 11-1)

Napoleons Mistress(IRE), out of a Lancashire Oaks winner and a half-sister to six winners, showed ability on her debut but could not pick up in the straight. She will appreciate middle distances in time. (op 9-1)

Antique Diamond(IRE) Official explanation: jockey said filly was slowly away from the stalls

6390 HANDEPAY MERCHANT SERVICES MAIDEN STKS 1m 75y

4:35 (4:36) (Class 5) 3-Y-O+ **£2,590** (£770; £385; £192) **Stalls** Low

Form RPR

0223 **1** **Mr Udagawa**[12] 6073 3-8-10 70 (p) JPFahy(7) 14 76+
(R M Beckett) *led 1f: trckd ldrs: wnt 2nd over 3f out: led over 1f out: pushed clr: readily* **11/4**[1]

4450 **2** 2½ **Olive Green (USA)**[62] 4473 3-8-12 71 TedDurcan 11 64
(Pat Eddery) *t.k.h in midfield: hdwy over 2f out: styd on to take 2nd ins fnl f* **9/2**[3]

0 **3** 3½ **Falcon's Tribute (IRE)**[13] 6022 7-9-2 0 GregFairley 1 56
(P Salmon) *drvn to make hdwy and led after 1f: hdd over 1f out: one pce* **66/1**

5224 **4** 2¼ **Papyrian**[39] 5242 3-9-3 76 (b) LiamJones 15 56
(W Jarvis) *chsd ldrs on outer: hung rt and one pce fnl 2f* **7/2**[2]

66- **5** 1¼ **Beat Faster**[285] 7726 3-8-12 0 TomEaves 4 48
(J G Given) *mid-div: drvn over 3f out: one pce* **20/1**

00 **6** ½ **Marina's Ocean**[12] 6073 5-9-2 0 (t) AmirQuinn 3 47
(S R Bowring) *chsd ldrs: one pce fnl 2f* **66/1**

50 **7** *hd* **Choosy Floosy**[27] 5614 3-8-5 0 TobyAtkinson(7) 8 47
(Pat Eddery) *in rr: styd on fnl 2f: nvr nr ldrs* **50/1**

0 **8** ½ **Suburbia (USA)**[22] 5747 3-9-3 0 StephenDonohoe 16 50
(M A Jarvis) *chsd ldrs: drvn 3f out: one pce* **14/1**

9 3½ **Stargazing (IRE)** 3-8-12 0 MartinDwyer 13 37
(B J Meehan) *chsd ldrs: wknd over 1f out* **7/1**

0 **10** 3¼ **Kilmun**[27] 5599 3-9-3 0 NCallan 12 35
(K A Ryan) *chsd ldrs: wknd over 1f out* **18/1**

0000 **11** 1 **Lady Dinsdale (IRE)**[31] 5470 3-8-12 40 SilvestreDeSousa 17 28
(T Keddy) *in rr: sme hdwy over 3f out: sn wknd* **50/1**

060 **12** ¾ **Mistic Academy (IRE)**[13] 6022 4-9-2 30 SimonWhitworth 7 26
(Miss J E Foster) *mid-div: drvn over 3f out: sn wknd* **125/1**

0005 **13** 1½ **A Lot Of Red (IRE)**[1] 6365 3-8-12 47 (bt) AshleyMorgan(5) 6 27
(P J O'Gorman) *in rr: sme hdwy over 3f out: sn wknd* **50/1**

-000 **14** *4* **Black Salix (USA)**[44] 5111 3-8-12 47.................................. PaulEddery 9 13
(Mrs P Sly) *s.i.s: a towards rr* **28/1**

04 **15** *6* **Forward Planning (USA)**[48] 4947 3-8-12 0.............. RoystonFfrench 5 —
(M Johnston) *s.s: t.k.h in rr: hung rt and eased over 1f out* **8/1**

1m 47.52s (1.92) **Going Correction** +0.226s/f (Good)
WFA 3 from 4yo+ 4lb **15** Ran SP% **120.5**
Speed ratings (Par 103): **99,96,93,90,89 89,88,88,84,81 80,79,78,74,68**
toteswingers: 1&2 £5.80, 1&3 £21.30, 2&3 £56.40 CSF £14.01 TOTE £3.00: £1.60, £2.30, £11.70; EX 17.90.

Owner B R Ingram **Bred** Richard C J Manning **Trained** Whitsbury, Hants

FOCUS

This older-horse maiden often falls to a late-developer, the best of those recently successful being subsequent Group winner Pride of Nation, although Tazeez was beaten in this on his debut in 2007 before going on to win last year's Cambridgeshire. The withdrawal of the 85-rated Capeability weakened the race and it looked pretty uncompetitive. The form is rated athrough the winner to his previous best.

Forward Planning(USA) Official explanation: jockey said filly ran too free

6391 HAPPY BIRTHDAY JUDITH DUFFY 40 TODAY - NEVER! NURSERY 1m 2f 50y
5:10 (5:11) (Class 5) (0-75,73) 2-Y-O £2,590 (£770; £385; £192) **Stalls** Low

Form RPR

000 **1** **Bateau Bleu**[106] 2997 2-8-0 **55**..................................(v[1]) KellyHarrison(3) 8 62+
(P C Haslam) *s.i.s: t.k.h in rr: gd hdwy on outer 2f out: hung lft: styd on strly to ld wl ins fnl f: wnt rt: kpt on wl* **66/1**

0011 **2** *1 ½* **Fantastic Pick**[7] 6215 2-9-3 **69** 6ex.................................. MartinDwyer 4 73
(B J Meehan) *trckd ldrs: pushed along over 5f out: chal over 2f out: edgd rt and led over 1f out: hdd and no ex last 75yds* **4/5**[1]

6533 **3** *2 ½* **Whiepa Snappa (IRE)**[28] 5573 2-8-12 **64**.......................... IanMongan 5 64
(P M Phelan) *in rr: hdwy over 3f out: styd on same pce appr fnl f* **12/1**

4002 **4** *1 ¼* **Ella Grace (USA)**[7] 6215 2-8-6 **58**............................ RoystonFfrench 10 56
(R A Fahey) *led 1f: t.k.h: trckd ldr: led over 2f out: hung rt and hdd over 1f out: fdd* **7/1**[2]

0614 **5** *1 ¾* **Leitzu (IRE)**[12] 6067 2-9-4 **70**.. ChrisCatlin 6 64
(M R Channon) *hld up in rr: effrt over 3f out: one pce fnl 2f* **10/1**

500 **6** *7* **Themanforacrisis (IRE)**[30] 5527 2-8-4 **63**.......................... JPFahy(7) 9 45
(R M Beckett) *chsd ldrs: lost pl over 1f out* **40/1**

0030 **7** *3 ¼* **Mary Celest (IRE)**[14] 5985 2-8-6 **58**......................(p) SilvestreDeSousa 1 34
(K A Ryan) *led after 1f: hdd over 2f out: hung rt and wknd over 1f out* **33/1**

1533 **8** *nk* **Diamond Duchess (IRE)**[7] 6211 2-9-7 **73**...................... TedDurcan 11 48
(D R Lanigan) *mid-div: effrt over 3f out: wknd over 1f out* **9/1**[3]

0542 **9** *¾* **Storm Command (IRE)**[16] 5951 2-8-10 **62**.......................... TomEaves 2 36
(B Smart) *s.i.s: hdwy and prom 5f out: lost pl over 2f out* **14/1**

2400 **10** *3* **Brunette (IRE)**[12] 6067 2-8-11 **66**.............................. PatrickHills(3) 7 35
(R Hannon) *mid-div: drvn over 4f out: lost pl 2f out* **33/1**

0360 **11** *¾* **Sixpenny Moon (USA)**[28] 5573 2-8-8 **60**............................ PatDobbs 3 27
(R Hannon) *in rr: hdwy 4f out: lost pl over 2f out* **33/1**

2m 15.02s (3.32) **Going Correction** +0.225s/f (Good) **11** Ran SP% **114.3**
Speed ratings (Par 95): **95,93,91,90,89 83,81,80,80,77 77**
toteswingers: 1&2 £17.90, 1&3 £41.00, 2&3 £5.30 CSF £115.51 CT £773.29 TOTE £66.00: £11.00, £1.10, £2.40; EX 326.10.

Owner Mrs Sheila Mason & Robert Stipetic **Bred** Llety Stud **Trained** Middleham Moor, N Yorks

FOCUS

An ordinary-looking nursery run over the maximum trip for juveniles. Much-improved form from the visored winner with the third close to his mark.

NOTEBOOK

Bateau Bleu swept into the lead inside the final furlong and scored going away. Fitted with a visor on this handicap debut, he had been well held in three starts over shorter trips, and again missed the break. However, despite being still last at the quarter-mile pole, his stamina then kicked in and he picked up well to cut down the favourite. He was rated just 55 here and clearly appreciates this sort of trip. Official explanation: trainer said, regarding apparent improvement in form, that since its last run it had been gelded, first time over 1m 2f, stepping up 3f and was wearing a visor for the first time. (tchd 80-1)

Fantastic Pick was carrying a 6lb penalty on this bid for a hat-trick. He had to be niggled at halfway, but got to the front well over a furlong out and looked sure to score, only to be collared by the winner who came from way back. He confirmed previous form with the fourth on 6lb worse terms. (op 5-6 tchd 8-13)

Whiepa Snappa(IRE) was held up out the back alongside the winner, but made his move sooner than that rival and could never quite reach the leaders. He might not have quite got home. (tchd 16-1)

Ella Grace(USA) put up an improved effort behind today's runner-up on her handicap debut last time. She was given a positive ride and went for home fairly early in the straight, but could not respond when the favourite went by. Official explanation: jockey said filly hung right (op 8-1 tchd 13-2)

Leitzu(IRE) was another held up and put up a decent effort, if unable to find an extra gear on this slight step up in trip but finished a fair way clear of the remainder. (op 8-1 tchd 7-1)

Mary Celest(IRE) was given a positive ride but faded in the straight. Official explanation: jockey said filly hung right (op 28-1)

Diamond Duchess(IRE) Official explanation: jockey said filly had no more to give

6392 AMATEUR JOCKEYS' ASSOCIATION H'CAP (FOR GENTLEMAN AMATEUR RIDERS) 1m 2f 50y
5:40 (5:40) (Class 5) (0-70,73) 3-Y-O+ £2,637 (£811; £405) **Stalls** Low

Form RPR

0202 **1** **Astronomical (IRE)**[13] 6017 7-10-7 **61**...........(p) MrStephenHarrison(5) 2 71
(R Hollinshead) *mde all: edgd lft over 1f out: jst hld on* **2/1**[1]

1023 **2** *shd* **Free Tussy (ARG)**[20] 5802 5-11-1 **67**.................(bt) MrJoshuaMoore(3) 8 77
(G L Moore) *hld up in tch: effrt over 3f out: styd on ins fnl f: jst hld* **7/2**[2]

3100 **3** *6* **Bavarica**[17] 5910 7-10-12 **66**.. MrRBirkett(5) 3 64
(Miss J Feilden) *trckd ldrs: effrt and upsides over 1f out: kpt on one pce* **8/1**

0030 **4** *2 ¾* **Efidium**[1] 6369 11-10-7 **63** ow5.............................. MrSebSpencer(7) 4 55
(N Bycroft) *hld up in rr: hdwy over 3f out: upsides 2f out: wknd appr fnl f* **8/1**

1204 **5** *hd* **Dragon Slayer (IRE)**[31] 5473 7-11-4 **67**............................ MrSWalker 9 59
(John A Harris) *s.i.s: hld up: effrt to chse ldrs over 3f out: wknd over 1f out* **4/1**[3]

1020 **6** *10* **Gallego**[19] 5833 7-11-2 **70**.. MrMPrice(5) 6 42
(R J Price) *stdd s: hld up wl detached: hdwy on wd outside 3f out: hung rt and wknd over 1f out* **12/1**

0-40 **7** *7* **Domesday (UAE)**[56] 4667 8-10-0 **56** oh11..............(v) MrJMQuinlan(7) 5 14
(T T Clement) *chsd wnr: drvn over 3f out: wknd 2f out* **33/1**

0 **8** *12* **Star Of Memory (FR)**[45] 5061 5-11-4 **70**.......... MrSTwiston-Davies(3) 7 4
(D G Bridgwater) *chsd ldrs: drvn over 4f out: lost pl 3f out: sn bhd* **22/1**

2m 15.48s (3.78) **Going Correction** +0.225s/f (Good) **8** Ran SP% **112.8**
Speed ratings (Par 103): **93,92,88,85,85 77,72,62**
toteswingers: 1&2 £2.30, 1&3 £5.90, 2&3 £7.50 CSF £8.72 CT £43.41 TOTE £2.70: £1.20, £1.50, £2.60; EX 7.70 Place 6: £63.47, Place 5: £6.14.

Owner FWH Partnership **Bred** Pollards Stables **Trained** Upper Longdon, Staffs

■ Stewards' Enquiry : Mr J M Quinlan one-day ban: used whip when out of contention and above shoulder height (Oct 26)

FOCUS

A modest amateurs' handicap that produced a close finish and the form is rated around the first two.

Gallego Official explanation: jockey said gelding hung right

T/Plt: £119.30 to a £1 stake. Pool: £46,904.50. 286.88 winning tickets. T/Qpdt: £4.30 to a £1 stake. Pool: £4,694.06. 791.90 winning tickets. WG

5602 SALISBURY (R-H)
Wednesday, September 30

OFFICIAL GOING: Good to firm (9.0)

Wind: Virtually nil Weather: Overcast but warm

6393 E B F MOLSON COORS MAIDEN STKS 1m
1:25 (1:25) (Class 4) 2-Y-O £4,695 (£1,397; £698; £348) **Stalls** High

Form RPR

4 **1** **Spoken**[19] 5831 2-9-3 0.. SteveDrowne 8 76+
(R Charlton) *lw: cl up: led over 1f out: kpt on wl: rdn out* **11/4**[3]

2 *¾* **Youm Jamil (USA)** 2-9-3 0.. EddieAhern 4 74+
(B J Meehan) *w'like: bit bkwd: trckd ldr: led 3f out: rdn and hdd over 1f out: kpt on but no ex* **12/1**

3 *nk* **Longliner** 2-9-3 0.. RyanMoore 2 74+
(Sir Michael Stoute) *str: scope: bit bkwd: hld up: hdwy 3f out: sn rdn: styd on: wnt 3rd ins fnl f: clsng at fin* **2/1**[1]

05 **4** *½* **Seaside Sizzler**[20] 5785 2-9-3 0.................................... SebSanders 6 73
(R M Beckett) *lw: s.i.s: towards rr: rdn 1/2-way: styd on fr over 1f out: clsng at fin* **28/1**

5 *1* **Golden Waters** 2-8-12 0.. RobertWinston 10 65
(Eve Johnson Houghton) *w'like: scope: bit bkwd: trckd ldrs: rdn wl over 2f out: kpt on same pce* **33/1**

0 **6** *1 ½* **Viviani (IRE)**[11] 6109 2-9-3 0.................................... JimCrowley 12 67
(Mrs A J Perrett) *swtg: led: rdn and hdd 3f out: one pce fnl 2f* **22/1**

7 *nk* **Gardening Leave** 2-9-3 0.. WilliamBuick 3 66+
(A M Balding) *w'like: scope: tall: lenghty: bit bkwd: s.i.s: mid-div: struggling to hold pl 1/2-way: sme late prog* **14/1**

05 **8** *1 ¼* **Quick Reaction**[20] 5793 2-9-3 0................................ RichardHughes 9 64+
(R Hannon) *trckd ldrs: rdn 3f out: wknd ent fnl f* **5/2**[2]

9 *1 ½* **Baltic Ben (USA)** 2-9-3 0.. HayleyTurner 7 60
(Eve Johnson Houghton) *lengthy: unf: scope: s.i.s: mid-div tl wknd over 2f out* **66/1**

10 *shd* **Steely Bird** 2-9-3 0.. RobertHavlin 1 60
(Miss Jo Crowley) *str: bit bkwd: s.i.s: a towards rr* **150/1**

00 **11** *2 ½* **Lisahane Bog**[20] 5807 2-9-3 0.................................. TGMcLaughlin 11 55
(P R Hedger) *a towards rr* **100/1**

1m 45.51s (2.01) **Going Correction** 0.0s/f (Good) **11** Ran SP% **116.8**
Speed ratings (Par 97): **89,88,87,87,86 84,84,83,81,81 79**
toteswingers: 1&2 £6.50, 1&3 £1.60, 2&3 £5.30 CSF £32.53 TOTE £4.00: £1.30, £2.80, £1.50; EX 31.40.

Owner Lady Rothschild **Bred** The Rt Hon Lord Rothschild **Trained** Beckhampton, Wilts

FOCUS

The ground was officially on the fast side, with the GoingStick reading 9.1, but the times suggested it wasn't quite as quick as that and clearly the track had been well watered. The rails on the inside had been moved out by around eight feet between the 6f and 2f poles. This maiden was run at a steady pace but there were some nice types on show.

NOTEBOOK

Spoken, who'd clearly learnt plenty from his debut at Sandown, travelled kindly for the most part and picked up when asked. He should make up into a decent middle-distance colt next season, although his Derby entry looks a bit optimistic. (tchd 3-1 in places)

Youm Jamil(USA) ◆, a half-brother to six winners, was weak in the betting beforehand but he holds a Racing Post Trophy entry and knew his job first time up. He travelled like the best horse in the race before finding the more experienced winner too strong for him, and should in theory have few problems going one better with this run under his belt. However, on a note of caution, his sire's progeny often go well fresh and don't always build on early promise. (op 8-1)

Longliner, who is out of a half-sister to Russian Rhythm, was quite keen early but stayed on well at the finish without being given a hard time and looks sure to come on a bundle for his debut. He will be a 1m2f-plus horse next season. (tchd 9-4)

Seaside Sizzler, having recorded RPRs in the low 60s on his previous two starts, looks to have run his best race to date on his third start, clearly appreciating the step up to a mile. He can go the handicapping route now. (op 25-1 tchd 33-1)

Golden Waters, a half-sister to Oaks runner-up Something Exciting, flashed her tail when the whip was used and looked in need of the experience. It was a sound effort in the circumstances and there should be better to come from her with time. (tchd 40-1)

Viviani(IRE) stepped up considerably on his debut effort when not unfancied, making much of the running. He looks one for handicaps after one more run. (op 20-1)

Quick Reaction, fifth behind Derby hype horse Coordinated Cut at Doncaster last time, was well backed but proved disappointing, failing to give that form much of a boost. (op 100-30)

Baltic Ben(USA) was very much on his toes beforehand.

6394 FRANCIS CLARK CHARTERED ACCOUNTANTS H'CAP (DIV I) 1m
2:00 (2:00) (Class 6) (0-65,64) 3-Y-O+ £2,719 (£809; £404; £202) **Stalls** High

Form RPR

3201 **1** **Seasonal Cross**[17] 5905 4-9-6 **61**.................................... HayleyTurner 4 74
(S Dow) *hld up in last pair: swtchd to centre and hdwy fr over 2f out: chal over 1f out: led narrowly ins fnl f: rdn out* **11/4**[1]

1443 **2** *shd* **Solo River**[28] 5569 4-9-5 **60**.. RyanMoore 6 72
(P J Makin) *trckd ldrs: rdn to ld over 1f out: hdd narrowly ins fnl f: kpt on* **10/3**[2]

40-3 **3** *3 ¼* **Mighty Mover (IRE)**[26] 5630 7-8-9 **50**............................ DavidProbert 3 55
(B Palling) *trckd ldr: rdn to ld over 2f out: hdd over 1f out: kpt on same pce* **7/1**

0140 **4** *¾* **Aine's Delight (IRE)**[41] 5179 3-8-9 **59**........................ SimonPearce(5) 9 62
(Andrew Turnell) *mid-div: rdn over 2f out: styd on same pce* **10/1**

0-00 **5** *1 ¼* **My Jeanie (IRE)**[18] 5883 5-8-8 **49** oh3.......................... RichardSmith 7 49
(J C Fox) *mid-div: rdn 3f out: styd on same pce* **50/1**

0240 6 ½ **Fire King**[6] 6224 3-9-3 62........................ RobertHavlin 10 61
(J A Geake) *hld up in last pair: swtchd to centre and rdn 2f out: sme late prog: nvr a danger* 11/2[3]

0000 7 hd **Prince Of Thebes (IRE)**[17] 5914 8-9-8 63........................(v) LukeMorris 1 62
(M J Attwater) *sn led: rdn and hdd over 2f out: wknd ent fnl f* 8/1

6420 8 2¾ **Shared Moment (IRE)**[9] 6174 3-9-2 61........................(p) TPO'Shea 5 53
(J Gallagher) *hld up: hung rt u.p over 2f out: no imp* 8/1

0560 9 13 **Double Valentine**[21] 5779 6-8-10 51........................ KirstyMilczarek 2 14
(R Ingram) *mid-div: effrt 3f out: wknd 2f out* 33/1

1m 43.23s (-0.27) **Going Correction** 0.0s/f (Good)
WFA 3 from 4yo+ 4lb 9 Ran SP% **113.8**
Speed ratings (Par 101): **101,100,97,96,95 95,94,92,79**
toteswingers: 1&2 £2.70, 1&3 £2.80, 2&3 £4.10 CSF £11.71 CT £56.04 TOTE £4.10: £1.20, £1.40, £2.80; EX 11.80.
Owner Mrs Alicia Aldis **Bred** Adrienne And Michael Barnett **Trained** Epsom, Surrey

FOCUS
The free-going Prince Of Thebes ensured this handicap was run at a decent clip and it was very much set up for a closer. The form is tricky to pin down and is best rated through the third to his latest turf form.
Double Valentine Official explanation: jockey said mare moved poorly throughout

6395 KATHRYN PEATY CLAIMING STKS 1m 1f 198y
2:30 (2:31) (Class 5) 3-4-Y-0 **£3,238** (£963; £481; £240) **Stalls** High

Form RPR

2431 1 **Bagber**[37] 5314 3-9-5 77........................ RyanMoore 3 72
(H J L Dunlop) *trckd ldr: led over 5f out: rdn over 2f out: a doing enough* 8/13[1]

2502 2 1¾ **Sixties Swinger (USA)**[31] 5482 3-9-0 65........................(tp) PhilipRobinson 1 63
(M A Jarvis) *led tl over 5f out: rdn whn lost 2nd 3f out: regained 2nd over 1f out: a being hld* 11/2[3]

0242 3 8 **Salybia Bay**[6] 6226 3-7-12 59........................ CharlesEddery(7) 4 38
(R Hannon) *trckd ldrs: rdn to chse wnr 3f out tl over 1f out: sn btn and edgd rt* 4/1[2]

0030 4 ½ **By Command**[12] 6074 4-9-2 61........................(p) SebSanders 2 42
(J W Hills) *cl 4th: effrt over 3f out: btn 2f out* 9/1

2m 9.97s (0.07) **Going Correction** 0.0s/f (Good)
WFA 3 from 4yo 6lb 4 Ran SP% **107.3**
Speed ratings (Par 103): **99,97,91,90**
CSF £4.28 TOTE £1.40; EX 3.10.Bagber was claimed by Peter Monteith for £30,000.
Owner R J McCreery & Major & Mrs R B Kennard **Bred** Stowell Hill Ltd & Major & Mrs R B Kennard **Trained** Lambourn, Berks

FOCUS
These four had only won two races between them from 54 previous starts, and the form looks decidedly ordinary, with the runner-up the best guide.

6396 BILL GARNETT MEMORIAL H'CAP 6f
3:05 (3:05) (Class 4) (0-85,84) 3-Y-0+ **£4,857** (£1,445; £722; £360) **Stalls** High

Form RPR

1153 1 **Royal Intruder**[19] 5830 4-9-1 77........................ RichardHughes 9 86+
(S Donohoe, Ire) *hld up: rdn and hdwy over 1f out: r.o wl: led towards fin* 5/1[3]

1211 2 ½ **Triple Dream**[7] 6220 4-8-13 75 6ex........................(p) RyanMoore 7 82
(J M Bradley) *lw: disp ld: overall ldr over 2f out: sn rdn: kpt on but no ex whn hdd towards fin* 9/4[1]

2031 3 nse **Steelcut**[14] 5989 5-8-8 70........................ StephenCarson 2 77
(Andrew Reid) *fly-leapt leaving stalls: towards rr: hdwy over 2f out: sn rdn: kpt on fnl f* 20/1

0000 4 ¾ **Princess Valerina**[12] 6050 5-9-1 77........................ FrankieMcDonald 3 81
(D Haydn Jones) *s.i.s: towards rr: rdn over 2f out: no imp tl r.o ins fnl f: nrst fin* 33/1

1463 5 hd **Victoria Sponge (IRE)**[9] 6167 3-9-6 84........................ DaneO'Neill 6 88
(R Hannon) *trckd ldrs: rdn 3f out: kpt on same pce fnl f* 11/2

6000 6 ¾ **Phantom Whisper**[35] 5349 6-9-5 81........................ JimCrowley 1 82
(B R Millman) *mid-div: effrt 3f out: one pce fr over 1f out* 11/1

0005 7 1½ **Vhujon (IRE)**[8] 6187 4-9-5 81........................ GeorgeBaker 4 78
(P D Evans) *hld up: chsd ldrs 3f out: rdn over 2f out: wknd over 1f out* 9/2[2]

3231 8 shd **Maverin (IRE)**[93] 3460 3-9-0 78........................ RichardKingscote 8 74
(Tom Dascombe) *disp ld tl over 2f out: wknd fnl f* 8/1

1445 9 3¼ **Francis Walsingham (IRE)**[48] 4952 3-8-8 72........................ SteveDrowne 5 58
(H Morrison) *cl up: rdn over 2f out: wknd ent fnl f* 14/1

1m 15.37s (0.57) **Going Correction** 0.0s/f (Good)
WFA 3 from 4yo+ 2lb 9 Ran SP% **114.8**
Speed ratings (Par 105): **96,95,95,94,94 93,91,90,86**
toteswingers: 1&2 £3.40, 1&3 £16.50, 2&3 £7.30 CSF £16.54 CT £206.56 TOTE £5.60: £1.80, £1.40, £4.60; EX 15.70.
Owner Mrs Anna McDwyer **Bred** Farmers Hill Stud **Trained** Cootehill Road, Co. Cavan

FOCUS
A decent sprint handicap, but the early pace wasn't that strong and a couple were inclined to take a grip. The proximity of the fourth running her best race for a long time, raises doubts about the form.
Princess Valerina Official explanation: jockey said mare was slowly away
Maverin(IRE) Official explanation: jockey said colt ran too free

6397 EUROPEAN BREEDERS' FUND NOVICE STKS 6f 212y
3:40 (3:40) (Class 4) 2-Y-0 **£6,476** (£1,927; £963; £481) **Stalls** High

Form RPR

104 1 **Fremont (IRE)**[20] 5795 2-9-5 103........................ RichardHughes 2 96+
(R Hannon) *lw: trckd ldr: hanging lft whn taking the ld wl over 1f out: sn drifted across trck to stands' side rail: rdn and r.o wl* 8/13[1]

1 2 2½ **Side Glance**[12] 6061 2-9-5 0........................ LPKeniry 4 90
(A M Balding) *lw: trckd ldrs: rdn to dispute 2nd fr wl over 1f out: kpt on but nt pce of wnr* 5/1[3]

31 3 ½ **Folly Bridge**[22] 5749 2-8-11 81........................ SteveDrowne 3 80
(R Charlton) *racd in cl 4th: rdn to dispute 2nd fr wl over 1f out: kpt on but no ex towards fin* 7/2[2]

3204 4 shd **Antonius Moris (IRE)**[18] 5853 2-9-2 82........................ RichardKingscote 1 85
(Tom Dascombe) *racd in cl 5th: rdn to dispute 2nd fr wl over 1f out: kpt on but no ex towards fin* 25/1

061 5 5 **Kumbeshwar**[18] 5852 2-9-0 81........................ RichardEvans(5) 5 75
(P D Evans) *led: rdn over 3f out: hdd wl over 1f out: sn wknd* 25/1

1m 29.17s (0.17) **Going Correction** 0.0s/f (Good) 5 Ran SP% **108.5**
Speed ratings (Par 97): **99,96,95,95,89**
CSF £3.99 TOTE £1.60: £1.10, £1.70; EX 4.00.
Owner Mrs J Wood **Bred** Peter Gibbons And Dermot Forde **Trained** East Everleigh, Wilts

FOCUS
A decent novice event. The fourth limits the form and the winner did not need to reproduce his Doncaster run.

NOTEBOOK
Fremont(IRE) looked to hold very strong claims in this company. That form had been boosted by the third Lucky General winning the Goffs Million Sprint next time out, and the fifth Take Ten finishing a close second in the Tattersalls Timeform Million Sprint, so it was understandable when he was backed into 8-13. He drifted right across the track to the stands' side from two furlongs out, but he had so much in hand it didn't matter, and he kept on well to win by a cosy margin. He didn't need to improve to win this, though, so little new was learnt. That's probably it for him for this season, and he's apparently likely to reappear in a Guineas trial. (op 8-11)
Side Glance, a shock winner on his debut, has stamina in his pedigree and was expected to appreciate the step up to 7f. It's questionable whether he improved greatly on his Newmarket form, given the proximity of the exposed Antonius Moris in fourth, but he got the trip well and looks the type to do much better at three. (op 9-2 tchd 11-2)
Folly Bridge won nicely at Lingfield last time and the way she saw her race out that day suggested she might be suited by a step up to 7f. Her pedigree raised question marks, though, and having raced keenly through the early stages she failed to quite see it out. There is better to come from her, but perhaps as a sprinter. (tchd 3-1)
Antonius Moris(IRE), the most exposed runner in the line-up, had run to similar marks in three of his previous four starts, and his performance gives a pretty good guide to the level of the form. (op 16-1)
Kumbeshwar, who made all from the one box at Chester last time, was always going to find it harder repeating the trick in this better company. (op 18-1)

6398 AXA WINTERTHUR WEALTH MANAGEMENT CONDITIONS STKS 6f
4:15 (4:15) (Class 2) 2-Y-0
£8,411 (£2,519; £1,259; £630; £314; £157) **Stalls** High

Form RPR

210 1 **Mon Cadeaux**[22] 5743 2-9-1 94........................ WilliamBuick 4 99+
(A M Balding) *lw: trckd ldrs: nt clr run 2f out: squeezed through gap to ld over 1f out: r.o strly: readily* 5/2[1]

1036 2 2¾ **Chaperno (USA)**[25] 5661 2-9-1 95........................ LDettori 1 91
(Saeed Bin Suroor) *lw: hld up last: smooth hdwy over 2f out: rdn whn edgd rt and ev ch over 1f out: kpt on but nt pce of wnr* 6/1[3]

1 3 hd **San Cassiano (IRE)**[21] 5778 2-8-12 0........................ SebSanders 6 88
(R M Beckett) *w'like: scope: str: prom: rdn and ev ch over 1f out: kpt on but nt pce of wnr ins fnl f* 5/2[1]

4101 4 ½ **Marcus Cicero (IRE)**[11] 6104 2-8-12 86........................ JimCrowley 3 86
(P Winkworth) *in tch: effrt 2f out: nvr quite ev ch but kpt on fnl f* 6/1[3]

2030 5 hd **Di Stefano**[20] 5795 2-9-1 97........................ RyanMoore 7 88
(M R Channon) *lw: chsd ldrs tl lost position over 3f out: sn rdn: styd on fr 2f out but unable to mount chal* 4/1[2]

4346 6 ½ **Footstepsofspring (FR)**[21] 5763 2-9-1 89........................ RichardHughes 5 87
(R Hannon) *restrained s: rdn 3f out: swtchd lft 2f out: styd on late: nvr a threat* 20/1

1045 7 8 **Anjomarba (IRE)**[51] 4850 2-8-10 78........................ JackDean 2 58
(W G M Turner) *prom: rdn over 2f out: wknd over 1f out* 66/1

6211 8 ½ **Italian Tom (IRE)**[14] 5992 2-8-12 80........................ RobertWinston 8 58
(R A Harris) *sn led: drifted lft u.p over 2f out: hdd over 1f out: wknd* 16/1

1m 14.93s (0.13) **Going Correction** 0.0s/f (Good) 8 Ran SP% **117.9**
Speed ratings (Par 101): **99,95,95,94,94 93,82,82**
toteswingers: 1&2 £3.30, 1&3 £3.30, 2&3 £4.90 CSF £19.01 TOTE £3.90: £1.40, £1.40, £1.60; EX 14.30.
Owner Mick and Janice Mariscotti **Bred** Stourbank Stud **Trained** Kingsclere, Hants

FOCUS
An interesting conditions event, won last year by subsequent Jersey Stakes winner Ouqba. Improvement from Mon Cadeaux, with Chaperno not far off his best.

NOTEBOOK
Mon Cadeaux ♦ had won his maiden in ready fashion here in August, but failed to run up to expectations when upped in both trip and grade in a Listed race at Goodwood last time. Back down to 6f here, he showed his true ability, brushing the Godolphin horse aside from a furlong out and running out a convincing winner. His pedigree suggests he should have no trouble getting further next year, and easier ground shouldn't be a concern at all. The Horris Hill will be considered, but it's just as likely he'll be put away for the year now. He should develop into a Pattern-class performer next term, though. (op 11-4)
Chaperno(USA) hasn't gone on since winning his maiden. He travelled well here but, not first the first time, didn't fancy it at all once asked to battle, hoisting the white flag pronto. He continues to look one to oppose, especially in running. (op 11-2 tchd 5-1)
San Cassiano(IRE), whose maiden form is working out well, still looked a bit green but shaped well on this rise in class. There should be better to come from this big gelding especially as a three-year-old. (op 3-1)
Marcus Cicero(IRE), who got up in a bunch finish to win a nursery off 83 last time out, had more on his plate in this company and didn't run too badly. (op 7-1 tchd 15-2)
Di Stefano, who came into the race with the highest official rating, was again disappointing and looks to have had enough for the season now. Official explanation: jockey said colt hung left-handed (op 9-2 tchd 7-2)
Footstepsofspring(FR) struggled to get involved from off the pace and looks exposed now. (tchd 18-1)
Italian Tom(IRE) Official explanation: jockey said colt hung left-handed

6399 FRANCIS CLARK CHARTERED ACCOUNTANTS H'CAP (DIV II) 1m
4:50 (4:50) (Class 6) (0-65,65) 3-Y-0+ **£2,719** (£809; £404; £202) **Stalls** High

Form RPR

0052 1 **Dichoh**[21] 5779 6-9-5 58........................(v) GeorgeBaker 8 64
(M Madgwick) *in tch: nt clr run over 2f out: rdn and r.o alone on far side rails whn field drifted lft fnl f: edgd lft fnl 75yds: led cl home* 9/1[3]

00-4 2 ½ **In The Mood (IRE)**[15] 5965 3-9-8 65........................ AlanMunro 2 70
(W Jarvis) *lw: bmpd leaving stalls: prom: led over 2f out: sn rdn: drifted lft over 1f out: hdd cl home* 11/1

5000 3 nk **Batchworth Blaise**[32] 5429 6-8-9 48........................ DavidProbert 11 53
(E A Wheeler) *hld up towards rr: gd hdwy fr over 2f out: sn rdn: ch over 1f out: styd on but no ex* 12/1

0200 4 1¼ **Annes Rocket (IRE)**[7] 6213 4-9-2 55........................ SamHitchcott 5 58+
(J C Fox) *t.k.h in mid-div: nt clrest of runs but travelling ok over 1f out: r.o jst ins fnl f: fining wl whn stopped in cl 3rd fnl 30yds* 12/1

5 ¾ **Orpen Winger (IRE)**[24] 5702 4-9-3 56........................ LDettori 7 56
(A J Martin, Ire) *hld up towards rr: rdn and stdy prog fr over 2f out: styd on fnl f* 5/1[2]

-662 6 1 **Foxtrot Bravo (IRE)**[28] 5574 3-9-4 61........................ SteveDrowne 9 59
(Miss S L Davison) *trckd ldrs: rdn over 2f out: kpt on same pce fnl f* 9/1[3]

2144 7 ¾ **Dr Wintringham (IRE)**[17] 5905 3-9-3 60........................ RyanMoore 10 56
(Karen George) *hld up bhd: rdn 2f out: styd on fnl f: nvr a danger* 2/1[1]

4-06 8 nk **Pagan Force (IRE)**[15] 5965 3-9-7 64........................(b[1]) JimCrowley 4 59
(Mrs A J Perrett) *wnt sltly lft s: mid-div: rdn and hdwy over 2f out: fdd ins fnl f* 16/1

-606 9 1 ½ **Highland Starlight (USA)**[25] 5683 3-8-12 **55**............ PhilipRobinson 1 47
(C G Cox) *led tl hung lft u.p over 2f out: wknd ent fnl f* **12/1**
0000 10 1 **Iron Man Of Mersey (FR)**[17] 5905 3-8-4 **47** oh2.........(b[1]) LukeMorris 3 37
(A W Carroll) *t.k.h: a towards rr* **50/1**
360- 11 nk **Christophers Quest**[404] 5218 4-9-7 **60**............ RichardKingscote 6 49
(Miss N A Lloyd-Beavis) *chsd ldrs: rdn 3f out: wknd over 1f out* **11/1**
1m 44.98s (1.48) **Going Correction** 0.0s/f (Good)
WFA 3 from 4yo+ 4lb 11 Ran SP% **117.6**
Speed ratings (Par 101): **92,91,91,89,89 88,87,87,85,84 84**
toteswingers: 1&2 £6.60, 1&3 £22.40, 2&3 £28.80 CSF £103.84 CT £1219.05 TOTE £8.90: £2.30, £2.60, £4.60; EX 62.50.
Owner Derek J Willis **Bred** Red House Stud **Trained** Denmead, Hants
■ Stewards' Enquiry : George Baker one-day ban: careless riding (Oct 14)
FOCUS
The slower of the two divisions by 1.75sec. The form is muddling but best rated around the placed horses.
Highland Starlight(USA) Official explanation: jockey said filly hung left-handed

6400 HORSESFIRSTRACING.COM H'CAP 1m 6f 21y
5:20 (5:20) (Class 5) (0-75,74) 3-Y-0+ £3,238 (£963; £481; £240)

Form RPR
4142 1 **Mykingdomforahorse**[18] 5876 3-9-7 **72**............ RyanMoore 4 81+
(M R Channon) *lw: hld up last: hdwy over 2f out: burst through to ld wl over 1f out: styd on strly: readily* **5/2**[1]
6523 2 2 **Theologist (IRE)**[32] 5430 3-9-5 **70**............(v[1]) JimCrowley 2 76
(Mrs A J Perrett) *trckd ldr: rdn and ev ch 2f out: sn no ch w wnr* **3/1**[2]
-060 3 3 ¾ **Whenever**[24] 5696 5-9-10 **65**............ GeorgeBaker 6 66
(R T Phillips) *led: rdn over 2f out: hdd wl over 1f out: no ex* **17/2**
2030 4 1 ¼ **Warrior Conquest**[26] 5642 4-9-4 **64**............ Louis-PhilippeBeuzelin[(5)] 5 63
(W J Knight) *cl up: rdn 3f out: hung rt 2f out: one pce after* **11/1**
53-4 5 1 ½ **Wester Ross (IRE)**[30] 5122 5-9-5 **60**............ LukeMorris 8 57
(J M P Eustace) *mid-div: rdn 3f out: styd on same pce fnl 2f* **9/2**[3]
0005 6 5 **Sufad**[20] 5802 4-9-6 **61**............(b[1]) KirstyMilczarek 1 51
(T D McCarthy) *mid-div: effrt 3f out: wknd ent fnl f* **25/1**
10 7 ¾ **Drussell (IRE)**[18] 5857 3-9-9 **74**............ SteveDrowne 9 63
(S Donohoe, Ire) *hld up: effrt over 2f out: wknd over 1f out* **20/1**
0210 8 4 **Fantino**[15] 5975 3-9-2 **67**............ DavidProbert 7 50
(J Mackie) *w ldr: slipped on bnd 7f out: rdn 3f out: wknd over 1f out* **6/1**
0340 9 ½ **Royal Willy (IRE)**[27] 5593 3-9-3 **68**............ AlanMunro 3 51
(W Jarvis) *lw: hld up: rn wd on bnd 7f out: rdn over 5f out: wknd 2f out* **12/1**
3m 8.76s (1.36) **Going Correction** 0.0s/f (Good)
WFA 3 from 4yo+ 10lb 9 Ran SP% **121.2**
Speed ratings (Par 103): **96,94,92,92,91 88,87,85,85**
toteswingers: 1&2 £3.20, 1&3 £4.30, 2&3 £10.00 CSF £10.70 CT £56.71 TOTE £2.50: £1.10, £1.50, £3.40; EX 7.60 Place 6: £5.64, Place 5: £3.85.
Owner C C Buckley **Bred** Hunscote House Farm Stud **Trained** West Ilsley, Berks
FOCUS
A modest handicap but the winner is unexposed at the trip and can do better, although there is little solid behind the front pair.
Whenever Official explanation: jockey said gelding hung left-handed
T/Plt: £5.40 to a £1 stake. Pool: £49,124.31. 6,604.77 winning tickets. T/Qpdt: £4.20 to a £1 stake. Pool: £3,001.36. 522.88 winning tickets. TM

4678 SLIGO (R-H)
Wednesday, September 30
OFFICIAL GOING: Good to yielding (yielding in places) changing to yielding (soft in places) after race 4 (4.45)

6401a IRISH STALLION FARMS EUROPEAN BREEDERS FUND MEDIAN AUCTION MAIDEN 6f 110y
3:10 (3:11) 2-Y-0 £7,715 (£1,797; £792; £457)

RPR
1 **Thunder Bridge (USA)** 2-9-3............ PJSmullen 1 105+
(D K Weld, Ire) *trckd ldrs: 6th 1/2-way: hdwy in 4th 2f out: rdn to ld over 1f out: kpt on strly to go clr fnl f: impressive* **4/1**[2]
2 13 **Dinger Belle (IRE)**[19] 5843 2-8-12............ CDHayes 14 66+
(Andrew Oliver, Ire) *chsd ldrs: led after 2f: rdn and hdd over 1f out: no ex and kpt on same pce* **3/1**[1]
3 3 **Sailors Warn (IRE)**[20] 5817 2-9-3............ WJLee 5 61
(Timothy Doyle, Ire) *towards rr: 10th 2f out: rdn into 5th 1f out: kpt on fnl f* **16/1**
4 3 **Duchess Of Foxland (IRE)**[5] 6261 2-8-9............ EJMcNamara[(3)] 3 48
(Mark L Fagan, Ire) *chsd ldrs: 5th 1/2-way: rdn in 3rd 2f out: no ex over 1f out: kpt on same pce* **8/1**
5 shd **Killeeter (IRE)** 2-8-12............ DPMcDonogh 4 47
(Kevin Prendergast, Ire) *chsd ldrs: 3rd 1/2-way: 2nd 2f out: rdn and no ex over 1f out: kpt on same pce* **11/2**[3]
6 2 ½ **Rye Rhythm (IRE)**[39] 5273 2-8-9............ PBBeggy[(3)] 7 41
(P Cluskey, Ire) *mid-div: rdn in mod 6th 2f out: kpt on one pce* **33/1**
7 2 ½ **East Of Tara (IRE)**[18] 5893 2-8-12............ DJMoran 9 34
(Desmond McDonogh, Ire) *mid-div: rdn and no imp over 2f out: kpt on one pce* **20/1**
8 4 ½ **Elusive Art (IRE)**[48] 4959 2-8-12............ CO'Donoghue 13 21
(David Marnane, Ire) *led: hdd after 2f: 2nd 1/2-way: rdn in 5th 2f out: sn no ex* **16/1**
9 6 **Debbie Harri (IRE)**[19] 5845 2-8-7............ GFCarroll[(5)] 15 5
(Michael Mulvany, Ire) *towards rr: sme late hdwy st: nvr a factor* **25/1**
10 4 ½ **Tj's Joy (IRE)**[85] 3723 2-8-10............ KarenKenny[(7)] 12 —
(Patrick Martin, Ire) *chsd ldrs: 4th 1/2-way: rdn and wknd over 2f out* **50/1**
11 5 **Mac Tiernan (IRE)** 2-8-10............ RobbieEgan[(7)] 10 —
(P J Lally, Ire) *s.i.s: towards rr for most* **14/1**
12 ¾ **Lily Of Laguna (IRE)** 2-8-12............ PShanahan 11 —
(Tracey Collins, Ire) *a towards rr* **10/1**
13 2 ½ **Intomeisee (IRE)** 2-8-7............ DEMullins[(5)] 8 —
(Daniel Miley, Ire) *mid-div: rdn and wknd over 2f out* **16/1**
14 9 **Xtraxtra (IRE)**[17] 5920 2-9-3 **72**............ KLatham 2 —
(M J Grassick, Ire) *prom on outer early: rdn in 7th 1/2-way: sn wknd* **7/1**
1m 31.34s (-1.76) 14 Ran SP% **130.9**
CSF £17.32 TOTE £3.80: £2.40, £1.30, £5.60; DF 13.50.
Owner K Abdulla **Bred** Millsec, Ltd **Trained** The Curragh, Co Kildare

FOCUS
A seriously impressive performance from the winner, worthy of a rating equal to that given to Grey Swallow when he won by ten lengths on his debut in 2003. He looks Group class alerady.
NOTEBOOK
Thunder Bridge(USA) powered right away from his rivals once asked for an effort and ran out a visually very impressive debut winner. Using the placed horses as a guide this was a seriously decent initial effort and, while he has no entries, his next appearance is eagerly anticipated. His pedigree suggests 1m should be within his compass next year. (op 5/2)

6402 - 6407a (Foreign Racing) - See Raceform Interactive

6088 AYR (L-H)
Thursday, October 1
OFFICIAL GOING: Good to firm (good in places; 7.8)
False rail used on both sides of straight course and rail realignment on round course increased distances by about 10yds.
Wind: Slight against Weather: Fine and dry

6408 UP TO £125 FREE BET AT VICTORCHANDLER.COM MEDIAN AUCTION MAIDEN STKS 6f
1:50 (1:51) (Class 5) 2-Y-0 £2,914 (£867; £433; £216) Stalls High

Form RPR
1 **Amitola (IRE)** 2-8-12 0............ PhillipMakin 2 89+
(T D Barron) *cl up gng wl: shkn up to ld wl over 1f out: clr ins fnl f and styd on wl* **6/1**
4 2 6 **Kellys Eye (IRE)**[24] 5728 2-9-3 0............ TomEaves 3 76
(B Smart) *chsd ldrs: rdn along and sltly outpcd 2f out: kpt on u.p ins fnl f: no ch w wnr* **5/2**[1]
3405 3 3 ¼ **Olympic Ceremony**[16] 5957 2-9-3 68............ PaulHanagan 10 66
(R A Fahey) *led: rdn along 2f out: hdd wl over 1f out and grad wknd* **15/2**
0363 4 ½ **Mercers Row**[15] 5977 2-9-3 69............ DanielTudhope 9 65
(A Dickman) *prom: rdn along 2f out: drvn wl over 1f out: kpt on same pce* **7/2**[2]
5 5 4 ½ **Dies Solis**[13] 6047 2-9-3 0............ TonyHamilton 4 51
(I Semple) *in tch: rdn along over 2f out and sn wknd* **10/1**
6 1 **Bobby McGee** 2-8-12 0............ AndrewElliott 5 43+
(Jedd O'Keeffe) *chsd ldrs: rdn along: rn green and lost pl 1/2-way: sn bhd: swtchd lftand hdwy wl over 1f out: kpt on ins fnl f: nrst fin* **33/1**
40 7 1 ¾ **Wing N Prayer (IRE)**[39] 5290 2-8-5 0............ BillyCray[(7)] 1 38
(A Berry) *sn rdn along and a towards rr* **100/1**
0 8 2 **Goodison Goal (IRE)**[21] 5785 2-8-12 0............ SJCraine 6 32
(Patrick Morris) *a in rr* **25/1**
55 9 2 ¾ **Silver Socks**[13] 6046 2-9-3 0............ DavidAllan 8 29
(I Semple) *in tch: rdn along over 2f out and sn wknd* **5/1**[3]
0 10 1 ¼ **Thescottishsoldier**[68] 4308 2-9-3 0............ AndrewMullen 11 25
(A G Foster) *dwlt: in tch on stands' rail: rdn along wl over 2f out and sn wknd* **28/1**
00 11 nk **Sumay Buoy (IRE)**[14] 6009 2-8-12 0............ LanceBetts[(5)] 7 24
(Mrs J C McGregor) *midfield: rdn along 1/2-way: sn wknd* **66/1**
1m 11.77s (-1.83) **Going Correction** -0.225s/f (Firm) 11 Ran SP% **115.3**
Speed ratings (Par 95): **103,95,90,90,84 82,80,77,74,72 71**
toteswingers: 1&2 £5.40, 1&3 £10.80, 2&3 £3.60 CSF £20.17 TOTE £6.10: £1.80, £1.60, £2.80; EX 16.90.
Owner J Browne **Bred** Patrick J Monahan **Trained** Maunby, N Yorks
FOCUS
On a breezy day the ground was very much on the quick side of good. A modest maiden but a useful winner of real potential and the form is worth rating at face value around the third and fourth.
NOTEBOOK
Amitola(IRE), a half-sister to three winners including the one-time useful sprinter Damika, came in for plenty of market support and certainly knew her job. She had the leader covered and after hitting the front came right away for quite an impressive success. Her nursery mark will be in the high 80s so if she runs again this season it may have to be the novice route. (op 14-1 tchd 11-2)
Kellys Eye(IRE), fourth on his debut at Newcastle, stepped up on that effort and should be able to go one better. (op 9-4)
Olympic Ceremony, having his eighth start, is officially rated 68. After taking them along he was swept aside by the winner and struggled to hang on to third. He looks fully exposed. (op 8-1)
Mercers Row, having his seventh start, is another who seems to have reached the limit of his improvement. He will struggle in nursery company from a mark of 69. (op 100-30 tchd 3-1)
Dies Solis, who showed a glimmer of ability over 7f here two weeks ago, looks more of a type for handicaps at three. (op 8-1 tchd 11-1)

6409 VICTORCHANDLER.COM NURSERY 5f
2:20 (2:20) (Class 5) (0-75,70) 2-Y-0 £2,914 (£867; £433; £216) Stalls High

Form RPR
5013 1 **Bossy Kitty**[15] 5992 2-9-3 **66**............ AndrewElliott 1 68
(N Tinkler) *chsd ldrs: swtchd lft to outer and hdwy 2f out: rdn wl over 1f out: styd on to ld ins fnl f* **7/1**
0602 2 nk **Powerful Pierre**[15] 5976 2-9-3 **66**............(v) TonyHamilton 3 67
(Jedd O'Keeffe) *chsd ldr: rdn along 2f out: styd on to chal ent fnl f and evch tl drvn and kpt on same pce towards fin* **7/1**
3520 3 2 ¼ **Silver Linnet (IRE)**[21] 5797 2-8-11 **60**............ DavidAllan 7 53
(T D Easterby) *chsd ldrs: hdwy 1/2-way: sn rdn and hung rt over 1f out: kpt on u.p ins fnl f* **11/4**[1]
5232 4 nk **Bronze Beau**[28] 5596 2-8-13 **69**............ KristinStubbs[(7)] 5 61
(Mrs L Stubbs) *t.k.h: led and sn clr: rdn along over 2f out: drvn and hung bdly lft over 1f out: hdd & wknd ins fnl f* **5/1**[3]
4635 5 1 ½ **Jack Luey**[27] 5620 2-9-7 **70**............ DuranFentiman 8 56
(L A Mullaney) *chsd ldrs: rdn along 1/2-way: sn drvn and one pce* **20/1**
0360 6 nk **Flow Chart (IRE)**[28] 5595 2-9-2 **65**............ PhillipMakin 10 50
(T D Barron) *chsd ldrs: rdn along over 2f out: sn drvn and kpt on same pce* **9/2**[2]
0064 7 ¾ **Kristen Jane (USA)**[11] 6134 2-8-4 **53**............ PaulHanagan 9 36
(Miss L A Perratt) *dwlt and a towards rr* **13/2**
050 8 1 ¼ **Classlin**[12] 6090 2-8-11 **60**............ DanielTudhope 6 38
(J S Goldie) *s.i.s and bhd: swtchd to wd outside and sme hdwy 1/2-way: rdn wl over 1f out and sn btn* **20/1**
300 9 11 **Safari Camp (IRE)**[27] 5620 2-7-11 **53**............(t) BillyCray[(7)] 4 —
(A Berry) *chsd ldrs: rdn along bef 1/2-way and sn wknd* **50/1**
59.64 secs (-0.46) **Going Correction** -0.225s/f (Firm) 9 Ran SP% **111.3**
Speed ratings (Par 95): **94,93,89,89,87 86,85,83,65**
toteswingers: 1&2 £7.10, 1&3 £6.20, 2&3 £6.50 CSF £51.33 CT £163.45 TOTE £4.40: £1.50, £2.50, £1.70; EX 41.90.
Owner Leeds Plywood And Doors Ltd **Bred** J P Coggan **Trained** Langton, N Yorks
FOCUS
A very modest nursery handicap with only one previous winner in the line-up.

NOTEBOOK

Bossy Kitty, now rated 66, she stuck on in most willing fashion to enjoy quite a decisive success. She seems to handle both quick and easy ground equally well. (op 6-1)

Powerful Pierre, runner-up in a selling nursery at Beverley when visored for the first time, ran from a 3lb higher mark and stuck on to finish a highly creditable second. (op 8-1 tchd 9-1)

Silver Linnet(IRE), closely matched with the winner on Ripon easy ground form, struggled to keep up then showed a tendency to edge right. The ground may have been quicker than she prefers. (tchd 3-1)

Bronze Beau, runner-up three times from eight previous outings, showed bags of speed to take them along. He hung away from the fence and seemed to fold very tamely. (tchd 9-2)

Jack Luey looked to have been given a stiff mark on his nursery bow and never threatened. (op 16-1)

Flow Chart(IRE), already tried in blinkers, had run over 7f on his previous starts and he looks to have connections scratching their heads.

6410 BEN H'CAP 5f
2:55 (2:55) (Class 6) (0-58,57) 3-Y-0+ **£2,729** (£806; £403) **Stalls High**

Form RPR

5332 **1** **Lost In Paris (IRE)**[4] 6308 3-9-2 **57**.....(b) DavidAllan 10 70+
(T D Easterby) *mde all: rdn clr wl over 1f out: kpt on* **2/1**[1]

0600 **2** *3* **Hosanna**[17] 5946 3-8-6 **47**..... PaulHanagan 6 49
(J Barclay) *cl up: rdn along 2f out: drvn and sltly outpcd over 1f out: kpt on u.p ins fnl f* **40/1**

1040 **3** *shd* **Darcy's Pride (IRE)**[1] 6380 5-9-2 **57**.....(t) TonyHamilton 3 59
(P T Midgley) *chsd ldrs on outer: rdn along 2f out: drvn and edgd lft over 1f out: kpt on same pce ins fnl f* **11/1**

0301 **4** *nk* **Half A Crown (IRE)**[24] 5727 4-9-2 **57**.....(v) PhillipMakin 14 58+
(M Dods) *hld up towards rr: smooth hdwy 1/2-way: chsd ldrs over 1f out: sn rdn and edgd lft ins fnl f: sn drvn and one pce* **6/1**[2]

623 **5** *shd* **Lake Chini (IRE)**[38] 5309 7-9-2 **57**.....(b) DaleGibson 8 57
(M W Easterby) *dwlt and sn rdn along towards rr: hdwy and in tch 1/2-way: drvn along wl over 1f out: kpt on same pce* **12/1**

4621 **6** *nk* **Captain Royale (IRE)**[10] 6161 4-8-10 **56** 6ex....(p) AndrewHeffernan(5) 4 55
(Miss Tracy Waggott) *chsd ldrs: rdn along 2f out: drvn over 1f out: kpt on same pce* **6/1**[2]

0003 **7** *½* **Star Addition**[1] 6379 3-8-4 **45**..... DuranFentiman 11 43+
(E J Alston) *dwlt and towards rr: hdwy 2f out: n.m.r and swtchd lft over 1f out: sn rdn and kpt on: nrst fin* **22/1**

3040 **8** *½* **Fern House (IRE)**[4] 6314 7-8-4 **45**.....(b) AndrewMullen 7 41
(Bruce Hellier) *s.i.s and bhd: rdn and sme hdwy fnl 2f: nvr a factor* **20/1**

010/ **9** *3 ½* **Blue Cross Boy (USA)**[20] 5846 4-8-9 **50**.....(b) CDHayes 15 33
(Adrian McGuinness, Ire) *in tch on outer: rdn along 1/2-way: nvr a factor* **8/1**[3]

4 **10** *¾* **San Diego Prince**[17] 5946 5-8-13 **54**.....(tp) JohnEgan 2 34
(Muredach Kelly, Ire) *chsd ldrs on outer: rdn along 2f out and sn wknd* **10/1**

665 **11** *¾* **Frisky Queen (IRE)**[36] 5336 3-7-13 **45**..... BACurtis(5) 13 23
(T G McCourt, Ire) *midfield: rdn along 2f out and nvr a factor* **33/1**

0000 **12** *2 ¾* **Blazing Heights**[4] 6314 6-8-9 **55**.....(v) GaryBartley(5) 9 23
(J S Goldie) *chsd ldrs: rdn along wl over 1f out and sn wknd* **14/1**

0000 **13** *nk* **Miacarla**[38] 5309 6-7-11 **45**.....(tp) JamesPSullivan(7) 5 12
(H A McWilliams) *s.i.s: hdwy and in tch 1/2-way: sn rdn and wknd* **66/1**

4600 **14** *5* **Tarus (IRE)**[24] 5727 5-7-11 **45**..... BillyCray(7) 12 —
(A Berry) *bhd fr 1/2-way* **80/1**

58.83 secs (-1.27) **Going Correction** -0.225s/f (Firm) **14** Ran SP% **122.0**

Speed ratings (Par 101): **101,96,96,95,95 94,94,93,87,86 85,80,80,72**

toteswingers: 1&2 £20.10, 1&3 £12.90, 2&3 £48.40 CSF £118.86 CT £777.99 TOTE £2.70: £1.30, £5.50, £3.50; EX 131.80.

Owner W H Ponsonby **Bred** Yeomanstown Stud **Trained** Great Habton, N Yorks

FOCUS

A low-grade sprint handicap and the action was all middle-to-far side. The form looks pretty solid rated around the third and fourth.

Miacarla Official explanation: jockey said he was slow to remove blind and mare missed the break

6411 NEW WEBSITE AT VICTORCHANDLER.COM H'CAP 1m
3:30 (3:30) (Class 6) (0-65,65) 3-Y-0+ **£2,729** (£806; £403) **Stalls Low**

Form RPR

-165 **1** **Social Rhythm**[10] 6157 5-8-10 **54**..... PaulHanagan 10 65
(A C Whillans) *hld up in rr: hdwy on wd outside over 2f out: rdn to chal 1f out: drvn to ld and hung lft ins fnl f: kpt on wl towards fin* **8/1**

0064 **2** *hd* **French Art**[8] 6218 4-9-3 **61**..... AndrewElliott 6 72
(N Tinkler) *hld up in rr: gd hdwy 3f out: rdn to ld wl over 1f out: drvn and hdd ins fnl f: kpt on gamely u.p* **6/1**[3]

1044 **3** *3 ½* **Moonage Daydream (IRE)**[10] 6157 4-9-4 **62**.....(b) DavidAllan 2 64
(T D Easterby) *in tch: hdwy 3f out: rdn along to chse ldrs 3f out: drvn and kpt on ins fnl f* **5/1**[1]

0060 **4** *1* **This Ones For Eddy**[19] 5884 4-9-4 **62**..... JohnEgan 14 62+
(J Balding) *chsd ldrs: hdwy 3f out: rdn to chse ldr over 2f out: effrt and ev ch over 1f out: sn drvn and one pce* **11/2**[2]

2500 **5** *1 ¼* **Jamieson Gold (IRE)**[17] 5941 6-8-8 **52**.....(p) TonyHamilton 12 49
(Miss L A Perratt) *midfield: hdwy over 2f out: sn rdn and kpt on same pce appr fnl f* **20/1**

6540 **6** *½* **Woodsley House (IRE)**[10] 6157 7-9-2 **65**.....(p) BMcHugh(5) 5 61
(A G Foster) *bhd: hdwy on inner over 2f out: sn rdn and kpt on ins fnl f: nrst fin* **20/1**

1260 **7** *¾* **Botham (USA)**[10] 6157 5-9-6 **64**..... DanielTudhope 9 58
(J S Goldie) *s.i.s and bhd: swtchd to wd outside and hdwy over 2f out: sn rdn and kpt on ins fnl f: nrst fin* **20/1**

4044 **8** *1* **Red Skipper (IRE)**[14] 6012 4-9-0 **58**..... AndrewMullen 11 50
(N Wilson) *chsd ldrs: rdn along 3f out and sn wknd* **8/1**

4301 **9** *1 ¾* **Pokfulham (IRE)**[13] 6052 3-8-11 **61**.....(v) KellyHarrison(3) 13 49
(J S Goldie) *chsd ldrs: rdn along 3f out: wknd over 2f out* **12/1**

1450 **10** *1 ¼* **Royal Premium**[12] 6103 3-8-5 **57**.....(v) LanceBetts(5) 1 42
(Mrs G S Rees) *led: clr 1/2-way: rdn along over 2f out: drvn and hdd wl over 1f out: sn wknd* **10/1**

-444 **11** *3 ¼* **Battle Royal (IRE)**[30] 5544 3-8-13 **60**..... TomEaves 4 38
(B Smart) *trckd ldr: rdn along 3f out: drvn over 2f out and sn wknd* **8/1**

4260 **12** *1 ¼* **Apache Nation (IRE)**[35] 5364 6-8-12 **56**..... PhillipMakin 3 31
(M Dods) *chsd ldrs: rdn along over 3f out: sn wknd* **10/1**

6-00 **13** *shd* **Toberogan (IRE)**[19] 5872 8-8-8 **52**..... RoystonFfrench 8 27
(W A Murphy, Ire) *s.i.s: a in rr* **66/1**

1m 40.71s (-3.09) **Going Correction** -0.225s/f (Firm) **13** Ran SP% **121.3**

WFA 3 from 4yo+ 3lb

Speed ratings (Par 101): **106,105,102,101,100 99,98,97,96,94 91,90,90**

toteswingers: 1&2 £20.30, 1&3 £14.40, 2&3 £2.30 CSF £53.58 CT £279.12 TOTE £10.40: £3.30, £2.20, £2.10; EX 80.10.

Owner Mrs L M Whillans **Bred** A And B Fairfields **Trained** Newmill-On-Slitrig, Borders

■ Stewards' Enquiry : Paul Hanagan caution: careless riding

FOCUS

Due to a re-alignment of the rails the round course was about 12 yards longer than the advertised distances. A very modest handicap run at a very strong gallop and the first two came from off the pace. The third looks a sound-enough guide.

6412 VICTORCHANDLER.COM H'CAP 1m 5f 13y
4:05 (4:05) (Class 3) (0-95,93) 3-Y-0+ **£7,771** (£2,312; £1,155; £577) **Stalls Low**

Form RPR

5055 **1** **Quai D'Orsay**[19] 5865 3-9-6 **93**..... RoystonFfrench 5 99+
(M Johnston) *chsd ldr: pushed along 3f out and sn lost pl: rdn and rallied to squeeze through and chal ent fnl f: sn drvn and hung rt: styd on to ld last 75yds* **7/2**[2]

56/5 **2** *½* **Hunting Tower**[12] 6095 5-9-1 **80**..... JohnEgan 8 85
(J J Lambe, Ire) *hld up in rr: hdwy 3f out: effrt on outer to chal 2f out: rdn to ld over 1f out: drvn and edgd lft ins fnl f: hdd and no ex last 75yds* **6/1**

5000 **3** *2 ¾* **King's Head (IRE)**[4] 6313 6-8-11 **76**.....(p) PhillipMakin 7 77
(Miss L A Perratt) *hld up: hdwy over 3f out: rdn to chal 2f out: drvn and led briefly over 1f out: sn hdd and keeping on whn n.m.r ins fnl f* **33/1**

0032 **4** *hd* **Dazzling Light (UAE)**[5] 6280 4-8-10 **75**..... DanielTudhope 4 76+
(J S Goldie) *hld up in tch: hdwy to trck ldrs over 2f out: effrt whn n.m.r over 1f out: rdn and styng on whn hmpd ins fnl f: nt rcvr* **7/2**[2]

0661 **5** *hd* **Amanda Carter**[12] 6095 5-9-8 **87**..... PaulHanagan 3 88
(R A Fahey) *trckd ldng pair: hdwy to chse ldr over 4f out: rdn to ld briefly 2f out: sn drvn and hdd: edgd rt and one pce ins fnl f* **11/2**[3]

-223 **6** *2 ½* **Wells Lyrical (IRE)**[89] 3642 4-10-0 **93**..... TomEaves 1 90
(B Smart) *led: rdn along 3f out: hdd 2f out: wkng whn n.m.r on inner over 1f out* **2/1**[1]

2m 53.5s (-0.50) **Going Correction** -0.225s/f (Firm)

WFA 3 from 4yo+ 8lb **6** Ran SP% **110.4**

Speed ratings (Par 107): **92,91,90,89,89 88**

toteswingers: 1&2 £4.50, 1&3 £9.20, 2&3 £6.60 CSF £23.11 CT £547.09 TOTE £5.20: £2.80, £3.00; EX 23.80.

Owner Sheikh Hamdan Bin Mohammed Al Maktoum **Bred** Miss K Rausing **Trained** Middleham Moor, N Yorks

■ Stewards' Enquiry : John Egan three-day ban: used whip with excessive frequency (Oct 15,16,18)

FOCUS

Despite the withdrawals a competitive handicap run at a sound pace. The form is a bit messy and best rated through the winner.

NOTEBOOK

Quai D'Orsay, back on his last winning mark, had to squeeze through the eye of a needle to deliver his challenge. Once ahead he edged right but did more than enough to outbattle the runner-up. He is notably tough, a typical inmate of his stable. (op 4-1 tchd 3-1 in places)

Hunting Tower, well beaten fifth behind Amanda Carter here two weeks earlier, enjoyed a stone pull. Happy to sit last, he moved up down the outside to look a major threat but upsides, he edged left and found the winner too tough. No doubt he will soon revert to hurdles. (op 13-2 tchd 5-1, 7-1 in places and 15-2 in a place)

King's Head(IRE), well beaten just four days earlier, has been struggling to find form for this yard and as a result has come tumbling down the ratings. He was held when tightened up by the first two inside the last but this was a lot more encouraging. (op 25-1)

Dazzling Light(UAE), third in Amanda Carter's race here, had finished runner-up at Chester five days previously. Quite keen, she was going nowhere when tightened up a furlong out but continues in good heart and likes fast ground. (op 4-1)

Amanda Carter, hammered with a 12lb weight rise after her runaway win here, looked the one to beat when mastering Wells Lyrical but in the end she came up some way short. This career-high mark simply looked beyond her. (op 5-1)

Wells Lyrical(IRE), runner-up twice and third in three starts in stronger company, was back after a three-month break. After setting the pace he had no more to give when tightened up by the winner, and was allowed to come home in his own time. This will have blown away the cobwebs and the Northumberland Plate runner-up should give a good account of himself in the Cesarewitch. (tchd 9-4)

6413 VICTOR CHANDLER CASINO H'CAP 6f
4:40 (4:42) (Class 5) (0-70,71) 3-Y-0+ **£2,914** (£867; £433; £216) **Stalls High**

Form RPR

5311 **1** **Milton Of Campsie**[10] 6160 4-9-4 **68** 6ex..... JohnEgan 3 79+
(J Balding) *trckd ldrs: hdwy to ld 2f out: sn rdn and hung rt over 1f out: drvn ins fnl f and hld on wl* **13/2**[1]

6516 **2** *shd* **Yorkshire Blue**[8] 6221 10-8-3 **56**.....(p) KellyHarrison(3) 5 65
(J S Goldie) *midfield: hdwy over 2f out: rdn wl over 1f out: styd on wl fnl f: jst failed* **28/1**

333 **3** *½* **John Keats**[4] 6309 6-8-10 **67**.....(p) JamesPSullivan(7) 6 74
(J S Goldie) *midfield: hdwy over 2f out: rdn to chal over 1f out: drvn and ev ch ins fnl f: nt qckn towards fin* **8/1**[3]

0321 **4** *¾* **Daring Dream (GER)**[36] 5332 4-9-1 **65**..... DanielTudhope 4 70
(J S Goldie) *midfield: hdwy 2f out: rdn to chal over 1f out: drvn and kpt on same pce ins fnl f* **10/1**

0216 **5** *1 ¼* **Liberty Trail (IRE)**[11] 6140 3-9-3 **68**..... PhillipMakin 10 69
(I Semple) *cl up: rdn along 2f out: drvn whn n.m.r and swtchd lft ins fnl f: drvn and kpt on same pce* **16/1**

4052 **6** *shd* **Maison Dieu**[8] 6221 6-8-9 **59**..... DavidAllan 13 59
(E J Alston) *midfield: swtchd rt towards stands' rail and gd hdwy 2f out: sn rdn and chsng ldrs over 1f out: drvn and one pce ins fnl f* **7/1**[2]

306 **7** *1* **Pickering**[33] 5421 5-9-0 **69**.....(p) GaryBartley(5) 7 66
(E J Alston) *led: rdn along and hdd 2f out: sn drvn and wknd ent fnl f* **16/1**

3004 **8** *1* **Hansomis (IRE)**[8] 6221 5-9-1 **65**..... PaulHanagan 12 59
(B Mactaggart) *chsd ldrs: rdn along wl over 2f out and grad wknd* **12/1**

0513 **9** *1 ¼* **Obe Brave**[12] 6120 6-8-9 **59**.....(p) TonyHamilton 15 49
(Lee Smyth, Ire) *hmpd s: a in rr* **18/1**

1104 **10** *½* **The Bear**[10] 6161 6-8-9 **64**..... AndrewHeffernan(5) 14 52
(Miss L A Perratt) *racd alone towards stands' rail: cl up tl rdn along 2f out and grad wknd appr fnl f* **25/1**

1245 **11** *½* **Steel Blue**[21] 5804 9-8-3 **58**.....(p) AmyRyan(5) 1 45
(R M Whitaker) *chsd ldrs: rdn along 1/2-way and sn wknd* **28/1**

0040 **12** *1* **Piste**[15] 5978 3-8-8 **64**..... BMcHugh(5) 11 48
(Miss T Jackson) *chsd ldrs: rdn along over 2f out and grad wknd* **33/1**

5300 **13** *½* **Elijah Pepper (USA)**[17] 5955 4-8-10 **65**.....(b[1]) DeanHeslop(5) 2 47
(T D Barron) *chsd ldrs on outer: rdn along bef 1/2-way and sn wknd* **8/1**[3]

6-00 **14** *1 ½* **Almost Married (IRE)**[54] 4772 5-8-0 **55** oh1..... PaulPickard(5) 9 32
(J S Goldie) *a in rr* **33/1**

2502 **15** *nk* **Jack Rackham**[54] 4783 5-9-3 **67**.....(v) TomEaves 16 43
(B Smart) *s.i.s: a in rr* **7/1**[2]

0041 **16** *1 ¾* **Distant Sun (USA)**[4] 6314 5-9-0 **71** 6ex..... IJBrennan(7) 17 42
(Miss L A Perratt) *a towards rr* **7/1**[2]

400 **U** **Top Bid**[26] 5675 5-8-10 **60**....(b) DuranFentiman 8 —
(T D Easterby) *rrd and uns rdr at s* **33/1**
1m 11.93s (-1.67) **Going Correction** -0.225s/f (Firm)
WFA 3 from 4yo+ 1lb **17** Ran SP% **126.4**
Speed ratings (Par 103): **102,101,101,100,98 98,97,95,94,93 92,91,90,88,88 86,—**
toteswingers: 1&2 £40.10, 1&3 £11.30, 2&3 £45.10 CSF £197.79 CT £991.33 TOTE £4.40: £1.80, £4.60, £2.40, £2.70; EX 226.90.
Owner Willie McKay **Bred** Slatch Farm Stud **Trained** Scrooby, Notts
■ Stewards' Enquiry : Kelly Harrison two-day ban: used whip with excessive frequency (Oct 15-16)
FOCUS
Another modest sprint handicap. The pace was centre to far side but the winner drifted right and ended up under the stands'-side rail. The form is sound enough rated around the placed horses.
Maison Dieu Official explanation: vet said gelding had been struck into from behind
Top Bid Official explanation: gelding reared on leaving the stalls, causing the jockey to lose his irons and become unseated

6414 BEST ODDS GUARANTEED VICTOR CHANDLER H'CAP (DIV I) 7f 50y
5:15 (5:16) (Class 6) (0-60,57) 3-Y-O+ **£2,388** (£705; £352) **Stalls** Low

Form RPR
6040 **1** **Finsbury**[17] 5948 6-9-0 **56**.... GaryBartley(5) 2 66
(J S Goldie) *in tch on inner: hdwy 2f out: rdn to chal ent fnl f: sn drvn to ld and styd on wl* **8/1**
4354 **2** *1 1/2* **Soto**[12] 6103 6-8-13 **57**....(b) JamesPSullivan(7) 5 63
(M W Easterby) *in tch: hdwy over 2f out: effrt and nt clr run over 1f out: swtchd rt and rdn ent fnl f: kpt on* **9/2**[3]
6-00 **3** *1 3/4* **Ros Cuire (IRE)**[19] 5869 4-8-12 **49**.... DavidAllan 11 51
(W A Murphy, Ire) *stdd s and hld up towards rr: hdwy 1/2-way: rdn to chse ldrs and n.m.r over 1f out: swtchd rt and drvn ins fnl f: kpt on wl towards fin* **25/1**
1042 **4** *nse* **Ask Dan (IRE)**[27] 5621 3-9-3 **56**....(p) PhillipMakin 6 57+
(M Dods) *led: rdn along 3f out: hdd over 1f out: sn drvn and one pce* **7/2**[1]
0/ **5** *hd* **Diamond Fire (IRE)**[20] 5846 5-9-0 **51**.... CDHayes 12 52
(Adrian McGuinness, Ire) *hld up towards rr: smooth hdwy 3f out: swtchd rt and effrt to chal on bit over 1f out: sn led: rdn and hdd jst ins fnl f: fnd little u.p* **7/1**
5544 **6** *shd* **Ingleby Princess**[17] 5953 5-8-6 **48**.... DeanHeslop(5) 9 49
(T D Barron) *chsd ldrs: rdn along wl over 2f out: sn drvn and wknd* **4/1**[2]
0000 **7** *1/2* **Glenluji**[10] 6161 4-9-1 **52**.... DanielTudhope 1 51
(J S Goldie) *chsd ldng pair on inner: rdn along over 2f out and gradsually wknd* **16/1**
0006 **8** *8* **Mister Biscuit (USA)**[10] 6158 3-8-6 **45**.... RoystonFfrench 3 24
(Miss L A Perratt) *a towards rr* **66/1**
455 **9** *hd* **Bertie Vista**[41] 5225 4-9-4 **55**....(b) DuranFentiman 10 33
(T D Easterby) *in tch: rdn along 1/2-way and sn wknd* **8/1**
0-05 **10** *2* **No Nightmare (USA)**[36] 5338 3-8-6 **45**.... AndrewElliott 8 18
(A P Jarvis) *chsd ldr: rdn along 3f out: sn wknd* **33/1**
0030 **11** *nk* **Obe One**[36] 5332 9-8-1 **45**....(p) BillyCray(7) 7 17
(A Berry) *s.i.s: a in rr* **40/1**
050 **12** *1/2* **Duke Of Bothwell (USA)**[34] 5394 3-8-8 **47**.... PaulHanagan 4 18
(R A Fahey) *midfield: rdn along 1/2-way and sn wknd* **16/1**
1m 31.93s (-1.47) **Going Correction** -0.225s/f (Firm)
WFA 3 from 4yo+ 2lb **12** Ran SP% **117.6**
Speed ratings (Par 101): **99,97,95,95,95 94,94,85,84,82 82,81**
toteswingers: 1&2 £10.90, 1&3 £37.40, 2&3 £26.60 CSF £42.38 CT £884.83 TOTE £9.10: £2.70, £1.90, £7.30; EX 57.60.
Owner M Mackay & S Bruce **Bred** O Pointing **Trained** Uplawmoor, E Renfrews
■ Stewards' Enquiry : Royston Ffrench one-day ban: used whip when out of contention (Oct 15)
FOCUS
Part one of a divided 7f handicap, both sellers in all but name. This division was a 45-57 affair run at a very strong pace and the form is best rated through the winner.
Finsbury Official explanation: trainer said, regarding apparent improvement in form, that the gelding was suited by the better draw.

6415 BEST ODDS GUARANTEED VICTOR CHANDLER H'CAP (DIV II) 7f 50y
5:50 (5:50) (Class 6) (0-60,56) 3-Y-O+ **£2,388** (£705; £352) **Stalls** Low

Form RPR
0006 **1** **Mr Lu**[28] 5601 4-9-0 **53**.... KellyHarrison(3) 9 61
(J S Goldie) *hld up towards rr: stdy hdwy on outer over 2f out: rdn and hung bdly lft: led 1f out: drvn and hdd wl ins fnl f: rallied to ld nr fin* **9/2**[2]
0603 **2** *nk* **Shunkawakhan (IRE)**[17] 5948 6-8-13 **54**....(p) BMcHugh(5) 5 61
(Miss L A Perratt) *trckd ldrs: hdwy 3f out: rdn to ld 2f out: drvn and hdd 1f out: rallied to ld again wl ins fnl f: hdd and no ex nr fin* **13/2**
300 **3** *1/2* **Mister Jingles**[14] 6023 6-9-0 **55**....(v) AmyRyan(5) 2 61+
(R M Whitaker) *trckd ldrs on inner: hdwy to chse ldng pair wl over 1f out: sn rdn and nt clr run ent fnl f: sn swtchd rt and drvn: styd on strly towards fin* **3/1**[1]
4350 **4** *3* **Imperial Echo (USA)**[15] 6005 8-8-9 **50**.... DeanHeslop(5) 11 48
(T D Barron) *hld up in rr: hdwy over 2f out: rdn to chse ldrs over 1f out: drvn and no imp whn n.m.r ins fnl f* **5/1**[3]
0/0- **5** *1 1/4* **King's Jester (IRE)**[31] 7401 7-9-6 **56**.... JohnEgan 1 51
(J J Lambe, Ire) *dwlt and hld up in rr: hdwy 3f out: rdn along wl over 1f out: drvn ent fnl f and sn no imp* **8/1**
4000 **6** *1 1/2* **Nino Zachetti (IRE)**[28] 5599 3-8-7 **45**....(p) DavidAllan 7 36
(E J Alston) *cl up: rdn along and ev ch over 2f out: drvn and wkng whn hmpd appr fnl f* **25/1**
4226 **7** *1 1/4* **Carnival Dream**[31] 5514 4-9-2 **52**....(b) PhillipMakin 4 40
(H A McWilliams) *midfield: rdn along 3f out: drvn over 2f out and n.d* **6/1**
6000 **8** *3 3/4* **Dolly No Hair**[52] 4845 4-8-3 **46**....(t) ShirleyTeasdale(7) 6 24
(N Wilson) *led: rdn along and hdd 2f out: sn drvn and wknd* **25/1**
5033 **9** *hd* **Positivity**[35] 5373 3-8-12 **50**.... TomEaves 10 27
(B Smart) *in tch on outer: rdn along wl over 2f out and sn wknd* **12/1**
0505 **10** *3* **Trade Price (GR)**[10] 6158 3-8-9 **47**....(b) RoystonFfrench 8 16
(I Semple) *trckd ldrs: effrt 3f out: rdn along over 2f out: sn drvn and wknd* **33/1**
1m 32.19s (-1.21) **Going Correction** -0.225s/f (Firm)
WFA 3 from 4yo+ 2lb **10** Ran SP% **116.9**
Speed ratings (Par 101): **97,96,96,92,91 89,88,83,83,80**
toteswingers: 1&2 £7.90, 1&3 £5.10, 2&3 £7.00 CSF £33.16 CT £103.49 TOTE £6.50: £1.60, £3.10, £1.50; EX 44.60 Place 6: £111.93 Place 5: £57.38 .
Owner The Greens Committee **Bred** Whitwell Bloodstock **Trained** Uplawmoor, E Renfrews
■ Stewards' Enquiry : Dean Heslop caution: careless riding
Kelly Harrison one-day ban: careless riding (Oct 18); one-day ban: used whip with excessive frequency (Oct 19)
FOCUS
A 45-56 handicap in part two and again the pace was strong, suggesting the form is sound.

T/Plt: £113.70 to a £1 stake. Pool: £53,602.65. 343.90 winning tickets. T/Qpdt: £89.00 to a £1 stake. Pool: £3,803.16. 31.60 winning tickets. JR

6199 GOODWOOD (R-H)
Thursday, October 1

OFFICIAL GOING: Good to firm (9.0)
Lower bend dolled out 7yds from 6f marker to winning post increasing distances by about 12yds.
Wind: Moderate, across Weather: Fine

6416 E B F BUY A £10,000 RACING POST BONUS YEARLING MEDIAN AUCTION MAIDEN STKS 7f
2:10 (2:12) (Class 5) 2-Y-O **£3,238** (£963; £481; £240) **Stalls** High

Form RPR
223 **1** **Awesome Act (USA)**[26] 5664 2-9-3 **85**.... DarryllHolland 8 93+
(J Noseda) *t.k.h: cl up: wnt 2nd 3f out and stalked ldr: plld out over 1f out: shkn up and fnd decent turn of foot to ld last 100yds* **3/1**[2]
2 **2** *1 1/4* **Morana (IRE)**[20] 5831 2-9-3 **0**.... AlanMunro 7 90+
(P W Chapple-Hyam) *racd freely: led: kicked on over 2f out: hdd and outpcd last 100yds* **4/9**[1]
30 **3** *9* **Christopher Wren (USA)**[38] 5312 2-9-0 **0**.... MarcHalford(3) 2 68
(J R Best) *chsd ldr to 3f out: sn rdn and steadily lft wl bhd by first pair* **40/1**
4 **4** *1/2* **Santa Margherita**[16] 5966 2-8-12 **0**.... MickyFenton 1 61
(H J L Dunlop) *hld up in tch: effrt to dispute modest 3rd on outer 2f out: one pce* **18/1**[3]
00 **5** *6* **Mystic Millie (IRE)**[23] 5749 2-8-12 **0**.... AdamKirby 4 46+
(C G Cox) *mostly in last pair: pushed along 1/2-way: wl outpcd over 2f out: wknd over 1f out* **100/1**
00 **6** *shd* **Atakora (IRE)**[10] 6163 2-8-12 **0**.... JimCrowley 9 46+
(Mrs A J Perrett) *fractious bef ent stalls: dwlt and awkward s: in tch: nudged along and wl outpcd fr over 2f out: edgd lft fr over 1f out* **22/1**
7 *3 3/4* **Cunning Plan (IRE)** 2-9-3 **0**.... PatDobbs 5 42
(P W Chapple-Hyam) *a in last pair: rdn 1/2-way: struggling after* **33/1**
8 *2 1/2* **Sonny G (IRE)** 2-9-3 **0**.... LiamJones 6 35
(J R Best) *plld hrd: in tch: effrt to dispute 3rd on outer over 2f out: wknd rapidly wl over 1f out* **66/1**
1m 27.6s (0.20) **Going Correction** -0.10s/f (Good) **8** Ran SP% **111.7**
Speed ratings (Par 95): **94,92,82,81,74 74,70,67**
toteswingers: 1&2 £1.40, 1&3 £6.90, 2&3 £7.50 CSF £4.45 TOTE £3.30: £1.20, £1.02, £6.50; EX 5.90.
Owner Mrs Susan Roy & Tom Ludt **Bred** Flaxman Holdings Ltd **Trained** Newmarket, Suffolk
FOCUS
The first pair came clear in this maiden and both look smart. The fifth sets the level backed up by the third.
NOTEBOOK
Awesome Act(USA) ◆ was undoubtedly suited best by the way the race was run. Despite pulling hard and taking his time to settle, he got plenty of cover and showed a good turn of foot when pulled out to make his challenge. This quick ground seems to suit him and on this evidence his Group 1 entries are merited, and it would not be a surprise if he was given his chance in the Dewhurst. He should make up into a Pattern performer next season and 1m looks well within his compass. (op 11-4 tchd 7-2)
Morana(IRE) was strong in the market and headstrong on the track, pulling hard. There was no pace to aim at, so this galloping type elected to make it, which set up the race for the winner. He showed plenty of pace but had no answer once Awesome Act swept past. This was only his second start and he won't be long in winning a maiden. (op 1-2 tchd 2-5 and 4-7 in places)
Christopher Wren(USA) was another who didn't settle that well. Once he did, he helped set the pace, such as it was, but after being one of the first off the bridle, he stayed on again. (op 50-1)
Santa Margherita shaped promisingly enough on her second start and needs one more run for a mark. (op 20-1)
Mystic Millie(IRE) never really got into this and looked one paced. She is bred for shorter trips.
Atakora(IRE) showed greenness at the start and didn't settle early on. There is a modicum of ability there and she will now be eligible for a handicap mark. She will be better with experience, probably over further. (op 16-1)
Cunning Plan(IRE) was always labouring on his debut and doesn't look very fast.
Sonny G(IRE) didn't get the trip after pulling hard early on. The pace of the race was against him. Official explanation: jockey said colt hung left (op 100-1)

6417 TOTEEXACTA MAIDEN STKS 1m 6f
2:45 (2:46) (Class 5) 3-Y-O+ **£3,238** (£963; £481; £240) **Stalls** Low

Form RPR
5420 **1** **Sana Abel (IRE)**[24] 5718 3-8-10 **70**....(p) TPO'Shea 3 73
(M A Jarvis) *chsd ldr: rdn wl over 3f out: clsd to ld jst over 2f out: styd on dourly* **15/8**[2]
3062 **2** *2 1/2* **Alhaque (USA)**[7] 6225 3-9-1 **77**.... DarryllHolland 1 75
(W J Haggas) *led at decent pce: gng bttr than wnr 4f out: rdn and hdd jst over 2f out: nt qckn* **8/11**[1]
00/0 **3** *21* **Double Exposure**[218] 670 5-9-10 **0**.... IanMongan 2 45
(Jamie Poulton) *hld up in last: lft wl bhd fr 5f out and sn pushed along: plugged on slowly to take remote 3rd 1f out* **33/1**
6 **4** *5* **Slick Mover (IRE)**[10] 6166 4-9-5 **0**.... DaneO'Neill 5 33
(B G Powell) *chsd ldng pair: rdn over 4f out and sn lft wl bhd: wknd and lost remote 3rd 1f out* **11/1**[3]
0000 **5** *17* **Miss Jodarah (USA)**[10] 6166 3-8-7 **38**.... MarcHalford(3) 4 9
(J R Best) *chsd ldng trio: pushed along over 6f out: dropped to last and wknd over 4f out: t.o* **66/1**
3m 1.74s (-1.86) **Going Correction** -0.10s/f (Good)
WFA 3 from 4yo+ 9lb **5** Ran SP% **105.5**
Speed ratings (Par 103): **101,99,87,84,75**
CSF £3.22 TOTE £2.70: £1.50, £1.10; EX 3.50.
Owner Hamdan Al Maktoum **Bred** Shadwell Estate Company Limited **Trained** Newmarket, Suffolk
■ Stewards' Enquiry : Darryll Holland two-day ban: used whip with excessive frequency down shoulder in the forehand (Oct 15-16)
FOCUS
A weak staying maiden and very few got into it. Straightforward form rated around the first two.

6418 OAKENHURST NURSERY STKS (H'CAP) 6f
3:20 (3:20) (Class 4) (0-80,76) 2-Y-O **£3,885** (£1,156; £577; £288) **Stalls** Low

Form RPR
3230 **1** **Chips O'Toole (IRE)**[31] 5526 2-9-6 **75**.... EddieAhern 10 82
(B J Meehan) *mde virtually all: edgd lft u.p fr over 1f out: hld on wl* **7/1**[2]

1 **2** *nk* **Gouray Girl (IRE)**[13] 6069 2-9-6 **75**.................................... AdamKirby 3 82+
(W R Swinburn) *w.w bhd ldrs gng wl: effrt over 1f out: drvn and prog to press wnr last 100yds: jst hld* **8/1**

016 **3** *1* **Katehari (IRE)**[18] 5899 2-8-13 **68**.................................... NeilChalmers 12 71
(A M Balding) *prom on outer: pressed wnr over 2f out tl ins fnl f: one pce* **14/1**

6241 **4** *shd* **Freeforaday (USA)**[9] 6185 2-9-3 **75** 6ex........................ MarcHalford(3) 2 78
(J R Best) *hld up bhd ldrs: effrt over 1f out: rdn and styd on fnl f: nrst fin* **8/1**

4245 **5** *¾* **Pose (IRE)**[6] 6241 2-9-1 **70**.. PatDobbs 6 71
(R Hannon) *w ldrs: rdn and hung lft over 1f out: nt qckn and hld fnl f: kpt on* **7/4**[1]

6422 **6** *2 ¾* **Battlemaiden (IRE)**[21] 5808 2-9-7 **76**.......................... DO'Donohoe 8 68
(Saeed Bin Suroor) *pressed wnr to over 2f out: wknd fnl f* **15/2**[3]

5345 **7** *¾* **Admirable Duchess**[18] 5899 2-8-13 **68**.............................. AlanMunro 4 59+
(D J S Ffrench Davis) *w ldrs: rdn 2f out: wl hld whn sltly hmpd jst over 1f out* **20/1**

4136 **8** *¾* **Watch Chain (IRE)**[17] 5950 2-8-5 **65**........................ AshleyMorgan(5) 11 53
(M H Tompkins) *w.w bhd ldrs: cl enough 2f out: wknd over 1f out* **10/1**

5416 **9** *3 ½* **Pherousa**[9] 6185 2-8-13 **68**.. LiamJones 1 51+
(M Blanshard) *t.k.h early: hld up bhd ldrs: shkn up and no prog 2f out: btn whn hmpd 1f out: eased* **66/1**

0452 **10** *3* **Jessica Hayllar (USA)**[73] 4153 2-8-5 **65**...... Louis-PhilippeBeuzelin(5) 5 33
(G L Moore) *hld up bhd ldrs: rdn over 2f out: wknd over 1f out* **16/1**

3303 **11** *1* **Bandear (IRE)**[14] 6035 2-8-8 **63**.. ChrisCatlin 9 28
(C E Brittain) *in tch: rdn over 2f out: wknd wl over 1f out* **12/1**

1m 11.25s (-0.95) **Going Correction** -0.10s/f (Good) **11** Ran SP% **118.4**
Speed ratings (Par 97): **102,101,100,100,99 95,94,93,88,84 83**
toteswingers: 1&2 £8.50, 1&3 £15.40, 2&3 £12.20 CSF £62.48 CT £787.89 TOTE £8.30: £2.70, £2.30, £4.30; EX 89.80.
Owner Abbott Racing Limited **Bred** Lynn Lodge Stud **Trained** Manton, Wilts
■ Stewards' Enquiry : Pat Dobbs two-day ban: careless riding (Oct 15-16)

FOCUS
A reasonable nursery, run at a good pace with few hard-luck stories, but they finished in a bit of a heap. The form looks fair though.

NOTEBOOK
Chips O'Toole(IRE) clearly has plenty of pace and had been somewhat unfortunate to bump into a couple of decent winners on a few starts previously. Front-running tactics on a speed-favouring track certainly didn't hurt is cause. He hung left and idled in the closing stages when under pressure and had to dig deep to hold on. With a confidence-boosting win under his belt, he should continue to progress. (op 8-1 tchd 10-1)
Gouray Girl(IRE) showed plenty of promise on her debut in a fillies' auction maiden at Wolverhampton (form boosted by the winner) and she improved on that here. She travelled powerfully, and though she showed a little inexperience when asked to make her challenge between horses, she stayed on in quite taking fashion. This 6f looks her trip for the time being. (op 17-2 tchd 15-2)
Katehari(IRE) was always up with the pace from her unfavourable wide draw and held every chance inside the final half-furlong, but her run flattened out. She may be seen in a better light when stepped up in trip. (tchd 16-1)
Freeforaday(USA), shouldering a 6lb penalty for wining at Folkestone last week, ran another fine race in defeat. That victory was over 5f, but he was staying on really well over a furlong further here and he looks fairly treated at present. (op 10-1)
Pose(IRE), who had little to spare when having the winner in behind her at Chepstow over 5f in August, looked well in on her run in a valuable 6½f sales race at Ascot over last week. However, after breaking smartly and settling well, she hung left and didn't find much. The track didn't suit her and her jockey reported that she didn't move well, particularly when coming downhill. (op 6-4 tchd 15-8 in places)
Battlemaiden(IRE) had no real excuses and was beaten when he had to check slightly inside the last furlong. He is bred for further. (op 5-1 tchd 8-1)

6419 BUTLINS BOGNOR REGIS FILLIES' STKS (H'CAP) 1m 4f
3:55 (3:55) (Class 3) (0-95,90) 3-Y-O+ **£9,714** (£2,890; £1,444; £721) **Stalls** Low

Form RPR

1102 **1** **Rosika**[18] 5904 3-9-0 **86**.................................. Louis-PhilippeBeuzelin(5) 3 99
(Sir Michael Stoute) *settled in 5th: clsd on ldrs 3f out: stl plenty to do and n.m.r over 2f out: rdn and prog to take 2nd 1f out: swept into the ld last 100yds: powered clr* **4/1**[3]

2611 **2** *2 ½* **Qelaan (USA)**[16] 5964 3-9-2 **83**.. TPO'Shea 2 92
(M P Tregoning) *led: drew 6 l clr 1/2-way: breather and c bk to field 3f out: shkn up and 3 l clr 2f out: hdd and outpcd last 100yds* **3/1**[2]

1111 **3** *2 ½* **Acquisition**[26] 5660 3-9-7 **88**.. EddieAhern 4 93
(H R A Cecil) *trckd ldr: clsd over 3f out: sn u.p: no imp over 2f out: one pce and lost 2nd 1f out* **9/4**[1]

1613 **4** *3* **Hollow Green (IRE)**[5] 6277 3-9-2 **83**........................ CatherineGannon 5 83
(P D Evans) *hld up in last: drvn 3f out: outpcd sn after: plugged on to take 4th nr fin* **12/1**

5021 **5** *¾* **Anice Stellato (IRE)**[12] 6113 3-9-9 **90**.............................. JimCrowley 7 89
(R M Beckett) *chsd ldng pair: rdn 3f out: no imp after: fdd over 1f out* **6/1**

0151 **6** *7* **Sweet Hollow**[13] 6060 3-8-12 **79**......................................(b) AdamKirby 1 67
(C G Cox) *chsd ldng pair to over 3f out: sn rdn and wknd* **8/1**

2m 35.9s (-2.50) **Going Correction** -0.10s/f (Good)
WFA 3 from 5yo 7lb **6** Ran SP% **108.9**
Speed ratings (Par 104): **104,102,100,98,98 93**
toteswingers: 1&2 £2.30, 2&3 £2.10, 1&3 not won. CSF £15.28 TOTE £4.90: £2.50, £1.70; EX 19.00.
Owner Sir Evelyn De Rothschild **Bred** Southcourt Stud **Trained** Newmarket, Suffolk
■ Stewards' Enquiry : Louis-Philippe Beuzelin caution: careless riding

FOCUS
A decent fillies' handicap full of progressive types and run at a true pace. Form worth treating positively with the first three on the upgrade.

NOTEBOOK
Rosika had been upped 3lb by the handicapper after chasing home an odds-on shot at Bath last time over 1m2f. Upped in trip under her claimer, she travelled well but still had plenty to do when extricating herself from a pocket approaching the furlong pole. Yet under a well-timed run, she sailed past the long-time leader to score decisively. Her trainer has a happy knack of improving 3-y-o fillies, and this one is clearly on an upward curve. (op 5-1)
Qelaan(USA) ran another fine race. Front-running tactics appeared to have worked when she held a clear lead approaching the final furlong, but she laboured in the last 300 yards and was collared. This progressive filly, who is versatile as regards to ground, simply has the misfortune to bump into a fast-improving rival at the trip. (op 11-4 tchd 7-2)
Acquisition had shown plenty of improvement to notch up a four-timer, but the extra 7lb appeared to anchor her this time. (op 5-2 tchd 2-1)
Hollow Green(IRE) stayed on quite well in the closing stages, having looked well beaten with 2f to run. She may be hard to win with off her current mark of 83 on this evidence, however. She is holding her form well, though, and is not one to write off yet. (op 8-1)
Anice Stellato(IRE), who had shown progressive form in handicaps, was on a 4lb higher mark. She ran quite free and as a result, she was a spent force approaching 1f out. She can be forgiven this below-par run and should remain competitive. (op 11-2)
Sweet Hollow could not match the class of her rivals and was under pressure approaching 3f out. She dropped out tamely. (tchd 15-2)

6420 SUBSCRIBE TO RACING UK STKS (H'CAP) 1m 3f
4:30 (4:31) (Class 4) (0-80,79) 3-Y-O **£6,476** (£1,927; £963; £481) **Stalls** Low

Form RPR

1621 **1** **Caster Sugar (USA)**[29] 5567 3-9-0 **75**.................................... PatDobbs 3 84
(R Hannon) *trckd ldrs: gng strly 3f out: effrt and pushed into ld over 1f out: sn jnd: shkn up and r.o wl fnl f* **7/2**[1]

6065 **2** *nk* **Sam Sharp (USA)**[19] 5876 3-8-13 **74**................................ IanMongan 1 82
(H R A Cecil) *t.k.h early: hld up: trckd ldrs 4f out: prog on outer to chal 2f out: coaxed along to join wnr over 1f out: nt qckn fnl f* **5/1**[3]

1033 **3** *3* **Andhaar**[19] 5876 3-9-2 **77**.. TPO'Shea 9 80
(E A L Dunlop) *hld up in last pair: sme prog 3f out but stl wl off the pce: rdn 2f out: gd hdwy over 1f out: wnt 3rd last 100yds: r.o but no ch of catching ldng pair* **13/2**

2135 **4** *2 ¾* **Bomber Brown (IRE)**[8] 6209 3-9-2 **77**.............................. AlanMunro 7 75
(P W Chapple-Hyam) *trckd ldr: drvn to ld over 2f out to over 1f out: sn outpcd: lost 3rd last 100yds* **8/1**

5511 **5** *hd* **Rockfella**[19] 5876 3-8-10 **71**.. EddieAhern 8 69
(D J Coakley) *led: tended to hang lft: rdn and hdd over 2f out: steadily fdd* **9/2**[2]

0004 **6** *3 ¼* **Saa'Ida (IRE)**[17] 5940 3-8-9 **70**..(b) ChrisCatlin 2 62
(C E Brittain) *hld up in last pair: effrt 4f out: chsd ldrs over 2f out: sn fdd* **11/1**

0-1 **7** *1* **Tahkeem**[23] 5744 3-8-11 **72**..(p) DaneO'Neill 5 62
(M P Tregoning) *trckd ldng pair to 4f out: sn rdn: wknd 2f out* **8/1**

0-10 **8** *14* **Brooklyn Spirit**[19] 5876 3-9-1 **76**.................................... AdamKirby 6 41
(C G Cox) *in tch in rr: rdn over 3f out: sn wknd and bhd* **28/1**

012- **9** *12* **Hurakan (IRE)**[367] 6344 3-9-4 **79**...................................... JimCrowley 4 22
(Mrs A J Perrett) *trckd ldrs: hmpd on inner over 5f out and over 4f out: sn dropped out: t.o* **8/1**

2m 24.62s (-3.68) **Going Correction** -0.10s/f (Good) **9** Ran SP% **115.5**
Speed ratings (Par 103): **109,108,106,104,104 102,101,91,82**
toteswingers: 1&2 £4.40, 1&3 £5.70, 2&3 £6.30 CSF £20.95 CT £108.45 TOTE £3.80: £1.60, £2.10, £1.90; EX 22.60.
Owner Mrs James Wigan **Bred** Mrs James Wigan & London TB Services Ltd **Trained** East Everleigh, Wilts

FOCUS
A tight handicap with the third and fifth to form.
Brooklyn Spirit Official explanation: jockey said gelding stopped quickly

6421 TURFTV FOR BETTING SHOPS STKS (H'CAP) 1m
5:05 (5:07) (Class 5) (0-75,75) 3-Y-O **£3,238** (£963; £481; £240) **Stalls** High

Form RPR

5300 **1** **Swift Chap**[20] 5834 3-8-13 **70**.. DarryllHolland 2 78
(B R Millman) *trckd ldr: rdn over 2f out: clsd u.p to ld over 1f out: sn drvn clr* **8/1**

1225 **2** *2* **Play It Sam**[29] 5575 3-9-1 **72**..(t) AdamKirby 5 75+
(W R Swinburn) *hld up in 6th: looking for room on inner fr 3f out tl prog wl over 1f out: r.o to take 2nd last 100yds: no ch to chal* **5/2**[1]

0132 **3** *1 ¼* **Wilbury Star (IRE)**[19] 5858 3-9-4 **75**............................(b) PatDobbs 4 75
(R Hannon) *led: drvn and hdd over 1f out: one pce and lost 2nd fnl 100yds* **5/1**[2]

6134 **4** *nk* **Fajita**[15] 5999 3-9-1 **72**..(b[1]) GeorgeBaker 7 71
(G L Moore) *trckd ldng pair on inner: rdn over 2f out: hanging and nt qckn after: one pce* **5/1**[2]

5323 **5** *¾* **Layer Cake**[7] 6223 3-8-4 **68**.. KierenFox(7) 8 66
(J W Hills) *hmpd on inner after 1f: sn taken to outer in last pair: effrt 2f out: kpt on fnl f: n.d* **8/1**

4502 **6** *½* **Fazbee (IRE)**[21] 5803 3-9-4 **75**.. EddieAhern 3 72
(P W D'Arcy) *trckd ldrs: shkn up over 2f out: no imp wl over 1f out: fdd* **13/2**[3]

1000 **7** *4 ½* **Diapason (IRE)**[17] 5940 3-8-10 **67**.................................. RichardSmith 6 53
(Tom Dascombe) *t.k.h early: hld up in last pair: shkn up over 2f out: no prog and sn btn* **14/1**

3650 **8** *4 ½* **Young Dottie**[29] 5570 3-8-5 **67**...................... Louis-PhilippeBeuzelin(5) 1 43
(P M Phelan) *plld hrd in 4th on outer to 1/2-way: rdn 3f out: sn wknd* **16/1**

1m 38.95s (-0.95) **Going Correction** -0.10s/f (Good) **8** Ran SP% **110.0**
Speed ratings (Par 101): **100,98,96,96,95 95,90,86**
toteswingers: 1&2 £4.20, 1&3 £7.00, 2&3 £2.70 CSF £26.19 CT £102.90 TOTE £10.20: £2.80, £1.40, £1.30; EX 33.60.
Owner M A Swift and A J Chapman **Bred** D R Tucker **Trained** Kentisbeare, Devon

FOCUS
A modest handicap in which the first pair remain progressive but the form is ordinary rated around the fourth and fifth.

6422 COME RACING ON SUNDAY 11TH OCTOBER APPRENTICE H'CAP 5f
5:40 (5:40) (Class 5) (0-70,75) 3-Y-O+ **£3,238** (£963; £481; £240) **Stalls** Low

Form RPR

0606 **1** **Even Bolder**[8] 6205 6-9-0 **65**.. LeeNewnes 9 76
(E A Wheeler) *racd towards centre: cl up: gng wl 1/2-way: pushed into ld over 1f out: edgd lft after but styd on wl* **8/1**

2006 **2** *1 ¾* **Namir (IRE)**[12] 6118 7-9-5 **70**..(vt) SimonPearce 5 74
(H J Evans) *walked to post: hld up bhd ldrs towards outer: rdn and effrt over 1f out: styd on to take 2nd wl ins fnl f: unable to chal* **10/1**

2112 **3** *nk* **Triple Dream**[1] 6396 4-9-7 **75** 6ex..................................(p) SPRyan(3) 3 78
(J M Bradley) *hld up bhd ldrs: trying to squeeze through fr 3f out: hanging and bmpd 2f out: styd on to take 3rd wl ins fnl f* **2/1**[1]

0402 **4** *nk* **Tiger Trail (GER)**[8] 6205 5-8-5 **56** oh2.................................... JPFahy 7 58+
(Mrs N Smith) *stdd s: racd towards centre: hld up last: plld out wd and prog 2f out: styd on fnl f: nvr able to chal* **7/1**[3]

5221 **5** *nse* **Brandywell Boy (IRE)**[8] 6205 6-9-3 **68** 6ex.................. TobyAtkinson 4 70
(D J S Ffrench Davis) *pressed ldrs: upsides and bmpd 2f out: chsd wnr over 1f out tl ins fnl f: one pce* **7/1**[3]

0010 **6** *1 ½* **Colorus (IRE)**[8] 6205 6-8-12 **70**..............................(p) LeonnaMayor(7) 6 67
(W J H Ratcliffe) *mde most towards centre: bmpd 2f out: hdd over 1f out: fdd ins fnl f* **16/1**

0033 **7** *hd* **Piazza San Pietro**[24] 5719 3-8-12 **68**.......................... RyanPowell(5) 2 64
(A B Haynes) *chsd ldrs and racd towards nr side rail: on terms 2f out: fdd fnl f* **9/1**

0000 8 3/4 **Sherjawy (IRE)**[32] 5477 5-8-5 **56** oh3........................(b) DebraEngland 10 49
(Miss Z C Davison) *dwlt: sn wl in tch in centre: nt qckn over 1f out: fdd fnl f* **25/1**

5100 9 2 1/4 **Ishibee (IRE)**[39] 5287 5-8-0 **56** oh7........................(v[1]) DannyBrock(5) 8 41
(J J Bridger) *taken down early: dwlt: cl up bhd ldrs in centre: fdd over 1f out* **33/1**

1413 10 1/2 **Lithaam (IRE)**[8] 6205 5-9-1 **66**........................(p) MatthewDavies 1 49
(J M Bradley) *racd against nr side rail: on terms w ldr to 2f out: sn wknd* **11/2**[2]

58.22 secs (-0.18) **Going Correction** -0.10s/f (Good) **10** Ran SP% **116.6**
Speed ratings (Par 103): **97,94,93,93,93 90,90,89,85,84**
toteswingers: 1&2 £20.10, 1&3 £6.20, 2&3 £7.10 CSF £85.03 CT £226.39 TOTE £9.80: £3.10, £3.80, £1.30; EX 111.70 Place 6: £25.17 Place 5: £22.32.
Owner Astrod TA Austin Stroud & Co **Bred** Raffin Bloodstock **Trained** Whitchurch-on-Thames, Oxon

FOCUS
A modest sprint handicap in which the fifth looks the best guide.
Colorus(IRE) Official explanation: jockey said gelding hung left
T/Plt: £44.90 to a £1 stake. Pool: £49,126.24. 797.37 winning tickets. T/Qpdt: £32.10 to a £1 stake. Pool: £2,953.20. 68.05 winning tickets. JN

6112 NEWMARKET (R-H)
Thursday, October 1

OFFICIAL GOING: Good to firm (8.4)
Far-side course used all three days.
Wind: Light half-behind Weather: Cloudy with sunny spells

6423 E B F BUY A RACING POST YEARLING BONUS CANDIDATE MAIDEN STKS (C&G) 1m
2:00 (2:01) (Class 4) 2-Y-O **£5,180** (£1,541; £770; £384) **Stalls** Low

Form RPR

1 **Fareej (USA)** 2-9-0 0........................ LDettori 7 85+
(Saeed Bin Suroor) *w'like: scope: str: attractive: chsd ldrs: pushed along over 2f out: rdn over 1f out: sn edgd lft: led ins fnl f: styd on wl* **6/5**[1]

2 2 1/4 **William Van Gogh** 2-9-0 0........................ RichardMullen 9 80
(J H M Gosden) *unf: scope: lengthy: led: shkn up over 2f out: rdn and edgd lft over 1f out: hdd and unable qck ins fnl f* **14/1**

3 1 1/4 **Theology** 2-9-0 0........................ ShaneKelly 4 77+
(J Noseda) *unf: scope: hld up: pushed along and hdwy over 2f out: r.o ins fnl f: nt rch ldrs* **10/1**

4 1/2 **Blissful Moment (USA)** 2-9-0 0........................ RyanMoore 1 76+
(Sir Michael Stoute) *w'like: scope: bit bkwd: s.i.s: hld up: hdwy over 2f out: shkn up over 1f out: r.o ins fnl f: nrst fin* **5/1**[2]

0 5 1 **Mass Rally (IRE)**[111] 2889 2-9-0 0........................ RobertHavlin 2 74+
(J H M Gosden) *prom: rdn and ev ch over 1f out: sn hung lft: wknd ins fnl f* **25/1**

6 4 1/2 **Balierus (GER)** 2-8-11 0........................ AhmedAjtebi(3) 11 64
(Saeed Bin Suroor) *w'like: scope: str: wnt rt s: sn chsng ldr: pushed along 3f out: rdn: edgd lft and wknd over 1f out* **12/1**

7 3/4 **Protaras (USA)** 2-9-0 0........................ TPQueally 5 62+
(H R A Cecil) *w'like: str: prom: rdn over 3f out: sn lost pl* **11/1**

8 nk **Knockdolian (IRE)** 2-9-0 0........................ SteveDrowne 6 62+
(R Charlton) *w'like: str: bit bkwd: s.s: hld up: a in rr* **20/1**

9 3/4 **Istidlaal** 2-9-0 0........................ RHills 10 60
(Sir Michael Stoute) *w'like: bit bkwd: prom: rdn over 3f out: wknd 2f out* **8/1**[3]

10 32 **Filibuster** 2-9-0 0........................ TGMcLaughlin 3 —
(Mrs C A Dunnett) *w'like: bit bkwd: hld up: rdn and wknd 1/2-way* **150/1**

1m 38.87s (0.27) **Going Correction** +0.025s/f (Good) **10** Ran SP% **114.3**
Speed ratings (Par 97): **99,96,95,95,94 89,88,88,87,55**
toteswingers: 1&2 £9.30, 1&3 £5.80, 2&3 £24.90 CSF £19.46 TOTE £2.00: £1.10, £4.00, £2.70; EX 24.20.
Owner Godolphin **Bred** Darley **Trained** Newmarket, Suffolk

FOCUS
An interesting maiden, won by Twice Over two years ago, and again some of the very top stables were represented. Only one of the ten runners had seen the racecourse before and half the field were entered for the Derby. The pace looked only a fair one but they look a decent bunch with potential.

NOTEBOOK
Fareej(USA) ◆, a full-brother to the useful Bergamask and a half-brother to the winning juvenile Alderney, was all the rage in the market beforehand. He needed to be slightly niggled along in midfield after halfway, but got stronger as the race progressed and he really took off once taking over in front around a furlong from home. One of those entered for next year's Derby, connections believe that he will be better over further next year, though he may have another run before the end of this season. (op 11-8 tchd 6-4, 13-8 in a place)
William Van Gogh ◆, another Derby entrant, had the run of the race out in front and kept on well, though he had no answer to the winner's late surge. A brother to a winner over 7f and a half-brother to three other winners at up to 1m4f, including the high-class Eco Friendly, he too should improve for further in due course. (tchd 16-1)
Theology ◆, out of a 1m2f winner in Italy, was held up and became outpaced entering the last 3f, but he stayed on up the final climb to snatch third. Entered for the Racing Post Trophy and the Irish Derby, he should come on a fair bit for this. (op 9-1 tchd 17-2)
Blissful Moment(USA) ◆, a $380,000 good-bodied colt out of a winner over 1m, raced a little green off the pace early but stayed on in pleasing style once he realised what was required. Connections had warned that he might just need it, so he is likely to progress a good deal from this. (op 6-1 tchd 8-1)
Mass Rally(IRE), off three months since a disappointing debut at Sandown when missing the break, ran much better here and nothing was travelling better than him when he loomed up to challenge coming to the last furlong, but he then hung away to his left and was run right out of the placings. There should be races to be won with him. (op 16-1)
Balierus(GER), a 49,000euros half-brother to three winners at up to 1m5f and stablemate of the winner, swerved out to his right exiting the stalls and then raced keenly in a handy position. Having got tired he was eventually eased right off, but there was enough promise here to build on. (op 10-1 tchd 17-2)
Protaras(USA), whose dam is from the family of Miesque, showed up prominently early but then ran very green when put under pressure and faded right out of it. His trainer had stated beforehand that the colt was still immature so he is probably capable of better, though he holds no big-race entries at this stage. (op 9-1 tchd 12-1)
Knockdolian(IRE), a half-brother to the useful Humungous, fluffed the start and then ran green at the back of the field. He looks to need more time.

6424 WEATHERBYS MAIDEN STKS 6f
2:35 (2:35) (Class 4) 2-Y-O **£5,180** (£1,541; £770; £384) **Stalls** Low

Form RPR

03 1 **Rum King (USA)**[23] 5749 2-9-3 0........................ RichardHughes 3 82+
(R Hannon) *w'like: racd alone against nr side rail: w ldr tl led overall 2f out: sn rdn and r.o wl* **11/4**[1]

2 2 **Chat De La Burg (USA)** 2-9-3 0........................ SteveDrowne 10 76
(J R Best) *unf: racd centre: trckd ldr: racd keenly: rdn and swtchd lft over 1f out: chsd wnr and hung lft ins fnl f: no imp* **7/2**[2]

3 1 1/2 **Brannagh (USA)** 2-9-3 0........................(t) LDettori 6 74+
(J Noseda) *str: scope: s.s: racd centre: hld up: hdwy and edgd lft over 2f out: rdn over 1f out: swished tail ins fnl f: nt trble ldrs* **5/1**[3]

04 4 2 1/2 **Aldorable**[21] 5800 2-8-12 0........................ NCallan 5 59
(R A Teal) *led centre 4f: sn rdn: wknd ins fnl f* **18/1**

00 5 shd **Great Intrigue (IRE)**[105] 3064 2-9-3 0........................ LPKeniry 9 64
(J S Moore) *racd centre: hld up in tch: racd keenly: rdn over 1f out: hung lft and no ex ins fnl f* **8/1**

6 3 3/4 **Bobby's Doll** 2-8-12 0........................ TGMcLaughlin 1 48+
(T T Clement) *leggy: angular: dwlt: racd centre: hld up: last 4f out: sme hdwy over 2f out: wknd wl over 1f out* **100/1**

0 7 1/2 **Rock A Doodle Doo (IRE)**[122] 2533 2-9-3 0........................ J-PGuillambert 4 51
(W Jarvis) *w'like: racd centre: sn pushed along and prom: lost pl 1/2-way: n.d after* **12/1**

8 nk **Joe Rua (USA)** 2-9-3 0........................ KFallon 7 53+
(J Ryan) *w'like: leggy: s.i.s: racd centre: sn pushed along in rr: wknd 2f out* **7/2**[2]

045 9 3/4 **Sassanian (IRE)**[13] 6065 2-9-3 65........................ IvaMilickova 2 48
(Jane Chapple-Hyam) *racd centre: a in rr: bhd fr 1/2-way* **28/1**

1m 13.12s (0.92) **Going Correction** +0.025s/f (Good) **9** Ran SP% **116.3**
Speed ratings (Par 97): **94,91,89,86,85 80,80,79,78**
toteswingers: 1&2 £3.60, 1&3 £2.90, 2&3 £4.60 CSF £12.57 TOTE £3.80: £1.40, £1.70, £1.60; EX 17.10.
Owner Sir David Seale **Bred** Ocala Stud **Trained** East Everleigh, Wilts

FOCUS
This looked an ordinary maiden, especially after the likely short-priced favourite was taken out in the morning. The winner left his previous form behind.

NOTEBOOK
Rum King(USA) was strong in the market despite only possessing modest previous form but, after coming down the stands'-side rail alone, he won this a bit to spare. A horse with a bit of size and scope, his future lies in how the Handicapper views his efforts. (op 5-2 tchd 9-4)
Chat De La Burg(USA), a $130,000 colt out of a triple sprint winner in America, does not look overly big but did enough on his debut to suggest races can be won with him. (op 4-1)
Brannagh(USA), a half-brother to Group 1 performer Lord Shanakill, was wearing a tongue tie for his first outing and did not seem that fancied, considering his family relation and the trainer he represented. Slowly away, he got the hang of things late on and stayed on nicely to catch the eye, although the swishing of his tail could be construed as a worry. (op 4-1 tchd 11-2)
Aldorable was quickly sent into the lead towards the middle of the course and led that bunch along at a respectable gallop. She did not completely cave in when joined and deserves some respect if tried in a low-grade handicap next. Her dam was smart when in training, and she looks to have passed some of that ability on. (op 12-1 tchd 20-1)
Great Intrigue(IRE), not seen since the middle of June, showed his best piece of form to date but did not look like a winner waiting to happen. (op 9-1 tchd 7-1)
Bobby's Doll went off at a long price but showed some ability.
Joe Rua(USA) is related to a few winners and hails from the stable responsible for the smart juvenile Silver Grecian. He attracted market support but showed little. (op 6-1)

6425 DIRECTA SIGNS NOEL MURLESS STKS (LISTED RACE) 1m 6f
3:10 (3:10) (Class 1) 3-Y-O **£22,708** (£8,608; £4,308; £2,148; £1,076) **Stalls** Centre

Form RPR

1511 1 **Akmal**[14] 6036 3-9-0 102........................ RHills 5 109
(J L Dunlop) *lw: mde all: rdn over 1f out: hung lft nr fin: a doing enough* **3/1**[2]

-100 2 3/4 **Nehaam**[104] 3087 3-9-0 103........................ RyanMoore 4 108
(J H M Gosden) *a.p: rdn to chse wnr fnl f: styd on* **6/1**[3]

21 3 1 1/2 **Manifest**[54] 4798 3-9-0 100........................ TPQueally 3 106
(H R A Cecil) *hld up in tch: rdn to chse wnr 3f out: styd on same pce fnl f* **4/6**[1]

4443 4 37 **Free Agent**[28] 5609 3-9-0 103........................(b) RichardHughes 1 54
(R Hannon) *chsd wnr: given reminders over 6f out: lost pl 3f out: sn wknd: eased fnl 2f: t.o* **9/1**

5 15 **Owls FC (IRE)** 3-8-9 0........................ TolleyDean 2 28
(M C Chapman) *w'like: sn pushed along in rr: rdn and lost tch 6f out: sn hung rt: t.o* **200/1**

2m 54.43s (-4.07) **Going Correction** +0.025s/f (Good) **5** Ran SP% **109.8**
Speed ratings (Par 109): **112,111,110,89,81**
CSF £19.68 TOTE £3.30: £1.40, £2.70; EX 18.00.
Owner Hamdan Al Maktoum **Bred** Shadwell Estate Company Limited **Trained** Arundel, W Sussex

FOCUS
An interesting Listed staying event won by the likes of Tungsten Strike and Lion Sands in recent years. Despite the small field, the pace was sound and the form looks worth being positive about.

NOTEBOOK
Akmal, winner of five of his last seven starts including three over this trip, was stepping up in class. Soon in front, his rider wisely made this a true test and he proved very game when challenged inside the last half-mile, pulling out more when asked and running all the way to the line. His rider believes that he could make up into a Cup horse for next year. (tchd 5-2)
Nehaamhad twice been disappointing at Group 2 level since beating Monitor Closely in a valuable sales race here in April and was having his first start since being gelded. Stepping up in trip, he plugged on from off the pace over the last couple of furlongs, but could never quite get on terms with the winner. This was a fair effort considering he was entitled to have just needed it. (op 7-1 tchd 15-2)
Manifest was taking a big step up in class on this third start after winning a weak Newmarket maiden over 1m4f by 19l, but he was nonetheless sent off at very cramped odds. Having been held up early, he made his move on the outside of the field coming to the last 3f and had every chance, but the winner kept finding more and he was made to look a little one-paced inside the final furlong. This ground may have been too quick for him and he is still very inexperienced, so he may well be capable of much more as a 4-y-o. (op 4-5 tchd 5-6)

Free Agent, proven at this level and far from disgraced against some useful older stayers over this trip at Salisbury last time, was the major disappointment of the race. Having tracked the winner early, he had to be given reminders passing the 7f pole and, after coming under even more severe pressure inside the last half-mile, eventually dropped right out. (op 7-1 tchd 10-1)

6426 SOMERVILLE TATTERSALL STKS (GROUP 3) (COLTS & GELDINGS) 7f

3:45 (3:46) (Class 1) 2-Y-O

£34,062 (£12,912; £6,462; £3,222; £1,614; £810) **Stalls** Low

Form				RPR
3106	**1**		**Sir Parky (IRE)**[23] 5743 2-8-12 94 RichardHughes 7	104
			(R Hannon) *mde all: clr 1/2way: rdn and hung rt fr over 1f out: jst hld on* **33/1**	
3	**2**	½	**Sebastian Flyte**[32] 5486 2-8-12 0 WJSupple 4	103
			(Francis Ennis, Ire) *chsd wnr: rdn and edgd rt fr over 2f out: styd on wl* **16/1**	
3262	**3**	1 ½	**Mata Keranjang (USA)**[23] 5743 2-8-12 103 MartinDwyer 5	99
			(P F I Cole) *chsd ldrs: rdn over 1f out: edgd rt and r.o: snatched 3rd on line* **5/1**[3]	
2011	**4**	shd	**Audacity Of Hope**[13] 6063 2-8-12 95 (t) KFallon 2	99
			(P J McBride) *hld up: rdn over 2f out: hdwy and hung rt over 1f out: r.o* **9/1**	
4112	**5**	shd	**Nideeb**[26] 5659 2-8-12 106 NCallan 9	99
			(C E Brittain) *lw: chsd ldrs: rdn over 1f out: styd on* **7/2**[1]	
1	**6**	1 ¾	**Khattaab (USA)**[55] 4738 2-8-12 0 RHills 8	94
			(B W Hills) *w'like: scope: hld up: hdwy 2f out: sn rdn: no ex ins fnl f* **4/1**[2]	
021	**7**	1	**Manhattan Fox (USA)**[19] 5879 2-8-12 82 LDettori 3	92
			(B J Meehan) *hld up: rdn over 2f out: nt trble ldrs* **20/1**	
1	**8**	nse	**Hunting Tartan**[21] 5785 2-8-12 0 RyanMoore 6	92
			(J H M Gosden) *w'like: scope: athletic: lw: hld up: racd keenly: rdn over 2f out: nvr trbld ldrs* **4/1**[2]	
3341	**9**	2 ¼	**Swilly Ferry (USA)**[21] 5795 2-8-12 97 WilliamBuick 1	86
			(B W Hills) *hld up: hdwy over 2f out: rdn and wknd over 1f out* **13/2**	

1m 24.59s (-0.81) **Going Correction** +0.025s/f (Good) **9** Ran SP% **115.8**
Speed ratings (Par 105): **105,104,102,102,102 100,99,99,96**
toteswingers: 1&2 £26.90, 1&3 £27.70, 2&3 £16.30 CSF £471.80 TOTE £39.00: £6.90, £3.30, £1.90; EX 388.70.
Owner Sir David Seale **Bred** Swordlestown Stud **Trained** East Everleigh, Wilts

FOCUS
This contest has produced the odd very good performer, most notably Milk It Mick and Aussie Rules in recent years. However, the 2009 running did not look a good renewal for a couple of reasons and probably form to be against.

NOTEBOOK
Sir Parky(IRE) had been running to a decent standard but was more exposed than the majority of his rivals. Richard Hughes deserves plenty of credit for the success, as he quickly got his mount to the front and kept increasing the pace to win by a narrow margin, despite hanging right across to the far rail. He finished behind Mata Keranjang last time, so it is difficult to put this victory in a really positive light. That said, connections will be rightly pleased with their horse, who has done them proud throughout the season.
Sebastian Flyte, an Irish raider stepping up to 7f for the first time, chased the winner at a respectable distance and kept on well once under pressure. He was closing in on the winner in the final furlong and seems sure to be competitive at this distance. (op 14-1 tchd 12-1)
Mata Keranjang(USA), whose trainer had produced two winners from two runners in this race since 2002, has been running consistently but never looked like taking a hand in the finish. (op 9-2 tchd 11-2, 4-1 in a place)
Audacity Of Hope was chasing a hat-trick after winning two nurseries (both wins at that level had come when a tongue tie was fitted) and ran well on this step up in grade, finishing strongly after being held up. (tchd 11-1)
Nideeb, who had landed a Listed race at Ascot before being beaten by recent Godolphin purchase Emerald Commander at that level over 1m, was given every chance but did not have a change of gear when needed. (op 4-1 tchd 9-2 in places)
Khattaab(USA), absent since bolting up on his debut at the start of August, travelled strongly but found disappointingly little off the bridle. He does deserve another chance but it might be that he's a sprinter. (op 9-2)
Manhattan Fox(USA) won an ordinary 1m maiden at Goodwood last time after a couple of defeats and did not feature in this after sitting off the pace. (op 25-1)
Hunting Tartan comfortably landed a Chepstow maiden on his only previous outing but found this all too much. One of the first to be ridden along, he got going late on and may have learnt more here than he did on his first outing. (op 9-2 tchd 5-1)
Swilly Ferry(USA) started his season in the Brocklesby way back in March and came back to prominence with a win in a valuable contest at Doncaster last time. However, he offered little in Group company. (op 6-1 tchd 5-1)

6427 NEWSELLS PARK STUD "GOLDEN BONUS" ROUS STKS (LISTED RACE) 5f

4:20 (4:21) (Class 1) 3-Y-O+

£22,708 (£8,608; £4,308; £2,148; £1,076; £540) **Stalls** Low

Form				RPR
0526	**1**		**Spin Cycle (IRE)**[12] 6107 3-8-12 105 RichardMullen 12	111
			(B Smart) *hld up in tch: outpcd 1/2-way: hdwy over 1f out: sn rdn: r.o to ld wl ins fnl f* **7/1**	
2114	**2**	nk	**Noble Storm (USA)**[33] 5420 3-8-12 105 GrahamGibbons 11	110+
			(E S McMahon) *lw: w ldrs: led over 1f out: sn rdn: hdd wl ins fnl f* **3/1**[1]	
-006	**3**	1 ½	**Run For The Hills**[54] 4771 3-8-12 88 RobertHavlin 4	105
			(J H M Gosden) *hld up: swtchd rt over 1f out: sn rdn: hung lft and r.o ins fnl f: wnt 3rd towards fin* **20/1**	
5014	**4**	½	**Dandy Man (IRE)**[22] 5765 6-8-12 106 (t) LDettori 9	103
			(Saeed Bin Suroor) *lw: trckd ldrs: carried hd to one side over 1f out: sn rdn: no ex ins fnl f* **4/1**[2]	
1335	**5**	hd	**Inxile (IRE)**[22] 5765 4-9-1 106 AdrianTNicholls 3	105
			(D Nicholls) *s.i.s: sn rcvrd to ld: rdn and hdd over 1f out: styd on same pce ins fnl f* **9/2**[3]	
14-6	**6**	¾	**Himalya (IRE)**[19] 5862 3-8-12 108 RyanMoore 5	99
			(J Noseda) *stdd s: bhd: pushed along 1/2-way: disputing last and plenty too do over 1f out: r.o strly ins fnl f: nt rch ldrs* **14/1**	
0004	**7**	½	**Matsunosuke**[9] 6180 7-8-12 99 TPQueally 2	98
			(A B Coogan) *prom: rdn over 1f out: styd on same pce* **40/1**	
0-30	**8**	hd	**Excellerator (IRE)**[41] 5233 3-8-7 96 (t) TedDurcan 6	92
			(George Baker) *hld up: pushed along 1/2-way: disputing last and plenty too do over 1f out: r.o strly ins fnl f: eased last strides: nt trble ldrs* **25/1**	
4010	**9**	¾	**Siren's Gift**[22] 5765 5-8-7 94 (b) DavidProbert 10	89
			(A M Balding) *w ldrs: rdn 1/2-way: no ex fnl f* **16/1**	
4103	**10**	½	**Sugar Free (IRE)**[32] 5491 3-8-10 0 WMLordan 7	90
			(T Stack, Ire) *hld up in tch: racd keenly: rdn over 1f out: no ex* **16/1**	
2060	**11**	1 ½	**Captain Gerrard (IRE)**[12] 6107 4-8-12 101 KFallon 8	87
			(B Smart) *chsd ldrs: rdn 1/2-way: swtchd rt over 1f out: sn wknd* **10/1**	
0100	**12**	½	**Group Therapy**[19] 5860 4-8-12 102 NCallan 1	85
			(N P Littmoden) *mid-div: rdn 2f out: wknd over 1f out* **25/1**	

58.25 secs (-0.85) **Going Correction** +0.025s/f (Good) **12** Ran SP% **118.1**
Speed ratings (Par 111): **107,106,104,103,103 101,101,100,99,98 96,95**
toteswingers: 1&2 £6.80, 1&3 £34.90, 2&3 £18.90 CSF £26.82 TOTE £8.00: £2.70, £1.70, £4.90; EX 34.10.
Owner H E Sheikh Rashid Bin Mohammed **Bred** Mrs Lisa Kelly **Trained** Hambleton, N Yorks

FOCUS
A competitive Listed sprint and with a couple of established trailblazers taking part, a strong pace was always likely. This proved a triumph for the younger generation who filled the first three places and is rated through the runner-up at face value.

NOTEBOOK
Spin Cycle(IRE) had been a bit disappointing in a first-time visor last time following his decent effort in a similar event at Doncaster last month when he had four of today's rivals behind him, but the removal of the headgear saw him bounce back to form. Held up on the wide outside of the field from his high draw, he was brought with his effort entering the Dip and battled on well up the hill to just deny the favourite. (op 8-1)
Noble Storm(USA), who didn't quite get home when bidding for a hat-trick at Beverley last time, showed his usual decent early speed though the presence of Inxile meant that he was never able to dominate on his own. He managed to burn that rival off, but the winner just outstayed him up the hill and it does appear that he is best suited by tracks without an uphill finish. (op 7-2 tchd 4-1)
Run For The Hills, by far the worst in at the weights, was down to the minimum trip for the first time and he made up a lot of late ground having been well off the pace early. This was much better following three disappointing efforts so far this year and he will be of interest back over 6f.
Dandy Man(IRE), behind the winner at Doncaster last time, was produced to hold every chance passing the furlong pole but had no more to offer up the final climb. Despite his success in a Leicester conditions event at Leicester two starts back, he is hard to win with these days. (op 7-2)
Inxile(IRE), already a dual winner at this level this season and conceding weight all round as a result, is at his best when able to dominate but he company right from the start here and had run his race on reaching the furlong pole. (op 5-1 tchd 4-1, 11-2 in a place)
Himalya(IRE) ◆ had a real problem going the early gallop and was still a long way off the pace passing the furlong pole, but he took off up the hill and was flying at the finish. He had finished tailed-off in a Doncaster Group 2 last month on his first start since finishing fourth in last year's Coventry Stakes, so he was entitled to still need this and is one to look out for next time, possibly back over 6f. (op 9-1)
Excellerator(IRE) ◆, out of her depth in the Nunthorpe last time, was another who seemed to find everything happening too quickly for her but she finished well without offering a threat. She is yet to win on turf, but is perfectly capable of putting that right when returned to further. (op 33-1 tchd 40-1)

6428 EUROPEAN BREEDERS' FUND FILLIES' H'CAP 6f

4:55 (4:55) (Class 2) (0-100,97) 3-Y-O+

£12,462 (£3,732; £1,866; £934; £466; £234) **Stalls** Low

Form				RPR
5200	**1**		**Sea Of Leaves (USA)**[12] 6089 3-8-11 **90** KFallon 7	99
			(J S Goldie) *lw: hld up: hdwy over 1f out: sn rdn: r.o to ld nr fin* **6/1**[3]	
-311	**2**	nk	**Bounty Box**[47] 5032 3-8-13 **92** TedDurcan 5	100
			(C F Wall) *lw: hld up in tch: rdn to ld ins fnl f: r.o: hdd nr fin* **15/8**[1]	
2621	**3**	2 ½	**Vitoria (IRE)**[10] 6155 3-9-1 **94** 6ex RichardMullen 6	94
			(B Smart) *lw: a.p: chsd ldr 1/2-way: rdn to ld 1f out: hdd and unable qck ins fnl f* **7/2**[2]	
1003	**4**	¾	**Carcinetto (IRE)**[19] 5855 7-9-0 **97** RichardEvans(5) 4	95
			(P D Evans) *chsd ldr tl rdn 1/2-way: outpcd over 1f out: styd on ins fnl f* **33/1**	
0000	**5**	hd	**Favourite Girl (IRE)**[16] 5959 3-8-8 **87** (b[1]) WJSupple 1	84
			(T D Easterby) *chsd ldrs: rdn over 2f out: styd on same pce fnl f* **20/1**	
3335	**6**	¾	**Angus Newz**[14] 6020 6-8-10 **88** MartinDwyer 3	83
			(M Quinn) *led: rdn and hdd 1f out: wknd towards fin* **16/1**	
410	**7**	½	**Filligree (IRE)**[5] 6282 4-8-7 **88** WilliamCarson(3) 9	81
			(Rae Guest) *lw: prom: rdn over 1f out: wknd ins fnl f* **15/2**	
0124	**8**	nse	**Artistic License (IRE)**[14] 6020 4-8-11 **89** RyanMoore 8	82
			(M R Channon) *sn outpcd and bhd: plenty too do over 1f out: r.o towards fin* **13/2**	
1040	**9**	1 ½	**Bahamian Babe**[42] 5203 3-8-8 **87** HayleyTurner 2	75
			(M L W Bell) *s.i.s: hld up: effrt: nt clr run and swtchd rt over 2f out: wknd over 1f out* **25/1**	

1m 11.13s (-1.07) **Going Correction** +0.025s/f (Good)
WFA 3 from 4yo+ 1lb **9** Ran SP% **113.8**
Speed ratings (Par 96): **108,107,104,103,103 102,101,101,99**
toteswingers: 1&2 £4.30, 1&3 £4.40, 2&3 £2.50 CSF £16.97 CT £45.05 TOTE £6.60: £2.10, £1.50, £1.40; EX 19.20.
Owner Frank & Annette Brady **Bred** Juddmonte Farms Inc **Trained** Uplawmoor, E Renfrews

FOCUS
A strong-looking handicap for fillies. The pace seemed strong and the form should prove reliable.

NOTEBOOK
Sea Of Leaves(USA) had been running well since leaving John Gosden for Jim Goldie, and the booking of Kieren Fallon caught the eye. A small type, she was ridden with restraint and got her nose in front at the right time. It was a good, well-executed ride, as she looks the type that needs to hit the front at the last moment. (op 11-2 tchd 5-1, 13-2 in a place)
Bounty Box, whose trainer won this race in the past with back-to-back winner Paradise Isle, got the better of Sea The Leaves last time they met and ran really well again on worse terms. She remains one to follow despite being beaten, as the ground may have been a bit quick for her. (op 2-1 tchd 9-4)
Vitoria(IRE), carrying a penalty, was always close up and kept on in resolute fashion, but was soundly held by the first two. (tchd 4-1, 9-2 in places)
Carcinetto(IRE) looked like dropping away under pressure over a furlong out, but she rallied and stayed on again up the hill. (op 25-1)
Favourite Girl(IRE), wearing blinkers for the first time, has hit a disappointing run of form and did not obviously improve for headgear.
Angus Newz, the winner of this race in 2007, weakened late on after showing her usual speed against the stands'-side rail. (op 14-1 tchd 12-1)
Filligree(IRE) was comfortably held again. (op 7-1 tchd 8-1)
Artistic License(IRE) got badly outpaced, as seems usual for her nowadays, before running on in the later stages. (op 8-1 tchd 6-1)

6429 RACING UK SKY 432 H'CAP 1m

5:30 (5:31) (Class 3) (0-95,92) 3-Y-O+

£8,723 (£2,612; £1,306; £653; £326; £163) **Stalls** Low

Form				RPR
3206	**1**		**Proponent (IRE)**[19] 5880 5-9-7 **92** (t) LDettori 6	104+
			(R Charlton) *lw: racd centre: hld up in tch: led over 1f out: sn rdn: styd on wl* **7/2**[1]	

3036 **2** ¾ **Legislate**[30] 5551 3-8-8 **82**.................................. MichaelHills 7 91
(B W Hills) *racd centre: overall ldr to over 6f out: chsd ldr tl led again overall over 3f out: rdn and hdd over 1f out: styd on* **15/2**

16 **3** 1½ **Namibian Orator (IRE)**[130] 2296 3-8-12 **86**.................... RyanMoore 11 92
(Sir Michael Stoute) *racd centre: stdd s: hld up: hdwy 2f out: styd on same pce ins fnl f* **7/1**[3]

2356 **4** 5 **Vainglory (USA)**[26] 5663 5-9-1 **86**...................... RichardMullen 2 80
(D M Simcock) *racd stands' side: chsd ldr: rdn and hung rt fr over 2f out: no imp fnl f* **13/2**[2]

-140 **5** 2 **African Art (USA)**[103] 3144 3-8-11 **85**...................... MartinDwyer 14 75
(B J Meehan) *racd centre: hld up: rdn over 2f out: n.d* **12/1**

0006 **6** ¾ **Lucky Dance (BRZ)**[68] 4310 7-9-1 **86**.......................... RobertHavlin 12 74
(A G Foster) *racd centre: slipped s: rcvrd to ld overall over 6f out: hdd over 3f out: sn rdn: hung lft and wknd over 1f out* **25/1**

3300 **7** nk **Nightjar (USA)**[28] 5615 4-8-12 **83**............................ GregFairley 8 70
(M Johnston) *racd centre: chsd ldrs: rdn over 2f out: wknd over 1f out* **22/1**

000 **8** 2¾ **Final Verse**[75] 4091 6-9-3 **88**.................................... LPKeniry 3 69
(Matthew Salaman) *sn led stands' side pair: rdn over 2f out: wknd over 1f out* **17/2**

2146 **9** ¾ **Dingaan (IRE)**[23] 5745 6-8-8 **79**........................... DavidProbert 4 58
(A M Balding) *swtg: s.i.s: racd centre: hdwy over 5f out: rdn and hung lft over 1f out: sn wknd* **11/1**

0045 **10** nk **Ellemujie**[12] 6117 4-9-1 **86**..................................... TPQueally 9 65
(D K Ivory) *s.i.s: racd centre: sn pushed along in rr: sme hdwy 1/2-way: rdn and wknd over 2f out* **11/1**

4000 **11** 1 **Flipando (IRE)**[12] 6094 8-9-3 **91**........................... NeilBrown(3) 1 67
(T D Barron) *swtchd to racd centre after 1f: hld up: rdn over 2f out: a in rr* **16/1**

0015 **12** nk **Mount Hadley (USA)**[15] 6002 5-9-3 **88**......................... NCallan 5 64
(G A Butler) *lw: racd centre: prom tl rdn and wknd over 1f out* **8/1**

1m 37.24s (-1.36) **Going Correction** +0.025s/f (Good)
WFA 3 from 4yo+ 3lb **12** Ran SP% **119.9**
Speed ratings (Par 107): **107,106,104,99,97 97,96,93,93,92 91,91**
toteswingers: 1&2 £6.80, 1&3 £5.30, 2&3 £7.60 CSF £29.44 CT £178.50 TOTE £3.80: £1.60, £2.90, £2.30; EX 28.60 Trifecta £196.50 Pool: £584.38 - 2.20 winning units. Place 6: £137.19 Place 5: £82.44.
Owner B E Nielsen **Bred** Fortbarrington Stud **Trained** Beckhampton, Wilts

FOCUS
A fair handicap run at a solid pace, but the field split early with the bulk racing up the centre, while two made for the stands' rail. The form looks pretty straightforward for the grade.

NOTEBOOK
Proponent(IRE) was without a success since winning here in May of last year and was still 2lb higher, but he had been successful in two of his three previous starts here and the market support suggested that a big run was expected. He travelled like a dream just behind the leaders in the main group and once produced with his effort in the Dip, there was only going to be one winner. The first-time tongue tie might also have been significant. (op 5-1 tchd 11-2 in a place)
Legislate, down to this trip for the first time since winning his maiden on the Lingfield Polytrack in March, was always up with the pace in the centre of the track and had every chance, but the winner proved much the better up the hill. A return to further won't hurt him. (op 8-1 tchd 17-2)
Namibian Orator(IRE), not seen since a disappointing last of six over 2f further here in May, stayed on well from off the pace over the last couple of furlongs and, though he lacked the speed to bother the front two, pulled a long way clear of the rest. He remains unexposed and should benefit from a return to 1m2f. (op 6-1 tchd 15-2)
Vainglory(USA), well-backed, may have done too much too soon on the Kempton Polytrack last time and was ridden with a bit more restraint here, tracking the only other horse to race up the stands' rail. He plugged on well to win the separate race for fourth, but was never able to get near the leading trio. (op 9-1)
African Art(USA), twice disappointing after a convincing success in a Haydock maiden in April, was on his toes beforehand. He wasn't disgraced, especially as he may have just needed it after three months off. (op 11-1 tchd 10-1)
Lucky Dance(BRZ) ◆, mainly out of form so far this season, showed up for a long way at the front of the main group. He is now on the same mark as when winning over course and distance last November, so is worth keeping an eye out for back on easier ground. (op 20-1)
Nightjar(USA), below form in his last two starts, ran well for a long way in the main group. He has form under these conditions, but does seem a much better horse on Fibresand and is one to be interested in back at Southwell. (op 14-1 tchd 25-1)
Ellemujie Official explanation: jockey said gelding was unsuited by the good to firm ground
T/Jkpt: Not won. T/Plt: £104.30 to a £1 stake. Pool: £76,237.93. 533.59 winning tickets. T/Qpdt: £30.30 to a £1 stake. Pool: £4,251.78. 103.50 winning tickets. CR

6342 WOLVERHAMPTON (A.W) (L-H)
Thursday, October 1
OFFICIAL GOING: Standard
Wind: Almost nil Weather: Fine

6430 BETDAQ THE BETTING EXCHANGE MAIDEN STKS 7f 32y(P)
5:45 (5:47) (Class 5) 3-4-Y-O £3,238 (£963; £481; £240) Stalls High

Form RPR

1 **Mr Rainbow** 3-9-3 0.. PJMcDonald 6 79+
(G A Swinbank) *hld up in mid-div: hdwy over 2f out: nt clr run and swtchd rt wl over 1f out: rdn to ld ins fnl f: r.o wl* **5/1**[2]

03 **2** 3½ **Anagram**[19] 5882 3-8-12 0.............................(b) RobertWinston 4 65
(W R Muir) *led early: a.p: led over 1f out: rdn and hdd ins fnl f: one pce* **6/1**[3]

02 **3** ¾ **Sometsuke**[24] 5717 3-9-3 0...............................(t) FergusSweeney 7 68
(P J Makin) *sn led: hung rt bnd over 2f out: hdd wl over 1f out: rdn and one pce ins fnl f* **5/2**[1]

4 hd **Serious Drinking (USA)** 3-8-12 0............................. ShaneKelly 11 62
(W R Swinburn) *hld up towards rr: stdy prog on outside 5f out: pushed along over 1f out: one pce fnl f* **16/1**

33 **5** 1¾ **Totalitarian**[17] 5954 3-9-3 0.................................. JerryO'Dwyer 12 63
(S A Callaghan, U.S.A) *sn chsng ldr: pushed along and led wl over 1f out: sn edgd rt and hdd: rdn and wknd ins fnl f* **5/2**[1]

5 **6** 2 **Magic Queen (IRE)**[12] 6101 3-8-7 0........................ MartinLane(5) 10 52
(A P Jarvis) *prom: pushed along over 2f out: wknd wl over 1f out* **40/1**

50 **7** ¾ **Fine Art Collector (IRE)**[7] 6223 3-9-3 0..................... PatCosgrave 3 55
(G L Moore) *hld up towards rr: pushed along wl over 1f out: no rspnse* **20/1**

8 1¼ **Big Sur** 3-9-3 0... KirstyMilczarek 8 52
(T Keddy) *s.i.s: hld up and bhd: pushed along over 2f out: c wd st: sn struggling* **20/1**

0 **9** 7 **She's Pivotal (IRE)**[136] 2139 3-8-12 0........................ SamHitchcott 5 28
(J A Osborne) *hld up in mid-div: pushed along over 2f out: rdn and wknd wl over 1f out* **33/1**

10 8 **Spirit Child (USA)** 3-8-12 0..................................... JamieSpencer 2 —
(J A Osborne) *s.s: a in rr* **16/1**

1m 28.83s (-0.77) **Going Correction** -0.15s/f (Stan)
WFA 3 from 4yo 2lb **10** Ran SP% **114.8**
Speed ratings (Par 103): **98,94,93,92,90 88,87,86,78,69**
toteswingers: 1&2 £4.60, 1&3 £3.80, 2&3 £3.00. CSF £32.59 TOTE £6.50: £1.70, £2.00, £1.20; EX 43.00.
Owner Guy Reed **Bred** G Reed **Trained** Melsonby, N Yorks

FOCUS
An ordinary maiden, featuring only a small group with worthwhile form, but they went a sound pace. The winner looks sure to do better and the runner-up sets the standard.
Sometsuke Official explanation: jockey said gelding hung badly right
Big Sur Official explanation: jockey said gelding ran green

6431 STAY AT THE WOLVERHAMPTON HOLIDAY INN CLAIMING STKS 1m 141y(P)
6:15 (6:15) (Class 6) 2-Y-O £2,388 (£705; £352) Stalls Low

Form RPR

1245 **1** **Daniella De Bruijn (IRE)**[77] 4017 2-9-1 77...................... SebSanders 3 72
(A B Haynes) *sn led: hdd after 1f: a.p: rdn to ld over 1f out: hung lft ins fnl f: drvn out* **9/2**[2]

1612 **2** ½ **Gold Fix (IRE)**[12] 6099 2-8-11 68.............................. TonyCulhane 7 67
(M R Channon) *hld up in mid-div: hdwy 3f out: sn rdn: c wd st: r.o u.p ins fnl f: tk 2nd nr fin* **5/1**[3]

3641 **3** ½ **Al Khimiya (IRE)**[7] 6228 2-8-10 69............................ JamieSpencer 11 65
(S A Callaghan, U.S.A) *led after 1f: rdn and edgd rt wl over 1f out: sn hdd: carried rt ins fnl f: nt qckn cl home* **6/4**[1]

33 **4** 1 **Springwell Giant (IRE)**[12] 6122 2-8-9 0..................... AndreaAtzeni(3) 9 65
(A J McCabe) *hld up in mid-div: pushed along over 2f out: swtchd rt and hdwy over 1f out: rdn and kpt on same pce fnl f* **10/1**

0041 **5** 2 **Underworld Dandy**[15] 5985 2-9-1 65............................ PatCosgrave 12 64
(P D Evans) *hld up towards rr: pushed along and effrt on outside over 2f out: c wd st: swtchd rt ins fnl f: rdn and edgd lft towards fin: nt rch ldrs* **10/1**

005 **6** 2½ **Pollan Bay (IRE)**[19] 5868 2-8-10 58................................ JamesDoyle 5 53
(S Kirk) *n.m.r s: hld up in rr: rdn over 2f out: nvr trbld ldrs* **25/1**

066 **7** ½ **Dinkie Short**[21] 5801 2-9-0 63................................ RobertWinston 1 56
(W R Muir) *led early: hld up in mid-div: rdn over 2f out: sn bhd* **20/1**

50 **8** nse **Elie Shore**[11] 6136 2-8-2 0.....................................(v[1]) MartinLane(5) 6 54+
(P C Haslam) *hld up in tch: pushed along over 2f out: rdn and cl 3rd whn bdly hmpd ins fnl f: nt rcvr* **50/1**

445 **9** 2¼ **Empressofboogie**[17] 5942 2-8-9 55............................ PJMcDonald 8 47
(M Dods) *prom: pushed along over 2f out: rdn and wknd wl over 1f out* **33/1**

10 1¾ **Square Pants (IRE)** 2-8-12 0.. ShaneKelly 4 46
(J A Osborne) *a towards rr* **33/1**

05 **11** nse **Al Zaeem**[38] 5319 2-8-13 0................................(v) KirstyMilczarek 2 47
(Miss D Mountain) *hld up in rr: rdn over 3f out: sn struggling* **50/1**

3506 **12** 2½ **Miss Taken (IRE)**[7] 6232 2-8-7 58................................(b) JoeFanning 13 36
(D Carroll) *prom: chsd ldr 7f out: ev ch over 2f out: wknd over 1f out* **66/1**

13 10 **Colonel Munro (IRE)** 2-9-7 0....................................... FrancisNorton 10 29
(D Nicholls) *s.i.s: a in rr: eased whn no ch ins fnl f* **16/1**

1m 50.95s (0.45) **Going Correction** -0.15s/f (Stan) **13** Ran SP% **118.8**
Speed ratings (Par 93): **92,91,91,90,88 86,85,85,83,82 82,79,71**
toteswingers: 1&2 £7.30, 1&3 £2.20, 2&3 £2.60. CSF £25.32 TOTE £6.90: £2.30, £1.90, £1.10; EX 35.40.
Owner Ms J Loylert **Bred** Manister House Stud **Trained** Limpley Stoke, Bath

FOCUS
A competitive claimer, with a clutch of previous winners in the line-up. The winner is rated to recent form.

NOTEBOOK
Daniella De Bruijn(IRE), who had posted several prominent efforts in fair company in the first half of the season, was returning from a 77-day layoff. She was entitled to go close if fully tuned-up for this comeback though, and, after chasing the pace from the outset, stayed on dourly. She jinked left in the closing stages, so may not be entirely straightfoward, but she looks worth something close to her official rating of 77. (tchd 4-1 and 5-1)
Gold Fix(IRE), winner of a 7f Epsom nursery early in September and rated 68, apeared to run right up to her best. She too stayed on in the closing stages, but never looked likely to catch the winner. (op 13-2 tchd 7-1)
Al Khimiya(IRE) had made much of the running when successful over 7f at Kempton on his previous start and attempted to employ similar tactics here. He put in a bold show, quickening off the home turn, but had nothing left when the winner went past approaching the furlong marker. (op 15-8)
Springwell Giant(IRE) had marred his first two outings with slow starts, but he broke much more professionally this time and showed improved form. In midfield for much of the journey, he battled on bravely, suggesting this distance is no problem for him. (op 12-1)
Underworld Dandy had taken advantage of a drop in his rating when landing a 1m Kempton nursery on his latest start, but that form did not look the strongest in the book and he was never in a position to make a serious bid to land this. (op 7-1)
Miss Taken(IRE) showed her best form so far in sprint maidens early in the season and, judged on her run here, she will benefit from a drop back in trip.

6432 WOLVERHAMPTON - THE BLACK COUNTRY'S ONLY RACECOURSE H'CAP 2m 119y(P)
6:45 (6:45) (Class 5) (0-70,70) 3-Y-O+ £3,238 (£963; £481; £240) Stalls Low

Form RPR

5213 **1** **John Forbes**[27] 5625 7-9-9 **70**................................ MartinLane(5) 4 76
(B Ellison) *chsd ldr 3f: a.p: rdn over 2f out: led over 1f out: styd on* **7/1**[2]

0005 **2** nk **King In Waiting (IRE)**[24] 5734 6-9-1 **57**............(vt) SilvestreDeSousa 13 63
(J Hetherton) *hld up towards rr: stdy prog over 3f out: rdn wl over 1f out: swtchd lft 1f out: rdn and ev ch whn edgd lft ins fnl f: styd on* **9/1**

5006 **3** 1 **Wester Lodge (IRE)**[23] 5740 7-8-9 **51** oh2........................ LukeMorris 3 55
(J M P Eustace) *hld up in mid-div: pushed along and hdwy 2f out: rdn wl over 1f out: ev ch ins fnl f: nt qckn cl home* **20/1**

2043 **4** ¾ **Mymateeric**[15] 5990 3-7-12 **51** oh1........................(b) AdrianMcCarthy 12 55
(J Pearce) *hld up towards rr: stdy hdwy on outside 5f out: ev ch wl over 1f out: sn rdn: nt qckn ins fnl f* **14/1**

2123 **5** nk **Deuce**[12] 6121 3-9-0 **67**.....................................(b) RobertWinston 9 70
(Eve Johnson Houghton) *hld up in mid-div: hdwy over 5f out: rdn to ld wl over 1f out: sn hdd: no ex ins fnl f* **10/1**

1240 **6** 2 **Black Or Red (IRE)**[27] 5625 4-9-8 **64**.......................(b) SebSanders 5 65+
(I A Wood) *hld up towards rr: nt clr run and swtchd rt over 2f out: hdwy on ins over 1f out: sn rdn: no further prog fnl f* **5/1**[1]

1145 **7** 3/4 **Baan (USA)**[25] [5696] 6-9-9 **65**.......................(p) JimmyQuinn 10 65
(H J Collingridge) *wnt prom after 3f: rdn over 1f out: wknd ins fnl f* **15/2**[3]

2443 **8** 1 1/4 **Sir Sandicliffe (IRE)**[12] [6097] 5-9-5 **61**.......................... TGMcLaughlin 8 59
(W M Brisbourne) *hld up in rr: pushed along 3f out: rdn wl over 1f out: n.d* **8/1**

5163 **9** 4 **Golden Future**[24] [5732] 6-8-9 **51**............................ JoeFanning 11 45
(P D Niven) *prom: chsd ldr after 3f: led over 3f out: pushed along and hdd wl over 1f out: rdn and wknd fnl f* **9/1**

440/ **10** 3/4 **Sa Nau**[677] [6131] 6-8-11 **53**................................ KirstyMilczarek 7 46
(T Keddy) *prom: lost pl wl over 3f out: bhd fnl 2f* **9/1**

0503 **11** 9 **The Quiet Genius**[24] [5733] 3-8-1 **54**........................ FrancisNorton 2 36
(Jedd O'Keeffe) *sn led: hdd over 3f out: wknd over 2f out* **10/1**

000 **12** 69 **Just Call Me Dave (USA)**[17] [5939] 3-7-12 **51** oh3.......... NickyMackay 1 —
(Paul Green) *led early: hld up in tch: rdn over 4f out: wknd wl over 3f out: eased whn no ch fnl 2f* **33/1**

/0-0 **13** 140 **City Well**[20] [5837] 6-9-7 **68**.......................(b[1]) ByronMoorcroft[(5)] 6 —
(Mrs L J Young) *hld up in tch: lost pl after 5f: bhd fnl 8f: t.o fnl 6f* **33/1**

3m 39.98s (-1.82) **Going Correction** -0.15s/f (Stan)
WFA 3 from 4yo+ 11lb **13** Ran SP% **117.5**
Speed ratings (Par 103): **98,97,97,97,96 95,95,95,93,92 88,56,—**
toteswingers: 1&2 £29.90, 1&3 £31.80, 2&3 £49.60. CSF £66.02 CT £1196.58 TOTE £8.00: £2.40, £3.60, £3.40; EX 115.00.
Owner R Wagner **Bred** Northmore Stud **Trained** Norton, N Yorks

■ Stewards' Enquiry : Adrian McCarthy two-day ban: used whip with excessive frequency down ther shoulder in the forehand (Oct 15-16)

FOCUS
A modest staying event, with the top weight rated 70 and three racing from out of the handicap, but it looked competitive on paper. The form is hard to rate positively considering the proximity of the third, fourth and fifth.

6433 BETDAQ.CO.UK H'CAP 5f 216y(P)
7:15 (7:16) (Class 6) (0-52,52) 3-Y-O+ **£2,388** (£705; £352) **Stalls** Low

Form RPR

2406 **1** **Briannsta (IRE)**[3] [6340] 7-8-12 **50**.......................(b) RichardThomas 10 57
(J E Long) *led early: w ldr: rdn wl over 1f out: led cl home: jst hld on* **10/1**

0636 **2** hd **Welcome Approach**[28] [5610] 6-9-0 **52**........................ JimmyQuinn 2 58
(J R Weymes) *hld up in mid-div: hdwy over 1f out: sn rdn: r.o wl towards fin: jst failed* **13/2**[3]

4000 **3** nk **Malapropism**[21] [5792] 9-8-10 **51**................................ MCGeran[(3)] 6 56
(M R Channon) *sn led: rdn over 1f out: hdd cl home* **14/1**

1506 **4** nk **All You Need (IRE)**[62] [4508] 5-8-7 **52**.....................(p) DavidKenny[(7)] 5 56
(R Hollinshead) *a.p: pushed along jst over 1f out: r.o one pce ins fnl f* **7/1**

02 **5** 1 **Battimoore (IRE)**[58] [4633] 3-8-9 **51**........................... AndreaAtzeni[(3)] 4 52
(Daniel Mark Loughnane, Ire) *a.p: rdn over 1f out: one pce fnl f* **5/1**[1]

0400 **6** hd **Minnola**[8] [6213] 4-9-0 **52**......................................(b) SaleemGolam 12 52
(Rae Guest) *hld up towards rr: pushed along wl over 1f out: r.o wl towards fin: nvr nrr* **16/1**

0060 **7** 1/2 **Commander Wish**[7] [6233] 6-9-0 **52**...............................(p) DNolan 7 51
(Lucinda Featherstone) *hld up in rr: pushed along wl over 1f out: kpt on ins fnl f: nvr trbld ldrs* **11/2**[2]

6-00 **8** hd **Our Wee Girl (IRE)**[12] [6119] 3-8-13 **52**........................ JamesDoyle 9 50
(Miss Tor Sturgis) *hld up in mid-div: n.m.r briefly over 3f out: rdn wl over 1f out: n.d* **33/1**

0100 **9** nk **Scruffy Skip (IRE)**[3] [6340] 4-9-0 **52**.....................(b) TGMcLaughlin 11 49
(Mrs C A Dunnett) *in rr: rdn 3f out: c wd st: edgd rt over 1f out: n.d* **10/1**

4066 **10** 1 3/4 **Davids Mark**[55] [4748] 9-8-13 **51**.............................. SimonWhitworth 3 42
(J R Jenkins) *s.i.s: hld up towards rr: rdn wl over 1f out: no rspnse* **8/1**

0020 **11** 1/2 **Head To Head (IRE)**[24] [5729] 5-8-12 **50**...............(bt) SilvestreDeSousa 8 40
(A D Brown) *t.k.h: prom: hung lft over 3f out: rdn and wkng whn hung lft wl over 1f out* **9/1**

1m 14.32s (-0.68) **Going Correction** -0.15s/f (Stan)
WFA 3 from 4yo+ 1lb **11** Ran SP% **112.7**
Speed ratings (Par 101): **98,97,97,96,95 95,94,94,94,91 91**
toteswingers: 1&2 £15.20, 1&3 £26.90, 2&3 £11.70. CSF £70.46 CT £924.48 TOTE £11.30: £3.40, £2.80, £4.40; EX 79.50.
Owner P Saxon **Bred** Anthony M Cahill **Trained** Caterham, Surrey

FOCUS
A poor race, with the top weight rated only 52, and few in the line-up had shown consistency. Despite that, the form looks straightforward, rated around the runner-up and fifth.

6434 GREAT OFFERS AT WOLVERHAMPTON-RACECOURSE.CO.UK H'CAP 5f 216y(P)
7:45 (7:46) (Class 4) (0-80,79) 3-Y-O+ **£5,046** (£1,510; £755; £377; £188) **Stalls** Low

Form RPR

3536 **1** **Green Park (IRE)**[63] [4469] 6-8-11 **71** ow1.......................(b) DNolan 13 82
(D Carroll) *hld up towards rr: hdwy wl over 1f out: r.o wl to ld towards fin* **40/1**

2124 **2** 1/2 **Lochan Mor**[76] [4044] 3-9-2 **77**.................................... JamieSpencer 8 86
(M L W Bell) *led over 1f: chsd ldr: rdn to ld ins fnl f: sn hdd: kpt on* **7/2**[1]

5-03 **3** 1 1/2 **Hazelrigg (IRE)**[10] [6159] 4-8-13 **73**.......................(p) GrahamGibbons 11 78
(T D Easterby) *hld up in rr: pushed along and swtchd rt jst over 1f out: rdn and r.o wl to take 3rd post* **10/1**

0315 **4** shd **Bonnie Prince Blue**[27] [5623] 6-9-2 **76**.....................(b) FrancisNorton 1 80
(D Nicholls) *racd keenly: led over 4f out: rdn jst over 1f out: hdd ins fnl f: no ex* **6/1**[3]

2223 **5** hd **Kingswinford (IRE)**[5] [6279] 3-8-10 **76**........................ MartinLane[(5)] 5 80
(P D Evans) *chsd ldrs: pushed along over 3f out: kpt on ins fnl f* **11/2**[2]

200 **6** 1/2 **Imprimis Tagula (IRE)**[2] [6359] 5-9-4 **78**.....................(v) NeilChalmers 3 80
(A Bailey) *a.p: rdn jst over 1f out: one pce* **14/1**

-405 **7** 1 3/4 **Sharp Bullet (IRE)**[22] [5777] 3-9-3 **78**............................ ShaneKelly 4 74
(W R Swinburn) *hld up in mid-div: pushed along wl over 1f out: nt clr run and swtchd rt ins fnl f: no hdwy* **16/1**

2052 **8** hd **Dvinsky (USA)**[7] [6230] 8-9-1 **75**.............................(b) PatCosgrave 9 71
(P Howling) *prom tl wknd ins fnl f* **12/1**

4036 **9** 1/2 **Artsu**[15] [5978] 4-8-13 **73**...................................... PJMcDonald 10 67
(M Dods) *hld up in rr: sme prog jst ins fnl f: n.d* **16/1**

3051 **10** 1/2 **Bahamian Lad**[12] [6120] 4-9-5 **79**............................... JerryO'Dwyer 12 72
(R Hollinshead) *hld up in rr: c wd st: nvr nr ldrs* **10/1**

1041 **11** 1 3/4 **Rio Cobolo (IRE)**[9] [6178] 3-9-1 **76** 6ex..................(v) SilvestreDeSousa 2 63
(Paul Green) *s.i.s: sn mid-div: rdn wl over 1f out: sn wknd* **6/1**[3]

2-05 **12** hd **Guertino (IRE)**[9] [6180] 4-9-4 **78**............................. J-PGuillambert 6 64
(C J Teague) *hld up in mid-div: rdn and c wd st: sn bhd* **25/1**

2020 **13** 3/4 **Mey Blossom**[49] [4929] 4-8-6 **69**........................ MichaelJStainton[(3)] 7 53
(R M Whitaker) *prom tl wknd over 2f out* **20/1**

1m 12.94s (-2.06) **Going Correction** -0.15s/f (Stan)
WFA 3 from 4yo+ 1lb **13** Ran SP% **121.5**
Speed ratings (Par 105): **107,106,104,104,103 103,100,100,100,99 97,96,95**
toteswingers: 1&2 £16.20, 1&3 £29.10, 2&3 £12.40. CSF £176.42 CT £1574.25 TOTE £24.40: £7.50, £2.20, £3.10; EX 91.20.
Owner G A Fixings Ltd **Bred** James Burns And A Moynan **Trained** Sledmere, E Yorks

FOCUS
A competitive sprint handicap bringing together a clutch of relatively lightly-raced three-year-olds and some established older performers. The time was decent and the form looks solid despite the surprise winner.
Guertino(IRE) Official explanation: trainer said gelding lost a shoe

6435 BET CAMBRIDGESHIRE H'CAP - BETDAQ HANDICAP 1m 1f 103y(P)
8:15 (8:15) (Class 4) (0-85,85) 3-Y-O+ **£5,046** (£1,510; £755; £377; £188) **Stalls** Low

Form RPR

6023 **1** **Farleigh House (USA)**[9] [6190] 5-9-0 **79**........................ SebSanders 5 89
(Sir Mark Prescott) *hld up in mid-div: hdwy whn nt clr run wl over 1f out: pushed along and qcknd to ld wl ins fnl f: r.o* **7/2**[2]

2131 **2** 3/4 **Ordoney (IRE)**[24] [5725] 4-9-3 **82**.................................... KFallon 1 90
(L M Cumani) *a.p: rdn to ld 1f out: edgd rt and hdd wl ins fnl f: nt qckn* **5/2**[1]

4263 **3** nk **Dear Maurice**[15] [6004] 5-8-10 **75**........................... JamieSpencer 13 83
(E A L Dunlop) *swtchd lft sn after s: hld up in rr: c v wd st: rdn and hdwy 1f out: edgd lft ins fnl f: r.o* **18/1**

1-04 **4** nk **Mannlichen**[115] [2767] 3-8-5 **74**.................................... JoeFanning 12 81+
(M Johnston) *hld up towards rr: c wd st: hung lft wl over 1f out: hdwy whn hung lft ins fnl f: kpt on* **9/1**[3]

0641 **5** 2 **Admiral Dundas (IRE)**[11] [6137] 4-8-13 **81** 6ex.............. AndreaAtzeni[(3)] 2 84
(W Jarvis) *a.p: rdn over 2f out: nt clr run and swtchd lft jst over 1f out: nt qckn ins fnl f* **12/1**

0502 **6** hd **Turn Me On (IRE)**[14] [6019] 6-9-3 **82**...................... GrahamGibbons 10 85
(T D Walford) *hld up towards rr: pushed along over 2f out: hdwy over 1f out: rdn and kpt on one pce ins fnl f* **20/1**

4022 **7** nk **Brouhaha**[13] [6059] 5-9-6 **85**............................. RichardKingscote 11 87
(Tom Dascombe) *hld up in tch: pushed along over 2f out: rdn wl over 1f out: wkng whn n.m.r ins fnl f* **12/1**

5015 **8** 2 **Daaweitza**[28] [5598] 6-8-10 **75**...............................(b) J-PGuillambert 6 73
(B Ellison) *w ldr: rdn and ev ch wl over 1f out: wknd wl ins fnl f* **25/1**

0-45 **9** 1/2 **Penchesco (IRE)**[22] [5780] 4-8-6 **71** oh1........................ PaulEddery 3 68
(Pat Eddery) *led: rdn and hdd 1f out: wknd wl ins fnl f* **20/1**

0200 **10** hd **Ilie Nastase (FR)**[54] [4781] 5-9-1 **85**......................... MartinLane[(5)] 9 81
(D M Simcock) *hld up in mid-div: pushed along over 2f out: btn whn nt clr run jst over 1f out* **10/1**

0042 **11** 2 **Stand Guard**[27] [5640] 5-9-5 **84**................................. JerryO'Dwyer 7 76
(P Howling) *prom: rdn over 2f out: wkng whn n.m.r wl ins fnl f* **10/1**

2460 **12** hd **Dream Of Fortune (IRE)**[31] [5509] 5-8-11 **81** ow1.......(t) JamieJones[(5)] 8 73
(M G Quinlan) *hld up towards rr: pushed along whn carried lft over 1f out: eased ins fnl f* **50/1**

06-5 **13** 4 **Cupid's Glory**[152] [1666] 7-9-3 **82**.......................... FergusSweeney 4 65
(G L Moore) *hld up in mid-div: wknd over 1f out* **40/1**

1m 59.01s (-2.69) **Going Correction** -0.15s/f (Stan)
WFA 3 from 4yo+ 4lb **13** Ran SP% **117.4**
Speed ratings (Par 105): **105,104,104,103,102 101,101,99,99,99 97,97,93**
toteswingers: 1&2 £2.00, 1&3 £18.20, 2&3 £13.90. CSF £11.42 CT £137.58 TOTE £4.90: £1.60, £1.60, £3.20; EX 12.10.
Owner Lordship Stud **Bred** Lordship Stud **Trained** Newmarket, Suffolk

FOCUS
An interesting contest and very competitive on paper. The form is rated at face value around the winner and third.

6436 EUROPEAN BREEDERS' FUND MAIDEN FILLIES' STKS 7f 32y(P)
8:45 (8:47) (Class 5) 2-Y-O **£3,561** (£1,059; £529; £264) **Stalls** High

Form RPR

22 **1** **Alice Alleyne (IRE)**[16] [5969] 2-9-0 0.............................. RyanMoore 12 77+
(Sir Michael Stoute) *broke wl: mde all: rdn and edgd rt ins fnl f: r.o wl* **2/1**[1]

23 **2** 1 1/4 **Pictures (IRE)**[13] [6069] 2-9-0 0....................................... KFallon 1 73
(L M Cumani) *chsd wnr: rdn over 1f out: kpt on same pce* **8/1**

022 **3** 1/2 **Whirly Dancer**[15] [5980] 2-9-0 70.................................... TPQueally 8 72
(H R A Cecil) *hld up towards rr: c wd st: hdwy wl over 1f out: sn rdn: kpt on ins fnl f* **5/1**[3]

2 **4** 1/2 **Arte Viva (USA)**[27] [5639] 2-9-0 0..................................... NCallan 9 70
(G A Butler) *a.p: rdn wl over 1f out: one pce fnl f* **9/4**[2]

06 **5** 3/4 **Angelena Ballerina (IRE)**[14] [6009] 2-9-0 77...............(p) DavidProbert 7 69
(A Bailey) *hld up in mid-div: rdn wl over 1f out: kpt on ins fnl f* **20/1**

6 1/2 **Athenian Garden (USA)** 2-9-0 0.................................. JimmyQuinn 2 67
(H R A Cecil) *s.i.s: hld up towards rr: pushed along and hdwy on ins whn n.m.r over 2f out: rdn jst over 1f out: no further prog* **20/1**

00 **7** 3 3/4 **Motrice**[10] [6163] 2-9-0 0.. SebSanders 3 63+
(Sir Mark Prescott) *s.i.s: hld up in rr: pushed along wl over 1f out: nvr nr ldrs* **50/1**

0 **8** 2 1/4 **Vanilla Loan (IRE)**[27] [5639] 2-9-0 0............................. JerryO'Dwyer 5 53
(M Botti) *hld up in tch: rdn over 1f out: wknd fnl f* **33/1**

60 **9** shd **Ellen Vannin (IRE)**[31] [5528] 2-9-0 0............................... ShaneKelly 6 54+
(Eve Johnson Houghton) *hld up: stdy prog over 5f out: hmpd jst over 2f out: n.d after* **80/1**

10 4 1/2 **Denton Ryal** 2-8-7 0.. MJMurphy[(7)] 11 41
(S W James) *s.i.s: a in rr* **100/1**

6 **11** 2 1/2 **China Lily (USA)**[15] [5980] 2-8-11 0.......................... AhmedAjtebi[(3)] 4 45+
(Saeed Bin Suroor) *prom tl pushed along and wknd 2f out* **12/1**

0PP **12** 10 **Scintillating (IRE)**[28] [5613] 2-9-0 0............................. PaulEddery 10 11
(R Hollinshead) *bhd fnl 3f* **66/1**

1m 28.6s (-1.00) **Going Correction** -0.15s/f (Stan) **12** Ran SP% **117.7**
Speed ratings (Par 92): **99,97,97,96,95 95,90,88,88,82 80,68**
toteswingers: 1&2 £2.10, 1&3 £4.10, 2&3 £3.60. CSF £17.55 TOTE £2.80: £1.10, £1.90, £2.00; EX 14.70.
Owner Plantation Stud **Bred** Plantation Stud **Trained** Newmarket, Suffolk

FOCUS
Several powerful stables were represented by well-bred two-year-olds in this interesting fillies' maiden. The form is rated around the placed horses.

NOTEBOOK
Alice Alleyne(IRE), runner-up on Polytrack on her first start, had, as is usual with her trainer's juveniles, improved on her second outing when pipped at Yarmouth 16 days before this. How much she needed to progress again is a moot point, as her main market rival was disappointing, but there is no doubt that she was given a fine ride. Smartly out of the stalls from her wide draw, she soon established a clear lead and was never headed. (op 5-2)
Pictures(IRE), whose third over 6f of this course 13 days previously looked solid-enough form, seemed likely to find the step up in trip in her favour. She certainly had no trouble with the distance, staying on well towards the finish, but she was comprehensively outpointed by the winner. (tchd 9-1)
Whirly Dancer had shown improved form on the latest of three previous starts, when third at Beverley, but another step forward seemed needed to take this stronger race. She almost certainly progressed again here, but, as even this effort may not indicate she is quite good enough to take an average maiden, her immediate future will probably be in nurseries. (op 9-1 tchd 9-2)
Arte Viva(USA), backed against a previous winner when second on her Kempton debut 27 days previously, looked sure to come on for that run. She was most disappointing though, never being able to get closer than fourth, and this moderate display represents a significant step backwards. (op 5-4)
Angelena Ballerina(IRE) lined up with some fair form and an official rating of 77, but she no longer looks progressive and had run poorly last time out. She will struggle to win a nursery from her current mark and consequently may be difficult to place profitably, unless her connections resort to claimers.
China Lily(USA), held up when showing a little promise behind Whirly Dancer on her Beverley debut, was given a much more positive ride here but still fell a long way short of turning the form around. (op 14-1)

6437 HOTEL & CONFERENCING AT WOLVERHAMPTON H'CAP 7f 32y(P)
9:15 (9:16) (Class 6) (0-65,65) 3-Y-O+ £2,388 (£705; £352) Stalls High

Form				RPR
6102	1		**Peper Harow (IRE)**[13] 6070 3-9-4 **65** DavidProbert 2 *(M D I Usher) hld up and bhd: hdwy wl over 1f out: rdn to ld ins fnl f: drvn out* **8/1**	74
5523	2	½	**Stanley Goodspeed**[21] 5813 6-9-6 **65** (tp) JamieSpencer 3 *(J W Hills) hld up in mid-div: hdwy wl over 1f out: rdn and r.o to take 2nd nr fin* **11/2**[2]	74
0000	3	hd	**A Big Sky Brewing (USA)**[28] 5612 5-9-2 **64** (b) NeilBrown(3) 12 *(T D Barron) sn w ldr: rdn over 1f out: ev ch ins fnl f: kpt on* **8/1**	72
6006	4	½	**Just Timmy Marcus**[13] 6070 3-9-2 **63** CatherineGannon 1 *(B P J Baugh) hld up wl in rr: hdwy on ins wl over 1f out: rdn and kpt on ins fnl f* **14/1**	69
5060	5	2 ½	**Valfurva (IRE)**[7] 6224 3-9-4 **65** KFallon 4 *(L M Cumani) led early: hld up in tch: rdn and one pce fnl f* **6/1**[3]	64
0003	6	½	**Diego Rivera**[12] 6123 4-9-3 **62** FergusSweeney 9 *(P J Makin) hld up in mid-div: hdwy wl over 1f out: sn rdn: one pce fnl f* **16/1**	61
0502	7	hd	**Sea Land (FR)**[12] 6123 5-9-3 **62** J-PGuillambert 10 *(B Ellison) sn wl in rr: pushed along over 2f out: hdwy 1f out: nt rch ldrs* **16/1**	60
6000	8	shd	**Fine Ruler (IRE)**[7] 6224 5-9-2 **61** VinceSlattery 5 *(M R Bosley) hld up in mid-div: pushed along over 2f out: c wd st: rdn and btn over 1f out* **50/1**	59
5062	9	hd	**Tri Chara (IRE)**[26] 5678 5-8-9 **61** (p) DavidKenny(7) 7 *(R Hollinshead) sn led: rdn over 1f out: hdd ins fnl f: sn wknd* **14/1**	59
435	10	1 ¾	**Chief Red Cloud (USA)**[13] 6070 3-8-13 **65** MartinLane(5) 11 *(A P Jarvis) prom: rdn over 2f out: wknd ins fnl f* **11/4**[1]	57
0610	11	1 ¼	**Bermondsey Girl**[13] 6070 3-9-4 **65** SebSanders 8 *(C F Wall) hld up towards rr: pushed along over 2f out: c v wd st: hung lft fr over 1f out: n.d* **7/1**	54
5100	12	2 ½	**Rabbit Fighter (IRE)**[12] 6123 5-9-3 **62** GrahamGibbons 6 *(D Shaw) sn prom: wkng whn n.m.r over 1f out* **33/1**	45

1m 27.73s (-1.87) **Going Correction** -0.15s/f (Stan)
WFA 3 from 4yo+ 2lb 12 Ran SP% 121.1
Speed ratings (Par 101): **104,103,103,102,99 99,98,98,98,96 95,92**
toteswingers: 1&2 £5.20, 1&3 £16.70, 2&3 £9.40. CSF £52.75 CT £376.88 TOTE £10.90: £3.00, £1.90, £2.90; EX 53.50 Place 6 £120.23, Place 5 £72.58..
Owner Mr & Mrs Richard Hames & Friends 1 **Bred** R And Mrs Hames **Trained** Upper Lambourn, Berks

FOCUS
Not a great race, with the top-weight rated 65, but there were plenty of interlocking formlines to evaluate, and there was plenty of pace. The time was decent for the grade and the form looks sound.
T/Plt: £184.60 to a £1 stake. Pool: £71,802.02. 283.85 winning tickets. T/Qpdt: £121.10 to a £1 stake. Pool: £7,757.13. 47.40 winning tickets. KH

5963 LINGFIELD (L-H)
Friday, October 2

OFFICIAL GOING: Standard to slow
Wind: Moderate, across towards stands Weather: Fine

6439 C BREWER & SONS H'CAP (DIV I) 1m 2f (P)
1:35 (1:35) (Class 6) (0-65,66) 3-Y-O £1,706 (£503; £252) Stalls Low

Form				RPR
3240	1		**Transformer (IRE)**[16] 5988 3-8-11 **58** (p) SebSanders 3 *(W J Knight) sn trckd ldr: led over 3f out: drvn over 2f out: edgd rt fnl f: kpt on* **5/2**[1]	62
0361	2	1 ½	**Waahej**[7] 6257 3-9-5 **66** 6ex ChrisCatlin 2 *(P W Hiatt) trckd ldng pair: wnt 2nd over 2f out: nt qckn u.p over 1f out: no imp on wnr after* **3/1**[2]	67
4150	3	hd	**Hold The Bucks (USA)**[30] 5574 3-9-4 **65** (p) LukeMorris 7 *(J S Moore) reminders in last trio over 6f out: nt gng wl after: prog u.p 2f out: styd on to press for 2nd ins fnl f* **12/1**	66
0001	4	½	**Night Knight (IRE)**[16] 6001 3-9-3 **64** (v) HayleyTurner 8 *(M L W Bell) trckd ldng trio: u.p over 3f out: lost pl over 2f out: rallied over 1f out: disp 2nd fnl f: one pce* **6/1**[3]	64
6340	5	¾	**Join Up**[33] 5470 3-8-4 **51** oh3 LiamJones 1 *(W M Brisbourne) hld up in 5th: nt qckn over 2f out and outpcd: tried to rally over 1f out: kpt on same pce* **11/1**	49
0400	6	½	**Order Order**[56] 4749 3-8-10 **57** MickyFenton 4 *(H J L Dunlop) hld up in 6th: prog on outer to dispute 2nd over 2f out: hanging and fnd nil over 1f out* **20/1**	54
660	7	4	**Queen Of Thebes (IRE)**[22] 5813 3-9-1 **62** (t) GeorgeBaker 5 *(G L Moore) stdd s: hld up last: gng wl 3f out: prog 2f out: fnd nil whn shkn up over 1f out* **12/1**	51
405	8	2 ¾	**Lady's Art (FR)**[42] 5215 3-8-13 **60** RichardKingscote 6 *(E F Vaughan) stdd s: hld up in last trio: effrt on inner whn n.m.r over 2f out: sn wknd* **8/1**	44
	9	14	**Four Mirrors (CAN)**[63] 4512 3-8-10 **57** (tp) LPKeniry 10 *(David P Myerscough, Ire) led to over 3f out: wknd rapidly over 2f out: t.o* **14/1**	13

2m 7.17s (0.57) **Going Correction** +0.125s/f (Slow) 9 Ran SP% 114.1
Speed ratings (Par 99): **102,100,100,100,99 99,96,93,82**
toteswingers: 1&2 £2.50, 1&3 £3.90, 2&3 £5.10 CSF £9.83 CT £72.37 TOTE £3.40: £1.20, £1.40, £2.70; EX 15.10 Trifecta £141.80 Part won. Pool: £191.69 - 0.10 winning units..
Owner Miss S Bowles **Bred** Bryan Ryan **Trained** Patching, W Sussex

FOCUS
This was the first meeting on the Polytrack circuit here since recent work to try and rejuvenate the surface. The official description was standard to slow and a winning time 3.37 seconds outside standard suggests that was about right. A poor handicap, though at least it was run at a good pace thanks to Four Mirrors, but not a race to rate positively.
Join Up Official explanation: jockey said gelding lost its action final bend

6440 C BREWER & SONS H'CAP (DIV II) 1m 2f (P)
2:05 (2:05) (Class 6) (0-65,65) 3-Y-O £1,706 (£503; £252) Stalls Low

Form				RPR
6653	1		**Quinsman**[7] 6248 3-9-3 **64** LPKeniry 7 *(J S Moore) trckd ldrs: rdn and prog on outer wl over 2f out: drvn ahd over 1f out: kpt on u.p* **3/1**[2]	67
0550	2	¾	**Chanrossa (IRE)**[16] 5988 3-8-11 **58** TGMcLaughlin 5 *(E A L Dunlop) no room and snatched up after 100yds: in last trio tl rdn and prog on outer over 2f out: styd on to take 2nd last 150yds: a hld* **12/1**	59
50	3	½	**Persian Tomcat (IRE)**[10] 6183 3-8-4 **51** oh5 CatherineGannon 1 *(Miss J Feilden) s.i.s and rousted along early: mostly last to 1/2-way: rdn and prog on inner over 2f out: pressed ldrs fnl f: kpt on* **16/1**	51
0000	4	1	**Rockabout (IRE)**[22] 5790 3-8-5 **52** (b[1]) HayleyTurner 9 *(B J Meehan) t.k.h early: trckd ldr: hrd rdn and upsides over 1f out: fnd nil: fdd last 100yds* **14/1**	50
4510	5	¾	**Primo Dilettante**[20] 5873 3-9-4 **65** ShaneKelly 8 *(W J Knight) led: rdn over 2f out: hdd over 1f out: fdd ins fnl f* **11/2**[3]	62
6-62	6	1 ½	**Rosco Flyer (IRE)**[8] 6224 3-9-4 **65** PatCosgrave 4 *(J R Boyle) trckd ldrs: rdn over 3f out: outpcd and struggling over 2f out: no ch after: styd on ins fnl f* **2/1**[1]	59
1000	7	7	**Montmartre (USA)**[19] 5905 3-8-9 **56** FergusSweeney 6 *(David Pinder) trckd ldng pair tl wknd 2f out* **10/1**	36
0456	8	¾	**Final Drive (IRE)**[30] 5582 3-8-11 **58** MickyFenton 2 *(E J Creighton) in tch in rr: rdn over 3f out: wknd 2f out* **14/1**	36
4060	9	15	**Solo Choice**[109] 2982 3-9-0 **61** TonyCulhane 3 *(I W McInnes) dropped to rr bef 1/2-way: t.o fnl 3f* **14/1**	9

2m 8.37s (1.77) **Going Correction** +0.125s/f (Slow) 9 Ran SP% 116.4
Speed ratings (Par 99): **97,96,96,95,94 93,87,87,75**
toteswingers: 1&2 £12.40, 1&3 £12.30, 2&3 £31.80 CSF £39.04 CT £498.17 TOTE £4.10: £1.70, £4.60, £4.00; EX 52.60.
Owner Donald M Kerr **Bred** Mr & Mrs G Middlebrook **Trained** Upper Lambourn, Berks

FOCUS
Another moderate handicap and, with the pace much less solid than the first division, the winning time was 1.2 seconds slower and another race to treat negatively, with the winner not needing to improve on recent selling-race form.

6441 DOUGLAS REGAN MAIDEN AUCTION FILLIES' STKS 1m (P)
2:40 (2:40) (Class 6) 2-Y-O £2,729 (£806; £403) Stalls High

Form				RPR
0	1		**Ravens Rose**[101] 3248 2-8-4 0 SaleemGolam 5 *(J G Portman) narrow ld tl wd bnd 2f out and hdd: rallied u.p fnl f: led post* **25/1**	62
2050	2	nse	**Folletta (IRE)**[9] 6211 2-8-6 67 PatDobbs 3 *(R Hannon) w ldr: led on inner 2f out: hrd rdn and kpt on fnl f: hdd post* **7/2**[2]	64
06	3	¾	**Charpoy Cobra**[16] 5984 2-8-4 0 KirstyMilczarek 8 *(J A R Toller) dwlt: sn prom on outer: effrt to chse ldng pair over 2f out: nt qckn u.p over 1f out: kpt on nr fin: a hld* **7/4**[1]	60
	4	nk	**Madame Roulin (IRE)** 2-8-12 0 HayleyTurner 11 *(M L W Bell) trckd ldrs: effrt over 2f out: tried to cl over 1f out: kpt on one pce fnl f* **11/2**[3]	68
	5	1 ¾	**Ermyntrude** 2-8-4 0 CatherineGannon 2 *(P M Phelan) hld up towards rr: effrt over 2f out: rdn and kpt on same pce fr over 1f out* **11/1**	56
	6	nk	**Lady Cavendish (IRE)** 2-8-10 0 JamieMackay 6 *(A Bailey) hld up in rr: effrt over 2f out on outer: shkn up over 1f out: styd on ins fnl f: nrst fin* **25/1**	61+
600	7	½	**Meer Und Wind (GER)**[32] 5527 2-8-12 54 (b[1]) SebSanders 1 *(P R Webber) s.s: hld up in last pair: pushed along in 8th over 2f out on inner: drvn and plugged on one pce over 1f out* **33/1**	62?
00	8	2 ¾	**Silvermine Bay (IRE)**[15] 6009 2-8-4 0 LiamJones 4 *(A P Jarvis) chsd ldng pair tl wknd over 2f out* **16/1**	48
	9	1 ¼	**Sharp And Chic** 2-8-6 0 JimmyQuinn 7 *(M L W Bell) dwlt: hld up in last pair: pushed along over 2f out: nvr on terms* **8/1**	47
6	10	19	**Fraamtaaztiic**[34] 5445 2-8-4 0 ow1 WilliamCarson(3) 9 *(R J Hodges) in tch: rdn 1/2-way: wknd sn after: t.o* **20/1**	6

1m 43.04s (4.84) **Going Correction** +0.125s/f (Slow) 10 Ran SP% 114.7
Speed ratings (Par 90): **80,79,79,78,77 76,76,73,72,53**
toteswingers: 1&2 £17.10, 1&3 £3.50, 2&3 £15.50 CSF £105.33 TOTE £42.40: £8.60, £1.20, £1.20; EX 281.40 Trifecta £392.30 Part won. Pool: £530.18 - 0.20 winning units..
Owner Hydraulic Component Services Ltd **Bred** Hydraulic Component Services Ltd **Trained** Compton, Berks

FOCUS
Probably only a modest maiden as the front pair dominated throughout and there wasn't much covering the first four at the line.

NOTEBOOK
Ravens Rose had been absent for three months since finishing a well-beaten last of 13 over 6f on her Newbury debut, but the layoff and this longer trip brought about plenty of improvement. Soon in front, she looked to have blown it when hanging off the final bend, handing the advantage to the runner-up, but to her great credit she battled back to snatch the race on the line. The form may not amount to much, but she is entitled to improver further. (op 20-1 tchd 33-1 in a place)
Folletta(IRE), by far the most exposed in the field, set the standard here with an official mark of 67. She was always close to the winner against the inside rail and looked to have been presented with a golden opportunity when her rival went wide off the bend, but though she kept on running she had the race snatched from her. She is the benchmark to the form, but this looks to be about as good as she is. (op 3-1)

Charpoy Cobra, who met trouble in running before finishing a staying-on sixth at Kempton last time, was always thereabouts on the wide outside and may not have been helped by the winner carrying her even wider rounding the home bend, so she did well to finish where she did. She needed this for a mark. (tchd 6-4, 15-8 in a place)

Madame Roulin(IRE), a 17,000gns yearling out of a half-sister to the useful juvenile sprinter Sir Xaar, was always prominent and stayed on well up the inside in the straight to fare best of the newcomers. (tchd 13-2)

Ermyntrude, out of a winning sister to the smart Catwalk, plugged on late having come off the bridle a fair way out and is entitled to improve from this debut. (op 16-1 tchd 20-1)

Lady Cavendish(IRE), related to three winners at up to 1m4f on the dam's side, looked green but made some late progress and should improve with experience as she goes up in trip. (tchd 20-1)

6442 BUXTON BUILDIT (S) STKS 7f (P)

3:15 (3:18) (Class 6) 3-Y-O **£2,047** (£604; £302) **Stalls** Low

Form RPR

1 **Rudolph Schmidt (IRE)**[6] 6296 3-8-7 75.................(bt[1]) HayleyTurner 13 79+
(David P Myerscough, Ire) *hld up in midfield on outer: pushed along and prog over 2f out: led over 1f out: cantered clr: outclassed rivals* **5/2[1]**

0402 2 *7* **King's Sabre**[11] 6170 3-8-12 65.......................... SebSanders 8 62
(W R Muir) *disp ld tl def advantage over 3f out: kicked at least 2 l clr over 2f out: hdd and totally outpcd over 1f out* **7/2[2]**

550 3 *1 3/4* **Capo Regime**[7] 6243 3-9-4 79.......................... IanMongan 14 63
(P Howling) *dropped in fr wd draw and hld up last: prog and cajoled along on outer 3f out: looked reluctant u.p but kpt on to take 3rd ins fnl f* **17/2[3]**

600 4 *3/4* **Cool Art (IRE)**[30] 5584 3-8-12 60.......................... JamieMackay 2 55
(Peter Grayson) *hld up wl in rr: gng strly but only 9th and plenty to do over 2f out: prog and shkn up 1f out: wnt 4th nr fin: nvr nr ldrs* **25/1**

4235 5 *1 1/2* **Vamos (IRE)**[30] 5581 3-8-12 58.......................... SteveDrowne 1 51
(J R Gask) *pushed along towards rr over 4f out: struggling after: 10th over 2f out: styd on fr over 1f out: no ch* **7/2[2]**

4000 6 *hd* **Dicey Affair**[16] 6005 3-8-7 52.......................(t) FergusSweeney 12 46
(G L Moore) *hld up in midfield: effrt over 2f out: one pce and nvr threatened ldrs* **20/1**

0045 7 *3/4* **Deckchair**[11] 6170 3-8-13 49.......................(v) KirstyMilczarek 10 50
(S Curran) *trckd ldrs: rdn to go 2nd wl over 2f out: no imp over 1f out: wknd* **16/1**

0000 8 *2 3/4* **Love Allowed**[28] 5647 3-8-7 50.......................... PaulDoe 11 36
(Jamie Poulton) *prom: rdn to go 3rd over 2f out: wknd over 1f out* **16/1**

0045 9 *2* **Ridgeway Silver**[28] 5644 3-8-0 49.......................... RachelKing(7) 5 31
(M D I Usher) *prom: chsd ldrs on inner over 2f out: wknd over 1f out* **16/1**

000- 10 *nk* **Die Haard**[280] 7783 3-8-7 59 ow2.......................... LukeKilgarriff(7) 9 37
(J R Gask) *last fr 1/2-way: sn wl t.o* **25/1**

6000 11 *18* **Thurston (IRE)**[14] 6070 3-8-12 55.......................(bt) SamHitchcott 7 —
(D J S Ffrench Davis) *disp ld to over 3f out: steadily wknd* **50/1**

2000 12 *15* **Sky High Kid (IRE)**[22] 5809 3-8-12 55.......................... TonyCulhane 4 —
(M R Channon) *disp ld to over 4f out: wknd u.p: t.o* **25/1**

1m 25.84s (1.04) **Going Correction** +0.125s/f (Slow) 12 Ran SP% **119.5**
Speed ratings (Par 99): **99,91,89,88,86 86,85,82,79,79 59,41**
.The winner was bought by D Ffrench Davis for 8,600gns. Cool Art was claimed by J. S. Wainwright for £6000. King's Sabre was claimed by R. C. Guest for £6000.\n\x\x
Owner Fergus Jones **Bred** Dr Dean Harron **Trained** Newbridge, Co Kildare
■ Stewards' Enquiry : Ian Mongan caution: used whip without giving gelding time to respond

FOCUS
Definitely a case of 'no contest' in this moderate seller, with the winner in a different class and not needing to run to her best Irish form to score.

6443 CHILANO MEDIAN AUCTION MAIDEN STKS 5f (P)

3:50 (3:50) (Class 6) 2-Y-O **£2,729** (£806; £403) **Stalls** High

Form RPR

1 **Bellini Rose (IRE)** 2-8-12 0.......................... RichardKingscote 7 65
(Tom Dascombe) *chsd ldrs on wd outside: rdn 2f out: sustained effrt fnl f to ld nr fin* **14/1**

3264 2 *nk* **Bush Master**[7] 6247 2-9-3 67.......................... PatDobbs 4 70+
(R Hannon) *trckd ldrs: cl up whn nt clr run 1f out: swtchd rt and fin best of all to snatch 2nd on post* **8/1[3]**

202 3 *nse* **Noble Greek (USA)**[42] 5234 2-9-3 86.......................... RobertWinston 2 69
(J R Best) *pressed ldr: hanging but led over 1f out: drvn and kpt on fnl f: hdd nr fin: lost 2nd post* **4/7[1]**

2522 4 *1/2* **Key Art (IRE)**[15] 6018 2-9-3 72.......................... SebSanders 10 67
(J Noseda) *narrow ld to over 1f out: kpt on but lost pls ins fnl f* **4/1[2]**

03 5 *1 1/4* **Pirate's Song**[15] 6032 2-9-3 0.......................... RobertHavlin 3 63
(J A R Toller) *dwlt: hld up in tch: effrt on inner 2f out: rdn and cl enough ent fnl f: nt qckn* **8/1[3]**

06 6 *13* **Ajara Boy**[8] 6231 2-9-3 0.......................... RichardSmith 5 16
(Tom Dascombe) *in tch: sn wl bhd: t.o* **50/1**

7 *13* **Stoneacre Joe (IRE)** 2-9-3 0.......................... JamieMackay 8 —
(Peter Grayson) *bhd after 2f: hanging bdly bnd 2f out: wl t.o* **66/1**

4323 P **Art Summer**[22] 5800 2-8-12 69.......................... LiamJones 1 —
(D M Simcock) *sn last: p.u after 2f: lame* **12/1**

60.14 secs (1.34) **Going Correction** +0.125s/f (Slow) 8 Ran SP% **123.7**
Speed ratings (Par 93): **94,93,93,92,90 69,49,—**
toteswingers: 1&2 £8.10, 1&3 £5.30, 2&3 £2.60 CSF £128.26 TOTE £23.70: £4.80, £2.40, £1.02; EX 118.50 Trifecta £260.00 Pool: £643.17 - 1.83 winning units..
Owner Five Horses Ltd **Bred** Five Horses Ltd **Trained** Lambourn, Berks

FOCUS
An ordinary sprint maiden and there was barely a length covering the front four at the line. It was also something of a rough race, but after a lengthy stewards' enquiry the result was allowed to stand.

NOTEBOOK
Bellini Rose(IRE) was soon ridden into a handy position on the outside and did very well to keep battling away for a narrow success, as she looked a little green during the contest and was up against some streetwise rivals. A half-sister to a bumper winner out of a high-class performer at up to 1m4f, she may have won this despite the trip and might be capable of even more over further. (tchd 16-1)

Bush Master was undoubtedly unlucky, however. He travelled well behind the leaders and looked a big threat when aiming between the winner and Key Art entering the last furlong, but the gap closed and he was forced to snatch up and switch wide. He ran on strongly when in the clear, but the damage had been done and he just failed. He has now been placed a few times on turf and on Polytrack over trips ranging from 5f to 7f and this was a decent effort considering he had a bit to find with the others holding official marks, but he lacks scope and this was surely one that got away. (op 9-1 tchd 10-1)

Noble Greek(USA), runner-up in two hot maidens at Kempton and York, was out of his depth in the July Stakes in between those efforts and this looked a much easier task despite dropping to the minimum trip for the first time. Always close to the pace, he fought his way to the front a furlong out and seemed likely to score, but lost two places in the last 25 yards. He has the ability to win a race, but on this evidence ran below his official mark of 86. (op 4-6 tchd 8-11, 4-5 in places)

Key Art(IRE), runner-up in three turf maidens over this trip, made much of the running and kept staying on, but was run out of it inside the last furlong. He seemed to handle the surface alright, but is now looking exposed. (op 5-1)

Pirate's Song, down to the minimum trip for this sand debut after not appearing to see out 6f in a couple of starts on turf, came from off the pace to hold every chance on the inside passing the furlong pole, but then couldn't quicken further. He now qualifies for a nursery mark. (tchd 9-1)

Art Summer Official explanation: vet said filly pulled up lame

6444 NATIONAL CENTRE FOR YOUNG PEOPLE WITH EPILEPSY H'CAP 6f (P)

4:25 (4:25) (Class 5) (0-75,74) 3-Y-O+ **£3,412** (£1,007; £504) **Stalls** Low

Form RPR

6041 1 **Billy Red**[15] 6028 5-8-13 **68**.......................(b) FergusSweeney 5 80
(J R Jenkins) *mde all: rdn and maintained gallop fnl 2f: unchal* **9/2[3]**

01 2 *2 3/4* **Poppanan (USA)**[25] 5717 3-9-2 **72**.......................... TonyCulhane 7 75
(S Dow) *trckd ldng pair: rdn 2f out: wnt 2nd over 1f out: one pce and no imp on wnr fnl f* **5/2[1]**

5002 3 *nk* **Hellbender (IRE)**[13] 6120 3-9-4 **74**.......................... GeorgeBaker 1 76
(S Kirk) *w.w: effrt on inner 2f out: kpt on u.p fr over 1f out but no real imp on wnr* **7/2[2]**

6120 4 *1/2* **Speak The Truth (IRE)**[44] 5164 3-8-6 **67**.............(p) MatthewDavies(5) 6 68+
(J R Boyle) *s.i.s: hld up in last trio: effrt and v wd bnd 2f out: r.o fnl f to snatch 4th last stride* **8/1**

0203 5 *shd* **Izzi Mill (USA)**[22] 5789 3-9-0 **70**.......................... HayleyTurner 10 70
(D R C Elsworth) *t.k.h: chsd wnr: hung rt bnd 2f out: sn lost 2nd and btn* **7/1**

1004 6 *2 1/4* **Carmenero (GER)**[16] 5991 6-8-12 **67**.......................... SimonWhitworth 2 60
(C R Dore) *hld up in last trio: nudged along over 1f out: nvr remotely nr ldrs* **12/1**

0065 7 *nse* **Musical Script (USA)**[9] 6212 6-9-1 **70**.......................(b) SebSanders 12 63
(Mouse Hamilton-Fairley) *hld up on outer: prog bef 1/2-way: disp 2nd and wd bnd 2f out: sn nt qckn and btn* **8/1**

P550 8 *22* **The Magic Of Rio**[23] 5777 3-8-13 **69**.......................... JamieMackay 8 —
(Peter Grayson) *chsd ldrs tl wknd rapidly over 2f out: t.o* **40/1**

1m 12.25s (0.35) **Going Correction** +0.125s/f (Slow)
WFA 3 from 4yo+ 1lb 8 Ran SP% **113.8**
Speed ratings (Par 103): **102,98,97,97,97 94,94,64**
toteswingers: 1&2 £3.00, 1&3 £4.30, 2&3 £3.20 CSF £16.02 CT £43.31 TOTE £5.30: £1.60, £1.40, £1.40; EX 15.40 Trifecta £28.80 Pool: £495.52 - 12.69 winning units..
Owner Mrs Irene Hampson **Bred** D R Tucker **Trained** Royston, Herts

FOCUS
An ordinary sprint handicap in which the first three raced on the inside rail up until the entrance to the straight. The form looks reasonable with the winner rated to his best form and the placed horses not far off recent marks.

Izzi Mill(USA) Official explanation: jockey said filly hung right

6445 NCYPE H'CAP (DIV I) 1m 4f (P)

5:00 (5:00) (Class 6) (0-60,63) 3-Y-O **£1,706** (£503; £252) **Stalls** Low

Form RPR

1112 1 **Arty Crafty (USA)**[2] 6376 3-9-8 **63** 6ex.......................... SebSanders 14 82+
(Sir Mark Prescott) *led after 1 1/2f: mde rest: pushed clr over 3f out: briefly threatened 1f out: drvn and styd on wl* **1/1[1]**

066 2 *3 3/4* **D'Artagnans Dream**[14] 6073 3-9-1 **56**.......................(b) HayleyTurner 11 63
(G D Blake) *s.s: hld up in last pair: sme prog gng wl but plenty to do 3f out: gd hdwy to chse wnr over 1f out and briefly looked like clsng: sn no imp* **14/1**

-606 3 *4* **Champagne Fizz (IRE)**[51] 4904 3-9-4 **59**.......................... FergusSweeney 5 60
(Miss Jo Crowley) *trckd ldng quartet: prog over 3f out to chse wnr wl over 2f out: nt qckn wl over 1f out: sn lost 2nd: one pce* **16/1**

4202 4 *hd* **Honorable Endeavor**[16] 5990 3-9-4 **59**.......................(p) GeorgeBaker 8 59
(E F Vaughan) *hld up in 8th: rdn and prog fr 3f out: wnt 4th over 1f out: kpt on same pce on inner* **11/4[2]**

0004 5 *2 1/4* **Pursuit Of Purpose**[89] 3661 3-7-12 **46**.......................... HarryBentley(7) 9 43
(G L Moore) *settled in 6th: rdn and prog 3f out: chsd ldng pair over 2f out: fdd fnl f* **33/1**

000 6 *8* **Dayanara (USA)**[25] 5718 3-9-2 **57**.......................... IanMongan 13 41
(C G Cox) *hld up in 7th: rdn and effrt 3f out: chsd ldrs over 2f out: sn btn: wknd over 1f out* **28/1**

7 *1 1/2* **Slicker (IRE)**[93] 3519 3-9-3 **58**.......................(p) RichardKingscote 4 39
(David P Myerscough, Ire) *dwlt: hld up in last: u.p and struggling 1/2-way: passed toiling rivals fnl 3f* **12/1[3]**

0003 8 *9* **Flirty (IRE)**[13] 6098 3-8-5 **46**.......................... AdrianMcCarthy 6 13
(Rae Guest) *led for over 1f: chsd wnr to wl over 2f out: wknd rapidly: t.o* **16/1**

506 9 *11* **Cecily Parsley**[47] 5061 3-9-2 **57**.......................... SteveDrowne 1 6
(H Morrison) *prom: pushed along in 3rd 7f out: wknd 3f out: t.o* **20/1**

000 10 *3* **Sula Dream**[18] 5939 3-8-7 **48**.......................... LiamJones 3 —
(J Pearce) *chsd ldng trio: rdn 5f out: wknd over 3f out: t.o* **33/1**

0500 11 *3 1/2* **Sparkling Suzie**[28] 5644 3-8-8 **49**.......................... GregFairley 7 —
(J S Moore) *a last trio: rdn over 5f out: sn wknd: t.o* **50/1**

2m 34.34s (1.34) **Going Correction** +0.125s/f (Slow) 11 Ran SP% **118.8**
Speed ratings (Par 99): **100,97,94,94,93 87,86,80,73,71 69**
toteswingers: 1&2 £4.40, 1&3 £6.90, 2&3 £13.10 CSF £16.84 CT £154.50 TOTE £1.90: £1.30, £2.50, £3.90; EX 17.10 Trifecta £145.00 Pool: £580.10 - 2.96 winning units..
Owner Mrs Sonia Rogers **Bred** Airlie Stud **Trained** Newmarket, Suffolk

FOCUS
They bet 12-1 bar two here, which shows how uncompetitive this moderate handicap was. Ten of the 11 runners were maidens coming into it and they remain so. The winner looks better than the bare form and the race could be rated higher.

Slicker(IRE) Official explanation: jockey said gelding missed the break

6446 NCYPE H'CAP (DIV II) 1m 4f (P)

5:35 (5:35) (Class 6) (0-60,60) 3-Y-O **£1,706** (£503; £252) **Stalls** Low

Form RPR

3304 1 **Tinkerbelle (IRE)**[21] 5838 3-8-11 **53**.......................(p) JimmyQuinn 13 64
(J L Dunlop) *hld up in midfield: smooth prog 4f out: led wl over 2f out: drvn and drew rt away fr over 1f out* **10/1**

3506 2 *7* **M'Lady Rousseur (IRE)**[23] 5782 3-9-4 **60**.......................... RobertHavlin 10 60
(D R C Elsworth) *hld up in last trio: stdy prog over 3f out: rdn 2f out: styd on to take 2nd ins fnl f w wnr already wl clr* **8/1**

3043 **3** *1 ¼* **Valkyrie (IRE)**[38] 5328 3-8-8 **50** SteveDrowne 12 48
(N P Littmoden) *settled midfield: prog on outer over 3f out: wd bnd u.p 2f out: kpt on fnl f to take 3rd nr fin* **20/1**

-051 **4** *¾* **Largem**[21] 5838 3-9-3 **59** SimonWhitworth 1 56
(J R Jenkins) *hld up in last trio: stl there 3f out: prog on inner after: rdn to go 2nd over 1f out: no ch w wnr: wknd ins fnl f* **9/2**[1]

3336 **5** *nk* **Good Buy Dubai (USA)**[93] 3511 3-9-2 **58** RobertWinston 11 54
(J R Best) *hld up in last trio: prog on outer over 3f out: rdn and v wd bnd 2f out: hanging and btn after: kpt on* **5/1**[2]

4001 **6** *¾* **Arlene Phillips**[20] 5873 3-8-6 **48** PatDobbs 6 43
(R Hannon) *hld up towards rr: dropped to last pair wl over 2f out: shkn up and prog 2f out: kpt on but no ch* **12/1**

0003 **7** *3 ¼* **Saute**[21] 5838 3-9-0 **56** ShaneKelly 2 46
(W R Swinburn) *dwlt: midfield: lost pl and pushed along 5f out: wl in rr over 2f out: plugged on fr over 1f out* **16/1**

-355 **8** *2 ¼* **Peintre D'Argent (IRE)**[94] 3482 3-9-1 **57** RichardKingscote 5 43
(Tom Dascombe) *chsd ldr after 4f: chal 3f out: chsd wnr over 2f out to over 1f out: wknd* **11/2**[3]

5125 **9** *1 ½* **Primera Rossa**[30] 5579 3-8-7 **49** GregFairley 8 33
(J S Moore) *chsd clr ldrs: rdn over 4f out: sn lost pl: struggling over 2f out* **14/1**

1545 **10** *5* **The Saucy Snipe**[16] 5990 3-8-11 **53** ow1 SebSanders 9 29
(P Winkworth) *chsd ldr 4f: rdn over 5f out: sn lost pl: struggling in rr over 2f out* **10/1**

2333 **11** *2 ¾* **Dhania (IRE)**[40] 5286 3-8-11 **56** (b) JackMitchell(3) 4 28
(R A Teal) *led: clr after 3f: c bk to field 5f out: hdd & wknd wl over 2f out* **6/1**

0506 **12** *3 ½* **Tiffany Lady**[193] 938 3-7-11 **46** oh1 RachelKing(7) 3 12
(M D I Usher) *hld up: prog on wd outside fr over 3f out: lost grnd whn v wd bnd 2f out: wknd and eased* **66/1**

2m 34.69s (1.69) **Going Correction** +0.125s/f (Slow) **12** Ran SP% **120.3**
Speed ratings (Par 99): **99,94,93,93,92 92,90,88,87,84 82,80**
toteswingers: 1&2 £14.50, 1&3 £18.70, 2&3 £29.20 CSF £89.08 CT £1587.08 TOTE £8.30: £3.00, £4.10, £5.70; EX 58.30 TRIFECTA Not won. Place 6: £12.40 Place 5: £8.12 .
Owner Windflower Overseas Holdings Inc **Bred** Windflower Overseas **Trained** Arundel, W Sussex

FOCUS
Another moderate handicap, but at least more of these were previous winners than in the first division. The early pace was strong with Dhania soon tearing off into a clear lead, but he surely did far too much too soon and had run himself into the ground before reaching the 2f pole. The pace seemed to collapse, suiting those held up early, and the winning time was 0.35 seconds slower than division one. the form is best rated around the placed horses.
T/Plt: £15.50 to a £1 stake. Pool: £48,045.49. 2,261.82 winning tickets. T/Qpdt: £1.90 to a £1 stake. Pool: £4,078.84. 1,577.02 winning tickets. JN

6423 NEWMARKET (R-H)

Friday, October 2

OFFICIAL GOING: Good to firm
Wind: Fresh behind Weather: Overcast

6447 SAKHEE OH SO SHARP STKS (GROUP 3) (FILLIES) 7f

1:25 (1:28) (Class 1) 2-Y-O

£28,385 (£10,760; £5,385; £2,685; £1,345; £675) **Stalls** Centre

Form RPR

1 **1** **Tabassum (IRE)**[55] 4797 2-8-12 0 RHills 2 108+
(Sir Michael Stoute) *free to post: sn trcking ldr and keen enough: led 3f out: rdn and hung lft fr over 1f out: r.o wl* **5/2**[2]

163 **2** *4* **Electric Feel**[97] 3396 2-8-12 0 MartinDwyer 1 98
(M Botti) *hld up: hdwy over 2f out: rdn to chse wnr and hung rt 1f out: styd on same pce* **12/1**

2215 **3** *2 ¾* **Hasty (IRE)**[22] 5797 2-8-12 86 MichaelHills 7 90
(B W Hills) *chsd ldrs: rdn over 2f out: no ex fnl f* **10/1**

3215 **4** *1* **Bella Swan**[34] 5427 2-8-12 84 AdamKirby 3 88
(W R Swinburn) *hld up in tch: rdn 2f out: styd on same pce appr fnl f* **7/1**[3]

212 **5** *shd* **Blue Maiden**[55] 4795 2-8-12 105 EdwardCreighton 8 88
(P J McBride) *hld up: hdwy 1/2-way: rdn 2f out: no ex fnl f* **2/1**[1]

120 **6** *4* **Amary (IRE)**[13] 6090 2-8-12 89 NCallan 6 77
(C E Brittain) *chsd ldrs: rdn over 2f out: wknd over 1f out* **20/1**

014 **7** *shd* **Fairy Promises (USA)**[16] 5994 2-8-12 79 SPasquier 4 77
(Pat Eddery) *led 4f: sn rdn: wknd wl over 1f out* **50/1**

0554 **8** *90* **Crown (IRE)**[42] 5208 2-8-12 89 RichardHughes 5 —
(R Hannon) *hld up: wknd 1/2-way: eased: t.o* **20/1**

1m 23.9s (-1.50) **Going Correction** -0.10s/f (Good) **8** Ran SP% **102.7**
Speed ratings (Par 102): **104,99,96,95,95 90,90,—**
toteswingers: 1&2 £4.80, 1&3 £3.40, 2&3 £7.70 CSF £23.33 TOTE £2.80: £1.20, £2.60, £2.30; EX 25.60 Trifecta £122.60 Pool: £381.15 - 2.30 winning units..
Owner Hamdan Al Maktoum **Bred** Shadwell Estate Company Limited **Trained** Newmarket, Suffolk
■ Stewards' Enquiry : Edward Creighton one-day ban: used whip with excessive frequency (Oct 16)

FOCUS
This has been an ordinary Group 3 in the past decade, but this year's winner impressed and can rate higher. The form is rated around the third and fourth.

NOTEBOOK
Tabassum(IRE) ◆ came into this with a very similar profile to that of the stable's two previous winners in the last decade. Returning from a 55-day break, she ran out an impressive winner despite still showing signs of inexperience. She raced prominently, as she had done on her debut, and came right away from her rivals after travelling best throughout. Despite her dam being a 6f juvenile winner, she is related to winners over further, and her sire Nayef injects the stamina influence, and she clearly stays well. . She has reportedly been tricky at home, but she obviously has a lot of talent and a crack at the Group 2 Rockfel back over this C&D looks an obvious next step. Both Skybet and Blue Square introduced her into the ante-post market for the 1000 Guineas at 14/1, which puts her near the top of the betting, and her trainer later admitted he will now have to give it some consideration. (op 2-1 tchd 11-4 in places)
Electric Feel, whose stable took this event with Rami Coya in 2007, was returning from a 97-day layoff having sustained a leg injury after her previous outing on the July course. She looked a big player when making her move from off the pace, but was ultimately outstayed by the winner over this extra furlong. Her maiden win came on this track and she has progressed into a smart filly, but the trip looked to stretch her stamina at this stage. (op 16-1)
Hasty(IRE), stepping up half a furlong, puts the form into some perspective with an official mark of 86 next to her name. Her yard is always to be respected in such events at this venue, however, and this should rate a personal-best effort in defeat. (op 12-1)
Bella Swan was very well backed to show her true colours. She had her chance, but lacked an extra gear and this looks as good as she is. She performed close enough to her debut form with the runner-up. (op 14-1)
Blue Maiden set the standard on her third over this trip in the Sweet Solera last time and proved popular in the betting ring. She had reportedly suffered an interrupted preparation due to problems with her feet, and the way her effort petered out here would suggest the run may have been needed as she was well below her previous level. (op 11-4)
Amary(IRE) showed her previous outing to be wrong but felt the pinch from halfway on this step up to 7f and found it too hot. (op 25-1)
Fairy Promises(USA) cut out the running, but was a sitting duck nearing the 2f marker and was another that got outclassed. (tchd 40-1)
Crown(IRE) failed to run her race and presumably something was amiss. Official explanation: jockey said filly never travelled

6448 NAYEF JOEL STKS (GROUP 3) 1m

1:55 (1:56) (Class 1) 3-Y-O+

£36,900 (£13,988; £7,000; £3,490; £1,748; £877) **Stalls** Centre

Form RPR

2211 **1** **Confront**[27] 5655 4-9-0 116 RyanMoore 1 117
(Sir Michael Stoute) *chsd ldr tl led 3f out: rdn over 1f out: styd on wl* **7/4**[1]

03-0 **2** *½* **Rio De La Plata (USA)**[27] 5655 4-9-0 116 LDettori 5 116+
(Saeed Bin Suroor) *hld up in tch: n.m.r over 2f out: rdn over 1f out: r.o* **4/1**[2]

1445 **3** *½* **Forgotten Voice (IRE)**[42] 5231 4-9-0 113 JMurtagh 3 115
(J Noseda) *trckd ldrs: rdn over 2f out: r.o* **5/1**[3]

5155 **4** *¾* **Donativum**[33] 5496 3-8-11 106 TedDurcan 8 113
(Saeed Bin Suroor) *s.i.s: hld up: nt clr run over 2f out: swtchd lft and hdwy over 1f out: sn rdn and edgd rt: r.o* **9/1**

/53- **5** *hd* **Young Pretender (FR)**[483] 2788 4-9-0 0 AhmedAjtebi 4 112
(Saeed Bin Suroor) *plld hrd and prom: rdn and hung rt fr over 1f out: no ex towards fin* **20/1**

1200 **6** *2 ¾* **Captain Brilliance (USA)**[43] 5200 4-9-0 101 TPQueally 2 106
(J Noseda) *s.i.s: sn pushed along in rr: hdwy over 2f out: sn rdn: edgd rt and no ex ins fnl f* **33/1**

1010 **7** *1 ½* **We'll Come**[20] 5863 5-9-0 108 (b) DarryllHolland 9 102
(M A Jarvis) *hld up: rdn over 2f out: n.d* **10/1**

6310 **8** *20* **Ordnance Row**[27] 5655 6-9-3 112 RichardHughes 7 57
(R Hannon) *led 1f: chsd ldrs: rdn over 2f out: wknd over 1f out* **16/1**

1014 **9** *7* **Khateeb (IRE)**[50] 4949 4-9-0 109 (t) RHills 6 37
(M A Jarvis) *led 7f out: hdd 3f out: rdn and wknd 2f out* **9/1**

1m 36.18s (-2.42) **Going Correction** -0.10s/f (Good)
WFA 3 from 4yo+ 3lb **9** Ran SP% **115.7**
Speed ratings (Par 113): **108,107,107,106,106 103,101,81,74**
toteswingers: 1&2 £4.00, 2&3 £3.00, 1&3 not won. CSF £8.58 TOTE £2.50: £1.10, £1.70, £1.90; EX 8.50 Trifecta £30.80 Pool: £759.82 - 18.21 winning units..
Owner K Abdulla **Bred** Juddmonte Farms Ltd **Trained** Newmarket, Suffolk

FOCUS
This looked a decent and pretty competitive renewal of this Group 3, although a number of these had questions to answer. The form is ordinary for the grade but makes sense rated around the placed horses.

NOTEBOOK
Confront ◆, a dual Listed winner who was on a hat-trick, having improved for the fitting of earplugs, was a course winner over 1m1f and as such there were no stamina doubts. The only question was whether he could cope with the slight rise in grade, and he answered that conclusively. Ryan Moore was always close to the pace and he kicked on around 3f out, soon establishing an advantage which he held all the way to the line. He held off several challenges in game style and, clearly on the up, could return here for the Darley Stakes or even go to Hong Kong at the end of the year, if invited. Whatever the plans, he looks the sort who could make an impression in top company next season. (op 6-4 tchd 11-8)
Rio De La Plata(USA), a Group 1 winner as a juvenile and placed at the same level last season, had finished well beaten behind today's winner on his return from 14 months off last month. He improved considerably on that effort but was always being held in the last furlong. He has yet to win beyond 7f and might be suited by the Challenge Stakes back here on Champions' Day. (tchd 9-2)
Forgotten Voice(IRE) had scored on fast ground on his turf debut but had been held on his only tries in Group company. Dropping in trip, he came to have a chance in the Dip but could not produce another gear up the hill. He has only had eight races and there may be more to come. (op 11-2 tchd 7-1)
Donativum, the winner of a valuable sales race here and the Breeders' Cup Juvenile Turf on fast ground last year, had been held at Group 3 level this season and was so again. He is another who might appreciate a drop back in distance. (op 12-1)
Young Pretender(FR), the third Godolphin representative, a Group 3 juvenile winner but lightly raced since, had not been seen since finishing third in the Diomed Stakes in June 2008. Despite being keen early, he came to deliver a challenge before wandering out to the centre of the track in the closing stages. This was creditable and, as he might need time to get over it, connections may opt to prepare him for the Dubai carnival. (op 22-1 tchd 25-1)
Captain Brilliance(USA), a 6f and 7f winner on the July course, was well beaten on his previous try at 1m and could never land a blow this time. A return to handicaps seems likely. (op 40-1)
We'll Come, a high-class handicapper having his first try at this level, was never able to land a blow. (op 9-1)
Ordnance Row ran his second below-par race in a row and has probably had enough for the time being. Official explanation: jockey said gelding was unsuited by the good to firm ground (op 14-1 tchd 20-1)
Khateeb(IRE) likes to make the running but was taken on early by the winner and dropped right away. (op 12-1 tchd 14-1)

6449 ELECTROLUX CHEVELEY PARK STKS (GROUP 1) (FILLIES) 6f

2:30 (2:31) (Class 1) 2-Y-O

£96,509 (£36,584; £18,309; £9,129; £4,573; £2,295) **Stalls** Centre

Form RPR

212 **1** **Special Duty**[40] 5299 2-8-12 0 SPasquier 7 117
(Mme C Head-Maarek, France) *led 5f out: rdn whn chal over 1f out: r.o wl ins fnl f: edgd rt towards fin* **3/1**[2]

1210 **2** *2 ¾* **Misheer**[21] 5822 2-8-12 109 NCallan 6 109
(C E Brittain) *plld hrd: led 1f: trckd ldrs: outpcd over 1f out: hung rt and rallied to go 2nd on line* **9/1**

1611 **3** *hd* **Lady Of The Desert (USA)**[43] 5199 2-8-12 113 MartinDwyer 3 108
(B J Meehan) *ponied to the s: trckd ldrs: plld hrd: rdn and ev ch over 1f out: no ex ins fnl f* **11/8**[1]

142 **4** *¾* **Puff (IRE)**[14] 6049 2-8-12 93 JimCrowley 4 106
(R M Beckett) *hld up: hdwy over 2f out: sn rdn: r.o: nt rch ldrs* **50/1**

2211 **5** *3 ½* **Shamandar (FR)**[7] 6241 2-8-12 104 MichaelHills 1 97
(W J Haggas) *sn pushed along in rr: hdwy 1/2-way: rdn over 1f out: sn edgd rt and wknd* **12/1**

1 **6** *9* **Song Of My Heart (IRE)**[20] 5895 2-8-12 0 JMurtagh 5 73
(David Wachman, Ire) *chsd ldrs: pushed along and hung rt fr over 3f out: wknd over 2f out* **14/1**

1311 **7** *5* **Sand Vixen**[21] 5822 2-8-12 107 LDettori 2 58
(Saeed Bin Suroor) *hld up: hdwy over 2f out: rdn: hung rt and wknd over 1f out* **6/1**[3]

3112 **8** *9* **Habaayib**[86] 3748 2-8-12 107 RHills 8 36
(E A L Dunlop) *s.i.s: hdwy over 4f out: rdn and wknd over 2f out* **14/1**

1m 10.38s (-1.82) **Going Correction** -0.10s/f (Good) **8** Ran SP% **114.4**
Speed ratings (Par 106): **108,104,104,103,98 86,79,67**
toteswingers: 1&2 £6.60, 1&3 £2.50, 2&3 £4.40 CSF £29.92 TOTE £3.00: £1.20, £2.40, £1.30; EX 24.30 Trifecta £89.40 Pool: £18474.29 - 152.80 winning units..

Owner K Abdulla **Bred** Juddmonte Farms Ltd **Trained** Chantilly, France

FOCUS

A quality renewal of this most important Group 1. It was run at a sound pace and the form looks very solid, with the runner-up returning to her peak form.

NOTEBOOK

Special Duty ◆ completed the task in fine style. She had split Arcano and Canford Cliffs on her previous outing in the Prix Morny 40 days earlier, when she attempted to make all, and she again set off in front here. Having been allowed a fairly easy lead, her jockey was able to hold on to her until her main market rival emerged out of the pack. Her response when asked to win the race was most taking and, after shaking off the challenge of Lady Of The Desert, she was going away again at the finish. This was the quickest ground she had encountered and it proved no bother, so her versatility on that front should continue to prove a notable advantage. It was her stable's fourth winner of this event and two of the previous three went on to take the 1000 Guineas the following season (the other finished fourth). She was also taking a very similar path here to that of the 2007 winner, Natagora, another French filly that went on to land the Classic here as a 3-y-o. All that considered, it was natural for her to be promoted to clear favourite in the ante-post betting for next season's Guineas, with most offering around 5/1 but Ladbrokes going a generous looking 8/1. As with every winner of this most important event, the pedigree must be examined with a view to her stepping up to 1m. Her sire is best known for speedy juveniles, but her unraced dam is a sister to multiple US 7f-9f Grade 1 winner Sightseek and half-sister to US 9f-1m2f Grade 1 winner Tates Creek. That is not conclusive, but the manner in which she outstayed her rivals was very encouraging. At this stage she is a very worthy favourite, and her trainer intends to train her for the race. (op 9-4 tchd 100-30 in places)

Misheer came unstuck back over the minimum trip in the Flying Childers, but had taken the Cherry Hinton on her previous start and was bidding to emulate her trainer's previous winner of this contest, Sayeddati, who had also taken that event. The step back up to this trip showed her in a much better light again, indeed the way she kept on suggested she needed every yard, but she was found wanting when the two market leaders began their battle. She again took a keen hold through the early parts and hung right when put under maximum pressure, but is no doubt a high-class filly in her own right. It wouldn't be at all surprising to see her re-oppose the winner in the 1000 Guineas next year, with a trial probable along the way. She is not totally without hope of getting 1m on breeding, but one cannot see the form being reversed. (op 11-1)

Lady Of The Desert(USA), whose only previous defeat came when racing too hard early on in the Queen Mary, was bidding to emulate her dam, who also won this race. She proved very popular to make it four wins from five outings on this debut at the top level and was delivered to challenge Special Duty around halfway. Her battle with that rival told inside the final furlong, and running a little freely through the early parts wouldn't have helped her cause. She also didn't appear as suited by the Dip as that one, but she comes out of this still looking the second-best filly in the race. Her trainer reckoned she was unhappy on the undulations, so the French Guineas is her likely target, but while the dam has already produced a winning miler at three, this filly looks all speed. Still, her mother landed the 7f Fred Darling on her 3-y-o debut before injury curtailed her career, and that is a possible starting point next season. (op 7-4)

Puff(IRE) had plenty to find on paper and had finished just over seven lengths behind Lady Of The Desert in the Lowther on her penultimate outing. The return to this trip proved right up her street and she ran by far her best race to date without ever threatening. She could be used to hold the form down somewhat, but it is worth chancing she is an improver and, on this showing, a drop back down in grade can see her go in again before the season's end. (op 40-1)

Shamandar(FR) had her chance more towards the near side, but was done with shortly after the furlong marker. This big step up in grade came just a week after she endured a fairly hard race in the Watership Down Stud Sales Race, but she still performed close enough to her recent best and helps to set the level. (tchd 14-1)

Song Of My Heart(IRE) arrived here on the back of a comfortable win in Listed company 20 days previously. It was her first outing on ground so quick, though, and the way she came off the bridle early on would suggest she failed to enjoy it. (op 12-1)

Sand Vixen landed the Flying Childers on her previous outing and was backed on this return to the extra furlong. She gave herself little chance of lasting out the distance by refusing to settle early on, however, and was well below her recent level. Official explanation: jockey said filly ran flat (op 8-1)

Habaayib, the Albany winner, was last seen finishing second to Misheer in the Cherry Hinton in July when her connections believed the race had come too soon for her. She dropped out very quickly here when the race began to hot up and was eased right off in the end. Something was clearly not right with her. Official explanation: jockey said filly ran flat (op 12-1)

6450 SHADWELL MIDDLE PARK STKS (GROUP 1) (ENTIRE COLTS) 6f

3:05 (3:07) (Class 1) 2-Y-O **£104,116** (£39,467; £19,752; £9,848; £4,933) **Stalls** Centre

Form RPR

111 **1** **Awzaan**[13] 6105 2-8-12 113 RHills 5 119
(M Johnston) *chsd ldrs: rdn to ld and hung lft fr over 1f out: r.o* **4/1**[3]

1134 **2** *3/4* **Radiohead**[13] 6105 2-8-12 113 (t) MartinDwyer 1 117
(B J Meehan) *ponied to the s: broke wl: stdd and dropped in rr: rdn: hung lft and outpcd over 1f out: r.o strly u.p ins fnl f to take 2nd nr fin* **14/1**

211 **3** *nk* **Showcasing**[44] 5172 2-8-12 113 JimmyFortune 2 116
(J H M Gosden) *prom: chsd ldr 1/2-way: rdn and ev ch over 1f out: styd on: lost 2nd nr fin* **2/1**[2]

3131 **4** *1* **Poet's Voice**[20] 5859 2-8-12 112 (t) LDettori 3 113
(Saeed Bin Suroor) *sn led: racd keenly: rdn and hdd over 1f out: hmpd ins fnl f: styd on same pce* **15/8**[1]

11 **5** *2 3/4* **Arctic (IRE)**[33] 5486 2-8-12 0 PJSmullen 4 107
(Tracey Collins, Ire) *chsd ldr to 1/2-way: remained handy: rdn and ev ch over 1f out: no ex ins fnl f: eased nr fin* **6/1**

1m 10.11s (-2.09) **Going Correction** -0.10s/f (Good) **5** Ran SP% **109.1**
Speed ratings (Par 109): **109,108,107,106,102**
CSF £45.01 TOTE £5.00: £2.20, £3.30; EX 33.10.

Owner Hamdan Al Maktoum **Bred** Shadwell Estate Company Limited **Trained** Middleham Moor, N Yorks

■ Stewards' Enquiry : R Hills one-day ban: careless riding (Oct 16)

FOCUS

This Group 1 is usually won by a speedy and experienced juvenile. The last ten winners had all scored on their previous start and included subsequent champion sprinter Oasis Dream and Breeders' Cup Juvenile winner Johannesburg, both of whom were represented as sires in this year's renewal. This looked a high-class and intriguing contest, despite the small field, although there were several reasons to suspect that it might have more bearing on next season's sprint championship rather than the classics. The time was 0.27secs faster than the Cheveley Park and the third sets the standard.

NOTEBOOK

Awzaan maintained his unbeaten record and equalled the feat of Dark Angel and Primo Valentino, who both took the Mill Reef Stakes before winning this race. Never far away, he came to deliver his challenge running into the Dip and always looked like holding his rivals, despite edging to his left under pressure, something he had also done at Newbury. He scored a shade cosily and looks a decent prospect for the top sprint races, although it is always hard for 3-y-os to take on their elders. On breeding he could stay the Guineas trip, a race for which he is quoted at between 8-1 and 16-1, but he looks to be all speed and his owner also has Arcano in the race. (op 7-2)

Radiohead, winner of the Norfolk Stakes and third in the Nunthorpe, looked a non-stayer when a beaten favourite in the Mill Reef. However, connections clearly believed stamina was not the issue and he proved them right, keeping on strongly up the hill having been held up early. He is likely to try to emulate his sire by going for the Breeders' Cup Juvenile. (op 12-1)

Showcasing, narrowly beaten by Arcano (who beat the Cheveley Park winner in the Prix Morny) on his debut, had won the Gimcrack since. Trying to emulate his sire by winning this race, he had every chance but could not find an extra gear up the hill. Connections accept he is a sprinter pure and simple, and they plan to prep him for Royal Ascot in the Duke Of York. (tchd 15-8, 9-4 in places)

Poet's Voice, a dual winner at 7f, including the Group 2 Champagne Stakes, was tried in a tongue tie for this drop in trip and made the running, despite jumping awkwardly from the stalls. He had been headed and was on the retreat when hampered by the winner. He might get 1m next season but that is not guaranteed on pedigree. (op 5-2 tchd 11-4)

Arctic(IRE), the Irish challenger and winner of all three previous starts, including at Listed and Group 3 level, had gained those successes on good and softer ground. Tackling fast turf for the first time, he ran creditably but was weakening out of contention when crossed by the winner. He could still make his mark back on an easier surface. (op 9-2 tchd 7-1)

6451 NUNNERY STUD E B F MAIDEN STKS 7f

3:40 (3:40) (Class 4) 2-Y-O **£6,476** (£1,927; £963; £481) **Stalls** Centre

Form RPR

53 **1** **Swiss Cross**[21] 5829 2-9-3 0 KFallon 7 86
(G A Butler) *chsd ldrs: rdn over 1f out: styd on u.p to ld nr fin* **10/1**

3 **2** *1/2* **Esaar (USA)**[49] 4986 2-9-3 0 RHills 5 85
(B W Hills) *sn led: hdd 1/2-way: rdn to ld over 1f out: edgd lft and hdd nr fin* **10/11**[1]

00 **3** *1 1/2* **Invincible Soul (IRE)**[49] 4985 2-9-3 0 RichardHughes 1 81
(R Hannon) *chsd ldr tl led 1/2-way: rdn and hdd over 1f out: styd on same pce ins fnl f* **20/1**

4 **4** *1/2* **Tartan Trip**[111] 2936 2-9-3 0 DavidProbert 6 80
(A M Balding) *sn pushed along in rr: hdwy 1/2-way: rdn over 1f out: styd on same pce ins fnl f* **14/1**

4 **5** *4 1/2* **Mushreq (USA)**[35] 5400 2-9-3 0 TPO'Shea 8 69
(Sir Michael Stoute) *hld up: hdwy over 2f out: wknd over 1f out* **9/2**[2]

6 *7* **Total Command** 2-9-3 0 RyanMoore 2 51+
(Sir Michael Stoute) *chsd ldrs: sn pushed along: wknd over 2f out* **5/1**[3]

7 *4* **Toy Razor (IRE)** 2-9-3 0 DaneO'Neill 9 41
(H Candy) *mid-div: rdn and wknd over 2f out* **20/1**

8 *1 1/4* **Indigo Ink** 2-8-12 0 TedDurcan 3 33
(S A Callaghan, U.S.A) *s.s: sn pushed along and a in rr: lost tch over 2f out* **50/1**

1m 24.72s (-0.68) **Going Correction** -0.10s/f (Good) **8** Ran SP% **114.5**
Speed ratings (Par 97): **99,98,96,96,91 83,78,77**
toteswingers: 1&2 £3.50, 1&3 £13.00, 2&3 £6.20 CSF £19.32 TOTE £9.90: £1.80, £1.10, £4.30; EX 24.90.

Owner A D Spence **Bred** Lordship Stud **Trained** Newmarket, Suffolk

FOCUS

Decent maiden form with the first four coming clear and the fifth sets the level.

NOTEBOOK

Swiss Cross ◆ opened his account at the third time of asking under a strong ride. He had raced over sprint distances in his first two outings, which considering he is out of the speedy Swiss Lake makes sense. However, it was the step up to this longer trip that made all the difference as he ultimately came out on top by outstaying his rivals. That shows his sire of the moment to be the leading influence and he has the scope to keep improving as he matures. There was also plenty to like about his attitude when under maximum pressure and he looks one to follow.

Esaar(USA) was well backed when a close third on his debut at Newbury in August and proved all the rage to open his account here. That form was the best on offer in this field and things looked good for him coming out of the Dip, but he was unable to cope with the renewed challenge of the winner. That may well have been due to him running a bit freely through the early stages and, while he should have little trouble finding a maiden, his Group 1 entries appear far too ambitious. (tchd 5-6 and Evens)

Invincible Soul(IRE) ◆, who was held up in his two previous outings, made his way to the front early on and produced a far better effort as a result. He kept on gamely once headed and is evidently coming good. He is now eligible for a mark and looks well up to winning this term, but is really bred to come into his own at around 1m2f as a 3-y-o. (op 25-1)

Tartan Trip was having his first outing since finishing fourth over 6f at York in August. He had his chance and shaped with definite ability, but failed to see out the longer distance like the principals. This was a definite step in the right direction. Official explanation: jockey said the colt ran green (tchd 16-1)

Mushreq(USA), whose stable have won this four times in the past decade, finished fourth in what is working out to be a decent maiden on the July course last time out. He appeared a threat to all 2f out, but didn't handle the Dip at all well and was soon in trouble. He is better than this and a move to a flatter track is what he wants. (tchd 4-1)

Total Command ◆ was the second from Sir Michael Stoute's yard and the betting suggested this debut run would be needed. That proved to be the case as he ran too green to do himself justice. It is very interesting that his siblings Arabian Gulf and the classy Quiff both finished unplaced on their sole runs at two before going onto better things the following season. With that in mind he is one for the notebook. (op 6-1 tchd 9-2)

Toy Razor(IRE) is a 90,000gns yearling whose pedigree suggests a mix of speed and stamina. He showed up well enough before weakening tamely, which indicates the run was needed, and he should be a deal sharper for this initial experience.

Indigo Ink was the first beaten and finished well out the back. She is bred for 1m and is surely capable of better in due course.

6452 HAAFHD GODOLPHIN STKS (LISTED RACE) 1m 4f

4:15 (4:15) (Class 1) 3-Y-O+ **£22,708** (£8,608; £4,308; £2,148) **Stalls** Centre

Form RPR

53 **1** **Chock A Block (IRE)**[23] 5764 3-8-7 106 LDettori 1 110
(Saeed Bin Suroor) *chsd ldrs in 3rd pl tl wnt 2nd 2f out: shkn up to ld over 1f out: rdn ins fnl f: jst hld on* **7/4**[2]

3240 **2** *shd* **Drill Sergeant**[5] 6303 4-9-0 108 JoeFanning 2 110
(M Johnston) *chsd ldr tl led wl over 2f out: rdn and hdd over 1f out: r.o gamely: edgd lft towards fin* **11/8**[1]

3421 **3** *8* **Funday**[23] 5771 3-8-2 82 TPO'Shea 3 92
(G L Moore) *s.i.s: hld up: rdn and hung rt fr over 4f out: wkng whn wnt 3rd 1f out* **8/1**

3023 **4** *22* **Classic Punch (IRE)**[34] 5446 6-9-0 102 ... RyanMoore 4 62
(D R C Elsworth) *led: rdn and hdd wl over 2f out: wknd over 1f out: eased* **9/2[3]**

2m 29.27s (-4.23) **Going Correction** -0.10s/f (Good)
WFA 3 from 4yo+ 7lb 4 Ran SP% **107.8**
Speed ratings (Par 111): **110,109,104,89**
CSF £4.51 TOTE £2.70; EX 5.80.
Owner Godolphin **Bred** Kilfrush And Waterside Studs **Trained** Newmarket, Suffolk

FOCUS
A small field for this Listed contest which often falls to an improving type, although none of the trainers represented had been responsible for a winner in the last ten years. Despite the small field and the form not being entirely solid, it provided an exciting contest between the market leaders.

NOTEBOOK
Chock A Block(IRE) was an appropriate winner of this Listed race. Sold out of Robert Collet's yard to Godolphin after winning his sole start as a juvenile over 1m1f in France, he had improved on his debut for the yard last time but was held up on this step up in trip with two confirmed pace-setters in the line-up. He travelled well into contention and looked likely to score comfortably when hitting the front, but was forced to pull out all the stops by the game runner-up. He should have more to offer next season and, now proven on both fast and easy ground, that increases connections' options and he is to go for the St Simon Stakes next. (tchd 13-8 and 15-8)
Drill Sergeant is a typically game and tough inmate of his yard and proved it here. Unable to make the running with Classic Punch in opposition, he travelled well before going on and rallied bravely to stretch the winner to the limit. He put a below-par effort behind him and may be able to win again before the season is out. (tchd 7-4)
Funday is a genuine sort but had a lot to find with the other three on official ratings. She was always in rear and never got in a blow, but did run on to take the minor placing and earn valuable black type in the process. (op 9-1 tchd 7-1)
Classic Punch(IRE) had conditions to suit (1m4f and a small field) and made the running. However, he was given no peace in front and dropped away when the runner-up re-took the lead over 2f out. (op 4-1)

6453 STANDING FOR SUCCESS H'CAP — 1m 2f
4:50 (4:50) (Class 2) (0-100,97) 3-Y-O — **£12,462** (£3,732; £1,866) **Stalls** Centre

Form — RPR
21 **1** **Alainmaar (FR)**[15] 6022 3-9-4 97 ... RHills 1 110+
(M A Jarvis) *chsd ldr over 8f out: shkn up over 2f out: rdn to ld wl over 1f out: styd on wl* **1/1[1]**
1022 **2** *2 1/2* **Rumble Of Thunder (IRE)**[41] 5266 3-8-4 83 ... MartinDwyer 3 88
(D W P Arbuthnot) *led: qcknd over 3f out: rdn and hdd over 2f out: styd on same pce ins fnl f* **7/1[3]**
-111 **3** *11* **Bab Al Salam (USA)**[19] 5904 3-9-2 95 ... LDettori 5 90
(Saeed Bin Suroor) *chsd ldr to over 8f out: remained handy: shkn up to ld over 2f out: rdn and hdd wl over 1f out: wknd and eased ins fnl f* **11/8[2]**

2m 3.93s (-1.87) **Going Correction** -0.10s/f (Good) 3 Ran SP% **104.6**
Speed ratings (Par 107): **103,101,92**
CSF £6.08 TOTE £1.80; EX 5.30.
Owner Hamdan Al Maktoum **Bred** Fares Stables Ltd **Trained** Newmarket, Suffolk

FOCUS
An interesting little handicap despite the small field. The winner is progressing fast and the runner-up represents a solid guide.

NOTEBOOK
Alainmaar(FR) ◆ followed up his impressive Pontefract maiden win 15 days previously with a ready effort under top weight on this handicap debut, landing strong support in the process. He tracked the runner-up until being asked for maximum effort 2f out and was always doing enough after hitting the front. He still looked inexperienced here so improvement is likely again from this, just his third outing so far. His trainer excels with such types so bigger and better things surely lie in waiting for this son of Johar. (op 10-11)
Rumble Of Thunder(IRE), another 3lb higher, has now finished second on his last three outings, but there should be no questioning his attitude. Time will likely tell he faced an impossible task with the winner, and he richly deserves to go one better, but he could well go up again for this. (op 11-2)
Bab Al Salam(USA) came into this unbeaten in his four starts to date and still looked feasibly handicapped off a 4lb higher mark for winning at Bath 19 days earlier. A change of tactics was deployed as he allowed the first two to go on, and he came there going nicely 2f out. He was disappointingly cooked soon after push came to shove, however, and was eventually eased to a near walk in the closing stages. This was not his true form and the track may have been to blame, but he does now have something to prove. (op 13-8 tchd 7-4 in a place)

6454 NEWMARKET CHALLENGE WHIP (A H'CAP) — 1m 2f
5:25 (5:25) (Class 6) (0-85,87) 3-Y-O+ — **£0** **Stalls** Centre

Form — RPR
4420 **1** **Dreamwalk (IRE)**[19] 5915 3-8-9 78 ... (v) JimCrowley 4 82
(R M Beckett) *racd apart tl merged 7f out: chsd ldr tl led 7f out: rdn over 1f out: hung lft and styd on wl* **4/11[1]**
-50 **2** *8* **Beauchamp Wizard**[9] 6212 4-8-10 74 ... (t) KFallon 1 62
(G A Butler) *racd apart tl merged 7f out: led 3f: chsd wnr: rdn over 1f out: sn outpcd* **2/1[2]**

2m 4.28s (-1.52) **Going Correction** -0.10s/f (Good)
WFA 3 from 4yo 5lb 2 Ran SP% **106.6**
Speed ratings (Par 101): **102,95**
TOTE £1.40 Place 6: £115.94 Place 5: £46.50 .
Owner P D Savill **Bred** Peter Savill **Trained** Whitsbury, Hants

FOCUS
The field for this historic race was cut in half by morning withdrawals, resulting in a match and the winner only had to match previous form to score.
T/Jkpt: £8,089.80 to a £1 stake. Pool: £51,273.72. 4.50 winning tickets. T/Plt: £54.30 to a £1 stake. Pool: £99,858.47. 1,340.66 winning tickets. T/Qpdt: £27.90 to a £1 stake. Pool: £5,830.76. 154.60 winning tickets. CR

6430 WOLVERHAMPTON (A.W) (L-H)
Friday, October 2

OFFICIAL GOING: Standard
Wind: Light behind Weather: Fine

6455 LADBROKES.COM H'CAP — 7f 32y(P)
5:50 (5:52) (Class 5) (0-70,71) 3-Y-O — **£2,914** (£867; £433; £216) **Stalls** High

Form — RPR
1500 **1** **Gassin**[49] 5003 3-9-1 67 ... (v[1]) ChrisCatlin 12 75+
(M L W Bell) *s.i.s: sn hld up in tch: led wl over 1f out: sn clr: drvn out ins fnl f* **25/1**
6460 **2** *3/4* **Kersivay**[27] 5677 3-9-4 70 ... TonyHamilton 8 79+
(Ollie Pears) *hld up towards rr: nt clr run fr over 3f out tl swtchd rt and hdwy over 1f out: r.o wl towards fin: nt rch wnr* **8/1**
1350 **3** *1 1/2* **All For You (IRE)**[27] 5677 3-9-0 66 ... (p) JerryO'Dwyer 6 68
(M Botti) *s.i.s: hld up in rr: c wd st: hdwy wl over 1f out: sn rdn: r.o ins fnl f* **8/1**
0-60 **4** *2* **Especially Special (IRE)**[36] 5370 3-9-4 70 ... JamesDoyle 10 67
(S Kirk) *hld up towards rr: hdwy on outside over 2f out: rdn wl over 1f out: one pce ins fnl f* **33/1**
0303 **5** *3/4* **Markhesa**[22] 5806 3-8-13 65 ... AlanMunro 5 60
(C F Wall) *hld up towards rr: nt clr run on ins over 2f out: sn swtchd rt: nt clr run wl over 1f out: kpt on fnl f: n.d* **9/1**
150 **6** *1/2* **Here Comes Danny**[131] 2300 3-9-3 69 ... PaulHanagan 4 62
(M Wigham) *hld up in tch: pushed along 2f out: rdn and edgd lft over 1f out: wknd ins fnl f* **11/2[2]**
0351 **7** *1 1/4* **Integria**[8] 6224 3-9-5 71 6ex ... (b) LukeMorris 3 61
(J M P Eustace) *hld up in mid-div: pushed along over 3f out: rdn and hdwy on ins over 1f out: wknd ins fnl f* **9/2[1]**
1440 **8** *shd* **Crystallize**[12] 6140 3-9-1 67 ... StephenDonohoe 9 57
(A B Haynes) *hld up in mid-div: nt clr run briefly jst over 2f out: rdn over 1f out: no hdwy* **16/1**
0000 **9** *2 3/4* **Amber Sunset**[27] 5677 3-9-3 69 ... LPKeniry 2 51
(J Jay) *sn led: rdn over 2f out: hdd wl over 1f out: wknd ent fnl f* **14/1**
4451 **10** *1 3/4* **Quiquillo (USA)**[50] 4937 3-8-12 69 ... AndrewHeffernan[(5)] 1 46
(P D Evans) *led early: prom: pushed along over 3f out: hmpd on ins over 2f out: rdn and wknd wl over 1f out* **9/2[1]**
3000 **11** *3/4* **Smalljohn**[29] 5601 3-8-9 68 ... (v) AdamCarter[(7)] 11 43
(B Smart) *sn prom: rdn and wknd over 1f out* **28/1**
401 **12** *14* **Whisky Jack**[30] 5582 3-9-2 68 ... (b) DarryllHolland 7 —
(W R Muir) *prom: rdn over 2f out: wknd wl over 1f out: eased whn no ch ins fnl f* **13/2[3]**

1m 27.84s (-1.76) **Going Correction** -0.225s/f (Stan) 12 Ran SP% **120.1**
Speed ratings (Par 101): **101,100,98,96,95 94,93,93,90,88 87,71**
toteswingers: 1&2 £38.80, 1&3 £42.00, 2&3 £14.70 CSF £212.94 CT £1795.19 TOTE £25.60: £6.90, £3.00, £2.90; EX 375.20.
Owner J L C Pearce **Bred** J L C Pearce **Trained** Newmarket, Suffolk

FOCUS
A shock result, compounded by the poor performances of the joint-favourites. Those in the frame behind the winner came from off the pace, and the lack of recent form of the third and fourth raises doubts over the strength of the form.

6456 GREAT OFFERS AT WOLVERHAMPTON-RACECOURSE.CO.UK H'CAP — 5f 20y(P)
6:20 (6:20) (Class 6) (0-60,60) 3-Y-O+ — **£2,729** (£806; £403) **Stalls** Low

Form — RPR
0501 **1** **Metal Guru**[29] 5610 5-8-11 56 ... (p) RussellKennemore[(3)] 3 67
(R Hollinshead) *led 1f: chsd ldr: rdn wl over 1f out: led ins fnl f: r.o* **11/4[1]**
532 **2** *nk* **Monsieur Reynard**[13] 6119 4-8-9 54 ... MCGeran[(3)] 4 64
(J M Bradley) *s.i.s: sn hld up in tch: swtchd rt ins fnl f: r.o to take 2nd last strides* **7/2[2]**
0605 **3** *hd* **Monte Major (IRE)**[181] 1134 8-9-2 58 ... (v) AdamKirby 2 67
(D Shaw) *hld up in mid-div: rdn and r.o ins fnl f: tk 3rd last strides* **14/1**
3520 **4** *nk* **Cayman Fox**[15] 6010 4-9-4 60 ... (e) PJMcDonald 6 68
(James Moffatt) *s.i.s: sn rcvrd: led after 1f: rdn and hdd ins fnl f: kpt on but lost two pls nr post* **9/2[3]**
0506 **5** *1 1/4* **Wreningham**[16] 5989 4-9-3 59 ... PatCosgrave 8 62
(P Leech) *a.p: rdn and one pce ins fnl f* **16/1**
4055 **6** *3/4* **Forever's Girl**[27] 5678 3-8-13 60 ... LanceBetts[(5)] 7 61
(G R Oldroyd) *hld up in mid-div: rdn over 1f out: no hdwy* **20/1**
604 **7** *1* **Dilli Dancer**[9] 6213 4-8-8 55 ... GabrielHannon[(5)] 1 52
(G D Blake) *hld up towards rr: pushed along over 2f out: rdn over 1f out: nvr trbld ldrs* **14/1**
6030 **8** *nk* **Maryolini**[9] 6216 4-8-12 59 ... RossAtkinson[(5)] 9 55
(Tom Dascombe) *s.i.s: sn swtchd lft: hld up in rr: c v wd st: rdn over 1f out: n.d* **12/1**
0505 **9** *shd* **Lady Vivien**[20] 5881 3-9-4 60 ... (t) PhillipMakin 12 56
(D H Brown) *s.i.s: hld up and bhd: pushed along wl over 1f out: no rspnse* **25/1**
55 **10** *3/4* **Josiah Bartlett (IRE)**[71] 4237 3-8-13 55 ... StephenDonohoe 10 48
(Ian Williams) *a in rr* **33/1**
3350 **11** *2* **Cheshire Rose**[9] 6205 4-8-13 58 ... (bt[1]) AndreaAtzeni[(3)] 5 44
(A M Hales) *hld up in tch: rdn 3f out: wknd wl over 1f out* **8/1**

61.12 secs (-1.18) **Going Correction** -0.225s/f (Stan) 11 Ran SP% **116.6**
Speed ratings (Par 101): **100,99,99,98,96 95,93,93,93,92 88**
toteswingers: 1&2 £2.30, 1&3 £9.00, 2&3 £8.00 CSF £11.63 CT £108.74 TOTE £3.60: £1.60, £1.80, £3.10; EX 13.60.
Owner Moores Metals Ltd **Bred** Reg Hollinshead **Trained** Upper Longdon, Staffs

FOCUS
A good sprint gallop, but the finish was largely fought out by horses who had raced handily. The form is modest but solid.

6457 BET IN PLAY AT LADBROKES.COM H'CAP — 1m 5f 194y(P)
6:50 (6:52) (Class 6) (0-65,65) 3-Y-O+ — **£2,729** (£806; £403) **Stalls** Low

Form — RPR
0102 **1** **Cape Marien (IRE)**[16] 5988 3-9-3 63 ... DarryllHolland 6 72
(D R Lanigan) *a.p: led ent fnl f: styd on wl* **7/2[1]**
5101 **2** *4* **Leyte Gulf (USA)**[15] 6025 6-9-10 61 ... DaneO'Neill 12 67+
(C C Bealby) *s.i.s: hld up in rr: pushed along and hdwy over 1f out: styd on wl to take 2nd nr fin* **11/1**
6225 **3** *nk* **Galiotto (IRE)**[21] 5838 3-8-6 52 ... AlanMunro 10 55
(C F Wall) *chsd ldr: led jst over 2f out: rdn and hdd ent fnl f: no ex and lost 2nd nr fin* **9/1**
0453 **4** *1/2* **Pertemps Power**[27] 3223 5-8-10 50 ... (t) RussellKennemore[(3)] 13 52
(B G Powell) *a.p: pushed along 2f out: one pce* **20/1**
6016 **5** *3/4* **Sitwell**[31] 5545 3-9-3 63 ... (v[1]) LPKeniry 4 64
(J R Fanshawe) *hld up in mid-div: pushed along over 2f out: rdn over 1f out: styd on ins fnl f* **10/1**
5031 **6** *hd* **Dazzling Begum**[10] 6188 4-8-13 55 7ex ... (p) SimonPearce[(5)] 9 56
(J Pearce) *hld up in tch: rdn and one pce fnl f* **9/1**
4010 **7** *3/4* **Stormy Morning**[16] 5990 3-9-3 63 ... AdamKirby 2 63
(W R Swinburn) *led: rdn and hdd jst over 2f out: wknd ins fnl f* **17/2[3]**
13/0 **8** *1/2* **Silent Lucidity (IRE)**[49] 4972 5-8-12 52 ... FrederikTylicki[(3)] 5 51
(P D Niven) *hld up towards rr: pushed along over 2f out: c wd st: rdn over 1f out: nvr trbld ldrs* **6/1[2]**
4334 **9** *4* **Fenners (USA)**[13] 6097 6-8-5 49 ... (p) JamesPSullivan[(7)] 1 43
(M W Easterby) *hld up in rr: rdn over 2f out: wknd wl over 1f out* **9/1**
025 **10** *1 1/4* **Mae Cigan (FR)**[56] 4737 6-9-6 57 ... FrancisNorton 11 49
(M Blanshard) *hld up in mid-div: stdy prog over 5f out: pushed along over 2f out: wknd wl over 1f out* **14/1**

6405 **11** ¾ **Apache Fort**[20] 5885 6-8-9 **53**........(bt) TobyAtkinson(7) 3 44
(T Keddy) *hld up in mid-div: pushed along and bhd fnl 3f* **16/1**
2664 **12** ¾ **Bold Adventure**[126] 2445 5-9-11 **62**........ ChrisCatlin 8 52
(W J Musson) *broke wl: stdd s: sn hld up in rr: c wd st: sn struggling* **12/1**

3m 4.85s (-1.15) **Going Correction** -0.225s/f (Stan)
WFA 3 from 4yo+ 9lb 12 Ran SP% **119.5**
Speed ratings (Par 101): **94,91,91,91,90 90,90,90,87,87 86,86**
toteswingers: 1&2 £6.70, 1&3 £9.50, 2&3 £24.10. CSF £43.28 CT £326.70 TOTE £3.70: £1.80, £4.70, £3.00; EX 23.40.
Owner Saif Ali **Bred** Darley **Trained** Newmarket, Suffolk
■ Stewards' Enquiry : Alan Munro caution: entered wrong stall

FOCUS
In theory, a sedate tempo should have favoured those who raced prominently. There was a relatively bunched finish and the form is not the most reliable.

6458 STAY AT THE WOLVERHAMPTON HOLIDAY INN CLAIMING STKS 5f 216y(P)
7:20 (7:21) (Class 6) 3-Y-0+ £2,729 (£806; £403) Stalls Low

Form RPR
2500 **1** **River Kirov (IRE)**[35] 5404 6-9-9 76........ DarryllHolland 4 85
(M Wigham) *hld up: hdwy on ins wl over 1f out: rdn to ld ins fnl f: r.o wl* **7/2**[2]
3006 **2** 1¼ **Onceaponatime (IRE)**[8] 6230 4-9-1 68........ AlanMunro 2 73
(M D Squance) *a.p: wnt 2nd 3f out: led jst over 1f out: rdn and hdd ins fnl f: nt qckn* **12/1**
1000 **3** nk **Mocha Java**[28] 5634 6-8-2 58........(b[1]) RossAtkinson(5) 3 64
(Matthew Salaman) *hld up towards rr: rdn and hdwy fnl f: nvr nrr* **16/1**
5001 **4** 1 **Desperate Dan**[4] 6329 8-8-12 73........(v) AmyBaker(5) 8 71
(A B Haynes) *hld up in mid-div: hdwy and pushed along over 2f out: rdn and one pce fnl f* **7/2**[2]
0251 **5** nk **Come On Buckers (IRE)**[22] 5809 3-8-8 60........(b) EdwardCreighton 11 62
(E J Creighton) *led: rdn and hdd jst over 1f out: no ex ins fnl f* **18/1**
0352 **6** 1¾ **Charles Parnell (IRE)**[27] 5676 6-8-13 70........(b) PhillipMakin 1 60
(M Dods) *chsd ldr 3f: rdn over 1f out: wknd ins fnl f* **3/1**[1]
0300 **7** ¾ **Klynch**[11] 6167 3-9-4 82........(b) PaulHanagan 10 64
(B J Meehan) *hld up towards rr: rdn jst over 1f out: n.d* **6/1**[3]
00 **8** 6 **Poppy Morris (IRE)**[4] 6329 4-7-11 0........ RyanPowell(7) 5 30
(A B Haynes) *n.m.r sn after s: hld up in rr: short-lived effrt on ins wl over 1f out* **100/1**
2300 **9** 3 **High Curragh**[16] 5989 6-9-0 65........(v[1]) AmyRyan(5) 6 35
(K A Ryan) *prom tl wknd over 2f out* **10/1**

1m 13.54s (-1.46) **Going Correction** -0.225s/f (Stan)
WFA 3 from 4yo+ 1lb 9 Ran SP% **112.6**
Speed ratings (Par 101): **100,98,97,96,96 93,92,84,80**
toteswingers: 1&2 £4.70, 1&3 £10.60, 2&3 £14.90. CSF £43.34 TOTE £4.60: £1.60, £3.40, £4.10; EX 49.90.
Owner A Darke T Matthews M Wigham **Bred** Kildaragh Stud **Trained** Newmarket, Suffolk
■ Stewards' Enquiry : Edward Creighton one-day ban: did not keep straight from stalls (Oct 18)

FOCUS
A fair-quality claimer. As usual, Come On Buckers pinged out and set a strong gallop, which suited the winner ideally. The form makes sense with the first three and the fifth to their marks.

6459 BET AFTER THE OFF AT LADBROKES.COM H'CAP 5f 20y(P)
7:50 (7:52) (Class 4) (0-85,90) 3-Y-0+ **£5,046** (£1,510; £755; £377; £188) Stalls Low

Form RPR
2361 **1** **Le Toreador**[11] 6171 4-9-5 **90** 6ex........(tp) AmyRyan(5) 3 99
(K A Ryan) *mde all: rdn 1f out: drvn out* **4/1**[3]
2204 **2** nk **Garstang**[7] 6253 6-8-12 **78**........(b) AdamKirby 1 86
(J Balding) *hld up in tch: reminder over 2f out: chsd wnr fnl f: rdn and kpt on* **6/1**
6036 **3** 1¼ **Chjimes (IRE)**[7] 6253 5-9-2 **82**........ LPKeniry 4 86+
(C R Dore) *t.k.h towards rr: swtchd rt wl over 1f out: sn rdn: hdwy whn edgd lft wl ins fnl f: r.o* **18/1**
5345 **4** ¾ **Nickel Silver**[11] 6171 4-8-13 **79**........(p) TomEaves 2 80
(B Smart) *chsd wnr to 1f out: rdn and one pce fnl f* **7/2**[2]
4020 **5** hd **The Jobber (IRE)**[11] 6171 8-9-2 **82**........ FrancisNorton 10 82
(M Blanshard) *hld up towards rr: swtchd rt over 1f out: r.o ins fnl f* **22/1**
0322 **6** hd **Feelin Foxy**[7] 6253 5-8-12 **78**........ AlanMunro 5 77
(J G Given) *hld up in tch: no imp fnl f* **3/1**[1]
4-00 **7** 1¼ **Moscow Eight (IRE)**[11] 6167 3-8-7 **78**........ RossAtkinson(5) 6 73
(Tom Dascombe) *s.i.s: hld up in rr: swtchd rt jst over 1f out: nvr trbld ldrs* **14/1**
0000 **8** ¾ **Almaty Express**[7] 6253 7-8-9 **75**........(b) DarryllHolland 8 67
(J R Weymes) *hld up towards rr: c wd st: pushed along wl over 1f out: n.d* **33/1**
1264 **9** shd **Dametime (IRE)**[11] 6167 3-8-12 **78**........(t) PatCosgrave 9 70
(Daniel Mark Loughnane, Ire) *prom: rdn over 1f out: wknd ins fnl f* **25/1**
0054 **10** 3 **Supermassive Muse (IRE)**[20] 5856 4-8-7 **73**........(p) GrahamGibbons 7 54
(E S McMahon) *prom: rdn over 1f out: wknd ins fnl f* **8/1**

60.48 secs (-1.82) **Going Correction** -0.225s/f (Stan) 10 Ran SP% **115.7**
Speed ratings (Par 105): **105,104,102,101,101 100,98,97,97,92**
toteswingers: 1&2 £4.30, 1&3 £14.60, 2&3 £12.90. CSF £27.31 CT £315.32 TOTE £3.20: £2.00, £1.90, £4.20; EX 32.00.
Owner Guy Reed **Bred** G Reed **Trained** Hambleton, N Yorks
■ Stewards' Enquiry : Francis Norton caution: careless riding

FOCUS
A competitive sprint on paper, but the winner comfortably outspeeded more exposed rivals. The runner-up to his recent form, sets the standard.

6460 HOTEL & CONFERENCING AT WOLVERHAMPTON H'CAP 1m 1f 103y(P)
8:20 (8:20) (Class 5) (0-75,75) 3-Y-0+ £3,238 (£963; £481; £240) Stalls Low

Form RPR
011 **1** **Denton (NZ)**[52] 4880 6-8-11 **66**........(t) PatCosgrave 5 73+
(J R Gask) *chsd ldr: led on bit over 2f out: hrd rdn fnl f: r.o* **6/4**[1]
5046 **2** nk **Quick Release (IRE)**[28] 5640 4-8-12 **72**........ MartinLane(5) 10 79
(D M Simcock) *hld up in tch: chsd wnr wl over 1f out: sn rdn: r.o ins fnl f* **9/1**[3]
5164 **3** 1¼ **Merrymadcap (IRE)**[17] 5964 7-9-5 **74**........ LPKeniry 6 78
(Matthew Salaman) *hld up in tch: rdn and edgd rt ins fnl f: nt qckn* **18/1**
4100 **4** 2¾ **Supercast (IRE)**[19] 5915 6-9-6 **75**........ LukeMorris 3 73
(N J Vaughan) *a.p: rdn over 1f out: sn edgd lft: one pce fnl f* **10/1**
3251 **5** shd **Tiger Dream**[7] 6250 4-8-9 **69**........(p) AmyRyan(5) 8 67
(K A Ryan) *hld up in mid-div: pushed along over 2f out: hdwy jst over 1f out: one pce ins fnl f* **5/1**[2]
0445 **6** 3¼ **Full Of Nature**[25] 5726 3-8-9 **68**........ JamesDoyle 2 59
(S Kirk) *dwlt: hld up in rr: rdn wl over 1f out: nvr nr ldrs* **20/1**
6600 **7** nk **Nevada Desert (IRE)**[7] 6250 9-8-8 **66**........ MichaelJStainton(3) 4 57
(R M Whitaker) *led: pushed along and hdd over 2f out: rdn and wknd over 1f out* **16/1**
2202 **8** nk **Benedict Spirit (IRE)**[125] 2499 4-9-3 **72**........ ChrisCatlin 9 62
(D Burchell) *hld up in mid-div: pushed along over 2f out: btn over 1f out* **12/1**
0505 **9** 1 **Tourist**[11] 6174 4-9-5 **74**........ GrahamGibbons 7 62
(D Shaw) *hld up in mid-div: pushed along wl over 1f out: rdn ins fnl f: n.d* **12/1**
1004 **10** 2¼ **Uncle Bertie**[129] 2362 4-8-8 **68**........ RossAtkinson(5) 11 51
(Tom Dascombe) *hld up in rr: pushed along over 3f out: rdn and struggling over 2f out* **12/1**
6-56 **11** nse **Boo**[32] 5503 7-9-5 **74**........(v) TGMcLaughlin 1 57
(J W Unett) *a in rr* **33/1**

1m 59.23s (-2.47) **Going Correction** -0.225s/f (Stan)
WFA 3 from 4yo+ 4lb 11 Ran SP% **117.7**
Speed ratings (Par 103): **101,100,99,97,97 94,93,93,92,90 90**
toteswingers: 1&2 £6.70, 1&3 £7.70, 2&3 £55.90. CSF £15.63 CT £180.23 TOTE £2.10: £1.80, £3.30, £3.60; EX 25.10.
Owner Horses First Racing Limited **Bred** Windsor Park Stud Ltd **Trained** Sutton Veny, Wilts

FOCUS
Just an ordinary gallop, making it hard to come from off the pace. The placed horses set the level in a muddling race.
Full Of Nature Official explanation: jockey said filly was slowly away

6461 LADBROKESCASINO.COM MAIDEN AUCTION STKS 1m 141y(P)
8:50 (8:51) (Class 6) 2-Y-0 £2,729 (£806; £403) Stalls Low

Form RPR
332 **1** **Venutius**[21] 5839 2-8-8 75........ GrahamGibbons 3 78+
(E S McMahon) *mde all: rdn over 1f out: eased cl home* **7/4**[1]
5226 **2** 1¾ **Flaming Miracle**[13] 6088 2-8-9 75........ LPKeniry 1 74
(A M Balding) *chsd wnr to 6f out: wnt 2nd again 3f out: rdn wl over 1f out: no imp* **7/4**[1]
04 **3** 7 **Magneto (IRE)**[22] 5811 2-8-9 65........ EdwardCreighton 5 60
(E J Creighton) *hld up in tch: rdn over 2f out: wknd wl over 1f out* **22/1**
03 **4** 2 **Golden Emperor (IRE)**[40] 5290 2-8-11 0........ PJMcDonald 7 57
(G A Swinbank) *hld up in tch: pushed along and wknd 2f out* **9/1**[3]
5 1¼ **Brink** 2-8-3 0........ LukeMorris 9 47
(T J Pitt) *s.i.s: hld up in rr: short-lived effrt on outside over 2f out* **40/1**
56 **6** 1 **Firehawk**[50] 4946 2-8-9 0 ow1........ PatCosgrave 6 51
(J G Portman) *prom chsd wnr 6f out tl rdn 3f out: sn wknd* **20/1**
7 1 **Xtreme (IRE)** 2-9-0 0........ NeilChalmers 4 54
(A Bailey) *s.i.s: a in rr* **33/1**
23 **8** 3¾ **Forshour**[53] 4847 2-8-9 0........ AlanMunro 8 46+
(E S McMahon) *a towards rr* **7/1**[2]
9 25 **Avon Called** 2-8-3 0........ PaulHanagan 2 —
(W M Brisbourne) *s.i.s: in rr: t.o fnl 5f* **33/1**

1m 48.29s (-2.21) **Going Correction** -0.225s/f (Stan) 9 Ran SP% **112.7**
Speed ratings (Par 93): **100,98,92,90,89 88,87,84,62**
toteswingers: 1&2 £1.20, 1&3 £4.50, 2&3 £12.90. CSF £4.13 TOTE £3.00: £1.50, £1.10, £4.20; EX 6.50.
Owner Mrs Fiona Williams **Bred** Mrs F S Williams **Trained** Lichfield, Staffs

FOCUS
A good pace, so the form should be reliable.

NOTEBOOK
Venutius, despite setting a good tempo, travelled well in front and found plenty off the turn. Though he had to be ridden out, he was never in danger of being caught and looks a useful juvenile at a realistic level. (op 13-8 tchd 15-8)
Flaming Miracle is rated 75, so he is capable of winning many a maiden and was unlucky to run into an above-average winner. Now winless in seven races, he can be placed to get off the mark. (op 15-8 tchd 2-1)
Magneto(IRE), keen to post, has looked better since being raised in trip, though this appeared to be stretching him a bit at present. He is not in the same league as the first two, so it was a creditable effort and a drop back to claimers would help. (op 25-1)
Golden Emperor(IRE) has done well enough in three maidens to suggest he can make his mark in nurseries. (tchd 8-1 and 10-1)
Brink fared best of the three newcomers. An 8,000gns half-sister to a 5-7f juvenile winner, she looks one for the longer term. (op 50-1)
Forshour had shown much more promise in his two previous races, one of them at this track, but at least he now has a handicap mark. (op 6-1 tchd 8-1)

6462 LADBROKESPOKER.COM H'CAP 1m 141y(P)
9:20 (9:20) (Class 4) (0-80,80) 3-Y-0+ **£5,046** (£1,510; £755; £377; £188) Stalls Low

Form RPR
0-50 **1** **Spate River**[28] 5640 4-9-6 **80**........ GeorgeBaker 8 93+
(C F Wall) *hld up: stdy hdwy 5f out: led jst over 1f out: rdn and r.o wl* **5/4**[1]
0000 **2** 1½ **Spinning**[20] 5887 6-9-1 **78**........(b) NeilBrown(3) 3 85
(T D Barron) *s.i.s: hld up in rr: rdn and struggling over 2f out: gd hdwy fnl f: nt trble wnr* **5/1**[2]
2655 **3** 2½ **Common Diva**[121] 2607 3-8-5 **74**........ MartinLane(5) 4 76
(A J McCabe) *chsd ldr 7f out: led over 2f out: rdn and hdd jst over 1f out: lost 2nd and no ex wl ins fnl f* **14/1**
5-60 **4** hd **Ektimaal**[27] 5665 6-9-6 **80**........ PaulHanagan 5 81
(E A L Dunlop) *hld up: pushed along and hdwy wl over 1f out: sn rdn: one pce ins fnl f* **11/1**
3000 **5** 6 **Kildare Sun (IRE)**[11] 6174 7-8-9 **69**........(p) GrahamGibbons 6 57
(J Mackie) *prom: pushed along over 2f out: rdn and wknd over 1f out* **18/1**
0635 **6** 1 **Perfect Citizen (USA)**[33] 5475 3-8-13 **77**........(p) AdamKirby 2 63
(W R Swinburn) *prom: rdn 5f out: wknd 4f out* **5/1**[2]
4630 **7** hd **Ultimate Respect (USA)**[10] 6178 3-8-5 **69**........(b[1]) RoystonFfrench 7 54
(M Johnston) *hld up towards rr: rdn over 3f out: sn struggling* **8/1**[3]
0100 **8** 6 **Glenridding**[14] 6072 5-9-3 **77**........(p) J-PGuillambert 1 49
(J G Given) *led: pushed along and hdd over 2f out: rdn and wknd over 1f out: eased fnl f* **9/1**

1m 47.22s (-3.28) **Going Correction** -0.225s/f (Stan)
WFA 3 from 4yo+ 4lb 8 Ran SP% **119.2**
Speed ratings (Par 105): **105,103,101,101,95 95,94,89**
toteswingers: 1&2 £9.20, 1&3 £11.30, 2&3 £11.50. CSF £8.22 CT £62.06 TOTE £2.10: £1.10, £2.40, £3.30; EX 11.40 Place 6: £306.22, Place 5: £54.31..
Owner Firman Webster Racing **Bred** Firman And Webster Bloodstock **Trained** Newmarket, Suffolk

FOCUS
A good gallop gave the hold-up horses a chance and a race to rate at face value with the runner-up having a good course record.
T/Plt: £1,299.40 to a £1 stake. Pool: £88,025.94. 49.45 winning tickets. T/Qpdt: £180.70 to a £1 stake. Pool: £10,514.93. 43.06 winning tickets. KH

6463 - 6466a (Foreign Racing) - See Raceform Interactive

6259 DUNDALK (A.W) (L-H)
Friday, October 2

OFFICIAL GOING: Standard

6467a DIAMOND STKS (GROUP 3) 1m 2f 150y(P)
8:30 (8:31) 3-Y-0+ £39,126 (£11,436; £5,417; £1,805)

RPR

1 **Mastercraftsman (IRE)**[27] 5688 3-9-2 125 JMurtagh 6 121+
(A P O'Brien, Ire) *trckd ldrs in mod 3rd: asked to cl over 2f out: led 1 1/2f out: kpt on strly fnl f to go clr: eased cl home* **2/9**[1]

2 *5* **Fiery Lad (IRE)**[27] 5685 4-9-2 109 KLatham 4 101+
(G M Lyons, Ire) *mid-div: mod 6th 1/2-way: rdn over 2f out: styd on to 3rd 1f out: 2nd ins fnl f: no ch w wnr* **9/1**[2]

3 *1 1/2* **Augustusthestrong (USA)**[7] 6264 3-8-11 95 (b) CO'Donoghue 2 99
(A P O'Brien, Ire) *chsd ldr in cl 2nd clr of field: rdn to ld 2f out: hdd 1 1/2f out: no ex in 2nd 1f out: lost 2nd ins fnl f* **25/1**

4 *1/2* **Man Of Iron (USA)**[26] 5704 3-8-11 101 JAHeffernan 3 98
(A P O'Brien, Ire) *hld up towards rr: sme hdwy in mod 7th 2f out: rdn into 5th 1f out: kpt on same pce fnl f* **33/1**

5 *3 1/2* **Lord Admiral (USA)**[27] 5688 8-9-2 108 (b) MJKinane 10 90
(Charles O'Brien, Ire) *mid-div: mod 8th 1/2-way: rdn into 5th over 2f out: no imp and kpt on same pce* **16/1**[3]

6 *1 1/2* **Wymering File (IRE)**[15] 6030 4-8-13 NGMcCullagh 11 84
(M J Grassick, Ire) *hld up towards rr: sme late hdwy in mod 8th 1f out: kpt on same pce fnl f* **66/1**

7 *nk* **Big Robert**[188] 1003 5-9-2 94 WJSupple 5 87
(P D Deegan, Ire) *chsd ldrs: mod 5th 1/2-way: rdn in 4th 2 1/2f out: no imp and kpt on one pce* **66/1**

8 *1 1/2* **Via Galilei (IRE)**[16] 6008 4-9-2 105 (t) KJManning 9 84
(J S Bolger, Ire) *led: rdn and hdd 2f out: no ex and wknd over 1f out* **33/1**

9 *1* **Cilium (IRE)**[22] 5798 3-8-8 88 WMLordan 7 80
(Andrew Oliver, Ire) *a towards rr* **66/1**

10 *shd* **Northgate (IRE)**[7] 6264 4-9-2 96 CDHayes 8 82
(Joseph G Murphy, Ire) *chsd ldrs: mod 4th 1/2-way: rdn 3f out: sn no ex and wknd over 2f out* **33/1**

11 *20* **Suailce (IRE)**[64] 4458 4-8-13 98 (b) PJSmullen 1 40
(D K Weld, Ire) *mid-div: mod 7th 1/2-way: rdn and wknd over 3f out: t.o* **25/1**

2m 12.18s (132.18)
WFA 3 from 4yo+ 6lb **11** Ran SP% **118.7**
CSF £2.34 TOTE £1.20: £1.02, £1.50, £4.10; DF 3.10.
Owner D Smith, Mrs J Magnier, M Tabor **Bred** Lynch Bages Ltd **Trained** Ballydoyle, Co Tipperary

FOCUS
A straightforward success for the favourite, and the form looks sound rated around the runner-up, fourth and sixth.

NOTEBOOK
Mastercraftsman(IRE) had an awful lot in hand here and he won accordingly in a race connections picked for him as a trial for the Breeders' Cup Classic. Held up in third place, he allowed the leaders, Via Galilei and Augustusthestrong, to race 12 lengths ahead of him leaving the back straight, but when asked to close early in the straight he did so with ease, hitting the front one and a half furlongs out before being allowed coast home. (op 1/4)
Fiery Lad(IRE), all but one of whose six wins have come at this track, had, like all of Mastercraftsman's rivals, a lot on his plate here. He acquitted himself well, making headway from 2f out and staying on to go second inside the final furlong without making any impression on the winner. (op 8/1)
Augustusthestrong(USA), runner-up here either side of a maiden win over 1m at the Listowel festival, would probably have won over the course and distance a week previously but for his rider losing his whip 2f out. A stablemate of the winner, he was a close second, and clear of the rest, until going to the front early in the straight. However, the winner picked him up in a hurry and, once headed one and a half furlongs out, he kept on at the same pace and just held on for third.
Man Of Iron(USA), winner of a handicap over the course and trip on his previous start, made headway from behind early in the straight and kept on inside the final furlong.
Lord Admiral(USA), over 13 lengths behind Mastercraftsman when they ran fifth and third respectively in the Irish Champion Stakes, made some progress early in the straight but never posed any sort of threat. (op 12/1)
Suailce(IRE), who finished tailed off, was reported to be "clinically abnormal" following veterinary examination. Official explanation: vet said filly was found to be clinically abnormal post race

6468 - 6469a (Foreign Racing) - See Raceform Interactive

5800 EPSOM (L-H)
Saturday, October 3

OFFICIAL GOING: Good to firm (good in home straight; overall 8.5; home straight: stands' side 8.4; far side 8.3)
Rail dolled out by up to 7yds from 6f pole to winning post, increasing distances by about 12yds.
Wind: Very strong, half against Weather: Cloudy

6470 BLUE SQUARE H'CAP 1m 2f 18y
2:05 (2:07) (Class 3) (0-95,92) 3-Y-0+ £9,714 (£2,890; £1,444; £721) Stalls Low

Form RPR

5131 1 **Kaleo**[18] 5963 5-8-7 75 HayleyTurner 11 84
(S Dow) *mde virtually all: kicked 3l clr 2f out: rdn out* **7/2**[1]

4665 2 *1 3/4* **Hunterview**[9] 6229 3-8-11 84 (b) RichardMullen 9 89
(M A Jarvis) *hld up in 4th: rdn over 2f out: hd high but prog to chse wnr over 1f out: styd on but unable to chal* **14/1**

3423 3 *1 1/2* **Can Can Star**[24] 5781 6-8-7 82 DebraEngland(7) 1 84
(A W Carroll) *trckd ldrs: 5th st: gng strly over 2f out: rdn to dispute 2nd over 1f out: nt qckn* **10/1**

5000 4 *hd* **King Charles**[16] 6013 5-9-10 92 (b[1]) TGMcLaughlin 3 94
(E A L Dunlop) *hld up in 6th: rdn over 2f out: sme prog over 1f out: kpt on to press for 3rd nr fin* **14/1**

125 5 *2 1/4* **Jo'Burg (USA)**[51] 4930 5-8-5 78 MartinLane(5) 4 75
(Lady Herries) *dwlt: hld up in 7th: pushed along ent st: no prog tl styd on fr over 1f out: n.d* **13/2**

4633 6 *1* **Red Jade**[17] 6002 4-9-1 83 TonyHamilton 2 78
(R A Fahey) *chsd ldng pair: rdn on inner to dispute 2nd wl over 1f out: sn wknd* **4/1**[2]

0-50 7 *5* **Dani's Girl (IRE)**[20] 5912 6-8-11 79 IanMongan 7 64
(P M Phelan) *chsd wnr to over 1f out: wknd rapidly* **50/1**

5040 8 *nk* **Bound By Honour (SAF)**[14] 6106 6-9-4 91 (b) JamieJones(5) 8 76
(G L Moore) *hld up in 8th: rdn 3f out: no prog and sn struggling* **13/2**

0321 9 *6* **Elna Bright**[6] 6307 4-9-5 90 6ex JackMitchell(3) 6 63
(B R Johnson) *hld up in last: losing tch ent st: hanging 3f out: sn bhd and no ch* **7/1**

3311 10 *1/2* **Potentiale (IRE)**[24] 5772 5-9-0 82 (p) EddieAhern 10 54
(J W Hills) *a in last pair: 9th st: sn wknd and bhd* **5/1**[3]

2m 7.94s (-1.76) **Going Correction** 0.0s/f (Good)
WFA 3 from 4yo+ 5lb **10** Ran SP% **122.4**
Speed ratings (Par 107): **107,105,104,104,102 101,97,97,92,92**
toteswingers: 1&2 £12.90, 1&3 £17.70, 2&3 £34.10. CSF £56.86 CT £463.44 TOTE £5.20: £1.80, £4.50, £3.90; EX 78.40 Trifecta £208.60 Pool: £423.03 - 1.50 winning units..
Owner John Robinson and Derek Stubbs **Bred** Gestut Hof Ittlingen **Trained** Epsom, Surrey

FOCUS
A windy day began with a decent handicap, the top weight being rated 92. It looked competitive on paper, but the winner made a mockery of any preconceptions about that. The placed horses are rated close to their recent marks.

NOTEBOOK
Kaleo had made all to land claimers at Folkestone and over this course and distance on two of his last three starts, but he had been beaten behind Potentiale in between. He was not weighted to ensure an overturning of that form, but he did so comprehensively after being allowed an easy time in front. He had a healthy advantage coming down the hill and never looking likely to be caught. (op 5-1 tchd 11-2)
Hunterview, who has been dropping down the ratings recently after a series of beaten efforts, stayed on strongly towards the finish and, although he was unable to get near the winner, did enough to suggest he is now on a fair mark. (tchd 16-1)
Can Can Star is largely consistent and appeared to run his race again, figuring towards the front of the group chasing the all-the-way winner from the outset and battling on bravely in the closing stages. (tchd 9-1 and 11-1)
King Charles, successful over this trip at Newbury in July, was fitted with first-time blinkers. He ran better in them than he had at Ayr on his previous run, but they did not improve him enough to indicate he is likely to score again in the immediate future. (tchd 12-1)
Elna Bright arrived bang in form, having won a 1m handicap at Ascot just six days previously, but a 6lb penalty made her task a tough one in this seemingly more competitive contest over a longer trip. She never seemed likely to overcome her impost, struggling from the top of the hill and perhaps not handling this track's idiosyncratic undulations. Official explanation: trainer said gelding was unsuited by the track (op 6-1 tchd 11-2)
Potentiale(IRE) lined up looking for a hat-trick, after wins at Goodwood and over this course and distance, but was racing from a 5lb higher mark than for the second of those recent victories. Even allowing for the extra weight, though, this was a disappointing performance, as, after being held up as usual, he failed to pick up at all when asked. (op 6-1)

6471 BLUE SQUARE CASINO NURSERY 7f
2:35 (2:35) (Class 3) (0-90,85) 2-Y-0 £7,771 (£2,312; £1,155; £577) Stalls Low

Form RPR

510 1 **Lord Aeryn (IRE)**[46] 5136 2-7-13 68 MartinLane(5) 1 72
(R A Fahey) *cl up: 3rd st: led on inner over 2f out: hrd pressed after: jst hld on* **11/4**[2]

051 2 *shd* **Constant Contact**[33] 5505 2-9-7 85 DavidProbert 6 89
(A M Balding) *led: rdn and hdd over 2f out: pressed wnr after w tail swishing: clsng at fin: jst failed* **15/8**[1]

6210 3 *1* **Trailblazing**[23] 5795 2-9-7 85 AndrewElliott 4 86
(M Johnston) *chsd ldr to over 3f out: nt qckn over 2f out: hld after: hung lft but kpt on fnl f* **17/2**[3]

3163 4 *hd* **Universal Circus**[15] 6063 2-9-1 79 SamHitchcott 7 80
(M R Channon) *hld up in 4th: rdn 3f out: no imp tl styd on ins fnl f* **10/1**

0134 5 *1 3/4* **Kurtanella**[20] 5913 2-9-7 85 EddieAhern 5 81
(R Hannon) *hld up in last but cl up: nt qckn over 2f out: kpt on ins fnl f as ldrs tired* **14/1**

01 6 *nk* **Dylanesque**[18] 5969 2-9-0 78 JimCrowley 2 79+
(M A Jarvis) *dwlt: slipped after 1f: hld up in 5th: hanging over 2f out: nt pushed but lost no grnd on rivals after: squeezed out nr fin* **11/4**[2]

1m 24.71s (1.41) **Going Correction** 0.0s/f (Good) **6** Ran SP% **114.4**
Speed ratings (Par 99): **91,90,89,89,87 87**
toteswingers: 1&2 £1.40, 1&3 £5.30, 2&3 £3.70. CSF £8.60 TOTE £3.70: £2.10, £1.80; EX 6.00.
Owner Mrs H Steel **Bred** Woodhouse Syndicate **Trained** Musley Bank, N Yorks

FOCUS
A decent nursery, featuring some experienced juvenile handicappers and a clutch of lightly raced potential improvers.

NOTEBOOK
Lord Aeryn(IRE), successful in a 6f Ayr maiden in July and not beaten far in a decent nursery at York the following month, promised to stay this longer distance. He needed too with a strong wind blowing into the runners' faces in the home straight, and, after making progress from midfield to engage in a dour battle with the second over the final 2f, he just prevailed. (op 100-30 tchd 7-2 in a place)
Constant Contact had shown improved form when breaking his duck over this course and distance on his latest start and made his handicap debut from what looked a reasonable mark. He ran a cracker in defeat, making much of the running and then rallying when headed, but will probably pay the price when the Handicapper assesses this contest. (tchd 2-1)
Trailblazing, snug winner of a maiden at Ascot in July, was attempting to bounce back after finishing last, albeit on unfavourable terms, in a valuable sales race at Doncaster. He showed that latest run was not his form, but could not quite cope with the first two on these terms. (op 10-1 tchd 11-1)
Universal Circus had a course-and-distance win to her credit, but needed to step up on her latest third-placed effort in order to take this from a rating of 79 and was unable to do so. (op 11-1)
Kurtanella seemed handicapped right up to her best and, after disappointing slightly at Goodwood on her latest outing, she appeared to have a tough task under top weight. It proved beyond her. (tchd 12-1)
Dylanesque, with just two races under her belt, seemed to have the potential to improve. The Handicapper had taken no chances with her after her narrow maiden win at Yarmouth though, and on this evidence, she is overrated, although she slipped in the early stages which might have had an effect. Official explanation: trainer's rep said filly was unsuited by the track (tchd 5-2 and 3-1)

6472 BLUE SQUARE SP CONDITIONS STKS 1m 114y
3:10 (3:10) (Class 3) 2-Y-0 £7,477 (£2,239; £1,119; £560; £279) Stalls Low

Form RPR

1 1 **Zeitoper**[17] 5993 2-8-11 0 AhmedAjtebi(3) 6 98
(Saeed Bin Suroor) *wnt rt s: hld up: wnt 3rd st and gng easily: pressed ldr over 2f out: shkn up to ld over 1f out: readily* **2/1**[1]

4341 2 *1 1/2* **Raine's Cross**[30] 5603 2-9-0 95 JimCrowley 4 95
(P Winkworth) *pressed ldr: led over 2f out: rdn and hdd over 1f out: one pce* **4/1**

1 3 *nk* **Layline (IRE)**[29] 5627 2-8-8 0 JackMitchell(3) 2 92+
(R M Beckett) *dwlt: nvr gng fluently in last: rdn to go 3rd 2f out: styd on u.p and nrly snatched 2nd* **3/1**[3]

3311 4 15 **Mingun Bell (USA)**[39] 5324 2-9-0 93 EddieAhern 3 63
(H R A Cecil) *led to over 2f out: wknd rapidly* 5/2[2]
10 5 23 **Ishtar Gate (USA)**[66] 4418 2-9-0 90 HayleyTurner 1 14
(P F I Cole) *chsd ldng pair tl wknd ent st: t.o* 12/1
1m 44.69s (-1.41) **Going Correction** 0.0s/f (Good) 5 Ran SP% 114.6
Speed ratings (Par 99): **106,104,104,91,70**
toteswingers: 1&2 £9.10. CSF £10.78 TOTE £3.10: £1.60, £2.40; EX 15.40.
Owner Godolphin **Bred** Darley **Trained** Newmarket, Suffolk

NOTEBOOK
Zeitoper had scored by just a nose on his debut at Sandown 17 days earlier and needed to step up on that form to take this much tougher contest. He did so convincingly, however, tracking the leaders from the start and quickly getting the better of the runner-up when they locked horns at the 2f pole. Beautifully bred, as a brother to the smart Eastern Anthem he should stay at least 1m2f as a three-year-old.It to place (op 3-1)
Raine's Cross lined up with the highest official rating, his 95 mark being earned at Listed level, and had proved his wellbeing with a last-time-out success at Salisbury. He was always towards the head of affairs and looks a sound guide to the form. (op 5-2)
Layline(IRE), the only gelding in the line-up and receiving 3lb from all his rivals, was attempting to follow up a Chepstow debut victory. He still looked green here, though, racing on and off the bridle and, not cornering entirely convincingly, can probably be rated slightly better than the bare form indicates. (op 5-1 tchd 11-4)
Mingun Bell(USA) had been steadily improving, romping to victory over 1m at Southwell on his latest start, but faced a very different test on this undulating turf course. He set out to make all the running, but came under the pump 2f from home and faded when the first three really got going. Official explanation: vet said colt had lost a front shoe (op 11-4)
Ishtar Gate(USA), winner of a Leicester maiden in June with Mingun Bell back in third, appeared to have had his limitations exposed when beaten more than eight lengths in a Goodwood Group 2 event second time out. He was again comprehensively outpointed and, unless his rating drops markedly, he will be difficult to place. (op 9-1 tchd 17-2)

6473 BLUE SQUARE APPRENTICES' DERBY H'CAP 1m 4f 10y
3:45 (3:46) (Class 4) (0-80,80) 3-Y-O+ £6,476 (£1,927; £963; £481) Stalls Centre

Form RPR
4341 1 **Worth A King'S**[16] 6027 3-9-6 80 (v) Louis-PhilippeBeuzelin 7 91
(Sir Michael Stoute) *led after 1f tl after 4f: trckd ldng pair after: clsd to ld again wl over 1f out: styd on wl* 11/2[3]
5104 2 2 **Ethics Girl (IRE)**[26] 5725 3-9-0 74 MarcHalford 8 82
(John Berry) *hld up in rr: 6th st and off the pce: prog wl over 2f out: rdn to go 2nd ent fnl f: styd on but no imp* 17/2
0303 3 3 ¾ **Tilos Gem (IRE)**[15] 6060 3-9-2 76 DavidProbert 3 78
(M Johnston) *disp ld 1f: w ldr again after 4f: upsides 2f out: chsd wnr wl over 1f out tl ent fnl f: fdd* 8/1
0232 4 ½ **Free Tussy (ARG)**[3] 6392 5-8-11 67 (bt) RossAtkinson(3) 5 68
(G L Moore) *s.s: hld up in rr: 8th st and off the pce: drvn over 2f out: styd on fr over 1f out: nrst fin* 10/3[1]
1135 5 5 **Turjuman (USA)**[20] 5912 4-8-13 66 RussellKennemore 9 59
(W J Musson) *disp ld 1f: w ldr tl ld again after 4f: increased the pce fr 1/2-way: hdd & wknd wl over 1f out* 17/2
6000 6 5 **Sir Boss (IRE)**[15] 6059 4-9-5 77 RosieJessop(5) 2 62
(D E Cantillon) *hld up in last pair: last st and outpcd: effrt and modest prog 3f out: no imp on ldrs 2f out: fdd* 14/1
1313 7 7 **Epsom Salts**[14] 6115 4-9-12 79 JackMitchell 1 53
(P M Phelan) *dwlt: a in rr: shkn up over 7f out: 7th and nt gng wl st: sn no ch* 7/2[2]
2444 8 ½ **Locum**[8] 6244 4-8-7 65 oh1 SimonPearce(5) 6 38
(M H Tompkins) *t.k.h early: sn restrained bhd ldrs: 5th st: wknd 3f out* 9/1
5056 9 8 **Taste The Wine (IRE)**[36] 5382 3-8-5 65 oh1 WilliamCarson 4 25
(J S Moore) *chsd ldrs: 4th and u.p st: sn wknd: eased whn no ch fnl f* 14/1
2m 39.54s (0.64) **Going Correction** 0.0s/f (Good)
WFA 3 from 4yo+ 7lb 9 Ran SP% 116.2
Speed ratings (Par 105): **97,95,93,92,89 86,81,81,75**
toteswingers: 1&2 £48.40, 1&3 £11.80, 2&3 £15.70. CSF £51.63 CT £374.07 TOTE £7.70: £2.00, £2.70, £2.30; EX 61.50.
Owner Mrs Denis Haynes **Bred** Wretham Stud **Trained** Newmarket, Suffolk
FOCUS
A competitive handicap run at a decent gallop and sound form rated through the runner-up.

6474 BLUE SQUARE EXCLUSIVE LIVE SHOWS H'CAP 1m 114y
4:20 (4:21) (Class 3) (0-90,90) 3-Y-O £7,771 (£2,312; £1,155; £577) Stalls Low

Form RPR
3033 1 **Roar Of Applause**[8] 6243 3-8-8 80 (b) EddieAhern 6 91
(B J Meehan) *sltly hmpd s: hld up: 6th st: smooth prog over 2f out: led 1f out: shkn up and sn in command* 9/2[2]
1632 2 1 ¾ **Sovereign Remedy (USA)**[70] 4316 3-9-1 90 AhmedAjtebi(3) 8 97
(Saeed Bin Suroor) *trckd ldng trio: n.m.r whn cl up over 2f out: rdn to ld over 1f out: hdd and outpcd fnl f* 11/10[1]
0006 3 ½ **Tudor Key (IRE)**[14] 6117 3-8-11 83 JimCrowley 5 89
(Mrs A J Perrett) *trckd ldr: led over 2f out to over 1f out: one pce* 12/1
140 4 nk **Mutawarath (IRE)**[17] 5986 3-8-10 82 HayleyTurner 3 87
(W J Haggas) *trckd ldng pair: effrt against rail over 2f out and cl up: nt qckn over 1f out: one pce after* 6/1[3]
2156 5 5 **Eastern Warrior**[57] 4741 3-7-13 78 ow2 KierenFox(7) 7 72
(J W Hills) *awkward s: racd wd: pressed ldrs: cl 5th st: hanging and wknd over 1f out* 20/1
510 6 ¾ **Amazing Tiger (GER)**[24] 5781 3-8-5 77 AndrewElliott 4 69
(M Johnston) *led to over 2f out: wknd over 1f out* 13/2
6014 7 1 **Chadwell Spring (IRE)**[16] 6023 3-8-1 76 oh5 Louis-PhilippeBeuzelin(3) 2 65
(Miss J Feilden) *hld up: slipped downhill 4f out: last st and rdn: struggling after* 12/1
1m 45.74s (-0.36) **Going Correction** 0.0s/f (Good) 7 Ran SP% 113.6
Speed ratings (Par 105): **101,99,99,98,94 93,92**
toteswingers: 1&2 £1.60, 1&3 £5.80, 2&3 £3.70. CSF £9.73 CT £53.04 TOTE £5.00: £2.30, £1.50; EX 7.50.
Owner Raymond Tooth **Bred** Southcourt Stud **Trained** Manton, Wilts
FOCUS
A decent handicap and a cosy winner. The form looks sound rated around those in the frame behind the winner.
NOTEBOOK
Roar Of Applause, a good third over this course and distance in August, had posted sound efforts since, including another third at Ascot only eight days before this. He does not always produce a great deal when let down but here, beautifully ridden, he was encouraged to creep into contention, going easily, before quickening between rivals and staying on for a cosy success. (op 5-1 tchd 4-1)
Sovereign Remedy(USA), who had made the first three in decent handicaps at Newmarket in July, was returning from a 70-day layoff. He looked fit enough and his stable is in cracking form, but he was unable to quicken when the winner went past him 1f out. (op 6-4 tchd 13-8 in places)
Tudor Key(IRE), whose official mark has dropped from a summer high in the 90s, is not entirely consistent, but he posted one of his better recent performances, figuring prominently from the start and keeping on in the closing stages. (op 10-1)
Mutawarath(IRE) had been progressive early in the season, breaking his duck at York in June, but his two subsequent attempts in handicaps had suggested a mark in the 80s flattered him slightly. That again looked the case as he tried hard but was unable to cope with the first three. (op 13-2)
Eastern Warrior is not straightforward and did his chance no good by cocking his jaw shortly after the start. He made some late progress, but was never in a position to mount a serious challenge. (op 14-1)
Amazing Tiger(GER), comfortable winner of a 1m Musselburgh maiden in June, had flopped when trying 1m4f on Polytrack next time out and ran moderately again here, leading deep into the home straight but producing only one pace after being headed. (op 5-1 tchd 7-1)
Chadwell Spring(IRE), a course-and-distance winner in mid-September, was encountering a better grade here and racing from 5lb out of the handicap. He lost his footing at the top of the hill and, after that incident, was unable to mount a challenge. Official explanation: jockey said filly lost its action 4f out (tchd 14-1)

6475 BLUE SQUARE POKER MAIDEN STKS 1m 2f 18y
4:55 (4:57) (Class 5) 3-Y-O £3,885 (£1,156; £577; £288) Stalls Low

Form RPR
2 1 **Feathered Crown (FR)**[16] 6022 3-9-3 0 HayleyTurner 3 80
(H R A Cecil) *pressed ldr: led 3f out: sn jnd and rdn: gained narrow advantage fnl f: hld on wl* 5/2[1]
35 2 nk **Deportment**[50] 4991 3-8-12 0 EddieAhern 5 74+
(J R Fanshawe) *in tch: 5th and pushed along st: rdn and kpt on fr over 2f out: clsd fnl f: tk 2nd last stride* 4/1
2332 3 hd **Mefraas (IRE)**[11] 6190 3-9-3 75 TGMcLaughlin 6 79
(E A L Dunlop) *trckd ldng pair: jnd wnr over 2f out: stl upsides jst over 1f out: nt qckn and hld fnl f: lost 2nd last stride* 11/4[2]
-334 4 1 ½ **Ebiayn (FR)**[56] 4798 3-9-0 80 JackMitchell(3) 2 76
(M A Jarvis) *trckd ldrs: 4th st: outpcd over 2f out: kpt on fr over 1f out: unable to chal* 7/2[3]
5 13 **Dubai Creek (IRE)** 3-9-3 0 JimCrowley 7 50+
(M Johnston) *s.s: mostly in last pair: in tch tl over 3f out: sn wknd* 8/1
0446 6 7 **Millharbour (IRE)**[14] 6124 3-9-3 61 (b[1]) PaulEddery 1 36
(B W Hills) *led to 3f out: wknd v rapidly: t.o* 33/1
7 11 **Uncle Keef (IRE)** 3-9-3 0 RichardMullen 4 14+
(M P Tregoning) *s.s: v green in last and detached to 6f out: jst in tch: sn wknd: t.o* 14/1
2m 9.59s (-0.11) **Going Correction** 0.0s/f (Good) 7 Ran SP% 118.2
Speed ratings (Par 101): **100,99,99,98,88 82,73**
toteswingers: 1&2 £3.50, 1&3 £2.00, 2&3 £2.20. CSF £13.66 TOTE £3.40: £2.30, £2.60; EX 19.90.
Owner H E Sheikh Sultan Bin Khalifa Al Nahyan **Bred** Sheikh Sultan Bin Khalifa Al Nayan **Trained** Newmarket, Suffolk
FOCUS
Just an ordinary maiden, but made a little more interesting by some well-bred newcomers. The third is a sound guide on recent form.

6476 BLUE SQUARE GAMES H'CAP 7f
5:30 (5:30) (Class 4) (0-85,84) 3-Y-O+ £6,476 (£1,927; £963; £481) Stalls Low

Form RPR
6406 1 **Lindoro**[28] 5665 4-9-3 83 JackMitchell(3) 13 93
(W R Swinburn) *awkward s: hld up wl off the pce: 10th st: stdy prog on outer fr 2f out: clsd to ld 150yds out: hung rt but sn clr* 8/1
4431 2 2 **Leadenhall Lass (IRE)**[23] 5805 3-8-0 72 (v) KierenFox(7) 6 76
(P M Phelan) *hld up bhd ldrs: 6th st: prog to ld 2f out: idled in front: hdd and outpcd last 150yds* 17/2
-064 3 1 **Frognal (IRE)**[14] 6112 3-9-5 84 EddieAhern 7 88+
(B J Meehan) *hld up off the pce: 8th st: prog over 2f out: disp 2nd jst over 1f out: 3rd and hld whn hmpd last 100yds* 8/1
02 4 1 **Space Station**[18] 5965 3-8-2 70 Louis-PhilippeBeuzelin(3) 5 68
(S Dow) *chsd ldrs: 7th st: hrd rdn fr 3f out: grad clsd on ldrs but nvr cl enough to chal* 7/1[3]
2312 5 ¾ **Hi Shinko**[24] 5774 3-8-13 78 TGMcLaughlin 10 74
(B R Millman) *led at fast pce: edgd rt and hdd 2f out: grad fdd* 5/1[1]
0115 6 ½ **Indy Driver**[17] 6004 4-9-0 77 (p) HayleyTurner 8 73+
(J R Fanshawe) *hld up: sn wl bhd: 11th and wl off the pce st: rdn 3f out: sme prog fr over 2f out: styd on fnl f: no ch* 6/1[2]
2106 7 3 ¼ **My Learned Friend (IRE)**[44] 5182 5-8-12 75 (v[1]) DavidProbert 3 62
(A M Balding) *prom: 3rd st: chsd ldr 3f out to over 2f out: wknd jst over 1f out* 8/1
4502 8 ½ **King Columbo (IRE)**[17] 6004 4-8-6 72 WilliamCarson(3) 9 58
(Miss J Feilden) *prom: 4th st: sing to lose pl whn sltly hmpd 2f out: fdd* 6/1[2]
6150 9 2 **Koraleva Tectona (IRE)**[27] 5697 4-9-0 77 PaulEddery 4 57
(Pat Eddery) *hld up: hmpd and snatched up after 2f: 9th st: no prog u.p over 2f out* 15/2
0160 10 7 **Tikka Masala (IRE)**[98] 3408 3-8-7 72 (t) RichardSmith 11 32
(Tom Dascombe) *s.v.s and lost all ch: last and wl bhd st* 33/1
0601 11 2 **Ginobili (IRE)**[7] 6293 3-8-10 75 (b) StephenCarson 1 30
(Andrew Reid) *plld hrd: hld up but sn trckd ldrs: 5th st and taken towards nr side rail: sn btn* 20/1
0610 12 16 **Cordell (IRE)**[44] 5190 4-8-9 72 RichardMullen 12 —
(R Ingram) *chsd ldr to 3f out: wknd rapidly: t.o* 20/1
1m 23.61s (0.31) **Going Correction** 0.0s/f (Good)
WFA 3 from 4yo+ 2lb 12 Ran SP% 125.8
Speed ratings (Par 105): **98,95,94,93,92 92,88,87,85,77 75,56**
toteswingers: 1&2 £20.80, 1&3 £19.40, 2&3 £21.60. CSF £77.14 CT £587.55 TOTE £11.00: £2.50, £3.60, £3.70; EX 173.80 Place 6: £52.10, Place 5: £16.62..
Owner P W Harris **Bred** Pigeon House Stud **Trained** Aldbury, Herts
■ Stewards' Enquiry : Jack Mitchell three-day ban: careless riding (Oct 18-20)
T G McLaughlin one-day ban: careless riding (Oct 18)
FOCUS
A run-of-the-mill handicap, with the top weight rated 84, but plenty could be given a chance and several had solid course form. The winner is the best guide to the level.
Space Station Official explanation: jockey said gelding became unbalanced on home turn
Ginobili(IRE) Official explanation: jockey said gelding ran too free and hung right
T/Plt: £106.30 to a £1 stake. Pool: £64,423.38. 442.18 winning tickets. T/Qpdt: £22.20 to a £1 stake. Pool: £3,227.70. 107.20 winning tickets. JN

6447 NEWMARKET (R-H)

Saturday, October 3

OFFICIAL GOING: Good to firm (8.1)

Wind: Strong across Weather: Overcast

6477 TATTERSALLS TIMEFORM FILLIES' 800 7f

1:50 (1:51) (Class 2) 2-Y-O

£433,360 (£177,280; £78,880; £39,360; £19,680; £7,840) **Stalls** High

Form				RPR
1213	**1**		**Lillie Langtry (IRE)**[34] 5488 2-9-0 0 ... JMurtagh 7 (A P O'Brien, Ire) *hld up: hdwy over 2f out: swtchd lft over 1f out: shkn up to ld ins fnl f: r.o wl* **8/11**[1]	99+
0532	**2**	*2 1/4*	**Dubawi Heights**[8] 6241 2-9-0 99 ... RyanMoore 15 (S A Callaghan, U.S.A) *led 1f: chsd ldr tl led again over 1f out: rdn and hdd ins fnl f: styd on same pce* **4/1**[2]	90
3310	**3**	*1 3/4*	**Waveband**[15] 6064 2-9-0 75 ... RoystonFfrench 16 (M Johnston) *chsd ldr tl led after 1f: rdn and hdd over 1f out: no ex ins fnl f* **66/1**	86
52	**4**	*1*	**Pink Symphony**[36] 5398 2-9-0 0 ... MartinDwyer 2 (P F I Cole) *hld up: hdwy 1/2-way: rdn over 1f out: hung rt and styd on same pce fnl f* **18/1**	84+
4043	**5**	*1/2*	**Jira**[15] 6064 2-9-0 100 ... NCallan 4 (C E Brittain) *prom: rdn over 1f out: no ex ins fnl f* **10/1**[3]	82+
10	**6**	*1 1/4*	**Siyaadah**[35] 5427 2-9-0 0 ... TedDurcan 13 (Saeed Bin Suroor) *chsd ldrs: rdn over 2f out: styd on same pce appr fnl f* **16/1**	79
0015	**7**	*1*	**Cracking Lass (IRE)**[15] 6064 2-9-0 79 ... PaulHanagan 1 (R A Fahey) *hld up: hdwy u.p over 1f out: nt rch ldrs* **40/1**	77+
0	**8**	*2 1/4*	**Contredanse (IRE)**[14] 6108 2-9-0 0 ... JimmyFortune 5 (B J Meehan) *mid-div: rdn over 2f out: nt trble ldrs* **40/1**	71+
	9	*2 3/4*	**Footsie (IRE)** 2-9-0 0 ... SebSanders 3 (J G Given) *dwlt: sn pushed along in rr: nvr nrr* **100/1**	64+
	10	*1/2*	**Sunarise (IRE)** 2-9-0 0 ... RichardHughes 12 (R Hannon) *s.s: hdwy over 5f out: lost pl 1/2-way: wknd over 2f out* **33/1**	63
2	**11**	*1/2*	**Sing Sweetly**[12] 6163 2-9-0 0 ... KFallon 9 (G A Butler) *dwlt: hld up: nt clr run 1/2-way: sn pushed along: n.d* **16/1**	62
340	**12**	*2*	**Iptkaar (USA)**[15] 6064 2-9-0 75 ... JoeFanning 11 (C E Brittain) *prom: rdn 1/2-way: wknd over 2f out* **33/1**	57
	13	*hd*	**Song To The Moon (IRE)** 2-9-0 0 ... WilliamBuick 6 (A M Balding) *sn pushed along: a in rr* **100/1**	56
40	**14**	*14*	**Al Joza**[15] 6062 2-9-0 0 ... ChrisCatlin 10 (C E Brittain) *chsd ldrs tl rdn and wknd over 2f out* **100/1**	21

1m 23.26s (-2.14) **Going Correction** -0.175s/f (Firm) **14** Ran SP% **117.8**

Speed ratings (Par 98): **105,102,100,99,98 97,96,93,90,89 89,87,86,70**

toteswingers: 1&2 £1.60, 1&3 £17.90, 2&3 £43.20. CSF £3.21 TOTE £1.80: £1.10, £1.50, £17.90; EX 4.40 Trifecta £204.50 Pool: £74.10 - 2.80 winning units..

Owner M Tabor, D Smith & Mrs John Magnier **Bred** K B Lynch **Trained** Ballydoyle, Co Tipperary

FOCUS

With no overnight rain, 4mm of water had been applied to the last six furlongs to ease the ground. However, a strong crosswind had caused conditions to dry out. The consensus amongst the jockeys was that the going was pretty fast but safe. Although the initial running of this valuable sales race in 2008 was won by the ill-fated Tiger Eye, it threw up a number of subsequent winners, including the Group 2 winner The Miniver Rose and several Listed winners. This looked to concern just three on previous form, and it worked out more or less that way. The seventh helps set the level of the form.

NOTEBOOK

Lillie Langtry(IRE), the form horse having been a Group 2 winner over 7f on easy ground and third in Moyglare, had also proved she handles fast ground and was sent off at odds on. Settled in the pack, she still had a bit to do running into the Dip, but found plenty up the hill to sweep past her market rival and score easily in the end. The winner's price for the 1000 Guineas was trimmed slightly to 7-1, although 10-1 is available in some places, and she looks worthy of her taking her chance, although appears to have a bit to find to match the Cheveley Park winner Special Duty. (tchd 4-5 and 5-6 in a place)

Dubawi Heights, third in Lowther and runner-up to Shamandar in Ascot fillies' sales race, was taking a slight step up in trip. After leading early, she settled just behind the leader and then went on again running into the Dip. For a few moments it looked as though she would hold on, but the winner swept past up the hill and she could not respond. She has already earned black type and has picked up more than three times her yearling price, so owes connections nothing; the only thing missing is a victory. She is in the December sales, but could possibly go with her trainer when he moves to the USA. (op 9-2)

Waveband, the winner of a 5f maiden on Polytrack and placed over 6f, is rated just 75 so had a lot to find with the principals. She soon showed in front and stuck on well to reverse form with a couple of these from a previous sales race over 6f here. (tchd 80-1)

Pink Symphony ◆ had run well on her debut at Goodwood before being touched off on the July course next time on easy ground. Tackling a fast surface for the first time, she ran creditably as she had to race on the outside of her field throughout, and this well-bred filly can pick up a maiden before long. (op 16-1 tchd 20-1)

Jira, a Listed winner in July who had run creditably in Group and Listed company since, had been well beaten on her only previous try at 7f and had a bit to find with today's runner-up on a line through Shamandar. She showed up until fading in the closing stages as if the trip was beyond her. (op 14-1 tchd 9-1)

Siyaadah, the winner of 7f maiden on her debut, had finished last in an ordinary looking Group 3 since. She showed up early, but was under pressure and looked to be fading over a quarter of a mile from home, before staying on again.

Cracking Lass(IRE), who stayed on when it was all too late in a sales race over 6f, appreciated the step back up in trip, keeping on late, but never landed a blow. It was still a creditable effort.

Contredanse(IRE) showed some promise on this second start and should sdo better in time. (op 33-1)

Footsie(IRE) showed signs of ability without playing anything other than a minor role.

6478 TATTERSALLS TIMEFORM MILLION 7f

2:25 (2:28) (Class 2) 2-Y-O

£541,700 (£221,600; £98,600; £49,200; £24,600; £9,800) **Stalls** High

Form				RPR
02	**1**		**Oasis Dancer**[10] 6199 2-9-3 0 ... SebSanders 22 (R M Beckett) *racd far side: hld up in tch: rdn to ld ins fnl f: r.o* **66/1**	95
6510	**2**	*nk*	**Kona Coast**[15] 6064 2-9-3 77 ... (p) JimmyFortune 20 (J H M Gosden) *racd far side: trckd ldrs: led that gp over 1f out: rdn and hdd whn rdr had whip knocked out of hand ins fnl f: r.o: 2nd of 9 in gp* **50/1**	94
1152	**3**	*hd*	**Take Ten**[15] 6064 2-9-3 92 ... RyanMoore 17 (M Johnston) *racd far side: hld up in tch: rdn and ev ch fr over 1f out: r.o: 3rd of 9 in gp* **15/2**[3]	94
2100	**4**	*4*	**Lowdown (IRE)**[15] 6064 2-9-3 90 ... RoystonFfrench 14 (M Johnston) *racd far side: hld up: pushed along 1/2-way: hdwy over 1f out: nt rch ldrs: 4th of 9 in gp* **66/1**	84
116	**5**	*1*	**Alfred Nobel (IRE)**[21] 5892 2-9-3 0 ... JMurtagh 3 (A P O'Brien, Ire) *racd stands' side: hld up: hdwy over 2f out: nt clr run and swtchd rt over 1f out: led that gp ins fnl f: r.o: no ch w far side: 1st of 13 in gp* **9/2**[2]	93+
010	**6**	*nk*	**Magnus Thrax (USA)**[15] 6064 2-9-3 81 ... RichardHughes 18 (R Hannon) *racd far side: trckd ldrs: rdn over 1f out: no ex fnl f: 5th of 9 in gp* **28/1**	81
511	**7**	*1 1/2*	**Society Rock (IRE)**[15] 6064 2-9-3 94 ... GeorgeBaker 10 (J R Fanshawe) *racd stands' side: stdd s: hld up: hdwy 1/2-way: rdn to ld that gp 1f out: sn hdd and unable qck: 2nd of 13 in gp* **15/2**[3]	84+
	8	*hd*	**Dynasty**[28] 5690 2-9-3 0 ... JAHeffernan 12 (A P O'Brien, Ire) *racd stands' side: s.i.s: sn prom: rdn over 1f out: styd on same pce: 3rd of 13 in gp* **14/1**	83+
54	**9**	*1*	**Rasselas (IRE)**[70] 4314 2-9-3 0 ... MichaelHills 23 (B W Hills) *racd far side: led: racd keenly: rdn and hdd over 1f out: wknd fnl f: 6th of 9 in gp* **20/1**	74
22	**10**	*1 1/4*	**Golden Shaheen (IRE)**[23] 5807 2-9-3 0 ... (v[1]) AlanMunro 13 (Saeed Bin Suroor) *racd stands' side: chsd ldrs: led that gp over 2f out: rdn and hdd 1f out: sn wknd: 4th of 13 in gp* **33/1**	78+
21	**11**	*hd*	**Markazzi**[32] 5542 2-9-3 92 ... RHills 5 (Sir Michael Stoute) *racd stands' side: s.i.s: sn prom: rdn and nt clr run over 2f out: edgd rt over 1f out: wknd fnl f: 5th of 13 in gp* **3/1**[1]	77+
24	**12**	*nk*	**Gritstone**[15] 6046 2-9-3 0 ... PaulHanagan 19 (R A Fahey) *racd far side: prom: lost pl 1/2-way: wknd over 1f out: 7th of 9 in gp* **100/1**	69
434	**13**	*2*	**Saboteur**[15] 6064 2-9-3 85 ... DO'Donohoe 1 (Saeed Bin Suroor) *racd stands' side: chsd ldrs: rdn and ev ch that gp 2f out: wknd fnl f: 6th of 13 in gp* **28/1**	71+
4	**14**	*1 1/4*	**Karaka Jack**[9] 6231 2-9-3 0 ... JimmyQuinn 6 (M Johnston) *racd stands' side: prom: rdn whn n.m.r over 2f out: sn wknd: 7th of 13 in gp* **66/1**	68+
	15	*2 1/2*	**Meezaan (IRE)** 2-9-3 0 ... TPO'Shea 9 (J H M Gosden) *racd stands' side: s.i.s: rdn over 2f out: hung rt over 1f out: nvr on terms: 8th of 13 in gp* **25/1**	62+
2	**16**	*hd*	**Bab Al Shams (IRE)**[16] 6033 2-9-3 0 ... NCallan 4 (Saeed Bin Suroor) *racd stands' side: sn pushed along: a in rr: 9th of 13 in gp* **33/1**	62+
123	**17**	*nk*	**Atlantis Star**[25] 5743 2-9-3 103 ... (t) TedDurcan 2 (Saeed Bin Suroor) *racd stands' side: hld up: hdwy over 2f out: sn rdn: wknd over 1f out: 10th of 13 in gp* **10/1**	61+
5565	**18**	*3/4*	**Ice Viking (IRE)**[15] 6071 2-9-3 69 ... ChrisCatlin 16 (J G Given) *racd far side: sn pushed along in rr: lost tch fr over 2f out: 8th of 9 in gp* **150/1**	52
2322	**19**	*8*	**Yarra River**[45] 5153 2-9-3 80 ... WilliamBuick 11 (A M Balding) *racd stands' side: chsd ldrs tl rdn and wknd over 2f out: 11th of 13 in gp* **50/1**	39+
3150	**20**	*4 1/2*	**Barzan (IRE)**[81] 3967 2-9-3 91 ... KFallon 7 (Tom Dascombe) *racd stands' side: led stands' side tl rdn and hdd over 2f out: wknd over 1f out: 12th of 13 in gp* **66/1**	28+
6	**21**	*3 3/4*	**Stormglass**[10] 6200 2-9-3 0 ... MartinDwyer 21 (W R Muir) *racd far side: s.i.s: sn pushed along: a in rr: bhd fr over 2f out: last of 9 in gp* **100/1**	11
0	**22**	*17*	**Darshonin**[15] 6054 2-9-3 0 ... DarryllHolland 8 (J Noseda) *racd stands' side: s.i.s: a in rr: lost tch fnl 3f: last of 13 in gp* **100/1**	—

1m 23.45s (-1.95) **Going Correction** -0.175s/f (Firm) **22** Ran SP% **117.4**

Speed ratings (Par 101): **104,103,103,98,97 97,95,95,94,92 92,92,90,88,85 85,85,84,75,70 65,46**

toteswingers: 1&2 £125.60, 1&3 £125.60, 2&3 £125.60 CSF £1836.12 TOTE £69.80: £13.60, £12.90, £3.10; EX 1840.00 TRIFECTA Not won..

Owner Mrs M E Slade **Bred** Whitsbury Manor Stud And Mrs M E Slade **Trained** Whitsbury, Hants

FOCUS

If last year's race is anything to go by then the form of this sales race should throw up some decent horses to follow. Last season's first and second (Donativum and Crowded House) went on to record success at the Breeders' Cup and in the Racing Post Trophy respectively, while back in sixth was subsequent Great Voltigeur victor Monitor Closely, so this second renewal has a good deal to live up to. The race contained a host of well-bred, lightly-raced individuals representing prominent connections, but it was an unsatisfactory race with the field splitting into two and the far-side group, containing the lesser-fancied runners, coming out well on top. It was run in a time marginally slower than the fillies' version earlier on the card and there has to be a big question mark over the bare form, with the sixth probably the best guide.

NOTEBOOK

Oasis Dancer looked to have a mountain to climb in this company having been easily seen off by impressive newcomer Workforce in a Goodwood maiden last time out. He handed Sir Michael Stoute's well-bred colt a compliment with this success, but the conclusion must be that he benefited from racing on a quicker strip of ground bang on the far rail. A half-brother to Smart Enough, a very useful multiple scorer over 1m, that trip should be within the winner's compass, too. (tchd 80-1)

Kona Coast, slowly away and last in another one of these races here last time, clearly didn't run his race that day, but he bounced back to form here returned to 7f, and his rider may have been disadvantaged by having his whip accidentally knocked out of his hand by the winning rider entering the final furlong.

Take Ten, beaten a head in the 6f version of this race here last month, had a stamina query next to his name over this longer trip. On reflection his rider might have wish he'd delayed his challenge a bit longer, but a drop back to sprinting looks the way to go now. (op 9-1 tchd 10-1)

Lowdown(IRE) had looked to be progressing nicely prior to his last two starts, when fast ground had possibly been the reason for his defeats, but he coped with conditions well enough to stay on for a never nearer fourth this time, looking for all the world as though he'll be suited by a step up to 1m.

Alfred Nobel(IRE) stood out on paper as the likeliest winner based on his Group 1 success in the Phoenix Stakes, but he'd finished last in the National Stakes on his previous start. He came back with swelling on a hock that day but had apparently recovered quite quickly and this quicker ground promised to suit him better. He travelled like the best horse in the contest and quickened in great style to win his race on his side, and his overall finishing position doesn't do him justice. (op 7-2, tchd 5-1 in places)

Magnus Thrax(USA), another who finished down the field in the 6f version of this race here 15 days earlier, was another to benefit from racing in the far-side group, but having travelled kindly his stamina failed him over this longer trip. He's another bred for sprinting. (op 25-1)

Society Rock(IRE) was another with a stamina query next to his name. He hadn't got home on his debut over this trip but had won both his starts since over 6f. It's too early to say for sure that he didn't get home, as he only found Group 1 winner Alfred Nobel too strong for him on the stands' side. (op 7-1)

Dynasty, third to subsequent National Stakes runner-up Chabal in a maiden last time out, ran perfectly well and can be expected to improve for 1m-plus next season. It's worth remembering, however, that his dam, despite being very able, was not all that straightforward. (tchd 12-1)

Rasselas(IRE), who hasn't impressed with his head carriage, raced keenly and didn't see his race out having made the running on the favoured far side. (op 28-1 tchd 33-1)

Golden Shaheen(IRE) did best of the four Godolphin colts, all of whom raced on the stands' side. Visored for the first time, he was prominent throughout and kept up the gallop, but there's plenty of speed in his pedigree and it's doubtful he wants to go this far at this stage of his career. (tchd 28-1)

Markazzi, one of three entries for his stable in the Dewhurst, was popular in the market having had his maiden form boosted by the subsequent success of the runner-up. Clearly well regarded, he didn't run up to scratch here, but it would be unwise to write him off and he should make a much better three-year-old in any case. Official explanation: jockey said colt ran flat (tchd 5-2 and 100-30 in places)

Meezaan(IRE), the only newcomer in the field, is by Medicean out of a half-sister to Steinbeck. This was a tough race in which to make his introduction, but he didn't run badly for a long way.

Atlantis Star, wearing a tongue-tie for the first time and carrying his owner's first colours, could never land a blow from off the pace, but he is another who we know is capable of better than this.

Stormglass Official explanation: trainer said jockey sustained a shoulder injury

Darshonin Official explanation: trainer's rep said colt was unsuited by the good to firm ground

6479 KINGDOM OF BAHRAIN SUN CHARIOT STKS (GROUP 1) (F&M) 1m

3:00 (3:02) (Class 1) 3-Y-O+

£113,540 (£43,040; £21,540; £10,740; £5,380; £2,700) **Stalls** High

Form				RPR
-242	**1**		**Sahpresa (USA)**[34] 5496 4-9-2 110 TedDurcan 2	119
			(Rod Collet, France) *prom: hdwy 2f out: rdn to ld ins fnl f: kpt on strly* **16/1**
-113	**2**	1 1/2	**Ghanaati (USA)**[66] 4419 3-8-13 119 RHills 5	115
			(B W Hills) *chsd ldrs: wnt 2nd after 2f: effrt and chal over 1f out to ins fnl f: edgd lft and kpt on same pce* **6/5**[1]
3130	**3**	1 1/2	**Spacious**[63] 4522 4-9-2 113 JMurtagh 3	112
			(J R Fanshawe) *dictated ordinary gallop: rdn over 2f out: hdd ins fnl f: kpt on same pce* **14/1**
1111	**4**	1 1/4	**Strawberrydaiquiri**[42] 5260 3-8-13 113 RyanMoore 6	109+
			(Sir Michael Stoute) *hld up towards rr: drvn and outpcd over 2f out: rallied over 1f out: nrst fin* **7/2**[2]
2202	**5**	*shd*	**Heaven Sent**[28] 5686 6-9-2 114 JimmyFortune 4	109
			(Sir Michael Stoute) *trckd ldrs: effrt over 2f out: kpt on same pce fnl f* **12/1**
1301	**6**	2 1/2	**Fantasia**[23] 5798 3-8-13 113 KFallon 8	103
			(L M Cumani) *bhd and sn niggled along: drvn 3f out: plugged on fnl f: nvr able to chal* **6/1**[3]
2521	**7**	12	**Alnadana (IRE)**[56] 4-9-2 112 RichardHughes 1	76
			(A De Royer-Dupre, France) *racd keenly: trckd ldr 2f: cl up tl rdn and wknd over 2f out: eased whn no ch fnl f* **14/1**
0311	**8**	1 1/4	**Nashmiah (IRE)**[17] 6003 3-8-13 107 NCallan 10	73
			(C E Brittain) *hld up in tch on ins: drvn over 2f out: sn btn: eased whn no ch fnl f* **33/1**

1m 34.4s (-4.20) **Going Correction** -0.175s/f (Firm) course record

WFA 3 from 4yo+ 3lb **8** Ran SP% **111.8**

Speed ratings (Par 117): **114,112,111,109,109 107,95,93**

toteswingers: 1&2 £6.30, 1&3 £19.90, 2&3 £5.00. CSF £34.28 TOTE £17.90: £3.80, £1.10, £3.60; EX 48.50 Trifecta £828.60 Pool: £16,908.69 - 15.10 winning units..

Owner D O McIntyre **Bred** Douglas McIntyre **Trained** France

FOCUS

This Group 1 has fallen to Classic winners Attraction and Halfway To Heaven in recent years but has also produced its share of surprise winners and did so again. The third looks the best guide to the form, and although the apparent improvement shown by the winner was slightly surprising, she had not had many chances. The third looks the best guide to the form.

NOTEBOOK

Sahpresa(USA) ◆, fourth in a soft-ground Deauville Group 1 behind Goldikova in August, had also been held at Group 3 level but was previously a dual winner in Listed company. The fast ground was an unknown, but her trainer believed beforehand that she would be suited by it. She was settled off the pace and moved up going well, then found plenty up the hill to get the better of the favourite. She is clearly progressive and will probably stay in training next season, when she can be expected to return for some of the big fillies' races here. (op 20-1)

Ghanaati(USA), the only Group 1 winner in the line-up having taken the 1000 Guineas and Coronation Stakes and finished third in the Sussex Stakes, appeared to have an outstanding chance with the ground in her favour. She was never far away and showed in front running into the Dip. However, she had to battle to get past the long-time leader and could not respond when the winner made her challenge. (op 6-4)

Spacious, a dual winner at Group 2 level over this trip, had finished fourth in this in 2008 and again ran with credit. She made the running and kept battling away when the favourite took her on. She has never won at this level, but has run well enough to deserve to have done so.

Strawberrydaiquiri ◆, a progressive filly and triple Listed winner, was stepping up in grade and was settled off the pace. She stayed on without ever looking likely to trouble the principals, but has not had much racing and looks the sort that can win in Group company if kept in training next season. (tchd 4-1)

Heaven Sent, a consistent performer who stays 1m1f and acts on fast ground, finished fifth in this last year. She was just touched off for fourth by her stablemate this time, but ran well enough without being able to land a serious blow. She was retired afterwards. (op 14-1 tchd 10-1)

Fantasia, a dual Group 3 winner who had not come up to expectations this season despite finishing third in the French 1000 Guineas, had not won beyond 7f and was another who was held up. She stayed on as if the trip was not a problem, but never got into contention. (op 4-1)

Alnadana(IRE), the other French challenger, a winner at Group 3 level last time, had questions to answer regarding the fast ground and, despite showing up early, never looked to be travelling that well and dropped away rather tamely, as if she would not let herself down on the going. Official explanation: jockey said filly lost its action (op 16-1 tchd 12-1)

Nashmiah(IRE), a progressive filly who stays 1m2f, had a bit to find with several of these and, after being restrained early, was the first under pressure. She may have had enough for the season. (op 40-1)

6480 TOTESPORT.COM CAMBRIDGESHIRE (HERITAGE H'CAP) 1m 1f

3:40 (3:41) (Class 2) 3-Y-O+

£99,696 (£29,856; £14,928; £7,472; £3,728; £1,872) **Stalls** High

Form				RPR
0065	**1**		**Supaseus**[42] 5262 6-9-1 100 TravisBlock 26	109
			(H Morrison) *mde all: rdn over 2f out: styd on gamely: all out* **16/1**
4020	**2**	*nse*	**Tartan Gigha (IRE)**[21] 5863 4-8-5 90 JoeFanning 32	99
			(M Johnston) *a.p: rdn and ev ch fr over 1f out: r.o gamely* **33/1**
2414	**3**	1 1/4	**Nanton (USA)**[14] 6093 7-9-3 102 4ex DanielTudhope 4	108+
			(J S Goldie) *hld up: hdwy and edgd rt fr over 1f out: r.o wl: nt rch ldrs* **33/1**
-116	**4**	*nk*	**Applause (IRE)**[7] 6267 3-8-3 92 WilliamBuick 14	98+
			(J Noseda) *hld up: hdwy over 2f out: rdn over 1f out: edgd rt fnl f: r.o* **10/1**[2]
1405	**5**	1 1/4	**Shavansky**[9] 6234 5-8-1 86 KirstyMilczarek 24	89
			(B R Millman) *chsd ldrs: rdn over 2f out: styd on same pce fnl f* **100/1**
4025	**6**	3/4	**Stevie Thunder**[16] 6013 4-8-1 89 (v[1]) AndreaAtzeni[(3)] 29	90
			(Ian Williams) *prom: rdn over 2f out: styd on same pce fnl f* **33/1**
1060	**7**	1 1/4	**Swop (IRE)**[21] 5863 6-9-6 105 KFallon 16	104+
			(L M Cumani) *hld up: hdwy over 3f out: rdn and ev ch 2f out: no ex ins fnl f* **16/1**
1146	**8**	1	**The Cayterers**[8] 6249 7-8-1 91 AmyBaker[(5)] 15	88
			(A W Carroll) *hld up: hdwy 3f out: rdn over 1f out: styd on* **100/1**
2-03	**9**	1 1/2	**Howdigo**[4] 6368 4-8-1 86 PaulQuinn 20	80+
			(J R Best) *hld up: plld hrd: r.o ins fnl f: nvr nrr* **66/1**
4515	**10**	1 1/2	**Charm School**[14] 6106 4-8-10 95 4ex JimmyFortune 21	85
			(J H M Gosden) *hld up: hdwy u.p over 2f out: edgd rt over 1f out: no imp* **14/1**
-501	**11**	*nk*	**Almiqdaad**[14] 6106 3-8-8 97 4ex RHills 22	87
			(M A Jarvis) *chsd ldrs: rdn and ev ch 2f out: wknd ins fnl f* **8/1**[1]
2111	**12**	5	**Wannabe King**[33] 5522 3-8-9 98 4ex (p) TedDurcan 37	77
			(D R Lanigan) *prom: rdn over 2f out: wknd over 1f out* **8/1**[1]
5662	**13**	1/2	**Alfathaa**[6] 6307 4-9-2 101 (p) TPO'Shea 9	79
			(W J Haggas) *hld up: rdn over 2f out: n.d* **33/1**
5206	**14**	1/2	**Kay Gee Be (IRE)**[21] 5863 5-8-2 92 GFCarroll[(5)] 23	69
			(W Jarvis) *chsd ldrs: rdn over 2f out: wknd over 1f out* **25/1**
0224	**15**	1 3/4	**Moynahan (USA)**[33] 5522 4-8-12 97 AlanMunro 18	70
			(P F I Cole) *hld up: hdwy over 3f out: rdn over 2f out: sn hung rt and wknd* **28/1**
1510	**16**	3/4	**Marajaa (IRE)**[43] 5221 7-8-5 90 ChrisCatlin 35	62
			(W J Musson) *mid-div: sme hdwy over 2f out: wknd fnl f* **40/1**
0024	**17**	*nk*	**Alazeyab (USA)**[21] 5863 3-9-0 103 NCallan 27	74
			(M A Jarvis) *chsd wnr: rdn and ev ch 2f out: wknd fnl f* **33/1**
5061	**18**	2	**The Which Doctor**[15] 6059 4-8-6 91 4ex JimmyQuinn 33	58
			(J Noseda) *hld up: rdn over 3f out: edgd rt and wknd over 1f out* **33/1**
0206	**19**	3/4	**Granston (IRE)**[16] 6013 8-8-3 88 RoystonFfrench 25	54
			(J D Bethell) *prom: rdn over 2f out: sn wknd* **100/1**
-123	**20**	1 1/2	**Tryst**[8] 6239 4-8-5 90 PaulHanagan 28	52
			(Sir Michael Stoute) *s.i.s: hdwy 5f out: rdn and wknd over 1f out* **10/1**[2]
1625	**21**	2	**Brief Encounter (IRE)**[21] 5863 3-8-11 100 LPKeniry 31	58
			(A M Balding) *pushed along early in rr: rdn over 3f out: wknd 2f out* **14/1**
0450	**22**	2 3/4	**Ellemujie**[2] 6429 4-8-2 87 AdrianMcCarthy 19	39
			(D K Ivory) *pushed along in rr early: nvr on terms* **100/1**
/0-3	**23**	3/4	**Salute Him (IRE)**[106] 3089 6-9-5 104 RichardHughes 12	55
			(A J Martin, Ire) *hld up: rdn over 3f out: wknd over 2f out* **12/1**[3]
2115	**24**	*nk*	**Kaolak (USA)**[7] 6277 3-8-3 92 7ex (v) LukeMorris 13	42
			(J Ryan) *s.i.s: pushed along in rr early: hdwy u.p 3f out: hung rt and wknd 2f out* **33/1**
-105	**25**	2 1/2	**General Eliott (IRE)**[14] 6110 4-9-10 109 JMurtagh 11	54
			(P F I Cole) *hld up: rdn over 2f out: nvr on terms* **50/1**
1111	**26**	3/4	**Sirvino**[84] 3873 4-9-2 101 PhillipMakin 5	44
			(T D Barron) *hld up: rdn 3f out: sn hung rt and wknd* **12/1**[3]
0332	**27**	3 1/4	**Greylami (IRE)**[8] 6239 4-8-6 91 ow1 MichaelHills 7	28
			(T G Mills) *hld up: a in rr: rdn: hung rt and wknd over 2f out* **20/1**
1310	**28**	3/4	**Royal Destination (IRE)**[14] 6106 4-9-0 99 DaleGibson 10	34
			(J Noseda) *in rr and pushed along at various stages: rdn and wknd over 2f out* **33/1**
006-	**29**	1 1/2	**Fight Club (GER)**[456] 3683 8-8-13 98 VinceSlattery 36	30
			(Evan Williams) *mid-div: rdn and lost pl over 4f out: wknd over 2f out* **100/1**
3350	**30**	1/2	**Docofthebay (IRE)**[44] 5200 5-8-12 97 RyanMoore 3	28
			(J A Osborne) *s.i.s: hld up and a in rr* **33/1**
0013	**31**	3/4	**Bencoolen (IRE)**[56] 4768 4-8-9 94 DO'Donohoe 8	23
			(D Nicholls) *s.i.s: a in rr: bhd fnl 3f* **66/1**
5000	**32**	6	**Smokey Oakey (IRE)**[28] 5655 5-8-12 102 AshleyMorgan[(5)] 30	19
			(M H Tompkins) *s.i.s: hld up: hdwy over 3f out: wknd over 2f out* **66/1**

1m 47.48s (-4.22) **Going Correction** -0.175s/f (Firm)

WFA 3 from 4yo+ 4lb **32** Ran SP% **133.2**

Speed ratings (Par 109): **111,110,109,109,108 107,106,105,104,103 102,98,97,97,95 95,95,93,92,91 89,87,86,86,83 83,80,7**

toteswingers: 1&2 £88.20, 1&3 £231.60, 2&3 £555.90. CSF £484.72 CT £15920.08 TOTE £21.40: £4.80, £8.50, £5.80, £3.90; EX 933.80 Trifecta £46355.40 Part won. Pool: £62,642.47 - 0.80 winning units..

Owner Ben & Sir Martyn Arbib **Bred** Arbib Bloodstock Partnership **Trained** East Ilsley, Berks

FOCUS

A good mix of tough, older handicappers meeting some unexposed, lighter-raced types, including six three-year-olds. It was questionable beforehand, however, whether there were any potential 'Group horses in disguise' in the field, and it was no great surprise when one of the more grizzled campaigners came out on top. Earlier races had suggested that a high draw would prove an advantage, and that is the way things worked out, with the first two benefiting greatly from running right next to the far rail. The whole field shunned the stands' side and the reliability of the form is compromised by the draw bias, with the first two rated close to their best.

NOTEBOOK

Supaseus had shaped as though returning to form last time out at Sandown and got to race off a 1lb lower mark here. Relatively fresh as a result of being lightly raced since picking up an injury when travelling to Dubai earlier in the year, he was undoubtedly fairly handicapped on his best form, which included a close third to Pipedreamer in a Group 2 at York last summer. Bagging the all-important far rail, he made every yard of the running, hanging on by the skin of his teeth at the finish from a strong challenge put down by Tartan Gigha. This was the winner's second success over this particular course and distance, having won the Suffolk Stakes earlier in his career, but it's difficult to say we learnt anything new about him, as he was fully entitled to go close if returning to his best. (op 20-1)

Tartan Gigha(IRE), who is an inconsistent sort but had ground conditions to suit, was 3lb well in at the weights and, crucially, took up a fine position from his high draw, tracking the leader on the far rail. He had every chance and was only denied by the narrowest of margins. (op 40-1)

Nanton(USA), second in this race last year when blessed with a good draw, has had a terrific season and as a result was racing off a 12lb higher mark. Not so fortunate with the draw this time, he ended up racing towards the centre of the track and made his challenge widest of all. He was undoubtedly disadvantaged by the way things worked out and put up a great effort to take third. He might still take in the Cesarewitch, over double this distance, if the ground remains quick.

Applause(IRE) looked an interesting contender on paper having given Wannabe King (winner three times since) a thrashing at Redcar two starts previously. She had also caught the eye running on late at Ascot last time and looked likely to be suited by this longer trip. Racing more towards the centre of the pack, she might have been suited by getting more cover, but nevertheless she still picked up well in the closing stages and looks a filly with plenty more to offer. This was only her sixth start and she can certainly win off her current sort of mark. (tchd 17-2)
Shavansky, all the better for his return from a seven-week break at Pontefract last time, bounced back to form despite being 2lb wrong at the weights. He stays 1m2f well, so a strongly run race over this distance proved right up his street.
Stevie Thunder took to the first-time visor and also had the benefit of racing not too far off the far-side rail. He has run well on fast ground before, but arguably he's at his best with a little cut. (op 40-1)
Swop(IRE), third from a good draw when sent off favourite for this race last year, was 7lb higher this time around and he didn't quite see it out as well as some of his rivals. The bare mile is probably his trip. (tchd 14-1 in places)
The Cayterers, who has improved a good deal this season, made ground from off the pace, but he never really threatened to land a blow. He goes on the Polytrack and is the type to keep going through the winter.
Howdigo, who stays further than this, didn't help his chance by failing to settle. He did pass a few late on, though, and will be suited by a return to a longer trip.
Charm School, who caught the eye running on late in the John Smith's Stakes - traditionally a strong trial for this race - last time out, was representing John Gosden, who'd sent out the last two winners of this race. Although drawn in stall 21, he ended up racing more towards the centre of the track, which was no help.
Almiqdaad, who won the John Smith's Stakes and had initially been a doubtful runner in this race, was up there for a long way, but didn't see it out. He might need a longer trip and/or a flatter track. (op 13-2)
Wannabe King, on a roll since having cheekpieces slapped on, was able to race on the rail throughout and looked to have the race run to suit. The question was whether he would stay the trip in a strongly run race and he answered in the negative. He needs to drop back to 1m. (op 11-1)
Alfathaa struggled to get involved from his single-figure draw.
Tryst, who is due to go to the sales, was done with over two furlongs out. (op 11-1)
Salute Him(IRE) Official explanation: jockey said gelding lost its action halfway
Sirvino came into the race unbeaten in five starts this season and had been given a break since his last start in July. He was disadvantaged by his draw in stall five and never got in a blow. (tchd 14-1)
Docofthebay(IRE) Official explanation: jockey said horse never travelled

6481 EUROPEAN BREEDERS' FUND JERSEY LILY FILLIES' NURSERY 7f

4:15 (4:17) (Class 2) 2-Y-O

£18,693 (£5,598; £2,799; £1,401; £699; £351) **Stalls** High

Form	Pos	Dist	Horse / Trainer / Comment	Jockey	RPR
3101	1		**Bab At The Bowster (IRE)**[21] 5853 2-8-11 **79** (W J Haggas) *trckd ldrs: rdn to ld 2f out: edgd lft ins fnl f: hld on wl* **4/1**[1]	RyanMoore 13	83
3221	2	shd	**Cash Queen Anna (IRE)**[10] 6214 2-8-7 **75** (B W Hills) *disp ld to 2f out: rdn over 2f out: kpt on wl fnl f: jst hld* **9/2**[2]	MichaelHills 8	79
135	3	nk	**Dark Eyes (IRE)**[31] 5580 2-8-10 **78** (D J Coakley) *slt ld to 2f out: sn drvn and outpcd: kpt on wl u.p fnl f* **33/1**	DarryllHolland 1	81
410	4	1 ½	**Mistic Magic (IRE)**[72] 4245 2-9-5 **87** (P F I Cole) *trckd ldrs: effrt and rdn over 2f out: kpt on same pce fnl f* **20/1**	JimmyFortune 14	87
614	5	½	**Transvaal Sky**[24] 5763 2-9-7 **89** (Tom Dascombe) *dwlt and blkd s: hdwy and in tch 3f out: sn rdn: kpt on u.p fnl f* **20/1**	NCallan 2	87+
0225	6	nk	**Pastello**[15] 6066 2-8-3 **71** ow1 (R Hannon) *bhd: rdn over 3f out: hdwy u.p over 1f out: nrst fin* **12/1**	RoystonFfrench 16	69+
3153	7	hd	**Candyfloss Girl**[9] 6227 2-7-13 **67** oh1 ow1 (H J L Dunlop) *midfield: outpcd 3f out: rallied and flashed tail fr over 1f out: no imp ins fnl f* **33/1**	JimmyQuinn 10	64+
6423	8	1 ¼	**Texas Queen**[14] 6096 2-8-5 **73** (M R Channon) *in tch: rdn over 2f out: one pce over 1f out* **16/1**	TPO'Shea 9	67
6100	9	1	**Velvet Band**[33] 5526 2-8-3 **71** (P F I Cole) *trckd ldrs: rdn and edgd rt 2f out: wknd ins fnl f* **28/1**	JoeFanning 12	62
0013	10	1 ¾	**Paleo (IRE)**[23] 5797 2-9-1 **83** (R Hannon) *wnt lft s: hld up: sme hdwy u.p over 2f out: btn ins fnl f* **5/1**[3]	RichardHughes 3	70
2506	11	hd	**Catbells (IRE)**[14] 6090 2-8-0 **75** (A Bailey) *hld up: drvn over 2f out: nvr able to chal* **16/1**	TobyAtkinson(7) 5	62
0452	12	1	**Kinky Afro (IRE)**[15] 6071 2-8-3 **71** ow1 (J S Moore) *dwlt: bhd and rdn over 3f out: nvr on terms* **16/1**	WilliamBuick 4	55
232	13	1	**L'Enchanteresse (IRE)**[23] 5800 2-8-7 **75** (M L W Bell) *t.k.h: hld up in tch: rdn over 2f out: wknd over 1f out* **9/1**	KFallon 7	57
033	14	6	**Hot Pursuits**[87] 3745 2-8-11 **79** (H Morrison) *dwlt: bhd: rdn over 3f out: nvr on terms* **16/1**	TravisBlock 15	46
0224	15	1	**Keyta Bonita (IRE)**[17] 5981 2-8-5 **73** (M G Quinlan) *chsd ldrs tl rdn and wknd 3f out* **33/1**	PaulHanagan 11	37

1m 24.4s (-1.00) **Going Correction** -0.175s/f (Firm) **15** Ran SP% **117.9**
Speed ratings (Par 98): **98,97,97,95,95 94,94,93,92,90 89,88,87,80,79**
toteswingers: 1&2 £4.60, 1&3 £33.50, 2&3 £28.40 CSF £17.77 CT £453.04 TOTE £5.20: £2.20, £2.60, £6.40; EX 26.60.
Owner Findlay & Bloom **Bred** Raymond P Doyle **Trained** Newmarket, Suffolk
■ Stewards' Enquiry : Ryan Moore caution: careless riding

FOCUS
A competitive fillies' nursery in which it is not essential to have been a previous winner to score. It produced a good finish, but the time was nearly a second slower than the slowest of the two sales races over the trip earlier in the day.

NOTEBOOK
Bab At The Bowster(IRE), both of whose wins had been at 7f on fast ground, was sent off favourite. However, those successes were both on sharp, turning tracks and this offered a very different test. She was always in the leading group, though, and got to the front entering the final furlong before just holding the renewed efforts of the placed horses. (op 5-1)
Cash Queen Anna(IRE) was drawn more towards the centre of the track but raced up with the pace and gradually edged across to join those nearer the far rail. Leading from halfway until headed by the winner, she kept battling and only went down narrowly. She is progressing and this is her trip. (op 5-1 tchd 4-1 and 11-2 in a place)
Dark Eyes(IRE) ◆ overcame being carried wide leaving the stalls and, despite her outside draw, was disputing the lead before halfway. She did not appear to come down the hill too well and lost ground on the first two before rallying once meeting the rising ground to join in the photo-finish. This proved the trip was no problem and she can gain compensation on a flatter track.
Mistic Magic(IRE) had five subsequent winners behind when taking her maiden over 7f on fast ground at Newbury, but was down in grade after finishing last in Listed company next time. She ran pretty well on this return from a break. (op 16-1)
Transvaal Sky, carrying the winning owners' second colours, was gradually switched to the far rail from her low draw and did not run badly giving weight all round. (op 16-1)
Pastello, placed in maidens at 7f and 1m on fast ground, was 11lb better off with today's winner for a two-and-a- quarter-length beating and was dropping back in trip. However, she could make no impression after tracking the pace. (tchd 14-1)
Candyfloss Girl, all of whose best form has been over 5-6f on Kempton's Polytrack, did not run badly on this fast ground and kept going despite showing her regular tail-flashing trait under pressure.
Paleo(IRE) beat two subsequent winners when taking her maiden (the runner-up finished fourth in the fillies' sales race earlier), and was third in the good fillies' nursery at Doncaster subsequently - a race from which the first two have both scored since. She was held up off the pace and never got involved here, so perhaps that was not the place to be with the first three all ridden prominently. (op 9-2)
Kinky Afro(IRE) Official explanation: trainer said filly was unsuited by the good to firm ground
L'Enchanteresse(IRE), placed all four starts at five and 6f on varying ground, was up in trip for this handicap debut and was backed. She was not far away early, but was a little keen and dropped away from over a furlong out. Official explanation: jockey said filly ran too free (op 12-1 tchd 8-1)

6482 BEST ODDS GUARANTEED AT TOTESPORT.COM H'CAP 7f

4:50 (4:51) (Class 2) (0-100,100) 3-Y-O+

£12,462 (£3,732; £1,866; £934; £466; £234) **Stalls** High

Form	Pos	Dist	Horse / Trainer / Comment	Jockey	RPR
0000	1		**Aldermoor (USA)**[27] 5695 3-8-4 **84** (S C Williams) *trckd ldr: led over 1f out: rdn and edgd rt ins fnl f: edgd lft and hld on wl* **25/1**	RoystonFfrench 7	94
1260	2	hd	**One Way Or Another (AUS)**[33] 5522 6-8-7 **90** (J R Gask) *hld up in midfield: hdwy 2f out: edgd rt and styd on wl fnl f: jst hld* **7/1**[3]	GFCarroll(5) 14	99+
0004	3	¾	**Celtic Sultan (IRE)**[7] 6278 5-8-9 **87** (T P Tate) *led to over 1f out: rallied u.p: one pce wl ins fnl f* **5/1**[1]	DarryllHolland 8	94
0000	4	1 ½	**Thebes**[14] 6089 4-8-10 **88** (M Johnston) *trckd ldrs: effrt over 1f out: cl 3rd and styng on whn hmpd ins fnl f: nt rcvr* **17/2**	JoeFanning 13	95+
5003	5	1 ½	**Something (IRE)**[7] 6270 7-9-2 **94** (D Nicholls) *bhd tl hdwy and edgd rt over 1f out: kpt on fnl f: nrst fin* **14/1**	(p) PaulQuinn 1	93
0304	6	½	**Spirit Of Sharjah (IRE)**[14] 6117 4-8-9 **87** (Miss J Feilden) *midfield: rdn over 2f out: kpt on same pce ins fnl f* **16/1**	JimmyQuinn 3	85
10-1	7	1	**Intense**[14] 6117 3-8-10 **90** (B W Hills) *cl up: rdn and hung lft appr fnl f: wknd ins fnl f* **11/2**[2]	MichaelHills 2	85
0600	8	½	**Dhaular Dhar (IRE)**[7] 6270 7-9-3 **95** (J S Goldie) *hld up: rdn over 2f out: kpt on fnl f: nvr rchd ldrs* **9/1**	DanielTudhope 11	93+
0565	9	1	**Pearly Wey**[7] 6282 6-8-7 **85** (C G Cox) *missed break: bhd: rdn over 3f out: styd on fnl f: n.d* **12/1**	TPO'Shea 4	76+
0400	10	1 ¼	**Spanish Bounty**[22] 5826 4-9-0 **92** (J G Portman) *hld up: hdwy on outside over 2f out: wknd appr fnl f* **20/1**	(p) KFallon 9	79
0020	11	1 ¼	**Fishforcompliments**[23] 5799 5-8-8 **86** (R A Fahey) *dwlt: bhd: rdn 3f out: nvr on terms* **16/1**	PaulHanagan 12	70
6220	12	2 ¼	**Zowington**[25] 5746 7-8-7 **85** (S C Williams) *midfield: drvn and outpcd 3f out: n.d after* **28/1**	ChrisCatlin 6	63
1000	13	4 ½	**Oceana Blue**[70] 4317 4-8-6 **84** oh4 (A M Balding) *towards rr: drvn over 3f out: nvr on terms* **20/1**	(t) WilliamBuick 17	50
-036	14	1 ½	**Wildcat Wizard (USA)**[24] 5766 3-9-2 **96** (P F I Cole) *dwlt: sn in tch: struggling 3f out: sn btn* **16/1**	NCallan 15	58
1030	15	15	**Pravda Street**[70] 4293 4-8-11 **89** (P F I Cole) *prom tl rdn and wknd qckly over 2f out* **12/1**	RyanMoore 10	10

1m 22.72s (-2.68) **Going Correction** -0.175s/f (Firm)
WFA 3 from 4yo+ 2lb **15** Ran SP% **121.6**
Speed ratings (Par 109): **108,107,106,105,103 102,101,101,100,98 97,94,89,87,70**
toteswingers: 1&2 £73.90, 1&3 £37.70, 2&3 £17.90. CSF £184.55 CT £1063.21 TOTE £40.90: £10.30, £3.00, £2.50; EX 518.70.
Owner Phil & Frances Kendall **Bred** Gulf Coast Farms LLC **Trained** Newmarket, Suffolk

FOCUS
A decent-quality handicap, but most of the field looked pretty exposed. Once again they raced towards the favoured far rail and, with the exception of the runner-up, the principals were in the front rank throughout. The winning time was the quickest of the four races run over the trip on the card. There was a controversial finish and the runner-up looks the best guide.

NOTEBOOK
Aldermoor(USA), one of only three three-year-olds in the field, hung badly right under a left-hand drive, hampering Celtic Sultan and, in turn, Thebes, next to the far rail. The interference was enough to prevent those two from rallying, which they were still in a position to do, and, having switched his whip and straightened his mount up, Royston Ffrench was able to hold off the challenge of One Way Or Another, who arrived late on the scene. Inevitably, a stewards' enquiry followed, but under the current rules the result could not be altered. From a handicapping perspective, the winner deserved to be considered as he'd won a nursery at about this time last year off a mark of 90 and got to race off 84 here, but he'd shown very little since the spring and was understandably sent off a big price. The step up to 7f clearly benefited him, though, and even a rise in the weights for this will leave him fairly handicapped on his best form. Official explanation: trainer said, regarding marked improvement in form, that the colt appeared suited by being raced over a longer trip.
One Way Or Another(AUS), who had a valid excuse last time when poorly drawn, was dropping back a furlong in distance and was very well backed. He ran well, closing down Aldermoor near the line, but ultimately this trip looked to be on the short side for him. (op 14-1 tchd 13-2 and 6-1 in places)
Celtic Sultan(IRE) is dangerous when allowed his own way in front. He made all in this race in 2007 and went close to repeating the trick. He'd been headed but hadn't been seen off entirely when hampered by the winner. (op 7-1 tchd 15-2)
Thebes tracked the leader and had just taken advantage of a gap between him and the rail when the winner edged over, squeezing them both up. The worst sufferer in the incident, his rider had to snatch up and lost all chance. He's well handicapped on his best form, being 2lb lower than for his last win, and while he's done most of his winning over 6f, he was in the process of seeing this trip out well. Official explanation: jockey said colt suffered interference in running (op 16-1)
Something(IRE), third in a competitive handicap over this trip at Ascot the previous week, again had the cheekpieces on. Poorly drawn, he was held up for a late run and made some really good late headway. However, the leaders weren't coming back and he remains a difficult horse to win with. (op 9-1)
Spirit Of Sharjah(IRE), drawn low, raced towards the outside of the bunch, which meant he didn't encounter any trouble this time, but it also meant he didn't get any cover, which he probably needs to be seen at his best. (op 12-1)
Intense had created a good impression when winning over 1m here a fortnight earlier, but she was poorly drawn this time and weak in the market. She used up some energy early getting over towards the far rail and probably paid for that in the closing stages. It's also possible that the race simply came too soon following her belated seasonal reappearance. (op 4-1, tchd 6-1 in places)
Dhaular Dhar(IRE) didn't get much of a run at Ascot a week earlier and it was the same story here. He got going late after running into the back of the weakening Pravda Street but was never a danger in a race in which the pace held up pretty well. (op 15-2)
Pearly Wey Official explanation: jockey said gelding missed the break

Fishforcompliments Official explanation: jockey said gelding fly-jumped leaving stalls

6483 VIEW TATTERSALLS LOT 5 & 39 H'CAP 1m 4f
5:25 (5:26) (Class 3) (0-95,91) 3-Y-O-**£8,723** (£2,612; £1,306; £653; £326) **Stalls** Centre

Form RPR
U01 **1** **Lochiel**[7] 6281 5-9-7 **87** .... PJMcDonald 1 96
(G A Swinbank) *chsd ldr tl led over 2f out: rdn over 1f out: r.o wl* **3/1**[2]
3203 **2** *4 ½* **Resplendent Light**[20] 5909 4-9-9 **89** .... NCallan 7 91
(W R Muir) *led: rdn and hdd over 2f out: no ex fnl f* **4/1**[3]
1451 **3** *1 ½* **Senses (USA)**[22] 5834 3-8-9 **82** .... DarryllHolland 8 82
(J Noseda) *hld up: hdwy over 3f out: sn pushed along: styd on same pce appr fnl f* **5/2**[1]
4000 **4** *nse* **Camps Bay (USA)**[20] 5909 5-9-11 **91** .... RyanMoore 6 91
(Mrs A J Perrett) *chsd ldrs: rdn over 3f out: styd on same pce appr fnl f* **3/1**[2]
2100 **5** *3 ¼* **Lord Theo**[17] 6002 5-9-4 **84** .... RobertHavlin 3 78
(N P Littmoden) *hld up: rdn over 2f out: sn outpcd* **9/1**

2m 31.67s (-1.83) **Going Correction** -0.175s/f (Firm)
WFA 3 from 4yo+ 7lb **5** Ran SP% **108.6**
Speed ratings (Par 107): **99,96,95,94,92**
toteswinger: 1&2 £6.60. CSF £14.44 TOTE £3.90: £1.90, £2.20; EX 15.30 Place 6: £401.70, Place 5: £323.66..
Owner G Hawkes & Partner **Bred** D W Barker **Trained** Melsonby, N Yorks

FOCUS
Withdrawals reduced the field size in this decent handicap by half and in the end only two were ever seriously involved with the runner-up setting the standard.

NOTEBOOK
Lochiel ◆ has his quirks but is capable on his day and stays further than this. Just a 1lb higher than for his success over 1m6f a week previously, he was taken down early to settle him before entering the stalls and behaved impeccably in the race. Never far away, he was upsides the leader at halfway and, going on over 2f out, it was pretty straightforward from then on. He looks capable of completing the hat-trick on this evidence. (op 5-2)
Resplendent Light has been running well of late without winning as a result of which he was back to his highest rating since June, and that was 7lb above his last successful mark. With conditions to suit, he made the running and, although he rallied briefly when the winner went on, he was no match in the end, despite holding off the remainder comfortably enough. (tchd 9-2)
Senses(USA), a dual 1m2f winner at Sandown, was backed into favouritism despite having yet to prove he stays this distance. He was held up off the pace, but tried to make ground as the leaders were quickening and could making only limited ground in the closing stages. (op 11-4, tchd 3-1 in places)
Camps Bay(USA), narrowly beaten on his only run here in May 2008, had dropped to his lowest mark in two years and was down in grade. He tracked the leaders but his rider was getting after him with half a mile left to run and he could only stay on at the one speed. (op 7-2, tchd 4-1 in places)
Lord Theo, a three-time winner over 1m2f on the July Course was 5lb above last his last winning mark. He was settled in rear, but was another who found the leaders quickening when he was trying to make ground, and could make no impression. (op 15-2 tchd 7-1)
T/Jkpt: Not won. T/Plt: £1,051.40 to a £1 stake. Pool: £181,363.06. 125.92 winning tickets.
T/Qpdt: £106.20 to a £1 stake. Pool: £11,924.01. 83.02 winning tickets. CR

6214 REDCAR (L-H)
Saturday, October 3

OFFICIAL GOING: Good to firm (firm in places; 10.3)
Wind: strong, half behind Weather: fine but very windy

6484 EUROPEAN BREEDERS' FUND MAIDEN STKS 7f
2:10 (2:15) (Class 4) 2-Y-O **£5,180** (£1,541; £770; £384) **Stalls** Centre

Form RPR
0 **1** **Mr Irons (USA)**[32] 5542 2-9-3 0 .... PatDobbs 8 80
(Sir Michael Stoute) *trckd ldrs: effrt on inner over 2f out: edgd lft ins fnl f: led nr fin* **8/1**
0 **2** *hd* **Tesslam**[57] 4756 2-9-3 0 .... PhilipRobinson 2 80
(M A Jarvis) *chsd ldrs on outer: edgd rt over 2f out: styd on to ld wl ins fnl f: hdd nr fin* **1/1**[1]
23 **3** *1* **Antoniola (IRE)**[16] 6009 2-9-3 0 .... DavidAllan 13 77
(T D Easterby) *w ldrs: led over 2f out: hdd and no ex last 75yds* **3/1**[2]
0 **4** *7* **Always De One**[17] 5980 2-8-12 0 .... GregFairley 4 55
(M Johnston) *w ldrs: outpcd over 3f out: rdr lost whip and lost pl over 2f out* **5/1**[3]
6 **5** *nk* **Tres Amigos**[15] 6047 2-9-3 0 .... AdrianTNicholls 1 59
(D Nicholls) *led tl over 2f out: wknd over 1f out* **50/1**
6 *8* **Smayal (USA)** 2-8-12 0 .... J-PGuillambert 3 34+
(C E Brittain) *in rr: outpcd and hung bdly rt 3f out: sn bhd* **28/1**
7 *8* **Rebel Chieftain (IRE)** 2-9-3 0 .... DaneO'Neill 12 19+
(Saeed Bin Suroor) *s.s: in rr and sn drvn along: bhd fnl 3f* **5/1**[3]

1m 24.6s (0.10) **Going Correction** -0.025s/f (Good) **7** Ran SP% **110.6**
Speed ratings (Par 97): **98,97,96,88,88 79,70**
toteswingers: 1&2 £2.50, 1&3 £3.30, 2&3 £1.40. CSF £15.54 TOTE £8.90: £2.60, £1.50; EX 18.30.
Owner Mrs Elizabeth Moran **Bred** Hunter Valley Farm & Hatta Bldstk **Trained** Newmarket, Suffolk
■ Stewards' Enquiry : Philip Robinson two-day ban: excessive use of the whip (Oct 18-19)

FOCUS
A fair maiden with the first three coming clear. The race was run in a strong headwind.

NOTEBOOK
Mr Irons(USA) narrowly got off the mark at the second time of asking and enhanced his leading yard's decent record at this venue. He proved somewhat free early on and still looked green, but the further he went, the better he looked. He ultimately scored with a little in reserve and thise $425,000 purchase looks a useful prospect for next year, when he should relish being upped to 1m. (op 17-2 tchd 9-1)
Tesslam ◆ made his debut in a decent affair at Newmarket 55 days earlier and proved very popular to shed his maiden tag. He had every chance and was only just held, but lacked the resolution of the winner. He will appreciate stepping up in trip and shouldn't remain a maiden for long. (op 11-8 tchd 6-4 in places)
Antoniola(IRE), up in trip, has now been placed on each of his three outings, so rates a sound benchmark. There was little faulting his attitude and time will likely show this was a fair contest. He now has the option of nurseries. (op 100-30 tchd 7-2)
Always De One again needed to be ridden from an early stage and looked green. She was keeping on when the race was effectively over and will be of more interest when qualifying for a mark after her next assignment (op 28-1)
Tres Amigos was put in his place in between the final two furlongs. This was an improvement on his debut and he too looks one to be more interested in when becoming eligible for nurseries. It also wouldn't be surprising to see him enjoy a sharper test in that sphere. (op 33-1)
Rebel Chieftain(IRE), a 220,000gns purchase who holds a Derby entry, simply lost all chance at the start. Official explanation: jockey said colt missed the break (op 7-2)

6485 BODDINGTONS REDCAR STRAIGHT-MILE CHAMPIONSHIP FINAL H'CAP 1m
2:40 (2:41) (Class 2) 3-Y-O+
£18,693 (£5,598; £2,799; £1,401; £699; £351) **Stalls** Centre

Form RPR
4111 **1** **Collateral Damage (IRE)**[16] 6016 6-7-12 **85** ow3...(t) KellyHarrison(3) 7 92
(T D Easterby) *hld up in midfield: hdwy whn nt clr run over 1f out: led wl ins fnl f: kpt on wl* **15/2**
0150 **2** *hd* **Daaweitza**[2] 6435 6-7-6 **83** oh4 ow1 .... (b) RyanPowell(7) 9 89
(B Ellison) *hld up: hdwy over 2f out: edgd lft u.p and ev ch wl ins fnl f: jst hld* **20/1**
2000 **3** *hd* **Charlie Tipple**[37] 5361 5-7-12 **82** oh2 .... (p) DuranFentiman 8 87
(T D Easterby) *in tch: effrt over 2f out: led briefly ins fnl f: hld towards fin* **14/1**
4425 **4** *¾* **Dream Lodge (IRE)**[14] 6093 5-9-7 **108** .... FrederikTylicki(3) 13 111
(R A Fahey) *bhd: rdn and hdwy over 2f out: kpt on wl fnl f: nrst fin* **4/1**[1]
3302 **5** *½* **Opus Maximus (IRE)**[10] 6217 4-8-2 **86** .... GregFairley 1 88
(M Johnston) *cl up: rdn and ev ch over 1f out to ins fnl f: no ex* **8/1**
3311 **6** *1 ¾* **Arizona John (IRE)**[17] 6004 4-7-12 **82** oh3 .... NickyMackay 5 80
(J Mackie) *cl up: led 1/2-way to ins fnl f: no ex last 75yds* **8/1**
1034 **7** *nse* **Reel Buddy Star**[8] 6249 4-8-0 **84** ow2 .... FrancisNorton 11 82
(G M Moore) *in tch: effrt over 2f out: kpt on same pce fnl f* **10/1**
1003 **8** *2* **Summer Gold (IRE)**[7] 6286 5-7-12 **82** oh2 .... CatherineGannon 10 75
(E J Alston) *trckd ldrs: drvn over 2f out: one pce over 1f out* **16/1**
5213 **9** *1 ½* **Mountain Cat (IRE)**[14] 6117 5-7-11 **86** ow2 .... AndrewHeffernan(5) 14 75
(G A Swinbank) *t.k.h early: chsd ldrs: lost pl over 2f out: n.d after* **5/1**[2]
1620 **10** *3 ½* **Celtic Change (IRE)**[16] 6014 5-7-9 **82** .... (bt) DominicFox(3) 4 63
(M Dods) *s.i.s: hdwy and prom 1/2-way: wknd over 2f out* **18/1**
0001 **11** *5* **White Deer (USA)**[10] 6217 5-7-13 **83** .... (p) SilvestreDeSousa 12 52
(G A Harker) *bhd: drvn 3f out: nvr able to chal* **7/1**[3]
1050 **12** *1 ½* **Just Bond (IRE)**[8] 6249 7-7-13 **83** .... JamieMackay 3 48
(G R Oldroyd) *s.i.s: rdn in rr over 3f out: nvr on terms* **25/1**
3000 **13** *6* **Toledo Gold (IRE)**[56] 4801 3-7-6 **86** oh10 ow1 .... MatthewLawson(7) 2 37
(E J Alston) *led to 1/2-way: lost pl and btn whn hung rt over 2f out* **50/1**

1m 35.84s (-2.16) **Going Correction** -0.025s/f (Good)
WFA 3 from 4yo+ 3lb **13** Ran SP% **120.6**
Speed ratings (Par 109): **109,108,108,107,107 105,105,103,102,98 93,92,86**
toteswingers: 1&2 £32.60, 1&3 £28.20, 2&3 £65.20. CSF £152.63 CT £2064.33 TOTE £7.20: £2.50, £6.70, £3.10; EX 237.20 TRIFECTA Not won..
Owner Middleham Park Racing Xxv **Bred** Minch Bloodstock And Castletown Stud **Trained** Great Habton, N Yorks

FOCUS
A very competitive handicap in which six were out of the weights. The first three fought out a tight finish and the form looks a bit messy.

NOTEBOOK
Collateral Damage(IRE) made it four wins from his last four outings with another gutsy effort off a mark 2lb higher than when completing the hat-trick at Ayr 16 days earlier. He is clearly at his peak and this rates a career-best effort. He is versatile as regards underfoot conditions and, as he shouldn't be going up too much for this, further improvement is not ruled out while he remains in this mood. It should also be noted his rider put up 3lb overweight and thus cancelled out her claim. (op 6-1)
Daaweitza had finished three lengths behind the winner on his penultimate outing and was better off here. He was produced on the near side with what appeared to be a winning run, but just got edged out at the line. This was a sterling effort from 4lb out of the weights. (op 16-1)
Charlie Tipple, 2lb out of the handicap and a stablemate of the winner, won this off a 2lb lower mark last season. He came into the race looking out of sorts, but the return to this course brought him back to his old self and he was only just held. (op 12-1 tchd 16-1)
Dream Lodge(IRE) was well backed despite conceding upwards of 22lb all round. He lacked the tactical speed to get seriously involved on this drop back in trip, and was getting there all too late inside the final furlong. (op 11-2 tchd 6-1)
Opus Maximus(IRE) was never far away and ran very close to his recent level, so rates the benchmark for the form. (op 7-1)
Mountain Cat(IRE) spoilt his chance by refusing to settle and was beaten some way out. Official explanation: jockey said gelding hung right final 2 1/2f (op 15-2)

6486 TOTEPOOL TWO-YEAR-OLD TROPHY (LISTED RACE) 6f
3:15 (3:20) (Class 1) 2-Y-O
£94,692 (£35,895; £17,964; £8,957; £4,486; £2,251) **Stalls** Centre

Form RPR
2415 **1** **Lucky Like (FR)**[36] 5416 2-8-6 0 .... FrancisNorton 10 104+
(E J O'Neill) *racd far side: chsd ldrs: edgd lft and led over 1f out: drew clr ins fnl f: 1st of 10 that gp* **20/1**
1116 **2** *4* **Kaptain Kirkup (IRE)**[28] 5658 2-8-7 95 ow1 .... TomEaves 11 90
(M Dods) *racd far side: hld up: hdwy 2f out: styd on ins fnl f to take modest 2nd nr line: 2nd of 10 that gp* **20/1**
0655 **3** *shd* **Nosedive**[16] 6044 2-8-6 97 .... LiamJones 9 89
(W J Haggas) *racd far side: chsd ldrs: kpt on wl ins fnl f: 3rd of 10 that gp* **25/1**
0260 **4** *¾* **Kingdom Of Light**[44] 5198 2-9-0 87 .... FrederikTylicki 7 94
(J Howard Johnson) *overall ldr far side: edgd rt and hdd over 1f out: kpt on same pce: 4th of 10 that gp* **33/1**
1221 **5** *¾* **Mister Hughie (IRE)**[8] 6247 2-9-0 89 .... TonyCulhane 23 92
(M R Channon) *s.s: hdwy over 2f out: styd on fnl f: nt rch ldrs* **28/1**
2241 **6** *nse* **Secret Queen**[19] 5949 2-8-1 85 .... NickyMackay 18 79
(B J Meehan) *w ldrs: styd on same pce fnl f* **16/1**
2012 **7** *1* **Angel's Pursuit (IRE)**[14] 6105 2-8-6 109 .... PatDobbs 19 81
(R Hannon) *chsd ldrs: effrt 2f out: kpt on same pce* **15/8**[1]
412 **8** *1* **Secret Millionaire (IRE)**[20] 5908 2-9-0 87 .... SJCraine 8 86
(Patrick Morris) *racd far side: hld up in midfield: hdwy over 2f out: chsng ldrs 1f out: wknd fnl 150yds: 5th of 10 that gp* **66/1**
1652 **9** *½* **Roodle**[24] 5763 2-8-4 90 .... SilvestreDeSousa 2 75
(Eve Johnson Houghton) *racd far side: chsd ldrs: kpt on same pce fnl 2f: 6th of 10 that gp* **16/1**
6310 **10** *hd* **Vanishing Grey (IRE)**[15] 6049 2-8-7 83 .... ShaneKelly 17 77
(B J Meehan) *mid-div: kpt on fnl 2f: nvr trbld ldrs* **80/1**
1114 **11** *nk* **Singeur (IRE)**[45] 5174 2-8-6 98 .... RobertWinston 21 75
(R Bastiman) *hld up in midfield: effrt over 2f out: nvr trbld ldrs* **14/1**[3]
0140 **12** *1 ½* **Exotic Beauty**[15] 6049 2-8-4 85 .... (v[1]) AdrianTNicholls 5 69
(M R Channon) *racd far side: w ldrs: wknd over 1f out: 7th of 10 that gp* **40/1**
410 **13** *½* **Star Rover (IRE)**[22] 5822 2-8-12 108 .... JohnEgan 13 75
(P D Evans) *led stands' side gp: wknd over 1f out* **16/1**

0032 **14** *2 ¾* **Confessional**[18] 5957 2-9-2 80........................(b¹) DavidAllan 6 71
(T D Easterby) *racd far side: chsd ldrs: wknd over 1f out: 8th of 10 that gp* **100/1**

2620 **15** *2 ¼* **Avonrose**[23] 5797 2-8-4 86........................ GregFairley 16 52
(M Johnston) *a towards rr: nvr a factor* **50/1**

1U **16** *2 ¼* **Rodrigo De Torres**[44] 5198 2-9-0 0........................ TPQueally 14 55
(H R A Cecil) *mid-div: edgd lft and lost pl 2f out* **7/1²**

0605 **17** *½* **Dancing Freddy (IRE)**[15] 6068 2-8-6 79........................ JamieMackay 1 46
(J G Given) *slowly away: racd far side: nvr on terms: 9th of 10 that gp* **100/1**

1660 **18** *nk* **Jack My Boy (IRE)**[28] 5658 2-8-3 80........................ CatherineGannon 12 42
(P D Evans) *mid-div: bhd fnl 2f* **100/1**

2243 **19** *1 ¾* **Walkingonthemoon**[48] 5085 2-9-0 99........................ RichardKingscote 22 48
(Tom Dascombe) *chsd ldrs: wknd 2f out* **33/1**

50 **20** *3 ¼* **Schoolboy Champ**[44] 5198 2-8-6 77........................ GrahamGibbons 20 30
(Patrick Morris) *chsd ldrs: wknd over 2f out* **100/1**

2120 **21** *8* **The Hermitage (IRE)**[109] 2995 2-8-7 85........................ PhilipRobinson 4 7
(M Johnston) *racd far side: mid-div: rdn 3f out: sn lost pl: last of 10 that gp* **25/1**

01 **22** *hd* **Bathwick Gold (IRE)**[19] 5934 2-8-9 79........................ StephenDonohoe 15 8
(P D Evans) *dwlt: in rr: bhd fnl 2f* **100/1**

1m 10.29s (-1.51) **Going Correction** -0.025s/f (Good) **22** Ran SP% **110.2**
Speed ratings: **109,103,103,102,101 101,100,98,98,97 97,95,94,91,88 85,84,84,81,77 66,66**
toteswingers: 1&2 not won, 1&3 not won, 2&3 £6.90. CSF £265.62 TOTE £26.60: £6.60, £4.40, £6.20; EX 271.10 Trifecta £282.60 Pool: £382.00 - 1 winning unit..
Owner Victory Racing & Partners **Bred** Paul Nataf **Trained** Southwell, Notts
■ Pastoral Player was withdrawn (9/2, ref to ent stalls). Deduct 15p in the £ under R4.

FOCUS
Despite the large numbers this was not a strong race for the grade. The winner proved in a different class and the form is rated around the third.

NOTEBOOK
Lucky Like(FR) ◆ was having just his second outing in Britain, having done most of his racing in France, and had shown himself to be smart when finishing fourth to Dick Turpin in the Richmond Stakes three runs back. Dropping back a furlong here, he fairly bolted up and had plenty in hand at the finish despite failing to settle through the early parts. As it transpired, this was not a strong race for the class, but he was in a different league and rates a decent prospect for next season, as he has plenty of scope. (tchd 22-1)
Kaptain Kirkup(IRE), drawn next to the winner in 11, puts the form into some perspective. That said, he travelled nicely before being found out by the Lucky Like's turn of foot and again did more than enough to suggest he is crying out for a stiffer test. This also confirmed his versatility as regards underfoot conditions. (op 14-1)
Nosedive was also drawn next door to Lucky Like. He bounced back to his best and turned in a solid effort, performing right up to his Richmond form with the winner. (op 20-1)
Kingdom Of Light helped to cut out the early running and kept on gamely when put under maximum pressure. He was another who ran close to his recent level.
Mister Hughie(IRE) fared best of those to come from behind and also those drawn towards the stands' side. He remains progressive. (op 33-1)
Secret Queen got off the mark over course and distance in maiden company 19 days previously and may well have stepped up on that a little without looking a serious threat. (tchd 12-1)
Angel's Pursuit(IRE) had a gilt-edged opportunity at the weights after being raised 9lb for finishing second to Awzaan in the Mill Reef a fortnight previously. His chance was enhanced after Awzaan extended his unbeaten run in the Group 1 Middle Park the previous day, and when his main market rival Pastoral Player refused to load into the stalls. However, he posted a laboured effort from off the pace and ran miles below expectations. Conditions may not have been ideal for one who enjoys coming late, but it was still most disappointing. (op 9-4 tchd 13-8)
Exotic Beauty Official explanation: jockey said filly hung right final 4f
Rodrigo De Torres was making his debut for Henry Cecil after a 44-day absence and attracted support. He was never involved from out the back though, and now has it to prove. (op 12-1 tchd 14-1)
Walkingonthemoon Official explanation: trainer's rep said colt was unsuited by the good to firm (firm in places) ground

6487 GUISBOROUGH STKS (LISTED RACE) 7f
3:55 (3:56) (Class 1) 3-Y-O+
£22,708 (£8,608; £4,308; £2,148; £1,076; £540) **Stalls** Centre

Form RPR

0104 **1** **Musaalem (USA)**[22] 5826 5-9-0 98........................ LiamJones 5 110
(W J Haggas) *hld up: hdwy over 2f out: led over 1f out: hld on towards fin* **14/1**

0331 **2** *nk* **Able Master (IRE)**[27] 5695 3-8-12 103........................ TomEaves 8 108
(B Smart) *hld up: hdwy to ld 2f out: sn hdd: kpt on wl: no ex nr fin* **11/2³**

2601 **3** *3 ½* **Taqdeyr**[33] 5529 4-9-0 102........................ PhilipRobinson 1 100+
(M A Jarvis) *tk fierce hold: w ldr: hung bdly lft then rt: kpt on fnl f* **6/1**

0356 **4** *shd* **Royal Confidence**[7] 6272 4-8-9 102........................(p) RobertWinston 10 94
(B W Hills) *chsd ldrs: kpt on same pce over 1f out* **7/1**

5002 **5** *½* **Kaabari (USA)**[11] 6187 3-8-7 82........................ SilvestreDeSousa 4 92
(C E Brittain) *sn outpcd and in rr: hdwy and edgd lft over 2f out: kpt on: nvr rchd ldrs* **80/1**

0034 **6** *2* **Carcinetto (IRE)**[2] 6428 7-8-9 97........................ TPQueally 3 88
(P D Evans) *chsd ldrs: sn drvn along: wknd over 1f out* **40/1**

-252 **7** *½* **Huntdown (USA)**[15] 6058 3-8-12 111........................ DaneO'Neill 11 90
(Saeed Bin Suroor) *trckd ldrs: rdn 2f out: sn wknd* **13/8¹**

6606 **8** *6* **Tombi (USA)**[14] 6091 5-9-0 103........................ FrederikTylicki 7 75
(J Howard Johnson) *w ldrs: rdn over 2f out: sn wknd: bhd whn eased ins fnl f* **7/2²**

4060 **9** *1 ¾* **Abbondanza (IRE)**[14] 6091 6-9-0 100........................(p) DavidAllan 12 70
(I Semple) *drvn to ld on stands' side: hdd 2f out: sn lost pl: eased ins fnl f* **33/1**

1m 22.97s (-1.53) **Going Correction** -0.025s/f (Good)
WFA 3 from 4yo+ 2lb **9** Ran SP% **115.8**
Speed ratings (Par 111): **107,106,102,102,101 99,99,92,90**
toteswingers: 1&2 £8.00, 1&3 £13.00, 2&3 £4.80. CSF £88.07 TOTE £18.00: £3.30, £1.80, £2.10; EX 142.70.
Owner Hamdan Al Maktoum **Bred** Shadwell Farm LLC **Trained** Newmarket, Suffolk

FOCUS
This average Listed event proved to be a messy race with the proximity of the fifth raising doubts about the form. There was a sound pace, though, and the first pair drew clear.

NOTEBOOK
Musaalem(USA) had plenty to find with the market leaders according to official figures on this step up in class, but the race was run to suit him and he came home a game winner. The handicap in which he finished fourth at Doncaster on his previous outing was a strong affair, however, and he had run well above his mark. The key to him is quick ground and a decent early pace and he should be high on confidence after this. (op 11-1)
Able Master(IRE) got back to winning ways in a decent handicap at York 27 days earlier and had been raised 8lb for that. He too enjoyed the way the race unfolded and vindicated the Handicapper's decision with a brave effort. He was nicely clear of the remainder and continues on an upward curve. (op 5-1)
Taqdeyr again raced freely on the early lead, but he hung markedly right from halfway and looked a nightmare ride. The fact he stayed on to bag third highlights his talent, but he is one to tread carefully with all the same. Official explanation: jockey said gelding hung both ways early stages (op 11-2 tchd 7-1)
Royal Confidence lacked the required gear change, but gave her running and is a solid Listed-class performer, so helps to set the level. (op 10-1)
Kaabari(USA) got badly outpaced at halfway and looked like finishing out the back. Once brought to the far side she motored home however, and turned in by far her best effort on paper. (op 66-1)
Carcinetto(IRE), fourth in a handicap over 6f two days earlier, had it to do on official figures and ran a solid enough race in the circumstances. (op 33-1)
Huntdown(USA), who was bidding to give his stable a fourth win in the race, was the one to beat with an official mark of 111. He raced handily, but came under pressure 2f out and ultimately posted a laboured effort. He does appear flattered by his mark and only has a maiden win to his name, but is better than this on his day. Official explanation: trainer's rep had no explanation for the poor form shown (op 2-1 tchd 6-4)
Tombi(USA) was well backed, but his supporters knew their fate soon after halfway and he ran well below his recent level on this step back up a furlong. (tchd 4-1)

6488 HOLD YOUR CHRISTMAS PARTY @ REDCAR RACECOURSE (S) STKS 1m 2f
4:30 (4:30) (Class 5) 3-5-Y-O
£3,238 (£963; £481; £240) **Stalls** Low

Form RPR

0031 **1** **Traphalgar (IRE)**[12] 6172 4-9-6 79........................ TPQueally 5 66
(Ollie Pears) *trckd ldrs: led 3f out: hld on wl towards fin* **15/8¹**

6240 **2** *¾* **Mount Hermon (IRE)**[48] 5062 5-9-0 71........................(b) PhilipRobinson 12 59
(H Morrison) *trckd ldrs: drvn 3f out: chsng wnr and edgd lft over 1f out: styd on ins fnl f* **2/1²**

2322 **3** *½* **Bold Indian (IRE)**[10] 6219 5-9-0 56........................ DavidAllan 9 58
(M E Sowersby) *mid-div: hdwy over 2f out: chsng ldrs over 1f out: kpt on same pce ins fnl f* **13/2**

0055 **4** *¾* **Flora's Pride**[10] 6219 5-8-12 46 ow3........................ TonyCulhane 2 54
(K G Reveley) *hld up in last: styd on fnl 2f: nt rch ldrs* **28/1**

-004 **5** *nk* **Moscow Oznick**[12] 6172 4-9-0 59........................(v) RichardKingscote 8 55
(Tom Dascombe) *chsd ldrs: chalng whn hung bdly rt over 2f out: kpt on ins fnl f* **9/2³**

4524 **6** *12* **Freda's Rose (IRE)**[16] 6022 5-8-9 53........................ StephenDonohoe 1 26
(J Mackie) *mid-div: effrt 4f out: lost pl over 2f out: eased ins fnl f* **16/1**

0000 **7** *9* **Adozen Dreams**[17] 5983 3-7-12 44 ow1........................ TerenceFury[(7)] 4 9
(N Bycroft) *t.k.h: led 3f: chsd ldrs: lost pl over 2f out: sn bhd* **80/1**

0000 **8** *nk* **Tump Mac**[19] 5954 5-8-9 39........................ PaulPickard[(5)] 6 13
(N Bycroft) *t.k.h in rr: edgd rt and lost pl over 2f out* **100/1**

-000 **9** *17* **Reel Bluff**[93] 3541 3-8-9 45........................ DuranFentiman 3 —
(N Wilson) *trckd ldr: led after 3f: hdd 3f out: sn lost pl: bhd whn eased fnl f* **66/1**

2m 6.65s (-0.45) **Going Correction** -0.075s/f (Good)
WFA 3 from 4yo+ 5lb **9** Ran SP% **112.7**
Speed ratings (Par 103): **98,97,97,96,96 86,79,79,65**
toteswingers: 1&2 £2.10, 1&3 £3.00, 2&3 £3.20. CSF £5.64 TOTE £2.90: £1.10, £1.60, £2.20; EX 6.30.There was no bid for the winner.
Owner We-Know Partnership **Bred** Deepwood Farm Stud **Trained** Norton, N Yorks

FOCUS
A weak affair and the winner did not have to run up to his mark to score with the third and fourth better guides to the form.

6489 11.52AM NO MORE CARDS TO DO H'CAP 5f
5:05 (5:06) (Class 5) (0-75,75) 3-Y-O+
£3,238 (£963; £481; £240) **Stalls** Centre

Form RPR

1020 **1** **Select Committee**[9] 6233 4-8-11 **68**........................(v) GrahamGibbons 1 75
(J J Quinn) *towards rr: rdn 1/2-way: led ins fnl f: hld on wl* **16/1**

0631 **2** *shd* **Hawkeyethenoo (IRE)**[6] 6308 3-8-1 **60** 6ex........................(v) KellyHarrison[(3)] 4 68+
(J S Goldie) *bhd: pushed along 1/2-way: gd hdwy over 1f out: chal wl ins fnl f: jst hld* **2/1¹**

010 **3** *nk* **Blown It (USA)**[36] 5405 3-8-12 **74**........................ BMcHugh[(5)] 8 80
(I Semple) *hld up: hdwy 2f out: led briefly ins fnl f: kpt on fin* **12/1**

5050 **4** *1 ¼* **Under Review (IRE)**[10] 6220 3-8-6 **68**........................ DeanHeslop[(5)] 10 70
(T D Barron) *hld up in midfield gng wl: hdwy to ld over 1f out: hdd ins fnl f: kpt on same pce* **16/1**

6040 **5** *nse* **Kyzer Chief**[10] 6220 4-8-5 **62**........................ DuranFentiman 6 63
(R E Barr) *chsd ldrs: effrt and ev ch over 1f out: one pce ins fnl f* **14/1**

2140 **6** *hd* **Ingleby Star (IRE)**[9] 6233 4-8-11 **73**........................(p) GaryBartley[(5)] 5 74
(N Wilson) *prom: effrt and ev ch over 1f out: no ex ins fnl f* **12/1**

0010 **7** *1 ¼* **Mandarin Spirit (IRE)**[6] 6309 9-8-11 **68**........................(b) RobertWinston 2 64
(Miss L A Perratt) *led to over 1f out: no ex fnl f* **16/1**

6006 **8** *1* **Pacific Pride**[9] 6233 6-8-4 **61** oh2........................(b) SilvestreDeSousa 11 54
(J J Quinn) *hld up bhd main gp: effrt over 1f out: sn no imp* **20/1**

1220 **9** *½* **Cape Royal**[8] 6253 9-9-4 **75**........................(bt) RichardKingscote 16 66
(J M Bradley) *racd towards stands' side: in tch: rdn 1/2-way: sn no imp* **16/1**

2500 **10** *1* **Miss Daawe**[16] 6010 5-7-11 **61** oh4........................(bt¹) RyanPowell[(7)] 7 48
(B Ellison) *hld up: hdwy whn nt clr run over 1f out: drifted lft and sn no imp* **33/1**

5100 **11** *1 ½* **Speedy Senorita (IRE)**[24] 5767 4-8-13 **70**........................ GregFairley 9 52
(J J Quinn) *chsd ldrs: ev ch over 1f out: sn rdn and wknd* **28/1**

040 **12** *¾* **Baybshambles (IRE)**[52] 4891 5-8-7 **69**........................ PaulPickard[(5)] 17 48
(R E Barr) *bhd stands' side: sn drvn along: no imp fr 1/2-way* **7/1²**

5210 **13** *nse* **Nomoreblondes**[22] 5830 5-8-13 **70**........................(p) TonyCulhane 13 49
(P T Midgley) *cl up: drvn 1/2-way: wknd appr fnl f* **16/1**

1040 **14** *2 ¼* **Bravely (IRE)**[24] 5768 5-9-2 **73**........................ DavidAllan 14 44
(T D Easterby) *in tch: drvn 1/2-way: wknd wl over 1f out* **17/2³**

1300 **15** *15* **Guest Connections**[16] 6010 6-8-9 **66**........................(v) AdrianTNicholls 12 —
(D Nicholls) *dwlt: sn struggling: no ch fr 1/2-way* **14/1**

57.60 secs (-1.00) **Going Correction** -0.025s/f (Good) **15** Ran SP% **125.6**
Speed ratings (Par 103): **107,106,106,104,104 103,101,100,99,97 95,94,94,90,66**
toteswingers: 1&2 £13.30, 1&3 £44.20, 2&3 £9.10. CSF £48.59 CT £441.44 TOTE £23.60: £5.90, £1.70, £4.10; EX 67.70.
Owner Which Bits Mine Syndicate **Bred** Llety Stud **Trained** Settrington, N Yorks

FOCUS
A moderate handicap, run at a sound pace, and the form looks solid enough. The main action developed on the far side inside the final furlong, despite the field having merged more towards the near rail from halfway.

Select Committee Official explanation: trainer's rep said, regarding apparent improvement in form, that the gelding had previously had three runs in eight days.

6490 WEDDING RECEPTIONS @ REDCAR RACECOURSE H'CAP 1m 2f
5:40 (5:40) (Class 5) (0-75,75) 3-Y-O+ **£3,238** (£963; £481; £240) **Stalls** Low

Form RPR
3052 **1** **Follow The Flag (IRE)**[12] 6174 5-9-4 **70**..........(p) TPQueally 9 79
(A J McCabe) *chsd ldrs: effrt over 4f out: sn rdn: styd on to ld 1f out: edgd lft nr fin: jst hld on* **12/1**
40/1 **2** *hd* **Bollin Dolly**[55] 4822 6-8-13 **65**.......... DavidAllan 8 73
(T D Easterby) *chsd ldrs: chal over 2f out: styd on wl ins fnl f: jst hld* **13/2**[2]
1311 **3** *¾* **Baltimore Jack (IRE)**[10] 6218 5-9-3 **69**.......... GrahamGibbons 2 76
(T D Walford) *uns rdr and rn briefly loose on way to s: led: edgd rt and hdd 1f out: no ex ins fnl f* **6/4**[1]
0044 **4** *1 ½* **Templetuohy Max (IRE)**[35] 5441 4-9-3 **69**..........(v) PhilipRobinson 3 73
(J D Bethell) *trckd ldrs: effrt over 2f out: same pce fnl f* **13/2**[2]
1-04 **5** *1 ¾* **Lilac Moon (GER)**[105] 3151 5-9-1 **67**.......... RichardKingscote 7 67
(Tom Dascombe) *trckd ldrs: chal over 2f out: one pce appr fnl f* **14/1**
6015 **6** *3* **Wovoka (IRE)**[6] 6312 6-9-4 **75**.......... AmyRyan(5) 5 69
(K A Ryan) *hld up towards rr: hdwy on ins 3f out: nvr nr ldrs* **12/1**
3105 **7** *nk* **Destinys Dream (IRE)**[7] 6280 4-9-1 **70**.......... KellyHarrison(3) 15 63
(Miss Tracy Waggott) *mid-div: effrt over 2f out: sn fdd* **22/1**
2063 **8** *6* **Eijaaz (IRE)**[10] 6218 8-8-12 **64**.......... DuranFentiman 1 45
(G A Harker) *in rr: lost pl over 2f out* **16/1**
0056 **9** *2* **Dialogue**[70] 4299 3-9-2 **73**.......... SilvestreDeSousa 10 50
(G A Harker) *dwlt: a bhd* **9/1**[3]
0-36 **10** *¾* **Green Passion (USA)**[253] 272 3-9-1 **72**.......... GregFairley 12 48
(M Johnston) *mid-div: drvn over 3f out: lost pl over 2f out* **20/1**
/00- **11** *13* **Along The Nile**[216] 6862 7-9-6 **72**.......... TonyCulhane 13 22
(K G Reveley) *in rr: bhd fnl 3f* **25/1**

2m 5.60s (-1.50) **Going Correction** -0.075s/f (Good)
WFA 3 from 4yo+ 5lb **11 Ran SP% 117.6**
Speed ratings (Par 103): **103,102,102,101,99 97,97,92,90,90 79**
toteswingers: 1&2 £10.70, 1&3 £3.10, 2&3 £3.70. CSF £85.48 CT £186.96 TOTE £14.90: £3.10, £2.90, £1.30; EX 51.50 Place 6: £1,775.36, Place 5: £1,097.45..
Owner S Gillen **Bred** Martin Francis **Trained** Averham Park, Notts

FOCUS
A modest handicap but the form looks sound rated around those in the frame behind the winner.
T/Plt: £890.50 to a £1 stake. Pool: £66,021.34. 54.12 winning tickets. T/Qpdt: £122.10 to a £1 stake. Pool: £4,059.10. 24.60 winning tickets. WG

6455 WOLVERHAMPTON (A.W) (L-H)
Saturday, October 3
OFFICIAL GOING: Standard changing to standard to fast after race 2 (6.15)
Wind: Moderate half behind Weather: Fine

6491 GMS GROUP NURSERY 1m 141y(P)
5:45 (5:47) (Class 4) (0-85,77) 2-Y-O **£5,046** (£1,510; £755; £377; £188) **Stalls** Low

Form RPR
51 **1** **Wild Rose**[17] 5984 2-9-7 **77**.......... SaleemGolam 6 82+
(M L W Bell) *s.i.s: hld up: hdwy whn nt clr run briefly over 2f out: nt clr run wl over 1f out: sn swtchd lft: rdn and r.o wl to ld last strides* **4/1**[2]
4201 **2** *hd* **Sejanus**[22] 5839 2-9-6 **76**.......... TonyHamilton 12 81
(K A Ryan) *led: hdd over 6f out: a.p: led wl over 1f out: rdn and edgd rt ins fnl f: hdd last strides* **12/1**
651 **3** *2 ¼* **Epic (IRE)**[17] 5981 2-9-6 **76**.......... AndrewMullen 10 76
(M Johnston) *a.p: wnt 2nd over 4f out: rdn and ev ch wl over 1f out: nt qckn ins fnl f* **6/1**
3361 **4** *½* **Llandovery**[28] 5682 2-8-13 **69**.......... EdwardCreighton 9 68
(P J McBride) *hld up towards rr: pushed along over 3f out: rdn over 2f out: c wd st: hdwy 1f out: kpt on one pce ins fnl f* **5/1**[3]
6213 **5** *2* **Luminous Star (USA)**[28] 5682 2-8-13 **76**.......... JPFahy(7) 3 71
(R M Beckett) *hld up: pushed along and hdwy on ins wl over 1f out: rdn and wknd ins fnl f* **3/1**[1]
6210 **6** *1 ¼* **Tanto Quanto (IRE)**[14] 6088 2-9-7 **77**..........(b) SebSanders 8 69
(W R Muir) *pushed along to sn chse ldr: led over 6f out: hdd wl over 1f out: wknd ins fnl f* **12/1**
01 **7** *¾* **Dr Mathias**[21] 5868 2-9-2 **72**.......... DNolan 1 62
(P D Evans) *hld up in rr: short-lived effrt 2f out* **9/1**
206 **8** *1 ¾* **Ragsta (IRE)**[9] 6228 2-8-1 **64**.......... RichardRowe(7) 4 51
(C A Dwyer) *hld up in tch: wknd over 2f out* **14/1**
0332 **9** *½* **High Resolution**[16] 6034 2-8-3 **59**.......... WandersonD'Avila 7 45
(Miss L A Perratt) *hld up: stdy prog on outside over 3f out: rdn and wknd wl over 1f out* **16/1**

1m 49.78s (-0.72) **Going Correction** -0.30s/f (Stan) **9 Ran SP% 113.9**
Speed ratings (Par 97): **91,90,88,88,86 85,84,83,82**
toteswingers: 1&2 £7.80, 1&3 £2.10, 2&3 £10.00. CSF £49.95 CT £285.12 TOTE £3.20: £1.50, £3.00, £2.60; EX 45.90.
Owner Saif Ali & Saeed H Altayer **Bred** Biddestone Stud **Trained** Newmarket, Suffolk

FOCUS
Other than half an hour of rain from around 4.30pm, conditions on the run-up to this meeting had been dry and windy. Five of the nine runners to stand their ground had won last time, so this looked a competitive nursery even after the defections.

NOTEBOOK
Wild Rose's mark of 77 for this nursery debut didn't look too prohibitive judged on her commanding victory at Kempton last time. Very weak in the market, she looked to have her work cut out after a slow start (her second in three runs), but she stayed on really takingly once she finally got a clear run. She will need to learn to break smarter as she ascends the ranks, but that is entirely possible just three starts into her career. (op 5-2 tchd 9-2)
Sejanus, who just held on to make all in a C&D maiden last time, was matched at 1.03 in running close home. Arguably he might have been deprived of victory a few strides sooner had Wild Rose's surge not been checked twice, but it was a third solid effort from as many all-weather starts and he can go in again at this level. (op 11-1)
Epic(IRE), for whom even the longer trip couldn't prevent rom getting outpaced from the furlong pole, and a return to stiffer courses seems advisable for now. (op 9-2 tchd 13-2)
Llandovery could have been worse treated than a 3lb rise for beating a 13lb superior rival over C&D last time, but he never threatened to do more than just staying on past toiling rivals late on in this better contest. (op 8-1)
Luminous Star(USA), 12lb better off here inclusive of jockeys' claims, was already in trouble leaving the back straight. (op 4-1)

6492 GREAT OFFERS AT WOLVERHAMPTON-RACECOURSE.CO.UK H'CAP 5f 216y(P)
6:15 (6:15) (Class 6) (0-60,61) 3-Y-O+ **£2,388** (£705; £352) **Stalls** Low

Form RPR
4316 **1** **Mayoman (IRE)**[14] 6103 4-9-3 **58**..........(b) DNolan 1 64
(D Carroll) *a.p: led jst over 1f out: sn rdn: drvn out* **9/2**[1]
0045 **2** *hd* **Shakespeare's Son**[16] 6038 4-9-3 **58**..........(v[1]) FergusSweeney 7 64
(H J Evans) *hld up towards rr: hdwy jst over 1f out: rdn and r.o ins fnl f: tk 2nd cl home* **10/1**
2156 **3** *½* **Titus Gent**[16] 6039 4-9-3 **58**.......... IanMongan 10 62
(J Ryan) *a.p: rdn and ev ch over 1f out: kpt on ins fnl f* **9/1**[3]
2043 **4** *nk* **Bold Ring**[4] 6362 3-9-4 **60**.......... EdwardCreighton 4 63
(E J Creighton) *hld up towards rr: hdwy wl over 1f out: rdn and ev ch ins fnl f: nt qckn towards fin* **6/1**[2]
3020 **5** *hd* **Loyal Royal (IRE)**[28] 5678 6-9-0 **58**..........(b) JackDean(3) 6 60
(J M Bradley) *s.i.s: hld up in rr: c wd st: nt clr run and swtchd lft over 1f out: gd late hdwy: nrst fin* **6/1**[2]
0036 **6** *½* **Running Flush (USA)**[29] 5632 3-9-2 **58**.......... LukeMorris 9 59
(J R Gask) *hld up towards rr: pushed along over 3f out: c v wd st: rdn wl over 1f out: kpt on ins fnl f* **16/1**
2515 **7** *2* **Come On Buckers (IRE)**[1] 6458 3-9-2 **61** ow1...(b) AlanCreighton(3) 13 55
(E J Creighton) *led: hdd over 3f out: rdn wl over 1f out: wknd ins fnl f* **16/1**
5235 **8** *2* **Exceed Elegance (IRE)**[69] 4343 3-8-12 **59**.......... MartinLane(5) 2 47
(D Shaw) *hld up in tch: pushed along over 2f out: rdn and wknd over 1f out* **16/1**
1034 **9** *¾* **Optical Illusion (USA)**[19] 5941 5-9-2 **57**.......... TonyHamilton 3 43
(R A Fahey) *hld up in mid-div: pushed along over 2f out: rdn and short-lived effrt on ins wl over 1f out* **9/2**[1]
0050 **10** *1 ½* **Fortina's Boy (USA)**[23] 5813 3-9-4 **60**..........(t) LPKeniry 11 41
(W R Swinburn) *s.i.s: hld up in rr: hrd rdn and struggling wl over 1f out* **22/1**
06-6 **11** *nk* **Philmack Dot Com**[259] 201 3-9-3 **59**.......... JamesDoyle 8 39
(D Donovan) *hld up in mid-div: pushed along over 2f out: rdn and wknd over 1f out* **22/1**
5603 **12** *hd* **One Cool Kitty**[23] 5809 3-9-2 **58**.......... JerryO'Dwyer 5 37
(M G Quinlan) *w ldr: led over 3f out: rdn and hdd over 1f out: wknd ins fnl f* **16/1**

1m 13.34s (-1.66) **Going Correction** -0.30s/f (Stan)
WFA 3 from 4yo+ 1lb **12 Ran SP% 116.3**
Speed ratings (Par 101): **99,98,98,97,97 96,94,91,90,88 88,87**
toteswingers: 1&2 £7.00, 1&3 £7.30, 2&3 £18.20. CSF £48.79 CT £387.80 TOTE £5.90: £2.50, £2.90, £3.10; EX 48.90.
Owner Tom Tuohy **Bred** James Cosgrove **Trained** Sledmere, E Yorks
■ Stewards' Enquiry : Alan Creighton one-day ban: failed to keep straight from stalls (Oct 18)

FOCUS
The clerk of the course changed the official going to standard following feedback from the riders after this second contest. The first six finished clear and the form is rated around the runner-up and fourth.

6493 ROYAL AIR FORCE ASSOCIATION MEDIAN AUCTION MAIDEN STKS 5f 216y(P)
6:45 (6:45) (Class 5) 2-Y-O **£3,238** (£963; £481; £240) **Stalls** Low

Form RPR
6 **1** **Never The Waiter**[50] 4986 2-9-3 0.......... LPKeniry 12 86+
(B J Meehan) *hld up in mid-div: hdwy on outside 3f out: led over 1f out: sn rdn: r.o wl* **7/4**[2]
6 **2** *3 ¼* **Hot Spark**[37] 5360 2-9-3 0.......... FergusSweeney 3 75
(K A Ryan) *led: rdn and hdd over 1f out: no ex ins fnl f* **33/1**
33 **3** *hd* **San Jemeniano (IRE)**[70] 4318 2-9-3 0.......... SebSanders 2 75
(P W Chapple-Hyam) *hld up in tch: nt clr run on ins after 1f: n.m.r on ins briefly over 1f out: sn rdn: one pce* **13/8**[1]
4 *nk* **Gramercy (IRE)** 2-9-3 0.......... SaleemGolam 7 74+
(M L W Bell) *s.i.s: sn hld up in mid-div: pushed along and hdwy 1f out: kpt on towards fin* **28/1**
44 **5** *1 ¼* **Tartufo Dolce (IRE)**[15] 6069 2-8-12 0.......... LeeVickers 4 65
(J G Given) *a.p: rdn jst over 1f out: one pce* **16/1**
36 **6** *2 ¾* **Wriggle (IRE)**[73] 4200 2-9-3 0..........(p) IanMongan 10 62
(W J Haggas) *hld up in mid-div: rdn wl over 1f out: no hdwy* **15/2**[3]
0 **7** *nk* **Little Garcon (USA)**[15] 6061 2-9-0 0.......... AndreaAtzeni(3) 5 61
(M Botti) *t.k.h: sn chsng ldr: ev ch wl over 1f out: sn rdn: wknd ins fnl f* **16/1**
0 **8** *¾* **Whipper's Delight (IRE)**[34] 5478 2-8-12 0.......... JamesDoyle 8 55+
(D Donovan) *hld up in rr: pushed along over 2f out: nvr nr ldrs* **100/1**
0 **9** *hd* **Woldgate**[17] 5977 2-8-12 0.......... LanceBetts(5) 13 58
(G R Oldroyd) *hld up: sn towards rr: pushed along over 2f out: sn struggling* **100/1**
5 **10** *hd* **City Gossip (IRE)**[15] 6069 2-8-12 0.......... JerryO'Dwyer 6 52
(M G Quinlan) *prom: pushed along over 2f out: wknd wl over 1f out* **25/1**
11 *1 ¼* **Singin' The Blues** 2-9-3 0.......... LukeMorris 9 54
(J M P Eustace) *s.i.s: in rr: rdn over 3f out: sn struggling* **40/1**
12 *½* **Mosqueta** 2-8-12 0.......... CatherineGannon 11 47
(P D Evans) *s.i.s: pushed along over 3f out: a in rr* **40/1**
4 **13** *1 ½* **Servetius (USA)**[16] 6026 2-9-3 0.......... TonyHamilton 1 48
(G A Butler) *s.i.s: pushed along over 3f out: a in rr* **33/1**

1m 13.67s (-1.33) **Going Correction** -0.30s/f (Stan) **13 Ran SP% 118.0**
Speed ratings (Par 95): **96,91,91,91,89 85,85,84,84,83 82,81,79**
toteswingers: 1&2 £10.80, 1&3 £1.80, 2&3 £5.40. CSF £69.12 TOTE £2.70: £1.20, £6.20, £1.40; EX 55.90.
Owner R P Foden **Bred** Barton Stud Partnership **Trained** Manton, Wilts

FOCUS
Few got into a race won in a time just 0.34 seconds slower than the older horses' handicap which preceded it.

NOTEBOOK
Never The Waiter, a half-brother to three multiple winners at 5f-6f, had been the subject of early money despite his unfavourable draw. He confirmed the impression he had shown when putting in good late work at Newbury on debut, and his rider had time for a look around close home. A well-run race at this trip looks about right on this evidence, and he could be a fair prospect. (op 15-8 tchd 2-1)
Hot Spark stepped up markedly on his soft-ground debut at Ayr, breaking smarter and showing good speed, yet still having enough left to repel challengers for second spot once the winner had flown. He could be worth a try around a fast 5f.
San Jemeniano(IRE), not seen since pulling a muscle at Newmarket 70 days previously, was twice short of room but appeared to find it all happening a bit too quickly notwithstanding. He looked in need of a touch further than 6f last time and still does. (op 7-4 tchd 6-4)

Gramercy(IRE) endured a problematic debut, slowest out of the stalls and checked when making his move turning in. It's doubtful that these hindrances cumulatively cost him a winning chance, but he would most likely have placed otherwise and he is worth keeping in mind for something similar next time. (op 25-1)

Wriggle(IRE) attracted appreciable late support prior to this first try in cheekpieces, but didn't finish any more purposefully than on his two previous outings. (op 12-1)

6494 BOOK NOW FOR CHRISTMAS (S) STKS — 5f 20y(P)

7:15 (7:15) (Class 6) 2-Y-O — £2,388 (£705; £352) Stalls Low

Form — RPR

3060 **1** **Fasilight**[29] 5636 2-8-3 69 .... AndreaAtzeni(3) 1 — 65
(M Botti) *a.p: rdn to ld over 1f out: rdn out* — 10/3[2]

3443 **2** *hd* **Chocolate Cookie (IRE)**[23] 5811 2-8-6 64 .... FrancisNorton 6 — 64
(R Hannon) *a.p: rdn over 1f out: wnt 2nd ins fnl f: r.o* — 9/2[3]

6000 **3** *1 ½* **Pepi Royal (IRE)**[19] 5938 2-8-2 56 ow1 .... MartinLane(5) 9 — 62+
(Pat Eddery) *towards rr: n.m.r on ins 2f out: hdwy over 1f out: rdn and r.o to take 3rd cl home* — 25/1

2444 **4** *1* **Yeadon**[14] 6096 2-8-8 74 .... FrederikTylicki(3) 8 — 60
(R A Fahey) *hld up towards rr: hdwy on outside over 2f out: rdn and one pce ins fnl f* — 11/4[1]

5466 **5** *1* **Tucker's Law**[24] 5776 2-8-11 66 .... FergusSweeney 4 — 57
(B R Millman) *mid-div: nt clr run 2f out: rdn over 1f out: kpt on ins fnl f* 9/1

100 **6** *nk* **Mahiki**[49] 5033 2-8-4 69 .... JPFahy(7) 11 — 56
(S A Callaghan, U.S.A) *hld up in tch: n.m.r briefly 2f out: carried hd high and hung lft over 1f out: no imp* — 12/1

6324 **7** *2* **Devassa**[11] 6185 2-8-6 62 .... LukeMorris 3 — 43
(C G Cox) *hld up in tch: rdn wl over 1f out: wknd ins fnl f* — 8/1

450 **8** *hd* **Starburst Excel**[86] 3772 2-8-7 69 ow1 .... (t[1]) JerryO'Dwyer 12 — 46+
(M G Quinlan) *s.i.s whn rdr sltly late removing blindfold: sn swtchd lft to ins: hld up in rr: nt clr run 2f out: rdn wl over 1f out: nvr nr ldrs* — 28/1

6100 **9** *3* **Wanchai Whisper**[15] 6068 2-8-11 64 .... CatherineGannon 13 — 37
(P D Evans) *w ldr: led over 3f out: rdn and hdd over 1f out: wknd ins fnl f* — 20/1

050 **10** *3* **Croft Bridge**[33] 5519 2-8-11 56 .... TomEaves 2 — 26
(M Dods) *led over 1f: prom: n.m.r and lost pl 2f out: n.d after* — 25/1

00 **11** *5* **Green Shoots**[66] 4430 2-8-5 0 ow4 .... LanceBetts(5) 5 — 7
(M E Sowersby) *hld up in mid-div: pushed along over 2f out: sn bhd* — 100/1

00 **12** *7* **Lady Zoe (IRE)**[10] 6207 2-7-13 0 .... (vt[1]) RichardRowe(7) 10 — —
(D Donovan) *sn outpcd* — 100/1

61.54 secs (-0.76) **Going Correction** -0.30s/f (Stan) — 12 Ran SP% 114.6
Speed ratings (Par 93): **94,93,91,89,88 87,84,84,79,74 66,55**
toteswingers: 1&2 £2.30, 1&3 £24.60, 2&3 £27.90. CSF £16.58 TOTE £4.20: £1.80, £1.70, £6.80; EX 18.00.The winner was bought in for 4,000gns.
Owner Giuliano Manfredini **Bred** David John Brown **Trained** Newmarket, Suffolk

FOCUS
A reasonable juvenile seller.

NOTEBOOK
Fasilight never strayed further than one horse's width from the inner rail out of stall one and didn't compromise her chance with over-keenness as at Kempton last month. It will be interesting to see whether she is returned to nurseries at this trip, as recent defeats in that discipline have all been recorded over 6f-7f. Connections went to 4,000gns to retain her. (tchd 7-2)

Chocolate Cookie(IRE) hasn't really gone on as expected from her good third to subsequent Group 2 winner Dick Turpin on debut in June, but showed the heart was still willing in running Faslight mightily close here. There should be a race at this level in her at least, and like the winner she is probably best kept to the minimum for now. (op 4-1)

Pepi Royal(IRE) appeared late on the scene to record a career-best effort without ever looking the likely winner. A try in a 6f seller might reap dividends, with all previous runs at the trip having been either in maidens or off too high a mark in nurseries. (op 22-1)

Yeadon placed on each of his first three starts but hasn't gone on since, and his challenge petered out disappointingly once again here. His current mark flatters him on this evidence. (op 100-30 tchd 9-4)

Mahiki is unbeaten in two starts on Southwell's Fibresand but threw her head up late on here and hasn't seemed happy on Polytrack either time she's been tried on it. (tchd 14-1)

Devassa continues to look a short-runner even over the sharpest of 5f tracks. (op 15-2 tchd 9-1)

Starburst Excel, on whom the blindfold was late to come off, lost his chance with a slow start. (op 25-1 tchd 40-1)

6495 RINGSIDE CONFERENCE SUITE - 700 THEATRE STYLE CLAIMING STKS — 7f 32y(P)

7:45 (7:46) (Class 5) 3-Y-O+ — £3,238 (£963; £481; £240) Stalls High

Form — RPR

6504 **1** **Capucci**[11] 6178 4-8-12 80 .... (p) IJBrennan(7) 6 — 88
(J J Quinn) *hld up in mid-div: hdwy whn nt clr run and swtchd rt jst over 1f out: rdn to ld towards fin: r.o* — 15/2

0604 **2** *¾* **Beauchamp Viceroy**[16] 6024 5-9-5 79 .... (bt[1]) FrederikTylicki(3) 3 — 89
(G A Butler) *led: rdn over 1f out: hdd towards fin* — 6/1[2]

6302 **3** *1 ¾* **Orpenindeed (IRE)**[16] 6024 6-9-4 87 .... SebSanders 7 — 80
(M Botti) *w ldr: ev ch 2f out: rdn over 1f out: lost 2nd and no ex wl ins fnl f* — 10/11[1]

0005 **4** *½* **Jack Junior (USA)**[13] 6137 5-8-12 87 .... FrancisNorton 8 — 73
(D Nicholls) *hld up in mid-div: c wd st: hdwy 1f out: rdn and kpt on one pce ins fnl f* — 15/2

0300 **5** *2 ½* **Ingleby Arch (USA)**[71] 4285 6-9-6 83 .... JimmyQuinn 12 — 74
(T D Barron) *hld up: sn in tch: rdn wl over 1f out: wknd ins fnl f* — 25/1

0-00 **6** *4 ½* **Burning Incense (IRE)**[27] 5697 6-9-5 73 .... (b) TomEaves 1 — 61
(M Dods) *hld up towards rr: rdn over 1f out: no rspnse* — 33/1

4002 **7** *2 ½* **Hits Only Jude (IRE)**[4] 6361 6-9-2 74 .... DNolan 5 — 51
(D Carroll) *prom: rdn wl over 1f out: sn wknd* — 7/1[3]

0060 **8** *4 ½* **Dorn Dancer (IRE)**[64] 4504 7-8-5 60 .... LukeMorris 11 — 28
(W M Brisbourne) *in rr: pushed along over 3f out: rdn and struggling wl over 1f out* — 100/1

2600 **9** *3 ¾* **The Staffy (IRE)**[110] 2975 4-8-7 60 .... RossAtkinson(5) 2 — 25
(Tom Dascombe) *hld up in mid-div: lost pl and pushed along over 3f out: sn struggling* — 40/1

1m 26.65s (-2.95) **Going Correction** -0.30s/f (Stan)
WFA 3 from 4yo+ 2lb — 9 Ran SP% 112.9
Speed ratings (Par 103): **104,103,101,100,97 92,89,84,80**
toteswingers: 1&2 £5.30, 1&3 £1.80, 2&3 £2.70. CSF £48.75 TOTE £8.30: £1.80, £1.60, £1.10; EX 56.50.
Owner Ross Harmon **Bred** Meon Valley Stud **Trained** Settrington, N Yorks

FOCUS
Recent winning form in the line-up for this claimer was in very short supply, and over half the field never figured. The winner is rated to his best with the runner-up a length below his optimum.

6496 RAFA H'CAP — 1m 141y(P)

8:15 (8:15) (Class 5) (0-75,76) 3-Y-O+ — £3,238 (£963; £481; £240) Stalls Low

Form — RPR

2202 **1** **Handsome Falcon**[8] 6250 5-9-6 76 .... FrederikTylicki(3) 9 — 86
(R A Fahey) *hld up in mid-div: pushed along and hdwy wl over 1f out: sn rdn: r.o to ld towards fin* — 5/1[2]

3012 **2** *1 ¼* **Tamasou (IRE)**[10] 6212 4-9-0 72 .... MartinLane(5) 5 — 79
(A J McCabe) *w ldr: led over 2f out: rdn wl over 1f out: hdd towards fin* — 3/1[1]

0220 **3** *2 ¾* **Luck Will Come (IRE)**[33] 5511 5-9-7 74 .... JimmyQuinn 1 — 75
(H J Collingridge) *led early: a.p: hrd rdn over 1f out: no ex ins fnl f* — 5/1[2]

5126 **4** *1 ¾* **Striding Edge (IRE)**[17] 5986 3-9-4 75 .... FrancisNorton 12 — 72
(W R Muir) *hld up in rr: hdwy over 1f out: rdn and no imp fnl f* — 14/1

2450 **5** *3* **Forbidden (IRE)**[11] 6190 6-9-0 70 .... (t) AndreaAtzeni(3) 2 — 60
(Daniel Mark Loughnane, Ire) *hld up in tch: rdn over 2f out: wknd over 1f out* — 10/1[3]

6055 **6** *2* **Hucking Heat (IRE)**[58] 4710 5-9-0 67 .... FergusSweeney 7 — 52
(R Hollinshead) *hld up in mid-div: rdn and btn jst over 1f out* — 11/1

0000 **7** *2 ½* **Hyde Lea Flyer**[21] 5887 4-9-4 71 .... TonyHamilton 11 — 50
(E S McMahon) *hld up in mid-div: pushed along over 2f out: c wd st: sn wknd* — 22/1

000 **8** *1 ¼* **Ansells Pride (IRE)**[30] 5598 6-9-5 72 .... TomEaves 3 — 48
(B Smart) *sn led: hdd over 2f out: rdn and wknd wl over 1f out* — 14/1

6000 **9** *4* **Elusive Fame (USA)**[12] 6168 3-9-1 72 .... (b) AndrewMullen 4 — 39
(M Johnston) *dwlt: hld up towards rr: nt clr run on ins 2f out: rdn wl over 1f out: no rspnse* — 14/1

0502 **10** *hd* **Omnium Duke (IRE)**[14] 6124 3-9-0 71 .... SebSanders 10 — 38
(J W Hills) *a towards rr* — 11/1

1000 **11** *¾* **Hilbre Court (USA)**[85] 3811 4-9-5 72 .... IanMongan 6 — 37
(B P J Baugh) *prom tl pushed along and wknd over 1f out* — 33/1

2230 **12** *¾* **Eastern Gift**[24] 5780 4-9-7 74 .... JerryO'Dwyer 13 — 37
(Miss Gay Kelleway) *a in rr* — 25/1

1m 46.96s (-3.54) **Going Correction** -0.30s/f (Stan)
WFA 3 from 4yo+ 4lb — 12 Ran SP% 115.2
Speed ratings (Par 103): **103,101,99,97,95 93,91,90,86,86 85,85**
toteswingers: 1&2 £1.80, 1&3 £5.50, 2&3 £4.70. CSF £19.17 CT £79.90 TOTE £5.50: £2.30, £1.90, £1.70; EX 25.10.
Owner B Shaw **Bred** Miss D Fleming **Trained** Musley Bank, N Yorks

FOCUS
One of three races run in a time quicker than standard, and the faster of the 2m contests by 2.82 seconds. The market leaders filled the frame between them and the form looks solid and good for the grade.

6497 ENJOY LUCKY 7 GROUP OFFER H'CAP — 1m 1f 103y(P)

8:45 (8:46) (Class 6) (0-55,65) 3-Y-O — £2,388 (£705; £352) Stalls Low

Form — RPR

4U04 **1** **Granny McPhee**[5] 6338 3-9-0 55 .... NeilChalmers 7 — 63+
(A Bailey) *half-rrd s: hld up towards rr: swtchd rt to outside bnd over 2f out: c v wd st: hdwy over 1f out: led ins fnl f: readily* — 13/2[3]

105 **2** *3 ¾* **Fleur De'Lion (IRE)**[12] 6172 3-8-13 54 .... JamesDoyle 6 — 54
(S Kirk) *a.p: rdn over 1f out: hdd ins fnl f: one pce* — 8/1

0604 **3** *¾* **Dramatic Jewel (USA)**[7] 6287 3-9-3 65 .... KierenFox(7) 2 — 64
(J W Hills) *hld up in mid-div: hdwy over 2f out: rdn jst over 1f out: one pce* — 6/1[2]

0450 **4** *¾* **Feet Of Fury**[36] 5384 3-9-0 55 .... SebSanders 4 — 52
(W M Brisbourne) *hld up in mid-div: c wd st: hdwy over 1f out: kpt on same pce ins fnl f* — 15/2

3000 **5** *1 ½* **One Scoop Or Two**[22] 5838 3-8-12 53 .... (t) SJCraine 3 — 47
(F Sheridan) *t.k.h early: led 1f: a.p: rdn wl over 1f out: wknd ins fnl f* 14/1

0600 **6** *hd* **Luthien (IRE)**[3] 6371 3-8-7 55 .... (p) JPFahy(7) 12 — 48
(A M Hales) *led after 1f: hdd 5f out: led 2f out: rdn and hdd over 1f out: wknd ins fnl f* — 33/1

3450 **7** *½* **Paint Splash**[17] 5983 3-9-0 55 .... TomEaves 1 — 47
(T D Barron) *hld up in tch: pushed along and lost pl over 3f out: rdn over 1f out: no hdwy* — 8/1

5006 **8** *1* **Flute Magic**[31] 5584 3-8-13 54 .... FrankieMcDonald 5 — 44
(W S Kittow) *hld up towards rr: pushed along over 2f out: nvr trbld ldrs* — 25/1

5000 **9** *1 ¾* **Bromhead (USA)**[18] 5972 3-8-13 54 .... (t) JerryO'Dwyer 13 — 41
(Mrs C A Dunnett) *prom: led 5f out to 2f out: rdn and wkng whn hmpd on ins 1f out* — 14/1

5500 **10** *1 ¼* **La Diosa (IRE)**[18] 5975 3-8-8 54 .... AndrewHeffernan(5) 8 — 38
(Mrs S Lamyman) *hld up towards rr: pushed along 3f out: no rspnse* 14/1

0000 **11** *1 ½* **Novastasia (IRE)**[43] 5229 3-8-11 55 .... (p) AndreaAtzeni(3) 9 — 36
(W R Swinburn) *hld up in tch: pushed along over 3f out: rdn 2f out: wknd wl over 1f out* — 14/1

0000 **12** *hd* **Brad's Luck (IRE)**[22] 5838 3-8-13 54 .... FrancisNorton 11 — 34
(M Blanshard) *hld up towards rr: pushed along and struggling over 2f out* — 5/1[1]

0-05 **13** *16* **Rumramah (USA)**[23] 5789 3-8-9 55 .... MartinLane(5) 10 — 2
(D M Simcock) *a in rr: pushed along 3f out: sn lost tch* — 14/1

1m 59.42s (-2.28) **Going Correction** -0.30s/f (Stan) — 13 Ran SP% 118.4
Speed ratings (Par 99): **98,94,94,93,92 91,91,90,88,87 86,86,72**
toteswingers: 1&2 £16.10, 1&3 £8.30, 2&3 £28.10. CSF £57.23 CT £332.28 TOTE £8.40: £2.90, £3.00, £1.80; EX 71.40.
Owner Middleham Park Racing XXVI & Alan Bailey **Bred** Sugar Puss Corporation **Trained** Newmarket, Suffolk
■ Stewards' Enquiry : S J Craine one-day ban: careless riding (Oct 18)

FOCUS
A moderate handicap rated around those in the frame behind the winner.
Flute Magic Official explanation: jockey said gelding ran too freely

6498 WOLVERHAMPTON HOSPITALITY - A PLEASURE H'CAP — 1m 4f 50y(P)

9:15 (9:15) (Class 5) (0-70,70) 3-Y-O+ — £3,238 (£963; £481; £240) Stalls Low

Form — RPR

105/ **1** **Ahmedy (IRE)**[902] 6076 6-9-4 70 .... IJBrennan(7) 9 — 77
(J J Quinn) *t.k.h in mid-div: pushed along over 2f out: hdwy wl over 1f out: rdn to ld cl home* — 10/1

0003 **2** *½* **Wind Flow**[28] 5679 5-9-7 66 .... (v) CatherineGannon 8 — 72
(C A Dwyer) *led: rdn wl over 1f out: hdd cl home* — 7/1[3]

5523 **3** 3/4 **Too Tall**[8] 6257 3-9-2 68 ... SebSanders 1 73
(L M Cumani) hld up in mid-div: hdwy on ins over 2f out: rdn and chal over 1f out: nt qckn wl ins fnl f **10/3**[2]

0331 **4** shd **Bramalea**[14] 6126 4-9-6 65 ... JamesDoyle 6 70+
(B W Duke) hld up towards rr: hdwy wl over 1f out: sn swtchd rt: rdn 1f out: kpt on towards fin **15/2**

153 **5** 1 3/4 **Birkside**[6] 6310 6-9-3 65 ... FrederikTylicki(3) 4 67
(Miss L A Perratt) hld up towards rr: hdwy on ins 2f out: rdn wl over 1f out: no ex wl ins fnl f **5/2**[1]

5000 **6** 1 1/4 **Paint The Town Red**[30] 5594 4-9-7 66 ... JerryO'Dwyer 10 66
(H J Collingridge) hld up in rr: pushed along and hdwy over 1f out: rdn and one pce ins fnl f **28/1**

5206 **7** 1 3/4 **Polish Power (GER)**[50] 4987 9-9-8 67 ... LPKeniry 7 64
(J S Moore) hld up towards rr: rdn over 1f out: nvr nr ldrs **20/1**

3602 **8** nk **Seventh Hill**[14] 6126 4-9-0 59 ... JimmyQuinn 11 56
(M Blanshard) hld up in tch: rdn over 1f out: wknd ins fnl f **11/1**

6-00 **9** 2 3/4 **Duneen Dream (USA)**[27] 1496 4-8-4 56 oh6 ... RachelKing(7) 3 48
(Mrs N S Evans) hld up in mid-div: forced wd bnd over 2f out: c v wd st: sn bhd **80/1**

0606 **10** nk **Royal Keva (IRE)**[14] 6102 3-8-10 62 ... TomEaves 12 54
(A D Brown) chsd ldr tl pushed along wl over 1f out: sn rdn and wknd **40/1**

3044 **11** 2 1/4 **Favours Brave**[54] 4838 3-8-10 67 ... AndrewHeffernan(5) 5 55
(Mrs S Lamyman) prom tl rdn and wknd over 2f out **12/1**

0000 **12** 3 1/4 **Parisian Dream**[32] 5548 5-9-4 63 ... LukeMorris 2 46
(T J Pitt) prom: rdn whn n.m.r 2f out: sn wknd **33/1**

2m 38.83s (-2.27) **Going Correction** -0.30s/f (Stan)
WFA 3 from 4yo+ 7lb **12** Ran SP% **115.9**
Speed ratings (Par 103): **95,94,94,94,92 92,90,90,88,88 87,85**
toteswingers: 1&2 £16.10, 1&3 £7.00, 2&3 £7.60. CSF £72.52 CT £285.63 TOTE £14.80: £4.50, £2.70, £1.50; EX 98.40 Place 6: £34.21 Place 5: £8.74.
Owner Exors Of The Late Lady Anne Bentinck **Bred** Tareq Al Mazeedi **Trained** Settrington, N Yorks

FOCUS
A moderately run contest, and the field remained tightly packed until past halfway. The third and fourth look the best guides to the form.
T/Plt: £22.40 to a £1 stake. Pool: £66,377.45. 2,161.35 winning tickets. T/Qpdt: £3.40 to a £1 stake. Pool: £8,030.55. 1,724.54 winning tickets. KH

6323 COLOGNE (R-H)
Saturday, October 3

OFFICIAL GOING: Good

6499a EBF KOLNER SPRINT-PREIS (LISTED RACE) 5f
3:55 (4:13) 3-Y-O+ **£12,621** (£3,883; £1,942; £971)

RPR

1 **Best Joking (GER)**[29] 5651 4-8-8 ... JanPalik 1 102
(W Hefter, Germany)

2 3 **Look Busy (IRE)**[14] 6107 4-9-1 ... SladeO'Hara 9 98
(A Berry) pushed along fr outside draw to r in midfield on outside: wdst of all ent st: wnt distant 2nd over 1f out: kpt on **9/5**[1]

3 1 1/4 **Le Big (GER)**[20] 5-9-4 ... JiriPalik 8 97
(U Stoltefuss, Germany)

4 1 **Pareia (GER)**[29] 5651 5-8-8 ... RPiechulek 5 83
(Uwe Ostmann, Germany)

5 3 1/2 **Ceodora (GER)**[32] 4-9-1 ... WMongil 3 77
(W Baltromei, Germany)

6 1 1/4 **Laokoon (GER)**[140] 4-9-0 ...(b) MariaPapke 4 72
(Mario Hofer, Germany)

7 nk **Fareion (GER)**[42] 6-9-4 ... HGrewe 2 75
(S Smrczek, Germany)

8 nk **Sacho (GER)**[60] 4637 11-9-4 ... THellier 6 74
(W Kujath, Germany)

9 8 **New Fan**[126] 2513 5-8-11 ... NRichter 7 38
(D Baltromei, Germany)

10 7 **Nadal (IRE)**[42] 6-9-0 ...(b) ABest 10 16
(Frau Doris Smith, Germany)

55.16 secs (-1.77) **10** Ran SP% **35.7**
(including 10 Euro stake): WIN 176; PL 19, 14, 11; SF 1270.
Owner Stall Feeling **Bred** Gestut Riepegrund & Frau H Seegelken **Trained** Germany

NOTEBOOK
Look Busy(IRE), whose rider was soon pushing along, was forced widest of all around the home bend and could not reel in Best Joking, who enjoyed a dream passage against the rail. She stayed on gamely to take second, albeit three lengths adrift.

2524 HOPPEGARTEN (R-H)
Saturday, October 3

OFFICIAL GOING: Good

6500a WESTMINSTER PREIS DER DEUTSCHEN EINHEIT (GROUP 3) 1m 2f
3:45 (3:58) 3-Y-O+ **£31,068** (£9,709; £4,854; £2,913)

RPR

1 **Antara (GER)**[20] 3-8-10 ... APietsch 10 115
(R Dzubasz, Germany) bhd in last: smooth hdwy through field fr over 2f out: led 1 1/2f out: sn clr: impressive **22/5**[3]

2 8 **Liang Kay (GER)**[35] 5461 4-9-4 ... YLerner 5 102
(Uwe Ostmann, Germany) midfield: 4th st: hdwy on ins rail to go 2nd over 1f out: no ch w wnr **37/10**[2]

3 1 **Tempelstern (GER)**[114] 5-9-4 ... ASuborics 2 100
(M Delzangles, France) hld up in 8th: kpt on steadily fnl 2f **116/10**

4 2 **Palermo (GER)**[31] 5585 3-9-0 ... JBojko 1 97
(C Zschache, Germany) led to 1 1/2f out: one pce **63/10**

5 3/4 **Titurel (GER)**[65] 4-9-4 ... ADeVries 4 94
(J Hirschberger, Germany) hld up in 7th: nvr a factor **13/10**[1]

6 1 3/4 **Duellant (IRE)**[35] 5461 4-9-4 ... AStarke 6 91
(P Schiergen, Germany) racd in 2nd: one pce fr over 2f out **21/1**

7 1/2 **White Lightning (GER)**[343] 6992 7-9-4 ... PJWerning 9 90
(U Stech, Germany) prom on outside: 3rd st: sn rdn and btn **28/1**

8 hd **Walzertraum (USA)**[13] 6152 4-9-4 ... JLermyte 3 89
(J Hirschberger, Germany) trckd ldrs on ins: 5th st: rdn and unable qck 2f out **106/10**

9 nk **Panyu (GER)**[31] 5585 3-9-0 ...(b) FilipMinarik 7 90
(P Schiergen, Germany) racd freely on outside: cl up to over 2f out **26/1**

10 1 1/2 **Assahab (GER)**[35] 5461 6-9-4 ... EFrank 11 86
(U Stech, Germany) racd in 9th: a in rr **28/1**

2m 6.90s (0.20)
WFA 3 from 4yo+ 5lb **10** Ran SP% **128.7**
(including 10 Euro stake): WIN 54; PL 19, 16, 26; SF 279.
Owner T Gehrig **Bred** T Gehrig **Trained** Germany

6131 LONGCHAMP (R-H)
Saturday, October 3

OFFICIAL GOING: Good to soft

6501a PRIX HORSE RACING ABROAD (CLAIMER) 1m
1:05 (1:05) 2-Y-O **£12,136** (£4,854; £3,641; £2,427; £1,214)

RPR

1 **Ayun Tara (FR)**[27] 5713 2-9-5 ...(p) TThulliez 85
(P Khozian, France)

2 2 **Wolverine (FR)**[15] 6080 2-9-2 ... FLeroy(3) 81
(Mme C Head-Maarek, France)

3 1/2 **Toxeas (FR)**[45] 2-8-9 ... JClaudic(6) 76
(C Laffon-Parias, France)

4 nse **Verglacial (IRE)** 2-9-2 ... 76
(C Lerner, France)

5 nk **Bubble Zack (FR)**[19] 2-9-2 ... 76
(D Prod'Homme, France)

6 hd **Help From Heaven (IRE)**[66] 4448 2-8-13 ... 72
(R Gibson, France)

7 hd **Issacar (IRE)** 2-8-12 ...(p) 71
(A De Watrigant, France)

8 snk **Emotional Rescue (FR)** 2-8-13 ... 72
(Y Durepaire, Spain)

9 1 **Tropico (FR)**[19] 2-9-2 ... 72
(S Wattel, France)

10 1/2 **Ascot And Co (IRE)**[57] 2-8-8 ...(p) 63
(S Wattel, France)

11 3 **Solarea (FR)**[19] 2-8-8 ... 57
(T Clout, France)

12 1 **Belle Amie (IRE)**[19] 2-8-8 ... 54
(C Boutin, France)

13 hd **Caunton Beck (FR)**[14] 6131 2-9-6 ... JAuge 66
(E J O'Neill) niggled along to gain prom position fr outside draw: 3rd st: led 2 1/2f out to 2f out: wknd **45/1**[1]

14 hd **Clegan (FR)** 2-9-2 ... 62
(J Bertran De Balanda, France)

15 1 1/2 **Le Grenelle (FR)** 2-9-6 ... 62
(F Doumen, France)

16 3/4 **Terradelice (FR)**[27] 5713 2-8-13 ... 54
(Mme L Audon, France)

17 1/2 **Une Autre Aventure (FR)**[27] 5713 2-8-8 ...(p) 47
(C Boutin, France)

18 10 **Million Kiss (IRE)**[69] 2-9-1 ... 32
(C Von Der Recke, Germany)

19 10 **Suerte Loca (IRE)**[53] 2-9-2 ... 11
(Mario Hofer, Germany)

1m 41.5s (3.10) **19** Ran SP% **2.2**
PARI-MUTUEL (Including 1 Euro stake): WIN 5.30; PL 2.20, 2.20, 3.20;DF 10.40.
Owner P Dreux **Bred** Earl Haras Du Camp Benard **Trained** France

6502a QATAR PRIX CHAUDENAY (GROUP 2) 1m 7f
1:35 (1:35) 3-Y-O **£71,942** (£27,767; £13,252; £8,835; £4,417)

RPR

1 **Manighar (FR)**[27] 5711 3-9-2 ... GMosse 2 114
(A De Royer-Dupre, France) racd in 3rd: 4th 1/2-way: 3rd and pushed along st: drvn to chal 1 1/2f out: led appr fnl f: styd on wl **11/4**[3]

2 1/2 **Los Cristianos (FR)**[26] 3-9-2 ... THuet 6 113
(A Couetil, France) hld up in last: 5th st: sn pushed along: rdn and 3rd 1 1/2f out: styd on wl fnl 150yds: nrest at fin **14/1**

3 2 1/2 **Aizavoski (IRE)**[20] 5930 3-9-2 ... ACrastus 1 110
(E Lellouche, France) led: r.o 1 1/2f out: drvn and hdd appr fnl f: no ex fnl 100yds **5/2**[2]

4 5 **Claremont (IRE)**[20] 5930 3-9-2 ... LDettori 5 104
(A Fabre, France) racd in 2nd: drvn st: rdn over 1 1/2f out: nt pce of ldrs **7/4**[1]

5 6 **Loch Long (IRE)**[28] 5688 3-9-2 ... PShanahan 3 97
(Tracey Collins, Ire) in tch in 5th early: 3rd 1/2-way: drvn 3f out: 4th and one pce fr early st **16/1**

6 10 **Amico Mio (FR)**[27] 5711 3-9-2 ... OPeslier 4 85
(J-M Beguigne, France) 5th 1/2-way: pushed along 4f out: last and sn btn st **16/1**

3m 11.0s (-5.00) **Going Correction** +0.125s/f (Good) **6** Ran SP% **110.0**
Speed ratings: **118,117,116,113,110 105**
PARI-MUTUEL: WIN 2.70; PL 1.70, 6.00; SF 24.40.
Owner H H Aga Khan **Bred** Haras De Son Altesse L'Aga Khan Scea **Trained** Chantilly, France

NOTEBOOK
Manighar(FR) is a really decent stayer in the making and has now won six of his seven starts. Fourth in the straight, he quickened impressively from one and a half out to lead shortly afterwards and had plenty in hand to hold off the fast-finishing runner-up. There are no definite plans for the moment but it would be no surprise if the gelding lined up for the Prix Royal-Oak.
Los Cristianos(FR). held up for much of this race, came with a blistering late challenge but could never get to the winner. He may well win a similar race in the future and certainly looks Group 3 level.
Aizavoski(IRE) tried to lead from pillar to post but was under pressure at the furlong marker when passed by the winner. He will certainly turn into a decent 4-y-o and would have preferred more cut in the ground.

Claremont(IRE), supplemented into this event, followed the long-time leader for much of the time but was in trouble halfway up the straight before finishing a remote fourth. This was certainly not his true form.

6503a TOTAL PRIX DE LA FORET (GROUP 1) 7f

2:40 (2:42) 3-Y-0+ **£138,689** (£55,485; £27,743; £13,859; £6,942)

RPR

1 **Varenar (FR)**[27] 5709 3-9-0 ... SPasquier 13 120+
(A De Royer-Dupre, France) *hld up: 7th st: styd on wl down outside fnl 2f to ld cl home* **20/1**

2 *shd* **Sweet Hearth (USA)**[29] 5653 3-8-10 ... GMosse 1 116
(A De Royer-Dupre, France) *disp 3rd trcking ldrs wl clr of remainder: wnt 2nd over 2f out : chal ins fnl f: led 50yds out: hdd cl home* **40/1**

3 *½* **Goldikova (IRE)**[48] 5086 4-8-13 ... OPeslier 14 118
(F Head, France) *racd in cl 2nd bhd scorching pce: led over 2 1/2f out: 1 1/2 l clr gng wl 1 1/2f out: rdn over 1f out: hdd 50yds out* **4/9[1]**

4 *3* **Cat Junior (USA)**[21] 5862 4-9-2 ... LDettori 10 113
(B J Meehan) *prom in main field bhd four ldrs: 5th st: styd on u.p fnl 2f* **25/1**

5 *¾* **Balthazaar's Gift (IRE)**[27] 5710 6-9-2 ... AdamKirby 2 111
(C G Cox) *prom in main field bhd four ldrs: 6th st: kpt on u.p fnl 2f* **16/1[3]**

6 *hd* **Dunkerque (FR)**[55] 4837 4-9-2 ...(p) DBoeuf 4 110
(Mme C Head-Maarek, France) *midfield: pushed along on ins in 10th ent st: kpt on at same pce u.p fnl 2f: fin 7th: plcd 6th* **50/1**

7 *1 ½* **Smooth Operator (GER)**[34] 5493 3-9-0 ... MGuyon 12 108
(Mario Hofer, Germany) *in rr: 8th st: sn one pce: fin 8th: plcd 7th* **25/1**

8 *nk* **Calrissian (GER)**[20] 5-9-2 ... JVictoire 8 109
(F Reuterskiold, Sweden) *a in rr: fin 9th: plcd 8th* **66/1**

9 *nk* **Border Patrol**[20] 5924 3-9-0 ... KJManning 3 106
(R Charlton) *hld up in rr: 11th on ins st: nvr a factor: fin 10th: plcd 9th* **7/1[2]**

10 *2 ½* **Mariol (FR)**[6] 6304 6-9-2 ... FBlondel 11 102
(Robert Collet, France) *hmpd after 2f: a in rr: fin 11th: plcd 10th* **33/1**

11 *¾* **Soneva (USA)**[51] 4971 3-8-10 ... IMendizabal 9 94
(Y De Nicolay, France) *hmpd after 2f: a in rr: fin 12th: plcd 11th* **20/1**

12 *8* **Welsh Emperor (IRE)**[77] 4077 10-9-2 ...(b) MickyFenton 5 78
(T P Tate) *set rapid pce tl hdd 2 1/2f out wknd: fin 13th: plcd 12th* **80/1**

13 *3* **Opera Comica (BRZ)**[63] 3-8-7 ... TJPereira 6 61
(G Duarte, Brazil) *prom: 4th whn rn wd ent st: wknd qckly: fin 14th: plcd 13th* **33/1**

D *hd* **Oiseau De Feu (USA)**[27] 5710 3-9-0 ... CSoumillon 7 109
(J-C Rouget, France) *hld up: edgd sltly lft hampering two rivals after 2f: 9th st: nvr a factor: fin 6th: disqualified and plcd last* **18/1**

1m 19.2s (-1.50) **Going Correction** +0.125s/f (Good)
WFA 3 from 4yo+ 2lb **14 Ran SP% 123.1**
Speed ratings: **113,112,112,108,108 107,105,105,105,102 101,92,88,107**
PARI-MUTUEL: WIN 20.60; PL 2.70, 6.20, 1.20; DF 220.20.
Owner H H Aga Khan **Bred** Haras De Son Altesse L'Aga Khan Scea **Trained** Chantilly, France

NOTEBOOK

Varenar(FR) had no real pretensions to a Group 1 success, his best previous effort having been when fourth in a weak Prix Maurice de Gheest. He is surely flattered to have claimed such a major prize, but he is clearly a colt on the upgrade, and it was no surprise that connections decided to pull him out that evening's Arc sale. That said, the very fact that he was entered for the auction confirms that he was not held in the highest regard before the Foret. However, he will remain in training as a 4-y-o and might be capable of winning a similar event next year.

Sweet Hearth(USA), a stablemate of the winner, had posted a cosy Listed success coming into the Foret, but this was light years in advance of that form. This was an excellent display, but it is hard to believe that the previously unheralded filly is as good as she seemed to show here. She will remain in training as a 4-y-o but is unlikely to travel being a nervous individual.

Goldikova(IRE) had been expected to cement her status as red-hot odds-on favourite for the Breeders' Cup Mile with an easy victory. However that wasn't the case as, racing over 7f for the first time in her career, she tired in the closing stages after racing prominently. Having been handed a horribly wide draw in stall 14, Olivier Peslier decided to let his mount roll along from the gate, but she then ended up at the head of a frantic gallop and one which took its toll in the final furlong. It trainer Freddie Head perplexed, but the 4-y-o bounced back from a disappointing seasonal reappearance and she will very likely do so again. Although a wide-margin winner of two Deauville Group 1s during the summer, Goldikova must have been drained by those wins, so much so that she might well have been feeling the effects here. She will undergo tests but came out of the race in good condition and, if back to her best at Santa Anita, where the round 1m track plays to her strengths, she will still be very much the one to beat.

Cat Junior(USA), with the tongue tie left off, had his chance and ran another respectable race but is not easy to place successfully.

Balthazaar's Gift(IRE) was not at his very best, but still performed creditably on this return to suitably quicker ground.

Border Patrol, taking a big step up in Grade, was allowed to take his chance despite his preference for cut underfoot. He was never in the hunt, but remains a smart prospect for next year when a return to softer ground should see him back in a better light.

Welsh Emperor(IRE) was having his first outing since winning at Haydock 77 days previously and had run well in this race three times in the past. With the blinkers back on he simply went off far too quickly, however.

6504a QATAR PRIX DE ROYALLIEU (GROUP 2) (F&M) 1m 4f 110y

3:15 (3:14) 3-Y-0+ **£71,942** (£27,767; £11,044; £11,044; £4,417)

RPR

1 **Daryakana (FR)**[31] 5586 3-8-7 ... GMosse 6 115+
(A De Royer-Dupre, France) *hld up in last: shkn up st: hdwy down outside over 1 1/2f out: rdn to ld 1f out: r.o wl* **5/2[2]**

2 *2 ½* **Peinture Rare (IRE)**[51] 4969 3-8-7 ... ACrastus 4 110
(E Lellouche, France) *in tch: 4th 1/2-way: r.o 2f out: qcknd to ld over 1 1/2f out to ld 1f out: nt pce of wnr ins fnl f* **10/1**

3 *¾* **Tanoura (IRE)**[23] 5796 3-8-7 ... MJKinane 5 109
(John M Oxx, Ire) *hld up in 6th: drvn on outside 2f out: styd on fnl f: dead-heated for 3rd on line* **5/1[3]**

3 *dht* **Plumania**[20] 5929 3-8-7 ... OPeslier 1 109
(A Fabre, France) *in tch: 5th 1/2-way: rdn 2f out: hdwy to go 3rd fnl f: kpt on wout troubling ldrs* **9/4[1]**

5 *1 ½* **Charity Belle (USA)**[41] 5298 3-8-7 ... LDettori 2 106
(J H M Gosden) *led: r.o st: hdd over 1 1/2f out: no ex fnl f* **5/1[3]**

6 *1* **Burn The Breeze (IRE)**[31] 5586 4-9-1 ... TJarnet 7 105
(Mlle H Van Zuylen, France) *racd in 5th early tl prog and 2nd 1/2-way: pushed along early st: u.p 2f out: one pce* **14/1**

7 *20* **Valletta**[21] 5896 3-8-7 ... DBoeuf 3 73
(H-A Pantall, France) *prom: 3rd 1/2-way: shkn up 2f out: sn btn* **16/1**

2m 38.4s (-1.50) **Going Correction** +0.125s/f (Good)
WFA 3 from 4yo 7lb **7 Ran SP% 114.3**
Speed ratings: **109,107,107,107,106 105,93**
PARI-MUTUEL: WIN 2.90 (coupled with Tanoura); PL 2.20, 3.20; SF 30.20.
Owner H H Aga Khan **Bred** H H The Aga Khan's Studs S C **Trained** Chantilly, France

NOTEBOOK

Daryakana(FR), a rapidly improving filly, posted an extremely impressive victory. Having been held up early on in last place, she came with a sweeping late run up the centre of the track and completely outclassed her rivals. She looks ure to turn into a very smart 4-y-o and looks cut out for next year's Prix Vermeille.

Peinture Rare(IRE), fourth for most of the race before taking over the lead halfway up the straight, could do absolutely nothing when the winner came sweeping past her.

Tanoura(IRE), second last in the early stages, came with a late run but didn't have the acceleration of the winner. She will now be retired to stud.

Plumania once again was disappointing and didn't stretch out in the straight as she had done in the Vermeille. Fifth in the early part of the race, she just stayed on one paced.

Charity Belle(USA) tried to make all the running and stayed at the head of affairs until halfway up the straight. She didn't appear to get this longer distance.

6505a QATAR PRIX DANIEL WILDENSTEIN (GROUP 2) 1m

3:45 (3:48) 3-Y-0+ **£71,942** (£27,767; £13,252; £8,835; £4,417)

RPR

1 **Tamazirte (IRE)**[41] 5298 3-8-8 ... CSoumillon 11 108+
(J-C Rouget, France) *hld up: 8th and prog st: gd hdwy fr 1 1/2f out to ld 100yds out: comf* **11/2[2]**

2 *1* **Danse Grecque (USA)**[41] 5300 4-8-11 ... ACrastus 3 106
(E Lellouche, France) *prom: disputing 3rd st: pushed along over 1 1/2f out: led jst ins fnl f to 100yds out: jst hld 2nd* **16/1**

3 *hd* **Murcielago (FR)**[33] 4-9-1 ...(b) TCastanheira 1 109
(T Castanheira, France) *prom: cl 5th on ins st: hdwy in centre 2f out: ev ch appr fnl f: kpt on: jst missed 2nd* **25/1**

4 *nk* **Handsome Maestro (IRE)**[34] 5496 3-8-11 ... SPasquier 4 108
(D Smaga, France) *prom: disputing 3rd st: drvn and 3rd 2f out: rdn 1 1/2f out: styd on steadily u.p* **16/1**

5 *1* **Beacon Lodge (IRE)**[35] 5426 4-9-1 ... AdamKirby 2 106+
(C G Cox) *mid-div: hrd drvn to chse ldrs over 1 1/2f out: nvr nrr* **5/1[1]**

6 *shd* **Reggane**[62] 4580 3-8-8 ... GMosse 8 102+
(A De Royer-Dupre, France) *in tch: 6th st: effrt in centre 2f out: no ex fr over 1f out* **5/1[1]**

7 *½* **Shamwari Lodge (IRE)**[7] 6267 3-8-8 ... MJKinane 9 101
(R Hannon) *mid-div: effrt 2f out: styd on in centre but n.d* **11/1[3]**

8 *nk* **Kachgai (IRE)**[34] 5496 6-9-1 ... IMendizabal 15 104
(Y De Nicolay, France) *towards rr: drvn and unable qck st* **14/1**

9 *nk* **Racinger (FR)**[34] 5496 6-9-1 ... DBonilla 12 103
(F Head, France) *in tch: 6th st: effrt in centre 2f out: no ex fr over 1f out* **11/2[2]**

10 *1 ½* **Golden Century (USA)**[34] 5496 3-8-11 ... MGuyon 5 99
(A Fabre, France) *racd in cl 2nd: led over 1 1/2f out: hdd jst ins fnl f: no ex fnl 150 yds* **12/1**

11 *5* **Spring Of Fame (USA)**[43] 5231 3-8-11 ... LDettori 10 88
(Saeed Bin Suroor) *hld up towards rr: pushed along st: unable qck* **12/1**

12 *4* **Earl Of Fire (GER)**[6] 6323 4-9-1 ... DBoeuf 6 79
(W Baltromei, Germany) *led to over 1 1/2f out: sn wknd* **16/1**

13 *nse* **Uncle Tom (BRZ)**[62] 3-8-13 ...(b) TJPereira 14 80
(G Duarte, Brazil) *a bhd* **28/1**

14 *nse* **Oroveso (BRZ)**[62] 3-8-8 ... BReis 7 75
(G Duarte, Brazil) *towards rr: rdn on outside st: no imp* **33/1**

15 *2 ½* **Sharpour (IRE)**[13] 5-9-1 ... VJanacek 13 73
(Z Koplik, Czech Republic) *a bhd* **50/1**

1m 38.6s (0.20) **Going Correction** +0.125s/f (Good)
WFA 3 from 4yo+ 3lb **15 Ran SP% 124.3**
Speed ratings: **104,103,102,102,101 101,100,100,100,98 93,89,89,89,87**
PARI-MUTUEL: WIN 4.20; PL 1.90, 3.10, 6.80; DF 23.70.
Owner Ecurie Vallee Martigny & Mme L Rabineau **Bred** Churchtown Bloodstock Ltd **Trained** Pau, France

NOTEBOOK

Tamazirte(IRE), who has been on the go since the beginning of the year, gained a well-deserved victory, having had been runner-up in two classics earlier in the season. Given a waiting ride, she came with a well-timed challenge and quickened well to eventually win with something in hand. Unlikely to race again this season, she may well be around as a 4-y-o.

Danse Grecque(USA) ran a solid race, was always well up and found a nice gap at the furlong marker. She then battled on gamely to hold second place.

Murcielago(FR) raced just behind the leading group, she went into the lead at the furlong marker but was then outpaced as the race came to a finish.

Handsome Maestro(IRE), another who was always well up with the pace and given every possible chance, just lacked a little finishing speed as the race came to an end.

Beacon Lodge(IRE) didn't start too well and was towards the tail of the field for much of the race. He did run on in the straight but never looked like finishing in the frame.

Reggane runner-up in the Coronation Stakes earlier in the season, would have preferred a sounder surface and could not pick up in the straight.

Shamwari Lodge(IRE), making her run up the centre of the track, had every chance at the furlong marker but could not quicken.

Spring Of Fame(USA) was never seen with a chance and made no show on this occasion.

6506a QATAR PRIX DOLLAR (GROUP 2) 1m 1f 165y

4:20 (4:19) 3-Y-0+ **£71,942** (£27,767; £13,252; £8,835; £4,417)

RPR

1 **Pipedreamer**[128] 2410 5-9-0 ... DBoeuf 6 115+
(J H M Gosden) *in tch: 5th and pushed along st: rdn and 3rd 2f out: r.o to ld 1f out: drvn out* **4/1[2]**

2 *nk* **Gris De Gris (IRE)**[27] 5709 5-9-0 ... GMosse 4 114
(A De Royer-Dupre, France) *led: pushed along 2f out: hdd 1f out: kpt on: pressed wnr to line* **8/1**

3 *nk* **Famous Name**[27] 5710 4-9-0 ... PJSmullen 10 114+
(D K Weld, Ire) *towards rr of mid-div: hdwy on outside 2f out to chal 1f out: ev ch fnl f: styd on* **15/8[1]**

4 *nk* **Stotsfold**[21] 5875 6-9-0 ... AdamKirby 9 113+
(W R Swinburn) *hld up: rdn and hdwy on outside 1 1/2f out: styd on fnl f: nrest at fin* **8/1**

5 *nk* **Starlish (IRE)**[27] 5712 4-9-0 ... ACrastus 5 113
(E Lellouche, France) *mid-div: hdwy through field over 1 1/2f out: disputing 4th 150yds out: styd on* **20/1**

6 1 1/2 **Mundybash**[27] 5712 4-9-0 TThulliez 13 109+
(N Clement, France) *hld up in rr: effrt down outside 2f out: kpt on steadily: nrest at fin* **20/1**
7 1/2 **Bon Grain (FR)**[27] 5712 4-9-0 FBlondel 3 108
(J J Napoli, France) *racd in 3rd on rail: pushed along 2f out: nt pce of ldrs* **40/1**
8 3 **Suits Me**[14] 6110 6-9-0 MickyFenton 7 102
(T P Tate) *racd in 2nd: pushed along appr st: r.o tl lost pl 1 1/2f out: no ex fnl f* **66/1**
9 2 1/2 **Estejo (GER)**[27] 5-9-0 IMendizabal 2 97
(R Rohne, Germany) *mid-div: disputing 6th on ins st: outpcd fr 2f out* **33/1**
10 1 1/2 **City Leader (IRE)**[15] 6056 4-9-0 DBonilla 12 94
(B J Meehan) *in tch towards outside: 4th st: sn pushed along: unable qck* **14/1**
11 snk **Balius (IRE)**[31] 5587 6-9-4 (b) LDettori 11 98
(Saeed Bin Suroor) *in tch: disputing 6th st: u.p 2f out: nt qckn* **7/1**[3]
12 1/2 **Adelar (GER)**[27] 5707 4-9-0 OPeslier 1 93
(W Baltromei, Germany) *mid-div: nvr in chalng position* **20/1**
13 8 **Estrela Anki (BRZ)**[63] 4-8-10 TJPereira 8 72
(G Duarte, Brazil) *a in rr* **40/1**

2m 0.30s (-2.60) **Going Correction** +0.125s/f (Good) **13** Ran SP% **119.8**
Speed ratings: **115,114,114,114,114 112,112,110,108,106 106,106,99**
PARI-MUTUEL: WIN 9.30; PL 3.10, 1.70, 1.30; DF 32.20.
Owner Cheveley Park Stud **Bred** Cheveley Park Stud Ltd **Trained** Newmarket, Suffolk

NOTEBOOK
Pipedreamer was given a beautiful ride by his replacement jockey on his first start since May. He was being kicked along early in the straight, and then ran on really well to take the lead halfway through the final furlong. He has been entered in the Champion Stakes.
Gris De Gris(IRE) made a very brave attempt to make all the running on a surface which was too firm for his liking. He fended off all attacks apart from that of the winner, which came inside the final furlong. He has plenty of races coming up for him and the ground is sure to be softer, which will suit.
Famous Name found the going was too firm. He was held up in the early stages and brought with a well-timed challenge, but would not let himself down and just stayed on one paced inside the final furlong.
Stotsfold, one of the last coming into the straight, was putting in his best work at the finish and was beaten under a length.
Suits Me, well up from the start, was in trouble halfway up the straight.
City Leader(IRE) had his nose in the air on the outside when racing in fourth place early on. Still well there in the straight, he was going nowhere during the final furlong and a half.
Balius(IRE) was in mid-division early on but was then beaten early in the straight.

6237 SAINT-CLOUD (L-H)
Friday, October 2

OFFICIAL GOING: Good

6507a PRIX NINO (C&G) 1m
1:05 (1:05) 2-Y-O **£16,505** (£6,602; £4,951; £3,301; £1,650)

RPR
1 **Maroon Machine (IRE)**[41] 5280 2-9-4 OPeslier 95
(E J O'Neill) *mid-div: hdwy to chal 2f out: tk narrow ld 1f out: drvn out and r.o wl* **5/2**[1]
2 snk **Marceti (IRE)** 2-8-13 GMosse 90
(E Leenders, France)
3 snk **Grand Duc (USA)**[37] 2-8-10 DBoeuf 86
(Mme C Head-Maarek, France)
4 2 1/2 **Battlecat**[28] 2-8-13 84
(A Fabre, France)
5 1 1/2 **Style De Lois (FR)**[26] 5713 2-8-10 78
(Robert Collet, France)
6 2 **Kaage (IRE)** 2-8-4 MBarzalona(3) 70
(F Head, France)
7 4 **Existes Ons Nous (FR)** 2-8-4 (3) 61
(J-M Lefebvre, France)

1m 43.1s (-4.40) 7 Ran SP% **28.6**
PARI-MUTUEL: WIN 3.50; PL 2.00, 3.30; SF 21.00.
Owner G A Lucas & A E Hunt **Bred** G Brochard **Trained** Southwell, Notts

2734 BELMONT PARK (L-H)
Saturday, October 3

OFFICIAL GOING: Dirt course - fast changing to sloppy after 8.23; turf course - soft
Torrential rain during the meeting got into the ground, turning the dirt sloppy and the turf very testing.

6508a BELDAME STKS (GRADE 1) (F&M) (DIRT) 1m 1f (D)
8:23 (8:23) 3-Y-O+ **£250,000** (£83,333; £41,667; £20,833; £12,500)

RPR
1 **Music Note (USA)**[35] 4-8-11 RMaragh 1 121
(Saeed Bin Suroor) **1/4**[1]
2 2 1/4 **Unbridled Belle (USA)**[34] 6-8-11 RADominguez 3 117
(Todd Pletcher, U.S.A) **14/5**[2]
3 9 1/4 **Copper State (USA)**[98] 5-8-11 SXBridgmohan 4 98
(Steven Asmussen, U.S.A) **128/10**[3]
4 13 3/4 **Captain's Lover (SAF)**[35] 5-8-11 JRVelazquez 2 71
(Todd Pletcher, U.S.A) **14/5**[2]
5 15 **With Flying Colors (USA)**[34] 4-8-11 JJCastellano 5 43
(Todd Pletcher, U.S.A) **159/10**

1m 48.49s (0.69) 5 Ran SP% **145.8**
PARI-MUTUEL (Including $2 stake): WIN 2.50; PL (1-2) 2.10, 2.10(Unbridled Belle coupled with Captain's Lover); SF 3.70.
Owner Godolphin Racing LLC **Bred** Gainsborough Farm Llc **Trained** Newmarket, Suffolk

FOCUS
A trial for the Breeders' Cup Ladies Classic.

NOTEBOOK
Music Note(USA) had no trouble in following up her success in the Ballerina Stakes, finding plenty for pressure having briefly looked set for a battle. Although her very best form is on dirt, she ran third in last year's Ladies Classic on the Pro-Ride at Santa Anita and that race is the target once again. Stan James make her a 7/1 shot and she's not to be underestimated for a yard enjoying a terrific time of things Stateside.
Unbridled Belle(USA), winner of this in 2007, had the blinkers left off this time and left behind a couple of sub-standard efforts. She was no match for the winner, though.

6509a VOSBURGH STKS (GRADE 1) (DIRT) 6f (D)
8:59 (8:59) 3-Y-O+ **£166,667** (£55,556; £27,778; £13,889)

RPR
1 **Kodiak Kowboy (USA)**[28] 4-8-12 SXBridgmohan 3 123
(Steven Asmussen, U.S.A) **48/10**[3]
2 1/2 **Fabulous Strike (USA)**[55] 6-8-12 RADominguez 4 122
(Todd M Beattie, U.S.A) **13/20**[1]
3 3 1/2 **Munnings (USA)**[35] 3-8-10 JRVelazquez 2 110
(Todd Pletcher, U.S.A) **12/5**[2]
4 8 **Go Go Shoot (USA)**[55] 4-8-12 RMaragh 1 87
(Bruce N Levine, U.S.A) **69/10**

1m 10.08s (0.88)
WFA 3 from 4yo+ 1lb 4 Ran SP% **119.9**
PARI-MUTUEL: WIN 11.60; PL (1-2) 3.00, 2.10; SF 20.40.
Owner Vinery Stables and Fox Hill Farm **Bred** Hartwell Farm **Trained** USA

FOCUS
The winner is a possible for the Breeders' Cup Sprint, but the runner-up is likely to look elsewhere.

NOTEBOOK
Kodiak Kowboy(USA) ♦, having his first run back with Steve Asmussen, was detached in last early on, upwards of 3l off his rivals, but powered home in the straight to improve on last season's third in this race. Already a winner on synthetics, he might run in the Breeders' Cup Sprint, for which he is 6/1 with Ladbrokes, and his run style promises to be well suited to a strongly run race on Pro-Ride.
Fabulous Strike(USA), winner of this in 2007 and runner-up last year, had every chance after tracking early leader Go Go Shoot. It's apparently unlikely that he'll try and improve on last season's fifth in the Breeders' Cup Sprint.

6510a FLOWER BOWL INVITATIONAL STKS (GRADE 1) (F&M) (TURF) 1m 2f (T)
9:35 (9:36) 3-Y-O+
£250,000 (£83,333; £41,667; £20,833; £12,500; £4,167)

RPR
1 **Pure Clan (USA)**[56] 4-8-9 (b) JRLeparoux 2 114
(Robert E Holthus, U.S.A) **13/5**[3]
2 2 3/4 **Criticism**[63] 5-8-9 JJCastellano 4 108
(Thomas Albertrani, U.S.A) **102/10**
3 1 1/4 **Queen Of Hearts (USA)**[26] 4-8-7 (b) JLEspinoza 6 104
(James Jerkens, U.S.A) **27/1**
4 2 3/4 **Moneycantbuymelove (IRE)**[63] 4522 3-8-5 ow2 JamieSpencer 7 103
(M L W Bell) *held up, effort and headway on wide outside 2f out, 5th straight, no impression on leaders closing stages* **49/20**[2]
5 3 3/4 **Leamington (USA)**[459] 3586 4-8-7 EPrado 1 91
(H Graham Motion, U.S.A) **143/10**
6 10 1/4 **Dynaforce (USA)**[56] 6-8-11 KDesormeaux 3 75
(William Mott, U.S.A) **23/10**[1]
7 3 1/4 **Beauty O' Gwaun (IRE)**[61] 4609 3-8-3 (b) RADominguez 5 65
(Christophe Clement, U.S.A) **61/10**

2m 12.43s (11.14)
WFA 3 from 4yo+ 5lb 7 Ran SP% **120.2**
PARI-MUTUEL: WIN 7.20; PL (1-2) 3.50, 7.80; SHOW (1-2-3) 2.50, 4.10,7.10; SF 72.00.
Owner Lewis Lakin **Bred** A Lakin And Sons Inc **Trained** North America

FOCUS
Something of a trial for the Breeders' Cup Filly & Mare Turf, but unless the ground is testing at Santa Anita, this is form to treat with real caution. The pace was steady, even allowing for the conditions, with the first 6f being covered in 1m20.43secs.

NOTEBOOK
Pure Clan(USA) had finished third behind Dynaforce in the Beverley D Stakes, but this ground was clearly to her liking. It will be a surprise if she follows up in the Filly & Mare Turf considering she failed to beat a rival in last year's running, but that race is said to be the target.
Criticism, who has form on soft ground from her days when trained in France, handled the conditions and trainer Tom Albertrani said he was pleased with the mare's effort. The Filly & Mare Turf is under consideration.
Moneycantbuymelove(IRE), carrying 2lb overweight, should not have minded the conditions, as although her two Listed wins so far were gained on good to firm, she was third in the Nassau on an easy surface, and is by Pivotal, whose progeny often favour easy going. As it turned out, the ground might have been deeper than ideal, but still, she was set plenty to do before trying to make her move five-wide around the bend. She soon tired and can be given another chance.
Dynaforce(USA), successful in this race 12 months ago and ahead of today's winner last time, is another with soft ground form to her name, having also started her career in France, but she ran no sort of race.

6511a JOE HIRSCH TURF CLASSIC INVITATIONAL STKS (GRADE 1) 1m 4f
10:09 (12:00) 3-Y-O+
£250,000 (£83,333; £41,667; £20,833; £12,500; £8,333)

RPR
1 **Interpatation (USA)**[14] 7-9-0 RAlbarado 1 114
(Robert Barbara, U.S.A) **44/1**
2 1 3/4 **Gio Ponti (USA)**[56] 4809 4-9-0 RADominguez 5 111+
(Christophe Clement, U.S.A) **17/20**[1]
3 1/2 **Grand Couturier**[20] 8900 6-9-0 AGarcia 6 110+
(Robert Ribaudo, U.S.A) *finished 4th, placed 3rd* **13/5**[2]
4 1 3/4 **Telling (USA)**[49] 5-9-0 JJCastellano 3 106
(Steve Hobby, U.S.A) *finished 3rd, placed 4th* **68/10**
5 7 1/4 **Al Khali (USA)**[27] 3-8-9 KDesormeaux 2 96+
(William Mott, U.S.A) **19/2**
6 3 1/2 **Musketier (GER)**[49] 7-9-0 EPrado 4 89
(Roger L Attfield, Canada) **67/10**[3]

2m 41.22s (12.64)
WFA 3 from 4yo+ 7lb 6 Ran SP% **119.4**
PARI-MUTUEL: WIN 89.50; PL (1-2) 14,40, 2.80; SHOW (1-2-3) 4.30, 2.10,2.40; SF 230.50.
Owner Elliot Mavorah **Bred** Larry Cassaday & Jack O Thompson **Trained** North America

FOCUS
Supposedly a Breeders' Cup Turf trial, but the unconsidered winner set extremely slow fractions, even allowing for the ground, and anyway the beaten favourite is most likely being pointed towards the Classic.

NOTEBOOK
Interpatation(USA), who had gone 17 races and over two years without success, clearly relished the soft ground, but in truth he stole this Grade 1 contest. Soon in front, he was able to cover the first 6f in a yawning 1m22.20secs, and although he looked beaten when headed by the runner-up early in the straight, on reflection it is no surprise he had sufficient reserves to rally. He's not even quoted in the betting for the Breeders' Cup Turf.
Gio Ponti(USA) ◆, bidding for a fifth straight Grade 1 success, his latest having come in the Arlington Million, was upset at odds on but this was a commendable effort in defeat. Trying his furthest trip to date and racing on ground this testing for the first time, he travelled strongly as usual and made up a few lengths on the early leader to take over at the top of straight. However, once under maximum pressure, he soon floundered and became unbalanced, clearly getting tired, and that handed the initiative back to Interpatation. It's likely he'll skip the Breeders' Cup Turf - he's now out to 8/1 - and the Classic is probably going to be his target. That looks a good decision, as grass form translates well to Pro-Ride (in actual fact he's already won on the synthetics at Santa Anita), and this high-class performer is ideally suited by a strongly run 1m2f. If Sea The Stars stays at home, the 20/1 offered by Coral will look big.
Grand Couturier, with conditions to suit, would probably have been third had been not been short of room at the top of the straight, and he was subsequently handed that position.
Telling(USA) ◆ couldn't sustain his run after coming from last and travelling four wide around the turn into the straight. Don't rule out much better back on quick turf in a strongly run race at the Breeders' Cup.

6512a JOCKEY CLUB GOLD CUP STKS (GRADE 1) (DIRT) 1m 2f (D)
10:43 (10:47) 3-Y-O+
£312,500 (£104,167; £52,083; £26,042; £15,625; £5,208)

			RPR
1		**Summer Bird (USA)**[35] 3-8-10 ....(b) KDesormeaux 3	127
		(Tim Ice, U.S.A) **5/4**[1]	
2	1	**Quality Road (USA)**[35] 3-8-10 .... JRVelazquez 7	125+
		(Todd Pletcher, U.S.A) **53/20**[2]	
3	4 ½	**Tizway (USA)**[56] 4-9-0 ....(b) RMaragh 4	115
		(Harold James Bond, U.S.A) **234/10**	
4	6 ½	**Macho Again (USA)**[28] 4-9-0 ....(b) RAlbarado 2	102+
		(Dallas Stewart, U.S.A) **53/20**[2]	
5	5 ½	**Dry Martini (USA)**[56] 6-9-0 ....(b) EPrado 6	92
		(Barclay Tagg, U.S.A) **153/10**	
6	9 ½	**Sette E Mezzo (USA)**[36] 4-9-0 .... RADominguez 1	74
		(William Mott, U.S.A) **38/1**	
7	28	**Asiatic Boy (ARG)**[28] 6-9-0 ....(b) AGarcia 5	23
		(Kiaran McLaughlin, U.S.A) **117/10**[3]	

2m 2.51s (1.89)
WFA 3 from 4yo+ 5lb **7** Ran SP% **119.9**
PARI-MUTUEL: WIN 4.50; PL (1-2) 2.80, 3.80; SHOW (1-2-3) 2.10, 3.80,6.30; SF 15.20.
Owner Kalarikkal K & Vilasini D Jayaraman **Bred** Dr K Jayaraman & V Jayaraman **Trained** North America

■ Summer Bird became the first horse since Easy Goer in 1989 to win the Belmont Stakes, the Travers and this race in one year.

FOCUS
This cannot be described as a Breeders' Cup trial - it's one of the most prestigious races in the US calendar in its own right, and in any case the Classic will again be run on a completely different surface this season. The race lacked strength in depth this year, with no outstanding older horse in the line up, but two top notch 3-y-os came clear.

NOTEBOOK
Summer Bird(USA) cemented his position as the leading 3-y-o colt in the US, confirming Travers Stakes form with Quality Road to secure his third Grade 1 success of the season. Indeed, his only defeat in four outings since the Kentucky Derby came at the hands of Rachel Alexandra over an inadequate 1m1f. He got shuffled back a bit early on and could have found himself in trouble, with the leaders setting modest fractions, but with his stamina assured (the same couldn't be said about the runner-up), Desormeaux shrewdly moved the colt into a challenging position leaving the back straight, before committing for home fully 4f out. A protracted battle with the only other 3-y-o ensued, but the pre-race market leader always remained favourite to come out on top and duly saw the race out best. Provided he comes out of this okay - said to be bouncing the day after - he is likely to be aimed at the Breeders' Cup Classic, where a potentially thrilling clash with the likes of Sea The Stars and Rip Van Winkle may await him. However, it's on dirt - both fast and sloppy - that he's proved himself a top-class racehorse, and the Pro-Ride at Santa Anita must put him at a big disadvantage against the European runners, even though he apparently trains on the surface. If he pulls it off, it will be quite a feat - even the great Curlin couldn't manage it after his success in this race 12 months ago.
Quality Road(USA) got closer to Summer Bird than when 5l behind in the Travers Stakes, and his jockey feels he can do better again, arguing that the winner had the advantage of more race-conditioning, as well as a proven ability to handle a sloppy surface. However, as valid as both of those points undoubtedly are, it's worth pointing out Quality Road enjoyed an advantage of his own by racing up with modest fractions, and if the winning rider is to be believed, then Summer Bird was idling in front. Whatever the case, the runner-up should come on again for this, and while doubts remain over his stamina for a strongly run 1m2f right now, he can be expected to improve next year, when he might just be a stronger stayer as well. No decision has yet been made on whether he'll tackle the Classic.
Macho Again(USA) is flattered by his recent close second to Rachel Alexandra in the Woodward. He needs the leaders to go too fast, which didn't happen this time.

6513 - 6520a (Foreign Racing) - See Raceform Interactive

3201 DORTMUND (R-H)
Sunday, October 4

OFFICIAL GOING: Soft

6521a GROSSER PREIS VON DSW21 DEUTSCHES ST LEGER (GROUP 3) 1m 6f
4:15 (4:26) 3-Y-O+ **£31,068** (£12,621; £6,311; £3,398)

			RPR
1		**Sassoaloro (GER)**[31] 5619 5-9-6 .... THellier 3	110
		(H Blume, Germany) *a cl up: 3rd st: led wl over 1f out: r.o wl* **22/5**[3]	
2	4	**Night Of Magic (IRE)**[70] 4367 3-8-8 .... HGrewe 1	101
		(H Steinmetz, Germany) *hld up in rr: last st: stdy prog on outside fnl 2f: nvr rchd wnr* **81/10**	
3	1 ½	**Tarkheena Prince (USA)**[32] 4-9-6 .... WMongil 6	102
		(C Von Der Recke, Germany) *in rr to st: hdwy wl over 1f out: disp 2nd ins fnl f: one pce* **171/10**	
4	shd	**Caudillo (GER)**[32] 6-9-6 .... ASuborics 7	102
		(Dr A Bolte, Germany) *hld up towards rr: hdwy wl over 1f out: disp 2nd ins fnl f: one pce* **11/2**	
5	1 ¼	**El Comodin (IRE)**[32] 5-9-6 .... JLermyte 2	100
		(J Hirschberger, Germany) *led 2f: settled in 3rd: lost pl over 3f out: rallied 1 1/2f out: no ex fnl f* **11/2**	
6	3 ½	**La Tournesol (GER)**[32] 4-9-3 .... AStarke 5	92
		(P Schiergen, Germany) *hld up: hdwy 1/2-way: 6th st: nvr nr to chal* **39/10**[2]	
7	2 ½	**Ordenstreuer (IRE)**[91] 3670 3-8-11 .... APietsch 4	92
		(R Dzubasz, Germany) *pressed ldrs: 2nd st: wknd over 1 1/2f out: eased fnl f* **33/10**[1]	
8	3 ½	**Valdino (GER)**[32] 4-9-6 ....(b) DPorcu 9	87
		(Uwe Ostmann, Germany) *led after 2f to wl over 1f out: wknd qckly* **49/10**	
9	nse	**Ruten (USA)**[32] 4-9-6 ....(b) AGoritz 8	87
		(Andreas Lowe, Germany) *mid-div: hdwy 1/2-way: 4th st: sn btn* **16/1**	

3m 2.73s (-2.77)
WFA 3 from 4yo+ 9lb **9** Ran SP% **132.3**
TOTE: WIN 54; PL 19, 25, 37; DF 593.
Owner Stall Life Style **Bred** Dr Werner Spengler **Trained** Germany

6501 LONGCHAMP (R-H)
Sunday, October 4

OFFICIAL GOING: Good

6522a QATAR PRIX DE L'ABBAYE DE LONGCHAMP (GROUP 1) 5f (S)
12:45 (12:46) 2-Y-O+ **£138,689** (£55,485; £27,743; £13,859; £6,942)

			RPR
1		**Total Gallery (IRE)**[15] 6107 3-9-11 .... JMurtagh 3	121
		(J S Moore) *trckd ldrs on rails: led over 1f out: r.o wl* **10/1**	
2	nk	**Fleeting Spirit (IRE)**[29] 5657 4-9-7 .... TPQueally 8	116
		(J Noseda) *lw: s.i.s: edgd to rails after 2f and trckd wnr: rdn wl over 1f out: r.o fnl f to take 2nd cl home* **11/8**[1]	
3	½	**War Artist (AUS)**[21] 5928 6-9-11 .... OPeslier 9	118
		(J M P Eustace) *lw: a in tch: rdn and kpt on u.str.p fnl f to take 3rd last strides* **6/1**[2]	
4	hd	**Benbaun (IRE)**[21] 5928 8-9-11 ....(v) PJSmullen 12	117
		(K A Ryan) *prom: disp ld after 2f: led 2f out to over 1f out: lost 3rd last strides* **16/1**	
5	¾	**Black Mambazo (IRE)**[14] 4-9-11 .... LDettori 2	115
		(L Riccardi, Italy) *in rr tl 1/2-way: gd hdwy fnl 2f: nrest at fin* **25/1**	
6	½	**Borderlescott**[44] 5233 7-9-11 .... NCallan 7	113
		(R Bastiman) *trckd ldrs: drvn wl over 1f out: 3rd ins fnl f: no ex cl home* **6/1**[2]	
7	nk	**Tax Free (IRE)**[44] 5233 7-9-11 .... AdrianTNicholls 1	112
		(D Nicholls) *a in tch: rdn over 2f out: kpt on same pce* **8/1**[3]	
8	hd	**Monsieur Chevalier (IRE)**[29] 5661 2-8-7 .... RichardHughes 5	106
		(R Hannon) *lw: s.i.s: last for 2f: prog fnl 2f: fin wl but n.d* **18/1**	
9	1	**Stern Opinion (USA)**[21] 5928 4-9-11 .... SPasquier 14	108
		(P Bary, France) *chsd ldrs on outside tl wknd 1f out* **20/1**	
10	hd	**Strike Up The Band**[29] 5654 6-9-11 .... DO'Donohoe 4	107
		(D Nicholls) *disp ld on rails: wknd wl over 1f out* **40/1**	
11	2 ½	**Equiano (FR)**[29] 5657 4-9-11 .... KFallon 15	98
		(B W Hills) *lw: disp ld: led 3f out to 2f out: wknd qckly appr fnl f* **33/1**	
12	¾	**Exhibition (IRE)**[21] 4-9-11 .... ManuelMartinez 11	95
		(F Castro, Sweden) *nvr in contention* **150/1**	
13	1 ½	**Reverence**[35] 5491 8-9-11 .... MJKinane 13	90
		(E J Alston) *in tch tl over 1f out* **66/1**	
14	3	**Sohraab**[15] 6107 5-9-11 .... DarryllHolland 16	79
		(H Morrison) *disp ld on outside to 1/2-way* **66/1**	
15	2 ½	**Atlantic Wave (USA)**[35] 4-9-11 .... MKappushev 6	70
		(R Tugusev, Slovakia) *a outpcd* **100/1**	
16	¾	**Another True Story**[7] 5-9-11 .... VJanacek 10	67
		(Z Koplik, Czech Republic) *bhd fr 1/2-way* **300/1**	

55.10 secs (-1.20) **Going Correction** +0.15s/f (Good) **16** Ran SP% **121.0**
Speed ratings: **115,114,113,113,112 111,110,110,109,108 104,103,101,96,92 91**
PARI-MUTUEL: WIN 14.40; PL 3.60, 1.60, 1.90; DF 23.10.
Owner Coleman Bloodstock Limited **Bred** Michael Woodlock And Seamus Kennedy **Trained** Upper Lambourn, Berks

FOCUS
A dry night and the ground remained officially good. They went a solid pace, a low draw was a help, and the form looks sound.

NOTEBOOK
Total Gallery(IRE) got a great lead into the race from Strike Up The Band. The only 3-y-o in the field, Stan Moore's colt became the first of his age to win this race since Carmine Lake in 1997, and confirmed the improvement he's made this season by taking another big step up and claiming his first success in Group company at the very top level. In fairness to his trainer, he has long been of the opinion that the colt was worthy of his place in the best races, as this was the plan way back in July when he took a handicap at Newmarket. His success does, however, once again underline the narrowness of the gap between the top handicappers and Group-class sprinters. Another year should see him strengthen up further and he should be a major player in all the big sprints next season.
Fleeting Spirit(IRE) arrived with a Group 1 success already under her belt, having captured the July Cup, and, if anything, the drop back to 5f promised to suit her even better. The only filly in the field, the ground was ideal for her, in contrast to Haydock last time, and she ran a fine race towards the stands' rail, but despite being given every chance she was just being held at the line. Her connections are tempted to keep going with her, with a trip to the Breeders' Cup a possibility.
War Artist(AUS), who finished well to take a Group 3 over course and distance last time out, again put his best work in at the end of the race. He's now been placed in each of his three starts at the top level since coming over to Europe, and deserves a change of fortune.
Benbaun(IRE), who won this race in 2007, was drawn out wide and used up energy early getting a prominent position nearer the stands' side. He ran well for a long way but his early exertions eventually cost him.
Black Mambazo(IRE), a consistent performer with three wins at Listed level to his name, was outpaced through the early stages but finished better than anything. He should be able to break his duck at Group level at some point on this evidence.
Borderlescott, a dual winner of the Nunthorpe, was the unlucky horse of the race. He was staying on strongly with a furlong and a half to race when the gap he was going for was blocked by Benbaun. Forced to snatch up, he lost all momentum and quickly dropped out of contention. He would probably have been placed at worst with a clear run.
Tax Free(IRE) looked to have a good draw in stall one, but he didn't break from the stalls as well as he can and was being vigorously ridden along at halfway. He kept on late but was never a danger to the principals.
Monsieur Chevalier(IRE), the only juvenile in the race, was at the tail of the field through the early stages, but his finishing effort has been the hallmark of his performances this season and he again saw his race out well. However, it only took him into midfield as those up front were not stopping over this easy 5f.
Stern Opinion(USA), the sole French-trained horse in the race, struggled to land a blow from his disadvantageous high draw.

Equiano(FR) had too much use made of him early in an attempt to overcome his wide draw and weakened badly in the closing stages.

Reverence is no longer up to this level, and in any case the ground was much too fast for him to show his best.

Sohraab, burdened with the worst stall of all, was a little out of his depth.

6523a TOTAL PRIX MARCEL BOUSSAC (GROUP 1) (FILLIES) 1m

1:20 (1:21) 2-Y-0 **£166,427** (£66,583; £33,291; £16,631; £8,330)

RPR

1 **Rosanara (FR)**[33] 2-8-11 .... CSoumillon 3 114+
(A De Royer-Dupre, France) *w'like: athletic: stmbld strt: in tch: cl 6th st: shkn up and hdwy down outside fr over 1 1/2f out: rdn to chal fnl f: r.o to ld cl home: comf* **2/1**[1]

2 2 **On Verra (IRE)**[17] 6045 2-8-11 .... TThulliez 6 107+
(F Doumen, France) *leggy: hld up: disputing 7th st: pushed along over 1 1/2f out: styd on strly in centre fnl 100yds to take 2nd on line* **33/1**

3 *nse* **Joanna (IRE)**[43] 5279 2-8-11 .... DVargiu 5 107
(B Grizzetti, Italy) *str: lw: prom: disputing 3rd st: drvn 2f out: rdn and chalng 1f out: r.o: jst missed 2nd on line* **14/1**

4 *hd* **Wedding March (IRE)**[15] 2-8-11 .... LDettori 1 107
(A Fabre, France) *w'like: scope: prom: 5th on ins st: pushed along 2f out: rdn to chal over 1f out: led 150yds out: hdd cl home* **3/1**[2]

5 1 1/2 **Green Dandy (IRE)**[20] 5956 2-8-11 .... KFallon 9 103
(E J O'Neill) *settled in tch: 9th towards outside st: pushed along 2f out: sn rdn and kpt on steadily in centre: nrest at fin* **66/1**

6 1 1/2 **American Nizzy (FR)**[17] 6045 2-8-11 .... IMendizabal 8 100
(Y De Nicolay, France) *w'like: bustled up to go 2nd after 2f: drvn 2f out: styd on tl no ex fr appr fnl f* **33/1**

7 3/4 **Olvia (IRE)**[54] 2-8-11 .... GMosse 4 98
(C Laffon-Parias, France) *unf: prom: disputing 3rd st: sn pushed along: wknd over 1f out* **20/1**

8 3/4 **Baahama (IRE)**[17] 6045 2-8-11 .... OPeslier 2 100+
(A Fabre, France) *w'like: hld up: disputing 7th st: pushed along to chse ldrs 2f out: no imp* **13/2**

9 1 1/2 **Kilo Alpha**[11] 2-8-11 .... SPasquier 11 97+
(Mme C Head-Maarek, France) *unf: scope: led: pushed along 2f out: rdn and r.o 1 1/2f out: hdd 150yds out: eased once hdd* **14/1**

10 1 1/2 **Hard Life (IRE)**[21] 2-8-11 .... MJKinane 7 90
(A Candi, Italy) *w'like: hld up: 10th st: nvr able to chal* **40/1**

11 *dist* **Cabaret (IRE)**[80] 4028 2-8-11 .... JMurtagh 10 —
(A P O'Brien, Ire) *w'like: hld up: last st: nvr a factor: sddle slipped* **9/2**[3]

1m 37.2s (-1.20) **Going Correction** +0.15s/f (Good) 11 Ran SP% **117.8**
Speed ratings: **112,110,109,109,108 106,106,105,103,102** —
PARI-MUTUEL: WIN 1.90; PL 1.30, 5.80, 3.00; DF 45.00.

Owner H H Aga Khan **Bred** Haras De Son Altesse L'Aga Khan Scea **Trained** Chantilly, France

FOCUS
This is always a fascinating and highly informative Group 1 and again it was made up of choicely bred and unexposed fillies. There was just a moderate early pace on, however, which caused most to run freely and it certainly didn't suit those racing from off the pace. As a result there were plenty of chances down the home straight, but the form looks solid enough on paper. Rosanara ran to a level bettered only by Finsceal Beo and Zarkava in recent years and looks a high class prospect. On Verra is improving and can do better again.

NOTEBOOK
Rosanara(FR) ◆ ran out an impressive debut winner over course and distance last month and was the one the locals all wanted to be with on this eagerly anticipated step up in class. She stumbled coming out of the gates and raced in mid-field until being wound up with her effort in the home straight. Despite the race not being run to suit, she picked up strongly around 2f out and was well on top at the finish. She immediately drew comparison with the brilliant Zarkava, who also took this for the stable on the back of one run two seasons ago before going on to a stunning 3-y-o campaign which culminated in an Arc success last year. There should be a lot more to come from his daughter of Sinndar as she matures. She is likely to tread a similar path to Zarkava at three, so a return in the Group 3 Prix de La Grotte before heading to the Pouliches looks firmly on the cards. However, while her pedigree gives some hope - she is by Sinndar out of a mare won over 1m2f - her trainer feels she is unlikely to stay beyond the 1m2f of the Prix de Diane. A sound surface is clearly to her liking, but the dam scored on testing ground so it is may not be a problem.

On Verra(IRE) was motoring home from off the pace and was the chief sufferer with the lack of early pace. She reversed her Group 3 form with Baahama, who also raced out the back, and is clearly an improving filly. It could be the Breeder's Cup Juvenile Fillies' Turf next for her and one could see her running a big race at Santa Anita. She ought to relish a stiffer test next year and this effort paid a compliment to her previous conqueror, the Richard Hannon-trained Middle Club.

Joanna(IRE) had been purchased by Hamdan Al Maktoum and was having her first run over the trip. She was suited by racing handily and held every chance, but was made to look one paced by the winner. She lost second near the line and the distance was probably far enough for her at this stage, but she is bred to enjoy around 1m2f as a 3-y-o.

Wedding March(IRE), like Rosanara, had also scored on her debut over course and distance last month yet that form wasn't as strong as the winner's. She proved keen, just off the ordinary pace and although she gave her all when asked to win the race, that ultimately blunted her finishing effort. Surprisingly her trainer has a moderate recent record in this event and this beautifully bred filly still rates a very decent prospect for next year.

Green Dandy(IRE) posted a very respectable effort , having been runner-up on both her previous outings. She too was somewhat free in the race and had to make her challenge wide in the home straight. She lacked the tactical pace to get seriously involved, but still did more than enough to suggest she can make her mark in Group company at some stage.

American Nizzy(FR) is the key to the form. She had finished behind On Verra on her previous outing and also behind Joanna at Deauville two runs back. She ran her race here and helps set the level.

Olvia(IRE) was another who proved free through the early parts and that didn't help her chances of seeing out the slightly longer trip.

Kilo Alpha, who proved reluctant to load up, was representing the stable that took this race last year. She was responsible for setting the moderate pace and was cooked shortly after the race became serious.

Hard Life(IRE) was settled in last place through the first few furlongs and the race was not really run to suit. This still looked too hot for her in any case.

Cabaret(IRE) had made all when comfortably winning a Group 3 at Leopardstown in July and looked a big player in this field. She was surprisingly ridden with restraint this time, despite the fact she was housed wide, and she never appeared happy. Her fate was sealed soon after the home turn and Johnny Murtagh looked down more than once in the home straight, nearly pulling her up in the end. Something obviously went wrong. Murtagh later reported her saddle slipped.

6524a PRIX JEAN-LUC LAGARDERE (GRAND CRITERIUM) (GROUP 1) (C&F) 7f

1:55 (1:54) 2-Y-0 **£194,165** (£77,680; £38,840; £19,403; £9,718)

RPR

1 **Siyouni (FR)**[28] 5708 2-9-0 .... GMosse 6 119+
(A De Royer-Dupre, France) *w'like: scope: tall: athletic: racd in 4th: hdwy 2f out to ld 1 1/2f out: comf* **7/1**

2 1 1/2 **Pounced (USA)**[51] 4985 2-9-0 .... JimmyFortune 2 115
(J H M Gosden) *lw: pushed along to ld: hdd 1 1/2f out: kpt on fnl f* **12/1**

3 1/2 **Buzzword**[28] 5708 2-9-0 .... AhmedAjtebi 3 115+
(Saeed Bin Suroor) *lw: racd in 3rd: 4th and pushed along over 2f out: r.o fr appr fnl f: wnt 3rd cl home: nrst at fin* **6/1**[3]

4 3/4 **Lope De Vega (IRE)**[21] 5927 2-9-0 .... MGuyon 4 112
(A Fabre, France) *w'like: scope: lw: racd in 2nd: rdn and lost pl over 1 1/2f out: one pce* **7/4**[1]

5 1 **Dick Turpin (IRE)**[43] 5274 2-9-0 .... RichardHughes 5 112+
(R Hannon) *settled in 5th: last and pushed along over 2f out: nvr able to chal* **15/8**[2]

6 *nse* **Beethoven (IRE)**[7] 6317 2-9-0 .... JMurtagh 7 110
(A P O'Brien, Ire) *racd in 6th: effrt 1 1/2f out: nvr in chalng position* **16/1**

7 6 **Roi De Vitesse (IRE)**[22] 5859 2-9-0 .... JamesMillman 1 95
(B R Millman) *racd in last: pushed along over 3f out: disputing 4th over 2f out: sn no ex* **100/1**

1m 19.5s (-1.20) **Going Correction** +0.15s/f (Good) 7 Ran SP% **112.5**
Speed ratings: **112,110,109,108,107 107,100**
PARI-MUTUEL: WIN 7.00; PL 3.30, 5.70; SF 49.90.

Owner H H Aga Khan **Bred** Haras De Son Altesse L'Aga Khan Scea **Trained** Chantilly, France

FOCUS
On paper this didn't look a particularly strong renewal of a race billed as the most important juvenile race in the French calendar. None of the last four winners managed to win another race, although previous winners this decade have included Rock Of Gibraltar, American Post and Oratorio, who all went on to record Group 1 success at three. The bare form doesn't look that hot, and it was a bit of a tactical affair. The runner-up has been rated a huge improver, with the third the benchmark.

NOTEBOOK
Siyouni(FR) was building a big reputation before being turned over by Special Duty in the Prix Robert Papin, and although that form has since been given a boost by the filly's success in the Cheveley Park, a defeat to Buzzword over course and distance last time out suggested his form may have plateaued a touch. He reversed form with the Godolphin colt here, though, aided by a shrewd ride from Gerald Mosse, who kept his rival boxed in and got first run on him. He quickened up well to take the measure of Pounced, and promises to have no trouble getting 1m next season. Presumably he'll be aimed at the Poulains, and one would imagine that he'll appreciate more cut in the ground as he's by Pivotal out of a half-sister to multiple Group 1 winner Slickly.

Pounced(USA) had the ground to suit and broke well, dictating things from an early stage. In the prime position to kick from the front, he found a more experienced rival too strong at the finish, but it was a good effort in defeat, justifying the big step up in class. The Dewhurst remains a possible target for him, and so does a trip to the Breeders' Cup. He should get 1m2f next year.

Buzzword was trapped with nowhere to go a furlong and a half out. The winner got first run on him and had gone beyond recall by the time he was switched and began to make up ground.

Lope De Vega(IRE) had been supplemented for this race following his success on Arc trials Sunday three weeks earlier. He chased the leader for much of the way, was given every chance, and it was slightly disappointing that he couldn't find a similar turn of foot to that which he showed here last time out. Perhaps the leap in grade was just too big this early in his career.

Dick Turpin(IRE), unbeaten in his four previous starts, including the Richmond Stakes and a valuable sales race in Ireland, was stepping up to 7f for the first time. The longer trip was a bit of a concern because there's plenty of speed in his pedigree, but the way he'd been seeing out his races over 6f suggested he'd have no trouble with it. Keen through the early stages, he was denied a clear run inside the final three furlongs and dropped back to last place, just as the others were beginning to quicken up. He could never get back into it and to a certain extent this run can be excused. However, he still has to prove he's not purely a sprinter, and might get his chance to do that in the Dewhurst.

Beethoven(IRE), representing a trainer responsible for sending out six of the last ten winners of this race, came here looking pretty exposed and established as one of the lesser lights of the yard. He ran a race in keeping with his place in the pecking order at Ballydoyle and did no more than give his stable a guide to the level of some of the opposition.

Roi De Vitesse(IRE) came into the race with clear limitations and was predictably outclassed on this step up in grade.

6525a QATAR PETROLEUM PRIX DE L'OPERA (GROUP 1) (F&M) 1m 2f

2:30 (2:33) 3-Y-0+ **£138,689** (£55,485; £27,743; £13,859; £6,942)

RPR

1 **Shalanaya (IRE)**[33] 5562 3-8-11 .... MGuyon 4 115+
(M Delzangles, France) *str: athletic: hld up: last st: pushed along and hdwy on outside 2f out: rdn to chal fnl f: led 100yds out: r.o wl* **20/1**

2 1 1/2 **Board Meeting (IRE)**[21] 5929 3-8-11 .... ACrastus 8 111
(E Lellouche, France) *w'like: scope: lw: hld up: 7th 1/2-way: disputing 7th st: pushed along and hdwy in centre 1 1/2f out: wnt 3rd 100yds out: styd on to take 2nd on line* **10/1**

3 *shd* **Midday**[64] 4522 3-8-11 .... TPQueally 7 111
(H R A Cecil) *lw: 4th 1/2-way: 3rd st: rdn to chal 2f out: led over 1f out: hdd 100yds out: kpt on u.p: lost 2nd on line* **11/4**[1]

4 3/4 **Alpine Rose (FR)**[42] 5300 4-9-2 .... GMosse 3 109
(A De Royer-Dupre, France) *3rd 1/2-way: 4th st: pushed along 1 1/2f out: kpt on steadily fnl f* **7/2**[2]

5 1 1/2 **Crystal Capella**[143] 2013 4-9-2 .... RyanMoore 5 106
(Sir Michael Stoute) *lw: 5th 1/2-way: 6th st: effrt over 1 1/2f out: styd on steadily to go 5th cl home* **9/2**[3]

6 1/2 **Lady Marian (GER)**[22] 5890 4-9-2 .... LDettori 10 105
(Saeed Bin Suroor) *hld up: disputing 7th st: pushed along 2f out: rdn and hdwy 1 1/2f out: disputing 3rd briefly 1f out: no ex fnl 100yds* **14/1**

7 1 1/2 **Again (IRE)**[29] 5686 3-8-11 ....(p) JMurtagh 9 102
(David Wachman, Ire) *racd in 2nd: pushed along st: rdn over 1 1/2f out: sn one pce* **20/1**

8 1 1/2 **Article Rare (USA)**[42] 5298 3-8-11 ....(p) OPeslier 2 99
(E Lellouche, France) *6th on ins 1/2-way: 5th st: rdn and r.o 2f out: disputing 2nd over 1f out: one pce fnl 100yds* **40/1**

9 ½ **Night Magic (GER)**[63] 4583 3-8-11 .... KKerekes 6 98
(W Figge, Germany) *leggy: led: pushed along and r.o over 2f out: rdn 1 1/2f out: hdd over 1f out: wknd* **9/2**[3]

2m 1.80s (-2.20) **Going Correction** +0.15s/f (Good)
WFA 3 from 4yo 5lb **9** Ran SP% **113.0**
Speed ratings: **114,112,112,112,110 110,109,108,107**
PARI-MUTUEL: WIN 19.50; PL 4.50, 2.70, 2.30; DF 50.40.
Owner H H Aga Khan **Bred** H H The Aga Khan's Studs S C **Trained** France

FOCUS
A quality field lined up for this top fillies' prize and it was highly competitive. The race was run at an uneven pace, but the winner came from right out the back. 3-y-os took the first three places.

NOTEBOOK
Shalanaya(IRE) made it three wins from six career starts and completed the task in great style. She was settled in last place for most of the contest and travelled beautifully into the home straight. Once angling out with her challenge, she picked up most strongly and showed a great attitude to get on top inside the final furlong. She has progressed with every outing to date and, while this was a massive step up in class, there was no fluke about it. She also didn't have too hard a race here, so the Breeders' Cup Filly & Mare Turf looks a most viable target now, although the extra distance would be an unknown. However, she may be put away, as she is likely to stay in training.
Board Meeting(IRE) came third in the controversial Prix Vermeille here 21 days earlier and had finished well in front of Shalanaya when winning a Group 3 at Deauville on her penultimate outing. She came from a similar position to the winner and ran a gallant race, but more positive tactics on this drop back from 1m4f would have suited ideally. With that in mind, she would also not be without a chance of reversing form if heading to Santa Anita next month.
Midday had been kept for this after taking the Nassau at Glorious Goodwood in August. She was asked for maximum effort nearing 2f out and gave her all in defeat, but was unable to cope with the winner's late surge. She is a most adaptable filly and has been a credit to connections this year, but was somewhat below her previous best here. She is likely now to head to Santa Anita and wouldn't be without hope of reversing form should the winner re-oppose, as she has already proven herself over the added distance of that contest and is entitled to improve for this outing.
Alpine Rose(FR), who swerved the Arc for this race, fared best of those to race prominently and confirmed her last-time-out form with Lady Marian. Connections are still hoping that she will turn out for the Emirates Champion Stakes at Newmarket later in the month.
Crystal Capella was having her first outing since she extended her winning sequence to six when beating the highly progressive Dar Re Mi at York back in May. She was well placed through the first half of the race, but found trouble when trying to improve in the home straight so should be rated better than the bare form. The best of her has probably still to be seen yet and she deserves to take her chance at the Breeders' Cup.
Lady Marian(GER) ran better here, but is still searching for a first success since winning this last year for another stable.
Again(IRE) was equipped with first-time cheekpieces for this step up in trip and had to be ridden early to attain a handy position. She had her chance, but was done with before the final furlong and failed to see it out under such tactics. The ground would also have been quick enough for her.
Article Rare(USA) had plenty to find on paper and was one of the first beaten.
Night Magic(GER) had made all over an extra furlong on her last two starts, most recently when slamming her rivals in the German Oaks, and proved popular to become the second straight German-trained winner of this race. She had her own way out in front, but ultimately disappointed.

6526a QATAR PRIX DE L'ARC DE TRIOMPHE (GROUP 1) (C&F) 1m 4f
3:15 (3:17) 3-Y-O **£2,219,029** (£887,767; £443,883; £221,748; £111,068)

RPR

1 **Sea The Stars (IRE)**[29] 5688 3-8-11 .... MJKinane 6 132+
(John M Oxx, Ire) *lw: t.k.h: restrained after 1f and sn dropped to 9th: gd prog on inner 2f out: led just over 1f out and qcknd clr: impressive* **4/6**[1]

2 2 **Youmzain (IRE)**[28] 5707 6-9-5 ....(v) KFallon 1 125
(M R Channon) *broke wl: settled in mid-div: 11th st: clsng up fr over 2f out: qcknd through gap 1 1/2f out: drvn to take 2nd wl ins fnl f* **20/1**

3 hd **Cavalryman**[21] 5930 3-8-11 .... LDettori 19 125
(A Fabre, France) *w'like: lw: sn prom: 5th st: drvn 2f out: 4th 1f out: 2nd 100yds out: kpt on steadily u.p* **12/1**

4 hd **Conduit (IRE)**[71] 4298 4-9-5 .... RyanMoore 12 124
(Sir Michael Stoute) *mid-div: 10th st: stdy prog fnl 2f: tk 4th cl home* **8/1**[3]

5 1 **Dar Re Mi**[21] 5929 4-9-2 .... JimmyFortune 2 119
(J H M Gosden) *lw: first to show: racd in 4th to st: disp 2nd over 1f out: 2nd 150yds out: one pce* **25/1**

6 1 **Fame And Glory**[29] 5688 3-8-11 .... JMurtagh 10 121
(A P O'Brien, Ire) *plld early: 6th and racing keenly 1/2-way: 8th st: styd on one pce fnl 2f: nvr able to chal* **6/1**[2]

7 ½ **La Boum (GER)**[42] 5300 6-9-2 .... TJarnet 8 117
(Robert Collet, France) *towards rr to st: swtchd outside 1 1/2f out: styd on: nvr a factor* **500/1**

7 dht **Stacelita (FR)**[21] 5929 3-8-8 .... CSoumillon 16 117
(J-C Rouget, France) *leggy: racd in 3rd ldng main gp: 3rd st: led wl over 1f: hdd just over 1f out: one pce* **20/1**

9 ¾ **Magadan (IRE)**[98] 3443 4-9-5 .... ACrastus 17 119
(E Lellouche, France) *towards rr to st: sme prog on outside fnl 2f: nvr a factor* **150/1**

10 ½ **Vision D'Etat (FR)**[21] 5931 4-9-5 .... OPeslier 9 118
(E Libaud, France) *a.p: 6th st: drvn over 1f out: one pce fnl f* **14/1**

11 ¾ **Tangaspeed (FR)**[21] 5929 4-9-2 .... IMendizabal 11 114
(R Laplanche, France) *last early: styd on u.str.p fnl 1 1/2f: nvr a factor* **500/1**

12 shd **Beheshtam (FR)**[21] 5930 3-8-11 .... GMosse 15 117
(A De Royer-Dupre, France) *w'like: scope: lw: mid-div: 7th st: one pce fnl 2f* **16/1**

13 3 **Getaway (GER)**[28] 5707 6-9-5 .... SPasquier 3 112+
(J Hirschberger, Germany) *14th 1/2-way: tried to get through on ins of wnr over 2f out: drvn and hdwy over 1f out: nt clr run ins fnl f: eased* **33/1**

14 snk **The Bogberry (USA)**[28] 5712 4-9-5 .... MKappushev 18 112
(A De Royer-Dupre, France) *a towards rr* **250/1**

15 8 **Hot Six (BRZ)**[63] 4-9-4 .... TJPereira 4 98
(G Duarte, Brazil) *bhd and rdn st: nvr a factor* **250/1**

16 2 **Tullamore (USA)**[63] 4-9-5 .... VJanacek 13 96
(Z Koplik, Czech Republic) *a bhd* **500/1**

17 4 **Grand Ducal (IRE)**[29] 5688 3-8-11 .... PJSmullen 5 89
(A P O'Brien, Ire) *sn led: hdd after 2f: 2nd st: wknd qckly wl over 1f out* **300/1**

18 2 **Set Sail (IRE)**[29] 5688 3-8-11 .... SMLevey 14 86
(A P O'Brien, Ire) *led after 2f to wl over 1f out: wknd qckly* **500/1**

19 15 **Steele Tango (USA)**[92] 3640 4-9-5 .... DarryllHolland 7 62
(R A Teal) *a bhd: last st: t.o* **500/1**

2m 26.3s (-4.10) **Going Correction** +0.15s/f (Good)
WFA 3 from 4yo+ 7lb **19** Ran SP% **124.7**
Speed ratings: **119,117,117,117,116 116,115,115,115,114 114,114,112,112,106 105,102,101,91**
PARI-MUTUEL: WIN 1.80; PL 1.40, 3.30, 3.70; DF 14.30.
Owner Christopher Tsui **Bred** Sunderland Holdings **Trained** Currabeg, Co Kildare

FOCUS
A thrilling Arc won in extraordinary style by a horse set to enter history as one of the greatest, if not the greatest racehorse of all time. The early gallop was set by the Ballydoyle pacemakers Set Sail and Grand Ducal, but they were given no respect by the opposition and, despite winding things up from a long way out, they were ignored, and the main bunch went about following the no-more-than-fair pace set by Stacelita. Judged strictly on RPRs, Sea The Stars ran to a figure some 5lb or more below his upgraded Irish Champion Stakes figure of 138. It was nevertheless a truly remarkable performance.

NOTEBOOK
Sea The Stars(IRE), who'd carried all before him in England and Ireland this term, winning five times in the space of five months, all at the top level, took another giant leap towards racing immortality. His task was a formidable one on several counts, for he was at a disadvantage in having not enjoyed a mid-season break, which has become the norm for Arc winners in recent years, and there were still some who doubted his stamina for a strongly run 1m4f. In addition, the stats backed up the view that what he was attempting was something out of the ordinary. Since Sea-Bird in 1965, only three horses had completed the Epsom Derby/Arc double in the same season (Mill Reef, Lammtarra and Sinndar), while 17 others had tried and failed. He was also trying to emulate the great Dancing Brave in becoming just the second winner in the previous 40 years to have taken the Guineas en route. A big field also threatened to make things tricky for him, but on the plus side was that the weights favour the 3-y-os in this race, evidenced by the fact that 12 of the previous 15 winners were representatives of the Classic generation, the ground had come right for him, he'd bagged a good draw, and he'd enjoyed a trouble-free preparation. Very little went right for him for much of the race as he got warm beforehand, pulled for his head through the early stages and got shuffled back in the pack as Kinane tried to restrain him. He continued to race very keenly to the entrance to the straight, was then hampered and lost his footing momentarily on straightening up before going for his run up the inside rail. Finding the rapidly weakening Grand Ducal falling back towards him, Kinane quickly switched Sea The Stars around the pacemaker and the colt then found the most electrifying turn of foot to leave the fillies Dar Re Mi and Stacelita for dead inside the last. Kinane didn't even have to get that serious with him, and he won with a ton in hand, leaving genuine Group 1 horses looking like slow old boats. The first horse ever to complete the Guineas/Derby/Arc treble, he has it all - stamina, speed, durability, and above all class. It was a truly sensational performance, the kind that will live long in the memory, and future champions will no doubt have to get used to being compared unfavourably with him. Whether or not he goes to Santa Anita for the Breeders' Cup Classic, for which he's a best-priced 4-5, hardly matters to his reputation, but success in America would undoubtedly cap a most incredible career, for which his trainer John Oxx deserves the utmost credit.
Youmzain(IRE) comes alive in this race and, visored for the first time, ran another screamer to finish runner-up for the third year in succession. From a good draw, he saved ground on the inside for most of the way and, angled out with 2f to run, stayed on strongly under the Fallon drive to grab second close home. An unlucky horse in many ways, he deserves to have won more than one of his last 16 starts, but he doesn't get his conditions - a strongly run 1m4f on fast ground - that often.
Cavalryman came here following wins in the Grand Prix de Paris and Prix Niel, just like Rail Link, who won the Arc for Andre Fabre in 2006. The Niel has been the best trial for this race in recent years, providing ten of the last 15 winners, and this son of Halling boasted the classic French preparation, having enjoyed a mid-season break to keep him fresh. Considering he was badly drawn in stall 19, Dettori did really well to get him over into a prominent position early and, all things considered, he ran a fine race to finish third given that early work. Had he been better drawn he might have given the winner a tiny bit more to do. One would like to think there's more to come from him, and he appeals strongly as the type to come back next year an even stronger contender. He was cut to a best price of 8-1 for the Breeders' Cup Turf afterwards, although he has the Champion Stakes as an alternative.
Conduit(IRE) was beaten over five lengths by Sea The Stars in the Eclipse, but he's a proper 1m4f horse, at his best running on late from off a strong pace at this trip, so there were reasons to expect him to get closer to the 3-y-o this time. He had a double-figure draw to overcome, though, and tended to race a shade keenly and could have done with Stacelita setting a higher tempo. For the last furlong he kept Youmzain company as they both stayed on to get in the mix for the places, and if he goes to America to try and win the Breeders' Cup Turf for a second year in succession (best price 3-1), connections will be hoping for a repeat of the end-to-end gallop he enjoyed last season.
Dar Re Mi, moral winner of the Prix Vermeille last time out, confirmed her status as Europe's top middle-distance filly on her first outing against the colts. Prominent throughout from her favourable low draw, she enjoyed a dream run through the race and ran right up to her best, getting some sort of revenge on Stacelita in the process. The Breeders' Cup Filly & Mare Turf, for which she's a best-priced 4-1, looks an attractive option now.
Fame And Glory had his chance of beating Sea The Stars in the Derby compromised by the apparent decision of his stable to run the race to suit the speedier Rip Van Winkle, while his trainer had left a bit to work on when he was once again beaten by John Oxx's stable star in the Irish Champion, over a trip short of his best. With two pacemakers in the field there should have been no excuses this time, but the decision of the others to ignore the pace set by Set Sail and Grand Ducal compromised his chance. He was keen early then took quite a while to pick up in the straight, in stark contrast to the winner, and tended to hang right under pressure. He remains an exciting horse for next season, however, when races like the Coronation Cup and King George should be right up his street. The Breeders' Cup Turf remains an option for him next month.
La Boum(GER) ran well for a 500-1 shot, especially as conditions were hardly ideal for her. Soft ground had seen her at her best in the past and it'll be interesting to see if she can now build on this, or whether it was something of a fluke.
Stacelita(FR), flattered to be still in possession of an unblemished record coming into this race, enjoyed the run of things, leading the main field for most of the way, and she was the first to quicken up in the straight, but she was swamped inside the last and just didn't see it out. The ground was undoubtedly quicker than she would have liked, but talk of her being the next Zarkava after her success in the Prix de Diane was wildly premature.
Magadan(IRE) had won three of his previous four starts at this track, but he faced a tough task in this company, especially as he was drawn in stall 17. He raced freely out wide, merely plugged on one-paced in the straight and is another who would probably have preferred more cut in the ground.
Vision D'Etat(FR), not at all knocked about when second in his prep race, the Prix Foy, three weeks earlier, was bidding to improve on his fifth in this race last year. He pulled hard early though, tracking Dar Re Mi, and was beaten and just plugging on at the finish when crossed by Fame And Glory. His one win over 1m4f came in a steadily run race and the suspicion is that his best trip is 1m2f.
Tangaspeed(FR) merely stayed on past horses that were being eased down.
Beheshtam(FR) had a bad draw and raced widest of all for much of the way. He had little chance the way the race unfolded, but he was the least-experienced runner in the line-up and will be open to improvement as a 4-y-o.
Getaway(GER), fourth and eighth in this race the previous two years, was outmanoeuvred by Sea The Stars turning into the straight and had his momentum checked, after which he just kept on steadily until running into a wall of horses inside the last.
Steele Tango(USA), always towards the rear, was completely outclassed.

6527a QATAR PRIX DU CADRAN (GROUP 1) 2m 4f
4:45 (4:44) 4-Y-O+ **£138,689** (£55,485; £27,743; £13,859; £6,942)

RPR

1 **Alandi (IRE)**[22] 5891 4-9-2 .... MJKinane 3 114
(John M Oxx, Ire) *a wl plcd: 3rd st: led 1 1/2f out: drvn out* **5/1**

2 *shd* **Kasbah Bliss (FR)**21 5932 7-9-2 .... TThulliez 5 114
(F Doumen, France) *mid-div: 6th st: 3rd 1 1/2f out: r.o wl fnl f: jst failed* **10/3**1

3 *1 1/2* **Yeats (IRE)**22 5891 8-9-2 .... JMurtagh 4 112
(A P O'Brien, Ire) *trckd his pcemaker tl wnt on 5f out: hdd 1 1/2f out: drvn and ev ch 1f out: one pce* **4/1**2

4 *2 1/2* **Pouvoir Absolu**35 5497 4-9-2 ....(b) ACrastus 8 110
(E Lellouche, France) *hld up: 8th st: hdwy on outside fr 2f out: 4th 1f out: one pce* **16/1**

5 *3* **Askar Tau (FR)**23 5824 4-9-2 ....(v) RyanMoore 11 107
(M P Tregoning) *hld up in rr: 9th st: kpt on one pce on outside: nvr nrr* **11/2**

6 *1/2* **Orion Star (FR)**365 6497 7-9-2 .... DBoeuf 12 106
(H-A Pantall, France) *hld up in rr: 11th st: hdwy on rail wl over 1f out: 5th 1f out: one pce* **25/1**

7 *1* **Armure**21 5929 4-8-13 .... GMosse 2 102
(A De Royer-Dupre, France) *hld up: 10th st: effrt on outside over 2f out: sn rdn: n.d* **14/1**

8 *2 1/2* **Incanto Dream**21 5932 5-9-2 .... YLerner 1 103
(C Lerner, France) *t.k.h early in mid-div: plld his way up to dispute 3rd at 1/2-way: 2nd st: wknd 1 1/2f out* **9/2**3

9 *3* **Bluefields (FR)**21 5932 8-9-2 .... DBonilla 7 100
(E Leray, France) *prom to 5f out: 7th and wkng st* **200/1**

10 *snk* **Pointilliste (USA)**21 5932 6-9-2 .... OPeslier 10 100
(E Lellouche, France) *a in tch: 4th st: rdn and btn wl over 1f out* **14/1**

P **Windsor Palace (IRE)**7 6320 4-9-2 .... SMLevey 9 —
(A P O'Brien, Ire) *led to 5f out: sn bhd: p.u* **200/1**

P **Bassel (FR)**21 5932 4-9-2 .... MGuyon 6 —
(H-A Pantall, France) *prom: 5th st: sn wknd: p.u* **100/1**

4m 12.7s (-5.30) **Going Correction** +0.15s/f (Good) **12** Ran SP% **118.4**
Speed ratings: **116,115,115,114,113 112,112,111,110,110 —,—**
PARI-MUTUEL: WIN 5.90; PL 1.90, 1.80, 1.80; DF 8.80.
Owner H H Aga Khan **Bred** Hh The Aga Khan's Studs Sc **Trained** Currabeg, Co Kildare

FOCUS
This was run at a fair pace and the first three came nicely clear. The form looks solid, rated around the runner-up and ninth.

NOTEBOOK
Alandi(IRE) just held off Kasbah Bliss to follow up his win in the Irish St Leger last month, capping off a brilliant day for his connections in the process. One unknown was the quicker surface, as he has long been thought of as a mud-lover, but he was allowed to take his chance here with a view to testing his credentials for a crack at the Gold Cup at Royal Ascot next year. The added distance was also a doubt, but he was ridden as though it wouldn't be a problem and answered his rider's every call. He took time to get the better of Yeats down the home straight and then proved game in fending off the runner-up. This was his best effort to date and now that he has confirmed his versatility it would be no surprise if he was next year's Gold Cup winner.
Kasbah Bliss(FR), fourth in this last season, beat a number of these when landing back-to-back wins in the Group 3 Prix Gladiateur 21 days previously. He had his ground here and was confidently ridden off the pace on this return to further. He took time to pick up and may well have been better suited by a stronger overall pace, but still was only beaten by a very narrow margin and was in front a stride after the line. He is likely to stay away from hurdling for now and the Breeders' Cup Marathon, where the drop back in trip shouldn't be of concern, could be next. Paddy Power promoted him to 7-2 market leader for that, while Bet 365 kept him at 5-1. He has the Prix Royal-Oak as an alternative.
Yeats(IRE) had run no sort of race behind the winner in the Irish St Leger on his first run back since landing a magnificent fourth Gold Cup, but we all know that he cannot operate on testing ground and much better was expected over the longer trip with the surface in his favour. Show his true colours he did, as he tracked his pace-making stablemate until taking it up over half a mile out. He gave his all under pressure down the home straight, but was eventually done with shortly after passing the furlong marker. This was a very honourable performance in defeat and he will be sorely missed in the staying division as he now heads off to stud as one of the best-ever stayers.
Pouvoir Absolu, who was in front of the runner-up over 1m4f last time out, was ridden to get the longer trip and posted a solid effort without ever threatening.
Askar Tau(FR) had won the Group 2 Yorkshire Cup and Doncaster Cup on his two previous outings. Ridden right out the back, he came under pressure nearing the final bend and had plenty on. He finished strongly once straightening up, however, and a more positive ride would have surely been more in his favour. He should be a player in the Gold Cup next term.
Incanto Dream had finished in front of Kasbah Bliss when going down narrowly in this event last season. This was only his second outing of the year though, so perhaps it came a little too soon.
Pointilliste(USA) had finished second behind the runner-up on his previous start but had yet to race over this far. He looked a non stayer.

6528 - 6529a (Foreign Racing) - See Raceform Interactive

5814 TIPPERARY (L-H)
Sunday, October 4
OFFICIAL GOING: Good to firm (good in places on jumps courses)

6530a COOLMORE STUD HOME OF CHAMPIONS CONCORDE STKS (GROUP 3) 7f 100y
3:25 (3:25) 3-Y-0+ **£45,436** (£13,281; £6,291; £2,097)

RPR

1 **Duff (IRE)**22 5862 6-9-8 114 .... FMBerry 2 117
(Edward Lynam, Ire) *led early: sn trckd ldr: on terms 1/2-way: rdn to ld bef st: clr over 1f out: reduced ld and styd on wl ins fnl f* **5/2**2

2 *3/4* **Dohasa (IRE)**7 6320 4-9-3 109 .... KLatham 1 110
(G M Lyons, Ire) *trckd ldrs: u.p in mod 3rd over 1f out: 2nd and kpt on ins fnl f: nt rch wnr* **9/4**1

3 *3/4* **Three Rocks (IRE)**49 5080 4-9-6 108 .... KJManning 6 111
(J S Bolger, Ire) *sn chsd ldrs in 5th: clsr in 3rd bef st: rdn in mod 4th over 1f out: kpt on wout threatening fnl f* **9/2**

4 *hd* **Advanced**8 6270 6-9-3 .... AmyRyan 8 108
(K A Ryan) *prom: sn led: jnd 1/2-way: hdd bef st: no imp u.p and kpt on same pce fr over 1f out* **4/1**3

5 *3 1/2* **Totally Devoted (USA)**8 6272 3-8-12 100 .... JAHeffernan 3 96
(A P O'Brien, Ire) *towards rr: rdn into mod 5th over 1f out: sn no imp: kpt on same pce* **12/1**

6 *nk* **King Jock (USA)**21 5924 8-9-3 98 .... PShanahan 7 98
(R J Osborne, Ire) *dwlt sltly: in rr: 6th bef st: sn no imp u.p and kpt on same pce* **20/1**

7 *4 1/2* **Maundy Money**18 6007 6-9-3 97 .... JohnEgan 4 87
(David Marnane, Ire) *trckd ldrs: 5th bef st: sn no imp u.p* **14/1**

1m 31.89s (91.89)
WFA 3 from 4yo+ 2lb **7** Ran SP% **116.6**
CSF £8.92 TOTE £3.50: £2.30, £1.40; DF 5.50.
Owner Kilboy Estate **Bred** Kilboy Estate **Trained** Dunshaughlin, Co Meath

FOCUS
The winner and third have been rated to their recent best, with the runner-up rated back to his early-season level.

NOTEBOOK
Duff(IRE) led early before his rider elected to settle him behind Advanced. Soon disputing again, he kicked rounding the home turn to seize the initiative and stuck to his job well under a good ride from Berry. His trainer is looking towards Hong Kong next for the 114-rated gelding, who needs to go up just 1lb, when the choice of the sprint or the mile will be open to him in December. On this evidence he's entitled to take his chance. (op 11/4)
Dohasa(IRE) had solid credentials to record his first Pattern win. He had finished behind Duff when they clashed in the Group 3 Ballycorus Stakes at Leopardstown in June but was 5lb better off this time, and was turning out again after winning at the Curragh over a marginally shorter trip. He went in pursuit of the winner when they straightened for home but just couldn't get there despite every call from the saddle. (op 2/1)
Three Rocks(IRE) was another who held every chance turning for home but couldn't quicken enough to get there on ground that was probably on the lively side for him. (op 7/2 tchd 5/1)
Advanced led until the winner took over after halfway, but to his credit he plugged on in the straight to hold on for fourth (op 9/2 tchd 7/2)

6531 - 6532a (Foreign Racing) - See Raceform Interactive

6231 PONTEFRACT (L-H)
Monday, October 5
OFFICIAL GOING: Good to firm (8.5)
Wind: Virtually nil Weather: Fine and dry

6533 E B F SATURDAY RACING AT SANTA ROSA MAIDEN STKS 1m 2f 6y
2:10 (2:10) (Class 4) 2-Y-O **£5,180** (£1,541; £770; £384) **Stalls** Low

Form RPR

03 **1** **Futurist**7 6331 2-9-0 0 .... AhmedAjtebi(3) 5 79+
(Saeed Bin Suroor) *trckd ldr on inner: hdwy over 2f out: swtchd rt and rdn to ld wl over 1f out: sn edgd lft: clr ins fnl f: kpt on* **4/1**3

54 **2** *1 1/2* **Indochina**21 5951 2-9-3 0 .... JoeFanning 7 73
(M Johnston) *led: rdn along 3f out: drvn and hdd wl over 1f out: kpt on u.p ins fnl f* **12/1**

5406 **3** *2* **Dream Spinner**12 6211 2-9-3 68 .... EddieAhern 4 70
(J L Dunlop) *in tch: hdwy over 3f out: rdn to chse ldng pair over 1f out: kpt on same pce* **17/2**

4 *1 1/4* **Golden Gates (IRE)** 2-9-3 0 .... TonyCulhane 3 67+
(Mrs A Duffield) *hld up in rr: hdwy on inner over 2f out: rdn to chse ldrs over 1f out: kpt on same pce* **50/1**

52 **5** *1/2* **Pena Dorada (IRE)**15 6136 2-9-3 0 .... AndrewElliott 1 71+
(A P Jarvis) *hld up: hdwy 1/2-way: trcking ldrs whn bdly hmpd 3f out: sn rdn and kpt on fnl 2f* **7/2**2

3 **6** *3 1/2* **Loyaliste (FR)**12 6200 2-9-3 0 .... RyanMoore 2 61+
(R Hannon) *dwlt and sn pushed along in rr: rdn and sme hdwy whn sltly hmpd 3f out: nvr a factor* **5/2**1

7 *14* **Always Roses** 2-8-12 0 .... RoystonFfrench 8 30
(C C Bealby) *a towards rr* **100/1**

063 **8** *1 1/2* **Green For Luck (IRE)**18 6033 2-9-3 66 .... NCallan 6 32
(S Gollings) *t.k.h: prom: rdn along over 2f out: wknd wl over 1f out* **25/1**

000 **9** *43* **Fireflash (IRE)**30 5674 2-9-3 47 ....(p) TomEaves 10 —
(Mrs A Duffield) *cl up on outer: rdn along 1/2-way: sn lost pl and bhd fnl 3f* **200/1**

56 **P** **Karamojo Bell**25 5793 2-9-3 0 .... MickyFenton 9 —
(T P Tate) *t.k.h: trckd ldrs: hdwy 1/2-way: disputing ld 3f out and gng wl whn broke leg and p.u: dead* **13/2**

2m 15.27s (1.57) **Going Correction** -0.025s/f (Good) **10** Ran SP% **109.6**
Speed ratings (Par 97): **92,90,89,88,87 85,73,72,38,—**
toteswinger: 1&2 £9.70, 1&3 £8.50, 2&3 £20.30. CSF £45.56 TOTE £5.10: £2.20, £3.70, £2.20; EX 46.80.
Owner Godolphin **Bred** Darley **Trained** Newmarket, Suffolk

FOCUS
After a sustained dry spell between 1 and 1½" of water was put on the track over the last week. The ground was quick but a good cover of grass. The gallop was just steady but even so this modest 1m2f maiden event was a stiff test of stamina for 2-y-os. The form is straightforward rated through the third.

NOTEBOOK
Futurist, quite a big son of Halling, was quite keen on his third start. He swept to the front once in line for home and, despite a tendency to hang left, he soon drew away. He should make a useful middle-distance handicapper at three. (tchd 7-2)
Indochina, who still looks very immature, helped set the pace but was left for dead by the winner in the home straight. He too should do better next year. (op 8-1 tchd 18-1)
Dream Spinner, having his sixth outing and rated 68, is already looking fully exposed. (op 9-1 tchd 10-1)
Golden Gates(IRE), whose dam won over 5f at two, kept on in good style from off the pace on his debut and clearly stays well. (op 66-1)
Pena Dorada(IRE) was knocked right back when another horse had to be pulled up. He could never recover but is well worth another chance. (op 9-2)
Loyaliste(FR) looked really well beforehand. He was given some sharp reminders soon after the start and was under pressure and going nowhere fully half a mile from home. This was very disappointing after his good third first time. (op 9-4)

6534 SOCA WARRIORS NURSERY 6f
2:40 (2:40) (Class 5) (0-85,83) 2-Y-O **£3,238** (£963; £481; £240) **Stalls** Low

Form RPR

4324 **1** **Edgewater (IRE)**25 5787 2-9-0 76 .... EddieAhern 2 78
(B J Meehan) *trckd ldrs: hdwy to chse wnr wl over 1f out and sn rdn: drvn ins fnl f: styd on wl to ld nr line* **11/1**

0314 **2** *shd* **Shibhan**27 5748 2-8-9 71 .... NCallan 1 73
(C E Brittain) *cl up: led 1/2-way: qcknd clr wl over 1f out and sn rdn: drvn ins fnl f: hdd nr line* **7/1**3

4043 **3** *2* **Reeds Bay (IRE)**15 6134 2-9-4 80 ....(b) RobertWinston 7 78+
(E S McMahon) *dwlt and sn pushed along in rr: rdn along and hdwy over 2f out: drvn over 1f out: kpt on ins fnl f: nrst fin* **7/1**3

412 **4** *7* **Yaa Wayl (IRE)**30 5658 2-9-7 83 ....(t) PhilipRobinson 4 58
(M A Jarvis) *trckd ldrs: effrt over 2f out and sn rdn: drvn wl over 1f out and kpt on same pce* **1/1**1

6243 **5** *2* **Lava Lamp (GER)**10 6247 2-8-13 75 .... JoeFanning 8 44
(M Johnston) *dwlt and sn rdn along in rr: bhd over 2f out: styd on ins fnl f: nvr nr ldrs* **6/1**2

3504 **6** *2 3/4* **Kakapuka**18 6018 2-8-9 71 .... TedDurcan 6 31
(Mrs A L M King) *in tch: effrt over 2f out: sn rdn and no imp* **22/1**

063 **7** *1* **Frontline Boy (IRE)**20 5958 2-8-13 75 .... AndrewElliott 5 32
(A P Jarvis) *chsd ldrs on inner: rdn along over 2f out and grad wknd* **20/1**

1500 **8** *12* **Monalini (IRE)**[36] 5467 2-9-0 **76**.. TomEaves 3 —
(B Smart) *led to 1/2-way: sn rdn and wknd 2f out* **40/1**
4005 **9** *nk* **Little Perisher**[15] 6134 2-8-9 **76**....................................... MartinLane(5) 9 —
(A P Jarvis) *in tch on outer: rdn along over 2f out and sn wknd* **40/1**
1m 17.41s (0.51) **Going Correction** -0.025s/f (Good) **9** Ran SP% **111.6**
Speed ratings (Par 95): **95,94,92,82,80 76,75,59,58**
toteswinger: 1&2 £6.40, 1&3 £7.80, 2&3 £6.70. CSF £77.65 CT £575.87 TOTE £11.90: £3.30, £2.10, £2.00; EX 71.80.
Owner Mrs B V Sangster **Bred** R Ahamad & P Scott **Trained** Manton, Wilts

FOCUS
A much more competitive 71-83 nursery handicap than the betting suggested and the form looks solid.

NOTEBOOK
Edgewater(IRE), fourth in a maiden over a mile at Chepstow, went in pursuit of the leader turning in and ran on to lead right on the post. A return to 7f might be even more in his favour. (op 12-1 tchd 10-1)
Shibhan, 3lb higher than when opening her account over 7f at Chester, took it up going into the final turn and soon skipped three lengths clear. She was nailed right on the line and possibly a shade unlucky she deserves another success. (op 9-1)
Reeds Bay(IRE), having his eighth start, is another already tried over further. After missing a beat at the start he put in some good work once in line for home and the first three pulled some way clear. (op 15-2 tchd 10-1)
Yaa Wayl(IRE), raised 2lb after finishing a well beaten runner-up in a stronger nursery at Haydock, was in trouble soon after halfway and never looked like justifying his market position. He may not want the ground as quick as this. (op 10-11)
Lava Lamp(GER) didn't have the best of breaks and was never travelling at any stage. (tchd 13-2)

6535 TRINIDAD & TOBAGO H'CAP — 1m 4y
3:10 (3:10) (Class 3) (0-95,91) 3-Y-O
£7,477 (£2,239; £1,119; £560; £279; £140) **Stalls** Low

Form RPR
1460 **1** **Good Again**[89] 3746 3-9-4 **91**.. TomEaves 3 99
(G A Butler) *dwlt: hld up in rr: hdwy 3f out: swtchd to inner and rdn to chal 1f out: styd on to ld ins fnl f: drvn out* **14/1**
-522 **2** *1 1/2* **Truism**[22] 5914 3-9-0 **87**.. NCallan 1 92+
(Mrs A J Perrett) *trckd ldng pair: hdwy over 2f out: rdn to ld wl over 1f out: jnd and drvn over 1f out: hdd ins fnl f: kpt on* **9/4**[2]
1405 **3** *hd* **African Art (USA)**[4] 6429 3-8-12 **85**.............................. RyanMoore 2 89
(B J Meehan) *hld up in tch: hdwy over 2f out: rdn to chal over 1f out and ev ch tl drvn and nt qckn ins fnl f* **6/1**
3-11 **4** *4* **My Verse**[19] 5996 3-8-8 **81**.. PhilipRobinson 4 76
(M A Jarvis) *towards rr: pushed along and outpcd over 3f out: rdn and hdwy 2f out: drvn over 1f out and nvr nr ldrs* **2/1**[1]
0055 **5** *6* **Yorgunnabelucky (USA)**[10] 6249 3-8-8 **81**..................(b[1]) JoeFanning 6 62
(M Johnston) *led: rdn along 3f out: drvn and hdd wl over 1f out: sn wknd* **9/1**
4442 **6** *1 3/4* **Laudatory**[19] 5986 3-8-12 **85**.. EddieAhern 5 62
(W R Swinburn) *chsd ldr: rdn along 3f out: sn drvn and wknd 2f out* **5/1**[3]
1m 43.69s (-2.21) **Going Correction** -0.025s/f (Good) **6** Ran SP% **111.7**
Speed ratings (Par 105): **110,108,108,104,98 96**
toteswinger: 1&2 £4.70, 1&3 £6.00, 2&3 £2.20. CSF £45.26 TOTE £18.60: £4.90, £1.50; EX 50.20.
Owner Future In Mind Partnership **Bred** L A Garfield **Trained** Newmarket, Suffolk

FOCUS
A competitive 81-91 3-y-o handicap and the pace was strong. The form looks sound rated around the placed horses.

NOTEBOOK
Good Again, 5lb higher than her last success at Ascot in May, was settled off the pace. Enjoying a dream run through, she went on inside the last and was right on top at the line. She has clearly come back better than ever after a three-month break. (op 11-1)
Truism, raised 2lb after just failing to get there at Goodwood, had the leader covered. He is clearly in very good heart but seems likely to continue his war with the assessor. (tchd 3-1)
African Art(USA), having his second outing in five days after over three months on the sidelines, showed ahead for a few strides but the winner swept by on the inner. In the end he just failed to hang on to second spot. (op 8-1)
My Verse, raised 6lb after winning on her handicap debut at Sandown, was being pushed along at the foot of the hill and never threatened to take a hand. (tchd 15-8)
Yorgunnabelucky(USA), in first time blinkers, set a strong pace but when collared once in line for home he soon dropped right away. He doesn't seem to be progressing at all. (op 8-1)

6536 PHIL BULL TROPHY CONDITIONS STKS — 2m 1f 216y
3:40 (3:40) (Class 3) 3-Y-O+ **£9,346** (£2,799; £1,399; £700) **Stalls** Low

Form RPR
1366 **1** **Urban Poet (USA)**[23] 5854 3-8-5 105.................................. TedDurcan 1 100+
(Saeed Bin Suroor) *trckd ldr: led 1/2-way: pushed along over 2f out: sn rdn: drvn over 1f out and styd on wl* **5/4**[1]
0666 **2** *5* **Dolly Penrose**[24] 5823 4-8-12 82..................................(v) TonyCulhane 2 87
(M R Channon) *hld up in rr: hdwy on inner over 3f out: trckd wnr 2f out: swtchd rt: rdn and ch wl over 1f out: sn drvn and one pce* **15/2**
2104 **3** *6* **Just Lille (IRE)**[15] 6138 6-8-12 91............................(p) RoystonFfrench 5 80
(Mrs A Duffield) *led: hdd 1/2-way: cl up tl rdn along 3f out and grad wknd* **7/4**[2]
1220 **4** *5* **Mr Crystal (FR)**[87] 3793 5-9-3 77.. JoeFanning 3 80
(Micky Hammond) *trckd ldng pair: pushed along 4f out: rdn wl over 2f out and sn wknd* **11/2**[3]
4m 3.88s (-0.02) **Going Correction** -0.025s/f (Good)
WFA 3 from 4yo+ 12lb **4** Ran SP% **108.0**
Speed ratings (Par 107): **99,96,94,91**
toteswinger: 1&2 £5.40. CSF £9.84 TOTE £1.90; EX 8.30.
Owner Godolphin **Bred** Claiborne Farm **Trained** Newmarket, Suffolk

FOCUS
A depleted field because of the quick ground and a there was just a sedate pace to the halfway mark. The form is best rated through the runner-up.

NOTEBOOK
Urban Poet(USA), a good third in the Group 3 Gordon Stakes after making a winning bow in maiden company at Hamilton, has flopped twice since in Listed company. Happy to accept a lead he went on over a mile out and stepped up the gallop markedly at the foot of the hill. He came right away once in line for home and won eased down, value double the official margin. He still looks under-developed and, bred in the purple, might yet make a high-class stayer at four. (tchd 11-10 and 11-8)
Dolly Penrose, with the visor retained, was put to sleep at the back. She took second travelling almost as well as the winner going into the final turn, but meeting him on 18lb worse terms than a handicap, she was soon put in her place. Her two career wins were in the mud but she didn't seem to find this lively surface a problem. (op 8-1 tchd 7-1)
Just Lille(IRE), attempting this marathon trip for the first time, dropped anchor in front. She came under pressure when the pace increased half a mile from home and she does not look a real stayer. (op 13-8 tchd 15-8)
Mr Crystal(FR), who likes it here, had much the least chance on official ratings and after racing quite keenly he was struggling to keep up half a mile out. Back here after a three month break, easier opportunities will come his way either on the Flat or over hurdles. (op 7-1 tchd 5-1)

6537 BUCCOO REEF "PREMIER" CLAIMING STKS — 1m 4y
4:10 (4:10) (Class 4) 3-Y-O **£5,180** (£1,541; £770; £384) **Stalls** Low

Form RPR
5123 **1** **Bea Menace (USA)**[53] 4940 3-8-4 72.................................. JoeFanning 3 83
(P F I Cole) *trckd ldrs on inner: hdwy 3f out: swtchd rt and effrt to chal wl over 1f out: rdn to ld appr fnl f: kpt on wl* **8/1**
0331 **2** *3/4* **Roar Of Applause**[2] 6474 3-8-9 80..............................(b) EddieAhern 7 86
(B J Meehan) *hld up in rr: hdwy 2f out: chsd ldrs over 1f out: rdn to chse wnr ins fnl f: sn drvn and kpt on* **11/8**[1]
4504 **3** *1 1/2* **All About You (IRE)**[16] 6111 3-8-6 78..............................(b) LiamJones 5 80
(W J Haggas) *led: rdn along over 2f out: drvn and hdd over 1f out: kpt on u.p fnl f* **7/2**[2]
1606 **4** *4* **Helieorbea**[6] 6357 3-8-7 73..(p) DavidAllan 6 72
(T D Easterby) *trckd ldr: effrt 3f out: rdn along 2f out: drvn and edgd lft over 1f out: wknd* **14/1**
3462 **5** *5* **Pyrus Time (IRE)**[10] 6248 3-8-8 70 ow1..............................(p) NCallan 4 61
(J S Moore) *dwlt: sn in tch: rdn along over 2f out: drvn and wknd wl over 1f out* **11/1**
6400 **6** *1 3/4* **Star Links (USA)**[10] 6243 3-8-4 78.............................. RoystonFfrench 8 53
(R Hannon) *chsd ldrs: rdn along over 2f out: sn drvn and wknd* **9/2**[3]
3050 **7** *2 1/2* **Charismatic Lady**[7] 6339 3-7-13 60.............................. AdrianMcCarthy 1 42
(Jane Chapple-Hyam) *in tch on inner: rdn along 3f out: drvn over 2f out and sn wknd* **33/1**
1m 44.8s (-1.10) **Going Correction** -0.025s/f (Good) **7** Ran SP% **111.6**
Speed ratings (Par 103): **104,103,101,97,92 91,88**
toteswinger: 1&2 £2.70, 1&3 £5.00, 2&3 £1.10. CSF £18.56 TOTE £10.10: £2.70, £1.60; EX 18.80.
Owner The Comic Strip Heroes **Bred** Stuart McPhee **Trained** Whatcombe, Oxon

FOCUS
A disappointing turn-out for this premier claimer with a minimum claiming price of £20,000, and the pace was very modest until the final 3f, so this is probably not form to be too positive about.

6538 DEM WINDOW SOLUTIONS H'CAP — 1m 4f 8y
4:40 (4:41) (Class 5) (0-70,70) 3-Y-O **£3,885** (£1,156; £577; £288) **Stalls** Low

Form RPR
3044 **1** **Bow To No One (IRE)**[15] 6139 3-8-5 **62** ow2................ MartinLane(5) 8 69+
(A P Jarvis) *hld up towards rr: hdwy 2f out: swtchd rt and rdn over 1f out: sn hung rt: drvn and styd on ins fnl f to ld last 75yds* **10/1**
2043 **2** *1/2* **Silent Act (USA)**[19] 5988 3-8-8 **60**.. NCallan 1 66
(Mrs A J Perrett) *trckd ldrs: hdwy over 2f out: swtchd lft to inner and rdn over 1f out: led jst ins fnl f and sn drvn: hdd and no ex last 75yds* **10/3**[1]
0242 **3** *1/2* **Regal Lyric (IRE)**[15] 6139 3-8-10 **62**.............................. MickyFenton 6 67
(T P Tate) *hld up in rr: hdwy on outer over 3f out: rdn to chal over 1f out and ev ch tl drvn: edgged lft and one pce wl ins fnl f* **11/2**
1506 **4** *2* **Bubses Boy**[19] 5988 3-8-4 **56** oh1.................................... JoeFanning 4 58
(P Howling) *prom: led after 2f: rdn along 3f out: hdd briefly over 1f out: drvn and rallied to ld again ent fnl f: sn hdd and kpt on same pce* **16/1**
2350 **5** *shd* **Persian Memories (IRE)**[19] 5990 3-8-9 **61**.......................... EddieAhern 5 63
(J L Dunlop) *trckd ldrs: hdwy 3f out: rdn on outer whn bmpd over 1f out: kpt on same pce after* **5/1**[3]
1634 **6** *1 1/2* **Drum Dragon**[32] 5594 3-9-3 **69**.. TedDurcan 7 68
(M H Tompkins) *in tch: hdwy on inner to chse ldrs over 2f out: rdn whn nt clr run and swtchd rt over 1f out: n.m.r ins fnl f: kpt on* **9/1**
5334 **7** *1 1/4* **Oriental Cavalier**[10] 6248 3-9-4 **70**..............................(p) RobertWinston 2 67
(R Hollinshead) *led 2f: cl up: effrt over 2f out: rdn to ld briefly over 1f out: drvn and hdd ent fnl f: sn wknd* **7/2**[2]
2265 **8** *1* **Punch Drunk**[23] 5858 3-9-3 **69**..................................(p) TomEaves 9 65
(J G Given) *a towards rr* **16/1**
3053 **9** *5* **Acquavella**[15] 6139 3-8-12 **64**...................................... TonyHamilton 10 52
(R A Fahey) *trckd ldrs: rdn along 3f out: sn wknd* **12/1**
2m 40.1s (-0.70) **Going Correction** -0.025s/f (Good) **9** Ran SP% **115.9**
Speed ratings (Par 101): **101,100,100,99,98 97,97,96,93**
toteswinger: 1&2 £10.20, 1&3 £10.20, 2&3 £3.50. CSF £43.57 CT £206.14 TOTE £13.50: £3.70, £1.30, £2.30; EX 61.30.
Owner Geoffrey Bishop **Bred** Albert Conneally **Trained** Middleham Moor, N Yorks
■ Stewards' Enquiry : N CallanM two-day ban: careless riding (Oct 19-20)
Martin LaneM one-day ban: used whip with excessive frequency (Oct 19)

FOCUS
A modest 56-70 3-y-o handicap and the pace was just steady until the final 3f. The form looks sound enough rated around the placed horses.

6539 MARACAS BAY MAIDEN STKS — 1m 4y
5:10 (5:10) (Class 5) 3-Y-O **£3,238** (£963; £481; £240) **Stalls** Low

Form RPR
5233 **1** **Ithinkbest**[74] 4246 3-9-3 78.. RyanMoore 4 75
(Sir Michael Stoute) *trckd ldr: hdwy to chal and carried wd home turn: rdn to ld wl over 1f out: edgd lft ins fnl f: drvn out* **7/2**[2]
36 **2** *1/2* **Laazim (USA)**[50] 5070 3-9-3 77.. JoeFanning 3 74
(M Johnston) *chsd ldng pair: hdwy 3f out: rdn along 2f out: drvn over 1f out: kpt on wl u.p ins fnl f* **7/1**
3 **3** *2 1/2* **Localiser (IRE)**[158] 1625 3-9-3 0.................................... AndrewMullen 7 68
(D Nicholls) *chsd ldrs on inner: rdn along over 2f out: drvn over 1f out: kpt on u.p fnl f* **33/1**
2630 **4** *nk* **Kloof**[7] 6348 3-9-3 75.. NCallan 2 67
(K A Ryan) *t.k.h: sn led and clr: pushed along and jnd whn rn wd home turn: sn rdn and hdd wl over 1f out: wknd ins fnl f* **13/2**
5 *1/2* **Black Eagle (IRE)** 3-9-3 0.. TedDurcan 6 66+
(Saeed Bin Suroor) *towards rr: hdwy 3f out: rdn wl over 1f out: kpt on ins fnl f: nrst fin* **10/11**[1]
605 **6** *14* **Convitezza**[18] 6022 3-8-12 40.. TomEaves 1 27
(M E Sowersby) *dwlt: a in rr* **125/1**
2266 **7** *7* **Capeability (IRE)**[18] 6022 3-9-3 85.............................. TonyCulhane 5 16
(M R Channon) *a in rr* **6/1**[3]
4340 **8** *12* **Georgie Bee**[36] 5470 3-8-12 48...................................... DuranFentiman 8 —
(T D Walford) *chsd ldrs on outer: rdn along 3f out: sn drvn and wknd 2f out* **80/1**
1m 46.16s (0.26) **Going Correction** -0.025s/f (Good) **8** Ran SP% **119.7**
Speed ratings (Par 101): **97,96,94,93,93 79,72,60**
toteswinger: 1&2 £12.30, 1&3 £8.00, 2&3 £14.50. CSF £29.13 TOTE £3.50: £1.40, £2.20, £4.50; EX 23.30 Place 6: £204.37 Place 5: £61.64.
Owner Saeed Suhail **Bred** Highbury Stud Ltd **Trained** Newmarket, Suffolk

FOCUS
A modest maiden run at a sound pace. The form looks ordianry rated through the runner-up to previous course handicap form.

T/Plt: £368.50 to a £1 stake. Pool: £57,008.78. 112.92 winning tickets. T/Qpdt: £13.00 to a £1 stake. Pool: £4,260.08. 241.70 winning tickets. JR

6362 WARWICK (L-H)

Monday, October 5

OFFICIAL GOING: Good to firm (good in places on round course; 8.7)
Wind: Nil Weather: Cloudy

6540 WARWICKRACECOURSE.CO.UK H'CAP 6f
2:20 (2:21) (Class 4) (0-85,85) 3-Y-0+ **£5,180** (£1,541; £770; £384) **Stalls** Low

Form RPR
0050 **1** **Methaaly (IRE)**[9] 6279 6-8-8 **74**.........................(be) EdwardCreighton 4 84
(M Mullineaux) *hld up in mid-div: pushed along over 3f out: hdwy wl over 1f out: sn rdn: led ins fnl f: r.o* **16/1**
-21 **2** *nk* **Leverage (IRE)**[87] 3813 3-8-13 **80**.................................. KFallon 5 89
(L M Cumani) *hld up in rr: swtchd lft over 2f out: pushed along and hdwy over 1f out: ev ch ins fnl f: ev ch whn edgd rt wl ins fnl f: kpt on* **10/3**[2]
0000 **3** *nk* **Orpsie Boy (IRE)**[9] 6279 6-9-3 **83**.............................. TPQueally 1 91
(N P Littmoden) *chsd ldrs: c to stands' rail 2f out: chal ins fnl f: rdn and edgd lft towards fin: nt qckn* **9/2**[3]
0400 **4** *3* **Earlsmedic**[9] 6279 4-8-12 **81**...............................(v) WilliamCarson(3) 3 79
(S C Williams) *led: carried hd high whn rdn and hdd jst over 1f out: wknd towards fin* **5/2**[1]
1400 **5** *3/4* **Dancing Maite**[25] 5799 4-8-12 **81**....................... RussellKennemore(3) 7 77
(S R Bowring) *a.p: rdn to ld jst over 1f out: hdd & wknd ins fnl f* **14/1**
0446 **6** *1 1/2* **Barons Spy (IRE)**[20] 5959 8-9-5 **85**.......................... HayleyTurner 8 76
(R J Price) *chsd ldrs: pushed along over 2f out: wknd wl over 1f out* **10/1**
5013 **7** *nk* **Fesko**[14] 6155 3-8-13 **80**.. GregFairley 2 70
(M Johnston) *bhd: pushed along over 4f out: rdn over 1f out: no rspnse* **15/2**
0202 **8** *3/4* **Bel Cantor**[9] 6279 6-8-11 **77**...................................(p) ChrisCatlin 9 65
(W J H Ratcliffe) *chsd ldr tl wl over 1f out: sn wknd* **14/1**
5230 **9** *27* **Memphis Man**[9] 6279 6-8-3 **74**............................ SimonPearce(5) 6 —
(P D Evans) *bolted a complete circ of rnd crse bef s: s.i.s: sn struggling: lost tch over 3f out* **28/1**

1m 11.08s (-0.72) **Going Correction** +0.025s/f (Good) course record
WFA 3 from 4yo+ 1lb **9** Ran SP% **113.4**
Speed ratings (Par 105): **105,104,104,100,99 97,96,95,59**
toteswinger: 1&2 £11.90, 1&3 £21.80, 2&3 £5.50. CSF £67.67 CT £287.24 TOTE £15.90: £5.10, £1.20, £2.00; EX 86.50.
Owner A Jones **Bred** Scuderia Golden Horse S R L **Trained** Alpraham, Cheshire

FOCUS
Ahead of the first race, the ground was changed slightly to good to firm (good in places on the round course). Not surprisingly, with three regular front-runners in the field, this race was run at a strong gallop and by and large favoured those held up, and the winner is the best guide on this year's form. The field came stands' side in the straight.
Memphis Man Official explanation: jockey said gelding bolted to post

6541 TURFTV BETTING SHOP SERVICE NURSERY 6f
2:50 (2:52) (Class 3) (0-95,88) 2-Y-0 **£8,095** (£2,408; £1,203; £601) **Stalls** Low

Form RPR
5210 **1** **Comedy Hall (USA)**[17] 6048 2-9-6 **87**............................ GregFairley 6 93
(M Johnston) *w ldr over 2f: pushed along to ld over 1f out: rdn ins fnl f: r.o* **11/1**
031 **2** *1/2* **Ongoodform (IRE)**[18] 6032 2-9-4 **85**................................ KFallon 9 90
(P W D'Arcy) *hld up and bhd: hdwy over 1f out: edgd lft ins fnl f: sn rdn and ev ch: r.o* **3/1**[1]
1616 **3** *3 1/2* **Radio City**[17] 6068 2-8-12 **79**...................................... TPQueally 1 73
(R M Beckett) *hld up in tch: chal over 1f out: rdn and one pce ins fnl f* **9/2**[3]
1010 **4** *1* **Yer Woman (IRE)**[25] 5797 2-9-1 **82**.............................. PatDobbs 2 73
(R Hannon) *s.i.s: hld up in rr: pushed along over 2f out: rdn and hdwy over 1f out: one pce ins fnl f* **17/2**
1020 **5** *1 1/2* **Mdawee (IRE)**[69] 4407 2-9-7 **88**........................... RichardSmith 3 75
(Tom Dascombe) *led: rdn and hdd over 1f out: wknd ins fnl f* **16/1**
1001 **6** *2 3/4* **Angel Of Fashion (IRE)**[14] 6169 2-8-10 **77**.............. MichaelHills 4 55
(B W Hills) *prom: jnd ldr over 3f out: pushed along and wknd over 1f out* **10/3**[2]
6303 **7** *nse* **Craicattack (IRE)**[16] 6104 2-8-9 **76**............................ LPKeniry 7 54
(J S Moore) *hld up: pushed along over 2f out: struggling whn rdn over 1f out* **5/1**
0051 **8** *2 1/2* **Existentialist**[24] 5835 2-8-6 **73**........................... HayleyTurner 8 44
(A E Price) *hld up: pushed along over 2f out: struggling over 1f out* **20/1**

1m 11.73s (-0.07) **Going Correction** +0.025s/f (Good) 2y crse rec **8** Ran SP% **112.4**
Speed ratings (Par 99): **101,100,95,94,92 88,88,85**
toteswinger: 1&2 £5.30, 1&3 £7.50, 2&3 £3.80. CSF £42.63 CT £173.31 TOTE £13.50: £3.00, £1.40, £1.80; EX 43.90.
Owner Sheikh Hamdan Bin Mohammed Al Maktoum **Bred** Stoneside Stable **Trained** Middleham Moor, N Yorks
■ Mark Johnston's 190th winner of the year, breaking the Flat record set by Richard Hannon in 1993.

FOCUS
An ordinary nursery run at a decent clip and few obvious excuses for any of the runners, so the form looks decent. The runners stayed more towards the middle/far side on this occasion.

NOTEBOOK
Comedy Hall(USA) put his recent Ayr flop behind him with a hard-earned success. Never far away, he saw his race out strongly despite tending to carry his head slightly awkwardly and left the impression he will improve again. Another furlong won't come amiss either, and given his pedigree he could be seen to good effect on the all-weather this winter. (op 15-2 tchd 7-1)
Ongoodform(IRE) hadn't won much of a race at Yarmouth and this was a step forward. He was set a bit more to do, and had a less clear run, than the winner, but he left the impression he was just second best anyway. He will be just as effective at 7f. (op 4-1 tchd 9-2)
Radio City will fare best kept to 6f for now. He looked set to play a big part entering the last but weakened noticeably late on. (op 6-1)
Yer Woman(IRE) never landed a blow and seemed to find the combination of the sharp track and fast ground against her. (op 7-1)
Mdawee(IRE) didn't seem to get home on his first try at the trip and might appreciate more give in the ground judged on his pounding action. (op 14-1)
Angel Of Fashion(IRE) dropped away tamely up in the weights in what was a warmer race than last time. (op 4-1)
Craicattack(IRE) never looked happy. He has form under these conditions before, and perhaps just had an off day. (op 4-1)
Existentialist had only won a claimer on the all weather last time and looked outclassed back on turf. (op 16-1)

6542 E B F BUY A RACING POST YEARLING BONUS CANDIDATE MAIDEN STKS 6f
3:20 (3:21) (Class 5) 2-Y-O **£4,209** (£1,252; £625; £312) **Stalls** Low

Form RPR
0 **1** **Regency Art (IRE)**[160] 1590 2-9-3 0................................. KFallon 5 72+
(D R C Elsworth) *chsd ldr: pushed along over 1f out: rdn and c to stands' rail jst ins fnl f: r.o u.p to ld towards fin* **17/2**[3]
5 **2** *1/2* **Libertino (IRE)**[133] 2328 2-9-3 0.............................. HayleyTurner 3 69+
(B J Meehan) *hld up: hdwy over 1f out: led ins fnl f: hdd towards fin* **5/2**[2]
052 **3** *3 3/4* **Sharp Shoes**[10] 6246 2-9-3 0... TPQueally 4 57
(Mrs A Duffield) *led: rdn and hdd ins fnl f: no ex towards fin* **14/1**
0 **4** *nk* **Taeping (IRE)**[45] 5234 2-9-3 0.................................... ChrisCatlin 6 56
(R Hollinshead) *hld up in tch: rdn and ev ch jst over 1f out: one pce ins fnl f* **18/1**
5 *3 3/4* **Tadhkeer** 2-9-3 0.. RHills 1 45
(W J Haggas) *prom: pushed along over 2f out: wknd jst over 1f out* **10/11**[1]
0 **6** *1 3/4* **Sonny G (IRE)**[4] 6416 2-9-0 0...................................... MarcHalford(3) 7 40
(J R Best) *prom tl pushed along and wknd wl over 1f out* **50/1**
7 *14* **Destiny Rules** 2-8-12 0.. CatherineGannon 2 —
(John Berry) *s.i.s: outpcd: no ch fnl 3f* **33/1**

1m 13.71s (1.91) **Going Correction** +0.025s/f (Good) **7** Ran SP% **108.3**
Speed ratings (Par 95): **88,87,82,81,76 74,55**
toteswinger: 1&2 £3.00, 1&3 £3.70, 2&3 £2.10. CSF £26.92 TOTE £10.00: £3.10, £1.30; EX 34.30.
Owner Matthew Green **Bred** Rathasker Stud **Trained** Newmarket, Suffolk

FOCUS
A weak maiden run at a steady pace until halfway and, behind the first two, little of real interest for the future, with the bare form modest.

NOTEBOOK
Regency Art(IRE) still looked green at stages through the race and ended up drifting across to the stands' rail, but he was only just getting going as he passed the line and looked to have plenty left in the tank. Off the track since the spring, he was the subject of an eye-catching jockey booking and is probably capable of a fair bit better. The Handicapper can't be too harsh on him for this, and, if so, will be an interesting runner in a nursery over an extra furlong. (tchd 12-1)
Libertino(IRE) was also making a comeback from a lengthy break and showed a fair turn of foot to come through and dispute the lead briefly inside the last. He might just have needed this, and looks best kept to this trip for now, though he won't find many easier opportunities than this. (op 3-1)
Sharp Shoes had shown only poor form so far and his proximity in third after getting the run of the race from the front rather puts the form into context. (op 17-2 tchd 16-1)
Taeping(IRE) had made his debut in a good maiden at York but is clearly only modest, though he might do better stepped up to 7f. (op 16-1 tchd 14-1)
Tadhkeer was sent off favourite but his yard gets few first-time-out 2-y-o winners and after pressing the leaders, was soon put in his place once the race begin in earnest without his rider being hard on him. He looks very much one of the stable lesser lights. Official explanation: jockey said gelding was unsuited by the good to firm ground (op 11-10 tchd 8-11)
Sonny G(IRE) finished his race off very weakly for the second race in succession. (op 25-1)
Destiny Rules showed little and is bred to need much more of a test. (op 18-1)

6543 CLEANEVENT H'CAP 1m 6f 213y
3:50 (3:50) (Class 5) (0-75,75) 3-Y-O **£2,729** (£806; £403) **Stalls** Low

Form RPR
3203 **1** **Khayar (IRE)**[5] 6384 3-8-9 **61** ow1.............................. DarryllHolland 2 67
(M H Tompkins) *sn led: rdn 2f out: drvn out* **7/2**[3]
1262 **2** *1/2* **Dice (IRE)**[18] 6027 3-9-9 **75**.. KFallon 4 80
(L M Cumani) *hld up in tch: rdn wl over 1f out: ev ch ins fnl f: nt qckn towards fin* **11/8**[1]
5232 **3** *1 1/2* **Theologist (IRE)**[5] 6400 3-9-4 **70**..............................(v) TPQueally 5 73
(Mrs A J Perrett) *hld up in tch: jnd ldr over 9f out: pushed along over 2f out: sltly outpcd wl over 1f out: sn rdn: styd on to take 3rd towards fin* **11/4**[2]
0560 **4** *1* **Taste The Wine (IRE)**[2] 6473 3-8-12 **64**............................ LPKeniry 3 66
(J S Moore) *led early: chsd ldr tl over 9f out: rdn over 3f out: hrd rdn and wnt 2nd again briefly wl over 1f out: wknd towards fin* **14/1**
0002 **5** *15* **Am I Blue**[13] 6188 3-8-4 **56** oh1.................................. ChrisCatlin 1 38
(H J L Dunlop) *hld up in last: pushed along over 7f out: rdn over 5f out: struggling 3f out* **7/1**

3m 20.64s (1.64) **Going Correction** -0.10s/f (Good) **5** Ran SP% **110.2**
Speed ratings (Par 101): **91,90,89,89,81**
CSF £8.81 TOTE £4.80: £1.90, £1.50; EX 10.70.
Owner Mrs S Lloyd **Bred** Mrs S Lloyd And Dr M Klay **Trained** Newmarket, Suffolk

FOCUS
A modest staying handicap run at a stop-start gallop. The form looks a bit muddling wioth the winner and third the best guides.

6544 BUY A RACING POST YEARLING BONUS CANDIDATE MAIDEN AUCTION STKS 7f 26y
4:20 (4:21) (Class 5) 2-Y-O **£3,238** (£963; £481; £240) **Stalls** Low

Form RPR
1 **Thrust Control (IRE)** 2-8-11 0............................... CatherineGannon 5 74
(M R Channon) *mde all: pushed along over 1f out: hld on wl fnl f* **10/1**
4 **2** *hd* **Pan American**[84] 3925 2-8-10 0................................. FergusSweeney 13 73+
(P J Makin) *hld up in mid-div: smooth prog 2f out: sustained chal fnl f: rdn and r.o* **7/1**[3]
5 **3** *2* **Cat Hunter**[39] 5368 2-8-6 0 ow1............................... EdwardCreighton 7 64
(Mrs A J Perrett) *hld up in tch: rdn wl over 1f out: nt qckn ins fnl f* **7/1**[3]
3 **4** *3/4* **Kenyan Cat**[21] 5934 2-8-7 0.. DO'Donohoe 8 63+
(George Baker) *a.p: rdn wl over 1f out: kpt on same pce fnl f* **9/2**[2]
0 **5** *nse* **Soho Theatre**[38] 5400 2-8-13 0.................................... TPQueally 6 69
(D R C Elsworth) *a.p: pushed along over 1f out: one pce ins fnl f* **14/1**
5 **6** *1 1/4* **Miss Zooter (IRE)**[60] 4688 2-8-5 0.............................. RichardSmith 11 58+
(R M Beckett) *s.i.s: sn swtchd lft: hld up in rr: pushed along over 2f out: rdn and kpt on fnl f: nvr trbld ldrs* **10/1**
0 **7** *1 1/4* **During The War (USA)**[25] 5807 2-8-13 0........................... KFallon 12 65+
(L M Cumani) *hld up in mid-div: reminder over 5f out: rdn jst over 1f out: no hdwy* **17/2**
4 **8** *nse* **Sidney Melbourne (USA)**[21] 5934 2-8-11 0.................... ChrisCatlin 10 61
(J R Best) *chsd wnr tl pushed along wl over 1f out: sn wknd* **4/1**[1]
05 **9** *2 3/4* **Spirit Land (IRE)**[11] 6235 2-8-4 0........................... AshleyMorgan(5) 3 52
(M H Tompkins) *hld up: sn towards rr: pushed along wl over 1f out: no rspnse* **33/1**

56 **10** *1* **Hathaway (IRE)**[10] 6245 2-8-4 0 .... PaulQuinn 4 44
(W M Brisbourne) *hld up towards rr: pushed along over 2f out: no rspnse* **16/1**

0 **11** *hd* **Chichina (USA)**[18] 6009 2-8-6 0 .... GregFairley 9 46
(M Johnston) *hld up towards rr: pushed along over 2f out: sn struggling* **20/1**

0 **12** *4 1/2* **Universal Pride**[25] 5800 2-8-4 0 .... HayleyTurner 2 33
(J Gallagher) *hld up in mid-div: pushed along over 2f out: sn bhd* **28/1**

1m 26.37s (1.77) **Going Correction** -0.10s/f (Good) **12** Ran SP% **115.6**
Speed ratings (Par 95): **85,84,82,81,81 80,78,78,75,74 74,69**
toteswinger: 1&2 £19.40, 1&3 £17.90, 2&3 £10.40. CSF £74.58 TOTE £10.50: £3.70, £2.70, £2.70; EX 101.10.
Owner Mrs T Burns **Bred** Rathasker Stud **Trained** West Ilsley, Berks

FOCUS
An ordinary maiden auction run at just a fair gallop, and not form to be getting carried away with, though the winner and second, as well as a couple behind, are open to improvement. It was an advantage to race up with the pace, so the runner-up deserves extra credit but the form looks limited rated around the third and fourth.

NOTEBOOK
Thrust Control(IRE) was nibbled at in the betting and proved game in the finish after seemingly being headed inside the last. For all he had the run of the race out in front and was clearly ready first time up, he is entitled to improve and seems likely to stay 1m before too long. (op 16-1)
Pan American ◆ looked an unlucky loser. Drawn widest of all, he travelled eye-catchingly well before showing a good turn of foot to dispute the lead inside the last, but the effort of getting there took its toll and he was just denied on the line. He looks a sure winner of a similar event, and will be just as effective back at 6f. (op 8-1 tchd 9-1)
Cat Hunter stepped up on his promising debut with a sound effort. His dam was a middle-distance winner, and he will be more effective this year at 1m. (op 4-1)
Kenyan Cat and Sydney Melbourne were very closely matched on their debut and that form seemed to set the standard, but it may be that was a weak race as neither threatened much once into the straight. The former showed more on this occasion and once again left the impression he needs more of a test of stamina. (op 4-1 tchd 7-2 and 5-1 in places)
Soho Theatre made a promising debut without being given a hard time and seems likely to step up on this next time. (op 16-1 tchd 12-1)
Miss Zooter(IRE) was noted keeping on well from an unpromising position entering the straight and will be interesting in staying nurseries. (op 9-1)
During The War(USA) still looked green and never threatened. He looks a slow learner and likely to come into his own next year. (op 12-1 tchd 14-1)

6545 CE PROPERTY SERVICES GROUP H'CAP 1m 22y
4:50 (4:52) (Class 5) (0-75,78) 3-Y-0+ **£3,885** (£1,156; £577; £288) **Stalls** Low

Form RPR

0663 **1** **Muftarres (IRE)**[9] 6294 4-9-5 **69** .... (t) TPQueally 2 78
(G A Butler) *hld up in rr: hdwy wl over 1f out: sn rdn: edgd rt ins fnl f: led cl home* **6/1**[2]

6611 **2** *nk* **Sham Sheer**[16] 6124 3-9-2 **69** .... KFallon 3 77+
(L M Cumani) *racd keenly: led: rdn and hung rt to stands' rail over 1f out: hdd cl home* **6/5**[1]

1316 **3** *1/2* **Darcey**[11] 6224 3-9-4 **71** .... HayleyTurner 4 78
(Miss Amy Weaver) *hld up: hdwy on ins 2f out: edgd rt over 1f out: rdn and ev ch ins fnl f: no ex nr fin* **7/1**

1331 **4** *3 1/2* **Cheam Forever (USA)**[6] 6365 3-9-6 **78** 6ex .... AshleyMorgan(5) 7 77
(R Charlton) *w ldrs: rdn and ev ch wl over 1f out: wknd ins fnl f* **6/1**[2]

0304 **5** *nse* **Bere Davis (FR)**[6] 6365 4-9-2 **71** .... RichardEvans(5) 1 70
(P D Evans) *w ldr tl reminder over 5f out: prom tl rdn and wknd jst over 1f out* **13/2**[3]

6606 **6** *1 1/4* **West End Lad**[13] 6178 6-9-4 **71** .... (b) RussellKennemore(3) 5 67
(S R Bowring) *hld up and bhd: pushed along over 2f out: struggling whn rdn over 1f out* **14/1**

3006 **7** *3 1/4* **Very Well Red**[14] 6174 6-9-2 **66** .... ChrisCatlin 6 55
(P W Hiatt) *broke wl: sn hld up in tch: pushed along 3f out: wknd wl over 1f out* **20/1**

0311 **8** *18* **Lordship (IRE)**[31] 5634 5-8-6 **63** .... JakePayne(7) 8 10
(A W Carroll) *t.k.h: sn w ldrs: pushed along and wknd over 2f out* **22/1**

1m 40.25s (-0.75) **Going Correction** -0.10s/f (Good)
WFA 3 from 4yo+ 3lb **8** Ran SP% **115.6**
Speed ratings (Par 103): **99,98,98,94,94 93,90,72**
toteswinger: 1&2 £3.70, 1&3 £4.20, 2&3 £2.40. CSF £13.79 CT £52.19 TOTE £7.80: £1.90, £1.20, £2.10; EX 20.50.
Owner Beetle N Wedge Partnership **Bred** Shadwell Estate Company Limited **Trained** Newmarket, Suffolk
■ Stewards' Enquiry : Hayley Turner one-day ban: used whip with excessive frequency (Oct 19)

FOCUS
Several recent winners in opposition but no more than a fair handicap for the grade. Despite the presence of several front runners, the pace took a while to pick up but, even when it did, was never breakneck. The field came stands' side in the straight and the third is the best guide to the form.

6546 RACING UK £12.99 PER MONTH H'CAP 1m 2f 188y
5:20 (5:20) (Class 3) (0-95,90) 3-Y-0+ **£9,714** (£2,890; £1,444; £721) **Stalls** Low

Form RPR

0200 **1** **Alcalde**[24] 5828 3-8-9 **83** .... GregFairley 2 93+
(M Johnston) *a.p: rdn to ld over 1f out: sn hung lft: r.o* **8/1**

1-20 **2** *3/4* **Crackentorp**[107] 3142 4-9-8 **90** .... KFallon 5 99+
(R M Beckett) *hld up: hdwy over 2f out: chsd wnr over 1f out: sn rdn: nt qckn ins fnl f* **6/4**[1]

2234 **3** *5* **Sequillo**[24] 5834 3-8-8 **82** .... PatDobbs 1 82
(R Hannon) *hld up: hdwy 2f out: swtchd rt over 1f out: sn rdn: wknd ins fnl f* **13/2**

1312 **4** *4* **Mick's Dancer**[28] 5725 4-9-0 **82** .... DarryllHolland 3 74
(W R Muir) *led: pushed along over 2f out: hdd over 1f out: wknd fnl f* **3/1**[2]

1646 **5** *1 1/4* **Dubai Crest**[10] 6239 3-8-12 **86** .... TPQueally 4 76
(Mrs A J Perrett) *hld up in last: rdn over 1f out: no rspnse* **5/1**[3]

0600 **6** *3 1/2* **Cheshire Prince**[16] 6100 5-9-3 **88** .... WilliamCarson(3) 6 71
(W M Brisbourne) *chsd ldr: rdn wl over 1f out: sn wknd and n.m.r* **18/1**

2m 17.84s (-3.26) **Going Correction** -0.10s/f (Good)
WFA 3 from 4yo+ 6lb **6** Ran SP% **111.4**
Speed ratings (Par 107): **107,106,102,99,99 96**
toteswinger: 1&2 £3.40, 1&3 £5.10, 2&3 £4.10. CSF £20.27 TOTE £10.70: £3.50, £1.80; EX 29.70 Place 6: £55.69 Place 5: £27.62..
Owner Sheikh Hamdan Bin Mohammed Al Maktoum **Bred** Miss K Rausing And Mrs S Rogers **Trained** Middleham Moor, N Yorks

FOCUS
Most of these had a question mark over them coming into this and, for all the first two pulled clear at the end of a well-run race and could still be on the upgrade, the form may not be totally what it seems. The field ended up on the stands' rail again.

NOTEBOOK
Alcalde has something of an in and out profile but he had looked a good prospect as a 2-y-o and put a modest run at Doncaster last time behind him with a ready victory despite a rather ungainly head carriage. Connections have had trouble establishing his best trip, but this is as well as he has ever run and he wasn't stopping at the end, so is likely to be just as effective back at 1m4f. (op 7-1 tchd 13-2)
Crackentorp was having his first run since starting favourite for the Duke Of Edinburgh Stakes at Royal Ascot but he looked just a touch rusty and wasn't able to find a change of gear late on. He's up to winning a race off this mark with this behind him, and a return to 1m4f will help as well. He might be an interesting runner in the November Handicap if he gets in. (op 9-4)
Sequillo didn't get the clearest of runs at one point but it made no difference to the result and he was readily held once in line for home. He needs a career best to get his head back in front from his current mark, though. (op 6-1 tchd 8-1)
Mick's Dancer has made hay this summer making the running in smallish fields on fast ground, but he is much higher in the weights now and was a sitting duck in the straight after being harried early. (op 5-2 tchd 9-4 and 100-30 in places)
Dubai Crest hasn't made the progress he promised to at one point and turned in a very disappointing effort trailing throughout. (tchd 11-2)
Cheshire Prince has been running better than his form figures suggest but didn't achieve much, already beaten when squeezed out early in the straight. (op 12-1)
T/Plt: £65.90 to a £1 stake. Pool: £46,351.12. 512.83 winning tickets. T/Qpdt: £18.00 to a £1 stake. Pool: £3,259.89. 133.90 winning tickets. KH

5444 WINDSOR (R-H)
Monday, October 5

OFFICIAL GOING: Good (8.3)
Top bend dolled out 2yds increasing distances of races over 1m plus by 7yds.
Wind: Almost nil Weather: Steady rain before meeting and for 1st 2 races

6547 GETREADING.CO.UK H'CAP 1m 67y
2:30 (2:31) (Class 5) (0-70,70) 3-Y-0+ **£2,729** (£806; £403) **Stalls** High

Form RPR

5000 **1** **Sapphire Prince (USA)**[58] 4791 3-9-3 **67** .... SteveDrowne 13 74
(J R Best) *chsd ldr: hrd rdn to cl 2f out: styd on fnl f to ld last 75yds* **10/1**

1000 **2** *1/2* **Compton Blue**[10] 6243 3-9-2 **66** .... RichardHughes 12 72
(R Hannon) *hld up in 5th: reminders over 3f out: prog u.p 2f out: styd on fnl f to grab 2nd on post* **7/1**[2]

3131 **3** *shd* **King Of The Moors (USA)**[8] 6312 6-9-9 **70** 6ex .... (b) FrancisNorton 9 76
(R C Guest) *racd freely: led: taken to far rail 2f out: sn rdn: hdd and no ex last 75yds: lost 2nd post* **8/1**

0212 **4** *1* **Magroom**[7] 6337 5-9-4 **68** .... MCGeran(3) 2 74+
(R J Hodges) *hld up in rr: prog fr 3f out: grabbed far rail 2f out but hmpd sn after: kpt on same pce fnl f* **13/2**[1]

0-40 **5** *1/2* **Transfer**[12] 6212 4-9-4 **65** .... WilliamBuick 10 68+
(A M Balding) *t.k.h: hld up in 8th: nt qckn 3f out and dropped to last pair: effrt on outer over 1f out: styd on fnl f: nrst fin* **8/1**

2-50 **6** *2 1/2* **Ibbetson (USA)**[23] 5869 4-9-5 **66** .... AdamKirby 5 63
(W R Swinburn) *chsd ldng pair: rdn over 2f out: grad wknd over 1f out* **14/1**

2006 **7** *nk* **Onenightinlisbon (IRE)**[12] 6208 5-8-4 **54** oh1 Louis-PhilippeBeuzelin(3) 8 50
(J R Boyle) *hld up in 9th: hrd rdn and no prog over 2f out: plugged on* **11/1**

5036 **8** *2* **Aggravation**[44] 4060 7-9-1 **62** .... JimmyFortune 4 54
(D R C Elsworth) *hld up in rr: effrt on outer over 2f out: no prog over 1f out: wknd fnl f* **7/1**[2]

4003 **9** *1/2* **Binfield (IRE)**[25] 5791 4-9-0 **61** .... AlanMunro 1 51
(B G Powell) *chsd ldng trio tl wknd fr 2f out* **13/2**[1]

5036 **10** *2 3/4* **Margarita (IRE)**[23] 5886 3-9-2 **66** .... DaneO'Neill 6 50
(J R Fanshawe) *hld up in 6th: rdn over 2f out: nt qckn whn short of room wl over 1f out: wknd* **15/2**[3]

1006 **11** *1/2* **Brer Rabbit**[18] 6031 3-9-1 **65** .... JamieSpencer 7 48
(B W Hills) *dwlt: hld up: a in last pair: rdn and no prog over 2f out* **25/1**

0060 **R** **The Winged Assasin (USA)**[13] 6190 3-9-4 **68** .... SimonWhitworth 11 —
(J Akehurst) *ref to r* **33/1**

1m 45.31s (0.61) **Going Correction** +0.10s/f (Good)
WFA 3 from 4yo+ 3lb **12** Ran SP% **116.5**
Speed ratings (Par 103): **100,99,99,98,97 95,95,93,92,89 89,—**
toteswinger: 1&2 £28.20, 1&3 £23.30, 2&3 £16.60 CSF £77.01 CT £593.44 TOTE £18.90: £4.70, £2.60, £2.50; EX 146.10 TRIFECTA Not won..
Owner Ian Beach & John Fletcher **Bred** Bruce Moriarty & Jill Moriarty **Trained** Hucking, Kent
■ Stewards' Enquiry : Richard Hughes caution: used whip with excessive frequency

FOCUS
Persistent rain throughout the morning meant ground conditions were an unknown and the fact that the entire field went over to the far side suggests conditions were now on the slow side. This isn't form to be getting too excited about as the early pace wasn't strong and several were quite keen through the early stages.
Magroom Official explanation: jockey said gelding slipped on path crossing approaching furlong mark
Brer Rabbit Official explanation: jockey said filly ran too free

6548 EUROPEAN BREEDERS' FUND MAIDEN STKS 1m 67y
3:00 (3:04) (Class 4) 2-Y-O **£5,018** (£1,493; £746; £372) **Stalls** High

Form RPR

3 **1** **Mont Agel**[19] 6000 2-9-3 0 .... JamieSpencer 8 89+
(M L W Bell) *trckd ldng pair to over 3f out: styd cl up: smooth prog on outer to ld jst over 1f out: bounded clr* **11/8**[1]

622 **2** *3 1/2* **Fine Sight**[67] 4451 2-9-3 83 .... RichardHughes 10 76
(R Hannon) *led: rdn 2f out: hdd jst over 1f out: no ch w wnr after: kpt on* **7/4**[2]

4 **3** *3/4* **Guidecca Ten**[60] 4713 2-9-3 0 .... WilliamBuick 5 75
(A M Balding) *trckd ldrs: pushed along over 3f out: rdn and prog on outer over 1f out: kpt on to take 3rd last strides* **10/1**

54 **4** *hd* **Henry San (IRE)**[19] 5993 2-9-3 0 .... DaneO'Neill 6 74
(A King) *chsd ldr to over 1f out: one pce* **33/1**

5 *1* **Paschendale** 2-9-3 0 .... TPO'Shea 7 72+
(Saeed Bin Suroor) *s.v.s: detached in last pair: shkn up 2f out: kpt on steadily* **8/1**[3]

4 **6** *1/2* **Persona Non Grata (IRE)**[14] 6162 2-9-3 0 .... (b) RichardKingscote 3 71+
(R Charlton) *in tch towards rr: shkn up 2f out: kpt on one pce* **33/1**

02 **7** *shd* **Banana Republic (IRE)**[39] 5371 2-9-3 0 .... AlanMunro 2 71
(P F I Cole) *t.k.h: cl up: wnt 3rd over 3f out to 2f out: fdd over 1f out* **16/1**

02 **8** 1/2 **First In The Queue (IRE)**[25] 5787 2-9-3 0 JamesDoyle 1 70+
(S Kirk) *stdd s fr wd draw: hld up and sn detached in last: shkn up over 2f out: keeping on whn n.m.r ins fnl f: nrst fin* **33/1**

50 **9** 4 **Power Of Dreams (IRE)**[38] 5400 2-9-3 0 SaleemGolam 4 61
(M H Tompkins) *t.k.h: in tch towards rr tl wknd wl over 1f out* **100/1**

1m 45.39s (0.69) **Going Correction** +0.10s/f (Good) **9** Ran SP% **114.4**
Speed ratings (Par 97): **100,96,95,95,94 94,93,93,89**
toteswinger: 1&2 £1.10, 1&3 £5.70, 2&3 £3.90 CSF £3.76 TOTE £2.20: £1.30, £1.10, £2.50; EX 5.10 Trifecta £31.10 Pool: £649.59 - 16.48 winning units..
Owner J L C Pearce **Bred** J L C Pearce **Trained** Newmarket, Suffolk

FOCUS
There didn't look much depth to this maiden but the 83-rated Fine Sight set a decent enough standard. The winner can rate higher.

NOTEBOOK
Mont Agel laughed at his rivals, cruising through the contest in the style of a well above-average colt, and Spencer only had to briefly shake the reins to send his mount clear in the final furlong, before easing up close home. This Derby entry has clearly learned plenty from his debut and is value for plenty more than the winning margin, so it would be no surprise were he to be stepped up to Pattern company next time. Spencer said afterwards that the colt appreciates some juice in the ground and he will improve a lot over the winter. (op 13-8, tchd 7-4 in a place)
Fine Sight appreciated the step up in trip but he was flat to the boards when the winner sauntered past and, although he'll be unfortunate to bump into such a classy rival again, his future looks to be in nurseries. (tchd 2-1)
Guidecca Ten is bred to want middle distances (Derby entry), so this would be plenty sharp enough around here, but he finished his race nicely to grab third and build on an encouraging debut. He looks sure to win races when tackling a stiffer test of stamina. (op 11-1 tchd 12-1)
Henry San(IRE) was made to look a bit one-paced in the closing stages and will probably do better when sent handicapping (now qualified for a mark).
Paschendale was pretty friendless in the market which wasn't a good sign and he made the worst possible start by missing the break and losing three to four lengths as the gates opened. He made some good headway in the straight and looks sure to benefit a good deal from this initial experience. Official explanation: jockey said colt was slowly away (op 13-2)
First In The Queue(IRE) Official explanation: jockey said colt was unsuited by the good ground

6549 WOKINGHAM & BRACKNELL TIMES CLAIMING STKS 1m 2f 7y
3:30 (3:33) (Class 6) 3-Y-O **£2,047** (£604; £302) **Stalls** Centre

Form RPR
0346 **1** **Lucy's Perfect**[28] 5720 3-8-2 45 (b[1]) DavidProbert 7 59
(B R Millman) *hld up in tch: effrt on outer 3f out: prog wl over 1f out: drvn and styd on wl to ld last strides* **28/1**

0233 **2** nk **Tiger Flash**[17] 6075 3-8-9 67 JamieSpencer 9 66
(W J Haggas) *led after 2f: hrd rdn over 2f out: kpt on fnl f: hdd last strides* **11/4**[2]

2046 **3** 1 1/2 **Navajo Nation (IRE)**[10] 6257 3-8-5 66 TPO'Shea 4 59
(B J Meehan) *t.k.h: hld up in tch: hanging bnd 6f out: prog to chal 2f out: nt qckn 1f out and sn lost 2nd* **4/1**[3]

02 **4** nk **Everaard (USA)**[16] 6116 3-9-3 70 JimmyFortune 5 70
(D R C Elsworth) *led 2f: mostly chsd ldr tl nt qckn u.p 2f out: one pce after* **13/2**

5545 **5** 3/4 **Orthology (IRE)**[27] 5751 3-8-13 66 (b) SaleemGolam 8 65
(M H Tompkins) *t.k.h: prom: tried to chal over 3f out: rdn and fnd nil wl over 2f out: one pce after* **20/1**

2362 **6** nk **Cloudesley (IRE)**[11] 6223 3-9-1 70 WilliamBuick 6 66
(A M Balding) *trckd ldrs: reminder 4f out: rdn on outer 3f out: nt qckn 2f out and sn lost pl: one pce* **5/2**[1]

064 **7** hd **Secret Desert**[33] 5578 3-8-2 65 AndreaAtzeni[(3)] 3 56
(D M Simcock) *dwlt: rousted along early in rr: u.p and struggling 4f out: kpt on fr over 1f out* **20/1**

4500 **8** 3 **Hip Hip Hooray**[9] 6289 3-8-2 64 (p) LukeMorris 1 47
(L A Dace) *hld up in last: effrt against far rail 3f out: wknd over 1f out* **15/2**

2m 9.15s (0.45) **Going Correction** +0.10s/f (Good) **8** Ran SP% **113.3**
Speed ratings (Par 99): **102,101,100,100,99 99,99,96**
toteswinger: 1&2 £11.40, 1&3 £38.90, 2&3 £3.80. CSF £101.00 TOTE £40.70: £6.90, £1.30, £1.80; EX 85.90 TRIFECTA Not won..Navajo Nation was claimed by Mr. P. Butler for £8,000.
Owner Avalon Surfacing Ltd **Bred** Avalon Surfacing Ltd & East Burrow Farm **Trained** Kentisbeare, Devon

FOCUS
These modest performers had managed just three wins between them going into this claimer, so it shouldn't have been the biggest surprise that it threw up a big-priced winner. The fourth is the guide to the level, rated to his recent best.

6550 READING POST NURSERY 5f 10y
4:00 (4:04) (Class 4) (0-95,91) 2-Y-O **£5,180** (£1,541; £770; £384) **Stalls** High

Form RPR
21 **1** **Citrus Star (USA)**[18] 6018 2-9-4 88 AlanMunro 4 102+
(C F Wall) *s.i.s: hld up last: gd prog fr 2f out: rdn to ld 1f out: bounded clr* **9/2**[1]

31 **2** 3 1/4 **Felsham**[12] 6207 2-8-1 71 FrankieMcDonald 9 73+
(H Candy) *in tch: rdn on outer 2f out: hanging after but r.o to take 2nd last 100yds: no ch w wnr* **15/2**

5U51 **3** 2 1/2 **Wellington Fair**[24] 5829 2-8-11 81 (b) LukeMorris 2 74
(C G Cox) *mde most: rdn 2f out: hdd and easily outpcd 1f out* **6/1**[3]

6420 **4** 1 **Leleyf (IRE)**[9] 6275 2-8-8 78 RichardHughes 3 67
(M R Channon) *pressed ldr: upsides jst over 1f out: nudged along and fdd* **14/1**

2311 **5** 1/2 **Monsieur Joe (IRE)**[17] 6068 2-9-1 85 AdamKirby 5 73
(W R Swinburn) *in rr: effrt against far rail 2f out: no prog whn rn short of room jst over 1f out: no ch after* **5/1**[2]

251 **6** nse **Micky's Knock Off (IRE)**[21] 5945 2-8-7 77 FrancisNorton 6 64
(R C Guest) *plld hrd early: hld up in tch: rdn and no prog 2f out: kpt on nr fin* **17/2**

4203 **7** 1 1/2 **Soccer (USA)**[44] 5241 2-9-7 91 (t) RichardKingscote 11 73
(Tom Dascombe) *in tch on outer: effrt 2f out: no prog over 1f out: fdd* **17/2**

2642 **8** 1/2 **Bush Master**[3] 6443 2-7-13 69 DavidProbert 10 49
(R Hannon) *sn pushed along in rr: nvr on terms* **5/1**[2]

5030 **9** hd **Here Now And Why (IRE)**[17] 6049 2-8-12 85 Louis-PhilippeBeuzelin[(3)] 8 65
(K A Ryan) *chsd ldrs: lost pl u.p 2f out: n.d after* **14/1**

3202 **10** 1 **Kings Of Leo**[81] 3993 2-8-13 83 PatCosgrave 1 59
(J R Boyle) *pressed ldng pair to wl over 1f out: wknd* **33/1**

60.39 secs (0.09) **Going Correction** +0.10s/f (Good) **10** Ran SP% **114.9**
Speed ratings (Par 97): **103,97,93,92,91 91,88,88,87,86**
toteswinger: 1&2 £8.70, 1&3 £8.40, 2&3 £11.60. CSF £37.64 CT £208.48 TOTE £5.90: £1.90, £2.70, £2.70; EX 46.00 Trifecta £138.50 Pool: £385.69 - 2.06 winning units..
Owner Induna Racing Partners Two **Bred** Stephen McDonald **Trained** Newmarket, Suffolk

FOCUS
This looked quite a competitive nursery on paper, but it was turned into a procession. The form looks solid.

NOTEBOOK
Citrus Star(USA) who absolutely bolted up despite being saddled with a mark of 88 for his Pontefract maiden win. Despite missing the break at the start and having to come from off the pace, he scorched through rivals to hit the front inside the final furlong and scoot clear to win like a horse ready for the step up into Pattern company. He doesn't have any immediate entries, but it would be no surprise if connections tried to get him out quickly under a penalty, as he's sure to be hit with a steep rise in the weights for this, before stepping him up in grade. (tchd 4-1 and 5-1)
Felsham had been awarded a mark of just 71 for his Kempton maiden win, and this half-brother to smart sprinter Oldjoesaid is well up to winning a race off this sort of mark judging by this effort. He stayed on well down the outside and looks an improving colt. (op 8-1)
Wellington Fair was always close to the pace and he kept on well enough without having a turn of foot to cope with the winner in the closing stages. (op 9-2 tchd 4-1)
Leleyf(IRE) ran her race but is exposed and her form has flattened out now. (op 20-1)
Monsieur Joe(IRE) can be rated a bit better than the bare form, for he was stopped in his run up the far rail and had to be switched out. He kept on well thereafter and would have finished a bit closer with a clear run. Official explanation: jockey said colt suffered interference in running (op 6-1)
Micky's Knock Off(IRE) Official explanation: jockey said gelding hung right

6551 ST JOHN AMBULANCE BERKSHIRE MAIDEN STKS 6f
4:30 (4:31) (Class 5) 3-Y-O+ **£2,729** (£806; £403) **Stalls** High

Form RPR
42-2 **1** **Hajoum (IRE)**[155] 1704 3-9-3 83 JamieSpencer 5 83+
(Saeed Bin Suroor) *wnt lft s: hld up: trckd ldrs bef 1/2-way: clsd 2f out: shkn up to ld 1f out: styd on wl* **7/4**[2]

034 **2** 2 **Ponting (IRE)**[76] 4172 3-9-0 57 JackMitchell[(3)] 8 72
(R M Beckett) *mde most: drvn and hdd 1f out: one pce* **10/1**[3]

22 **3** 1 1/4 **Bended Knee**[25] 5789 3-8-12 0 DaneO'Neill 11 63
(H Candy) *taken steadily to post: pressed ldr: chal 2f out: nt qckn over 1f out: fdd ins fnl f* **6/5**[1]

4 1/2 **Jonny Mudball** 3-9-3 0 RichardKingscote 6 66+
(Tom Dascombe) *pressed ldrs: clr in ldng quartet fr over 2f out: fdd fnl f* **11/1**

5 7 **Clincher** 3-8-12 0 RichardHughes 9 39+
(J A Osborne) *hld up wl in rr and wl off the pce: nudged along and kpt on steadily fnl 2f: tk modest 5th last stride: do bttr* **25/1**

6 shd **Jack Galvin (IRE)** 3-9-3 0 SteveDrowne 13 44
(J R Gask) *s.s: wl in rr: prog bef 1/2-way: mostly chsd clr ldng quartet fr over 2f out: no imp* **25/1**

0 **7** 1 **Dajen**[116] 2862 3-9-3 0 PatCosgrave 10 40
(D M Simcock) *wl off the pce after 2f: modest late prog: nvr a factor* **50/1**

U556 **8** 3 1/4 **Louise Sauvage**[25] 5789 3-8-7 0 LeeNewnes[(5)] 14 25
(M D I Usher) *drvn to chse ldrs to 1/2-way: wknd* **66/1**

000 **9** 5 **Day In Dubai**[20] 5965 3-8-9 47 MCGeran[(3)] 12 9
(J J Bridger) *sn struggling and wl off the pce: nvr a factor* **100/1**

10 3/4 **Stratford Bridge**[326] 6-9-4 0 FrankieMcDonald 3 12
(J L Spearing) *dwlt and hmpd s: a wl in rr: nvr a factor* **40/1**

0 **11** 2 3/4 **Dancing Again**[154] 1752 3-8-12 0 StephenCarson 1 —
(E A Wheeler) *prom to 1/2-way: wknd rapidly* **100/1**

0004 **12** 1 **Divine White**[20] 5971 6-8-13 45 (v) AdamKirby 7 —
(G P Enright) *sn struggling: a wl in rr* **100/1**

1m 12.88s (-0.12) **Going Correction** +0.10s/f (Good)
WFA 3 from 6yo 1lb **12** Ran SP% **115.8**
Speed ratings (Par 103): **104,101,99,99,89 89,88,83,77,76 72,71**
toteswinger: 1&2 £4.00, 1&3 £1.50, 2&3 £4.80 CSF £17.85 TOTE £2.60: £1.40, £2.30, £1.10; EX 22.10 Trifecta £27.10 Pool: £525.02 - 14.30 winning units..
Owner Godolphin **Bred** Darley **Trained** Newmarket, Suffolk

FOCUS
A pretty modest maiden in which the proximity of 57-rated Ponting gives the form a very shaky look, with the third appearing to be going backwards from his debut.
Clincher Official explanation: jockey said, regarding running and riding, that his orders were to ride the filly as he found it, adding that it had broken well and then ran too freely before becoming unbalanced.

6552 GET READING H'CAP 1m 3f 135y
5:00 (5:00) (Class 4) (0-85,84) 3-Y-O **£5,180** (£1,541; £770; £384) **Stalls** Centre

Form RPR
2003 **1** **Lively Fling (USA)**[26] 5771 3-9-4 84 (b[1]) JimmyFortune 6 90
(J H M Gosden) *led: set stdy pce to 1/2-way: rdn and hdd 2f out and looked btn: rallied u.p 1f out: drvn ahd last strides* **6/1**

1323 **2** nk **Souter Point (USA)**[22] 5904 3-9-3 83 RichardKingscote 1 89
(R Charlton) *hld up in last: trckd ldrs fr 3f out: produced to ld over 1f out: hrd rdn fnl f: hdd last strides* **9/2**[3]

4324 **3** 1 1/2 **Non Dom (IRE)**[23] 5870 3-8-13 79 SteveDrowne 4 82
(H Morrison) *trckd ldr: rdn to ld 2f out: hdd and nt qckn over 1f out: one pce* **7/2**[2]

4615 **4** 3/4 **Master Fong (IRE)**[28] 5725 3-8-9 75 WilliamBuick 7 77
(B W Hills) *trckd ldng pair: shkn up 4f out: rdn to chal 2f out: stl upsides jst over 1f out: nt qckn* **13/2**

31 **5** 4 **Hajmah (IRE)**[28] 5718 3-9-1 81 JamieSpencer 5 76
(Saeed Bin Suroor) *s.s: hld up in 4th: rdn and no rspnse over 2f out: last and btn after* **6/4**[1]

2m 29.66s (0.16) **Going Correction** +0.10s/f (Good) **5** Ran SP% **108.0**
Speed ratings (Par 103): **103,102,101,101,98**
toteswinger: 1&2 £6.30. CSF £30.03 TOTE £7.00: £2.50, £2.00; EX 31.50 Place 6: £95.80 Place 5: £26.31.
Owner George Strawbridge **Bred** George Strawbridge Jr **Trained** Newmarket, Suffolk

■ Stewards' Enquiry : Jimmy Fortune one-day ban: used whip with excessive frequency (Oct 19)

FOCUS
A fair handicap which saw plenty of chances and the form is a bit muddling, with the exposed fourth the best guide.
Hajmah(IRE) Official explanation: jockey said filly was unsuited by the good ground
T/Jkpt: Not won. T/Plt: £51.00 to a £1 stake. Pool: £75,494.71. 1,078.72 winning tickets. T/Qpdt: £12.80 to a £1 stake. Pool: £6,029.81. 346.70 winning tickets. JN

6096 CATTERICK (L-H)

Tuesday, October 6

OFFICIAL GOING: Good to firm (firm in places) changing to good after race 2 (2.30)

Wind: almost nil Weather: rain 1st 4 races

6553 AMATEUR JOCKEYS ASSOCIATION INSURE THEIR MEMBERS AMATEUR RIDERS' H'CAP 5f

2:00 (2:02) (Class 6) (0-55,57) 3-Y-0+ **£2,307** (£709; £354) **Stalls** Low

Form RPR

0322 **1** **The Name Is Frank**[8] 6340 4-11-0 **55**..............................(t) MrSWalker 2 62
(Mark Gillard) *stmbld s: sn chsng ldrs: wnt 2nd 1f out: styd on to ld nr fin* **11/8**[1]

426 **2** 3/4 **Strensall**[9] 6314 12-10-5 **51**.. MissVBarr(5) 1 56
(R E Barr) *mde most: hdd towards fin* **9/1**

6406 **3** 3/4 **Alacity (IRE)**[32] 5624 3-10-9 **57** ow4.......................... MrSebSpencer(7) 4 59
(N Bycroft) *w ldrs: kpt on same pce ins fnl f: 3rd and hld whn eased towards fin* **22/1**

3000 **4** 1 1/2 **Sandy Par**[26] 5792 4-10-1 **47**..............................(b) MissSBradley(5) 12 44+
(J M Bradley) *chsd ldrs: kpt on wl fnl f* **25/1**

0050 **5** 1 **Admiral Bond (IRE)**[11] 6251 4-10-6 **52**.........................(p) DaleSwift(5) 5 45
(G R Oldroyd) *mid-div: hdwy 2f out: edgd lft and kpt on: nvr trbld ldrs* **18/1**

2354 **6** 3 **Towy Boy (IRE)**[11] 6251 4-10-8 **54**..............................(vt) MrCMartin(5) 9 36
(I A Wood) *w ldrs: wknd appr fnl f* **15/2**[3]

322 **7** 3/4 **Monsieur Reynard**[4] 6456 4-10-6 **54**........................ MissHDavies(7) 10 34
(J M Bradley) *t.k.h: chsd ldrs: wknd appr fnl f* **11/2**[2]

5560 **8** 5 **Andrasta**[19] 6010 4-10-4 **50**..................................(p) MrCAHarris(5) 11 12
(S A Harris) *s.s: in rr: kpt on fnl f: nvr on terms* **25/1**

0000 **9** 1/2 **Molly Two**[9] 6314 4-10-7 **55**.. MissRWilson(7) 3 15
(L A Mullaney) *mid-div: edgd rt over 2f out: nvr nr ldrs* **28/1**

0500 **10** 1/2 **Gower**[151] 1846 5-10-3 **49**... MrMPrice(5) 7 7
(R J Price) *hmpd s: a in rr* **20/1**

0300 **11** 3/4 **Red Cell (IRE)**[8] 6341 3-10-5 **53**...............................(p) MissHBethell(7) 6 8
(I W McInnes) *wnt rt s: a in rr* **40/1**

1000 **12** 3/4 **Princess Charlmane (IRE)**[6] 6379 6-10-13 **54**..........(p) MrSDobson 15 7
(C J Teague) *sn w ldrs: lost pl over 1f out* **28/1**

4040 **13** 1 1/4 **Excitable (IRE)**[41] 5341 3-10-0 **48**..............................(p) MissDLenge(7) 8 —
(Mrs D J Sanderson) *hmpd s: in rr: wnt rt over 3f out: nvr on terms* **28/1**

0-50 **14** hd **Bettys Touch**[6] 6380 4-9-13 **47** oh1 ow1................. MrJMThomas(7) 13 —
(K G Reveley) *a in rr* **33/1**

61.42 secs (1.62) **Going Correction** +0.10s/f (Good) **14 Ran SP% 117.0**

Speed ratings (Par 101): **91,89,88,86,84 79,78,70,69,69 67,66,64,64**

toteswingers: 1&2 £2.90, 1&3 £5.00, 2&3 £6.10 CSF £10.81 CT £187.19 TOTE £2.10: £1.30, £2.40, £5.70; EX 12.20.

Owner Don Hazzard **Bred** Fifehead Farms M C Denning **Trained** Holwell, Dorset

■ Stewards' Enquiry : Miss S Bradley caution: careless riding

Mr C Martin three-day ban: careless riding (Oct 28, Nov 18 & 24)

Mr Seb Spencer seven-day ban: failed to ride out for second (Oct 28, Nov 18, 24, 30, Dec 1 & 7, Jan 2)

FOCUS

A weak handicap, confined to amateur riders and the winner did not need to improve to score, with thopse drawn low seemingly having an advantage.

6554 RACING UK NURSERY (DIV I) 5f

2:30 (2:31) (Class 6) (0-65,65) 2-Y-0 **£2,047** (£604; £302) **Stalls** Low

Form RPR

033 **1** **Night Trade (IRE)**[13] 6207 2-9-4 **65**.......................... RussellKennemore(3) 1 75+
(Mrs D J Sanderson) *mde virtually all: edgd rt 2f out: styd on wl ins fnl f: won gng away* **7/2**[1]

5530 **2** 1 3/4 **Love Match**[12] 6227 2-9-7 **65**...(b[1]) NCallan 5 69
(R Charlton) *chsd ldrs: swtchd ins to chse wnr 2f out: upsides 1f out: kpt on same pce* **7/2**[1]

4050 **3** 5 **Vilnius**[20] 5976 2-8-12 **56**.. CatherineGannon 6 42
(M R Channon) *swvd rt s: sn trcking ldrs: one pce fnl 2f* **5/1**[3]

000 **4** 4 1/2 **Satin Princess (IRE)**[25] 5829 2-8-10 **54** ow2............ StephenDonohoe 3 24
(A M Hales) *chsd ldrs: outpcd over 2f out: edgd lft over 1f out* **17/2**

5054 **5** 3/4 **Oondiri (IRE)**[22] 5950 2-9-2 **60**... DavidAllan 10 27+
(T D Easterby) *chsd ldrs: wknd over 1f out* **9/2**[2]

060 **6** 1 3/4 **Selina Rio**[55] 4889 2-8-1 **45**... DuranFentiman 2 6
(L A Mullaney) *chsd ldrs: outpcd over 2f out: keeping on whn n.m.r over 1f out* **100/1**

4060 **7** 2 1/4 **Dispol Kabira**[20] 5976 2-8-6 **50**... GregFairley 8 —+
(D W Thompson) *hmpd s: a towards rr* **20/1**

0000 **8** 2 1/4 **Diamond Affair (IRE)**[14] 6185 2-8-10 **54**................. GrahamGibbons 11 —+
(M G Quinlan) *chsd ldrs on outer: outpcd and lost pl over 2f out* **22/1**

5000 **9** 3/4 **Turf Time**[22] 5950 2-8-1 **45**...(p) SilvestreDeSousa 4 —
(J A Glover) *w ldrs: lost pl over 2f out: sltly hmpd over 1f out* **17/2**

3560 **10** 4 **Sweet Mirasol (IRE)**[11] 6245 2-8-11 **60**.........................(p) AmyRyan(5) 9 —+
(K A Ryan) *hmpd s: a in rr* **22/1**

60.59 secs (0.79) **Going Correction** +0.10s/f (Good) **10 Ran SP% 114.8**

Speed ratings (Par 93): **97,94,86,79,77 75,71,67,66,60**

toteswingers: 1&2 £2.90, 1&3 £5.00, 2&3 £6.10 CSF £14.54 CT £61.74 TOTE £4.20: £1.40, £1.80, £2.30; EX 11.30.

Owner R J Budge **Bred** John Foley **Trained** Wiseton, Notts

FOCUS

A moderate nursery and not a race to go overboard about.

NOTEBOOK

Night Trade(IRE) made virtually all from her favourable draw. She showed a willing attitude last time on the AW at Kempton and showed her tenacity again here. This was only her fourth start and this very genuine sort can go on from this. (op 9-2 tchd 5-1)

Love Match seemed suited by the first-time blinkers even though she hung a bit towards the rail near the finish. This was her first run over 5f and she is worth another try over it. She simply bumped into an improving and relatively unexposed filly. (op 5-2)

Vilnius, who made an awkward break, was beaten a long way yet still helps to set the level. (op 13-2 tchd 9-2)

Satin Princess(IRE) had shown ability in 5f maidens, but never got competitive. This was only her fourth start, however, and she's still learning. (tchd 9-1)

Oondiri(IRE) was disappointing. He wasn't done any favours by the draw, but was beaten a long way and weakened late on. There were no obvious excuses. (tchd 5-1 in places)

6555 RACING UK NURSERY (DIV II) 5f

3:00 (3:01) (Class 6) (0-65,65) 2-Y-0 **£2,047** (£604; £302) **Stalls** Low

Form RPR

5203 **1** **Silver Linnet (IRE)**[5] 6409 2-9-2 **60**.................................(b[1]) DavidAllan 1 68+
(T D Easterby) *mde all: drvn clr over 1f out: eased towards fin: unchal* **7/4**[1]

402 **2** 3 **Gower Sophia**[8] 6343 2-9-5 **63**..............................(v) SilvestreDeSousa 6 60
(M Brittain) *chsd ldrs: wnt 2nd 1f out: no imp* **5/1**[2]

4050 **3** 3 1/4 **Zaskia (IRE)**[8] 6345 2-8-10 **54**... NCallan 2 40
(K A Ryan) *dwlt: sn chsng ldrs: kpt on same pce fnl 2f* **9/1**

0520 **4** 2 **Prettiest Star (IRE)**[20] 5976 2-8-9 **53**..........................(p) TonyHamilton 4 31
(K A Ryan) *chsd ldrs: outpcd and lost pl over 2f out: kpt on fnl f* **8/1**[3]

5101 **5** 1/2 **On The Piste (IRE)**[22] 5950 2-9-2 **65**............................ GaryBartley(5) 7 42+
(L A Mullaney) *in rr div: kpt on fnl 2f: nvr nr ldrs* **8/1**[3]

000 **6** 2 1/4 **Social Grace**[22] 5950 2-9-5 **63**... PhillipMakin 10 31+
(D H Brown) *in rr on outer: kpt on fnl f: nvr a factor* **10/1**

0600 **7** 1 **Jigajig**[22] 5950 2-8-1 **45**...(v) AndrewMullen 5 10
(N Wilson) *dwlt: sn chsng ldrs: wknd over 1f out* **25/1**

000 **8** 2 1/2 **Lady Compton**[11] 6245 2-8-4 **48** ow1................................ GregFairley 9 4+
(R Bastiman) *in rr on outer: nvr on terms* **20/1**

6630 **9** shd **Kirkby's Gem**[22] 5950 2-8-0 **51**....................................... BillyCray(7) 8 6+
(A Berry) *in rr on outer: nvr on terms* **20/1**

0000 **10** 6 **Burtondale Boy (IRE)**[7] 6354 2-8-1 **45**.....................(p) DuranFentiman 3 —
(P T Midgley) *sn outpcd in rr: bhd fnl 2f* **16/1**

60.68 secs (0.88) **Going Correction** +0.10s/f (Good) **10 Ran SP% 113.6**

Speed ratings (Par 93): **96,91,86,82,82 78,76,72,72,63**

toteswingers: 1&2 £3.10, 1&3 £5.40, 2&3 £8.70 CSF £9.34 CT £61.15 TOTE £1.90: £1.60, £2.60, £2.30; EX 10.50.

Owner Liam Mulryan **Bred** L Mulryan **Trained** Great Habton, N Yorks

FOCUS

This second division was another moderate heat but the stall bias was again significant.

NOTEBOOK

Silver Linnet(IRE), dropped in grade and making the most of her plum draw, made all. The first-time blinkers may have helped, but she appears genuine enough. (op 9-4)

Gower Sophia showed signs of a return to form last week on the AW at Wolverhampton and confirmed that impression with a promising run here. The return to the minimum trip didn't appear to have hurt her chances, although she would have found this ground a shade lively. She is capable of winning races. (op 7-2)

Zaskia(IRE), who came in for some market support, missed the break from her good draw and it lost her a length and a half. She was never able to make it up and the ground could have been quick enough, but she is moderate. (op 16-1)

Prettiest Star(IRE) could not dictate matters but, although tapped for speed midway through the race, she stuck on well, despite being beaten a long way. (tchd 15-2)

On The Piste(IRE) came here in great form, winning three of her last six, but never got into it. A combination of the draw and her 5lb rise in the weights anchored her. (op 11-2 tchd 5-1)

6556 EUROPEAN BREEDERS' FUND MAIDEN STKS 5f

3:30 (3:30) (Class 5) 2-Y-0 **£4,209** (£1,252; £625; £312) **Stalls** Low

Form RPR

4 **1** **Commanche Raider (IRE)**[140] 2153 2-9-3 0.................. PhillipMakin 4 73+
(M Dods) *w ldr: led 2f out: drew clr ins fnl f* **9/2**[2]

4250 **2** 4 **Il Forno**[24] 5853 2-9-3 74.. TomEaves 8 59+
(D Nicholls) *chsd ldrs: rdn and outpcd 2f out: styd on wl ins fnl f: tk modest 2nd nr fin* **9/2**[2]

000 **3** 1/2 **Safari Camp (IRE)**[5] 6409 2-9-3 53........................... StephenDonohoe 1 52
(A Berry) *led tl 2f out: kpt on same pce fnl f* **100/1**

4 shd **Set Back** 2-9-3 0.. AndrewMullen 3 52
(D Nicholls) *dwlt and wnt lft s: sn chsng ldrs: kpt on same pce appr fnl f* **14/1**

63 **5** shd **Fear Nothing**[21] 5957 2-9-3 0.. RichardMullen 9 56+
(E S McMahon) *chsd ldrs: one pce fnl 2f* **7/2**[1]

6 3 1/4 **Giptar (IRE)** 2-9-3 0... DavidAllan 2 40
(E F Vaughan) *hmpd s: hdwy to chse ldrs over 2f out: wknd fnl 100yds* **9/2**[2]

00 **7** 2 3/4 **Show Willing (IRE)**[10] 6292 2-8-12 0............................ AndrewElliott 7 25
(A P Jarvis) *in tch: outpcd over 2f out: no threat after* **50/1**

6240 **8** 1 **Trinder**[45] 5256 2-9-3 72.. TonyHamilton 11 26+
(R A Fahey) *blind lft eye: reminders sn after s: racd wd: nvr a factor* **12/1**

9 4 1/2 **Young George** 2-9-3 0.. PJMcDonald 12 10+
(C W Fairhurst) *in rr on outer: hung bdly lft 2f out: nvr on terms* **50/1**

5 **10** 3 **Princess Lexi (IRE)**[11] 6245 2-8-12 0................................. NCallan 6 —
(K A Ryan) *sn outpcd and in rr* **13/2**[3]

0042 **11** 3/4 **Final Ovation (IRE)**[20] 5977 2-9-3 69........................ GrahamGibbons 10 —
(J J Quinn) *stmbld s: a towards rr* **7/1**

60.54 secs (0.74) **Going Correction** +0.10s/f (Good) **11 Ran SP% 121.9**

Speed ratings (Par 95): **98,91,90,90,90 85,80,79,72,67 66**

toteswingers: 1&2 £5.90, 1&3 £45.20, 2&3 £20.20 CSF £26.06 TOTE £5.90: £2.60, £1.10, £20.10; EX 33.10.

Owner Doug Graham **Bred** Epona Bloodstock Ltd **Trained** Denton, Co Durham

FOCUS

A modest maiden where the track bias again played a part. The third sets the level.

NOTEBOOK

Commanche Raider(IRE) ◆, making his first start for 140 days, having shown plenty of ability on his Musselburgh debut, won decisively. Always up with the pace, he travelled well and stayed on well for a professional and fluent performance. He is bred for further and he is open to plenty of progression. (op 3-1)

Il Forno didn't really handle this undulating track and became unbalanced on a number of occasions, but he stayed on really well to grab second. He has had a few chances, but there are races to be won with him. He ran too freely over 7f, but a return to a sharp 6f might be the way to go. (op 7-1)

Safari Camp(IRE) clouds the form somewhat, but he made the most of his low draw and stuck on doggedly. He is modest but this was much his best display to date. (op 80-1)

Set Back, a cheap purchase and a half-brother to prolific winners New Options and Steely Dan, made a highly promising debut. He stayed on well under a sympathetic ride and would have learned plenty. There are races to be won with him. (op 12-1)

Fear Nothing couldn't get into it. The ability is there and he is not one to write off yet. (op 4-1)

Giptar(IRE), a half-brother to multiple 5f-6f winner Charles Parnell, was very slowly away and looked green. He ran enthusiastically enough, without getting competitive. (op 7-1 tchd 15-2)

Young George Official explanation: jockey said bit slipped through gelding's mouth

Final Ovation(IRE) Official explanation: jockey said gelding slipped leaving stalls

6557 SATURDAY 17TH OCTOBER IS TOTESPORT DAY NURSERY STKS (H'CAP) 7f

4:00 (4:01) (Class 4) (0-85,81) 2-Y-O **£4,079** (£1,214; £606; £303) **Stalls** Centre

Form RPR

464 **1** **Bahraj (USA)**[54] 4928 2-8-3 **63** ow2 GregFairley 7 67
(M Johnston) *mde all: kpt on wl fnl 2f: hld on towards fin* **6/1**[2]

521 **2** ¾ **Unshakable Will (IRE)**[18] 6047 2-9-2 **77** TomEaves 12 79
(B Smart) *trckd wnr: t.k.h: effrt 2f out: styd on ins fnl f: a jst hld* **7/1**

0615 **3** 3 ¼ **Kumbeshwar**[6] 6397 2-9-2 **81** RichardEvans(5) 4 75
(P D Evans) *chsd ldng pair: hung lft over 1f out: kpt on same pce* **8/1**

2014 **4** 2 **Pure Nostalgia (IRE)**[43] 5303 2-7-13 **64** MartinLane(5) 8 53
(J Howard Johnson) *chsd ldrs: drvn over 2f out: one pce* **10/1**

543 **5** 2 ¼ **Pepper Lane**[8] 6345 2-7-12 **58** oh1 CatherineGannon 2 41
(J Hetherton) *mid-div: one pce fnl 2f* **13/2**[3]

5332 **6** 1 ½ **Jehu**[12] 6228 2-9-3 **77** TonyCulhane 10 57+
(M R Channon) *in rr: hdwy over 2f out: hung lft over 1f out: nvr nr ldrs* **5/1**[1]

21 **6** dht **Living It Large (FR)**[68] 4463 2-8-13 **73** TonyHamilton 3 53
(R F Fisher) *sn mid-div: hdwy over 2f out: nvr nr ldrs* **13/2**[3]

2533 **8** 4 ½ **Cassidy K**[94] 3605 2-7-12 **58** DuranFentiman 9 26
(J Howard Johnson) *in rr: sme hdwy 2f out: nvr on terms* **22/1**

5221 **9** 2 ¾ **Saxby (IRE)**[10] 6292 2-8-10 **70** SilvestreDeSousa 6 32
(G A Harker) *dwlt: hld up in rr: shkn up over 1f out: nvr a factor: eased nr fin* **6/1**[2]

2300 **10** 13 **William Arnold**[17] 6099 2-7-12 **58** oh5 JamieMackay 11 —
(C W Fairhurst) *dwlt: a in rr: bhd whn eased ins fnl f* **33/1**

0000 **11** 22 **Ron The Don**[80] 4101 2-7-9 **58** oh13 (p) DominicFox(3) 1 —
(A Berry) *rr-div: lost pl over 4f out: bhd fnl 2f: t.o* **125/1**

1m 27.72s (0.72) **Going Correction** +0.10s/f (Good) **11** Ran SP% **112.7**
Speed ratings (Par 97): **99,98,94,92,89 87,87,82,79,64 39**
toteswingers: 1&2 £7.70, 1&3 £13.40, 2&3 £11.50 CSF £44.79 CT £341.68 TOTE £6.20: £2.40, £2.30, £4.00; EX 39.50.
Owner Hamdan Al Maktoum **Bred** Shadwell Farm LLC **Trained** Middleham Moor, N Yorks

FOCUS
A modest nursery which saw the first pair come clear. The winner improved for the longer trip.

NOTEBOOK
Bahraj(USA) ◆, whose jockey carried 2lb overweight, could hardly have been more impressive. Pitched into sprint maidens for her first three runs, the step up in trip on this sharp track clearly suited her on her nursery debut. She is a keen filly, but she is on a mark of 61, so there is every reason to think connections can exploit that. (tchd 11-2 and 13-2)
Unshakable Will(IRE) ◆, who made all the running to win at Ayr last time, was drawn wide here so probably did better than the bare form indicates. He tracked the winner from the stalls and showed a thoroughly likeable attitude in defeat. Like the winner, he is progressive and lightly raced. (op 11-2)
Kumbeshwar had made all to win a Chester maiden, but could not dictate here. He remained third throughout and the front two were drawing away from him at the end. He had plenty on his plate off this mark but is not to be written off just yet. (op 15-2)
Pure Nostalgia(IRE) was fourth entering the straight and never made much impression thereafter to finish in that position. This was her first try at 7f and she may be worth another try over it. (op 11-1 tchd 12-1)
Pepper Lane shaped as though this trip would suit her last time, but looked one-paced. This ground might have been a bit lively for her. (op 6-1)
Jehu never got competitive, although made a bit of headway from the back. The draw was against him, though the same could be said for the runner-up. He looks exposed. (op 13-2)
Saxby(IRE) Official explanation: jockey said, regarding running and riding, that his orders were to drop the colt in and do his best, adding that it became unbalanced between 2f and 3f out and lost its action; trainer confirmed, adding that the colt had only been in his care ten days; vet said it had problems with its shins in the past and was suffering from a sore left front shin post-race

6558 SKYRAM H'CAP (DIV I) 1m 7f 177y

4:30 (4:31) (Class 6) (0-60,60) 3-Y-O+ **£2,047** (£604; £302) **Stalls** Centre

Form RPR

0000 **1** **Ingenue**[14] 6188 3-8-2 **46** oh1 (b) SilvestreDeSousa 11 59+
(Sir Mark Prescott) *w ldr: drvn over 4f out: led 2f out: drew clr: eased ins fnl f* **7/1**[3]

2625 **2** 6 **Goldan Jess (IRE)**[7] 5600 5-8-13 **46** oh1 LeeVickers 1 51
(P A Kirby) *trckd ldrs: effrt over 1f out: chsd wnr 1f out: no imp* **4/1**[1]

000/ **3** 2 **Ishismart**[16] 2654 5-8-10 **46** oh1 RussellKennemore(3) 9 49
(R Hollinshead) *trckd ldrs: drvn over 4f out: one pce fnl 3f* **15/2**

0054 **4** nk **Shanavaz**[6] 6384 3-8-2 **46** oh1 (p) JamieMackay 2 48
(C J Teague) *s.s: t.k.h in rr: hdwy over 3f out: kpt on fnl f* **17/2**

5-00 **5** ¾ **Hernando's Boy**[17] 6097 8-9-13 **60** TomEaves 7 61
(K G Reveley) *mid-div: hdwy over 4f out: one pce fnl 2f* **10/1**

503 **6** ½ **Obara D'Avril (FR)**[9] 6022 7-9-6 **53** MHNaughton 4 54
(S G West) *hld up in rr: hdwy and swtchd outside over 2f out: kpt on: nvr a threat* **12/1**

2043 **7** nk **Mystified (IRE)**[19] 6021 6-9-7 **54** (tp) TonyHamilton 6 54
(R F Fisher) *led: shkn up over 4f out: hdd 2f out: fdd last 100yds* **5/1**[2]

8 22 **Lost In France (IRE)**[38] 5457 4-8-13 **46** oh1 (v[1]) CatherineGannon 12 20
(T G McCourt, Ire) *sn trcking ldrs: t.k.h: lost pl over 1f out: sn eased and bhd* **20/1**

0130 **9** 1 ½ **Jordan's Light (USA)**[29] 5733 6-9-7 **59** (v) LanceBetts(5) 10 31
(T J Pitt) *mid-div: pushed along 9f out: lost pl over 2f out: sn bhd* **17/2**

3340 **10** 13 **Fenners (USA)**[4] 6457 6-9-2 **49** (v) DaleGibson 5 6
(M W Easterby) *s.i.s: in rr: drvn 9f out: reminders 5f out: bhd and eased 2f out* **9/1**

0-00 **11** 4 ½ **Firestorm (IRE)**[17] 6097 5-8-13 **46** oh1 (b) PJMcDonald 8 —
(C W Fairhurst) *hld up in midfield: effrt over 3f out: lost pl over 2f out: sn bhd* **50/1**

3m 33.43s (1.43) **Going Correction** +0.10s/f (Good)
WFA 3 from 4yo+ 11lb **11** Ran SP% **115.5**
Speed ratings (Par 101): **100,97,96,95,95 95,95,84,83,76 74**
toteswingers: 1&2 £5.80, 1&3 £15.50, 2&3 £8.60 CSF £34.43 CT £217.71 TOTE £7.80: £2.60, £1.80, £2.30; EX 48.40.
Owner Miss K Rausing **Bred** Miss K Rausing **Trained** Newmarket, Suffolk
■ Stewards' Enquiry : Jamie Mackay 14-day ban: breach of Rule (B) 59.4 (Oct 20-24, 26-Nov 3)

FOCUS
A very weak handicap with thmore than half the field out of te handicap. The runner-up was rated close to his recent best.
Ingenue ◆ Official explanation: trainer's rep said, regarding apparent improvement in form, that the filly had benefited from the fitting of blinkers on its last few runs and felt this was a weaker race.

Shanavaz Official explanation: jockey said, regarding running and riding, that his orders were to jump out and get a good position, adding that trainer said if he had a poor start to make up ground going down the back straight for the last time, however, he was unable to do so unless he went around horses going down the outside; trainer confirmed adding that he considered that the rider should have made up more ground going down the back straight final time and therefore was dissatisfied with the ride.

6559 SKYRAM H'CAP (DIV II) 1m 7f 177y

5:00 (5:00) (Class 6) (0-60,60) 3-Y-O+ **£2,047** (£604; £302) **Stalls** Centre

Form RPR

4224 **1** **Jackday (IRE)**[19] 6021 4-9-8 **60** BMcHugh(5) 3 70
(T D Easterby) *hld up in rr: hdwy over 4f out: wnt 2nd over 2f out: rdn to ld over 1f out: styd on* **6/4**[1]

0042 **2** 2 **Park's Prodigy**[17] 6102 5-9-0 **47** PAspell 1 55
(G A Harker) *w ldrs: led 8f out: hdd over 6f out: led over 3f out: hung rt and hdd over 1f out: styd on same pce* **7/1**

1505 **3** 2 ½ **They All Laughed**[17] 6102 6-9-6 **58** (p) PatrickDonaghy(5) 6 63
(Mrs Marjorie Fife) *trckd ldrs: effrt over 2f out: styd on same pce* **20/1**

4611 **4** 3 ¾ **Simple Jim (FR)**[17] 6097 5-9-7 **54** SilvestreDeSousa 4 54
(J Hetherton) *hld up in rr: hdwy to trck ldrs after 6f: effrt over 2f out: fdd fnl f* **9/2**[2]

2600 **5** 5 **Moon Money (IRE)**[14] 6184 3-8-10 **54** TonyHamilton 10 48
(K A Ryan) *in rr: pushed along after 6f: in tch and drvn over 5f out: nvr a factor* **12/1**

0003 **6** 4 ½ **Blue Jet (USA)**[17] 6102 5-8-13 **46** oh1 PaulQuinn 7 35
(R M Whitaker) *dwlt: sn t.k.h in midfield: effrt and c wd bnd over 2f out: racd stands' side: nvr trbld ldrs* **12/1**

0030 **7** 1 ½ **Bright Sparky (GER)**[35] 5554 6-8-13 **46** oh1 (v) DaleGibson 9 33
(M W Easterby) *chsd ldrs: led over 6f out: hdd over 3f out: lost pl over 1f out* **28/1**

0064 **8** 33 **Markadam**[38] 5442 3-8-6 **50** AndrewMullen 11 —
(Miss S E Hall) *trckd ldrs on outer: t.k.h: lost pl over 3f out: bhd whn eased 2f out* **13/2**[3]

0030 **9** 6 **Art Gallery**[38] 5307 5-8-13 **46** oh1 StephenDonohoe 5 —
(D W Thompson) *led: hdd 8f out: sn drvn along: lost pl over 5f out: wl bhd whn brought wd to r stands' side over 2f out: t.o* **25/1**

4060 **10** 17 **Katie Girl**[29] 5732 3-8-2 **46** oh1 (p) CatherineGannon 2 —
(Mrs G S Rees) *tk fierce hold: trckd ldrs: lost pl over 6f out: bhd 4f out: sn t.o* **18/1**

3m 34.46s (2.46) **Going Correction** +0.10s/f (Good)
WFA 3 from 4yo+ 11lb **10** Ran SP% **116.7**
Speed ratings (Par 101): **97,96,94,92,90 88,87,70,67,59**
toteswingers: 1&2 £3.90, 1&3 £10.10, 2&3 £16.00 CSF £12.00 CT £151.82 TOTE £2.60: £1.40, £1.70, £7.30; EX 16.80.
Owner Mrs Jean P Connew **Bred** Mrs H D McCalmont **Trained** Great Habton, N Yorks

FOCUS
Another very weak handicap with a slight persoanal best from the winner and the runner-up to his recent mark.
Blue Jet(USA) Official explanation: jockey said gelding slipped on bend turning for home

6560 BOOK ON-LINE AT CATTERICKBRIDGE.CO.UK H'CAP 1m 3f 214y

5:30 (5:30) (Class 5) (0-75,75) 3-Y-O+ **£2,914** (£867; £433; £216) **Stalls** Low

Form RPR

0000 **1** **Rayhani (USA)**[17] 6095 6-9-9 **75** AndrewMullen 10 84
(D Nicholls) *mde all: edgd lft over 1f out: hld on wl* **28/1**

3240 **2** 1 ¼ **Saloon (USA)**[52] 5034 5-9-7 **73** (p) SilvestreDeSousa 7 80
(Jane Chapple-Hyam) *chsd ldrs: drvn and outpcd over 6f out: hdwy to chse ldrs over 4f out: swtchd rt and 2nd over 1f out: carried hd high: no real imp* **8/1**

1514 **3** 4 ½ **Patavium (IRE)**[22] 5947 6-8-9 **61** oh4 DavidAllan 5 61
(E W Tuer) *hld up in rr: hdwy over 4f out: sn drvn along: kpt on one pce fnl 2f: tk 3rd last 50yds* **12/1**

1R44 **4** 1 **Inspirina (IRE)**[26] 5802 5-9-3 **69** TonyHamilton 6 67
(R Ford) *t.k.h: hdwy over 4f out: sn chsng ldrs: one pce fnl 2f* **10/1**

1443 **5** 2 ¾ **African Cheetah**[6] 6385 3-9-2 **75** GregFairley 9 69
(M Johnston) *dwlt: sn chsng ldrs: chal over 2f out: wknd over 1f out* **9/4**[1]

0112 **6** 15 **Rosewin (IRE)**[20] 5979 3-8-4 **68** BMcHugh(5) 8 38
(A Dickman) *awkward to load: in rr: sme hdwy over 4f out: nvr on terms* **9/2**[2]

2444 **7** 14 **Nawamees (IRE)**[24] 5857 11-8-9 **61** (p) CatherineGannon 2 8
(P D Evans) *in tch: drvn and lost pl after 4f: bhd fnl 4f* **11/1**

1323 **8** 7 **Air Maze**[19] 6027 3-9-0 **73** StephenDonohoe 11 9
(Sir Mark Prescott) *chsd ldrs: drvn 4f out: lost pl over 2f out: sn bhd and eased* **11/2**[3]

2240 **9** dist **Maslak (IRE)**[13] 6204 5-9-6 **72** TonyCulhane 4 —
(P W Hiatt) *mid-div: drvn and lost pl after 4f: bhd 6f out: sn t.o: virtually p.u* **8/1**

2m 39.15s (0.25) **Going Correction** +0.10s/f (Good)
WFA 3 from 4yo+ 7lb **9** Ran SP% **115.1**
Speed ratings (Par 103): **103,102,99,98,96 86,77,72,—**
toteswingers: 1&2 £14.40, 1&3 £20.30, 2&3 £16.10 CSF £234.21 CT £2837.23 TOTE £35.70: £6.70, £2.30, £4.70; EX 220.30 Place 6: £56.21 Place 5: £34.07 .
Owner Leavy,McManus,Flood,Devaney & Reynolds **Bred** Darley **Trained** Sessay, N Yorks
■ Stewards' Enquiry : Silvestre De Sousa two-day ban: used whip with excessive force (Oct 20-21)

FOCUS
A modest handicap. The form looks fair for the class, rated through the second.
Rosewin(IRE) Official explanation: jockey said filly ran flat
Maslak(IRE) Official explanation: trainer had no explanation for the poor form shown
T/Jkpt: Not won. T/Plt: £45.30 to a £1 stake. Pool: £60,714.71. 977.41 winning tickets. T/Qpdt: £38.70 to a £1 stake. Pool: £3,087.48. 58.90 winning tickets. WG

6185 FOLKESTONE (R-H)

Tuesday, October 6

OFFICIAL GOING: Good changing to good to soft after race 1 (2.20)
Wind: medium, across Weather: showers (5mm rain this morning)

6561 LIPSCOMB.CO.UK MAIDEN STKS 7f (S)

2:20 (2:21) (Class 5) 2-Y-O **£2,729** (£806; £403) **Stalls** Low

Form RPR

1 **Bint Doyen** 2-8-12 0 ChrisCatlin 6 79+
(C E Brittain) *chsd ldng trio: shkn up and sltly outpcd over 1f out: rallied and hdwy jst ins fnl f: rdn to ld fnl 75yds: edgd lft nr fin: r.o wl* **25/1**

03 **2** ¾ **Old Money**[26] 5786 2-8-12 0 .... JamesDoyle 4 77
(H J L Dunlop) *chsd ldng pair: rdn and unable qck wl over 1f out: hdwy jst ins fnl f: ev ch ins fnl f: one pce fnl 75yds* **8/1**[3]

2 **3** 2 **Govern**[20] 6000 2-9-3 0 .... TPQueally 1 77
(H R A Cecil) *racd keenly: led: hrd pressed and rdn over 1f out: hdd fnl 75yds: and no ex: wknd towards fin* **11/10**[1]

2452 **4** 1 ½ **Cansili Star**[23] 5913 2-9-3 82 .... PhilipRobinson 7 73
(M A Jarvis) *racd keenly: chsd ldr: pushed along over 2f out: rdn and ev ch wl over 1f out tl wknd fnl 75yds* **7/4**[2]

5 16 **Tuscan King** 2-9-3 0 .... GeorgeBaker 2 35+
(W R Muir) *stdd s: hld up in last pair: pushed along 3f out: sn lost tch* **14/1**

6 13 **Appeal To Reason (USA)** 2-9-0 0 .... MarcHalford(3) 5 —
(J R Best) *s.i.s: sn bustled along and struggling to go pce: lost tch 4f out: t.o* **50/1**

7 8 **Eclipsed (USA)** 2-9-3 0 .... SteveDrowne 3 —
(J R Best) *in tch towards rr: pushed along 1/2-way: sn struggling bdly: lost tch qckly over 2f out: t.o* **25/1**

1m 28.78s (1.48) **Going Correction** +0.275s/f (Good) **7** Ran SP% **111.4**
Speed ratings (Par 95): **102,101,98,97,78 64,54**
toteswingers: 1&2 £34.70, 1&3 £8.60, 2&3 £2.40 CSF £193.68 TOTE £22.50: £13.90, £3.20; EX 84.90.

Owner Mohammed Al Nabouda **Bred** Rabbah Bloodstock Limited **Trained** Newmarket, Suffolk

FOCUS
The rain over the previous 24 hours had eased the ground from that forecast and was now described as good to soft, good in places on the round course and good on the straight. This looked an uncompetitive maiden with only two seriously fancied according to the betting, but the market got it wrong and the race produced a shock result. The form is rated at face value around the third and fourth.

NOTEBOOK
Bint Doyen ◆ was making her debut, but she certainly seemed to know her job and having never been too far off the pace, produced a nice turn of foot down the outside to hit the front inside the last half-furlong and win a shade cosily. A half-sister to four winners including the very useful Zoning, she should have little trouble staying a mile and looks to have a future. (tchd 33-1)
Old Money, a fair third at Chepstow last time, raced prominently all the way and may have hit the front briefly when switched around the two weakening market leaders half a furlong from home, but no sooner had she done so than the winner pounced. She needed this for a mark, so has a few more options now. (op 9-1 tchd 10-1 and 15-2)
Govern, in front of two subsequent winners when a promising runner-up over this trip on his Yarmouth debut, made the running but was a little keen and he always had his main market rival snapping at his heels. It was disappointing that he wasn't able to see his race out, but perhaps the easing ground was against him and he is worth another chance, providing he settles a bit better. (op 10-11 tchd 5-6 and 6-5)
Cansili Star, runner-up a couple of times including behind the smart Showcasing on debut, set the standard here with an official mark of 82. He was always up there and had every chance, but had run his race entering the last half-furlong and previous efforts suggest that he could probably have done without the rain. (op 2-1 tchd 9-4 and 13-8 and 5-2 in a place)

6562 GARDEN OF ENGLAND H'CAP — 7f (S)
2:50 (2:52) (Class 5) (0-75,75) 3-Y-O+ — **£2,729** (£806; £201; £201) **Stalls** Low

Form — RPR

100 **1** **Arteus**[14] 6178 3-8-13 **72** ....(p) PatCosgrave 5 79
(Jane Chapple-Hyam) *mde all: rdn over 1f out: styd on wl u.p fnl f* **22/1**

0334 **2** 1 **Lodi (IRE)**[14] 6187 4-9-4 **75** ....(t) AdamKirby 3 80
(J Akehurst) *in tch: chsd ldrs 4f out: rdn and n.m.r ent fnl f: drvn ins fnl f: chsd wnr fnl 100yds: kpt on same pce* **7/2**[2]

2230 **3** nk **Black N Brew (USA)**[148] 1930 3-9-0 **73** .... KirstyMilczarek 6 76+
(J R Best) *in tch towards rr: pushed along and outpce 1/2-way: rdn and hdwy over 1f out: swtchd rt ent fnl f: kpt on wl: nt rch ldrs* **20/1**

0460 **3** dht **Al Sabaheya**[14] 6190 3-9-1 **74** ....(b) ChrisCatlin 7 77
(C E Brittain) *chsd wnr: rdn and ev ch over 1f out: nt qckn u.p 1f out: lost 2nd fnl 100yds* **13/2**

3-13 **5** 2 ¾ **Zero Money (IRE)**[17] 6111 3-9-2 **75** .... SteveDrowne 11 71+
(R Charlton) *in tch on outer: pushed along and outpcd 1/2-way: rallied over 1f out: chsd ldrs and rdn ent fnl f: btn fnl 100yds: eased towards fin* **6/4**[1]

5515 **6** ¾ **Hobson**[8] 6337 4-9-1 **72** .... WilliamBuick 9 67
(Eve Johnson Houghton) *t.k.h: hld up towards rr: rdn and hdwy on outer 2f out: chsd ldrs ent fnl f: wknd fnl 100yds* **5/1**[3]

1620 **7** 1 ¾ **Cut And Thrust (IRE)**[34] 5575 3-9-0 **73** ....(p) PhilipRobinson 1 62
(M A Jarvis) *s.i.s: a bhd: rdn and struggling over 3f out: edging out rt wl over 1f out: swtchd rt over 1f out: nvr on terms* **13/2**

6000 **8** 5 **Super Frank (IRE)**[37] 5477 6-8-2 **62** ....(p) AndreaAtzeni(3) 10 39
(J Akehurst) *in tch on outer: chsd ldrs tl rdn and wknd wl over 1f out* **14/1**

6510 **9** ½ **Choreography**[8] 6337 6-8-10 **70** ....(b) RobertLButler(3) 8 45
(Jim Best) *dwlt: a bhd* **22/1**

1m 28.64s (1.34) **Going Correction** +0.275s/f (Good)
WFA 3 from 4yo+ 2lb **9** Ran SP% **125.7**
Speed ratings (Par 103): **103,101,101,101,98 97,95,89,89**PL: Al Sabaheya £1.30, Black N Brew £2.30 TRI: Ateus/Lodi /AS: £291.57 A/L/BNB: £812.37 toteswingers: 1&2 £15.10, 1& Black N Brew £26.50, 1& Al Sabaheya £17.60. 2& Black N Brew £3.80, 2& Al Sabaheya £3.70 CSF £103.68 TOTE £26.40: £7.60, £1.60; EX 142.40 Trifecta £189.20 Art27 Owner.

FOCUS
The ground was changed to good to soft all round before this race. Just an ordinary handicap, but unlike in the opening contest this result seemed to confirm that the stands' rail was favoured. The form is rated around the principals with a slight personal best from the winner.
Al Sabaheya Official explanation: jockey said filly hung right
Cut And Thrust(IRE) Official explanation: jockey said gelding was unsuited by the ground

6563 HYTHE MAIDEN FILLIES' STKS — 6f
3:20 (3:22) (Class 5) 2-Y-O — **£2,729** (£806; £403) **Stalls** Low

Form — RPR

24 **1** **Flip Flop (IRE)**[15] 6164 2-9-0 0 .... MichaelHills 7 72+
(B W Hills) *racd in centre gp: chsd ldr: rdn and ev ch over 1f out: led fnl 75yds: styd on* **5/1**[3]

55 **2** ½ **Caramelita**[21] 5969 2-8-7 0 .... DannyBrock(7) 1 71
(J R Jenkins) *racd in centre gp: led: rdn and edgd lft over 1f out: kpt on wl tl hdd and no ex fnl 75yds* **20/1**

52 **3** hd **Excellent Thought**[99] 3458 2-9-0 0 .... LiamJones 11 70
(W J Haggas) *racd alone on far side: cl up: ev ch and rdn jst over 2f out: drvn over 1f out: kpt on same pce fnl 100yds* **6/1**

0 **4** 3 ½ **Trade Name (IRE)**[28] 5752 2-9-0 0 .... DaneO'Neill 9 59
(H Candy) *racd in centre gp: chsd ldrs: rdn and unable qck ent fnl 2f: plugged on same pce fr over 1f out* **18/1**

00 **5** 1 ¼ **Rosa Gurney (IRE)**[68] 4460 2-9-0 0 .... SteveDrowne 2 56
(J R Best) *racd alone on stands' rail: s.i.s: towards rr: hdwy u.p over 1f out: styd on fnl f: nvr trbld ldrs* **33/1**

65 **6** 2 **Angelena Ballerina (IRE)**[5] 6436 2-9-0 77 ....(p) WilliamBuick 5 50
(A Bailey) *racd in centre gp: awkward leaving stalls: hld up towards rr: rdn and no prog over 2f out* **10/3**[1]

0 **7** shd **Tudor Princess**[21] 5969 2-9-0 0 .... MartinDwyer 3 49
(W R Muir) *racd in centre gp: chsd ldrs: rdn and struggling over 2f out: sn wknd* **13/2**

8 2 ¼ **Rathbawn Girl (IRE)** 2-9-0 0 .... KirstyMilczarek 8 43
(M D Squance) *racd in centre gp: s.i.s: hld up in rr: short-lived effrt over 2f out: n.d* **12/1**

420 **9** 6 **Emma Jean Lass (IRE)**[57] 4850 2-9-0 67 .... LukeMorris 10 25
(J S Moore) *racd in centre gp: towards rr: rdn and effrt wl over 2f out: no hdwy and wl btn fnl 2f* **12/1**

0 **10** 8 **Sard**[38] 5431 2-9-0 0 .... PhilipRobinson 4 1
(M A Jarvis) *racd in centre gp: dwlt: sn rcvrd and chsd ldrs: rdn and wknd wl over 2f out* **7/2**[2]

1m 14.64s (1.94) **Going Correction** +0.275s/f (Good) **10** Ran SP% **117.9**
Speed ratings (Par 92): **98,97,97,92,90 88,87,84,76,66**
toteswingers: 1&2 £9.70, 1&3 £3.10, 2&3 £9.60 CSF £99.73 TOTE £4.90: £1.50, £6.30, £2.40; EX 86.50 Trifecta £217.50 Part won. Pool: £294.02 - 0.60 winning units..

Owner J Acheson **Bred** Kilcarn Stud **Trained** Lambourn, Berks
■ Stewards' Enquiry : Michael Hills caution: used whip with excessive frequency

FOCUS
A modest maiden and they used the whole width of the track with the main bulk coming centre-to-stands' side, while one went up the far rail. The form looks just fair for the grade.

NOTEBOOK
Flip Flop(IRE), who had run well in both her first two starts and was back down to this trip after tackling an extra furlong last time, was always handy and was delivered to win her race half a furlong from home. She needed every yard of this trip and may have more to offer in nurseries back over further. (op 100-30)
Caramelita, held in a Windsor conditions event and a Yarmouth maiden in her first two starts, showed much more here and led the main group towards the nearside until the winner pounced inside the last furlong. She also now qualifies for a mark. (op 33-1)
Excellent Thought ◆, absent for three months since coming up against a decent sort in a Windsor maiden last time, was stepping up in trip here. The only one to race up the far rail from her high draw, she tended to hang about due to lack of company but still looked a possible winner until the very late stages. Another to qualify for nurseries after this, she looks up to winning a race or two. (op 11-2 tchd 8-1)
Trade Name(IRE), very green and badly drawn when well beaten on her Lingfield Polytrack debut last month, showed a bit more here but was eventually left behind by the front trio and probably needs more time. (op 25-1 tchd 16-1)
Rosa Gurney(IRE), beaten a long way in her first two starts, made some late progress up the stands' rail and is another who now gets a handicap mark. (op 28-1, tchd 40-1 in a place)
Angelena Ballerina(IRE), disappointing in her last two starts having not been disgraced in a couple of Listed events earlier in the season, never looked like winning here either and seems to have gone the wrong way. (tchd 11-4 and 7-2)
Emma Jean Lass(IRE) Official explanation: jockey said filly was unsuited by the good to soft ground
Sard, not knocked about after misbehaving before her debut at Newmarket last month, was very disappointing as she came off the bridle at halfway and dropped herself right out. She looks one to avoid. (tchd 4-1)

6564 BURGESS HODGSON CHARTERED ACCOUNTANTS H'CAP — 6f
3:50 (3:50) (Class 4) (0-80,79) 3-Y-O+ — **£5,180** (£1,541; £770; £384) **Stalls** Low

Form — RPR

1221 **1** **We Have A Dream**[13] 6201 4-9-4 **79** .... MartinDwyer 1 92
(W R Muir) *mde all: gng best 2f out: rdn and edgd rt over 1f out: clr fnl f: r.o wl* **2/1**[1]

031 **2** 3 ¼ **Idle Power (IRE)**[33] 5592 11-8-13 **74** .... PatCosgrave 2 77
(J R Boyle) *chsd wnr: rdn and edgd lft over 1f out: sn outpcd by wnr: wl hld but kpt on to hold 2nd fnl f* **13/2**

4036 **3** 1 ¼ **The Galloping Shoe**[14] 6187 4-9-3 **78** .... TPQueally 6 77+
(J Noseda) *s.i.s: sn swtchd lft: bhd: effrt and hdwy on stands' rail wl over 1f out: nt clr run and hmpd over 1f out: sn rdn: edgd rt u.p fnl f: wnt 3rd on nr fin: nvr threatened wnr* **9/2**[3]

4340 **4** hd **Last Sovereign**[13] 6212 5-9-4 **79** .... RobertHavlin 4 77
(Jane Chapple-Hyam) *chsd ldrs: rdn and effrt wl over 1f out: outpcd by wnr over 1f out: lost 3rd nr fin* **7/2**[2]

1100 **5** 8 **C'Mon You Irons (IRE)**[38] 5424 4-8-12 **76** .... JackMitchell(3) 7 48
(M R Hoad) *chsd ldrs: rdn ent fnl 2f: wknd u.p over 1f out: wl btn fnl f* **9/2**[3]

425 **6** 12 **White Shift (IRE)**[23] 5902 3-9-2 **78** .... IanMongan 5 12
(P Howling) *hld up in tch in last pair: swtchd rt and effrt 2f out: wknd over 1f out: wl bhd and virtually p.u fnl 100yds* **12/1**

1m 13.53s (0.83) **Going Correction** +0.275s/f (Good)
WFA 3 from 4yo+ 1lb **6** Ran SP% **112.9**
Speed ratings (Par 105): **105,100,99,98,88 72**
toteswingers: 1&2 £1.10, 1&3 £2.20, 2&3 £7.50 CSF £15.66 TOTE £3.80: £1.20, £4.40; EX 7.70.

Owner The Dreaming Squires **Bred** Whitsbury Manor Stud **Trained** Lambourn, Berks
■ Stewards' Enquiry : Pat Cosgrave two-day ban: careless riding (Oct 20-21)

FOCUS
A fair sprint handicap with the winner better than ever recently. The form could be a few pounds out either way.

6565 WESTENHANGER H'CAP — 1m 1f 149y
4:20 (4:20) (Class 6) (0-65,65) 3-Y-O+ — **£2,047** (£604; £302) **Stalls** Centre

Form — RPR

0331 **1** **Florentia**[8] 6333 3-9-1 **63** .... LiamJones 9 71+
(Sir Mark Prescott) *chsd ldng pair: rdn to chse ldr over 2f out: led 1f out: drvn and forged ahd ins fnl f: in command whn edgd lft towards fin* **11/8**[1]

1211 **2** 1 ¼ **Recalcitrant**[26] 5790 6-9-3 **60** .... SaleemGolam 2 64
(S Dow) *chsd ldr: rdn to ld jst over 2f out: hdd and drvn 1f out: kpt on same pce fnl f* **5/1**[2]

0055 **3** nse **Oronsay**[34] 5567 4-8-4 **50** oh5 ....(t) AndreaAtzeni(3) 10 54
(B R Millman) *taken down early: t.k.h: hld up in last trio: swtchd lft and hdwy 2f out: sn rdn: edgd rt u.p fnl f: kpt on* **11/2**[3]

0453 **4** 3 **Dancer's Legacy**[13] 6208 4-8-11 **54** ....(p) PatCosgrave 3 52
(J R Boyle) *in tch: rdn to chse ldr jst over 2f out tl over 1f out: wknd fnl f* **7/1**

1604 **5** 5 **Inquisitress**[33] 5602 5-8-7 **50** oh1 .... LukeMorris 7 37
(J J Bridger) *t.k.h: hld up in last trio: hdwy on outer over 2f out: chsd ldrs and rdn jst over 2f out: wknd over 1f out* **16/1**

1000 **6** 8 **Rosy Dawn**[34] 5577 4-8-4 **50**.. MarcHalford(3) 5 20
(J J Bridger) *led: rdn and hdd jst over 2f out: wknd qckly 2f out: eased fnl f* **12/1**
4543 **7** 3/4 **Nassar (IRE)**[40] 5365 6-9-7 **64**...................................(v) KirstyMilczarek 4 33
(G Prodromou) *s.i.s: a bhd: lost tch over 2f out* **8/1**
2m 9.70s (4.80) **Going Correction** +0.425s/f (Yiel)
WFA 3 from 4yo+ 5lb **7** Ran SP% **111.3**
Speed ratings (Par 101): **97,96,95,93,89 83,82**
toteswingers: 1&2 £2.40, 1&3 £2.80, 2&3 £5.00 CSF £7.94 CT £26.72 TOTE £2.10: £1.40, £2.40; EX 6.60 Trifecta £31.90 Pool: £399.25 - 9.24 winning units..
Owner Neil Greig **Bred** W N Greig **Trained** Newmarket, Suffolk

FOCUS
A modest handicap weakened by three non-runners, though the pace was solid enough. The winner did not need to improve and the runner-up is rated to form.
Rosy Dawn Official explanation: jockey said filly lost its action
Nassar(IRE) Official explanation: jockey said horse was unsuited the good to soft ground

6566 ROMNEY MARSH H'CAP 1m 4f
4:50 (4:50) (Class 5) (0-70,69) 3-Y-O+ **£2,729** (£806; £403) **Stalls** Low

Form RPR
4042 **1** **Dove Cottage (IRE)**[23] 5912 7-9-8 **66**...................... FergusSweeney 10 79
(W S Kittow) *taken down early: mde all: rdn jst over 2f out: clr over 1f out: styd on strly* **5/1**[3]
4505 **2** 6 **Vinces**[40] 5365 5-9-4 **62**... GeorgeBaker 9 65
(T D McCarthy) *chsd ldrs: wnt 2nd 3f out: rdn and effrt 2f out: drvn and no prog over 1f out: wl hld fnl f* **8/1**
1221 **3** 3 3/4 **Squad**[8] 6338 3-8-11 **65**.................................... Louis-PhilippeBeuzelin(3) 3 62+
(S Dow) *bhd: rdn and effrt jst over 3f out: swtchd lft 2f out: kpt on to go modest 3rd fnl 75yds: nvr nr ldng pair* **5/2**[1]
3365 **4** 3/4 **Good Buy Dubai (USA)**[4] 6446 3-8-8 **59** ow1................ SteveDrowne 7 55
(J R Best) *towards rr: niggled along 8f out: rdn over 4f out: sme hdwy to chse clr ldng pair wl over 1f out: no imp: lost 3rd fnl 75yds* **9/2**[2]
1121 **5** 6 **Sagunt (GER)**[11] 4263 6-9-4 **69**.. AFreeman(7) 4 56
(S Curran) *s.i.s: a bhd: rdn and struggling 3f out: plugged on past btn horses fnl 2f: n.d* **8/1**
0603 **6** 2 **Evident Pride (USA)**[32] 5649 6-9-7 **68**.......................... JackMitchell(3) 6 51
(B R Johnson) *hld up in last trio: hdwy into midfield over 5f out: rdn and effrt on inner over 2f out: no prog and wl btn fnl 2f* **7/1**
150 **7** 4 **Rough Sketch (USA)**[21] 5975 4-8-12 **56**....................(v[1]) PatCosgrave 5 33
(Sir Mark Prescott) *chsd ldrs: rdn to chse ldng pair over 2f out tl wl over 1f out: sn wknd* **12/1**
0056 **8** 17 **Sufad**[6] 6400 4-9-3 **61**...(b) KirstyMilczarek 1 11
(T D McCarthy) *chsd ldrs: rdn and struggling 3f out: wknd qckly over 2f out: eased ins fnl f: t.o* **25/1**
1005 **9** 23 **Madam President**[21] 5975 4-9-6 **64**.............................. AdamKirby 8 —
(W R Swinburn) *chsd ldr tl 3f out: wknd qckly: wl bhd and eased fnl f: t.o* **9/1**
2m 45.02s (4.12) **Going Correction** +0.425s/f (Yiel)
WFA 3 from 4yo+ 7lb **9** Ran SP% **119.7**
Speed ratings (Par 103): **103,99,96,96,92 90,88,76,61**
toteswingers: 1&2 £5.80, 1&3 £4.50, 2&3 £4.30 CSF £46.25 CT £124.87 TOTE £6.90: £2.00, £2.90, £1.60; EX 53.40 Trifecta £176.80 Pool: £420.54 - 1.76 winning units. Place 6: £697.77 Place 5: £48.67 .
Owner Reg Gifford **Bred** D R Tucker **Trained** Blackborough, Devon

FOCUS
A modest handicap, but they went a decent pace and very few ever got into it. Probably not form to take at face value with the runner-up the best guide.
Evident Pride(USA) Official explanation: jockey said saddle slipped
Sufad Official explanation: jockey said gelding was unsuited by the good to soft ground
Madam President Official explanation: jockey said filly stopped quickly
T/Plt: £229.10 to a £1 stake. Pool: £60,897.48. 194.01 winning tickets. T/Qpdt: £3.30 to a £1 stake. Pool: £5,977.02. 1,334.11 winning tickets. SP

6169 LEICESTER (R-H)
Tuesday, October 6

OFFICIAL GOING: Good to firm (firm in places; 8.4)
Wind: Fresh behind Weather: Overcast

6567 E B F LADBROKES.COM MAIDEN FILLIES' STKS 7f 9y
2:10 (2:12) (Class 4) 2-Y-O **£5,180** (£1,541; £770; £384) **Stalls** Low

Form RPR
33 **1** **Marie De Medici (USA)**[88] 3823 2-9-0 0.......................... JoeFanning 17 94+
(M Johnston) *led to 1/2-way: chsd ldr tl led again 1f out: r.o wl* **5/1**
22 **2** 2 **Faithful One (IRE)**[15] 6164 2-9-0 0.................................... TedDurcan 2 89+
(D R Lanigan) *chsd ldr tl led 1/2-way: rdn and hdd 1f out: styd on same pce* **9/2**[3]
320 **3** 8 **Boogie Diva**[18] 6055 2-9-0 81.. JerryO'Dwyer 7 69
(M Botti) *hld up: hdwy 1/2-way: rdn over 2f out: wknd fnl f* **4/1**[2]
0 **4** 2 1/4 **Sign Of Life**[28] 5752 2-9-0 0.. DavidProbert 18 63
(W R Swinburn) *chsd ldrs: rdn over 2f out: edgd rt and wknd over 1f out* **14/1**
5 1 **Al Jaadl** 2-9-0 0... HayleyTurner 15 61+
(W Jarvis) *mid-div: rdn over 2f out: nvr on terms* **33/1**
6 3 **Queen's Envoy** 2-9-0 0... KFallon 13 55+
(L M Cumani) *hld up in tch: racd keenly: edgd rt and outpcd over 2f out: n.d after* **12/1**
7 1 **Ice Diva** 2-9-0 0.. DarrylHolland 16 51
(P W D'Arcy) *prom: rdn over 2f out: wknd wl over 1f out* **9/1**
8 3/4 **Child Of Our Time (IRE)** 2-9-0 0...................................... AlanMunro 1 49+
(P W Chapple-Hyam) *dwlt: hld up: pushed along 1/2-way: nt clr run wl over 1f out: n.d* **33/1**
6 **9** 4 1/2 **Eleanora Duse (IRE)**[15] 6164 2-9-0 0................................ RyanMoore 5 38+
(Sir Michael Stoute) *mid-div: sn pushed along: hdwy 1/2-way: wknd wl over 1f out: eased fnl f* **11/4**[1]
0 **10** *hd* **Banco Busto (IRE)**[15] 6164 2-9-0 0.................................. MickyFenton 12 37
(H S Howe) *sn pushed along and a in rr* **200/1**
6 **11** *shd* **Hold Me**[25] 5839 2-9-0 0.. JimmyQuinn 6 37
(H R A Cecil) *chsd ldrs: rdn 1/2-way: wknd over 2f out* **25/1**
12 2 1/2 **Miss California** 2-9-0 0.. TravisBlock 14 31
(Miss Tor Sturgis) *s.i.s: a outpcd* **100/1**
5 **13** 5 **Persian Heroine (IRE)**[61] 4701 2-9-0 0.......................... DO'Donohoe 10 18
(J L Dunlop) *dwlt: sn pushed along in rr: outpcd* **66/1**
0 **14** 24 **Lady Brickhouse**[19] 6032 2-9-0 0.................................... RoystonFfrench 3 —
(M D Squance) *chsd ldrs: rdn 1/2-way: sn wknd: t.o* **200/1**

00 **P** **Miss Isle Control**[14] 6181 2-8-11 0......................... NataliaGemelova(3) 8 —
(A J McCabe) *sn pushed along in rr: lost tch 1/2-way: t.o whn p.u over 2f out* **200/1**
1m 22.6s (-3.60) **Going Correction** -0.325s/f (Firm) 2y crse rec **15** Ran SP% **119.6**
Speed ratings (Par 94): **107,104,95,93,91 88,87,86,81,81 80,78,72,44,—**
toteswingers: 1&2 £3.50, 1&3 £7.30, 2&3 £5.70 CSF £26.62 TOTE £5.90: £1.70, £1.70, £2.00; EX 26.70.
Owner Sheikh Hamdan Bin Mohammed Al Maktoum **Bred** Flaxman Holdings Ltd **Trained** Middleham Moor, N Yorks

FOCUS
There looked to be more strength in depth to this fillies' maiden than the beaten distances might suggest, the form looks strong and the front two look very useful, particularly the winner. For example, not only does the 81-rated third give the form real substance, but the juvenile course record, dating back to 1997, was lowered by 0.20 seconds, and the time, easily the quickest of three 7f races on the card, was also 2.32 seconds quicker than the 58-rated Averoo, a 4-y-o carrying 5lb less, managed in the following race.

NOTEBOOK
Marie De Medici(USA) ◆, back after nearly three months off, improved on her two previous efforts with a likeable performance. She showed good speed more towards the centre of the track than the runner-up and sustained her run all the way to the line. She is probably worthy of a step up to Pattern company and is likely to stay at least 1m. (op 6-1 tchd 9-2)
Faithful One(IRE) ◆ soon grabbed the stands' rail and went off quickly, although not too fast judged by where the winner raced. She ran on to the line, pulling well clear of the remainder, but was simply beaten by a better one on the day. Although she might be beginning to frustrate, with this being her third consecutive runners-up placing, this was still a decent effort in defeat. (tchd 4-1)
Boogie Diva never looked a threat to the front two but still finished in a clear third. Even if her official mark is a little high, the RPRs she recorded on her first three starts suggest she's worthy of a rating in the 70s at least and she gives the form a solid look. (op 11-2 tchd 6-1)
Sign Of Life is extremely well bred, being a half-sister to Victory Note, and she stepped up on her debut effort. She should continue to progress and we probably won't see the best of her until next year. (op 20-1 tchd 11-1)
Al Jaadl, a 40,000gns half-sister to a 1m1f winner in France, was stuck out towards the middle of the track and never threatened, but she made some encouraging late headway. She should be all the better for this experience. (op 40-1)
Queen's Envoy, the first foal of a 7f winner, she should have learnt plenty. (op 11-1 tchd 9-1)
Ice Diva was popular in the market but she was another who ran as though in need of the experience. Many of her sire's progeny favour soft ground. (tchd 8-1)
Eleanora Duse(IRE), a half-sister to 2006 Irish Oaks runner-up Scottish Stage, was a major disappointment considering she had shown ability when not too far behind Faithful One on debut at Kempton, and was representing a trainer who had won a division of this maiden for the last two years. Official explanation: jockey said filly never travelled (op 9-4 tchd 7-2)
Miss Isle Control Official explanation: jockey said filly lost its action; vet said filly returned slightly lame left-fore

6568 LADBROKES.COM APPRENTICE H'CAP 7f 9y
2:40 (2:40) (Class 5) (0-70,70) 3-Y-O+ **£2,590** (£770; £385; £192) **Stalls** Low

Form RPR
212 **1** **Averoo**[19] 6039 4-8-9 **58**..(p) PaulPickard 8 67
(M D Squance) *chsd ldrs: rdn to ld ins fnl f: hung rt: r.o* **10/3**[1]
0350 **2** 1 1/2 **Kheskianto (IRE)**[7] 6358 3-8-4 **60**............................... RachelKing(5) 5 64
(M C Chapman) *w ldr tl led 3f out: rdn and hdd ins fnl f: edgd rt and styd on same pce* **11/1**
0001 **3** 1 1/4 **Sairaam (IRE)**[21] 5972 3-8-4 **58** oh1 ow2.................... DebraEngland(3) 6 59
(C Smith) *hld up: hdwy over 2f out: rdn over 1f out: styd on same pce fnl f* **4/1**[2]
5054 **4** 1 1/4 **Goodbye Cash (IRE)**[8] 6339 5-8-6 **58**................. AndrewHeffernan(3) 1 56
(P D Evans) *led: racd keenly: hdd 3f out: sn rdn and hung rt: outpcd wl over 1f out: styd on towards fin* **5/1**
2060 **5** 1 1/2 **Compton's Eleven**[26] 5804 8-9-3 **66**............................ MatthewDavies 9 60
(M R Channon) *chsd ldrs: rdn over 1f out: wknd ins fnl f* **9/2**[3]
00/0 **6** 3 3/4 **Sir Orpen (IRE)**[24] 5869 6-8-4 **56** oh2....................... TobyAtkinson(3) 7 40
(J F Panvert) *s.s: hld up: rdn over 2f out: edgd lft fnl f: nvr trbld ldrs* **9/1**
3600 **7** 7 **Thunder Gorge (USA)**[28] 5745 4-9-4 **70**........................ IJBrennan(3) 2 35
(Mouse Hamilton-Fairley) *s.s: hld up: plld hrd: rdn and hung rt fr 1/2-way: nt run on* **13/2**
000 **8** 54 **Torquemada (IRE)**[44] 5287 8-8-7 **56** oh6.................(tp) RossAtkinson 10 —
(M J Attwater) *hld up in tch: racd keenly: wknd wl over 2f out: eased: t.o* **33/1**
1m 24.92s (-1.28) **Going Correction** -0.325s/f (Firm)
WFA 3 from 4yo+ 2lb **8** Ran SP% **112.5**
Speed ratings (Par 103): **94,92,90,89,87 83,75,13**
toteswingers: 1&2 £6.80, 1&3 £2.30, 2&3 £8.30 CSF £39.04 CT £148.93 TOTE £2.70: £1.30, £3.40, £1.90; EX 36.00.
Owner M D Squance **Bred** Mrs H Johnson Houghton & Mrs R F Johnson Hought **Trained** Newmarket, Suffolk
■ Stewards' Enquiry : I J Brennan one-day ban: used whip without giving gelding time to respond (Oct 20)

FOCUS
An ordinary handicap best rated around the placed horses. They raced towards the stands' side early on, before ending up in the middle of the track.

6569 LADBROKES.COM SQUIRREL CONDITIONS STKS 1m 1f 218y
3:10 (3:10) (Class 3) 2-Y-O **£6,854** (£2,052; £1,026) **Stalls** High

Form RPR
31 **1** **Al Ghazal (USA)**[55] 4908 2-8-11 87.. LDettori 1 92+
(Saeed Bin Suroor) *led after 1f: pushed along over 3f out: rdn clr over 1f out: eased ins fnl f* **1/1**[1]
331 **2** 5 **Realisation (USA)**[27] 5770 2-8-13 80................................. JoeFanning 3 82+
(M Johnston) *led 1f: chsd ldrs: rdn over 3f out: wnt 2nd again over 1f out: no imp* **2/1**[2]
314 **3** 11 **Shaayeq (IRE)**[18] 6057 2-8-13 85.......................................(v) RHills 2 65+
(M P Tregoning) *chsd wnr after 1f: rdn over 2f out: wknd and eased over 1f out* **7/2**[3]
2m 5.80s (-2.10) **Going Correction** -0.175s/f (Firm) **3** Ran SP% **105.6**
Speed ratings (Par 99): **101,97,88**
CSF £3.14 TOTE £1.50; EX 3.30.
Owner Godolphin **Bred** Darley **Trained** Newmarket, Suffolk

FOCUS
Only three runners and the best horse in the race, Al Ghazal, was allowed an easy lead.

NOTEBOOK
Al Ghazal(USA), reappearing nearly two months after winning a 7f maiden at Sandown, this scopey son of Motivator enjoyed himself in front and stayed on strongly in the straight, never being seriously challenged and eventually winning eased down. A big colt, he is understandably still considered to be on the weak side by Saeed Bin Suroor, who expects him to be suited by 1m-1m2f. He holds some Group-race entries and something better probably awaits - maybe the Zetland Stakes at Newmarket could be a suitable target - but whatever, we're unlikely to see the best of him until next year and beyond. (op 4-5)
Realisation(USA), a recent Epsom maiden winner, surprisingly raced last of all in the three-runner field. The way he stayed on in the straight suggests he might have finished closer under a more positive ride, although it's extremely unlikely he would have troubled the winner. (op 11-4)
Shaayeq(IRE) was no sure thing to stay the trip judged on breeding and he burnt himself out after racing keenly. (tchd 3-1)

6570 LADBROKES.COM STOAT (S) STKS — 1m 1f 218y
3:40 (3:41) (Class 6) 3-Y-O — **£1,942** (£578; £288; £144) **Stalls High**

Form — RPR
5225 **1** **Kyle Of Bute**[8] 6338 3-8-11 53 .... TedDurcan 3 — 67
(J L Dunlop) *hld up: hdwy 2f out: rdn to ld and edgd rt over 1f out: styd on wl* **8/1**
341 **2** *4 1/2* **Kind Heart**[22] 5953 3-8-11 70 .... KFallon 2 — 58
(P Howling) *a.p: led 3f out: rdn and hdd over 1f out: no ex ins fnl f* **9/4**[1]
0230 **3** *1 1/4* **Abulharith**[15] 6172 3-8-11 56 .... RobertWinston 7 — 55
(R A Harris) *chsd ldrs: rdn over 1f out: styd on same pce fnl f* **12/1**
6-6 **4** *2 1/4* **Private Equity (IRE)**[20] 5999 3-8-6 0 .... JoeFanning 9 — 46
(W Jarvis) *s.i.s: hld up: hdwy over 2f out: sn rdn: kpt on: nt trble ldrs* **14/1**
0-00 **5** *nk* **Red Horse (IRE)**[32] 5644 3-8-11 48 .... HayleyTurner 13 — 50
(M L W Bell) *mid-div: rdn over 2f out: styd on u.p fr over 1f out: nt trble ldrs* **20/1**
1052 **6** *5* **Jeronimo Joe**[58] 4818 3-8-11 56 .... AmyBaker(5) 6 — 45
(A B Haynes) *hld up: hdwy over 3f out: sn rdn: wknd 2f out* **14/1**
0365 **7** *nse* **Nouailhas**[17] 6098 3-8-11 50 .... RoystonFfrench 10 — 40
(R Hollinshead) *led 1f: chsd ldr tl led again over 3f out: sn hdd: rdn and wknd over 1f out* **66/1**
0004 **8** *3/4* **Yeoman Of England (IRE)**[20] 6001 3-8-11 52 .... AlanMunro 4 — 38
(C F Wall) *hld up in tch: plld hrd: hdwy on outer over 2f out: rdn and wknd over 1f out* **9/1**
503 **9** *2 1/2* **Dream On Connie**[20] 6001 3-8-11 56 .... (vt[1]) JimCrowley 8 — 33
(W J Knight) *hld up: hdwy 1/2-way: wknd over 1f out* **6/1**[2]
5444 **10** *1 1/4* **Location**[7] 6369 3-8-6 51 .... AndrewHeffernan(5) 5 — 31
(P D Evans) *dwlt: hld up: hmpd over 6f out: rdn over 2f out: a in rr* **14/1**
4245 **11** *5* **Brooksby**[26] 5806 3-8-6 64 .... (b) RichardSmith 1 — 16
(L A Dace) *prom: rdn over 3f out: sn edgd rt and wknd* **7/1**[3]
160 **12** *17* **Jenny's Pride (IRE)**[15] 6170 3-8-11 54 .... DavidProbert 11 — —
(John A Harris) *chsd ldrs tl rdn and wknd over 2f out: t.o* **33/1**
0000 **13** *16* **Bahamian Ceilidh**[7] 6362 3-8-6 53 .... JimmyQuinn 12 — —
(B N Pollock) *led after 1f: rdn and hdd over 3f out: sn wknd: t.o* **40/1**

2m 6.34s (-1.56) **Going Correction** -0.175s/f (Firm) — **13** Ran SP% **118.0**
Speed ratings (Par 99): **99,95,94,92,92 88,88,87,85,84 80,67,54**
toteswingers: 1&2 £3.70, 1&3 £13.60, 2&3 £8.50 CSF £25.05 TOTE £8.50: £2.20, £1.70, £3.60; EX 30.50.The winner was bought by B. Baugh for 5,200gns. Kind Heart was claimed by D. McCain Jnr for £6000.
Owner J L Dunlop **Bred** Chippenham Lodge Stud Ltd **Trained** Arundel, W Sussex
FOCUS
A standard seller that makes sense rate around the third and fifth.
Jenny's Pride(IRE) Official explanation: jockey said filly was unsuited by the good to firm (firm in places) ground
Bahamian Ceilidh Official explanation: jockey said filly ran too free

6571 LADBROKES.COM QUORN H'CAP — 1m 3f 183y
4:10 (4:13) (Class 2) (0-100,97) 3-Y-O — **£11,215** (£3,358; £1,679) **Stalls High**

Form — RPR
1661 **1** **Highland Glen**[15] 6165 3-9-2 95 .... RyanMoore 5 — 102+
(Sir Michael Stoute) *difficult to load into stalls: sn led at brisk pce: rdn and hld on wl ins fnl f: edgd rt nr fin* **1/2**[1]
3232 **2** *1/2* **Souter Point (USA)**[1] 6552 3-8-4 83 .... HayleyTurner 1 — 89
(R Charlton) *chsd wnr: appeared to be gng wl enough ent fnl f: rdn and didn't find what seemed likely towards fin* **7/2**[2]
1024 **3** *43* **Clerk's Choice (IRE)**[20] 6002 3-8-6 85 .... AlanMunro 3 — 22
(W Jarvis) *chsd ldrs: pushed along over 3f out: wknd over 2f out: eased: t.o* **4/1**[3]

2m 30.34s (-3.56) **Going Correction** -0.175s/f (Firm) — **3** Ran SP% **108.9**
Speed ratings (Par 107): **104,103,75**
CSF £2.60 TOTE £1.30; EX 2.20.
Owner The Queen **Bred** The Queen **Trained** Newmarket, Suffolk
FOCUS
A thoroughly unconvincing performance from the winner in this three-runner race. The runner-up offers the best guide to the level.
NOTEBOOK
Highland Glen again showed an aversion to the starting stalls (refused to load at Goodwood earlier in the season) and must have been on his last chance when finally consenting to step forward. In the race itself he was free in the lead, despite the fitting of a cross-noseband, and was ultimately all out to hang on, albeit he was willing enough, from his only serious rival, Souter Point, who has a reputation of finding little for pressure. The winner is now 2-2 since being gelded, this success coming off a 6lb higher mark than when winning at Kempton a couple of weeks earlier, and he is game under pressure, but he's obviously got an issue with the stalls and runs like a horse keen to get it all over and done with. He could go either way, but he's obviously with the right trainer and certainly has the ability to make it at a decent level as he gets older. (tchd 8-13)
Souter Point(USA) filled the same position at Windsor the previous day. Sensibly held up off the quick gallop set by the winner, he travelled well but couldn't find enough for pressure to get by. (op 4-1 tchd 100-30)
Clerk's Choice(IRE) was never out of last place following a slow start and seemed to lose his action after stumbling in the straight. (op 9-2 tchd 7-2)

6572 LADBROKESCASINO.COM FILLIES' H'CAP — 5f 218y
4:40 (4:41) (Class 5) (0-70,70) 3-Y-O+ — **£3,238** (£963; £481; £240) **Stalls Low**

Form — RPR
1-05 **1** **Speedy Guru**[81] 4061 3-8-9 67 .... AmyScott(7) 1 — 75+
(H Candy) *chsd ldr: rdn to ld over 1f out: r.o: hung rt nr fin* **10/1**
0004 **2** *hd* **Gower Valentine**[39] 5405 3-9-3 68 .... JoeFanning 7 — 74
(D Nicholls) *led: rdn and hdd over 1f out: rallied ins fnl f: r.o: carried rt nr fin* **7/1**[3]
-044 **3** *2 1/2* **One Cool Dream**[28] 5747 3-8-11 62 .... DavidProbert 5 — 60
(W R Swinburn) *chsd ldrs: rdn 1/2-way: styd on u.p* **14/1**
3215 **4** *nse* **Weet A Surprise**[25] 5836 4-8-6 63 .... (v) AlexEdwards(7) 2 — 61
(J W Unett) *hld up: rdn over 2f out: hdwy over 1f out: styd on* **5/1**[1]
2406 **5** *1 1/2* **Joyeaux**[15] 6159 7-8-10 60 .... RoystonFfrench 4 — 53
(Ollie Pears) *hld up: rdn and nt clr run over 1f out: swtchd lft: r.o: nt trble ldrs* **8/1**
0210 **6** *1 1/2* **Timeless Dream**[17] 6120 3-9-5 70 .... AlanMunro 10 — 58
(P W Chapple-Hyam) *mid-div: outpcd 1/2-way: r.o ins fnl f: nt trble ldrs* **11/2**[2]
500 **7** *1 3/4* **Leading Edge (IRE)**[12] 6230 4-9-1 65 .... KFallon 12 — 48+
(M R Channon) *s.s: outpcd: nvr nrr* **8/1**
1200 **8** *1* **Dancing Wave**[77] 4172 3-8-2 58 .... AndrewHeffernan(5) 13 — 37
(M C Chapman) *s.i.s: hdwy over 4f out: rdn over 1f out: wknd fnl f* **16/1**
350 **9** *1 1/4* **Leftontheshelf (IRE)**[29] 5719 3-9-5 70 .... (p) JimCrowley 8 — 45
(Miss T Spearing) *chsd ldrs: rdn over 1f out: wknd fnl f* **9/1**
36F1 **10** *5* **Romantic Queen**[11] 6252 3-8-12 68 .... (t) MatthewDavies(5) 6 — 27
(George Baker) *chsd ldrs tl rdn and wknd over 1f out* **25/1**
4202 **11** *8* **Dressed To Dance (IRE)**[26] 5788 5-9-4 68 .... (v) RobertWinston 3 — 2
(R A Harris) *sed slow: outpcd: eased fr over 1f out* **15/2**

1m 11.04s (-1.96) **Going Correction** -0.325s/f (Firm)
WFA 3 from 4yo+ 1lb — **11** Ran SP% **114.0**
Speed ratings (Par 100): **100,99,96,96,94 92,90,88,87,80 69**
toteswingers: 1&2 £18.00, 1&3 £26.50, 2&3 £19.10 CSF £75.89 CT £996.29 TOTE £11.50: £3.50, £3.30, £2.80; EX 108.80.
Owner Henry Candy **Bred** Miss M Cornell **Trained** Kingston Warren, Oxon
■ Stewards' Enquiry : Amy Scott caution: careless riding
FOCUS
A modest fillies' handicap best rated around the third and fourth. They raced towards the stands' side.
Dressed To Dance(IRE) Official explanation: vet said mare finished sore

6573 LADBROKES.COM DORMOUSE MAIDEN STKS — 7f 9y
5:10 (5:12) (Class 5) 3-Y-O — **£2,590** (£770; £385; £192) **Stalls Low**

Form — RPR
-333 **1** **Euston Square**[135] 2298 3-9-3 85 .... JimmyFortune 9 — 71+
(J H M Gosden) *trckd ldrs: shkn up to ld 1f out: r.o wl* **1/4**[1]
-600 **2** *2 3/4* **Contemplate**[20] 5998 3-8-12 43 .... (b[1]) JoeFanning 3 — 59
(Dr J D Scargill) *sn led: rdn: edgd rt and hdd 1f out: styd on same pce* **100/1**
3 *2 3/4* **Montego Breeze** 3-8-12 0 .... MickyFenton 1 — 51+
(John A Harris) *chsd ldrs: rdn over 2f out: sn outpcd: r.o wl towards fin* **66/1**
6 **4** *3/4* **Cheers Big Ears (IRE)**[11] 6255 3-9-3 0 .... RobertWinston 8 — 54+
(J R Best) *dwlt: hld up: hdwy 2f out: rdn over 1f out: no ex ins fnl f* **8/1**[3]
5 **5** *1 1/2* **Mydy Easy (USA)**[57] 4854 3-9-3 0 .... AlanMunro 7 — 50
(P W Chapple-Hyam) *chsd ldrs: pushed along 1/2-way: wknd fnl f* **6/1**[2]
00 **6** *1 3/4* **She's Pivotal (IRE)**[5] 6430 3-8-12 0 .... JimCrowley 5 — 40
(J A Osborne) *hld up: rdn over 1f out: wknd fnl f* **50/1**
7 *9* **Bawdsey Bank** 3-8-12 0 .... MarkCoumbe(5) 6 — 21
(John A Harris) *s.i.s: a outpcd in rr* **100/1**
8 *2* **Amazing Memories (IRE)**[345] 7002 3-9-3 0 .... FrankieMcDonald 2 — 16
(John A Harris) *hld up: rdn and edgd rt over 2f out: sn wknd* **100/1**
0 **9** *1 1/4* **Spirit Child (USA)**[5] 6430 3-8-12 0 .... DavidProbert 4 — 7
(J A Osborne) *prom tl rdn and wknd over 2f out* **40/1**

1m 24.86s (-1.34) **Going Correction** -0.325s/f (Firm) — **9** Ran SP% **114.3**
Speed ratings (Par 101): **94,90,87,86,85 83,72,70,69**
toteswingers: 1&2 £6.20, 1&3 £6.90, 2&3 £28.50 CSF £70.57 TOTE £1.40: £1.02, £9.30, £8.10; EX 25.80 Place 6: £70.25 Place 5: £30.19.
Owner K Abdulla **Bred** Juddmonte Farms Ltd **Trained** Newmarket, Suffolk
FOCUS
A very weak maiden that is best rated around the fourth and fifth.
Cheers Big Ears(IRE) Official explanation: jockey said colt hung left
T/Plt: £53.10 to a £1 stake. Pool: £60,000.87. 823.65 winning tickets. T/Qpdt: £28.40 to a £1 stake. Pool: £3,493.30. 90.80 winning tickets. CR

6574 - 6575a (Foreign Racing) - See Raceform Interactive

SEGRE (R-H)
Monday, October 5

OFFICIAL GOING: Good to soft

6576a PRIX JEAN DE JOURDAN (MAIDEN) — 1m 2f
2:00 (12:00) 2-Y-O — **£4,854** (£1,942; £1,456; £971; £485)

RPR
1 **Breizh Touch (FR)** 2-8-8 .... MAndrouin — 72
(J Boisnard, France)
2 *2 1/2* **Plume Du Peintre (FR)** 2-8-10 ow2 .... ABourgeais — 68
(N Leenders, France) *finished 3rd, placed 2nd*
3 *1 1/2* **Idothea (IRE)** 2-8-13 .... LHuart — 68
(D Sepulchre, France) *finished 4th, placed 3rd*
4 *2 1/2* **Dimoitoo (FR)** 2-8-8 .... — 55
(J Boisnard, France) *finished 6th, placed 4th*
5 *hd* **Letcho (FR)**[39] 5378 2-9-2 .... — 63
(D Leblond, France) *finished 7th, placed 5th*
6 **Askabad Maybe (FR)** 2-8-8 .... — —
(C Plisson, France) *finished 8th, placed 6th*
D *5* **Apollo Blues (IRE)** 2-8-9 .... WSaraiva(1) — 58
(E J O'Neill) *close up when went wrong side of marker early stages, outpaced final 1 1/2f, finished 5th, beaten 7 1/2 lengths, disqualified, placed last*
D *1* **Scheibenhard (FR)** 2-9-2 .... FVeron — 78
(J-L Guillochon, France) *finished 2nd, disqualified, placed last*
8 Ran

Owner D Cherdo **Bred** D Cherdo **Trained** France

6198 CHANTILLY (R-H)
Tuesday, October 6

OFFICIAL GOING: Soft changing to very soft after race 1 (12.40)

6578a PRIX DE LA PISTE RODOSTO (MAIDEN) 1m
1:45 (1:45) 2-Y-O **£11,650** (£4,660; £3,495; £2,330; £1,165)

RPR
1 **Simon De Montfort (IRE)** 2-8-10 MBarzalona(6) 86
(A Fabre, France)
2 2 1/2 **Philander**25 5831 2-9-2 OPeslier 80
(E J O'Neill)
3 snk **Precipitate**35 2-8-13 SPasquier 77
(D Smaga, France)
4 1 **Ajdaad (USA)**32 2-9-2 77
(J E Hammond, France)
5 1 1/2 **At Least (FR)**11 2-8-8 (8) 74
(Robert Collet, France)
6 3/4 **Croix Madame (FR)** 2-8-10 (3) 70
(F Doumen, France)
7 3 **Trofee Dore (FR)**22 5956 2-8-13 63
(Mme R-W Allen, France)
8 2 1/2 **Feuille De Route (FR)**32 2-8-13 57
(Mlle S-V Tarrou, France)

1m 45.0s (7.00) **8** Ran
PARI-MUTUEL: WIN 3.60; PL 1.60, 1.70, 1.50; DF 13.20.
Owner Sheikh Mohammed **Bred** Darley **Trained** Chantilly, France

6579a PRIX DE BONNEVAL (LISTED RACE) 5f 110y
2:50 (2:51) 3-Y-O+ **£25,243** (£10,097; £7,573; £5,049; £2,524)

RPR
1 **Peace Camp (USA)**14 3-8-8 JVictoire 7 100
(A Fabre, France)
2 hd **Tayseer**37 5495 4-9-2 FBlondel 1 106
(J E Hammond, France)
3 snk **Bluster (FR)**23 5928 3-9-2 OPeslier 5 107
(Robert Collet, France)
4 1/2 **Blue Cayenne (FR)**37 5495 4-8-8 TJarnet 11 96
(Mlle S-V Tarrou, France)
5 1 1/2 **Planet Five (USA)**86 3908 3-8-11 TThulliez 6 95
(P Bary, France)
6 2 1/2 **Doriana (FR)**149 1918 3-8-8 J-BEyquem 10 84
(A De Royer-Dupre, France)
7 3/4 **Peach Pearl**32 5653 3-8-12 ACrastus 3 85
(Y De Nicolay, France)
8 4 **Cadeau For Maggi**45 4-8-11 MGuyon 14 70
(H-A Pantall, France)
9 1 1/2 **Capone (IRE)**59 4783 4-8-11 DBoeuf 13 65
(R Curtis)
10 nse **Zalka (FR)**35 4-8-8 FLefebvre 9 62
(Jean-Francois Clais, France)
11 **Contest (IRE)**30 5709 5-9-2 (b) THuet 2 70
(C Theodorakis, Greece)
12 **Higha (FR)**37 5495 3-8-8 SPasquier 8 63
(P Demercastel, France)
13 **Parfum Des Dieux**129 2513 4-8-11 IMendizabal 4 65
(J-C Rouget, France)
14 **Blue And Gold (FR)**37 5495 3-8-8 RMarchelli 12 63
(Mlle S-V Tarrou, France)

65.30 secs (0.80) **14** Ran
PARI-MUTUEL: WIN 12.20; PL 3.00, 1.80, 2.10; DF 26.10.
Owner Godolphin S N C **Bred** Darley **Trained** Chantilly, France

NOTEBOOK
Capone(IRE) was never seen with a chance of finishing in the frame. He raced on the outside of the pack in mid-division early on and was beaten by the furlong marker.

6370 KEMPTON (A.W) (R-H)
Wednesday, October 7

OFFICIAL GOING: Standard
Wind: Moderate, across towards stands Weather: Raining races 1-5; overcast remainder

6581 PANORAMIC BAR & RESTAURANT H'CAP 5f (P)
5:50 (5:51) (Class 7) (0-50,50) 3-Y-O+ **£2,047** (£604; £302) **Stalls** High

Form RPR
0005 1 **Best One**24 5911 5-8-13 **50** (v) KevinGhunowa 6 58
(R A Harris) *pressed ldr: rdn to chal over 1f out: edgd ahd ins fnl f* **7/2**1
0000 2 3/4 **Sonhador**62 4718 3-8-13 **50** SaleemGolam 11 58+
(G Prodromou) *trckd ldng pair: trapped bhd them fr 2f out tl ins fnl f: r.o to take 2nd nr fin* **5/1**2
0200 3 1/2 **Head To Head (IRE)**6 6433 5-8-13 **50** (tp) SteveDrowne 10 54
(A D Brown) *led: drvn over 1f out: hdd and no ex ins fnl f: lost 2nd nr fin* **5/1**2
5400 4 3/4 **Rhapsilian**20 6039 5-8-12 **49** (v) RobertWinston 5 50
(J R Jenkins) *awkward s: plld hrd early: chsd ldrs and racd wd: cl enough over 1f out: fnd nil u.p* **7/2**1
0053 5 1 **Nawaaff**93 3671 4-8-12 **49** DavidProbert 8 46
(M Quinn) *chsd ldrs: nt qckn wl over 1f out: one pce and no real imp after* **6/1**3
0/0- 6 1 1/4 **Granakey (IRE)**475 3162 6-8-13 **50** JimmyQuinn 9 43
(Ian Williams) *in tch: outpcd and rdn 1/2-way: no ch after: plugged on* **12/1**
0000 7 6 **Lily Jicaro (IRE)**9 6340 3-8-13 **50** LukeMorris 2 21
(Mrs L Williamson) *s.s: a detached in last pair* **33/1**
356- 8 7 **Franchesca's Gold**368 6489 3-8-12 **49** LPKeniry 12 —
(Jane Southcombe) *a in rr: wknd 1/2-way: t.o* **16/1**
0034 P **Rapanui Belle**14 6206 3-8-12 **49** (b) FergusSweeney 3 —
(G L Moore) *lost action after 1f and p.u: dismntd* **14/1**

60.13 secs (-0.37) **Going Correction** -0.075s/f (Stan) **9** Ran SP% **115.2**
Speed ratings (Par 97): **99,97,97,95,94 92,82,71,—**
toteswingers: 1&2 £7.60, 1&3 £4.60, 2&3 £9.30 CSF £20.96 CT £87.19 TOTE £4.60: £2.00, £1.60, £2.10; EX 27.60.
Owner The Govin Partnership **Bred** Darley **Trained** Earlswood, Monmouths
■ Stewards' Enquiry : Saleem Golam one-day ban: careless riding (Oct 21)

FOCUS
A moderate and tight handicap with every horse rated either 49 or 50. The pace was sound and the prominent racers held the edge. The winner raced just off the inside rail in the straight. The winner only had to run to something like her summer form.
Rhapsilian Official explanation: one-day ban: careless riding (Oct 21)
Franchesca's Gold Official explanation: trainer said filly was found to be in season the following day

6582 "BUY A £10,000 RACING POST BONUS YEARLING" MAIDEN FILLIES' STKS 5f (P)
6:20 (6:23) (Class 5) 2-Y-O **£2,590** (£770; £385; £192) **Stalls** High

Form RPR
62 1 **Desert Poppy (IRE)**9 6328 2-9-0 0 AdamKirby 7 73
(W R Swinburn) *chsd ldr: rdn over 1f out: gradual inroads ins fnl f: r.o to ld last strides* **7/2**2
3453 2 hd **La Fortunata**45 5282 2-9-0 66 JimmyQuinn 11 72
(J R Jenkins) *mounted on crse: led: rdn and kpt on fr over 1f out: looked likely wnr tl fdd and ct last strides* **16/1**
226 3 nk **Baby Dottie**12 6241 2-9-0 77 IanMongan 9 71
(P M Phelan) *chsd ldng trio: drvn to go 3rd over 1f out: kpt on wl fnl f but nvr quite able to chal* **11/2**3
3 4 1 **Forest Crown**105 3277 2-9-0 0 SteveDrowne 6 67
(R M Beckett) *nt wl away: rchd 6th by 1/2-way: shkn up over 1f out: wnt 4th ins fnl f: pushed along and nvr on terms* **7/2**2
02 5 2 **Posy Fossil (USA)**12 6245 2-9-0 0 SaleemGolam 12 60
(S C Williams) *chsd ldng pair to over 1f out: grad fdd* **9/1**
0 6 nk **Elsie's Orphan**27 5808 2-9-0 0 DavidProbert 2 59
(P R Chamings) *in tch and racd wd: shkn up and outpcd wl over 1f out: kpt on steadily* **25/1**
00 7 1 1/2 **Dreamy Eyed (IRE)**34 5604 2-9-0 0 FergusSweeney 10 54
(Mrs P N Dutfield) *rousted along on inner early: chsd ldng quartet: fdd over 1f out* **100/1**
20 8 3/4 **Nimue (USA)**48 5199 2-9-0 0 ChrisCatlin 4 51+
(P F I Cole) *mounted on crse: blanket and blindfold on for entry: blindfold late off and slowest away: last in pair and nvr on terms: pushed along and modest late prog: shambles* **2/1**1
00 9 2 **Ramayana (IRE)**12 6245 2-8-11 0 MCGeran(3) 3 44
(M R Channon) *mounted on crse: nvr beyond midfield: rdn and struggling 1/2-way: sn btn* **50/1**
00 10 3 3/4 **Rightcar Marian**14 6207 2-9-0 0 FrankieMcDonald 5 30
(Peter Grayson) *dwlt: in tch at rr of main gp: shkn up and flashed tail over 1f out: fnd nil* **200/1**
11 2 1/2 **Kummel Excess (IRE)** 2-9-0 0 TedDurcan 1 21
(George Baker) *dwlt: a outpcd: wl bhd 1/2-way* **28/1**

59.90 secs (-0.60) **Going Correction** -0.075s/f (Stan) **11** Ran SP% **119.8**
Speed ratings (Par 92): **101,100,100,98,95 94,92,91,88,82 78**
toteswingers: 1&2 £9.30, 1&3 £6.20, 2&3 £9.90 CSF £55.79 TOTE £3.90: £1.10, £2.50, £2.20; EX 51.00.
Owner Oasis Dreamers **Bred** Kildaragh Stud **Trained** Aldbury, Herts

FOCUS
A race lacking much in the way of strength, like most 5f maidens at this time of year, and one that did not take as much winning as seemed likely with the market leader disappointing. The pace was sound and the winner raced towards the centre in the straight.

NOTEBOOK
Desert Poppy(IRE) ◆ is a steadily progressive sort who showed a good attitude returned to Polytrack to get off the mark at the third attempt. She left the strong impression the return to 6f would suit and she should be able to win a handicap on this surface. (op 4-1 tchd 9-2)
La Fortunata, a consistent sort on turf, ran well on this all-weather debut. She looks all about speed and will be one to look out for in ordinary handicaps back over this course and distance when favourably drawn. (op 20-1)
Baby Dottie was far from disgraced returned to Polytrack and shaped as though the return to 6f would suit but she is vulnerable to the more progressive sorts in this grade and her current mark of 77 offers no margin for error. (op 6-1 tchd 13-2)
Forest Crown, who divided subsequent winners when showing promise on her debut in June, was on her toes in the preliminaries on this first run since but probably ran to a similar level and she should do better in due course when stepped up to 6f. (op 11-4)
Posy Fossil(USA), very well backed when showing much improved form on her previous start, was fairly easy to back this time but was far from disgraced on this first run over 5f on this all-weather debut. She will be of more interest back over further in ordinary nurseries. (op 10-1 tchd 11-1)
Nimue(USA), tailed off in the Lowther Stakes after playing up in the stalls, was loaded with a blanket and fitted with a blindfold for this all-weather debut in this much more realistic grade but was again restless in the traps and lost all chance with a tardy start. Her debut run showed she has plenty of ability but she looks one to have reservations about at present. Official explanation: jockey said the filly missed the break (op 9-4 tchd 5-2)

6583 KIA SOUL, SAFE BET H'CAP 1m 2f (P)
6:50 (6:52) (Class 4) (0-80,80) 3-Y-O+ **£4,727** (£1,406; £702; £351) **Stalls** High

Form RPR
2120 1 **Uncle Fred**63 4641 4-9-8 **79** RichardKingscote 2 91+
(P R Chamings) *hld up in last pair: racd wd fr 4f out: prog and brought v wd in st: led jst over 1f out: sn clr* **11/2**3
6436 2 2 3/4 **Sharpazmax (IRE)**19 6060 5-9-6 **77** SteveDrowne 1 83
(P J Makin) *in tch: prog on outer 1/2-way: wnt 3rd 3f out: sn rdn: tried to mount a chal over 1f out: kpt on to take 2nd ins fnl f* **6/1**
2314 3 3/4 **Putra One (IRE)**33 5649 3-9-4 **80** PhilipRobinson 8 85
(M A Jarvis) *chsd ldr 2f: wnt 2nd again over 3f out: rdn to ld briefly over 1f out: sn outpcd by wnr: one pce* **7/2**1
1052 4 1/2 **Hallingdal (UAE)**9 6346 4-9-2 **73** LPKeniry 5 77
(J J Bridger) *s.s: hld up in last: prog on inner and looking for room wl over 1f out: nt pce to threaten after* **10/1**
4315 5 1/2 **Woodlark Island (IRE)**12 6243 3-8-13 **75** TedDurcan 4 78
(M P Tregoning) *chsd ldrs: tended to run-in snatches fr 6f out: nt qckn u.p over 1f out: plugged on* **9/2**2
0020 6 2 1/2 **Eseej (USA)**48 5185 4-9-3 **74** DarryllHolland 6 72
(P W Hiatt) *led at gd pce: rdn over 2f out: hdd over 1f out: wknd fnl f* **8/1**

315 7 3 1/2 **Racing Hero (IRE)**[100] 3461 3-9-2 78 AdamKirby 9 69
(J Noseda) *hld up in tch: prog to go 4th on inner 2f out: cl up over 1f o ut: wknd rapidly* **7/2**[1]
5043 8 25 **Ballyalla**[45] 5285 3-9-0 76 PatDobbs 3 17
(R Hannon) *chsd ldr after 2f to over 3f out: wknd rapidly: t.o* **20/1**
2m 5.82s (-2.18) **Going Correction** -0.075s/f (Stan)
WFA 3 from 4yo+ 5lb **8** Ran SP% **117.3**
Speed ratings (Par 105): **105,102,102,101,101 99,96,76**
toteswingers: 1&2 £6.30, 1&3 £7.00, 2&3 £7.30 CSF £39.25 CT £132.82 TOTE £8.50: £2.40, £2.00, £1.80; EX 42.00.
Owner P R Chamings M A Kirby **Bred** Netherfield House Stud **Trained** Baughurst, Hants

FOCUS
A decent handicap for the grade and the form looks sound. It was run at just an ordinary gallop. The winner came wide of the rest - who stayed towards the inside rail - in the straight.
Ballyalla Official explanation: jockey said the filly stopped very quickly

6584 DIGIBET H'CAP 1m 4f (P)
7:20 (7:25) (Class 6) (0-65,71) 3-Y-0+ **£2,047** (£604; £302) **Stalls** Centre

Form RPR
1021 1 **Cape Marien (IRE)**[5] 6457 3-9-7 69 6ex TedDurcan 9 84+
(D R Lanigan) *dwlt: rousted along to take prom position and sn trckd ldng pair: led over 2f out: drvn and in command wl over 1f out: styd on wl* **7/4**[1]
6120 2 2 **Resplendent Ace (IRE)**[11] 6288 5-9-10 65 IanMongan 14 74
(P Howling) *hld up in last pair: stdy prog fr over 3f out: rdn over 2f out: styd on to take 2nd ent fnl f: no imp on wnr* **6/1**[2]
4044 3 2 3/4 **Smooth As Silk (IRE)**[18] 6126 4-9-3 58 (p) SteveDrowne 4 63
(C R Egerton) *dwlt: sn in midfield: rdn and prog over 3f out and sn prom: chsd wnr over 1f out tl ent fnl f: one pce* **16/1**
0100 4 1 3/4 **Inch Lodge**[10] 6303 7-9-1 63 (t) TobyAtkinson(7) 2 65
(Miss D Mountain) *dwlt: t.k.h early: hld up in rr: reminder 5f out: prog on inner over 2f out: kpt on: nvr able to threaten* **14/1**
-456 5 2 1/2 **Silken Promise (USA)**[100] 3462 3-9-2 64 AdamKirby 10 62
(W R Swinburn) *hld up in last quartet: wd bnd over 3f out: sharp reminder 2f out: kpt on after: n.d* **8/1**[3]
3010 6 1/2 **Blue Tango (IRE)**[9] 6342 3-9-3 65 (b) JimmyQuinn 6 62
(Mrs A J Perrett) *trckd ldrs: prog and cl up 3f out: chsd wnr over 2f out to over 1f out: wknd* **25/1**
0631 7 3/4 **Capable Guest (IRE)**[7] 6385 7-10-2 71 6ex TonyCulhane 7 67
(M R Channon) *last pair and nt gng wl early: taken wdst of all in st: kpt on fnl 2f: nvr nrr* **6/1**[2]
3036 8 1/2 **Act Three**[74] 4325 5-9-2 57 (e[1]) LPKeniry 8 52
(Mouse Hamilton-Fairley) *cl up: rdn to go 4th over 3f out: lost pl over 2f out: no prog after* **33/1**
0-31 9 shd **Ardmaddy (IRE)**[133] 534 5-9-4 59 FergusSweeney 1 54
(G L Moore) *hld up in midfield: shuffled along over 2f out: reminder over 1f out: nvr nr ldrs* **25/1**
5000 10 nk **Zaif (IRE)**[11] 6288 6-9-4 59 ChrisCatlin 13 54
(D J S Ffrench Davis) *hld up in last quartet: shkn up over 2f out: plugged on: nvr any ch* **25/1**
0015 11 1/2 **Megalala (IRE)**[72] 4382 8-9-6 64 MarcHalford(3) 12 58
(J J Bridger) *led to over 2f out: wknd rapidly over 1f out* **25/1**
0354 12 1 3/4 **King Of The Beers (USA)**[41] 5377 5-9-3 58 (p) LukeMorris 5 49
(R A Harris) *hld up in midfield: hrd rdn and sme prog over 2f out: wknd over 1f out* **28/1**
6035 13 8 **Yvonne Evelyn (USA)**[22] 5964 4-9-7 62 WilliamBuick 11 40
(J R Gask) *restless stalls: chsd ldr to 3f out: sn wknd: eased over 1f out* **16/1**
44/0 14 19 **Croon**[128] 2552 7-9-10 65 (p) KirstyMilczarek 3 13
(Andrew Turnell) *prom on outer tl wknd rapidly over 3f out: t.o* **33/1**
2m 33.46s (-1.04) **Going Correction** -0.075s/f (Stan)
WFA 3 from 4yo+ 7lb **14** Ran SP% **119.2**
Speed ratings (Par 101): **100,98,96,95,94 93,93,92,92,92 92,91,85,73**
toteswingers: 1&2 £4.60, 1&3 £11.10, 2&3 £15.60 CSF £10.08 CT £126.86 TOTE £2.70: £1.30, £2.30, £5.10; EX 14.20.
Owner Saif Ali **Bred** Darley **Trained** Newmarket, Suffolk

FOCUS
An ordinary handicap but fair form for the grade. The progressive winner raced in the centre in the straight.
Act Three Official explanation: jockey say that the mare hung left

6585 DIGIBET.COM NOVICE STKS 6f (P)
7:50 (7:54) (Class 5) 2-Y-0 **£2,590** (£770; £385; £192) **Stalls** High

Form RPR
1525 1 **Treadwell (IRE)**[21] 5994 2-9-2 98 TPQueally 2 90
(J A Osborne) *trckd ldng pair: effrt on outer to ld wl over 1f out: drvn and styd on wl* **7/2**[3]
132 2 3/4 **Bagamoyo**[28] 5769 2-9-5 88 AdamKirby 6 91
(J R Fanshawe) *trckd ldng pair: chal on inner 2f out: pressed wnr fr over 1f out: styd on but hld last 100yds* **15/8**[2]
14 3 4 **I Am That (IRE)**[39] 5445 2-9-2 79 HayleyTurner 3 76
(S A Callaghan, U.S.A) *led 1f: pressed ldr: led again briefly 2f out: edgd lft and wl outpcd over 1f out* **16/1**
1300 4 1 **Perfect Ch'I (IRE)**[12] 6241 2-9-2 81 MartinDwyer 1 73
(I A Wood) *led after 1f to 2f out: sn wl outpcd* **12/1**
1 5 3/4 **Goodwood Maestro**[139] 2187 2-9-2 0 TedDurcan 5 71
(J L Dunlop) *dwlt: hld up in 5th: pushed along and no prog over 2f out: sn lft bhd* **11/10**[1]
5006 6 4 1/2 **King's Approach (IRE)**[24] 5908 2-9-2 74 PatDobbs 4 57
(R Hannon) *hld up in last: rdn and struggling 1/2-way: sn no ch* **25/1**
1m 13.41s (0.31) **Going Correction** -0.075s/f (Stan) **6** Ran SP% **122.0**
Speed ratings (Par 95): **94,93,87,86,85 79**
toteswingers: 1&2 £3.10, 1&3 £4.40, 2&3 £2.50 CSF £11.68 TOTE £4.80: £2.00, £1.50; EX 13.50.
Owner Mrs F Walwyn & A Taylor **Bred** Liberty Road Stables **Trained** Upper Lambourn, Berks

FOCUS
A couple of interesting performers in a fair novice event but a race that took less winning than had seemed likely with the market leader disappointing. The gallop was reasonable and the first two, who raced towards the far rail in the straight, pulled clear. The winner was just short of his best.

NOTEBOOK
Treadwell(IRE) had disappointed on his previous start but didn't have to better his previous best efforts for this all-weather debut to break a losing run since June for the stable. The return to 7f should not inconvenience and his trainer is reportedly eyeing a minor Group race abroad. (tchd 4-1)
Bagamoyo, conceding weight all round, was meeting the winner on considerably worse terms than in a handicap but he showed himself to be equally as good on this surface as on turf after travelling strongly. He pulled clear of the remainder and appeals as the sort to win more races on either turf or Polytrack. (op 11-4)
I Am That(IRE) had a fair bit to find at the weights but ran as well as could be expected on this all-weather debut. He is open to further progress and should be seen to better effect when switched to handicaps. (op 14-1 tchd 12-1)
Perfect Ch'I(IRE) had not been seen to best from an unfavourable draw at Ascot on her previous start but had her limitations firmly exposed on this all-weather debut. She may not be the easiest to place. (op 16-1)
Goodwood Maestro was well supported, despite being absent since creating a very favourable impression on turf in May. He found very little for pressure on this all-weather debut but, while too soon to write off, he is probably one to watch rather than bet on next time. (op 11-8, tchd 6-4 in places)
King's Approach(IRE) had been soundly beaten in nurseries and was soundly beaten in the face of a stiff task on this all-weather debut. He remains one to have reservations about.

6586 DIGIBET CASINO CLAIMING STKS 7f (P)
8:20 (8:21) (Class 6) 2-Y-0 **£2,047** (£604; £302) **Stalls** High

Form RPR
0500 1 **Shark Man (IRE)**[22] 5970 2-8-11 69 (p) JackMitchell(3) 3 69
(P J McBride) *wl in rr: pushed along 1/2-way: rdn and prog over 2f out: clsd on ldrs 1f out: sustained effrt between rivals to ld last strides* **10/1**
04 2 shd **Pont D'Avignon**[13] 6228 2-8-5 0 FrankieMcDonald 1 60
(F J Brennan) *racd wd: sn prom fr low draw: pressed ldr over 2f out: drvn ahd ins fnl f: edgd lft and hdd last strides* **20/1**
0051 3 3/4 **Newton Circus**[27] 5811 2-8-12 70 DaneO'Neill 6 65
(Ollie Pears) *trckd ldrs: prog on outer and cl up 2f out: chal over 1f out: nt qckn ins fnl f* **5/1**[2]
2451 4 1/2 **Daniella De Bruijn (IRE)**[6] 6431 2-8-12 77 SebSanders 14 64
(A B Haynes) *mde most but a pressed: drvn over 2f out: hanging rt and hdd ins fnl f: nt qckn* **11/10**[1]
3600 5 3/4 **Sixpenny Moon (USA)**[7] 6391 2-8-9 60 (b[1]) PatDobbs 2 59
(R Hannon) *wl in rr on outer: rdn and prog over 2f out: clsd on ldrs 1f out: nvr quite pce to chal* **20/1**
0056 6 1/2 **Lofthouse**[23] 5942 2-8-10 56 TonyCulhane 9 59
(M R Channon) *stdd s: t.k.h and hld up towards rr: prog on inner over 2f out: drvn to cl on ldrs 1f out: nt qckn last 150yds* **33/1**
0200 7 1/2 **Timelord (IRE)**[13] 6228 2-8-10 66 LPKeniry 13 57
(S Kirk) *chsd ldrs: rdn 1/2-way: stl cl up over 1f out: one pce fnl f* **7/1**[3]
1260 8 hd **Michaelmas Daisy**[49] 5166 2-8-5 66 MartinDwyer 5 52
(Miss Amy Weaver) *w ldr to over 2f out: lost pl but stl cl up over 1f out: fdd ins fnl f* **9/1**
2040 9 9 **Lochbroom Sunset**[11] 6292 2-8-4 56 WilliamCarson(3) 10 31
(S C Williams) *chsd ldrs: rdn 1/2-way: wknd rapidly wl over 1f out: t.o* **20/1**
0660 10 3 1/4 **Dinkie Short**[6] 6431 2-9-0 63 (b[1]) RobertWinston 11 30
(W R Muir) *nvr bttr than midfield: struggling u.p 1/2-way: sn wknd: t.o* **16/1**
11 1 **Brenda Duke** 2-8-3 0 ow1 ChrisCatlin 12 17
(J G Portman) *completely missed break and lft abt 15 l: t.o and mde no grnd: passed two wkng rivals nr fin* **33/1**
0600 12 1/2 **Campaigner**[24] 5913 2-9-2 55 LiamJones 4 29
(J W Hills) *t.k.h: hld up wl in rr: v wd bnd 3f out: sn bhd: t.o* **66/1**
6500 13 1 **Reel Credit Crunch**[21] 5976 2-8-5 56 HayleyTurner 7 15
(I W McInnes) *a wl in rr: wknd over 2f out: t.o* **66/1**
1m 26.5s (0.50) **Going Correction** -0.075s/f (Stan) **13** Ran SP% **124.9**
Speed ratings (Par 93): **94,93,93,92,91 91,90,90,79,76 75,74,73**
toteswingers: 1&2 £21.20, 1&3 £8.20, 2&3 £18.70 CSF £198.97 TOTE £16.30: £4.40, £5.80, £1.60; EX 383.50.
Owner J Burns **Bred** John Grimes **Trained** Newmarket, Suffolk

FOCUS
Mainly exposed types in a modest claimer. The pace was sound and the first eight finished in a heap. The principals raced in the centre in the straight.

NOTEBOOK
Shark Man(IRE) appreciated the decent gallop and returned to form dropped in grade and back on sand with cheekpieces fitted for the first time. He fared easily the best of those coming from off the pace but his record suggests he would not be an obvious one to follow up. (op 11-1)
Pont D'Avignon, having her first run for a new stable, turned in her best effort yet. Modest handicaps around this trip on Polytrack will be the way forward with her.
Newton Circus, a recent course and distance winner, had a decent chance at the weights and was not disgraced on this first start for a trainer that does well with this type. He should be placed to best effect. (op 6-1)
Daniella De Bruijn(IRE) looked to have solid claims following a recent Wolverhampton win but proved disappointing after attracting plenty of support. This may have come too quickly though and, although she may not be entirely straightforward she may be worth another chance in this grade. (op Evens, tchd 5-4 and 6-5 in places)
Sixpenny Moon(USA), tried in blinkers, was not totally disgraced in the face of a stiffish task from a low draw after taking plenty of stoking up returned to Polytrack but she does not look one to place maximum faith in. (op 25-1)
Michaelmas Daisy, who had claims at the weights, was nibbled at in the market in this lower grade but was again below her best. She has something to prove at present. (op 12-1)

6587 CALLUM LEE H'CAP 7f (P)
8:50 (8:51) (Class 6) (0-55,55) 3-Y-0+ **£2,047** (£604; £302) **Stalls** High

Form RPR
2004 1 **Annes Rocket (IRE)**[7] 6399 4-9-4 55 PatDobbs 10 67+
(J C Fox) *hld up in last trio: stl there wl over 1f out: gd prog after: scythed through rivals to ld ins fnl f: in command after* **15/2**
0053 2 1 **Vanadium**[12] 6256 7-9-4 55 (p) GeorgeBaker 7 61
(G L Moore) *t.k.h: stdd s: t.k.h: 7hld up bhd ldrs: effrt to ld jst over 1f out: hdd and outpcd ins fnl f: styd on* **13/2**[2]
3122 3 nk **Who's Winning (IRE)**[9] 6335 8-9-4 55 (t) KirstyMilczarek 8 60
(B G Powell) *plld hrd: bmpd after 1f: sn chsd ldr: carried lft over 2f out: stl chalng over 1f out: kpt on* **8/1**
5000 4 nk **My Flame**[45] 5287 4-9-4 55 RobertWinston 3 59
(J R Jenkins) *racd freely: led after 1f: hung bdly lft fr over 2f out: hdd jst over 1f out: nt qckn* **33/1**
300 5 1 **Madhal**[124] 2652 3-9-2 55 WilliamBuick 12 56
(Matthew Salaman) *plld hrd: sn restrained towards rr: prog on inner 2f out to chal over 1f out: one pce fnl f* **7/1**[3]
3035 6 nk **Pipers Piping (IRE)**[21] 5989 3-9-2 55 TPQueally 2 55
(J A Osborne) *prom on outer: carried lft over 2f out: nt qckn over 1f out: kpt on* **17/2**
0003 7 nse **Only A Game (IRE)**[9] 6339 4-9-4 55 (t) AdamKirby 1 56
(I W McInnes) *hld up in last trio: gd prog fr 2f out to chal on inner over 1f out: fdd ins fnl f* **20/1**
5005 8 nk **Dark Camellia**[12] 6255 4-9-3 54 (t) DaneO'Neill 11 54
(H J L Dunlop) *hld up in midfield: nt qckn 2f out: one pce after: no imp on ldrs* **9/1**

4063 9 3/4 **Shake On It**[14] 6213 5-8-13 **53** AndreaAtzeni(3) 9 51
(M R Hoad) *dwlt: t.k.h: hld up wl in rr on inner: effrt and sme prog 2f out: one pce and no imp jst over 1f out* 9/1

6302 10 nk **Miss Firefly**[12] 6251 4-9-0 **54** WilliamCarson(3) 4 51
(R J Hodges) *racd wd in midfield: nt qckn over 1f out: one pce after* 12/1

501 11 nk **Straight Face (IRE)**[14] 6213 5-9-4 **55** (b) DarryllHolland 14 51
(Miss Gay Kelleway) *t.k.h: led 1f: bmpd sn after: trckd ldrs after: hrd rdn 2f out: sn btn* 11/2[1]

000 12 1/2 **Prince De Fortune**[29] 5747 3-9-2 **55** TGMcLaughlin 6 49
(Mrs C A Dunnett) *s.i.s: hld up in last trio: effrt on outer over 2f out: no prog over 1f out: btn after* 66/1

0000 13 1/2 **H Harrison (IRE)**[9] 6339 9-8-11 **53** AndrewHeffernan(5) 5 47
(I W McInnes) *chsd ldr after 1f to over 2f out: sn lost pl and btn* 40/1

0 14 1 **Clearing House**[27] 5813 4-9-4 **55** SaleemGolam 13 46
(R W Price) *nvr beyond midfield: dropped to rr 2f out: sn struggling* 10/1

1m 27.01s (1.01) **Going Correction** -0.075s/f (Stan)
WFA 3 from 4yo+ 2lb 14 Ran SP% **123.0**
Speed ratings (Par 101): **91,89,89,89,88 87,87,87,86,86 85,85,84,83**
toteswingers: 1&2 £14.80, 1&3 £13.00, 2&3 £11.30 CSF £55.24 CT £412.30 TOTE £7.50: £1.80, £2.30, £3.10; EX 44.30.

Owner The Cross Keys Racing Club **Bred** S Coughlan **Trained** Collingbourne Ducis, Wilts

FOCUS
A low-grade handicap in which a 3lb range covered the whole field. An ordinary early gallop picked up around halfway and, although the field fanned across the course in the closing stages, the winner came down the centre. He is rated a bit better than the bare form.

Who's Winning(IRE) Official explanation: jockey said that the gelding was hampered at the start

My Flame Official explanation: jockey said the colt hung left

Only A Game(IRE) Official explanation: jockey said the gelding hung left turning into the home straight

Straight Face(IRE) Official explanation: jockey said that the gelding was hampered at the start

6588 KEMPTON.CO.UK H'CAP 1m (P)
9:20 (9:20) (Class 6) (0-60,60) 3-Y-O+ **£2,047** (£604; £302) **Stalls** High

Form RPR

0132 1 **Cadeaux Fax**[9] 6339 4-9-2 **60** JamesMillman(3) 12 72+
(B R Millman) *sn trckd ldrs: prog over 3f out: led wl over 2f out gng easily: drvn out to hold on fnl f* 9/1

0642 2 1 **French Art**[6] 6411 4-9-4 **59** JimCrowley 5 69
(N Tinkler) *hld up in rr: rdn and hanging over 2f out: no prog tl over 1f out: r.o to take 2nd ins fnl f: unable to chal* 15/8[1]

4355 3 1/2 **The Grey One (IRE)**[19] 6074 6-9-4 **59** (p) KevinGhunowa 11 68
(J M Bradley) *trckd ldrs: prog 3f out: drvn over 2f out: chsd wnr wl over 1f out tl ins fnl f: styd on* 14/1

201 4 2 1/4 **Blue Turk**[11] 6288 4-9-5 **60** PatCosgrave 4 64
(J R Boyle) *hld up towards rr: rdn over 2f out: sme prog over 1f out: kpt on fnl f: n.d* 9/2[2]

-056 5 1/2 **Indian Tonic (IRE)**[23] 5940 3-9-2 **60** HayleyTurner 8 63
(W Jarvis) *mostly in midfield: nt qckn over 2f out: kpt on fr over 1f out: nvr gng pce to threaten* 9/1

3630 6 shd **Mister Trickster (IRE)**[91] 3735 8-9-2 **57** TonyCulhane 10 59
(R Dickin) *slowest away: mostly in last pair: taken wdst of all st: rdn and kpt on fnl 2f: n.d* 14/1

0000 7 nk **Fine Ruler (IRE)**[6] 6437 5-9-4 **59** GeorgeBaker 1 61
(M R Bosley) *dropped in fr wd draw and hld up last: effrt on inner over 2f out: no imp jst over 1f out* 12/1

0030 8 1/2 **Hereford Boy**[60] 4791 5-9-5 **60** TPQueally 2 61
(D K Ivory) *hld up towards rr: prog on outer 3f out: drvn to try to cl on ldrs over 1f out: hanging and fnd nil: fdd* 16/1

0000 9 hd **Sign Of The Cross**[9] 6349 5-9-3 **58** LiamJones 6 58
(C R Dore) *t.k.h: hld up in midfield: prog to chse ldrs over 2f out and cl up: nt qckn over 1f out: wknd* 33/1

0064 10 6 **Divertimenti (IRE)**[29] 5750 5-9-5 **60** LPKeniry 7 46
(C R Dore) *led 1f: chsd ldr: clsd and upsides wl over 2f out: wknd rapidly wl over 1f out* 20/1

5-00 11 9 **Spinning Ridge (IRE)**[240] 478 4-9-2 **57** RobertWinston 9 23
(R A Harris) *hld up: hmpd and dropped in rr 1/2-way: effrt on inner whn hmpd over 2f out: no ch* 40/1

5053 12 1 3/4 **Sovereignty (JPN)**[13] 6224 7-9-5 **60** DaneO'Neill 13 22
(D K Ivory) *nt wl away but pushed up on inner to ld after 1f: sn clr: hdd & wknd rapidly wl over 2f out* 8/1[3]

0000 13 10 **Romantic Verse**[27] 5813 4-9-2 **57** JamesDoyle 3 —
(S Curran) *chsd ldrs tl wknd rapidly over 3f out: t.o* 50/1

1m 39.1s (-0.70) **Going Correction** -0.075s/f (Stan)
WFA 3 from 4yo+ 3lb 13 Ran SP% **123.1**
Speed ratings (Par 101): **100,99,98,96,95 95,95,94,94,88 79,77,67**
toteswingers: 1&2 £4.40, 1&3 £15.40, 2&3 £13.60 CSF £26.10 CT £258.84 TOTE £12.10: £3.30, £1.40, £3.40; EX 26.60 Place 6: £113.94 Place 5: £68.18.

Owner Mrs Mette Campbell-Andenaes **Bred** Mrs S Halliwell **Trained** Kentisbeare, Devon

■ Stewards' Enquiry : Kevin Ghunowa two-day ban: use of whip (Oct 21-22nd)

Robert Winston one-day ban: careless riding (Oct 21-22)

FOCUS
Another tight handicap (comprising mainly exposed horses rated 57-60) in which the gallop was soon sound. The first three, who finished clear, raced in the centre. The form could have been rated a little higher.

Sovereignty(JPN) Official explanation: jockey said gelding ran too freely

Romantic Verse Official explanation: jockey said filly had a breathing problem

T/Plt: £104.40 to a £1 stake. Pool: £70,357.95. 491.59 winning tickets. T/Qpdt: £24.00 to a £1 stake. Pool: £9,235.38. 284.30 winning tickets. JN

The Form Book, Raceform Ltd, Compton, RG20 6NL

6386 NOTTINGHAM (L-H)
Wednesday, October 7

OFFICIAL GOING: Good to soft changing to good to soft (soft in places) after race 2 (2.40)
Rail moved out 4.5m from 1m start to 4f marker adding circa 8yds to advertised distances on round course.
Wind: Virtually nil Weather: Overcast, sunny periods

6589 BOOK YOUR CHRISTMAS PARTY AT NOTTINGHAM RACECOURSE NURSERY (DIV I) 6f 15y
2:10 (2:11) (Class 6) (0-60,60) 2-Y-O **£1,706** (£503; £252) **Stalls** High

Form RPR

300 1 **Gypsy Jazz (IRE)**[19] 6069 2-9-6 **59** SJCraine 9 66+
(Jennie Candlish) *dwlt and towards rr stands' side: swtchd rt and hdwy over 2f out: rdn to chal and edgd lft over 1f out: led ent fnl f and kpt on strly* 33/1

010 2 2 1/4 **Dragonessa (IRE)**[9] 6343 2-9-4 **57** NeilChalmers 14 57
(B Palling) *b.nr hind: prom stands' side: hdwy to ld that gp and overall ldr over 2f out: rdn wl over 1f out: hdd ent fnl f and one pce: 2nd of 9 in gp* 14/1

6000 3 hd **Black Daddy**[23] 5938 2-9-2 **55** RichardHughes 15 54
(R Hannon) *trckd ldrs stands' side: hdwy 1/2-way: effrt over 2f out and sn rdn: drvn over 1f out: edgd lft and one pce ins fnl f: 3rd of 9 in gp* 4/1[1]

0000 4 2 1/4 **Email Exit (IRE)**[34] 5596 2-9-5 **58** AlanMunro 11 51
(C F Wall) *wnt lft s: in tch stands' side: hdwy 1/2-way: rdn along to chse ldrs 2f out: sn drvn and kpt on same pce appr fnl f: 4th of 9 in gp* 12/1

000 5 nk **Until The Man (IRE)**[14] 6199 2-9-7 **60** (p) KirstyMilczarek 17 52
(R Ingram) *in rr stands' side: hdwy 2f out: sn rdn and kpt on ins fnl f: nrst fin: 5th of 9 in gp* 10/1

345 6 1/2 **Blue Rum (IRE)**[143] 2100 2-9-1 **59** PatrickDonaghy(5) 16 49
(P C Haslam) *t.k.h: cl up stands' side: led that gp briefly 1/2-way: rdn and hung lft wl over 2f out: sn drvn and kpt on same pce* 22/1

4340 7 nk **Cygnet Committee (IRE)**[21] 5976 2-8-13 **52** (b) RichardKingscote 10 41
(J S Wainwright) *s.i.s and in rr stands' side: swtchd rt and rdn along over 2f out: drvn over 1f out: plugged on: nvr nr ldrs: 7th of 9 in gp* 50/1

6063 8 1 3/4 **Nabrina (IRE)**[23] 5950 2-8-8 **54** JohnCavanagh(7) 4 44+
(M Brittain) *prom far side: effrt over 2f out and ev ch: sn rdn and kpt on: no ch w stands' side: 1st of 8 in gp* 14/1

0040 9 1 **Thewinnatakesitall**[21] 5985 2-9-5 **58** KevinGhunowa 3 45+
(H J Evans) *swtg: sn led far side and overall ldr tl rdn along and hdd over 2f out: sn drvn and grad wknd: 2nd of 8 in gp* 33/1

060 10 hd **Althabea**[37] 5527 2-9-1 **54** StephenDonohoe 7 41+
(Ian Williams) *s.i.s and in rr far side: hdwy over 2f out: sn rdn and kpt on same pce: 3rd of 8 in gp* 50/1

5400 11 1/2 **Acting Elegant**[23] 5935 2-8-10 **49** CatherineGannon 12 28
(P D Evans) *chsd ldrs stands' side: rdn along 1/2-way: grad wknd: 8th of 9 in gp* 28/1

2466 12 nse **Daisy Brown**[21] 5976 2-9-2 **55** AndrewElliott 13 34
(N Tinkler) *prom stands' side: rdn along bef 1/2-way: sn lost pl and bhd: last of 9 in gp* 12/1

0150 13 nk **Kapelad Junior (IRE)**[22] 5967 2-9-7 **60** PaulEddery 2 44+
(Pat Eddery) *prom far side: rdn along wl over 2f out and grad wknd: 4th of 8 in gp* 12/1

6630 14 nse **Dixi Heights**[37] 5526 2-9-7 **60** PatCosgrave 6 44+
(J R Boyle) *bmpd s: a towards rr far side: 5th of 8 in gp* 11/1

6540 15 hd **The Shuffler**[57] 4868 2-9-4 **57** RyanMoore 5 40+
(G L Moore) *dwlt and towards rr far side: hdwy and in tch 1/2-way: rdn along over 2f out and sn wknd: 6th of 8 in gp* 7/1[3]

3426 16 3 1/2 **Drinking Buddy**[18] 6096 2-9-4 **57** PJMcDonald 8 30+
(D W Thompson) *chsd ldrs far side: rdn along wl over 2f out and sn wknd: 7th of 8 in gp* 16/1

040 17 7 **Bojangles Andrews**[39] 5431 2-8-8 **50** PatrickHills(3) 1 —+
(B G Powell) *a in rr far side: last of 8 in gp* 11/2[2]

1m 17.2s (2.30) **Going Correction** +0.30s/f (Good) 17 Ran SP% **125.2**
Speed ratings (Par 93): **96,93,92,89,89 88,88,85,84,84 83,83,83,83,82 78,68**
toteswingers: 1&2 £133.10, 1&3 £50.00, 2&3 £20.50 CSF £432.61 CT £2270.69 TOTE £44.50: £6.80, £4.20, £1.50, £3.60; EX 640.10.

Owner P and Mrs G A Clarke **Bred** David Barry **Trained** Basford Green, Staffs

FOCUS
The field predictably split into two fairly equal-sized groups, but those who raced on the stands' side dominated with the first seven home coming from that group.

NOTEBOOK
Gypsy Jazz(IRE) had been disappointing in two starts since showing some ability on her Carlisle debut, but returned to form on this easier ground. She was drawn right in the middle, which gave her rider the choice of which side to go, and crucially he made the right one. Dropped out early, she made her ground gradually and though she did hang about a bit when taking over in front a furlong out, found more than enough to score. She can probably build on this granted similar conditions. (op 40-1)
Dragonessa(IRE), well beaten on Polytrack since winning a Lingfield nursery on turf off 5lb lower, was always up with the pace on the nearside and this was much more like it. This trip on easy ground seems to bring out the best in her. (op 12-1 tchd 11-1)
Black Daddy, over this trip for the first time after two starts over 5f and two over 7f, ran his best race so far but on this evidence seems to need a return to further. (op 9-2 tchd 6-1)
Email Exit(IRE), making his nursery debut after showing little in four maidens, improved plenty on previous efforts and was doing all his best work late. (op 14-1)
Until The Man(IRE), back down to 6f for this nursery debut, had cheekpieces on for the first time and was another noted staying on in the latter stages. On this evidence a return to further looks needed. (tchd 12-1)
Blue Rum(IRE), not seen since showing some ability in two sellers and a claimer in the spring, took quite a hold at the front of the nearside group early and wasn't disgraced in the circumstances. He should come on for this, but will need to settle better. (op 28-1)
Nabrina(IRE) deserves credit for winning the race on the far side of the track. (op 16-1)
Thewinnatakesitall was another to run well on the far side.

6590 BOOK YOUR CHRISTMAS PARTY AT NOTTINGHAM RACECOURSE NURSERY (DIV II) 6f 15y
2:40 (2:43) (Class 6) (0-60,60) 2-Y-O **£1,706** (£503; £252) **Stalls** High

Form RPR

660 1 **North Shadow**[23] 5951 2-8-9 **53** DeanHeslop(5) 15 62+
(A D Brown) *mde all: shkn up and clr over 2f out: drvn out* 8/1[3]

4305 **2** 2 3/4 **Saint Sebastian (IRE)**[21] 5976 2-9-2 **55**........................(p) SebSanders 3 56
(E S McMahon) *racd towards far side: swtchd rt to r stands' side after 1f: chsd ldrs: wnt 2nd over 1f out: no imp* **10/1**

654 **3** 1 1/4 **Cane Cat (IRE)**[9] 6343 2-8-8 **54**.......................... DebraEngland(7) 2 51
(A W Carroll) *racd towards far side: lft alone in centre after 1f: chsd ldrs: wnt 3rd over 1f out: kpt on same pce* **14/1**

2364 **4** nk **Izuizorizuain't (IRE)**[18] 6099 2-9-5 **58**.......................... JamieSpencer 13 54
(K A Ryan) *chsd wnr: kpt on same pce appr fnl f* **9/2**[1]

4050 **5** 3/4 **Almuntaser (IRE)**[12] 6247 2-9-3 **56**........................(b[1]) StephenDonohoe 7 50+
(Ian Williams) *s.i.s: drvn and hdwy over 3f out: edgd rt over 1f out: kpt on same pce* **25/1**

0603 **6** 2 1/4 **Take My Hand**[9] 6343 2-9-7 **60**.......................... RyanMoore 6 47+
(M R Channon) *in rr: hdwy 2f out: kpt on: nt rch ldrs* **13/2**[2]

5050 **7** 3/4 **Bustard Bay (IRE)**[34] 5595 2-9-6 **59**.......................... TPQueally 12 44
(J G Given) *chsd ldrs: wknd over 1f out* **14/1**

0600 **8** 1/2 **Dispol Kabira**[1] 6554 2-8-11 **50**.......................... PJMcDonald 17 35+
(D W Thompson) *t.k.h in rr: hdwy and swtchd lft 2f out: nvr nr ldrs* **16/1**

034 **9** 2 **Bothwell Castle (IRE)**[113] 2996 2-9-2 **60**.......... PatrickDonaghy(5) 10 37+
(P C Haslam) *hld up in rr: sme hdwy 2f out: nvr a factor* **12/1**

004 **10** 1 1/2 **Slasi**[33] 5637 2-9-6 **59**.......................... NCallan 9 32
(C E Brittain) *trckd ldrs: t.k.h: hung rt: hmpd and lost pl over 1f out* **10/1**

430 **11** 1 1/2 **Peter's Follie**[30] 5714 2-9-4 **57**.......................... RichardKingscote 5 25
(Tom Dascombe) *chsd ldrs: drvn over 2f out: sn lost pl* **16/1**

600 **12** shd **Bazsharani**[24] 5899 2-9-0 **58**.......................... MartinLane(5) 8 26
(P D Evans) *prom: lost pl over 2f out* **20/1**

0002 **13** 1/2 **Kilmanseck**[8] 6364 2-9-6 **59**.......................... WilliamBuick 1 26
(Eve Johnson Houghton) *lw: racd towards far side: swtchd rt after 1f and racd towards stands' side: mid-div: lost pl and eased over 1f out* **17/2**

5040 **14** 1 3/4 **Flapjack**[11] 6292 2-9-1 **57**.......................... PatrickHills(3) 14 18
(R Hannon) *a in rr* **12/1**

0060 **15** 3 1/4 **Teeraha (IRE)**[16] 6169 2-8-10 **49**.......................... AlanMunro 11 —
(D Shaw) *chsd ldrs: lost pl 3f out: sn bhd* **50/1**

1m 16.47s (1.57) **Going Correction** +0.30s/f (Good) **15** Ran SP% **122.4**
Speed ratings (Par 93): **101,97,95,95,94 91,90,89,86,84 82,82,82,79,75**
toteswingers: 1&2 £15.50, 1&3 £33.70, 2&3 £20.20 CSF £84.80 CT £1141.74 TOTE £9.60: £3.50, £3.50, £5.60; EX 104.80.
Owner G Morrill **Bred** Cheveley Park Stud Ltd **Trained** Yedingham, N Yorks

FOCUS
With the evidence of the first race fresh in their minds, the jockeys all made for the stands' side, though one came alone down the middle. Remarkably few ever got into this race and the winning time was 0.73 seconds faster than the first division.

NOTEBOOK
North Shadow had been well held in three maidens and was dropping to this trip for the first time on this nursery debut, having been tried over 3f further last time, but he was well backed beforehand. Freely sweating, he soon bagged the stands' rail in front and, with his stamina assured on breeding, he basically ran his rivals into the ground. He can expect a hefty rise for this, but has plenty of scope and can probably go on to better things. Official explanation: trainer said, regarding the apparent improvement of form, that the gelding had taken time to mature, benefitted from a good draw and appreciated the drop in trip to 6f (op 12-1)
Saint Sebastian(IRE), placed a few times in modest company, can be given plenty of credit as he had to give away plenty of ground to take a handy position towards the nearside from his low draw, but never stopped trying. He can win a similar event on this performance, but is more exposed than most. (op 11-1 tchd 12-1)
Cane Cat(IRE) ran an even more remarkable race, as she was brought to race down the middle of the track in isolation from her low draw, but kept on going for longer than might have been expected. This was a good effort, but she is already exposed as modest. (tchd 16-1)
Izuizorizuain't(IRE), in the frame over 5f in her first two starts, was over 7f for her last two outings. She seemed to have every chance on the nearside, but she was quite weak in the market beforehand and she may prefer better ground. (op 7-2 tchd 5-1)
Almuntaser(IRE), disappointing since an encouraging debut, was down 7lb here and also seemed to have every chance. The first-time blinkers didn't appear to have too much of an effect.
Take My Hand, who ran her best race so far on her Polytrack/nursery debut at Wolverhampton last time, tried to come from well back and though she never got into the race, still did best of those held up. (op 6-1 tchd 8-1)
Kilmanseck, 13lb well in compared to his new mark after showing huge improvement to finish runner-up at 66-1 in a 7f Warwick maiden eight days earlier, was disappointing and his number one stall can't really be used as an excuse with the pair drawn right next to him both making the frame. Official explanation: jockey said gelding was unsuited by the going (op 9-1 tchd 10-1)
Joan's Legacy Official explanation: jockey said that the filly hung right

6591 EUROPEAN BREEDERS' FUND MAIDEN STKS 6f 15y
3:10 (3:10) (Class 4) 2-Y-O **£5,180** (£1,541; £770; £384) **Stalls** High

Form RPR

00 **1** **No Explaining (IRE)**[40] 5397 2-8-12 0.......................... TPQueally 12 76
(B J Curley) *a.p: cl up 1/2-way: led jst over 2f out: rdn appr fnl f and kpt on wl* **25/1**

2 2 1/4 **Skyrider (IRE)** 2-8-12 0.......................... JimmyFortune 10 75+
(R Charlton) *unf: scope: trckd ldrs: pushed along 1/2-way: rdn: grren and edgd lft wl over 1f out: styd on strly ins fnl f: tk 2nd towards fin* **16/1**

0 **3** 1 **Olney Lass**[16] 6163 2-8-7 0.......................... PaulPickard(5) 13 66
(W J H Ratcliffe) *cl up: rdn to ld briefly over 2f out: sn hdd and drvn wl over 1f out: kpt on same pce ins fnl f* **33/1**

4 1/2 **High Comedy** 2-9-3 0.......................... LDettori 2 70+
(Saeed Bin Suroor) *w'like: scope: wnt lft s and towards rr: hdwy on outer 1/2-way: rdn along to chse ldrs over 2f out: kpt on same pce appr fnl f* **8/1**

5 3/4 **Deacon Blues** 2-9-3 0.......................... GeorgeBaker 6 68+
(J R Fanshawe) *str: towards rr: hdwy wl over 2f out: rdn to chse ldrs over 1f out: kpt on same pce* **25/1**

6 shd **Picnic Party** 2-8-12 0.......................... RyanMoore 4 62+
(J Noseda) *w'like: leggy: chsd ldrs: hdwy over 2f out: sn rdn and one pce appr fnl f* **9/2**[3]

7 4 **Frequency** 2-9-3 0.......................... JamieSpencer 7 55+
(E A L Dunlop) *w'like: bit bkwd: s.i.s and swtchd rt s: bhd: hdwy 1/2-way: n.m.r andswtchd lft over 2f out: sn rdn and no imp* **25/1**

5 **8** 3 **Ostentation**[15] 6181 2-9-3 0.......................... JoeFanning 1 46
(M Johnston) *unf: sltly hmpd s and towards rr: hdwy and in tch on outer 1/2-way: sn rdn along and grad wknd* **12/1**

32 **9** shd **Merchant Of Medici**[23] 5934 2-9-3 0.......................... MartinDwyer 14 46
(W R Muir) *lw: trckd ldrs towards stands' rail: pushed along 1/2-way: rdn over 2f out and sn btn* **2/1**[1]

0000 **10** 1 1/2 **Gessabelle**[8] 6355 2-8-5 46.......................... CarolineKelly(7) 16 36
(P S McEntee) *led: rdn along and hdd over 2f out: sn wknd* **100/1**

6 **11** 3/4 **Midwestern (USA)**[19] 6054 2-9-3 0.......................... HayleyTurner 9 39
(M L W Bell) *b: in tch: rdn along wl over 2f out and sn wknd* **4/1**[2]

60 **12** 1 3/4 **Lord Victor**[18] 6125 2-9-3 0..........................(b[1]) SebSanders 17 34
(A J McCabe) *plld hrd: chsd ldrs on stands' rail: rdn along 1/2-way and sn wknd* **28/1**

0 **13** 1/2 **Bullet Duck (IRE)**[12] 6245 2-8-7 0.......................... RossAtkinson(5) 5 27
(Tom Dascombe) *a towards rr* **100/1**

0 **14** hd **Gee Major**[96] 3571 2-9-3 0.......................... RichardKingscote 15 32
(Tom Dascombe) *w'like: cl up: rdn along 1/2-way: sn wknd* **40/1**

15 5 **Pink Please (IRE)** 2-8-12 0.......................... RichardSmith 3 12
(Tom Dascombe) *leggy: dwlt: a in rr* **100/1**

1m 16.5s (1.60) **Going Correction** +0.30s/f (Good) **15** Ran SP% **119.5**
Speed ratings (Par 97): **101,98,96,96,95 94,89,85,85,83 82,80,79,79,72**
toteswingers: 1&2 £31.60, 1&3 £108.10, 2&3 £61.10 CSF £351.61 TOTE £60.90: £14.30, £4.40, £15.00; EX 444.30.
Owner P Byrne **Bred** P Byrne, Eimear Mulhern & B Grassick **Trained** Newmarket, Suffolk

FOCUS
The ground was changed to good to soft, soft in places before this race. Again they all wanted to come over to the stands' side. There were a few interesting types in this maiden, but the winning time was fractionally slower than the second division of the nursery, which suggests the form is nothing special.

NOTEBOOK
No Explaining(IRE) had been well beaten on her first two starts, but had run well for a long way behind the subsequent May Hill winner Pollenator over 7f at Newmarket last time and this drop back in trip and slower ground brought about a much better effort. The market didn't really suggest that she was fancied here and the form may not add up to much, but she obviously possesses plenty of ability. (op 20-1)
Skyrider(IRE) ran a debut full of promise, staying on very nicely from the middle of the field late on. An 85,000euros 2-y-o and half-brother to the 1m winner Flying Silks, she can be expected to come on for this. (op 12-1 tchd 11-1)
Olney Lass, last of 14 when 66-1 for her Kempton Polytrack debut, improved a ton from that having been prominent from the start. She is related to several winners on the dam's side and on this evidence looks likely to carry on the family tradition. (tchd 40-1)
High Comedy, out of a winning juvenile sprinter, was weak in the market and wasn't well drawn as things turned out, but he made some fair late progress and should have benefited from this. (op 5-1)
Deacon Blues, out of a winning sister to the smart Heretic, was right out the back early but was noted staying on late without being by any means knocked about. He is one to keep a close eye on. (op 33-1)
Picnic Party, first foal of the very useful Antediluvian, ran well for a very long way on this debut before lack of a previous run took its toll. She can do better. (op 5-1 tchd 4-1)
Frequency, a 13,000gns half-brother to the winning sprinter Sloop Johnb, never got into the race but he had to be switched around weakening rivals and was not given a hard time. There is much better to come from him. (op 20-1)
Merchant Of Medici, absent for four months after finishing lame on debut when narrowly beaten by a 66-1 shot at Leicester last month, didn't look happy at any stage here and has questions to answer now. (op 9-4 tchd 5-2)

6592 BUY A RACING POST YEARLING BONUS CANDIDATE MAIDEN STKS (DIV I) 1m 75y
3:40 (3:40) (Class 5) 2-Y-O **£2,914** (£867; £433; £216) **Stalls** Low

Form RPR

1 **Anhar (USA)** 2-9-3 0.......................... LDettori 11 79+
(Saeed Bin Suroor) *w'like: scope: str: s.i.s: effrt on outer and hung lft over 3f out: styd on to ld over 1f out: hld on towards fin* **4/1**[3]

2 1/2 **Desert Sage** 2-8-12 0.......................... JimCrowley 1 73+
(R M Beckett) *gd sort: rangy: lw: s.s: green in last: swtchd rt and gd hdwy on outer over 2f out: chal ins fnl f: styd on towards fin: will improve* **22/1**

06 **3** 1 1/4 **Mawaddah (IRE)**[21] 5993 2-9-3 0.......................... RichardHughes 7 75
(R Hannon) *mid-div: hdwy over 2f out: styd on to chal 1f out: kpt on same pce* **33/1**

3 **4** 1 1/2 **Colonel Carter (IRE)**[18] 6109 2-9-3 0.......................... MartinDwyer 8 72+
(B J Meehan) *lw: rn in snatches: chsd ldrs: drvn over 4f out: one pce fnl 2f* **11/8**[1]

5 2 1/4 **Shernando** 2-9-3 0.......................... JoeFanning 6 67+
(M Johnston) *w'like: bit bkwd: w ldrs: led after 1f: hdd after 2f: led over 2f out: sn hdd: edgd rt and wknd appr fnl f* **20/1**

0 **6** 5 **Varachi**[19] 6066 2-9-3 0.......................... TGMcLaughlin 12 56
(E A L Dunlop) *mid-div: drvn over 3f out: kpt on fnl f: nvr nr ldrs* **66/1**

02 **7** 1 3/4 **Krymian**[18] 6125 2-9-3 0.......................... RyanMoore 9 53
(Sir Michael Stoute) *led 1f: w ldrs: led 2f out: sn hdd & wknd* **3/1**[2]

06 **8** hd **King's Realm (IRE)**[11] 6285 2-9-3 0.......................... SebSanders 10 52
(Sir Mark Prescott) *sn drvn in rr: nvr on terms* **66/1**

9 1 **Calm And Serene (USA)** 2-8-12 0.......................... NCallan 5 45
(Rae Guest) *w'like: mid-div: effrt over 3f out: lost pl over 2f out* **14/1**

00 **10** 3 3/4 **Eltheeb**[22] 5966 2-9-3 0.......................... RHills 4 46+
(J L Dunlop) *w ldrs: led after 2f: hdd over 2f out: wkng whn hmpd over 1f out* **25/1**

0 **11** 7 **Hannah Greeley (USA)**[27] 5807 2-8-12 0.......................... PatCosgrave 2 22
(J R Boyle) *leggy: chsd ldrs: drvn over 3f out: wknd 2f out* **100/1**

12 2 1/4 **Dubawi King** 2-9-3 0.......................... AndrewElliott 3 22+
(N Tinkler) *str: bit bkwd: s.i.s: sme hdwy over 3f out: sn wknd* **100/1**

1m 51.38s (5.78) **Going Correction** +0.75s/f (Yiel) **12** Ran SP% **114.6**
Speed ratings (Par 95): **101,100,99,97,95 90,88,88,87,83 76,74**
toteswingers: 1&2 £12.00, 1&3 £13.20, 2&3 £17.90 CSF £87.72 TOTE £6.70: £1.60, £2.50, £7.40; EX 55.10 TRIFECTA Not won..
Owner Godolphin **Bred** Daylesford Stud **Trained** Newmarket, Suffolk

FOCUS
An interesting maiden run at a generous pace and several of these are likely to improve a good deal from two to three.

NOTEBOOK
Anhar(USA) ◆ managed to make a winning debut and can be given plenty of credit for the way he went about it. By no means best away, he was soon ridden into a handy position and was sent to the front inside the last 2f. He looked like finishing third when headed briefly a furlong from home, but pulled out a bit more under pressure to record a very game victory. A $950,000 colt out of a sister to Yesterday and Quarter Moon, he looks a very nice prospect for decent middle-distance contests next year. (op 100-30 tchd 9-2)
Desert Sage ◆, related to several winners over middle-distances on the dam's side, was a major eyecatcher on this debut. Slowest from the stalls, she looked green out the back early but got stronger as the race progressed and looked like coming to beat them all down the outside coming to the last furlong, but the Godolphin colt found a bit more and just held her off. She will get further and is a filly to keep in mind for next season. (op 33-1 tchd 20-1)
Mawaddah(IRE), well beaten in his first two starts, took a big step forward here and having been pulled out for his effort, looked a big danger when possibly hitting the front for a few strides passing the furlong pole, but his effort then flattened out. He will win races and nurseries now also become an option for him. (tchd 28-1)

The Form Book, Raceform Ltd, Compton, RG20 6NL

Colonel Carter(IRE), a very promising third over 7f on his Newbury debut, was inclined to race in snatches behind the leaders and though he was close enough against the inside rail passing the 2f pole, could never really land a telling blow. Perhaps the easier ground wasn't for him and he is worth another chance. (op 15-8 tchd 2-1 in places)

Shernando, a 22,000gns half-brother to six winners including the smart Starlit Sands, was always up there and hit the front 3f from home, but he lost the advantage soon afterwards and he then had little left to offer. There should be improvement in him. (op 16-1)

Krymian, just caught after looking sure to win over a similar trip on the Wolverhampton Polytrack last time, raced handily and hit the front briefly over 2f from home but then weakened noticeably.
Official explanation: jockey said the colt had no more to give (op 100-30 tchd 7-2)

6593 BUY A RACING POST YEARLING BONUS CANDIDATE MAIDEN STKS (DIV II) 1m 75y

4:10 (4:11) (Class 5) 2-Y-O **£2,914** (£867; £433; £216) **Stalls** Low

Form RPR

1 **Ceilidh House** 2-8-12 0 ..... SebSanders 6 80+
(R M Beckett) *lengthy: scope: lw: s.i.s and sn pushed along: hdwy on outer 1/2-way: effrt on outer to ld over 2f out: qcknd clr appr fnl f: impressive* **11/4²**

0 2 4 **Life And Soul (IRE)**[14] 6199 2-9-3 0 ..... JimCrowley 5 75
(Mrs A J Perrett) *trckd ldr: hdwy to chal 3f out: sn rdn and ev ch: drvn over 1f out: kpt on: no ch w wnr* **6/1**

3 2 ¼ **Retrato (USA)** 2-8-12 0 ..... NCallan 1 65
(Rae Guest) *leggy: hld up in tch: hdwy whn hmpd over 3f out: rdn over 2f out: styd on ent fnl f: nrst fin* **22/1**

0 4 1 ¼ **Liberty Square (USA)**[21] 6000 2-9-3 0 ..... LDettori 4 67
(Saeed Bin Suroor) *w'like: trckd ldr on inner: swtchd rt and effrt over 3f out: rdn along over 2f out: drvn wl over 1f out and sn wknd* **5/1³**

026 5 4 ½ **Comradeship (IRE)**[24] 5907 2-9-3 78 ..... JimmyFortune 8 57+
(J H M Gosden) *lw: led: rdn along 3f out: hdd over 2f out: sn drvn and wknd wl over 1f out* **9/4¹**

00 6 nk **All Moving Parts (USA)**[20] 6009 2-9-3 0 ..... AlanMunro 12 57
(J S Wainwright) *lengthy: unf: chsd ldrs: rdn along 3f out: drvn and edgd lft over 2f out: sn wknd* **40/1**

0 7 ½ **Cordiality**[11] 6291 2-9-3 0 ..... GeorgeBaker 2 56+
(J R Fanshawe) *w'like: in tch: effrt 3f out and sn rdn along: drvn over 2f out and n.d* **16/1**

0 8 3 ¼ **Kahfre**[19] 6066 2-9-3 0 ..... TGMcLaughlin 7 49+
(E A L Dunlop) *a towards rr* **22/1**

0 9 2 ½ **Persian Poet**[27] 5787 2-9-3 0 ..... JoeFanning 9 43+
(M Johnston) *w'like: midfield: rdn along over 3f out and sn wknd* **14/1**

6 10 3 **Henry Havelock**[15] 6181 2-9-3 0 ..... TonyHamilton 11 37
(C Grant) *w'like: tall: dwlt: a in rr* **100/1**

00 11 37 **Securitisation (IRE)**[76] 4243 2-9-3 0 ..... TPQueally 10 —
(B J Curley) *dwlt: a bhd* **28/1**

1m 52.57s (6.97) **Going Correction** +0.75s/f (Yiel) 11 Ran SP% **116.5**
Speed ratings (Par 95): **95,91,88,87,83 82,82,78,76,73 36**
toteswingers: 1&2 £5.30, 1&3 £14.00, 2&3 £24.50 CSF £18.24 TOTE £3.80: £1.50, £1.90, £8.10; EX 26.50.
Owner J H Richmond-Watson **Bred** Lawn Stud **Trained** Whitsbury, Hants

FOCUS
The second division of this maiden didn't look as strong as the first and it was a four-horse race according to the market. The winning time was also 1.19 seconds slower then division one, but the winner was visually more impressive.

NOTEBOOK
Ceilidh House ◆, representing the same owner/trainer combination as Desert Sage in the first division, made a remarkable winning debut and was backed to do so. She walked out of the stalls, looked clueless out the back early, and was then forced to race wide in order to make up ground. However, she produced a very impressive turn of speed down the wide outside to hit the front over 2f from home and maintained her momentum to forge clear and eventually win hard-held. The winning time casts some doubt over the true value of the form, but she should be given the benefit of the doubt and looks a high-class prospect for next season. (op 4-1)

Life And Soul(IRE), who showed a little ability though eventually well beaten on his Goodwood debut, lasted much longer this time and had every chance passing the 2f pole, but was firmly put in his place by a very classy filly. He is likely to improve again and shouldn't take long in going one better. (tchd 11-2 and 13-2)

Retrato(USA), a half-sister to a couple of winners in the US and the only other debutante apart from the winner, stayed on well from the middle of the field under pressure in the latter stages and is sure to come on from this. (op 25-1 tchd 20-1)

Liberty Square(USA), seventh of eight on debut in a Yarmouth maiden that has produced a couple of winners, ran without his declared tongue-tie. Weak in the market beforehand, he ran well for a long way and should be up to winning an ordinary maiden, but doesn't look one of the stable's stars. (op 3-1)

Comradeship(IRE), a good second at Chepstow two starts back, may have found the ground too quick when disappointing at Ffos Las last time. He made much of the running on this easier surface, but had nothing left when headed 2f from home and he may be worth a try in a nursery. (op 5-2 tchd 3-1)

All Moving Parts(USA), who was well held though staying on at the end in his first two starts over 6f, saw plenty of daylight on the outside over this longer trip, but again wasn't disgraced and may have more to offer now that he now qualifies for a nursery mark. (op 66-1)

6594 EVENT GUARD STAFF H'CAP 1m 2f 50y

4:40 (4:41) (Class 4) (0-85,85) 3-Y-O+ **£6,476** (£1,927; £963; £481) **Stalls** Low

Form RPR

044 1 **Ellmau**[124] 2666 4-9-5 **82** ..... RichardMullen 9 90
(E S McMahon) *sn trcking ldrs: t.k.h: effrt over 2f out: styd on u.p fnl f: led post* **8/1³**

0030 2 hd **Watergate (IRE)**[21] 5986 3-8-12 **80** ..... SebSanders 2 88
(Sir Mark Prescott) *trckd ldrs: drvn 3f out: led 1f out: hdd fnl strides* **12/1**

5204 3 ½ **Dark Prospect**[26] 5828 4-9-7 **84** ..... (b¹) NCallan 12 91
(M A Jarvis) *led 1f: racd wd: t.k.h: led over 3f out: edgd rt and hdd 1f out: no ex* **12/1**

-450 4 1 ¼ **Penchesco (IRE)**[6] 6435 4-8-4 **70** ..... AndreaAtzeni(3) 4 75
(Pat Eddery) *trckd ldrs: t.k.h: drvn over 4f out: outpcd over 2f out: styd on fnl f* **14/1**

2103 5 ¾ **Wing Play (IRE)**[19] 6059 4-9-5 **82** ..... (p) GeorgeBaker 11 85+
(H Morrison) *hld up in rr: hdwy over 2f out: hung lft and one pce fnl f* **9/1**

1252 6 4 ½ **Lady Artemisia (IRE)**[26] 5828 3-9-3 **85** ..... JamieSpencer 1 80
(M L W Bell) *s.i.s: sn mid-div: effrt over 3f out: nvr nr ldrs* **2/1¹**

6641 7 1 ¼ **Special Reserve (IRE)**[44] 5321 4-9-7 **84** ..... RichardHughes 10 76+
(R Hannon) *lw: stdd s: hld up in rr: hdwy over 3f out: nvr nr ldrs* **9/1**

1301 8 5 **Agilete**[21] 6002 7-9-1 **83** ..... SimonPearce(5) 8 66
(J Pearce) *mid-div: effrt over 3f out: wknd over 1f out* **22/1**

100 9 2 ¼ **Dome Rocket**[14] 6209 3-8-11 **79** ..... (p) ShaneKelly 6 58
(W J Knight) *led after 1f: hdd over 3f out: wknd over 1f out* **20/1**

200 10 ¾ **Satwa Gold (USA)**[33] 5648 3-8-12 **80** ..... RyanMoore 5 57
(E A L Dunlop) *mid-div: drvn 4f out: sn btn* **25/1**

-000 11 4 ½ **Unshakable (IRE)**[46] 5262 10-9-4 **81** ..... PaulEddery 7 50
(Bob Jones) *hld up in rr: lost pl over 3f out: sn bhd* **22/1**

4555 12 1 ¾ **Muraweg (IRE)**[14] 6203 3-9-0 **82** ..... (b) RHills 15 47
(J H M Gosden) *trckd ldrs: hung lft and lost pl over 2f out* **7/1²**

2m 17.73s (6.03) **Going Correction** +0.75s/f (Yiel)
WFA 3 from 4yo+ 5lb 12 Ran SP% **116.3**
Speed ratings (Par 105): **105,104,104,103,102 99,98,94,92,91 88,86**
toteswingers: 1&2 £17.70, 1&3 £14.30, 2&3 £24.40 CSF £91.91 CT £1147.32 TOTE £10.30: £2.70, £4.20, £4.40; EX 191.50.
Owner Premspace Ltd **Bred** Lady Hardy **Trained** Lichfield, Staffs
■ Stewards' Enquiry : Seb Sanders one-day ban: used whip with excessive frequency (Oct 21)

FOCUS
A fair, competitive handicap, but the pace was steady early on, resulting in a few of these racing keenly and it proved difficult to make up ground. They raced up the middle of the track in the straight.
Satwa Gold(USA) Official explanation: jockey said thecolt was unsuited by the going

6595 EVENT GUARD SECURITY RATING RELATED MAIDEN STKS 1m 2f 50y

5:10 (5:11) (Class 5) 3-Y-O+ **£2,590** (£770; £385; £192) **Stalls** Low

Form RPR

1 **Gunslinger (FR)**[336] 4-9-5 78 ..... PatCosgrave 9 81
(M J Scudamore) *w'like: hld up towards rr: hdwy wl over 2f out: n.m.r 2f out and sn rdn: drvn to chal ent fnl f: styd on wl to ld nr fin* **16/1**

2625 2 nse **Cotillion**[65] 4599 3-9-0 77 ..... JamieSpencer 7 81
(W J Haggas) *lw: dwlt: sn in midfield: hdwy on outer 4f out: effrt wl over 2f out: rdn to chal over 1f out: drvn ins fnl f and ev ch tl no ex nr line* **9/4¹**

3435 3 shd **Bruton Street (USA)**[75] 4270 3-9-0 76 ..... JimmyFortune 8 81
(J H M Gosden) *trckd ldng pair: hdwy over 3f out: chal over 2f out: rdn to ld wl over 1f out: drvn ins fnl f: hdd and no ex nr line* **8/1**

26 4 4 ½ **Lilly Royal (IRE)**[48] 5181 3-8-11 65 ..... NeilChalmers 2 69
(B Palling) *bhd: pushed along 1/2-way: hdwy on outer 3f out: rdn along 2f out: styd on ins fnl f: nrst fin* **40/1**

3-33 5 ¾ **Meyyal (USA)**[11] 6287 3-9-0 77 ..... RHills 10 71
(B W Hills) *lw: chsd ldr: hdwy to ld 3f out: sn jnd and rdn: drvn and hdd wl over 1f out: grad wknd* **6/1³**

622 6 2 ¼ **Duke Of Burgundy (FR)**[30] 5731 6-9-5 74 ..... SJCraine 1 66
(Jennie Candlish) *lw: hld up in rr: stdy hdwy on inner over 3f out: rdn to chse ldrs 2f out: sn drvn and btn over 1f out* **9/2²**

404 7 6 **Charger**[29] 5744 3-9-0 75 ..... LDettori 3 55
(J Noseda) *midfield: hdwy to trck ldrs on inner 1/2-way: rdn along 3f out: wknd over 2f out* **9/2²**

3236 8 1 **Merdaam**[73] 4354 3-9-0 78 ..... TPO'Shea 4 53
(J L Dunlop) *chsd ldrs: rdn along over 3f out and sn wknd* **16/1**

-563 9 ¾ **Custody (IRE)**[13] 6225 3-9-0 70 ..... RyanMoore 11 52
(Sir Michael Stoute) *led: rdn along and hdd 3f out: sn wknd* **9/1**

10 14 **Apurna**[716] 6395 4-8-11 60 ..... MarkCoumbe(5) 5 22
(John A Harris) *a towards rr: rdn along 1/2-way and sn bhd* **100/1**

2m 17.81s (6.11) **Going Correction** +0.75s/f (Yiel)
WFA 3 from 4yo+ 5lb 10 Ran SP% **117.7**
Speed ratings (Par 103): **105,104,104,101,100 98,94,93,92,81**
toteswingers: 1&2 £9.70, 1&3 £12.40, 2&3 £5.70 CSF £52.69 TOTE £20.70: £4.30, £1.40, £2.10; EX 80.70.
Owner S Smith, K Hunter, P Duffen **Bred** Dayton Investments Ltd **Trained** Bromsash, Herefordshire
■ Stewards' Enquiry : Jamie Spencer one-day ban: used whip with excessive frequency (Oct 21)

FOCUS
A modest rating related maiden and several of these have had plenty of chances. It was a competitive race, though, with seven of the ten runners covered by just 4lb. The field were kept well away from the inside rail throughout and it produced a thrilling finish with nothing separating the front three at the line.
Charger Official explanation: jockey said that the gelding was unsuited by the going

6596 BOOK YOUR 2010 HOSPITALITY AT NOTTINGHAM RACECOURSE APPRENTICE H'CAP 6f 15y

5:40 (5:40) (Class 5) (0-70,71) 3-Y-O+ **£2,590** (£770; £385; £192) **Stalls** High

Form RPR

4101 1 **Simple Rhythm**[9] 6341 3-9-1 **71** 6ex ..... RyanPowell(5) 11 87+
(J Ryan) *cl up: led wl over 2f out and sn clr: edgd lft ent fnl f: eased towards fin* **14/1**

0060 2 1 ¾ **Eastern Hills**[20] 6015 4-9-3 **67** ..... (v¹) LanceBetts 3 72
(J S Wainwright) *in tch: hdwy over 2f out: rdn to chse wnr over 1f out: styd on ins fnl f* **12/1**

0320 3 1 **Micky Mac (IRE)**[34] 5601 5-8-7 **57** ..... PatrickDonaghy 8 59
(C J Teague) *in tch: hdwy 2f out: swtchd lft and rdn wl over 1f out: kpt on ins fnl f: nrst fin* **20/1**

0235 4 3 ¼ **The History Man (IRE)**[12] 6251 6-8-1 **56** ..... (b) RachelKing(5) 6 48
(B D Leavy) *led: rdn along 1/2-way: hdd wl over 2f out and sn drvn: grad wknd* **14/1**

041 5 ¾ **Castano**[12] 6251 5-8-6 **56** ..... RossAtkinson 13 45+
(B R Millman) *towards rr: rdn along and hdwy wl over 1f out: kpt on ins fnl f: nvr rchd ldrs* **9/2¹**

4122 6 hd **Ghost Dancer**[8] 6362 5-9-4 **68** ..... (p) MartinLane 1 57
(J M Bradley) *chsd ldrs: rdn over 2f out: drvn and hung bdly rt over 1f out: n.d* **7/1²**

0160 7 nk **Downhill Skier (IRE)**[42] 5332 5-9-1 **65** ..... AmyRyan 9 53
(W M Brisbourne) *sltly hmpd s and towards rr: hdwy 1/2-way: rdn wl over 1f out and sn no imp* **12/1**

0000 8 shd **Alan Devonshire**[20] 6024 4-9-5 **69** ..... AshleyMorgan 16 56
(M H Tompkins) *midfield: rdn along 1/2-way: sme hdwy wl over 1f out: n.d* **16/1**

4000 9 nk **Grey Boy (GER)**[53] 5031 8-8-6 **63** ..... GeorgeDowning(7) 5 49
(A W Carroll) *s.i.s and bhd tl sme late hdwy* **33/1**

0040 10 6 **Flashy Photon**[39] 5429 4-8-3 **56** ..... AmyScott(3) 15 23
(H Candy) *s.i.s and bhd: swtchd lft and rdn 1/2-way: nvr a factor* **8/1³**

-000 11 1 **Sawpit Sunshine (IRE)**[117] 2880 4-8-4 **57** ..... (b) AndrewHeffernan(3) 4 21
(J L Spearing) *midfield: rdn along 1/2-way: nvr a factor* **40/1**

2060 12 5 **Forward Feline (IRE)**[117] 2879 3-8-13 **67** ..... DeclanCannon(3) 17 15
(B Palling) *in tch: rdn along over 2f out and sn wknd* **12/1**

0000 13 ¾ **Chartist**[111] 3065 4-9-6 **70** ..... PaulPickard 7 16
(B P J Baugh) *cl up: rdn along 1/2-way: sn wknd* **25/1**

5530 14 4 **Ice Planet**[63] 4654 8-8-9 **59** ..... DeanHeslop 14 —
(Mrs R A Carr) *a bhd* **10/1**

001 15 ½ **Whiteoak Lady (IRE)**[40] 5406 4-9-6 **70**......................(b) RichardEvans 10 1
(J L Spearing) *in tch: rdn along 1/2-way and sn wknd* **7/1**[2]
1m 16.13s (1.23) **Going Correction** +0.30s/f (Good)
WFA 3 from 4yo+ 1lb **15** Ran SP% **119.7**
Speed ratings (Par 103): **103,100,99,95,94 93,93,93,92,84 83,76,75,70,69**
toteswingers: 1&2 £31.90, 1&3 £19.60, 2&3 £46.90 CSF £163.42 CT £3413.01 TOTE £13.40: £2.90, £4.40, £6.30; EX 286.50 Place 6: £16571.41 Place 5: £5079.04.
Owner J Ryan **Bred** P Quinlan **Trained** Newmarket, Suffolk

FOCUS
A big field, but a modest sprint handicap. They raced centre-to-stands' side this time, but those who came down the middle very much held the advantage and very few ever got into it.
Whiteoak Lady(IRE) Official explanation: jockey said tha the filly was never travelling
T/Jkpt: Not won. T/Plt: £49,067.30 to a £1 stake. Pool: £67,215.58. 0.45 winning tickets. T/Qpdt: £979.30 to a £1 stake. Pool: £4,631.88. 3.50 winning tickets. JR

6597 - 6604a (Foreign Racing) - See Raceform Interactive

1268 HANOVER (L-H)
Sunday, October 4

OFFICIAL GOING: Good

6605a GROSSER PREIS DES HANNOVER AIRPORT (LISTED RACE) (F&M) 7f
4:00 (4:03) 3-Y-0+ **£11,650** (£4,272; £2,330; £1,165)

			RPR
1		**Bella Platina (GER)**[30] 5651 5-9-5 .... FilipMinarik 8 (U Stoltefuss, Germany) **47/10**[3]	97
2	2	**Mambo Light (USA)**[21] 3-9-1 .... EPedroza 9 (A Wohler, Germany) **21/10**[2]	90
3	1 ½	**Margie's World (GER)**[21] 5-8-13 .... ABest 5 (S Wegner, Germany) **23/1**	82
4	1	**Say No Now (IRE)**[24] 5798 3-9-3 .... ChrisCatlin 11 (D R Lanigan) *drawn on outside: sn led: c towards stands' side in st: hdd appr fnl f: wknd last 100yds* **11/10**[1]	85
5	4	**Addicted (GER)**[95] 3520 3-9-3 .... EFrank 7 (T Mundry, Germany) **56/10**	74
6	6	**Irika (GER)** 4-9-3 .... WPanov 2 (H J Groschel, Germany) **175/10**	56
7	½	**Abbielou**[808] 6-9-1 .... MariaPapke 4 (H I Larsen, Sweden) **26/1**	53
8	13	**Lacy Sunday (USA)**[371] 3-8-10 .... GMasure 3 (A Trybuhl, Germany) **226/10**	15
9	2	**Zarah Top (GER)**[65] 3-8-10 .... JiriPalik 1 (Dr A Bolte, Germany) **30/1**	9
10	3	**Namastee (GER)** 3-8-10 .... MissSReichert 6 (F Kurz, Germany) **84/1**	1

1m 27.36s (87.36)
WFA 3 from 4yo+ 2lb **10** Ran SP% **134.5**
TOTE: WIN 57; PL 21, 14, 34; DF 226.
Owner Galoppgemeinschaft Bad Harzburg **Bred** Galoppgemeinschaft Bad Harzburg **Trained** In Germany

NOTEBOOK
Say No Now(IRE), her trainer's first runner in Germany, once again adopted front-running tactics, but she might have done a bit too much too soon.

LE MANS (R-H)
Sunday, October 4

OFFICIAL GOING: Firm

6606a PRIX D'AUTOMNE (MAIDEN) 7f
2:00 (2:00) 3-Y-0 **£4,854** (£1,942; £1,408; £971; £485)

			RPR
1		**Smart Diplomacy (USA)**[164] 3-8-10 .... SMoulin(6) (A De Royer-Dupre, France) *437/10*	85
2	1 ½	**Dame Anouska (IRE)**[25] 5783 3-8-13 .... JAuge (E J O'Neill) *led, clear well over 1f out, caught inside final f, one pace* **44/1**[1]	78
3	3	**Olga D'Or (USA)**[77] 4130 3-8-13 .... WVion (R Gibson, France)	70
4	nse	**Beguiler**[60] 3-8-13 .... (H-A Pantall, France)	70
5	shd	**Collimateur (FR)** 3-9-2 .... ABourgeais (A Lamotte D'Argy, France)	73
6	1	**Order Me (USA)**[358] 3-8-13 .... (F Head, France)	67
7	1	**Alpina (FR)** 3-8-8 .... (J-V Toux, France)	59
8	nk	**Don Salsa (FR)**[12] 3-9-2 .... (C Diard, France)	67
9	1	**Glimmer**[57] 4810 3-8-10 .... (3) (H-A Pantall, France)	61
10	1	**Speed Pearl (FR)**[66] 3-8-13 .... (L Viel, France)	58
0		**Chamir (FR)**[60] 3-9-2 .... (C Martens, France)	—
0		**Martalina (FR)** 3-8-0 .... (8) (S Wattel, France)	—

12 Ran SP% **2.2**
PARI-MUTUEL (including one euro stakes): WIN 44.70; PL 10.10, 2.70, 2.20; DF 262.40.
Owner H Guy **Bred** Gaines Gentry Thoroughbreds & S & H Thoroughbreds **Trained** Chantilly, France

6581 KEMPTON (A.W) (R-H)
Thursday, October 8

OFFICIAL GOING: Standard
Wind: virtually nil Weather: sunny and bright (dark later)

6607 KEMPTON.CO.UK MEDIAN AUCTION MAIDEN STKS 1m (P)
5:30 (5:33) (Class 6) 2-Y-O **£2,047** (£604; £302) **Stalls** High

Form				RPR
6	1		**Art Excellence**[15] 6214 2-9-3 0 .... JamieSpencer 5 (S A Callaghan, U.S.A) *s.i.s: gd hdwy on outer to ld 6f out: mde rest: rdn clr ent fnl 2f: drvn fnl f: a jst holding on* **7/2**[1]	73
63	2	hd	**Magnetic Force (IRE)**[26] 5879 2-9-3 0 .... RichardMullen 3 (Sir Michael Stoute) *t.k.h: stdd to trck ldrs after 1f: chsd wnr over 4f out: rdn and sltly outpcd jst over 2f out: rallied gamely fnl f: nvr quite getting to wnr* **5/1**[2]	73
54	3	½	**Ipswich Lad**[20] 6066 2-9-3 0 .... LPKeniry 6 (A M Balding) *towards rr: hdwy and pushed along on outer over 3f out: drvn to chse ldng pair over 2f out: kpt on wl fnl f: nvr quite pce to rch ldng pair* **13/2**	72
	4	¾	**Arctic Cosmos (USA)** 2-9-3 0 .... RobertHavlin 8 (J H M Gosden) *s.i.s: bhd: pushed along jst over 3f out: hdwy on outer over 1f out: edging rt but styd on wl fnl f: nt rch ldrs* **15/2**	72+
	5	½	**Khajaaly (IRE)** 2-9-3 0 .... TPO'Shea 10 (E A L Dunlop) *s.i.s: towards rr: hdwy on outer over 3f out: rdn to chse ldrs 2f out: kpt on fnl f: nt quite pce to rch ldrs* **16/1**	69+
34	6	1 ¼	**Milnagavie**[34] 5627 2-8-12 0 .... PatDobbs 12 (R Hannon) *led tl 6f out: chsd ldrs after tl rdn and unable qck jst over 2f out: kpt on again u.p fnl f* **11/2**[3]	61
	7	¾	**Bonnie Brae** 2-8-12 0 .... DaneO'Neill 14 (G G Margarson) *in tch in midfield: effrt towards inner over 2f out: n.m.r over 1f out: keeping on but n.d whn sltly hmpd ins fnl f* **66/1**	61+
	8	1 ¼	**Jinto** 2-9-3 0 .... HayleyTurner 11 (R M H Cowell) *s.i.s: bhd in last pair: rdn and swtchd lft over 2f out: sme late hdwy: nvr trbld ldrs* **33/1**	62+
0	9	nk	**Tammela**[12] 6291 2-8-12 0 .... LiamJones 4 (A P Jarvis) *t.k.h: hld up in midfield on outer: hdwy to chse ldrs and rdn wl over 2f out: wkng whn edgd rt over 1f out* **66/1**	56
5	10	1 ¼	**Tom Wade (IRE)**[17] 6162 2-9-3 0 .... PhilipRobinson 9 (M A Jarvis) *in tch: pushed along 4f out: rdn and hanging rt over 2f out: sn outpcd and btn fnl 2f* **5/1**[2]	59
	11	¾	**Wide Ranging** 2-9-3 0 .... SteveDrowne 13 (R Charlton) *in tch in midfield: rdn and effrt on inner over 2f out: wknd over 1f out* **14/1**	57
0	12	2	**Feel The Magic (IRE)**[20] 6069 2-8-12 0 .... JamesDoyle 7 (S Kirk) *chsd ldrs tl wknd u.p jst over 2f out: wl btn fnl f* **66/1**	48
	13	7	**Abigails Angel** 2-8-12 0 .... FrankieMcDonald 2 (B R Johnson) *v.s.a: a bhd* **50/1**	32

1m 40.39s (0.59) **Going Correction** -0.05s/f (Stan) **13** Ran SP% **118.0**
Speed ratings (Par 93): **95,94,94,93,93 91,91,89,89,88 87,85,78**
toteswingers: 1&2 £5.60, 1&3 £5.90, 2&3 £4.50. CSF £19.82 TOTE £4.80: £1.60, £1.80, £1.90; EX 27.70.
Owner Matthew Green **Bred** Darley **Trained**
■ Stewards' Enquiry : Robert Havlin caution: careless riding

FOCUS
There was an open market for this fair maiden. The first six in the betting were priced between 7-2 and 15-2. The pace was steady and they finished in a bit of a bunch. The form may not be particularly strong but the winner is a likeable type and there was promise from a few newcomers.

NOTEBOOK
Art Excellence drifted over from stall five to grab the early lead, kicked clear early in the straight and had enough left to hang on from several finishers. He shaped with promise when 9-2 in a 7f Redcar maiden and found improvement to take this contest. He is a half-brother to Dignify, a dual 7f winner at two who was later fourth in the Italian Oaks. He should continue to progress and seems to have plenty of natural pace, so could prove equally effective at 7f at this early stage of his career. (op 3-1)
Magnetic Force(IRE) was reluctant to go in the stalls but stuck to his task really well in the race and gave the winner a scare in the closing stages. The 160,000euros colt is going the right way and has stacks of useful middle-distance winners on the dam's side of his pedigree. (op 11-2)
Ipswich Lad stayed on well out wide and has now shaped with promise on all three of his runs. He has a decent pedigree and could do well when sent handicapping off a mark possibly in the low-70s. (op 7-1 tchd 11-2)
Arctic Cosmos(USA), who ran very green and looked to be going nowhere at the 2f before finding a strong finishing burst. The 47,000gns son of North Light is a first foal of a 1m2f winner in US. He should have learned a lot from this debut run and the support he attracted in the morning suggests he has been doing good things at home. (op 7-1 tchd 8-1)
Khajaaly(IRE) price rocketed to 140,000gns as a yearling and he showed plenty of promise on this debut run. He has a speedy pedigree, so it was slightly surprising to see him starting off over 1m, but he stayed on nicely and should improve for the experience.
Milnagavie set the standard on her debut third behind Dyna Waltz, a subsequent fifth in the Group 1 Fillies' Mile at Ascot, but she could not convert favouritism on easy turf last time and put in another lacklustre effort here. (op 5-1)
Bonnie Brae does not have the most appealing pedigree and attracted little interest at the sales or in the market for this debut. However, she showed definite signs of ability and was not given a hard time.
Jinto looked very inexperienced on his first outing but seemed to get the hang of things late and is another who offered encouragement for the future. (op 40-1)

6608 RACING UK MEDIAN AUCTION MAIDEN STKS 1m (P)
6:00 (6:16) (Class 6) 3-5-Y-0 **£2,047** (£604; £302) **Stalls** High

Form				RPR
0003	1		**Classically (IRE)**[35] 5614 3-9-3 71 .... SteveDrowne 5 (R Charlton) *chsd ldr after 1f: rdn and effrt over 2f out: led over 1f out: styd on wl and in command fnl f:* **3/1**[2]	73
2	2	2	**Illuminative (USA)**[20] 6073 3-9-3 0 .... RichardMullen 10 (J H M Gosden) *hld up towards rr: hdwy over 3f out: rdn to chse ldng pair wl over 1f out: wnt 2nd ins fnl f: nvr had pce to rch wnr* **4/5**[1]	68
4450	3	1	**Dom Polski**[19] 6124 3-9-3 67 .... (t) AdamKirby 11 (W R Swinburn) *broke v fast: led: rdn over 2f out: drvn and hdd over 1f out: one pce after: lost 2nd ins fnl f* **10/1**	66
4	4	½	**Bowsers Beau**[48] 5215 3-9-3 0 .... PatDobbs 3 (M P Tregoning) *in tch in midfield: pushed along over 3f out: racd awkwardly and outpcd over 2f out: edgd lft but kpt on ins fnl f: styng on fin* **7/1**	65

2 **5** 2 ¼ **Ask The Oracle**[167] 1490 3-9-3 0........................ TravisBlock 4 59+
(H Morrison) *towards rr: rdn and hdwy on outer over 3f out: carried lft over 2f out: plugged on but nvr had pce to threaten ldrs* **9/2**[3]

646 **6** ½ **Herecomethegirls**[21] 6029 3-8-12 0........................ HayleyTurner 2 53
(M L W Bell) *t.k.h: hld up in last pair: rdn and effrt on inner over 2f out: nvr gng pce to rch ldrs* **16/1**

05 **7** 8 **Barathea's Acclaim**[21] 6029 3-8-12 0........................ DaneO'Neill 6 34
(P R Hedger) *chsd ldr for 1f: styd handy tl wknd u.p ent fnl 2f* **50/1**

0 **8** 3 ¾ **Silvester**[30] 5751 3-9-3 0........................ J-PGuillambert 9 30
(R M H Cowell) *s.i.s: a bhd lost tch over 2f out* **66/1**

550- **9** 1 ¾ **Balais Folly (FR)**[350] 6927 4-9-6 47........................ JamieMackay 1 26
(D Haydn Jones) *chsd ldrs: rdn and struggling whn edgd lft over 2f out: wknd qckly 2f out* **66/1**

1m 39.03s (-0.77) **Going Correction** -0.05s/f (Stan)
WFA 3 from 4yo 3lb **9** Ran SP% **131.2**
Speed ratings (Par 101): **101,99,98,97,95 94,86,83,81**
toteswingers: 1&2 £2.00, 1&3 £6.40, 2&3 £4.90 CSF £6.66 TOTE £3.90: £1.40, £1.10, £2.90; EX 10.10.
Owner P Gleeson **Bred** Bridgewater Equine Ltd **Trained** Beckhampton, Wilts

FOCUS
There was a long delay before this maiden auction, due to Edward Creighton being injured when thrown off Final Drive (33/1, withdrawn). The pace was decent but it went to one of the most exposed runners and the form looks suspect. The third helps with the standard and the winner did not need to match his best.

6609 PANORAMIC BAR & RESTAURANT NURSERY 7f (P)
6:30 (6:44) (Class 6) (0-65,68) 2-Y-O **£2,047** (£604; £302) **Stalls** High

Form RPR

4450 **1** **Ever So Bold**[20] 6071 2-9-6 64........................(b[1]) HayleyTurner 9 68
(W R Muir) *chsd ldr: rdn to ld over 1f out: drvn and hrd pressed ins fnl f: fnd ex and hld on wl fnl 100yds* **9/1**

2344 **2** nk **Maoi Chinn Tire (IRE)**[42] 5369 2-9-6 64........................(p) LPKeniry 8 68
(J S Moore) *hld up in tch: rdn and effrt jst over 2f out: rdn to chse wnr ent fnl f: ev ch fnl 150yds: r.o but hld fnl 100yds* **11/2**[2]

0004 **3** 3 **Boycott (IRE)**[22] 5985 2-9-5 63........................(b) RichardMullen 10 59
(J H M Gosden) *racd keenly: led: rdn ent fnl 2f: hdd over 1f out: wknd ins fnl f* **11/2**[2]

066 **4** nk **Lost Cause**[45] 5317 2-9-7 65........................ EddieAhern 5 60+
(R Charlton) *t.k.h: hld up in tch in midfield: swtchd lft and rdn 2f out: kpt on steadily fnl f: nt rch ldrs* **5/1**[1]

605 **5** 1 ¼ **Magnificence**[21] 6032 2-9-5 63........................ RyanMoore 4 55
(Sir Michael Stoute) *t.k.h: hld up in tch towards rr: rdn and hdwy jst over 2f out: kpt on same pce u.p fnl f* **11/2**[2]

060 **6** 2 ¼ **Glamour Profession (IRE)**[30] 5741 2-9-4 62........................ PatDobbs 7 49
(R Hannon) *s.i.s: sn swtchd rt: in tch in rr: rdn and no real prog over 2f out: plugged on fnl f: nvr trbld ldrs* **33/1**

0602 **7** nk **Thaliwarru**[55] 4973 2-9-2 60........................ SteveDrowne 12 46
(J R Gask) *trckd ldng pair: gng wl over 2f out: swtchd lft and rdn jst over 2f out: fnd little and edgd lft over 1f out: wl hld fnl f* **8/1**[3]

5041 **8** nk **Chandrayaan**[10] 6343 2-9-10 68 6ex........................(v) TGMcLaughlin 1 53
(E A L Dunlop) *s.i.s: sn swtchd rt: t.k.h in rr: rdn and effrt over 2f out: no real prog* **8/1**[3]

0050 **9** 1 **D'Urberville**[20] 6066 2-9-7 65........................ RobertHavlin 13 48
(J R Jenkins) *wnt lft s: sn in tch: rdn and unable qck over 2f out: wl hld fnl 2f* **25/1**

060 **10** ½ **Dutiful**[20] 6054 2-9-2 60........................ ChrisCatlin 14 41
(M R Channon) *t.k.h: hld up in tch in rr: rdn and effrt wl over 2f out: no prog* **14/1**

2060 **11** ¾ **Ragsta (IRE)**[5] 6491 2-8-13 64........................ RichardRowe(7) 2 43
(C A Dwyer) *in tch in midfield on outer: rn v wd and dropped to rr bnd 3f out: no ch and continued to edge lft after* **25/1**

206 **12** 3 ¼ **Bideeya (USA)**[66] 4603 2-9-7 65........................(p) NCallan 3 36
(C E Brittain) *t.k.h: chsd ldrs tl wknd qckly u.p 2f out* **9/1**

1m 27.37s (1.37) **Going Correction** -0.05s/f (Stan) **12** Ran SP% **122.3**
Speed ratings (Par 93): **90,89,86,85,84 81,81,81,80,79 78,74**
toteswingers: 1&2 £8.80, 1&3 £15.50, 2&3 £8.40 CSF £58.65 CT £307.08 TOTE £12.80: £3.00, £1.90, £1.90; EX 83.60.
Owner North Farm Partnership **Bred** North Farm Stud **Trained** Lambourn, Berks

FOCUS
An ordinary nursery, involving a number of exposed types. The runners had managed just two wins in a combined total of 55 runs. The pace was modest and it was an advantage to race prominently. The first two, who finished clear, both showed a bit of improvement.

NOTEBOOK
Ever So Bold, for whom the switch to more positive tactics and application of first-time blinkers spurred a revival, put in a gritty display to get off the mark on his eighth start. He was always in the right place in a steadily run event and could shoot up the weights after this win, but he is relatively unexposed on this surface and could find further progress in his newly acquired headgear. (op 11-1)
Maoi Chinn Tire(IRE) looked a huge threat at the furlong marker but could not get past the feisty winner. He can look a tricky ride and has been expensive to follow in nurseries, but this effort with cheekpieces applied is right up near his best form and he pulled some way clear of the third. (tchd 6-1)
Boycott(IRE) was allowed a soft lead for most of the way and settled better than he has done on occasions, but it was disappointing that he faded away in the closing stages. He has a six-figure price-tag but has struggled to progress in six runs. (op 9-2)
Lost Cause was tapped for speed when the pace quickened but eventually found a sweeping run out wide. He should be a more potent force in a strongly run race. (op 11-2 tchd 6-1 in a place)
Magnificence, who is bred to be much better than her rating of 63. The switch to patient tactics on her nursery/AW debut backfired but she showed some promise staying on late and it is still relatively early in her career, so it would be no surprise if she found a bit more off a stronger tempo over a slightly stiffer test. (tchd 5-1)
Thaliwarru Official explanation: jockey said gelding hung left

6610 BOOK KEMPTON TICKETS ON 0844 579 3008 NURSERY 6f (P)
7:00 (7:09) (Class 6) (0-65,65) 2-Y-O **£2,047** (£604; £302) **Stalls** High

Form RPR

6002 **1** **Kilt Rock (IRE)**[10] 6345 2-9-5 63........................ JamesDoyle 9 71+
(T G Mills) *wnt sltly lft s: hld up in tch: swtchd ins: rdn and gd hdwy jst over 2f out: led over 1f out: drvn and edgd lft ins fnl f: r.o wl and asserted fnl 100yds* **1/2**[1]

0004 **2** 1 ½ **Speedyfix**[10] 6345 2-8-3 47........................(tp) JimmyQuinn 8 47
(Mrs C A Dunnett) *bmpd s: hld up in tch in rr: hdwy on inner jst over 2f out: wnt 2nd 1f out: pressed wnr fnl 150yds: nt pce of wnr fnl 100yds* **12/1**

400 **3** ½ **Ballyvonane (USA)**[29] 5778 2-8-3 47........................(b[1]) LukeMorris 4 46
(L A Dace) *t.k.h: chsd ldr tl rdn to ld 2f out: drvn and hdd over 1f out: kpt on same pce fnl f* **33/1**

4020 **4** 2 **Wing Of Faith**[23] 5967 2-9-1 59........................ GeorgeBaker 5 52
(S Kirk) *in tch: rdn and effrt ent fnl 2f: chsd ldng trio 1f out: no imp fnl f* **6/1**[2]

0430 **5** 1 ¾ **Wigan Lane**[10] 6343 2-9-7 65........................ IanMongan 6 52
(P Howling) *hld up in tch in rr: rdn and effrt over 2f out: hdwy u.p over 1f out: kpt on but nvr had pce to threaten ldrs* **14/1**

065 **6** nk **Pursuit Of Gold**[143] 2135 2-9-6 64........................ RobertWinston 3 50
(J R Best) *chsd ldng pair: rdn and effrt jst over 2f out: unable qck u.p wl over 1f out: one pce and hld fnl f* **10/1**[3]

40 **7** ¾ **Yeah**[42] 5372 2-8-12 56........................ SJCraine 11 40
(Patrick Morris) *t.k.h: hld up wl in tch: n.m.r ent fnl 2f: rdn and unable qck wl over 1f out: no prog after* **11/1**

600P **8** 6 **Saachi's Vision (IRE)**[84] 4018 2-8-3 47........................(b) AdrianMcCarthy 10 13
(D K Ivory) *led: rdn and hdd 2f out: wknd qckly over 1f out: wl btn fnl f* **40/1**

6540 **9** 2 ¼ **Split The Pot (IRE)**[36] 5573 2-8-12 56........................ JimCrowley 2 15
(P R Chamings) *wnt lft s: hld up in rr on outer: struggling wl over 2f out: n.d* **33/1**

005 **10** 8 **The Two G'S**[15] 6207 2-9-2 60........................ NCallan 7 —
(P D Evans) *chsd ldrs: hung lft bnd jst over 3f out: drvn and wknd jst over 2f out* **20/1**

1m 13.69s (0.59) **Going Correction** -0.05s/f (Stan) **10** Ran SP% **125.8**
Speed ratings (Par 93): **94,92,91,88,86 85,84,76,73,63**
toteswingers: 1&2 £3.20, 1&3 £8.40, 2&3 £40.80. CSF £8.95 CT £130.22 TOTE £1.50: £1.10, £2.90, £8.40; EX 11.40.
Owner Mrs L M Askew **Bred** Strategy Bloodstock **Trained** Headley, Surrey

FOCUS
A modest nursery without much strength in depth. Ten of the 11 runners were maidens, but the pace was decent and the winner looks on the upgrade.

NOTEBOOK
Kilt Rock(IRE) had strong claims on his narrow defeat off this mark when a springer in the market on nursery debut at Wolverhampton last week. He was heavily backed again and stormed up the far rail to win with more in hand than the margin suggests. He looks a determined character who has scope for further improvement, and his good US pedigree suggests he may prove best on this surface. (op 4-6 tchd 8-11 in places)
Speedyfix received a bump at the start and could not quite match the winner's turn of foot against the far rail but did well to get as close as he did from an unpromising position. He still needs to learn to break with a bit more urgency but should be able to win a similar event when things go his way. (op 14-1)
Ballyvonane(USA) seemed energized by the first-time blinkers on his nursery debut. He had shown nothing at big prices in three maidens but shaped with quite a bit of promise switched to more aggressive tactics. (op 25-1)
Wing Of Faith put in a tame effort when favourite on easy turf last time, but looked more convincing back on Polytrack. He has a patchy profile but has gone close off similar marks and should be able to win at this level. (op 7-1 tchd 11-2)
Wigan Lane stayed on from a long way back. She has partially bounced back from a disappointment at Wolverhampton last time but has been an expensive one to follow and has not really progressed since a maiden win at Doncaster in June. Official explanation: jockey said filly hung left in the home straight. (op 10-1)
The Two G'S Official explanation: jockey said filly hung left

6611 RACING UK IN YOUR PUB 0870 351 8834 MEDIAN AUCTION MAIDEN STKS 7f (P)
7:30 (7:37) (Class 5) 3-4-Y-O **£2,590** (£770; £385; £192) **Stalls** High

Form RPR

0203 **1** **Leelu**[30] 5751 3-8-12 56........................ HayleyTurner 5 62
(D W P Arbuthnot) *taken down early: chsd ldrs: wnt 2nd wl over 2f out: led jst over 2f out: sn rdn: drvn and hrd pressed ins fnl f: hld on wl* **12/1**

0522 **2** nk **Sermons Mount (USA)**[15] 6213 3-9-3 57........................(p) NCallan 4 66
(Mouse Hamilton-Fairley) *plld hrd: hld up wl in tch: hdwy to chse wnr wl over 1f out: rdn to chal ins fnl f: nt qckn and hld fnl 50yds* **8/1**

0-3 **3** 2 ½ **Lord Of The Dance (IRE)**[13] 6255 3-9-3........................ LukeMorris 9 59+
(J M P Eustace) *t.k.h: hld up in tch in midfield: rdn and unable qck over 2f out: hrd drvn and hdwy over 1f out: wnt 3rd ins fnl f: kpt on* **7/2**[2]

05 **4** 1 ¾ **Suzi's Dancer**[20] 6073 3-8-12........................ JimmyQuinn 12 49
(H J Collingridge) *chsd ldrs: effrt on inner to chse ldng pair wl over 1f out: sn rdn: outpcd by ldng pair ent fnl f: lost 3rd fnl 150yds* **9/1**

00 **5** 1 ½ **Madame Guillotine (USA)**[105] 3297 3-8-12........................ SebSanders 7 45
(R M Beckett) *t.k.h early: hld up towards rr: hdwy towards inner jst over 2f out: chsd ldng trio over 1f out: outpcd ent fnl f: plugged on same pce after* **7/1**

033 **6** ½ **Farncombe (IRE)**[57] 4913 3-8-12 70........................ PatDobbs 11 44
(M P Tregoning) *s.i.s and n.m.r sn after s: bhd: rdn over 2f out: styd on fnl f but n.d* **9/4**[1]

0402 **7** 3 ½ **Hay Fever (IRE)**[10] 6344 3-9-3 70........................(b) WilliamBuick 10 39
(Eve Johnson Houghton) *hld up in rr: effrt on inner jst over 2f out: no real prog and n.d* **13/2**[3]

0-00 **8** ½ **Chatterszaha**[26] 5881 3-8-9 52........................ WilliamCarson(3) 2 33
(C Drew) *led: hung lft fr wl over 2f out: hdd jst over 2f out: steadily wknd* **66/1**

00-0 **9** ¾ **Miss Jabba (IRE)**[22] 6005 3-8-12 45........................ JimCrowley 1 31
(Miss J Feilden) *chsd ldr tl wl over 2f out: wknd fnl 2f* **66/1**

0000 **10** 5 **Improper (USA)**[48] 5217 3-9-3 40........................ DaneO'Neill 3 23
(Mouse Hamilton-Fairley) *a towards rr: wd bnd and rdn 3f out: nvr on terms* **66/1**

56 **11** 1 ¼ **Magic Queen (IRE)**[7] 6430 3-8-12........................ LiamJones 6 14
(A P Jarvis) *t.k.h: in tch: rdn and unable qck over 2f out: hrd drvn and wknd wl over 1f out* **33/1**

0000 **12** 8 **Any Secrets**[35] 5614 3-9-3 37........................(v[1]) ChrisCatlin 8 —
(Karen George) *a towards rr: wd and rdn bnd 3f out: sn toiling and bhd* **80/1**

1m 25.86s (-0.14) **Going Correction** -0.05s/f (Stan) **12** Ran SP% **116.3**
Speed ratings (Par 103): **98,97,94,92,91 90,86,85,85,79 77,68**
toteswingers: 1&2 £6.60, 1&3 £8.00, 2&3 £5.30. CSF £100.66 TOTE £15.60: £4.10, £1.60, £2.00; EX 69.00.
Owner Philip Banfield **Bred** P Banfield **Trained** Compton, Berks

FOCUS
An uncompetitive maiden that threw up a surprise. Modest form, with the first pair pretty exposed.
Farncombe(IRE) Official explanation: jockey said filly suffered interference leaving the stalls

Chatterszaha Official explanation: jockey said filly hung left

6612 TURFTV BETTING SHOP SERVICE CLAIMING STKS 1m 4f (P)

8:00 (8:07) (Class 6) 3-Y-O+ £2,047 (£604; £302) Stalls Centre

Form RPR

0-50 **1** **Bandama (IRE)**[124] 2706 6-9-10 85 JimCrowley 2 74
(Mrs A J Perrett) *hld up in tch towards rr: hdwy to trck ldrs gng wl over 2f out: shkn up to ld 2f out: clr ent fnl f: rdn out* **13/8**[1]

3020 **2** 1 ¾ **Quince (IRE)**[15] 6218 6-9-6 68 (v) SebSanders 3 67
(J Pearce) *dwlt: sn bustled along: chsd ldrs: rdn over 2f out: chsd wnr ent fnl f: r.o but a comf hld* **10/3**[2]

6015 **3** 3 ¾ **Ghufa (IRE)**[15] 6210 5-9-8 65 TedDurcan 4 63
(George Baker) *hld up in last pair: rdn and hanging rt over 2f out: swtchd lft 2f out: kpt on u.p to go 3rd towards fin: nvr trbld ldrs* **9/2**[3]

3000 **4** ½ **Little Sark (IRE)**[15] 6210 4-9-5 50 PatCosgrave 6 59
(P D Evans) *chsd ldrs: rdn to chse ldng pair over 3f out: hmpd fr over 2f out tl swtchd rt over 1f out: plugged on same pce* **18/1**

0/50 **5** 1 ½ **Iffy**[15] 6210 8-8-12 60 AmyBaker(5) 7 55
(A B Haynes) *towards rr: hdwy 6f out: edgd rt over 4f out: sn chsng ldr: rdn and ev ch over 2f out: edging lft wout correction after: wknd over 1f out* **25/1**

5310 **6** 3 ½ **New England**[48] 5227 7-9-5 59 LukeMorris 8 51
(F Sheridan) *s.i.s: hld up in last pair: hdwy wl over 2f out: rdn and chsd wnr on inner wl over 1f out: sn outpcd: wknd fnl f* **9/1**

260- **7** 17 **Kilmeena Magic**[230] 5020 7-8-10 45 GabrielHannon(5) 9 20
(J C Fox) *a towards rr: lost tch over 2f out: eased fnl f: t.o* **20/1**

0043 **8** 2 **Felicia**[22] 5987 4-9-0 45 NataliaGemelova(3) 1 19
(J E Long) *chsd ldr after 2f tl over 4f out: wknd wl over 2f out: t.o and eased fnl f* **16/1**

0040 **9** 19 **Gasat (IRE)**[30] 5750 8-9-5 60 JamieSpencer 5 —
(A B Haynes) *sn rdn along and led after 1f: rdn and hdd 2f out: sn btn: virtually p.u fnl f* **9/1**

60-0 **10** 17 **Lord Orpen (IRE)**[28] 5788 5-8-10 38 TobyAtkinson(7) 10 —
(Patrick Morris) *led for 1f: chsd ldrs after tl rdn and hmpd bnd over 4f out: sn dropped to last and lost tch: t.o and virtually p.u fnl 2f* **66/1**

2m 33.03s (-1.47) **Going Correction** -0.05s/f (Stan) 10 Ran SP% 120.6
Speed ratings (Par 101): **102,100,98,98,97 94,83,82,69,58**
toteswingers: 1&2 £2.20, 1&3 £2.70, 2&3 £3.70. CSF £7.06 TOTE £2.40: £1.20, £1.40, £1.60; EX 8.20.
Owner Mrs S L Whitehead **Bred** Newberry Stud Farm Ltd **Trained** Pulborough, W Sussex
■ Stewards' Enquiry : Pat Cosgrave caution: careless riding

FOCUS
There did not seem to be much strength in depth in this claimer. The pace was decent and the two market leaders pulled a long way clear of the rest. The winner did not need to be anywhere near his best.

6613 LEVY BOARD H'CAP 1m 4f (P)

8:30 (8:37) (Class 4) (0-80,80) 3-Y-O £4,727 (£1,406; £702; £351) Stalls Centre

Form RPR

2452 **1** **Incendo**[23] 5975 3-8-8 70 (t) HayleyTurner 10 86+
(J R Fanshawe) *hld up towards rr: hdwy on bit wl over 1f out: upsides ldr stl cruising ent fnl f: led narrowly ins fnl f: cheekily* **12/1**

015 **2** hd **Itlaaq**[68] 4520 3-9-2 78 RHills 4 89
(J L Dunlop) *dwlt: bhd in last pair: rdn and gd hdwy on outer wl over 2f out: led over 1f out: hdd ins fnl f: kpt on trying but a hld by cruising wnr* **5/2**[2]

1264 **3** 4 **Halfway House**[29] 5771 3-9-2 78 JamieSpencer 2 83
(M L W Bell) *stdd after s: hld in last: hdwy ent fnl 2f: swtchd lft and rdn over 1f out: r.o to go 3rd fnl 100yds: nvr threatened ldng pair* **11/1**

04 **4** ½ **Bourne**[38] 5531 3-8-12 74 WilliamBuick 9 78+
(L M Cumani) *chsd ldrs: rdn over 2f out: ev ch and drvn over 1f out: outpcd fnl f* **6/1**[3]

3134 **5** 1 ½ **Going For Gold**[26] 5876 3-9-3 79 (e[1]) SteveDrowne 7 80
(R Charlton) *led tl after 1f: chsd ldr after: rdn and pressed ldr over 2f out: ev ch and drvn wl over 1f out: wknd ent fnl f* **12/1**

4025 **6** hd **Nawaadi (USA)**[27] 5834 3-8-13 75 (v) TPO'Shea 3 76
(J H M Gosden) *pushed up to ld after 1f: rdn ent fnl 3f: hdd over 1f out: wknd fnl f* **20/1**

3213 **7** nk **Monetary Fund (USA)**[9] 6360 3-9-2 78 (t) NCallan 5 79
(G A Butler) *t.k.h: hld up in tch: rdn and unable qck over 2f out: one pce after* **13/2**

0000 **8** 1 ¾ **Admirable Duque (IRE)**[35] 5593 3-8-4 66 oh1 ChrisCatlin 8 64
(D J S Ffrench Davis) *sn niggled along towards rr: rdn and no imp fnl 3f* **50/1**

1 **9** 22 **Tripitaka**[169] 1464 3-9-4 80 PhilipRobinson 1 43
(M A Jarvis) *hld up towards rr on outer: rdn and no rspnse over 2f out: sn wl btn: eased ins fnl f: t.o* **2/1**[1]

4525 **10** 12 **Calaloo (IRE)**[20] 6059 3-9-3 79 (b) JimCrowley 6 22
(C R Egerton) *t.k.h: chsd ldrs: rdn and struggling over 3f out: wl bhd fnl 2f: t.o and eased fnl f* **25/1**

2m 31.19s (-3.31) **Going Correction** -0.05s/f (Stan) 10 Ran SP% 123.8
Speed ratings (Par 103): **109,108,106,105,104 104,104,103,88,80**
toteswingers: 1&2 £5.80, 1&3 £11.60, 2&3 £7.50. CSF £44.16 CT £361.57 TOTE £11.80: £2.60, £1.40, £3.20; EX 57.00.
Owner Andrew & Julia Turner **Bred** London Thoroughbred Services Ltd **Trained** Newmarket, Suffolk

FOCUS
A decent three-year-old handicap and good form for the grade, in a fast time. The pace was fairly strong and the first two came from some way back and finished clear of the rest. The winner scored under a very cool and motionless ride from Hayley Turner and is rated value for 3l.
Tripitaka Official explanation: jockey said gelding stopped quickly

6614 JUMP RACING HERE OCTOBER 20TH H'CAP 1m (P)

9:00 (9:06) (Class 4) (0-80,85) 3-Y-O+ £4,727 (£1,406; £702; £351) Stalls High

Form RPR

1044 **1** **Audemar (IRE)**[17] 6168 3-9-2 78 JamieSpencer 7 90+
(E F Vaughan) *in tch: rdn and qcknd to ld 2f out: clr over 1f out: r.o strly* **3/1**[2]

2130 **2** 2 ½ **Block Party**[19] 6111 3-9-3 79 RichardMullen 12 85+
(R Charlton) *hld up in tch towards rr: rdn and effrt whn nt clr run and hmpd wl over 1f out: swtchd lft over 1f out: r.o wl fnl f to go 2nd towards fin: no ch w wnr* **6/1**[3]

3045 **3** nk **Suzi Spends (IRE)**[10] 6346 4-9-7 80 JimmyQuinn 4 85
(H J Collingridge) *hmpd sn after s: racd in last trio: clsd and in tch over 4f out: hdwy and rdn 2f out: swtchd lft ent fnl f: r.o to chse clr wnr fnl 150yds: lost 2nd towards fin* **16/1**

4001 **4** 1 ¼ **Mcconnell (USA)**[9] 6357 4-9-9 82 6ex GeorgeBaker 6 84
(G L Moore) *hmpd sn after s: sn in tch in midfield: rdn and effrt over 2f out: chsd clr wnr wl over 1f out: no imp: lost 2 pls fnl 150yds* **8/1**

4411 **5** ¾ **King's Colour**[28] 5804 4-9-1 77 JackMitchell(3) 11 77+
(B R Johnson) *hmpd sn after s: racd in last trio: clsd and in tch over 4f out: effrt whn nt clr run and hmpd 2f out: swtchd lft and gd hdwy on outer over 1f out: pressing for pls 1f out: no ex fnl 100yds* **11/4**[1]

3140 **6** ¾ **Fancy Footsteps (IRE)**[17] 6168 4-8-10 76 JPFahy(7) 14 75
(C G Cox) *in tch: rdn over 2f out: n.m.r briefly over 1f out: kpt on same pce u.p fnl f* **10/1**

-144 **7** 2 **Conry (IRE)**[15] 6212 3-9-2 78 EddieAhern 3 72
(Patrick Morris) *t.k.h: hld up in tch on outer: rdn and effrt 2f out: sn unable qck: wknd ent fnl f* **12/1**

55P- **8** hd **Dubai Meydan (IRE)**[391] 5858 4-9-6 79 SteveDrowne 9 73
(Miss Gay Kelleway) *v.s.a: bhd: clsd and in tch over 4f out: rdn and hanging rt over 2f out: sn swtchd lft: no imp after* **25/1**

0000 **9** ¾ **Resplendent Nova**[33] 5676 7-9-5 78 IanMongan 1 70
(P Howling) *sn outpcd in last pair: clsd and in tch over 4f out: effrt on inner and rdn 2f out: no real prog* **40/1**

4305 **10** 2 ½ **Buxton**[22] 5991 5-8-10 69 (t) PatDobbs 10 55
(R Ingram) *chsd ldrs: rdn and unable qck over 2f out: wkng whn n.m.r over 1f out* **14/1**

2366 **11** 1 **Pegasus Lad (USA)**[28] 5803 3-9-0 76 RoystonFfrench 8 60
(M Johnston) *chsd ldr: rdn and ev ch 2f out: sn outpcd: wknd over 1f out* **14/1**

-100 **12** 6 **Haakima (USA)**[152] 1860 3-9-4 80 NCallan 13 50
(C E Brittain) *led: stdd pce over 4f out: rdn over 2f out: hdd 2f out: sn outpcd by wnr: wknd over 1f out* **16/1**

1m 39.0s (-0.80) **Going Correction** -0.05s/f (Stan)
WFA 3 from 4yo+ 3lb 12 Ran SP% 125.2
Speed ratings (Par 105): **102,99,99,97,97 96,94,94,93,91 90,84**
toteswingers: 1&2 £5.10, 1&3 £10.20, 2&3 £22.90. CSF £23.05 CT £264.56 TOTE £4.00: £1.80, £2.20, £6.90; EX 27.10 Place 6: £26.36, Place 5: £15.15..
Owner Gute Freunde Partnership **Bred** Mrs Amanda Brudenell And Mr & Mrs R A **Trained** Newmarket, Suffolk

FOCUS
A reasonable handicap that was run at a steady pace and the hold-up performers struggled to get into contention. A personal best from the winner with the next two close to their marks.
Suzi Spends(IRE) Official explanation: jockey said filly was hampered at the start
T/Plt: £29.00 to a £1 stake. Pool: £64,987.22. 1,630.27 winning tickets. T/Qpdt: £11.50 to a £1 stake. Pool: £6,792.10. 435.10 winning tickets. SP

6104 NEWBURY (L-H)

Thursday, October 8

OFFICIAL GOING: Good (good to soft in places; 7.6)
Rail on back straight moved out but on inside line on bends and distances as advertised.
Wind: Moderate behind Weather: Sunny

6615 EUROPEAN BREEDERS' FUND MAIDEN STKS (DIV I) 6f 110y

1:35 (1:38) (Class 4) 2-Y-O £4,857 (£1,445; £722; £360) Stalls High

Form RPR

23 **1** **Exceedingly Bold**[17] 6154 2-9-3 0 DarryllHolland 9 85+
(Miss Gay Kelleway) *trckd ldrs: led jst ins fnl 2f: pushed clr 1f out: easily* **5/1**[2]

5 **2** 3 ½ **Strictly Dancing (IRE)**[20] 6054 2-8-12 0 WilliamBuick 3 70
(A M Balding) *chsd ldrs: rdn 2f out: chsd wnr jst ins fnl f but nvr any ch: kpt on wl to hold 2nd* **6/1**[3]

00 **3** 1 ¼ **Scottish Boogie (IRE)**[10] 6334 2-9-3 0 JamesDoyle 2 72
(S Kirk) *chsd ldrs: rdn 2f out: disp 2nd jst ins fnl f but nvr any ch w wnr: one pce into 3rd fnl 50yds* **20/1**

0 **4** 2 ¼ **Galatian**[19] 6108 2-9-0 0 JamesMillman(3) 10 66
(B R Millman) *led tl hdd jst ins fnl 2f: styd chsng wnr tl jst ins fnl f: sn wknd* **20/1**

5 shd **Count Of Anjou (USA)** 2-9-3 0 RyanMoore 6 65+
(R Hannon) *in rr: pushed along 3f out: drvn and styd on fr over 1f out: fin wl and gng on cl home but nvr a threat* **13/2**

6 ¾ **Grey Bunting** 2-9-3 0 MichaelHills 14 63+
(B W Hills) *in rr: pushed along over 2f out: kpt on wl fnl f and gng on cl home but nvr a threat* **8/1**

0 **7** 3 **Avon Rock**[20] 6054 2-9-3 0 (t) SebSanders 13 55+
(J W Hills) *s.i.s: in rr: hdwy 2f out: nt clr run over 1f out: kpt on again ins fnl f but nvr nr ldrs* **50/1**

8 ½ **Sweet Pilgrim** 2-8-12 0 DavidProbert 5 49
(M D I Usher) *chsd ldrs: rdn over 2f out: wknd fnl f* **100/1**

9 nk **State Gathering** 2-9-3 0 DaneO'Neill 8 53
(H Candy) *chsd ldrs: drvn over 2f out: wknd fnl f* **17/2**

10 nse **Aultcharn (FR)** 2-9-3 0 MartinDwyer 11 53
(B J Meehan) *s.i.s: sn rcvrd and in tch: rdn 2f out: sn green: wknd fnl f* **9/2**[1]

11 ¾ **Sweet Secret** 2-8-12 0 RichardHughes 7 46
(R Hannon) *v.s.a: rcvrd and in tch 1/2-way: rdn 2f out: n.d after* **12/1**

12 6 **Farmers Dream (IRE)** 2-8-12 0 NCallan 1 29
(J L Spearing) *chsd ldrs: rdn 3f out: wknd fr 2f out* **50/1**

13 7 **Green Energy** 2-9-3 0 JimCrowley 4 15
(Mrs A J Perrett) *slowly away: rdn over 2f out: green and a bhd* **28/1**

14 8 **Aleqa** 2-8-12 0 AlanMunro 12 —
(C F Wall) *pushed along: hung lft and green 2f out: a in rr* **16/1**

1m 20.32s (1.02) **Going Correction** +0.075s/f (Good) 14 Ran SP% 115.6
Speed ratings (Par 97): **97,93,91,89,88 88,84,84,83,83 82,75,67,58**
toteswingers: 1&2 £2.70, 1&3 £21.40, 2&3 £24.30 CSF £30.99 TOTE £5.10: £1.90, £1.80, £6.70; EX 19.00.
Owner Exceedingly Hopeful Partnership **Bred** Andrea Wilkinson Gay Kelleway **Trained** Exning, Suffolk

FOCUS
The ground was officially described as good, good to soft in places following 16.3mm of rain in the last day or so. The rail had been moved out on the back straight but was on the inside line around the bends. It's hard to get too excited about the form of this maiden but the winning time was 0.29 seconds quicker than Noafal (raced up the middle of the track) managed in the second division. They raced towards the stands' side in the closing stages, and the rail was no disadvantage. The winner impressed and the form seems sound.

NOTEBOOK

Exceedingly Bold failed to build on his debut promise when too keen at Hamilton last time, but he showed himself to be pretty useful on this occasion with a decisive success. Always handy, he travelled well before running on strongly for pressure. Gay Kelleway said afterwards that she was tempted to look for a suitable race in France for this colt, but also mentioned that Darryll Holland reckons he should be aimed at the Horris Hill. It's interesting to note that the 2007 winner of that Group 3, Beacon Lodge, had won a division of this maiden, while Mythical Kid, who also landed a version of this race in 2006, ran second in the same pattern race next time. (tchd 9-2)

Strictly Dancing(IRE) confirmed the ability she showed over 6f here on debut but still looked inexperienced. She should continue to progress with time. (op 9-2 tchd 13-2)

Scottish Boogie(IRE) ran poorly at Brighton last time, but he had previously shown ability when three places behind Strictly Dancing on his debut. This probably represents his best effort yet and he might do better again now that handicaps are an option. (op 40-1)

Galatian, too green on his debut over 7f here, fared a little better this time. He showed good speed against the possibly favoured stands' rail but couldn't sustain his challenge. He might still be on the weak side, although it may also be that he'll prove better suited by even shorter. (tchd 22-1)

Count Of Anjou(USA) ◆, a 140,000 euros half-brother to Listed-placed juvenile Roof Fiddle, apparently did some impressive work earlier in the year, but suffered from some niggling problems when just about ready to go in July. This was an eyecatching effort on his belated debut, as he lost his place when running green and coming off the bridle at about halfway, before gradually getting the idea and making good late headway out widest of all. Expect a lot better next time. (op 5-1)

Grey Bunting, a half-brother to a 6f winner, took a while to pick up and never posed a threat but he did make some modest progress in the latter stages. (op 11-1 tchd 7-1)

Avon Rock, again equipped with a tongue-tie, didn't enjoy the clearest of runs through and was not given anything like a hard time. He might be one to look out for in handicaps.

Aultcharn(FR), a 120,000gns purchase, was solid in the market for this racecourse debut but he looked clueless when placed under pressure and made no progress. (op 7-2)

6616 EUROPEAN BREEDERS' FUND MAIDEN STKS (DIV II) 6f 110y

2:10 (2:11) (Class 4) 2-Y-O **£4,857** (£1,445; £722; £360) **Stalls** High

Form RPR

3 **1** **Noafal (IRE)**[40] 5431 2-9-3 0 RHills 10 82+
(M A Jarvis) *t.k.h: trckd ldrs: travelling wl fr 2f out: tk narrow ld 1f out: shkn up ins fnl f: edgd lft cl home but a in control* **9/4**[2]

04 **2** ½ **The Rectifier (USA)**[19] 6108 2-9-3 0 MickyFenton 6 79
(Stef Liddiard) *led: rdn ins fnl 2f: hdd 1f out: styd on wl u.p but a hld by wnr* **10/1**

6 **3** 1¼ **Free For All (IRE)**[20] 6061 2-9-3 0 GeorgeBaker 2 75
(S Kirk) *stdd s: sn in tch: trckd ldrs 2f out: hung bdly lft to far rail and racd alone but styd chsng ldrs: kpt on wl thrght fnl f but nt pce of ldng duo* **7/1**[3]

4 2¼ **Quite Something** 2-8-12 0 WilliamBuick 3 64+
(A M Balding) *t.k.h and stdd in rr: hdwy over 1f out: swtchd rt and styd on ins fnl f: fin strly* **50/1**

5 1¾ **Mutafajer** 2-9-3 0 LDettori 1 64
(Saeed Bin Suroor) *chsd ldrs: drvn to chal 2f out: wknd fnl f* **15/8**[1]

6 2½ **Adventure Story** 2-8-12 0 RyanMoore 13 52
(R Hannon) *s.i.s: sn in tch: rdn over 2f out: wknd over 1f out* **33/1**

33 **7** 1¼ **Exceedthewildman**[15] 6199 2-9-3 0 JimmyFortune 12 54+
(J S Moore) *chsd ldrs: rdn over 2f out: wknd wl over 1f out* **7/1**[3]

0 **8** ½ **Celtic Ransom**[19] 6109 2-9-3 0 EddieAhern 9 53
(J W Hills) *t.k.h: in tch: shkn up 2f out: wknd over 1f out* **50/1**

9 ½ **Kings 'n Dreams** 2-9-3 0 TPQueally 11 51
(D K Ivory) *s.i.s: outpcd most of way* **150/1**

0 **10** *shd* **Monograph**[20] 6054 2-9-3 0 SebSanders 7 51
(J W Hills) *t.k.h: chsd ldrs: rdn 2f out: wknd over 1f out* **100/1**

00 **11** 4 **Novillero**[19] 6108 2-9-3 0 LPKeniry 8 40
(J C Fox) *outpcd most of way* **200/1**

12 3¼ **Swish Dish (CAN)** 2-8-12 0 RichardHughes 4 26+
(R Hannon) *s.i.s: in rr: n.m.r over 2f out: outpcd most of way* **28/1**

1m 20.61s (1.31) **Going Correction** +0.075s/f (Good) **12** Ran SP% **112.1**

Speed ratings (Par 97): **95,94,93,90,88 85,84,83,83,82 78,74**

toteswingers: 1&2 £5.70, 1&3 £5.40, 2&3 £9.90 CSF £22.55 TOTE £3.20: £1.20, £2.60, £2.20; EX 27.60.

Owner Hamdan Al Maktoum **Bred** J Egan, J Corcoran And J Judd **Trained** Newmarket, Suffolk

FOCUS

The winning time was 0.29 seconds slower than Exceedingly Bold managed in the first division. The main action took place up the middle of the track and, off a steady pace, very few were ever involved. Noafal is rated a bit better than the bare form, and the third helps set the level.

NOTEBOOK

Noafal(IRE) was plenty keen enough early on, but his cruising speed enabled him to stay on the bridle for longer than most, allowing Richard Hills to get a breather into the colt, and he found enough under pressure, despite edging left near the line. This one-time Mill Reef entrant, who is in the Irish 2,000 Guineas, is evidently well regarded and showed himself to be pretty useful, confirming the promise he showed on debut at the Newmarket July course. (op 2-1 tchd 15-8)

The Rectifier(USA), who was a bit too keen over 7f here last time but still showed progression from his debut, responded kindly to a more positive ride on this slight drop in trip and ran well, again improving. The type to keep going the right way, he looks just the sort his small stable will do well with and handicaps are now an option. (op 12-1)

Free For All(IRE) again hung left under pressure, this time quite badly, and that compromised his chance. He ended up against the far rail late on and obviously has some sort of issue, but he has plenty of ability as well. Official explanation: jockey said colt hung left (tchd 6-1)

Quite Something, a first foal, was keen enough early on and then became outpaced, before making some encouraging headway. (op 66-1)

Mutafajer got tired quite quickly when coming under pressure and was looked after by Dettori. (op 2-1)

Adventure Story was outpaced in the closing stages and should be better for the experience.

Swish Dish(CAN) Official explanation: jockey said filly stopped quickly

6617 PINKE JOBS MAIDEN STKS (DIV I) 1m (S)

2:45 (2:47) (Class 4) 2-Y-O **£4,857** (£1,445; £722; £360) **Stalls** High

Form RPR

33 **1** **Kalypso King (USA)**[20] 6054 2-9-3 0 RichardHughes 15 98+
(R Hannon) *mde all: shkn up and qcknd wl clr over 1f out: eased fnl 75yds: v impressive* **11/2**[2]

3 **2** 7 **Centurio**[22] 5993 2-9-3 0 RichardKingscote 11 78
(R Charlton) *rr-div: hdwy over 2f out: tk 2nd appr fnl f: no ch w wnr* **9/1**

3 *nk* **Database (IRE)** 2-9-3 0 LDettori 10 77
(Saeed Bin Suroor) *mid-div: hdwy and n.m.r over 2f out: styd on to take 3rd appr fnl f* **7/1**[3]

2 **4** 6 **Tactician**[28] 5793 2-9-3 0 HayleyTurner 2 64
(M L W Bell) *hld up towards rr: effrt over 2f out: hung lft over 1f out: kpt on to take modest 4th ins fnl f* **7/4**[1]

5 2½ **Regal Park (IRE)** 2-9-3 0 RyanMoore 5 60+
(J Noseda) *in rr: kpt on fnl 2f: nvr nr ldrs* **9/1**

5 **6** 1 **Primary Colors**[41] 5400 2-9-3 0 AdamKirby 16 56
(C G Cox) *trckd ldrs: effrt over 2f out: one pce* **12/1**

0 **7** *shd* **Zagarock**[37] 5547 2-8-12 0 DavidProbert 14 51
(B Palling) *dwlt: sn in tch: drvn 3f out: one pce* **100/1**

8 ½ **Mount Athos (IRE)** 2-9-3 0 SebSanders 4 59+
(J W Hills) *dwlt: in rr: drvn over 3f out: kpt on fnl 2f: nvr a factor* **66/1**

06 **9** 1½ **Kingston Acacia**[28] 5807 2-8-12 0 WilliamBuick 8 46
(A M Balding) *chsd wnr: drvn over 3f out: lost pl over 1f out* **50/1**

0 **10** *nk* **Trovare (USA)**[19] 6108 2-9-3 0 JimCrowley 6 51
(Mrs A J Perrett) *mid-div: effrt on outer over 2f out: lost pl over 1f out* **20/1**

00 **11** 3½ **Desert Aisling (IRE)**[118] 2889 2-8-12 0 JerryO'Dwyer 7 38
(Edgar Byrne) *chsd ldrs: wknd over 2f out* **150/1**

12 *nk* **Taqleed (IRE)** 2-9-3 0 RHills 1 42
(J H M Gosden) *mid-div on outer: effrt over 3f out: wknd over 1f out* **14/1**

13 1½ **On Khee** 2-8-12 0 TravisBlock 3 34
(H Morrison) *trckd ldrs on outer: lost pl over 1f out* **66/1**

14 2¼ **Bombadero (IRE)** 2-9-3 0 EddieAhern 17 34
(J L Dunlop) *a in rr: reminders after s* **16/1**

0 **15** *hd* **Stadium Of Light (IRE)**[110] 3160 2-9-3 0 SteveDrowne 9 34
(H Morrison) *in rr: rdn over 3f out: nvr on terms* **50/1**

0 **16** 3¾ **Passionate Cry (USA)**[28] 5807 2-9-3 0 TPQueally 13 25
(W J Knight) *chsd ldrs: wknd 2f out* **80/1**

1m 39.6s (-0.10) **Going Correction** +0.075s/f (Good) **16** Ran SP% **119.0**

Speed ratings (Par 97): **103,96,95,89,87 86,86,85,84,83 80,80,78,76,76 72**

toteswingers: 1&2 £7.90, 1&3 £4.00, 2&3 £6.50 CSF £51.12 TOTE £6.50: £2.40, £3.00, £1.80; EX 33.60.

Owner Sir David Seale **Bred** Chelston **Trained** East Everleigh, Wilts

FOCUS

The two divisions of this race last year were won by Skanky Biscuit, third next time in the Racing Post Trophy, and the subsequent Group 3 winner Palavicini. This season's race looked a potentially strong maiden, with several major trainers and owners represented, but it's hard to know what to make of the form. Unfortunately the official racecourse timing mechanism failed, so a 100% accurate comparison with the second division (only other race run over the straight 1m) is not possible, but hand times suggest Kalypso King went almost a second and a half quicker than Racing Post Trophy possible Dancing David. Flattered by the bare result or not, this son of Giant's Causeway travelled and quickened like a decent horse, and he's bred to be smart considering his dam won a Musidora before placing in the Oaks. He certainly deserves his chance in something better now, although he doesn't hold any Group-race entries.

NOTEBOOK

Kalypso King(USA) had already been beaten twice, but following his encouraging debut over 6f at Windsor, Richard Hannon apparently blamed himself for the next defeat, reasoning that he should have stepped the colt up in trip. Allowed his chance over further this time, he won in most impressive fashion and looked value for more like 10l. However, while he's evidently very good, plenty went his way and it might just be that he's a little flattered. For a start he was probably on the best ground against the stands' rail (winner of second division, who recorded a slower time, came up middle), and he was allowed his own way in front from a favourable draw (front-running tactics employed as he can be keen). And while he set quite a strong pace according to his rider, Richard Hughes admitted that put the colt at an advantage over those without previous racecourse experience, especially as the ground was on the easy ground. (op 5-1)

Centurio floundered under pressure on ground that could have been expected to suit, and struggled to confirm his debut promise, although he did finally run on into second. He's likely to want further next year. (tchd 10-1)

Database(IRE) came under pressure over 2f out and took a while to understand what was required, displaying a knee action in the process. He looks as though he will want 1m2f-plus before long. (op 8-1)

Tactician, second behind the much-hyped Coordinated Cut on debut at Doncaster, did little for that form, even allowing for being drawn poorly. He didn't enjoy the clearest of runs through, but that's no real excuse - he just didn't have the tactical speed - and he made only modest late progress. He'll want at least 1m4f next season. (op 9-4)

Regal Park(IRE) ◆, a £180,000 brother to 2005 Derby runner-up Walk In The Park, and Crimson Sky, a Navan maiden winner (1m2f) the previous day, looks one to take from the race. He was never competitive, racing well out the back and having to be niggled along from a fair way out to stay in touch, but he made good late headway. There should be any amount of improvement to come and he might be able to win a maiden this year, but it's over further next season that we're likely to see him fulfil his potential. (op 15-2 tchd 11-1)

Primary Colors failed to improve on his debut effort. (tchd 14-1)

Mount Athos(IRE), who is closely related to The Great Gatsby, probably needs time and distance. He ended up towards the stands' side from stall four and was not given a hard time late on.

Trovare(USA) ◆ is one to look out for when he's handicapped. He charted an extremely wide course and could never get involved. (op 16-1)

Taqleed(IRE) ◆ had the worst draw and should be capable of a lot better. (op 12-1)

On Khee ◆, also drawn low, is another likely to leave this form behind in time.

6618 MALONE ROOFING FILLIES' H'CAP 1m 2f 6y

3:20 (3:22) (Class 4) (0-85,84) 3-Y-O+ **£4,857** (£1,445; £722; £360) **Stalls** Low

Form RPR

1065 **1** **Natural Flair (USA)**[54] 5027 3-8-12 **79** AlanMunro 1 85
(P W Chapple-Hyam) *chsd ldrs: led appr fnl 2f: kpt slt advantage whn strly chal appr fnl f: asserted fnl 100yds: styd on wl* **16/1**

2-21 **2** 1 **Flora Trevelyan**[48] 5222 3-9-2 **83** AdamKirby 6 87+
(W R Swinburn) *plld hrd early: stdd in tch: stdy hdwy over 2f out to trck ldrs gng wl whn nt clr run over 1f out: swtchd rt: rdn and styd on fnl f: tk 2nd last strides but a hld by wnr* **3/1**[1]

0031 **3** *shd* **Fanditha (IRE)**[15] 6203 3-9-3 **84** RichardHughes 10 88
(R Hannon) *trckd ldr: drvn to chal appr fnl f tl ins fnl f: outstyd by wnr fnl 110yds and lost 2nd last strides* **5/1**[2]

6503 **4** ¾ **Trumpet Lily**[52] 5099 4-9-7 **83** JimCrowley 15 86+
(J G Portman) *hld up in rr: stdy hdwy fr 3f out: trckd ldrs travelling wl 2f out: drvn and styd on appr fnl f: chsd ldrs ins fnl f: styd on same pce* **20/1**

310 **5** ½ **Crimson Ribbon (USA)**[22] 6003 3-9-2 **83** JimmyFortune 3 85
(J H M Gosden) *in tch: hdwy to chse ldrs fr 4f out: rdn over 2f out: one pce ins fnl f* **12/1**

6410 **6** *nse* **Liberally (IRE)**[74] 4365 4-9-6 **82** EddieAhern 7 83
(B J Meehan) *chsd ldrs: rdn and one pce 3f out: styd on u.p fr over 1f out but no imp on ldrs fnl 100yds* **11/1**

0225 **7** *hd* **Accede**[55] 5009 3-9-1 **82** RyanMoore 14 83+
(J G Portman) *in rr: rdn and hdwy fr 2f out: nt clr run and swirchd rt jst ins fnl f: fin wl but nt rch ldrs* **8/1**[3]

0462 **8** *hd* **Presbyterian Nun (IRE)**[12] 6286 4-9-7 **83** (p) RichardMullen 5 84
(J L Dunlop) *in rr tl hdwy into mid-div: drvn to chse ldrs over 2f out: kpt on same pce ins fnl f* **9/1**

512 **9** 1¾ **Mildoura (FR)**[173] 1357 4-9-6 **82** IanMongan 8 79
(Mrs L J Mongan) *chsd ldrs: rdn over 2f out: wkng whn hmpd jst ins fnl f* **12/1**

5060 **10** *hd* **Latin Tinge (USA)**[15] 6209 3-8-10 **77** NCallan 11 74
(P F I Cole) *in rr: hrd drvn over 3f out: styd on u.p fnl 2f: kpt on ins fnl f but nvr a threat* **33/1**

0P **11** *3/4* **Ocean Transit (IRE)**[21] 6016 4-9-5 **81** JamesDoyle 4 76
(R J Price) *led tl hdd appr fnl f: wknd appr fnl f* **25/1**

6134 **12** *1/2* **Hollow Green (IRE)**[7] 6419 3-8-11 **83** MartinLane(5) 2 77
(P D Evans) *hmpd in rr sn after s: rdn along and sme hdwy ins fnl 3f: nvr rchd ldrs and wknd ins fnl 2f* **16/1**

1232 **13** *3 1/2* **Full Of Love (IRE)**[71] 4422 3-9-2 **83** MichaelHills 13 70
(B W Hills) *towards rr on outside: rdn ins fnl 3f: a bhd* **8/1**[3]

-006 **14** *15* **Nora Mae (IRE)**[22] 5996 3-9-1 **82** GeorgeBaker 16 39
(S Kirk) *plld hrd: in rr: lost tch fnl 3f: eased fnl 2f* **20/1**

2m 8.83s (0.03) **Going Correction** +0.075s/f (Good)
WFA 3 from 4yo 5lb **14** Ran SP% **125.7**
Speed ratings (Par 102): **102,101,101,100,100 100,99,99,98,98 97,97,94,82**
toteswingers: 1&2 £26.20, 1&3 £37.30, 2&3 £5.50 CSF £63.37 CT £293.01 TOTE £23.10: £6.70, £2.10, £2.60; EX 144.90.
Owner M Al-Qatami & K M Al-Mudhaf **Bred** Georgica Stable Llc & Andrew Rosen **Trained** Newmarket, Suffolk

FOCUS
A fair fillies' handicap. They went just a modest pace, and the main action took place centre field in the straight. The winner ran to the form of her C&D maiden win in April.

6619 SIR GERALD WHENT MEMORIAL NURSERY 6f 8y
3:55 (3:55) (Class 4) (0-85,85) 2-Y-O £5,180 (£1,541; £770; £384) Stalls High

Form RPR

2414 **1** **Freeforaday (USA)**[7] 6418 2-8-11 **75** RobertWinston 1 86
(J R Best) *rr-div: hdwy on outside 2f out: edgd rt: styd on wl fnl f: led towards fin* **7/1**[2]

4130 **2** *3/4* **Fleeting Echo**[33] 5658 2-8-12 **76** JimmyFortune 15 85
(R Hannon) *trckd ldrs: led jst ins fnl f: hdd towards fin* **17/2**

6600 **3** *3* **Jack My Boy (IRE)**[5] 6486 2-9-2 **80** GeorgeBaker 7 80
(P D Evans) *led 3f: led appr fnl f: sn hdd: kpt on same pce* **25/1**

1215 **4** *1/2* **Astonishment (IRE)**[11] 6305 2-9-0 **85** JPFahy(7) 14 84
(S Kirk) *chsd ldrs: effrt over 2f out: kpt on same pce fnl f* **11/2**[1]

1162 **5** *1 1/2* **Farmers Wish (IRE)**[18] 6134 2-9-3 **81** FrancisNorton 8 75
(J L Spearing) *t.k.h: w ldr: led 3f out: hdd & wknd appr fnl f* **10/1**

315 **6** *3/4* **Moonline Dancer (FR)**[20] 6055 2-9-6 **84** RichardHughes 4 76
(R Hannon) *chsd ldrs: fdd appr fnl f* **10/1**

310 **7** *3/4* **La Pantera**[19] 6104 2-9-4 **82** RyanMoore 9 72
(R Hannon) *in rr: swtchd rt and styd on wl stands' side rail fnl f* **9/1**

6300 **8** *1* **Imperial Warrior**[69] 4488 2-8-8 **72** SteveDrowne 3 59
(H Morrison) *dwlt: hdwy over 2f out: nvr nr ldrs* **16/1**

0210 **9** *hd* **Fardyieh**[13] 6241 2-9-0 **78** NCallan 11 64
(C E Brittain) *chsd ldrs: drvn over 2f out: wknd over 1f out* **15/2**[3]

0205 **10** *hd* **Transfixed (IRE)**[12] 6275 2-8-6 **75** MartinLane(5) 5 60
(P D Evans) *chsd ldrs: rdn over 2f out: wknd 2f out* **28/1**

3513 **11** *1* **Our Dream Queen**[62] 4739 2-8-7 **71** MichaelHills 6 53
(B W Hills) *mid-div: effrt over 2f out: sn wknd* **10/1**

0016 **12** *2 3/4* **Monte Mayor One**[48] 5218 2-8-1 **65** JamieMackay 16 39
(D Haydn Jones) *t.k.h in rr: nvr on terms* **50/1**

2215 **13** *1/2* **Miss Lesley**[68] 4539 2-9-0 **78** ChrisCatlin 13 51
(D K Ivory) *a in rr* **14/1**

224 **14** *7* **Lutine Charlie (IRE)**[29] 5778 2-9-3 **81** JimCrowley 17 33
(P Winkworth) *s.i.s: hld up in rr: bhd fnl 2f: eased* **11/1**

3432 **15** *7* **Mr Corby (IRE)**[14] 6227 2-8-7 **71** TonyCulhane 10 2
(M R Channon) *chsd ldrs: lost pl 3f out: bhd whn eased 1f out* **16/1**

1m 13.68s (0.68) **Going Correction** +0.075s/f (Good) **15** Ran SP% **123.5**
Speed ratings (Par 97): **98,97,93,92,90 89,88,87,86,86 85,81,80,71,62**
toteswingers: 1&2 £12.70, 1&3 £32.50, 2&3 £55.00 CSF £65.56 CT £1463.95 TOTE £9.00: £2.90, £3.20, £7.50; EX 81.90 TRIFECTA Not won..
Owner John Best **Bred** Susan Mauer **Trained** Hucking, Kent

FOCUS
A decent nursery. The first two came clear and the form looks sound. They raced middle to stands' side.

NOTEBOOK
Freeforaday(USA) ◆ produced a likeable effort off a mark 8lb higher than when winning over 5f at Folkestone two starts back. He still had a couple of lengths to make up on the leaders over 1f out, and had to switch a couple of times, but he quickened up in the style of a useful type. He can rate quite a bit higher. (op 6-1)
Fleeting Echo did little wrong. Although ultimately readily held by the winner, she pulled clear of the remainder having travelled strongly. She has the speed for 5f on this evidence. (tchd 9-1)
Jack My Boy(IRE), having his tenth start, was given a positive ride and ran well. He's due to be eased 3lb, which will help. (op 28-1)
Astonishment(IRE) ran okay, without improving for the drop in trip and switch to easy ground. He's a tough sort but is due to go up 2lb. (op 8-1)
Farmers Wish(IRE) showed a lot of speed and was a little keen but she ran respectably. She has won on soft ground but might be best suited by a quick surface, and a drop to 5f might help at some point as well.
Moonline Dancer(FR) couldn't sustain her run and might want better ground. (op 17-2)
La Pantera didn't show much on her return from a break last time but this was better. She was never seen with a chance but finished well against the stands' rail and looks ready for 7f. (op 10-1)
Imperial Warrior is entitled to come on for this first run in over two months. (op 20-1)

6620 PINKE JOBS MAIDEN STKS (DIV II) 1m (S)
4:25 (4:26) (Class 4) 2-Y-O £4,857 (£1,445; £722; £360) Stalls High

Form RPR

2 **1** **Dancing David (IRE)**[35] 5603 2-9-3 0 MartinDwyer 12 85+
(B J Meehan) *mde virtually all: racd stands' side tl field merged over 4f out: drvn fr over 2f out: forged clr ins fnl f* **7/4**[1]

2 *2 3/4* **Tamaathul** 2-9-3 0 RHills 9 79+
(B W Hills) *in tch: pushed along and hdwy fr 3f out: rn green ins fnl 2f: rdn and styd on to chse wnr ins fnl f but nvr any ch* **12/1**

3 *1 1/4* **Tenessee** 2-9-3 0 AdamKirby 3 76
(C G Cox) *chsd ldrs: rdn along fr 3f out: styd on to chal over 2f out: styd chsng wnr tl outpcd into 3rd fnl f* **12/1**

3 **4** *1 1/4* **Lunar Victory (USA)**[20] 6057 2-9-3 0 JimmyFortune 7 73
(J H M Gosden) *chsd ldrs: travelling ok over 2f out: sn rdn and no imp on wnr: wknd ins fnl f* **15/8**[2]

5 *3/4* **London Stripe (IRE)** 2-9-3 0 RyanMoore 6 72
(Sir Michael Stoute) *in tch: rdn and styd on to chse ldrs over 1f out: one pce ins fnl f* **9/1**[3]

6 *2* **First Fandango** 2-9-3 0 SebSanders 4 67
(J W Hills) *s.i.s: in tch 1/2-way: rdn 3f out: swtchd rt over 2f out: styd on same pce* **66/1**

0 **7** *2 1/2* **Veni Vedi Veci (IRE)**[45] 5312 2-8-12 0 WilliamBuick 11 57
(A M Balding) *racd promly stands' side tl field merged over 4f out: styd wl there tl wknd over 1f out* **66/1**

8 *2 1/4* **Green Moon (IRE)** 2-9-3 0 EddieAhern 16 57+
(H J L Dunlop) *in rr and racd stands' side tl field merged over 4f out: sn reminders: styd on fnl 2f: nvr in contention* **66/1**

9 *3 1/4* **Street Entertainer (IRE)** 2-9-3 0 JimCrowley 10 50+
(Mrs A J Perrett) *s.i.s: racd stands' side and bhd tl field merged over 4f out: hdwy to trck ldrs travelling wl ins fnl 3f: shkn up: green and hung lft 2f out: sn btn* **40/1**

10 *2 3/4* **Alfonso The Wise (IRE)** 2-9-3 0 ShaneKelly 14 44
(J Noseda) *racd stands' side and in tch whn field merged over 4f out: rdn: hung lft and wknd over 2f out* **16/1**

50 **11** *1 3/4* **Pont De Nuit**[19] 6108 2-9-3 0 RichardHughes 5 40
(R Hannon) *chsd ldrs: chal fr 3f out tl rdn: hung lft and wknd ins fnl 2f* **28/1**

12 *4 1/2* **Goldtrek (USA)** 2-8-12 0 RichardKingscote 2 25
(R Charlton) *s.i.s: towards rr most of way* **66/1**

00 **13** *5* **The Mighty Mod (USA)**[25] 5907 2-9-3 0 JoeFanning 15 19
(M Johnston) *racd stands' side tl field merged over 4f out and styd front rnk tl wknd over 2f out* **33/1**

14 *8* **Falahill** 2-9-3 0 AlanMunro 8 —
(R Hannon) *chsd ldrs tl wknd qckly 1/2-way* **50/1**

15 *3/4* **Serious Spirit** 2-8-12 0 SaleemGolam 13 —
(Rae Guest) *racd stands' side gp tl field merged over 4f out: sn rdn: a in rr* **100/1**

16 *7* **French Fantasy** 2-8-12 0 TravisBlock 1 —
(H Morrison) *chsd ldrs: rdn 3f out and wknd qckly* **50/1**

1m 40.99s (1.29) **Going Correction** +0.075s/f (Good) **16** Ran SP% **122.1**
Speed ratings (Par 97): **96,93,92,90,90 88,85,83,80,77 75,71,66,58,57 50**
toteswingers: 1&2 £9.60, 1&3 £10.20, 2&3 £16.70 CSF £22.91 TOTE £2.30: £1.60, £3.20, £2.90; EX 30.60.
Owner Catesby W Clay **Bred** Runnymede Farm Inc **Trained** Manton, Wilts

FOCUS
This looked a strong maiden beforehand, but the time was pretty ordinary, especially compared with the first division, although that race was hand-timed. It is doubtful if the winner had to improve. They split into two groups early on but were racing as one up the middle soon enough.

NOTEBOOK
Dancing David(IRE) ◆ produced an impressive performance and was ridden out with mainly hands and heels to defeat a potentially decent field. This confirmed the promise he showed on his debut at Salisbury and he could be quite smart. His stable won a division of this race with Skanky Biscuit, who then ran third in the Racing Post Trophy, and that race is apparently the target for this one. (op 9-4 tchd 6-4 and 5-2 in places)
Tamaathul, the first foal of a useful dual 7f winner, made a pleasing debut. He couldn't land a serious blow on the winner after running green when first coming under pressure, but he stayed on in quite taking style. (tchd 11-1 and 16-1)
Tenessee, a half-brother to dual 7f winner Hazytoo, out of a useful dual 5f-6f scorer at two, made a creditable introduction. Being a son of Nayef, he should do better given more time. (op 16-1 tchd 18-1)
Lunar Victory(USA) seemed to travel well but his finishing effort was disappointing and he didn't confirm the promise he showed when third in what is usually a decent conditions event at this track on his debut. He might want better ground. (tchd 9-4)
London Stripe(IRE), the first foal of a 1m2f winner, was easy to back and probably needed this. (op 7-1 tchd 10-1)
First Fandango showed ability but is likely to need 1m2f at the very least. (op 100-1)

6621 WISE CATERING H'CAP 1m 7y(R)
5:00 (5:01) (Class 5) (0-75,76) 3-Y-O £2,590 (£770; £385; £192) Stalls Low

Form RPR

3001 **1** **Swift Chap**[7] 6421 3-9-5 **76** 6ex DarryllHolland 7 85
(B R Millman) *mde all: shkn up and qcknd 2f out: edgd lft and sn clr: unchal* **11/2**[2]

3002 **2** *3* **Piccolo Mondo**[96] 3630 3-9-1 **72** IanMongan 1 74
(P Winkworth) *hld up in midfield: hdwy over 2f out: chsd wnr ins fnl f: styd on same pce* **20/1**

035 **3** *hd* **Day Of The Eagle (IRE)**[30] 5744 3-9-1 **72** WilliamBuick 5 74+
(L M Cumani) *s.i.s: in rr: drvn 4f out: hdwy and hung rt 2f out: veered lft and styd on strly ins fnl f* **11/1**

551- **4** *1 3/4* **Reaction**[361] 6673 3-9-2 **73** ChrisCatlin 4 71
(M R Channon) *trckd ldrs: effrt and chsd wnr 2f out: kpt on same pce* **11/1**

2000 **5** *1* **Perfect Friend**[28] 5810 3-9-4 **75** EddieAhern 12 70
(S Kirk) *trckd ldrs: effrt 2f out: one pce* **12/1**

2216 **6** *shd* **Implication**[17] 6168 3-9-4 **75** SebSanders 11 70
(E A L Dunlop) *hld up in rr: effrt over 2f out: kpt on nvr on terms* **7/2**[1]

34 **7** *nk* **Silent Oasis**[97] 3574 3-9-3 **74** MartinDwyer 2 68
(B J Meehan) *s.s: in rr: drvn over 2f out: kpt on fnl f: nvr nr ldrs* **14/1**

2-41 **8** *3/4* **Great Art (IRE)**[19] 6101 3-9-4 **75** AlanMunro 6 68
(P W Chapple-Hyam) *trckd ldrs: t.k.h: effrt over 2f out: wknd over 1f out* **11/2**[2]

61 **9** *3/4* **Diktat Queen**[28] 5789 3-9-4 **75** SaleemGolam 10 66
(Rae Guest) *s.i.s: mid-div: nt clr run 2f out: nvr a factor* **8/1**[3]

5601 **10** *hd* **Illusive Spirit (IRE)**[70] 4472 3-9-1 **72** JimmyFortune 9 62
(J H M Gosden) *hld up towards rr: effrt over 2f out: nvr nr ldrs* **11/1**

31-0 **11** *1 3/4* **Dialect**[40] 5449 3-9-1 **72** JimCrowley 3 58
(Mrs A J Perrett) *hld up in rr: effrt over 2f out: sn btn* **16/1**

3423 **12** *3 3/4* **Yellow Printer**[37] 3309 3-9-3 **74** TonyCulhane 8 52
(F J Brennan) *sn trcking ldrs: drvn over 2f out: sn lost pl* **25/1**

1m 39.94s (99.94) **12** Ran SP% **118.0**
toteswingers: 1&2 £17.70, 1&3 £11.60, 2&3 £32.50 CSF £109.37 CT £1191.62 TOTE £5.80: £1.70, £5.60, £3.80; EX 148.50.
Owner M A Swift and A J Chapman **Bred** D R Tucker **Trained** Kentisbeare, Devon

FOCUS
The first race staged on the round 1m at this track since 2001. This looked a fair 3-y-o handicap, but the pace was steady. They raced up the middle of the track in the straight. The runner-up is the best guide to the form.

6622 EVENTS BAR MANAGEMENT APPRENTICE H'CAP 2m
5:35 (5:35) (Class 5) (0-75,72) 4-Y-O+ £2,590 (£770; £385; £192) Stalls High

Form RPR

2213 **1** **Arab League (IRE)**[23] 5962 4-8-11 **59** AndreaAtzeni 1 68+
(R J Price) *trckd ldrs: led ins fnl 3f: rdn over 2f out: styd on wl u.p whn strly chal ins fnl f* **7/2**[1]

004- **2** *1/2* **Bugsy's Boy**[177] 6861 5-9-3 **68** MatthewDavies(3) 2 77
(George Baker) *in rr: hdwy on outside fr 3f out: rdn to chse wnr 1f out and chal ins fnl f: sn no ex and one pce fnl 110yds* **11/1**

42 **3** *3* **Whitcombe Spirit**[31] 5734 4-8-6 **57** MartinLane(3) 9 62
(Jamie Poulton) *chsd ldrs: hrd rdn and hung lft fr ins fnl 3f: n.m.r and swtchd lft jst ins fnl f and sn outpcd by ldng duo* **5/1**[3]

3-45 **4** *5* **Wester Ross (IRE)**[8] 6400 5-8-12 **60** WilliamCarson 6 59
(J M P Eustace) *trckd ldr tl wnt upsides fr 1/2-way: rdn 4f out: hung lft and wknd fr 2f out* **15/2**

0464 **5** *1 ¼* **Absolut Power (GER)**[25] 5917 8-9-8 **70** MarcHalford 7 68
(J A Geake) *chsd ldrs: rdn 4f out: styd wl there tl wknd qckly over 1f out* **7/1**

1250 **6** *3 ¼* **Star Of Pompey**[40] 5425 5-8-5 **56** AmyBaker(3) 12 50
(A B Haynes) *chsd ldrs: rdn and wkng whn n.m.r ins fnl 3f* **12/1**

0/51 **7** *2 ½* **Gandalf**[34] 5642 7-9-4 **71** JPFahy(5) 11 62
(Miss Amy Weaver) *in rr tl hdwy 3f out: drvn to chse ldrs over 2f out: wknd over 1f out* **5/1**[3]

22-0 **8** *26* **General Ting (IRE)**[34] 5649 4-9-9 **71** JackMitchell 5 30
(Sir Mark Prescott) *in tch: rdn 4f out: hung bdly lft and wknd ins fnl 3f* **9/2**[2]

3m 36.0s (4.00) **Going Correction** +0.075s/f (Good) **8** Ran SP% **114.0**
Speed ratings (Par 103): **93,92,91,88,88 86,85,72**
toteswingers: 1&2 £5.60, 1&3 £3.30, 2&3 £8.70 CSF £42.19 CT £190.83 TOTE £3.70: £1.20, £4.40, £2.20; EX 65.20 Place 6: £153.8, Place 5: £62.47.
Owner Mrs P A Wallis **Bred** D G Iceton **Trained** Ullingswick, H'fords

FOCUS
A modest apprentice handicap, and muddling form. The main action was up the middle of the track in the straight.
General Ting(IRE) Official explanation: trainer's rep had no explanation for the poor form shown
T/Jkpt: Not won. T/Plt: £262.70 to a £1 stake. Pool: £193,721.55. 538.31 winning tickets. T/Qpdt: £59.60 to a £1 stake. Pool: £4,780.52. 59.30 winning tickets. ST

6623 - 6626a (Foreign Racing) - See Raceform Interactive

6439 LINGFIELD (L-H)
Friday, October 9

OFFICIAL GOING: Standard to slow
Wind: Light, across away from stands Weather: Overcast, rain from race 4 onwards

6627 CROWHURST MAIDEN STKS (DIV I) 7f (P)
1:50 (1:52) (Class 4) 2-Y-O £3,561 (£1,059; £529; £264) Stalls Low

Form RPR

2 **1** **Verdant**[21] 6065 2-9-3 0 RyanMoore 11 80+
(Sir Michael Stoute) *trckd ldng pair: chal on outer 2f out: led over 1f out: edgd rt but styd on wl* **6/4**[1]

0 **2** *1 ¼* **Shamir**[20] 6109 2-9-3 0 FergusSweeney 14 75
(Miss Jo Crowley) *chsd ldrs on outer: effrt to chal and wdst of all 2f out: pressed wnr 1f out: stl green and nt qckn* **22/1**

3043 **3** *hd* **Sheer Force (IRE)**[26] 5913 2-9-3 72 JimCrowley 8 74
(W J Knight) *lw: dwlt: towards rr: prog 1/2-way to go 7th over 2f out: hdwy over 1f out: rdn and styd on fnl f* **5/1**[3]

6 **4** *1 ¾* **Beaumont's Party (IRE)**[20] 6109 2-9-3 0 RichardHughes 1 70
(R Hannon) *lw: led to over 1f out: hung rt and fdd fnl f* **3/1**[2]

5 *3 ¼* **Illustrious Prince (IRE)** 2-9-3 0 EddieAhern 13 62
(J Noseda) *w'like: scope: tall: dwlt: hld up: stdy prog after 3f: 6th and wl in tch 2f out: pushed along over 1f out: wknd* **14/1**

0 **6** *3* **Vito Volterra (IRE)**[61] 4825 2-9-3 0 TonyCulhane 10 54+
(J R Best) *str: settled in last trio: shuffled along fr 2f out: kpt on steadily: nvr nr ldrs: do bttr* **100/1**

06 **7** *½* **Foxtrot Delta (IRE)**[13] 6291 2-9-3 0 FrankieMcDonald 3 53
(P Winkworth) *w'like: chsd ldng trio: cl enough on inner 2f out: wknd over 1f out* **40/1**

00 **8** *nk* **Old Devil Moon (IRE)**[16] 6199 2-9-3 0 JamesDoyle 7 52
(T G Mills) *chsd ldr: upsides 2f out: sn wknd* **50/1**

06 **9** *2 ½* **Luck Of The Draw (IRE)**[22] 6026 2-9-3 0 SebSanders 9 46
(Sir Mark Prescott) *bit bkwd: racd wd in midfield: rdn and effrt on outer over 2f out and jst in tch w ldrs: sn wknd* **50/1**

00 **10** *1 ¾* **Belle Zorro**[13] 6291 2-8-12 0 J-PGuillambert 12 37
(M L W Bell) *swtg: sn pushed along: struggling fr 1/2-way: no ch after* **66/1**

11 *3* **Moobeyn** 2-9-3 0 MartinDwyer 5 34+
(M P Tregoning) *w'like: dwlt: rn v green and sn struggling in last: nvr a factor* **11/2**

12 *6* **Optimistic Duke (IRE)** 2-9-3 0 NCallan 2 19+
(W R Muir) *w'like: str: bit bkwd: nvr bttr than midfield: pushed along 1/2-way: wkng in last pair over 2f out* **25/1**

0 **13** *nk* **Finch Flyer (IRE)**[28] 5829 2-9-3 0 GeorgeBaker 6 19+
(G L Moore) *sn pushed along to stay in tch: struggling after 3f: wl bhd fnl 2f* **50/1**

1m 25.87s (1.07) **Going Correction** +0.15s/f (Slow) **13** Ran SP% **122.7**
Speed ratings (Par 97): **99,97,97,95,91 88,87,87,84,82 79,72,71**
toteswingers: 1&2 £15.90, 2&3 £21.50, 2& 3 not won. CSF £44.89 TOTE £2.50: £1.10, £3.60, £1.70; EX 43.60 TRIFECTA Not won..
Owner K Abdulla **Bred** Juddmonte Farms Ltd **Trained** Newmarket, Suffolk

FOCUS
Following the refurbishment of the Polytrack course, the going was "standard to slow" for the second meeting running. This first race contained several unexposed types with potential, and there was a better gallop than average for the track. Solid form, with the third the key.

NOTEBOOK
Verdant had been edgy in the paddock on his debut but was more relaxed this time. He had learnt from that first run but still gave the impression that there is more to come as he matures. He should stay at least 1m next year. (op 13-8 tchd 2-1 and 9-4 in places)
Shamir holds the form down to some extent, having finished only seventh on his debut, but he showed promise that day and has probably improved. A relatively inexpensive Dubai Destination half-brother to three winners, he is capable of winning a similar event and should stay 1m. (op 20-1)
Sheer Force(IRE), the most exposed of these, helps to put the race into perspective. He could still win a maiden, but his handicap mark is not far wrong so a return to nurseries is an even more attractive option, with 1m likely to suit. (op 9-2 tchd 4-1)
Beaumont's Party(IRE), who pulled too hard when held up on his debut, switched to front-running here but he probably went a fraction too quick. He should find a race when he calms down a bit. (op 4-1)
Illustrious Prince(IRE), a 72,000gns brother to a good 7f winner, was drawn wide and had a satisfactory spin round. He looks likely to improve on this encouraging first effort. (op 12-1)
Vito Volterra(IRE) looks to be heading for handicaps after one more run, and can probably improve on his two efforts to date.
Foxtrot Delta(IRE) will now get a handicap mark and, having shown some minor ability in three maidens, will be more competitive in that company. (op 50-1)
Old Devil Moon(IRE) has yet to prove he stays 7f but needs to switch to handicaps before more can be deduced.
Moobeyn appears to need more time to justify the price he went off at here. (op 8-1 tchd 5-1)

6628 ST PIERS MAIDEN FILLIES' STKS 1m (P)
2:20 (2:22) (Class 4) 2-Y-O £3,885 (£1,156; £577; £288) Stalls High

Form RPR

2 **1** **Timepiece**[21] 6062 2-9-0 0 TPQueally 3 80
(H R A Cecil) *lw: mde all: drvn clr over 1f out: styd on wl* **5/2**[2]

4 **2** *1 ¾* **Shimmering Surf (IRE)**[31] 5752 2-9-0 0 JimCrowley 5 76
(P Winkworth) *w'like: str: chsd wnr: rdn to chal 2f out: nt qckn over 1f out: kpt on* **14/1**

3 **3** *shd* **Gertrude Bell**[21] 6062 2-9-0 0 JimmyFortune 2 76
(J H M Gosden) *trckd ldng pair on inner: rdn and nt qckn wl over 1f out: kpt on fnl f to press for 2nd* **9/4**[1]

4 *1 ½* **Nouriya** 2-9-0 0 RyanMoore 12 76+
(Sir Michael Stoute) *w'like: str: scope: hld up and sn in last trio: stl wl off the pce over 2f out: gd prog wl over 1f out: clsng and looked likely to fin 2nd whn no room ins fnl f* **16/1**

3 **5** *1 ¾* **Maristar (USA)**[21] 6055 2-9-0 0 NCallan 7 69
(G A Butler) *chsd ldng pair: rdn to chal on outer 2f out: fdd over 1f out* **4/1**[3]

52 **6** *nk* **A Pocketful Of Rye (IRE)**[13] 6274 2-9-0 0 ShaneKelly 8 68
(J A Osborne) *w'like: leggy: wl in tch on outer: rdn and effrt over 2f out: wd bnd sn after: outpcd over 1f out: plugged on* **40/1**

3 **7** *nk* **Verity Lane (USA)**[34] 5681 2-9-0 0 EddieAhern 4 67
(R M H Cowell) *unf: dwlt: t.k.h and sn trckd ldrs: cl enough and rdn 2f out: fdd* **33/1**

4 **8** *1 ¾* **Mirabella (IRE)**[18] 6163 2-9-0 0 RichardHughes 11 65+
(R Hannon) *w'like: str: rn in snatches and pushed along in midfield: rdn over 2f out: no imp on ldrs over 1f out: eased last 100yds* **7/1**

04 **9** *hd* **Sparkling Smile (IRE)**[13] 6274 2-9-0 0 TedDurcan 6 63
(D R Lanigan) *nvr beyond midfield: rdn 3f out: no prog: plugged on* **66/1**

10 *hd* **Ildiko (USA)** 2-9-0 0 SebSanders 10 63
(Sir Mark Prescott) *tall: dropped in fr quite a wd draw and hld up in last: taken to wd outside bnd 2f out: pushed along and kpt on one pce* **66/1**

40 **11** *10* **Momtaz**[18] 6164 2-9-0 0 LiamJones 9 41
(C E Brittain) *racd wd: a in rr: struggling 3f out: bhd over 1f out* **40/1**

12 *21* **Danvilla** 2-9-0 0 PatCosgrave 1 —
(P R Webber) *w'like: bit bkwd: s.s: a in rr: t.o* **100/1**

1m 39.15s (0.95) **Going Correction** +0.15s/f (Slow) **12** Ran SP% **116.2**
Speed ratings (Par 94): **101,99,99,97,95 95,95,93,93,93 83,62**
toteswingers: 1&2 £20.10, 1&3 £1.20, 2&3 not won. CSF £34.58 TOTE £2.80: £1.80, £3.00, £1.30; EX 39.70 Trifecta £52.10 Pool: £442.25 - 6.28 winning units..
Owner K Abdulla **Bred** Juddmonte Farms Ltd **Trained** Newmarket, Suffolk

FOCUS
This looked a decent race of its sort for the track, but the pace was average at best. The winner was close to her debut form.

NOTEBOOK
Timepiece impressed in the way she took control from the front early in the straight. Connections reported that the ground was too fast for her on her debut and that this surface - particularly the way it was riding on this occasion - suited her much better. She still looks to have plenty to learn and has the physique to make up into a good filly next year. (op 15-8 tchd 7-4)
Shimmering Surf(IRE), stepped up a furlong from her debut, ran a solid race in defeat. There are maidens to be won with her at either trip. (op 20-1 tchd 25-1)
Gertrude Bell, just behind the winner when both made their debuts, was beaten further this time. She had looked unlucky that day, so it must be assumed that the winner has made more progress since then, but she is capable of winning races in her own right. (op 5-2 tchd 3-1)
Nouriya ◆, a Danehill Dancer debutante from a good family at trips from 6f to 1m4f, made a promising debut and is one to note next time. Drawn wide, this Irish 1000 Guineas entry was finding her stride late on and will need at least this trip as she matures. (op 14-1)
Maristar(USA) had run creditably on her debut, which was on turf. She is capable of winning races on either surface. (op 11-2)
A Pocketful Of Rye(IRE) is now qualified for nurseries and should be interesting when making the switch.
Verity Lane(USA) will be at home in handicaps after one more run. She was too headstrong here, so a stronger pace would help.
Mirabella(IRE) looked happier making the running over 7f on her debut. Official explanation: jockey said filly resented the kickback (op 15-2)

6629 CROWHURST MAIDEN STKS (DIV II) 7f (P)
2:55 (2:57) (Class 4) 2-Y-O £3,561 (£1,059; £529; £264) Stalls Low

Form RPR

1 **Sahara Kingdom (IRE)** 2-9-3 0 TedDurcan 10 80+
(Saeed Bin Suroor) *unf: scope: s.s: mostly in last pair tl gd prog on wd outside fr over 2f out: shkn up and r.o to ld ent fnl f: sn clr* **6/4**[1]

4 **2** *3 ¼* **Essexbridge**[21] 6065 2-9-3 0 RichardHughes 2 72
(R Hannon) *lw: chsd ldrs: drvn in 3rd over 2f out: styd on ins fnl f to snatch 2nd on post* **4/1**[2]

00 **3** *nk* **Round Won (USA)**[26] 5907 2-9-3 0 JimCrowley 8 71
(W J Knight) *str: lw: sn trckd ldr: wnt 2nd over 3f out: rdn to ld over 1f out: hdd and outpcd ent fnl f: lost 2nd post* **12/1**

4 *¾* **High Importance (USA)** 2-9-3 0 RyanMoore 12 69+
(J Noseda) *w'like: str: scope: hld up towards rr: prog on outer and in tch 2f out: outpcd over 1f out: shkn up and kpt on* **4/1**[2]

5 *1 ¼* **Moose Moran (USA)** 2-9-3 0 TPQueally 7 66+
(H R A Cecil) *w'like: str: bit bkwd: chsd ldrs: pushed along fr 1/2-way: effrt to dispute 3rd 2f out: sn outpcd: fdd fnl f* **11/1**

0 **6** *nk* **Tamarind Hill (IRE)**[21] 6054 2-9-3 0 MartinDwyer 9 65
(C R Egerton) *trckd ldr: led 1/2-way: hdd over 1f out: wknd fnl f* **66/1**

05 **7** *3* **Baralaka**[30] 5778 2-9-3 0 SebSanders 6 58
(Sir Mark Prescott) *settled in rr: outpcd in 9th 2f out and pushed along: kpt on steadily fnl f* **8/1**[3]

8 *2* **Fivefold (USA)** 2-9-3 0 J-PGuillambert 3 53
(J Akehurst) *w'like: bit bkwd: dwlt: t.k.h in midfield: rn green but stl in tch over 2f out: wknd over 1f out* **66/1**

06 **9** *1 ¼* **Sonny G (IRE)**[4] 6542 2-9-0 0 MarcHalford(3) 5 50
(J R Best) *hld up at bk of main gp but wl in tch: outpcd over 2f out: no ch after* **66/1**

00 **10** *4 ½* **Foxtrot Foxtrot**[18] 6162 2-9-3 0 FrankieMcDonald 11 39
(P Winkworth) *awkward s: mostly in last: detached fr 3f out* **66/1**

4 **11** *2 ½* **Call Of The Kings**[126] 2676 2-9-3 0 (b[1]) LPKeniry 1 32
(R A Teal) *in tch on inner: losing pl whn hmpd over 2f out: wknd* **33/1**

00 **12** *5* **Draco Boy**[39] 5528 2-9-3 0........................ StephenCarson 4 20
(Andrew Turnell) *led to 1/2-way: wknd rapidly: t.o* **100/1**
1m 26.32s (1.52) **Going Correction** +0.15s/f (Slow) 12 Ran SP% **117.0**
Speed ratings (Par 97): **97,93,92,92,90 90,86,84,83,78 75,69**
toteswingers: 1&2 £3.00, 1&3 £5.50, 2&3 £5.10 CSF £7.10 TOTE £2.70: £1.20, £1.60, £3.10; EX 10.40 Trifecta £69.80 Pool: £303.11 - 3.21 winning units..
Owner Godolphin **Bred** John O'Connor **Trained** Newmarket, Suffolk

FOCUS
A slow pace until the first turn and the form is limited as a result. The winner was impressive.

NOTEBOOK
Sahara Kingdom(IRE) ◆ was slowly out but his raking stride left the others standing in the straight. Ted Durcan reported that he had missed the break because a horse in an adjacent stall had been playing up but that in the end he had won like a "nice horse". A 200,000euro Cozzene half-brother to three winners in the US, his superiority was accentuated by challenging wide, but he has immense potential and could develop into a high-class 3yo. (op 7-4 tchd 2-1)
Essexbridge followed up a good turf debut with another fine run, only to be outspeeded by a classy debutant. He is well up to winning a typical maiden and should be suited by 1m. (op 100-30 tchd 3-1)
Round Won(USA) ran his best race to date and looks closer to winning now. His opening handicap mark is likely to be higher following this, but he is progressive and one to keep an eye on. (op 11-1 tchd 8-1 and 14-1)
High Importance(USA) ◆, a son of the 1m2f Group 1 dirt winner Arch, is related to several good winners worldwide. He made an encouraging debut, picking up well when switched outside in the straight, and this Irish Derby entry should improve plenty. (op 11-2)
Moose Moran(USA), a son of the Belmont Stakes winner Lemon Drop Kid out of a maiden sprinter, was one of the first off the bridle but should be suited by 1m (op 10-1 tchd 12-1)
Tamarind Hill(IRE), last on his debut, ran much better here. However, he faded badly late on and may not quite have stayed 7f at this stage of his career.
Baralaka is now qualified for handicaps, and he will be one for close consideration when making the switch. (op 7-1 tchd 9-1)

6630 MARSH GREEN H'CAP 7f (P)
3:30 (3:30) (Class 4) (0-80,80) 3-Y-O+ **£6,476** (£1,927; £963; £481) **Stalls** Low

Form RPR
56 **1** **Ravi River (IRE)**[21] 6072 5-9-2 76........................ PatCosgrave 8 84
(J R Boyle) *hld up in midfield on outer: prog over 2f out: drvn ahd ent fnl f: styd on* **20/1**
0000 **2** *1/2* **Trafalgar Square**[16] 6212 7-9-3 77........................ JimCrowley 14 84
(M J Attwater) *dwlt: hld up in rr and racd wd: prog on outer fr 3f out: rdn to chal ent fnl f: nt qckn last 100yds* **16/1**
0001 **3** *nk* **Trade Centre**[13] 6294 4-8-11 71........................ MartinDwyer 7 77
(W R Muir) *prom on outer: effrt over 2f out: drvn to press ldrs over 1f out: kpt on same pce nr fin* **12/1**
0000 **4** *nk* **Alfresco**[26] 5914 5-9-6 80........................(b) TonyCulhane 12 85
(J R Best) *hld up wl in rr: prog on outer over 2f out: cruising bhd ldrs but nowhere to go over 1f out: rdn and r.o lasst 150yds: hopeless task* **33/1**
2120 **5** *shd* **Indian Art (IRE)**[37] 5575 3-9-1 77........................ RichardHughes 2 81
(R Hannon) *dwlt: hld up in last quartet: stl there 2f out: pushed along and gd prog over 1f out: clsd on ldrs ins fnl f: one pce nr fin* **10/1**
6050 **6** *nk* **Spiritual Art**[20] 6111 3-8-8 70........................(p) PaulDoe 11 73
(L A Dace) *hld up in last quartet: prog on wd outside 2f out: rdn and styd on fnl f: nvr quite rchd ldrs* **66/1**
3345 **7** *1 3/4* **I Confess**[13] 6279 4-8-13 78........................(b) RichardEvans(5) 10 77
(P D Evans) *mde most to jst over 2f out: led again over 1f out: wknd and hdd ent fnl f* **7/1**
5543 **8** *1 1/2* **Hustle (IRE)**[16] 6212 4-9-6 80........................(p) GeorgeBaker 13 75
(Miss Gay Kelleway) *sn c across fr outside draw to press ldr: rdn to ld jst over 2f out: fnd nil in front: hdd & wknd over 1f out* **14/1**
2122 **9** *3/4* **Hightime Heroine (IRE)**[11] 6348 3-9-1 77........................ RyanMoore 9 80+
(J Noseda) *lw: hld up wl in rr: stl there 2f out: prog towards inner over 1f out: styng on whn no room and eased ins fnl f: would have fin much clsr* **4/1**[1]
6060 **10** *1/2* **Shamrock Lady (IRE)**[31] 5746 4-9-0 74........................ TPO'Shea 6 66
(J Gallagher) *hld up in last quartet: last and detached over 2f out: being nudged along whn rdr dropped whip over 1f out: styd on last 100yds* **25/1**
5400 **11** *1/2* **Valatrix (IRE)**[44] 5349 4-9-1 75........................ AlanMunro 4 66
(C F Wall) *chsd ldrs: rdn over 2f out: stl cl enough over 1f out: wknd fnl f* **14/1**
4310 **12** *1/2* **Intolerable (IRE)**[86] 3982 3-8-12 74........................ SebSanders 5 62
(R M Beckett) *chsd ldng pair tl lost pl u.p 2f out* **20/1**
0032 **13** *nse* **Mark Of Meydan**[27] 5884 4-9-1 75........................ PhillipMakin 3 64
(M Dods) *nvr beyond midfield: u.p 3f out: no prog 2f out: wknd* **11/2**[3]
0122 **14** *shd* **Tamasou (IRE)**[6] 6496 4-8-12 72........................ TPQueally 1 61
(A J McCabe) *cl up on inner: u.p over 2f out: wknd over 1f out* **9/2**[2]
1m 24.76s (-0.04) **Going Correction** +0.15s/f (Slow)
WFA 3 from 4yo+ 2lb 14 Ran SP% **119.9**
Speed ratings (Par 105): **106,105,105,104,104 104,102,100,99,99 98,98,97,97**
toteswingers: 1&2 £3.00, 1&3 £5.50, 2&3 £5.10 CSF £292.76 CT £4082.04 TOTE £23.00: £6.60, £4.10, £4.40; EX 391.60 TRIFECTA Not won..
Owner M Khan X2 **Bred** Gainsborough Stud Management Ltd **Trained** Epsom, Surrey

FOCUS
A lively gallop helped the hold-up horses, and several of those involved in the blanket finish came from a long way back. The winner is a fair guide to the form.
Hightime Heroine(IRE) Official explanation: jockey said filly was denied a clear run

6631 SANDHAWES HILL H'CAP 6f (P)
4:05 (4:06) (Class 3) (0-90,90) 3-Y-O+ **£8,418** (£2,505; £1,251; £625) **Stalls** Low

Form RPR
3114 **1** **Lemon N Sugar (USA)**[91] 3795 4-8-11 82........................ RyanMoore 8 92+
(J Noseda) *lw: hld up in midfield: prog on outer fr 2f out: r.o wl to ld ins fnl f: sn clr* **2/1**[1]
0-00 **2** *1 3/4* **Masamah (IRE)**[154] 1824 3-9-4 90........................ TPO'Shea 11 95
(E A L Dunlop) *t.k.h: trckd ldr after 2f: rdn to ld on outer jst ins fnl f: sn hdd and outpcd* **12/1**
-540 **3** *hd* **Beat The Bell**[13] 6278 4-9-4 89........................ ShaneKelly 10 93
(J A Osborne) *hld up in rr: effrt on outer over 2f out: styd on fr over 1f out to press for 2nd nr fin: no imp on wnr* **18/1**
0254 **4** *1/2* **Crystal Moments**[18] 6155 3-9-3 89........................ EddieAhern 6 91
(E A L Dunlop) *hld up in midfield: prog on inner fr 2f out: cl enough ent fnl f: one pce after* **14/1**
-110 **5** *3/4* **Tagula Night (IRE)**[29] 5799 3-8-12 84........................(vt) TedDurcan 7 84
(W R Swinburn) *chsd ldr 2f: styd prom: outpcd over 1f out* **4/1**[2]
2040 **6** *nk* **Macdillon**[14] 6240 3-9-4 90........................ FergusSweeney 1 89
(W S Kittow) *trckd ldrs: effrt on inner 2f out: cl enough over 1f out: one pce* **12/1**
0305 **7** *hd* **Diriculous**[35] 5646 5-9-5 90........................(b) JimmyFortune 9 88
(T G Mills) *s.s and urged along early: last tl pushed along and styd on wl fnl f: nrst fin* **7/1**
0054 **8** *3/4* **Dazed And Amazed**[28] 5830 5-8-10 81........................ RichardHughes 5 77
(R Hannon) *mde most tl hdd & wknd jst ins fnl f* **8/1**
6416 **9** *5* **Mutamared (USA)**[13] 6293 9-8-8 79........................(t) StephenCarson 3 59
(Andrew Reid) *t.k.h: hld up in midfield on inner: snatched up over 4f out: snatched up again over 2f out: sn bhd* **20/1**
0001 **10** *shd* **Good Gorsoon (USA)**[20] 6112 4-8-9 85........................ AshleyMorgan(5) 2 65
(B W Hills) *lw: hld up: plld hrd and snatched up after 1f: stl pulling after: dropped away over 2f out* **6/1**[3]
1m 12.39s (0.49) **Going Correction** +0.15s/f (Slow)
WFA 3 from 4yo+ 1lb 10 Ran SP% **123.3**
Speed ratings (Par 107): **102,99,99,98,97 97,97,96,89,89**
toteswingers: 1&2 £3.40, 1&3 £20.30, 2&3 not won. CSF £30.60 CT £315.83 TOTE £2.20: £1.50, £3.40, £5.60; EX 69.00 TRIFECTA Not won..
Owner The Searchers **Bred** Establo Madoca Corp **Trained** Newmarket, Suffolk

FOCUS
A decent sprint, but the pace soon steadied and only quickened going into the final bend. The form is not rock solid but the progressive winner can rate higher still.

NOTEBOOK
Lemon N Sugar(USA) has had a fine season and is useful enough on turf, but she is particularly effective on Polytrack. Though favoured by challenging wide, she finished full of running and is one to treat with respect in good company. (op 3-1 tchd 100-30 and 7-2 in places)
Masamah(IRE) had been off since two flops on turf in the spring, but this showed he still has plenty to offer. Already a winner on this track, he was only beaten by a smart and improving filly. (tchd 11-1)
Beat The Bell appreciated the drop back to 6f and is gradually inching back towards a fifth win. Three of his four to date have been on Polytrack. (op 20-1 tchd 16-1)
Crystal Moments could yet win off this mark now she is back on Polytrack. (op 12-1)
Tagula Night(IRE), who has had a tougher task at the weights since winning twice in August, needs the handicapper to relent a fraction. (tchd 7-2 and 9-2)
Macdillon made a respectable all-weather debut. Lightly-raced, he has shown some form in decent company on turf and should build on this. (tchd 11-1)
Good Gorsoon(USA) pulled so hard he kept running into the back-end of his rivals early on and is probably best when trying to make all, something that he achieved in style last time out. Official explanation: jockey said colt hung right on the first bend (op 11-2 tchd 13-2)

6632 FELCOURT H'CAP 5f (P)
4:40 (4:40) (Class 4) (0-80,80) 3-Y-O+ **£6,476** (£1,927; £722; £722) **Stalls** High

Form RPR
0005 **1** **Lucky Leigh**[24] 5974 3-8-10 72........................ SamHitchcott 5 81
(M R Channon) *hld up: in last pair 2f out: prog on inner over 1f out: led ins fnl f: drvn out and hld on* **25/1**
3064 **2** *1/2* **Our Piccadilly (IRE)**[26] 5919 4-9-0 76........................ FergusSweeney 3 83
(W S Kittow) *hld up and sn last: prog on outer over 1f out: r.o fnl f to take 2nd on post: nt rch wnr* **8/1**
2042 **3** *hd* **Garstang**[7] 6459 6-9-1 77........................(b) GeorgeBaker 2 83
(J Balding) *sn trckd ldrs gng strly: nt clr run briefly over 1f out: got through to chal ins fnl f: hung bdly rt and fnd nil: lost 2nd on post* **11/4**[1]
0516 **3** *dht* **Make My Dream**[18] 6171 6-8-6 68........................ TPO'Shea 8 74
(J Gallagher) *chsd ldrs: shkn up over 2f out: prog on outer over 1f out: r.o and clsd on ldrs fin: a jst hld* **12/1**
1-4 **5** *1 3/4* **Todber**[174] 1360 4-8-4 66 oh1........................(v) MartinDwyer 6 66+
(M P Tregoning) *hld up bhd ldrs: nt clr run over 1f out and dropped bk to 9th: plld out ins fnl f: r.o wl nr fin* **8/1**
0363 **6** *nse* **Chjimes (IRE)**[7] 6459 5-9-4 80........................ LPKeniry 4 80
(C R Dore) *hld up bhd ldrs: effrt over 1f out: one pce and no imp fnl f* **4/1**[2]
242- **7** *1/2* **Master Lightfoot**[357] 6769 3-9-1 77........................ EddieAhern 9 75
(W R Swinburn) *disp ld: narrow advantage over 1f out: hdd & wknd ins fnl f* **7/1**[3]
0313 **8** *1/2* **Steelcut**[9] 6396 5-8-8 70........................ StephenCarson 10 66
(Andrew Reid) *lw: rousted along early: pressed ldrs on outer: fdd jst over 1f out* **8/1**
0025 **9** *1 3/4* **Fault**[11] 6329 3-9-4 80........................(t) TPQueally 1 70
(Stef Liddiard) *lw: disp ld to over 1f out: wknd rapidly ins fnl f* **14/1**
-600 **10** *1/2* **Asaint Needs Brass (USA)**[18] 6167 3-8-5 70........................ MarcHalford(3) 7 58
(J R Best) *a in rr: last and losing tch over 1f out* **20/1**
59.40 secs (0.60) **Going Correction** +0.15s/f (Slow) 10 Ran SP% **110.7**
Speed ratings (Par 105): **101,100,99,99,97 97,96,95,92,91**PL: Garstang £0.60, Make My Dream £2.20, TRI: Lucky Leigh/Our Piccadilly/Garstang £366.56 LL/OP/MMD £1,286.08 toteswingers: 1&2 not won, 1&G £7.50, 1&MMD £7.50, 2&G £7.50, 2&MMD not won. CSF £205.51 TOTE £11.80: £2.70, £2.90; EX 94.40 Trifecta £91.30 Part won. Pool: £246.827 Owner.

FOCUS
A good sprint gallop enabled the winner to make late ground from second-last. On an afternoon where it had paid to challenge wide, she arrived closest to the inside rail and won convincingly. Ordinary but sound handicap form.

6633 TANDRIDGE H'CAP 1m (P)
5:10 (5:11) (Class 3) (0-95,95) 3-Y-O+ **£9,066** (£2,697; £1,348; £673) **Stalls** Low

Form RPR
0000 **1** **Rock Ascot (URU)**[13] 6290 5-9-0 90........................(b[1]) PatCosgrave 5 100
(G L Moore) *t.k.h early: hld up bhd ldrs: prog 2f out: chsd ldr ins fnl f: r.o wl to ld last strides* **20/1**
6114 **2** *nk* **Sarah Park (IRE)**[13] 6267 4-8-13 89........................ MartinDwyer 10 98
(B J Meehan) *pressed ldr: led wl over 1f out and sn 2 l clr: styd on fnl f: hdd last strides* **9/1**
0366 **3** *1 3/4* **Spitfire**[55] 5025 4-8-11 87........................ JimCrowley 4 92+
(J R Jenkins) *stdd s: hld up in last: gd prog over 1f out: hd high and looked v awkward but r.o to snatch 3rd nr fin* **8/1**
0001 **4** *nk* **Hurricane Spirit (IRE)**[18] 6168 5-8-8 84........................ TedDurcan 1 88
(J R Best) *lw: s.s: hld up in rr: prog on inner over 1f out: styd on ins fnl f but nvr able to chal* **13/2**[3]
0532 **5** *1/2* **Osteopathic Remedy (IRE)**[20] 6092 5-8-10 86........................ PhillipMakin 2 89
(M Dods) *lw: chsd ldrs: 3rd jst over 2f out: rdn and nt qckn over 1f out: one pce after* **9/2**[2]
-000 **6** *hd* **Willow Dancer (IRE)**[73] 4409 5-8-10 86........................(p) EddieAhern 3 88
(W R Swinburn) *hld up in midfield: gng strly 2f out: asked for effrt over 1f out: nt qckn and no imp* **10/1**
6100 **7** *3/4* **Cordell (IRE)**[6] 6476 4-9-2 92........................ JimmyFortune 12 93
(R Ingram) *led to wl over 1f out: wknd fnl f* **40/1**
5-20 **8** *hd* **Multakka (IRE)**[34] 5663 6-8-12 88........................ TPO'Shea 8 88+
(M P Tregoning) *hld up in rr: sit in last pair 2f out: nt clr run over 1f out: styd on ins fnl f but no ch by then* **9/1**
0100 **9** *1 1/2* **Uniquely Poised (USA)**[113] 3049 3-8-9 88........................(p) RyanMoore 6 84+
(J H M Gosden) *nvr bttr than midfield: hmpd wl over 1f out: sn n.d* **4/1**[1]

0004 **10** 2 1/4 **Orchard Supreme**[31] 5745 6-9-4 **94** .... RichardHughes 9 85
(R Hannon) *lw: hld up in rr: pushed along on wd outside over 2f out: limited prog over 1f out: heavily eased ins fnl f* **10/1**

3640 **11** 4 1/2 **Red Somerset (USA)**[153] 1861 6-9-2 **95** .... MCGeran(3) 7 75
(R J Hodges) *chsd ldrs: rdn over 2f out: no prog whn hmpd wl over 1f out: no ch after* **16/1**

11-0 **12** *nse* **Novikov**[167] 1527 5-8-12 **88** .... (p) FergusSweeney 11 68
(G L Moore) *chsd ldrs: hung lft u.p wl over 1f out: wknd* **33/1**

1m 38.87s (0.67) **Going Correction** +0.15s/f (Slow)
WFA 3 from 4yo+ 3lb **12** Ran SP% **116.8**
Speed ratings (Par 107): **102,101,99,99,99 98,98,98,96,94 89,89**
toteswingers: 1&2 £0.00, 2&3 £7.60 1&3 not won. CSF £184.44 CT £1594.69 TOTE £32.50: £7.60, £2.60, £2.50; EX 242.20 TRIFECTA Not won..
Owner Ramzan Kadyrov **Bred** Haras Gavroche **Trained** Lower Beeding, W Sussex

FOCUS
A medium tempo for an above-average event. Decent form, if not the most solid.

NOTEBOOK
Rock Ascot(URU), sharpened up by the application of blinkers, finished off the race to good effect and looks a useful sort for the winter. He two previous wins were in Uruguay, one at 1m4f, so he should stay further if asked. (tchd 25-1)
Sarah Park(IRE) has developed into a reliable performer on turf, but she is also effective on Polytrack. She is on a testing mark since winning at Goodwood but continues to give it everything. (op 13-2 tchd 6-1)
Spitfire, trying a longer trip, picked up in the straight but continues to give the impression that he needs humouring. He tends to come late and would probably be best suited by a flat-out gallop. (op 7-1 tchd 6-1)
Hurricane Spirit(IRE) has come back to form since stepping up to 1m. (op 8-1 tchd 6-1)
Osteopathic Remedy(IRE) should have appreciated the return from 7f but has yet to win in 13 races this year. (op 5-1)
Uniquely Poised(USA), off since Royal Ascot, posed more questions than he answered. His previous appearance on Polytrack was impressive, but he has been disappointing since, though on this occasion his jockey reported than he had suffered two doses of interference, so there may be better to come. Official explanation: jockey said colt suffered interference shortly after the start and coming off the final bend (op 8-1)

6634 BLACKBERRY LANE H'CAP — 1m 4f (P)
5:40 (5:40) (Class 4) (0-80,80) 3-Y-0+ **£6,476** (£1,927; £963; £481) **Stalls** Low

Form RPR

5611 **1** **Rowan Tiger**[9] 6376 3-8-9 **69** 6ex .... PatCosgrave 3 79+
(J R Boyle) *trckd ldrs gng wl: prog to go 3rd 2f out: clsd to ld ent fnl f: drvn out* **11/4**[1]

0032 **2** 1 1/4 **Wind Flow**[6] 6498 5-8-8 **66** .... (v) AshleyMorgan(5) 10 74
(C A Dwyer) *chsd ldr: pushed along 4f out: outpcd over 2f out: rallied to chal 1f out: pressed wnr after: no ex last 100yds* **7/1**

1643 **3** 3 **Merrymadcap (IRE)**[7] 6460 7-9-7 **74** .... LPKeniry 9 77
(Matthew Salaman) *led: drew more than 2 l in front over 2f out: idled over 1f out: hdd & wknd ent fnl f* **14/1**

4153 **4** 1/2 **Formula (USA)**[16] 6209 3-9-5 **79** .... RichardHughes 2 81
(R Hannon) *hld up in last trio: prog fr 3f out to go 4th 2f out: sn nt qckn: clsd grad on 3rd nr fin* **7/1**

1-60 **5** 1 1/2 **Hazy Dancer**[27] 5876 3-9-1 **75** .... MartinDwyer 4 75
(M P Tregoning) *chsd ldng pair to 2f out: grad fdd on inner over 1f out* **25/1**

5015 **6** 1/2 **Soundbyte**[24] 5962 4-9-0 **67** .... TPO'Shea 5 66
(J Gallagher) *racd wd in midfield: rdn and prog to dispute 4th 2f out: nt qckn over 1f out* **12/1**

0200 **7** 2 3/4 **Bassinet (USA)**[111] 3169 5-9-8 **75** .... JimCrowley 1 70
(J A R Toller) *hld up in last: effrt on inner 2f out: sn rdn and no imp on ldrs* **20/1**

1126 **8** 6 **El Diego (IRE)**[175] 1319 5-9-11 **78** .... GeorgeBaker 6 63
(J R Gask) *hld up in last trio: effrt on wd outside 2f out: hanging and wknd over 1f out* **13/2**[3]

13 **9** 1 **Mary Goodnight**[61] 4827 3-9-6 **80** .... RyanMoore 8 63
(J Noseda) *chsd ldrs: rdn 5f out: sn lost pl: struggling fnl 3f* **4/1**[2]

0040 **10** 1/2 **Maxwil**[21] 6059 4-9-5 **72** .... EddieAhern 7 55
(P M Phelan) *s.s: sn in midfield: pushed along and lost pl over 3f out: wl in rr after* **16/1**

0-00 **11** 1 **Fantasy Princess (USA)**[11] 6346 4-9-10 **77** .... (tp) TPQueally 11 58
(G A Butler) *chsd ldng pair tl wknd rapidly 2f out* **25/1**

2m 32.76s (-0.24) **Going Correction** +0.15s/f (Slow)
WFA 3 from 4yo+ 7lb **11** Ran SP% **117.7**
Speed ratings (Par 105): **106,105,103,102,101 101,99,95,95,94 94**
toteswingers: 1&2 £4.50, 1&3 £7.40, 2&3 £8.30 CSF £21.57 CT £225.87 TOTE £4.10: £1.10, £3.20, £3.70; EX 20.30 Trifecta £109.40 Pool: £204.12 - 1.38 winning units. Place 6: £119.29 Place 5: £71.57.
Owner Rowan Stud Partnership 1 **Bred** Rowan Farm Stud **Trained** Epsom, Surrey

FOCUS
Just a fair gallop. The runner-up and third look the best guides to the form.
T/Plt: £92.90 to a £1 stake. Pool: £60,566.71. 475.54 winning tickets. T/Qpdt: £67.80 to a £1 stake. Pool: £3,898.20. 42.50 winning tickets. JN

6491 WOLVERHAMPTON (A.W) (L-H)
Friday, October 9

OFFICIAL GOING: Standard
Wind: Almost nil Weather: Overcast, raining for ther last two

6635 CORAL H'CAP — 5f 20y(P)
5:50 (5:51) (Class 5) (0-70,70) 3-Y-0+ **£3,238** (£963; £481; £240) **Stalls** Low

Form RPR

60/ **1** **Liberty Island (IRE)**[41] 5455 4-9-4 **70** .... DO'Donohoe 10 80
(W McCreery, Ire) *chsd ldrs: pushed along over 3f out: edgd lft bnd over 2f out: rdn over 1f out: r.o wl to ld wl ins fnl f* **16/1**

235 **2** 3/4 **Femme De Fer**[32] 5717 3-9-1 **67** .... AdamKirby 4 75
(C G Cox) *a.p: rdn over 1f out: ev ch wl ins fnl f: kpt on* **9/2**[2]

0120 **3** 1 1/4 **Silver Prelude**[20] 6118 8-9-1 **67** .... (t) ChrisCatlin 9 70
(S C Williams) *chsd ldr: rdn to ld ins fnl f: sn hdd: no ex* **10/1**

6022 **4** *nk* **Figaro Flyer (IRE)**[43] 5374 6-9-4 **70** .... JimmyQuinn 1 72
(P Howling) *mid-div: pushed along over 3f out: sme hdwy on ins over 2f out: rdn wl over 1f out: r.o towards fin* **9/4**[1]

0100 **5** 1/2 **Mandarin Spirit (IRE)**[6] 6489 9-9-2 **68** .... (b) PaulMulrennan 7 68
(Miss L A Perratt) *a.p: rdn over 1f out: one pce* **14/1**

1040 **6** *nse* **Island Legend (IRE)**[20] 6120 3-9-4 **70** .... (t) RichardKingscote 2 70
(J M Bradley) *led: rdn over 1f out: hdd ins fnl f: no ex* **25/1**

4130 **7** *nse* **Lithaam (IRE)**[8] 6422 5-8-12 **67** .... (p) KellyHarrison(3) 12 67
(J M Bradley) *hld up in mid-div: pushed along over 2f out: c wd st: hung lft and rdn over 1f out: kpt on towards fin* **20/1**

0000 **8** 1 1/4 **Divine Spirit**[22] 6010 8-9-2 **68** .... RoystonFfrench 8 63
(M Dods) *in rr: pushed along over 3f out: nvr nrr* **16/1**

4020 **9** 1/2 **Grudge**[22] 6010 4-8-12 **64** .... PJMcDonald 6 66+
(Ollie Pears) *hld up towards rr: pushed along over 2f out: rdn and hdwy fnl f: nt clr run towards fin* **14/1**

5150 **10** 1/2 **Steel City Boy (IRE)**[22] 6028 6-9-2 **68** .... DaneO'Neill 11 60
(D Shaw) *hld up towards rr: rdn wl over 1f out: no rspnse* **25/1**

0000 **11** 1 3/4 **First Order**[18] 6159 8-8-12 **69** .... (v) AnnStokell(5) 3 66+
(Miss A Stokell) *in rr: nt clr run on ins over 2f out: hdwy wl over 1f out: sn rdn: running on whn bdly hmpd towards fin* **11/1**

0005 **12** 1/2 **Kyle (IRE)**[16] 6220 5-9-1 **67** .... TravisBlock 13 51
(C R Dore) *s.i.s: hld up: pushed along over 3f out: c v wd st: a in rr* **20/1**

6224 **13** 2 1/4 **Quasi Congaree (GER)**[15] 6230 3-9-2 **68** .... (t) JoeFanning 5 43
(I A Wood) *mid-div: pushed along over 3f out: sltly hmpd jst over 2f out: sn bhd: eased ins fnl f* **13/2**[3]

62.49 secs (0.19) **Going Correction** 0.0s/f (Stan) **13** Ran SP% **122.0**
Speed ratings (Par 103): **98,96,94,94,93 93,93,91,90,89 86,86,82**
toteswingers: 1&2 £12.80, 2&3 £18.70, 1&3 £8.60. CSF £83.98 CT £797.98 TOTE £19.40: £5.10, £2.10, £3.40; EX 115.40.
Owner Iona Equine Syndicate **Bred** Pat Grogan **Trained** Maynooth, Co.Kildare
■ Stewards' Enquiry : P J McDonald four-day ban: careless riding (Oct 23, 26 -28)

FOCUS
As expected there was no hanging about in this modest sprint handicap and there was a tight finish. Straightforward form.
Quasi Congaree(GER) Official explanation: jockey said colt hung right three furlongs out

6636 WOLVERHAMPTON-RACECOURSE.CO.UK H'CAP — 1m 5f 194y(P)
6:20 (6:21) (Class 4) (0-80,80) 3-Y-0+ **£5,046** (£1,510; £755; £377; £188) **Stalls** Low

Form RPR

25 **1** **Dayia (IRE)**[132] 2486 5-9-12 **78** .... SaleemGolam 10 92+
(J Pearce) *hld up in mid-div: hdwy on ins over 2f out: nt clr run and swtchd rt ent st: chsd ldr and edgd lft wl over 1f out: rdn to ld towards fin* **14/1**

3411 **2** 1/2 **Worth A King'S**[6] 6473 3-9-5 **80** .... (v) NCallan 1 93
(Sir Michael Stoute) *a.p: led on bit 2f out: hung lft into rail over 1f out: rdn and hdd towards fin* **11/8**[1]

5006 **3** 5 **Chookie Hamilton**[19] 6138 5-9-1 **72** .... PatrickDonaghy(5) 4 78
(I Semple) *hld up in mid-div: nt clr run over 2f out: sn pushed along: hdwy wl over 1f out: rdn and one pce fnl f* **14/1**

0112 **4** 3/4 **Rose Row**[14] 6258 5-10-0 **80** .... HayleyTurner 7 85
(Mrs Mary Hambro) *hld up in rr: hdwy on ins over 2f out: rdn wl over 1f out: wknd ins fnl f* **8/1**[3]

1012 **5** 4 **Leyte Gulf (USA)**[7] 6457 6-8-11 **63** ow2 .... DaneO'Neill 3 62
(C C Bealby) *s.i.s: hld up towards rr: hdwy on outside over 2f out: c wd st: rdn and hung lft fr over 1f out: wknd fnl f* **10/1**

4022 **6** *shd* **Fin Vin De Leu (GER)**[11] 6330 3-8-12 **73** .... JoeFanning 9 72
(M Johnston) *led: hdd 2f out: sn wknd* **6/1**[2]

3624 **7** 3 3/4 **Force Group (IRE)**[24] 5961 5-9-5 **71** .... (b[1]) JimmyQuinn 5 65
(M H Tompkins) *t.k.h in mid-div: pushed along over 3f out: hdwy on outside over 2f out: rdn and wknd wl over 1f out* **11/1**

5051 **8** 6 **Bushy Dell (IRE)**[14] 6258 4-8-13 **70** .... AmyBaker(5) 8 56
(Miss J Feilden) *hld up in tch: pushed along over 3f out: wknd over 2f out* **14/1**

0256 **9** 5 **Haarth Sovereign (IRE)**[24] 5961 5-9-12 **78** .... (t) AdamKirby 6 57
(W R Swinburn) *chsd ldr: pushed along over 3f out: wknd 2f out* **16/1**

6000 **10** 48 **Aegean Prince**[83] 4098 5-9-11 **77** .... StephenDonohoe 2 —
(P Howling) *s.i.s: hld up in rr: lost tch 5f out: t.o* **50/1**

3m 1.87s (-4.13) **Going Correction** 0.0s/f (Stan)
WFA 3 from 4yo+ 9lb **10** Ran SP% **112.8**
Speed ratings (Par 105): **111,110,107,107,105 105,102,99,96,69**
toteswingers: 1&2 £6.30, 2&3 £26.40, 1&3 £9.60. CSF £32.49 CT £285.10 TOTE £16.00: £3.90, £1.30, £4.00; EX 53.40.
Owner Lady Green **Bred** Shadwell Estate Company Limited **Trained** Newmarket, Suffolk

FOCUS
This was run at a sound pace and the first pair had it to themselves inside the final furlong. Good form for the grade, with the winner capable of better.

6637 CARLSBERG H'CAP — 7f 32y(P)
6:50 (6:51) (Class 6) (0-65,65) 3-Y-0+ **£2,388** (£705; £352) **Stalls** High

Form RPR

0040 **1** **Silver Guest**[16] 6201 4-9-6 **65** .... ChrisCatlin 2 76
(M R Channon) *hld up in mid-div: hdwy on ins 2f out: led ins fnl f: drvn out* **12/1**

0064 **2** 1 3/4 **Just Timmy Marcus**[8] 6437 3-9-2 **63** .... CatherineGannon 1 68
(B P J Baugh) *a.p: led wl over 1f out: sn rdn: hdd ins fnl f: nt qckn* **6/1**[2]

1005 **3** 1 **The Happy Hammer (IRE)**[20] 6124 3-9-1 **62** .... AdamKirby 11 64
(E V Stanford) *hld up towards rr: stdy hdwy on ins over 2f out: rdn over 1f out: sn swtchd rt: kpt on same pce ins fnl f* **8/1**

66-2 **4** 1 1/4 **Cape Cobra**[49] 5211 5-9-1 **60** .... TravisBlock 7 60
(H Morrison) *w ldr tl rdn wl over 1f out: one pce* **9/2**[1]

534 **5** 3/4 **Tripbiyah (USA)**[32] 5727 3-9-3 **64** .... PJMcDonald 5 61
(G A Swinbank) *prom: lost pl over 3f out: pushed along over 2f out: rallied on ins wl over 1f out: sn rdn: no imp fnl f* **13/2**[3]

5232 **6** 1 3/4 **Stanley Goodspeed**[8] 6437 6-9-6 **65** .... (tp) HayleyTurner 9 58
(J W Hills) *in rr: pushed along over 3f out: rdn wl over 1f out: nvr nr ldrs* **9/2**[1]

5130 **7** *nk* **Obe Brave**[8] 6413 6-9-0 **59** .... (p) LukeMorris 3 51
(Lee Smyth, Ire) *led: rdn and hdd wl over 1f out: wknd fnl f* **10/1**

3000 **8** *shd* **Glasshoughton**[30] 5767 6-9-6 **65** .... RoystonFfrench 8 57
(M Dods) *anticipated s and s.i.s: hld up in mid-div: pushed along over 2f out: wknd wl over 1f out* **25/1**

6032 **9** 1 1/2 **Shunkawakhan (IRE)**[8] 6415 6-9-2 **61** .... (p) PaulMulrennan 4 49
(Miss L A Perratt) *t.k.h: prom: pushed along wl over 1f out: wknd fnl f* **9/1**

2020 **10** 15 **Sampower Rose (IRE)**[17] 6182 3-9-2 **63** .... DNolan 6 10
(D Carroll) *sn prom: pushed along over 3f out: wknd wl over 2f out* **12/1**

0600 **11** 1 **Dorn Dancer (IRE)**[6] 6495 7-9-1 **60** .... TGMcLaughlin 12 5
(W M Brisbourne) *a in rr* **50/1**

1m 29.17s (-0.43) **Going Correction** 0.0s/f (Stan)
WFA 3 from 4yo+ 2lb **11** Ran SP% **115.4**
Speed ratings (Par 101): **102,100,98,97,96 94,94,94,92,75 74**
toteswingers: 1&2 £17.40, 2&3 £17.20, 1&3 £12.70. CSF £80.79 CT £629.22 TOTE £18.90: £4.50, £2.80, £2.80; EX 112.20.
Owner John Guest **Bred** Timber Hill Racing Partnership **Trained** West Ilsley, Berks

FOCUS
A moderate, but tight-looking handicap. It was another race run at a decent clip. Straightforward form, the winner taking advantage of a declining mark.
The Happy Hammer(IRE) Official explanation: jockey said gelding stumbled leaving the stalls
Glasshoughton Official explanation: jockey said gelding stumbled leaving the stalls

6638 STAY AT THE WOLVERHAMPTON HOLIDAY INN MEDIAN AUCTION MAIDEN STKS — 7f 32y(P)
7:20 (7:22) (Class 6) 2-Y-O — **£2,047** (£604; £302) **Stalls** High

Form — RPR

3 **1** **Chardonnay**[25] 5949 2-8-12 0 ... PJMcDonald 3 — 74
(G A Swinbank) *hld up in tch: pushed along wl over 1f out: rdn to ld ins fnl f: drvn out* — **7/1**

43 **2** ¾ **Serafina's Flight**[23] 5984 2-8-12 0 ... ChrisCatlin 6 — 72
(W R Muir) *a.p: pushed along over 2f out: rdn over 1f out: r.o to take 2nd towards fin* — **13/2**

3 1 **Juicy Pear (IRE)** 2-9-3 0 ... HayleyTurner 11 — 75
(M L W Bell) *hld up in rr: hdwy on ins wl over 1f out: sn pushed along: swtchd rt ins fnl f: kpt on to take 3rd nr fin* — **16/1**

3 **4** ½ **Major Maximus**[14] 6254 2-9-3 0 ... DaneO'Neill 7 — 73
(George Baker) *hld up: hdwy on outside 5f out: rdn wl over 1f out: led ins fnl f: sn hdd: no ex* — **10/3**[1]

22 **5** 1¼ **Duster**[60] 4839 2-9-3 0 ... TravisBlock 2 — 70
(H Morrison) *t.k.h: a.p: rdn over 1f out: fdd towards fin* — **7/2**[2]

54 **6** ¾ **Temple Queen**[13] 6291 2-8-12 0 ... JamesDoyle 5 — 63
(S Kirk) *led: rdn over 1f out: hdd ins fnl f: wknd* — **10/1**

3 **7** 2 **Cotton Top (IRE)**[10] 6363 2-8-12 0 ... CatherineGannon 1 — 59
(M R Channon) *t.k.h in mid-div: pushed along wl over 1f out: no hdwy* — **9/2**[3]

3 **8** 6 **Princess Emma**[17] 6181 2-8-12 0 ... PaulHanagan 10 — 44
(R A Fahey) *t.k.h towards rr: pushed along 3f out: c wd st: struggling whn hung lft over 1f out* — **16/1**

9 shd **Honoured (IRE)** 2-9-3 0 ... SebSanders 9 — 49
(Sir Mark Prescott) *n.m.r sn after s: a in rr* — **22/1**

0 **10** 14 **Bom Boms (IRE)**[11] 6347 2-9-3 0 ... RichardKingscote 8 — 14
(Tom Dascombe) *chsd ldr after 1f tl over 3f out: wknd 2f out* — **66/1**

1m 30.71s (1.11) **Going Correction** 0.0s/f (Stan) — **10** Ran SP% **116.0**
Speed ratings (Par 93): **93,92,91,90,89 88,85,79,78,62**
toteswingers: 1&2 £9.60, 2&3 £16.70, 1&3 £11.30. CSF £51.70 TOTE £8.50: £2.70, £1.80, £4.50; EX 39.50.
Owner Guy Reed **Bred** Guy Reed **Trained** Melsonby, N Yorks

FOCUS
This modest juvenile maiden was wide-open as seven of the runners had either made the frame or be placed on their previous outings. It was run at an uneven pace and the form is limited, rated around the runner-up and fifth.

NOTEBOOK
Chardonnay travelled nicely into the home straight and stayed on to open her account at the second attempt. The step up in trip was a big help, indeed she shaped as though 1m will suit before long, and she looks sure to improve again for the experience. (op 11-2 tchd 5-1)
Serafina's Flight was upsides the winner at the top of the home straight, but was under pressure at that stage and didn't prove suited by the drop back to this trip. She was coming back at that rival late in the day, now qualifies for nurseries and should be placed to strike when reverting to further. (op 9-2)
Juicy Pear(IRE) ◆, a half-brother to the formerly very useful Jewelled Dagger, caught the eye staying on from way off the pace on this racecourse bow. He proved distinctly green under pressure and ought to prove plenty sharper next time, so looks one to take from the race. Official explanation: jockey said gelding hung left (op 14-1)
Major Maximus, third over C&D on debut a fortnight previously, again had to come wide with his effort round the home bend and paid the price inside the final furlong. He helps to set the standard. (op 5-1)
Duster proved keen early on due to the uneven pace. He ran close to his recent level on this return to Polytrack and is entitled to come on somewhat for the run, so could be better off switching to nurseries now he is eligible. (op 9-2)
Temple Queen had the run of things on this drop back from 1m, but could offer just the same pace when asked for maximum effort. She is now qualified for nurseries and will appreciate reverting to further. (op 12-1)
Cotton Top(IRE) would have enjoyed a more truly-run race and may even now be ready to tackle another furlong as she is bred for further. Official explanation: jockey said filly ran keen (op 11-2 tchd 4-1)

6639 BOOK NOW FOR CHRISTMAS NURSERY — 1m 141y(P)
7:50 (7:50) (Class 6) (0-65,65) 2-Y-O — **£2,729** (£806; £403) **Stalls** Low

Form — RPR

000 **1** **Fine Lace (IRE)**[13] 6284 2-9-1 59 ... AdamKirby 3 — 63
(D J S Ffrench Davis) *hld up towards rr: reminders over 3f out: pushed along and hdwy over 2f out: plld out wl over 1f out: sn rdn: led ins fnl f: edgd lft: drvn out* — **25/1**

5606 **2** 2 **Bubbly Braveheart (IRE)**[42] 5399 2-9-7 65 ... (b) JoeFanning 8 — 65
(A Bailey) *hld up: hdwy on outside over 6f out: rdn and ev ch ins fnl f: nt qckn* — **9/1**

4606 **3** nk **Execution (IRE)**[23] 5985 2-9-2 60 ... TGMcLaughlin 2 — 59
(E A L Dunlop) *hld up towards rr: stdy prog over 3f out: led wl over 1f out: sn rdn and hung rt: hdd ins fnl f: no ex* — **15/2**[3]

0001 **4** ½ **Bateau Bleu**[9] 6391 2-8-12 61 6ex ... (v) PatrickDonaghy(5) 11 — 59
(P C Haslam) *hld up in rr: pushed along 4f out: n.m.r on ins briefy over 2f out: hdwy wl over 1f out: sn rdn: kpt on one pce ins fnl f* — **4/1**[1]

0415 **5** 1½ **Underworld Dandy**[8] 6431 2-9-6 64 ... DaneO'Neill 6 — 59
(P D Evans) *hld up towards rr: pushed along and hdwy over 2f out: c wd st: rdn and edgd lft fr over 1f out: one pce* — **4/1**[1]

406 **6** ½ **Apostle Of Rome (IRE)**[61] 4825 2-9-7 65 ... RichardKingscote 10 — 59
(Tom Dascombe) *prom: rdn over 2f out: ev ch over 1f out: sn carried rt: one pce* — **5/1**[2]

0340 **7** 6 **Bothwell Castle (IRE)**[2] 6590 2-8-13 60 ... KellyHarrison(3) 5 — 41
(P C Haslam) *led: hdd over 5f out: led over 3f out: rdn and hdd wl over 1f out: wknd ins fnl f* — **12/1**

0056 **8** 1¼ **Pollan Bay (IRE)**[8] 6431 2-9-0 58 ... JamesDoyle 4 — 37
(S Kirk) *hld up in rr: rdn over 2f out: no rspnse* — **11/2**

0100 **9** nk **Dear Mr Fantasy (IRE)**[23] 5985 2-9-4 62 ... SebSanders 1 — 40
(J W Hills) *hld up in tch: pushed along whn n.m.r on ins briefly 2f out: sn wknd* — **10/1**

5000 **10** hd **Dixie Bright (USA)**[15] 6227 2-9-4 62 ... TomEaves 13 — 40
(J G Given) *a towards rr* — **16/1**

060 **11** 9 **Alotago (IRE)**[22] 6011 2-9-2 60 ... AdrianTNicholls 12 — 19
(D Nicholls) *prom: led over 5f out tl over 3f out: wknd over 2f out* — **16/1**

066 **12** 5 **Young Firth**[64] 4705 2-8-13 57 ... PaulMulrennan 7 — 5
(J R Norton) *hld up in tch: pushed along over 5f out: sn lost pl: bhd fnl 3f* — **50/1**

1m 51.96s (1.46) **Going Correction** 0.0s/f (Stan) — **12** Ran SP% **118.7**
Speed ratings (Par 93): **93,91,90,90,89 88,83,82,82,81 73,69**
toteswingers: 1&2 £67.60, 2&3 £46.40, 1&3 £10.60. CSF £235.54 CT £1897.87 TOTE £22.50: £4.00, £3.60, £2.30; EX 628.80.
Owner Miss A Jones **Bred** R A Major **Trained** Lambourn, Berks

FOCUS
A modest nursery in which five of the runners were making their handicap debuts. The form is fairly solid. There was just an ordinary pace on.

NOTEBOOK
Fine Lace(IRE) ◆ showed her true colours on this nursery debut and opened her account at the fourth time of asking. She got a nice passage in mid-field from her low draw, but met traffic turning for home and was forced to come very wide with her challenge once straightening up. She was still nicely on top at the finish and obviously rates value for further, so this improving filly could defy a higher mark next time. Official explanation: trainer's representative said, regarding the apparent improvement of form, that the filly may have been unsuited by the firm going on her last run.
Bubbly Braveheart(IRE) was ridden more patiently on this return to the AW and posted a much-improved display for this drop in class. He too had to come wide on the home turn and is worth persevering with in this company. (op 14-1)
Execution(IRE) hung markedly left under maximum pressure once hitting the front, but didn't cause any real interference and reversed his last-time-out form with Underworld Dandy on 6lb better terms. (op 7-1)
Bateau Bleu, penalised for his surprise Nottingham success six days earlier, hit a flat spot before staying on with purpose again down the home straight. He found the drop in trip against him and remains open to more improvement back over 1m2f. (tchd 7-2)
Underworld Dandy could not confirm Kempton superiority over Execution on these 6lb worse terms. (op 9-2)
Apostle Of Rome(IRE) was fancied to go well on this switch to a nursery, but he spent up too much energy early on from his wide draw and didn't see out the longer trip.
Pollan Bay(IRE) Official explanation: jockey said gelding felt wrong behind on pulling up; vet said gelding returned sound

6640 CORAL.CO.UK H'CAP — 1m 1f 103y(P)
8:20 (8:20) (Class 5) (0-70,70) 3-Y-O+ — **£3,238** (£963; £481; £240) **Stalls** Low

Form — RPR

3300 **1** **Intersky Charm (USA)**[22] 6019 5-9-0 64 ... TonyCulhane 5 — 73
(R M Whitaker) *hld up in tch: squeezed through over 1f out: rdn to ld jst ins fnl f: drvn out* — **11/1**

6000 **2** nk **Nevada Desert (IRE)**[7] 6460 9-8-13 63 ... DO'Donohoe 10 — 71
(R M Whitaker) *hld up towards rr: hdwy over 1f out: swtchd rt jst ins fnl f: rdn and r.o* — **20/1**

0100 **3** 1 **Becuille (IRE)**[11] 6346 4-9-6 70 ... (b) JoeFanning 6 — 76
(B J Meehan) *a.p: rdn to ld over 1f out: sn hung rt: hdd jst ins fnl f: nt qckn cl home* — **16/1**

3066 **4** 2¾ **La Rosa Nostra**[26] 5910 4-9-6 70 ... AdamKirby 7 — 70
(W R Swinburn) *chsd ldr after 1f: rdn 3f out: ev ch whn edgd lft over 1f out: one pce ins fnl f* — **8/1**

4602 **5** ¾ **Nisaal (IRE)**[18] 6157 4-9-4 68 ... (p) SebSanders 13 — 67
(J J Quinn) *hld up and bhd: hdwy on outside over 2f out: rdn and wknd ins fnl f* — **13/2**[3]

1505 **6** 2 **Dr Jameson (IRE)**[14] 6250 3-9-0 68 ... PaulHanagan 11 — 62
(R A Fahey) *hld up in rr: pushed along over 3f out: rdn wl over 1f out: nvr nrr* — **12/1**

0060 **7** nse **Avoir Choisi (IRE)**[21] 6052 3-9-2 70 ... TomEaves 2 — 64
(I Semple) *t.k.h: a.p: ev ch whn n.m.r on ins briefly over 1f out: rdn and wknd ins fnl f* — **40/1**

20-0 **8** ½ **Maximus Aurelius (IRE)**[87] 3960 4-9-4 68 ... (t) LukeMorris 3 — 61
(J Jay) *hld up in tch: rdn over 2f out: wknd over 1f out* — **22/1**

0030 **9** 1¾ **Khun John (IRE)**[74] 4378 6-9-2 66 ... ChrisCatlin 9 — 56
(W J Musson) *sn wl in rr: pushed along over 2f out: swtchd lft ins fnl f: nvr nr ldrs* — **12/1**

6023 **10** 1 **Bid For Glory**[21] 6074 5-9-4 68 ... (v) JimmyQuinn 4 — 56
(H J Collingridge) *hld up and bhd: effrt wl over 1f out: sn rdn and btn* — **10/3**[2]

-550 **11** 3¼ **Four Tel**[15] 6224 5-9-0 64 ... RichardKingscote 1 — 45
(Tom Dascombe) *led: rdn and hdd over 1f out: wknd fnl f* — **3/1**[1]

0010 **12** 2 **Kings Topic (USA)**[188] 1122 9-9-2 66 ... StephenDonohoe 8 — 42
(A B Haynes) *pushed along over 7f out: a in rr* — **25/1**

2m 1.13s (-0.57) **Going Correction** 0.0s/f (Stan)
WFA 3 from 4yo+ 4lb — **12** Ran SP% **117.5**
Speed ratings (Par 103): **102,101,100,98,97 95,95,95,93,93 90,88**
toteswingers: 1&2 £58.40, 2&3 £5.70, 1&3 £52.40. CSF £214.85 CT £3476.11 TOTE £13.50: £2.90, £4.70, £4.90; EX 85.30.
Owner R M Whitaker **Bred** Phil Booker **Trained** Scarcroft, W Yorks

FOCUS
A moderate handicap which saw the first three come clear. The market leaders disappointed and the form is ordinary.

6641 SPONSOR A RACE BY CALLING 01902 390000 MAIDEN STKS — 5f 20y(P)
8:50 (8:51) (Class 5) 3-Y-O+ — **£2,729** (£806; £403) **Stalls** Low

Form — RPR

04 **1** **Tongalooma**[27] 5882 3-8-12 0 ... PJMcDonald 3 — 56
(James Moffatt) *led over 1f: chsd ldr: rdn to ld wl ins fnl f: r.o* — **5/1**[3]

-005 **2** 1¼ **Shirley High**[53] 5105 3-8-12 43 ... JimmyQuinn 5 — 51
(P Howling) *chsd ldrs: wnt 2nd wl over 1f out: rdn and ev ch ins fnl f: nt qckn* — **16/1**

0065 **3** shd **Sorrel Point**[24] 5971 6-9-3 45 ... (vt[1]) SebSanders 11 — 56
(H J Collingridge) *s.i.s: sn swtchd lft: hld up in rr: hdwy jst over 1f out: rdn and r.o ins fnl f* — **14/1**

2643 **4** hd **Majestic Lady (IRE)**[45] 5326 3-8-12 54 ... ChrisCatlin 6 — 50
(B W Hills) *a.p: rdn over 2f out: kpt on towards fin* — **11/4**[1]

4-3 **5** 1 **Acrosstheuniverse (USA)**[266] 188 3-8-12 0 ... LukeMorris 12 — 46
(J R Gask) *chsd ldrs: c wd st: rdn wl over 1f out: one pce fnl f* — **11/2**

436 **6** ¾ **Fatal Attraction**[32] 5727 4-8-12 55 ... SaleemGolam 2 — 44
(Rae Guest) *w ldr: led over 3f out: rdn over 1f out: hdd ins fnl f: wknd* **4/1**[2]

0-40 **7** ½ **Winterbourne**[113] 3071 3-8-12 47 ... FrancisNorton 7 — 42
(M Blanshard) *hld up in mid-div: swtchd lft and hdwy over 1f out: one pce fnl f* — **15/2**

06-0 **8** nse **Rightcar Dominic**[268] 166 4-9-3 47 ... AdamKirby 1 — 47
(Peter Grayson) *hld up in mid-div: hdwy on ins wl over 1f out: sn rdn: no imp fnl f* — **20/1**

000 **9** 4 **Mrs Medley**[11] 6344 3-8-12 0 ... DaneO'Neill 9 — 27
(D Shaw) *a towards rr* — **66/1**

0050 **10** 1 ¾ **Little Lost (IRE)**[35] 5645 3-8-12 41.............................. TGMcLaughlin 10 21
(Karen George) *hld up in mid-div: hdwy on ins over 2f out: rdn over 1f out: wknd fnl f* **25/1**

11 7 **Mycana (IRE)**[44] 5353 3-9-3 0...............................(p) CatherineGannon 8 1
(Lee Smyth, Ire) *s.i.s: a in rr* **40/1**

62.92 secs (0.62) **Going Correction** 0.0s/f (Stan) 11 Ran SP% **115.6**
Speed ratings (Par 103): **95,93,92,92,90 89,88,88,82,79 68**
toteswingers: 1&2 £10.70, 2&3 £9.20, 1&3 £13.80. CSF £75.87 TOTE £7.10: £1.90, £4.90, £4.70; EX 117.30.
Owner Mrs Jennie Moffatt **Bred** Mrs J A Moffatt And Brian T Clark **Trained** Cartmel, Cumbria

FOCUS
A weak maiden. Little got into it from the rear.

6642 RINGSIDE CONFERENCE SUITE - 700 THEATRE STYLE H'CAP 5f 216y(P)

9:20 (9:22) (Class 5) (0-75,76) 3-Y-0+ **£3,238** (£963; £481; £240) **Stalls** Low

Form RPR

431P **1** **Gwilym (GER)**[41] 5436 6-8-11 **68**.............................. HayleyTurner 7 76
(D Haydn Jones) *chsd ldr: rdn over 1f out: led ins fnl f: drvn out* **11/1**

0030 **2** *nk* **Legal Eagle (IRE)**[13] 6279 4-9-4 **75**.............................. SilvestreDeSousa 5 82
(Paul Green) *led: rdn and hdd ins fnl f: r.o* **8/1**

0023 **3** ¾ **Hellbender (IRE)**[7] 6444 3-8-11 **74**.............................. LeeNewnes(5) 6 79
(S Kirk) *hld up in mid-div: hdwy on ins 2f out: rdn and kpt on ins fnl f* **6/1**[3]

0024 **4** *hd* **Jordaura**[25] 5937 3-9-3 **75**.............................. AdamKirby 4 79+
(W R Swinburn) *hld up towards rr: hdwy on ins wl over 1f out: rdn and kpt on ins fnl f* **8/1**

0005 **5** 1 ¾ **Spiritofthewest (IRE)**[15] 6233 3-9-0 **72**.............................. PhillipMakin 2 71
(D H Brown) *hld up towards rr: hdwy wl over 1f out: rdn ins fnl f: nvr trbld ldrs* **28/1**

0411 **6** ½ **Billy Red**[7] 6444 5-9-3 **74** 6ex..............................(b) FergusSweeney 1 71
(J R Jenkins) *a.p: rdn over 1f out: one pce* **9/2**[1]

5361 **7** 2 ¼ **Green Park (IRE)**[8] 6434 6-9-5 **76** 6ex..............................(b) DNolan 10 66
(D Carroll) *hld up towards rr: pushed along over 2f out: n.d* **11/2**[2]

0 **8** 1 **Little Arrows (IRE)**[55] 5042 3-9-1 **73**..............................(b) DO'Donohoe 3 60
(W McCreery, Ire) *s.i.s: sn wl outpcd: kpt on fnl f: nrst fin* **16/1**

0004 **9** 3 **Not My Choice (IRE)**[30] 5768 4-8-11 **68**.............................. JohnEgan 12 45
(J Balding) *chsd ldrs: rdn over 2f out: wknd over 1f out* **10/1**

26 **10** *hd* **Milne Bay (IRE)**[20] 6120 4-8-10 **72**..............................(t) MartinLane(5) 9 49
(D M Simcock) *mid-div: rdn over 2f out: wknd wl over 1f out* **12/1**

000 **11** 2 ¼ **Great Charm (IRE)**[77] 4285 4-9-3 **74**.............................. MickyFenton 13 43
(M L W Bell) *s.i.s: c wd st: a in rr* **12/1**

1645 **12** 1 ¼ **Hysterical Lady**[23] 5978 3-8-13 **71**.............................. AdrianTNicholls 11 36
(D Nicholls) *prom: rdn over 2f out: wknd wl over 1f out* **6/1**[3]

050 **13** 2 ¼ **Cheap Thrills**[16] 6212 3-9-1 **73**.............................. ChrisCatlin 8 31
(J A Osborne) *mid-div: pushed along over 3f out: bhd fnl 2f* **22/1**

1m 14.28s (-0.72) **Going Correction** 0.0s/f (Stan)
WFA 3 from 4yo+ 1lb 13 Ran SP% **130.8**
Speed ratings (Par 103): **104,103,102,102,100 99,96,95,91,90 87,86,83**
toteswingers: 1&2 £22.50, 2&3 £19.80, 1&3 £13.90. CSF £105.59 CT £600.90 TOTE £15.80: £4.90, £3.40, £1.80; EX 216.70 Place 6: £4,163.43 Place 5: £1,239.90..
Owner S Kon, D Llewelyn and J Runeckles **Bred** B Krutmann **Trained** Efail Isaf, Rhondda C Taff

FOCUS
Another wide-open race. It was run at a decent pace yet it still paid to race handily and the front pair were always 1-2. There is a slight doubt over the form as a result.
Great Charm(IRE) Official explanation: jockey said gelding stumbled leaving the stalls
T/Plt: £15,833.60 to a £1 stake. Pool: £86,759.47. 4.00 winning tickets. T/Qpdt: £1,206.50 to a £1 stake. Pool: £7,989.16. 4.90 winning tickets. KH

5692 YORK (L-H)

Friday, October 9

OFFICIAL GOING: Good (7.4)
Rail realignment reduced advertised distances on round course by 27yds.
Wind: Virtually nil Weather: Overcast

6643 GARBUTT & ELLIOTT STKS (NURSERY H'CAP) 6f

2:10 (2:10) (Class 3) 2-Y-0 **£4,327** (£4,327; £991; £495) **Stalls** High

Form RPR

0131 **1** **Bossy Kitty**[8] 6409 2-7-12 **72** 6ex.............................. SilvestreDeSousa 10 77
(N Tinkler) *midfield: pushed along and hdwy 1/2-way: rdn to ld wl over 1f out: drvn ins fnl f: kpt on: jnd on line* **11/1**

6231 **1** *dht* **Jeannie Galloway (IRE)**[22] 6009 2-7-13 **73**.............................. DaleGibson 7 78
(R A Fahey) *cl up: effrt wl over 1f out: sn rdn and ev ch: drvn ins fnl f and styd on to join ldr on line* **8/1**

1200 **3** 1 **Flaneur**[30] 5762 2-8-0 **74**..............................(b) DuranFentiman 3 76
(T D Easterby) *prom: rdn along 2f out: drvn and ev ch over 1f out tl no ex wl ins fnl f* **25/1**

1351 **4** 2 **Emerald Girl (IRE)**[19] 6134 2-8-0 **74**.............................. PaulHanagan 8 70
(R A Fahey) *prom: pushed along and lost pl after 1 1/2f: outpcd and towards rr 1/2-way: rdn and hdwy over 2f out: styd on u.p appr fnl f: nrst fin* **6/1**[3]

201 **5** *hd* **Colepeper**[20] 6096 2-9-7 **95**.............................. GregFairley 2 90
(M Johnston) *dwlt and wnt lft s: hdwy to chse ldrs 1/2-way: sn rdn along: drvn wl over 1f out and kpt on same pce* **5/1**[2]

4312 **6** *nk* **Marine Spirit (GER)**[44] 5344 2-8-11 **85**.............................. LDettori 6 80
(Saeed Bin Suroor) *towards rr: pushed along and hdwy 1/2-way: rdn to chse ldrs 2f out: sn drvn and edgd rt over 1f out: sn no imp* **7/2**[1]

1454 **7** 3 ¾ **Haltela (IRE)**[22] 6011 2-9-2 **90**..............................(p) DarryllHolland 1 73
(K A Ryan) *dwlt and outpcd in rr: pushed along and hdwy 1/2-way: rdn to chse ldrs whn n.m.r and swtchd lft over 1f out: sn edgd rt and wknd* **22/1**

1502 **8** 7 **Coolree Star (IRE)**[14] 6247 2-7-10 **73** oh2 ow1.......... AndreaAtzeni(3) 4 35
(J A Glover) *prom: rdn along 1/2-way and sn wknd* **12/1**

0335 **9** *nse* **Bell's Ocean (USA)**[15] 6227 2-7-6 **73** oh3 ow1............ RyanPowell(7) 5 35
(J Ryan) *chsd ldrs: rdn along wl over 2f out and sn wknd* **20/1**

4411 **10** *shd* **Wasmi (IRE)**[15] 6227 2-8-3 **77**.............................. ChrisCatlin 9 39
(C E Brittain) *chsd ldrs: swtchd lft and rdn over 2f out: sn drvn and wknd* **12/1**

0023 **11** 5 **Gertmegalush (IRE)**[21] 6048 2-8-8 **82**..............................(b) GrahamGibbons 11 29
(J D Bethell) *led and sn clr: rdn along over 2f out: hdd wl over 1f out and wknd qckly* **7/1**

034 **12** 5 **Almadaa**[43] 5368 2-7-12 **72**.............................. JimmyQuinn 12 4
(E A L Dunlop) *chsd ldrs: rdn along 1/2-way: sn wknd* **12/1**

1m 11.81s (-0.09) **Going Correction** +0.15s/f (Good) 12 Ran SP% **121.2**
Speed ratings (Par 99): **106,106,104,102,101 101,96,87,86,86 80,73**WIN: Jeannie Galloway £4.80, Bossy Kitty £5.90 PL: JG £2.90, BK £2.60, F £8.00 EX JG/BK £60.00, BK/JG £61.30 CSF: JG/BK £46.13 BK/JG £47.85 TRI: JG/BK/Flaneur £1,075.69 BK/JG/F £1,102.55 toteswingers: JG&3 not won, BK&3 not won, JG&BK £15.0027 Owner Trifecta £David Renwick Bred G And J Bloodstock.
Owner Leeds Plywood And Doors Ltd **Bred** J P Coggan **Trained** Langton, N Yorks
■ Stewards' Enquiry : Silvestre De Sousa caution: excessive use of the whip

FOCUS
A competitive nursery featuring five last-time-out winners, and the front two could not be separated. They came up the stands' rail.

NOTEBOOK
Bossy Kitty is a tough filly and was having her 13th outing of the campaign. All but one of her previous starts had been over the minimum trip and she was 3lb wrong under her penalty for her Ayr win, but she got the longer trip well and is clearly progressing this autumn. Her versatility with regard to ground conditions will continue to help her cause. (tchd 7-1)
Jeannie Galloway(IRE) was always up there and responded well to pressure. Both her pedigree and win on easy ground at Ayr suggest that softer going will be in her favour in the coming weeks, but apparently that's going to be it for her this season. (tchd 7-1)
Flaneur, also prominent from the off, bounced back from a couple of poor efforts to show his true form. (op 20-1)
Emerald Girl(IRE) put in some good work at the finish having struggled to go the pace early. A stiffer track seems to suit her better, a view supported by the fact that she's won at Beverley and Hamilton previously. (op 13-2 tchd 7-1)
Colepeper had been given a stiff task off a mark of 95 on his handicap debut, and in the circumstances he didn't run too badly. (op 6-1 tchd 7-1)
Marine Spirit(GER) missed the break slightly and was held up. He got a bit outpaced halfway before trying to challenge wide, and his effort soon petered out. It might be that he needs it rattling to be at his best.

6644 ACORN WEB OFFSET CONDITIONS STKS 1m 2f 88y

2:45 (2:45) (Class 3) 3-Y-0+ **£9,714** (£2,890; £1,444; £721) **Stalls** Low

Form RPR

-263 **1** **Peligroso (FR)**[20] 6110 3-8-11 106.............................. LDettori 3 103
(Saeed Bin Suroor) *mde all: qcknd 3f out: rdn 2f out: hung rt over 1f out: kpt on* **3/1**[2]

0122 **2** 2 ¼ **Wasan**[13] 6290 4-9-4 110.............................. RHills 7 100
(E A L Dunlop) *hld up: hdwy 4f out: rdn to chse wnr 2f out: sn drvn and kpt on ins fnl f* **11/4**[1]

1 **3** *nk* **Blizzard Blues (USA)**[93] 3751 3-8-11 85.............................. IanMongan 2 98
(H R A Cecil) *pushed along sn after s: trckd ldr tl rdn along and outpcd 3f out: in rr and drvn over 2f out: styd on u.p to chse ldrs appr fnl f: kpt on towards fin* **11/2**

3412 **4** 1 ¼ **Demolition**[20] 6095 5-8-11 89..............................(p) GaryBartley(5) 4 95
(N Wilson) *chsd wnr: rdn along over 3f out: drvn 2f out: kpt on same pce* **14/1**

0304 **5** 2 ¾ **Kings Gambit (SAF)**[30] 5764 5-9-2 110.............................. MickyFenton 6 90
(T P Tate) *hld up in rr: pushed along 1/2-way: hdwy on outer over 3f out: rdn to chse ldrs over 2f out: drvn wl over 1f out and wknd ent fnl f* **4/1**[3]

-535 **6** 26 **Once More Dubai (USA)**[137] 2327 4-8-13 107.......(bt) AhmedAjtebi(3) 1 38
(Saeed Bin Suroor) *t.k.h: trckd ldng pair: hdwy to chse wnr over 3f out and sn rdn: drvn and wknd over 2f out: sn bhd and eased* **11/2**

2m 12.5s **Going Correction** 0.0s/f (Good)
WFA 3 from 4yo+ 5lb 6 Ran SP% **109.1**
Speed ratings (Par 107): **100,98,97,96,94 73**
toteswingers: 1&2 £1.10, 1&3 £1.90, 2&3 £2.00 CSF £10.95 TOTE £3.60: £2.00, £2.20; EX 8.70.
Owner Godolphin **Bred** S R L Undosa **Trained** Newmarket, Suffolk
■ Stewards' Enquiry : R Hills two-day ban: excessive use of the whip (Oct 23, 26)

FOCUS
There wasn't a lot between four of these on the ratings. The winner made all in a moderate time and did not need to be at his best. The fourth limits the form.

NOTEBOOK
Peligroso(FR), one of two 3-y-os in the field, had the potential to be a bit better than he had shown previously. A colt that has been twice placed in Group company in Germany, he has apparently been physically immature and needed time to strengthen up, hence the three months off during the summer. He ran a promising race on his return at Newbury, was fully entitled to be fitter for that outing and, allowed an uncontested lead here, travelled kindly in front. He edged over to the stands' rail inside the final 2f but kept on well, and won with a nice bit up his sleeve. He can make the move up to Listed company next, when softer ground will be very much in his favour, but the best of him won't be seen until next year. (op 11-4 tchd 100-30 and 7-2 in a place)
Wasan, another who was entitled to have come on for a recent return from a three-month break, ran a sound race after being held up off the pace, especially as the winner very much enjoyed the run of things. (op 100-30 tchd 5-2)
Blizzard Blues(USA), not seen since he beat his stablemate Manifest in a Newmarket maiden back in July, came into the race with an official mark of 85. On this evidence he could have hacked up in a handicap, but his connections clearly have loftier ambitions for him and this was a good effort up in grade. He ran as though he'll get another 2f. (op 6-1 tchd 9-2)
Demolition, who tracked the leader for much of the race, ran above himself in defeat and will probably pay for his decent effort with a modest rise in the weights. (tchd 16-1)
Kings Gambit(SAF), who was keen early, just couldn't pick up under pressure and proved disappointing. (op 7-2)
Once More Dubai(USA), who'd been off the track since May, raced with the choke out and hopefully this run will have taken the freshness out of him. (op 13-2 tchd 7-1)

6645 BEST ODDS GUARANTEED AT TOTESPORT.COM STKS (H'CAP) 7f

3:20 (3:21) (Class 4) (0-85,84) 3-Y-0+ **£7,641** (£2,273; £1,136; £567) **Stalls** High

Form RPR

4040 **1** **Feldday**[21] 6050 3-9-4 **82**.............................. SteveDrowne 3 97
(H Morrison) *trckd ldrs: smooth hdwy 3f out: cl up 2f out: sn led: rdn and qckndclr appr fnl f: kpt on strly* **11/2**[1]

5161 **2** 3 ¾ **Balata**[17] 6187 4-9-2 **78**.............................. TGMcLaughlin 1 83
(B R Millman) *towards rr: hdwy 3f out: rdn over 2f out: drvn to chse ldrs over 1f out: kpt on ins fnl f: no ch w wnr* **20/1**

0241 **3** *shd* **Kiwi Bay**[22] 6019 4-9-6 **82**.............................. DarryllHolland 8 87
(M Dods) *hld up in rr: hdwy over 2f out: swtchd lft and rdn over 1f out: styd on ins fnl f: nrst fin* **14/1**

3141 **4** 1 ½ **Medicean Man**[39] 5523 3-9-5 **83**.............................. LukeMorris 5 84
(J R Gask) *dwlt and towards rr: hdwy 1/2-way: rdn to chse ldrs over 2f out: sn drvn and kpt on same pce appr fnl f* **13/2**[2]

0563 **5** 2 ¾ **Ezdeyaad (USA)**[14] 6249 5-9-5 **81**.............................. IanMongan 16 74
(G A Swinbank) *cl up: led over 4f out: rdn along 3f out: drvn 2f out: sn hdd and grad wknd* **16/1**

The Form Book, Raceform Ltd, Compton, RG20 6NL

4052 **6** *1 ½* **Grazeon Gold Blend**[40] 5465 6-8-9 **78**..........................(p) IJBrennan(7) 9 67
(J J Quinn) *towards rr: hdwy 1/2-way: rdn along over 2f out: kpt on appr fnl f: nt rch ldrs* **20/1**

2021 **7** *1 ¾* **Handsome Falcon**[6] 6496 5-9-3 **82** 6ex..................... FrederikTylicki(3) 4 66
(R A Fahey) *in tch: hdwy wl over 2f out: rdn wl over 1f out: sn no imp* **17/2**[3]

5026 **8** *nse* **Turn Me On (IRE)**[8] 6435 6-9-6 **82**.......................... GrahamGibbons 14 66+
(T D Walford) *midfield: rdn along 3f out: nt clr run and swtchd lft wl over 1f out: rdn and kpt on appr fnl f: n.d* **20/1**

2622 **9** *shd* **Hail Promenader (IRE)**[58] 4909 3-9-6 **84**...................... MichaelHills 13 68
(B W Hills) *trckd ldrs: hdwy 1/2-way: rdn and cl up over 2f out: sn ev ch tl wknd over 1f out* **12/1**

U030 **10** *2 ¼* **South Cape**[26] 5914 6-8-13 **80**..........................(p) MartinLane(5) 19 58
(G L Moore) *hld up in rr: hdwy 3f out: rdn along over 2f out and n.d* **20/1**

000 **10** *dht* **Knavesmire (IRE)**[78] 4228 3-9-2 **80**............................. FrancisNorton 2 58
(M Brittain) *towards rr: hdeadway 3f out: sn rdn and nvr a factor* **66/1**

4030 **12** *hd* **Orpen Wide (IRE)**[17] 4501 7-8-11 **80**..........................(b) JPFahy(7) 11 57
(M C Chapman) *bhd: rdn along 4f out: sme hdwy on wd outside fnl 2f: nvr a factor* **50/1**

003 **13** *1 ¼* **Silver Rime (FR)**[22] 6016 4-9-6 **82**........................ PaulHanagan 10 56
(Miss L A Perratt) *trckd ldrs: effrt over 2f out: sn rdn and nt clr run wl over 1f out: wknd* **12/1**

3000 **14** *nk* **Bond City (IRE)**[21] 6050 7-9-1 **82**.............................. LanceBetts(5) 15 55
(G R Oldroyd) *in tch: rdn along over 3f out: wkng whn hmpd 2f out* **33/1**

3505 **15** *¾* **Kashimin (IRE)**[42] 5404 4-9-1 **77**................................. TonyHamilton 18 48
(G A Swinbank) *dwlt: sn in tch: rdn along to chse ldrs 1/2-way: wknd wl over 2f out* **16/1**

0010 **16** *¾* **White Deer (USA)**[6] 6485 5-9-7 **83**......................(p) SilvestreDeSousa 20 52
(G A Harker) *swtchd lft s: a in rr* **28/1**

0241 **17** *4 ½* **Malcheek (IRE)**[12] 6309 7-9-2 **78** 6ex................................ DavidAllan 17 35
(T D Easterby) *cl up: rdn along 3f out: drvn 2f out and sn wknd* **13/2**[2]

1124 **18** *1 ½* **Legal Legacy**[41] 5432 3-9-2 **80**.. TomEaves 12 33
(M Dods) *chsd ldrs: rdn along 3f out: drvn whn n.m.r 2f out and sn wknd* **16/1**

-055 **19** *2* **Cara's Request (AUS)**[55] 5031 4-9-1 **77**.................... AdrianTNicholls 6 25
(D Nicholls) *led: hdd over 4f out and cl up: tl rdn along wl over 2f out and sn wknd* **16/1**

1m 24.49s (-0.81) **Going Correction** 0.0s/f (Good)
WFA 3 from 4yo+ 2lb **19** Ran **SP% 127.0**
Speed ratings (Par 105): **104,99,99,97,94 93,91,90,90,88 88,88,86,86,85 84,79,77,75**
toteswingers: 1&2 £45.70, 1&3 £36.50, 2&3 £52.20 CSF £121.08 CT £1502.80 TOTE £7.00: £2.40, £5.80, £3.40, £2.40; EX 358.60.
Owner Exors Of The Late Mrs R C A Hammond **Bred** Rockwell Bloodstock **Trained** East Ilsley, Berks

FOCUS
There was a good gallop on here and they migrated towards the stands' rail after turning into the straight. A low draw proved an advantage, with six of the first seven drawn in single figures. Felday produced a personal best.
Malcheek(IRE) Official explanation: trainer had no explanation for the poor form shown
Legal Legacy Official explanation: jockey said gelding ran flat
Cara's Request(AUS) Official explanation: jockey said colt had no more to give

6646 EUROPEAN BREEDERS' FUND MAIDEN STKS 6f
3:55 (3:57) (Class 4) 2-Y-O **£6,605** (£1,965; £982; £490) **Stalls** High

Form RPR

25 **1** **Walvis Bay (IRE)**[22] 6009 2-9-3 0.................................... MickyFenton 3 81+
(T P Tate) *cl up: shkn up to ld 2f out: rdn clr over 1f out: edgd rt ins fnl f: styd on* **2/1**[1]

3322 **2** *3* **George Benjamin**[21] 6046 2-9-3 71........................... AdrianTNicholls 4 72
(D Nicholls) *towards rr: pushed along 1/2-way: rdn and hdwy 2f out: styd on to chse wnr ins fnl f: no imp towards fin* **9/2**[3]

4 **3** *2* **Excellent Vision**[18] 6154 2-9-3 0.................................. RichardMullen 8 70+
(B Smart) *v.s.a and bhd: swtchd wd and hdwy 1/2-way: rdn: rn green and edgd lft wl over 1f out: styd on u.p appr fnl f: nrst fin* **11/2**

003 **4** *1 ½* **Fair Bunny**[17] 6179 2-8-12 70.................................. GrahamGibbons 1 57
(A D Brown) *chsd ldrs: rdn 2f out: swtchd rt and drvn ent fnl f: kpt on same pce* **50/1**

5 *1 ¾* **Orchid Wing** 2-9-3 0... PaulHanagan 5 56
(R A Fahey) *dwlt: sn chsng ldrs: rdn along 2f out and grad wknd* **4/1**[2]

2425 **6** *¾* **Trade Secret**[97] 3606 2-9-3 75.. TomEaves 6 54
(M Brittain) *led: rdn along and hdd 2f out: sn drvn and wknd over 1f out* **11/1**

4 **7** *½* **Lucky Windmill**[104] 3392 2-9-3 0............................... RobertWinston 9 54+
(G A Swinbank) *chsd ldrs: rdn along over 2f out: n.m.r and swtchd lft over 1f out: wknd* **9/1**

50 **8** *1* **Sir Louis**[48] 5256 2-9-3 0.. TonyHamilton 7 50
(R A Fahey) *midfield: rdn along 1/2-way: no imp* **33/1**

6 **9** *8* **Layla's Prince (IRE)**[48] 5253 2-9-3 0......................... FrancisNorton 10 26+
(D Nicholls) *a towards rr* **20/1**

0 **10** *15* **Media Jury**[23] 5977 2-9-3 0.. DanielTudhope 2 —
(J S Wainwright) *chsd ldrs to 1/2-way: sn wknd and bhd* **100/1**

1m 13.21s (1.31) **Going Correction** +0.15s/f (Good) **10** Ran **SP% 115.9**
Speed ratings (Par 97): **97,93,90,88,86 85,84,83,72,52**
toteswingers: 1&2 £1.10, 1&3 £12.10, 2&3 £3.80 CSF £10.62 TOTE £3.20: £1.60, £1.50, £2.30; EX 9.70.
Owner Mrs Sylvia Clegg and Louise Worthington **Bred** Swordlestown Stud **Trained** Tadcaster, N Yorks

FOCUS
Just a fair maiden. Walvis Bay was bacl to his debut form, with the runner-up helping to set the level.

NOTEBOOK
Walvis Bay(IRE) set the standard on his two previous efforts - both those races had worked out from a form perspective - and this looked a fine opportunity to finally get off the mark. Prominent from the off, he got the job done in a professional manner and, not over-big, looks the type to keep going with this term. A nursery will be next for him. (op 9-4 tchd 15-8 and 5-2 in a place)
George Benjamin made the frame for the sixth time in succession, but he never looked like winning. Shoved along at halfway, he stumbled at one point and took an age to get into full stride, but he finished his race in good style and has the potential to do better as a 3-y-o. (op 5-1 tchd 4-1)
Excellent Vision, who was green on his debut, again showed signs of inexperience, being slowest away from the stalls and getting detached in last early. He made relentless progress from halfway, though, despite hanging left and eventually finishing his race wide of the others. Another run will qualify him for a mark and he'll be interesting as a handicapper next season. (op 6-1 tchd 9-2)
Fair Bunny, who looked to be crying out for a return to 6f when doing her best work late over 5f at Beverley last time, will be of more interest in modest handicap company. (tchd 66-1)
Orchid Wing, whose dam was unraced but is a sister to high-class dual 5f-winning juvenile Mrs P, and a half-sister to eight other winners, is bred to be fast, and he travelled like a good horse for a long way. He didn't see it out but is entitled to come on a bundle for his debut and is one to keep in mind. (op 100-30 tchd 9-2)
Trade Secret, returning from a three-month break, showed early speed but didn't see it out. He was entitled to need the run, but still has to prove he gets this trip. (op 16-1)

6647 PARSONAGE COUNTRY HOUSE HOTEL STKS (H'CAP) 5f
4:30 (4:36) (Class 4) (0-85,85) 3-Y-O+ **£6,540** (£1,946; £972; £485) **Stalls** High

Form RPR

2123 **1** **Russian Spirit**[22] 6020 3-9-2 **80**..................................... PhilipRobinson 2 90
(M A Jarvis) *chsd ldrs: rdn wl over 1f out: styng on whn n.m.r and swtchd lft wl ins fnl f: drvn and led nr fin* **6/1**[2]

5120 **2** *nk* **Hotham**[21] 6050 6-8-12 **81**.. GaryBartley(5) 1 90
(N Wilson) *in rr: hdwy over 2f out: rdn over 1f out: styd on strly ins fnl f: jst hld* **16/1**

5600 **3** *nk* **Equuleus Pictor**[34] 5654 5-9-4 **85**...................................... JackDean(3) 3 93
(J L Spearing) *led: rdn along wl over 1f out: drvn ins fnl f: edgd rt: hdd and no ex towards fin* **22/1**

0601 **4** *nse* **Go Go Green (IRE)**[15] 6233 3-8-10 **77**...................... FrederikTylicki(3) 8 85
(D H Brown) *in tch: hdwy 2f out: rdn and styd on to have ev ch ins fnl f: sn drvn: edgd lft and nt qckn towards fin* **5/1**[1]

5202 **5** *2 ½* **Taurus Twins**[22] 6010 3-8-4 **73**....................................(b) MartinLane(5) 6 72
(R J Price) *prom: rdn along wl over 1f out: drvn and ev ch ent fnl f: sn edgd rt and one pce* **20/1**

5116 **6** *1* **Ocean Blaze**[10] 6359 5-9-3 **81**.. DarryllHolland 14 76+
(B R Millman) *prom stands' rail: rdn along 2f out and ev ch tl drvn and wkndent fnl f* **12/1**

0005 **7** *nk* **Mandurah (IRE)**[13] 6283 5-9-2 **85**............................ MarkCoumbe(5) 12 79+
(B P J Baugh) *in tch: effrt 2f out: sn rdn and kpt on ins fnl f: nrst fin* **20/1**

4510 **7** *dht* **Discanti (IRE)**[41] 5436 4-8-13 **77**...................................... DavidAllan 9 71
(T D Easterby) *towards rr: hdwy 2f out: sn rdn and nt clr run over 1f out: kpt on ins fnl f: nrst fin* **20/1**

3533 **9** *½* **Excellent Show**[27] 5856 3-9-0 **78**................................. RichardMullen 10 70
(B Smart) *towards rr: swtchd rt and hdwy 2f out: sn rdn and kpt on ins fnl f: nrst fin* **16/1**

1511 **10** *½* **Mythical Blue (IRE)**[27] 5877 3-8-12 **76**........................... DavidProbert 5 66
(J M Bradley) *chsd ldrs: rdn along 2f out: grad wknd* **12/1**

0644 **11** *nk* **Spring Green**[21] 6051 3-8-12 **76**...................................... SteveDrowne 7 65
(H Morrison) *chsd ldrs: hdwy 2f out: sn rdn and ch over 1f out: drvn and wknd ent fnl f* **20/1**

6435 **12** *½* **Northern Bolt**[21] 6050 4-8-13 **77**...........................(v) AdrianTNicholls 19 65
(D Nicholls) *racd towards stands' side: a midfield* **12/1**

2601 **13** *¾* **Rasaman (IRE)**[13] 6279 5-9-5 **83**.............................(v) DanielTudhope 20 68
(J S Goldie) *racd towards stands' rail: chsd ldrs: rdn along over 2f out and sn wknd* **14/1**

0205 **14** *1 ½* **The Jobber (IRE)**[7] 6459 8-9-4 **82**................................ FrancisNorton 17 61
(M Blanshard) *racd towards stands' rail: in tch: rdn along 1/2-way: sn wknd* **28/1**

2614 **15** *hd* **Incomparable**[18] 6171 4-8-13 **82**.................................(b) BMcHugh(5) 4 61
(J A Glover) *s.i.s: a in rr* **12/1**

-050 **16** *3 ½* **Guertino (IRE)**[8] 6434 4-8-11 **80**.................................. LanceBetts(5) 11 46
(C J Teague) *s.i.s: a bhd* **66/1**

0034 **17** *1 ¼* **Ebraam (USA)**[58] 4891 6-9-5 **83**................................... JerryO'Dwyer 16 45
(P Howling) *racd towards stands' rail: chsd ldrs: rdn along over 2f out and sn wknd* **16/1**

2101 **18** *1 ¼* **Medici Time**[22] 6010 4-8-10 **74**...........................(v) GrahamGibbons 18 31
(T D Easterby) *a in rr* **8/1**[3]

59.39 secs (0.09) **Going Correction** +0.15s/f (Good) **18** Ran **SP% 125.5**
Speed ratings (Par 105): **105,104,104,103,99 98,97,97,97,96 95,95,93,91,91 85,83,81**
toteswingers: 1&2 £29.20, 1&3 £24.10, 2&3 £111.10 CSF £89.54 CT £1257.02 TOTE £5.50: £1.90, £3.90, £6.90, £1.90; EX 120.70.
Owner Cromhall Stud **Bred** Derek R Price **Trained** Newmarket, Suffolk
■ Stewards' Enquiry : Philip Robinson five-day ban: excessive use of th whip (Oct 23-24, 26-28)

FOCUS
There was a bit of a split in this sprint handicap, and the best pace appeared to be up the centre of the track. The first three home were drawn in the lowest three boxes. The form looks sound enough, though, amongst the principals.
Ocean Blaze Official explanation: jockey said mare was unsuited by the good ground
Discanti(IRE) Official explanation: jockey said gelding was denied a clear run
Guertino(IRE) Official explanation: jockey said gelding missed the break
Medici Time Official explanation: jockey said gelding was never travelling.

6648 WEWILLBUYYOURCAR.COM APPRENTICE STKS (H'CAP) 1m 2f 88y
5:00 (5:01) (Class 4) (0-85,85) 4-Y-O+ **£5,180** (£1,541; £770; £384) **Stalls** Low

Form RPR

5605 **1** **Veiled Applause**[22] 6014 6-8-6 **73**.. IJBrennan 6 85
(J J Quinn) *hld up towards rr: swtchd lft over 4f out and gd hdwy on inner over 3f out: sn swtchd rt: led 2f out and sn rdn: drvn ent fnl f and kpt on wl towards fin* **6/1**[3]

300 **2** *nk* **Persian Peril**[34] 5671 5-8-7 **81** ow1.............................. JoshuaCrane(7) 3 92
(G A Swinbank) *hld up in tch: hdwy 4f out: effrt to chal 2f out: sn rdn and ev ch tl no ex last 100yds* **20/1**

6336 **3** *7* **Red Jade**[6] 6470 4-8-11 **83**.. LeeTopliss(5) 5 80
(R A Fahey) *trckd ldrs on inner: hdwy over 4f out: led over 3f out: rdn and hdd 2f out: sn drvn and kpt on same pce* **5/1**[2]

5400 **4** *¾* **Rosbay (IRE)**[34] 5671 5-8-5 **77**...................................... AdamCarter(5) 11 73
(T D Easterby) *dwlt and towards rr: hdwy on outer 3f out: rdn and hung lft over 2f out: drvn to chse ldrs wl over 1f out: sn no imp* **14/1**

0200 **5** *8* **King Olav (UAE)**[41] 5437 4-9-3 **84**................................. DebraEngland 13 64
(A W Carroll) *towards rr: hdwy over 3f out: rdn over 2f out: plugged on but nvr nr ldrs* **16/1**

2163 **6** *¾* **Golden Button (IRE)**[11] 6346 4-8-5 **72**................................. JPFahy 15 50
(Sir Mark Prescott) *plld hrd: chsd ldrs: rdn along over 3f out and sn outpcd* **7/2**[1]

5342 **7** *nk* **Bavarian Nordic (USA)**[35] 5622 4-8-2 **72**....................... LauraPike(3) 14 49
(Mrs A Duffield) *trckd ldrs: hdwy 4f out: rdn along over 3f out and sn outpcd* **8/1**

3140 **8** *5* **Charlie Tokyo (IRE)**[22] 6013 6-8-13 **85**..................(v) FrazerWilliams(5) 4 52
(R A Fahey) *v.s.a and bhd: bdly hmpd home turn over 4f out: kpt on fnl 3f but nvr a facgtor* **8/1**

2003 **9** *1 ½* **Motafarred (IRE)**[15] 6234 7-8-11 **81** ow3........................ NSLawes(3) 12 45
(Micky Hammond) *a towards rr* **33/1**

0001 **10** *nk* **Shy Glance (USA)**[18] 6157 7-8-7 **74**................................ TobyAtkinson 8 38
(P Monteith) *chsd ldrs: effrt over 4f out: rdn along over 3f out and grad wknd* **16/1**

0466 **11** *11* **Hurlingham**[34] 5671 5-8-2 **72**..............................(p) MatthewLawson(3) 2 14
(M W Easterby) *led: rdn along over 4f out: hdd over 3f out and sn wknd* **16/1**

30-0 **12** *2 ¾* **Holiday Cocktail**[34] 5671 7-8-4 **71**................................ DeclanCannon 9 7
(J J Quinn) *bhd whn hmpd home bnd over 4f out: no ch after* **33/1**

-610 **13** *11* **Northern Jem**[70] 4502 5-8-10 **77**.................................. SimonPearce 1 —
(Jane Chapple-Hyam) *towards rr on inner: bdly hmpd home bnd over 4f out: no ch after* **16/1**

4406 **14** *4 ½* **Casino Night**[9] 6385 4-8-2 **74**............................... RyanPowell(5) 10 —
(F P Murtagh) *s.i.s: rapid hdwy to join ldrs after 1f: cl up tl rdn along over 3f out and grad wknd* **25/1**

000 **15** *52* **Sri Kuantan (IRE)**[23] 6002 5-8-7 **74** ow1.......................(b[1]) JPHamblett 7 —
(R C Guest) *dwlt: sn cl up: rdn along over 4f out and wknd qckly* **33/1**

2m 11.02s (-1.48) **Going Correction** 0.0s/f (Good) **15** Ran SP% **123.0**
Speed ratings (Par 105): **105,104,99,98,92 91,91,87,86,85 77,74,66,62,20**
toteswingers: 1&2 £66.00, 1&3 £3.00, 2&3 £11.00 CSF £129.77 CT £646.80 TOTE £7.90: £2.40, £6.80, £2.10; EX 237.00 Place 6: £269.24 Place 5: £29.73.
Owner Far 2 Many Sues **Bred** P J McCalmont **Trained** Settrington, N Yorks
■ Stewards' Enquiry : I J Brennan five-day ban: careless riding (Oct 23-24, 26-28)
Simon Pearce £290 fine: left course within five minutes of race and unavailable for stewards' inquiry

FOCUS
A decent apprentice handicap in which the first pair came clear. The form has been taken at something like face value.
T/Jkpt: £9,277.70 to a £1 stake. Pool: £26,134.62. 2.00 winning tickets. T/Plt: £269.20 to a £1 stake. Pool: £105,973.25. 287.36 winning tickets. T/Qpdt: £17.60 to a £1 stake. Pool: £8,060.26. 337.70 winning tickets. JR

6649 - 6655a (Foreign Racing) - See Raceform Interactive

6507 SAINT-CLOUD (L-H)

Friday, October 9

OFFICIAL GOING: Very soft

6656a PRIX THOMAS BRYON (GROUP 3) 1m
1:40 (1:41) 2-Y-O **£38,835** (£15,534; £11,650; £7,767)

RPR

1 **Circumvent**[18] 6173 2-8-11 .... IMendizabal 1 104
(P F I Cole) *racd in 3rd: pushed along after 3f and dropped bk to last: rdn 2 1/2f out: styd on down outside fr over 1f out to ld last 100yds: r.o* **42/10**[3]

2 *1 ½* **Silver Grey (IRE)**[31] 5743 2-8-8 .... RobertHavlin 2 98
(R Ingram) *racd in 2nd: cl 3rd whn rdn 1 1/2f out: styd on fnl f to take 2nd cl home* **14/1**

3 *shd* **Ameer (IRE)**[21] 6057 2-8-11 .... OPeslier 3 100
(Saeed Bin Suroor) *led: rdn 2f out: hdd 100yds out: lost 2nd cl home* **1/1**[1]

4 *½* **Rajsaman (FR)**[21] 6080 2-8-11 .... SPasquier 4 99
(A De Royer-Dupre, France) *racd in 4th: wnt 3rd bef 1/2-way: hdwy on ins to press ldr 1 1/2f out: wknd ins fnl f* **7/5**[2]

1m 45.1s (-2.40) **4** Ran SP% **117.6**
PARI-MUTUEL: WIN 5.20; PL 2.40, 3.60; SF 15.70.
Owner The Fairy Story Partnership **Bred** Deepwood Farm Stud **Trained** Whatcombe, Oxon

NOTEBOOK
Circumvent seemed to appreciate the cut in the ground and put up a game effort. He was in last position rounding the final turn and, pushed along coming into the straight, was outpaced two and a half out. He gradually built up momentum and hit the lead a furlong out and was going away from the field in the final stages. He won a little cosily in the end and should definitely stay further. There are no real plans but he could be supplemented into the Prix de Conde.
Silver Grey(IRE) battled on very gamely throughout the straight and only pinched second place in the final few strides. This was her best ever performance and she may well come back to France for the Poule d'Essai des Pouliches next year.
Ameer(IRE) tried to make every yard of the running and set a respectable pace early on. Still in the lead at the 2f marker, he was then attacked by the other three runners. He battled on gamely but was dominated by the winner inside the final furlong and then lost second place at the end of the mile.
Rajsaman(FR), last in the early stages, moved up closer to the lead rounding the final turn. He started his challenge for the lead on the inside and battled on gamely before finally going under by just over two lengths.

6657a PRIX DU RANELAGH (LISTED RACE) 1m
2:10 (2:13) 3-Y-O+ **£25,243** (£10,097; £7,573; £5,049; £2,524)

RPR

1 **Usbeke (GER)**[33] 3-8-11 .... TThulliez 3 98
(J-P Carvalho, Germany)

2 *shd* **Skins Game**[42] 3-8-11 .... IMendizabal 8 97
(J-C Rouget, France)

3 *2* **Ideology**[75] 4367 3-8-11 .... SPasquier 9 93
(A Fabre, France)

4 *1* **Cheyrac (FR)**[143] 3-8-8 .... GBenoist 1 87
(X Nakkachdji, France)

5 *½* **Accord Secret (FR)**[65] 4685 3-8-11 .... FBlondel 11 89
(J-C Rouget, France)

6 *1* **Ogre (USA)**[29] 5804 4-8-11 .... AndrewHeffernan 4 84
(P D Evans) *led to 1 1/2f out: one pce* **14/1**[1]

7 *1* **Polarix**[18] 6176 3-8-11 .... MGuyon 12 85
(H-A Pantall, France)

8 *2* **Chopastair (FR)**[18] 6176 8-9-5 .... J-BEyquem 10 85
(T Lemer, France)

9 *1* **Konig Bernard (FR)**[54] 5083 3-8-11 .... DBoeuf 7 78
(W Baltromei, Germany)

10 *hd* **Saphir River (FR)**[18] 6176 3-8-11 ....(p) YLerner 2 77
(C Lerner, France)

0 **Partner Shift (IRE)**[97] 3649 3-8-11 .... OPeslier 13 —
(H-A Pantall, France)

0 **Isaonor (FR)**[15] 6237 3-8-8 .... TJarnet 6 —
(Mlle S-V Tarrou, France)

1m 43.6s (-3.90)
WFA 3 from 4yo+ 3lb **12** Ran SP% **6.7**
PARI-MUTUEL: WIN 61.30; PL 8.80, 1.80, 1.90; DF 73.60.
Owner Stall Lucky Owner **Bred** Gestut Rottgen **Trained** Germany

NOTEBOOK
Ogre(USA) made a very game effort to go from pillar to post. Several lengths clear of the field coming into the straight, she was still galloping on strongly at the furlong marker and was then swamped by her opponents.

6658a PRIX TANTIEME (LISTED RACE) 1m 2f 110y
2:40 (2:46) 4-Y-O+ **£25,243** (£10,097; £7,573; £5,049; £2,524)

RPR

1 **Capitaine Courage (IRE)**[20] 4-8-11 .... TThulliez 3 104
(F Doumen, France)

2 *1 ½* **Moyenne Corniche**[34] 5655 4-8-11 .... IMendizabal 4 101
(M L W Bell) *broke wl then restrained in midfield on ins: 6th st: rdn in 3rd 2 1/2f out: styd on to dispute ld briefly 100yds out: kpt on* **12/1**[1]

3 *snk* **Mr Brock (SAF)**[14] 6327 6-9-2 .... DBoeuf 1 106
(Mme C Head-Maarek, France)

4 *½* **Rainbow Dancing**[33] 5712 4-8-8 .... TJarnet 5 97
(Mlle H Van Zuylen, France)

5 *1 ½* **Satwa Prince (FR)**[16] 6-8-11 .... JVictoire 8 97
(J De Roualle, France)

6 *1 ½* **Thanatos**[9] 4-8-11 .... GMasure 11 94
(P Schiergen, Germany)

7 *hd* **Tau**[16] 4-8-11 .... OPeslier 2 94
(J E Pease, France)

8 *2* **Porgy**[33] 5712 4-8-11 .... SPasquier 10 90
(Mme C Head-Maarek, France)

9 *15* **All The Winds (GER)**[405] 5529 4-8-11 .... MGuyon 9 60
(T Mundry, Germany)

10 *2* **Boytard (FR)**[15] 4-8-11 .... FBlondel 7 57
(F Belmont, France)

2m 17.3s (-2.30) **10** Ran SP% **7.7**
PARI-MUTUEL: WIN 4.30; PL 1.80, 3.20, 2.00; DF 22.90.
Owner J Vasicek **Bred** Vision Bloodstock **Trained** Bouce, France

NOTEBOOK
Moyenne Corniche was tucked in behind the leading group in the early stages, made a forward move from halfway up the straight and took second place with 50 yards left to run.

6302 ASCOT (R-H)

Saturday, October 10

OFFICIAL GOING: Good to soft(soft in places on round course; 8.4; good in places on straight course; stands' side 7.6, centre 8.3, far side 8.0)
Wind: Medium, half against Weather: Bright, partly cloudy

6660 WILLMOTT DIXON CORNWALLIS STKS (GROUP 3) 5f
2:15 (2:16) (Class 1) 2-Y-O
£31,223 (£11,836; £5,923; £2,953; £1,479; £742) **Stalls** Centre

Form RPR

3110 **1** **Our Jonathan**[29] 5822 2-9-0 98.................................. JamieSpencer 1 110+
(K A Ryan) *stdd s: hld up in rr: grad crossed to far rail: hdwy over 2f out: swtchd lft 1f out: swtchd bk to rail ins fnl f: forced way through to ld last strides* **5/1**[2]

2122 **2** *nk* **Taajub (IRE)**[30] 5795 2-9-0 108.................................. RHills 2 108
(W J Haggas) *chsd ldrs: rdn and clsd 2f out: ev ch ent fnl f: kpt on* **11/4**[1]

1026 **3** *nse* **Iver Bridge Lad**[14] 6275 2-9-0 104.............................. MichaelHills 5 108
(J Ryan) *towards rr: hdwy on outer ent fnl 2f: rdn to chal jst ins fnl f: led narrowly fnl 100yds: edgd rt and hdd nr fin: lost 2nd on line* **12/1**

502 **4** *1 ¼* **Bould Mover**[29] 5822 2-9-0 107............................... DarryllHolland 4 103
(R Curtis) *chsd clr ldr: rdn and clsd 2f out: led over 1f out: sn hrd pressed: edgd lft u.p and hdd fnl 100yds: edgd rt and wknd towards fin* **14/1**

1305 **5** *1 ¼* **Tawaabb**[39] 5552 2-9-0 96.. RyanMoore 15 99
(M R Channon) *chsd ldrs: rdn and effrt ent fnl 2f: kpt on same pce u.p fnl f* **16/1**

6033 **6** *nk* **Above Limits (IRE)**[31] 5765 2-8-11 102.................... CatherineGannon 3 95
(Tom Dascombe) *chsd ldrs: rdn and clsd 2f out: ev ch over 1f out: wknd ins fnl f* **12/1**

100 **7** *hd* **Star Rover (IRE)**[7] 6486 2-9-0 107............................. JimmyFortune 11 97
(P D Evans) *racd in midfield: shuffled bk and lost pl over 2f out: swtchd lft and rdn 2f out: styd on wl fnl f: nt rch ldrs* **18/1**

23 **8** *1 ½* **Sole Power**[51] 5198 2-9-0 0...................................... PJSmullen 10 92
(Edward Lynam, Ire) *towards rr: hdwy on outer 2f out: rdn and plugged on steadily fr over 1f out: nvr gng pce to rch ldrs* **11/2**[3]

3115 **9** *1 ¾* **Monsieur Joe (IRE)**[5] 6550 2-9-0 85.............................. AdamKirby 7 85
(W R Swinburn) *in tch in midfield: rdn and unable qck over 2f out: no ch w ldrs fr over 1f out* **20/1**

0160 **10** *2 ¼* **Hairspray**[21] 6090 2-8-11 94...................................... ChrisCatlin 8 74
(M R Channon) *v.s.a: bhd and sn pushed along: n.d* **100/1**

4435 **11** *nse* **Red Avalanche (IRE)**[35] 5661 2-9-0 100......................... LDettori 16 77
(P F I Cole) *racd in midfield: rdn and unable qck over 2f out: no ch w ldrs fr over 1f out* **20/1**

5424 **12** *1* **Fratellino**[14] 6275 2-9-0 98...................................... TPQueally 9 73
(A J McCabe) *chsd ldrs: rdn and struggling over 2f out: wknd 2f out* **25/1**

2116 **13** *shd* **Piccadilly Filly (IRE)**[29] 5822 2-8-11 98................. EdwardCreighton 18 70
(E J Creighton) *led and sn clr: rdn and hdd over 1f out: wknd qckly* **16/1**

110 **14** *nk* **Don't Tell Mary (IRE)**[115] 3015 2-8-11 99.................. RichardKingscote 12 69
(Tom Dascombe) *a in rr: rdn and no prog over 2f out* **14/1**

3100 **15** *1 ¾* **Vanishing Grey (IRE)**[7] 6486 2-8-11 83.....................(b[1]) TedDurcan 14 63
(B J Meehan) *hmpd s: a towards rr: rdn and no prog whn hmpd over 2f out* **80/1**

1212 **16** *2 ½* **Yurituni**[14] 6275 2-8-11 84...................................... TonyCulhane 17 54
(Eve Johnson Houghton) *racd in midfield: rdn and struggling whn hmpd over 1f out: wl btn after* **40/1**

2223 **17** *11* **Aalsmeer**[22] 6049 2-8-11 92..................................... RichardMullen 13 14
(E S McMahon) *restless in stalls: wnt rt s: sn in midfield: rdn and struggling over 2f out: wl bhd fnl f* **20/1**

61.29 secs (0.79) **Going Correction** +0.425s/f (Yiel) **17** Ran SP% **127.3**
Speed ratings (Par 105): **110,109,109,107,105 104,104,102,99,95 95,94,94,93,90 86,69**
toteswingers: 1&2 £5.20, 2&3 £46.30, 1&3 £19.00. CSF £18.19 TOTE £5.50: £2.20, £1.90, £4.70; EX 16.20 Trifecta £413.20 Pool: £815.35 - 1.46 winning units..
Owner Dr Marwan Koukash **Bred** W G M Turner **Trained** Hambleton, N Yorks
■ Stewards' Enquiry : Darryll Holland three-day ban: careless riding (Oct 26-28)
Jamie Spencer one-day ban: careless riding (Oct 26)

FOCUS
This was certainly a competitive contest and the form looks solid rated around the runner-up. Our Jonathan built on his Flying Childers form. The pace predictably was strong. They all raced towards the far side, and the rail looked advantageous, yet surprisingly five of the first six finishers emerged from the bottom five boxes.

NOTEBOOK
Our Jonathan was dropped in from stall one and sat second last after a couple of furlongs or so, before enjoying a dream run through towards the far rail under an ambitious ride to get up in the final strides. All things considered, even though the next three home were also drawn low, the winner looks better than the bare result. Following a Listed win in Ireland, he wasn't beaten very far in the Flying Childers when losing many lengths with a slow start, and this success confirms him a pretty smart sprinter. His jockey thinks he will make a 3-y-o, provided he continues to relax and doesn't get wound up going to the start and in the stalls, like he did last time. It's true he missed the kick here as well, but that was probably by design. He might not run again this year but should stay 6f next season. (op 9-2 tchd 11-2)
Taajub(IRE) travelled well, displaying plenty of speed, and that enabled him to get a decent, handy position from stall two. He battled on well to narrowly get the better of a prolonged duel with Iver Bridge Lad, but was caught with a sucker punch near the line. He didn't run up to his Gimcrack form when runner-up over 6.5f in a sales race last time, but this drop in trip suited and he looks all speed. (op 3-1 tchd 7-2 and 4-1 in places)
Iver Bridge Lad looked the winner when moving into a threatening position late on, and he briefly hit the front inside the final 1f, but he couldn't quite sustain his run. He was caught a little wide throughout but looked to be beaten fair and square. (op 25-1)
Bould Mover, runner-up in the Flying Childers, again displayed plenty of speed, but the easy ground placed more emphasis on stamina than was ideal, and he didn't quite get home. He was bumped by the winner late on, but it made no difference. (op 12-1)
Tawaabb returned to something like his Norfolk form, although he did have the benefit of a favourable draw, unlike those ahead of him. He's probably not easy to place. (op 25-1)
Above Limits(IRE) ran well for a long way, showing lots of natural speed from stall three. She simply got tired and looks better than the beaten margin suggests. (op 10-1)
Star Rover(IRE), having his 14th start, couldn't hold his position at a crucial stage. (op 20-1)
Sole Power got quite far back, albeit the winner did as well, and made only moderate progress before flattening out. His trainer suggested beforehand that the colt didn't want the ground too soft. (op 7-1)
Piccadilly Filly(IRE) has a serious amount of natural speed and went off too fast.
Don't Tell Mary(IRE) didn't show much at all on her first start since returning home lame from the Queen Mary. She probably wants quick ground. (op 16-1)

6661 WILLMOTT DIXON BENGOUGH MEMORIAL STKS (GROUP 3) 6f
2:55 (2:55) (Class 1) 3-Y-O+

£36,900 (£13,988; £7,000; £3,490; £1,313; £1,313) Stalls Centre

Form RPR
-164 1 **Royal Rock**[27] 5921 5-9-1 105 GeorgeBaker 5 115
(C F Wall) *stdd after s: hld up in rr: hdwy wl over 1f out: rdn to chal ent fnl f: led narrowly fnl 100yds: kpt on wl* **11/1**
2124 2 *hd* **Triple Aspect (IRE)**[21] 6107 3-9-0 112 LiamJones 18 114
(W J Haggas) *hld up in tch: hdwy to ld gng wl 2f out: rdn over 1f out: hdd narrowly fnl 100yds: kpt on but a jst hld after* **11/2**[1]
0010 3 *1 1/4* **Brave Prospector**[21] 6091 4-9-1 102 (t) JamieSpencer 9 110
(P W Chapple-Hyam) *hld up towards rr: hdwy and edging rt jst over 2f out: swtchd lft and rdn over 1f out: chsd ldng pair ins fnl f: kpt on* **28/1**
6044 4 *nk* **Bonnie Charlie**[15] 6240 3-9-0 100 PatDobbs 3 109
(R Hannon) *hld up bhd: hdwy over 1f out: r.o wl u.p fnl f: nt rch ldrs* **33/1**
4331 5 *1 3/4* **Jimmy Styles**[21] 6091 5-9-1 106 (p) PhilipRobinson 14 103
(C G Cox) *hld up in midfield: edging rt and hdwy 2f out: chsd ldrs and drvn over 1f out: one pce fnl f* **12/1**
4410 5 *dht* **Markab**[28] 5860 6-9-1 104 PatCosgrave 7 103+
(H Candy) *racd in centre: in midfield tl converged w field and chsng ldrs over 2f out: drvn to chse ldng pair jst over 1f out: wknd fnl 100yds* **11/1**
2110 7 *nse* **Golden Desert (IRE)**[14] 6270 5-9-1 105 AlanMunro 11 103
(T G Mills) *hld up in tch: rdn and effrt wl over 1f out: kpt on u.p fnl f but nt gng pce to threaten ldrs* **25/1**
2410 8 *1 3/4* **Palace Moon**[13] 6304 4-9-1 107 SteveDrowne 19 98
(H Morrison) *chsd ldrs: ev ch 2f out: wknd u.p fnl f* **11/1**
1330 9 *nk* **Knot In Wood (IRE)**[13] 6304 7-9-5 110 TonyHamilton 12 101
(R A Fahey) *racd in midfield: rdn and effrt jst over 2f out: kpt on but nvr threatened ldrs fnl 2f* **16/1**
0133 10 *3/4* **Mullein**[13] 6304 4-8-12 105 JimCrowley 15 91
(R M Beckett) *hld up in midfield: rdn and effrt on far rail ent fnl 2f: no prog fr over 1f out* **9/1**[2]
6660 11 *1/2* **Rowe Park**[28] 5878 6-9-1 103 TedDurcan 1 93
(Mrs L C Jewell) *stdd s: jnd main gp over 4f out: bhd: nt clr run 2f out: rdn wl over 1f out: nvr trbld ldrs* **66/1**
1031 12 *1/2* **Golden Stream (IRE)**[14] 6272 3-8-11 103 RyanMoore 4 94
(Sir Michael Stoute) *sn bhd: hdwy on far rail whn nt clr run and bdly hmpd over 1f out: swtchd lft ent fnl f: n.d* **12/1**
3501 13 *hd* **Awinnersgame (IRE)**[25] 5973 3-9-0 105 DarryllHolland 8 90
(J Noseda) *hld up in midfield: rdn and effrt ent fnl 2f: no prog* **20/1**
23 14 *shd* **Icelandic**[55] 5079 7-9-1 105 (t) HayleyTurner 6 90
(F Sheridan) *bhd: rdn 3f out: swtchd rt ent fnl 2f: nvr trbld ldrs* **20/1**
2055 15 *1 1/2* **Prime Defender**[13] 6304 5-9-1 107 (b) MichaelHills 16 85
(B W Hills) *s.i.s and hmpd sn after s: bhd: hdwy over 3f out: ev ch and rdn 2f out: sn wknd* **10/1**[3]
2412 16 *2* **Tamagin (USA)**[13] 6304 6-9-1 109 (p) StephenDonohoe 10 79
(J Pearce) *taken down v early: restless in stalls: led tl over 3f out: pressed ldr after tl rdn and wknd qckly ent fnl 2f* **9/1**[2]
1300 17 *7* **Enderby Spirit (GR)**[56] 5032 3-9-0 104 RichardMullen 20 57
(B Smart) *a towards rr and niggled along: nvr trbld ldrs: wl bhd fnl f* **20/1**
2-52 18 *1 3/4* **Waffle (IRE)**[136] 2373 3-9-0 102 TPQueally 2 51
(J Noseda) *racd in centre pair: a towards rr: no ch fr wl over 1f out: eased ins fnl f* **40/1**
0310 19 *5* **Ancien Regime (IRE)**[42] 5434 4-9-1 105 LDettori 17 35
(Saeed Bin Suroor) *chsd ldr tl led over 3f out: hdd 2f out: sn dropped out: wl bhd and eased ins fnl f* **16/1**
53 20 *hd* **Festoso (IRE)**[22] 6058 4-8-12 101 (b) JimmyFortune 13 31
(H J L Dunlop) *chsd ldrs: rdn and lost pl qckly wl over 1f out: wl bhd and eased ins fnl f* **33/1**

1m 14.99s (0.59) **Going Correction** +0.425s/f (Yiel)
WFA 3 from 4yo+ 1lb **20 Ran SP% 128.0**
Speed ratings (Par 113): **113,112,111,110,108 108,108,105,105,104 103,103,102,102,100 98,88,86,79,79**
toteswingers: 1&2 £14.00, 2&3 £254.50, 1&3 £44.40. CSF £63.15 TOTE £15.30: £5.40, £2.90, £11.60; EX 111.80 Trifecta £1232.90 Part won. Pool: £1,666.13 - 0.50 winning units..
Owner Ms Aida Fustoq **Bred** Deerfield Farm **Trained** Newmarket, Suffolk

FOCUS
A good, competitive Group 3 run at a strong pace. A small group raced up the centre of the track through the first couple of furlongs, but soon enough the field were as one towards the far side. A clear personal best from Royal Rock, with the third and fourth the best guides.

NOTEBOOK
Royal Rock had the ground to suit, and he was said by George Baker to have improved for his recent run in Ireland, when he was returning from more than three months off, but he got warm beforehand, which tempered enthusiasm somewhat. In the race itself, he travelled strongly off the decent pace and, once getting a gap, he stayed on relentlessly to get the better of Triple Aspect. This was only his fourth start of the season, and just his 13th in total, and it's understandable his connections hope he can step up again. A trip to Dubai for the carnival is apparently unlikely, as he needs soft ground, but he has won on Polytrack and it's by no means out of the question the Tapeta surface at Meydan would suit. Whatever, he is one to have on side when he gets suitable conditions. (op 10-1)
Triple Aspect(IRE) was gradually worn down after travelling strongly close enough to the pace. Although he appreciates a bit of cut in the ground, these conditions placed more emphasis on stamina than was ideal. And considering a quick 5f usually finds him out, he's not the easiest to place, but perhaps he'll come back a stronger horse next year. He does give the impression he has the potential to progress beyond this level.
Brave Prospector ◆, who lost a shoe in the Ayr Gold Cup, travelled just about as well as anything, but he was messed about a bit when trying to find room to make a move and couldn't muster the pace to threaten the front two. This was a good effort considering his connections stated after his Doncaster win two starts back that he needs quick ground. (op 25-1 tchd 33-1)
Bonnie Charlie appreciated the return to easy ground and came back to something like the form he showed when runner-up in last season's Horris Hill. He was set quite a bit to do, although in fairness stall three was no help at all, and he did his best work late on.
Jimmy Styles was up in grade after winning the Ayr Gold Cup and he performed with credit, without ever looking likely to win. (op 16-1)
Markab might have been at a disadvantage in joining the main group later than most, after racing up the middle early. He ran well in the circumstances. (op 16-1)
Golden Desert(IRE) has made good progress this season but he was comfortably held on this rise in class, with the ground probably not in his favour. (tchd 28-1)
Palace Moon seemed to travel quite well but he struggled to go through the ground under pressure. (op 14-1)
Knot In Wood(IRE) could have been expected to finish closer with the ground to suit.
Mullein handles easy ground but she ran nowhere near the form she showed when third in the Diadem over this C&D last time. (op 8-1)
Rowe Park found only the one pace after being denied a clear run. (op 80-1)
Golden Stream(IRE), who was drawn in four and struggled to lay up through the early stages on this drop in trip, went for an ambitious run near the far rail, but she had her path blocked from around 2f out until just over 1f from the finish. She looked to have something to offer at the time, despite having got warm at the start, but her chance had passed by the time she was finally in the clear. Official explanation: jockey said filly was denied a clear run
Tamagin(USA) was unsuited by the ground. Official explanation: jockey said the colt was unsuited by the ground (op 8-1)
Ancien Regime(IRE) Official explanation: jockey said colt stopped quickly

6662 LADBROKES.COM HERITAGE H'CAP 1m 4f
3:30 (3:30) (Class 2) (0-105,102) 3-Y-O+

£46,732 (£13,995; £6,997; £3,502; £1,747; £877) Stalls High

Form RPR
-310 1 **Opinion Poll (IRE)**[114] 3051 3-8-10 95 LDettori 1 109+
(M A Jarvis) *racd alone on far rail for 3f: chsd ledaers: rdn to chse ldr 2f out: sn ev ch and drvn: led ins fnl f: styd on strly* **15/2**[2]
4214 2 *3 1/2* **Kings Destiny**[35] 5656 3-8-13 98 PhilipRobinson 12 106
(M A Jarvis) *led: rdn and clr w wnr wl over 1f out: hdd ins fnl f: nt pce of wnr fnl 150yds* **11/1**
2332 3 *1 1/4* **Safari Sunup (IRE)**[36] 5641 4-9-0 97 AshleyMorgan(5) 4 103
(P Winkworth) *hld up in tch: rdn and effrt over 2f out: chsd ldng pair over 1f out: kpt on but no imp* **40/1**
6001 4 *nk* **Pevensey (IRE)**[21] 6100 7-8-8 93 (p) IJBrennan(7) 10 99+
(J J Quinn) *s.i.s and pushed along early: bhd: 18th and rdn 3f out: hdwy on outer over 1f out: styd on wl fnl f: nvr trbld ldrs* **11/1**
5041 5 *1 1/2* **Record Breaker (IRE)**[13] 6302 5-9-10 102 (b) RHills 9 106
(M Johnston) *dwlt and niggled along early: rdn and hdwy on outer over 2f out: kpt on but nvr gng pce to trble ldrs* **10/1**[3]
4-00 6 *1* **Siberian Tiger (IRE)**[26] 5173 4-9-1 98 (b[1]) GFCarroll(5) 3 100
(A J Martin, Ire) *t.k.h: hld up in midfield: steadily lost pl and bhd 3f out: rdn: no hdwy and hung rt over 2f out: swtchd lft over 1f out: styd on steadily fnl f: nvr trbld ldrs* **16/1**
0434 7 *1/2* **Young Mick**[112] 3142 7-9-4 96 (v) JohnEgan 19 97
(G G Margarson) *in tch on inner: rdn and switching lft off rail 3f out: outpcd and edgd lft by ldng pair over 2f out: plugged on same pce after* **12/1**
3164 8 *1/2* **Classic Vintage (USA)**[42] 5425 3-8-12 97 JimCrowley 2 97
(Mrs A J Perrett) *hld up towards rr: effrt and rdn over 2f out: sme hdwy over 1f out: nvr trbld ldrs* **14/1**
0551 9 *1 1/4* **Quai D'Orsay**[9] 6412 3-8-13 98 JoeFanning 6 96
(M Johnston) *chsd ldr: rdn wl over 2f out: lost 2nd 2f out and nt pce of ldng pair: wknd jst over 1f out* **20/1**
110 10 *1 1/2* **Lethal Glaze (IRE)**[28] 5870 3-9-0 99 PatDobbs 8 95
(R Hannon) *racd in tch in midfield: rdn and struggling to hold pl 3f out: n.d after* **33/1**
0321 11 *hd* **Rangefinder**[35] 5671 5-8-12 90 JamieSpencer 13 88
(L M Cumani) *hld up in tch: rdn and effrt 3f out: hanging rt and no prog ent fnl 2f: btn and eased ins fnl f* **12/1**
1324 12 *1/2* **Class Is Class (IRE)**[21] 6106 3-8-12 97 RyanMoore 18 92
(Sir Michael Stoute) *a bhd: rdn and no prog over 3f out: hanging rt u.p over 1f out: n.d* **11/4**[1]
316- 13 *3/4* **First Avenue**[156] 7244 4-9-2 94 (p) GeorgeBaker 7 88
(G L Moore) *t.k.h: trckd ldrs: rdn and unable qck over 2f out: wknd over 1f out* **80/1**
2623 14 *1/2* **Mystery Star (IRE)**[23] 6036 4-9-6 98 (p) TedDurcan 16 91
(M H Tompkins) *a towards rr: pushed along 8f out: rdn and effrt on inner over 2f out: no real prog* **33/1**
3503 15 *1 3/4* **Unleashed (IRE)**[13] 6302 4-9-7 99 (b) TPQueally 11 89
(H R A Cecil) *dwlt and sn pushed along: rn in snatches: in tch in midfield: rdn and nt qckn over 2f out: btn whn short of room wl over 1f out* **20/1**
2300 16 *hd* **Magicalmysterytour (IRE)**[35] 5656 6-9-4 96 ChrisCatlin 14 86
(W J Musson) *hld up in midfield: rdn and no prog over 2f out: nvr trbld ldrs* **20/1**
-410 17 *3* **Coin Of The Realm (IRE)**[52] 5170 4-8-11 89 RichardMullen 5 74
(G L Moore) *s.i.s: a bhd: rdn and no rspnse over 2f out* **33/1**
4-5 18 *1 3/4* **Inventor (IRE)**[35] 5662 4-9-8 100 JimmyFortune 15 82
(B J Meehan) *chsd ldrs: rdn and wknd over 2f out: bhd fr over 1f out* **16/1**

6404 **19** *13* **Yellowstone (IRE)**[105] 3397 5-9-7 99 DarryllHolland 17 60
(P F I Cole) *s.i.s a bhd: lost tch over 2f out: eased fr over 1f out* **33/1**

2m 34.06s (1.56) **Going Correction** +0.425s/f (Yiel)
WFA 3 from 4yo+ 7lb **19** Ran SP% **127.7**
Speed ratings (Par 109): **111,108,107,107,106 105,105,105,104,103 103,103,102,102,101 100,98,97,89**
toteswingers: 1&2 £44.30, 2&3 £165.80, 1&3 £152.40. CSF £79.62 CT £3146.44 TOTE £8.80: £2.50, £3.10, £7.70, £3.10; EX 71.60 Trifecta £4962.10 Pool: £65,044.05 - 9.70 winning units..
Owner Sheikh Ahmed Al Maktoum **Bred** Darley **Trained** Newmarket, Suffolk
■ A 1-2 for trainer Michael Jarvis.
■ Stewards' Enquiry : I J Brennan two-day ban: used whip with excessive frequency (Oct 29-30); two-day ban: careless riding (Oct 31-Nov 1)

FOCUS
This was a decent, competitive handicap, but the winner, who was getting weight all round, was much too good and looks a potential Group horse. The fifth is the best guide to the form. A time nearly four seconds slower than standard confirms the ground on the round course was on the soft side.

NOTEBOOK
Opinion Poll(IRE) ◆ impressed when winning a decent handicap on testing ground at Haydock back in May, and on his only run since then he was unsuited by fast ground over this C&D in the King George V Stakes. With conditions to suit on his return from nearly four months off, he was given an intelligent ride by Frankie Dettori, who overcame a potentially tricky draw in stall one by taking the colt towards the far rail under the trees before the first bend, which is often a good move when the ground is soft. By the time he joined the rest of the field, the winner was in a handy position and travelled well. After taking a while to respond when first coming under pressure in the straight, he gradually drew nicely clear and was an impressive winner. He looks likely to progress into a Group horse when the ground is soft, but before then the November Handicap could be on the agenda. (op 8-1 tchd 9-1 in a place)
Kings Destiny, dropped in trip, was given a good ride from the front and had his chance. He remains progressive and, like his winning stablemate, may go for the November Handicap. (op 12-1)
Safari Sunup(IRE) moved into contention travelling well, but was forced wider than ideal around the final bend. He ran on and this was a very useful effort off a career-high mark. (op 50-1)
Pevensey(IRE), 7lb higher than when winning at Catterick, didn't travel all that well towards the rear and only had one or two behind at the top of the straight, but he made good progress out wide to finish much closer than had appeared likely at one stage.
Record Breaker(IRE) ran a good race off a mark 6lb higher than when winning over C&D on his previous start, especially as he ideally wants quicker ground. (op 9-1)
Siberian Tiger(IRE), back on the Flat, had blinkers on in place of cheekpieces and did not look an easy ride. It's true he didn't enjoy the clearest of runs in the straight, but he didn't help his rider by hanging right.
Young Mick seemed to have his chance but he wasn't at his best. Official explanation: jockey said gelding hung left (op 14-1)
Rangefinder hung under pressure. Official explanation: jockey said horse hung right in the straight (op 11-1)
Class Is Class(IRE) should have been suited by the return to 1m4f, as well as easy ground, but he was a major disappointment. He was never going from the moment the stalls opened, not responding to being niggled along, and having been poorly placed as a result, he didn't pick up for more urgent riding when the race got serious. While he has the physical scope to make a fine 4-y-o, this is not the first time he's failed to travel well enough to get a good position (York two runs back) and he's not straightforward. (op 7-2)

6663 CARRAIG INSURANCE HYPERION CONDITIONS STKS 7f
4:05 (4:06) (Class 2) 2-Y-O £8,411 (£2,519; £1,259; £630; £314) Stalls Centre

Form RPR
1336 **1** **Corporal Maddox**[52] 5172 2-9-4 101 TPQueally 1 104
(H R A Cecil) *hld up wl in tch: hdwy to ld on bit jst over 2f out: rdn over 1f out: drvn and edgd rt ins fnl f: kpt on and jst lasted* **7/2**[3]
11 **2** *hd* **Quadrille**[35] 5664 2-9-2 96 RyanMoore 2 102
(R Hannon) *w ldr: rdn ent fnl 2f: chsd wnr clr of rivals over 1f out: rallied u.p ent fnl f: edgd rt but kpt on wl and pressing wnr nr fin* **6/4**[1]
4 **3** *6* **Vimiero (USA)**[21] 6109 2-9-0 0 AdamKirby 5 85
(W R Swinburn) *led at stdy gallop: hdd and rdn jst over 2f out: wknd and edgd lft over 1f out: no ch w ldng pair fnl f: wnt 3rd nr fin* **14/1**
1436 **4** *3/4* **Lamh Albasser (USA)**[30] 5795 2-9-0 99 (p) LDettori 4 83
(Saeed Bin Suroor) *t.k.h: hld up wl in tch: rdn and immediately outpcd 2f out: modest 3rd but no ch w ldng pair over 1f out: lost 3rd nr fin* **5/1**
01 **5** *14* **Wigmore Hall (IRE)**[22] 6066 2-9-0 86 JamieSpencer 3 73+
(M L W Bell) *sltly hmpd s: hdwy to press ldrs 3f out: rdn over 2f out: wknd qckly over 1f out: eased fnl f* **9/4**[2]

1m 30.62s (2.62) **Going Correction** +0.425s/f (Yiel) **5** Ran SP% **116.3**
Speed ratings (Par 101): **102,101,94,94,78**
CSF £9.83 TOTE £4.30: £1.40, £1.60; EX 9.60.
Owner Mogeely Stud & Mrs Maura Gittins **Bred** Theobalds Stud **Trained** Newmarket, Suffolk

FOCUS
A good conditions contest, although the early pace was steady. They raced up the middle of the track early but gradually drifted towards the far rail. The first pair came clear and the form is sound.

NOTEBOOK
Corporal Maddox, back up in trip after finishing last in the Gimcrack on his final start for Alan Jarvis, made a winning debut for the Cecil yard after nearly two months off. He probably made his ground up quicker than ideal, as he was in front about 2f out, but he had just enough left to hold on, despite edging right. (tchd 4-1)
Quadrille, the winner of his first two starts, only just failed to maintain his unbeaten record. He handled the ground well, pulling clear of the remainder, and ran right up to his mark considering he had 3lb to find with the winner on official figures. (tchd 13-8 and 7-4 in places)
Vimiero(USA) ◆ is a very big colt and, after leading, he still looked weak when coming under pressure, with easy ground probably not ideal at this stage of his career. He should do better when he strengthens up next year and beyond. (op 16-1)
Lamh Albasser(USA) was the best off at the weights but he ruined his chance by racing too keenly and was well below his official mark of 99. (tchd 9-2)
Wigmore Hall(IRE) is a fine-looking colt with plenty of scope, and had won his maiden at Newmarket last time, albeit under different conditions, but he ran no sort of race this time. Official explanation: jockey said colt lost two shoes (op 100-30 tchd 7-2)

6664 JAGUAR ALL-NEW XJ AUTUMN STKS (GROUP 3) 1m (R)
4:40 (4:40) (Class 1) 2-Y-O £28,385 (£10,760; £5,385; £2,685; £1,345; £675) Stalls High

Form RPR
22 **1** **Morana (IRE)**[9] 6416 2-9-0 0 AlanMunro 9 108+
(P W Chapple-Hyam) *t.k.h: trckd ldrs: nt clr run over 1f out: swtchd lft and hdwy to chal 1f out: led fnl 50yds: styd on wl* **9/1**
216 **2** *hd* **Prompter**[49] 5261 2-9-0 98 HayleyTurner 6 108+
(M L W Bell) *led: pressed and rdn wl over 1f out: kpt on wl u.p tl hdd and no ex fnl 50yds* **15/2**[3]
3151 **3** *4 1/2* **Simenon (IRE)**[23] 6011 2-9-0 101 LPKeniry 2 98
(A M Balding) *chsd ldr: rdn whn bdly hmpd and lost pl 2f out: drvn and edgd rt over 1f out: plugged on to go 3rd on post* **9/2**[2]
1121 **4** *nse* **Azizi**[28] 5864 2-9-0 98 RHills 5 98
(W J Haggas) *hld up in tch in last trio: plld out and effrt over 2f out: plugging on whn sltly hmpd jst ins fnl f: chsd ldng pair fnl 150yds: no imp: lost 3rd on post* **6/4**[1]
412 **5** *shd* **Togiak (IRE)**[25] 5970 2-9-0 88 TPQueally 8 98
(E A L Dunlop) *stdd after s: hld up in tch in last trio: swtchd lft and effrt over 2f out: rdn wl over 1f out: pressing for placings fnl f but nvr trbld ldrs* **8/1**
6213 **6** *2 1/4* **Dubawi Phantom**[49] 5261 2-9-0 102 (b) AhmedAjtebi 1 93
(D M Simcock) *t.k.h: hld up wl in tch: hdwy and edgd rt ent fnl 2f: ev ch over 1f out: rdn and edgd lft 1f out: wknd qckly: eased towards fin* **8/1**
511 **7** *2 1/2* **Stags Leap (IRE)**[45] 5347 2-9-0 92 RyanMoore 4 87
(R Hannon) *w ldrs for 2f: lost pl and pushed along 1/2-way: rdn and no prog wl over 2f out* **11/1**
13 **8** *1/2* **Blakey's Boy**[56] 5022 2-9-0 90 TedDurcan 7 86
(J L Dunlop) *s.i.s: hld up wl in tch in rr: short-lived effrt on inner over 2f out: no ch w ldrs fnl 2f* **16/1**

1m 43.51s (2.81) **Going Correction** +0.425s/f (Yiel) **8** Ran SP% **116.4**
Speed ratings (Par 105): **102,101,97,97,97 94,92,91**
toteswingers: 1&2 £12.00, 2&3 £7.00, 1&3 £6.60. CSF £75.02 TOTE £13.10: £3.30, £1.60, £2.00; EX 66.80 Trifecta £1021.60 Part won. Pool: £1,380.57 - 0.50 winning units..
Owner A Black **Bred** S Murphy **Trained** Newmarket, Suffolk

FOCUS
This is often a very good race - recent winners include Kite Wood, Ibn Khaldun and, a bit further back, Nayef - and this edition looked up to standard if not an outstanding renewal. The form should work out. The pace was only steady early on.

NOTEBOOK
Morana(IRE) was beaten at odds of 4-9 in a maiden last time, when failing to confirm his debut promise after racing too freely, but he left that running well behind. It's to his credit he managed to win as, with the pace far steadier than ideal, he was again keen and he didn't get in the clear until being switched right off the rail 1f out. Peter Chapple-Hyam is apparently not that bothered about running the colt again this year, and believes he's more of a 3-y-o type, but both the Racing Post Trophy and the Criterium de Saint-Cloud were mentioned as possible targets if he is given another run. (op 10-1 tchd 11-1)
Prompter, who apparently found the ground too quick in the Solario, ran a little better under these vastly different conditions, although he very much enjoyed the run of the race. He should make a nice 3-y-o and the Dee Stakes has already been mentioned as a likely target for next year. (op 8-1 tchd 7-1)
Simenon(IRE) is better than he showed as he took a while to reorganise himself after being squeezed up between horses inside the final 2f, and, all things considered, he did well to get up for third. (op 13-2 tchd 7-1)
Azizi, a clear-cut nursery winner off 89 on his previous start, was faced with easy ground for the first time. He ran okay but couldn't muster the required speed having been held up, and a stronger pace would probably have suited better. (tchd 11-8, 13-8 and 7-4 in places)
Togiak(IRE)'s proximity puts the form into perspective considering he was beaten in a nursery off 82 last time, even though that was a good effort in defeat. (op 9-1)
Dubawi Phantom got warm beforehand and may not have appreciated the easy ground. (tchd 7-1)
Stags Leap(IRE) came off the bridle early on and offered little. The ground shouldn't have been a problem. (op 9-1)
Blakey's Boy was another who got warm and he never featured after a slow start. Official explanation: jockey said colt had no more to give

6665 DAVID & TONI EYLES H'CAP 1m 2f
5:15 (5:17) (Class 2) (0-105,102) 3-Y-O+
£11,215 (£3,358; £1,679; £840; £419; £210) Stalls High

Form RPR
1216 **1** **Cill Rialaig**[21] 6106 4-8-7 86 SteveDrowne 4 96
(H Morrison) *hld up in midfield: pushed along 3f out: hdwy on outer over 2f out: str run to ld jst ins fnl f: edgd rt u.p after: hld on wl nr fin* **7/2**[1]
0300 **2** *shd* **Espiritu (FR)**[13] 6307 3-8-13 97 (p) RyanMoore 3 107
(J Noseda) *stdd and swtchd rt sn after s: hld up bhd: stl 11th over 2f out: hdwy over 1f out: swtchd lft and squeezed between horses 1f out: chsd wnr ins fnl f: r.o wl u.p: jst hld* **11/1**
0321 **3** *2 1/2* **Mutamaashi**[14] 6277 3-8-10 94 RHills 5 99
(W J Haggas) *hld up towards rr: hdwy over 5f out: swtchd lft and hdwy over 2f out: rdn and ev ch ent fnl f: carried rt and one pce fnl 150yds* **7/2**[1]
0515 **4** *1 1/4* **Tartan Gunna**[13] 6307 3-8-7 91 JoeFanning 11 93
(M Johnston) *s.i.s: towards rr: prog over 3f out: switching rt and hdwy on inner over 1f out: kpt on fnl f but nvr gng pce to rch ldrs* **8/1**[3]
4-60 **5** *1* **Ezdiyaad (IRE)**[161] 1673 5-9-7 100 PatDobbs 6 100+
(M P Tregoning) *chsd ldr: rdn and unable qck 3f out: lost 2nd wl over 1f out: stl pressing ldrs whn hmpd and swtchd rt 1f out: kpt on same pce after* **10/1**
1432 **6** *3/4* **Mountain Pride (IRE)**[70] 4526 4-8-12 91 TedDurcan 9 90
(J L Dunlop) *hld up in tch in midfield: hdwy to chse ldrs 4f out: c wd over 2f out: sn rdn and hld hd awkwardly: led over 1f out: hdd jst ins fnl f: wknd fnl 150yds* **10/1**
5044 **7** *1 3/4* **Bucked Off (SAF)**[13] 6307 5-8-9 88 DarryllHolland 14 83
(T P Tate) *racd keenly: led: rdn and forged clr over 2f out: hung lft u.p and hdd over 1f out: wknd qckly fnl f* **14/1**
0256 **8** *3/4* **Stevie Thunder**[7] 6480 4-8-7 89 (v) AndreaAtzeni(3) 13 83
(Ian Williams) *chsd ldng pair: rdn and effrt over 2f out: styd handy but looked btn whn jostled 1f out: n.d after* **9/1**
1000 **9** *shd* **Kavachi (IRE)**[21] 6106 6-8-10 89 FergusSweeney 8 82
(G L Moore) *hld up towards rr: rdn and no prog over 2f out: nvr trbld ldrs* **16/1**
3522 **10** *1/2* **Wintercast**[105] 3399 4-9-0 93 AdamKirby 1 89+
(W R Swinburn) *chsd ldng trio: rdn and unable qck jst over 2f out: keeping on same pce whn bdly hmpd over 1f out: no ch after* **15/2**[2]
5200 **11** *15* **Checklow (USA)**[119] 2933 4-9-0 93 LDettori 10 55
(J Noseda) *hld up in tch in midfield: rdn and wknd over 2f out: eased ins fnl f* **14/1**
00 **12** *5* **Doubnov (FR)**[14] 6290 6-8-11 90 StephenDonohoe 7 42
(Ian Williams) *stdd s: t.k.h: hld up in rr: rdn and lost tch over 2f out* **40/1**

2m 10.04s (3.04) **Going Correction** +0.425s/f (Yiel)
WFA 3 from 4yo+ 5lb **12** Ran SP% **125.5**
Speed ratings (Par 109): **104,103,101,100,100 99,98,97,97,97 85,81**
toteswingers: 1&2 £18.00, 2&3 £4.90, 1&3 £10.10. CSF £47.57 CT £151.20 TOTE £4.40: £1.80, £4.10, £1.90; EX 58.10 TRIFECTA Not won..
Owner Pangfield Partners **Bred** T J Billington **Trained** East Ilsley, Berks
■ Stewards' Enquiry : Steve Drowne caution: used whip with excessive frequency.

FOCUS
A decent handicap and good form, with the winner continuing to progress. They raced towards the far rail in search of better ground in the stretch before the final bend into the straight.

NOTEBOOK
Cill Rialaig, racing off the same mark as when a good sixth in the John Smith's Stakes at Newbury, continued her progression with a hard-earned victory. She looked set to win quite well when picking up in good style towards the outside in the straight, but the runner-up was also motoring and narrowed the gap quickly late on. She's one to keep on side. (op 9-2 tchd 11-2)
Espiritu(FR) is not an easy ride. Trying 1m2f for the first time, he had it all to do at the top of the straight and took an age to pick up, but he finally got going inside the final 2f and, after squeezing through a narrow gap over 1f out, he produced a sustained challenge, just failing to get up. (op 10-1 tchd 12-1)
Mutamaashi ran with credit off a mark 3lb higher than when successful at Chester last time. The easy ground didn't seem to bother him. (op 9-2)
Tartan Gunna did well to finish so close considering he compromised his chance with a slow start and might have preferred quicker ground. (tchd 7-1)
Ezdiyaad(IRE) was always well placed but he simply wasn't good enough. He met some trouble about 1f out but wasn't unlucky. (tchd 8-1)
Mountain Pride(IRE) carried his head high and made little progress for pressure. (tchd 9-1)
Bucked Off(SAF) was sweating and raced much too freely in front. It was a surprise he stayed there for so long. (op 16-1 tchd 12-1)
Wintercast didn't look unlucky but he's a lot better than he showed as he was badly hampered over 1f out and couldn't recover. Official explanation: jockey said gelding suffered interference in running (op 8-1)
Checklow(USA) Official explanation: jockey said gelding found nothing

6666 GOODING GROUP APPRENTICE H'CAP — 5f
5:50 (5:50) (Class 4) (0-85,85) 3-Y-0+
£6,231 (£1,866; £933; £467; £233; £117) **Stalls** Centre

Form				RPR
6061	**1**		**Even Bolder**[9] 6422 6-8-0 71 oh1 .... KierenFox(5) 6 (E A Wheeler) *hld up towards rr: gd hdwy 2f out: rdn to chal over 1f out: led ins fnl f: r.o wl* **20/1**	79
0056	**2**	*nk*	**Servoca (CAN)**[15] 6240 3-9-2 85 .... (t) AshleyMorgan(3) 9 (B W Hills) *towards rr: hdwy jst over 2f out: edging rt u.p over 1f out: r.o wl fnl f to go 2nd towards fin: nt rch wnr* **9/1**	92
2426	**3**	*nk*	**Magical Speedfit (IRE)**[25] 5974 4-7-12 71 oh3........ RyanPowell(7) 12 (G G Margarson) *in tch: rdn to chal wl over 1f out: led jst over 1f out: hdd ins fnl f: kpt on same pce fnl 100yds* **33/1**	77
1102	**4**	*1*	**Step It Up (IRE)**[21] 6118 5-8-0 71 .... JPFahy(5) 3 (J R Boyle) *hld up towards rr: rdn and hdwy wl over 1f out: styd on wl fnl f: nt rch ldrs* **8/1**[3]	73
2330	**5**	*½*	**The Tatling (IRE)**[19] 6171 12-9-0 80 .... JackDean 5 (J M Bradley) *racd in midfield: pushed along 1/2-way: hdwy 2f out: chsd ldrs and drvn over 1f out: no ex ins fnl f* **20/1**	81
1212	**6**	*¾*	**King Of Swords (IRE)**[16] 6233 5-8-5 71 oh1........ (p) KellyHarrison 14 (N Tinkler) *towards rr: hdwy 2f out: n.m.r fr over 1f out: swtchd lft ins fnl f: kpt on but nvr able to chal* **7/1**[2]	69
1044	**7**	*hd*	**Rocker**[37] 5592 5-8-8 77 .... JamieJones(3) 17 (G L Moore) *hld up in rr: hdwy and rdn over 1f out: chsd ldrs ent fnl f: no prog fnl f* **20/1**	74
2200	**8**	*hd*	**Zowington**[7] 6482 7-9-4 84 .... (v) WilliamCarson 10 (S C Williams) *s.i.s: bhd: effrt and edging rt over 1f out: kpt on fnl f but nvr gng pce to threaten ldrs* **25/1**	80
0606	**9**	*nk*	**Sands Crooner (IRE)**[42] 5436 6-8-9 75 .... (v) AndreaAtzeni 7 (J G Given) *s.i.s: bhd: hdwy jst over 2f out: chsd ldrs and rdn over 1f out: wknd jst ins fnl f* **20/1**	70
2010	**10**	*1 ¼*	**Bertoliver**[35] 5654 5-9-5 85 .... MarcHalford 2 (S C Williams) *led: rdn and hung rt fr 2f out: hdd jst over 1f out: wknd fnl f* **25/1**	76
4333	**11**	*shd*	**Luminous Gold**[21] 6118 4-8-6 72 .... JackMitchell 15 (C F Wall) *in tch: hdwy over 2f out: ev ch and rdn over 1f out: wknd ent fnl f* **4/1**[1]	62
1123	**12**	*hd*	**Triple Dream**[9] 6422 4-8-10 79 .... (p) RossAtkinson(3) 13 (J M Bradley) *a bhd: rdn and effrt 2f out: nt clr run wl over 1f out tl 1f out: nvr a threat* **11/1**	73+
1152	**13**	*nk*	**Whiskey Junction**[25] 5974 5-8-11 77 .... RussellKennemore 11 (M Quinn) *pressed ldrs tl rdn jst over 2f out: wknd over 1f out* **14/1**	66
2-00	**14**	*1 ¼*	**Fantasy Explorer**[160] 1699 6-9-0 85 .... IJBrennan(5) 18 (J J Quinn) *chsd ldrs: ev ch over 1f out: wknd u.p ent fnl f* **11/1**	69
2015	**15**	*¾*	**Brunelleschi**[21] 6112 6-8-8 79 .... (b) JosephineBruning(5) 1 (P L Gilligan) *a in rr: pushed along and struggling over 2f out: n.d* **16/1**	60
6343	**16**	*34*	**Sharpened Edge**[28] 5871 3-8-11 80 .... DeanHeslop(3) 16 (B Palling) *rrd as stalls opened and rdr unable to remove hood: lost many l and a t.o* **12/1**	—
430	**P**		**Kay Two (IRE)**[28] 5871 7-8-13 84 .... (p) TobyAtkinson(5) 4 (R J Price) *w ldr: ev ch and rdn 2f out: wknd rapidly over 1f out: p.u and dismntd ins fnl f: burst blood vessel* **10/1**	—

61.95 secs (1.45) **Going Correction** +0.425s/f (Yiel) **17 Ran SP% 129.3**
Speed ratings (Par 105): **105,104,104,102,101 100,100,99,99,97 97,96,96,94,93 38,—**
toteswingers: 1&2 £58.60, 2&3 £82.50, 1&3 £97.80. CSF £184.37 CT £5891.59 TOTE £29.80: £4.40, £4.00, £9.00, £2.80; EX 223.80 TRIFECTA Not won. Place 6: £247.00 Place 5: £117.03 .
Owner Astrod TA Austin Stroud & Co **Bred** Raffin Bloodstock **Trained** Whitchurch-on-Thames, Oxon
FOCUS
A competitive sprint handicap but an ordinary race for the track. The third is the best guide to the form.
Bertoliver Official explanation: jockey said gelding hung right
Sharpened Edge Official explanation: jockey said filly reared as the stalls opened
Kay Two(IRE) Official explanation: jockey said gelding bled from the nose
T/Plt: £248.00 to a £1 stake. Pool: £119,882.29. 352.85 winning tickets. T/Qpdt: £69.50 to a £1 stake. Pool: £6,492.92. 69.04 winning tickets. SP

6635 WOLVERHAMPTON (A.W) (L-H)
Saturday, October 10
OFFICIAL GOING: Standard
Wind: Light behind Weather: Overcast

6667 BET SUPER LEAGUE GRAND FINAL - BETDAQ FILLIES' H'CAP — 7f 32y(P)
5:45 (5:46) (Class 4) (0-85,83) 3-Y-0+ **£5,046** (£1,510; £755; £377; £188) **Stalls** High

Form				RPR
0340	**1**		**Beautiful Filly**[12] 6333 3-7-13 67 .... (b) MartinLane(5) 4 (D M Simcock) *dwlt: hld up: hdwy over 1f out: rdn to ld ins fnl f: r.o wl* **16/1**	71
4000	**2**	*1 ¼*	**Luckier (IRE)**[11] 6361 3-8-9 72 .... JamesDoyle 1 (S Kirk) *led: hdd over 6f out: chsd ldrs: led again over 1f out: rdn and hdd ins fnl f: styd on same pce* **20/1**	73
514	**3**	*hd*	**Ursula (IRE)**[77] 4309 3-9-3 80 .... SebSanders 5 (R M Beckett) *hld up: hdwy over 2f out: rdn and swtchd rt over 1f out: edgd lft ins fnl f: r.o* **7/2**[1]	86+
-146	**4**	*½*	**Sakhee's Pearl**[19] 6155 3-9-6 83 .... LukeMorris 2 (Miss Gay Kelleway) *chsd ldrs: rdn over 1f out: edgd lft ins fnl f: styd on* **13/2**[2]	82
4256	**5**	*nk*	**My Best Bet**[12] 6348 3-8-11 77 .... MCGeran(3) 3 (M R Channon) *chsd ldrs: rdn over 1f out: kpt on* **9/1**	75
5422	**6**	*½*	**Leonid Glow**[23] 6015 4-8-12 73 .... TonyHamilton 7 (M Dods) *hld up: rdn and r.o ins fnl f: nt rch ldrs* **12/1**	70
1021	**7**	*hd*	**Peper Harow (IRE)**[9] 6437 3-8-5 68 .... DavidProbert 11 (M D I Usher) *hld up: hdwy over 1f out: sn rdn: nt rch ldrs* **13/2**[2]	64
041	**8**	*2*	**Moojeh (IRE)**[38] 5572 3-9-0 77 .... JerryO'Dwyer 10 (M Botti) *mid-div: rdn 1/2-way: styd on ins fnl f: n.d* **12/1**	68
6553	**9**	*1 ½*	**Common Diva**[8] 6462 3-8-10 73 .... PatCosgrave 6 (A J McCabe) *prom: chsd ldr over 5f out: rdn over 1f out: wknd ins fnl f* **11/1**	60
026	**10**	*¾*	**Respite**[38] 5575 3-8-12 75 .... LiamJones 9 (W J Haggas) *prom: rdn 1/2-way: wknd 2f out* **15/2**[3]	60
-550	**11**	*1 ¾*	**Borasco (USA)**[135] 2402 4-9-0 78 .... NeilBrown(3) 12 (T D Barron) *plld hrd: hdwy to ld over 6f out: rdn and hdd over 1f out: wknd fnl f* **12/1**	58
	12	*1 ¼*	**Keyala (IRE)**[12] 6351 4-9-3 78 .... RichardKingscote 8 (David P Myerscough, Ire) *hld up: a in rr: rdn over 2f out: sn wknd* **16/1**	55

1m 28.91s (-0.69) **Going Correction** -0.05s/f (Stan)
WFA 3 from 4yo 2lb **12 Ran SP% 118.6**
Speed ratings (Par 102): **101,99,99,98,98 97,97,95,93,92 90,89**
toteswingers: 1&2 £72.00, 1&3 £20.80, 2&3 £32.70 CSF £300.43 CT £1381.54 TOTE £23.30: £5.90, £8.30, £1.70; EX 508.60.
Owner Dr Ali Ridha **Bred** Mrs C C Regalado-Gonzalez **Trained** Newmarket, Suffolk
FOCUS
A decent pace, but not as strong as looked likely when the headstrong Borasco swept up wide to take an early lead. Modest but sound form.

6668 BET MULTIPLES - BETDAQ H'CAP — 1m 1f 103y(P)
6:15 (6:15) (Class 6) (0-65,65) 3-Y-0+ **£2,388** (£705; £352) **Stalls** Low

Form				RPR
-602	**1**		**Naheell**[18] 6189 3-9-4 65 .... SaleemGolam 4 (G Prodromou) *chsd ldrs: rdn to ld ins fnl f: jst hld on* **12/1**	71
2030	**2**	*hd*	**Snow Dancer (IRE)**[15] 6250 5-9-3 65 .... SladeO'Hara(5) 10 (H A McWilliams) *hld up: nt clr run over 1f out: r.o wl ins fnl f: jst failed to get there* **13/2**	74+
0004	**3**	*½*	**Sullenberger (IRE)**[23] 6031 3-9-0 61 .... ChrisCatlin 6 (J A Osborne) *racd keenly: trckd ldr to over 5f out: remained handy: rdn over 1f out: r.o* **6/1**[3]	66
03	**4**	*1*	**Ermine Grey**[36] 5631 8-9-1 58 .... (b) SebSanders 13 (S Gollings) *hld up: hdwy to chse ldr over 5f out: led 4f out: rdn and hdd over 1f out: styd on same pce ins fnl f* **8/1**	60
0503	**5**	*nse*	**Prince Golan (IRE)**[11] 6358 5-9-0 57 .... (p) TGMcLaughlin 3 (J W Unett) *hld up: hdwy over 5f: chsd ldr tl led again over 1f out: rdn and hdd ins fnl f: unable qck* **9/2**[1]	59
4/04	**6**	*¾*	**Easterly Breeze (IRE)**[12] 6342 5-8-12 62 .... (bt) AlexEdwards(7) 7 (Mrs L J Young) *a.p: rdn over 1f out: styd on same pce ins fnl f* **8/1**	63
5	**7**	*shd*	**Sotelo**[80] 4197 7-9-8 65 .... PatCosgrave 11 (S Gollings) *hld up: r.o ins fnl f: nt rch ldrs* **33/1**	66
0025	**8**	*2 ¼*	**Clipperdown (IRE)**[32] 5750 8-9-2 62 .... (bt[1]) AlanCreighton(3) 8 (E J Creighton) *hld up: hdwy over 1f out: rdn and no ex ins fnl f* **20/1**	58
4210	**9**	*1 ½*	**King Of Connacht**[41] 5479 6-9-1 58 .... (p) LiamJones 9 (M Wellings) *hld up: hdwy over 2f out: rdn over 1f out: wknd ins fnl f* **6/1**[3]	51
2413	**10**	*½*	**Our Kes (IRE)**[21] 6126 7-9-0 57 .... JerryO'Dwyer 12 (P Howling) *chsd ldrs: rdn over 2f out: wknd fnl f* **11/2**[2]	49
/200	**11**	*5*	**Castellina**[123] 2785 5-9-3 60 .... (t) EdwardCreighton 5 (E J Creighton) *dwlt: hld up: hdwy on outer over 2f out: sn rdn and wknd* **25/1**	41

2m 2.72s (1.02) **Going Correction** -0.05s/f (Stan)
WFA 3 from 5yo+ 4lb **11 Ran SP% 116.9**
Speed ratings (Par 101): **93,92,92,91,91 90,90,88,87,86 82**
toteswingers: 1&2 £22.60, 1&3 £17.00, 2&3 £17.90 CSF £85.38 CT £521.84 TOTE £13.30: £4.50, £2.10, £2.90; EX 91.20.
Owner P Hajipiery **Bred** Darley **Trained** East Harling, Norfolk
FOCUS
A modest gallop which quickened 3f out favoured those near the front. It is hard to rate the form positively given the lack of pace.

6669 ENJOY THE LUCKY 7 GROUP OFFER H'CAP — 5f 20y(P)
6:45 (6:45) (Class 5) (0-75,73) 3-Y-0+ **£3,238** (£963; £481; £240) **Stalls** Low

Form				RPR
36	**1**		**Misaro (GER)**[12] 6329 8-9-3 72 .... (b) DavidProbert 3 (R A Harris) *prom: rdn 1/2-way: edgd lft and r.o to ld wl ins fnl f* **6/1**[2]	84
0003	**2**	*1 ¾*	**Bookiesindex Boy**[36] 5629 5-8-10 65 .... FrancisNorton 2 (J R Jenkins) *chsd ldrs: swtchd lft over 1f out: rdn and ev ch ins fnl f: unable qck* **8/1**	71
3045	**3**	*shd*	**Mazzola**[12] 6341 3-8-8 63 .... SamHitchcott 8 (M R Channon) *chsd ldrs: led over 1f out: rdn and hdd wl ins fnl f* **9/1**	68
0014	**4**	*nk*	**Desperate Dan**[8] 6458 8-8-13 73 .... (v) AmyBaker(5) 9 (A B Haynes) *hld up: rdn and r.o ins fnl f: nt rch ldrs* **15/2**	77
0000	**5**	*1 ¼*	**Punching**[23] 6028 5-8-7 62 .... SimonWhitworth 10 (C R Dore) *hld up: hdwy over 1f out: edgd lft ins fnl f: nt rch ldrs* **33/1**	62
0600	**6**	*shd*	**Blades Princess**[29] 5830 3-9-4 73 .... (p) SebSanders 1 (E S McMahon) *hld up: hdwy and nt clr run over 1f out: sn rdn: styd on* **8/1**	72
2200	**7**	*1*	**Cape Royal**[7] 6489 9-9-3 72 .... (bt) KevinGhunowa 7 (J M Bradley) *chsd ldr tl led 1/2-way: rdn and hdd over 1f out: no ex ins fnl f* **11/1**	68
6204	**8**	*1 ½*	**Peninsular War**[16] 6233 3-9-2 71 .... TonyHamilton 6 (R A Fahey) *hld up: rdn over 1f out: nvr nrr* **5/1**[1]	61
0000	**9**	*1 ¼*	**Almaty Express**[8] 6459 7-9-1 70 .... (b) ChrisCatlin 12 (J R Weymes) *mid-div: rdn 2f out: wknd over 1f out* **20/1**	56
012	**10**	*¾*	**Green Lagonda (AUS)**[12] 6329 7-8-5 65 .... MartinLane(5) 11 (P D Evans) *mid-div: rdn 1/2-way: in rr and no ch whn hmpd ins fnl f* **6/1**[2]	48
3430	**11**	*2 ¾*	**Spic 'n Span**[12] 6329 4-8-9 64 .... (b) KirstyMilczarek 5 (R A Harris) *unruly to post: chsd ldrs: rdn over 1f out: wknd fnl f* **13/2**[3]	37

5500 12 3¾ **The Magic Of Rio**[8] 6444 3-8-10 **65**..........................(b[1]) JamieMackay 4 25
(Peter Grayson) *led to 1/2-way: rdn over 1f out: sn wknd* **33/1**

61.59 secs (-0.71) **Going Correction** -0.05s/f (Stan) 12 Ran SP% **121.5**
Speed ratings (Par 103): **103,100,100,99,97 97,95,93,91,90 85,79**
toteswingers: 1&2 £11.20, 1&3 £15.40, 2&3 £18.40 CSF £53.72 CT £440.99 TOTE £6.60: £2.90, £3.80, £3.40; EX 70.00.
Owner Messrs Criddle Davies Dawson & Villa **Bred** Wilhelm Fasching **Trained** Earlswood, Monmouths

FOCUS
A good sprint pace in this ordinary handicap. The form is rated around the third.
The Magic Of Rio Official explanation: jockey said filly stopped quickly

6670 BOOK NOW FOR CHRISTMAS (S) STKS 5f 216y(P)
7:15 (7:15) (Class 6) 3-Y-O+ **£2,047** (£604; £302) **Stalls** Low

Form RPR
1563 1 **Titus Gent**[7] 6492 4-9-3 59.. KirstyMilczarek 4 75
(J Ryan) *chsd ldrs: rdn over 1f out: r.o to ld wl ins fnl f* **9/1**
1305 2 ¾ **Swinbrook (USA)**[27] 5900 8-9-3 72..............................(v) DavidProbert 1 73
(R A Harris) *chsd ldr: rdn to ld ins fnl f: sn hdd and unable qck* **7/2**[1]
315- 3 1¾ **Absa Lutte (IRE)**[14] 6296 6-7-13 68.......................(t) JamesPSullivan(7) 5 56
(J A Nash, Ire) *hld up: hdwy over 2f out: rdn over 1f out: styd on same pce ins fnl f* **7/2**[1]
5011 4 1¼ **Bertie Southstreet**[37] 5612 6-9-3 67................................(v) ChrisCatlin 2 63
(Karen George) *led: rdn over 1f out: edgd lft: hdd and no ex ins fnl f* **6/1**[3]
3526 5 6 **Charles Parnell (IRE)**[8] 6458 6-8-11 68...................(p) TonyHamilton 13 38
(M Dods) *mid-div: rdn over 2f out: wknd over 1f out* **8/1**
6036 6 hd **Interactive (IRE)**[12] 6335 6-9-3 65.......................... RichardKingscote 10 44
(Andrew Turnell) *chsd ldrs: rdn over 2f out: wknd over 1f out* **16/1**
0004 7 1¾ **Tournedos (IRE)**[57] 4976 7-8-11 81...........................(p) FrancisNorton 6 32
(D Nicholls) *dwlt: rdn over 2f out: n.d* **11/2**[2]
5301 8 9 **Rio Sands**[10] 6379 4-9-3 60.. MartinDwyer 9 9
(R M Whitaker) *chsd ldrs: hmpd 1/2-way: sn rdn and wknd* **16/1**
060 9 1 **Fyodor (IRE)**[23] 6028 8-8-11 60..................................(v) PatCosgrave 3 —
(P D Evans) *hld up: rdn over 2f out: a in rr* **9/1**
0-0 10 27 **Jung (USA)**[147] 2070 3-8-10 0...(bt[1]) LukeMorris 8 —
(J R Gask) *mid-div: wknd 1/2-way: t.o* **66/1**

1m 13.91s (-1.09) **Going Correction** -0.05s/f (Stan)
WFA 3 from 4yo+ 1lb 10 Ran SP% **118.5**
Speed ratings (Par 101): **105,104,101,100,92 91,89,77,76,40**
toteswingers: 1&2 £10.90, 1&3 £4.20, 2&3 £6.50 CSF £41.27 TOTE £10.40: £2.50, £1.90, £1.90; EX 46.10.The winner was bought by R Harris for 7,000gns.
Owner G Wilson **Bred** Heather Raw **Trained** Newmarket, Suffolk

FOCUS
Not much early pace on here for a sprint, and it was hard to come from too far back. Improvement from the winner but probably not form to take at face value.
Interactive(IRE) Official explanation: jockey said gelding ran flat
Fyodor(IRE) Official explanation: jockey said gelding fly lept leaving the stalls

6671 WOLVERHAMPTON-RACECOURSE.CO.UK H'CAP 1m 5f 194y(P)
7:45 (7:47) (Class 4) (0-85,85) 3-Y-O **£5,046** (£1,510; £755; £377; £188) **Stalls** Low

Form RPR
111 1 **Royal Diamond (IRE)**[28] 5870 3-9-7 **85**.......................... SebSanders 1 101+
(Sir Mark Prescott) *hld up: hdwy over 4f out: led over 3f out: sn pushed clr: eased towards fin* **4/7**[1]
3232 2 10 **Ramora (USA)**[14] 6287 3-8-8 **72**.. TPQueally 5 71
(H R A Cecil) *led 1f: chsd ldr tl led 4f out: sn rdn and hdd: outpcd fnl 2f* **7/2**[2]
4325 3 3¾ **Onemix**[81] 4166 3-8-12 **76**.. RobertWinston 4 70
(B W Hills) *hld up: hdwy over 4f out: rdn over 2f out: sn btn: no ch whn hung lft over 1f out* **8/1**
5203 4 1½ **Battle Planner (USA)**[24] 5979 3-9-2 **80**............................(p) TomEaves 3 72
(I Semple) *chsd ldrs: rdn 6f out: sn lost pl: wknd over 3f out* **15/2**[3]
1336 5 3¼ **Straits Of Hormuz (USA)**[31] 5771 3-9-1 **79**............. RoystonFfrench 2 66
(M Johnston) *led after 1f: hdd 4f out: sn rdn and wknd* **10/1**

3m 3.62s (-2.38) **Going Correction** -0.05s/f (Stan) 5 Ran SP% **117.8**
Speed ratings (Par 103): **104,98,96,95,93**
CSF £3.33 TOTE £1.30: £1.50, £1.50; EX 2.90.
Owner E B Rimmer-Osborne House **Bred** Moyglare Stud Farm Ltd **Trained** Newmarket, Suffolk

FOCUS
A modest tempo gave the winner the chance to seize the initiative at the end of the back straight. The winner impressed but may not have had much to beat.

6672 SPONSOR A RACE BY CALLING 01902 390000 MAIDEN STKS 1m 141y(P)
8:15 (8:16) (Class 5) 2-Y-O **£2,729** (£806; £403) **Stalls** Low

Form RPR
6232 1 **Start Right**[14] 6285 2-9-3 81.. WilliamBuick 6 82
(L M Cumani) *chsd ldrs: led over 1f out: hung lft ins fnl f: r.o* **7/4**[1]
5 2 1¼ **Plato (JPN)**[36] 5637 2-9-3 0.. TPQueally 2 79+
(H R A Cecil) *a.p: rdn over 1f out: r.o* **10/1**
5 3 nk **Christmas Carnival**[21] 6108 2-9-3 0.................................. MartinDwyer 7 79
(B J Meehan) *chsd ldrs: sn pushed along: rdn over 1f out: r.o* **2/1**[2]
62 4 2¼ **Music Maestro (IRE)**[35] 5674 2-9-3 0............................ RobertWinston 12 74
(B W Hills) *sn chsng ldr: led over 2f out: rdn and hdd over 1f out: no ex ins fnl f* **12/1**
23 5 1 **King's Parade**[40] 5528 2-9-3 0...................................... RichardMullen 10 72
(Sir Michael Stoute) *prom: rdn over 1f out: styd on* **8/1**
6 1 **Psychic Ability (USA)** 2-9-3 0...................................... TedDurcan 3 70
(Saeed Bin Suroor) *s.i.s: sn pushed along in rr: styd on ins fnl f: nvr nrr* **7/1**[3]
7 ½ **Franki J** 2-8-12 0.. JerryO'Dwyer 5 64
(D Donovan) *mid-div: rdn over 2f out: wknd fnl f* **100/1**
6 8 2¼ **Lady Cavendish (IRE)**[8] 6441 2-8-12 0.......................... JamieMackay 8 59
(A Bailey) *mid-div: rdn over 2f out: wknd over 1f out* **50/1**
9 hd **Hail Bold Chief (USA)** 2-9-3 0.. TomEaves 1 64
(G A Swinbank) *s.i.s: a in rr* **16/1**
5 10 2 **Baraconti (IRE)**[17] 6214 2-9-3 0.................................... TonyHamilton 13 59
(R A Fahey) *s.i.s: hld up: sme hdwy on outer over 2f out: sn wknd* **25/1**
6 11 1¼ **Let Them Eat Cake**[14] 6274 2-8-9 0........................ FrederikTylicki(3) 4 52
(R A Fahey) *hld up: a in rr: wknd over 2f out* **50/1**
33 12 7 **Ting Ting (USA)**[26] 5951 2-8-12 0.................................... MickyFenton 11 37
(T P Tate) *led: rdn and hdd over 2f out: wknd over 1f out* **40/1**

1m 51.03s (0.53) **Going Correction** -0.05s/f (Stan) 12 Ran SP% **127.2**
Speed ratings (Par 95): **95,93,93,91,90 89,89,87,87,85 84,78**
toteswingers: 1&2 £18.00, 1&3 £1.10, 2&3 £14.50 CSF £22.06 TOTE £2.60: £1.10, £3.20, £1.70; EX 23.20.
Owner L Marinopoulos **Bred** Dukes Stud & Overbury Stallions Ltd **Trained** Newmarket, Suffolk

FOCUS
A lively gallop made this above-average maiden a good test and the form, which makes plenty of sense, should be reliable.

NOTEBOOK
Start Right made a fine first appearance on sand, winning convincingly despite being keen and having to be settled behind the leaders early on. His turf form was solid and he looks a decent recruit to the all-weather. (op 2-1)
Plato(JPN) ◆ is gradually coming on and got much closer than he had on his debut. He should stay farther and can win soon. (op 16-1)
Christmas Carnival showed promise on his debut and this switch to the all-weather showed his potential. He is capable of winning a maiden and going on from there. (op 9-4 tchd 5-2)
Music Maestro(IRE) looked the likely winner when being dashed ahead turning for home but did not quite make it after helping to set a good tempo. Ridden positively like this, 1m would be his limit for now but he is capable of winning races. (op 11-1)
King's Parade, who has shown ability in his three races, made a satisfactory first appearance on sand if not setting the world alight. He could probably win a routine maiden but nurseries are an option now. (tchd 15-2 and 9-1)
Psychic Ability(USA) took ages to get going but there were more encouraging signs in the home straight. Purchased for 200,000gns this year, this Kingmambo son of a winning miler probably needs further than his parents and should improve greatly with this first experience behind him. (op 8-1 tchd 13-2)

6673 BET IN RUNNING - BETDAQ MAIDEN STKS 1m 1f 103y(P)
8:45 (8:47) (Class 5) 3-Y-O+ **£2,729** (£806; £403) **Stalls** Low

Form RPR
44 1 **At Wits End**[22] 6073 3-9-3 0.. KirstyMilczarek 4 75
(J A R Toller) *chsd ldrs: rdn to ld ins fnl f: jst hld on* **16/1**
3454 2 nk **Burma Rock (IRE)**[15] 6250 3-9-3 75................................. TPQueally 11 74
(L M Cumani) *hld up in tch: rdn over 1f out: r.o* **4/1**[3]
4342 3 3¾ **Demeanour (USA)**[23] 6031 3-8-12 72..............................(p) SebSanders 2 61
(E A L Dunlop) *led over 7f out: rdn over 1f out: hdd and no ex ins fnl f* **11/4**[2]
4 2 **Muzo (USA)** 3-9-3 0.. WilliamBuick 5 62+
(J Noseda) *hld up in tch: outpcd over 2f out: r.o ins fnl f* **7/4**[1]
5 5 shd **Dubai Creek (IRE)**[7] 6475 3-9-3 0................................ RoystonFfrench 9 62+
(M Johnston) *s.i.s: hld up: r.o ins fnl f: nvr nrr* **8/1**
2- 6 nk **Lilly Grove**[383] 6163 4-9-2 0... RobertWinston 13 56
(G A Swinbank) *sn led: hdd over 7f out: chsd ldr: rdn and ev ch over 1f out: wknd ins fnl f* **16/1**
7 ½ **Magistrate (IRE)**[35] 4-9-7 0.................................... RichardKingscote 3 60
(Andrew Turnell) *chsd ldrs: rdn over 2f out: wknd over 1f out* **66/1**
5 8 4½ **Big Whitfield**[113] 3120 3-9-3 0.. TomEaves 7 51
(M Dods) *hld up: racd keenly: sme hdwy over 2f out: sn rdn and wknd* **40/1**
00 9 2 **Fulfilment (IRE)**[22] 6073 3-8-12 0....................................... ChrisCatlin 10 41
(W J Musson) *s.i.s: a in rr* **50/1**
10 1¼ **Supplementary (IRE)**[208] 7-8-9 0............................... RichardRowe(7) 8 39
(M J Coombe) *prom: rdn and wknd wl over 2f out* **100/1**
11 2 **Red Hot Desert** 3-9-3 0... AdamKirby 12 40
(W R Swinburn) *s.i.s: sn pushed along in rr: wknd wl over 2f out* **16/1**
12 23 **Madman (FR)**[40] 5-9-7 0.. KevinGhunowa 6 —
(C N Kellett) *s.i.s: hld up: hdwy over 4f out: rdn and wknd wl over 2f out: t.o* **100/1**
- 13 35 **Varah** 3-9-3 0... LukeMorris 1 —
(R A Harris) *hld up: rdn over 4f out: sn weakene: t.o* **66/1**

2m 0.68s (-1.02) **Going Correction** -0.05s/f (Stan)
WFA 3 from 4yo+ 4lb 13 Ran SP% **121.2**
Speed ratings (Par 103): **102,101,98,96,96 96,95,91,90,88 87,66,35**
toteswingers: 1&2 £6.90, 1&3 £5.20, 2&3 £3.00 CSF £79.71 TOTE £20.00: £3.90, £1.90, £1.60; EX 68.10.
Owner George Materna **Bred** George Materna **Trained** Newmarket, Suffolk

FOCUS
Just a medium gallop for these late developers. No beter than fair maiden form, rated around the runner-up.
Varah Official explanation: jockey said colt lost its action

6674 DINE IN THE HORIZONS RESTAURANT H'CAP 7f 32y(P)
9:15 (9:15) (Class 7) (0-50,56) 3-Y-O+ **£2,183** (£644; £322) **Stalls** High

Form RPR
003 1 **Mister Jingles**[9] 6415 6-8-6 **50**..................................(v) AmyRyan(5) 1 61
(R M Whitaker) *chsd ldrs: led over 1f out: rdn ins fnl f: r.o* **4/1**[2]
0004 2 ½ **Herbert Crescent**[28] 5883 4-8-8 **50**.......................... FrederikTylicki(3) 5 60
(Ollie Pears) *hld up in tch: rdn to chse wnr over 1f out: r.o* **13/2**[3]
4302 3 4½ **Mansii**[28] 5883 4-8-8 **50**.. AndreaAtzeni(3) 10 48
(P J McBride) *chsd ldrs: rdn over 1f out: styd on same pce* **7/1**
4006 4 1¼ **Minnola**[9] 6433 4-8-11 **50**.......................................(b) SaleemGolam 8 44+
(Rae Guest) *s.i.s: hld up: hdwy over 1f out: nt trble ldrs* **20/1**
6000 5 1½ **Bentley**[66] 4654 5-8-10 **49**.. TPQueally 12 39+
(J G Given) *s.i.s: hld up: rdn over 1f out: hung lft and styd on ins fnl f: nvr nrr* **20/1**
0005 6 5 **Heavenly Saint**[28] 5872 4-8-11 **50**.......................... RichardThomas 3 27
(C Roberts) *hld up: rdn over 2f out: a in rr* **16/1**
0051 7 ½ **Best One**[3] 6581 5-9-3 **56** 6ex..................................(v) KevinGhunowa 2 32
(R A Harris) *sn led: hdd over 5f out: led again over 3f out: rdn and hdd over 1f out: wknd fnl f* **8/1**
0510 8 5 **Union Jack Jackson (IRE)**[54] 5111 7-8-7 **49**........(v) KellyHarrison(3) 6 11
(John A Harris) *mid-div: rdn over 2f out: wknd sn after* **16/1**
0500 9 3 **Danzig Fox**[33] 5729 4-8-11 **50**....................................(be[1]) SebSanders 7 4
(M Mullineaux) *s.i.s: hdwy over 5f out: rdn over 2f out: sn wknd* **33/1**
2445 10 10 **Dubai To Barnsley**[72] 4467 4-8-11 **50**.......................... TGMcLaughlin 9 —
(D A Nolan) *racd keenly: led over 5f out: hdd over 3f out: rdn and wknd over 1f out: t.o* **25/1**
3 11 23 **Read The Script (IRE)**[28] 5883 4-8-11 **50**............... RichardKingscote 4 —
(Tom Dascombe) *trckd ldrs: plld hrd: rdn and wknd over 2f out: t.o* **15/8**[1]

1m 29.04s (-0.56) **Going Correction** -0.05s/f (Stan) 11 Ran SP% **119.8**
Speed ratings (Par 97): **101,100,95,93,92 86,85,80,76,65 39**
toteswingers: 1&2 £4.70, 1&3 £7.60, 2&3 £10.10 CSF £29.13 CT £182.96 TOTE £5.50: £2.00, £2.30, £2.60; EX 32.90 Place 6: £75.85 Place 5: £26.04.
Owner James Marshall & Mrs Susan Marshall **Bred** Catridge Farm Stud Ltd **Trained** Scarcroft, W Yorks

FOCUS
Little pace in this low-grade contest, but some of these do have ability at this level. The winner ran to his turf latest.
Heavenly Saint Official explanation: jockey said filly suffered interference in running
Read The Script(IRE) Official explanation: vet said gelding bled from the nose
T/Plt: £128.60 to a £1 stake. Pool: £64,691.46. 367.07 winning tickets. T/Qpdt: £12.50 to a £1 stake. Pool: £7,888.28. 463.90 winning tickets. CR

6643 YORK (L-H)

Saturday, October 10

OFFICIAL GOING: Good (7.4)

Rail realignment reduced advertised distances on round course by 27yds.

Wind: Moderate 1/2 against Weather: Fine

6675 BEST PRICE GUARANTEE AT CORAL.CO.UK H'CAP — 7f

2:05 (2:05) (Class 2) (0-100,99) 3-Y-O+ **£11,656** (£3,468; £1,733; £865) **Stalls** High

Form — RPR

0332 **1** **Light From Mars**[15] 6249 4-8-13 **94** .... JamesMillman(3) 2 106
(B R Millman) *in tch: hdwy 3f out: rdn to chse ldr over 1f out: styd on to ld jst ins fnl f: r.o wl* **11/1**

0206 **2** 2 3/4 **Everymanforhimself (IRE)**[14] 6282 5-9-2 **99** ....(v) AmyRyan(5) 5 104
(K A Ryan) *hld up in midfield: hdwy 3f out: rdn to ld wl over 1f out: drvn and hdd jst ins fnl f: kpt on same pce* **20/1**

2440 **3** 1/2 **Webbow (IRE)**[28] 5863 7-8-12 **90** .... EddieAhern 17 94+
(N Tinkler) *towards rr: hdwy on outer over 2f out: rdn wl over 1f out: styd on ins fnl f: nrst fin* **12/1**

6000 **4** 2 1/2 **Dhaular Dhar (IRE)**[7] 6482 7-8-10 **93** .... GaryBartley(5) 8 90
(J S Goldie) *in rr: hdwy on inner 2f out: rdn over 1f out: styd on strly ins fnl f: nrst fin* **10/1**[3]

5361 **5** 1/2 **Harrison George (IRE)**[21] 6092 4-9-3 **95** .... PaulHanagan 7 91
(R A Fahey) *in tch: hdwy over 2f out: rdn wl over 1f out: kpt on under perssure ins fnl f: nrst fin* **8/1**[1]

0035 **6** nk **Something (IRE)**[7] 6482 7-9-2 **94** ....(p) PaulQuinn 11 89
(D Nicholls) *dwlt and towards rr: hdwy 1/2-way: rdn to chse ldrs over 1f out: sn drvn and one pce* **16/1**

0010 **7** 1 1/2 **Baldemar**[14] 6270 4-8-8 **91** .... BMcHugh(5) 3 82
(R A Fahey) *prom: hdwy to ld wl over 2f out and sn rdn: hdd and drvn wl over 1f out: wknd appr fnl f* **16/1**

1100 **8** 2 1/2 **The Osteopath (IRE)**[21] 6094 6-9-1 **93** .... PhillipMakin 19 77+
(M Dods) *hld up in rr: hdwy 3f out: swtchd to wd outside over 2f out and sn rdn: kpt on ins fnl f: n.d* **40/1**

005 **9** 1/2 **Fullandby (IRE)**[21] 6089 7-9-2 **94** .... GregFairley 15 77
(T J Etherington) *in tch: hdwy to chse ldrs wl over 2f out: sn rdn and edgd rt over 1f out: wknd* **16/1**

6004 **10** 3/4 **Mastership (IRE)**[21] 6089 5-8-11 **89** ....(p) GrahamGibbons 6 70
(J J Quinn) *hld up: hdwy wl over 2f out: sn rdn and no imp* **11/1**

3553 **11** 2 **Appalachian Trail (IRE)**[21] 6094 8-9-6 **98** ....(b) TomEaves 10 73
(I Semple) *hld up in midfield: swtchd rt and hdwy 2f out: rdn and n.m.r over 1f out: no imp after* **12/1**

-110 **12** 4 **Makaamen**[140] 2270 3-9-1 **95** .... TPO'Shea 14 59
(B W Hills) *prom: led 1/2-way: rdn and hdd wl over 2f out: grad wknd* **10/1**[3]

0020 **13** shd **Beckermet (IRE)**[13] 6304 7-8-12 **90** .... RoystonFfrench 1 54
(R F Fisher) *chsd ldrs on inner: rdn along wl over 2f out: grad wknd* **25/1**

0043 **14** 1/2 **Celtic Sultan (IRE)**[7] 6482 5-8-12 **90** .... MickyFenton 18 53
(T P Tate) *a towards rr* **14/1**

106 **15** 3/4 **Invincible Force (IRE)**[14] 6278 5-9-1 **93** ....(b) SilvestreDeSousa 16 54
(Paul Green) *led: pushed along and hdd 1/2-way: sn rdn and wknd wl over 2f out* **33/1**

2222 **16** 3 3/4 **Billy Dane (IRE)**[21] 6094 5-8-6 **89** ....(p) MartinLane(5) 20 40
(F P Murtagh) *prom: rdn along 3f out and sn wknd* **16/1**

0610 **17** 1 1/2 **Medici Pearl**[40] 5522 5-8-11 **89** .... DavidAllan 9 36
(T D Easterby) *a towards rr* **33/1**

1000 **18** nse **City Of The Kings (IRE)**[15] 6249 4-8-9 **92** .... PatrickDonaghy(5) 13 38
(G A Harker) *a in rr* **40/1**

4000 **19** 3 1/2 **Joseph Henry**[21] 6089 7-8-12 **90** .... AdrianTNicholls 12 27
(D Nicholls) *a in rr* **25/1**

-213 **20** 12 **Splendorinthegrass (IRE)**[63] 4796 3-9-2 **96** .... SebSanders 4 1
(R Charlton) *chsd ldrs: rdn along 1/2-way: sn wknd* **9/1**[2]

1m 24.92s (-0.38) **Going Correction** +0.175s/f (Good)

WFA 3 from 4yo+ 2lb **20** Ran SP% **124.8**

Speed ratings (Par 109): **109,105,105,102,101 101,99,96,96,95 93,88,88,87,87 82,81,81,77,63**

toteswingers: 1&2 £47.60, 1&3 £55.40, 2&3 £99.30 CSF £222.74 CT £2741.17 TOTE £13.20: £3.50, £5.00, £3.30, £2.80; EX 363.70 Trifecta £712.50 Part won. Pool: £962.89 - 0.10 winning units..

Owner R K Arrowsmith **Bred** Harts Farm And Stud **Trained** Kentisbeare, Devon

FOCUS

The going was given as good on the final meeting at York this season but a couple of jockeys said it was a bit loose on top and on the dead side.This looked an impossible race to work out, as it contained a few talented three-year-olds taking on their elders. However, it did have plenty of horses who found 7f their ideal distance, so the form should be relatively sound. The winner produced a personal best.

NOTEBOOK

Light From Mars, 11lb above his previous highest winning mark, hit the front late on and seemed to relish the test in the ground. He will find it difficult when hiked in the weights again but connections believe a fast-run 7f is his ideal, as he doesn't quite get 1m. If he comes out of this win unscathed, he could run again this season. (op 16-1)

Everymanforhimself(IRE) has never won over this trip and did not quite get home after travelling well. This was by far his best effort over the distance. (op 18-1)

Webbow(IRE) was behind but stayed on quite well in the final stages. He is such a consistent performer and seems to like York. (op 16-1)

Dhaular Dhar(IRE) looked to be going nowhere two furlongs out but rallied and claimed fourth up the inside rail. He is only fairly weighted on his wins. (op 9-1)

Harrison George(IRE), raised 5lb for winning last time, usually does his best work in the final stages and that was the case again.

Something(IRE) weaved his way into contention and looked like getting placed at least when tacking on to the leaders, but his effort soon petered out and he looked tired.

Baldemar came through to have his chance but failed to get home. It seems fair to say 7f stretches his stamina too far. (op 18-1)

The Osteopath(IRE) never looked like winning but finished well through the also-rans.

Makaamen, absent since May, looked a fascinating contender on his best pieces of form and had been gelded since his last run. Quickly away, he sat in front for much of the race but was always doing too much, and weakened under pressure. (op 12-1)

Invincible Force(IRE) Official explanation: vet said gelding was lame

Joseph Henry Official explanation: jockey said gelding had no more to give

Splendorinthegrass(IRE), who was only due to run if significant rain came, faded early and dropped away after hanging under pressure from around halfway. Official explanation: vet said colt finished sore behind (op 17-2)

6676 10% CASHBACK AT CORAL.CO.UK H'CAP — 2m 2f

2:40 (2:40) (Class 4) (0-85,85) 3-Y-O+ **£7,641** (£2,273; £1,136; £567) **Stalls** Low

Form — RPR

3221 **1** **Theola (IRE)**[23] 6021 3-8-8 **75** .... JimmyQuinn 6 85+
(M H Tompkins) *hld up in tch: hdwy over 3f out: rdn over 1f out: styd on strly ins fnl f to ld last 100yds* **9/4**[1]

0-13 **2** 1 1/4 **Mith Hill**[14] 6273 8-9-7 **76** ....(vt) TPO'Shea 11 83
(Ian Williams) *chsd ldr: hdwy 5f out: led 4f out: rdn clr over 2f out: drvn ent fnl f: hdd and no ex last 100yds* **12/1**

2204 **3** 1 **Mr Crystal (FR)**[5] 6536 5-9-5 **77** .... FrederikTylicki(3) 9 83
(Micky Hammond) *hld up in midfield: stdy hdwy 4f out: rdn to chse ldr 2f out: drvn and ev ch ent fnl f: kpt on same pce* **14/1**

423 **4** 6 **Murcar**[14] 6281 4-9-4 **73** ....(b) IanMongan 3 72
(C G Cox) *hld up in midfield: hdwy 5f out: rdn to chse ldrs 3f out: drvn and kpt on same pce fnl 2f* **8/1**

0052 **5** 1 3/4 **King In Waiting (IRE)**[9] 6432 6-8-9 **64** oh6 ....(vt) SilvestreDeSousa 15 61
(J Hetherton) *t.k.h: hld up towards rr: hdwy 4f out: rdn along wl over 2f out: drvn and kpt on: nt rch ldrs* **20/1**

2146 **6** 3/4 **Perfect Shot (IRE)**[14] 6273 3-9-4 **85** .... EddieAhern 14 82
(J L Dunlop) *in tch: hdwy 4f out: rdn to chse ldrs 3f out: drvn over 2f out and grad wknd* **6/1**[3]

2542 **7** 3 3/4 **Danzatrice**[22] 6053 7-9-0 **69** .... PaulHanagan 7 61
(C W Thornton) *bhd: hdwy 5f out: rdn 3f out: swtchd lft and drvn over 2f out: n.d* **10/1**

54-0 **8** 1/2 **According To Pete**[22] 6053 8-8-10 **65** .... TomEaves 8 57
(J M Jefferson) *led: rdn along over 4f out: sn hdd and grad wknd fnl 2f* **12/1**

1421 **9** 6 **Mykingdomforahorse**[10] 6400 3-8-10 **77** .... SamHitchcott 12 62
(M R Channon) *hld up and bhd: sme hdwy 4f out: effrt on inner 3f out: sn rdn along and nvr a factor* **11/2**[2]

4-00 **10** 12 **Sphinx (FR)**[22] 6053 11-9-3 **72** ....(b) PaulMulrennan 5 44
(E W Tuer) *trckd ldrs: hdwy over 4f out: rdn over 3f out and sn wknd* **25/1**

000- **11** 9 **Daltaban (FR)**[399] 5699 5-9-4 **73** .... DaleGibson 4 35
(P Salmon) *chsd ldng pair: rdn along 5f out and sn wknd* **50/1**

0-6 **12** 11 **Royal Entourage**[21] 6100 4-10-0 **83** .... RobertWinston 1 33
(C A Mulhall) *trckd ldrs: rdn along 4f out: sn wknd and eased whn bhd fnl 2f* **20/1**

4m 1.35s (2.95) **Going Correction** +0.175s/f (Good)

WFA 3 from 4yo+ 12lb **12** Ran SP% **118.0**

Speed ratings (Par 105): **100,99,99,96,95 95,93,93,90,85 81,76**

toteswingers: 1&2 £8.70, 2&3 £11.80, 1&3 £17.10. CSF £29.53 CT £315.48 TOTE £3.10: £1.50, £3.80, £3.40; EX 31.30 Trifecta £419.40 Part won. Pool: £566.84 - 0.50 winning units..

Owner E Buddle **Bred** Richard Klay And Dr M Klay **Trained** Newmarket, Suffolk

FOCUS

Plenty of these had a negative or two attached to their chance, so despite the number of runners, this was probably an ordinary staying handicap. The winner has more to offer granted a suitable test. A lot of those held up were quite keen during the race.

Mykingdomforahorse Official explanation: jockey said colt failed to stay the trip

6677 CORAL ROCKINGHAM STKS (LISTED RACE) — 6f

3:10 (3:11) (Class 1) 2-Y-O **£17,778** (£6,723; £3,360; £1,680) **Stalls** High

Form — RPR

2101 **1** **Layla's Hero (IRE)**[35] 5658 2-9-0 96 .... EddieAhern 12 103+
(D Nicholls) *stdd s and swtchd lft: hld up and bhd: hdwy on wd outside wl over 1f out: rdn ent fnl f: qcknd to ld last 100yds: comf* **7/2**[1]

11 **2** 2 1/4 **Coolminx (IRE)**[18] 6179 2-8-9 90 .... PaulHanagan 1 91
(R A Fahey) *trckd ldrs: hdwy 2f out: rdn to ld over 1f out: drvn and edgd rt ins fnl f: hdd and one pce last 100yds* **8/1**

61 **3** nk **Never The Waiter**[7] 6493 2-9-0 88 .... MartinDwyer 2 95
(B J Meehan) *hld up in tch on outer: hdwy 2f out: rdn and ev ch over 1f out: drvn and edgd rt ins fnl f: kpt on same pce* **6/1**[2]

1140 **4** 2 **Singeur (IRE)**[7] 6486 2-9-0 95 .... DanielTudhope 8 89
(R Bastiman) *slt ld: rdn along over 2f out: drvn and hdd over 1f out: wknd ins fnl f* **14/1**

31 **5** 2 **Sunnandaeg**[63] 4774 2-9-0 85 .... PhillipMakin 9 83
(I Semple) *hld up towards rr: hdwy on outer 2f out: sn rdn and ch ent fnl f: sn drvn and wknd* **14/1**

2115 **6** 4 **Duchess Dora (IRE)**[22] 6049 2-8-9 94 .... GrahamGibbons 11 66
(J J Quinn) *cl up: rdn 2f out and ev ch tl drvn and wknd appr fnl f* **16/1**

162 **7** 1 1/4 **Dorback**[18] 6179 2-9-0 95 .... DaneO'Neill 4 69
(H Candy) *hld up towards rr: hdwy whn nt clr run and bmpd 2f out: sn wknd* **9/1**

1144 **8** 3/4 **Capercaillie (USA)**[94] 3748 2-8-9 95 .... GregFairley 3 60
(M Johnston) *cl up: rdn and ev ch 2f out: sn wknd* **6/1**[2]

3410 **9** 1 **Swilly Ferry (USA)**[9] 6426 2-9-0 97 .... WilliamBuick 10 62
(B W Hills) *chsd ldrs: effrt 2f out: sn rdn and wknd over 1f out* **7/1**[3]

5500 **10** 12 **Ghostwing**[30] 5795 2-9-0 94 .... FrederikTylicki 7 26
(R A Fahey) *cl up: rdn along 1/2-way: wknd over 2f out* **28/1**

3654 **11** 4 **Archers Road (IRE)**[22] 6049 2-9-0 97 .... SamHitchcott 6 17
(M R Channon) *chsd ldrs effrt and swtchd lft over 2f out: sn rdn and n.m.r: sn drvn and wknd* **9/1**

31 **12** 8 **Fenella Rose**[30] 5800 2-8-9 76 ....(v) SaleemGolam 5 —
(S C Williams) *prom: rdn along over 2f out and sn wknd* **66/1**

1m 13.02s (1.12) **Going Correction** +0.30s/f (Good) **12** Ran SP% **118.6**

Speed ratings (Par 103): **104,101,100,97,95 89,88,87,85,69 64,53**

toteswingers: 1&2 £4.10, 2&3 £6.50, 1&3 £8.60. CSF £31.37 TOTE £4.40: £1.70, £1.90, £2.70; EX 21.00 Trifecta £272.30 Pool: £662.44 - 1.80 winning units..

Owner Dr Marwan Koukash **Bred** Epona Bloodstock Ltd **Trained** Sessay, N Yorks

FOCUS

Some talented horses have taken this race, so the winner should go on to do well if following a similar path. He built on his impressive nursery win.

NOTEBOOK

Layla's Hero(IRE) ◆, switched after leaving the stalls, has enjoyed a profitable juvenile campaign and continued it after showing a fantastic turn of foot. That is probably it for this season but he should strengthen up into a tough campaigner at three. (op 4-1)

Coolminx(IRE) came into the race unbeaten but was upped in trip. She travelled really well and looked the likely winner but could not hold the fast-finishing winner. She would have no problem being dropped back to 5f, as she has lots of pace. (op 10-1)

Never The Waiter ◆ made his debut in a hot contest and duly got off the mark at Wolverhampton on his next start. Up in grade, he was far from disgraced and can continue to improve. (op 5-1)

Singeur(IRE) won four races in a row during the summer and bounced back to something close to his best after moving strongly. (op 18-1 tchd 20-1)

Sunnandaeg finished well towards the stands' side and appeared to maintain his upward curve. (op 16-1)
Duchess Dora(IRE) was quite keen throughout and possibly failed to get home.
Dorback was behind Coolminx last time and played no significant part here. He has hampered when making his final challenge, but the interference did not stop him from winning. (op 17-2)
Capercaillie(USA), given a break since the Group 2 Cherry Hinton, showed speed but was ultimately disappointing. (op 11-2)
Swilly Ferry(USA), who seemed to struggle in the ground at the business end of the contest. (op 9-1)
Archers Road(IRE) Official explanation: jockey said colt got tired and became unbalanced inside the final two furlongs

6678 CORAL SPRINT TROPHY (HERITAGE H'CAP) 6f
3:45 (3:46) (Class 2) (0-105,100) 3-Y-O+**£25,904** (£7,708; £3,852; £1,924) **Stalls** High

Form RPR

421 **1** **Kaldoun Kingdom (IRE)**[21] 6089 4-8-13 **93** BMcHugh(5) 9 106
(R A Fahey) *hld up in mid-div: str run to ld 1f out: styd on wl* **6/1**[1]

0501 **2** 1 3/4 **Cheveton**[35] 5654 5-9-6 **95** RobertWinston 13 102
(R J Price) *w ldrs: upsides over 1f out: no ex ins fnl f* **22/1**

0601 **3** 1/2 **Hitchens (IRE)**[14] 6282 4-9-9 **98** PhillipMakin 17 104+
(T D Barron) *hld up in mid-div: smooth hdwy 2f out: shkn up appr fnl f: r.o same pce ins fnl f* **11/1**

0431 **4** nk **Green Manalishi**[14] 6283 8-9-5 **94** (p) EddieAhern 4 99
(K A Ryan) *trckd ldrs towards far side: effrt over 1f out: edgd rt: kpt on same pce* **9/1**[3]

0200 **5** shd **Wi Dud**[21] 6091 5-9-4 **98** AmyRyan(5) 1 103
(K A Ryan) *dwlt sn chsd ldrs on outside: kpt on same pce fnl f* **25/1**

0216 **6** nk **Quest For Success (IRE)**[21] 6089 4-9-6 **95** PaulHanagan 5 99
(R A Fahey) *w ldrs towards far side: led 2f out: hdd 1f out: no ex* **12/1**

5631 **7** hd **Captain Dunne (IRE)**[18] 6180 4-9-7 **96** DavidAllan 10 99
(T D Easterby) *trckd ldrs: nt clr run and swtchd rt appr fnl f: kpt on same pce* **11/1**

34 **8** 1/2 **Irish Heartbeat (IRE)**[13] 6315 4-9-2 **91** (p) WilliamBuick 14 92
(David P Myerscough, Ire) *mid-div: effrt over 2f out: kpt on: nvr trbld ldrs* **17/2**[2]

30U0 **9** nk **Excusez Moi (USA)**[29] 5826 7-9-3 **92** SilvestreDeSousa 12 92
(Mrs R A Carr) *in rr: kpt on fnl 2f: nvr nr ldrs* **22/1**

1100 **10** nk **Johannes (IRE)**[21] 6089 6-9-3 **95** FrederikTylicki(3) 3 99+
(R A Fahey) *trckd ldrs far side: nt clr run fr 1f out: nt rcvr: eased towards fin* **14/1**

2600 **11** 1/2 **Hamish McGonagall**[14] 6283 4-9-8 **97** GrahamGibbons 16 95
(T D Easterby) *mid-div: effrt over 2f out: nvr nr ldrs* **16/1**

6000 **12** 1/2 **Hogmaneigh (IRE)**[21] 6091 6-9-10 **99** DanielTudhope 11 95
(J S Goldie) *dwlt: in rr: hdwy over 1f out: nvr trbld ldrs* **14/1**

13 nk **Toufan Express**[13] 6315 7-9-3 **92** CDHayes 8 87
(Adrian McGuinness, Ire) *in rr: kpt on fnl 2f: nvr a factor* **12/1**

1002 **14** nk **Global City (IRE)**[25] 5973 3-9-10 **100** (t) MartinDwyer 7 94
(Saeed Bin Suroor) *hld up in mid-div: effrt over 2f out: edgd lft and wknd over 1f out* **25/1**

6560 **15** 3 3/4 **Confuchias (IRE)**[14] 6282 5-9-6 **95** PaulEddery 18 77
(Pat Eddery) *mid-div stands' side: effrt over 2f out: sn wknd* **33/1**

1100 **16** 5 **My Gacho (IRE)**[14] 6278 7-9-3 **92** (v) RoystonFfrench 2 58
(M Johnston) *charged gate and stall opened fractionally early: chsd ldrs: sn drvn along: lost pl over 2f out* **25/1**

0600 **17** nk **Captain Gerrard (IRE)**[9] 6427 4-9-8 **97** TomEaves 15 62
(B Smart) *t.k.h in rr: bhd fnl 2f* **25/1**

3611 **18** 1 1/4 **Le Toreador**[8] 6459 4-9-3 **92** (tp) PaulMulrennan 6 53
(K A Ryan) *led tl 2f out: sn wknd* **20/1**

5000 **19** 3 **Parisian Pyramid (IRE)**[35] 5654 3-9-3 **93** AdrianTNicholls 19 45
(D Nicholls) *chsd ldrs stands' side: lost pl over 2f out* **10/1**

000 **20** 2 1/4 **Magic Cat**[21] 6091 3-9-5 **95** AndrewElliott 20 40
(A P Jarvis) *chsd ldrs stands' side: lost pl over 3f out* **50/1**

1m 12.34s (0.44) **Going Correction** +0.30s/f (Good)
WFA 3 from 4yo+ 1lb **20** Ran SP% **128.9**
Speed ratings (Par 109): **109,106,106,105,105 105,104,104,103,103 102,102,101,101,96 89,89,87,83,80**
toteswingers: 1&2 £30.80, 2&3 £9.40, 1&3 £58.60. CSF £144.85 CT £1487.74 TOTE £7.70: £2.50, £6.10, £3.30, £2.50; EX 229.80 Trifecta £618.00 Pool: £2,422.16 - 2.90 winning units..
Owner P D Smith Holdings Ltd **Bred** Gainsborough Stud Management Ltd **Trained** Musley Bank, N Yorks

FOCUS
This big field of talented handicappers mostly came up the middle of the course, but those that stayed towards the centre to far side prospered at the end. Pretty straightforward form.

NOTEBOOK
Kaldoun Kingdom(IRE), raised 4lb for landing the Ayr Silver Cup, got the job done nicely once striking the front. His trainer feels that the winner is at his best when there is a bit of ease in the ground, so one would imagine he could be seen again this season if remaining in good heart. A gelding operation is also in his future. (op 13-2)
Cheveton, unproven at this distance, made his bid at around the furlong marker but could not contain the winner. (op 20-1)
Hitchens(IRE) was on the bridle longer than most of his rivals but could find only one pace under pressure. (op 12-1)
Green Manalishi was far from disgraced off a high-enough mark. He is in good heart. (op 8-1)
Wi Dud has not won for a long time and finished upsides his stablemate in this.
Quest For Success(IRE) did not quite get home after racing prominently.
Captain Dunne(IRE) travelled well in behind but could not get out when the jockey needed room. (op 12-1)
Johannes(IRE) ◆ would have almost certainly been placed had he not run into a wall of horses inside the final furlong. Official explanation: jockey said gelding was denied a clear run (op 12-1)
Hogmaneigh(IRE) finished strongly after being well behind. (op 12-1)

6679 GALA CORAL CONQUER EVEREST - SUE RYDER CARE E B F MAIDEN STKS 7f
4:20 (4:21) (Class 3) 2-Y-O **£7,317** (£2,177; £1,088; £271; £271) **Stalls** High

Form RPR

40 **1** **Karaka Jack**[7] 6478 2-9-3 0 GregFairley 7 76
(M Johnston) *mde all: edgd rt fnl f: jst hld on* **6/1**[2]

2 shd **Taste The Victory (USA)** 2-9-3 0 PJMcDonald 8 76+
(G A Swinbank) *in rr: hdwy 2f out: styd on strly ins fnl f: jst failed* **14/1**

2654 **3** 1 **Count Bertoni (IRE)**[22] 6047 2-9-3 70 IanMongan 4 73
(S Gollings) *chsd ldrs: effrt over 2f out: styd on wl fnl f* **20/1**

2 **4** 1/2 **Lay Claim (USA)**[21] 6109 2-9-3 0 WilliamBuick 3 72
(Sir Michael Stoute) *trckd ldrs: effrt 2f out: sn rdn: kpt on same pce fnl f* **8/15**[1]

0 **4** dht **Tewin Wood**[57] 5000 2-9-3 0 NeilChalmers 10 72
(A Bailey) *chsd ldrs: styd on same pce fnl f* **25/1**

6 7 **Lost In The Moment (IRE)** 2-9-3 0 ShaneKelly 2 55+
(J Noseda) *s.i.s: hdwy over 3f out: edgd rt over 1f out: sn wknd* **13/2**[3]

0 **7** 1 **Caldercruix (USA)**[40] 5512 2-9-3 0 MickyFenton 13 52
(T P Tate) *hld up in rr: effrt over 2f out: sn wknd* **40/1**

0606 **8** 5 **Meetings Man (IRE)**[16] 6235 2-9-3 65 DaleGibson 12 40
(Micky Hammond) *chsd ldrs: lost pl over 2f out* **66/1**

00 **9** 7 **Woldgate**[7] 6493 2-8-12 0 LanceBetts(5) 5 22+
(G R Oldroyd) *rdr lost iron s: chsd ldrs: rcvrd iron over 3f out: sn lost pl* **80/1**

10 nk **Batgirl** 2-8-12 0 TPO'Shea 9 16
(John Berry) *s.s: a outpcd and in rr* **33/1**

11 9 **Roman Sioux (IRE)** 2-9-3 0 DanielTudhope 11 —
(R Bastiman) *in tch: lost pl over 4f out: bhd fnl 2f* **50/1**

1m 27.58s (2.28) **Going Correction** +0.175s/f (Good) **11** Ran SP% **118.2**
Speed ratings (Par 99): **93,92,91,91,91 83,82,76,68,67 57**
toteswingers: 1&2 £9.50, 2&3 £11.00, 1&3 £10.30. CSF £77.15 TOTE £7.30: £2.10, £3.50, £5.90; EX 112.60.
Owner Sheikh Hamdan Bin Mohammed Al Maktoum **Bred** Tarworth Bloodstock Investments Ltd **Trained** Middleham Moor, N Yorks

FOCUS
Not many of these made any obvious appeal for various reasons but there was a very exciting finish. There are doubts over the form but the race has been rated at face value.

NOTEBOOK
Karaka Jack, well beaten in the previous weekend's Timeform Million after coming down the 'wrong' side, was quickly away and held on by the skin of his teeth. He will need to find more to win in handicap company. (op 8-1)
Taste The Victory(USA) ◆, a half-brother to a top-class US sprinter, didn't seem to have a clue when asked for his effort but flew home once the penny dropped. He would have been in front in another stride or two. (op 16-1)
Count Bertoni(IRE), who had the highest official mark of the two with one, was never far away and plugged on to catch a couple of tired horses.
Lay Claim(USA) ◆ showed plenty of promise at Newbury on his debut and was sent off at short odds. A leggy sort, he came upsides the winner inside the final furlong but did not get home. He should be given another chance and could be a handicap type next season. (op 4-7 tchd 8-13 and 4-6 in places)
Tewin Wood showed a lot of early pace but could not sustain it in the last half-furlong. It was a big improvement on his debut, however. (op 4-7 tchd 8-13 and 4-6 in places)
Lost In The Moment(IRE), a 380,000-euro half-brother to Irish 1,000 Guineas third Luas Line, looked very green but ran on to the line once getting the idea. He is probably better than his position suggests. (op 6-1 tchd 11-2)

6680 PLAY JEFF OR REF AT CORAL H'CAP 1m 2f 88y
4:55 (4:56) (Class 4) (0-80,80) 3-Y-O **£6,476** (£1,927; £963; £481) **Stalls** Low

Form RPR

2244 **1** **Starla Dancer (GER)**[15] 6257 3-8-11 **70** PaulHanagan 12 82
(R A Fahey) *chsd ldrs: led 2f out: edgd lft: styd on wl* **20/1**

4200 **2** 2 1/2 **Paquerettza (FR)**[15] 6243 3-9-3 **79** FrederikTylicki(3) 1 86
(D H Brown) *mid-div: hdwy on ins over 3f out: chsd wnr 1f out: kpt on same pce* **8/1**[3]

2414 **3** 3/4 **Embsay Crag**[21] 6100 3-9-1 **79** PaulPickard(5) 11 85
(Mrs K Walton) *s.i.s: hdwy 3f out: swtchd rt and styd on strly fnl f: fin wl* **14/1**

0652 **4** 3 **Sam Sharp (USA)**[9] 6420 3-9-6 **79** (t) IanMongan 15 79
(H R A Cecil) *in rr: hdwy to trck ldrs over 3f out: edgd lft over 1f out: sn wknd* **6/1**[1]

4211 **5** 1/2 **Some Sunny Day**[27] 5910 3-9-2 **75** TravisBlock 8 74
(H Morrison) *trckd ldrs: led over 2f out: sn hdd: fdd over 1f out* **8/1**[3]

422 **6** 2 3/4 **Citizenship**[65] 4709 3-9-2 **75** ShaneKelly 13 69
(Ian Williams) *mid-div: hdwy on outer 3f out: kpt on: nvr nr ldrs* **11/1**

4030 **7** 1/2 **Mt Kintyre (IRE)**[60] 4867 3-9-2 **75** JimmyQuinn 17 68
(M H Tompkins) *in rr: hdwy over 2f out: n.m.r over 1f out: kpt on: nvr nr ldrs* **33/1**

-154 **8** 7 **Ultimate**[148] 2038 3-9-4 **77** RobertHavlin 5 57
(H Morrison) *trckd ldrs: t.k.h: led 3f out: sn hdd & wknd* **14/1**

4212 **9** 1 1/2 **Veroon (IRE)**[17] 6209 3-9-5 **78** (p) RoystonFfrench 6 55
(J G Given) *chsd ldrs: wkng whn hmpd over 1f out* **12/1**

01-0 **10** 1 3/4 **Wee Giant (USA)**[138] 2341 3-9-4 **77** PaulMulrennan 16 51
(K A Ryan) *hld up in rr: sme hdwy over 3f out: sn wknd* **66/1**

1515 **11** 1 3/4 **Upton Seas**[31] 5771 3-9-3 **76** DaleGibson 3 46
(M W Easterby) *towards rr: sn drvn along: nvr on terms* **7/1**[2]

1354 **12** 2 3/4 **Bomber Brown (IRE)**[9] 6420 3-9-2 **75** WilliamBuick 4 49
(P W Chapple-Hyam) *mid-div: hdwy over 3f out: sn chsng ldrs: one pce whn hmpd and eased ins fnl f* **12/1**

140- **13** 2 1/4 **Dream In Waiting**[343] 7144 3-9-4 **77** EddieAhern 7 38
(B J Meehan) *mid-div: effrt over 3f out: sn wknd* **16/1**

0420 **14** hd **Russian George (IRE)**[29] 5834 3-9-7 **80** AdrianTNicholls 10 40
(S Gollings) *rrd s: in rr: hdwy on outside over 2f out: wknd over 1f out* **33/1**

5605 **15** 3 **Striker Torres (IRE)**[73] 4433 3-8-11 **70** TomEaves 9 25
(B Smart) *t.k.h: led: hdd 3f out: sn wknd* **33/1**

-400 **16** 1 **Albaher**[15] 6243 3-8-11 **70** TPO'Shea 20 23
(J L Dunlop) *hld up in rr: nvr on terms* **33/1**

1153 **17** 1 1/4 **Aldaado (IRE)**[64] 4741 3-9-2 **75** PhillipMakin 14 26
(M Dods) *wnt rt s: a in rr* **16/1**

4546 **18** 4 **Tarzan (IRE)**[23] 6019 3-9-3 **76** (b) GregFairley 18 19
(M Johnston) *drvn to sn chse ldrs: lost pl over 3f out: sn bhd* **16/1**

1000 **P** **State General (IRE)**[68] 4602 3-8-8 **67** MickyFenton 2 —
(Miss J Feilden) *prom: eased and lost pl over 3f out: p.u and dismntd over 2f out* **50/1**

2m 11.42s (-1.08) **Going Correction** +0.175s/f (Good) **19** Ran SP% **123.7**
Speed ratings (Par 103): **111,109,108,106,105 103,103,97,96,94 93,91,89,89,86 86,85,81,—**
toteswingers: 1&2 £35.80, 2&3 £42.00, 1&3 £27.00. CSF £164.44 CT £2347.82 TOTE £22.70: £3.80, £2.30, £3.10, £2.00; EX 326.20.
Owner Aricabeau Racing Limited **Bred** Hof Ittlingen & Morton Bloodstock **Trained** Musley Bank, N Yorks

■ Dale Gibson, whose first ride was at York 24 years ago, hung up his boots after partnering Upton Seas.
■ Stewards' Enquiry : Ian Mongan four-day ban: careless riding (Oct 26-29)
Paul Hanagan one-day ban: careless riding (Oct 26)
Phillip Makin caution: entered wrong stall
Travis Block caution: used whip down shoulder in the forehand

FOCUS
Only a fair handicap for three-year-olds, and it was hardly surprising that bookmakers went 6/1 the field considering how open it looked. Despite the surprise winner the form looks pretty solid.
Russian George(IRE) Official explanation: jockey said gelding had no more to give
Aldaado(IRE) Official explanation: jockey said gelding was never travelling

State General(IRE) Official explanation: vet said gelding lost its action but returned sound

6681 COLDSTREAM GUARDS ASSOCIATION H'CAP 1m 4f
5:30 (5:30) (Class 4) (0-85,85) 3-Y-0+ £6,476 (£1,927; £963; £481) Stalls Centre

Form RPR
2435 1 **Trip The Light**[25] 5961 4-9-5 81 PaulHanagan 2 89
(R A Fahey) *drvn to ld 1f: chsd ldrs: led 2f out: sn hdd: rallied to ld post* 10/1[3]
6204 2 shd **Snoqualmie Boy**[28] 5865 6-9-7 83 MickyFenton 1 91
(T P Tate) *in rr: hdwy over 3f out: slt ld over 1f out: edgd rt: hdd post* 16/1
1330 3 1 1/2 **Zaaqya**[31] 5771 3-9-2 85 TPO'Shea 4 90+
(J L Dunlop) *mid-div: hmpd and lost pl after 2f: gd hdwy on outside over 2f out: styd on wl* 12/1
6666 4 3/4 **Goodwood Starlight (IRE)**[18] 6190 4-8-12 74 (t) DaneO'Neill 20 78
(G L Moore) *in rr: gd hdwy and nt clr run over 2f out: swtchd outside over 1f out: styd on wl* 25/1
0616 5 1 **Puzzlemaster**[47] 5315 3-9-2 85 JimmyQuinn 7 87
(Jane Chapple-Hyam) *s.i.s: hdwy over 3f out: chal over 1f out: one pce* 16/1
4113 6 3/4 **Lady Luachmhar (IRE)**[70] 4520 3-8-10 82 FrederikTylicki(3) 17 83
(R A Fahey) *t.k.h: sn trcking ldrs: wnt 2nd over 3f out: fading whn n.m.r over 1f out* 3/1[1]
000 7 1 **Hindu Kush (IRE)**[20] 6138 4-9-9 85 CDHayes 3 85
(D Nicholls) *trckd ldrs: outpcd over 2f out: kpt on fnl f* 8/1[2]
2520 8 3 1/2 **Shaloo Diamond**[35] 5671 4-9-6 85 MichaelJStainton(3) 18 79
(R M Whitaker) *mid-div: hdwy on outer 3f out: nvr nr ldrs* 25/1
400/ 9 shd **My Arch**[514] 4388 7-8-13 80 BMcHugh(5) 14 74
(Ollie Pears) *dwlt: in rr: hdwy on outside over 3f out: nvr nr ldrs* 50/1
4035 10 1 **Lost Soldier Three (IRE)**[14] 6281 8-9-3 79 AdrianTNicholls 13 71
(D Nicholls) *w ldrs: led after 2f: hdd 2f out: sn wknd* 12/1
4016 11 2 3/4 **Devotion To Duty (IRE)**[70] 4518 3-8-11 80 EddieAhern 5 68
(B W Hills) *t.k.h in mid-div: effrt over 2f out: hung lft and sn wknd* 20/1
0035 12 1 **Full Speed (GER)**[21] 6100 4-9-7 83 PJMcDonald 8 69
(G A Swinbank) *in rr: hdwy on ins 3f out: wknd over 1f out* 12/1
-140 13 2 1/4 **Hollins**[45] 5334 5-8-11 73 GregFairley 10 56
(Micky Hammond) *mid-div: sn drvn along: nvr nr ldrs* 28/1
0055 14 7 **King Fingal (IRE)**[35] 5671 4-8-13 75 GrahamGibbons 6 46
(J J Quinn) *in rr: sme hdwy 3f out: sn wknd* 8/1[2]
0640 15 1/2 **Bugaku**[29] 5823 4-9-9 85 (t) PhillipMakin 16 56
(Sir Michael Stoute) *chsd ldrs: drvn over 3f out: lost pl over 1f out* 11/1
0120 16 30 **Bajan Parkes**[14] 6281 6-9-5 81 DavidAllan 9 4
(E J Alston) *w ldr: led after 1f: hdd after 2f and sn given reminders: lost pl over 3f out: sn bhd and eased: t.o* 33/1
-150 17 11 **Scarab (IRE)**[25] 5961 4-9-3 79 DuranFentiman 12 —
(T D Walford) *w ldrs: lost pl over 3f out: sn bhd: t.o* 25/1
03-2 18 29 **Long Distance (FR)**[174] 139 4-9-1 77 PaulMulrennan 11 —
(Miss Lucinda V Russell) *chsd ldrs: reminders over 4f out: sn lost pl and bhd: virtually p.u: wl t.o* 33/1

2m 33.77s (0.57) **Going Correction** +0.175s/f (Good)
WFA 3 from 4yo+ 7lb 18 Ran SP% 127.1
Speed ratings (Par 105): **105,104,103,103,102 102,101,99,99,98 96,96,94,89,89 69,62,42**
toteswingers: 1&2 £30.40, 2&3 £24.70, 1&3 £28.40. CSF £148.88 CT £1970.66 TOTE £9.60: £1.90, £4.00, £3.80, £6.40; EX 184.00 TRIFECTA £28.40. Place 6: £487.82 Place 5: £94.27.
Owner The Matthewman One Partnership **Bred** Darley **Trained** Musley Bank, N Yorks
■ Stewards' Enquiry : Micky Fenton caution: careless riding.

FOCUS
A competitive handicap. The game winner produced a personal best with the runner-up the best guide.
Bugaku Official explanation: jockey said gelding had a breathing problem
T/Jkpt: Not won. T/Plt: £1,386.70 to a £1 stake. Pool: £138,484.31. 72.90 winning tickets. T/Qpdt: £139.50 to a £1 stake. Pool: £7,183.85. 38.10 winning tickets. WG

6326 MAISONS-LAFFITTE (R-H)
Saturday, October 10

OFFICIAL GOING: Very soft

6682a PRIX DE BEZONS (CLAIMER) (RIGHT-HANDED) 1m 7f
2:40 (2:45) 3-Y-0 £10,194 (£4,077; £3,058; £2,039; £1,019)

RPR
1 **Salt River (FR)**[10] 3-8-8 (b) GMasure 70
(J Bertran De Balanda, France)
2 3 **Lips Motion (GER)** 3-8-8 JVictoire 66
(Andreas Lowe, Germany)
3 3 **Victorian Tycoon (IRE)**[20] 6149 3-8-11 (b) JAuge 66
(E J O'Neill) *in tch: 5th 1/2-way: 3rd st: drvn and kpt on fr 2f out: nt pce of ldrs: jst hld 3rd cl home* 24/1[1]
4 hd **Mafra (IRE)**[10] 3-9-3 72
(Y Fouin, France)
5 3/4 **Phoenix King (FR)**[18] 3-9-4 72
(E Lellouche, France)
6 1/2 **Silver Valny (FR)** 3-9-1 68
(Mlle M-L Mortier, France)
7 snk **Less Moi Rire (FR)**[17] 3-9-6 73
(Y Fouin, France)
8 4 **Canmoss (USA)**[21] 3-9-1 (b) 63
(A Bonin, France)
9 nk **L'Impetueux (FR)**[21] 3-9-1 63
(U Suter, France)
10 1 1/2 **Mister Humphrey (FR)**[26] 3-9-2 62
(J-P Carvalho, Germany)
0 **Mr Sir (USA)**[390] 3-9-1 —
(X Nakkachdji, France)
0 **Aussie Pearl (FR)**[26] 3-8-11 (b) —
(C Boillot, France)
0 **Counterbid (IRE)**[21] 3-8-11 —
(C Laffon-Parias, France)
0 **Narjan**[18] 3-8-11 —
(D Prod'Homme, France)
0 **Ransom Demand**[21] 3-8-11 —
(P Chevillard, France)
0 **Tap Tip (USA)**[10] 3-8-8 (b) —
(F Danloux, France)
0 **Lorroy (FR)**[52] 3-8-11 —
(Mlle M-L Mortier, France)
0 **Piteur (FR)**[26] 3-8-11 —
(E Leenders, France)
0 **Racing Along (FR)** 3-9-1 —
(C Boillot, France)
0 **Topix (FR)** 3-8-11 —
(Mlle M-L Mortier, France)

3m 24.6s (204.60) 20 Ran SP% 4.0
PARI-MUTUEL: WIN 51.00; PL 13.40, 6.30, 7.80; DF 424.40.
Owner Prime Equestrian SARL **Bred** Earl Haras De Nonant Le Pin & Georges Real **Trained** France

6684 - 6686a (Foreign Racing) - See Raceform Interactive

6531 SANTA ANITA (L-H)
Saturday, October 10

OFFICIAL GOING: All-weather - fast; turf course - firm

6687a GOODWOOD STKS (GRADE 1) (PRO-RIDE) 1m 1f (D)
11:30 (11:56) 3-Y-0+ £114,583 (£48,611; £29,167; £14,583; £4,861)

RPR
1 **Gitano Hernando**[23] 6030 3-8-9 KFallon 8 122
(M Botti) *pulled early, always close up, 4th & moved outside straight, led inside final f, driven out* 18/1
2 nk **Colonel John (USA)**[34] 4-8-12 GKGomez 4 121
(Eoin Harty, U.S.A) 5/2[1]
3 3/4 **Richard's Kid (USA)**[34] 4-8-12 (b) ASolis 3 119
(Bob Baffert, U.S.A) 68/10
4 3/4 **Parading (USA)**[34] 6-8-12 (b) RBejarano 7 118
(Claude McGaughey III, U.S.A) 22/5[3]
5 1 3/4 **Chocolate Candy (USA)**[35] 3-8-9 VEspinoza 1 115
(Jerry Hollendorfer, U.S.A) 117/10
6 nk **Mine That Bird (USA)**[70] 3-8-9 CHBorel 10 114+
(Bennie L Woolley Jr, U.S.A) 17/5[2]
7 3/4 **Monzante (USA)**[35] 5-8-12 JRosario 6 112
(Mike Mitchell, U.S.A) 164/10
8 hd **Informed (USA)**[34] 5-8-12 (b) MCBaze 9 111
(Doug O'Neill, U.S.A) 34/1
9 7 1/4 **Tres Borrachos (USA)**[34] 4-8-12 JTalamo 5 96
(C Beau Greely, U.S.A) 248/10
10 3 **Tiago (USA)**[45] 5-8-12 MESmith 2 90
(John Shirreffs, U.S.A) 79/10

1m 48.39s (-0.51)
WFA 3 from 4yo+ 4lb 10 Ran SP% 119.5
PARI-MUTUEL: WIN 38.00; PL (1-2) 14.40, 4.40; SHOW (1-2-3) 9.40, 3.20,4.40; SF 199.80.
Owner Team Valor Intl & Gary Barber **Bred** Newsells Park Stud Limited **Trained** Newmarket, Suffolk

FOCUS
A trial for the Breeders' Cup Classic, but they went steady.

NOTEBOOK
Gitano Hernando stepped up from what the Americans call an allowance race, when he broke the 1m 1/2f track record at Wolverhampton, to Grade 1 winner, and was given a lovely ride by Fallon to do so. Never too far away from the modest pace, he was well positioned for the dash in the straight and, displaying a good attitude, was always doing enough. He has long been well regarded by Marco Botti, who was originally keen for him to take part in the Triple Crown, and this victory confirms he is a high-class colt. He's earned an automatic berth in the Classic, and the extra furlong, combined with a stronger pace, seems sure to suit, but as he's not nominated for the race his owners will have to pay a $250,000 supplementary fee. Whatever is decided as far as his next race is concerned, he's staying Stateside.
Colonel John(USA), beaten 5l into sixth in last year's Classic, ran close to his best in defeat. There seems no reason why he'll improve significantly on his 2008 placing if he again takes his chance in the big one next month, however.
Richard's Kid(USA) landed a Grade 1 on Polytrack last time and gives the form a solid look.
Mine That Bird(USA) ◆ was set a virtually impossible task and his seemingly one-dimensional running style is playing a big part in his regression since the Preakness. His jockey blamed the surface, reasoning that it wasn't quick enough for this gelding, but considering he was a top 2-y-o on Polytrack in Canada, it's hard to use that as an excuse, and he basically got too far out of his ground off steady fractions. In the circumstances he ran a creditable race after over two months off, and this could even be described as a reasonable trial for the Classic, which is apparently still the target. For a start, if he's once again dropped out next time, the likely strong pace will play to his strengths, as will the extra furlong. He is also entitled to strip fitter for the run, so it might pay to keep him on side next month, in case everything falls kindly.

6416 GOODWOOD (R-H)
Sunday, October 11

OFFICIAL GOING: Good to soft (7.5)
Top bend dolled out 3yds increasing distances by 7yds.
Wind: Mostly against; moderate, Races 1-3; almost nil, Races 4-5; moderate again, Races 6-7 Weather: Overcast, drizzly, becoming bright, Race 7

6692 THREE MUSKETEERS TROPHY H'CAP (FOR NATIONAL HUNT JOCKEYS) 2m
2:00 (2:00) (Class 5) (0-70,69) 4-Y-0+ £3,238 (£963; £481; £240) Stalls High

Form RPR
4506 1 **Kokkokila**[68] 4625 5-11-0 57 (p) LeightonAspell 6 66+
(Lady Herries) *s.s: hld up in last trio: smooth prog on outer fr 4f out: led main gp wl over 1f out: rdn and styd on to ld wl ins fnl f* 8/1
2406 2 3/4 **Black Or Red (IRE)**[10] 6432 4-11-5 62 (b) AlanO'Keeffe 10 70
(I A Wood) *awkward s: hld up in rr: wd bnd 5f out: prog and taken alone to r nr side 4f out: sn led: clr over 2f out: wknd fnl f: hdd nr fin* 13/2[3]
00 3 6 **Blockley (USA)**[43] 5444 5-11-5 62 (tp) DougieCostello 13 63
(Ian Williams) *in tch: rdn over 5f out: outpcd over 4f out: styd on u.p fr 3f out: wnt 3rd ins fnl f* 20/1
5/1- 4 2 1/2 **Hawridge Star (IRE)**[390] 5993 7-11-10 67 AndrewThornton 8 65
(W S Kittow) *hld up wl in rr: prog on inner 6f out to trck ldrs 4f out: led main gp over 2f out to wl over 1f out: fdd* 4/1[1]
3120 5 nk **No Rules**[23] 6053 4-11-9 66 DaveCrosse 4 63
(M H Tompkins) *prom: disp ld in main gp 4f out to over 2f out: fdd u.p* 13/2[3]
23 6 4 **Whitcombe Spirit**[3] 6622 4-11-0 57 MattieBatchelor 11 50
(Jamie Poulton) *pressed ldr: led 6f out to 4f out: wknd over 2f out* 6/1[2]

The Form Book, Raceform Ltd, Compton, RG20 6NL

-036 **7** 1 1/2 **Ned Ludd (IRE)**[135] 2429 6-11-12 **69** SJCraine 9 60
(J G Portman) *trckd ldrs: disp ld in main gp 4f out to over 2f out: wknd* **10/1**

4403 **8** 1 3/4 **The Composer**[13] 6330 7-10-7 **50** oh5 JAMcCarthy 2 39
(M Blanshard) *racd wd bnd after 4f: wl in tch: steadily wknd fr over 3f out* **25/1**

0410 **9** 8 **Trempari**[24] 6021 6-10-9 **52** AndrewTinkler 7 31
(Mike Murphy) *mde most to 6f out: on terms w ldrs 4f out: sn wknd* **28/1**

40-0 **10** 13 **Damascus Gold**[33] 5740 5-10-11 **54** OwynNelmes 14 18
(Miss Z C Davison) *in tch: rdn 5f out: steadily wknd over 3f out: t.o* **66/1**

1300 **11** 10 **Swordsman (GER)**[16] 4793 7-11-11 **68** (t) ColinBolger 5 20
(C Gordon) *pressed ldrs tl wknd u.p 5f out: t.o* **10/1**

220- **12** 1 1/4 **Forget It**[226] 7216 4-11-7 **64** PhilipHide 12 14
(G L Moore) *w ldrs to over 4f out: sn wknd: t.o* **9/1**

0026 **13** 13 **Hill Of Clare (IRE)**[59] 4935 7-10-7 **50** oh5 MarkGrant 3 —
(G H Jones) *s.s: a in last trio: lost tch over 5f out: t.o* **50/1**

/500 **14** 12 **Enthusius**[39] 5579 6-10-7 **50** oh4 EamonDehdashti 1 —
(G L Moore) *racd wd on bnds: in tch to over 4f out: sn wknd: t.o* **33/1**

3m 40.66s (11.66) **Going Correction** +0.50s/f (Yiel) **14** Ran SP% **118.7**
Speed ratings (Par 103): **90,89,86,85,85 83,82,81,77,71 66,65,58,52**
toteswingers: 1&2 £16.80, 1&3 £38.40, 2&3 £39.50 CSF £54.22 CT £1015.58 TOTE £9.90: £3.30, £2.50, £5.30; EX 71.80.

Owner Lady Mary Mumford **Bred** Lady Mary & Group Captain A Mumford **Trained** Patching, W Sussex

■ Stewards' Enquiry : Leighton Aspell one-day ban: used whip in incorrect place (Oct 25)

FOCUS
The time suggested the ground was softer than advertised and the jockeys reported it was good jumping ground. The pace was strong early on and the majority finished tired. The winner returned to form.
Swordsman(GER) Official explanation: jockey said gelding ran flat

6693 EBF RUK NURSERY 7f
2:35 (2:36) (Class 4) (0-85,85) 2-Y-O **£5,504** (£1,637; £818; £408) **Stalls High**

Form RPR
010 **1** **Ransom Note**[32] 5762 2-8-8 **72** MichaelHills 11 77
(B W Hills) *trckd ldrs in 6th: stdy prog on outer to ld 2f out: rdn and pressed jst over 1f out: jst hld on* **4/1**[1]

016 **2** nse **Brick Red**[32] 5762 2-9-1 **79** WilliamBuick 10 84
(A M Balding) *trckd ldng quartet: eased out over 2f out: rdn to chse wnr over 1f out: str chal fnl f: jst pipped* **8/1**[3]

3642 **3** 1 3/4 **Jairzihno**[11] 6373 2-9-3 **81** TonyCulhane 8 82
(J R Best) *hld up wl in rr: rdn and prog fr over 2f out: styd on u.p to dispute 3rd fnl f: kpt on* **14/1**

5044 **4** hd **Master Of Dance (IRE)**[22] 6104 2-9-0 **78** PatDobbs 15 78
(R Hannon) *trckd ldng trio: chal and upsides jst over 2f out: nt qckn w ldng pair sn after: kpt on* **10/1**

315 **5** 3 3/4 **Five Cents**[16] 6247 2-9-1 **79** TedDurcan 3 70
(Saeed Bin Suroor) *hld up in 9th: prog on outer fr 3f out: wl in tch 2f out: wknd jst over 1f out* **7/1**[2]

353 **6** 2 1/4 **If I Were A Boy (IRE)**[31] 5808 2-8-11 **75** JamesDoyle 7 60
(S Kirk) *settled in 8th: rdn 1/2-way: effrt on wd outside over 2f out: no prog over 1f out: wknd* **20/1**

2004 **7** 3 1/2 **Reddy To Star (IRE)**[13] 6328 2-8-8 **72** TPO'Shea 6 48
(C G Cox) *chsd ldrs in 7th: effrt on outer over 2f out: wknd over 1f out* **22/1**

3105 **8** 4 1/2 **Toga Tiger (IRE)**[29] 5864 2-9-7 **85** SamHitchcott 2 50
(M R Channon) *awkward s: wl in rr: rdn 1/2-way: trying to make grnd whn hmpd wl over 1f out: no prog after* **25/1**

016 **9** 1 1/2 **Celestial Tryst**[50] 5280 2-9-0 **78** PJMcDonald 1 39
(G M Moore) *dropped in fr wd draw: sn detached in last: rdn bef 1/2-way: effrt on outer 3f out: no prog 2f out: wknd* **12/1**

510 **10** 5 **Giulietta Da Vinci**[70] 4565 2-8-9 **73** ow1 DaneO'Neill 4 22+
(R Hannon) *trckd ldng pair: losing pl whn n.m.r on nr side rail 2f out: wknd rapidly* **16/1**

0244 **11** 5 **Fawley Green**[26] 5957 2-8-11 **75** DarryllHolland 14 11
(W R Muir) *led at gd pce to 2f out: wknd rapidly* **20/1**

4005 **12** shd **Danzoe (IRE)**[12] 6366 2-8-7 **71** DavidProbert 13 7+
(D Donovan) *chsd ldr: upsides over 2f out: losing pl whn n.m.r sn after: wknd rapidly* **14/1**

0366 **13** 7 **Professor John (IRE)**[26] 5970 2-9-1 **79** MickyFenton 9 —
(M L W Bell) *a wl in rr: last and tailing off 3f out* **33/1**

4551 **14** 1 3/4 **Pintura**[12] 6367 2-8-10 **74** ChrisCatlin 5 —
(M R Channon) *awkward s: a wl in rr: wknd over 2f out: t.o* **4/1**[1]

1m 30.4s (3.00) **Going Correction** +0.50s/f (Yiel) **14** Ran SP% **120.3**
Speed ratings (Par 97): **102,101,99,99,95 92,88,83,82,76 70,70,62,60**
toteswingers: 1&2 £11.20, 1&3 £10.60, 2&3 £23.20 CSF £32.32 CT £416.46 TOTE £4.10: £1.70, £3.30, £4.30; EX 41.00.

Owner H R Mould **Bred** Rabbah Bloodstock Limited **Trained** Lambourn, Berks

FOCUS
A decent nursery and as with the preceding race, it was run at a stiff pace early on. They all elected to come up the stands' side. The third and fourth set the level.

NOTEBOOK
Ransom Note, a scopey son of Red Ransom, who was a game winner at Chester on his second start, 'wasn't right' last time at Doncaster, according to his rider. But having hit the front perhaps sooner than he would have wished, he dug deep once again to get the verdict in a head-bobbing finish. He is still an immature colt but he handled the ground well and looks a nice prospect. (op 100-30 tchd 3-1)
Brick Red joined the battle approaching the furlong pole and the pair came very close on a couple of occasions. Though he looked to have got the better of his rival, the winner, who had finished behind him at Doncaster, just turned the tables. Dropped 1lb here, he stayed on gallantly, and has the scope to progress. (op 10-1)
Jairzihno had not looked particularly straightforward in his first two starts, but certainly ran like he'd learned plenty. Dropped back to 7f here and having the early pace to aim at seemed to suit him. He handled this ground well. (op 12-1)
Master Of Dance(IRE) seemed to handle this trip in conditions that would not really have suited him and stayed on nicely. He doesn't have as much scope as some, but is up to winning a nursery. (op 9-1)
Five Cents did not seem to progress from his Epsom victory last month when dropped in trip at Haydock next time, and although back up in trip here, he was labouring a bit in this ground. He will be better with racing. (op 8-1)
Giulietta Da Vinci Official explanation: jockey said filly was unsuited by the good to soft ground
Fawley Green Official explanation: jockey said colt was unsuited by the good to soft ground

Pintura was slowly out of the stalls and never got competitive. This was not his true form and this run is best ignored. (op 6-1 tchd 13-2)

6694 JENNY ALLEN BIRTHDAY CELEBRATION H'CAP 6f
3:10 (3:11) (Class 3) (0-95,91) 3-Y-O+ **£7,771** (£2,312; £1,155; £577) **Stalls Low**

Form RPR
0502 **1** **Arthur's Edge**[18] 6201 5-8-5 **77** oh3 DavidProbert 14 87
(B Palling) *prom on outer: led over 2f out: hrd pressed fr over 1f out: kpt on gamely* **11/1**

4153 **2** 1/2 **Son Of The Cat (USA)**[16] 6240 3-8-11 **91** (t) JPFahy[(7)] 13 100
(B Gubby) *trckd ldrs gng wl: cl up fr 2f out: wouldn't go through gap over 1f out: styd on to take 2nd ins fnl f: a hld* **15/2**

1440 **3** 1/2 **Aye Aye Digby (IRE)**[22] 6089 4-9-5 **91** DaneO'Neill 10 98
(H Candy) *settled in rr: outpcd 2f out: rdn and prog over 1f out: clsd and looked threatening ins fnl f: nt qckn last 100yds* **11/1**

0410 **4** 1 1/4 **Seamus Shindig**[31] 5799 7-8-9 **88** AmyScott[(7)] 8 91
(H Candy) *prom on outer: pressed wnr wl over 1f out: cajoled along and hld ent fnl f: wknd last 100yds* **14/1**

0006 **5** nk **Phantom Whisper**[11] 6396 6-8-5 **80** AndreaAtzeni[(3)] 11 82
(B R Millman) *dwlt: wl in rr: rdn and effrt on outer 1/2-way: styd on fr over 1f out: nvr able to chal* **9/2**[2]

0204 **6** 3 3/4 **Viking Spirit**[37] 5646 7-9-3 **89** (t) EddieAhern 4 79
(W R Swinburn) *hld up in midfield: outpcd 2f out: rdn and hanging rt fr over 1f out: no imp on ldrs* **12/1**

2010 **7** nse **Haajes**[23] 6050 5-9-0 **86** (t) TedDurcan 7 76
(J Balding) *towards rr in centre: outpcd over 2f out: nvr on terms after* **7/1**[3]

6110 **8** 1 1/4 **Mujood**[15] 6278 6-9-2 **91** (b) PatrickHills[(3)] 9 77
(Eve Johnson Houghton) *racd on outer: a struggling to go the pce: nvr on terms* **20/1**

2300 **9** 2 3/4 **Rash Judgement**[23] 6050 4-8-13 **85** FergusSweeney 1 62
(W S Kittow) *reluctant to enter stalls: wl in rr against nr side rail: no prog and bhd 2f out: modest late hdwy* **12/1**

2211 **10** 1 1/4 **We Have A Dream**[5] 6564 4-8-13 **85** 6ex DarryllHolland 6 58
(W R Muir) *led against nr side rail: edgd rt bef 1/2-way: hdd over 2f out: wknd over 1f out* **4/1**[1]

-406 **11** 1 1/4 **Perfect Flight**[38] 5607 4-9-1 **87** KirstyMilczarek 3 56
(M Blanshard) *in tch in midfield: wknd fr 2f out* **14/1**

0050 **12** 18 **Osiris Way**[43] 5424 7-8-13 **85** JimCrowley 5 —
(P R Chamings) *w ldrs to jst over 2f out: wknd rapidly over 1f out: eased: t.o* **14/1**

0562 **13** 4 1/2 **Kerrys Requiem (IRE)**[20] 6155 3-8-12 **85** TonyCulhane 2 —
(M R Channon) *a in rr: wknd 2f out: t.o* **16/1**

010- **14** 10 **Cerito**[372] 6483 3-9-1 **88** PatCosgrave 12 —
(J R Boyle) *pressed ldrs to over 2f out: wknd rapidly: t.o* **40/1**

1m 14.12s (1.92) **Going Correction** +0.50s/f (Yiel)
WFA 3 from 4yo+ 1lb **14** Ran SP% **127.6**
Speed ratings (Par 107): **107,106,105,104,103 98,98,96,93,91 89,65,59,46**
toteswingers: 1&2 £20.40, 1&3 £33.80, 2&3 £13.10 CSF £96.71 CT £662.48 TOTE £13.10: £4.00, £3.00, £3.20; EX 118.60.

Owner Mrs Annabelle Mason **Bred** Christopher J Mason **Trained** Tredodridge, Vale Of Glamorgan

FOCUS
A decent handicap run at a sensible pace for the conditions. They elected to come stands' side as they had done in the previous races. A personal best from the winner.

NOTEBOOK
Arthur's Edge had run well over C&D last month, so it was not a great surprise to see him score off a career-best mark. Drawn widest of all, he was given a positive ride and had just enough in hand to repel his rivals. He is a consistent sort and was recording his fifth career victory in 20 starts (the second on turf), and there is no reason to think he won't keep paying his way. There are not too many 0-80 6f handicaps to run in this month – something which probably needs looking at. (op 12-1)
Son Of The Cat(USA), who looked well beforehand, was also drawn wide. He made a sustained bid and stayed on well under a good ride from his young claimer. Like the winner, he is holding his form well and is another who appears to like getting his toe in. He is useful in this grade. (op 10-1)
Aye Aye Digby(IRE) had the benefit of a good draw, something he did not have in the Silver Cup at Ayr last time, and underfoot conditions to suit. He stayed on well and he continues to be a credit to his connections. He remains an in-form handicapper, but has not won off a mark this high. (op 12-1 tchd 10-1)
Seamus Shindig was running off a career-high mark and, although he came with a promising run, it petered out. This was a stronger race than he won at Newmarket in August and, in the circumstances, he ran up to his mark in conditions that would have played to his strengths. (op 16-1)
Phantom Whisper was getting the ground he likes for the first time in a while. Though a winner of this race off an 11lb higher mark last year, he couldn't match the pace of the winner, having dwelt at the start. He stayed on well though, and can be considered in autumn ground. (op 13-2)
Viking Spirit was similarly a bit outpaced when the winner kicked on. He had won here off a 9lb higher mark on his last visit (May 2008), but he has not been in that sort of form since. He has not had too many chances on this type of ground and remains largely consistent.
We Have A Dream didn't have the ideal draw up the slower, near-side rail. Though he was given a positive ride, he faded. This was a tougher race than he won at Folkestone on Tuesday and the penalty found him out. (op 9-2 tchd 5-1 in places)
Perfect Flight Official explanation: jockey said filly stopped very quickly

6695 TABLE 6 H'CAP 1m
3:45 (3:46) (Class 4) (0-85,85) 3-Y-O+ **£5,180** (£1,541; £770; £384) **Stalls High**

Form RPR
4205 **1** **Cape Hawk (IRE)**[28] 5914 5-9-0 **81** PatrickHills[(3)] 15 91
(R Hannon) *mde all: set stdy pce to 1/2-way: led majority of field down centre in st: rdn and hld on wl fnl 2f* **8/1**

0300 **2** 3/4 **Key Signature**[60] 4909 3-8-10 **77** (b) DarryllHolland 1 85
(Pat Eddery) *t.k.h: hld up in tch: prog to chse wnr 3f out: clr of rest 2f out: ev ch but hanging and ref to throw down proper chal* **33/1**

400 **3** 3/4 **The Fifth Member (IRE)**[120] 2933 5-9-7 **85** PatCosgrave 14 91
(J R Boyle) *cl up: rdn 3f out: chsd clr ldng pair 2f out: kpt on but nvr able to chal* **13/2**[3]

2000 **4** 3/4 **Kinsya**[24] 6014 6-8-13 **77** JimmyQuinn 11 82+
(M H Tompkins) *hld up in last quartet: outpcd 3f out: rdn and prog over 2f out: styd on to press ldrs ins fnl f: one pce last 100yds* **9/1**

1300 **5** 1 3/4 **Wellington Square**[59] 4954 4-9-5 **83** TravisBlock 9 83
(H Morrison) *stdd s: hld up in last quartet: outpcd whn rdn and effrt over 2f out: kpt on fr over 1f out: n.d* **10/1**

3322 **6** 1 **Effigy**[33] 5745 5-9-1 **79** DaneO'Neill 4 77
(H Candy) *sweating: trckd ldrs: rdn 3f out: nt qckn and outpcd over 2f out: no imp after* **9/2**[1]

00 **7** ½ **Opera Prince**[79] 4262 4-9-0 **78** .... LPKeniry 10 75
(S Kirk) *hld up in midfield: outpcd fr 3f out: rdn and one pce after: nvr on terms w ldrs* **16/1**

6430 **8** 4½ **Salient**[14] 6307 5-9-4 **82** .... KirstyMilczarek 13 68
(M J Attwater) *hld up in midfield: outpcd fr 3f out: no prog after: wknd* **16/1**

1156 **9** 1½ **Indy Driver**[8] 6476 4-8-12 **76** .... (p) EddieAhern 17 58
(J R Fanshawe) *hld up in midfield: outpcd fr 3f out: no prog after: wknd* **6/1**[2]

2245 **10** ½ **Happy Anniversary (IRE)**[53] 5175 3-9-1 **82** .... TedDurcan 3 63
(Mrs D J Sanderson) *s.i.s: hld up in last quartet on outer: no prog over 2f out: sn no ch* **8/1**

6000 **11** 4½ **Mishrif (USA)**[25] 5986 3-8-12 **79** .... FergusSweeney 5 49
(J R Jenkins) *t.k.h: w ldrs: c across to nr side in striaght: sn btn and bhd* **25/1**

0000 **12** 2¼ **Weald Park (USA)**[64] 4794 3-9-4 **85** .... PatDobbs 12 50
(R Hannon) *hld up: a in last quartet: lft bhd fr 3f out* **25/1**

4452 **13** 2¼ **Northern Spy (USA)**[20] 6168 5-8-9 **73** .... ChrisCatlin 2 33
(S Dow) *chsd ldrs: c towards nr side in st: sn btn and bhd* **14/1**

1350 **14** 7 **Pearl Of Manacor (IRE)**[25] 6004 3-8-8 **75** .... TonyCulhane 8 18
(M R Channon) *chsd wnr to 3f out: wknd rapidly over 2f out: t.o* **40/1**

1m 42.83s (2.93) **Going Correction** +0.50s/f (Yiel)
WFA 3 from 4yo+ 3lb **14** Ran SP% **118.6**
Speed ratings (Par 105): **105,104,103,102,101 100,99,95,93,93 88,86,84,77**
toteswingers: 1&2 £53.70, 2&3 £10.10, 1&3 not won. CSF £256.73 CT £1862.46 TOTE £7.40: £2.40, £11.30, £3.10; EX 272.60.
Owner Thurloe Thoroughbreds XVII **Bred** John And Leslie Young **Trained** East Everleigh, Wilts

FOCUS
They elected to come up the middle of the track for the first time looking for better ground. Fair form for the grade.

6696 CELER ET AUDAX MEDIAN AUCTION MAIDEN STKS 6f
4:20 (4:22) (Class 5) 2-Y-O **£3,238** (£963; £481; £240) **Stalls** Low

Form RPR

2020 **1** **Carnaby Street (IRE)**[31] 5795 2-9-3 88 .... PatDobbs 11 88+
(R Hannon) *pressed ldr: rdn to ld wl over 1f out: steadily drew clr* **11/10**[1]

4 **2** 5 **London Gold**[23] 6054 2-9-3 0 .... DaneO'Neill 13 73+
(H Candy) *narrow ld: rdn and hdd wl over 1f out: sn no ch w wnr: wknd fnl f: jst hld on for 2nd* **5/2**[2]

0 **3** nk **The Confessor**[102] 3500 2-9-3 0 .... FrankieMcDonald 4 72
(H Candy) *w ldng pair to 1/2-way: sn rdn and outpcd: kpt on again fnl f* **33/1**

00 **4** ½ **Cereal Killer (IRE)**[22] 6108 2-9-3 0 .... TedDurcan 9 71+
(R Hannon) *outpcd and bhd: shkn up 1/2-way: prog over 2f out: styd on: nrst fin* **16/1**

433 **5** nk **Warning Song (USA)**[129] 2636 2-9-3 88 .... JimCrowley 2 70
(Mrs A J Perrett) *racd against nr side rail 1f: chsd ldrs: outpcd over 2f out: kpt on again fr over 1f out* **6/1**[3]

0 **6** 8 **Joe Rua (USA)**[10] 6424 2-9-3 0 .... JerryO'Dwyer 10 46
(J Ryan) *dwlt: sn outpcd: a bhd* **16/1**

0 **7** 1 **Sapphire Spirit (USA)**[130] 2595 2-9-0 0 .... MarcHalford(3) 8 43
(J R Best) *taken down early: chsd ldrs tl wknd u.p over 2f out: sn bhd* **33/1**

8 3 **Rolling Hills (IRE)** 2-9-3 0 .... FergusSweeney 1 34+
(H Candy) *racd against nr side rail 1f: a bhd* **12/1**

00 **9** ¾ **Barafundle Boy**[22] 6108 2-9-0 0 .... MCGeran(3) 6 31
(J J Bridger) *outpcd and a bhd* **200/1**

0 **10** 3¾ **Wannabee (IRE)**[31] 5808 2-8-12 0 .... LPKeniry 5 15
(J J Bridger) *reluctant to enter stalls: chsd ldrs to 1/2-way: wknd rapidly: t.o* **100/1**

1m 15.48s (3.28) **Going Correction** +0.50s/f (Yiel) **10** Ran SP% **117.3**
Speed ratings (Par 95): **98,91,90,90,89 79,77,73,72,67**
toteswingers: 1&2 £2.00, 1&3 £13.50, 2&3 £18.20 CSF £3.82 TOTE £2.00: £1.10, £1.50, £6.60; EX 4.50.
Owner Noodles Racing **Bred** D And Mrs D Veitch **Trained** East Everleigh, Wilts

FOCUS
An uncompetitive maiden and they finished strung out off a fair pace in the conditions. They elected to come up the faster centre of the track.

NOTEBOOK
Carnaby Street(IRE), who had gone close in the St Leger Yearling Sales race at York in August, was well backed. That support was justified as he won with plenty to spare. Though he looked set for a battle 2f from home against a rival who was seemingly travelling better, he forged clear in the manner of a good horse to break his maiden. It wouldn't do to get too carried away, because most of these rivals appeared ordinary at best. (op 5-4 tchd 11-8 and 6-4 in a place)
London Gold shaped well on his debut when an unfancied fourth in a well-contested Newbury maiden. He underlined that potential with another pleasing performance, travelling very well before finding little off the bridle. He bumped into a decent colt and looks capable of breaking his maiden tag soon. (op 3-1)
The Confessor, who raced widest of all, stayed on quite well without ever looking like getting on terms. This was only his second start and he will have learned plenty. (op 25-1)
Cereal Killer(IRE) is now qualified for a handicap mark and he finished to good effect. He had shown precious little in Sandown (5f) and Newbury (7f) maidens previously, but he could be interesting if upped in trip.
Warning Song(USA), one of the more experienced, but having his first run since June, was doing his best work late on and will be interesting next time. This ground would be soft enough for him. (op 5-1 tchd 9-2)

6697 EBF GOODWOOD RACEHORSE OWNERS' GROUP MAIDEN STKS 1m 1f
4:55 (5:01) (Class 4) 2-Y-O **£5,180** (£1,541; £770; £384) **Stalls** High

Form RPR

0 **1** **Ted Spread**[78] 4314 2-9-3 0 .... JimmyQuinn 14 78
(M H Tompkins) *trckd ldng trio: prog to ld narrowly 2f out: sn drvn: gained uppper hand ins fnl f* **4/1**[1]

02 **2** 1½ **Regal Guest**[18] 6200 2-9-3 0 .... ChrisCatlin 5 75
(M R Channon) *chsd ldng pair: rdn 4f out: chal w wnr and upsides 2f out: nt qckn u.p ins fnl f* **10/1**

65 **3** 1½ **Berling (IRE)**[29] 5879 2-9-3 0 .... EddieAhern 3 72
(J L Dunlop) *off the pce in abt 8th: gd prog over 3f out: jnd ldng pair wl over 1f out: sn rdn and nt qckn: one pce fnl f* **16/1**

4 1¼ **Domination** 2-9-3 0 .... TravisBlock 9 70+
(H Morrison) *s.s: last and wl off the pce: gd prog rnd outside of field oer 3f out to go modest 6th over 2f out: rdn and styd on: nrst fin* **18/1**

0 **5** 5 **Cast Of Stars (IRE)**[41] 5499 2-9-3 0 .... RichardKingscote 10 60+
(R M Beckett) *w ldr: styd far side in st: lost pl 2f out: grad fdd* **11/2**[3]

053 **6** nk **Another Magic Man (USA)**[26] 5966 2-9-0 77 .... MarcHalford(3) 7 59+
(J R Best) *led at decent pce: styd faar side in st: lost ld 2f out: grad fdd* **9/1**

03 **7** 6 **Phonic (IRE)**[23] 6066 2-9-3 0 .... TedDurcan 12 48+
(J L Dunlop) *hld up in last trio and wl off the pce: modest prog past toiling rivals fr 2f out* **9/2**[2]

00 **8** 1¼ **Harry Paget (IRE)**[18] 6200 2-9-3 0 .... TonyCulhane 1 44
(J R Best) *reluctant to enter stalls: a towards rr and off the pce: rdn 4f out: no prog* **66/1**

0 **9** nk **Helaku (IRE)**[23] 6066 2-9-3 0 .... PatDobbs 8 45+
(R Hannon) *s.i.s: pushed up to chse ldrs: 6th and nt on terms 4f out: no prog and btn 3f out: wknd* **9/1**

0 **10** 2½ **Big Talk**[37] 5627 2-9-3 0 .... JamesDoyle 15 40+
(S Kirk) *a in rr and wl off the pce: struggling over 3f out* **50/1**

0 **11** 1 **Lis Pendens**[25] 5993 2-9-3 0 .... DaneO'Neill 6 39+
(W R Muir) *late to post after last minute jockey replment: reluctant to enter stalls: midfield: 7th and nt on terms 4f out: wknd* **25/1**

06 **12** 10 **Viviani (IRE)**[11] 6393 2-9-3 0 .... JimCrowley 11 17
(Mrs A J Perrett) *reminder after 1f: a in rr: t.o* **14/1**

000 **13** 15 **Lisahane Bog**[11] 6393 2-9-3 60 .... (p) TGMcLaughlin 13 —
(P R Hedger) *chsd clr ldrs: 5th and nt on terms 4f out: sn wknd: t.o* **100/1**

2m 1.21s (4.91) **Going Correction** +0.50s/f (Yiel) **13** Ran SP% **108.8**
Speed ratings (Par 97): **98,96,95,94,89 89,84,83,82,80 79,70,57**
toteswingers: 1&2 £8.00, 1&3 £12.60, 2&3 £10.00 CSF £35.60 TOTE £4.30: £1.80, £2.30, £3.20; EX 45.30.
Owner False Nose 'N Glasses Partnership **Bred** Pollards Stables **Trained** Newmarket, Suffolk

FOCUS
An interesting maiden, run at a decent early gallop for the conditions and they finished well strung out. The front trio all improved.

NOTEBOOK
Ted Spread stepped up on his Newmarket debut seventh in July to score readily. He was one of a quartet that elected to come up the centre of the track and wore down Regal Guest inside the last half furlong. He does not lack for stamina and he should be a horse to follow. (op 5-1 tchd 7-2)
Regal Guest, who was a fair second over C&D last time on his second start, elected to come up the middle of the track in search of better ground and produced a similar level of form to his last run. He has now qualified for a handicap mark. (op 11-1 tchd 9-1)
Berling(IRE) cost 650,000gns as a yearling. He travelled well and loomed large approaching the final furlong. He wasn't given a particularly tough time of it and he ran to a level one would expect, considering his shrewd trainer is now likely to pitch him into handicap company. He is bred for middle-distances and will be a nice horse next year. His trainer could also target 1m2f nurseries in the meantime. There is one at Nottingham later in the month that may be interesting. (op 14-1)
Domination, who broke slowly, losing two or three lengths on the field, but was never nearer than at the finish, staying on well. He has plenty of scope for improvement. (op 20-1 tchd 16-1)
Cast Of Stars(IRE) appears to have a future and will get better with racing. (op 7-1)
Another Magic Man(USA) helped set the pace and elected to stay close to the far rail, tactics that didn't pan out. Stepped up in trip, he improved on what he achieved on his debut, though he was beaten a long way. (op 10-1 tchd 12-1)

6698 LAST CHANCE TOTEEXACTA H'CAP 1m 4f
5:30 (5:32) (Class 5) (0-75,75) 3-Y-O **£3,238** (£963; £481; £240) **Stalls** Low

Form RPR

-560 **1** **Scene Two**[67] 4650 3-9-0 **71** .... WilliamBuick 7 78
(L M Cumani) *prom: trckd ldr 1/2-way: rdn to ld 2f out: wandered bdly in all directions u.p: kpt on* **5/1**[2]

24 **2** 1½ **Gaselee (USA)**[58] 5009 3-8-10 **67** .... ChrisCatlin 4 72
(Rae Guest) *led: rdn and hdd 2f out: plugged on but a hld after* **11/2**[3]

256 **3** 3 **Lady Rusty (IRE)**[36] 5666 3-8-10 **67** .... LukeMorris 6 67
(P Winkworth) *mostly in last: rdn over 3f out: prog over 2f out: kpt on to take 3rd fnl f: no imp ldng pair* **13/2**

0023 **4** 1½ **Cherish The Moment (IRE)**[39] 5578 3-9-2 **73** .... (p) MichaelHills 8 71
(B W Hills) *chsd ldr to 1/2-way: styd cl up: rdn over 2f out: one pce u.p after* **7/1**

-626 **5** 7 **Rosco Flyer (IRE)**[9] 6440 3-8-10 **67** .... PatCosgrave 9 54
(J R Boyle) *wl in tch: rdn over 3f out: no imp ldrs 2f out: hung bdly lft over 1f out* **12/1**

004 **6** 5 **Princability (IRE)**[60] 4910 3-8-11 **68** .... TonyCulhane 5 47
(M R Channon) *in tch: pushed along 5f out: no prog u.p 3f out: sn btn* **7/1**

625 **7** 8 **Reset City**[34] 5718 3-9-1 **72** .... RobertHavlin 1 38
(A B Haynes) *hld up in tch: cl up fr 1/2-way: gng bttr than most 3f out: sn rdn and wknd tamely* **15/2**

0-42 **8** ¾ **Beauchamp Xiara**[20] 6166 3-8-13 **70** .... DaneO'Neill 2 35
(H Candy) *hld up in tch: gng wl enough 4f out: wknd rapidly 3f out* **3/1**[1]

2m 43.78s (5.38) **Going Correction** +0.50s/f (Yiel) **8** Ran SP% **114.8**
Speed ratings (Par 101): **102,101,99,98,93 90,84,84**
toteswingers: 1&2 £4.80, 1&3 £6.80, 2&3 £9.90 CSF £32.64 CT £180.15 TOTE £5.40: £1.90, £2.50, £2.10; EX 35.20 Place 6: £522.58 Place 5: £136.93 .
Owner Team Spirit 2 **Bred** R E Crutchley **Trained** Newmarket, Suffolk

FOCUS
A modest handicap run at a good pace for the conditions and they finished very leg-weary. Not form to be too positive about.
Beauchamp Xiara Official explanation: jockey said filly was unsuited by the good to soft ground
T/Jkpt: Not won. T/Plt: £387.90 to a £1 stake. Pool: £80,713.40. 151.87 winning tickets. T/Qpdt: £35.70 to a £1 stake. Pool: £7,167.42. 148.35 winning tickets. JN

6627 LINGFIELD (L-H)
Sunday, October 11

OFFICIAL GOING: Standard to slow
Wind: fresh, across Weather: overcast

6699 BET HEINEKEN CUP - BETDAQ H'CAP (DIV I) 7f (P)
1:50 (1:50) (Class 5) (0-70,72) 3-Y-O **£2,914** (£867; £433; £216) **Stalls** Low

Form RPR

6640 **1** **Finnegan McCool**[18] 6201 3-8-13 **65** .... (p) SebSanders 11 77
(R M Beckett) *stdd after s: in rr: rdn along over 4f out: gd hdwy on outer over 2f otu: hanging lft but rdn to chal ins fnl f: led fnl 75yds: r.o wl* **9/1**

0-30 **2** nk **King Of Defence**[124] 2797 3-8-7 **59** .... PaulHanagan 7 70
(M A Jarvis) *s.i.s: hdwy into midfield: over 4f out: hdwy on outer over 3f out: rdn to ld 2f out: hrd pressed ins fnl f: hdd and unable qck fnl 75yds* **9/2**[2]

5001 **3** 3 **Gassin**[9] 6455 3-9-6 **72** .... (v) HayleyTurner 2 75
(M L W Bell) *t.k.h: trckd ldrs: rdn to press ldng pair ent fnl f: nt qckn u.p ins fnl f: wknd fnl 75yds* **9/4**[1]

0000 **4** *4* **Amber Sunset**[9] 6455 3-8-12 **67** WilliamCarson(3) 10 59
(J Jay) *t.k.h: chsd ldrs: wnt 2nd over 3f out: rdn to ld over 2f out: hdd 2f out: wknd and edgd rt fnl f* **20/1**

0111 **5** *½* **La Gifted**[22] 6103 3-8-9 **61** CatherineGannon 8 52
(M R Channon) *in tch: rdn and outpcd wl over 2f out: plugged on steadily fr over 1f out: no ch w ldrs* **11/2**[3]

6034 **6** *¾* **Safari Guide**[66] 4700 3-9-2 **68** LukeMorris 4 57
(P Winkworth) *t.k.h: hld up in tch: rdn and struggling to hold pl over 2f out: no ch w ldrs fnl 2f* **10/1**

1450 **7** *nk* **Russian Rave**[43] 5449 3-9-3 **69** TPQueally 9 57
(J G Portman) *chsd ldrs: rdn and struggling over 2f out: n.d whn hung lft wl over 1f out* **9/2**[2]

605 **8** *12* **Shadow Bay (IRE)**[15] 6293 3-8-13 **65** IanMongan 6 21
(Miss Z C Davison) *a towards rr: rdn over 4f out: lost tch wl over 2f out* **20/1**

6000 **9** *10* **Badtanman**[20] 6161 3-8-4 **56** oh11 JamieMackay 1 —
(Peter Grayson) *dwlt: sn rcvrd to ld 6f out: hdd over 3f out: sn struggling: wl bhd fnl 2f: t.o* **100/1**

040- **10** *2¼* **Sienna Lake (IRE)**[361] 6730 3-8-6 **58** LiamJones 5 —
(T D McCarthy) *a in rr: rdn and struggling over 3f out: t.o* **66/1**

0315 **11** *2½* **Hatman Jack (IRE)**[39] 5584 3-8-9 **61** ow1 (p) StephenDonohoe 3 —
(B G Powell) *t.k.h: led for 1f: w ldr tl led again over 3f out: hdd over 2f out: wknd rapidly: eased fr over 1f out: t.o* **12/1**

1m 24.62s (-0.18) **Going Correction** +0.075s/f (Slow) **11** Ran SP% **121.3**
Speed ratings (Par 101): **104,103,100,95,95 94,93,80,68,66 63**
toteswingers: 1&2 £9.30, 1&3 £7.50, 2&3 £4.50 CSF £49.37 CT £127.70 TOTE £13.70: £2.80, £2.40, £1.40; EX 83.70 Trifecta £168.70 Part won. Pool of £228.04 - 0.76 winning units..
Owner Lawrence & Wilkinson **Bred** D J And Mrs Deer **Trained** Whitsbury, Hants

FOCUS
The pace seemed steady early before quickening up a long way out, and the winning time was 0.48 seconds faster than the second division, which was won by Kuanyao. The first two came well clear of a recent winner, and with the time respectable as well, this is probably reasonable form for the grade. The runner-up is the best guide.
Finnegan McCool Official explanation: trainer said, regarding the apparent improvement of form, the gelding had benefitted from a return to running on the all weather surface
Shadow Bay(IRE) Official explanation: jockey said gelding did not face the kickback.
Sienna Lake(IRE) Official explanation: jockey said filly did not handle the track
Hatman Jack(IRE) Official explanation: jockey said gelding ran too free

6700 OXTED MAIDEN STKS 5f (P)

2:25 (2:25) (Class 5) 2-Y-O **£3,238** (£963; £481; £240) **Stalls** High

Form RPR

5223 **1** **Admin (IRE)**[52] 5194 2-9-3 79 SebSanders 7 71
(R M Beckett) *trckd ldrs: rdn and effrt 2f out: led ent fnl f: kpt on* **8/13**[1]

06 **2** *1¼* **Robens Rock (IRE)**[29] 5867 2-9-3 0 GeorgeBaker 6 67
(A B Haynes) *stdd after s: hld up in last pair: hdwy over 1f out: chsd wnr ins fnl f: no imp fnl 100yds* **12/1**

3453 **3** *nk* **My Mandy (IRE)**[12] 6354 2-8-12 63 (p) ShaneKelly 4 60
(Ian Williams) *in tch: effrt and rdn 2f out: no prog tl styd on u.p ins fnl f: nvr gng pce to rch wnr* **9/1**

4032 **4** *1½* **Dusty Spirit**[19] 6185 2-9-0 68 JackDean(3) 3 60
(W G M Turner) *chsd ldrs: pushed along over 3f out: drvn and unable qck jst over 2f out: no one pce after* **5/1**[2]

02 **5** *¾* **Fazza**[11] 6386 2-9-3 0 HayleyTurner 5 57
(D W P Arbuthnot) *led for 1f: chsd ldr after: hung rt bnd ent fnl 2f: lost 2nd over 1f out: outpcd ent fnl f* **7/1**[3]

000 **6** *1* **Rightcar**[13] 6345 2-9-3 50 (b[1]) AdamKirby 2 54
(Peter Grayson) *sn pushed along: led after 1f: rdn ent fnl 2f: hdd ent fnl f: wknd fnl 150yds* **66/1**

050 **7** *4½* **L'Isle Joyeuse**[34] 5714 2-8-12 45 LukeMorris 1 33
(P Winkworth) *a in last pair: struggling over 2f out: wl bhd fr over 1f out* **66/1**

59.20 secs (0.40) **Going Correction** +0.075s/f (Slow) **7** Ran SP% **111.8**
Speed ratings (Par 95): **99,97,96,94,92 91,84**
toteswingers: 1&2 £2.50, 1&3 £2.00, 2&3 £7.10 CSF £9.13 TOTE £1.60: £1.40, £4.80; EX 10.90.
Owner The Anagram Partnership **Bred** M J Halligan **Trained** Whitsbury, Hants

FOCUS
A weak juvenile maiden with the fourth and sixth limiting the form.

NOTEBOOK
Admin(IRE), a beaten favourite on his last four starts, gained an overdue first success at the sixth attempt. He travelled well but didn't find quite as much as had looked likely, basically just doing enough to keep some inferior rivals at bay. (op 8-11, tchd 4-5 in places)
Robens Rock(IRE), too keen over further on both his previous starts, proved suited by the minimum trip. He never seriously threatened the winner but showed enough to suggest he might be able to make his mark, particularly considering handicaps are now an option. (op 9-1)
My Mandy(IRE) is now 0-11 but she would have been 11lb better off with the winner in a nursery. (op 13-2 tchd 6-1)
Dusty Spirit was slightly below his rating of 68 considering he had the same chance as the third-placed finisher judged on official figures. (op 6-1)
Fazza kept the leader honest but dropped away in the straight and was nowhere near the form he showed when runner-up over 6f at Nottingham on his previous start. (tchd 15-2)

6701 BET HEINEKEN CUP - BETDAQ H'CAP (DIV II) 7f (P)

3:00 (3:00) (Class 5) (0-70,70) 3-Y-O **£2,914** (£867; £433; £216) **Stalls** Low

Form RPR

1332 **1** **Kuanyao (IRE)**[39] 5581 3-8-9 **61** SteveDrowne 8 68
(P J Makin) *awkward leaving stalls: sn chsng ldr: rdn to ld over 1f out: r.o wl fnl f* **2/1**[1]

0506 **2** *1½* **Spiritual Art**[2] 6630 3-9-4 **70** (p) PaulDoe 1 73
(L A Dace) *chsd ldrs: rdn and pressed wnr on inner over 1f out: no ex and btn fnl 75yds: hld on for 2nd* **6/1**[3]

3221 **3** *hd* **Miss Frangipane (IRE)**[26] 5971 3-8-13 **65** ShaneKelly 6 67
(J Noseda) *in tch on outer: hdwy to chse ldrs over 2f out: unable qck and outpcd over 1f out: kpt on again ins fnl f: pressing for 2nd nr fin* **5/1**[2]

0640 **4** *¾* **Imperial Skylight**[13] 6339 3-8-5 **57** CatherineGannon 3 57
(M R Channon) *in tch: rdn and unable qck 3f out: kpt on u.p to chse ldng pair ins fnl f: no imp and lost 3rd fnl 75yds* **16/1**

5016 **5** *nk* **Pacific Bay (IRE)**[13] 6333 3-8-8 **60** PaulHanagan 2 60
(R A Fahey) *led: rdn ent fnl 2f: hdd over 1f out: one pce after* **12/1**

6-65 **6** *1* **Lindy Hop (IRE)**[160] 1743 3-9-1 **67** AdamKirby 10 64
(W R Swinburn) *wnt rt s: sn swtchd lft and racd in rr: rdn and effrt jst over 2f out: styd on and hdwy fnl f: n.d* **12/1**

-604 **7** *3* **Especially Special (IRE)**[9] 6455 3-9-3 **69** GeorgeBaker 9 58
(S Kirk) *stdd after s: hld up towards rr: hdwy over 2f out: rdn and unable qck wl over 1f out: wl hld after* **9/1**

0540 **8** *1* **Satwa Star (IRE)**[15] 6294 3-9-2 **68** TGMcLaughlin 5 54
(E A L Dunlop) *hmpd s: hld up in rr: drvn over 1f out: n.d* **6/1**[3]

0040 **9** *5* **Quick Single (USA)**[39] 5581 3-8-3 **58** (v) KellyHarrison(3) 4 31
(P S McEntee) *wnt rt s: t.k.h: in tch tl dropped towards rr over 4f out: rdn and struggling 3f out* **40/1**

-060 **10** *4* **Pagan Force (IRE)**[11] 6399 3-8-8 **60** (b) TPQueally 7 22
(Mrs A J Perrett) *stmbld s: hld up in midfield: rdn: hung lft and nt run on wl over 1f out: bhd and esaed ins fnl f* **16/1**

1m 25.1s (0.30) **Going Correction** +0.075s/f (Slow) **10** Ran SP% **118.2**
Speed ratings (Par 101): **101,99,99,98,97 96,93,92,86,81**
toteswingers: 1&2 £5.40, 1&3 £2.70, 2&3 £7.50 CSF £14.19 CT £55.32 TOTE £2.30: £1.40, £2.00, £1.70; EX 16.50 Trifecta £28.90 Pool: £332.44 - 8.49 winning units..
Owner D M Ahier **Bred** Newlands House Stud **Trained** Ogbourne Maisey, Wilts

FOCUS
A modest 3-y-o handicap run in a time 0.48 seconds slower than the first division. The winner is rated in line with his previous C&D form.
Lindy Hop(IRE) ◆ Official explanation: jockey said filly had no more to give

6702 BET WORLD CUP FOOTBALL - BETDAQ H'CAP 7f (P)

3:35 (3:37) (Class 3) (0-95,94) 3-Y-O+ **£8,871** (£2,619; £1,310) **Stalls** Low

Form RPR

305 **1** **Kyllachy Star**[22] 6092 3-8-12 **88** PaulHanagan 1 98
(R A Fahey) *hld up in midfield: switching out rt fr over 2f out: rdn and hdwy over 1f out: drvn to ld fnl 75yds: r.o wl* **15/2**

3046 **2** *1* **Spirit Of Sharjah (IRE)**[8] 6482 4-8-13 **87** RoystonFfrench 12 95
(Miss J Feilden) *t.k.h: hld up in tch: hdwy over 2f out: rdn to chse ldrs 2f out: led 1f out: hdd and no ex fnl 75yds* **25/1**

612 **3** *shd* **Prescription**[55] 5104 4-9-6 **94** SebSanders 13 102
(Sir Mark Prescott) *stdd s: t.k.h: hld up towards rr: hdwy on outer over 3f out: chsd ldrs and drvn wl over 1f out: kpt on wl fnl f* **7/2**[1]

1310 **4** *1½* **Broad Cairn**[32] 5766 3-8-12 **88** SteveDrowne 4 91
(R Charlton) *chsd ldrs: rdn and effrt jst over 2f out: drvn and ev ch ent fnl f tl wknd fnl 100yds* **11/1**

0056 **5** *1¼* **King's Wonder**[29] 5874 4-8-13 **87** HayleyTurner 11 87
(W R Muir) *chsd ldrs: wnt 2nd 3f out tl over 1f out: drvn and nt qckn ent fnl f: wknd ins fnl f* **14/1**

6001 **6** *shd* **Desert Dreamer (IRE)**[15] 6278 8-8-11 **85** CatherineGannon 6 85+
(P D Evans) *taken down early: hld up in rr: stl 11th whn nt clr run jst over 1f out: r.o fnl f: nvr trbld ldrs* **20/1**

0422 **7** *shd* **Satwa Laird**[16] 6243 3-8-11 **87** TPQueally 5 86
(E A L Dunlop) *hld up in rr: rdn and effrt 2f out: drvn over 1f out: kpt on but nvr pce to rch ldrs* **7/1**[3]

-110 **8** *hd* **Crown Choice**[29] 5874 4-9-2 **90** AdamKirby 2 89+
(W R Swinburn) *in tch on inner : shuffled bk and lost pl over 2f out: switching out rt fr 2f out: kpt on fnl f but nvr able to chal* **10/1**

1410 **9** *hd* **Without Prejudice (USA)**[15] 6270 4-8-11 **88** (v) FrederikTylicki(3) 7 87
(J Noseda) *chsd ldr tl led 3f out: rdn ent fnl 2f: hdd 1f out: wknd ins fnl f* **4/1**[2]

0050 **10** *hd* **Archie Rice (USA)**[30] 5832 3-8-6 **82** LiamJones 10 79
(W Jarvis) *racd in midfield: rdn over 2f out: no prog* **20/1**

0500 **11** *2¼* **Internationaldebut (IRE)**[31] 5799 4-9-2 **90** JohnEgan 8 82
(J Balding) *t.k.h: hld up in tch in rr: c towards outer over 2f out: rdn and no prog fr wl over 1f out* **14/1**

20-0 **12** *1* **Oratory (IRE)**[35] 5695 3-9-4 **94** ShaneKelly 9 82
(R Hannon) *s.i.s: sn rdn along and nvr gng: n.d* **8/1**

1000 **13** *16* **Cordell (IRE)**[2] 6633 4-9-4 **92** PaulDoe 3 38
(R Ingram) *sn rdn up to ld: hdd 3f out and immediately dropped out: wl bhd fnl 2f* **33/1**

1m 23.88s (-0.92) **Going Correction** +0.075s/f (Slow)
WFA 3 from 4yo+ 2lb **13** Ran SP% **124.7**
Speed ratings (Par 107): **108,106,106,105,103 103,103,103,102,102 100,98,80**
toteswingers: 1&2 £34.50, 1&3 £9.10, 2&3 £19.20 CSF £193.12 CT £809.82 TOTE £11.90: £2.60, £8.90, £1.90; EX 316.60 TRIFECTA Not won..
Owner Dr Marwan Koukash **Bred** John James **Trained** Musley Bank, N Yorks

FOCUS
A good, competitive handicap, and the pace seemed fair enough by this track's usual standards. Improved form from the winner back on Polytrack.

NOTEBOOK
Kyllachy Star's improvement looked to have levelled off recently, but in fairness he shaped quite well at Ayr on his latest start and built on that with what must be a career-best performance. A tough colt, there could well be better to come again. (op 9-1)
Spirit Of Sharjah(IRE) briefly looked the winner about 1f out but tired late on. This was a good effort considering he was drawn in stall 12 and was a little keen early. (op 28-1)
Prescription's outside draw meant she was stuck slightly wider than ideal, but she by no means endured a terrible trip. Whatever the case, this was still a useful effort under top weight and the distance (only her second try at 7f) wasn't an issue. (op 3-1 tchd 4-1)
Broad Cairn, trying Polytrack for the first time, left behind a disappointing run at Doncaster. He seemed to have his chance but wasn't quite good enough. (tchd 10-1)
King's Wonder was another far from ideally drawn but he managed to get a decent enough pitch. He's probably high enough in the weights. (op 16-1 tchd 12-1)
Desert Dreamer(IRE), 4lb higher than when winning at Chester, made up a lot of ground late on and would have been even closer with a clearer run. He's a hold-up horse who needs the leaders to come back to him, and this occasion that didn't happen fast enough, but he still ran well. Official explanation: jockey said gelding was denied a clear run
Crown Choice, the winner of both his previous starts on Polytrack (at Kempton), is better than he showed as he lost his place at a crucial stage. (op 7-1)
Without Prejudice(USA) dropped away disappointingly. (op 5-1 tchd 11-2)
Cordell(IRE) Official explanation: jockey said gelding stopped quickly

6703 TRY BETDAQ FOR AN EXCHANGE (S) STKS 1m (P)

4:10 (4:13) (Class 6) 3-Y-O+ **£2,047** (£604; £302) **Stalls** High

Form RPR

3000 **1** **Ocean Legend (IRE)**[12] 6361 4-8-13 63 CatherineGannon 3 73
(Miss J Feilden) *t.k.h: hld up towards rr of main gp: hdwy to chse ldrs 2f out: swtchd rt ent fnl f: r.o wl to ld wl ins fnl f* **13/2**

0006 **2** *1¼* **Geezers Colours**[83] 4154 4-8-8 80 MartinLane(5) 7 70
(A P Jarvis) *chsd ldrs: hdwy to chse ldr over 2f out: ev ch and wanting to hang lft over 1f out: nt pce of wnr wl ins fnl f* **11/4**[1]

2250 **3** *nk* **Northern Desert (IRE)**[37] 5634 10-9-4 68 (p) PaulDoe 11 74
(S Curran) *in tch: hdwy to chse ldrs over 2f out: rdn and led narrowly jst over 1f out: hdd and nt pce of wnr wl ins fnl f: lost 2nd nr fin* **11/1**

4600 **4** *2* **Dream Of Fortune (IRE)**[10] 6435 5-8-13 78 (t) JamieJones(5) 1 69
(M G Quinlan) *s.i.s: hld up in rr of main gp: nt clr run bnd jst over 2f out: hdwy and rdn over 1f out: chsd ldng trio ins fnl f: nvr pce to chal* **6/1**

0630 **5** *shd* **Fiefdom (IRE)**[19] 6178 7-8-6 69.. IJBrennan(7) 4 64
(I W McInnes) *hld up in rr of main gp: rdn 2f out: wanting to hang lft over 1f out: styd on fnl f: nvr trbld ldrs* **9/2**[3]

3160 **6** *2 3/4* **Dabbers Ridge (IRE)**[18] 6217 7-8-13 67............ AndrewHeffernan(5) 10 62
(I W McInnes) *t.k.h: chsd ldr tl led 3f out: rdn and hdd jst over 1f out: wknd fnl f* **16/1**

6044 **7** *3/4* **Digger Derek (IRE)**[23] 6052 3-8-10 60........................ PaulHanagan 5 56
(R A Fahey) *t.k.h: chsd ldrs tl rdn and outpcd over 2f out: no ch w ldrs fr over 1 fout* **4/1**[2]

2050 **8** *1 1/2* **Bookiebasher Babe (IRE)**[13] 6346 4-8-13 71.............. FrancisNorton 8 52
(M Quinn) *sn pushed up to ld: hdd 3f out: sn rdn : wknd over 2f out* **12/1**

00 **9** *14* **Copper Sovereign**[33] 5747 7-8-13 0.............................. SteveDrowne 12 18
(Jamie Poulton) *slwoly into stride: a wl bhd in last pair* **66/1**

10 *2 3/4* **Escape Wall**[616] 8-8-10 0.. WilliamCarson(3) 6 12
(R J Hodges) *v.s.a: a wl bhd in last* **100/1**

1m 39.6s (1.40) **Going Correction** +0.075s/f (Slow)
WFA 3 from 4yo+ 3lb **10** Ran SP% **116.9**
Speed ratings (Par 101): **96,94,94,92,92 89,88,87,73,70**
toteswingers: 1&2 £5.10, 1&3 £12.90, 2&3 £6.20 CSF £24.75 TOTE £8.20: £2.50, £1.50, £3.10; EX 32.10 TRIFECTA Not won..There was no bid for the winner.
Owner Ocean Trailers Ltd **Bred** Mark Commins **Trained** Exning, Suffolk

FOCUS
A reasonable race for the grade at face value but there were doubts over plenty of these. The form makes sense.

6704 HOLLOW LANE H'CAP — 1m 5f (P)
4:45 (4:47) (Class 5) (0-75,80) 3-Y-O+ **£3,238** (£963; £481; £240) **Stalls Low**

Form RPR

4465 **1** **Bell Island**[33] 5740 5-9-5 67..(v) SebSanders 10 75
(Lady Herries) *chsd ldrs tl wnt 2nd 10f out: rdn over 2f out: clsd on ldr ins fnl f: pushed ahd towards fin* **5/1**[3]

5216 **2** *1/2* **Jadalee (IRE)**[16] 6258 6-9-12 74................................(tp) HayleyTurner 12 81
(G A Butler) *taken down early: chsd ldr tl led after 1f: clr 9f out: rdn 2f out: edgd rt u.p fnl f: hdd towards fin* **4/1**[2]

3521 **3** *1 1/2* **Buckie Boy (IRE)**[11] 6375 3-9-10 80................................. TPQueally 11 85
(H R A Cecil) *dwlt and bustled along early:racd in midfield: hdwy to chse clr ldng pair 3f out: rdn ent fnl 2f: plugged on same pce u.p after* **11/4**[1]

6620 **4** *nk* **Little Carmela**[24] 6025 5-8-10 58.................................... SaleemGolam 9 62
(S C Williams) *s.i.s: towards rr: pushed along 5f out: hdwy into midfield but stl wl off the pce 3f out: kpt plugging on to chse ldrs over 1f out: pressing for 3rd nr fin* **14/1**

6514 **5** *9* **Trachonitis (IRE)**[18] 6204 5-9-8 70............................ AdrianMcCarthy 4 61
(J R Jenkins) *stdd s: hld up in rr: hedaway over 3f out: chsd ldrs and rdn on inner wl over 1f out: no prog and wknd fnl f* **8/1**

13 **6** *2 1/2* **Sheila's Castle**[40] 5545 5-8-12 65............................... LeeNewnes(5) 6 52
(S Regan) *t.k.h: hld up off the pce towards rr: rdn and effrt on outer 3f out: no prog u.p 2f out: wl btn fnl f* **17/2**

7 *8* **Gamedor (FR)**[113] 4-9-5 67.. GeorgeBaker 7 42
(G L Moore) *stdd s: hld up in rr: hdwy on outer 3f out: drvn and no prog 2f out: wl btn fnl f* **9/1**

3650 **8** *1 1/4* **Zalkani (IRE)**[13] 6342 9-8-3 56.............................. SimonPearce(5) 1 29
(J Pearce) *stdd s: hld up in rr: rdn and no prog over 2f out:nvr a factor* **20/1**

4440 **9** *1 3/4* **Nawamees (IRE)**[5] 6560 11-8-13 61..............................(p) PaulHanagan 5 32
(P D Evans) *led for 1f: chsd ldr tl 10f out: chsd ldrs after tl wknd u.p over 2f out* **14/1**

0 **10** *7* **Father Figure (USA)**[15] 6287 3-8-9 65.......................... SteveDrowne 3 25
(Heather Dalton) *racd in midfield: rdn over 4f out: wl bhd fnl 2f* **40/1**

600P **11** *16* **Mixing**[17] 6226 7-8-1 56 oh2.. KierenFox(7) 8 —
(M J Attwater) *racd in midfield: rdn and lost pl 5f out: wl bhd fnl 3f: t.o* **33/1**

2m 45.94s (-0.06) **Going Correction** +0.075s/f (Slow)
WFA 3 from 4yo+ 8lb **11** Ran SP% **118.4**
Speed ratings (Par 103): **103,102,101,101,96 94,89,88,87,83 73**
oteswingers: 1&2 £6.00, 1&3 £4.10, 2&3 £3.80 CSF £25.01 CT £66.73 TOTE £6.20: £1.90, £1.80, £1.80; EX 25.50 Trifecta £43.70 Pool: £411.39 - 6.96 winning units..
Owner L G Lazarus **Bred** Juddmonte Farms Ltd **Trained** Patching, W Sussex
■ Stewards' Enquiry : Hayley Turner one-day ban: used whip with excessive frequency (Oct 26)

FOCUS
A modest staying handicap run at a good pace. Ordinary but sound form.
Mixing Official explanation: trainer said gelding bled from the nose

6705 DORMANSLAND APPRENTICE H'CAP — 1m 2f (P)
5:20 (5:20) (Class 6) (0-60,61) 3-Y-O **£1,942** (£578; £288; £144) **Stalls Low**

Form RPR

6005 **1** **Mellow Mixture**[25] 5988 3-9-2 57...................................(t) LeeNewnes 7 65
(S Kirk) *in tch towards rr: gd hdwy on outer over 3f out: clr w runner up 2f out: led over 1f out: clr fnl f: pushed out* **7/1**[3]

2401 **2** *2 1/2* **Transformer (IRE)**[9] 6439 3-9-6 61.................................(p) JPFahy 13 64
(W J Knight) *chaesd ldr 9f out: led over 2f out: clr w wnr and rdn 2f out: hdd and drvn over 1f out: btn 1f out: jst hld on for 2nd* **5/2**[1]

4440 **3** *shd* **Location**[5] 6570 3-8-9 53.. HollyHall(3) 6 58+
(P D Evans) *racd in last trio: hdwy whn sltly hmpd bnd 2f out: str run on outer ent fnl f: nrly snatched 2nd: nvr gng to rch wnr* **12/1**

6032 **4** *1/2* **Triple Cee (IRE)**[13] 6338 3-9-5 60................................. IJBrennan 14 62
(M R Channon) *hld up in tch: rdn to chse clr ldng pair 2f out: edgd rt u.p wl over 1f out: kpt on fnl f: nvr a threat to wnr* **5/1**[2]

503 **5** *hd* **Persian Tomcat (IRE)**[9] 6440 3-8-2 50............(v[1]) MatthewCosham(7) 5 51
(Miss J Feilden) *hld up in tch in midfield: n.m.r and swtchd rt over 2f out: chsng clr ldrs and carried rt wl over 1f out: kpt on but nvr pce to chal wnr* **9/1**

0044 **6** *6* **Bicksta**[25] 5983 3-8-9 50..(v) JPHamblett 1 39
(E F Vaughan) *led tl 9f out: chsd ldrs after: rdn and struggling to hold pl whn jostled bnd 2f out: wl hld after* **12/1**

060 **7** *1 3/4* **Laura Land**[41] 5531 3-8-8 52.............................. RichardRowe(3) 12 38
(W M Brisbourne) *s.i.s: hdwy on outer to chse ldrs over 8f out tl 2f out: sn wknd* **20/1**

5040 **8** *1/2* **Kristopher James (IRE)**[46] 5331 3-8-12 53.................. TobyAtkinson 9 38
(W M Brisbourne) *t.k.h: hld up in tch towards rr: rdn over 4f out: hmpd and dropped to last over 3f out: n.d after: sme hdwy fnl f* **12/1**

3405 **9** *nk* **Join Up**[9] 6439 3-8-3 49...................................... AlexEdwards(5) 4 33
(W M Brisbourne) *t.k.h: led 9f tl 6f out: sn wknd: sddle slipped* **11/1**

0000 **10** *3 1/4* **Errol Flynn (IRE)**[8] 5381 3-8-11 52 ow2....................(t) KylieManser 2 30
(B G Powell) *a rr and rn in snatches: nvr trbld ldrs* **66/1**

600 **11** *1/2* **Innactualfact**[156] 1834 3-9-5 60..................................(p) SimonPearce 8 37
(L A Dace) *t.k.h: hld up in tch in midfield: rdn whn hmpd bnd 2f out: no ch after* **25/1**

010 **12** *1* **Molly The Witch (IRE)**[22] 6124 3-8-9 57..................... RosePearson(7) 3 32
(W J Musson) *in tch in midfield: shuffled bk over 2f out: n.d fnl 2f* **16/1**

5060 **13** *8* **Suhailah**[25] 5988 3-8-11 55...(p) KierenFox(3) 11 14
(M J Attwater) *chsd ldrs tl rdn and losing pl whn hmpd over 2f out:: wl bhd fnl 2f* **40/1**

0-20 **14** *1 1/2* **Prince Andjo (USA)**[179] 1281 3-9-5 60.................(t) AndrewHeffernan 10 16
(I W McInnes) *stdd s: t.k.h: hld up in rr: rdn and effrt on outer over 2f out: sn struggling: nvr a factor* **20/1**

2m 8.45s (1.85) **Going Correction** +0.075s/f (Slow) **14** Ran SP% **122.3**
Speed ratings (Par 99): **95,93,92,92,92 87,86,85,85,82 82,81,75,74**
toteswingers: 1&2 £11.60, 1&3 £4.80, 2&3 £14.80 CSF £23.60 CT £216.91 TOTE £8.40: £2.30, £1.30, £4.00; EX 29.10 Trifecta £220.70 Part won. Pool: £298.31 - 0.46 winning units. Place 6: £11.97 Place 5: £7.44.
Owner Ben CM Wong **Bred** Paramount Bloodstock **Trained** Upper Lambourn, Berks

FOCUS
A moderate handicap for apprentices who had not ridden more than 25 winners. Somewhat muddling form.
T/Plt: £9.80 to a £1 stake. Pool: £57,999.55. 4,286.64 winning tickets. T/Qpdt: £4.40 to a £1 stake. Pool: £5,165.94. 859.90 winning tickets. SP

6706 - (Foreign Racing) - See Raceform Interactive

[6315] CURRAGH (R-H)
Sunday, October 11

OFFICIAL GOING: Soft
The ground changed to soft following 2.9mm of rain overnight which led to 25 non-runners primarily due to the ground.

6707a GO RACING IN KILDARE FESTIVAL WATERFORD TESTIMONIAL STKS (LISTED RACE) — 6f
3:00 (3:01) 3-Y-O+ **£26,861** (£7,881; £3,754; £1,279)

RPR

1 **Rayeni (IRE)**[28] 5924 3-9-2 113....................................... MJKinane 4 107+
(John M Oxx, Ire) *led and disp: 2nd 1/2-way: led 2 1/2f out: rdn and hdd 1 1/2f out: led again 1f out: disp fnl f: asserted cl home* **5/4**[1]

2 *nk* **Luisant**[14] 6320 6-9-3 103.. WJSupple 14 106
(J A Nash, Ire) *hld up: hdwy to 5th 1/2-way: 3rd 2f out: rdn to chal 1f out: disp fnl f: no ex cl home* **14/1**

3 *4 1/2* **Genki (IRE)**[22] 6091 5-9-3 .... KJManning 12 92
(R Charlton) *mid-div: hdwy in 7th 1/2-way: 4th 2f out: rdn over 1f out: kpt on same pce fnl f: no imp on ldrs* **7/2**[2]

4 *shd* **Perfect Polly**[42] 5491 4-9-3 104................................. DPMcDonogh 5 91
(James M Ryan, Ire) *chsd ldrs: 3rd 1/2-way: impr to chal 2f out: led 1 1/2f out: rdn and hdd 1f out: no ex and kpt on same pce fnl f* **6/1**[3]

5 *3/4* **Russian Empress (IRE)**[14] 6315 5-9-0 94............................ RMBurke 1 86
(David P Myerscough, Ire) *s.i.s: sn chsd ldrs: 4th 1/2-way: rdn in 5th 1 1/2f out: kpt on same pce fr over 1f out* **33/1**

6 *nk* **Six Of Hearts**[14] 6320 5-9-3 94..(p) JAHeffernan 11 88
(Cecil Ross, Ire) *hld up towards rr: sme late hdwy in 9th 1f out: kpt on same pce fnl f* **20/1**

7 *nk* **Three Way Stretch (IRE)**[14] 6320 3-9-2 86....................(b[1]) DMGrant 2 87
(J T Gorman, Ire) *chsd ldrs: lost pl 1/2-way: rdn 2f out: 8th 1f out: kpt on same pce fnl f* **50/1**

8 *1* **Snaefell (IRE)**[28] 5921 5-9-8 108.....................................(b) FMBerry 10 89
(M Halford, Ire) *mid-div: 8th 2f out: rdn in 7th 1f out: no ex fnl f* **7/1**

9 *1 1/4* **Ohiyesa (IRE)**[14] 6315 3-8-13 94.....................................(b[1]) KLatham 13 77
(G M Lyons, Ire) *sn chsd ldrs: 6th 1/2-way: rdn 2f out: no ex over 1f out* **20/1**

10 *5 1/2* **Cnocan Gold (IRE)**[132] 2555 3-8-13 92............................... PJSmullen 6 59
(D K Weld, Ire) *a towards rr* **16/1**

11 *2* **Le Cadre Noir (IRE)**[168] 1543 5-9-3 104........................ PShanahan 15 56
(D K Weld, Ire) *hld up towards rr: clsr in 8th 1/2-way: 7th 2f out: rdn in 8th 1 1/2f out: sn no ex* **10/1**

12 *5 1/2* **Gluteus Maximus (IRE)**[2] 6649 3-9-2 92...........................(b) JMurtagh 3 38
(A P O'Brien, Ire) *chsd ldr in cl 2nd: led after 2f: rdn and hdd 2 1/2f out: sn wknd* **16/1**

1m 15.28s (0.58) **Going Correction** +0.375s/f (Good)
WFA 3 from 4yo+ 1lb **12** Ran SP% **135.4**
Speed ratings: **111,110,104,104,103 103,102,101,99,92 89,82**
CSF £26.22 TOTE £2.20: £1.10, £5.90, £1.50; DF 25.60.
Owner H H Aga Khan **Bred** Hh The Aga Khan's Studs Sc **Trained** Currabeg, Co Kildare

FOCUS
The runner-up has been rated to his AW best, with the seventh closer to his juvenile level.

NOTEBOOK
Rayeni(IRE) registered a battling success. The drop back to this trip wasn't guaranteed to suit, but he showed plenty of early speed and then got into top gear inside the final furlong when the runner-up headed him to get back up to win on the line. A step back up to 7f will suit him ideally. (op 5/4 tchd 11/8)
Luisant ran the race of his career and showed that this is probably his optimum trip. Racing handily, he travelled to challenge and led inside the last before being outpointed close home. He is one to look forward to next year as an improving horse. The way he pulled clear of the remainder showed this to be a high-class display.
Genki(IRE) ran respectably but probably below his best. Covered up behind the leaders, he didn't have the pace to mount a challenge when asked and the first two pulled clear of him inside the last. There didn't appear to be too many excuses. (op 9/2)
Perfect Polly travelled well to be in a challenging position over a furlong out. She ran out of steam a little bit up the hill, though, giving the impression that 5f might be her optimum trip. (op 8/1)
Russian Empress(IRE) ran above her rating, but she might be flattered by her proximity, which was probably helped by her draw next to the rails. She ran on well inside the last but was never really competitive.
Six Of Hearts did his best work late.
Three Way Stretch(IRE) showed a good bit of early pace.
Snaefell(IRE) did not enjoy the best of luck in running but may just have been feeling the effects of a long season. (op 6/1)

Le Cadre Noir(IRE) was very disappointing and was sending out the distress signals well over a furlong from the finish. (op 8/1)

6708a LANWADES & STAFFORDSTOWN STUDS STKS (LISTED RACE) (FILLIES) 1m

3:30 (3:30) 2-Y-O £29,389 (£8,622; £4,108; £1,399)

				RPR
1		**Lady Lupus (IRE)**[4] 6600 2-8-12 ... JMurtagh 5		98
		(A P O'Brien, Ire) *chsd ldr in 2nd: pushed along 3f out: rdn 2f out: stdy on to chal 1f out: sn led: kpt on wl u.p fnl f*	**9/2**	
2	3/4	**Atasari (IRE)**[15] 6299 2-8-12 88 ... DEMullins 6		96
		(J S Bolger, Ire) *led: rdn 2f out: chal 1f out: sn hdd: no ex and kpt on same pce*	**8/1**	
3	1 1/2	**Akdarena**[28] 5922 2-8-12 92 ... KJManning 7		93
		(J S Bolger, Ire) *chsd ldrs: 5th 1/2-way: rdn 2f out: styd on to 3rd 1f out: no imp ldrs fnl f: kpt on same pce*	**3/1**[2]	
4	4	**Berg Bahn (IRE)**[19] 6193 2-8-12 ... KLatham 1		84
		(G M Lyons, Ire) *hld up: clsr in 6th 3f out: rdn 1 1/2f out: 4th 1f out: no ex fnl f and kpt on same pce*	**7/2**[3]	
5	1/2	**Crystal Gal (IRE)**[14] 6319 2-8-12 ... DPMcDonogh 3		83
		(Kevin Prendergast, Ire) *chsd ldrs: 4th 1/2-way: rdn 2f out: no ex in 5th 1f out: kpt on same pce*	**9/4**[1]	
6	2 1/2	**Cornakill (USA)**[14] 6316 2-8-12 89 ... CDHayes 8		78
		(Kevin Prendergast, Ire) *chsd ldrs: 3rd 1/2-way: rdn 2f out: no ex over 1f out*	**10/1**	
7	1/2	**Moonlight Rock (IRE)**[13] 6350 2-8-12 ... WJSupple 2		77
		(P D Deegan, Ire) *hld up: rdn in 7th 2f out: no imp and kpt on one pce*	**20/1**	
8	25	**Lombrici (IRE)**[7] 6514 2-8-12 ... NGMcCullagh 10		22
		(M J Grassick, Ire) *hld up: trailing 3f out: t.o*	**66/1**	

1m 47.18s (5.28) **Going Correction** +0.675s/f (Yiel) **8** Ran SP% **122.6**
Speed ratings: **100,99,97,93,93 90,90,65**
CSF £43.00 TOTE £4.70: £1.70, £2.50, £1.10; DF 53.70.
Owner Mrs A M O'Brien **Bred** Whisperview Trading Ltd **Trained** Ballydoyle, Co Tipperary

FOCUS
This may have been a Listed contest but it looked an ordinary one.

NOTEBOOK
Lady Lupus(IRE) had looked reasonably exposed, having been beaten in a Navan maiden last Wednesday. She showed a good attitude here, though, tracking the runner-up most of the way and running on well inside the last to get up, having had to be switched to the inside. Once again she ran into a bit of trouble in running, as she did the previous Wednesday, but got out of it this time. She will stay middle distances without much trouble next season. (op 5/1 tchd 6/1)
Atasari(IRE) attempted to make all and stuck to her task very well. However, having won a nursery off 82 last time, it probably puts the quality of this contest into some sort of perspective. The step up to a mile, though, has brought improvement from this filly and she can be considered a bit unlucky to be worn down close home. (op 11/1)
Akdarena ran a perfectly respectable race and, even at this stage, is crying out for a trip in excess of a mile. Caught a little bit for tactical speed in the straight, she kept staying on all the way to the line and was never nearer. (op 4/1)
Berg Bahn(IRE) betrayed a little bit of inexperience late on and it would be no real surprise if she proved to be the filly to take out of this race in due course. She travelled quite well most of the way and began her effort early in the straight, which saw her with every chance a furlong out. Her effort flattened out up the hill, but she still ran a little bit green. (op 7/2 tchd 3/1)
Crystal Gal(IRE) looked a potentially decent filly when landing something of a gamble on her debut at this track the previous month, but she hasn't really progressed in two runs since. She was handy enough most of the way and moved up to challenge in the straight, but found little inside the last furlong or so. (op 7/4)
Cornakill(USA) faded inside the last furlong, having travelled just behind the leaders to that point. (op 12/1)

6151 DUSSELDORF (R-H)

Sunday, October 11

OFFICIAL GOING: Soft

6713a GROSSER PREIS DER LANDESHAUPTSTADT DUSSELDORF (GROUP 3) 1m 110y

4:10 (4:21) 3-Y-O+ £31,068 (£12,621; £6,311; £3,398)

				RPR
1		**Schutzenjunker (GER)**[43] 5461 4-9-2 ... DPorcu 4		105
		(Uwe Ostmann, Germany) *made all, driven out*	**8/1**	
2	2 1/2	**Iolith (GER)**[42] 4-9-2 ... FilipMinarik 2		100
		(J Hirschberger, Germany) *disputed 2nd, 2nd straight, chasing winner and hard ridden over 1f out, one pace final f*	**17/5**[2]	
3	7	**Globus (GER)**[14] 6323 3-8-13 ... YLerner 5		85
		(Uwe Ostmann, Germany) *always in touch, 4th straight, went 3rd over 1f out, never near to challenge*	**58/10**[3]	
4	1	**Torres (GER)**[42] 3-8-13 ... VSchulepov 1		83
		(Frau E Mader, Germany) *mid-division, 6th straight, kept on one pace final 2f*	**13/1**	
5	3	**Ottomax (GER)**[77] 4-9-2 ... HGrewe 3		75
		(Andreas Lowe, Germany) *7th straight, never a factor*	**29/1**	
6	8	**Forthe Millionkiss (GER)**[84] 4129 5-9-2 ... RPiechulek 6		58
		(Uwe Ostmann, Germany) *disputed 2nd, 3rd straight, weakened well over 1f out*	**189/10**	
7	5	**Sehrezad (IRE)**[84] 4129 4-9-4 ... JiriPalik 7		49
		(Andreas Lowe, Germany) *in touch, 5th straight, weakened quickly*	**3/5**[1]	
8	9	**Caro Jina (FR)**[40] 5563 3-8-11 ... JBojko 8		26
		(A Trybuhl, Germany) *always towards rear, last & beaten straight*	**117/10**	

1m 46.8s (-0.78)
WFA 3 from 4yo+ 3lb **8** Ran SP% **134.4**
TOTE: WIN 90; PL 31, 28, 42; SF 285.
Owner W Busch **Bred** W Busch **Trained** Germany

6152 FRANKFURT (L-H)

Sunday, October 11

OFFICIAL GOING: Soft

6714a FRANKFURTER STUTENPREIS (GROUP 3) (F&M) 1m 2f 165y

3:20 (3:34) 3-Y-O+ £31,068 (£12,621; £6,311; £3,398)

				RPR
1		**Norderney (GER)**[21] 6152 3-8-11 ... AStarke 6		102
		(P Schiergen, Germany) *always prominent, 3rd straight, led inside final f, ridden out*	**13/10**[1]	
2	1 1/4	**Sworn Pro (GER)**[35] 3-8-11 ... AHelfenbein 7		100
		(Mario Hofer, Germany) *led til inside final furlong, kept on one pace*	**37/10**[2]	
3	nk	**Themelie Island (IRE)**[21] 6153 4-9-4 ... THellier 2		100
		(A Trybuhl, Germany) *a cl up: 4th st: wnt 3rd over 1f out: kpt on*	**101/10**	
4	1 1/4	**La Bamba (GER)**[14] 5-9-4 ... JVictoire 1		98
		(A Wohler, Germany) *6th st on ins: 4th over 1f out: one pce*	**37/10**[2]	
5	1 1/4	**Sakza (IRE)**[77] 4365 4-9-4 ... GMasure 4		96
		(M Delzangles, France) *mid-division, close 7th straight, one pace from over 1f out*	**237/10**	
6	1 3/4	**All Annalena (IRE)**[35] 3-8-11 ... NRichter 5		91
		(Andreas Lowe, Germany) *pressed leader, 2nd straight, no extra from well over 1f out*	**73/10**[3]	
7	hd	**Irish Queen (FR)**[59] 4969 3-8-11 ... DBoeuf 9		91
		(H-A Pantall, France) *mid-division, 5th straight on outside, soon one pace*	**74/10**	
8	1 3/4	**Promesse De L'Aube (FR)**[43] 5461 4-9-4 ...(b) AGoritz 3		89
		(P Schiergen, Germany) *a in rr*	**30/1**	
9	hd	**Lilia (GER)**[63] 5-9-4 ... APietsch 8		88
		(W Hickst, Germany) *a in rr*	**147/10**	

2m 24.37s (144.37)
WFA 3 from 4yo+ 6lb **9** Ran SP% **132.6**
TOTE: WIN 23; PL 17, 20, 25; SF 114.
Owner Gestut Bona **Bred** Gestut Bona **Trained** Germany

6153 SAN SIRO (R-H)

Sunday, October 11

OFFICIAL GOING: Soft

6715a PREMIO VERZIERE (GROUP 3) (F&M) 1m 2f

2:35 (2:37) 3-Y-O+ £43,340 (£20,467; £11,573; £5,786)

				RPR
1		**Cottonmouth (IRE)**[57] 5-9-0 ... NPinna 7		103
		(S Botti, Italy) *led over 4f: 2nd st: styd on far rail and led again 4f out: rdn out*	**41/20**[1]	
2	1 1/2	**Allegoria (IRE)**[7] 4-9-0 ... CColombi 9		100
		(V Valiani, Italy) *a in tch: 5th st: styd on far rail: r.o fnl 2f: nvr rchd wnr*	**165/10**	
3	1 1/4	**Lady Alida**[39] 5585 3-8-13 ... KKerekes 5		102
		(W Figge, Germany) *hld up: c to middle in st: hdwy over 1f out: r.o to take 3rd cl home*	**13/5**[3]	
4	shd	**Ephigenie (GER)**[21] 6152 3-8-9 ... SPasquier 6		97
		(T Mundry, Germany) *mid-div: 6th st: trckd gp ldr in middle: tk 4th 1f out: kpt on same pce*	**68/10**	
5	1	**Laguna Salada (IRE)**[140] 2310 3-8-9 ... SLandi 2		95
		(R Feligioni, Italy) *pressed wnr on outside tl led over 5f out: c to middle ent st: hdd 4f out: one pce fnl 2f*	**16/1**	
6	2	**Near Galante (GER)**[70] 4583 3-8-9 ... EPedroza 8		91
		(A Wohler, Germany) *prom: 3rd st: styd on far rail: one pce fr over 1f out*	**23/10**[2]	
7	2 1/4	**Makoto**[14] 4-9-0 ... GArena 10		87
		(B Grizzetti, Italy) *hld up: last st: hrd rdn and swished tail over 1f out: sme late prog*	**54/1**	
8	1	**Radhakunda**[483] 3076 4-9-0 ... OPeslier 4		85
		(C Laffon-Parias, France) *a towards rr*	**25/1**	
9	hd	**Balilla (ITY)**[14] 4-9-0 ... MDemuro 1		84
		(Laura Grizzetti, Italy) *prom: 5th st: btn over 1f out: eased*	**38/1**	
10	3/4	**Rosa Del Dubai (IRE)**[7] 4-9-0 ... DVargiu 3		83
		(B Grizzetti, Italy) *mid-div to st: bhd fnl 3f*	**67/10**	

2m 8.00s (1.30)
WFA 3 from 4yo+ 5lb **10** Ran SP% **136.5**
TOTE (including one euro stakes): WIN 3.05; PL 1.50, 2.88, 1.54; SF21.06.
Owner Effevi Snc **Bred** Cloneen Stud **Trained** Italy

6716a GRAN CRITERIUM (GROUP 1) (C&F) 1m

3:10 (3:16) 2-Y-O £178,121 (£92,960; £54,983; £27,492)

				RPR
1		**Hearts Of Fire**[37] 5652 2-8-11 ... OPeslier 9		117
		(Pat Eddery) *hld up: 9th st: hdwy fr over 2f out: led ins fnl f: r.o wl (2.36/1)*	**12/5**[2]	
2	nk	**Vale Of York (IRE)**[15] 6268 2-8-11 ... AhmedAjtebi 7		116
		(Saeed Bin Suroor) *led 1 1/2f: 2nd st: led 3f out: hdd ins fnl f: r.o*	**7/2**[3]	
3	5	**Mata Keranjang (USA)**[10] 6426 2-8-11 ... MDemuro 1		105
		(P F I Cole) *hld up: 8th st on outside: hdwy over 1f out: tk 3rd ins fnl f: nvr nr first two*	**63/10**	
4	3	**Ladiesandgentlemen (ITY)**[21] 2-8-11 ... SLandi 4		98
		(R Feligioni, Italy) *6th st: styd on one pce fnl 2f*	**29/1**	
5	4 1/2	**Marshade (ITY)**[21] 2-8-11 ... URispoli 10		89
		(S Botti, Italy) *7th st: rdn 2f out: nvr nr to chal*	**23/10**[1]	
6	2 1/4	**Blow Up (IRE)**[21] 2-8-11 ... GMarcelli 8		84
		(R Menichetti, Italy) *3rd st: rdn and btn wl over 1f out*	**92/10**	
7	nk	**Air Crew (USA)**[28] 2-8-11 ... LManiezzi 3		83
		(R Menichetti, Italy) *a towards rr*	**92/10**	
8	2 1/4	**Dancer Cat (ITY)**[21] 2-8-11 ... SUrru 5		78
		(B Grizzetti, Italy) *led after 1 1/2f to 3f out: bhd fnl 2f*	**58/10**	
9	1 3/4	**Fantastic Shift** 2-8-11 ... DVargiu 11		74
		(B Grizzetti, Italy) *plld hrd early: 6th st: btn 2f out*	**58/10**	

10 nk **Collesano (IRE)**[36] 2-8-11 .... MMonteriso 6 73
(R Biondi, Italy) *prom: 4th st: btn 2f out* **97/10**

11 3 ¼ **Davie's Story** 2-8-11 .... SPasquier 2 66
(B Grizzetti, Italy) *a bhd* **58/10**

1m 38.9s (-3.20) **11** Ran SP% **172.0**
WIN 3.36; PL 1.48, 1.66, 1.82; DF 10.80.
Owner Pat Eddery Racing (Detroit) **Bred** Bearstone Stud **Trained** Nether Winchendon, Bucks

NOTEBOOK
Hearts Of Fire, who won a Group 3 in Germany last time out, stayed on well from well off the pace to run down the long-time leader inside the last. He provided Pat Eddery with his first Group 1 winner as a trainer, and may return to Italy next season for the Guineas.
Vale Of York(IRE), third in the Royal Lodge last time out, made most of the running but was worn down late on. The ground might have been softer than ideal for this son of Invincible Spirit.
Mata Keranjang(USA), third in the Somerville Tattersall Stakes last time out, stayed on to take third without ever really threatening to win. He boasts an official rating of 104 but remains a maiden.

6717a PREMIO SERGIO CUMANI (GROUP 3) (F&M) 1m
3:55 (3:56) 3-Y-0+ **£43,184** (£20,350; £11,495; £5,748)

RPR

1 **Ravenel (GER)**[14] 3-8-9 .... MEsposito 5 99
(R Rohne, Germany) *led after 1f, made rest, driven out (12.69/1)* **127/10**

2 nk **Annabelle's Charm (IRE)**[15] [6267] 4-8-13 .... JamieSpencer 7 99
(L M Cumani) *held up, last straight, headway on inside over 2f out, driven final f to take 2nd 150yds out, ran on* **67/10**

3 ½ **Fabiana**[126] [2757] 3-8-9 .... GBietolini 9 97
(Andreas Lowe, Germany) *mid-division, 7th straight, ridden 2f out, stayed on dwon outside, nearest at finish* **11/2**[3]

4 1 ¾ **Emergency**[35] [5709] 3-8-9 .... SPasquier 4 93
(D Smaga, France) *held up, 9th straight, 10th & switched outside 2f out, driven well over 1f out, kept on to take 4th well inside final f* **11/20**[1]

5 snk **My Sweet Baby (USA)**[14] 3-8-13 .... LManiezzi 2 96
(R Menichetti, Italy) *4th straight, one pace final 2f* **122/10**

6 2 **Silent Sunday (IRE)**[20] [6176] 4-8-13 .... MGuyon 11 89
(H-A Pantall, France) *in rear to straight, stayed on from over 1f out, never dangerous* **137/10**

7 hd **Vattene (IRE)**[98] 4-8-13 .... MMonteriso 10 88
(M Gasparini, Italy) *never nearer than mid-division* **237/10**

8 1 ¼ **Alta Fedelta**[14] 3-8-9 .... MDemuro 1 85
(V Caruso, Italy) *6th straight on inside, headway to go 2nd over 2f out, weakened inside final f, eased* **51/10**[2]

9 6 **Zaya (GER)**[28] 4-8-13 .... EPedroza 6 72
(A Wohler, Germany) *5th straight on outside, beaten over 2f out* **215/10**

10 ¾ **L'Indiscreta**[119] 4-9-2 .... DVargiu 3 73
(B Grizzetti, Italy) *led 1f, 3rd straight, weakened well over 1f out* **51/1**

11 ½ **Magritte (ITY)**[140] 4-8-13 .... GMarcelli 8 69
(R Menichetti, Italy) *prominent, 2nd straight, ridden & weakened quickly well over 1f out* **122/10**

1m 39.4s (-2.70)
WFA 3 from 4yo 3lb **11** Ran SP% **149.0**
WIN 13.69; PL 3.68, 3.09, 2.93; SF 73.87.
Owner Gestut Ohlerweiherhof **Bred** Gestut Ohlerweiherhof **Trained** Germany

NOTEBOOK
Annabelle's Charm(IRE) had never run on ground this soft before but she is a daughter of Indian Ridge, stays further than this and, having been given a patient ride out the back, saw her race out strongly to take second.

6718a PREMIO VITTORIO DI CAPUA (GROUP 1) 1m
4:25 (4:28) 3-Y-0+ **£158,102** (£78,018; £45,022; £22,511)

RPR

1 **Gladiatorus (USA)**[35] [5710] 4-9-0 .... AhmedAjtebi 11 115
(Saeed Bin Suroor) *led after 1f, 3 lengths clear 2f out, ridden out, unchallenged (1.83/1)* **9/5**[1]

2 4 ½ **Win For Sure (GER)**[35] 4-9-0 .... EPedroza 7 104
(A Wohler, Germany) *always in touch, 5th straight, went 2nd over 3f out, 3 lengths down 2f out, never able to threaten winner* **48/10**

3 hd **Rockhorse (IRE)**[98] 4-9-0 .... DVargiu 2 104
(B Grizzetti, Italy) *led 1f, 2nd straight, outpaced over 2f out, rallied to regain 3rd 1f out, ran on* **45/1**

4 ¾ **King Of Sydney (USA)**[39] [5585] 3-8-10 .... MGuyon 1 101
(Mario Hofer, Germany) *7th straight on inside, 6th & ridden 1f out, never nearer* **123/10**

5 1 ½ **Major Cadeaux**[21] [6135] 5-9-0 .... OPeslier 8 99
(R A Fahey) *towards rear to straight, kept on from over 2f out, disputed 4th 1f out, one pace* **53/10**

6 shd **Blue Coral (IRE)**[21] 5-9-0 .... MTellini 6 99
(T Satra, Czech Republic) *towards rear to straight, some headway final 2f, never nearer* **33/1**

7 ½ **Freemusic (IRE)**[119] [2955] 5-9-0 .... GMarcelli 5 97
(L Riccardi, Italy) *behind to straight, last 4f out, never a factor* **28/1**

8 hd **Precious Boy (GER)**[57] [5059] 4-9-0 .... ASuborics 3 97
(W Hickst, Germany) *held up, 8th straight, soon pushed along, beaten over 2f out* **39/10**[2]

9 ¾ **Aspectus (IRE)**[40] [5563] 6-9-0 .... MDemuro 10 95
(T Mundry, Germany) *prominent, 3rd straight, beaten over 2f out* **154/10**

10 snk **Miles Gloriosus (USA)**[35] 6-9-0 .... LManiezzi 9 95
(R Menichetti, Italy) *6th straight on outside, 3rd 3f out til weakening over 1f out* **33/1**

11 dist **Wilside (IRE)**[39] [5588] 3-8-7 .... SPasquier 4 —
(M Delzangles, France) *prominent, 4th straight, soon weakened, tailed off* **9/2**[3]

1m 38.0s (-4.10)
WFA 3 from 4yo+ 3lb **11** Ran SP% **132.5**
WIN 2.83; PL 1.74, 2.50, 7.58; SF 23.18.
Owner Godolphin **Bred** Az Agr Le Ferriere Di Raponi Giampaolo **Trained** Newmarket, Suffolk

NOTEBOOK
Gladiatorus(USA), who won six times in Italy earlier in his career, bounced back to winning form on his return visit. Very effective on a turning track, he made most of the running and won easily, despite the ground being softer than ideal. There are no definite plans but he might have another run this season, and the Breeders' Cup Mile would be an attractive target as conditions would play to his strengths.
Major Cadeaux did not improve as expected from his Hamilton outing and never really threatened to land a major blow.

6607 KEMPTON (A.W) (R-H)
Monday, October 12

OFFICIAL GOING: Standard
Wind: Very moderate across Weather: Bright

6719 VISIT THE NEW SPREADEX.COM H'CAP (DIV I) 1m (P)
2:20 (2:21) (Class 6) (0-65,65) 3-Y-0+ **£1,706** (£503; £252) **Stalls** High

Form RPR

4345 1 **Red Suede Shoes**[12] [6370] 3-9-1 **65** .... (p) JamesMillman(3) 3 75
(B R Millman) *in tch: hdwy towards outer over 2f out: led appr fnl f: styd on strly* **5/1**[1]

2460 2 ¾ **Diamond Twister (USA)**[17] [6257] 3-9-0 **64** .... (t) MarcHalford(3) 13 72
(J R Best) *in rr tl: hdwy on ins over 2f out: styd on wl to chse wnr jst ins fnl f: edgd lft and no imp fnl 75yds* **11/2**[2]

0506 3 2 **Djalalabad (FR)**[19] [6213] 5-8-9 **53** ow1 .... (tp) MickyFenton 8 56
(Mrs C A Dunnett) *stmbld s: towards rr: hdwy over 2f out: swtchd lft to outside and styd on fr over 1f out: kpt on ins fnl f but nt trble ldng duo* **20/1**

-650 4 hd **Burnbrake**[150] [2039] 4-9-2 **60** .... RobertHavlin 11 63
(L Montague Hall) *chsd ldrs: rdn 2f out: nvr quite gng pce to chal over 1f out: one pce ins fnl f* **16/1**

3553 5 ½ **The Grey One (IRE)**[5] [6588] 6-9-1 **59** .... (p) KevinGhunowa 6 61
(J M Bradley) *chsd ldrs in 3rd: rdn to chse ldr 2f out: no imp on wnr 1f out: wknd ins fnl f* **5/1**[1]

0030 6 nse **Binfield (IRE)**[7] [6547] 4-9-4 **65** .... RussellKennemore(3) 5 67
(B G Powell) *led: 3 l clr 3f out: rdn 2f out: hdd appr fnl f and sn wknd* **10/1**

00-0 7 7 **Under Fire (IRE)**[18] [6224] 6-8-10 **57** .... JackDean(3) 9 42
(A W Carroll) *in rr: rdn on outside and sme hdwy 2f out: nvr rchd ldrs and wknd ins fnl f* **13/2**[3]

00-0 8 hd **Josr's Magic (IRE)**[16] [6288] 5-8-12 **56** .... TPO'Shea 7 40
(T E Powell) *in tch: rdn over 2f out: wknd over 1f out* **16/1**

421- 9 ½ **Sunny Spells**[389] [6044] 4-9-7 **65** .... SaleemGolam 4 48
(S C Williams) *a towards rr* **8/1**

0010 10 2 **Artesium**[19] [6213] 3-8-8 **55** .... LPKeniry 12 33
(Patrick Morris) *chsd ldrs: rdn over 2f out: sn btn* **16/1**

3000 11 2 **Takitwo**[19] [6213] 6-8-9 **53** .... SimonWhitworth 2 27
(P D Cundell) *chsd ldrs 5f: wkng towards rr whn n.m.r 2f out* **16/1**

0000 12 1 **Marmooq**[18] [6224] 6-9-5 **63** .... (e) LiamJones 1 34
(M J Attwater) *in tch on outside: rdn and effrt 3f out: wknd over 2f out* **14/1**

0-00 13 2 ½ **Professor Malone**[14] [6344] 4-8-7 **51** oh2 .... (p) SamHitchcott 10 16
(M S Tuck) *chsd ldr tl wknd over 2f out* **50/1**

1m 38.9s (-0.90) **Going Correction** 0.0s/f (Stan)
WFA 3 from 4yo+ 3lb **13** Ran SP% **119.2**
Speed ratings (Par 101): **104,103,101,101,100 100,93,93,92,90 88,87,85**
toteswingers: 1&2 £7.90, 1&3 £16.60, 2&3 £29.00 CSF £31.57 CT £530.24 TOTE £6.10: £1.50, £2.50, £7.40; EX 43.10.
Owner Essex Racing Club & Partners **Bred** Mrs M Campbell-Andenaes **Trained** Kentisbeare, Devon

FOCUS
An ordinary handicap won by an 11-race maiden, which underlines the weak nature of the contest. The pace was decent and the first six pulled a long way clear of the rest. The time was quicker than division 2 and the form is probably sound enough.

6720 VISIT THE NEW SPREADEX.COM H'CAP (DIV II) 1m (P)
2:55 (2:55) (Class 6) (0-65,65) 3-Y-0+ **£1,706** (£503; £252) **Stalls** High

Form RPR

0332 1 **Dinner Date**[16] [6288] 7-9-7 **65** .... LPKeniry 3 74
(T Keddy) *hld up in tch: hdwy travelling wl appr fnl 2f: led wl over 1f out: drvn out ins fnl f* **9/2**[2]

5105 2 1 ¼ **Having A Ball**[18] [6224] 5-9-6 **64** .... SimonWhitworth 9 70
(P D Cundell) *in rr: rdn over 2f out: hdwy over 1f out: styd on u.p fnl f: tk 2nd last strides but no imp on wnr* **7/1**

4444 3 hd **Freedom Fire (IRE)**[16] [6289] 3-9-1 **62** .... MickyFenton 4 68
(J M P Eustace) *trckd ldrs: slt ld ins fnl 2f: hdd wl over 1f out: styd chsng wnr tl last 2nd last strides* **7/2**[1]

0000 4 2 ¼ **Highland River**[22] [5444] 3-9-2 **63** .... RobertHavlin 10 63
(D R C Elsworth) *chsd ldrs: rdn over 2f out: styd on same pce fnl f* **28/1**

1115 5 hd **La Gifted**[1] [6699] 3-9-0 **61** .... SamHitchcott 11 61
(M R Channon) *chsd ldrs: rdn to chal fr 2f out: wknd 1f out: edgd lft u.p ins fnl f* **6/1**[3]

5060 6 1 **Inside Story (IRE)**[14] [6349] 7-9-4 **62** .... (b) RichardMullen 2 59
(C R Dore) *slowly away: in rr: rdn and hdwy over 1f out: styng on whn swtchd rt ins fnl f: one pce cl home* **16/1**

3002 7 hd **Ymir**[38] [5647] 3-8-8 **55** .... (p) LiamJones 6 52
(M J Attwater) *chsd ldrs: rdn over 2f out: wknd and edgd lft fnl f* **9/1**

6626 8 shd **Foxtrot Bravo (IRE)**[12] [6399] 3-8-13 **60** .... PaulHanagan 12 57
(Miss S L Davison) *led tl hdd jst ins fnl 2f: wknd fnl f* **8/1**

5400 9 ¾ **Lopinot (IRE)**[124] [2824] 6-9-4 **62** .... (v) GeorgeBaker 1 57
(M R Bosley) *t.k.h towards rr: racd towards outside: rdn and hung lft fr 2f out: nvr in contention* **12/1**

6060 10 1 ½ **Inside Trade (IRE)**[46] [5367] 3-8-9 **56** .... JerryO'Dwyer 8 47
(N P Mulholland) *s.i.s: sn mid-div: rdn 3f out: wknd fr 2f out* **25/1**

5600 11 3 ½ **Double Valentine**[12] [6394] 6-8-7 **49** .... PaulDoe 7 34
(R Ingram) *s.i.s: in rr: rdn and effrt on inner over 2f out: nvr in contention and sn wknd* **40/1**

-640 12 ¾ **Trusted Venture (USA)**[236] [586] 3-8-8 **58** .... MarcHalford(3) 5 39
(J R Best) *in rr: hung bdly lft and no ch fr over 2f out* **28/1**

1m 39.38s (-0.42) **Going Correction** 0.0s/f (Stan)
WFA 3 from 5yo+ 3lb **12** Ran SP% **115.1**
Speed ratings (Par 101): **102,100,100,98,98 97,96,96,96,94 91,90**
toteswingers: 1&2 £7.40, 1&3 £3.50, 2&3 £7.90 CSF £33.36 CT £123.54 TOTE £5.20: £1.40, £2.90, £1.90; EX 34.70.
Owner Mrs H Keddy **Bred** J M Greetham **Trained** Newmarket, Suffolk

FOCUS
The second division of a modest handicap. The pace was solid and the winner was fairly impressive. The form looks fairly straightforward.
Freedom Fire(IRE) Official explanation: jockey said the gelding hung right

Foxtrot Bravo(IRE) Official explanation: jockey said the gelding hung right

6721 SPREADEX SPORTS SPREAD BETTING EXPERTS CLAIMING STKS 1m (P)

3:25 (3:25) (Class 5) 2-Y-O **£2,590** (£770; £385; £192) **Stalls** High

Form RPR

6413 **1** **Al Khimiya (IRE)**[11] 6431 2-8-4 70 RichardMullen 13 58+
(S A Callaghan, U.S.A) *chsd ldr: led over 2f out: rdn over 1f out: styd on strly ins fnl f* **7/4**[1]

4000 **2** 1 ½ **Carnaval Court (IRE)**[13] 6366 2-8-6 60 ow2 (b[1]) LPKeniry 12 57
(A M Balding) *led tl hdd over 2f out: styd chsng wnr and kpt on u.p fnl f but a hld* **14/1**

4514 **3** 1 ¾ **Daniella De Bruijn (IRE)**[5] 6586 2-8-13 77 RobertHavlin 10 60
(A B Haynes) *chsd ldng pair thrght: rdn over 2f out: styd on same pce fr over 1f out* **4/1**[2]

0060 **4** nk **Alfalevva**[14] 6334 2-8-6 50 SamHitchcott 6 52
(M R Channon) *chsd ldrs: drvn along fr 3f out: styd on fnl 2f but nvr gng pce to trble ldng trio* **80/1**

3054 **5** 1 ¼ **Lady Lefroy (IRE)**[25] 6034 2-8-4 56 PaulHanagan 11 47
(R A Fahey) *chsd ldrs: rdn 3f out: outpcd 2f out: styd on again ins fnl f but nvr any danger* **16/1**

6 ½ **No One Likes Us** 2-8-6 0 PaulDoe 5 49+
(S Curran) *hmpd s: in rr tl hdwy over 2f out: green and nt clr run over 1f out: styd on strly ins fnl f: gng on cl home* **66/1**

0005 **7** 1 **Mrs Puff (IRE)**[21] 6169 2-7-13 47 MartinLane(5) 9 44
(P D Evans) *in rr: rdn and hdwy on outside 3f out: styd on fr over 1f out but nvr gng pce to get into contention* **50/1**

40U6 **8** hd **Proper Littlemadam**[32] 5811 2-8-7 64 JerryO'Dwyer 3 47
(M Botti) *chsd ldrs: rdn 3f out: wknd fnl f* **25/1**

6005 **9** ¾ **Sixpenny Moon (USA)**[5] 6586 2-8-6 56 (b) SaleemGolam 14 44
(R Hannon) *s.i.s: sn in tch: wknd over 2f out* **12/1**

0230 **10** 1 **Rainsborough**[18] 6228 2-8-13 68 JamesDoyle 4 50
(S Curran) *a in rr* **16/1**

46 **11** shd **Persona Non Grata (IRE)**[7] 6548 2-8-12 0 (b) LiamJones 7 48
(R Charlton) *in rr: hung lft on outside and rdn 3f out: no rspnse* **9/2**[3]

0356 **12** shd **George Baker (IRE)**[16] 6292 2-8-6 68 (p) MatthewDavies(5) 2 46
(George Baker) *in rr: effrt on ins over 2f out: nvr in contention and sn wknd* **10/1**

4061 **13** 3 **Rakhine (IRE)**[25] 6034 2-8-11 62 TPO'Shea 8 40
(P F I Cole) *in rr: rdn over 3f out and no rspnse* **14/1**

1m 39.68s (-0.12) **Going Correction** 0.0s/f (Stan) 13 Ran SP% **125.0**
Speed ratings (Par 95): **100,98,96,96,95 94,93,93,92,91 91,91,88**
toteswingers: 1&2 £10.00, 1&3 £2.90, 2&3 £13.60 CSF £31.62 TOTE £2.30: £1.10, £4.20, £1.80; EX 40.10.Al Khimiya claimed by S. Woodman for £6000.
Owner David F O'Rourke **Bred** Plantation Stud **Trained**

FOCUS
A modest claimer for juveniles. The first four were always prominent and nothing got into it from behind. The winner did not need to be near her best, with th second and fourth grounding the form.

NOTEBOOK
Al Khimiya(IRE) had a leading chance at the weights on her 7f claiming win here last month and was 4lb better off with Daniella De Bruijn for a 1l beating at Wolverhampton last time. She tracked the leader for most of the way, eased her way to the front inside the final 2f and scored in professional and fairly decisive style. She has a good attitude and decent cruising speed at this trip and should be able to win more races. (op 2-1 tchd 5-2)
Carnaval Court(IRE), fitted with first-time blinkers and switched to positive tactics, ran well. He may get punished for chasing home a rival with a 10lb higher rating but could have more to offer in headgear. (op 16-1 tchd 12-1)
Daniella De Bruijn(IRE) has hung and not looked entirely straightforward and was turned over at a short price in a 7f claimer her last Wednesday, but she ran a creditable race back up in trip and got near the form of her 8.5f Wolverhampton win early this month. She is fairly consistent but needs to improve to justify a mark of 77 in handicaps and her future depends on whether a few kinks can be ironed out. (tchd 7-2)
Alfalevva had not shown much at increasingly big prices in four maidens but put in a much better effort stepped up to 1m and switched to claiming company on her AW debut.
Lady Lefroy(IRE) lacked the pace to pose a threat.
No One Likes Us Official explanation: jockey said that the gelding hung left
Persona Non Grata(IRE) had a fair chance on adjusted figures but looked an uncooperative character and was never anywhere near the leaders. (op 5-1 tchd 4-1)
Rakhine(IRE) Official explanation: jockey said the gelding was never travelling

6722 SPREADEX 10TH ANNIVERSARY E B F MAIDEN FILLIES' STKS 6f (P)

4:00 (4:03) (Class 4) 2-Y-O **£4,533** (£1,348; £674; £336) **Stalls** High

Form RPR

3 **1** **Cloud's End**[12] 6386 2-9-0 0 LiamJones 9 73
(W J Haggas) *led: shkn up fnl f: edgd lft and narrowly hdd nr fin: rallied: wl and led again last stride* **3/1**[2]

2 nse **Basle** 2-9-0 0 JerryO'Dwyer 8 73
(Miss Gay Kelleway) *in rr tl: hdwy and nt clr run over 2f out: swtchd rt over 1f out and str run fnl f to take slt ld nr fin: ct last stride* **25/1**

0 **3** 1 ¾ **Hulcote Rose (IRE)**[94] 3810 2-9-0 0 JamesDoyle 4 68
(S Kirk) *in rr: hdwy over 2f out: styd on to chse ldng duo 1f out: one pce ins fnl f* **7/1**

2 **4** 3 **Tatiana Romanova (USA)**[21] 6154 2-9-0 0 PaulHanagan 7 61+
(R A Fahey) *chsd ldrs: rdn and struggling to go pce over 3f out: styd on again ins fnl f but nvr a threat* **13/8**[1]

2200 **5** ¾ **Magic Lantern**[17] 6241 2-8-11 78 PatrickHills(3) 1 56
(R Hannon) *s.i.s: in rr: hdwy ins fnl 2f: styd on fnl f but nvr a threat* **4/1**[3]

5300 **6** shd **Dancing Poppy**[41] 5543 2-9-0 54 SamHitchcott 6 56
(M R Channon) *chsd ldrs: rdn along ins fnl 3f: wknd ins fnl f* **50/1**

0 **7** ½ **Bird On The Wire**[24] 6069 2-8-11 0 JackDean(3) 11 55
(W G M Turner) *chsd ldrs: rdn 3f out: wknd 2f out* **66/1**

8 4 **Totally Ours** 2-9-0 0 RichardMullen 10 43
(W R Muir) *s.i.s: a towards rr* **20/1**

0 **9** ¾ **Vert Chapeau**[21] 6163 2-9-0 0 LPKeniry 3 40
(E F Vaughan) *s.i.s: a in rr* **14/1**

6 **10** 4 ½ **Winifred Jo**[19] 6207 2-9-0 0 TPO'Shea 2 27
(J R Gask) *chsd ldrs: rdn 3f out: wknd qckly 2f out* **25/1**

1m 13.01s (-0.09) **Going Correction** 0.0s/f (Stan) 10 Ran SP% **118.2**
Speed ratings (Par 94): **100,99,97,93,92 92,91,86,85,79**
toteswingers: 1&2 £9.00, 1&3 £7.30, 2&3 £18.90 CSF £80.78 TOTE £3.60: £1.60, £4.50, £2.20; EX 54.20.
Owner Manor Farm Stud & Miss S Hoare **Bred** R T And Mrs Watson **Trained** Newmarket, Suffolk

FOCUS
There was a lively market for this ordinary fillies' maiden which produced an exciting finish. The winner ran to her pre-race mark.

NOTEBOOK
Cloud's End ◆ ran green but finished strongly when close third at 6-4 in a 6f Nottingham maiden on debut late last month. She looked a strong contender given normal improvement and showed a gritty attitude under forcing tactics to get the better of a tight duel with the runner-up. The half-sister to Group 1 winning sprinter Airwave has a good physique and looks a nice prospect. (op 5-2 tchd 7-2)
Basle had to negotiate her way through some traffic problems but stayed on strongly and was just denied, despite being matched at 1.01 in running on the exchanges. This was an excellent debut run for a yard not renowned for winning newcomers. The half-sister to useful sprinting 2-y-o Queen's Victory could improve significantly for the experience and looks a bargain at £15,000. (op 16-1)
Hulcote Rose(IRE) was a springer in the market and deserves plenty of credit for a much improved display on her second run and first try on Polytrack. She cost 95,000euros and has some high-class milers on the dam's side of her pedigree. (op 25-1)
Tatiana Romanova(USA)'s second behind an odds-on rival on debut last month was a good performance but she put in a very laboured effort in her own bid to justify favouritism here. She is bred to want a bit further than this but this still has to rate as a disappointment from the form pick. (op 15-8 tchd 6-4 and 2-1 in a place)
Magic Lantern had decent claims on her runner-up efforts over 7f here and at Salisbury in the summer but her form had dipped since and she was never a factor from a low draw on this switch back to sprinting. (op 7-2)

6723 SPREADEX - SPORTS AND FINANCIAL SPREAD BETTING H'CAP 6f (P)

4:30 (4:31) (Class 4) (0-85,85) 3-Y-O+ **£4,727** (£1,406; £702; £351) **Stalls** High

Form RPR

0510 **1** **Bahamian Lad**[11] 6434 4-8-12 78 JerryO'Dwyer 8 86
(R Hollinshead) *trckd ldr: rdn 2f out: styd on u.p fnl f to ld fnl 20yds* **8/1**[3]

5005 **2** ½ **Little Pete (IRE)**[17] 6253 4-9-3 83 (t) LPKeniry 2 89
(A M Balding) *led: drvn and styd on wl fr 2f out: edgd rt appr fnl f: hdd and no ex fnl 20yds* **9/1**

0400 **3** ¾ **Baby Strange**[13] 6359 5-9-0 85 MartinLane(5) 1 89
(D Shaw) *chsd ldrs: rdn and one pce fr 2f out tl styd on wl fnl f but nt trble ldng duo* **10/1**

6000 **4** ¾ **Drawnfromthepast (IRE)**[16] 6282 4-9-5 85 (t) PaulHanagan 7 86+
(J A Osborne) *in rr: pushed along 2f out: styd on ins fnl f: fin wl* **8/1**[3]

0-60 **5** hd **Carved Emerald**[12] 6374 4-9-2 82 RobertHavlin 9 83
(D R C Elsworth) *towards rr tl hdwy on ins over 2f out: chsd ldrs u.p over 1f out: outpcd ins fnl f* **20/1**

1304 **6** ½ **My Kingdom (IRE)**[16] 6279 3-9-2 83 (t) GeorgeBaker 6 82
(H Morrison) *chsd ldrs: rdn and carried rt appr fnl f: wknd ins fnl f* **7/4**[1]

0024 **7** nk **Bobbie Soxer (IRE)**[29] 5901 3-8-11 78 TPO'Shea 3 76
(J L Dunlop) *in rr and pushed along over 3f out: hdwy appr fnl f: one pce ins fnl f* **8/1**[3]

0000 **8** 1 ½ **Mogok Ruby**[19] 6201 5-8-13 79 LiamJones 4 72
(L Montague Hall) *s.i.s: in rr: rdn over 2f out: sme prog fnl f* **14/1**

0050 **9** nk **Vhujon (IRE)**[12] 6396 4-8-7 80 HollyHall(7) 5 72
(P D Evans) *s.i.s: in rr: sme prog over 2f out: nvr in contention* **6/1**[2]

1m 13.45s (0.35) **Going Correction** 0.0s/f (Stan)
WFA 3 from 4yo+ 1lb 9 Ran SP% **114.5**
Speed ratings (Par 105): **97,96,95,94,94 93,93,91,90**
toteswingers: 1&2 £8.00, 1&3 £12.80, 2&3 £7.30 CSF £76.55 CT £733.06 TOTE £11.70: £2.90, £2.50, £3.40; EX 115.00.
Owner Graham Brothers Racing Partnership **Bred** J D Graham **Trained** Upper Longdon, Staffs

FOCUS
A decent-grade handicap but the majority of runners were struggling for form. The pace was very steady and the first two filled those positions for most of the way. The winner ran a clear personal best but the form may not be reliable.
Vhujon(IRE) Official explanation: jockey said the gelding missed the break and ran flat

6724 SPREADEX £400 NEW ACCOUNT OFFERS H'CAP 1m 4f (P)

5:00 (5:03) (Class 4) (0-85,84) 3-Y-O+ **£4,727** (£1,406; £702; £351) **Stalls** Centre

Form RPR

1200 **1** **Thin Red Line (IRE)**[31] 5828 3-9-2 82 PaulHanagan 12 92
(E A L Dunlop) *in tch: drvn along over 3f out: styd on to ld wl over 1f out: pushed along and styd on strly fnl f* **9/2**[2]

-030 **2** 1 ½ **Howdigo**[9] 6480 4-9-8 84 MarcHalford(3) 8 92+
(J R Best) *hld up in rr: stl plenty to do over 2f out: hdwy sn after: edgd rt and quicked fnl f to go 2nd nr fin but no ch w wnr* **7/1**[3]

0005 **3** nk **Mister New York (USA)**[38] 5649 4-9-3 76 (b) GeorgeBaker 10 83
(Noel T Chance) *hld up in rr: hdwy over 2f out: swtchd lft but hung rt sn after and kpt edging that way but styd on to chse wnr wout holding any ch fnl f: lost 2nd nr fin* **20/1**

1535 **4** 1 **Cyborg**[45] 5402 5-9-5 78 RobertHavlin 11 84
(D R C Elsworth) *t.k.h: in tch tl chsd ldr over 7f out: chal 4f out to 3f out: styd chsng wnr tl wknd ins fnl f* **7/1**[3]

1542 **5** 2 **Summer Lodge**[12] 6385 6-8-9 73 BMcHugh(5) 5 75
(J A Glover) *chsd ldrs: drvn along fr 3f out: wknd fnl f* **8/1**

2103 **6** 1 ¾ **Balnagore**[17] 6244 5-8-11 75 MartinLane(5) 7 75
(J L Dunlop) *led: rdn fr 3f out: hdd wl over 1f out: sn wknd* **10/1**

3003 **7** ½ **Tanto Faz (IRE)**[23] 6116 4-9-5 78 LiamJones 2 77
(W J Haggas) *stdd s and swtchd rt to rail: t.k.h: hdwy over 2f out but hung continually rt and no imp* **14/1**

0442 **8** hd **Sehoy (USA)**[29] 5909 3-9-4 84 RichardMullen 3 82
(J H M Gosden) *chsd ldrs: rdn and swtchd rt to ins rail over 2f out: wknd over 1f out* **3/1**[1]

2305 **9** 1 **Encircled**[107] 3406 5-9-11 84 SimonWhitworth 1 81
(J R Jenkins) *in rr: shkn up ins fnl 3f and no prog* **50/1**

-000 **10** 2 ¼ **Pinch Of Salt (IRE)**[38] 5641 6-9-11 84 (v[1]) LPKeniry 13 77
(A M Balding) *chsd ldrs: rdn 3f out: wknd 2f out* **7/1**[3]

0602 **11** 7 **Buddy Holly**[19] 6204 4-9-9 82 TPO'Shea 4 64
(Pat Eddery) *mid-div: rdn and sme hdwy whn nt clr run over 2f out: sn dropped away* **15/2**

310/ **12** 21 **Urban Tiger (GER)**[15] 1922 6-9-2 75 KevinGhunowa 6 23
(Tim Vaughan) *bhd fr 1/2-way* **40/1**

2m 34.63s (0.13) **Going Correction** 0.0s/f (Stan)
WFA 3 from 4yo+ 7lb 12 Ran SP% **128.5**
Speed ratings (Par 105): **99,98,97,97,95 94,94,94,93,92 87,73**
toteswingers: 1&2 £6.30, 1&3 £21.90, 2&3 £33.60 CSF £38.94 CT £602.11 TOTE £6.30: £2.50, £2.40, £5.70; EX 35.00.
Owner Byculla Thoroughbreds **Bred** Peter Jones And G G Jones **Trained** Newmarket, Suffolk
■ Stewards' Enquiry : George Baker caution: careless riding

FOCUS
A decent handicap, but the pace was not great. The form is ordinary for the grade with the fourth the best guide.
Encircled Official explanation: jockey said that the mare lost a shoe

Buddy Holly Official explanation: jockey said that the gelding ran flat

6725 SPREADEX.COM H'CAP (DIV I) 7f (P)
5:30 (5:31) (Class 5) (0-75,75) 3-Y-0+ £2,266 (£674; £337; £168) Stalls High

Form RPR

3512 1 **Millfield (IRE)**[16] 6294 6-9-2 71 GeorgeBaker 5 80+
(P R Chamings) *stdd s: t.k.h in rr: hrd rdn 2f out: styd on over 1f out: str run fnl f to ld fnl 20yds: won gng away* **4/1**[1]

4015 2 ¾ **Defector (IRE)**[13] 6361 3-9-0 71 RichardMullen 10 77
(W R Muir) *t.k.h early: sn chsng ldr: rdn 2f out: styd on to ld fnl 110yds: hdd and outpcd fnl 20yds* **8/1**

0512 3 1½ **Black Dahlia**[13] 6365 4-8-11 71 BMcHugh(5) 7 74
(J A Glover) *sn led: rdn and styd alone on far rail fr 2f out: edgd lft ins fnl f and hdd fnl 110yds: wknd nr fin* **7/1**[2]

130 4 ¾ **Tuxedo**[34] 5746 4-9-3 72 LPKeniry 3 73
(P W Hiatt) *chsd ldrs: rdn over 2f out: styd on same pce fr over 1f out* **7/1**[2]

045 5 ½ **Izzibizzi**[25] 6015 4-8-13 68 (p) PaulHanagan 4 68
(E A L Dunlop) *wnt rt s: sn in tch: chsd ldrs and rdn 3f out: one pce fnl 2f* **15/2**[3]

0000 6 3 **Grey Boy (GER)**[5] 6596 8-8-13 75 GeorgeDowning(7) 12 66+
(A W Carroll) *towards rr: hdwy on ins over 2f out: kpt on but nvr gng pce to rch ldrs* **16/1**

0135 7 ½ **Gurteen Diamond**[19] 6216 3-8-5 67 MartinLane(5) 1 56
(P D Evans) *in rr: hdwy on outside over 2f out: kpt on fnl f but nvr in contention* **14/1**

-000 8 nk **Retro (IRE)**[18] 6230 3-8-8 68 PatrickHills(3) 11 56
(R Hannon) *chsd ldrs: rdn 3f out: wknd over 1f out* **20/1**

0500 9 nk **Silver Hotspur**[12] 6374 5-9-0 74 SimonPearce(5) 8 62
(C R Dore) *slowly away: in rr: sme prog fr over 1f out* **20/1**

0530 10 1 **Aflaam (IRE)**[44] 5441 4-9-4 73 (t) JerryO'Dwyer 6 59
(P Howling) *a towards rr* **17/2**

1060 11 1¼ **Bahamian Kid**[17] 6250 4-9-0 69 (p) TPO'Shea 2 51
(R Hollinshead) *a towards rr* **16/1**

0203 12 18 **Gazboolou**[12] 6374 5-9-6 75 LiamJones 9 9
(David Pinder) *chsd ldrs to 1/2-way: sn wknd and wl bhd* **15/2**[3]

1m 25.52s (-0.48) **Going Correction** 0.0s/f (Stan)
WFA 3 from 4yo+ 2lb **12** Ran SP% **118.1**
Speed ratings (Par 103): **102,101,99,98,98 94,94,93,93,92 90,70**
toteswingers: 1&2 £5.70, 1&3 £3.10, 2&3 £4.40 CSF £35.17 CT £218.19 TOTE £4.60: £2.10, £3.40, £1.80; EX 39.10.

Owner Inhurst Players **Bred** Limestone Stud **Trained** Baughurst, Hants

FOCUS
A minor handicap, but the first five were all prominent in the market and pulled clear of the rest, so the form could work out. The winner is rated back to his best.

Gazboolou Official explanation: jockey said the gelding had no more to give

6726 SPREADEX.COM H'CAP (DIV II) 7f (P)
6:00 (6:01) (Class 5) (0-75,75) 3-Y-0+ £2,266 (£674; £337; £168) Stalls High

Form RPR

0520 1 **Dvinsky (USA)**[11] 6434 8-9-5 74 (b) PaulDoe 5 82
(P Howling) *sn trcking ldr: led appr fnl 2f: rdn and styd on gamely whn strly chal thrght fnl f: jst hld on* **5/1**[2]

0200 2 shd **Shaded Edge**[34] 5753 5-8-13 68 JamesDoyle 7 76
(D W P Arbuthnot) *in tch: rdn and one pce 2f out: styd on u.p appr fnl f: fin strly: nt quite get up* **10/1**

3031 3 ½ **Autumn Blades (IRE)**[14] 6336 4-9-6 75 (p) RobertHavlin 10 82
(A Bailey) *hld up in tch: hdwy on bit fr 2f out: rdn to chal fr 1f out: no ex ins fnl f and fdd cl home* **13/2**

3342 4 shd **Lodi (IRE)**[6] 6562 4-9-6 75 (t) GeorgeBaker 9 81
(J Akehurst) *chsd ldrs: rdn to chal 1f out: no ex and outpcd cl home* **4/1**[1]

0326 5 hd **Billberry**[16] 6294 4-8-12 67 (t) SaleemGolam 12 73
(S C Williams) *in rr tl hdwy on ins over 2f out: pressed ldrs u.p 1f out: wknd ins fnl f* **13/2**

2300 6 1¼ **Eastern Gift**[9] 6496 4-8-12 72 KylieManser(5) 11 74
(Miss Gay Kelleway) *stdd s: in rr: styd on fnl f but nvr rchd ldrs* **16/1**

0065 7 1¾ **Woolston Ferry (IRE)**[62] 4872 3-8-11 68 LiamJones 4 66
(David Pinder) *in rr: rdn over 2f out: styd on fr over 1f out but nt rch ldrs* **20/1**

4140 8 1¾ **Ivory Lace**[20] 6187 8-8-13 73 BMcHugh(5) 6 66
(S Woodman) *towards rr: rdn and outpcd fnl 3f* **16/1**

2545 9 2 **Sweet Gale (IRE)**[12] 6374 5-9-2 71 LPKeniry 3 59
(Mike Murphy) *s.i.s: a towards rr* **10/1**

0650 10 3 **Musical Script (USA)**[10] 6444 6-9-0 69 (b) JerryO'Dwyer 2 49
(Mouse Hamilton-Fairley) *fast s fr outside and sn led: t.k.h: hdd appr fnl 2f: sn wknd* **6/1**[3]

/160 11 nk **Expensive Problem**[53] 5190 6-9-0 69 IvanLopez 1 48
(R J Smith) *s.i.s: sn rcvrd to chse ldrs: wknd ins fnl 3f* **12/1**

0004 12 hd **Chosen Son (IRE)**[32] 5813 3-7-13 61 AmyBaker(5) 8 39
(P J O'Gorman) *outpcd* **10/1**

1m 25.38s (-0.62) **Going Correction** 0.0s/f (Stan)
WFA 3 from 4yo+ 2lb **12** Ran SP% **129.1**
Speed ratings (Par 103): **103,102,102,102,101 100,98,96,94,90 90,90**
toteswingers: 1&2 £15.30, 1&3 £5.00, 2&3 £20.00 CSF £59.80 CT £348.70 TOTE £5.60: £2.10, £3.80, £1.90; EX 96.60 Place 6: £238.17 Place 5: £106.66.

Owner Richard Berenson **Bred** Eclipse Bloodstock & Tipperary Bloodstock **Trained** Newmarket, Suffolk

FOCUS
A modest handicap. There was a thrilling finish but the first five finished in a bunch. Sound form.

Eastern Gift Official explanation: jockey said the gelding resented the kickback in the early stages

Sweet Gale(IRE) Official explanation: jockey said the mare was never travelling

T/Plt: £244.60 to a £1 stake. Pool: £51,469.49. 153.56 winning tickets. T/Qpdt: £104.90 to a £1 stake. Pool: £4,168.76. 29.40 winning tickets. ST

6393 SALISBURY (R-H)
Monday, October 12

OFFICIAL GOING: Soft (good to soft in places) changing to soft after race 5 (3.45)
Wind: virtually nil Weather: Sunny

6727 BATHWICK TYRES MAIDEN AUCTION STKS (DIV I) 1m
1:35 (1:36) (Class 5) 2-Y-0 £2,914 (£867; £433; £216) Stalls High

Form RPR

2262 1 **Flaming Miracle**[10] 6461 2-8-10 74 DavidProbert 3 76+
(A M Balding) *mde all: qcknd clr 4f out: a in command after: eased nr fin* **9/2**[3]

2 nk **Donna Elvira** 2-8-8 0 RyanMoore 6 72+
(R Hannon) *mid-div: running green and dropped to rr u.p over 4f out: swtchd to centre over 1f out: styd on wl ins fnl f but nvr gng to catch wnr* **14/1**

2044 3 2¾ **Layla's Boy**[22] 6136 2-8-10 75 FrederikTylicki(3) 2 71
(R A Fahey) *s.i.s: towards rr: rdn and hdwy over 3f out: styd on fnl f* **8/1**

0 4 ½ **Jasmeno**[29] 5906 2-8-4 0 GregFairley 12 61
(H Morrison) *s.i.s: towards rr: rdn 3f out: stdy hdwy: styd on fnl f* **33/1**

022 5 ¾ **Inside Track (IRE)**[16] 6291 2-8-11 82 LDettori 5 67
(B J Meehan) *mid-div: hdwy to chse clr ldr over 3f out: sn rdn: fdd ins fnl f* **11/4**[2]

0 6 ½ **Strike A Deal (IRE)**[83] 4176 2-8-8 0 AlanMunro 4 62
(C F Wall) *mid-div: rdn 3f out: short of room briefly over 1f out: styd on same pce* **28/1**

4 7 2¼ **Madame Roulin (IRE)**[10] 6441 2-8-8 0 HayleyTurner 10 57
(M L W Bell) *t.k.h early: mid-div: hdwy u.p 3f out: wknd ins fnl f* **12/1**

6553 8 3¼ **Lenkiewicz**[17] 6241 2-8-6 77 KirstyMilczarek 1 48
(B R Millman) *sn chsng ldr: rdn 3f out: fdd fnl f* **2/1**[1]

5 9 2½ **Ermyntrude**[10] 6441 2-8-4 0 CatherineGannon 8 41
(P M Phelan) *chsd ldr: rdn over 3f out: wknd 2f out* **33/1**

0 10 ¾ **Roybuoy**[19] 6199 2-8-13 0 EddieAhern 7 48
(H J L Dunlop) *chsd ldrs: rdn over 3f out: wknd over 2f out* **100/1**

0 11 8 **Reve De Mardi**[31] 5839 2-8-9 0 DO'Donohoe 9 27
(George Baker) *a bhd* **100/1**

0 12 hd **River Landing**[19] 6199 2-8-13 0 (t) JimCrowley 11 30
(R M Beckett) *mid-div tl 3f out* **66/1**

1m 48.08s (4.58) **Going Correction** +0.20s/f (Good) **12** Ran SP% **116.5**
Speed ratings (Par 95): **85,84,81,81,80 80,77,74,72,71 63,63**
toteswingers: 1&2 £11.40, 1&3 £6.30, 2&3 £10.30 CSF £60.17 TOTE £5.70: £1.80, £3.80, £2.40; EX 72.60.

Owner M A L Evans **Bred** M A L Evans **Trained** Kingsclere, Hants

FOCUS
A fair maiden but without much strength in depth. There was no pace on early and the winner was able to dictate. Suspect form.

NOTEBOOK
Flaming Miracle got to the front early on and skipped clear entering the home straight, catching his rivals out in the process. It was clear passing the furlong pole he was not for catching and his rider got it spot on, before prematurely easing him down in the closing stages. His supporters had a scare as the runner-up motored home and closed right up near the line, but he had just done enough. The winner has to rate flattered by this as he nicked it, but it was still a much-deserved win and he seemed to enjoy the cut underfoot. (op 5-1 tchd 6-1)
Donna Elvira ◆, a 20,000gns purchase, looked like finishing out the back when becoming badly outpaced as the tempo became serious. The further she went the more she picked up for pressure, however, and she gave the winner a scare at the business end. She was in front shortly after the line and, with plenty of stamina on her dam's side of the pedigree, looks sure to appreciate a further step up in trip this year. (op 16-1 tchd 11-1)
Layla's Boy was one of many than proved totally unsuited by being held up off the sedate pace. He is better than the bare form, but is exposed and likely still needs some respite from the handicapper. (op 15-2 tchd 7-1)
Jasmeno pulled hard early on due to the lack of real pace on and still showed signs of greenness. She finished her race nicely, however, and this was a definite step in the right direction. (tchd 28-1)
Inside Track(IRE) was the first to try and keep tabs with the winner when that one kicked clear, but his effort proved one-paced. He was a little below his recent level here, but still helps to put the form into some perspective. (op 9-4 tchd 3-1)
Strike A Deal(IRE) was having his first outing since finishing out the back on debut at Yarmouth over 6f 83 days previously. He was never a player here, but still posted an improved display for the step up in distance and will look more interesting after his next outing. (op 16-1)
Madame Roulin(IRE) was another not seen at her best due to the way the race unfolded and looks to be going the right way. (op 14-1 tchd 9-1)
Lenkiewicz ran her best race to date in the Watership Down Stud Sales Race last time and was well backed on this return to further. She could have done with a better pace like the majority here, but still turned in a laboured performance. (op 11-4)

6728 BATHWICK TYRES MAIDEN AUCTION STKS (DIV II) 1m
2:10 (2:11) (Class 5) 2-Y-0 £2,914 (£867; £433; £216) Stalls High

Form RPR

5 1 **Soul Station (FR)**[12] 6372 2-8-11 0 RichardKingscote 12 84
(R Charlton) *mde all: rdn whn hrd pressed fr 3f out: styd on strly to assert fnl 100yds: rdn out* **17/2**

3 2 2 **Flouncing (IRE)**[21] 6163 2-8-8 0 MichaelHills 8 77+
(W J Haggas) *hld up towards rr: hdwy wl over 3f out: rdn to chal wl over 2f out: ev ch ent fnl f: no ex fnl 100yds* **11/4**[2]

00 3 3 **High On A Hill (IRE)**[21] 6162 2-8-12 0 DavidProbert 11 74
(S Kirk) *w wnr: rdn and ev ch 3f out tl over 1f out: kpt on same pce* **100/1**

0 4 2¼ **Sabatini (IRE)**[111] 3248 2-8-8 0 RyanMoore 10 65
(R Hannon) *trckd ldrs: rdn 3f out: styd on same pce fnl 2f* **15/2**[3]

6222 5 3¼ **Baltimore Clipper (USA)**[30] 5864 2-8-12 76 JimmyFortune 1 62
(P F I Cole) *trckd ldrs: effrt over 3f out: fdd over 1f out* **13/8**[1]

0 6 2 **Wavertree Bounty**[32] 5785 2-8-7 0 ow2 AlanMunro 6 53
(C F Wall) *s.i.s: towards rr: rdn and styd on same pce fnl 2f: nvr threatened* **100/1**

00 7 8 **Seeking Rose**[26] 5984 2-8-5 0 DO'Donohoe 5 33
(E A L Dunlop) *mid-div tl wknd 2f out* **100/1**

0 8 1¼ **Set To Go**[16] 6291 2-8-11 0 DaneO'Neill 9 36
(H J L Dunlop) *trckd ldrs: rdn 4f out: wknd 2f out* **100/1**

9 ¾ **Shoot The Pot (IRE)** 2-8-9 0 JimCrowley 4 33
(R M Beckett) *a towards rr* **9/1**

05 10 ½ **Sundream**[42] 5528 2-8-4 0 CatherineGannon 2 26
(Tom Dascombe) *towards rr: hdwy over 4f out: wknd wl over 2f out* **16/1**

0 **11** *shd* **Baltic Ben (USA)**[12] 6393 2-8-10 0 EddieAhern 3 32
(Eve Johnson Houghton) *mid-div: rdn over 3f out: wknd 2f out* **20/1**
0 **12** *5* **Sharp And Chic**[10] 6441 2-8-5 0 HayleyTurner 7 16
(M L W Bell) *mid-div tl wknd over 2f out* **33/1**
1m 45.72s (2.22) **Going Correction** +0.20s/f (Good) **12** Ran SP% **114.6**
Speed ratings (Par 95): **96,94,91,88,85 83,75,74,73,73 72,67**
toteswingers: 1&2 £6.60, 1&3 £42.50, 2&3 £33.40 CSF £30.27 TOTE £11.10: £2.30, £1.70, £10.00; EX 35.60.
Owner Michael Pescod **Bred** Sugar Puss Corporation **Trained** Beckhampton, Wilts

FOCUS
The second division of the 1m maiden and again the winner made all, although he may not have been flattered. The runner-up did best from the rear.

NOTEBOOK
Soul Station(FR) looked sure to appreciate a stiffer test when fifth on debut at Kempton 12 days earlier and this extra furlong saw him off the mark. He was no doubt at a big advantage racing on the pace from his decent draw and, like the winner of the first, caught most of his rivals flat-footed when asserting for home. However, he still completed the task in good fashion, showing a willing attitude and looks a nice handicapper in the making. (op 8-1 tchd 9-1)
Flouncing(IRE) ◆ finished a promising third on debut at Kempton 21 days previously and was better than the bare form on that occasion as she met some trouble. She got a clear passage on this turf debut and did well as she raced off the ordinary early pace, but still failed to see out the extra furlong like the winner. A clear-second best, she should soon be winning. (op 2-1 tchd 3-1)
High On A Hill(IRE) showed his most worthwhile form to date on this switch to the turf. He was another at a real advantage under a positive ride from a good draw and is likely somewhat flattered, but could be able to build on this now he can enter nurseries.
Sabatini(IRE) met support on this return from a 111-day layoff and step up from 6f. His effort flattened out from the 2f marker and he likely found the distance a bit stiff at this stage, so a drop to 7f could suit better. (op 10-1 tchd 7-1)
Baltimore Clipper(USA) came into this having finished runner-up on his last three outings and set the standard. He lacked any sort of gear change and may have found the ground easier ground against him. (tchd 11-8 and 7-4 in places)
Wavertree Bounty was one of the chief sufferers due to the lack of early pace and she stayed on well in the circumstances. This was an improvement on her initial run and she is one to become more interested in after her next assignment.

6729 BATHWICK TYRES MAIDEN FILLIES' STKS (DIV I) 6f 212y
2:40 (2:42) (Class 5) 2-Y-O **£2,914** (£867; £433; £216) **Stalls** High

Form RPR
3 **1** **Thrill**[21] 6164 2-9-0 0 JimmyFortune 14 81+
(J H M Gosden) *mde all: styd on wl to draw clr ent fnl f: pushed out* **11/8**[1]
54 **2** *3* **Opera Gal (IRE)**[39] 5603 2-9-0 0 DavidProbert 13 74
(A M Balding) *chsd wnr thrght: rdn and ev ch over 2f out tl over 1f out: kpt on for clr 2nd but sn hld* **10/3**[2]
3 *1 1/2* **Revered** 2-9-0 0 RyanMoore 9 70
(Sir Michael Stoute) *mid-div: swtchd lft and hdwy 2f out: sn rdn: styd on* **15/2**
4 *1* **Roxy Flyer (IRE)** 2-9-0 0 JimCrowley 11 67
(Mrs A J Perrett) *trckd ldrs: rdn over 3f out: styd on same pce* **33/1**
5 *hd* **Thaahira (USA)** 2-9-0 0 RHills 15 67
(M A Jarvis) *in tch: rdn and hung lft fr 2f out: kpt on same pce* **14/1**
6 *hd* **Leaving Alone (USA)** 2-9-0 0 DaneO'Neill 4 66+
(R Hannon) *hld up towards rr: rdn and stdy prog fr 3f out: nvr trbld ldrs* **33/1**
3 **7** *3/4* **Shimmering Moment (USA)**[62] 4869 2-9-0 0 EddieAhern 7 64
(H R A Cecil) *chsd ldrs: rdn 3f out: fdd ent fnl f* **7/1**[3]
8 *hd* **Issabella Gem (IRE)** 2-9-0 0 PhilipRobinson 10 64
(C G Cox) *chsd ldrs: rdn over 3f out: wknd ent fnl f* **25/1**
0 **9** *3 3/4* **Scarcity (IRE)**[27] 5969 2-9-0 0 JamieSpencer 1 55+
(E A L Dunlop) *mid-div: hdwy 2f out: sn rdn and wknd* **33/1**
6 **10** *1/2* **Madam Ruby (IRE)**[42] 5498 2-9-0 0 RichardKingscote 5 53
(A King) *a towards rr* **25/1**
11 *1* **Centime** 2-9-0 0 AlanMunro 3 51+
(B J Meehan) *s.i.s: a towards rr* **40/1**
05 **12** *12* **Mini Max**[38] 5639 2-8-9 0 GabrielHannon(5) 16 21
(B W Duke) *mid-div tl wknd over 2f out* **66/1**
0 **13** *3 1/2* **Lily Rio (IRE)**[16] 6284 2-9-0 0 HayleyTurner 8 12
(W R Muir) *in tch tl wknd over 2f out* **40/1**
14 *1 1/2* **Celebrian** 2-9-0 0 AdamKirby 2 8
(W R Swinburn) *a towards rr* **66/1**
15 *15* **Lauren's Kitty (IRE)** 2-9-0 0 CatherineGannon 12 —
(J C Fox) *s.i.s: a bhd* **100/1**
1m 29.94s (0.94) **Going Correction** +0.20s/f (Good) **15** Ran SP% **121.5**
Speed ratings (Par 92): **102,98,96,95,95 95,94,94,89,89 88,74,70,68,51**
toteswingers: 1&2 £3.50, 1&3 £5.30, 2&3 £6.30 CSF £4.98 TOTE £2.40: £1.20, £1.80, £2.30; EX 7.90.
Owner Cheveley Park Stud **Bred** Cheveley Park Stud Ltd **Trained** Newmarket, Suffolk

FOCUS
This should work out to be an above-average maiden. Thrill was the third consecutive winner to make all and Opera Gal was always in second.

NOTEBOOK
Thrill ◆ confirmed the promise of her debut third at Kempton 21 days earlier and made all in determined fashion. She got an easy time out in front, but did the business in great style and had no trouble on the contrasting surface. She is a sister to Infallible, who took the Nell Gwynn on her 3-y-o debut for the stable a few years back, and it wouldn't be surprising to see her take in that race when reappearing next year. (op 2-1)
Opera Gal(IRE), the second favourite, tracked the winner from the off and failed to find the required gear change to trouble that rival when it mattered. It is not hard to see why she was tried over 1m last time as that would now appear to be the trip she wants and she should be placed to deservedly strike before the season's end. (op 7-2 tchd 3-1)
Revered ◆ is a half-sister to two decent fillies that were trained by her leading stable, the Group 1-winning Promising Lead and Visit, who landed two Group 3s. She proved easy to back for this racecourse debut, but still ran a big race and would have very likely got closer under a more prominent ride. This experience should mean she proves very hard to stop next time out. (op 13-2 tchd 8-1)
Roxy Flyer(IRE) is out of a multiple winner in the US and did not go unbacked for this initial outing. She was never far away, but got outpaced 2f out before keeping on resolutely towards the finish. Another furlong will suit before long and she is well up to winning races. (op 50-1)
Thaahira(USA) proved friendless in the betting ring and ran as though this debut experience was needed. She showed more than enough to suggest she will get a deal closer next time out. (op 11-1)
Leaving Alone(USA) ◆ fared best of those ridden out the back and caught the eye staying on with promise under a hands-and-heels ride. This 120,000gns purchase should repay her rider's kindness sooner rather than later. (op 40-1)
Shimmering Moment(USA), stepping up in trip, proved one paced when it mattered on this return from a 62-day break and first outing for Henry Cecil. Her pedigree suggests the ground would have been soft enough and she is not one to abandon. (op 13-2)
Issabella Gem(IRE) knew her job as she was well away and she shaped like a horse that will appreciate stepping up in trip, something that her breeding fully backs up. (op 22-1 tchd 20-1)
Celebrian Official explanation: jockey said the filly ran green

6730 BATHWICK TYRES MAIDEN FILLIES' STKS (DIV II) 6f 212y
3:15 (3:17) (Class 5) 2-Y-O **£2,914** (£867; £433; £216) **Stalls** High

Form RPR
23 **1** **Qaraaba**[45] 5397 2-9-0 0 RHills 15 76+
(J L Dunlop) *awkward leaving stalls: sn mid-div: hung lft but hdwy fr 2f out: sn rdn: styd on: led fnl stride* **11/4**[2]
6 **2** *shd* **Cojo (IRE)**[27] 5969 2-9-0 0 EddieAhern 16 76
(B J Meehan) *trckd ldr: rdn to chal over 2f out: kpt on to ld ins fnl f: hdd fnl stride* **8/1**
3 *1 1/4* **Vegas Palace (IRE)** 2-9-0 0 RichardKingscote 4 73+
(Tom Dascombe) *prom: rdn to ld 2f out: hdd ins fnl f: no ex* **33/1**
4 *3/4* **Scorn (USA)** 2-9-0 0 JimmyFortune 8 72+
(J H M Gosden) *s.i.s: towards rr: pushed along and stdy prog fr over 2f out: styd on fnl f* **12/1**
5 *1/2* **Flambeau** 2-9-0 0 DaneO'Neill 1 71+
(H Candy) *trckd ldrs: rdn over 2f out: styd on same pce* **14/1**
6 *1/2* **Naddwah** 2-9-0 0 LDettori 2 68
(M A Jarvis) *mid-div: rdn over 2f out: styd on fr over 1f out* **7/1**[3]
7 *shd* **Starclass** 2-9-0 0 AdamKirby 3 68+
(W R Swinburn) *s.i.s: towards rr: styd on fr over 1f out but nvr threatened* **66/1**
0 **8** *1 1/4* **Kai Mook**[19] 6207 2-9-0 0 CatherineGannon 9 65
(R Ingram) *led tl 2f out: remained pressing ldrs u.p: fdd fnl 100yds* **100/1**
0 **9** *4* **Highland Jewel (IRE)**[39] 5604 2-9-0 0 PhilipRobinson 14 55
(C G Cox) *mid-div tl 2f out* **20/1**
10 *shd* **Sweet Clementine (IRE)** 2-9-0 0 HayleyTurner 5 55+
(W J Knight) *nvr bttr than mid-div* **25/1**
11 *nk* **Hidden Fire** 2-9-0 0 AlanMunro 11 54
(D R C Elsworth) *mid-div: rdn 4f out: wknd 2f out* **33/1**
02 **12** *nk* **Lost Horizon (IRE)**[24] 6055 2-9-0 0 RyanMoore 13 53
(R Hannon) *s.i.s: sn in tch: effrt over 2f out: wknd 1f out* **5/2**[1]
13 *1 1/2* **Night Sky** 2-9-0 0 DavidProbert 6 50
(P J Makin) *s.i.s: a towards rr* **40/1**
14 *1/2* **Penderyn** 2-9-0 0 JimCrowley 12 48
(Mrs A J Perrett) *s.i.s: a towards rr* **50/1**
15 *2* **Lady Of Garmoran (USA)** 2-9-0 0 GregFairley 10 43
(P F I Cole) *prom: rdn 3f out: sn wknd* **40/1**
16 *11* **Deora De** 2-9-0 0 TGMcLaughlin 7 16
(E A L Dunlop) *mid-div tl wknd over 2f out* **66/1**
1m 31.89s (2.89) **Going Correction** +0.20s/f (Good) **16** Ran SP% **118.5**
Speed ratings (Par 92): **91,90,89,88,88 87,87,85,81,81 80,80,78,78,75 63**
toteswingers: 1&2 £5.20, 1&3 £26.40, 2&3 £28.50 CSF £21.97 TOTE £4.00: £1.50, £2.80, £6.90; EX 30.80.
Owner Hamdan Al Maktoum **Bred** Shadwell Estate Company Limited **Trained** Arundel, W Sussex

FOCUS
This second division of the fillies' maiden looked the weaker of the two and that was reflected by the slower winning time. There was a bunch finish for the final placing. The bare form is limited but there were some promising performances.

NOTEBOOK
Qaraaba, placed on her two previous outings, made it third time lucky with a last-gasp success. She was covered up through the early parts on the inside and was asked for an effort around 2f out. She took an age to pick up, however, and did little to help her rider by wanting to hang throughout the final furlong. She still stuck her head out where it mattered, however, and it is probably best to give her the benefit of the doubt regarding her attitude at this early stage. A step up in trip is really going to suit her next season and her best two performances have now both been on easy ground, but this surface was probably softer than she really cares for. (tchd 9-4)
Cojo(IRE) stepped up markedly on the level of her debut at Yarmouth 27 days earlier and only failed narrowly. The step up a furlong was much to her liking and she shouldn't remain a maiden for long. (op 15-2 tchd 7-1)
Vegas Palace(IRE) ◆ posted a solid debut display. She was able to race prominently and, although one-paced when asked for maximum effort 2f out, she kept on resolutely for pressure. She deserves extra credit as she was drawn wide and clearly has a future.
Scorn(USA) ◆, easy to back, is out of a high-class juvenile winner but her two previous foals to date have needed much more time. She left the impression there would be plenty better to come for this debut experience and is definitely one to take from the race. (op 9-1)
Flambeau, half-sister to two winning juveniles, turned in a pleasing introduction and deserves extra credit as she was drawn widest of all. She was not given too hard a time of it late on and ought to prove sharper for the run, but her pedigree suggests this trip is far enough at present. (tchd 16-1)
Naddwah boasts a choice pedigree, but is another for whom this trip looks far enough at present. She should come on nicely for the run and is in the right hands. (op 8-1)
Starclass ◆ did well on this debut outing. She is bred to enjoy middle-distances next year, so it was very pleasing that she made up her ground from off the pace to finish so close here. Her rider was not hard on her nearing the finish and she is one to take from the race. Official explanation: jockey said that the filly ran green (tchd 80-1)
Lost Horizon(IRE) was very popular in the betting, but she was done with before the furlong marker and the return to softer ground was likely to blame Official explanation: jockey said the filly was unsuited by the ground.(Soft, Good to Soft in places) (op 3-1)
Night Sky Official explanation: jockey said that the filly ran green

6731 BATHWICK TYRES BOURNEMOUTH H'CAP 6f 212y
3:45 (3:49) (Class 4) (0-85,85) 3-Y-O **£4,857** (£1,445; £722; £360) **Stalls** High

Form RPR
4635 **1** **Victoria Sponge (IRE)**[12] 6396 3-9-2 **83** DaneO'Neill 13 94
(R Hannon) *hld up towards rr: weaved way through field fr 2f out: r.o to ld ins fnl f: rdn clr* **14/1**
1 **2** *1 1/4* **Mr Rainbow**[11] 6430 3-9-1 **82** PJMcDonald 17 90
(G A Swinbank) *chsd ldr: rdn to ld 2f out: hdd ins fnl f: no ex* **10/1**
2235 **3** *1* **Kingswinford (IRE)**[11] 6434 3-8-8 **75** CatherineGannon 11 80
(P D Evans) *mid-div: hung rt and reminders 4f out: hdwy 3f out: sn rdn: disp 2nd briefly ins fnl f: no ex towards fin* **8/1**[3]
5163 **4** *1/2* **Shangani**[29] 5916 3-8-6 **80** AmyScott(7) 4 84+
(H Candy) *hld up towards rr: hdwy over 2f out: rdn over 1f out: styd on same pce* **16/1**
01-0 **5** *3/4* **Captain Dancer (IRE)**[164] 1656 3-8-8 **75** MichaelHills 2 77+
(B W Hills) *s.i.s: towards rr: hdwy over 3f out: sn rdn: styd on same pce fnl f* **9/1**
2-1 **6** *1/2* **Bawaardi (IRE)**[27] 5965 3-8-7 **74** ow1 RHills 5 74
(J H M Gosden) *hld up towards rr: hdwy over 2f out: sn rdn: styd on same pce* **7/1**[2]
3000 **7** *1/2* **Lovely Thought**[84] 4148 3-8-11 **78** (b) RichardKingscote 10 77
(W J Haggas) *led tl rdn 2f out: remained cl up: fdd fnl 100yds* **20/1**

-006 **8** *2 ½* **Miss Eze**[89] 3981 3-8-10 **77** .... JamieSpencer 15 69
(M L W Bell) *hld up towards rr: rdn and stdy prog 2f out: no further imp ins fnl f* **16/1**

1205 **9** *hd* **Indian Art (IRE)**[3] 6630 3-9-4 **85** .... RyanMoore 8 77
(R Hannon) *nvr bttr than mid-div* **12/1**

5350 **10** *1 ½* **Thousand Miles (IRE)**[25] 6014 3-8-13 **80** .... AlanMunro 14 68
(P W Chapple-Hyam) *rdn 3f out: a mid-div* **14/1**

3510 **11** *3 ¾* **Justonefortheroad**[12] 6374 3-8-8 **78** ow3 .... FrederikTylicki(3) 1 55
(R A Fahey) *mid-div: rdn over 2f out: wknd over 1f out* **16/1**

4312 **12** *6* **Leadenhall Lass (IRE)**[9] 6476 3-7-13 **73** .... (v) KierenFox(7) 6 34
(P M Phelan) *trckd ldrs: rdn over 2f out: wknd over 1f out* **16/1**

0400 **13** *3* **Global**[17] 6243 3-8-11 **78** .... (b¹) JimCrowley 16 31
(R Hannon) *mid-div: effrt 3f out: wknd 2f out: eased* **33/1**

3125 **14** *2* **Hi Shinko**[9] 6476 3-8-11 **78** .... TGMcLaughlin 9 26
(B R Millman) *chsd ldrs: rdn over 3f out: wknd 2f out* **10/1**

0115 **15** *½* **Poppet's Lovein**[15] 6311 3-8-12 **79** .... LDettori 3 25
(A B Haynes) *chsd ldrs: rdn over 2f out: wknd over 1f out: eased* **10/1**

2404 **16** *7* **Laurie Grove (IRE)**[17] 6243 3-9-2 **83** .... JimmyFortune 12 11
(T G Mills) *mid-div: rdn over 2f out: sn wknd: eased* **5/1**¹

1m 29.81s (0.81) **Going Correction** +0.20s/f (Good) **16** Ran SP% **129.8**
Speed ratings (Par 103): **103,101,100,99,99 98,97,95,94,93 88,81,78,76,75 67**
toteswingers: 1&2 £37.10, 1&3 £30.20, 2&3 £11.60 CSF £156.56 CT £1229.89 TOTE £17.80: £3.60, £2.60, £2.70, £5.00; EX 163.50.
Owner Simon Leech **Bred** Corrin Stud & Peter McCutcheon **Trained** East Everleigh, Wilts

FOCUS
A wide-open handicap. A high draw was an advantage. The winner was back to form, with the the third and fourth sound guides.
Kingswinford(IRE) Official explanation: jockey said that the gelding hung right handed
Poppet's Lovein Official explanation: jockey said filly was unsuited by the ground. (Soft)
Laurie Grove(IRE) Official explanation: jockey said the gelding was unsuited by the ground (Soft)

6732 BATHWICK TYRES FREE ADMISSION RACEDAY H'CAP — 1m

4:20 (4:20) (Class 2) (0-105,104) 3-Y-O+
£11,215 (£3,358; £1,679; £840; £419; £210) **Stalls** High

Form RPR

1 **1** **Prince Of Dance**[149] 2080 3-9-2 **94** .... RichardKingscote 11 106
(Tom Dascombe) *a.p: rdn 2f out: led jst over 1f out: drifted rt ins fnl f: r.o wl* **6/1**²

-413 **2** *1 ¾* **Prime Exhibit**[23] 6092 4-8-13 **88** .... JimmyFortune 6 96
(R Charlton) *led tl 3f out: styd pressing ldrs: rdn over 2f out: kpt on: 2nd and hld whn hmpd ins fnl f* **7/1**³

12-3 **3** *½* **Secrecy**[30] 5863 3-9-10 **102** .... LDettori 15 112+
(Saeed Bin Suroor) *mid-div: hdwy 3f out: sn rdn: kpt on but unable to mount chal* **5/2**¹

4110 **4** *1* **Marching Time**[16] 6270 3-9-4 **96** .... RyanMoore 2 101
(Sir Michael Stoute) *mid-div: hdwy to ld 3f out: sn rdn: hdd jst over 1f out: no ex* **8/1**

0540 **5** *nk* **Vitznau (IRE)**[16] 6270 5-9-6 **95** .... EddieAhern 5 99+
(R Hannon) *hld up towards rr: hdwy over 2f out: sn rdn: styd on same pce fnl f* **25/1**

2200 **6** *½* **Signor Peltro**[16] 6270 6-9-11 **100** .... DaneO'Neill 1 103+
(H Candy) *hld up towards rr: hdwy 3f out: sn rdn: styd on same pce fnl f* **11/1**

0 **7** *¾* **Salden Licht**[25] 6030 5-9-7 **96** .... LukeMorris 14 97
(J M P Eustace) *chsd ldrs: rdn over 2f out: one pce fr over 1f out* **100/1**

5545 **8** *1* **Sohcahtoa (IRE)**[76] 4409 3-8-12 **90** .... JamieSpencer 3 89
(R Hannon) *squeezed out s: bhd: rdn 2f out: styd on fnl f: nvr a danger* **14/1**

4000 **9** *3 ¼* **Huzzah (IRE)**[15] 6307 4-9-6 **95** .... MichaelHills 13 86
(B W Hills) *hld up towards rr: sme late prog: n.d* **11/1**

5343 **10** *nse* **Derbaas (USA)**[37] 5655 3-9-12 **104** .... RHills 4 95
(E A L Dunlop) *mid-div: rdn 3f out: sn hung rt: no imp* **14/1**

1225 **11** *1* **Russian Jar (IRE)**[33] 5766 3-8-8 **86** .... PhilipRobinson 7 75
(M A Jarvis) *trckd ldrs: rdn 3f out: wknd over 1f out* **12/1**

0020 **12** *shd* **Bolodenka (IRE)**[23] 6094 7-8-12 **90** .... FrederikTylicki(3) 8 79
(R A Fahey) *mid-div: rdn over 3f out: wknd 2f out* **12/1**

00 **13** *shd* **Pride Of Nation (IRE)**[109] 3301 7-8-7 **82** oh5 .... HayleyTurner 16 70
(J W Hills) *trckd ldrs: rdn over 3f out: wknd wl over 1f out* **50/1**

1500 **14** *3 ¾* **Stevie Gee (IRE)**[70] 4597 5-8-9 **84** .... JimCrowley 9 64
(Ian Williams) *mid-div tl 2f out* **28/1**

100P **15** *½* **Dubai Dynamo**[135] 2480 4-8-12 **87** .... GregFairley 12 66
(P F I Cole) *dwlt: bhd: t.k.h and hdwy whn swtchd to centre after 2f: rdn 3f out: sn btn* **33/1**

1m 45.63s (2.13) **Going Correction** +0.20s/f (Good)
WFA 3 from 4yo+ 3lb **15** Ran SP% **125.0**
Speed ratings (Par 109): **97,95,94,93,93 92,92,91,87,87 86,86,86,82,82**
toteswingers: 1&2 £8.50, 1&3 £7.30, 2&3 £7.70 CSF £47.41 CT £139.21 TOTE £9.60: £3.00, £2.30, £1.70; EX 53.00.
Owner Five Horses Ltd **Bred** Five Horses Ltd **Trained** Lambourn, Berks
■ Stewards' Enquiry : Richard Kingscote caution: careless riding

FOCUS
A decent and very competitive handicap. The early pace was only modest, but this is still form to rate positively. The winner should do better still.

NOTEBOOK
Prince Of Dance was having his first run since scoring comfortably on debut at Newbury back in May, when he suffered a hairline fracture of his pelvis, and had been allotted a tough-looking mark for this switch to a handicap. He followed up and confirmed himself a smart performer with a gutsy effort. He did well to find extra under maximum pressure considering he took a keen hold early on and the step up a furlong proved right up his street. On this showing he is a Pattern performer in the making, he clearly enjoys some juice in the ground and should go forward again for the experience. He may have one more run before being put away and connections are reportedly thinking about the Lincoln next season. (op 8-1)
Prime Exhibit, 6lb higher, was responsible for the slow early pace. He kept on gamely after being headed around 3f out and is evidently still on a fair mark. He helps to set the standard. (op 8-1)
Secrecy ◆ had every chance after making up his ground near the 2f pole and ran another solid race on this return to soft ground. He would have ideally preferred a more end-to-end gallop and there will be other days for him. (tchd 11-4)
Marching Time showed his Ascot flop 16 days earlier to be wrong, but failed to see out the extra furlong as well as the principals. This was the first time he had encountered ground this soft, though, so that was the likely cause for his effort petering out. (op 9-1)
Vitznau(IRE) ◆ did best of those coming from off the pace and this was his most encouraging display for a while. He is now on a fair mark, enjoys this sort of ground and a drop back to 7f could see him get closer again.
Signor Peltro was ridden to get this first ever run over the extra furlong and thus also had to come from behind. He performed respectably and is versatile as regards underfoot conditions. (op 10-1)
Huzzah(IRE) Official explanation: jockey said the colt hung right handed
Russian Jar(IRE) had yet to race away from a quick surface and his stamina looked stretched on this ground, but he again didn't help his cause by running freely early on. (op 11-1)

6733 BATHWICK TYRES ANDOVER H'CAP — 1m 1f 198y

4:50 (4:50) (Class 4) (0-85,85) 3-Y-O+ **£4,857** (£1,445; £722; £360) **Stalls** High

Form RPR

401 **1** **Hanoverian Baron**[26] 5997 4-9-0 **76** .... JamieSpencer 9 84+
(A G Newcombe) *hld up: nudged along over 4f out: rdn 3f out: hdwy fr over 2f out: styd on strly to ld ins fnl f* **9/2**²

0252 **2** *1 ¼* **Goliaths Boy (IRE)**[16] 6277 3-8-12 **82** .... FrederikTylicki(3) 7 87
(R A Fahey) *hld up: hdwy 6f out: chal 3f out: sn rdn: remained w ev ch tl fnl 75yds* **4/1**¹

44-2 **3** *hd* **Finney Hill**[139] 2351 4-8-13 **75** .... DaneO'Neill 2 80
(H Candy) *trckd ldr: rdn to take narrow advantage over 2f out: remained hrd pressed: no ex whn hdd wl ins fnl f* **6/1**³

6031 **4** *1* **Featherweight (IRE)**[29] 5915 3-9-0 **81** .... MichaelHills 10 84
(B W Hills) *led: rdn and narrowly hdd over 2f out: styd pressing ldr: ev ch ins fnl f: no ex fnl 75yds* **12/1**

2500 **5** *1 ¾* **Resurge (IRE)**[30] 5880 4-9-8 **84** .... AdamKirby 1 84
(W S Kittow) *mid-div: effrt 3f out: styd on same pce fnl f* **12/1**

6415 **6** *hd* **Admiral Dundas (IRE)**[11] 6435 4-9-2 **78** .... JimmyFortune 4 77
(W Jarvis) *cl up: rdn over 2f out: sn one pce* **11/1**

4321 **7** *shd* **Heritage Coast (USA)**[52] 5205 4-8-11 **73** .... RyanMoore 5 75+
(H Morrison) *trckd ldrs: rdn 3f out: kpt chsng ldrs but n.m.r on far rails: kpt on same pce: short of room and eased towards fin* **4/1**¹

0202 **8** *3 ¾* **Oriental Girl**[29] 5915 4-8-9 **71** oh8 .... (v) HayleyTurner 6 62
(J A Geake) *cl up: rdn over 2f out: fdd ent fnl f* **25/1**

3551 **9** *3 ¼* **Pelham Crescent (IRE)**[19] 6204 6-9-3 **79** .... DavidProbert 8 64
(B Palling) *hld up: hdwy over 4f out: rdn over 2f out: wknd over 1f out* **12/1**

000 **10** *1 ¼* **Final Verse**[11] 6429 6-9-9 **85** .... AlanMunro 11 67
(Matthew Salaman) *hld up: swtchd to centre and tk clsr order over 3f out: sn rdn: wknd wl over 1f out* **16/1**

-600 **11** *8* **Shooting Party (IRE)**[26] 5997 3-8-6 **73** .... EddieAhern 3 39
(R Hannon) *mid-div: rdn over 3f out: wknd 2f out* **18/1**

2m 13.3s (3.40) **Going Correction** +0.20s/f (Good)
WFA 3 from 4yo+ 5lb **11** Ran SP% **118.9**
Speed ratings (Par 105): **94,93,92,92,90 90,90,87,84,83 77**
toteswingers: 1&2 £4.40, 1&3 £9.70, 2&3 £9.40 CSF £23.14 CT £110.64 TOTE £6.40: £2.30, £1.70, £2.70; EX 21.50.
Owner Paul Moulton **Bred** S Coughlan **Trained** Yarnscombe, Devon

FOCUS
A fair handicap. It was steadily-run and the form looks ordinary, but the winner shaped a bit better than the bare form.
Heritage Coast(USA) Official explanation: jockey said the filly was denied a clear run
Pelham Crescent(IRE) Official explanation: jockey said the gelding was unsuited by the ground (Soft)
Shooting Party(IRE) Official explanation: jockey said the colt was unsuited by the ground (Soft)

6734 BATHWICK TYRES "SEASON FINALE" H'CAP — 1m 6f 21y

5:20 (5:21) (Class 3) (0-95,92) 3-Y-O+ **£7,771** (£2,312; £1,155; £577) **Stalls** High

Form RPR

3022 **1** **Overturn (IRE)**[16] 6281 5-9-12 **88** .... AdamKirby 6 101
(W R Swinburn) *prom: led after 3f: rdn whn narrowly hdd 2f out: rallied gamely: regained ld ins fnl f: styd on wl* **17/2**

2122 **2** *½* **Omokoroa (IRE)**[37] 5660 3-8-2 **78** .... AshleyMorgan(5) 4 90
(M H Tompkins) *hld up towards rr: gd hdwy fr over 3f out: tk narrow advantage 2f out: sn hung rt and rdn: hdd ins fnl f: no ex towards fin* **7/2**²

4-20 **3** *2 ¾* **Sleepy Hollow**[33] 5781 4-9-9 **85** .... RyanMoore 1 93
(H Morrison) *mid-div: hdwy over 2f out: sn rdn: styd on* **12/1**

4254 **4** *5* **Hawridge King**[13] 6368 7-9-0 **76** .... AlanMunro 2 77
(W S Kittow) *mid-div: hdwy over 2f out: sn rdn: styd on same pce* **25/1**

0051 **5** *1* **Crossbow Creek**[17] 6244 11-9-3 **79** .... JamieSpencer 3 79
(M G Rimell) *hld up: rdn over 2f out: styd on fr wl over 1f out but nvr trbld ldrs* **25/1**

154 **6** *hd* **Malt Or Mash (USA)**[23] 6116 5-9-4 **80** .... JimmyFortune 10 80
(R Hannon) *led for 3f: chsd ldrs: rdn 3f out: one pce fnl 2f* **25/1**

0-20 **7** *1* **Ruler Of All (IRE)**[178] 1328 3-8-7 **78** .... FrankieMcDonald 8 76
(H Candy) *in tch: rdn 3f out: sn one pce: fdd ins fnl f* **9/1**

6001 **8** *4 ½* **Kimberley Downs (USA)**[16] 6273 3-9-3 **88** .... (v) GregFairley 13 80
(M Johnston) *trckd ldrs: rdn to chal 3f out tl 2f out: wknd* **8/1**³

2113 **9** *1* **Brief Look**[23] 6113 3-8-13 **84** .... EddieAhern 12 75
(H R A Cecil) *trckd ldrs: rdn over 3f out: wknd over 2f out: hmpd whn btn* **10/3**¹

1513 **10** *4* **Times Up**[30] 5870 3-9-7 **92** .... JimCrowley 5 77
(J L Dunlop) *in tch: rdn 3f out: wknd over 1f out* **8/1**³

/0-0 **11** *2 ½* **Misty Dancer**[15] 6302 10-9-3 **82** .... FrederikTylicki(3) 11 64
(Miss Venetia Williams) *mid-div tl wknd 2f out* **33/1**

06/0 **12** *1* **Sagredo (USA)**[16] 6273 5-10-0 **90** .... RichardKingscote 9 70
(Jonjo O'Neill) *a towards rr* **50/1**

216- **13** *72* **Okafranca (IRE)**[221] 6390 4-8-9 **71** oh1 .... HayleyTurner 14 —
(J A B Old) *a bhd: detached fnl 4f* **33/1**

/505 **P** **Alessano**[33] 5781 7-8-13 **75** .... (b) DaneO'Neill 7 —
(G L Moore) *in tch: rdn 3f out: eased over 2f out: p.u ins fnl f: lame* **25/1**

3m 7.42s (0.02) **Going Correction** +0.20s/f (Good)
WFA 3 from 4yo+ 9lb **14** Ran SP% **119.0**
Speed ratings (Par 107): **107,106,105,102,101 101,101,98,97,95 94,93,52,—**
toteswingers: 1&2 £9.60, 1&3 £17.00, 2&3 £15.30 CSF £34.86 CT £366.60 TOTE £9.60: £3.10, £1.90, £3.70; EX 43.20 Place 6: £131.27 Place 5: £44.98.
Owner P W Harris **Bred** Pendley Farm **Trained** Aldbury, Herts

FOCUS
A decent staying handicap for the grade. A personal best from the winner and the first three finished clear.

NOTEBOOK
Overturn(IRE) opened his account for the season at the sixth time of asking and did the job in most game fashion. He made most and repelled numerous challenges down the home straight, but his attitude in fending off the runner-up late on was admirable. He had been placed on three of his last four outings so success was deserved and it confirms his versatility regarding ground conditions. It was also just his second outing at the trip and he should have more to offer as a stayer. (op 9-1 tchd 10-1)
Omokoroa(IRE) finished second on his debut over this distance on testing ground off a 1lb lower mark 37 days previously and was well backed on this return. He emerged with a strong challenge from 2f out, but found the winner too resolute and has now finished a runner-up on three of his last four runs. (op 11-2 tchd 3-1)
Sleepy Hollow was produced with his chance and stuck gamely to his task inside the final furlong. This was much more like it from him, but the soft ground over this trip looked to stretch his stamina.

Hawridge King plugged on at the same pace and really wants better ground, so was not disgraced. (op 20-1)
Crossbow Creek, back to winning ways at Ascot last time, was 6lb higher and despite having twice raced over further in the past had yet to prove his stamina for this distance. He finished well from off the pace, but never looked a serious danger and very probably find this too testing. (op 22-1 tchd 20-1)
Malt Or Mash(USA), stepping up from 1m4f, was taken back after initially adopting a positive position and never seriously threatened but this was one of his better runs. (tchd 22-1)
Ruler Of All(IRE) was returning from a 178-day layoff and got supported for this handicap debut. He spoilt his chance of getting home by refusing to settle, but still showed enough to suggest he has begun life in this sphere on a fair mark. (op 20-1 tchd 22-1)
Brief Look was backed to resume winning ways, but her fate over this longer trip on such ground was apparent some way out due to her refusal to settle early on. Official explanation: jockey said that the filly was unsuited by the ground (Soft) (op 7-2 tchd 3-1)
Alessano Official explanation: jockey said that the gelding finished lame
T/Plt: £182.30 to a £1 stake. Pool: £61,267.64. 245.30 winning tickets. T/Qpdt: £14.00 to a £1 stake. Pool: £5,857.47. 309.45 winning tickets. TM

6547 WINDSOR (R-H)

Monday, October 12

OFFICIAL GOING: Good to soft (soft in places)

Top bend dolled out 2yds increasing distances of races over 1m plus by 7yds.
Wind: light, across Weather: sunny

6735 WINDSOR & ETON EXPRESS NURSERY (DIV I) — 1m 67y

2:00 (2:02) (Class 5) (0-75,75) 2-Y-O — £2,388 (£705; £352) Stalls High

Form — RPR

6515 **1** — **Agony And Ecstasy**[19] 6211 2-9-7 **75** .... SebSanders 2 — 78
(R M Beckett) *mde all: wnt towards far side st: rdn over 2f out: drvn ent fnl f: a doing enough to hold on* — **8/1**[3]

5532 **2** shd **Mountrath**[24] 6066 2-9-2 **73** ....(p) JackMitchell(3) 8 — 76
(B R Johnson) *hld up towards rr: effrt in centre over 2f out: hung lft after but kpt on to chse wnr over 1f out: kpt on wl but nvr quite getting there* — **4/1**[1]

5333 **3** 1 ½ **Whiepa Snappa (IRE)**[12] 6391 2-8-11 **65** .... IanMongan 10 — 64
(P M Phelan) *in tch: rdn to chse wnr wl over 2f out: lost 2nd over 1f out: kpt on same pce fnl f* — **4/1**[1]

4050 **4** 2 ¼ **Cafe Greco**[19] 6211 2-9-3 **71** ....(v[1]) TedDurcan 14 — 65
(P J Makin) *s.i.s: sn bustled along and in tch: rdn and wanting to hang lft ent fnl 2f: keeping on same pce whn hmpd over 1f out* — **12/1**

1600 **5** 2 **Emma Dora (IRE)**[19] 6211 2-8-10 **64** .... RobertWinston 13 — 54
(D R C Elsworth) *chsd ldr after 1f tl wl over 2f out: wknd u.p 2f out: hung lft after* — **16/1**

4505 **6** nse **My Sister**[14] 6343 2-8-7 **61** .... NeilChalmers 7 — 51
(M D I Usher) *bhd: rdn and effrt towards centre over 2f out: hung lft but kpt on steadily fnl 2f: nvr trbld ldrs* — **16/1**

000 **7** ½ **Bun Oir (USA)**[45] 5400 2-9-0 **68** .... PatDobbs 3 — 57
(R Hannon) *chsd ldrs: rdn 3f out: drvn and unable qck ent fnl 2f: swtchd lft and btn over 1f out* — **8/1**[3]

0340 **8** 2 **Fire And Stone (IRE)**[71] 4565 2-8-13 **67** .... RichardSmith 6 — 53
(Tom Dascombe) *hld up towards rr: rdn and effrt 3f out: nvr trbld ldrs* — **25/1**

0361 **9** 4 **Green Earth (IRE)**[13] 6366 2-9-6 **74** .... SteveDrowne 9 — 50
(Mrs A J Perrett) *s.i.s: sn in midfield: rdn and hdwy over 3f out: chsd ldrs and drvn over 2f out: wknd qckly and hung lft over 1f out* — **5/1**[2]

0304 **10** 2 **Whipperway (IRE)**[19] 6199 2-9-2 **70** .... ChrisCatlin 1 — 41
(M R Channon) *chsd ldrs tl wknd u.p over 2f out* — **14/1**

006 **11** shd **Petite Mambo**[86] 4086 2-8-11 **65** .... FrancisNorton 4 — 38
(W De Best-Turner) *a bhd: rdn and struggling wl over 3f out: no ch whn hmpd ins fnl f* — **33/1**

0660 **12** 2 **Calm Storm (IRE)**[26] 5985 2-8-8 **62** ....(v[1]) ShaneKelly 5 — 29
(J Noseda) *a towards rr: rdn and no rspnse over 2f out* — **16/1**

0005 **13** 5 **Carlcol Girl**[25] 6033 2-7-8 **55** .... RyanPowell(7) 12 — 17
(Mrs C A Dunnett) *s.i.s: t.k.h and hld up in tch in midfield: rdn and struggling over 2f out* — **66/1**

600 **14** 8 **The Frying Pan (IRE)**[68] 4666 2-7-12 **52** oh7........(b) AdrianMcCarthy 11 — —
(Dr J D Scargill) *a bhd: lost tch over 2f out: eased fnl f* — **100/1**

1m 47.46s (2.76) **Going Correction** +0.25s/f (Good) — **14** Ran SP% **120.2**
Speed ratings (Par 95): **96,95,94,92,90 90,89,87,83,81 81,79,74,66**
toteswingers: 1&2 £4.20, 1&3 £5.90, 2&3 £3.30 CSF £39.06 CT £155.50 TOTE £7.10: £2.60, £1.40, £1.80; EX 32.20 Trifecta £204.60 Part won. Pool: £276.49 - 0.40 winning units..
Owner Miss Rachel Tregaskes **Bred** Downfield Cottage Stud **Trained** Whitsbury, Hants

FOCUS
The first division of a modest nursery. The winner dictated and the form looks solid.

NOTEBOOK
Agony And Ecstasy led soon after the off and holding on well from the wayward runner-up. She had gone too fast when finishing fifth at Kempton last time and received a better-judgedride on this occasion, but it remains to be seen whether she can go on and score off a higher mark. (op 4-1)
Mountrath, 14lb higher than when finishing third in a 7f nursery at Epsom two starts back, showed improved form when second in a Newmarket maiden over this trip last time and he ran another improved race in the first-time cheekpieces, just failing to get there having hung left from inside the final 2f. (op 9-1)
Whiepa Snappa(IRE) has now finished third on all four starts in handicaps. Tried over 1m2f at Nottingham last time, he was just found wanting for a bit of speed on this return to 1m, but should find a race eventually if holding his form. (op 6-1 tchd 13-2)
Cafe Greco, never involved at Kempton last time, got a bit behind in the first-time visor, but he was going on at the finish and would have been closer but for getting hampered 1f out. (tchd 14-1)
Emma Dora(IRE) continues to slide in the weights and this was a step back in the right direction. (tchd 14-1)
Green Earth(IRE), up 6lb for winning at Warwick last time, was faced with slower ground conditions on this occasion and was found out by the extra furlong. (op 9-2 tchd 4-1)
The Frying Pan(IRE) Official explanation: jockey said the filly lost its action

6736 WINDSOR & ETON EXPRESS NURSERY (DIV II) — 1m 67y

2:30 (2:30) (Class 5) (0-75,74) 2-Y-O — £2,388 (£705; £352) Stalls High

Form — RPR

303 **1** — **Christopher Wren (USA)**[11] 6416 2-9-2 **69** .... RobertWinston 14 — 73
(J R Best) *in tch: hmpd bnd on inner 6f out: hdwy to chse ldrs over 3f out: ev ch wl over 1f out: led 1f out: styd on wl and clr ins fnl f* — **9/1**

040 **2** 2 ¼ **Wild Rockette**[21] 6164 2-9-6 **73** .... TedDurcan 6 — 72
(B J Meehan) *hld up bhd: hdwy towards centre wl over 1f out: drvn and styd on wl fnl f to chse wnr fnl 75yds: nvr gng to rch wnr* — **7/1**[3]

0002 **3** ¾ **Edward Whymper**[39] 5595 2-8-12 **65** .... SebSanders 11 — 62
(M H Tompkins) *chsd ldrs over 6f out: ev ch and rdn over 2f out: hrd drvn 2f out: no ex and outpcd ins fnl f* — **4/1**[1]

0625 **4** hd **Rodrigo De Freitas (IRE)**[26] 5985 2-8-10 **63** .... NickyMackay 8 — 60
(J R Boyle) *dwlt and bustled along early: in tch: hdwy and edging lft fr 2f out: chsd ldrs over 1f out: one pce fnl f* — **4/1**[1]

044 **5** 2 ¾ **Deely Plaza**[30] 5852 2-9-7 **74** .... IanMongan 13 — 66
(R Hannon) *chsd ldrs tl led after 1f: hrd pressed and rdn over 2f out: hdd 1f out: wknd ins fnl f* — **16/1**

0340 **6** 1 ¼ **Machine Gun Kelly (IRE)**[15] 6305 2-8-12 **65** .... TomEaves 3 — 53
(G L Moore) *led for 1f: styd handy: effrt to press ldrs 2f out: wknd u.p jst over 1f out* — **12/1**

354 **7** ¾ **Banks And Braes**[30] 5879 2-9-6 **73** .... PatDobbs 9 — 60
(R Hannon) *in tch tl lost pl u.p over 2f out: no ch w ldrs after* — **5/1**[2]

0000 **8** hd **Vadition (IRE)**[19] 6200 2-7-7 **51** oh6........ AmyBaker(5) 5 — 37
(J J Bridger) *s.i.s: wl in tch in rr: pushed along and no hdwy 3f out: plugged on fr over 1f out: nt trble ldrs* — **100/1**

6063 **9** ¾ **Execution (IRE)**[3] 6639 2-8-7 **60** ....(b[1]) ChrisCatlin 12 — 44
(E A L Dunlop) *s.i.s and pushed along early: in tch in midfield whn hmpd bnd over 5f out: drvn and effrt ent fnl 2f: no prog* — **8/1**

006 **10** ¾ **Knockback (IRE)**[58] 5017 2-8-2 **55** .... FrancisNorton 10 — 39
(P R Chamings) *chsd ldrs: rdn and struggling jst over 2f out: wkng whn hmpd over 1f out: wl btn fnl f* — **25/1**

2000 **11** 2 ¾ **New York Lights (IRE)**[25] 6034 2-7-10 **56** oh1 ow5...... RachelKing(7) 2 — 33
(M D I Usher) *taken down early: a in rr: nvr a factor* — **66/1**

3200 **12** 6 **Storm Hawk (IRE)**[28] 5935 2-8-10 **68** ....(v) MartinLane(5) 1 — 32
(Pat Eddery) *in tch in midfield tl carried v wd and lost pl bnd 6f out: bhd after: rdn and no rspnse 3f out: bhd fnl 2f* — **18/1**

304 **13** 6 **Saint Thomas (IRE)**[23] 6125 2-9-3 **70** ....(b[1]) SteveDrowne 4 — 20
(J A Osborne) *chsd ldrs tl nt handle bnd and rn wd bnd 6f out: bhd after: rdn and no rspnse 3f out: wl bhd fnl 2f* — **22/1**

1m 47.84s (3.14) **Going Correction** +0.25s/f (Good) — **13** Ran SP% **119.8**
Speed ratings (Par 95): **94,91,91,90,88 86,86,85,85,84 81,75,69**
toteswingers: 1&2 £14.60, 1&3 £8.00, 2&3 £7.00 CSF £69.08 CT £308.72 TOTE £10.00: £3.10, £3.10, £1.70; EX 98.30 Trifecta £187.40 Pool: £344.46 - 1.36 winning units..
Owner Kingsgate Racing **Bred** Rod D'Elia **Trained** Hucking, Kent
■ Stewards' Enquiry : Nicky Mackay one-day ban: careless riding

FOCUS
This was just as competitive as the first division. Fair and reliable nursery form.

NOTEBOOK
Christopher Wren(USA), expected to be suited by the return to 1m for this nursery debut, was slightly interfered with after a couple of furlongs, but it didn´t affect him and, having hit the front over 1f out, he stayed on strongly to win with a bit in hand. There may well be more to come at this distance. (op 11-1 tchd 14-1)
Wild Rockette was always likely to improve once going handicapping and she stayed on well inside the final furlong to take second. The step up to this trip clearly helped and she should find a small race before long. (op 9-2 tchd 15-2)
Edward Whymper, raised 2lb for finishing third at Redcar last time, couldn´t quicken on this first try at 1m and may be better back on faster ground. (op 9-2 tchd 5-1)
Rodrigo De Freitas(IRE), a non-runner at Goodwood the previous day, bounced back to the sort of form that saw him finish second at Kempton last month. (op 7-1)
Deely Plaza didn´t get home on this first try at 1m, but is probably capable of winning a small race back in trip. (op 14-1)
Machine Gun Kelly(IRE) didn´t get home on this first try at 1m. (op 10-1)
Banks And Braes failed to build on the form shown in maidens, being beaten with 2f to run. (tchd 9-2)
Saint Thomas(IRE) Official explanation: jockey said colt failed handle the bend

6737 E B F CAYLEY RAYERS LOYAL ROYALS MAIDEN STKS — 6f

3:05 (3:06) (Class 5) 2-Y-O — £3,885 (£1,156; £577; £288) Stalls High

Form — RPR

5 **1** — **Za Za Zoom (IRE)**[58] 5021 2-8-12 0 .... RobertWinston 1 — 75+
(B W Hills) *in tch in midfield: hdwy to chse ldrs and rdn wl over 1f out: nt clr run and swtchd rt over 1f out: r.o wl u.p to ld towards fin* — **9/4**[1]

0 **2** ½ **Humidor (IRE)**[77] 4377 2-9-3 0 .... SteveDrowne 4 — 78
(R Charlton) *chsd ldrs: rdn and effrt 2f out: drvn through gap on far rail to ld jst ins fnl f: no ex towards fin* — **12/1**

4 **3** nk **Imperial Delight**[71] 4568 2-9-3 0 .... SebSanders 15 — 77
(H Candy) *chsd ldrs: rdn 2f out: ev ch wl over 1f out: led ent fnl f: hdd jst ins fnl f: kpt on same pce fnl 100yds* — **15/2**[3]

03 **4** ½ **Pin Cushion**[58] 5021 2-8-12 0 .... TedDurcan 8 — 70+
(B J Meehan) *dwlt: bhd: lost tch 1/2-way: hdwy ent fnl 2f: styd on wl fnl f: gng on fin but nt rch ldrs* — **11/4**[2]

0240 **5** 1 ¾ **West Leake Star (IRE)**[48] 5325 2-9-3 72 .... FrancisNorton 14 — 70
(B W Hills) *w ldrs: rdn ent fnl 2f: drvn over 1f out: wknd ins fnl f* — **8/1**

0 **6** 1 **Brave Ghurka**[93] 3867 2-9-3 0 .... ShaneKelly 10 — 67
(S Kirk) *led tl over 3f out: led again wl over 1f out tl ent fnl f: wknd fnl 150yds* — **33/1**

7 3 **Erebus (IRE)** 2-9-3 0 .... PatDobbs 6 — 58
(S Kirk) *dwlt: towards rr: pushed along and struggling 4f out: hdwy into midfield 2f out: nvr trbld ldrs* — **66/1**

0266 **8** hd **Starwatch**[24] 6057 2-9-0 70 .... MCGeran(3) 13 — 57
(J J Bridger) *in tch tl struggling and rdn wl over 2f out: no ch fnl 2f* — **10/1**

9 1 ½ **Micky P** 2-9-0 0 .... WilliamCarson(3) 9 — 57+
(S C Williams) *s.i.s: bhd: sme modest late hdwy: nvr a factor* — **66/1**

06 **10** 1 ¼ **Pie Poudre**[12] 6386 2-9-3 0 .... TomEaves 7 — 49
(R Brotherton) *v.s.a: a bhd* — **100/1**

0 **11** 2 ¼ **Valmina**[108] 3344 2-9-3 0 .... RichardSmith 12 — 42
(Tom Dascombe) *w ldrs tl led over 3f out: rdn and hdd wl over 1f out: wknd rapidly over 1f out* — **33/1**

00 **12** 6 **Rock A Doodle Doo (IRE)**[11] 6424 2-9-3 0 .... J-PGuillambert 3 — 28+
(W Jarvis) *racd off the pce in midfield: struggling bef 1/2-way: wl bhd fnl 2f* — **50/1**

0 **13** 1 ½ **Eclipsed (USA)**[6] 6561 2-9-3 0 .... TonyCulhane 11 — 20
(J R Best) *racd off the pce in midfield: struggling 1/2-way: sn bhd* — **33/1**

14 ¾ **Swansea Jack** 2-9-3 0 .... ChrisCatlin 2 — 18
(S C Williams) *s.i.s: rn green and a bhd* — **16/1**

1m 15.16s (2.16) **Going Correction** +0.25s/f (Good) — **14** Ran SP% **117.7**
Speed ratings (Par 95): **95,94,93,93,90 89,85,85,83,81 78,70,68,67**
toteswingers: 1&2 £11.90, 1&3 £4.00, 2&3 £12.80 CSF £28.90 TOTE £3.70: £1.70, £3.30, £1.70; EX 38.00 Trifecta £230.50 Part won. Pool: £304.50 - 0.50 winning units..
Owner Simon Brooke & Steve Smith **Bred** Rathbarry Stud **Trained** Lambourn, Berks

FOCUS
This was a modest maiden. The form is limited, but solid enough.

NOTEBOOK

Za Za Zoom(IRE), a promising fifth in a fair race at Newbury on debut, had to be switched into the clear, but picked up well and stayed on well to get on top close home. There is more to come from her at 7f. (op 5-2)

Humidor(IRE) improved markedly on his debut effort over C&D, coming through to lead inside the final furlong before being run down close home. (op 14-1 tchd 16-1)

Imperial Delight stepped up on his initial effort and is the type to find a small race once handicapping. He will do better back on faster ground. (op 6-1 tchd 11-2)

Pin Cushion got behind following a sluggish start and looked to be going nowhere at halfway, but really started to run on well down the straight and she was going on close home. She is qualified for a mark now and should find a race before long. (op 2-1 tchd 15-8)

West Leake Star(IRE) ran no sort of race on the Fibresand last time and this was better, but he is well exposed and shall remain vulnerable. (op 12-1)

6738 AT THE RACES SKY 415 H'CAP (DIV I) — 6f

3:35 (3:36) (Class 5) (0-70,70) 3-Y-O+ — £2,388 (£705; £352) Stalls High

Form — RPR

040 **1** **Efisio Princess**[59] 5008 6-8-5 **56** oh2 .... RichardThomas 6 — 72
(J E Long) *mde all: rdn and clr over 1f out: unchal after* **8/1**

0300 **2** *3* **Hereford Boy**[5] 6588 5-8-6 **60** ....(p) JackMitchell(3) 7 — 66
(D K Ivory) *stdd s: hld up in rr: hdwy over 2f out: chsd clr wnr over 1f out: no imp* **7/1**[3]

000 **3** *3/4* **Leading Edge (IRE)**[6] 6572 4-9-0 **65** .... ChrisCatlin 13 — 69
(M R Channon) *s.i.s: bhd: rdn over 2f out: styd on to chse ldng pair ins fnl f: nvr nr wnr* **20/1**

0504 **4** *1 1/2* **Rough Rock (IRE)**[26] 5998 4-8-2 **56** oh5 .... KellyHarrison(3) 8 — 55
(C A Dwyer) *chsd ldrs: rdn and struggling to hold pl wl over 2f out: kpt on same pce fr over 1f out* **7/1**[3]

0046 **5** *3/4* **Carmenero (GER)**[10] 6444 6-9-1 **66** .... SJCraine 2 — 62
(C R Dore) *bhd: rdn and no prog jst over 2f out: kpt on ins fnl f: n.d* **25/1**

5406 **6** *1 1/2* **Dream Express (IRE)**[23] 6112 4-9-3 **68** .... IanMongan 11 — 60
(P Howling) *hld up towards rr: styd towards stands' side and rdn over 2f out: edgd lft fr over 1f out: nvr trbld ldrs* **14/1**

2034 **7** *1 1/2* **Espy**[25] 6028 4-8-9 **67** .... JPFahy(7) 3 — 54
(S Kirk) *chsd wnr: ev ch and rdn 2f out: nt qckn and wanting to hang rt after: fdd tamely over 1f out* **13/2**[2]

2035 **8** *1 1/4* **Izzi Mill (USA)**[10] 6444 3-9-2 **68** .... TedDurcan 5 — 51
(D R C Elsworth) *t.k.h: in tch: rdn and effrt 2f out: wknd over 1f out: eased ins fnl f* **9/1**

060 **9** *3 1/2* **Caledonia Princess**[13] 6361 3-9-4 **70** .... TonyCulhane 9 — 42
(R Curtis) *in tch: rdn and unable qck over 2f out: no ch fnl 2f* **16/1**

4002 **10** *1 1/4* **Tudor Prince (IRE)**[25] 6028 5-9-1 **66** .... ShaneKelly 4 — 34
(A W Carroll) *stdd s: hld up in rr: hdwy into midfield 1/2-way: rdn and struggling jst over 2f out: wl btn and eased ins fnl f* **5/1**[1]

2003 **11** *3 1/4* **Foxtrot Alpha (IRE)**[54] 5167 3-9-1 **67** .... StephenCarson 12 — 24
(P Winkworth) *chsd ldrs tl wknd u.p 2f out: wl btn fnl f* **9/1**

5504 **12** *shd* **Golden Dixie (USA)**[13] 6362 10-8-12 **63** .... RobertWinston 10 — 20
(R A Harris) *a in rr: pushed along over 3f out: no ch fnl 2f* **12/1**

1m 13.93s (0.93) **Going Correction** +0.25s/f (Good)
WFA 3 from 4yo+ 1lb — **12** Ran SP% **115.0**
Speed ratings (Par 103): **103,99,98,96,95 93,91,89,84,83 78,78**
toteswingers: 1&2 £7.50, 1&3 £35.30, 2&3 £37.00 CSF £61.07 CT £1096.04 TOTE £9.60: £2.80, £2.90, £5.50; EX 55.80 Trifecta £195.90 Part won. Pool: £264.81 - 0.10 winning units..
Owner Miss M B Fernandes **Bred** Mrs A Yearley **Trained** Caterham, Surrey

FOCUS
A moderate sprint handicap run in thre quickest of the three C&D times. The winner reproduced something like her AW best.
Dream Express(IRE) Official explanation: jockey said gelding hung right
Izzi Mill(USA) Official explanation: jockey said gelding hung right
Golden Dixie(USA) Official explanation: trainer said gelding was unsutied by the Good to Soft, Soft in places going

6739 AT THE RACES SKY 415 H'CAP (DIV II) — 6f

4:10 (4:12) (Class 5) (0-70,69) 3-Y-O+ — £2,388 (£705; £352) Stalls High

Form — RPR

1300 **1** **Fyelehk (IRE)**[31] 5836 3-8-11 **62** .... TedDurcan 1 — 74
(B R Millman) *taken down early: in tch: hdwy towards far side over 2f out: led 2f out: edgd rt over 1f: pushed clr fnl f* **10/1**

1345 **2** *3* **Solemn**[19] 6201 4-8-12 **65** ....(b) MCGeran(3) 8 — 67
(J M Bradley) *in tch: rdn and effrt 2f out: hung bdly lft over 1f out: chsd wnr fnl f: no imp: jst hung on for 2nd* **11/2**[2]

1400 **3** *shd* **Ben's Dream (IRE)**[18] 6230 3-9-3 **68** ....(tp) PatDobbs 9 — 70
(A M Balding) *in tch in midfield: rdn ent fnl 2f: carried lft and hmpd over 1f out: kpt on to press for 2nd nr fin: no ch w wnr* **14/1**

4440 **4** *1* **Top Town Girl**[18] 6230 3-9-2 **67** ....(p) SebSanders 7 — 66
(R M Beckett) *chsd ldr tl rdn to ld over 2f out: hdd 2f out: btn whn carried lft and hmpd 1f out* **8/1**[3]

U060 **5** *nk* **Pinball (IRE)**[12] 6377 3-8-7 **58** ....(v) NeilChalmers 13 — 56
(Mrs L Williamson) *in tch in midfield: effrt u.p 2f out: chsd ldrs over 1f out: kpt on same pce fnl f* **25/1**

3500 **6** *2 1/2* **Kipchak (IRE)**[23] 6120 4-9-3 **67** ....(p) AdrianMcCarthy 4 — 57
(C R Dore) *taken down early: led tl over 2f out: wknd u.p wl over 1f out* **20/1**

-536 **7** *1* **Golden Rosie (IRE)**[28] 5937 3-9-2 **67** .... RobertWinston 3 — 54
(B W Hills) *bhd: hdwy and rdn towards far side over 2f out: nvr gng pce to threaten wnr* **12/1**

0603 **8** *2* **Style Award**[14] 6341 4-8-7 **60** ....(p) KellyHarrison(3) 10 — 40
(W J H Ratcliffe) *hmpd sn after s: bhd: sme hdwy 2f out: nvr trbld ldrs* **11/1**

4515 **9** *nse* **Bermondsey Bob (IRE)**[14] 6340 3-8-4 **55** oh5 .... FrancisNorton 2 — 35
(J L Spearing) *chsd ldrs: rdn ent fnl 2f: wknd over 1f out: eased whn btn ins fnl f* **8/1**[3]

1065 **10** *2* **Chasca (IRE)**[25] 6028 3-9-0 **65** .... SteveDrowne 5 — 39
(Mrs A J Perrett) *chsd ldrs: drvn and no rspnse over 2f out: wknd 2f out* **11/1**

2206 **11** *nse* **Ken's Girl**[32] 5804 5-9-4 **68** .... ChrisCatlin 12 — 42
(W S Kittow) *chsd ldrs: struggling 1/2-way: wl bhd fnl 2f* **5/1**[1]

4-00 **12** *hd* **Mugeba**[30] 5883 8-7-13 **56** oh10 ow1 .... JPFahy(7) 14 — 29
(C A Dwyer) *a in rr: rdn and no prog over 2f out: eased ins fnl f* **66/1**

1100 **13** *1/2* **Realt Na Mara (IRE)**[35] 5719 6-9-5 **69** .... TravisBlock 6 — 40
(H Morrison) *s.i.s: a bhd* **16/1**

2020 **14** *3 1/2* **Dressed To Dance (IRE)**[6] 6572 5-8-13 **68** ....(b) RichardEvans(5) 11 — 28
(R A Harris) *awkward s: a in rr* **10/1**

1m 15.09s (2.09) **Going Correction** +0.25s/f (Good)
WFA 3 from 4yo+ 1lb — **14** Ran SP% **119.5**
Speed ratings (Par 103): **96,92,91,90,90 86,85,82,82,80 80,79,79,74**
toteswingers: 1&2 £20.50, 1&3 £34.10, 2&3 £16.70 CSF £62.38 CT £806.05 TOTE £10.70: £2.90, £1.90, £5.90; EX 97.80 TRIFECTA Not won..
Owner The Links Partnership **Bred** Camogue Stud Ltd **Trained** Kentisbeare, Devon

FOCUS
This was probably just the stronger of the two divisions, although the time was more thana second slower. Ordinary form.
Solemn Official explanation: jockey said gelding hung left
Dressed To Dance(IRE) Official explanation: trainer said gelding was unsutied by the Good to Soft, Soft in places going

6740 SLOUGH & SOUTH BUCKS EXPRESS H'CAP — 1m 2f 7y

4:40 (4:40) (Class 4) (0-85,85) 3-Y-O — £4,857 (£1,445; £722; £360) Stalls Low

Form — RPR

315 **1** **Splinter Cell (USA)**[37] 5670 3-9-3 **84** .... TedDurcan 7 — 91+
(M Botti) *hld up in last trio: hdwy over 3f out: rdn to chse ldrs 2f out: hanging lft and swtchd rt 1f out: kpt hanging lft but drvn to chal ins fnl f: led on post* **5/1**[3]

4100 **2** *nse* **History Lesson**[64] 4827 3-9-3 **84** .... PatDobbs 5 — 91
(R Hannon) *chsd ldr tl led after 1f: rdn and hdd 2f out: 3rd and looked btn 1f out: rallied gamely to ld again nr fin: hdd on post* **16/1**

5326 **3** *1/2* **Call It On (IRE)**[23] 6114 3-9-4 **85** .... SebSanders 1 — 91
(M H Tompkins) *chsd ldrs: rdn to ld on far side 2f out: drvn over 1f out: hdd and lost 2 pls nr fin* **9/2**[2]

4316 **4** *3* **Critical Path (IRE)**[26] 5997 3-8-9 **76** .... FrancisNorton 6 — 76
(A M Balding) *t.k.h: hld up towards rr: hdwy and rdn ent fnl 2f: keeping on same pce whn nt clr run and swtchd rt ins fnl f: snatched 4th on post* **11/1**

225 **5** *nse* **Tinshu (IRE)**[26] 5996 3-8-11 **78** .... ChrisCatlin 3 — 78
(D Haydn Jones) *t.k.h: led for 1f: chsd ldr after: rdn and ev ch 2f out: drvn and one pce over 1f out: btn whn squeezed and hmpd ins fnl f* **12/1**

4216 **6** *1/2* **Vivachi (IRE)**[54] 5168 3-8-1 **75** .... JPFahy(7) 2 — 74
(R M Beckett) *dwlt: in tch in midfield: rdn and unable qck jst over 2f out: jinked rt 1f out: plugged on same pce* **10/1**

3521 **7** *1* **Silverglas (IRE)**[20] 6190 3-8-9 **76** .... ShaneKelly 11 — 73+
(M P Tregoning) *hld up in tch: rdn and unable qck over 2f out: hanging lft and real prog after* **9/4**[1]

4050 **8** *1 3/4* **Norwegian Dancer (UAE)**[17] 6239 3-9-3 **84** .... RobertWinston 8 — 77
(E S McMahon) *t.k.h: chsd ldrs: rdn and unable qck ent fnl 2f: wknd qckly jst over 1f out* **12/1**

3302 **9** *5* **In Secret**[29] 5910 3-8-4 **71** oh1 .... NickyMackay 4 — 54
(J L Dunlop) *dwlt: in tch: rdn and struggling to hold pl over 3f out: wl btn fnl 2f: eased ins fnl f* **11/1**

0166 **10** *2 3/4* **Directorship**[31] 5834 3-8-13 **80** .... TonyCulhane 9 — 58
(P R Chamings) *t.k.h: hld up in last pair: rdn and toiling bdly 3f out* **20/1**

12-0 **11** *3/4* **Hurakan (IRE)**[11] 6420 3-8-10 **77** .... SteveDrowne 10 — 53
(Mrs A J Perrett) *hld up in last pair: rdn and toiling bdly 3f out* **22/1**

2m 9.98s (1.28) **Going Correction** +0.25s/f (Good) — **11** Ran SP% **121.8**
Speed ratings (Par 103): **104,103,103,101,101 100,99,98,94,92 91**
toteswingers: 1&2 £17.80, 1&3 £5.80, 2&3 £11.40 CSF £85.11 CT £393.90 TOTE £7.00: £2.10, £5.40, £2.00; EX 132.50 TRIFECTA Not won..
Owner Op - Center **Bred** Old Carhue Stud **Trained** Newmarket, Suffolk

FOCUS
A good handicap for the grade. The first three finished clear.

6741 BAYLIS MEDIA MAIDEN STKS — 1m 67y

5:10 (5:10) (Class 5) 3-Y-O+ — £2,729 (£806; £403) Stalls High

Form — RPR

1 **Rainbow Desert (USA)** 3-8-12 0 .... TedDurcan 8 — 90+
(Saeed Bin Suroor) *mde all: gng much the best over 2f out: c clr wl over 1f out: v easily* **15/8**[1]

20/ **2** *5* **Etruscan (IRE)**[712] 6592 4-9-6 0 .... ChrisCatlin 7 — 74
(C Gordon) *chsd wnr thrght: rdn jst over 2f out: no ch w wnr fr wl over 1f out: kpt on for 2nd* **16/1**

4 **3** *1 1/4* **Serious Drinking (USA)**[11] 6430 3-8-12 0 .... ShaneKelly 5 — 66
(W R Swinburn) *in tch: chsd ldng pair over 2f out: wl outpcd by wnr wl over 1f out: plugged on for 3rd* **4/1**[2]

4 *4* **Owen Jones (USA)** 3-9-0 0 .... WilliamCarson(3) 13 — 61
(P W Hiatt) *in tch in midfield: rdn and effrt wl over 2f out: kpt on same pce and no ch w wnr fnl 2f* **28/1**

5 *1/2* **Silken Sands (IRE)** 3-8-12 0 .... IanMongan 14 — 55
(C G Cox) *chsd ldrs tl rdn and btn over 2f out: one pce fnl 2f* **16/1**

3 **6** *1/2* **Parallel (IRE)**[52] 5222 3-8-12 0 .... NickyMackay 12 — 54
(J H M Gosden) *in tch in midfield: hdwy to chse ldrs and rdn 3f out: sn struggling and no ch fnl 2f* **4/1**[2]

7 *1* **Jafir (USA)** 3-9-3 0 .... RobertWinston 3 — 57+
(B J Meehan) *s.i.s: bhd: sme modest hdwy fnl f: n.d* **13/2**[3]

5 **8** *nk* **Lean Burn (USA)**[38] 5628 3-9-3 0 ....(t) RichardThomas 2 — 56
(A G Newcombe) *chsd ldrs early: lost pl and shuffled bk over 6f out: sme modest late hdwy: nvr a factor* **14/1**

9 *3 1/4* **Miskin Spirit** 3-8-12 0 .... NeilChalmers 10 — 43
(B Palling) *s.i.s: a bhd: nvr on terms* **100/1**

64 **10** *6* **Slick Mover (IRE)**[11] 6417 4-8-12 0 .... RobertLButler(3) 1 — 29
(B G Powell) *in tch on outer: rdn and struggling over 3f out: wl bhd fnl 2f* **50/1**

11 *4* **Pivotal Express (IRE)** 3-9-3 0 .... J-PGuillambert 9 — 24
(J F Panvert) *v.s.a: rn green and a bhd* **25/1**

12 *5* **Albiera (IRE)** 4-9-1 0 .... TravisBlock 4 — 7
(H Morrison) *v.s.a: nvr on terms* **20/1**

0-4 **13** *3/4* **Bonnie Bea**[25] 6029 3-8-12 0 .... MickyFenton 6 — 5
(B I Case) *chsd ldrs tl over 3f out: sn dropped out* **25/1**

0 **14** *1 1/2* **Bengers Lass (USA)**[16] 6287 3-8-12 0 .... TonyCulhane 11 — —
(R Curtis) *off the pce in midfield: struggling over 3f out: eased fr over 1f out* **100/1**

1m 47.22s (2.52) **Going Correction** +0.25s/f (Good)
WFA 3 from 4yo 3lb — **14** Ran SP% **126.4**
Speed ratings (Par 103): **97,92,90,86,86 85,84,84,81,75 71,66,65,63**
toteswingers: 1&2 £7.30, 1&3 £3.50, 2&3 £8.00 CSF £37.45 TOTE £2.40: £1.30, £3.90, £1.90; EX 39.20 Trifecta £170.70 Part won. Pool: £230.81 - 0.73 winning units..
Owner Godolphin **Bred** Arthur Hancock **Trained** Newmarket, Suffolk

FOCUS
A weak maiden that was won with ease by a Godolphin newcomer, who was value for 9l. The bare form does not amount to much.

Miskin Spirit Official explanation: jockeys said filly ran green

6742 MAIDENHEAD ADVERTISER H'CAP 1m 3f 135y
5:40 (5:41) (Class 5) (0-70,68) 3-Y-O £2,729 (£806; £403) Stalls Low

Form RPR
0500 1 **Windpfeil (IRE)**26 5990 3-8-4 54 oh2 (b) NickyMackay 4 64
(J H M Gosden) t.k.h and racd freely: mde all: rdn and clr 2f out: styd on wl 16/1
5116 2 2 3/4 **Sparkaway**25 6027 3-8-9 59 MickyFenton 3 64
(W J Musson) chsd ldrs: chsd clr wnr and rdn over 3f out: no imp but battled on to hold 2nd 13/2[3]
3216 3 shd **Broughtons Paradis (IRE)**24 6075 3-8-12 62 ChrisCatlin 9 67+
(W J Musson) stdd s: hld up in rr: hdwy on far side 3f out: drvn to press for 2nd ent fnl f: kpt on but no ch w wnr 7/1
2004 4 6 **Nice Time (IRE)**18 6236 3-9-2 66 SebSanders 6 61
(M H Tompkins) chsd ldrs: rdn and unable qck 3f out: drvn and btn 2f out 14/1
5020 5 1 1/4 **Whisky Galore**44 5430 3-9-4 68 (v) IanMongan 14 61
(C G Cox) a towards rr: hung lft u.p and sme hdwy over 1f out: nvr trbld ldrs 6/1[2]
4206 6 2 1/2 **Sunceleb (IRE)**40 5567 3-9-4 68 TravisBlock 5 57
(H Morrison) hld up in tch in midfield: rdn and btn over 3f out: no ch fnl 2f 28/1
035 7 1/2 **Amroth**16 6276 3-8-9 59 TomEaves 12 47
(P D Evans) in tch in midfield tl drvn and struggling over 3f out: sn wl btn 14/1
2003 8 nse **Cayman Sky**19 6210 3-8-9 59 (b) PatDobbs 10 47
(R Hannon) trckd ldrs: rdn and nt qckn wl over 2f: sn btn 9/1
3654 9 nse **Good Buy Dubai (USA)**6 6566 3-8-7 57 ow1 TonyCulhane 1 45
(J R Best) bhd and rdn 1/2-way: sme modest hdwy but no ch whn hmpd 1f out: n.d 15/2
0052 10 3/4 **Sea Lavender**41 5548 3-9-4 68 SteveDrowne 13 54
(R Charlton) hld up in tch in midfield: effrt and hrd rdn over 2f out: sn btn: eased ins fnl f 4/1[1]
500- 11 1 1/2 **Meirig's Dream (IRE)**457 3968 3-8-9 59 PaulFitzsimons 2 43
(Miss N A Lloyd-Beavis) t.k.h: hld up in rr: rdn and short-lived effrt over 3f out: sn wl bhd 66/1
052 12 7 **Fleur De'Lion (IRE)**9 6497 3-8-4 54 RichardSmith 8 26
(S Kirk) hld up in rr: rdn and lost tch over 3f out 25/1
000 13 6 **Emerald Hawk (IRE)**43 5465 3-8-1 54 oh4 (v) KellyHarrison(3) 7 16
(D H Brown) t.k.h: sn chsng wnr tl over 3f out: sn dropped out and wl bhd 66/1
-344 14 33 **Cluny**35 5726 3-9-0 64 FrancisNorton 11 —
(J R Fanshawe) in tch in midfield tl lost pl and bhd 1/2-way: t.o 14/1
000 15 15 **Hard Ball**123 2863 3-8-9 59 TedDurcan 15 —
(M Quinn) hld up in midfield on outer: lost pl over 3f out: t.o and eased fnl f 25/1

2m 33.24s (3.74) **Going Correction** +0.25s/f (Good) **15** Ran SP% **121.9**
Speed ratings (Par 101): **97,95,95,91,90 88,88,88,88,87 86,82,78,56,46**
toteswingers: 1&2 £41.20, 1&3 £41.10, 2&3 £10.60 CSF £112.57 CT £812.39 TOTE £19.30: £5.30, £2.40, £3.70; EX 190.20 TRIFECTA Not won. Place 6: £204.93 Place 5: £125.70.
Owner L Kirk & C J Murfitt **Bred** Gainsborough Stud Management Ltd **Trained** Newmarket, Suffolk
■ Stewards' Enquiry : Ian Mongan one-day ban: careless riding (Oct 30)

FOCUS
A modest handicap run at a good pace. Once again they went far side in the straight. The first three finished clear but it is doubtful if this is form to be too positive about.
Hard Ball Official explanation: jockey said gelding had a breathing problem
T/Jkpt: Not won. T/Plt: £381.30 to a £1 stake. Pool: £70,822.70. 135.59 winning tickets. T/Qpdt: £161.40 to a £1 stake. Pool: £5,608.64. 25.70 winning tickets. SP

6748 - 6750a (Foreign Racing) - See Raceform Interactive

6577 CHANTILLY (R-H)
Monday, October 12

OFFICIAL GOING: Very soft

6751a PRIX DE L'ALLEE TENEBREUSE (CLAIMER) 1m 1f 110y
12:55 (12:55) 2-Y-O £8,738 (£3,495; £2,621; £1,748; £874)

RPR
1 **Marina (GER)** 2-8-11 GMasure 78
(C Von Der Recke, Germany)
2 1/2 **Scandola (USA)** 2-9-1 SPasquier 81
(G Botti, Italy)
3 4 **Mana Kourou (FR)**12 2-8-11 RMarchelli 69
(D Windrif, France)
4 3 **Tinder Ball (FR)**12 2-9-4 70
(J Van Handenhove, France)
5 2 **The Miss McArdle (GER)** 2-9-1 63
(Dr A Bolte, Germany)
6 2 **Nice Girl (FR)**12 2-8-11 54
(F Cohen, France)
7 1 1/2 **Quillin**15 6322 2-9-4 DBonilla 58
(E J O'Neill) led tl hdd over 1f out: wknd 48/10[1]
8 2 1/2 **Miss Kamikaze (FR)**93 2-8-11 46
(M Boutin, France)
9 3/4 **Shining Sun (FR)** 2-8-11 45
(J Bertran De Balanda, France)
10 3/4 **Darwind (FR)**28 2-9-1 (b) 47
(J-L Pelletan, France)
0 **Tryanon (FR)**12 2-9-1 —
(C Boutin, France)
0 **Convocation (IRE)**12 2-8-11 —
(Mme M Bollack-Badel, France)
0 **Money For Nothing (FR)**91 3935 2-9-1 (p) —
(R Pritchard-Gordon, France)
0 **Marly Gomont (FR)** 2-8-11 (b) —
(S Jesus, France)
0 **Pinkiskass (FR)**19 2-8-8 (p) —
(J-P Gallorini, France)
0 **Tout Chocolat (FR)** 2-9-1 —
(Robert Collet, France)
F **Tarzane (FR)** 2-9-1 —
(F Foresi, France)
F **El Milagro (SPA)** 2-8-11 —
(C Laffon-Parias, France)

2m 1.80s (121.80) **18** Ran SP% **17.2**
PARI-MUTUEL (Including 1 Euro stake): WIN 4,50; PL 2.20, 5.70, 2.80;DF 51.20.
Owner C Von Der Recke **Bred** P Heitmann **Trained** Weilerswist, Germany

6752a PRIX ECLIPSE (GROUP 3) 6f
1:25 (1:27) 2-Y-O £38,835 (£15,534; £11,650; £7,767; £3,883)

RPR
1 **Eightfold Path (USA)**36 5708 2-8-11 SPasquier 1 105
(P Bary, France) mde all: rdn out: jst hld on 8/5[1]
2 hd **Irish Cat (IRE)**6 2-8-8 GBenoist 4 101
(Robert Collet, France) hld up in rr: hdwy on ins to go 4th whn n.m.r and sltly hmpd 1 1/2f out: wnt 2nd ins fnl f: jst failed 18/1
3 1 **Absolute Music (USA)**41 5552 2-8-8 IMendizabal 6 98
(R M H Cowell) sn pushed along towards rr: rdn on outside over 2f out: disp 2nd 1 1/2f out to ins fnl f: one pce 17/1
4 snk **Kelty In Love (FR)**25 6044 2-8-8 FBlondel 2 98
(T Larriviere, France) trckd wnr in 3rd: wnt 2nd under 2f out: lost 2nd ins fnl f: one pce 10/1
5 3 **Duplicity**87 4049 2-8-11 TThulliez 5 92
(R Hannon) pressed wnr in 2nd tl effrt and nt qckn 2f out 13/5[2]
6 1 1/2 **Wonderfilly (FR)**17 6326 2-8-8 OPeslier 7 84
(P Demercastel, France) a in rr 58/10[3]
7 nk **Forum Magnum (USA)**17 6326 2-8-11 MGuyon 8 86
(A Fabre, France) cl up on outside to 2f out 63/10
8 1 1/2 **Too Nice Name (FR)**17 6326 2-8-11 TJarnet 3 82
(Robert Collet, France) a towards rr 22/1

1m 13.8s (2.40) **8** Ran SP% **118.9**
PARI-MUUTEL: WIN 2.60; PL 1.40, 3.40, 3.30; DF 21.30.
Owner Niarchos Family **Bred** Flaxman Holdings Ltd **Trained** Chantilly, France

LE PIN AU HARAS
Sunday, October 11

OFFICIAL GOING: Good

6753a PRIX DU HARAS DU MEZERAY (MAIDEN) (FILLIES) 1m 3f
1:00 (12:00) 3-Y-O £5,825 (£2,330; £1,748; £1,165; £583)

RPR
1 **Fastback (IRE)**94 3-9-2 JCabre 77
(S Wattel, France)
2 2 **Rouge Emery (FR)** 3-8-7 MDelalande(5) 69
(A Couetil, France)
3 2 1/2 **Khazina (FR)**159 3-9-2 WVion 69
(R Gibson, France)
4 1 **Barlia (IRE)** 3-8-12 63
(C Laffon-Parias, France)
5 3/4 **Kalasi (FR)** 3-8-12 62
(Mme J Hendriks, France)
6 1 **Manresa (IRE)**399 5728 3-8-12 60
(F Belmont, France)
7 3/4 **Andraste (USA)** 3-8-12 59
(N Clement, France)
8 nk **Bedawina (FR)**116 3-8-12 59
(Mme P Alexanian, France)
9 1 **Aumale (FR)** 3-8-12 57
(H-A Pantall, France)
10 nse **Guendalina (FR)** 3-8-12 57
(J-M Beguigne, France)
0 **Repetischa (IRE)**64 4799 3-8-12 JAuge —
(E J O'Neill)
0 **Red Ballerina (IRE)**118 3-8-12 —
(D Sepulchre, France)
0 **Golos** 3-8-12 —
(A Couetil, France)
0 **Strataciella (USA)** 3-8-12 —
(G Henrot, France)
0 **Tirovia (FR)** 3-8-12 —
(J-M Plasschaert, Belgium)
0 **Comedie Francaise** 3-8-12 —
(J Bertran De Balanda, France)

16 Ran
PARI-MUTUEL (including 1 Euro stake): WIN 5.70; PL 1.60, 14.20, 1.70;DF 40.20.
Owner Ecurie Skymarc Farm **Bred** Newsells Park Stud **Trained** France

6567 LEICESTER (R-H)
Tuesday, October 13

OFFICIAL GOING: Good (good to firm in places; 7.8)
Wind: Almost nil Weather: Fine and sunny

6754 E B F REFERENCE POINT MAIDEN STKS (C&G) 7f 9y
2:10 (2:11) (Class 4) 2-Y-O £5,180 (£1,541; £770; £384) Stalls Low

Form RPR
32 1 **Mufarrh (IRE)**24 6108 2-9-0 0 RHills 7 89+
(J L Dunlop) w ldr tl led 2f out: shkn up and r.o wl fnl f: readily 2/1[2]
03 2 4 **Official Style**24 6108 2-9-0 0 RyanMoore 14 78
(Sir Michael Stoute) hld up: hdwy over 2f out: rdn to chse wnr fnl f: no imp 6/4[1]
523 3 1 1/2 **State Fair**136 2477 2-9-0 87 NCallan 18 74
(P F I Cole) mid-div: hdwy over 2f out: sn rdn: styd on and hung rt ins fnl f: wnt 3rd nr fin 15/2
4 nk **Hidden Glory** 2-9-0 0 MickyFenton 17 74+
(Pat Eddery) s.s: in rr: hdwy over 2f out: rdn over 1f out: styd on same pce ins fnl f: lost 3rd nr fin 33/1
5 2 **Hypnotized (USA)** 2-9-0 0 HayleyTurner 16 69+
(M L W Bell) s.s: sn pushed along in rr: hdwy over 2f out: styd on: nt rch ldrs 25/1

23 6 *hd* **Poor Prince**[73] 4524 2-9-0 0 PhilipRobinson 13 68
(C G Cox) *chsd ldrs: rdn over 1f out: no ex fnl f* **6/1**[3]

00 7 *2* **Painswick (USA)**[24] 6109 2-9-0 0 TPQueally 2 63
(J L Dunlop) *sn pushed along in rr: swtchd rt over 2f out: styd on fr over 1f out: nvr nrr* **100/1**

06 8 *1 1/2* **Imjin River (IRE)**[37] 5693 2-8-9 0 AshleyMorgan(5) 15 59
(M H Tompkins) *prom: rdn over 2f out: wknd fnl f* **200/1**

9 *1/2* **Penrod Ballantyne (IRE)** 2-9-0 0 EddieAhern 6 58
(B J Meehan) *prom: rdn whn n.m.r over 1f out: sn wknd* **66/1**

10 *6* **Donair** 2-9-0 0 StephenDonohoe 10 43
(P F I Cole) *hld up: rdn over 2f out: n.d* **80/1**

11 *1 1/4* **Breakheart (IRE)** 2-9-0 0 LPKeniry 5 40
(A M Balding) *dwlt: a outpcd and bhd* **50/1**

00 12 *3/4* **Captain Clint (IRE)**[46] 5401 2-9-0 0 LiamJones 12 38
(M H Tompkins) *sn pushed along: a in rr* **250/1**

6000 13 *hd* **Polebrook**[20] 6200 2-8-7 30 (v1) DannyBrock(7) 8 38
(J R Jenkins) *chsd ldrs tl rdn and wknd over 2f out* **250/1**

0 14 *3/4* **Al Khawarezmi**[73] 4515 2-9-0 0 RoystonFfrench 3 36
(M Johnston) *mid-div: sn pushed along: wknd over 2f out* **33/1**

02 15 *7* **Sixties Rock**[13] 6381 2-9-0 0 PaulHanagan 9 28+
(J A Glover) *free to post: led 5f: sn wknd* **50/1**

6 16 *13* **Appeal To Reason (USA)**[7] 6561 2-9-0 0 SteveDrowne 4 —
(J R Best) *sn outpcd and bhd* **200/1**

1m 24.39s (-1.81) **Going Correction** -0.325s/f (Firm) **16** Ran SP% **118.5**
Speed ratings (Par 97): **97,92,90,90,88 87,85,83,83,76 75,74,73,73,65 50**
toteswingers: 1&2 £2.30, 1&3 £3.30, 2&3 £6.10 CSF £4.88 TOTE £3.20: £1.10, £1.30, £2.40; EX 5.60 Trifecta £18.40 Pool: £164.19 - 6.60 winning units..
Owner Hamdan Al Maktoum **Bred** Kenilworth House Stud **Trained** Arundel, W Sussex

FOCUS
There was a false rail from the round course bend to the 1f pole, out approximately ten yards. This was a decent maiden that should produce a few winners. The winner impressed and decisively confirmed form with the runner-up. They raced up the middle of the track.

NOTEBOOK
Mufarrh(IRE) had no trouble confirming recent Newbury form with Official Style and was a most decisive winner. Having travelled strongly on the pace for most of the way, he found plenty for pressure and looks a very useful type. (op 15-8)
Official Style ◆ was not given a hard time after finding trouble when 4 1/2l behind today's winner at Newbury last time, and was clearly fancied by many to reverse form, but he didn't have the required pace. Some might consider this disappointing, but he is quietly progressive and will be of real interest if taking the handicap route over 1m-plus next year. (op 2-1 tchd 85-40 in places)
State Fair, up in trip after over four months off, ran a good race in third. He lacked the sharpness of the winner but finished strongly after initially taking a while to pick up. He didn't quite run up to his official mark of 87 but there should be better to come. (op 13-2)
Hidden Glory was green in the preliminaries but fared best of the newcomers. This £26,000 half-brother to a winner in Hong Kong should progress. (op 25-1)
Hypnotized(USA) ◆ made a noteworthy debut. Although by no means unlucky, he never had much room to play with inside the final 2f but still finished nicely. A $110,000 half-brother to a 6f winner, he should improve enough to a similar event, maybe next time.
Poor Prince is expected by his trainer to make a nice 3-y-o, but the colt was much too keen on this return from over two months off. This isn't the first time he's looked a free-going sort but he should still be kept on side for the time being now that handicaps are an option. Official explanation: jockey said colt ran too keen (tchd 13-2)
Painswick(USA), reported to have stopped quickly at Newbury last time, hinted that he might do better, possibly at three, now that he's qualified for a handicap mark.
Imjin River(IRE) is now eligible for an official rating and he should find his level, possibly back over shorter trips. (op 150-1)
Penrod Ballantyne(IRE) ◆ made a better debut than his finishing position suggests. Keen early, he was soon travelling strongly, before his lack of experience told, but he would still have finished closer had he not been squeezed out between horses around 1f from the finish.
Donair ◆ travelled well to a point and is one to keep in mind for when he's stepped up to middle-distances next year. (op 100-1 tchd 66-1)
Sixties Rock Official explanation: jockey said gelding hung right-handed

6755 WHISSENDINE (S) STKS — 7f 9y
2:40 (2:41) (Class 6) 3-4-Y-O **£1,942** (£578; £288; £144) **Stalls** Low

Form RPR

3035 1 **Markhesa**[11] 6455 3-8-5 63 AlanMunro 9 64
(C F Wall) *hld up towards rr: swtchd rt and hdwy 2f out: sn rdn: r.o to ld wl ins fnl f* **4/1**[1]

4160 2 *1 1/2* **Indian Skipper (IRE)**[24] 6112 4-8-12 75 AshleyMorgan(5) 18 71
(M H Tompkins) *s.i.s: hld up in rr: hdwy over 2f out: rdn wl over 1f out: kpt on ins fnl f* **5/1**[2]

0103 3 *1* **Stand In Flames**[39] 5628 4-8-12 60 TonyCulhane 6 63
(George Baker) *hld up in rr: pushed along over 3f out: rdn and hdwy over 1f out: fin wl to take 3rd towards fin* **20/1**

0400 4 *2 1/4* **Well Of Echoes**[18] 6251 3-8-5 53 (bt1) PaulHanagan 12 51
(J A Glover) *racd centre: sn clr: rdn over 1f out: hdd and no ex wl ins fnl f* **40/1**

0046 5 *1* **Fathey (IRE)**[13] 6383 3-8-5 60 BMcHugh(5) 16 53
(R A Fahey) *hld up in tch: pushed along over 3f out: rdn over 2f out: one pce* **10/1**

0/1- 6 *1 1/4* **Sir George (IRE)**[556] 1215 4-8-12 0 CatherineGannon 8 51
(P D Evans) *hld up in mid-div: pushed along and hdwy over 2f out: rdn jst over 1f out: no imp* **6/1**[3]

503 7 *1* **Capo Regime**[11] 6442 3-9-1 64 (v) IanMongan 5 52
(P Howling) *s.i.s: hld up in rr: pushed along over 3f out: short-lived effrt wl over 1f out* **33/1**

600 8 *2 1/4* **Enhancing**[25] 6070 3-7-12 55 (v1) JamesPSullivan(7) 13 36
(J A Glover) *hld up in mid-div: rdn over 3f out: no hdwy fnl 2f* **66/1**

0000 9 *1/2* **Kannon**[15] 6339 4-8-12 55 RoystonFfrench 7 41
(I W McInnes) *hld up in rr: hdwy over 2f out: wknd over 1f out* **80/1**

5245 10 *1 3/4* **Cardinal**[39] 5633 4-8-12 57 (t) DavidProbert 4 36
(R A Harris) *hld up in tch: pushed along over 3f out: rdn over 2f out: wknd over 1f out* **16/1**

-030 11 *1 3/4* **Tina's Best (IRE)**[43] 5514 4-8-7 63 EddieAhern 2 26
(E J Alston) *hld up in mid-div: swtchd rt over 2f out: sn btn* **33/1**

0030 12 *5* **Only A Game (IRE)**[6] 6587 4-9-3 55 AdamKirby 15 23
(I W McInnes) *a in rr* **33/1**

1410 13 *1 3/4* **Sir Ike (IRE)**[38] 5676 4-9-3 67 (tp) ShaneKelly 11 18
(W S Kittow) *prom: pushed along over 3f out: rdn and wknd 2f out* **14/1**

4506 14 *4 1/2* **Migliori**[36] 5716 3-8-10 54 MickyFenton 3 —
(Rae Guest) *s.i.s: hld up towards rr: pushed along over 3f out: no rspnse* **66/1**

0 15 *hd* **Soul Murmur (IRE)**[172] 1493 4-8-12 72 (t) JamesDoyle 1 —
(F Sheridan) *hld up in tch: rdn and wknd over 2f out* **13/2**

4510 16 *8* **Equipe De Nuit**[14] 6362 3-8-12 67 WilliamCarson(3) 17 —
(S C Williams) *chsd clr ldr: sn c to stands' rail: wknd over 2f out* **15/2**

6 17 *9* **Donny Bowl**[28] 5971 4-8-12 0 PatrickMathers 14 —
(I W McInnes) *s.s: a wl in rr* **250/1**

1m 25.22s (-0.98) **Going Correction** -0.325s/f (Firm)
WFA 3 from 4yo 2lb **17** Ran SP% **118.3**
Speed ratings (Par 101): **92,90,89,86,85 84,82,80,79,77 75,70,68,62,62 53,43**
toteswingers: 1&2 £5.00, 1&3 £25.80, 2&3 £32.50 CSF £20.47 TOTE £5.30: £1.80, £1.90, £6.20; EX 21.70 Trifecta £109.40 Part won. Pool: £147.84 - 0.10 winning units..The winner was sold to Jim Boyle for £5,800. Indian Skipper was claimed by Richard Guest for £6,000.
Owner The National Stud Never Say Die Club Ltd **Bred** The National Stud Never Say Die Club Ltd **Trained** Newmarket, Suffolk

■ Stewards' Enquiry : Ashley Morgan one-day ban: used whip with excessive frequency (Oct 27)
William Carson two-day ban: careless riding (Oct 27-28)

FOCUS
A standard seller run at a very strong pace. The majority of these raced towards the stands' side early but the main action was ultimately up the middle of the track. The form is rated around the third.

6756 BLACKBERRY SOLUTIONS FROM 21C TELECOM CONDITIONS STKS — 7f 9y
3:10 (3:12) (Class 3) 2-Y-O **£6,938** (£2,076; £1,038; £519; £258) **Stalls** Low

Form RPR

12 1 **Hafawa (IRE)**[59] 5038 2-8-11 86 RHills 4 93
(M Johnston) *trckd ldr: racd keenly: rdn to ld and hung rt fr over 1f out: r.o wl to go clr wl ins fnl f* **8/13**[1]

16 2 *4* **Dawnbreak (USA)**[25] 6055 2-8-11 81 LDettori 5 86+
(Saeed Bin Suroor) *led: rdn and hdd over 1f out: no ex wl ins fnl f* **4/1**[3]

1203 3 *1 3/4* **Cumulus Nimbus**[27] 5994 2-9-2 88 RyanMoore 2 84
(R Hannon) *hld up: hdwy 1/2-way: rdn over 2f out: styd on same pce appr fnl f* **3/1**[2]

4 *18* **Premium Charge** 2-8-13 0 JerryO'Dwyer 1 41+
(C A Dwyer) *sn pushed along and a in rr: lost tch fnl 3f* **100/1**

0 5 *11* **Rosie's Magic**[25] 6055 2-8-8 0 RobertHavlin 3 3
(W De Best-Turner) *chsd ldrs tl wknd 3f out* **400/1**

0 6 *10* **Bravo Blue (IRE)**[18] 6245 2-8-8 0 PaulHanagan 6 —
(T H Caldwell) *chsd ldrs: pushed along 1/2-way: wknd 3f out* **250/1**

1m 23.77s (-2.43) **Going Correction** -0.325s/f (Firm) **6** Ran SP% **108.6**
Speed ratings (Par 99): **100,95,93,72,60 48**
toteswingers: 1&2 £1.10, 1&3 £1.10, 2&3 £1.40 CSF £3.28 TOTE £1.50: £1.10, £2.40; EX 2.20.
Owner Hamdan Al Maktoum **Bred** Shadwell Estate Company Limited **Trained** Middleham Moor, N Yorks

FOCUS
This only concerned three of the six runners, but the form amongst those who mattered is useful. The time was very good; easily the quickest of the three 7f races on the card, including 0.62 seconds faster than the promising-looking colt, Mufarrh, managed in an earlier maiden. They raced up the middle of the track. The form is rated around the winner and third.

NOTEBOOK
Hafawa(IRE) got rid of her rider on more than one occasion before the off, and was keen in the race itself. But while she obviously has the odd quirk, she again showed herself to be quite a decent filly with a clear-cut success. (op 4-6 tchd 8-11)
Dawnbreak(USA) was a little free in front, not really managing to get much of a breather in, and proved no match for the winner. Her limitations on turf are becoming clear, but she won her maiden on Polytrack and is bred to be suited by artificial surfaces considering both her sire and dam won on dirt, as well as a couple of her siblings. (op 100-30 tchd 3-1)
Cumulus Nimbus had no easy task conceding weight all round and never threatened. He looks to need further. (op 4-1)
Premium Charge ran green throughout but hinted at ability and should do better given time and distance.

6757 WREAKE FILLIES' CONDITIONS STKS — 1m 60y
3:40 (3:40) (Class 3) 3-Y-O+ **£7,569** (£2,265; £1,132; £566; £282) **Stalls** High

Form RPR

5-20 1 **Moonlife (IRE)**[118] 3016 3-8-9 100 (t) LDettori 3 102+
(Saeed Bin Suroor) *led 7f out: pushed clr fr over 1f out: eased towards fin* **15/8**[1]

4 2 *4* **Perfect Star**[81] 4259 5-8-12 97 AdamKirby 5 89
(C G Cox) *prom: rdn over 2f out: chsd wnr over 1f out: no imp* **15/8**[1]

440- 3 *nse* **Farley Star**[391] 6034 5-8-12 86 RyanMoore 2 89
(M G Quinlan) *hld up: hdwy u.p over 1f out: styd on: nrst fin* **14/1**

5005 4 *3/4* **First City**[17] 6272 3-8-9 93 StephenDonohoe 1 87
(D M Simcock) *hld up: hdwy u.p fr over 1f out: nt rch ldrs* **7/2**[2]

0240 5 *3 1/4* **Dixey**[24] 6092 4-8-12 88 PhilipRobinson 6 79
(M A Jarvis) *led: hdd 7f out: chsd ldrs: rdn over 2f out: wknd over 1f out* **11/1**[3]

140 6 *hd* **Multiplication**[18] 6242 3-8-12 76 ShaneKelly 4 82?
(W J Knight) *chsd wnr 7f out tl rdn over 1f out: wknd fnl f* **66/1**

1m 42.27s (-2.83) **Going Correction** -0.125s/f (Firm)
WFA 3 from 4yo+ 3lb **6** Ran SP% **108.3**
Speed ratings (Par 104): **109,105,104,104,100 100**
toteswingers: 1&2 £1.60, 1&3 £4.10, 2&3 £4.60 CSF £5.06 TOTE £2.40: £1.50, £1.70; EX 4.30.
Owner Godolphin **Bred** M Parola **Trained** Newmarket, Suffolk

FOCUS
A decent conditions race but muddling form. The winner did not need to improve to beat the below-par second.

NOTEBOOK
Moonlife(IRE) ◆, the best off at the weights, was allowed to dominate and, after travelling strongly into the straight, won pretty much unchallenged. It's true plenty went her way, but there was much to like about this performance and she looks a likely type for the 2010 Dubai Carnival. (op 5-4)
Perfect Star came under pressure about 3f out but, although never a match for the winner, she kept responding. That said, she seemingly ran below her official mark of 97 considering she would have been 11lb worse off with the third-placed finisher in a handicap, even though that one probably improved a little. (op 5-2 tchc 11-4 in places)
Farley Star, who has apparently only been with her current yard for a couple of months, having left Roger Charlton since she was last seen over a year previously, ran above her official mark of 86. She may be open to improvement fitness-wise, and when stepped up in trip, and it would be no surprise if she's placed to try and nick a bit of black type at some point. (op 16-1 tchd 12-1)
First City, a touch keen in rear early on, was never competitive, only running on when the race was all but over. (op 11-2)
Dixey looks better suited by 7f. (op 7-1)

Multiplication, who was keen, had a lot to find at the weights.

6758 LYME DISEASE ACTION CLASSIFIED CLAIMING STKS 1m 3f 183y
4:10 (4:10) (Class 5) 3-5-Y-O **£2,590** (£770; £385; £192) **Stalls** High

Form RPR
0165 **1** **Sitwell**[11] 6457 3-8-11 62..................(v) LPKeniry 13 66
(J R Fanshawe) *a.p: chsd ldr 6f out: rdn to ld over 1f out: hung rt ins fnl f: styd on* **6/1**[3]
0045 **2** *1* **Moscow Oznick**[10] 6488 4-9-3 59..................(b[1]) RichardKingscote 10 63
(Tom Dascombe) *hld up in tch: racd keenly: rdn over 1f out: hung rt ins fnl f: styd on* **9/1**
2600 **3** *1 ½* **Graylyn Ruby (FR)**[13] 6385 4-9-7 65.................. LukeMorris 1 65+
(J Jay) *hld up: hdwy 3f out: rdn and hung rt ins fnl f: styd on* **14/1**
2332 **4** *1 ¼* **Tiger Flash**[8] 6549 3-9-0 67.................. RyanMoore 9 63
(W J Haggas) *a.p: rdn to chse wnr over 1f out: no ex wl ins fnl f* **11/4**[1]
5455 **5** *½* **Orthology (IRE)**[8] 6549 3-8-12 66..................(b) TPQueally 12 60
(M H Tompkins) *led after 1f: rdn and hdd over 1f out: no ex fnl f* **17/2**
4355 **6** *1 ½* **Hucking Hero (IRE)**[40] 5594 4-9-3 66.................. PatCosgrave 11 55
(J R Boyle) *s.i.s: hld up: hdwy 3f out: sn rdn: hung rt over 1f out: nt trble ldrs* **7/1**
0351 **7** *hd* **Mista Rossa**[20] 6210 4-9-10 68.................. TravisBlock 2 62
(H Morrison) *prom: rdn over 2f out: hung rt over 1f out: no ex* **9/2**[2]
0000 **8** *3 ¾* **Bromhead (USA)**[10] 6497 3-8-6 51..................(t) RoystonFfrench 3 45
(Mrs C A Dunnett) *hld up: racd keenly: hdwy u.p over 1f out: nt rch ldrs* **50/1**
0600 **9** *6* **Refuse Toulouse (IRE)**[17] 6289 3-8-10 52..................(b[1]) PhilipRobinson 14 39
(C G Cox) *hld up: rdn over 3f out: nvr on terms* **28/1**
000/ **10** *3 ¼* **Remark (IRE)**[777] 4920 5-8-7 42..................(t) JamesPSullivan[(7)] 4 31
(M W Easterby) *mid-div: rdn over 3f out: wknd over 2f out* **150/1**
0-04 **11** *7* **Alannah (IRE)**[46] 5381 4-8-9 44.................. JackMitchell[(3)] 6 18
(Mrs P N Dutfield) *chsd ldrs: rdn over 3f out: wknd over 2f out* **50/1**
0600 **12** *1 ½* **La Columbina**[42] 5549 4-9-1 59.................. MickyFenton 5 19
(G A Harker) *s.i.s: hld up: rdn and hung rt 4f out: sn wknd* **28/1**
-000 **13** *1 ¼* **Shape Shifter (USA)**[21] 6188 3-8-10 40.................. SteveDrowne 7 19
(J R Best) *led 1f: chsd ldr to 6f out: wknd over 3f out* **100/1**
0500 **14** *115* **Carnival Fair**[136] 2473 4-8-10 44..................(t) SPRyan[(7)] 8 —
(S Wynne) *prom: rdn and lost pl 1/2-way: bhd fnl 4f: t.o* **200/1**

2m 32.78s (-1.12) **Going Correction** -0.125s/f (Firm)
WFA 3 from 4yo+ 7lb 14 Ran SP% **111.8**
Speed ratings (Par 103): **98,97,96,95,95 94,94,91,87,85 80,79,78,—**
toteswingers: 1&2 £10.00, 1&3 £14.50, 2&3 £20.60 CSF £52.79 TOTE £6.30: £2.00, £3.60, £6.40; EX 56.00 Trifecta £372.21 Part won. Pool: £372.21 - 0.90 winning units..
Owner Rupert Hambro & Nigel & Carolyn Elwes **Bred** Aylesfield Farms Stud Ltd **Trained** Newmarket, Suffolk

FOCUS
A modest claimer run at a fair pace. It is doubtful this is form to be too positive about.
Orthology(IRE) Official explanation: jockey said gelding hung right-handed
Bromhead(USA) Official explanation: jockey said gelding ran too keen
Remark(IRE) Official explanation: jockey said gelding had a breathing problem

6759 E B F SOAR MAIDEN STKS 1m 60y
4:40 (4:42) (Class 4) 2-Y-O **£5,180** (£1,541; £770; £384) **Stalls** High

Form RPR
02 **1** **Botanist**[27] 5993 2-9-3 0.................. RyanMoore 3 82+
(Sir Michael Stoute) *hld up: hdwy over 3f out: led over 1f out: sn hung rt and r.o wl* **4/6**[1]
0 **2** *2 ¾* **Protaras (USA)**[12] 6423 2-9-3 0.................. EddieAhern 9 74+
(H R A Cecil) *chsd ldr: rdn and ev ch over 1f out: edgd rt: styd on* **18/1**
3 *nk* **Treasure Town** 2-9-3 0.................. LDettori 14 73
(Saeed Bin Suroor) *led: rdn and hdd over 1f out: edgd rt: styd on* **9/1**[3]
4 *2 ½* **Capital Attraction (USA)** 2-9-3 0.................. TPQueally 5 68
(H R A Cecil) *prom: outpcd over 2f out: hung rt and styd on ins fnl f* **20/1**
04 **5** *1* **Isdaar (IRE)**[17] 6285 2-9-3 0.................. TPO'Shea 7 66
(J H M Gosden) *chsd ldrs: rdn over 2f out: hung rt over 1f out: no ex* **20/1**
6 **6** *½* **Green Lightning (IRE)**[25] 6046 2-9-3 0.................. RoystonFfrench 13 64
(M Johnston) *chsd ldrs: rdn over 3f out: styd on same pce appr fnl f* **33/1**
3 **7** *nk* **Argaum (IRE)**[22] 6162 2-9-3 0.................. AdamKirby 10 64+
(W R Swinburn) *prom: rdn over 2f out: styd on same pce appr fnl f* **5/1**[2]
8 *3* **Highland Knight (IRE)** 2-9-3 0..................(t) LPKeniry 11 57
(A M Balding) *prom: rdn and hung lft over 2f out: wknd over 1f out* **100/1**
0 **9** *½* **Mme De Stael**[13] 6389 2-8-12 0.................. StephenDonohoe 6 53+
(Sir Mark Prescott) *hld up: pushed along over 2f out: n.d* **150/1**
0 **10** *1 ¾* **Azaday (IRE)**[35] 5741 2-8-12 0.................. AlanMunro 8 49+
(C F Wall) *hld up: rdn over 2f out: a in rr* **150/1**
11 *¾* **Mataaleb** 2-9-3 0.................. RHills 4 51
(M A Jarvis) *s.i.s: hld up: a in rr* **14/1**
12 *1 ¾* **Yes Chef** 2-9-3 0.................. NCallan 2 47
(J Gallagher) *hld up: effrt over 2f out: sn wknd* **150/1**
0 **13** *4* **Daryainur (IRE)**[24] 6109 2-8-12 0.................. RobertHavlin 1 33
(W De Best-Turner) *hld up: rdn over 2f out: a in rr* **250/1**
14 *½* **The Blue Dog (IRE)** 2-8-12 0.................. TonyCulhane 12 32
(George Baker) *s.s: rn green and a in rr* **150/1**

1m 47.36s (2.26) **Going Correction** -0.125s/f (Firm) 14 Ran SP% **115.1**
Speed ratings (Par 97): **83,80,79,77,76 75,75,72,72,70 69,67,63,63**
toteswingers: 1&2 £7.10, 1&3 £3.40, 2&3 £15.00 CSF £13.73 TOTE £1.60: £1.10, £5.20, £1.70; EX 17.90 Trifecta £102.60 Pool: £388.30 - 2.80 winning units..
Owner Cheveley Park Stud **Bred** Cheveley Park Stud Ltd **Trained** Newmarket, Suffolk

FOCUS
This looked a potentially decent maiden, although the early pace was steady. The winner was quite impressive but the form is limited.

NOTEBOOK
Botanist ◆ continued his improvement with quite an impressive success, quickening up well of the modest gallop to draw clear, despite still showing signs of inexperience when edging slightly right after the false rail disappeared late on. He looks very useful. (op 8-11 tchd 4-5)
Protaras(USA) was always well placed and, although no match for the winner, this was a marked improvement on his debut effort, when he ran green at Newmarket. He should continue to progress. (tchd 20-1)
Treasure Town set off in front, with nothing else particularly keen to lead, and he went a modest pace. He was quickly held when strongly challenged but kept on and is open to improvement. (tchd 8-1)
Capital Attraction(USA), a $95,000 purchase, out of a quite useful multiple winner at around 6f-1m1f on dirt in the US, was keeping on in the closing stages and should do better. (op 16-1)
Isdaar(IRE) again showed ability without making a telling impression. He might do better in handicaps next year. (tchd 22-1)
Green Lightning(IRE) is likely to do much better over middle-distances next year. (op 28-1)
Argaum(IRE) failed to build on the form he showed on his debut. (op 11-2 tchd 6-1 and 4-1)

Highland Knight(IRE) Official explanation: jockey said colt hung left

6760 STEWARDS H'CAP (DIV I) 1m 1f 218y
5:10 (5:11) (Class 5) (0-75,75) 3-Y-O+ **£2,914** (£867; £433; £216) **Stalls** High

Form RPR
0506 **1** **Spensley (IRE)**[67] 4759 3-8-9 65.................. EddieAhern 4 79
(J R Fanshawe) *hld up towards rr: hdwy 3f out: rdn wl over 1f out: edgd rt and led wl ins fnl f: r.o* **16/1**
6631 **2** *hd* **Muftarres (IRE)**[8] 6545 4-9-10 75 6ex..................(t) NCallan 14 89
(G A Butler) *racd keenly: sn hld up in mid-div: hdwy over 3f out: rdn to ld over 1f out: hdd wl ins fnl f: edgd rt: r.o* **5/1**[1]
6603 **3** *3 ¼* **Society Venue**[22] 6157 4-9-5 70.................. PaulHanagan 15 77
(Jedd O'Keeffe) *chsd ldr: led over 3f out: rdn and hdd over 1f out: no ex wl ins fnl f* **5/1**[1]
0521 **4** *7* **Follow The Flag (IRE)**[10] 6490 5-9-8 73.................. TPQueally 1 66
(A J McCabe) *hld up in rr: pushed along 3f out: rdn and hdwy 2f out: sn hung rt and btn* **8/1**[3]
03-0 **5** *¾* **Starburst**[181] 1287 4-8-9 60 oh1.................. DavidProbert 8 52
(A M Balding) *hld up in mid-div: rdn 3f out: styd on ins fnl f: n.d* **16/1**
211 **6** *1 ½* **Sceilin (IRE)**[14] 6369 5-8-10 64..................(t) JackMitchell[(3)] 2 53
(J Mackie) *hld up in rr: sme prog on ins over 3f out: pushed along over 2f out: rdn and btn over 1f out* **9/1**
4000 **7** *2* **Addikt (IRE)**[26] 6019 4-9-7 72.................. MickyFenton 6 57
(G A Harker) *s.i.s: hld up towards rr: pushed along 3f out: rdn and sme prog 2f out: sn wknd* **15/2**[2]
1-16 **8** *2* **Lyra's Daemon**[145] 2212 3-9-4 74.................. HayleyTurner 10 55
(W R Muir) *hld up in tch: pushed along and wknd over 2f out* **9/1**
0200 **9** *2* **Kool Katie**[22] 6157 4-8-9 60 oh7.................. CatherineGannon 9 37
(Mrs G S Rees) *a towards rr* **33/1**
2021 **10** *¾* **Astronomical (IRE)**[13] 6392 7-8-7 65..................(p) DavidKenny[(7)] 3 40
(R Hollinshead) *prom tl rdn and wknd over 2f out* **9/1**
1004 **11** *1* **Supercast (IRE)**[11] 6460 6-9-2 74.................. JosephineBruning[(7)] 11 47
(N J Vaughan) *hld up in tch: rdn and wknd 2f out* **18/1**
1313 **12** *11* **King Of The Moors (USA)**[8] 6547 6-9-2 67..................(b) PhilipRobinson 7 18
(R C Guest) *t.k.h: led: racd wd 3f: hdd over 3f out: wknd over 2f out* **15/2**[2]

2m 5.78s (-2.12) **Going Correction** -0.125s/f (Firm)
WFA 3 from 4yo+ 5lb 12 Ran SP% **117.9**
Speed ratings (Par 103): **103,102,100,94,94 92,91,89,88,87 86,77**
toteswingers: 1&2 £26.20, 1&3 £22.20, 2&3 £10.10 CSF £93.71 CT £469.44 TOTE £26.00: £6.80, £3.90, £2.00; EX 167.20 Trifecta £162.80 Part won. Pool: £220.06 - 0.30 winning units..
Owner Axom (XV) **Bred** Mount Coote Stud And M H Dixon **Trained** Newmarket, Suffolk

FOCUS
A modest handicap run at a decent enough pace. The winning time was 0.47 seconds quicker than the second division and the form looks good for the grade, rated around the third.
Spensley(IRE) Official explanation: trainer's rep said, regarding apparent improvement in form, that it had been gelded since its last run.
Kool Katie Official explanation: jockey said filly ran too keen

6761 STEWARDS H'CAP (DIV II) 1m 1f 218y
5:40 (5:40) (Class 5) (0-75,75) 3-Y-O+ **£2,914** (£867; £433; £216) **Stalls** High

Form RPR
021 **1** **Tanfidh**[15] 6332 3-9-4 75.................. RHills 5 94+
(M P Tregoning) *chsd ldr: led over 2f out: rdn clr fnl f* **9/4**[2]
4250 **2** *6* **Gross Prophet**[20] 6204 4-9-6 72.................. SteveDrowne 14 74
(A J Lidderdale) *prom: rdn over 3f out: styd on same pce fnl f* **16/1**
6051 **3** *nk* **Veiled Applause**[4] 6648 6-9-0 73.................. IJBrennan[(7)] 9 74
(J J Quinn) *hld up: hdwy over 2f out: sn rdn: nt clr run ins fnl f: styd on same pce* **7/4**[1]
1006 **4** *½* **So Blissful (IRE)**[66] 4799 3-9-3 74.................. HayleyTurner 7 74
(Mrs L Wadham) *chsd ldrs: rdn over 2f out: one pce fnl f* **16/1**
-500 **5** *½* **Decameron (USA)**[14] 6357 4-9-9 75.................. DavidProbert 15 74
(R A Harris) *led: rdn and hdd over 2f out: no ex fnl f* **28/1**
3626 **6** *1* **Cloudesley (IRE)**[8] 6549 3-8-13 70..................(v[1]) LPKeniry 11 67
(A M Balding) *chsd ldrs: lost pl over 6f out: rdn over 2f out: kpt on ins fnl f* **10/1**[3]
0443 **7** *¾* **Moonage Daydream (IRE)**[12] 6411 4-8-9 61..................(b) PaulHanagan 2 57
(T D Easterby) *prom: rdn over 3f out: wknd fnl f* **12/1**
-160 **8** *5* **Agapanthus (GER)**[76] 4426 4-9-5 71.................. TPQueally 13 57
(B J Curley) *dwlt: hld up: n.d* **40/1**
6 **9** *1 ¼* **Active Asset (IRE)**[42] 5548 7-8-10 67..................(t) BMcHugh[(5)] 8 50
(J A Glover) *hld up: hdwy 1/2-way: rdn 4f out: wknd over 2f out* **25/1**
0006 **10** *4* **Paint The Town Red**[10] 6498 4-8-8 63.................. JackMitchell[(3)] 3 38
(H J Collingridge) *hld up: a in rr* **16/1**
3260 **11** *12* **Pitbull**[68] 4710 6-8-9 61 oh5..................(p) LiamJones 12 12
(Mrs G S Rees) *dwlt: hld up: a in rr: t.o* **50/1**
/0-0 **12** *17* **Cape Greko**[139] 1356 7-8-13 65.................. FergusSweeney 4 —
(B G Powell) *s.i.s: hdwy 7f out: wknd 4f out: t.o* **66/1**

2m 6.25s (-1.65) **Going Correction** -0.125s/f (Firm)
WFA 3 from 4yo+ 5lb 12 Ran SP% **114.7**
Speed ratings (Par 103): **101,96,95,95,95 94,93,89,88,85 75,62**
toteswingers: 1&2 £8.70, 1&3 £2.40, 2&3 £9.10 CSF £34.62 CT £75.67 TOTE £3.60: £1.80, £3.80, £1.10; EX 30.10 Trifecta £238.90 Part won. Pool: £322.89 - 0.74 winning units. Place 6: £11.88, Place 5: £10.05..
Owner Hamdan Al Maktoum **Bred** Shadwell Estate Company Limited **Trained** Lambourn, Berks

FOCUS
An ordinary handicap but an impressive winner in the context of the grade. The time was 0.47 seconds slower than the first division. The form is rated around the runner-up.
Pitbull Official explanation: jockey said gelding hung left
T/Plt: £13.20 to a £1 stake. Pool: £54,722.82. 3,009.86 winning tickets. T/Qpdt: £7.10 to a £1 stake. Pool: £3,899.47. 401.70 winning tickets. CR

6378 NEWCASTLE (L-H)
Tuesday, October 13

OFFICIAL GOING: Straight course - good; round course - good to soft
Wind: Almost nil Weather: Overcast

6762 EUROPEAN BREEDERS' FUND MAIDEN FILLIES' STKS 1m (R)
1:50 (1:51) (Class 5) 2-Y-O **£3,885** (£1,156; £577; £288) **Stalls** Low

Form RPR
5 **1** **Deirdre**[22] 6163 2-9-0 0.................. JimmyFortune 6 78+
(J H M Gosden) *set stdy pce: qcknd over 2f out: rdn along over 1f out: kpt on* **9/4**[2]

003 **2** *3 1/4* **Anaya**[17] 6284 2-9-0 71 .... KFallon 5 71
(M R Channon) *trckd ldng pair: effrt 2f out: rdn to chse wnr over 1f out: no imp ins fnl f* **7/1**

5 **3** *2 1/4* **Yankee Bright (USA)**[17] 6284 2-8-11 0 .... FrederikTylicki(3) 1 67+
(J G Given) *trckd ldrs: hdwy 2f out: sn rdn: drvn and kpt on ins fnl f: nrst fin* **12/1**

4 **4** *1/2* **Woodford Belle (USA)**[25] 6062 2-9-0 0 .... RobertWinston 7 65
(B J Meehan) *trckd wnr: effrt over 2f out and sn rdn: wknd appr fnl f* **15/8**[1]

5 *shd* **Addahab (USA)** 2-9-0 0 .... TedDurcan 2 65+
(Saeed Bin Suroor) *s.i.s and towards rr: hdwy on inner 2f out: kpt on ins fnl f: nrst fin* **12/1**

52 **6** *shd* **Michevious Spirit (IRE)**[13] 6389 2-9-0 0 .... PhillipMakin 8 64
(K A Ryan) *trckd ldrs: hdwy 3f out: rdn along over 2f out: drvn and wknd over 1f out* **11/2**[3]

5 **7** *2 1/4* **Shayla**[22] 6154 2-9-0 0 .... PJMcDonald 9 59
(G A Swinbank) *towards rr: sme hdwy over 2f out: sn rdn and no imp* **25/1**

04 **8** *1/2* **Goodison Park**[45] 5440 2-9-0 0 .... AndrewMullen 10 58
(A G Foster) *trckd ldrs on outer: effrt over 3f out: sn rdn and wknd 2f out* **150/1**

9 *5* **Pathway To Heaven (IRE)** 2-9-0 0 .... GrahamGibbons 4 47
(J J Quinn) *s.i.s: a in rr* **100/1**

10 *1* **Bollin Julie** 2-9-0 0 .... DavidAllan 3 45
(T D Easterby) *s.i.s: a in rr* **80/1**

1m 46.91s (3.51) **Going Correction** -0.075s/f (Good) **10** Ran SP% **115.6**
Speed ratings (Par 92): **79,75,73,73,72 72,70,70,65,64**
toteswingers: 1&2 £5.30, 1&3 £7.20, 2&3 £11.10 CSF £18.13 TOTE £3.00: £1.10, £2.40, £3.00; EX 23.00.
Owner Normandie Stud Ltd **Bred** Normandie Stud Ltd **Trained** Newmarket, Suffolk

FOCUS
An average fillies' maiden. Sound form, with improvement from the winner.

NOTEBOOK
Deirdre, related to a couple of very useful sorts, is still on the leg. After a promising first run on the all-weather she dictated things from the front. She stepped up the gallop at the three furlongs from home marker and, driven out, ran out a most decisive winner. She was very professional and should do even better at three. (op 7-4 tchd 5-2 and 11-4 in places)
Anaya, having her fourth start and rated 71, did nothing wrong and finished clear second best but she is looking fully exposed. (tchd 8-1)
Yankee Bright(USA), only seventh at the furlong pole, finished with quite a flourish. She should make a decent handicapper at three. (op 14-1 tchd 16-1)
Woodford Belle(USA), fourth at Newmarket first time, kept tabs on the winner. She was soon being niggled along and tired noticeably in the closing stages. She still looks very immature. (op 3-1)
Addahab(USA), a big, rangy newcomer, missed the break and looked very inexperienced. Picking up ground nicely late on she will do much better next year. (op 10-1)
Michevious Spirit(IRE) ◆, having her third run, was tightened up when starting her final effort. She could never take a hand but should make her mark in handicap company next year. (op 13-2)

6763 EUROPEAN BREEDERS' FUND MAIDEN STKS (C&G) 1m (R)
2:20 (2:21) (Class 5) 2-Y-0 **£3,885** (£1,156; £577; £288) **Stalls** Low

Form RPR

1 **Burnett (IRE)** 2-9-0 0 .... TedDurcan 8 85+
(Saeed Bin Suroor) *in tch: stdy hdwy over 2f out: shkn up to ld over 1f out: styd on strly fnl f* **11/4**[2]

2032 **2** *4* **Pytheas (USA)**[38] 5682 2-9-0 80 .... GregFairley 1 76
(M Johnston) *led: rdn over 2f out: hdd over 1f out: kpt on same pce ins fnl f* **15/8**[1]

3 *1 3/4* **Palawi (IRE)** 2-9-0 0 .... GrahamGibbons 11 72+
(J J Quinn) *midfield: rdn and outpcd over 2f out: rallied fnl f: r.o* **25/1**

56 **4** *hd* **Danceintothelight**[23] 6136 2-9-0 0 .... PhillipMakin 4 72
(K A Ryan) *trckd ldrs: effrt over 2f out: one pce fnl f* **10/1**

5 *hd* **Sir Pitt** 2-9-0 0 .... JimmyFortune 7 75+
(J H M Gosden) *sn niggled in rr: hdwy and edgd lft 2f out: styd on wl fnl f: improve* **4/1**[3]

0 **6** *nk* **Molon Labe (IRE)**[60] 5000 2-9-0 0 .... RobertWinston 6 71
(T P Tate) *trckd ldrs: rdn 3f out: one pce over 1f out* **10/1**

7 *4* **Dandino** 2-9-0 0 .... PaulMulrennan 2 62
(J G Given) *s.i.s: hld up: pushed along 3f out: hdwy 2f out: nvr rchd ldrs* **20/1**

00 **8** *6* **Edward Longshanks (USA)**[29] 5951 2-9-0 0 .... DNolan 9 49
(T P Tate) *towards rr: rdn over 3f out: nvr on terms* **66/1**

6 **9** *6* **Fusenam**[46] 5408 2-9-0 0 .... TomEaves 5 35+
(Miss J A Camacho) *hld up: rdn over 3f out: sn btn* **50/1**

60 **10** *10* **Hotgrove Boy**[26] 6011 2-9-0 0 .... TonyHamilton 13 13
(A G Foster) *prom tl drvn and wknd fr 3f out* **100/1**

0 **11** *6* **Tantsor (FR)**[44] 5466 2-8-9 0 .... PaulPickard(5) 3 —
(P T Midgley) *in tch tl rdn and wknd 3f out* **200/1**

0 **12** *1 1/2* **Acol**[25] 6046 2-9-0 0 .... AndrewMullen 12 —
(A G Foster) *t.k.h: in tch tl wknd 3f out* **150/1**

0 **13** *3* **Timetowynagain**[45] 5439 2-9-0 0 .... PJMcDonald 10 —
(C W Fairhurst) *t.k.h: midfield: struggling 1/2-way: sn btn* **200/1**

1m 44.55s (1.15) **Going Correction** -0.075s/f (Good) **13** Ran SP% **114.3**
Speed ratings (Par 95): **91,87,85,85,84 84,80,74,68,58 52,51,48**
toteswingers: 1&2 £2.90, 1&3 £12.40, 2&3 £12.00 CSF £7.54 TOTE £3.90: £1.20, £1.20, £6.40; EX 8.00.
Owner Godolphin **Bred** Swettenham Stud **Trained** Newmarket, Suffolk

FOCUS
An interesting maiden run at a sound pace and a debut winner of real potential. The runner-up is rated to the balance of his form.

NOTEBOOK
Burnett(IRE) ◆, a 460,000gns purchase, is a big and well-made colt. He moved up on the bridle to take second place 2f out and, when sent about his busniness, had his race won in a matter of strides. An Epsom Derby entry, he will be even better suited by quicker ground and could prove very useful next year. (op 4-1 tchd 5-2)
Pytheas(USA), having his fifth start, is rated 80. He made this a true test but in the end was no match for the winner. He deserves to break his duck. (op 13-8 tchd 6-4 and 2-1)
Palawi(IRE) picked up ground once in line for home and this newcomer put in some pleasing late work. He may not be at his best until next year. (op 28-1 tchd 20-1)
Danceintothelight, clear second at one stage, tied up badly in the closing stages. He still looks on the weak side and should make his presence felt in handicap company at three. (op 11-1 tchd 9-1)
Sir Pitt ◆, out of a Coronation Stakes winner, is a robust, well-made type. After a tardy start under a patient ride he picked up nicely late in the day and was not given a hard time. He can be expected to do a lot better with another year over his head. Official explanation: jockey said, regarding running and riding, that his orders were to jump out and do his best, adding that the colt was very green and was off the bridle a long way out and became short of room final furlong. (op 3-1)
Molon Labe(IRE) improved on his debut effort and is another for handicaps next year. (op 12-1)
Acol Official explanation: jockey said gelding stumbled early; trainer said gelding had knocked right-fore

6764 DALES BROADCAST TELEVISION FACILITY H'CAP (DIV I) 6f
2:50 (2:51) (Class 5) (0-75,75) 3-Y-O+ **£2,525** (£751; £375; £187) **Stalls** High

Form RPR

3462 **1** **Misplaced Fortune**[26] 6020 4-9-2 75 .... (v) Louis-PhilippeBeuzelin(3) 13 84
(N Tinkler) *cl up stands' side: hdwy to ld that gp over 2f out: rdn and overall ldr ent fnl f: drvn and kpt on wl towards fin* **8/1**

4226 **2** *1/2* **Leonid Glow**[3] 6667 4-9-3 73 .... PhillipMakin 16 80
(M Dods) *hld up in tch stands' side: hdwy to chse wnr 2f out: rdn to chal and ev ch ent fnl f: sn drvn and no ex last 100yds: 2nd of 7 in gp* **6/1**[2]

4120 **3** *2 1/2* **Avontuur (FR)**[28] 5960 7-8-8 69 .... (b) DeanHeslop(5) 5 68
(Mrs R A Carr) *overall ldr far side: rdn along and hdd over 2f out: drvn over 1f out: kpt on same pce u.p ins fnl f: 1st of 9 in gp* **18/1**

-343 **4** *nk* **Verinco**[20] 6221 3-8-1 65 .... (p) AdamCarter(7) 2 63
(B Smart) *cl up far side: effrt to ld that gp and overall ldr over 2f out: sn rdn: drvn and hdd ent fnl f: kpt on same pce: 2nd of 9 in gp* **33/1**

6031 **5** *nk* **Revue Princess (IRE)**[13] 6380 4-8-10 66 .... (b) DavidAllan 3 63
(T D Easterby) *trckd ldrs far side: effrt over 2f out and sn rdn along and sltly outpcd tl kpt on u.p ins fnl f: 3rd of 9 in gp* **16/1**

400U **6** *1 1/4* **Top Bid**[12] 6413 5-8-2 61 oh1 .... (b) KellyHarrison(3) 6 54
(T D Easterby) *dwlt and swtchd lft s: sn in tch far side: effrt 2f out and sn rdn: kpt on same pce u.p ins fnl f: 4th of 9 in gp* **50/1**

0142 **7** *hd* **Sea Salt**[16] 6309 6-8-12 73 .... PaulPickard(5) 11 66
(R E Barr) *led stands' side: gp: pushed along 1/2-way: sn rdn and hung lft towards far side gp over 2f out: drvn and one pce appr fnl f: 3rd of 7 in gp* **8/1**

0000 **8** *1* **Glasshoughton**[4] 6637 6-8-9 65 .... PJMcDonald 1 55
(M Dods) *s.i.s and bhd far side: hdwy 2f out: sn rdn and kpt on same pce fnl f: 5th of 9 in gp* **22/1**

50-0 **9** *nse* **Geojimali**[25] 6050 7-8-13 74 .... (p) GaryBartley(5) 9 63
(J S Goldie) *dwlt and in rr far side: hdwy 2f out: sn rdn and kpt on ins fnl f: 6th of 9 in gp* **25/1**

0200 **10** *1* **Mey Blossom**[12] 6434 4-8-4 65 .... AmyRyan(5) 14 51
(R M Whitaker) *prom stands' side: rdn along over 2f out and grad wknd: 4th of 7 in gp* **14/1**

-410 **11** *1/2* **Dance Card**[26] 6015 4-9-2 72 .... (t) PaulMulrennan 12 57
(A G Foster) *dwlt: hld up towards rr stands' side: hdwy 1/2-way: rdn along 2f out: sn edgd lft and wknd: 5th of 7 in gp* **15/2**[3]

1000 **12** *1* **Rabbit Fighter (IRE)**[12] 6437 5-8-1 62 .... (v) MartinLane(5) 7 43
(D Shaw) *trckd ldrs far side: rdn along 2f out: drvn and wknd appr fnl f: 7th of 9 in gp* **33/1**

333 **13** *3 1/2* **John Keats**[12] 6413 6-8-11 67 .... (p) DanielTudhope 4 37
(J S Goldie) *a towards rr far side: 8th of 9 in gp* **12/1**

103 **14** *6* **Blown It (USA)**[10] 6489 3-9-4 75 .... TomEaves 17 26
(I Semple) *s.i.s and a towards rr stands' side: 6th of 7 in gp* **16/1**

3111 **15** *2* **Milton Of Campsie**[12] 6413 4-9-1 71 .... KFallon 15 52
(J Balding) *in tch stands' side: effrt over 2f out: sn rdn and btn: eased over 1f out: last of 7 in gp* **7/2**[1]

221- **16** *29* **Frisbee**[451] 4207 5-8-13 69 .... RobertWinston 8 —
(C J Teague) *chsd ldrs far side: rdn along wl over 2f out: sn wknd and bhd whn eased over 1f out: last of 9 in gp* **14/1**

1m 14.18s (-1.02) **Going Correction** -0.075s/f (Good)
WFA 3 from 4yo+ 1lb **16** Ran SP% **124.6**
Speed ratings (Par 103): **103,102,99,98,98 96,96,94,94,93 92,91,86,78,76 37**
toteswingers: 1&2 £16.50, 1&3 £42.40, 2&3 £33.10 CSF £53.54 CT £896.12 TOTE £9.30: £2.60, £2.00, £4.00, £6.30; EX 83.40.
Owner W F Burton **Bred** Adrian Smith **Trained** Langton, N Yorks

FOCUS
A moderate sprint handicap. Six set off racing towards the stands' side but two of them elected to join the other ten on the far side. The first two home raced exclusively on the stands' side. The second looks the best guide to the form.
Sea Salt Official explanation: jockey said gelding hung left throughout
Milton Of Campsie Official explanation: jockey said filly lost its action final 1 1/2f
Frisbee Official explanation: jockey said mare had no more to give

6765 DALES BROADCAST TELEVISION FACILITY H'CAP (DIV II) 6f
3:20 (3:20) (Class 5) (0-75,75) 3-Y-O+ **£2,525** (£751; £375; £187) **Stalls** High

Form RPR

6-22 **1** **Viva Volta**[40] 5601 6-9-0 72 .... (v1) FrederikTylicki(3) 8 79
(A C Whillans) *racd far side: mde all: clr 2f out: hld on wl:* **10/1**

2100 **2** *nk* **Noodles Blue Boy**[17] 6279 3-9-4 74 .... FrancisNorton 11 80
(Ollie Pears) *prom stands' side: rdn over 2f out: styd on to ld that gp towards fin: jst hld by far side wnr: 1st of 9 in gp* **9/1**[3]

3005 **3** *nk* **Ingleby Arch (USA)**[10] 6495 6-9-0 72 .... NeilBrown(3) 3 77
(T D Barron) *dwlt: hld up far side: rdn over 2f out: hdwy to chse wnr 1f out: kpt on wl: jst hld: 2nd of 7 in gp* **16/1**

1145 **4** *nse* **Bid For Gold**[40] 5597 5-8-13 73 .... PatrickDonaghy(5) 10 78
(Jedd O'Keeffe) *cl up stands' side: rdn 1/2-way: led that gp over 1f out: hdd nr fin: 2nd of 9 in gp* **14/1**

0003 **5** *1* **Rising Shadow (IRE)**[26] 6015 8-9-0 74 .... DeanHeslop(5) 17 79
(A D Brown) *hld up towards rr stands' side: hdwy whn nt clr run over 1f out: rdn and r.o fnl f: 3rd of 9 in gp* **5/1**[1]

0401 **6** *hd* **Finsbury**[12] 6414 6-8-3 61 .... KellyHarrison(5) 15 62
(J S Goldie) *hld up stands' side: hdwy over 1f out: swtchd lft and kpt on towards fin: 4th of 9 in gp* **12/1**

0000 **7** *1 3/4* **Sea Rover (IRE)**[29] 5955 5-8-10 65 .... RobertWinston 13 61
(M Brittain) *cl up stands' side: effrt and ev ch that gp over 1f out: no ex ins fnl f: 5th of 9 in gp* **28/1**

1012 **8** *1 1/4* **Midnight Fantasy**[40] 5591 3-9-5 75 .... SaleemGolam 5 67
(Rae Guest) *hld up far side: hdwy over 1f out: no imp fnl f: 3rd of 7 in gp* **9/1**[3]

2000 **9** *1 1/2* **Sandwith**[25] 6051 6-9-1 70 .... AndrewMullen 1 57
(A G Foster) *cl up far side: rdn over 2f out: one pce over 1f out: 4th of 7 in gp* **40/1**

3460 **10** *3/4* **Jonny Lesters Hair (IRE)**[14] 6361 4-8-12 67 .... DavidAllan 2 51
(T D Easterby) *trckd far side ldrs: drvn and outpcd over 2f out: no imp fnl f: 5th of 7 in gp* **11/1**

006 **11** *hd* **Burning Incense (IRE)**[10] 6495 6-9-0 69 .... (b) PhillipMakin 14 53
(M Dods) *hld up stands' side: rdn over 2f out: sme late hdwy: nvr rchd ldrs: 6th of 9 in gp* **16/1**

3010 **11** *dht* **Rio Sands**[3] 6670 4-8-5 60 .... PaulQuinn 12 44
(R M Whitaker) *prom stands' side: rdn over 2f out: no ex over 1f out: 7th of 9 in gp* **18/1**

3214 **13** 1/2 **Daring Dream (GER)**[12] 6413 4-8-10 **65** .... DanielTudhope 9 47
(J S Goldie) *hld up on outside of stands' side gp: rdn over 2f out: sn wknd: 8th of 9 in gp* **6/1**[2]

0021 **14** 3 3/4 **Just Sam (IRE)**[20] 6216 4-8-8 **68** .... PaulPickard(5) 4 38
(R E Barr) *cl up far side tl rdn and wknd over 1f out: 6th of 7 in gp* **10/1**

3000 **15** 3/4 **Sir Geoffrey (IRE)**[18] 6253 3-9-0 **70** ....(bt) PaulMulrennan 16 38
(J A Glover) *led stands' side to over 1f out: sn wknd: last of 9 in gp* **28/1**

0040 **16** 1 **Hansomis (IRE)**[12] 6413 5-8-9 **64** .... TomEaves 6 29
(B Mactaggart) *hld up in tch far side: rdn and outpcd over 2f out: sn wknd: last of 7 in gp* **33/1**

1m 13.71s (-1.49) **Going Correction** -0.075s/f (Good)
WFA 3 from 4yo+ 1lb **16** Ran SP% **121.1**
Speed ratings (Par 103): **106,105,105,105,103 103,101,99,97,96 96,96,95,90,89 88**
toteswingers: 1&2 £22.90, 1&3 £50.40, 2&3 £45.50 CSF £93.13 CT £1507.05 TOTE £12.30: £2.80, £2.20, £3.50, £4.10; EX 116.20.
Owner Mrs L Irving **Bred** T W H And Mrs Dancer **Trained** Newmill-On-Slitrig, Borders

FOCUS
The second division of the sprint handicap. There was no real bias in the draw and the first four were very closely covered at the finish. The form makes a fair bit of sense.
Rising Shadow(IRE) ◆ Official explanation: jockey said gelding was denied a clear run
Rio Sands Official explanation: jockey said gelding ran flat

6766 WIN A 308 CC MEDIAN AUCTION MAIDEN STKS 1m 4f 93y
3:50 (3:50) (Class 6) 3-4-Y-0 **£2,590** (£770; £385; £192) **Stalls** Low

Form RPR

0606 **1** **Zelos Diktator**[24] 6116 3-8-12 47 ....(p) MartinLane(5) 1 63
(Rae Guest) *mde all: rdn along wl over 2f out: drvn over 1f out: kpt on gamely u.p ins fnl f* **20/1**

3334 **2** 1 **Astrodiva**[27] 5987 3-8-12 67 .... TedDurcan 2 56
(M H Tompkins) *trckd wnr: hdwy to chal over 2f out and ev ch: rdn wl over 1f out and kpt on same pce* **5/4**[1]

0634 **3** 2 **Melkatant**[20] 6219 3-8-12 47 .... FrancisNorton 7 53
(N Bycroft) *t.k.h: hld up: hdwy on inner over 3f out: rdn to chse ldng pair over 2f out: drvn wl over 1f out and no imp fnl f* **14/1**

30-3 **4** 1 1/4 **Lisbon Lion (IRE)**[235] 623 4-9-7 58 .... FrederikTylicki(3) 9 56
(James Moffatt) *dwlt: hld up in rr: hdwy over 4f out: rdn along wl over 2f out: drvn and kpt on same pce appr fnl f* **7/1**

6354 **5** 2 1/2 **Gosforth Park**[74] 4491 3-9-3 54 .... RobertWinston 5 52
(M Brittain) *trckd ldrs: hdwy 4f out: rdn along over 2f out: sn drvn and plugged on same pce* **4/1**[2]

025 **6** 7 **Aven Mac (IRE)**[21] 6177 3-8-12 44 ....(p) DavidAllan 8 36
(N Bycroft) *hld up towards rr: hdwy to chse ldrs on outer 5f out: rdn along over 3f out: sn drvn and wknd* **25/1**

4-40 **7** 8 **Gulnaz**[71] 4593 4-9-5 41 .... DNolan 10 23
(C J Teague) *midfield: hdwy to trck ldrs 1/2-way: rdn along over 4f out: sn drvn and wknd 3f out* **80/1**

6334 **8** 1 1/4 **Quick Gourmet**[55] 5158 3-8-12 58 .... PJMcDonald 11 21
(G A Swinbank) *s.i.s: plld hrd and rapid prog to chse ldrs after 4f: rdn along 4f out: drvn 3f out and sn wknd* **13/2**[3]

0 **9** 3 **Haunting**[71] 4599 3-8-12 0 .... AndrewMullen 3 16
(A G Foster) *nvr bttr than midfield* **100/1**

4040 **10** *nk* **Bogula (IRE)**[21] 6183 3-8-12 55 .... SJCraine 13 16
(Mrs A Duffield) *in tch: rdn along over 4f out: sn wknd* **18/1**

11 25 **Subasta**[16] 4-8-12 0 .... JohnCavanagh(7) 12 —
(M Brittain) *s.i.s and rdn sn after s: a bhd* **100/1**

0-00 **12** 58 **Ugly Betty**[108] 3379 4-9-5 30 .... PaulMulrennan 6 —
(Bruce Hellier) *chsd ldrs: pushed along 1/2-way: sn lost pl and bhd fnl 3f* **200/1**

2m 45.32s (-0.28) **Going Correction** -0.075s/f (Good)
WFA 3 from 4yo 7lb **12** Ran SP% **114.5**
Speed ratings (Par 101): **97,96,95,94,92 87,82,81,79,79 62,24**
toteswingers: 1&2 £7.40, 1&3 £21.70, 2&3 £6.10 CSF £43.36 TOTE £20.20: £4.60, £1.10, £2.90; EX 50.20.
Owner Tremousser Partnership **Bred** The Duke Of Roxburghe's Stud **Trained** Newmarket, Suffolk

FOCUS
A weak maiden and not form to be too positive about. The front pair were always 1-2.

6767 3008 LAUNCH H'CAP 2m 19y
4:20 (4:22) (Class 5) (0-75,72) 3-Y-0+ **£2,978** (£886; £442; £221) **Stalls** Low

Form RPR

4001 **1** **Unawatuna**[42] 5554 4-8-7 **54** .... KellyHarrison(3) 16 64
(Mrs K Walton) *prom: hdwy to ld 2f out: sn hrd pressed: hld on gamely fnl f* **11/1**

1252 **2** 1/2 **Outland (IRE)**[40] 5600 3-7-13 **54** .... NickyMackay 2 63
(M H Tompkins) *settled midfield: swtchd rt and smooth hdwy over 2f out: ev ch appr fnl f: kpt on: hld towards fin* **5/2**[1]

5611 **3** *nk* **Puy D'Arnac (FR)**[39] 5622 6-9-12 **70** .... RobertWinston 11 81+
(G A Swinbank) *t.k.h: prom: nt clr run fr 3f out to over 1f out: kpt on fnl f: hld towards fin* **7/1**[3]

1633 **4** 7 **Simonside**[25] 6053 6-10-0 **72** .... TomEaves 1 73
(B Ellison) *prom: drvn and outpcd over 2f out: rallied fnl f: nt rch ldng trio* **8/1**

4636 **5** *nk* **Red Wine**[39] 5625 10-9-5 **66** .... FrederikTylicki(3) 10 66
(J A Glover) *hld up: stdy hdwy into midfield 4f out: rdn and one pce fnl 2f* **20/1**

1334 **6** 1 1/2 **Summer Soul (IRE)**[25] 6053 7-9-9 **70** ....(p) ClGillies(3) 4 68
(Miss Lucinda V Russell) *cl up: led after 3f: rdn and hdd 2f out: sn outpcd* **16/1**

002 **7** 1 1/2 **Orsippus (USA)**[13] 6384 3-8-10 **65** .... DavidAllan 7 62
(Michael Smith) *t.k.h: prom: effrt over 2f out: outpcd over 1f out* **10/1**

-200 **8** 1 1/4 **Baaher (USA)**[25] 6053 5-9-0 **58** .... DanielTudhope 8 53
(J S Goldie) *cl up tl rdn and no ex fr 2f out* **20/1**

0404 **9** 1 1/4 **Dechiper (IRE)**[13] 6385 7-9-7 **65** .... GrahamGibbons 14 59
(R Johnson) *hld up: rdn over 3f out: plugged on fnl f: nvr able to chal* **20/1**

5565 **10** *hd* **Lets Roll**[25] 6053 8-9-0 **58** .... PJMcDonald 5 51
(C W Thornton) *hld up: rdn over 3f out: nvr rchd ldrs* **16/1**

3005 **11** 1 **Rapid Desire (IRE)**[42] 5554 3-7-12 **53** oh3........ DuranFentiman 6 45
(J R Weymes) *midfeld: drvn fr 1/2-way: rallied: outpcd fnl 3f* **33/1**

/426 **12** 1 **Pagan Starprincess**[25] 6053 5-8-12 **56** .... PhillipMakin 15 47
(G M Moore) *hld up: rdn over 3f out: nvr on terms* **9/2**[2]

3060 **13** 1 3/4 **Rare Coincidence**[43] 4862 8-9-3 **61** ....(tp) TonyHamilton 9 50
(R F Fisher) *led 3f: cl up tl rdn and wknd fr 2f out* **40/1**

0030 **14** 16 **Uptown Lad (IRE)**[3] 5734 10-8-4 **53** oh8........ PaulPickard(5) 12 23
(R Johnson) *missed break: bhd: rdn over 4f out: sn wknd: t.o* **100/1**

4000 **15** 24 **Merrion Tiger (IRE)**[25] 6053 4-8-11 **55** ....(p) AndrewMullen 3 —
(A G Foster) *midfield: struggling over 5f out: sn btn: t.o* **66/1**

3m 35.56s (-3.84) **Going Correction** -0.075s/f (Good)
WFA 3 from 4yo+ 11lb **15** Ran SP% **121.7**
Speed ratings (Par 103): **106,105,105,102,101 101,100,99,99,99 98,98,97,89,77**
toteswingers: 1&2 £7.70, 1&3 £18.60, 2&3 £4.80 CSF £36.04 CT £217.91 TOTE £13.60: £3.10, £1.70, £2.50; EX 56.50.
Owner Trainers House Enterprises Ltd **Bred** Trainers House Enterprises Limited **Trained** Middleham Moor, N Yorks

FOCUS
A moderate handicap which saw the first three finish clear. Sound form among them, the winner back to his best.

6768 SPOOKY SPECTACULAR ON 31ST OCTOBER H'CAP (FOR AMATEUR RIDERS) (DIV I) 1m 4f 93y
4:50 (4:50) (Class 6) (0-65,65) 3-Y-0+ **£1,747** (£537; £268) **Stalls** Low

Form RPR

-440 **1** **Nakoma (IRE)**[51] 5291 7-10-1 **57** .... DaleSwift(5) 4 64+
(B Ellison) *trckd ldrs on inner: hdwy 3f out: swtchd rt and rdn over 1f out: squeezed through on inner ent fnl f: styd on to ld last 100yds* **25/1**

204 **2** 1/2 **Rudry World (IRE)**[50] 5307 6-9-13 **55** .... MissMMullineaux(5) 3 61
(M Mullineaux) *hld up in rr: stdy hdwy 3f out: effrt on outer 2f out and sn chsng ldrs: styd on wl fnl f* **16/1**

0233 **3** 3/4 **Front Rank (IRE)**[9] 5734 9-9-9 **51** .... MissECSayer(5) 11 56
(Mrs Dianne Sayer) *trckd ldrs: effrt 3f out: rdn 2f out: styd on to ld ent fnl f: hdd and no ex last 100yds* **11/1**

3204 **4** 3/4 **Greenbelt**[133] 2580 8-9-8 **52** .... MrSWelton(7) 13 56
(G M Moore) *prom on outer: hdwy to chal 3f out: rdn to ld 2f out: hdd ent fnl f: kpt on same pce* **25/1**

0000 **5** 3/4 **Charging Indian (IRE)**[13] 6370 3-10-0 **63** .... MissWGibson(5) 12 66
(P T Midgley) *in tch: hdwy 4f out: rdn to chse ldrs over 2f out: kpt on same pce u.p ins fnl f* **14/1**

3212 **6** *hd* **Grandad Bill (IRE)**[29] 5947 6-10-10 **61** .... MrsCBartley 7 63
(J S Goldie) *t.k.h: led 4f: cl up tl effrt over 3f out and ev ch tl rdn along 2f out and grad wknd appr fnl f* **7/4**[1]

5440 **7** 2 **Royal Flynn**[35] 5307 7-9-11 **55** ....(p) MrJHBrooke(7) 9 54
(Mrs K Walton) *hld up in rr: hdwy over 3f out: rdn 2f out: styd on appr fnl f: nt rch ldrs* **25/1**

3462 **8** *hd* **Edas**[45] 5438 7-10-9 **65** .... MissHCuthbert(5) 14 64
(T A K Cuthbert) *hld up: hdwy over 4f out: rdn along over 2f out: n.m.r wl over 1f out: kpt on same pce* **14/1**

0360 **9** 1 **Shadows Lengthen**[32] 5838 3-9-5 **54** ow2........ MrJakeGreenall(5) 6 51
(M W Easterby) *hld up: hdwy 5f out: rdn along and in tch 3f out: drvn 2f out and sn one pce* **17/2**

0612 **10** 1 1/2 **Hurricane Thomas (IRE)**[14] 6369 5-10-3 **59** .... MissPhillipaTutty(5) 2 54
(R A Fahey) *cl up: led 5f out: rdn along 3f out: hdd 2f out and grad wknd* **8/1**[3]

0006 **11** 1 1/2 **Cripsey Brook**[40] 5600 11-10-1 **59** oh6 ow8........ MrJMThomas(7) 1 51
(K G Reveley) *a in rr* **40/1**

6122 **12** 5 **Amazing King (IRE)**[17] 4755 5-10-7 **65** .... MrATBrook(7) 8 49
(P A Kirby) *cl up: led after 4f: hdd 1/2-way and styd cl up: rdn and ev ch 2f out: sn drvn and wknd* **9/2**[2]

0304 **13** 11 **Efidium**[13] 6392 11-10-5 **63** ow3........ MrSebSpencer(7) 10 30
(N Bycroft) *t.k.h: hld up: a in rr* **20/1**

2m 48.06s (2.46) **Going Correction** -0.075s/f (Good)
WFA 3 from 5yo+ 7lb **13** Ran SP% **122.5**
Speed ratings (Par 101): **88,87,87,86,86 86,84,84,83,82 81,78,71**
toteswingers: 1&2 £15.20, 1&3 £37.80, 2&3 £16.70 CSF £366.20 CT £4615.39 TOTE £41.60: £9.30, £4.30, £2.80; EX 405.50.
Owner Racing Management & Training, K & BGM **Bred** John Davison **Trained** Norton, N Yorks

FOCUS
A moderate handicap, confined to amatuer riders, and the slowest of the three C/D times. Due to the steady early pace there was a bunched finish between the first six. The form is modest and somewhat muddling.
Charging Indian(IRE) Official explanation: jockey said colt stumbled on bend approx 1f after start

6769 SPOOKY SPECTACULAR ON 31ST OCTOBER H'CAP (FOR AMATEUR RIDERS) (DIV II) 1m 4f 93y
5:20 (5:21) (Class 6) (0-65,65) 3-Y-0+ **£1,747** (£537; £268) **Stalls** Low

Form RPR

0615 **1** **Rossini's Dancer**[26] 6012 4-10-9 **65** .... MissPhillipaTutty(5) 11 73
(R A Fahey) *hld up: hdwy and in tch over 2f out: rdn to ld ins fnl f: r.o wl* **13/2**[3]

5143 **2** 1 3/4 **Patavium (IRE)**[7] 6560 6-10-6 **57** .... MissSBrotherton 9 62+
(E W Tuer) *prom: led over 1f out to ins fnl f: kpt on u.p* **3/1**[2]

5036 **3** 2 3/4 **Obara D'Avril (FR)**[7] 6558 7-9-11 **53** .... MissEStead(5) 2 54
(S G West) *hld up: hdwy over 2f out: kpt on same pce fnl f* **12/1**

3625 **4** 1 1/2 **Hawkit (USA)**[22] 6156 8-9-12 **56** .... MrMEnnis(7) 12 54
(P Monteith) *hld up: stdy hdwy and in tch over 2f out: one pce fnl f* **12/1**

0003 **5** *nk* **Mehendi (IRE)**[15] 6342 3-10-4 **62** .... MissLEllison 10 60
(B Ellison) *chsd clr ldr: led over 2f out to over 1f out: no ex* **2/1**[1]

0/0- **6** 3 1/2 **Sea Storm (IRE)**[145] 6056 11-10-2 **60** .... MissRebeccaSparkes(7) 4 52
(James Moffatt) *bhd tl hdwy over 2f out: nvr able to chal* **16/1**

1066 **7** 5 **Realism (FR)**[37] 5694 9-10-3 **59** ....(tp) MrJakeGreenall(5) 14 43
(M W Easterby) *dwlt and almost ref to r: bhd: sme hdwy 2f out: nvr rchd ldrs* **14/1**

0160 **8** 4 **Monfils Monfils (USA)**[19] 5438 7-10-9 **65** .... MissVBarr(5) 7 43
(R E Barr) *led and clr to st: hdd over 2f out: sn wknd* **16/1**

-000 **9** 6 **Firestorm (IRE)**[7] 6558 5-9-7 **51** oh6........(b) MrJHBrooke(7) 1 19
(C W Fairhurst) *hld up: rdn 4f out: sn btn* **100/1**

0061 **10** 1 1/4 **Phantom Serenade (IRE)**[20] 6219 4-10-2 **60** .... MrJMullaney(7) 13 26
(M Dods) *t.k.h: prom tl edgd lft and wknd wl over 2f out* **9/1**

/555 **11** 3 1/4 **Samizdat (FR)**[11] 3314 6-9-9 **51** ....(tp) MissECSayer(5) 5 12
(Mrs Dianne Sayer) *chsd ldrs to 3f out: sn struggling* **40/1**

00-0 **12** 2 3/4 **Skylarker (USA)**[137] 2442 11-9-9 **51** oh1........ MissHCuthbert(5) 8 8
(T A K Cuthbert) *midfield: outpcd 3f out: sn btn* **100/1**

1600 **13** 24 **Media Stars**[13] 6383 4-9-7 **51** oh2........(p) MrTSpeke(7) 6 —
(R Johnson) *dwlt: hld up: rdn 4f out: sn lost tch* **33/1**

2m 46.9s (1.30) **Going Correction** -0.075s/f (Good)
WFA 3 from 4yo+ 7lb **13** Ran SP% **122.8**
Speed ratings (Par 101): **92,90,89,88,87 85,82,79,75,74 72,70,54**
toteswingers: 1&2 £6.40, 1&3 £14.30, 2&3 £10.90 CSF £26.76 CT £237.85 TOTE £6.10: £1.50, £2.30, £4.60; EX 33.70 Place 6: £134.48, Place 5: £54.09..
Owner Lets Go Racing 1 **Bred** Heather Raw **Trained** Musley Bank, N Yorks
■ Stewards' Enquiry : Mr T Speke caution: used whip when out of contention.

FOCUS
This second division of the handicap for amatuer riders was run at a decent pace thanks to the tearaway leader. The time was quicker than the first division but the form is limited.
T/Jkpt: Not won. T/Plt: £223.70 to a £1 stake. Pool: £72,722.09. 237.28 winning tickets. T/Qpdt: £82.70 to a £1 stake. Pool: £5,668.07. 50.70 winning tickets. RY

6719 KEMPTON (A.W) (R-H)
Wednesday, October 14

OFFICIAL GOING: Standard
Wind: Moderate, across towards stands Weather: Overcast

6770 TURFTV H'CAP — 1m 4f (P)
5:45 (5:45) (Class 7) (0-50,50) 3-Y-0+ — **£2,047** (£604; £302) Stalls Centre

Form — RPR

0004 **1** **Little Sark (IRE)**[6] 6612 4-9-2 **50** PatCosgrave 7 — 57
(P D Evans) *led 1f: settled in 3rd: rdn to chse clr ldr over 2f out: clsd fnl f: led last stride* **9/2**[1]

5000 **2** *shd* **It's Josr**[34] 5790 4-9-1 **49** (b) TPQueally 4 — 56
(I A Wood) *t.k.h early: trckd ldr after 1f: led 3f out and kicked clr: stl 3 l up ins fnl f: ct post* **16/1**

2523 **3** *hd* **Tivers Song (USA)**[15] 6369 5-9-2 **50** (b) HayleyTurner 9 — 57
(John A Harris) *hld up in last pair: stl there wl over 2f out as ldr wnt clr: gd prog after: bdly bmpd wl over 1f out: r.o fnl f: jst hld* **6/1**[2]

-034 **4** *1 3/4* **Mr Plod**[14] 6371 4-9-2 **50** (v) StephenCarson 14 — 54
(Andrew Reid) *hld up in last quartet: prog wl over 2f out: swtchd lft wl over 1f out: styd on fnl f: nvr able to chal* **12/1**

-000 **5** *nk* **Duneen Dream (USA)**[11] 6498 4-8-7 **48** RachelKing(7) 6 — 52
(Mrs N S Evans) *t.k.h early: trckd ldrs: trapped bhd struggling rival over 3f out: prog on inner over 2f out: disp 2nd wl over 1f out: pushed along and nt qckn fnl f* **50/1**

3330 **6** *3* **Dontpaytheferryman (USA)**[20] 6025 4-8-11 **48** FrederikTylicki(3) 5 — 47
(B Ellison) *racd wd: trckd ldrs: rdn and nt qckn over 2f out: outpcd and struggling after* **9/2**[1]

5600 **7** *2* **Medieval Maiden**[20] 6226 6-9-2 **50** (p) IanMongan 10 — 46
(Mrs L J Mongan) *a in midfield: effrt on outer over 2f out: no prog and wl outpcd after* **16/1**

0500 **8** *1/2* **Desert Hawk**[41] 5617 8-9-0 **48** LiamJones 11 — 43
(W M Brisbourne) *stdd s: hld up in abt 10th: rdn and keeping on at one pce whn bmpd and squeezed out wl over 1f out: no ch after* **20/1**

3003 **9** *1 1/4* **Uig**[34] 5790 8-9-2 **50** KirstyMilczarek 13 — 43
(H S Howe) *settled bhd ldrs: pushed along 4f out: effrt u.p to dispute 3rd over 2f out: sn wknd* **16/1**

2244 **10** *1/2* **Fantasy Ride**[41] 5617 7-8-10 **49** SimonPearce(5) 1 — 41
(J Pearce) *stdd s: t.k.h and hld up in last pair: taken v wd bnd 3f out: brief effrt over 2f out: sn no prog* **8/1**[3]

050- **11** *3 1/2* **Celtic Charlie (FR)**[408] 5574 4-8-11 **48** JackMitchell(3) 8 — 34
(P M Phelan) *hld up in last quartet: rdn on outer wl over 2f out: fnd nil* **16/1**

0006 **12** *1 1/4* **Rosy Dawn**[8] 6565 4-8-13 **50** MarcHalford(3) 2 — 34
(J J Bridger) *rdn to ld after 1f: hdd 3f out: sn wknd* **33/1**

00-0 **13** *1 1/2* **Petroglyph**[267] 224 5-9-2 **50** (p) EddieAhern 3 — 32
(M G Quinlan) *trckd ldrs: rdn 4f out: wknd over 2f out: sn bhd* **8/1**[3]

3500 **14** *20* **Touch Of Style (IRE)**[15] 6369 5-9-2 **50** (p) KFallon 12 — —
(T D McCarthy) *nvr bttr than midfield: rdn 4f out: sn wknd: eased: t.o* **12/1**

2m 33.71s (-0.79) **Going Correction** -0.125s/f (Stan) — **14** Ran SP% **121.4**
Speed ratings (Par 97): **97,96,96,95,95 93,92,91,90,90 88,87,86,73**
toteswingers: 1&2 £14.40, 1&3 £3.50, 2&3 £20.30 CSF £78.86 CT £445.42 TOTE £5.70: £2.30, £6.40, £1.60; EX 120.30.
Owner Trevor Gallienne **Bred** A Pereira **Trained** Pandy, Monmouths
■ Stewards' Enquiry : Stephen Carson four-day ban: careless riding (Oct 28-31)

FOCUS
A poor, but tight-knit handicap with just 2lb separating the field. They went a level gallop and the time suggested that the track was riding quickly. The form looks sound.
Touch Of Style(IRE) Official explanation: jockey said gelding felt wrong behind

6771 GROOMED TO PERFECTION, KIA SOUL CLASSIFIED STKS — 1m (P)
6:20 (6:20) (Class 6) 3-Y-0+ — **£2,047** (£604; £302) Stalls High

Form — RPR

4050 **1** **Lady's Art (FR)**[12] 6439 3-9-0 55 (v[1]) KFallon 6 — 62
(E F Vaughan) *hld up: prog on outer to trck ldrs 1/2-way: hdwy to ld jst over 2f out: rdn over 1f out: styd on wl* **4/1**[2]

000 **2** *1 1/2* **Rebel Woman**[34] 5789 3-9-0 52 TPQueally 14 — 58
(J A Osborne) *hld up: n.m.r and dropped in rr over 6f out: prog over 2f out to trck ldrs: drvn to chse wnr fnl f: nt qckn* **11/1**

0463 **3** *1* **Winterfell**[40] 5647 3-9-0 52 AlanMunro 1 — 56
(C F Wall) *trckd ldr: rdn to chal over 2f out but sn nt qckn w wnr: chsng tl one pce fnl f* **7/2**[1]

-066 **4** *3 1/2* **Mountain Forest (GER)**[101] 3661 3-9-0 47 TravisBlock 11 — 47
(H Morrison) *hld up in rr: rdn and c v wd bnd 3f out: sme prog over 2f out: no imp on ldrs fnl f* **14/1**

-000 **5** *4 1/2* **Hardanger (IRE)**[40] 5624 4-9-3 51 RobertWinston 8 — 36
(T J Fitzgerald) *led to jst over 2f out: wknd over 1f out* **20/1**

605 **6** *3/4* **Black Stocking**[29] 5965 4-9-3 55 MickyFenton 7 — 35
(Rae Guest) *mostly in midfield: pushed along 1/2-way: struggling over 2f out: sn lft bhd* **4/1**[2]

0000 **7** *1 1/2* **Cardenio (USA)**[40] 5647 3-9-0 47 SteveDrowne 12 — 31
(J R Gask) *bmpd and hit rail after 1f: dropped to rr and nvr gng wl after: last over 2f out: plugged on* **20/1**

0 **8** *3/4* **Four Mirrors (CAN)**[12] 6439 3-9-0 54 (bt[1]) LPKeniry 10 — 29
(C R Dore) *t.k.h: hld up: effrt on inner and cl enough 3f out: hanging and nt run on after* **16/1**

6060 **9** *shd* **Highland Starlight (USA)**[14] 6399 3-9-0 51 AdamKirby 9 — 29
(C G Cox) *nvr beyond midfield: rdn sn after 1/2-way: lft bhd fr over 2f out* **13/2**[3]

0-06 **10** *2* **Richardlionheart (USA)**[107] 3459 3-9-0 48 RobertHavlin 5 — 24
(M Madgwick) *nt that wl away but keen early and sn prom on outer: rdn and wknd rapidly over 2f out* **25/1**

5060 **P** **Cake Stand**[28] 5998 3-9-0 50 (v) EddieAhern 3 — —
(J A R Toller) *s.s: wl bhd tl p.u 1/2-way* **12/1**

1m 39.0s (-0.80) **Going Correction** -0.125s/f (Stan)
WFA 3 from 4yo 3lb — **11** Ran SP% **117.5**
Speed ratings (Par 101): **99,97,96,93,88 87,86,85,85,83 —**
toteswingers: 1&2 £10.80, 1&3 £2.50, 2&3 £9.10 CSF £45.93 TOTE £5.50: £1.50, £4.30, £1.60; EX 60.40.
Owner Matthew Green **Bred** Mme Anne De Clermont Tonnerre **Trained** Newmarket, Suffolk

FOCUS
A poor race, though they went an even pace and put up a fair time for the grade. The form is probably fair for the level, with the first four clear.
Black Stocking Official explanation: jockey said filly hung left-handed
Cardenio(USA) Official explanation: jockey said filly suffered interference in running
Highland Starlight(USA) Official explanation: jockey said filly hung left-handed
Cake Stand Official explanation: jockey said gelding lost its action; vet said gelding returned lame left-hind

6772 "BUY A £10,000 RACING POST BONUS YEARLING" MAIDEN STKS — 1m (P)
6:50 (6:51) (Class 4) 2-Y-0 — **£3,885** (£1,156; £577; £288) Stalls High

Form — RPR

22 **1** **Dahaam**[23] 6162 2-9-3 0 LDettori 13 — 79
(Saeed Bin Suroor) *mde all: stretched clr fr 2f out: rdn fnl f: a holding on* **11/8**[1]

02 **2** *1/2* **Robust Wish (USA)**[19] 6254 2-9-3 0 EddieAhern 5 — 78
(B J Meehan) *hld up in 5th: effrt over 2f out: chsd wnr over 1f out: edgd rt but clsd fnl f: a hld* **11/2**[3]

00 **3** *1* **Red Intrigue (IRE)**[15] 6363 2-8-12 0 JimCrowley 10 — 71+
(Mrs A J Perrett) *hld up in 6th: shkn up and prog over 2f out: wnt 3rd 1f out: clsd grad: wl hld whn n.m.r nr fin* **25/1**

0 **4** *3 1/2* **Monterey (IRE)**[33] 5831 2-9-3 0 AlanMunro 7 — 68+
(T G Mills) *trckd ldng trio: effrt over 2f out: rdn in 3rd over 1f out: wknd fnl f* **11/2**[3]

0 **5** *1 3/4* **Rakhapura (IRE)**[30] 5934 2-9-3 0 SebSanders 8 — 64
(P R Webber) *mounted on crse: racd wd: mostly chsd wnr to over 1f out: wknd* **80/1**

6 *3/4* **Dynamic Drive (IRE)** 2-9-3 0 AdamKirby 9 — 63+
(W R Swinburn) *s.i.s: hld up in rr: shkn up over 2f out: prog over 1f out: kpt on one pce fnl f* **25/1**

4 **7** *nk* **Christmas Coming**[14] 6372 2-9-3 0 DaneO'Neill 2 — 62
(D R C Elsworth) *t.k.h: hld up in midfield: shkn up over 2f out: no prog and btn after: one pce* **4/1**[2]

8 *3 1/2* **Midfielder (USA)** 2-9-3 0 JimmyFortune 4 — 54
(J H M Gosden) *hld up in rr and racd wd: shkn up and no prog over 2f out: no ch after* **12/1**

00 **9** *1/2* **Dauntsey Park (IRE)**[34] 5785 2-9-3 0 FergusSweeney 6 — 53
(Miss Tor Sturgis) *plld hrd: hld up: shkn up and no prog over 2f out* **100/1**

00 **10** *1* **Sefton Park**[29] 5966 2-9-3 0 SteveDrowne 1 — 51
(C R Egerton) *racd wd early: hld up in rr: brought wdst of all in st: no prog* **100/1**

0 **11** *1 1/4* **Jennerous Blue**[23] 6163 2-8-9 0 JackMitchell(3) 3 — 43
(D K Ivory) *hld up last of main gp: effrt on inner over 2f out: sn wknd* **100/1**

00 **12** *1 1/4* **Ibn Hiyyan (USA)**[61] 5002 2-9-3 0 JoeFanning 12 — 45
(M Johnston) *pressed ldng pair to over 2f out: steadily wknd* **25/1**

13 *30* **Another Character (USA)** 2-9-3 0 FrancisNorton 11 — —
(M Blanshard) *s.s: sn t.o* **80/1**

1m 39.29s (-0.51) **Going Correction** -0.125s/f (Stan) — **13** Ran SP% **117.5**
Speed ratings (Par 97): **97,96,95,92,90 89,89,85,85,84 82,81,51**
toteswingers: 1&2 £2.60, 1&3 £9.90, 2&3 £22.40 CSF £8.48 TOTE £2.00: £1.10, £1.90, £5.00; EX 11.60.
Owner Godolphin **Bred** Shadwell Estate Co Ltd **Trained** Newmarket, Suffolk

FOCUS
A decent maiden, contested by some powerful yards, although there didn't appear to be any superstars among them and it is doubtful the form will turn out much better than this . The pace was even, though the time was a shade slow compared to the previous two races.

NOTEBOOK
Dahaam, who hung right over C&D last time, was very well drawn and his rider made the most of that fact. Under a positive ride, he pinged out in front and set his own fractions. He got first run turning for home and soon put daylight between himself and his rivals. But in the end, edging right again, he was hanging on. He may not be up to Group-race standards next year, but he is still on the weak side and looks to have scope for progression. (tchd 13-8)
Robust Wish(USA) had shown ability on his previous two starts and, stepping up in trip here, he handled it very well. He stayed on late and was never nearer than at the finish. He looks set to break his maiden shortly. This looks his trip for now. (op 9-2)
Red Intrigue(IRE) improved again. She showed a winning attitude and stayed on in good style. She has a bright future on this showing. (op 20-1)
Monterey(IRE) is bred for further. He looks a nice horse for next year. (op 5-1 tchd 6-1)
Rakhapura(IRE) showed plenty of early dash, but faded. This was a step up from his debut effort. (op 66-1)
Dynamic Drive(IRE) ◆, a Motivator colt out of a half-sister to Irish 1,000 Guineas winner Tarascon, looked well beforehand, but was very green and on his hind legs in the paddock. His trainer is not known for first-time out juvenile winners and he will have learned plenty. He was given an educational ride but showed distinct ability. (op 33-1 tchd 22-1)
Christmas Coming was well backed, despite having a poor draw. He stayed on well enough, but didn't really have the run of the race. His Derby entry looks a little ambitious, but he's not one to write off yet. He has a bit of scope. (op 8-1)
Dauntsey Park(IRE) took a strong hold early and, as a result, expended his energy before it mattered. This was his bet run so far, however. The promise is evident. Official explanation: jockey said colt ran too free

6773 DIGIBET H'CAP — 1m (P)
7:20 (7:21) (Class 4) (0-85,85) 3-Y-0 — **£4,727** (£1,406; £702; £351) Stalls High

Form — RPR

-203 **1** **Burgundy Ice (USA)**[17] 6311 3-9-2 **83** LDettori 13 — 95+
(Saeed Bin Suroor) *mounted on crse: trckd ldrs: smooth prog over 2f out: led over 1f out: shkn up and in command after: eased nr fin* **5/2**[1]

20 **2** *nk* **Thunderball**[27] 6019 3-8-7 **77** FrederikTylicki(3) 10 — 86
(J A Glover) *t.k.h: hld up in rr: rdn and prog over 2f out: wnt 2nd ins fnl f: r.o and tried to press wnr: a readily hld* **14/1**

0441 **3** *3 3/4* **Audemar (IRE)**[6] 6614 3-9-3 **84** 6ex JimmyFortune 7 — 84
(E F Vaughan) *hld up in rr: gng strly 3f out: sme prog over 2f out: shkn up over 1f out: styd on wl to take 3rd nr fin* **4/1**[2]

6100 **4** *1/2* **Chapter And Verse (IRE)**[33] 5832 3-8-13 **80** RobertWinston 9 — 79
(B W Hills) *t.k.h: trckd ldng pair: rdn and nt qckn over 2f out: one pce after and sn no ch* **16/1**

1546 **5** *3/4* **Palacefield (IRE)**[33] 5833 3-8-10 **77** AlanMunro 12 — 74
(P W Chapple-Hyam) *mde most at decent pce to over 1f out: wknd fnl f* **33/1**

4132 **6** *1* **Sunshine Always (IRE)**[14] 6374 3-9-2 **83** KirstyMilczarek 1 — 78+
(T D McCarthy) *allowed to s slowly fr wd draw: dropped in last and detached early: t.k.h and in tch after 2f: prog on inner over 2f out: wknd over 1f out* **14/1**

2403 **7** 2 ¾ **Maswerte (IRE)**[22] 6187 3-9-1 **82**.. KFallon 4 70
(L M Cumani) *hld up in midfield on outer: rdn wl over 2f out: sme prog over 1f out: sn wknd* **12/1**[3]

362 **8** 3 ¼ **Laazim (USA)**[9] 6539 3-8-10 **77**.. JoeFanning 3 57
(M Johnston) *sn last: pushed along 1/2-way: struggling after* **14/1**

3320 **9** 1 **Something Perfect (USA)**[28] 5996 3-8-13 **80**.................... TPQueally 5 58
(H R A Cecil) *dwlt: a in rr: rdn on wd outside 3f out: no prog* **20/1**

5610 **10** 2 ¾ **Edgeworth (IRE)**[19] 6243 3-8-10 **77**................................ SebSanders 14 48
(B G Powell) *w ldr: led briefly 1/2-way: wknd rapidly over 2f out* **12/1**[3]

1302 **11** 1 ¾ **Block Party**[6] 6614 3-8-12 **79**.. EddieAhern 11 46
(R Charlton) *dwlt: rcvrd and trckd ldrs on inner fr 1/2-way: wknd over 2f out* **4/1**[2]

1m 37.35s (-2.45) **Going Correction** -0.125s/f (Stan) **11** Ran SP% **117.5**
Speed ratings (Par 103): **107,106,102,102,101 100,97,94,93,90 89**
toteswingers: 1&2 £11.10, 1&3 £2.00, 2&3 £10.90 CSF £37.30 CT £110.28 TOTE £3.80: £1.30, £3.90, £1.60; EX 46.30.
Owner Godolphin **Bred** Darley **Trained** Newmarket, Suffolk
■ Laudatory was withdrawn after proving unruly in the stalls (9/1, deduct 10p in the £.)

FOCUS
A decent handicap and the time was solid. The first two finished clear.

6774 DIGIBET.COM CLAIMING STKS 6f (P)
7:50 (7:50) (Class 6) 2-Y-O **£2,047** (£604; £302) **Stalls** High

Form RPR

355 **1** **Safari Special**[98] 3745 2-8-7 70.. LukeMorris 4 67
(P Winkworth) *t.k.h early: trckd ldng trio on outer: wnt 2nd over 1f out: chal fnl f: led last 50yds* **12/1**

5001 **2** nk **Shark Man (IRE)**[7] 6586 2-8-6 69.............................. JackMitchell(3) 5 68
(P J McBride) *trckd ldrs: shkn up on outer over 2f out: clsd fr over 1f out: styd on to take 2nd last strides* **13/2**[3]

1265 **3** nk **Six Wives**[40] 5650 2-8-9 77.. FrederikTylicki(3) 1 70
(J A Glover) *fast away fr wd draw: led: rdn and pressed over 1f out: looked like holding on tl hdd and no ex last 50yds* **15/2**

1000 **4** ½ **Velvet Band**[11] 6481 2-9-0 68.. NCallan 7 72
(P F I Cole) *prom: chsd ldr 1/2-way: sltly hmpd 2f out and lost pl: styd on again ins fnl f* **11/1**

6533 **5** hd **Lady Pattern (IRE)**[18] 6292 2-8-11 75................................ EddieAhern 2 67
(P W D'Arcy) *wl away fr wd draw: chsd ldr to 1/2-way: styd cl up: pressing ins fnl f: nt qckn* **4/1**[2]

0020 **6** ½ **Public Service (IRE)**[26] 6071 2-9-5 74.................................... KFallon 11 74
(B J Meehan) *trckd ldng quartet: n.m.r 2f out: lost pl and swtchd outside over 1f out: styd on fnl f but unable to chal* **15/2**

2241 **7** nse **Zelos Dream (IRE)**[28] 5976 2-8-4 67.......................... SilvestreDeSousa 12 58
(Rae Guest) *hld up in midfield on inner: prog 2f out: pressed ldrs fnl f: no ex last 100yds* **4/1**[2]

6420 **8** nse **Bush Master**[9] 6550 2-9-2 74.. PatDobbs 10 70
(R Hannon) *rrd s: hld up in last trio: shkn over 2f out: styd on fr over 1f out: clsng grad to the line but nvr able to chal* **7/2**[1]

00 **9** 4 ½ **Naseby (USA)**[20] 6228 2-9-3 0.. FergusSweeney 9 58
(Miss S L Davison) *hld up in last trio: rdn 3f out: no prog and lft bhd fnl 2f* **50/1**

00 **10** 2 ½ **Theladyisatramp**[20] 6228 2-8-6 0.. HayleyTurner 3 39
(M L W Bell) *dwlt: a last: rdn 1/2-way: no prog* **20/1**

1m 13.52s (0.42) **Going Correction** -0.125s/f (Stan) **10** Ran SP% **121.8**
Speed ratings (Par 93): **92,91,91,90,90 89,89,89,83,80**
toteswingers: 1&2 £49.40, 1&3 £25.50, 2&3 £17.80 CSF £91.80 TOTE £15.00: £3.70, £3.00, £2.80; EX 164.20.
Owner P Winkworth **Bred** Redhill Bloodstock And Dr Bruno Bardi **Trained** Chiddingfold, Surrey

FOCUS
A competitive, if low-grade claimer, run in a solid time, but they all finished in a heap and the form is limited.

NOTEBOOK
Safari Special, coming here off a three-month break travelled very well, having raced four-wide off the turn and took his time to get past the eventual third, just getting up in the shadow of the post. This was as far as he would have wanted, but this confidence-booster would not have hurt and since it was only his fourth race, he could be open to progression. (op 16-1)
Shark Man(IRE) was never nearer than at the finish, sweeping up the outside. The suspicion beforehand was that he wanted further and this genuine animal did nothing to dispel that notion. (op 5-1 tchd 7-1)
Six Wives made a gallant effort from the front from a very poor draw and was only headed inside the last 75yds. She has done most of her best work at 5f, but she is worth another try over this trip. (op 8-1 tchd 7-1)
Velvet Band, always to the fore, got squeezed for room at the 2f marker and had to be switched. He momentarily lost momentum, but picked up again and could be deemed a little unlucky. He's worth keeping an eye on in this company. (op 12-1)
Lady Pattern(IRE) responded to pressure 2f out up the far rail, but never managed to reduce the margin with the main protagonists. The draw didn't help her cause, but she was given every assistance and there were no real excuses. Official explanation: jockey said filly hung left-handed (op 6-1)
Public Service(IRE) also found a little trouble and had to be switched wide. He was staying on well at the finish, but that was no surprise since his best form has come over further. (op 13-2 tchd 8-1)
Bush Master has had plenty of chances. Dropped in grade here, having found life tough in a warm nursery last time, he had a good draw, but was unable to make the most of it. He ran on well, however, and there's every reason to think he can pick up a race or two. The race just didn't pan out for him. Official explanation: jockey said gelding left the stalls awkwardly (op 9-2)

6775 DIGIBET CASINO NURSERY 6f (P)
8:20 (8:20) (Class 6) (0-65,65) 2-Y-O **£2,047** (£604; £302) **Stalls** High

Form RPR

0003 **1** **Pepi Royal (IRE)**[11] 6494 2-8-12 **62**.............................. MartinLane(5) 8 68
(Pat Eddery) *prom: chsd ldr 1/2-way: rdn over 2f out: styd on fnl f to ld last 100yds* **12/1**

4665 **2** 1 ¼ **Tucker's Law**[11] 6494 2-9-4 **63**.. FergusSweeney 3 65
(B R Millman) *hld up in midfield on outer: rdn and nt qckn over 2f out: prog over 1f out: styd on to take 2nd last 50yds* **14/1**

640 **3** 1 **Admiral Cochrane (IRE)**[30] 5934 2-9-4 **63**........................ JoeFanning 9 62
(W Jarvis) *t.k.h early: hld up in midfield: nt qckn over 2f out: urged along and styd on wl fnl f to take 3rd post* **6/1**[3]

5302 **4** nse **Love Match**[8] 6554 2-9-6 **65**..............................(v[1]) SteveDrowne 4 64
(R Charlton) *led: pushed 2 l clr 2f out and looked in command: wknd and hdd last 100yds* **2/1**[1]

533 **5** nk **Dream Number (IRE)**[16] 6328 2-9-3 **65**.................. RussellKennemore(3) 10 63
(W R Muir) *chsd ldr to 1/2-way: stl disputing 2nd over 1f out: nt qckn u.p: one pce* **11/2**[2]

2340 **6** 1 ¾ **Out The Ring (IRE)**[16] 6343 2-9-2 **61**.. AdamKirby 5 54+
(Miss Gay Kelleway) *hld up in last trio: swtchd ins 2f out: 2 reminders jst over 1f out: running on at fin: nvr nr ldrs* **12/1**

0665 **7** ½ **Kate Skate**[20] 6228 2-9-2 **61**.. KFallon 2 52
(Miss Gay Kelleway) *t.k.h: trckd ldrs: cl enough over 2f out: nt qckn after: wknd fnl f* **8/1**

3066 **8** nk **Bathwick Xaara**[23] 6169 2-8-13 **65**.............................. JPFahy(7) 11 55
(J G Portman) *settled in midfield on inner: effrt over 2f out: no real imp on ldrs over 1f out* **8/1**

640 **9** ¾ **Three's A Crowd**[96] 3810 2-9-3 **62**................................ DaneO'Neill 12 50
(D R C Elsworth) *hld up in last trio: shuffled along bhd rivals fnl 2f: nvr nr ldrs* **14/1**

0656 **10** ½ **Pursuit Of Gold**[6] 6610 2-9-2 **64**.............................. MarcHalford(3) 1 51
(J R Best) *racd wd and hld up in last trio: no prog over 2f out* **33/1**

044 **11** 10 **Aldorable**[13] 6424 2-9-3 **62**.. NCallan 7 19
(R A Teal) *chsd ldrs tl wknd over 2f out: t.o* **14/1**

1m 13.33s (0.23) **Going Correction** -0.125s/f (Stan) **11** Ran SP% **123.6**
Speed ratings (Par 93): **93,91,90,89,89 87,86,86,85,84 71**
toteswingers: 1&2 £32.30, 1&3 £16.10, 2&3 £12.90 CSF £176.44 CT £1140.48 TOTE £13.20: £4.20, £4.00, £2.60; EX 165.80.
Owner Aitken & Phillips **Bred** Mrs Fiona Gordon And Charles Carter **Trained** Nether Winchendon, Bucks

FOCUS
A poor race but competitive, with just 4lb splitting the field, and it was run at a true pace. The form is little better than plating grade but sound enough.

NOTEBOOK
Pepi Royal(IRE) gave Pat Eddery's in-form stable another success. Always prominent for her first attempt on Polytrack, and a return to a trip that suits, she had the run of the race, getting a nice tow from Love Match. She stayed on nicely but it would not do to get carried away. It was a weak race and she is modest. Connections will think about bringing her back here. (op 9-1)
Tucker's Law had to come round rivals, but he swept down the outside late on and was doing his best work at the finish. Although a nine-race maiden, this was another fair effort and he shouldn't be too long breaking his duck. (op 12-1)
Admiral Cochrane(IRE) was also doing his best work late on. He didn't get a lot of room 2f out and took his time to find his feet, but once in the clear, he came with a steady surge to grab third. He wants further. (op 11-2 tchd 7-1)
Love Match produced a game effort from the front under a positive ride. However, she ran out of gas late on. There were no obvious excuses. This is probably as good as she is. (op 100-30)
Dream Number(IRE) had a reasonable draw and held every chance, but looked one-paced. This was just her fourth start and she handled her first try on the AW surface well. She can win races if she continues to progress. (op 9-2 tchd 6-1)
Out The Ring(IRE), last turning for home, stayed on nicely under a considerate ride. He has ability, albeit limited. (op 14-1)

6776 LEVY BOARD H'CAP 7f (P)
8:50 (8:50) (Class 4) (0-80,80) 3-Y-O+ **£4,727** (£1,406; £702; £351) **Stalls** High

Form RPR

05 **1** **Dance And Dance (IRE)**[25] 6111 3-8-12 **79**.............. MartinLane(5) 10 91
(E F Vaughan) *hld up in midfield: lost pl sltly 2f out: gd prog over 1f out and weaved through: r.o to ld last 100yds: sn clr* **11/1**[3]

3236 **2** 1 ¾ **Yankee Storm**[41] 5612 4-8-8 **68**.. JimmyQuinn 2 75
(H J Collingridge) *hld up: last 1/2-way: rapid prog on inner over 2f out to ld over 1f out: hdd and outpcd last 100yds* **33/1**

05 **3** 1 ¼ **Toto Skyllachy**[89] 4064 4-9-6 **80**.. IanMongan 1 84
(S Gollings) *sn prom fr wd draw: outpcd 2f out: styd on and wnt 2nd briefly 1f out: one pce after* **33/1**

1540 **4** 2 ½ **Seek The Fair Land**[119] 3028 3-9-1 **77**............................ PatCosgrave 9 73
(J R Boyle) *trckd ldrs: lost pl over 2f out and sn in rr: kpt on again fnl f: n.d* **20/1**

3506 **5** ½ **Solar Spirit (IRE)**[18] 6279 4-8-13 **80**.............................. IJBrennan(7) 7 76
(J J Quinn) *plld hrd: hld up and racd wd: nt qckn over 2f out: sn outpcd: plugged on fnl f* **8/1**[2]

-604 **6** 1 ½ **Ektimaal**[12] 6462 6-9-4 **78**.. EddieAhern 11 69
(E A L Dunlop) *hld up bhd ldrs: prog on inner to chal 2f out: chsd ldr over 1f out: wknd fnl f* **14/1**

1014 **7** ¾ **Perfect Silence**[14] 6374 4-9-4 **78**..............................(b) AdamKirby 6 67
(C G Cox) *barged way through to ld after 2f: hdd & wknd over 1f out* **12/1**

1240 **8** nk **Arabian Pearl (IRE)**[14] 6374 3-8-13 **75**.............................. AlanMunro 12 63
(P W Chapple-Hyam) *led 2f: styd prom tl wknd over 1f out* **25/1**

-212 **9** nk **Leverage (IRE)**[9] 6540 3-9-4 **80**.. KFallon 5 67
(L M Cumani) *hld up in rr: racd wdst of all bnd 4f out to 3f out: struggling after: no ch over 1f out* **4/5**[1]

0020 **10** 3 **Secret Witness**[21] 6212 3-9-2 **78**.. SebSanders 4 57
(J Noseda) *chsd ldr after 2f to over 2f out: sn wknd* **14/1**

4454 **11** 2 **Restless Genius (IRE)**[15] 6361 4-8-6 **66**.............. SilvestreDeSousa 14 40
(B Ellison) *plld hrd: hld up in rr: brief effrt on inner over 2f out: sn wknd* **8/1**[2]

5P-0 **U** **Dubai Meydan (IRE)**[6] 6614 4-9-5 **79**.............................. SteveDrowne 3 —
(Miss Gay Kelleway) *dwlt: hld up in rr: at bk of tightly gped field whn stmbld and uns rdr wl over 1f out* **33/1**

1m 24.33s (-1.67) **Going Correction** -0.125s/f (Stan)
WFA 3 from 4yo+ 2lb **12** Ran SP% **124.6**
Speed ratings (Par 105): **104,102,100,97,97 95,94,94,93,90 88,—**
toteswingers: 1&2 £32.30, 1&3 £70.00, 2&3 £170.80 CSF £343.86 CT £11241.39 TOTE £13.80: £3.30, £8.20, £11.70; EX 383.20.
Owner Mohammed Rashid **Bred** Darley **Trained** Newmarket, Suffolk
■ Stewards' Enquiry : Adam Kirby four-day ban: careless riding (Oct 28-31)
Pat Cosgrave three-day ban: careless riding (Oct 28-30)

FOCUS
A modest handicap for the grade and run at a true pace, although it proved a rough race. They fanned out across the track to avoid the kickback. The runner-up is a clear guide to the form.

6777 RACING UK H'CAP 6f (P)
9:20 (9:22) (Class 6) (0-52,56) 3-Y-O+ **£2,047** (£604; £302) **Stalls** High

Form RPR

4200 **1** **Charlie Delta**[23] 6175 6-9-0 **52**..............................(b) LukeMorris 11 61
(R A Harris) *trckd ldng pair: led on inner 2f out: rdn and styd on wl fnl f* **5/1**[2]

0003 **2** 1 ¼ **Malapropism**[13] 6433 9-8-11 **52**.. MCGeran(3) 6 57
(M R Channon) *trckd ldrs: nt qckn 2f out: lost pl and nt clr run over 1f out: r.o wl again fnl f to snatch 2nd on post* **6/1**[3]

0000 **3** hd **Fantasy Fighter (IRE)**[63] 4894 4-9-0 **52**.............................. JimmyQuinn 3 56
(J J Quinn) *hld up bhd ldrs: gng strly over 2f out: chsd wnr over 1f out: no imp fnl f: lost 2nd on post* **8/1**

30-0 **4** 3 1/4 **Gracie's Games**[19] 6251 3-8-8 52 .... MartinLane(5) 9 46
(R J Price) *hld up in rr: rdn over 2f out: styd on fr over 1f out: nt gng pce to trble ldrs* **12/1**

6040 **5** *nk* **Dilli Dancer**[12] 6456 4-9-0 52 .... AdamKirby 5 45
(G D Blake) *dwlt: hld up in rr: pushed along over 2f out: trying to cl whn rn into trble over 1f out: no real imp ins fnl f* **13/2**

3000 **6** *nk* **Mr Rio (IRE)**[47] 5406 4-9-0 52 .... (v1) AlanMunro 10 44
(A P Jarvis) *hld up: sed pulling furiously after 1f to 3f out: nt qckn 2f out: n.d after* **11/1**

1000 **7** 2 **Scruffy Skip (IRE)**[13] 6433 4-9-0 52 .... (b) TGMcLaughlin 8 38
(Mrs C A Dunnett) *sltly hmpd s: last and struggling after 2f: got in tch w main gp over 2f out: no hdwy after* **16/1**

0226 **8** 3/4 **Cavitie**[120] 3010 3-8-13 52 .... SebSanders 4 35
(Andrew Reid) *a in rr: struggling in last over 2f out: no ch after* **9/2**[1]

3/00 **9** 1 1/4 **Tan Bonita (USA)**[51] 5323 4-9-0 52 .... IvanLopez 12 31
(R J Smith) *chsd ldr to jst over 2f out: wknd over 1f out* **25/1**

0000 **10** 2 3/4 **Zim Ho**[40] 5644 3-8-13 52 .... (v1) DaneO'Neill 1 22
(J Akehurst) *led to 2f out: wknd rapidly* **12/1**

1m 12.38s (-0.72) **Going Correction** -0.125s/f (Stan)
WFA 3 from 4yo+ 1lb **10** Ran SP% **107.0**
Speed ratings (Par 101): **99,97,97,92,92 91,89,88,86,82**
toteswingers: 1&2 £5.90, 1&3 £5.10, 2&3 £5.70 CSF £29.28 CT £177.27 TOTE £4.80: £2.10, £1.60, £2.60; EX 19.30 Place 6: £217.63 Place 5: £90.77 .
Owner Robert & Nina Bailey **Bred** P K Gardner **Trained** Earlswood, Monmouths
■ Sherjawy was withdrawn (13/2, unruly in stalls). Deduct 10p in the £ under R4.

FOCUS
A desperate handicap, with all participants having an official rating of 52, and it is hard to rate the form positively. The pace was true, however.
T/Plt: £104.80 to a £1 stake. Pool: £74,844.63. 521.23 winning tickets. T/Qpdt: £33.20 to a £1 stake. Pool: £7,286.03. 162.02 winning tickets. JN

6699 LINGFIELD (L-H)
Wednesday, October 14

OFFICIAL GOING: Standard to slow
Wind: modest, half against Weather: overcast

6778 NEWS INTERNATIONAL H'CAP (DIV I) 1m (P)
1:30 (1:32) (Class 5) (0-75,75) 3-Y-0+ **£2,729** (£806; £403) **Stalls** High

Form RPR

632- **1** **Penton Hook**[420] 5184 3-8-13 70 .... JimCrowley 9 82+
(P Winkworth) *t.k.h: hld up in tch in midfield: hdwy over 3f out: chsd ldr over 2f out: rdn to ld jst ins fnl f: drvn and kpt on wl* **20/1**

5106 **2** 1 **Amazing Tiger (GER)**[11] 6474 3-9-4 75 .... JoeFanning 7 85+
(M Johnston) *t.k.h: hld up towards rr: hdwy to chse ldng pair over 2f out: chsd wnr ins fnl f: one pce* **5/1**[2]

4603 **3** 2 **Al Sabaheya**[8] 6562 3-9-3 74 .... (b) NCallan 2 79
(C E Brittain) *racd keenly: led tl 4f out: chsd ldr tl led again over 2f out: c to centre st: sn rdn: drvn and hdd jst ins fnl f: one pce* **5/1**[2]

0000 **4** 2 3/4 **Prince Of Thebes (IRE)**[14] 6394 8-9-7 75 .... PaulDoe 10 74
(M J Attwater) *sn bustled along: chsd ldrs: rdn over 3f out: drvn and nt pce of ldng trio ent fnl 2f: one pce after* **10/1**

2303 **5** *nk* **Black N Brew (USA)**[8] 6562 3-9-2 73 .... RobertWinston 6 71
(J R Best) *hld up in midfield: rdn and outpcd over 2f out: no ch w ldrs fnl 2f: plugged on* **4/1**[1]

-446 **6** 1/2 **Trueblue Wizard (IRE)**[21] 6209 3-8-11 71 ...... (b) RussellKennemore(3) 3 68
(W R Muir) *sn niggled along: in tch: rdn and struggling wl over 2f out: styd on ins st and wl btn after* **9/1**

0-00 **7** 1 1/2 **Daniel Thomas (IRE)**[15] 6365 7-9-2 70 .... JimmyQuinn 8 63
(Mrs A L M King) *v.s.a: hld up in last trio: clsd over 4f out: rdn and btn whn hung lft over 1f out* **7/1**[3]

0-42 **8** 1/2 **In The Mood (IRE)**[14] 6399 3-8-9 66 .... AlanMunro 4 58
(W Jarvis) *v.s.a: t.k.h: hld up in last trio: rdn and struggling over 2f out: n.d* **15/2**

601 **9** 18 **You've Been Mowed**[16] 6337 3-8-3 63 .... KellyHarrison(3) 1 12
(R J Price) *racd keenly: chsd ldr tl led 4f out: hdd over 2f out: styd on ins and sn dropped out: wl btn fnl 2f* **14/1**

06-6 **10** 6 **Shannersburg (IRE)**[37] 5725 4-9-6 74 .... (bt) SebSanders 5 8
(A B Haynes) *v.s.a: styd wd: a bhd: rdn and struggling 3f out: sn wl bhd: t.o* **12/1**

1m 37.3s (-0.90) **Going Correction** +0.025s/f (Slow)
WFA 3 from 4yo+ 3lb **10** Ran SP% **115.8**
Speed ratings (Par 103): **105,104,102,99,98 98,96,96,78,72**
toteswingers: 1&2 £16.50, 1&3 £13.20, 2&3 £8.80 CSF £116.42 CT £603.73 TOTE £24.70: £5.00, £2.20, £2.70; EX 109.70 TRIFECTA Not won..
Owner Mrs Tessa Winkworth **Bred** A H Munnis **Trained** Chiddingfold, Surrey

FOCUS
A rather messy race with a few completely blowing their chances at the start. The early pace seemed only ordinary but the race produced the clear pick of the three C/D times. Fair form for the grade.
In The Mood(IRE) Official explanation: jockey said filly was slowly away
Shannersburg(IRE) Official explanation: jockey said gelding was slowly away

6779 E B F SMITHS NEWS NOVICE STKS 1m (P)
2:00 (2:01) (Class 4) 2-Y-0 **£5,180** (£1,541; £770) **Stalls** High

Form RPR

1 **1** **Fareej (USA)**[13] 6423 2-9-5 0 .... LDettori 1 92
(Saeed Bin Suroor) *styd wd tl 5f out: chsd ldr tl hdwy to go upsides and rdn 2f out: led jst over 1f out: r.o wl* **5/4**[1]

1 **2** 2 1/4 **Business As Usual**[28] 6000 2-9-5 0 .... PhilipRobinson 2 87
(M A Jarvis) *led: jnd and rdn 2f out: hdd jst over 1f out: kpt on same pce fnl f* **5/4**[1]

1 **3** 1 **Magician's Cape (IRE)**[29] 5966 2-9-5 0 .... RyanMoore 3 85
(Sir Michael Stoute) *styd wd tl 5f out: hld up in 3rd: rdn jst over 2f out: kpt on but nvr gng pce to chal rivals* **5/1**[2]

1m 38.36s (0.16) **Going Correction** +0.025s/f (Slow) **3** Ran SP% **105.6**
Speed ratings (Par 97): **100,97,96**
CSF £3.02 TOTE £1.80; EX 2.80.
Owner Godolphin **Bred** Darley **Trained** Newmarket, Suffolk

FOCUS
Very much the race of the day despite just the three runners. Each had won their only previous starts, all on turf, and the only problem was that this was always likely to become a tactical affair. The form makes sense.

NOTEBOOK
Fareej(USA) ◆, who looked a smart prospect when winning over this trip on his Newmarket debut, proved fractious in the preliminaries but settled well enough in second place behind Business As Usual once under way, and it was noticeable that he was kept wide of the leader in the early stages. Set alight around the outside to lead rounding the home bend, he quickened up very nicely to put the race to bed and remains a very nice prospect, though there are no specific plans for him at this stage. (tchd 6-5)
Business As Usual ◆, who had a couple of subsequent winners behind him when winning in decent style over 7f at Yarmouth on debut, soon found himself in front but never looked that happy and was also keen enough. Having slowed things up before halfway, he was completely out-speeded by the winner over the last 2f, but this tight track may not have been ideal for such a big horse and he is still a promising colt. (op 6-5, tchd 11-8 in places)
Magician's Cape(IRE), who overcame market weakness to make a winning debut over 7f on turf here last month, was always in last place and became outpaced when the tempo quickened approaching the home bend. He stayed on again up the straight, though, and he too may have found this too sharp. Bred to stay further, he will be much better served by middle distances next season. (tchd 11-2)

6780 NEWS INTERNATIONAL H'CAP (DIV II) 1m (P)
2:30 (2:30) (Class 5) (0-75,75) 3-Y-0+ **£2,729** (£806; £403) **Stalls** High

Form RPR

6544 **1** **Hawaana (IRE)**[86] 4149 4-9-7 75 .... JerryO'Dwyer 10 82
(Miss Gay Kelleway) *stdd after s: hld up in rr: hdwy and swtchd lft over 1f out: qcknd to ld ins fnl f: r.o gamely and a jst holding runner- up after* **15/2**

4054 **2** *hd* **Murrin (IRE)**[16] 6337 5-9-0 68 .... (p) StephenDonohoe 3 75
(T G Mills) *hld up in last trio: hdwy and swtchd lft over 1f out: ev ch ins fnl f: r.o but a jst hld* **5/1**[3]

6216 **3** 1 1/2 **Astrodonna**[55] 5190 4-9-4 72 .... TedDurcan 7 75
(M H Tompkins) *hld up in midfield: hdwy jst over 2f otu: chsd ldng pair over 1f out: ev ch briefly ins fnl f: nt pce of ldng pair fnl 150yds* **10/1**

4 *nk* **Napa Starr (FR)**[25] 6128 5-9-3 71 .... JamesDoyle 6 78+
(C Byrnes, Ire) *stdd after s: hld up in last: nt clr run 2f out: stl nowhere to go and swtchd sharply rt ins fnl f: stl nt clr run and swtchd lft ins fnl100yds: wnt 4th fnl 50yds: nvr able to chal* **11/4**[2]

0000 **5** 3/4 **Baariq**[16] 6348 3-9-2 73 .... JimmyFortune 8 74
(P W Chapple-Hyam) *chsd ldrs: rdn to chse ldr wl over 1f out: ev ch briefly ins fnl f: sn outpcd* **14/1**

4230 **6** 3/4 **Yellow Printer**[6] 6621 3-9-3 74 .... ChrisCatlin 9 73
(F J Brennan) *dwlt: sn bustled up to chse ldrs: rdn over 3f out: kpt on same pce fnl 2f* **16/1**

02-0 **7** 3 **Invincible Joe (IRE)**[74] 4414 4-9-1 74 .... (b) DEMullins(5) 1 66
(John Joseph Hanlon, Ire) *t.k.h: chsd ldr tl led ent fnl 2f: sn rdn: hdd ins fnl f: wknd qckly* **25/1**

000 **8** 2 **Bull Market (IRE)**[19] 6258 6-8-13 67 .... VinceSlattery 2 54
(M S Tuck) *chsd ldrs: n.m.r bnd ent fnl 2f: wknd over 1f out* **40/1**

3322 **9** 4 1/2 **El Ameen**[30] 5954 3-9-2 73 .... (b1) RHills 4 49
(M Johnston) *racd freely: sn led: rdn and hdd ent fnl 2f: btn and eased ins fnl f* **9/4**[1]

5000 **10** 1 1/4 **Hip Hip Hooray**[9] 6549 3-8-7 64 .... (p) LukeMorris 5 37
(L A Dace) *in tch tl rdn and struggling over 2f out: wl btn whn bdly hmpd and snatched up jst ins fnl f* **20/1**

1m 38.5s (0.30) **Going Correction** +0.025s/f (Slow)
WFA 3 from 4yo+ 3lb **10** Ran SP% **118.6**
Speed ratings (Par 103): **99,98,97,97,96 95,92,90,86,84**
toteswingers: 1&2 £8.10, 1&3 £9.70, 2&3 £4.70 CSF £44.62 CT £392.98 TOTE £8.90: £2.10, £2.20, £3.20; EX 60.00 Trifecta £215.30 Part won. Pool: £290.97 - 0.7 winning units..
Owner Kings Club Syndicate II **Bred** Norelands Bloodstock, J Hanly & H Lascelles **Trained** Exning, Suffolk
■ Stewards' Enquiry : R Hills two-day ban: careless riding (Oct 28-29)

FOCUS
Like the first division, a modest early gallop and a messy contest. Despite that, most of the principals came from well off the pace. The winning time was 1.2 seconds slower than division one and also 0.14 seconds slower than the 2-y-o race. Ordinary form.
Napa Starr(FR) Official explanation: jockey said gelding was denied a clear run

6781 EBF MENZIES DISTRIBUTION MAIDEN STKS 7f (P)
3:05 (3:06) (Class 5) 2-Y-O **£3,885** (£1,156; £577; £288) **Stalls** Low

Form RPR

0 **1** **Meezaan (IRE)**[11] 6478 2-9-3 0 .... TPO'Shea 2 84+
(J H M Gosden) *mde all: t.k.h: rdn and pushed 2 l clr 2f out: rdn and edgd rt 1f out: pressed jst ins fnl f: styd on strly and wl in command fnl 75yds* **9/2**[3]

05 **2** 2 1/4 **Mass Rally (IRE)**[13] 6423 2-9-3 0 .... JimmyFortune 13 78
(J H M Gosden) *chsd ldng trio: rdn to chse wnr 2f out: edgd lft u.p ent fnl f: pressed wnr briefly jst ins fnl f: sn outpcd* **3/1**[1]

05 **3** 2 1/2 **Soho Theatre**[9] 6544 2-9-3 0 .... DaneO'Neill 10 72
(D R C Elsworth) *dwlt: hdwy into midfield 5f out: rdn and edgd lft over 1f out: kpt on to go 3rd fnl 100yds: no ch w ldng pair* **25/1**

05 **4** 1/2 **First Instance**[28] 5993 2-9-3 0 .... JoeFanning 7 71
(M Johnston) *chsd wnr tl 2f out: outpcd by ldng pair over 1f out: lost 3rd fnl 100yds* **9/1**

5 1 **Quick Wit** 2-9-3 0 .... LDettori 3 70+
(Saeed Bin Suroor) *v.s.a: racd in last pl: hdwy on inner over 2f out: swtchd rigth 1f out: styd on steadily but nvr nr ldrs* **7/2**[2]

06 **6** 1 **Tamtara**[36] 5741 2-8-12 0 .... JimCrowley 11 61+
(Mrs A J Perrett) *hld up towards rr: hdwy on outer into midfield over 3f out: outpcd bnd 2f out: rdn and kpt on on fnl f: nvr trbld ldrs* **14/1**

2 **7** *nk* **Serhaal (IRE)**[69] 4717 2-9-3 0 .... RHills 4 65+
(Sir Michael Stoute) *chsd ldng pair tl over 2f out: wknd over 1f out* **9/2**[3]

00 **8** 3/4 **Astronomer's Dream**[74] 4542 2-8-12 0 .... LPKeniry 12 58+
(E F Vaughan) *stdd after s: towards rr: rdn and struggling over 2f out: kpt on ins fnl f: nvr trbld ldrs* **100/1**

6 **9** *hd* **Calypso Star (IRE)**[152] 2037 2-9-3 0 .... RyanMoore 5 62
(R Hannon) *racd in midfield: rdn 5f out: nvr gng pce to threaten ldrs* **14/1**

0 **10** 2 **Lady Hetherington**[36] 5752 2-8-12 0 .... IanMongan 9 52
(Jamie Poulton) *a towards rr: rdn and no prog 3f out* **66/1**

0 **11** 3/4 **Allannah Abu**[23] 6164 2-8-12 0 .... SebSanders 8 51
(Sir Mark Prescott) *stdd after s: a bhd: rdn and toiling wl over 2f out* **66/1**

00 **12** 1/2 **Hayek**[26] 6061 2-9-3 0 .... AlanMunro 1 54
(W Jarvis) *dwlt: a towards rr: n.m.r bnd 5f out: no ch fnl 2f* **66/1**

0 **13** 1 **Professor Bollini (IRE)**[42] 5571 2-9-3 0 .... LukeMorris 6 52
(H J L Dunlop) *in tch in midfield: rdn and lost pl 3f out: wl bhd fnl 2f* **100/1**

1m 25.56s (0.76) **Going Correction** +0.025s/f (Slow) **13** Ran SP% **117.2**
Speed ratings (Par 95): **96,93,90,90,88 87,87,86,86,84 83,82,81**
totewingers: 1&2 £4.80, 1&3 £26.70, 2&3 £14.60 CSF £17.63 TOTE £5.40: £1.80, £1.60, £4.50; EX 19.60 TRIFECTA Not won..

Owner Hamdan Al Maktoum **Bred** Epona Bloodstock Ltd **Trained** Newmarket, Suffolk

FOCUS

An interesting maiden, though it was steadily run and few ever got into it. The form seems pretty solid.

NOTEBOOK

Meezaan(IRE) ◆, who hadn't been completely disgraced in the Timeform Tattersalls Million on debut earlier this month, found this a rather easier task. In front within a furlong of breaking from the stalls, he did show a strange head-carriage which gives the impression he is pulling hard. Despite that, he still kept on pulling out more when challenged as the race progressed and he was well on top at the line. He can probably go on to better things. (tchd 5-1)

Mass Rally(IRE), who ran well despite hanging when fifth behind Fareej at Newmarket last time, travelled well behind the leaders but although he had every chance turning in, he hung away to his left once again and ended up against the inside rail. He has ability, but is not proving the most straightforward. (op 7-2 tchd 4-1)

Soho Theatre, a fair fifth at Warwick earlier this month, was never far away and ran well especially as he didn't seem to handle the home bend too well. He now qualifies for a mark, so could be interesting in a nursery. (tchd 33-1)

First Instance, not disgraced in a decent Sandown maiden last time, was another to race handily throughout and also now qualifies for a mark. (op 17-2 tchd 8-1)

Quick Wit, a 190,000gns half-brother to four winners including the high-class Gallagher, basically lost his race at the start and though he stayed on late he was never going to get amongst the leaders. He is better than this. Official explanation: jockey said colt was slowly away (op 4-1)

Tamtara, who ran much better when sixth behind a couple of subsequent winners at Goodwood last month, travelled powerfully behind the leaders but she became outpaced rounding the home bend and there was no way back. She may fare better now that she qualifies for handicaps. (tchd 16-1)

Serhaal(IRE), very green when second of four on his Yarmouth debut and the choice of Richard Hills over the winner, had his chance on the inside rail turning for home but was then comfortably seen off.

6782 MAIL NEWSPAPERS CLASSIFIED CLAIMING STKS (DIV I) 7f (P)

3:35 (3:36) (Class 6) 3-Y-O+ **£1,706** (£503; £252) **Stalls** Low

Form RPR

5010 **1** **Straight Face (IRE)**[7] 6587 5-8-1 55....................(b) CatherineGannon 10 60
(Miss Gay Kelleway) *hld up towards rr: hdwy on outer over 3f out: c wdst st: rdn to chal jst over 1f out: led ins fnl f: r.o strly to draw clr fnl 75yds* **6/1**[3]

5235 **2** 2 ¼ **Whitbarrow (IRE)**[201] 980 10-9-0 70.................... JamesMillman(3) 11 70
(B R Millman) *led: rdn ent fnl 2f: hdd ins fnl f: no ex fnl 75yds: jst hld on for 2nd* **15/2**

2450 **3** hd **Brooksby**[8] 6570 3-8-1 66...(v) LukeMorris 12 54
(L A Dace) *dwlt: sn pushed up to chse ldrs: edgd lft u.p and chsd ldrs over 1f out: one pce fnl f* **9/2**[2]

3634 **4** hd **Monashee Rock (IRE)**[14] 6370 4-8-7 64................................ LPKeniry 6 59+
(Matthew Salaman) *hld up in last trio: nt clr run on inner 2f out tl over 1f out: sn rdn and hdwy: kpt on to press for 2nd at fin: nvr threatened wnr* **9/2**[2]

0-10 **5** 1 **The Mumbo**[135] 2548 3-8-9 65....................................(b[1]) JoeFanning 4 62+
(W Jarvis) *s.i.s: hld up in rr: rdn and hdwy wl over 1f out: sltly hmpd and swtchd rt 1f out: r.o fnl f but nvr able to chal* **9/1**

-600 **6** nk **Miracle Baby**[127] 2794 7-8-3 43 ow1............................. MarcHalford(3) 9 54
(J A Geake) *in tch: rdn and unable qck ent fnl 2f: kpt on u.p fnl f: nt pce to threaten ldrs* **80/1**

50-0 **7** 2 ¼ **Balais Folly (FR)**[6] 6608 4-8-1 47.............................. FrankieMcDonald 8 43
(D Haydn Jones) *s.i.s: hld up in rr: rdn and effrt bnd 2f out: no real prog* **33/1**

6F10 **8** 2 **Romantic Queen**[8] 6572 3-8-3 68....................................(t) DO'Donohoe 2 41
(George Baker) *hld up in midfield on inner: rdn and no prog 2f out: swtchd rt ins fnl f: nvr gng pce to trble ldrs* **10/1**

0102 **9** ½ **Royal Challenge**[16] 6336 8-8-1 62.......................... SilvestreDeSousa 5 36
(I W McInnes) *chsd ldr tl over 3f out: rdn and wknd wl over 1f out* **4/1**[1]

6000 **10** 1 ¾ **Asaint Needs Brass (USA)**[5] 6632 3-8-9 70.............. RobertWinston 7 40
(J R Best) *t.k.h: in tch: rdn and struggling 2f out: btn whn edgd rt 1f out: eased ins fnl f* **14/1**

1m 25.56s (0.76) **Going Correction** +0.025s/f (Slow)

WFA 3 from 4yo+ 2lb **10** Ran SP% **112.3**

Speed ratings (Par 101): **96,93,93,92,91 91,88,86,86,84**

toteswingers: 1&2 £8.80, 1&3 £16.60, 2&3 £12.20 CSF £48.48 TOTE £5.30: £1.90, £2.80, £1.50; EX 55.50 Trifecta £96.90 Pool: £192.50 - 1.47 winning units..

Owner KingsClubSyndicate I **Bred** P J Towell **Trained** Exning, Suffolk

FOCUS

A moderate classified claimer which was slowly run. The bare form looks shaky.

Romantic Queen Official explanation: jockey said filly was denied a clear run

6783 MAIL NEWSPAPERS CLASSIFIED CLAIMING STKS (DIV II) 7f (P)

4:10 (4:10) (Class 6) 3-Y-O+ **£1,706** (£503; £252) **Stalls** Low

Form RPR

0521 **1** **Dichoh**[14] 6399 6-9-5 69...(v) AdamKirby 8 82+
(M Madgwick) *stdd after s: hld up wl off the pce in rr: stl plenty to do wl over 1f out: rdn and gd hdwy 1f out: led ins fnl f: sn in command: comf* **5/1**[2]

2402 **2** 1 **Kingsgate Castle**[19] 6252 4-8-1 56.........................(v) CatherineGannon 9 61
(Miss Gay Kelleway) *hld up towards rr: hdwy over 2f out: rdn to chse ldng trio jst over 2f out: chsd wnr ins fnl f: kpt on but readily hld* **6/1**[3]

0226 **3** 2 ½ **Art Market (CAN)**[34] 5813 6-8-7 59...............................(p) FergusSweeney 1 60
(Miss Jo Crowley) *led at gd gallop: rdn ent fnl 2f: hdd ins fnl f: sn outpcd* **8/1**

1606 **4** hd **Dabbers Ridge (IRE)**[3] 6703 7-8-7 67...................... SilvestreDeSousa 6 60
(I W McInnes) *hld up off the pce in midfield: hdwy ent fnl 2f: pressed ldrs ent fnl f: one pce fnl 150yds* **9/2**[1]

0236 **5** ½ **Napoletano (GER)**[16] 6337 8-8-11 64...................................(p) NCallan 3 62
(S Dow) *chsd ldng trio: rdn to chse ldr wl over 1f out: pressed ldrs and edgd rt u.p 1f out: wknd fnl 100yds* **6/1**[3]

6620 **6** 1 **Royal Envoy (IRE)**[27] 6024 6-8-4 66.......................... TobyAtkinson(7) 5 60
(P Howling) *stdd s: hld up in last: rdn 2f out: kpt on u.p fnl f: nvr nr ldrs* **6/1**[3]

0- **7** 1 **Magic Cloud**[8] 6076 4-8-2 58 ow1...................................(tp) ChrisCatlin 7 48
(John Joseph Hanlon, Ire) *chsd ldng trio tl 1/2-way: sn struggling u.p: one pce fnl 2f* **16/1**

2400 **8** 5 **My Sweet Georgia (IRE)**[14] 6370 3-8-5 64.................... DO'Donohoe 11 39
(Stef Liddiard) *s.i.s: a bhd* **20/1**

065/ **9** 1 ½ **Tango Step (IRE)**[129] 2749 9-7-13 44 ow1..............(b) KellyHarrison(3) 4 30
(D Carroll) *chsd ldr tl wl over 1f out: sn wknd* **33/1**

0000 **10** 3 ¾ **Love Allowed**[12] 6442 3-8-1 47.. LukeMorris 2 21
(Jamie Poulton) *a towards rr: struggling and bhd over 2f out* **66/1**

500 **R** **Lady Micklegate (USA)**[146] 2206 3-8-5 66.................... JimmyQuinn 12 —
(J R Best) *taken down early and led to s: ref to r* **8/1**

1m 24.6s (-0.20) **Going Correction** +0.025s/f (Slow)

WFA 3 from 4yo+ 2lb **11** Ran SP% **115.0**

Speed ratings (Par 101): **102,100,98,97,97 96,94,89,87,83** —

toteswingers: 1&2 £3.80, 1&3 £10.70, 2&3 £8.00 CSF £33.61 TOTE £6.70: £2.20, £1.80, £2.70; EX 19.80 Trifecta £127.80 Pool: £328.37 - 1.90 winning units..

Owner Derek J Willis **Bred** Red House Stud **Trained** Denmead, Hants

FOCUS

Like the first division, a moderate classified claimer. The early pace looked a bit more solid than in division one, however, and the winning time was nearly a second quicker. The winner is rated back to something like last winter's form.

6784 BEDFORDS H'CAP 1m 2f (P)

4:45 (4:45) (Class 5) (0-70,70) 3-Y-O **£2,729** (£806; £403) **Stalls** Low

Form RPR

2442 **1** **Global Conquest (IRE)**[19] 6255 3-8-11 70................ TobyAtkinson(7) 2 79+
(Pat Eddery) *stdd s: t.k.h: hld up in rr: gd hdwy on outer 3f out: led 2f out: sn rdn clr: in n.d fnl f* **12/1**

024 **2** 3 ¼ **Everaard (USA)**[9] 6549 3-9-4 70... DaneO'Neill 4 70
(D R C Elsworth) *chsd ldrs: rdn over 2f out: kpt on u.p to chse clr wnr ins fnl f: no imp* **12/1**

002 **3** 2 **Noble Dictator**[18] 6289 3-8-10 62...................................... JimmyQuinn 1 58+
(E F Vaughan) *t.k.h: hld up in midfield: shuffled bk and rdn over 2f out: drvn and hdwy over 1f out: swtchd rt ins fnl f: r.o to go 3rd nr fin: nvr nr wnr* **3/1**[2]

1042 **4** hd **Evening Sunset (GER)**[24] 5567 3-9-0 66................................ NCallan 3 62
(M G Quinlan) *hld up in tch in midfield: rdn and unable qck ent fnl 2f: kpt on same pce u.p fnl f* **5/2**[1]

4033 **5** ½ **Vita Mia**[16] 6338 3-8-5 57... CatherineGannon 5 52
(P D Evans) *restless in stalls: chsd ldrs: rdn and chsd wnr 2f out: edgd lft u.p and wl outpcd over 1f out: lost 3 pls ins fnl f* **7/1**

3400 **6** ½ **Royal Willy (IRE)**[14] 6400 3-8-13 65.................................. AlanMunro 9 59+
(W Jarvis) *stdd s: t.k.h: hld up in rr: rdn and effrt ent fnl 2f: keeping on but no ch w wnr whn swtchd rt ins fnl f* **5/1**[3]

060 **7** 4 **Colangnik (USA)**[14] 6376 3-8-11 63............................... RobertWinston 7 49
(J R Best) *hld up towards rr on outer: rdn and no prog over 2f out: no ch fnl 2f* **12/1**

2000 **8** nk **Jazacosta (USA)**[16] 6333 3-8-13 65.................................. JimCrowley 10 50
(Mrs A J Perrett) *chsd ldr tl led 3f out: drvn and hdd 2f out: wknd qckly over 1f out* **12/1**

0340 **9** 7 **Countenance**[90] 4004 3-9-4 70.. MichaelHills 8 41
(W J Haggas) *led tl 3f out: sn lost pl: bhd fnl 2f* **8/1**

0-00 **U** **Ausonius**[16] 6339 3-8-4 56 oh1.. ChrisCatlin 6 —
(L M Cumani) *stmbld and uns rdr leaving stalls* **25/1**

2m 6.31s (-0.29) **Going Correction** +0.025s/f (Slow) **10** Ran SP% **128.5**

Speed ratings (Par 101): **102,99,97,97,97 96,93,93,87,**—

toteswingers: 1&2 £11.60, 1&3 £5.20, 2&3 £7.50 CSF £160.89 CT £558.04 TOTE £11.10: £2.40, £3.10, £1.30; EX 89.20 Trifecta £289.90 Part won. Pool: £391.82 - 0.93 winning units..

Owner Ms J F Harrison **Bred** Carrigbeg Stud And Gavan Kinch **Trained** Nether Winchendon, Bucks

FOCUS

Although a low-grade handicap, it certainly seemed competitive. The bare form is ordinary but the winner may do better.

6785 CITIPOST DIRECT DISTRIBUTION H'CAP 2m (P)

5:15 (5:15) (Class 6) (0-65,65) 3-Y-O+ **£2,047** (£604; £302) **Stalls** Low

Form RPR

0445 **1** **Ja One (IRE)**[85] 4168 3-9-0 62... MichaelHills 4 68
(B W Hills) *led for 1f: chsd ldrs after: rdn to chal and flashed tail over 1f out: led jst ins fnl f: styd on wl* **14/1**

0001 **2** 2 **Ingenue**[8] 6558 3-8-3 51 6ex....................................(b) SilvestreDeSousa 6 55
(Sir Mark Prescott) *sn bustled up to ld after 1f tl hdd 11f out: led again 6f out: rdn over 2f out: drvn and hdd ins fnl f: one pce after* **7/4**[1]

1-10 **3** hd **Don't Stop Me Now (IRE)**[27] 6042 4-9-9 65..............(p) DEMullins(5) 2 68
(John Joseph Hanlon, Ire) *hmpd after 1f: w.w in midfield: hdwy to chse ldr 3f out: drvn and ev ch 2f out: edgd lft u.p and one pce ent fnl f* **3/1**[2]

0004 **4** 1 ¼ **Benozzo Gozzoli**[32] 5872 3-7-13 48 oh1 ow1................. JimmyQuinn 7 49
(H Morrison) *t.k.h: chsd ldrs tl hdwy to ld 11f out: hdd 6f out: lost 2nd 3f out but stl handy: kpt on same pce u.p fnl 2f* **16/1**

1030 **5** shd **Astroleo**[28] 5990 3-8-0 48... NickyMackay 10 50
(M H Tompkins) *t.k.h: chsd ldrs: rdn over 3f out: drvn and plugged on same pce fnl 2f* **20/1**

000/ **6** nk **Isle De Maurice**[166] 6131 7-9-4 55..................................(b) PatDobbs 13 56+
(G L Moore) *stdd and dropped in bhd s: hld up towards rr: rdn an effrt on inner wl over 1f out: r.o fnl f: nvr threatened ldrs* **16/1**

2506 **7** shd **Star Of Pompey**[6] 6622 5-9-5 56.. SebSanders 3 57
(A B Haynes) *hmpd after 1f: hld up in midfield: drvn and unable qck over 2f out: plugged on one pce after* **14/1**

0000 **8** nk **Brad's Luck (IRE)**[11] 6497 3-8-3 51................................ FrancisNorton 11 52
(M Blanshard) *hld up in midfield on outer: lost pl and dropped towards rr 3f out: sme hdwy ent fnl f: styd on: nvr trbld ldrs* **25/1**

0434 **9** ¾ **Mymateeric**[13] 6432 3-8-2 50...(b) ChrisCatlin 12 51+
(J Pearce) *wnt rt s: hld up in last trio: rdn over 2f out: kpt on u.p ent fnl f: n.m.r towards fin: n.d* **5/1**[3]

-000 **10** hd **Stagecoach Emerald**[99] 3714 7-8-2 46 oh1..........(v[1]) TobyAtkinson(7) 9 46
(R W Price) *in tch in midfield: chsd ldrs 7f out: rdn and nt qckn over 3f out: no ch w ldrs fnl 2f* **40/1**

6060 **11** 6 **Cragganmore Creek**[85] 4170 6-8-9 47 oh1........... CatherineGannon 14 39
(D Morris) *hld up in last trio: short lived effrt on outer 3f out: n.d* **50/1**

106- **12** ¾ **Highland Homestead**[157] 7216 4-9-10 61............................ JimCrowley 1 53
(M R Hoad) *stdd s: hld up in last pl: c wd st: no prog* **33/1**

40/0 **13** ½ **Sa Nau**[13] 6432 6-8-13 50.. J-PGuillambert 5 41
(T Keddy) *in tch tl lost pl u.p 3f out: bhd fnl 2f* **14/1**

3m 29.28s (3.58) **Going Correction** +0.025s/f (Slow)

WFA 3 from 4yo+ 11lb **13** Ran SP% **125.7**

Speed ratings (Par 101): **92,91,90,90,90 90,90,89,89,89 86,86,85**

toteswingers: 1&2 £5.80, 1&3 £13.80, 2&3 £4.60 Place 6: £171.37 Place 5: £74.42 CSF £38.99 CT £102.75 TOTE £13.20: £2.70, £1.60, £2.70; EX 36.60 Trifecta £132.20 Part won. Pool: £178.75 - 0.93 winning units..

Owner J Acheson **Bred** N Hartery **Trained** Lambourn, Berks

■ Stewards' Enquiry : D E Mullins three-day ban: careless riding (tbn)

FOCUS

A decent-sized field for this modest staying handicap, but the pace was very steady and that handed the advantage to those that raced prominently. Muddling form which may prove unreliable.

Stagecoach Emerald Official explanation: jockey said gelding was denied a clear run

T/Jkpt: Not won. T/Plt: £443.00 to a £1 stake. Pool: £66,754.73. 109.99 winning tickets. T/Qpdt: £53.80 to a £1 stake. Pool: £4,819.19. 66.20 winning tickets. SP

6334 BRIGHTON (L-H)

Thursday, October 15

OFFICIAL GOING: Good (good to soft in places)

Course dolled out 5m from 6f to 3f but impact on distances not quanitifed.
Wind: Moderate, half against Weather: Fine

6786 E B F / COMFORT CONTROLS 25TH JUBILEE CELEBRATION MEDIAN AUCTION MAIDEN STKS 7f 214y

2:30 (2:30) (Class 5) 2-Y-O **£3,532** (£1,057; £528; £264; £131) **Stalls** Low

Form RPR

6 **1** **Avon Lady**[38] 5722 2-8-12 0 PatCosgrave 6 69+
(J R Fanshawe) *hld up in rr: hdwy over 2f out: led wl over 1f out: drvn out: hld on wl fnl 50yds* **14/1**

043 **2** *nk* **Harlestone Times (IRE)**[32] 5907 2-9-3 74 JimmyQuinn 4 73
(J L Dunlop) *prom: rdn 2f out: kpt on wl fnl 100yds* **15/8**[2]

424 **3** *3/4* **Dr Finley (IRE)**[58] 5119 2-9-3 77 HayleyTurner 1 71
(M L W Bell) *led and set modest pce: hdd wl over 1f out: hrd rdn: kpt on* **7/4**[1]

44 **4** *1 1/4* **Santa Margherita**[14] 6416 2-8-12 0 LukeMorris 7 64
(H J L Dunlop) *sn prom: hrd rdn and styd on same pce fnl 2f* **10/1**

5 *4 1/2* **Maskan** 2-9-3 0 TPO'Shea 3 61+
(W J Haggas) *dwlt: sn chsng ldrs: wknd 2f out* **5/1**[3]

00 **6** *2 1/2* **Cool Kitten (IRE)**[114] 3249 2-8-12 0 ShaneKelly 5 48
(W J Knight) *prom 2f: lost pl over 4f out: rdn and n.d fnl 3f* **40/1**

0 **7** *1/2* **Calm And Serene (USA)**[8] 6592 2-8-12 0 RichardMullen 2 47
(Rae Guest) *prom and t.k.h early: stdd bk after 2f: rdn 3f out: n.d after* **20/1**

1m 37.72s (1.72) **Going Correction** 0.0s/f (Good) 7 Ran SP% **110.8**
Speed ratings (Par 95): **91,90,89,88,84 81,81**
toteswingers: 1&2 £2.20, 1&3 £4.00, 2&3 £1.40 CSF £38.23 TOTE £19.70: £5.70, £1.10; EX 48.90.
Owner Helena Springfield Ltd **Bred** Meon Valley Stud **Trained** Newmarket, Suffolk

FOCUS

This looked an ordinary juvenile maiden and they went a steady pace, resulting in a few of these racing keenly. As is usually the case when the going is on the easy side, they raced towards the stands' side in the straight. The form is rated around the second, third and sixth.

NOTEBOOK

Avon Lady improved significantly on the form she showed on her debut over 7f, proving well suited by the extra furlong. Having settled better than most under a hold up ride, she challenged three-horse widths off the stands' rail in the straight but found enough for pressure to gain a hard-fought success. She's by Avonbridge, but clearly gets plenty of stamina from the dam's side of her pedigree and might stay even further next season. (op 12-1)

Harlestone Times(IRE) had every chance if good enough but he was just held. He probably ran to something like his official mark of 74, but is likely to remain vulnerable in maidens. (op 2-1 tchd 9-4 and 13-8)

Dr Finley(IRE) sweated up beforehand and, despite leading at a steady pace and bagging the stands' rail in the straight, he didn't run up to official rating of 77. In fairness, he kept on for pressure, but he was always held late on. (op 13-8 tchd 2-1)

Santa Margherita had shown ability on her first two starts, including in a decent maiden at Goodwood last time, but she raced a little keenly on this occasion and found only the one pace in the straight. She should find her level now handicaps are an option. (op 9-1)

Maskan is nicely bred - out of a high-class multiple 7f-1m2f winner - and cost 55,000gns, but he's already been gelded and showed little. (op 15-2)

Cool Kitten(IRE) was well beaten after racing keenly. (op 33-1)

Calm And Serene(USA) also paid for racing too keenly. (op 25-1 tchd 16-1)

6787 COMFORT CONTROLS CELEBRATING 25 YEARS IN BUSINESS H'CAP 7f 214y

3:00 (3:00) (Class 6) (0-60,60) 3-Y-O **£2,590** (£770; £385; £192) **Stalls** Low

Form RPR

2601 **1** **Ocean Countess (IRE)**[17] 6339 3-9-2 **58** CatherineGannon 8 63
(Miss J Feilden) *hld up in midfield: hdwy over 2f out: led ins fnl f: drvn out* **5/1**[1]

1-00 **2** *nk* **Dream Huntress**[26] 6124 3-9-4 **60** GeorgeBaker 2 64
(J W Hills) *stdd s: hdwy over 2f out: led over 1f out tl ins fnl f: r.o* **16/1**

0-00 **3** *3* **Miss Jabba (IRE)**[7] 6611 3-8-4 **46** oh1 LukeMorris 13 43
(Miss J Feilden) *prom: rdn over 2f out: one pce appr fnl f* **50/1**

406- **4** *1 1/2* **Seaquel**[374] 6535 3-8-8 **55** AmyBaker(5) 12 49
(A B Haynes) *towards rr: rdn and styd on fnl 2f: nvr nrr* **22/1**

5310 **5** *1/2* **Fitz**[16] 6358 3-9-2 **58** (p) LPKeniry 9 51
(Matthew Salaman) *prom 2f: rdn and lost pl over 4f out: styd on fnl 2f* **7/1**[3]

0006 **6** *1/2* **Dicey Affair**[13] 6442 3-8-8 **50** (t) RichardMullen 14 42
(G L Moore) *dwlt: bhd tl hdwy over 2f out: hrd rdn over 1f out: one pce* **28/1**

0000 **7** *hd* **Montmartre (USA)**[13] 6440 3-8-10 **52** FergusSweeney 15 43
(David Pinder) *led: hung lft and hdd over 1f out: sn btn* **16/1**

0240 **8** *1/2* **Superstitious Me (IRE)**[124] 2910 3-8-13 **55** NeilChalmers 16 45
(B Palling) *hdwy to chse ldrs after 2f: wknd 2f out* **20/1**

0406 **9** *3 1/4* **Haling Park (UAE)**[17] 6338 3-8-5 **50** (p) Louis-PhilippeBeuzelin(3) 1 33
(G L Moore) *chsd ldrs towards ins tl wknd over 1f out* **12/1**

0433 **10** *2 3/4* **Jewelled Reef (IRE)**[17] 6333 3-9-3 **59** ShaneKelly 4 35
(Eve Johnson Houghton) *mid-div: outpcd 3f out: sn btn* **6/1**[2]

0000 **11** *1/2* **Wunder Strike (USA)**[45] 5506 3-8-13 **55** (p) PatCosgrave 7 30
(J R Boyle) *chsd ldrs: n.m.r and lost several pls 5f out: wknd over 2f out* **5/1**[1]

3404 **12** *1 1/4* **Miss Kittyhawk (IRE)**[26] 6101 3-9-4 **60** JimmyQuinn 3 32
(Rae Guest) *mid-div tl hrd rdn and wknd 2f out* **16/1**

1003 **13** *nse* **Eye For The Girls**[29] 5998 3-8-13 **55** TonyCulhane 5 27
(M R Channon) *prom: edgd rt over 2f out: sn lost pl* **12/1**

0005 **14** *3 3/4* **Royal Adelaide (IRE)**[24] 6175 3-7-11 **46** oh1 NathanAlison(7) 6 10
(J A Osborne) *chsd ldrs over 5f* **10/1**

1m 36.06s (0.06) **Going Correction** 0.0s/f (Good) 14 Ran SP% **116.8**
Speed ratings (Par 99): **99,98,95,94,93 93,93,92,89,86 86,84,84,80**
toteswingers: 1&2 £26.20, 1&3 £42.50, 2&3 £21.30 CSF £79.54 CT £3648.41 TOTE £6.60: £2.90, £7.00, £17.90; EX 86.10 TRIFECTA Not won..
Owner Ocean Trailers Ltd **Bred** Don Commins **Trained** Exning, Suffolk

FOCUS

A weak handicap in which they came centre-to-stands' side once into the straight and although things became a bit tight passing the 2f pole, it didn't appear to affect the result. The form is not too solid.

Eye For The Girls Official explanation: jockey said gelding hung both ways

6788 COMFORT CONTROLS 25TH ANNIVERSARY CELEBRATIONS (S) STKS 1m 3f 196y

3:30 (3:30) (Class 6) 3-Y-O **£1,942** (£578; £288; £144) **Stalls** High

Form RPR

0-50 **1** **My Les**[58] 5131 3-8-7 42 PaulDoe 3 65
(Jim Best) *chsd ldrs: led over 3f out: rdn clr over 1f out: comf* **14/1**

3330 **2** *10* **Dhania (IRE)**[13] 6446 3-8-12 53 (b) LukeMorris 2 54
(R A Teal) *mid-div: rdn and hdwy 5f out: chsd wnr over 2f out: no imp* **4/1**[1]

2030 **3** *shd* **Regal Blush**[29] 5990 3-8-7 60 LPKeniry 7 49
(A M Balding) *bhd: hdwy to chse ldrs 4f out: one pce fnl 2f* **5/1**[3]

0640 **4** *1/2* **Secret Desert**[10] 6549 3-8-12 65 PatCosgrave 10 53
(D M Simcock) *bhd: rdn and hdwy 4f out: one pce fnl 2f* **5/1**[3]

4-00 **5** *7* **Sixties Gift (UAE)**[118] 3117 3-8-7 54 RichardMullen 1 37
(Rae Guest) *early reminders in rr: sme hdwy into midfield 1/2-way: no prog fnl 4f* **12/1**

2340 **6** *1 1/2* **Fine Tolerance**[19] 6289 3-8-7 53 HayleyTurner 11 34
(J R Boyle) *chsd ldr: led 5f out tl over 3f out: sn hrd rdn and wknd* **9/1**

3324 **7** *22* **Tesserae**[18] 6310 3-8-7 52 FergusSweeney 8 —
(A B Haynes) *chsd ldrs tl wknd over 3f out: eased whn no ch fnl 2f* **9/2**[2]

6006 **8** *3* **Dalrymple (IRE)**[39] 4734 3-9-4 46 (t) GeorgeBaker 9 5
(M Madgwick) *mid-div: outpcd 4f out: n.d after* **14/1**

3650 **9** *13* **Nouailhas**[9] 6570 3-8-9 50 RussellKennemore(3) 13 —
(R Hollinshead) *led tl 5f out: styd alone far side st: wknd 4f out: hung lft* **20/1**

0-20 **10** *4 1/2* **Art Discovery (IRE)**[39] 4177 3-8-12 52 (b) JimmyQuinn 14 —
(M H Tompkins) *s.s and drvn along early: a wl bhd* **40/1**

-000 **11** *36* **Spin Sister**[28] 6029 3-8-8 40 ow1 ShaneKelly 4 —
(J Gallagher) *prom tl wknd 5f out* **50/1**

06- **12** *3 3/4* **Southoffrance (IRE)**[7] 4387 3-8-7 0 (p) CatherineGannon 5 —
(W G M Turner) *towards rr: rdn over 5f out: no ch fnl 4f* **80/1**

00- **13** *1 3/4* **Endeavoured (IRE)**[335] 7312 3-8-7 0 (bt[1]) AndrewHeffernan(5) 12 —
(D Carroll) *chsd ldrs: rdn and struggling to hold pl after 3f: wknd 1/2-way: sn t.o* **10/1**

2m 32.21s (-0.49) **Going Correction** 0.0s/f (Good) 13 Ran SP% **122.0**
Speed ratings (Par 99): **101,94,94,93,89 88,73,71,62,59 35,33,32**
toteswingers: 1&2 £29.20, 1&3 £10.00, 2&3 £8.10 CSF £69.26 TOTE £11.60: £3.10, £2.30, £2.10; EX 120.40 TRIFECTA Not won..There was no bid for the winner.
Owner SN Racing II **Bred** S Nunn **Trained** Lewes, E Sussex

FOCUS

A very poor seller and wide open according to the market. They finished spread out all over Sussex. The time was quicker tha the following maiden though and the winner's improved form has been taken at face value.

Art Discovery(IRE) Official explanation: jockey said gelding was slowly away

Spin Sister Official explanation: jockey said filly had a breathing problem

Southoffrance(IRE) Official explanation: jockey said filly was unsuited by the track

6789 COMFORT CONTROLS 25 YEARS IN HVAC CONTROLS MAIDEN STKS 1m 3f 196y

4:00 (4:02) (Class 5) 3-Y-O+ **£3,406** (£1,019; £509; £254; £126) **Stalls** High

Form RPR

4040 **1** **Charger**[8] 6595 3-9-3 75 ShaneKelly 2 76
(J Noseda) *hld up in tch: chsd ldr 3f out: led jst ins fnl f: edgd rt: rdn out* **10/3**[2]

3325 **2** *1 3/4* **Decorum (USA)**[82] 4319 3-9-3 76 (bt[1]) RichardMullen 4 73
(J H M Gosden) *led: qcknd 4f out: rdn and hdd jst ins fnl f: swtchd lft: one pce* **15/8**[1]

-330 **3** *12* **Daredevil Dan**[82] 4319 3-9-3 68 JimmyQuinn 7 53
(M H Tompkins) *towards rr: rdn 5f out: sn struggling: styd on to take mod 3rd wl ins fnl f* **5/1**

4352 **4** *1 1/4* **Nesayem (IRE)**[19] 6276 3-8-12 67 PatCosgrave 3 46
(D M Simcock) *prom: chsd ldr 6f out tl 3f out: wknd 2f out* **4/1**[3]

64 **5** *3 1/2* **Lilly Royal (IRE)**[8] 6595 3-8-12 65 NeilChalmers 6 40
(B Palling) *chsd ldr 6f: outpcd 4f out: sn btn* **8/1**

004 **6** *32* **Legend Of Greece (IRE)**[23] 6189 3-9-3 48 LukeMorris 8 —
(Mrs N Smith) *in tch: drvn along and wknd 5f out: sn bhd: eased over 1f out* **100/1**

0 **7** *38* **Lion Road (USA)**[24] 6158 3-9-3 0 RobertHavlin 1 —
(A B Haynes) *hld up in rr: hrd rdn 5f out: no ch fnl 4f* **66/1**

2m 33.14s (0.44) **Going Correction** 0.0s/f (Good) 7 Ran SP% **108.1**
Speed ratings (Par 103): **98,96,88,88,85 64,39**
CSF £8.85 TOTE £3.80: £1.90, £1.60; EX 9.80 Trifecta £42.50 Pool: £620.11 - 10.79 winning units..
Owner Cheveley Park Stud **Bred** Cheveley Park Stud Ltd **Trained** Newmarket, Suffolk

FOCUS

Only five counted in this moderate maiden and the winning time was nearly a second slower than the seller. Modest form.

6790 COMFORT CONTROLS 25 YEARS BMS ENGINEERING H'CAP 6f 209y

4:30 (4:30) (Class 5) (0-70,70) 3-Y-O+ **£3,154** (£944; £472; £236; £117) **Stalls** Low

Form RPR

0600 **1** **Rondeau (GR)**[21] 6230 4-9-1 **65** GeorgeBaker 10 76
(P R Chamings) *hld up in rr: hdwy wd of others on stands' rail 2f out: r.o to ld ins fnl f: rdn clr* **11/1**

2311 **2** *2 1/4* **Blue Noodles**[27] 6070 3-8-10 **67** AndrewHeffernan(5) 9 72
(P D Evans) *led after 1f: hrd rdn and hdd ins fnl f: one pce* **9/2**[1]

4060 **3** *3 1/4* **Lady Florence**[23] 6178 4-8-10 **63** Louis-PhilippeBeuzelin(3) 3 59
(A B Coogan) *w ldrs tl no ex fnl f* **17/2**

5240 **4** *nk* **Advertise**[26] 6111 3-9-1 **67** LPKeniry 6 62
(A M Balding) *chsd ldrs: sltly outpcd 4f out: styd on fnl f* **11/2**[2]

2011 **5** *1 3/4* **Seasonal Cross**[15] 6394 4-9-2 **66** HayleyTurner 11 57
(S Dow) *bhd: hdwy over 2f out: chsng ldrs whn bmpd over 1f out: one pce* **9/2**[1]

004 **6** *hd* **Phluke**[21] 6224 8-9-3 **67** StephenCarson 7 57
(Eve Johnson Houghton) *led 1f: pressed ldrs tl wknd wl over 1f out* **10/1**

6145 **7** *1 1/4* **Outer Hebrides**[35] 5788 8-8-1 **56** (v) AmyBaker(5) 4 43
(J M Bradley) *chsd ldrs: rdn 3f out: btn whn bmpd over 1f out* **20/1**

610 **8** *2 1/4* **Miss Bootylishes**[38] 5723 4-9-4 **68** KevinGhunowa 13 49
(A B Haynes) *chsd ldrs: drvn along over 2f out: wknd wl over 1f out* **11/1**

0560 **9** *nk* **Mick Is Back**[22] 6208 5-8-2 **59** (p) RyanPowell(7) 14 39
(G G Margarson) *sn bhd on outer: rdn over 3f out: hung lft fnl 2f: n.d* **16/1**

0300 **10** *shd* **Driven (IRE)**[17] 6337 4-9-5 **69** ShaneKelly 2 55+
(Mrs A J Perrett) *s.i.s: bhd: sme hdwy into midfield whn bdly hmpd over 1f out: nt rcvr* **8/1**[3]

0060 **11** *4* **Purus (IRE)**[35] 5804 7-9-6 **70** .... LukeMorris 5 39
(R A Teal) *chsd ldrs 2f: sn rdn along and lost pl* **12/1**

1m 22.4s (-0.70) **Going Correction** 0.0s/f (Good)
WFA 3 from 4yo+ 2lb **11** Ran SP% **117.5**
Speed ratings (Par 103): **104,101,97,97,95 95,93,91,90,90 86**
toteswingers: 1&2 £15.60, 1&3 £26.20, 2&3 £8.60 CSF £59.91 CT £459.13 TOTE £15.60: £4.50, £2.00, £2.40; EX 105.00 Trifecta £344.10 Part won. Pool: £465.00 - 0.50 winning units..
Owner The Foxford House Partnership **Bred** Ippotour Stud **Trained** Baughurst, Hants

FOCUS
An ordinary handicap and further evidence that a position close to the stands' rail was the place to be. The runner-up looks the best guide to this form.

6791 COMFORT CONTROLS 25 YEARS SAVING YOU ENERGY H'CAP 5f 59y
5:00 (5:01) (Class 5) (0-75,75) 3-Y-0+ **£3,280** (£981; £490; £245; £122) **Stalls** Low

Form RPR

4263 **1** **Magical Speedfit (IRE)**[5] 6666 4-8-4 **68** .... RyanPowell(7) 12 76
(G G Margarson) *towards rr: swtchd left and hdwy over 1f out: r.o to ld fnl strides* **7/1**[3]

3521 **2** *shd* **Edith's Boy (IRE)**[22] 6206 3-8-5 **62** .... HayleyTurner 10 70
(S Dow) *led: c to stands' rail st: hrd rdn fnl f: ct fnl strides* **12/1**

120 **3** *1 ¾* **Green Lagonda (AUS)**[5] 6669 7-8-12 **69** .... PaulDoe 1 71
(P D Evans) *mid-div: hdwy to chse ldrs 2f out: one pce fnl f* **16/1**

1011 **4** *1 ¼* **Simple Rhythm**[8] 6596 3-8-10 **70** .... Louis-PhilippeBeuzelin(3) 5 67+
(J Ryan) *chsd ldrs: styd far side st: led gp 1f out: one pce* **2/1**[1]

1300 **5** *shd* **Lithaam (IRE)**[6] 6635 5-8-7 **67** ....(p) JackDean(3) 3 64
(J M Bradley) *in tch: pressed ldr 2f out: no ex fnl f* **14/1**

0366 **6** *nk* **Raimond Ridge (IRE)**[15] 6387 3-8-10 **67** .... CatherineGannon 13 63
(M R Channon) *s.s: bhd tl hdwy 2f out: kpt on fnl f* **25/1**

0400 **7** *nk* **Cosmic Destiny (IRE)**[17] 6341 7-7-11 **61** oh3 .... NoelGarbutt(7) 14 56+
(E F Vaughan) *bhd tl r.o appr fnl f: nvr nrr* **40/1**

040 **8** *nk* **Requisite**[32] 5919 4-8-12 **69** .... PatCosgrave 4 63
(I A Wood) *outpcd in rr: rapid hdwy 2f out: no ex fnl f* **12/1**

2436 **9** *hd* **Forest Dane**[22] 6201 9-8-5 **62** .... LukeMorris 6 55
(Mrs N Smith) *chsd ldrs over 3f* **16/1**

2000 **10** *¾* **Cape Royal**[5] 6669 9-9-3 **74** ....(bt) KevinGhunowa 8 64+
(J M Bradley) *w ldrs: styd far side st: wknd fnl f* **28/1**

0106 **11** *½* **Colorus (IRE)**[14] 6422 6-8-7 **69** ....(p) PaulPickard(5) 9 58+
(W J H Ratcliffe) *w ldrs: styd far side st: wknd fnl f* **22/1**

0611 **12** *nk* **Even Bolder**[5] 6666 6-8-13 **70** .... StephenCarson 7 58+
(E A Wheeler) *sn outpcd towards rr* **5/1**[2]

-336 **13** *6* **Stash**[222] 784 3-9-1 **75** .... RussellKennemore(3) 11 42
(R Hollinshead) *dwlt: sn in tch: wknd 2f out* **25/1**

1610 **14** *nse* **Guto**[16] 6359 6-9-3 **74** .... TravisBlock 2 40
(W J H Ratcliffe) *chsd ldrs: styd far side st: hrd rdn and wknd wl over 1f out* **14/1**

62.73 secs (0.43) **Going Correction** 0.0s/f (Good) **14** Ran SP% **120.9**
Speed ratings (Par 103): **96,95,93,91,90 90,89,89,89,87 87,86,77,76**
toteswingers: 1&2 £21.40, 1&3 £17.80, 2&3 £11.40 CSF £82.60 CT £1344.25 TOTE £8.70: £2.50, £2.90, £3.20; EX 97.00 TRIFECTA Not won. Place 6: £291.78 Place 5: £88.02.
Owner John Guest **Bred** John Malone **Trained** Newmarket, Suffolk

FOCUS
This looked a good handicap for the grade - three of the runners were officially well in - and the pace was strong, but the noticeable track bias played its part. They majority of these raced middle to stands' side in the straight, and again that proved the place to be. A length personal best from the winner.

T/Plt: £357.20 to a £1 stake. Pool: £60,382.62. 123.39 winning tickets. T/Qpdt: £54.00 to a £1 stake. Pool: £4,525.02. 61.90 winning tickets. LM

6589 NOTTINGHAM (L-H)
Thursday, October 15

OFFICIAL GOING: (outer course) soft (good to soft in places) changing to soft after race 5 (4.10)
Wind: Light against Weather: Drizzle

6792 EUROPEAN BREEDERS' FUND MAIDEN STKS 1m 75y
2:10 (2:12) (Class 5) 2-Y-O **£3,753** (£1,108; £554) **Stalls** Low

Form RPR

4340 **1** **Saboteur**[12] 6478 2-9-3 84 .... LDettori 9 89+
(Saeed Bin Suroor) *mde all: pushed clr fr over 1f out: eased ins fnl f* **5/4**[1]

6 **2** *7* **Readymade (IRE)**[29] 6000 2-9-3 0 .... RyanMoore 3 72
(Sir Michael Stoute) *chsd wnr: rdn over 3f out: lost 2nd over 1f out: sn outpcd: wnt 2nd again nr fin* **5/1**[2]

063 **3** *hd* **Mawaddah (IRE)**[8] 6592 2-9-3 0 .... EddieAhern 4 72
(R Hannon) *prom: rdn to chse wnr over 1f out: sn outpcd: lost 2nd nr fin* **6/1**[3]

4 *4 ½* **Countess Comet (IRE)** 2-8-12 0 .... SebSanders 17 57+
(R M Beckett) *hld up: hdwy over 3f out: rdn and wknd over 1f out* **25/1**

04 **5** *3 ½* **Shelfah (IRE)**[20] 6245 2-8-12 0 .... PhilipRobinson 13 49+
(M A Jarvis) *chsd ldrs: rdn over 2f out: wknd wl over 1f out* **16/1**

0 **6** *3 ¼* **Flag Of Glory**[87] 4152 2-9-3 0 .... AlanMunro 10 47
(C F Wall) *broke wl: sn lost pl: rdn over 2f out: nvr trbld ldrs* **100/1**

7 *1 ¼* **Sadler's Mark** 2-9-3 0 .... RobertWinston 12 45+
(T P Tate) *s.s: styd on fr over 2f out: nvr nrr* **14/1**

0 **8** *2 ¼* **The Love Guru**[24] 6162 2-9-3 0 ....(b[1]) SJCraine 1 40
(J R Boyle) *chsd ldrs: rdn over 3f out: wknd over 2f out* **150/1**

9 *2* **A P Ling** 2-8-12 0 .... JerryO'Dwyer 6 31
(C N Kellett) *dwlt: hld up: rdn over 2f out: n.d* **250/1**

10 *hd* **Idealism** 2-9-3 0 .... JimmyFortune 5 35+
(J H M Gosden) *broke wl: sn lost pl: hdwy over 5f out: rdn and wknd wl over 2f out* **10/1**

11 *1* **Inshaallah** 2-9-3 0 .... TPQueally 8 33
(J G Given) *hld up: nt clr run over 4f out: n.d* **100/1**

0 **12** *2* **Khazara**[29] 5984 2-8-12 0 .... DaneO'Neill 2 24
(A King) *prom: rdn and wknd over 2f out* **100/1**

13 *½* **Home Advantage** 2-9-3 0 .... ChrisCatlin 15 28
(R Charlton) *broke wl: sn lost pl: in rr fr 1/2-way* **12/1**

0 **14** *1 ½* **Star Of Kalani (IRE)**[46] 5466 2-9-3 0 .... PJMcDonald 11 24
(G M Moore) *hld up: a in rr: wknd 1/2-way* **150/1**

15 *3 ¾* **Master Of Song** 2-9-3 0 .... AmirQuinn 7 16
(S R Bowring) *s.s: a in rr* **100/1**

0 **16** *1 ¼* **Set To Rock**[49] 5371 2-9-3 0 .... JamesDoyle 14 14
(J G Portman) *mid-div: sn pushed along: hdwy 1/2-way: wknd over 2f out* **150/1**

P **Dovedon Diva** 2-8-12 0 .... KirstyMilczarek 16 —
(T Keddy) *s.s: hung rt thrght: a in rr: rn v wd turning for home: sn p.u* **150/1**

1m 49.63s (4.03) **Going Correction** +0.475s/f (Yiel) **17** Ran SP% **115.6**
Speed ratings (Par 95): **98,91,90,86,82 79,78,76,74,73 72,70,70,68,65 63,—**
toteswingers: 1&2 £2.70, 1&3 £4.40, 2&3 £5.00 CSF £6.52 TOTE £1.90: £1.10, £2.80, £2.00; EX 8.50.
Owner Godolphin **Bred** Usk Valley Stud **Trained** Newmarket, Suffolk

FOCUS
An average maiden. It paid to race up front and the winner was value for 2l extra. The form makes sense looking at the placed horses.

NOTEBOOK
Saboteur easily opened his account by making every yard. He got a freebie on the lead, under one of the best front-running jockeys in the world, and had the race in the bag passing the two-furlong marker. Officially rated 84, he was entitled to win this and rates a little flattered as he was pretty much gifted the race, but it was much deserves all the same. He had no trouble with the easier surface and clearly stays well, so there should be more to come after this confidence booster. (op 11-10)

Readymade(IRE) first began to feel the pinch nearing the three-furlong pole and was never a serious threat to the winner. He got the trip well enough, though, and looks the type to progress through the handicap ranks as he matures. (op 13-2)

Mawaddah(IRE) had run his best race to date when third over C&D eight days previously and was proven on easy ground. He took time to pick up once asked for his effort, but still gives the form a sound look. (tchd 11-2 and 13-2)

Countess Comet(IRE) fared best of the newcomers and, having made her effort on the outer with 3f to run, ultimately shaped as though the run would bring her on a good deal. She is bred to relish stepping up in trip as she matures. (tchd 22-1)

Shelfah(IRE) failed to see out the longer trip on this ground and ought to appreciate a return to a sounder surface. She also now has the option of nurseries. (op 10-1)

Idealism Official explanation: jockey said colt kept stumbling

Dovedon Diva Official explanation: jockey said filly was unsteerable

6793 DG TAXIS GET YOU HOME SAFELY NURSERY 1m 75y
2:40 (2:42) (Class 5) (0-70,70) 2-Y-O **£2,590** (£770; £385; £192) **Stalls** Low

Form RPR

5623 **1** **Rezwaan**[27] 6067 2-9-5 **68** .... RHills 3 75+
(E A L Dunlop) *chsd ldrs: effrt over 2f out: styd on to ld ins fnl f: hld on towards fin* **3/1**[1]

5601 **2** *½* **Pullyourfingerout (IRE)**[31] 5938 2-9-7 **70** .... KFallon 5 76
(B G Powell) *in tch: sn drvn along: hdwy over 2f out: chal ins fnl f: no ex* **10/1**

4246 **3** *1 ½* **Dolphin Rock**[40] 5682 2-9-2 **65** .... TedDurcan 8 68
(Mrs G S Rees) *trckd ldrs: led over 1f out: hdd and no ex ins fnl f* **16/1**

3340 **4** *½* **Nina Rose**[31] 5938 2-9-5 **68** .... AdamKirby 2 70
(C G Cox) *s.i.s: sn mid-div: hdwy over 3f out: edgd rt and styd on wl fnl f* **18/1**

0001 **5** *6* **Fine Lace (IRE)**[6] 6639 2-9-2 **65** 6ex .... JamesDoyle 13 53
(D J S Ffrench Davis) *chsd ldrs: wknd appr fnl f* **25/1**

5650 **6** *¾* **Ice Viking (IRE)**[12] 6478 2-9-5 **68** .... TPQueally 17 55
(J G Given) *mid-div on outer: drvn over 5f out: sme hdwy over 2f out: nvr nr ldrs* **25/1**

2506 **7** *¾* **Chairman Pat (USA)**[32] 5913 2-9-2 **70** .... RossAtkinson(5) 14 55
(Tom Dascombe) *s.i.s: hld up in rr on outer: hdwy over 2f out: nvr nr ldrs* **50/1**

035 **8** *2* **Spinning Spirit (IRE)**[33] 5852 2-9-1 **67** .... FrederikTylicki(3) 4 48
(J G Given) *led early: trckd ldr: led over 2f out: hdd over 1f out: sn wknd* **18/1**

6062 **9** *6* **Bubbly Braveheart (IRE)**[6] 6639 2-9-2 **65** ....(b) RobertWinston 10 33+
(A Bailey) *sn led: hdd over 2f out: sn wknd* **16/1**

0664 **10** *¾* **Lost Cause**[7] 6609 2-9-2 **65** .... LDettori 7 35+
(R Charlton) *hld up in rr: effrt over 3f out: wknd over 2f out* **9/2**[2]

6545 **11** *1 ½* **Sounds Of Thunder**[31] 5938 2-9-5 **68** .... DaneO'Neill 6 35+
(H J L Dunlop) *in rr: effrt on ins 3f out: sn btn* **16/1**

453 **12** *3 ½* **Turf Trivia**[82] 4308 2-9-3 **66** .... JimmyFortune 15 21
(G M Moore) *trckd ldrs on outer: rdn 3f out: sn btn* **16/1**

2256 **13** *4 ½* **Pastello**[12] 6481 2-9-7 **70** .... RyanMoore 9 15
(R Hannon) *t.k.h in rr: effrt 3f out: sn btn* **7/1**[3]

6254 **14** *3* **Rodrigo De Freitas (IRE)**[9] 6736 2-9-0 **63** .... NickyMackay 1 23+
(J R Boyle) *dwlt: in rr: lost pl 4f out: sn bhd: eased* **10/1**

1m 49.29s (3.69) **Going Correction** +0.475s/f (Yiel) **14** Ran SP% **117.6**
Speed ratings (Par 95): **100,99,98,97,91 90,90,88,82,81 79,76,71,68**
toteswingers: 1&2 £8.30, 1&3 £14.70, 2&3 £31.20 CSF £31.64 CT £417.50 TOTE £3.50: £1.50, £2.10, £6.30; EX 19.80.
Owner Hamdan Al Maktoum **Bred** Shadwell Estate Company Limited **Trained** Newmarket, Suffolk

FOCUS
A modest nursery. The first four came clear and showed fair form.

NOTEBOOK
Rezwaan had been placed on both his outings since switching to this sphere and he ran out a deserved winner, opening his account at the sixth attempt in the process. He tracked the early leaders and moved nicely, but took time to pick up when asked to improve. His rider always looked confident enough, however, and he showed a resolute attitude to repel the runner-up where it mattered. This proves his versatility as regards underfoot conditions and he should at least continue to hold his own after another likely rise. (op 100-30 tchd 7-2)

Pullyourfingerout(IRE) first came under pressure nearing 3f out, but he kept going under strong driving to make the winner work for his prize. He got the longer trip without fuss and remains in good heart. (op 9-1 tchd 11-1)

Dolphin Rock was never far away and bounced back to form, but this distance on such ground looked to find out his stamina. (op 25-1)

Nina Rose finished a lot closer to the runner-up than had been the case when disappointing on her previous start and she enjoyed the step up in trip. She is in good hands and can be placed to strike before the year is out. (op 16-1 tchd 14-1)

Fine Lace(IRE) posted a sound effort under her penalty on this return to turf and she continues in good form. (op 28-1 tchd 33-1)

Lost Cause, stepping up a furlong, struggled to make up his ground from off the pace on this return from the AW and disappointed. Official explanation: jockey said colt never travelled (op 4-1)

Pastello was another who failed to make any sort of impact from out the back and she was eased off before the furlong pole. The ground was most likely to blame. Official explanation: jockey said filly was unsuited by the soft (good to soft places) ground (op 17-2)

Rodrigo De Freitas(IRE) Official explanation: jockey said gelding was unsuited by the soft (good to soft places) ground

6794 DG TAXIS NOTTINGHAM'S MOST RELIABLE MAIDEN STKS 1m 2f 50y
3:10 (3:13) (Class 5) 3-Y-O **£3,238** (£963; £481; £240) **Stalls** Low

Form				RPR
5	**1**		**Black Eagle (IRE)**[10] 6539 3-9-3 0 ... LDettori 6 (Saeed Bin Suroor) *sn led: hdd over 3f out: led again over 2f out: shkn up and styd on wl: eased nr fin* **5/2**[2]	91+
22	**2**	*1 ½*	**Troopingthecolour**[75] 4519 3-9-3 0 ... JimmyFortune 1 (J H M Gosden) *trckd ldrs: led over 3f out: rdn and hdd over 2f out: hung lft over 1f out: styd on same pce ins fnl f* **7/4**[1]	83
0	**3**	*1 ¾*	**Time Book (IRE)**[181] 1328 3-9-3 0 ... NickyMackay 16 (J H M Gosden) *a.p: rdn over 2f out: edgd lft fr over 1f out: styd on same pce fnl f* **16/1**	79+
02	**4**	*nk*	**Starkat**[87] 4151 3-8-12 0 ... TPQueally 5 (Jane Chapple-Hyam) *chsd ldrs: rdn over 3f out: styd on same pce fnl f* **16/1**	74
32	**5**	*¾*	**Panto Princess**[37] 5744 3-8-12 0 ... FrankieMcDonald 10 (H Candy) *hld up in tch: outpcd over 3f out: styd on ins fnl f* **12/1**	72+
03	**6**	*12*	**Country Road (IRE)**[45] 5531 3-9-3 0 ... AlanMunro 11 (P W Chapple-Hyam) *chsd ldrs: rdn over 2f out: edgd lft and wknd over 1f out* **9/2**[3]	53
	7	*2 ¾*	**Two Together (USA)** 3-9-3 0 ... TedDurcan 12 (D R Lanigan) *dwlt: wl in rr: mod late prog: nrst fin* **50/1**	48+
0	**8**	*2*	**Uncle Keef (IRE)**[12] 6475 3-9-3 0 ... DaneO'Neill 4 (M P Tregoning) *s.i.s: wl in rr: mod late prog: nvr nrr* **66/1**	44+
	9	*1 ½*	**Simulate** 3-9-3 0 ... RyanMoore 8 (Sir Michael Stoute) *mid-div: lost pl 1/2-way: sn bhd* **12/1**	41
00	**10**	*10*	**Silvester**[7] 6608 3-9-3 0 ... GrahamGibbons 14 (R M H Cowell) *s.i.s: hdwy over 7f out: rdn and wknd 3f out* **250/1**	21
-	**11**	*2 ½*	**Bella Fighetta** 3-8-12 0 ... JamesDoyle 13 (Ms J S Doyle) *mid-div: rdn 1/2-way: sn wknd* **250/1**	11
0	**12**	*¾*	**Stardust Memories (UAE)**[37] 5751 3-8-12 0 ... TGMcLaughlin 3 (John Berry) *hld up: rdn and wknd over 3f out* **250/1**	—
	13	*1 ½*	**Kashubian Quest** 3-9-3 0 ... ChrisCatlin 9 (D R Lanigan) *s.s: a outpcd* **80/1**	11
0	**14**	*nk*	**Swirl Tango**[21] 6223 3-8-9 0 ... FrederikTylicki(3) 7 (F Jordan) *w wnr over 5f: sn rdn: wknd over 3f out* **250/1**	—
	15	*10*	**Little Billie** 3-8-7 0 ow2 ... BarryAdams(7) 2 (Mike Murphy) *s.s: a bhd: detached 1/2-way* **200/1**	—

2m 15.64s (3.94) **Going Correction** +0.475s/f (Yiel) **15** Ran SP% **117.0**
Speed ratings (Par 101): **103,101,100,100,99 89,87,86,84,76 74,74,73,72,64**
toteswingers: 1&2 £1.90, 1&3 £7.80, 2&3 £8.30 CSF £7.01 TOTE £3.40: £1.30, £1.30, £4.00; EX 7.20.
Owner Godolphin **Bred** Darley **Trained** Newmarket, Suffolk

FOCUS
An interesting maiden in which they came down the cente of the home straight. The winner is value for 4l+ and the first five came clear. The form makes a fair bit of sense.

6795 T DENMAN & SONS H'CAP 1m 2f 50y
3:40 (3:40) (Class 3) (0-95,92) 3-Y-O+ **£7,771** (£2,312; £1,155; £577) **Stalls** Low

Form				RPR
1036	**1**		**Fastnet Storm (IRE)**[29] 6002 3-8-10 **86** ... AlanMunro 4 (T P Tate) *sn led: rdn over 2f out: hdd jst ins fnl f: kpt on bravely to ld towards fin* **12/1**	95
2302	**2**	*nk*	**Gala Casino Star (IRE)**[28] 6016 4-8-11 **85** ... FrederikTylicki(3) 2 (R A Fahey) *trckd ldrs: chal over 1f out: slt ld jst ins fnl f: hdd and no ex towards fin* **15/2**[3]	93
04	**3**	*1 ¼*	**Ella**[44] 5551 5-9-3 **88** ... RobertWinston 16 (G A Swinbank) *led early: t.k.h and sn stdd: trckd ldrs: ev ch over 1f out: no ex ins fnl f* **9/1**	94
2-16	**4**	*¾*	**Bothy**[153] 2029 3-8-11 **87** ... PhillipMakin 15 (R M Beckett) *trckd ldrs: chal over 2f out: styd on same pce fnl f* **7/1**[2]	91
4010	**5**	*1 ¾*	**Marvo**[28] 6013 5-8-7 **83** ... AshleyMorgan(5) 3 (M H Tompkins) *s.i.s: hdwy over 3f out: sn chsng ldrs: wknd towards fin* **20/1**	84
2001	**6**	*1 ½*	**Alcalde**[10] 6546 3-8-13 **89** 6ex ... JoeFanning 7 (M Johnston) *t.k.h: trckd ldrs: chal over 2f out: fdd appr fnl f* **7/1**[2]	87
1502	**7**	*4 ½*	**Daaweitza**[12] 6485 6-8-8 **84** ... (b) MartinLane(5) 11 (B Ellison) *in rr: hdwy over 3f out: sn chsng ldrs: wknd over 1f out* **22/1**	73
0020	**8**	*4 ½*	**Charlie Cool**[20] 6239 6-9-2 **87** ... (tp) SilvestreDeSousa 5 (Mrs R A Carr) *chsd ldrs: wknd over 1f out* **12/1**	67
112	**9**	*½*	**Ottoman Empire (FR)**[24] 6165 3-9-1 **91** ... TedDurcan 8 (D R Lanigan) *trckd ldrs: drvn over 3f out: lost pl 2f out* **3/1**[1]	70
0000	**10**	*8*	**Ra Junior (USA)**[58] 5137 3-9-0 **90** ... (tp) EddieAhern 14 (B J Meehan) *chsd ldrs on outer: lost pl over 2f out* **25/1**	53
0005	**11**	*8*	**Bon Spiel**[33] 5880 5-9-5 **90** ... KFallon 12 (L M Cumani) *hld up in rr: bhd fnl 3f* **16/1**	37
1005	**12**	*¾*	**Lord Theo**[12] 6483 5-8-11 **82** ... TGMcLaughlin 9 (N P Littmoden) *in rr div: drvn over 5f out: bhd fnl 3f* **50/1**	27
5204	**13**	*¾*	**Trans Siberian**[108] 3461 5-8-13 **84** ... JimmyFortune 1 (P F I Cole) *dwlt: in rr and brought wd 4f out: nvr on terms* **33/1**	28
0	**14**	*15*	**Body Gold (ARG)**[18] 6302 6-9-7 **92** ... ChrisCatlin 13 (P J Makin) *in rr: lost pl after 3f: t.o 4f out* **125/1**	6
36	**15**	*9*	**Elliptical (USA)**[21] 6229 3-8-11 **87** ... (tp) TPQueally 6 (G A Butler) *t.k.h in midfield: effrt over 3f out: sn wknd: bhd whn heavily eased: t.o* **12/1**	—

2m 14.64s (2.94) **Going Correction** +0.475s/f (Yiel)
WFA 3 from 4yo+ 5lb **15** Ran SP% **119.4**
Speed ratings (Par 107): **107,106,105,105,103 102,98,95,94,88 82,81,80,68,61**
toteswingers: 1&2 £24.70, 1&3 £25.50, 2&3 £12.10 CSF £90.97 CT £861.94 TOTE £17.50: £4.80, £2.50, £3.30; EX 129.50.
Owner The Kittywake Partnership **Bred** Norelands Bloodstock **Trained** Tadcaster, N Yorks
■ Stewards' Enquiry : Alan Munro one-day ban: used whip without giving gelding time to respond (Oct 29)

FOCUS
A cracking handicap. The early pace was sound and the field again came down the middle of the home straight. The winner made all and is rated back to his best. Nothing got into it from the rear.

NOTEBOOK
Fastnet Storm(IRE), whose yard sent out Suits Me to finish second in this last year before he begun a winning sequence, bounced back to form with a very gutsy effort from the front. He wasn't guaranteed to get an easy lead here and had to go off fast enough early on, but he repelled numerous challenges down the home straight. This was his third win of the season and he was only 2lb higher than when registering the last of them in June, but hadn't looked at his happiest on this sort of ground in the past. He is evidently versatile on that front, though, and this has to rate a career-best effort. (tchd 14-1)

Gala Casino Star(IRE) was produced with every chance, but found the winner too resolute and again managed to find one too good. He is adaptable regarding underfoot conditions and rates the benchmark, but has become tricky to actually win with. (op 7-1 tchd 13-2)

Ella was produced with every chance, but found the winner too resolute and again managed to find one too good. He is adaptable regarding underfoot conditions and rates the benchmark, but has become tricky to actually win with. (tchd 17-2)

Bothy ◆ was last seen flopping in the Glasgow Stakes in May, but was well backed for this handicap debut. He had his chance and shaped as though a return to further, with this outing now under his belt, can see him back to winning ways. (tchd 8-1)

Marvo posted a much better effort and moved nicely into the race, but the manner in which he levelled out inside the final furlong would suggest he is just held by the handicapper. A slight drop back in trip could help, however. (op 16-1)

Alcalde showed last season he enjoyed cut underfoot and came here under a penalty for resuming winning ways at Warwick ten days earlier. He lacked the tactical pace to land a telling blow and again carried his head awkwardly under pressure, but wasn't disgraced. (tchd 13-2 and 15-2)

Ottoman Empire(FR) Official explanation: jockey said colt had no more to give

Bon Spiel was well backed on this drop back in trip and return to the turf. He failed to pick up when asked for an effort in the home straight and really looked as though he found the ground too easy for his liking. (op 14-1)

6796 GALLIFORD TRY RENEWABLES MAIDEN AUCTION STKS (DIV I) 6f 15y
4:10 (4:12) (Class 5) 2-Y-O **£2,388** (£705; £352) **Stalls** High

Form				RPR
22	**1**		**Horseradish**[16] 6356 2-8-11 0 ... KFallon 9 (M L W Bell) *chsd ldr tl led over 2f out: shkn up over 1f out: styd on wl* **4/11**[1]	77+
	2	*1 ½*	**Silk Street (USA)** 2-8-13 0 ... FrederikTylicki(3) 4 (R A Fahey) *mid-div: hdwy over 2f out: styd on to go 2nd ins fnl f: no ch w wnr* **12/1**	76+
4405	**3**	*2*	**Kalahari Desert (IRE)**[16] 6355 2-8-7 58 ... MichaelJStainton(3) 7 (R M Whitaker) *chsd ldrs: rdn over 1f out: styd on same pce ins fnl f* **33/1**	64
3240	**4**	*1*	**Pinnacle Lad (IRE)**[17] 6347 2-8-9 68 ... FrancisNorton 6 (J L Spearing) *led: rdn and hdd over 2f out: no ex ins fnl f* **16/1**	60
6355	**5**	*½*	**Jack Luey**[14] 6409 2-8-11 67 ow2 ... PaulMulrennan 10 (L A Mullaney) *prom: rdn 1/2-way: styd on same pce fnl f* **18/1**	60
4004	**6**	*8*	**Avec Moi**[16] 6355 2-8-4 48 ... FrankieMcDonald 5 (Mrs C A Dunnett) *s.i.s: sn pushed along in rr: hdwy over 1f out: sn rdn and hung rt: n.d* **100/1**	29
0P50	**7**	*½*	**Ochilview Warrior (IRE)**[29] 5981 2-8-10 40 ... GregFairley 11 (R Bastiman) *s.i.s: sn pushed along: a in rr* **150/1**	34
	8	*2*	**Zelos Spirit** 2-8-5 0 ... ChrisCatlin 8 (Rae Guest) *s.s: sn pushed along: a on rr* **33/1**	23
00	**9**	*11*	**Atherton (IRE)**[16] 6356 2-8-13 0 ... TPQueally 2 (J G Given) *sn prom: pushed along 1/2-way: wknd over 2f out* **100/1**	—
54	**10**	*1 ¼*	**Diman Waters (IRE)**[123] 2940 2-8-12 0 ... TomEaves 1 (E J Alston) *mid-div: hdwy 1/2-way: sn rdn and wknd* **8/1**[2]	—
	11	*5*	**Gojeri (IRE)** 2-9-1 0 ... PhilipRobinson 3 (M A Jarvis) *mid-div: pushed along and wknd 1/2-way* **11/1**[3]	—

1m 16.64s (1.74) **Going Correction** +0.25s/f (Good) **11** Ran SP% **120.1**
Speed ratings (Par 95): **98,96,93,92,91 80,80,77,62,61 54**
toteswingers: 1&2 £3.00, 1&3 £6.40, 2&3 £28.80 CSF £6.29 TOTE £1.30: £1.02, £3.00, £5.60; EX 8.10.
Owner Mrs G Rowland-Clark **Bred** Mrs F A Veasey **Trained** Newmarket, Suffolk

FOCUS
A moderate maiden. A high draw proved crucial. The third is the key to the form and the winner can rate higher.

NOTEBOOK
Horseradish had proved a costly failure on Fibresand 16 days previously, but he was again sent off a very short-priced favourite and this time made amends. He made his way over to the stands' rail 3f out to hit the front and was soon in command. He can now expect a mark in the high 70s for nurseries and soft ground evidently suits him well, so he will likely be kept on the go (op 1-2 tchd 8-15 in a place)

Silk Street(USA) ◆, whose dam was a triple winner on turf in the US, proved distinctly green through the first half of the race. He finished most pleasingly once the penny dropped, however, and was eating into the winner's advantage in the closing stages. This should put him spot on for his next assignment and he looks one to side with when reappearing.

Kalahari Desert(IRE), who got warm beforehand, kept on at the same pace to bag third and never seriously got involved but he proved better suited by the longer trip. This was his sixth outing and he helps to put the form into some perspective. (op 40-1)

Pinnacle Lad(IRE) helped to cut out the pace with the winner and was a spent force from the furlong marker. The extra furlong on this ground found him out. Official explanation: jockey said gelding ran too free (op 25-1)

Jack Luey, whose rider put up 2lb overweight, plugged on to finish clear of the remainder in fifth and seemed to get the longer trip. A return to quick ground and low-grade nurseries should see him fare better. (op 14-1)

Diman Waters(IRE) turned in a lifeless performance on this return from a 123-day break and it leaves him with plenty to prove. (tchd 9-1)

Gojeri(IRE) Official explanation: jockey said gelding was unsuited by the soft (good to soft places) ground

6797 GALLIFORD TRY RENEWABLES MAIDEN AUCTION STKS (DIV II) 6f 15y
4:40 (4:40) (Class 5) 2-Y-O **£2,388** (£705; £352) **Stalls** High

Form				RPR
0	**1**		**Dormer Fleet**[15] 6372 2-8-11 0 ... JimmyFortune 11 (J H M Gosden) *led to 1/2-way: led again over 2f out: shkn up and styd on strly: eased towards fin* **8/1**	78+
0220	**2**	*3 ¼*	**Jozafeen**[20] 6241 2-8-4 63 ... GregFairley 1 (R Bastiman) *chsd ldrs: rdn over 2f out: styd on same pce fnl f* **9/2**[2]	60+
500	**3**	*nk*	**Pont De Nuit**[7] 6620 2-9-1 0 ... RyanMoore 10 (R Hannon) *chsd ldrs: rdn over 2f out: sn hung lft: styd on same pce fnl f* **3/1**[1]	70
	4	*hd*	**Kenswick** 2-8-2 0 ... MartinLane(5) 6 (Pat Eddery) *hld up: outpcd 1/2-way: swtchd lft over 1f out: styd on ins fnl f: nt rch ldrs* **15/2**	62+
0	**5**	*3*	**Singin' The Blues**[12] 6493 2-8-7 0 ... WilliamCarson(3) 2 (J M P Eustace) *s.i.s: hdwy over 4f out: rdn 1/2-way: wknd over 1f out* **33/1**	56
	6	*½*	**Vanilla Rum** 2-8-12 0 ... DaneO'Neill 5 (H Candy) *chsd ldrs: rdn 1/2-way: wknd over 1f out* **13/2**	56
	7	*1*	**Mighty Aphrodite** 2-8-5 0 ... JoeFanning 4 (Rae Guest) *plld hrd and prom: rdn over 2f out: wknd over 1f out* **12/1**	46
604	**8**	*½*	**Cookie Galore**[16] 6356 2-8-4 56 ... SilvestreDeSousa 9 (J A Glover) *dwlt: plld hrd: hdwy over 4f out: led 1/2-way: sn rdn and hdd: hung lft over 1f out: wknd fnl f* **5/1**[3]	44

5050 9 2 3/4 **Pavement Games**20 6241 2-8-4 0 PaulEddery 8 35
(R C Guest) *hld up: sme hdwy 1/2-way: rdn and wknd wl over 1f out* **14/1**

1m 17.85s (2.95) **Going Correction** +0.25s/f (Good) **9** Ran SP% **113.4**
Speed ratings (Par 95): **90,85,85,85,81 80,79,78,74**
oteswingers: 1&2 £7.40, 1&3 £5.90, 2&3 £2.90 CSF £43.02 TOTE £11.30: £2.80, £1.70, £1.50; EX 42.10.
Owner C J Murfitt **Bred** C J Murfitt **Trained** Newmarket, Suffolk

FOCUS
The ground was unsurprisingly changed to soft before this second division of the sprint maiden. It was another moderate affair and as with the preceding race it saw another winner come up the stands' rail. The form is rated around the second and third.

NOTEBOOK
Dormer Fleet ◆ proved clueless on his debut at Kempton 15 days earlier, but had obviously learnt a great deal from that experience and he ran out a ready winner. He was no doubt in the place to be on the rail, but the way he travelled through the race was taking and he was no doubt the best horse on show. The drop in trip on such ground proved right up his street and he should go on from this. (op 7-1)
Jozafeen proved easy to back on this slight drop back in trip. She showed her tame effort in the Watership Down Stud Sales Race last time to be wrong and wasn't at all helped by having to race on the outside from her low draw here. She really deserves to get her head in front. (op 7-2 tchd 100-30)
Pont De Nuit was well backed on this drop back in distance and he ran a lot better, but shaped as though he now wants a stiffer test. (op 9-2)
Kenswick is sprint-bred and she put in some decent late work after taking time to get the hang of things. She should prove a deal sharper next time out. (op 8-1 tchd 10-1)
Cookie Galore Official explanation: jockey said filly ran too free

6798 MOORES CONSTRUCTION H'CAP 6f 15y
5:10 (5:12) (Class 5) (0-75,75) 3-Y-O **£2,590** (£770; £385; £192) **Stalls** High

Form RPR
3200 1 **Cawdor (IRE)**45 5506 3-9-1 **72** DaneO'Neill 14 83
(H Candy) *w ldrs racing against stands' side rail: led over 1f out: sn drew clr* **14/1**
1341 2 3 **Cheyenne Red (IRE)**25 6140 3-8-12 **69** PhillipMakin 13 70
(M Dods) *trckd ldrs against stands' side rail: kpt on to take 2nd wl ins fnl f: no ch w wnr* **8/1**2
3160 3 3/4 **Lucky Art (USA)**15 6387 3-9-1 **72** AndrewElliott 5 71
(Mrs R A Carr) *led tl over 1f out: kpt on same pce* **66/1**
0244 4 shd **Jordaura**6 6642 3-9-4 **75** AdamKirby 12 74+
(W R Swinburn) *dwlt: in rr: hdwy and nt clr run over 1f out: fin strly* **9/1**
4510 5 nk **Quiquillo (USA)**13 6455 3-8-7 **69** MartinLane(5) 8 67+
(P D Evans) *chsd ldrs: outpcd over 2f out: hdwy over 1f out: kpt on wl* **25/1**
1204 6 3/4 **Speak The Truth (IRE)**13 6444 3-8-13 **70** (p) SJCraine 11 65
(J R Boyle) *towards rr: hdwy over 2f out: kpt on fnl f* **25/1**
0055 7 nse **Spiritofthewest (IRE)**6 6642 3-9-1 **72** (v1) PaulMulrennan 6 67
(D H Brown) *chsd ldrs: edgd lft jst ins fnl f: one pce* **25/1**
0624 8 1 1/4 **Reject**22 6201 3-8-13 **70** KFallon 16 61
(W J Haggas) *towards rr: hdwy and edgd lft over 1f out: nvr nr ldrs* **5/1**1
5160 9 1 1/2 **Captain Scooby**29 5978 3-8-11 **71** MichaelJStainton(3) 17 57
(R M Whitaker) *bhd: hdwy on stands' side rail and nt clr run over 1f out: kpt on: nvr nr ldrs* **9/1**
0410 10 1 **Rio Cobolo (IRE)**14 6434 3-9-3 **74** (v) SilvestreDeSousa 3 57
(Paul Green) *mid-div on outer: effrt over 2f out: wknd over 1f out* **18/1**
4223 11 1/2 **Lucky Dan (IRE)**31 5937 3-8-13 **70** JamesDoyle 2 52
(Paul Green) *dwlt: swtchd rt after 100yds: hdwy and swtchd lft over 1f out: nvr on terms* **22/1**
4101 12 1/2 **Mamlakati (IRE)**17 6335 3-8-11 **68** RyanMoore 1 48
(R Hannon) *racd alone far side over 1f: brought stands' side: racd wd: chsd ldrs: wknd fnl f* **16/1**
333 13 1 1/2 **La Capriosa**29 5978 3-8-8 **68** FrederikTylicki(3) 7 43
(J A Glover) *chsd ldrs: wknd over 1f out* **17/2**3
2126 14 3/4 **George Thisby**26 6111 3-9-1 **75** JamesMillman(3) 9 48
(B R Millman) *sn detached in rr and drvn along* **8/1**2
023 15 4 1/2 **Sometsuke**14 6430 3-9-0 **71** (t) JimmyFortune 10 29
(P J Makin) *mid-div: effrt and edgd lft over 1f out: sn wknd: eased* **8/1**2
1050 16 7 **Dubai Legend**46 5471 3-9-2 **73** J-PGuillambert 4 9
(D M Simcock) *mid-div on outer: nvr trbld ldrs: eased over 1f out* **20/1**

1m 15.93s (1.03) **Going Correction** +0.25s/f (Good) **16** Ran SP% **120.5**
Speed ratings (Par 101): **103,99,98,97,97 96,96,94,92,91 90,90,88,87,81 71**
toteswingers: 1&2 £24.50, 1&3 £76.80, 2&3 £66.50 CSF £109.63 CT £7311.58 TOTE £15.70: £3.20, £2.00, £9.90, £3.60; EX 119.70.
Owner Thurloe Thoroughbreds XIV **Bred** Mrs D J Hughes **Trained** Kingston Warren, Oxon

FOCUS
A tight 3-y-o sprint handicap, run at a sound pace and once more the stands' rail was the place to be. The form looks sound amongst the principals.
George Thisby Official explanation: jockey said gelding was restless in stalls and never travelled
Sometsuke Official explanation: jockey sasid gelding stopped quickly

6799 MOORES ELECTRICAL H'CAP 5f 13y
5:40 (5:41) (Class 6) (0-65,65) 3-Y-O+ **£2,047** (£604; £302) **Stalls** High

Form RPR
3452 1 **Solemn**3 6739 4-9-1 **65** (b) MCGeran(3) 4 76
(J M Bradley) *chsd ldrs: rdn to ld and hung lft fr over 1f out: r.o wl* **7/1**3
4065 2 1 3/4 **Joyeaux**9 6572 7-8-10 **60** FrederikTylicki(3) 8 65+
(Ollie Pears) *hld up: rdn over 1f out: r.o ins fnl f: nt rch wnr* **7/1**3
0453 3 shd **Mazzola**5 6669 3-8-9 **63** IJBrennan(7) 16 68
(M R Channon) *led: rdn and hdd over 1f out: styd on* **8/1**
0003 4 nk **Chosen One (IRE)**28 6010 4-8-13 **60** TomEaves 9 64
(B Smart) *prom: rdn over 1f out: styd on* **13/2**2
6400 5 nk **Jilly Why (IRE)**24 6175 8-9-2 **63** (b) SilvestreDeSousa 2 65
(Paul Green) *mid-div: pushed along 1/2-way: hdwy over 1f out: nt rch ldrs* **14/1**
2030 6 nk **Compton Classic**29 5989 7-8-10 **62** (p) JemmaMarshall(5) 12 63
(J R Boyle) *chsd ldrs: rdn over 1f out: styd on* **16/1**
5052 7 nk **Tartatartufata**40 5675 7-9-3 **64** (v) J-PGuillambert 13 64
(J G Given) *trckd ldrs: rdn 1/2-way: kpt on* **9/1**
000 8 1/2 **After The Show**134 2596 8-9-4 **65** PhilipRobinson 11 64
(Rae Guest) *sn pushed along in mid-div: swtchd rt and hdwy over 1f out: nvr nr to ldrs* **20/1**
3600 9 nse **Russian Rocket (IRE)**30 5974 7-9-0 **61** TGMcLaughlin 6 59
(Mrs C A Dunnett) *chsd ldr tl rdn over 1f out: styd on same pce* **14/1**
3014 10 3/4 **Half A Crown (IRE)**14 6410 4-8-10 **57** (v) PhillipMakin 7 53
(M Dods) *s.i.s: hld up: hdwy whn nt clr run ins fnl f: nvr trbld ldrs* **17/2**
0405 11 1 **Pic Up Sticks**23 6186 10-8-12 **59** KirstyMilczarek 3 51
(B G Powell) *prom: rdn over 1f out: no ex fnl f* **40/1**
0403 12 shd **Lord Of The Reins (IRE)**47 5421 5-9-4 **65** PaulMulrennan 10 57
(J G Given) *s.i.s: sn pushed along in rr: n.d* **16/1**
-360 13 3/4 **Queen Sally (IRE)**29 5991 3-9-1 **62** RichardKingscote 1 51
(Tom Dascombe) *s.i.s: sn pushed along in rr: nvr trbld ldrs* **33/1**
0324 14 1/2 **Rosie Says No**15 6377 4-8-13 **60** (p) GrahamGibbons 15 47
(R M H Cowell) *s.i.s: rdn along thrght: a in rr* **6/1**1
5000 15 1 1/2 **Miss Daawe**12 6489 5-8-10 **57** (bt) TonyHamilton 14 39
(B Ellison) *n.m.r sn after s: sn pushed along in rr: bhd fr 1/2-way* **22/1**
105 16 1 **Greek Secret**62 4998 6-8-10 **57** (b) TolleyDean 17 35
(J O'Reilly) *chsd ldrs tl rdn and wknd over 1f out* **28/1**

62.07 secs (1.07) **Going Correction** +0.25s/f (Good) **16** Ran SP% **127.3**
Speed ratings (Par 101): **101,98,98,97,97 96,96,95,95,94 92,92,91,90,87 86**
toteswingers: 1&2 £13.90, 1&3 £13.70, 2&3 £14.60 CSF £54.25 CT £432.88 TOTE £9.00: £1.80, £1.80, £2.20, £2.40; EX 66.90 Place 6: £24.59 Place 5: £20.05 .
Owner E A Hayward **Bred** Cheveley Park Stud Ltd **Trained** Sedbury, Gloucs

FOCUS
This was wide-open. The field again came stands' side, but the winner prevailed despite hanging all the way over to the far rail. Straightforward form, with the winner better than ever.
Mazzola Official explanation: jockey said reins snapped shortly after start
T/Jkpt: £7,611.20 to a £1 stake. Pool: £58,960.50. 5.50 winning tickets. T/Plt: £10.60 to a £1 stake. Pool: £70,988.26. 4,855.35 winning tickets. T/Qpdt: £5.50 to a £1 stake. Pool: £3,457.41. 461.24 winning tickets. CR

6667 WOLVERHAMPTON (A.W) (L-H)
Thursday, October 15

OFFICIAL GOING: Standard
Wind: Nil Weather: Drizzle

6800 DINE IN THE HORIZONS RESTAURANT APPRENTICE H'CAP 1m 141y(P)
5:30 (5:30) (Class 7) (0-50,50) 3-Y-O+ **£2,183** (£644; £322) **Stalls** Low

Form RPR
263 1 **Gifted Heir (IRE)**33 5888 5-8-9 **50** NatashaEaton(5) 10 61
(A Bailey) *sn chsng ldr: lost 2nd over 4f out: chsd ldr again wl over 1f out: pushed along to ld ins fnl f: r.o wl* **15/2**
0042 2 2 3/4 **Herbert Crescent**5 6674 4-9-0 **50** JohnCavanagh 3 55
(Ollie Pears) *a.p: rdn 2f out: edgd lft over 1f out: r.o to take 2nd towards fin: nt trble wnr* **11/4**1
00/2 3 1/2 **Insomnitas**9 5846 4-9-0 **50** SPRyan 5 54
(Seamus Fahey, Ire) *s.i.s: hld up towards rr: hdwy on ins over 2f out: sn rdn: kpt on ins fnl f* **8/1**
0-60 4 2 1/4 **Private Soldier**119 3077 6-8-13 **49** SoniaEaton 1 47
(Tom Dascombe) *led: pushed along and hdd ins fnl f: wknd towards fin* **11/2**3
0245 5 1 1/4 **Emperor's Well**23 6184 10-8-12 **48** (b) MatthewLawson 2 43
(M W Easterby) *plld hrd in tch: lost pl 5f out: pushed along over 2f out: rdn over 1f out: edgd lft ins fnl f: kpt on* **4/1**2
0000 6 3/4 **Kannon**2 6755 4-8-9 **48** AdamCarter(3) 9 42
(I W McInnes) *hld up in rr: pushed along and struggling 3f out: rdn and edgd lft over 1f out: swtchd rt ins fnl f: nvr nrr* **20/1**
0 7 2 1/4 **Fathzo (IRE)**39 5702 5-8-9 **50** LeeTopliss(5) 6 39
(Gerard Keane, Ire) *hdwy over 6f out: wknd 2f out* **8/1**
3500 8 1 **Gracechurch (IRE)**22 6208 6-9-0 **50** RichardRowe 4 36
(R J Hodges) *hld up in mid-div: rdn over 2f out: c wd st: sn bhd* **8/1**
-060 9 hd **Minwir (IRE)**33 5883 4-8-12 **48** NSLawes 8 34
(W M Brisbourne) *prom: chsd ldr over 4f out tl pushed along wl over 1f out: sn wknd* **25/1**
0 10 36 **Polar Gold**24 6175 7-8-10 **49** AlexEdwards(3) 7 —
(A J Chamberlain) *s.i.s: a in rr: t.o fnl 3f* **100/1**

1m 50.77s (0.27) **Going Correction** -0.075s/f (Stan) **10** Ran SP% **116.7**
Speed ratings (Par 97): **95,92,92,90,89 88,86,85,85,53**
toteswingers: 1&2 £5.10, 1&3 £10.70, 2&3 £5.10 CSF £27.99 CT £176.81 TOTE £6.10: £2.00, £1.10, £2.70; EX 17.60.
Owner A Bailey **Bred** A Malone **Trained** Newmarket, Suffolk

FOCUS
This was a weak handicap. The winner is rated to his best.
Emperor's Well Official explanation: jockey said gelding ran too free

6801 BOS MAGAZINE FILLIES' H'CAP 5f 20y(P)
6:00 (6:01) (Class 4) (0-80,79) 3-Y-O+ **£5,046** (£1,510; £755; £377; £188) **Stalls** Low

Form RPR
3226 1 **Feelin Foxy**13 6459 5-9-3 **78** AlanMunro 7 87
(J G Given) *sn chsng ldr: rdn to ld wl ins fnl f: r.o wl* **8/1**
5204 2 1 3/4 **Cayman Fox**13 6456 4-7-11 **65** oh5 (e) MatthewLawson(7) 5 68
(James Moffatt) *led: clr over 2f out: rdn over 1f out: ct wl ins fnl f* **7/1**
5133 3 1 **Welsh Opera**17 6335 4-8-0 **66** oh1 ow1 (v) SophieDoyle(5) 9 65+
(S C Williams) *outpcd in rr: hdwy on ins wl over 1f out: kpt on u.p to take 3rd wl ins fnl f* **14/1**
0520 4 3/4 **Sweet Applause (IRE)**28 6010 3-8-4 **70** ow3 MatthewDavies(5) 2 67
(A P Jarvis) *hld up and bhd: hdwy on ins over 2f out: rdn over 1f out: r.o towards fin* **9/1**
0315 5 1/2 **Revue Princess (IRE)**2 6764 4-8-5 **66** (b) DuranFentiman 1 61
(T D Easterby) *a.p: pushed along 2f out: rdn jst over 1f out: kpt on same pce* **5/2**1
2154 6 3 1/2 **Weet A Surprise**9 6572 4-8-3 **71** (v) AlexEdwards(7) 10 53
(J W Unett) *hld up: pushed along 2f out: c wd st: rdn jst over 1f out: n.d* **7/1**
00 7 3/4 **Drifting Gold**47 5436 5-8-12 **73** (b) EddieAhern 4 53
(C G Cox) *hld up in tch: rdn and wknd over 1f out* **13/2**3
5044 8 1 1/2 **Jord (IRE)**78 4435 5-8-5 **66** (p) SaleemGolam 8 40
(J A Glover) *hld up: pushed along 3f out: bhd fnl 2f* **20/1**
212- 9 6 **Anne Of Kiev (IRE)**355 6990 4-9-4 **79** NCallan 6 32
(J R Gask) *hld up in tch: wknd wl over 1f out* **5/1**2

61.18 secs (-1.12) **Going Correction** -0.075s/f (Stan) **9** Ran SP% **116.1**
Speed ratings (Par 102): **105,102,100,99,98 93,91,89,79**
toteswingers: 1&2 £5.90, 1&3 £6.40, 2&3 £9.20 CSF £63.02 CT £780.10 TOTE £6.10: £1.90, £3.30, £3.60; EX 18.20.
Owner Danethorpe Racing Partnership **Bred** Bearstone Stud **Trained** Willoughton, Lincs

FOCUS
A fair sprint handicap. The first pair were always 1-2.

6802 EUROPEAN BREEDERS' FUND MAIDEN STKS 5f 216y(P)
6:30 (6:31) (Class 5) 2-Y-O **£3,561** (£1,059; £529; £264) **Stalls** Low

Form RPR

402 **1** **I'Malwaysright (IRE)**[36] 5776 2-9-3 72 RobertWinston 1 72
(D R C Elsworth) *sn led: rdn over 1f out: drvn out* **10/1**[3]

4323 **2** *nk* **Barlaman (USA)**[17] 6347 2-9-3 72 (t) TedDurcan 11 71
(Saeed Bin Suroor) *hld up in mid-div: hdwy and n.m.r briefly 2f out: rdn and r.o to take 2nd nr fin* **7/2**[2]

03 **3** *hd* **Autocracy**[75] 4546 2-9-3 0 LiamJones 3 71
(W J Haggas) *a.p: chsd wnr over 2f out: rdn and kpt on ins fnl f* **10/1**[3]

4 *hd* **Tomatin** 2-9-3 0 AlanMunro 5 70
(P W Chapple-Hyam) *s.s: hld up and bhd: hdwy on ins wl over 1f out: sn rdn: kpt on ins fnl f* **10/1**[3]

42 **5** *1 1/4* **King Of Windsor (IRE)**[55] 5212 2-8-12 0 LanceBetts(5) 9 66
(R M Beckett) *a.p: pushed along over 2f out: rdn wl over 1f out: kpt on same pce* **4/6**[1]

00 **6** *2 3/4* **Goodison Goal (IRE)**[14] 6408 2-8-12 0 SaleemGolam 8 53
(Patrick Morris) *s.i.s: sn chsng ldrs: rdn over 1f out: wknd ins fnl f* **100/1**

7 *6* **Princess Mandy (IRE)** 2-8-12 0 NCallan 4 35
(K A Ryan) *s.s: in rr: pushed along 3f out: struggling fnl 2f* **33/1**

0 **8** *3/4* **True To Form (IRE)**[16] 6356 2-9-3 0 StephenDonohoe 10 41+
(Sir Mark Prescott) *sn in rr: pushed along and struggling over 2f out* **66/1**

9 *7* **Rafiki (IRE)** 2-9-3 0 EddieAhern 2 17
(W R Swinburn) *s.v.s: a in rr* **28/1**

10 *3 1/4* **Bertie Buckle (IRE)** 2-9-3 0 DuranFentiman 7 7
(J R Gask) *led early: chsd wnr tl rdn over 2f out: wknd wl over 1f out* **66/1**

1m 15.46s (0.46) **Going Correction** -0.075s/f (Stan) **10** Ran SP% **119.8**
Speed ratings (Par 95): **93,92,92,92,90 86,78,77,68,64**
toteswingers: 1&2 £5.90, 1&3 £11.80, 2&3 £4.40 CSF £45.38 TOTE £3.90: £2.10, £1.10, £2.30; EX 39.50.
Owner Yan Wah Wu **Bred** Liam Ormsby **Trained** Newmarket, Suffolk

FOCUS
Nothing more than a modest maiden. The form is rated around the principals.

NOTEBOOK
I'Malwaysright(IRE), second from a mark of 70 on his recent nursery debut, looked vulnerable to some of these, but he found improvement for the return to 6f and made a lot of the running to score. He is clearly going the right way now and should continue to progress back in handicaps.
Barlaman(USA), slightly disappointing when third at the course last time, may well have been an unlucky loser on this occasion, for he was short of room at a key stage and couldn´t quite get there in time. He should benefit from a step up to 7f, but clearly isn´t one of his yard's better prospects. (op 100-30 tchd 3-1)
Autocracy, most disappointing over 5f at Thirsk last time, was always likely to appreciate the extra furlong of this contest and ran easily his best effort to date. He is now qualified for a handicap mark. (op 15-2)
Tomatin, a newcomer by Kyllachy, made a really promising debut back in fourth, keeping on nicely having been slowly away and got behind. This was a promising start and he should be able to win something similar. (op 8-1)
King Of Windsor(IRE) had twice shown a fair level of ability in Salisbury maidens. He was always nicely positioned, but simply couldn´t quicken under pressure and the surface evidently didn´t suit. On the plus side, he is now qualified for a handicap mark. (op 10-11)

6803 ELBO BETTING SERVICE FOR INDEPENDENT BOOKMAKERS H'CAP 2m 119y(P)
7:00 (7:00) (Class 4) (0-85,81) 3-Y-O+ **£5,046** (£1,510; £755; £377) **Stalls** Low

Form RPR

5/6- **1** **Monahullan Prince**[28] 6042 8-9-2 68 ChrisCatlin 4 76+
(Gerard Keane, Ire) *s.i.s: hld up in tch: pushed along over 5f out: led 4f out: rdn wl over 1f out: styd on* **5/1**[3]

2131 **2** *3/4* **John Forbes**[14] 6432 7-9-2 73 LanceBetts(5) 1 79
(B Ellison) *led early: led after 3f: hdd over 6f out: outpcd 5f out: sn rdn: rallied wl over 1f out: edgd lft and styd on to take 2nd ins fnl f: nt rch wnr* **9/1**

110 **3** *3 1/4* **Penang Princess**[55] 5230 3-9-4 81 RobertWinston 3 83
(R M Beckett) *sn led: hdd after 3f: chsd ldr: led briefly over 6f out: chsd wnr: pushed along 5f out: rdn 2f out: edgd rt over 1f out: lost 2nd and no ex ins fnl f* **4/5**[1]

2214 **4** *50* **Spiekeroog**[68] 4785 3-9-3 80 (b[1]) TPQueally 2 22
(H R A Cecil) *hld up in tch: led over 6f out to 4f out: wknd over 3f out: eased wl over 1f out: lame* **11/4**[2]

3m 40.35s (-1.45) **Going Correction** -0.075s/f (Stan)
WFA 3 from 7yo+ 11lb **4** Ran SP% **108.9**
Speed ratings (Par 105): **100,99,98,74**
CSF £35.20 TOTE £4.30; EX 15.00.
Owner Mrs E Keane **Bred** Templeton Stud **Trained** Trim, Co Meath

FOCUS
Only the four runners, but this was still a competitive event. The front pair in the market disappointed though and it is doubtful this took much winning.
Spiekeroog Official explanation: vet said colt was lame behind

6804 ENJOY THE LUCKY 7 GROUP OFFER CLAIMING STKS 1m 1f 103y(P)
7:30 (7:30) (Class 6) 3-Y-O **£2,388** (£705; £352) **Stalls** Low

Form RPR

2454 **1** **Gaily Noble (IRE)**[25] 6137 3-9-7 80 KFallon 8 79
(A B Haynes) *sn led: drvn out fnl f* **11/4**[1]

2066 **2** *1 3/4* **Johnmanderville**[20] 6250 3-9-2 76 (p) MartinLane(5) 7 76
(A P Jarvis) *a.p: chsd wnr over 3f out: rdn over 2f out: styd on same pce fnl f* **7/1**[3]

0336 **3** *1 3/4* **Farncombe (IRE)**[7] 6611 3-8-12 70 TedDurcan 4 63
(M P Tregoning) *hld up in tch: rdn and lost pl over 3f out: styd on on ins fr over 1f out: tk 3rd towards fin* **8/1**

000 **4** *hd* **Enhancing**[2] 6755 3-8-3 55 (v) ChrisCatlin 1 54
(J A Glover) *hld up in mid-div: n.m.r on ins bnd over 6f out: hdwy over 2f out: rdn over 1f out: styd on same pce* **25/1**

0001 **5** *2 1/2* **Why Nee Amy**[29] 5982 3-7-12 56 LauraPike(7) 5 50
(T Keddy) *hld up in mid-div: stdy prog over 6f out: rdn and edgd lft over 1f out: no imp* **16/1**

0000 **6** *3 3/4* **Ay Tay Tate (IRE)**[41] 5624 3-8-13 50 GrahamGibbons 9 50
(D Shaw) *hld up in rr: pushed along and hdwy on ins over 2f out: sn rdn: no further prog* **66/1**

3000 **7** *3/4* **Andean Margin (IRE)**[23] 6178 3-9-1 73 PaulMulrennan 3 51
(M W Easterby) *hld up in tch: rdn over 2f out: wknd over 1f out* **16/1**

0010 **8** *3 1/4* **Inconspicuous Miss (USA)**[15] 6376 3-8-5 68 MatthewDavies(5) 13 39
(George Baker) *hld up in rr: nt clr run briefly over 2f out: sme prog on ins wl over 1f out: n.d* **9/1**

2303 **9** *5* **Abulharith**[9] 6570 3-8-13 59 RobertWinston 12 32
(R A Harris) *hld up towards rr: pushed along and c wd bnd over 2f out: sn struggling* **16/1**

0600 **10** *1 1/2* **Latin Tinge (USA)**[7] 6618 3-8-12 77 (b[1]) NCallan 2 27
(P F I Cole) *hld up in mid-div: pushed along over 3f out: sn bhd* **4/1**[2]

0005 **11** *2 1/4* **Royal Crest**[40] 5683 3-8-10 57 FrancisNorton 6 21
(J A Osborne) *a in rr* **11/1**

5060 **12** *2 1/2* **Fortunate Flame**[26] 6123 3-8-11 60 (v[1]) PhillipMakin 10 16
(K A Ryan) *prom: pushed along over 3f out: sn wknd* **25/1**

0000 **13** *3/4* **Red Reef**[21] 6226 3-8-7 55 (v[1]) EddieAhern 11 11
(D J Coakley) *prom: chsd wnr over 6f out tl over 3f out: wknd wl over 2f out* **25/1**

1m 59.96s (-1.74) **Going Correction** -0.075s/f (Stan) **13** Ran SP% **119.3**
Speed ratings (Par 99): **104,102,100,100,98 95,94,91,87,85 83,81,80**
toteswingers: 1&2 £6.40, 1&3 £3.50, 2&3 £16.80 CSF £20.93 TOTE £3.20: £1.90, £2.00, £3.40; EX 26.50.
Owner Ms J Loylert **Bred** Garry Chong **Trained** Limpley Stoke, Bath

FOCUS
This was a fair claimer but it is probably not form to take too positively. The fourth is the most likely guide.

6805 INDEPENDENT BOOKMAKERS SERVICE ELBO LAUNCHES TODAY NURSERY 1m 141y(P)
8:00 (8:01) (Class 4) (0-85,85) 2-Y-O **£4,533** (£1,348; £674; £336) **Stalls** Low

Form RPR

5421 **1** **Spanish Duke (IRE)**[17] 6334 2-9-0 78 EddieAhern 6 82+
(J L Dunlop) *hld up: smooth prog over 2f out: carried hd awkwardly and rdn to ld 1f out: rdn out* **4/1**[2]

1 **2** *3/4* **Diam Queen (GER)**[38] 5722 2-9-0 78 KFallon 7 80+
(L M Cumani) *n.m.r s: hld up and bhd: rdn 3f out: hdwy on outside 2f out: rdn and chsd wnr ins fnl f: nt qckn* **4/1**[2]

053 **3** *1 1/4* **Architrave**[21] 6235 2-8-8 72 ChrisCatlin 9 72
(Sir Mark Prescott) *chsd ldr after 1f: rdn over 2f out: ev ch over 1f out: no ex ins fnl f* **14/1**

61 **4** *1/2* **Graymalkin (IRE)**[19] 6285 2-9-5 83 TedDurcan 2 82
(Saeed Bin Suroor) *chsd ldr 1f: a.p: rdn and ev ch over 1f out: one pce ins fnl f* **6/4**[1]

0144 **5** *1* **Flipping**[24] 6173 2-9-2 80 IanMongan 3 77
(W S Kittow) *hld up: pushed along over 2f out: hdwy and swtchd rt over 1f out: rdn and one pce ins fnl f* **5/1**[3]

1634 **6** *1* **Universal Circus**[12] 6471 2-9-1 79 SamHitchcott 1 74
(M R Channon) *led: rdn and hdd 1f out: wknd ins fnl f* **14/1**

1020 **7** *1/2* **The Starboard Bow**[18] 6305 2-9-2 85 LeeNewnes(5) 10 79
(S Kirk) *hld up in rr: pushed along over 2f out: rdn wl over 1f out: n.d* **28/1**

2012 **8** *3* **Sejanus**[12] 6491 2-9-1 79 NCallan 4 66
(K A Ryan) *prom: pushed along over 2f out: wknd wl over 1f out* **11/2**[3]

1m 49.89s (-0.61) **Going Correction** -0.075s/f (Stan) **8** Ran SP% **114.6**
Speed ratings (Par 97): **99,98,97,96,95 95,94,91**
toteswingers: 1&2 £5.00, 1&3 £9.10, 2&3 £12.00 CSF £20.45 CT £201.38 TOTE £5.70: £2.00, £1.90, £3.30; EX 26.40.
Owner Windflower Overseas Holdings Inc **Bred** Windflower Overseas Holdings Inc **Trained** Arundel, W Sussex

FOCUS
This was probably a fair nursery. The first two improved and the form should work out.

NOTEBOOK
Spanish Duke(IRE), easy winner of a 7f maiden at Brighton last time, looked open to further improvement on this step back up in trip and, despite looking a little awkward by way of a funny head carriage, he found enough to score. He is clearly going the right way and will improve for a further step up in trip. (op 9-2)
Diam Queen(GER), winner of a 7f maiden at Folkestone on her debut, was always likely to benefit from the extra furlong and may well have won had she not been squeezed for room at the start. Forced to be held up, she came through wide to take second and should be capable of gaining compensation. (op 11-4)
Architrave was always likely to improve once going handicapping and he ran well, but couldn't quicken at the business end and was ultimately unable to match the front pair. We have still to see the best of him. (op 16-1 tchd 12-1)
Graymalkin(IRE) looked to be making his handicap debut from a fair mark and was understandably made favourite, but he just lacked that vital change of pace when it mattered. (op 7-4)
Flipping made some late headway having been held up on this handicap debut, but it remains to be seen if he is capable of winning off this mark. Official explanation: jockey said gelding suffered interference in running

6806 SPONSOR A RACE BY CALLING 01902 390000 H'CAP 1m 1f 103y(P)
8:30 (8:30) (Class 5) (0-70,66) 3-Y-O+ **£2,914** (£867; £433; £216) **Stalls** Low

Form RPR

0005 **1** **Kildare Sun (IRE)**[13] 6462 7-9-6 66 (p) GrahamGibbons 8 74
(J Mackie) *a.p: wnt 2nd jst over 3f out: pushed along over 2f out: led wl over 1f out: drvn out* **12/1**

6206 **2** *1/2* **Lunar River (FR)**[17] 6346 6-9-6 66 (t) EddieAhern 5 73
(David Pinder) *hld up in tch: chsd wnr ins fnl f: sn rdn: nt qckn* **12/1**

4032 **3** *3 1/2* **Arashi**[17] 6349 3-9-2 66 (p) KFallon 2 66+
(Lucinda Featherstone) *led early: led 7f out: hdd wl over 1f out: sn rdn: no ex ins fnl f* **15/8**[1]

2100 **4** *3 1/4* **King Of Connacht**[5] 6668 6-8-12 58 (p) LiamJones 6 51
(M Wellings) *hld up towards rr: pushed along over 3f out: hdwy over 2f out: wknd over 1f out* **12/1**

0556 **5** *5* **Hucking Heat (IRE)**[12] 6496 5-9-6 66 (p) ChrisCatlin 9 48
(R Hollinshead) *hld up in rr: pushed along and hdwy on ins over 2f out: rdn and wknd over 1f out* **7/1**[3]

2000 **6** *13* **Top Seed (IRE)**[26] 6126 8-8-10 56 SamHitchcott 4 11
(M S Tuck) *n.m.r s: in rr: pushed along 4f out: struggling over 2f out* **33/1**

005- **7** *18* **Chia (IRE)**[486] 3089 6-9-5 65 (p) NCallan 3 —
(D Haydn Jones) *sn led: hdd 7f out: chsd ldr tl rdn jst over 3f out: wknd over 2f out: eased wl over 1f out* **12/1**

0060 **8** *53* **Brer Rabbit**[10] 6547 3-9-1 65 RobertWinston 1 —
(B W Hills) *prom: rdn over 4f out: sn wknd: eased over 3f out* **12/1**

00-5 **9** *3 1/4* **Flodden Field**[91] 4022 3-8-13 63 AlanMunro 7 —
(P W Chapple-Hyam) *hld up in rr: eased whn btn 3f out: lame* **11/4**[2]

2m 0.96s (-0.74) **Going Correction** -0.075s/f (Stan)
WFA 3 from 5yo+ 4lb **9** Ran SP% **115.4**
Speed ratings (Par 103): **100,99,96,93,89 77,61,14,11**
toteswingers: 1&2 £13.00, 1&3 £14.40, 2&3 £3.50 CSF £144.78 CT £392.49 TOTE £17.00: £2.60, £2.50, £1.10; EX 108.20.

Owner Mrs Barbara Woodworth **Bred** Gordan Woodworth **Trained** Church Broughton , Derbys

FOCUS

This was a moderate handicap in which the first pair chased a strong pace. The winner was back to something like his best.

Kildare Sun(IRE) Official explanation: trainer said, regarding apparent improvement in form, that the gelding was better suited by the step up in trip.

Brer Rabbit Official explanation: jockey said filly lost its action

Flodden Field Official explanation: vet said gelding finished lame

6807 ENJOY RINGSIDE ENTERTAINMENT AFTER RACING H'CAP 1m 4f 50y(P)

9:00 (9:00) (Class 6) (0-65,65) 3-Y-O **£2,388** (£705; £352) **Stalls** Low

Form RPR

0000 **1** **Admirable Duque (IRE)**[7] 6613 3-8-11 **65**....................(p) BillyCray(7) 4 76
(D J S Ffrench Davis) *hld up towards rr: pushed along over 3f out: hdwy wl over 1f out: rdn to ld ins fnl f: r.o wl* **14/1**

00-0 **2** *2 ½* **Kazbow (IRE)**[37] 5744 3-9-3 **64**.................................... KFallon 6 71+
(L M Cumani) *a.p: chsd ldr over 7f out: led wl over 1f out: sn rdn: hdd and no ex ins fnl f* **2/1**[1]

0506 **3** *5* **Supernoverre (IRE)**[15] 6376 3-9-4 **65**.............................. IanMongan 1 64
(P Howling) *a.p: rdn over 1f out: wknd ins fnl f* **15/2**

5062 **4** *2* **M'Lady Rousseur (IRE)**[13] 6446 3-8-12 **59**.............. DaneO'Neill 8 55
(D R C Elsworth) *hld up in mid-div: hdwy over 6f out: pushed along over 3f out: rdn and wknd fnl f* **13/2**[3]

3041 **5** *2 ¼* **Tinkerbelle (IRE)**[13] 6446 3-9-4 **65**.............................(p) EddieAhern 11 57
(J L Dunlop) *hld up towards rr: stdy hdwy on outside over 3f out: rdn over 1f out: wknd fnl f* **9/2**[2]

0000 **6** *½* **Bessie Lou (IRE)**[27] 6052 3-9-1 **62**............................(p) PhillipMakin 12 53
(K A Ryan) *led: rdn over 2f out: hdd wl over 1f out: wknd ins fnl f* **25/1**

6060 **7** *½* **Royal Keva (IRE)**[12] 6498 3-8-8 **60**.............................. DeanHeslop(5) 2 51
(A D Brown) *hld up in rr: pushed along on outside over 2f out: c wd st: rdn wl over 1f out: edgd lft ent fnl f: nvr nr ldrs* **14/1**

0460 **8** *nk* **Clippity Clop (IRE)**[28] 6031 3-9-4 **65**.............................. ChrisCatlin 5 55
(J A Osborne) *hld up in tch: pushed along and lost pl over 3f out: sn bhd* **12/1**

6-00 **9** *1 ½* **Great Bounder (CAN)**[57] 5152 3-9-3 **64**.................. RobertWinston 7 52
(J R Best) *chsd ldr over 4f: prom: pushed along over 3f out: rdn over 2f out: wknd 1f out* **12/1**

2006 **10** *2* **Hold The Star**[17] 6349 3-9-0 **61**.................................... TPQueally 9 46
(E F Vaughan) *hld up towards rr: pushed along 2f out: rdn and struggling jst over 1f out* **10/1**

2m 39.89s (-1.21) **Going Correction** -0.075s/f (Stan) **10** Ran SP% **118.3**

Speed ratings (Par 99): **101,99,96,94,93 92,92,92,91,89**

toteswingers: 1&2 £29.30, 1&3 £10.60, 2&3 £9.90 CSF £42.90 CT £238.67 TOTE £16.80: £4.20, £1.50, £2.20; EX 73.60 Place 6: £835.39, Place 5: £373.79..

Owner Brian W Taylor **Bred** Airlie Stud And R N Clay **Trained** Lambourn, Berks

FOCUS

A modest handicap. The winner is rated back to his early-season form.

Bessie Lou(IRE) Official explanation: jockey said filly hung right

T/Plt: £274.00 to a £1 stake. Pool: £67,839.35. 180.69 winning tickets. T/Qpdt: £44.10 to a £1 stake. Pool: £7,854.01. 131.60 winning tickets. KH

6477 NEWMARKET (R-H)

Friday, October 16

OFFICIAL GOING: Good (8.3)

Far-side track in use.

Wind: Fresh behind Weather: Overcast

6809 E B F FEDERATION OF BLOODSTOCK AGENTS MAIDEN STKS 6f

1:30 (1:32) (Class 4) 2-Y-O **£5,828** (£1,734; £866; £432) **Stalls** High

Form RPR

1 **Inler (IRE)** 2-9-3 0.. TonyCulhane 4 93+
(J R Best) *w'like: scope: str: mde all: shkn up over 1f out: rdn and r.o wl ins fnl f* **1/1**[1]

03 **2** *4* **Chaussini**[31] 5969 2-8-12 0.................................. JimmyFortune 11 76
(J A R Toller) *w'like: attractive: bit bkwd: a.p: chsd wnr over 2f out: rdn over 1f out: outpcd ins fnl f* **7/2**[2]

0 **3** *2 ½* **Maashooq**[53] 5311 2-9-3 0.. TPO'Shea 1 74
(M P Tregoning) *str: lw: chsd ldrs: rdn over 2f out: styd on same pce appr fnl f* **25/1**

333 **4** *½* **San Jemeniano (IRE)**[13] 6493 2-9-3 **87**.......................... RyanMoore 9 72
(P W Chapple-Hyam) *chsd wnr tl rdn 1/2-way: styd on same pce appr fnl f* **6/1**[3]

5 *¾* **Progress (IRE)** 2-8-12 0.. KFallon 5 65+
(J Noseda) *w'like: cl-cpld: s.i.s: sn pushed along in rr: styd on fr over 2f out: nt trble ldrs* **14/1**

663 **6** *1 ½* **Kerchak (USA)**[28] 6061 2-9-3 **79**.................................. JoeFanning 8 65
(W Jarvis) *lw: chsd ldrs: rdn over 2f out: wknd over 1f out* **9/1**

7 *1* **En Fuego** 2-9-3 0.. AlanMunro 10 62+
(P W Chapple-Hyam) *w'like: athletic: bit bkwd: s.i.s and rn green in rr: nvr nrr* **20/1**

8 *nk* **House Point** 2-8-9 0.. WilliamCarson(3) 2 56
(S C Williams) *s.i.s: hld up: swtchd rt over 2f out: n.d* **66/1**

04 **9** *3* **Taeping (IRE)**[11] 6542 2-9-3 0.................................... ChrisCatlin 7 52
(R Hollinshead) *lw: prom: rdn over 2f out: sn wknd* **100/1**

0 **10** *19* **Chorus Boy**[53] 5318 2-9-3 0.. TPQueally 3 —
(G G Margarson) *leggy: mid-div: sn pushed along: wknd over 3f out* **150/1**

1m 12.55s (0.35) **Going Correction** +0.05s/f (Good) **10** Ran SP% **114.9**

Speed ratings (Par 97): **99,93,90,89,88 86,85,84,80,55**

toteswingers: 1&2 £3.40, 1&3 £7.80, 2&3 £10.60 CSF £4.21 TOTE £2.20: £1.30, £1.50, £4.40; EX 6.60.

Owner Mrs M Findlay **Bred** D And J Cantillon & C & K Canning **Trained** Hucking, Kent

FOCUS

This is often a fair juvenile maiden and the form looks sound rated through the runner-up. The winner impressed.

NOTEBOOK

Inler(IRE) ◆ arrived at the track with a tall reputation with his trainer stating before the race "he is as nice a 2-y-o that I have had through my hands", which is some statement remembering he handled Kingsgate Native as a juvenile. He has had problems this year with sore shins, hence the late debut, but was ready to run earlier this month and well fancied before the ground went against him. He got backed accordingly here and didn't disappoint, doing the job comfortably. Despite taking time to load up, he pinged out when the stalls opened before being restrained into a share of the lead. It was clear coming to the furlong marker he was still full of running and he quickened clear to settle the issue when asked for an effort. He jinked when right out in front, but that was due to greenness and he will no doubt learn plenty for this initial experience. It also bodes very well for his future that he showed the speed to win so well over this trip first time up, considering he is bred to enjoy around 1m as a 3-y-o and he rates a decent prospect for next year. (op 5-4 after early 13-8 6-4 and 11-8 in places)

Chaussini has to be considered unfortunate to have bumped into the winner as she finished a clear second-best. She shaped better than the bare form on her previous outing at Yarmouth (form working out nicely) and was not surprisingly fancied to go well here. She had the benefit of the far rail to race against, but did things nicely through the race and time will likely tell there was certainly no disgrace in losing out to Inler. She now qualifies for nurseries and should soon be found an opening. (op 4-1)

Maashooq was having his first run since running distinctly green on debut at Kempton 53 days earlier and, while he was not easy to fancy on paper, his trainer's past record in this race had to make him of interest. He looks to have done well physically since his debut and confirmed he is an improver with a much more encouraging display in defeat. The way he stayed on suggests another would suit ideally now, something his breeding backs up, and he can be placed to get off the mark before the season is out. (op 33-1)

San Jemeniano(IRE) set the standard with an official mark of 87. He raced handily, but got outpaced nearing the 2f pole and lacked any sort of gear change. He is flattered by his current mark and isn't going to prove simple to place. (op 9-2)

Progress(IRE) kept on nicely without ever threatening after making a tardy start. She ought to improve a bundle for the experience and looks sure to relish a stiffer test. (op 16-1 tchd 12-1)

Kerchak(USA) ran his race and is probably a touch flattered by his mark, but his optimum trip is uncertain at this stage. (op 7-1)

En Fuego was the second-string from his stable according to the betting and proved too green to do himself justice. The manner in which he finished his race is an indication that better should be expected next time, however.

House Point was never going the pace to get seriously involved, but left the impression she would benefit a good deal for the run. She is another that will come into her own over further according to pedigree.

Taeping(IRE) dropped out from halfway and found it too hot, but now has the option of nurseries.

6810 ANGLO HIBERNIAN BLOODSTOCK INSURANCE E B F MAIDEN STKS 1m

2:00 (2:03) (Class 4) 2-Y-O **£5,828** (£1,734; £866; £432) **Stalls** High

Form RPR

003 **1** **Invincible Soul (IRE)**[14] 6451 2-9-3 **77**.......................... RichardHughes 8 85
(R Hannon) *chsd ldrs: led over 1f out: sn rdn and hung rt: r.o* **7/1**

2 *hd* **Fair Trade** 2-9-3 0.. EddieAhern 10 85
(D R C Elsworth) *tall: str: bit bkwd: a.p: pushed along over 2f out: rdn and hung lft over 1f out: r.o wl* **40/1**

34 **3** *2* **Munsarim (IRE)**[36] 5793 2-9-3 0.................................... TPO'Shea 9 80
(J L Dunlop) *b: chsd ldr: rdn and ev ch over 1f out: edgd rt and no ex ins fnl f* **7/1**

4 *3* **Nibani (IRE)** 2-9-3 0.. RyanMoore 11 74+
(Sir Michael Stoute) *s.i.s: sn pushed along in rr: styd on fr over 1f out: nt rch ldrs* **20/1**

2 **5** *¾* **William Van Gogh**[15] 6423 2-9-3 0.............................. JimmyFortune 12 72
(J H M Gosden) *lw: led: rdn and hdd over 1f out: wknd ins fnl f* **5/2**[1]

6 *½* **Pekan Three (IRE)** 2-9-3 0.. NCallan 13 71+
(P F I Cole) *str: bit bkwd: s.i.s: sn pushed along in rr: styd on fr over 1f out: nvr nrr* **16/1**

7 *nk* **Fatanah (IRE)** 2-8-12 0.. TedDurcan 4 65+
(M P Tregoning) *unf: s.i.s: sn pushed along in rr: hdwy fr over 1f out: n.d* **33/1**

2 **8** *nk* **Judiciary (IRE)**[16] 6382 2-9-3 0.................................... LDettori 2 69
(Saeed Bin Suroor) *w'like: scope: sn chsng ldrs: rdn over 2f out: wknd fnl f* **9/2**[2]

540 **9** *3 ¾* **Rasselas (IRE)**[13] 6478 2-9-3 **83**.................................. MichaelHills 6 61
(B W Hills) *prom: rdn over 2f out: wknd over 1f out* **11/1**

10 *6* **Sour Mash (IRE)** 2-9-3 0.. KFallon 5 48
(L M Cumani) *w'like: bit bkwd: hld up: pushed along 1/2-way: wknd 2f out* **18/1**

11 *1 ¾* **Yorksters Prince (IRE)** 2-9-3 0.................................. RobertWinston 7 44
(M G Quinlan) *leggy: athletic: s.s: sn in mid-div: rdn and wknd over 2f out* **100/1**

12 *10* **Mejd (IRE)** 2-9-3 0.. ChrisCatlin 3 22
(M R Channon) *w'like: lengthy: hld up: rdn: hung rt and wknd over 2f out* **100/1**

3 **13** *¾* **Theology**[15] 6423 2-9-3 0.. ShaneKelly 1 21
(J Noseda) *hld up: a in rr: hung rt and wknd 2f out* **13/2**[3]

1m 38.17s (-0.43) **Going Correction** +0.05s/f (Good) **13** Ran SP% **116.7**

Speed ratings (Par 97): **104,103,101,98,98 97,97,96,93,87 85,75,74**

toteswingers: 1&2 £58.00, 1&3 £10.50, 2&3 £54.50 CSF £269.33 TOTE £8.90: £2.50, £10.10, £2.90; EX 351.30.

Owner Patrick J Fahey **Bred** Mrs Ann Marie O'Brien **Trained** East Everleigh, Wilts

FOCUS

This looked a hot maiden and the time, marginally quicker than Champagne Style recorded when carrying 5lb less in the following conditions race, seems to confirm that. Plenty of winners should come out of it.

NOTEBOOK

Invincible Soul(IRE) proved well suited by the step up to 1m and produced an improved performance, building on his recent third over 7f at this track to run well above his official mark of 77. Having been well placed throughout, he briefly looked set to win quite well when getting to the front inside the final furlong, but he was being closed down fast by the runner-up near the line. He has the scope to make a very useful 3-y-o. (op 6-1 tchd 8-1)

Fair Trade ◆, an 80,000gns half-brother to, among others, useful multiple 1m-1m2f winner Island Sound, is a fine, big colt, although he was keen to post. In the race itself he was being pushed along over 3f out but he gradually got the idea and finished well, closing down the winner, who in turn was extending his advantage over the third. He might win a maiden this year but looks all over a 3-y-o and rates a very useful prospect.

Munsarim(IRE) was always handy after breaking sharply and had his chance, but he didn't see the race out as well as the front two, weakening late on. He now has the option of handicaps. (op 6-1)

Nibani(IRE) ◆, the first foal of a half-sister to Spectrum, is one to take from the race. He missed the break and was being niggled along from an early stage, but finished strongly as he got the hang of things and his stamina kicked in, and this was a taking debut. He should do really well over further next year. (op 14-1)

William Van Gogh is a big colt whom John Gosden believes will be well suited by middle-distances next year, so it was no surprise to see him given a positive ride, but he was soon well held. This wasn't a step forward from his debut. (op 11-4 tchd 9-4 and 3-1 in a place)
Pekan Three(IRE) ◆ ran a similar race to Nibani, lacking the experience and speed to threaten, but keeping on nicely late on. This 175,000gns half-brother to a 1m4f winner is another who should come into his own over further at three. (op 40-1)
Fatanah(IRE) ◆, the only filly, made a likeable debut and clearly has plenty of ability. She was pretty much clueless throughout and should do a lot better. (op 25-1)
Judiciary(IRE) failed to build on the form he showed in an ordinary Newcastle maiden on his debut. (op 4-1 tchd 11-2)
Rasselas(IRE) was a long way below his official rating of 83. (op 12-1)
Theology, green beforehand, was only 1 1/4l behind William Van Gough on debut over this C&D but he ran poorly this time. His draw was no help but he should still have fared a lot better. Official explanation: trainer had no explasnation for the poor form shown (op 8-1 tchd 6-1)

6811 SARISKA HOUGHTON CONDITIONS STKS — 1m

2:35 (2:35) (Class 2) 2-Y-O
£9,346 (£2,799; £1,399; £700; £349) **Stalls** High

Form — RPR

22 **1** — **Champagne Style (USA)**[44] 5580 2-8-12 0 .... RyanMoore 6 100
(B J Meehan) *lw: chsd ldrs: sn pushed along: rdn over 2f out: r.o u.p to ld ins fnl f: drvn clr: hung lft towards fin* **8/1**[3]

331 **2** 3 ¾ **Kalypso King (USA)**[8] 6617 2-9-3 0 .... RichardHughes 4 97
(R Hannon) *lw: sn led: rdn and edgd lft over 1f out: hdd and no ex ins fnl f* **6/4**[2]

143 **3** 2 ¾ **Emirates Dream (USA)**[27] 6133 2-9-3 104 .... LDettori 5 91
(Saeed Bin Suroor) *sn chsng ldr: rdn 2f out: wknd ins fnl f* **1/1**[1]

1U0 **4** 1 **Rodrigo De Torres**[13] 6486 2-9-3 88 .... TPQueally 1 89+
(H R A Cecil) *trckd ldrs: racd keenly: rdn over 1f out: wknd ins fnl f* **16/1**

105 **5** 13 **Invincible Prince (IRE)**[43] 5603 2-9-3 82 ....(b[1]) RichardKingscote 2 60
(R M Beckett) *pushed along in rr early: rdn over 3f out: wknd over 2f out* **66/1**

1m 38.23s (-0.37) **Going Correction** +0.05s/f (Good) **5** Ran SP% **108.5**
Speed ratings (Par 101): **103,99,96,95,82**
toteswingers: 1&2 £4.20 CSF £20.01 TOTE £10.70: £2.80, £1.30; EX 29.50.
Owner Roldvale Limited **Bred** Southern Chase Farm Inc Et Al **Trained** Manton, Wilts

FOCUS

A conditions event that is very often won by a promising 3-y-o prospect, but the rollcall of winners in the past ten years isn't very inspiring and this season's race looks no more than decent. The winning time was marginally slower than the preceding maiden.

NOTEBOOK

Champagne Style(USA) opened his account at the third time of asking with a greatly improved display on this step up grade. He became outpaced around 3f out and had to be hard-ridden, but once coming out of the Dip he motored home on the fair rail to win with something to spare. Having finished second in maiden company on both his previous outings he had plenty to find with the market leaders coming into this, but he has always been well regarded and the step up in trip saw him prove a totally different proposition. There should be more to come still looking at the way he raced here and he remains in the Racing Post Trophy, which his yard took last season with Crowded House and also saddled the third. They also have the progressive Dancing David as a possible for that, however, and this colt would need to step up a great deal again in order to take a hand in that. (op 10-1 tchd 12-1)
Kalypso King(USA) routed the opposition when taking a maiden on his debut over this trip eight days earlier and was well backed here. He set out to repeat the feat and gave his all, but got readily outstayed by the winner in the closing stages. It may be that this came a bit quick for him and a return to slightly easier ground could be what he wants. However, he doesn't have the most scope and it remains to be seen how much more there is to come. (op 7-4 tchd 11-8)
Emirates Dream(USA) was the clear form pick on the level of his two previous efforts in Group company in France. He ran a little freely just off the early leader, but still came there with every chance only to flatten out under pressure. The track may not have suited this big colt, but it has to rate as disappointing. (op 5-6 tchd 11-10 in places)
Rodrigo De Torres was bidding to give his stable a third consecutive win in the race. He showed his run in the Redcar Two-Year-Old Trophy to be wrong and performed a lot more encouragingly, but didn't help his chances of lasting out the extra distance by refusing to settle. (op 14-1)
Invincible Prince(IRE), on his toes beforehand, fluffed the start and looked a very tricky ride in the first-time blinkers. He needs his sights lowering again, but can only be watched until showing more enthusiasm. (op 80-1)

6812 THURLOW NUNN STANDEN DARLEY STKS (GROUP 3) — 1m 1f

3:10 (3:10) (Class 1) 3-Y-O+
£36,900 (£13,988; £7,000; £3,490; £1,748; £877) **Stalls** High

Form — RPR

0050 **1** — **Steele Tango (USA)**[12] 6526 4-9-3 110 .... LPKeniry 7 113
(R A Teal) *b: chsd ldrs: rdn to ld over 1f out: r.o gamely* **25/1**

5614 **2** hd **Glass Harmonium (IRE)**[27] 6110 3-8-13 112 .... RyanMoore 11 113
(Sir Michael Stoute) *chsd ldrs: nt clr run and swtchd lft 2f out: rdn and ev ch ins fnl f: r.o* **4/1**[2]

0146 **3** 2 ½ **Palavicini (USA)**[19] 6303 3-9-3 113 .... EddieAhern 6 111
(J L Dunlop) *lw: a.p: rdn over 2f out: styd on same pce fnl f* **9/1**[3]

3561 **4** hd **Charlie Farnsbarns (IRE)**[27] 6110 5-9-3 110 .... TPO'Shea 13 109+
(B J Meehan) *lw: chsd ldrs: rdn over 1f out: styd on* **11/1**

3-02 **5** 4 ½ **Rio De La Plata (USA)**[14] 6448 4-9-3 115 .... LDettori 9 98
(Saeed Bin Suroor) *s.s: hld up: hdwy and hung rt fr 2f out: wknd ins fnl f* **9/4**[1]

1324 **6** ¾ **Stotsfold**[13] 6506 6-9-7 116 .... AdamKirby 5 100
(W R Swinburn) *lw: mid-div: rdn whn hmpd wl over 1f out: n.d after* **9/1**[3]

2200 **7** nk **Russian Sage (SAF)**[56] 5231 5-9-3 113 .... PatCosgrave 1 96
(M F De Kock, South Africa) *chsd ldr tl led over 2f out: rdn and hdd over 1f out: wknd ins fnl f* **28/1**

1520 **8** hd **Balcarce Nov (ARG)**[20] 6270 4-9-3 105 .... RobertWinston 12 95
(T P Tate) *hld up: hdwy over 2f out: sn rdn: wknd ins fnl f* **16/1**

512 **9** nk **Bushman**[41] 5655 5-9-3 107 .... GeorgeBaker 3 95
(D M Simcock) *hld up: hdwy over 1f out: wknd ins fnl f* **10/1**

0651 **10** 4 ½ **Supaseus**[13] 6480 6-9-3 108 .... TravisBlock 14 85
(H Morrison) *led: rdn and hdd over 2f out: wknd fnl f* **10/1**

3045 **11** 6 **Ballinteni**[21] 6239 7-9-3 87 .... JerryO'Dwyer 2 73
(M G Quinlan) *hld up: rdn 1/2-way: wknd 3f out* **200/1**

030- **12** 1 **Hebridean (IRE)**[197] 6816 4-9-3 112 .... KFallon 4 71
(L M Cumani) *hld up: rdn: hung rt and wknd over 2f out* **20/1**

1m 49.55s (-2.15) **Going Correction** +0.05s/f (Good)
WFA 3 from 4yo+ 4lb **12** Ran SP% **115.7**
Speed ratings (Par 113): **111,110,108,108,104 103,103,103,103,99 93,92**
toteswingers: 1&2 £34.30, 1&3 £54.00, 2&3 £8.20 CSF £116.90 TOTE £29.10: £6.60, £1.90, £3.20; EX 278.50.
Owner The Thirty Acre Racing Partnership **Bred** Tom Zwiesler **Trained** Ashtead, Surrey
■ Roger Teal's first Group winner.
■ Stewards' Enquiry : Ryan Moore caution: careless riding.

FOCUS

A decent, competitive Group 3 contest although the form is not as strong as it might of been with several below par at the end of a long season. The pace was strong and the time was good.

NOTEBOOK

Steele Tango(USA) failed to beat a rival in the Arc at odds of 500/1 two weeks earlier, but on his penultimate outing he had finished a highly creditable fifth in a brilliant renewal of the Eclipse. This represented a return to his best form, and he showed a really game attitude to hold off the runner-up's persistent challenge inside the final furlong. He may now be aimed at the Hong Kong Cup, but it will be a major surprise if he's up to that level. (op 22-1)
Glass Harmonium(IRE) ◆ seemed to find 1m1f too short on his return from a break when unfavoured by the weights in a conditions event at Newbury, but he had sufficient speed this time. Once switched around 2f from the finish, he finished well and looked likely to win late on, but was just worried out of it. He was clear of the remainder and promises to do even better back over 1m2f, particularly next year. (op 7-2)
Palavicini(USA) appreciated the drop back from 1m4f and ran well, although he probably wasn't at his absolute best. He's had quite a long season. (op 11-1 tchd 12-1)
Charlie Farnsbarns(IRE), 50/1 when winning this race last year, had finished just over 1l ahead of today's runner-up (when in receipt of 4lb) in a conditions race at Newbury on his previous start. He did little wrong but simply wasn't good enough this time. (op 10-1)
Rio De La Plata(USA) was no sure thing to be suited by this extra furlong judged on his recent course effort when he was plenty keen enough, and he failed to prove his stamina. He can be given another chance back over 1m, or even 7f. Official explanation: jockey said colt stumbled on leaving stalls and lost its action (tchd 11-4)
Stotsfold looked in trouble when hampered over 1f out and proved unsuited by this drop in trip. (tchd 7-1)
Russian Sage(SAF) was well below his best on his British debut in August when returning from around five months off, and he had been off for a further 56 days since then, but this was a little better from a poor draw. It would be no surprise at all if he goes back to Dubai this winter. (op 25-1)
Balcarce Nov(ARG) couldn't handle the step back up in grade.
Bushman was a surprise runner considering he was taken out of the Cambridgeshire on account of the quick ground. Unsurprisingly he was well beaten. (op 11-1 tchd 12-1)
Supaseus tried to repeat the front-running tactics that saw him land the Cambridgeshire off a mark a 100 over C&D two weeks earlier, but he was below form and didn't cope with the step back up in class. (tchd 11-1)
Hebridean(IRE) Official explanation: trainer said gelding was unsuited by the good ground

6813 LANWADES STUD SEVERALS STKS (LISTED RACE) (F&M) — 1m 2f

3:45 (3:46) (Class 1) 3-Y-O+
£22,708 (£8,608; £4,308; £2,148; £1,076; £540) **Stalls** High

Form — RPR

1-30 **1** — **Enticement**[110] 3442 3-8-11 102 .... JimmyFortune 11 100
(Sir Michael Stoute) *a.p: rdn to ld 2f out: r.o: jst hld on* **12/1**

-552 **2** shd **Pachattack (USA)**[27] 6114 3-8-11 95 ....(b[1]) RichardHughes 15 100
(G A Butler) *trckd ldrs: outpcd over 1f out: r.o wl ins fnl f: jst failed* **33/1**

1523 **3** 1 ½ **Splashdown**[30] 6003 3-9-0 102 .... KFallon 1 100
(L M Cumani) *a.p: outpcd over 1f out: rallied ins fnl f: no ex nr fin* **8/1**[3]

144 **4** ½ **Queen Of Pentacles (IRE)**[30] 6003 3-8-11 92 .... EddieAhern 5 96+
(J Noseda) *lw: hld up: swtchd lft over 4f out: hdwy u.p over 1f out: sn edgd rt: styd on same pce ins fnl f* **25/1**

1410 **5** nk **Kaloni (IRE)**[30] 6003 3-8-11 88 .... MickyFenton 13 95
(Mrs P Sly) *chsd ldr tl led 3f out: rdn and hdd 2f out: styd on same pce ins fnl f* **33/1**

1212 **6** ½ **Plaisterer**[29] 6013 4-9-2 94 .... JackMitchell 10 98+
(C F Wall) *lw: hld up: rdn over 2f out: nt clr run and hmpd 1f out: r.o ins fnl f: nvr able to chal* **14/1**

3-63 **7** 1 **Copperbeech (IRE)**[20] 6290 3-8-11 106 .... LDettori 4 92
(Saeed Bin Suroor) *hld up in tch: rdn over 2f out: styd on same pce fnl f* **8/1**[3]

-142 **8** nk **Leocorno (IRE)**[57] 5202 3-8-11 103 .... RyanMoore 7 92+
(Sir Michael Stoute) *trckd ldrs: stdd and lost pl over 7f out: rdn: nt clr run and swtchd lft over 1f out: r.o: hopeless task* **9/4**[1]

4002 **9** ½ **Mooakada (IRE)**[30] 6003 3-8-11 99 .... TPO'Shea 9 91
(J H M Gosden) *s.s: hdwy over 3f out: sn rdn: hung rt over 1f out: no ex ins fnl f* **16/1**

61 **10** nse **Benedicte (IRE)**[20] 6276 3-8-11 73 .... TedDurcan 12 91
(M Botti) *hld up: rdn over 3f out: nvr trbld ldrs* **100/1**

1421 **11** 2 ½ **Honimiere (IRE)**[27] 6114 3-8-11 94 .... NCallan 16 86
(G A Swinbank) *led: rdn and hdd 3f out: wknd ins fnl f* **14/1**

141 **12** nse **Gripsholm Castle (USA)**[20] 6286 3-8-11 99 .... TPQueally 3 86
(H R A Cecil) *chsd ldrs: rdn and ev ch 2f out: wkng whn n.m.r 1f out* **4/1**[2]

-212 **13** 1 **Flora Trevelyan**[8] 6618 3-8-11 83 .... AdamKirby 2 84
(W R Swinburn) *lw: hld up: rdn and edgd rt over 1f out: wknd fnl f* **14/1**

2m 3.92s (-1.88) **Going Correction** +0.05s/f (Good)
WFA 3 from 4yo 5lb **13** Ran SP% **117.3**
Speed ratings (Par 111): **109,108,107,107,107 106,105,105,105,105 103,103,102**
toteswingers: 1&2 £36.50, 1&3 £13.10, 2&3 £25.90 CSF £362.58 TOTE £15.70: £4.80, £5.70, £2.60; EX 315.10.
Owner The Queen **Bred** Ecoutila Partnership **Trained** Newmarket, Suffolk

FOCUS

An open-looking Listed event for fillies and mares. There was just an average pace on, which meant those racing prominently were at an advantage and it proved a messy race as a number of runners found trouble in running. The winner is rated to her Musidora form.

NOTEBOOK

Enticement was very much the second string for her leading stable, but she got no-nonsense ride and just did enough to open her account for the season. She came here with plenty to prove on this return from a 110-day absence, but it was easier than her two previous starts this season and it must be remembered she was sent off favourite for the Musidora on her 3-y-o return. She had also signed off as a juvenile with success at this track and so is now two from two here. It will be interesting to see whether connections bring her back next year, as she likely has more to offer, especially when stepping back up in distance. (op 11-1)
Pachattack(USA), second to Honimiere over C&D on her handicap debut last time, didn't enjoy the same sort of passage through the race as the winner and only just lost out. The suspicion is the winner was always just holding her, but this was no doubt a personal-best display and she is evidently now coming good for connections. She wore blinkers for the first time.
Splashdown, just behind the winner over C&D last year, got a nice run through from off the pace and ran very close to her best. This consistent filly helps to put the form into some perspective. (op 10-1)
Queen Of Pentacles(IRE) turned in a very similar effort to when behind Splashdown at Yarmouth last time out, so also helps to set the standard. She again shaped as though a more positive ride over this trip or indeed stepping up in trip is ideally required, however.
Kaloni(IRE) finished a little too close for comfort. However, she finished fifth behind Splashdown and Queen Of Pentacles on her previous outing so it shouldn't be considered too surprising.
Plaisterer ran a solid race on this step up from handicap company considering she met trouble. She has developed into a likeable performer. (op 12-1)

Copperbeech(IRE), a market drifter, was representing a leading stable that had won this three times in the past ten years. She didn't get the best of runs in mid-field and should be rated better than the bare form. (op 13-2 tchd 17-2)

Leocorno(IRE), just run out of it in this grade over 1m4f at York 57 days earlier, looked sure to enjoy this drop back in distance and was very well backed. She endured a nightmare passage from off the pace, however, and was simply not able to show her true colours. It is hard to explain why she was taken so far back off the average early pace, as it was never likely to suit and she is no doubt capable of leaving this behind when ridden more positively over this trip. (op 11-4 tchd 3-1 in places)

Mooakada(IRE) had finished in front of the third and fourth at Yarmouth 30 days earlier, but she failed to repeat that form and has become hard to predict. (op 14-1)

Benedicte(IRE) wasn't at all disgraced considering she was stepping up from a maiden success and having just her third run to date. A step up in trip could see her progress again.

Gripsholm Castle(USA) looked a big player on this step back up in class and had scored over C&D on debut back in May. She was held when tight for room at the furlong pole, but would have enjoyed a more truly-run race so she is not one to judge too harshly. (op 7-2 tchd 100-30)

6814 E B F NATIONAL STUD BOADICEA FILLIES' STKS (LISTED RACE) 6f

4:20 (4:20) (Class 1) 3-Y-O+

£22,708 (£8,608; £4,308; £2,148; £1,076; £540) **Stalls** High

Form RPR

2420 **1** **Damaniyat Girl (USA)**[20] 6267 3-8-12 104........................(b) LDettori 14 103+
(W J Haggas) *hld up: hdwy over 1f out: str run to ld post* **6/1**

6213 **2** *hd* **Vitoria (IRE)**[15] 6428 3-8-12 96..................................... RichardMullen 11 102
(B Smart) *lw: led: rdn clr 1f out: hdd post* **9/1**

5122 **3** *1* **Enact**[21] 6240 3-8-12 95.. RyanMoore 7 99+
(Sir Michael Stoute) *lw: hld up: hdwy over 1f out: r.o wl: nt rch ldrs* **11/4**[1]

2001 **4** *1 1/4* **Sea Of Leaves (USA)**[15] 6428 3-8-12 94..................................... KFallon 12 95
(J S Goldie) *lw: trckd ldrs: racd keenly: rdn over 1f out: styd on same pce ins fnl f* **5/1**[2]

1026 **5** *shd* **Iasia (GR)**[36] 5798 3-8-12 89.. TPQueally 10 94+
(Jane Chapple-Hyam) *s.i.s: hld up: r.o wl ins fnl f: nrst fin* **20/1**

3112 **6** *1* **Bounty Box**[15] 6428 3-8-12 95... TedDurcan 1 91
(C F Wall) *lw: prom: rdn over 2f out: edgd rt over 1f out: no ex ins fnl f* **11/2**[3]

6000 **7** *3* **Madame Trop Vite (IRE)**[27] 6091 3-8-12 97........................... NCallan 5 82
(K A Ryan) *trckd ldrs: racd keenly: rdn over 1f out: wknd fnl f* **25/1**

-500 **8** *3/4* **Undaunted Affair (IRE)**[33] 5921 3-8-12 94........................... EddieAhern 9 79
(K A Ryan) *trckd ldrs: racd keenly: n.m.r and lost pl over 3f out: rdn and wknd over 1f out* **33/1**

4060 **9** *1 1/4* **King's Starlet**[36] 5798 3-8-12 95..................................... RobertWinston 3 75
(H Morrison) *chsd ldrs: rdn over 1f out: wknd ins fnl f* **20/1**

5050 **10** *3 1/2* **Pusey Street Lady**[27] 6089 5-8-13 92................................. TPO'Shea 8 64
(J Gallagher) *chsd ldrs tl rdn and wknd over 1f out* **12/1**

4005 **11** *1 3/4* **Never Lose**[69] 4771 3-8-12 90... JimmyFortune 4 58
(C E Brittain) *s.i.s: hld up: hmpd 5f out: a in rr* **16/1**

1m 12.3s (0.10) **Going Correction** +0.05s/f (Good)
WFA 3 from 5yo 1lb 11 Ran SP% **112.9**
Speed ratings (Par 108): **101,100,99,97,97 96,92,91,89,84 82**
toteswingers: 1&2 £8.30, 1&3 £5.30, 2&3 £6.40 CSF £52.90 TOTE £6.60: £2.30, £2.70, £1.30; EX 54.50.
Owner Mohamed Obaida **Bred** Gainsborough Farm Llc **Trained** Newmarket, Suffolk
■ Stewards' Enquiry : Richard Mullen one-day ban: used whip in incorrect place (Oct 30)

FOCUS

An ordinary fillies' Listed sprint and they went steady early. A high draw was advantageous and the form looks ordinary for the grade.

NOTEBOOK

Damaniyat Girl(USA), well drawn, ended a losing run stretching back to her maiden success in this month of last year, and this was the first time she had raced over 6f since that win. She did well considering the race did not unfold to suit, as having come under pressure over 2f out, she still had around 3l to find on the runner-up at the furlong pole, who had been allowed an easy lead, but she was able to bridge the gap, eventually getting up in the final stride. That said, she was the best off at the weights, having upwards of 7lb in hand. She does stay further but may be best kept to this trip, as there might be more to come in a stronger-run race. (op 7-1 tchd 9-1)

Vitoria(IRE) was allowed a surprisingly easy lead from a handy draw and was at least 2l clear inside the final furlong, looking certain to score, but she was pegged back literally on the post. This was a good effort strictly on the weights considering she had 8lb to find with the winner, but she did have the run of things. (op 10-1 tchd 8-1)

Enact gave the impression she would benefit from a positive ride over this trip when a fast-finishing second at Ascot on her latest start, but she again raced further back than ideal, especially considering the modest gallop. Once more she was doing all her best work at the finish, having briefly had to wait for a run around 2f out. (op 3-1 tchd 5-2)

Sea Of Leaves(USA), successful in a C&D handicap off 90 on her previous start, was well positioned considering the lack of pace and ran her race, but she wasn't good enough. (op 6-1 tchd 13-2)

Iasia(GR) ◆ raced keenly out the back off the steady tempo and had too much ground to make up late on. She finished with something left. (op 25-1 tchd 18-1)

Bounty Box was closely matched with Sea Of Leaves on their recent meeting at this track, but the widest draw was no help at all. (op 7-2)

Madame Trop Vite(IRE), another drawn lower than ideal, was too keen. (op 33-1)

Pusey Street Lady Official explanation: jockey said mare hung left

6815 VISIT ALL-NEW SPREADEX.COM H'CAP 7f

4:55 (4:58) (Class 2) (0-105,100) 3-Y-O+

£11,215 (£3,358; £1,679; £840; £419; £105) **Stalls** High

Form RPR

5640 **1** **Esoterica (IRE)**[20] 6278 6-8-13 87.......................................(v) TPQueally 7 97
(J S Goldie) *chsd ldrs: rdn to ld ins fnl f: r.o wl* **25/1**

0444 **2** *1 1/2* **Bonnie Charlie**[6] 6661 3-9-10 100................................ RichardHughes 4 106
(R Hannon) *lw: a.p: rdn and nt clr run over 1f out: styd on* **8/1**

0643 **3** *nk* **Frognal (IRE)**[13] 6476 3-8-9 85..................................... EddieAhern 5 89
(B J Meehan) *mid-div: hdwy over 2f out: rdn over 1f out: r.o* **25/1**

0606 **4** *hd* **Mister Hardy**[20] 6270 4-9-0 93.. BMcHugh(5) 14 98
(R A Fahey) *a.p: rdn over 1f out: kpt on* **8/1**

5040 **5** *1 1/4* **Marine Boy (IRE)**[139] 2500 3-9-10 100........................ RichardKingscote 6 100
(Tom Dascombe) *chsd ldrs: led 3f out: rdn over 1f out: hdd and unable qck ins fnl f* **33/1**

4100 **6** *nk* **Without Prejudice (USA)**[5] 6702 4-9-0 88..................(v) RyanMoore 17 90+
(J Noseda) *dwlt: hld up: rdn and r.o ins fnl f: nt rch ldrs* **15/2**[3]

1205 **6** *dht* **Photographic**[100] 3746 3-9-4 94..................................... RobertWinston 8 93+
(B W Hills) *lw: s.i.s: hld up: hdwy over 2f out: rdn over 1f out: r.o* **16/1**

1005 **8** *3/4* **Giganticus (USA)**[20] 6270 6-9-11 99................................ MichaelHills 12 97+
(B W Hills) *mid-div: pushed along and lost pl over 4f out: rdn and swtchd lft over 1f out: r.o: nt trble ldrs* **12/1**

1550 **9** *shd* **Big Noise**[20] 6270 5-9-0 91........................... Louis-PhilippeBeuzelin(3) 15 89+
(Dr J D Scargill) *s.i.s: hld up: nt clr run and r.o ins fnl f: nvr nrr* **7/1**[2]

0401 **10** *nk* **Felday**[7] 6645 3-8-12 88 6ex.. TravisBlock 1 84
(H Morrison) *swtg: hld up: hdwy over 2f out: no ex ins fnl f* **13/2**[1]

1516 **11** *1/2* **Zomerlust**[27] 6092 7-8-13 87....................................(v) GrahamGibbons 16 83
(J J Quinn) *mid-div: rdn over 2f out: styd on ins fnl f: n.d* **20/1**

0004 **12** *nk* **Thebes**[13] 6482 4-9-4 92.. JoeFanning 3 87
(M Johnston) *hld up: hdwy 1/2-way: rdn and ev ch over 1f out: no ex ins fnl f* **16/1**

40 **13** *3/4* **Shallal**[90] 4087 4-9-8 96.. JimmyFortune 13 89
(P W Chapple-Hyam) *led: hdd over 5f out: rdn over 1f out: wknd ins fnl f* **20/1**

0-06 **14** *1/2* **Classic Descent**[121] 3030 4-8-8 82.................................(t) TedDurcan 11 74
(P J Makin) *s.s: bhd: nvr nrr* **16/1**

0040 **15** *3 1/2* **Thunderous Mood (USA)**[21] 6240 3-8-9 85........................(b) NCallan 2 66
(P F I Cole) *chsd ldrs: rdn: hung rt and ev ch over 1f out: wknd ins fnl f* **50/1**

216 **16** *1 1/4* **Foolin Myself**[29] 6030 4-9-11 99..(b) LDettori 9 78
(M L W Bell) *led over 5f out: hdd 3f out: wknd and eased ins fnl f* **12/1**

543 **17** *22* **Agente Parmigiano (IRE)**[37] 5766 3-8-12 88....................(t) KFallon 10 7
(G A Butler) *lw: a in rr: rdn and wknd over 2f out* **12/1**

1m 24.29s (-1.11) **Going Correction** +0.05s/f (Good)
WFA 3 from 4yo+ 2lb 17 Ran SP% **122.7**
Speed ratings (Par 109): **108,106,105,105,104 103,103,103,102,102 102,101,100,100,96 94,69**
toteswingers: 1&2 £42.50, 1&3 £112.50, 2&3 £20.90 CSF £200.46 CT £5039.21 TOTE £30.70: £6.10, £2.20, £5.20, £2.30; EX 303.70.
Owner Mrs S E Bruce **Bred** A Lyons Bloodstock **Trained** Uplawmoor, E Renfrews

FOCUS

Not the strongest handicap for the class with the joint-top weights being rated 6lb below the race's ceiling. There was a solid pace on and the form is rated around the placed horses.

NOTEBOOK

Esoterica(IRE) bounced right back to his best and ran out a ready winner. He found a gap 3f out, but had to briefly wait for his challenge coming to the 2f pole. His response thereafter was immediate and he motored up the rising finish. This was his first victory since landing back-to-back wins earlier in the season, the last of them off a 7lb lower mark, so this must rate his best display to date. (op 22-1 tchd 20-1)

Bonnie Charlie was upsides the winner and moved nicely through the race. He lacked the turn of foot displayed by that one, but did not get the best of runs late on and ran another honest race. He rates the benchmark and deserves another opening, but the handicapper knows all about him now. (op 9-1)

Frognal(IRE) caught the eye going well in midfield and posted another improved effort from a 1lb higher mark. He looks a winner waiting to happen when eased in grade and a return to a sharper test over this trip should be ideal.

Mister Hardy met support and turned in another solid effort from a good draw. He is just held by the handicapper and is another who helps to set the form. (op 11-1 tchd 7-1)

Marine Boy(IRE) was given a positive ride showed up far more encouragingly on this return from a 139-day absence. His stable have now emerged from a recent quiet spell and he is entitled to come on a deal for the run, but his handicap mark will not make him simple to place. Official explanation: jockey said gelding hung left (op 40-1)

Photographic had to come from behind after a tardy start, but the sound pace helped on that front and she posted a respectable return to the track. She could well be ready to tackle 1m again. (op 11-1 tchd 12-1)

Without Prejudice(USA), well backed, was staying on with purpose before meeting some trouble and is a touch better than this. He does not look the easiest of rides, though. (op 11-1 tchd 12-1)

Giganticus(USA) was always getting there too late having been set plenty to do and he failed to conform last-time-out form with Mister Hardy on 2lb worse terms. (op 11-1 tchd 10-1)

Big Noise didn't help his cause with a sluggish start, but he would have been closer at the finish with a clearer passage inside the final furlong. (tchd 15-2)

Felday was popular under his penalty for winning readily at York a week previously, but he was on his toes beforehand, wasn't helped by his outside draw and raced without cover. (op 11-2 tchd 5-1)

6816 BRITISH BLOODSTOCK MARKETING H'CAP 1m 4f

5:30 (5:31) (Class 2) (0-105,99) 3-Y-O+

£11,215 (£3,358; £1,679; £840; £419; £210) **Stalls** Centre

Form RPR

6342 **1** **Becausewecan (USA)**[53] 5315 3-8-7 85.............................. JoeFanning 10 94
(M Johnston) *mde all: rdn over 1f out: styd on gamely* **7/1**

-260 **2** *1* **Hevelius**[82] 4340 4-9-2 87... AdamKirby 9 94+
(W R Swinburn) *s.i.s: hdwy over 7f out: rdn: edgd lft and outpcd over 1f out: rallied and r.o wl ins fnl f: hung rt and wnt 2nd wl ins fnl f: nt rch wnr* **9/2**[1]

3230 **3** *1 1/4* **Final Victory**[56] 5230 3-8-6 84.. DavidProbert 4 89
(A M Balding) *lw: chsd wnr: rdn over 2f out: styd on same pce ins fnl f* **11/2**[2]

0004 **4** *1/2* **Camps Bay (USA)**[13] 6483 5-9-4 89................................(p) TPQueally 13 93
(Mrs A J Perrett) *chsd ldrs: rdn over 1f out: styd on same pce ins fnl f* **14/1**

0004 **5** *nk* **King Charles**[13] 6470 5-9-7 92.................................(b) RichardHughes 6 96+
(E A L Dunlop) *s.i.s: hld up: r.o wl ins fnl f: nrst fin* **10/1**

0332 **6** *3/4* **William Blake**[22] 6234 4-9-3 88...................................... JimmyFortune 8 91
(M Johnston) *chsd ldrs: rdn over 1f out: no ex ins fnl f* **13/2**[3]

-620 **7** *3/4* **Meethaaq (USA)**[111] 3390 4-9-3 88...................................... TPO'Shea 11 89
(Sir Michael Stoute) *hld up: hdwy over 1f out: styd on same pce ins fnl f* **12/1**

0120 **8** *1 1/4* **Gifted Leader (USA)**[98] 3797 4-8-12 83............................ EddieAhern 1 82
(Ian Williams) *hld up: rdn over 1f out: n.d* **12/1**

40 **9** *6* **Rendezvous (IRE)**[63] 5004 3-8-12 90..........................(v[1]) RyanMoore 12 80
(Sir Michael Stoute) *hld up in tch: rdn over 2f out: wknd over 1f out* **8/1**

0424 **10** *1 1/2* **Dance The Star (USA)**[33] 5909 4-9-3 88............................ TedDurcan 5 75
(D M Simcock) *hld up: rdn: hung rt and wknd over 1f out* **14/1**

0005 **11** *24* **Philatelist (USA)**[20] 6290 5-9-12 97....................................... NCallan 3 46
(M A Jarvis) *hld up: rdn over 2f out: wknd over 1f out* **16/1**

2m 31.11s (-2.39) **Going Correction** +0.05s/f (Good)
WFA 3 from 4yo+ 7lb 11 Ran SP% **114.2**
Speed ratings (Par 109): **109,108,107,107,106 106,105,105,101,100 84**
toteswingers: 1&2 £10.10, 1&3 £6.80, 2&3 £7.90 CSF £37.33 CT £186.15 TOTE £8.30: £2.80, £1.90, £2.60; EX 43.00 Place 6: £360.79 Place 5: £266.20.
Owner Douglas Livingston **Bred** Tony Holmes & Walter Zent **Trained** Middleham Moor, N Yorks

FOCUS

A good handicap, but the pace was ordinary and the winner was allowed the run of things in front. He is rated to a personal best.

NOTEBOOK

Becausewecan(USA) won a shade cosily, needing mainly hands-and-heels riding until very late on, and this was a useful effort off a 6lb higher mark than when runner-up at Kempton on his previous start, but everything went his way. (op 9-2)

Hevelius, eased 3lb since his last run in July, finished well after having to be switched into the clear around 2f out. He took a while to pick up when initially in the clear and could have done with a stronger pace. (tchd 4-1 and 5-1)
Final Victory was given a handy ride on this drop in trip and had his chance. He'll probably benefit from a stronger-run race and/or a return to further. (op 13-2)
Camps Bay(USA) ran okay without improving for the fitting of first-time cheekpieces. (op 11-1)
King Charles isn't the easiest to win with these days, so Richard Hughes was probably keen to deliver him late, but but on this occasion the steady pace was no use to him and he was left with too much to do by the time he got in the clear. Official explanation: jockey said gelding was denied a clear run (op 11-1 tchd 12-1)
William Blake remains too high in the weights. (op 8-1 tchd 6-1)
Rendezvous(IRE) offered nothing in a first-time visor on this step up in trip. (op 10-1 tchd 12-1)
T/Jkpt: Not won. T/Plt: £891.50 to a £1 stake. Pool: £85,855.58. 70.30 winning tickets. T/Qpdt: £68.50 to a £1 stake. Pool: £6,277.08. 67.80 winning tickets. CR

6484 **REDCAR** (L-H)
Friday, October 16

OFFICIAL GOING: Ggod to firm (firm in places; 8.7)

6817 AJA DANCE 21ST NOVEMBER SCOTCH CORNER LADIES' H'CAP (FOR LADY AMATEUR RIDERS) (DIV I) — 1m 2f
1:40 (1:40) (Class 6) (0-60,60) 3-Y-0+ — **£1,648** (£507; £253) **Stalls** Low

Form — RPR

1222 **1** **Zaplamation (IRE)**[30] 5982 4-10-2 **55** ... MissADeniel 3 — 63
(J J Quinn) *in tch: hdwy 3f out: rdn to chse ldr over 1f out: styd on ins fnl f to ld last 100yds* **5/1**[1]

-444 **2** *1* **Follow The Sun (IRE)**[24] 6184 5-10-0 **53** ... (p) MissGAndrews 4 — 59
(Ronald O'Leary, Ire) *trckd ldrs: smooth hdwy to ld over 2f out: rdn clr over 1f out: drvn ins fnl f: hdd and no ex fnl 100yds* **6/1**[2]

0554 **3** *1* **Flora's Pride**[13] 6488 5-9-11 **50** ... MrsCBartley 9 — 54
(K G Reveley) *hld up towards rr: hdwy over 3f out: rdn wl over 1f out: kpt on ins fnl f: nrst fin* **17/2**

0215 **4** *5* **Chichen Daawe**[24] 6183 3-9-7 **51** ... MissLEllison 13 — 45
(B Ellison) *chsd ldr: hdwy and slt ld 4f out: rdn along 3f out: sn hdd and drvn: plugged on same pce* **13/2**[3]

2056 **5** *nk* **Gala Sunday (USA)**[17] 6369 9-10-3 **56** ... (bt) MissSBrotherton 6 — 49
(M W Easterby) *trckd ldng pair: hdwy on inner 4f out and sn cl up: rdn along and ev ch over 2f out: sn drvn and wknd over 1f out* **5/1**[1]

4062 **6** *1* **Trouble Mountain (USA)**[71] 4710 12-10-0 **58**(t) MissJoannaMason(5) 1 — 49
(M W Easterby) *dwlt and hld up in rr: hdwy 3f out: n.m.r over 2f out: sn rdn and kpt on: nvr nr ldrs* **7/1**

000 **7** *4 ½* **Treetops Hotel (IRE)**[29] 6017 10-9-0 **46** oh1 ... MissVCoates(7) 10 — 28
(L R James) *midfield: rdn along over 3f out: sn no hdwy* **100/1**

30/0 **8** *¾* **Chicamia**[64] 4932 5-9-2 **46** oh1 ... MissMMullineaux(5) 11 — 27
(M Mullineaux) *bhd tl sme late hdwy* **50/1**

000 **9** *1 ¾* **Rainbow Zest**[48] 5441 6-9-6 **50** ... MissPhillipaTutty(5) 5 — 27
(W Storey) *nvr bttr than midfield* **33/1**

0005 **10** *½* **Houri (IRE)**[26] 5469 4-9-8 **50** ... (b) MissZoeLilly(3) 7 — 26
(J T Stimpson) *chsd ldrs: rdn along 3f out: grad wknd* **22/1**

0600 **11** *1* **Solo Choice**[14] 6440 3-9-13 **57** ... (b) MissEJJones 14 — 31
(I W McInnes) *led: rdn along and hdd 4f out: sn wknd* **25/1**

0610 **12** *½* **Phantom Serenade (IRE)**[3] 6769 4-10-7 **60** ... MissLHorner 12 — 33
(M Dods) *midfield: hdwy on outer o4f out: chsd ldrs 3f out: sn rdn and wknd 2f out* **15/2**

0000 **13** *½* **Hunting Haze**[63] 4972 6-9-0 **46** oh1 ... (b[1]) MrsDWilkinson(7) 2 — 18
(A Crook) *a in rr* **100/1**

0600 **14** *nk* **Second Reef**[46] 5513 7-9-2 **46** oh1 ... MissHCuthbert(5) 15 — 18
(T A K Cuthbert) *in tch: rdn along over 3f out and sn wknd* **14/1**

00 **15** *5* **Scotty's Future (IRE)**[74] 4588 11-9-0 **46** oh1 ... MissDLenge(7) 8 — 8
(A Berry) *a towards rr* **66/1**

2m 10.94s (3.84) **Going Correction** +0.275s/f (Good)
WFA 3 from 4yo+ 5lb — **15** Ran SP% **114.8**
Speed ratings (Par 101): **95,94,93,89,89 88,84,84,82,82 81,81,80,80,76**
toteswingers: 1&2 £6.00, 1&3 £8.60, 2&3 £12.10 CSF £30.25 CT £247.67 TOTE £5.00: £1.30, £2.40, £2.70; EX 31.30.
Owner Andrew Turton & David Barker **Bred** Mesnil Investments Ltd And Deerpark Stud **Trained** Settrington, N Yorks
■ Stewards' Enquiry : Miss D Lenge one-day ban: used whip when out of contention (tbn)

FOCUS
A cool and cloudy autumn day and the ground was just on the easy side of good. Part one of a low-grade ladies' handicap, run at a sound pace. The form is sound.

6818 AJA DANCE 21ST NOVEMBER SCOTCH CORNER LADIES' H'CAP (FOR LADY AMATEUR RIDERS) (DIV II) — 1m 2f
2:10 (2:13) (Class 6) (0-60,60) 3-Y-0+ — **£1,648** (£507; £253) **Stalls** Low

Form — RPR

000 **1** **Tres Froide (FR)**[40] 5698 4-10-0 **52** ... MissEJJones 13 — 67
(N Tinkler) *in tch: hdwy over 3f out: swtchd rt and effrt 2f out: rdn to ld over 1f out: clr ins fnl f* **28/1**

0004 **2** *5* **Thunderstruck**[24] 6183 4-10-7 **59** ... (p) MissADeniel 14 — 64
(J A Glover) *trckd ldrs: smooth hdwy and cl up over 3f out: led 2f out: sn rdn and hdd over 1f out: kpt on same pce* **14/1**

0131 **3** *1 ¾* **Tropical Duke (IRE)**[24] 6184 3-9-12 **60** ... MissVBarr(5) 4 — 62+
(R E Barr) *bhd: rdn and hung bdly lft 4f out: hdwy 3f out: styd on to chse ldrs over 1f out: sn one pce* **2/1**[1]

0F0- **4** *½* **Nayessence**[386] 6230 3-9-12 **55** ... (t) MissSBrotherton 9 — 56
(M W Easterby) *trckd ldrs: hdwy 4f out: effrt over 2f out: sn rdn and hung lft: no imp* **4/1**[2]

4640 **5** *4 ½* **Emerald Rock (CAN)**[27] 6126 4-9-13 **58** ... (p) MissDLJSharp(7) 2 — 50
(Tom Dascombe) *trckd ldrs: effrt over 3f out: rdn along over 2f out and grad wknd* **14/1**

2340 **6** *1 ½* **Terminate (GER)**[27] 6102 7-10-3 **55** ... MrsCBartley 6 — 44
(A Berry) *midfield: rdn along over 3f out: drvn 2f out and no imp* **14/1**

0002 **7** *¾* **Fitzwarren**[24] 6184 8-9-7 **45** ... (tp) MissLEllison 1 — 32
(A D Brown) *cl up: led 4f out: rdn along 3f out: hdd 2f out and grad wknd* **9/1**[3]

0-00 **8** *3* **Intavac Boy**[80] 4402 8-9-2 **45** ... MissERamstrom(5) 5 — 26
(S P Griffiths) *led: rdn along and hdd 4f out: cl up tl drvn over 2f out and grad wknd* **100/1**

4440 **9** *2* **Rain Stops Play (IRE)**[24] 6184 7-9-7 **50** ... MissJRRichards(5) 11 — 27
(N G Richards) *midfield: hdwy over 3f out: in tch and rdn over 2f out: sn wknd* **14/1**

000 **10** *¾* **Kirstys Lad**[21] 6256 7-9-8 **51** ... MissMMullineaux(5) 7 — 27
(M Mullineaux) *a towards rr* **20/1**

00-6 **11** *2* **Govenor Eliott (IRE)**[30] 5982 4-9-5 **48** ... MissPhillipaTutty(5) 12 — 20
(A J Lockwood) *chsd ldng pair: rdn along over 3f out and sn wknd* **16/1**

S060 **12** *5* **Neon Blue**[40] 5694 8-9-1 **46** ow1 ... (p) MissCharlotteHolmes(7) 3 — 8
(R M Whitaker) *s.i.s: a bhd* **12/1**

2345 **13** *2 ½* **Byron Bay**[17] 6358 7-9-7 **45** ... MissLHorner 8 — —
(R Johnson) *towards rr: hdwy on wd outside 3f out: rdn over 2f out and sn wknd* **16/1**

0-0 **14** *3 ¼* **Revolving World (IRE)**[161] 1851 6-9-7 **45** ... (t) MissGAndrews 10 — —
(L R James) *s.i.s: a bhd* **50/1**

2m 11.21s (4.11) **Going Correction** +0.275s/f (Good)
WFA 3 from 4yo+ 5lb — **14** Ran SP% **120.6**
Speed ratings (Par 101): **94,90,88,88,84 83,82,80,78,78 76,72,70,68**
toteswingers: 1&2 £34.70, 1&3 £17.50, 2&3 £3.90 CSF £372.16 CT £1156.20 TOTE £42.10: £9.20, £2.50, £1.30; EX 401.60.
Owner Leeds Plywood And Doors Ltd **Bred** Wertheimer Et Frere **Trained** Langton, N Yorks
■ Stewards' Enquiry : Miss E J Jones caution: used whip when clearly winning

FOCUS
Part two and another very moderate event. The pace was not quite as strong. The winner was up 3lb on her previous British form.
Tres Froide(FR) Official explanation: trainer had no explanation for the apparent improvement in form

6819 MARKET CROSS JEWELLERS CLAIMING STKS — 7f
2:45 (2:47) (Class 6) 2-Y-0 — **£2,047** (£604; £302) **Stalls** Centre

Form — RPR

06 **1** **Vito Volterra (IRE)**[7] 6627 2-8-9 0 ... HayleyTurner 6 — 73+
(J R Best) *overall ldr: mde all towards far side: pushed along 2f out: styd on strly fnl f* **13/2**[3]

0513 **2** *2* **Newton Circus**[9] 6586 2-8-9 70 ... FrancisNorton 13 — 68
(Ollie Pears) *prom main gp: led that gp and chsd wnr over 1f out: edgd lft: kpt on same pce fnl f* **9/1**

3644 **3** *1 ¾* **Izuizorizuain't (IRE)**[9] 6590 2-8-0 58 ... JimmyQuinn 1 — 55
(K A Ryan) *hld up in tch far side: rdn over 2f out: styd on wl fnl f: nrst fin* **8/1**

3326 **4** *½* **Jehu**[10] 6557 2-8-9 77 ... SamHitchcott 19 — 63
(M R Channon) *in tch main gp: effrt over 2f out: one pce appr fnl f* **5/1**[2]

5435 **5** *shd* **Pepper Lane**[10] 6557 2-8-2 58 ... DO'Donohoe 18 — 56
(J Hetherton) *cl up in main gp: led over 2f out to over 1f out: sn no ex* **18/1**

3400 **6** *1* **Cygnet Committee (IRE)**[9] 6589 2-8-0 52 ... (b) AndrewMullen 5 — 51
(J S Wainwright) *trckd far side ldrs gng wl: rdn over 1f out: sn no ex* **80/1**

600 **7** *¾* **Labretella (IRE)**[49] 5397 2-7-12 58 ... PaulQuinn 7 — 47
(M Dods) *midfield main gp: drvn and outpcd over 2f out: kpt on u.p fnl f* **20/1**

6000 **8** *½* **Dispol Kabira**[9] 6590 2-7-8 50 ow1 ... RyanPowell(7) 17 — 49
(D W Thompson) *dwlt: bhd main gp: effrt and hung lft 2f out: kpt on fnl f: nvr rchd ldrs* **100/1**

623 **9** *1 ¾* **Precious Coral (IRE)**[32] 5935 2-7-12 70 ... CatherineGannon 3 — 42
(S A Callaghan, U.S.A) *trckd far side ldrs: rdn over 2f out: wknd over 1f out* **2/1**[1]

650 **10** *nk* **Sydney Bridge**[29] 6009 2-7-10 64 ... (p) JamesPSullivan(7) 9 — 46
(I Semple) *t.k.h: led main gp to over 2f out: sn rdn and wknd* **14/1**

006 **11** *6* **Social Grace**[10] 6555 2-8-4 63 ... SaleemGolam 12 — 32
(D H Brown) *midfield main gp: outpcd over 2f out: n.d after* **28/1**

00 **12** *1 ¼* **Shercon (IRE)**[76] 4515 2-8-5 0 ... GregFairley 20 — 30
(N Tinkler) *bhd main gp: shortlived effrt over 2f out: sn btn* **50/1**

13 *10* **Better Be Blue (IRE)**[35] 5845 2-8-0 0 ... DuranFentiman 16 — —
(Miss S Collins, Ire) *w ldrs main gp tl wknd over 2f out* **20/1**

5204 **14** *hd* **Prettiest Star (IRE)**[10] 6555 2-7-12 53 ... (p) JamieMackay 10 — —
(K A Ryan) *cl up main gp tl rdn and wknd over 2f out* **50/1**

5 **15** *3 ¼* **Fond**[122] 2996 2-7-12 0 ... SilvestreDeSousa 8 — —
(Ollie Pears) *bhd main gp: rdn over 2f out: sn btn* **22/1**

0000 **16** *12* **Ron The Don**[10] 6557 2-8-0 38 ... (b[1]) DominicFox(3) 15 — —
(A Berry) *t.k.h: towards rr main gp: struggling 1/2-way: sn lost tch* **200/1**

000 **17** *2 ¼* **Keithshazel (IRE)**[101] 3709 2-7-7 0 ow2 ... MatthewLawson(7) 4 — —
(R C Guest) *prom far side tl rdn and wknd over 2f out* **150/1**

1m 29.59s (5.09) **Going Correction** +0.50s/f (Yiel) — **17** Ran SP% **121.0**
Speed ratings (Par 93): **90,87,85,85,85 83,83,82,80,80 73,71,60,60,56 42,40**
toteswingers: 1&2 £12.50, 1&3 £15.60, 2&3 £6.90 CSF £58.05 TOTE £7.80: £2.20, £3.10, £3.10; EX 73.20.Newton Circus claimed by Mr D. Redvers for £8,000. Precious Coral claimed by Mrs Ruth A. Carr for £5,000. Vito Volterra claimed by Mr A. B. Haynes for £8,000.
Owner Findlay & Bloom **Bred** O McElroy **Trained** Hucking, Kent

FOCUS
An ordinary juvenile claimer with plenty of dead wood. Half-a-dozen elected to race wide towards the far side but in the end they converged into one group. The second and thid set a solid but limited level.

NOTEBOOK
Vito Volterra(IRE), who had shown definite promise in two previous starts in maiden company, seized the initiative towards the far side. Edging right and in the end joining the main body of the field, he was driven out for a most decisive success. He is clearly capable of holding his own in nursery company and was claimed by Andy Haynes. (op 12-1 tchd 14-1)
Newton Circus, from a stable that does especially well in sellers and claimers, is rated 69 after his victory in a claimer on the all-weather at Kempton. He finished clear second best behind something of a tartar and he should have no difficulty going one better for his third set of connections. (tchd 17-2)
Izuizorizuain't(IRE), rated 58, was another to initially race towards the far side. She was putting in her best work at the finish and is worth another try over 7f. (op 7-1 tchd 17-2)
Jehu, rated 75, had a poor draw when only sixth in nursery company at Catterick last time, finished second best of those who raced towards the stands' side. This was his 13th start and he already looks fully exposed. (op 9-2 tchd 6-1)
Pepper Lane is also rated just 58 and seemed to run well above herself. She finished one place ahead of Jehu at Catterick, but was meeting him on 12lb worse terms here. (op 20-1)
Precious Coral(IRE), rated 70 and clear top on official ratings, chased the winner from halfway on the far side but weakened noticeably in the final furlong. She seems to be going the wrong way, but Ruth Carr thought it was worth taking a chance on her. (op 5-2 tchd 15-8)
Fond Official explanation: jockey said filly never travelled

6820 EUROPEAN BREEDERS' FUND MAIDEN FILLIES' STKS — 6f
3:20 (3:21) (Class 5) 2-Y-0 — **£3,885** (£1,156; £577; £288) **Stalls** Centre

Form — RPR

3 **1** **Coin From Heaven (IRE)**[21] 6245 2-8-11 0 ... FrederikTylicki(3) 3 — 81+
(R A Fahey) *hld up: hdwy 2f out: qcknd to ld over 1df out: rdn clr ent fnl f* **11/4**[2]

2	4	**Briary Mac** 2-8-9 0 ... GaryBartley(5) 4 (N Bycroft) *led: rdn along 2f out: drvn and hdd over 1f out: kpt on u.p ins fnl f* **33/1**	68
2320 3	1 ½	**L'Enchanteresse (IRE)**[13] 6481 2-9-0 75 ... HayleyTurner 9 (M L W Bell) *hld up: hdwy on outer whn hmpd 2f out: sn rdn and kpt on same pce appr fnl f* **5/2[1]**	64
444 4	1 ½	**Seven Of Diamonds (IRE)**[84] 4278 2-9-0 64 ... DavidAllan 1 (T D Easterby) *trckd ldrs: hdwy 1/2-way: rdn along 2f out: sn drvn and wknd over 1f out* **9/2[3]**	59
5	1 ¼	**As You Like It (IRE)**[16] 6402 2-9-0 0 ... StephenDonohoe 6 (John Joseph Murphy, Ire) *trckd ldrs: effrt over 2f out: sn rdn and kpt on same pce* **12/1**	55
0034 6	4	**Fair Bunny**[7] 6646 2-9-0 70 ... SilvestreDeSousa 8 (A D Brown) *trckd ldrs: effrt whn bmpd and pushed rt 2f out: sn rdn and wknd* **8/1**	43
4230 7	3	**Royal Record**[21] 6241 2-8-7 65 ... JohnCavanagh(7) 7 (M Brittain) *cl up: rdn and hung rt 2f out: sn drvn and wknd* **5/1**	34
5660 8	24	**Bonasera (IRE)**[39] 5728 2-9-0 40 ... DanielTudhope 2 (A Berry) *a in rr: outpcd and wl bhd fr 1/2-way* **100/1**	—

1m 14.91s (3.11) **Going Correction** +0.50s/f (Yiel) **8** Ran SP% **112.8**
Speed ratings (Par 92): **99,93,91,89,88 82,78,46**
toteswingers: 1&2 £13.60, 1&3 £2.70, 2&3 £12.60 CSF £78.76 TOTE £3.40: £1.40, £5.00, £1.20; EX 82.40.
Owner G Morrin **Bred** Camogue Stud Ltd **Trained** Musley Bank, N Yorks

FOCUS
A very modest maiden but a ready winner of some potential who won with a fair bit in hand.

NOTEBOOK
Coin From Heaven(IRE), third first time in a maiden at Haydock that has not worked out at all, took charge coming to the final furlong and ran out a most decisive winner. She will improve again and should make a fair handicapper at three. (op 9-4 tchd 3-1)
Briary Mac, from a stable without a two-year-old maiden race winner in the last five years, showed bags of toe to take them along. She looks immature and ought to do better next year.
L'Enchanteresse(IRE), having her sixth start and rated 73, was dropped in at the start. She was just starting her finishing effort when knocked out of her stride. She kept on without ever threatening the winner and looked second best on the day. (op 9-4 tchd 11-4)
Seven Of Diamonds(IRE), rated 64, had no excuse. (op 7-1)
As You Like It(IRE), who contested a Listed race in the summer, is now rated just 56 and looks regressive. (op 14-1)
Fair Bunny made a violent jink right soon after halfway, hampering the eventual third. (tchd 7-1)

6821 HOLD YOUR CHRISTMAS PARTY HERE MEDIAN AUCTION MAIDEN STKS 1m
3:55 (3:55) (Class 6) 2-Y-O £2,047 (£604; £302) **Stalls** Centre

Form			RPR
32 1		**Medicinal Compound**[34] 5852 2-9-3 0 ... PhillipMakin 4 (K A Ryan) *trckd ldrs: hdwy to ld 3f out: rdn wl over 1f out: drvn ins fnl f: hld on gamely* **5/2[1]**	79
0 2	shd	**Fourth Generation (IRE)**[41] 5674 2-9-3 0 ... PJMcDonald 6 (G A Swinbank) *trckd ldrs: hdwy over 2f out: swtchd lft and effrt wl over 1f out: rdn to chal ins fnl f and ev ch tl drvn and nt qckn nr line* **25/1**	79
00 3	3	**Master Leon**[30] 5981 2-9-3 0 ... TomEaves 8 (B Smart) *a.p: effrt and cl up over 2f out: sn rdn and ev ch tl drvn and edgd rt: ins fnl f: one pce* **100/1**	72
4 4	1 ¼	**Arctic Cosmos (USA)**[8] 6607 2-9-3 0 ... RobertHavlin 18 (J H M Gosden) *dwlt and wnt rt s: in tch on wd outside: hdwy 3f out: rdn along to chse ldrs over 2f out: drvn wl over 1f out and one pce* **10/3[2]**	69
5	nse	**Mountain Quest** 2-9-3 0 ... HayleyTurner 2 (M L W Bell) *towards rr: stdy hdwy over 2f out: hmpd wl over 1f out: kpt on ins fnl f: nrst fin* **25/1**	69+
63 6	2 ½	**Blue Lyric**[29] 6026 2-8-12 0 ... FrancisNorton 14 (L M Cumani) *trckd ldrs: hdwy 3f out: rdn along 2f out: drvn and wknd appr fnl f* **8/1**	59
04 7	½	**Always De One**[13] 6484 2-8-12 0 ... GregFairley 16 (M Johnston) *towards rr: hdwy 3f out: rdn along 2f out: kpt on ins fnl f: nrst fin* **25/1**	58
000 8	2 ¼	**Forethought**[28] 6062 2-8-12 64 ... JimmyQuinn 13 (P Howling) *in rr tl styd on fnl 2f: nrst fin* **66/1**	53
5 9	½	**Paschendale**[11] 6548 2-9-3 0 ... DO'Donohoe 9 (Saeed Bin Suroor) *chsd ldrs: rdn along wl over 2f out and sn no prog* **7/2[3]**	57
2224 10	2 ½	**Desert Forest (IRE)**[72] 4651 2-9-0 70 ...(p) FrederikTylicki(3) 1 (J Howard Johnson) *cl up: rdn along 3f out: wkng whn bmpd wl over 1f out* **12/1**	51+
00 11	2 ¾	**Persian Poet**[9] 6593 2-9-3 0 ... AdrianTNicholls 5 (M Johnston) *led: rdn along 1/2-way: hdd 3f out and grad wknd* **33/1**	45
12	1 ½	**Green Army** 2-9-3 0 ... SamHitchcott 3 (M R Channon) *in tch on wd outside: rdn along wl over 2f out: sn wknd* **66/1**	42
4640 13	¾	**Abbi Jicaro**[25] 6169 2-8-12 49 ... SilvestreDeSousa 17 (Mrs L Williamson) *a towards rr* **150/1**	35
0400 14	2 ¾	**War Wolf**[62] 5036 2-9-3 35 ... DNolan 12 (T D Easterby) *cl up: rdn along over 3f out and sn wknd* **200/1**	34
15	hd	**Myraid** 2-9-3 0 ... PaulMulrennan 11 (Ollie Pears) *dwlt: sn in midfield: effrt and in tch 3f out: sn rdn and wknd* **100/1**	34
16	4 ½	**Broctune Papa Gio** 2-9-3 0 ... TonyHamilton 7 (K G Reveley) *dwlt: a bhd* **150/1**	24
000 17	35	**Green Shoots**[13] 6494 2-8-5 20 ... JamesPSullivan(7) 10 (M E Sowersby) *prom: rdn along and wknd bef 1/2-way: sn bhd* **200/1**	—

1m 42.79s (4.79) **Going Correction** +0.50s/f (Yiel) **17** Ran SP% **114.4**
Speed ratings (Par 93): **96,95,92,91,91 89,88,86,85,83 80,79,78,75,75 70,35**
toteswingers: 1&2 £13.60, 1&3 £2.70, 2&3 £12.60 CSF £72.38 TOTE £3.30: £1.20, £6.80, £13.10; EX 65.10.
Owner Hambleton Racing Ltd XIII **Bred** Mr & Mrs G Middlebrook **Trained** Hambleton, N Yorks
■ Stewards' Enquiry : P J McDonald one-day ban: careless riding (Oct 30)

FOCUS
A median auction maiden event with solid form thin on the ground. The winner is the best guide, rated to his Chester form.

NOTEBOOK
Medicinal Compound, who achieved an RPR of 79 when narrowly out-pointed at Chester, travelled strongly but had to dig deep in the end to repel Fourth Generation. (op 11-4)
Fourth Generation(IRE) stepped up markedly on his soft-ground debut effort. A grand type, he should make a fair handicapper at three.
Master Leon, who showed little after starting slowly on his first two starts, turned in a much improved effort but this will have blown a possible lenient handicap mark out of the water.
Arctic Cosmos(USA), who showed promise when fourth on his debut on the all-weather at Kempton just eight days earlier, stayed on in his own time from off the pace down the stands' side. He will do much better over a fair bit further next year. (op 9-4)
Mountain Quest, bred to make a middle-distance three-year-old, made a pleasing start. (op 33-1)
Blue Lyric, having her third outing, will hopefully improve over the winter and make her mark in modest handicap company at three. (op 9-1 tchd 7-1)
Always De One, a slow learner, ran easily her best race on her third start and she now qualified for nurseries.
Paschendale, who lost his chance when starting slowly first time, was very lit up and simply would not settle this time.
Green Army Official explanation: jockey said colt suffered interference in runing

6822 SAM HALL MEMORIAL H'CAP 1m 6f 19y
4:30 (4:30) (Class 5) (0-75,75) 3-Y-O+ £2,590 (£770; £385; £192) **Stalls** Low

Form			RPR
3362 1		**Bollin Judith**[32] 5952 3-8-3 **59** ... FrancisNorton 6 (T D Easterby) *hld up in tch: hdwy over 3f out: led over 1f out: drew clr ent fnl f: eased wl ins fnl f* **4/1[2]**	73+
454 2	5	**Abstract Folly (IRE)**[19] 6313 7-8-12 **59** ... JimmyQuinn 2 (J D Bethell) *hld up in tch: effrt whn n.m.r over 2f out: hdwy to chse wnr 1f out: kpt on: no imp* **12/1**	64
5133 3	½	**Dramatic Solo**[32] 5943 4-9-4 **65** ...(b) AndrewElliott 1 (A P Jarvis) *led: rdn over 2f out: hdd over 1f out: kpt on same pce* **11/1**	70
2-00 4	1 ½	**General Ting (IRE)**[8] 6622 4-9-10 **71** ... StephenDonohoe 10 (Sir Mark Prescott) *hld up: rdn over 3f out: plugged on fnl 2f: nrst fin* **14/1**	74
0126 5	nse	**Bergonzi (IRE)**[23] 5235 5-9-11 **75** ...(p) FrederikTylicki(3) 4 (J Howard Johnson) *prom: rdn 3f out: kpt on same pce wl over 1f out* **9/2[3]**	77
0-3 6	nk	**Summercove (IRE)**[26] 6147 4-8-6 **56** oh8 ... DominicFox(3) 3 (John Joseph Murphy, Ire) *hld up on outside: hdwy to chse ldrs over 2f out: edgd lft and no ex over 1f out* **40/1**	58
6613 7	¾	**Ifatfirst (IRE)**[19] 6313 6-9-3 **64** ... DanielTudhope 5 (J S Goldie) *trckd ldrs: drvn and outpcd over 2f out: n.d after* **11/1**	65
5300 8	7	**Drop The Hammer**[16] 6384 3-8-0 **56** oh1 ... SilvestreDeSousa 7 (T P Tate) *midfield: lost pl 1/2-way: n.d after* **18/1**	47
161 9	hd	**Lady Hestia (USA)**[18] 6330 4-9-5 **66** ... HayleyTurner 9 (M P Tregoning) *chsd ldr: rdn over 3f out: lost pl 2f out* **9/4[1]**	57
4400 10	½	**Royal Flynn**[3] 6768 7-8-11 **58** oh1 ow2 ...(p) PaulMulrennan 8 (Mrs K Walton) *dwlt: bhd: drvn over 3f out: nvr on terms* **22/1**	48

3m 7.29s (2.59) **Going Correction** +0.275s/f (Good)
WFA 3 from 4yo+ 9lb **10** Ran SP% **112.0**
Speed ratings (Par 103): **103,100,99,99,98 98,98,94,94,93**
toteswingers: 1&2 £7.30, 1&3 £7.10, 2&3 £14.20 CSF £48.96 CT £481.48 TOTE £5.10: £1.50, £2.50, £2.70; EX 48.70.
Owner Sir Neil Westbrook **Bred** Sir Neil & Exors Of Late Lady Westbrook **Trained** Great Habton, N Yorks

FOCUS
A modest 56-75 handicap run at a strong pace. The third seems the best guide to the form.
Lady Hestia(USA) Official explanation: trainer's rep said filly was unsuited by the good to firm ground

6823 HAPPY BIRTHDAY SARA MAIDEN STKS 6f
5:05 (5:08) (Class 5) 3-Y-O+ £2,590 (£770; £385; £192) **Stalls** Centre

Form			RPR
23 1		**Primaeval**[64] 4947 3-9-3 0 ... HayleyTurner 19 (J R Fanshawe) *hld up: stdy hdwy wl over 2f out: n.m.r and swtchd rt over 1f out: rdn and qcknd to ld ins fnl f: kpt on wl* **5/2[1]**	77+
0030 2	2 ½	**Star Addition**[15] 6410 3-8-12 44 ... GaryBartley(5) 14 (E J Alston) *in tch: hdwy to chse ldrs 2f out: swtchd lft and rdn over 1f out: kpt on wl fnl f: nrst fin* **66/1**	61
550 3	nk	**Bertie Vista**[15] 6414 4-9-4 52 ...(p) DNolan 16 (T D Easterby) *chsd ldrs: pushed along 1/2-way: rdn to chal 2f out: drvn and edgd lft over 1f out: ev ch tl hrd drvn and one pce ins fnl f* **16/1**	60
2342 4	shd	**Wilfred Pickles (IRE)**[27] 6111 3-9-3 76 ... JimmyQuinn 12 (Mrs A J Perrett) *trckd ldrs: hdwy over 2f out: rdn to ld over 1f out: drvn and hdd ins fnl f: one pce* **3/1[2]**	59
5400 5	3 ¼	**King Of Eden (IRE)**[58] 5158 3-9-3 55 ... DavidAllan 9 (E J Alston) *prom: led wl over 2f out and sn rdn: drvn and hdd over 1f out: wknd ent fnl f* **66/1**	49
4063 6	¾	**Alacity (IRE)**[10] 6553 3-8-12 53 ... FrancisNorton 8 (N Bycroft) *led: rdn along 1/2-way: hdaed over 2f out and sn drvn: wknd over 1f out* **12/1**	42
2000 7	5	**Sleepy Valley (IRE)**[19] 6308 3-8-12 45 ...(p) DanielTudhope 1 (A Dickman) *in tch towards outer: hdwy to chse ldrs over 2f out: sn rdn and wknd over 1f out* **80/1**	26
4 8	½	**Abbashinko**[21] 6255 3-8-12 0 ... RichardSmith 5 (Tom Dascombe) *in tch: rdn along over 2f out: sn edgd rt and wknd* **16/1**	24
6304 9	½	**Kloof**[11] 6539 3-9-3 74 ... PhillipMakin 20 (K A Ryan) *cl up: rdn along over 2f out and grad wknd* **5/1[3]**	27
56 10	1	**Camomile**[76] 4531 3-8-12 0 ... PJMcDonald 6 (K A Ryan) *chsd ldrs: rdn along wl over 2f out and sn wknd* **50/1**	19
33 11	4	**Localiser (IRE)**[11] 6539 3-9-3 0 ... AdrianTNicholls 4 (D Nicholls) *midfield: swtchd lft to outer and hdwy 1/2-way: prom and rdn 2f out: sn wknd* **7/1**	11
64 12	½	**Cheers Big Ears (IRE)**[10] 6573 3-9-0 0 ... FrederikTylicki(3) 2 (J R Best) *prom: rdn along 1/2-way: sn wknd* **14/1**	10
13	½	**Champagne All Day** 3-9-0 0 ... MichaelJStainton(3) 15 (S P Griffiths) *dwlt: a in rr* **200/1**	8
00 14	1 ½	**Kilmun**[16] 6390 3-9-3 0 ... PaulMulrennan 18 (K A Ryan) *cl up: rdn along 1/2-way: a towards rr* **100/1**	3
0000 15	½	**Another Luke (IRE)**[88] 4133 3-9-3 48 ... GregFairley 13 (T J Etherington) *s.i.s: a bhd* **150/1**	2
00 16	¾	**Spiosra (USA)**[32] 5954 3-8-12 0 ...(t) AndrewElliott 10 (C J Teague) *chsd ldrs: rdn along and lost pl 1/2-way: bhd fnl 2f* **200/1**	—
0 17	½	**Aquapark**[43] 5599 3-9-3 0 ... TonyHamilton 3 (R Craggs) *a in rr* **200/1**	—
18	24	**Grant Me A Wish** 3-9-3 0 ... AndrewMullen 17 (S P Griffiths) *dwlt: a in rr: bhd fr 1/2-way* **200/1**	—

1m 14.53s (2.73) **Going Correction** +0.50s/f (Yiel)
WFA 3 from 4yo 1lb **18** Ran SP% **118.7**
Speed ratings (Par 103): **101,97,97,97,92 91,85,84,83,82 77,76,75,73,73 72,71,39**
toteswingers: 1&2 £40.90, 1&3 £11.60, 2&3 £99.40 CSF £192.81 TOTE £3.40: £1.40, £9.20, £5.10; EX 130.60.
Owner Lord Vestey **Bred** Stowell Park Stud **Trained** Newmarket, Suffolk

FOCUS
A very modest sprint maiden and only eight of the 18 runners have qualified for a handicap mark. The winner did not have to repeat his earlier form, with the second and third the keys to this race.

6824 THANKS & SEE YOU NEXT SEASON H'CAP 7f
5:40 (5:42) (Class 5) (0-70,70) 3-Y-O £2,590 (£770; £385; £192) **Stalls** Centre

Form RPR

2165 **1** **Liberty Trail (IRE)**[15] 6413 3-9-1 **67** .... PhillipMakin 13 74
(I Semple) *mde all: pushed along over 1f out: hld on wl fnl f* **12/1**

0006 **2** *1* **Jimwil (IRE)**[25] 6170 3-8-13 **65** ....(p) HayleyTurner 10 69
(M Dods) *s.i.s: hld up: hdwy over 2f out: chsd wnr ins fnl f: r.o* **14/1**

6100 **3** *1/2* **Imperial House**[41] 5672 3-8-12 **64** .... SamHitchcott 3 67
(M R Channon) *sn midfield: effrt over 2f out: edgd lft and kpt on ins fnl f* **12/1**

0013 **4** *4* **Sairaam (IRE)**[10] 6568 3-8-4 **56** oh1 .... FrancisNorton 7 48
(C Smith) *cl up: rdn over 2f out: outpcd fnl f* **14/1**

2024 **5** *3/4* **Two Turtle Doves (IRE)**[26] 6140 3-8-6 **58** .... GregFairley 1 48
(M Mullineaux) *prom tl edgd lft and outpcd over 1f out* **10/1**

2106 **6** *nk* **Timeless Dream**[10] 6572 3-9-4 **70** .... RobertHavlin 16 59
(P W Chapple-Hyam) *midfield: drvn over 2f out: kpt on fnl f: nvr rchd ldrs* **12/1**

-105 **7** *nk* **Ykikamoocow**[67] 4846 3-9-1 **67** .... SilvestreDeSousa 8 60+
(G A Harker) *towards rr: edgd rt over 3f out: sn blkd and outpcd: kpt on fnl f: n.d* **14/1**

5430 **8** *1 3/4* **Doric Echo**[17] 6361 3-8-10 **69** .... AdamCarter(7) 2 53
(B Smart) *prom tl rdn and wknd wl over 1f out* **14/1**

5022 **9** *1* **Amethyst Dawn (IRE)**[16] 6383 3-8-10 **62** .... DavidAllan 18 43
(T D Easterby) *cl up: rdn over 2f out: wknd wl over 1f out* **6/1**[1]

0443 **10** *4* **One Cool Dream**[10] 6572 3-8-10 **62** .... SaleemGolam 4 32
(W R Swinburn) *midfield: drvn and outpcd over 2f out: n.d after* **12/1**

6056 **11** *6* **Convitezza**[11] 6539 3-7-11 **56** oh11 .... JamesPSullivan(7) 12 10
(M E Sowersby) *bhd: bdly hmpd over 3f out: nvr on terms* **100/1**

1122 **12** *3/4* **Future Gem**[26] 6140 3-8-11 **66** ....(p) FrederikTylicki(3) 5 18
(A Dickman) *dwlt: sn in tch: drvn and outpcd over 2f out: sn btn* **8/1**[3]

0002 **13** *hd* **Cook's Endeavour (USA)**[30] 5999 3-9-4 **70** .... TonyHamilton 14 22+
(K A Ryan) *rdr slow to remove blindfold: missed break and wnt bdly rt s: nvr on terms* **12/1**

0000 **14** *2 3/4* **Lily Jicaro (IRE)**[9] 6581 3-8-1 **56** oh8 ....(v[1]) DominicFox(3) 6 —
(Mrs L Williamson) *hld up: rdn over 2f out: nvr on terms* **80/1**

010 **15** *1 1/4* **Sleepy Blue Ocean**[26] 6140 3-8-11 **63** .... AndrewElliott 15 4
(J Balding) *cl up tl rdn and wknd over 2f out* **25/1**

4600 **16** *3 3/4* **Wotatomboy**[24] 6182 3-8-4 **56** oh1 .... DO'Donohoe 11 —
(R M Whitaker) *towards rr: struggling 1/2-way: nvr on terms* **33/1**

0042 **17** *10* **Gower Valentine**[10] 6572 3-9-2 **68** .... AdrianTNicholls 17 —
(D Nicholls) *cl up: rdn 3f out: sn wknd* **7/1**[2]

0000 **F** **Seldom (IRE)**[43] 5601 3-8-5 **64** .... JohnCavanagh(7) 9 —
(M Brittain) *midfield: outpcd whn bdly hmpd and fell over 3f out* **33/1**

1m 28.58s (4.08) **Going Correction** +0.50s/f (Yiel) **18 Ran SP% 124.1**
Speed ratings (Par 101): **96,94,94,89,88 88,88,86,85,80 73,72,72,69,67 63,52,—**
toteswingers: 1&2 £42.20, 1&3 £49.20, 2&3 £59.50 CSF £165.60 CT £2131.44 TOTE £20.50: £4.60, £3.70, £3.50, £4.00; EX 119.20 Place 6: £185.10 Place 5: £266.20.
Owner G L S Partnership **Bred** Clougher Partnership **Trained** Carluke, S Lanarks
■ Stewards' Enquiry : Silvestre De Sousa five-day ban: careless riding (Oct 30-Nov 3)

FOCUS
A modest 56-70 handicap and an eventful end to the 2009 season at Redcar. The winner probably did not need to improve.
Cook's Endeavour(USA) Official explanation: jockey said gelding missed the break
T/Plt: £98.10 to a £1 stake. Pool: £42,162.86. 313.48 winning tickets. T/Qpdt: £25.70 to a £1 stake. Pool: £3,948.24. 113.60 winning tickets. JR

6800 WOLVERHAMPTON (A.W) (L-H)
Friday, October 16

OFFICIAL GOING: Standard changing to standard to fast after race 1 (5.45)
Wind: Nil Weather: Fine

6825 TOTESPORTBINGO.COM APPRENTICE H'CAP 5f 216y(P)
5:45 (5:47) (Class 6) (0-65,71) 3-Y-O+ £2,388 (£705; £352) **Stalls** Low

Form RPR

0401 **1** **Silver Guest**[7] 6637 4-9-9 **71** 6ex .... IJBrennan(3) 2 79+
(M R Channon) *sn hld up in mid-div: hdwy on ins 3f out: wnt 2nd wl over 1f out: rdn to ld cl home* **7/2**[1]

0004 **2** *hd* **Yanza**[21] 6252 3-9-0 **60** ....(b[1]) AshleyMorgan 1 67
(J R Gask) *sn led: rdn wl over 1f out: hdd cl home* **25/1**

5631 **3** *1/2* **Titus Gent**[6] 6670 4-9-1 **65** 6ex .... SPRyan(5) 10 70
(R A Harris) *hld up in mid-div: hdwy on ins wl over 1f out: sn rdn: r.o ins fnl f* **4/1**[2]

0241 **4** *1 1/2* **Rainy Night**[34] 5881 3-8-13 **64** .... DavidKenny(5) 6 65
(R Hollinshead) *a.p: n.m.r briefly 2f out: rdn over 1f out: nt qckn fnl f* **12/1**

0000 **5** *1 3/4* **Rabbit Fighter (IRE)**[3] 6764 5-8-13 **61** ow2 ....(v) ByronMoorcroft(3) 3 56
(D Shaw) *s.i.s: hld up in rr: hdwy on ins over 1f out: rdn and kpt on one pce fnl f* **12/1**

6000 **6** *nse* **Grimes Faith**[29] 6010 6-9-6 **65** ....(p) AmyRyan 11 60
(K A Ryan) *hld up towards rr: nt clr run on ins briefly jst over 2f out: hdwy wl over 1f out: rdn and one pce fnl f* **25/1**

-203 **7** *2* **Witchry**[25] 6175 7-9-3 **62** .... PaulPickard 5 50
(A G Newcombe) *hld up in tch: lost pl over 3f out: rdn over 2f out: no hdwy* **8/1**[3]

5040 **8** *shd* **Golden Dixie (USA)**[4] 6738 10-8-13 **63** ....(p) JakePayne(5) 4 51
(R A Harris) *chsd ldr: ev ch over 2f out: rdn and wknd fnl f* **18/1**

500 **9** *1 1/4* **Weekend Away (IRE)**[46] 5503 3-9-1 **64** .... LeeNewnes(3) 8 48
(S Kirk) *a in rr* **14/1**

0/ **10** *nk* **Doorock (IRE)**[4] 6747 5-9-3 **62** ....(p) RossAtkinson 7 45
(S T Nolan, Ire) *t.k.h: prom: pushed along over 2f out: rdn and wknd wl over 1f out* **9/1**

0161 **11** *shd* **Boho Chic**[18] 6340 3-9-5 **65** ....(p) MatthewDavies 9 48
(George Baker) *prom tl pushed along and wknd wl over 1f out* **14/1**

0600 **12** *2 1/2* **Grand Palace (IRE)**[27] 6120 6-9-1 **63** ....(v) SimonPearce(3) 13 38
(H J Evans) *in rr: pushed along wl over 3f out: struggling over 2f out* **33/1**

0526 **13** *nk* **Maison Dieu**[15] 6413 6-9-2 **61** ....(b) AmyBaker 12 35
(E J Alston) *hld up in mid-div on outside: rdn over 2f out: c v wd st: sn bhd* **16/1**

1m 14.4s (-0.60) **Going Correction** -0.15s/f (Stan)
WFA 3 from 4yo+ 1lb **13 Ran SP% 113.8**
Speed ratings (Par 101): **98,97,97,95,92 92,90,89,88,87 87,84,83**
toteswingers: 1&2 £48.00, 1&3 £2.10, 2&3 £49.60 CSF £93.99 CT £374.31 TOTE £2.90: £1.70, £10.00, £1.20; EX 87.10.
Owner John Guest **Bred** Timber Hill Racing Partnership **Trained** West Ilsley, Berks

FOCUS
A modest apprentice handicap, but there were four last-time-out winners in the line-up and three of them finished in the first four. Ordinary form, the runner-up the best guide.

6826 TOTESPORTGAMES.COM MEDIAN AUCTION MAIDEN STKS 5f 216y(P)
6:15 (6:16) (Class 6) 2-Y-O £2,388 (£705; £352) **Stalls** Low

Form RPR

3000 **1** **So Surreal (IRE)**[21] 6241 2-8-12 **71** ....(b) FergusSweeney 6 73
(G L Moore) *a.p: hrd rdn to ld nr fin* **15/2**

6 **2** *nk* **Suranam**[29] 6018 2-9-3 **0** .... KirstyMilczarek 9 77
(W J Haggas) *a.p: edgd lft over 1f out: rdn to ld wl ins fnl f: edgd lft: hdd nr fin* **5/2**[1]

6 **3** *1 1/4* **Goddess Of Light (IRE)**[12] 6514 2-8-12 **0** .... ShaneKelly 4 68
(Daniel Mark Loughnane, Ire) *led: rdn over 1f out: hdd wl ins fnl f: nt qckn* **11/2**[3]

34 **4** *1 1/2* **Major Maximus**[7] 6638 2-8-12 **0** .... MatthewDavies(5) 11 69
(George Baker) *hld up: pushed along and hdwy over 1f out: rdn and one pce fnl f* **9/2**[2]

5 **5** *2* **Notte Di Note (IRE)**[18] 6334 2-8-12 **0** .... ChrisCatlin 13 58
(L M Cumani) *w ldr: ev ch over 2f out: pushed along and wknd over 1f out* **10/1**

6 *nse* **Blast**[62] 5044 2-8-12 **0** ....(b[1]) LukeMorris 8 58
(J R Gask) *hld up: hdwy wl over 1f out: sn hrd rdn: wknd ins fnl f* **40/1**

6 **7** *nk* **Bobby's Doll**[15] 6424 2-8-12 **0** .... TGMcLaughlin 12 57
(T T Clement) *hld up: pushed along 3f out: no hdwy fnl 2f* **66/1**

533 **8** *1 1/2* **One Good Emperor (IRE)**[16] 6372 2-9-0 **78** .... MarcHalford(3) 7 57
(J R Best) *prom: pushed along over 2f out: wknd wl over 1f out* **5/2**[1]

4034 **9** *2 1/2* **Bitter Honey**[77] 4493 2-8-5 **64** .... BillyCray(7) 2 45
(Mrs G S Rees) *prom: pushed along on ins over 2f out: rdn and wknd wl over 1f out* **22/1**

0 **10** *1/2* **Flash For Freedom (USA)**[95] 3920 2-9-3 **0** .... PaulHanagan 1 49+
(J R Best) *s.i.s: pushed along 3f out: a in rr* **16/1**

1m 15.11s (0.11) **Going Correction** -0.15s/f (Stan) **10 Ran SP% 125.7**
Speed ratings (Par 93): **93,92,90,88,86 86,85,83,80,79**
toteswingers: 1&2 £4.60, 1&3 £7.90, 2&3 £6.00 CSF £28.51 TOTE £8.00: £2.50, £1.40, £1.90; EX 30.40.
Owner R Henderson & B Cunningham **Bred** Rathasker Stud **Trained** Lower Beeding, W Sussex

FOCUS
The going was changed to standard to fast. Not a great maiden, but several were closely matched on form and the winner had a BHA rating of 71. Limited form but it makes sense.

NOTEBOOK
So Surreal(IRE) had a leading chance on her third to quite useful Puff at Lingfield in July and showed signs of a revival with blinkers applied faced with a very stiff task in an Ascot sales race last time. The headgear was back on here, and she found a sustained run in the straight to cut down the leaders who had been fighting it out for a couple of furlongs. She does not look an easy ride, but there is quite a bit of ability there and she should be competitive back in handicaps off her current mark. (op 7-1 tchd 13-2)
Suranam had quite a bit to find here but ran a huge race stepped up in trip and showed some good fighting qualities to overhaul the third before being picked off by the late raider. (op 7-2)
Goddess Of Light(IRE) was a bit keen up with the pace but showed a good attitude to keep battling. She was clear fourth behind a pair rated in the 70s in a 6f Dundalk maiden this month and adds some solidity to the form. (op 6-1 tchd 7-1)
Major Maximus could never get into it after being switched to the inside from a wide draw but did do some good late work. He is out of a multiple sprint winner but could stay a bit further than this and should be able to make an impact when sent handicapping. (tchd 4-1 and 5-1)
Notte Di Note(IRE) ran well for a long way and showed a similar hint of ability as she did when a fading fifth behind a 70-rated rival in a 7f Brighton maiden on her debut. (op 11-1 tchd 9-1)
Blast, regressive at big prices in three runs in Ireland, took a minor step back in the right direction with blinkers applied on her debut for a new yard after two months off. (op 28-1)
One Good Emperor(IRE) was in serious trouble turning for home and toiled after that. (op 7-2 tchd 4-1)

6827 WOLVERHAMPTON-RACECOURSE.CO.UK NURSERY 5f 20y(P)
6:45 (6:45) (Class 4) (0-85,82) 2-Y-O £3,885 (£1,156; £577; £288) **Stalls** Low

Form RPR

3423 **1** **Lewyn**[17] 6355 2-8-7 **68** .... FergusSweeney 11 72
(K A Ryan) *t.k.h: a.p: c wd st: pushed along over 1f out: edgd lft and led ins fnl f: r.o* **16/1**

2653 **2** *1 1/4* **Six Wives**[2] 6774 2-9-2 **77** .... JamesDoyle 6 76
(J A Glover) *led: rdn over 1f out: hdd ins fnl f: nt qckn* **11/1**

6050 **3** *nk* **Dancing Freddy (IRE)**[13] 6486 2-9-3 **78** .... PatCosgrave 8 76
(J G Given) *s.i.s: hld up in rr: hdwy on ins over 2f out: pushed along wl over 1f out: rdn and r.o to take 3rd last strides* **16/1**

5413 **4** *shd* **Ruthie Babe**[24] 6185 2-8-7 **68** .... KirstyMilczarek 2 66
(W J Haggas) *hld up in mid-div: hdwy on ins to chse ldr 2f out: ev ch over 1f out: rdn fnl f: kpt on* **4/1**[1]

4022 **5** *1/2* **Gower Sophia**[10] 6555 2-8-1 **67** .... AndrewHeffernan(5) 4 63
(M Brittain) *a.p: rdn wl over 1f out: kpt on towards fin* **8/1**

4204 **6** *2* **Leleyf (IRE)**[11] 6550 2-9-3 **78** .... ChrisCatlin 7 67
(M R Channon) *hld up towards rr: hdwy on ins wl over 1f out: rdn and wknd ins fnl f* **13/2**[2]

1333 **7** *1 1/4* **Any Day (IRE)**[33] 5899 2-8-3 **71** .... JPFahy(7) 13 55
(R M Beckett) *hld up in tch: pushed along wl over 1f out: rdn and btn ent fnl f* **12/1**

2516 **8** *1/2* **Micky's Knock Off (IRE)**[11] 6550 2-9-2 **77** .... J-PGuillambert 9 59
(R C Guest) *hld up towards rr: pushed along over 2f out: sn struggling* **16/1**

2110 **9** *3/4* **Italian Tom (IRE)**[16] 6398 2-9-5 **80** .... LukeMorris 10 60
(R A Harris) *chsd ldr tl pushed along 2f out: sn rdn and wknd* **7/1**[3]

012 **10** *1* **Star Promise**[66] 4875 2-8-10 **76** .... DeanHeslop(5) 12 52
(T D Barron) *a in rr* **8/1**

0231 **11** *3 1/4* **Morgans Choice**[34] 5866 2-8-12 **73** .... DaneO'Neill 5 37
(J L Spearing) *hld up in mid-div: pushed along 2f out: rdn and wknd over 1f out* **13/2**[2]

61.67 secs (-0.63) **Going Correction** -0.15s/f (Stan) **11 Ran SP% 115.1**
Speed ratings (Par 97): **99,97,96,96,95 92,90,89,88,86 81**
toteswingers: 1&2 £63.90, 1&3 £29.30, 2&3 £28.00 CSF £176.92 CT £2891.40 TOTE £21.50: £5.80, £4.20, £3.90; EX 161.30.

Owner N Cable & M Smith **Bred** Mrs S J Walker **Trained** Hambleton, N Yorks

FOCUS

A decent nursery. The pace looked solid but the hold-up performers struggled to land a blow. The form has a solid but limited feel.

NOTEBOOK

Lewyn had shaped like a future winner on a few occasions and found a sweeping run out wide to get the job done in good style on her sixth attempt. She has hung and looked a bit quirky at times but she has steadily improved since blinkers have been applied. She should not go up much for this win and there could be more to come. (op 12-1)

Six Wives gave it a good shot under trailblazing tactics on her 14th start of the season. (op 9-1 tchd 12-1)

Dancing Freddy(IRE) deserves credit for doing best of those who came from some way back.

Ruthie Babe made a successful start to her nursery career at Ffos Las last month and was unlucky not to finish closer at Folkestone last time. She avoided trouble back on the all-weather and put in another decent effort, particularly as she was a bit keen early on. She remains capable of better. (op 7-2)

Gower Sophia never really looked like justifying support switched to more patient tactics with a visor removed but she did stay on strongly after being switched wide at the furlong marker. (op 11-1 tchd 15-2)

Leleyf(IRE) usually likes to attack up front but could not get near the pace here. However, she did quite well in the circumstances to plug on from some way back on her 17th run since March. She is a likeable type who has won three times this year but this mark may represent the ceiling of her ability. (op 10-1)

6828 HOTEL & CONFERENCING AT WOLVERHAMPTON H'CAP 7f 32y(P)

7:15 (7:15) (Class 6) (0-60,60) 3-Y-O+ £2,388 (£705; £352) Stalls High

Form	Pos	Btn	Horse / Comment	RPR
0120	1		**Connor's Choice**[16] 6377 4-8-13 **60**........ SimonPearce(5) 2 (Andrew Turnell) *led 1f: a.p: shkn up to ld over 1f out: readily* **14/1**	68
0205	2	½	**Loyal Royal (IRE)**[13] 6492 6-8-13 **58**........(b) JackDean(3) 1 (J M Bradley) *t.k.h towards rr: hdwy on ins wl over 1f out: chsd wnr ins fnl f: rdn and nt qckn* **5/1**	65
0353	3	1 ¼	**Turkish Lokum**[18] 6344 3-9-1 **59**........ LukeMorris 12 (J M P Eustace) *swtchd lft sn after s: hld up towards rr: c wd st: hdwy wl over 1f out: sn rdn and edgd lft: nt qckn ins fnl f* **20/1**	63
121	4	1 ¼	**Averoo**[10] 6568 4-9-2 **58**........(p) ShaneKelly 4 (M D Squance) *hld up in mid-div: hdwy 2f out: nt clr run ent st: swtchd rt over 1f out: rdn and kpt on to take 4th post* **10/3**[1]	61+
0135	5	hd	**Golden Prospect**[18] 6339 5-9-0 **59**........ PatrickHills(3) 5 (J W Hills) *hld up towards rr: hdwy and swtchd lft wl over 1f out: rdn and one pce fnl f* **4/1**[3]	59
0544	6	nk	**Goodbye Cash (IRE)**[10] 6568 5-8-11 **58**........ RichardEvans(5) 3 (P D Evans) *hld up in tch: nt clr run on ins 2f out: swtchd lft 1f out: rdn and one pce ins fnl f* **11/1**	57+
-560	7	1 ½	**The City Kid (IRE)**[42] 5634 6-9-1 **57**........ ChrisCatlin 9 (G D Blake) *hld up in rr: hdwy on ins whn nt clr run over 1f out: sn swtchd rt: nvr trbld ldrs* **33/1**	52
-003	8	3 ¾	**Ros Cuire (IRE)**[15] 6414 4-9-1 **57**........ PaulHanagan 6 (W A Murphy, Ire) *prom: pushed along and wknd over 1f out* **20/1**	42
6-24	9	½	**Cape Cobra**[7] 6637 5-9-4 **60**........(b) GeorgeBaker 7 (H Morrison) *led after 1f: rdn and hdd over 1f out: wknd fnl f* **7/2**[2]	43
6004	10	9	**Norcroft**[18] 6336 7-9-3 **59**........(v) TGMcLaughlin 11 (Mrs C A Dunnett) *hld up: hdwy on outside over 5f out: rdn and wknd 2f out* **33/1**	18
5000	11	hd	**Greystoke Prince**[30] 5991 4-9-3 **59**........ PaulQuinn 10 (W R Swinburn) *prom: jnd ldr over 5f out: ev ch over 2f out: wknd wl over 1f out* **33/1**	18

1m 28.81s (-0.79) **Going Correction** -0.15s/f (Stan)

WFA 3 from 4yo+ 2lb 11 Ran SP% **115.3**

Speed ratings (Par 101): **98,97,96,94,94 94,92,88,87,77 76**

toteswingers: 1&2 £9.90, 1&3 £36.40, 2&3 £18.80 CSF £75.51 CT £1428.67 TOTE £18.20: £2.80, £2.50, £3.00; EX 115.70.

Owner Andrew Turnell **Bred** Mrs Claire Hollowood **Trained** Broad Hinton, Wilts

FOCUS

An ordinary handicap run at a decent pace. Sound form.

The City Kid(IRE) Official explanation: jockey said mare was denied a clear run

6829 TOTESPORTCASINO.COM NURSERY 7f 32y(P)

7:45 (7:45) (Class 5) (0-70,71) 2-Y-O £2,914 (£867; £433; £216) Stalls High

Form	Pos	Btn	Horse / Comment	RPR
065	1		**Be A Devil**[21] 6254 2-9-4 **67**........ DaneO'Neill 7 (W R Muir) *hld up in mid-div: hdwy over 2f out: rdn wl over 1f out: r.o to ld wl ins fnl f* **12/1**	73
0604	2	2	**Pat Seamur**[28] 6071 2-9-3 **66**........ PaulHanagan 4 (E A L Dunlop) *led: rdn 2f out: clr over 1f out: hdd and no ex wl ins fnl f* **4/1**[2]	67
3652	3	½	**Ginger Grey (IRE)**[17] 6366 2-9-3 **66**........(p) GeorgeBaker 8 (S A Callaghan, U.S.A) *hld up towards rr: hdwy wl over 1f out: sn rdn and edgd lft: kpt on ins fnl f* **6/1**[3]	66
0306	4	1 ½	**Nave (USA)**[72] 4647 2-9-1 **64**........ J-PGuillambert 12 (M Johnston) *s.i.s: hld up in rr: pushed along 3f out: c v wd st: rdn and styd on fnl f: nrst fin* **16/1**	60
0021	5	nk	**Kilt Rock (IRE)**[8] 6610 2-9-8 **71** 6ex........ JamesDoyle 1 (T G Mills) *s.i.s: sn hld up in mid-div: hdwy wl over 1f out: sn rdn: one pce fnl f* **2/1**[1]	66
4613	6	2 ¼	**Russian Davis (IRE)**[35] 5841 2-9-5 **68**........ ShaneKelly 10 (R M H Cowell) *t.k.h: hdwy on outside over 5f out: ev ch over 2f out: rdn and wknd ins fnl f* **8/1**	58
6430	7	nk	**Jimmy The Poacher (IRE)**[40] 5692 2-9-5 **68**........ DuranFentiman 9 (T D Easterby) *hld up towards rr: pushed along over 3f out: nvr nr ldrs* **25/1**	57
404	8	2	**Rigid**[83] 4308 2-9-5 **68**........ PatCosgrave 2 (J G Given) *chsd ldr 1f: prom tl rdn and wknd over 1f out* **20/1**	52
0000	9	½	**Rosiliant (IRE)**[17] 6367 2-9-2 **65**........(b[1]) LukeMorris 11 (C G Cox) *prom: rdn over 3f out: c wd st: wkng whn edgd lft wl over 1f out* **66/1**	48
01	10	2	**Royal Holiday (IRE)**[67] 4839 2-9-7 **70**........ TomEaves 5 (B Ellison) *hld up towards rr: pushed along and short-lived effrt over 2f out* **14/1**	48
043	11	4 ½	**Magneto (IRE)**[14] 6461 2-9-1 **64**........ CatherineGannon 6 (E J Creighton) *chsd ldr after 1f tl rdn over 2f out: wknd wl over 1f out* **20/1**	31
030	12	3	**Rockweiller**[43] 5611 2-9-3 **66**........(b[1]) ChrisCatlin 3 (C R Egerton) *s.i.s: a in rr* **25/1**	26

1m 29.44s (-0.16) **Going Correction** -0.15s/f (Stan) 12 Ran SP% **117.7**

Speed ratings (Par 95): **94,91,91,89,89 86,86,83,83,81 75,72**

toteswingers: 1&2 £18.50, 1&3 £13.70, 2&3 £5.10 CSF £55.20 CT £324.79 TOTE £13.90: £2.70, £2.40, £2.00; EX 75.20.

Owner Foursome Thoroughbreds **Bred** Darley **Trained** Lambourn, Berks

FOCUS

A fair nursery. The third sets a solid level and the winner was much improved.

NOTEBOOK

Be A Devil looked on a difficult rating for his nursery debut and did not attract much interest in the market but he responded really well to pressure and found a storming run to get off the mark on his fourth attempt. He is a half-brother to high-class 6f-7f performer Miss Lucifer and could be capable of quite a bit of progress at this trip and a bit further. Official explanation: trainer's rep said, regarding apparent improvement in form, that the gelding had improved with time.

Pat Seamur ◆ ensured a good pace and looked the likely winner when kicking clear early in the straight but he was just reeled in. His sire is an influence for speed and he showed plenty of natural pace here, so may be hard to catch if allowed to dominate back at 6f. (op 9-2 tchd 7-2)

Ginger Grey(IRE) added another creditable run to his sequence of good efforts with and without cheekpieces in turf/AW nurseries at 6f-1m. He should be able to win one of these but does have a habit of finding trouble, is now 0-12 and could be the type who needs exact timing. (op 7-1 tchd 5-1)

Nave(USA) stayed on well from a long way back and has finished quite a bit closer to Ginger Grey than he did over a furlong shorter at Kempton on his previous run 72 days earlier. The $100,000 colt should be sharper next time and is open to improvement at this trip. (op 14-1)

Kilt Rock(IRE) looked highly progressive when storming up the far rail to land a massive gamble in 6f Kempton nursery last week. He had a penalty and an extra 2lb to deal with over this longer trip but he seemed to lack a bit of spark and this run may have come too soon. (op 9-4)

6830 BEST ODDS AT TOTESPORT.COM H'CAP 1m 141y(P)

8:15 (8:17) (Class 4) (0-85,85) 3-Y-O+ £5,046 (£1,510; £755; £377; £188) Stalls Low

Form	Pos	Btn	Horse / Comment	RPR
2331	1		**Ithinkbest**[11] 6539 3-9-0 **84** 6ex........ Louis-PhilippeBeuzelin(3) 6 (Sir Michael Stoute) *led early: a.p: chsd ldr jst over 3f out: rdn to ld 1f out: r.o* **12/1**	91
0231	2	nk	**Farleigh House (USA)**[15] 6435 5-9-6 **83**........ ChrisCatlin 2 (Sir Mark Prescott) *hld up in tch: pushed along over 1f out: rdn and kpt on to take 2nd last strides* **15/8**[1]	89
3005	3	nse	**Wellington Square**[5] 6695 4-9-6 **83**........ GeorgeBaker 4 (H Morrison) *s.i.s: hld up in mid-div: hdwy on ins wl over 1f out: sn rdn: styd on to take 3rd last strides* **15/2**[3]	89
0002	4	shd	**Spinning**[14] 6462 6-9-0 **80**........(b) NeilBrown(3) 5 (T D Barron) *s.i.s: hld up in rr: rdn and hdwy whn swtchd rt over 1f out: fin wl* **14/1**	86
4353	5	nse	**Emperor Court (IRE)**[25] 6168 5-9-6 **83**........ FergusSweeney 12 (P J Makin) *sn led: rdn and hdd 1f out: r.o but lost 3 pls last strides* **25/1**	89
0210	6	4	**Bomber Command (USA)**[25] 6168 6-9-5 **85**........(v) PatrickHills(3) 8 (J W Hills) *hld up in tch: pushed along over 2f out: wknd over 1f out* **28/1**	81
010-	7	1 ½	**Rising Prospect**[356] 6973 3-9-2 **83**........ KFallon 1 (L M Cumani) *hld up in mid-div: pushed along and hdwy on ins 2f out: rdn over 1f out: wknd ins fnl f* **3/1**[2]	76
4000	8	nk	**Maze (IRE)**[76] 4549 4-9-3 **80**........ TomEaves 3 (B Smart) *hld up in mid-div: pushed along over 2f out: rdn and btn jst over 1f out* **33/1**	72
0055	9	1	**Gallantry**[29] 6024 7-9-8 **85**........ JerryO'Dwyer 9 (P Howling) *s.i.s: hld up in rr: pushed along 3f out: rdn wl over 1f out: no rspnse* **33/1**	75
5006	10	½	**Arabian Spirit**[16] 6374 4-9-5 **82**........ TGMcLaughlin 7 (E A L Dunlop) *hld up in mid-div: pushed along over 3f out: bhd fnl 2f* **22/1**	71
3010	11	3 ¾	**Agilete**[9] 6594 7-9-1 **83**........ SimonPearce(5) 13 (J Pearce) *hld up in mid-div: pushed along 2f out: rdn and wknd over 1f out* **28/1**	63
0220	P		**Brouhaha**[15] 6435 5-9-7 **84**........ RichardKingscote 10 (Tom Dascombe) *sn chsng ldr: lost 2nd over 3f out: pushed along and lost action 2f out: sn eased: p.u ins fnl f* **12/1**	—
0240	P		**Clientele (USA)**[27] 6092 3-9-1 **82**........ J-PGuillambert 11 (M Johnston) *s.i.s: a in rr: pushed along over 3f out: sn eased: p.u ins fnl f* **16/1**	—

1m 47.9s (-2.60) **Going Correction** -0.15s/f (Stan)

WFA 3 from 4yo+ 4lb 13 Ran SP% **120.5**

Speed ratings (Par 105): **105,104,104,104,104 101,99,99,98,98 94,—,—**

toteswingers: 1&2 £3.10, 1&3 £9.50, 2&3 £3.80 CSF £32.37 CT £189.47 TOTE £12.80: £3.00, £1.30, £3.40; EX 26.70.

Owner Saeed Suhail **Bred** Highbury Stud Ltd **Trained** Newmarket, Suffolk

■ Stewards' Enquiry : Louis-Philippe Beuzelin one-day ban: failed to ride to draw (Oct 30)

FOCUS

A decent handicap. It was fast and furious and produced an exciting finish. The first five finished in a bunch and the bare form is only ordinary for the grade but the winner and runner-up are both progressive types and the form could work out.

Brouhaha Official explanation: jockey said gelding lost its action

Clientele(USA) Official explanation: jockey said gelding's fore-lef became caught in the stalls prior to race

6831 BETXTRA WIN ONLY AT TOTESPORT.COM CLASSIFIED STKS 1m 1f 103y(P)

8:45 (8:49) (Class 6) 3-Y-O+ £2,047 (£604; £302) Stalls Low

Form	Pos	Btn	Horse / Comment	RPR
	1		**Mondego (GER)**[610] 5479 7-8-11 55........ MatthewDavies(5) 5 (George Baker) *hld up in mid-div: rdn over 2f out: c wd st: edgd lft and hdwy over 1f out: led ins fnl f: rdn out* **15/8**[1]	56+
3600	2	1 ½	**Rascal In The Mix (USA)**[30] 5982 3-8-7 54........ AmyRyan(5) 8 (R M Whitaker) *hld up towards rr: rdn over 2f out: hdwy over 1f out: r.o to take 2nd nr fin* **9/1**	53
000-	3	¾	**Bourn Fair**[335] 7337 3-8-12 55........ DaneO'Neill 3 (P J McBride) *a.p: led wl over 1f out: sn rdn: hdd ins fnl f: no ex* **8/1**	51
0500	4	hd	**Head First**[16] 6371 3-8-12 49........ PaulHanagan 13 (W Jarvis) *a.p: led over 3f out: c wd st: rdn and hdd wl over 1f out: no ex towards fin* **7/1**[3]	51
5000	5	5	**Qualitas**[76] 4552 3-8-12 52........ PaulMulrennan 12 (M W Easterby) *hld up in tch: pushed along over 3f out: rdn wl over 2f out: wknd ins fnl f* **6/1**[2]	41
0-00	6	¾	**Yaldas Girl (USA)**[42] 5644 3-8-9 50........ MarcHalford(3) 11 (J R Best) *prom: pushed along wl over 2f out: rdn and wknd wl over 1f out* **18/1**	39
6-00	7	¾	**Anasy (USA)**[36] 5789 3-8-9 48 ow2........ KylieManser(5) 9 (T Keddy) *hld up in rr: pushed along over 3f out: rdn and hdwy on ins over 1f out: n.d* **40/1**	39

0 **8** 2¼ **A Chailin Mo Chroi (IRE)**[70] 4755 4-9-2 44....................(p) ChrisCatlin 7 33
(Aidan Anthony Howard, Ire) *t.k.h: stdd into mid-div after 2f: pushed along over 3f out: sn bhd* **22/1**

400- **9** ¾ **Lunar Romance**[439] 4659 3-8-7 49.................................. RossAtkinson(5) 6 31
(T J Pitt) *hld up towards rr: sme prog on ins over 3f out: rdn over 2f out: wknd wl over 1f out* **40/1**

\- **10** 2¼ **Tumblecloud (IRE)**[404] 5724 4-9-2 44.............................. TomEaves 4 26
(W A Murphy, Ire) *hld up in rr: sme hdwy on ins over 2f out: rdn and wknd over 1f out* **20/1**

0000 **11** 9 **Vigorosa (IRE)**[113] 3303 3-8-12 42.................................. JerryO'Dwyer 1 7
(P Howling) *led: hdd over 3f out: sn rdn: wknd wl over 1f out: sn eased* **14/1**

6000 **P** **The Staffy (IRE)**[13] 6495 4-9-2 55........................(v[1]) RichardKingscote 10 —
(Tom Dascombe) *hdwy over 6f out: prom whn wnt lame and p.u over 3f out* **6/1**[2]

2m 2.50s (0.80) **Going Correction** -0.15s/f (Stan)
WFA 3 from 4yo+ 4lb **12** Ran SP% **122.9**
Speed ratings (Par 101): **90,88,88,87,83 82,82,80,79,77 69,—**
toteswingers: 1&2 £11.10, 1&3 £9.70, 2&3 £9.10 CSF £19.66 TOTE £2.80: £2.00, £2.10, £3.40; EX 26.60.
Owner Lady Forwood & Partners **Bred** S Pavenstedt And J Th Pavenstedt **Trained** Moreton Morrell, Warwicks

FOCUS
A very poor race and weak form even for the grade. It was hard to find a positive angle on many of the runners but the market proved highly informative.
Vigorosa(IRE) Official explanation: jockey said filly had no more to give

6832 BET ON LIVE SPORT AT TOTESPORT.COM H'CAP 1m 4f 50y(P)
9:15 (9:16) (Class 5) (0-70,70) 3-Y-0+ **£2,914** (£867; £433; £216) **Stalls** Low

Form RPR

000 **1** **Black Rain**[25] 6174 4-9-10 **69**.................................. TGMcLaughlin 4 79+
(M Wigham) *hld up in tch: led wl over 1f out: drvn out* **9/2**[2]

5030 **2** 1¼ **Shady Gloom (IRE)**[31] 5962 4-9-1 **65**..........................(v[1]) AmyRyan(5) 3 71
(K A Ryan) *s.i.s: hld up towards rr: hdwy on ins over 3f out: pushed along and n.m.r 2f out: ev ch over 1f out: rdn and nt qckn ins fnl f* **14/1**

6506 **3** 3 **Dubburg (USA)**[28] 6074 4-9-2 **61**.................................. ChrisCatlin 2 62
(W J Musson) *hld up in rr: rdn and hdwy wl over 1f out: one pce ins fnl f* **10/1**

5350 **4** 5 **Strike Force**[17] 6369 5-8-11 **56** oh1................................ TomEaves 7 49
(Miss J Feilden) *hld up towards rr: pushed along and hdwy over 2f out: hrd rdn over 1f out: wknd ins fnl f* **15/2**[3]

120- **5** 2½ **Covert Mission**[270] 7272 6-8-11 **56**.............................. PatCosgrave 8 45
(P D Evans) *hld up in mid-div: hdwy 4f out: rdn wl over 1f out: wknd ins fnl f* **16/1**

1062 **6** 3 **Moonshine Creek**[123] 2983 7-9-3 **65**.................... WilliamCarson(3) 1 49
(P W Hiatt) *led 2f: chsd ldr: led over 3f out: rdn and hdd wl over 1f out: sn wknd* **8/1**

1513 **7** 6 **Oddsmaker (IRE)**[25] 6156 8-9-3 **67**....................(t) AndrewHeffernan(5) 5 42
(M A Barnes) *led after 2f: rdn and hdd over 3f out: sn wknd* **15/2**[3]

2-00 **8** 1¾ **Desert Vision**[41] 5673 5-9-11 **70**..............................(t) PaulMulrennan 6 51
(M W Easterby) *prom: ev ch 2f out: wknd wl over 1f out: eased fnl f* **16/1**

0322 **9** 16 **Wind Flow**[7] 6634 5-9-8 **67**..................................(v) CatherineGannon 11 13
(C A Dwyer) *bhd fnl 7f: lost tch over 3f out* **7/2**[1]

-050 **10** 66 **Spiritual Treasure (USA)**[77] 4481 3-9-2 **68**................. PaulHanagan 12 —
(M A Magnusson) *s.i.s: hdwy 8f out: lost pl over 6f out: rdn over 5f out: lost tch and eased 3f out* **9/2**[2]

2m 37.68s (-3.42) **Going Correction** -0.15s/f (Stan)
WFA 3 from 4yo+ 7lb **10** Ran SP% **120.7**
Speed ratings (Par 103): **105,104,102,98,97 95,91,90,79,35**
toteswingers: 1&2 £19.70, 1&3 £17.00, 2&3 £22.20 CSF £68.05 CT £610.60 TOTE £4.90: £2.30, £4.80, £3.30; EX 119.00 Place 6: £1027.31 Place 5: £537.06.
Owner R Morecombe, SP Racing Investments SA **Bred** Kirtlington Stud And Gilridge Bloodstock **Trained** Newmarket, Suffolk

FOCUS
A minor handicap run at a fair pace. A few of the in-form runners were disappointing but the winner was quite impressive, and they finished strung out, so the form could be reliable.
Wind Flow Official explanation: jockey said gelding never travelled
T/Plt: £378.00 to a £1 stake. Pool: £75,851.10. 146.46 winning tickets. T/Qpdt: £495.90 to a £1 stake. Pool: £8,310.64. 12.40 winning tickets. KH

6833 - 6839a (Foreign Racing) - See Raceform Interactive

[6553] CATTERICK (L-H)
Saturday, October 17

OFFICIAL GOING: Good (8.3)
Wind: Light, half against Weather: Fine

6840 BET ON TODAY'S FOOTBALL AT TOTESPORT.COM APPRENTICE CLAIMING STKS 1m 3f 214y
1:40 (1:40) (Class 6) 3-Y-0+ **£2,729** (£806; £403) **Stalls** Low

Form RPR

6346 **1** **Drum Dragon**[12] 6538 3-8-9 67.................................. AshleyMorgan(3) 1 72+
(M H Tompkins) *trckd ldrs: smooth hdwy over 3f out: led on bit 2f out: pushed clr ent fnl f: styd on* **2/1**[1]

0350 **2** 3 **Lost Soldier Three (IRE)**[7] 6681 8-9-9 76........................ NSLawes(5) 2 72
(D Nicholls) *hld up in tch: hdwy on inner over 3f out: chsd ldrs 2f out: rdn to chse wnr ent fnl f: sn drvn and no imp* **2/1**[1]

0200 **3** 2¼ **Cecina Marina**[18] 6369 6-8-9 44.................................. AmyRyan(3) 4 52
(Mrs K Walton) *chsd ldng pair: effrt whn nt clr run 2f out: swtchd rt and rdn over 1f out: kpt on same pce ent fnl f* **14/1**

1200 **4** 7 **Bajan Parkes**[7] 6681 6-9-12 79.................................. DavidProbert 13 55
(E J Alston) *towards rr: hdwy 4f out and sn pushed along: rdn wl over 2f out: drvn and edgd lft over 1f out: nvr rchd ldrs* **7/1**[2]

256 **5** 3 **Aven Mac (IRE)**[4] 6766 3-7-13 44.................................. TerenceFury(7) 8 37
(N Bycroft) *in rr: sme hdwy over 2f out: sn rdn and nvr a factor* **28/1**

2043 **6** nk **Moggy (IRE)**[24] 6219 3-8-4 50 ow1.............................. PaulPickard(3) 3 38
(G A Harker) *led: pushed along 4f out: rdn over 3f out: drvn and hdd 2f out: sn wknd* **12/1**[3]

0066 **7** 2¼ **Grethel (IRE)**[20] 6310 5-8-8 42.................................. BillyCray(5) 9 33
(A Berry) *trckd ldrs: hdwy and cl up 1/2-way: rdn along over 3f out: drvn and edgd lft 2f out: sn wknd* **50/1**

2060 **8** 2¼ **Dream In Blue**[74] 4617 4-8-13 55.............................. JonathanHinch(7) 10 36
(J A Glover) *a in rr* **40/1**

3030 **9** 7 **Another Decree**[19] 6349 4-9-5 57..............................(p) NeilBrown 11 24
(M Dods) *hld up: a in rr* **12/1**[3]

0000 **10** 1 **Boy Dancer (IRE)**[49] 5423 6-8-13 47.............................. IJBrennan(5) 14 22
(J J Quinn) *plld hrd: cl up: rdn along 1/2-way: wknd wl over 3f out* **28/1**

4-00 **11** nk **Bigalo's Star (IRE)**[28] 6098 3-8-6 60....................(p) JamesPSullivan(5) 12 21
(L A Mullaney) *in tch: rdn along 1/2-way: wknd 4f out* **80/1**

2m 38.95s (0.05) **Going Correction** +0.05s/f (Good)
WFA 3 from 4yo+ 7lb **11** Ran SP% **113.7**
Speed ratings (Par 101): **101,99,97,92,90 90,89,87,82,82 82**
toteswingers: 1&2 £2.40, 1&3 £8.10, 2&3 £8.40 CSF £4.98 TOTE £3.20: £1.40, £1.40, £3.40; EX 8.50.The winner was the subject of a friendly claim.
Owner David P Noblett **Bred** Ian Lochhead **Trained** Newmarket, Suffolk

FOCUS
This apprentice riders' claimer featured mainly horses on the downgrade, but the winner was a notable exception. Muddling form.

6841 BET LIVE IN PLAY AT TOTESPORT.COM NOVICE STKS 5f
2:15 (2:16) (Class 4) 2-Y-0 **£4,209** (£1,252; £625; £312) **Stalls** Low

Form RPR

51 **1** **The Only Boss (IRE)**[17] 6381 2-9-5 0.............................. LiamJones 6 90+
(W J Haggas) *led tl over 1f out: led ins fnl f: drvn out* **9/2**[2]

2301 **2** ½ **Chips O'Toole (IRE)**[16] 6418 2-9-5 79.............................. AlanMunro 7 88
(B J Meehan) *w ldrs: slt advantage over 1f out: hdd and no ex ins fnl f* **7/2**[1]

0331 **3** 3¾ **Night Trade (IRE)**[11] 6554 2-8-7 73 ow1........... RussellKennemore(3) 13 68+
(Mrs D J Sanderson) *chsd ldrs: hung lft 1f out: kpt on same pce* **13/2**

31 **4** 1½ **Durham Express (IRE)**[44] 5596 2-9-0 74.......................... PhillipMakin 10 64
(M Dods) *sn outpcd: hdwy and edgd rt over 1f out: kpt on: nvr trbld ldrs* **11/2**

5 **5** 2½ **As You Like It (IRE)**[1] 6820 2-8-7 0.............................. GregFairley 3 48
(John Joseph Murphy, Ire) *chsd ldrs: outpcd over 2f out: kpt on fnl f* **20/1**

0215 **6** 2¾ **Hold On Tiger (IRE)**[29] 6048 2-9-2 77.............................. PJMcDonald 4 50+
(I Semple) *w ldrs: wknd 1f out* **11/2**

7 1 **Dispol Fay (IRE)** 2-8-4 0.................................. DuranFentiman 5 32
(P T Midgley) *s.i.s: sme hdwy 2f out: nvr nr ldrs* **100/1**

1005 **8** 1¾ **Mijas Playa**[34] 5908 2-9-0 77.................................. DavidProbert 14 36
(C A Dwyer) *mid-div: outpcd over 2f out* **28/1**

1303 **9** nse **Ramamara (IRE)**[21] 6275 2-8-11 81.......................... CatherineGannon 2 32
(P D Evans) *chsd ldrs: wknd over 1f out* **5/1**[3]

5106 **10** 1 **Camacho Flyer (IRE)**[25] 6179 2-8-9 68.......................(t) PaulPickard(5) 1 32
(P T Midgley) *w ldrs: wknd appr fnl f* **28/1**

0004 **11** 3 **Lees Anthem**[18] 6354 2-8-5 60.............................. JamesPSullivan(7) 12 19
(C J Teague) *s.i.s: jinked rt sn after s: a bhd* **66/1**

00 **12** 4 **Baze Mac**[47] 5519 2-8-7 0......................................(b[1]) SilvestreDeSousa 8 —
(N Bycroft) *in rr: bhd fnl 2f* **200/1**

60.69 secs (0.89) **Going Correction** +0.20s/f (Good) **12** Ran SP% **115.8**
Speed ratings (Par 97): **100,99,93,90,86 82,80,78,77,76 71,65**
toteswingers: 1&2 £3.70, 1&3 £12.40, 2&3 £6.70 CSF £19.09 TOTE £3.00: £1.60, £1.90, £2.50; EX 12.10.
Owner Mohammed Jaber **Bred** Ms Natalie Cleary **Trained** Newmarket, Suffolk

FOCUS
This looked quite a competitive heat on paper but very few got into it, as the front two had it to themselves from a fair way out. They have been rated positively.

NOTEBOOK
The Only Boss(IRE) appeared to have done his chance no good by almost bolting going to post, but he clearly has some engine because, under just hands-and-heels riding, he hung in there to outbattle Chips O'Toole in the closing stages and make it two wins from three starts. He is a very buzzy sort, so the drop back to the minimum trip was a good move and he is open to stacks more improvement. He looks a sprinter to follow. (op 100-30 tchd 3-1)
Chips O'Toole(IRE) ran very well in defeat. The drop back to 5f wasn't sure to suit the colt but he showed good speed to get to the front by the time they straightened up for home, and only found a less exposed rival too strong. (op 9-2 tchd 100-30)
Night Trade(IRE) had a bit to find with a few of these at the weights and she was parked out wide in stall 13 (although she did edge across to the inside rail in the closing stages), so in the circumstances she ran very well and this marks her down as a filly on the upgrade. (tchd 6-1)
Durham Express(IRE) didn't have the speed to keep tabs on the principals early, but he finished to good effect from a long way back. He looks one to keep a close eye on back up to 6f. (op 6-1 tchd 15-2)
As You Like It(IRE) wasn't disgraced dropped back in trip, but she needs to be competing at a slightly lower level. (op 18-1 tchd 25-1)
Lees Anthem Official explanation: jockey said gelding lost its action

6842 BET TOTEPOOL AT TOTESPORT.COM MEDIAN AUCTION MAIDEN STKS 7f
2:50 (2:54) (Class 5) 2-Y-0 **£2,729** (£806; £403) **Stalls** Centre

Form RPR

1 **Madam Macie (IRE)** 2-8-12 0.................................. SilvestreDeSousa 9 77
(J Hetherton) *mde all: pushed along 2f out: rdn wl over 1f out: kpt on strly ins fnl f* **66/1**

2 **2** 3¼ **Huntingfortreasure**[29] 6047 2-9-3 0.............................. PhillipMakin 2 74
(M Dods) *in tch on inner: rdn along 3f out: swtchd rt and drvn over 1f out: styd on to chse wnr ins fnl f: no imp* **11/4**[1]

5 **3** 2 **Brink**[15] 6461 2-8-12 0.................................. TonyHamilton 1 64
(T J Pitt) *chsd ldrs: rdn along over 2f out: drvn over 1f out: kpt on same pce* **40/1**

6042 **4** nk **Brinscall**[17] 6378 2-8-9 72.................................. FrederikTylicki(3) 8 63+
(R A Fahey) *dwlt and towards rr: swtchd outside and hdwy over 2f out: sn rdn and kpt on appr fnl f: nrst fin* **4/1**[2]

5 2¾ **Alsufooh (USA)** 2-8-12 0.................................. GregFairley 12 56
(M Johnston) *chsd wnr: rdn along 2f out: sn drvn and edgd lft over 1f out: wknd* **7/1**[3]

5 **6** ½ **Jupiter Fidius**[159] 1920 2-9-3 0.................................. PaulMulrennan 14 60+
(Mrs K Walton) *dwlt and in rr: hdwy on inner over 2f out: sn rdn and kpt on appr fnl f: nrst fin* **16/1**

4 **7** 1¼ **Honest Broker (IRE)**[17] 6381 2-9-3 0.......................... J-PGuillambert 13 57
(M Johnston) *chsd ldrs: rdn along over 2f out: sn drvn and no hdwy* **25/1**

00 **8** 4 **Mr Mohican (IRE)**[17] 6382 2-9-3 0..............................(p) SJCraine 6 47
(Mrs A Duffield) *mid-div: rdn along over 3f out and sn wknd* **150/1**

30 **9** 1¾ **Cotton Top (IRE)**[8] 6638 2-8-12 0.............................. SamHitchcott 3 38
(M R Channon) *chsd ldrs: rdn along 3f out: drvn over 2f out and sn wknd* **14/1**

5 **10** ½ **Tadhkeer**[12] 6542 2-9-3 0.................................. LiamJones 11 41
(W J Haggas) *a towards rr* **14/1**

524 **11** hd **Onyx Of Arabia (IRE)**[37] 5786 2-9-3 77.......................... AlanMunro 10 41
(B J Meehan) *midfield: effrt 3f out: sn rdn along and nvr a factor* **11/4**[1]

5 **12** 4½ **Madame Excelerate**[21] 6274 2-8-12 0.............................. DuranFentiman 4 25
(W M Brisbourne) *dwlt: a in rr* **125/1**

06 **13** *10* **Gazamali (IRE)**[185] 1275 2-8-12 0 PatrickDonaghy(5) 15 5
(G A Harker) *dwlt: a in rr* **150/1**

0 **14** *1 ½* **Edward Lear**[43] 5643 2-9-3 0 RichardKingscote 7 1
(E F Vaughan) *in tch on outer: rdn along 1/2-way: sn wknd* **80/1**

1m 27.54s (0.54) **Going Correction** +0.05s/f (Good) **14** Ran SP% **116.2**
Speed ratings (Par 95): **98,94,92,91,88 87,86,81,79,79 79,74,62,60**
toteswingers: 1&2 £20.00, 1&3 £107.80, 2&3 £27.60 CSF £235.53 TOTE £39.80: £5.20, £1.30, £9.20; EX 432.70.
Owner R Fell & K Everitt **Bred** Michael McGlynn **Trained** Nawton, N Yorks

FOCUS
A real turn-up in this maiden, the surprise winner making all. The form makes sense at face value but is obviously limited.

NOTEBOOK
Madam Macie(IRE) ◆ defied her inexperience and lack of market confidence to blast out and make all the running. The daughter of Bertolini cost only 4,000 euros but she is related to winners and has clearly inherited a great deal of speed. Having straightened up for home, it looked momentarily like she had only set up the race for the finishers, but she kicked again and was not for catching in the final furlong. Her stable does not get many first-time-out two-year-old winners, so it's likely this filly is pretty decent and on this evidence, she might prove just as effective at sprint trips. (op 100-1)
Huntingfortreasure was the only one to emerge from the pack and make any inroads on the leader, but he was never going to reel her in. A slightly stiffer track would probably suit him better and he has potential granted such conditions. (op 2-1 tchd 3-1 in places)
Brink didn't show a great deal at Wolverhampton on her debut, but she stepped up on that here, racing in touch with the pace and keeping on well enough to hold on for third. It's likely low-grade handicaps will be her bag. (op 66-1 tchd 80-1 and 100-1 in a place)
Brinscall finished well but she could never land a blow and although she has ability, her losing run now stands at seven. (tchd 11-4)
Alsufooh(USA) tried to keep tabs on the winner in the early stages and shaped well for a long way before tiring in the final furlong. She can only improve for this. (op 11-1)

6843 TOTESPORT.COM CATTERICK DASH H'CAP STKS 5f
3:25 (3:28) (Class 3) (0-95,94) 3-Y-0+ **£9,714** (£2,890; £1,444; £721) **Stalls** Low

Form RPR

1254 **1** **The Nifty Fox**[18] 6359 5-8-6 82 DavidAllan 5 93
(T D Easterby) *chsd ldrs: hmpd on inner over 2f out: led jst ins fnl f: r.o strly* **11/2**[2]

1210 **2** *1 ¼* **Cape Vale (IRE)**[28] 6089 4-8-11 87 AdrianTNicholls 15 93
(D Nicholls) *w ldrs: led over 1f out: hdd jst ins fnl f: no ex* **16/1**

0605 **3** *2 ¼* **Fathom Five (IRE)**[42] 5654 5-9-3 93 AlanMunro 13 91
(C F Wall) *chsd ldrs towards outside: kpt on same pce appr fnl f* **10/1**

6003 **4** *1 ½* **Equuleus Pictor**[8] 6647 5-8-8 87 JackDean(3) 10 80+
(J L Spearing) *s.i.s: hdwy on outer over 1f out: kpt on: nvr trbld ldrs* **16/1**

060 **5** *hd* **Toms Laughter**[28] 6107 5-9-0 90 (b) KevinGhunowa 4 82
(R A Harris) *chsd ldrs on inner: edgd rt over 2f out: kpt on same pce* **12/1**

0302 **6** *½* **Legal Eagle (IRE)**[8] 6642 4-8-4 80 oh2 SilvestreDeSousa 9 70
(Paul Green) *prom: effrt 2f out: one pce appr fnl f* **14/1**

0053 **7** *nk* **Isheto**[25] 6180 5-8-13 94 (v[1]) BMcHugh(5) 1 83+
(A Dickman) *stmbld s: in rr: hdwy 2f out: kpt on: nvr nr ldrs* **9/2**[1]

0005 **8** *¾* **Favourite Girl (IRE)**[16] 6428 3-8-9 85 (b) PJMcDonald 14 71
(T D Easterby) *in rr on outer: kpt on fnl 2f: nvr a factor* **33/1**

05-1 **9** *½* **Mondovi**[22] 6253 5-8-13 89 RichardKingscote 7 74
(Tom Dascombe) *in rr: kpt on fnl 2f: nvr a factor* **12/1**

1210 **10** *nse* **Pavershooz**[35] 5860 4-9-4 94 DuranFentiman 12 78
(N Wilson) *chsd ldrs: wknd appr fnl f* **12/1**

3356 **11** *½* **Angus Newz**[16] 6428 6-8-9 85 (v) StephenDonohoe 6 68
(M Quinn) *mid-div: stmbld over 2f out* **16/1**

030 **12** *2* **Hypnosis**[18] 6359 6-8-7 83 oh3 ow3 TonyHamilton 8 58
(N Wilson) *t.k.h towards rr: nvr on terms* **25/1**

2300 **13** *2 ½* **Northern Dare (IRE)**[35] 5860 5-8-12 91 FrederikTylicki(3) 11 57
(D Nicholls) *s.i.s: a in rr* **9/1**[3]

6610 **14** *3 ¾* **Stolt (IRE)**[29] 6051 5-8-6 87 GaryBartley(5) 2 40
(N Wilson) *chsd ldrs on inner: hung bdly rt 2f out: sn lost pl and heavily eased* **16/1**

6110 **15** *6* **Le Toreador**[7] 6678 4-8-11 92 (tp) AmyRyan(5) 3 23
(K A Ryan) *led tl hdd and lost pl over 1f out: heavily eased ins fnl f: b.b.v* **9/1**[3]

59.86 secs (0.06) **Going Correction** +0.20s/f (Good) **15** Ran SP% **122.7**
Speed ratings (Par 107): **107,105,101,99,98 97,97,96,95,95 94,91,87,81,71**
toteswingers: 1&2 £21.90, 1&3 £20.90, 2&3 £34.90 CSF £92.10 CT £891.65 TOTE £8.00: £2.30, £4.00, £3.50; EX 142.80.
Owner Roy Peebles **Bred** Mrs Norma Peebles **Trained** Great Habton, N Yorks

FOCUS
A competitive sprint in which prominent runners gain did best. The form is rated through the runner-up.

NOTEBOOK
The Nifty Fox, who has an excellent record at the track, was never far away and took advantage of a nice gap up the inside to hit the front inside the final furlong. Although the winner ideally wants softer ground, there was enough give underfoot for him to produce something like his best and win his second race off this mark of 82. He doesn't have much leeway in terms of handicap mark but is a consistent sort. (op 10-1)
Cape Vale(IRE) showed good speed to take a prominent position from his wide draw and he kept on well to bounce back from a disappointing run in the Ayr Silver Cup. (tchd 14-1)
Fathom Five(IRE) won off this mark at Epsom earlier in the year and, given a break ahead of this, he kept on well to run to somewhere near his best. (tchd 11-1)
Equuleus Pictor stayed on well from a long way off the pace down the middle of the track despite being weighted up to the hilt. He prefers more testing conditions, so this was an encouraging run.
Toms Laughter was bang there with every chance at the furlong pole, but he too is on the wrong side of the assessor. (tchd 10-1)
Isheto blew his chance at the start and was never a factor. (op 11-2 tchd 4-1)
Angus Newz Official explanation: jockey said mare stumbled 3f out
Stolt(IRE) Official explanation: jockey sdaid gelding hung right
Le Toreador Official explanation: jockey said gelding bled from the nose

6844 TOTESPORT.COM HOME OF POOL BETTING FILLIES' NURSERY 7f
4:00 (4:01) (Class 4) (0-85,81) 2-Y-0 **£4,533** (£1,348; £674; £336) **Stalls** Centre

Form RPR

2050 **1** **Transfixed (IRE)**[9] 6619 2-8-13 73 CatherineGannon 9 77
(P D Evans) *mde all: rdn wl over 1f out: drvn ins fnl f: hld on gamely* **12/1**

0223 **2** *½* **Whirly Dancer**[16] 6436 2-8-12 72 IanMongan 12 75
(H R A Cecil) *chsd ldrs: hdwy 1/2-way: chsd wnr and brought wd home turn: rdn wl over 1f out: drvn to chal and edgd lft ins fnl f: ev ch tl no ex nr fin* **3/1**[1]

130 **3** *1 ½* **Gobama**[34] 5913 2-9-1 75 LiamJones 11 74
(J W Hills) *dwlt and in rr: hdwy on wd outside 2f out: sn rdn and styd on u.p ins fnl f: nrst fin* **40/1**

0405 **4** *1 ¼* **Baileys Vision**[30] 6035 2-8-4 64 (v[1]) GregFairley 3 60
(M Johnston) *chsd ldrs: hdwy on inner over 2f out: rdn wl over 1f out: drvn and one pce ent fnl f* **16/1**

3004 **5** *nk* **Perfect Ch'I (IRE)**[10] 6585 2-9-5 79 TonyHamilton 1 74
(I A Wood) *chsd ldrs on inner: hdwy over 2f out: rdn wl over 1f out: kpt on same pce* **10/1**

6122 **6** *2 ¾* **Gold Fix (IRE)**[16] 6431 2-8-9 69 SamHitchcott 7 57
(M R Channon) *in tch: hdwy to chse ldrs 1/2-way: rdn over 2f out: drvn wl over 1f out and grad wknd* **15/2**

2160 **7** *3* **Water Biscuit**[37] 5797 2-9-6 80 AlanMunro 4 61
(B J Meehan) *dwlt: a towards rr* **7/2**[2]

01 **8** *4 ½* **Interlace**[37] 5808 2-9-7 81 StephenDonohoe 6 61+
(Sir Mark Prescott) *chsd wnr: rdn along over 2f out: sn drvn and wknd wl over 1f out* **4/1**[3]

0340 **9** *6* **Suzi's A Smartlady (IRE)**[44] 5595 2-8-4 64 SilvestreDeSousa 2 19
(M Johnston) *a towards rr* **13/2**

1m 28.45s (1.45) **Going Correction** +0.05s/f (Good) **9** Ran SP% **117.4**
Speed ratings (Par 94): **93,92,90,89,88 85,82,77,70**
toteswingers: 1&2 £8.10, 1&3 £25.80, 2&3 £13.90 CSF £48.90 CT £1116.42 TOTE £16.10: £3.70, £1.90, £9.30; EX 63.00.
Owner Mrs I M Folkes **Bred** Rathasker Stud **Trained** Pandy, Monmouths

FOCUS
Just a fair nursery. The winner returned to her best under a good front-running ride.

NOTEBOOK
Transfixed(IRE) made all the running under an excellent ride. Allowed a breather going downhill before being asked to kick on again, that enterprise was probably the main reason she had enough in reserve to see off the strong challenge of Whirly Dancer in the final furlong. She is admirably tough and despite her long season looking like it may have caught up with her recently, she bounced right back to her best to win her fifth race of the year on her 20th start. (op 18-1)
Whirly Dancer looked like she had produced a race-winning challenge inside the final furlong, but she was outbattled by a seriously courageous rival close home. This was her first try in handicaps and although her mark seems about right, she looks capable of getting off the mark soon. (op 7-2)
Gobama ◆ was the big eyecatcher of the race, as she was tardily away and nearly last turning for home but took off in the final furlong and finished better than anything. She had gone backwards since making a winning debut, but this was much more like it and ground with a bit of juice in it seems to suit her. Official explanation: jockey said filly hung right throughout (op 33-1)
Baileys Vision seemed to run better in a first-time visor and kept on well up the inside, although without landing a blow. She is proving disappointing.
Perfect Ch'I(IRE) couldn't take advantage of the drop in grade, despite getting a nice tow into the race. She is fully exposed. (op 11-1 tchd 9-1)
Interlace, easy to back, was in trouble early in the straight. Official explanation: trainer had no explanation for the poor form shown (op 2-1)

6845 BEST ODDS AT TOTESPORT.COM H'CAP 1m 5f 175y
4:35 (4:35) (Class 6) (0-60,60) 3-Y-0+ **£2,590** (£770; £385; £192) **Stalls** Low

Form RPR

6114 **1** **Simple Jim (FR)**[11] 6559 5-9-2 51 SilvestreDeSousa 5 59
(J Hetherton) *hld up towards rr: effrt over 2f out: styd on wl to ld jst ins fnl f: kpt on strly* **11/4**[1]

053 **2** *1 ½* **Dimashq**[65] 4927 7-9-1 50 PJMcDonald 4 56
(P T Midgley) *trckd ldrs: effrt over 2f out: chsng ldrs appr fnl f: styd on same pce ins fnl f* **14/1**

1630 **3** *¾* **Golden Future**[16] 6432 6-8-10 50 BMcHugh(5) 6 55+
(P D Niven) *trckd ldrs: led over 2f out: hdd jst ins fnl f: no ex* **6/1**[2]

-005 **4** *3 ½* **Hernando's Boy**[11] 6558 8-9-7 56 PhillipMakin 13 56
(K G Reveley) *in rr: hdwy on outside over 2f out: kpt on: nvr threatened ldrs* **10/1**

5 *1 ¼* **Sovento (GER)**[73] 4683 5-9-6 55 DavidProbert 14 53
(Shaun Harley, Ire) *trckd ldrs: led after 2f: hdd over 2f out: wknd appr fnl f* **14/1**

3561 **6** *1* **Andorn (GER)**[18] 6310 5-9-11 60 LeeVickers 8 57
(P A Kirby) *chsd ldrs: outpcd over 3f out: kpt on fnl 2f: no threat* **11/1**

0431 **7** *½* **Sphere (IRE)**[25] 6177 4-9-10 59 SJCraine 10 55
(J Mackie) *sn trcking ldrs: effrt over 2f out: wknd over 1f out* **10/1**

3260 **8** *¾* **Tender Moments**[51] 5359 5-9-1 50 GregFairley 3 45
(B Smart) *t.k.h: trckd ldrs: drvn over 5f out: outpcd over 3f out: wknd 2f out* **7/1**[3]

3/00 **9** *4* **Silent Lucidity (IRE)**[15] 6457 5-9-1 50 DavidAllan 9 40
(P D Niven) *hld up in rr: drvn over 4f out: nvr a factor* **9/1**

2054 **10** *18* **Astroangel**[48] 5479 5-8-12 52 (p) AshleyMorgan(5) 12 16
(M H Tompkins) *hld up in rr: effrt over 3f out: lost pl over 2f out: sn bhd and eased: t.o* **14/1**

5022 **11** *3 ½* **Tropical Bachelor (IRE)**[25] 6177 3-9-0 58 (b) TonyHamilton 1 17
(T J Pitt) *led 2f: jnd ldr 5f out: lost pl over 2f out: sn bhd and eased: t.o* **15/2**

3m 5.93s (2.33) **Going Correction** +0.05s/f (Good)
WFA 3 from 4yo+ 9lb **11** Ran SP% **121.7**
Speed ratings (Par 101): **95,94,93,91,91 90,90,89,87,77 75**
toteswingers: 1&2 £13.40, 1&3 £5.80, 2&3 £26.10 CSF £46.66 CT £223.11 TOTE £3.30: £2.20, £5.20, £2.60; EX 52.30.
Owner R G Fell **Bred** Snc Haras Des Peltrais, Laurent Thibault **Trained** Nawton, N Yorks

FOCUS
A poor staying handicap in which the pace was strong and that allowed the hold-up horses to dominate in the closing stages. Solid form amongst the first two.

6846 BETXTRA WIN ONLY AT TOTESPORT.COM H'CAP (DIV I) 7f
5:10 (5:11) (Class 5) (0-75,77) 3-Y-0+ **£2,914** (£867; £433; £216) **Stalls** Centre

Form RPR

4312 **1** **Ancient Cross**[26] 6175 5-9-1 70 (t) PhillipMakin 10 83+
(M W Easterby) *hld up towards rr: gd hdwy on inner 2f out: n.m.r over 1f out: squeezed through and swtchd rt ins fnl f: qcknd to ld last 100yds* **7/2**[1]

-123 **2** *2* **Ishiadancer**[18] 6361 4-8-12 67 CatherineGannon 15 75+
(E J Alston) *cl up: led over 2f out: rdn clr wl over 1f out: drvn and edgd lft ent fnl f: hdd and one pce last 100yds* **12/1**

1100 **3** *2 ¼* **Tangerine Trees**[23] 6233 4-9-2 71 PaulMulrennan 6 73
(B Smart) *trckd ldrs: hdwy over 2f out: rdn wl over 1f out: drvn ent fnl f and kpt on same pce* **20/1**

2100 **4** *¾* **Island Chief**[30] 6014 3-8-11 73 (b) AmyRyan(5) 12 72
(K A Ryan) *in tch: hdwy over 2f out: swtchd lft and rdn whn hmpd over 1f out: kpt on same pce* **22/1**

5041 **5** *2* **Capucci**[14] 6495 4-8-11 73 (p) IJBrennan(7) 4 68
(J J Quinn) *midfield: hdwy over 2f out and sn rdn: swtchd lft and drvn ent fnl f: nt rch ldrs* **4/1**[2]

0030 **6** *½* **Nuit Sombre (IRE)**[25] 6178 9-8-12 67 (p) SilvestreDeSousa 3 60
(G A Harker) *led: rdn along and hdd over 2f out: sn wknd* **14/1**

0-4 **7** *4 1/2* **Belle Noverre (IRE)**[15] 6465 5-8-13 68......................(p) DavidProbert 11 49
(Shaun Harley, Ire) *midfield: effrt and sme hdwy over 2f out: sn rdn and n.d* **20/1**

2033 **8** *1/2* **Azure Mist**[40] 5723 4-8-3 63.............................. AshleyMorgan(5) 14 43
(M H Tompkins) *a towards rr* **16/1**

6000 **9** *1/2* **Dorn Dancer (IRE)**[8] 6637 7-8-7 62 oh1 ow1................ TonyHamilton 2 40
(W M Brisbourne) *a in rr* **66/1**

-033 **10** *shd* **Hazelrigg (IRE)**[16] 6434 4-9-3 72.......................................(p) DavidAllan 1 50
(T D Easterby) *towards rr: hdwy and wd st: sn rdn and nvr a factor* **6/1**

-000 **11** *1/2* **Sadeek**[41] 5697 5-9-3 72.. PJMcDonald 7 49
(B Smart) *a towards rr* **16/1**

1062 **12** *shd* **Amazing Tiger (GER)**[3] 6778 3-9-4 75............................... GregFairley 9 50
(M Johnston) *trckd ldng pair: effrt over 2f out: sn rdn and wknd over 1f out* **9/2[3]**

3203 **13** *4* **Micky Mac (IRE)**[10] 6596 5-7-13 61 oh4................. DeclanCannon(7) 13 27
(C J Teague) *in tch: rdn along 1/2-way: sn wknd* **33/1**

1m 26.69s (-0.31) **Going Correction** +0.05s/f (Good)
WFA 3 from 4yo+ 2lb **13** Ran SP% **119.1**
Speed ratings (Par 103): **103,100,98,97,95 94,89,88,88,88 87,87,82**
toteswingers: 1&2 £7.00, 1&3 £11.00, 2&3 £24.20. CSF £42.90 CT £773.88 TOTE £4.50: £1.60, £3.60, £5.50; EX 41.10.
Owner P J Bown **Bred** Darley **Trained** Sheriff Hutton, N Yorks

FOCUS
Another race in which they went too hard in front, although the time was still quicker than division II. The winner may be capable of better.
Hazelrigg(IRE) Official explanation: jockey said gelding slipped on leaving stalls; trainer said gelding was unsuited by the track
Micky Mac(IRE) Official explanation: trainer said felding was unsuited by the good ground

6847 BETXTRA WIN ONLY AT TOTESPORT.COM H'CAP (DIV II) 7f
5:40 (5:44) (Class 5) (0-75,74) 3-Y-0+ **£2,914** (£867; £433; £216) **Stalls** Centre

Form RPR

0160 **1** **Mujaadel (USA)**[30] 6015 4-9-5 73.................................(p) AndrewMullen 1 80
(D Nicholls) *chsd ldrs: hrd drvn over 2f out: led over 1f out: hld on towards fin* **10/1**

3- **2** *nk* **Rum Raisin**[25] 6195 3-8-4 60 oh2............................ CatherineGannon 5 65
(John Joseph Murphy, Ire) *stdd s: hld up in last: gd hdwy and swtchd outside over 1f out: edgd lft ins fnl f: fin wl: jst hld* **28/1**

0604 **3** *1* **This Ones For Eddy**[16] 6411 4-8-2 61............................ PaulPickard(5) 2 64
(J Balding) *prom: wnt 2nd appr fnl f: kpt on same pce* **5/1[2]**

0602 **4** *1 1/4* **Eastern Hills**[10] 6596 4-8-13 67.................................(v) PaulMulrennan 7 67
(J S Wainwright) *in rr: hdwy on ins over 2f out: styd on fnl f* **11/1**

3031 **5** *3/4* **Salerosa (IRE)**[18] 6361 4-9-1 69.............................. SilvestreDeSousa 4 67
(Mrs A Duffield) *hld up in midfield: effrt over 2f out: kpt on fnl f: nvr nr to chal* **4/1[1]**

1110 **6** *2 1/2* **Dark Moment**[20] 6309 3-9-1 74..............................(p) FrederikTylicki(3) 11 64
(A Dickman) *chsd ldrs: chal over 2f out: wknd fnl f* **17/2**

5120 **7** *hd* **Allformary**[18] 6357 3-8-11 74.................................... AdamCarter(7) 13 64
(B Smart) *chsd ldrs: chal over 2f out: wknd fnl f* **18/1**

203 **8** *1/2* **Mr Wolf**[23] 6233 8-8-8 69...(p) IJBrennan(7) 12 58
(J J Quinn) *led tl over 1f out: sn wknd* **22/1**

6405 **9** *1/2* **Zabeel Tower**[20] 6309 6-8-12 66................................(v) TonyHamilton 14 54
(R Allan) *hld up in midfield: effrt over 2f out: nvr a factor* **18/1**

50 **10** *shd* **Misphire**[51] 5363 6-9-4 72...(p) PhillipMakin 9 60
(M Dods) *t.k.h in rr: effrt over 2f out: nvr on terms* **16/1**

0035 **11** *shd* **Rising Shadow (IRE)**[4] 6765 8-9-1 74........................ DeanHeslop(5) 3 62
(A D Brown) *s.i.s: hdwy on ins 3f out: wknd over 1f out* **7/1[3]**

3542 **12** *nk* **Soto**[16] 6414 6-7-13 60 oh1.................................. JamesPSullivan(7) 10 47
(M W Easterby) *in rr-div: brief effrt on outer 2f out: sn wknd* **9/1**

0056 **13** *3/4* **Cornus**[32] 5960 7-9-3 71...(be) JamesDoyle 6 56
(J A Glover) *trckd ldrs: chal over 2f out: wknd over 1f out* **10/1**

0-00 **14** *12* **Billy Cadiz**[86] 4225 4-8-6 63 oh15 ow3.................... MichaelJStainton(3) 15 15
(N Tinkler) *s.i.s: a in rr: drvn over 3f out: lost pl and eased over 1f out* **125/1**

1m 27.75s (0.75) **Going Correction** +0.05s/f (Good)
WFA 3 from 4yo+ 2lb **14** Ran SP% **121.2**
Speed ratings (Par 103): **97,96,95,94,93 90,90,89,89,88 88,88,87,73**
toteswingers: 1&2 £31.70, 1&3 £9.80, 2&3 £21.60. CSF £269.42 CT £1100.24 TOTE £12.60: £4.90, £6.60, £2.20; EX 302.40 Place 6 £87.82, Place 5 £65.85.
Owner W R B Racing 49 **Bred** Lawrence Goichman **Trained** Sessay, N Yorks

FOCUS
The pace held up this time although the time was slower than the first division. Rather muddling form with the winner the best guide.
T/Plt: £72.50 to a £1 stake. Pool: £44,493.78. 447.45 winning tickets. T/Qpdt: £68.30 to a £1 stake. Pool: £2,617.40. 28.35 winning tickets. WG

6809 NEWMARKET (R-H)
Saturday, October 17

OFFICIAL GOING: Good (good to firm in places) (straight 8.0, beacon 8.3)
Stands'-side track in use.
Wind: Strong, behind Weather: Overcast, Chilly

6848 VICTOR CHANDLER CHALLENGE STKS (GROUP 2) 7f
1:50 (1:50) (Class 1) 3-Y-0+
£60,829 (£23,058; £11,540; £5,753; £2,882; £1,446) **Stalls** Low

Form RPR

303 **1** **Arabian Gleam**[35] 5862 5-9-3 114.....................................(p) JMurtagh 8 118
(J Noseda) *t.k.h: chsd ldng pair: rdn to ld over 1f out: drvn and styd on wl fnl f* **7/1**

0164 **2** *nk* **Ouqba**[35] 5862 3-9-1 114... RHills 4 116+
(B W Hills) *lw: bmpd s: hld up in tch: nt clr run 2f out: sn swtchd rt: hdwy and drvn jst over 1f out: r.o wl ins fnl f: wnt 2nd towards fin: gng on fin but nvr quite gng to rch wnr* **5/1[3]**

1554 **3** *3/4* **Donativum**[15] 6448 3-9-1 108.. TedDurcan 10 114
(Saeed Bin Suroor) *hld up towards rr on outer: hdwy over 2f out: rdn to chse wnr jst over 1f out drvn and nt qckn ins fnl f: lost 2nd towards fin* **9/1**

4200 **4** *1/2* **Main Aim**[42] 5657 4-9-3 120.. RyanMoore 7 114
(Sir Michael Stoute) *swtg: midfield: niggled along after 2f: rdn and unable qck 2f out: swtchd rt jst ins fnl f: styd on but nvr gng pce to chal* **5/1[3]**

2011 **5** *1 1/2* **Ashram (IRE)**[29] 6058 3-9-1 115..................................(v) LDettori 6 109
(Saeed Bin Suroor) *bmpd s: sn rcvrd and chsd ldr: ev ch 2f out: drvn and unable qck over 1f out: wknd ins fnl f* **7/2[1]**

0266 **6** *1/2* **Asset (IRE)**[20] 6304 6-9-3 110.......................................(b) RichardHughes 3 108
(Saeed Bin Suroor) *lw: wnt rt s: t.k.h: hld up in rr: hdwy and swtchd rt over 1f out: rdn to chse ldrs ent fnl f: wknd fnl 100yds* **8/1**

0-20 **7** *4 1/2* **Cuis Ghaire (IRE)**[146] 2304 3-8-12 110.............................. KJManning 1 93
(J S Bolger, Ire) *ponied to s: led: rdn ent fnl 2f: drvn and hdd over 1f out: sn wknd* **9/2[2]**

-606 **8** *3/4* **Tariq**[29] 6058 5-9-3 108.. KFallon 2 94
(P W Chapple-Hyam) *stdd s: hld up in rr: rdn and no rspnse jst over 2f out: wl btn after* **20/1**

-640 **9** *9* **Al Qasi (IRE)**[42] 5657 6-9-3 107...................................... JimmyFortune 9 70
(P W Chapple-Hyam) *chsd ldrs: rdn over 2f out: wknd 2f out and sn bhd* **28/1**

1m 23.81s (-1.59) **Going Correction** +0.05s/f (Good)
WFA 3 from 4yo+ 2lb **9** Ran SP% **115.6**
Speed ratings (Par 115): **111,110,109,109,107 106,101,100,90**
toteswingers: 1&2 £7.10, 1&3 £10.70, 2&3 £9.10 CSF £41.90 TOTE £8.60: £2.60, £2.20, £2.90; EX 42.10 Trifecta £295.10 Pool: £3,788.94 - 9.50 winning units.
Owner Saeed Suhail **Bred** P And Mrs A G Venner **Trained** Newmarket, Suffolk
■ Stewards' Enquiry : R Hills caution: used whip without giving colt time to respond.

FOCUS
Drying conditions overnight saw the official going description amended slightly from good all round. They were racing on fresh ground up the straight that had not been used since May, and the stalls were on the stands' side. This had the look of a fairly ordinary renewal of this Group 2 prize. The pace was sound and the time was 0.61 seconds outside standard, suggesting the ground was fairly quick. The winner looks the best guide to the form, and there were slight personal bests from the second and third.

NOTEBOOK
Arabian Gleam would ideally have preferred a bit of give, but after being let down to lead going to the furlong pole, he saw it out well. This was his third victory at this level to go with two editions of the Park Stakes at Doncaster, in which he was a narrow third to Duff this year, a neck in front of Ouqba, who was beaten the same margin here after having to wait for a run. The winner won't be seen again this season, but may head for Dubai in the new year, where the Tapeta surface at Meydan is expected to suit him. (tchd 13-2)
Ouqba, who won the Free Handicap over course and distance six months ago, was arguably unlucky not to add this Group 2 as he was short of room behind Ashram and Cuis Ghaire at around the two pole. He ran on strongly when in the clear, but the winner had taken first run and the line just beat him. A bump at the start did not help his cause as the intention had been to make more use of him. That will be it for the season, but he stays in training. (op 13-2 tchd 7-1)
Donativum fared best of the three Godolphin runners, going after the winner down the outside a furlong out and only being caught for second late on. The drop back from 1m was not a problem and this was a slight personal best from a gelding whose golden autumn last year was always going to be difficult to emulate. (tchd 8-1)
Main Aim, on his toes beforehand, was found to be suffering badly with ulcers after his disappointing effort in the Haydock Sprint Cup six weeks previously. Having been treated he ran a better race, staying on for pressure, but he was still below the level he showed in the July Cup. (tchd 11-2 and 6-1 in places)
Ashram(IRE), the Godolphin first string, was bidding for a hat-trick after wins in lesser company, but was one-paced when let down and faded out of the places inside the last. There seemed no obvious excuse, with a bump as he left the stalls unlikely to have made any difference. (op 4-1)
Asset(IRE), the third Godolphin runner, was reunited with Richard Hughes, who rode him regularly in his Richard Hannon days. Reverting to hold-up tactics, he ran on a bit when let down but could never mount a challenge. (op 11-1)
Cuis Ghaire(IRE), the 1,000 Guineas runner-up, reportedly pulled muscles in the heavy ground when beating just one home in the Irish equivalent, and this was her first appearance since. Wintry in her coat, she has not grown much since the spring and, ponied to the start, had the run of the race against the rail but weakened a little tamely. The drop in trip was perhaps not in her favour, but this was still disappointing. (op 4-1 tchd 5-1 in places)
Tariq was well beaten on this second run back after a break. (tchd 22-1)
Al Qasi(IRE), runner-up in this two years ago, was the first beaten. (op 25-1)

6849 JUMEIRAH DEWHURST STKS (GROUP 1) (ENTIRE COLTS & FILLIES) 7f
2:25 (2:26) (Class 1) 2-Y-0
£180,159 (£68,293; £34,178; £17,041; £8,536; £4,284) **Stalls** Low

Form RPR

5346 **1** **Beethoven (IRE)**[13] 6524 2-9-1 0..................................(v[1]) RyanMoore 3 118
(A P O'Brien, Ire) *chsd ldrs: rdn and sltly outpcd 2f out: switching out rt and rdn over 1f out: hdwy ent fnl f: edgd rt u.str.p but r.o wl to ld fnl 50yds* **33/1**

2 *nk* **Fencing Master**[41] 5700 2-9-1 0.................................. CO'Donoghue 13 117+
(A P O'Brien, Ire) *str: hmpd s: bhd and pushed along 4f out: rdn and hdwy on outer over 2f out: relentless prog to chal jst ins fnl f: no ex towards fin* **20/1**

121 **3** *nse* **Xtension (IRE)**[80] 4418 2-9-1 108.................................. AdamKirby 11 117
(C G Cox) *lw: hld up in rr: swtchd rt and hdwy on outer over 2f out: rdn and ev ch 1f out: led fnl 100yds tl hdd and no ex towards fin* **6/1[3]**

1 **4** *nk* **Steinbeck (IRE)**[157] 1994 2-9-1 0...................................... JMurtagh 1 116+
(A P O'Brien, Ire) *led: rdn 2f out: kpt on wl u.p tl hdd and no ex fnl 100yds* **4/1[2]**

2213 **5** *1 3/4* **Buzzword**[13] 6524 2-9-1 114...................................... AhmedAjtebi 7 112
(Saeed Bin Suroor) *lw: in tch: hdwy over 2f out: rdn and hung rt 2f out: ev ch ent fnl f tl wknd fnl 150yds* **14/1**

1115 **6** *2* **Dick Turpin (IRE)**[13] 6524 2-9-1 112.......................... RichardHughes 5 107
(R Hannon) *in tch: rdn and effrt ent fnl 2f: drvn to chse ldrs ent fnl f: wknd fnl 150yds* **8/1**

1113 **7** *1* **Silver Grecian**[35] 5859 2-9-1 112.................................... MichaelHills 15 105
(J Ryan) *sltly hmpd s: bhd: hdwy into midfield 3f out: rdn and effrt jst over 2f out: plugged on same pce after* **13/2**

0 **8** *nk* **Free Judgement (USA)**[8] 6651 2-9-1 0.............................. DJMoran 14 104
(J S Bolger, Ire) *w'like: tall: racd keenly: chsd ldr tl jst over 2f out: rdn to press ldr again over 1f out: wknd ins fnl f* **66/1**

2231 **9** *1 1/2* **Awesome Act (USA)**[16] 6416 2-9-1 98........................ DarryllHolland 10 100+
(J Noseda) *dwlt and hmpd s: t.k.h: hld up in tch in midfield: rdn and unable qck jst over 2f out: wl hld fnl f* **14/1**

2 **10** *1/2* **Chabal (IRE)**[35] 5892 2-9-1 0..................................... KJManning 4 99
(J S Bolger, Ire) *lengthy: lean: t.k.h: chsd ldng pair: wnt 2nd jst over 2f out: sn ev ch and rdn: btn whn rdr dropped whip 1f out: sn fdd* **7/2[1]**

1321 **11** *hd* **Maroon Machine (IRE)**[15] 6507 2-9-1 0........................ CSoumillon 2 98
(E J O'Neill) *hld up in tch: rdn and edgd rt over 1f out: no prog and wl btn after* **33/1**

214 **12** *3* **High Twelve (IRE)**[21] 6268 2-9-1 102.............................. KFallon 6 91
(J H M Gosden) *lw: taken down early: stdd s: hld up in tch in midfield: rdn and no rspnse over 2f out: wl btn after* **9/1**

2140 **13** *nk* **Timely Jazz (IRE)**[21] 6268 2-9-1 101............................ EddieAhern 9 90
(B J Meehan) *lw: wnt rt s: plld hrd: stdd and grad crossed to stands' rail: a bhd* **66/1**

0 **14** *7* **Lord High Admiral (IRE)**[20] 6319 2-9-1 0 SMLevey 8 73
(A P O'Brien, Ire) *sn pushed along in midfield: rdn and struggling towards rr 3f out: sn bhd* **66/1**

0210 **15** *1 1/4* **Manhattan Fox (USA)**[16] 6426 2-9-1 97 LDettori 12 69+
(B J Meehan) *stdd s and grad crossed to stands' rail: hld up in rr: a bhd: lost tch and eased over 1f out* **66/1**

1m 23.49s (-1.91) **Going Correction** +0.05s/f (Good) **15** Ran SP% **120.9**
Speed ratings (Par 109): **112,111,111,111,109 106,105,105,103,103 102,99,99,91,89**
toteswingers: 1&2 £61.20, 1&3 £38.40, 2&3 £29.90 CSF £561.95 TOTE £37.00: £8.90, £8.20, £3.10; EX 616.80 TRIFECTA Not won..

Owner M Tabor, D Smith & Mrs John Magnier **Bred** Whisperview Trading Ltd **Trained** Ballydoyle, Co Tipperary

■ Only the second Dewhurst for Aidan O'Brien, who saddled three of the first four. The first and second are both by Oratorio.

■ Stewards' Enquiry : Ryan Moore two-day ban: used whip with excessive frequency without giving colt time to respond (Oct 31-Nov 1)

FOCUS

The likes of Arcano, Awzaan, Canford Cliffs and Kingsfort were all missing, so this didn't look a strong Dewhurst. The result would seem to confirm that it was an unspectacular, renewal, with the fifth helping to set the level, but the time - 0.32 seconds quicker than Arabian Gleam clocked in the Group 2 Challenge Stakes - was very good, suggesting it would be unwise to be too dismissive, and there were at least a couple of potentially high-class colts among the beaten runners. They raced stands' side, but the first three finishers were positioned away from the rail.

NOTEBOOK

Beethoven(IRE), whose only previous success in nine starts came in maiden company, had looked shy of this level on his three previous tries, including in France last time, and his best placing in a Group 1 came when third in an ordinary-looking National Stakes last month. However, he has clearly improved for the fitting of a first-time visor. Having broken alertly, he got a good lead close to the pace and travelled well. Once coming under pressure and switched right into the clear around 2f out, he picked up well, displaying a game attitude under very strong driving to get up in the final few strides and scoring in the manner of a colt who will do even better over a strongly run 1m. Although prior to this success he was not as classy as his sire, he's similarly tough, and like Oratorio, who also had a busy juvenile campaign, he may go on improving at three, provided the headgear continues to work. However, the suspicion is he'll find one or two too good in the 2,000 Guineas, and it's off-putting as far as that race is concerned that he may go to the US for one of the Breeders' Cup Juvenile races.

Fencing Master ◆, the winner of a Polytrack maiden on his only previous start, ran a fine race in second. He was green throughout, lacking the sharpness of most of his rivals and racing well off the pace, but he gradually got the idea when switched out very wide. It remains to be seen whether he runs again this season, but whatever, he's open to significant improvement. He looks one to have on side for the Guineas, with that race remaining wide open, and the 20-1 available with a number of firms appeals as worth taking. (op 25-1 tchd 33-1)

Xtension(IRE), who backed up his 6l second to Canford Cliffs in the Coventry with victory in the Group 2 Vintage Stakes when last seen in July, ran a game race in defeat. He didn't look totally at ease on the undulations, but he ran as though he'll appreciate a step up to 1m and he'll be aimed at the Guineas. He's probably not open to as much improvement as the two O'Brien runners he separated at the finish, however. (op 11-2 tchd 5-1)

Steinbeck(IRE) ◆, along with stablemate Fencing Master, looks worth taking from the race. He's always been well regarded - the impression is his connections have very high hopes for him - but had been off since landing a decent race on his debut over 6f at Naas in May, having obviously had his problems. He broke well, almost too well, and as a result Johnny Murtagh let him bowl along, rather than interrupt his stride. Ideally, though, he probably would have benefited from getting a lead considering he wasn't race-fit, and after setting a strong pace, he simply ran out of energy inside the final furlong. He promises to make up into a top-class 3-y-o and, like the runner-up, he looks worth getting on side for the Guineas, with 16-1 appealing as a very fair price. (tchd 5-1)

Buzzword couldn't confirm Prix Jean-Luc Lagardere form with Beethoven, but he still ran close to his best. He should be capable of even better back on easy ground, but his powerful stable surely have better colts at home. (op 12-1)

Dick Turpin(IRE) failed to reverse recent form from France with Buzzword and, like that one, he probably found the ground quicker than ideal. He may ultimately prove best over sprint trips when the going is on the easy side. (op 10-1)

Silver Grecian was caught a bit wider than ideal throughout but he basically wasn't up to this level. (op 6-1)

Free Judgement(USA), one of two colts attempting to provide Jim Bolger with a fourth straight win in the race, went off a much bigger price than his stablemate. He was a little keen but was another basically not good enough. (op 100-1)

Awesome Act(USA), slightly bumped at the start, didn't have much cover early on and was too keen. Official explanation: jockey sasid colt ran too free (op 16-1, tchd 25-1 in a place)

Chabal(IRE), who was to join Godolphin after this race, was too keen and failed to reproduce the form he showed when runner-up in the National Stakes. It's true he had today's winner 1 3/4l behind last time, but that one has clearly improved significantly since then and it remains to be seen what the bare form of that Irish Group 1 is worth. Whatever, he will need to learn to settle for his new connections if he's to progress. (op 4-1 tchd 100-30)

Maroon Machine(IRE), the winner of two of his four starts in France, including over 1m last time, was unsuited by the drop in trip and failed to prove himself up to this sort of level. (tchd 40-1 in places)

High Twelve(IRE), who misbehaved before the start in the Royal Lodge, went to post early this time. He proved rather disappointing in the race itself and was seemingly unsuited by the drop in trip. He has loads of scope, but it remains to be seen which way he'll go. (op 10-1 tchd 12-1)

6850 EMIRATES AIRLINE CHAMPION STKS (GROUP 1) 1m 2f

3:00 (3:07) (Class 1) 3-Y-O+

£213,739 (£81,022; £40,549; £20,218; £10,127; £5,082) **Stalls** Low

Form RPR

4011 **1** **Twice Over**[24] 6202 4-9-3 119 TPQueally 8 123
(H R A Cecil) *lw: hld up off the pce in midfield: hdwy over 2f out: led 2f out: rdn and hung rt fr over 1f out: styd on wl fnl f: all out* **14/1**

-011 **2** *1/2* **Mawatheeq (USA)**[20] 6303 4-9-3 117 RHills 13 122+
(M P Tregoning) *lw: hld up off the pce in midfield: hdwy and rdn 2f out: chsd ldng pair and carried rt over 1f out: nt clr run and swtchd lft ins fnl f: r.o to go 2nd fnl 75yds* **7/1**[3]

1112 **3** *1* **Sariska**[58] 5201 3-8-9 120 KFallon 2 117+
(M L W Bell) *lw: awkward s: wl bhd: swtchd to outer and niggled along over 5f out: rdn and prog over 2f out: drvn and styd on relentlessly fr over 1f out: wnt 3rd nr fin: nt rch ldrs* **8/1**

-251 **4** *1/2* **Pipedreamer**[14] 6506 5-9-3 118 SebSanders 4 119
(J H M Gosden) *swtg: hld up wl bhd: hdwy on outer over 2f out: rdn and ev ch ent fnl f: wknd fnl 75yds* **25/1**

0-40 **5** *3/4* **City Leader (IRE)**[14] 6506 4-9-3 110 (b[1]) TedDurcan 11 118
(B J Meehan) *handy in main gp: rdn and unable qck and edgd lft 2f out: hdwy u.p over 1f out: no imp ins fnl f* **100/1**

2126 **6** *1 1/2* **Fame And Glory**[13] 6526 3-8-12 129 JMurtagh 5 115
(A P O'Brien, Ire) *chsd ldng pair: wnt 2nd jst over 3f out: rdn to ld over 2f out: hdd 2f out: drvn and one pce after: btn fnl f* **6/4**[1]

1144 **7** *3/4* **Barshiba (IRE)**[58] 5201 5-9-0 110 PaulHanagan 12 110
(D R C Elsworth) *chsd clr ldr tl jst over 3f out: rdn wl over 2f out: kpt on gamely but no threat to ldrs fnl f* **33/1**

1633 **8** *1 1/4* **Virtual**[41] 5710 4-9-3 117 JimmyFortune 6 111+
(J H M Gosden) *lw: chsd clr ldng trio: rdn and unable qck whn nt clr run and swtchd rt 2f out: no prog after* **33/1**

2132 **9** *11* **Campanologist (USA)**[20] 6303 4-9-3 115 LDettori 7 89
(Saeed Bin Suroor) *hld up off the pce in midfield: rdn and effrt over 2f out: no hdwy and btn wl over 1f out: eased ins fnl f* **25/1**

5130 **10** *1 3/4* **Never On Sunday (FR)**[62] 5086 4-9-3 120 C-PLemaire 14 85
(J-C Rouget, France) *s.i.s: hld up in rr: nvr on terms: eased whn wl btn ins fnl f* **5/1**[2]

1011 **11** *5* **Doctor Fremantle**[29] 6056 4-9-3 115 RyanMoore 3 75
(Sir Michael Stoute) *t.k.h: hld up in wl off the pce towards rr: rdn and no prog over 2f out: eased whn no ch ins fnl f* **8/1**

4453 **12** *5* **Forgotten Voice (IRE)**[15] 6448 4-9-3 113 RichardHughes 1 65
(J Noseda) *t.k.h: hld up in rr: rdn and btn over 2f out: wl bhd and eased ins fnl f* **66/1**

1214 **13** *9* **Alpine Rose (FR)**[13] 6525 4-9-0 115 CSoumillon 9 44
(A De Royer-Dupre, France) *awkward leaving stalls: hld up in rr: rdn and btn over 2f out: wl bhd and eased fnl f: t.o* **16/1**

0300 **14** *1 1/4* **Set Sail (IRE)**[13] 6526 3-8-12 100 CO'Donoghue 10 45
(A P O'Brien, Ire) *led at fast gallop and sn clr: hdd over 2f out: sn dropped out: eased fnl f: t.o* **200/1**

2m 1.31s (-4.49) **Going Correction** +0.05s/f (Good)
WFA 3 from 4yo+ 5lb **14** Ran SP% **120.5**
Speed ratings (Par 117): **119,118,117,117,116 115,115,114,105,103 99,95,88,87**
toteswingers: 1&2 £15.20, 1&3 £13.80, 2&3 £8.40 CSF £104.58 CT £854.65 TOTE £19.50: £4.80, £3.50, £1.70; EX 114.00 Trifecta £696.40 Pool: £13,834.15 - 14.70 winning units..

Owner K Abdulla **Bred** Juddmonte Farms Ltd **Trained** Newmarket, Suffolk

■ Stewards' Enquiry : T P Queally one-day ban: careless riding (Oct 31)

FOCUS

This was a decent enough renewal of this prestigious event, with two of this year's Classic winners among five Group 1 scorers in all, but the fourth and fifth suggest the form is limited for the grade and the winner has been rated only 2lb higher than when trounced by New Approach here in 2008. Some of the field were below par at the end of a busy campaign, but the pace was very strong, and the time was almost exactly on the standard. The first eight finished a long way clear.

NOTEBOOK

Twice Over, who was a 6l second to New Approach in this last year, went one better to post a deserved first Group 1 victory at the sixth attempt. Given a break after a disappointing run in the Eclipse then two confidence boosters in lesser company, he travelled well, in touch without chasing the strong pace, before running on bravely once striking for home despite drifting right. His trainer thinks he is a better horse than he was a year ago and this was a slight personal best. He could well run in the Breeders' Cup Classic and probably stays in training. (tchd 16-1 and 20-1 in places)

Mawatheeq(USA) ◆, supplemented following his impressive Cumberland Lodge win, required two handlers in the paddock and was a little reluctant to load. He found it difficult to go the pace and was niggled along at halfway, but was beginning to run on when he was forced to switch left as a gap between Pipedreamer and the winner closed. He ran on strongly once gathering momentum again, as befits one who is well at home over 1m4f, and was reeling in Twice Over at the line. This was a fine effort from this lightly-raced colt, who will be a contender for top middle distance races next year. (tchd 6-1)

Sariska was not best suited by the drying ground on this first run against colts. The dual Oaks winner, on whom Kieren Fallon replaced the suspended Jamie Spencer, was slow to leave the stalls and raced in rear, before making her way over to the outside of the pack before halfway. She looked well held with two to run, but then began to find her stride and stayed on powerfully down the centre of the track for third. She is obviously effective at this trip but 1m4f is ideal, and this was a good effort in the circumstances. Granted some cut in the ground she will be a major player in races like the Coronation Cup and King George next year. (op 7-1 tchd 9-1)

Pipedreamer, winner of a Longchamp Group 2 a fortnight previously, came through to look a threat and was only run out of second inside the last. This most likeable colt does not quite see out 1m2f. (op 20-1)

City Leader(IRE), having only his third run since finishing tenth in this last year, and well behind Pipedreamer in France, travelled kindly in the first-time blinkers and stuck on well for a creditable fifth.

Fame And Glory, the form pick, raced in third place behind the searching gallop set by his pacemaker Set Sail, and the writing was on the wall as he was being niggled along by halfway. He did show briefly in front, but his exertions had told and he was a spent force inside the last. He has had a long season and this came quick enough after his Arc sixth to nemesis Sea The Stars in the Arc. Likely to stay in training, he will not mind a return to 1m4f. (op 7-4)

Barshiba(IRE) raced close to the pace, as she often does these days, and ran her race with no excuses. She has enjoyed a rewarding season. (tchd 40-1)

Virtual, representing the same connections as Pipedreamer, was having only his second run at 1m2f and this ground was against him. He ran respectably but this trip just stretches him. He has been found wanting in top company since his Lockinge win.

Campanologist(USA), noisy in the paddock, was 3lb better off with Mawatheeq compared to Ascot but failed to fire in the face of a stiff task. (op 33-1)

Never On Sunday(FR), whose French yard won this two years ago with Literato, was always at the back of the field and merely passed a few eased-down rivals when it was as good as over. (op 7-1)

Doctor Fremantle, in the second colours of the winning over, was always in the rear division. He was reported to have boiled over in the preliminaries, and probably needs further these days in any case. Official explanation: jockey said colt boiled over in the preliminaries and did not run its usual race (tchd 9-1)

Forgotten Voice(IRE), who had a lot to do in this company, was keen in the early stages and was always towards the rear. Official explanation: jockey said colt had no more to give (tchd 100-1 in a place)

Alpine Rose(FR) needs softer ground and was always out the back. (op 14-1)

6851 TOTESPORT.COM CESAREWITCH (HERITAGE H'CAP) 2m 2f

3:40 (3:52) (Class 2) 3-Y-O+

£99,696 (£29,856; £14,928; £7,472; £3,728; £1,872) **Stalls** High

Form RPR

1212 **1** **Darley Sun (IRE)**[36] 5824 3-8-6 **94** AndreaAtzeni[(3)] 25 111+
(D M Simcock) *lw: t.k.h: hld up in midfield: hdwy over 3f out: swtchd rt and str run on far rail over 2f out: led over 1f out: clr 1f out: r.o strly: readily* **9/2**[1]

/23- **2** *5* **Mamlook (IRE)**[197] 6817 5-9-1 **89** RichardHughes 16 100
(D E Pipe) *hld up wl bhd: stl plenty to do 4f out: weaved through horses and hdwy 3f out: stl 7th 1f out: r.o wl to go 2nd nr fin: nvr nr wnr* **14/1**[3]

0005 **3** *1/2* **Sereth (IRE)**[85] 4274 6-8-13 **87** JMurtagh 8 97+
(B J Curley) *lw: hld up in tch: jnd ldr gng wl over 3f out: rdn to ld over 2f out: hdd and nt pce of wnr over 1f out: lost 2nd nr fin* **16/1**

51 **4** *1* **Dayia (IRE)**[8] 6636 5-8-8 **82** 4ex................................ SaleemGolam 35 91
(J Pearce) *in tch: swtchd lft and hdwy 4f out: ev ch and rdn over 2f out: edgd lft u.p and outpcd by wnr over 1f out: plugged on same pce fnl f* **16/1**

204 **5** *2 ½* **Ajaan**[44] 5609 5-9-10 **98**..(b) TPQueally 31 105
(H R A Cecil) *chsd ldrs: rdn and effrt 3f out: swtchd lft jst over 2f out: drvn and btn wl over 1f out* **20/1**

3534 **6** *½* **Gordonsville**[21] 6281 6-8-5 **82**.......................... KellyHarrison(3) 33 88
(J S Goldie) *t.k.h: hld up wl bhd: hdwy on far rail over 4f out: rdn 3f out: chsd ldrs and drvn wl over 1f out: no hdwy ent fnl f* **33/1**

1013 **7** *2 ¾* **Aaim To Prosper (IRE)**[57] 5235 5-8-11 **85**..............(b[1]) NickyMackay 19 88
(B J Meehan) *t.k.h: chsd ldrs tl wnt 2nd 7f out: led over 5f out: rdn 3f out: sn hdd: wknd wl over 1f out* **33/1**

6/0- **8** *2 ¼* **Bahrain Storm (IRE)**[15] 6468 6-9-5 **98**.........................(b) GFCarroll(5) 5 99
(Patrick J Flynn, Ire) *dropped in bhd after s: hld up towards rr: hdwy 6f out: rdn and edging rt 4f out: no prog over 2f out* **22/1**

4143 **9** *3* **Nanton (USA)**[14] 6480 7-10-0 **102** 4ex..................... DanielTudhope 7 99
(J S Goldie) *dropped in bhd after s: hld up wl in rr: prog on far rail over 5f out: nt clr run and switching out lft and on outer over 2f out: sme late hdwy: n.d* **28/1**

0-40 **10** *1 ½* **Highland Legacy**[42] 5656 5-9-2 **90**...................................(v) NCallan 30 86
(M L W Bell) *lw: wl in tch: rdn and unable qck over 2f out: struggling whn hmpd jst over 2f out: sn btn* **40/1**

1400 **11** *2 ¼* **Judgethemoment (USA)**[57] 5235 4-9-5 **93**.................... EddieAhern 18 86
(Jane Chapple-Hyam) *swtg: hld up in midfield: rdn and effrt 4f out: sn struggling: no ch fnl 2f* **33/1**

4214 **12** *1 ½* **Sweetheart**[21] 6273 5-8-6 **80**.. DJMoran 23 71
(Jamie Poulton) *hld up in midfield: swtchd to outer and rdn over 4f out: no prog and wl hld fnl 3f* **16/1**

56- **13** *½* **Dirar (IRE)**[28] 6130 4-9-2 **90**... CSoumillon 6 81
(Gordon Elliott, Ire) *hld up in midfield: rdn and effrt 4f out: no prog and btn whn hmpd over 2f out: eased fnl f* **33/1**

6422 **14** *2 ½* **Woolfall Treasure**[21] 6273 4-9-0 **88**..............................(b) RyanMoore 21 76
(G L Moore) *hld up in midfield: hdwy over 5f out: in tch and rdn 3f out: sn btn: eased fnl f* **14/1**[3]

1000 **15** *2 ¼* **Som Tala**[42] 5656 6-9-6 **94**... TonyCulhane 32 80
(M R Channon) *racd in midfield: rdn and no prog 4f out: wl btn fnl 3f* **66/1**

6232 **16** *1 ½* **Alanbrooke**[28] 6115 3-8-11 **96**...(b) LDettori 13 80
(M Johnston) *in tch: hdwy and swtchd lft 4f out: wanting to hang rt after: pressed ldrs u.p 3f out: wknd rapidly over 2f out: eased ent fnl f* **12/1**[2]

12/3 **17** *½* **Royal Rationale (IRE)**[36] 2994 5-8-12 **86**..................(b) SebSanders 28 70
(D E Pipe) *t.k.h: hld up in rr: n.m.r fr 5f out tl swtchd lft over 3f out: no hdwy: n.d* **16/1**

5P0- **18** *hd* **Silk Affair (IRE)**[220] 7487 4-9-1 **89**................................. PaulHanagan 15 72
(M G Quinlan) *hld up towards rr: rdn and effrt over 4f out: wl btn fnl 3f* **33/1**

2236 **19** *4 ½* **Wells Lyrical (IRE)**[16] 6412 4-9-5 **93**................................ TomEaves 26 71
(B Smart) *t.k.h: chsd ldrs: swtchd lft and rdn over 4f out: struggling over 3f out: no ch fnl 2f* **20/1**

20 *1 ¼* **Truckers Delight (IRE)**[28] 4391 8-8-12 **86**.................. CO'Donoghue 36 63
(John Joseph Hanlon, Ire) *hld up in midfield: rdn and btn over 3f out* **40/1**

6605 **21** *13* **Bulwark (IRE)**[45] 4769 7-8-11 **88**..............(v) Louis-PhilippeBeuzelin(3) 17 51
(Ian Williams) *sn niggled along towards rr: rdn and effrt on outer over 4f out: nvr trbld ldrs: t.o and eased over 1f out* **40/1**

-451 **22** *nk* **Electrolyser (IRE)**[20] 6306 4-9-11 **99** 4ex.................. PhilipRobinson 11 61
(C G Cox) *in tch tl lost pl and edgd lft over 4f out: wl btn after: eased fnl f: t.o* **25/1**

060- **23** *1 ½* **Horseford Hill**[23] 6361 5-8-7 **81**.............................(b[1]) PaulFitzsimons 14 42
(Miss J R Tooth) *hld up in rr: rdn and no rspnse 6f out: wl bhd fnl 4f: t.o and eased fnl 2f* **150/1**

1313 **24** *shd* **Swingkeel (IRE)**[20] 6306 4-9-9 **97**................................ JimmyFortune 10 58
(J L Dunlop) *hld up in midfield: rdn and btn 4f out: eased over 1f out: t.o* **14/1**[3]

3/0- **25** *½* **Fair Along (GER)**[170] 1916 7-9-6 **94**...................................(p) KFallon 29 54
(P J Hobbs) *t.k.h: hld up in rr: swtchd lft and effrt u.p 5f out: no real hdwy: wl btn fnl 3f: eased over 1f out: t.o* **12/1**[2]

336 **26** *2* **Tilt**[112] 3390 7-8-11 **90**.. MartinLane(5) 2 48
(B Ellison) *hld up in midfield: rdn and no prog whn bmpd over 4f out: n.d: eased fnl f: t.o* **50/1**

00/3 **27** *26* **Raslan**[34] 5903 6-8-9 **83**..(vt) HayleyTurner 9 12
(D E Pipe) *chsd ldr tl led 7f out: rdn and over 5f out: sn dropped out: wl bhd fnl 3f: t.o and eased over 1f out* **40/1**

02 **28** *3 ½* **Nemo Spirit (IRE)**[42] 5656 4-9-1 **89**.............................. RichardMullen 3 14
(W R Muir) *lw: chsd ldrs tl wknd qckly over 6f out: wl bhd fnl 4f: eased fnl f: t.o* **66/1**

4544 **29** *8* **Keenes Day (FR)**[20] 6306 4-9-4 **92**...................................... RHills 20 9
(M Johnston) *stdd s: hld up in rr: nvr a factor: t.o fnl 3f: eased over 1f out* **25/1**

40-6 **30** *13* **Enjoy The Moment**[34] 5903 6-9-6 **94**............................... ShaneKelly 24 —
(J A Osborne) *a bhd: lost tch over 4f out: eased over 1f out: wl t.o* **66/1**

4231 **31** *16* **Yes Mr President (IRE)**[42] 5656 4-9-6 **94** 4ex................ JoeFanning 12 —
(M Johnston) *t.k.h: chsd ldrs tl lost pl qckly over 4f out: wl t.o fnl 3f: eased over 1f out: fin lame* **16/1**

11-0 **32** *105* **Viper**[142] 2409 7-9-2 **90**... ChrisCatlin 27 —
(R Hollinshead) *led tl 7f out: sn dropped out: wl t.o fnl 4f: bbv* **33/1**

3m 50.27s (-4.53) **Going Correction** +0.05s/f (Good)
WFA 3 from 4yo+ 11lb **32 Ran SP% 142.5**
Speed ratings (Par 109): **112,109,109,109,108 107,106,105,104,103 102,101,101,100,99 98,98,98,96,96 90,90,89,89,89 88,7**
toteswingers: 1&2 £35.20, 1&3 £101.80, 2&3 £55.10 CSF £53.04 CT £1004.51 TOTE £6.30: £3.10, £4.00, £5.50, £7.10; EX 119.20 Trifecta £5672.10 Pool: £26,827.74 - 3.50 winning units..
Owner Abdullah Saeed Belhab **Bred** Manfred Hoffer & Ballygrelihan Farm **Trained** Newmarket, Suffolk
■ Darley Sun was the first 3-y-o winner since 1998, but few get into the race nowadays.

FOCUS
A fine performance from the progressive 3-y-o Darley Sun, though he was 12lb well in and so entitled to win. The form has been rated around the fourth and fifth, with Mamlook running his best race yet on the Flat and Sereth his best race since he arrrived from Germany.

NOTEBOOK
Darley Sun(IRE) ◆ was 12lb ahead of the handicapper, having earned his impending weight rise with a fine second behind Askar Tau over this trip in the Doncaster Cup, and he confirmed himself very much a Group-class stayer with a really smart performance. He was a bit keen early on but that made no difference whatsoever, as having come under pressure a fair way out, he stayed on strongly once switched on to the far rail inside the final 3f. His challenge was relentless and he looked better the further he went. It remains to be seen whether he runs again this season, but his main target for 2010 is the Ascot Gold Cup and even at this early stage he has to be considered a major player. He will absolutely relish the 2m4f trip in a race where few rarely stay, and was a 10l winner on his only previous start at the track. (op 13-2)
Mamlook(IRE), 4lb higher than when third in this race last year, his last run on the Flat, did well to get up for second as he was set an awful lot to do and was searching for room over 3f out, at which point the winner was already building up his momentum. (op 16-1)
Sereth(IRE), the subject of an ante-post gamble at big prices, landed the each-way money with a good effort in defeat, proving his stamina on this first run beyond 2m. A dual Listed winner over 1m6f when trained in Germany last year, he had been struggling since joining Barney Curley but he was fully 17lb lower than when first contesting a handicap in Britain and much better was clearly expected this time. This performance is all the more creditable considering no winner of the race has been drawn lower than 11 in the last ten years. (op 14-1)
Dayia(IRE), 3lb well in under her penalty, travelled well for much of the way but lacked the finishing kick of some of these. It was a fine effort nonetheless.
Ajaan was 3lb higher than when runner-up in the Chester Cup, but still 4lb well in. He ran well but struggles to win these days.
Gordonsville, a bit keen early, travelled well for much of the way but could not make an impression once coming under pressure.
Aaim To Prosper(IRE), with blinkers replacing a visor on his first start since leaving Mick Channon, ran okay after about two months off. He was given a positive ride but didn't see his race out. (op 50-1)
Bahrain Storm(IRE) made some progress from the rear but was never seen with a winning chance. (op 20-1)
Nanton(USA), who was third in the Cambridgeshire but had earlier won over 1m6f, found all sorts of trouble under his usual hold-up ride and as such it's impossible to know whether he stayed. He's due to go up 5lb. (tchd 25-1)
Highland Legacy probably wants easier ground. (tchd 50-1)
Judgethemoment(USA) is a proven stayer who was only 2lb higher than when winning at Royal Ascot, and better could have been expected from him.
Woolfall Treasure Official explanation: jockey said gelding had no more to give
Alanbrooke Official explanation: jockey said colt hung right
Royal Rationale(IRE) Official explanation: jockey said gelding was denied a clear run
Electrolyser(IRE) Official explanation: jockey said colt suffered interference in running
Yes Mr President(IRE) Official explanation: vet said gelding returned lame
Viper Official explanation: trainer's rep said gelding bled from the nose

6852 LOTUS EVORA ROCKFEL STKS (GROUP 2) (FILLIES) 7f
4:15 (4:26) (Class 1) 2-Y-O

£45,416 (£17,216; £8,616; £4,296; £2,152; £1,080) **Stalls** Centre

Form RPR

110 **1** **Music Show (IRE)**[28] 6090 2-8-12 89.. KFallon 4 110
(M R Channon) *midfield early: rdn over 2f out: swtchd rt and hdwy over 1f out: r.o strly to ld cl home* **25/1**

052 **2** *nk* **Atasari (IRE)**[6] 6708 2-8-12 0.. KJManning 5 109
(J S Bolger, Ire) *t.k.h early: sn trcking ldrs: rdn to chal 1f out: led briefly ins fnl f: nt able to repel wnr* **16/1**

11 **3** *¾* **Tabassum (IRE)**[15] 6447 2-8-12 108.. RHills 1 107
(Sir Michael Stoute) *lw: broke wl: sn led against stands' rails: rdn over 1f out: hdd and no ex fnl 75yds* **4/6**[1]

0 **4** *6* **Gibraltar Blue (IRE)**[20] 6317 2-8-12 0.............................. ShaneKelly 9 94+
(T Stack, Ire) *w'like: carried rt s: swtchd to nr side gp early: hld up: kpt hanging rt: rdn over 2f out: hdwy over 1f out: styd on: nvr nr ldrs* **33/1**

13 **5** *1 ¼* **Astrophysical Jet**[28] 6090 2-8-12 90........................... GrahamGibbons 6 89
(E S McMahon) *w'like: slowly away: swtchd to trck ldrs on stands' side rail: rdn over 2f out: sn btn but plugged on* **33/1**

5322 **6** *1* **Dubawi Heights**[14] 6477 2-8-12 99.. LDettori 8 87
(S A Callaghan, U.S.A) *wnt rt s: led centre trio tl joining main gp 4f out: rdn over 2f out: grad wknd ins fnl f* **8/1**[2]

311 **7** *¾* **Distinctive**[28] 6090 2-8-12 101.. TomEaves 10 85
(B Smart) *str: lw: carried rt s: racd keenly in centre trio: rdn over 2f out: grad wknd and hung lft ins fnl f* **8/1**[2]

1 **8** *4 ½* **Silver Rock (IRE)**[29] 6055 2-8-12 0.............................. JimmyFortune 2 79+
(M A Magnusson) *w'like: athletic: racd keenly in midfield: rdn w no rspnse over 2f out: sn btn* **16/1**

0130 **9** *1 ¾* **Paleo (IRE)**[14] 6481 2-8-12 83... RichardHughes 7 71+
(R Hannon) *t.k.h in midfield: racd rather awkwardly: rdn over 2f out: sn wknd* **66/1**

1 **10** *6* **Champagnelifestyle**[92] 4055 2-8-12 0............................. MichaelHills 3 59+
(B W Hills) *t.k.h: trckd ldrs: rdn over 2f out: no rspnse: wl btn whn eased ins fnl f* **9/1**[3]

1 **11** *4* **Bint Doyen**[11] 6561 2-8-12 0.. NCallan 11 44
(C E Brittain) *w'like: carried rt s: plld hrd in midfield: rdn and dropped out qckly over 2f out* **33/1**

1m 23.83s (-1.57) **Going Correction** +0.05s/f (Good) **11 Ran SP% 118.1**
Speed ratings (Par 104): **110,109,108,101,100 99,98,93,91,84 79**
toteswingers: 1&2 £27.20, 1&3 £8.90, 2&3 £5.20 CSF £357.22 TOTE £25.30: £4.40, £3.80, £1.20; EX 522.20.
Owner Jaber Abdullah **Bred** Darley **Trained** West Ilsley, Berks
■ Stewards' Enquiry : K J Manning one-day ban: used whip with excessive frequency (Oct 31)

FOCUS
This race has gone to 1,000 Guineas winners Speciosa and Finsceal Beo and runner-up Maids Causeway in recent years, and with the front three clear in a time only 0.63 seconds outside standard it is form to be positive about. The winner is back on the right trail and it was much improved form from the second.

NOTEBOOK
Music Show(IRE), whose yard won this with Lahaleeb a year ago, was drawn on the wrong side in the Firth Of Clyde at Ayr but comfortably reversed the form with the winner that day, Distinctive. Well suited by this step up to 7f, she responded to pressure to get past the first two close home. Available at between 16-1 and 33-1 for the 1,000 Guineas, it is not hard to envisage her taking in a similar campaign early next season to Lahaleeb, who won the Fred Darling first time out before running in the Guineas. Official explanation: trainer had no explanation for the apparent improvement in form (tchd 22-1 and 33-1)
Atasari(IRE), from the same stable as Finsceal Beo, who won this in 2006, had every chance and went down fighting. This was the best run yet from this tough filly, who was runner-up in a Gowran Listed race just six days earlier. She has already shown that she stays a mile and that she is at home in soft ground. (op 20-1)

Tabassum(IRE) was prominent in the 1,000 Guineas betting after her impressive win in the Group 3 Oh So Sharp Stakes over this course and distance, for which she picked up no penalty. Drawn against the rail, she tried to make all but, after kicking over a furlong out, she could never shake off the two fillies who beat her and was caught close home. She did not do much wrong and remains a promising filly, with the Guineas still the plan. She is not the biggest, though. (op 4-5)

Gibraltar Blue(IRE) was not disgraced in a valuable sales race over 6f last time. At the back of the field when her run was blocked over a quarter of a mile out, she ran on when it was all over. She reportedly joins Mike de Kock in South Africa now. (op 20-1)

Astrophysical Jet, ahead of Music Show at Ayr last time, travelled quite well behind the favourite on the rail but was outpaced by the principals from the two pole. (op 25-1)

Dubawi Heights, who has picked up £238,000 in prize-money despite remaining a maiden, faded rather disappointingly when the race developed. It remains to be seen whether she will join her trainer when he relocates to the US. Official explanation: jockey said filly hung left (op 10-1 tchd 11-1)

Distinctive was a disappointment following her impressive Group 3 win in Ayr's Firth of Clyde Stakes, where she had today's winner back in seventh. She failed to get cover and didn't settle, and was unable to pick up when required. She may need dropping back to 6f. (tchd 15-2)

Silver Rock(IRE)'s Newbury debut form has been let down and she failed to handle this rise in grade. She was reported to have run too free. Official explanation: jockey said filly ran too free (op 20-1)

Paleo(IRE) held only a very slim chance on official figures. (op 50-1)

Champagnelifestyle back-pedalled quickly on this first start since her winning debut on the July course three months ago. (op 8-1)

Bint Doyen, a surprise Redcar winner on her debut, was not up to this rise in grade. (op 25-1)

6853 PRIDE STKS (GROUP 2) (F&M) 1m 4f

4:50 (4:58) (Class 1) 3-Y-O+

£56,770 (£21,520; £10,770; £5,370; £2,690; £1,350) Stalls High

Form RPR

12 **1** **Ashalanda (FR)**[27] 6153 3-8-12 110 ..... C-PLemaire 2 115
(A De Royer-Dupre, France) *w'like: athletic: t.k.h: hld up wl in tch: rdn ent fnl 2f: chsd clr ldr wl over 1f out: r.o wl fnl f to ld last stride* **11/2**[2]

1-15 **2** *shd* **Crystal Capella**[13] 6525 4-9-3 116 ..... RyanMoore 3 113
(Sir Michael Stoute) *lw: t.k.h: hld up in rr tl plld wy into 2nd over 7f out: led jst over 2f out: rdn clr wl over 1f out: hrd drvn fnl f: hdd last stride* **7/4**[1]

-506 **3** *1 ½* **Saphira's Fire (IRE)**[58] 5201 4-9-3 99 ..... HayleyTurner 5 111+
(W R Muir) *stdd s: t.k.h: racd in last: effrt on far rail 3f out: nt clr run and swtchd lft wl over 1f out: switching rt and hdwy ent fnl f: r.o wl to chse ldng pair ins fnl f: nt rch ldrs* **50/1**

3315 **4** *1 ½* **High Heeled (IRE)**[77] 4522 3-8-10 114 ..... MichaelHills 8 108
(B W Hills) *dwlt: t.k.h: hld up wl in tch: rdn to chse ldng pair wl over 1f out: plugged on same pce fr over 1f out: lost 3rd ins fnl f* **7/1**[3]

51 **5** *1 ¼* **Arwaah (IRE)**[64] 4991 3-8-10 98 ..... RHills 10 106+
(M P Tregoning) *lw: t.k.h: chsd ldrs early: steadily eased bk and towards rr 6f out: nt clr run 3f out tl wl over 1f out: edgd rt but hdwy to chse ldrs ent fnl f: no imp and btn jst ins fnl f* **8/1**

01-2 **6** *4* **Baila Me (GER)**[28] 6093 4-9-3 111 ..... LDettori 9 100
(Saeed Bin Suroor) *set stdy gallop tl over 7f out: styd chsng ldrs: rdn and unable qck whn n.m.r and looking to switch lft jst over 2f out: keeping on same pce whn hmpd over 1f out: wl hld after* **15/2**

5416 **7** *1 ¾* **Snoqualmie Girl (IRE)**[22] 6242 3-8-10 105 ..... KFallon 11 97
(D R C Elsworth) *t.k.h: hld up in midfield early: stdd bk to last trio 7f out: swtchd lft and rdn jst over 2f out: edging rt u.p and no hdwy over 1f out* **20/1**

1211 **8** *1 ¾* **Ave**[21] 6298 3-8-10 108 ..... RichardMullen 6 94
(Sir Michael Stoute) *stdd s: hld up in tch in last trio: effrt and rdn 2f out: no hdwy and wl btn fnl f* **7/1**[3]

4215 **9** *1 ¼* **Charity Belle (USA)**[14] 6504 3-8-10 107 ..... JimmyFortune 7 92
(J H M Gosden) *lw: chsd ldr tl led over 7f out: hdd jst over 2f out: rdn and nt pce of ldr wl over 1f out: wknd over 1f out* **25/1**

2435 **10** *20* **Flame Of Gibraltar (IRE)**[31] 6003 3-8-10 100 ..... TPQueally 1 60
(H R A Cecil) *stdd s: t.k.h: hld up towards rr early: hdwy to chse ldrs 7f out: wknd ent fnl 2f: wl btn and eased fnl f* **20/1**

2m 31.55s (-1.95) **Going Correction** +0.05s/f (Good)
WFA 3 from 4yo 7lb **10** Ran SP% **115.0**
Speed ratings (Par 115): **108,107,106,105,105 102,101,100,99,85**
toteswingers: 1&2 £4.10, 1&3 £33.40, 2&3 £14.70 CSF £14.53 TOTE £5.50: £2.10, £1.50, £7.00; EX 16.50.
Owner H H Aga Khan **Bred** Haras De Son Altesse L'Aga Khan **Trained** Chantilly, France

FOCUS
The second running of this distaff Group 2. The pace was very steady through the first part of the race and a number pulled for their heads. Decent form for the grade nevertheless.

NOTEBOOK
Ashalanda(FR), ostensibly the pacemaker when winning in this grade in Saint-Cloud before a good effort in defeat at San Siro, was an appropriate winner of a race named after Pride, who won the Champion Stakes for the Royer-Dupre yard. One of those who was keen early, she went after the winner from the two-pole and seemed held for a time, but gradually gathered her in and snatched the race on the line. Probably best with a bit of cut in the ground, she is a very smart filly who may stay in training next year. (op 6-1 tchd 15-2)

Crystal Capella ◆, last year's winner, failed to settle early on and soon moved up to track the pace. She went on over a quarter of a mile out and soon pulled perhaps three lengths clear, but was caught right on the line. Previously unbeaten over this trip, she was injured in her box after her narrow defeat of Dar Re Mi, who received 4lb, at York in May, and was sharper for her return at Longchamp. A tough and genuine filly, she will be back next season. (tchd 2-1 and 9-4 in places)

Saphira's Fire(IRE), third to Crystal Capella a year ago, ran perhaps her best race since, finishing well from the back of the field after encountering traffic problems. She has been ill for most of the year and should do well next season now that she is over her problems.

High Heeled(IRE), running over this trip for the first time since her Oaks third, disputed second over a furlong out but lacked a change of pace from that point. She prefers some give in the ground. (op 8-1 tchd 13-2)

Arwaah(IRE)'s Newbury maiden win has worked out well and she was not at all disgraced on this big rise in grade, keeping on again after losing her pitch and then encountering a bit of trouble.

Baila Me(GER), runner-up to stablemate Prince Siegfried on her British debut at Ayr, cut out the early running and eventually dropped away inside the last 2f. She is going to prove difficult to place. (op 7-1 tchd 8-1)

Snoqualmie Girl(IRE) had plenty to find with the principals on these terms and did not prove up to the task. (op 33-1)

Ave has shown progressive form of late, winning in Listed and Group 3 company since finishing second to High Heeled at York, but she was the Stoute second string here and she never looked like completing a hat-trick. (op 13-2 tchd 6-1)

Charity Belle(USA) managed to get to the front early in the long home straight but her stamina ultimately looked to give out. (op 20-1)

Flame Of Gibraltar(IRE) has proved a disappointment since finishing second in the Ribblesdale at Ascot and was beaten a long way here.

6854 JOCKEY CLUB CUP (GROUP 3) 2m

5:25 (5:34) (Class 1) 3-Y-O+

£36,900 (£13,988; £7,000; £3,490; £1,748; £877) Stalls High

Form RPR

5111 **1** **Akmal**[16] 6425 3-8-4 107 ..... RHills 3 106
(J L Dunlop) *lw: mde all: rdn ent fnl 2f: 2 l clr 1f out: edgd lft and all out fnl 50yds: a gng to hold on: v gamely* **9/4**[1]

1002 **2** *½* **Nehaam**[16] 6425 3-8-4 103 ..... TPO'Shea 6 106
(J H M Gosden) *t.k.h: hld up in midfield: hemmed in whn swtchd lft and forced way out over 3f out: sn rdn: chsd wnr ent fnl f: styd on u.p fnl 100yds: nvr quite getting to wnr* **9/2**[3]

0350 **3** *½* **Above Average (IRE)**[35] 5861 3-8-7 102 ..... MichaelHills 2 108
(B W Hills) *lw: t.k.h: hld up in last trio: hdwy jst over 2f out: swtchd lft over 1f out: drvn ins fnl f: styd on fnl 100yds: wnt 3rd nr fin* **12/1**

0/24 **4** *½* **Blue Bajan (IRE)**[35] 5854 7-9-0 111 ..... LDettori 1 104
(Andrew Turnell) *t.k.h: hld up in last pair: swtchd lft and effrt over 2f out: drvn and kpt on ins fnl f: unable to rch ldrs* **13/2**

0132 **5** *nk* **Oasis Knight (IRE)**[20] 6306 3-8-4 98 ..... (v) KFallon 7 104
(M P Tregoning) *t.k.h: sn chsng ldrs: wnt 2nd and rdn jst over 2f out: drvn wl over 2f out: plugging on but hld whn swtchd rt wl ins fnl f: lost 2 pls nr fin* **4/1**[2]

3002 **6** *6* **Starfala**[37] 5796 4-8-11 105 ..... NCallan 5 94
(P F I Cole) *swtg: t.k.h: chsd ldrs: rdn and unable qck whn bmpd over 3f out: bhd whn edgd rt 2f out* **10/1**

2003 **7** *19* **Mischief Making (USA)**[22] 6242 4-8-11 98 ..... TGMcLaughlin 4 71
(E A L Dunlop) *lw: hld up in last pair: pushed along 4f out: rdn and btn wl over 2f out: eased fnl f* **25/1**

3661 **8** *1 ½* **Urban Poet (USA)**[12] 6536 3-8-4 105 ..... AhmedAjtebi 8 72
(Saeed Bin Suroor) *chsd ldr tl jst over 2f out: sn edgd lft and wknd: eased fr over 1f out* **7/1**

3m 31.9s (1.10) **Going Correction** +0.05s/f (Good)
WFA 3 from 4yo+ 10lb **8** Ran SP% **115.4**
Speed ratings (Par 113): **99,98,98,98,98 95,85,84**
toteswingers: 1&2 £3.00, 1&3 £7.90, 2&3 £10.70. CSF £12.63 TOTE £2.90: £1.40, £1.90, £2.90; EX 10.70 Place 6 £383.84, Place 5 £115.70.
Owner Hamdan Al Maktoum **Bred** Shadwell Estate Company Limited **Trained** Arundel, W Sussex
■ Akmal provided John Dunlop with his 250th winner at Newmarket.

FOCUS
The 3yos dominated what looked an ordinary running of this Group 3, which was run in a time nearly 12 seconds above standard. Muddling form.

NOTEBOOK
Akmal, making the running for the third race in succession, dictated just a steady pace and once again displayed terrific battling qualities when challenged. He only won his maiden in May, a success that came at the sixth attempt, but he has made great progress since then, adding four handicaps and a Listed win, and he handled this further rise in class to gain his seventh success from his last nine outings. It's true he enjoyed the run of things, and that his stamina wasn't severely tested on this first run at 2m, but he's always looked likely to stay this sort of trip and doesn't appear particularly flattered. He may make further progress this year, but repeating these sort of tactics will get tougher as he continues to go up in grade. (tchd 11-4)

Nehaam, trying 2m for the first time, had to be switched into the clear about 3f out but he was in the open for long enough if good enough. He stayed on but was always being held by the winner. (op 5-1)

Above Average(IRE) ◆, like the front two trying this trip for the first time, appeared to get unbalanced when coming under pressure over 2f out and, displaying a knee action, he took a while to respond to pressure. The way he finished suggests he would have gone even closer had his rider got after him sooner, but whatever, he'll surely appreciate some cut in the ground. (op 18-1 tchd 10-1)

Blue Bajan(IRE) was surprisingly trying this trip for the first time on the Flat. He travelled well but, rather like the third-placed finisher, took too long to pick up when placed under pressure. (op 11-2 tchd 7-1)

Oasis Knight(IRE) was a bit disappointing. He was well enough placed but was inclined to hang right in behind the winner when Fallon looked to angle him out. (op 5-1)

Starfala was warm and raced too keenly on this first try at the trip. (tchd 17-2)

Urban Poet(USA) won a very weak conditions race at Pontefract last time, but prior to that he had run two abysmal races. This was another one. (op 17-2 tchd 9-1)

T/Jkpt: Not won. T/Plt: £214.60 to a £1 stake. Pool: £194,186.72. 660.52 winning tickets. T/Qpdt: £13.30 to a £1 stake. Pool: £11,520.41. 640.60 winning tickets. SP

6825 WOLVERHAMPTON (A.W) (L-H)

Saturday, October 17

OFFICIAL GOING: Standard
Wind: Nil Weather: Fine

6855 LADBROKES.COM H'CAP 1m 4f 50y(P)

5:50 (5:52) (Class 4) (0-85,85) 3-Y-O+ £5,046 (£1,510; £755; £377; £188) Stalls Low

Form RPR

051 **1** **Akbabend**[64] 4974 3-8-13 77 ..... RobertWinston 2 86+
(M Johnston) *led early: chsd ldr: lft in ld over 5f out: rdn over 1f out: drvn out* **9/4**[1]

0434 **2** *2 ¼* **Secret Life**[64] 4979 3-8-12 76 ..... AdamKirby 4 81
(J Noseda) *hld up: pushed along over 2f out: hdwy over 1f out: rdn to take 2nd wl ins fnl f: nt trble wnr* **6/1**

1042 **3** *1* **Ethics Girl (IRE)**[14] 6473 3-8-11 75 ..... RobertHavlin 5 78
(John Berry) *hld up: stdy prog over 5f out: chsd wnr over 3f out tl rdn 1f out: one pce* **4/1**[2]

2020 **4** *¾* **Benedict Spirit (IRE)**[15] 6460 4-9-0 71 ..... JimmyQuinn 8 73
(D Burchell) *a.p: rdn to chse wnr 1f out: lost 2nd and no ex wl ins fnl f* **12/1**

332 **5** *½* **Phoenix Flight (IRE)**[38] 5781 4-9-11 82 ..... (p) J-PGuillambert 7 83
(H J Evans) *racd keenly in rr: pushed along and effrt over 2f out: rdn over 1f out: one pce* **9/2**[3]

5200 **6** *27* **Valdan (IRE)**[72] 4696 5-8-12 74 ..... (t) AndrewHeffernan(5) 1 32
(M A Barnes) *hld up in rr: pushed along and lost tch fnl 3f* **12/1**

1020 **P** **Geneva Geyser (GER)**[36] 5828 3-9-7 85 ..... MickyFenton 3 —
(J M P Eustace) *sn led: lost action and hdd over 5f out: sn p.u* **13/2**

2m 39.67s (-1.43) **Going Correction** -0.025s/f (Stan)
WFA 3 from 4yo+ 7lb **7** Ran SP% **112.0**
Speed ratings (Par 105): **103,101,100,100,100 82,—**
toteswingers: 1&2 £3.70, 1&3 £2.70, 2&3 £1.70 CSF £15.42 CT £49.23 TOTE £2.70: £1.40, £3.40; EX 14.10.
Owner Markus Graff **Bred** Miss K Rausing **Trained** Middleham Moor, N Yorks

FOCUS
Just an ordinary gallop set by Geneva Geyser until he pulled up at halfway. The winner is rated to a similar level to his 'win' last time.
Geneva Geyser(GER) Official explanation: jockey said colt lost its action

6856 BET IN PLAY AT LADBROKES.COM MAIDEN STKS 5f 20y(P)
6:20 (6:20) (Class 5) 3-Y-O+ £2,729 (£806; £403) Stalls Low

Form RPR
0 **1** **Fourtowns Flyer (IRE)**[27] 6135 5-9-3 0........................(tp) GeorgeBaker 4 72
(Lee Smyth, Ire) *mde virtually all: rdn fnl f: r.o wl* **4/1**[2]
0-52 **2** 3 **Westwood Dawn**[246] 540 4-9-3 55........................(v) DaneO'Neill 3 61
(D Shaw) *a.p: rdn to chse wnr wl over 1f out: no imp* **5/1**[3]
366 **3** 1 3/4 **Fatal Attraction**[8] 6641 4-8-12 53........................ AdamKirby 9 50+
(Rae Guest) *hld up towards rr: hdwy wl over 1f out: rdn to take 3rd ins fnl f: kpt on one pce* **16/1**
2432 **4** 1 1/2 **Avrilo**[43] 5645 3-8-12 53........................ FergusSweeney 12 44
(M S Saunders) *chsd ldrs: rdn over 2f out: c wd st: kpt on to take 4th wl ins fnl f* **10/1**
20 **5** 1 1/2 **Distant Vision (IRE)**[69] 4823 6-8-8 49 ow1........................ SladeO'Hara(5) 7 40
(H A McWilliams) *w wnr: pushed along and lost 2nd wl over 1f out: sn rdn: wknd ins fnl f* **22/1**
44-5 **6** 1 **Strategic Mover (USA)**[192] 1185 4-9-3 75........................(b[1]) JimmyQuinn 11 40
(P F I Cole) *hld up towards rr: swtchd rt over 1f out: sn rdn: nvr nr ldrs* **7/2**[1]
0503 **7** 1/2 **Green Poppy**[17] 6380 3-8-12 52........................ RobertWinston 6 34
(B Smart) *prom: rdn and wknd over 1f out* **7/2**[1]
00 **8** nk **Hayley's Girl**[31] 5998 3-8-7 44........................ AmyBaker(5) 8 32
(S W James) *mid-div: pushed along over 3f out: wknd wl over 1f out* **50/1**
5 **9** 1 3/4 **Clincher**[12] 6551 3-8-12 0........................ FrancisNorton 10 26
(J A Osborne) *s.i.s: sn outpcd* **16/1**
6 **10** 3/4 **Jack Galvin (IRE)**[12] 6551 3-9-3 0........................ RobertHavlin 5 28
(J R Gask) *hld up in mid-div: short-lived effrt on ins wl over 1f out* **12/1**
0-06 **11** 3/4 **Place The Duchess**[19] 6344 3-8-12 50........................(t) WandersonD'Avila 13 21
(A J Lidderdale) *prom tl rdn and wknd wl over 1f out* **50/1**
12 2 1/2 **Across The Sands** 3-9-3 0........................ FrankieMcDonald 2 17
(C N Kellett) *s.i.s: sn mid-div: wkng whn n.m.r on ins over 2f out* **66/1**
00 **13** 2 **Dancing Again**[12] 6551 3-8-12 0........................ StephenCarson 1 5
(E A Wheeler) *in rr: sltly hmpd on ins sn after s: sn outpcd* **66/1**

61.64 secs (-0.66) **Going Correction** -0.025s/f (Stan) **13** Ran SP% **120.9**
Speed ratings (Par 103): **104,99,96,94,91 90,89,88,85,84 83,79,76**
toteswingers: 1&2 £7.60, 1&3 £16.10, 2&3 £15.70 CSF £23.95 TOTE £5.00: £1.50, £1.70, £4.50; EX 27.00.
Owner C G Bryson **Bred** Corduff Stud **Trained** Dungannon, Co Tyrone

FOCUS
A strong gallop, and many of these were quickly taken off their feet. Just a modest maiden, rated around the runner-up.
Green Poppy Official explanation: jockey said filly hung right
Clincher Official explanation: jockey said filly was denied a clear run

6857 WOLVERHAMPTON-RACECOURSE.CO.UK CLAIMING STKS 5f 20y(P)
6:50 (6:51) (Class 6) 3-Y-O+ £2,388 (£705; £352) Stalls Low

Form RPR
0114 **1** **Bertie Southstreet**[7] 6670 6-8-5 67........................(v) KirstyMilczarek 5 73
(Karen George) *w ldr: led 2f out: rdn over 1f out: drvn out* **9/2**[2]
0200 **2** 2 **Grudge**[8] 6635 4-8-9 64........................ FrancisNorton 3 70
(Ollie Pears) *a.p: pushed along on ins over 2f out: chsd wnr jst ins fnl f: rdn and no imp* **10/1**
6240 **3** 1 **Fivefootnumberone (IRE)**[29] 6051 3-9-1 72........................(v) J-PGuillambert 6 72
(J J Quinn) *mid-div: pushed along over 3f out: c wd st: rdn and hdwy whn edgd lft over 1f out: r.o to take 3rd nr fin* **12/1**
0144 **4** nk **Desperate Dan**[7] 6669 8-8-4 73........................(v) AmyBaker(5) 1 65
(A B Haynes) *towards rr: pushed along over 3f out: hdwy on ins over 2f out: rdn wl over 1f out: kpt on one pce u.str.p fnl f* **11/4**[1]
-000 **5** nk **Moscow Eight (IRE)**[15] 6459 3-9-0 78........................ RossAtkinson(5) 12 74
(Tom Dascombe) *led: hdd 2f out: rdn over 1f out: one pce* **9/1**
0250 **6** nse **Fault**[8] 6632 3-8-13 72........................(t) MickyFenton 7 68+
(Stef Liddiard) *hld up towards rr: c v wd st: hdwy u.p fnl f: r.o* **10/1**
0565 **7** 3/4 **Kheylide (IRE)**[17] 6379 3-8-2 62........................(v[1]) DominicFox(3) 2 57
(Mrs D J Sanderson) *hld up towards rr: pushed along on ins over 2f out: swtchd rt and sme prog over 1f out: one pce fnl f* **12/1**
3052 **8** 1/2 **Swinbrook (USA)**[7] 6670 8-8-11 72........................(v) RobertWinston 8 61+
(R A Harris) *s.i.s: in rr: pushed along over 3f out: swtchd lft over 1f out and ins fnl f: nvr nrr* **11/2**[3]
4300 **9** 3/4 **Handsome Cross (IRE)**[28] 6118 8-8-11 70........................ ChrisCatlin 9 59
(W J Musson) *prom tl rdn and wknd over 1f out* **22/1**
00 **10** 1 **Jeannie (IRE)**[35] 5882 3-8-0 0........................ JimmyQuinn 10 44
(A Bailey) *s.i.s: t.k.h in rr: pushed wd over 3f out: n.d* **66/1**
0000 **11** 1 1/4 **Divine Spirit**[8] 6635 8-8-11 67........................ TomEaves 4 51
(M Dods) *hld up in tch: pushed along and wknd over 2f out* **25/1**
5426 **12** 5 **Godfrey Street**[51] 5374 6-8-7 71........................(p) FergusSweeney 11 29
(A G Newcombe) *chsd ldrs tl rdn and wknd wl over 1f out* **16/1**

61.54 secs (-0.76) **Going Correction** -0.025s/f (Stan) **12** Ran SP% **119.4**
Speed ratings (Par 101): **105,101,100,99,99 99,97,97,95,94 92,84**
toteswingers: 1&2 £8.90, 1&3 £21.90, 2&3 £25.50 CSF £48.53 TOTE £4.90: £1.50, £3.30, £4.10; EX 53.30.Moscow Eight was claimed by E. J. O'Neill for £12,000.
Owner Eastington Racing Club **Bred** B Whitehouse **Trained** Higher Eastington, Devon

FOCUS
For the second race running a 5f sprint went to a front-runner even though there were plenty of speedsters in this line-up. The front pair are the most likefly guide to the form.
Swinbrook(USA) Official explanation: jockey said gelding was denied a clear run

6858 ENJOY THE LUCKY 7 GROUP OFFER MAIDEN AUCTION STKS 1m 141y(P)
7:20 (7:22) (Class 6) 2-Y-O £2,388 (£705; £352) Stalls Low

Form RPR
1 **Brooklands Bay (IRE)** 2-8-12 0........................ LukeMorris 4 68+
(J R Weymes) *hld up and bhd: pushed along 3f out: rdn and hdwy on ins 2f out: edgd rt and led ins fnl f: r.o* **33/1**
656 **2** 3/4 **Angelena Ballerina (IRE)**[11] 6563 2-8-5 69........................(p) JimmyQuinn 2 60
(A Bailey) *a.p: led wl over 1f out: hrd rdn and edgd rt jst ins fnl f: sn hdd: kpt on* **7/2**[2]
05 **3** 1 3/4 **Dubai Phantom (USA)**[21] 6291 2-9-0 0........................ FergusSweeney 7 66+
(D M Simcock) *s.i.s: hld up in rr: c wd st: rdn and hdwy over 1f out: edgd rt ins fnl f: one pce* **6/1**[3]
0005 **4** 1 **Noverre Over There (IRE)**[30] 6034 2-8-2 55........................ TobyAtkinson(7) 3 58
(M E Rimmer) *hld up: rdn over 3f out: hdwy whn n.m.r briefly jst over 2f out: nt clr run and swtchd rt wl over 1f out: nt clr run and swtchd rt ins fnl f: kpt on* **20/1**
3 **5** 2 **Inpursuitoffreedom**[64] 5000 2-8-1 0........................ AndreaAtzeni(3) 6 49
(P J McBride) *hld up and bhd: hdwy on outside 3f out: sn rdn: hung lft over 1f out: fdd towards fin* **10/11**[1]
40 **6** 3 1/2 **One Cool Poppy (IRE)**[22] 6241 2-8-8 0 ow1........................ MickyFenton 5 45
(H J L Dunlop) *chsd ldr: ev ch over 2f out: wknd over 1f out* **12/1**
00 **7** 3 **Chichina (USA)**[12] 6544 2-8-8 0........................ RobertWinston 8 39
(M Johnston) *prom: pushed along over 3f out: rdn whn hmpd and lost pl over 2f out: sn bhd* **16/1**
060 **8** 4 1/2 **Crystal Bridge**[81] 4398 2-8-6 30 ow2........................ NeilChalmers 1 28
(Mrs L Williamson) *led: rdn and hdd wl over 1f out: sn wknd* **80/1**
066 **9** 30 **Ajara Boy**[15] 6443 2-8-7 45........................(v[1]) RossAtkinson(5) 9 —
(Tom Dascombe) *bhd: rdn 3f out: sn struggling: eased whn no ch fnl 2f* **33/1**

1m 52.04s (1.54) **Going Correction** -0.025s/f (Stan) **9** Ran SP% **114.3**
Speed ratings (Par 93): **92,91,89,88,87 84,81,77,50**
toteswingers: 1&2 £5.30, 1&3 £17.70, 2&3 £3.50 CSF £141.03 TOTE £44.50: £6.20, £1.50, £1.80; EX 262.50.
Owner High Moor Racing 1 **Bred** Michael Rourke **Trained** Middleham Moor, N Yorks

FOCUS
A shock result, with an unfancied debutant winning, and the hot favourite out of the frame. Really modest form.

NOTEBOOK
Brooklands Bay(IRE) is a relatively cheap Pyrus colt out of a maiden who is closely related to several winners up to 1m. Time will tell how good he is but, with the favourite running moderately, this race took little winning.
Angelena Ballerina(IRE)'s recent form has not built on early promise. While she has a fair record, she has run often enough to put the quality of the race into perspective. (tchd 4-1)
Dubai Phantom(USA), who has been showing gradual improvement in maidens, had the blinkers left off here after wearing them in his first two races. He does not appear to need them and will be at home in low-grade handicaps at this trip and beyond. (op 7-1 tchd 8-1)
Noverre Over There(IRE) lacks tactical speed at this distance and again ran into trouble at a crucial stage, as he had in his previous race. He is modest but longer trips look within reach.
Official explanation: jockey said gelding was denied a clear run
Inpursuitoffreedom had made a fine debut on turf two months earlier, so this was disappointing. It remains to be seen whether she is at her best on sand. (tchd 4-5, Evens in places)
One Cool Poppy(IRE) was well beaten and needs to look outside maiden company. (tchd 11-1)

6859 BET AFTER THE OFF AT LADBROKES.COM H'CAP 2m 119y(P)
7:50 (7:51) (Class 6) (0-65,59) 3-Y-O+ £2,388 (£705; £352) Stalls Low

Form RPR
/003 **1** **Bute Street**[30] 6025 4-8-13 47........................ MCGeran(3) 8 53
(R J Hodges) *sn led: rdn and edgd rt over 1f out: drvn out* **9/1**
0000 **2** 1 1/2 **Brad's Luck (IRE)**[3] 6785 3-8-10 51........................ FrancisNorton 1 55
(M Blanshard) *led early: a.p: rdn and edgd rt over 1f out: styd on to take 2nd post* **17/2**
0063 **3** shd **Wester Lodge (IRE)**[16] 6432 7-9-6 51........................ LukeMorris 10 55
(J M P Eustace) *chsd wnr after 2f: rdn over 2f out: nt qckn ins fnl f: lost 2nd post* **11/2**[1]
0604 **4** 3/4 **Squirtle (IRE)**[35] 5885 6-9-8 53........................ KirstyMilczarek 13 56+
(W M Brisbourne) *hld up in mid-div: rdn and hdwy over 2f out: styd on ins fnl f* **9/1**
005/ **5** 2 **Cry Presto (USA)**[68] 4866 5-9-0 45........................(b) RobertWinston 4 46
(S T Nolan, Ire) *hld up in mid-div: hdwy over 4f out: rdn over 2f out: one pce fnl f* **20/1**
04-1 **6** 4 1/2 **Market Watcher (USA)**[28] 5054 8-9-11 56........................ JerryO'Dwyer 5 51
(Seamus Fahey, Ire) *hld up in mid-div: hdwy on ins 3f out: sn rdn: wknd over 1f out* **13/2**[3]
060 **7** 3 1/4 **Be Kind**[23] 6225 3-8-7 48........................(p) JamieMackay 3 39
(Karen George) *s.i.s: hld up towards rr: nt clr run and swtchd rt over 2f out: rdn over 1f out: nvr nr ldrs* **40/1**
00/4 **8** 3/4 **Menelaus**[85] 4264 8-9-3 48........................(p) JimmyQuinn 12 39
(K A Morgan) *a in rr* **12/1**
4430 **9** 1 1/4 **Sir Sandicliffe (IRE)**[16] 6432 5-10-0 59........................ SebSanders 9 48
(W M Brisbourne) *s.s: rel to r early on: a in rr* **6/1**[2]
P-06 **10** 4 1/2 **Bundle Up**[56] 3950 6-9-0 45........................ KevinGhunowa 2 29
(J L Flint) *prom: pushed along over 3f out: rdn and wknd wl over 2f out* **16/1**
0316 **11** 17 **Dazzling Begum**[15] 6457 4-9-1 51........................(b[1]) SimonPearce(5) 6 14
(J Pearce) *hld up in mid-div: hdwy over 5f out: rdn and wknd 3f out* **11/2**[1]
006/ **12** 13 **Yellow Ridge (IRE)**[454] 4227 6-8-9 45........................(bt) MartinLane(5) 11 —
(Luke Comer, Ire) *a in rr* **14/1**

3m 43.04s (1.24) **Going Correction** -0.025s/f (Stan)
WFA 3 from 4yo+ 10lb **12** Ran SP% **116.4**
Speed ratings (Par 101): **96,95,95,94,93 91,90,89,89,87 79,73**
toteswingers: 1&2 £16.00, 1&3 £9.20, 2&3 £9.10 CSF £81.82 CT £463.99 TOTE £10.40: £3.70, £2.60, £2.60; EX 80.30.
Owner J W Mursell **Bred** J W Mursell **Trained** Charlton Mackrell, Somerset

FOCUS
A well-judged ride by Geran, who dictated a weak gallop and wound it up from 5f out. The winner probably did not need to improve to win this weak race.

6860 LADBROKESCASINO.COM H'CAP 1m 1f 103y(P)
8:20 (8:21) (Class 6) (0-65,68) 3-Y-O+ £2,388 (£705; £352) Stalls Low

Form RPR
0002 **1** **Nevada Desert (IRE)**[8] 6640 9-9-10 67........................ DO'Donohoe 3 76
(R M Whitaker) *hld up in mid-div: hdwy over 2f out: swtchd rt ent st: led jst over 1f out: rdn out* **11/2**[1]
2 1 1/2 **Earmark**[122] 3040 6-8-10 53........................ JerryO'Dwyer 12 58
(Seamus Fahey, Ire) *hld up in mid-div: rdn and hdwy on outside over 2f out: c wd st: hung lft jst over 1f out: tk 2nd wl ins fnl f: nt trble wnr* **9/1**
0302 **3** 2 1/4 **Snow Dancer (IRE)**[7] 6668 5-9-6 68........................ SladeO'Hara(5) 9 69
(H A McWilliams) *a.p: chsd ldr over 3f out: pushed along and ev ch over 1f out: one pce ins fnl f* **13/2**[2]
5430 **4** 1/2 **Nassar (IRE)**[11] 6565 6-9-7 64........................(p) SaleemGolam 11 64+
(G Prodromou) *hld up towards rr: pushed along over 2f out: hdwy wl over 1f out: rdn and swtchd rt ins fnl f: kpt on* **20/1**
0104 **5** 1 1/4 **Eightdaysaweek**[28] 6121 3-9-2 63........................(p) ChrisCatlin 2 60
(A J McCabe) *hld up in mid-div: pushed along and hdwy wl over 1f out: wknd wl ins fnl f* **22/1**
1202 **6** 3 1/4 **Resplendent Ace (IRE)**[10] 6584 5-9-10 67........................ IanMongan 6 57
(P Howling) *hld up in rr: pushed along over 3f out: styng on whn swtchd rt jst ins fnl f: n.d* **11/2**[1]

0063 **7** *nk* **Ella Woodcock (IRE)**[17] 6383 5-9-6 **63**.................(b) GrahamGibbons 10 53
(E J Alston) *sn led: clr over 5f out: rdn over 2f out: hdd jst over 1f out: wknd qckly ins fnl f* **8/1**[3]
4153 **8** *¾* **Mohawk Ridge**[29] 6052 3-9-4 **65**.................... TomEaves 5 53
(M Dods) *hld up in tch: pushed along 3f out: wknd wl over 1f out* **11/2**[1]
5- **9** *2 ¾* **Honkey Tonk Tony (IRE)**[502] 2687 4-8-9 **52**.................... LukeMorris 1 34
(Luke Comer, Ire) *hld up in tch: rdn and wknd wl over 1f out* **14/1**
6010 **10** *1* **Hits Only Cash**[21] 6288 7-9-0 **62**.................(p) SimonPearce(5) 7 42
(J Pearce) *a in rr* **10/1**
400 **11** *½* **Lyrical Intent**[19] 6349 3-8-9 **56**.................... JimmyQuinn 13 35
(P Howling) *dwlt: a towards rr* **50/1**
6-54 **12** *18* **Womaniser (IRE)**[19] 6349 5-8-13 **56**.................... J-PGuillambert 8 —
(T Keddy) *s.i.s: a in rr: lost tch fnl 3f* **14/1**
4400 **13** *13* **Park Melody (IRE)**[31] 5988 3-8-11 **58**.................(b[1]) RobertWinston 4 —
(B J Meehan) *led early: chsd ldr tl rdn and wknd qckly over 2f out: eased wl over 1f out* **22/1**

2m 0.23s (-1.47) **Going Correction** -0.025s/f (Stan)
WFA 3 from 4yo+ 4lb **13** Ran SP% **118.4**
Speed ratings (Par 101): **105,103,101,101,100 97,96,96,93,92 92,76,64**
toteswingers: 1&2 £11.70, 1&3 £7.30, 2&3 £17.50 CSF £51.35 CT £332.82 TOTE £6.00: £2.00, £2.50, £2.50; EX 87.60.
Owner J Barry Pemberton **Bred** Bryan Ryan **Trained** Scarcroft, W Yorks

FOCUS
A hair-raising gallop set the race up for the finishers. Pretty ordinary form for the grade.
Resplendent Ace(IRE) Official explanation: jockey said gelding never travelled
Hits Only Cash Official explanation: trainer said that the gelding was found to be lame
Park Melody(IRE) Official explanation: jockey said filly lost its action

6861 LADBROKESPOKER.COM H'CAP 1m 141y(P)
8:50 (8:50) (Class 5) (0-70,70) 3-Y-O+ **£3,561** (£1,059; £529; £264) **Stalls** Low

Form RPR
021- **1** **Alqaahir (USA)**[5] 6746 7-9-0 **62**.................... RobertWinston 1 72+
(Lee Smyth, Ire) *a.p: nt clr run and swtchd over 1f out: rdn to ld wl ins fnl f: r.o wl* **10/1**
5050 **2** *2* **Tourist**[15] 6460 4-9-8 **70**.................... DaneO'Neill 2 75
(D Shaw) *led 1f: chsd ldr: rdn to ld jst over 1f out: hdd wl ins fnl f: no ex* **6/1**[3]
3311 **3** *hd* **Florentia**[11] 6565 3-9-1 **67**.................... SebSanders 9 72
(Sir Mark Prescott) *hld up in tch: hdwy over 6f out: rdn over 1f out: kpt on ins fnl f* **5/2**[1]
4034 **4** *¾* **Chatanoogachoochoo**[26] 6166 4-8-9 **62**.................... RossAtkinson(5) 8 65+
(M Hill) *s.i.s: hld up towards rr: rdn over 1f out: r.o ins fnl f: nrst fin* **16/1**
0000 **5** *nse* **Hyde Lea Flyer**[14] 6496 4-9-4 **66**.................... GrahamGibbons 6 69
(E S McMahon) *hld up in mid-div: hdwy over 2f out: rdn over 1f out: one pce fnl f* **8/1**
4505 **6** *nk* **Forbidden (IRE)**[14] 6496 6-9-1 **70**.................(t) JamesPSullivan(7) 12 72+
(Daniel Mark Loughnane, Ire) *hld up towards rr: rdn wl over 1f out: kpt on ins fnl f: nrst fin* **20/1**
5020 **7** *hd* **Omnium Duke (IRE)**[14] 6496 3-9-4 **70**.................(v) JimmyQuinn 10 72
(J W Hills) *hld up towards rr: sme prog whn n.m.r briefly wl over 1f out: rdn ins fnl f: nvr trbld ldrs* **20/1**
P035 **8** *nk* **Captain Imperial (IRE)**[43] 5621 3-9-1 **67**.................... MickyFenton 3 68
(T P Tate) *t.k.h in tch: rdn over 1f out: one pce fnl f* **20/1**
34 **9** *1* **Full Victory (IRE)**[79] 4473 7-9-0 **67**.................... AndrewHeffernan(5) 4 66
(R A Farrant) *prom: rdn and lost pl over 2f out: n.d after* **11/1**
5020 **10** *1 ¾* **Sea Land (FR)**[16] 6437 5-8-9 **62**.................... MartinLane(5) 11 57
(B Ellison) *hld up towards rr: pushed along over 2f out: c v wd st: rdn over 1f out: no rspnse* **16/1**
3011 **11** *½* **Lujano**[17] 6383 4-9-5 **70**.................... FrederikTylicki(3) 7 63
(Ollie Pears) *led after 1f: rdn and hdd jst over 1f out: wknd ins fnl f* **5/1**[2]
1000 **11** *dht* **Petsas Pleasure**[17] 6383 3-9-0 **66**.................... TomEaves 5 59
(Ollie Pears) *hld up in mid-div: lost pl on ins over 3f out: short-lived effrt wl over 1f out* **28/1**
4/30 **13** *36* **Bold Diktator**[98] 3863 7-9-3 **65**.................... DO'Donohoe 13 —
(R M Whitaker) *a in rr: lost tch over 3f out: t.o* **33/1**

1m 50.29s (-0.21) **Going Correction** -0.025s/f (Stan)
WFA 3 from 4yo+ 4lb **13** Ran SP% **120.5**
Speed ratings (Par 103): **99,97,97,96,96 96,95,95,94,93 92,92,60**
toteswingers: 1&2 £13.00, 1&3 £9.90, 2&3 £4.10 CSF £64.09 CT £207.37 TOTE £10.90: £2.90, £2.00, £1.60; EX 74.30.
Owner Leslie Laverty **Bred** Shadwell Farm LLC **Trained** Dungannon, Co Tyrone

FOCUS
The winner returned to form on a surface that suits in a race where it paid to race handily. The form makes sense although may not be the most solid give the steady pace and bunch finish.

6862 STAY AT THE WOLVERHAMPTON HOLIDAY INN H'CAP 1m 141y(P)
9:20 (9:22) (Class 6) (0-65,65) 3-Y-O+ **£2,388** (£705; £352) **Stalls** Low

Form RPR
2355 **1** **Vamos (IRE)**[15] 6442 3-8-10 **57**.................... RobertHavlin 1 65
(J R Gask) *hld up in mid-div: hdwy on ins over 2f out: rdn wl over 1f out: led wl ins fnl f: r.o* **12/1**
0043 **2** *¾* **Sullenberger (IRE)**[7] 6668 3-9-1 **62**.................... ChrisCatlin 3 68
(J A Osborne) *hld up in mid-div: hdwy whn nt clr run briefly jst over 2f out: rdn jst over 1f out: r.o to take 2nd cl home* **7/2**[1]
460 **3** *½* **Clear Sailing**[30] 6012 6-9-5 **65**.................(p) FrederikTylicki(3) 9 70
(Ollie Pears) *prom: chsd ldr over 6f out: rdn to ld over 1f out: hdd and no ex wl ins fnl f* **5/1**[2]
5260 **4** *nk* **Island Music (IRE)**[24] 6218 4-8-10 **60**.................(p) IJBrennan(7) 7 64
(J J Quinn) *hld up in rr: rdn over 2f out: hdwy on ins wl over 1f out: kpt on ins fnl f* **12/1**
3154 **5** *1 ¾* **Petomic (IRE)**[21] 6288 4-9-0 **62**.................... RossAtkinson(5) 5 62
(M Hill) *a.p: rdn 2f out: hung rt jst over 1f out: one pce* **11/2**[3]
143- **6** *nk* **Wakita (IRE)**[176] 1499 6-8-12 **55**.................(t) JerryO'Dwyer 12 55
(Aidan Anthony Howard, Ire) *hld up towards rr: pushed along over 2f out: hdwy over 1f out: kpt on one pce ins fnl f* **12/1**
6155 **7** *2* **Neo's Mate (IRE)**[59] 5145 3-8-8 **55**.................... SilvestreDeSousa 4 50
(Paul Green) *hld up towards rr: pushed along over 3f out: nvr nrr* **22/1**
000/ **8** *nse* **Oversighted (GER)**[22] 6262 8-8-9 **52**.................... RobertWinston 13 47
(Mrs Y Dunleavy, Ire) *sn led: pushed along over 2f out: rdn and hdd over 1f out: wknd wl ins fnl f* **12/1**
5201 **9** *6* **Pianoforte (USA)**[22] 6256 7-8-12 **55**.................(b) GrahamGibbons 10 36
(E J Alston) *hld up in mid-div: rdn over 2f out: wknd wl over 1f out* **8/1**
0-00 **10** *4 ½* **Nesno (USA)**[29] 6074 6-9-5 **62**.................(p) JimmyQuinn 8 33
(J D Bethell) *hld up in tch: rdn over 2f out: wknd wl over 1f out* **11/1**
0466 **11** *¾* **Ten Pole Tudor**[110] 3467 4-8-4 **54**.................... JakePayne(7) 2 23
(R A Harris) *s.v.s: a in rr* **25/1**
0020 **12** *½* **Transmission (IRE)**[26] 6157 4-9-6 **63**.................... TomEaves 11 31
(B Smart) *prom: rdn 4f out: sn wknd* **25/1**
2300 **13** *64* **Sularno**[95] 3946 5-8-12 **55**.................... SebSanders 6 —
(J Pearce) *a towards rr: pushed along over 3f out: sn struggling: eased whn no ch wl over 1f out* **12/1**

1m 49.46s (-1.04) **Going Correction** -0.025s/f (Stan)
WFA 3 from 4yo+ 4lb **13** Ran SP% **124.2**
Speed ratings (Par 101): **103,102,101,101,100 99,98,97,92,88 87,87,30**
toteswingers: 1&2 £8.40, 1&3 £11.60, 2&3 £7.60 CSF £54.59 CT £253.90 TOTE £14.90: £4.30, £2.10, £2.70; EX 94.10 Place 6 £287.85, Place 5 £152.40.
Owner Horses First Racing Limited **Bred** Jeremy Gompertz **Trained** Sutton Veny, Wilts
■ Stewards' Enquiry : Robert Havlin one-day ban: used whip with excessive frequency (Oct 31)

FOCUS
A decent gallop to this weakish handicap. The form seems sound enough.
Petomic(IRE) Official explanation: jockey said gelding hung right-handed
Neo's Mate(IRE) Official explanation: jockey said filly suffered interference in running
Sularno Official explanation: trainer said reported that the gelding finished distressed
T/Plt: £987.60 to a £1 stake. Pool: £66,511.16. 49.16 winning tickets. T/Qpdt: £89.70 to a £1 stake. Pool: £9,605.31. 79.20 winning tickets. KH

6863 - 6866a (Foreign Racing) - See Raceform Interactive

5267 CORK (R-H)
Saturday, October 17

OFFICIAL GOING: Round course - good (good to yielding in places); sprint course - good to yielding (yielding in places)

6867a NAVIGATION STKS (LISTED RACE) 1m 100y
4:10 (4:10) 3-Y-O+ **£26,861** (£7,881; £3,754; £1,279)

RPR
1 **Alaiyma (IRE)**[20] 6320 3-8-12 96.................(b) MJKinane 2 98
(John M Oxx, Ire) *a.p: rdn fr 2f out: styd on wl fnl f to ld cl home* **9/1**
2 *1* **Jumbajukiba**[75] 4608 6-9-7 110.................(p) FMBerry 11 102
(Mrs John Harrington, Ire) *attempted to make all: strly pressed fr over 1f out: hdd and dropped to 3rd ins fnl f: kpt on wout matching wnr* **5/1**[2]
3 *nk* **Six Of Hearts**[6] 6707 5-9-4 94.................(p) WJSupple 14 98
(Cecil Ross, Ire) *mid-div: hdwy travelling wl fr 2f out: 3rd over 1f out: rdn to ld ins fnl f: hdd and dropped to 3rd cl home* **10/1**
4 *2* **Scarlet O'Hara (IRE)**[37] 5815 4-9-1 92.................... KLatham 13 90
(D K Weld, Ire) *towards rr: rdn fr 2f out: r.o wl wout threatening fr over 1f out* **16/1**
5 *hd* **Libano (IRE)**[34] 5924 3-9-6 111.................... PJSmullen 8 98+
(D K Weld, Ire) *chsd ldrs: 6th bef st: 4th and kpt on same pce u.p fr over 1f out* **7/1**[3]
6 *nk* **Indiana Gal (IRE)**[15] 6468 4-9-4 99.................(p) DPMcDonogh 12 92
(Patrick Martin, Ire) *towards rr: r.o wl wout threatening u.p fr over 1f out* **14/1**
7 *hd* **Windsor Palace (IRE)**[13] 6527 4-9-4 102.................... JPO'Brien 15 92+
(A P O'Brien, Ire) *trckd ldrs: short of room 1 1/2f out: sn no imp and kpt on wout threatening* **7/1**[3]
8 *nk* **Worldly Wise**[20] 6320 6-9-4 104.................(p) DMGrant 5 91
(Patrick J Flynn, Ire) *mid-div: 8th bef st: no imp u.p in 5th and kpt on same pce fr over 1f out* **9/2**[1]
9 *½* **Via Galilei (IRE)**[15] 6467 4-9-4 105.................(t) DEMullins 7 90
(J S Bolger, Ire) *prom: sn 2nd: lost pl and wknd fr over 1f out* **14/1**
10 *nk* **Chief Lone Eagle (USA)**[10] 6603 3-9-1 102.................(b) JAHeffernan 10 89
(A P O'Brien, Ire) *trckd ldrs: pushed along 1/2-way: 7th bef st: sn no imp* **5/1**[2]
11 *1 ½* **Bravely Fought (IRE)**[34] 5926 4-9-4 96.................... CPGeoghegan 6 86
(Sabrina J Harty, Ire) *trckd ldrs: 4th bef st: lost pl and wknd fr over 1f out* **25/1**
12 *hd* **Belle's Ridge**[13] 5490 5-9-4 96.................... WJLee 9 85
(Timothy Doyle, Ire) *nvr bttr than mid-div: no imp fr 2f out* **33/1**
13 *1* **Peter Tchaikovsky**[42] 5685 3-9-1 102.................... DavidMcCabe 4 83
(A P O'Brien, Ire) *s.i.s and a towards rr* **20/1**
14 *4* **Three Way Stretch (IRE)**[6] 6707 3-9-1 92.................(b) CDHayes 1 74
(J T Gorman, Ire) *a towards rr* **20/1**
15 *15* **Thewaytosanjose (IRE)**[40] 5735 3-8-12.................... MCHussey 3 36
(Patrick J Flynn, Ire) *a towards rr: no ex fr over 2f out* **50/1**

1m 45.77s (105.77)
WFA 3 from 4yo+ 3lb **15** Ran SP% **133.1**
CSF £55.59 TOTE £14.70: £3.70, £1.50, £4.70; DF 100.40.
Owner H H Aga Khan **Bred** Hh The Aga Khan's Studs S C **Trained** Currabeg, Co Kildare

FOCUS
The rating bands were fairly tight for this open contest.

NOTEBOOK
Alaiyma(IRE) wasn't able to go with the runner-up when he attempted to go for his race early in the straight, but the rider remained patient and in the end she outstayed her rivals and won going away. She'll get further and if it didn't come too soon, one would imagine that a race like the Trigo Stakes at Leopardstown would suit her ideally. (op 8/1)
Jumbajukiba ran one of his better races outside of the Curragh. Attempting to make all, he went for his race early in the straight but couldn't really shake off his rivals. To his credit though he battled on well and got back up for second place close home. (op 9/2 tchd 4/1)
Six Of Hearts ran the race of his life and looked the likely winner over a furlong out. He's a horse that comes with one run, and while it was good enough to get him almost to the front over a furlong out he couldn't sustain it inside the last half furlong. His ability to stay a mile would have been far from certain either so it was a particularly good effort in the circumstances. (op 14/1)
Scarlet O'Hara(IRE) has run well in Listed company a couple of times since winning her maiden and this was another of those. She was never competitive before running on well inside the last to be nearest at the finish.
Libano(IRE) took a walk in the market but looked likely to throw down a challenge when ridden to chase the leader early in the straight. He might not be the bravest horse in the world, though, as he seemed reluctant to go through a gap inside the last and had to be switched, although it was of little consequence in the end.

(Foreign Racing) - See Raceform Interactive

CAULFIELD (R-H)

Saturday, October 17

OFFICIAL GOING: Good to soft

6871a BMW CAULFIELD CUP (H'CAP) (GROUP 1) — 1m 4f

6:05 (6:05) 3-Y-O+

£754,854 (£182,039; £97,087; £53,398; £43,689; £36,408)

			RPR
1		**Viewed (AUS)**14 6-9-0 ....(b) BradRawiller 13 (Bart Cummings, Australia) **12/1**	124
2	2 1/4	**Roman Emperor (NZ)**14 4-8-7 ....(b¹) HughBowman 4 (Bart Cummings, Australia) **14/1**	114
3	1/2	**Vigor (NZ)**14 5-8-1 ....(b) CoreyBrown 18 (Danny O'Brien, Australia) **14/1**	107+
4	nk	**Daffodil (NZ)**14 4-8-2 .... ChrisMunce 3 (Kevin Gray, New Zealand) **10/1**	108+
5	nk	**Fiumicino (NZ)**14 6-8-11 .... DwayneDunn 17 (Michael, Wayne & John Hawkes, Australia) **80/1**	116
6	3/4	**Master O'Reily (NZ)**7 7-8-10 .... VladDuric 15 (Danny O'Brien, Australia) **14/1**	114+
7	hd	**Kirklees (IRE)**42 [5662] 5-8-12 .... KerrinMcEvoy 6 (Saeed Bin Suroor) *racd in 10th or 11th: pushed along 2 1/2f out: rdn towards rr on outside ent st: kpt on steadily fnl 1 1/2f* **8/1²**	116
8	nk	**Allez Wonder (AUS)**7 4-7-13 ....(b) MichellePayne 5 (Bart Cummings, Australia) **9/1³**	102+
9	nk	**Zavite (NZ)**7 7-8-5 ....(b) MarkZahra 7 (Anthony Cummings, Australia) **40/1**	108
10	1/2	**Harris Tweed (NZ)**14 4-8-4 ....(b) CraigNewitt 1 (Murray & Bjorn Baker, New Zealand) **40/1**	106
11	3/4	**Ready To Lift (AUS)**14 6-8-2 ....(b) GlenBoss 10 (Gerald Ryan, Australia) **40/1**	103
12	nk	**Predatory Pricer (AUS)**14 4-8-6 .... StevenKing 14 (Paul Murray, Australia) **6/1¹**	106
13	1 1/2	**Cima De Triomphe (IRE)**70 [4809] 4-8-11 .... DamienOliver 9 (L M Cumani) *racd keenly in 8th or 9th on outside: rdn 2f out: dropped to rr ent st: kpt on again clsng stages* **8/1²**	109
14	hd	**Red Lord (AUS)**14 6-8-2 .... GlynSchofield 2 (Anthony Cummings, Australia) **40/1**	99
15	3/4	**C'Est La Guerre (NZ)**14 5-8-11 .... StevenArnold 11 (John D Sadler, Australia) **20/1**	107
16	3/4	**Sarrera (AUS)**14 9-8-7 .... NicholasHall 8 (Michael Moroney, Australia) **66/1**	102
17	3/4	**Light Vision (NZ)**14 6-8-4 .... LukeNolen 16 (Robert Smerdon, Australia) **14/1**	98
18	1 1/4	**Red Ruler (NZ)**14 5-8-6 ....(b) DannyNikolic 12 (John Sargent, New Zealand) **16/1**	98

2m 29.7s (149.70) **18 Ran SP% 113.1**

Owner Dato Tan Chin Nam **Bred** I Johnson **Trained** Australia

FOCUS

A strong-looking renewal of this famous and valuable handicap. The pace looked sound and it proved to be yet another feather in the cap of the legend that is Bart Cummings, who collected his seventh Caulfield Cup. His first victory in the race came in the same year that England last won the World Cup.

NOTEBOOK

Viewed(AUS) ◆ took another big prize. His most recent effort in the Turnbull caught the eye in a big way but his burden, as well as an awkward draw, did not make his chance look obvious against some tough rivals. Given an inspired ride by Brad Rawiller, who got fined for his whip use, he sneaked up the inside rail and won by a decisive margin, enhancing his already obvious chance in retaining his Melbourne Cup crown. He will be penalised for this but that should not stop his going well at Flemington, although it should be remembered that Efficient, another previous winner of the Melbourne Cup, comfortably held him in the Turnbull.

Roman Emperor(NZ) is a talented individual when the mood takes him and he had a going day, but was never going to hang on once his stablemate threaded his way up his inside.

Vigor(NZ) had been fancied for this race for quite a while but his stalls position looked daunting. He worked his way to the front about 300 metres out but then tended to wander under pressure. His rider got fined for his use of the whip.

Daffodil(NZ) ◆ is a multiple Group 1 winner in New Zealand and did not disappoint her supporters with a valiant effort. She finished really well (the jockey got a hefty ban for whip infringements however), shaping like a horse that should stay further.

Fiumicino(NZ) falls into a similar category as the runner-up, capable on his day but those days are infrequent. He raced at the head of affairs and responded to pressure.

Master O'Reilly(NZ) came home well but never had a chance of getting on terms. He had every rival to pass off the home bend.

Kirklees(IRE) stayed on to be a strong-finishing seventh but his chance had been more or less blown at the stalls, as his good draw was soon negated by a sluggish start. Soon behind, his rider drove him along leaving the back straight before the combination was forced wide turning in. Connections were initially disappointed with the effort, but they reasoned that the run had put him right and it appears as though he is still on target for the Melbourne Cup.

Allez Wonder(AUS), the third of the Bart Cummings-trained trio, was well placed turning in but found her third big race in the space of 17 days a bit too much for her. She weakened inside the final 100 metres.

Predatory Pricer(AUS) was the subject of strong home support in the minutes before the off but he looked to be ridden with the trip in mind (he was completely unproven at the distance) and kept on but never featured. The jockey reported afterwards that the horse was much too keen.

Cima De Triomphe(IRE) had been the subject of good reports since arriving in Australia but he ran flat for some reason. He moved well until the tempo increased, but did not look happy once Damien Oliver got stuck into him. It was interesting to note afterwards that the rider said he felt there were no excuses.

WOODBINE (R-H)

Saturday, October 17

OFFICIAL GOING: Firm

6872a E P TAYLOR STKS (GRADE 1) (F&M) (TURF) — 1m 2f (T)

10:03 (10:04) 3-Y-O+

£338,983 (£112,994; £62,147; £33,898; £16,949; £226)

			RPR
1		**Lahaleeb (IRE)**34 [5924] 3-8-6 .... WilliamBuick 3 (M R Channon) *held up in 6th but always well in touch, 5th straight, switched outside well over 1f out, driven to lead distance, ran on strongly (44.35/1)* **44/1**	115
2	1 3/4	**Rainbow View (USA)**42 [5686] 3-8-6 ....(p) JRLeparoux 2 (J H M Gosden) *disputed early lead, settled in 3rd, close 4th straight, led briefly over 1f out, headed distance, ran on one pace* **9/4¹**	112
3	2 1/4	**Princess Haya (USA)**27 4-8-12 .... RBejarano 5 (Michael Matz, U.S.A) *held up in 7th, closed up on final turn, 7th straight, headway well over 1f out, reached 3rd just inside final f, kept on same pace* **76/10**	108
4	2 1/4	**Eastern Aria (UAE)**23 [6238] 3-8-6 .... RoystonFfrench 4 (M Johnston) *raced in close 5th, went 3rd on inside approaching straight, 6th 1f out, driven to take 4th close home* **182/10**	103
5	1 3/4	**Salve Germania (IRE)**49 4-8-12 .... JJCastellano 8 (Todd Pletcher, U.S.A) *held up, last to straight, brought wide, never able to challenge* **63/10**	101
6	nse	**Treat Gently**377 [6521] 4-8-12 .... GKGomez 1 (Robert Frankel, U.S.A) *always prominent, pressed leader on inside after 3f, led 4f out to over 1f out, soon weakened* **49/20²**	101
7	3/4	**Look Here**29 [6056] 4-8-12 .... JimCrowley 6 (R M Beckett) *disputed 3rd on outside, close 5th straight, soon beaten* **63/20³**	99
8	2 1/4	**Roses 'N' Wine (CAN)**40 4-8-12 ....(b) ChantalSutherland 7 (David R Bell, Canada) *led to 4f out, 2nd straight, driven & every chance over 1f out, weakened quickly* **217/10**	95

2m 2.89s (-1.13)

WFA 3 from 4yo 5lb **8 Ran SP% 121.0**

PARI-MUTUEL (including $2 stakes): WIN 90.70; PL (1-2) 32.90, 3.70;SHOW (1-2-3) 12.80, 2.60, 4.60; SF 310.00.

Owner M Al-Qatami & K M Al-Mudhaf **Bred** Tom Twomey **Trained** West Ilsley, Berks

FOCUS

The pace was steady in this weak Grade 1 for fillies.

NOTEBOOK

Lahaleeb(IRE), who got no run at all at the Curragh last time out, had a different jockey on board here and, stepping up to 1m2f for the first time, caused a shock by staying on strongly to defy long odds. Her pace was an asset considering how the race unfolded, but that's not to say this was a fluke. She's now likely to be aimed at the Hong Kong Cup in December.

Rainbow View(USA) won the Matron Stakes on her previous start, but that was an ordinary race for the top level and she found one too good this time. She's not as good as many might have expected after a brilliant juvenile campaign and is hard to fancy for her next intended target, the Breeders' Cup Ladies Classic.

Eastern Aria(UAE) won a French Listed race well enough last time out but this was a much tougher assignment. In the circumstances she ran about as well as one could expect.

Look Here once again proved disappointing. The 2008 Oaks winner has now been retired.

6873a PATTISON CANADIAN INTERNATIONAL (GRADE 1) (TURF) — 1m 4f (T)

10:40 (10:44) 3-Y-O+

£677,966 (£225,989; £124,294; £67,797; £33,898; £226)

			RPR
1		**Champs Elysees**27 6-9-0 .... GKGomez 1 (Robert Frankel, U.S.A) *held up in 7th, 6th straight, headay on outside from well over 1f out, driven to lead well inside final f, ran on* **13/5¹**	121
2	1/2	**Jukebox Jury (IRE)**20 [6324] 3-8-7 .... RoystonFfrench 7 (M Johnston) *slowly into stride, raced in 2nd after 1f, pushed along 4f out, led entering straight, driven over 1f out, caught well inside final f, ran on* **69/20³**	120
3	2	**Buccellati**34 [5931] 5-9-0 ....(v) WilliamBuick 6 (A M Balding) *always close up, disputed 3rd half-way, 3rd straight on outside, 2nd & driven over 1f out, kept on same pace under pressure* **94/10**	117
4	hd	**Marsh Side (USA)**27 6-9-0 .... JJCastellano 5 (Neil Drysdale, U.S.A) *led, steady pace, quickened over 4f out, headed entering straight, kept on same pace* **49/10**	116
5	6 3/4	**Just As Well (USA)**27 6-9-0 .... JRLeparoux 4 (Jonathan Sheppard, U.S.A) *held up in rear, closed up over 3f out, 7th straight, never dangerous* **13/4²**	106
6	nse	**Spice Route**83 5-9-0 ....(b) JMcAleney 8 (Roger L Attfield, Canada) *5th half-way, 4th straight, ridden & beaten over 1f out* **158/10**	106
7	1 3/4	**Allied Powers (IRE)**42 [5685] 4-9-0 .... JimCrowley 2 (M L W Bell) *raced in 6th, ridden & close 5th 4f out, 5th straight, soon beaten* **27/1**	103
P		**Quijano (GER)**27 7-9-0 .... AStarke 3 (P Schiergen, Germany) *raced in 3rd, weakened 4f out, last straight, soon well behind, pulled up* **78/10**	—

2m 28.36s (-1.24)

WFA 3 from 4yo+ 7lb **8 Ran SP% 121.2**

PARI-MUTUEL: WIN 7.20; PL (1-2) 4.00, 5.40; SHOW (1-2-3) 3.00, 3.20,5.10; SF 38.60.

Owner Juddmonte Farms **Bred** Juddmonte Farms Ltd **Trained** USA

FOCUS

This year's Canadian International lacked a stand-out performer and, as such, it was an ordinary but competitive race for the level. The pace was steady.

NOTEBOOK

Champs Elysees came with a late run down the outside from well off the pace to mug Jukebox Jury inside the last, and deserves extra credit considering he would have preferred a stronger gallop. A winner of three Grade 1 races, he has now been retired and will stand at stud in Newmarket.

Jukebox Jury(IRE), who has improved this autumn and found his trip at 1m4f, ran a fine race in defeat. He came off the bridle a fair way out but kept responding to pressure and gave the impression he will stay further. This tough sort should do even better as a 4-y-o.

Buccellati looked to have plenty going for him, and he was well ridden, but when produced with his chance he wouldn't go through with his effort. His rider thought that slightly easier ground would have been in his favour, but even so this was a little disappointing.

Allied Powers(IRE) had a bit to do in this company and is arguably at his best over 1m2f.

6354 SOUTHWELL (L-H)

Sunday, October 18

OFFICIAL GOING: Standard

Wind: Light 1/2 behind Weather: Fine

6874 EBF BUY A RACING POST YEARLING BONUS CANDIDATE MAIDEN STKS 7f (F)

2:10 (2:12) (Class 5) 2-Y-O **£3,885** (£1,156; £577; £288) **Stalls** Low

Form RPR

65 **1** **Tres Amigos**15 6484 2-9-3 0 AdrianTNicholls 1 75
(D Nicholls) *mde all: pushed along 3f out: styd on wl: unchal* **12/1**3

03 **2** *4* **Primo De Vida (IRE)**79 4478 2-9-3 0 SebSanders 5 65
(R M Beckett) *chsd wnr: effrt 3f out: kpt on: no imp* **4/1**2

60 **3** *4* **Let Them Eat Cake**8 6672 2-8-12 0 PaulHanagan 4 50
(R A Fahey) *chsd ldrs: edgd lft 2f out: one pce* **25/1**

0323 **4** *1 1/2* **Demonstrative (USA)**36 5853 2-9-3 71 GregFairley 3 51
(M Johnston) *s.i.s: in rr and sn drvn along: kpt on fnl 2f: nvr on terms* **4/9**1

000 **5** *7* **Wedding Dream**34 5949 2-8-12 0 (p) TomEaves 2 29
(K A Ryan) *chsd ldrs: wknd 2f out* **100/1**

6 *1/2* **Consult** 2-9-3 0 StephenDonohoe 8 33+
(Sir Mark Prescott) *s.i.s: in rr: nvr on terms* **12/1**3

00 **7** *4* **The Ducking Stool**79 4497 2-8-12 0 DarryllHolland 6 18
(H J Collingridge) *chsd ldrs: drvn and outpcd over 3f out: hung bdly lft and lost pl over 1f out* **25/1**

8 *9* **Red Valerian Two (IRE)** 2-9-3 0 PaulMulrennan 9 —
(P T Midgley) *dwlt: a in rr: bhd fnl 3f* **40/1**

00P **9** *12* **Miss Isle Control**12 6567 2-8-5 0 DeclanCannon(7) 7 —
(A J McCabe) *sn drvn along in midfield: lost pl over 4f out: sn bhd* **150/1**

1m 29.75s (-0.55) **Going Correction** -0.15s/f (Stan) **9** Ran SP% **116.4**

Speed ratings (Par 95): **97,92,87,86,78 77,73,62,49**

toteswingers: 1&2 £3.00, 1&3 £8.70, 2&3 £5.20 CSF £57.55 TOTE £13.20: £3.80, £1.70, £7.30; EX 69.30 Trifecta £253.40 Part won. Pool £342.54 - 0.91 winning units..

Owner Dab Hand Racing **Bred** Eagle Bloodstock & Racing **Trained** Sessay, N Yorks

■ Stewards' Enquiry : Darryll Holland caution: used whip down shoulder in the forehand

FOCUS

A weak and uncompetitive juvenile maiden in which the odds-on favourite was a major disappointment. The winner stepped forward and the form seems sound enough.

NOTEBOOK

Tres Amigos, who avoided the kickback out in front on first try on Fibresand, stayed on strongly in the straight and was never seriously threatened. This wasn't much of a race, but he's progressed with every run so far and should cope with the switch to handicaps. (op 14-1)

Primo De Vida(IRE), returning from over two months off, ran to just a modest level at best on this step up in trip and switch from turf. (tchd 9-2)

Let Them Eat Cake didn't offer a great deal but she's from a respected yard and should find her level, maybe in handicaps. (op 20-1)

Demonstrative(USA)'s supporters knew their fate almost immediately, with this colt looking beaten after less than a furlong. He got out of the stalls on terms but struggled badly to find his stride and was soon out the back, being scrubbed along into a wall of kickback. He eventually ran on past, beaten, moderate rivals in the straight, but he was a long way below form and this track seemingly didn't suit at all. Official explanation: trainer had no explanation for the poor form shown (tchd 2-5 and 1-2 in places)

The Ducking Stool Official explanation: jockey said filly hung left

6875 BRAMLEY APPLE BI-CENTENARY CELEBRATION H'CAP 1m 6f (F)

2:40 (2:40) (Class 4) (0-85,82) 3-Y-O+ **£5,504** (£1,637; £818; £408) **Stalls** Low

Form RPR

221 **1** **Blue Nymph**24 6225 3-9-3 80 SebSanders 3 93+
(R M Beckett) *trck ldrs: led over 4f out: shkn up and qcknd 3f out: rdn and 4 l clr whn edgd rt over 1f out: styd on grimly* **10/3**2

6066 **2** *2 1/2* **Dunaskin (IRE)**21 5837 9-9-2 75 LanceBetts(5) 1 82
(B Ellison) *in rr and sn pushed along: plld wd and hdwy to trck ldrs 7f out: rdn over 3f out: kpt on to chse wnr over 2f out: no imp* **12/1**3

0226 **3** *3/4* **Fin Vin De Leu (GER)**9 6636 3-8-9 72 GregFairley 5 78
(M Johnston) *chsd ldrs: sn pushed along: hung lft over 2f out: one pce* **10/3**2

2505 **4** *19* **Dart**132 2766 5-8-9 63 oh1 RobertWinston 2 42
(Mrs S Lamyman) *dwlt: hdwy to trck ldrs after 4f: outpcd over 2f out: sn lost pl* **16/1**

21 **5** *nk* **Feathered Crown (FR)**15 6475 3-8-13 76 TPQueally 4 55
(H R A Cecil) *racd keenly: slt ld: hdd over 4f out: wknd over 2f out* **3/1**1

000 **6** *10* **Hindu Kush (IRE)**8 6681 4-10-0 82 StephenDonohoe 7 47
(D Nicholls) *w ldr: lost pl over 4f out: bhd and eased 3f out* **10/3**2

3m 7.19s (-1.11) **Going Correction** -0.15s/f (Stan)

WFA 3 from 4yo+ 9lb **6** Ran SP% **107.8**

Speed ratings (Par 105): **97,95,95,84,84 78**

toteswingers: 1&2 £5.70, 1&3 £2.00, 2&3 £5.30 CSF £35.80 TOTE £3.50: £2.10, £4.50; EX 24.60.

Owner J H Richmond-Watson **Bred** Lawn Stud **Trained** Whitsbury, Hants

FOCUS

Only three of the six runners ran close to form. The pace was fair. The winner was value for 4l.

6876 CORAL BACKING SUE RYDER CARE H'CAP 1m (F)

3:15 (3:16) (Class 2) (0-100,96) 3-Y-O+ **£12,304** (£3,661; £1,829; £913) **Stalls** Low

Form RPR

6322 **1** **Sovereign Remedy (USA)**15 6474 3-8-12 90 TedDurcan 12 111+
(Saeed Bin Suroor) *trckd ldrs: rdn to ld 2f out: styd on strly: eased towards fin: v readily* **5/1**1

2121 **2** *2 1/4* **Penitent**24 6229 3-9-1 93 ShaneKelly 11 107+
(W J Haggas) *trckd ldrs: nt clr run over 2f out: rdn to chse wnr over 1f out: no imp* **5/1**1

1111 **3** *4* **Collateral Damage (IRE)**15 6485 6-8-13 88 (t) DavidAllan 5 92
(T D Easterby) *led early: w ldrs: led 3f out: hdd 2f out: kpt on same pce* **12/1**

3000 **4** *2 3/4* **Nightjar (USA)**17 6429 4-9-5 94 GregFairley 2 92
(M Johnston) *sn led: hdd 3f out: fdd appr fnl f* **9/1**

3564 **5** *1/2* **Vainglory (USA)**17 6429 5-8-5 85 MartinLane(5) 6 82
(D M Simcock) *chsd ldrs: lost pl over 4f out: kpt on fnl 2f* **11/1**

0066 **6** *1/2* **Lucky Dance (BRZ)**17 6429 7-8-9 84 RobertHavlin 9 80
(A G Foster) *in rr and sn drvn along: drvn over 4f out: kpt on fnl 2f: nvr nr ldrs* **28/1**

3210 **7** *1/2* **Faithful Ruler (USA)**23 6249 5-9-0 89 PaulHanagan 3 84
(R A Fahey) *drvn to chse ldrs: lost pl over 4f out: kpt on fnl 2f* **14/1**

2025 **8** *nk* **Lowther**22 6278 4-9-6 95 (be) RobertWinston 10 89
(A Bailey) *sn drvn along to chse ldrs: wknd over 1f out* **6/1**2

0000 **9** *2 1/4* **Flipando (IRE)**17 6429 8-9-0 89 PhillipMakin 4 78
(T D Barron) *hld up towards rr: sme hdwy on inner 2f out hung rt: nvr a factor* **20/1**

2240 **10** *2 1/2* **Moynahan (USA)**15 6480 4-9-7 96 TPQueally 8 79
(P F I Cole) *s.i.s: hdwy over 3f out: lost pl over 1f out* **12/1**

-440 **11** *12* **Tactful (IRE)**98 3894 4-9-1 90 SebSanders 13 45
(R M Beckett) *drvn along to sn chse ldrs on outer: lost pl over 2f out: eased* **20/1**

13 **12** *5* **More Time Tim (IRE)**45 5615 4-8-12 87 PatCosgrave 14 31
(J R Boyle) *w ldrs on outer: lost pl 2f out: eased* **7/1**3

0000 **13** *7* **Wise Dennis**31 6013 7-8-12 87 (v) DarryllHolland 7 15
(A P Jarvis) *s.i.s: racd v wd in last: wl bhd 3f out* **20/1**

1m 40.68s (-3.02) **Going Correction** -0.15s/f (Stan)

WFA 3 from 4yo+ 3lb **13** Ran SP% **118.2**

Speed ratings (Par 109): **109,106,102,100,99 99,98,98,95,93 81,76,69**

toteswingers: 1&2 £4.00, 1&3 £6.10, 2&3 £5.50 CSF £26.64 CT £296.65 TOTE £5.70: £2.20, £1.80, £2.80; EX 28.80 Trifecta £46.40 Pool £332.99 - 5.31 winning units..

Owner Godolphin **Bred** Gainsborough Farm Llc **Trained** Newmarket, Suffolk

FOCUS

This looks like strong form, with two progressive, well-handicapped runners pulling clear of a gelding who had won his last four starts, and that one was in turn nicely ahead of a colt previously unbeaten on Fibresand. The pace was good. Prominent runners dominated but the form has been rated at face value.

NOTEBOOK

Sovereign Remedy(USA) ◆ won in the style of a smart colt. He had been beaten in four straight handicaps since winning his maiden, but this was easily a career best, and the surface obviously suited. It's impossible to know whether his improvement was simply a consequence of the switch to Fibresand, but his dam was high class on turf and it may be that he is now just beginning to fulfil his potential. He could do well at the 2010 Dubai Carnival. (op 13-2)

Penitent ◆, 7lb higher than when dead-heating at Kempton on his previous start, travelled very nicely throughout but the winner got first run, as this gelding was short of room and forced to switch two furlongs out, with Shane Kelly taking his time getting serious. In fairness, though, he was simply beaten by a better rival on the day. There should be much more to come and, while he clearly stays this trip, he's a horse with plenty of speed, as his breeding suggests. He may ultimately prove best back over shorter. (op 4-1 tchd 7-2 and 11-2)

Collateral Damage(IRE), successful in four straight turf handicaps, the first in that sequence coming off a mark of 70, the latest off 85, ran well on what was his first Fibresand start since running third on his debut in 2005. He was simply beaten by two very useful types. (op 10-1)

Nightjar(USA) was 4-4 on Fibresand coming into this, but he's yet to win beyond 7f. He had to work hard enough to lead and was in trouble when strongly challenged turning into the straight. (op 8-1 tchd 11-1)

Vainglory(USA) ◆ did not look to enjoy the kickback one little bit, and he performed creditably in the circumstances. He's not badly handicapped and can win when things fall a bit more kindly. (tchd 10-1)

Lucky Dance(BRZ) ◆ was another who got plenty of sand in his face. He is on a very fair mark and is one to keep in mind.

Lowther didn't face the kickback early on and had to be pulled wide. This surface didn't seem to suit. (op 15-2)

Flipando(IRE) Official explanation: jockey said gelding hung badly right

Moynahan(USA) Official explanation: jockey said gelding never travelled

More Time Tim(IRE), 3-4 on Fibresand prior to this, broke well and raced handy but he dropped away as though something was amiss. (op 17-2 tchd 9-1)

Wise Dennis Official explanation: jockey said gelding was unable to face the kick back

6877 MERCEDES BENZ OF DERBY H'CAP 5f (F)

3:50 (3:50) (Class 5) (0-70,80) 3-Y-O+ **£3,412** (£1,007; £504) **Stalls** High

Form RPR

1060 **1** **Colorus (IRE)**3 6791 6-8-12 69 (p) PaulPickard(5) 6 77
(W J H Ratcliffe) *mde all: edgd rt ins fnl f: jst hld on* **5/1**2

500 **2** *shd* **Loose Caboose (IRE)**116 3268 4-9-2 68 (b) RobertWinston 5 76
(A J McCabe) *w ldrs: edgd rt wl ins fnl f: kpt on wl: jst failed* **16/1**

3402 **3** *3 3/4* **Halaak (USA)**20 6341 3-8-10 62 (b) ChrisCatlin 13 57
(D M Simcock) *dwlt: hdwy stands' side over 2f out: styd on same pce* **7/1**

0000 **4** *1 1/4* **First Order**9 6635 8-8-11 68 (v) AnnStokell(5) 8 58
(Miss A Stokell) *in rr: hdwy 2f out: kpt on ins fnl f* **11/1**

0-03 **5** *1/2* **Danum Dancer**43 5675 5-8-11 63 LeeVickers 10 51
(N Bycroft) *s.s: styd on fnl 2f: nt rch ldrs* **14/1**

5143 **6** *1 1/4* **First Blade**18 6387 3-8-11 63 (b) AmirQuinn 7 47+
(S R Bowring) *dwlt: in rr and edgd lft over 2f out: racd far side: kpt on: nvr nr ldrs* **7/1**

0114 **7** *1* **Simple Rhythm**3 6791 3-9-7 80 RyanPowell(7) 4 60+
(J Ryan) *chsd ldrs: hmpd after 1f: lost pl over 1f out* **4/1**1

235 **8** *1/2* **Lake Chini (IRE)**17 6410 7-8-4 56 (b) AndrewElliott 3 34
(M W Easterby) *w ldrs: edgd rt over 2f out: wknd over 1f out: b.b.v* **14/1**

1500 **9** *1 1/2* **Steel City Boy (IRE)**9 6635 6-8-10 67 MartinLane(5) 2 40
(D Shaw) *rrd s: sn w ldrs: wknd 2f out* **6/1**3

0000 **10** *4* **Molly Two**12 6553 4-8-4 56 oh4 (p) PaulHanagan 1 15
(L A Mullaney) *chsd ldrs on outside: lost pl over 1f out* **20/1**

00-2 **11** *1* **Tanley**18 6380 4-8-1 58 oh4 ow2 (p) AndrewHeffernan(5) 12 13
(J F Coupland) *chsd ldrs: lost pl and in rr whn hmpd over 2f out* **25/1**

1045 **12** *3/4* **Silvanus (IRE)**21 6314 4-8-11 63 ow3 (p) PaulMulrennan 11 15
(P T Midgley) *mid-div: hung lft and lost pl over 2f out* **18/1**

59.19 secs (-0.51) **Going Correction** -0.025s/f (Stan) **12** Ran SP% **117.4**

Speed ratings (Par 103): **103,102,96,94,94 92,90,89,87,80 79,78**

toteswingers: 1&2 £20.10, 1&3 £5.90, 2&3 £20.80 CSF £81.56 CT £572.46 TOTE £6.40: £2.20, £5.60, £1.90; EX 93.30 Trifecta £189.50 Part won. Pool £256.11 - 0.30 winning units..

Owner J Sheard & W J S Ratcliffe **Bred** M Ervine **Trained** Newmarket, Suffolk

■ Stewards' Enquiry : Paul Pickard caution: careless riding.

FOCUS

A modest sprint handicap in which the first pair were always 1-2. The winner is rated to his recent turf best.

Lake Chini(IRE) Official explanation: vet said gelding bled from the nose

6878 JOHN CARTER H'CAP 1m 3f (F)

4:25 (4:25) (Class 4) (0-85,87) 3-Y-O+ **£5,504** (£1,637; £818; £408) **Stalls** Low

Form RPR

0206 **1** **Eseej (USA)**11 6583 4-8-9 72 DarryllHolland 3 83
(P W Hiatt) *mde all: qcknd over 4f out: styd on fnl 2f: hld on wl* **20/1**

1101 **2** *2* **Lucky Punt**19 6360 3-8-10 79 FergusSweeney 7 86
(B G Powell) *a chsng wnr: drvn over 3f out: kpt on same pce fnl f: no imp ins fnl f* **7/1**

002 **3** *3 1/4* **Persian Peril**9 6648 5-9-8 85 RobertWinston 4 87
(G A Swinbank) *chsd ldrs: kpt on same pce fnl 2f* **5/1**3

-044 **4** *nk* **Mannlichen**^{17} 6435 3-8-5 74 .... GregFairley 2 75
(M Johnston) *chsd ldrs: drvn over 3f out: hung rt and one pce fnl 2f* **5/2**^{1}

4232 **5** *14* **Ours (IRE)**^{19} 6357 6-8-11 74 .... (p) ChrisCatlin 6 50
(John A Harris) *sn pushed along: hdwy to chse ldrs 7f out: wknd 3f out* **14/1**

0660 **6** *½* **Realism (FR)**^{5} 6769 9-8-11 74 ow1 .... PaulMulrennan 1 49
(M W Easterby) *s.i.s: sme hdwy on outer 7f out: lost pl over 3f out* **25/1**

4230 **7** *3¾* **Laughing Boy (IRE)**^{23} 6243 3-8-7 76 .... TedDurcan 5 44
(L M Cumani) *chsd ldrs: drvn over 3f out: lost pl over 2f out* **10/1**

0113 **8** *1¼* **High Ambition**^{63} 5067 6-8-6 72 .... FrederikTylicki(3) 8 38
(R A Fahey) *dwlt: hdwy on outer to chse ldrs 7f out: wknd over 2f out* **9/2**^{2}

2042 **9** *34* **Snoqualmie Boy**^{8} 6681 6-9-10 87 .... TPQueally 9 —
(T P Tate) *in rr: sn pushed along: lost pl over 4f out: bhd fnl 3f: heavily eased: t.o* **6/1**

2m 23.32s (-4.68) **Going Correction** -0.15s/f (Stan)
WFA 3 from 4yo+ 6lb **9** Ran SP% **114.6**
Speed ratings (Par 105): **111,109,107,106,96 96,93,92,68**
toteswingers: 1&2 £10.80, 1&3 £17.70, 2&3 £8.00 CSF £151.48 CT £817.84 TOTE £23.40: £4.70, £1.70, £2.00; EX 116.40 Trifecta £295.50 Part won. Pool £399.35 - 0.40 winning units..
Owner P W Hiatt **Bred** Shadwell Farm LLC **Trained** Hook Norton, Oxon

FOCUS
An ordinary handicap for the grade and form to treat with caution as the winner got the run of the race in front and the next three home were always prominent too.
High Ambition Official explanation: jockey said gelding was unsuited by the all-weather surface

6879 CORAL.CO.UK H'CAP 6f (F)
5:00 (5:02) (Class 4) (0-85,85) 3-Y-0+ **£5,504** (£1,637; £818; £408) **Stalls** Low

Form RPR

0053 **1** **Ingleby Arch (USA)**^{5} 6765 6-9-2 82 .... PhillipMakin 9 96
(T D Barron) *w ldr: led over 1f out: styd on wl ins fnl f* **4/1**^{2}

0130 **2** *1¾* **Fesko**^{13} 6540 3-8-12 79 .... GregFairley 2 87
(M Johnston) *drvn along to chse ldrs: kpt on same pce fnl f* **12/1**

000 **3** *nk* **Great Charm (IRE)**^{9} 6642 4-8-6 72 .... HayleyTurner 5 79+
(M L W Bell) *t.k.h: trckd ldrs: effrt over 2f out: kpt on same pce* **6/1**

006 **4** *2½* **Imprimis Tagula (IRE)**^{17} 6434 5-8-10 76 .... (v) RobertWinston 7 75
(A Bailey) *chsd ldrs: effrt over 2f out: one pce* **7/1**

3014 **5** *1* **Invincible Isle (IRE)**^{20} 6348 3-9-0 81 .... TPQueally 1 77
(H R A Cecil) *hld up: effrt on ins over 2f out: sn chsng ldrs: wknd fnl 150yds* **7/2**^{1}

4005 **6** *shd* **Dancing Maite**^{13} 6540 4-8-13 79 .... DarryllHolland 3 75+
(S R Bowring) *in rr: sme hdwy on outside over 2f out: nvr trbld ldrs* **5/1**^{3}

6062 **7** *¾* **Lesley's Choice**^{19} 6359 3-8-10 77 .... (b) FrankieMcDonald 8 71
(R Curtis) *led tl over 1f out: wandered and sn wknd* **13/2**

00 **8** *8* **Suzie Quw**^{48} 5523 3-8-11 78 .... AndrewElliott 6 46
(A P Jarvis) *in rr on outer: sme hdwy on wd outside over 2f out: sn lost pl* **33/1**

5525 **9** *1* **Pawan (IRE)**^{19} 6359 9-9-0 85 .... (b) AnnStokell(5) 4 50
(Miss A Stokell) *dwlt: in rr: reminders after 1f and over 3f out: sme hdwy on ins over 2f out: sn wknd* **18/1**

1m 15.0s (-1.50) **Going Correction** -0.15s/f (Stan)
WFA 3 from 4yo+ 1lb **9** Ran SP% **114.9**
Speed ratings (Par 105): **104,101,101,97,96 96,95,84,83**
toteswingers: 1&2 £6.70, 1&3 £6.90, 2&3 £8.20 CSF £50.45 CT £286.00 TOTE £5.30: £1.80, £2.30, £2.30; EX 46.90 Trifecta £188.20 Pool £437.44 - 1.72 winning units..
Owner Dave Scott **Bred** Alexander-Groves Thoroughbreds **Trained** Maunby, N Yorks

FOCUS
This looked an ordinary handicap for the level. Front runners were again favoured and the winner is probably the best guide.

6880 LORNA CARTER MEDIAN AUCTION MAIDEN STKS 7f (F)
5:30 (5:32) (Class 6) 3-5-Y-0 **£2,047** (£604; £302) **Stalls** Low

Form RPR

1 **Skysurfers** 3-9-3 0 .... TedDurcan 8 92+
(Saeed Bin Suroor) *sn trcking ldrs: led on bit 2f out: sn wnt effrtlessly clr: eased ins fnl f: v easily* **8/13**^{1}

0330 **2** *10* **Positivity**^{17} 6415 3-8-12 50 .... TomEaves 11 52
(B Smart) *chsd ldrs: reminders over 3f out: outpcd over 2f out: kpt on to take remote 2nd ins fnl f* **12/1**

3546 **3** *2* **Towy Boy (IRE)**^{12} 6553 4-9-5 53 .... (vt) SebSanders 2 52
(I A Wood) *w ldrs: kpt on same pce fnl 2f* **7/1**^{2}

5505 **4** *1½* **Dark Echoes**^{55} 5306 3-9-3 46 .... (b^{1}) AndrewElliott 7 48
(Jedd O'Keeffe) *drvn to chse ldrs: lost pl over 4f out: sn bhd: hrd rdn and hung lft over 2f out: styd on fnl f* **25/1**

0440 **5** *1¾* **Abu Derby (IRE)**^{38} 5809 3-9-3 58 .... (bt^{1}) TPQueally 4 43
(J G Given) *chsd ldrs: one pce fnl 2f* **11/1**^{3}

0000 **6** *shd* **Dolly No Hair**^{17} 6415 4-9-0 40 .... (tp) GaryBartley(5) 5 43
(N Wilson) *w ldrs: one pce fnl 2f* **66/1**

335 **7** *1¾* **Catchpenny**^{20} 6344 3-8-12 51 .... PaulMulrennan 3 33
(K A Ryan) *in rr: reminders over 3f out: kpt on fnl 2f: nvr on terms* **12/1**

5000 **8** *6* **Scotch And Soda (IRE)**^{44} 5621 3-8-5 44 .... EleanorMcGowan(7) 9 17
(Jedd O'Keeffe) *chsd ldrs: lost pl over 4f out* **100/1**

9 *¾* **Peachey Moment (USA)**^{22} 4-9-5 0 .... DarryllHolland 10 20
(H J Collingridge) *s.i.s: sme hdwy on outer over 3f out: wknd over 2f out* **11/1**^{3}

00 **10** *1½* **Elevate Bobbob**^{37} 5840 3-8-10 0 .... BillyCray(7) 13 16
(A Berry) *hld up in rr: sme hdwy over 3f out: lost pl over 2f out* **100/1**

005 **11** *1¼* **Meydan Style (USA)**^{52} 5373 3-9-3 41 .... (p) MickyFenton 14 12
(J Balding) *swtchd lft after s: led tl hdd & wknd 2f out* **50/1**

000- **12** *5* **Elizabeth's Quest**^{445} 4533 4-8-9 45 .... (p) AndrewHeffernan(5) 1 —
(Miss N A Lloyd-Beavis) *mid-div: drvn over 2f out: sn lost pl* **100/1**

00/ **13** *21* **Petidium**^{730} 6306 4-9-0 0 .... LeeVickers 6 —
(N Bycroft) *t.k.h and wnt long way to s: hld up in rr: bhd fnl 2f: t.o* **100/1**

1m 29.11s (-1.19) **Going Correction** -0.15s/f (Stan)
WFA 3 from 4yo 2lb **13** Ran SP% **117.7**
Speed ratings (Par 101): **100,88,86,84,82 82,80,73,72,71 69,63,39**
toteswingers: 1&2 £4.40, 1&3 £3.70, 2&3 £7.20. CSF £8.94 TOTE £1.60: £1.20, £2.80, £1.70; EX 12.90 Trifecta £53.10 Pool £580.79 - 8.08 winning units. Place 6 £675.76, Place 5 £180.29..
Owner Godolphin **Bred** Darley **Trained** Newmarket, Suffolk

FOCUS
An extremely weak maiden - the highest official rating any of these could boast was just 58 - and the Godolphin newcomer always had the potential to be in a different league. He looks potentially smart.
T/Plt: £453.30 to a £1 stake. Pool: £64,039.63. 103.11 winning tickets. T/Qpdt: £40.40 to a £1 stake. Pool: £6,739.86. 123.40 winning tickets. WG

6881 - 6885a (Foreign Racing) - See Raceform Interactive

6499 COLOGNE (R-H)
Sunday, October 18

OFFICIAL GOING: Soft

6886a WETTEM-SIEBERTS-NEUSS-WUPPERTAL-STUTENPREIS (LISTED RACE) (F&M) 1m
3:40 (3:50) 3-Y-0+ **£12,621** (£3,883; £1,942; £971)

RPR

1 **Rock My Soul (IRE)**^{21} 3-8-13 .... YLerner 5 100
(Uwe Ostmann, Germany) **13/5**^{1}

2 *3* **Masquenada (FR)**^{21} 4-9-2 .... WMongil 3 93
(W Baltromei, Germany) **76/10**

3 *1½* **Red Dune (IRE)**^{22} 6272 4-9-2 .... NCallan 7 90
(M A Jarvis) *mid-div: hdwy fr 3f out: disp 2nd fr 2f out to 1f out: one pce* **13/5**^{1}

4 *½* **Novita (FR)**^{35} 3-8-13 .... AStarke 10 89
(P Schiergen, Germany) **73/10**^{3}

5 *1¼* **Wildfahrte (GER)**^{42} 3-8-13 .... EFrank 9 86
(T Mundry, Germany) **19/1**

6 *2* **Irini (GER)**^{42} 3-8-13 .... WPanov 4 82
(H J Groschel, Germany) **27/1**

7 *2* **Cent Cheveux Blanc (GER)**^{35} 3-8-13 .... THellier 1 77
(W Hickst, Germany) **22/1**

8 *1* **Manipura (GER)**^{21} 4-9-2 .... AGoritz 2 75
(H Steguweit, Germany) **16/1**

9 *hd* **Jeninsky (USA)**^{71} 4796 4-9-2 .... JimmyQuinn 6 75
(Rae Guest) *hld up: rdn 2f out: sn btn* **101/10**

10 *1½* **Ainia**^{49} 5472 4-9-2 .... LPKeniry 12 72
(D M Simcock) *a towards rr* **43/1**

11 *6* **Prema (GER)**^{35} 3-8-13 .... ASuborics 11 58
(W Hickst, Germany) **59/10**^{2}

12 *1½* **Picobella (GER)**^{21} 4-9-2 .... EPedroza 8 55
(A Wohler, Germany) **137/10**

1m 40.0s (1.61)
WFA 3 from 4yo 3lb **12** Ran SP% **130.6**
(including ten euro stakes): WIN 36; PL 16, 18, 18; SF 200.
Owner G Merkel **Bred** G Kredel **Trained** Germany

6887a LITEX COMMERCE - PREIS DES WINTERFAVORITEN (GROUP 3) 1m
4:15 (4:25) 2-Y-0 **£82,524** (£30,097; £19,903; £10,000; £5,340; £2,621)

RPR

1 **Glad Tiger (GER)** 2-9-2 .... YLerner 3 103
(Uwe Ostmann, Germany) *sn led: narrowly hdd appr fnl f: drvn to ld again 100yds out: all out* **61/10**

2 *nk* **Noble Alpha (IRE)**^{44} 5652 2-9-2 .... ASuborics 7 102
(Mario Hofer, Germany) *hld up in 6th: 5th st: drvn to chal 2f out: tk narrow ld appr fnl f: hdd 100yds out: r.o u.p* **7/5**^{1}

3 *1¼* **Kite Hunter (IRE)**^{28} 6151 2-9-2 .... EPedroza 1 99
(Mario Hofer, Germany) *first to show: trckd ldr to over 3f out: 3rd st: ev ch on rails wl over 1f out: kpt on u.p* **131/10**

4 *1¾* **Nightdance Paolo (GER)** 2-9-2 .... AStarke 5 95
(P Schiergen, Germany) *racd in 4th tl lost pl over 3f out: last st: rallied ins fnl f to take 4th cl home* **22/5**^{3}

5 *½* **Angolaner (GER)** 2-9-2 .... THellier 4 94
(H Blume, Germany) *hld up in rr tl hdwy 1/2-way: 2nd st: 4th 2f out: rdn and btn wl over 1f out* **61/10**

6 *1¼* **Santino (GER)** 2-9-2 .... JimmyQuinn 6 92
(J-P Carvalho, Germany) *racd in 3rd to over 3f out: 5th st: disp 4th over 1f out: one pce* **102/10**

7 *6* **Fierce Storm (IRE)** 2-9-2 .... ADeVries 2 78
(J Hirschberger, Germany) *hld up: last 1/2-way: 6th st: rdn and btn 2f out* **14/5**^{2}

1m 44.05s (5.66) **7** Ran SP% **130.7**
WIN 71; PL 22, 12, 27; SF 183.
Owner Gestut Auenquelle **Bred** Gestuet Auenquelle **Trained** Germany

6522 LONGCHAMP (R-H)
Sunday, October 18

OFFICIAL GOING: Good to soft

6889a PRIX DE CONDE (GROUP 3) 1m 1f
2:50 (2:56) 2-Y-0 **£38,835** (£15,534; £11,650; £7,767; £3,883)

RPR

1 **Zeitoper**^{15} 6472 2-8-11 .... AhmedAjtebi 4 102
(Saeed Bin Suroor) *trckd ldr: drvn to take narrow ld wl over 1f out: rdn out* **15/8**^{1}

2 *snk* **Circumvent**^{9} 6656 2-9-1 .... IMendizabal 1 106
(P F I Cole) *led to wl over 1f out: ev ch 1f out: kpt on u.p* **11/4**^{2}

3 *¾* **Shamalgan (FR)**^{14} 2-8-11 .... TJarnet 3 101
(A Savujev, Czech Republic) *last to st: drvn 2f out: hdwy on rails over 1f out: r.o fnl f: nrest at fin* **25/1**

4 *½* **Kartica**^{38} 2-8-8 .... SPasquier 5 97
(P Demercastel, France) *disp 3rd: cl 4th st: 3rd and rdn 1 1/2f out: one pce* **10/1**

5 *snk* **Anzas (IRE)**^{57} 5280 2-8-11 .... OPeslier 6 99
(R Gibson, France) *s.i.s: disp 3rd at 1/2-way: 3rd on outside st: 5th and rdn wl over 1f out: kpt on same pce u.p* **8/1**^{3}

1m 57.9s (1.90) **Going Correction** +0.275s/f (Good) **5** Ran SP% **85.5**
Speed ratings: **102,101,101,100,100**
PARI-MUTUEL: WIN 2.30; PL 1.50, 1.50; SF 4.50.
Owner Godolphin **Bred** Darley **Trained** Newmarket, Suffolk
■ The Mark Johnston-trained Layali Al Andalus was withdrawn after being found to be lame at the start.

NOTEBOOK

Zeitoper was always well up in a race which was run at a snail's pace early on. Having tracked the long-time leader, he began his challenge for the lead early in the straight. He hit the front at the furlong marker and then idled as the race came to an end. Certainly a very nice colt in the making, the lack of early pace was a disadvantage and he can probably be rated better than the bare form. Sure to stay further, he has already been talked about as a classic prospect.

Circumvent gave a very brave performance in defeat. A reluctant leader as there were no takers for this task, he set a moderate gallop early on and quickened things up early in the straight. He looked beaten running into the final furlong but ran on again close to home. Considering he was conceding 3lbs to the winner it was a really decent effort from this juvenile, who had one a similar race just nine days before. He is finished for the season and something like the Prix La Force back here next April might fit the bill.

Shamalgan(FR) was last for much of the early stages and caught out for speed when things suddenly quickened up early in the straight. He really began to run on well up the far rail throughout the final furlong, though, and was closest at the line.

Kartica was fourth virtually throughout the race. She ran on but lost third place running into the final furlong. A longer trip would certainly be an advantage in the future.

6890a PRIX DU CONSEIL DE PARIS (GROUP 2) 1m 4f

3:20 (3:24) 3-Y-0+ **£71,942** (£27,767; £13,252; £8,835; £4,417)

RPR

1 **Cirrus Des Aigles (FR)**[29] [6132] 3-8-11 .... FBlondel 8 115
(Mme C Barande-Barbe, France) *trckd ldr to 4f out: 4th st: qcknd on rails wl over 1f out: led appr fnl f: drvn out* **6/1**

2 6 **Makt (FR)**[26] [6198] 3-8-9 .... KFallon 3 104
(T Doumen, France) *a cl up: wnt 2nd 4f out: led ent st to appr fnl f: one pce* **12/1**

3 3/4 **Shahwardi (FR)**[26] [6198] 3-8-9 .... C-PLemaire 2 103
(A De Royer-Dupre, France) *mid-div: 5th st: disp 3rd 2f out to 1f out: kpt on one pce* **5/2[1]**

4 nk **Court Canibal**[196] [1144] 4-9-4 .... MGuyon 6 104
(M Delzangles, France) *mid-div: 6th st on outside: disp 3rd 2f out to 1f out: one pce* **14/1**

5 6 **Not Just Swing (IRE)**[36] [5898] 5-9-2 .... OPeslier 9 93
(J-M Beguigne, France) *towards rr tl hdwy 4f out: 3rd st: ev ch wl over 1f out: wknd over 1f out* **9/2[2]**

6 8 **Scintillo**[85] [4298] 4-9-6 .... RichardHughes 4 85
(R Hannon) *mid-div: 7th st on ins: rdn and btn 2f out* **14/1**

7 1 **Puchet (ARG)**[41] 5-9-2 ....(b) TThulliez 10 80
(J-M Beguigne, France) *led to st: sn wknd* **33/1**

8 shd **Traffic Guard (USA)**[36] [5854] 5-9-2 .... IMendizabal 5 80
(P F I Cole) *hld up: last st: nvr a factor* **5/1[3]**

9 shd **Camill (IRE)**[28] [6153] 5-9-2 .... GHind 7 80
(P Kalas, Slovakia) *8th st: a in rr* **33/1**

10 3/4 **The Bogberry (USA)**[14] [6526] 4-9-2 .... CSoumillon 1 79
(A De Royer-Dupre, France) *hld up: 9th st: rdn and 6th 1 1/2f out: sn eased* **11/2**

2m 33.5s (3.10) **Going Correction** +0.65s/f (Yiel)
WFA 3 from 4yo+ 7lb 10 Ran SP% **120.0**
Speed ratings: **115,111,110,110,106 100,100,100,100,99**
PARI-MUTUEL: WIN 8.60; PL 1.80, 2.70, 1.30; DF 30.90.
Owner J-C Dupouy **Bred** Yvon Lelimouzin & Benoit Deschamps **Trained** France

NOTEBOOK

Cirrus Des Aigles(FR) was never far from the leading group and didn't have too much room coming into the straight. Once in the clear, he quickened impressively and drew clear of his nine rivals to pass the post on his own. This was his 16th run of the season and his second consecutive group event. His trainer now has several options and they include going to California for the Hollywood Derby, a run in the Premio Roma and a trip to Hong Kong for either the Cup or the Vase. This horse appears to be improving with every outing.

Makt(FR), never far from the leaders, he made a forward move before the straight and started his charge to the line from one and a half out. He had nothing in hand to tackle the winner but still stayed on courageously for second place and reversed some previous form with the third. A very consistent individual, his trainer will see how he comes out of the race before making any plans. He acts well on soft ground and will remain in training as a 4yo.

Shahwardi(FR), mid division in the early stages, came with a run from halfway up the straight and stayed on albeit a little one paced. His trainer felt he acts better on good ground, so wasn't totally at home on this occasion. He should turn into a really decent 4yo over middle distances.

Court Canibal was fifth running down the hill before the straight and ran on throughout the final furlong and a half. He only missed third place by a narrow margin. He has been engaged in a Group 3 race at Frankfort in mid November.

Scintillo galloped in sixth position virtually throughout. He was unable to quicken when things warmed up in the straight and never looked like taking a place in the frame. It was his first outing since July and the ground was probably softer than he liked.

Traffic Guard(USA) made no show on this occasion and was beaten early in the straight. Did have some interference on the run down the hill.

6891a PRIX LE FABULEUX (LISTED RACE) 1m 1f

3:55 (3:56) 3-Y-O **£26,699** (£10,680; £8,010; £5,340; £2,670)

RPR

1 **Lungwa (IRE)**[24] [6237] 3-8-8 .... ACrastus 3 103
(E Lellouche, France)

2 1/2 **Konig Bernard (FR)**[9] [6657] 3-8-12 .... DBoeuf 1 106
(W Baltromei, Germany)

3 1 1/2 **Lady Francesca**[22] [6267] 3-8-8 .... OPeslier 5 99
(W R Muir) *racd in 6th to st: u.p 1f out: r.o wl to take 3rd nr fin* **13/1[1]**

4 1 1/2 **Broken In Light (FR)**[37] [5851] 3-9-2 ....(b) GMillet 6 104
(T Larriviere, France)

5 1 1/2 **Mistaken Identity (FR)**[189] [1239] 3-8-12 .... TThulliez 2 97
(P Bary, France)

6 1 1/2 **Sokar (FR)**[159] [1979] 3-8-12 .... IMendizabal 7 94
(J Boisnard, France)

7 4 **Double Handful (GER)**[15] 3-8-12 .... SPasquier 4 86
(M Figge, Germany)

8 hd **Belango (GER)** 3-8-12 .... GMasure 8 86
(F Willenbrock, Germany)

1m 56.3s (0.30) **Going Correction** +0.275s/f (Good) **8** Ran SP% **7.1**
Speed ratings: **109,108,107,105,104 103,99,99**
PARI-MUTUEL: WIN 2.80; PL 1.30, 1.90, 3.10; SF 7.30.
Owner Ecurie Wildenstein **Bred** Dayton Investments Ltd **Trained** Lamorlaye, France

NOTEBOOK

Lady Francesca, towards the tail of the field early on, she was a bit outpaced early in the straight before running on in the final stages. Connections hope to come back to France and find a similar race later in the year.

6715 SAN SIRO (R-H)

Sunday, October 18

OFFICIAL GOING: Good

6892a PREMIO DORMELLO (GROUP 3) (FILLIES) 1m

3:05 (3:09) 2-Y-0 **£58,311** (£27,180; £15,272; £7,636)

RPR

1 **Blessed Luck (IRE)** 2-8-11 .... NPinna 1 102
(S Botti, Italy) *a.p: 3rd on ins st: outpcd over 2f out: drvn 1f out: led 100yds out: drvn out (exact SP 7.79/1)* **78/10**

2 1/2 **Nantha (IRE)** 2-8-11 .... MDemuro 3 101
(S Botti, Italy) *trckd ldr to st: led wl over 2f out: drvn over 1f out: hdd 100yds out: r.o* **54/10[2]**

3 shd **Cronsa (GER)** 2-8-11 .... URispoli 6 101
(S Botti, Italy) *first to show: settled in 3rd: 3rd st: styd on u.p fnl f: nrest at fin* **68/10[3]**

4 2 1/2 **Parisella (IRE)**[63] [5085] 2-8-11 .... LDettori 9 95
(Mario Hofer, Germany) *sn led: hdd wl over 2f out: drvn and stl 2nd 1f out: one pce* **143/10**

5 nk **Nicea (GER)**[21] 2-8-11 .... GBietolini 10 94
(P Schiergen, Germany) *hld up: 9th st: rdn and hdwy on outside 2f out: kpt on fnl f but nvr nr to chal* **4/5[1]**

6 1/2 **Chikorita (IRE)** 2-8-11 .... GMarcelli 4 93
(L Riccardi, Italy) *towards rr to st: hdwy on ins and 6th over 3f out: kpt on one pce fnl 2f* **127/10**

7 snk **Biancarosa (IRE)**[15] 2-8-11 .... DVargiu 8 93
(B Grizzetti, Italy) *6th st: rdn over 2f out: one pce* **139/10**

8 3/4 **Letizia Relco (IRE)**[63] 2-8-11 .... CColombi 5 91
(B Grizzetti, Italy) *in rr to st: hdwy on rails 3f out: 5th over 1f out: sn wknd* **72/1**

9 hd **Train Deal (IRE)** 2-8-11 .... Flovine 7 91
(F Jovine, Italy) *hld up in rr: nvr a factor* **89/10**

10 3 1/2 **Gemma Dell'Olmo (USA)** 2-8-11 .... LManiezzi 11 83
(R Menichetti, Italy) *a in rr* **52/1**

11 8 **Alpacina (GER)** 2-8-11 .... MEsposito 12 66
(H Blume, Germany) *last most of way* **125/10**

1m 38.6s (-3.50) 11 Ran SP% **136.7**
(including ten euro stake): WIN 8.79; PL 2.40, 2.24, 2.47; SF 25.51.
Owner Scuderia Effevi SNC **Bred** Scuderia Dioscuri Srl **Trained** Italy

6893a GRAN PREMIO DEL JOCKEY CLUB E COPPA D'ORO (GROUP 1) 1m 4f

3:45 (3:49) 3-Y-O+ **£155,709** (£76,150; £43,777; £21,888)

RPR

1 **Schiaparelli (GER)**[36] [5891] 6-9-4 .... LDettori 4 117
(Saeed Bin Suroor) *mde all: rdn over 1f out: r.o wl (exact SP 46/100)* **9/20[1]**

2 1 3/4 **Sant'Antonio (ITY)**[42] 4-9-4 .... URispoli 2 114
(S Botti, Italy) *racd in 5th to st: hdwy wl over 1f out: fin wl to snatch 2nd last strides* **25/1**

3 1/2 **Voila Ici (IRE)**[28] [6153] 4-9-4 .... MDemuro 5 114
(V Caruso, Italy) *disp 2nd: wnt 2nd 1/2-way: rdn and 2 l bhd wnr 2f out: sn btn: lost 2nd last strides* **2/1[2]**

4 3 **Halicarnassus (IRE)**[30] [6056] 5-9-4 .... AlanMunro 1 109
(M R Channon) *trckd ldr: 3rd st: stl 3rd tl no ex appr fnl f* **51/10[3]**

5 1/2 **Papetti (ITY)**[42] 4-9-4 .... DVargiu 3 108
(B Grizzetti, Italy) *racd in 4th to st: disp 3rd fr 3f out to 2f out: one pce* **27/1**

6 3 **Jakkalberry (IRE)**[162] [1904] 3-8-13 .... MMonteriso 6 106
(E Botti, Italy) *last thrght* **21/1**

2m 28.2s (-3.30)
WFA 3 from 4yo+ 7lb 6 Ran SP% **130.7**
WIN 1.46; PL 1.27, 3.43; SF 20.39.
Owner Godolphin **Bred** Gestut Karlshof **Trained** Newmarket, Suffolk

6894a PREMIO OMENONI (GROUP 3) 5f

5:35 (5:42) 3-Y-O+ **£40,893** (£18,631; £10,350; £5,175)

RPR

1 **Titus Shadow (IRE)**[28] 5-9-0 .... DVargiu 4 106
(B Grizzetti, Italy) *a.p: led over 1f out: pushed out and r.o wl (exact SP 58/100)* **3/5[1]**

2 nk **Morgan Drive (IRE)**[126] 4-9-0 .... LDettori 1 105
(M Gasparini, Italy) *hld up: last to over 1f out: drvn to go 2nd ins fnl f: rdr lost whip 100yds out: r.o* **9/5[2]**

3 1/2 **L'Indiscreta**[7] [6717] 4-9-0 .... SUrru 2 103
(B Grizzetti, Italy) *hld up: 5th to over 1 1/2f out: swtchd rt and hdwy 1f out: r.o* **3/5[1]**

4 3/4 **Xenes**[28] 5-9-0 .... LManiezzi 6 100
(R Menichetti, Italy) *led to over 1f out: one pce* **16/1**

5 2 1/4 **Air Ransom (ITY)**[28] 3-9-0 .... MDemuro 5 92
(V Caruso, Italy) *pressed ldr on outside tl wknd over 1f out* **9/2[3]**

6 2 **Derek**[28] 3-9-0 .... MEsposito 3 85
(H Blume, Germany) *cl up tl wknd fr dist* **155/10**

59.30 secs (0.10) 6 Ran SP% **190.8**
WIN 1.58 (coupled with L'Indiscreta); PL 1.21, 1.33; SF 2.58.
Owner Scuderia Blueberry **Bred** Scuderia Blueberry **Trained** Italy

6533 PONTEFRACT (L-H)

Monday, October 19

OFFICIAL GOING: Good to firm (good in places; 8.1)

Wind: Light, half behind Weather: Dry with sunny periods

6895 TOTEPLACEPOT NURSERY (DIV I) 1m 4y

2:10 (2:11) (Class 5) (0-75,74) 2-Y-O **£2,914** (£867; £433; £216) **Stalls** Low

Form RPR

41 **1** **Landowner**[20] 6364 2-9-4 **74** AhmedAjtebi(3) 8 89+
(Saeed Bin Suroor) *cl up: led over 4f out: rdn along wl over 1f out: drvn: edgd rt and hdd briefly ins fnl f: sn rallied to regain initiative: kpt on wl* **9/2**[1]

0604 **2** *nk* **Mason Hindmarsh**[26] 6215 2-8-0 **53** SilvestreDeSousa 1 67+
(Karen McLintock) *sn led on inner: hdd over 4f out: cl up and rdn wl over 1f out: drvn to ld briefly ins fnl f: sn hdd and ev ch tl no ex last 50yds* **11/2**[3]

0034 **3** *15* **Mighty Clarets (IRE)**[35] 5935 2-9-1 **68** PaulHanagan 4 48
(R A Fahey) *in tch: hdwy over 3f out: rdn along over 2f out: kpt on same pce u.p* **5/1**[2]

0445 **4** *nse* **Deely Plaza**[7] 6736 2-9-5 **72** PatDobbs 2 52
(R Hannon) *chsd ldng pair: rdn along over 2f out: sn drvn and kpt on same pce* **9/1**

0303 **5** *2 1/2* **We'll Deal Again**[43] 5692 2-8-5 **65** JamesPSullivan(7) 10 39
(M W Easterby) *t.k.h early: midfield: hdwy 1/2-way: rdn along 3f out: plugged on same pce fnl 2f* **7/1**

0400 **6** *3 1/2* **Bintalaleumydarlin (IRE)**[22] 6319 2-8-4 **57** JoeFanning 5 23
(M Johnston) *towards rr: pushed along 1/2-way: n.d* **20/1**

4260 **7** *1/2* **Drinking Buddy**[12] 6589 2-8-4 **57** AndrewElliott 3 22
(D W Thompson) *sn rdn along and a in rr* **40/1**

050 **8** *1/2* **Scooby Dee**[35] 5949 2-7-12 **51** oh1 PaulQuinn 6 15
(R M Whitaker) *a towards rr* **40/1**

0614 **9** *1 1/2* **Truly Magic**[20] 6367 2-8-10 **63** ChrisCatlin 13 23
(H J L Dunlop) *midfield: rdn along 1/2-way: nvr a factor* **15/2**

6621 **10** *9* **Raleigh Quay (IRE)**[57] 5290 2-9-3 **73** FrederikTylicki(3) 9 12
(Micky Hammond) *in tch: rn wd bnd after 1 1/2f: effrt over 3f out and sn rdn: wknd over 2f out* **10/1**

0060 **11** *7* **Red Eddie**[20] 6367 2-8-6 **59** (b[1]) MartinDwyer 12 —
(B J Meehan) *midfield: rdn along 1/2-way: sn wknd* **22/1**

4205 **12** *1 1/4* **Music Of The Moor (IRE)**[23] 6285 2-9-7 **74** RobertWinston 11 —
(T P Tate) *chsd ldrs on outer: rdn along over 3f out: sn wknd* **12/1**

500 **13** *14* **Elie Shore**[18] 6431 2-8-13 **66** (v) TonyHamilton 7 —
(P C Haslam) *a in rr* **66/1**

1m 46.99s (1.09) **Going Correction** +0.15s/f (Good) **13 Ran SP% 116.8**
Speed ratings (Par 95): **100,99,84,84,82 78,78,77,76,67 60,58,44**
toteswingers: 1&2 £6.90, 1&3 £4.90, 2&3 £8.40 CSF £26.45 CT £132.97 TOTE £3.90: £1.70, £2.30, £2.10; EX 39.70.
Owner Godolphin **Bred** Compagnia Generale S R L **Trained** Newmarket, Suffolk

FOCUS
A moderate nursery. The first pair came a long way clear and the form could be better than rated.

NOTEBOOK
Landowner ◆, who improved significantly on his debut effort when winning a 7f Warwick maiden last time, stepped forward considerably once again on this step up 1m. He was a little keen under a positive ride but kept responding to pressure to get the better of a prolonged dual with the runner-up in the straight. Clearly much better than his current mark, he should keep progressing. (op 7-2)
Mason Hindmarsh ◆ produced his best form to date with a gutsy effort in defeat. He'll be hammered by the Handicapper for this, though. (op 7-1)
Mighty Clarets(IRE) could make no impression whatsoever on this step up in trip and is best watched until racing on easier ground. (op 11-2 tchd 9-2)
Deely Plaza didn't improve for the switch to quicker ground. (op 10-1)
We'll Deal Again, up in trip, was well held after racing keenly. (op 8-1)
Bintalaleumydarlin(IRE) Official explanation: jockey said the filly ran too free
Music Of The Moor(IRE) Official explanation: jockey said the gelding hung left-handed in the straight

6896 TOTESWINGER MAIDEN AUCTION STKS 6f

2:40 (2:42) (Class 5) 2-Y-O **£3,238** (£963; £481; £240) **Stalls** Low

Form RPR

1 **Rock 'N' Royal** 2-8-7 0 ow1 FrederikTylicki(3) 6 79+
(R A Fahey) *towards rr: pushed along and hdwy 1/2-way: effrt on inner over 1f out: rdn and squeezed through ins fnl f: sn led and styd on wl* **8/1**

5220 **2** *1 3/4* **Filwa (IRE)**[35] 5934 2-8-8 75 MartinDwyer 3 72
(B J Meehan) *led: rdn along 2f out: drvn and edgd rt ent fnl f: hdd and no ex last 100yds* **7/2**[1]

03 **3** *2 1/4* **The Confessor**[8] 6696 2-8-11 0 FrankieMcDonald 7 68
(H Candy) *cl up: rdn along over 2f out: drvn wl over 1f out and grad wknd* **10/1**

04 **4** *1/2* **Sabatini (IRE)**[7] 6728 2-8-7 0 PatDobbs 8 63
(R Hannon) *s.i.s and bhd: hdwy 3f out: rdn and wd home turn: styd on appr fnl f: nrst fin* **7/1**[3]

42 **5** *9* **Kellys Eye (IRE)**[18] 6408 2-8-13 0 TomEaves 10 42
(B Smart) *cl up: rdn over 2f out: sn drvn and wknd* **7/2**[1]

60 **6** *3/4* **House Of Rules**[20] 6356 2-8-9 0 TonyHamilton 4 36
(Miss J A Camacho) *bhd: hdwy over 2f out: swtchd lft over 1f out: styd on on inner appr fnl f: nrst fin* **22/1**

7 *1* **Singing Scott (IRE)** 2-8-10 0 DanielTudhope 2 34
(R Bastiman) *towards rr: pushed along 1/2-way: styd on fnl 2f: nrst fin* **28/1**

0 **8** *1 1/2* **Monsieur Pontaven**[46] 5596 2-8-9 0 SilvestreDeSousa 9 28
(R Bastiman) *a towards rr* **66/1**

025 **9** *1/2* **Fazza**[8] 6700 2-8-10 0 KFallon 12 28
(D W P Arbuthnot) *racd wd: in tch: rdn along 1/2-way and sn outpcd* **8/1**

0 **10** *2* **Kintyre Bay**[44] 5668 2-8-10 0 ow1 PhillipMakin 1 31+
(T D Barron) *chsd ldrs on inner: rdn along over 2f out: sn drvn and wknd* **25/1**

11 *16* **Tealing** 2-8-4 0 DeanHeslop(5) 11 —
(T D Barron) *chsd ldrs: rdn along wl over 2f out and sn wknd* **33/1**

4 **12** *7* **Set Back**[13] 6556 2-8-10 0 AdrianTNicholls 5 —
(D Nicholls) *chsd ldrs: rdn along over 2f out: sn pushed wd home turn and wkng whn hung lft and lost action wl over 1f out: eased* **6/1**[2]

1m 18.5s (1.60) **Going Correction** +0.15s/f (Good) **12 Ran SP% 118.6**
Speed ratings (Par 95): **95,92,89,89,77 76,74,72,72,69 48,38**
toteswingers: 1&2 £6.90, 1&3 £10.60, 2&3 £10.20 CSF £34.22 TOTE £8.60: £2.80, £1.50, £3.80; EX 53.40.
Owner Mr & Mrs G Calder **Bred** Mr & Mrs G Calder **Trained** Musley Bank, N Yorks

FOCUS
An ordinary juvenile maiden rated around those in the frame behind the winner, who looks to have more to offer.

NOTEBOOK
Rock 'N' Royal ◆ cost only £2,500 and is the first foal of a dual 7f-1m winner. She raced well off the pace through the early stages, but after coming under pressure a long way out she stayed on relentlessly in the straight, eventually squeezing through between the inside rail and the runner-up inside the final furlong. There should be more to come. (op 10-1)
Filwa(IRE) was reported to have been unsuited by quick ground at Leicester last time, but she handled these conditions okay. She ran her race under a positive ride but was picked off late on. (op 5-1 tchd 6-1)
The Confessor didn't really build on his recent third at Goodwood but handicaps are now an option. (op 8-1)
Sabatini(IRE), fourth on soft ground over 1m last time, lost her chance with a slow start under these vastly different conditions. She should benefit from more of a stamina test and handicaps are now an option. (op 6-1 tchd 11-2)
Kellys Eye(IRE) got warm and wasn't good enough to concede weight all round, running well below expectations. (op 4-1 tchd 9-2)
House Of Rules might do better now he can switch to handicaps, but he'll need to sharpen up. (tchd 20-1 and 25-1)
Set Back Official explanation: jockey said the colt was never travelling

6897 TOTESUPER7 H'CAP (DIV I) 5f

3:10 (3:10) (Class 4) (0-85,85) 3-Y-O+ **£4,857** (£1,445; £722; £360) **Stalls** Low

Form RPR

1202 **1** **Hotham**[10] 6647 6-8-12 **84** GaryBartley(5) 4 91
(N Wilson) *dwlt and in rr: hdwy 2f out: swtchd ins over 1f out and sn rdn: drvn ins fnl f: styd on strly to ld nr line* **7/2**[1]

0400 **2** *hd* **Bravely (IRE)**[16] 6489 5-8-5 **72** DuranFentiman 3 78
(T D Easterby) *chsd ldr: swtchd rt and hdwy over 1f out: sn rdn: drvn ins fnl f and styd on to ld towards fin: hdd nr line* **25/1**

41-0 **3** *hd* **Master Rooney (IRE)**[43] 5695 3-9-4 **85** RichardMullen 1 93+
(B Smart) *t.k.h early: trckd ldrs on inner: hdwy and ev ch whn nt clr run and swtchd rt over 1f out: rdn and hmpd ent fnl f: drvn and styd on strly towards fin* **5/1**[2]

040 **4** *1/2* **Tabaret**[20] 6359 6-9-4 **85** TonyHamilton 9 88
(R M Whitaker) *led: rdn over 1f out: drvn ins fnl f: hdd & wknd nr fin* **13/2**

0053 **5** *1* **Ivory Silk**[24] 6253 4-8-7 **74** (b) MartinDwyer 2 74
(J R Gask) *in tch: rdn along 2f out: swtchd outside and drvn over 1f out: kpt on ins fnl f: nrst fin* **6/1**[3]

0000 **6** *1* **Northern Fling**[31] 6051 5-8-12 **79** DanielTudhope 8 75
(J S Goldie) *dwlt and in rr tl styd on appr fnl f: nrst fin* **8/1**

2126 **7** *1/2* **King Of Swords (IRE)**[9] 6666 5-8-4 **71** (p) AndrewElliott 7 65
(N Tinkler) *prom: hdwy to chse ldr 2f out: sn rdn and ch whn hung rt ent fnl f: sn drvn and wknd* **6/1**[3]

3610 **8** *1 3/4* **Green Park (IRE)**[10] 6642 6-8-9 **76** (b) KFallon 5 64
(D Carroll) *hld up: hdwy 2f out: sn rdn and wknd over 1f out* **12/1**

1040 **9** *nk* **Argentine (IRE)**[91] 4134 5-8-8 **78** (b) FrederikTylicki(3) 6 65
(J A McShane) *chsd ldrs on outer: hdwy 2f out and sn rdn: drvn and ch whn bmpd ent fnl f: nt rcvr* **14/1**

6060 **10** *4* **Sands Crooner (IRE)**[9] 6666 6-8-6 **73** (v) PaulHanagan 10 46
(J G Given) *dwlt: a in rr* **12/1**

64.12 secs (0.82) **Going Correction** +0.15s/f (Good) **10 Ran SP% 117.8**
Speed ratings (Par 105): **99,98,98,97,95 94,93,90,90,83**
toteswingers: 1&2 £19.10, 1&3 £3.30, 2&3 £22.50 CSF £97.01 CT £373.99 TOTE £4.70: £1.60, £8.70, £2.50; EX 98.50.
Owner Far 2 Many Sues **Bred** Capt J H Wilson **Trained** Flaxton, N Yorks

FOCUS
A fair sprint and this looked the stronger of the two divisions and could be rated a little higher.
King Of Swords(IRE) Official explanation: jockey said gelding hung left in the straight

6898 TOTEPOOL SILVER TANKARD STKS (LISTED RACE) 1m 4y

3:40 (3:40) (Class 1) 2-Y-O

£19,869 (£7,532; £3,769; £1,879; £941; £472) **Stalls** Low

Form RPR

1454 **1** **Gallic Star (IRE)**[38] 5825 2-8-11 98 ChrisCatlin 8 93
(M R Channon) *towards rr: hdwy over 2f out: rdn to chse ldrs over 1f out: drvn ins fnl f: kpt on wl u.p to ld last stride* **11/2**[3]

2161 **2** *shd* **Tominator**[30] 6099 2-9-2 86 GrahamGibbons 5 98
(R Hollinshead) *led: rdn 2f out: drvn ent fnl f: kpt on gamely: hdd on line* **20/1**

31 **3** *shd* **Namecheck (GER)**[27] 6181 2-9-2 DO'Donohoe 4 98
(Saeed Bin Suroor) *prom: effrt on outer 2f out: sn rdn and chal ins fnl f: drvn and evch tl nt qckn nr line* **9/1**

2154 **4** *3/4* **Astonishment (IRE)**[11] 6619 2-9-2 85 PatDobbs 2 96
(S Kirk) *chsd ldr: rdn 2f out: styd on and ev ch ent fnl f: sn drvn and edgd rt: no ex last 75yds* **16/1**

1334 **5** *1 1/4* **Black Snowflake (USA)**[30] 6133 2-9-2 97 AhmedAjtebi 3 93
(Saeed Bin Suroor) *chsd ldrs: effrt over 2f out and sn rdn: drvn over 1f out and kpt on same pce ins fnl f* **13/2**

21 **6** *1 3/4* **Hot Prospect**[38] 5831 2-9-2 94 KFallon 9 89
(M A Jarvis) *plld hrd: in tch: effrt over 2f out: sn rdn btn over 1f out* **11/8**[1]

110 **7** *8* **Frozen Power (IRE)**[23] 6268 2-9-5 109 TedDurcan 10 81
(Saeed Bin Suroor) *hld up and bhd on outer: effrt over 2f out: sn rdn and nvr a factor* **7/2**[2]

30 **8** *1/2* **Top Spin (IRE)**[22] 6318 2-9-2 StephenDonohoe 6 71
(John Joseph Murphy, Ire) *in tch: rdn along wl over 2f out: sn wknd* **66/1**

1m 46.94s (1.04) **Going Correction** +0.15s/f (Good) **8 Ran SP% 115.2**
Speed ratings (Par 103): **100,99,99,99,97 96,88,87**
toteswingers: 1&2 £7.80, 1&3 £8.30, 2&3 £6.80 CSF £103.26 TOTE £6.80: £2.00, £3.30, £2.80; EX 103.20.
Owner Jon and Julia Aisbitt **Bred** J M Beever **Trained** West Ilsley, Berks

FOCUS
A weak race for the class which produced a blanket finish. The winner is rated 6lb below her May Hill form.

NOTEBOOK
Gallic Star(IRE), whose yard has a great record in this, didn't have to run up to the form she showed when fourth in the May Hill on her previous start, but she still did well to win as she raced well off a modest gallop and the runner-up had been allowed a clear lead. A daughter of Galileo who now has a Listed win to her name, this will have boosted her paddock value considerably. (op 13-2 tchd 9-2)
Tominator, successful in a 7f Catterick nursery off a mark of 81 on his previous start, was bred to appreciate this longer trip and ran a fine race, but he does have to be considered flattered, as he was allowed a soft lead. He might not be the easiest to place from now on, but his breeding suggests he'll continue to progress as he keeps going up in trip. (op 33-1 tchd 16-1)

Namecheck(GER), a Beverley maiden winner on his previous start, was the Godolphin third-string judged on jockey bookings and his position in the market in relation to his stalemates, but he fared best of Saeed Bin Suroor's trio. He briefly looked set to win when staying on for strong pressure around 1f out, but his run flattened out near the line. (op 16-1)

Astonishment(IRE), trying 1m for the first time, was a bit keen early and basically wasn't good enough. Rated just 85, his proximity would seem to confirm this was a weak race for the grade (op 28-1)

Black Snowflake(USA) didn't run up to his official mark of 97 and has to be considered somewhat disappointing. (op 10-1)

Hot Prospect looked a smart type on his first two starts, particularly last time when defeating subsequent Autumn Stakes winner Morana in a Sandown maiden, but he let himself down on this occasion. On edge beforehand, he was noticeably sweating and pulled much too hard in the race itself. Official explanation: jockey said that the colt ran too free (op 10-11 tchd 6-4 and 5-6 in places)

Frozen Power(IRE) had been progressing nicely prior to his slightly unlucky run in the Royal Lodge, but this was very disappointing. He was given quite a negative ride, but in fairness he seemingly just had nothing to offer. (op 4-1 tchd 100-30)

6899 TOTEEXACTA BLUFF COVE H'CAP — 2m 1f 216y

4:10 (4:10) (Class 5) (0-75,74) 3-Y-0+ — £3,238 (£963; £481; £240) Stalls Low

Form — RPR

-425 **1** **Ragamuffin Man (IRE)**[30] 6115 4-10-0 **74**....................(p) KFallon 2 — 83
(W J Knight) *trckd ldr: effrt over 3f out: rdn to ld wl over 2f out: drvn clr ent fnl f: styd on wl* **6/4**[1]

1110 **2** *4* **Markington**[12] 4417 6-9-8 **71**....................(b) WilliamCarson(3) 1 — 76
(P Bowen) *dwlt and in rr: pushed along 1/2-way: hdwy on outer 4f out: rdn along to chse ldng pair over 2f out: drvn over 1f out: kpt on to take 2nd ins fnl f* **7/2**[2]

1450 **3** *1* **Baan (USA)**[18] 6432 6-9-4 **64**....................(p) JimmyQuinn 4 — 68
(H J Collingridge) *trckd ldrs: hdwy gng wl over 2f out and sn chsng wnr: rdn wl over 1f out: swtchd lft and drvn ent fnl f: one pce* **9/2**[3]

4040 **4** *30* **Dechiper (IRE)**[6] 6767 7-9-5 **65**.................... GrahamGibbons 6 — 36
(R Johnson) *in tch: effrt 4f out and sn rdn along: drvn 3f out and sn outpcd* **8/1**

0000 **5** *7* **Emerald Hawk (IRE)**[7] 6742 3-7-12 **55** oh5........(b[1]) SilvestreDeSousa 3 — 18
(D H Brown) *led: rdn along 4f out: hdd wl over 2f out and sn wknd* **20/1**

0300 **6** *55* **Uptown Lad (IRE)**[6] 6767 10-8-2 **55** oh10............. MatthewLawson(7) 5 — —
(R Johnson) *hld up: a bhd* **50/1**

6201 **7** *9* **Terenzium (IRE)**[56] 5307 7-8-10 **56**....................(p) PaulHanagan 7 — —
(Micky Hammond) *t.k.h: prom tl rdn along and wknd qckly over 3f out: eased over 2f out* **7/1**

4m 3.32s (-0.58) **Going Correction** +0.15s/f (Good)
WFA 3 from 4yo+ 11lb — **7** Ran SP% **110.7**
Speed ratings (Par 103): **107,105,104,91,88 63,59**
toteswingers: 1&2 £2.50, 1&3 £3.30, 2&3 £3.30 CSF £6.37 TOTE £2.10: £1.20, £2.10; EX 5.60.

Owner M Hutton & B Spiers **Bred** D G Hardisty Bloodstock **Trained** Patching, W Sussex

■ Stewards' Enquiry : Matthew Lawson caution: use of whip

FOCUS
A weak staying handicap. The runner-up is the best guide to the form.

Terenzium(IRE) Official explanation: jockeu said that the gelding ran too free

6900 TOTETRIFECTA H'CAP — 1m 2f 6y

4:40 (4:43) (Class 5) (0-75,75) 3-Y-0+ — £3,238 (£963; £481; £240) Stalls Low

Form — RPR

0/12 **1** **Bollin Dolly**[16] 6490 6-8-13 **67**.................... DavidAllan 4 — 74
(T D Easterby) *trckd ldrs: hdwy 3f out: led wl over 1f out and sn rdn clr: drvn ins fnl f and hld on wl* **9/2**[1]

1625 **2** *hd* **Addwaitya**[27] 6190 4-9-7 **75**.................... KFallon 5 — 82+
(C F Wall) *hld up in rr: hdwy over 2f out: swtchd outside and effrt over 1f out: sn rdn and hung bdly lft ent fnl f drvn to chse wnr last 100yds: jst hld* **13/2**[3]

3212 **3** *2 1/4* **Safebreaker**[24] 6244 4-8-12 **71**....................(p) AmyRyan(5) 6 — 73
(K A Ryan) *midfield: hdwy over 2f out: rdn to chse ldrs over 1f out: styng on whn n.m.r ins fnl f: one pce after* **6/1**[2]

2000 **4** *1 1/4* **Kool Katie**[6] 6760 4-8-7 **61** oh8.................... AndrewElliott 2 — 61
(Mrs G S Rees) *towards rr: gd hdwy on inner wl over 1f out: rdn and kpt on ins fnl f: nrst fin* **50/1**

5244 **5** *2 1/4* **Maybeme**[33] 5979 3-8-10 **69** ow2.................... LeeVickers 7 — 69+
(N Bycroft) *hld up: effrt whn n.m.r 2f out: swtchd outside and rdn wl over 1f out: styd on ins fnl f: nrst fin* **12/1**

4435 **6** *2 1/2* **African Cheetah**[13] 6560 3-9-1 **74**.................... JoeFanning 15 — 64
(M Johnston) *prom: effrt to ld 4f out: rdn along and hdd wl over 1f out: sn drvn and wknd* **13/2**[3]

0001 **7** *1/2* **Black Rain**[3] 6832 4-8-11 **72** 6ex.................... TobyAtkinson(7) 9 — 61
(M Wigham) *trckd ldrs: n.m.r and swtchd rt bnd after 1 1/2f: effrt over 2f out: rdn whn hmpd over 1f out and no ch after* **6/1**[2]

60 **8** *4 1/2* **Active Asset (IRE)**[6] 6761 7-8-13 **67**....................(t) PaulMulrennan 3 — 47
(J A Glover) *trckd ldrs: hdwy 3f out: rdn to chal over 2f out and ev ch: sn drvn and grad wknd* **33/1**

5200 **9** *1* **Diamond Lass (IRE)**[32] 6023 4-8-7 **61** oh3.................... PaulHanagan 1 — 39
(R A Fahey) *prom: rdn along 4f out: drvn 3f out and sn wknd* **16/1**

065 **10** *3/4* **Sarwin (USA)**[32] 6019 6-8-13 **67**.................... RobertWinston 8 — 44
(G A Swinbank) *led: rdn along and hdd 4f out: sn wknd* **9/1**

060 **11** *hd* **Blue Spinnaker (IRE)**[44] 5673 10-8-1 **62**............. JamesPSullivan(7) 10 — 38
(M W Easterby) *hld up: a in rr* **33/1**

00-0 **12** *17* **Along The Nile**[16] 6490 7-9-1 **69**.................... TomEaves 11 — 11
(K G Reveley) *dwlt: a towards rr* **66/1**

3105 **13** *14* **Danehillsundance (IRE)**[62] 5126 5-9-3 **74**..........(t) FrederikTylicki(3) 12 — —
(D H Brown) *in tch on outer: rdn along over 3f out and sn wknd* **14/1**

1/0 **14** *22* **Come April**[26] 6204 5-9-2 **70**.................... MartinDwyer 13 — —
(P R Webber) *midfield whn hmpd bnd after 1 1/2f: sn lost pl: rdn along bef 1/2-way: sn bhd and eased* **16/1**

2m 14.33s (0.63) **Going Correction** +0.15s/f (Good)
WFA 3 from 4yo+ 5lb — **14** Ran SP% **118.9**
Speed ratings (Par 103): **103,102,101,100,98 96,95,92,91,90 90,77,65,48**
toteswingers: 1&2 £6.20, 1&3 £3.20, 2&3 £13.50 CSF £31.57 CT £179.63 TOTE £5.40: £2.00, £2.80, £2.00; EX 32.20 Trifecta £118.60 Pool: £288.52 - 1.80 winning units.

Owner Sir Neil Westbrook **Bred** Sir Neil And Lady Westbrook **Trained** Great Habton, N Yorks

FOCUS
A fair handicap and the form looks sound despite the proximity of the fourth from out of the handicap.

6901 TOTEPLACEPOT NURSERY (DIV II) — 1m 4y

5:10 (5:12) (Class 5) (0-75,74) 2-Y-O — £2,914 (£867; £433; £216) Stalls Low

Form — RPR

256 **1** **Beat The Rush**[52] 5407 2-8-12 **65**.................... TomEaves 7 — 74
(Miss J A Camacho) *midfield: hdwy over 2f out: effrt over 1f out: swtchd lft and rdn to ld ins fnl f: styd on strly* **9/1**

2463 **2** *2 1/2* **Dolphin Rock**[4] 6793 2-8-12 **65**.................... TedDurcan 6 — 68
(Mrs G S Rees) *trckd ldrs: hdwy wl over 2f out: rdn to ld over 1f out: drvn and edgd rt ins fnl f: sn hdd and one pce* **7/2**[2]

2040 **3** *1 1/2* **Tres Coronas (IRE)**[30] 6088 2-9-7 **74**.................... PhillipMakin 2 — 74
(T D Barron) *led: rn wd bnd after 1 1/2f: hdd 5f out: cl up and led again over 2f out: sn rdn and hdd over 1f out: kpt on same pce* **11/2**[3]

2000 **4** *2 1/4* **Storm Hawk (IRE)**[7] 6736 2-8-12 **68**.................... AndreaAtzeni(3) 1 — 63
(Pat Eddery) *chsd ldrs on inner: rdn along and outpcd over 2f out: drvn and rallied over 1f out: wknd ent fnl f* **20/1**

056 **5** *5* **Vittachi**[33] 5981 2-8-0 **53** oh1 ow2....................(p) JimmyQuinn 12 — 37
(J D Bethell) *dwlt and in rr: hdwy over 2f out: sn rdn and styd on ins fnl f: nt rch ldrs* **66/1**

241 **6** *3 3/4* **Rescent**[52] 5393 2-8-4 **57**.................... SilvestreDeSousa 4 — 33
(Mrs R A Carr) *chsd ldrs: rdn along wl over 2f out and sn no imp* **12/1**

4535 **7** *1/2* **Aattash (IRE)**[41] 5742 2-9-5 **72**....................(v[1]) ChrisCatlin 11 — 46
(M R Channon) *t.k.h and cl up: rn wd bnd after 1 1/2f: led over 5f out: rdn and hdd over 2f out: sn wknd* **7/1**

0050 **8** *1 1/4* **Moonlight Blaze**[49] 5515 2-8-9 **62**.................... PJMcDonald 10 — 34
(C W Fairhurst) *in tch: rdn along over 3f out and sn wknd* **66/1**

0112 **9** *1* **Fantastic Pick**[19] 6391 2-9-7 **74**.................... MartinDwyer 9 — 43
(B J Meehan) *prom: effrt 2f out and sn rdn: drvn and wknd over 1f out* **11/4**[1]

230 **10** *4 1/2* **Forshour**[17] 6461 2-9-0 **67**.................... GrahamGibbons 5 — 27
(E S McMahon) *a towards rr* **12/1**

000 **11** *4* **The Mighty Mod (USA)**[11] 6620 2-8-5 **58**.................... JoeFanning 8 — 9
(M Johnston) *dwlt: a towards rr* **14/1**

5600 **12** *29* **Sweet Mirasol (IRE)**[13] 6554 2-8-2 **55**.................... PaulHanagan 3 — —
(K A Ryan) *a towards rr* **50/1**

1m 48.03s (2.13) **Going Correction** +0.15s/f (Good) — **12** Ran SP% **118.5**
Speed ratings (Par 95): **95,92,91,88,83 80,79,78,77,72 68,39**
toteswingers: 1&2 £8.20, 1&3 £13.30, 2&3 £8.50 CSF £39.70 CT £196.59 TOTE £11.00: £2.90, £1.70, £2.30; EX 50.50.

Owner Axom (XX) **Bred** David Brown & G B Turnbull Ltd **Trained** Norton, N Yorks

FOCUS
This is ordinary nursery form, with the favourite disappointing and the time being 1.04 seconds slower than the first division. The runner-up is the best guide and the form looks pretty solid.

NOTEBOOK
Beat The Rush showed himself reasonably treated on this nursery debut. He kept on in relentless fashion in the straight, despite having to be switched, and is considered to be very much a stayer according to his connections. (op 15-2)

Dolphin Rock, back on quicker ground, ran his race but simply found one too good. (op 6-1)

Tres Coronas(IRE) was wanting to hang right early on and went wide around the first bend. He did well to recover his composure and remain handy, before finishing a creditable third. (op 6-1 tchd 9-2)

Storm Hawk(IRE) ran a little better with the visor left off but was still well held.

Fantastic Pick, runner-up at odds on over 1m2f on his previous start, was well held off a 5lb higher mark and seemed to run flat. Official explanation: vet said the gelding finished distressed (op 5-2 tchd 3-1)

6902 TOTESUPER7 H'CAP (DIV II) — 5f

5:40 (5:41) (Class 4) (0-85,85) 3-Y-O+ — £4,857 (£1,445; £722; £360) Stalls Low

Form — RPR

6014 **1** **Go Go Green (IRE)**[10] 6647 3-8-9 **79**.................... FrederikTylicki(3) 6 — 96
(D H Brown) *chsd ldr: hdwy 2f out: rdn to ld over 1f out: drvn clr ins fnl f: kpt on* **15/8**[1]

2025 **2** *2 3/4* **Taurus Twins**[10] 6647 3-8-3 **75** ow3....................(b) PaulPickard(5) 10 — 82
(R J Price) *sn led: clr 1/2-way: rdn 2f out: hdd over 1f out: sn drvn and kpt on same pce ins fnl f* **9/1**[3]

1135 **3** *1 1/4* **Gilt Edge Girl**[24] 6240 3-9-4 **85**.................... KFallon 1 — 88
(C G Cox) *in tch: hdwy to chse ldrs wl over 1f out: sn rdn and no imp ins fnl f* **5/2**[2]

0050 **4** *1 3/4* **Mandurah (IRE)**[10] 6647 5-8-12 **84**.................... MarkCoumbe(5) 2 — 80
(B P J Baugh) *trckd ldrs: hdwy 2f out: rdn wl over 1f out: drvn and one pce ent fnl f* **10/1**

6442 **5** *nk* **Inter Vision (USA)**[27] 6178 9-8-10 **77**.................... PaulHanagan 7 — 72
(A Dickman) *in rr: hdwy 2f out: sn rdn and styd on ins fnl f: nrst fin* **10/1**

6036 **6** *2 1/2* **Mullglen**[49] 5523 3-8-7 **74**....................(t) DavidAllan 8 — 60
(T D Easterby) *chsd ldrs: rdn along wl over 2f out and sn wknd* **11/1**

0005 **7** *1 3/4* **Rothesay Dancer**[28] 6155 6-8-8 **80**.................... GaryBartley(5) 4 — 60
(J S Goldie) *a towards rr* **16/1**

0051 **8** *nk* **Lucky Leigh**[10] 6632 3-8-9 **76**.................... ChrisCatlin 9 — 55
(M R Channon) *midfield: effrt 1/2-way: sn rdn along and n.d* **14/1**

1406 **9** *2 3/4* **Ingleby Star (IRE)**[16] 6489 4-7-12 **72**.................... ShirleyTeasdale(7) 5 — 41
(N Wilson) *chsd ldng pair: rdn along over 2f out: sn wknd* **20/1**

2030 **10** *dist* **Monte Cassino (IRE)**[64] 5073 4-8-5 **72** oh14 ow1...... AdrianTNicholls 3 — —
(J O'Reilly) *a in rr* **50/1**

63.75 secs (0.45) **Going Correction** +0.15s/f (Good) — **10** Ran SP% **119.1**
Speed ratings (Par 105): **102,97,95,92,92 88,85,85,80,—**
toteswingers: 1&2 £8.20, 1&3 £2.10, 2&3 £3.90 CSF £20.55 CT £45.67 TOTE £2.60: £1.60, £2.60, £1.40; EX 23.80 Place 6: £61.06 Place 5: £37.78.

Owner S Bolland P Holling **Bred** Edmond And Richard Kent **Trained** Maltby, S Yorks

FOCUS
The second division of the sprint handicap was the weaker of the pair despite being run in a faster winning time. The placed horses set the level.

T/Plt: £319.90 to a £1 stake. Pool: £64,820.19. 147.90 winning tickets. T/Qpdt: £52.00 to a £1 stake. Pool: £4,667.25. 66.30 winning tickets. JR

6735 WINDSOR (R-H)

Monday, October 19

OFFICIAL GOING: Good (8.2)

Top bend rail was dolled out 5yds from innermost line increasing distances of races over 1m plus by 10yards. Full width of straight utilised.

Wind: Virtually nil Weather: Overcast

6903 GETREADING.CO.UK MEDIAN AUCTION MAIDEN STKS — 5f 10y

2:00 (2:02) (Class 5) 2-Y-O — **£2,729** (£806; £403) **Stalls** High

Form — RPR

0330 **1** **Hot Pursuits**[16] 6481 2-8-12 79 ... SteveDrowne 11 62+
(H Morrison) *trckd ldrs: led ins fnl 2f: drvn and asserted over 1f out: styd on strly fnl f* **17/2**

6 **2** 1 1/2 **Adventure Story**[11] 6616 2-8-12 0 ... RichardHughes 15 60+
(R Hannon) *bmpd s: sn rr: wl bhd after 2f and hung lft: stl plenty to do whn hung lft 2f out: styd on strly fr over 1f out and stl green: fin wl: to take 2nd last strides but nt trble wnr* **15/2**[2]

2324 **3** hd **Bronze Beau**[18] 6409 2-9-3 67 ... TGMcLaughlin 3 61
(Mrs L Stubbs) *drvn to chse ldrs after 2f: wnt 2nd wl over 1f out but no imp: lost 2nd cl home* **15/2**[2]

5500 **4** 3/4 **Master Mylo (IRE)**[74] 4699 2-9-3 53 ... (b[1]) AlanMunro 5 58
(D K Ivory) *mid-div: pushed along and hdwy over 2f out: kpt on ins fnl f but nvr gng pce to rch ldrs* **40/1**

5 nk **Mr Money Maker** 2-9-3 0 ... RichardKingscote 10 57
(Tom Dascombe) *chsd ldrs: rdn 2f out: kpt on same pce ins fnl f* **3/1**[1]

0200 **6** 2 **Gooseberry Bush**[24] 6241 2-8-12 66 ... EddieAhern 8 45
(P J Makin) *chsd ldrs: rdn over 2f out: wknd ins fnl f* **15/2**[2]

02 **7** 2 1/4 **Young Simon**[63] 5109 2-9-3 0 ... TPQueally 9 42
(G G Margarson) *in rr: pushed along 1/2-way: hdwy over 1f out and kpt on but nvr a threat* **12/1**

606 **8** hd **Casanova Kid**[41] 5749 2-9-3 45 ... EdwardCreighton 1 41
(E J Creighton) *towards rr: hdwy 1/2-way: kpt on fr over 1f out but nvr in contention* **100/1**

5 **9** shd **Fire Raiser**[23] 6292 2-9-3 0 ... DavidProbert 6 41
(A M Balding) *in tch: pushed along 3f out: wknd fnl f* **8/1**[3]

2404 **10** 2 1/2 **Pinnacle Lad (IRE)**[4] 6796 2-9-3 68 ... (b[1]) FrancisNorton 12 32
(J L Spearing) *led tl hdd ins fnl 2f: sn wknd* **9/1**

0 **11** 3 **Mosqueta**[16] 6493 2-8-12 0 ... CatherineGannon 14 16
(P D Evans) *wnt rt s: a in rr* **33/1**

00 **12** 1 **Rosetta Hill**[34] 5969 2-8-5 0 ... DannyBrock(7) 13 12
(J R Jenkins) *early spd: sn bhd: no ch whn hung lft over 2f out* **50/1**

4024 **13** 1/2 **Papageno**[40] 5776 2-9-3 64 ... JimCrowley 2 16
(J R Jenkins) *chsd ldrs to 1/2-way* **18/1**

14 1 3/4 **Dane Cottage** 2-8-12 0 ... DarryllHolland 16 4
(Miss Gay Kelleway) *green and bhd most of way* **33/1**

15 1 3/4 **Petit Belle** 2-8-12 0 ... LukeMorris 4 —
(N P Littmoden) *sn bhd* **66/1**

00 **16** nk **Sapphire Spirit (USA)**[8] 6696 2-9-0 0 ... MarcHalford(3) 7 6+
(J R Best) *sn rdn: bhd after 2f* **100/1**

60.74 secs (0.44) **Going Correction** +0.075s/f (Good) **16** Ran SP% **118.6**

Speed ratings (Par 95): **99,96,96,95,94 91,87,87,87,83 78,76,76,73,70 70**

toteswingers: 1&2 £15.00, 1&3 £11.20, 2&3 £8.10 CSF £66.80 TOTE £10.40: £3.10, £3.40, £2.50; EX 64.90 Trifecta £191.30 Part won. Pool: £258.54 - 0.20 winning units..

Owner Mrs I Eavis **Bred** M Channon B/Stck & G Richardson B/Stck **Trained** East Ilsley, Berks

FOCUS

An ordinary backend maiden run at a fair clip. The third and fourth look the best guides to the level.

NOTEBOOK

Hot Pursuits, with the highest official rating in the field, possessing a mark of 79, won decisively. This was her first attempt at the minimum trip, having had four previous starts over 6f and 7f, and she made the most of a favourable draw, scooting clear from the 1f marker. She is a gutsy filly but does not have a great deal of scope. (tchd 11-1)

Adventure Story didn't show a lot on her 7f Newbury debut. She was drawn against the rail, but looked green beforehand and was reluctant to enter the stalls. Dropped in trip here, she stayed on really well from the back and looks to have a future on this evidence. She is now eligible for a handicap mark. (op 5-1 tchd 8-1)

Bronze Beau, a runner-up on three occasions, didn't have a good draw and, while he doesn't always find a lot of the bridle, he showed plenty of resolution on this occasion, without ever looking like troubling the winner. He has had plenty of chances and his proximity to the winner underlines the modest form of the contest as a whole. (op 8-1)

Master Mylo(IRE) did not have the best draw, either. Coming off a two-month break, he stayed on quite well, but is exposed. (op 50-1)

Mr Money Maker was very well backed (double figures in the morning), but looked green in the early stages, wandering about. He clearly has ability and was doing his best work at the finish. He will certainly come on for the experience. (op 11-4 tchd 5-2)

Gooseberry Bush, last seen running with credit in a valuable 7f sales race at Ascot, found this trip a bit sharp. (op 11-1)

Pinnacle Lad(IRE), blinkered for the first time, set off like a scalded cat and was beaten at the furlong pole. (op 14-1)

6904 READING POST CLAIMING STKS — 6f

2:30 (2:31) (Class 6) 3-Y-O+ — **£2,047** (£604; £302) **Stalls** High

Form — RPR

2353 **1** **Kingswinford (IRE)**[7] 6731 3-8-11 75 ... AndrewHeffernan(5) 14 82
(P D Evans) *chsd ldrs: rdn 2f out: led ins fnl f: styd on wl* **11/4**[1]

0000 **2** 3/4 **Mango Music**[30] 6118 6-8-10 73 ... FrancisNorton 10 73
(M Quinn) *w ldr tl rdn and outpcd over 2f out: styd on again to take 2nd wl ins fnl f but no imp on wnr* **8/1**[3]

2/00 **3** 1 **Jimmy Ryan (IRE)**[36] 5919 8-8-6 75 ... GregFairley 12 65
(T D McCarthy) *slt ld: rdn over 2f out: hdd ins fnl f: lost 2nd sn after and no ex nr fin* **12/1**

0004 **4** 1 3/4 **Esteem Machine (USA)**[23] 6293 5-8-9 82 ... LukeMorris 4 63
(R A Teal) *s.i.s: bhd: hrd rdn and hdwy 2f out: kpt on same pce fnl f* **8/1**[3]

3250 **5** 2 1/2 **Desert Strike**[19] 6387 3-8-10 72 ... EddieAhern 15 57
(P F I Cole) *chsd ldrs: pushed along over 2f out: wknd fnl f* **25/1**

0/10 **6** shd **Matuza (IRE)**[77] 4607 6-8-9 68 ... LPKeniry 13 54
(P R Chamings) *chsd ldrs: rdn over 2f out: wknd fnl f* **9/2**[2]

0036 **7** 1 3/4 **Diego Rivera**[18] 6437 4-8-13 62 ... FergusSweeney 8 53
(P J Makin) *mid-div: rdn and hung lft over 2f out: sme prog fnl f* **12/1**

0006 **8** shd **Mr Rio (IRE)**[5] 6777 4-8-9 52 ... AlanMunro 7 49
(A P Jarvis) *in rr: shkn up and r.o fr over 1f out: kpt on cl home* **40/1**

0000 **9** 4 1/2 **Retro (IRE)**[7] 6725 3-8-11 69 ow1 ... RichardHughes 9 37
(R Hannon) *chsd ldrs: rdn 2f out: no imprssion: wknd qckly fnl f* **10/1**

0530 **10** 1/2 **Sovereignty (JPN)**[12] 6588 7-8-4 59 ... SophieDoyle(5) 2 33
(D K Ivory) *in rr: mod prog fnl f* **33/1**

003 **11** 4 **Sweet Kiss (USA)**[23] 6293 4-8-2 50 ow1 ... LiamJones 1 13
(M J Attwater) *chsd ldrs tl wknd over 2f out* **33/1**

1560 **12** 1 **Keep Dancing (IRE)**[47] 5584 3-8-3 67 ... (p) DavidProbert 6 12
(A M Balding) *s.i.s: outpcd most of way on outside* **8/1**[3]

0204 **13** 2 1/2 **Cocktail Party (IRE)**[36] 5911 3-7-12 46 ... (t) Louis-PhilippeBeuzelin(3) 3 2
(J W Hills) *in tch on outside over 3f* **25/1**

0200 **14** 2 1/4 **Joss Stick**[26] 6205 4-8-7 55 ... CatherineGannon 11 —
(J J Bridger) *a in rr* **33/1**

1m 12.84s (-0.16) **Going Correction** +0.075s/f (Good)

WFA 3 from 4yo+ 1lb **14** Ran SP% **121.6**

Speed ratings (Par 101): **104,103,101,99,96 95,93,93,87,86 81,80,76,73**

toteswingers: 1&2 £9.50, 1&3 £9.60, 2&3 £25.10 CSF £23.17 TOTE £3.30: £1.40, £3.40, £5.30; EX 31.90 TRIFECTA Not won..

Owner Nick Shutts **Bred** J Costello **Trained** Pandy, Monmouths

■ Stewards' Enquiry : Andrew Heffernan one-day ban: used whip with excessive frequency

FOCUS

A modest claimer run at a fair pace with the winner looking th best guide to the form.

Esteem Machine(USA) Official explanation: jockey said gelding missed the break

Diego Rivera Official explanation: jockey said gelding hung left

Retro(IRE) Official explanation: jockey said colt was unsuited by the good ground

Keep Dancing(IRE) Official explanation: jockey said filly hung left; vet said filly cut to the right fore coronet post race

Joss Stick Official explanation: trainer said colt was unsuited by the good ground

6905 AT THE RACES VIRGIN 534 NURSERY (DIV I) — 6f

3:00 (3:01) (Class 5) (0-75,75) 2-Y-O — **£2,388** (£705; £352) **Stalls** High

Form — RPR

5020 **1** **Coolree Star (IRE)**[10] 6643 2-9-3 **71** ... JimCrowley 5 73
(J A Glover) *chsd ldr 4f out tl outpcd 2f out: styd on u.p fnl f to ld cl home* **12/1**

425 **2** 1/2 **Bonheurs Art (IRE)**[51] 5431 2-9-1 **69** ... MichaelHills 1 70
(B W Hills) *in tch: pushed along and hdwy 1/2-way: led jst ins fnl 2f: drvn and kpt on ins fnl f: hdd and no ex cl home* **5/2**[1]

0324 **3** 1 **Lucky Mellor**[31] 6068 2-9-5 **73** ... AlanMunro 3 71
(D K Ivory) *chsd ldrs: rdn 2f out: wnt 2nd appr fnl f: no imp and one pce ins fnl f* **9/1**[3]

6022 **4** nk **Powerful Pierre**[18] 6409 2-8-12 **71** ... (v) PatrickDonaghy(5) 10 68
(Jedd O'Keeffe) *t.k.h: led after 2f: hung lft ins fnl 3f and hdd jst ins fnl 2f and continued to hang: styd on same pce fnl f* **9/1**[3]

100 **5** 1/2 **Giulietta Da Vinci**[8] 6693 2-9-4 **72** ... RichardHughes 6 67
(R Hannon) *hld up towards rr: hdwy ins fnl 2f: kpt on fnl f but nvr a threat* **11/2**[2]

6560 **6** hd **Pursuit Of Gold**[5] 6775 2-8-9 **63** ... TonyCulhane 13 58
(J R Best) *trckd ldrs: swirchd lft to outside 3f out: shkn up and hdwy 2f out and edgd lft: kpt on fnl f but nvr a threat* **20/1**

3350 **7** 1 1/2 **Bell's Ocean (USA)**[10] 6643 2-8-13 **67** ... JerryO'Dwyer 8 57
(J Ryan) *in tch: rdn over 2f out: styd on same pce fnl f* **11/1**

0505 **8** 3/4 **Almuntaser (IRE)**[12] 6590 2-7-12 **55** ow1..(b) Louis-PhilippeBeuzelin(3) 2 43
(Ian Williams) *in rr tl sme hdwy on outside over 2f out but nvr rchd ldrs* **16/1**

225 **9** hd **Duster**[10] 6638 2-9-7 **75** ... SteveDrowne 4 62
(H Morrison) *chsd ldrs: rdn over 2f out: wknd over 1f out* **12/1**

600 **10** 3/4 **Ellen Vannin (IRE)**[18] 6436 2-8-8 **62** ... WilliamBuick 12 47
(Eve Johnson Houghton) *led 2f: styd chsng ldrs: rdn over 2f out: sn btn* **25/1**

546 **11** 3 **Temple Queen**[10] 6638 2-8-13 **67** ... JamesDoyle 11 49
(S Kirk) *chsd ldrs and rdn 3f out: wknd 2f out* **14/1**

4320 **12** 6 **Mr Corby (IRE)**[11] 6619 2-9-0 **68** ... SamHitchcott 7 29
(M R Channon) *rdn 1/2-way: a in rr* **16/1**

5604 **13** 6 **Oasis Jade**[25] 6227 2-8-11 **65** ... FergusSweeney 14 14
(G L Moore) *chsd ldrs to 1/2-way* **12/1**

5505 **14** 25 **Princess Shamal**[20] 6354 2-8-4 **58** ... FrancisNorton 9 —
(J R Jenkins) *rrd bdly s: rdn lost irons and a wl bhd* **33/1**

1m 13.39s (0.39) **Going Correction** +0.075s/f (Good) **14** Ran SP% **125.3**

Speed ratings (Par 95): **100,99,98,97,96 96,94,93,93,92 88,80,72,39**

toteswingers: 1&2 £10.00, 1&3 £20.40, 2&3 £8.30 CSF £42.74 CT £262.35 TOTE £16.30: £4.10, £1.70, £3.70; EX 70.90 Trifecta £258.30 Part won. Pool: £349.06 - 0.40 winning units..

Owner Sexy Six Partnership **Bred** D Johnson **Trained** Babworth, Notts

FOCUS

The first division of this 6f nursery was run at a true pace and the handicapper will be chuffed, since the majority finished in a heap. The form is limited and best rated around the third and fourth.

NOTEBOOK

Coolree Star(IRE) won a seller back in July and looked to have a bit to find on the book, yet he was given every assistance from the saddle under a typically forceful ride. He does not look an easy ride and looked beaten approaching 1f out, but he found more despite hanging left under pressure, and his late lunge gave him his second career victory on his seventh start. It would not do to get carried away with the form, though. (op 16-1)

Bonheurs Art(IRE) got first run on the winner and looked to be going much the best entering the final furlong, but didn't find much until the winner came alongside. She idled a bit in front, but is up to winning races on this evidence. This was only her fourth start and she looks progressive. (op 11-4 tchd 7-2)

Lucky Mellor needed to be cajoled under much tender handling to show his best. He travelled well up front and held every chance but didn't finish his race as well as some. The blinkers were off this time, yet he looked in need of some assistance. He is consistent, however, as this was his third placing in four nurseries. (op 12-1)

Powerful Pierre came here in good form, having gone close twice in nurseries in the north, but despite having a decent draw and running up the stands' rail, he hit a flat spot before running on again. The 5lb extra appeared to anchor him, rather than the extended trip. (tchd 10-1)

Giulietta Da Vinci, who had won a Leicester maiden in June, caught the eye. She found herself shuffled back turning for home having been run off her feet early on, but she stayed on nicely past beaten horses and was never nearer than at the finish. She has been running over further and a return to 7f might be on the cards. (op 8-1)

Pursuit Of Gold was unable to take advantage of a favourable draw and had to come wide to challenge. He has had three chances in this company now and has had excuses in each one. The potential is there, but he is becoming frustrating. (op 16-1)

Duster Official explanation: jockey said gelding hung left

Oasis Jade Official explanation: jockey said saddle slipped

Princess Shamal Official explanation: jockey said the filly had plunged leaving the stalls and he lost his irons

6906 AT THE RACES VIRGIN 534 NURSERY (DIV II) 6f
3:30 (3:30) (Class 5) (0-75,79) 2-Y-O £2,388 (£705; £352) Stalls High

Form RPR

4260 1 **Poppy N'Penny (IRE)**[24] 6241 2-9-1 **69** KirstyMilczarek 7 80
(W J Haggas) *in tch: rdn and hdwy to ld ins fnl 2f: drvn clr fnl f: readily* **10/3**[2]

00 2 4 ½ **Schoolboy Champ**[16] 6486 2-9-3 **71** SJCraine 12 68
(Patrick Morris) *chsd ldrs: rdn over 2f out: styd on to chse wnr fnl f but nvr any ch* **22/1**

4520 3 ¾ **Jessica Hayllar (USA)**[18] 6418 2-8-11 **65** FergusSweeney 11 60
(G L Moore) *chsd ldrs: led over 2f out: hdd ins fnl quarter m: lost 2nd and one pce fnl f* **16/1**

0460 4 1 **Reach For The Sky (IRE)**[25] 6227 2-8-13 **67** RichardHughes 13 59
(R Hannon) *in rr: rdn over 2f out: styd on fnl f but nvr gng pce to get into contention* **7/1**[3]

3321 5 ¾ **Masked Dance (IRE)**[49] 5519 2-9-0 **75** (p) JPFahy[(7)] 8 65
(K A Ryan) *sn slt ld: rdn and hdd over 2f out: sn hung lft: one pce appr fnl f* **9/4**[1]

6543 6 ¾ **Cane Cat (IRE)**[12] 6590 2-8-0 **54** LukeMorris 1 41
(A W Carroll) *chsd ldrs: rdn over 2f out: wknd fnl f* **12/1**

3600 7 1 ½ **Super Duplex**[34] 5967 2-8-10 **64** IanMongan 4 47
(P M Phelan) *in rr: pushed along 1/2-way: mod prog fnl f* **33/1**

0050 8 hd **Little Perisher**[14] 6534 2-9-2 **70** AlanMunro 14 52+
(A P Jarvis) *in rr: sme hdwy on outside whn nt clr run over 2f out: mod prog fnl f* **16/1**

0605 9 ½ **Greek Key (IRE)**[20] 6367 2-9-0 **68** WilliamBuick 9 52+
(M L W Bell) *stmbld s and towards rr: sme prog over 2f out: nver in contention* **8/1**

1506 10 10 **Deloria**[30] 6104 2-9-4 **72** (b[1]) DaneO'Neill 2 23
(Eve Johnson Houghton) *w ldrs: led 4f out: hdd over 2f out: sn wknd* **10/1**

0600 11 3 ¼ **Althabea**[12] 6589 2-7-12 **52** oh1 (b[1]) CatherineGannon 3 —
(Ian Williams) *disp ld and sn rdn: wknd qckly ins fnl 3f* **40/1**

1m 12.72s (-0.28) **Going Correction** +0.075s/f (Good) **11** Ran SP% **115.7**
Speed ratings (Par 95): **104,98,97,95,94 93,91,91,90,77 73**
toteswingers: 1&2 £24.00, 1&3 £14.60, 2&3 £43.00 CSF £76.57 CT £1030.65 TOTE £4.80: £1.40, £5.50, £4.10; EX 108.10 TRIFECTA Not won..
Owner M Scotney/ D Asplin/ A Symonds **Bred** Tally-Ho Stud **Trained** Newmarket, Suffolk

FOCUS
They went a decent pace for the second division of the nursery, which looked a weaker race. The form looks quite solid though, rated around the placed horses.

NOTEBOOK
Poppy N'Penny(IRE) came here off the back of a modest run in a valuable sales race and was 6lb higher than when finishing sixth in a 7f AW nursery at Lingfield on her penultimate start in August. Dropped in trip, she looked a totally different proposition here, scooting clear to land a comfortable victory. This will have not harmed her confidence but she heads to the sales next week. This race was very much the plan, according to connections. (op 7-2 tchd 4-1)
Schoolboy Champ is clearly well thought of, having been pitched into the St Leger Yearling Sales race at York and Redcar's Two-Year-Old Trophy. Dropped in class here, he was well beaten off. He may just have bumped into a highly progressive animal, but the overriding feeling is that he probably isn't that quick. (op 20-1 tchd 25-1)
Jessica Hayllar(USA) finished her race better than some, but was beaten a long way. She won a Yarmouth seller in July, but she is still lightly raced and may progress. (tchd 20-1)
Reach For The Sky(IRE) is starting to prove disappointing. He was off a 4lb lower mark than when going down here narrowly in August and though he stayed on from the back, the fact that he finished so far adrift of the winner makes him look regressive. (op 8-1 tchd 6-1)
Masked Dance(IRE) was given a positive ride, but faded. He was given a 12lb hike in the handicap after hosing up at Ripon and looked anchored by it. (op 5-2)
Cane Cat(IRE) made ground to 2f out, but was made to look one-paced and she weakened late on. She is starting to look exposed after nine runs and a drop in class is required. (op 10-1)
Greek Key(IRE) Official explanation: jockey said colt stumbled leaving the stalls

6907 HARLEQUINS BIG GAME 2 H'CAP 1m 2f 7y
4:00 (4:01) (Class 4) (0-85,85) 3-Y-O+ £4,857 (£1,445; £722; £360) Stalls Low

Form RPR

2300 1 **Decision**[38] 5834 3-8-6 **75** LukeMorris 2 85
(C G Cox) *led: rdn and edgd lft ins fnl 2f: narrowly hdd jst ins fnl f: rallied to ld again cl home* **20/1**

003 2 nk **The Fifth Member (IRE)**[8] 6695 5-9-7 **85** PatCosgrave 16 94
(J R Boyle) *chsd ldrs: rdn to chse wnr over 1f out: led jst ins fnl f: hdd and no ex cl home* **11/1**

6410 3 1 ¾ **Special Reserve (IRE)**[12] 6594 4-9-5 **83** RichardHughes 11 89+
(R Hannon) *hld up in rr: styd on fr 2f out: kpt on wl to take 3rd ins fnl f but nt rch ldng duo* **8/1**[2]

1312 4 nk **Ordoney (IRE)**[18] 6435 4-9-5 **83** WilliamBuick 5 88
(L M Cumani) *in tch: rdn to chse ldrs ins fnl 3f: no imp u.p over 1f out: styd on same pce ins fnl f* **3/1**[1]

6000 5 nse **Aurorian (IRE)**[79] 4520 3-8-9 **78** DaneO'Neill 4 83
(R Hannon) *in tch: rdn and hdwy 2f out: styd on fnl f but nvr gng pce to chal* **12/1**

000 6 hd **Opera Prince**[8] 6695 4-9-0 **78** LPKeniry 10 83
(S Kirk) *chsd ldrs: rdn fr 4f out: styd on fnl 2f: nvr gng pce to chal* **16/1**

4005 7 ½ **Burns Night**[24] 6257 3-8-5 **74** GregFairley 1 78
(M Johnston) *chsd ldr: rdn and outpcd 3f out: edgd lft u.p over 1f out but styd on again ins fnl f* **16/1**

2043 8 1 ¼ **Dark Prospect**[12] 6594 4-9-7 **85** (b) GeorgeBaker 8 86
(M A Jarvis) *chsd ldrs: drvn to chal over 3f out tl veered lft u.p over 2f out: wknd over 1f out* **9/1**[3]

0044 9 1 ¼ **Lady Brora**[56] 5321 4-8-7 **71** DavidProbert 6 70
(A M Balding) *mid-div: rdn: hung lft and no prog over 2f out* **16/1**

5620 10 ½ **Golden Rock (IRE)**[79] 4518 3-8-3 **75** Louis-PhilippeBeuzelin[(3)] 15 73
(R Charlton) *in rr: mod prog on outside over 2f out: nvr in contention* **16/1**

4233 11 2 **Can Can Star**[16] 6470 6-8-11 **82** DebraEngland[(7)] 3 76
(A W Carroll) *trckd ldrs: n.m.r 3f out: wknd 2f out* **12/1**

221 12 1 ¼ **Rocky's Pride (IRE)**[38] 3472 3-8-11 **80** FergusSweeney 9 71
(G L Moore) *in rr: sme hdwy on outside over 2f out but nvr anywhere nr ldrs* **25/1**

6465 13 ½ **Dubai Crest**[14] 6546 3-9-2 **85** JimCrowley 7 75
(Mrs A J Perrett) *a towards rr* **12/1**

2231 14 7 **Mr Udagawa**[19] 6390 3-8-0 **76** ow2 (p) JPFahy[(7)] 14 52
(R M Beckett) *in rr: sme prog over 3f out: nvr rchd ldrs and sn bhd* **8/1**[2]

2300 15 1 ¼ **Charlotte Point (USA)**[33] 5986 3-8-13 **82** EddieAhern 12 56
(P F I Cole) *chsd ldrs: hmpd after 3f: styd in tch tl wknd over 3f out* **25/1**

2m 7.53s (-1.17) **Going Correction** +0.075s/f (Good)
WFA 3 from 4yo+ 5lb **15** Ran SP% **124.6**
Speed ratings (Par 105): **107,106,105,105,105 104,104,103,102,102 100,99,99,93,92**
toteswingers: 1&2 £71.80, 1&3 £40.10, 2&3 £15.70 CSF £226.99 CT £1924.30 TOTE £32.60: £7.90, £4.40, £2.50; EX 305.70 TRIFECTA Not won..Whooshka was withdrawn. Price at time of withdrawal 16/1. Rule 4 does not apply.
Owner A D Spence **Bred** D D And Mrs Jean P Clee **Trained** Lambourn, Berks

FOCUS
A sensible gallop for this reasonably competitive handicap with the runner-up rated close to his best.
Decision Official explanation: trainer said, regarding the apparent improvement of form, that the colt had benefitted from a short break
Ordoney(IRE) Official explanation: jockey said colt hung left

6908 STEVE HAGGER HAPPY 70TH BIRTHDAY H'CAP (DIV I) 1m 67y
4:30 (4:34) (Class 5) (0-70,70) 3-Y-O+ £2,388 (£705; £352) Stalls High

Form RPR

0002 1 **Compton Blue**[14] 6547 3-9-1 **68** (b[1]) RichardHughes 10 78
(R Hannon) *trckd ldrs: rdn over 2f out: led jst ins fnl f: sn asserted: readily* **6/1**[3]

6422 2 1 ½ **French Art**[12] 6588 4-9-1 **65** EddieAhern 5 72
(N Tinkler) *chsd ldrs: rdn to take slt ld over 1f out: hdd jst ins fnl f: sn no ch w wnr but kpt on wl for clr 2nd* **3/1**[1]

340 3 2 ½ **Full Victory (IRE)**[2] 6861 7-8-12 **67** AndrewHeffernan[(5)] 13 68
(R A Farrant) *led after 2f: rdn 3f out: hdd over 1f out: wknd ins fnl f* **8/1**

3050 4 1 **El Libertador (USA)**[30] 6111 3-9-0 **67** StephenCarson 7 66
(E A Wheeler) *slt ld 2f: styd chsing ldrs: rdn 3f out: ev ch over 1f out: wknd ins fnl f* **10/1**

2113 5 1 ½ **Morocchius (USA)**[37] 5869 4-8-9 **64** (p) BMcHugh[(5)] 1 60
(Miss J A Camacho) *t.k.h: chsd ldrs after 2f: rdn and ev ch ins fnl 2f: wknd fnl f* **11/2**[2]

1052 6 ½ **Having A Ball**[7] 6720 5-8-6 **56** oh2 WilliamBuick 8 50+
(P D Cundell) *in rr: rdn and hdwy over 2f out: styd on fr over 1f out but nvr in contention* **7/1**

5240 7 1 **Fortunate Bid (IRE)**[31] 6052 3-9-2 **69** TGMcLaughlin 2 61
(Mrs L Stubbs) *s.i.s: in rr: sme hdwy on outside over 2f out: nt trble ldrs* **14/1**

0002 8 3 ¼ **Trafalgar Square**[10] 6630 7-9-6 **70** JimCrowley 12 55
(M J Attwater) *in tch: rdn over 3f out: sn wknd* **10/1**

530- 9 1 ¼ **Candilejas**[323] 7505 3-8-2 **62** KierenFox[(7)] 6 44
(R J Smith) *a towards rr* **40/1**

0001 10 shd **Sapphire Prince (USA)**[14] 6547 3-9-3 **70** TonyCulhane 9 51
(J R Best) *chsd ldrs: rdn over 3f out: wknd over 2f out* **10/1**

2100 11 7 **Voortrekker**[36] 5915 3-9-3 **70** DarryllHolland 11 35
(D J Coakley) *a in rr* **10/1**

60-0 12 12 **Christophers Quest**[19] 6399 4-8-8 **58** PaulFitzsimons 3 —
(Miss N A Lloyd-Beavis) *led part of way to s: unruly to load: sn bhd* **66/1**

1m 44.61s (-0.09) **Going Correction** +0.075s/f (Good)
WFA 3 from 4yo+ 3lb **12** Ran SP% **125.2**
Speed ratings (Par 103): **103,101,99,98,96 96,95,91,90,90 83,71**
toteswingers: 1&2 £6.10, 1&3 £13.00, 2&3 £9.80 CSF £25.74 CT £154.88 TOTE £5.20: £2.30, £2.00, £3.00; EX 24.40 Trifecta £234.40 Pool: £339.00 - 1.07 winning units.
Owner Godfrey Wilson **Bred** Caroline Wilson **Trained** East Everleigh, Wilts

FOCUS
A relatively competitive handicap for poor prizemoney and it was run at a decent pace. The form does not look anything special, however, with the placed horses the best guides.

6909 STEVE HAGGER HAPPY 70TH BIRTHDAY H'CAP (DIV II) 1m 67y
5:00 (5:00) (Class 5) (0-70,70) 3-Y-O+ £2,388 (£705; £352) Stalls High

Form RPR

204 1 **Miss Sophisticat**[25] 6223 3-9-2 **68** (v) JimCrowley 8 77
(W J Knight) *pressed ldrs tl rdn and outpcd ins fnl 2f: rallied u.p to ld ins fnl f: kpt on wl* **14/1**

5640 2 1 ¼ **Bosamcliff (IRE)**[26] 6218 4-8-4 **58** AndrewHeffernan[(5)] 12 64
(P D Evans) *in tch: rdn and outpcd over 2f out: hdwy over 1f out: styd on wl to go 2nd ins fnl f but no imp on wnr* **7/1**[3]

5252 3 nk **Jewelled**[21] 6333 3-9-4 **70** EddieAhern 10 75
(J W Hills) *led and kpt slt advantage whn rdn over 2f out: hdd and one pce ins fnl f* **7/1**[3]

0610 4 1 **Pha Mai Blue**[37] 5886 4-9-0 **63** PatCosgrave 6 66
(J R Boyle) *chsd ldrs: rdn and ev ch over 1f out: outpcd ins fnl f* **10/1**

1321 5 hd **Cadeaux Fax**[12] 6588 4-8-12 **64** JamesMillman[(3)] 5 66+
(B R Millman) *in rr: swtchd towards outside and hdwy over 2f out: nvr quite gng pce to chal but styd on fnl f* **7/2**[1]

5210 6 ½ **Secret Hero**[30] 6111 3-9-3 **69** (b) RichardHughes 9 70
(R Hannon) *chsd ldrs: rdn over 2f out: styd wl there tl n.m.r 1f out: no ex ins fnl f* **7/1**[3]

5332 7 ¾ **Manere Bay**[67] 4936 4-9-2 **65** ShaneKelly 2 71+
(J L Dunlop) *hld up in rr: effrt on rails but nt room fr 2f out and nt rcvr* **13/2**[2]

6000 8 1 ½ **Mr Hichens**[51] 5448 4-9-6 **69** (p) AlanMunro 1 65
(Karen George) *hdwy to chse ldrs 4f out: rdn over 2f out: wknd appr fnl f* **11/1**

000 9 1 **Mississippian (IRE)**[23] 6288 5-8-11 **60** CatherineGannon 7 54
(C J Mann) *v.s.a: in rr tl hdwy over 3f out: in tch w ldrs u.p over 2f out: wknd over 1f out* **16/1**

6306 10 shd **Mister Trickster (IRE)**[12] 6588 8-8-6 **55** KirstyMilczarek 11 48
(R Dickin) *slowly away: nvr beyond mid-div and bhd fr over 2f out* **11/1**

0000 11 1 ½ **Sammy The Snake (IRE)**[44] 5676 4-9-5 **68** (p) DaneO'Neill 4 58
(B W Duke) *towards rr most of way* **40/1**

6504 12 3 ¼ **Komreyev Star**[45] 5631 7-8-6 **55** oh9 (p) FrancisNorton 3 37
(R E Peacock) *hdwy to chse ldrs 4f out: wknd wl over 2f out* **50/1**

1m 44.91s (0.21) **Going Correction** +0.075s/f (Good)
WFA 3 from 4yo+ 3lb **12** Ran SP% **115.8**
Speed ratings (Par 103): **101,99,99,98,98 97,97,95,94,94 92,89**
toteswingers: 1&2 £26.00, 1&3 £11.40, 2&3 £12.50 CSF £106.28 CT £752.53 TOTE £19.10: £3.90, £3.10, £2.20; EX 123.80 TRIFECTA Not won..
Owner Mrs Sheila Mitchell **Bred** Newsells Park Stud Limited **Trained** Patching, W Sussex

FOCUS
A modest handicap run at a decent pace but the merit of the form is open to question, since little separated the first half dozen home. The placed horses set the level of the form.
Manere Bay Official explanation: jockey said filly was denied a clear run
Mississippian(IRE) Official explanation: jockey said gelding was slowly away

Komreyev Star Official explanation: trainer said gelding suffered an overreach on its off fore

6910 DORIS HORTON MEMORIAL VASE H'CAP 1m 2f 7y
5:30 (5:31) (Class 6) (0-65,65) 3-Y-O £2,047 (£604; £302) Stalls Low

Form RPR

1404 **1** **Aine's Delight (IRE)**[19] 6394 3-8-6 58 .... SimonPearce(5) 2 67
(Andrew Turnell) *in rr: hdwy on outside over 2f out: hung bdly lft to r alone but led over 2f out: pushed clr fr over 1f out* **22/1**

2163 **2** *2* **Broughtons Paradis (IRE)**[7] 6742 3-9-1 62 .... AlanMunro 14 67+
(W J Musson) *in tch: hdwy over 4 out: styd on fnl 2f and r.o to take 2nd cl home but no ch w wnr on far side* **5/1**[2]

2423 **3** *hd* **Salybia Bay**[19] 6395 3-8-11 58 .... RichardHughes 7 63
(R Hannon) *in tch: styd on to chse ldrs 2f out and led main gp over 1f out but no ch w wnr far side: one pce and lost 2nd cl home* **8/1**[3]

6500 **4** *1 ½* **Young Dottie**[18] 6421 3-9-3 64 .... IanMongan 4 66
(P M Phelan) *in rr: hdwy fr 3f out: drvn to chse ldrs 2f out: one pce ins fnl f* **33/1**

2251 **5** *hd* **Kyle Of Bute**[13] 6570 3-9-4 65 .... J-PGuillambert 11 66+
(B P J Baugh) *in rr: rdn and hdwy fr 3f out: swtchd lft and styd on fr over 1f out but nvr quite gng pce to rch ldrs* **16/1**

0-33 **6** *2 ¼* **Lord Of The Dance (IRE)**[11] 6611 3-9-1 62 .... LukeMorris 3 59
(J M P Eustace) *in rr tl hdwy 4f out: chsd ldrs: rdn and hung lft u.p over 2f out: styd wl there tl wknd ins fnl f* **16/1**

6042 **7** *nk* **Garter Knight**[123] 3054 3-9-3 64 .... MickyFenton 9 60
(Mrs P Sly) *t.k.h towards rr: hdwy 3f out: pressed ldrs 2f out tl wknd ins fnl f* **16/1**

3461 **8** *2* **Lucy's Perfect**[14] 6549 3-8-12 59 .... (b) DavidProbert 16 51
(B R Millman) *chsd ldrs: led 4f out: hdd over 2f out: wknd ins fnl 2f* **14/1**

2100 **9** *3 ½* **Fantino**[19] 6400 3-9-3 64 .... GeorgeBaker 5 49
(J Mackie) *led 2f: styd chsng ldrs tl wknd 2f out* **14/1**

0106 **10** *nk* **Blue Tango (IRE)**[12] 6584 3-9-2 63 .... (b) JimCrowley 10 48
(Mrs A J Perrett) *chsd ldrs: rdn 3f out: wknd over 2f out* **20/1**

5030 **11** *5* **Major Value**[39] 5790 3-8-0 52 .... (p) SophieDoyle(5) 15 27
(C G Cox) *chsd ldrs: rdn 3f out: sn wknd* **40/1**

006 **12** *19* **Catchmeifyoucan (FR)**[23] 6287 3-9-2 63 .... (b[1]) AdamKirby 6 —
(C G Cox) *chsd ldrs: rdn 4f out: wknd qckly* **20/1**

300 **13** *1* **Iketi (GR)**[49] 5531 3-8-9 56 ow1 .... PatCosgrave 1 —
(Jane Chapple-Hyam) *a in rr* **33/1**

4330 **14** *5* **Jewelled Reef (IRE)**[4] 6787 3-8-12 59 .... WilliamBuick 8 —
(Eve Johnson Houghton) *a in rr* **20/1**

5125 **15** *¾* **My Girl Jode**[29] 6139 3-9-1 62 .... TPQueally 13 —
(M H Tompkins) *led after 2f: hdd 4f out: sn btn* **9/1**

060- **16** *26* **Aestival**[363] 6879 3-8-6 53 .... EddieAhern 12 —
(Sir Mark Prescott) *s.i.s: sn in tch: wknd 5f out* **9/4**[1]

2m 8.67s (-0.03) **Going Correction** +0.075s/f (Good) **16 Ran SP% 126.5**
Speed ratings (Par 99): **103,101,101,100,99 98,97,96,93,93 89,74,73,69,68 47**
toteswingers: 1&2 £36.70, 1&3 £42.00, 2&3 £8.00 CSF £124.20 CT £995.35 TOTE £30.90: £4.90, £1.50, £2.30, £7.70; EX 142.10 TRIFECTA Not won. Place 6: £275.15 Place 5: £100.32.
Owner Dave Murray, Joe Mallon & Peter Ross **Bred** Dr John Hollowood And Aiden Murphy **Trained** Broad Hinton, Wilts

FOCUS
A weak handicap finale to Windsor's Flat season, run at a sensible clip. The form looks sound if limited.
My Girl Jode Official explanation: jockey said filly ran too free
T/Jkpt: Not won. T/Plt: £423.30 to a £1 stake. Pool: £67,812.43. 116.93 winning tickets. T/Qpdt: £127.60 to a £1 stake. Pool: £6,156.34. 35.70 winning tickets. ST

6778 LINGFIELD (L-H)
Tuesday, October 20

OFFICIAL GOING: Standard
Wind: Moderate across Weather: Dull

6911 BET CHAMPIONS LEAGUE FOOTBALL - BETDAQ MAIDEN AUCTION STKS (DIV I) 7f (P)
2:00 (2:00) (Class 5) 2-Y-O £2,388 (£705; £352) Stalls Low

Form RPR

53 **1** **Cat Hunter**[15] 6544 2-8-6 0 .... JimCrowley 5 65+
(Mrs A J Perrett) *chsd ldrs: rdn 2f out: str run centre of crse to ld fnl 110yds: drvn out* **4/1**[2]

0 **2** *1 ½* **Fivefold (USA)**[11] 6629 2-9-1 0 .... J-PGuillambert 6 70
(J Akehurst) *led 1f: styd chsng ldrs: rdn 2f out: led jst ins fnl f: hrd rdn: hdd and hung bdly rt fnl 110yds* **11/1**

0040 **3** *1 ¼* **Reddy To Star (IRE)**[9] 6693 2-8-11 72 .... AdamKirby 4 63
(C G Cox) *chsd ldrs: rdn 2f out: hung lft u.p fr over 1f out: styd on to take 3rd cl home but nvr gng pce of ldng duo* **5/1**[3]

320 **4** *1 ¼* **Merchant Of Medici**[13] 6591 2-8-11 73 .... MartinDwyer 3 60+
(W R Muir) *in rr: pushed along over 2f out: styd on u.p and prog on rail ins fnl f: gng on cl home but nvr a threat* **7/2**[1]

06 **5** *1 ¼* **Brave Ghurka**[8] 6737 2-8-13 0 .... RichardHughes 11 59
(S Kirk) *w ldr: slt advantage after 1f: styd in front and pushed along wl over 1f out: hdd jst ins fnl f: wknd fnl 75yds* **15/2**

050 **6** *1* **Light The Way**[22] 6334 2-8-11 55 .... (t) FergusSweeney 10 54
(P J Makin) *wiith ldr: rdn over 2f out: wknd appr fnl f* **12/1**

56 **7** *1* **Louisiana Gift (IRE)**[25] 6254 2-8-11 0 .... WilliamBuick 7 52+
(J W Hills) *broke wl: sn in rr: pushed along 2f out: styd on in middle of crse fnl f: nvr a factor* **11/2**

8 *hd* **Ermyn Express** 2-8-4 0 .... CatherineGannon 9 44+
(P M Phelan) *in rr: sn pushed along: styd on towards fin but nvr anywhere nr ldrs* **16/1**

00 **9** *1* **Goodwood Diva**[89] 4239 2-8-8 0 .... EddieAhern 8 46+
(J L Dunlop) *chsd ldrs tl wknd ins fnl 2f* **25/1**

0 **10** *½* **Tregony Bridge**[46] 5627 2-8-11 0 .... FrancisNorton 2 47
(M Blanshard) *rdn 1/2-way: a bhd* **100/1**

0 **11** *3 ¾* **Wee Bobbie**[43] 5714 2-8-6 0 ow2 .... NeilChalmers 1 33
(Mrs P N Dutfield) *a in rr* **100/1**

1m 25.81s (1.01) **Going Correction** +0.025s/f (Slow) **11 Ran SP% 113.8**
Speed ratings (Par 95): **95,93,91,90,89 87,86,86,85,84 80**
toteswingers: 1&2 £18.40, 1&3 £7.90, 2&3 £15.80 CSF £45.39 TOTE £4.00: £1.60, £4.10, £2.30; EX 47.20.
Owner David Cohen **Bred** Sunny Days Ltd **Trained** Pulborough, W Sussex

FOCUS
Not the strongest of maidens ever run on the Polytrack here and it paid to race handily. This looks form to treat with caution.

NOTEBOOK
Cat Hunter, who had shown progressive form in her first two starts, improved again on this return to Polytrack. She was always stalking the leaders and the key to this victory was that she was produced with her effort down the wide outside, and as was the case at the last meeting here that did appear the place to be. She now gets an official mark and should improve for further, but at this stage it's not clear whether she will run again during the winter. (tchd 7-2)
Fivefold(USA) ◆, green when well beaten over C&D on his debut earlier this month, was a springer in the market here but he again appeared to run green in a handy position. He also made his effort up the inside of the hanging Brave Ghurka once into the home straight, which probably wasn't ideal, so he can be given extra credit for this effort. With further improvement to come, it shouldn't be long before he goes one better. (op 16-1 tchd 10-1)
Reddy To Star(IRE) plugged on to grab third after coming off the bridle rounding the home turn, but he was by far the most experienced in the field and now looks totally exposed. (op 6-1)
Merchant Of Medici, a very disappointing favourite at Nottingham last time after showing ability in his first two starts, was weak in the market beforehand. He made some late headway up the inside rail over the last furlong or so, but never looked like winning and the jury is still out on him. (op 11-4 tchd 4-1)
Brave Ghurka, far from disgraced though unplaced at Windsor on his second outing, made most of the running but he started to hang passing the furlong pole and finished very weakly. He needed this for a mark and may improve for a switch to nurseries. Official explanation: jockey said gelding hung left in straight (op 8-1)
Light The Way, unplaced in his first three starts and rated just 55, had a tongue tie on for the first time and he showed up for a long way, but he eventually faded and looks very moderate. (op 14-1)

6912 BET CHAMPIONS LEAGUE FOOTBALL - BETDAQ MAIDEN AUCTION STKS (DIV II) 7f (P)
2:30 (2:31) (Class 5) 2-Y-O £2,388 (£705; £352) Stalls Low

Form RPR

0 **1** **Sunarise (IRE)**[17] 6477 2-8-10 0 .... RichardHughes 4 80+
(R Hannon) *trckd ldrs: drvn to ld 1f out: kpt on wl: readily* **11/4**[2]

2263 **2** *1 ¼* **Baby Dottie**[13] 6582 2-8-4 74 .... CatherineGannon 6 68
(P M Phelan) *chsd ldrs: rdn 2f out: chsd wnr ins fnl f but no imp* **3/1**[3]

42 **3** *½* **Pan American**[15] 6544 2-8-11 0 .... FergusSweeney 8 74
(P J Makin) *in rr but in tch: rdn: hung lft and styd on fr over 1f out: kpt on ins fnl f: gng on cl home* **5/2**[1]

0 **4** *2 ¾* **Classical Piece (USA)**[20] 6372 2-8-13 0 .... EdwardCreighton 5 69+
(Mrs D J Sanderson) *outpcd in rr: pushed along 1/2-way: hdwy in middle of crse over 1f out: kpt on ins fnl f but nvr nr ldrs* **100/1**

000 **5** *½* **Show Willing (IRE)**[14] 6556 2-8-0 50 ow1 .... MartinLane(5) 10 60
(A P Jarvis) *t.k.h early: chsd ldr: rdn 2f out: slt ld appr fnl f: hdd & wknd sn after* **66/1**

00 **6** *2 ¼* **Tuscan Gold**[20] 6372 2-8-13 0 .... StephenDonohoe 1 62
(Sir Mark Prescott) *s.i.s: in rr: pushed along 1/2-way: rdn and kpt on fnl f but nvr a threat* **25/1**

3 **7** *2* **Gifted Apakay (USA)**[46] 5643 2-8-8 0 .... WilliamBuick 2 53
(E A L Dunlop) *chsd ldrs: pushed along 2f out: n.m.r and wknd over 1f out* **7/2**

06 **8** *3 ¼* **Antoella (IRE)**[21] 6363 2-8-4 0 .... DO'Donohoe 9 40
(Ian Williams) *led tl hdd appr fnl f: wknd qckly* **40/1**

0 **9** *2* **Lady Christie**[47] 5605 2-8-4 0 .... FrancisNorton 3 35
(M Blanshard) *a towards rr* **50/1**

1m 25.99s (1.19) **Going Correction** +0.025s/f (Slow) **9 Ran SP% 113.2**
Speed ratings (Par 95): **94,92,92,88,88 85,83,79,77**
toteswingers: 1&2 £2.90, 1&3 £3.10, 2&3 £1.10 CSF £10.85 TOTE £2.90: £1.30, £1.20, £1.10; EX 11.30.
Owner Mrs J Wood **Bred** Gigginstown House Stud & Lynn Lodge Stud **Trained** East Everleigh, Wilts

FOCUS
Only four mattered according to the market in this and the winning time was 0.18 seconds slower than the first division. The form makes sense and the winner may have more to offer.

NOTEBOOK
Sunarise(IRE), unplaced in the Tattersalls Timeform Fillies' 800 at Newmarket on debut, found this a whole lot easier. She was always travelling well behind the leaders and the only question was whether she would get the gap when she needed it. Fortunately she got one coming to the last furlong and, even though it meant that she made her effort closer to the inside rail than ideal, she found plenty once in front. Still considered green by connections, she may be aimed at the Tattersalls Timeform 3-y-o Trophy at next year's Craven meeting. (op 3-1 tchd 100-30 and 5-2)
Baby Dottie, placed three times from her first four starts and currently rated 74, was trying this trip for the first time. She was inclined to take a keen grip on the outside in a handy position early, but still had every chance all the way up the home straight and never stopped trying. She is more exposed than the winner, but she has the ability to win a race and may be worth a try in a nursery. (tchd 5-2)
Pan American, narrowly denied stepped up to this trip at Warwick last time when in front of the winner of the first division Cat Hunter, had his chance turning for home but hung once into the straight and, although he ran on down the outside, he wasn't doing enough. He now qualifies for a nursery mark. (op 11-4 tchd 100-30)
Classical Piece(USA), green when well beaten on his Kempton debut last month, raced in last place for much of the way but he stayed on well once in line for home and this was a major step forward. (op 66-1)
Show Willing(IRE), well beaten in her first three starts and rated just 50, took a strong hold up with the pace but lasted much longer than might have been expected. She may be worth a try in a nursery off her current modest mark.
Tuscan Gold plugged on without offering a threat, but he now qualifies for a handicap mark and is one to watch out for in that sphere when stepped up to a trip more in line with his breeding.
Gifted Apakay(USA), an encouraging third over a furlong further on debut here last month, was hampered when trying to creep up the inside of the weakening Antoella passing the furlong pole and he is worth another chance. (tchd 4-1)

6913 BET IN RUNNING - BETDAQ MEDIAN AUCTION MAIDEN STKS 6f (P)
3:00 (3:00) (Class 5) 2-Y-O £2,729 (£806; £403) Stalls Low

Form RPR

2 **1** **Oil Strike**[171] 1669 2-9-3 0 .... LukeMorris 2 79+
(P Winkworth) *t.k.h: led tl narrowly hdd over 4f out: pushed along to ld again ins fnl 2f: rdn and hung rt fnl f: comf* **15/8**[1]

0 **2** *1 ¾* **Frequency**[13] 6591 2-9-3 0 .... EddieAhern 4 73+
(E A L Dunlop) *chsd ldrs tl rn wd and lost position ins fnl 2f: styd on wl to take 2nd ins fnl f but no imp on wnr* **5/2**[2]

3 *¾* **Lago Indiano (IRE)** 2-9-3 0 .... JimCrowley 6 71+
(Mrs A J Perrett) *s.i.s: bhd: pushed along and hdwy fr 2f out: styd on to briefly chse wnr jst ins fnl f: one pce nr fin* **9/1**

4533 **4** *2* **My Mandy (IRE)**[9] 6700 2-8-12 63 .... (p) ShaneKelly 3 60
(Ian Williams) *w ldr: led over 4f out: rn wd and hdd ins fnl 2f: nvr a danger after* **10/1**

6352 **5** *2 ¼* **Could It Be Magic**[68] 4933 2-9-0 75 .... (p) JackDean(3) 8 58
(W G M Turner) *chsd ldrs: rdn 1/2-way: wknd fr 2f out* **7/2**[3]

6 2 3/4 **Hot Form** 2-8-12 0 JerryO'Dwyer 5 45
(M Botti) *sn pushed along in rr: rcvrd and in tch 1/2-way: chsd ldrs 2f out: wknd appr fnl f* **12/1**

60 7 11 **Fraamtaaztiic**[18] 6441 2-8-9 0 MCGeran(3) 7 12
(R J Hodges) *a in rr* **100/1**

0 P **Roar Talent (USA)**[24] 6291 2-9-3 0 RobertWinston 1 —
(J R Best) *a bhd: p.u 2f out* **66/1**

1m 12.48s (0.58) **Going Correction** +0.025s/f (Slow) 8 Ran SP% **114.8**
Speed ratings (Par 95): **97,94,93,91,88 84,69,—**
toteswingers: 1&2 £2.20, 1&3 £7.00, 2&3 £10.20 CSF £6.77 TOTE £3.00: £1.70, £1.60, £3.00; EX 10.50.
Owner David Holden **Bred** Cobhall Court Stud **Trained** Chiddingfold, Surrey

FOCUS
An ordinary maiden, but they seemed to go a decent pace. The proximity of the fourth limits the form.

NOTEBOOK
Oil Strike hadn't been seen since going down narrowly on his Goodwood debut in May due to a chipped bone in his foreleg and one or two other problems, but the layoff obviously hadn't done him any harm. Having disputed the lead with My Mandy throughout and racing tight against the inside rail, he had the lead on his own coming to the last furlong. He did hang away to his right in the latter stages and ended up in the centre of the track, but that is no bad thing here and he always had matters under control. He is entitled to step up again from this, but is likely to be put away now. (op 7-4 tchd 2-1)
Frequency ◆, who showed some ability on his Nottingham debut earlier this month when by no means knocked about, travelled very sweetly behind the leaders, but he took time to find his stride once into the straight and by the time he did it was too late. He seems to be improving and should be suited by a return to a more galloping track. (op 3-1)
Lago Indiano(IRE) ◆ ran a debut full of promise, especially as he got messed about soon after the start and found himself well off the pace. Even so, he managed to get himself into a challenging position off the final bend before lack of a recent run took its toll. His sire was a top-class sprinter, but he is a half-brother to five winners on the dam's side including the Irish Oaks-winner Winona, so there is plenty of stamina there and the way he performed suggests that he will appreciate further. (op 8-1)
My Mandy(IRE), by far the most exposed in the field having raced 11 times already and rated 63, making the frame in nine of those, was racing beyond the minimum trip for the first time. She mixed it with the winner until fading inside the last furlong and may not have quite seen out the trip, but lacks anything in the way of scope. (op 8-1)
Could It Be Magic, placed a couple of times in four previous outings on turf, came off the bridle on the outside rounding the home turn and was soon beaten. He isn't progressing and on a line through My Mandy doesn't seem that well treated off a mark of 75 either. (op 9-2)
Hot Form, a half-sister to the 7f winner Maggie The Cat, was too green to do herself justice on this debut even though she managed to give herself a glimmer of a chance against the inside rail once into the straight. (op 14-1 tchd 11-1)

6914 MARKETFORM TEAM D&O (S) STKS 6f (P)
3:30 (3:31) (Class 6) 3-Y-O £2,047 (£604; £302) Stalls Low

Form RPR

005 1 **Athaakeel (IRE)**[25] 6252 3-9-0 60 CatherineGannon 11 64
(R A Harris) *s.i.s: bhd tl rn wd into st and str run centre of crse to ld fnl 110yds: drvn out* **22/1**

1610 2 1 1/2 **Boho Chic**[4] 6825 3-9-0 65 DO'Donohoe 7 59
(George Baker) *trckd ldrs: drvn to ld appr fnl f: hdd and one pce fnl 110yds* **13/2[3]**

F100 3 shd **Romantic Queen**[6] 6782 3-8-9 65 (t) MatthewDavies(5) 10 59
(George Baker) *mid-div: pushed along and styd on to chal 1f out: styd on same pce ins fnl f* **9/1**

0434 4 1 1/2 **Bold Ring**[17] 6492 3-9-0 60 EdwardCreighton 4 54
(E J Creighton) *in rr: n.m.r over 3f out: hdwy in centre of crse over 1f out: styd on ins fnl f but nvr gng pce to be competitive* **6/1[2]**

005 5 1 3/4 **True Decision**[22] 6349 3-9-5 58 JamesDoyle 2 53
(S Kirk) *in rr: pushed along and stl last over 1f out: kpt on u.p ins fnl f but nvr a threat* **9/1**

0366 6 1/2 **Running Flush (USA)**[17] 6492 3-9-0 57 LukeMorris 3 47
(J R Gask) *chsd ldrs: rdn and one pce over 2f out: styd on again fnl f* **11/2[1]**

3150 7 nk **Hatman Jack (IRE)**[9] 6699 3-9-5 60 GeorgeBaker 6 51
(B G Powell) *hld up in rr: pushed along ins fnl 2f: styd on same pce* **10/1**

3020 8 1 1/2 **Kings Ace (IRE)**[30] 6140 3-9-5 60 (v) JimCrowley 9 46
(A P Jarvis) *chsd ldrs: rdn over 2f out: wknd ins fnl 2f* **11/1**

0444 9 hd **Flamsteed (IRE)**[48] 5581 3-9-5 64 MartinDwyer 5 45
(M Quinn) *w ldr: slt advantage fr 4f out: rdn 2f out: hdd appr fnl f: sn btn* **11/2[1]**

4022 10 6 **King's Sabre**[18] 6442 3-9-0 63 FrancisNorton 1 21
(R C Guest) *slt ld 2f: styd w ldr tl wknd 2f out: hung lft fr over 1f out* **7/1**

1m 12.36s (0.46) **Going Correction** +0.025s/f (Slow) 10 Ran SP% **112.7**
Speed ratings (Par 99): **97,95,94,92,90 89,89,87,87,79**
toteswingers: 1&2 £36.00, 1&3 £47.50, 2&3 £4.30 CSF £153.42 TOTE £21.90: £7.30, £2.60, £4.10; EX 203.10.There was no bid for the winner.
Owner Mrs J Bloomfield **Bred** Shadwell Estate Company Limited **Trained** Earlswood, Monmouths

FOCUS
A very moderate seller and the form probably amounts to little. The pace was decent enough though, with a three-way battle for the early lead.

6915 THREE BRIDGES H'CAP 6f (P)
4:00 (4:01) (Class 5) (0-70,70) 3-Y-O+ £3,070 (£906; £453) Stalls Low

Form RPR

6033 1 **Perfect Act**[26] 6230 4-9-4 68 AdamKirby 10 78
(C G Cox) *t.k.h: hld up in rr: hdwy 2f out: swtchd lft to ins rail and qcknd to ld fnl 75yds: drvn out* **13/2[3]**

1250 2 1/2 **Sister Clement (IRE)**[67] 5007 3-9-5 70 RichardHughes 4 78+
(R Hannon) *trckd ldrs: shkn up and n.m.r over 1f out: qcknd ins fnl f: fin wl to take 2nd cl home but no imp on wnr* **9/2[1]**

2240 3 3/4 **Quasi Congaree (GER)**[11] 6635 3-9-2 67 (t) CatherineGannon 3 73
(I A Wood) *led: rdn 2f out: kpt slt advantage tl hdd and outpcd fnl 75yds: lost 2nd cl home* **16/1**

3265 4 1/2 **Billberry**[8] 6726 4-9-3 67 (t) JimCrowley 11 74+
(S C Williams) *in rr: drvn and hdwy over 1f out: styng on wl fnl f whn nt clr run cl home: nt rcvr* **11/2[2]**

024 5 hd **Space Station**[17] 6476 3-9-5 70 TonyCulhane 5 74
(S Dow) *chsd ldr: rdn over 2f out: no ex fnl 75yds* **7/1**

0062 6 hd **Onceaponatime (IRE)**[18] 6458 4-9-3 67 RobertWinston 2 70
(M D Squance) *chsd ldrs: rdn 2f out: styd chsng ldrs tl wknd fnl 75yds* **8/1**

206 7 1 1/4 **Kyllachy Storm**[37] 5901 5-9-2 66 GeorgeBaker 7 65
(R J Hodges) *sn chsng ldrs: rdn over 2f out: wknd ins fnl f* **12/1**

6500 8 1 1/2 **Musical Script (USA)**[8] 6726 6-9-5 69 (b) LPKeniry 6 63
(Mouse Hamilton-Fairley) *t.k.h early: chsd ldrs: rdn over 2f out: wknd ins fnl f* **16/1**

6450 9 shd **Gentle Guru**[24] 6294 5-9-3 67 JamesDoyle 8 61
(R T Phillips) *chsd ldrs: rdn over 3f out: wknd appr fnl f* **11/1**

400 10 1 1/4 **Requisite**[5] 6791 4-9-0 69 MartinLane(5) 12 59
(I A Wood) *sn outpcd* **11/1**

2213 11 shd **Diamond Surprise**[236] 689 3-9-3 68 IvanLopez 9 58
(R J Smith) *mid-div: pushed along 1/2-way: sn outpcd* **28/1**

0605 12 1 3/4 **Song Of Praise**[26] 6230 3-9-3 68 FrancisNorton 1 52
(M Blanshard) *mid-div 1/2-way: sn rdn and wknd* **16/1**

1m 11.65s (-0.25) **Going Correction** +0.025s/f (Slow)
WFA 3 from 4yo+ 1lb 12 Ran SP% **116.0**
Speed ratings (Par 103): **102,101,100,99,99 99,97,95,95,93 93,91**
toteswingers: 1&2 £4.50, 1&3 £13.70, 2&3 £20.70 CSF £34.95 CT £457.10 TOTE £7.20: £2.20, £2.30, £5.70; EX 26.80.
Owner Dr Bridget Drew & E E Dedman **Bred** Howard Barton Stud **Trained** Lambourn, Berks

FOCUS
This was a tight little handicap with just 3lb separating the top and bottom weights. It was also a typically competitive Lingfield sprint with racing room at a premium and a bunched finish. The pace was strong and the winning time was 0.71 seconds faster than the seller, suggesting the form is reasonably sound.
Quasi Congaree(GER) Official explanation: jockey said colt yung right
Billberry ◆ Official explanation: jockey said gelding denied a clear run

6916 BETDAQ ON 0870 178 1221 H'CAP 5f (P)
4:30 (4:30) (Class 5) (0-75,75) 3-Y-O+ £3,412 (£1,007; £504) Stalls High

Form RPR

1024 1 **Step It Up (IRE)**[10] 6666 5-8-13 70 SJCraine 7 83+
(J R Boyle) *trckd ldrs: rdn to ld appr fnl f: sn in command: comf* **11/4[1]**

2215 2 1 3/4 **Brandywell Boy (IRE)**[19] 6422 6-8-13 70 RichardThomas 5 73
(D J S Ffrench Davis) *in rr: pushed along and hdwy on outside fnl f: str run ins fnl f to take 2nd last stride but no ch w wnr* **8/1[3]**

0040 3 nse **Chosen Son (IRE)**[8] 6726 3-8-4 61 WilliamBuick 3 64
(P J O'Gorman) *in tch: rdn and hdwy towards outer 1f out: styd on to chse wnr ins fnl f: no imp and lost 2nd last stride* **10/1**

0050 4 3/4 **Kyle (IRE)**[11] 6635 5-8-8 65 LPKeniry 9 65
(C R Dore) *in rr: hdwy on outside over 1f out: styd on wl ins fnl f: gng on cl home but nvr gng pce to trble wnr* **14/1**

012 5 1/2 **Poppanan (USA)**[18] 6444 3-9-1 72 TonyCulhane 8 71
(S Dow) *in rr: hdwy on outside over 1f out: styd on ins fnl f but nvr a threat* **13/2[2]**

5150 6 1 **Come On Buckers (IRE)**[17] 6492 3-7-13 61 oh1 SophieDoyle(5) 6 56
(E J Creighton) *chsd ldrs: rdn over 2f out: no ex ins fnl f* **22/1**

42-0 7 nk **Master Lightfoot**[11] 6632 3-9-4 75 AdamKirby 10 69
(W R Swinburn) *sn led: narrowly hdd 2f out: styd upsides and ev ch over 1f out: wknd ins fnl f* **13/2[2]**

003 8 1 **Love You Louis**[41] 5777 3-9-1 72 (b) EddieAhern 2 62
(J R Jenkins) *chsd ldrs: rdn over 2f out: wknd 1f out* **11/1**

0450 9 1 3/4 **Rio Royale (IRE)**[35] 5968 3-8-9 66 JimCrowley 1 50
(Mrs A J Perrett) *in rr: sme hdwy on ins over 1f out: nvr quite rchd ldrs and wknd ins fnl f* **12/1**

0030 10 2 **Ten Down**[28] 6186 4-8-5 62 MartinDwyer 4 39
(M Quinn) *w ldr: slt advantage fr 2f out tl hdd & wknd qckly appr fnl f: sn btn* **13/2[2]**

58.83 secs (0.03) **Going Correction** +0.025s/f (Slow) 10 Ran SP% **113.9**
Speed ratings (Par 103): **100,97,97,95,95 93,93,91,88,85**
toteswingers: 1&2 £3.60, 1&3 £6.90, 2&3 £15.50 CSF £24.23 CT £189.92 TOTE £3.30: £1.10, £3.10, £4.30; EX 32.90.
Owner The Vine Associates **Bred** David Fitzgerald **Trained** Epsom, Surrey

FOCUS
A disputed early lead produced a strong pace but the form is not that solid with the third the best guide.

6917 SPELDHURST H'CAP (DIV I) 1m 4f (P)
5:00 (5:01) (Class 6) (0-60,66) 3-Y-O+ £1,706 (£503; £252) Stalls Low

Form RPR

1 1 **Mondego (GER)**[4] 6831 7-9-5 61 6ex MatthewDavies(5) 6 69+
(George Baker) *towards rr: clsd on ldrs over 4f out: str run on outside: hung lft and led 1f out: rdn and fnd ex whn chal fnl 75yds* **4/1[2]**

4130 2 1/2 **Our Kes (IRE)**[10] 6668 7-9-5 56 IanMongan 12 63
(P Howling) *in rr: hdwy on outside wl over 1f out: str run ins fnl f and tk 2nd cl home but a jst hld by wnr* **14/1**

0400 3 1/2 **Kames Park (IRE)**[58] 5294 7-9-5 56 JimCrowley 13 62
(R C Guest) *stdd and swtchd lft to ins s: in rr: gd hdwy on outside wl over 1f out: chsd wnr and carried lft ins fnl f: almost on terms fnl 100yds: sn no ex and lost 2nd cl home* **11/1**

662 4 2 3/4 **D'Artagnans Dream**[18] 6445 3-9-1 59 (b) CatherineGannon 2 65+
(G D Blake) *in rr: stl bhd whn effrt and nt clr run ins fnl 2f: styd on wl fnl f: gng on cl home but nvr a threat* **7/2[1]**

3230 5 2 3/4 **Prince Charlemagne (IRE)**[24] 6288 6-9-9 60 GeorgeBaker 5 57
(G L Moore) *chsd ldrs: rdn over 2f out: wknd appr fnl f* **7/1[3]**

0006 6 1/2 **Dayanara (USA)**[18] 6445 3-8-8 52 (b[1]) LukeMorris 10 49
(C G Cox) *led 1f: chsd ldrs: rdn 3f out: styd pressing ldrs tl wknd ins fnl f* **16/1**

5020 7 hd **Diktalina**[20] 6384 3-8-7 51 MartinDwyer 14 47
(W R Muir) *led after 1f: hdd 1f out and wknd qckly* **8/1**

2440 8 1 1/4 **Fantasy Ride**[6] 6770 7-8-7 49 SimonPearce(5) 4 43+
(J Pearce) *in rr: pushed along over 2f out: styng on whn nt clr run over 1f out: kpt on again fnl 100yds* **9/1**

5060 9 nk **Tiffany Lady**[18] 6446 3-7-9 46 oh1 RyanPowell(7) 11 40
(M D I Usher) *chsd ldrs: rdn 3f out: wknd appr fnl f* **66/1**

000 10 1 **Innactualfact**[9] 6705 3-9-2 60 (p) ShaneKelly 15 52
(L A Dace) *chsd ldrs: ev ch 2f out: wknd over 1f out* **40/1**

02 11 shd **Arabian Silk (IRE)**[38] 5873 3-8-3 52 MartinLane(5) 3 44
(D M Simcock) *in tch: rdn 3f out: wknd 2f out* **11/1**

06/0 12 3 3/4 **Yellow Ridge (IRE)**[3] 6859 6-8-9 46 oh1 (t) JerryO'Dwyer 9 32
(Luke Comer, Ire) *chsd ldrs: wknd wl over 1f out* **33/1**

5006 13 9 **Bridge Of Fermoy (IRE)**[122] 3158 4-8-11 48 (p) SamHitchcott 7 20
(D C O'Brien) *in tch: rdn and hdwy 7f out: nvr rchd ldrs and wknd over 2f out* **25/1**

-000 **14** *14* **Fantastic Morning**[26] 6226 5-8-13 **50**....................(p) TravisBlock 8 —
(F Jordan) *a bhd* **66/1**
2m 35.98s (2.98) **Going Correction** +0.025s/f (Slow)
WFA 3 from 4yo+ 7lb **14** Ran SP% **117.3**
Speed ratings (Par 101): **91,90,90,88,86 86,86,85,85,84 84,81,75,66**
toteswingers: 1&2 £9.30, 1&3 £9.80, 2&3 £21.00 CSF £55.00 CT £571.70 TOTE £4.30: £1.70, £3.20, £3.60; EX 59.40.
Owner Lady Forwood & Partners **Bred** S Pavenstedt And J Th Pavenstedt **Trained** Moreton Morrell, Warwicks
■ Stewards' Enquiry : Matthew Davies three-day ban: careless riding (Nov 3-5)
FOCUS
A modest but competitive middle-distance handicap run at just a fair gallop. The first four all came from off the pace and the placed horses are rated close to recent form.
D'Artagnans Dream Official explanation: jockey said gelding was slowly away

6918 SPELDHURST H'CAP (DIV II) 1m 4f (P)
5:30 (5:31) (Class 6) (0-60,60) 3-Y-O+ **£1,706** (£503; £252) **Stalls** Low

Form RPR
0601 **1** **Giant Sequoia (USA)**[20] 6371 5-9-9 **60**....................(t) EddieAhern 14 76+
(Jane Chapple-Hyam) *hld up in rr: stdy hdwy fr 5f out: chsd ldr towards outside over 1f out: qcknd ahd ins fnl f: comf* **5/2**[1]
0002 **2** *2 ½* **It's Josr**[6] 6770 4-8-12 **49**....................(b) CatherineGannon 13 58
(I A Wood) *in rr: hdwy and rdn 3f out: str run on outside over 1f out and kpt on wl fnl f to take 2nd cl home but nvr any ch w wnr* **8/1**
-501 **3** *nk* **My Les**[5] 6788 3-8-7 **51** 6ex.................... PaulDoe 11 60
(Jim Best) *chsd ldrs: led over 2f out: sn rdn: hdd jst ins fnl f: sn no ch w wnr: lost 2nd cl home* **11/2**[2]
6540 **4** *3 ½* **Good Buy Dubai (USA)**[8] 6742 3-8-11 **55**....................(v[1]) TonyCulhane 5 58
(J R Best) *in rr: hdwy 4f out: racd towards outside fr wl over 1f out: one pce ins fnl f* **8/1**
-310 **5** *2 ¼* **Ardmaddy (IRE)**[13] 6584 5-9-6 **57**....................(b) GeorgeBaker 15 56
(G L Moore) *chsd ldrs: wnt 2nd and no imp over 2f out: wknd over 1f out* **8/1**
6500 **6** *6* **Zalkani (IRE)**[9] 6704 9-9-0 **56**.................... SimonPearce(5) 3 46
(J Pearce) *in rr tl hdwy fr ins fnl 2f: fin wl but nvr anywhere nr ldrs* **18/1**
060 **7** *½* **Jezza**[42] 5751 3-8-8 **52**.................... NickyMackay 9 41
(Karen George) *mid-div whn drvn along fr over 4f out: wknd 2f out* **80/1**
0610 **8** *hd* **New World Order (IRE)**[25] 6256 5-9-9 **60**....................(t) RobertWinston 2 49
(Edgar Byrne) *sn led: hdd over 3f out: wknd over 2f out* **15/2**[3]
0600 **9** *2* **Suhailah**[9] 6705 3-8-11 **55**....................(p) LukeMorris 8 40
(M J Attwater) *chsd ldrs: rdn along after 4f: styd chsng ldrs tl wknd ins fnl 3f* **100/1**
6063 **10** *7* **Champagne Fizz (IRE)**[18] 6445 3-8-13 **57**.................... IanMongan 4 31
(Miss Jo Crowley) *chsd ldr: led over 3f out tl over 2f out: sn wknd* **12/1**
00-0 **11** *3 ¼* **The Beat Is On**[26] 6225 3-7-11 **46** oh1.................... AmyBaker(5) 12 15
(A W Carroll) *in tch to 1/2-way* **100/1**
0640 **12** *15* **Divertimenti (IRE)**[13] 6588 5-9-5 **56**.................... LPKeniry 10 1
(C R Dore) *chsd ldrs tl wknd qckly over 3f out* **33/1**
0016 **13** *1 ½* **Arlene Phillips**[18] 6446 3-8-3 **47**.................... WilliamBuick 6 —
(R Hannon) *sn bhd* **12/1**
5-0 **14** *13* **Honkey Tonk Tony (IRE)**[3] 6860 4-9-1 **52**.................... JerryO'Dwyer 7 —
(Luke Comer, Ire) *chsd ldrs over a m* **33/1**
4500 **15** *23* **Summer Bounty**[134] 2762 13-8-11 **48** oh1 ow2.................... TravisBlock 1 —
(F Jordan) *a in rr* **100/1**
2m 30.87s (-2.13) **Going Correction** +0.025s/f (Slow)
WFA 3 from 4yo+ 7lb **15** Ran SP% **119.8**
Speed ratings (Par 101): **108,106,106,103,102 98,97,97,96,91 89,79,78,70,54**
toteswingers: 1&2 £6.60, 1&3 £3.80, 2&3 £11.60 CSF £21.77 CT £102.82 TOTE £3.00: £1.60, £2.50, £2.30; EX 20.50 Place 6 £79.23, Place 5 £28.25..
Owner Mrs Jane Chapple-Hyam **Bred** Strategy Bloodstock **Trained** Newmarket, Suffolk
FOCUS
They seemed to go no pace at all early on here, but they must have really quickened up in the second half of the contest as the winning time was over five seconds faster than the first division. Again those held up were favoured and the front five pulled clear, suggesting the form is solid.
T/Plt: £66.90 to a £1 stake. Pool: £60,061.65. 655.31 winning tickets. T/Qpdt: £40.60 to a £1 stake. Pool: £4,195.53. 76.40 winning tickets. ST

6032 YARMOUTH (L-H)
Tuesday, October 20
OFFICIAL GOING: Good to firm (good in places; 7.2)
Wind: strong, against Weather: bright but breezy

6919 CRYSTAL CLEANING (S) STKS 1m 3f 101y
1:50 (1:51) (Class 6) 3-Y-O **£1,942** (£578; £288; £144) **Stalls** Low

Form RPR
6204 **1** **Extremely So**[58] 5286 3-8-7 57.................... ChrisCatlin 5 56
(P J McBride) *chsd ldng pair: hdwy to trck ldr ent fnl 3f: led over 2f out: clr and drvn over 1f out: in command and pushed out fnl f* **11/4**[1]
6404 **2** *2 ¾* **Secret Desert**[5] 6788 3-8-5 63.................... LauraPike(7) 1 57
(D M Simcock) *dwlt: hld up in rr: rdn along 3f out: swtchd to outer and hdwy jst over 2f out: chsd clr wnr and edgd lft over 1f out: no imp* **4/1**[2]
0000 **3** *5* **Bromhead (USA)**[7] 6758 3-9-5 51....................(t[1]) SaleemGolam 12 55
(Mrs C A Dunnett) *t.k.h: chsd ldrs: drvn ent fnl 2f: modest 3rd and wl hld fnl f: plugged on* **40/1**
2056 **4** *1 ¼* **Rose Of Coma (IRE)**[51] 5470 3-8-7 48.................... DavidKenny(7) 8 48
(A G Juckes) *hld up in tch in midfield: hdwy 4f out: chsd ldrs and rdn 2f out: fnd little and btn over 1f out* **14/1**
0040 **5** *1* **Yeoman Of England (IRE)**[14] 6570 3-8-12 52.................... AlanMunro 11 44
(C F Wall) *t.k.h: hld up in tch in midfield: pushed along and effrt 3f out: rdn and no prog fnl 2f* **10/1**
-366 **6** *hd* **Game Roseanna**[31] 6098 3-8-7 55.................... LiamJones 2 39
(W M Brisbourne) *bhd: rdn after 3f out: plugged on past btn horses fr over 1f out: n.d* **9/1**
0030 **7** *1 ¼* **Flirty (IRE)**[18] 6445 3-8-0 44.................... NoelGarbutt(7) 3 37
(Rae Guest) *led: rdn 3f out: hdd over 2f out: steadily wknd* **12/1**
4535 **8** *3 ¼* **Intikama (IRE)**[56] 5327 3-8-7 60....................(b[1]) JimmyQuinn 7 31
(M H Tompkins) *dwlt: sn pushed up and in tch: rdn and strugging 4f out: wl bhd fnl 2f* **7/1**[3]
0430 **9** *1* **Flying Phoebe**[23] 6310 3-8-10 52 ow3.................... TGMcLaughlin 9 32
(Mrs L Stubbs) *stdd s: hld up wl in rr: rdn and no prog 3f out: n.d* **11/1**
450 **10** *nk* **Rebel Prince (IRE)**[56] 5328 3-8-10 46 ow3.................... JamieJones(5) 6 37
(M G Quinlan) *stdd s: hld up wl in rr: rdn and effrt on outer 3f out: n.d* **22/1**

0000 **11** *¾* **Sampower Quin (IRE)**[39] 5838 3-8-12 51....................(b[1]) DNolan 10 33
(D Carroll) *chsd ldr tl ent fnl 3f: sn wknd u.p: bhd and eased ins fnl f* **33/1**
0406 **12** *1 ½* **Wicklewood**[35] 5972 3-8-12 45.................... MickyFenton 4 30
(Mrs C A Dunnett) *in tch in midfield: rdn and dropped to rr 4f out: no ch after* **25/1**
2m 28.47s (-0.23) **Going Correction** -0.025s/f (Good) **12** Ran SP% **114.5**
Speed ratings (Par 99): **99,97,93,92,91 91,90,88,87,87 86,85**
toteswingers: 1&2 £2.70, 1&3 £19.90, 2&3 £26.10 CSF £11.90 TOTE £3.00: £1.60, £1.20, £6.20; EX 12.50 TRIFECTA Not won..There was no bid for the winner.
Owner N Davies **Bred** Kirtlington Stud And Gilridge Bloodstock **Trained** Newmarket, Suffolk
■ Stewards' Enquiry : Laura Pike one-day ban: careless riding (Nov 3)
FOCUS
A very poor affair and the winner did not need to match earlier course form to score.

6920 EUROPEAN BREEDERS' FUND MAIDEN FILLIES' STKS (DIV I) 1m 3y
2:20 (2:25) (Class 5) 2-Y-O **£4,100** (£1,227; £613; £306; £152) **Stalls** High

Form RPR
1 **Hymnsheet** 2-9-0 0.................... RyanMoore 2 83+
(Sir Michael Stoute) *s.i.s: hld up in tch in rr: hdwy 3f out: pushed along to chse ldr jst ins fnl f: led fnl 100yds: r.o wl* **10/3**[1]
0 **2** *1* **Thousandkissesdeep (IRE)**[50] 5498 2-9-0 0.................... RichardMullen 6 77
(J H M Gosden) *led for 2f: chsd ldr after tl led again 2f out: sn rdn: kpt on wl tl hdd and no ex fnl 100yds* **22/1**
3 *1 ¼* **Radio Wave** 2-9-0 0.................... RobertHavlin 7 78+
(J H M Gosden) *s.i.s: bhd: nt clr run ent fnl 2f: stl plenty to do over 1f out: hdwy ent fnl f: styd on fnl f: gng on fin* **11/1**
34 **4** *1* **Miss Antonia (IRE)**[24] 6284 2-9-0 0.................... TPQueally 9 75+
(H R A Cecil) *in tch: short of room and hmpd ent fnl 2f: hdwy between horses over 1f out: kpt on same pce ins fnl f* **5/1**[2]
5 *½* **Strictly Lambada** 2-9-0 0.................... JimmyFortune 8 71+
(J H M Gosden) *in tch: effrt to chse ldr wl over 1f out: sn rdn: wknd fnl 150yds* **12/1**
3 **6** *¾* **Granite Girl**[66] 5029 2-8-11 0.................... AndreaAtzeni(3) 5 69
(P J McBride) *in tch in midfield: effrt to chse ldng pair and rdn over 1f out: wknd ins fnl f* **10/1**[3]
7 *nk* **Towbaat** 2-9-0 0.................... PhilipRobinson 1 69+
(M A Jarvis) *s.i.s: bhd and rn green: grad crossed towards stands' rail: nudged along and styd on steadily fnl f: nvr trbld ldrs* **12/1**
8 *3 ¼* **Pleasant Way (IRE)** 2-9-0 0.................... TedDurcan 4 61
(D R Lanigan) *t.k.h: hld up in tch in midfield: rdn and unable qck ent fnl 2f: wl hld fnl f* **50/1**
6 **9** *½* **Nefyn**[37] 5906 2-9-0 0.................... DarryllHolland 3 60+
(W R Muir) *t.k.h: hld up in tch towards rr: rdn and no prog ent fnl 2f: plugged on same pce after* **33/1**
0 **10** *1* **Denton Ryal**[19] 6436 2-8-7 0.................... MJMurphy(7) 12 58
(S W James) *in tch: hdwy to chse ldrs 1/2-way: rdn and wknd wl over 1f out* **200/1**
11 *3* **Up At Last** 2-9-0 0.................... MichaelHills 11 54+
(W J Haggas) *stdd s: t.k.h: hld up in tch: effrt and rdn over 2f out: wknd wl over 1f out* **25/1**
00 **12** *¾* **Mme De Stael**[7] 6759 2-9-0 0.................... SebSanders 14 50
(Sir Mark Prescott) *uns rdr and galloped off on way to s: in tch in rr: pushed along 3f out: no hdwy* **100/1**
13 *2 ¼* **Twilight Tear** 2-9-0 0.................... HayleyTurner 10 45
(M L W Bell) *chsd ldr for 2f: styd chsng ldrs tl wknd qckly ent fnl 2f* **16/1**
24 **14** *2 ¼* **Arte Viva (USA)**[19] 6436 2-9-0 0.................... KFallon 13 46+
(G A Butler) *t.k.h: chsd ldrs tl led 6f out tl hung lft and hdd 2f out: sn wknd: eased ins fnl f* **10/3**[1]
1m 44.25s (3.65) **Going Correction** +0.225s/f (Good) **14** Ran SP% **116.1**
Speed ratings (Par 92): **90,89,87,86,86 85,85,81,81,80 77,76,74,72**
toteswingers: 1&2 £22.40, 1&3 £11.30, 2&3 £45.80 CSF £85.16 TOTE £3.90: £1.80, £6.90, £4.70; EX 86.80 TRIFECTA Not won..
Owner Cheveley Park Stud **Bred** Cheveley Park Stud Ltd **Trained** Newmarket, Suffolk
FOCUS
Despite the modest early pace, this is a fillies' maiden that should throw up plenty of future winners. The fourth helps set the level.
NOTEBOOK
Hymnsheet ◆ responded to pressure nearing the 2f marker and was always going to get up in the closing stages to post a winning debut. A half-sister to the high-class Chorist, this trip looked plenty far enough on breeding but she evidently stays well. Another 2f shouldn't pose her any problems next season and her 3-y-o debut will be eagerly anticipated. (tchd 11-4 and 4-1)
Thousandkissesdeep(IRE) had disappointed on her debut 50 days earlier, but was sent off as favourite that day and she showed her true colours here with a solid effort from the front. There should be an opening for her this term.
Radio Wave ◆ has a lovely staying pedigree, being out of an Ebor winner, and did not go unbacked for this racecourse debut. She kept on most promisingly albeit all too late in the day, and should improve a great deal for the run. She is one to side with next time out. (op 20-1)
Miss Antonia(IRE) had made the frame on her two previous runs and again came in for solid support. She got hampered 3f out and lost vital momentum, before staying on with purpose after getting reorganised inside the final furlong. The best of this daughter of Antonius Pius has yet to be seen. Official explanation: jockey said filly suffered interference in running (tchd 9-2 and 11-2)
Strictly Lambada, a half-sister to this year's progressive 3-y-o stayer Yankee Doodle, was the number one from her yard according to jockey bookings. She lacked a gear change when it mattered most, but still turned in a nice debut effort and is sure to be sharper with the experience behind her. (op 14-1)
Granite Girl, third on debut at Newmarket 66 days previously, got outstayed by the principals over this longer trip yet still posted an improved effort. She should be getting off the mark before too long and a drop back to 7f should prove ideal in the short term. (op 12-1)
Towbaat, half-sister to a useful miler, proved distinctly green on this introduction and it is a good bet she will get closer on her next assignment. (tchd 14-1)
Arte Viva(USA), ponied down to the start early, proved keen early on and, after pulling her way to a share of the lead, was taken over for a solo on the stands' rail. She eventually dropped right out and this has to rate as very disappointing. Official explanation: jockey said filly ran too freely (op 5-2 tchd 7-2)

6921 EUROPEAN BREEDERS' FUND MAIDEN FILLIES' STKS (DIV (II) 1m 3y
2:50 (2:56) (Class 5) 2-Y-O **£4,100** (£1,227; £613; £306; £152) **Stalls** High

Form RPR
1 **Principal Role (USA)** 2-9-0 0.................... TPQueally 8 80+
(H R A Cecil) *rrd as stalls opened and slowly away: hld up in rr: swtchd rt and smooth hdwy over 2f out: pushed into narrow ld ent fnl f: rdn and hld on wl fnl 100yds* **5/1**[3]
2 *hd* **Tomodachi (IRE)** 2-8-11 0.................... AndreaAtzeni(3) 13 78+
(M Botti) *t.k.h: hld up in tch: hdwy to chse ldrs 2f out: rdn and ev ch whn racd awkwardly 1f out: edging lft but kpt on fnl f: a jst hld* **66/1**

3 **3** 3/4 **Meeznah (USA)**[73] 4797 2-9-0 0........................ TedDurcan 12 76
(D R Lanigan) *chsd ldr tl led 2f out: sn rdn: hdd narrowly 1f out: carried sltly lft and no ex fnl 150yds* **11/4**[1]

0 **4** shd **Wulfrida (IRE)**[32] 6066 2-9-0 0........................ DavidProbert 6 76+
(J R Fanshawe) *chsd ldng trio: rdn whn short of room and swtchd lft ent fnl f: kpt on wl but nt quite pce to chal* **18/1**

5 nse **Mujdeya** 2-9-0 0........................ RHills 10 79+
(J H M Gosden) *s.i.s: hld up in rr: hdwy jst over 2f out: nt clr run and swtchd 2f out: sn swtchd rt and hdwy to chse ldrs 1f out: pushed along and kpt on steadily: nt rch ldrs* **15/2**

6 5 **Choice** 2-9-0 0........................ RyanMoore 14 67+
(Sir Michael Stoute) *s.i.s: rn green in rr: pushed along 1/2-way: hdwy and in tch 2f out: no prog and btn over 1f out* **12/1**

6 **7** 1/2 **Aktia (IRE)**[24] 6284 2-9-0 0........................ KFallon 5 65+
(L M Cumani) *in tch in midfield: pushed along 1/2-way: edging out rt and hdwy over 2f out: chsd ldrs and drvn 2f out: wknd over 1f out* **4/1**[2]

0 **8** 1 1/4 **Child Of Our Time (IRE)**[14] 6567 2-9-0 0........................ AlanMunro 2 61
(P W Chapple-Hyam) *hld up in tch towards rr: effrt over 2f out: rdn and no hdwy 2f out* **17/2**

635 **9** 4 1/2 **La Ville Lumiere (USA)**[37] 5906 2-8-11 68........................ AhmedAjtebi(3) 7 53
(Saeed Bin Suroor) *chsd ldr tl over 2f out: sn rdn and wknd* **14/1**

10 3 **Empress Leizu (IRE)** 2-9-0 0........................ TGMcLaughlin 9 44+
(E A L Dunlop) *a towards rr: rdn over 4f out: wl bhd fnl 2f* **100/1**

000 **11** 1 3/4 **Motrice**[19] 6436 2-9-0 0........................ SebSanders 4 40
(Sir Mark Prescott) *in tch tl struggling u.p over 2f out: wl bhd fnl 2f* **40/1**

12 nk **Cardossi** 2-9-0 0........................ HayleyTurner 1 40
(M L W Bell) *s.i.s: a bhd: struggling 1/2-way* **33/1**

13 3/4 **Choir Solo** 2-9-0 0........................(b[1]) RobertHavlin 11 38
(J H M Gosden) *led tl 2f out: sn wknd: wl bhd over 1f out* **33/1**

1m 42.01s (1.41) **Going Correction** +0.225s/f (Good) **13** Ran SP% **116.1**
Speed ratings (Par 92): **101,100,100,99,99 94,94,93,88,85 83,83,82**
toteswingers: 1&2 £50.50, 1&3 £3.00, 2&3 £36.60 CSF £316.29 TOTE £6.30: £1.70, £16.60, £1.70; EX 293.90 TRIFECTA Not won..
Owner K Abdulla **Bred** Juddmonte Farms Inc **Trained** Newmarket, Suffolk

FOCUS
This second division was run at a stronger pace, yet produced a blanket finish. It is another race that should prove informative with the first five drawing clear.

NOTEBOOK
Principal Role(USA) ◆ went in at the first time of asking and completed the task in taking fashion. She looked up against it after rearing as the gates went back and lost ground, but as the race developed she came there going easily on the near side. Once asked to win the race she put her head down and obviously rates a good bit better than the bare margin. Her dam has now produced seven winners and the pick of her progeny to date has been Midships, who developed into a classy performer at up to 1m6f after being sent to the US. A stiffer test will be right up her street next term and it wouldn't be surprising to see this well-regarded filly return next season in something like the Lingfield Oaks Trial. While her sire isn't the greatest stamina influence for 1m4f, her dam's side offers plenty of hope on that front. (op 13-2 tchd 9-2)
Tomodachi(IRE) ◆ posted a big effort on her racecourse bow and looks a lovely prospect. Her pedigree suggests 1m is too far for her, but she got every yard and considering she was sent off at odds of 66/1 there should be a lot of improvement in her. (tchd 50-1)
Meeznah(USA) set the standard on her debut third to subsequent Group 3 winner Tabassum, but had been off for 73 days since then. She probably ran very close to that form over this extra furlong, so represents a decent benchmark. (op 5-2 tchd 3-1)
Wulfrida(IRE) ◆, from an in-form stable, stepped up markedly on the level of her Newmarket debut and had clearly come on a bundle for that run. She is progressive and shouldn't remain a maiden for long. Official explanation: jockey said filly was denied a clear run (op 16-1 tchd 20-1)
Mujdeya ◆, whose stable sent out the second, third and fourth in the first division, would have probably won this had she not endured a troubled passage. She caught the eye off the pace, but as the first pair came over to the near side she was forced to stay central and by the time she hit top gear it was all too late. Being by Linamix an easier surface will probably suit her best and, another sure to benefit from further next season, she should soon find compensation. (op 8-1)
Choice, representing the connections that took the first division, ran too green and lacked the pace to land a telling blow. The betting suggested this would be needed, however, and this well-bred filly should leave the form behind as she matures. (op 8-1)
Aktia(IRE) was backed to step up on her debut sixth at Haydock where she ran green pretty much throughout. She broke a lot better this time, but couldn't find any extra in between the final 2f. (op 5-1 tchd 11-2)

6922 EUROPEAN BREEDERS' FUND MAIDEN STKS 6f 3y
3:20 (3:25) (Class 5) 2-Y-O **£3,784** (£1,132; £566; £283; £141) **Stalls** High

Form RPR

2 **1** **Rule Of Nature**[21] 6363 2-8-12 0........................ RyanMoore 2 77+
(Sir Michael Stoute) *chsd ldrs: effrt to chal 2f out: rdn to ld over 1f out: styd on wl u.p to assert fnl 100yds* **5/6**[1]

30 **2** 1 **Dherghaam (IRE)**[32] 6061 2-9-3 0........................ RHills 5 79+
(E A L Dunlop) *led: rdn wl over 1f out: hdd narrowly over 1f out: kpt on gamely tl no ex and btn fnl 100yds* **4/1**[2]

04 **3** 2 1/2 **Tewin Wood**[10] 6679 2-9-3 0........................ TPQueally 1 72
(A Bailey) *chsd ldr tl 2f out: sn drvn and outpcd by ldng pair: kpt on to hold 3rd towards fin* **11/1**[3]

60 **4** nk **Midwestern (USA)**[13] 6591 2-9-3 0........................ HayleyTurner 8 71+
(M L W Bell) *bhd: sme prog over 2f out: kpt on steadily to press for 3rd towards fin: nvr trbld ldrs* **14/1**

60 **5** 2 1/2 **Laureldean Desert**[36] 5949 2-8-12 0........................ PaulHanagan 9 58+
(R A Fahey) *racd in midfield: pushed along and unable qckn over 3f out: kpt on same pce fnl 2f* **33/1**

0 **6** 4 1/2 **Cunning Plan (IRE)**[19] 6416 2-9-3 0........................ AlanMunro 10 50+
(P W Chapple-Hyam) *sn outpcd in rr: rdn 1/2-way: nvr trbld ldrs* **33/1**

4 **7** 1/2 **High Comedy**[13] 6591 2-9-0 0........................ AhmedAjtebi(3) 6 48+
(Saeed Bin Suroor) *chsd ldrs: hanging rt to stands' rail and rdn looking down over 2f out: rdn and unbalanced 2f out: sn btn and eased fnl f* **4/1**[2]

0 **8** hd **Swansea Jack**[8] 6737 2-9-0 0........................ WilliamCarson(3) 4 48
(S C Williams) *stdd s: a in rr: lost tch 3f out: n.d* **66/1**

0000 **9** 3 1/4 **Antique Diamond (IRE)**[20] 6389 2-8-12 31........................ DNolan 7 33
(Lucinda Featherstone) *a towards rr: rdn and struggling 1/2-way: no ch fnl 2f* **200/1**

000 **10** 8 **Rufus Roughcut**[98] 3957 2-9-3 0........................(t) SaleemGolam 3 14
(S C Williams) *racd in midfield: rdn and struggling 1/2-way: wl bhd fnl 2f* **100/1**

1m 15.12s (0.72) **Going Correction** +0.225s/f (Good) **10** Ran SP% **118.4**
Speed ratings (Par 95): **104,102,99,98,95 89,88,88,84,73**
toteswingers: 1&2 £1.70, 1&3 £3.00, 2&3 £5.60 CSF £4.46 TOTE £1.80: £1.10, £1.40, £2.30; EX 5.40 Trifecta £18.10 Pool £799.86 - 32.65 winning units..
Owner K Abdulla **Bred** Millsec Limited **Trained** Newmarket, Suffolk

FOCUS
A fair maiden in which the first pair dominated. The winner is value for a little further with the placed horses setting the level.

NOTEBOOK
Rule Of Nature came in for plenty of support and she went one better than her debut second at Warwick with a game display. She showed the natural pace required for this shorter test, but had to get serious in order to master the runner-up and probably found it sharp enough. A decent surface clearly suits and she is in the right hands to reach greater heights as a 3-y-o (op Evens)
Dherghaam(IRE) was most disappointing at Newmarket on his previous outing, but he has been freshened up since then and showed it to be wrong with a much better effort on this return to a flatter track. He now qualifies for a mark and can be placed to strike before the season's end. (op 9-2 tchd 5-1)
Tewin Wood, dropping back a furlong, posted another sound effort and has progressed with each of his three outings to date. He is one to look out for when switching to a nursery, for which he is now eligible. (op 9-1)
Midwestern(USA) ◆ finished with plenty left in the tank after being given a lot to do and is no doubt better than he showed. It may be that he now wants another furlong, though, and he has more options now he is qualified for nurseries. (op 16-1)
High Comedy looked to hold decent claims on the level of his debut effort at Nottingham 13 days earlier, when he finished well in front of Midwestern. He raced handily, but still looked very green as he drifted over to the stands' rail. His rider began to look down at halfway as though something was amiss, but he kept putting his horse under pressure in between doing so. It was a disappointing run come what may. Official explanation: jockey said bit slipped through colt's mouth (op 7-2 tchd 9-2)

6923 FIRSTBET.COM £50 MATCHED BET 0800 230 0800 NURSERY 1m 3y
3:50 (3:52) (Class 5) (0-75,75) 2-Y-O **£3,885** (£1,156; £577; £288) **Stalls** High

Form RPR

6566 **1** **Number One Guy**[32] 6067 2-9-0 **68**........................ JimmyQuinn 7 72+
(M H Tompkins) *bmpd s: t.k.h: hld up in tch: hdwy to chse ldrs and nt clr run wl over 1f out: swtchd lft and rdn jst over 1f out: str chal ins fnl f: led on post* **12/1**

0005 **2** nse **Until The Man (IRE)**[13] 6589 2-7-13 **58** ow1.....(p) AndrewHeffernan(5) 4 61+
(R Ingram) *chsd ldrs: ev ch and rdn wl over 1f out: led ins fnl f: battled on wl tl hdd on post* **18/1**

3354 **3** 1 3/4 **City Vaults Girl (IRE)**[20] 6382 2-8-13 **70**........................ FrederikTylicki(3) 5 69
(R A Fahey) *t.k.h: hld up in tch in midfield: rdn over 2f out: swtchd lft wl over 1f out: rdn to ld ent fnl f: hdd ins fnl f: one pce after* **6/1**[2]

0600 **4** 1 1/4 **Ragsta (IRE)**[12] 6609 2-8-6 **60**........................ DavidProbert 3 56
(C A Dwyer) *in tch in midfield: rdn and effrt ent fnl 2f: ev ch over 1f out: wknd ins fnl f* **16/1**

6055 **5** 1 1/2 **Magnificence**[12] 6609 2-8-7 **61** ow1........................ RyanMoore 11 54
(Sir Michael Stoute) *hld up towards rr: hdwy 3f out: chsd ldrs and rdn wl over 1f out: drvn and kpt on same pce fr over 1f out* **7/1**[3]

006 **6** 3/4 **All Moving Parts (USA)**[13] 6593 2-8-11 **65**........................ AlanMunro 9 56
(J S Wainwright) *hld up in tch in rr: rdn and effrt 3f out: prog u.p to chse ldrs wl over 1f out: wknd over 1f out* **33/1**

353 **7** 1 1/4 **Branderburgo (IRE)**[35] 5970 2-9-4 **75**........................(p) AndreaAtzeni(3) 1 64
(M Botti) *hld up towards rr: hdwy on far side over 2f out: hung rt u.p and no hdwy over 1f out: wl hld fnl f* **7/1**[3]

6631 **8** 3/4 **Baby Judge (IRE)**[33] 6035 2-7-11 **58**........................ RachelKing(7) 6 45
(M C Chapman) *wnt rt and barged rival s: led: rdn wl over 1f out: hdd ent fnl f: wknd qckly* **14/1**

5002 **9** 2 **Creevy (IRE)**[21] 6367 2-7-13 **56**........................ Louis-PhilippeBeuzelin(3) 8 40
(S Kirk) *in tch in midfield: j. path 6f out: dropped to rr and rdn over 2f out: n.d after* **16/1**

063 **10** 3 3/4 **Charpoy Cobra**[18] 6441 2-8-11 **65**........................ KirstyMilczarek 2 39
(J A R Toller) *hld up in tch in rr: rdn and effrt over 2f out: no real hdwy: wl btn whn eased ins fnl f* **12/1**

61 **11** 2 **Chain Of Office**[37] 5906 2-9-5 **73**........................ RHills 13 43+
(W J Haggas) *racd freely early: sn chsng ldr: rdn and immediately btn wl over 1f out: wl bhd and eased ins fnl f* **15/8**[1]

600 **12** 3 1/2 **Sweet Baby Jane (IRE)**[112] 3487 2-8-3 **57**........................ PaulHanagan 12 19
(R A Fahey) *chsd ldrs: rdn and struggling 3f out: bhd fnl 2f* **25/1**

1m 43.2s (2.60) **Going Correction** +0.225s/f (Good) **12** Ran SP% **119.9**
Speed ratings (Par 95): **96,95,94,92,91 90,89,88,86,82 80,77**
toteswingers: 1&2 £26.80, 1&3 £13.70, 2&3 £22.20 CSF £212.14 CT £1433.73 TOTE £14.90: £3.70, £7.00, £2.30; EX 141.60 Trifecta £333.00 Part won. Pool £450.02 - 0.61 winning units..
Owner GPD Ltd **Bred** Floors Farming **Trained** Newmarket, Suffolk

FOCUS
A moderate nursery but the form looks solid rated around the first two.

NOTEBOOK
Number One Guy didn't get home over 1m1f in a stronger nursery at Newmarket last time but he'd been eased 4lb since, and a drop back to 1m in this company saw him off the mark. He did well to win considering he was keen early, and would not be denied in a driving finish, so there might be a bit more to come from him. Official explanation: trainers rep had no explanation regarding apparent improvement in form (op 11-1)
Until The Man(IRE), who found the drop back to 6f against him on his handicap debut, posted an improved effort for his first try over 1m. In theory his rider's 1lb overweight was the difference, and there should be a similar race to be won with him before the season is out. (op 16-1)
City Vaults Girl(IRE), who had been as big as 14-1 in the morning, landed the each-way money. She is a good guide to the form, having shown a fair level of consistency in her starts to date. (op 13-2 tchd 7-1 and 11-2)
Ragsta(IRE), dropped 4lb, looked happier back on turf and on a straight track, but she found a few too good at the weights. (tchd 20-1)
Magnificence looked sure to appreciate the step up to 1m considering her pedigree, but she could never really muster the pace to land a blow and perhaps she needs softer ground. (op 8-1 tchd 9-1)
All Moving Parts(USA), who had been keen when winning her maiden at Ffos Las, pulled much too hard through the early stages here and gave herself little chance of seeing out her race. She is going to need to learn to settle if she is to fulfil her potential.
Chain Of Office Official explanation: jockey said filly ran too freely

6924 LISA AND TONY BOGGIS WEDDING DAY CLAIMING STKS 1m 3y
4:20 (4:23) (Class 6) 3-Y-O+ **£2,266** (£674; £337; £168) **Stalls** High

Form RPR

6606 **1** **Spring Goddess (IRE)**[33] 6012 8-8-12 70........................ RichardMullen 15 62
(A P Jarvis) *hld up towards rr: hdwy 3f out: chsd ldrs 2f out: rdn to ld jst over 1f out: hld on wl u.p fnl 100yds* **9/1**

0002 **2** 1/2 **Musigny (USA)**[35] 5972 3-8-6 54........................ AlanMunro 11 56
(W Jarvis) *bhd: hdwy over 2f out: rdn 2f out: drvn to chse ldrs over 1f out: edgd rt and hld hd high ins fnl f: r.o u.p to go 2nd nr fin: nt quite rch wnr* **20/1**

0015 **3** hd **Why Nee Amy**[5] 6804 3-8-3 56 ow2........................ ChrisCatlin 6 53
(T Keddy) *in tch in midfield: rdn and effrt over 1f out: pressed wnr ins fnl f: unable qck u.p fnl 100yds: lost 2nd nr fin* **9/1**

0540 **4** 1 1/4 **Al Rayanah**[64] 5111 6-8-6 49........................(p) SaleemGolam 9 51
(G Prodromou) *hld up in rr: hdwy over 2f out: rdn to chse ldrs wl over 1f out: kpt on same pce u.p fnl f* **25/1**

5 **5** ½ **West Kirk**[262] 356 3-9-7 0 FrederikTylicki(3) 4 70
(W Jarvis) *dwlt and short of room sn after s: hld up towards rr: hdwy on far side 3f out: drvn to press ldrs jst over 1f out: one pce ins fnl f* **25/1**

0313 **6** ¾ **Autumn Blades (IRE)**[8] 6726 4-9-3 75 (p) DavidProbert 16 59
(A Bailey) *hld up in tch: rdn and nt qckn jst over 1f out: no imp fnl f* **11/4**[1]

0030 **7** 2¼ **Pressing Matters (IRE)**[41] 5779 3-9-0 70 (p) JimmyQuinn 7 53
(M Botti) *hld up in tch in midfield: hdwy to join ldrs on bit 2f out: pushed into ld over 1f out: sn hdd and fnd nil u.p: btn fnl f* **12/1**

0156 **8** 1¾ **Wovoka (IRE)**[17] 6490 6-9-2 72 AmyRyan(5) 1 53
(K A Ryan) *in tch: effrt 3f out: ev ch and rdn wl over 1f out: wknd u.p ent fnl f* **15/2**[3]

-000 **9** 2 **Bahama Baileys**[22] 6335 4-8-4 46 KellyHarrison(3) 10 35
(C A Dwyer) *bhd: hdwy and in tch 3f out: rdn and no prog wl over 1f out: wl btn fnl f* **100/1**

3000 **10** *hd* **High Curragh**[18] 6458 6-8-11 63 DarryllHolland 8 38
(K A Ryan) *led tl rdn and hdd wl over 1f out: wknd u.p over 1f out* **12/1**

0565 **11** 3½ **Indian Tonic (IRE)**[13] 6588 3-8-0 63 AndreaAtzeni(3) 3 24
(W Jarvis) *hld up in tch in midfield: effrt and rdn jst over 2f out: wknd qckly over 1f out* **11/2**[2]

0000 **12** *15* **Alan Devonshire**[13] 6596 4-8-8 65 AshleyMorgan(5) 14 —
(M H Tompkins) *pressed ldr tl 3f out: sn struggling u.p: wl bhd over 1f out* **16/1**

0000 **13** *6* **Cordell (IRE)**[9] 6702 4-9-8 70 AndrewHeffernan(5) 12 —
(R Ingram) *t.k.h: chsd ldrs tl 3f out: sn lost pl u.p: wl bhd fr over 1f out* **33/1**

0500 **14** ½ **Charismatic Lady**[15] 6537 3-8-5 57 (b[1]) AdrianMcCarthy 5 —
(Jane Chapple-Hyam) *chsd ldrs tl wknd u.p over 3f out: wl bhd fnl 2f* **28/1**

000- **15** *nse* **Ensign's Trick**[383] 6409 5-8-2 50 LiamJones 13 —
(W M Brisbourne) *chsd ldrs tl 1/2-way: sn struggling: wl bhd fnl 2f* **66/1**

0200 **16** 3¾ **Sampower Rose (IRE)**[11] 6637 3-7-13 63 (b[1]) PaulHanagan 2 —
(D Carroll) *racd in midfield: rdn and struggling over 3f out: wl bhd fnl 2f* **10/1**

1m 42.03s (1.43) **Going Correction** +0.225s/f (Good)
WFA 3 from 4yo+ 3lb **16** Ran SP% **125.5**
Speed ratings (Par 101): **101,100,100,99,98 97,95,93,91,91 88,73,67,66,66 62**
toteswingers: 1&2 £32.20, 1&3 £19.20, 2&3 £33.90 CSF £185.86 TOTE £10.30: £2.80, £6.50, £2.80; EX 129.80 TRIFECTA Not won..High Curragh was claimed by David Barlow for £7,000.
Owner Grant & Bowman Limited **Bred** Ballyhane Stud **Trained** Middleham Moor, N Yorks

FOCUS
A weak claimer and the form is muddling, with the fourth probably the best guide, rated to her summer course form.
High Curragh Official explanation: jockey said gelding hung right

6925 FIRSTBET.COM £50 MATCHED BET 0800 230 0800 H'CAP 7f 3y
4:50 (4:54) (Class 6) (0-65,65) 3-Y-0+ **£2,331** (£693; £346; £173) **Stalls** High

Form RPR

0330 **1** **Azure Mist**[3] 6846 4-9-6 63 JimmyQuinn 4 73
(M H Tompkins) *stdd s: t.k.h: hld up in tch in rr: hdwy 3f out: trckd ldrs gng wl 2f out: pushed into ld 1f out: rdn out* **13/2**

1202 **2** 2 **Many Welcomes**[34] 5998 4-8-9 57 JemmaMarshall(5) 5 62
(B P J Baugh) *chsd ldrs: rdn ent fnl 2f: led over 1f out: hdd 1f out: no ch w wnr after but kpt on for clr 2nd* **5/1**[2]

6100 **3** 2¼ **Bermondsey Girl**[19] 6437 3-9-6 65 TedDurcan 11 64+
(C F Wall) *taken down early: rrd as stalls opened and slowly away: t.k.h: hld up in rr: hdwy over 2f out: swtchd rt and drvn over 1f out: wnt 3rd ins fnl f: no ch w ldng pair* **11/2**[3]

4 3½ **Soul Sista (IRE)**[53] 5405 3-9-5 64 LiamJones 13 53
(J L Spearing) *chsd ldrs: pushed along over 4f out: drvn and wknd over 1f out* **25/1**

0340 **5** ½ **Optical Illusion (USA)**[17] 6492 5-8-13 56 PaulHanagan 14 44
(R A Fahey) *taken down early: hld up towards rr: hdwy and edging lft jst over 2f out: no hdwy and wl hld over 1f out* **10/1**

-142 **6** ½ **Vogarth**[16] 224 5-8-12 62 (b) RachelKing(7) 6 49
(M C Chapman) *led tl rdn and hdd over 1f out: fdd* **40/1**

0-10 **7** 1½ **Bob Stock (IRE)**[158] 2048 3-9-4 63 ChrisCatlin 8 46
(W J Musson) *hld up in tch in midfield: rdn and nt qckn over 2f out: drvn and no prog fr 2f out and wl btn after* **5/2**[1]

0103 **8** 2½ **Registrar**[34] 6005 7-9-0 57 (p) SaleemGolam 3 33
(Mrs C A Dunnett) *in tch in midfield: rdn and no rspnse ent fnl 2f: no ch fnl f* **10/1**

0360 **9** 2¼ **Margarita (IRE)**[15] 6547 3-9-5 64 (vt[1]) DavidProbert 10 34
(J R Fanshawe) *in tch in midfield tl dropped to rr and rdn over 2f out: sn wl btn: no ch whn swtchd rt ins fnl f* **7/1**

35-0 **10** 2¾ **Time To Play**[242] 618 4-9-0 57 MickyFenton 7 19
(T T Clement) *s.i.s: a bhd: struggling bdly fr 1/2-way* **33/1**

6002 **11** 1¾ **Contemplate**[14] 6573 3-8-7 55 (b) Louis-PhilippeBeuzelin(3) 12 13
(Dr J D Scargill) *chsd ldr tl over 2f out: sn struggling u.p: wl bhd fnl f* **25/1**

1m 28.76s (2.16) **Going Correction** +0.225s/f (Good)
WFA 3 from 4yo+ 2lb **11** Ran SP% **117.7**
Speed ratings (Par 101): **96,93,91,87,86 86,84,81,78,75 73**
toteswingers: 1&2 £7.20, 1&3 £7.80, 2&3 £9.00 CSF £37.54 CT £197.00 TOTE £7.90: £2.70, £1.90, £2.30; EX 47.00 Trifecta £252.70 Part won. Pool £341.56 - 0.46 winning units..
Owner David P Noblett **Bred** Worksop Manor Stud **Trained** Newmarket, Suffolk

FOCUS
A weak handicap, run at a fair pace. The first three came clear and the runner-up looks the best guide to the form.
Azure Mist Official explanation: trainer said, regarding apparent improvement in form, that the filly was better suited by the track
Time To Play Official explanation: jockey said gelding hung left

6926 SCROBY SANDS FARMS WIND FARM H'CAP 6f 3y
5:20 (5:21) (Class 6) (0-60,60) 3-Y-0+ **£2,331** (£693; £346; £173) **Stalls** High

Form RPR

345 **1** **Another Try (IRE)**[45] 5675 4-9-5 60 TPQueally 9 70
(A P Jarvis) *chsd ldr tl led 2f out: sn rdn: battled on wl fnl f* **5/1**[2]

2000 **2** ¾ **Dancing Wave**[14] 6572 3-8-8 57 RachelKing(7) 1 65
(M C Chapman) *chsd ldrs: ev ch and rdn over 1f out: unable qck ins fnl f* **40/1**

2463 **3** 2 **Elkhorn**[27] 6216 7-8-11 52 (b) TomEaves 7 54
(Miss J A Camacho) *travelled wl: hld up in tch: effrt to chse ldng pair jst over 1f out: rdn 1f out: nt qckn fnl 150yds: btn after* **11/2**[3]

646 **4** *nk* **Eliza Doolittle**[38] 5882 3-9-2 58 HayleyTurner 6 59
(J R Fanshawe) *hld up in tch towards rr: hdwy over 2f out: drvn to chse ldrs ent fnl f: kpt on but nvr quite pce to chal* **8/1**

3600 **5** ¾ **Divine Force**[97] 3989 3-9-2 58 SimonWhitworth 3 56
(M Wigham) *hld up towards rr: effrt on outer over 2f out: chsd ldrs and rdn over 1f out: no imp ins fnl f* **50/1**

5040 **6** ½ **Naomh Geileis (USA)**[29] 6156 4-9-5 60 (b) GregFairley 5 57
(M Johnston) *towards rr: rdn over 3f out: hdwy u.p over 1f out: swtchd lft ins fnl f: styd on but nvr gng to rch ldrs* **16/1**

5105 **7** *nk* **Secret City (IRE)**[31] 6103 3-9-3 59 (b) DanielTudhope 2 55
(R Bastiman) *chsd ldrs: rdn 2f out: styd chsng ldrs tl wknd u.p 1f out* **18/1**

0600 **8** ¾ **Commander Wish**[19] 6433 6-9-0 55 (p) LiamJones 4 48
(Lucinda Featherstone) *chsd ldrs: rdn over 2f out: wknd u.p over 1f out* **10/1**

5201 **9** 2¼ **Fuzzy Cat**[56] 5326 3-8-6 53 (b) DeanHeslop(5) 8 39
(T D Barron) *hld up in tch in midfield: hung rt and racd awkwardly over 1f out: no prog* **12/1**

1333 **10** *shd* **Welsh Opera**[5] 6801 4-9-1 59 WilliamCarson(3) 13 45
(S C Williams) *hld up in tch towards rr: rdn and effrt 2f out: no prog* **7/2**[1]

0400 **11** ¾ **Flashy Photon**[13] 6596 4-8-12 53 (b[1]) FrankieMcDonald 11 36
(H Candy) *v.s.a: detached in last pl tl past btn rivals fnl f: nvr on terms* **16/1**

/060 **12** *1* **So Glamorous**[34] 6005 4-8-13 54 TedDurcan 14 34
(C F Wall) *a in rr of main gp: rdn and no rspnse ent fnl 2f* **16/1**

0000 **13** *5* **Scruffy Skip (IRE)**[6] 6777 4-8-11 52 TGMcLaughlin 12 16
(Mrs C A Dunnett) *chsd ldrs: rdn over 2f out: struggling whn hmpd and swtchd lft over 1f out: no ch after* **25/1**

6004 **14** 2½ **Cool Art (IRE)**[18] 6442 3-9-4 60 (b) AlanMunro 16 16
(J S Wainwright) *chsd ldrs tl wknd qckly wl over 2f out: wl bhd fnl 2f* **18/1**

5030 **15** *2* **Star Strider**[66] 5031 5-8-9 55 ow1 (b) KylieManser(5) 10 5
(T Keddy) *led tl 2f out: sn wknd: wl bhd fnl f* **25/1**

1m 15.51s (1.11) **Going Correction** +0.225s/f (Good)
WFA 3 from 4yo+ 1lb **15** Ran SP% **122.4**
Speed ratings (Par 101): **101,100,97,96,95 95,94,93,90,90 89,88,81,78,75**
toteswingers: 1&2 £44.60, 1&3 £8.40, 2&3 £58.30 CSF £206.86 CT £1186.51 TOTE £5.30: £2.30, £15.70, £2.40; EX 172.80 Trifecta £193.30 Part won. Pool £261.29 - 0.10 winning units..
Place 6 £202.24, Place 5 £112.60..
Owner The Twyford Partnership **Bred** Jarvis Associates **Trained** Middleham Moor, N Yorks

FOCUS
A wide-open handicap, run at a fair pace. Moderate form but sound enough if ignoring the winner.
Flashy Photon Official explanation: jockey said gelding was slowly away
T/Jkpt: Not won. T/Plt: £363.20 to a £1 stake. Pool: £66,089.64. 132.81 winning tickets. T/Qpdt: £44.90 to a £1 stake. Pool: £5,367.61. 88.30 winning tickets. SP

ANGERS (R-H)
Tuesday, October 20

OFFICIAL GOING: Good to soft

6927a PRIX BRANTOME 1m 2f
12:55 (12:58) 2-Y-0 **£13,107** (£5,243; £3,932; £2,621; £1,311)

RPR

1 **Ucandri (IRE)** 2-9-2 JAuge 86
(C Ferland, France)

2 *5* **Argun River (IRE)**[48] 2-8-12 RonanThomas 73
(R Gibson, France)

3 ½ **Fylarchos (FR)**[23] 6322 2-8-12 GMasure 72
(C Laffon-Parias, France)

4 ½ **Ma Dauphine (FR)** 2-8-12 71
(Y Barberot, France)

5 *4* **Lovely Samantha** 2-8-6 (b) 58
(Mario Hofer, Germany)

6 1½ **Freedom Light (FR)**[36] 2-8-12 61
(C Boutin, France)

7 ½ **Le Grenelle (FR)**[17] 6501 2-8-9 57
(F Doumen, France)

8 *6* **Impressioniste (IRE)**[43] 5739 2-9-2 MAndrouin 54
(E J O'Neill) *bhd: last 1/2-way: nvr a factor* **6/1**[1]

9 *nk* **Existes Ons Nous (FR)**[18] 6507 2-8-9 46
(J-M Lefebvre, France)

2m 6.50s (126.50) **9** Ran SP% **14.3**
PARI-MUTUEL (Including 1 Euro stake): WIN 3.60; PL 1.30, 1.20, 1.50;DF 5.60.
Owner V Laumaille **Bred** D, P & Mrs P Gibbons **Trained** France

6928a PRIX LUNA WELLS (MAIDEN) 1m 2f
1:25 (1:32) 2-Y-0 **£6,796** (£2,718; £2,039; £1,359; £680)

RPR

1 **Mogadishio (FR)** 2-9-2 FLefebvre 78
(A Couetil, France)

2 ½ **Caunton Beck (FR)**[17] 6501 2-9-2 JAuge 77
(E J O'Neill) *pressed ldr: led after 3f to ins fnl f: r.o* **11/1**[1]

3 ½ **Okadoun (FR)** 2-8-13 GAvranche 73
(C Lotoux, France)

4 *2* **Croix Madame (FR)**[14] 6578 2-8-13 70
(F Doumen, France)

5 *3* **Ched (USA)** 2-9-2 67
(F-X De Chevigny, France)

6 1½ **Singapore Fun (FR)** 2-8-12 60
(C Laffon-Parias, France)

7 *8* **Nuit D'Ete (GER)** 2-8-8 42
(H-A Pantall, France)

8 *2* **Appia Nova (FR)** 2-8-12 42
(G Botti, Italy)

9 *10* **El Jahid (FR)** 2-8-12 24
(P Monfort, France)

10 *3* **Plume Du Peintre (FR)**[15] 6576 2-8-13 20
(N Leenders, France)

11 **Divine Summer (FR)**[20] 2-8-13 20
(C Boutin, France)

2m 7.34s (127.34) **11** Ran SP% **8.3**
PARI-MUTUEL: WIN 2.60; PL 1.20, 2.50, 1.80; DF 15.00.
Owner F Carre **Bred** Pierre Camus Denais **Trained** France

[5494]DEAUVILLE (R-H)

Tuesday, October 20

OFFICIAL GOING: Turf course - good to soft; all-weather - standard

6929a PRIX DES RESERVOIRS - HARAS D'ETREHAM (GROUP 3) (FILLIES) (ROUND) 1m (R)

1:40 (2:20) 2-Y-0 £38,835 (£13,592; £13,592; £7,767; £3,883)

RPR

1 **Barouda (FR)**[26] 2-8-9 .... OPeslier 5 105
(J-M Beguigne, France) *racd in 4th: 3rd and pushed along st: r.o fnl f to ld last strides* **4/1**[3]

2 ½ **Marie De Medici (USA)**[14] 6567 2-8-9 .... JoeFanning 4 104
(M Johnston) *led: pushed along and r.o st: kpt on gamely: hdd fnl strides* **29/10**[2]

2 *dht* **Ayun Tara (FR)**[17] 6501 2-8-9 ....(p) GBenoist 2 104
(X Nakkachdji, France) *racd in 3rd: 2nd st: pushed along and pressing ldr over 1 1/2f out: kpt on u.p: dead-heated for 2nd on line* **10/1**

4 1 **Zagora (FR)**[48] 2-8-9 .... CSoumillon 6 102
(Y De Nicolay, France) *hld up in last: effrt over 1f out: styd on in centre to go 4th 100yds out: nvr in chalng position* **8/5**[1]

5 1 **American Nizzy (FR)**[16] 6523 2-8-9 .... IMendizabal 3 100
(Y De Nicolay, France) *settled in 5th: pushed along 1 1/2f out: n.d* **48/10**

6 6 **Xaarienne**[43] 5739 2-8-9 .... MGuyon 1 86
(H-A Pantall, France) *racd in 2nd: 4th st: sn pushed along: rdn and one pce fr 1 1/2f out* **16/1**

1m 44.6s (3.60) **6 Ran SP% 116.3**
PARI-MUTUEL: WIN 5.00; PL 1.80, 1.30 (Marie de Medici), 2.00 (AyunTara); SF 12.50 (with Marie de Medici), 17.80 (with Ayun Tara).
Owner H De La Chauvelais **Bred** Comtesse M-F De La Chauvelais **Trained** France

NOTEBOOK
Barouda(FR), given a finely judged waiting ride, this filly showed outstanding late acceleration to win this Group 3 event. She was held up early on and produced at exactly the right time, taking the lead well inside the final furlong. The winner of two of her three races she is now finished for the season, and will start 2010 with a run in the Prix de la Grotte. If all goes well she will be aimed for the Poule d'Essai des Pouliches.
Marie De Medici(USA) made a brave effort to lead from pillar to post. She set a respectable pace from the start and quickened things up early in the straight but was passed by the winner inside the final furlong. She stayed on bravely to share second spot and her trainer will see how she comes out of the race before making any further plans, although she could return to France for another Group event.
Ayun Tara(FR) having her first try at this level after running in claimers, put up an an excellent performance. She was in third place virtually throughout and ran a little free early on. She moved up to the leader rounding the final turn and kept up the good work to the finish. She might turn out for the Prix Miesque at Maisons-Laffitte at the beginning of next month.
Zagora(FR) put up a rather a disappointing performance and never looked like finishing in the first three. Held up virtually last in the early stages, she was outpaced early in the straight when brought with a run up the centre of the track.

[6328]BATH (L-H)

Wednesday, October 21

OFFICIAL GOING: Good (good to soft in places; 8.0)
Wind: quite strong behind Weather: overcast with sunny periods, heavy shower after the 3rd.

6930 JOHN SMITH'S MAIDEN STKS (DIV I) 1m 5y

2:00 (2:00) (Class 5) 2-Y-0 £2,266 (£674; £337; £168) Stalls Low

Form RPR

5 1 **Rasmy**[32] 6109 2-9-3 0 .... RHills 6 85+
(M P Tregoning) *chsd ldng pair: led over 1f out: rdn clr: comf* **9/4**[1]

0 2 5 **Breakheart (IRE)**[8] 6754 2-9-3 0 .... LPKeniry 15 74
(A M Balding) *mid-div: pushed along and hdwy 3f out: rdn to chse wnr over 1f out but nvr any ch* **18/1**

020 3 ¾ **First In The Queue (IRE)**[16] 6548 2-9-3 76 .... JamesDoyle 3 72
(S Kirk) *in tch: hung rt on bnd over 4f out: sn rdn: hdwy 3f out: styd on fnl 2f: wnt 3rd ent fnl f* **7/1**[3]

04 4 2¼ **Liberty Square (USA)**[14] 6593 2-9-0 0 ....(t) AhmedAjtebi(3) 8 67
(Saeed Bin Suroor) *chsd ldrs: rdn over 3f out: styd on same pce fnl 2f* **8/1**

3 5 2 **Yabtree (IRE)**[41] 5785 2-9-3 0 .... SteveDrowne 10 63
(R Charlton) *chsng ldrs whn hmpd and snatched up after 1f: dropped to mid-div: rdn and hdwy over 2f out: styd on* **7/1**[3]

6 2½ **Tayacoba (CAN)** 2-9-3 0 .... JimmyFortune 13 57+
(J H M Gosden) *s.i.s: rn green towards rr and sn nudged along: styd on fr 2f out: nvr nrr* **12/1**

7 1 **Paydaar**[82] 4509 2-9-3 0 .... MartinDwyer 16 55
(B J Meehan) *plld hrd: hung lft most of way: sn led: rdn and hdd over 1f out: fading in 5th whn squeezed out on rails jst ins fnl f* **6/1**[2]

6 8 ¾ **Specialising**[84] 4421 2-8-12 0 .... SamHitchcott 9 50
(M R Channon) *mid-div: effrt u.p over 2f out wout ever threatening: fdd ent fnl f* **14/1**

60 9 2¾ **Calypso Star (IRE)**[7] 6781 2-9-3 0 .... RichardHughes 2 47
(R Hannon) *a towards rr* **14/1**

0006 10 2 **Expensive Legacy**[22] 6366 2-8-12 54 .... JimmyQuinn 4 38
(H J L Dunlop) *a towards rr* **100/1**

00 11 2¾ **Khazara**[6] 6792 2-8-12 0 .... DaneO'Neill 7 32
(A King) *led early: chsd ldr: rdn over 3f out: wknd 2f out* **150/1**

0060 12 *nse* **Petite Mambo**[9] 6735 2-9-3 65 .... TolleyDean 1 37
(W De Best-Turner) *a bhd* **200/1**

00 13 1½ **Moonbalej**[31] 6136 2-9-3 0 .... RoystonFfrench 12 42
(M Johnston) *chsng ldrs whn hmpd and snatched up after 1f: bhd and nvr bk on terms after* **22/1**

14 24 **First Post (IRE)** 2-9-3 0 .... HayleyTurner 11 —
(D Haydn Jones) *a bhd: t.o fnl 2f* **40/1**

0 15 ½ **Green Energy**[13] 6615 2-9-3 0 .... JimCrowley 5 —
(Mrs A J Perrett) *slowly away: a bhd: t.o* **33/1**

1m 41.33s (0.53) **Going Correction** +0.175s/f (Good) **15 Ran SP% 119.3**
Speed ratings (Par 95): **104,99,98,96,94 91,90,89,87,85 82,82,80,56,56**
toteswinger: 1&2 £17.00, 1&3 £5.90, 2&3 £23.80. CSF £46.92 TOTE £2.60: £1.10, £6.20, £2.60; EX 66.70 TRIFECTA Not won..
Owner Hamdan Al Maktoum **Bred** Minster Stud And Mrs H Dalgety **Trained** Lambourn, Berks

FOCUS
Following 15mm of rain in the previous 24 hours, the ground had officially eased to good, good to soft in places, though the riders in the first race felt it was a bit softer than that. The first division of this maiden was big on numbers, but looked short on quality. The early pace was decent, though, and the field was soon well spread out. The form looks reasonable with the winner building on his debut.

NOTEBOOK
Rasmy, who showed ability on his Newbury debut last month, is bred to have been suited by this extra furlong but he was fairly easy in the market beforehand. Having settled in a handy early position, albeit a few lengths off the runaway leader, he moved smoothly into contention as the race developed and once sent on inside the last 2f, absolutely bolted up. He may not have beaten much here, but he is highly regarded and looks a nice type for decent middle-distance contests next year. (op 15-8 tchd 5-2 in places)
Breakheart(IRE), outpaced over 7f on debut, came off the bridle in midfield some way out, but he stayed on down the wide outside to snatch second place at a respectful distance behind the winner. He is likely to step up again from this. (tchd 20-1)
First In The Queue(IRE), officially rated 76 after showing some ability in three maidens, plugged on from the middle of the field to make the frame but he lacks the scope of the pair who beat him and may be worth switching to nurseries. (op 15-2 tchd 8-1)
Liberty Square(USA), mildly progressive in ordinary maidens, was never too far away and was close enough 2f out, but he was then made to look one-paced. He needed this for a nursery mark and that may be his best option now. (op 7-1)
Yabtree(IRE), a fair third in an ordinary Chepstow maiden on debut, was forced to make his effort widest of all in the home straight but he had run his race on reaching the furlong pole. He only looks modest. (op 17-2)
Paydaar, in the frame in a couple of Irish maidens, was making his debut for the yard after three months off. After carting himself to the front after a furlong, he then did far too much and had run himself into the ground entering the final quarter-mile. (op 10-1)
Moonbalej Official explanation: jockey said colt hung left-handed

6931 JOHN SMITH'S MAIDEN STKS (DIV II) 1m 5y

2:30 (2:33) (Class 5) 2-Y-0 £2,266 (£674; £337; £168) Stalls Low

Form RPR

3 1 **Database (IRE)**[13] 6617 2-9-0 0 .... AhmedAjtebi(3) 4 77
(Saeed Bin Suroor) *mde all: rdn and hrd pressed fr 3f out: asserted ent fnl f: drvn out* **1/1**[1]

2 ¾ **Whistleinthewind (IRE)** 2-9-3 0 .... RyanMoore 8 75+
(G L Moore) *rn green: s.i.s: towards rr: swtchd to centre and prog fr over 2f out: styd on wl fnl f but nvr gng to quite catch wnr* **8/1**[3]

402 3 2½ **Spa's Dancer (IRE)**[35] 5994 2-9-3 87 .... MichaelHills 14 70
(J W Hills) *trckd ldr: rdn to chal 3f out tl no ex ent fnl f: sn edgd lft* **3/1**[2]

4 1½ **Jazz Age (IRE)** 2-9-3 0 ....(b[1]) JimmyFortune 3 68+
(J H M Gosden) *s.i.s: sn pushed into midfield: rdn and hdwy 3f out to chse ldng pair: no ex whn squeezed up ins fnl f* **8/1**[3]

00 5 4½ **Zagarock**[13] 6617 2-8-12 0 .... DavidProbert 9 52
(B Palling) *trckd ldrs: rdn over 2f out: wknd fnl f* **50/1**

60 6 2½ **Madam Ruby (IRE)**[9] 6729 2-8-12 0 .... DaneO'Neill 11 46+
(A King) *mid-div: rdn over 3f out: no imp* **18/1**

060 7 4½ **Set In Ice**[58] 5319 2-8-12 37 .... SimonPearce(5) 1 41
(Mark Gillard) *dwlt: bhd: hdwy into midfield over 5f out: rdn over 3f out: no further imp fnl 2f* **200/1**

00 8 7 **Liebelei (USA)**[26] 6254 2-8-12 0 .... JamesDoyle 5 21
(H J L Dunlop) *chsd ldrs: rdn over 3f out: wknd over 2f out* **66/1**

9 2 **Annelko** 2-9-3 0 .... SteveDrowne 15 21
(A B Haynes) *a towards rr* **66/1**

0 10 2¾ **Steely Bird**[21] 6393 2-9-3 0 .... RobertHavlin 10 15
(Miss Jo Crowley) *mid-div: rdn 4f out: wknd over 2f out* **80/1**

04 11 3 **Temple Fair (USA)**[34] 6033 2-9-3 0 .... RoystonFfrench 12 9
(M Johnston) *prom: rdn over 3f out: sn wknd* **20/1**

12 21 **Laid Bare** 2-8-12 0 .... FergusSweeney 6 —
(Mrs P N Dutfield) *s.i.s: a bhd* **100/1**

1m 42.69s (1.89) **Going Correction** +0.175s/f (Good) **12 Ran SP% 114.9**
Speed ratings (Par 95): **97,96,93,92,87 85,80,73,71,69 66,45**
toteswinger: 1&2 £4.90, 1&3 £1.10, 2&3 £5.10. CSF £9.42 TOTE £2.10: £1.10, £2.90, £1.10; EX 13.30 Trifecta £27.40 Pool: £485.52 - 13.08 winning units..
Owner Godolphin **Bred** Mount Coote Stud **Trained** Newmarket, Suffolk

FOCUS
Like the first division this didn't look a competitive maiden and only a couple had shown much in the way of ability. The winning time was 1.36 seconds slower than division one and the together with the proximity of the fifth and seventh limits the form.

NOTEBOOK
Database(IRE), a fair third over this trip on his Newbury debut earlier this month, was well backed to confirm that promise but he made very hard work of it. Soon in front, he was put under severe pressure by Spa's Dancer passing the 3f pole and for a while he seemed to be getting the worse of the argument. He managed to get the better of a protracted duel with that rival on reaching the furlong pole and had just about enough in hand to hold on from thereon in. His rider felt that he was still a bit babyish, but he doesn't look a superstar and nurseries are probably his best option now. (op 6-5 tchd 5-4 in a place)
Whistleinthewind(IRE), an already gelded 55,000gns two-year-old, is a half-brother to the multiple winning sprinter Sunrise Safari and is probably the one to take from the race. Out the back early, he was being niggled along at halfway but he took off down the wide outside once into the straight and was cutting into the favourite's advantage at the line. He is sure to come on from this and should go one better before too long. (op 9-1 tchd 7-1)
Spa's Dancer(IRE), gradually improving and only just beaten at Sandown last time after trying to make all, had to settle for a prominent early position this time and he didn't take the home bend too well. However, he still managed to serve it up to the winner passing the 3f pole and may even have hit the front for a few strides, but he had run his race inside the last furlong. Already rated 87, he has a race in him but doesn't have as much potential improvement as the first two. (tchd 7-2)
Jazz Age(IRE), an 85,000gns half-brother to three winners at up to this trip, had blinkers on for this debut which suggested he wasn't considered straightforward. He did show some ability, though, and looked a danger when sent after the two leaders inside the last 3f, but he could never quite get there. He doesn't look anything special, but is entitled to improve and should find an opportunity at some stage. (tchd 9-1)
Zagarock, well beaten in her first two starts, showed a bit more this time and will have more options now that she is qualifies for a mark.
Madam Ruby(IRE), disappointing last time but far from disgraced on her debut, is another for whom nurseries now become an option. (op 14-1 tchd 12-1)
Set In Ice Official explanation: jockey said gelding was slowly away

6932 E.B.F./FREEBETS.CO.UK ONLINE CASINO OFFERS MAIDEN STKS 5f 11y

3:00 (3:05) (Class 5) 2-Y-0 £3,561 (£1,059; £529; £264) Stalls Centre

Form RPR

0324 1 **Dusty Spirit**[10] 6700 2-9-0 68 .... JackDean(3) 1 76
(W G M Turner) *a.p: rdn into narrow advantage over 2f out: hung on gamely: all out* **20/1**

523 **2** *hd* **Excellent Thought**[15] 6563 2-8-12 73 MichaelHills 8 70
(W J Haggas) *led for 2f: prom: rdn and ev ch fr over 2f out: stl level thrght fnl f: kpt on: jst hld* **6/5**[1]
5 **3** *1 ½* **Memorandum**[23] 6328 2-8-12 0 SteveDrowne 4 65
(R Charlton) *chsd ldrs: rdn over 2f out: chal ent fnl f: no ex fnl 75yds* **9/1**
0622 **4** *1 ¾* **Dimaire**[22] 6354 2-8-12 66 HayleyTurner 9 59
(D Haydn Jones) *chsd ldrs rdn over 2f out: sn edgd lft: kpt on same pce* **8/1**
062 **5** *1 ¼* **Robens Rock (IRE)**[10] 6700 2-9-3 0 RichardHughes 7 59
(A B Haynes) *chsd ldrs: rdn over 2f out: nt pce to mount chal* **7/1**[3]
55 **6** *1 ¼* **Be Grateful (IRE)**[23] 6347 2-8-12 0 EddieAhern 5 54+
(H Morrison) *chsd ldrs tl wknd 2f out* **16/1**
0 **7** *4 ½* **Belle Park**[28] 6207 2-8-12 0 DarryllHolland 6 33
(Karen George) *awkward leaving stalls: struggling in rr after 2f* **100/1**
8 *1 ¾* **Youcanalwaysdream (IRE)** 2-8-12 0 FergusSweeney 2 27+
(K A Ryan) *s.i.s and hmpd: gd spd to ld after 2f: rdn and hdd over 2f out: sn wknd* **25/1**
0555 **9** *5* **Grace Jicaro**[29] 6185 2-8-7 47 (b[1]) DeanHeslop(5) 3 9
(Mrs L Williamson) *wnt lft and s.i.s: a bhd* **100/1**
10 *1 ½* **Clifton Encore (USA)** 2-8-12 0 RichardKingscote 10 4
(Tom Dascombe) *s.i.s: a bhd* **3/1**[2]

61.73 secs (-0.77) **Going Correction** -0.075s/f (Good) **10** Ran SP% **120.5**
Speed ratings (Par 95): **103,102,100,97,95 93,86,83,75,73**
toteswinger: 1&2 £6.90, 1&3 £15.00, 2&3 £3.60. CSF £45.35 TOTE £30.10: £3.40, £1.10, £2.70; EX 68.30 Trifecta £352.80 Part won. Pool: £476.79 - 0.76 winning units..
Owner T.O.C.S. Ltd **Bred** T O C S Limited **Trained** Sigwells, Somerset

FOCUS
A modest maiden and this time the jockeys decided to come up the stands' rail. A contested lead meant that the pace was decent, however. the form looks fair, rated around the runner-up, fourth, sixth and seventh.

NOTEBOOK
Dusty Spirit had already made the frame a few times in maiden and nursery company and had finished a couple of lengths behind Robens Rock on Polytrack last time, but he reversed that form in no uncertain terms here. One of those to dispute the early pace, he battled on really well to break his duck at the eighth attempt with nothing to spare. He looks a tough sort and just the type to keep on going well into the winter. (op 14-1 tchd 12-1)
Excellent Thought, dropping back in trip and a close third after having to race alone on her third start at Folkestone last time, was another to be up there from the start and she never stopped trying, but she may need to step back up in trip. (op 6-4)
Memorandum, who shaped as though in need of further rather than shorter when fifth over a slightly longer trip here on debut, swerved away to her left exiting the stalls but it wasn't long before she was in touch with the leaders. She had every chance, but couldn't quicken where it mattered and it still looks as though she needs a stiffer test. (op 8-1)
Dimaire, who has improved since dropping to the minimum trip having finished runner-up in a Ffos Las maiden and a Southwell nursery on her last two starts, showed good pace up the stands' rail for a long way, but was held entering the last furlong. (op 9-1 tchd 15-2)
Robens Rock(IRE) proved suited by the drop to this trip when runner-up on Polytrack last time, but although close enough for much of the way he couldn't pick up sufficiently and may need a return to sand. (op 8-1)
Be Grateful(IRE), unplaced though not disgraced in her first two starts, wasn't totally disgraced here either, but she may come into her own now that she gets a mark. (tchd 14-1)
Youcanalwaysdream(IRE), a 27,000gns half-sister to a couple of winners at up to 1m2f, ended up well beaten but she showed decent early pace to get to the front after being hampered at the start, so it wasn't a surprise when those exertions eventually took their toll. There was enough here to build on.
Clifton Encore(USA), out of a half-sister to the Gimcrack-winner Country Reel, was very well backed throughout the day but she swerved away to her left leaving the stalls and was never in the race. (op 4-1 tchd 9-2)

6933 FREEBETS.CO.UK FREE CASINO OFFERS H'CAP 5f 161y
3:30 (3:31) (Class 6) (0-58,58) 3-Y-O+ **£1,878** (£558; £279; £139) **Stalls** Centre

Form RPR
2354 **1** **The History Man (IRE)**[14] 6596 6-9-1 55 (p) HayleyTurner 3 64
(B D Leavy) *led for over 2f: styd prom and sn u.p: rallied to regain ld jst ins fnl f: kpt on wl* **9/1**
3221 **2** *½* **The Name Is Frank**[15] 6553 4-9-3 57 (t) EddieAhern 7 64
(Mark Gillard) *prom: led over 2f out: sn rdn: hdd jst ins fnl f: kpt on: hld towards fin* **3/1**[1]
0046 **3** *¾* **Billy Beetroot (USA)**[41] 5809 3-9-3 58 (p) LukeMorris 8 63
(R A Harris) *chsd ldrs: rdn wl over 2f out: kpt on ins fnl f* **16/1**
0034 **4** *¾* **Diane's Choice**[23] 6335 6-9-1 55 (e) DavidProbert 5 57
(Miss Gay Kelleway) *chsd ldrs: rdn over 2f out: swtchd lft jst over 1f out: kpt on* **6/1**[3]
546 **5** *½* **Desert Pride**[21] 6377 4-9-4 58 (v) FergusSweeney 2 59
(W S Kittow) *trckd ldrs: rdn and ev ch ent fnl f: no ex* **8/1**
1450 **6** *½* **Outer Hebrides**[6] 6790 8-8-11 56 (v) AmyBaker(5) 11 55
(J M Bradley) *hld up: rdn over 2f out: nt pce to chal* **12/1**
0532 **7** *½* **Vanadium**[14] 6587 7-9-2 56 (tp) RichardHughes 9 53
(A J Lidderdale) *hld up bhd: hdwy in centre over 2f out: sn rdn: one pce fnl f* **11/2**[2]
0035 **8** *1 ¼* **Namu**[21] 6377 6-9-2 56 (p) DaneO'Neill 4 49
(Miss T Spearing) *cl up: rdn over 2f out: fdd ent fnl f* **12/1**
5334 **9** *1* **Dualagi**[34] 6039 5-9-2 56 JimCrowley 10 45
(M R Bosley) *hld up: short lived effrt over 2f out* **13/2**
0605 **10** *1 ¾* **Pinball (IRE)**[9] 6739 3-9-3 58 (v) NeilChalmers 12 42
(Mrs L Williamson) *hld up: nt clr run on ins rail over 2f out: rdn over 1f out: sn wknd* **16/1**
0030 **11** *2 ¾* **Triumphant Welcome**[121] 3227 4-9-2 56 VinceSlattery 6 30
(H J Evans) *s.i.s: a towards rr* **33/1**

1m 11.7s (0.50) **Going Correction** -0.075s/f (Good)
WFA 3 from 4yo+ 1lb **11** Ran SP% **119.2**
Speed ratings (Par 101): **93,92,91,90,89 89,88,86,85,83 79**
toteswinger: 1&2 £8.80, 1&3 £10.00, 2&3 £16.40. CSF £36.64 CT £446.89 TOTE £9.80: £2.90, £1.30, £4.10; EX 35.80 Trifecta £176.20 Part won. Pool: £238.22 - 0.10 winning units..
Owner D E Simpson & R Farrington-Kirkham **Bred** J Beckett **Trained** Forsbrook, Staffs

FOCUS
A modest sprint handicap and not the most straightforward bunch with ten of the 12 runners requiring some sort of headgear. Again they came over towards the stands' rail and this that raced handily dominated throughout. The form appears fairly solid rated around the first three.

6934 FREEBETS.CO.UK HORSE RACING FREE BETS MAIDEN FILLIES' STKS 1m 2f 46y
4:00 (4:00) (Class 5) 3-Y-O+ **£2,590** (£770; £385; £192) **Stalls** Low

Form RPR
4-23 **1** **Finney Hill**[9] 6733 4-9-3 75 DaneO'Neill 7 76
(H Candy) *mde all: styd on wl fnl f: drvn out* **11/4**[1]
3020 **2** *nk* **In Secret**[9] 6740 3-8-12 69 EddieAhern 11 76
(J L Dunlop) *mid-div: smooth hdwy on ins rail fr over 3f out: rdn to chse wnr: styd on: clsng at fin* **9/1**
6-50 **3** *1 ¾* **Capitelli (IRE)**[148] 2356 3-8-12 73 RichardHughes 2 72
(R Hannon) *chsd wnr most of way: effrt to chal over 2f out: styd on same pce fnl f* **13/2**[2]
3432 **4** *shd* **Insolence (USA)**[26] 6257 3-8-12 72 RyanMoore 1 72
(Sir Michael Stoute) *chsd ldrs: hrd rdn 3f out: styd on same pce fnl 2f* **11/4**[1]
24 **5** *½* **Crazy Chris**[25] 6276 4-9-3 0 RichardKingscote 10 71
(Tom Dascombe) *trckd ldrs: rdn wl over 2f out: styd on same pce fnl f* **10/1**
6 *11* **Spring Fashion (IRE)** 3-8-9 0 AndreaAtzeni(3) 12 49
(M Botti) *in tch: rdn 3f out: wknd over 1f out* **25/1**
7 *11* **Gaditana** 3-8-12 0 DavidProbert 3 27+
(Pat Eddery) *racd green: slowly away: a in rr* **12/1**
0 **8** *½* **Stage Performance (IRE)**[68] 4991 3-8-12 0 JimmyFortune 14 26+
(J H M Gosden) *trckd ldrs: rdn over 2f out: eased whn btn over 1f out* **8/1**[3]
04 **9** *hd* **Denices Desert**[23] 6332 3-8-12 0 JimmyQuinn 9 26
(M Botti) *in tch tl wknd over 2f out* **40/1**
10 *6* **Blue Celeste** 3-8-12 0 SteveDrowne 8 14
(R T Phillips) *unsettled in stalls: slowly away: a bhd* **66/1**
0 **11** *½* **Berkalani (IRE)**[47] 5628 3-8-12 0 CatherineGannon 4 13
(P D Evans) *mid-div: reminders after 2f: bhd fnl 3f* **40/1**
5-0 **12** *3 ¾* **Devon Diva**[121] 3228 3-8-12 0 SimonWhitworth 6 5
(J F Panvert) *a towards rr* **100/1**
13 *1 ¼* **Seren Arian** 3-8-12 0 NeilChalmers 13 3
(B Palling) *s.i.s: a towards rr* **100/1**
00 **14** *nk* **Bengers Lass (USA)**[9] 6741 3-8-12 0 DarryllHolland 15 2
(R Curtis) *a towards rr* **125/1**

2m 11.27s (0.27) **Going Correction** +0.175s/f (Good)
WFA 3 from 4yo 5lb **14** Ran SP% **117.6**
Speed ratings (Par 100): **105,104,103,103,102 94,85,84,84,79 79,76,75,75**
toteswinger: 1&2 £8.80, 1&3 £6.60, 2&3 £14.50. CSF £28.07 TOTE £3.40: £1.50, £3.20, £2.70; EX 27.60 Trifecta £215.30 Part won. Pool: £291.05 - 0.96 winning units..
Owner Major M G Wyatt **Bred** Dunchurch Lodge Stud Company **Trained** Kingston Warren, Oxon

FOCUS
An ordinary fillies' maiden but the form looks straightforward enough rated around those in the frame behind the winner.
Gaditana Official explanation: jockey said filly was slowly away and ran green
Stage Performance(IRE) Official explanation: jockey said filly stumbled approaching final furlong

6935 FREEBETS.CO.UK FREE BETS H'CAP 2m 1f 34y
4:30 (4:30) (Class 5) (0-75,69) 3-Y-O **£2,590** (£770; £385; £192) **Stalls** Centre

Form RPR
4112 **1** **Saborido (USA)**[34] 6037 3-9-4 66 JimCrowley 5 71
(Mrs A J Perrett) *trckd ldr: led over 2f out: styd on wl: rdn out* **15/8**[1]
4034 **2** *2 ¾* **Wightgold**[29] 6188 3-8-2 50 oh3 JimmyQuinn 7 52
(H J L Dunlop) *wnt rt s: racd in cl 4th: wnt 3rd 6f out: effrt 2f out: styd on wout mounting serious chal* **4/1**[2]
2323 **3** *nk* **Theologist (IRE)**[16] 6543 3-9-7 69 RyanMoore 6 70
(Mrs A J Perrett) *led: rdn and hdd over 2f out: styd on* **15/8**[1]
0605 **4** *1 ¾* **Brandy Butter**[21] 6375 3-8-7 55 (v) WilliamBuick 1 54
(A M Balding) *trckd ldng pair tl 6f out: remained cl enough: rdn 3f out: no imp* **5/1**[3]
5 *10* **Emily Harley (IRE)**[37] 3-8-4 55 WilliamCarson(3) 4 42
(W G M Turner) *racd in cl 5th: effrt 3f out: wknd over 1f out* **16/1**

3m 58.68s (6.78) **Going Correction** +0.175s/f (Good) **5** Ran SP% **112.1**
Speed ratings (Par 101): **91,89,89,88,84**
toteswinger: 1&2 £9.20. CSF £9.96 TOTE £2.60: £1.50, £2.10; EX 12.50.
Owner Tracey, Cotton, James, Slade **Bred** R D Hubbard And R Masterson **Trained** Pulborough, W Sussex

FOCUS
An ordinary 3-y-o staying handicap, especially after the withdrawal of the likely favourite Khayar, and they went no pace early with the field in single file for the first 1m3f. The form is limited by the proximity of the third and fourth.

6936 FREEBETS.CO.UK ONLINE BETTING H'CAP 1m 3f 144y
5:00 (5:00) (Class 4) (0-80,80) 3-Y-O+ **£4,727** (£1,406; £702; £351) **Stalls** Low

Form RPR
5115 **1** **Rockfella**[20] 6420 3-8-7 71 AlanMunro 11 82
(D J Coakley) *hld up towards rr: gd hdwy on nrside rail fr 3f out: rdn to ld ins fnl f: r.o wl* **14/1**
51-1 **2** *2* **Foxhaven**[65] 5097 7-9-9 80 (v) RichardKingscote 1 88
(P R Chamings) *trckd ldrs: led 3f out: sn rdn: hdd ins fnl f: no ex* **9/2**[2]
1516 **3** *1 ¼* **Sweet Hollow**[20] 6419 3-8-13 77 (b) AdamKirby 14 83
(C G Cox) *trckd ldrs: rdn over 2f out: styd on same pce fnl f* **22/1**
1506 **4** *1 ¼* **King Supreme (IRE)**[46] 5667 4-9-3 74 (b) RyanMoore 10 78
(R Hannon) *hld up towards rr: rdn and hdwy fr 2f out: swtchd to nrside rail ent fnl f: styd on* **14/1**
6240 **5** *2* **Force Group (IRE)**[12] 6636 5-8-13 70 (b) JimmyQuinn 5 71
(M H Tompkins) *mid-div: rdn over 2f out: styd on fnl f* **8/1**
3245 **6** *shd* **Solar Graphite (IRE)**[61] 5216 3-8-8 72 EddieAhern 12 73
(J L Dunlop) *hld up towards rr: hdwy 6f out: rdn to chal over 3f out: wknd ent fnl f* **3/1**[1]
250 **7** *3* **Mae Cigan (FR)**[19] 6457 6-8-6 66 oh7 Louis-PhilippeBeuzelin(3) 2 62
(M Blanshard) *towards rr: sme late prog past btn horses: nvr a factor* **33/1**
0421 **8** *1 ¼* **Dove Cottage (IRE)**[15] 6566 7-9-3 74 FergusSweeney 6 68
(W S Kittow) *prom: rdn and ev ch 3f out tl wknd jst over 1f out* **14/1**
0111 **9** *nk* **Denton (NZ)**[19] 6460 6-9-0 71 (t) SteveDrowne 3 64
(J R Gask) *mid-div: in tch whn rdn 3f out: wknd over 1f out* **7/1**[3]
5510 **10** *½* **Pelham Crescent (IRE)**[9] 6733 6-9-8 79 DavidProbert 7 72
(B Palling) *mid-div: rdn 4f out: wknd over 1f out* **14/1**
6664 **11** *½* **Goodwood Starlight (IRE)**[11] 6681 4-9-5 76 (t) DarryllHolland 8 68
(G L Moore) *a towards rr* **9/1**
-200 **12** *5* **Ruler Of All (IRE)**[9] 6734 3-9-0 78 DaneO'Neill 13 62
(H Candy) *led tl 3f out: sn wknd* **11/1**
1142 **13** *2* **Run For Ede's**[81] 4544 5-9-7 78 IanMongan 4 59
(P M Phelan) *towards rr: hdwy 6f out: rdn 3f out: wknd 2f out* **14/1**
5250 **14** *17* **Calaloo (IRE)**[13] 6613 3-8-12 76 (b) WilliamBuick 9 29
(C R Egerton) *chsd ldrs tl wknd over 2f out* **28/1**

2m 31.13s (0.53) **Going Correction** +0.175s/f (Good)
WFA 3 from 4yo+ 7lb **14** Ran SP% **129.2**
Speed ratings (Par 105): **105,103,102,102,100 100,98,97,97,97 96,93,92,80**
toteswinger: 1&2 £20.40, 1&3 £65.30, 2&3 £25.50. CSF £80.02 CT £1442.98 TOTE £20.00: £5.80, £2.20, £6.30; EX 153.30 TRIFECTA Not won..

Owner L M A Hurley **Bred** Ascagnano S P A **Trained** West Ilsley, Berks

FOCUS

A competitive handicap and a race of changing fortunes in which the third is the best guide to the level. Again the runners came up the stands' rail in the straight.

Denton(NZ) Official explanation: jockey said gelding had a breathing problem

Pelham Crescent(IRE) Official explanation: jockey said he lost an iron 2f out; trainer's rep said gelding was unsuited by the good (good to soft places) ground

6937 FREEBETS.CO.UK ONLINE FREE BETS APPRENTICE H'CAP — 1m 5y

5:30 (5:30) (Class 5) (0-75,74) 3-Y-0+ — **£2,590** (£770; £385; £192) **Stalls** Low

Form — RPR

2224 **1** **Truly Asia (IRE)**[40] 5833 3-9-5 **74**....(t) JPFahy 4 82
(R Charlton) *trckd ldrs: c to nr side 3f out: sn rdn: r.o ins fnl f: drifted lft: led nr fin* **4/1**[2]

6035 **2** 3/4 **Support Fund (IRE)**[25] 6294 5-9-7 **73**.... SimonPearce 7 80
(Eve Johnson Houghton) *hld up bhd: hdwy in centre fr 3f out: rdn 2f out: led wl ins fnl f: hdd nr fin* **13/2**[3]

1565 **3** 1 **Eastern Warrior**[18] 6474 3-9-2 **74**.... KierenFox(3) 1 78
(J W Hills) *led: racd alone on far side fr over 3f out: kpt on but no ex whn wl ins fnl f* **17/2**

2124 **4** 1 1/4 **Magroom**[16] 6547 5-8-12 **69**.... RyanPowell(5) 2 71
(R J Hodges) *trckd ldrs: short of room and lost pl over 5f out: hdwy 3f out: drifted rt to nr side u.p sn after: kpt on same pce* **3/1**[1]

0006 **5** 1 1/4 **Grey Boy (GER)**[9] 6725 8-8-1 **60**.... GeorgeDowning(7) 9 59
(A W Carroll) *trckd ldrs: c nr side 3f out: rdn over 2f out: sn one pce* **11/1**

3403 **6** 2 **Full Victory (IRE)**[2] 6908 7-9-1 **67**.... AndrewHeffernan 10 61
(R A Farrant) *trckd ldr: c nrside 3f out: sn rdn: one pce fnl 2f* **4/1**[2]

6-60 **7** 2 **Shannersburg (IRE)**[7] 6778 4-9-8 **74**.... ByronMoorcroft 6 64
(A B Haynes) *struggling on nr side 3f out: a towards rr* **28/1**

610 **8** 3/4 **Diktat Queen**[13] 6621 3-9-4 **73**.... TobyAtkinson 5 60
(Rae Guest) *t.k.h: mid-div: c nr side over 2f out: wknd over 1f out* **8/1**

3110 **9** 2 1/4 **Lordship (IRE)**[16] 6545 5-8-6 **63**.... JakePayne(5) 8 46
(A W Carroll) *stdd s: effrt 3f out on nr side: wknd over 1f out* **14/1**

1m 42.48s (1.68) **Going Correction** +0.175s/f (Good)

WFA 3 from 4yo+ 3lb — **9** Ran SP% **118.4**

Speed ratings (Par 103): **98,97,96,95,93 91,89,89,86**

toteswinger: 1&2 £5.20, 1&3 £7.30, 2&3 £11.50. CSF £31.07 CT £213.42 TOTE £4.20: £1.20, £2.90, £2.90; EX 26.50 Trifecta £289.20 Part won. Pool: £390.83 - 0.86 winning units. Place 6: £16.92, Place 5: £8.54..

Owner H R H Sultan Ahmad Shah **Bred** Forenaghts Stud **Trained** Beckhampton, Wilts

■ Stewards' Enquiry : J P Fahy one-day ban: careless riding (Nov 4)

FOCUS

A modest apprentice handicap in which the pace was ordinary and a few of these were inclined to take a grip. The bulk of the field followed the trend of previous races by coming up the stands' rail in the home straight, but Eastern Warrior stayed to race alone up the inside. The form is straightforward rated around the placed horses.

Diktat Queen Official explanation: vet said filly bled from the nose

T/Jkpt: £25,232.90 to a £1 stake. Pool: £71,078.71. 2.00 winning tickets. T/Plt: £22.20 to a £1 stake. Pool: £63,497.72. 2,079.50 winning tickets. T/Qpdt: £15.20 to a £1 stake. Pool: £4,127.10. 200.84 winning tickets. TM

6770 KEMPTON (A.W) (R-H)

Wednesday, October 21

OFFICIAL GOING: Standard

Wind: Moderate behindh Weather: Overcast

6938 KEMPTON.CO.UK NURSERY — 5f (P)

5:50 (5:51) (Class 6) (0-60,60) 2-Y-0 — **£2,047** (£604; £302) **Stalls** High

Form — RPR

060 **1** **Blue Neptune**[23] 6347 2-9-2 **56**.... MartinDwyer 7 64+
(W R Muir) *led: drvn clr appr fnl f: unchal* **4/1**[1]

2305 **2** 2 1/2 **True Red (IRE)**[23] 6345 2-8-11 **58**.... RachelKing(7) 4 57
(Mrs N S Evans) *sn chsng wnr: rdn 2f out: no imp fr over 1f out but styd on for clr 2nd* **14/1**

6040 **3** 2 **Cookie Galore**[6] 6797 2-8-13 **56**.... FrederikTylicki(3) 3 48
(J A Glover) *s.i.s: in rr: hdwy 2f out: styd on wl fr over 1f out to chse ldng duo fnl f but no imp* **8/1**[3]

5040 **4** 1 **Exceed Power**[42] 5776 2-8-11 **56**....(t) MartinLane(5) 5 44
(D M Simcock) *in rr: rdn 2f out: hdwy u.p appr fnl f but nvr gng pce to rch ldrs* **8/1**[3]

604 **5** nk **Chinese Democracy (USA)**[130] 2907 2-9-4 **58**.... TomEaves 8 45+
(P F I Cole) *bmpd s: in rr: rdn and hdwy towards outside wl over 1f out: fin wl but nvr a threat* **10/1**

506 **6** 1 **Caol Ila (IRE)**[23] 6347 2-9-4 **58**.... J-PGuillambert 9 42
(J G Given) *chsd ldrs: rdn and hung rt over 1f out: wknd ins fnl f* **7/1**[2]

000 **7** 1 **Dreamy Eyed (IRE)**[14] 6582 2-9-5 **59**.... TGMcLaughlin 6 40+
(Mrs P N Dutfield) *t.k.h: towards rr but in tch: rdn and sme hdwy whn hmpd over 1f out: nvr a threat after* **16/1**

000 **8** 2 1/2 **Titoli Di Coda (IRE)**[26] 6245 2-9-2 **56**.... KFallon 11 27
(L M Cumani) *chsd ldrs: rdn 2f out: wknd appr fnl f* **8/1**[3]

0006 **9** nk **Beyond The City (USA)**[21] 6373 2-9-2 **56**.... PatDobbs 12 26
(R Hannon) *in tch: rdn 2f out: no imp on ldrs and wknd over 1f out* **4/1**[1]

006 **10** 6 **Avon Grounds**[22] 6364 2-9-0 **57**.... MCGeran(3) 10 5
(J M Bradley) *s.i.s: sn rdn and a in rr* **20/1**

405 **11** 3 1/4 **Phoenix Rose (IRE)**[22] 6356 2-9-6 **60**.... RobertWinston 2 —
(J R Best) *chsd ldrs: rdn and wknd 1/2-way* **10/1**

60.63 secs (0.13) **Going Correction** 0.0s/f (Stan) — **11** Ran SP% **121.3**

Speed ratings (Par 93): **98,94,90,89,88 87,85,81,81,71 66**

toteswinger: 1&2 £18.10, 1&3 £10.00, 2&3 £20.40. CSF £66.18 CT £439.02 TOTE £4.30: £1.70, £3.90, £3.00; EX 76.30.

Owner Martin P Graham **Bred** T E Pocock And C M Oakshott **Trained** Lambourn, Berks

FOCUS

The course had been power-harrowed to a depth of 75mm the previous day and the going was described as standard. A very ordinary nursery devoid of a single previous winner and the exposed runner-up puts the form into perspective.

NOTEBOOK

Blue Neptune had excuses for being beaten on his previous three starts, as there was a bug in the stable after his first outing, he paid for trying to keep tabs with a useful sort at Sandown on his second start, and he was drawn wide and gave away plenty of ground at Wolverhampton last time. Backed into joint-favouritism for this handicap debut, he was quickly away and had secured the lead by the time they got to the first turn. It was easy for him from there, and he might be up to defying a little rise in the weights. Official explanation: trainer said, regarding apparent improvement in form, that the colt ran quite well on its previous run despite being badly drawn. (op 9-2 tchd 7-2)

True Red(IRE), the most experienced runner in the race, likes to make the running but, being drawn lower than the winner, wasn't quite up to taking the outright lead. She ran a solid race, but the Handicapper knows all about her.

Cookie Galore, dropping back from 6f, settled better this time and ran a sound race considering she was poorly drawn and ended up racing wide throughout. She'll be interesting for a similarly modest affair when faring better with the draw. (op 9-1 tchd 10-1)

Exceed Power, not for the first time, was doing her best work at the finish, but she remains opposable. (tchd 9-1)

Chinese Democracy(USA) got outpaced before running on again at the finish. This trip looked on the short side for her and she'll be more interesting back over 6f, especially having been off the track for 130 days prior to this handicap debut. (op 12-1 tchd 9-1)

Beyond The City(USA) had the best draw but, although he'd shown good early speed over 1m last time, he found the early pace over this trip all too much. (tchd 9-2)

6939 SYLVIA BAKER 60TH BIRTHDAY H'CAP — 5f (P)

6:20 (6:20) (Class 6) (0-55,55) 3-Y-0+ — **£2,047** (£604; £302) **Stalls** High

Form — RPR

4556 **1** **Spoof Master (IRE)**[105] 3735 5-9-1 **54**.... LPKeniry 12 60
(C R Dore) *mde virtually all: hld on gamely u.p fnl f* **15/2**

4324 **2** hd **Avrilo**[4] 6856 3-9-0 **53**.... RobertWinston 10 58
(M S Saunders) *chsd ldrs: rdn to go narrow 2nd ins fnl f: styd on but jst hld by wnr* **4/1**[1]

0032 **3** hd **Jolly Ranch**[39] 5881 3-8-10 **54**.... MartinLane(5) 2 58+
(A G Newcombe) *in tch towards outside: rdn and gd hdwy over 1f out: styd on strly ins fnl f but nt quite get to ldng duo* **16/1**

4040 **4** nk **Ask Jenny (IRE)**[113] 3471 7-9-1 **54**.... RichardHughes 3 57+
(Patrick Morris) *bmpd and stdd in rr s and stl plenty to do appr fnl f: sn str run and rapid hdwy ins fnl f: fin fast but nt quite rch ldrs* **14/1**

3500 **5** 1/2 **Cheshire Rose**[19] 6456 4-9-0 **53**....(p) LiamJones 11 54
(A M Hales) *chsd ldrs: rdn over 1f out: outpcd cl home* **14/1**

01 **6** shd **Chantilly Jewel (USA)**[47] 5645 4-9-2 **55**....(b) RichardMullen 4 56+
(R M H Cowell) *in rr: wd into st and hdwy appr fnl f: fin wl: nt rch ldrs* **14/1**

0510 **7** 1 1/2 **Best One**[11] 6674 5-8-13 **52**....(v) LukeMorris 7 47
(R A Harris) *chsd ldrs: rdn over 1f out: wknd wl ins fnl f* **5/1**[3]

4004 **8** nk **Well Of Echoes**[8] 6755 3-8-11 **53**....(bt) FrederikTylicki(3) 9 47
(J A Glover) *pressed ldr and upsides 1/2-way: rdn ins fnl 2f: wknd ins fnl f* **9/2**[2]

3220 **9** 1 1/4 **Monsieur Reynard**[15] 6553 4-8-13 **55**....(b) MCGeran(3) 5 45
(J M Bradley) *chsd ldrs: rdn 2f out: wkng whn n.m.r jst ins fnl f* **11/2**

0300 **10** 1 **Maryolini**[19] 6456 4-8-11 **55**.... RossAtkinson(5) 8 41
(Tom Dascombe) *rdn 2f out and outpcd most of way* **8/1**

0000 **11** 2 3/4 **Woodcote (IRE)**[48] 5610 7-8-13 **52**....(v) FrankieMcDonald 6 28
(Peter Grayson) *rrd bdly s and a outpcd in rr* **40/1**

60.46 secs (-0.04) **Going Correction** 0.0s/f (Stan) — **11** Ran SP% **121.4**

Speed ratings (Par 101): **100,99,99,98,98 97,95,95,93,91 87**

toteswinger: 1&2 £6.20, 1&3 £23.70, 2&3 £7.60. CSF £38.87 CT £488.52 TOTE £6.90: £2.60, £1.70, £4.60; EX 42.60.

Owner Mrs Jennifer Marsh **Bred** Chris McHale And Oghill House Stud **Trained** Cowbit, Lincs

FOCUS

With the top-weight rated just 55 this looked a moderate handicap and the form is very ordinary rated around the first two.

6940 KIA SOUL, SAFE BET CLAIMING STKS — 1m 2f (P)

6:50 (6:50) (Class 6) 3-4-Y-0 — **£2,047** (£604; £302) **Stalls** High

Form — RPR

000 **1** **Satwa Gold (USA)**[14] 6594 3-9-2 77.... KFallon 6 73+
(E A L Dunlop) *hld up in mid-div: hdwy: nt clr run and swtchd lft wl over 1f out: str run to peg bk clr ldr ins fnl f: led last strides* **9/2**[2]

2-00 **2** hd **Hurakan (IRE)**[9] 6740 3-9-0 77.... LPKeniry 2 71
(Mrs A J Perrett) *trckd ldr tl led over 2f out: rdn 4 l clr appr fnl f: shkn up ins fnl f: ct last strides* **14/1**

0100 **3** 3 1/2 **Inconspicuous Miss (USA)**[6] 6804 3-8-2 68.... MatthewDavies(5) 11 57
(George Baker) *chsd ldrs: wnt 2nd but no ch w ldr wl over 1f out: styd on same pce fnl f* **15/2**

0304 **4** 1 1/2 **By Command**[21] 6395 4-9-5 60....(p) MichaelHills 8 61
(J W Hills) *in rr: hdwy and nt clr run wl over 1f out: styd on fnl f but no ch w ldng trio* **16/1**

5003 **5** 3/4 **The Dial House**[25] 6289 3-9-3 72.... ShaneKelly 4 63
(J A Osborne) *s.i.s: in rr tl hdwy and n.m.r wl over 1f out: kpt on fnl f: nvr a threat* **4/1**[1]

0640 **6** 1 1/2 **Candy Rose**[28] 6213 4-8-10 52....(t) PatDobbs 10 48
(M P Tregoning) *chsd ldrs: rdn along fr 4f out: wknd ins fnl f* **14/1**

5030 **7** 1/2 **Interchoice Star**[170] 1741 4-8-12 47.... RussellKennemore(3) 3 52
(R Hollinshead) *s.i.s: in rr: hdwy and n.m.r wl over 1f out and again by wkng horse appr fnl f: kpt on but nvr a threat* **25/1**

0456 **8** hd **Harting Hill**[65] 5113 4-9-1 45.... RichardMullen 7 51
(M P Tregoning) *mid-div: rdn 4f out: nvr gng pce to get into contention and wknd fnl f* **16/1**

5022 **9** 4 1/2 **Sixties Swinger (USA)**[21] 6395 3-9-4 65....(bt[1]) PhilipRobinson 5 50
(M A Jarvis) *in tch: hrd rdn over 3f out: hung lft: nt keen and wknd qckly 2f out* **9/2**[2]

200- **10** 1 3/4 **Little Finch (IRE)**[314] 7637 4-8-8 45.... CatherineGannon 9 32
(S Curran) *chsd ldrs: rdn over 3f out: wknd qckly 2f out* **16/1**

100 **11** 22 **Drussell (IRE)**[21] 6400 3-8-12 70.... RichardHughes 1 —
(S Donohoe, Ire) *led tl hdd over 2f out: lost 2nd wl over 1f out: wknd rapidly and eased fnl f* **11/2**[3]

2m 7.25s (-0.75) **Going Correction** 0.0s/f (Stan)

WFA 3 from 4yo 5lb — **11** Ran SP% **118.3**

Speed ratings (Par 101): **103,102,100,98,98 97,96,96,92,91 73**

toteswinger: 1&2 £15.60, 1&3 £17.50, 2&3 £16.70. CSF £66.44 TOTE £4.70: £1.40, £5.60, £3.40; EX 38.90.Hurakan was claimed by David Evans for £12,000.

Owner The Lamprell Partnership **Bred** B P Walden, L Taylor Et Al **Trained** Newmarket, Suffolk

FOCUS

The two who were best in at the weights finished clear in this claimer and there re doubts over the form.

Interchoice Star Official explanation: jockey said gelding was denied a clear run early in home straight

Drussell(IRE) Official explanation: jockey said gelding lost its action

6941 DIGIBET MEDIAN AUCTION MAIDEN STKS — 1m 4f (P)

7:20 (7:21) (Class 5) 3-5-Y-0 — **£2,590** (£770; £385; £192) **Stalls** Centre

Form — RPR

3-23 **1** **Count Of Tuscany (USA)**[43] 5744 3-9-3 75.... JimCrowley 9 78+
(Mrs A J Perrett) *trckd ldrs: led appr fnl 2f: hung lft fr 1f out: easily* **6/4**[1]

44 **2** *6* **Bowsers Beau**[13] 6608 3-9-3 0 .... PatDobbs 4 65
(M P Tregoning) *mid-div: pushed along 3f out: edgd lft and r.o wl fnl f to take a n.d 2nd* **5/1**[3]

0030 **3** *3/4* **Cayman Sky**[9] 6742 3-9-3 59 .... (b) RichardHughes 3 64
(R Hannon) *hld up in rr: hdwy fr 3f out: drvn over 1f out and sn edgd lft: disp 2nd ins fnl f but nvr any ch w wnr and sn one pce* **8/1**

2203 **4** *1* **Storming Sioux**[21] 6375 3-8-12 65 .... KFallon 7 57
(W J Haggas) *hld up in tch: hdwy to chse ldrs 3f out: disp n.d 2nd and edgd lft ins fnl f: wknd cl home* **11/2**

0035 **5** *shd* **Holden Eagle**[28] 6204 4-9-10 73 .... RussellKennemore 8 62
(A G Newcombe) *chsd ldrs: led ins fnl 3f: rdn and hdd appr fnl 2f and sn bmpd: styd disputing wl hld 2nd ins fnl f and hung rt: wknd nr fin* **11/4**[2]

0-05 **6** *16* **Desert Fairy**[109] 3610 3-8-12 48 .... RobertWinston 5 32
(J W Unett) *towards rr: sme prog on outside 3f out: sn hung rt and bhd* **50/1**

0430 **7** *4 1/2* **Felicia**[13] 6612 4-9-2 45 .... NataliaGemelova(3) 10 24
(J E Long) *chsd ldr tl led after 4f: hdd & wknd ins fnl 3f* **40/1**

0-00 **8** *2 1/4* **Reel Man**[35] 5987 4-9-5 45 .... MarkCoumbe(5) 2 26
(D K Ivory) *in rr: rdn 6f out: chsd ldrs 3f out: sn wknd* **66/1**

00 **9** *8* **Set Em Up Mo**[27] 6223 3-8-12 47 .... (v1) LiamJones 1 8
(M J Attwater) *sn led: hdd after 4f: wknd over 3f out* **66/1**

10 *84* **Miss Blueandblack (IRE)**[60] 3-8-12 0 .... LPKeniry 6 —
(Jean-Rene Auvray) *rdn 5f out: a wl bhd: t.o fnl 4f* **66/1**

2m 33.38s (-1.12) **Going Correction** 0.0s/f (Stan)
WFA 3 from 4yo 7lb **10** Ran SP% **118.7**
Speed ratings (Par 103): **103,99,98,97,97 87,84,82,77,—**
toteswinger: 1&2 £2.10, 1&3 £4.30, 2&3 £4.40. CSF £9.68 TOTE £2.20: £1.10, £1.70, £2.30; EX 11.10.
Owner K Abdulla **Bred** Juddmonte Farms Inc **Trained** Pulborough, W Sussex
■ Stewards' Enquiry : Russell Kennemore three-day ban: failed to ride out for 4th (Nov 4-6)

FOCUS
The proximity of Cayman Sky at the finish suggests this was a fairly modest maiden. The third looks the best guide to the form.

6942 DIGIBET.COM MAIDEN FILLIES' STKS 6f (P)
7:50 (7:55) (Class 5) 2-Y-O **£2,590** (£770; £385; £192) **Stalls** High

Form RPR

03 **1** **Hulcote Rose (IRE)**[9] 6722 2-9-0 0 .... JimmyFortune 6 71+
(S Kirk) *trckd ldrs: pushed along to ld 1f out: drvn and styd on strly ins fnl f* **10/11**[1]

2 *1* **Merton Matriarch** 2-9-0 0 .... JimCrowley 12 67
(P Winkworth) *led: rdn 2f out: hdd 1f out: styd on fnl f: sn nt pce of wnr but hld on wl for 2nd* **6/1**[3]

0 **3** *nse* **May Chorus (IRE)**[41] 5808 2-9-0 0 .... SJCraine 10 67
(J R Boyle) *chsd ldrs: rdn and hung lft appr fnl 3f: nt pce of wnr ins fnl f but rallied wl to press for 2nd last strides* **33/1**

0 **4** *3/4* **Kummel Excess (IRE)**[14] 6582 2-8-9 0 .... MatthewDavies(5) 3 65
(George Baker) *t.k.h: stdd towards rr but in tch: hdwy on outside over 1f out: kpt on ins fnl f but no imp on ldrs nr fin* **66/1**

5 *1 1/2* **Alinghi (IRE)** 2-9-0 0 .... RichardHughes 9 60
(R Hannon) *s.i.s: in rr early: hdwy to chse ldrs over 2f out: sn rdn: no imp and wknd fnl f* **7/1**

6 *1* **Akamon** 2-9-0 0 .... KFallon 7 58+
(E A L Dunlop) *chsd ldrs: pushed along: hung rt and green 2f out: sme prog whn carried lft over 1f out: n.d after* **11/2**[2]

7 *1 1/2* **Gibraltar Lass (USA)** 2-9-0 0 .... DarryllHolland 2 53
(H J Collingridge) *chsd ldrs: rdn over 2f out: wknd over 1f out* **16/1**

8 *7* **Krysanthe** 2-9-0 0 .... RichardThomas 11 32
(J A Geake) *v.s.a: a in rr* **40/1**

0 **9** *2 1/2* **Sandfairyann**[68] 4980 2-9-0 0 .... LPKeniry 1 24
(B R Johnson) *slowly away: plld hrd: a in rr* **40/1**

1m 14.41s (1.31) **Going Correction** 0.0s/f (Stan) **9** Ran SP% **109.7**
Speed ratings (Par 92): **91,89,89,88,86 85,83,73,70**
toteswinger: 1&2 £1.80, 1&3 £8.10, 2&3 £19.70. CSF £5.86 TOTE £1.60: £1.10, £1.80, £5.80; EX 7.80.
Owner The Kathryn Stud **Bred** Ecurie Des Monceaux **Trained** Upper Lambourn, Berks
■ Stewards' Enquiry : S J Craine three-day ban: careless riding (Nov 4-6)

FOCUS
Experience paid in this fillies' maiden and the winner did not need to improve much on recent form.

NOTEBOOK
Hulcote Rose(IRE) failed to land a gamble when backed in from 25-1 to 7s and only third over this C&D last time out, but she gave her supporters few worries on this occasion and, having been solidly supported into odds-on, got the job done in professional style. She had to be kept up to her work to beat the newcomers, though, and it's questionable whether she improved from her second start, so she'll have to step up on this if she's to make her mark in handicaps. (op 11-8 tchd 5-6, 13-8 in a place and 6-5 in a place)
Merton Matriarch, representing a stable that sends out first-time-out winners from time to time, knew her job and, from the best draw, made most of the running. With a little improvement she will be dangerous in similar company next time. (op 7-1 tchd 15-2)
May Chorus(IRE) showed little on her debut but the benefit of a previous outing is worth plenty in this sort of company, and a double-figure draw was no handicap either. Tracking the pace on the rail, she enjoyed a good run through and duly improved significantly. (op 25-1)
Kummel Excess(IRE), last on her debut here over 5f, was another to show improved form for that experience. A half-sister to Lethal, who won five times on the AW, including twice at this track, out of a mare who won three times on Fibresand, she's bred to enjoy the artificial surfaces. (op 40-1)
Alinghi(IRE) should be better for the run and will appreciate a stiffer test in time. (op 5-1)

6943 DIGIBET CASINO MAIDEN STKS 7f (P)
8:20 (8:24) (Class 4) 2-Y-O **£3,885** (£1,156; £577; £288) **Stalls** High

Form RPR

220 **1** **Golden Shaheen (IRE)**[18] 6478 2-9-3 84 .... (v) TedDurcan 1 86
(Saeed Bin Suroor) *wnt lft s: sn rcvrd to ld: shkn up 2f out: sn styd on to go clr: comf* **5/4**[1]

4335 **2** *3 1/2* **Warning Song (USA)**[10] 6696 2-9-3 88 .... JimCrowley 7 77
(Mrs A J Perrett) *in tch: pushed along over 2f out: styd on wl thrght fnl f to take 2nd cl home but nvr any ch w wnr* **14/1**

44 **3** *nk* **Tartan Trip**[19] 6451 2-9-3 0 .... DavidProbert 5 77
(A M Balding) *disp 2nd tl chsd wnr over 2f out but nvr any ch: styd on same pce u.p and lost 2nd cl home* **9/4**[2]

4 *nk* **Julienas (IRE)** 2-9-3 0 .... AdamKirby 10 77+
(W R Swinburn) *in rr: pushed along and green ins fnl 3f: styd on fr over 1f out and kpt on ins fnl f: gng on cl home* **20/1**

43 **5** *2 3/4* **Nizaa (USA)**[54] 5401 2-9-3 0 .... RHills 2 69
(B W Hills) *disp 2nd tl over 2f out: wknd appr fnl f* **9/1**[3]

06 **6** *1* **Tamarind Hill (IRE)**[12] 6629 2-9-3 0 .... SteveDrowne 3 66
(C R Egerton) *in tch: rdn 3f out: and nvr rchd ldrs: one pce u.p over 2f out: wknd ins fnl f* **50/1**

7 *3 1/4* **Harris Tweed** 2-9-3 0 .... StephenDonohoe 9 58
(Sir Mark Prescott) *bhd: pushed along over 2f out: sme prog fnl f* **50/1**

8 *2* **Baibars (USA)** 2-9-3 0 .... KFallon 11 53
(G A Butler) *a towards rr* **12/1**

9 *7* **Ocean Club** 2-9-3 0 .... MichaelHills 8 36
(B W Hills) *v.s.a: rcvrd into mid-div 1/2-way: sn wknd* **16/1**

1m 26.04s (0.04) **Going Correction** 0.0s/f (Stan) **9** Ran SP% **114.1**
Speed ratings (Par 97): **99,95,94,94,91 90,86,84,76**
toteswinger: 1&2 £5.50, 1&3 £1.10, 2&3 £9.40. CSF £20.53 TOTE £2.10: £1.10, £2.90, £1.20; EX 24.60.
Owner Godolphin **Bred** Peter Gibbons And Dermot Forde **Trained** Newmarket, Suffolk

FOCUS
A decent maiden rated around the placed horses.

NOTEBOOK
Golden Shaheen(IRE), fourth on the wrong side in the draw-bias ravaged Tattersalls Timeform Million last time out, set a pretty good standard here and, despite being a bit awkward from the stalls, had no trouble at all tacking over to lead by the first bend in a race in which few seemed keen to take him on for the role. Moving easily in front with 2f to run, he stretched clear for a commanding win, and perhaps a nursery will be found for him before the end of the year as he's clearly very effective on this surface. (op 11-8 tchd 11-10 and 6-4 in a place)
Warning Song(USA), whose sire and dam were both dirst sprinters in the US, handled this surface well and saw out the seventh furlong in good style. His official rating looks ridiculous based on what he's achieved to date so handicaps look a tough option, but a maiden should come his way on this evidence. (op 12-1 tchd 16-1)
Tartan Trip had seen his Newmarket fourth boosted by the subsequent success of the third, but he was up against a useful rival here and was made to look one-paced. He has the option of handicaps now but is another who might be better off trying to pick up an ordinary maiden first. (op 2-1 tchd 5-2)
Julienas(IRE), who's out of a Cherry Hinton winner, was unfancied on this debut but he shaped with encouragement. He looks sure to come on for the run. (tchd 16-1)
Nizaa(USA) weakened after racing prominently for a long way. He needed this for a mark and will be seen to better effect in handicaps. (op 8-1)
Tamarind Hill(IRE) is another now eligible for handicaps and might show a bit more in that sphere.
Harris Tweed, who is in the Derby and once held a Racing Post Trophy entry, has bucketloads of stamina in his pedigree and is the type to make his mark in handicaps over a lot further next year.

6944 LEVY BOARD H'CAP 7f (P)
8:50 (8:51) (Class 4) (0-85,85) 3-Y-O+ **£4,727** (£1,406; £702; £351) **Stalls** High

Form RPR

1210 **1** **Captain Macarry (IRE)**[25] 6270 4-9-6 85 .... (v) TomEaves 9 96
(B Smart) *t.k.h: chsd ldrs: drvn to ld ins fnl f: rdn out* **4/1**[1]

0540 **2** *1* **Thief Of Time (IRE)**[32] 6117 3-9-3 84 .... AlanMunro 4 92
(P W Chapple-Hyam) *hld up in rr: hdwy on outside over 2f out: str run fnl f: gng on cl home but nt rch wnr* **9/1**

P-0U **3** *1 3/4* **Dubai Meydan (IRE)**[7] 6776 4-9-0 79 .... SteveDrowne 2 83
(Miss Gay Kelleway) *s.i.s: in rr: nt clr run and swtchd lft to outside wl over 2f out: styd on wl fr over 1f out: kpt on to take 3rd cl home but no ch w ldng duo* **14/1**

1651 **4** *nk* **Arachnophobia (IRE)**[28] 6212 3-9-0 81 .... RobertWinston 11 83
(Pat Eddery) *disp ld tl def advantage ins fnl 3f: sn hrd drvn: hdd ins fnl f: wknd nr fin* **4/1**[1]

3001 **5** *1 1/4* **Highly Regal (IRE)**[46] 5663 4-9-4 83 .... (b) LPKeniry 6 83
(R A Teal) *chsd ldrs: rdn over 2f out: wknd ins fnl f* **7/1**[3]

3331 **6** *hd* **Euston Square**[15] 6573 3-9-4 85 .... JimmyFortune 3 83
(J H M Gosden) *in tch: hdwy towards outside over 2f out: styd on fnl f but nvr gng pce to rch ldrs* **9/1**

3450 **7** *3/4* **I Confess**[12] 6630 4-8-5 77 .... (v) HollyHall(7) 5 74
(P D Evans) *disp ld tl ins fnl 3f: styd w ldr tl wknd appr fnl 2f* **12/1**

0016 **8** *1/2* **Desert Dreamer (IRE)**[10] 6702 8-9-1 85 .... RichardEvans(5) 7 81
(P D Evans) *hld up in rr: pushed along over 2f out: styd on fnl f: nvr a threat* **20/1**

060 **9** *hd* **Classic Descent**[5] 6815 4-9-3 82 .... (t) KFallon 13 77
(P J Makin) *s.i.s: sn trcking ldrs: rdn over 2f out: wknd fnl f* **6/1**[2]

4003 **10** *nk* **Baby Strange**[9] 6723 5-9-1 85 .... MartinLane(5) 10 80
(D Shaw) *s.i.s: t.k.h: chsd ldrs over 3f out: wknd appr fnl f* **16/1**

0150 **11** *dist* **Brunelleschi**[11] 6666 6-8-5 77 .... (b) JosephineBruning(7) 8 —
(P L Gilligan) *struck into and a bhd: virtually p.u fnl 2f* **25/1**

1m 25.0s (-1.00) **Going Correction** 0.0s/f (Stan)
WFA 3 from 4yo+ 2lb **11** Ran SP% **115.6**
Speed ratings (Par 105): **105,103,101,101,100 99,99,98,98,97 —**
toteswinger: 1&2 £9.10, 1&3 £15.00, 2&3 £27.90. CSF £39.73 CT £465.49 TOTE £5.10: £1.90, £3.20, £4.50; EX 49.90.
Owner Anthony D Gee **Bred** Humphrey Okeke **Trained** Hambleton, N Yorks

FOCUS
This looked pretty competitive on paper and the form looks sound, but the winner scored quite readily.
Brunelleschi Official explanation: vet said gelding was struck into

6945 BOXINGDAYRACES.CO.UK H'CAP 1m (P)
9:20 (9:20) (Class 6) (0-52,52) 3-Y-O+ **£2,047** (£604; £302) **Stalls** High

Form RPR

-303 **1** **Signora Frasi (IRE)**[77] 4667 4-9-1 52 .... FergusSweeney 10 62
(A G Newcombe) *t.k.h: trckd ldrs: rdn 2f out: led wl ins fnl f: hld on wl* **4/1**[2]

4200 **2** *nk* **Just Jimmy (IRE)**[47] 5634 4-9-0 51 .... CatherineGannon 12 60
(P D Evans) *chsd ldrs: n.m.r on ins over 2f out: sn drvn to chal: slt ld jst ins fnl f: hdd and no ex wl ins fnl f* **9/1**

0630 **3** *1 1/4* **Shake On It**[14] 6587 5-9-1 52 .... JimCrowley 3 58
(M R Hoad) *hld up in rr: str run on outside fr 2f out: styd on to chse ldrs ins fnl f: one pce cl home* **12/1**

5063 **4** *1* **Djalalabad (FR)**[9] 6719 5-9-1 52 .... (tp) TGMcLaughlin 6 56
(Mrs C A Dunnett) *t.k.h chsd ldrs and n.m.r over 2f out: styd on u.p fnl f nt gng pce to rch ldrs* **12/1**

0410 **5** *1 1/4* **Copper King**[98] 3980 5-8-13 50 .... KFallon 9 52
(Miss Tor Sturgis) *led 3f: styd chsng ldr: led again 2f out: hdd jst ins fnl f: sn wknd* **7/1**[3]

5006 **6** *hd* **Party In The Park**[23] 6339 4-9-0 51 .... SJCraine 1 51
(J R Boyle) *in rr: hdwy and n.m.r 2f out: kpt on ins fnl f but nt rch ldrs* **20/1**

2631 **7** *nk* **Gifted Heir (IRE)**[6] 6800 5-8-13 50 .... NeilChalmers 5 49
(A Bailey) *in rr: hdwy on outside 2f out: kpt on: nvr a threat* **3/1**[1]

1656 **8** *3 1/4* **Broughtons Silk**[26] 6256 4-9-1 52 .... ChrisCatlin 7 44
(W J Musson) *in tch: chsd ldrs and rdn over 2f out: sn wknd* **8/1**

0440 **9** 2 3/4 **Artreju (GER)**[22] 6369 6-8-10 **50**.................................. RobertLButler(3) 8 35
(P Butler) *mid-div: rdn over 3f out: sn wknd* **25/1**
405 **10** *hd* **Tyrana (GER)**[125] 3074 6-9-1 **52**.............................. StephenDonohoe 13 37
(Ian Williams) *in rr tl mod prog fnl f* **8/1**
2000 **11** 1/2 **Cavalry Guard (USA)**[102] 3863 5-8-8 **50**........................ AmyBaker(5) 11 33
(T D McCarthy) *led 3f: styd pressing ldr and led again briefly over 2f out: sn hdd & wknd* **33/1**
5064 **12** 1 1/4 **All You Need (IRE)**[20] 6433 5-8-12 **52**..........(p) RussellKennemore(3) 14 32
(R Hollinshead) *led after 3f: kpt slt ld tl hdd & wknd over 2f out* **20/1**
0056 **13** 1 1/2 **Heavenly Saint**[11] 6674 4-8-13 **50**.............................. RichardThomas 4 27
(C Roberts) *in rr: sme hdwy on outside 3f out: sn wknd* **66/1**

1m 40.09s (0.29) **Going Correction** 0.0s/f (Stan) **13** Ran SP% **122.9**
Speed ratings (Par 101): **98,97,96,95,94 94,93,90,87,87 87,85,84**
toteswinger: 1&2 £11.80, 1&3 £17.20, 2&3 £31.30. CSF £38.42 CT £423.29 TOTE £5.70: £2.20, £3.50, £5.60; EX 60.50 Place 6: £35.89, Place 5: £13.11..
Owner A G Newcombe **Bred** Mrs Clodagh McStay **Trained** Yarnscombe, Devon
■ Stewards' Enquiry : Catherine Gannon one-day ban: used whip with excessive frequency (Nov 4)

FOCUS
A moderate handicap but sound enough form rated around the placed horses.
Copper King Official explanation: jockey said gelding finished lame
T/Plt: £79.30 to a £1 stake. Pool: £69,780.05. 641.69 winning tickets. T/Qpdt: £8.20 to a £1 stake. Pool: £6,728.19. 602.31 winning tickets. ST

6874 SOUTHWELL (L-H)
Wednesday, October 21

OFFICIAL GOING: Standard
Wind: virtually nil Weather: Overcast and showers

6946 BETDAQ ASIAN H'CAPS - BETDAQ HANDICAP 1m (F)
2:10 (2:10) (Class 4) (0-85,89) 3-Y-O+ **£5,828** (£1,734; £866; £432) **Stalls** Low

Form RPR
1540 **1** **Ultimate**[11] 6680 3-8-11 **76**.. RobertWinston 1 94+
(H Morrison) *mde all: rdn along 2f out: styd on strly and clr ins fnl f* **13/2**[2]
2031 **2** 4 1/2 **Burgundy Ice (USA)**[7] 6773 3-9-10 **89** 6ex........................... LDettori 11 96
(Saeed Bin Suroor) *prom: hdwy to chse wnr 3f out: rdn wl over 1f out: hung lft appr fnl f and sn one pce* **9/4**[1]
0000 **3** 2 1/4 **Hilbre Court (USA)**[18] 6496 4-8-9 **71**......................... GrahamGibbons 3 73
(B P J Baugh) *prom: effrt over 2f out and sn: rdn: drvn wl over 1f out: kpt on same pce* **40/1**
0122 **4** *nse* **Sunnyside Tom (IRE)**[24] 6312 5-9-6 **82**......................... PaulHanagan 5 84
(R A Fahey) *trckd ldrs on inner: hdwy 3f out: rdn along 2f out: drvn over 1f out and sn one pce* **8/1**
0014 **5** *hd* **Mcconnell (USA)**[13] 6614 4-9-6 **82**.. NCallan 7 84
(G L Moore) *midfield: hdwy 1/2-way: rdn to chse ldrs wl over 1f out: sn no imp* **8/1**
5033 **6** 1 3/4 **Silent Hero**[23] 6348 3-9-3 **82**.......................................(p) PhilipRobinson 8 80+
(M A Jarvis) *towards rr: hdwy 3f out: rdn along over 2f out: sn drvn and nvr rchd ldrs* **15/2**[3]
3526 **7** 1/2 **Xpres Maite**[48] 5615 6-9-6 **82**..(b) AmirQuinn 10 78
(S R Bowring) *s.i.s and in rr: swtchd wd and hdwy over 2f out: sn rdn and kpt on: nvr nr ldrs* **20/1**
1420 **8** *nk* **Jack Cool (IRE)**[81] 4540 3-9-4 **83**............................... AdrianMcCarthy 2 82
(P W Chapple-Hyam) *prom: rdn along wl over 2f out: grad wknd* **18/1**
1000 **9** 3 3/4 **Betteras Bertie**[27] 6236 6-8-3 **70** oh2 ow1........................ PaulPickard(5) 9 57
(M Brittain) *s.i.s: a towards rr* **50/1**
0434 **10** 13 **Swiss Art (IRE)**[22] 6357 3-8-8 **73**....................................(p) AndrewElliott 12 30
(Mrs R A Carr) *nvr bttr than midfield* **22/1**
13 **11** 1 1/4 **Life's Challenge (USA)**[40] 5834 3-9-3 **82**......................... GregFairley 4 36
(M Johnston) *sn rdn along and a in rr* **10/1**
1004 **12** 2 **Keys Of Cyprus**[34] 6016 7-9-0 **76**............................. AdrianTNicholls 13 26
(D Nicholls) *a towards rr* **10/1**
1500 **13** 8 **Electric Warrior (IRE)**[193] 1213 6-8-11 **73**..................... TravisBlock 6 4
(C R Dore) *prom: rdn along over 3f out and sn wknd* **80/1**

1m 40.02s (-3.68) **Going Correction** -0.30s/f (Stan)
WFA 3 from 4yo+ 3lb **13** Ran SP% **116.3**
Speed ratings (Par 105): **106,101,99,99,99 97,96,96,92,79 78,76,68**
toteswinger: 1&2 £5.30, 1&3 £64.90, 2&3 £52.30. CSF £19.73 CT £565.52 TOTE £6.40: £2.30, £1.70, £12.60; EX 29.90.
Owner Gillian, Lady Howard De Walden **Bred** Avington Manor Stud **Trained** East Ilsley, Berks

FOCUS
A decent handicap and the form looks reasonable with several course winners reasonably close.
Jack Cool(IRE) Official explanation: vet said colt returned lame in front
Swiss Art(IRE) Official explanation: jockey said gelding was unsteerable
Keys Of Cyprus Official explanation: jockey said gelding never travelled

6947 EUROPEAN BREEDERS' FUND MAIDEN FILLIES' STKS 7f (F)
2:40 (2:40) (Class 5) 2-Y-O **£3,885** (£1,156; £577; £288) **Stalls** Low

Form RPR
35 **1** **Maristar (USA)**[12] 6628 2-9-0 0... LDettori 1 77
(G A Butler) *trckd ldr: hdwy over 2f out: rdn to ld wl over 1f out: styd on* **13/8**[1]
3 **2** 1 1/4 **Vegas Palace (IRE)**[9] 6730 2-9-0 0................................ RichardSmith 6 74
(Tom Dascombe) *trckd ldng pair: effrt over 2f out: rdn wl over 1f out: kpt on u.p ins fnl f: nt trble wnr* **13/8**[1]
00 **3** 6 **Vanilla Loan (IRE)**[20] 6436 2-9-0 0.............................. JerryO'Dwyer 5 62+
(M Botti) *led: rdn along over 2f out: drvn and hdd wl over 1f out: grad wknd* **9/1**[3]
0 **4** 7 **The Blue Dog (IRE)**[8] 6759 2-9-0 0............................... TonyCulhane 2 41
(George Baker) *chsd ldrs: rdn along 1/2-way: drvn and outpcd fr wl over 2f out* **50/1**
5 5 **Cheyenne Chant** 2-9-0 0....................................... StephenDonohoe 3 29+
(Sir Mark Prescott) *sn pushed along and a outpcd in rr* **20/1**
6 2 **Three Times** 2-9-0 0.. ChrisCatlin 4 24
(D R Lanigan) *swtchd rt after s: in tch on outer: rdn along 1/2-way: sn wknd* **5/1**[2]

1m 28.67s (-1.63) **Going Correction** -0.30s/f (Stan) **6** Ran SP% **109.6**
Speed ratings (Par 92): **97,95,88,80,75 72**
toteswinger: 1&2 £1.20, 1&3 £3.20, 2&3 £7.30. CSF £4.06 TOTE £2.30: £1.50, £1.10; EX 6.60.
Owner M V Deegan **Bred** Barnett Enterprises **Trained** Newmarket, Suffolk

FOCUS
A modest and uncompetitive fillies' maiden and the form is solid but limited.

NOTEBOOK
Maristar(USA), a promising fifth first time at Newbury, had failed to see out the mile when stepped up in trip next time at Lingfield. She had the pacesetter covered and after taking charge merely had to be kept up to her work. Handicaps presumably beckon next year. (op 7-4)
Vegas Palace(IRE), unfancied when a good third on her debut at Salisbury, was tapped for toe when the pace increased turning in. She stayed on to take second spot and will be suited by a step up to a mile. (op 6-4 tchd 11-8)
Vanilla Loan(IRE), having her third outing, stepped up the pace from the front but in the end her stamina seemed to give out. A 6f nursery might be the next port of call. (op 8-1)
The Blue Dog(IRE), tailed off last in a maiden on her debut, looks no better than selling class. (op 100-1)
Cheyenne Chant, soon struggling in the rear, will no doubt tackle middle distances next year after two more mandatory outings. (tchd 18-1)
Three Times, who did not go unsupported on her debut, tended to race wide and flat out at halfway, she soon dropped away once in line for home. (op 13-2 tchd 7-1)

6948 BET MULTIPLES - BETDAQ NURSERY 7f (F)
3:10 (3:10) (Class 4) (0-85,81) 2-Y-O **£5,504** (£1,637; £818; £408) **Stalls** Low

Form RPR
401 **1** **Karaka Jack**[11] 6679 2-9-2 **76**... GregFairley 6 90+
(M Johnston) *mde all: rdn clr wl over 1f out: edgd rt ins fnl f: unchal* **11/8**[1]
301 **2** 8 **Stef And Stelio**[48] 5613 2-9-4 **78**..(b) NCallan 5 72
(G A Butler) *trckd ldrs: hdwy to chse wnr over 2f out and sn rdn: drvn wl over 1f out and kpt on same pce* **7/1**
3000 **3** 1 3/4 **Imperial Warrior**[13] 6619 2-8-8 **68**................................... TravisBlock 1 58
(H Morrison) *s.i.s and in rr: hdwy on outer 3f out: rdn to chse ldng pair 2f out: sn drvn and outpcd* **6/1**
6543 **4** 1 **Count Bertoni (IRE)**[11] 6679 2-8-13 **73**.........................(b[1]) TPQueally 2 60
(S Gollings) *wnt rt and reminders s: sn cl up: rdn along 3f out: drvn over 2f out and sn wknd* **5/1**[3]
6601 **5** 17 **North Shadow**[14] 6590 2-8-3 **63**...................................... PaulHanagan 3 8
(A D Brown) *chsd wnr on inner: rdn along 3f out: sn wknd and bhd fnl 2f* **10/3**[2]

1m 27.66s (-2.64) **Going Correction** -0.30s/f (Stan) **5** Ran SP% **108.6**
Speed ratings (Par 97): **103,93,91,90,71**
toteswinger: 1&2 £6.10. CSF £10.95 TOTE £1.70: £1.10, £2.60; EX 4.50.
Owner Sheikh Hamdan Bin Mohammed Al Maktoum **Bred** Tarworth Bloodstock Investments Ltd **Trained** Middleham Moor, N Yorks

FOCUS
The market told the tale here in this ultimately very one-sided nursery. The winner was impressive on his first start on sand.

NOTEBOOK
Karaka Jack, off the mark at the third attempt with a last breath victory at York, was backed to the exclusion of his four opponents. Asked to race from a mark of 76, he made every yard and came right away for a facile success. A grand, big type, he can run under a penalty if he returns in the next nine days. He should make a useful handicapper at three. (op 7-4)
Stef And Stelio, raised 7lb after taking a claimer in first-time blinkers on his fifth start, did enough to secure a remote second spot. (op 13-2 tchd 6-1)
Imperial Warrior, last away, was flat out before halfway and looks very one paced. (op 11-2)
Count Bertoni(IRE), in first-time blinkers, was switched wide to avoid the kick back. Runner-up on his debut for a different yard, he does not look to have progressed at all. (tchd 6-1)
North Shadow, who had the advantage of racing against the favoured stands' side when making all from a 10lb lower mark at Nottingham, raced keenly upsides the winner but dropped right away once in line for home. Turf seems to suit him a lot better, but he was almost certainly flattered by his Nottingham success. (op 3-1)

6949 WRIGHT VIGAR 30TH CELEBRATION H'CAP 6f (F)
3:40 (3:40) (Class 3) (0-95,95) 3-Y-O+
£9,346 (£2,799; £1,399; £700; £349; £175) **Stalls** Low

Form RPR
0531 **1** **Ingleby Arch (USA)**[3] 6879 6-8-13 **88** 6ex........................ PhillipMakin 6 99
(T D Barron) *chsd ldrs: rdn along and sltly outpcd 2f out: hdwy to chse ldr over 1f out: drvn and styd on wl fnl f to ld last 100yds* **7/2**[1]
0004 **2** 1 1/4 **Nightjar (USA)**[3] 6876 4-9-5 **94**.. GregFairley 7 101
(M Johnston) *midfield: hdwy over 2f out: rdn and n.m.r whn swtchd rt ent fnl f: sn drvn and styd on wl towards fin* **11/2**[3]
6061 **3** 1/2 **Invincible Lad (IRE)**[22] 6359 5-9-1 **90**............................ DavidAllan 13 95+
(E J Alston) *cl up: led 1/2-way: rdn clr over 1f out: drvn ins fnl f: hdd and no ex last 100yds* **5/1**[2]
2166 **4** 3 3/4 **Quest For Success (IRE)**[11] 6678 4-9-1 **90**................. PaulHanagan 10 83
(R A Fahey) *cl up: chal over 2f out and ev ch tl rdn wl over 1f out and kpt on same pce* **5/1**[2]
0343 **5** 1 3/4 **Masai Moon**[36] 5959 5-8-12 **90**................................. JamesMillman(3) 3 78
(B R Millman) *towards rr: pushed along 1/2-way: rdn and hdwy 2f out: kpt on appr fnl f: nvr nr ldrs* **6/1**
4510 **6** *hd* **Coleorton Choice**[130] 2934 3-8-11 **87**.................................(t) NCallan 11 74
(K A Ryan) *chsd ldrs: hdwy and ev ch 2f out: sn rdn and wknd over 1f out* **22/1**
0000 **7** *nk* **Bond City (IRE)**[12] 6645 7-8-8 **88**.................................. LanceBetts(5) 1 74
(G R Oldroyd) *chsd ldrs on inner: rdn along over 2f out: sn drvn and wknd* **33/1**
3026 **8** *nk* **The Kyllachy Kid**[107] 3688 3-8-11 **87**................................ DO'Donohoe 4 72
(S Gollings) *a towards rr* **33/1**
3050 **9** *hd* **Diriculous**[12] 6631 5-8-13 **88**..(p) TPQueally 8 73
(T G Mills) *towards rr: hdwy over 2f out: sn rdn and no imp* **8/1**
0501 **10** 1 1/4 **Methaaly (IRE)**[16] 6540 6-8-2 **80** oh3.....................(be) KellyHarrison(3) 5 61
(M Mullineaux) *a towards rr* **20/1**
0100 **11** 1 1/4 **Raggle Taggle (IRE)**[38] 5902 3-8-11 **87**........................... ChrisCatlin 2 64
(R M Beckett) *led to 1/2-way: sn rdn along and wknd over 2f out* **40/1**
0-60 **12** 6 **Galpin Junior (USA)**[24] 6304 3-9-5 **95**.........................(bt[1]) TPO'Shea 9 52
(B J Meehan) *stdd and swtchd outside s: hdwy to chse ldrs 1/2-way: rdn along over 2f out: sn wknd* **25/1**

1m 14.33s (-2.17) **Going Correction** -0.30s/f (Stan)
WFA 3 from 4yo+ 1lb **12** Ran SP% **117.6**
Speed ratings (Par 107): **102,100,99,94,92 92,91,91,91,89 87,79**
toteswinger: 1&2 £1.90, 1&3 £3.40, 2&3 £7.90. CSF £20.24 CT £98.36 TOTE £4.40: £1.70, £1.80, £2.80; EX 20.20.
Owner Dave Scott **Bred** Alexander-Groves Thoroughbreds **Trained** Maunby, N Yorks

FOCUS
A highly competitive 81-94 sprint handicap and the complexion changed radically late on. The form looks pretty decent.

NOTEBOOK
Ingleby Arch(USA), penalised 6lb for his win here last Sunday, had to race from a mark of 88. He had defied a mark of 87 in the past and really knuckled down to run down Invincible Lad inside the last. He is just the tough sort of sprinter his trainer excels with. (op 4-1 tchd 9-2 and 5-1 in a place)
Nightjar(USA), fourth over 1m here last Sunday, finished with a rattle to snatch second spot near the line. 7f might prove a happy medium. (op 6-1 tchd 7-1)

Invincible Lad(IRE), a highly progressive individual 7lb higher after making it two from two here over 5f three weeks ago, had the outside stall to overcome. He took command once in line for home and looked like taking a lot of catching until tiring badly inside the last. He stays six but is much better suited by 5f and should soon regain the winning thread. (op 9-2 tchd 4-1)
Quest For Success(IRE), having just his third start on the all-weather and just his second try here, is 5lb better treated on the all-weather compared with turf but on the day he looked to have no excuse.
Masai Moon had won his only previous outing on the Fibresand but that was over seven and he never threatened to take a hand.
Galpin Junior(USA) Official explanation: jockey said colt hung right-handed throughout

6950 BET CHAMPIONS LEAGUE FOOTBALL - BETDAQ MEDIAN AUCTION MAIDEN STKS — 1m (F)
4:10 (4:10) (Class 6) 3-4-Y-O — **£2,729** (£806; £403) **Stalls** Low

Form / RPR
2643 **1** **Bennelong**[118] 3319 3-9-3 75 ....(p) LDettori 6 76+
(R M Beckett) *trckd ldng pair: smooth hdwy to ld over 2f out: sn clr: comf* **13/8**[1]
55 **2** *2* **Tobrata**[51] 5520 3-9-0 0 .... MichaelJStainton(3) 2 64
(M Brittain) *sn pushed along to trck ldrs: hdwy to chse wnr over 2f out and sn rdn: drvn wl over 1f out and kpt on same pce* **9/1**
25 **3** *½* **Ask The Oracle**[13] 6608 3-9-3 0 .... TravisBlock 5 63+
(H Morrison) *sn pushed along and outpcd in rr: rdn and hdwy 2f out: kpt on fnl f: nrst fin* **11/4**[2]
5660 **4** *5* **Noche De Reyes**[48] 5617 4-9-6 48 .... DavidAllan 4 51
(E J Alston) *cl up: led over 3f out: sn rdn and hdd over 2f out: sn drvn and wknd* **14/1**
66-5 **5** *2¼* **Beat Faster**[21] 6390 3-8-12 53 .... TPQueally 7 41
(J G Given) *in tch: rdn along 1/2-way: drvn 3f out and sn wknd* **8/1**
050 **6** *6* **Meydan Style (USA)**[3] 6880 3-9-3 41 ....(p) DO'Donohoe 8 31
(J Balding) *chsd ldrs: rdn along over 3f out: sn drvn and outpcd* **50/1**
0-00 **7** *13* **Valentine Bay**[23] 6344 3-8-12 40 ....(be) GregFairley 3 —
(M Mullineaux) *led: rdn along and hdd 3f out: sn wknd* **100/1**
055 **8** *28* **Severio (IRE)**[44] 5731 3-8-12 60 .... NCallan 1 —
(A P Jarvis) *chsd ldrs on inner: rdn along 1/2-way and sn wknd* **5/1**[3]

1m 42.91s (-0.79) **Going Correction** -0.30s/f (Stan)
WFA 3 from 4yo 3lb — **8** Ran SP% **112.2**
Speed ratings (Par 101): **91,89,88,83,81 75,62,34**
toteswinger: 1&2 £3.70, 1&3 £2.10, 2&3 £3.10. CSF £16.85 TOTE £1.90: £1.10, £3.30, £1.10; EX 14.90.
Owner R A Pegum **Bred** The National Stud **Trained** Whitsbury, Hants

FOCUS
A very weak maiden and the form looks shaky with the runner-up far from solid.
Severio(IRE) Official explanation: jockey said filly hung right-handed throughout

6951 DINE IN THE QUEEN MOTHER RESTAURANT H'CAP — 1m 3f (F)
4:40 (4:40) (Class 5) (0-75,74) 3-Y-O — **£3,561** (£1,059; £529; £264) **Stalls** Low

Form / RPR
0005 **1** **Charging Indian (IRE)**[8] 6768 3-8-7 63 ....(p) TonyCulhane 6 71
(P T Midgley) *hld up in rr: stdy hdwy 4f out: chsd ldrs over 2f out and sn rdn: chal on inner ent fnl f: sn led and drvn out* **9/1**
42 **2** *2¼* **Gaselee (USA)**[10] 6698 3-8-11 67 .... NCallan 8 71
(Rae Guest) *prom: led 1/2-way: rdn along over 2f out: drvn over 1f out: hdd jst ins fnl f and kpt on same pce* **11/4**[2]
3612 **3** *2* **Waahej**[19] 6439 3-8-10 66 .... ChrisCatlin 1 67
(P W Hiatt) *trckd ldrs: hdwy 4f out: rdn to chse ldr over 2f out: drvn wl over 1f out and kpt on same pce* **5/1**
022- **4** *4* **Inflammable**[354] 7126 3-9-0 70 .... StephenDonohoe 4 66
(Sir Mark Prescott) *trckd ldrs: hdwy to chse ldr 4f out: rdn over 2f out: sn drvn and wknd wl over 1f out* **2/1**[1]
5260 **5** *3½* **Barbarian**[33] 6052 3-8-11 67 ....(p) PaulHanagan 2 55
(A D Brown) *led to 1/2-way: prom and pushed along 4f out: rdn over 3f out: sn drvn and wknd over 2f out* **14/1**
5150 **6** *1½* **Upton Seas**[11] 6680 3-9-4 74 .... PhillipMakin 7 60
(M W Easterby) *hld up in rr: effrt and sme hdwy over 4f out: sn rdn along and nvr a factor* **9/2**[3]
0440 **7** *41* **Favours Brave**[18] 6498 3-8-9 65 .... GrahamGibbons 3 —
(Mrs S Lamyman) *cl up: pushed along and lost pl 1/2-way: sn bhd* **16/1**
-334 **8** *1¼* **Mile High Lad (USA)**[88] 4320 3-9-0 70 .... DO'Donohoe 5 —
(George Baker) *dwlt and sn rdn along: a towards rr: wl bhd fnl 3f* **14/1**

2m 24.79s (-3.21) **Going Correction** -0.30s/f (Stan) — **8** Ran SP% **124.1**
Speed ratings (Par 101): **99,97,95,93,90 89,59,58**
toteswinger: 1&2 £4.50, 1&3 £7.40, 2&3 £3.30. CSF £37.09 CT £145.65 TOTE £10.60: £2.80, £1.80, £1.60; EX 34.70 Place 6: £12.00, Place 5: £6.37..
Owner David Mann **Bred** Samac Ltd **Trained** Westow, N Yorks

FOCUS
A modest 63-74 handicap, run at a sound pace and the placed horses set the standard.

6958 - 6959a (Foreign Racing) - See Raceform Interactive

6929 DEAUVILLE (R-H)
Wednesday, October 21

OFFICIAL GOING: Turf course - soft; all-weather - standard

6960a PRIX DES GLAZIERES (CLAIMER) (ALL-WEATHER) — 1m 1f 110y
1:55 (1:56) 2-Y-O — **£10,194** (£4,077; £3,058; £2,039; £1,019)

RPR
1 **Scandola (USA)**[9] 6751 2-8-11 .... SPasquier 73
(G Botti, Italy)
2 *½* **Asoraya (IRE)**[37] 2-8-8 ....(p) JVictoire 69
(F-X De Chevigny, France)
3 *1½* **Je Suis La (FR)** 2-9-4 .... TJarnet 76
(D Guillemin, France)
4 *nse* **Poletto** 2-9-4 76
(Mario Hofer, Germany)
5 *¾* **Ascot And Co (IRE)**[18] 6501 2-9-1 72
(S Wattel, France)
6 *1½* **Arrieta (IRE)**[21] 2-9-1 ....(b) 69
(Y Durepaire, Spain)
7 *shd* **Campanaca (FR)**[54] 2-9-10 78
(C Boutin, France)
8 *2½* **Fei Fei (FR)** 2-8-8 57
(Mlle A Imaz-Ceca, France)
9 *nse* **Sir Des Brousses (FR)**[12] 2-9-4 67
(F Chappet, France)
10 *1½* **Talka (FR)**[21] 2-8-8 ....(p) 54
(J-L Guillochon, France)
11 **Belle Eponine**[24] 6325 2-8-8 .... JAuge 54
(E J O'Neill) *racd in 2nd: rdn 1 1/2f out: wknd* **62/1**[1]
0 **Al Munadel (FR)**[28] 2-9-4 .... —
(C Boutin, France)
0 **El Miesquo (FR)**[21] 2-8-11 .... —
(Robert Collet, France)
0 **Run To Win (FR)**[37] 2-8-11 .... —
(H Billot, France)
0 **Pink Flower (IRE)**[12] 2-8-11 ....(p) —
(J-L Pelletan, France)
0 **Scheibenhard (FR)**[16] 6576 2-8-11 ....(p) —
(J-L Guillochon, France)
0 **Darli Girl (FR)** 2-8-8 .... —
(C Aubert, France)

2m 2.80s (122.80) — **17** Ran SP% **1.6**
PARI-MUTUEL: WIN 5.00; PL 2.00, 2.70, 3.50; DF 20.90.
Owner Stromboli Farm Limited **Bred** Stromboli Farm Ltd & Aleyrion Bloodstock Ltd **Trained** Italy

GEELONG (L-H)
Wednesday, October 21

OFFICIAL GOING: Good

6961a CENTREBET.COM GEELONG CUP (GROUP 3) (H'CAP) — 1m 4f 7y
6:00 (12:00) 3-Y-O+
£65,533 (£17,476; £8,738; £4,369; £2,427; £1,942)

RPR
1 **Leica Ding (AUS)**[39] 5-8-5 .... DannyNikolic 20 109
(Darren Weir, Australia) **12/1**
2 *nk* **Dandaad (NZ)**[11] 6-8-5 ....(b) ClareLindop 1 108
(Bart Cummings, Australia) **9/1**
3 *shd* **Sterling Prince (NZ)**[18] 6-8-8 .... HughBowman 10 110
(Wayne Hillis, New Zealand) **5/1**[1]
4 *1¼* **Stormhill (AUS)**[508] 8-8-8 ....(b) BradRawiller 8 109
(Clinton McDonald, Australia) **15/2**
5 *hd* **Hoorang (NZ)**[11] 7-8-5 .... MichellePayne 9 106
(Ian Shaw, New Zealand) **20/1**
6 *shd* **Crime Scene (IRE)**[82] 4484 6-9-1 .... KerrinMcEvoy 3 116
(Saeed Bin Suroor) *in tch: wnt 3rd 3 1/2f out: disp 2nd briefly 2f out: kpt on at one pce* **11/1**
7 *2¼* **Basaltico (IRE)**[48] 5609 5-8-10 .... DamienOliver 13 107
(L M Cumani) *last and struggling to go the pce: stl last 2 1/2f out: keeping on whn nt clr run and swtchd rt over 1f out: r.o: nrst fin* **6/1**[2]
8 *hd* **Cats Fun (AUS)**[32] 7-8-7 ....(b) LukeNolen 15 104
(Jarrod McLean, Australia) **40/1**
9 *hd* **Six O'Clock News (NZ)**[18] 5-8-5 ....(b) NoelHarris 18 101
(P & T Busuttin, New Zealand) **12/1**
10 *3¼* **Spin Around (AUS)**[193] 9-8-10 .... MarkDuPlessis 14 101
(Steven Cooper, Australia) **50/1**
11 *1½* **Young Centaur (AUS)**[11] 7-8-9 ....(b) CraigAWilliams 7 98
(John Sargent, New Zealand) **12/1**
12 *hd* **Guyno (NZ)**[18] 6-8-10 ....(b) JasonWhiting 6 98
(Lou Luciani, Australia) **7/1**[3]
13 *2* **Gallions Reach (NZ)**[18] 7-8-10 .... GlenBoss 19 95
(Richard Yuill, New Zealand) **60/1**
14 *2½* **Arapaho Miss (AUS)**[11] 5-8-5 ....(b) DeanHolland 16 86
(Pat Carey, Australia) **20/1**
15 *2¾* **Zacroona (NZ)** 5-8-5 ....(b) DwayneDunn 4 82
(Lee Freedman, Australia) **15/1**
16 *30* **Maestro Of Murano (AUS)** 4-8-5 ....(b) AdrianPatterson 21 34
(Roslyn Day, Australia) **40/1**
17 *12* **Completion (NZ)**[715] 6711 7-8-5 ....(b) DanielMoor 2 15
(Brendan Woodman, Australia) **25/1**

2m 27.52s (147.52) — **17** Ran SP% **124.7**
Owner T Macknamara, N McInnes, P Wheelahan et al **Bred** Riversdale Stud **Trained** Australia

NOTEBOOK
Crime Scene(IRE), off the course since finishing down the field in a Group 3 at Goodwood in July, handled the track, ran a sound race in defeat and will join stablemate Kirklees in the Melbourne Cup.
Basaltico(IRE), whose stable took this last year with Bauer, missed the break and got shuffled back to the tail of the field. He put in some really good work late, without getting the best of luck in running, and shaped with real promise. The intention is to run in the Melbourne Cup providing he makes the cut, but otherwise he'll run in a race over 1m4f the previous day.

6786 BRIGHTON (L-H)
Thursday, October 22

OFFICIAL GOING: Good (good to soft in places; 7.5)
Wind: Fresh, against Weather: Mainly cloudy

6962 WEST SUSSEX SIGNS - RACECOURSE SIGNAGE SPECIALISTS MEDIAN AUCTION MAIDEN STKS — 6f 209y
2:00 (2:02) (Class 5) 2-Y-O — **£3,784** (£1,132; £566; £283; £141) **Stalls** Low

Form / RPR
42 **1** **Essexbridge**[13] 6629 2-9-3 0 .... RichardHughes 4 77+
(R Hannon) *chsd ldr: hrd rdn over 1f out: led jst ins fnl f: edgd lft: drvn out* **10/3**[2]
0 **2** *1¾* **Bonnie Brae**[14] 6607 2-8-12 0 .... DaneO'Neill 2 67
(G G Margarson) *chsd ldng pair: edgd lft and hrd rdn over 1f out: kpt on to take 2nd ins fnl f* **14/1**
4 **3** *½* **High Importance (USA)**[13] 6629 2-9-3 0 .... RyanMoore 1 71
(J Noseda) *led tl jst ins fnl f: one pce* **8/11**[1]
5 **4** *1½* **Tahseen**[34] 6057 2-9-3 0 .... TPO'Shea 7 67+
(M P Tregoning) *s.i.s: sn t.k.h and chsng ldrs: hung lft and rdn 3f out: styd on same pce fnl 2f* **7/1**[3]

06 5 *hd* **Varachi**[15] 6592 2-9-3 0 TGMcLaughlin 5 66+
(E A L Dunlop) *hld up in rr: rdn over 2f out: hdwy over 1f out: no imp* **33/1**
0 6 *10* **Penderyn**[10] 6730 2-8-12 0 JimCrowley 3 36
(Mrs A J Perrett) *dwlt: a in rr: bhd fnl 2f* **25/1**
00 7 *nk* **Avon Rock**[14] 6615 2-9-3 0 (t) LiamJones 6 40
(J W Hills) *in tch: rdn 4f out: wknd over 2f out* **50/1**

1m 24.11s (1.01) **Going Correction** +0.10s/f (Good) 7 Ran SP% **108.9**
Speed ratings (Par 95): **98,96,95,93,93 82,81**
toteswinger: 1&2 £5.30, 1&3 £1.40, 2&3 £1.60. CSF £39.47 TOTE £3.70: £1.50, £4.10; EX 31.70.
Owner Morecombe Elsom Notley Burnham **Bred** Whatton Manor Stud **Trained** East Everleigh, Wilts

FOCUS
An ordinary juvenile maiden, run at a sound pace. The field came more towards the near side after straightening for home. Limited form, with the first five compressed.

NOTEBOOK
Essexbridge opened his account at the third time of asking and enhanced his stable's decent record in the race. He had finished in front of High Importance last time out at Lingfield and it was surprising to see such a difference in their respective odds as the money came for the favourite. He confirmed the form in game fashion and looks the sort to relish another furlong. This likeable son of Avonbridge can build on this in nurseries. (op 3-1)
Bonnie Brae posted a big run in defeat and performed better than the bare form of her recent debut at Kempton a fortnight previously. It isn't hard to see why she started off over 1m as she was doing her best work towards the finish here, and there should be more to come from her after this experience. (op 12-1 tchd 11-1)
High Importance(USA) ultimately got outstayed by the first pair after adopting front-running tactics. He raced behind the winner at Lingfield on debut and, while he was the one open to more improvement of the pair, he hardly finished full of running there. Perhaps the ground was easier than he cares for and he should find his feet when going handicapping in due course. (op 5-6 tchd 10-11 in a place)
Tahseen, fifth on debut at Newbury last month, again proved too inexperienced to do himself full justice. He was staying on again at the finish, suggesting another furlong will suit him ideally, and he should learn again from this. (op 9-1 tchd 10-1)
Varachi was never seriously in the hunt from out the back and a more positive ride over this shorter trip would have helped, but still posted another improved effort in defeat. He now has the option of nurseries. (op 40-1)

6963 DIGIBET NURSERY 6f 209y
2:30 (2:31) (Class 5) (0-75,79) 2-Y-O £3,784 (£1,132; £566; £283; £141) Stalls Low

Form RPR
040 1 **Whistle Blower**[34] 6066 2-8-10 63 RobertHavlin 9 67
(J H M Gosden) *wnt lft s: chsd ldrs: drvn to ld ins fnl f: rdn out* **4/1**[1]
0501 2 *1 ½* **Transfixed (IRE)**[5] 6844 2-9-7 79 6ex RichardEvans(5) 10 79
(P D Evans) *led: rdn and edgd rt 2f out: hdd ins fnl f: one pce* **8/1**[3]
6523 3 *1 ½* **Ginger Grey (IRE)**[6] 6829 2-8-11 64 (b) PatCosgrave 3 60
(S A Callaghan, U.S.A) *towards rr: rdn over 2f out: hdwy and hung bdly lft fr over 1f out: one pce fnl f* **9/2**[2]
0650 4 *nse* **Captain Cool (IRE)**[45] 5715 2-7-12 51 oh1 CatherineGannon 11 48
(R Hannon) *dwlt: sn chsng ldrs: rdn over 4f out: rallied and nt clr run on stands' rail over 1f out: swtchd lft: styd on* **9/1**
2000 5 *2 ½* **Timelord (IRE)**[15] 6586 2-8-12 65 LPKeniry 5 55
(S Kirk) *mid-div: rdn to chse ldrs 2f out: no ex fnl f* **14/1**
0066 6 *nse* **Queen's Hawk**[23] 6367 2-8-11 64 (v[1]) TPO'Shea 2 54
(D J Coakley) *mid-div: outpcd and struggling towards rr 3f out: styd on fnl f* **12/1**
3406 7 *nse* **Machine Gun Kelly (IRE)**[10] 6736 2-8-12 65 FergusSweeney 13 55
(G L Moore) *prom tl wknd over 1f out* **8/1**[3]
4155 8 *3 ¼* **Underworld Dandy**[13] 6639 2-8-12 65 (v[1]) DaneO'Neill 1 48
(P D Evans) *chsd ldrs: hrd rdn and edgd rt over 2f out: edgd lft wl over 1f out: sn wknd* **16/1**
0502 9 *1 ¾* **Folletta (IRE)**[20] 6441 2-9-1 68 RyanMoore 8 47
(R Hannon) *bmpd s: sn detached last: rdn over 2f out: nvr nr ldrs* **10/1**
3610 10 *2* **Green Earth (IRE)**[10] 6735 2-9-7 74 JimCrowley 7 48
(Mrs A J Perrett) *squeezed s: bhd: mod effrt over 3f out: wknd over 2f out: eased* **11/1**
0400 11 *29* **Gold Diamond (USA)**[32] 6134 2-8-12 65 GregFairley 12 —
(M Johnston) *chsd ldr 4f: sn wknd* **12/1**

1m 23.49s (0.39) **Going Correction** +0.10s/f (Good) 11 Ran SP% **115.8**
Speed ratings (Par 95): **101,99,97,97,94 94,94,90,88,86 53**
toteswinger: 1&2 £7.50, 1&3 £2.60, 2&3 £5.10. CSF £35.32 CT £152.48 TOTE £5.90: £1.90, £3.70, £1.50; EX 51.60 Trifecta £159.40 Part won. Pool: £215.48 - 0.80 winning units..
Owner H R H Princess Haya Of Jordan **Bred** New England Stud Farm Ltd **Trained** Newmarket, Suffolk

FOCUS
A wide-open nursery and again the field shunned the near side in the home straight. The form is rated around the winner, second and fourth.

NOTEBOOK
Whistle Blower had not done enough on paper to suggest he was quite up to a mark of 63 for this nursery debut, but he showed his true colours and proved the best handicapped horse in the race. He did too much from the front in first-time blinkers on his previous outing but, with the headgear dispensed with and under more patient tactics, he came good. The drop back in trip also helped and he could go on from this career-first success. (op 5-1 tchd 6-1)
Transfixed(IRE) turned in a very brave effort from the front under top weight and rates a solid benchmark. This was her 22nd outing of the campaign and this tough performer remains in great heart. (op 5-1)
Ginger Grey(IRE) had the blinkers back on and met support. He came through with his chance as he hung towards the centre of the track, but again didn't look willing and was well held by the first two. It is a little surprising he has yet to be gelded. (op 5-1 tchd 11-2 and 4-1)
Captain Cool(IRE), 1lb out of the weights, came in for support and posted a much-improved display. He wasn't done too many favours when the runner-up bagged the stands' rail and this easier ground looked more to his liking. (op 16-1)
Timelord(IRE) ran a little more encouragingly but didn't do enough to suggest he'll be getting off the mark anytime soon. (op 12-1)
Queen's Hawk was another who stayed on inside the final furlong after hitting a flat spot and it isn't hard to see why connections reached for the visor. (tchd 10-1)
Machine Gun Kelly(IRE) showed good early speed from the outside gate, but hit a flat spot at a crucial stage before staying on again and appeared to find the drop back a furlong round here too sharp. (op 10-1)
Folletta(IRE)'s rider reported that his filly was interfered with at the start. Official explanation: jockey said filly suffered interference in running (op 15-2)
Green Earth(IRE) was later reported to have hung left. Official explanation: jockey said colt hung left (op 10-1 tchd 9-1)

6964 CONNOLLY'S RED MILLS TRAINERS CHAMPIONSHIP H'CAP 5f 213y
3:05 (3:05) (Class 4) (0-80,80) 3-Y-O- £8,831 (£2,643; £1,321; £660; £329) Stalls Low

Form RPR
5021 1 **Arthur's Edge**[11] 6694 5-9-5 80 6ex DavidProbert 11 94+
(B Palling) *chsd ldrs: led 1f out: rdn out* **9/2**[1]
1242 2 *1 ½* **Lochan Mor**[21] 6434 3-9-3 79 HayleyTurner 12 86
(M L W Bell) *sn chsng ldrs: rdn to chal over 1f out: one pce fnl f* **11/2**[3]
0210 3 *½* **Zebrano**[64] 5154 3-9-2 78 RichardHughes 7 83
(Miss E C Lavelle) *mid-div: rdn and hdwy over 1f out: r.o fnl f* **18/1**
0363 4 *1 ½* **The Galloping Shoe**[16] 6564 4-9-2 77 RyanMoore 14 78+
(J Noseda) *bhd: rdn and r.o fnl 2f: nrst fin* **5/1**[2]
0440 5 *¾* **Rocker**[12] 6666 5-8-9 75 JamieJones(5) 3 73
(G L Moore) *chsd ldrs: hld whn edgd lft ins fnl f* **14/1**
312 6 *1 ½* **Idle Power (IRE)**[16] 6564 11-8-13 74 PatCosgrave 2 67
(J R Boyle) *chsd ldrs: hrd rdn over 1f out: one pce* **16/1**
00 7 *1 ½* **Doric Lady**[31] 6171 4-9-2 77 KirstyMilczarek 9 66+
(J A R Toller) *s.s: towards rr: promising effrt whn squeezed and bmpd over 2f out: hmpd wl over 1f out: sme late hdwy* **16/1**
0340 8 *nk* **Ebraam (USA)**[13] 6647 6-9-5 80 JerryO'Dwyer 5 68
(P Howling) *towards rr: rdn and hdwy over 1f out: no imp fnl f* **25/1**
2300 9 *1* **Memphis Man**[17] 6540 6-8-13 74 PaulDoe 10 58
(P D Evans) *bhd: c to stands' rail 3f out: rdn over 2f out: styng on at fin* **22/1**
6254 10 *hd* **Cape Melody**[37] 5968 3-8-11 73 TravisBlock 13 57+
(H Morrison) *mid-div: hmpd and dropped to rr over 2f out: n.d after* **16/1**
1245 11 *nse* **Patavium Prince (IRE)**[50] 5565 6-9-0 75 DaneO'Neill 4 59
(Miss Jo Crowley) *chsd ldrs tl n.m.r and wknd 2f out* **14/1**
2020 12 *1* **Bel Cantor**[17] 6540 6-8-12 76 (p) KellyHarrison(3) 1 56
(W J H Ratcliffe) *prom 4f* **12/1**
2631 13 *¾* **Elusive Hawk (IRE)**[87] 4374 5-8-9 70 TPQueally 15 48
(B J Curley) *mid-div: rdn 4f out: outpcd fnl 2f* **9/1**
0603 14 *½* **Peter Island (FR)**[42] 5805 6-9-1 76 (v) NCallan 6 52
(J Gallagher) *led and set gd pce tl wknd 1f out* **20/1**
0200 15 *½* **Highland Harvest**[39] 5916 5-8-10 71 RobertHavlin 8 46+
(Jamie Poulton) *towards rr: effrt whn hmpd over 2f out: n.d* **20/1**

69.96 secs (-0.24) **Going Correction** +0.10s/f (Good)
WFA 3 from 4yo+ 1lb 15 Ran SP% **121.9**
Speed ratings (Par 105): **105,103,102,100,99 97,95,94,93,93 93,91,90,90,89**
toteswinger: 1&2 £4.80, 1&3 £30.50, 2&3 £21.40. CSF £26.65 CT £418.04 TOTE £6.10: £2.70, £1.90, £8.00; EX 33.90 TRIFECTA Not won. Pool: £464.65..
Owner Mrs Annabelle Mason **Bred** Christopher J Mason **Trained** Tredodridge, Vale Of Glamorgan

FOCUS
As expected there was no hanging about here and the main action developed in the centre of the track late on.
Lochan Mor Official explanation: jockey said colt hung left
Doric Lady Official explanation: jockey said filly was hampered 1f out
Cape Melody Official explanation: jockey said filly was denied a clear run
Highland Harvest Official explanation: jockey said gelding was denied a clear run

6965 EBF / SAPPHIRE ANNIVERSARY MAIDEN STKS 7f 214y
3:35 (3:36) (Class 4) 2-Y-O
£5,452 (£1,632; £816; £408; £203; £102) Stalls Low

Form RPR
1 **Tertiary (USA)** 2-9-0 0 AhmedAjtebi(3) 11 71
(Saeed Bin Suroor) *trckd ldrs: led 4f out tl 2f out: led ins fnl f: shkn up and kpt on: jst hld on* **11/2**[2]
06 2 *hd* **Activate**[52] 5499 2-9-3 0 HayleyTurner 9 71
(M L W Bell) *mid-div: rdn over 4f out: hdwy 2f out: styd on strly fnl f: clsng at fin: jst failed* **7/2**[1]
000 3 *2 ¼* **Eltheeb**[15] 6592 2-9-3 60 NCallan 3 66
(J L Dunlop) *chsd ldrs: rdn over 2f out: one pce fnl f* **40/1**
6 4 *¾* **Athenian Garden (USA)**[21] 6436 2-8-12 0 TPQueally 12 59
(H R A Cecil) *chsd ldrs: led 2f out: hung lft and hdd ins fnl f: no ex* **7/2**[1]
060 5 *2* **Viviani (IRE)**[11] 6697 2-9-3 0 (b[1]) JimCrowley 10 60+
(Mrs A J Perrett) *hld up towards rr: c to stands' rail 3f out: rdn and styd on appr fnl f: nvr nrr* **25/1**
00 6 *5* **Finch Flyer (IRE)**[13] 6627 2-9-3 0 GeorgeBaker 4 49
(G L Moore) *towards rr: rdn 5f out: nvr rchd ldrs* **100/1**
0 7 *6* **Extreme Green**[23] 6363 2-8-12 0 DavidProbert 6 31
(A M Balding) *prom tl hrd rdn and lost pl over 3f out* **12/1**
00 8 *3 ¾* **Stadium Of Light (IRE)**[14] 6617 2-9-3 0 TravisBlock 2 28+
(H Morrison) *led tl 4f out: wknd over 2f out* **50/1**
0 9 *3 ¾* **Moobeyn**[13] 6627 2-9-3 0 MartinDwyer 1 19
(M P Tregoning) *s.i.s: towards rr: rdn and rn green 6f out: n.d* **12/1**
0 10 *shd* **Abigails Angel**[14] 6607 2-8-12 0 FrankieMcDonald 8 14
(B R Johnson) *s.s: hld up in rr: rdn 4f out: nvr trbld ldrs* **150/1**
045 11 *4* **Isdaar (IRE)**[9] 6759 2-9-3 0 (b[1]) TPO'Shea 13 10
(J H M Gosden) *dwlt: sn chsng ldrs: wknd over 2f out* **8/1**[3]
12 *¾* **Silent Dancer (IRE)**[36] 6006 2-9-3 0 RichardHughes 5 9
(S Donohoe, Ire) *hld up in tch: effrt and wandered over 2f out: wknd wl over 1f out: eased whn wl btn fnl f* **7/2**[1]
0 13 *26* **Zazy's Gift**[23] 6363 2-8-7 0 MatthewDavies(5) 7 —
(George Baker) *s.i.s: drvn along and a bhd: no ch fnl 4f* **200/1**

1m 36.93s (0.93) **Going Correction** +0.10s/f (Good) 13 Ran SP% **118.9**
Speed ratings (Par 97): **99,98,96,95,93 88,82,79,75,75 71,70,44**
toteswinger: 1&2 £7.80, 1&3 £7.00, 2&3 £65.50. CSF £24.48 TOTE £5.40: £2.20, £1.80, £8.50; EX 31.90 Trifecta £282.70 Part won. Pool: £382.13 - 0.90 winning units..
Owner Godolphin **Bred** Darley **Trained** Newmarket, Suffolk

FOCUS
The first four came clear and the race is best viewed through the second and third. Limited form.

NOTEBOOK
Tertiary(USA) is a half-brother to the top-class Anabaa Blue and was representing a leading stable still banging out the winners, so it was surprising he proved a market drifter. Despite taking a keen hold to post, he settled nicely just off the early pace and knuckled down like a professional when asked to win the race from 2f out. He is value for a little further as his rider took it a little easy inside the closing stages and was unaware of the fast-finishing runner-up. He should make up into a nice middle-distance performer at three. (op 7-2 tchd 100-30)
Activate was eating into the winner's advantage in the closing stages and could have given that one even more to think about under a slightly more positive ride, but he does not appear the easiest of rides. He has now improved with each of his three starts to date, now has the option of handicaps and should be found an opening in maiden company. (op 11-2)
Eltheeb kept on gamely under pressure and turned in by far his most encouraging effort so far. He already looks in need of a stiffer test and should build on this. (op 50-1)

Athenian Garden(USA) showed the benefit of her debut experience at Wolverhampton and had every chance, but was outstayed by the principals over this extra furlong. A return to a sounder surface should enhance her chances of getting home better and she is entitled to go forward again for the run. (op 3-1 tchd 4-1)
Viviani(IRE) didn't look the easiest of rides in the first-time blinkers. He was keeping on late in the day though and, as a son of Galileo, he should relish a stiffer test in due course. (op 22-1)
Silent Dancer(IRE), for whom there was money, travelled sweetly into contention but found very little when push came to shove. (op 4-1)

6966 BLAKES BUTCHERS (S) H'CAP 1m 1f 209y
4:05 (4:06) (Class 6) (0-60,60) 3-Y-O+ £2,072 (£616; £308; £153) Stalls High

Form RPR
1050 1 **Hector Spectre (IRE)**[22] 6370 3-9-0 **56**.................. PaulDoe 8 64
(P D Evans) *chsd ldrs: rdn 4f out: led ins fnl f: drvn out* **4/1**[2]
5105 2 *nk* **Primo Dilettante**[20] 6440 3-9-2 **58**..................(p) JimCrowley 14 65
(W J Knight) *led: hrd rdn over 1f out: hung lft and hdd ins fnl f: r.o* **7/2**[1]
5-00 3 *3* **Awatuki (IRE)**[70] 4957 6-9-9 **60**.................. PatCosgrave 3 61
(J R Boyle) *prom: hrd rdn and hung lft over 1f out: one pce* **5/1**[3]
0036 4 *1 ½* **Prince Valentine**[50] 5569 8-8-12 **49**..................(p) FergusSweeney 7 47
(G L Moore) *hld up towards rr: rdn 3f out: styd on fnl 2f: nt rch ldrs* **16/1**
6-00 5 *1* **Spanish Cross (IRE)**[146] 2458 4-9-0 **51**.................. SaleemGolam 12 47
(G Prodromou) *in tch: rdn 3f out: styd on same pce* **20/1**
6430 6 *2 ¼* **Ocean Of Peace (FR)**[28] 6226 6-8-10 **47**.................. HayleyTurner 6 39
(M R Bosley) *chsd ldrs: hrd rdn 2f out: wknd over 1f out* **11/2**
0553 7 *nk* **Oronsay**[16] 6565 4-8-13 **50**..................(t) NickyMackay 10 41
(B R Millman) *dwlt: sn in rr of midfield: effrt over 2f out: hrd rdn over 1f out: one pce* **7/1**
-060 8 *6* **Richardlionheart (USA)**[8] 6771 3-8-9 **51** ow3.................. RobertHavlin 5 30
(M Madgwick) *plld hrd in rr: rdn 3f out: nvr trbld ldrs* **66/1**
5600 9 *3 ¾* **Mick Is Back**[7] 6790 5-9-8 **59**..................(v) DaneO'Neill 9 30
(G G Margarson) *mid-div: hrd rdn over 3f out: sn wknd: eased whn wl btn over 1f out: lame* **14/1**
0000 10 *4 ½* **Cranworth Blaze**[55] 5406 5-8-4 **46** oh1.................. SimonPearce(5) 1 8
(A G Newcombe) *sn detached in last: rdn 1/2-way: no ch fnl 4f* **33/1**
1033 11 *1 ¾* **Stand In Flames**[9] 6755 4-9-4 **60**.................. MatthewDavies(5) 13 19
(George Baker) *prom tl wknd 3f out* **11/1**

2m 3.87s (0.27) **Going Correction** +0.10s/f (Good)
WFA 3 from 4yo+ 5lb 11 Ran SP% **116.9**
Speed ratings (Par 101): **102,101,99,98,97 95,95,90,87,83 82**
toteswinger: 1&2 £4.80, 1&3 £8.50, 2&3 £8.80. CSF £17.93 CT £71.45 TOTE £5.00: £1.80, £2.30, £2.20; EX 20.10 Trifecta £102.70 Pool: £256.95 - 1.85 winning units..The winner was bought in for 5,000gns.
Owner Mrs I M Folkes **Bred** D & R Burns **Trained** Pandy, Monmouths
■ Stewards' Enquiry : Jim Crowley caution: careless riding.
Paul Doe caution: used whip without giving colt time to respond

FOCUS
This weak selling handicap was run at a fair pace and the first pair fought it out in a driving finish. Straightforward form.
Mick Is Back Official explanation: vet said gelding finished lame

6967 BRIGHTON SQUARE H'CAP (DIV I) 7f 214y
4:40 (4:40) (Class 6) (0-63,66) 3-Y-O+ £2,590 (£770; £385; £192) Stalls Low

Form RPR
4465 1 **Piquante**[26] 6289 3-9-3 **63**.................. HayleyTurner 13 73+
(M L W Bell) *hld up in midfield: smooth hdwy over 2f out: led 1f out: styd on wl: rdn out* **4/1**[1]
3000 2 *1 ¼* **Ede's Dot Com (IRE)**[28] 6226 5-8-12 **55**.................. IanMongan 1 63
(P M Phelan) *prom: led briefly over 1f out: kpt on u.p* **12/1**
6402 3 *2 ½* **Bosamcliff (IRE)**[3] 6909 4-8-10 **58**.................. AndrewHeffernan(5) 5 60
(P D Evans) *chsd ldr: led over 2f out tl over 1f out: one pce* **4/1**[1]
5211 4 *½* **Dichoh**[8] 6783 6-9-9 **66** 6ex..................(v) GeorgeBaker 10 67
(M Madgwick) *hld up in rr: pushed along 4f out: hdwy 2f out: drvn into 4th 1f out: styd on same pce* **5/1**[2]
4050 5 *3* **Pippbrook Gold**[56] 5365 4-9-4 **61**.................. PatCosgrave 6 55
(J R Boyle) *mid-div: effrt over 2f out: no imp* **8/1**
0150 6 *¾* **Megalala (IRE)**[15] 6584 8-9-5 **62**.................. NeilChalmers 11 54
(J J Bridger) *led tl over 2f out: sn btn* **12/1**
0030 7 *¾* **Bidable**[42] 5791 5-8-7 **50**.................. DavidProbert 3 41
(B Palling) *prom over 5f* **20/1**
604 8 *2 ½* **Croeso Cusan**[48] 5630 4-8-9 **57**.................. SophieDoyle(5) 7 42
(J L Spearing) *hld up in rr: effrt and hrd rdn 2f out: nt pce to chal* **7/1**[3]
4022 9 *4 ½* **Kingsgate Castle**[8] 6783 4-8-13 **56**..................(v) CatherineGannon 9 31
(Miss Gay Kelleway) *t.k.h towards rr: drvn along over 3f out: n.d* **15/2**
0066 10 *1 ¼* **Dicey Affair**[7] 6787 3-8-4 **50**..................(t) NickyMackay 8 21
(G L Moore) *mid-div: effrt over 2f out: wknd wl over 1f out* **28/1**
6006 11 *1 ½* **Luthien (IRE)**[19] 6497 3-8-1 **54** ow2..................(p) JPFahy(7) 12 21
(A M Hales) *chsd ldrs 4f: sn lost pl* **40/1**

1m 35.53s (-0.47) **Going Correction** +0.10s/f (Good)
WFA 3 from 4yo+ 3lb 11 Ran SP% **118.1**
Speed ratings (Par 101): **106,104,102,101,98 98,97,94,90,89 87**
toteswinger: 1&2 £13.20, 1&3 £6.40, 2&3 £16.60. CSF £52.40 CT £209.82 TOTE £5.30: £1.90, £4.30, £1.70; EX 60.40 TRIFECTA Not won. Pool: £381.02..
Owner Highclere Thoroughbred Racing(Persimmon) **Bred** Aston House Stud **Trained** Newmarket, Suffolk
■ Stewards' Enquiry : Andrew Heffernan one-day ban: used whip with excessive frequency (Nov 5)

FOCUS
A moderate handicap but a pleasing performance from Piquante who is rated back to her eearly-season best. The quickest of the three C/D races.
Kingsgate Castle Official explanation: jockey said gelding never travelled

6968 BRIGHTON SQUARE H'CAP (DIV II) 7f 214y
5:10 (5:10) (Class 6) (0-63,64) 3-Y-O+ £2,590 (£770; £385; £192) Stalls Low

Form RPR
6011 1 **Ocean Countess (IRE)**[7] 6787 3-9-3 **64** 6ex.................. CatherineGannon 2 72
(Miss J Feilden) *hld up in rr: hdwy over 2f out: drvn to ld over 1f out: rdn out* **4/1**[1]
0603 2 *1 ¼* **Lady Florence**[7] 6790 4-9-2 **63**.................. Louis-PhilippeBeuzelin(3) 3 69
(A B Coogan) *chsd ldrs: chal over 1f out: hung lft: kpt on* **11/2**[3]
2330 3 *1* **Kassuta**[40] 5888 5-8-7 **51** oh3.................. NickyMackay 7 55
(R M H Cowell) *disp ld tl over 1f out: one pce: tk 3rd nr fin* **12/1**
6401 4 *½* **King's Masque**[22] 6370 3-8-11 **58**.................. MartinDwyer 9 59
(W R Muir) *disp ld tl over 1f out: no ex fnl 100yds: lost 3rd nr fin* **7/1**
-002 5 *½* **Dream Huntress**[7] 6787 3-8-13 **60**.................. LiamJones 5 60
(J W Hills) *hld up in rr: hdwy and hrd rdn 2f out: one pce appr fnl f* **9/2**[2]
6045 6 *1 ¾* **Inquisitress**[16] 6565 5-8-4 **51** oh3.................. MarcHalford(3) 4 48
(J J Bridger) *bhd: drvn along and sme hdwy over 1f out: nt rch ldrs* **33/1**
2406 7 *¾* **Fire King**[22] 6394 3-8-12 **59**..................(p) RobertHavlin 8 53
(J A Geake) *in tch: hrd rdn 2f out: no imp* **12/1**
2002 8 *1 ¼* **Just Jimmy (IRE)**[1] 6945 4-8-2 **51**.................. AndrewHeffernan(5) 13 43
(P D Evans) *prom: hrd rdn 3f out: sn btn* **8/1**
0406 9 *nse* **Dancing Storm**[63] 5179 6-8-11 **55** ow1.................. IanMongan 11 47
(W S Kittow) *dwlt: hdwy to chse ldrs after 2f: wknd 2f out* **10/1**
0-00 10 *13* **Under Fire (IRE)**[10] 6719 6-8-13 **57**.................. HayleyTurner 6 18
(A W Carroll) *mid-div: dropped to rr 4f out: n.d after* **10/1**
4056 11 *½* **Kina Jazz**[232] 758 3-8-4 **51** oh3.................. KirstyMilczarek 1 10
(M Botti) *bhd: j. road after 2f: sme hdwy 2f out: sn wknd* **22/1**
0-00 12 *4 ½* **Leptis Magna**[15] 4645 5-9-2 **60**.................. FrankieMcDonald 10 9
(R H York) *t.k.h: chsd ldrs: lost pl after 3f: sn rdn in rr* **28/1**

1m 36.49s (0.49) **Going Correction** +0.10s/f (Good)
WFA 3 from 4yo+ 3lb 12 Ran SP% **121.5**
Speed ratings (Par 101): **101,99,98,98,97 96,95,94,93,80 80,75**
toteswinger: 1&2 £4.50, 1&3 £12.20, 2&3 £13.60. CSF £25.87 CT £253.30 TOTE £5.30: £2.10, £2.50, £4.70; EX 25.30 TRIFECTA Not won. Pool: £456.63..
Owner Ocean Trailers Ltd **Bred** Don Commins **Trained** Exning, Suffolk
■ Stewards' Enquiry : Catherine Gannon two-day ban: used whip with excessive frequency (Nov 5-6)

FOCUS
The second division of the 7f handicap and another moderate heat. The form looks sound enough, with a personal best from the winner.

6969 STREAMLINE TAXIS - BRIGHTON'S BEST FOR TAXIS APPRENTICE H'CAP 1m 3f 196y
5:40 (5:42) (Class 6) (0-55,55) 3-Y-O+ £2,590 (£770; £385; £192) Stalls High

Form RPR
0000 1 **Zaif (IRE)**[15] 6584 6-9-4 **55**..................(p) BillyCray(3) 10 65
(D J S Ffrench Davis) *bhd: rdn early: gd hdwy 5f out: led 2f out: drvn out* **25/1**
6343 2 *½* **Sinbad The Sailor**[28] 6226 4-9-2 **55**..................(v) KierenFox(5) 7 64
(J W Hills) *prom: led after 3f tl 2f out: kpt on* **11/4**[1]
4403 3 *1 ½* **Location**[11] 6705 3-8-7 **53**.................. HollyHall(5) 5 60
(P D Evans) *hld up towards rr: smooth hdwy 3f out: rdn to chse ldrs over 1f out: hung lft: nt qckn* **13/2**[2]
210 4 *2 ¼* **Iguacu**[101] 3929 5-9-5 **53**.................. MatthewDavies 11 56
(George Baker) *sn in tch: clsd on ldrs 5f out: hrd rdn 2f out: one pce appr fnl f* **11/1**
4455 5 *½* **Bernabeu (IRE)**[35] 6025 7-9-4 **52**.................. RichardEvans 1 54
(S Curran) *led 3f: pressed ldr after: cl 3rd whn squeezed for room 1f out* **16/1**
020 6 *7* **Arabian Silk (IRE)**[2] 6917 3-8-6 **52**.................. LauraPike(5) 14 43
(D M Simcock) *mid-div: rdn and lost pl 1/2-way: sn struggling in rr: sme hdwy 2f out: n.d* **15/2**
0645 7 *hd* **Turner's Touch**[78] 4640 7-8-7 **48**..................(b) HarryBentley(7) 8 39
(G L Moore) *t.k.h in midfield: lost pl 5f out: sme hdwy 2f out: no further prog* **16/1**
500 8 *6* **Choosy Floosy**[22] 6390 3-8-8 **52**.................. TobyAtkinson(3) 13 33
(Pat Eddery) *wl bhd: hrd rdn over 2f out: passed btn horses* **9/1**
3266 9 *1 ¼* **Sand Repeal (IRE)**[27] 6244 7-9-7 **55**.................. AmyBaker 4 34
(Miss J Feilden) *chsd ldrs: rdn 5f out: wknd over 3f out* **8/1**
0002 10 *1* **Hidden Door (IRE)**[36] 6001 4-8-13 **54**.................. RichardOld(7) 12 31
(G Prodromou) *towards rr: sme hdwy 5f out: wknd 3f out* **20/1**
4300 11 *1* **Channel Crossing**[37] 5962 7-9-2 **50**.................. PaulPickard 6 26
(S Wynne) *prom 7f* **20/1**
433 12 *¾* **Corrib (IRE)**[40] 5872 6-8-10 **47**.................. LeeNewnes(3) 9 22
(B Palling) *mid-div on outer: clsd on ldrs 5f out: hrd rdn and wknd over 2f out* **7/1**[3]
4650 13 *4 ½* **Red Army Commander (IRE)**[50] 5579 4-8-10 **49**.................. RyanPowell(5) 2 16
(J A Geake) *prom: n.m.r 5f out: sn struggling to hold pl* **33/1**

2m 34.65s (1.95) **Going Correction** +0.10s/f (Good)
WFA 3 from 4yo+ 7lb 13 Ran SP% **121.8**
Speed ratings (Par 101): **97,96,95,94,93 89,89,85,84,83 82,82,79**
toteswinger: 1&2 £31.20, 1&3 £48.30, 2&3 £3.70. CSF £91.08 CT £529.63 TOTE £33.10: £7.70, £1.80, £2.80; EX 148.50 TRIFECTA Not won. Place 6: £52.42 Place 5: £10.87.
Owner Miss R Wakeford **Bred** Bobby Donworth And Miss Honora Corridan **Trained** Lambourn, Berks
■ Stewards' Enquiry : Billy Cray one-day ban: used whip with excessive frequency (Nov 6); one-day ban: careless riding (Nov 5)

FOCUS
This weak handicap for apprentice riders was run at just an ordinary pace. The first five came clear of the remainder and the form is straightforward.
Choosy Floosy Official explanation: jockey said filly never travelled
T/Jkpt: Not won. T/Plt: £143.10 to a £1 stake. Pool: £68,927.58. 351.60 winning tickets. T/Qpdt: £22.00 to a £1 stake. Pool: £6,075.29. 204.30 winning tickets. LM

6938 KEMPTON (A.W) (R-H)
Thursday, October 22

OFFICIAL GOING: Standard
Race times suggest the track was riding very fast.
Wind: modest, half behind Weather: dry

6970 WILLIAM HILL WINTER FESTIVAL - BOOK NOW CLAIMING STKS 5f (P)
5:50 (5:52) (Class 6) 2-Y-O £2,047 (£604; £302) Stalls High

Form RPR
1000 1 **Wanchai Whisper**[19] 6494 2-8-7 59.................. MartinLane(5) 10 62
(P D Evans) *in tch: hung lft and racd awkwardly bnd over 3f out: rdn and effrt wl over 1f out: led 1f out: drvn and kpt on fnl f* **10/1**
00 2 *nk* **Cyan Eyed**[27] 6241 2-9-2 0.................. RichardKingscote 2 65
(Tom Dascombe) *dwlt: sn in tch in midfield: drvn and effrt over 1f out: chsd wnr ins fnl f: kpt on wl u.p* **9/1**
2410 3 *1 ½* **Zelos Dream (IRE)**[8] 6774 2-8-13 67.................. FrederikTylicki(3) 9 60
(Rae Guest) *in tch: carried lft bnd over 3f out: drvn and hdwy ent fnl f: wnt 3rd fnl 100yds: nt pce to rch ldrs* **11/4**[2]
0206 4 *1* **Point To Prove**[28] 6227 2-9-1 66.................. KFallon 8 55
(Miss Amy Weaver) *stdd s: t.k.h: hld up in rr: hdwy on outer over 2f out: drvn wl over 1f out: kpt on fnl f: nvr gng pce to chal* **5/2**[1]
0204 5 *shd* **Wing Of Faith**[14] 6610 2-9-3 56.................. RichardHughes 3 57
(S Kirk) *chsd ldr: rdn and effrt ent fnl 2f: ev ch and hrd drvn jst over 1f out: wknd ins fnl f* **13/2**

0 **6** *1 ¼* **Graceandgratitude**[105] 3772 2-8-13 0 WilliamCarson(3) 12 52
(S C Williams) *s.i.s: in tch in rr: rdn and edging out lft over 1f out: kpt on same pce u.p fnl f* 20/1
3240 **7** *1 ¾* **Devassa**[19] 6494 2-8-6 59 LukeMorris 11 35
(C G Cox) *led: rdn wl over 1f out: hdd 1f out: wknd fnl f* 4/1[3]
4500 **8** *2 ½* **Starburst Excel**[19] 6494 2-8-12 62 (t) JerryO'Dwyer 6 32
(M G Quinlan) *taken down early: chsd ldrs: rdn and nt qckn wl over 1f out: wknd ent fnl f* 25/1
6030 **9** *8* **Usquaebach**[23] 6356 2-8-4 55 (b) RichardThomas 5 —
(S Curran) *s.i.s: sn detached in last and rdn: nvr a factor* 33/1
60.75 secs (0.25) **Going Correction** -0.125s/f (Stan) 9 Ran SP% 119.2
Speed ratings (Par 93): **93,92,90,88,88 86,83,79,66**
toteswinger: 1&2 £14.10, 1&3 £8.00, 2&3 £6.40. CSF £95.65 TOTE £14.30: £3.20, £3.10, £1.10; EX 125.60.
Owner M&R Refurbishments Ltd **Bred** Mike Smith **Trained** Pandy, Monmouths

FOCUS
This was a moderate juvenile claimer and the form is weak and of little interest with the future in mind.

NOTEBOOK
Wanchai Whisper had shown very little since being sold out of William Haggas's yard for 11,500gns after winning a seller in August, but she was well suited by the combination of a favourable draw and the return to patient tactics. Once in front, she was always doing enough. (tchd 9-1)
Cyan Eyed, although down the field on her first two starts, had shown ability, including in a valuable sales races last time. Dropped in grade, she was forced three wide into the straight and lacked the winner's sharpness, but the way she kept on suggests she'll have little bother finding a similar race. (op 6-1)
Zelos Dream(IRE) didn't seem to have too many excuses but she probably didn't run up to her official mark of 67. (op 100-30 tchd 7-2)
Point To Prove was fractious on entering the stalls and, not best away, he raced wider than ideal pretty much throughout and could never muster the required speed. (op 7-2 tchd 9-4)
Wing Of Faith had a bit of a task on at the figures and was not given a hard time once held. (op 7-1 tchd 11-2)
Devassa, ahead of today's winner in a Wolverhampton seller last time, switched to front-running tactics on this occasion and seemed to enjoy a soft-enough lead, but her finishing effort was tame, suggesting she'll be hard to place. (op 5-1)

6971 KEMPTON.CO.UK MAIDEN STKS 5f (P)
6:20 (6:21) (Class 5) 2-Y-O £2,590 (£770; £385; £192) Stalls High

Form RPR
2 **1** **Chat De La Burg (USA)**[21] 6424 2-9-3 0 RobertWinston 9 76+
(J R Best) *chsd ldrs: outpcd by ldr and rdn wl over 1f out: wnt 4 l 2nd jst over 1f out: storming run ins fnl f to ld towards fin* 1/1[1]
4532 **2** *¾* **La Fortunata**[15] 6582 2-8-12 74 JimmyQuinn 10 68
(J R Jenkins) *led: pushed along and wnt clr wl over 1f out: 4 l clr jst over 1f out: rdn ins fnl f: fdd and ct towards fin* 15/8[2]
220 **3** *1* **Lexi's Layla (IRE)**[55] 5379 2-8-12 65 JamieSpencer 2 64
(D M Simcock) *t.k.h: hld up towards rr: swtchd lft and effrt over 1f out: r.o u.p fnl f: nt rch ldrs* 12/1
5224 **4** *nk* **Key Art (IRE)**[20] 6443 2-9-3 70 TPQueally 8 68
(J Noseda) *chsd ldr: rdn and outpcd by wnr wl over 1f out: lost 2nd jst over 1f out: plugged on same pce fnl f* 9/2[3]
0 **5** *1* **The Strig**[91] 4243 2-9-3 0 SaleemGolam 7 65+
(S C Williams) *wnt lft s and s.i.s: in rr: pushed along over 3f out: carried lft over 1f out: hdwy ent fnl f: r.o but nvr able to chal* 25/1
6 *2 ¼* **Fair Passion** 2-8-12 0 DaneO'Neill 1 52
(D Shaw) *v.s.a: wl detached in last: hdwy over 2f out: tagged on to rr of field and edgd rt over 1f out: nvr trbld ldrs* 50/1
7 *2 ½* **Ahwahnee** 2-8-12 0 SebSanders 6 43
(R M Beckett) *bmpd s: sn rcvrd to chse ldng trio: rdn jst over 2f out: wknd over 1f out* 13/2
60.31 secs (-0.19) **Going Correction** -0.125s/f (Stan) 7 Ran SP% 129.8
Speed ratings (Par 95): **96,94,93,92,91 87,83**
toteswinger: 1&2 £1.20, 1&3 £3.70, 2&3 £4.70. CSF £3.85 TOTE £1.90: £1.60, £1.60; EX 4.70.
Owner Kent Bloodstock **Bred** S M D Ltd **Trained** Hucking, Kent

FOCUS
An ordinary 2-y-o maiden run in a time 0.44sec quicker than the earlier juvenile claimer won by the 59-rated Wanchai Whisper. The placed horses set the level and the form could be rated higher.

NOTEBOOK
Chat De La Burg(USA) ◆'s trainer expressed concerns beforehand that this colt, who ran second over 6f at Newmarket on his debut, would not be totally suited by this drop in trip, suggesting he'll soon want 7f, but he was still good enough to win. Having come off the bridle over 2f out, he had 3l to find on the runner-up passing the furlong pole, but that one slowed noticeably late on, allowing this son of Johannesburg to get up near the line. He may get a workable handicap mark with improvement to come when he goes up in trip, and he has the scope to make a nice 3-y-o. (tchd 11-8)
La Fortunata ran a very similar race to the way she performed over this course and distance last time, showing loads of natural speed and looking the winner for much of the straight, only to empty late on. And on this occasion she may even have been a little unfortunate as she was reported to have lost an off-fore shoe, apparently inside the final furlong. Her raw pace should see her win eventually, especially if she can get a breather in. Official explanation: jockey said filly lost an off-fore shoe (op 3-1)
Lexi's Layla(IRE), returning from nearly two months off, was bit keen under restraint, with stall two no help, but she kept on in the straight. Granted a better draw next time, she might benefit from having more use made of her. (op 14-1)
Key Art(IRE) is already looking pretty exposed and there wasn't a great deal of encouragement in this performance. (op 6-1)
The Strig ◆ caught the eye under a considerate ride, being waited with early and not hit with the whip in the straight, and he's one to keep in mind. (op 33-1 tchd 20-1)
Fair Passion ◆ is quite a big filly and she was extremely green, but she hinted at ability. There should be a lot better to come.

6972 LEVY BOARD H'CAP 5f (P)
6:50 (6:51) (Class 4) (0-85,85) 3-Y-O+ £4,727 (£1,406; £702; £351) Stalls High

Form RPR
1531 **1** **Royal Intruder**[22] 6396 4-9-0 81 RichardHughes 10 92
(S Donohoe, Ire) *in tch in midfield: looking for run over 1f out: swtchd rt jst ins fnl f and qcknd between horses: led fnl 75yds: sn in command: comf* 11/2[3]
1166 **2** *1 ½* **Ocean Blaze**[13] 6647 5-8-11 78 ChrisCatlin 9 83
(B R Millman) *led: hrd pressed and rdn over 1f out: kpt on wl tl hdd fnl 75yds: no ch w wnr but hld on wl for 2nd* 5/1[2]
0241 **3** *hd* **Step It Up (IRE)**[2] 6916 5-8-6 76 6ex AndreaAtzeni(3) 11 81
(J R Boyle) *chsd ldrs: swtchd lft and effrt wl over 1f out: drvn and styd on same pce fnl f* 7/4[1]
2152 **4** *hd* **Brandywell Boy (IRE)**[2] 6916 6-8-4 71 oh1 RichardThomas 6 75
(D J S Ffrench Davis) *sn outpcd and niggled along in rr: hdwy on inner over 1f out: r.o wl fnl f: swtchd lft fnl 100yds: nt rch ldrs* 12/1
-200 **5** *½* **Sir Edwin Landseer (USA)**[48] 5646 9-9-2 83 (v[1]) GeorgeBaker 5 85
(G L Moore) *taken down early: chsd ldng trio: rdn and unable qck over 1f out: kpt on same pce after* 25/1
0460 **6** *¾* **Lochstar**[103] 3844 5-9-4 85 DavidProbert 8 85
(A M Balding) *chsd ldr: rdn and chal over 1f out tl wknd ins fnl f* 13/2
0642 **7** *1 ½* **Our Piccadilly (IRE)**[13] 6632 4-8-11 78 FergusSweeney 2 72
(W S Kittow) *s.i.s: a in rr: n.d* 20/1
3636 **8** *½* **Chjimes (IRE)**[13] 6632 5-8-12 79 LPKeniry 7 71
(C R Dore) *racd in midfield: rdn over 2f out: struggling over 1f out: n.d after* 16/1
2050 **9** *2 ¼* **The Jobber (IRE)**[13] 6647 8-8-13 80 DaneO'Neill 1 64
(M Blanshard) *a towards rr: effrt u.p wl over 1f out: nvr trbld ldrs* 25/1
61 **10** *nk* **Misaro (GER)**[12] 6669 8-8-10 77 (v) LukeMorris 3 60
(R A Harris) *a in rr: drvn on outer jst over 2f out: nvr on terms* 14/1
0010 **11** *2* **Good Gorsoon (USA)**[13] 6631 4-8-13 85 AshleyMorgan(5) 4 61
(B W Hills) *dwlt: a in last pair: wd and rdn over 2f out: nvr a factor* 14/1
59.07 secs (-1.43) **Going Correction** -0.125s/f (Stan) 11 Ran SP% 121.1
Speed ratings (Par 105): **106,103,103,102,102 100,98,97,94,93 90**
toteswinger: 1&2 £5.70, 1&3 £3.00, 2&3 £3.60. CSF £33.35 CT £67.70 TOTE £6.50: £2.00, £1.50, £1.30; EX 45.20.
Owner Mrs Anna McDwyer **Bred** Farmers Hill Stud **Trained** Cootehill Road, Co. Cavan

FOCUS
A fair sprint handicap and the time was not far outside the track record.
Good Gorsoon(USA) Official explanation: jockey said colt failed to handle the bend

6973 KIA SOUL, SAFE BET H'CAP 1m 2f (P)
7:20 (7:22) (Class 4) (0-80,80) 3-Y-O+ £4,727 (£1,406; £702; £351) Stalls High

Form RPR
3213 **1** **Poyle Meg**[41] 5833 3-8-7 76 (p) JPFahy(7) 5 86
(R M Beckett) *chsd ldrs: rdn over 2f out: chsd clr ldr ins fnl f: drvn and r.o strly to ld nr fin* 14/1
0022 **2** *nk* **Mafeking (UAE)**[77] 4716 5-9-9 80 ChrisCatlin 2 89
(M R Hoad) *crossed over to rail and led over 8f out: set str gallop: clr 4f out: rdn wl over 1f out: kpt on tl hdd and no ex nr fin* 14/1
100 **3** *1* **Al Qeddaaf (IRE)**[29] 6209 3-9-0 76 RHills 11 83+
(W J Haggas) *hld up in midfield: swtchd lft and effrt u.p over 2f out: styd on u.p to go 3rd ins fnl f: nt rch ldng pair* 2/1[1]
02 **4** *1 ½* **Thunderball**[8] 6773 3-8-12 77 FrederikTylicki(3) 6 81
(J A Glover) *in tch in midfield: rdn and sltly hmpd ent fnl 2f: swtchd lft over 1f out: kpt on u.p: nvr rchd ldrs* 4/1[2]
0462 **5** *½* **Quick Release (IRE)**[20] 6460 4-8-13 75 MartinLane(5) 9 78
(D M Simcock) *chsd ldrs untl wnt 2nd over 4f out: rdn and no imp over 2f out: hanging u.p over 1f out: lost 3 pls ins fnl f* 8/1
4500 **6** *1 ¾* **Ellemujie**[19] 6480 4-9-9 80 MartinDwyer 7 80+
(D K Ivory) *sn bhd in last pair: pushed along over 7f out: hdwy over 1f out: styd on wl fnl f: nvr trbld ldrs* 16/1
1534 **7** *1 ¼* **Formula (USA)**[13] 6634 3-9-2 78 RichardHughes 4 75
(R Hannon) *s.i.s: hld up in rr: rdn and hdwy on inner 2f out: swtchd lft over 1f out: nvr trbld ldrs* 12/1
6315 **8** *1 ¾* **Sahaal (USA)**[42] 5803 3-9-3 79 (t) TPO'Shea 14 73
(M P Tregoning) *chsd ldrs: rdn and unable qck over 2f out: wknd u.p over 1f out* 20/1
0524 **9** *hd* **Hallingdal (UAE)**[15] 6583 4-9-4 75 LPKeniry 10 68
(J J Bridger) *dwlt: sn pushed up into midfield: n.m.r and shuffled bk 3f out: swtchd lft over 1f out: nvr trbld ldrs* 25/1
15 **10** *4* **Laafet**[72] 4881 4-9-4 75 JimmyQuinn 12 60
(K A Morgan) *led tl over 8f out: chsd ldr after tl over 4f out: wknd qckly u.p wl over 1f out* 20/1
545- **11** *3 ¼* **Motarjm (USA)**[382] 4726 5-9-7 78 SaleemGolam 8 57
(J Pearce) *stdd s: hld up in last pl: nvr on terms* 50/1
5506 **12** *nk* **Kidlat**[12] 6059 4-9-3 74 (t) KFallon 1 52
(B G Powell) *hld up in midfield on outer: rdn and no prog 3f out: no ch fnl 2f* 25/1
2633 **13** *2* **Dear Maurice**[21] 6435 5-9-5 76 JamieSpencer 13 50
(E A L Dunlop) *a bhd: nt clr run and hmpd bnd 2f out: switching lft after: n.d* 13/2[3]
6004 **14** *14* **Dream Of Fortune (IRE)**[11] 6703 5-9-2 78 (bt) JamieJones(5) 3 24
(M G Quinlan) *stdd s: hld up in rr: hdwy on outer 5f out: wknd over 2f out: wl bhd and eased ins fnl f* 50/1
2m 5.15s (-2.85) **Going Correction** -0.125s/f (Stan)
WFA 3 from 4yo+ 5lb 14 Ran SP% 125.8
Speed ratings (Par 105): **106,105,104,103,103 101,100,99,99,96 93,93,91,80**
toteswinger: 1&2 £14.90, 1&3 £18.20, 2&3 £12.50. CSF £187.48 CT £568.67 TOTE £16.90: £4.80, £3.60, £2.00; EX 243.40.
Owner Cecil Wiggins **Bred** Miss Alison Wiggins **Trained** Whitsbury, Hants

FOCUS
A fair handicap and the time was well under standard.
Kidlat Official explanation: jockey said gelding had a breathing problem
Dear Maurice Official explanation: jockey said gelding was denied a clear run

6974 TRY OUR NEW BISTRO MENU MAIDEN STKS 1m 3f (P)
7:50 (7:54) (Class 5) 3-Y-O+ £2,590 (£770; £385; £192) Stalls High

Form RPR
1 **King's Salute (USA)**[219] 3-9-3 0 RoystonFfrench 13 77+
(M Johnston) *chsd ldr tl 4f out: styd chsng ldrs: effrt u.p to press ldr over 1f out: lft in ld 1f out: clr and r.o strly fnl f* 1/1[1]
2 *2 ¾* **Shubbaan (USA)** 4-9-9 0 RHills 4 72+
(M P Tregoning) *hld up in midfield on outer: hdwy over 2f out: rdn to chse ldrs whn carried lft and sltly hmpd 1f out: sn chsng wnr: r.o but no imp* 4/1[3]
4 **3** *1 ¼* **Muzo (USA)**[12] 6673 3-9-3 0 TPQueally 11 70
(J Noseda) *chsd ldrs: wnt 2nd 4f out: drvn and ev ch jst over 2f out: keeping on same pce whn carried lft and sltly hmpd 1f out: kpt on same pce after* 10/3[2]
0 **4** *hd* **Alpha Vega (IRE)**[156] 2165 3-8-12 0 (v[1]) LPKeniry 8 65
(J R Fanshawe) *hld up in tch in midfield: hdwy on inner to chse ldrs ent fnl 2f: edgd lft u.p over 1f out: one pce after* 20/1
036 **5** *1* **Country Road (IRE)**[7] 6794 3-9-3 0 AlanMunro 5 68+
(P W Chapple-Hyam) *led: rdn and edging lft 2f out: hung bdly lft and hdd 1f out: lost all ch: wknd towards fin* 9/2

00 **6** 3½ **Franco Is My Name**[36] 5987 3-9-3 0 .... FergusSweeney 1 62
(P R Hedger) *stdd and swtchd rt after s: hld up in rr: nt clr run wl over 2f out: hdwy and in tch wl over 1f out: pushed along and outpcd jst over 1f out* **100/1**

05 **7** ½ **Court Princess**[28] 6225 6-9-4 0 .... DaneO'Neill 3 56
(George Baker) *dwlt: towards rr: rdn and effrt over 2f out: kpt on u.p but nvr gng pce to threaten ldrs* **66/1**

00 **8** ½ **Uncle Keef (IRE)**[7] 6794 3-9-3 0 .... MartinDwyer 14 60
(M P Tregoning) *dwlt: sn bustled along: hdwy into midfield 6f out: rdn and struggling to hold pl 4f out: hdwy on inner over 2f out: no prog and btn over 1f out* **50/1**

0 **9** nse **Red Hot Desert**[12] 6673 3-9-3 0 .... AdamKirby 2 60
(W R Swinburn) *racd in tch in midfield: n.m.r and swtchd lft over 2f out: sn drvn and no real prog: n.d fnl f* **66/1**

4 **10** ½ **Summer Affair (IRE)**[22] 6375 4-9-9 0 .... ShaneKelly 7 59
(B I Case) *t.k.h: chsd ldrs: ev ch and rdn over 2f out: wknd qckly over 1f out* **33/1**

0 **11** 3¾ **Two Together (USA)**[7] 6794 3-9-3 0 ....(t) ChrisCatlin 10 52
(D R Lanigan) *s.i.s: a bhd: wd and rdn 3f out: no hdwy and wl btn after* **20/1**

0 **12** 2¾ **Keepholdin (IRE)**[22] 6375 4-9-9 0 .... JimCrowley 9 47
(N P Mulholland) *s.i.s: a bhd* **66/1**

0 **13** 6 **Supplementary (IRE)**[12] 6673 7-8-11 0 .... RichardRowe(7) 6 31
(M J Coombe) *t.k.h: hld up in midfield on outer: rn wd and lost pl bnd 3f out: hung bdly lft and wl bhd after* **100/1**

2m 22.33s (0.43) **Going Correction** -0.125s/f (Stan)
WFA 3 from 4yo+ 6lb **13 Ran SP% 132.1**
Speed ratings (Par 103): **93,91,90,89,89 86,86,85,85,85 82,80,76**
toteswinger: 1&2 £2.60, 1&3 £2.40, 2&3 £3.60. CSF £5.88 TOTE £1.80: £1.10, £2.00, £1.60; EX 9.90.
Owner Sheikh Hamdan Bin Mohammed Al Maktoum **Bred** Darley **Trained** Middleham Moor, N Yorks

FOCUS
A reasonable maiden featuring some extremely well-bred types, but the pace was steady.
Country Road(IRE) Official explanation: jockey said colt hung left under pressure
Two Together(USA) Official explanation: trainer's rep said colt had been struck into

6975 CHRISTMAS PARTY NIGHTS AT KEMPTON PARK H'CAP 1m 4f (P)
8:20 (8:23) (Class 5) (0-75,74) 3-Y-O **£2,590** (£770; £385; £192) **Stalls** Centre

Form RPR

0441 **1** **Bow To No One (IRE)**[17] 6538 3-8-9 70 .... MartinLane(5) 5 82
(A P Jarvis) *hld up in rr: stl plenty to do and c wd 3f out: rdn and gd hdwy over 2f out: led over 1f out: r.o strly* **13/2**[2]

3033 **2** 2½ **Tilos Gem (IRE)**[19] 6473 3-9-4 74 .... RoystonFfrench 9 82
(M Johnston) *chsd ldr tl 6f out: hmpd sn after: rdn to ld over 2f out: hdd over 1f out: no ch w wnr fnl f but kpt on for clr 2nd* **7/1**[3]

3423 **3** 3½ **Demeanour (USA)**[12] 6673 3-9-2 72 .... JamieSpencer 10 75
(E A L Dunlop) *s.i.s: sn in tch: rdn over 2f out: chsd ldr briefly 2f out: drvn and wl outpcd by ldng pair over 1f out* **7/1**[3]

-605 **4** 7 **Hazy Dancer**[13] 6634 3-9-1 71 .... RichardHughes 8 62
(M P Tregoning) *hld up towards rr: rdn over 2f out: nvr nr ldrs: plugged on to go poor 4th ins fnl f* **10/1**

242 **5** ½ **Everaard (USA)**[8] 6784 3-9-0 70 .... KFallon 4 61
(D R C Elsworth) *chsd ldrs: rdn over 3f out: drvn and wknd ent fnl 2f: wl btn after* **8/1**

62-3 **6** hd **Attainable**[59] 5314 3-9-0 70 .... JimCrowley 6 60
(Mrs A J Perrett) *chsd ldrs early: grad lost pl: towards rr and rdn wl over 2f out: no ch w ldrs fnl 2f* **14/1**

5530 **7** 5 **Sparkling Crystal (IRE)**[39] 5910 3-9-3 73 .... MichaelHills 14 55
(B W Hills) *t.k.h: chsd ldrs: rdn and effrt on inner over 2f out: chsd ldrs and drvn ent fnl 2f: sn wknd* **16/1**

0020 **8** ½ **Danse On Wood**[47] 5666 3-9-2 72 .... ShaneKelly 7 53
(J Noseda) *hld up in rr: hmpd and dropped to last over 6f out: sme late hdwy but n.d* **25/1**

213 **9** 3 **Key Regard (IRE)**[28] 865 3-9-4 74 .... MartinDwyer 1 51
(P F I Cole) *hld up in midfield: hdwy to press ldr over 5f out tl over 2f out: sn wknd: eased ins fnl f* **20/1**

064- **10** nk **Rawaaj**[390] 6282 3-8-9 65 .... RHills 2 41
(Sir Michael Stoute) *racd in midfield on outer: struggling wl over 2f out: wl btn fnl f* **8/1**

046 **11** 5 **Princability (IRE)**[11] 6698 3-8-12 68 .... SamHitchcott 11 36
(M R Channon) *in tch in midfield on inner: rdn and struggling wl over 2f out: sn wl bhd* **10/1**

0520 **12** 7 **Sea Lavender**[10] 6742 3-8-12 68 ....(b[1]) SteveDrowne 3 25
(R Charlton) *stdd s: hld up in rr: pushed along and no hdwy over 3f out: wl bhd fr over 2f out* **25/1**

2322 **13** 9 **Ramora (USA)**[12] 6671 3-9-1 71 .... TPQueally 13 14
(H R A Cecil) *led tl rdn and hdd over 2f out: wkng whn hmpd 2f out: eased fnl f* **7/2**[1]

2m 32.01s (-2.49) **Going Correction** -0.125s/f (Stan) **13 Ran SP% 126.0**
Speed ratings (Par 101): **103,101,99,94,94 93,90,90,88,88 84,80,74**
toteswinger: 1&2 £13.20, 1&3 £9.50, 2&3 £11.60. CSF £53.19 CT £336.66 TOTE £8.00: £3.00, £2.80, £2.90; EX 36.70.
Owner Geoffrey Bishop **Bred** Albert Conneally **Trained** Middleham Moor, N Yorks
■ Stewards' Enquiry : Martin Dwyer caution: careless riding.

FOCUS
An ordinary handicap, and with the pace good they finished strung out.
Tilos Gem(IRE) Official explanation: jockey said colt clipped heels

6976 BISTRO PRICES FROM £37 H'CAP 7f (P)
8:50 (8:51) (Class 5) (0-75,75) 3-Y-O+ **£2,590** (£770; £385; £192) **Stalls** High

Form RPR

5622 **1** **Berbice (IRE)**[22] 6370 4-9-1 70 ....(b) RichardHughes 10 79
(S Donohoe, Ire) *awkward and wnt lft leaving stalls: stdd and hld up wl in rr: hdwy to chse ldrs on bit over 1f out: rdn: edgd rt but qcknd ent fnl f: led ins fnl f: edgd lft and a holding rival fnl 75yds* **3/1**[1]

3136 **2** ½ **Autumn Blades (IRE)**[2] 6924 4-9-6 75 ....(p) DavidProbert 13 83
(A Bailey) *chsd ldng trio: clsd 3f out: ev ch and stl on bit 2f out: rdn 1f out: pressed wnr fnl 100yds: nt qckn and a hld* **7/1**

0152 **3** 1¾ **Defector (IRE)**[10] 6725 3-9-0 71 .... MartinDwyer 2 74
(W R Muir) *chsd ldrs and clr of field: ev ch and rdn 2f out: led over 1f out: hedaed ins fnl f: sn outpcd* **12/1**

304 **4** ¾ **Tuxedo**[10] 6725 4-9-3 72 .... LukeMorris 3 73
(P W Hiatt) *racd off the pce in midfield: clsd and rdn 3f out: kpt on u.p fnl f but nvr able to chal* **16/1**

-135 **5** nk **Zero Money (IRE)**[16] 6562 3-9-4 75 .... RichardKingscote 5 75
(R Charlton) *towards rr: rdn along over 4f out: hdwy u.p over 1f out: styd on fnl f: nvr able to chal* **10/3**[2]

2002 **6** ¾ **Shaded Edge**[10] 6726 5-8-13 68 .... HayleyTurner 9 66
(D W P Arbuthnot) *racd off the pce in midfield: rdn over 3f out: hdwy u.p over 2f out: ev ch over 1f out: wknd jst ins fnl f* **12/1**

6401 **7** nk **Finnegan McCool**[11] 6699 3-9-0 71 6ex ....(p) SebSanders 4 69
(R M Beckett) *wl off the pce towards rr: swtchd to outer and hdwy over 2f out: kpt on u.p but nvr gng pce to chal ldrs* **14/1**

2362 **8** 1 **Yankee Storm**[8] 6776 4-8-13 68 .... JimmyQuinn 11 63
(H J Collingridge) *hld up off the pce in midfield: hdwy over 2f out: swtchd ins and hdwy to chse ldrs over 1f out: wknd ent fnl f* **6/1**[3]

0000 **9** 1¾ **Resplendent Nova**[14] 6614 7-9-6 75 .... IanMongan 7 65
(P Howling) *stdd s: hld up in last pl: rdn and effrt over 2f out: edging out lft after: n.d* **33/1**

5123 **10** hd **Black Dahlia**[10] 6725 4-8-13 71 .... FrederikTylicki(3) 1 61
(J A Glover) *chsd ldr: rdn over 2f out: ev ch 2f out tl wknd qckly ent fnl f* **20/1**

1004 **11** hd **Bold Marc (IRE)**[26] 6294 7-9-0 69 .... AndrewElliott 14 58
(A P Jarvis) *led at fast gallop: rdn jst over 2f out: hdd over 1f out: wknd qckly ent fnl f* **7/1**

1m 25.0s (-1.00) **Going Correction** -0.125s/f (Stan)
WFA 3 from 4yo+ 2lb **11 Ran SP% 123.0**
Speed ratings (Par 103): **100,99,97,96,96 95,95,93,91,91 91**
toteswinger: 1&2 £7.00, 1&3 £5.70, 2&3 £14.00. CSF £25.80 CT £233.96 TOTE £3.80: £1.80, £1.60, £3.80; EX 35.50.
Owner Mrs Samantha Donohoe **Bred** William Flynn **Trained** Cootehill Road, Co. Cavan

FOCUS
A moderate handicap for the class dominated by horses with suspect attitudes. The pace was strong.

6977 BOXINGDAYRACES.CO.UK H'CAP 1m (P)
9:20 (9:21) (Class 5) (0-75,75) 3-Y-O **£2,590** (£770; £385; £192) **Stalls** High

Form RPR

6112 **1** **Sham Sheer**[17] 6545 3-9-4 75 .... KFallon 13 82+
(L M Cumani) *in tch: chsd ldrs and rdn jst over 2f out: drvn to ld over 1f out: styd on wl and a in command fnl f* **5/4**[1]

3451 **2** 1 **Red Suede Shoes**[10] 6719 3-8-11 71 6ex ....(p) JamesMillman(3) 3 76
(B R Millman) *hld up in midfield: rdn and effrt jst over 2f out: hdwy over 1f out: chsd wnr fnl 100yds: kpt on but nt pce to threaten wnr* **15/2**[3]

2244 **3** ½ **Papyrian**[22] 6390 3-9-2 73 .... AlanMunro 12 77
(W Jarvis) *hld up towards rr: effrt on inner jst over 2f out: drvn and hdwy over 1f out: styd on wl to go 3rd fnl 100yds: nt pce to chal wnr* **16/1**

0031 **4** 1 **Classically (IRE)**[14] 6608 3-9-1 72 .... SteveDrowne 8 73
(R Charlton) *chsd ldrs: rdn to chse wnr briefly 2f out: plugged on same pce u.p fnl f* **3/1**[2]

0022 **5** nk **Piccolo Mondo**[14] 6621 3-9-1 72 .... JimCrowley 2 73
(P Winkworth) *stdd and dropped in bhd after s: hld up wl in rr: hdwy over 2f out: chsd ldrs and drvn over 1f out: no prog fnl f* **10/1**

3235 **6** ¾ **Layer Cake**[21] 6421 3-8-12 69 ....(p) SebSanders 4 68
(J W Hills) *t.k.h: hld up in last trio on outer: effrt and hanging rt wl over 2f out: swtchd lft sn after: hdwy and chsng ldrs over 1f out: no prog fnl f* **16/1**

4330 **7** ½ **Spring Adventure**[44] 5745 3-9-4 75 .... JamieSpencer 14 73
(E A L Dunlop) *led: rdn over 2f out: hdd over 1f out: wknd ins fnl f* **10/1**

0-10 **8** 3 **Altimatum (USA)**[91] 4246 3-9-3 74 .... TPQueally 6 64
(P F I Cole) *a towards rr: rdn and effrt over 2f out: no real hdwy and nvr trbld ldrs* **50/1**

51-4 **9** 9 **Reaction**[14] 6621 3-9-2 73 .... ChrisCatlin 10 42
(M R Channon) *chsd ldrs: rdn and unable qck over 2f out: wknd u.p wl over 1f out* **12/1**

4466 **10** 6 **Trueblue Wizard (IRE)**[8] 6778 3-9-0 71 ....(b) MartinDwyer 7 25
(W R Muir) *t.k.h: hld up in midfield early: hdwy to chse ldr over 4f out tl over 2f out: sn wknd u.p: wl bhd over 1f out* **14/1**

3510 **11** 3½ **Integria**[20] 6455 3-8-13 70 ....(b) LukeMorris 5 16
(J M P Eustace) *racd in midfield on outer: lost pl qckly u.p over 2f out: wl bhd fnl 2f* **12/1**

0-0 **12** 5 **Warrior Nation (FR)**[37] 5964 3-8-10 67 .... NeilChalmers 9 1
(A J Chamberlain) *towards rr on inner: rdn and lost tch qckly over 2f out: t.o fnl f* **100/1**

1m 38.78s (-1.02) **Going Correction** -0.125s/f (Stan) **12 Ran SP% 136.2**
Speed ratings (Par 101): **100,99,98,97,97 96,95,92,83,77 74,69**
toteswinger: 1&2 £7.80, 1&3 £16.40, 2&3 £23.90. CSF £14.16 CT £129.80 TOTE £2.70: £1.70, £2.40, £6.90; EX 24.10 Place 6: £23.34 Place 5: £6.01.
Owner Sheikh Mohammed Obaid Al Maktoum **Bred** Brook Stud Bloodstock Ltd **Trained** Newmarket, Suffolk

FOCUS
A modest handicap run at a steady gallop.
T/Plt: £26.60 to a £1 stake. Pool: £72,671.40. 1,988.52 winning tickets. T/Qpdt: £10.20 to a £1 stake. Pool: £7,375.67. 533.60 winning tickets. SP

6978 - (Foreign Racing) - See Raceform Interactive

6960 DEAUVILLE (R-H)
Thursday, October 22

OFFICIAL GOING: Turf course - good; all-weather - standard

6979a PRIX DE LA POMMERAIE (UNRACED COLTS & GELDINGS) (ALL-WEATHER) 7f 110y
1:40 (1:50) 2-Y-O

£11,650 (£4,660; £4,660; £3,495; £2,330; £1,165)

RPR

1 **Lui Seul (IRE)** 2-9-2 .... IMendizabal 78
(J-C Rouget, France)

2 ¾ **Classic Hero (GER)** 2-9-2 .... WMongil 76
(H Hiller, Germany)

3 ½ **Army Scout (USA)** 2-9-2 .... CSoumillon 75
(J-C Rouget, France)

4 hd **Paris Vegas (USA)** 2-9-2 75
(F Chappet, France)

5 ¾ **Docteur Carter (FR)** 2-8-13 .... (3) 73
(J De Chevigny, France)

6 ¾ **Oui Non (IRE)** 2-9-2 71
(Y De Nicolay, France)

7 3/4 **Rubacuori (FR)** 2-9-2 69
(J Rossi, France)
8 2 **Bilyboy (FR)** 2-9-2 65
(J-L Pelletan, France)
9 nk **Makani (GER)** 2-9-2 64
(J E Pease, France)
10 2 1/2 **Yosolito (FR)** 2-9-2 58
(L A Urbano-Grajales, France)
0 **Atlantic Mist (FR)** 2-9-2 —
(Y De Nicolay, France)
0 **Escape To Freedom (IRE)** 2-9-2 —
(E J O'Neill)
0 **Darielli (USA)** 2-9-2 —
(F Head, France)
0 **Amour Sacre (FR)** 2-9-2 (p) —
(Robert Collet, France)
0 **Tag's Book (IRE)** 2-8-10 (6) —
(U Suter, France)
0 **My Boy Davis (IRE)** 2-9-2 —
(N Clement, France)

1m 33.2s (93.20) 16 Ran
PARI-MUTUEL: WIN 11.80; PL 2.90, 4.90, 2.10; DF 102.80.
Owner G Augustin-Normand **Bred** Petra Bloodstock Agency Ltd **Trained** Pau, France

LYON VILLEURBANNE (R-H)
Thursday, October 22

OFFICIAL GOING: Standard

6980a PRIX DE LA CONFLUENCE (CLAIMER) (ALL-WEATHER) 1m 1f
12:20 (12:20) 3-Y-O **£5,825** (£2,330; £1,748; £1,165; £583)

RPR
1 **Huangdi (FR)**[53] 3-9-4 JBensimon 69
(M Boutin, France)
2 snk **Derringbay (IRE)**[33] 3-8-11 MSautjeau 60
(Mme G Rarick, France) *fin 3rd: plcd 2nd*
3 nse **Flying Shadow (SWI)**[82] 5118 3-8-8 (b) CCare 57
(H-A Pantall, France) *fin 3rd: plcd 4th*
4 2 **Lilly Gold (FR)**[43] 5784 3-8-11 (b) 55
(Mlle S-V Tarrou, France) *fin 5th: plcd 4th*
5 3 **Ligne Claire (FR)**[104] 3-8-8 46
(Y De Nicolay, France)
6 shd **Salsavana (FR)**[33] 3-8-11 49
(Rod Collet, France)
7 1 1/2 **Mayouta (FR)**[52] 3-9-1 50
(B Goudot, France)
8 2 **High Ville (FR)** 3-8-8 39
(N Bertran De Balanda, France)
9 5 **Kidogo (FR)** 3-9-1 35
(E Drai, France)
10 **Sabelotodo (FR)**[104] 3-8-11 31
(M Boutin, France)
0 **Roi De Slic (FR)** 3-8-11 (b) —
(J-P Roman, France)
0 **Ange Doree (FR)** 3-9-5 —
(Frau Carmen Bocksai, Germany)
D 1 **Dame Anouska (IRE)**[18] 6606 3-8-11 J-BEyquem 60
(E J O'Neill) *led: pushed along 1 1/2f out: rdn and r.o fnl f: hdd 50yds out: disqualified and plcd last (blamed for horses falling bhd)* **7/2**[1]
F **Diamantino (FR)**[50] 3-8-11 —
(B Goudot, France)
F **Let's Go Outside (FR)**[110] 3-8-11 —
(J Heloury, Italy)
F **Cyrnea (FR)**[10] 3-9-5 —
(C Boutin, France)

1m 48.08s (108.08) **16** Ran SP% **22.2**
PARI-MUTUEL (Including 1 Euro stake): WIN 11.50 (coupled with Sabelotodo); PL 5.80, 5.60, 8.70; DF 191.10.
Owner M Boutin **Bred** Mme Marie-Carmen Boutin **Trained** France

6981a PRIX DU PARC DE LA TETE D'OR (H'CAP) (F&M) (ALL-WEATHER) 1m 2f 165y
1:25 (1:25) 3-Y-O+ **£8,738** (£3,495; £2,621; £1,748; £874)

RPR
1 **Naranja (GER)**[29] 6-9-0 ALarue 74
(J-P Gauvin, France)
2 1 **Royale Again (FR)**[12] 4-8-13 AClement 71
(P Monfort, France)
3 3/4 **Manita (IRE)**[62] 4-8-13 AlexisBadel 70
(C Boutin, France)
4 nse **Mageska (FR)**[224] 4-9-2 72
(J-P Gauvin, France)
5 snk **Diner En Ville (FR)**[446] 5-8-9 65
(F Pardon, France)
6 nk **Reve D'Ailleur (FR)**[53] 5-9-1 71
(J-V Toux, France)
7 1 1/2 **Happy Fellow (FR)**[109] 5-9-3 70
(P Lefevre, France)
8 1 1/2 **Riotista (IRE)**[32] 6150 3-9-6 J-BEyquem 76
(E J O'Neill) *hld up in 8th: tried to improve over 1 1/2f out: sn one pce* **12/1**[1]
9 2 **Space Tune (FR)** 3-9-0 66
(M Pimbonnet, France)
10 nk **Royaline (IRE)**[33] 4-8-6 (b) 52
(A Spanu, France)

2m 13.59s (133.59)
WFA 3 from 4yo+ 6lb **10** Ran SP% **7.7**
PARI-MUTUEL: WIN 6.10; PL 2.40, 3.10, 3.70; DF 44.30.
Owner S Henriroux **Bred** Frau M Niebuhr **Trained** France

6408 AYR (L-H)
Friday, October 23

OFFICIAL GOING: Good (5.7)
False rail in use on both sides of straight course and rail on home bend dolled out on home bend increasing distances on round course by about 10yds.
Wind: Fresh, half behind Weather: Cloudy

6982 EUROPEAN BREEDERS' FUND MAIDEN STKS 1m
1:40 (1:42) (Class 4) 2-Y-O **£5,180** (£1,541; £770; £384) **Stalls** Low

Form RPR
255 1 **Corsica (IRE)**[42] 5831 2-9-3 77 RoystonFfrench 4 74
(M Johnston) *chsd ldr: rdn and led over 1f out: kpt on wl fnl f* **2/1**[1]
564 2 3/4 **Danceintothelight**[10] 6763 2-9-0 0 FrederikTylicki(3) 2 72
(K A Ryan) *led to over 1f out: rallied: kpt on ins fnl f* **6/1**[3]
3 3 **Mr Emirati (USA)** 2-9-3 0 RichardMullen 9 66+
(B Smart) *hld up in tch: effrt over 2f out: kpt on same pce fnl f* **12/1**
4 1 1/2 **La Di Da** 2-8-12 0 TomEaves 8 57+
(I Semple) *s.i.s: hld up: hdwy over 2f out: edgd lft and no imp over 1f out* **20/1**
0 5 1 1/4 **Mrs E**[27] 6284 2-8-12 0 PaulMulrennan 3 55
(M W Easterby) *s.i.s: sn in tch: rdn over 2f out: one pce over 1f out* **80/1**
3 6 8 **Monkton Vale (IRE)**[35] 6046 2-9-3 0 DanielTudhope 1 42
(N Wilson) *sn trcking ldrs: rdn over 2f out: wknd wl over 1f out* **9/2**[2]
6 7 18 **Balierus (GER)**[22] 6423 2-9-3 0 DO'Donohoe 7 3
(Saeed Bin Suroor) *prom on outside: drvn 1/2-way: wknd wl over 2f out* **2/1**[1]
0006 8 1 **Stanley Bridge**[84] 4492 2-8-10 32 BillyCray(7) 6 —
(A Berry) *hld up: rdn after 3f: sn wknd* **100/1**
9 13 **One Cat Diesel (IRE)** 2-9-3 0 DuranFentiman 5 —
(N Wilson) *t.k.h: hld up in tch: struggling 1/2-way: sn btn* **50/1**

1m 45.62s (1.82) **Going Correction** -0.05s/f (Good) **9** Ran SP% **115.8**
Speed ratings (Par 97): **88,87,84,82,81 73,55,54,41**
toteswinger: 1&2 £2.80, 1&3 £4.70, 2&3 £5.40. CSF £14.91 TOTE £2.80: £1.10, £1.40, £2.30; EX 11.50.
Owner Sheikh Hamdan Bin Mohammed Al Maktoum **Bred** Epona Bloodstock Ltd And P A Byrne **Trained** Middleham Moor, N Yorks
■ Mark Johnston's 200th British winner of the calendar year. He is the first Flat trainer to reach this milestone.

FOCUS
Just a fair maiden and the pace seemed ordinary. The front pair dominated from the start.

NOTEBOOK
Corsica(IRE) had twice been disappointing since an encouraging racecourse debut, but he got it right here. On the shoulder of the leader from the off, he was sent for home coming to the last furlong but with his rival rallying, he had to be kept up to his work to make sure of it. He would have been 9lb worse off with runner-up so did little more than he was entitled to, but he is probably capable of building on this. (op 15-8)
Danceintothelight, whose three efforts to date have been fair at best, had the run of the race out in front and to his great credit he battled back very gamely after being headed. He seems to be gradually progressing and looks one for handicaps in due course. (op 13-2)
Mr Emirati(USA) ◆, a 140,000gns half-brother to a triple sprint winner in the US, stayed on well from off the pace over the last couple of furlongs and there is likely much better to come from him. (op 10-1)
La Di Da ◆, a £27,000 half-sister to a winner over 1m2f, missed the break and raced out the back early, but she showed definite signs of ability when making an effort down the wide outside in the straight despite also looking a little green. There should be better to come from her. (op 18-1)
Mrs E ran well for a long way and this was much better than when well beaten on her Haydock debut, but the way she hung all over the place inside the last 2f suggests that the experience was still needed. She may come into her own once handicapped after one more run. (op 66-1)
Monkton Vale(IRE), a staying-on third on debut here last month when shaping as though this longer trip would suit, showed up for a long way but folded very tamely inside the last 2f and this was a step backwards. Official explanation: jockey said gelding had suffered interference on bend leave back straight (op 13-2)
Balierus(GER), who showed some ability on his Newmarket debut, was bitterly disappointing as he was off the bridle and going nowhere at halfway. (tchd 9-4)

6983 VICTOR CHANDLER NURSERY 6f
2:10 (2:13) (Class 5) (0-75,73) 2-Y-O **£3,238** (£963; £481; £240) **Stalls** High

Form RPR
216 1 **Living It Large (FR)**[17] 6557 2-9-7 73 TonyHamilton 4 78
(R F Fisher) *mde all: rdn over 2f out: kpt on strly fnl f* **20/1**
P500 2 3/4 **Ochilview Warrior (IRE)**[8] 6796 2-7-12 50 oh5..(b[1]) SilvestreDeSousa 1 52
(R Bastiman) *prom: rdn and outpcd over 1f out: r.o ins fnl f* **100/1**
4321 3 3/4 **Newbury Street**[25] 6345 2-8-12 67 FrederikTylicki(3) 13 67+
(R A Fahey) *in tch: rdn and hdwy 2f out: kpt on fnl f: hld nr fin* **2/1**[1]
020 4 1 1/4 **Lieu Day Louie (IRE)**[50] 5596 2-8-12 64 DanielTudhope 5 60
(N Wilson) *hld up in tch: effrt over 2f out: one pce over 1f out* **20/1**
6136 5 3/4 **Russian Davis (IRE)**[7] 6829 2-9-2 68 RichardMullen 14 62+
(R M H Cowell) *dwlt: bhd: rdn 1/2-way: hdwy over 1f out: kpt on strly fnl f* **8/1**
4653 6 2 1/4 **Ya Boy Sir (IRE)**[39] 5942 2-8-2 54 DuranFentiman 9 41
(I Semple) *chsd ldrs: hung lft thrght: rdn 1/2-way: wknd over 1f out* **16/1**
0300 7 shd **Charity Fair**[30] 6215 2-7-12 57 oh1 ow7 (p) BillyCray(7) 16 44
(A Berry) *missed break: bhd and outpcd: styd on fnl f: nvr rchd ldrs* **66/1**
043 8 1 1/4 **Besty**[29] 6231 2-9-2 68 TomEaves 6 51
(B Smart) *prom tl rdn and no ex over 1f out* **12/1**
02 9 nk **Schoolboy Champ**[4] 6906 2-9-5 71 (t) SJCraine 8 53
(Patrick Morris) *midfield: effrt over 2f out: btn over 1f out* **11/1**
6500 10 1 **Sydney Bridge**[7] 6819 2-8-12 64 (p) PaulMulrennan 10 43
(I Semple) *in tch tl rdn and wknd wl over 1f out* **25/1**
0050 11 3 1/2 **Thinking**[24] 6355 2-8-9 61 DavidAllan 12 30
(T D Easterby) *dwlt: bhd and drvn along: nvr wnt pce* **9/2**[2]
3320 12 5 **High Resolution**[20] 6491 2-8-2 59 MartinLane(5) 2 13
(Miss L A Perratt) *chsd ldrs tl rdn and wknd fr 2f out* **18/1**
550 13 3 1/2 **Silver Socks**[22] 6408 2-8-9 66 PatrickDonaghy(5) 7 9
(Miss L A Perratt) *dwlt: t.k.h and sn in tch: wknd fr 2f out* **25/1**
21 14 1 **Tell Me A Story**[87] 4398 2-9-6 72 RoystonFfrench 15 12
(M Brittain) *midfield: drvn 1/2-way: btn over 1f out* **15/2**[3]
0640 15 3 **Kristen Jane (USA)**[22] 6409 2-8-0 52 AndrewMullen 3 —
(Miss L A Perratt) *dwlt: sn midfield: rdn and wknd fr 2f out* **33/1**

0060 **16** 1 1/4 **Maiwand**[37] 5980 2-8-0 **55** oh5 ow5............................ KellyHarrison(3) 11 —
(Mrs R A Carr) *bhd and sn drvn along: no ch fr 1/2-way* **40/1**

1m 13.34s (-0.26) **Going Correction** -0.05s/f (Good) **16** Ran SP% **126.6**
Speed ratings (Par 95): **99,98,97,95,94 91,91,89,89,87 83,76,71,70,66 64**
toteswinger: 1&2 £38.50, 1&3 £11.90, 2&3 £22.70. CSF £1276.88 CT £5902.26 TOTE £24.40: £3.70, £8.80, £1.10, £5.00; EX 686.70.
Owner Des Johnston **Bred** Sunny Days Limited **Trained** Ulverston, Cumbria

FOCUS
Quite a competitive nursery, but those that raced down the centre of the track seemed to hold the advantage and low-drawn horses filled three of the first four places. The big-priced runner-up apart the form makes plenty of sense.

NOTEBOOK
Living It Large(FR) ◆ was back down in trip after finishing well beaten over 7f on his nursery debut last time and it did the trick. He made just about every yard down the centre of the track and showed a good attitude, so probably still has more to offer. He was already due to be dropped 5lb before this, so would be of obvious interest if turned out again quickly under a penalty. (op 16-1)
Ochilview Warrior(IRE), beaten out of sight all five previous starts and effectively 10lb wrong, had blinkers on for the first time and he left that previous form well behind. Admittedly he was probably racing on the best part of the track, but even so this was a massive leap forward. The main question is whether the headgear was responsible for the improvement and, if so, whether it will work again. (op 66-1)
Newbury Street, raised 5lb after making a successful Polytrack debut at Wolverhampton, was sent off quite a warm favourite and had every chance, but it did appear that he was at a disadvantage in racing close to the stands' rail from his high draw so he is well worth another chance. (op 5-2 tchd 11-4)
Lieu Day Louie(IRE), making his nursery debut but disappointing last time after a much-improved effort on his second start, returned to form here and was always close to the pace down the centre of the track. He should be up to winning a race like this. (op 16-1)
Russian Davis(IRE), trying this trip for the first time after three runs over 5f and three over 7f, was returning to turf for the first time since his second outing and deserves a lot of credit as he was given a lot to do from his high draw, but was noted putting in some solid late work up the stands' rail. On this evidence a return to further is required. (op 15-2 tchd 7-1)
Ya Boy Sir(IRE), making his nursery debut after finishing a well-beaten third in a Musselburgh seller last time, showed good speed from the off towards the nearside, but he tended to hang under pressure and had no more to offer inside the last furlong.
Charity Fair, whose best effort by far came in a soft-ground nursery over course and distance three starts back, ran an almost identical race here, walking out of the stalls and becoming outpaced before hanging away to her left and finishing strongly down the centre of the track. She has the ability when she puts her mind to it, but looks a horrendously hard ride.
Thinking, well held after meeting trouble at the start on his nursery debut on Fibresand last time, had looked mildly progressive on turf before that and he was the subject of quite a plunge here, but after missing the break he was soon being niggled along and never got into the race at any stage. (op 14-1)
Tell Me A Story Official explanation: trainer had no explanation for the poor form shown

6984 VICTORCHANDLER.COM H'CAP (DIV I) 7f 50y
2:45 (2:46) (Class 5) (0-70,69) 3-Y-O+ **£2,914** (£867; £433; £216) **Stalls** Low

Form RPR
1232 **1** **Ishiadancer**[6] 6846 4-9-4 **67**.. DuranFentiman 4 80
(E J Alston) *mde all: rdn clr fr wl over 1f out: styd on strly fnl f* **5/2[1]**
4600 **2** 5 **Jonny Lesters Hair (IRE)**[10] 6765 4-9-4 **67**.......................... DavidAllan 10 66
(T D Easterby) *chsd wnr thrght: rdn over 2f out: one pce fr over 1f out* **8/1[3]**
1050 **3** 1/2 **Ykikamoocow**[7] 6824 3-9-2 **67**................................ SilvestreDeSousa 11 64+
(G A Harker) *bhd: rdn 3f out: hdwy over 1f out: nrst fin* **10/1**
0040 **4** 1/2 **Nacho Libre**[93] 4191 4-8-1 **55** oh1..............................(b[1]) MartinLane(5) 3 51
(M W Easterby) *prom: effrt over 2f out: one pce fr over 1f out* **7/1[2]**
5406 **5** nk **Woodsley House (IRE)**[22] 6411 7-8-11 **63**............(p) FrederikTylicki(3) 6 58
(A G Foster) *midfield: effrt over 2f out: edgd lft: no imp wl over 1f out* **10/1**
2140 **6** 2 **Daring Dream (GER)**[10] 6765 4-9-2 **65**...................... DanielTudhope 13 55
(J S Goldie) *in tch: effrt and hung lft over 2f out: no ex over 1f out* **8/1[3]**
0030 **7** hd **Ros Cuire (IRE)**[7] 6828 4-7-13 **55** oh6................................ BillyCray(7) 7 45
(W A Murphy, Ire) *bhd: rdn over 2f out: nvr able to chal* **66/1**
0600 **8** 2 1/2 **Avoir Choisi (IRE)**[14] 6640 3-8-11 **62**.................................. TomEaves 9 44
(I Semple) *hld up: rdn 3f out: nvr rchd ldrs* **20/1**
6006 **9** 1/2 **Distant Pleasure**[58] 5332 5-8-6 **55** oh3..................(p) RoystonFfrench 12 36
(M Dods) *hld up: rdn 3f out: nvr on terms* **16/1**
3330 **10** 5 **John Keats**[10] 6764 6-8-13 **67**.. GaryBartley(5) 5 35
(J S Goldie) *t.k.h early: in tch: outpcd over 2f out: sn btn* **10/1**
1203 **11** 4 1/2 **Avontuur (FR)**[10] 6764 7-9-1 **69**...............................(b) DeanHeslop(5) 1 25
(Mrs R A Carr) *hld up in midfield: rdn 3f out: sn wknd* **10/1**
0066 **12** 35 **Cold Quest (USA)**[26] 6312 5-9-2 **65**.........................(p) PaulMulrennan 2 —
(Miss L A Perratt) *trckd ldrs to 3f out: wknd qckly: t.o* **40/1**
0061 **U** **Mr Lu**[22] 6415 4-8-3 **55**.. KellyHarrison(3) 8 —
(J S Goldie) *stmbld and uns rdr leaving stalls* **12/1**

1m 32.42s (-0.98) **Going Correction** -0.05s/f (Good)
WFA 3 from 4yo+ 2lb **13** Ran SP% **121.9**
Speed ratings (Par 103): **103,97,96,96,95 93,93,90,89,84 79,36,—**
toteswinger: 1&2 £7.60, 1&3 £8.60, 2&3 £16.30. CSF £22.28 CT £183.90 TOTE £3.20: £1.40, £2.60, £3.60; EX 27.70.
Owner Racing Shares Nuppend **Bred** Southern Seafoods **Trained** Longton, Lancs

FOCUS
An ordinary handicap and very few ever got into it with the winner making all and the runner-up always second. The time was much quicker than division II. The form is rated through the third.
Daring Dream(GER) Official explanation: jockey said colt hung left throughout
Avontuur(FR) Official explanation: trainer had no explanation for the poor form shown
Cold Quest(USA) Official explanation: trainer said gelding lost its action but returned sound

6985 VICTORCHANDLER.COM H'CAP (DIV II) 7f 50y
3:20 (3:20) (Class 5) (0-70,69) 3-Y-O+ **£2,914** (£867; £433; £216) **Stalls** Low

Form RPR
2600 **1** **Botham (USA)**[22] 6411 5-8-13 **62**................................ DanielTudhope 7 71
(J S Goldie) *t.k.h: hld up in tch: hdwy 2f out: led ins fnl f: drvn out* **14/1**
2204 **2** 3/4 **Stellite**[26] 6309 9-9-1 **69**.. GaryBartley(5) 5 76
(J S Goldie) *prom: hdwy to ld over 1f out: hdd ins fnl f: kpt on u.p* **6/1**
0605 **3** 2 1/4 **Compton's Eleven**[17] 6568 8-8-13 **65**................................ MCGeran(3) 10 66
(M R Channon) *hld up in tch: hdwy and cl up over 1f out: sn rdn: one pce fnl f* **7/1**
6024 **4** 1 3/4 **Eastern Hills**[6] 6847 4-8-13 **67**.................................(v) LanceBetts(5) 4 63
(J S Wainwright) *prom: effrt and swtchd rt over 1f out: sn rdn and one pce* **3/1[1]**
0000 **5** 1 1/4 **Glenluji**[22] 6414 4-8-3 **55** oh5.. KellyHarrison(3) 8 48
(J S Goldie) *hld up: hdwy over 1f out: kpt on fnl f: no ex* **18/1**
0610 **6** 1 1/2 **Young Gladiator (IRE)**[50] 5601 4-8-8 **60** ow1.....(b) FrederikTylicki(3) 12 49
(Miss J A Camacho) *pressed ldr: outpcd 2f out: no imp fnl f* **10/3[2]**

0424 **7** 1/2 **Ask Dan (IRE)**[22] 6414 3-8-5 **56**.................................(p) RoystonFfrench 6 43
(M Dods) *led to 1f rdn and hdd over 1f out: sn wknd* **11/2[3]**
000 **8** 1 3/4 **Mission Impossible**[30] 6221 4-8-2 **56** oh2 ow1.... PatrickDonaghy(5) 13 39
(Miss Tracy Waggott) *hld up: drvn over 2f out: nvr able to chal* **66/1**
1005 **9** 3/4 **Mandarin Spirit (IRE)**[14] 6635 9-9-4 **67**....................(b) PaulMulrennan 3 48
(Miss L A Perratt) *trckd ldrs tl rdn and wknd wl over 1f out* **14/1**
000 **10** 2 3/4 **Mozayada (USA)**[24] 6357 5-9-2 **65**...................................... DavidAllan 11 38
(M Brittain) *bhd: drvn over 3f out: sn btn* **12/1**

1m 33.79s (0.39) **Going Correction** -0.05s/f (Good)
WFA 3 from 4yo+ 2lb **10** Ran SP% **118.0**
Speed ratings (Par 103): **95,94,91,89,88 86,85,83,83,79**
toteswinger: 1&2 £13.10, 1&3 £20.70, 2&3 £8.80. CSF £96.82 CT £650.07 TOTE £21.30: £4.80, £2.10, £3.00; EX 78.60.
Owner Caledonia Racing **Bred** France Weiner & Neal Hayias **Trained** Uplawmoor, E Renfrews

FOCUS
Another ordinary handicap and the pace looked nothing special. The entire field were within a couple of lengths of each other passing the furlong pole and the winning time was 1.37 seconds slower than the first division. Straightforward form.
Ask Dan(IRE) Official explanation: jockey said gelding ran too free

6986 KAREN KENNEDY AND FRIENDS CELEBRATION H'CAP 1m 2f
3:55 (3:55) (Class 4) (0-85,85) 3-Y-O+ **£4,857** (£1,445; £722; £360) **Stalls** Low

Form RPR
1-5 **1** **Emirates Champion**[161] 2029 3-9-5 **85**..........................(t) DO'Donohoe 8 104+
(Saeed Bin Suroor) *prom: smooth hdwy to ld 2f out: sn pushed clr* **5/4[1]**
1400 **2** 6 **Charlie Tokyo (IRE)**[14] 6648 6-9-6 **84**....................(v) FrederikTylicki(3) 6 91
(R A Fahey) *t.k.h: trckd ldrs: effrt over 2f out: kpt on fnl f: no ch w wnr* **5/1[2]**
4105 **3** 3 1/4 **Wee Charlie Castle (IRE)**[26] 6313 6-9-1 **76**............... PaulMulrennan 3 77
(I Semple) *hld up: rdn 3f out: hdwy over 1f out: n.d* **14/1**
4311 **4** 1/2 **Bagber**[23] 6395 3-8-11 **77**.. TonyHamilton 5 77
(P Monteith) *cl up: led over 3f to 2f out: sn outpcd* **13/2**
5130 **5** 3 **Oddsmaker (IRE)**[7] 6832 8-8-9 **70** oh3.................................. DavidAllan 2 64
(M A Barnes) *led to over 3f out: rallied: wknd wl over 1f out* **16/1**
0003 **6** 1 1/4 **King's Head (IRE)**[22] 6412 6-9-0 **75**..........................(p) RoystonFfrench 4 66
(Miss L A Perratt) *in tch: drvn over 2f out: sn wknd* **20/1**
0655 **7** 1 3/4 **Magic Echo**[36] 6016 5-9-4 **79**... TomEaves 1 67
(M Dods) *t.k.h: hld up: rdn 3f out: sn btn* **6/1[3]**
2515 **8** 3/4 **Tiger Dream**[21] 6460 4-8-6 **72**... AmyRyan(5) 9 58
(K A Ryan) *hld up towards rr: struggling over 4f out: nvr on terms* **10/1**

2m 11.94s (-0.06) **Going Correction** -0.05s/f (Good)
WFA 3 from 4yo+ 5lb **8** Ran SP% **115.1**
Speed ratings (Par 105): **98,93,90,90,87 86,85,84**
toteswinger: 1&2 £3.20, 1&3 £7.10, 2&3 £10.90. CSF £7.74 CT £58.33 TOTE £2.30: £1.20, £2.10, £2.60; EX 9.70.
Owner Godolphin **Bred** Gainsborough Stud Management Ltd **Trained** Newmarket, Suffolk

FOCUS
A decent little handicap run at just a fair pace, but ultimately a one-horse race. The form is rated through the fourth.

6987 DAILY RECORD CLASSIFIED CLAIMING STKS 1m 1f 20y
4:30 (4:32) (Class 5) 3-Y-O+ **£3,238** (£963; £481; £240) **Stalls** Low

Form RPR
43 **1** **Cool Baranca (GER)**[32] 6158 3-8-13 62............................ TonyHamilton 8 74
(P Monteith) *hld up: hdwy 2f out: led ins fnl f: styd on wl* **11/1**
2212 **2** 2 **Graceful Descent (FR)**[26] 6310 4-8-11 65........................ GaryBartley(5) 4 69
(J S Goldie) *hld up: hdwy 3f out: led over 1f out to ins fnl f: kpt on* **7/2[1]**
2015 **3** 3 1/2 **Applaude**[28] 6248 4-8-12 68...........................(b) SilvestreDeSousa 12 57
(R C Guest) *missed break: bhd: hdwy and in tch whn hung bdly rt to stands' rail over 1f out: r.o fnl f* **7/2[1]**
3045 **4** 1 **Bere Davis (FR)**[18] 6545 4-9-3 70..................................(t) TomEaves 1 60
(M A Barnes) *trckd ldrs: effrt over 2f out: one pce over 1f out* **7/1[3]**
6254 **5** 1 1/2 **Hawkit (USA)**[10] 6769 8-8-7 56.................................... RoystonFfrench 3 47
(P Monteith) *midfield: n.m.r and lost pl over 2f out: rallied fnl f: r.o* **7/1[3]**
5446 **6** hd **Ingleby Princess**[22] 6414 5-8-2 48.................................... DeanHeslop(5) 10 46
(T D Barron) *cl up: led 3f to over 1f out: sn outpcd* **16/1**
3034 **7** hd **Rowan Lodge (IRE)**[28] 6256 7-8-8 65..................(b) FrederikTylicki(3) 13 50
(Ollie Pears) *in tch: rdn and hung lft over 2f out: sn outpcd* **4/1[2]**
0100 **8** 7 **Barataria**[36] 6023 7-9-0 70... DanielTudhope 2 38
(R Bastiman) *hld up: rdn over 2f out: nvr on terms* **16/1**
060 **9** 1 **Kingsholm**[36] 6012 7-8-7 53... DuranFentiman 9 28
(N Wilson) *trckd ldrs tl rdn and wknd wl over 1f out* **25/1**
5004 **10** 12 **Sharp Sovereign (USA)**[32] 6156 3-8-2 46 ow2....... PatrickDonaghy(5) 6 6
(Miss L A Perratt) *trckd ldrs tl rdn and wknd over 2f out* **33/1**
6000 **11** 19 **Elements (IRE)**[42] 5840 3-8-7 52 ow1................................ DavidAllan 7 —
(E J Alston) *led to 3f out: sn rdn and wknd* **25/1**
000 **12** 15 **Royal Society**[58] 5331 3-8-11 49 ow1........................... PaulMulrennan 11 —
(Miss L A Perratt) *cl up tl rdn and wknd fr 3f out* **25/1**

1m 59.42s (1.02) **Going Correction** -0.05s/f (Good)
WFA 3 from 4yo+ 4lb **12** Ran SP% **124.0**
Speed ratings (Par 103): **93,91,88,87,85 85,85,79,78,67 50,37**
toteswinger: 1&2 £5.50, 1&3 £11.70, 2&3 £4.40. CSF £49.73 TOTE £13.30: £3.60, £1.70, £1.80; EX 56.10.
Owner Dennis J Coppola **Bred** Stiftung Gestut Fahrhof **Trained** Rosewell, Midlothian

FOCUS
A fair claimer and reasonably competitive judged on official ratings, but the time was slow and the form is unconvincing.
Applaude Official explanation: jockey said gelding hung right-handed

6988 NEW WEBSITE AT VICTORCHANDLER.COM H'CAP 5f
5:00 (5:02) (Class 5) (0-70,69) 3-Y-O **£2,914** (£867; £433; £216) **Stalls** Centre

Form RPR
6312 **1** **Hawkeyethenoo (IRE)**[20] 6489 3-8-10 **63**.................... GaryBartley(5) 1 78
(J S Goldie) *hld up in rr: smooth hdwy 2f out: led ins fnl f: sn clr: readily* **3/1[1]**
4533 **2** 3 **Mazzola**[8] 6799 3-8-12 **63**.. MCGeran(3) 4 67
(M R Channon) *mde most to ins fnl f: kpt on: nt pce of wnr* **6/1**
5330 **3** 1 **Musical Bridge**[79] 4653 3-9-7 **69**.. TonyHamilton 2 69
(Mrs L Williamson) *chsd ldrs: drvn 2f out: kpt on fnl f* **20/1**
0504 **4** 1 3/4 **Under Review (IRE)**[20] 6489 3-9-0 **67**........................ DeanHeslop(5) 5 61
(T D Barron) *s.i.s: hdwy 1/2-way: effrt 2f out: one pce fnl f* **5/1[2]**
0302 **5** 2 **Star Addition**[7] 6823 3-8-2 **50** oh5.................................. DuranFentiman 3 37
(E J Alston) *midfield: sn outpcd and drvn along: plugged on fnl f: no imp* **11/2[3]**
4161 **6** 1/2 **Scrapper Smith (IRE)**[58] 5336 3-9-0 **65**................ FrederikTylicki(3) 11 50
(A C Whillans) *bhd: drvn along 1/2-way: kpt on fnl f: nrst fin* **11/2[3]**

3260 **7** ¾ **Sea Crest**[55] 5422 3-8-10 **58** DavidAllan 7 40
(M Brittain) *chsd ldrs: drvn 1/2-way: wknd over 1f out* **20/1**

3434 **8** 1 **Verinco**[10] 6764 3-9-3 **65** (p) TomEaves 10 44
(B Smart) *in tch: rdn and edgd lft 2f out: sn outpcd* **10/1**

0065 **9** 1 ¼ **Madame Jourdain (IRE)**[57] 5362 3-7-9 **50** oh5 CharlotteKerton(7) 9 24
(S A Harris) *in tch tl hung lft and wknd fr 1/2-way* **66/1**

0250 **10** 1 **Fasliyanne (IRE)**[23] 6387 3-9-0 **62** (b) SilvestreDeSousa 8 33
(K A Ryan) *cl up tl rdn and wknd wl over 1f out* **14/1**

4200 **11** 1 ¾ **Officer Mor (USA)**[43] 5809 3-8-0 **55** BillyCray(7) 6 19
(A Berry) *sn outpcd and bhd: no ch fr 2f out* **50/1**

58.84 secs (-1.26) **Going Correction** -0.05s/f (Good) **11** Ran SP% **115.5**
Speed ratings (Par 101): **108,103,101,98,95 94,93,92,90,88 85**
toteswinger: 1&2 £4.40, 1&3 £10.50, 2&3 £19.10. CSF £19.64 CT £259.04 TOTE £3.70: £1.60, £2.10, £4.90; EX 15.90.
Owner J S Goldie, F Connor, G Brown **Bred** S Leigh & R Leigh & Islandmore Stud **Trained** Uplawmoor, E Renfrews

FOCUS
A fair sprint handicap run at a decent pace and more evidence that the centre of the track was favoured. Another clear personal best from the winner.

6989 VICTOR CHANDLER CASINO H'CAP 6f
5:30 (5:35) (Class 6) (0-65,65) 3-Y-0+ **£1,942** (£433; £433; £144) **Stalls** Centre

Form RPR

0140 **1** **Half A Crown (IRE)**[8] 6799 4-8-11 **57** (v) TomEaves 12 64
(M Dods) *t.k.h: hld up: hdwy over 1f out: styd on to ld cl home* **16/1**

6043 **2** *shd* **This Ones For Eddy**[6] 6847 4-8-12 **61** FrederikTylicki(3) 17 68
(J Balding) *dwlt: towards rr: hdwy over 1f out: disp ld cl home: jst hld* **9/4**[1]

3006 **2** *dht* **First Swallow**[60] 5309 4-8-7 **53** (t) AndrewMullen 8 60
(D H Brown) *mde most: rdn 2f out: hdd cl home* **25/1**

003 **4** *nk* **Leading Edge (IRE)**[11] 6738 4-9-0 **63** MCGeran(3) 4 69
(M R Channon) *hld up: hdwy and ev ch over 1f out: hung lft ins fnl f: kpt on* **11/2**[2]

6216 **5** ¾ **Captain Royale (IRE)**[22] 6410 4-8-3 **54** (p) PatrickDonaghy(5) 15 57
(Miss Tracy Waggott) *trckd ldrs: checked 1/2-way: effrt over 1f out: kpt on u.p ins fnl f* **12/1**

5162 **6** ¾ **Yorkshire Blue**[22] 6413 10-8-9 **58** (p) KellyHarrison(3) 2 59
(J S Goldie) *bhd: drvn 1/2-way: hdwy over 1f out: r.o fnl f* **8/1**[3]

0006 **7** *nk* **Grimes Faith**[7] 6825 6-8-4 **55** (p) AmyRyan(5) 9 55
(K A Ryan) *in tch: effrt 2f out: one pce fnl f* **14/1**

0-46 **8** *hd* **Lambrini Lace (IRE)**[46] 5729 4-8-8 **54** SilvestreDeSousa 14 53
(Mrs L Williamson) *cl up: ev ch over 1f out: no ex ins fnl f* **11/1**

6210 **9** *hd* **Imperial Sword**[53] 5516 6-9-0 **65** (b) DeanHeslop(5) 11 64
(T D Barron) *missed break: bhd tl styd on fnl f: nrst fin* **14/1**

00U6 **10** *hd* **Top Bid**[10] 6764 5-9-0 **60** (b) DavidAllan 7 58
(T D Easterby) *hld up on outside: rdn over 2f out: no ex appr fnl f* **8/1**[3]

0040 **11** 3 ¾ **Cool Art (IRE)**[3] 6926 3-8-8 **60** LanceBetts(5) 3 46
(J S Wainwright) *towards rr: drvn and outpcd over 3f out: n.d after* **40/1**

6020 **12** ½ **No Grouse**[34] 6103 9-8-12 **58** DuranFentiman 10 42
(E J Alston) *trckd ldrs tl rdn and wknd over 1f out* **25/1**

0003 **13** ½ **Embra (IRE)**[23] 6377 4-8-8 **59** MartinLane(5) 1 42
(T J Etherington) *hld up in tch: outpcd 2f out: sn btn* **8/1**[3]

0000 **14** ½ **Blazing Heights**[22] 6410 6-8-5 **51** oh1 RoystonFfrench 13 32
(J S Goldie) *midfield: struggling over 2f out: sn btn* **33/1**

1m 13.25s (-0.35) **Going Correction** -0.05s/f (Good)
WFA 3 from 4yo+ 1lb **14** Ran SP% **127.8**
Speed ratings (Par 101): **100,99,99,99,98 97,97,96,96,96 91,90,89,89**PL: Half A Crown £6.00,This Ones For Eddy £1.50 First Swallow £6.50. Tote Ex: HAC,TOFE £64.50 HAC,FS £291.30. CSF: HAC,TOFE £24.53 HAC,FS £168.75. Tricast: HAC,TOFE,FS £379.84 HAC,FS,TOFE £488.50. toteswinger: HAC-TOFE £20.50 HAC-FS £164.60 TOFE-FS £30.9027 CSF £Owner CT £G N Parker TOTE £Bred: £Burns Farm Stud, £Trained, £Denton, Co Durham.
■ Stewards' Enquiry : M C Geran one-day ban: careless riding (Nov 6)

FOCUS
An ultra-competitive sprint handicap with the principals finishing in a heap, and the result seemed to buck the trend of the previous sprint contests with the first three horses all finishing towards the stands' rail. The fourth is the best guide to the form.
T/Plt: £45.40 to a £1 stake. Pool: £61,129.17. 981.64 winning tickets. T/Qpdt: £10.40 to a £1 stake. Pool: £4,188.50. 296.70 winning tickets. RY

5859 DONCASTER (L-H)
Friday, October 23

OFFICIAL GOING: Straight course - good (good to soft in places) round course - good to soft (good in places)
Wind: light 1/2 against Weather: fine

6990 CROWNHOTEL-BAWTRY.COM EBF MAIDEN STKS (DIV I) 7f
1:15 (1:16) (Class 4) 2-Y-0 **£4,533** (£1,348; £674; £336) **Stalls** High

Form RPR

2 **1** **Tamaathul**[15] 6620 2-9-3 0 TPO'Shea 2 84+
(B W Hills) *racd centre: mde all: clr 1/2-way: rdn over 1f out and kpt on strly* **5/4**[1]

5 **2** 1 ½ **Quick Wit**[9] 6781 2-9-3 0 LDettori 14 80+
(Saeed Bin Suroor) *racd towards stands' rail: in tch: hdwy 1/2-way: rdn to chse wnr and edgd lft wl over 1f out: kpt on* **2/1**[2]

00 **3** 4 ½ **Caldercruix (USA)**[13] 6679 2-9-3 0 DarryllHolland 8 67
(T P Tate) *chsd wnr centre: rdn along over 2f out: sn drvn and kpt on same pce* **80/1**

0 **4** 2 **Yes Chef**[10] 6759 2-9-3 0 FergusSweeney 13 62
(J Gallagher) *racd towards stands' rail: prom: rdn along wl over 2f out: sn edgd lft and kpt on same pce* **200/1**

5 1 ¾ **Silent Majority (IRE)** 2-9-3 0 PaulHanagan 7 58
(E A L Dunlop) *in tch: effrt and hdwy 3f out: rdn along over 2f out and sn no imp* **50/1**

6 ¾ **Oriental Cat** 2-9-3 0 JimmyFortune 10 57+
(J H M Gosden) *dwlt and towards rr: hdwy 3f out: sn rdn along and kpt on fnl 2f: nrst fin* **9/1**[3]

6 **7** 2 ¾ **Path Of Peace**[23] 6378 2-8-12 0 JimmyQuinn 6 44
(J D Bethell) *chsd ldrs: rdn along wl over 2f out: sn drvn and grad wknd* **100/1**

8 *nk* **Brananx (USA)** 2-9-3 0 JamieSpencer 12 48+
(K A Ryan) *dwlt and in rr: hdwy 3f out: kpt on fnl 2f: nrst fin* **20/1**

50 **9** ¾ **On The Cusp (IRE)**[26] 6319 2-9-3 0 NCallan 1 46
(M A Jarvis) *nvr bttr than midfield* **20/1**

10 ½ **Signor Verdi** 2-9-3 0 MartinDwyer 4 45
(B J Meehan) *dwlt: a towards rr* **40/1**

11 3 **Russian Brigadier** 2-9-3 0 AlanMunro 15 38
(M Brittain) *s.i.s and a towards rr* **100/1**

12 1 ¼ **Falakee** 2-9-3 0 KFallon 3 34+
(P W Chapple-Hyam) *in tch on outer: rdn along wl over 2f out: sn wknd* **12/1**

13 *nse* **Vumbura (IRE)** 2-9-3 0 TedDurcan 9 34
(W J Knight) *nvr nr ldrs* **33/1**

14 12 **Grams And Ounces** 2-9-3 0 JerryO'Dwyer 5 4
(Miss Amy Weaver) *s.i.s: a in rr* **100/1**

15 8 **Priestley (IRE)** 2-9-3 0 TPQueally 11 —
(J G Given) *chsd ldrs to 1/2-way: sn lost pl and bhd* **100/1**

1m 25.5s (-0.80) **Going Correction** -0.05s/f (Good) **15** Ran SP% **118.0**
Speed ratings (Par 97): **102,100,95,92,90 90,86,86,85,85 81,80,80,66,57**
toteswinger: 1&2 £2.00, 1&3 £39.50, 2&3 £26.60. CSF £3.24 TOTE £2.10: £1.30, £1.10, £8.80; EX 4.40 Trifecta £58.60 Pool: £262.12 - 3.31 winning units..
Owner Hamdan Al Maktoum **Bred** Shadwell Estate Company Limited **Trained** Lambourn, Berks

FOCUS
Very few got into this and those with previous experience dominated. The first two finished clear and are better than the bare facts.

NOTEBOOK
Tamaathul gave a nice boost to the chances of Dancing David in Saturday's Racing Post Trophy with a comfortable success. He'd found Brian Meehan's colt too good for him on his debut at Newbury but wasn't up against anything of that calibre here and duly made every yard, only having to be pushed out to score cosily. He should stay further than a mile next season. (tchd 11-8 and 6-4 in a place)

Quick Wit ◆ didn't shape too badly on his debut after giving away ground with a slow start. Sharper away this time, he raced in a group of three nearer the stands' side while the majority followed the winner up the centre. He kept on well to secure second, but is flattered to finish as close as he did to the winner, whose rider was taking things pretty easily in the closing stages. He can break his maiden tag on the Polytrack if given the opportunity. (op 11-4)

Caldercruix(USA) is improving with racing and posted his best effort so far on this third run. He was not cheap at $140,000 but he's a half-brother to six winners and should do better next year in handicaps. (op 50-1 tchd 100-1)

Yes Chef was well beaten on his debut but showed the benefit of that experience and gave a lead to the runner-up on the stands' side. His dam, who is by Double Trigger, won over this trip at two and he should appreciate further next season.

Silent Majority(IRE) ◆, who hails from a stable whose juveniles usually need their debut outings, did best of the newcomers and should come on a bundle for the experience.

Oriental Cat, who is by the same sire as the winner, was green and took a while to get the hang of what was required. There should be better to come with this run under his belt. (op 7-1)

6991 CROWNHOTEL-BAWTRY.COM EBF MAIDEN STKS (DIV II) 7f
1:50 (1:51) (Class 4) 2-Y-0 **£4,533** (£1,348; £674; £336) **Stalls** High

Form RPR

1 **Rashaad (USA)** 2-9-3 0 TPO'Shea 12 81+
(B W Hills) *sn trcking ldrs: effrt over 2f out: r.o fnl f: led nr fin* **3/1**[2]

26 **2** ½ **Robinson Cruso**[35] 6064 2-9-3 0 NCallan 10 80
(M A Jarvis) *t.k.h: trckd ldrs: led after 3f: hdd and no ex towards fin* **9/4**[1]

3 2 ¾ **Jack O'Lantern** 2-9-3 0 JimmyFortune 5 73
(J H M Gosden) *led 3f: chsd ldrs: kpt on same pce appr fnl f* **10/1**

4 3 ¼ **Strong Vigilance (IRE)** 2-9-3 0 KFallon 13 65
(P W Chapple-Hyam) *in rr: hdwy 3f out: sn chsng ldrs: wknd over 1f out* **13/2**

5 *nk* **Oriental Scot** 2-9-3 0 JoeFanning 11 64+
(W Jarvis) *t.k.h in rr: styd on fnl 2f: nt rch ldrs* **18/1**

2 **6** 1 ¼ **Much Acclaimed (IRE)**[30] 6214 2-9-3 0 MickyFenton 1 61
(T P Tate) *chsd ldrs: wknd over 1f out* **11/2**[3]

6 **7** *hd* **Redden**[38] 5958 2-9-3 0 MichaelHills 15 61+
(W J Haggas) *in rr: hdwy over 2f out: kpt on steadily: nvr trbld ldrs* **20/1**

2 **8** 2 ¾ **Stefanki (IRE)**[41] 5867 2-9-3 0 TonyCulhane 14 54
(R Curtis) *stdd s: t.k.h in rr: swtchd lft sn after s: nvr nr ldrs* **7/1**

4 **9** 9 **Second Brook (IRE)**[127] 3052 2-9-3 0 GeorgeBaker 8 31
(R Hollinshead) *mid-div: effrt over 2f out: sn wknd* **80/1**

000 **10** 2 ¼ **Securitisation (IRE)**[16] 6593 2-9-3 0 TPQueally 4 26
(B J Curley) *s.s: hdwy after 3f: lost pl over 2f out* **125/1**

06 **11** 6 **Bravo Blue (IRE)**[10] 6756 2-8-7 0 RossAtkinson(5) 6 6
(T H Caldwell) *chsd ldrs 4f: sn wknd* **200/1**

12 2 ½ **Cross The Boss (IRE)** 2-9-3 0 PhillipMakin 9 4
(P C Haslam) *s.s: hdwy 3f out: edgd lft and sn wknd* **100/1**

13 2 ½ **Crystal Glass** 2-9-3 0 DNolan 3 —
(T D Easterby) *chsd ldrs: sn pushed along: lost pl over 2f out* **100/1**

1m 27.03s (0.73) **Going Correction** -0.05s/f (Good) **13** Ran SP% **120.6**
Speed ratings (Par 97): **93,92,89,85,85 83,83,80,70,67 60,57,55**
toteswinger: 1&2 £4.00, 1&3 £17.30, 2&3 £3.90. CSF £10.14 TOTE £4.20: £1.70, £1.40, £3.10; EX 10.40 Trifecta £228.90 Part won. Pool: £309.33 - 0.85 winning units..
Owner Hamdan Al Maktoum **Bred** G Watts Humphrey Jr **Trained** Lambourn, Berks

FOCUS
A steady early pace resulted in a 1.53sec slower winning time than the first division. There is more to come from the winner and the second helps with the level.

NOTEBOOK
Rashaad(USA) ◆, backed in from as big as 10-1 in the morning, looked fit beforehand and landed a bit of a punt. A $650,000 brother to a dual Grade 3 winning mare on turf in the US, he tracked the more experienced favourite for much of the race and just ran him down inside the last. He will get middle distances next season and has the makings of a very useful performer. (op 9-2, tchd 5-1 in a place)

Robinson Cruso had shown in his first two starts enough to suggest a race of this nature was within his ability, but he was stepping up to 7f for the first time, was on edge beforehand and drifted in the betting. A touch keen through the early stages, he found the Barry Hills-trained newcomer too strong late on but probably ran up to his previous form in defeat. (op 7-4)

Jack O'Lantern ◆, a half-brother to a couple of winners over a mile, shaped with promise on his debut, racing up with the pace throughout and only weakening from a furlong out. He will be difficult to beat next time if allowed to take his chance in a Polytrack maiden. (op 16-1)

Strong Vigilance(IRE), who showed signs of greenness, is the type to do better in time, especially on quicker ground. Despite a Derby entry, he looks like a miler on pedigree. (op 5-1)

Oriental Scot, one of the slowest away from the stalls, raced keenly through the early stages and in the circumstances didn't shape at all badly. Bred to appreciate further in time, he can only improve for this debut effort. (op 33-1 tchd 16-1)

Much Acclaimed(IRE) is by Sulamani and was probably unsuited by the relatively steady early pace. A stronger gallop would have seen him in a better light. (op 7-1)

6992 UK COAL EBF MAIDEN FILLIES' STKS 1m (R)
2:20 (2:25) (Class 4) 2-Y-O £5,180 (£1,541; £770; £384) Stalls Low

Form RPR

1 **Modeyra** 2-9-0 0 LDettori 16 83+
(Saeed Bin Suroor) *trckd ldrs: smooth hdwy on outer 3f out: chal 2f out: sn led and rdn over 1f out: styd on strly ins fnl f* **9/2**[3]

33 2 ½ **Gertrude Bell**[14] 6628 2-9-0 0 JimmyFortune 8 82
(J H M Gosden) *midfield: hdwy 3f out: swtchd lft and effrt 2f out: rdn to chse wnr over 1f out: drvn ins fnl f: kpt on* **3/1**[2]

2 3 1¾ **Cheetah**[40] 5906 2-9-0 0 KFallon 21 78
(L M Cumani) *in tch: hdwy on outer 3f out: rdn to chse wnr wl over 1f out: drvn ins fnl f: no imp* **17/2**

2 4 ¾ **Giants Play (USA)**[70] 4980 2-9-0 0 RyanMoore 18 76
(Sir Michael Stoute) *midfield: effrt 3f out and sn pushed along: rdn and hdwy 2f out: sn drvn and styd on same pce* **2/1**[1]

0 5 2¾ **Ice Diva**[17] 6567 2-9-0 0 DarryllHolland 15 70
(P W D'Arcy) *prom: led 3f out: rdn along 2f out: sn hdd and drvn: grad wknd* **33/1**

6 ¾ **Bebopalula (IRE)** 2-9-0 0 MichaelHills 9 69+
(B W Hills) *dwlt and towards rr: n.m.r over 3f out: swtchd rt and hdwy over 2f out: sn rdn and kpt on appr fnl f: nrst fin* **33/1**

0 7 1¾ **Song To The Moon (IRE)**[20] 6477 2-9-0 0 DavidProbert 3 65
(A M Balding) *trckd ldrs: hdwy and cl up 3f out: rdn along 2f out: sn drvn and grad wknd* **20/1**

8 1½ **Craighall** 2-9-0 0 NickyMackay 20 62
(D M Simcock) *s.i.s and towards rr: hdwy over 2f out: rdn and styd on appr fnl f: nrst fin* **100/1**

9 hd **Fantastic Cuix (FR)** 2-9-0 0 JamieSpencer 12 64+
(L M Cumani) *dwlt and hit hd on stalls: swtchd rt and hdwy over 3f out: rdn over 2f out: kpt on appr fnl f: nrst fin* **40/1**

00 10 ½ **Albeed**[24] 6363 2-9-0 0 TPO'Shea 2 60
(J L Dunlop) *in tch: hdwy over 3f out: rdn and ev ch 2f out: sn hung lft and wknd over 1f out* **66/1**

11 1¾ **Ellbeedee (IRE)** 2-9-0 0 NCallan 10 56
(M A Jarvis) *chsd ldrs: rdn along wl over 2f out: sn wknd* **20/1**

6 12 ½ **Little Oz (IRE)**[35] 6062 2-9-0 0 PaulHanagan 13 57+
(E A L Dunlop) *nvr bttr than midfield* **16/1**

0 13 nk **Footsie (IRE)**[20] 6477 2-9-0 0 TPQueally 11 54
(J G Given) *midfield whn hmpd and pushed wd home turn: sn lost pl and rdn along: n.d* **20/1**

14 1 **That's My Style** 2-9-0 0 RobertHavlin 22 52+
(J H M Gosden) *s.i.s and towards rr: sme hdwy 3f out: sn rdn along and nvr nr ldrs* **33/1**

0 15 3 **Centime**[11] 6729 2-9-0 0 MartinDwyer 4 46
(B J Meehan) *chsd ldrs: swtchd lft and rdn wl over 2f out: sn wknd* **40/1**

16 ½ **Babycakes (IRE)** 2-9-0 0 MickyFenton 6 45
(M L W Bell) *chsd ldrs: rdn along 3f out: sn wknd* **50/1**

00 17 nk **Azaday (IRE)**[10] 6759 2-9-0 0 TedDurcan 1 46+
(C F Wall) *a towards rr* **100/1**

18 1 **Straversjoy** 2-9-0 0 GrahamGibbons 5 44+
(R Hollinshead) *s.i.s: a in rr* **100/1**

19 4 **Causeway Coast (USA)** 2-9-0 0 AlanMunro 19 36+
(P W Chapple-Hyam) *a in rr* **20/1**

0 20 5 **Ildiko (USA)**[14] 6628 2-9-0 0 SebSanders 14 22
(Sir Mark Prescott) *a towards rr* **100/1**

0PP0 21 1½ **Scintillating (IRE)**[22] 6436 2-9-0 0 PaulEddery 7 19
(R Hollinshead) *led: rdn along and hdd 3f out: sn wknd* **150/1**

1m 38.89s (-0.81) **Going Correction** -0.125s/f (Firm) **21 Ran SP% 133.7**
Speed ratings (Par 94): **99,98,96,96,93 92,90,89,89,88 86,86,86,85,82 81,81,80,76,71 69**
toteswinger: 1&2 £6.70, 1&3 £6.10, 2&3 £3.70. CSF £17.03 TOTE £5.90: £3.00, £1.90, £2.50; EX 32.70 Trifecta £61.30 Pool: £303.68 - 3.66 winning units..
Owner Godolphin **Bred** Darley **Trained** Newmarket, Suffolk

FOCUS
An interesting fillies' maiden. The winner looks potentially smart and the placed horses set the level.

NOTEBOOK
Modeyra ◆, who was solidly backed, could be a decent filly in the making. She travelled well throughout the contest and, when shaken up, quickened up to put the race to bed. It was a professional display and, being a well-bred daughter of Shamardal out of a mare who won the Musidora, was third in the Oaks and then won the Nassau, it was understandable that she was given a quote by Victor Chandler of 33-1 for Epsom. She wouldn't be a lock to get further than 1m2f next season on pedigree, though. (op 6-1 tchd 4-1)
Gertrude Bell, with two runs already under her belt, already needs every yard of this trip and will be seen to better effect when sent over middle distances next season. (op 4-1 tchd 9-2)
Cheetah, who raced wider than most throughout, is another with plenty of stamina in her pedigree and she can only improve for a winter on her back. (op 9-1 tchd 8-1)
Giants Play(USA), off for ten weeks since running a promising race on her debut at Kempton, was expected to appreciate the step up to a mile. She got the trip well but found the competition a little too hot. (op 15-8 tchd 9-4)
Ice Diva lasted longer than on her debut at Leicester and is clearly going the right way. She is out of a mare who is a half-sister to a German Derby winner, so there's a fair amount of stamina in her pedigree.
Bebopalula(IRE) was unfancied on her debut and shaped with encouragement in the circumstances. She was green but ran on late and this daughter of Galileo looks the type to do much better at three. (tchd 40-1)
Song To The Moon(IRE), who had been set a stiff task on her debut, was more effective in this class, but she looks one for handicaps after one more outing. (op 16-1)
Craighall, who was running on at the finish having been towards the back of the field early on, is a half-sister to seven winners and looks to have a future.
Fantastic Cuix(FR) was reported to have hit his head on the stalls and returned with a mouthful of blood. Official explanation: jockey said filly banged its head on leaving stalls (op 33-1)

6993 RACING & FOOTBALL OUTLOOK NURSERY 1m (R)
2:55 (2:59) (Class 3) 2-Y-O £7,771 (£2,312; £1,155; £577) Stalls Low

Form RPR

233 1 **Antoniola (IRE)**[20] 6484 2-8-6 76 GrahamGibbons 20 83
(T D Easterby) *hld up in tch: hdwy and hung lft 2f out: led 1f out: kpt on wl towards fin* **16/1**

2100 2 1 **Alrasm (IRE)**[64] 5198 2-9-3 87 NCallan 6 92
(M A Jarvis) *chsd ldrs on inner: kpt on to take 2nd cl home* **18/1**

4443 3 hd **Keen Bidder**[26] 6305 2-7-12 68 NickyMackay 13 72
(D M Simcock) *hld up in rr: hdwy and swtchd rt over 2f out: kpt on wl fnl f* **22/1**

1 4 hd **Layla's Dancer**[48] 5674 2-8-7 77 PaulHanagan 5 81+
(R A Fahey) *in tch: effrt and outpcd over 2f out: hdwy over 1f out: styd on wl ins fnl f* **9/2**[2]

0221 5 ½ **Navy List (FR)**[39] 5951 2-9-0 87 AhmedAjtebi(3) 17 90
(Saeed Bin Suroor) *trckd ldrs: led over 1f out: sn hdd: stl hanging on to 2nd whn hmpd last 50yds* **12/1**

1050 6 2¾ **Toga Tiger (IRE)**[12] 6693 2-9-1 85 TonyCulhane 1 82
(M R Channon) *hmpd on ins and lost pl after 1f: hdwy over 2f out: nvr nr ldrs* **66/1**

3401 7 ½ **Saboteur**[8] 6792 2-9-6 90 6ex LDettori 11 86
(Saeed Bin Suroor) *trckd ldrs: smooth hdwy to chal over 1f out: sn fdd* **3/1**[1]

1445 8 ½ **Flipping**[8] 6805 2-8-10 80 FergusSweeney 8 75
(W S Kittow) *chsd ldrs: wknd fnl f* **80/1**

010 9 ¾ **Dromore (IRE)**[41] 5864 2-8-8 78 DavidProbert 7 71
(A M Balding) *s.i.s: in rr: hdwy 3f out: nvr nr ldrs* **33/1**

001 10 hd **Arlequin**[23] 6382 2-8-10 80 JamieSpencer 3 72
(J D Bethell) *hld up in midfield: effrt over 2f out: nvr threatened ldrs* **25/1**

060 11 ½ **Miniyamba (IRE)**[35] 6062 2-8-1 71 JimmyQuinn 4 62
(J L Dunlop) *chsd ldrs: wknd over 1f out* **16/1**

4034 12 ½ **Farmer Giles (IRE)**[26] 6305 2-9-2 86 KFallon 2 76
(M L W Bell) *hld up in rr: hdwy on ins over 3f out: wknd 2f out* **12/1**

13 13 ¾ **Layline (IRE)**[20] 6472 2-9-7 91 SebSanders 16 80
(R M Beckett) *unruly s: in rr: nvr on terms* **7/1**

51 14 6 **Sharaayeen**[40] 5907 2-8-9 79 TPO'Shea 18 54
(B W Hills) *in rr: rn wd st: sme hdwy on outer whn hmpd over 2f out: sn wknd* **6/1**[3]

1110 15 1¾ **Mister Angry (IRE)**[41] 5864 2-9-4 88 GregFairley 10 60
(M Johnston) *led tl 3f out: sn wknd* **33/1**

3114 16 4 **Whippers Love (IRE)**[41] 5864 2-8-10 80 J-PGuillambert 15 43
(M Johnston) *chsd ldrs: led 3f out: sn rdn: hdd & wknd over 1f out* **20/1**

443 17 1½ **Iron Condor**[64] 5192 2-8-1 71 LukeMorris 19 30
(J M P Eustace) *s.i.s: in rr whn rn wd st: nvr on terms* **80/1**

614 18 3¾ **Llandovery**[20] 6491 2-7-9 68 AndreaAtzeni(3) 9 19
(P J McBride) *a in rr* **50/1**

6203 19 ½ **Butch And Sundance**[34] 6088 2-9-3 87 (b) MartinDwyer 14 37
(B J Meehan) *in rr: wd st: sme hdwy on outer whn hmpd over 2f out: sn wknd* **33/1**

1m 38.37s (-1.33) **Going Correction** -0.125s/f (Firm) **19 Ran SP% 130.1**
Speed ratings (Par 99): **101,100,99,99,99 96,95,95,94,94 93,93,92,86,84 80,79,75,75**
toteswinger: 1&2 £76.70, 1&3 £52.30, 2&3 £136.90. CSF £267.98 CT £6380.10 TOTE £19.80: £4.50, £4.70, £6.00, £1.80; EX 533.70 TRIFECTA Not won..
Owner Mrs Jennifer E Pallister **Bred** George Williams Jnr **Trained** Great Habton, N Yorks
■ Stewards' Enquiry : Nicky Mackay two-day ban: careless riding (Nov 6-7)
Graham Gibbons two-day ban: careless riding (Nov 6-7)
Ahmed Ajtebi one-day ban: careless riding (Nov 6)

FOCUS
A competitive nursery run in a decent time, and the form looks solid.

NOTEBOOK
Antoniola(IRE), who is out of a mare who won twice over middle distances in Italy, so the fact that he improved for a step up to a mile for the first time shouldn't have come as a surprise. He only cost 7,500gns but looks a useful sort who will pay his way in decent handicaps next season. (op 22-1)
Alrasm(IRE), who apparently found the ground too quick for him at York last time, ran in the Coventry two starts ago. The trip was a concern for this son of Acclamation, but he got it well despite perhaps not being helped by racing nearest the far-side rail in the straight. (op 20-1)
Keen Bidder, one of the more exposed in the line-up, has performed to a consistent level since going handicapping and this looked a step up on his first try at a mile. He finished well down the centre of the track and looks the type that could well be kept on the go on the Polytrack over the winter. (op 28-1)
Layla's Dancer ◆, who made a winning debut over 7f last month, promised to be suited by the step up to a mile. Much like on his debut, he took a long while to get into top gear but, once rolling, stayed on strongly. He is very much the type to do better as a 3-y-o. (op 7-2 tchd 5-1)
Navy List(FR), whose rider wore the owner's second colours, wasn't going to have any trouble with stamina as he won over 1m1f last time. He gave a lead to his stablemate for much of the race and kept plugging away after being headed. By Nayef, he's bred to improve with time.
Toga Tiger(IRE), who is due to be dropped 3lb, is a winner of his only start on Polytrack and could be another who pays his way on the artificial surfaces over the winter. (tchd 80-1)
Saboteur, who was officially 4lb well in under his penalty, went to the front with 2f to run, but he didn't find a great deal and, after being bumped by the winner, was soon backpedaling. Perhaps the race came too soon after his maiden win. (op 5-1)

6994 AUKER RHODES BLUE PARROT H'CAP 6f
3:30 (3:33) (Class 2) (0-105,103) 3-Y-O+ £11,656 (£3,468; £1,733; £865) Stalls High

Form RPR

0562 1 **Servoca (CAN)**[13] 6666 3-8-6 86 (t) JimmyQuinn 4 98
(B W Hills) *hld up towards rr: hdwy 1/2-way: swtchd lft to outer and rdn over 1f out: styd on to ld ent fnl f: sn drvn and kpt on strly* **16/1**

2110 2 1¾ **We Have A Dream**[12] 6694 4-8-6 85 MartinDwyer 1 91
(W R Muir) *racd wd: cl up: rdn 2f out and ev ch tl drvn ent fnl f and nt qckn* **33/1**

1000 3 ¾ **Johannes (IRE)**[13] 6678 6-8-9 95 LeeTopliss(7) 12 99
(R A Fahey) *hmpd s and bhd: hdwy 1/2-way: swtchd rt and rdn 2f out: styd on wl fnl f: nrst fin* **12/1**

2021 4 nk **Hotham**[4] 6897 6-8-6 90 6ex PaulPickard(5) 13 93
(N Wilson) *wnt lft s: cl up: effrt over 2f out: sn rdn and ev ch tl drvn ent fnl f and kpt on same pce* **16/1**

6013 5 1 **Hitchens (IRE)**[13] 6678 4-9-6 99 PhillipMakin 22 99+
(T D Barron) *racd wd: in tch: hdwy 3f out: rdn to chse ldrs 2f out: sn edgd lft and drvn over 1f out: kpt on same pce ins fnl f* **8/1**[2]

0540 6 nse **Sunrise Safari (IRE)**[35] 6050 6-8-6 85 (v) PaulHanagan 9 85
(R A Fahey) *chsd ldrs: rdn along 2f out: drvn over 1f out and kpt on same pce* **11/1**

0000 7 shd **River Falcon**[27] 6283 9-8-9 88 KFallon 8 87
(J S Goldie) *towards rr: hdwy wl over 2f out: sn swtchd lft and rdn over 1f out: styd on wl fnl f: nrst fin* **14/1**

0100 8 nk **Baldemar**[13] 6675 4-8-7 91 BMcHugh(5) 15 89
(R A Fahey) *prom: rdn along over 2f out: sn drvn and kpt on same pce appr fnl f* **9/1**

1231 9 1¼ **Russian Spirit**[14] 6647 3-8-4 84 WilliamBuick 10 78
(M A Jarvis) *led: rdn along and hrd pressed 2f out: sn drvn and edgd lft: hdd ent fnl f and wknd* **11/2**[1]

4104 10 nk **Seamus Shindig**[12] 6694 7-8-2 88 AmyScott(7) 16 81
(H Candy) *dwlt and in rr: swtchd rt and rdn over 2f out: sme late hdwy* **33/1**

0250 **11** *shd* **Lowther**[5] 6876 4-9-2 **95**..............................(be) JimmyFortune 7 88
(A Bailey) *unruly s and loaded late: in tch: rdn along 2f out: sn drvn and wknd* **17/2**[3]

4403 **12** *shd* **Aye Aye Digby (IRE)**[12] 6694 4-8-12 **91**.............................. DaneO'Neill 2 84
(H Candy) *in tch: rdn along over 2f out: sn drvn and wknd wl over 1f out* **16/1**

0150 **13** *1 ¾* **Zidane**[34] 6091 7-9-7 **100**.............................. GeorgeBaker 5 87
(J R Fanshawe) *dwlt and in rr: hdwy whn n.m.r 2f out: sn rdn and nvr a factor* **12/1**

5100 **14** *2* **Silver Wind**[27] 6282 4-8-5 **84**..............................(v) CatherineGannon 21 65
(P D Evans) *chsd ldrs on wd outside: rdn along over 2f out and sn wknd* **25/1**

5600 **15** *nk* **Confuchias (IRE)**[13] 6678 5-8-13 **92**.............................. RobertWinston 19 72
(Pat Eddery) *dwlt: a towards rr* **16/1**

0001 **16** *¾* **Aldermoor (USA)**[20] 6482 3-8-10 **90**.............................. SaleemGolam 11 67
(S C Williams) *wnt rt s: chsd ldrs: rdn along over 2f out: sn drvn and wknd* **25/1**

2003 **17** *11* **Red Cape (FR)**[27] 6282 6-8-9 **88**.............................. AndrewElliott 17 30
(Mrs R A Carr) *midfield: rdn along 1/2-way: sn wknd* **33/1**

-061 **18** *25* **Sundae**[88] 4387 5-8-8 **87**.............................. TedDurcan 18 —
(C F Wall) *in tch on outer: rdn along 1/2-way: sn wknd* **8/1**[2]

1m 11.9s (-1.70) **Going Correction** -0.05s/f (Good)
WFA 3 from 4yo+ 1lb **18** Ran SP% **128.6**
Speed ratings (Par 109): **109,106,105,105,103 103,103,103,101,101 101,101,98,96,95 94,79,46**
toteswinger: 1&2 £117.80, 1&3 £78.50, 2&3 £117.80. CSF £496.13 CT £6592.59 TOTE £17.50: £6.30, £5.60, £3.00, £5.40; EX 494.10 TRIFECTA Not won..
Owner A L R Morton **Bred** Dermot Carty **Trained** Lambourn, Berks

FOCUS
A high-class and competitive sprint handicap that looks pretty sound with several in-form horses close up. The field raced up the centre and, although the first two home were drawn low, there did not appear to be much of a draw advantage, as the next three were drawn in double figures.

NOTEBOOK
Servoca(CAN) has been knocking at the door in decent sprints all season and looked unlucky when narrowly beaten over 5f at Ascot last time, a race from which the next two home had scored subsequently. Settled off the pace, he came through to lead entering the final furlong and scored with something in hand. He looks to be finishing the year in good heart and can score again, especially as he has the option of Polytrack if the turf turns soft.
We Have A Dream had been running well until disappointing at Goodwood last time, but bounced back here without being able to hold the winner. He raced wide of the remainder early before tucking in and responded well for pressure in the closing stages. He handles cut so there may be more to come. (op 28-1)
Johannes(IRE) ◆ has been running well without having the best of luck in recent runs but got a clear passage this time and was staying on for pressure late. He can be given extra credit as he missed the break. (tchd 14-1)
Hotham, another who has been running well of late, was penalised for his recent success. He raced close to the pace and kept going while the others that raced prominently early faded out of contention. (tchd 20-1)
Hitchens(IRE) also came into this in good form and ran his race, but ideally prefers faster ground and the ease in the ground might have gone against him. (op 7-1)
Sunrise Safari(IRE) had finished ahead of today's winner over C&D at the St Leger meeting and could not reverse form from that race with Hotham either, despite being better off. That said, he performed with credit having been up with the leaders throughout. Official explanation: jockey said gelding was denied a clear run (op 14-1)
River Falcon is always capable of running creditably in this sort of contest but had not scored for over two years. He finished well from off the pace and has dropped to his lowest mark for a long time. (op 16-1)
Baldemar had been twice beaten over 7f since winning the Ayr Bronze Cup and was backed on this return to his optimum trip. He ran his race but was already held when short of room near the finish. (op 14-1)
Russian Spirit had beaten Hotham over 5f earlier in the month and made a bold bid to lead all the way. However, she folded pretty quickly when taken on and might be best ridden slightly more conservatively in future. She has only had seven races and could be the sort that really comes to herself next season. (tchd 6-1)
Silver Wind Official explanation: jockey said gelding hung left
Sundae paid for racing up with the early pace towards the stands' side. Official explanation: trainer's rep had no explanation for the poor form shown (op 15-2 tchd 13-2 and 9-1)

6995 RACING POST / SIS BETTING SHOP MANAGER H'CAP — 1m 6f 132y
4:05 (4:06) (Class 4) (0-85,83) 3-Y-0+ **£6,476** (£1,927; £963; £481) **Stalls** Low

Form RPR

3213 **1** **Crocus Rose**[48] 5666 3-8-7 **71**.............................. JimmyQuinn 1 82
(H J L Dunlop) *trckd ldrs: swtchd outside over 2f out: r.o gamely: led nr fin* **15/2**

442 **2** *nk* **Mubrook (USA)**[23] 6375 4-9-10 **79**.............................. KFallon 15 90
(L M Cumani) *sn trcking ldr: drvn over 4f out: led over 2f out: hdd and no ex towards fin* **13/2**[3]

3412 **3** *1 ¼* **Deauville Flyer**[47] 5696 3-8-13 **77**.............................. PaulHanagan 8 86
(T D Easterby) *trckd ldrs: upsides over 1f out: kpt on same pce ins fnl f* **3/1**[1]

0156 **4** *5* **Soundbyte**[14] 6634 4-8-10 **65**.............................. FergusSweeney 11 67
(J Gallagher) *in rr: effrt towards inner over 2f out: kpt on: nvr nr ldrs* **25/1**

0044 **5** *hd* **Royal Trooper (IRE)**[24] 6360 3-8-7 **71**.............................. AlanMunro 4 75+
(J G Given) *rr-div: hdwy over 3f out: nt clr run over 2f out: kpt on: nvr nr ldrs* **33/1**

6113 **6** *1 ¾* **Puy D'Arnac (FR)**[10] 6767 6-9-1 **70**.............................. RobertWinston 17 70
(G A Swinbank) *trckd ldrs: effrt 3f out: wknd over 1f out* **11/2**[2]

2402 **7** *shd* **Saloon (USA)**[17] 6560 5-9-6 **75**..............................(p) JamieSpencer 2 75
(Jane Chapple-Hyam) *trckd ldrs: effrt on outer over 3f out: hung lft: one pce* **14/1**

0306 **8** *½* **Dar Es Salaam**[83] 4541 5-9-9 **78**.............................. PhillipMakin 5 77
(James Moffatt) *hld up in rr: kpt on fnl 3f: nvr nr ldrs* **50/1**

/1-4 **9** *1* **Hawridge Star (IRE)**[12] 6692 7-8-12 **67**.............................. TPO'Shea 10 65
(W S Kittow) *hld up in rr: sme hdwy whn nt clr run over 2f out: nvr a factor* **22/1**

6014 **10** *shd* **Herrera (IRE)**[44] 5781 4-8-9 **69**.............................. BMcHugh(5) 6 67
(R A Fahey) *mid-div: hdwy on inner over 3f out: fdd over 1f out* **20/1**

1220 **11** *1* **Devil To Pay**[72] 4911 3-8-12 **76**.............................. TedDurcan 13 72
(J L Dunlop) *in rr: effrt over 2f out: swtchd wd over 1f out: nvr on terms* **12/1**

3236 **12** *nse* **Cleaver**[97] 4092 8-9-9 **78**.............................. RyanMoore 16 74
(Lady Herries) *hld up in rr: effrt 3f out: nvr a factor* **12/1**

546 **13** *1 ½* **Malt Or Mash (USA)**[11] 6734 5-9-11 **80**.............................. RichardHughes 12 74
(R Hannon) *led: hdd over 2f out: lost pl over 1f out* **16/1**

1200 **14** *¾* **Gifted Leader (USA)**[7] 6816 4-10-0 **83**.............................. StephenDonohoe 9 76
(Ian Williams) *in tch: effrt on outside over 2f out: wkng whn hmpd over 1f out* **10/1**

3m 9.73s (3.03) **Going Correction** -0.125s/f (Firm)
WFA 3 from 4yo+ 9lb **14** Ran SP% **120.4**
Speed ratings (Par 105): **86,85,85,82,82 81,81,81,80,80 80,80,79,78**
toteswinger: 1&2 £5.20, 1&3 £7.10, 2&3 £5.40. CSF £51.97 CT £181.98 TOTE £8.20: £2.40, £2.40, £1.90; EX 79.40 Trifecta £336.50 Pool: £454.80 - 1 winning unit..
Owner When Harry Met Rosie Partnership **Bred** Biddestone Stud **Trained** Lambourn, Berks

FOCUS
A modest staying handicap run at a fairly steady pace. The form has been rated at face value.
Royal Trooper(IRE) Official explanation: jockey said colt was denied a clear run
Hawridge Star(IRE) Official explanation: jockey said gelding was denied a clear run

6996 WEATHERBYS BANK H'CAP — 1m 2f 60y
4:40 (4:42) (Class 4) (0-85,90) 3-Y-O **£6,476** (£1,927; £963; £481) **Stalls** Low

Form RPR

3211 **1** **Luc Jordan**[30] 6209 3-9-0 **81**.............................. KFallon 4 92+
(L M Cumani) *hld up: swtchd outside and gd hdwy over 2f out: str run to ld and hung lft appr fnl f: sn rdn and kpt on wl towards fin* **8/1**[2]

4353 **2** *nk* **Bruton Street (USA)**[16] 6595 3-8-10 **77**.............................. JimmyFortune 10 85
(J H M Gosden) *hld up in midfield: hdwy 3f out: effrt 2f out: rdn over 1f out: styd on to chse wnr ins fnl f: sn drvn and kpt on* **12/1**

1002 **3** *1 ¼* **History Lesson**[11] 6740 3-9-3 **84**.............................. RichardHughes 5 90
(R Hannon) *chsd ldr: effrt 3f out: rdn 2f out: ev ch over 1f out: sn drvn and kpt on u.p ins fnl f* **10/1**[3]

151 **4** *shd* **Splinter Cell (USA)**[11] 6740 3-9-6 **90** 6ex.............................. AndreaAtzeni(3) 6 96
(M Botti) *trckd ldrs: hdwy 3f out: rdn wl over 1f out: drvn and n.m.r ent fnl f: kpt on same pce* **16/1**

0500 **5** *¾* **Norwegian Dancer (UAE)**[11] 6740 3-9-3 **84**.............................. GrahamGibbons 13 88
(E S McMahon) *trckd ldrs: hdwy 3f out: rdn over 2f out: drvn and ev ch over 1f out: n.m.r and one pce ins fnl f* **66/1**

0211 **6** *¾* **Tanfidh**[10] 6761 3-9-0 **81** 6ex.............................. TPO'Shea 1 84
(M P Tregoning) *led: rdn along over 2f out: drvn and hdd appr fnl f: wknd* **5/4**[1]

6165 **7** *nk* **Puzzlemaster**[13] 6681 3-9-4 **85**.............................. JamieSpencer 14 87
(Jane Chapple-Hyam) *hld up in rr: swtchd outside and hdwy over 2f out: rdn over 1f out: kpt on ins fnl f: nrst fin* **8/1**[2]

3263 **8** *½* **Call It On (IRE)**[11] 6740 3-9-4 **85**.............................. JimmyQuinn 9 86+
(M H Tompkins) *trckd ldrs: smooth hdwy 3f out: effrt 2f out: sn rdn and n.m.r appr fnl f: wknd* **14/1**

1340 **9** *¾* **Hollow Green (IRE)**[15] 6618 3-8-10 **82**.............................. BMcHugh(5) 3 82
(P D Evans) *hld up: a towards rr* **33/1**

4143 **10** *1 ½* **Embsay Crag**[13] 6680 3-8-8 **80**.............................. PaulPickard(5) 15 77
(Mrs K Walton) *s.i.s and bhd: hdwy into midfield after 2f: effrt to chse ldrs 3f out: rdn along over 2f out and sn wknd* **8/1**[2]

2660 **11** *3* **Capeability (IRE)**[18] 6539 3-8-13 **80**.............................. TonyCulhane 11 72
(M R Channon) *a in rr* **100/1**

0000 **12** *1* **Mishrif (USA)**[12] 6695 3-8-12 **79**..............................(v[1]) RobertWinston 7 69
(J R Jenkins) *trckd ldrs on inner: effrt 3f out: sn rdn along and n.m.r 2f out: sn wknd* **66/1**

140 **13** *3 ¾* **Whooshka (USA)**[78] 4709 3-8-11 **78**.............................. AlanMunro 8 60
(P W Chapple-Hyam) *a towards rr* **33/1**

2343 **14** *3 ¼* **Sequillo**[18] 6546 3-9-1 **82**.............................. RyanMoore 12 58
(R Hannon) *hld up: a in rr* **12/1**

1-00 **15** *3* **Wee Giant (USA)**[13] 6680 3-8-5 **72**.............................. PaulHanagan 2 43
(K A Ryan) *a towards rr* **66/1**

2m 9.15s (-2.05) **Going Correction** -0.125s/f (Firm) **15** Ran SP% **126.2**
Speed ratings (Par 103): **103,102,101,101,101 100,100,99,99,98 95,94,91,89,86**
toteswinger: 1&2 £15.40, 1&3 £10.70, 2&3 £17.70. CSF £101.86 CT £993.83 TOTE £8.00: £3.00, £3.50, £3.00; EX 136.40 Trifecta £560.60 Part won. Pool: £757.63 - 0.10 winning units..
Owner Equibreed S.R.L. **Bred** Equibreed S R L **Trained** Newmarket, Suffolk

FOCUS
A fair race for the grade. The winner was value for a bit extra.

6997 DRANSFIELD NOVELTY COMPANY "HANDS AND HEELS" APPRENTICE SERIES FINAL H'CAP — 7f
5:10 (5:15) (Class 5) (0-75,75) 3-Y-O **£5,180** (£1,541; £770; £384) **Stalls** High

Form RPR

4222 **1** **Steel Stockholder**[34] 6101 3-7-13 **61** oh1.............................. NoraLooby(5) 5 70
(M Brittain) *chsd ldrs: led over 2f out: hld on towards fin* **16/1**

2424 **2** *½* **Iron Out (USA)**[43] 5806 3-8-10 **67**.............................. PaulPickard 13 75
(R Hollinshead) *racd stands' side: hdwy over 2f out: styd on wl ins fnl f* **12/1**

2565 **3** *1 ¾* **My Best Bet**[13] 6667 3-9-2 **73**.............................. CharlesEddery 6 76
(M R Channon) *hld up: hdwy over 2f out: kpt on fnl f* **20/1**

0564 **4** *shd* **Hypnotist (UAE)**[32] 6174 3-8-5 **62**..............................(p) DebraEngland 12 65
(C E Brittain) *racd towards stands' side: hdwy over 2f out: kpt on fnl f* **6/1**[3]

0664 **5** *2 ½* **Steel Free (IRE)**[36] 6015 3-8-11 **73**.............................. MalinHolmberg(5) 8 69
(M L W Bell) *in rr: hdwy over 2f out: nvr trbld ldrs* **18/1**

1-05 **6** *½* **Captain Dancer (IRE)**[11] 6731 3-9-4 **75**.............................. DavidKenny 1 70
(B W Hills) *hmpd s: hdwy over 2f out: nvr nr ldrs* **9/2**[2]

-410 **7** *1 ½* **Great Art (IRE)**[15] 6621 3-9-2 **73**.............................. TobyAtkinson 4 64
(P W Chapple-Hyam) *in rr: hdwy over 2f out: nvr nr ldrs* **9/1**

0000 **8** *½* **Woteva**[154] 2236 3-8-6 **66** ow5.............................. LeeTopliss(3) 3 56
(T P Tate) *dwlt: in rr and pushed along: kpt on fnl 2f: nvr on terms* **50/1**

6150 **9** *shd* **Miss Hollybell**[95] 4148 3-9-1 **72**.............................. JPFahy 11 61
(J Gallagher) *chsd ldrs: outpcd over 2f out: wknd fnl f* **25/1**

6050 **10** *2* **Striker Torres (IRE)**[13] 6680 3-8-6 **66**.............................. AdamCarter(3) 14 50
(B Smart) *w ldrs: lost pl over 2f out* **10/1**

3010 **11** *¾* **Pokfulham (IRE)**[22] 6411 3-8-1 **61**..............................(v) RyanPowell(3) 2 43
(J S Goldie) *wnt lft s: sn chsng ldrs: hung lft and lost pl over 2f out* **14/1**

441 **12** *3 ¼* **Tiddliwinks**[28] 6255 3-9-1 **72**.............................. JamesPSullivan 7 45
(K A Ryan) *mde most tl over 2f out: sn wknd* **7/2**[1]

-051 **13** *¾* **Speedy Guru**[17] 6572 3-9-1 **72**.............................. AmyScott 10 43
(H Candy) *chsd ldrs: hung lft and lost pl over 1f out* **12/1**

0560 **14** *20* **Convitezza**[7] 6824 3-8-6 **63** oh16 ow2.............................. DTDaSilva 9 —
(M E Sowersby) *chsd ldrs: lost pl 3f out: sn bhd: t.o* **100/1**

1m 27.35s (1.05) **Going Correction** -0.05s/f (Good) **14** Ran SP% **118.5**
Speed ratings (Par 101): **92,91,89,89,86 85,84,83,83,81 80,76,75,52**
toteswinger: 1&2 £16.10, 1&3 £22.20, 2&3 £29.10. CSF £187.12 CT £3928.49 TOTE £12.00: £3.00, £4.50, £4.70; EX 141.70 Trifecta £325.90 Part won. Pool: £440.45 - 0.30 winning units. Place 6: £102.02 Place 5: £81.56.
Owner Mel Brittain **Bred** Mrs Joan M Langmead **Trained** Warthill, N Yorks
■ David Kenny was the series winner.

FOCUS
The Final of this hands and heels series for apprentices. The form looks fairly sound.

Speedy Guru Official explanation: jockey said filly hung left inside final furlong
T/Jkpt: Not won. T/Plt: £194.60 to a £1 stake. Pool: £85,533.27. 320.84 winning tickets. T/Qpdt: £82.80 to a £1 stake. Pool: £6,390.30. 57.10 winning tickets. JR

6855 WOLVERHAMPTON (A.W) (L-H)

Friday, October 23

OFFICIAL GOING: Standard
Wind: Nil Weather: Fine

6998 WOLVERHAMPTON-RACECOURSE.CO.UK H'CAP — 1m 1f 103y(P)
5:40 (5:41) (Class 6) (0-60,67) 3-Y-0+ **£2,217** (£654; £327) **Stalls** Low

Form — RPR

5535 **1** **The Grey One (IRE)**[11] 6719 6-9-8 **60**....(p) KevinGhunowa 5 — 69
(J M Bradley) *hld up in tch: n.m.r briefly 3f out: pushed along to ld over 1f out: sn rdn: drvn out* **7/1**[2]

0042 **2** *shd* **Thunderstruck**[7] 6818 4-9-7 **59**....(p) ChrisCatlin 3 — 68
(J A Glover) *hld up: hdwy over 6f out: pushed along over 3f out: rdn wl over 1f out: ev ch ins fnl f: r.o* **5/2**[1]

3504 **3** *1 ½* **Strike Force**[7] 6832 5-9-3 **55**....(p) DarryllHolland 1 — 61
(Miss J Feilden) *hld up in tch: pushed along and swtchd rt over 2f out: rdn to chal over 1f out: edgd rt ins fnl f: no ex towards fin* **5/2**[1]

1004 **4** *5* **King Of Connacht**[8] 6806 6-9-5 **57**....(p) AdamKirby 7 — 52
(M Wellings) *hld up towards rr: stdy prog over 3f out: nt clr run and swtchd rt over 1f out: rdn and wknd ins fnl f* **10/1**

5 *4* **Vaporetto (IRE)**[75] 4162 7-9-3 **55**....(p) LPKeniry 13 — 42
(P J Rothwell, Ire) *w ldr: led over 6f out: rdn over 2f out: hdd over 1f out: wknd fnl f* **16/1**

0300 **6** *12* **Devinius (IRE)**[39] 5941 4-9-3 **55**.... PatCosgrave 6 — 17
(G A Swinbank) *chsd ldrs: n.m.r on ins briefly over 2f out: rdn and wknd over 1f out* **10/1**

0000 **7** *7* **Parisian Dream**[20] 6498 5-9-8 **60**....(b[1]) ShaneKelly 8 — 7
(T J Pitt) *led: hdd over 6f out: chsd ldr tl rdn and wknd over 2f out* **16/1**

0 **8** *4 ½* **Forced Opinion (USA)**[78] 4721 4-9-4 **56**.... JamesDoyle 11 — —
(K A Morgan) *s.v.s: hld up in rr: pushed along 3f out: sn struggling* **20/1**

6400 **9** *3 ¼* **Trusted Venture (USA)**[11] 6720 3-9-2 **58**.... SteveDrowne 9 — —
(J R Best) *hld up towards rr: pushed along over 4f out: rdn and struggling over 3f out: eased fnl 2f* **33/1**

3106 **10** *4* **New England**[15] 6612 7-9-6 **58**.... LukeMorris 10 — —
(F Sheridan) *hld up in rr: pushed along over 5f out: struggling over 3f out: eased wl over 1f out* **8/1**[3]

2m 1.77s (0.07) **Going Correction** +0.025s/f (Slow)
WFA 3 from 4yo+ 4lb — **10** Ran SP% **118.4**
Speed ratings (Par 101): **100,99,98,94,90 79,73,69,66,63**
toteswinger: 1&2 £5.60, 1&3 £3.70, 2&3 £1.90. CSF £25.23 CT £57.24 TOTE £8.80: £1.80, £1.20, £2.30; EX 23.20.
Owner R Miles **Bred** Blackdown Stud **Trained** Sedbury, Gloucs
■ Stewards' Enquiry : Chris Catlin one-day ban: used whip without giving gelding time to respond (Nov 6)

FOCUS
The pace looked strong in this modest handicap, and Vaporetto and Parisian Dream ruined their chances by taking each other on through the early stages. Straightforward form.

6999 ENJOY THE LUCKY 7 GROUP OFFER H'CAP — 1m 141y(P)
6:10 (6:11) (Class 6) (0-55,55) 3-Y-0+ **£2,388** (£705; £352) **Stalls** Low

Form — RPR

655 **1** **Confide In Me**[37] 6005 5-9-3 **55**....(tp) HayleyTurner 4 — 61
(G A Butler) *hld up in mid-div: hdwy 3f out: rdn to ld ins fnl f: sn edgd lft and hdd: led post* **3/1**[1]

0422 **2** *nse* **Herbert Crescent**[8] 6800 4-9-0 **52**.... SebSanders 3 — 58
(Ollie Pears) *a.p: pushed along wl over 1f out: rdn to ld ins fnl f: hdd post* **9/2**

4010 **3** *nse* **Whipma Whopma Gate (IRE)**[39] 5953 4-9-2 **54**....(b) DNolan 6 — 59
(D Carroll) *hld up in tch: led wl over 1f out: rdn and edgd lft ins fnl f: sn hdd: r.o* **14/1**

0043 **4** *1 ½* **Bestowed**[32] 6172 4-8-12 **55**.... AndrewHeffernan(5) 2 — 57
(P D Evans) *hld up in mid-div: hdwy over 2f out: rdn and edgd lft over 1f out: swtchd rt ins fnl f: kpt on* **7/2**[2]

3606 **5** *2 ½* **Sion Hill (IRE)**[32] 6175 8-9-3 **55**....(p) ChrisCatlin 10 — 51
(John A Harris) *sn chsng ldr: led 5f out: pushed along and hdd wl over 1f out: cl 4th whn hmpd on ins ins fnl f: sn btn* **16/1**

0050 **6** *6* **Dark Camellia**[16] 6587 4-9-1 **53**....(t) DaneO'Neill 13 — 35
(H J L Dunlop) *s.s: hld up in rr: sme prog on ins over 2f out: rdn wl over 1f out: sn wknd* **16/1**

1500 **7** *4 ½* **Natural Rhythm (IRE)**[36] 6023 4-9-1 **53**....(b) LukeMorris 5 — 25
(Mrs R A Carr) *led: hdd 5f out: rdn over 3f out: wknd over 2f out* **25/1**

-000 **8** *3* **Spinning Ridge (IRE)**[16] 6588 4-9-3 **55**.... DavidProbert 11 — 20
(R A Harris) *hld up towards rr: nt clr run over 2f out: rdn and struggling wl over 1f out* **40/1**

3-00 **9** *hd* **Sir Billy Nick**[25] 6342 4-9-0 **52**.... LPKeniry 8 — 17
(S Wynne) *hld up in rr: hrd rdn 4f out: struggling 3f out* **33/1**

0-00 **10** *2 ¾* **Roman Maze**[34] 6123 9-9-3 **55**.... ShaneKelly 1 — 13
(W M Brisbourne) *hld up in rr: pushed along and hdwy over 2f out: wknd wl over 1f out* **28/1**

5500 **11** *2 ¾* **Kalhan Sands (IRE)**[53] 5518 4-9-2 **54**.... PatCosgrave 7 — 6
(J J Quinn) *hld up in mid-div: short-lived effrt on outside over 2f out* **20/1**

5/ **12** *25* **Leap The Liffey (IRE)**[47] 5702 6-9-2 **54**.... JoeFanning 9 — —
(Mrs Valerie Keatley, Ire) *hld up in tch: pushed along 3f out: bmpd twice over 2f out: sn eased* **4/1**[3]

1m 51.11s (0.61) **Going Correction** +0.025s/f (Slow) — **12** Ran SP% **121.3**
Speed ratings (Par 101): **98,97,97,96,94 89,85,82,82,79 77,55**
toteswinger: 1&2 £3.70, 1&3 £10.00, 2&3 £11.80. CSF £15.89 CT £168.59 TOTE £3.50: £1.60, £1.20, £3.40; EX 20.70.
Owner A D Spence & Mr And Mrs P Hargreaves **Bred** Cheveley Park Stud Ltd **Trained** Newmarket, Suffolk

FOCUS
A moderate handicap run at a steady pace and the principals got a bit close in the straight. The first three finished in a line and the form is rated around the runner-up. An objection by the rider of the third to the winner was overruled.

Leap The Liffey(IRE) Official explanation: jockey said gelding lost its action and hung left

7000 BOOK NOW FOR CHRISTMAS AT WOLVERHAMPTON H'CAP — 7f 32y(P)
6:40 (6:40) (Class 4) (0-80,80) 3-Y-0+ **£5,046** (£1,510; £755; £377; £188) **Stalls** High

Form — RPR

0013 **1** **Gassin**[12] 6699 3-8-10 **72**....(v) HayleyTurner 10 — 83
(M L W Bell) *chsd ldr after 1f: led over 3f out: clr wl over 1f out: rdn and edgd lft jst ins fnl f: r.o* **8/1**

5050 **2** *2* **Kashimin (IRE)**[14] 6645 4-9-2 **76**.... PatCosgrave 7 — 82
(G A Swinbank) *hld up in tch: chsd wnr over 2f out: rdn over 1f out: kpt on same pce ins fnl f: jst hld on for 2nd* **12/1**

6402 **3** *nse* **Chief Exec**[35] 6072 7-9-1 **75**....(b) AdamKirby 3 — 81+
(J R Gask) *hld up in rr: pushed along over 2f out: nt clr run briefly ent st: hdwy over 1f out: r.o wl ins fnl f: jst failed to take 2nd* **6/1**[3]

4011 **4** *nk* **Silver Guest**[7] 6825 4-8-10 **70**.... ChrisCatlin 8 — 75
(M R Channon) *hld up towards rr: c wd st: hdwy wl over 1f out: edgd lft and rdn ins fnl f: kpt on one pce* **4/1**[1]

3250 **5** *5* **Kensington (IRE)**[200] 1152 8-8-13 **73**.... SebSanders 5 — 65
(A J McCabe) *led early: prom: pushed along and btn over 1f out* **22/1**

5430 **6** *½* **Hustle (IRE)**[14] 6630 4-9-5 **79**....(e[1]) DarryllHolland 1 — 69
(Miss Gay Kelleway) *hld up towards rr: nt clr run wl over 1f out: sn pushed along: swtchd lft jst over 1f out: nvr nr ldrs* **11/2**[2]

0-33 **7** *shd* **Avertis**[24] 6357 4-9-6 **80**....(t) MickyFenton 2 — 70
(Stef Liddiard) *hld up in tch: rdn over 1f out: btn whn sltly hmpd ins fnl f* **6/1**[3]

1010 **8** *¾* **Ninth House (USA)**[36] 6016 7-9-0 **74**....(t) LukeMorris 4 — 62
(Mrs R A Carr) *a towards rr* **9/1**

0210 **9** *2* **Peper Harow (IRE)**[13] 6667 3-8-6 **68**.... DavidProbert 11 — 50
(M D I Usher) *hld up in mid-div: rdn wl over 1f out: wknd ins fnl f* **12/1**

0000 **10** *6* **Elusive Fame (USA)**[20] 6496 3-8-8 **70**....(b) JoeFanning 9 — 35
(M Johnston) *sn led: hdd over 3f out: wknd 2f out* **14/1**

4010 **11** *2 ¼* **Whisky Jack**[21] 6455 3-8-6 **68**....(b) MartinDwyer 6 — 27
(W R Muir) *hld up in mid-div: hdwy 3f out: sn rdn: wknd 2f out* **28/1**

1m 28.83s (-0.77) **Going Correction** +0.025s/f (Slow)
WFA 3 from 4yo+ 2lb — **11** Ran SP% **114.9**
Speed ratings (Par 105): **105,102,102,102,96 96,95,95,92,85 83**
toteswinger: 1&2 £22.70, 1&3 £8.90, 2&3 £20.80. CSF £97.61 CT £625.86 TOTE £9.20: £2.90, £4.10, £2.50; EX 133.30.
Owner J L C Pearce **Bred** J L C Pearce **Trained** Newmarket, Suffolk

FOCUS
A fair handicap for the grade. The winner produced a clear personal best.

Hustle(IRE) Official explanation: jockey said gelding was denied a clear run

7001 THE BLACK COUNTRY'S ONLY RACECOURSE MAIDEN STKS — 5f 216y(P)
7:10 (7:12) (Class 5) 2-Y-0 **£3,238** (£963; £481; £240) **Stalls** Low

Form — RPR

00 **1** **Little Garcon (USA)**[20] 6493 2-9-0 0.... AndreaAtzeni(3) 8 — 82+
(M Botti) *hld up and bhd: hdwy over 2f out: rdn whn nt clr run on ins wl over 1f out: sn plld out: rdn to ld wl ins fnl f: edgd lft: r.o wl* **25/1**

0320 **2** *1 ¼* **Confessional**[20] 6486 2-9-3 80.... DarryllHolland 5 — 75
(T D Easterby) *led early: a.p: pushed along and edgd lft wl over 1f out: rdn to ld ins fnl f: sn hdd: nt qckn* **7/1**[3]

4230 **3** *¾* **Texas Queen**[20] 6481 2-8-12 70.... ChrisCatlin 10 — 68
(M R Channon) *sn chsng ldr: led over 1f out: sn edgd lft: hdd ins fnl f: nt qckn* **9/2**[2]

52 **4** *4* **Sophie's Beau (USA)**[35] 6061 2-9-3 0.... MartinDwyer 2 — 64+
(B J Meehan) *sn led: rdn and hdd over 1f out: hmpd ins fnl f: nt rcvr* **8/13**[1]

5 *½* **Super Yellow** 2-9-3 0.... SteveDrowne 11 — 59+
(J A Osborne) *in rr: pushed along over 3f out: rdn and kpt on fr wl over 1f out: nvr nr ldrs* **66/1**

6 *1 ¼* **Layla's Lad (USA)** 2-9-3 0.... PatCosgrave 7 — 56
(R A Fahey) *prom tl rdn and wknd wl over 1f out* **12/1**

00 **7** *4 ½* **Lady Brickhouse**[17] 6567 2-8-12 0.... LukeMorris 4 — 37
(M D Squance) *hld up in tch: pushed along and wknd over 2f out* **150/1**

00 **8** *nk* **True To Form (IRE)**[8] 6802 2-9-3 0.... SebSanders 9 — 44+
(Sir Mark Prescott) *in rr: pushed along over 3f out: no ch whn c wd st* **66/1**

9 *3 ½* **Kidnap (IRE)** 2-9-3 0.... JerryO'Dwyer 3 — 31
(M G Quinlan) *s.i.s: hld up towards rr: pushed along over 2f out: sn struggling* **66/1**

10 *3* **Mnasikia (USA)** 2-8-12 0.... WilliamBuick 12 — 19
(L M Cumani) *hld up in mid-div: pushed along over 3f out: bhd fnl 2f* **16/1**

11 *12* **Special Betty** 2-8-12 0.... AdamKirby 6 — —
(D Haydn Jones) *s.i.s: sn wl outpcd* **100/1**

1m 14.96s (-0.04) **Going Correction** +0.025s/f (Slow) — **11** Ran SP% **116.2**
Speed ratings (Par 95): **101,99,98,93,92 90,84,84,79,75 59**
toteswinger: 1&2 £10.20, 1&3 £13.20, 2&3 £3.10. CSF £185.27 TOTE £28.60: £4.20, £2.00, £1.20; EX 124.70.
Owner Joseph Barton **Bred** Castleton Lyons **Trained** Newmarket, Suffolk

FOCUS
The front three in the betting went off plenty fast enough and there was a surprise result. The form seems pretty solid though, and is best viewed through the runner-up.

NOTEBOOK
Little Garcon(USA) appreciated the strong pace and stepped up considerably on his two previous efforts. The race unfolded to suit, so he might be a little flattered, but that said, he did have to be switched four wide in the straight when his attempted run against the inside rail was blocked. (tchd 20-1)

Confessional, without the blinkers this time, emerges with credit considering he fared best of those to race handy. He was slightly short of room against the inside rail in the straight, but was not unlucky. (op 6-1 tchd 11-2)

Texas Queen looked the winner when taking over from the favourite early in the straight, but she ruined her chance by edging left, and was held when then heading in the other direction late on. Although her pedigree suggests otherwise, she showed enough speed for 5f. (tchd 5-1)

Sophie's Beau(USA) was well below the form he showed when runner-up at Newmarket on his previous start, and that race is not really working out. He was badly squeezed out in the straight when the third home went left, but he was beaten at the time. He'll probably benefit from a drop to the minimum trip. (op 4-5 tchd 5-6, 10-11 in places)

Super Yellow ◆ cost 58,000euros and is bred to sprint. He was very green, starting sluggishly and racing out the back for the most part, but he made pleasing late headway, albeit the leaders were stopping. There should be better to come from him.

Layla's Lad(USA) ◆ ran as though he needed this after chasing the hot pace, but he has ability. (op 11-1)

Special Betty Official explanation: jockey said filly ran green

7002 WOLVERHAMPTON HOSPITALITY - A PLEASURE CLASSIFIED STKS 5f 216y(P)

7:40 (7:41) (Class 6) 3-Y-O+ **£2,047** (£604; £302) **Stalls** Low

Form RPR

0500 **1** **Shannon Golden**[59] 5326 3-9-0 52..............................(t) AmirQuinn 2 61
(S R Bowring) *in rr: pushed along over 2f out: hdwy wl over 1f out: rdn and edgd lft 1f out: led wl ins fnl f: r.o* **28/1**

-522 **2** ½ **Westwood Dawn**[6] 6856 4-9-1 55..............................(v) DaneO'Neill 3 59
(D Shaw) *hld up and bhd: stdy prog on ins over 3f out: swtchd rt over 2f out: rdn to ld and hung lft 1f out: hdd wl ins fnl f: kpt on* **5/2**[1]

0000 **3** 2 **Deo Valente (IRE)**[28] 6252 4-9-1 54..............................(bt[1]) DavidProbert 5 53
(J M Bradley) *led: rdn and hdd 1f out: no ex towards fin* **11/1**

16 **4** 1 **Chantilly Jewel (USA)**[2] 6939 4-9-1 55..............................(b) GrahamGibbons 6 50
(R M H Cowell) *hld up and bhd: hdwy on ins over 2f out: rdn over 1f out: swtchd rt wl ins fnl f: nt qckn* **5/1**[3]

6550 **5** 4 ½ **Davids Matador**[25] 6339 3-8-9 55..............................(p) AndrewHeffernan[(5)] 9 35
(Eve Johnson Houghton) *prom tl rdn and wknd wl over 1f out* **9/1**

3005 **6** nk **Madhal**[16] 6587 3-9-0 54.............................. WilliamBuick 10 36
(Matthew Salaman) *prom: hung rt bnd over 2f out: c wd st: btn over 1f out* **4/1**[2]

0-60 **7** ¾ **Anfield Star (IRE)**[30] 6213 3-9-0 50.............................. JamesDoyle 1 32
(Patrick Morris) *prom tl rdn and wknd over 1f out* **33/1**

0220 **8** 1 **Monte Mayor Eagle**[49] 5632 3-9-0 54..............................(b) AdamKirby 13 29
(D Haydn Jones) *hld up in mid-div: lost pl wl over 3f out: c wd st: sn rdn: n.d after* **11/1**

0500 **9** shd **Kingsgate Storm (IRE)**[25] 6340 3-9-0 53.............................. SteveDrowne 4 29
(J R Best) *a bhd* **16/1**

0364 **10** 1 ½ **Pepin (IRE)**[59] 5326 3-9-0 54.............................. FrankieMcDonald 7 24
(D Haydn Jones) *prom: pushed along over 3f out: wknd over 2f out* **11/1**

0100 **11** nse **Artesium**[11] 6719 3-8-7 55..............................(p) AlexEdwards[(7)] 11 24
(Patrick Morris) *hld up in mid-div: pushed along and wknd 2f out* **20/1**

12 4 **Right Of Veto**[16] 6604 3-9-0 44.............................. LPKeniry 12 11
(P J Rothwell, Ire) *outpcd* **33/1**

5650 **13** 2 ¾ **Lana's Charm**[49] 5647 3-9-0 52..............................(t) SebSanders 8 —
(P J Makin) *prom tl rdn and wknd wl over 1f out* **33/1**

1m 15.56s (0.56) **Going Correction** +0.025s/f (Slow)
WFA 3 from 4yo 1lb **13** Ran SP% **123.2**
Speed ratings (Par 101): **97,96,93,92,86 85,84,83,83,81 81,76,72**
toteswinger: 1&2 £20.70, 1&3 £76.20, 2&3 £8.90. CSF £96.18 TOTE £33.10: £9.40, £1.10, £3.90; EX 211.60.
Owner P O'Boyle **Bred** P O'Boyle **Trained** Edwinstowe, Notts

FOCUS

A very moderate contest run at a good pace. The runner-up looks the best guide.

Shannon Golden Official explanation: trainer said, regarding apparent improvement in form, that the gelding had returned fresh after a lay off and appreciated being held up.

Chantilly Jewel(USA) Official explanation: jockey said filly was denied a clear run closing stages

Madhal Official explanation: jockey said gelding lost its action but returned sound

Lana's Charm Official explanation: jockey said filly had no more to give

7003 SPONSOR A RACE BY CALLING 01902 390000 NURSERY 1m 141y(P)

8:10 (8:10) (Class 4) (0-80,78) 2-Y-O **£4,209** (£1,252; £625; £312) **Stalls** Low

Form RPR

500 **1** **Nafura**[37] 5980 2-8-8 **65**..............................(p) TedDurcan 11 76
(Saeed Bin Suroor) *sn chsng ldr: rdn over 2f out: led wl over 1f out: sn edgd lft: r.o wl* **9/1**

3536 **2** 4 ½ **If I Were A Boy (IRE)**[12] 6693 2-9-3 **74**.............................. JamesDoyle 1 76
(S Kirk) *led early: hld up: lost pl over 6f out: in rr whn pushed along 3f out: hdwy over 2f out: styd on to take 2nd wl ins fnl f: no ch w wnr* **10/1**

1544 **3** 1 **Miss Smilla**[29] 6232 2-9-4 **75**.............................. TonyCulhane 3 74
(K A Ryan) *hld up in tch: lost pl on ins wl over 3f out: pushed along and hdwy over 2f out: swtchd lft over 1f out: kpt on ins fnl f: tk 3rd towards fin* **14/1**

3321 **4** ½ **Venutius**[21] 6461 2-9-6 **77**.............................. GrahamGibbons 8 75
(E S McMahon) *sn led: rdn and hdd wl over 1f out: wknd wl ins fnl f* **11/4**[1]

0113 **5** 1 ¾ **Boquito (IRE)**[23] 6373 2-9-6 **77**.............................. JerryO'Dwyer 7 72
(Miss Amy Weaver) *hld up in mid-div: rdn and hdwy over 2f out: wknd ins fnl f* **6/1**[3]

352 **6** 5 **Kensei (IRE)**[64] 5192 2-9-7 **78**.............................. SebSanders 5 67+
(R M Beckett) *hld up in rr: nt clr run over 3f out: pushed along over 2f out: nvr nr ldrs* **9/1**

6513 **7** 2 ¾ **Epic (IRE)**[20] 6491 2-9-4 **75**.............................. JoeFanning 10 53
(M Johnston) *prom: pushed along whn n.m.r on ins briefly jst over 2f out: sn wknd* **5/1**[2]

334 **8** 8 **Springwell Giant (IRE)**[22] 6431 2-8-3 **67**.............................. DeclanCannon[(7)] 2 29
(A J McCabe) *hld up towards rr: rdn and struggling over 2f out* **40/1**

010 **9** 2 ¾ **Dr Mathias**[20] 6491 2-8-9 **71**.............................. AndrewHeffernan[(5)] 9 27
(P D Evans) *prom tl rdn and wknd 3f out* **33/1**

526 **10** 31 **A Pocketful Of Rye (IRE)**[14] 6628 2-9-0 **71**.............................. ShaneKelly 4 —
(J A Osborne) *hld up: hdwy over 5f out: rdn over 3f out: wknd over 2f out: eased whn no ch over 1f out* **14/1**

0651 **11** 3 **Be A Devil**[7] 6829 2-9-2 **73** 6ex.............................. DaneO'Neill 6 —
(W R Muir) *a towards rr: eased whn no ch fnl 2f* **5/1**[2]

1m 49.95s (-0.55) **Going Correction** +0.025s/f (Slow) **11** Ran SP% **122.1**
Speed ratings (Par 97): **103,99,98,97,96 91,89,82,79,52 49**
toteswinger: 1&2 £16.60, 1&3 £29.00, 2&3 £23.50. CSF £99.41 CT £1293.39 TOTE £14.70: £3.60, £4.10, £6.50; EX 102.30.
Owner Godolphin **Bred** Darley **Trained** Newmarket, Suffolk

FOCUS

An ordinary contest for the class. The winner was a big improver with the runner-up helping with the level.

NOTEBOOK

Nafura ◆ improved for the step up in trip, as well as the fitting of cheekpieces, and showed herself to be well handicapped on this nursery debut. Having been driven into second place from the widest stall, she looked to have gone off plenty quick enough (early leader Venutius dropped away), but she kept on well. A half-sister to Dubai Destination and Librettist, this success has boosted her paddock value, but she can win more races if persevered with on the track. Official explanation: trainer's rep said, regarding apparent improvement in form, that the filly was suited by a return to the all-weather and the application of first time cheekpieces. (op 8-1 tchd 15-2)

If I Were A Boy(IRE) stayed on from a long way back and would have been closer had she got in the clear sooner, but she still wouldn't have troubled the winner. (op 12-1)

Miss Smilla didn't get the clearest of runs into the straight, but she wasn't unlucky.

Venutius, a C&D maiden winner last time, went off plenty quick enough, but that can't really be used as an excuse seeing as the winner sat in second early on. (tchd 5-2 and 3-1)

Boquito(IRE)'s improvement seems to have levelled off. (op 10-1)

Kensei(IRE) ◆ can do better. He raced out the back after starting slowly and was continually denied a clear run rounding the final bend. (tchd 10-1)

Be A Devil Official explanation: jockey said colt suffered interference shortly after start

7004 STAY AT THE WOLVERHAMPTON HOLIDAY INN MEDIAN AUCTION MAIDEN STKS 1m 1f 103y(P)

8:40 (8:40) (Class 6) 3-5-Y-O **£2,047** (£604; £302) **Stalls** Low

Form RPR

22 **1** **Illuminative (USA)**[15] 6608 3-9-3 0.............................. JimmyFortune 1 74
(J H M Gosden) *s.i.s: hld up in mid-div: hdwy 2f out: carried hd high and led jst over 1f out: r.o wl* **1/4**[1]

2-6 **2** 7 **Lilly Grove**[13] 6673 4-9-2 0.............................. PatCosgrave 4 54
(G A Swinbank) *led 1f: chsd ldr: led wl over 1f out: sn rdn and hdd: one pce* **6/1**[2]

0605 **3** 3 ½ **Jobekani (IRE)**[109] 3680 3-9-3 54.............................. NeilChalmers 7 52
(Mrs L Williamson) *hld up in tch: rdn and wknd ins fnl f* **66/1**

606 **4** nse **Meml**[62] 5259 3-8-12 49.............................. DarryllHolland 2 47
(J D Bethell) *hld up towards rr: pushed along and hdwy on ins over 2f out: rdn and wknd fnl f* **33/1**

063 **5** ½ **Davana**[93] 4196 3-8-7 44.............................. PaulPickard[(5)] 5 46
(W J H Ratcliffe) *hld up in rr: pushed along over 2f out: sme late prog* **33/1**

6 ½ **Heathyards Junior** 3-9-3 0.............................. GrahamGibbons 12 50
(R Hollinshead) *s.i.s: hld up towards rr: short-lived effrt on outside 3f out* **25/1**

0006 **7** 1 **Very Distinguished**[29] 6223 3-8-7 49.............................. LeeNewnes[(5)] 6 43
(S Kirk) *s.i.s: hld up towards rr: pushed along over 2f out: sn struggling* **14/1**[3]

0006 **8** hd **Ay Tay Tate (IRE)**[8] 6804 3-9-3 50..............................(v[1]) DaneO'Neill 11 47
(D Shaw) *prom: rdn over 1f out: wknd fnl f* **50/1**

9 1 **Good Karma (IRE)**[56] 5-9-7 0.............................. LPKeniry 10 45
(P J Rothwell, Ire) *s.i.s: sn hld up in tch: rdn over 2f out: wknd wl over 1f out* **66/1**

0/00 **10** 3 ¼ **Chicamia**[7] 6817 5-9-2 44..............................(p) GregFairley 8 33
(M Mullineaux) *hld up towards rr: pushed along over 3f out: sn struggling* **100/1**

06- **11** 3 ½ **Tagula Minx (IRE)**[348] 7259 3-8-12 0.............................. JerryO'Dwyer 9 26
(J Pearce) *led after 1f: rdn and hdd wl over 1f out: sn wknd* **50/1**

560 **12** 9 **Magic Queen (IRE)**[15] 6611 3-8-12 57.............................. TedDurcan 3 7
(A P Jarvis) *prom: pushed along over 3f out: sn wknd: eased whn no ch over 1f out* **66/1**

2m 1.37s (-0.33) **Going Correction** +0.025s/f (Slow)
WFA 3 from 4yo+ 4lb **12** Ran SP% **120.1**
Speed ratings (Par 101): **102,95,92,92,92 91,90,90,89,86 83,75**
toteswinger: 1&2 £1.60, 1&3 £11.40, 2&3 £17.80. CSF £1.91 TOTE £1.60: £1.02, £1.40, £10.30; EX 3.20.
Owner Malih L Al Basti **Bred** Juddmonte Farms Inc **Trained** Newmarket, Suffolk

FOCUS

An uncompetitive maiden. The winner was a class above and the form is rated around the second, fourth and fifth.

7005 HORIZONS RESTAURANT - THE PLACE TO DINE H'CAP 2m 119y(P)

9:10 (9:10) (Class 4) (0-80,80) 3-Y-O+ **£5,046** (£1,510; £755; £377; £188) **Stalls** Low

Form RPR

234 **1** **Murcar**[13] 6676 4-9-6 **72**..............................(b) AdamKirby 6 82
(C G Cox) *hld up in tch: led after 4f: hdd 3f out: rdn to ld 2f out: drvn out* **9/4**[2]

603- **2** 1 **Basalt (IRE)**[405] 5887 5-9-9 **75**.............................. GregFairley 9 84
(T J Pitt) *a.p: rdn over 2f out: styd on to take 2nd wl ins fnl f: nt rch wnr* **14/1**

0211 **3** 3 ¼ **Cape Marien (IRE)**[16] 6584 3-9-0 **76**.............................. TedDurcan 10 81+
(D R Lanigan) *s.i.s: sn prom: led 3f out: rdn and hdd 2f out: one pce fnl f* **5/4**[1]

5130 **4** 1 ½ **Alnwick**[40] 5917 5-9-12 **78**.............................. DaneO'Neill 5 81
(P D Cundell) *led 4f: a.p: pushed along over 3f out: outpcd over 2f out: styd on one pce fnl f* **8/1**[3]

6640 **5** ½ **Bold Adventure**[21] 6457 5-8-9 **61** oh1.............................. ChrisCatlin 8 63
(W J Musson) *hld up towards rr: stdy prog over 5f out: outpcd over 3f out: styd on ins fnl f* **14/1**

6 ¾ **Eyeffess (IRE)**[20] 1906 8-8-9 **61** oh2.............................. LPKeniry 1 63
(P J Rothwell, Ire) *s.i.s: hld up in rr: pushed along over 2f out: rdn and styd on fnl f: n.d* **40/1**

1235 **7** 1 **Deuce**[22] 6432 3-7-13 **66**..............................(b) AndrewHeffernan[(5)] 3 66
(Eve Johnson Houghton) *hld up in mid-div: pushed along 3f out: rdn and struggling wl over 1f out* **11/1**

/54- **8** 15 **Tayman (IRE)**[19] 4365 7-8-9 **61**..............................(p) JamesDoyle 4 43
(N A Twiston-Davies) *prom: rdn over 3f out: wknd wl over 2f out* **16/1**

003/ **9** ½ **Pagan Sword**[85] 6439 7-10-0 **80**.............................. DNolan 7 62
(D G Bridgwater) *hld up towards rr: pushed along over 5f out: no ch fnl 4f* **66/1**

3m 41.0s (-0.80) **Going Correction** +0.025s/f (Slow)
WFA 3 from 4yo+ 10lb **9** Ran SP% **117.8**
Speed ratings (Par 105): **102,101,100,99,99 98,98,91,90**
toteswinger: 1&2 £13.80, 1&3 £2.10, 2&3 £8.00. CSF £34.71 CT £55.28 TOTE £2.90: £1.10, £3.20, £1.30; EX 45.10 Place 6: £538.72, Place 5: £422.19..
Owner Peter J Skinner **Bred** John W Ford And Peter J Skinner **Trained** Lambourn, Berks

FOCUS

An ordinary staying handicap for the grade. The fourth is probably the best guide.

T/Plt: £406.20 to a £1 stake. Pool: £75,080.69. 134.90 winning tickets. T/Qpdt: £175.10 to a £1 stake. Pool: £7,952.40. 33.60 winning tickets. KH

6833 DUNDALK (A.W) (L-H)

Friday, October 23

OFFICIAL GOING: Standard

7007a MERCURY STKS (LISTED RACE) 5f (P)

7:00 (7:01) 2-Y-O+ **£26,861** (£7,881; £3,754; £1,279)

RPR

1 **Arganil (USA)**[34] 6091 4-10-0.............................. KLatham 7 106
(K A Ryan) *chsd ldrs: 3rd 1/2-way: impr to chal 1 1/2f out: rdn to ld 1f out: kpt on wl u.p fnl f* **5/1**[2]

2 1 **Rain Delayed (IRE)**[64] 5203 3-9-11 103 JMurtagh 3 99
(G M Lyons, Ire) *sn led: rdn and disp 1 1/2f out: hdd 1f out: kpt on in 2nd fnl f: no imp on wnr* **11/4**[1]

3 shd **Perfect Polly**[12] 6707 4-9-11 102 FMBerry 6 99
(James M Ryan, Ire) *mid-div: 7th 1/2-way: hdwy in 5th 2f out: rdn 1 1/2f out: kpt on fnl f* **8/1**[3]

4 shd **Santo Padre (IRE)**[41] 5860 5-9-11 102 CO'Donoghue 10 98
(David Marnane, Ire) *hld up: rdn into 8th 1 1/2f out: 7th 1f out: kpt on wl fnl f* **5/1**[2]

5 shd **Green Manalishi**[13] 6678 8-9-11 (p) DPMcDonogh 5 98
(K A Ryan) *prom early: sn chsd ldrs: 5th 1/2-way: rdn in 6th 2f out: kpt on fnl f* **10/1**

6 1/2 **Luisant**[12] 6707 6-9-11 108 PJSmullen 8 96
(J A Nash, Ire) *mid-div: 6th 1/2-way: rdn and dropped to 10th 2f out: kpt on fnl f* **5/1**[2]

7 hd **Miss Gorica (IRE)**[26] 6315 5-9-8 102 WMLordan 1 92
(Ms Joanna Morgan, Ire) *prom: cl 2nd 1/2-way: chal 2f out: rdn to dispute 1 1/2f out: no ex in 3rd 1f out: kpt on same pce fnl f* **12/1**

8 1/2 **Invincible Ash (IRE)**[14] 6649 4-9-8 93 (b) GFCarroll 11 91
(M Halford, Ire) *towards rr for most: nvr a factor* **16/1**

9 1/2 **Mary Josephine (IRE)**[7] 6834 4-9-8 83 (tp) DEMullins 4 89
(H Rogers, Ire) *chsd ldrs: 4th 1/2-way: 3rd 2f out: rdn in cl 4th 1 1/2f out: no ex fnl f* **33/1**

10 1 3/4 **Calm Bay (IRE)**[14] 6649 3-9-11 92 WJSupple 9 86
(H Rogers, Ire) *hld up: hdwy into 7th 2f out: rdn in 9th 1 1/2f out: no imp and kpt on one pce* **20/1**

11 hd **Madame Trop Vite (IRE)**[7] 6814 3-9-8 KJManning 2 82
(K A Ryan) *hld up: hdwy in 8th 2f out: rdn in 7th 1 1/2f out: no ex and wknd 1f out* **25/1**

58.00 secs (58.00) **11 Ran SP% 122.0**
CSF £19.44 TOTE £5.20: £2.40, £1.10, £2.60; DF 23.30.
Owner The Big Moment **Bred** Colt Neck Stables, Llc **Trained** Hambleton, N Yorks

FOCUS
Two lengths separated the next nine horses behind the winner, emphasising the competitiveness of the contest.

NOTEBOOK
Arganil(USA) has been mostly campaigned in better company than this and showed a bit of class. Despite what the jockey described as a sluggish break, he was in an ideal position throughout and responded well to pressure inside the final furlong and a half to win going away. He races like he should be equally effective over another furlong. (op 9/2)
Rain Delayed(IRE) showed plenty of early dash, leading before the home bend until the winner took it up over 1f out. He kept on at the same pace and just managed to hold on to second place. (op 3/1)
Perfect Polly looked more at home over this trip than the 6f of the Curragh on her last start. She was a little outpaced in the early strides but came with a reasonable-looking effort over 1f out and was a shade unlucky not to be second as she just was a bit short of room inside the final furlong.
Santo Padre(IRE) also seemed to struggle fractionally to go the early pace and while she did make some headway inside the final furlong and a half she never looked like getting there. She found this trip on a quick surface in this company just beyond her. (op 9/2)
Green Manalishi ran a typical sort of race for him, showing early speed and keeping on again late, having been fractionally outpaced. (op 8/1)
Luisant ran on again late having been outpaced in the straight. (op 4/1)
Miss Gorica(IRE) showed lots of early speed before fading late. (op 12/1 tchd 14/1)

7008 - 7012a (Foreign Racing) - See Raceform Interactive

6990
DONCASTER (L-H)
Saturday, October 24

OFFICIAL GOING: Good to soft (good in places) changing to good to soft after race 1 (1.15)
Wind: Fresh across Weather: Dull and raining

7013 CROWNHOTEL-BAWTRY.COM NURSERY 7f
1:15 (1:17) (Class 3) 2-Y-O **£9,714** (£2,890; £1,444; £721) **Stalls** High

Form RPR

1530 1 **Leviathan**[48] 5692 2-9-1 82 MickyFenton 4 90
(T P Tate) *hld up towards rr: swtchd lft and gd hdwy on wd outside 2f out: rdn to ld over 1f out and hung bdly rt ent fnl f: sn drvn and kpt on wl* **25/1**

4124 2 1/2 **Yaa Wayl (IRE)**[19] 6534 2-9-2 83 (b[1]) LDettori 10 90
(M A Jarvis) *hld up: gd hdwy over 2f out: rdn to chal over 1f out: ev ch whn hung lft ent fnl f: sn drvn and nt qckn fnl 100yds* **7/1**[3]

421 3 2 3/4 **Sand Skier**[33] 6154 2-9-6 87 JoeFanning 6 87
(M Johnston) *cl up: led 1/2-way: rdn along over 2f out: sn drvn and hdd over 1f out: kpt on same pce* **10/3**[1]

315 4 shd **Sunnandaeg**[14] 6677 2-9-4 85 PhillipMakin 12 85
(I Semple) *hld up in rr: hdwy on outer wl over 2f out: rdn to chse ldrs over 1f out: sn drvn and one pce ins fnl f* **9/1**

1656 5 hd **Desert Auction (IRE)**[27] 6305 2-9-7 88 PatDobbs 11 87
(R Hannon) *hld up in rr: hdwy on outer over 2f out: rdn wl over 1f out: kpt on ins fnl f: nrst fin* **33/1**

531 6 1 **Swiss Cross**[22] 6451 2-9-0 81 KFallon 3 78
(G A Butler) *in tch: hdwy to chse ldrs wl over 2f out: rdn wl over 1f out: drvn appr fnl f and no imp* **4/1**[2]

251 7 hd **Subtefuge**[25] 6363 2-8-12 79 TPQueally 1 75
(H R A Cecil) *trckd ldrs: hdwy to chal wl over 2f out and ev ch tl rdn and wknd appr fnl f* **8/1**

13 8 3 1/4 **Be Invincible (IRE)**[155] 2247 2-9-2 83 RobertWinston 9 72
(B W Hills) *chsd ldrs: rdn along over 2f out: sn drvn and wknd over 1f out* **17/2**

016 9 2 1/2 **Dylanesque**[21] 6471 2-8-11 78 RichardMullen 8 62
(M A Jarvis) *wnt lft and dwlt s: sn in tch: rdn along 3f out and sn wknd* **16/1**

4540 10 5 **Haltela (IRE)**[15] 6643 2-9-6 87 (v[1]) NCallan 13 58
(K A Ryan) *chsd ldrs: rdn along wl over 2f out: sn edgd lft and wknd* **40/1**

5212 11 1 **Unshakable Will (IRE)**[18] 6557 2-9-0 81 TomEaves 7 48
(B Smart) *led: hdd 1/2-way: sn rdn along and wknd over 2f out* **16/1**

15 12 hd **Goodwood Maestro**[17] 6585 2-9-4 85 EddieAhern 15 51
(J L Dunlop) *in tch: rdn along 3f out: sn wknd* **20/1**

1002 13 4 **Sea Lord (IRE)**[36] 6063 2-9-7 88 RoystonFfrench 2 44
(M Johnston) *cl up: rdn along 1/2-way: wknd wl over 2f out* **16/1**

1m 26.03s (-0.27) **Going Correction** -0.05s/f (Good) **13 Ran SP% 118.9**
Speed ratings (Par 99): **99,98,95,95,94 93,93,89,87,81 80,79,75**
toteswinger: 1&2 £62.10, 1&3 £30.80, 2&3 £2.70. CSF £184.77 CT £749.97 TOTE £37.30: £9.40, £2.30, £1.60; EX 390.00 TRIFECTA Not won..
Owner Paul Moulton **Bred** Laundry Cottage Stud Farm **Trained** Tadcaster, N Yorks

FOCUS
Following 1.5mm of rain since early morning, the ground had eased slightly from the previous day and was described as good to soft, good in places on the straight course. As was the case the previous day, the runners raced more towards the centre of the track and they seemed to go a generous pace in this, with three vying for the early lead, but that seemed to play into the hands of the hold-up horses. Solid form.

NOTEBOOK
Leviathan ◆ had been slightly disappointing at York last time, but he was ridden much more patiently on this occasion and his rider was of the opinion that the easing ground was the key. Having been held up last early, he travelled into the race supremely well down the far side of the field to take it up over 1f out and, despite hanging away to his right, kept on finding what was required. He could make up into a nice handicapper at three, especially given similar conditions. (op 40-1)
Yaa Wayl(IRE), blinkered for the first time on this step up in trip, was another held up early before being produced with his effort more towards the near side of the track. He tended to edge away to his left and brushed the winner, but he looked to be getting the worse of the argument at the time.
Sand Skier ◆, making his nursery debut after showing progressive form in maidens, earns himself credit as he was the only one of the leading trio to still be in the thick of the action at the business end, and this unexposed sort can win more races. (op 3-1 tchd 4-1)
Sunnandaeg, making his nursery debut and not disgraced in a York Listed event last time, came through towards the near side to give himself every chance, but couldn't quicken again inside the final furlong. He still has some scope. (op 11-1)
Desert Auction(IRE), unplaced three times since winning a Newbury nursery off 2lb lower, had to be switched right over to the stands' rail to make his effort and finished in good style. He could probably have done without the rain, but is more exposed than many of these. (op 25-1)
Swiss Cross, making his nursery debut after showing progressive form in maidens, tracked the leaders down the centre of the track, but couldn't pick up sufficiently when asked. Another possibly not helped by the rain, he still has scope for further improvement. (op 7-2)
Subtefuge, making her nursery debut after beating a subsequent winner in a Warwick maiden last month, was produced to join the leaders towards the far side of the group coming to the last 2f, but once there she hung away to her right and had little more to offer. All of her previous starts had been on quick ground. (op 11-1)
Sea Lord(IRE) Official explanation: trainer had no explanation for the poor form shown

7014 LINCOLN RESTAURANT H'CAP (DIV I) 1m 2f 60y
1:50 (1:50) (Class 4) (0-80,80) 3-Y-O+ **£4,857** (£1,445; £722; £360) **Stalls** Low

Form RPR

0021 1 **Nevada Desert (IRE)**[7] 6860 9-9-0 73 DO'Donohoe 4 82
(R M Whitaker) *hld up towards rr: hdwy on inner 3f out: chsd ldrs wl over 1f out: swtchd rt and rdn ent fnl f: styd on wl u.p to ld nr line* **16/1**

2441 2 nk **Starla Dancer (GER)**[14] 6680 3-8-9 76 FrederikTylicki[(3)] 5 84
(R A Fahey) *trckd ldr: effrt and cl up 3f out: rdn to ld over 1f out: drvn ent fnl f: hdd and no ex nr line* **9/4**[1]

6100 3 1 3/4 **Northern Jem**[15] 6648 5-9-2 75 EddieAhern 2 80
(Jane Chapple-Hyam) *trckd ldng pair on inner: effrt over 2f out: rdn over 1f out: drvn ent fnl f and one pce* **16/1**

0513 4 nk **Veiled Applause**[11] 6761 6-9-0 78 BMcHugh[(5)] 8 82
(J J Quinn) *hld up towards rr: hdwy over 4f out: effrt to chse ldrs 3f out: rdn along 2f out: sn drvn and kpt on same pce appr fnl f* **15/2**[3]

2650 5 1 **Punch Drunk**[19] 6538 3-8-2 66 oh1 (p) PaulHanagan 1 68
(J G Given) *led: rdn along 3f out: drvn 2f out: hdd over 1f out and grad wknd* **7/1**[2]

2445 6 nse **Maybeme**[5] 6900 3-8-3 67 DuranFentiman 7 69
(N Bycroft) *hld up in rr: hdwy on outer over 3f out: rdn along over 2f out: sn drvn and kpt on ins fnl f: nrst fin* **10/1**

-000 7 1 3/4 **Desert Vision**[8] 6832 5-8-0 66 oh1 (t) JamesPSullivan[(7)] 10 65
(M W Easterby) *hld up in rr: hdwy wl over 2f out: sn rdn and nt rch ldrs* **28/1**

4156 8 2 1/2 **Admiral Dundas (IRE)**[12] 6733 4-9-4 77 JoeFanning 3 71
(W Jarvis) *chsd ldrs: rdn along 3f out: sn drvn and wknd* **9/1**

5010 9 5 **Middlemarch (IRE)**[30] 6012 9-8-8 72 ow2 (v) GaryBartley[(5)] 6 57
(J S Goldie) *hld up towards rr: hdwy over 3f out: rdn along over 2f out and sn wknd* **11/1**

3113 10 11 **Baltimore Jack (IRE)**[21] 6490 5-8-11 70 GrahamGibbons 11 34
(T D Walford) *chsd ldrs: rdn along 4f out: drvn over 3f out and sn wknd* **7/1**[2]

1600 11 1/2 **Agapanthus (GER)**[11] 6761 4-8-9 68 TPQueally 12 31
(B J Curley) *in tch: rdn along 4f out and sn wknd* **20/1**

2m 10.37s (-0.83) **Going Correction** +0.05s/f (Good)
WFA 3 from 4yo+ 5lb **11 Ran SP% 114.9**
Speed ratings (Par 105): **105,104,103,103,102 102,100,98,94,86 85**
toteswinger: 1&2 £19.60, 1&3 £42.20, 2&3 £9.60. CSF £50.86 CT £605.66 TOTE £11.30: £3.20, £1.40, £3.70; EX 49.80 Trifecta £183.80 Part won. Pool: £248.50 -0.46 winning units..
Owner J Barry Pemberton **Bred** Bryan Ryan **Trained** Scarcroft, W Yorks

FOCUS
The ground was changed to good to soft all round before this race. Just a fair handicap, but sound form with the winner rated to his best over the past year or so.
Baltimore Jack(IRE) Official explanation: trainer had no explanation for the poor form shown

7015 CORAL.CO.UK H'CAP 5f
2:20 (2:25) (Class 2) (0-100,100) 3-Y-O+
£31,155 (£9,330; £4,665; £2,335; £1,165; £585) **Stalls** High

Form RPR

1664 1 **Quest For Success (IRE)**[3] 6949 4-8-10 95 FrederikTylicki[(3)] 16 104+
(R A Fahey) *prom: hdwy and cl up 1/2-way: rdn to chal over 1f out: led ent fnl f: sn drvn and kpt on wl* **9/1**[2]

0U00 2 1/2 **Excusez Moi (USA)**[14] 6678 7-8-9 91 AndrewElliott 9 98
(Mrs R A Carr) *s.i.s and in rr: hdwy 2f out: str run appr fnl f: fin wl* **33/1**

-520 3 hd **Waffle (IRE)**[14] 6661 3-9-4 100 LDettori 7 106
(J Noseda) *hld up towards rr: hdwy 2f out: sn rdn and styd on to chse wnr ins fnl f: drvn and nt qckn last 75yds* **22/1**

0050 4 3/4 **Fullandby (IRE)**[14] 6675 7-8-7 94 MartinLane[(5)] 21 98
(T J Etherington) *dwlt and sn rdn along in rr: hdwy 2f out: styd on wl u.p ins fnl f: nrst fin* **10/1**[3]

0000 5 3/4 **Parisian Pyramid (IRE)**[14] 6678 3-8-8 90 JoeFanning 19 91
(D Nicholls) *towards rr: hdwy 2f out: rdn over 1f out: styd on ins fnl f: nrst fin* **25/1**

6000 6 nk **Captain Gerrard (IRE)**[14] 6678 4-8-13 95 (b) TomEaves 6 95
(B Smart) *led: rdn 2f out: drvn over 1f out: hdd ent fnl f and grad wknd* **25/1**

3020 7 shd **Judge 'n Jury**[42] 5860 5-9-4 100 (t) DavidProbert 15 100
(R A Harris) *cl up: rdn wl over 1f out and ev ch tl drvn ent fnl f and grad wknd* **10/1**[3]

0000 8 hd **River Falcon**[1] 6994 9-8-6 88 PaulHanagan 22 87
(J S Goldie) *qckly away: sn lost pl and towards rr tl hdwy over 1f out: rdn and styd on ins fnl f: nrst fin* **18/1**

0613 **9** *nse* **Invincible Lad (IRE)**[3] 6949 5-8-6 **88**........................ CatherineGannon 5 87
(E J Alston) *midfield: hdwy 2f out: sn rdn and chsd ldrs over 1f out: drvn and no imp ins fnl f* **14/1**

5012 **10** *1 ½* **Cheveton**[14] 6678 5-9-1 **97**............................ RobertWinston 11 90
(R J Price) *cl up: rdn along over 2f out: drvn wl over 1f out: sn edgd lft and wknd* **6/1**[1]

2005 **11** *nse* **Wi Dud**[14] 6678 5-9-2 **98**..(p) NCallan 13 91
(K A Ryan) *chsd ldrs: rdn along over 2f out and n.d* **11/1**

2102 **12** *hd* **Cape Vale (IRE)**[7] 6843 4-8-8 **90**..................... AdrianTNicholls 2 82
(D Nicholls) *prom: rdn along over 2f out: sn drvn and edgd lft: wknd* **16/1**

6053 **13** *shd* **Fathom Five (IRE)**[7] 6843 5-8-11 **93**................................ AlanMunro 14 85
(C F Wall) *cl up: edgd lft over 3f out: rdn over 2f out: drvn and wknd wl over 1f out* **14/1**

0034 **14** *hd* **Equuleus Pictor**[7] 6843 5-8-5 **87**........................ JimmyQuinn 18 78
(J L Spearing) *in tch on wd outside: hdwy to chse ldrs 2f out: sn rdn and wknd appr fnl f* **16/1**

6000 **15** *nk* **Hamish McGonagall**[14] 6678 4-8-8 **95**.................... BMcHugh(5) 12 85
(T D Easterby) *in tch whn n.m.r and checked over 3f out: sn rdn and n.d* **12/1**

3000 **16** *1* **Northern Dare (IRE)**[7] 6843 5-8-6 **88**............................ EddieAhern 20 75
(D Nicholls) *a towards rr* **16/1**

2541 **17** *1 ¾* **The Nifty Fox**[7] 6843 5-8-8 **90**...................................... DavidAllan 4 70
(T D Easterby) *nvr bttr than midfield* **14/1**

11-1 **18** *2 ½* **Rulesn'regulations**[29] 6240 3-8-9 **91**............................... KFallon 1 62
(Matthew Salaman) *dwlt: in tch on wd outside: rdn along over 2f out and sn wknd* **10/1**[3]

00 **19** *¾* **Canadian Danehill (IRE)**[63] 5263 7-8-11 **93**.................(p) PatCosgrave 8 62
(R M H Cowell) *nvr nr ldrs* **66/1**

0040 **20** *10* **Matsunosuke**[23] 6427 7-8-13 **95**............................... KJManning 3 28
(A B Coogan) *in tch: effrt over 2f out: sn rdn and wknd* **50/1**

59.60 secs (-0.90) **Going Correction** +0.05s/f (Good) **20** Ran SP% **128.9**
Speed ratings (Par 109): **109,108,107,106,105 105,104,104,104,102 101,101,101,101,100 99,96,92,91,75**
toteswingers: 1&2 £144.40, 1&3 £49.40, 2&3 £96.20 CSF £302.66 CT £6383.60 TOTE £11.70: £3.10, £7.40, £4.10, £2.90; EX 734.10 TRIFECTA Not won..
Owner Morebrooke Ltd **Bred** Desmond Monaghan **Trained** Musley Bank, N Yorks
■ Stewards' Enquiry : David Probert two-day ban: careless riding (Nov 7, 9)

FOCUS
A very competitive sprint handicap on the face of it and again the field came up the centre of the track, but remarkably very few ever managed to get into it. The winner produced a personal best and fared best of the prominent racers.

NOTEBOOK
Quest For Success(IRE), reappearing just three days after finishing behind Invincible Lad on the Southwell Fibresand, was trying the minimum trip for the first time since his racecourse debut and it worked a treat. Well backed, he was always up with the pace and, once taking over in front 1f out, the race was in the bag. He was 19lb higher than when winning over 7f on the Friday of this fixture last year, which shows how much he has improved, and it will be interesting to see if he can find another race over this trip before the turf seasons ends. (op 12-1)
Excusez Moi(USA), below form in recent months, was always likely to find things happening too quickly for him and the last thing he needed was to miss the break. However, he finished with a real rattle to snatch second and was catching the winner at the line. He is very hard to predict and there is no guarantee he will repeat this next time.
Waffle(IRE) ◆, lightly raced this season and making his handicap debut, was another to finish in good style having been held up early. He remains unexposed and may have even more to offer as a 4-y-o. (op 25-1 tchd 20-1)
Fullandby(IRE), back down in trip, fluffed the start and was soon being ridden along to go the pace, but he finished in decent style. He hasn't proved very consistent so far this season. (op 12-1 tchd 14-1)
Parisian Pyramid(IRE), whose only previous win came in August of last year, didn't find his stride until too late and ideally needs further. (op 20-1)
Captain Gerrard(IRE), a long way below his best of late including when dropped into a handicap last time, made much of the running and, though he couldn't respond once headed, this was a bit better.
Judge 'n Jury, 5lb lower than when winning this race last year, was in the firing line for a long way and ran his race. Official explanation: jockey said gelding hung left (op 11-1 tchd 9-1)
River Falcon, a staying-on seventh over a furlong further here the previous day, was another not to get going until it was far too late, and he hasn't won in well over two years. (op 20-1)
Invincible Lad(IRE), running well on Fibresand lately, was back down to his best trip, but could only plug on after coming off the bridle at halfway. He is currently 13lb higher than for his last win on turf. (op 10-1)
Cheveton, back down to the trip over which he has gained all seven of his career victories, should have appreciated the softening ground but although he was close to the pace early, he was under serious pressure just after halfway and dropped out. He is currently 6lb above his highest winning mark on turf and that may be the problem. (op 9-1)
Rulesn'regulations Official explanation: jockey said colt was unsuited by the good to soft ground
Matsunosuke Official explanation: jockey said gelding lost its action final 2f

7016 RACINGPOSTPOKER.COM STKS REGISTERED AS THE DONCASTER STAKES (LISTED RACE) 6f

2:55 (2:59) (Class 1) 2-Y-O **£20,741** (£7,843; £3,920; £1,960) **Stalls** High

Form RPR

1011 **1** **Layla's Hero (IRE)**[14] 6677 2-9-4 103................................ EddieAhern 4 105
(D Nicholls) *in tch: pushed along after 2f: hdwy to ld over 1f out: rdn and hld on wl fnl f* **13/8**[1]

1404 **2** *hd* **Singeur (IRE)**[14] 6677 2-9-1 93................................ DanielTudhope 2 101
(R Bastiman) *s.i.s: hld up: hdwy to chse wnr 1f out: kpt on u.p towards fin* **16/1**

211 **3** *nk* **Citrus Star (USA)**[19] 6550 2-9-1 99............................... AlanMunro 1 100
(C F Wall) *t.k.h: trckd ldrs: effrt 2f out: kpt on fnl f: hld nr fin* **7/2**[3]

6540 **4** *2 ¾* **Archers Road (IRE)**[14] 6677 2-9-1 97.................................... KFallon 8 92
(M R Channon) *cl up: led over 2f out to over 1f out: one pce u.p fnl f* **16/1**

3436 **5** *nk* **Colonel Mak**[35] 6105 2-9-1 92............................... PhillipMakin 6 91
(D H Brown) *hld up in tch: effrt over 2f out: one pce fnl f* **18/1**

3361 **6** *hd* **Corporal Maddox**[14] 6663 2-9-4 105............................. TPQueally 9 94+
(H R A Cecil) *dwlt: hld up: stdy hdwy over 2f out: sn drvn: one pce appr fnl f* **3/1**[2]

1 **7** *nk* **Tropical Treat**[103] 3918 2-8-10 0.................................. PatCosgrave 7 85
(R M Beckett) *trckd ldrs tl rdn and no ex over 1f out* **14/1**

4 **8** *3 ½* **Tomatin**[9] 6802 2-9-1 0.. RichardMullen 10 80
(P W Chapple-Hyam) *in tch: drvn and outpcd over 2f out: n.d after* **25/1**

2430 **9** *8* **Walkingonthemoon**[21] 6486 2-9-1 95............................ RichardSmith 11 55
(Tom Dascombe) *led 2f: cl up tl rdn and wknd over 2f out* **28/1**

324 **10** *7* **Al Naouwee (USA)**[29] 6254 2-9-1 79............................ RoystonFfrench 3 59
(B Smart) *t.k.h: led after 2f to over 2f out: sn hung lft and wknd: eased whn btn fr over 1f out* **66/1**

1m 14.21s (0.61) **Going Correction** +0.05s/f (Good) **10** Ran SP% **117.8**
Speed ratings (Par 103): **97,96,96,92,92 91,91,86,76,66**
toteswingers: 1&2 £5.50, 1&3 £3.10, 2&3 £17.90. CSF £31.57 TOTE £2.50: £1.30, £4.30, £1.60; EX 32.00 Trifecta £174.00 Pool: £1302.68 - 5.54 winning units..
Owner Dr Marwan Koukash **Bred** Epona Bloodstock Ltd **Trained** Sessay, N Yorks

FOCUS
A fair Listed race for juveniles run at a good pace and the main action unfolded towards the far side of the track, though to be fair the winner and third were rather carried there by the weakening and hanging Al Naouwee. Solid form with the winner going from strength to strength.

NOTEBOOK
Layla's Hero(IRE), who successfully stepped up to this level at York earlier this month when he had two of today's rivals behind, took a while to hit top stride and wasn't helped by being carried right over towards the far rail passing the 2f pole, but he still managed to produce a telling turn of foot to hit the front 1f out and kept on to win with little to spare. His trainer thinks he will stay 7f next year. (op 7-4 tchd 11-8)
Singeur(IRE) had looked held since stepping up into Listed company, including behind Layla's Hero at York last time, but he ran a blinder here. Not best away, he was soon being niggled to stay in touch, but he put in a strong effort to join the leaders 1f out and looked likely to score. However, despite trying hard, he could never quite get the better of the winner and it may be that this trip on the slowest ground he has encountered is right on the limit of his stamina. (op 20-1 tchd 25-1)
Citrus Star(USA), a progressive sort over 5f trying this trip for the first time, had to switch to the far side to avoid a weakening rival, but he had every chance and never stopped trying. (op 11-4)
Archers Road(IRE) was a long way behind Layla's Hero on his first attempt at the trip at York, but he ran well for a long way here. He was having his 16th outing of the campaign and was runner-up in the Brocklesby, so is as tough as old boots. (op 20-1 tchd 14-1)
Colonel Mak didn't run too badly considering he had a bit to find at this level, but lacks the scope of a few of these. (op 20-1 tchd 22-1 and 16-1)
Corporal Maddox, back down in trip after making a successful debut for the yard over 7f at Ascot earlier this month, missed the break and, though he tried to get into the race coming to the last 2f, he never really looked like taking a hand. Official explanation: jockey said colt missed the break (op 9-2)
Tropical Treat, not seen since making a winning debut in a Windsor maiden in July that has worked out quite well, was keen enough in a handy position early and was eventually put in her place, but she was entitled to need it and should be a better filly next season. (op 12-1)
Al Naouwee(USA) Official explanation: jockey said colt hung left-handed throughout

7017 RACING POST TROPHY (GROUP 1) 1m (S)

3:30 (3:32) (Class 1) 2-Y-O
£113,540 (£43,040; £21,540; £10,740; £5,380; £2,700) **Stalls** High

Form RPR

1 **1** **St Nicholas Abbey (IRE)**[27] 6318 2-9-0 0............................ JMurtagh 9 123+
(A P O'Brien, Ire) *hld up in rr: smooth hdwy over 2f out: effrt to ld appr fnl f: pushed along and sn qcknd clr* **13/8**[1]

11 **2** *3 ¾* **Elusive Pimpernel (USA)**[67] 5133 2-9-0 101................... EddieAhern 8 115
(J L Dunlop) *in tch: hdwy over 2f out: swtchd rt and effrt over 1f out: sn ev ch: rdn ent fnl f: kpt on: no ch w wnr* **4/1**[2]

11 **3** *2 ½* **Al Zir (USA)**[43] 5827 2-9-0 112.. LDettori 2 109
(Saeed Bin Suroor) *stdd s and trckd ldrs: hdwy 1/2-way: rdn and ev ch 2f out: sn drvn and kpt on same pce ent fnl f* **9/2**[3]

21 **4** *nk* **Dancing David (IRE)**[16] 6620 2-9-0 91............................ MartinDwyer 5 109
(B J Meehan) *trckd ldrs: pushed along wl over 2f out: rdn wl over 1f out: sn drvn and one pce appr fnl f* **12/1**

221 **5** *1 ¼* **Morana (IRE)**[14] 6664 2-9-0 107...................................... AlanMunro 10 106
(P W Chapple-Hyam) *t.k.h early: hld up towards rr: hdwy over 2f out: sn rdn and no imp appr fnl f* **18/1**

5311 **6** *nk* **Shakespearean (IRE)**[27] 6319 2-9-0 105........................... JoeFanning 7 105
(M Johnston) *led 2f: cl up tl rdn to ld again 2f out: sn drvn and hdd over 1f out: wknd ent fnl f* **14/1**

41 **7** *2* **Hanson'D (IRE)**[36] 6046 2-9-0 85.. NCallan 11 101
(K A Ryan) *prom: pushed along over 2f out: sn rdn and wknd wl over 1f out* **50/1**

311 **8** *¾* **Al Ghazal (USA)**[18] 6569 2-9-0 90.. AhmedAjtebi 4 100
(Saeed Bin Suroor) *cl up: led after 2f: rdn along 3f out: hdd and drvn 2f out: wknd appr fnl f* **40/1**

21 **9** *½* **Musaafer (IRE)**[30] 6235 2-9-0 95.. RHills 6 98
(M A Jarvis) *plld hrd: hld up in tch: effrt over 2f out: sn rdn and btn* **25/1**

1 **10** *2 ½* **Coordinated Cut (IRE)**[44] 5793 2-9-0 0.................................. KFallon 3 93
(P W Chapple-Hyam) *in tch on outer: rdn along over 2f out and sn wknd* **11/1**

11 *10* **Elusive Award (USA)**[48] 5701 2-9-0 0............................. KJManning 12 71
(Andrew Oliver, Ire) *in tch on outer: rdn along wl over 2f out and sn wknd* **50/1**

1m 39.62s (0.32) **Going Correction** +0.05s/f (Good) **11** Ran SP% **114.4**
Speed ratings (Par 109): **100,96,93,93,92 91,89,89,88,86 76**
toteswingers: 1&2 £4.10, 1&3 £2.70, 2&3 £6.60. CSF £7.24 TOTE £2.40: £1.40, £2.00, £2.00; EX 9.00 Trifecta £58.30 Pool: £44,190.02 - 560.01 winning units..
Owner D Smith, Mrs J Magnier, M Tabor **Bred** Barton Bloodstock & Villiers S **Trained** Ballydoyle, Co Tipperary
■ Stewards' Enquiry : Ahmed Ajtebi caution: allowed colt to coast home with no assistance

FOCUS
A race with a rich tradition of producing Classic winners with the Derby heroes High Chaparral (2001), Motivator (2004) and Authorized (at Newbury in 2006) all successful within the past 10 years, while the St Leger winner Brian Boru won it in 2002 and the subsequent French 2,000 Guineas winner American Post landed the contest the following year. This year's renewal probably took on even more significance than usual with the result of the Dewhurst the previous week muddying the waters rather than clarifying the 2-y-o pecking order, and the presence of the first four in the betting for next year's Derby added extra spice. All 11 runners had been successful in their most recent starts, five came into the race unbeaten, while four had already been successful at Group level. St Nicholas Abbey was most impressive and is rated the best winner of this since Celtic Swing in 1994. The overall form looks pretty solid.

NOTEBOOK
St Nicholas Abbey(IRE) ◆, one of six from the yard entered at the five-day stage and favourite for next year's Derby before the off, looked very much the one to beat after his two victories over this trip at the Curragh and he seemed to win the Group 2 Beresford Stakes last time with a lot more in hand than the winning margin would suggest. The rain here was never going to bother him and, despite getting a little edgy beforehand, he put up a performance that had to be seen to be believed. Johnny Murtagh was very happy to switch him right off out the back of the field from the start and he stayed there for most of the journey, but he travelled like a dream and it always looked as though his rider expected him to produce something special when the colt was asked. That is just what happened, as when he was delivered between the Godolphin pair to lead over 1f out, he then produced an absolutely devastating turn of foot to pull clear and win going away. He was immediately given quotes of between 5-2 and 3-1 for next year's Derby and is between 3-1 and 7-2 favourite for the 2000 Guineas. Provided he winters well, it's hard to imagine anything improving past him between now and then. (op 15-8)

Elusive Pimpernel(USA) ◆, encountering easy ground for the first time, had been given a short break since his victory in the Acomb at York in August and the form of that race, and the maiden he won on his Newmarket debut, have been handsomely advertised since. The way he won both contests strongly suggested that this extra furlong would suit and he was duly held up off the pace, with the favourite in his slipstream. Switched to make his effort towards the near side over 1f out just as the winner was being delivered towards the far side, he stayed on well to finish a clear second, but was blown away by his rival's turn of foot. His trainer had made no secret of the fact that he expected him to be a better horse next year, and while it seems inconceivable that he will ever beat a fit-and-well St Nicholas Abbey, he will surely win some decent races over further next year. (op 9-2)

Al Zir(USA) ◆ was still something of an unknown factor coming into this after easy victories in a Newmarket maiden and from two rivals in a conditions event here last month. The extra furlong was never going to be a problem, but this was a big step up in class. Soon tucked in from his low draw, he was bang there 1f out but, like everything else, was made to look very pedestrian by the winner. He remains a nice prospect, though. (op 5-1)

Dancing David(IRE) ◆, representing last year's winning stable and whose recent Salisbury win was given a boost with the victory of the runner-up Tamaathul here on Friday, raced handily but looked likely to drop out when getting outpaced 2f out. However, he then stayed on again to finish a very creditable fourth and looks a nice sort for next year. (op 14-1)

Morana(IRE) appeared to be the stable's second string, despite his victory in the Group 3 Autumn Stakes over this trip at Ascot a fortnight earlier. He was trying to make an effort when having a bit of trouble getting through between Hanson'd and the stands' rail, but it probably didn't make that much difference. This was still a good effort. (op 20-1)

Shakespearean(IRE) came into this in good heart following victories in the Solario and the Goffs Million Mile, in which his winning time was nearly three seconds faster than St Nicholas Abbey in the Beresford earlier on the same card. He helped force the pace from the start, but once the challengers arrived over 1f out he had little left to offer. (tchd 16-1)

Hanson'D(IRE) looked a nice sort when slamming a 68-rated rival by 6l on his second start at Ayr last month, but even that form left him with a mountain to climb here so under the circumstances this was a very commendable effort. He will find easier opportunities. (op 66-1)

Al Ghazal(USA), winner of his last two starts but officially rated 22lb inferior to his stable-companion Al Zir, showed to the fore until coming to the end of his tether over 1f out. (op 33-1)

Musaafer(IRE) ◆, another taking a major step up in class after thrashing a 76-rated rival by 6l in a Pontefract maiden last month, was keen enough and never got into the race, but he should be a better horse next year. (op 20-1)

Coordinated Cut(IRE), weak in the market beforehand, was the disappointment of the race. He was something of a talking horse even before he made a winning debut over C&D last month, but that form has been made to look ordinary since, and he was being asked a totally different question at this level. Held up towards the outside of the field, he came off the bridle fully 3f out and there was no response. He is surely better than this and we should see that next season. (op 8-1)

Elusive Award(USA), who only cost 7,000gns as a yearling, has more than repaid that after narrow victories in a Leopardstown maiden and a Dundalk conditions event, but he faced a very stiff task at this level and found it all too much. Official explanation: jockey said colt lost its action in last 2f

7018 RICHARD BONEY JAMES HONE MEMORIAL H'CAP — 1m 4f

4:05 (4:06) (Class 3) (0-95,95) 3-Y-O+ — **£7,771** (£2,312; £1,155; £577) **Stalls** Low

Form	Pos	Dist	Horse	RPR
6652	**1**		**Hunterview**[21] 6470 3-8-7 **86** ....(b) RHills 1 (M A Jarvis) *mde all: rdn along 3f out: drvn over 1f out: styd on gamely fnl f* **6/1**[2]	98
103	**2**	1 ¾	**Hillview Boy (IRE)**[37] 6013 5-9-1 **87** .... DanielTudhope 10 (J S Goldie) *hld up towards rr: hdwy over 3f out: effrt on inner to chse ldrs 2f out and sn rdn: drvn to chse wnr ent fnl f: kpt on* **7/1**[3]	96+
0016	**3**	1 ¾	**Alcalde**[9] 6795 3-8-10 **89** .... RoystonFfrench 2 (M Johnston) *trckd wnr: effrt 3f out: rdn along over 2f out: drvn over 1f out: kpt on same pce* **12/1**	95
441	**4**	shd	**Ellmau**[17] 6594 4-8-13 **85** .... RichardMullen 4 (E S McMahon) *prom: effrt over 2f out and sn rdn: drvn wl over 1f out and kpt on same pce* **14/1**	91
6615	**5**	5	**Amanda Carter**[23] 6412 5-8-11 **86** .... FrederikTylicki(3) 9 (R A Fahey) *midfield: hdwy to chse ldrs over 3f out: rdn along wl over 2f out: drvn and edgd lft wl over 1f out: sn no imp* **16/1**	84
3000	**6**	shd	**Magicalmysterytour (IRE)**[14] 6662 6-9-6 **95** .... NCallan 6 (W J Musson) *hld up: hdwy over 3f out: rdn 2f out: drvn and kpt on appr fnl f: nt rch ldrs* **10/1**	93
0302	**7**	4 ½	**Howdigo**[12] 6724 4-8-13 **85** .... RobertWinston 15 (J R Best) *hld up towards rr: hdwy over 3f out: rdn along over 2f out: nt rch ldrs* **12/1**	76
4062	**8**	nse	**Spring Jim**[37] 6036 8-9-1 **87** .... JMurtagh 11 (J R Fanshawe) *hld up towards rr: hdwy over 3f out: swtchd rt and rdn over 2f out: sn no further prog* **9/2**[1]	78
2005	**9**	6	**King Olav (UAE)**[15] 6648 4-8-10 **82** .... DavidProbert 13 (A W Carroll) *prom: rdn along 3f out: drvn over 2f out and sn wknd* **66/1**	63
011	**10**	6	**Lochiel**[21] 6483 5-9-7 **93** .... KFallon 8 (G A Swinbank) *hld up towards rr: hdwy on outer over 3f out: in tch and rdn over 2f out: sn wknd* **7/1**[3]	64
0430	**11**	3 ¼	**Heron Bay**[50] 5641 5-9-7 **93** .... AlanMunro 7 (C F Wall) *in tch: hdwy to chse ldrs over 4f out: rdn along over 3f out and sn wknd* **16/1**	59
0420	**12**	4	**Snoqualmie Boy**[6] 6878 6-9-1 **87** .... MartinDwyer 5 (T P Tate) *hld up: a in rr* **22/1**	47
0044	**13**	13	**Camps Bay (USA)**[8] 6816 5-9-3 **89** ....(p) TPQueally 14 (Mrs A J Perrett) *in tch: hdwy to chse ldrs over 4f out and sn rdn: drvn over 3f out and sn wknd* **16/1**	28
15-0	**14**	19	**Cape Tribulation**[147] 2486 5-8-13 **85** .... TomEaves 3 (J M Jefferson) *midfield: rdn along 1/2-way: sn lost pl and bhd fnl 3f* **14/1**	—
000-	**P**		**Greek Envoy**[350] 7244 5-9-0 **86** .... MickyFenton 12 (T P Tate) *a in rr: rdn along and lost tch 4f out: bhd whn lost action and p.u 2f out* **25/1**	—

2m 32.82s (-2.28) **Going Correction** +0.05s/f (Good)
WFA 3 from 4yo+ 7lb — **15** Ran SP% **122.6**
Speed ratings (Par 107): **109,107,106,106,103 103,100,100,96,92 90,87,78,66,—**
toteswingers: 1&2 £9.00, 1&3 £11.00, 2&3 £67.00. CSF £47.35 CT £501.56 TOTE £7.40: £2.70, £2.70, £5.20; EX 38.00 TRIFECTA Not won..
Owner Sheikh Ahmed Al Maktoum **Bred** Darley **Trained** Newmarket, Suffolk

FOCUS

This was a good handicap for the grade, but the pace was very modest which proved a major advantage to the pacesetters. The field gave the inside rail a wide berth turning into the straight and they came down the middle. The winner is rated up 2lb and the runner-up did much the best of those coming from the rear.

NOTEBOOK

Hunterview made every yard and his jockey judged the fractions perfectly. A winner on soft ground and on Fibresand before today, these conditions proved right up his street. He is now due to go to the sales. (op 13-2)

Hillview Boy(IRE) ◆, still 7lb higher than when winning over 1m2f on soft ground here in August, was the only one in this field to make any sort of impression from off the pace, but he could never quite get to the winner. His two wins on the Flat have been over shorter, but he is a bumper winner and stamina wasn't an issue here. (op 13-2 tchd 6-1)

Alcalde, back up in trip and with the ground in his favour, was always in a good position in a steadily run race, but he lacked the turn of foot required to get the better of the winner. This was a fair effort, but he may have been flattered by the way the race was run and he hasn't always looked the easiest of rides. (op 10-1)

Ellmau ◆, 3lb higher than when winning over a shorter trip at Nottingham earlier this month, was another to benefit from racing handily and he had every chance. He is unbeaten in two previous tries on Fibresand, so is very much one to look out for if returned to that surface in the next few weeks. (op 16-1)

Amanda Carter moved into a challenging position turning for home, but could make little impression and tended to hang inside the last 2f. Her best form has come on quicker ground and she still looks on a stiff mark.

Magicalmysterytour(IRE) had been disappointing lately, but he had conditions in his favour here and attracted market support. However, he ideally needed a strong pace to run at and when he didn't get it, all he could do was stay on late without offering a threat. (op 14-1)

Spring Jim, whose second to Akmal at Yarmouth last month looks very smart form now, was sent off a well-backed favourite, but he could never get into the race from off the pace. The ground shouldn't have been a problem. (op 13-2 tchd 7-1 in a place)

Greek Envoy Official explanation: jockey said gelding lost its action but returned sound

7019 ROBINHOODAIRPORT.COM CONDITIONS STKS — 7f

4:40 (4:42) (Class 2) 3-Y-O+
£12,462 (£3,732; £1,866; £934; £466; £234) **Stalls** High

Form	Pos	Dist	Horse	RPR
3002	**1**		**Mia's Boy**[37] 6030 5-8-11 104 .... EddieAhern 12 (C A Dwyer) *hld up: nt clr run over 2f out: squeezed through over 1f out: led ins fnl f: rdn out* **4/1**[2]	111
53-5	**2**	1 ¼	**Young Pretender (FR)**[22] 6448 4-8-11 107 .... LDettori 3 (Saeed Bin Suroor) *dwlt: sn trcking centre ldr: hdwy and overall ldr over 1f out: edgd rt and hdd ins fnl f: kpt on* **2/1**[1]	108
2006	**3**	shd	**Captain Brilliance (USA)**[22] 6448 4-8-11 101 ....(v[1]) TPQueally 8 (J Noseda) *hld up in midfield: hdwy to chse ldrs over 1f out: kpt on ins fnl f* **16/1**	108
3014	**4**	2 ½	**Advanced**[20] 6530 6-8-11 105 .... AmyRyan 2 (K A Ryan) *cl up: lft in ld and overall ldr in main gp over 5f out: hdd appr fnl f: kpt on same pce ins fnl f* **10/1**	101
3312	**5**	½	**Able Master (IRE)**[21] 6487 3-8-9 105 .... TomEaves 4 (B Smart) *dwlt: sn trckd centre ldrs: effrt over 2f out: kpt on same pce fnl f* **7/1**[3]	99+
3321	**6**	4	**Light From Mars**[14] 6675 4-8-11 100 .... JamesMillman 15 (B R Millman) *prom: effrt over 2f out: outpcd appr fnl f* **17/2**	89
-400	**7**	2 ¼	**Garnica (FR)**[34] 6135 6-8-11 102 .... AdrianTNicholls 11 (D Nicholls) *t.k.h: hld up: hdwy over 2f out: wknd over 1f out* **33/1**	83
-000	**8**	nse	**Protector (SAF)**[35] 6089 8-8-11 89 ....(t) PatCosgrave 10 (A G Foster) *cl up: rdn over 2f out: outpcd whn hmpd over 1f out* **33/1**	83
300	**9**	nse	**Courageous (IRE)**[90] 4352 3-8-9 98 .... RichardMullen 1 (B Smart) *t.k.h: led centre to over 1f out: sn wknd* **50/1**	81
5250	**10**	3 ½	**Pawan (IRE)**[6] 6879 9-8-11 85 .... AnnStokell 14 (Miss A Stokell) *prom tl rdn and wknd fr 2f out* **100/1**	73
1100	**11**	2 ¼	**Golden Desert (IRE)**[14] 6661 5-8-11 104 .... AlanMunro 5 (T G Mills) *t.k.h: prom: effrt and rdn over 2f out: wknd over 1f out* **14/1**	67
5530	**12**	20	**Appalachian Trail (IRE)**[14] 6675 8-8-11 97 ....(b) FrederikTylicki 6 (I Semple) *hld up in tch: bdly hmpd over 5f out: nt rcvr: lost tch over 2f out* **20/1**	13+
6010	**P**		**Welsh Emperor (IRE)**[21] 6503 10-9-4 105 ....(b) MickyFenton 13 (T P Tate) *led tl struck into and p.u over 5f out* **22/1**	—
2432	**U**		**Cyflymder (IRE)**[42] 5855 3-8-9 98 .... PatDobbs 7 (R Hannon) *cl up whn bdly hmpd and uns rdr over 5f out* **22/1**	—

1m 26.94s (0.64) **Going Correction** +0.05s/f (Good)
WFA 3 from 4yo+ 2lb — **14** Ran SP% **120.3**
Speed ratings (Par 109): **98,96,96,93,93 88,85,85,85,81 79,56,—,—**
toteswingers: 1&2 £2.80, 1&3 £17.90, 2&3 £14.10. CSF £11.32 TOTE £5.00: £2.30, £1.50, £4.90; EX 15.70 Trifecta £265.60 Pool: £782.70 - 2.18 winning units..
Owner Iraj Parvizi **Bred** Sir Eric Parker **Trained** Burrough Green, Cambs
■ Stewards' Enquiry : Amy Ryan one-day ban: failed to keep straight from stalls (Nov 7)

FOCUS

A decent conditions event, but one marred by an incident after more than a furlong when the leader Welsh Emperor lost his action and was immediately pulled up, in the process hampering Cyflymder who lost his rider, and also hampering Appalachian Trail, whose chance was ended there and then. The winner is rated back to his best but it is unwise to be too positive about late-season conditions form.

NOTEBOOK

Mia's Boy was without a win since May of last year, but his recent second to Gitano Hernando on the Wolverhampton Polytrack looks very good form now. Held up early, he had to wait for the gaps to appear but when they did he quickened up in very impressive style. He may turn out again soon in a Nottingham conditions event and next year's Lincoln, in which he finished fourth this year, would seem a suitable longer-term target. (op 5-1)

Young Pretender(FR), who ran really well in a Newmarket Group 3 on his return from a long layoff earlier this month, tracked the pace down the centre of the track and looked likely to score when taking it up over 1f out, but the winner's turn of foot proved too much. Perhaps this came a little quick and maybe the easing ground was against him. (op 11-4)

Captain Brilliance(USA), almost 3l behind Young Pretender at Newmarket last time, ran much better here in the first time visor and, having had every chance, finished much closer to his old rival this time. This was the slowest ground he had encountered, so he deserves plenty of credit. (op 12-1)

Advanced ran yet another fine race from the front and he seems as good as ever, but his current mark of 105 means that he will remain difficult to place. (op 8-1)

Able Master(IRE), back down in trip after being narrowly denied in a Listed race over a furlong further last time, wouldn't have minded this easier ground and he ran another solid race down the centre of the track. (op 6-1 tchd 11-2)

Light From Mars showed up for a long way towards the nearside of the track, but found this tougher on this step up from handicap company. (op 9-1)

Welsh Emperor(IRE), happily, was reported fine afterwards. (op 20-1 tchd 25-1)

7020 LINCOLN RESTAURANT H'CAP (DIV II) — 1m 2f 60y

5:15 (5:15) (Class 4) (0-80,80) 3-Y-O+ — **£4,857** (£1,445; £722; £360) **Stalls** Low

Form	Pos	Dist	Horse	RPR
3150	**1**		**Racing Hero (IRE)**[17] 6583 3-8-13 **75** .... LDettori 1 (J Noseda) *mde all: pushed along wl over 2f out: rdn over 1f out and styd on strly ins fnl f* **5/1**[2]	91+
R444	**2**	4	**Inspirina (IRE)**[18] 6560 5-8-10 **67** .... TonyHamilton 4 (R Ford) *trckd ldrs: hdwy 3f out: chal 2f out and ev ch tl rdn: edgd lft and one pce appr fnl f* **15/2**	73

-164 **3** *2 1/4* **Beau Fighter**[78] 4737 4-9-1 **72** .... KFallon 5 74
(C F Wall) *hld up in tch: hdwy over 3f out: rdn to chse ldrs wl over 1f out: sn edgd lft and no imp* **13/8**[1]

1506 **4** *1 1/4* **Upton Seas**[3] 6951 3-8-12 **74** .... PhillipMakin 8 73
(M W Easterby) *towards rr: hdwy on outer over 3f out: rdn along over 2f out: drvn and kpt on appr fnl f: nt rch ldrs* **16/1**

3061 **5** *2* **Jawaab (IRE)**[54] 5532 5-9-7 **78** .... RichardMullen 9 74
(Mark Buckley) *hld up: hdwy over 3f out: rdn to chse ldrs over 2f out: sn drvn and btn* **8/1**

01-0 **6** *1 1/2* **Maria Di Scozia**[137] 2796 4-9-6 **77** .... (t) AlanMunro 3 70
(P W Chapple-Hyam) *chsd wnr: rdn along 3f out: drvn jst over 2f out and grad wknd* **9/1**

1064 **7** *9* **Highkingofireland**[98] 4074 3-8-4 **66** .... AndrewElliott 2 42
(A P Jarvis) *chsd ldrs on inner: rdn along over 3f out: drvn over 2f out and sn wknd* **20/1**

05/1 **8** *6* **Ahmedy (IRE)**[21] 6498 6-8-13 **70** .... GrahamGibbons 10 34
(J J Quinn) *a towards rr* **11/2**[3]

2m 11.05s (-0.15) **Going Correction** +0.05s/f (Good)
WFA 3 from 4yo+ 5lb **8** Ran SP% **113.7**
Speed ratings (Par 105): **102,98,97,96,94 93,86,81**
toteswingers: 1&2 £4.70 1&3 £2.20, 2&3 £3.80. CSF £41.26 CT £85.65 TOTE £5.10: £1.90, £2.50, £1.10; EX 46.20 Trifecta £88.30 Pool: £ 914.57 - 7.66 winning units. Place 6: 100.67 Place 5: £47.81.
Owner Albert S N Hu **Bred** Lynch Bages Ltd **Trained** Newmarket, Suffolk

FOCUS
No more than a fair handicap, but again they rather gifted the race to the front-runner and the winning time was 0.68 seconds slower than division one. The winner apart the bare form is only ordinary.
T/Jkpt: Not won. T/Plt: £127.30 to a £1 stake. Pool: £116,263.51. 666.65 winning tickets. T/Qpdt: £31.50 to a £1 stake. Pool: £6,672.61. 156.40 winning tickets. JR

6970 KEMPTON (A.W) (R-H)
Saturday, October 24

OFFICIAL GOING: Standard
Wind: medium, across Weather: rain cleared, dry

7021 KEMPTON.CO.UK CLASSIFIED CLAIMING STKS 5f (P)
5:40 (5:40) (Class 6) 3-Y-O+ **£2,047** (£604; £302) **Stalls** High

Form RPR

15-3 **1** **Absa Lutte (IRE)**[14] 6670 6-8-12 65 .... (t) SJCraine 12 74+
(Patrick Morris) *trckd ldrs: clipped heels and unbalanced over 1f out: swtchd lft and qcknd to ld ins fnl f: sn clr: comf* **9/2**[2]

1506 **2** *1 3/4* **Come On Buckers (IRE)**[4] 6916 3-8-7 60 .... (b) EdwardCreighton 4 61
(E J Creighton) *chsd ldr: rdn and ev ch over 1f out: kpt on but no ch w wnr fnl 100yds* **12/1**

1P10 **3** *hd* **Kheley (IRE)**[37] 6028 3-9-0 69 .... LiamJones 9 67
(W M Brisbourne) *chsd ldrs: pushed along 1/2-way: kpt on u.p to press for 2nd fnl 75yds but no ch w wnr* **9/1**

6040 **4** *nk* **Especially Special (IRE)**[13] 6701 3-8-10 67 .... JamesDoyle 7 62+
(S Kirk) *hmpd and dropped to rr sn after s: rdn 4f out: no hdwy tl styd on strly ins fnl f: gng on fin: nt rch ldrs* **7/1**[3]

0000 **5** *hd* **Cape Royal**[9] 6791 9-9-4 68 .... (bt) KevinGhunowa 10 70
(J M Bradley) *led: rdn over 1f out: hdd ins fnl f: no ch w wnr after: lost 3 pls fnl 75yds* **4/1**[1]

0520 **6** *1* **Rebecca De Winter**[52] 5576 3-8-1 65 .... AndreaAtzeni(3) 8 52
(David Pinder) *s.i.s: a in rr: rdn and effrt wl over 1f out: kpt on but n.d* **9/2**[2]

5065 **7** *nk* **Wreningham**[22] 6456 4-8-7 59 .... TobyAtkinson(7) 5 61
(P Leech) *hmpd sn after s: in tch: rdn and unable qck wl over 1f out: one pce no ch w ldrs fnl f* **12/1**

5625 **8** *nk* **Bluebok**[31] 6205 8-8-11 61 .... (bt) JackDean(3) 11 60
(J M Bradley) *s.i.s: hdwy into midfield 1/2-way: no prog u.p over 1f out* **9/2**[2]

2100 **9** *3 3/4* **Five Gold Rings (IRE)**[122] 3281 3-9-0 65 .... ShaneKelly 6 46
(J A Osborne) *s.i.s: a detached in last* **33/1**

60.16 secs (-0.34) **Going Correction** +0.025s/f (Slow) **9** Ran SP% **115.4**
Speed ratings (Par 101): **103,100,99,99,99 97,97,96,90**
toteswingers: 1&2 £12.40, 1&3 £6.60, 2&3 £15.80 CSF £56.67 TOTE £6.30: £2.50, £4.40, £1.50; EX 77.70.
Owner I T Amond **Bred** Ian Amond **Trained** Tarporley, Cheshire
■ Stewards' Enquiry : Edward Creighton three-day ban: careless riding (Nov 7, 9, 11)

FOCUS
A modest classified event run at a sound pace. As usual over this course and distance, the prominent racers held a big edge over those attempting to come from off the pace and the winner raced just off the inside rail in the straight. The runner-up looks the best guide.
Rebecca De Winter Official explanation: trainer's rep said filly returned lame

7022 ELIZABETH JONES 90TH BIRTHDAY H'CAP 1m 2f (P)
6:10 (6:10) (Class 6) (0-60,60) 3-Y-O **£2,047** (£604; £302) **Stalls** High

Form RPR

4033 **1** **Location**[2] 6969 3-8-12 **54** .... PaulDoe 8 61
(P D Evans) *stdd s: hld up towards rr: hdwy over 2f out: swtchd lft over 1f out: str run to press ldrs ins fnl f: led nr fin* **7/2**[1]

-00U **2** *hd* **Ausonius**[10] 6784 3-8-13 **55** .... DaneO'Neill 5 62+
(L M Cumani) *in tch: hdwy to chse ldrs over 4f out: led wl over 1f out: drvn ins fnl f: kpt on wl tl hdd nr fin* **14/1**

050 **3** *nk* **Good Humoured**[75] 4843 3-9-1 **57** .... SebSanders 9 63
(Sir Mark Prescott) *t.k.h: hld up in midfield: rdn and effrt wl over 1f out: ev ch ins fnl f: kpt on wl* **17/2**

0400 **4** *2* **Kristopher James (IRE)**[13] 6705 3-8-10 **52** .... LiamJones 1 54
(W M Brisbourne) *led over 8f out tl rdn and hdd wl over 1f out: no ex ins fnl f* **28/1**

0324 **5** *1/2* **Triple Cee (IRE)**[13] 6705 3-9-4 **60** .... SamHitchcott 2 61
(M R Channon) *hld up in rr: hdwy on outer 3f out: kpt on same pce u.p over 1f out* **6/1**[3]

1056 **6** *1* **Carter**[34] 6139 3-9-1 **57** .... ShaneKelly 3 59+
(W M Brisbourne) *towards rr: nt clr run ent fnl 2f tl swtchd lft over 1f out: kpt on but nvr able to chal ldrs* **9/1**

000 **7** *1* **Lyrical Intent**[7] 6860 3-8-10 **52** .... JimmyQuinn 12 49
(P Howling) *wnt lft s and v.s.a: hld up in last: hdwy on outer over 2f out: styd on fnl f: nvr trbld ldrs* **25/1**

5030 **8** *1* **Dream On Connie**[18] 6570 3-8-11 **53** .... (p) JimCrowley 4 48
(W J Knight) *chsd ldrs: wnt 2nd 7f out tl 2f out: wknd u.p over 1f out* **10/1**

-005 **9** *1 1/2* **Red Horse (IRE)**[18] 6570 3-8-10 **52** .... HayleyTurner 14 44
(M L W Bell) *t.k.h: chsd ldrs: rdn over 2f out: unable qck and n.m.r wl over 1f out: n.d fnl f* **8/1**

5502 **10** *1 1/2* **Chanrossa (IRE)**[22] 6440 3-9-2 **58** .... TGMcLaughlin 13 47
(E A L Dunlop) *in tch: rdn over 2f out: losing pl whn n.m.r over 1f out: n.d fnl f* **4/1**[2]

00-0 **11** *1* **Marjury Daw (IRE)**[45] 5775 3-8-10 **52** .... J-PGuillambert 6 39
(J G Given) *led tl over 8f out: steadily lost pl: bhd whn swtchd lft over 1f out* **16/1**

0400 **12** *1 1/2* **Quick Single (USA)**[13] 6701 3-8-10 **55** .... KellyHarrison(3) 10 39
(P S McEntee) *hld up in rr: nvr a factor* **40/1**

2m 7.61s (-0.39) **Going Correction** +0.025s/f (Slow) **12** Ran SP% **119.5**
Speed ratings (Par 99): **102,101,101,100,99 98,98,97,96,94 94,92**
toteswingers: 1&2 £25.20, 1&3 £5.70, 2&3 £54.30 CSF £53.29 CT £395.22 TOTE £4.40: £1.30, £5.60, £2.00; EX 108.00.
Owner R Edwards, S Howell & J Swinnerton **Bred** Juddmonte Farms Ltd **Trained** Pandy, Monmouths

FOCUS
A moderate handicap in which the gallop was ordinary at best. The winner raced in the centre in the straight. Sound if limited form.
Lyrical Intent Official explanation: jockey said gelding was slowly away
Marjury Daw(IRE) Official explanation: jockey said filly was denied a clear run

7023 TRY OUR NEW BISTRO MENU APPRENTICE H'CAP 6f (P)
6:40 (6:40) (Class 5) (0-70,70) 4-Y-O+ **£2,590** (£770; £385; £192) **Stalls** High

Form RPR

5 **1** **Todber**[15] 6632 4-8-9 **65** .... (v) KatiaScallan(5) 4 78+
(M P Tregoning) *hld up towards rr on outer: hdwy and edgd rt over 2f out: chsd ldr and hanging rt ent fnl 2f: led over 1f out: r.o strly* **5/1**[1]

05-3 **2** *1 3/4* **Braddock (IRE)**[39] 6086 6-8-10 **66** .... (t) JakePayne(5) 3 73
(S Donohoe, Ire) *led: rdn and edgd lft over 2f out: hdd over 1f out: nvr gng pce of wnr ins fnl f* **5/1**[1]

1226 **3** *2 1/2* **Ghost Dancer**[17] 6596 5-9-2 **70** .... (p) RyanPowell(3) 5 69
(J M Bradley) *stdd s: hld up in last: swtchd to outer and effrt over 2f out: kpt on to go 3rd ins fnl f: no ch w ldng pair* **11/2**[2]

1600 **4** *1* **Downhill Skier (IRE)**[17] 6596 5-8-13 **64** .... KierenFox 10 60
(W M Brisbourne) *hld up in rr: effrt on inner over 2f out: kpt on to go 4th ins fnl f: nvr trbld ldrs* **6/1**[3]

6000 **5** *4* **Grand Palace (IRE)**[8] 6825 6-8-9 **60** .... (v) DavidKenny 9 43
(H J Evans) *in tch: rdn to dispute 2nd jst over 2f out: outpcd over 1f out: wknd fnl f* **8/1**

0340 **6** *1 1/2* **Espy**[12] 6738 4-9-1 **66** .... RichardRowe 6 44
(S Kirk) *in tch: effrt to dispute 2nd jst over 2f out: sn outpcd u.p: wknd fnl f* **5/1**[1]

6001 **7** *4* **Sam's Cross (IRE)**[24] 6377 4-8-9 **63** .... RyanClark(3) 2 28
(J J Bridger) *chsd ldr tl over 2f out: sn struggling u.p: wl bhd over 1f out* **7/1**

2000 **8** *2 1/4* **Joss Stick**[5] 6904 4-8-0 **56** oh1 .... (b) DannyBrock(5) 1 14
(J J Bridger) *t.k.h: chsd ldrs tl 1/2-way: wl bhd fnl 2f* **33/1**

4530 **U** **Radiator Rooney (IRE)**[144] 2564 6-8-7 **61** .... AlexEdwards(3) 7 —
(Patrick Morris) *stdd s: t.k.h: hld up in rr: clipped heels: stmbld bdly and uns rdr wl over 2f out* **12/1**

1m 12.77s (-0.33) **Going Correction** +0.025s/f (Slow) **9** Ran SP% **113.9**
Speed ratings (Par 103): **103,100,97,96,90 88,83,80,—**
toteswingers: 1&2 £5.30, 1&3 £3.30, 2&3 £7.60 CSF £29.40 CT £141.24 TOTE £4.90: £1.70, £2.00, £1.80; EX 21.90.
Owner Major & Mrs R B Kennard And Partner **Bred** Stowell Hill Ltd & Major & Mrs R B Kennard **Trained** Lambourn, Berks

FOCUS
A modest handicap run at a decent gallop and the quickest of the three races over the trip. Good form for the grade. The winner raced in the centre in the straight.
Sam's Cross(IRE) Official explanation: trainer said gelding was showing signs of abdominal pain after the race

7024 GROOMED TO PERFECTION, THE KIA SOUL MEDIAN AUCTION MAIDEN STKS 7f (P)
7:10 (7:11) (Class 6) 2-Y-O **£2,047** (£604; £302) **Stalls** High

Form RPR

6 **1** **Highland Quaich**[33] 6162 2-9-3 0 .... DaneO'Neill 4 75+
(D R C Elsworth) *t.k.h: in tch: hdwy to chse ldr over 4f out: rdn and ev ch ent fnl 2f: sustained chal fnl f to ld on post* **5/1**[2]

2 *nse* **Point Out (USA)** 2-9-3 0 .... JimmyFortune 8 75+
(J H M Gosden) *led: pressed and rdn 2f out: kpt on wl tl hdd on post* **1/1**[1]

4 **3** *2 3/4* **Plutocraft**[121] 3306 2-9-3 0 .... GeorgeBaker 5 68
(J R Fanshawe) *t.k.h: chsd ldrs: wnt 3rd 2f out: rdn and nt pce of ldng pair fnl f* **11/1**

0 **4** *1 1/4* **St Ignatius**[24] 6372 2-9-3 0 .... SebSanders 12 65
(R M Beckett) *in tch in midfield: pushed along over 3f out: rdn to chse ldrs and edgd rt jst over 2f out: outpcd by ldng pair jst over 1f out* **6/1**[3]

00 **5** *1/2* **State Visit**[28] 6285 2-9-3 0 .... (b[1]) WilliamBuick 1 64
(W R Muir) *in tch: rdn and unable qck ent fnl 2f: kpt on u.p fnl f: nt pce to chal ldrs* **25/1**

6 *1* **Hubble Space** 2-8-9 0 .... AndreaAtzeni(3) 7 56+
(M Botti) *racd in midfield: effrt and rdn over 2f out: no prog tl kpt on ins fnl f: nt pce to chal ldrs* **20/1**

00 **7** *1* **Set To Go**[12] 6728 2-9-3 0 .... SteveDrowne 14 59
(H J L Dunlop) *racd in midfield: rdn and effrt over 2f out: no real prog: edgd rt and kpt on fnl f* **100/1**

00 **8** *2 1/4* **Feel The Magic (IRE)**[16] 6607 2-8-12 0 .... JamesDoyle 10 48
(S Kirk) *towards rr: rdn and unable qck over 2f out: nvr trbld ldrs* **100/1**

9 *hd* **Chateau Zara** 2-8-12 0 .... AdamKirby 6 48+
(C G Cox) *a towards rr: rdn and struggling over 2f out: nvr trbld ldrs* **22/1**

10 *4 1/2* **Desert Recluse (IRE)** 2-9-3 0 .... DarryllHolland 9 41
(Pat Eddery) *v.s.a: rn green and sn detached in last pl: flashing tail over 2f out: past btn horses fnl f: n.d* **14/1**

00 **11** *1 3/4* **Bird On The Wire**[12] 6722 2-8-9 0 .... JackDean(3) 13 32
(W G M Turner) *chsd ldrs tl over 4f out: wknd qckly jst over 2f out* **33/1**

12 *hd* **Aintgottaname** 2-8-12 0 .... ShaneKelly 11 32
(M J McGrath) *a bhd: lost tch over 2f out: sn wl bhd* **40/1**

00 **13** *1 1/2* **Flash For Freedom (USA)**[8] 6826 2-9-0 0 .... MarcHalford(3) 3 33
(J R Best) *a bhd: lost tch and rn green u.p over 2f out: sn wl bhd* **100/1**

14 *dist* **Rusty Pelican** 2-9-3 0 .... FergusSweeney 2 —
(P J Makin) *s.i.s: a bhd and rn green: rn v wd bnd 3f out: t.o and eased fnl f* **33/1**

1m 27.66s (1.66) **Going Correction** +0.025s/f (Slow) **14** Ran SP% **120.2**
Speed ratings (Par 93): **91,90,87,86,85 84,83,80,80,75 73,73,71,—**
toteswingers: 1&2 £5.40, 1&3 £3.70, 2&3 £2.90 CSF £9.42 TOTE £6.90: £1.90, £1.10, £2.70; EX 15.30.
Owner J Wotherspoon **Bred** John Wotherspoon **Trained** Newmarket, Suffolk

FOCUS
A race lacking anything in the way of strength in depth, and no better than fair form. The pace was only fair and the first two, who raced centre to far side in the straight, pulled a few lengths clear in the closing stages.

NOTEBOOK
Highland Quaich, who showed ability at a modest level on his debut, was well supported and bettered that effort, despite dropping back in distance. The return to 1m should suit and, while he wouldn't be certain to confirm placings with the runner-up should they meet again, he is capable of better in handicaps back over 1m. (op 8-1 tchd 9-2)
Point Out(USA) ◆, a well-bred half-brother to a useful all-weather middle-distance winner, was a warm order on this debut and was just touched off after being allowed the run of the race. It will be a surprise if he does not prove to be easily the best of these and he is certain to make amends in similar company at least. (tchd 6-5)
Plutocraft, having his first run for four months and his first on an artificial surface, bettered the form of his debut. He will be well suited by the step up to 1m and will be one to keep an eye on in ordinary handicap company. (op 9-1)
St Ignatius probably ran to a similar level as on his debut over this course and distance in September. He was not knocked about and should do better in ordinary handicaps in due course. (op 11-2 tchd 13-2)
State Visit, dropping in trip and fitted with blinkers for this all-weather debut, again had his limitations exposed in maiden company but he wasn't disgraced after racing wide and may do better in run-of-the-mill handicaps. (tchd 22-1)
Hubble Space, a half-sister to a couple of winners over this trip and beyond, was easy to back but hinted at ability on this debut. She should have no problems with 1m and should be all the better for this experience. (tchd 18-1)
Desert Recluse(IRE) Official explanation: jockey said colt was slowly away
Rusty Pelican Official explanation: jockey said gelding pulled itself up in straight

7025 CAROLYN PERCHARD FABULOUS AT 50 H'CAP 2m (P)
7:40 (7:42) (Class 6) (0-65,65) 3-Y-O **£2,047** (£604; £302) **Stalls** High

Form RPR

0624 **1** **M'Lady Rousseur (IRE)**[9] 6807 3-9-1 **57** .... DaneO'Neill 2 61
(D R C Elsworth) *stdd s and dropped in bhd: rdn and hdwy on outer over 2f out: styd on wl to ld fnl 100yds: forged clr fnl 50yds* **8/1**

4451 **2** *1 3/4* **Ja One (IRE)**[10] 6785 3-9-9 **65** .... MichaelHills 3 67
(B W Hills) *hld up in last trio: rdn and gd hdwy to chse ldr over 2f out: led and edgd rt u.p over 1f out: hdd fnl 100yds: one pce* **15/8**[1]

0433 **3** *1 1/2* **Valkyrie (IRE)**[22] 6446 3-8-6 **48** .... LukeMorris 5 48
(N P Littmoden) *chsd ldrs: rdn and effrt to press ldrs jst over 2f out: no ex u.p fnl f* **7/1**

6005 **4** *nk* **Moon Money (IRE)**[18] 6559 3-8-9 **51** .... FergusSweeney 9 51
(K A Ryan) *in tch in midfield: effrt and nt clr run briefly jst over 2f out: sn rdn: kpt on u.p fnl f: unable to rch ldrs* **10/1**

5063 **5** *3/4* **Supernoverre (IRE)**[9] 6807 3-9-6 **62** .... IanMongan 7 61
(P Howling) *hld up in last pair: effrt and rdn over 2f out: no prog tl kpt on ins fnl f: nvr trbld ldrs* **5/1**[3]

4150 **6** *3* **Seminal Moment**[71] 5011 3-9-0 **56** .... SebSanders 6 51
(J G Given) *led: pushed on and clr 3f out: rdn and hdd over 1f out: sn btn* **9/1**

4340 **7** *5* **Mymateeric**[10] 6785 3-8-1 **48** ....(b) SimonPearce(5) 8 37
(J Pearce) *chsd ldng pair: rdn and struggling whn short of room on inner over 2f out: no ch fnl 2f* **9/2**[2]

-600 **8** *19* **Pezula**[24] 6371 3-8-9 **51** ow1 .... SteveDrowne 1 17
(R T Phillips) *chsd ldr: rdn over 4f out: wknd over 2f out: wl bhd and eased fnl f* **33/1**

3m 32.12s (2.02) **Going Correction** +0.025s/f (Slow) **8** Ran SP% **115.3**
Speed ratings (Par 99): **95,94,93,93,92 91,88,79**
toteswingers: 1&2 £3.70, 1&3 £3.90, 2&3 £5.00 CSF £23.67 CT £112.54 TOTE £9.30: £2.40, £1.40, £2.10; EX 28.60.
Owner Wyddial Racing **Bred** Eimear Mulhern **Trained** Newmarket, Suffolk

FOCUS
A modest handicap run at just a steady early gallop until increasing turning for home. The winner raced centre to far side in the straight. Muddling and limited form.

7026 DENISE SERVANTE'S WISH I WAS THERE H'CAP 6f (P)
8:10 (8:11) (Class 4) (0-85,84) 3-Y-O+ **£4,727** (£1,406; £702; £351) **Stalls** High

Form RPR

-000 **1** **Fantasy Explorer**[14] 6666 6-9-4 **83** .... DarryllHolland 8 94
(J J Quinn) *t.k.h: pressed ldr: pushed into ld jst over 1f out: hrd drvn fnl f: kpt on and a jst holding off runner-up* **10/1**

2-21 **2** *hd* **Hajoum (IRE)**[19] 6551 3-9-3 **83** .... TedDurcan 5 93
(Saeed Bin Suroor) *chsd ldrs: rdn and ev ch ent fnl f: kpt on u.p but nvr looked like getting up* **11/4**[1]

4004 **3** *2* **Earlsmedic**[19] 6540 4-8-12 **80** ....(v) WilliamCarson(3) 12 84
(S C Williams) *led at stdy gallop: rdn and qcknd jst over 2f out: hdd and hrd drvn jst over 1f out: kpt on same pce fnl f* **11/4**[1]

0004 **4** *1* **Drawnfromthepast (IRE)**[12] 6723 4-9-5 **84** ....(t) ShaneKelly 9 85
(J A Osborne) *t.k.h: chsd ldrs: rdn and unable qck over 2f out: kpt on same pce fr over 1f out* **10/1**

0400 **5** *nk* **Thunderous Mood (USA)**[8] 6815 3-9-0 **80** ....(b) WilliamBuick 10 80
(P F I Cole) *chsd ldng pair: rdn to press ldrs on inner 2f out: nt pce of ldng pair fnl f* **14/1**

5201 **6** *1 1/2* **Dvinsky (USA)**[12] 6726 8-8-11 **76** ....(b) IanMongan 2 71
(P Howling) *t.k.h: in tch on outer: rdn over 2f out: sn unable qck and no hdwy* **12/1**

-605 **7** *1/2* **Carved Emerald**[12] 6723 4-9-2 **81** .... DaneO'Neill 1 74+
(D R C Elsworth) *stdd s and hld up in last trio: plld out and rdn jst over 2f out: kpt on but nvr trbld ldrs* **6/1**[2]

0000 **8** *nk* **Mogok Ruby**[12] 6723 5-8-13 **78** ....(v[1]) LukeMorris 3 70
(L Montague Hall) *t.k.h: hld up in rr: rdn and effrt 2f out: no real prog and n.d* **25/1**

4 **9** *1/2* **Obe Gold**[57] 5406 7-8-10 **75** ....(v) J-PGuillambert 11 66+
(P Howling) *in tch in midfield on inner: rdn 1/2-way: struggling over 2f out: wl hld fnl f* **12/1**

0065 **10** *3/4* **Phantom Whisper**[13] 6694 6-8-13 **78** .... JimCrowley 4 66
(B R Millman) *hld up in rr: plld out and rdn over 2f out: no prog and nvr trbld ldrs* **8/1**[3]

4160 **11** *1 1/2* **Mutamared (USA)**[15] 6631 9-8-6 **78** ....(t) RosieJessop(7) 6 62
(Andrew Reid) *fly-jmpd and awkward leaving stalls: plld hrd and hld up in rr: n.d* **33/1**

0250 **12** *nk* **Harlech Castle**[102] 3956 4-9-0 **79** .... PatCosgrave 7 62
(J R Boyle) *in tch in midfield: rdn and struggling over 2f out: wl btn over 1f out* **16/1**

1m 13.11s (0.01) **Going Correction** +0.025s/f (Slow)
WFA 3 from 4yo+ 1lb **12** Ran SP% **131.6**
Speed ratings (Par 105): **100,99,97,95,95 93,92,92,91,90 88,88**
toteswingers: 1&2 £3.80, 1&3 £5.50, 2&3 £3.40 CSF £41.87 CT £106.13 TOTE £14.60: £3.50, £1.50, £1.80; EX 51.00.
Owner The Fantasy Fellowship E **Bred** Sexton Enterprises **Trained** Settrington, N Yorks

FOCUS
Mainly exposed performers in a fair handicap and an ordinary gallop saw those up with the pace holding the edge. Winner and second raced in the centre in the straight with the winner rated back to near his 3yo best.

7027 DALE BURR WIZARD OF OZ HEADMASTER H'CAP 7f (P)
8:40 (8:40) (Class 4) (0-85,85) 3-Y-O **£4,727** (£1,406; £702; £351) **Stalls** High

Form RPR

1231 **1** **Bea Menace (USA)**[19] 6537 3-8-12 **79** .... JimCrowley 7 90+
(P F I Cole) *hld up in tch: hdwy gng wl over 2f out: led wl over 1f out: sn rdn: clr ins fnl f: comf* **10/1**

051 **2** *1 3/4* **Dance And Dance (IRE)**[10] 6776 3-8-13 **85** .... MartinLane(5) 11 91
(E F Vaughan) *awkward leaving stalls and s.i.s: towards rr: swtchd lft and hdwy over 2f out: chsd wnr and drvn ent fnl f: r.o but no ch w wnr* **3/1**[1]

3602 **3** *1 3/4* **Ray Of Joy**[33] 6167 3-9-3 **84** .... JimmyQuinn 10 85
(J R Jenkins) *hld up towards rr: hdwy and rdn jst over 2f out: chsd ldng pair ent fnl f: one pce and no imp after* **14/1**

2120 **4** *3/4* **Leverage (IRE)**[10] 6776 3-9-1 **82** .... WilliamBuick 4 81
(L M Cumani) *s.i.s: hld up towards rr: shkn up and nt qckn over 2f out: rdn and hdwy over 1f out: kpt on steadily to go 4th fnl 100yds: nvr gng pce to trble ldrs* **7/1**

126 **5** *1* **Carbon Hoofprint**[41] 5914 3-9-0 **81** .... FergusSweeney 8 78
(P J Makin) *chsd ldrs: rdn and effrt jst over 2f out: pressed ldrs 2f out: wknd jst over 1f out* **11/2**[3]

5043 **6** *nk* **All About You (IRE)**[19] 6537 3-8-11 **78** ....(b) LiamJones 1 74
(W J Haggas) *s.i.s: wl bhd: hdwy on inner jst over 2f out: switching lft fr over 1f out: styd on but nvr able to chal* **16/1**

2 **7** *1 1/4* **Dukes Art**[71] 4984 3-8-13 **80** .... RobertHavlin 9 72
(J A R Toller) *in tch: rdn and effrt to chse ldrs jst over 2f out: wknd u.p over 1f out* **7/2**[2]

4053 **8** *2 1/4* **African Art (USA)**[19] 6535 3-9-4 **85** .... JimmyFortune 3 71
(B J Meehan) *wnt lft s: in tch in midfield on outer: lost pl and rdn over 2f out: sn hung lft and wl btn* **8/1**

1003 **9** *shd* **Imperial House**[8] 6824 3-8-4 **71** oh6 .... CatherineGannon 2 57
(M R Channon) *bmpd s: sn detached in last and rdn along: clsd and tagged on to field over 3f out: no real prog fnl 2f* **25/1**

3163 **10** *shd* **Darcey**[19] 6545 3-8-3 **73** .... Louis-PhilippeBeuzelin(3) 6 59
(Miss Amy Weaver) *led: rdn over 2f out: hdd wl over 1f out: sn wknd* **16/1**

0002 **11** *5* **Luckier (IRE)**[14] 6667 3-8-5 **72** .... ChrisCatlin 5 44
(S Kirk) *chsd ldr tl over 2f out: sn wknd: wl bhd fnl f* **16/1**

1m 25.15s (-0.85) **Going Correction** +0.025s/f (Slow) **11** Ran SP% **123.5**
Speed ratings (Par 103): **105,103,101,100,99 98,97,94,94,94 88**
toteswingers: 1&2 £3.80, 1&3 £26.10, 2&3 £4.40 CSF £42.16 CT £441.78 TOTE £13.20: £2.60, £1.80, £4.50; EX 43.80.
Owner The Comic Strip Heroes **Bred** Stuart McPhee **Trained** Whatcombe, Oxon

FOCUS
A fair handicap run at a reasonable gallop. Solid form. The winner raced towards the centre in the straight.
African Art(USA) Official explanation: jockey said colt hung badly

7028 TRY OUR NEW BISTRO MENU H'CAP 6f (P)
9:10 (9:10) (Class 5) (0-75,75) 3-Y-O **£1,680** (£1,680; £385; £192) **Stalls** High

Form RPR

2506 **1** **Fault**[7] 6857 3-8-11 **68** ....(t) MickyFenton 11 76
(Stef Liddiard) *hld up bhd: swtchd ins and hdwy jst over 2f out: rdn to chse ldng pair over 1f out: r.o wl to press ldr fnl f: jnd ldr on post* **9/2**[3]

0233 **1** *dht* **Hellbender (IRE)**[15] 6642 3-8-12 **74** .... LeeNewnes(5) 12 82
(S Kirk) *towards rr: pushed along over 4f out: hdwy on inner over 2f out: rdn to ld over 1f out: pushed along hands and heels ins fnl f: jnd on post* **5/2**[1]

500 **3** *1 1/2* **Cheap Thrills**[15] 6642 3-9-0 **71** .... ShaneKelly 3 74
(J A Osborne) *sn pushed up to ld and grad crossed to rail: rdn over 2f out: hdd over 1f out: drvn and no ex ins fnl f* **25/1**

3666 **4** *1 1/4* **Raimond Ridge (IRE)**[9] 6791 3-8-8 **65** .... ChrisCatlin 5 64
(M R Channon) *hld up wl bhd: hdwy over 1f out: r.o u.p fnl f: nt rch ldrs* **7/1**

0600 **5** *2* **Caledonia Princess**[12] 6738 3-8-10 **67** .... TonyCulhane 9 60
(R Curtis) *t.k.h: hld up in tch: rdn to chse ldrs 2f out: outpcd ent fnl f and wl hld after* **16/1**

3150 **6** *3 3/4* **Diddums**[31] 6201 3-8-4 **68** .... AmyScott(7) 4 49
(J W Hills) *hld up in midfield: rdn and wanting to hang rt over 2f out: no prog* **25/1**

1600 **7** *1* **Tikka Masala (IRE)**[21] 6476 3-8-13 **70** ....(vt[1]) RichardKingscote 6 48
(Tom Dascombe) *dwlt: sn rdn and hdwy to press ldrs after 1f: rdn and wknd qckly ent fnl 2f* **16/1**

2403 **8** *3 1/4* **Quasi Congaree (GER)**[4] 6915 3-8-10 **67** ....(t) CatherineGannon 10 34
(I A Wood) *chsd ldr: rdn over 2f out: wknd qckly wl over 1f out* **3/1**[2]

6010 **9** *25* **Ginobili (IRE)**[21] 6476 3-9-1 **72** ....(b) PatCosgrave 7 —
(Andrew Reid) *taken down early: pressed ldrs tl dropped out rapidly over 2f out: t.o* **8/1**

1m 12.82s (-0.28) **Going Correction** +0.025s/f (Slow) **9** Ran SP% **114.8**
Speed ratings (Par 101): **102,102,100,98,95 90,89,85,51**WIN: Hellbender £2.10 Fault £2.60 PL: H £1/60, F £2.30EX: Hellbender/Fault £7.60, F/H £8.40 CSF: H/F £6.95, F/H £8.03 TRI: H/F/Cheapthrills £109.11 F/H/CT £122.69 toteswingers: Hellbender&Fault £3.20, Hellbender&3 £16.50, Fault&3 £15.70, £6.20 Plac27 Owner.
Owner Mike Newbould **Bred** James Lombard **Trained** Upper Lambourn, Berks

FOCUS
An ordinary handicap but the decent gallop saw the finish fought out by those racing in the rear early on. The dead-heaters raced against and just off the inside rail in the straight. The third is rated around the third, who set the pace.
T/Plt: £27.00 to a £1 stake. Pool: £64,668.27. 1,744.60 winning tickets. T/Qpdt: £3.30 to a £1 stake. Pool: £7,319.47. 1,599.52 winning tickets. SP

6615 NEWBURY (L-H)

Saturday, October 24

OFFICIAL GOING: Soft

Rail realignment around the 5f and 7f bend increased distances on round course by about 33yards.

Wind: quite strong across Weather: overcast

7029 HILDON EBF MAIDEN STKS (DIV 1) 1m (S)

1:30 (1:32) (Class 4) 2-Y-O **£4,857** (£1,445; £722; £360) **Stalls** Centre

Form RPR

0 **1** **Multames (IRE)**[126] 3167 2-9-3 0 TedDurcan 8 93+
(Saeed Bin Suroor) *lw: cl up: shkn up to ld over 1f out: sn in command: styd on wl* **4/1**[2]

6 **2** *3 ½* **Total Command**[22] 6451 2-9-3 0 RyanMoore 18 85
(Sir Michael Stoute) *hld up towards rr: nudged along and weaved way through field fr 3f out: styd on to go 2nd jst ins fnl f but n.d to wnr* **7/1**

3 *2 ¼* **Latansaa** 2-9-3 0 TPO'Shea 4 80
(M P Tregoning) *w'like: str: athletic: trckd ldrs: effrt 2f out: styd on same pce: lost 2nd jst ins fnl f* **12/1**

0 **4** *¾* **Green Moon (IRE)**[16] 6620 2-9-3 0 JimCrowley 17 79
(H J L Dunlop) *lw: s.i.s: towards rr on stands' side rails: rdn and stdy prog fr over 2f out: styd on same pce fnl f: nvr trbld ldrs* **16/1**

0 **5** *2 ½* **Sweet Secret**[16] 6615 2-8-12 0 RichardHughes 14 68
(R Hannon) *s.i.s: towards rr: stdy prog u.p fr over 2f out: one pce fnl f* **28/1**

0 **6** *1* **Aultcharn (FR)**[16] 6615 2-9-3 0 PJSmullen 9 71
(B J Meehan) *prom: led over 2f out: rdn and hdd wl over 1f out: fdd ins fnl f* **13/2**

233 **7** *10* **State Fair**[11] 6754 2-9-3 85 GregFairley 3 49
(P F I Cole) *led tl over 2f out: sn rdn: grad fdd* **5/1**[3]

5 **8** *¾* **Sir Pitt**[11] 6763 2-9-3 0 JimmyFortune 10 48
(J H M Gosden) *w'like: scope: lw: chsd ldrs tl wknd over 2f out* **10/3**[1]

00 **9** *1 ¼* **Baoli**[35] 6109 2-8-12 0 DaneO'Neill 7 42
(R Hannon) *mid-div: rdn over 2f out: wknd over 1f out* **66/1**

10 *1 ¼* **Sea Of Heartbreak (IRE)** 2-8-12 0 SteveDrowne 2 37
(R Charlton) *unf: scope: bit bkwd: chsd ldrs tl 2f out* **25/1**

0 **11** *9* **Mount Athos (IRE)**[16] 6617 2-9-3 0 SebSanders 5 22
(J W Hills) *mid-div tl wknd 2f out* **33/1**

0 **12** *¾* **First Post (IRE)**[3] 6930 2-9-3 0 MichaelHills 16 20
(D Haydn Jones) *w'like: mid-div tl wknd over 2f out* **150/1**

13 *3* **Tappanappa (IRE)** 2-9-3 0 WilliamBuick 6 14
(A M Balding) *w'like: dwlt: a towards rr* **9/1**

00 **14** *1 ¼* **Big Talk**[13] 6697 2-9-3 0 GeorgeBaker 12 11
(S Kirk) *a towards rr* **100/1**

00 **15** *2 ½* **Oak Leaves**[70] 5026 2-8-12 0 JamesDoyle 13 1
(J G Portman) *mid-div: rdn over 2f out: sn wknd* **100/1**

1m 44.55s (4.85) **Going Correction** +0.75s/f (Yiel) **15 Ran SP% 123.5**
Speed ratings (Par 97): **105,101,99,98,96 95,85,84,83,81 72,72,69,67,65**
toteswinger: 1&2 £10.80, 1&3 £14.30, 2&3 £18.90. CSF £31.84 TOTE £5.40: £2.40, £2.30, £4.10; EX 49.80.
Owner Godolphin **Bred** Shadwell Estate Company Limited **Trained** Newmarket, Suffolk

FOCUS

This opening juvenile maiden was run in a time around eight and a half seconds slower than standard and the going was officially changed to soft soon after.

NOTEBOOK

Multames(IRE) ◆, never involved after a slow start on his debut over 7f at Newmarket in the summer, has clearly benefited from a break and he was seen to much better effect on this slower ground over 1m, staying on strongly having hit the front over 1f out and winning with plenty in hand. He gave a good blow afterwards, which suggests he will come on plenty for the run, and connections clearly think a lot of this Derby entry. (op 100-30 tchd 11-2)

Total Command, a son of Sadler's Wells who would have found 7f on fast ground too sharp a test on his debut, ran a really promising race, staying on well having weaved a way through to finish a clear second best. The conditions were evidently much more to his liking and he should have no trouble winning races. (op 6-1 tchd 15-2)

Latansaa, a half-brother to the yard's smart middle-distance filly Arwaah, seemed to know his job and was soon up near the leaders. He had his chance, but couldn't go on with the winner and was outstayed for second inside the final furlong. This was a pleasing enough start and he should win a standard maiden, with improvement likely. (op 16-1)

Green Moon(IRE), too inexperienced over C&D on his debut, didn't get the best of starts, but he came good inside the final 2f and was staying on rather nicely close home. He should continue to progress and looks to have a bright future as a middle-distance handicapper. (op 25-1 tchd 14-1)

Sweet Secret, who started very slowly before running green on her debut over 7f at the course, was again sluggish out of the gates, but she showed a lot more this time and is another likely handicap type for next season. (op 33-1)

Aultcharn(FR) showed a lot more than on his debut, but he stopped pretty quickly having been headed by the winner and the trip clearly stretched him. (op 6-1 tchd 11-2 and 15-2 in a place)

State Fair failed to run to form, dropping right out having been headed with around 2f to run. (op 9-2)

Sir Pitt caught the eye in a fair race at Newcastle on his debut, but he failed to confirm that promise with a laboured effort. (op 4-1 tchd 5-1)

7030 TOTESPORT 0800 221 221 STKS (REGISTERED AS THE HORRIS HILL STAKES) (GROUP 3) 7f (S)

2:05 (2:06) (Class 1) 2-Y-O

£28,385 (£10,760; £5,385; £2,685; £1,345; £675) **Stalls** Centre

Form RPR

0201 **1** **Carnaby Street (IRE)**[13] 6696 2-8-12 94 JimmyFortune 6 102
(R Hannon) *trckd ldrs: rdn wl over 1f out: kpt on to wear down ldr ins fnl f: led nr fin* **14/1**

0121 **2** *shd* **Pleasant Day (IRE)**[27] 6305 2-8-12 92 (b) PJSmullen 13 102
(B J Meehan) *in tch: hdwy to ld wl over 1f out: kpt on u.str.p: ct nr fin* **16/1**

0114 **3** *hd* **Audacity Of Hope**[23] 6426 2-8-12 104 (t) DaneO'Neill 15 101
(P J McBride) *hld up towards rr: hdwy 2f out: rdn whn short of room to chal jst over 1f out: squeezed through and kpt on wl ins: clsng at fin: jst failed* **12/1**

0263 **4** *1 ¼* **Iver Bridge Lad**[14] 6660 2-8-12 108 AdamKirby 5 98+
(J Ryan) *hld up bhd: nt clr run 2f out: sn swtchd to stands' side rails: rdn and styd on wl fnl f: nrst fin* **10/1**

31 **5** *¾* **Critical Moment (USA)**[35] 6109 2-8-12 0 MichaelHills 10 96+
(B W Hills) *in tch: nt clr run over 2f out: rdn whn short of room over 1f out: kpt on wout threatening* **14/1**

3126 **6** *¾* **Cadley Road (IRE)**[27] 6319 2-8-12 98 RichardHughes 9 95+
(R Hannon) *led: rdn 2f out: hdd sn after: cl 4th but hld whn squeezed out ins fnl f: lost 2 pls* **9/1**

2136 **7** *2* **Dubawi Phantom**[14] 6664 2-8-12 102 JimCrowley 3 90
(D M Simcock) *hld up towards rr: rdn and stdy prog but hung lft fr 2f out: hld in mid-div whn veered lft ins fnl f* **16/1**

1 **8** *shd* **Classic Colori (IRE)**[110] 3692 2-8-12 93 RichardKingscote 2 89
(Tom Dascombe) *in tch: rdn 2f out: kpt on same pce fnl f* **15/2**

231 **9** *½* **Exceedingly Bold**[16] 6615 2-8-12 82 DarryllHolland 7 88
(Miss Gay Kelleway) *t.k.h in mid-div: effrt 2f out: weakeend ins fnl f* **20/1**

1 **10** *1 ½* **Pastoral Player**[36] 6054 2-8-12 0 SteveDrowne 1 84+
(H Morrison) *hld up towards rr: hdwy 2f out: sn rdn: wknd fnl f* **5/1**[2]

61 **11** *¾* **Art Excellence**[16] 6607 2-8-12 77 HayleyTurner 12 82
(S A Callaghan, U.S.A) *trckd ldrs: rdn and ev ch 2f out: wknd fnl f* **40/1**

3261 **12** *hd* **Red Badge (IRE)**[56] 5433 2-8-12 92 RyanMoore 8 82
(R Hannon) *trckd ldrs: rdn 3f out: wknd over 1f out* **13/2**[3]

1 **13** *8* **Burnett (IRE)**[11] 6763 2-8-12 0 TedDurcan 4 62
(Saeed Bin Suroor) *mid-div: effrt 2f out: wknd jst over 1f out* **9/2**[1]

53 **14** *½* **Navajo Chief**[91] 4294 2-8-12 88 SebSanders 11 61
(A P Jarvis) *prom: rdn over 3f out: wknd 2f out* **66/1**

1m 29.96s (4.26) **Going Correction** +0.75s/f (Yiel) **14 Ran SP% 120.5**
Speed ratings (Par 105): **105,104,104,103,102 101,99,99,98,96 95,95,86,86**
toteswingers: 1&2 £50.90, 1&3 £42.80, 2&3 £46.10 CSF £217.80 TOTE £19.30: £4.70, £5.40, £4.70; EX 447.30 TRIFECTA Not won..
Owner Noodles Racing **Bred** D And Mrs D Veitch **Trained** East Everleigh, Wilts
■ Stewards' Enquiry : Dane O'Neill caution: careless riding

FOCUS

A wide-open running of a race that can throw up a smart performer, though rarely a high-class one.

NOTEBOOK

Carnaby Street(IRE), the apparent Hannon third string, has no pretensions of being any better than Group 3 level. Off the mark at the sixth attempt when easily winning a 6f maiden at Goodwood last time, he had earlier finished well held in a very valuable sales race at Doncaster and this improved effort has to be put down to the step up to 7f on soft ground. He had to really dig deep under strong pressure inside the final furlong, but always just looked to be getting there. (op 16-1)

Pleasant Day(IRE), a ready winner off a mark of 84 over this trip at Ascot last time, was tight against the stands' rail throughout on this rise in grade and he looked the winner going into the final furlong, but just couldn't repel Carnaby Street late on. The blinkers have been the making of him and he is evidently still progressing. (op 14-1)

Audacity Of Hope, who beat the runner-up in a Doncaster nursery last month, wasn't beaten far when upped to this level at Newmarket last time and he looked unlucky not to take this, being a bit short of room before running on well, only to find the line coming too soon. He is clearly on the up still and there is every chance of more to come at 1m. (tchd 14-1)

Iver Bridge Lad, a good third in the Cornwallis Stakes last time, was having his first try at 7f and, having been denied a clear run and forced to switch, he stayed on really well for fourth. A bit of cut in the ground is evidently to his liking and he looks capable of winning another Pattern contest. (op 9-1 tchd 8-1)

Critical Moment(USA), narrow winner of a C&D maiden last month, has more of a fast-ground pedigree, but he would have undoubtedly been involved in the finish had he not met with trouble in running. He can be rated better than the bare form and looks likely to improve for the step up to 1m. (tchd 12-1)

Cadley Road(IRE), sixth behind Shakespearean in the Goffs Million Mile at the Curragh last time, was made plenty of use of on this drop in trip, but had been brushed aside inside the two and was held when squeezed late on. He would have finished a shade closer. (op 12-1)

Dubawi Phantom was beginning to close when he started to hang quite badly left, ending any hope of reaching the frame. (op 14-1)

Classic Colori(IRE), winner of a 6f Windsor maiden in July, was faced with different conditions on this marked rise in grade and he simply couldn't quicken for pressure. (op 6-1 tchd 10-1)

Pastoral Player, who looked a decent horse when winning over 6f at the track on his debut, could never really get into it having been held up and forced to try to challenge wide. He wasn't overly punished and deserves another chance. Official explanation: jockey said colt was unsuited by the soft ground (op 9-2 tchd 11-2)

Red Badge(IRE), winner from a mark of 84 at Newmarket last time, failed to prove anywhere near as effective on this slower ground and was disappointing. (op 8-1)

Burnett(IRE) didn't have a gallop in him on this drop in trip/rise in grade. Official explanation: jockey said colt was unsuited by the soft ground (op 7-1)

7031 TOTESPORT.COM ST SIMON STKS (GROUP 3) 1m 4f 5y

2:35 (2:36) (Class 1) 3-Y-O+

£36,900 (£13,988; £7,000; £3,490; £1,748; £877) **Stalls** Low

Form RPR

3154 **1** **High Heeled (IRE)**[7] 6853 3-8-7 112 MichaelHills 13 117
(B W Hills) *hld up bhd: smooth hdwy fr 4f out to ld 2f out: sn clr: comf* **4/1**[1]

1313 **2** *6* **Tastahil (IRE)**[149] 2409 5-9-3 111 TPO'Shea 3 111
(B W Hills) *disp ld: rdn and hdd over 2f out: kpt on battling for 2nd but no ch w wnr sn after* **11/2**[2]

2110 **3** *hd* **Harbinger**[67] 5134 3-8-13 112 (t) RyanMoore 9 113
(Sir Michael Stoute) *mid-div: hdwy 3f out: rdn and ev ch briefly 2f out: sn hld by wnr but kpt chalng for 2nd* **6/1**[3]

6661 **4** *7* **Heliodor (USA)**[28] 6290 3-8-10 107 RichardHughes 4 99
(R Hannon) *trckd ldrs: short of room on bnd 7f out: rdn 4f out: kpt on but a 1 l down tl wknd ent fnl f* **20/1**

2402 **5** *1* **Drill Sergeant**[22] 6452 4-9-3 107 GregFairley 6 97
(M Johnston) *disp ld tl rdn over 2f out: sn one pce: fdd fnl f* **12/1**

1625 **6** *1 ½* **All The Aces (IRE)**[42] 5891 4-9-3 114 JimmyFortune 8 95
(M A Jarvis) *chsd ldrs: rdn whn lost pl 4f out: nvr bk on terms* **4/1**[1]

531 **7** *1 ¾* **Chock A Block (IRE)**[22] 6452 3-8-10 107 TedDurcan 12 92
(Saeed Bin Suroor) *mid-div: lost pl and rdn over 3f out: nvr threatened: wknd over 1f out* **8/1**

312 **8** *½* **Merchant Of Dubai**[34] 6138 4-9-3 97 WilliamBuick 10 91
(G A Swinbank) *hld up towards rr: hdwy 3f out: sn rdn: wknd wl over 1f out* **20/1**

4556 **9** *shd* **Enroller (IRE)**[27] 6324 4-9-6 110 DarryllHolland 11 94
(W R Muir) *mid-div: rdn 4f out: wknd 2f out* **8/1**

6150 **10** *19* **Illustrious Blue**[27] 6303 6-9-6 110 JimCrowley 5 64
(W J Knight) *s.i.s: towards rr: effrt 3f out but nvr trbld ldrs: eased whn btn fnl f* **16/1**

2154 **11** *30* **Halicarnassus (IRE)**[6] 6893 5-9-9 110 TonyCulhane 7 19
(M R Channon) *trckd ldrs: rdn 4f out: wknd 3f out: eased fr over 1f out* **25/1**

2m 40.91s (5.41) **Going Correction** +0.75s/f (Yiel)
WFA 3 from 4yo+ 7lb **11 Ran SP% 118.8**
Speed ratings (Par 113): **111,107,106,102,101 100,99,99,98,86 66**
toteswingers: 1&2 £5.70, 1&3 £5.50, 2&3 £4.60. CSF £25.09 TOTE £4.30: £2.10, £2.10, £2.10; EX 24.40 Trifecta £147.70 Pool: £499.20 - 2.50 winnin units..
Owner Mr And Mrs Steven Jenkins **Bred** Ballylinch Stud **Trained** Lambourn, Berks

FOCUS
This had looked a really competitive Group 3, but the 3yo filly High Heeled fairly destroyed her rivals.
NOTEBOOK
High Heeled(IRE) fairly destroyed her rivals. A real soft-ground lover, she ran a fine race when fourth in the Group 2 Pride Stakes at Newmarket on Champions Day and proved far too strong for the boys in this, travelling up well having been ridden with restraint and quickly bursting clear around 2f out. Third to Sariska in the Oaks earlier in the season, this will have to go down as a career-best and it was also her first win at Group level. She is in the December Sales, but her trainer would love to keep her and have another crack at a Group 1 in soft ground, on which her rider believes she is around half a stone better. One footnote - she did show signs of coming into season on returning to the paddock. (op 5-1)
Tastahil(IRE) , a Listed winner here back in May, had been given a break since finishing third to Geordieland in the Henry II Stakes over 2m later that month and he could really have done with making it more of a test at the distance. He was readily brushed side from 2f out, but battled it out in typically game fashion to hold second, suggesting a step back up in trip is what is needed. He is entitled to come on for this outing and should find another opening. (op 5-1 tchd 6-1)
Harbinger looked a horse of real class when winning the Gordon Stakes, but his subsequent flop in the Voltigeur left him with a lot to prove taking on his elders for the first time. Sporting a cross-noseband/tongue-tie combination, he moved comfortably into the straight, but couldn't quicken out of the ground and was just denied second. This was a step back in the right direction, but he is not looking the star he promised to be. (op 11-2 tchd 7-1)
Heliodor(USA) again ran reasonably faced with a stiff task. He was impeded before halfway, but it made no difference to his finishing position.
Drill Sergeant, narrowly denied by Chock A Block at Newmarket last time, was primarily responsible for the pace and, as with Tastahil, it was surprising he didn't try to make it more of a test given he stays 2m. (op 14-1)
All The Aces(IRE), below his best in the Irish St Leger last time, had conditions in his favour and should have run well, but he was under pressure and beaten by the time they hit the straight. He looks to have lost his form. (op 5-1)
Chock A Block(IRE) has still to fully fill his frame and he may have found the conditions too testing at this stage of his career, his Newmarket victory having come on a sound surface. (tchd 13-2)
Enroller(IRE) should have done a lot better with the ground having come in his favour. (op 10-1)

7032 EBF BATHWICK TYRES FILLIES' H'CAP 7f (S)
3:10 (3:11) (Class 3) (0-95,95) 3-Y-O+ **£9,066** (£2,697; £1,348; £673) **Stalls** Centre

Form				RPR
2544	**1**		**Crystal Moments**[15] 6631 3-8-9 **84** ow1 .... RichardHughes 3	93
			(E A L Dunlop) *trckd ldrs: rdn 2f out: led jst ins fnl f: kpt on: drvn out* **10/1**	
2405	**2**	*nk*	**Dixey**[11] 6757 4-9-0 **87** .... (p) TPO'Shea 2	96
			(M A Jarvis) *led: rdn over 2f out: hdd jst ins fnl f: kpt on but no ex* **16/1**	
P0	**3**	*2 ¾*	**Ocean Transit (IRE)**[16] 6618 4-8-6 **79** .... JamesDoyle 7	81+
			(R J Price) *little slowly away: sn prom: rdn over 2f out: kpt on same pce* **17/2**	
40-3	**4**	*nk*	**Farley Star**[11] 6757 5-9-6 **93** .... RyanMoore 11	94+
			(M G Quinlan) *hld up: rdn jst over 2f out: no imp tl styd on fnl f* **10/1**	
1634	**5**	*shd*	**Shangani**[12] 6731 3-7-12 **80** .... AmyScott(7) 14	79
			(H Candy) *hld up: hdwy over 3f out: rdn whn hung lft and chal over 2f out: one pce fnl f* **7/1**[3]	
0404	**6**	*¾*	**To Be Or Not To Be**[27] 6311 4-8-6 **79** oh5 .... LukeMorris 13	77
			(John Berry) *hld up: hdwy 3f out: effrt and edgd lft over 1f out: fdd ins fnl f* **16/1**	
2410	**7**	*nk*	**Glen Molly (IRE)**[71] 5005 3-9-1 **90** .... MichaelHills 9	87
			(B W Hills) *mid-div: effrt over 2f out: one pce fnl f* **5/2**[1]	
5000	**8**	*¾*	**Undaunted Affair (IRE)**[8] 6814 3-9-3 **92** .... JimmyFortune 5	87
			(K A Ryan) *awkward and slowly away: towards rr: hdwy over 2f out: sn rdn: nvr threatened ldrs: fdd ins fnl f:* **16/1**	
1464	**9**	*½*	**Sakhee's Pearl**[14] 6667 3-8-9 **84** ow1 .... DarryllHolland 10	77
			(Miss Gay Kelleway) *racd freely in tch: jnd ldrs over 3f out: effrt over 2f out: wknd fnl f* **8/1**	
5500	**10**	*1*	**Jet D'Eau (FR)**[28] 6267 3-9-6 **95** .... (b) GeorgeBaker 4	86
			(G L Moore) *hld up: rdn 3f out: nvr had pce to chal* **20/1**	
120-	**11**	*6*	**La Adelita (IRE)**[357] 7144 3-8-11 **86** .... HayleyTurner 12	60
			(M L W Bell) *trckd ldrs: rdn 3f out: sn btn* **5/1**[2]	

1m 31.12s (5.42) **Going Correction** +0.75s/f (Yiel)
WFA 3 from 4yo+ 2lb **11** Ran SP% **120.0**
Speed ratings (Par 104): **99,98,95,95,95 94,93,93,92,91 84**
toteswingers: 1&2 £15.80, 1&3 £21.90, 2&3 £35.80. CSF £161.63 CT £1427.26 TOTE £11.50: £3.30, £4.20, £2.30; EX 126.70 TRIFECTA Not won..
Owner Mohammed Jaber **Bred** Lady Jennifer Green And John Eyre **Trained** Newmarket, Suffolk
FOCUS
Two drew clear in what was a fair fillies' handicap.
NOTEBOOK
Crystal Moments, whose rider was putting up 1lb overweight, had finished well beaten on her one previous try at 7f, but that was as a 2-y-o and she improved for the longer trip here, leading inside the final furlong and keeping on well to hold the runner-up. There may be even better to come on a faster surface. (op 17-2)
Dixey is back on a decent mark and she returned to something like her best in the first-time cheekpieces, leading from an early stage and not giving in without a fight. (op 14-1 tchd 12-1)
Ocean Transit(IRE) has not been running that well, but the drop in trip seemed to help a little and she stayed on back in third. (op 16-1)
Farley Star remains 8lb above her last winning mark and she stayed on all too late, just missing third. (op 11-2)
Shangani made a swift forward move to dispute it with two to run, but she started to hang and couldn't race on in the end.
To Be Or Not To Be ran well considering she was racing from out of the weights and her rider was putting up overweight, only crying enough inside the final furlong.
Glen Molly(IRE), who has winning form with some cut in the ground, never got into it and has now flopped twice off this mark since winning at Newmarket in August. (op 7-2)

7033 RBL COUNTY POPPY APPEAL STKS REGISTERED AS THE RADLEY STAKES (LISTED RACE) 7f (S)
3:45 (3:47) (Class 1) 2-Y-O
£17,031 (£6,456; £3,231; £1,611; £807; £405) **Stalls** Centre

Form				RPR
1632	**1**		**Electric Feel**[22] 6447 2-8-12 98 .... AndreaAtzeni 11	100
			(M Botti) *mid-div: smooth hdwy over 2f out: led wl over 1f out: in command after: pushed out* **15/2**[3]	
51	**2**	*1 ¼*	**Za Za Zoom (IRE)**[12] 6737 2-8-12 75 .... MichaelHills 1	97
			(B W Hills) *hld up: hdwy 3f out: sn rdn: chsd wnr ent fnl f: a being hld* **10/1**	
1	**3**	*shd*	**Pipette**[51] 5605 2-8-12 0 .... WilliamBuick 16	97
			(A M Balding) *mid-div: rdn and stdy prog fr over 2f out: styng on at the fin: jst failed to snatch 2nd* **7/2**[1]	
01	**4**	*8*	**Fontley**[38] 5994 2-8-12 83 .... DarryllHolland 7	77
			(Eve Johnson Houghton) *mid-div: hdwy 2f out: sn rdn: swtchd lft then rt over 1f out: kpt on same pce* **20/1**	
1	**5**	*1 ½*	**Madam Macie (IRE)**[7] 6842 2-8-12 0 .... SilvestreDeSousa 10	73
			(J Hetherton) *led for 2f: chsd ldr: rdn over 2f out: wknd ent fnl f* **16/1**	
1100	**6**	*nk*	**Don't Tell Mary (IRE)**[14] 6660 2-9-1 95 .... RichardKingscote 9	75
			(Tom Dascombe) *hld up: rdn over 2f out: some late prog: nvr a threat* **20/1**	
21	**7**	*2*	**Jacqueline Quest (IRE)**[28] 6274 2-8-12 0 .... IanMongan 13	67
			(H R A Cecil) *chsd ldr: led over 2f out: rdn and hdd wl over 1f out: wknd ent fnl f* **9/2**[2]	
22	**8**	*3 ¼*	**Indian Valley (USA)**[24] 6372 2-8-12 0 .... AdamKirby 12	59
			(Rae Guest) *mid-div: hdwy over 2f out: sn rdn: wknd jst over 1f out* **40/1**	
1243	**9**	*3*	**Snow Fairy (IRE)**[56] 5427 2-8-12 102 .... PJSmullen 5	52
			(E A L Dunlop) *chsd ldrs: rdn over 2f out: wknd over 1f out* **7/1**	
4104	**10**	*nk*	**Mistic Magic (IRE)**[21] 6481 2-8-12 87 .... (p) JimmyFortune 14	51
			(P F I Cole) *trckd ldr: led after 2f: rdn and hdd over 2f out: wknd over 1f out* **20/1**	
1530	**11**	*3 ½*	**Candyfloss Girl**[21] 6481 2-8-12 65 .... SteveDrowne 15	42
			(H J L Dunlop) *mid-div for 4f: struggling in rr after* **80/1**	
5	**12**	*5*	**Tislimeen**[51] 5604 2-8-12 0 .... TonyCulhane 3	30
			(M R Channon) *chsd ldrs for 4f* **33/1**	
222	**13**	*6*	**Faithful One (IRE)**[18] 6567 2-8-12 81 .... TedDurcan 4	15
			(D R Lanigan) *chsd ldrs: effrt 2f out: sn wknd* **9/1**	
4321	**14**	*3*	**Silent Secret (IRE)**[38] 5980 2-8-12 77 .... RyanMoore 2	7
			(R Hannon) *chsd ldrs tl wknd 2f out* **16/1**	

1m 31.45s (5.75) **Going Correction** +0.75s/f (Yiel) **14** Ran SP% **126.1**
Speed ratings (Par 103): **97,95,95,86,84 84,81,78,74,74 70,64,57,54**
toteswingers: 1&2 £15.60, 1&3 £8.70, 2&3 £8.30. CSF £77.42 TOTE £10.10: £3.20, £2.40, £1.80; EX 103.70 TRIFECTA Not won..
Owner Joseph Barton **Bred** Bearstone Stud **Trained** Newmarket, Suffolk
■ Stewards' Enquiry : Michael Hills one-day ban: used whip with excessive frequency (Nov 7)
FOCUS
The front three came right away in what was probably a decent Listed race for fillies.
NOTEBOOK
Electric Feel, readily brushed aside by a smart filly in the Group 3 Oh So Sharp Stakes at Newmarket, had no problems dealing with this softer ground and, having moved up strongly to lead inside the final 2f, she stayed on well to score with a bit up her sleeve. There is plenty of speed in her pedigree, which would raise doubts about her getting 1m, but she would have a chance on the evidence of this. She was given a 50/1 quote for the Guineas by William Hill and expect to see her out early next season in the one of the trials. (tchd 7-1)
Za Za Zoom(IRE) had already won with some juice in the ground and she really improved for the step up to 7f, but just lacked the winner's acceleration in the ground. (op 7-1)
Pipette ◆ looked a filly of real potential when winning on soft ground on her debut at Salisbury last month and she would have won this in another half-furlong, running on well inside the final furlong having been outpaced. She will stay at least 1m and is definitely the one to take from the race, with her having plenty of physical scope for improvement. (op 5-1)
Fontley fared best of the remainder. Winner of a Sandown novice stakes, the daughter of Sadler's Wells was found wanting for speed in this stronger heat, but she should improve for 1m and beyond next season. (op 28-1)
Madam Macie(IRE), ready winner of a Catterick maiden only last week, showed up well for a long way on this sharp rise in grade and will obviously find easier opportunities. (op 20-1)
Don't Tell Mary(IRE) had proved a major flop on her last two starts and was having to concede weight all round, having already won at this level. She looked to be really struggling at one point, but stayed on nicely inside the final furlong and the step up from 5f was clearly a help. (op 22-1 tchd 25-1)
Jacqueline Quest(IRE), easy winner of a weak Chester maiden, stopped quickly once headed and may have found the ground too testing, while another to disappoint. (op 5-1 tchd 11-2)
Snow Fairy(IRE), couldn't run to the form that saw her finish third in a Group 3 at Goodwood last time. Official explanation: jockey said filly was unsuited by the soft ground (op 100-30 tchd 4-1)

7034 HILDON EBF MAIDEN STKS (DIV II) 1m (S)
4:20 (4:21) (Class 4) 2-Y-O **£4,857** (£1,445; £722; £360) **Stalls** Centre

Form				RPR
0	**1**		**Gardening Leave**[24] 6393 2-9-3 0 .... WilliamBuick 8	80+
			(A M Balding) *mde all: edgd sltly lft fr over 2f out: r.o strly to draw clr fnl f: rdn out* **8/1**	
	2	*3 ½*	**Prince Of Dreams** 2-9-3 0 .... JimCrowley 6	72
			(W J Knight) *trckd ldrs: rdn over 2f out: chsd wnr ent fnl f: kpt on but a hld* **16/1**	
0	**3**	*2 ¼*	**Knockdolian (IRE)**[23] 6423 2-9-3 0 .... RichardKingscote 10	67
			(R Charlton) *mid-div: rdn over 3f out: no imp tl styd on ent fnl f* **20/1**	
0	**4**	*hd*	**Bombadero (IRE)**[16] 6617 2-9-3 0 .... DaneO'Neill 5	67
			(J L Dunlop) *mid-div: rdn over 2f out: little imp tl styd on fnl f* **40/1**	
6	**5**	*2 ¼*	**First Fandango**[16] 6620 2-9-3 0 .... SebSanders 17	62
			(J W Hills) *prom: rdn wl over 2f out: kpt on tl no ex ent fnl f* **12/1**	
	6	*2 ¼*	**Streets Of War (USA)** 2-9-3 0 .... RobertHavlin 4	57
			(P W Chapple-Hyam) *hld up towards rr: hdwy over 2f out to chse ldrs: sn rdn for effrt: fdd ins fnl f* **8/1**	
	7	*½*	**High Ransom** 2-8-12 0 .... DarryllHolland 16	51+
			(M A Jarvis) *prom: rdn over 3f out: sn lost pl: nvr bk on terms* **16/1**	
	8	*½*	**Out Of Eden** 2-9-3 0 .... IanMongan 7	55
			(H R A Cecil) *mid-div: rdn over 2f out: wknd ent fnl f* **9/2**[3]	
5	**9**	*hd*	**Count Of Anjou (USA)**[16] 6615 2-9-3 0 .... RichardHughes 9	54+
			(R Hannon) *mid-div: rdn wl over 2f out: wknd ent fnl f* **3/1**[1]	
4	**10**	*hd*	**Domination**[13] 6697 2-9-3 0 .... SteveDrowne 13	54
			(H Morrison) *in tch: rdn over 2f out: wknd over 1f out* **7/2**[2]	
0	**11**	*nk*	**Optimistic Duke (IRE)**[15] 6627 2-9-3 0 .... HayleyTurner 1	53
			(W R Muir) *mid-div: rdn wl over 2f out: wknd over 1f out* **66/1**	
	12	*1 ¼*	**Bonded (IRE)** 2-9-3 0 .... PJSmullen 12	51
			(B J Meehan) *s.i.s: a in rr* **25/1**	
0	**13**	*5*	**Balsha (USA)**[36] 6062 2-8-12 0 .... TedDurcan 15	35
			(E A L Dunlop) *a towards rr* **25/1**	

1m 46.49s (6.79) **Going Correction** +0.75s/f (Yiel) **13** Ran SP% **123.5**
Speed ratings (Par 97): **96,92,90,90,87 85,85,84,84,84 83,82,77**
toteswingers: 1&2 £31.40, 1&3 £26.50, 2&3 £57.90. CSF £118.48 TOTE £10.00: £2.60, £4.70, £6.60; EX 178.00.
Owner Another Bottle Racing 2 **Bred** Darley **Trained** Kingsclere, Hants
FOCUS
There were a couple of key defectors in what was the weaker of the two divisions, that being backed up by the time, which was almost two seconds slower.\n\x\x There were three withdrawals - Blissful Moment (3/1, vet's advice, deduct 25p in the £ under R4), Tafawut (14/1, unruly in stalls, deduct 5p & High On A Hill (16/1, lost shoe, deduct 5p).
NOTEBOOK
Gardening Leave, never involved following a slow start on fast ground at Salisbury on his debut, was much better suited to these softer conditions and prospered under a positive ride, really finding his stride approaching the final furlong and coming clear. A fine, big son of Selkirk, the ground is clearly important to him and he should make up into a nice 3-y-o. (old market op 10-1)

Prince Of Dreams, related to a couple of useful middle-distance performers, emerged from the pack to go in pursuit of the winner, but he was left trailing from 1f out. This was a promising start and he can probably win an ordinary maiden. (old market op 22-1)

Knockdolian(IRE) was backed to improve on his debut effort and he duly did, staying on late having been outpaced to reward each-way backers. He is going to relish a step up to 1m2f and further next season, so look for him to develop into a useful handicapper. (old market op 50-1, new market op 25-1)

Bombadero(IRE) is another likely handicap prospect for next term, the son of Sadler's Wells leaving his debut effort well behind and looking certain to improve for middle distances in time. (old market op 66-1)

First Fandango showed up well for a long way before fading late on and can be expected to fare better back in faster ground in future. He is another likely handicap sort. (old market op 16-1, new market tchd 10-1)

Streets Of War(USA), a late-foaled American-bred, showed ability and ran well considering the ground would probably have been against him. (old market op 16-1)

High Ransom, a sister to Arkle winner Contraband, was up there until past halfway but she could not race on with the principals. (old market op 25-1, new market op 14-1 tchd 20-1)

Out Of Eden, who is reportedly well thought of and was backed, failed to make a show. (old market op 6-1)

Count Of Anjou(USA), who was well fancied by his trainer, failed to build on the promise of his intial outing and clearly had a problem with the ground. (old market tchd 9-2, new market op 11-4)

Domination was unable to build on the promise shown on his debut and had no obvious excuse. Official explanation: jockey said colt hung left-handed (old market op 8-1)

7035 WATCH THE JUMP SEASON ON RACING UK H'CAP — 1m 2f 6y

4:55 (4:56) (Class 2) (0-100,97) 3-Y-O+

£11,215 (£3,358; £1,679; £840; £419; £210) Stalls Low

Form — RPR

11 **1** **Rainbow Peak (IRE)**[29] 6239 3-9-5 **97** .... JimmyFortune 14 110+
(M A Jarvis) *hld up towards rr: gd hdwy over 2f out: led ent fnl f: sn rdn: kpt on wl* **3/1**[1]

-265 **2** *¾* **Dr Livingstone (IRE)**[50] 5641 4-9-0 **87** .... WilliamBuick 9 95
(C R Egerton) *led: rdn over 2f out: hdd ent fnl f: kpt on u.str.p but a being hld* **25/1**

00 **3** *1 ½* **Salden Licht**[12] 6732 5-9-7 **94** .... LukeMorris 6 102+
(J M P Eustace) *hld up towards rr: hdwy fr 3f out: nt clr run over 2f out: swtchd lft: sn rdn: styd on: wnt 3rd towards fin: nt rch ldng pair* **16/1**

163 **4** *1* **Namibian Orator (IRE)**[23] 6429 3-8-8 **86** .... RyanMoore 3 89
(Sir Michael Stoute) *hld up towards rr: hdwy 3f out: sn rdn: ch jst over 1f out: no ex fnl 100yds: lost 3rd towards fin* **7/2**[2]

0610 **5** *7* **The Which Doctor**[21] 6480 4-9-2 **89** .... DarryllHolland 13 78
(J Noseda) *hld up last: styd on past btn horses fr 2f out: nvr a danger* **20/1**

2161 **6** *1* **Cill Rialaig**[14] 6665 4-9-6 **93** .... SteveDrowne 2 80
(H Morrison) *cl up: rdn over 2f out: wknd ent fnl f* **8/1**

3326 **7** *2 ¼* **William Blake**[8] 6816 4-9-1 **88** .... GregFairley 16 71
(M Johnston) *w ldr: rdn over 3f out: grad fdd* **10/1**

0045 **8** *¾* **King Charles**[8] 6816 5-9-5 **92** ....(b) PJSmullen 12 73
(E A L Dunlop) *towards rr of midfield: rdn over 2f out: wknd over 1f out* **10/1**

0032 **9** *3 ¾* **The Fifth Member (IRE)**[5] 6907 5-8-9 **85** .... JackMitchell(3) 5 59
(J R Boyle) *mid-div: rdn over 2f out: no imp: wknd fnl f* **13/2**[3]

-425 **10** *nse* **Spell Caster**[105] 3840 4-8-12 **85** .... RichardKingscote 15 58
(R M Beckett) *chsd ldrs: rdn 3f out: wknd over 1f out* **18/1**

5220 **11** *8* **Wintercast**[14] 6665 4-9-6 **93** .... AdamKirby 10 50
(W R Swinburn) *mid-div: effrt 3f out: wknd over 1f out* **11/1**

5450 **12** *24* **Sohcahtoa (IRE)**[12] 6732 3-8-10 **88** .... RichardHughes 11 —
(R Hannon) *chsd ldrs: rdn 3f out: wknd 2f out* **16/1**

2m 13.99s (5.19) **Going Correction** +0.75s/f (Yiel)
WFA 3 from 4yo+ 5lb — **12** Ran SP% **123.8**
Speed ratings (Par 109): **109,108,107,106,100 100,98,97,94,94 88,68**
toteswingers: 1&2 £20.40, 1&3 £17.30, 2&3 £65.20. CSF £86.27 CT £1077.10 TOTE £3.30: £1.70, £6.20, £6.30; EX 98.00.
Owner P D Savill **Bred** P D Savill **Trained** Newmarket, Suffolk

FOCUS
This had the look of a good middle-distance handicap and they went a decent gallop.

NOTEBOOK
Rainbow Peak(IRE) maintained his unbeaten record and already looks to be better than a handicapper. Making his handicap debut off a mark of 97, having won a conditions race at Ascot last time, he made rapid headway closer to the stands' side in the straight and started to assert from over 1f out. This win showed him to be effective on a variety of surfaces and, with the likelihood of better to come as he goes up to 1m4f, he is definitely a horse to keep on-side. (op 11-4 tchd 7-2)

Dr Livingstone(IRE), though still 8lb above his last winning mark, looked capable of a good run if building on his recent return from a short break, and he made them all go, but in the end the winner possessed a bit too much class.

Salden Licht ran easily his best race since joining current connections. Down another 2lb having finished seventh at 100-1 at Salisbury last time, he was short of room over 2f out and had to switch, but once he did he started to run on really well and in the end just grabbed third. The step up in trip was clearly a help and he should go on again from this. (op 12-1)

Namibian Orator(IRE), third off this mark over 1m at Newmarket this month, has winning form with some cut in the ground and he made good progress towards the far side to challenge over 1f out, only to empty right out in the final 100 yards. He remains capable of better and perhaps slow ground over 1m may prove his ideal conditions. (op 4-1 tchd 9-2)

The Which Doctor, well beaten in the Cambridgeshire, made some headway from the rear without ever posing a threat. (op 33-1)

Cill Rialaig has had a profitable season and again looked a player despite being up 7lb for her recent Ascot victory. She was well held, though, being beaten over 2f out, and perhaps the ground proved too testing. (tchd 15-2)

Sohcahtoa(IRE) Official explanation: jockey said gelding had no more to give

7036 FRANK OSGOOD MEMORIAL LADY JOCKEYS' H'CAP — 1m 4f 5y

5:25 (5:25) (Class 5) (0-75,75) 4-Y-O+ £3,123 (£968; £484; £242) Stalls Low

Form — RPR

000/ **1** **Warne's Way (IRE)**[630] 2434 6-9-11 **65** .... MissSBrotherton 10 72+
(B G Powell) *towards rr: plenty to do 4f out: styd on fr 2f out: fin wl to squeeze through gap ins fnl f: led line* **6/1**[2]

3510 **2** *shd* **Mista Rossa**[11] 6758 4-9-8 **67** .... MissVCartmel(5) 13 75+
(H Morrison) *sn prom: rdn 3f out: led ent fnl f: 1 1/2 l clr whn rdr stopped riding fnl 30yds: pushed out nr fin but ct line* **7/1**

6310 **3** *1* **Capable Guest (IRE)**[17] 6584 7-9-13 **67** .... MissLEllison 15 72
(M R Channon) *led chsng gp of front trio: clsd on ldrs fr 3f out: rdn over 2f out: styd on fnl f* **5/1**[1]

20/2 **4** *nk* **Etruscan (IRE)**[12] 6741 4-10-4 **75** .... MissCAllen(3) 2 80
(C Gordon) *mid-div: rdn and hdwy fr 3f out: ch ent fnl f: no ex* **14/1**

2426 **5** *2 ¼* **Princess Flame (GER)**[16] 6236 7-9-9 **63** .... MissADeniel 14 64
(B G Powell) *mid-div: hdwy over 2f out: effrt over 1f out: no ex fnl f* **20/1**

4400 **6** *1* **Nawamees (IRE)**[13] 6704 11-9-0 **61** oh5 ....(p) MissHJones(7) 11 60
(P D Evans) *chsd clr ldrs: clsd on ldrs fr over 3f out: effrt to chal over 1f out: fdd and eased fnl 75yds* **33/1**

1-00 **7** *2 ¾* **Anfield Road**[29] 428 4-9-12 **73** ....(v) MissJBuck(7) 5 68
(L Corcoran) *s.i.s: towards rr: hdwy fr 5f out: rdn in 4th 3f out: one pce fnl f* **25/1**

02-2 **8** *½* **Benfleet Boy**[36] 6060 5-9-13 **72** .... MissCLWills(5) 12 66
(B G Powell) *led at decent pce: rdn over 2f out: hdd ent fnl f: wknd* **13/2**[3]

1663 **9** *4 ½* **Arctic Cape**[21] 3378 4-10-7 **75** ....(b[1]) MissEJJones 3 62
(D E Pipe) *mid-div tl wknd 2f out* **7/1**

212 **10** *nk* **Boundless Prospect (USA)**[37] 6012 10-9-13 **67** .... MissEFolkes 8 53
(P D Evans) *a bhd* **13/2**[3]

1506 **11** *½* **Megalala (IRE)**[2] 6967 8-9-3 **64** ow2 .... MrsNParry(7) 9 50
(J J Bridger) *prom tl wknd 2f out* **12/1**

600/ **12** *11* **Attorney General (IRE)**[224] 958 10-10-0 **75** .... MissKLoftus(7) 4 43
(C Gordon) *s.i.s: a bhd* **33/1**

042 **13** *19* **Rudry World (IRE)**[11] 6768 6-9-2 **61** oh4 .... MissMMullineaux(5) 1 —
(M Mullineaux) *s.i.s: clipped rails over 7f out: a bhd* **12/1**

2m 47.51s (12.01) **Going Correction** +0.75s/f (Yiel) — **13** Ran SP% **119.2**
Speed ratings (Par 103): **89,88,88,88,86 85,84,83,80,80 80,72,60**
toteswingers: 1&2 £11.50, 1&3 £8.00, 2&3 £8.00. CSF £45.36 CT £226.59 TOTE £7.70: £2.80, £2.60, £2.10; EX 56.80 Place 6: £5901.29 Place 5: £2145.95.
Owner Nigel Stafford **Bred** Mrs Ann Kennedy **Trained** Upper Lambourn, Berks
■ Stewards' Enquiry : Miss V Cartmel four-day ban: used whip with excesive frequency, down shoulder in the forehand without giving gelding time to respond (tbn); 28-day ban: dropped hands, failed to ride out for first (tbn)

FOCUS
A low-grade female jockeys' handicap that was run at a fast gallop thanks to Benfleet Boy, Megalala and Mista Rossa taking each other on from a very early stage. They fell in a heap in the straight, as one would have expected them to, but Mista Rossa somehow managed to battle her way back to the lead and looked to have it won nearing the line, only for her rider to ease for a few strides and gift victory to Warnes Way.

Warne's Way(IRE) Official explanation: trainer said, regasrding apparent improvement in form, that the gelding had not run for 630 days and was a reasonable hudler.

T/Plt: £29,510.10 to a £1 stake. Pool: £88,934.61. 2.20 winning tickets. T/Qpdt: £1,122.30 to a £1 stake. Pool: £6,066.80. 4.00 winning tickets. TM

5462 CLAIREFONTAINE (R-H)

Saturday, October 24

OFFICIAL GOING: Very soft

7037a PRIX TBA ESPAGNE (PRIX DES GERBERAS) (CLAIMER) — 1m 4f

12:15 (12:14) 3-Y-0 £5,825 (£2,330; £1,748; £1,165; £583)

RPR

1 **L'Aventurier (FR)**[10] 3-9-5 ....(p) JVictoire 78
(J De Roualle, France)

2 *2* **Frantz De Galais (FR)**[38] 3-9-4 .... P-CBoudot 74
(Y Fouin, France)

3 *3* **Folie Express (FR)**[24] 3-8-8 ....(b) ACrastus 59
(D Sepulchre, France)

4 *shd* **Wishlad (FR)** 3-8-12 63
(J De Roualle, France)

5 *3* **Archissime (FR)**[10] 3-9-9 ....(b) 69
(Y Barberot, France)

6 *½* **Etoile Du Ninian (FR)** 3-9-1 60
(D Windrif, France)

7 *2* **Saphir Du Vallon (FR)**[112] 3-9-1 57
(C Lotoux, France)

8 *3* **Counterbid (IRE)**[14] 6682 3-8-12 49
(C Laffon-Parias, France)

9 *4* **Victorian Tycoon (IRE)**[14] 6682 3-8-12 ....(b) JAuge 43
(E J O'Neill) *in tch: 5th 1/2-way: pushed along over 3f out: rdn and no imp st* **53/10**[1]

10 *3* **Malindi (FR)**[24] 3-9-1 ....(p) 41
(J Van Handenhove, France)

0 **Jumeirah Queen (FR)**[80] 3-8-8 ....(b) —
(B Dutruel, France)

0 **Full Of Honor (IRE)**[32] 3-9-1 ....(b) —
(J-Y Artu, France)

0 **Fils D'Helene (FR)**[99] 3-8-12 .... —
(J-P Delaporte, France)

0 **Viva Agrippina (USA)**[88] 3-8-13 .... —
(J Bertran De Balanda, France)

0 **Yashtrack (FR)** 3-8-8 ....(b) —
(M Rolland, France)

0 **Princess Lala (GER)** 3-8-8 ....(p) —
(Mario Hofer, Germany)

0 **Bagmati (FR)** 3-8-12 .... —
(M Droueche, France)

2m 42.1s (4.20) — **17** Ran SP% **15.9**
PARI-MUTUEL (Including 1 Euro stake): WIN 9.80 (coupled with Wishlad);PL 4.20, 4.00, 6.10; DF 36.20.
Owner D Guindon & P-N Rossier **Bred** Scea Des Bissons **Trained** France

7038a PRIX TBA TURQUIE (PRIX DE LA FORET VERTE) — 1m 6f 110y

1:15 (1:15) 4-Y-0+ £7,767 (£3,107; £2,330; £1,553; £777)

RPR

1 **Pluie D'Or (IRE)**[22] 4-8-8 .... ACrastus 72
(E Lellouche, France)

2 *2* **Yellowstone (IRE)**[14] 6662 5-9-0 ....(p) CSoumillon 75
(P F I Cole) *led: brought field wd 1/2-way: rdn and hdd over 1f out: styd on to hold 2nd fnl f: rr pce of wnr* **1/1**[1]

3 *nk* **Grande Haya (FR)**[125] 10-8-12 .... RMarchelli 73
(A Bonin, France)

4 *1 ½* **Spectaculaire**[48] 6-9-4 77
(J-J Boutin, France)

5 *4* **Superior Officer (FR)**[14] 7-8-12 65
(A Gilibert, France)

6 *8* **Sunrise Spirit (FR)**[74] 8-9-0 56
(F Doumen, France)

7 *5* **Ostella (GER)**[1161] 8-9-1 ....(p) 50
(Katja Gernreich, Germany)
8 *10* **Northwester (FR)**[465] 4-8-12 33
(L Viel, France)
9 *snk* **Kotmaille (FR)**[421] 4-8-12 33
(F Leralle, France)
10 *dist* **Grande Fortune (FR)** 4-8-8 .... —
(Mme O Rouleau, France)

3m 20.9s (200.90) **10** Ran SP% **50.0**
PARI-MUTUEL: WIN 5.50; PL 1.60, 1.30, 1.70; DF 6.80.
Owner Ecurie Wildenstein **Bred** Dayton Investments Ltd **Trained** Lamorlaye, France

5707 BADEN-BADEN (L-H)
Saturday, October 24

OFFICIAL GOING: Soft

7039a HEEL - BADEN-WURTTEMBERG-TROPHY (GROUP 3) 1m 3f
2:40 (2:43) 3-Y-O+ **£29,126** (£12,136; £4,854; £2,427)

RPR
1 **Liang Kay (GER)**[21] 6500 4-9-2 .... YLerner 3 105
(Uwe Ostmann, Germany) *hld up: 8th 1/2-way: prog appr st: cl 5th st: sn wnt 2nd: chal 1f out: rdn to ld ins fnl f: drvn out* **27/10**[2]
2 *1/2* **Pont Des Arts (FR)**[41] 5-9-2 .... FSpanu 6 104
(A Scharer, Germany) *led: jnd 1f out: hdd narrowly ins fnl f: styd on* **84/10**
3 *6* **Steuben (GER)**[149] 3-8-8 .... FilipMinarik 4 92
(J Hirschberger, Germany) *in tch: 5th 1/2-way: 6th and rdn st: wnt 3rd 1f out: nt pce of ldng pair* **19/10**[1]
4 *2 1/2* **Schiller Danon (GER)**[27] 6324 3-8-10 .... ASuborics 7 90
(W Hickst, Germany) *hld up in last: pushed along appr st: rdn and wnt 3rd briefly over 1f out: styd on same pce* **33/10**[3]
5 *2 1/2* **Ordenstreuer (IRE)**[20] 6521 3-8-9 ow1 .... APietsch 2 84
(R Dzubasz, Germany) *in tch: disputing 3rd 1/2-way: rdn 1 1/2f out: one pce* **145/10**
6 *1/2* **White Lightning (GER)**[21] 6500 7-9-0 .... PJWerning 10 83
(U Stech, Germany) *in tch: disputing 3rd 1/2-way: drvn appr st: unable qck* **26/1**
7 *3* **Ambassador (GER)**[27] 6324 5-9-6 .... EPedroza 8 84
(T Mundry, Germany) *hld up: pushed along appr st: n.d* **161/10**
8 *1 1/4* **Saphir (GER)**[69] 5082 3-8-13 .... AStarke 9 80
(P Schiergen, Germany) *racd in 2nd: drvn ent st: sn 3rd and one pce* **56/10**
9 *2 1/2* **Dwilano (GER)**[56] 5461 6-9-2 .... NRichter 5 73
(P Remmert, Germany) *towards rr: n.d* **238/10**

2m 24.65s (5.38)
WFA 3 from 4yo+ 6lb **9** Ran SP% **130.6**
(Including 10 Euro stake): WIN 37; PL 14, 20, 14; SF 338.
Owner Stall Emina **Bred** Frau I Zimmermann **Trained** Germany

MOONEE VALLEY (L-H)
Saturday, October 24

OFFICIAL GOING: Good

7040a TATTS COX PLATE (GROUP 1) 1m 2f 44y
6:30 (12:00) 3-Y-O+
£898,058 (£213,592; £106,796; £63,107; £53,398; £48,544)

RPR
1 **So You Think (NZ)**[14] 3-7-11 ....(b) GlenBoss 7 121+
(Bart Cummings, Australia) **12/1**
2 *2 1/2* **Manhattan Rain (AUS)**[14] 3-7-11 .... CraigAWilliams 13 116
(Mrs Gai Waterhouse, Australia) **20/1**
3 *1/2* **Zipping (AUS)**[21] 8-9-4 .... StevenArnold 2 120
(John D Sadler, Australia) **11/1**
4 *shd* **El Segundo (NZ)**[21] 8-9-4 .... LukeNolen 12 120+
(Colin Little, Australia) **15/1**
5 *3/4* **Scenic Shot (AUS)**[21] 7-9-4 .... ShaneScriven 6 118
(Daniel Morton, Australia) **20/1**
6 *shd* **Whobegotyou (AUS)**[14] 4-9-1 ....(b) DamienOliver 10 115
(Mark Kavanagh, Australia) **7/4**[1]
7 *1 3/4* **Heart Of Dreams (AUS)**[14] 4-9-1 .... CraigNewitt 3 112
(Mick Price, Australia) **13/2**[2]
8 *1 3/4* **Rock Kingdom (AUS)**[14] 4-9-1 ....(b) NashRawiller 9 108
(Mrs Gai Waterhouse, Australia) **15/1**
9 *3/4* **Black Piranha (AUS)**[14] 6-9-4 .... TyeAngland 8 110
(Con Karakatsanis, Australia) **20/1**
10 *1 3/4* **Road To Rock (AUS)**[21] 5-9-4 ....(b) GlynSchofield 1 106
(Anthony Cummings, Australia) **20/1**
11 *2* **Vision And Power (NZ)**[14] 7-9-4 ....(b) HughBowman 4 102
(Joseph Pride, Australia) **20/1**
12 *1/2* **Speed Gifted**[21] 5-9-4 .... DwayneDunn 11 101
(Lee Freedman, Australia) **10/1**[3]
13 *4* **Nom Du Jeu (NZ)**[14] 5-9-4 ....(b) MichaelRodd 5 93
(Murray & Bjorn Baker, New Zealand) **66/1**

2m 3.98s (123.98)
WFA 3 from 4yo+ 5lb **13** Ran SP% **112.6**

Owner Dato Tan Chin Nam & Tunku Ahmed Yahaya **Bred** M J Moran & Piper Farm Ltd **Trained** Australia

NOTEBOOK
So You Think(NZ) looks a horse of immense potential. Glen Boss quickly had his mount at the head of affairs and the combination repelled all challengers. There is a chance that the jockey stole it from the front, although the winning time was less than half a second outside the course record, but So You Think is a big, imposing sort that kept going at a relentless gallop. He will be difficult to beat for the rest of the season, although connections reported that he is unlikely to run in the Victoria Derby. 81-y-o Bart Cummings is now on some hat-trick after winning the Caulfield Cup the previous weekend with last season's Melbourne Cup winner Viewed who, incidentally, carries the same colours as So You Think. If any of his horses go on to win on the first Tuesday in November, it will have to go down as one of the training performances of all time.

Manhattan Rain(AUS) chased the winner from the outset and went someway to justifying the huge amount of money spent in supplementing him for this race. He was no match for the winner off the bridle but looks sure to develop into a top-class performer.
El Segundo(NZ), whose connections had stated that this race was the horse's target for most of the year, and that some modest performances leading up to it were best ignored, got an injury to his eye on his previous outing. Held up towards the rear after leaving the stalls, he was given a bit too much to do and also came wide off the bend. If there was an unlucky horse in the race, it was him.
Speed Gifted dropped out very tamely after taking a keen grip at the rear. He looked a very awkward ride with his head held high, but would have wanted a stronger gallop to chase and possibly softer ground.

7041 - 7043a (Foreign Racing) - See Raceform Interactive

7039 BADEN-BADEN (L-H)
Sunday, October 25

OFFICIAL GOING: Soft

7044a BADENER SPRINT CUP (GROUP 3) 7f
1:10 (1:18) 3-Y-O+ **£29,126** (£12,136; £4,854; £2,427)

RPR
1 **Walero (GER)**[71] 3-8-13 .... PJWerning 5 109
(Uwe Ostmann, Germany) *a cl up: 3rd st: chal 1f out: drvn to ld cl home: all out* **19/2**
2 *hd* **Le Big (GER)**[22] 6499 5-9-1 .... AStarke 3 108
(U Stoltefuss, Germany) *a cl up: wnt 2nd 1/2-way: led over 2f out: drvn fnl f: hdd cl home* **71/10**
3 *2* **Rock Of Rochelle (USA)**[52] 5618 4-8-13 .... GFCarroll 10 101
(A Kinsella, Ire) *sn racing in 3rd: 4th st: r.o one pce fr over 1f out* **8/1**
4 *2* **Smooth Operator (GER)**[22] 6503 3-9-1 .... AHelfenbein 11 99
(Mario Hofer, Germany) *towards rr early: hdwy 1/2-way: 5th st: c to stands' rails: kpt on one pce fr over 1f out* **9/5**[1]
5 *hd* **Nareion (GER)**[33] 3-8-10 .... KClijmans 1 94
(W Baltromei, Germany) *mid-div: 6th st: rdn and hung rt dist: kpt on but nvr able to chal* **41/5**
6 *9* **Chantilly Tiffany**[29] 6272 5-8-11 ow2 .... THellier 2 68
(E A L Dunlop) *towards rr tl styng on ins ent st: sn 6th: sn rdn and one pce: eased whn btn fnl f* **11/2**[3]
7 *4 1/2* **Contat (GER)**[56] 5493 6-9-3 .... EPedroza 13 62
(P Vovcenko, Germany) *sn led: hdd over 2f out: 2nd st: sn wknd* **15/1**
8 *hd* **Addicted (GER)**[21] 6605 3-8-11 .... EFrank 6 58
(T Mundry, Germany) *a towards rr: nvr a factor* **32/1**
9 *1 3/4* **Setareh (GER)**[98] 4129 4-9-1 .... APietsch 8 55
(P Olsanik, Germany) *first to show: cl up tl wkng wl over 2f out* **59/1**
10 *nk* **Aturo (FR)**[162] 2097 5-8-13 .... LennartHammer-Hansen 12 52
(C Sprengel, Germany) *dwlt: sn cl up on outside: wknd wl over 2f out* **40/1**
11 *1/2* **Key To Pleasure (GER)**[42] 9-8-13 .... ASuborics 9 51
(Mario Hofer, Germany) *hld up: last st: a in rr* **21/1**
12 *9* **Entre Deux Eaux (FR)**[49] 5709 3-8-9 .... FilipMinarik 4 24
(Robert Collet, France) *a in rr* **48/10**[2]

1m 28.14s (4.24)
WFA 3 from 4yo+ 2lb **12** Ran SP% **130.1**
TOTE (including 10 euro stake): WIN 105; PL 37, 23, 33; SF 1079.
Owner H Schroer-Dreesmann **Bred** H Schroer-Dreesmann **Trained** Germany

NOTEBOOK
Chantilly Tiffany, who won this race last year, was never a threat in her repeat bid. Her rider put up 2lb overweight.

7045a PREIS DER WINTERKONIGIN (GROUP 3) (FILLIES) 1m
2:20 (2:27) 2-Y-O
£58,252 (£22,330; £10,680; £5,825; £2,913; £1,942)

RPR
1 **Neon Light (GER)** 2-9-2 .... JBojko 10 108
(A Wohler, Germany) *mde all: rdn out: r.o wl* **61/10**[2]
2 *3/4* **Elle Shadow (IRE)** 2-9-2 .... AStarke 3 106
(P Schiergen, Germany) *trckd ldrs: wnt 2nd 3f out: chsd wnr fnl 2f: 1 1/2 l bhd 1f out: styd on but could nvr trble her* **4/5**[1]
3 *7* **Nianga (GER)** 2-9-2 .... ASuborics 6 91
(P Schiergen, Germany) *6th 1/2-way: hdwy and 3rd st: btn over 1f out* **15/2**[3]
4 *1 1/4* **Prakasa (FR)**[35] 6151 2-9-2 .... APietsch 5 88
(W Hickst, Germany) *a cl up: 4th st: one pce fr wl over 1f out* **8/1**
5 *2* **All I Want** 2-9-2 .... WMongil 4 84
(Andreas Lowe, Germany) *hld up in rr: 8th st: hdwy wl over 1f out: nvr nr to chal* **103/10**
6 *1/2* **Tech Exceed (GER)** 2-9-2 .... EPedroza 9 83
(A Wohler, Germany) *trckd wnr to 1/2-way: 5th and btn st* **138/10**
7 *7* **Ordensfrau (GER)** 2-9-2 .... AHelfenbein 7 67
(Mario Hofer, Germany) *disputing 4th on outside whn rn wd on turn over 3f out: 6th st: sn btn* **18/1**
8 *6* **Top Act (FR)** 2-9-2 .... FilipMinarik 2 54
(P Schiergen, Germany) *cl up early: bhd fr 1/2-way: last st* **77/10**
9 *3 1/2* **Artica (GER)** 2-9-2 .... THellier 1 46
(T Mundry, Germany) *dwlt: sn in tch: 7th and btn st* **168/10**

1m 43.65s (4.54) **9** Ran SP% **130.5**
WIN 71; PL 14, 14, 18; SF 119.
Owner Stall Titan **Bred** Pavel Kusmin **Trained** Germany

2586 CAPANNELLE (R-H)
Sunday, October 25

OFFICIAL GOING: Good to soft

7046a PREMIO LYDIA TESIO SHADWELL (GROUP 1) (F&M) 1m 2f
3:30 (3:39) 3-Y-O+ **£167,374** (£84,899; £49,609; £24,805)

RPR
1 **Eva's Request (IRE)**[53] 5588 4-8-13 .... AlanMunro 15 109
(M R Channon) *hld up: 11th st: brought wd: hdwy wl over 2f out: drvn to ld last strides (exact SP 11.44/1)* **114/10**

The Form Book, Raceform Ltd, Compton, RG20 6NL

2 hd **Night Magic (GER)**[21] 6525 3-8-10 KKerekes 8 111
(W Figge, Germany) *a.p: 4th st: led over 2f out: drvn over 1f out: ct last strides* **54/10[3]**
3 hd **Les Fazzani (IRE)**[50] 5689 5-8-13 PhillipMakin 12 108
(K A Ryan) *trckd ldr: 2nd st: ev ch wl over 1f out: r.o* **202/10**
4 nk **Nashmiah (IRE)**[22] 6479 3-8-10 NCallan 14 110
(C E Brittain) *a cl up: 7th st on outside: rdn 2f out: styd on wl u.p: nrest at fin* **205/10**
5 2 1/4 **Lady Marian (GER)**[21] 6525 4-8-13 HayleyTurner 13 103
(Saeed Bin Suroor) *hld up towards rr to st: hdwy on wd outside 3f out: kpt on u.p fnl 2f: nvr nrr (cpld w Flying Cloud)* **29/10[2]**
6 nse **Flying Cloud (IRE)**[129] 3047 3-8-10 TedDurcan 10 105
(Saeed Bin Suroor) *mid-div: hdwy on far side over 2f out: rdn wl over 1f out: one pce (cpld w Lady Marian)* **29/10[2]**
7 1 **Louise Aron (IRE)**[21] 3-8-10 SLandi 11 103
(Sante Zanardino, Italy) *nvr nrr than mid-div* **62/1**
8 1 3/4 **Quiza Quiza Quiza**[112] 3668 3-8-10 MDemuro 1 100
(L Riccardi, Italy) *led to over 2f out* **118/10**
9 1 1/4 **Allegoria (IRE)**[14] 6715 4-8-13 CColombi 9 95
(V Valiani, Italy) *prom: 6th st: btn wl over 1f out* **56/1**
10 3 **Chinese White (IRE)**[43] 5890 4-8-13 PJSmullen 6 89
(D K Weld, Ire) *prom: 3rd st: btn 2f out* **13/10[1]**
11 1/2 **Tapioka Express (IRE)**[127] 3186 3-8-10 ASanna 5 90
(F & L Camici, Italy) *a in rr* **114/1**
12 2 **Night Of Magic (IRE)**[21] 6521 3-8-10 DPorcu 2 86
(H Steinmetz, Germany) *last st: nvr a factor* **14/1**
13 2 **Suchita Devious (ITY)**[21] 3-8-10 MBelli 4 82
(G Cassanelli, Italy) *prom: 5th st: btn 3f out* **61/1**
14 2 1/4 **Cottonmouth (IRE)**[14] 6715 5-8-13 NPinna 7 76
(S Botti, Italy) *a bhd* **92/10**
15 15 **Rosa Del Dubai (IRE)**[14] 6715 4-8-13 DVargiu 3 46
(B Grizzetti, Italy) *a towards rr: wl bhd fnl 2f* **60/1**

2m 4.30s (1.00)
WFA 3 from 4yo+ 5lb **15 Ran SP% 159.6**
(including 1 Euro stake): WIN 12.44; PL 5.22, 2.96, 5.28; SF 94.70.
Owner Liam Mulryan **Bred** Ballylinch Stud **Trained** West Ilsley, Berks

NOTEBOOK
Eva's Request(IRE), successful in a Turkish Group 2 last time out, took her first win at Group 1 level and proved her stamina for 1m2f in no uncertain style.
Les Fazzani(IRE), winner of a handicap in Ireland off 103 last time out, stays further than this and appreciates plenty of give in the ground. She ran a solid race having been up there all the way.
Nashmiah(IRE) probably prefers the ground quicker than this but she still ran her best race of the campaign.
Lady Marian(GER) hasn't hit the heights of last season and was again below her best.
Flying Cloud(IRE), not seen since winning the Ribblesdale at Royal Ascot, suffered her first ever defeat but wasn't disgraced.

6888 LONGCHAMP (R-H)
Sunday, October 25

OFFICIAL GOING: Soft

7047a PRIX ROYAL-OAK (GROUP 1) 1m 7f 110y
1:35 (1:39) 3-Y-O+ **£138,689** (£55,485; £27,743; £13,859; £6,942)

RPR
1 **Ask**[92] 4298 6-9-4 RyanMoore 1 123
(Sir Michael Stoute) *broke wl: settled disputing 3rd: 3rd over 4f out: wnt 2nd ent st: led ins fnl 100yds: r.o wl* **7/4[1]**
2 1 1/2 **Schiaparelli (GER)**[7] 6893 6-9-4 LDettori 3 121
(Saeed Bin Suroor) *led: drvn 3 l clr over 1f out: ct ins fnl 100yds: r.o one pce* **7/2[2]**
3 3 **Manighar (FR)**[22] 6502 3-8-9 C-PLemaire 5 119
(A De Royer-Dupre, France) *hld up in 8th: 2nd st: hdwy on outside fr over 2f out: rdn wl over 1f out: 3rd 1f out: one pce* **9/2**
4 1 1/2 **Clowance**[43] 5891 4-9-1 KFallon 6 113
(R Charlton) *racd in 5th to st: rdn over 1 1/2f out: one pce* **4/1[3]**
5 6 **Pouvoir Absolu**[21] 6527 4-9-4 (b) ACrastus 7 110
(E Lellouche, France) *mid-div: 7th st: rdn over 2f out: sn btn* **14/1**
6 2 1/2 **Askar Tau (FR)**[21] 6527 4-9-4 (v) RichardHughes 2 107
(M P Tregoning) *disp 3rd: 4th over 4f out: clsd up on outside and hung in ent st: sn disputing 2nd: rdn and btn wl over 1f out* **14/1**
7 nk **Sassoaloro (GER)**[21] 6521 5-9-4 DBoeuf 4 107
(H Blume, Germany) *mid-div: 6th st: sn one pce* **28/1**
8 20 **The Miniver Rose (IRE)**[45] 5796 3-8-6 SPasquier 9 83
(R Hannon) *last virtually thrght* **28/1**
9 2 **Sevenna (FR)**[87] 4458 4-9-1 CSoumillon 8 80
(H R A Cecil) *sn trcking ldr: cl 3rd whn bmpd ent st: sn wknd* **25/1**

3m 32.17s (10.67) **Going Correction** +0.20s/f (Good)
WFA 3 from 4yo+ 9lb **9 Ran SP% 120.8**
Speed ratings: **81,80,78,78,75 73,73,63,62**
PARI-MUTUEL: WIN 3.40; PL 1.30, 1.40, 1.40; DF 6.20.
Owner Patrick J Fahey **Bred** Side Hill Stud **Trained** Newmarket, Suffolk

FOCUS
There was a lengthy stewards' enquiry before the result was confirmed.

NOTEBOOK
Ask took an age to hit top gear in the home straight, but eventually won this Group 1 contest with something in hand. He won't run again this year and is now being specifically targeted at the Dubai Sheema Classic before coming back to Europe for top-class middle-distance events.
Schiaparelli(GER) put in a game effort to make all the running. He set a reasonable pace early on and really quickened things up early in the straight. Looking the likely winner a furlong and a half out, his stride then began to shorten inside the final furlong. He loves cut in the ground and, while there are no plans for the moment, he will no doubt be raced where the going is suitable next year.
Manighar(FR) was held up in the early stages and not too lucky turning into the straight, but it didnt really make much difference. He engaged top gear from two out and was putting in his best work at the finish. Next year he will be aimed at races like the Prix de Barbeville and Prix Vicomtesse Vigier, and connections will also have a look at the Ascot Gold Cup.
Clowance, who ran such a huge race when second in the Irish St Leger on her belated reappearance, was a little disappointing, although only given how well she had performed at the Curragh. However, she behaved like a proper madam at the start and was very reluctant to load, which suggests that she might not have been at the top of her game. She will stay in training.
Askar Tau(FR) was never seen with a chance and made no show.

7021 KEMPTON (A.W) (R-H)
Monday, October 26

OFFICIAL GOING: Standard
Wind: Moderate behind Weather: Sunny

7048 BISTRO PRICES FROM £37 H'CAP 1m 2f (P)
2:10 (2:10) (Class 5) (0-75,75) 3-Y-O+ **£2,590** (£770; £385; £192) **Stalls High**

Form RPR
4542 1 **Burma Rock (IRE)**[16] 6673 3-9-6 **74** WilliamBuick 2 87+
(L M Cumani) *hld up in tch: hdwy 3f out: rdn 2f out: led appr fnl f: pushed out* **5/2[1]**
6154 2 1 3/4 **Master Fong (IRE)**[21] 6552 3-9-7 **75** AdamKirby 11 80
(B W Hills) *chsd ldrs: rdn along fr 5f out: kpt on fr over 1f out to chsd wnr ins fnl f: no ch but hld on wl for 2nd* **4/1[2]**
2026 3 nk **Resplendent Ace (IRE)**[9] 6860 5-9-4 **67** TonyCulhane 13 72
(P Howling) *in rr: hdwy towards outside wl over 1f out: styd on wl fnl f to press for 2nd cl home but no ch w wnr* **12/1**
0010 4 1 1/2 **Sapphire Prince (USA)**[7] 6908 3-8-13 **70** MarcHalford[(3)] 7 72
(J R Best) *in rr: hdwy on outside fr wl over 1f out: styd on ins fnl f but nvr a threat* **18/1**
0040 5 hd **Supercast (IRE)**[13] 6760 6-9-9 **72** LukeMorris 4 73
(N J Vaughan) *chsd ldrs: rdn over 2f out: wknd fnl f* **16/1**
-160 6 3/4 **Lyra's Daemon**[13] 6760 3-9-4 **72** GeorgeBaker 3 72
(W R Muir) *led after 1f: rdn over 2f out: hdd appr fnl f: wknd ins fnl f* **16/1**
-000 7 nk **Daniel Thomas (IRE)**[12] 6778 7-9-5 **68** EddieAhern 14 67
(Mrs A L M King) *s.i.s: sn in mid-div: rdn 3f out: no imp on ldrs 2f out tl kpt on ins fnl f: nvr a threat* **20/1**
4602 8 nse **Diamond Twister (USA)**[14] 6719 3-8-13 **67** (t) JimmyFortune 6 66
(J R Best) *chsd ldrs: wnt 2nd and rdn 3f out: ev ch ins fnl 2f: wknd fnl f* **8/1**
1000 9 nk **Drussell (IRE)**[5] 6940 3-9-2 **70** CatherineGannon 1 69+
(S Donohoe, Ire) *slowly int stride: in rr: impr 1/2-way: styng on whn nt clr run appr fnl f: nt rcvr but kpt on ins fnl f* **33/1**
21-0 10 nse **Sunny Spells**[14] 6719 4-8-13 **62** SaleemGolam 10 60
(S C Williams) *a towards rr but styd on fnl f* **20/1**
5300 11 1/2 **Aflaam (IRE)**[14] 6725 4-9-6 **69** (t) JerryO'Dwyer 8 66
(P Howling) *slowly away: a towards rr but sme prog fnl f* **14/1**
3210 12 shd **Heritage Coast (USA)**[14] 6733 4-9-9 **72** TravisBlock 12 69+
(H Morrison) *led 1f: styd chsng ldrs: rdn 3f out: wknd ins fnl f* **6/1[3]**

2m 7.17s (-0.83) **Going Correction** -0.025s/f (Stan)
WFA 3 from 4yo+ 5lb **12 Ran SP% 117.8**
Speed ratings (Par 103): **102,100,100,99,99 98,98,98,97,97 97,97**
toteswingers: 1&2 £5.30, 1&3 £6.90, 2&3 £14.80 CSF £11.28 CT £101.26 TOTE £3.30: £1.80, £1.40, £3.80; EX 17.90.
Owner Drones Racing **Bred** Philip Brady **Trained** Newmarket, Suffolk

FOCUS
A modest handicap. The winner got off the mark in good style and the third looks the best guide.
Aflaam(IRE) Official explanation: jockey said the gelding was never travelling

7049 DIGIBET H'CAP 1m 4f (P)
2:40 (2:40) (Class 6) (0-60,60) 3-Y-O **£2,047** (£604; £302) **Stalls Centre**

Form RPR
0030 1 **Saute**[24] 6446 3-8-12 **54** AdamKirby 2 60
(W R Swinburn) *sn led: mde rest and styd on u.p fr 2f out: edgd rt ins fnl f: r.o gamely* **16/1**
0566 2 1 1/4 **Carter**[2] 7022 3-9-1 **57** ShaneKelly 7 61
(W M Brisbourne) *chsd ldrs: rdn and ev ch 2f out: chsd wnr ins fnl f and hld whn crossed: hld on wl for 2nd* **9/1**
2550 3 nk **Pure Crystal**[74] 4470 3-8-8 **50** JerryO'Dwyer 3 53
(M G Quinlan) *in rr: hdwyfr 2f out: styd on u.p to press for 2nd cl home but no ch w wnr* **50/1**
0303 4 nse **Cayman Sky**[5] 6941 3-9-0 **59** (b) PatrickHills[(3)] 4 62
(R Hannon) *hld up in mid-div: hdwy over 3f out: styd on fr over 1f out: kpt on ins fnl f to press for 2nd cl home but no ch w wnr* **6/1**
6655 5 1 1/4 **Chateauneuf (IRE)**[47] 5775 3-8-11 **53** (p) MichaelHills 6 54
(B W Hills) *chsd ldrs tl rdn and lost position 4f out: hung rt u.p 2f out: styd on again fnl f but nvr a threat* **16/1**
3505 6 3 1/2 **Persian Memories (IRE)**[21] 6538 3-9-3 **59** (b[1]) EddieAhern 8 54
(J L Dunlop) *in rr: chsng ldrs: stdd in mid-div 1/2-way: hdwy on ins fr 3f out: rdn and ev ch over 1f out: wknd ins fnl f* **9/2[3]**
0022 7 7 **Sircozy (IRE)**[26] 6371 3-8-10 **55** WilliamCarson[(3)] 1 39
(S C Williams) *s.i.s: sn chsng ldrs: wnt 2nd 6f out: rdn 3f out: ev ch 2f out: wknd fnl f* **4/1[2]**
6624 8 3 **D'Artagnans Dream**[6] 6917 3-9-3 **59** (b) TravisBlock 5 38
(G D Blake) *slowly away: hdwy and wd on bnd after 2f: sn chsng ldrs but styd on: wknd 2f out* **7/2[1]**
000 9 1 1/4 **First Maid**[59] 5381 3-7-13 **46** oh1 AmyBaker[(5)] 10 23
(A B Haynes) *rdn 1/2-way: a bhd* **100/1**
3440 10 2 1/4 **Cluny**[14] 6742 3-9-4 **60** GeorgeBaker 11 34
(J R Fanshawe) *rdn 5f out: a in rr* **20/1**
5064 11 2 1/2 **Bubses Boy**[21] 6538 3-8-12 **54** TonyCulhane 9 24
(P Howling) *chsd ldrs: wknd qckly over 3f out* **12/1**

2m 34.89s (0.39) **Going Correction** -0.025s/f (Stan) **11 Ran SP% 111.9**
Speed ratings (Par 99): **97,96,95,95,95 92,88,86,85,83 82**
toteswingers: 1&2 £19.50, 1&3 £43.40, 2&3 £61.10 CSF £143.22 CT £6796.98 TOTE £16.50: £5.30, £1.30, £10.60; EX 155.30.
Owner The Lucky Few **Bred** Azienda Agricola Rosati Colarieti **Trained** Aldbury, Herts

FOCUS
A poor race run at a steady pace. The form appears sound.
Cluny Official explanation: joceky said filly was never travelling
Bubses Boy Official explanation: jockey said gelding hung left on the final bend

7050 DIGIBET.COM MAIDEN STKS 7f (P)
3:10 (3:13) (Class 4) 2-Y-O **£3,885** (£1,156; £577; £288) **Stalls High**

Form RPR
1 **Prizefighting (USA)** 2-9-3 0 JimmyFortune 12 80+
(J H M Gosden) *in rr: sme prog whn nt clr run and swtchd lft over 2f out: stl 8 l down whn hdwy to chse ldng duo over 1f out: rapid hdwy under hand riding ins fnl f to ld nr fin: won gng away impressive* **14/1**
2 2 3/4 **Silk Street (USA)**[11] 6796 2-9-0 0 FrederikTylicki[(3)] 11 78
(R A Fahey) *chsd ldrs: wnt 2nd over 3f out: drvn to chal ins fnl 2f: slt ld fnl 110yds: hdd and outpcd cl home* **7/2[2]**

5 **3** *1 1/4* **Mutafajer**[18] 6616 2-9-3 0 .... LDettori 10 75
(Saeed Bin Suroor) *led: drvn and styd on whn chal fr ins fnl 2f: hdd and no ex fnl 110yds* **4/6**[1]

6 **4** *7* **Grey Bunting**[18] 6615 2-9-3 0 .... MichaelHills 14 57
(B W Hills) *chsd ldrs: rdn over 2f out: styd on same pce and no ch w ldng duo fr over 1f out* **10/1**[3]

00 **5** *2 1/4* **Passionate Cry (USA)**[18] 6617 2-9-3 0 .... ShaneKelly 5 52
(W J Knight) *wnt lft s: sn chsng ldrs: rdn over 2f out: sn one pce* **100/1**

6 *1/2* **Alubari** 2-9-3 0 .... AdamKirby 4 51
(W R Swinburn) *bmpd s: bhd: pushed along over 3f: prog on ins fr 2f out but nvr in contention* **50/1**

0 **7** *2* **Silent Dancer (IRE)**[4] 6965 2-9-3 0 .... RichardHughes 3 46
(S Donohoe, Ire) *bmpd s: in rr: sme hdwy 2f out: nvr in contention* **28/1**

0 **8** *1/2* **Dhan Dhana (IRE)**[48] 5752 2-8-12 0 .... TonyCulhane 13 39
(W J Haggas) *in rr tl sme hdwy fnl 2f* **50/1**

9 *1* **Ana Moutabahi** 2-9-3 0 .... LukeMorris 7 42
(C G Cox) *in rr: pushed along over 4f out: nvr gng pce to get into contention* **66/1**

10 *nk* **Dame Shanakill (USA)** 2-8-12 0 .... TPQueally 8 36
(H R A Cecil) *t.k.h: in tch: pushed along over 3f out: wknd over 1f out* **12/1**

00 **11** *2* **Celtic Ransom**[18] 6616 2-9-3 0 .... EddieAhern 6 36
(J W Hills) *chsd ldrs on outside tl wknd over 2f out* **50/1**

005 **12** *6* **Joan's Legacy**[75] 4906 2-8-12 55 .... RichardSmith 1 16
(J C Fox) *a towards rr* **66/1**

00 **13** *4* **Roybuoy**[14] 6727 2-9-3 0 .... MickyFenton 9 11
(H J L Dunlop) *sn chsng ldr: lost pl on outside and wknd over 3f out* **100/1**

1m 25.64s (-0.36) **Going Correction** -0.025s/f (Stan) **13** Ran SP% **120.0**
Speed ratings (Par 97): **101,100,98,90,88 87,85,84,83,83 80,74,69**
toteswingers: 1&2 £5.20, 1&3 £4.60, 2&3 £1.70 CSF £61.73 TOTE £12.40: £2.80, £1.30, £1.10; EX 59.70.
Owner H R H Princess Haya Of Jordan **Bred** Allen E Paulson Living Trust **Trained** Newmarket, Suffolk

FOCUS
There was always the possibility of hype surrounding the winner of this maiden, considering Ghanaati landed the race last year, but even so it was hard not to be impressed with Prizefighting.

NOTEBOOK
Prizefighting(USA) ◆, a $500,000 purchase, produced a remarkable performance on his debut. Having been hampered over 2f out, he had around 8l to find on the runner-up and third-placed finisher when switched into the clear shortly after, but he found a stunning change of pace, without being hit with the whip, to score a most unlikely victory. Ultimately a cosy winner, this performance was all the more noteworthy given the next two home maintained their advantage over the remainder, and the final time was quicker than both divisions of the older-horse 46-60 handicap later on the card. He's a colt with size and scope and could well be a Group horse next year. (tchd 16-1)
Silk Street(USA) did really well to wear down the Godolphin runner and looked to have done enough, but he had no answer to the winner's late surge. This was a useful effort in defeat and he should soon be winning. (tchd 3-1)
Mutafajer ◆ improved on the form he showed on his debut at Newbury but still found a couple too good. He's a fine-looking colt and should go on improving. (op 8-11 tchd 8-13)
Grey Bunting ran okay without really building on the form he showed first time up at Newbury, although he still looked as though the race would do him good. (op 8-1 tchd 7-1)
Passionate Cry(USA) should find his level now handicaps are an option.
Alubari, a half-brother to Leporello, showed ability, keeping on nicely in the closing stages from well off the pace. However, he was a bit edgy beforehand and needed a blanket for stalls entry, so it's hoped he goes the right way.

7051 DIGIBET CASINO H'CAP (DIV I) 7f (P)
3:40 (3:40) (Class 6) (0-60,60) 3-Y-O+ **£1,706** (£503; £252) **Stalls High**

Form RPR

6464 **1** **Eliza Doolittle**[6] 6926 3-9-0 **56** .... AdamKirby 12 64
(J R Fanshawe) *chsd ldrs: hdwy on ins over 2f out: styd on u.p to chal thrght fnl f: led last strides* **15/2**

306 **2** *shd* **Copperwood**[150] 2459 4-8-10 **50** .... NCallan 13 58
(M Blanshard) *hld up in tch: hdwy over 1f out: chal ins fnl f: slt advantage fnl 110yds: hdd last strides* **16/1**

2031 **3** *1/2* **Leelu**[18] 6611 3-9-0 **56** .... EddieAhern 11 63
(D W P Arbuthnot) *led: rdn and styd on whn chal fr over 2f out: hdd fnl 110yds: styd upsides tl no ex nr fin* **9/2**[1]

5320 **4** *1* **Vanadium**[5] 6933 7-8-9 **56** ....(t) AmyScott(7) 5 60+
(A J Lidderdale) *mid-div: hdwy over 1f out: styd on fnl f: nt rch ldrs* **14/1**

3345 **5** *1* **Russian Angel**[46] 5791 5-8-9 **49** .... J-PGuillambert 9 50
(Jean-Rene Auvray) *chsd ldr: chal over 2f out tl over 1f out: styd wl there tl wknd fnl 110yds* **12/1**

6643 **6** *nk* **Rockfield Lodge (IRE)**[87] 4479 4-9-0 **54** .... StephenDonohoe 3 54
(Ian Williams) *in tch: pushed along and hdwy over 1f out: kpt on but nvr gng pce to rch ldrs* **7/1**[3]

1155 **7** *1* **La Gifted**[14] 6720 3-9-4 **60** .... CatherineGannon 8 58
(M R Channon) *chsd ldrs: hung bdly lft fr over 2f out: no ch w ldrs after but kpt on* **12/1**

2052 **8** *hd* **Loyal Royal (IRE)**[10] 6828 6-9-3 **60** ....(b) JackDean(3) 6 57
(J M Bradley) *hld up in rr: hdwy fnl f: gng on cl home* **8/1**

0634 **9** *1/2* **Djalalabad (FR)**[5] 6945 5-8-12 **52** ....(tp) MickyFenton 7 48
(Mrs C A Dunnett) *stdd and wnt rt s: sme prog on ins 2f out: nvr gng pce to rch ldrs* **11/1**

5642 **10** *3/4* **Boss Hog**[27] 6358 4-9-2 **56** .... TonyCulhane 14 50
(P T Midgley) *in tch: rdn 3f out: wknd over 1f out* **7/1**[3]

0041 **11** *1 3/4* **Annes Rocket (IRE)**[19] 6587 4-9-6 **60** .... RichardHughes 4 49
(J C Fox) *stdd s and wnt rt: sme prog fnl f* **5/1**[2]

1000 **12** *4* **Ishibee (IRE)**[25] 6422 5-8-2 **49** ow1 ....(p) RyanClark(7) 1 27
(J J Bridger) *a towards rr* **66/1**

460 **13** *1 3/4* **Moneysupermarket (IRE)**[44] 5881 3-8-1 **48** .... PaulPickard(5) 2 22
(Patrick Morris) *stdd s: a outpcd* **66/1**

0000 **14** *19* **Nun Today (USA)**[52] 5647 3-8-7 **49** ....(b) JerryO'Dwyer 10 —
(Karen George) *uns rdr and bolted 2f to s: rdn and bhd fr 1/2-way* **40/1**

1m 26.32s (0.32) **Going Correction** -0.025s/f (Stan)
WFA 3 from 4yo+ 2lb **14** Ran SP% **124.4**
Speed ratings (Par 101): **97,96,96,95,94 93,92,92,91,90 88,84,82,60**
toteswingers: 1&2 £31.20, 1&3 £11.60, 2&3 £12.40 CSF £125.31 CT £468.45 TOTE £9.50: £3.10, £5.50, £2.50; EX 146.60.
Owner Mrs C C Regalado-Gonzalez **Bred** Miss A J Rawding & P M Crane **Trained** Newmarket, Suffolk
■ Stewards' Enquiry : N Callan two-day ban: used whip with excessive frequency, and without giving time to respond.
Adam Kirby cauiton: use of whip

FOCUS
A moderate handicap in which those drawn high dominated. Nothing got into it from the rear. The winner stepped up on her maiden form.
La Gifted Official explanation: jockey said that the filly hung left
Loyal Royal(IRE) Official explanation: jockey said that the gelding ran too free
Annes Rocket(IRE) Official explanation: jockey said the colt hung left throughout
Nun Today(USA) Official explanation: jockey said that the filly was never travelling

7052 DIGIBET CASINO H'CAP (DIV II) 7f (P)
4:10 (4:12) (Class 6) (0-60,60) 3-Y-O+ **£1,706** (£503; £252) **Stalls High**

Form RPR

3002 **1** **Hereford Boy**[14] 6738 5-9-6 **60** ....(p) RobertHavlin 7 71
(D K Ivory) *hld up towards rr: drvn and gd hdwy over 1f out: styd on strly fnl f to ld fnl 100yds: readily* **9/2**[2]

5222 **2** *1* **Sermons Mount (USA)**[18] 6611 3-9-1 **57** ....(p) NCallan 1 65
(Mouse Hamilton-Fairley) *towards rr: gd hdwy over 2f out: drvn to ld over 1f out: hdd and nt qucknd fnl 100yds* **10/3**[1]

5000 **3** *1 1/2* **Kingsgate Storm (IRE)**[3] 7002 3-8-8 **53** .... MarcHalford(3) 13 57
(J R Best) *led: rdn over 2f out: hdd over 1f out: styd on same pce ins fnl f* **20/1**

055 **4** *shd* **True Decision**[6] 6914 3-9-2 **58** .... RichardHughes 9 62
(S Kirk) *chsd ldrs: rdn over 2f out: no imp appr fnl f: wknd fnl 110yds* **8/1**

0655 **5** *1 1/4* **Avoca Dancer (IRE)**[33] 6213 6-8-13 **53** ....(v) JerryO'Dwyer 6 54
(Karen George) *in rr: rdn over 2f out: sn hung lft: styd on fnl f: nt rch ldrs* **14/1**

3340 **6** *1/2* **Guildenstern (IRE)**[26] 6377 7-9-5 **59** .... TonyCulhane 8 58
(P Howling) *in rr tl hdwy on ins over 2f out: chsd ldrs 1f out: wknd qckly ins fnl f* **8/1**

6000 **7** *3/4* **Imperium**[32] 6226 8-9-0 **54** .... J-PGuillambert 4 51
(Jean-Rene Auvray) *chsd ldrs: rdn over 2f out: wknd ins fnl f* **25/1**

0034 **8** *1/2* **Commandingpresence (USA)**[28] 6344 3-8-3 **52** .... RyanClark(7) 12 48
(J J Bridger) *chsd ldrs: rdn over 2f out: wknd ins fnl f* **18/1**

3533 **9** *1* **Turkish Lokum**[10] 6828 3-9-3 **59** .... LukeMorris 11 52
(J M P Eustace) *chsd ldrs: rdn 3f out: sn one pce: wknd fnl f* **7/1**[3]

6404 **10** *nk* **Imperial Skylight**[15] 6701 3-9-0 **56** .... CatherineGannon 2 48
(M R Channon) *in rr: pushed along over 2f out: sme prog over 1f out: nvr anywhere nr ldrs* **12/1**

0000 **11** *3/4* **Jojesse**[147] 2532 5-8-6 **46** oh1 .... SimonWhitworth 10 36
(W Storey) *hit rails after 1f: a in rr* **40/1**

6245 **12** *3* **Roodee King**[33] 6206 3-8-2 **49** .... PaulPickard(5) 14 31
(Patrick Morris) *reluctant to load: t.k.h: chsd ldrs: rdn over 2f out: wknd qckly appr fnl f* **14/1**

-000 **13** *nse* **Time For Old Time**[39] 6039 3-7-11 **46** oh1 .... AmyScott(7) 3 28
(I A Wood) *slowly away: in rr: v wd and hung lft fr over 3f out: nt rcvr* **25/1**

1m 26.11s (0.11) **Going Correction** -0.025s/f (Stan)
WFA 3 from 5yo+ 2lb **13** Ran SP% **117.2**
Speed ratings (Par 101): **98,96,95,95,93 93,92,91,90,90 89,85,85**
toteswingers: 1&2 £3.20, 1&3 £25.60, 2&3 £16.30 CSF £18.39 CT £283.58 TOTE £5.30: £1.90, £1.70, £7.50; EX 20.20.
Owner Recycled Products Limited **Bred** Mrs L R Burrage **Trained** Radlett, Herts
■ Stewards' Enquiry : Catherine Gannon two-day ban: (Nov 9, 11)

FOCUS
The winning time was 0.21 seconds quicker than the first division. A similar level of form, rated through the runner-up.
Time For Old Time Official explanation: jockey said that the filly hung left

7053 KEMPTON.CO.UK CLASSIFIED CLAIMING STKS 6f (P)
4:40 (4:40) (Class 6) 3-Y-O+ **£2,047** (£604; £302) **Stalls High**

Form RPR

5-31 **1** **Absa Lutte (IRE)**[2] 7021 6-8-13 **65** ....(t) SJCraine 7 73+
(Patrick Morris) *hld up in rr: stdy hdwy over 1f out to ld ins fnl f: sn in control: comf* **9/4**[2]

0030 **2** *1 1/2* **Thunder Bay**[26] 6379 4-8-8 **56** ow2 .... FrederikTylicki(3) 8 64
(R A Fahey) *hld up in rr: hdwy whn n.m.r and swtchd lft 2f out: r.o wl fnl f to take 2nd cl home but no ch w wnr* **20/1**

2254 **3** *hd* **Lethal**[73] 4978 6-8-5 **63** .... RosieJessop(7) 1 64
(Andrew Reid) *sn led: rdn over 2f out: hdd ins fnl f: styd on same pce: lost 2nd cl home* **14/1**

0626 **4** *nk* **Onceaponatime (IRE)**[6] 6915 4-8-9 **67** ....(p) PaulPickard(5) 3 65
(M D Squance) *sn chsng ldrs: rdn over 2f out: kpt on same pce ins fnl f* **6/1**[3]

5000 **5** *3/4* **Musical Script (USA)**[6] 6915 6-9-2 **67** ....(p) NCallan 5 65
(Mouse Hamilton-Fairley) *in tch: hdwy 2f out: chsd ldrs 1f out: sn wknd* **8/1**

5-32 **6** *nk* **Braddock (IRE)**[2] 7023 6-9-0 **66** ....(t) RichardHughes 2 62
(S Donohoe, Ire) *chsd ldr: pushed along 2f out: fdd ins fnl f* **15/8**[1]

6206 **7** *2* **Royal Envoy (IRE)**[12] 6783 6-9-0 **65** .... JerryO'Dwyer 6 56
(P Howling) *s.i.s: rdn 1/2-way: a towards rr* **10/1**

050 **8** *nk* **Shadow Bay (IRE)**[15] 6699 3-8-11 **63** .... SamHitchcott 4 53
(Miss Z C Davison) *chsd ldrs tl wknd over 1f out* **66/1**

1m 12.65s (-0.45) **Going Correction** -0.025s/f (Stan)
WFA 3 from 4yo+ 1lb **8** Ran SP% **113.0**
Speed ratings (Par 101): **102,100,99,99,98 97,95,94**
toteswingers: 1&2 £9.20, 1&3 £7.80, 2&3 £13.70 CSF £43.79 TOTE £3.10: £1.40, £3.20, £2.50; EX 47.30.Absa Lutte was claimed by G Kelleway for £7,000.
Owner I T Amond **Bred** Ian Amond **Trained** Tarporley, Cheshire
■ Stewards' Enquiry : Rosie Jessop one-day ban: used whip with excessive frequency (remedial training centre)

FOCUS
An ordinary claimer. The favourite disappointed and the winner only had to repeat her recent 5f win here.
Braddock(IRE) Official explanation: jockey said that the gelding hung both ways

7054 BOXINGDAYRACES.CO.UK H'CAP 1m (P)
5:10 (5:10) (Class 4) (0-80,79) 3-Y-O+ **£4,727** (£1,406; £702; £351) **Stalls High**

Form RPR

6042 **1** **Beauchamp Viceroy**[23] 6495 5-9-4 **79** ....(bt) FrederikTylicki(3) 2 88
(G A Butler) *mde virtually all: rdn 2f out: styd on wl thrght fnl f* **5/1**[2]

1560 **2** *hd* **Indy Driver**[15] 6695 4-9-3 **75** ....(p) EddieAhern 7 84
(J R Fanshawe) *in rr: hdwy over 1f out: str run fnl f to cl on wnr nr fin but a hld* **8/1**[3]

3321 **3** *1* **Dinner Date**[14] 6720 7-8-11 **69** .... LPKeniry 3 75
(T Keddy) *chsd ldrs: wnt 2nd travelling wl appr fnl f: sn rdn and no imp: outpcd into 3rd nr fin* **14/1**

5441 **4** *nk* **Hawaana (IRE)**[12] 6780 4-9-7 **79** LDettori 10 85
(Miss Gay Kelleway) *in rr: hdwy over 1f out: styd on wl fnl f but nt rch ldrs* **5/1**[2]

6221 **5** *2 1/2* **Berbice (IRE)**[4] 6976 4-9-4 **76** 6ex (b) RichardHughes 8 76+
(S Donohoe, Ire) *missed break by 5 l: t.k.h and hld up in rr: styd on fr over 1f out: nvr in contention* **5/4**[1]

6550 **6** *1 1/2* **Justcallmehandsome**[38] 6072 7-8-6 **71** (v) BillyCray(7) 4 67
(D J S Ffrench Davis) *chsd ldrs: rdn over 2f out: wknd fnl f* **25/1**

0006 **7** *nk* **The Snatcher (IRE)**[33] 6212 6-9-2 **77** PatrickHills(3) 11 73
(R Hannon) *in rr: rdn and sme hdwy 2f out: nvr rchd ldrs* **14/1**

0013 **8** *2* **Trade Centre**[17] 6630 4-9-0 **72** WilliamBuick 1 63
(W R Muir) *chsd ldrs in 3rd: rdn over 2f out: sn btn* **12/1**

0542 **9** *2* **Murrin (IRE)**[12] 6780 5-8-13 **71** (p) StephenDonohoe 5 57
(T G Mills) *a towards rr* **12/1**

0004 **10** *shd* **Prince Of Thebes (IRE)**[12] 6778 8-9-2 **74** PaulDoe 6 60
(M J Attwater) *sn w wnr tl wknd ins fnl 2f* **16/1**

1m 38.15s (-1.65) **Going Correction** -0.025s/f (Stan) **10** Ran SP% **127.3**
Speed ratings (Par 105): **107,106,105,105,103 101,101,99,97,97**
toteswingers: 1&2 £14.90, 1&3 £13.00, 2&3 £17.80 CSF £49.25 CT £558.95 TOTE £6.30: £1.40, £3.00, £4.00; EX 63.40 Place 6: £236.56 Place 5: £156.40 .
Owner Erik Penser **Bred** E Penser **Trained** Newmarket, Suffolk

FOCUS
A fair handicap which was strong run. The form seems sound.
T/Jkpt: Not won. T/Plt: £2,209.20 to a £1 stake. Pool: £52,507.81. 17.35 winning tickets. T/Qpdt: £15.30 to a £1 stake. Pool: £4,687.04. 225.40 winning tickets. ST

6754 LEICESTER (R-H)
Monday, October 26

OFFICIAL GOING: Good to firm (8.7)
There was a false rail from the bend to the1f marker approx 8m from the far rail.
Wind: Light behind Weather: Overcast

7055 HAYMARKET NURSERY (DIV I) 7f 9y
1:00 (1:01) (Class 6) (0-65,65) 2-Y-O **£2,266** (£674; £337; £168) **Stalls** Low

Form RPR
0506 **1** **House Red (IRE)**[63] 5318 2-9-4 **62** RobertWinston 14 73
(B W Hills) *a.p: rdn to chse ldr over 2f out: led ins fnl f: styd on* **10/1**

500 **2** *1/2* **Power Of Dreams (IRE)**[21] 6548 2-9-5 **63** JimmyQuinn 9 72
(M H Tompkins) *hld up: hdwy over 2f out: rdn to chse wnr ins fnl f: r.o* **7/1**[3]

6310 **3** *4 1/2* **Baby Judge (IRE)**[6] 6923 2-8-9 **58** AndrewHeffernan(5) 12 56
(M C Chapman) *sn led: rdn and hdd ins fnl f: wknd towards fin* **7/1**[3]

000 **4** *hd* **Knowledgeable**[46] 5786 2-8-3 **47** DavidProbert 8 45
(B Palling) *s.i.s and hmpd s: outpcd: r.o u.p fnl f: nt rch ldrs* **25/1**

4260 **5** *1* **Crushing (IRE)**[31] 6247 2-9-6 **64** SteveDrowne 11 59
(A J McCabe) *hld up: hdwy over 1f out: r.o: nt trble ldrs* **3/1**[1]

4502 **6** *1 1/2* **Orpen Arms (IRE)**[42] 5942 2-9-2 **60** PaulMulrennan 6 51
(R A Fahey) *prom: rdn 1/2-way: wknd fnl f* **7/1**[3]

450 **7** *1/2* **Bramshill Lady (IRE)**[68] 5153 2-9-4 **65** AndreaAtzeni(3) 10 55
(Pat Eddery) *prom: rdn over 2f out: wknd over 1f out* **25/1**

2300 **8** *3/4* **Rainsborough**[14] 6721 2-9-6 **64** (b[1]) JamesDoyle 15 52
(S Curran) *s.i.s: sn chsng ldrs: rdn over 2f out: wknd fnl f* **10/1**

066 **9** *shd* **Bring Sweets (IRE)**[147] 2526 2-8-0 **49** ow3 MartinLane(5) 2 37
(B Ellison) *mid-div: rdn whn rdr dropped reins over 2f out: wknd over 1f out* **9/1**

2600 **10** *1/2* **Drinking Buddy**[7] 6895 2-8-13 **57** AlanMunro 5 44
(D W Thompson) *s.i.s: sn pushed along: a in rr* **40/1**

6443 **11** *6* **Izuizorizuain't (IRE)**[10] 6819 2-9-0 **58** TPO'Shea 4 30
(K A Ryan) *chsd ldrs: rdn over 4f out: wknd 2f out* **11/2**[2]

0005 **12** *1* **Welsh Legacy (IRE)**[91] 4371 2-8-3 **50** KellyHarrison(3) 3 19
(B W Duke) *prom: rdn 1/2-way: wknd over 2f out* **66/1**

0000 **13** *1 1/2* **Argyll**[33] 6215 2-8-12 **56** DaneO'Neill 13 21
(J Pearce) *mid-div: rdn over 2f out: sn wknd: eased fnl f* **25/1**

0433 **14** *10* **Ba Jetstream**[96] 4188 2-8-9 **53** LiamJones 7 —
(F Jordan) *s.i.s: sn drvn along: outpcd* **33/1**

1m 26.64s (0.44) **Going Correction** -0.125s/f (Firm) **14** Ran SP% **124.5**
Speed ratings (Par 93): **92,91,86,86,84 83,82,81,81,81 74,73,71,59**
toteswingers: 1&2 £17.60, 1&3 £17.90, 2&3 £15.20 CSF £75.89 CT £538.08 TOTE £11.80: £3.90, £1.90, £2.70; EX 50.20 Trifecta £188.00 Part won. Pool: £254.12 - 0.46 winning units..
Owner Richard Morecombe **Bred** P J Harrington **Trained** Lambourn, Berks

FOCUS
A low-grade nursery.

NOTEBOOK
House Red(IRE) was making his handicap bow after a two-month break. From a powerful stable ending the turf season on a high, he kept tabs on the leader and in the end did just enough. Reportedly the gelding operation has made the difference. Official explanation: trainer said, regarding the apparent improvement in form, that he had been gelded since his last run (op 7-1)
Power Of Dreams(IRE), from another stable in much better form now, was another making his nursery debut. He stayed on from way off the pace and, fast catching the winner at the line, will be suited by going back up to a mile. (op 9-1)
Baby Judge(IRE), who took a similar event from a 3lb lower mark at Yarmouth, tried to make all but was fading fast at the line. (op 9-1 tchd 13-2)
Knowledgeable, who showed precious little in three starts in maiden company, ran off just 47. He made up a deal of late ground and will be suited by a much stiffer test, but with such a low rating opportunities will be strictly limited. (op 22-1)
Crushing(IRE), who came in for plenty of market support. was having his second start for this stable and his second start after being gelded. Runner-up at Ripon on his second start, he has not progressed at all. (op 8-1)

7056 HAYMARKET NURSERY (DIV II) 7f 9y
1:30 (1:31) (Class 6) (0-65,65) 2-Y-O **£2,266** (£674; £337; £168) **Stalls** Low

Form RPR
5335 **1** **Dream Number (IRE)**[12] 6775 2-9-7 **65** PhillipMakin 6 71
(W R Muir) *trckd ldrs: rdn to ld over 1f out: r.o* **11/2**[3]

0000 **2** *1* **Dixie Bright (USA)**[17] 6639 2-9-0 **58** PaulMulrennan 2 61
(J G Given) *led: rdn and hdd over 1f out: unable qck towards fin* **33/1**

400 **3** *1/2* **Cuts Both Ways (USA)**[56] 5499 2-8-6 **50** (b[1]) MartinDwyer 1 52
(P F I Cole) *sn pushed along in rr: detached 1/2-way: r.o u.p ins fnl f: nrst fin* **15/2**

050 **4** *1 1/2* **Mini Max**[14] 6729 2-9-2 **60** DaneO'Neill 4 58
(B W Duke) *s.i.s: bhd 1/2-way: r.o ins fnl f: nvr nrr* **22/1**

0000 **5** *3/4* **Rosiliant (IRE)**[10] 6829 2-9-0 **58** (b) SteveDrowne 9 54
(C G Cox) *chsd ldrs: rdn over 2f out: no ex fnl f* **20/1**

1 **6** *6* **Push Me (IRE)**[37] 6122 2-9-6 **64** LiamJones 13 45
(M S Tuck) *s.i.s: hdwy u.p over 2f out: wknd over 1f out* **7/2**[2]

064 **7** *1/2* **Mr Harmoosh (IRE)**[28] 6334 2-9-6 **64** KFallon 10 44
(E F Vaughan) *s.i.s: sn prom: rdn over 2f out: wknd and eased fnl f* **3/1**[1]

0400 **8** *3/4* **Bojangles Andrews**[19] 6589 2-8-6 **50** (v[1]) DavidProbert 5 28
(B G Powell) *s.i.s: hdwy to chse ldr over 5f out: rdn over 2f out: wknd over 1f out* **12/1**

0000 **9** *3 1/2* **Dispol Kabira**[10] 6819 2-8-3 **47** FrancisNorton 11 17
(D W Thompson) *hld up: rdn over 4f out: wknd over 1f out* **25/1**

0400 **10** *7* **Thewinnatakesitall**[19] 6589 2-8-12 **56** KevinGhunowa 12 8
(H J Evans) *hld up: rdn 1/2-way: a in rr* **16/1**

006 **11** *14* **Regal Rave (USA)**[69] 5129 2-9-1 **59** RobertWinston 14 —
(J R Best) *sn pushed along in rr: wknd over 2f out: eased* **6/1**

1m 27.1s (0.90) **Going Correction** -0.125s/f (Firm) **11** Ran SP% **118.1**
Speed ratings (Par 93): **89,87,87,85,84 77,77,76,72,64 48**
toteswingers: 1&2 £11.90, 1&3 £10.20, 2&3 £35.40 CSF £180.95 CT £1372.05 TOTE £5.30: £2.10, £8.20, £3.20; EX 188.60 TRIFECTA Not won..
Owner Linkslade Lottery **Bred** James Waldron **Trained** Lambourn, Berks

FOCUS
Part two of this very modest nursery.

NOTEBOOK
Dream Number(IRE), who made her nursery debut on the all-weather, appreciated the step up in trip and got the better of the pacesetter to open her account at the fifth attempt. The extra furlong seemed very much in her favour. (op 5-1)
Dixie Bright(USA), struggling to make any impact since opening his account with an all-weather maiden race success at Wolverhampton in June on his second start, started life in nurseries from a 20lb higher mark. With the headgear dispensed with, he took them along at a strong pace and fought hard all the way to the line. He can certainly find a nursery from this sort of mark. (op 40-1)
Cuts Both Ways(USA), wearing blinkers on his handicap bow, came flying through from the rear in the closing stages. He will be suited by a return to a mile but, rated only 50, opportunities will be thin on the ground. (op 8-1 tchd 17-2)
Mini Max, on her third start, ran her best race so far on turf without ever really threatening after a tardy start. (tchd 16-1)
Rosiliant(IRE), wearing blinkers for a second time, does not seem to be progressing at all. (op 18-1 tchd 16-1)
Push Me(IRE), who took a Wolverhampton seller on her debut, was posted wide and could never take a hand. (op 9-2 tchd 5-1 and 100-30)
Mr Harmoosh(IRE), another making his handicap bow, found himself towards the far side and in the end was eased when all chance had gone. (op 4-1)

7057 GUMLEY CLAIMING STKS 7f 9y
2:00 (2:00) (Class 5) 3-4-Y-O **£2,590** (£770; £385; £192) **Stalls** Low

Form RPR
-600 **1** **Rioliina (IRE)**[139] 2794 3-8-2 75 FrankieMcDonald 16 74
(J G Portman) *chsd ldrs: led over 1f out: r.o wl* **33/1**

0330 **2** *3 1/4* **Piazza San Pietro**[25] 6422 3-8-9 68 KFallon 8 72
(A B Haynes) *hld up: hdwy over 1f out: wnt 2nd ins fnl f: no ch w wnr* **4/1**[2]

4-56 **3** *1 1/2* **Strategic Mover (USA)**[9] 6856 4-8-5 69 (t) MartinDwyer 17 62
(P F I Cole) *chsd ldrs: rdn over 2f out: styd on same pce fnl f* **9/1**

6032 **4** *1* **Lady Florence**[4] 6968 4-8-8 62 TPO'Shea 15 62
(A B Coogan) *led: rdn and hdd over 1f out: no ex ins fnl f* **8/1**

4602 **5** *3 1/2* **Kersivay**[24] 6455 3-9-3 72 FrancisNorton 12 64
(Ollie Pears) *hld up in tch: rdn over 2f out: wknd fnl f* **7/2**[1]

0330 **6** *3/4* **Stand In Flames**[4] 6966 4-7-13 60 AndreaAtzeni(3) 13 45
(George Baker) *mid-div: hdwy 1/2-way: rdn and wknd over 1f out* **17/2**

0000 **7** *1* **Alan Devonshire**[6] 6924 4-8-13 65 JimmyQuinn 3 53
(M H Tompkins) *prom: plld hrd: stdd and lost pl 5f out: rdn over 2f out: sn hung rt: n.d after* **18/1**

4020 **8** *1 1/4* **Hay Fever (IRE)**[18] 6611 3-8-7 62 AlanMunro 18 46
(Eve Johnson Houghton) *prom: rdn over 2f out: wknd over 1f out* **20/1**

6146 **9** *3/4* **Jeremiah (IRE)**[26] 6370 3-8-11 67 (v[1]) JamesDoyle 9 48
(J G Portman) *hmpd s: in rr: rdn over 2f out: nvr on terms* **12/1**

1004 **10** *1 1/4* **Island Chief**[9] 6846 3-8-6 71 (b) AmyRyan(5) 14 45
(K A Ryan) *chsd ldr: rdn over 2f out: sn ev ch: wknd fnl f* **5/1**[3]

0 **11** *12* **Deportista**[44] 5882 3-8-10 0 ow1 RussellKennemore(3) 6 14
(J A Pickering) *mid-div: sn pushed along: bhd fr 1/2-way* **100/1**

0220 **12** *3/4* **King's Sabre**[6] 6914 3-8-4 63 ow1 (p) PaulEddery 11 —
(R C Guest) *stdd and wnt lft s: plld hrd and sn prom: wknd over 2f out* **14/1**

1m 24.8s (-1.40) **Going Correction** -0.125s/f (Firm)
WFA 3 from 4yo 2lb **12** Ran SP% **118.8**
Speed ratings (Par 103): **103,99,97,96,92 91,90,89,88,86 73,72**
toteswingers: 1&2 £35.90, 1&3 £48.00, 2&3 £8.30 CSF £159.99 TOTE £37.80: £8.70, £1.90, £3.40; EX 256.40 TRIFECTA Not won..Strategic Mover was claimed by Patrick Butler for £6,000.
Owner Exors of the late A S B Portman **Bred** Catridge Farm Stud Ltd **Trained** Compton, Berks

FOCUS
A depleted field for this claimer. It was the quickest of the four 7f times and the runner-up seems the best guide to the form.
Alan Devonshire Official explanation: jockey said the gelding ran too freely

7058 EBF FOSSE WAY MAIDEN STKS 5f 218y
2:30 (2:30) (Class 4) 2-Y-O **£5,180** (£1,541; £770; £384) **Stalls** Low

Form RPR
5 **1** **Deacon Blues**[19] 6591 2-9-3 0 PhillipMakin 5 79
(J R Fanshawe) *trckd ldrs: racd keenly: led over 2f out: rdn over 1f out: edgd rt: r.o* **7/4**[1]

0 **2** *1 1/4* **Rolling Hills (IRE)**[15] 6696 2-9-3 0 DaneO'Neill 1 75
(H Candy) *led: hdd over 4f out: rdn over 1f out: edgd rt ins fnl f: styd on* **25/1**

02 **3** *nk* **Humidor (IRE)**[14] 6737 2-9-3 0 SteveDrowne 3 74
(R Charlton) *trckd ldrs: plld hrd: rdn over 1f out: no ex ins fnl f* **3/1**[2]

6 **4** *shd* **Vanilla Rum**[11] 6797 2-9-3 0 FrankieMcDonald 7 74
(H Candy) *prom: rdn over 2f out: sn outpcd: rallied fnl f: r.o* **20/1**

04 **5** *1/2* **Galatian**[18] 6615 2-9-0 0 JamesMillman(3) 4 72
(B R Millman) *chsd ldr tl led over 4f out: hdd and hung rt fr over 2f out: styd on same pce ins fnl f* **7/1**

6 *1 1/4* **Mint Whip (IRE)** 2-8-12 0 FrancisNorton 9 64
(R Hannon) *s.i.s: outpcd: rdn over 1f out: r.o wl ins fnl f: nrst fin* **22/1**

5 **7** *nk* **Orchid Wing**[17] 6646 2-9-3 0 TonyHamilton 2 68
(R A Fahey) *hld up: rdn and hung rt fr over 1f out: nt trble ldrs* **13/2**

0 **8** *8* **Master Of Song**[11] 6792 2-9-3 0 AmirQuinn 6 44
(S R Bowring) *s.s: hdwy 1/2-way: rdn and wknd over 2f out* **100/1**

24 **9** 1 ½ **Lady Slippers (IRE)**[27] 6363 2-8-12 0.......................... SebSanders 10 34
(H J L Dunlop) *in rr: wknd over 2f out* **6/1**[3]

1m 12.38s (-0.62) **Going Correction** -0.125s/f (Firm) **9** Ran SP% **115.4**
Speed ratings (Par 97): **99,97,96,96,96 94,94,83,81**
toteswingers: 1&2 £10.50, 1&3 £2.70, 2&3 £9.40 CSF £54.59 TOTE £3.10: £1.20, £6.90, £1.40; EX 44.40 Trifecta £207.20 Part won. Pool: £280.00 - 0.92 winning units..
Owner Jan & Peter Hopper & Michelle Morris **Bred** Mr & Mrs K W Grundy, Mr & Mrs P Hopper **Trained** Newmarket, Suffolk

FOCUS
A fair maiden.

NOTEBOOK
Deacon Blues had shown definite promise when fifth on his debut at Nottingham two weeks earlier and was reckoned to have improved a fair bit since. Well supported, he travelled strongly and after taking charge had only to be kept up to his work. His trainer has done very well with this family in the past - he is related to former course specialist Warningford - and he should make a useful sprinter at three. (op 5-2 tchd 11-4)
Rolling Hills(IRE), well beaten on his debut at Goodwood two weeks earlier, was never far behind the winner but nearer the rail could not hold that rival but kept on to grab second spot on the line. A son of Celtic Swing, he looks sure to improve and make his mark at three. (op 20-1)
Humidor(IRE), runner-up behind a useful type in a Windsor maiden on his second start, tended to race freely. After looking a major threat to the winner he did not find an awful lot, and in the end was pipped for second spot. He looks to have the mindset of a sprinter. (op 11-4 tchd 100-30)
Vanilla Rum, disappointing on his debut in soft ground at Nottingham 11 days earlier, kept on stoutly down the outside and is another who should improve at three. (op 16-1)
Galatian, fourth over slightly further on his second start at Newbury, was in the firing line throughout. This sets him up for handicaps at three. (op 9-1 tchd 6-1)
Mint Whip(IRE), bred purely for speed, made a pleasing debut putting in some eye-catching late work after a slow start. (op 20-1)
Orchid Wing was given a more patient ride this time. He will need another outing to qualify for a handicap mark at three. (op 4-1)

7059 SIR GORDON RICHARDS CONDITIONS STKS 1m 3f 183y
3:00 (3:00) (Class 3) 3-Y-0+ **£7,569** (£2,265; £1,132; £566) **Stalls** High

Form RPR
5356 **1** **Once More Dubai (USA)**[17] 6644 4-9-8 107.................(bt) AlanMunro 3 110
(Saeed Bin Suroor) *s.i.s: hld up: hdwy over 1f out: led and hung rt ins fnl f: drvn out* **17/2**[3]
-630 **2** *shd* **Copperbeech (IRE)**[10] 6813 3-8-4 99.......................... DO'Donohoe 2 99
(Saeed Bin Suroor) *chsd ldrs: rdn over 3f out: led over 1f out: hdd ins fnl f: styd on* **10/3**[2]
-605 **3** ¾ **Ezdiyaad (IRE)**[16] 6665 5-9-2 99.............................. TPO'Shea 5 103
(M P Tregoning) *sn led: rdn and hdd over 2f out: ev ch over 1f out: no ex ins fnl f* **10/3**[2]
4245 **4** 2 ¾ **Tactic**[53] 5609 3-8-13 105.. SteveDrowne 4 102
(J L Dunlop) *chsd ldr tl led over 2f out: rdn and hdd over 1f out: no ex fnl f* **1/1**[1]

2m 32.64s (-1.26) **Going Correction** +0.05s/f (Good)
WFA 3 from 4yo+ 7lb **4** Ran SP% **106.7**
Speed ratings (Par 107): **106,105,105,103**
CSF £32.60 TOTE £6.70; EX 13.20.
Owner Godolphin **Bred** Cashel Stud Inc **Trained** Newmarket, Suffolk

FOCUS
Just four runners, two from Godolphin and the other pair carrying the colours of Hamdan Al Maktoum. The pace was not bad for a small field but this is probably not form to take too literally. The winner is rated back to his 3yo best at face value.

NOTEBOOK
Once More Dubai(USA) had the same chance as the other three with the filly Copperbeech 3lb best in on official ratings. Put to sleep at the back and in no hurry to join issue, he swept down the outside entering the final furlong. He looked likely to win by a decisive margin, but the filly was very game and it was a very close call at the line, although his rider felt he got there too soon. This was his first try at this trip and the steady gallop was in his favour. (op 12-1 tchd 14-1)
Copperbeech(IRE), who is not very big, showed decent form in France at two but has rather struggled in three starts here this time. One of three in line coming to the final furlong she fought back hard when headed by the winner and would have snatched the prize in a few more strides. She is nothing if not game. (op 15-8)
Ezdiyaad(IRE), having his second outing after a five-month break, stepped up the gallop from the front with half-a-mile left to run. He battled on bravely but came up short in the end. He would not want the ground any quicker and is at his best on soft. (op 4-1 tchd 11-4)
Tactic, the last to come off the bridle, looked full of running when moving upsides but he was the first to crack. Suited by quick ground, this must go down as a disappointing effort. (op 5-4 tchd 11-8)

7060 LEICESTER RACECOURSE CONFERENCE CENTRE H'CAP 1m 60y
3:30 (3:30) (Class 3) (0-90,96) 3-Y-0+
£7,788 (£2,332; £1,166; £583; £291; £146) **Stalls** High

Form RPR
0011 **1** **Mabait**[28] 6348 3-9-1 **87**.. KFallon 9 97+
(L M Cumani) *a.p: rdn to ld and hung rt ins fnl f: r.o* **10/3**[2]
0011 **2** ¾ **Swift Chap**[18] 6621 3-8-11 **83**.................................... AlanMunro 8 92
(B R Millman) *chsd ldr tl led over 2f out: rdn over 1f out: hdd and edgd rt ins fnl f: styd on* **8/1**[3]
1102 **3** 1 ½ **Rock Anthem (IRE)**[45] 5833 5-8-4 **76** oh1.............. AndreaAtzeni(3) 10 81
(Mike Murphy) *s.i.s: hld up: hdwy over 1f out: hung rt ins fnl f: r.o: nt rch ldrs* **10/1**
5020 **4** *nse* **Daaweitza**[11] 6795 6-8-10 **84**.........................(b) MartinLane(5) 4 89
(B Ellison) *s.i.s: sn pushed into mid-div: outpcd over 2f out: rallied over 1f out: edgd rt ins fnl f: r.o* **12/1**
0003 **5** 1 ¼ **Charlie Tipple**[23] 6485 5-9-0 **83**...................(p) PaulMulrennan 2 85
(T D Easterby) *chsd ldrs: rdn over 2f out: edgd rt and styd on same pce fnl f* **16/1**
3221 **6** 6 **Sovereign Remedy (USA)**[8] 6876 3-9-10 **96** 6ex.......... DO'Donohoe 7 84
(Saeed Bin Suroor) *hld up: hdwy over 2f out: rdn over 1f out: wknd fnl f* **13/8**[1]
5000 **7** ½ **Stevie Gee (IRE)**[14] 6732 5-8-13 **82**.......................... TPO'Shea 3 69
(Ian Williams) *hld up: rdn over 2f out: nvr on terms* **20/1**
5160 **8** *shd* **Zomerlust**[10] 6815 7-9-3 **86**...........................(v) GrahamGibbons 11 73
(J J Quinn) *chsd ldrs: rdn over 2f out: wknd over 1f out* **16/1**
0000 **9** 1 ½ **City Of The Kings (IRE)**[16] 6675 4-9-2 **90**.......... PatrickDonaghy(5) 13 73
(G A Harker) *hld up: rdn over 4f out: wknd over 2f out* **25/1**
2200 **10** 2 **Guilded Warrior**[30] 6278 6-9-1 **87**.............. Louis-PhilippeBeuzelin(3) 12 66
(W S Kittow) *led: rdn and hdd over 2f out: wknd wl over 1f out* **16/1**

1m 43.95s (-1.15) **Going Correction** +0.05s/f (Good)
WFA 3 from 4yo+ 3lb **10** Ran SP% **115.3**
Speed ratings (Par 107): **107,106,104,104,103 97,96,96,95,93**
toteswingers: 1&2 £2.50, 1&3 £7.60, 2&3 £6.80 CSF £29.95 CT £241.21 TOTE £3.60: £1.90, £2.20, £2.90; EX 20.10 Trifecta £57.00 Pool: £276.24 - 3.58 winning units..

Owner Sheikh Mohammed Obaid Al Maktoum **Bred** L A C Ashby Newhall Estate Farm **Trained** Newmarket, Suffolk

FOCUS
A decent handicap in which the trio of 3-y-os dominated the betting and two of them had the finish to themselves. The pace looked solid and the form appears sound, with the first three in form coming into this. The favourite was a stone off his previous turf marks.

NOTEBOOK
Mabait has established a good partnership with Fallon and the pair completed the hat-trick in slightly comfortable fashion over the longest trip he has tackled so far. He won his previous two starts on Polytrack, so the winning run could well continue. (op 4-1 tchd 5-1)
Swift Chap, another bidding for a hat-trick, was always in the first two and did his best to resist the winner's challenge. He lost nothing in defeat off a mark 13lb higher than for the first of those successes, but will need the rain to keep away if he is to gain compensation. (op 7-1)
Rock Anthem(IRE) came into this having won his last three on turf, but including being 1lb wrong had gone up 19lb since the first of those wins. He was held up at the back before running on in the last 2f but could never get to the first two. (op 12-1 tchd 14-1)
Daaweitza appreciated the return to fast ground but had to be bustled along after missing the break. He was doing his best work at the finish as befits a horse that stays 1m2f.
Charlie Tipple has not won for over a year and is 5lb above his last winning mark but is running well at present and kept on after being close to the pace throughout. (op 14-1)
Sovereign Remedy(USA) was carrying a penalty for his success at Southwell but was well backed. He had every chance 2f out but the response was less than looked likely under pressure. Official explanation: jockey that the colt lost its action (op 7-4 after 2-1 in a place tchd 5-4)

7061 HOBY MEDIAN AUCTION MAIDEN FILLIES' STKS 5f 218y
4:00 (4:00) (Class 6) 2-Y-0 **£2,590** (£770; £385; £192) **Stalls** Low

Form RPR
56 **1** **Miss Zooter (IRE)**[21] 6544 2-9-0 0.......................... SebSanders 3 80+
(R M Beckett) *chsd ldrs: led over 3f out: rdn and hung rt fr over 1f out: r.o wl* **7/1**[3]
62 **2** 4 **Adventure Story**[7] 6903 2-9-0 0.............................. SteveDrowne 10 68
(R Hannon) *plld hrd and prom: led 5f out to over 3f out: rdn over 2f out: styd on same pce fnl f* **13/8**[1]
34 **3** 1 ¼ **Kenyan Cat**[21] 6544 2-9-0 0.. DO'Donohoe 4 64
(George Baker) *in rr whn hmpd 5f out: rdn 1/2-way: r.o ins fnl f: nrst fin* **9/1**
552 **4** ½ **Caramelita**[20] 6563 2-8-7 73.................................... DannyBrock(7) 12 63
(J R Jenkins) *led 1f: chsd ldrs: rdn over 1f out: no ex fnl f* **11/2**[2]
04 **5** *nk* **Trade Name (IRE)**[20] 6563 2-9-0 0.........................(b[1]) DaneO'Neill 7 62
(H Candy) *s.i.s: plld hrd and swtchd lft 5f out: hdwy sn after: rdn over 1f out: styd on same pce* **15/2**
4 **6** 6 **Kenswick**[11] 6797 2-8-9 0.. MartinLane(5) 6 44
(Pat Eddery) *mid-div: rdn over 3f out: wknd over 1f out* **8/1**
7 ¾ **Catawollow** 2-9-0 0... PaulEddery 1 42
(R C Guest) *s.s: outpcd: nvr nrr* **100/1**
00 **8** ¾ **Suzi's Challenger**[26] 6389 2-9-0 0............................. JimmyQuinn 11 39
(H J Collingridge) *prom: pushed along and lost pl over 3f out: n.d after* **66/1**
44 **9** 2 ½ **Via Aurelia (IRE)**[41] 5958 2-9-0 0.......................... RichardMullen 8 32
(J R Fanshawe) *prom: rdn 1/2-way: wknd wl over 1f out* **8/1**
0 **10** 1 ¼ **Keep Silent**[58] 5431 2-8-11 0.............................. AndreaAtzeni(3) 5 28
(W J H Ratcliffe) *mid-div: lost pl over 3f out: sn bhd* **100/1**
0 **11** ½ **Farmers Dream (IRE)**[18] 6615 2-9-0 0.......................... LiamJones 9 27
(J L Spearing) *plld hrd and prom: wknd over 2f out* **40/1**
12 *nse* **Sostenuto** 2-8-9 0.. RossAtkinson(5) 2 26
(T H Caldwell) *s.s: snpushed along in rr: rdn and wknd 1/2-way* **66/1**

1m 12.92s (-0.08) **Going Correction** -0.125s/f (Firm) **12** Ran SP% **117.4**
Speed ratings (Par 90): **95,89,88,87,86 78,77,76,73,71 71,71**
toteswingers: 1&2 £5.10, 1&3 £9.70, 2&3 £4.80 CSF £18.45 TOTE £8.00: £2.50, £1.20, £2.70; EX 27.40 Trifecta £81.20 Pool: £504.80 - 4.60 winning units..
Owner Timeform Betfair Racing Club Ltd **Bred** Rathyork Stud **Trained** Whitsbury, Hants

FOCUS
A fair fillies' maiden in which very few had much experience and Caramelita set the standard with an official mark of 73.

NOTEBOOK
Miss Zooter(IRE) was slightly surprisingly dropped in trip after running on well over 7f last time, but started much better than on her two previous outings and was in front at halfway going well. She ran on strongly under pressure and looks the sort to make her mark in handicaps. (op 8-1)
Adventure Story was stepping up in distance after finishing well over 5f last time. She showed plenty of pace towards the centre, but the winner had her measure in the last quarter-mile. (op 7-4 tchd 15-8 and 11-8)
Kenyan Cat looks one to be with now she qualifies for handicap mark. Given a bump early by the free-running fifth, she was near the back at halfway but really found her stride in the last furlong to snatch third near the line. A stiff test at this trip looks ideal. (tchd 10-1)
Caramelita had to race up the centre of the track from her outside draw and faded after showing up for a long way. Her best effort was on easier ground and, on a strict line through the fifth, did not run up to that form on this occasion. (op 9-2 tchd 4-1)
Trade Name(IRE) had a bit to find with today's fourth on previous form, but was fitted with blinkers for the first time and was backed. She was quite keen early, doing no favours to the third, and looked beaten 2f out before keeping on again for pressure. She is another that qualifies for handicaps now. (op 10-1)

7062 AMATEUR JOCKEYS ASSOCIATION INSURE THEIR MEMBERS H'CAP (FOR GENTLEMEN AMATEUR RIDERS) 7f 9y
4:30 (4:30) (Class 5) (0-70,69) 3-Y-0+ **£2,637** (£811; £405) **Stalls** Low

Form RPR
1000 **1** **Realt Na Mara (IRE)**[14] 6739 6-10-5 **65**.................... MrRPooles(5) 10 77
(H Morrison) *a.p: led over 2f out: pushed clr fr over 1f out* **8/1**[3]
4242 **2** 4 **Iron Out (USA)**[3] 6997 3-10-5 **67**.................. MrStephenHarrison(5) 6 68
(R Hollinshead) *mid-div: hdwy 4f out: outpcd over 2f out: r.o fr over 1f out: no ch w wnr* **11/4**[1]
0134 **3** ¾ **Sairaam (IRE)**[10] 6824 3-9-7 **55**.............................. MrAWedge(5) 17 54
(C Smith) *mid-div: hdwy 1/2-way: rdn over 1f out: styd on same pce* **9/1**
060- **4** 3 ¾ **Camerooney**[24] 3551 6-9-9 **55** oh9.............................. DaleSwift(5) 15 44
(B Ellison) *chsd ldr tl led over 5f out: hdd over 4f out: rdn over 2f out: sn edgd lft: styd on same pce* **16/1**
0415 **5** 1 ¾ **Castano**[19] 6596 5-9-10 **56**...................................... MrPMillman(5) 12 40
(B R Millman) *chsd ldrs: led over 4f out: hdd over 2f out: wknd fnl f* **10/1**
0001 **6** 2 **Ocean Legend (IRE)**[15] 6703 4-10-8 **68**.................. MrRBirkett(5) 2 47
(Miss J Feilden) *s.i.s: hld up: styd on fr over 1f out: n.d* **9/1**
3502 **7** 2 **Kheskianto (IRE)**[20] 6568 3-9-10 **60**............................ MrJBanks(7) 7 34
(M C Chapman) *prom: rdn over 2f out: wknd over 1f out* **14/1**
3040 **8** 6 **Efidium**[13] 6768 11-10-6 **68** ow11.....................(b) MrSebSpencer(7) 18 25
(N Bycroft) *s.i.s: nvr on terms* **25/1**
6066 **9** 6 **West End Lad**[21] 6545 6-10-11 **69**.........................(b) MrTRDavid(3) 11 10
(S R Bowring) *a in rr: bhd fnl 4f* **10/1**

0-00 **10** 1 1/2 **A One (IRE)**[42] 5936 10-9-7 **55** oh10.......................... MrSamPainting(7) 9 —
(Mrs H J Manners) *pushed along to ld: hdd over 5f out: wknd 1/2-way* **66/1**

214 **11** 4 **Averoo**[10] 6828 4-10-6 **61**..(p) MrSWalker 16 —
(M D Squance) *prom: rdn 1/2-way: sn wknd* **10/3**[2]

0-60 **12** 55 **Canary Girl**[130] 3076 6-9-7 **55** oh10...........................(v) MrPFerguson(7) 1 —
(G Prodromou) *sn outpcd: lost tch 4f out: eased fnl 2f* **100/1**

1m 25.54s (-0.66) **Going Correction** -0.125s/f (Firm)
WFA 3 from 4yo+ 2lb **12** Ran SP% **117.9**
Speed ratings (Par 103): **98,93,92,88,86 84,81,74,68,66 61,—**
toteswingers: 1&2 £8.60, 1&3 £14.70, 2&3 £6.60 CSF £29.78 CT £210.15 TOTE £5.70: £2.90, £1.90, £2.90; EX 31.30 TRIFECTA Not won. Place 6: £1290.11 Place 5: £409.50.
Owner H Morrison **Bred** J C Condon **Trained** East Ilsley, Berks

FOCUS
The field for this modest amateur riders' handicap was reduced by a third due to withdrawals. The winner is rated to his turf best.
Ocean Legend(IRE) Official explanation: jockey said that the gelding lost its near-fore plate
Canary Girl Official explanation: jockey said that the mare lost her action
T/Plt: £1,100.20 to a £1 stake. Pool: £56,141.78. 37.25 winning tickets. T/Qpdt: £126.90 to a £1 stake. Pool: £4,750.56. 27.70 winning tickets. CR

6911 LINGFIELD (L-H)
Monday, October 26

OFFICIAL GOING: Standard
Wind: fresh, across Weather: bright spells, breezy

7063 BETDAQ THE BETTING EXCHANGE NOVICE STKS 6f (P)
1:20 (1:21) (Class 4) 2-Y-O **£3,885** (£1,156; £577; £288) **Stalls** Low

Form RPR

0362 **1** **Chaperno (USA)**[26] 6398 2-9-2 **94**................................ AhmedAjtebi(3) 8 92
(Saeed Bin Suroor) *in tch in midfield: c wdst ent st: pushed along and hdwy over 1f out: pressed ldr ins fnl f: kpt on to ld last stride* **13/2**[3]

0312 **2** *shd* **Ongoodform (IRE)**[21] 6541 2-9-5 **89**.............................. NCallan 6 92
(P W D'Arcy) *wnt lft s: chsd ldrs: wnt 2nd over 2f out: rdn and ev ch wl over 1f out: led over 1f out: kpt on wl fnl f tl hdd fnl stride* **11/4**[2]

21 **3** 2 1/4 **Racy**[32] 6231 2-9-5 **86**... RyanMoore 7 85
(Sir Michael Stoute) *racd keenly: chsd ldr tl led 4f out: rdn ent fnl 2f: c centre st: hdd over 1f out: nt gng pce of ldng pair ins fnl f* **1/1**[1]

0106 **4** *nk* **Magnus Thrax (USA)**[23] 6478 2-9-2 **81**........................ RichardHughes 9 81
(R Hannon) *stdd and dropped in bhd after s: hld up in last trio: hdwy ent fnl 2f: chsd ldrs and drvn jst over 1f out: one pce fnl f* **15/2**

5251 **5** *nk* **Treadwell (IRE)**[19] 6585 2-9-9 **96**................................ TPQueally 1 87
(J A Osborne) *in tch on inner: rdn and effrt wl over 1f out: hanging rt ent fnl f: swtchd rt ins fnl f: r.o wl fnl 100yds: unable to chal* **11/1**

3030 **6** 7 **Ramamara (IRE)**[9] 6841 2-8-11 **79**.............................. PatCosgrave 2 54
(P D Evans) *led for 2f: chsd ldr tl over 2f out: sn rdn: wknd wl over 1f out* **33/1**

4003 **7** 3 1/4 **Ballyvonane (USA)**[18] 6610 2-8-12 **49**.....................(b) TGMcLaughlin 4 45
(L A Dace) *t.k.h early: a bhd struggling and rdn wl over 2f out: lost tch 2f out* **100/1**

8 14 **Billyonair** 2-8-8 0... GregFairley 5 —
(W De Best-Turner) *v.s.a: a bhd: rdn 4f out: lost tch 3f out* **100/1**

1m 11.36s (-0.54) **Going Correction** 0.0s/f (Stan) 2y crse rec **8** Ran SP% **115.0**
Speed ratings (Par 97): **103,102,99,99,99 89,85,66**
toteswingers: 1&2 £4.50, 2&3 £1.80, 1&3 not won. CSF £24.87 TOTE £8.00: £1.80, £1.50, £1.10; EX 33.20.
Owner Godolphin **Bred** Bruce Berenson & Laurie Berenson **Trained** Newmarket, Suffolk

FOCUS
A fair little novice stakes.

NOTEBOOK
Chaperno(USA) couldn't cut it at Group level earlier in the season, but he ran well when second in a fair conditions event at Salisbury last time and was the best in at the weights. He took a while to get on top, having come widest with his challenge, but stayed on well to get up close home. (tchd 15-2)
Ongoodform(IRE), second off a mark of 85 on his recent nursery debut, came through to lead over 1f out and briefly looked like holding on, but the winner's late charge proved too much for him (op 5-1)
Racy, who led throughout for an easy success at Pontefract last time, was a bit keen and went on after a couple of furlongs. He headed centre-track in the straight, but was readily done for speed once they started to sprint and ended up well held back in third. (op 4-5, tchd 11-10 in a place)
Magnus Thrax(USA), who has run respectably in a couple of big sales races since winning his maiden, was dropped in at the start and could never really get close enough to challenge. Official explanation: jockey said colt was unsettled in the starting stalls (op 11-2)
Treadwell(IRE), back to winning ways in a novice event at Kempton last time, was conceding weight all round and could never land a telling blow, keeping on despite hanging right. (op 12-1 tchd 17-2)

7064 DORMANS PARK MEDIAN AUCTION MAIDEN STKS 1m (P)
1:50 (1:51) (Class 6) 2-Y-O **£2,729** (£806; £403) **Stalls** High

Form RPR

3 **1** **Treasure Town**[13] 6759 2-9-3 0.................................... TedDurcan 6 79+
(Saeed Bin Suroor) *led tl over 6f out: chsd ldr after tl led again 2f out: clr ent fnl f: rdn out* **8/11**[1]

02 **2** 3 **Life And Soul (IRE)**[19] 6593 2-9-3 0............................ JimCrowley 1 72
(Mrs A J Perrett) *dwlt: sn rcvrd to trck ldrs: rdn and effrt 2f out: chsd clr wnr 1f out: no imp fnl f* **9/2**[2]

3 *nk* **Penangdouble O One** 2-9-3 0...........................(t) RichardKingscote 7 72
(R M Beckett) *s.i.s: towards rr: pushed along over 6f out: rdn and hdwy over 2f out: kpt on to go 3rd fnl 150yds: pressing for 2nd at fin but no ch w wnr* **11/2**[3]

4 2 1/2 **Boston Blue** 2-9-3 0.. LPKeniry 8 66
(W J Knight) *towards rr: niggled along over 5f out: hdwy and in tch over 2f out: outpcd by ldrs 2f out: kpt on again fnl f: nvr trbld ldrs* **14/1**

00 **5** 1 1/2 **Kahfre**[19] 6593 2-9-3 0.. TGMcLaughlin 5 63
(E A L Dunlop) *chsd ldrs: rdn over 3f out: drvn and outpcd ent fnl 2f: plugged on same pce after* **50/1**

05 **6** 1 **Rakhapura (IRE)**[12] 6772 2-9-3 0.................................. ChrisCatlin 9 61
(P R Webber) *taken down early: t.k.h: chsd ldrs tl led over 6f out: rdn and hdd 2f out: sn outpcd by wnr: wknd ent fnl f* **20/1**

43 **7** 6 **Patachou**[87] 4503 2-8-5 0.. KierenFox(7) 3 43
(R J Smith) *stdd s: hld up in rr: nvr a factor* **33/1**

00 **8** 1 1/4 **Daryainur (IRE)**[13] 6759 2-8-12 0.................................. GregFairley 12 40
(W De Best-Turner) *t.k.h: chsd ldrs tl rdn and wknd ent fnl 2f* **100/1**

60 **9** 8 **Lady Cavendish (IRE)**[16] 6672 2-8-12 0............................ JoeFanning 2 22
(A Bailey) *in tch in midfield: lost pl and rdn over 2f out: sn wl bhd* **50/1**

6 **10** 1 **Consult**[8] 6874 2-9-3 0.. StephenDonohoe 11 25
(Sir Mark Prescott) *s.i.s: sn rdn along in last pl: lost tch 3f out* **80/1**

11 3 1/4 **Big Hands Lynch (IRE)** 2-9-3 0................................... PatCosgrave 4 18
(J R Boyle) *v.s.a: a bhd: rdn 5f out: lost tch 3f out* **40/1**

1m 38.68s (0.48) **Going Correction** 0.0s/f (Stan) **11** Ran SP% **114.4**
Speed ratings (Par 93): **97,94,93,91,89 88,82,81,73,72 69**
toteswingers: 1&2 £1.20, 1&3 £3.20, 2&3 £5.20 CSF £3.65 TOTE £1.70: £1.02, £1.50, £2.20; EX 4.00.
Owner Godolphin **Bred** Darley **Trained** Newmarket, Suffolk

FOCUS
A fair juvenile maiden and a winner of potential.

NOTEBOOK
Treasure Town ◆, third behind a useful sort on his debut at Leicester, he was always well positioned and readily asserted over 1f out, winning with tons in hand. He is in next year's Derby and looks sure to go on to better things, so it will be interesting to see what mark he is given for handicaps. (op 5-6 tchd evens in places)
Life And Soul(IRE) improved on his debut effort when finishing second at Nottingham last time and he travelled really well in behind the speed, but couldn't match the winners acceleration and was left trailing. He is now qualified for a mark and should find a race at some stage, with better expected as he goes up to 1m2f. (op 11-4)
Penangdouble O One ◆, a half-brother to Harbinger who was sporting a tongue tie for this debut, had plenty of running to do rounding for home, but he stayed on well to bustle up the second. He should improve nicely. (op 10-1 tchd 11-1)
Boston Blue, a 52,000gns son of Halling, comes from a yard that can produce one to win first time up, but he looked in need of the experience, running on inside the final furlong having been green through the early stages. (op 12-1 tchd 9-1)
Kahfre is now qualified for a handicap mark and should fare better in that sphere.
Rakhapura(IRE) didn't get home having raced keenly, but he too now qualifies for a mark. (tchd 16-1)

7065 BETDAQ POKER H'CAP 1m (P)
2:20 (2:20) (Class 5) (0-70,70) 3-Y-O+ **£3,070** (£906; £453) **Stalls** High

Form RPR

4210 **1** **Ugenius**[27] 6361 5-9-6 **66**.. TGMcLaughlin 12 74
(Mrs C A Dunnett) *taken down early: in tch: rdn to chse ldng pair ent fnl 2f: styd on wl u.p fnl f to ld towards fin* **12/1**

5062 **2** 1/2 **Spiritual Art**[15] 6701 3-9-7 **70**....................................(p) PaulDoe 6 76
(L A Dace) *in tch: trckd ldr over 2f out: rdn and clr w ldr 2f out: led 1f out: hdd and no ex towards fin* **10/1**

3103 **3** 1/2 **Cavendish Road (IRE)**[28] 6337 3-9-6 **69**.............................. RyanMoore 10 74
(W R Muir) *in tch towards rr: rdn and effrt on outer 2f out: r.o wl u.p fnl f: nt rch ldrs* **6/1**[3]

6104 **4** 3 3/4 **Pha Mai Blue**[7] 6909 4-9-6 **66**.. PatCosgrave 11 63
(J R Boyle) *chsd ldrs tl led over 3f out: rdn and clr w rival 2f out: drvn and hdd 1f out: wknd ins fnl f* **11/2**[2]

0000 **5** 3/4 **Marmooq**[14] 6719 6-9-1 **61**... JimCrowley 8 57
(M J Attwater) *stdd s: hld up in last pair: rdn and hdwy over 1f out: styd on steadily fnl f: nvr trbld ldrs* **25/1**

0600 **6** *hd* **Colangnik (USA)**[12] 6784 3-8-11 **60**.................................. TedDurcan 1 54
(J R Best) *dwlt: sn in tch in midfield: n.m.r and pushed along over 4f out: drvn and outpcd over 2f out: n.d after* **16/1**

0432 **7** 3/4 **Sullenberger (IRE)**[9] 6862 3-9-0 **63**..............................(p) ChrisCatlin 4 55
(J A Osborne) *chsd ldrs: rdn and struggling jst over 3f out: wknd u.p jst over 2f out* **7/2**[1]

2306 **8** 6 **Yellow Printer**[12] 6780 3-9-7 **70**.. LPKeniry 5 49
(F J Brennan) *dwlt: sn pushed up to go prom: rdn and struggling 3f out: no ch fnl 2f* **7/1**

6006 **9** 2 **Sonny Parkin**[40] 6004 7-8-11 **62**...............................(v) SimonPearce(5) 2 37
(J Pearce) *stdd s: a bhd: n.d* **25/1**

0455 **10** 2 **Izzibizzi**[14] 6725 4-9-6 **66**......................................(p) KirstyMilczarek 7 36
(E A L Dunlop) *hld up in tch on inner: nt clr run bnd jst over 2f out: no ch after* **7/1**

0443 **11** 3 3/4 **Sunny Future (IRE)**[59] 5384 3-9-2 **65**................................ JoeFanning 3 26
(M S Saunders) *led tl over 3f out: wknd qckly jst over 2f out* **9/1**

0-00 **12** 8 **Warrior Nation (FR)**[4] 6977 3-9-4 **67**..........................(p) NeilChalmers 9 9
(A J Chamberlain) *a bhd: lost tch over 3f out* **66/1**

1m 37.95s (-0.25) **Going Correction** 0.0s/f (Stan)
WFA 3 from 4yo+ 3lb **12** Ran SP% **118.7**
Speed ratings (Par 103): **101,100,100,96,95 95,94,88,86,84 80,72**
toteswingers: 1&2 £40.40, 1&3 £24.50, 2&3 £5.50 CSF £124.62 CT £811.66 TOTE £21.30: £6.00, £3.50, £2.30; EX 200.10.
Owner Mrs Christine Dunnett **Bred** Three Acres Stud **Trained** Hingham, Norfolk

FOCUS
Ordinary handicap form, but sound enough.

7066 BETDAQ.CO.UK H'CAP 1m 4f (P)
2:50 (2:50) (Class 4) (0-85,85) 3-Y-O+ **£5,180** (£1,541; £770; £384) **Stalls** Low

Form RPR

0053 **1** **Mister New York (USA)**[14] 6724 4-9-0 **76**.....................(b) JimCrowley 5 89
(Noel T Chance) *hld up in last: swtchd to outer and gd hdwy over 2f out: led 2f out: rdn clr jst over 1f out: drvn out* **10/1**

113 **2** 1 **Tinaar (USA)**[35] 6165 3-9-1 **84**.. RyanMoore 7 95
(G A Butler) *t.k.h early: hld up in tch: chsd ldng pair and rdn ent fnl 2f: chsd wnr ent fnl f: kpt on u.p but nvr able to rch wnr* **13/8**[1]

511 **3** 5 **Akbabend**[9] 6855 3-9-1 **84**.. JoeFanning 6 87
(M Johnston) *chsd ldr for 2f and again 4f out: rdn and ev ch 2f out: outpcd by wnr over 1f out: wknd fnl f* **4/1**[2]

6036 **4** *hd* **Evident Pride (USA)**[20] 6566 6-9-9 **85**............................(v[1]) LPKeniry 4 88
(B R Johnson) *stdd s: t.k.h early: hld up in rr: hdwy 3f out: chsd ldng trio and drvn over 1f out: kpt on same pce* **14/1**

2335 **5** 2 1/2 **Colonel Flay**[38] 6060 5-8-7 **72**.. JackMitchell(3) 8 71
(Mrs P N Dutfield) *hld up in tch towards rr: rdn and effrt over 2f out: short of room on bnd ent fnl 2f: n.d after* **12/1**

5005 **6** 7 **Resurge (IRE)**[14] 6733 4-9-7 **83**.. ChrisCatlin 3 71
(W S Kittow) *hld up in tch towards rr: rdn and effrt over 2f out: sn struggling and wl btn whn nt clr run over 1f out* **16/1**

3220 **7** 5 **Wind Flow**[10] 6832 5-8-4 **71** oh2..............................(v) AshleyMorgan(5) 9 51
(C A Dwyer) *pushed along early: chsd ldr 10f out tl 4f out: wknd u.p ent fnl 2f* **20/1**

315 **8** 5 **Hajmah (IRE)**[21] 6552 3-8-9 **78**.. TedDurcan 1 50
(Saeed Bin Suroor) *led tl rdn and hdd 2f out: sn wknd* **9/2**[3]

016- **9** *10* **Shady Lady (IRE)**[358] 7158 3-8-11 **80** .... GregFairley 2 36
(M Johnston) *chsd ldrs: pushed along 6f out: dropped to rr over 3f out: sn lost tch* **25/1**

2m 31.16s (-1.84) **Going Correction** 0.0s/f (Stan)
WFA 3 from 4yo+ 7lb **9** Ran SP% **114.2**
Speed ratings (Par 105): **106,105,102,101,100 95,92,88,82**
toteswingers: 1&2 £3.80, 1&3 £4.90, 2&3 £2.40 CSF £26.35 CT £77.97 TOTE £12.50: £2.80, £1.30, £1.40; EX 32.50.
Owner Chance, Talbot & Taylor **Bred** J S McDonald **Trained** Upper Lambourn, Berks

FOCUS
Two drew clear in what was a fair handicap, although it was not slowly run. The form has been rated at face value.
Colonel Flay Official explanation: jockey said gelding suffered interference in running

7067 GRANTS LANE MAIDEN STKS 7f (P)
3:20 (3:21) (Class 5) 3-Y-0+ **£2,729** (£806; £403) **Stalls** Low

Form RPR

4 **1** **Jonny Mudball**[21] 6551 3-9-3 0 .... RichardKingscote 8 91+
(Tom Dascombe) *mde all: rdn clr ent fnl 2f: in n.d after: easily* **9/2**[2]

0320 **2** *5* **La Marseillaise (IRE)**[28] 6348 3-8-12 70 .... JoeFanning 3 68
(B W Hills) *chsd wnr thrght: rdn and nt qckn w wnr ent fnl 2f: no ch after but kpt on for clr 2nd* **6/1**[3]

64 **3** *4* **Massilah**[171] 1825 3-8-12 0 .... TedDurcan 5 57
(B W Hills) *chsd ldng pair: rdn and nt pce of ldng pair ent fnl 2f: wl hld after* **11/4**[1]

0- **4** *½* **First Service (IRE)**[367] 6944 3-9-0 0 .... JackMitchell(3) 13 61+
(R Charlton) *t.k.h: hld up in rr: swtchd to outer and effrt over 2f out: styd on u.p fr over 1f out: pressing for modest 3rd at fin: nvr trbld ldrs* **10/1**

05 **5** *1 ¼* **Luisa Tetrazzini (IRE)**[45] 5840 3-8-12 0 .... ChrisCatlin 1 52
(K A Ryan) *chsd ldrs: rdn and struggling wl over 2f out: no ch after* **33/1**

00 **6** *¾* **Dajen**[21] 6551 3-9-3 0 .... PatCosgrave 4 55+
(D M Simcock) *t.k.h: hld up towards rr: rdn and effrt over 2f out: no ch w ldrs fnl 2f* **66/1**

234 **7** *¾* **Major Lawrence (IRE)**[54] 5572 3-9-3 76 .... RyanMoore 11 53
(J Noseda) *in tch in midfield: rdn and fnd nil over 2f out: wl btn fnl 2f* **11/4**[1]

8 *½* **Princess Pivotal** 4-9-0 0 .... GregFairley 9 47
(G A Butler) *a towards rr: lost tch over 2f out* **14/1**

64- **9** *½* **Karashar (IRE)**[125] 2454 4-9-5 0 .... LPKeniry 12 51+
(Evan Williams) *t.k.h: hld up in rr: nt clr run bnd over 2f out: nvr a factor* **25/1**

10 *nse* **Katie The Hatter (IRE)** 3-8-12 0 .... JimCrowley 7 46
(Mike Murphy) *v.s.a: a wl bhd* **33/1**

0 **11** *2* **Miskin Spirit**[14] 6741 3-8-12 0 .... NeilChalmers 2 40
(B Palling) *in tch in midfield: rdn and struggling 3f out: wl bhd fnl 2f* **66/1**

0 **12** *shd* **Big Sur**[25] 6430 3-9-3 0 .... KirstyMilczarek 10 45
(T Keddy) *t.k.h: chsd ldrs tl wknd over 2f out* **33/1**

13 *1* **Wacato King (IRE)**[406] 5980 3-9-3 0 .... PaulDoe 14 42
(R A Farrant) *a towards rr: rdn and no prog on outer wl over 2f out* **66/1**

1m 24.66s (-0.14) **Going Correction** 0.0s/f (Stan)
WFA 3 from 4yo 2lb **13** Ran SP% **118.7**
Speed ratings (Par 103): **100,94,89,89,87 86,86,85,84,84 82,82,81**
toteswingers: 1&2 £3.80, 2&3 £8.30 1&3 not won. CSF £29.85 TOTE £4.60: £1.50, £2.20, £1.60; EX 32.10.
Owner Woodgate Family **Bred** Mrs P A Reditt And M J Reditt **Trained** Lambourn, Berks

FOCUS
A moderate maiden and a very easy winner. The first three were in their finishing positions throughout and this is perhaps not form to take too literally, although the winner certainly impressed.
Major Lawrence(IRE) Official explanation: jockey said the colt was never travelling
Katie The Hatter(IRE) Official explanation: jockey said, regarding the running and riding, that stated that his instructions were to try to achieve a position in mid-division and to ride a normal race and do his best from there on; the trainer confirmed these instructions, but added that the fact that the filly had missed the break had made it impossible for Mr Crowley to carry out the original instructions; jockey added that having missed the break, he moved to the outside to avoid the severe kick-back. He made an attempt to close down the hill from about three furlongs out and further added that the filly was green at this point. The filly then made some late progress in the straight despite having to weave through rivals. No action taken.
Wacato King(IRE) Official explanation: jockey said colt hung left

7068 TANDRIDGE APPRENTICE H'CAP (DIV I) 6f (P)
3:50 (3:53) (Class 6) (0-55,55) 3-Y-0+ **£1,706** (£503; £252) **Stalls** Low

Form RPR

0545 **1** **Cheery Cat (USA)**[40] 5998 5-8-7 **48** ....(p) DavidKenny(3) 6 56
(J Balding) *chsd ldrs: swtchd rt over 1f out: drvn ent fnl f: led fnl 100yds: r.o wl* **8/1**

66 **2** *nk* **Colombard (IRE)**[44] 5883 4-8-6 **49** ....(b) AlexEdwards(5) 5 56
(Patrick Morris) *hld up in tch in midfield: rdn and effrt on outer over 1f out: led ins fnl f: sn hdd and unable qck towards fin* **6/1**

0-00 **3** *shd* **Megalo Maniac**[51] 5678 6-8-9 **54** .... MarzenaJeziorek(7) 3 61+
(R A Fahey) *hld up in rr of main gp: hdwy on rail over 1f out: pushed along and edgd rt ins fnl f: pressed ldr fnl 100yds: one pce towards fin* **16/1**

0056 **4** *hd* **North South Divide (IRE)**[131] 3020 5-8-2 **45** .... RyanPowell(5) 7 51
(K A Ryan) *hld up in rr of main gp: hdwy and looking for run over 1f out: swtchd lft and squeezed between horses ins fnl f: r.o wl: nt quite rch ldrs* **7/2**[2]

0003 **5** *1 ½* **Fantasy Fighter (IRE)**[12] 6777 4-9-0 **52** .... JamesPSullivan 4 53
(J J Quinn) *chsd ldr tl 2f out: sn drvn: ev ch ins fnl f: wknd fnl 100yds* **9/2**[3]

300- **6** *1* **Edge End**[460] 4307 5-8-11 **52** .... HollyHall(3) 9 50
(P D Evans) *led: rdn over 1f out: hdd fnl 100yds: fdd towards fin* **9/1**

3242 **7** *½* **Avrilo**[5] 6939 3-8-13 **52** .... JPFahy 8 48
(M S Saunders) *chsd ldrs on outer: rdn to chse ldr 2f out tl 1f out: wknd u.p fnl 100yds* **3/1**[1]

0040 **8** *1 ½* **Stormburst (IRE)**[39] 6028 5-8-6 **47** .... RichardRowe(3) 10 39
(A J Chamberlain) *s.i.s: effrt and rdn over 1f out: no imp fnl f* **33/1**

-005 **9** *¾* **Station Place**[64] 5283 4-8-12 **50** .... ByronMoorcroft 1 39
(A B Haynes) *in tch towards rr of main gp: rdn and effrt on inner ent fnl 2f: drvn and no prog ent fnl f* **25/1**

1030 **10** *1 ¾* **May Martin**[140] 2776 3-9-2 **55** .... TobyAtkinson 2 39
(Rae Guest) *walked to s: v.s.a: a bhd* **12/1**

1m 12.21s (0.31) **Going Correction** 0.0s/f (Stan)
WFA 3 from 4yo+ 1lb **10** Ran SP% **121.2**
Speed ratings (Par 101): **97,96,96,96,94 92,92,90,89,86**
toteswingers: 1&2 £9.50, 1&3 £35.20, 2&3 £26.50 CSF £57.68 CT £766.23 TOTE £9.30: £2.30, £1.90, £5.70; EX 58.50.
Owner The Cataractonium Racing Syndicate **Bred** K L Ramsay & Sarah K Ramsay **Trained** Scrooby, Notts

FOCUS
A weak handicap which saw a blanket finish between the first four. The winner looks the best guide to the form.
May Martin Official explanation: jockey said the filly was slowly away

7069 TANDRIDGE APPRENTICE H'CAP (DIV II) 6f (P)
4:20 (4:21) (Class 6) (0-55,55) 3-Y-0+ **£1,706** (£503; £252) **Stalls** Low

Form RPR

0032 **1** **Malapropism**[12] 6777 9-8-12 **53** .... CharlesEddery(3) 2 60
(M R Channon) *mde all: rdn over 1f out: kpt on and a doing enough fnl f* **2/1**[1]

20-0 **2** *1* **Bountiful Bay**[121] 3407 4-9-0 **52** .... LeeNewnes 4 56
(Matthew Salaman) *chsd ldrs: rdn to chse wnr wl over 1f out: kpt on u.p but nvr able to chal wnr* **9/2**[2]

640 **3** *hd* **Cheers Big Ears (IRE)**[10] 6823 3-8-9 **53** .... RyanPowell(5) 5 56
(J R Best) *dwlt: sn in tch in midfield: hdwy to chse ldrs over 2f out: wating to hang lft over 1f out: swtchd rt jst ins fnl f: r.o wl to press for 2nd nr fin* **6/1**[3]

0300 **4** *1 ¼* **Danzadil (IRE)**[28] 6337 3-8-8 **50** .... KierenFox(3) 9 49+
(R A Teal) *bhd: swtchd rt 3f out: hdwy on outer bnd ent fnl 2f: edgd lft fr over 1f out: r.o but nvr a threat to wnr* **9/1**

-060 **5** *2* **Cullybackey (IRE)**[131] 3023 4-8-5 **48** .... NathanAlison(5) 1 41
(J R Boyle) *dwlt: towards rr: swtchd rt 3f out: effrt towards outer and n.m.r over 1f out: swtchd rt jst ins fnl f: r.o but nvr trbld ldrs* **13/2**

06-0 **6** *hd* **Beau Jazz**[126] 3211 8-8-4 **45** .... LauraPike(3) 6 37
(W De Best-Turner) *chsd wnr tl wl over 1f out: outpcd u.p over 1f out: one pce fnl f* **40/1**

065 **7** *nk* **Missed Mondays**[145] 2593 3-8-1 **45** .... AlexEdwards(5) 8 36
(Patrick Morris) *in tch: effrt over 2f out: one pce and no real hdwy fr over 1f out* **14/1**

-600 **8** *1* **Key To Love (IRE)**[174] 1772 3-8-13 **55** ....(p) RichardRowe(3) 7 43
(A J Chamberlain) *awkward leaving stalls: bhd: swtchd rt 3f out: effrt and rdn ent fnl 2f: nvr had pce to trble ldrs* **33/1**

4010 **9** *2 ½* **Equinity**[39] 6038 3-8-11 **50** ....(t) TobyAtkinson 10 30
(J Pearce) *towards rr on outer early: swtchd rt 3f out: no prog u.p fr over 1f out* **8/1**

5330 **10** *½* **Talamahana**[28] 6329 4-8-9 **47** ....(v) JPFahy 3 25
(A B Haynes) *midfield: pushed along whn clipped heels and stmbld 3f out: n.d after* **8/1**

1m 13.23s (1.33) **Going Correction** 0.0s/f (Stan)
WFA 3 from 4yo+ 1lb **10** Ran SP% **123.4**
Speed ratings (Par 101): **97,95,95,93,91 90,90,89,85,85**
toteswingers: 1&2 £3.70, 1&3 £5.30, 2&3 £5.60 CSF £11.59 CT £49.10 TOTE £3.60: £1.20, £1.70, £2.30; EX 17.40 Place 6: £46.41 Pklace 5: £40.89.
Owner Michael A Foy **Bred** Michael A Foy **Trained** West Ilsley, Berks
■ Stewards' Enquiry : Ryan Powell six-day ban: careless riding (Nov 9, 11-14, 16)

FOCUS
This looked slightly stronger than the first division and is rated around the second. The time was similar to the first division.
T/Plt: £99.30 to a £1 stake. Pool: £51,709.63. 380.14 winning tickets. T/Qpdt: £87.30 to a £1 stake. Pool: £3,666.00. 31.04 winning tickets. SP

7070 - 7071a (Foreign Racing) - See Raceform Interactive

5684 LEOPARDSTOWN (L-H)
Monday, October 26
OFFICIAL GOING: Yielding (yielding to soft in places)

7072a J.R.A. KILLAVULLAN STKS (GROUP 3) 7f
1:25 (1:30) 2-Y-0 **£39,186** (£11,497; £5,477; £1,866)

RPR

1 **Free Judgement (USA)**[9] 6849 2-9-1 105 .... KJManning 5 108
(J S Bolger, Ire) *trckd ldr: qcknd to ld over 1f out: sn clr: styd on wl* **7/1**[3]

2 *2* **Lord High Admiral (IRE)**[9] 6849 2-9-1 95 .... CO'Donoghue 3 103
(A P O'Brien, Ire) *led: drvn along fr early st: hdd over 1f out: no ch w wnr but kpt on same pce* **16/1**

3 *shd* **Keredari (IRE)**[28] 6350 2-9-1 .... MJKinane 7 103
(John M Oxx, Ire) *trckd ldrs in 4th: rdn over 2f out: kpt on one pce into 3rd fnl f* **4/1**[2]

4 *½* **Air Chief Marshal (IRE)**[29] 6317 2-9-1 110 .... JAHeffernan 6 102
(A P O'Brien, Ire) *in rr of mid-div: 8th ent st: kpt on wl u.p on outer fr 1f out to go 4th cl home* **7/1**[3]

5 *¾* **Thunder Bridge (USA)**[26] 6401 2-9-1 .... PJSmullen 1 100
(D K Weld, Ire) *trckd ldrs on inner in 3rd: rdn ent st: no imp fr over 1f out and dropped to 5th clsng stages* **6/4**[1]

6 *1* **Wrong Answer**[44] 5895 2-8-12 100 .... CDHayes 2 94
(Kevin Prendergast, Ire) *towards rr on inner: sme hdwy into 5th early st: no ex fr over 1f out* **10/1**

7 *3* **Utrillo (IRE)**[17] 6652 2-9-1 95 .... JMurtagh 4 90
(A P O'Brien, Ire) *chsd ldrs in 5th: pushed along appr st: 7th and no imp fr 2f out: kpt on one pce* **7/1**[3]

8 *1 ¾* **Moonreach (IRE)**[8] 6883 2-9-1 94 .... WJSupple 10 85
(P D Deegan, Ire) *chsd ldrs in 6th: no ex fr 1 1/2f out* **10/1**

9 *2* **Alshahbaa (IRE)**[81] 4726 2-8-12 97 .... DPMcDonogh 9 77
(Kevin Prendergast, Ire) *a towards rr* **16/1**

10 *5* **Timeless Whisper (IRE)**[9] 6870 2-8-12 .... KLatham 8 65
(J G Burns, Ire) *a bhd* **25/1**

1m 29.56s (0.86) **Going Correction** +0.275s/f (Good) **10** Ran SP% **131.3**
Speed ratings: **106,103,103,103,102 101,97,95,93,87**
CSF £125.91 TOTE £9.50: £3.00, £6.40, £2.00; DF 156.10.
Owner Mrs June Judd **Bred** Twin Hopes Farm Inc **Trained** Coolcullen, Co Carlow

NOTEBOOK
Free Judgement(USA), beaten six lengths when eighth in the Dewhurst Stakes on his previous start, ran out a decisive winner here. After tracking the leader, he responded well when asked to pick up over 1f out and was soon in front before keeping on well in the closing stages. Trainer Jim Bolger believes 1m will not be a problem for the winner, who will be trained for a 2,000 Guineas next season. (op 6/1)
Lord High Admiral(IRE), 12 lengths behind Free Judgement when a 66-1 shot for the Dewhurst, finished a lot closer to that rival here. He made the running and, after coming under pressure early in the straight, stuck to his task but lacked the pace of the winner when it mattered.
Keredari(IRE), an easy winner on fast ground on his debut at Roscommon last month, tracked the leaders and kept on in the closing stages, having been unable to make much impression over 1f out.

Air Chief Marshal(IRE), the highest rated in the race on official figures and whose participation had been in doubt 24 hours previously due to a stone bruise, was towards the back of the field until beginning to make headway on the outside under 2f out. He ran on well inside the final furlong. (op 6/1)
Thunder Bridge(USA), favourite on the strength of a 13-length debut win at Sligo last month, tracked the leaders but was done with early in the final furlong. (op 7/4)

7073 - 7078a (Foreign Racing) - See Raceform Interactive

6840 CATTERICK (L-H)

Tuesday, October 27

OFFICIAL GOING: Soft (good to soft in places; 7.3)
Wind: Light, half behind Weather: dull and damp, becoming very misty with limited visibility.

7079 COWTHORPE MEDIAN AUCTION MAIDEN STKS 5f 212y
1:00 (1:00) (Class 6) 2-Y-O £2,388 (£705; £352) Stalls Low

Form RPR
4 **1** **Revelator (IRE)**[81] 4738 2-9-3 0 ... AndrewElliott 6 74
(A P Jarvis) *mde all: drvn clr over 1f out: rdn out: unchal* **12/1**
4053 **2** 2 1/2 **Olympic Ceremony**[26] 6408 2-9-0 68 ... FrederikTylicki(3) 9 66
(R A Fahey) *t.k.h on outer: trckd ldrs: wnt 2nd over 1f out: no imp* **4/1[2]**
3555 **3** 3 1/2 **Jack Luey**[12] 6796 2-9-3 66 ...(p) DuranFentiman 4 56
(L A Mullaney) *chsd ldrs: drvn over 2f out: kpt on same pce* **10/1**
0 **4** 3/4 **Princess Mandy (IRE)**[12] 6802 2-8-12 0 ... TomEaves 3 48
(K A Ryan) *dwlt: in rr: hdwy and swtchd ins over 1f out: styd on: nvr nrr* **25/1**
2 **5** 1/2 **Briary Mac**[11] 6820 2-8-8 0 ow1 ... GaryBartley(5) 1 48
(N Bycroft) *in rr-div: drvn and wl outpcd over 2f out: kpt on fnl f* **2/1[1]**
6 1 3/4 **Bubber (IRE)** 2-8-12 0 ... PaulHanagan 7 42
(R A Fahey) *t.k.h: trckd ldrs: wknd over 1f out* **6/1[3]**
4054 **7** 1 3/4 **Baileys Vision**[10] 6844 2-8-12 62 ...(v) GregFairley 12 36
(M Johnston) *in rr-div: rdn over 2f out: nvr a factor* **13/2**
0 **8** 2 1/2 **Future Regime (IRE)**[29] 6347 2-8-12 0 ... SJCraine 10 29
(Patrick Morris) *hld up in midfield: effrt 2f out: sn fdd* **50/1**
0 **9** 1 1/2 **Dispol Fay (IRE)**[10] 6841 2-8-12 0 ... PhillipMakin 8 24
(P T Midgley) *trckd ldrs: t.k.h: wknd 2f out* **11/1**
00 **10** 4 1/2 **Choc'A'Moca (IRE)**[52] 5674 2-9-3 0 ...(b[1]) DavidAllan 5 16
(I W McInnes) *chsd ldrs: lost pl over 2f out* **66/1**
4 **11** 12 **Psychopathicsandra (IRE)**[72] 5066 2-8-5 45 ... BillyCray(7) 11 —
(A Berry) *in rr: bhd fnl 2f* **150/1**

1m 16.81s (3.21) **Going Correction** +0.50s/f (Yiel) 11 Ran SP% **114.0**
Speed ratings (Par 93): **98,94,90,89,88 86,83,80,78,72 56**
toteswinger: 1&2 £10.30, 1&3 £13.40, £8.20. CSF £57.04 TOTE £12.40: £4.20, £1.80, £2.60; EX 101.70.
Owner Cyril Wall **Bred** Castletown & Knighton House **Trained** Middleham Moor, N Yorks

FOCUS
The going was changed to soft, good to soft in places following a small amount of rain. This was a moderate maiden.

NOTEBOOK
Revelator(IRE), a well-beaten fourth on his debut at Haydock in August, was ridden more positively on this occasion and he cleared right away from over 1f out to win with a lot in hand. He showed plenty of pace and could be the sort to develop into a fair sprint handicapper next season. (tchd 10-1 and 14-1)
Olympic Ceremony, officially rated 68, ran better than she had done at Ayr last time, but was always likely to find at least one too good. He remains exposed. (op 3-1 tchd 5-1)
Jack Luey is another exposed sort and he failed to improve for the first-time cheekpieces, just keeping on at the one pace. (op 8-1 tchd 11-1)
Princess Mandy(IRE), never involved having been slowly away on debut, was again not the quickest away, but she stayed on late and clearly improved for the switch to turf. (op 20-1)
Briary Mac, whose rider was putting up 1lb overweight, failed to build on her debut effort and probably found the ground too soft as she was never really travelling. (op 3-1)
Bubber(IRE), a daughter of Westerner who is related to a 1m winner for the yard, showed a bit of early pace before fading from over 1f out. She should improve and can do better next time. (tchd 11-2)

7080 RACING UK ON SKY 432 H'CAP (DIV I) 1m 3f 214y
1:30 (1:30) (Class 6) (0-60,60) 3-Y-O+ £2,047 (£604; £302) Stalls Low

Form RPR
0422 **1** **Park's Prodigy**[21] 6559 5-8-12 48 ow1 ... DanielTudhope 10 63+
(G A Harker) *trckd ldrs: hung lft bnd over 4f out: led over 2f out: sn rdn clr: eased towards fin* **4/1[2]**
-310 **2** 6 **No Wonga**[32] 6258 4-9-4 59 ... RichardEvans(5) 6 68+
(P D Evans) *hld up in rr: outpcd over 3f out: hdwy on ins whn nt clr run and swtchd outside over 1f out: kpt on to take 2nd ins fnl f: no ch w wnr* **7/2[1]**
4442 **3** 2 1/4 **Follow The Sun (IRE)**[11] 6817 5-9-3 56 ...(p) FrederikTylicki(3) 14 56
(Ronald O'Leary, Ire) *hld up in rr: hdwy to trck ldrs 7f out: hung lft and wnt modest 2nd 1f out: one pce* **9/1**
1141 **4** 1 1/2 **Simple Jim (FR)**[10] 6845 5-9-1 56 ... BMcHugh(5) 9 53
(J Hetherton) *hld up towards rr: drvn and sme hdwy over 4f out: kpt on same pce fnl 2f: nvr a threat* **6/1[3]**
2003 **5** 2 1/4 **Cecina Marina**[10] 6840 6-8-7 48 ... PatrickDonaghy(5) 13 42
(Mrs K Walton) *w ldr: led over 4f out: hdd over 2f out: wknd over 1f out* **12/1**
F0-4 **6** 4 **Nayessence**[11] 6818 3-8-11 54 ...(t) PhillipMakin 11 41
(M W Easterby) *led tl over 4f out: wknd over 1f out* **11/1**
00-4 **7** shd **Dubai Diva**[189] 1441 3-9-3 60 ... GeorgeBaker 2 47
(C F Wall) *mid-div: outpcd and lost pl over 4f out: kpt on fnl 2f: nvr on terms* **7/2[1]**
006 **8** 6 **Marina's Ocean**[27] 6390 5-8-13 49 ...(t) AmirQuinn 4 27
(S R Bowring) *chsd ldrs: rdn and hung rt over 2f out: lost pl over 1f out* **33/1**
0006 **9** 25 **Kannon**[12] 6800 4-9-2 52 ...(p) DavidAllan 1 —
(I W McInnes) *trckd ldrs: rdn over 5f out: sn lost pl: bhd fnl 3f: t.o* **40/1**
0036 **10** 2 1/4 **Inside Knowledge (USA)**[88] 4491 3-8-7 50 ... AndrewElliott 12 —
(G Woodward) *in rr: bhd fnl 4f: t.o* **40/1**
0000 **11** 4 1/2 **Hunting Haze**[11] 6817 6-8-9 45 ...(b) FrancisNorton 7 —
(A Crook) *s.i.s: in rr: bhd fnl 4f: t.o* **100/1**
6000 **12** 44 **Media Stars**[14] 6769 4-8-10 46 ... GrahamGibbons 5 —
(R Johnson) *dwlt: sn mid-div: drvn 7f out: rdn and lost pl over 5f out: sn bhd: wl t.o* **50/1**

2m 44.47s (5.57) **Going Correction** +0.50s/f (Yiel)
WFA 3 from 4yo+ 7lb 12 Ran SP% **115.5**
Speed ratings (Par 101): **101,97,95,94,93 90,90,86,69,68 65,35**
toteswinger: 1&2 £4.50, 1&3 £7.40, £7.20. CSF £17.34 CT £118.01 TOTE £4.90: £1.90, £1.70, £2.00; EX 18.60.
Owner John J Maguire **Bred** P D And Mrs Player **Trained** Thirkleby, N Yorks

FOCUS
The first division of what was a low-grade handicap. A clear personal best from the winner.
No Wonga Official explanation: jockey said gelding was unsuited by the track

7081 COME RACING AGAIN NEXT TUESDAY H'CAP (DIV I) 5f
2:00 (2:02) (Class 6) (0-65,65) 3-Y-O+ £2,047 (£604; £302) Stalls Low

Form RPR
2240 **1** **Silk Gallery (USA)**[45] 5882 4-8-6 53 ...(t) GrahamGibbons 14 63
(E J Alston) *led stands' side gp: r.o to ld overall towards fin* **14/1**
0034 **2** 1 **Chosen One (IRE)**[12] 6799 4-8-13 60 ... TomEaves 3 66
(B Smart) *overall ldr far side: hdd and no ex wl ins fnl f: 1st of 6 that gp* **4/1[2]**
1436 **3** 1 **First Blade**[9] 6877 3-9-2 63 ...(b) AmirQuinn 11 65
(S R Bowring) *racd stands' side: w ldrs: hung lft 2f out: kpt on ins fnl f: nt rch ldrs* **8/1**
0652 **4** shd **Joyeaux**[12] 6799 7-8-11 61 ... FrederikTylicki(3) 10 63
(Ollie Pears) *racd stands' side: in rr: hdwy over 1f out: styd on ins fnl f* **7/2[1]**
0636 **5** 3/4 **Alacity (IRE)**[11] 6823 3-8-8 55 ... FrancisNorton 8 54
(N Bycroft) *racd stands' side side: chsd ldrs: kpt on same pce fnl f* **12/1**
5600 **6** nk **Andrasta**[21] 6553 4-7-11 51 oh1 ... CharlotteKerton(7) 1 49
(S A Harris) *racd far side: chsd ldrs: kpt on same pce appr fnl f: 2nd of 5 that gp* **50/1**
4066 **7** 3/4 **Foreign Rhythm (IRE)**[27] 6380 4-7-11 51 oh5 ... DeclanCannon(7) 13 47
(N Tinkler) *racd stands' side: mid-div: kpt on fnl 2f: nvr rchd ldrs* **28/1**
262 **8** 3/4 **Strensall**[21] 6553 12-8-4 51 oh1 ... DuranFentiman 2 44
(R E Barr) *racd far side: w ldrs: wknd fnl f: 3rd of 5 that gp* **11/1**
0602 **9** nk **Ursus**[27] 6379 4-8-8 55 ...(b[1]) PaulHanagan 5 47
(C R Wilson) *racd far side: sn outpcd: nvr on terms: 4th of 5 that gp* **6/1[3]**
0000 **10** 2 1/2 **Divine Spirit**[10] 6857 8-9-4 65 ... PhillipMakin 9 48
(M Dods) *racd stands' side: mid-div: nvr a factor* **14/1**
65/0 **11** 2 **Tango Step (IRE)**[13] 6783 9-7-11 51 oh6 ...(b) NeilFarley(7) 6 27
(D Carroll) *racd far side: sn outpcd and last in that gp: last of 5 that side* **80/1**
5005 **12** 3 **Highland Warrior**[36] 6159 10-9-4 65 ... MickyFenton 12 30
(P T Midgley) *racd stands' side: mid-div: drvn over 2f out: sn wknd* **14/1**
0503 **13** 2 3/4 **Killer Class**[30] 6314 4-8-10 62 ... GaryBartley(5) 7 17
(J S Goldie) *racd stands' side: sn in rr* **8/1**

61.72 secs (1.92) **Going Correction** +0.50s/f (Yiel) 13 Ran SP% **121.4**
Speed ratings (Par 101): **104,102,100,100,99 98,97,96,96,92 88,84,79**
toteswinger: 1&2 £16.50, 1&3 £22.70, £7.90. CSF £69.84 CT £511.96 TOTE £21.20: £5.50, £1.70, £2.70; EX 107.50.
Owner Mr & Mrs G Middlebrook **Bred** Barnett Enterprises **Trained** Longton, Lancs
■ Stewards' Enquiry : Charlotte Kerton five-day ban: excessive use of the whip (Nov 11-14, 16)

FOCUS
The mist had set in before this sprint handicap, in which the field split into two. There was very little in it, with Silk Gallery on the stands' side just emerging on top and Chosen One top on his side. The time was slower than division II.

7082 GO RACING AT WETHERBY THIS FRIDAY H'CAP 5f 212y
2:30 (2:30) (Class 5) (0-75,75) 3-Y-O £2,914 (£867; £433; £216) Stalls Low

Form RPR
0000 **1** **Lovely Thought**[15] 6731 3-9-4 75 ...(b) PaulHanagan 5 89
(W J Haggas) *w ldr: led over 4f out: edgd rt on to stands' side rail 2f out: rdn clr fnl f* **9/4[1]**
5000 **2** 4 **Real Diamond**[60] 5405 3-8-8 68 ...(p) FrederikTylicki(3) 2 69
(A Dickman) *chsd ldrs: chal over 2f out: kpt on same pce* **7/1[3]**
1603 **3** 1 1/2 **Lucky Art (USA)**[12] 6798 3-9-1 72 ... AndrewElliott 6 68
(Mrs R A Carr) *t.k.h: led tl over 4f out: rdn and hmpd 2f out: kpt on same pce* **8/1**
1002 **4** 1/2 **Noodles Blue Boy**[14] 6765 3-9-4 75 ... FrancisNorton 9 70
(Ollie Pears) *mid-div on outer: styd on fnl 2f: nvr trbld ldrs* **7/2[2]**
0245 **5** 3/4 **Two Turtle Doves (IRE)**[11] 6824 3-8-4 61 oh4 ... GregFairley 7 53
(M Mullineaux) *in rr: hdwy on outside over 2f out: kpt on fnl f* **8/1**
032 **6** 4 **Anagram**[26] 6430 3-8-10 67 ...(b) PhillipMakin 11 47
(W R Muir) *in rr on outer: come hdwy stands' side rail 2f out: nvr on terms* **12/1**
2000 **7** 1 1/2 **Officer Mor (USA)**[4] 6988 3-7-11 61 oh6 ...(b) BillyCray(7) 1 36
(A Berry) *in rr: sme hdwy on outer 2f out: nvr a factor* **66/1**
0600 **8** hd **Forward Feline (IRE)**[20] 6596 3-8-6 63 ...(p) DavidProbert 3 37
(B Palling) *chsd ldrs: outpcd over 2f out: sn wknd* **14/1**
14-2 **9** 1 1/4 **Final Salute**[219] 924 3-9-3 74 ... TomEaves 10 44
(B Smart) *hld up towards rr: nvr a factor* **12/1**
0005 **10** nk **Dark Velvet (IRE)**[87] 4528 3-8-4 61 oh11 ... AndrewMullen 4 30
(E J Alston) *mid-div: lost pl over 2f out* **100/1**
4005 **11** 7 **King Of Eden (IRE)**[11] 6823 3-8-4 61 oh8 ... DuranFentiman 8 8
(E J Alston) *chsd ldrs: sn drvn along: lost pl over 2f out: sn bhd* **33/1**

1m 16.25s (2.65) **Going Correction** +0.50s/f (Yiel) 11 Ran SP% **115.2**
Speed ratings (Par 101): **102,96,94,94,93 87,85,85,83,83 74**
toteswinger: 1&2 £6.10, 1&3 £4.60, £10.00. CSF £17.88 CT £107.04 TOTE £3.30: £1.30, £1.90, £2.70; EX 21.70.
Owner Liam Sheridan **Bred** Whitsbury Manor Stud **Trained** Newmarket, Suffolk
■ Stewards' Enquiry : Paul Hanagan two-day ban: careless riding (Nov 11-12)

FOCUS
As in the previous race, it was hard to make ground. The winner was back to his early-season form.

7083 TURFTV.CO.UK H'CAP 7f
3:00 (3:01) (Class 4) (0-85,82) 3-Y-O+ £5,180 (£1,541; £770; £384) Stalls Centre

Form RPR
1440 **1** **Conry (IRE)**[19] 6614 3-8-11 77 ... SJCraine 14 86
(Patrick Morris) *hld up: hdwy over 2f out: r.o to ld nr fin* **14/1**
4120 **2** 1/2 **Grissom (IRE)**[31] 6279 3-8-4 77 ... BillyCray(7) 7 85
(A Berry) *chsd ldrs: edgd rt and led ins fnl f: hdd nr fin* **16/1**
0550 **3** 1 **Cara's Request (AUS)**[18] 6645 4-8-10 74 ... FrancisNorton 11 80
(D Nicholls) *w ldr: led over 2f out: hdd and hmpd last 100yds* **11/2[2]**
53 **4** 1 **Toto Skyllachy**[13] 6776 4-8-13 80 ... FrederikTylicki(3) 13 84+
(S Gollings) *chsng ldrs over 2f out: keeping on same pce whn hmpd wl ins fnl f* **4/1[1]**
4425 **5** 2 1/4 **Inter Vision (USA)**[8] 6902 9-8-13 77 ... DanielTudhope 4 74+
(A Dickman) *in rr: styd on fnl 2f: nvr nr ldrs* **9/1[3]**
1420 **6** 1 1/4 **Sea Salt**[14] 6764 6-8-4 73 ... PaulPickard(5) 5 67
(R E Barr) *in tch: styd alone far side in home st: fdd fnl f* **9/1[3]**
0260 **7** 1 1/2 **Turn Me On (IRE)**[18] 6645 6-9-4 82 ... GrahamGibbons 8 72
(T D Walford) *towards rr: kpt on fnl 2f: nvr nr ldrs* **11/1**

3000 **8** *nse* **Memphis Man**[5] 6964 6-8-5 74 .... AndrewHeffernan(5) 9 64
(P D Evans) *in rr-div: hdwy over 2f out: nvr a factor* **18/1**

2410 **9** *3 ¾* **Malcheek (IRE)**[18] 6645 7-9-4 82 .... DavidAllan 12 61
(T D Easterby) *nvr bttr than mid-div* **16/1**

3400 **10** *nk* **Boy Blue**[28] 6357 4-9-0 78 .... GregFairley 10 57
(P Salmon) *mid-div: nvr a factor* **12/1**

0000 **11** *10* **Bond City (IRE)**[6] 6949 7-9-4 82 .... DavidProbert 3 34
(G R Oldroyd) *mid-div: lost pl over 2f out* **18/1**

0050 **12** *¾* **Favourite Girl (IRE)**[10] 6843 3-9-2 82 .... TomEaves 1 31
(T D Easterby) *in rr: bhd fnl 3f* **10/1**

1000 **13** *1 ½* **Glenridding**[25] 6462 5-8-13 77 .... (p) PaulHanagan 2 23
(J G Given) *led tl hdd & wknd over 2f out* **20/1**

0500 **14** *hd* **Guertino (IRE)**[18] 6647 4-8-8 72 .... DuranFentiman 6 17
(C J Teague) *wl bhd fnl 3f* **66/1**

1454 **15** *4* **Bid For Gold**[14] 6765 5-8-4 73 .... PatrickDonaghy(5) 15 7
(Jedd O'Keeffe) *in rr: bhd fnl 3f* **14/1**

1m 29.49s (2.49) **Going Correction** +0.50s/f (Yiel)
WFA 3 from 4yo+ 2lb **15 Ran SP% 122.4**
Speed ratings (Par 105): **105,104,103,102,99 98,96,96,92,91 80,79,77,77,72**
toteswinger: 1&2 £43.70, 1&3 £42.30, £42.60. CSF £223.47 CT £1423.05 TOTE £19.40: £6.30, £6.60, £2.70; EX 287.90.
Owner Mrs S J Kelly **Bred** Shay White **Trained** Tarporley, Cheshire
■ Stewards' Enquiry : Billy Cray two-day ban: careless riding (Nov 11-12)

FOCUS
Visibility was very limited for what was a competitive handicap. The winner was rated in line with his August C/D win.
Bond City(IRE) Official explanation: jockey said gelding ran flat

7084 CATTERICKBRIDGE.CO.UK H'CAP — 1m 7f 177y
3:30 (3:30) (Class 5) (0-70,68) 3-Y-0+ — **£2,914** (£867; £433; £216) **Stalls** Centre

Form — RPR

1205 **1** **No Rules**[16] 6692 4-9-6 65 .... SimonPearce(5) 3 75
(M H Tompkins) *trckd ldrs: led 3f out: edgd rt ins fnl f: hld on* **6/1**[2]

100 **2** *½* **Agglestone Rock**[96] 3760 4-9-8 62 .... LeeVickers 4 71
(P A Kirby) *mid-div: hdwy to chse ldrs over 2f out: upsides 1f out: edgd lft ins fnl f: no ex towards fin* **8/1**[3]

6365 **3** *6* **Red Wine**[14] 6767 10-9-11 65 .... PhillipMakin 9 67
(J A Glover) *hld up towards rr: smlooth hdwy to trck ldrs over 2f out: one pce over 1f out* **10/1**

2241 **4** *1 ¼* **Jackday (IRE)**[21] 6559 4-9-4 63 .... BMcHugh(5) 10 64
(T D Easterby) *mid-div: hdwy to chse ldrs over 3f out: one pce fnl 2f* **11/4**[1]

0000 **5** *6* **River Danube**[53] 5625 6-8-10 50 .... PaulHanagan 7 44
(T J Fitzgerald) *in rr: hdwy over 7f out: chsng ldrs over 3f out: wknd over 1f out* **22/1**

4 **6** *1* **Sergeant Pink (IRE)**[104] 3976 3-8-11 64 .... FrederikTylicki(3) 13 56
(S Gollings) *chsd ldrs: wknd 2f out* **8/1**[3]

1563 **7** *2* **Rare Ruby (IRE)**[42] 5961 5-10-0 68 .... SJCraine 11 58
(Jennie Candlish) *in rr-div: hdwy into midfield over 7f out: chsng ldrs 3f out: sn wknd* **10/1**

0544 **8** *7* **Shanavaz**[21] 6558 3-7-13 49 oh4 .... (p) DuranFentiman 8 31
(C J Teague) *hld up in rr: hdwy to chse ldrs over 3f out: wknd over 1f out* **20/1**

4503 **9** *1* **Baan (USA)**[8] 6899 6-9-5 64 .... (p) RichardEvans(5) 5 44
(H J Collingridge) *mid-div: chsng ldrs 3f out: sn wknd* **8/1**[3]

542 **10** *7* **Abstract Folly (IRE)**[11] 6822 7-9-6 60 .... GrahamGibbons 2 32
(J D Bethell) *led: hdd 3f out: sn wknd* **11/1**

/05- **11** *nk* **Starbougg**[205] 6725 5-8-9 49 oh4 .... TonyCulhane 14 21
(K G Reveley) *sn detached in rr: nvr on terms* **100/1**

00-0 **12** *5* **Daltaban (FR)**[17] 6676 5-9-13 67 .... GregFairley 12 33
(P Salmon) *chsd ldrs: lost pl 3f out* **66/1**

0050 **13** *6* **Rapid Desire (IRE)**[14] 6767 3-7-13 49 .... (p) DavidProbert 6 7
(J R Weymes) *chsd ldrs: lost pl over 3f out* **18/1**

3m 41.75s (9.75) **Going Correction** +0.50s/f (Yiel)
WFA 3 from 4yo+ 10lb **13 Ran SP% 117.7**
Speed ratings (Par 103): **95,94,91,91,88 87,86,83,82,79 78,76,73**
toteswinger: 1&2 £18.90, 1&3 £10.60, £25.40. CSF £50.81 CT £476.49 TOTE £7.70: £2.30, £3.30, £2.60; EX 65.80.
Owner M P Bowring **Bred** R F And S D Knipe **Trained** Newmarket, Suffolk

FOCUS
This was a moderate staying handicap and it is probably not form to be positive about despite the gap to the third. Visibility was poor once again due to mist.
Shanavaz Official explanation: jockey said filly had no more to give
Baan(USA) Official explanation: jockey said gelding was unsuited by the soft (good to soft places) ground

7085 RACING UK ON SKY 432 H'CAP (DIV II) — 1m 3f 214y
4:00 (4:01) (Class 6) (0-60,58) 3-Y-0+ — **£2,047** (£604; £302) **Stalls** Low

Form — RPR

6005 **1** **Beat The Shower**[43] 5952 3-8-8 50 .... PaulHanagan 4 57
(P D Niven) *chsd ldrs: styd on to ld 2f out: jst hld on* **6/1**[3]

5543 **2** *shd* **Flora's Pride**[11] 6817 5-9-2 51 .... TonyCulhane 10 58
(K G Reveley) *hld up towards rr: hdwy 3f out: sn chsng ldrs: chal 1f out: jst hld* **12/1**

0-40 **3** *1 ¾* **Amical Risks (FR)**[76] 4893 5-8-12 47 .... PhillipMakin 2 51
(W J Musson) *in rr: gd hdwy over 2f out: styd on fnl f* **7/1**

20-5 **4** *1 ¾* **Covert Mission**[11] 6832 6-9-0 54 .... RichardEvans(5) 8 55+
(P D Evans) *prom: upsides over 2f out: one pce over 1f out* **4/1**[1]

0625 **5** *7* **Jenny Soba**[50] 5733 6-9-7 56 .... DNolan 11 46
(Lucinda Featherstone) *in rr: sme hdwy over 2f out: nvr nr ldrs* **11/1**

0-34 **6** *2 ½* **Lisbon Lion (IRE)**[14] 6766 4-9-7 56 .... TomEaves 6 42
(James Moffatt) *prom: hdwy to chal over 2f out: wknd over 1f out* **8/1**

0000 **7** *1 ¼* **Mesbaah (IRE)**[14] 5423 5-9-6 58 .... FrederikTylicki(3) 9 42
(R A Fahey) *mid-div: sme hdwy over 2f out: sn btn* **9/2**[2]

-000 **8** *¾* **Intavac Boy**[11] 6818 8-8-10 45 .... (p) AndrewMullen 12 28
(S P Griffiths) *led tl over 2f out: sn wknd* **100/1**

532 **9** *6* **Dimashq**[10] 6845 7-9-3 52 .... MickyFenton 7 25
(P T Midgley) *hld up in rr: hdwy to take narrow ld 3f out: hdd 2f out: sn wknd* **7/1**

0-06 **10** *7* **Aspirational (IRE)**[155] 2323 3-8-12 54 .... DavidProbert 14 16
(B Palling) *chsd ldrs: wknd 3f out* **25/1**

-400 **11** *1 ¾* **Gulnaz**[14] 6766 4-8-10 45 .... DuranFentiman 3 4
(C J Teague) *chsd ldrs: upsides over 2f out: sn lost pl* **50/1**

5000 **12** *15* **Danzig Fox**[17] 6674 4-8-13 48 .... (b) GregFairley 13 —
(M Mullineaux) *trckd ldrs: t.k.h: lost pl over 3f out: sn wl bhd* **40/1**

2m 46.7s (7.80) **Going Correction** +0.50s/f (Yiel)
WFA 3 from 4yo+ 7lb **12 Ran SP% 113.8**
Speed ratings (Par 101): **94,93,92,91,86 85,84,83,79,75 74,64**
toteswinger: 1&2 £11.90, 1&3 £8.50, £15.10. CSF £70.67 CT £512.69 TOTE £7.70: £1.60, £3.60, £3.00; EX 54.90.
Owner Mrs Kate Young **Bred** C P E Brooks **Trained** Barton-le-Street, N Yorks

FOCUS
This was probably the stronger of the two divisions, although the time was slower. The first three raced nearest the stands' rail. Visibility was again limited.
Beat The Shower Official explanation: trainer said, regarding apparent improvement in form, that the gelding had run to its form having been beaten 4 1/2 lengths previously.
Aspirational(IRE) Official explanation: jockey said gelding was unsuited by the soft (good to soft places) ground
Danzig Fox Official explanation: jockey said gelding ran too free

7086 COME RACING AGAIN NEXT TUESDAY H'CAP (DIV II) — 5f
4:30 (4:30) (Class 6) (0-65,65) 3-Y-0+ — **£2,047** (£604; £302) **Stalls** Low

Form — RPR

0156 **1** **Spirit Of Coniston**[43] 5946 6-8-11 58 .... MickyFenton 10 73
(P T Midgley) *mde all sn racing against far side rail: clr over 1f out: eased towards fin* **8/1**

00 **2** *4 ½* **Bertbrand**[29] 6335 4-8-6 53 .... (b) GregFairley 6 52
(I W McInnes) *chsd ldrs: styd on same pce fnl 2f: no ch w wnr* **16/1**

0520 **3** *3* **Tartatartufata**[12] 6799 7-9-2 63 .... (v) PaulHanagan 9 51
(J G Given) *chsd ldrs: kpt on same pce fnl 2f* **9/2**[1]

3541 **4** *1 ½* **The History Man (IRE)**[6] 6933 6-8-9 61 6ex .... (p) AndrewHeffernan(5) 5 44
(B D Leavy) *chsd ldrs: kpt on same pce fnl 2f* **7/1**[3]

2002 **5** *¾* **Grudge**[10] 6857 4-9-4 65 .... FrancisNorton 13 45
(Ollie Pears) *chsd ldrs: one pce fnl 2f* **17/2**

6000 **6** *2* **Commander Wish**[7] 6926 6-8-3 55 .... (p) PatrickDonaghy(5) 14 28
(Lucinda Featherstone) *in rr on outside: stmbld over 2f out: kpt on: nt rch ldrs* **16/1**

0400 **7** *1* **Fern House (IRE)**[26] 6410 7-8-3 55 oh6 ow4 .... PaulPickard(5) 1 24
(Bruce Hellier) *in rr: styd on fnl 2f: nvr a factor* **20/1**

0060 **8** *½* **Grimes Faith**[4] 6989 6-8-6 53 .... (b) GrahamGibbons 2 20
(K A Ryan) *mid-div: effrt over 2f out: nvr nr ldrs* **6/1**[2]

3155 **9** *¾* **Revue Princess (IRE)**[12] 6801 4-9-4 65 .... (b) DavidAllan 8 30
(T D Easterby) *in rr: nvr on terms* **7/1**[3]

0205 **10** *2* **Tenancy (IRE)**[36] 6161 5-8-4 51 oh1 .... PaulQuinn 11 8
(S A Harris) *chsd ldrs: wknd 2f out* **16/1**

360 **11** *1 ¼* **Castlecarra (IRE)**[50] 5727 4-8-4 51 oh4 .... DuranFentiman 4 4
(J Hetherton) *a in rr* **14/1**

0000 **12** *4 ½* **Blazing Heights**[4] 6989 6-8-4 51 oh1 .... (b) DavidProbert 15 —
(J S Goldie) *mid-div on outside: lost pl over 2f out* **14/1**

0-20 **13** *shd* **Tanley**[9] 6877 4-8-5 52 .... (p) AndrewMullen 3 —
(J F Coupland) *in rr: bhd fnl 2f* **12/1**

5306 **U** **Paddy Jack**[69] 5159 4-8-4 51 oh6 .... (v[1]) AndrewElliott 7 —
(J R Weymes) *t.k.h: clipped heels and uns rdr over 3f out* **22/1**

61.22 secs (1.42) **Going Correction** +0.50s/f (Yiel) **14 Ran SP% 126.9**
Speed ratings (Par 101): **108,100,96,93,92 89,87,86,85,82 80,73,73,—**
toteswinger: 1&2 £40.20, 1&3 £8.70, £36.40. CSF £136.89 CT £662.96 TOTE £11.00: £3.70, £6.90, £2.90; EX 291.50 Place 6: £277.67, Place 5: £92.42..
Owner P O'Gara & N Kelly **Bred** Green Square Racing **Trained** Westow, N Yorks

FOCUS
Visibility was extremely poor for this moderate sprint handicap. The winning time was 0.50 seconds quicker than the first division and the first three were always 1-2-3. The winner is the best guide to the form.
Commander Wish Official explanation: jockey said gelding stumbled halfway
T/Jkpt: Not won. T/Plt: £805.30 to a £1 stake. Pool: £49,370.12. 44.75 winning tickets. T/Qpdt: £161.80 to a £1 stake. Pool: £5,401.92. 24.70 winning tickets. WG

6946 SOUTHWELL (L-H)
Tuesday, October 27

OFFICIAL GOING: Standard
Wind: Light across Weather: Overcast

7087 BETDAQ THE BETTING EXCHANGE MAIDEN AUCTION STKS — 6f (F)
1:20 (1:20) (Class 5) 2-Y-0 — **£3,412** (£1,007; £504) **Stalls** Low

Form — RPR

1 **Bowmaker** 2-8-12 0 .... RoystonFfrench 7 79
(M Johnston) *chsd ldrs: led wl over 1f out: pushed clr fnl f: impressive* **11/4**[2]

0002 **2** *7* **Clear Ice (IRE)**[28] 6355 2-8-10 58 .... AdrianTNicholls 6 56
(D Nicholls) *chsd ldr tl led over 2f out: rdn and hdd wl over 1f out: sn outpcd* **3/1**[3]

6 **3** *1 ¼* **Giptar (IRE)**[21] 6556 2-8-10 0 .... TedDurcan 2 52
(E F Vaughan) *dwlt: hld up: hdwy over 2f out: rdn over 1f out: styd on same pce* **13/8**[1]

0600 **4** *1 ¼* **Bookiesindex Girl (IRE)**[39] 6061 2-8-1 51 .... MartinLane(5) 8 45
(J R Jenkins) *sn led: rdn and hdd over 2f out: styd on same pce* **33/1**

63 **5** *nk* **Marjolly (IRE)**[28] 6356 2-8-9 0 .... AndreaAtzeni(3) 1 50
(M Botti) *prom: rdn 1/2-way: styd on same pce fnl 2f* **7/1**

6 *7* **Weimarland (IRE)** 2-8-13 0 .... SteveDrowne 3 30
(J A Osborne) *hld up in tch: rdn over 2f out: sn wknd* **25/1**

7 *2* **Plenty O'Toole** 2-8-13 0 .... EdwardCreighton 5 24
(Mrs D J Sanderson) *hld up: rdn 1/2-way: sn wknd* **25/1**

1m 15.32s (-1.18) **Going Correction** -0.15s/f (Stan) **7 Ran SP% 112.9**
Speed ratings (Par 95): **101,91,90,88,87 78,75**
toteswinger: 1&2 £2.10, 1&3 £2.50, £3.10. CSF £11.04 TOTE £4.60: £2.10, £1.50; EX 11.90.
Owner Sheikh Hamdan Bin Mohammed Al Maktoum **Bred** Brook Stud Bloodstock Ltd **Trained** Middleham Moor, N Yorks

FOCUS
A modest maiden and they finished very well spread out, but the winner was very impressive.

NOTEBOOK
Bowmaker, a 62,000gns foal and 20,000gns 2-y-o, is a half-brother to the recent Kempton winner Sham Sheer. Despite being fairly weak in the market, he travelled powerfully behind the leaders in the early stages before taking it up on the outside 2f from home and, once in front, he stretched further and further clear. The form probably doesn't amount to much with the runner-up rated 58, but the style of his victory was very impressive and there is probably much more to come. (tchd 5-2 and 100-30)

Clear Ice(IRE), the most experienced in the field who improved for the switch to this surface when only narrowly beaten off 55 in a 5f nursery here last time, was always handy. He may have hit the front for a few strides after sneaking up the inside of the leader off the final bend, but as soon as the winner was unleashed he was made to look extremely one-paced. He will always be vulnerable to unexposed sorts in races like this and he would probably be better off back in handicap company. (op 9-4)
Giptar(IRE), green when unplaced on his Catterick debut earlier this month, was the major mover in the market beforehand but he spoiled his chances by missing the break and then racing keenly out the back. He was travelling well against the inside rail starting up the home straight, but then found very little off the bridle as his earlier exertions took their toll. A half-brother to the dual course winner Charles Parnell, he should be able to find a race on this surface though the cat is now rather out of the bag. (op 4-1)
Bookiesindex Girl(IRE), unplaced all five starts so far including in selling company, set the early pace but after losing the advantage she had little left to offer over the last couple of furlongs. (op 25-1)
Marjolly(IRE), a well-beaten third in a similar event over C&D last month, ran to a similar level of form having raced keenly in midfield in the early stages. He needed this for a mark, but will still need to improve to make his mark in nurseries. (op 9-2)

7088 COME JUMP RACING 9TH NOVEMBER NURSERY (DIV I) 6f (F)

1:50 (1:50) (Class 6) (0-65,65) 2-Y-O **£2,524** (£745; £372) **Stalls** Low

Form				RPR
060	**1**		**Imjin River (IRE)**[14] 6754 2-9-7 **65** ... TedDurcan 3 (M H Tompkins) *chsd ldr: led 2f out: rdn out* **5/1**	71
3035	**2**	2 1/4	**We'll Deal Again**[8] 6895 2-9-0 **65** ... JamesPSullivan(7) 2 (M W Easterby) *dwlt: hld up: hdwy over 1f out: sn rdn: r.o: nt rch wnr* **9/2[3]**	64
0350	**3**	*hd*	**Spinning Spirit (IRE)**[12] 6793 2-9-7 **65** ... PaulMulrennan 6 (J G Given) *chsd ldrs: rdn: nt clr run and swtchd lft over 1f out: r.o* **8/1**	63
4053	**4**	1	**Kalahari Desert (IRE)**[12] 6796 2-9-1 **62** ... MichaelJStainton(3) 10 (R M Whitaker) *hld up: hdwy over 1f out: r.o: nt trble ldrs* **7/2[2]**	57
5060	**5**	3/4	**Miss Taken (IRE)**[26] 6431 2-8-5 **52** ... (b) KellyHarrison(3) 9 (D Carroll) *plld hrd: led 1f: chsd ldrs: rdn over 1f out: styd on same pce fnl f* **14/1**	45
0630	**6**	1	**Nabrina (IRE)**[20] 6589 2-8-10 **54** ... RobertWinston 8 (M Brittain) *sn pushed along to chse ldrs: rdn over 2f out: no ex fnl f* **9/1**	44
0040	**7**	2 1/2	**Lees Anthem**[10] 6841 2-8-9 **58** ... LanceBetts(5) 1 (C J Teague) *led 5f out: rdn and hdd 2f out: sn hung rt: wknd fnl f* **20/1**	41
0042	**8**	10	**Speedyfix**[19] 6610 2-8-3 **50** ... (tp) AndreaAtzeni(3) 4 (Mrs C A Dunnett) *prom: rdn over 2f out: wknd over 1f out: eased* **3/1[1]**	3
0600	**9**	2 1/4	**Maiwand**[4] 6983 2-8-1 **45** ... (b[1]) SilvestreDeSousa 7 (Mrs R A Carr) *sn outpcd and bhd* **66/1**	—
6600	**10**	14	**Bonasera (IRE)**[11] 6820 2-7-12 **45** ... DominicFox(3) 11 (A Berry) *sn outpcd and bhd* **125/1**	—

1m 16.37s (-0.13) **Going Correction** -0.15s/f (Stan) **10** Ran SP% **116.9**
Speed ratings (Par 93): **94,91,90,89,88 87,83,70,67,48**
toteswinger: 1&2 £5.60, 1&3 £3.70, £9.10. CSF £27.58 CT £178.63 TOTE £5.80: £2.00, £1.70, £3.30; EX 17.50.
Owner Miss Clare Hollest **Bred** Glending Bloodstock **Trained** Newmarket, Suffolk

FOCUS
A modest first division of the nursery and the winning time was over a second slower than the maiden.

NOTEBOOK
Imjin River(IRE), making his sand and nursery debuts, is a brother to the triple course-winner More Time Tim and he followed in the family tradition by stepping up considerably on the form he showed in three turf maidens. He could be spotted travelling best up with the pace from some way out and when asked to go and win his race entering the last 2f, he found plenty. He would be of obvious interest if returning here in the coming weeks. Official explanation: trainer's rep said, regarding apparent improvement in form, that the colt only came into training in August and benefited from the drop back to 6f. (op 11-2)
We'll Deal Again was back down in trip for this sand debut after failing to see out 1m last time. He gave himself plenty to do by fluffing the start, but he stayed on well over the last couple of furlongs despite being carried over to the inside rail. His sire relished this surface and he should be able to hit the target back here. (op 7-2)
Spinning Spirit(IRE), back to sprinting for this sand debut after failing to get home over 1m last time, also stayed on towards the inside of the track in the latter stages and it may be that 7f is his ideal trip. (op 15-2 tchd 17-2)
Kalahari Desert(IRE), not disgraced in a 5f nursery here last month, ran his best race so far when stepped up to this trip at Nottingham last time. He didn't have a great deal of room to play with when trying to launch an effort halfway up the home straight, but it would be pushing things to say that he was unlucky. (tchd 3-1)
Miss Taken(IRE), placed a couple of times over sprint trips early on this season, had been very disappointing over 1m in her recent starts and though she plugged on down the wide outside towards the end, she never looked like winning and her best trip remains a mystery.
Speedyfix, who had been mildly progressive in Polytrack nurseries of late and was well backed, was off the bridle gainst the inside rail passing halfway and when it became obvious that he wasn't going to figure in the finish, he was eased right off. He didn't seem to take to the surface at all. (op 11-2 tchd 6-1)

7089 COME JUMP RACING 9TH NOVEMBER NURSERY (DIV II) 6f (F)

2:20 (2:20) (Class 6) (0-65,65) 2-Y-O **£2,524** (£745; £372) **Stalls** Low

Form				RPR
6201	**1**		**Angie's Nap (USA)**[28] 6354 2-9-3 **61** ... (p) RobertWinston 7 (P S McEntee) *led: hdd over 2f out: rallied u.p to ld over 1f out: r.o* **7/2[2]**	67
4506	**2**	3/4	**Cape Kimberley**[28] 6355 2-9-7 **65** ... PaulMulrennan 10 (J G Given) *chsd ldrs: led over 2f out: rdn and hdd over 1f out: ev ch ins fnl f: styd on* **8/1**	68
0046	**3**	3 3/4	**Avec Moi**[12] 6796 2-8-1 **48** ... AndreaAtzeni(3) 5 (Mrs C A Dunnett) *s.i.s and hmpd s: sn pushed along in rr: styd on u.p fr over 1f out: nt rch ldrs* **9/2[3]**	40
000	**4**	1/2	**Old Devil Moon (IRE)**[18] 6627 2-8-10 **54** ... StephenDonohoe 3 (T G Mills) *prom: rdn 1/2-way: styd on same pce appr fnl f* **10/3[1]**	45
535	**5**	2 3/4	**Luv U Noo**[56] 5553 2-8-13 **62** ... MartinLane(5) 8 (A P Jarvis) *prom: rdn 1/2-way: hung lft 2f out: no ex* **17/2**	44
2600	**6**	1/2	**Michaelmas Daisy**[20] 6586 2-9-7 **65** ... (be[1]) HayleyTurner 2 (Miss Amy Weaver) *sn pushed along and prom: outpcd fr 1/2-way* **7/1**	46
0503	**7**	8	**Zaskia (IRE)**[21] 6555 2-8-7 **51** ... FergusSweeney 9 (K A Ryan) *chsd ldrs: rdn over 2f out: wknd over 1f out* **7/1**	8
000	**8**	5	**Polish Steps (IRE)**[34] 6207 2-8-9 **53** ... TedDurcan 4 (J A Osborne) *sn pushed along in rr: wknd 1/2-way* **12/1**	—

1m 17.17s (0.67) **Going Correction** -0.15s/f (Stan) **8** Ran SP% **117.8**
Speed ratings (Par 93): **89,88,83,82,78 78,67,60**
toteswinger: 1&2 £5.80, 1&3 £6.90, £12.20. CSF £32.46 CT £130.73 TOTE £4.40: £1.30, £2.60, £2.00; EX 39.20.
Owner Eventmaker Racehorses **Bred** James Millar & Janice Millar **Trained** Newmarket, Suffolk

FOCUS
This looked an even weaker nursery than the first division and very few ever got into it. The winning time was 0.8 seconds slower than division one and 1.85 seconds slower than the maiden.

NOTEBOOK
Angie's Nap(USA), whose best two previous efforts had come here including winning a 5f nursery off 7lb lower last month, didn't get home in her only previous try over this trip, but she was nonetheless ridden very positively here and showed real grit and determination to out-battle the runner-up after looking sure to be swallowed up. She looks well worth persevering with that this venue and may return here in a fortnight. (op 9-2)
Cape Kimberley, who has shown glimpses of ability on this surface, was back up to 6f after finding the drop to 5f against him last time. Prominent from the off, he looked likely to win when smoothly moving around the outside to challenge off the home bend, but although he never appeared to stop trying he was up against a dogged rival who just had the legs of him where it mattered. (op 13-2 tchd 6-1)
Avec Moi, whose close fourth in a 5f nursery here last month was by far her best effort so far in 12 attempts, not for the first time attracted market support but she had a real problem going the early pace and by the time she found her stride and stayed on it was far too late. (op 17-2)
Old Devil Moon(IRE), making his nursery debut after showing limited ability in three maidens, was another seriously off the bridle rounding the home bend and lacked the pace to make an serious impression. He hadn't got home over 7f in his last two starts, but this looked too sharp which gives connections a problem. (tchd 3-1 and 7-2)
Luv U Noo, making her sand and nursery debuts after showing some ability in turf maidens, was trying this extra furlong for the first time but she was yet another struggling to go the early pace and she had little to offer once into the home straight. (op 7-1 tchd 6-1)
Michaelmas Daisy Official explanation: trainer said filly was unsuited by the Fibresand

7090 SOUTHWELL-RACECOURSE.CO.UK CONDITIONS STKS 5f (F)

2:50 (2:53) (Class 3) 3-Y-0+ **£9,714** (£2,890; £1,444; £721) **Stalls** High

Form				RPR
6600	**1**		**Rowe Park**[17] 6661 6-9-5 102 ... SteveDrowne 2 (Mrs L C Jewell) *stmbld s: hdwy 1/2-way: rdn to ld over 1f out: all out* **5/2[1]**	108
-300	**2**	*nse*	**Excellerator (IRE)**[26] 6427 3-8-9 95 ... (t) TedDurcan 6 (George Baker) *chsd ldrs: rdn and hung lft fr 1/2-way: r.o wl ins fnl f: jst failed* **5/1**	98
4300	**3**	1 3/4	**Exclamation**[129] 3141 4-9-0 97 ... HayleyTurner 1 (B J Meehan) *chsd ldrs: rdn to ld over 1f out: sn hdd: styd on same pce ins fnl f* **11/2**	97
030	**4**	2 3/4	**Strike Up The Band**[23] 6522 6-9-0 102 ... AdrianTNicholls 7 (D Nicholls) *led: rdn and hdd over 1f out: no ex fnl f* **9/2[3]**	87
2500	**5**	*hd*	**Pawan (IRE)**[3] 7019 9-9-2 85 ... AnnStokell(5) 3 (Miss A Stokell) *sn outpcd: swtchd lft 1/2-way: styd on ins fnl f: nvr nrr* **28/1**	93
1-24	**6**	*nk*	**Turn On The Style**[255] 553 7-9-0 103 ... (b) PaulMulrennan 5 (J Balding) *reluctant to go to post: wnt lft s: sn w ldr: rdn and ev ch over 1f out: no ex* **7/2[2]**	85
5002	**7**	5	**Loose Caboose (IRE)**[9] 6877 4-8-9 68 ... (b) RobertWinston 8 (A J McCabe) *s.i.s: sn rdn along to chse ldrs: wknd over 1f out* **12/1**	62
1436	**8**	6	**Doubtful Sound (USA)**[234] 785 5-9-0 96 ... DavidKenny(7) 4 (R Hollinshead) *s.s: a outpcd* **22/1**	52

58.94 secs (-0.76) **Going Correction** +0.025s/f (Slow) **8** Ran SP% **116.5**
Speed ratings (Par 107): **107,106,104,99,99 98,90,81**
toteswinger: 1&2 £4.80, 1&3 £3.80, £4.30. CSF £15.75 TOTE £3.80: £1.50, £1.90, £2.10; EX 15.70.
Owner Mrs Sue Ashdown **Bred** J Baker **Trained** Sutton Valence, Kent
■ Stewards' Enquiry : Steve Drowne caution: excessive use of the whip

FOCUS
A decent conditions sprint, featuring a few that have been taking on some very decent company in their recent starts. The first two are the best guides to the form. They went a serious pace and the action unfolded down the centre of the track.

NOTEBOOK
Rowe Park, who has spent most of the last two years in Group and Listed company, had been successful in his only previous try over C&D. He looked to have blown it when stumbling at the gates and losing ground, which is usually fatal over this straight 5f, but he travelled into the race very powerfully and looked likely to win easily when taking it up over a furlong from home, but the runner-up gave him a real scare in the closing stages. He is likely to be aimed at a similar event at Lingfield next month. (op 11-4 tchd 100-30)
Excellerator(IRE), successful over C&D on her racecourse debut, had faced stiff tasks in her last couple of outings. Content to track the leaders early, she drifted over towards the far rail when asked for her effort, but still put in a powerful finish which only just failed by the narrowest of margins. She remains relatively unexposed, but it still seems that she needs a return to further. Official explanation: jockey said filly hung left throughout (op 11-2 tchd 9-2)
Exclamation, off since June, was trying Fibresand for the first time and this was also his first attempt at the minimum trip. He travelled well up with the leaders and had every chance a furlong out, but race-fit rivals then had his measure. (op 17-2 tchd 9-1)
Strike Up The Band, without a win in well over a year, was making his Fibresand debut after finishing tenth in the Prix de l'Abbaye. He showed his usual early pace to take the field along, but had nothing more to offer once collared over a furlong from home. (op 7-2)
Pawan(IRE), having his 17th start of the year, is fully effective here but not for the first time he had a mountain to climb at these weights. Strictly on the book he again ran above himself, but he never looked like figuring at the finish at any stage. Official explanation: jockey said gelding suffered interference at start (op 33-1)
Turn On The Style, very effective here and best in at the weights, was having his first outing since February and though he did win following a five-month layoff in his younger days, there was still a question mark against him after this longer absence. Not for the first time walked to start, he showed up for a fair way but came off the bridle passing the 2f pole and was soon beaten. He was entitled to need this, but will need to improve if he is to be aimed at Dubai. (op 11-4 tchd 5-2)

7091 ROTARY CLUB OF MAPPERLEY H'CAP 1m 6f (F)

3:20 (3:20) (Class 3) (0-95,92) 3-Y-0+ **£9,714** (£2,890; £1,444; £721) **Stalls** Low

Form				RPR
1012	**1**		**Lucky Punt**[9] 6878 3-8-6 **79** ... FergusSweeney 1 (B G Powell) *chsd ldr tl led over 7f out: shkn up over 2f out: clr over 1f out: eased towards fin* **85/40[1]**	91+
4351	**2**	3 3/4	**Trip The Light**[17] 6681 4-9-8 **86** ... TonyHamilton 5 (R A Fahey) *hld up: pushed along 10f out: hdwy 7f out: chsd wnr over 5f out: rdn over 2f out: sn hung lft: styd on same pce* **5/2[2]**	91
000	**3**	28	**Carte Diamond (USA)**[17] 3826 8-9-9 **92** ... (b[1]) LanceBetts(5) 2 (B Ellison) *led: hdd over 7f out: chsd wnr to over 5f out: rdn and wknd over 3f out: t.o* **10/1**	58
000	**4**	10	**Bogside Theatre (IRE)**[38] 6095 5-9-2 **80** ... RobertWinston 6 (G M Moore) *chsd ldrs: pushed along 8f out: hrd rdn over 5f out: wknd wl over 3f out: t.o* **8/1**	32
6/00	**5**	27	**Sagredo (USA)**[15] 6734 5-9-4 **82** ... RichardKingscote 4 (Jonjo O'Neill) *hld up: rdn over 7f out: sn lost tch: t.o fnl 4f* **10/1**	—
360	**R**		**Tilt**[10] 6851 7-9-5 **88** ... (b[1]) MartinLane(5) 3 (B Ellison) *ref to r: tk no part* **7/2[3]**	—

3m 3.62s (-4.68) **Going Correction** -0.15s/f (Stan)
WFA 3 from 4yo+ 9lb **6** Ran SP% **112.1**
Speed ratings (Par 107): **107,104,88,83,67** —
toteswinger: 1&2 £1.50, 1&3 £4.90, £5.30. CSF £7.69 TOTE £2.80: £1.30, £1.90; EX 5.70.

Owner I S Smith **Bred** S A Douch **Trained** Upper Lambourn, Berks

FOCUS

A decent handicap with good prize money, but only one of these had previous Fibresand experience and it showed, as Lucky Punt recorded another clear personal best.

NOTEBOOK

Lucky Punt, a winner three times and runner-up once from four previous outings on this surface, was racing beyond 1m4f for the first time on the Flat. Always in a handy position, he took over in front before the end of the back straight and, with only one serious rival within striking distance turning in, galloped on relentlessly to score. He is likely to keep on coming back here and if all goes well, he may travel to Dubai. (op 15-8 tchd 9-4)

Trip The Light, raised 5lb for his recent York victory and making his Fibresand debut, was travelling well enough turning for home but, despite coming under strong pressure, he could never get on terms with the winner though he pulled a mile clear of the others. He has won twice over this trip on turf, but this gruelling surface may have just found him out. (op 9-4 tchd 11-4 and 2-1 in a place)

Carte Diamond(USA), having his first start on the Flat since July but well beaten over hurdles earlier this month, had blinkers on for the first time on this Fibresand debut. He set the early pace, but once the winner had headed him at halfway the writing was soon on the wall. (op 18-1)

Bogside Theatre(IRE), disappointing on the Flat and over hurdles over the past year and without a win since July 2007, was another making her Fibresand debut. She likes to get her toe in on turf which offered some hope, but she was being niggled along at halfway and it wasn't long before she was really struggling. (op 17-2 tchd 15-2)

Sagredo(USA), well beaten both starts since returning to the Flat and making his Fibresand debut, completely lost touch soon after halfway. Official explanation: jockey said gelding never travelled (op 12-1 tchd 14-1)

Tilt, in first-time blinkers, planted himself as the stall opened and refused to race. (op 9-2 tchd 3-1)

7092 BETDAQ ON 0870 178 1221 FILLIES' H'CAP — 1m (F)

3:50 (3:51) (Class 4) (0-85,78) 3-Y-0+ — **£6,824** (£2,015; £1,008) **Stalls** Low

Form				RPR
0660	**1**		**Miss Glitters (IRE)**[61] 5375 4-9-3 **74** .... SteveDrowne 5 (H Morrison) *sn led: rdn and hdd over 1f out: rallied to ld ins fnl f: r.o* **7/2**[2]	87
0315	**2**	½	**Salerosa (IRE)**[10] 6847 4-8-12 **69** .... SilvestreDeSousa 4 (Mrs A Duffield) *trckd ldrs: plld hrd: led over 1f out: rdn and hdd ins fnl f: styd on* **11/8**[1]	81
2166	**3**	4 ½	**Implication**[19] 6621 3-9-1 **75** .... TedDurcan 2 (E A L Dunlop) *broke wl: stdd sn after s: hld up in tch: shkn up over 2f out: styd on same pce appr fnl f* **9/2**[3]	77
-000	**4**	*hd*	**Fantasy Princess (USA)**[18] 6634 4-9-1 **72** .... (t) HayleyTurner 1 (G A Butler) *chsd ldrs: rdn over 3f out: styd on same pce appr fnl f* **16/1**	73
0000	**5**	1	**Mozayada (USA)**[4] 6985 5-9-4 **75** .... RobertWinston 6 (M Brittain) *sn w wnr: rdn and ev ch over 2f out: wknd fnl f* **9/2**[3]	74
3100	**6**	3	**La Coveta (IRE)**[72] 5062 4-9-2 **78** .... GabrielHannon(5) 3 (B J Meehan) *sn pushed along in rr: bhd fnl 3f* **16/1**	70

1m 41.66s (-2.04) **Going Correction** -0.15s/f (Stan)

WFA 3 from 4yo+ 3lb — **6 Ran SP% 112.5**

Speed ratings (Par 102): **104,103,99,98,97 94**

toteswinger: 1&2 £1.80, 1&3 £2.70, £2.10. CSF £8.80 TOTE £5.20: £2.30, £1.40; EX 9.00.

Owner Mrs M D W Morrison **Bred** Roger And Henry O'Callaghan **Trained** East Ilsley, Berks

FOCUS

A fair fillies' handicap run at a good pace. The winner is rated up 3lb.

7093 BETDAQ.CO.UK H'CAP — 1m 3f (F)

4:20 (4:20) (Class 5) (0-70,73) 3-Y-0+ — **£3,238** (£963; £481; £240) **Stalls** Low

Form				RPR
0340	**1**		**Ibrox (IRE)**[42] 5962 4-9-8 **66** .... (p) SilvestreDeSousa 6 (A D Brown) *hld up: hdwy over 8f out: chsd ldr over 4f out: led over 2f out: drvn out* **7/1**	80
2-46	**2**	4 ½	**Wing Diva (IRE)**[102] 4071 4-9-0 **58** .... TonyHamilton 3 (B Smart) *led: rdn and hdd over 2f out: edgd rt and styd on same pce fnl f* **12/1**	64
2044	**3**	1	**Greenbelt**[14] 6768 8-8-8 **52** .... RoystonFfrench 8 (G M Moore) *sn pushed along in rr: hdwy over 3f out: rdn over 2f out: styd on same pce fnl f* **9/2**[2]	56
1045	**4**	4 ½	**Eightdaysaweek**[10] 6860 3-8-12 **62** .... (p) RobertWinston 5 (A J McCabe) *s.i.s: hdwy over 8f out: rdn over 2f out: wknd over 1f out* **13/2**	58
0146	**5**	1 ¾	**Astrolibra**[42] 5962 5-9-4 **62** .... TedDurcan 9 (M H Tompkins) *s.i.s: sn pushed along in rr: rdn over 4f out: nvr on terms* **5/2**[1]	55
36-1	**6**	¾	**Red Expresso (IRE)**[29] 6342 4-9-4 **65** .... KellyHarrison(3) 4 (Ollie Pears) *hld up: rdn 1/2-way: nvr on terms* **11/2**[3]	57
50	**7**	2 ½	**Plenilune (IRE)**[82] 4710 4-8-7 **54** .... MichaelJStainton(3) 1 (M Brittain) *chsd ldrs: rdn over 3f out: sn wknd* **12/1**	42
0626	**8**	9	**Trouble Mountain (USA)**[11] 6817 12-8-12 **56** .... (t) PaulMulrennan 2 (M W Easterby) *chsd ldrs tl rdn and wknd over 3f out* **12/1**	28
0620	**9**	22	**Echo Dancer**[95] 4275 3-9-2 **73** ow5 .... JoshWall(7) 7 (T Wall) *chsd ldrs: rdn over 4f out: wknd over 3f out* **14/1**	6

2m 25.95s (-2.05) **Going Correction** -0.15s/f (Stan)

WFA 3 from 4yo+ 6lb — **9 Ran SP% 117.7**

Speed ratings (Par 103): **101,97,97,93,92 91,90,83,67**

toteswinger: 1&2 £12.30, 1&3 £6.10, £6.60. CSF £88.18 CT £422.85 TOTE £7.60: £2.50, £3.60, £1.50; EX 98.20 Place 6: £32.85, Place 5: £15.58..

Owner sportaracing.com **Bred** Hellwood Stud Farm **Trained** Yedingham, N Yorks

FOCUS

An ordinary handicap. The form is rated at face value with the winner up 8lb.

Astrolibra Official explanation: jockey said mare never travelled

Red Expresso(IRE) Official explanation: jockey said gelding ran flat

Plenilune(IRE) Official explanation: vet said gelding lost a shoe

T/Plt: £47.60 to a £1 stake. Pool: £55,245.44. 845.65 winning tickets. T/Qpdt: £8.90 to a £1 stake. Pool: £4,449.00. 366.20 winning tickets. CR

6919 YARMOUTH (L-H)

Tuesday, October 27

OFFICIAL GOING: Good (good to soft in places in straight; 6.6)

Wind: Virtually nil Weather: light rain, clearing

7094 STRAIGHTFORWARDSOLUTIONS.CO.UK (S) STKS — 1m 2f 21y

12:40 (12:41) (Class 6) 3-4-Y-0 — **£1,942** (£578; £288; £144) **Stalls** Low

Form				RPR
4555	**1**		**Orthology (IRE)**[14] 6758 3-8-12 63 .... (p) NCallan 11 (M H Tompkins) *chsd ldrs: wnt 2nd 4f out: led narrowly wl over 2f out: sn rdn: kpt on wl fnl f* **11/4**[1]	60
4640	**2**	*nk*	**Lady Sorcerer**[38] 6102 4-8-12 47 .... (v) RichardMullen 10 (A P Jarvis) *hld up in midfield: hdwy over 3f out: ev ch over 2f out: drvn and pressed wnr fr over 1f out: a jst hld fnl f* **8/1**	54
-005	**3**	½	**Spanish Cross (IRE)**[5] 6966 4-8-12 51 .... KirstyMilczarek 8 (G Prodromou) *hld up towards rr: hdwy and forced way through 3f out: chsd ldng pair 2f out: kpt on same pce u.p fnl f* **8/1**	53
3340	**4**	6	**Mile High Lad (USA)**[6] 6951 3-8-12 70 .... (p) DaneO'Neill 7 (George Baker) *dwlt: sn pushed up into midfield: rdn 3f out: chsd clr ldng trio wl over 1f out: no imp* **8/1**	46
0020	**5**	½	**Hidden Door (IRE)**[5] 6969 4-8-12 54 .... SaleemGolam 2 (G Prodromou) *hld up towards rr: drvn and effrt over 2f out: plugged on to press for modest 4th fnl f: nvr trbld ldrs* **6/1**[2]	40
0564	**6**	4 ½	**Rose Of Coma (IRE)**[7] 6919 3-8-13 48 .... ChrisCatlin 5 (A G Juckes) *s.i.s: hld up in last pair: effrt u.p over 2f out: no prog fnl 2f* **11/1**	37
5350	**7**	2 ¼	**Intikama (IRE)**[7] 6919 3-8-7 60 .... (bt) JimmyQuinn 6 (M H Tompkins) *in tch: rdn and struggling whn jostling match w rival 3f out: wl bhd after* **7/1**[3]	27
0000	**8**	7	**Hard Ball**[15] 6742 3-8-12 53 .... SebSanders 4 (M Quinn) *chsd ldr tl led ent fnl 4f: rdn and hdd wl over 2f out: sn btn: eased fnl f* **16/1**	18
0003	**9**	¾	**Bromhead (USA)**[7] 6919 3-9-4 50 .... (t) TGMcLaughlin 3 (Mrs C A Dunnett) *sn bustled along to ld: rdn and hdd ent fnl 4f: sn struggling: wl bhd fr over 2f out* **12/1**	22
0000	**10**	2 ½	**Bahama Baileys**[7] 6924 4-9-3 46 .... CatherineGannon 12 (C A Dwyer) *tubed: stdd s: hld up in rr: rdn 5f out: nvr trbld ldrs* **40/1**	11
000-	**11**	1 ½	**Cape Roberto (IRE)**[321] 7629 4-9-3 49 .... AlanMunro 1 (John Berry) *t.k.h: chsd ldrs tl rdn and struggling 4f out: wl bhd fr over 2f out* **16/1**	8

2m 10.73s (0.23) **Going Correction** +0.025s/f (Good)

WFA 3 from 4yo 5lb — **11 Ran SP% 117.0**

Speed ratings (Par 101): **100,99,99,94,94 90,88,83,82,80 79**

toteswinger: 1&2 £7.40, 1&3 £4.80, £17.80. CSF £24.66 TOTE £3.30: £1.60, £3.50, £2.80; EX 35.10 Trifecta £130.40 Part won. Pool: £176.26 - 0.66 winning units..The winner was bought in for 5,800gns.

Owner M Winter **Bred** D And Mrs D Veitch **Trained** Newmarket, Suffolk

■ Stewards' Enquiry : Kirsty Milczarek one-day ban: careless riding (Nov 11)

FOCUS

The first three came clear in this open seller. Weak form with the runner-up perhaps the best guide.

Hard Ball Official explanation: jockey said gelding had no more to give

7095 EUROPEAN BREEDERS' FUND MAIDEN STKS (DIV I) — 1m 3y

1:10 (1:12) (Class 5) 2-Y-0 — **£3,469** (£1,038; £519; £259; £129) **Stalls** High

Form				RPR
	1		**Commissionaire** 2-9-3 0 .... JimmyFortune 7 (J H M Gosden) *s.i.s: rn green and sn nudged along in rr: hdwy and swtchd lft 2f out: chsd ldrs ent fnl f: rdn to ld fnl 75yds: sn in command and pushed out towards fin* **11/1**[3]	80
3	**2**	1 ¼	**Longliner**[27] 6393 2-9-3 0 .... RyanMoore 8 (Sir Michael Stoute) *chsd ldr: ev ch and rdn 2f out: drvn to ld jst over 1f out: hdd and no ex fnl 75yds* **1/2**[1]	77
	3	1 ½	**Sarrsar** 2-9-3 0 .... LDettori 10 (M A Jarvis) *chsd ldrs: rdn and sltly outpcd 2f out: rallied and edgd lft u.p 1f out: kpt on same pce fnl 150yds* **4/1**[2]	74
	4	1	**Solicitor** 2-9-3 0 .... JoeFanning 3 (M Johnston) *chsd ldrs tl rdn to ld 2f out: hdd jst over 1f out: rn green u.p ins fnl f: wknd fnl 100yds* **20/1**	72
06	**5**	2	**Strike A Deal (IRE)**[15] 6727 2-8-9 0 .... JackMitchell(3) 6 (C F Wall) *s.i.s: in tch tl pushed along and outpcd 3f out: hdwy and swtchd rt over 1f out: styd on steadily fnl f but nt pce to rch ldrs* **22/1**	62
0	**6**	1 ½	**Astromoon**[39] 6062 2-8-12 0 .... JimmyQuinn 2 (M H Tompkins) *chsd ldrs: pushed along and outpcd over 2f out: wandered and rn green over 1f out: plugged on steadily fnl f: nt pce to rch ldrs* **40/1**	59
053	**7**	3	**Soho Theatre**[13] 6781 2-9-3 76 .... DaneO'Neill 4 (D R C Elsworth) *led tl hdd and rdn 2f out: wknd qckly over 1f out* **14/1**	57
06	**8**	2	**Wavertree Bounty**[15] 6728 2-8-12 0 .... AlanMunro 1 (C F Wall) *in tch in midfield: rdn over 3f out: sn struggling: no ch fnl 2f* **66/1**	47
	9	1 ¾	**Doyenne Dream** 2-8-12 0 .... LukeMorris 12 (J M P Eustace) *s.i.s: sn rdn along in rr: nvr trbld ldrs* **100/1**	43
40	**10**	4	**Firefly Mustique**[56] 5542 2-9-3 0 .... DO'Donohoe 11 (George Baker) *in tch in midfield tl struggling u.p over 3f out: wl bhd fnl 2f* **150/1**	39
	11	25	**Ava Doll** 2-8-5 0 .... DannyBrock(7) 9 (J R Jenkins) *s.i.s: a bhd: lost tch 1/2-way: t.o and eased fnl f* **150/1**	—

1m 42.88s (2.28) **Going Correction** +0.20s/f (Good) — **11 Ran SP% 117.0**

Speed ratings (Par 95): **96,94,93,92,90 88,85,83,82,78 53**

toteswinger: 1&2 £3.00, 1&3 £3.40, £1.80. CSF £16.54 TOTE £13.70: £2.80, £1.02, £1.40; EX 25.90 Trifecta £77.80 Pool: £476.86 - 4.53 winning units..

Owner Cheveley Park Stud **Bred** Cheveley Park Stud Ltd **Trained** Newmarket, Suffolk

FOCUS

A fair maiden. Sound form with the first four, all from big stables, coming clear.

NOTEBOOK

Commissionaire ♦, a brother to Officer and half-brother to Battle Chant, got his career off to a flying start, despite falling out of the gates and running green through the early stages. He got the hang of things from halfway and made smooth headway to join the leaders. His attitude when under pressure was spot on and this effort is made more meritorious as nothing else managed to land a blow from off the pace. He wouldn't be certain to get further than 1m2f on breeding next year, but he evidently stays well and has a bright future. (op 7-1)

Longliner was all the rage to build on his debut third at Salisbury 27 days previously and open his account. He got a bit warm beforehand, though, and ran somewhat freely up with the early pace. That didn't help his finishing effort and he was laboured throughout the final furlong. There could still be an opening for him this term, but he really appeals as the sort to do a lot better with a winter on his back. (op 8-13 tchd 4-9 and 8-11 in a place)

Sarrsar, representing a yard that boasts a cracking record with juveniles at the course this term, got well backed but was awash with sweat. He helped to cut out the running and came under heavy pressure 2f out, but to his credit stuck on gamely. His dam was second in the Oaks and took the Ribblesdale, so 1m2f plus is going to be right up his street next season. (op 5-1 tchd 6-1 and 7-2)

Solicitor ♦ is a touch more speedily bred than the first three. He ran a very pleasing debut race and looks sure to go close next time out. (op 16-1)

Strike A Deal(IRE) was never seriously involved, but ran a similarly encouraging race to that of her previous Salisbury run and is now qualified for nurseries. (op 16-1)

7096 EBF / AYLSHAM SLURRY SERVICES MAIDEN STKS 7f 3y

1:40 (1:42) (Class 5) 2-Y-O **£3,974** (£1,189; £594; £297; £148) **Stalls** High

Form RPR

5 **1** **London Stripe (IRE)**[19] 6620 2-9-3 0 RyanMoore 11 79
(Sir Michael Stoute) *in tch in midfield: pushed along and hdwy 3f out: led 2f out: kpt edging lft u.p after but hld on wl fnl f* **10/11**[1]

052 **2** ½ **Mass Rally (IRE)**[13] 6781 2-9-3 81 JimmyFortune 6 78
(J H M Gosden) *wnt lft s: in tch: hdwy over 3f out: ev ch 2f out: hrd drvn and unable qck ins fnl f* **7/2**[2]

0 **3** *hd* **En Fuego**[11] 6809 2-9-3 0 AlanMunro 2 77
(P W Chapple-Hyam) *hmpd s: chsd ldr: ev ch and rdn ent fnl 2f: sltly outpcd by ldng pair over 1f out: rallied and swtchd rt ins fnl f: r.o fnl 50yds to press for 2nd at fin* **16/1**

4 *5* **Lileo (IRE)** 2-9-3 0 KFallon 3 64
(L M Cumani) *hmpd s: racd in midfield: pushed along 3f out: outpcd by ldrs over 2f out: plugged on to go 4th ins fnl f: nvr had pce to trble ldrs* **12/1**

5 *2 ½* **Bondage (IRE)** 2-9-3 0 AdamKirby 8 57
(J R Fanshawe) *bhd: pushed along and struggling 3f out: no ch w ldrs fnl 2f: sme modest late hdwy* **20/1**

002 **6** ½ **Notice Given**[40] 6032 2-9-3 71 TPQueally 9 56
(H R A Cecil) *in tch in midfield: rdn and unable qck over 2f out: no ch w ldrs fr wl over 1f out* **12/1**

0 **7** ¾ **Astrovenus**[58] 5478 2-8-12 0 JimmyQuinn 7 49
(M H Tompkins) *a in rr: struggling 1/2-way* **66/1**

523 **8** *2 ¾* **Swift Return**[31] 6291 2-9-3 78 NCallan 5 47
(S C Williams) *hmpd s: sn led tl rdn and hdd 2f out: wknd qckly over 1f out* **6/1**[3]

9 *7* **Eye Of Eternity** 2-8-12 0 ChrisCatlin 10 23
(Rae Guest) *sn detached in last pl: lost tch 4f out* **66/1**

P **10** *4* **Dovedon Diva**[12] 6792 2-8-12 0 J-PGuillambert 4 12
(T Keddy) *hmpd s: chsd ldrs tl wknd qckly over 2f out: sn bhd* **200/1**

00 **11** *nk* **No Complaining (IRE)**[59] 5431 2-8-12 0 JerryO'Dwyer 12 12
(B J Curley) *chsd ldrs tl 3f out: sn struggling: wl bhd fnl 2f* **66/1**

1m 28.62s (2.02) **Going Correction** +0.20s/f (Good) **11** Ran SP% **119.9**
Speed ratings (Par 95): **96,95,95,89,86 86,85,82,74,69 69**
toteswinger: 1&2 £2.50, 1&3 £8.00, £14.30. CSF £4.10 TOTE £2.00: £1.40, £1.20, £4.50; EX 5.60 Trifecta £54.10 Pool: £669.44 - 9.14 winning units..
Owner Takashi Watanabe **Bred** Takashi Watanabe **Trained** Newmarket, Suffolk

FOCUS
A good maiden which the the first three fight out a tight finish.

NOTEBOOK
London Stripe(IRE), whose leading stable had won three of the past five runnings of this event, showed the benefit of his debut experience at Newbury 19 days previously and did the job in workmanlike fashion. He was asked to close from 3f out and took time to hit the scene, plus he looked to idle when getting his head in front. This drop back a furlong probably wasn't totally to his liking, however, and he still looks a horse of potential for next season. It will be interesting to see how the handicapper assesses this performance. (op Evens, tchd 11-10 in places)
Mass Rally(IRE), having his fourth start, travelled more kindly into contention than the winner but couldn't master that rival when push came to shove. He may not be the most straightforward of rides, but a return to a sounder surface could prove ideal and he can win a race before the season is out. (op 4-1 tchd 100-30)
En Fuego ◆ ran a much-improved race on this step up in trip and had clearly improved a bundle from his debut outing at Newmarket. He again showed signs of inexperience late on and was coming back at the front pair at the business end, so he will hold strong claims on his next assignment.
Lileo(IRE) ◆, a stoutly bred son of Galileo who proved too green to do himself full justice after meeting some trouble at the start. He caught the eye running on when the penny dropped, though, and looks sure to relish another furlong. (op 9-1 tchd 17-2)
Bondage(IRE), half-brother to this term's Chester Cup winner Daraahem, was another that did his best work late in the day. His yard is in decent form at present and, with improvement forthcoming for the experience, he should get a deal closer next time out. Another furlong also looks sure to prove much to his liking. (op 25-1 tchd 28-1)
Notice Given was again ridden with restraint on this return to 7f, but again proved free and looked to find it too testing on this easy surface. Now looks the time to go into nurseries with him, but he is looking just modest. (op 10-1 tchd 9-1)
Swift Return, dropped back a furlong, failed to see it out after racing handily and disappointed. (op 15-2 tchd 11-2)

7097 THROWER AND RUTLAND BUILDING CONTRACTORS NURSERY 7f 3y

2:10 (2:12) (Class 5) (0-75,80) 2-Y-O **£3,238** (£963; £481; £240) **Stalls** High

Form RPR

003 **1** **Scottish Boogie (IRE)**[19] 6615 2-9-2 **70** RyanMoore 4 77
(S Kirk) *t.k.h: chsd ldr: rdn and ev ch 2f out: led over 1f out: drvn clr jst ins fnl f: r.o wl* **5/1**[3]

411 **2** *2 ¾* **Landowner**[8] 6895 2-9-12 **80** 6ex LDettori 9 80
(Saeed Bin Suroor) *in tch: rdn and effrt over 2f out: chsd ldng pair over 1f out: kpt on to go 2nd fnl stride but nvr had pce to threaten wnr* **13/8**[1]

232 **3** *shd* **Pictures (IRE)**[26] 6436 2-9-5 **73** KFallon 6 73
(L M Cumani) *prom: led 2f out: sn hrd pressed and drvn: hdd over 1f out: one pce fnl f: lost 2nd last stride* **4/1**[2]

1063 **4** *1 ¼* **Rosedale**[36] 6169 2-8-3 **57** AdrianMcCarthy 7 54
(J A R Toller) *dwlt: sn rcvrd to chse ldrs: rdn and outpcd ent fnl 2f: rallied u.p to chse ldng trio 1f out: no imp after* **12/1**

6530 **5** *2 ½* **Amno Dancer (IRE)**[54] 5596 2-9-4 **72** JimmyQuinn 2 62
(M H Tompkins) *chsd ldrs: rdn and unable qck ent fnl 2f: wl hld fnl f* **12/1**

6005 **6** *1 ½* **Emma Dora (IRE)**[15] 6735 2-8-6 **60** AlanMunro 3 46
(D R C Elsworth) *t.k.h: chsd ldrs: lost pl and towards rr 1/2-way: rdn and wl btn 2f out* **12/1**

01 **7** *1 ½* **Dormer Fleet**[12] 6797 2-9-7 **75** JimmyFortune 8 57
(J H M Gosden) *hld up in rr: swtchd rt and effrt u.p wl over 1f out: no prog over 1f out and wl hld fnl f* **11/2**

0050 **8** *1* **Carlcol Girl**[15] 6735 2-7-12 **52** oh4 (p) CatherineGannon 5 32
(Mrs C A Dunnett) *stdd s: hld up in last pair: rdn and struggling ent fnl 2f* **100/1**

0503 **9** *1 ¼* **Hellenio**[28] 6367 2-8-6 **60** ChrisCatlin 1 37
(S C Williams) *led tl rdn and hdd 2f out: wknd u.p over 1f out: wl bhd fnl f* **28/1**

1m 28.87s (2.27) **Going Correction** +0.20s/f (Good) **9** Ran SP% **117.7**
Speed ratings (Par 95): **95,91,91,90,87 85,84,82,81**
toteswinger: 1&2 £2.50, 1&3 £3.70, £2.80. CSF £13.79 CT £36.33 TOTE £6.00: £2.10, £1.10, £1.60; EX 15.80 Trifecta £58.30 Pool: £809.91 - 10.27 winning units..
Owner J C Smith **Bred** Littleton Stud **Trained** Upper Lambourn, Berks

FOCUS
Not a bad nursery.

NOTEBOOK
Scottish Boogie(IRE) ◆ proved suited by the step back up in trip on his nursery debut and was a convincing winner. He seems to be progressing into a useful type and will have an obvious chance of following up if turned out under a penalty. (op 7-1)
Landowner was 2lb well in under the penalty he picked up for his recent Pontefract nursery success, when there was a 15l gap back to the third. That hat win came over 1m on quick ground, though, and he was not as effective under these conditions. A mark in the low 80s will not look unreasonable when he steps back up in trip. (op 11-10)
Pictures(IRE) had every chance but was comfortably held and doesn't have much in hand off her current mark. (op 7-1)
Rosedale didn't improve for the step up in trip and needs to drop in class. (op 16-1 tchd 11-1)
Dormer Fleet failed to get home over this stiffer test. (op 7-1 tchd 15-2)

7098 AYLSHAM BATHROOM AND KITCHEN CENTRE CLAIMING STKS 7f 3y

2:40 (2:41) (Class 6) 2-Y-O **£1,942** (£578; £288; £144) **Stalls** High

Form RPR

061 **1** **Vito Volterra (IRE)**[11] 6819 2-8-13 72 RyanMoore 2 66
(A B Haynes) *mde all: rdn wl over 1f out: kpt on wl fnl f* **5/4**[1]

3040 **2** ¾ **Whipperway (IRE)**[15] 6735 2-8-8 66 ChrisCatlin 6 59
(M R Channon) *chsd ldrs: wnt 2nd 3f out: drvn and pressed wnr over 1f out: uanble to qckn and a hld fnl f* **9/1**

0 **3** ½ **Better Be Blue (IRE)**[11] 6819 2-8-0 0 NickyMackay 5 49
(H J L Dunlop) *hld up in midfield: rdn and effrt 2f out: hdwy u.p over 1f out: kpt on wl fnl f: nt quite pce to chal ldrs* **8/1**[3]

0050 **4** ½ **Mrs Puff (IRE)**[15] 6721 2-7-5 50 JosephineBruning(7) 7 46
(P D Evans) *in tch: hdwy to chse ldng pair wl over 2f out: rdn and one pce fr over 1f out* **16/1**

000 **5** *2 ¼* **Man In The Mirror (IRE)**[53] 5627 2-8-7 43 (v[1]) JerryO'Dwyer 3 49
(P L Gilligan) *chsd wnr tl 3f out: sn rdn: hrd drvn and one pce fr over 1f out* **125/1**

00 **6** *2* **Chorus Boy**[11] 6809 2-8-3 0 (b[1]) LukeMorris 1 40
(G G Margarson) *chsd ldrs: rdn 3f out: hrd drvn and no prog fr over 1f out* **50/1**

6004 **7** ½ **Ragsta (IRE)**[7] 6923 2-8-2 60 KirstyMilczarek 4 38
(C A Dwyer) *in tch in midfield: rdn and no hdwy over 2f out: plugged on same pce fnl 2f* **7/2**[2]

0000 **8** ½ **Walnut Rise**[76] 4915 2-8-0 41 ow2 JimmyQuinn 11 34
(M H Tompkins) *bhd: reminder after: struggling wl over 2f out: sme modest hdwy u.p over 1f out: nvr trbld ldrs* **100/1**

0000 **9** *2* **Rufus Roughcut**[7] 6922 2-8-5 0 (t) SaleemGolam 12 34
(S C Williams) *in tch in midfield tl struggling u.p 3f out: n.d fnl 2f* **33/1**

04 **10** *6* **Pearl Of Kent (IRE)**[45] 5868 2-7-12 0 CatherineGannon 9 12
(P D Evans) *in rr: rdn and effrt wl over 2f out: struggling 2f out and sn wl btn* **16/1**

4006 **11** *7* **Cygnet Committee (IRE)**[11] 6819 2-8-5 52 ow1 (b) AlanMunro 13 —
(J S Wainwright) *a bhd: edgd lft and lost tch over 2f out* **50/1**

3120 **12** *1 ¼* **Ibmab**[47] 5811 2-8-9 65 TGMcLaughlin 8 —
(Mrs L Stubbs) *hld up towards rr: lost tch over 2f out: wl bhd and eased ins fnl f* **8/1**[3]

1m 29.13s (2.53) **Going Correction** +0.20s/f (Good) **12** Ran SP% **119.3**
Speed ratings (Par 93): **93,92,91,91,88 86,85,85,82,75 67,66**
toteswinger: 1&2 £4.30, 1&3 £4.40, £12.60. CSF £13.80 TOTE £2.40: £1.30, £2.80, £1.90; EX 14.30 Trifecta £71.90 Pool: £540.92 - 5.56 winning units..Ragsta was claimed by Jeff Pearce for £7,000.
Owner Ms J Loylert **Bred** O McElroy **Trained** Limpley Stoke, Bath

FOCUS
The runners went towards the far side in this weak juvenile claimer and it proved hard to make up ground from out the back.

NOTEBOOK
Vito Volterra(IRE), narrowly best in at the weights, met plenty of support and made all to follow up his Redcar success 11 days earlier. His new stable has made a name for itself with such types in the past and look to have another little money spinner in this son of Antonius Pius. (op 6-4)
Whipperway(IRE), dropping back a furlong, was the next best in at the weights and ran a solid race under a prominent ride. She has now found her level and should be able to go one better in the coming weeks. (op 8-1 tchd 15-2)
Better Be Blue(IRE) fared best of those coming from off the pace and finished a lot closer to the winner than had been the case on her previous outing. This was her first run for a new stable so the switch looks to have had a positive effect and she is well suited by easy ground, so could build on this. (op 16-1 tchd 18-1)
Mrs Puff(IRE) found only the same pace for pressure and this is clearly very much her level. (tchd 12-1 and 18-1)
Man In The Mirror(IRE) showed his most worthwhile form to date on this drop in class and enjoyed the ground. However, it's not hard to see why connections reached for the visor as he appeared a tricky ride. (op 100-1)
Ragsta(IRE) didn't get the best of runs around halfway and was keeping on too late once in the clear. The drop back in trip on this ground really looked against her. (op 9-2 tchd 3-1)

7099 EUROPEAN BREEDERS' FUND MAIDEN STKS (DIV II) 1m 3y

3:10 (3:13) (Class 5) 2-Y-O **£3,469** (£1,038; £519; £259; £129) **Stalls** High

Form RPR

1 **Bullet Train** 2-9-3 0 TPQueally 5 77
(H R A Cecil) *hld up in tch: hdwy to trck ldrs over 2f out: chal and rdn ent fnl f: rn green but r.o to ld fnl 50yds: edgd lft nr fin* **2/1**[1]

2 *shd* **Lion Mountain** 2-9-3 0 LDettori 6 77
(Saeed Bin Suroor) *chsd ldr: rdn and ev ch wl over 1f out: led over 1f out: sn hrd pressed: kpt on wl tl hdd fnl 50yds: jst hld* **7/2**[2]

3 *3 ½* **Parvaaz (IRE)** 2-9-3 0 NCallan 3 69
(M A Jarvis) *t.k.h: chsd ldrs: rdn over 2f out: pressed ldrs over 1f out: wknd and edgd rt fnl 150yds* **12/1**

4 **4** *nse* **Zenarinda**[94] 4318 2-8-12 0 JimmyQuinn 7 64
(M H Tompkins) *t.k.h: hld up in tch in midfield: pushed along and outpcd over 2f out: hdwy and rdn jst over 1f out: styd on wl to press for 3rd at fin* **50/1**

5 *1 ¾* **Hayzoom** 2-9-3 0 RyanMoore 10 65
(P W Chapple-Hyam) *in tch in rr: rdn over 3f out: outpcd wl over 2f out: styd on steadily fnl f: unable to chal* **10/1**

0265 **6** ½ **Comradeship (IRE)**[20] 6593 2-9-3 75 JimmyFortune 11 64
(J H M Gosden) *hld up in tch in midfield: effrt ent fnl 2f: hung lft u.p and btn over 1f out* **9/1**

7 *1 ½* **Kathleen Frances** 2-8-12 0 SaleemGolam 1 55
(M H Tompkins) *s.i.s and dropped in bhd after s: pushed along and struggling over 2f out: nvr trbld ldrs* **100/1**

55 **8** ¾ **Snoqualmie Star**[60] 5398 2-8-12 0 DaneO'Neill 9 54
(D R C Elsworth) *chsd ldrs: rdn and fnd little 2f out: sn btn* **9/2**[3]

9 *shd* **Egyptology (IRE)** 2-9-3 0 .... JoeFanning 4 58
(M Johnston) *racd keenly: led hrd pressed and rdn ent fnl 2f: hdd over 1f out: wknd qckly fnl f* **12/1**

06 10 *4 1/2* **Flag Of Glory**[12] 6792 2-9-3 0 .... AlanMunro 2 48
(C F Wall) *t.k.h: hld up in tch: rdn and struggling whn edgd rt over 2f out: sn wl btn* **66/1**

11 *12* **Sory** 2-9-3 0 .... KFallon 8 20
(L M Cumani) *s.i.s: a bhd and sn niggled along: lost tch over 2f out: eased fr over 1f out* **16/1**

1m 43.26s (2.66) **Going Correction** +0.20s/f (Good) **11 Ran SP% 118.5**
Speed ratings (Par 95): **94,93,90,90,88 88,86,85,85,81 69**
toteswinger: 1&2 £3.10, 1&3 £8.00, £10.30. CSF £8.80 TOTE £3.10: £1.50, £1.70, £4.70; EX 11.40 Trifecta £89.90 Pool: £552.07 - 4.54 winning units..
Owner K Abdulla **Bred** Juddmonte Farms Ltd **Trained** Newmarket, Suffolk

FOCUS
This second division of the maiden saw the first two finish clear and both look potentially very useful.

NOTEBOOK
Bullet Train ◆ came in for plenty of support on this belated racecourse debut and just did enough to reward it. He travelled kindly in mid-field before being asked for an effort 2f out and knuckled down when it mattered at the business end. He is the first foal of Kind, a smart 6-7f winner, who is a half-sister to Powerscourt, and this son of Sadler's Wells clearly has a fair bit of stamina. With that in mind 1m2f-plus next term will see him come into his own and he is one for the notebooks. (op 11-4)
Lion Mountain ◆ cost 80,000gns and is half-brother to numerous winners, most notably Cheveley Park winner Donna Blini. He was never far away and enjoyed more like the run of the race than the winner, but still showed a game attitude to push that one to the line. He should prove very hard to stop on his next outing. (op 2-1)
Parvaaz(IRE) is a half-brother to three winners up to 1m2f and out of a dam that is a half-sister to the top-class 1m4f Italian winner Close Conflict. He posted a sound debut effort and did more than enough to suggest he will be going close next time, now that he has some experience under his belt. (op 9-1)
Zenarinda wasn't disgraced when last seen finishing fourth on debut at Newmarket when last seen 94 days earlier and enjoyed this step up in trip. She is entitled to come on for the run and may be able to find a small maiden before going handicapping. (tchd 66-1)
Hayzoom, whose dam was a smart 6f-7f winner at two, proved easy to back and shaped as though the race was needed. He stayed on encouragingly when the race was effectively over and should prove a lot sharper for the experience. (op 8-1 tchd 12-1)
Comradeship(IRE) effort flattened out inside the final furlong, but still bettered his Nottingham disappointment 20 days earlier and helps to set the level. (tchd 17-2 and 11-1)

7100 LOWESTOFT JOURNAL H'CAP 5f 43y
3:40 (3:40) (Class 6) (0-60,60) 3-Y-O+ £2,072 (£616; £308; £153) Stalls High

Form RPR
3240 1 **Rosie Says No**[12] 6799 4-9-2 58 ....(p) RichardMullen 8 68
(R M H Cowell) *in tch in midfield: pushed along early: shkn up and hdwy over 1f out: rdn ins fnl f: led fnl 50yds: rdn out* **8/1**[3]

5044 2 *1* **Rough Rock (IRE)**[15] 6738 4-8-9 51 .... JerryO'Dwyer 14 57
(C A Dwyer) *racd in midfield: rdn effrt 2f out: hdwy u.p ins fnl f: wnt 2nd towards fin* **7/1**[1]

6000 3 *1/2* **Russian Rocket (IRE)**[12] 6799 7-9-3 59 .... TGMcLaughlin 16 63
(Mrs C A Dunnett) *racd alone on stands' side: prom: hung lft fr 1/2-way: led 1f out: continued hanging lft: hdd and no ex fnl 50yds* **15/2**[2]

50-5 4 *3/4* **Irish Music (IRE)**[120] 3459 4-9-4 60 .... NCallan 2 62
(A P Jarvis) *chsd ldr tl rdn to ld wl over 1f out: hdd 1f out: carried lft and one pce fnl f* **8/1**[3]

0500 5 *3/4* **Sofinella (IRE)**[53] 5629 6-8-4 46 oh1 .... LukeMorris 12 45
(A W Carroll) *chsd ldrs: rdn ent fnl 2f: hrd drvn and one pce fr over 1f out* **16/1**

3544 6 *3/4* **Imaginary Diva**[35] 6186 3-9-2 58 .... ChrisCatlin 6 54
(G G Margarson) *chsd ldrs: rdn to press ldrs over 1f out: unable qck 1f out: wknd wl ins fnl f* **7/1**[1]

-000 7 *1/2* **Mugeba**[15] 6739 8-8-4 46 oh1 .... CatherineGannon 4 40
(C A Dwyer) *racd in midfield: rdn and effrt 2f out: kpt on u.p but nvr had pce to rch ldrs* **33/1**

0653 8 *2* **Sorrel Point**[18] 6641 6-8-13 55 ....(vt) SebSanders 3 42
(H J Collingridge) *dwlt: sn bustled along: hdwy into midfield 1/2-way: rdn and no prog 2f out* **14/1**

6053 9 *nse* **Monte Major (IRE)**[25] 6456 8-8-4 46 oh1 ....(v) JimmyQuinn 15 33
(D Shaw) *hld up towards rr: rdn and effrt over 1f out: nvr trbld ldrs* **7/1**[1]

630 10 *hd* **Taboor (IRE)**[98] 4182 11-8-4 46 .... NickyMackay 9 32
(R M H Cowell) *hld up in rr: nt clr run over 1f out: nvr a factor* **25/1**

-000 11 *3/4* **Gleaming Spirit (IRE)**[62] 5341 5-8-4 46 oh1 ....(v) KirstyMilczarek 1 30
(Peter Grayson) *led tl rdn and hdd wl over 1f out: wknd over 1f out* **14/1**

0-00 12 *1 1/2* **Wavertree Princess (IRE)**[47] 5792 4-8-11 53 .... AlanMunro 13 31
(C F Wall) *a bhd* **14/1**

-000 13 *1* **Chatterszaha**[19] 6611 3-8-5 47 .... SaleemGolam 7 22
(C Drew) *sn pushed along: racd in midfield: struggling fr 1/2-way* **66/1**

51-5 14 *1* **Summer Rose**[97] 4204 4-8-9 51 ....(b) EddieAhern 10 22
(R M H Cowell) *racd in midfield: rdn and fnd nil 2f out: wl btn after* **9/1**

3005 15 *2* **Town House**[27] 6380 7-8-4 46 oh1 .... JoeFanning 5 10
(B P J Baugh) *chsd ldrs: struggling 1/2-way: wl bhd fnl f* **16/1**

64.57 secs (2.37) **Going Correction** +0.20s/f (Good) **15 Ran SP% 121.5**
Speed ratings (Par 101): **89,87,86,85,84 83,82,79,78,78 77,75,73,71,68**
toteswinger: 1&2 £6.60, 1&3 £13.20, £9.60. CSF £62.30 CT £456.29 TOTE £8.20: £2.40, £2.00, £2.90; EX 47.60 Trifecta £108.50 Pool: £190.71 - 1.30 winning units..
Owner The Hercules Horseracing Syndicate **Bred** C R And Mrs Kennedy **Trained** Six Mile Bottom, Cambs
■ Stewards' Enquiry : T G McLaughlin two-day ban: careless riding (Nov 11-12); two-day ban: used whip down shoulder in forehand position (Nov 13-14)

FOCUS
A weak sprint, run at a decent early pace. The form is sound.

7101 FIRSTBET.COM £50 MATCHED BET 0800 230 0800 H'CAP 1m 2f 21y
4:10 (4:10) (Class 4) (0-80,81) 3-Y-O £5,051 (£1,503; £751; £375) Stalls Low

Form RPR
352 1 **Deportment**[24] 6475 3-9-4 75 .... EddieAhern 7 88+
(J R Fanshawe) *chsd ldrs: wnt 2nd over 6f out: rdn to press ldr 2f out: drvn to ld 1f out: forged ahd fnl 75yds* **11/4**[2]

1501 2 *1 3/4* **Racing Hero (IRE)**[3] 7020 3-9-10 81 6ex .... LDettori 8 91
(J Noseda) *led after 1f: rdn 3f out: clr w wnr over 1f out: hdd 1f out: btn fnl 75yds: eased nr fin* **15/8**[1]

5233 3 *2 1/2* **Too Tall**[24] 6498 3-8-11 68 .... KFallon 6 72
(L M Cumani) *t.k.h: led for 1f: chsd ldr after tl over 6f out: rdn 3f out: drvn and no imp on ldng pair over 1f out* **6/1**[3]

325 4 *1 3/4* **Panto Princess**[12] 6794 3-9-2 73 .... FrankieMcDonald 5 74
(H Candy) *hld up in tch towards rr: pushed along and hdwy 4f out: rdn 3f out: 4th and no imp fr over 1f out* **8/1**

2006 5 *2 3/4* **Green Agenda**[35] 6182 3-9-2 73 .... JoeFanning 1 68
(M Johnston) *dwlt: in tch towards rr: rdn and effrt over 4f out: wknd 2f out and wl btn after* **14/1**

0300 6 *6* **Mt Kintyre (IRE)**[17] 6680 3-9-1 72 .... JimmyQuinn 3 55
(M H Tompkins) *s.i.s: hld up in rr: rdn and effrt over 3f out: no prog and wl btn fnl 2f* **10/1**

-340 7 *3 1/2* **Group Leader (IRE)**[40] 6031 3-8-11 68 .... AdrianMcCarthy 4 44
(J R Jenkins) *hld up in tch towards rr: rdn and shot-lived effrt 3f out: wl btn fnl 2f: eased ins fnl f* **50/1**

6021 8 *6* **Naheell**[17] 6668 3-8-11 68 .... SaleemGolam 2 32
(G Prodromou) *t.k.h: chsd ldrs: rdn over 3f out: wknd qckly over 2f out: eased ins fnl f* **16/1**

2m 9.78s (-0.72) **Going Correction** +0.025s/f (Good) **8 Ran SP% 110.4**
Speed ratings (Par 103): **103,101,99,98,96 91,88,83**
toteswinger: 1&2 £2.50, 1&3 £8.00, £3.10. CSF £7.67 CT £24.35 TOTE £3.20: £1.50, £1.30, £1.40; EX 6.70 Trifecta £30.80 Pool: £540.51 - 12.97 winning units. Place 6: £3.99, Place 5: £2.17..
Owner Chippenham Lodge Stud **Bred** Chippenham Lodge Stud Ltd **Trained** Newmarket, Suffolk

FOCUS
An interesting 3-y-o handicap, run at a sound enough pace and the two unexposed market leaders dominated. The form is rated through the third.
T/Plt: £5.00 to a £1 stake. Pool: £43,481.04. 6,299.16 winning tickets. T/Qpdt: £2.90 to a £1 stake. Pool: £4,783.81. 1,193.71 winning tickets. SP

2694 LYON PARILLY (R-H)
Tuesday, October 27

OFFICIAL GOING: Good to soft

7102a PRIX ANDRE BABOIN (GRAND PRIX DES PROVINCES) (GROUP 3) 1m 2f
2:40 (2:42) 3-Y-O+ £38,835 (£15,534; £11,650; £7,767; £3,883)

RPR
1 **Starlish (IRE)**[24] 6506 4-9-1 .... ACrastus 8 109
(E Lellouche, France) *hld up: 6th st: drvn and r.o fr over 1 1/2f out: disputing ld 150yds out: styd on to ld fnl strides* **15/2**[3]

2 *nk* **Capitaine Courage (IRE)**[18] 6658 4-8-11 .... SPasquier 6 104
(F Doumen, France) *settled in tch disputing 4th: drvn ent st: r.o in centre to chal over 1f out: led 100yds out tl hdd fnl strides* **53/10**[2]

3 *1 1/2* **Gris De Gris (IRE)**[24] 6506 5-9-4 .... FBlondel 2 108
(A De Royer-Dupre, France) *racd in 2nd: 3rd st: stdy hdwy fr 2f out to ld narrowly 150yds out: hdd 100yds out: kpt on* **6/4**[1]

4 *2 1/2* **Ailton (GER)**[88] 5-8-11 ....(p) RJuteau 5 96
(G Raveneau, Switzerland) *towards rr: 7th st: late hdwy to go 4th but nvr a threat* **50/1**

5 *snk* **Ashaaq**[25] 3-8-7 .... DBonilla 4 97
(F Head, France) *led 6f: led again ent st: rdn and 1 1/2 l clr 1 1/2f out: hdd 150yds out: no ex* **53/10**[2]

6 *1/2* **Mundybash**[24] 6506 4-8-11 .... TThulliez 1 95
(N Clement, France) *settled disputing 4th: pushed along st: sn outpcd* **10/1**

7 *1 1/2* **Runaway**[30] 6323 7-9-1 .... TJarnet 3 96
(R Pritchard-Gordon, France) *cl 3rd: led 4f out to ent st: unable to go pce fr 2f out* **14/1**

8 *3/4* **Eire**[30] 5-8-8 .... GBenoist 9 87
(M Nigge, France) *towards rr: 8th st: nvr a factor* **22/1**

9 *6* **Sans Chichi (FR)**[32] 6327 5-8-11 ....(p) OPeslier 7 78
(Y Barberot, France) *hld up: last st: sn pushed along: no imp* **9/1**

2m 13.86s (133.86)
WFA 3 from 4yo+ 5lb **9 Ran SP% 115.6**
PARI-MUTUEL (Including 1 Euro stake): WIN 8.50; PL 1.90, 1.70, 1.20;DF 25.20.
Owner Mme D Malingue **Bred** D Malingue **Trained** Lamorlaye, France

3417 NANTES (R-H)
Tuesday, October 27

OFFICIAL GOING: Very soft

7103a PRIX DES SABLONNETS (LISTED RACE) 1m
12:50 (12:54) 2-Y-O £26,699 (£10,680; £8,010; £5,340; £2,670)

RPR
1 **Marceti (IRE)**[25] 6507 2-9-2 .... GAvranche 2 —
(E Leenders, France)

2 *1 1/2* **Itri (FR)**[53] 2-8-13 ....(b) THuet 1 —
(M Boutin, France)

3 *shd* **Saronsla Belle (FR)** 2-8-13 .... JCabre 3 —
(L Edon, France)

4 *5* **Green Dandy (IRE)**[23] 6523 2-8-13 .... J-BEyquem 7 —
(E J O'Neill) *in rr after stall opened sltly late: pushed along to go 4th 1 1/2f out: sn rdn and outpcd by first three* **6/4**[1]

5 *3/4* **Too Nice Name (FR)**[15] 6752 2-9-2 .... JVictoire 6 —
(Robert Collet, France)

6 *1* **Oranor (FR)**[35] 2-8-13 .... FVeron 5 —
(H-A Pantall, France)

7 *4* **Les Yeux Bleus (IRE)** 2-8-13 .... J-MBreux 4 —
(N Clement, France)

1m 42.64s (102.64) **7 Ran SP% 40.0**
PARI-MUTUEL (including 1 Euro stake): WIN 3.40; PL 2.00, 4.20;SF 38.30.
Owner E Leenders **Bred** Ecurie Skymarc Farm **Trained** France

7104 - (Foreign Racing) - See Raceform Interactive

[7048] KEMPTON (A.W) (R-H)

Wednesday, October 28

OFFICIAL GOING: Standard

Wind: Almost Nil Weather: Becoming very misty from Race 5 onwards

7105 GROOMED TO PERFECTION, THE KIA SOUL CLASSIFIED STKS 7f (P)

5:50 (5:53) (Class 6) 3-Y-O+ **£2,047** (£604; £302) **Stalls** High

Form				RPR
0002	**1**		**Ede's Dot Com (IRE)**[6] 6967 5-8-9 55 .... KierenFox(7) 11 (P M Phelan) *trckd ldrs: prog on inner over 2f out to ld over 1f out: rdn clr and in n.d fnl f* **6/4**[1]	64
0554	**2**	2 ¾	**Clerical (USA)**[48] 5809 3-9-0 55 .... (p) JimCrowley 2 (R M H Cowell) *racd wd thrght fr low draw: hld up in rr: rdn over 2f out: prog over 1f out: styd on to take 2nd last 50yds* **8/1**	56
2200	**3**	1	**Top Flight Splash**[112] 3727 3-9-0 53 .... (v) LiamJones 5 (Mrs G S Rees) *prom: hrd rdn over 2f out: chsd wnr briefly 1f out: kpt on same pce* **25/1**	53
0060	**4**	shd	**Mr Rio (IRE)**[9] 6904 4-9-2 50 .... AlanMunro 8 (A P Jarvis) *trckd ldrs on outer: rdn and nt qckn 2f out: styd on to go 2nd ins fnl f: no imp on wnr: wknd last 50yds* **12/1**	54
0340	**5**	1 ½	**Commandingpresence (USA)**[2] 7052 3-8-7 52 .... RyanClark(7) 7 (J J Bridger) *mostly in midfield: rdn over 2f out: kpt on same pce fr over 1f out* **16/1**	49
0336	**6**	½	**Versaki (IRE)**[29] 6358 3-9-0 55 .... (b[1]) SebSanders 13 (Ian Williams) *bmpd s: towards rr: prog on inner and drvn over 2f out: kpt on one pce after* **13/2**[3]	47
0004	**7**	shd	**My Flame**[21] 6587 4-9-2 55 .... LDettori 14 (J R Jenkins) *wnt lft s: pressed ldr: led 1/2-way to over 1f out: wknd fnl f* **7/2**[2]	48
0005	**8**	6	**One Scoop Or Two**[25] 6497 3-9-0 51 .... (t) EddieAhern 10 (F Sheridan) *led to 1/2-way: losing pl whn short of room over 2f out: wknd* **12/1**	31
0600	**9**	nk	**Inside Trade (IRE)**[16] 6720 3-9-0 54 .... JerryO'Dwyer 3 (N P Mulholland) *sn rdn to keep in tch w ldrs on outer: struggling 1/2-way: wknd over 2f out* **16/1**	30
500-	**10**	¾	**Seven Royals (IRE)**[386] 6560 4-9-2 55 .... FrankieMcDonald 4 (Miss A M Newton-Smith) *t.k.h: hld up in rr: nt clr run briefly over 2f out: no ch sn after* **33/1**	29
0050	**11**	6	**Royal Adelaide (IRE)**[13] 6787 3-9-0 42 .... SteveDrowne 12 (J A Osborne) *chsd ldrs on inner: wknd rapidly 2f out* **33/1**	12
000-	**12**	2 ½	**Ready To Prime**[319] 7666 3-8-7 39 .... BarryAdams(7) 6 (Mike Murphy) *pushed along in last after 3f: sn bhd* **150/1**	5

1m 25.71s (-0.29) **Going Correction** -0.10s/f (Stan)

WFA 3 from 4yo+ 2lb **12** Ran SP% **124.2**

Speed ratings (Par 101): **97,93,92,92,90 90,90,83,83,82 75,72**

toteswinger: 1&2 £3.60, 1&3 £11.60, £28.90. CSF £14.96 TOTE £2.70: £1.40, £2.10, £4.00; EX 15.50.

Owner Ede's (uk) Ltd **Bred** Maurice Burns **Trained** Epsom, Surrey

FOCUS

A typically very weak classified event to open proceedings. It was run at a sound pace. Straightforward form, the first four all close to their marks.

My Flame Official explanation: jockey said colt hung left-handed

7106 KEMPTON.CO.UK MAIDEN AUCTION FILLIES' STKS 1m (P)

6:20 (6:23) (Class 4) 2-Y-O **£3,885** (£1,156; £577; £288) **Stalls** High

Form				RPR
00	**1**		**Perfect Vision**[50] 5741 2-8-8 0 .... EddieAhern 12 (C G Cox) *chsd ldng quartet: shkn up and prog 2f out: pressed ldr over 1f out: styd on stoutly to ld last 50yds* **12/1**	72
0032	**2**	½	**Anaya**[15] 6762 2-8-8 72 ow2 .... LDettori 11 (M R Channon) *trckd ldng pair: prog to ld over 2f out: drvn over 1f out: styd on: collared last 50yds* **9/4**[2]	71
	3	¾	**Inner Angel** 2-8-8 0 .... AndreaAtzeni(3) 1 (M Botti) *towards rr: wl off the pce 1/2-way: prog on outer over 3f out despite looking green: shkn up over 2f out: styd on to cl on ldng pair fnl f: a hld* **9/1**[3]	72
50	**4**	5	**Ermyntrude**[16] 6727 2-8-4 0 .... JimmyQuinn 8 (P M Phelan) *sn off the pce in midfield: gd prog on inner fr 3f out: wnt 2nd briefly 2f out: wknd jst over 1f out* **28/1**	54
	5	3 ½	**Qaraqum (USA)** 2-8-11 0 .... AlanMunro 9 (D J Coakley) *slowest away: in last pair and wl off the pce 1/2-way: pushed along and gd prog on inner over 2f out: rchd 5th over 1f out: no further hdwy* **14/1**	53
650	**6**	11	**China Bay**[135] 2978 2-8-4 0 .... LiamJones 6 (P M Phelan) *chsd ldr to wl over 2f out: sn wknd and bhd* **125/1**	20
0	**7**	hd	**Philippa Jane**[42] 5984 2-8-4 0 .... LukeMorris 13 (P Winkworth) *t.k.h: mde most w tail swishing: hdd over 2f out: hung lft and wknd over 1f out* **40/1**	20
2	**8**	4	**Donna Elvira**[16] 6727 2-8-8 0 .... RichardHughes 2 (R Hannon) *chsd ldrs: pushed along firmly over 3f out: no prog and sn struggling: wknd over 2f out: t.o* **6/5**[1]	15
	9	¾	**Auburn Place** 2-8-11 0 .... SebSanders 5 (E F Vaughan) *racd wd in rr: wl off the pce 1/2-way: no prog 3f out: t.o* **25/1**	16
00	**10**	nk	**Sisters Warning**[124] 3356 2-8-4 0 ow3 .... MarcHalford(3) 3 (J Ryan) *nvr beyond midfield: rdn sn after 1/2-way: wknd over 2f out: t.o* **125/1**	11
0	**11**	¾	**Ermyn Express**[8] 6911 2-8-4 0 .... CatherineGannon 10 (P M Phelan) *struggling towards rr sn after 1/2-way: wknd over 2f out: t.o* **16/1**	7
00	**12**	3	**Sandfairyann**[7] 6942 2-8-6 0 .... FrankieMcDonald 7 (B R Johnson) *hld up: in last pair and wl off the pce 1/2-way: no prog and t.o over 2f out* **200/1**	2

1m 40.12s (0.32) **Going Correction** -0.10s/f (Stan) **12** Ran SP% **118.3**

Speed ratings (Par 94): **94,93,92,87,84 73,73,69,68,68 67,64**

toteswinger: 1&2 £7.50, 1&3 £11.90, £28.90. CSF £38.43 TOTE £15.70: £2.50, £1.30, £2.70; EX 56.40.

Owner Mildmay Racing **Bred** Cheveley Park Stud Ltd **Trained** Lambourn, Berks

FOCUS

An ordinary fillies' maiden. The first three came nicely clear.

NOTEBOOK

Perfect Vision put in a greatly improved effort to shed her maiden tag at the third time of asking. She moved fluently through the race and, despite still looking green when asked to win the race, was always going to get up. She had something in hand at the finish, looks to have benefited a great deal from her time off the track and certainly has the scope for further improvement.

Anaya looked a likely winner passing the furlong pole, but ultimately found another one too good. She is vulnerable to anything useful, but rates the benchmark and deserves an opening. (tchd 5-2)

Inner Angel finished clear of the remainder and emerges from her debut outing with plenty of credit. She had to race from the outside stall and came from behind, but still came there with her chance. A race can surely be found for her before the year is out and a stiffer test will suit in due course. (op 12-1)

Ermyntrude fared best of the three from her stable and ran much more encouragingly again for the return to an artificial surface. She is now eligible for nurseries. (op 33-1 tchd 25-1)

Qaraqum(USA), a US-bred debutante, would have finished a good bit closer had she not fluffed the start. She made up her ground well until just flattening out from the furlong pole, and could be better off dropping back to 7f in the short term. Official explanation: jockey said filly ran green (op 18-1)

Donna Elvira would have made a winning bow at Salisbury 16 days earlier but for running so green. She was more professional this time to hold a prominent position, but came under pressure turning for home and eventually dropped right out. She finished a long way in front of Ermyntrude on debut and something probably went amiss here. Official explanation: trainer's rep had no explanation for the poor form shown (op 5-4 tchd Evens and 11-8 in a place)

7107 DIGIBET MEDIAN AUCTION MAIDEN STKS 6f (P)

6:50 (6:52) (Class 5) 3-4-Y-O **£2,590** (£770; £385; £192) **Stalls** High

Form				RPR
22	**1**		**Wake Up Call**[50] 5747 3-8-9 0 .... JackMitchell(3) 1 (C F Wall) *trckd ldrs: prog to ld over 1f out: sn wl clr: eased last 75yds: impressive* **4/5**[1]	76+
20	**2**	5	**Nativity**[29] 6362 3-8-9 55 .... JackDean(3) 3 (J L Spearing) *sn pushed along in last pair on outer: prog fr 2f out: wnt 2nd 1f out: no ch w wnr but kpt on* **16/1**	56
40	**3**	2	**Abbashinko**[12] 6823 3-8-12 0 .... RichardKingscote 4 (Tom Dascombe) *chsd ldng pair: disp 2nd 2f out: wl outpcd over 1f out: plugged on* **10/1**[3]	50
3000	**4**	1	**Athboy Auction**[42] 6005 4-8-13 44 .... (t) JimmyQuinn 5 (H J Collingridge) *slowest away: mostly last tl prog on inner to dispute 2nd briefly wl over 1f out: sn outpcd: fdd* **33/1**	46
0-00	**5**	1 ¼	**Cativo**[102] 4097 3-8-9 44 .... (t) JamesMillman(3) 6 (B R Millman) *settled in last pair: stl last over 1f out: shuffled along and kpt on: no ch* **33/1**	42
2	**6**	1 ¼	**Looby Loo**[35] 6206 3-8-12 0 .... AlanMunro 8 (P W Chapple-Hyam) *racd freely in ld for 1 1/2f: settled bttr whn chsng: led again over 2f out to over 1f out: wknd tamely* **7/4**[2]	38
00	**7**	1 ¾	**Clever Omneya (USA)**[79] 4860 3-8-12 0 .... EddieAhern 7 (J R Jenkins) *s.i.s: chsd ldrs: disp 2nd 2f out: wknd over 1f out* **50/1**	33
0004	**8**	6	**Sandy Par**[22] 6553 4-9-4 45 .... (b) DavidProbert 2 (J M Bradley) *led over 4f out to over 2f out: hung lft and wknd rapidly* **20/1**	19

1m 11.73s (-1.37) **Going Correction** -0.10s/f (Stan)

WFA 3 from 4yo 1lb **8** Ran SP% **119.5**

Speed ratings (Par 103): **105,98,95,94,92 91,88,80**

toteswinger: 1&2 £4.30, 1&3 £2.40, £6.20. CSF £16.44 TOTE £1.90: £1.10, £2.80, £2.20; EX 16.50.

Owner J G Lambton **Bred** Whatton Manor Stud **Trained** Newmarket, Suffolk

FOCUS

A weak maiden with the second favourite disappointing, although Wake Up Call won easily in a fair time.

7108 DIGIBET.COM NURSERY 6f (P)

7:20 (7:22) (Class 4) (0-90,88) 2-Y-O **£3,885** (£1,156; £577; £288) **Stalls** High

Form				RPR
4141	**1**		**Freeforaday (USA)**[20] 6619 2-9-4 85 .... RobertWinston 3 (J R Best) *squeezed for room in midfield after 1f: rdn and effrt over 2f out: prog on outer over 1f out: sustained effrt to ld fnl 100yds: r.o wl* **10/1**[3]	94
12	**2**	1	**Gouray Girl (IRE)**[27] 6418 2-8-13 80 .... ShaneKelly 7 (W R Swinburn) *squeezed for room after 1f: chsd ldrs: prog on outer over 2f out: rdn to ld over 1f out: hdd and outpcd fnl 100yds* **3/1**[1]	86
1302	**3**	1 ¾	**Fleeting Echo**[20] 6619 2-9-1 82 .... RichardHughes 8 (R Hannon) *led 1f: styd prom: rdn to ld briefly wl over 1f out: outpcd fnl f: clung on for 3rd* **3/1**[1]	82
1625	**4**	nse	**Farmers Wish (IRE)**[20] 6619 2-8-11 78 .... LiamJones 9 (J L Spearing) *chsd ldrs: rdn and cl up over 1f out: sn outpcd: kpt on nr fin* **14/1**	78
043	**5**	1 ¼	**High Spice (USA)**[40] 6068 2-8-13 80 .... JimCrowley 4 (R M H Cowell) *stdd s: hld up in 8th: effrt over 2f out: rdn and kpt on fr over 1f out: nt pce to threaten* **12/1**	76
3012	**6**	½	**Chips O'Toole (IRE)**[11] 6841 2-9-7 88 .... EddieAhern 1 (B J Meehan) *t.k.h: c across fr wd draw to chse ldr over 4f out: tried to chal 2f out: wknd fnl f* **10/1**[3]	83
0001	**7**	hd	**So Surreal (IRE)**[12] 6826 2-8-8 75 .... (b) FergusSweeney 10 (G L Moore) *in tch on inner: prog over 2f out: cl enough over 1f out: sn fdd* **14/1**	69
3126	**8**	2	**Marine Spirit (GER)**[19] 6643 2-9-2 83 .... (b[1]) LDettori 2 (Saeed Bin Suroor) *led after 1f to wl over 1f out: wknd rapidly* **10/3**[2]	71
2020	**9**	3	**Kings Of Leo**[23] 6550 2-9-1 82 .... SJCraine 11 (J R Boyle) *awkward s: a abt same pl: struggling over 2f out* **33/1**	60
0010	**10**	7	**Avongate**[33] 6247 2-8-10 77 .... DaneO'Neill 6 (R Hannon) *sn struggling in last: wl bhd bef 1/2-way* **66/1**	33

1m 12.3s (-0.80) **Going Correction** -0.10s/f (Stan) **10** Ran SP% **116.7**

Speed ratings (Par 97): **101,99,97,97,95 94,94,92,88,78**

toteswinger: 1&2 £7.20, 1&3 £3.60, £3.60. CSF £40.18 CT £114.85 TOTE £11.20: £2.50, £1.80, £1.20; EX 40.20.

Owner Inside Track Racing Club **Bred** Susan Mauer **Trained** Hucking, Kent

■ Stewards' Enquiry : Eddie Ahern four-day ban plus four deferred; careless riding (Nov 11-14, 16-19)

FOCUS

A competitive nursery, run at a decent pace. Solid form.

NOTEBOOK

Freeforaday(USA) ◆ did the job readily on this all-weather debut and has now won three of his four outings since switching to nurseries. He confirmed his last-time-out form with the third despite racing on 4lb worse terms with that rival from his new 10lb higher mark and is clearly still improving. Granted another truly-run race over this trip again next time he ought to prove hard to beat again as he looked a little better than the bare margin here.

Gouray Girl(IRE) had finished in front of the winner on 5lb better terms at Goodwood on her previous outing, so some may deem it a little disappointing the form was not confirmed. It would be wrong to do so, however, as that rival is fast-progressing and she put in a gallant effort on this return to Polytrack. There should be another race for her in the coming weeks and now may be the time to step up a furlong. (op 5-2 tchd 100-30)
Fleeting Echo, who won on her only previous run here, was well backed to reverse her Newbury form with the winner and she held every chance. This was another solid effort from her and it vindicates the handicapper's decision to up her so much after her last run. (op 9-2)
Farmers Wish(IRE) was 3lb lower and ran close enough to her last-time-out form with the winner and third. She can find less competitive assignment in this sphere. (op 16-1)
High Spice(USA), back from a 40-day absence, didn't get the best of runs around 2f out but her effort thereafter was only one paced. A more positive ride over this extra furlong now appears required. (op 10-1)
Chips O'Toole(IRE), closely matched with some of these, was always likely to find things tricky from the outside stall and off an 11lb higher mark. He unsurprisingly paid for his early efforts before the final furlong.
So Surreal(IRE), 4lb higher, made her effort on the inside rail and lacked the pace to get seriously involved. (op 16-1)
Marine Spirit(GER), wearing first-time blinkers, was another to pay for doing too much early on from a poor draw. (op 3-1 tchd 7-2)

7109 DIGIBET CASINO H'CAP (DIV I) 1m (P)
7:50 (7:50) (Class 6) (0-60,66) 3-Y-O+ £1,706 (£503; £252) Stalls High

Form RPR
0000 1 **Fine Ruler (IRE)**[21] 6588 5-9-3 **56** GeorgeBaker 13 63
(M R Bosley) *hld up in midfield: prog on inner fr 3f out to ld jst over 2f out: drvn and hrd pressed fnl f: jst hld on* **5/1**[2]
4600 2 *hd* **King Of Legend (IRE)**[30] 6349 5-9-3 **59** JackMitchell(3) 9 66+
(D Morris) *stdd sn after s: hld up in last trio: gng easily whn nt clr run over 2f out: gd prog wl over 1f out: r.o to take 2nd nr fin: jst failed* **14/1**
5351 3 *3/4* **The Grey One (IRE)**[5] 6998 6-9-13 **66** 6ex (p) KevinGhunowa 14 71
(J M Bradley) *plld hrd early: prom: rdn to chse wnr 2f out: chal fnl f: a hld: lost 2nd nr fin* **4/1**[1]
6303 4 *1/2* **Shake On It**[7] 6945 5-8-13 **52** JimCrowley 4 56
(M R Hoad) *hld up towards rr: prog and gng strly whn checked and swtchd lft 2f out: tried to cl on ldrs fnl f: nvr able to chal* **5/1**[2]
6504 5 *nk* **Burnbrake**[16] 6719 4-9-7 **60** (v[1]) RobertHavlin 2 63
(L Montague Hall) *t.k.h: prom towards outer: hanging and nt qckn 2f out: kpt on fnl f* **6/1**[3]
5300 6 *1/2* **Sovereignty (JPN)**[9] 6904 7-9-1 **59** SophieDoyle(5) 1 61
(D K Ivory) *sn pressed ldng pair: hanging bdly and nt qckn 2f out: one pce after* **14/1**
0006 7 *1/2* **Binnion Bay (IRE)**[59] 5473 8-9-3 **56** (b) JerryO'Dwyer 11 57
(J J Bridger) *s.i.s: hld up in last trio: rdn and kpt on fr 2f out: nt pce to rch ldrs* **16/1**
0200 8 *5* **Rockson (IRE)**[37] 6175 3-8-10 **52** StephenDonohoe 3 41
(Ian Williams) *a towards rr: brought wd bnd 3f out: sn outpcd: no ch over 1f out* **33/1**
2300 9 *1 3/4* **Jiggalong**[42] 5988 3-9-1 **57** PaulDoe 10 42
(Jim Best) *hld up in last trio: taken wdst of all bnd 3f out: nvr on terms* **5/1**[2]
0 10 *1 1/4* **Sufficient Warning**[112] 3735 5-9-2 **55** (b) IvanLopez 8 37
(R J Smith) *led 1f: led again 1/2-way to jst over 2f out: wknd rapidly* **50/1**
0-00 11 *1/2* **Balais Folly (FR)**[14] 6782 4-8-8 **47** ChrisCatlin 7 28
(D Haydn Jones) *drvn to ld after 1f to 1/2-way: wknd rapidly wl over 2f out* **33/1**
0014 12 *3 1/2* **Simpsons Gamble (IRE)**[43] 5963 6-9-4 **57** (p) LPKeniry 5 30
(R A Teal) *t.k.h: trckd ldrs: wknd rapidly over 2f out* **12/1**

1m 39.32s (-0.48) **Going Correction** -0.10s/f (Stan)
WFA 3 from 4yo+ 3lb 12 Ran SP% **119.0**
Speed ratings (Par 101): **98,97,97,96,96 95,95,90,88,87 86,83**
toteswinger: 1&2 £19.00, 1&3 £5.10, £11.60. CSF £72.28 CT £310.77 TOTE £6.90: £2.30, £4.60, £1.80; EX 78.80.
Owner Mrs Jean M O'Connor **Bred** Gainsborough Stud Management Ltd **Trained** Chalfont St Giles, Bucks

FOCUS
A weak, but wide-open handicap. The race was run at a solid pace, but also in low visibility due to fog. The form is sound with the winner not needing to match last season's best.

7110 DIGIBET CASINO H'CAP (DIV II) 1m (P)
8:20 (8:20) (Class 6) (0-60,60) 3-Y-O+ £1,706 (£503; £252) Stalls High

Form RPR
0456 1 **Inquisitress**[6] 6968 5-8-6 **48** MarcHalford(3) 2 56
(J J Bridger) *hld up in 11th: gd prog over 2f out: swtchd to inner wl over 1f out: r.o to ld ins fnl f: in command after* **16/1**
0066 2 *1* **Party In The Park**[7] 6945 4-8-12 **51** SJCraine 10 57
(J R Boyle) *hld up in 6th early: gng strly over 2f out: effrt to ld over 1f out: hdd and nt qckn ins fnl f* **9/1**
0000 3 *shd* **Hi Spec (IRE)**[75] 4977 6-8-7 **46** oh1 (p) JimmyQuinn 8 52
(Miss M E Rowland) *hld up in 11th: prog on outer fr 2f out: drvn to cl on ldr fnl f: nt qckn last 100yds* **66/1**
0000 4 *nk* **Imperium**[2] 7052 8-9-1 **54** (p) DaneO'Neill 11 62+
(Jean-Rene Auvray) *pushed along in 10th early: stl pushed along over 2f out: prog and gng bttr whn nowhere to go and lost pl over 1f out: plld out wd and r.o fnl f* **16/1**
2263 5 *1 1/4* **Art Market (CAN)**[14] 6783 6-9-5 **58** (p) FergusSweeney 6 60
(Miss Jo Crowley) *mde most to over 1f out: fdd ins fnl f* **6/1**[1]
0002 6 *1/2* **Rebel Woman**[14] 6771 3-8-13 **55** ShaneKelly 12 56
(J A Osborne) *hld up in 7th early: chsng ldrs 2f out: rdn and nt qckn over 1f out: fdd* **8/1**
50 7 *1/2* **Josiah Bartlett (IRE)**[26] 6456 3-8-8 **50** StephenDonohoe 1 50
(Ian Williams) *hld up in 13th early: rdn in rr over 2f out: styd on ins fnl f* **12/1**
6344 8 *3/4* **Monashee Rock (IRE)**[14] 6782 4-9-7 **60** TGMcLaughlin 5 58
(Matthew Salaman) *s.s: last and sn rousted along: prog fr 2f out: drvn and kpt on: n.d* **13/2**[3]
4000 9 *1 3/4* **Lopinot (IRE)**[16] 6720 6-9-7 **60** (v) JimCrowley 9 54
(M R Bosley) *t.k.h: hld up in 8th: trying to cl on ldrs over 1f out: hld whn hmpd ent fnl f: eased* **8/1**
0046 9 *dht* **Phluke**[13] 6790 8-9-6 **59** SebSanders 14 53
(Eve Johnson Houghton) *cl up in 5th on inner 1st 3f: lost pl after 1/2-way: trapped bhd wkng rival over 2f out: nvr on terms after* **8/1**
4503 11 *nse* **Brooksby**[14] 6782 3-9-3 **59** (b) LukeMorris 3 53
(L A Dace) *trckd ldrs: hrd rdn in 3rd over 2f out: wkng whn short of room ent fnl f* **15/2**[3]
6260 12 *4* **Foxtrot Bravo (IRE)**[16] 6720 3-9-2 **58** RichardKingscote 7 43
(Miss S L Davison) *w ldr to 3f out: wknd over 2f out* **16/1**
000 13 *11* **Ryker (IRE)**[50] 5751 3-9-4 **60** EddieAhern 4 20
(J W Hills) *abt 9th in 1st 3f: struggling in rr on wd outside over 2f out: wknd: t.o* **12/1**
0000 14 *16* **Hilltop Alchemy**[28] 6375 3-7-11 **46** oh1 (v) DannyBrock(7) 13 —
(J R Jenkins) *t.k.h: chsd ldng pair early: wkng rapidly wl over 2f out: t.o* **100/1**

1m 39.16s (-0.64) **Going Correction** -0.10s/f (Stan)
WFA 3 from 4yo+ 3lb 14 Ran SP% **118.2**
Speed ratings (Par 101): **99,98,97,97,96 95,95,94,92,92 92,88,77,61**
toteswinger: 1&2 £34.90, 1&3 £57.90, £184.20. CSF £150.63 CT £9174.92 TOTE £23.00: £5.90, £3.00, £15.60; EX 289.20.
Owner C Marshall T Wallace J J Bridger **Bred** A Saccomando **Trained** Liphook, Hants

FOCUS
The second division of the 1m handicap and this time visibility was even worse due to the heavy fog. The race was run at a decent clip and it was marginally quicker than the first division. Straightforward but modest form.
Imperium Official explanation: jockey said gelding was denied a clear run

7111 KIA SOUL, SAFE BET H'CAP 7f (P)
8:50 (9:17) (Class 4) (0-80,80) 3-Y-O+ £4,727 (£1,406; £702; £351) Stalls High

Form RPR
-0U3 1 **Dubai Meydan (IRE)**[7] 6944 4-9-6 **79** SteveDrowne 4 90
(Miss Gay Kelleway) *most reluctant to go to post: dwlt: hld up in 5th: nt clr run over 2f out: gd prog over 1f out to ld ent fnl f: drvn and r.o wl* **9/2**[3]
4115 2 *1 1/4* **King's Colour**[20] 6614 4-9-4 **77** LPKeniry 3 85
(B R Johnson) *hld up in 4th: rdn over 2f out: prog to chal jst over 1f out: chsd wnr fnl f: r.o but a hld* **7/2**[2]
1523 3 *2 1/4* **Defector (IRE)**[6] 6976 3-8-11 **72** MartinDwyer 7 74
(W R Muir) *led: drew 3 l clr 1/2-way: hdd and outpcd ent fnl f* **9/2**[3]
5121 4 *3/4* **Millfield (IRE)**[16] 6725 6-9-1 **74** GeorgeBaker 2 74
(P R Chamings) *s.s: t.k.h in last: effrt on inner over 2f out: nt qckn over 1f out: pushed along and one pce* **5/1**
5143 5 *1/2* **Ursula (IRE)**[18] 6667 3-9-5 **80** SebSanders 1 79
(R M Beckett) *t.k.h: hld up in 6th: rdn and nt qckn over 2f out: no imp on ldrs after* **3/1**[1]
0142 6 *2 1/4* **Lucy Brown**[39] 6112 3-9-0 **75** RichardHughes 6 67
(R Hannon) *trckd ldng pair: disp 2nd fr 1/2-way to wl over 1f out: wknd fnl f* **8/1**
5222 7 *1/2* **Caprio (IRE)**[71] 5120 4-9-6 **79** SJCraine 5 70
(J R Boyle) *mostly chsd ldr to over 2f out: hanging and nt qckn: wknd fnl f* **12/1**

1m 24.47s (-1.53) **Going Correction** -0.10s/f (Stan)
WFA 3 from 4yo+ 2lb 7 Ran SP% **119.1**
Speed ratings (Par 105): **104,102,100,99,98 96,95**
toteswinger: 1&2 £1.20, 1&3 £1.90, £3.00. CSF £21.81 TOTE £5.30: £2.40, £3.20; EX 30.20.
Owner M K Armitt & N Spence **Bred** Crandon Park Stud **Trained** Exning, Suffolk

FOCUS
There was a delay prior to this race because of the foggy conditions. This was a tight handicap and the form looks sound enough, with a clear personal best from the winner.

7112 EPSOM OWNERS & TRAINERS AWARDS DINNER H'CAP 1m 4f (P)
9:20 (9:39) (Class 6) (0-65,66) 3-Y-O+ £2,047 (£604; £302) Stalls Centre

Form RPR
0432 1 **Silent Act (USA)**[23] 6538 3-9-3 **62** JimCrowley 2 69
(Mrs A J Perrett) *chsd clr ldr: clsd to dispute ld 2f out: asserted over 1f out: styd on wl* **5/1**[2]
0041 2 *3/4* **Little Sark (IRE)**[14] 6770 4-9-2 **54** GeorgeBaker 9 60
(P D Evans) *prom: rdn and nt qckn over 2f out: kpt on fr over 1f out: wnt 2nd nr fin* **8/1**[3]
6011 3 *1/2* **Giant Sequoia (USA)**[8] 6918 5-10-0 **66** 6ex (t) EddieAhern 13 71
(Jane Chapple-Hyam) *mostly trckd ldng pair: effrt to chal and upsides 2f out: nt qckn over 1f out: lost 2nd nr fin* **4/9**[1]
/046 4 *3/4* **Easterly Breeze (IRE)**[18] 6668 5-9-1 **60** (bt) AlexEdwards(7) 7 64
(Mrs L J Young) *hld up in last trio: pushed along over 2f out: gd prog over 1f out: styd on ins fnl f: nrst fin* **25/1**
640 5 *1* **Slick Mover (IRE)**[16] 6741 4-9-0 **55** RobertLButler(3) 10 57
(B G Powell) *3hld up in midfield: rdn and effrt over 2f out: kpt on same pce: nvr able to chal* **66/1**
050/ 6 *1/2* **Croix Rouge (USA)**[598] 7-9-4 **63** KierenFox(7) 12 65
(R J Smith) *hld up in last trio: pushed along over 2f out: prog over 1f out: styd on: nrst fin* **40/1**
0-00 7 *1 1/4* **Cape Greko**[15] 6761 7-9-5 **60** (v) RussellKennemore(3) 4 60
(B G Powell) *hld up towards rr: effrt over 2f out: no imp on ldrs over 1f out: one pce* **66/1**
6020 8 *1 1/2* **Seventh Hill**[25] 6498 4-9-6 **58** JimmyQuinn 14 55
(M Blanshard) *hld up in midfield: promising hdwy on inner over 2f out: nt qckn over 1f out: wknd fnl f* **14/1**
1004 9 *3 1/2* **Inch Lodge**[21] 6584 7-9-2 **61** (t) TobyAtkinson(7) 11 53
(Miss D Mountain) *led: sn clr: c bk to field 4f out: hdd & wknd 2f out* **14/1**
2014 10 *4 1/2* **Blue Turk**[21] 6588 4-9-8 **60** SJCraine 6 44
(J R Boyle) *a towards rr: struggling whn nt clr run over 2f out: no ch after* **10/1**
30-0 11 *3* **Candilejas**[9] 6908 3-9-3 **62** (t) IvanLopez 1 42
(R J Smith) *racd wd in midfield: struggling over 2f out: sn btn* **66/1**
0030 12 *nk* **Double Spectre (IRE)**[20] 6188 7-9-3 **55** (b[1]) DaneO'Neill 5 34
(Jean-Rene Auvray) *s.s: hld up in last: drvn over 3f out: no prog* **33/1**
4565 13 *21* **Silken Promise (USA)**[21] 6584 3-9-3 **62** ShaneKelly 8 8
(W R Swinburn) *prom: wknd rapidly over 3f out: t.o* **10/1**

2m 32.37s (-2.13) **Going Correction** -0.10s/f (Stan)
WFA 3 from 4yo+ 7lb 13 Ran SP% **142.2**
Speed ratings (Par 101): **103,102,102,101,101 100,99,98,96,93 91,91,77**
toteswinger: 1&2 £7.20, 1&3 £2.90, £3.70. CSF £52.25 CT £54.96 TOTE £7.50: £1.30, £3.00, £1.40; EX 24.00 Place 6: £210.66 Place 5: £100.92.
Owner Mr & Mrs R Scott **Bred** Allen E Paulson Living Trust **Trained** Pulborough, W Sussex

FOCUS
This moderate handicap was run at a fair pace, but those racing handily still held sway. Sound form but hard to rate positively.
Inch Lodge Official explanation: jockey said horse ran too free
T/Plt: £239.90 to a £1 stake. Pool: £75,927.75. 231.00 winning tickets. T/Qpdt: £29.20 to a £1 stake. Pool: £7,133.23. 180.30 winning tickets. JN

6308 **MUSSELBURGH** (R-H)

Wednesday, October 28

OFFICIAL GOING: Good to soft (good in places; 6.2)

Wind: Virtually nil Weather: Dry and bright

7113 SCOTTISH RACING AMATEUR RIDERS' H'CAP — 1m 1f

1:00 (1:00) (Class 6) (0-65,65) 3-Y-0+ **£2,498** (£774; £387; £193) **Stalls** High

Form RPR

4620 **1** **Edas**[15] 6768 7-10-8 **64** MissHCuthbert(5) 9 75
(T A K Cuthbert) *midfield: hdwy wl over 2f out: rdn to chal over 1f out: led ent fnl f: styd on wl* **16/1**

3520 **2** *2 1/4* **Bed Fellow (IRE)**[31] 6312 5-9-7 **51** oh1 MrCWhillans(7) 10 57
(P Monteith) *dwlt and towards rr: hdwy over 4f out: cl up over 2f out: sn rdn to chal and ev ch tl one pce ins fnl f* **22/1**

13 **3** *hd* **Vertigo On Course (IRE)**[30] 6349 4-10-3 **59** MrsVFahey(5) 8 68+
(R A Fahey) *trckd ldrs on inner: hdwy and cl up 3f out: effrt over 2f out: rdn and nt clr run appr fnl f: swtchd lft wl ins fnl f and kpt on* **4/1**[2]

4222 **4** *1/2* **French Art**[9] 6908 4-11-0 **65** MissSBrotherton 5 69
(N Tinkler) *trckd ldrs: hdwy 3f out: led over 2f out: rdn wl over 1f out: hdd ent fnl f and kpt on same pce* **11/4**[1]

0031 **5** *1 3/4* **Business Class (BRZ)**[29] 6358 4-10-7 **63** MissVBarr(5) 2 64
(D Nicholls) *led: rn wd home bnd and sn rdn along: hdd over 2f out and hanging rt: grad wknd* **13/2**[3]

2604 **6** *1* **Island Music (IRE)**[11] 6862 4-10-9 **60** MissADeniel 11 58
(J J Quinn) *hld up: effrt and sme hdwy over 2f out: sn rdn and no imp fr over 1f out* **11/1**

4065 **7** *2 1/2* **Woodsley House (IRE)**[5] 6984 7-10-5 **63** (p) MrMEnnis(7) 3 56
(A G Foster) *chsd ldrs: rdn along 3f out: drvn over 2f out and sn wknd* **12/1**

0020 **8** *1* **Fitzwarren**[12] 6818 8-9-9 **51** oh6 (tp) DaleSwift(5) 12 42
(A D Brown) *in tch: rdn along over 4f out and sn wknd* **50/1**

4233 **9** *2 3/4* **Grand Diamond (IRE)**[11] 5941 5-11-0 **65** (p) MrsCBartley 1 50
(J S Goldie) *hld up: a in rr* **8/1**

3406 **10** *2 1/2* **Terminate (GER)**[12] 6818 7-9-10 **52** (b) MissWGibson(5) 13 31
(A Berry) *a in rr* **25/1**

5202 **11** *6* **Ulysees (IRE)**[37] 6156 10-10-0 **51** oh1 MrSDobson 4 17
(I Semple) *a towards rr* **12/1**

0046 **12** *13* **Westport**[42] 5998 6-10-0 **56** (p) MissRBastiman(5) 6 —
(R Bastiman) *chsd ldrs: rdn along 3f out: sn wknd* **22/1**

1m 57.16s (2.46) **Going Correction** +0.325s/f (Good) **12** Ran SP% **115.2**

Speed ratings (Par 101): **102,100,99,99,97 96,94,93,91,89 83,72**

toteswinger: 1&2 £7.00, 1&3 £10.30, £4.10. CSF £325.13 CT £1678.40 TOTE £22.40: £3.50, £4.70, £1.90; EX 348.10.

Owner Mrs Joyce Cuthbert **Bred** Stilvi Compania Financiera Sa **Trained** Little Corby, Cumbria

■ Stewards' Enquiry : Miss H Cuthbert caution: used whip down shoulder in the forehand

Miss W Gibson caution: used whip when out of contention

FOCUS

The ground was reported by the amateurs in the first to be on the soft side of good or 'dead'. This modest handicap was run at only a steady pace. The form looks pretty straightforward.

7114 EUROPEAN BREEDERS' FUND MAIDEN FILLIES' STKS — 7f 30y

1:30 (1:31) (Class 5) 2-Y-0 **£3,885** (£1,156; £577; £288) **Stalls** High

Form RPR

24 **1** **Tatiana Romanova (USA)**[16] 6722 2-9-0 0 PaulHanagan 6 74
(R A Fahey) *mde all: pushed along and clr 2f out: shkn up appr fnl f and kpt on strly* **11/8**[2]

53 **2** *6* **Brink**[11] 6842 2-9-0 0 TonyHamilton 4 59
(T J Pitt) *trckd ldng pair: hdwy to chse wnr 3f out: rdn along over 2f out: sn drvn and no imp* **9/2**[3]

3 *1* **Infanta (IRE)** 2-8-11 0 AhmedAjtebi(3) 5 57
(Saeed Bin Suroor) *dwlt: in tch: pushed along and rn green over 3f out: swtchd lft and rdn over 2f out: kpt on ins fnl f* **5/4**[1]

3000 **4** *5* **Charity Fair**[5] 6983 2-8-7 49 BillyCray(7) 2 44
(A Berry) *a in rr* **66/1**

0000 **5** *2* **Dead Womans Pass (IRE)**[29] 6366 2-9-0 42 DanielTudhope 1 39
(N Wilson) *a towards rr* **50/1**

0 **6** *1/2* **Rubicon Bay (IRE)**[137] 2936 2-8-9 0 GaryBartley(5) 3 38
(C J Teague) *chsd wnr: rdn along over 3f out and sn wknd* **40/1**

1m 32.09s (1.79) **Going Correction** +0.325s/f (Good) **6** Ran SP% **110.6**

Speed ratings (Par 92): **102,95,94,88,86 85**

toteswinger: 1&2 £12.70, 1&3 £3.70, £8.50. CSF £7.61 TOTE £2.30: £1.10, £2.10; EX 7.70.

Owner Martin M Dempsey **Bred** W Lazy T Limited **Trained** Musley Bank, N Yorks

FOCUS

An uncompetitive fillies' maiden.

NOTEBOOK

Tatiana Romanova(USA), the form pick despite a disappointing effort at Kempton, was well away from the inside stall and set her own pace. Gradually stepping things up in the straight before drawing right away in the final furlong, she had no problem with this longer trip. She is a nice type of filly but much will depend on what sort of mark she is allotted. (op 13-8 tchd 7-4)

Brink, third at Catterick on her previous start, chased the winner in vain all the way up the home straight. A step up in trip will suit her next year. (tchd 5-1)

Infanta(IRE), a half-sister to Group 3 winner Utrecht out of a mare who was runner-up in Listed races, was green going to post and missed the break. Coming under pressure early in the home straight, she floundered in the ground and never looked like picking up until it was all over. She does not appear a potential star for her powerful yard but will definitely know more next time and can leave this form behind. (tchd 10-11 and 11-8)

Charity Fair, thoroughly exposed and rated only 49, proved best of the no-hopers. (tchd 80-1)

Rubicon Bay(IRE) gave trouble in the preliminaries. (tchd 50-1)

7115 WEATHERBYS BANK NURSERY — 5f

2:00 (2:00) (Class 4) (0-85,85) 2-Y-0 **£5,180** (£1,541; £770; £384) **Stalls** Low

Form RPR

0430 **1** **Besty**[5] 6983 2-8-4 **68** PaulHanagan 3 71
(B Smart) *led: pushed along and hdd wl over 1f out: rdn to chal ent fnl f: styd on wl to ld fnl 100yds* **11/2**

0503 **2** *1* **Dancing Freddy (IRE)**[12] 6827 2-8-11 **78** FrederikTylicki(3) 6 77
(J G Given) *cl up: rdn to ld wl over 1f out: drvn ent fnl f: hdd and no ex last 100yds* **3/1**[1]

5160 **3** *2 1/2* **Micky's Knock Off (IRE)**[12] 6827 2-8-13 **77** GrahamGibbons 2 67
(R C Guest) *chsd ldrs: hdwy 2f out: rdn over 1f out: kpt on same pce ins fnl f* **8/1**

3000 **4** *1 3/4* **Eternal Instinct**[39] 6090 2-8-9 **78** GaryBartley(5) 4 62
(J S Goldie) *in rr: hdwy 2f out: sn rdn and styd on ins fnl f: nrst fin* **5/1**[3]

0204 **5** *1/2* **Lieu Day Louie (IRE)**[5] 6983 2-8-0 **64** AndrewMullen 9 46
(N Wilson) *in tch: hdwy to chse ldrs 2f out: rdn along and n.m.r whn swtchd rt over 1f out: sn drvn and wknd* **12/1**

0346 **6** *nk* **Fair Bunny**[12] 6820 2-7-12 **62** SilvestreDeSousa 1 43
(A D Brown) *cl up on inner: rdn along 2f out and grad wknd* **14/1**

021 **7** *3 3/4* **Magical Macey (USA)**[43] 5957 2-9-7 **85** (b) PhillipMakin 7 53
(T D Barron) *prom: rdn along over 2f out: rdn wl over 1f out and sn wknd* **4/1**[2]

003 **8** *4* **Safari Camp (IRE)**[22] 6556 2-7-13 **70** ow6 BillyCray(7) 5 23
(A Berry) *a in rr* **66/1**

4231 **9** *3* **Lewyn**[12] 6827 2-8-10 **74** TomEaves 8 17
(K A Ryan) *prom on outer: rdn along 2f out: sn wknd* **7/1**

60.51 secs (0.11) **Going Correction** +0.075s/f (Good) **9** Ran SP% **116.5**

Speed ratings (Par 97): **102,100,96,93,92 92,86,79,75**

toteswinger: 1&2 £7.60, 1&3 £2.10, £8.00. CSF £22.59 CT £133.49 TOTE £7.80: £2.00, £1.60, £2.60; EX 26.30.

Owner A Turton & P Langford **Bred** Argosy Ltd **Trained** Hambleton, N Yorks

FOCUS

A fair nursery which was run at a strong pace. Nothing could get involved from the rear.

NOTEBOOK

Besty was always prominent one off the stands' rail and he battled on well enough to repel the runner-up. The drop back to 5f suited and he turned around Ayr form from the previous Friday with today's fifth. Official explanation: trainer said, regarding apparent improvement in form, that the colt was suited by the drop back to 5f. (op 13-2)

Dancing Freddy(IRE) had been a good third on his one previous vist to Musselburgh and he had every chance, handling the sharp five and softish ground well. (op 9-2)

Micky's Knock Off(IRE) posted his one win to date over course and distance and he ran respectably, keeping on for third and comfortably clear of the rest. (op 7-1)

Eternal Instinct, another course-and-distance winner, could never get involved but did make late headway. This company was more suitable but she found the trip on the sharp side. (op 9-2)

Lieu Day Louie(IRE) finished in front of today's winner at Ayr but things did not go his way here, as he missed the kick and was then denied a clear run entering the last. He would have finished closer otherwise.

Magical Macey(USA) showed pace on this nursery debut before fading. His high draw was no help. (op 11-2)

Lewyn was trapped wide after coming out of stall 8 and could not confirm her Wolverhampton superiority over Dancing Freddy on these 6lb worse terms. (op 6-1)

7116 EUROPEAN BREEDERS' FUND MAIDEN STKS — 1m

2:35 (2:35) (Class 5) 2-Y-0 **£3,885** (£1,156; £577; £288) **Stalls** High

Form RPR

56 **1** **Jupiter Fidius**[11] 6842 2-9-0 0 FrederikTylicki(3) 1 75
(Mrs K Walton) *trckd ldr: hdwy to ld wl over 2f out: rdn wl over 1f out: drvn and edgd lft ins fnl f: kpt on wl* **14/1**

2 **2** *1 1/4* **Taste The Victory (USA)**[18] 6679 2-9-3 0 PJMcDonald 4 73
(G A Swinbank) *trckd ldrs: effrt and hdwy 2f out: sn rdn and edgd rt over 1f out: drvn and wandered ins fnl f: hung lft and bmpd towards fin: kpt on* **11/10**[1]

3 **3** *1/2* **Palawi (IRE)**[15] 6763 2-9-3 0 GrahamGibbons 2 71
(J J Quinn) *chsd ldrs: rdn along and outpcd over 2f out: gd hdwy over 1f out: str run ins fnl f whn edgd rt and hmpd towards fin: kpt on* **4/1**[2]

003 **4** *1/2* **Master Leon**[12] 6821 2-9-3 74 TomEaves 10 70
(B Smart) *dwlt: sn chsng ldng pair on inner: rdn along wl over 2f out: drvn over 1f out and kpt on same pce ins fnl f* **16/1**

6042 **5** *shd* **Mason Hindmarsh**[9] 6895 2-9-3 53 PaulHanagan 8 70
(Karen McLintock) *led: rdn along 3f out and sn hdd: cl up and drvn 2f out and grad wknd appr fnl f* **7/1**

4 **6** *1 1/4* **Florensky (IRE)**[34] 6235 2-9-0 0 AhmedAjtebi(3) 3 67
(Saeed Bin Suroor) *midfield: hdwy 3f out and sn rdn along: drvn to chse ldrs 2f out: edgd lft and wknd wl over 1f out* **9/2**[3]

7 *10* **Bowdler's Magic** 2-9-3 0 JoeFanning 6 44
(M Johnston) *a towards rr* **14/1**

60 **8** *13* **Henry Havelock**[21] 6593 2-9-3 0 TonyHamilton 7 14
(C Grant) *a towards rr* **150/1**

00 **9** *nk* **Thescottishsoldier**[27] 6408 2-9-3 0 AndrewMullen 5 14
(A G Foster) *a in rr* **100/1**

1m 43.06s (1.86) **Going Correction** +0.325s/f (Good) **9** Ran SP% **119.2**

Speed ratings (Par 95): **103,101,101,100,100 99,89,76,76**

toteswinger: 1&2 £3.70, 1&3 £5.80, £4.90. CSF £30.89 TOTE £15.30: £3.50, £1.30, £1.70; EX 45.60.

Owner Tennant, Sharpe & Boston **Bred** A C Birkle **Trained** Middleham Moor, N Yorks

FOCUS

This looked a fair maiden on paper, but the market leaders disappointed and the first half-dozen finished somewhat compressed, so the form looks a little suspect.

NOTEBOOK

Jupiter Fidius had not shown a great deal in two previous starts, latterly at Catterick where Brink, runner-up earlier on this card, had been third. He broke better this time though and tacked over to race prominently from his outside stall. In front plenty soon enough, he kept up the gallop over this longer trip to hold on. The easier ground suited this small colt. Official explanation: trainer said, regarding apparent improvement in form, that the colt was better suited by being up with the pace and allowed to dominate. (tchd 16-1)

Taste The Victory(USA) looked the one to beat following his narrow York defeat by subsequent winner Karaka Jack. He travelled well enough but came under pressure with over two to run and did not pick up until it was too late, hanging left as he did so and colliding with the third. He is probably worth another chance. (op Evens tchd 6-5)

Palawi(IRE) found his stride entering the final furlong but veered left away from the whip before edging the other way when his rider pulled the stick through. He would have finished second but for his erratic course. (op 13-2)

Master Leon set the standard with an official rating of 74, but could only stay on at the same pace once brought under pressure. (op 14-1)

Mason Hindmarsh, who showed improved form when second at Pontefract, finishing 15l clear of the third, was headed by the winner early in the straight but remained in second place until inside the final furlong. (op 8-1 tchd 6-1)

Florensky(IRE) could not build on his debut effort and seemed ill at ease on the dead ground. (op 6-1)

Bowdler's Magic was notably green both in the preliminaries and the race. (op 12-1)

7117 WEATHERBYS BLOODSTOCK INSURANCE WILLIE PARK TROPHY H'CAP — 2m

3:05 (3:05) (Class 2) (0-100,98) 3-Y-0+

£12,462 (£3,732; £1,866; £934; £466; £234) **Stalls** High

Form RPR

5346 **1** **Gordonsville**[11] 6851 6-9-6 **82** DanielTudhope 4 91
(J S Goldie) *trckd ldrs: hdwy on outer 4f out: chal wl over 2f out: sn rdn and styd on to ld jst over 1f out: drvn and kpt on ins fnl f* **11/2**[3]

514 **2** *1* **Dayia (IRE)**[11] 6851 5-9-9 **85** .... SaleemGolam 7 93
(J Pearce) *trckd ldng pair: effrt on inner over 2f out and sn rdn: drvn over 1f out: n.m.r and swtchd lft wl ins fnl f: styd on wl towards fin* **9/4**[1]

2320 **3** *1 3/4* **Alanbrooke**[11] 6851 3-9-12 **98** ....(b) JoeFanning 3 104
(M Johnston) *trckd ldr: hdwy to ld 3f out: jnd and rdn over 2f out: drvn and hdd over 1f out: kpt on same pce ins fnl f* **11/4**[2]

5300 **4** *1* **Inchnadamph**[39] 6115 9-9-2 **78** ....(t) PaulHanagan 6 83
(T J Fitzgerald) *hld up in tch: hdwy 3f out: rdn along over 2f out: drvn wl over 1f out and kpt on same pce* **20/1**

0324 **5** *nk* **Dazzling Light (UAE)**[27] 6412 4-8-10 **77** .... GaryBartley(5) 9 81
(J S Goldie) *hld up in rr: hdwy on outer 3f out: rdn and in tch 2f out: sn drvn and kpt on same pce* **16/1**

0000 **6** *2 3/4* **Som Tala**[11] 6851 6-10-0 **90** .... TonyCulhane 5 91
(M R Channon) *trckd ldrs: effrt 3f out and sn rdn along: drvn wl over 1f out and sn wknd* **14/1**

1511 **7** *10* **Callisto Moon**[32] 5903 5-9-9 **85** ....(p) GrahamGibbons 8 74
(R Curtis) *led: rdn along over 3f out: sn hdd & wknd* **7/1**

5213 **8** *nk* **Buckie Boy (IRE)**[17] 6704 3-8-8 **80** .... PJMcDonald 2 68
(J S Goldie) *a in rr* **9/1**

3m 35.1s (1.60) **Going Correction** +0.325s/f (Good)
WFA 3 from 4yo+ 10lb **8 Ran SP% 112.6**
Speed ratings (Par 109): **109,108,107,107,106 105,100,100**
toteswinger: 1&2 £23.40, 1&3 £13.60, £8.20. CSF £17.72 CT £40.37 TOTE £6.60: £2.20, £1.40, £1.10; EX 22.70.
Owner Thomson & Fyffe Racing **Bred** George Strawbridge **Trained** Uplawmoor, E Renfrews

FOCUS
Half the field in this decent and quite valuable handicap contested the Cesarewitch earlier this month. The pace was fairly strong and the form appears sound.

NOTEBOOK
Gordonsville, winner of the Musselburgh Gold Cup back in the spring, finished sixth in the Cesarewitch and was meeting third home Dayia on 3lb better terms. One of three runners for his yard in this, he raced more prominently than usual before moving smoothly to the front. Fighting off Alanbrooke, he then held the mare late on. He has recently been sold to stay in the yard and will be campaigned over hurdles. (tchd 5-1)
Dayia(IRE) may not have been able to confirm her Cesarewitch superiority over Gordonsville on these 3lb worse terms but she ran another good race, hitting a bit of a flat spot before staying on stoutly in the final furlong. A little more rain would have helped her cause. (op 5-2 tchd 15-8)
Alanbrooke, only 16th in the Cesarewitch and 2lb higher here, harried Callisto Moon for the lead and took over in the straight. He could not hold on to his lead for long, but boxed on and was only caught for third inside the last. (op 3-1 tchd 100-30)
Inchnadamph was not discredited in fourth but he remains without a win for nearly two years. (op 18-1)
Dazzling Light(UAE), a stablemate of the winner and deserted by Danny Tudhope, made late progress from the back without threatening the leaders. (op 11-1)
Som Tala finished a place ahead of Alanbrooke in midfield in the Cesarewitch and was 4lb lower here, but he continues out of sorts since his Northumberland Plate win in June. (op 16-1)
Callisto Moon missed the Cesarewitch due to a bout of colic but came here with four wins from his last five Flat starts. On ground softer than he would care for, he was given no peace up front by Alanbrooke and dropped away quickly once headed. Official explanation: trainer said gelding was unsuited b y the good to soft (good in places) ground (op 8-1 tchd 12-1)
Buckie Boy(IRE), making his debut for the Goldie yard but still with the owners who had him with Henry Cecil, momentarily threatened a forward move but was soon toiling. He was worth a try at this trip on pedigree but has shown his best form on Polytrack. (op 17-2 tchd 10-1)

7118 RACING UK SKY 432 (S) STKS — 1m 4f 100y
3:40 (3:40) (Class 6) 3-Y-O+ **£1,942** (£578; £288; £144) **Stalls** Low

Form RPR

1305 **1** **Oddsmaker (IRE)**[5] 6986 8-9-1 65 ....(t) AndrewHeffernan(5) 3 71
(M A Barnes) *mde all: clr 1/2-way: pushed along 3f out: rdn over 2f out: rdr dropped whip wl over 1f out: hld on gamely ins fnl f* **5/1**[3]

3502 **2** *3/4* **Lost Soldier Three (IRE)**[11] 6840 8-9-0 74 .... AdrianTNicholls 7 64
(D Nicholls) *trckd ldng pair: hdwy to chse wnr after 4f: effrt 3f out and sn pushed along to take clsr order: rdn 2f out: drvn over 1f out: kpt on u.p ins fnl f* **11/10**[1]

3103 **3** *8* **Capable Guest (IRE)**[4] 7036 7-9-6 67 .... TonyCulhane 6 58
(M R Channon) *trckd ldrs: pushed along and outpcd over 4f out: rdn 3f out: drvn and plugged in fnl 2f: n.d* **7/2**[2]

1100 **4** *1 1/4* **Tufton**[41] 6012 6-9-6 72 .... PaulHanagan 8 56
(R A Fahey) *t.k.h: trckd wnr 4f: chsd ldng pair after: pushed along 3f out: rdn and hung rt 2f out: sn outpcd* **13/2**

0240 **5** *1 1/4* **Ballade De La Mer**[62] 5359 3-8-2 42 .... AndrewMullen 4 43
(A G Foster) *chsd ldrs: rdn along over 4f out and sn wknd* **33/1**

535 **6** *4 1/2* **Birkside**[25] 6498 6-9-6 62 .... PhillipMakin 2 47
(Miss L A Perratt) *hld up in rr: hdwy on inner 3f out: rdn to chse ldrs over 2f out: sn drvn and wknd* **9/1**

00-0 **7** *63* **Boy Racer (IRE)**[91] 4432 4-9-0 57 .... DanielTudhope 5 —
(C J Teague) *t.k.h: a towards rr* **80/1**

2m 45.24s (3.24) **Going Correction** +0.325s/f (Good)
WFA 3 from 4yo+ 7lb **7 Ran SP% 114.0**
Speed ratings (Par 101): **102,101,96,95,94 91,49**
toteswinger: 1&2 £10.50, 1&3 £8.10, £4.30. CSF £10.87 TOTE £6.00: £2.90, £1.30; EX 15.20.There was no bid for the winner.
Owner D Maloney **Bred** Margaret Conlon **Trained** Farlam, Cumbria
■ Stewards' Enquiry : Andrew Mullen caution: used whip with excessive frequency

FOCUS
A decent seller in which the winner set a decent gallop. He is probably the best guide.

7119 SUBSCRIBE ONLINE AT RACINGUK.COM H'CAP — 5f
4:10 (4:12) (Class 5) (0-75,72) 3-Y-O+ **£3,238** (£963; £481; £240) **Stalls** Low

Form RPR

1152 **1** **Igoyougo**[28] 6387 3-9-7 **72** .... SilvestreDeSousa 12 81
(G A Harker) *prom: effrt 2f out: rdn to chal over 1f out: drvn ins fnl f and kpt on wl to ld nr fin* **6/1**[2]

0050 **2** *nk* **Mandarin Spirit (IRE)**[5] 6985 9-9-2 **67** ....(b) TonyHamilton 9 75
(Miss L A Perratt) *led: rdn wl over 1f out: drvn ins fnl f: hdd and nt qckn nr fin* **33/1**

0410 **3** *3/4* **Distant Sun (USA)**[27] 6413 5-9-2 **70** .... FrederikTylicki(3) 5 75
(Miss L A Perratt) *towards rr: hdwy 1/2-way: and sn chsng ldrs: swtchd rt and rdn over 1f out: drvn to chal ins fnl f and ev ch tl no ex towards fin* **16/1**

3121 **4** *2 1/2* **Hawkeyethenoo (IRE)**[5] 6988 3-8-13 **69** 6ex .... GaryBartley(5) 11 65+
(J S Goldie) *dwlt and sn in rr: effrt and hdwy on wd outside 2f out: sn rdn and kpt on ins fnl f: nt rch ldrs* **5/6**[1]

0000 **5** *1 3/4* **Sandwith**[15] 6765 6-9-2 **67** .... AndrewMullen 13 57
(A G Foster) *cl up: rdn along 2f out: drvn over 1f out: wknd ent fnl f* **18/1**

0502 **6** *3/4* **Avertuoso**[60] 5421 5-9-0 **65** .... TomEaves 7 52
(B Smart) *in tch: rdn along over 2f out: drvn over 1f out: sn no imp* **11/1**[3]

4060 **7** *1/2* **Ingleby Star (IRE)**[9] 6902 4-9-2 **72** ....(p) AmyRyan(5) 1 57
(N Wilson) *chsd ldrs on inner: rdn along 2f out: sn drvn and grad wknd* **16/1**

2040 **8** *3/4* **Peninsular War**[18] 6669 3-9-4 **69** .... PaulHanagan 6 51
(R A Fahey) *a towards rr* **11/1**[3]

3102 **9** *4* **Wicked Wilma (IRE)**[31] 6314 5-8-5 **63** .... BillyCray(7) 4 50
(A Berry) *prom: rdn along 2f out: swtchd rt and drvn over 1f out: sddle slipped and qckly eased ent fnl f* **16/1**

0100 **10** *21* **Prince Namid**[60] 5421 7-9-4 **69** .... AdrianTNicholls 10 —
(D Nicholls) *chsd ldrs on outer: rdn along bef 1/2-way: sn wknd and heavily eased over 1f out* **16/1**

60.35 secs (-0.05) **Going Correction** +0.075s/f (Good) **10 Ran SP% 117.2**
Speed ratings (Par 103): **103,102,101,97,94 93,92,91,84,51**
toteswinger: 1&2 £3.50, 1&3 £1.90, £3.20. CSF £178.94 CT £3054.34 TOTE £6.50: £1.80, £6.00, £4.10; EX 247.90 Place 6: £35.61 Place 5: £6.71.
Owner Miss K Watson **Bred** Karen Watson **Trained** Thirkleby, N Yorks

FOCUS
Just a modest handicap, in which it proved difficult to make up ground from off the pace. Straightforward form.
Sandwith Official explanation: jockey said gelding hung left throughout
Wicked Wilma(IRE) Official explanation: jockey said mare lost its action but returned sound
Prince Namid Official explanation: jockey said gelding hung left and was whinnying from halfway
T/Plt: £29.80 to a £1 stake. Pool: £50,226.73. 1,226.72 winning tickets. T/Qpdt: £4.60 to a £1 stake. Pool: £4,140.21. 653.70 winning tickets. JR

6792 NOTTINGHAM (L-H)
Wednesday, October 28

OFFICIAL GOING: Good to firm (good in places) changing to good after race 2 (1.10)
Races on inner track. Race times and jockey opinion suggest the ground was riding on the slow side.
Wind: Light against Weather: Fine

7120 DG TAXIS FIRST PAST THE POST (S) STKS — 1m 75y
12:40 (12:42) (Class 6) 2-Y-O **£2,047** (£604; £302) **Stalls** Low

Form RPR

060 **1** **Glass Of Red (IRE)**[98] 4201 2-8-6 63 .... RichardKingscote 16 66
(R M Beckett) *chsd ldrs: led and edgd lft over 1f out: styd on wl* **8/1**

5422 **2** *3 3/4* **Zaffature**[55] 5613 2-8-3 62 .... AndreaAtzeni(3) 5 57
(M Botti) *hld up in tch: rdn to chse wnr fnl f: no imp* **3/1**[1]

0 **3** *3/4* **Indigo Ink**[26] 6451 2-8-6 0 .... HayleyTurner 6 55
(Miss Amy Weaver) *chsd ldr tl led over 2f out: hdd and edgd rt over 1f out: styd on same pce fnl f* **7/2**[2]

50 **4** *1 3/4* **City Gossip (IRE)**[25] 6493 2-8-1 0 .... MartinLane(5) 14 51
(M G Quinlan) *hld up in tch: rdn over 2f out: styd on same pce fnl f* **12/1**

600 **5** *1/2* **Lady Cavendish (IRE)**[2] 7064 2-8-6 0 ....(p) JimmyQuinn 17 50
(A Bailey) *hld up: hdwy over 2f out: sn rdn: nt rch ldrs* **12/1**

430 **6** *1* **Magneto (IRE)**[12] 6829 2-8-11 61 .... EdwardCreighton 11 53
(E J Creighton) *hld up: hdwy over 2f out: sn rdn and hung lft: no ex fnl f* **16/1**

0 **7** *3/4* **Xtreme (IRE)**[26] 6461 2-8-11 0 ....(be[1]) DavidProbert 12 51
(A Bailey) *led: rdn and hdd over 2f out: wknd fnl f* **12/1**

0 **8** *1 1/2* **Brenda Duke**[21] 6586 2-8-6 0 .... TPO'Shea 15 43
(J G Portman) *hld up: rdn over 2f out: nvr trbld ldrs* **66/1**

PP00 **9** *4* **Scintillating (IRE)**[5] 6992 2-8-6 0 .... PaulEddery 7 33
(R Hollinshead) *sn pushed along in rr: sme hdwy over 2f out: n.d* **100/1**

10 *1/2* **Develop U** 2-8-8 0 .... JackDean(3) 10 37
(W G M Turner) *hld up: sme hdwy u.p over 2f out: sn hung lft: n.d* **80/1**

06 **11** *3/4* **Generoso (USA)**[58] 5512 2-8-11 0 .... JimCrowley 1 36
(S C Williams) *chsd ldrs: pushed along over 2f out: wknd over 1f out* **16/1**

00 **12** *3 1/4* **Star Of Kalani (IRE)**[13] 6792 2-8-11 0 .... DavidAllan 8 28
(G M Moore) *sn pushed along: a in rr: bhd fr 1/2-way* **100/1**

06 **13** *1 1/2* **Bellaharry (IRE)**[39] 6122 2-8-6 0 .... ChrisCatlin 2 20
(Matthew Salaman) *hld up: sme hdwy over 2f out: sn wknd* **66/1**

0P0 **14** *6* **Rock Of Behistun (IRE)**[48] 5811 2-8-4 0 .... JosephineBruning(7) 4 11
(P L Gilligan) *chsd ldrs tl rdn and wknd over 2f out* **200/1**

15 *16* **Cayo Costa (IRE)** 2-7-13 0 .... DeclanCannon(7) 9 —
(A J McCabe) *dwlt: a outpcd* **33/1**

00 **16** *7* **Set To Rock**[13] 6792 2-8-11 0 .... TPQueally 13 —
(J G Portman) *sn pushed along in rr: bhd fr 1/2-way: no ch whn hung lft over 2f out* **150/1**

6 **17** *21* **No One Likes Us**[16] 6721 2-8-11 0 .... PaulDoe 3 —
(S Curran) *plld hrd and prom: wknd over 2f out: eased fnl f* **5/1**[3]

1m 47.49s (-2.11) **Going Correction** -0.375s/f (Firm) **17 Ran SP% 120.1**
Speed ratings (Par 93): **95,91,90,88,88 87,86,85,81,80 79,76,75,69,53 46,25**
toteswinger: 1&2 £7.00, 1&3 £10.30, £4.10. CSF £31.16 TOTE £9.50: £3.20, £1.20, £1.70; EX 24.10.The winner was bought in for 7,800gns.
Owner Richard Morecombe and Jamie Perryman **Bred** T J Rooney And Corduff Stud **Trained** Whitsbury, Hants

FOCUS
A big field for this seller, but it still looked a weak race and, with the pace strong, they were soon strung out.

NOTEBOOK
Glass Of Red(IRE) had an unconvincing profile, but she did hint at ability on her second outing, when beaten just over 3l in a Chepstow maiden, and she was a decisive winner on this drop in grade and step up in trip after over three months off. She deserves extra credit for overcoming a wide draw and might be competitive in low-grade handicaps. (op 15-2 tchd 11-2)
Zaffature, without the blinkers on her return from 55 days off, and trying her furthest trip to date, ran okay but it's debatable whether she quite performed up to her official mark. (op 7-2 tchd 9-2)
Indigo Ink looked one of the likelier winners when getting to the front travelling well over 2f out, but her response to pressure was a little disappointing. In fairness, though, this was only her second start, and she looked to lack the pace of the front two late on, giving the impression she'll stay further. (op 11-2 tchd 100-30)
City Gossip(IRE), upped significantly in trip, kept on without posing a threat and displayed a knee action, suggesting an easier surface will suit. (op 17-2)
Lady Cavendish(IRE), tried in cheekpieces just two days after being beaten a long way in a Polytrack maiden, was not helped by stall 17 and, although keeping on, couldn't muster the pace to challenge. (tchd 14-1)

No One Likes Us, reported to have hung left on his debut in a Polytrack claimer, was not without support but he played up beforehand and showed nothing in race itself, being heavily eased from over 2f out. (op 11-2 tchd 9-2)

7121 DG TAXIS FOR SPEED AND COMFORT MAIDEN STKS (C&G) 1m 75y
1:10 (1:11) (Class 4) 2-Y-O **£3,885** (£1,156; £577; £288) **Stalls** Low

Form RPR

6 **1** **Psychic Ability (USA)**[18] [6672] 2-9-0 0 (p) LDettori 13 85
(Saeed Bin Suroor) *chsd ldr: pushed along over 2f out: led wl over 1f out: sn rdn and edgd lft: drvn clr ins fnl f: r.o wl* **11/4**[1]

0 **2** 4 **Dandino**[15] [6763] 2-9-0 0 PaulMulrennan 10 76
(J G Given) *hld up in mid-div: hdwy on ins over 2f out: rdn wl over 1f out: r.o to take 2nd last strides* **20/1**

0322 **3** hd **Pytheas (USA)**[15] [6763] 2-9-0 79 GregFairley 7 75
(M Johnston) *led: pushed along and hdd wl over 1f out: rdn and no ex ins fnl f: lost 2nd last strides* **4/1**[3]

04 **4** hd **Palio Square (USA)**[63] [5347] 2-9-0 0 TPQueally 14 75
(H R A Cecil) *hld up in mid-div: hdwy 3f out: rdn jst over 2f out: kpt on same pce fnl f* **3/1**[2]

0 **5** 2½ **Hail Bold Chief (USA)**[18] [6672] 2-9-0 0 RobertWinston 4 69
(G A Swinbank) *a.p: pushed along over 2f out: rdn over 1f out: wknd wl ins fnl f* **8/1**

6 1 **Florentine Ruler (USA)** 2-9-0 0 EddieAhern 17 67
(H R A Cecil) *hld up in mid-div: prog over 3f out: pushed along wl over 1f out: sn btn* **14/1**

5 **7** 9 **Mountain Quest**[12] [6821] 2-9-0 0 HayleyTurner 12 46
(M L W Bell) *bhd: pushed along over 5f out: no ch fnl 2f* **7/1**

0 **8** 1¼ **Inshaallah**[13] [6792] 2-9-0 0 J-PGuillambert 11 43
(J G Given) *prom tl rdn and wknd over 2f out* **100/1**

0 **9** ½ **Dubawi King**[21] [6592] 2-9-0 0 DO'Donohoe 9 42
(N Tinkler) *s.i.s: sn wl bhd: short-lived effrt over 2f out* **150/1**

0 **10** 4 **Donair**[15] [6754] 2-9-0 0 StephenDonohoe 6 33
(P F I Cole) *s.i.s: bhd: rdn and short-lived effrt 2f out* **80/1**

11 4 **Sansili** 2-9-0 0 JimCrowley 2 24
(Pat Eddery) *s.v.s: a wl in rr* **33/1**

00 **12** 11 **Lord Wheathill**[87] [4557] 2-9-0 0 NeilChalmers 8 —
(Mrs L Williamson) *s.i.s: a bhd* **150/1**

06 **13** 1½ **Joe Rua (USA)**[17] [6696] 2-9-0 0 NCallan 15 —
(J Ryan) *hld up: sn in tch: wknd 3f out* **100/1**

1m 46.93s (-2.67) **Going Correction** -0.375s/f (Firm) 13 Ran SP% **114.2**
Speed ratings (Par 97): **98,94,93,93,91 90,81,79,79,75 71,60,58**
toteswinger: 1&2 £12.70, 1&3 £3.70, £8.50. CSF £60.27 TOTE £3.60: £1.50, £4.20, £1.20; EX 63.40.
Owner Godolphin **Bred** Flaxman Holdings Ltd **Trained** Newmarket, Suffolk

FOCUS
This looked a fair juvenile maiden, but the winning time was only 0.56 seconds quicker than the earlier seller, won by the 63-rated Glass Of Red, albeit that one carried 8lb less than this lot.

NOTEBOOK
Psychic Ability(USA) was originally the Godolphin second string, with Ted Durcan taking the ride, but the stable's apparent first choice, newcomer Burj Nahar, was declared a non-runner. As it turned out, this son of Kingmambo, who was fitted with cheekpieces for the first time, was always well placed and ran out a ready winner, improving on his debut performance. However, Frankie Dettori felt this wasn't a strong race, and that the winner is just a handicapper. (op 4-1 tchd 9-2)
Dandino ran an encouraging race, improving on the form he showed on debut. He lacked the tactical speed of some of these and didn't have a great deal of room to play with against the inside rail for much of the straight, but he finished well. There may be a race in him this year, but we're unlikely to see the best of him until he tackles further next season. (tchd 16-1 and 22-1)
Pytheas(USA) didn't run badly but he's not progressing and has now placed on five of his six starts. (op 100-30 tchd 11-4)
Palio Square(USA), debuting for Henry Cecil after two months off, was easy to back and proved a little disappointing, failing to build on the promise he showed on his first two starts. He got shuffled back a little further than ideal early on, but then looked to be hanging left when trying to make ground in the straight. Still, he's a horse with plenty of scope and it's possible he won't fulfil his potential until next year. (op 9-4 tchd 7-2)
Hail Bold Chief(USA) confirmed the ability he showed behind today's winner on his debut at Wolverhampton. He was an expensive yearling and should continue to progress. Official explanation: jockey said colt was denied a clear run (op 14-1)
Florentine Ruler(USA) ◆, described as a bit of a baby by connections beforehand, made a pleasing start from an unfavourable draw. He was inexperienced but showed ability and is open to plenty of improvement, especially over a little further. (tchd 16-1)
Mountain Quest was on and off the bridle and was basically still very green. He's going to want 1m4f-plus next year. (op 8-1 tchd 13-2)

7122 MOURDAKOTA HOTEL H'CAP (DIV I) 5f 13y
1:40 (1:41) (Class 5) (0-75,75) 3-Y-O+ **£2,266** (£674; £337; £168) **Stalls** High

Form RPR

0252 **1** **Taurus Twins**[9] [6902] 3-9-1 72 (b) RobertWinston 7 80
(R J Price) *mde all: rdn over 1f out: styd on wl* **9/4**[1]

21-0 **2** 1 **Frisbee**[15] [6764] 5-8-8 65 DuranFentiman 10 69
(D W Thompson) *a.p: rdn over 1f out: chsd wnr ins fnl f: r.o* **22/1**

5332 **3** 1½ **Mazzola**[5] [6988] 3-8-7 64 CatherineGannon 9 63
(M R Channon) *a.p: chsd wnr 3f out: sn rdn: styd on same pce ins fnl f* **3/1**[2]

0U60 **4** ½ **Top Bid**[5] [6989] 5-8-1 61 oh3 (b) KellyHarrison(3) 8 58
(T D Easterby) *s.i.s: sn pushed along in rr: rdn 1/2-way: styd on ins fnl f: nt rch ldrs* **7/1**[3]

0600 **5** 2¼ **Sands Crooner (IRE)**[9] [6897] 6-9-2 73 (v) TPQueally 1 62+
(J G Given) *dwlt and wnt lft s: bhd: swtchd lft over 1f out: rdn and hung lft ins fnl f: styd on: nrst fin* **11/1**

0062 **6** shd **Namir (IRE)**[27] [6422] 7-8-13 70 (vt) VinceSlattery 11 59
(H J Evans) *sn pushed along in mid-div: rdn over 1f out: no ex fnl f* **7/1**[3]

1000 **7** 1 **Speedy Senorita (IRE)**[25] [6489] 4-8-11 68 PaulMulrennan 5 53
(J J Quinn) *chsd wnr 2f: sn rdn: no ex fnl f* **16/1**

5000 **8** 4 **Steel City Boy (IRE)**[10] [6877] 6-8-10 67 JimCrowley 2 38
(D Shaw) *s.i.s: sn pushed along: a in rr* **16/1**

3360 **9** 7 **Stash**[13] [6791] 3-8-8 72 DavidKenny(7) 3 18
(R Hollinshead) *prom: rdn 3f out: sn lost pl* **33/1**

003 **10** ½ **Jimmy Ryan (IRE)**[9] [6904] 8-9-4 75 GregFairley 4 19
(T D McCarthy) *chsd ldrs: rdn 1/2-way: wknd wl over 1f out* **12/1**

60.20 secs (-0.80) **Going Correction** -0.075s/f (Good) 10 Ran SP% **115.8**
Speed ratings (Par 103): **103,101,99,98,94 94,92,86,75,74**
toteswinger: 1&2 £7.60, 1&3 £2.10, £8.00. CSF £55.28 CT £152.96 TOTE £2.60: £1.60, £5.50, £1.70; EX 42.40.
Owner G E Amey **Bred** G E Amey **Trained** Ullingswick, H'fords

FOCUS
A modest sprint handicap. The first three home raced nearest the rail with the third possibly the best guide.

7123 MOURDAKOTA HOTEL H'CAP (DIV II) 5f 13y
2:10 (2:10) (Class 5) (0-75,74) 3-Y-O+ **£2,266** (£674; £337; £168) **Stalls** High

Form RPR

3454 **1** **Nickel Silver**[26] [6459] 4-9-4 74 (p) RichardMullen 6 84
(B Smart) *mde all: rdn ins fnl f: r.o: hung lft towards fin* **11/4**[1]

5163 **2** hd **Make My Dream**[19] [6632] 6-8-13 69 TPO'Shea 7 78
(J Gallagher) *a.p: rdn to chse wnr fnl f: edgd lft: r.o* **5/1**[2]

2631 **3** 2¼ **Magical Speedfit (IRE)**[13] [6791] 4-8-8 71 RyanPowell(7) 8 72
(G G Margarson) *hld up: nt clr run over 1f out: rdn and r.o ins fnl f: nt rch ldrs* **9/1**

4005 **4** ½ **Jilly Why (IRE)**[13] [6799] 8-8-7 63 (b) DavidProbert 10 62
(Paul Green) *sn pushed along in rr but in tch: rdn over 1f out: no imp ins fnl f* **8/1**

330 **5** nk **La Capriosa**[13] [6798] 3-8-7 68 BMcHugh(5) 5 66
(J A Glover) *chsd wnr tl rdn over 1f out: wknd wl ins fnl f* **7/1**

1524 **6** 1¼ **Brandywell Boy (IRE)**[6] [6972] 6-8-10 66 RichardThomas 4 60
(D J S Ffrench Davis) *prom: rdn 1/2-way: wknd ins fnl f* **13/2**

4030 **7** ½ **Lord Of The Reins (IRE)**[13] [6799] 5-8-8 64 TPQueally 2 56
(J G Given) *s.i.s: sn chsng ldrs: rdn over 1f out: wknd ins fnl f* **12/1**

4002 **8** 8 **Bravely (IRE)**[9] [6897] 5-9-2 72 DuranFentiman 3 35
(T D Easterby) *s.i.s: hdwy 1/2-way: wknd over 1f out* **6/1**[3]

60.25 secs (-0.75) **Going Correction** -0.075s/f (Good) 8 Ran SP% **112.3**
Speed ratings (Par 103): **103,102,99,98,97 95,95,82**
toteswinger: 1&2 £3.70, 1&3 £5.80, £4.90. CSF £15.72 CT £105.30 TOTE £3.70: £1.30, £1.70, £2.90; EX 19.10.
Owner M Barber **Bred** Mrs Sheila White **Trained** Hambleton, N Yorks

FOCUS
Just as in the first division, the winner made all against near rail, suggesting those drawn low and/or stuck out wide were at a disadvantage. Sound form.
Magical Speedfit(IRE) Official explanation: jockey said gelding stopped very quickly

7124 HALLGARTEN DRUITT WINE H'CAP 2m 9y
2:45 (2:46) (Class 6) (0-65,64) 3-Y-O+ **£2,047** (£604; £302) **Stalls** Low

Form RPR

0044 **1** **Benozzo Gozzoli**[14] [6785] 3-8-0 46 NickyMackay 13 62
(H Morrison) *chsd ldrs: led after 2f: rdn clr over 1f out: styd on strly* **16/1**

1464 **2** 9 **Night Orbit**[138] [735] 5-9-13 63 CatherineGannon 6 69
(Miss J Feilden) *sn rdn to ld: hdd after 2f: remained handy tl outpcd over 4f out: rallied over 1f out: wnt 2nd nr fin but nvr any ch w wnr* **5/1**[3]

2131 **3** nk **Arab League (IRE)**[20] [6622] 4-9-11 64 AndreaAtzeni(3) 4 69
(R J Price) *chsd ldrs: n.m.r and lost pl after 2f: hld up: swtchd rt over 2f out: hdwy u.p over 1f out: nvr any ch w wnr* **3/1**[1]

5061 **4** 7 **Kokkokila**[17] [6692] 5-9-12 62 (p) JimmyFortune 2 58
(Lady Herries) *hld up in tch: rdn over 2f out: wknd over 1f out: fin 5th: plcd 4th* **11/2**

5650 **5** ¾ **Lets Roll**[15] [6767] 8-9-5 55 NCallan 7 51
(C W Thornton) *hld up: hdwy 10f out: rdn and wknd over 2f out: fin 6th: plcd 5th* **8/1**

-060 **6** 1 **Muntami (IRE)**[24] [5483] 8-8-10 46 ow1 (p) StephenDonohoe 11 41
(John A Harris) *hld up: hdwy over 2f out: sn wknd: fin 7th: plcd 6th* **66/1**

-004 **7** 2¼ **Present**[24] [6037] 5-8-9 45 TPQueally 10 37
(Miss Diana Weeden) *chsd wnr after 2f tl rdn over 3f out: wknd over 2f out: fin 8th: plcd 7th* **50/1**

4-64 **8** shd **Stoop To Conquer**[117] [3593] 9-9-12 62 VinceSlattery 8 54
(A W Carroll) *hld up: a in rr: fin 9th: plcd 8th* **25/1**

5002 **9** 2 **Petella**[71] [5131] 3-8-3 49 ChrisCatlin 9 39
(C W Thornton) *a in rr: bhd fnl 6f: fin 10th: plcd 9th* **14/1**

2522 **10** 1½ **Outland (IRE)**[15] [6767] 3-8-13 59 JimmyQuinn 14 47
(M H Tompkins) *prom: racd keenly: chsd wnr over 3f out to over 2f out: sn rdn and wknd: fin 11th: plcd 10th* **7/2**[2]

00 **11** 18 **Vertueux (FR)**[79] [4862] 4-9-8 58 ShaneKelly 1 24
(A W Carroll) *chsd ldrs tl wknd 3f out: fin 12th: plcd 11th* **50/1**

0-02 **12** 8 **Three Boars**[124] [967] 7-9-5 60 (b) JamieJones(5) 3 17
(S Gollings) *sn rdn along and a in rr: wknd over 3f out: eased over 1f out: fin 13th: pl 12th* **33/1**

4230 **D** ½ **Drawn Gold**[33] [6244] 5-9-8 61 RussellKennemore(3) 5 65
(R Hollinshead) *s.i.s: hld up: hdwy 4f out: rdn to chse wnr over 2f out: sn outpcd: fin 4th, 9l, nk, 1/2l: rdr failed to carry the correct weight: disq & plcd last* **20/1**

3m 34.39s (-1.61) **Going Correction** -0.375s/f (Firm)
WFA 3 from 4yo+ 10lb 13 Ran SP% **119.9**
Speed ratings (Par 101): **89,84,84,80,80 79,78,78,77,76 67,63,84**
toteswinger: 1&2 £23.40, 1&3 £13.60, £8.20. CSF £89.43 CT £314.66 TOTE £18.20: £4.60, £2.20, £1.90; EX 157.10.
Owner Miss B Swire **Bred** Miss B Swire **Trained** East Ilsley, Berks

FOCUS
A moderate staying handicap. The form is rated around the fourth, with a clear personal best from the winner.
Kokkokila Official explanation: jockey said mare hung right throughout

7125 MOUTARD CHAMPAGNE H'CAP 1m 75y
3:15 (3:15) (Class 4) (0-85,82) 3-Y-O+ **£6,476** (£1,927; £963; £481) **Stalls** Low

Form RPR

0300 **1** **South Cape**[19] [6645] 6-9-3 78 TPO'Shea 5 88
(G L Moore) *hld up: hdwy over 1f out: rdn to ld ins fnl f: r.o* **6/1**

2413 **2** ¾ **Kiwi Bay**[19] [6645] 4-9-7 82 ShaneKelly 12 90
(M Dods) *hld up: hdwy over 2f out: rdn to ld 1f out: hdd ins fnl f: styd on* **11/2**[3]

3263 **3** ½ **Observatory Star (IRE)**[52] [5697] 6-9-4 79 (bt) RobertWinston 6 88+
(T D Easterby) *hld up: hdwy over 2f out: nt clr run fr over 1f out: grad swtchd rt: r.o whn clr wl ins fnl f: nvr able to chal* **9/2**[2]

P03 **4** ¾ **Ocean Transit (IRE)**[4] [7032] 4-8-13 79 MartinLane(5) 10 84+
(R J Price) *led 3f: remained w ldr: rdn to ld 2f out: hdd over 1f out: styd on same pce* **8/1**

3116 **5** ½ **Arizona John (IRE)**[25] [6485] 4-9-4 79 DavidProbert 7 83
(J Mackie) *chsd ldrs: led over 1f out: sn hdd: styd on same pce* **7/2**[1]

2325 **6** ¾ **Ours (IRE)**[10] [6878] 6-8-7 68 (p) ChrisCatlin 9 71
(John A Harris) *hld up: bhd and rdn 1/2-way: r.o ins fnl f: nt trble ldrs* **9/1**

0100 **7** nk **Ninth House (USA)**[5] [7000] 7-8-10 71 (t) NeilChalmers 1 73
(Mrs R A Carr) *prom: rdn over 2f out: no ex fnl f* **12/1**

2103 **8** 13 **Harriet's Girl**[44] [5940] 3-8-10 74 AndrewElliott 8 46
(A P Jarvis) *w ldr tl led 5f out: rdn and hdd 2f out: wknd fnl f* **12/1**

5306 **9** *2½* **Brasingaman Hifive**[46] 5887 4-8-12 **73**.......................... JimmyQuinn 11 39
(Mrs G S Rees) *prom: rdn over 3f out: wknd over 2f out* **9/1**

1m 45.59s (-4.01) **Going Correction** -0.375s/f (Firm)
WFA 3 from 4yo+ 3lb **9** Ran SP% **116.6**
Speed ratings (Par 105): **105,104,103,103,102 101,101,88,85**
toteswinger: 1&2 £10.50, 1&3 £8.10, £4.30. CSF £39.31 CT £164.56 TOTE £9.30: £2.80, £2.30, £2.30; EX 48.60 Trifecta £25.90 Pool: £164.96 - 4.71 winning units..
Owner Heart Of The South Racing **Bred** John And Mrs Caroline Penny **Trained** Lower Beeding, W Sussex

FOCUS
The leaders went off a bit too fast, with Ocean Transit and Harriet's Girl taking each other on, and those held up dominated. Straightforward form.

7126 DG TAXIS "THE SAFE BET" MAIDEN STKS — 1m 75y
3:50 (3:51) (Class 5) 3-Y-O — **£3,238** (£963; £481; £240) **Stalls** Low

Form RPR

3320 **1** **Big Bay (USA)**[132] 3049 3-9-3 85.. NCallan 12 79
(Jane Chapple-Hyam) *a.p: chsd ldr over 6f out: led over 3f out: rdn and hdd over 1f out: rallied to ld wl ins fnl f: r.o* **2/1**[2]

0-20 **2** *½* **Aspro Mavro (IRE)**[34] 6223 3-9-3 75.............................. JimmyFortune 8 77
(J H M Gosden) *a.p: pushed along to chse wnr over 2f out: rdn to ld over 1f out: hrd rdn and hdd wl ins fnl f: styd on* **13/2**[3]

0-3 **3** *7* **Tafaool (IRE)**[60] 5435 3-8-12 0.. TPO'Shea 3 56
(M P Tregoning) *pushed along early: sn settled into mid-div: rdn and hung lft fr over 2f out: nvr nr ldrs* **11/10**[1]

-100 **4** *1¼* **Altimatum (USA)**[6] 6977 3-9-3 74..................................(b[1]) GregFairley 10 58
(P F I Cole) *prom: rdn over 3f out: hung lft fr over 2f out: wknd over 1f out* **11/1**

50 **5** *nk* **Big Whitfield**[18] 6673 3-9-3 0... ShaneKelly 6 57
(M Dods) *led after 1f: rdn and hdd over 3f out: wknd over 1f out* **33/1**

6 *1* **Lastroseofsummer (IRE)** 3-8-12 0.............................. RichardMullen 5 49
(Rae Guest) *prom: rdn over 4f out: wknd 2f out* **33/1**

3 **7** *3¾* **Montego Breeze**[22] 6573 3-8-12 0.................................. MickyFenton 9 40
(John A Harris) *broke wl: sn lost pl: n.d after* **25/1**

000- **8** *6* **Quadrifolio**[445] 4873 3-9-3 31.. NeilChalmers 7 31
(Paul Green) *led 1f: chsd ldrs tl rdn and wknd over 2f out* **150/1**

00- **9** *8* **Kabougg**[400] 6187 3-8-5 0... DeclanCannon(7) 11 —
(A J McCabe) *s.i.s: a in rr* **100/1**

0 **10** *½* **Bawdsey Bank**[22] 6573 3-8-12 0.................................... MarkCoumbe(5) 4 —
(John A Harris) *a in rr: wl bhd fnl 5f* **150/1**

0000 **11** *11* **Floods Of Tears**[140] 2820 3-8-12 45................................(b) DavidAllan 2 —
(I W McInnes) *hld up: rdn and wknd over 3f out* **150/1**

12 *8* **Lily Wood** 3-8-12 0.. PaulMulrennan 1 —
(J W Unett) *a in rr: wl bhd fnl 5f* **100/1**

1m 46.25s (-3.35) **Going Correction** -0.375s/f (Firm) **12** Ran SP% **116.3**
Speed ratings (Par 101): **101,100,93,92,91 90,87,81,73,72 61,53**
toteswinger: 1&2 £10.50, 1&3 £8.10, £4.30. CSF £14.61 TOTE £2.90: £1.40, £2.10, £1.10; EX 15.00.
Owner Jane Chapple-Hyam & Mrs B J Hirst **Bred** Hermitage Farm Llc **Trained** Newmarket, Suffolk

FOCUS
Not a maiden to dwell on. The favourite disappointed and it is doubtful if the winner had to match his early-summer form.
Tafaool(IRE) Official explanation: jockey said filly hung left under pressure
Lily Wood Official explanation: jockey said filly suffered interference at start

7127 AJA INSURE THEIR MEMBERS H'CAP (FOR LADY AMATEUR RIDERS) — 1m 2f 50y
4:20 (4:20) (Class 6) (0-65,65) 3-Y-O+ — **£1,977** (£608; £304) **Stalls** Low

Form RPR

2045 **1** **Dragon Slayer (IRE)**[28] 6392 7-10-1 **64**........................ MissABevan(5) 5 74
(John A Harris) *hld up: hdwy over 3f out: led over 2f out: drvn out* **12/1**

0420 **2** *½* **Garter Knight**[9] 6910 3-10-1 **64**.................................. MissGAndrews 16 73
(Mrs P Sly) *hld up: hdwy on outside over 1f out: edgd lft: rdn and ev ch ins fnl f: styd on* **11/1**

4023 **3** *2* **Bosamcliff (IRE)**[6] 6967 4-10-0 **58**................................... MissEFolkes 3 63
(P D Evans) *hld up: hdwy over 1f out: sn rdn and hung lft: styd on same pce ins fnl f* **5/1**[3]

560 **4** *2¼* **Boo**[12] 6460 7-9-6 **55**... MissJCWilliams(5) 6 56
(J W Unett) *hld up: r.o ins fnl f: nt rch ldrs* **20/1**

2515 **5** *1* **Kyle Of Bute**[9] 6910 3-9-9 **65**......................... MissStefaniaGandola(7) 10 64
(B P J Baugh) *hld up: hdwy over 3f out: rdn over 1f out: no ex ins fnl f* **11/1**

104 **6** *1¼* **Iguacu**[6] 6969 5-9-4 **53**.. MissJoannaMason(5) 2 50
(George Baker) *chsd ldrs: rdn over 2f out: wknd ins fnl f* **9/2**[2]

6000 **7** *½* **Mick Is Back**[6] 6966 5-9-7 **58**.............................. MissKMargarson(7) 15 54
(G G Margarson) *chsd ldrs: rdn over 1f out: wknd ins fnl f* **40/1**

6120 **8** *¾* **Hurricane Thomas (IRE)**[15] 6768 5-9-10 **59**...... MissPhillipaTutty(5) 11 53
(R A Fahey) *led 1f: chsd ldr: led again 3f out: rdn and hdd over 2f out: wknd ins fnl f* **17/2**

0210 **9** *1¼* **Astronomical (IRE)**[15] 6760 7-10-2 **65**.....................(p) MissRKneller(5) 8 57
(R Hollinshead) *led after 1f: hdd 3f out: wknd over 1f out* **8/1**

0001 **10** *1* **Tres Froide (FR)**[12] 6818 4-10-3 **61**.............................. MissEJJones 12 51
(N Tinkler) *prom: lost pl over 3f out: n.d after* **7/2**[1]

3030 **11** *½* **General Tufto**[50] 5740 4-9-12 **61**.........................(b) MissJennyCarr(5) 13 50
(C Smith) *hld up: hdwy over 2f out: wkng whn hmpd over 1f out* **18/1**

2506 **12** *9* **Turn To Dreams**[231] 808 3-8-13 **55**.............................. MissHJones(7) 9 27
(P D Evans) *mid-div: lost pl 6f out: bhd fnl 4f* **66/1**

0003 **13** *9* **Kingaroo (IRE)**[84] 4669 3-9-4 **53**...................................... MissLEllison 1 8
(G Woodward) *prom: rdn over 4f out: wknd over 3f out* **25/1**

2m 13.27s (-1.03) **Going Correction** -0.375s/f (Firm)
WFA 3 from 4yo+ 5lb **13** Ran SP% **120.9**
Speed ratings (Par 101): **89,88,87,85,84 83,83,82,81,80 80,73,65**
toteswinger: 1&2 £20.50, 1&3 £16.90, £9.10. CSF £134.24 CT £757.69 TOTE £15.90: £4.50, £3.80, £2.40; EX 126.80 Place 6: £18.29 Place 5: £11.84.
Owner Mrs A E Harris **Bred** Arandora Star Syndicate **Trained** Eastwell, Leics

FOCUS
A moderate contest and, as is usually the case in this type of race, form to treat with some caution. The first four came from well back off the pace and the third looks a sound guide.
Mick Is Back Official explanation: jockey said gelding hung badly left
T/Jkpt: Not won. T/Plt: £16.20 to a £1 stake. Pool: £51,590.01. 2,317.28 winning tickets. T/Qpdt: £6.70 to a £1 stake. Pool: £3,720.10. 405.20 winning tickets. CR

6656 SAINT-CLOUD (L-H)
Wednesday, October 28

OFFICIAL GOING: Very soft

7128a PRIX DE FLORE (GROUP 3) (F&M) — 1m 2f 110y
1:50 (1:50) 3-Y-O+ — **£38,835** (£15,534; £11,650; £7,767; £3,883)

RPR

1 **Celimene (IRE)**[87] 4583 3-8-10 .... YLerner 4 115
(C Lerner, France) *mid-div: 6th st: pushed along over 2f out: rdn and r.o 1 1/2f out: chal 100yds out: led cl home* **11/2**[3]

2 *½* **Shemiyla (FR)**[22] 6577 3-8-7 .... C-PLemaire 11 111
(A De Royer-Dupre, France) *in tch: 4th 1/2-way: cl 5th st: pushed along and 3rd 1 1/2f out: styd on to ld 150yds out tl hdd cl home* **11/5**[1]

3 *shd* **Rainbow Dancing**[19] 6658 4-8-11 .... TThulliez 12 109
(Mlle H Van Zuylen, France) *hld up on outside: disputing last st: pushed along 2f out: rdn and fin wl fnl f: nrest at fin* **44/1**

4 *hd* **La Boum (GER)**[24] 6526 6-8-11 .... TJarnet 2 109
(Robert Collet, France) *in tch: disp 3rd st: shkn up over 2f out: crossed by Take the Hint and sltly short of room 2f out: drvn and styd on steadily: fin 5th: promoted to 4th* **16/5**[2]

5 *2* **Take The Hint**[116] 3619 3-8-7 .... SPasquier 9 107
(J H M Gosden) *cl up: 2nd 1/2-way: sn drvn ent st: styd on to ld fr over 1f out to 150yds out: sn no ex: fin 4th: disqualified and plcd 5th* **17/1**

6 *2½* **One Clever Cat (IRE)**[88] 4578 3-8-7 .... FPrat 3 102
(T Clout, France) *hld up: disputing last st: drvn over 2f out: modest hdwy tl no ex fr 1 1/2f out* **19/1**

7 *¾* **Enticement**[12] 6813 3-8-7 .... RyanMoore 5 101
(Sir Michael Stoute) *led: drvn ent st: kpt on u.p tl hdd over 1f out: wknd* **16/1**

8 *½* **Terre Du Vent (FR)**[6] 6978 3-8-7 .... IMendizabal 1 100
(Y De Nicolay, France) *prom: 3rd 1/2-way: disputing 3rd st: rdn and u.p 2f out: steadily wknd* **17/1**

9 *½* **Andrea (GER)**[87] 4583 3-8-7 .... OPeslier 6 99
(F Head, France) *towards rr: disputing 8th st: sn pushed along: no imp* **10/1**

10 *hd* **Alpine Snow (IRE)**[138] 2989 3-8-7 .... RMarchelli 10 98
(S Wattel, France) *hld up: 11th st: n.d* **26/1**

11 *1* **Qertaas (IRE)**[57] 5562 3-8-7 .... DBonilla 8 96
(F Head, France) *hld up: disputing 8th st: pushed along 2f out: nvr in contention* **57/1**

12 *½* **Sworn Pro (GER)**[17] 6714 3-8-7 .... DBoeuf 7 95
(Mario Hofer, Germany) *mid-div: 7th st: sn drvn along: unable qck* **47/1**

13 *1* **Biased**[22] 6577 3-8-7 .... GMasure 13 93
(M Delzangles, France) *mid-div on outside: disputing 8th st: pushed along early: sn n.d* **21/1**

2m 19.4s (-0.20)
WFA 3 from 4yo+ 5lb **13** Ran SP% **115.8**
PARI-MUTUEL: WIN 6.50; PL 2.80, 1.60, 8.20; DF 11.60.
Owner G Laboureau **Bred** Petra Bloodstock Agency Ltd **Trained** France

NOTEBOOK
Take The Hint, off the track since July, returned to her best on this softer ground. She hung right 2f out and the Stewards decided she had stopped Le Boum obtaining the best possible prize money so they demoted her to fifth, one place behind that rival.
Enticement, bidding to follow up her Listed success at Newmarket, made the running but could not last home on this very soft surface. She may no be retired to stud.

7063 LINGFIELD (L-H)
Thursday, October 29

OFFICIAL GOING: Standard
This meeting marked the 20th anniversary of All-Weather racing in Britain.
Wind: Almost Nil Weather: Fine but cloudy, very mild

7129 TOTESPORT.COM ALL-WEATHER 20TH ANNIVERSARY APPRENTICE H'CAP — 7f (P)
1:10 (1:11) (Class 6) (0-60,60) 3-Y-O+ — **£2,047** (£604; £302) **Stalls** Low

Form RPR

1550 **1** **La Gifted**[3] 7051 3-9-2 **60**... CharlesEddery(5) 10 70
(M R Channon) *prom: trckd ldr over 3f out: pushed into ld over 1f out: rdn and kpt on fnl f* **4/1**[1]

0000 **2** *1½* **Cavalry Guard (USA)**[8] 6945 5-8-13 **50**..........................(b) AmyBaker 9 56
(T D McCarthy) *led: rdn and hdd over 1f out: kpt on one pce* **8/1**

0000 **3** *¾* **Sign Of The Cross**[22] 6588 5-9-4 **55**................................ JamieJones 13 59
(C R Dore) *dropped in fr wd draw and hld up in last trio: prog to 7th 2f out: effrt on inner over 1f out: styd on to take 3rd last 100yds* **13/2**[3]

003 **4** *½* **Mocha Java**[27] 6458 6-9-7 **58**.................................(b) RossAtkinson 12 61
(Matthew Salaman) *racd wd: prog and prom over 4f out: rdn to dispute 3rd 2f out: nt qckn over 1f out: kpt on* **11/2**[2]

000 **5** *nk* **Torquemada (IRE)**[23] 6568 8-8-8 **50**............................(tp) KierenFox(5) 8 52
(M J Attwater) *racd wd: hld up: prog over 2f out: disp 3rd over 1f out to ins fnl f: nt qckn* **16/1**

0000 **6** *¾* **Ardent Prince**[48] 5842 6-8-12 **52**.............................. DeclanCannon(3) 5 52
(A J McCabe) *rrd s and slowest away: in last trio: effrt over 2f out: kpt on fr over 1f out: n.d* **12/1**

4420 **7** *½* **One More Round (USA)**[86] 4621 11-9-0 **58**................ KevinLundie(7) 2 56
(P D Evans) *hld up and sn last: effrt on wd outside 2f out: styd on ins fnl f but no ch* **9/1**

500- **8** *1¼* **Nightstrike (IRE)**[546] 1747 6-8-6 **50**.................................. RPWalsh(7) 4 45
(Luke Comer, Ire) *chsd ldrs: drvn on inner 3f out: stl disputing 3rd over 1f out: wknd rapidly last 150yds* **14/1**

2350 **9** *½* **Exceed Elegance (IRE)**[26] 6492 3-9-5 **58**.......................... MartinLane 1 52
(D Shaw) *mostly in midfield: drvn on inner over 3f out: short of room briefly 2f out: no real prog* **10/1**

6-60 **10** *¾* **Philmack Dot Com**[26] 6492 3-9-4 **57**............................(t) AshleyMorgan 7 49
(D Donovan) *chsd ldrs: rdn to dispute 3rd wl over 1f out: wknd fnl f: sddle slipped* **9/1**

56-0 **11** *5* **Franchesca's Gold**[22] 6581 3-8-10 **49**............................ SimonPearce 6 27
(Jane Southcombe) *prom 2f: lost pl: struggling in rr 2f out* **66/1**

5-00 **12** *6* **Honkey Tonk Tony (IRE)**[9] 6918 4-8-8 50..................(p) JakePayne(5) 3 12
(Luke Comer, Ire) *chsd ldr to over 3f out: wknd rapidly 2f out: t.o* **25/1**

1m 25.77s (0.97) **Going Correction** +0.075s/f (Slow)
WFA 3 from 4yo+ 2lb **12** Ran SP% **114.5**
Speed ratings (Par 101): **97,95,94,93,93 92,92,90,90,89 83,76**
toteswinger: 1&2 £8.90, 1&3 £6.30, 2&3 £9.40. CSF £34.23 CT £173.08 TOTE £4.90: £1.60, £2.90, £2.60; EX 41.10 TRIFECTA Not won..
Owner Patrick and Simon Trant **Bred** Patrick & Simon Trant **Trained** West Ilsley, Berks

FOCUS
A moderate handicap, and these apprentice riders had not ridden more than 50 winners. The runner-up is a sound guide to the form.
Mocha Java Official explanation: jockey said gelding hung right
Philmack Dot Com Official explanation: jockey said saddle slipped

7130 E B F BARRY DENNIS ALL-WEATHER 20TH ANNIVERSARY MAIDEN STKS 7f (P)

1:40 (1:40) (Class 5) 2-Y-O **£4,403** (£1,310; £654; £327) **Stalls** Low

Form RPR
6222 **1** **Fine Sight**[24] 6548 2-9-3 83.................................. RichardHughes 5 79
(R Hannon) *lw: mde all: rdn and hrd pressed fr over 1f out: hld on wl* **5/1**

02 **2** *1/2* **Shamir**[20] 6627 2-9-3 0.................................. FergusSweeney 4 78
(Miss Jo Crowley) *lw: trckd ldng pair: rdn 2f out: wnt 2nd ins fnl f and pressed wnr: jst hld* **11/2**

3 **3** *3/4* **Brannagh (USA)**[28] 6424 2-9-3 0..............................(t) ShaneKelly 6 76
(J Noseda) *trckd ldng trio: effrt 2f out: hanging and nt qckn over 1f out: shkn up and styd on to take 3rd nr fin* **10/1**

24 **4** *1/2* **Lay Claim (USA)**[19] 6679 2-9-3 0.............................. RyanMoore 8 75
(Sir Michael Stoute) *chsd wnr: rdn to chal over 1f out: nt qckn and hld ent fnl f: fdd* **2/1**[1]

5 **5** *1* **Hypnotized (USA)**[16] 6754 2-9-3 0.............................. HayleyTurner 2 72
(M L W Bell) *w'like: lw: chsd ldng quartet: pushed along to cl over 2f out: effrt on inner over 1f out: grad wknd* **9/2**[3]

5 **6** *10* **Tuscan King**[23] 6561 2-9-3 0.............................. MartinDwyer 1 47
(W R Muir) *leggy: a in last trio: lost tch 3f out: t.o* **100/1**

23 **7** *6* **Govern**[23] 6561 2-9-3 0.................................. TPQueally 7 32
(H R A Cecil) *w'like: str: lw: u.p in last trio after 3f: sn btn: wl bhd 2f out: t.o* **3/1**[2]

00 **8** *hd* **Whipper's Delight (IRE)**[26] 6493 2-8-12 0..................... JimmyQuinn 3 27
(D Donovan) *leggy: a in last pair: lost tch fr 1/2-way: t.o* **100/1**

1m 25.05s (0.25) **Going Correction** +0.075s/f (Slow) **8** Ran SP% **119.6**
Speed ratings (Par 95): **101,100,99,99,97 86,79,79**
toteswinger: 1&2 £4.80, 1&3 £5.90, 2&3 £8.40. CSF £34.14 TOTE £6.00: £1.70, £1.70, £2.60; EX 48.00 Trifecta £366.10 Pool: £494.78 - 1.00 winning units..
Owner The Queen **Bred** The Queen **Trained** East Everleigh, Wilts

FOCUS
This looked a fair maiden beforehand, but there wasn't much change in the order throughout.

NOTEBOOK
Fine Sight played up a bit in the pre-parade ring but he proved suited by the drop back to 7f and was a game winner from the front. His breeding suggests he may improve with age, and he'll have another try over further in time, but a mark in the 80s probably doesn't leave him with much in hand just now. (op 9-2)
Shamir was behind Lay Claim on debut at Newbury but has subsequently made more progress than that one. He confirmed the promise of his recent second in a similar event over C&D and, although not that big, looks a fair type in the making, with handicaps now an option. (op 7-1)
Brannagh(USA) ◆, who showed ability on his debut over 6f at Newmarket, was very easy to back and ran an interesting race. A sizeable colt, he didn't look comfortable rounding the final bend and seemed unbalanced in the straight, but he ran on nicely near the line without being given a hard ride, displaying a raking stride. There should be more to come from this half-brother to Group 1 winner Lord Shanakill when he switches to a galloping track. (tchd 9-1)
Lay Claim(USA) was always well placed but his finishing effort was disappointing. He's failed to progress as expected since an encouraging debut (beaten at odds of 8-15 last time) and, while it would be silly to dismiss him completely now he's qualified for a handicap mark, he still doesn't appeal as worth following. (op 9-4 tchd 5-2, 3-1 in a place and 11-4 in places)
Hypnotized(USA) failed to confirm the promise he showed on his debut at Leicester and has to be considered disappointing. He came off the bridle over 2f out and made limited progress. (op 11-2)
Govern came under pressure before halfway and was a major disappointment. He's another who has failed to build on an encouraging first start, although he may do better when going up in trip when sent handicapping. (op 7-2 tchd 4-1)

7131 E B F ALL-WEATHER 20TH ANNIVERSARY RIVER EDEN FILLIES' STKS (LISTED RACE) 1m 5f (P)

2:10 (2:11) (Class 1) 3-Y-O+
£22,708 (£8,608; £4,308; £2,148; £1,076; £540) **Stalls** Low

Form RPR
1-26 **1** **Baila Me (GER)**[12] 6853 4-9-2 107.................................. LDettori 8 106
(Saeed Bin Suroor) *lw: trckd ldng trio: smooth prog to ld wl over 2f out: sn clr and in n.d: rdn out* **3/1**[1]

1021 **2** *4* **Rosika**[28] 6419 3-8-8 93.................................. RyanMoore 6 100+
(Sir Michael Stoute) *hld up in last trio: prog on wd outside 3f out: drvn and effrt 2f out: r.o to take 2nd last 150yds: no ch of delivering a chal* **10/3**[2]

6025 **3** *2 3/4* **Storyland (USA)**[32] 6302 4-9-2 88.............................. RichardHughes 5 96
(W J Haggas) *hld up in midfield: prog over 3f out: drvn to chse wnr wl over 1f out: no imp: lost 2nd last 150yds* **8/1**[3]

4554 **4** *1* **Princess Taylor**[34] 6242 5-9-2 98..............................(t) TedDurcan 4 94
(M Botti) *chsd ldng pair to 3f out: nt clr run over 2f out and outpcd: kpt on again fr over 1f out* **11/1**

4350 **5** *1 1/4* **Flame Of Gibraltar (IRE)**[12] 6853 3-8-8 98..................... TPQueally 3 93
(H R A Cecil) *lw: s.i.s: hld up in last trio: gng strly 3f out: prog over 2f out: pressing for a pl over 1f out: effrt flattened out* **16/1**

3105 **6** *1 3/4* **Crimson Ribbon (USA)**[21] 6618 3-8-8 83..................... NickyMackay 12 90+
(J H M Gosden) *lw: s.i.s: hld up in last trio: 10th and no ch whn nt clr run over 2f out: styd on fr over 1f out* **28/1**

3305 **7** *4 1/2* **Uvinza**[34] 6242 3-8-8 98.................................. JimCrowley 11 83
(W J Knight) *lw: trckd ldr to 3f out: chsd wnr shortly after tl wl over 1f out: wknd rapidly* **11/1**

1121 **8** *4 1/2* **Arty Crafty (USA)**[27] 6445 3-8-9 75 ow1.......................... SebSanders 7 77
(Sir Mark Prescott) *drvn to ld: reminder 4f out to maintain str pce: hdd wl over 2f out: wknd rapidly* **16/1**

5120 **9** *nk* **Mildoura (FR)**[21] 6618 4-9-2 80.................................. PaulDoe 2 76
(Mrs L J Mongan) *settled towards rr: shkn up over 3f out: losing pl whn squeezed out shortly after* **100/1**

02/1 **10** *4* **Dove (IRE)**[114] 3703 4-9-2 88.................................. JimmyFortune 1 70
(J H M Gosden) *chsd ldrs tl wknd rapidly over 2f out* **16/1**

1113 **11** *3* **Acquisition**[28] 6419 3-8-8 87.................................. JimmyQuinn 10 65
(H R A Cecil) *swtg: chsd ldrs on outer: lost pl 7f out: rdn and struggling 4f out: sn btn* **8/1**[3]

4160 **12** *nk* **Snoqualmie Girl (IRE)**[12] 6853 3-8-11 105.............................. KFallon 9 68
(D R C Elsworth) *hld up towards rr: prog on outer into midfield 7f out: rdn 4f out: wknd 3f out* **10/1**

2m 41.72s (-4.28) **Going Correction** +0.075s/f (Slow) course record
WFA 3 from 4yo+ 8lb **12** Ran SP% **118.1**
Speed ratings (Par 108): **116,113,111,111,110 109,106,103,103,101 99,99**
toteswinger: 1&2 £2.40, 1&3 £6.40, 2&3 £9.70. CSF £12.70 TOTE £3.60: £1.50, £1.80, £2.40; EX 12.30 Trifecta £56.10 Pool: £384.00 - 5.06 winning units..
Owner Godolphin **Bred** Gestut Karlshof **Trained** Newmarket, Suffolk
■ Stewards' Enquiry : Nicky Mackay One-day ban: careless riding (Nov 12)

FOCUS
An ordinary fillies' Listed contest but Baila Me, who had 14lb in hand over the runner-up based on official ratings, and 19lb over the third, totally outclassed her rivals and is better than this level. This was the only race on the card run in a time under standard, and it was not that far off the track record, so the form looks sound.

NOTEBOOK
Baila Me(GER) ◆, a sizeable individual, was given an uncomplicated ride and, after quickening clear early in the straight, had the race won from over 1f out. She avoided a penalty for last year's Group 1 win in Germany and this was her first success in three starts for Godolphin. The trip, a furlong longer that she had tried previously, clearly suited and she may stay even further. (op 7-2)
Rosika ◆, a progressive type whose latest win was gained off a mark of 86, did not have things go her way on this rise in class and did well to get second, although it's highly unlikely she would have troubled the winner whatever the case. After being bumped at the start and taking time to find her stride, she ended up last of all, much too far back, and then had to make her move four wide around the final bend. She should keep progressing and can earn more black type. (op 7-2)
Storyland(USA), sixth when joint-favourite for this race last year, was produced with her chance but couldn't match the winner's pace and this looks about as good as she is. (op 9-1)
Princess Taylor lost momentum when stopped in her run turning into the straight, and but for that she would have had a squeak of getting third. Even so, she was probably slightly below her official mark of 98. (tchd 10-1)
Flame Of Gibraltar(IRE) travelled well for a long way but after having to wait for a run she didn't find as much as had looked likely. She's a disappointing sort. (tchd 20-1)
Crimson Ribbon(USA) had a bit of a task on at the weights and didn't enjoy the clearest of runs. (op 25-1)
Uvinza could have been expected to fare better considering she was won a maiden on her only previous Polytrack start and was not that badly in at the weights. (op 10-1)
Arty Crafty(USA), a progressive handicapper who was carrying 1lb overweight, was driven to lead and, although getting her own way, was quickly beaten once challenged.
Dove(IRE), off since winning a Pontefract maiden over 1m2f in July, travelled well to a point but found nothing. (op 12-1)
Acquisition ran as though she's either had enough for the year, or didn't handle the Polytrack. (op 11-1)
Snoqualmie Girl(IRE) was the second best off at the weights, even allowing for her penalty, but she ran a long way below the pick of her turf form. Official explanation: jockey said filly had felt the effect of recent races (op 9-1 tchd 8-1)

7132 E B F ALL-WEATHER 20TH ANNIVERSARY FLEUR DE LYS FILLIES' STKS (LISTED RACE) 1m (P)

2:40 (2:40) (Class 1) 3-Y-O+
£22,708 (£8,608; £4,308; £2,148; £1,076; £540) **Stalls** High

Form RPR
-201 **1** **Moonlife (IRE)**[16] 6757 3-8-11 105..............................(t) LDettori 2 107+
(Saeed Bin Suroor) *lw: trckd ldrs: smooth prog 2f out: led over 1f out: wl in command fnl f: pushed out* **10/3**[2]

5041 **2** *2 1/4* **Ahla Wasahl**[33] 6267 3-9-0 101.............................. WilliamBuick 3 105
(D M Simcock) *settled towards rr: sme prog over 2f out and pushed along: effrt and hdwy to go 2nd jst ins fnl f: styd on wl but no ch w wnr* **8/1**

-112 **3** *2 1/2* **Apple Charlotte**[116] 3-9-0 105.................................. TPQueally 5 99
(H R A Cecil) *lw: trckd ldr: led over 2f out: brought wd in st: hdd over 1f out: sn outpcd* **9/4**[1]

0346 **4** *1* **Carcinetto (IRE)**[26] 6487 7-9-0 95.............................. CatherineGannon 9 94
(P D Evans) *lw: t.k.h: hld up in last trio: rousted along over 2f out: nt clr run briefly sn after: stl only 9th ent fnl f: r.o strly last 100yds* **33/1**

0530 **5** *1/2* **Rosaleen (IRE)**[68] 5260 4-9-3 96.............................. MartinDwyer 10 96
(B J Meehan) *chsd ldng trio: u.p wl over 2f out: outpcd over 1f out: kpt on* **20/1**

0005 **6** *3/4* **Russian Empress (IRE)**[18] 6707 5-9-0 94.............................. KFallon 12 91
(David P Myerscough, Ire) *dropped in fr wd draw and hld up in last trio: effrt over 2f out: sme prog over 1f out: kpt on same pce* **12/1**

2250 **7** *1/2* **Accede**[21] 6618 3-8-11 82.................................. TPO'Shea 7 90
(J G Portman) *hld up and sn last: urged along over 3f out: no prog tl styd on fnl f: nrst fin* **66/1**

0-10 **8** *nk* **Intense**[26] 6482 3-8-11 90.................................. MichaelHills 1 89
(B W Hills) *trckd ldrs on inner: effrt over 2f out: nt qckn sn after: kpt on fr over 1f out* **14/1**

6000 **9** *1 1/2* **Aroundthebay**[54] 5665 3-8-11 82.............................. DaneO'Neill 8 86
(H J L Dunlop) *mostly in midfield: rdn over 2f out: no prog: kpt on same pce* **66/1**

1142 **10** *shd* **Sarah Park (IRE)**[20] 6633 4-9-0 93.............................. RichardHughes 4 86
(B J Meehan) *chsd ldng pair: lost pl on inner 2f out: wknd fnl f* **9/1**

3003 **11** *1 1/2* **Greenisland (IRE)**[33] 6272 3-8-11 97.............................. SteveDrowne 6 82
(H Morrison) *led to over 2f out: wknd rapidly on inner jst over 1f out* **11/2**[3]

5034 **12** *7* **Trumpet Lily**[21] 6618 4-9-0 84.................................. JimCrowley 11 66
(J G Portman) *hld up on outer: prog 5f out: lost pl and rdn 3f out: wl bhd over 1f out* **33/1**

1m 36.93s (-1.27) **Going Correction** +0.075s/f (Slow)
WFA 3 from 4yo+ 3lb **12** Ran SP% **118.3**
Speed ratings (Par 108): **109,106,104,103,102 102,101,101,99,99 98,91**
toteswinger: 1&2 £6.30, 1&3 £2.60, 2&3 £6.10. CSF £28.70 TOTE £3.60: £1.90, £2.50, £1.80; EX 28.40 Trifecta £62.40 Pool: £375.76 - 4.45 winning units..
Owner Godolphin **Bred** M Parola **Trained** Newmarket, Suffolk

FOCUS
Just a fair fillies' Listed contest and the form is a bit muddling and ordinary for the grade overall.

NOTEBOOK
Moonlife(IRE) ◆ returned to form when a comfortable winner of a Leicester conditions race last time and built on that effort on this step back up in grade, in the process proving she doesn't have to lead. She was a convincing winner after travelling well and, considering she's not had much racing this year, it would be no surprise to see her at the Dubai Carnival. (op 5-2 tchd 7-2)
Ahla Wasahl, a surprise winner of a Listed handicap at Ascot off a mark of 97 on her previous start, for which she picked up a penalty, probably bettered that form but got going too late to threaten the winner, who was basically too good. (op 9-1)

Apple Charlotte had a tough time when contesting the Hollywood Oaks back in July and had taken time to come back to herself according to her connections. This was a respectable effort under a penalty and she might do even better when returned to slightly further. (op 11-4)
Carcinetto(IRE) got going too late after being getting behind and becoming outpaced at a crucial stage. (op 40-1)
Rosaleen(IRE), returning from over two months off, had no easy task conceding weight all round and was comfortably held. (op 25-1)
Russian Empress(IRE) can be given another chance as she did quite a bit of racing early, when dropped in from a wide draw before being rushed up to get a position towards the inside (op 20-1)
Accede ran on from an unpromising position and, officially rated 82, her proximity limits the form.
Greenisland(IRE) dropped away tamely after leading through the early stages. (op 15-2)

7133 CORAL ALL-WEATHER 20TH ANNIVERSARY H'CAP — 7f (P)
3:10 (3:10) (Class 3) (0-95,93) 3-Y-0+ **£7,771** (£2,312; £1,155; £577) **Stalls** Low

Form				RPR
10-	**1**		**Sirocco Breeze**[369] 6975 4-9-6 **93**........ LDettori 3 (Saeed Bin Suroor) *lw: t.k.h: hld up bhd ldng trio: prog to ld over 1f out: sn pushed clr: comf* **15/8**[1]	111+
0200	**2**	*4*	**Beckermet (IRE)**[19] 6675 7-9-1 **88**........ NCallan 8 (R F Fisher) *led: drvn and hdd over 1f out: no ch w wnr after: clung on for 2nd* **7/1**	93
5000	**3**	*½*	**Glow Star (SAF)**[33] 6270 5-9-0 **87**........ RyanMoore 7 (G L Moore) *hld up last: pushed along 3f out: drvn and prog on outer over 1f out: r.o wl to snatch 3rd nr fin* **9/2**[3]	91
0462	**4**	*hd*	**Spirit Of Sharjah (IRE)**[18] 6702 4-9-2 **89**........ JimmyQuinn 6 (Miss J Feilden) *t.k.h: hld up and racd on outer: rdn and effrt 2f out: hanging over 1f out: wnt 3rd briefly ins fnl f: styd on* **7/2**[2]	92
6520	**5**	*2¾*	**Cumana Bay**[61] 5432 3-8-11 **86**........ RichardHughes 9 (R Hannon) *lw: mostly chsd ldr to over 1f out: wknd fnl f* **12/1**	82
5403	**6**	*1¾*	**Beat The Bell**[20] 6631 4-9-2 **89**........ ShaneKelly 5 (J A Osborne) *t.k.h: hld up in last trio: rdn and no prog over 2f out: no ch after* **14/1**	80
4300	**7**	*¾*	**Salient**[18] 6695 5-8-7 **80**........ PaulDoe 2 (M J Attwater) *disp 2nd pl to over 1f out: wknd rapidly fnl f* **16/1**	69
6400	**8**	*¾*	**Red Somerset (USA)**[20] 6633 6-9-6 **93**........ GeorgeBaker 4 (R J Hodges) *s.i.s: a in last trio: lft wl bhd fr over 2f out* **16/1**	80
0160	**9**	*¾*	**Desert Dreamer (IRE)**[8] 6944 8-8-12 **85**........ CatherineGannon 1 (P D Evans) *s.i.s: rousted along to rch midfield: nvr gng wl: lost pl u.p over 2f out* **22/1**	70

1m 23.83s (-0.97) **Going Correction** +0.075s/f (Slow)
WFA 3 from 4yo+ 2lb — **9** Ran SP% **118.2**
Speed ratings (Par 107): **108,103,102,102,99 97,96,95,94**
toteswinger: 1&2 £4.40, 1&3 £3.20, 2&3 £6.60. CSF £16.23 CT £53.80 TOTE £2.70: £1.30, £2.80, £1.70; EX 16.20 Trifecta £91.80 Pool: £366.07 - 2.95 winning units..
Owner Godolphin **Bred** Gainsborough Stud Management Ltd **Trained** Newmarket, Suffolk

FOCUS
A decent handicap in which the winner was impressive and the form is rated around the placed horses.

NOTEBOOK
Sirocco Breeze ◆ had been off since being reported to have raced too freely in a conditions event a year previously, having apparently had problems with his hooves, and he took a strong hold once more on this belated return, only his third racecourse appearance, but he still picked up well to readily defy a mark of 93. He is clearly smart but will need to learn to settle if he's to fulfil his potential and may ultimately prove best suited by sprint trips. Whatever the case, expect to see him at Meydan in 2010. (op 6-4 tchd 11-8 and 2-1 in a place)
Beckermet(IRE) ◆, racing off a career-low mark on this return to Polytrack, was able to dominate and had his chance, but he's yet to win beyond 6f. He could pick up a nice prize or two if persevered with this winter, possibly back over a sprint trip. (op 9-1)
Glow Star(SAF), set a lot to do, became outpaced well before the straight and got going too late. He might be ready for another try at 1m. (op 15-2)
Spirit Of Sharjah(IRE), 2lb higher than when a good second over C&D from a wide draw last time, raced wider than ideal without cover pretty much throughout and that cannot have helped his chance. (op 9-2 tchd 5-1)
Cumana Bay was well held off a mark 16lb higher than when last seen on Polytrack.
Beat The Bell was a little keen under a hold-up ride and never got involved. He's probably better suited by 6f, but there still wasn't a great deal of encouragement in this effort. (op 12-1 tchd 11-1)

7134 LADBROKES ALL-WEATHER 20TH ANNIVERSARY H'CAP — 1m 2f (P)
3:40 (3:40) (Class 5) (0-75,75) 3-Y-0+ **£3,412** (£1,007; £504) **Stalls** Low

Form				RPR
2324	**1**		**Free Tussy (ARG)**[26] 6473 5-9-5 **70**........(bt) RyanMoore 1 (G L Moore) *hld up in 3rd tl jnd ldr over 4f out: sustained battle whn pce lifted 3f out: gained upper hand u.p fnl f* **15/8**[1]	78
32-1	**2**	*½*	**Penton Hook**[15] 6778 3-9-5 **75**........ JimCrowley 6 (P Winkworth) *led after 3f: jnd over 4f out: disp u.p tl nt qckn fnl f* **2/1**[2]	82
2115	**3**	*1*	**Some Sunny Day**[19] 6680 3-9-4 **74**........ TravisBlock 3 (H Morrison) *led at slow pce for 3f: dropped to 3rd 1/2-way: rdn and nt qckn 2f out: styd on ins fnl f w rdr juggling whip* **10/3**[3]	79
2062	**4**	*2¾*	**Lunar River (FR)**[14] 6806 6-9-4 **69**........(t) FergusSweeney 5 (David Pinder) *stdd s: hld up in last: cl enough over 2f out: sn rdn and fnd nil* **5/1**	69

2m 9.71s (3.11) **Going Correction** +0.075s/f (Slow)
WFA 3 from 5yo+ 5lb — 4 Ran SP% **107.9**
Speed ratings (Par 103): **90,89,88,86**
toteswinger: 1&2 £2.60. CSF £5.88 TOTE £2.40; EX 6.10.
Owner T Bowley **Bred** Antonio Carlos Iguacel Et Al **Trained** Lower Beeding, W Sussex

FOCUS
They went a slow pace for much of the way in this four-runner contest and the form probably isn't worth a great deal, although the form has been rated at face value.

7135 E B F WEATHERBYS PRINTING ALL-WEATHER 20TH ANNIVERSARY MAIDEN FILLIES' STKS — 7f (P)
4:10 (4:11) (Class 5) 2-Y-0 **£4,403** (£1,310; £654; £327) **Stalls** Low

Form				RPR
	1		**Padmini** 2-9-0 0........ LDettori 9 (Saeed Bin Suroor) *w'like: str: lw: sn prom on outer: wnt 3rd over 2f out: shkn up to chse ldr 1f out: r.o to ld last 100yds* **11/10**[1]	75
40	**2**	*1½*	**Mirabella (IRE)**[20] 6628 2-9-0 0........ RichardHughes 10 (R Hannon) *unf: led at stdy pce: kicked on 2f out: rdn over 1f out: hdd and outpcd last 100yds* **9/2**[3]	71
6	**3**	*1*	**Queen's Envoy**[23] 6567 2-9-0 0........ KFallon 14 (L M Cumani) *str: t.k.h early: chsd ldr: rdn 2f out: lost 2nd and one pce 1f out* **3/1**[2]	69
0	**4**	*shd*	**Dubai Media (CAN)**[82] 4792 2-9-0 0........ NCallan 11 (D M Simcock) *w'like: str: prom: rdn on inner and effrt 2f out: pressing for pl fr over 1f out: kpt on* **9/2**[3]	68
	5	*1¼*	**Mirror Lake** 2-9-0 0........ TPQueally 13 (Mrs A J Perrett) *str: bit bkwd: s.i.s: hld up wl in rr: stl only 9th 2f out: styd on wl on outer fnl f: nrst fin* **25/1**	65
4	**6**	*1¼*	**Roxy Flyer (IRE)**[17] 6729 2-9-0 0........ JimCrowley 3 (Mrs A J Perrett) *unf: mostly in midfield: rdn to dispute 6th 2f out: styd on fnl f: n.d* **11/1**	62
	7	*1*	**Faited To Pretend (IRE)** 2-9-0 0........ HayleyTurner 6 (M L W Bell) *unf: scope: dwlt: hld up in last pair: lft bhd by ldrs over 2f out: taken to outer over 1f out: shuffled along and kpt on steadily* **40/1**	60
0	**8**	*½*	**On Khee**[21] 6617 2-9-0 0........ TravisBlock 1 (H Morrison) *leggy: nvr bttr than midfield on inner: outpcd fr over 2f out: n.d after* **66/1**	58
0	**9**	*2¼*	**Celebrian**[17] 6729 2-9-0 0........ ShaneKelly 7 (W R Swinburn) *w'like: hld up in rr: lft bhd by ldrs over 2f out: pushed along and no prog over 1f out* **100/1**	53
0	**10**	*shd*	**Sweet Clementine (IRE)**[17] 6730 2-9-0 0........ JimmyFortune 2 (W J Knight) *w'like: mostly chsd ldng pair on inner to over 2f out: wknd over 1f out* **33/1**	52
00	**11**	*2¼*	**Allannah Abu**[15] 6781 2-8-7 0........ RosieJessop(7) 4 (Sir Mark Prescott) *w'like: dwlt: a wl in rr: lft bhd by ldrs fr over 2f out* **100/1**	47
	12	*1*	**Evening Tale (IRE)** 2-9-0 0........ RyanMoore 12 (B J Meehan) *w'like: plld hrd sn after s: hld up bhd ldrs: effrt and disp 6th 2f out: wknd fnl f and heavily eased* **14/1**	44
0	**13**	*1¼*	**French Fantasy**[21] 6620 2-9-0 0........ SteveDrowne 8 (H Morrison) *plld hrd sn after s: hld up in midfield: effrt and disp 6th 2f out: sn wknd rapidly* **100/1**	41
	14	*5*	**Strait Street (IRE)** 2-9-0 0........ DaneO'Neill 5 (P Winkworth) *leggy: dwlt: a wl in rr: lft bhd fr over 2f out* **100/1**	29

1m 26.37s (1.57) **Going Correction** +0.075s/f (Slow) — **14** Ran SP% **138.7**
Speed ratings (Par 92): **94,92,91,91,89 88,87,86,83,83 81,80,78,72**
toteswinger: 1&2 £3.80, 1&3 £3.10, 2&3 £4.50. CSF £7.81 TOTE £2.50: £1.60, £2.20, £1.60; EX 15.30 Trifecta £67.70 Pool: £473.57 - 5.17 winning units. Place 6: £42.40, Place 5: £21.40..
Owner Godolphin **Bred** Darley **Trained** Newmarket, Suffolk
■ A four-timer for Frankie Dettori, taking him to 100 winners for the season.

FOCUS
The bare form of this fillies' maiden is probably just fair, but Padmini is potentially above average.

NOTEBOOK
Padmini ◆, a big filly, is bred to come into her own over 1m4f next year and, although her dam, Petrushka, has yet to produce anything of note from her three previous foals, she was a top-class filly on the racetrack, and this one holds an entry in the Derby. She's obviously an exciting prospect. (op 5-4 tchd 11-8 and 13-8 in a place and 6-4 in places)
Mirabella(IRE) disappointed over 1m around here last time, but she had previously shown ability on her debut at Kempton and this was more like it. The drop in trip and return to front-running tactics suited and she had her chance. (op 11-2)
Queen's Envoy built on the form she showed on her debut and is going the right way. An entry in the Irish 1000 Guineas suggests she's well regarded. (op 9-2)
Dubai Media(CAN), who cost $250,000 and is a half-sister to US Grade 1 winner Square Eddie, was returning from nearly three months off and she showed enough to suggest she'll find a race to boost her paddock value. (op 6-1)
Mirror Lake made a pleasing introduction. She never threatened after a slow start but finished strongly and should have learnt plenty. (op 33-1)
Roxy Flyer(IRE) failed to build on an encouraging debut. (op 12-1)
Evening Tale(IRE) Official explanation: jockey said filly hung left in straight
T/Jkpt: £1,862.00 to a £1 stake. Pool: £64,252.77. 24.50 winning tickets. T/Plt: £68.10 to a £1 stake. Pool: £68,776.72. 737.21 winning tickets. T/Qpdt: £8.10 to a £1 stake. Pool: £5,407.50. 488.90 winning tickets. JN

6998 WOLVERHAMPTON (A.W) (L-H)
Thursday, October 29

OFFICIAL GOING: Standard
Wind: Almost nil Weather: Fine

7136 TRY BETDAQ FOR AN EXCHANGE H'CAP — 5f 20y(P)
4:30 (4:30) (Class 5) (0-70,68) 3-Y-0+ **£3,238** (£963; £481; £240) **Stalls** Low

Form				RPR
3005	**1**		**Lithaam (IRE)**[14] 6791 5-9-1 **65**........(p) DavidProbert 5 (J M Bradley) *hld up in mid-div: hdwy on ins 2f out: rdn wl over 1f out: led ins fnl f: r.o wl* **9/2**	74
2042	**2**	*¾*	**Cayman Fox**[14] 6801 4-8-5 **62**........(e) MatthewLawson(7) 8 (James Moffatt) *sn led: rdn wl over 1f out: hdd ins fnl f: nt qckn* **11/4**[1]	68
500	**3**	*1½*	**Leftontheshelf (IRE)**[23] 6572 3-9-3 **67**........ StephenDonohoe 11 (Miss T Spearing) *bhd: pushed along over 2f out: rdn and hdwy over 1f out: r.o wl to take 3rd last strides* **14/1**	68
0004	**4**	*nk*	**First Order**[11] 6877 8-8-13 **68**........(v) AnnStokell(5) 2 (Miss A Stokell) *sn chsng ldr: rdn and lost 2nd 1f out: no ex and lost 3rd last strides* **7/2**[2]	68
6250	**5**	*2¼*	**Bluebok**[5] 7021 8-8-8 **61**........(bt) JackDean(3) 9 (J M Bradley) *hld up in tch: rdn wl over 1f out: one pce fnl f* **7/1**	53
0000	**6**	*2½*	**Almaty Express**[19] 6669 7-9-3 **67**........(b) LukeMorris 3 (J R Weymes) *prom: sn rdn along: wknd over 1f out* **4/1**[3]	50
5000	**7**	*2*	**The Magic Of Rio**[19] 6669 3-8-10 **60**........(b) LPKeniry 10 (Peter Grayson) *bhd: pushed along over 2f out: rdn and effrt wl over 1f out: n.d* **33/1**	36
5/00	**8**	*4*	**Tango Step (IRE)**[2] 7081 9-7-11 **54** oh9........(b) NeilFarley(7) 1 (D Carroll) *pushed along 4f out: a bhd* **16/1**	15
0000	**9**	*2¾*	**Miacarla**[28] 6410 6-7-11 **54** oh9........ JamesPSullivan(7) 7 (H A McWilliams) *led early: prom tl rdn and wknd over 2f out* **80/1**	5
0000	**10**	*3½*	**Gleaming Spirit (IRE)**[2] 7100 5-8-4 **54** oh9........(b[1]) KirstyMilczarek 4 (Peter Grayson) *s.s: a in rr* **16/1**	—

62.36 secs (0.06) **Going Correction** 0.0s/f (Stan) — **10** Ran SP% **122.2**
Speed ratings (Par 103): **99,97,95,94,91 87,84,77,73,67**
toteswinger: 1&2 £4.30, 1&3 £13.40, 2&3 £6.60. CSF £18.22 CT £169.79 TOTE £5.50: £2.30, £1.50, £4.50; EX 20.10.
Owner JMB Racing.co.uk **Bred** Shadwell Estate Company Limited **Trained** Sedbury, Gloucs

FOCUS
Fast and furious stuff here with the race being set up for a horse running close to the pace. The runner-up is a pretty sound guide to the form of this ordinary contest.

7137 WOLVERHAMPTON-RACECOURSE.CO.UK (S) STKS 1m 5f 194y(P)
5:00 (5:00) (Class 6) 3-Y-0+ **£1,942** (£578; £288; £144) **Stalls** Low

Form RPR

3556 **1** **Hucking Hero (IRE)**[16] 6758 4-9-4 63 (p) SJCraine 8 59
(J R Boyle) *hld up: stdy prog 6f out: led wl over 1f out: sn edgd lft: hrd drvn fnl f: styd on* **11/2**[3]

4400 **2** *hd* **Fantasy Ride**[9] 6917 7-8-13 47 SimonPearce(5) 7 59
(J Pearce) *s.i.s: racd keenly in rr: hdwy over 2f out: sn rdn: styd on ins fnl f* **16/1**

0153 **3** *1 3/4* **Ghufa (IRE)**[21] 6612 5-9-10 65 MickyFenton 1 63
(George Baker) *s.i.s: hld up: swtchd rt and hdwy over 1f out: sn rdn: styd on to take 3rd wl ins fnl f* **4/1**[2]

1030 **4** *3/4* **Aureate**[40] 6095 5-9-5 79 MartinLane(5) 2 62
(B Ellison) *hld up in tch: nt clr run on ins and swtchd rt over 1f out: rdn and one pce fnl f* **10/11**[1]

5 *1 3/4* **Davids City (IRE)**[433] 5-9-4 0 SilvestreDeSousa 10 53
(G A Harker) *dwlt: hld up in rr: rdn and hdwy on ins wl over 1f out: sn swtchd rt: one pce fnl f* **33/1**

6-00 **6** *shd* **K'Gari (USA)**[15] 4943 3-8-5 41 ow1 (b1) LanceBetts(5) 6 54?
(B Ellison) *set modest pce: rdn 3f out: hdd wl over 1f out: wknd ins fnl f* **66/1**

4006 **7** *10* **Nawamees (IRE)**[5] 7036 11-9-5 56 (p) RichardEvans(5) 9 45
(P D Evans) *prom tl rdn and wknd over 2f out* **14/1**

0000 **8** *1 1/4* **First Maid**[3] 7049 3-7-13 35 AmyBaker(5) 5 32
(A B Haynes) *hld up in tch: rdn and lost pl 7f out: bhd fnl 6f* **66/1**

5000 **9** *1/2* **Desert Hawk**[15] 6770 8-9-10 47 LukeMorris 3 43
(W M Brisbourne) *hld up in tch: rdn and wknd wl over 2f out* **33/1**

3334 **10** *1 3/4* **Soul Singer**[43] 5990 3-8-10 50 FrankieMcDonald 4 35
(J G Portman) *chsd ldr: pushed along and ev ch 2f out: wknd wl over 1f out* **16/1**

3m 7.59s (1.59) **Going Correction** 0.0s/f (Stan)
WFA 3 from 4yo+ 9lb **10** Ran SP% **115.1**
Speed ratings (Par 101): **95,94,93,93,92 92,86,85,85,84**
toteswinger: 1&2 £17.00, 1&3 £3.40, 2&3 £11.20. CSF £83.14 TOTE £5.70: £2.10, £3.90, £1.40; EX 90.90.There was no bid for the winner. Aureate was claimed by Brian Forsey for £6,000.
Owner M Khan X2 **Bred** Mrs A Hughes **Trained** Epsom, Surrey

FOCUS
An ordinary seller and the form is muddling.

7138 BACK & LAY AT BETDAQ H'CAP 5f 216y(P)
5:30 (5:30) (Class 6) (0-65,65) 3-Y-0+ **£2,388** (£705; £352) **Stalls** Low

Form RPR

0520 **1** **Loyal Royal (IRE)**[3] 7051 6-8-11 **60** (b) JackDean(3) 9 69
(J M Bradley) *t.k.h early in mid-div: hdwy on ins over 2f out: hrd rdn 1f out: led wl ins fnl f: r.o* **10/1**

0042 **2** *1 1/4* **Yanza**[13] 6825 3-9-2 **63** (b) RobertHavlin 1 68
(J R Gask) *sn led: rdn wl over 1f out: sn edgd lft: hdd wl ins fnl f: no ex* **16/1**

0034 **3** *nk* **Leading Edge (IRE)**[6] 6989 4-9-0 **63** MCGeran(3) 6 67
(M R Channon) *hld up and bhd: hdwy on ins wl over 1f out: rdn ins fnl f: r.o to take 3rd towards fin* **13/2**[2]

51 **4** *3/4* **Todber**[5] 7023 4-9-2 **65** (v) AndreaAtzeni(3) 2 67
(M P Tregoning) *a.p on ins: rdn and chsd ldr wl over 1f out: nt qckn and lost 2nd ins fnl f* **5/4**[1]

0001 **5** *nk* **Charles Darwin (IRE)**[48] 5836 6-9-1 **61** FrancisNorton 7 62
(M Blanshard) *hld up in mid-div: rdn over 1f out: kpt on ins fnl f* **9/1**

0300 **6** *nk* **Timber Treasure (USA)**[34] 6250 5-9-2 **62** (b) SilvestreDeSousa 12 62
(Paul Green) *hld up and bhd: pushed along over 3f out: rdn and hdwy over 1f out: nt rch ldrs* **16/1**

1160 **7** *1 1/2* **Perlachy**[217] 971 5-9-5 **65** (v) LukeMorris 8 60
(J R Holt) *led early: chsd ldr tl rdn wl over 1f out: wknd ins fnl f* **40/1**

1003 **8** *1/2* **Romantic Queen**[9] 6914 3-9-2 **63** (t) MickyFenton 10 56
(George Baker) *hld up and sn bhd: c wd st: rdn and no real prog fnl f* **20/1**

3161 **9** *1 1/4* **Mayoman (IRE)**[26] 6492 4-9-1 **61** (b) DNolan 13 50
(D Carroll) *prom tl pushed along and wknd over 1f out* **16/1**

000 **10** *1* **Weekend Away (IRE)**[13] 6825 3-8-10 **62** LeeNewnes(5) 4 48
(S Kirk) *s.i.s: a in rr* **22/1**

0400 **11** *nk* **Golden Dixie (USA)**[13] 6825 10-9-0 **60** (p) DavidProbert 3 45
(R A Harris) *hld up in tch: pushed along over 2f out: rdn and wknd wl over 1f out* **25/1**

3231 **12** *3 1/4* **Milldown Story**[31] 6344 3-9-3 **64** ChrisCatlin 5 39
(B R Millman) *a bhd* **15/2**[3]

1m 14.92s (-0.08) **Going Correction** 0.0s/f (Stan)
WFA 3 from 4yo+ 1lb **12** Ran SP% **121.7**
Speed ratings (Par 101): **100,98,97,96,96 96,94,93,91,90 90,85**
toteswinger: 1&2 £26.80, 1&3 £13.00, 2&3 £11.80. CSF £154.25 CT £1146.42 TOTE £11.90: £3.00, £5.30, £2.60; EX 180.90.
Owner JMB Racing.co.uk **Bred** J F Tuthill **Trained** Sedbury, Gloucs

FOCUS
A modest handicap best rated around the placed horses.

7139 ENJOY THE LUCKY 7 GROUP OFFER CLAIMING STKS 1m 1f 103y(P)
6:00 (6:00) (Class 6) 2-Y-O **£2,388** (£705; £352) **Stalls** Low

Form RPR

6244 **1** **Mary Helen**[57] 5573 2-8-7 55 LiamJones 13 53
(W M Brisbourne) *wnt rt s: sn swtchd lft: hld up in rr: pushed along 3f out: hdwy whn nt clr run over 2f out: n.m.r briefly wl over 1f out: rdn to ld nr fin* **11/2**[3]

0604 **2** *nk* **Alfalevva**[17] 6721 2-8-12 62 ChrisCatlin 11 57
(M R Channon) *sn chsng ldr: led wl over 1f out: sn hrd rdn: hdd nr fin* **9/1**

1550 **3** *1/2* **Underworld Dandy**[7] 6963 2-8-9 63 MartinLane(5) 10 59
(P D Evans) *a.p: pushed along over 2f out: rdn wl over 1f out: edgd lft and ev ch ins fnl f: kpt on* **9/2**[2]

0000 **4** *5* **As Brave As You (IRE)**[63] 5358 2-8-11 45 LanceBetts(5) 12 51
(B Ellison) *hld up in mid-div: pushed along and sme prog on outside over 3f out: rdn over 2f out: wknd over 1f out* **66/1**

0054 **5** *3/4* **Noverre Over There (IRE)**[12] 6858 2-8-9 62 TobyAtkinson(7) 4 50
(M E Rimmer) *hld up towards rr: pushed along over 2f out: effrt on ins whn nt clr run and swtchd rt over 1f out: nvr nr ldrs* **8/1**

000 **6** *1* **Desert Aisling (IRE)**[21] 6617 2-8-11 52 JerryO'Dwyer 5 43
(Edgar Byrne) *hld up in rr: pushed along over 2f out: c wd st: rdn wl over 1f out: sn edgd lft: n.d* **16/1**

425 **7** *hd* **Dontbugthebunny (USA)**[40] 6122 2-8-5 57 ow2 MarkCoumbe(5) 2 41
(George Baker) *hld up in tch: rdn and slt ld jst over 2f out: hdd wl over 1f out: wknd ins fnl f* **14/1**

5143 **8** *1* **Daniella De Bruijn (IRE)**[17] 6721 2-8-13 73 SebSanders 3 42
(A B Haynes) *led early: prom: pushed along over 2f out: rdn wl over 1f out: wknd ins fnl f* **5/4**[1]

0300 **9** *5* **Mary Celest (IRE)**[29] 6391 2-8-9 54 (p) StephenDonohoe 6 29
(K A Ryan) *sn led: rdn and hdd jst over 2f out: wknd wl over 1f out* **25/1**

030 **10** *7* **Press To Reset**[58] 5543 2-8-8 52 JackDean(3) 9 18
(W G M Turner) *hld up in tch: pushed along and lost pl over 3f out: sn hung rt and lost tch* **40/1**

00 **U** **Typical Female**[49] 5786 2-8-5 0 AmyBaker(5) 8 —
(A B Haynes) *hld up in rr: stmbld and uns rdr on ins bnd over 6f out* **100/1**

2m 2.70s (1.00) **Going Correction** 0.0s/f (Stan) **11** Ran SP% **120.4**
Speed ratings (Par 93): **95,94,94,89,89 88,88,87,82,76** —
toteswinger: 1&2 £10.40, 1&3 £2.80, 2&3 £7.70. CSF £54.34 TOTE £6.10: £2.10, £2.40, £1.40; EX 57.00.Mary Halen was the subject of a friendly claim.
Owner P Mort & Mark Brisbourne **Bred** World Racing Network **Trained** Great Ness, Shropshire

FOCUS
With the exception of the favourite, adjusted official ratings suggested there wasn't a lot between a number of the main contenders at the weights, and with Daniella De Bruijn running way below her best, it wasn't a surprise to see a tight finish between her main market rivals. The race was hand timed.

NOTEBOOK
Mary Helen promised to be suited by the return to claiming grade and by the step up in trip, and she was given a good ride. Clearly a filly who doesn't want to be in front for long, her challenge was timed perfectly. Her trainer expects her to get 1m4f next season. (op 13-2 tchd 7-1 and 9-2)
Alfalevva, prominent throughout, reversed Kempton form with Daniella De Bruijn over this longer trip and appears to have found her level. (tchd 10-1)
Underworld Dandy ran much better with the headgear left off and, despite his pedigree, got the trip pretty well. (op 5-1 tchd 4-1)
As Brave As You(IRE), dropped into a claimer for the first time on his return from a two-month layoff, faced a very stiff task at the weights.
Noverre Over There(IRE) Official explanation: jockey said gelding waas denied a clear run
Desert Aisling(IRE) Official explanation: jockey said filly felt short upon pulling up
Daniella De Bruijn(IRE) disappointed, largely it seemed as a result of racing keenly over this longer trip. Her rider reported that the fillly was probably over the top. (tchd 6-4)

7140 EUROPEAN BREEDERS' FUND MAIDEN FILLIES' STKS 1m 141y(P)
6:30 (6:31) (Class 5) 2-Y-O **£3,561** (£1,059; £529; £264) **Stalls** Low

Form RPR

5 **1** **Addahab (USA)**[16] 6762 2-9-0 0 (p) TedDurcan 7 64+
(Saeed Bin Suroor) *sn chsng ldr: pushed along over 3f out: rdn wl over 1f out: edgd lft ins fnl f: styd on to ld towards fin* **5/2**[2]

4000 **2** *1* **Reallymissgreeley (USA)**[56] 5611 2-9-0 54 StephenDonohoe 6 62
(K A Ryan) *s.i.s: hld up: hdwy 3f out: rdn jst over 2f out: led over 1f out: hdd towards fin* **100/1**

3 *6* **Sister Earth (IRE)** 2-9-0 0 RichardMullen 5 49
(J H M Gosden) *wnt rt and s.s: hld up in rr: pushed along 3f out: styd on to take 3rd wl ins fnl f* **9/1**

3 **4** *1 1/4* **Shaluca**[29] 6389 2-9-0 0 GrahamGibbons 4 47
(E S McMahon) *s.i.s: t.k.h: sn in tch: pushed along over 2f out: hung lft and wknd over 1f out* **3/1**[3]

62 **5** *nse* **Cojo (IRE)**[17] 6730 2-9-0 0 LiamJones 3 47
(B J Meehan) *led: rdn and hdd over 1f out: wknd ins fnl f* **9/4**[1]

0 **6** *6* **Fringe Success (IRE)**[62] 5397 2-8-11 0 Louis-PhilippeBeuzelin(3) 8 34
(Sir Michael Stoute) *prom: pushed along and lost pl over 3f out: bhd fnl 2f* **5/1**

60 **7** *1 1/2* **Nefyn**[9] 6920 2-9-0 0 PhillipMakin 2 31
(W R Muir) *prom: pushed along over 3f out: wkng whn n.m.r briefly on ins over 2f out* **33/1**

1m 50.62s (0.12) **Going Correction** 0.0s/f (Stan) **7** Ran SP% **114.9**
Speed ratings (Par 92): **99,98,92,91,91 86,84**
toteswinger: 1&2 £45.30, 1&3 £3.70, 2&3 £28.10. CSF £138.18 TOTE £3.30: £1.60, £14.40; EX 132.50.
Owner Godolphin **Bred** Stoneside Stable **Trained** Newmarket, Suffolk

FOCUS
This maiden didn't take much winning.

NOTEBOOK
Addahab(USA), representing a stable that can do little wrong at present and that boasts a 32 per cent strike-rate at this track over the last five seasons, had shown enough on her debut to suggest that she would be competitive in this company. Although once again showing signs of inexperience, she stayed on that bit stronger than the runner-up to get off the mark in the first-time cheekpieces. She has the build to make a better 3-y-o, but whether she gets the chance to race at three remains to be seen. (op 11-4 tchd 3-1)
Reallymissgreeley(USA) came into the race with a mark of 54 and, even allowing for this being a modest heat, she clearly improved significantly for the step up in trip from sprint distances.
Sister Earth(IRE) was clueless at the start, missing the break badly and giving away several lengths. Very green, she stayed on from off the pace to take an unlikely third and looks sure to benefit considerably from the outing. A daughter of Galileo out of a filly who was second in the Prix de Diane, she won't be seen at her best until she tackles middle distances next season.
Shaluca pulled hard early and paid the price for wasting her energy in the straight. (op 4-1)
Cojo(IRE) was free to post and raced keenly through the early stages of the race itself. As a result she understandably got very tired in the closing stages. Now eligible for handicaps, a return to 7f won't hurt. (op 6-4)
Fringe Success(IRE), off for two months since her debut, is well related, but she looked very slow here. (op 13-2)

7141 WOLVERHAMPTON-RACECOURSE.CO.UK H'CAP 1m 141y(P)
7:00 (7:00) (Class 4) (0-85,81) 3-Y-O **£5,046** (£1,510; £755; £377; £188) **Stalls** Low

Form RPR

6321 **1** **Espero (IRE)**[41] 6073 3-9-2 **79** GrahamGibbons 1 86
(R A Farrant) *a.p: rdn to ld over 1f out: drvn out* **5/1**[3]

4040 **2** *1/2* **Laurie Grove (IRE)**[17] 6731 3-9-3 **80** StephenDonohoe 3 86+
(T G Mills) *hld up in mid-div: stdy prog over 3f out: rdn over 1f out: r.o to take 2nd last stride* **3/1**[2]

40-0 **3** *shd* **Dream In Waiting**[19] 6680 3-8-11 **74** MartinDwyer 7 80
(B J Meehan) *hld up towards rr: hdwy over 2f out: swtchd rt over 1f out: rdn to chse wnr ins fnl f: lost 2nd last stride* **8/1**

4541 **4** *2 1/4* **Gaily Noble (IRE)**[14] 6804 3-9-3 **80** RobertHavlin 4 81
(A B Haynes) *led: rdn and hdd over 1f out: no ex wl ins fnl f* **5/1**[3]

4100 **5** 5 **Rio Cobolo (IRE)**[14] 6798 3-8-10 **73**......................(v) SilvestreDeSousa 8 62
(Paul Green) *hld up in rr: pushed along over 3f out: nvr nr ldrs* **16/1**

-000 **6** 1 ½ **Wee Giant (USA)**[6] 6996 3-8-13 **76**.......................... PaulMulrennan 5 62
(K A Ryan) *chsd ldr: rdn and ev ch wl over 2f out: lost 2nd and wknd wl over 1f out* **20/1**

1011 **7** 7 **Just Five (IRE)**[37] 6182 3-8-12 **75**.......................... PhillipMakin 6 45
(M Dods) *hld up in mid-div: carried wd by rival pulling up over 5f out: short-lived effrt on outside wl over 2f out* **8/1**

10-0 **P** **Rising Prospect**[13] 6830 3-9-4 **81**.......................... WilliamBuick 2 —
(L M Cumani) *hld up in mid-div: p.u lame over 5f out* **5/2**[1]

1m 49.6s (-0.90) **Going Correction** 0.0s/f (Stan) **8** Ran SP% **119.8**
Speed ratings (Par 103): **104,103,103,101,97 95,89,—**
toteswinger: 1&2 £5.70, 1&3 £11.50, 2&3 £8.20. CSF £21.50 CT £122.04 TOTE £6.70: £1.60, £1.50, £3.20; EX 28.00.
Owner M Sawers **Bred** Derek Christopher Shields **Trained** East Garston, Berks

FOCUS
A competitive little handicap weakened by the favourite having pulled up. The form still looks sound rated through the runner-up. The race was hand timed.

7142 BET MULTIPLES - BETDAQ H'CAP (DIV I) 1m 1f 103y(P)
7:30 (7:30) (Class 6) (0-55,60) 3-Y-O+ **£2,047** (£604; £302) **Stalls** Low

Form RPR

4006 **1** **Mystic Touch**[47] 5873 3-8-10 **50**.......................... RobertHavlin 13 59
(A B Haynes) *stdd s: sn swtchd lft: hld up in rr: nt clr run on ins over 2f out: smooth hdwy wl over 1f out: r.o to ld nr fin: pushed out* **11/1**

0000 **2** nk **Castle Myth (USA)**[52] 5730 3-8-6 **51**..........(bt) MartinLane(5) 2 59
(B Ellison) *n.m.r s: hld up towards rr: stdy prog and squeezed through over 3f out: swtchd lft wl over 1f out: sn rdn: led wl ins fnl f: hdd nr fin* **16/1**

2455 **3** 1 ¼ **Emperor's Well**[14] 6800 10-8-12 **48**.......................... PaulMulrennan 10 53
(M W Easterby) *led after 1f: rdn and hdd wl ins fnl f: nt qckn* **16/1**

0331 **4** 4 **Location**[5] 7022 3-9-1 **60** 6ex.......................... RichardEvans(5) 8 57+
(P D Evans) *hld up towards rr: hdwy on wd outside over 2f out: c wd st: rdn wl over 1f out: kpt on u.p to take 4th towards fin* **7/2**[1]

35 **5** ¾ **Persian Tomcat (IRE)**[18] 6705 3-8-10 **50**..........(v) CatherineGannon 1 45
(Miss J Feilden) *hld up in mid-div: hdwy over 6f out: rdn wl over 1f out: wknd ins fnl f* **7/1**[2]

0000 **6** nk **Duke Of Normandy (IRE)**[40] 6124 3-9-1 **55**.......... GrahamGibbons 9 50
(B P J Baugh) *prom: chsd ldr 6f out: rdn over 2f out: lost 2nd over 1f out: wknd ins fnl f* **25/1**

6000 **7** ½ **Solo Choice**[13] 6817 3-8-11 **54**..........(b) AndreaAtzeni(3) 4 48
(I W McInnes) *hld up towards rr: sme prog 3f out: rdn wl over 1f out: no imp* **25/1**

4050 **8** 4 **Join Up**[18] 6705 3-8-9 **49**.......................... LiamJones 7 34
(W M Brisbourne) *hld up towards rr: hdwy on outside over 2f out: pushed along whn n.m.r wl over 1f out: n.d after* **14/1**

5246 **9** 3 **Freda's Rose (IRE)**[26] 6488 5-9-0 **50**.......................... SJCraine 5 29
(J Mackie) *led 1f: chsd ldr to 6f out: rdn and wknd over 2f out* **12/1**

030 **10** 3 **Tar (IRE)**[30] 6358 5-9-3 **53**..........(v) ChrisCatlin 6 26
(John A Harris) *hld up in tch: pushed along over 3f out: wkng whn n.m.r jst over 2f out* **7/2**[1]

6250 **11** 10 **Libre**[36] 6208 9-8-12 **51**..........(p) FrederikTylicki(3) 11 3
(F Jordan) *hld up in tch: pushed along over 3f out: wkng whn hmpd wl over 1f out* **10/1**[3]

12 60 **Stage Dream (IRE)**[17] 6748 4-9-2 **52**.......................... SebSanders 3 —
(Lee Smyth, Ire) *hld up in tch: rdn and wkng whn hmpd on ins over 3f out: eased whn no ch over 2f out* **7/1**[2]

2m 1.40s (-0.30) **Going Correction** 0.0s/f (Stan)
WFA 3 from 4yo+ 4lb **12** Ran SP% **120.7**
Speed ratings (Par 101): **101,100,99,96,95 95,94,91,88,85 76,23**
toteswinger: 1&2 £5.70, 1&3 £11.50, 2&3 £8.20. CSF £177.68 CT £2790.61 TOTE £15.30: £3.90, £5.10, £4.80; EX 278.40.
Owner Caloona Racing **Bred** R W Huggins **Trained** Limpley Stoke, Bath

FOCUS
There was a good gallop on here and it was set up for the hold-up horses. Nevertheless, the form looks sound for the grade. The race was hand timed.
Stage Dream(IRE) Official explanation: jockey said filly moved poorly throughout

7143 BET MULTIPLES - BETDAQ H'CAP (DIV II) 1m 1f 103y(P)
8:00 (8:02) (Class 6) (0-55,55) 3-Y-O+ **£2,047** (£604; £302) **Stalls** Low

Form RPR

4004 **1** **Kristopher James (IRE)**[5] 7022 3-8-11 **52**.......................... LiamJones 3 58
(W M Brisbourne) *led: hdd over 7f out: w ldr: led over 4f out: rdn clr over 2f out: hld on ins fnl f* **8/1**

0-00 **2** hd **Marjury Daw (IRE)**[5] 7022 3-8-11 **52**.......................... J-PGuillambert 7 59+
(J G Given) *a.p: rdn wl over 1f out: wnt 2nd ins fnl f: r.o* **28/1**

-036 **3** 1 ½ **Mojeerr**[29] 6371 3-8-9 **50**..........(p) DavidProbert 5 52
(A J McCabe) *hld up in mid-div: hdwy 3f out: chsd wnr wl over 1f out: sn rdn: lost 2nd ins fnl f: kpt on same pce* **12/1**

0600 **4** 2 ¾ **Royal Keva (IRE)**[14] 6807 3-9-0 **55**.......................... SilvestreDeSousa 6 51
(A D Brown) *hld up in mid-div: hdwy 2f out: rdn over 1f out: one pce* **10/1**

6056 **5** 2 ½ **Black Stocking**[15] 6771 4-9-1 **52**.......................... MickyFenton 2 43
(Rae Guest) *hld up in tch: pushed along over 2f out: swtchd rt over 1f out: edgd lft ins fnl f: no imp* **20/1**

455 **6** ½ **Casablanca Minx (IRE)**[77] 4927 6-8-3 **47**..........(v) DavidKenny(7) 4 37
(A G Juckes) *hld up towards rr: rdn over 2f out: hdwy on ins wl over 1f out: sn no imp* **16/1**

5043 **7** 2 ¾ **Strike Force**[6] 6998 5-9-2 **53**..........(p) TomEaves 11 37
(Miss J Feilden) *hld up towards rr: sme prog over 3f out: rdn and wknd 2f out* **3/1**[1]

00-3 **8** 2 **Bourn Fair**[13] 6831 3-8-13 **54**.......................... ChrisCatlin 13 34
(P J McBride) *hld up in rr: swtchd lft sn after s: pushed along over 2f out: no ch whn rdn jst over 1f out* **15/2**[3]

3550 **9** 14 **Peintre D'Argent (IRE)**[27] 6446 3-9-0 **55**.......... RichardKingscote 12 6
(Tom Dascombe) *prom: rdn over 2f out: wknd wl over 1f out* **8/1**

540 **10** 18 **Womaniser (IRE)**[12] 6860 5-9-3 **54**.......................... PaulDoe 10 —
(T Keddy) *s.i.s: in rr: pushed along over 7f out: short-lived effrt on outside 3f out* **12/1**

0004 **11** 2 **Rockabout (IRE)**[27] 6440 3-8-9 **50**..........(b) MartinDwyer 1 —
(B J Meehan) *w ldr: led over 7f out tl over 4f out: pushed along and wknd over 3f out* **8/1**

12 ½ **Little Opera (IRE)**[77] 4968 3-8-7 **48**..........(t) JerryO'Dwyer 9 —
(Aidan Anthony Howard, Ire) *a towards rr* **50/1**

13 3 ¾ **By The Sea (IRE)**[34] 6262 4-8-5 **47**.......................... MartinLane(5) 8 —+
(M P Sunderland, Ire) *half-rrd s: sn mid-div: hdwy over 5f out: chsd wnr over 3f out tl wl over 1f out: sn wknd and eased* **11/2**[2]

2m 1.85s (0.15) **Going Correction** 0.0s/f (Stan)
WFA 3 from 4yo+ 4lb **13** Ran SP% **126.0**
Speed ratings (Par 101): **99,98,97,95,92 92,89,88,75,59 57,57,54**
toteswinger: 1&2 £88.20, 1&3 £23.10, 2&3 £105.90. CSF £226.38 CT £2698.06 TOTE £10.30: £2.90, £7.10, £4.80; EX 270.00 Place 6: £293.04, Place 5: £139.53..
Owner Stephen Jones **Bred** County Down Bloodstock **Trained** Great Ness, Shropshire

FOCUS
The slower of the two divisions by 0.65sec and trhe form of this handicap looks weak and slightly muddling, with the winner probably the best guide.
By The Sea(IRE) Official explanation: jockey said filly lost its action
T/Plt: £475.70 to a £1 stake. Pool: £67,386.31. 103.40 winning tickets. T/Qpdt: £106.60 to a £1 stake. Pool: £9,765.50. 67.78 winning tickets. KH

6848 NEWMARKET (R-H)
Friday, October 30

OFFICIAL GOING: Good (7.7)
Far side course used.
Wind: Fresh, against Weather: Bright

7145 E B F PRESTIGE VEHICLES MAIDEN STKS 6f
12:40 (12:42) (Class 4) 2-Y-O **£5,180** (£1,541; £770; £384) **Stalls** High

Form RPR

1 **Asraab (IRE)** 2-9-3 0.......................... LDettori 11 82+
(Saeed Bin Suroor) *str: scope: lw: racd in far side gp: hld up in tch: chsd ldrs whn gp merged over 1f out: rdn to ld jst ins fnl f: eased nr fin* **6/4**[1]

5 **2** hd **Illustrious Prince (IRE)**[21] 6627 2-9-3 0.......................... RyanMoore 3 81
(J Noseda) *on toes: racd in centre gp: chsd ldrs: rdn to ld overall 2f out: hdd jst ins fnl f: kpt on gamely but a hld by wnr* **9/1**

3 ¾ **Hajjaan (USA)** 2-9-3 0.......................... TedDurcan 12 79+
(J L Dunlop) *w'like: bit bkwd: racd in far side gp: dwlt: hld up in rr: hdwy 2f out: chsd ldrs whn gp merged over 1f out: kpt on same pce ins fnl f* **16/1**

4 1 ¼ **Mawzoon (IRE)** 2-9-3 0.......................... RHills 2 75+
(M A Jarvis) *unf: racd in centre gp: chsd ldrs: rdn and ev ch wl over 1f out: no ex ins fnl f* **9/2**[2]

64 **5** 2 ¼ **Beaumont's Party (IRE)**[21] 6627 2-9-3 0.......................... RichardHughes 6 69
(R Hannon) *racd in centre gp: led that gp tl hdd 2f out: sn rdn: kpt on same pce whn gps merged fr over 1f out* **9/1**

0 **6** shd **Gojeri (IRE)**[15] 6796 2-9-3 0.......................... NCallan 7 68
(M A Jarvis) *w'like: str: bit bkwd: racd in centre gp: chsd ldr tl 2f out: rdn and unable qck whn gps merged over 1f out: plugged on same pce fnl f* **100/1**

423 **7** nk **Ghazwah**[77] 4980 2-8-12 75.......................... TPO'Shea 15 62
(J H M Gosden) *racd in far side gp: chsd ldr tl over 1f out: rdn and nt pce of ldrs whn gps merged over 1f out* **8/1**[3]

43 **8** 2 **Imperial Delight**[18] 6737 2-9-3 0.......................... DaneO'Neill 10 61
(H Candy) *w'like: athletic: racd in far side gp: led that gp: rdn and chsng overall ldng pair whn gp merged over 1f out: wknd fnl f* **12/1**

0 **9** 2 ¼ **State Gathering**[22] 6615 2-9-3 0.......................... FergusSweeney 16 55
(H Candy) *racd in far side gp: chsd ldrs: rdn and struggling ent fnl 2f: n.d after gps merged over 1f out* **33/1**

0 **10** 2 ¼ **Decency (IRE)**[80] 4869 2-8-12 0.......................... KFallon 9 43
(E A L Dunlop) *leggy; scope: racd in far side gp: hld up in tch tl wknd ent fnl 2f: wl btn whn gps merged over 1f out: eased ins fnl f* **33/1**

0 **11** 1 ½ **Billie Jean**[176] 1810 2-8-12 0.......................... MichaelHills 8 38
(B W Hills) *w'like: leggy: racd in centre gp: dwlt: a towards rr: struggling over 2f out: wl btn whn gps merged over 1f out* **50/1**

03 **12** nse **May Chorus (IRE)**[9] 6942 2-8-12 0.......................... SJCraine 4 38
(J R Boyle) *w'like: racd in centre gp: a in rr of that gp: wknd qckly 2f out: bhd whn gps merged over 1f out* **66/1**

13 1 ¼ **Compton Way** 2-9-3 0.......................... RobertWinston 13 40
(B W Hills) *w'like: bit bkwd: racd in far side gp: s.i.s: a towards rr: lost tch over 2f out: wl bhd whn gps merged over 1f out* **50/1**

14 10 **Hallucinating** 2-9-3 0.......................... FrankieMcDonald 5 10+
(H Candy) *cmpt: bit bkwd: racd in centre gp: a bhd: lost tch qckly over 2f out: t.o and eased ins fnl f* **100/1**

15 ¾ **Tell Halaf** 2-9-3 0.......................... HayleyTurner 14 7
(M L W Bell) *unf: scope: racd in far side gp: a bhd: t.o whn gps merged over 1f out* **50/1**

16 2 ¾ **Brody's Boy** 2-9-3 0.......................... GeorgeBaker 1 —
(G L Moore) *unf: bit bkwd: racd in centre gp: a bhd: lost tch over 2f out: t.o whn gps merged over 1f out* **150/1**

1m 14.15s (1.95) **Going Correction** +0.425s/f (Yiel) **16** Ran SP% **118.8**
Speed ratings (Par 97): **104,103,102,101,98 97,97,94,91,88 86,86,85,71,70 67**
toteswinger: 1&2 £7.10, 1&3 £11.30, 2&3 £20.40. CSF £14.53 TOTE £2.50: £1.30, £3.40, £4.60; EX 19.90.
Owner Godolphin **Bred** Mountarmstrong Stud **Trained** Newmarket, Suffolk

FOCUS
This maiden, run in a time only 0.14 seconds slower than Queen's Grace (carried 8st12lb) recorded in the later juvenile fillies' Listed race, should produce a host of winners. The field split into two groups early on but were spread out across the track in the closing stages and there was no obvious bias.

NOTEBOOK
Asraab(IRE), a 220,000euros first foal of a 5f juvenile winner, won a shade cosily on debut. Always travelling nicely towards the far side, he picked up well for pressure before being eased in the final strides. He has some size about him and should make a nice 3-y-o, probably over sprint trips. He'll winter in Dubai, but it remains to be seen whether he'll race out there. (tchd 7-4)
Illustrious Prince(IRE), who offered encouragement on his debut over 7f on Polytrack, built on that effort with a good run in defeat. Having been well placed up the centre, he kept on strongly for pressure, but was always just held. He ought to win a maiden before going handicapping and should be versatile with regards trip. (op 14-1)
Hajjaan(USA) ◆, a $400,000 half-brother to a number of winners in the US, including high-class dirt miler High Strike Zone, fared best of Hamdan Al Maktoum's trio, despite looking the third string on jockey bookings and sporting the pink cap. This was a pleasing debut, as he showed his inexperience with a slow start and raced off the pace, before finishing very nicely. There should be a lot better to come, and his breeding suggests he'll really come into his own on an artificial surface. (op 25-1)
Mawzoon(IRE) ◆ is evidently well regarded - Richard Hills's choice of the owner's three runners and entered in the Irish 2,000 Guineas - and this was a pleasing start. A 200,000gns half-brother to Group 1 winner Red Clubs, he's obviously bred to be pretty good and is one to keep on side.

Beaumont's Party(IRE) ◆ was not given a hard time once held and may do better now handicaps are an option. His optimum trip remains unclear, and his pedigree is a mix of speed and stamina, but he'll probably want further. (op 12-1 tchd 17-2)
Gojeri(IRE), reported to have been unsuited by soft ground on debut, ran an improved race.
Ghazwah, the owner's second string, fared best of the four fillies after 77 days off but was still well held. She's not progressing. (op 6-1)
Imperial Delight ◆ was not given a hard ride once his chance had passed and might do better now he can switch to handicaps. (op 14-1)
State Gathering ◆, who was always held, was another not knocked about. He needs one more run for a mark.
Decency(IRE) seemed to travel well towards the outer of the far-side group but she was quickly beaten once coming under pressure, running as though in need of this first start for 80 days. (op 25-1)
Billie Jean, representing a trainer who has won this maiden four times since 2002, was keen to post and never seen with a chance after a slow start. (tchd 66-1)

7146 E B F CLIFF LINES 60 YEARS IN RACING MAIDEN STKS (C&G) 7f
1:15 (1:16) (Class 4) 2-Y-O £5,180 (£1,541; £770; £384) Stalls High

Form RPR
52 **1** **Quick Wit**[7] 6990 2-9-0 0 ... LDettori 17 80
(Saeed Bin Suroor) *lw: racd in far side gp: mde all: rdn and clr overall ldr whn gps merged over 1f out: styd on wl* **10/11**[1]
2 **2** 1 ½ **Youm Jamil (USA)**[30] 6393 2-9-0 0 ... KFallon 4 76
(B J Meehan) *lw: racd in centre gp: in tch: chsd ldng pair whn gps merged over 1f out: chsd wnr ins fnl f: edgd rt u.p: r.o wl but unable to chal wnr* **4/1**[2]
3 1 **Man Of Action (USA)** 2-9-0 0 ... JimmyFortune 10 74
(J H M Gosden) *w'like: scope: racd in centre gp: dwlt: sn rcvrd to chsd ldr of that gp: chsd wnr 2f out: no imp and lost 2nd ins fnl f: kpt on same pce* **15/2**[3]
4 1 ¾ **King's Warrior (FR)** 2-9-0 0 ... RyanMoore 5 69
(G L Moore) *str: lw: racd in centre gp: in tch: chsd ldng trio and outpcd whn gps merged over 1f out: kpt on same pce after* **16/1**
5 nk **Huff And Puff** 2-9-0 0 ... PaulHanagan 7 69
(Mrs A J Perrett) *lengthy: scope: athletic: racd in centre gp: bhd and sn pushed along: hdwy and hanging rt whn gps merged over 1f out: kpt on wl but nvr able to chal* **50/1**
6 1 **Blitzed** 2-9-0 0 ... TPQueally 2 66
(G L Moore) *unf: racd in centre gp: s.i.s: racd in midfield: rdn and unable qck ent fnl 2f: midfield and btn whn gps merged over 1f out: styd on steadily ins fnl f: nt pce to trble ldrs* **125/1**
55 **7** 1 **Kajima**[50] 5786 2-9-0 0 ... RichardHughes 6 64
(R Hannon) *racd in centre gp: plld hrd: hld up in tch: rdn and unable qck 2f out: plugged on same pce whn gps merged over 1f out* **16/1**
8 hd **Brigadoon** 2-9-0 0 ... AlanMunro 9 63
(W Jarvis) *w'like: green: racd in centre gp: led that gp tl 2f out: sn rdn and rn green whn gps merged over 1f out: kpt on again ins fnl f* **100/1**
9 nk **Kakatosi** 2-9-0 0 ... WilliamBuick 12 62
(A M Balding) *w'like: bit bkwd: racd in centre gp: bdly hmpd s: pushed along and swtchd lft ent fnl 2f: no ch whn gps merged and rn green over 1f out: kpt on but nvr trbld ldrs* **66/1**
00 **10** ½ **Trovare (USA)**[22] 6617 2-9-0 0 ... JimCrowley 15 61
(Mrs A J Perrett) *racd in far side gp: chsd wnr tl over 2f out: sn struggling u.p: btn whn gps merged over 1f out: sltly short of room 1f out* **100/1**
11 hd **Awsaal** 2-9-0 0 ... RHills 14 61
(J L Dunlop) *w'like: scope: str: racd in far side gp: in tch: rdn and unable qck ent fnl 2f: one pce whn gps merged over 1f out: btn whn sltly hmpd 1f out* **14/1**
12 ½ **Pittodrie Star (IRE)** 2-9-0 0 ... DavidProbert 18 59
(A M Balding) *w'like: bit bkwd: racd in far side gp: hld up in tch towards rr: rdn and effrt 2f out: edgd lft whn gps merged over 1f out: kpt on same pce after* **66/1**
13 ½ **Uphold** 2-9-0 0 ... MichaelHills 13 58
(B W Hills) *w'like: scope: str: bit bkwd: :racd in centre gp: in tch: rdn and unable qck ent fnl 2f: btn whn gps merged over 1f out: sltly hmpd 1f out* **14/1**
14 nse **Battle Honour** 2-9-0 0 ... DaneO'Neill 1 58
(H Candy) *w'like: bit bkwd: racd in centre gp: in tch tl rdn and unable qck ent fnl 2f: no threat to ldrs whn gps merged over 1f out* **50/1**
0 **15** 4 **Micky P**[18] 6737 2-8-11 0 ... WilliamCarson(3) 19 48
(S C Williams) *w'like: bit bkwd: racd in far side gp: s.i.s: a bhd: struggling over 2f out: no ch whn gps merged over 1f out* **100/1**
0 **16** nk **Vumbura (IRE)**[7] 6990 2-9-0 0 ... ShaneKelly 16 47
(W J Knight) *racd in far side gp: chsd ldrs tl rdn to chse wnr over 2f out: sn struggling: wknd and wl hld whn gps merged over 1f out* **100/1**
17 3 **Beauchamp Yeoman** 2-9-0 0 ... FergusSweeney 3 40
(H Candy) *w'like: bit bkwd: racd in centre gp: in tch in midfield tl wknd and hung lft fnl 2f: no ch whn gps merged over 1f out* **100/1**
30 **18** 19 **Scarboro Warning (IRE)**[35] 6254 2-9-0 0 ... LeeVickers 11 —
(J G Given) *racd in centre: awkward and hmpd rival s: plld hrd: hld up in tch tl wknd qckly over 2f out: wl bhd whn gps merged over 1f out: eased ins fnl f: t.o* **66/1**

1m 28.71s (3.31) **Going Correction** +0.425s/f (Yiel) **18** Ran SP% **123.4**
Speed ratings (Par 97): **98,96,95,93,92 91,90,90,89,89 89,88,88,87,83 83,79,57**
toteswinger: 1&2 £3.00, 1&3 £4.60, 2&3 £7.00. CSF £4.21 TOTE £1.90: £1.20, £1.80, £2.70; EX 5.40.
Owner Godolphin **Bred** Ptarmigan Bloodstock Limited **Trained** Newmarket, Suffolk

FOCUS
Some smart types have won this maiden over the last decade, most notably Spanish Moon in 2006, but the bare form of this year's race looks useful at best. They split into two groups through the early stages, with the majority racing up the centre and only six towards the far side, but again, there was no apparent track bias.

NOTEBOOK
Quick Wit ◆ confirmed the promise of his recent second at Doncaster and probably did well to win this as, having led the far-side group, he was out on his own for a long time, with his main rivals racing more towards the centre. He could be quite useful at around this trip next year and will now go to Dubai, although like his stablemate who won the first, it's unclear whether he'll race out there. Incidentally, this was a seventh consecutive winner for his trainer. (op 6-5 tchd 5-4 in places)
Youm Jamil(USA), runner-up on debut over 1m, fared best of those who raced up the centre but could never quite get to the winner. He should win a maiden before making a useful handicapper. (op 3-1 tchd 11-4)
Man Of Action(USA) ◆ is one to take from the race. He looked very green on his way to the start, and reared slightly in the stalls before the off, but he showed a deal of ability in the race itself. There should be significant improvement to come from this $225,000 purchase, who is a half-brother to, among others, very useful US prolific-winning dirt sprinter Joe Six Pack. (op 10-1 tchd 12-1)
King's Warrior(FR) ◆, out of a winner in France, lacked the pace of the front three in the closing stages but this was still a pleasing debut. He displayed a long stride and looks a nice type. (op 20-1)
Huff And Puff, keen to post, did well to finish so close as he raced out the back after starting slowly and being bumped on leaving the stalls, and then didn't enjoy the clearest of runs. Official explanation: jockey said colt hung right (op 66-1 tchd 40-1)
Blitzed, a stablemate of the fourth, is already gelded, and was dismissed in the betting, but he showed ability. He might be one for handicaps over a little further in time. (op 100-1)
Kajima was much too keen on his return from nearly two months off, and although handicaps are now an option, he'll need to learn to settle if he's to progress. Official explanation: jockey said colt ran too free (op 12-1)
Brigadoon was keen to post and led the group up the centre before weakening. This might take the freshness out of him, but his pedigree is a real mix of speed and stamina and it's hard to know what trip he'll want.
Kakatosi ◆ was squeezed out at the start and ran green. He has quite a speedy pedigree and can do a lot better.
Trovare(USA) ◆ was unsuited by the drop in trip. He's one to keep in mind for 3-y-o handicaps.
Uphold ◆ was said to have been struck into, so he could do a lot better. Official explanation: jockey said colt was struck into (op 16-1)
Beauchamp Yeoman Official explanation: jockey said colt hung left

7147 E B F IGLOOS BOSRA SHAM FILLIES' STKS (LISTED RACE) 6f
1:50 (1:50) (Class 1) 2-Y-O
£17,031 (£6,456; £3,231; £1,611; £807; £405) Stalls High

Form RPR
013 **1** **Queen's Grace**[57] 5606 2-8-12 98 ... SteveDrowne 6 102
(H Morrison) *swtg: mde all: rdn jst over 1f out: hrd pressed ent fnl f: r.o gamely to assert fnl 100yds* **16/1**
1424 **2** 1 **Puff (IRE)**[28] 6449 2-8-12 108 ... JimCrowley 3 99
(R M Beckett) *hld up in tch towards rr: hdwy to chse ldrs 1/2-way: rdn to chal ent fnl f: ev ch tl no ex u.p fnl 100yds* **13/8**[1]
221 **3** hd **Tomintoul Singer (IRE)**[113] 3772 2-8-12 84 ... TPQueally 2 98
(H R A Cecil) *lw: hld up in tch in rr: gd hdwy on outer 2f out: chal and rdn 1f out: unable qck and btn fnl 100yds* **12/1**
155 **4** 1 ½ **Conniption (IRE)**[41] 6090 2-8-12 95 ... LDettori 4 94
(B J Meehan) *dwlt: hld up in last pair: hdwy and looking for a run 2f out: swtchd rt and qcknd between horses jst over 1f out: chsd ldng trio fnl f: no imp* **4/1**[2]
1 **5** 1 ¾ **Amitola (IRE)**[29] 6408 2-8-12 0 ... PhillipMakin 9 89
(T D Barron) *w'like: tall: chsd ldng pair: rdn ent fnl 2f: outpcd by ldng trio jst over 1f out: plugged on same pce fnl f* **9/2**[3]
6520 **6** nse **Roodle**[27] 6486 2-8-12 90 ... WilliamBuick 10 89+
(Eve Johnson Houghton) *stdd s: hld up in tch in rr: effrt and nt clr run 2f out: swtchd rt and hdwy jst over 1f out: edgd lft and no real imp ins fnl f* **40/1**
31 **7** ¾ **Coin From Heaven (IRE)**[14] 6820 2-8-12 82 ... PaulHanagan 5 86
(R A Fahey) *w'like: lw: in tch: rdn and unable qck ent fnl 2f: plugged on again u.p fnl f* **33/1**
1250 **8** 1 ½ **Jeanie Johnston (IRE)**[41] 6090 2-8-12 95 ... AndrewElliott 8 82
(A P Jarvis) *chsd ldr: rdn jst over 2f out: lost 2nd wl over 1f out: wknd ent fnl f* **25/1**
2114 **9** 2 ¾ **Seeking Dubai**[35] 6326 2-8-12 95 ... RyanMoore 7 74
(E F Vaughan) *t.k.h: in tch: rdn and unable qck over 2f out: sn struggling: n.d fnl f* **16/1**
10 6 **Manx Miss (USA)**[21] 6650 2-8-12 0 ... KFallon 1 56
(David P Myerscough, Ire) *s.i.s: grad crossed to r on far rail: niggled along 1/2-way: rdn and btn 2f out: wl bhd fnl f* **14/1**
2126 **11** nk **Skylla**[42] 6049 2-8-12 94 ... JerryO'Dwyer 12 55
(J R Holt) *dwlt: sn in tch in midfield: rdn and lost pl qckly over 2f out: wl bhd fnl f* **20/1**
032 **12** ¾ **Chaussini**[14] 6809 2-8-12 79 ... JimmyFortune 11 52
(J A R Toller) *in tch: rdn jst over 2f out: sn struggling: wl btn over 1f out: eased ins fnl f: fin lame* **28/1**

1m 14.01s (1.81) **Going Correction** +0.425s/f (Yiel) **12** Ran SP% **119.8**
Speed ratings (Par 100): **104,102,102,100,98 98,97,95,91,83 82,81**
toteswinger: 1&2 £6.30, 1&3 £10.00, 2&3 £5.60. CSF £40.51 TOTE £16.90: £2.60, £1.40, £2.90; EX 42.90.
Owner Miss B Swire **Bred** Miss B Swire **Trained** East Ilsley, Berks

FOCUS
The 84-rated third is clearly much better than her official mark suggests and this looked a reasonable enough fillies' Listed race.

NOTEBOOK
Queen's Grace apparently returned with a bit of a cough after her third in a Listed race at Salisbury and this was a fine effort after 57 days off. She came under pressure sooner than the runner-up and third-placed finisher but displayed a really likeable attitude to prevail. She is apparently likely to be given an entry in the 1,000 Guineas, but while it's not out the question she could progress into a very smart filly, she's not that big and there would have to be real doubts about her stamina for a strongly run 1m. (op 14-1 tchd 12-1)
Puff(IRE), fourth in the Cheveley Park on her previous start, seemed to run her race and gives the form a solid look. She again displayed a lot of speed, though, travelling well for a long way, and once more gave the impression she may prove best over the minimum trip. (op 6-4)
Tomintoul Singer(IRE) had been off for nearly four months, so might not have been at peak fitness, but she's looked all speed from day one and didn't get home this time after travelling best of all. This was still an excellent effort, and she'll do better again when dropped back to 5f. (tchd 11-1)
Conniption(IRE) looked unlucky not to finish closer as she got too far back after missing the break. She travelled well, but got going too late to challenge. She can do better. (op 9-2 tchd 5-1)
Amitola(IRE), who produced a useful performance to win over this trip on her debut at Ayr, found this tougher and still looked green. (op 6-1)
Roodle was denied a clear run at a crucial stage and was unlucky not to finish closer. (op 33-1)
Coin From Heaven(IRE) found this tougher than the Redcar maiden she won on her previous start.
Manx Miss(USA) missed the break and then didn't have much room after being switched all the way from stall one to the far rail. (op 16-1 tchd 20-1 in places)
Chaussini Official explanation: vet said filly finished lame

7148 E B F IGLOOS FILLIES' H'CAP 1m 4f
2:25 (2:26) (Class 3) (0-90,87) 3-Y-O+
£8,723 (£2,612; £1,306; £653; £326; £163) Stalls Centre

Form RPR
0125 **1** **Teeky**[55] 5666 3-8-12 76 ... JimmyFortune 4 85
(J H M Gosden) *lw: chsd clr ldr: clsd and rdn over 2f out: drvn to ld ent fnl f: styd on strly and drew clr* **9/2**[2]

0314 **2** *3* **Featherweight (IRE)**[18] 6733 3-9-3 **81** .... MichaelHills 3 85
(B W Hills) *b: stdd and dropped in bhd after s: nt clr run ent fnl 2f: swtchd rt and rdn over 1f out: styd on steadily to go 2nd nr fin: nvr able to chal wnr* **7/1**[3]

0313 **3** *½* **Fanditha (IRE)**[22] 6618 3-9-8 **86** .... RichardHughes 5 89
(R Hannon) *hld up in tch in midfield: hdwy to chse ldrs 2f out: rdn to chse wnr jst ins fnl f: sn edging rt and no imp* **8/1**

4620 **4** *nk* **Presbyterian Nun (IRE)**[22] 6618 4-9-11 **82** ....(b[1]) RyanMoore 6 85
(J L Dunlop) *lw: t.k.h: hld up in rr: hdwy 3f out: chsd ldrs and drvn over 1f out: racd awkwardly and hanging rt ent fnl f: no imp after* **8/1**

6112 **5** *2 ¾* **Qelaan (USA)**[29] 6419 3-9-7 **85** .... RHills 8 83
(M P Tregoning) *on toes: racd keenly: led and sn clr: rdn over 1f out: hdd ent fnl f: wknd qckly ins fnl f* **9/4**[1]

3303 **6** *2 ¼* **Zaaqya**[20] 6681 3-9-9 **87** .... TPO'Shea 2 82
(J L Dunlop) *on toes: t.k.h: chsd ldrs after 1f: rdn wl over 2f out: hanging rt u.p and wknd over 1f out* **7/1**[3]

6662 **7** *1* **Dolly Penrose**[25] 6536 4-9-11 **82** ....(v) WilliamBuick 1 75
(M R Channon) *swtg: stdd and dropped in bhd after s: hld up in rr: effrt and rdn over 2f out: sn hanging rt and no prog: wl btn fnl f* **20/1**

3400 **8** *nk* **Hollow Green (IRE)**[7] 6996 3-9-4 **82** .... GeorgeBaker 7 75
(P D Evans) *b: stdd s: hld up in rr: effrt and rdn over 2f out: swtchd rt and no prog over 1f out* **20/1**

-231 **9** *5* **Finney Hill**[9] 6934 4-9-10 **81** 6ex .... DaneO'Neill 9 66
(H Candy) *in tch: clsd and chsd ldrs 3f out: wknd u.p 2f out: wl bhd fnl f* **9/1**

2m 38.39s (4.89) **Going Correction** +0.425s/f (Yiel)
WFA 3 from 4yo 7lb **9** Ran SP% **115.7**
Speed ratings (Par 104): **100,98,97,97,95 94,93,93,89**
toteswinger: 1&2 £7.10, 1&3 £5.60, 2&3 £10.40. CSF £36.02 CT £240.64 TOTE £5.20: £1.60, £2.80, £2.60; EX 36.30.

Owner George Strawbridge **Bred** George Strawbridge **Trained** Newmarket, Suffolk

FOCUS

A reasonable fillies' handicap, but the pace was steady. The winner did not need to improve to score with the form rated around the placed horses.

NOTEBOOK

Teeky returned from a near two-month break with a convincing performance and has now won her last two starts on turf. Having been well placed throughout, she displayed plenty of speed to pick up off the modest tempo and she was clearly suited by the drop back from 2m. This half-sister to Sleeping Indian is now likely to be aimed at a Listed race at Fontainebleau before being retired. (op 7-2 tchd 100-30)

Featherweight(IRE), trying 1m4f for the first time, was seemingly ridden to get the trip, but as a result she was poorly placed considering the slow gallop. Although finally running on to take second, she was never seen with a winning chance. (op 8-1 tchd 17-2, 9-1 in places)

Fanditha(IRE), another racing over the longest trip she has tackled to date, was given a patient ride but didn't really pick up and failed to prove her stamina. A career-high mark didn't help matters. (op 9-1)

Presbyterian Nun(IRE), with blinkers replacing cheekpieces, raced keenly before failing to respond to pressure and, not for the first time, she looked ungenuine. There's a lot of speed in her pedigree (half-sister to 7f specialist Jedburgh, out of a 5f winner) and perhaps a significant drop in trip is worth a shot. Official explanation: jockey said filly hung both ways (op 17-2)

Qelaan(USA) was unchallenged in front, but she still refused to settle and that cost her any chance. (op 5-2 tchd 3-1)

Zaaqya was too keen. (op 8-1 tchd 17-2)

Dolly Penrose lacked the pace of some of these and needs a long trip and easier ground. (op 16-1)

7149 BETFAIR APPRENTICE TRAINING SERIES FINAL (H'CAP) 1m

3:00 (3:00) (Class 5) (0-75,74) 3-Y-O **£6,476** (£1,927; £963; £481) **Stalls High**

Form RPR

0353 **1** **Day Of The Eagle (IRE)**[22] 6621 3-8-12 **72** .... RyanPowell(5) 11 82+
(L M Cumani) *hld up wl in tch: chsd ldr over 2f out: rdn to ld over 1f out: hung bdly lft after and ended up racing on stands' rail: pushed along and a holding rivals fnl f* **3/1**[1]

0504 **2** *¾* **El Libertador (USA)**[11] 6908 3-8-9 **67** .... KierenFox(3) 8 72
(E A Wheeler) *lw: t.k.h: chsd ldrs: led over 2f out: hdd but clr w wnr over 1f out: kpt on but a hld fnl f* **8/1**

1030 **3** *¾* **Harriet's Girl**[2] 7125 3-9-5 **74** .... JamesPSullivan 6 77
(A P Jarvis) *stdd s: hld up in rr: hdwy and edging rt ent fnl 2f: chsd ldng pair over 1f out: kpt on fnl f but unable to chal ldng pair* **14/1**

0310 **4** *2 ¾* **Kiss A Prince**[58] 5575 3-9-4 **73** .... RosieJessop 7 70
(D K Ivory) *hld up in tch in midfield: pushed along 3f out: sn outpcd and rdn: edging lft fr over 1f out: styd on fnl f but nvr gng pce to rch ldrs* **22/1**

1020 **5** *3 ¼* **Flapper (IRE)**[33] 6311 3-9-1 **73** .... AmyScott(3) 4 62
(J W Hills) *led tl hdd and rdn over 2f out: wl outpcd by ldng pair 2f out: wl btn over 1f out* **10/1**

3400 **6** *4* **Moon Lightning (IRE)**[39] 6157 3-8-10 **65** .... AshleyMorgan 3 45
(M H Tompkins) *t.k.h: hld up in tch: rdn and hanging rt over 2f out: no ch w ldrs fnl 2f* **7/1**[3]

1005 **7** *nk* **Wood Fairy**[37] 6218 3-8-5 **65** .... LeeTopliss(5) 10 45
(R A Fahey) *lw: t.k.h: chsd ldrs tl lost pl qckly whn rdn over 2f out: no ch fnl 2f* **13/2**[2]

1630 **8** *1 ½* **Darcey**[6] 7027 3-9-1 **73** .... LauraPike(3) 5 49
(Miss Amy Weaver) *restless in stalls: dwlt: sn rcvrd and chsng ldr: lost 2nd 3f out: sn struggling and wl btn fnl 2f* **8/1**

230 **9** *10* **Atacama Sunrise**[50] 5791 3-8-9 **64** .... SimonPearce 1 17
(J Pearce) *a bhd: lost tch over 3f out* **20/1**

0351 **10** *½* **Markhesa**[17] 6755 3-8-3 **63** .... NathanAlison(5) 2 15
(J R Boyle) *in tch tl lost pl qckly 4f out: wl bhd fnl 3f* **7/1**[3]

-420 **11** *4* **In The Mood (IRE)**[16] 6778 3-8-11 **66** .... PaulPickard 9 9
(W Jarvis) *s.i.s: hdwy into midfield after 2f: rdn and wknd qckly wl over 2f out: sn wl bhd* **16/1**

1m 42.35s (3.75) **Going Correction** +0.425s/f (Yiel) **11** Ran SP% **116.3**
Speed ratings (Par 101): **98,97,96,93,90 86,86,84,74,74 70**
toteswinger: 1&2 £8.70, 1&3 £5.80, 2&3 £20.40. CSF £26.55 CT £296.45 TOTE £3.30: £1.90, £2.70, £3.30; EX 33.90.

Owner Chris Wright & Andy MacDonald **Bred** Swersky & Associates **Trained** Newmarket, Suffolk

FOCUS

A modest apprentice handicap and the form looks straightforward rated around the placed horses..

In The Mood(IRE) Official explanation: jockey said filly ran flat

7150 NGK SPARK PLUGS CONDITIONS STKS (RUN IN MEMORY OF REG DAY) 6f

3:35 (3:36) (Class 3) 2-3-Y-O

£7,477 (£2,239; £1,119; £560; £279; £140) **Stalls High**

Form RPR

031 **1** **Rum King (USA)**[29] 6424 2-8-7 80 ow1 .... RichardHughes 5 92
(R Hannon) *chsd ldr for 2f: styd chsng ldrs: swtchd rt and rdn jst over 1f out: led ins fnl f: r.o wl: edgd lft towards fin* **9/1**

0405 **2** *hd* **Marine Boy (IRE)**[14] 6815 3-9-11 100 .... RichardKingscote 1 95
(Tom Dascombe) *racd alone towards centre: prom: hung rt u.p and jnd remainder over 1f out: kpt on wl u.p to press wnr fnl 50yds: hld towards fin* **17/2**

4-66 **3** *1 ¼* **Himalya (IRE)**[29] 6427 3-9-11 108 .... RyanMoore 9 91
(J Noseda) *taken down early and ponied to s: stdd s: t.k.h: hld up in tch in last pair: rdn and unable qck over 1f out: hdwy on far rail ins fnl f: r.o but unable to rch ldng pair* **10/3**[2]

0126 **4** *nk* **Chips O'Toole (IRE)**[2] 7108 2-8-4 88 ow1 .... MartinDwyer 2 83
(B J Meehan) *racd freely: led: rdn and edgd lft u.p fr over 1f out: hdd ins fnl f: keeping on same pce and btn whn edgd rt and sltly hmpd nr fin* **8/1**[3]

1620 **5** *hd* **Dorback**[20] 6677 2-8-6 94 .... FergusSweeney 7 85
(H Candy) *lw: t.k.h: hld up wl in tch: nt clr run over 1f out tl ins fnl f: r.o fnl 100yds: unable to chal* **11/1**

12 **6** *nse* **Haadeeth**[41] 6104 2-8-6 81 .... RHills 8 85
(M P Tregoning) *lw: t.k.h: hld up in tch towards rr: swtchd lft over 3f out: hdwy to join ldr 2f out: rdn over 1f out: no ex and btn fnl 75yds* **3/1**[1]

10 **7** *½* **Pastoral Player**[6] 7030 2-8-6 0 .... SteveDrowne 4 83
(H Morrison) *on toes: restless in stalls: stdd s: t.k.h: chsd ldrs: wnt 2nd 4f out tl 2f out: ev ch and rdn over 1f out: nt qckn ent fnl f: no ex fnl 150yds* **3/1**[1]

540 **8** *10* **Always The Sun**[85] 4718 3-9-3 42 .... MickyFenton 6 50
(P Leech) *a in rr: toiling over 3f out: sn wl bhd* **200/1**

1m 14.73s (2.53) **Going Correction** +0.425s/f (Yiel) **8** Ran SP% **113.5**
Speed ratings: **100,99,98,97,97 97,96,83**
toteswinger: 1&2 £7.30, 1&3 £4.80, 2&3 £6.30. CSF £80.42 TOTE £8.70: £2.20, £2.20, £1.50; EX 88.50.

Owner Sir David Seale **Bred** Ocala Stud **Trained** East Everleigh, Wilts

FOCUS

This conditions race for 2-y-os & 3-y-os went to a juvenile for the seventh time in the last eight years, but only narrowly, and this is form to treat with caution, with the principals finishing in a bunch, and the 42-rated Always The Sun a bit close for comfort. The majority of these were positioned towards the far side, but the runner-up did much of his racing alone a bit wider.

NOTEBOOK

Rum King(USA), carrying 1lb overweight, was always well placed and followed up his C&D maiden success. His trainer won this race in 2007 with Paco Boy, who then reappeared as a 3-y-o with a win in the Spring Cup at Lingfield, and that Listed race is said to be the aim for this colt. He certainly has the size to progress and could make a smart type next season. (op 8-1 tchd 13-2)

Marine Boy(IRE) raced away from the others for much of the way but that didn't seem to harm his chance and he was only just denied. This was a good effort in defeat considering the weight-for-age scale seems to favour the 2-y-os in this race. (op 6-1 tchd 10-1)

Himalya(IRE) was a major eyecatcher over 5f here on his previous start, but he let himself down this time. After a sluggish start, he pulled much too hard, finding himself a bit squeezed for room at one stage as a result. It was a surprise he ran on to take third, and there's no denying his ability, but he's certainly not straightforward. (op 11-4 tchd 5-2)

Chips O'Toole(IRE), well held from a poor draw in a Kempton nursery two days earlier, had the run of the race in front but wandered around a bit under pressure. He's starting to look exposed. (op 12-1)

Dorback has not progressed as expected since a winning debut but he's better than he was able to show this time as he had nowhere to go when trying to make his move until inside the final furlong. Official explanation: jockey said colt was denied a clear run (op 12-1 tchd 14-1)

Haadeeth looked the type to keep progressing but he failed to build on his two previous efforts. He was a bit keen and a stronger pace would probably have suited better. (op 5-1 tchd 11-4)

Pastoral Player, reported to have been unsuited by soft ground in the Horris Hill, ran like a horse with issues this time and has not gone on as expected from his debut success. We know he has a problem with the stalls from when he refused to enter the gates for the Redcar Two-Year-Old Trophy, and he was again very restless on loading. Although he consented to step forward, he then missed the break, before racing keenly, and unsurprisingly failed to pick up for pressure. He's talented, but needs to learn to relax. (op 11-4 tchd 7-2)

7151 TURFTV H'CAP 2m

4:05 (4:08) (Class 3) (0-90,93) 3-Y-O+ **£7,771** (£2,312; £1,155; £577) **Stalls Centre**

Form RPR

0130 **1** **Aaim To Prosper (IRE)**[13] 6851 5-9-8 **84** .... LDettori 16 92
(B J Meehan) *lw: hld up in tch in midfield: rdn and effrt over 2f out: swtchd rt over 1f out: drvn to chal ins fnl f: r.o wl to ld fnl 50yds* **7/2**[1]

2544 **2** *hd* **Hawridge King**[18] 6734 7-8-13 **75** .... AlanMunro 13 83
(W S Kittow) *hld up in rr: swtchd to outer and pushed along 4f out: gd hdwy to chse ldrs but edging rt over 1f out: led ins fnl f: hdd and no ex fnl 50yds* **25/1**

1304 **3** *2* **Alnwick**[7] 7005 5-9-2 **78** .... DaneO'Neill 9 83
(P D Cundell) *chsd ldr: clr of remainder 12f out: led 4f out: rdn over 2f out: drvn and hdd ins fnl f: plugged on same pce after* **33/1**

6031 **4** *3 ½* **My Mate Max**[31] 6368 4-8-9 **71** oh2 ....(p) TPQueally 2 72
(R Hollinshead) *chsd ldng pair after 2f: clsd over 5f out: chsd ldr and rdn over 3f out: lost 2nd over 1f out: outpcd fnl f* **20/1**

100 **5** *1 ½* **Lethal Glaze (IRE)**[20] 6662 3-9-7 **93** .... RichardHughes 11 92
(R Hannon) *in tch in main gp: clsd on ldrs over 4f out: chsng ldrs and drvn over 1f out: wknd fnl f* **12/1**

6411 **6** *¾* **Spirit Of Adjisa (IRE)**[34] 6280 5-9-9 **85** .... RobertWinston 6 83
(Pat Eddery) *t.k.h: prom in main gp: rdn over 5f out: hdwy and chsng ldrs over 2f out: wknd u.p over 1f out* **12/1**

1466 **7** *1 ¼* **Perfect Shot (IRE)**[20] 6676 3-8-11 **83** .... TedDurcan 4 80
(J L Dunlop) *taken down early: hld up in midfield: gng wl whn nt clr run over 3f out tl swtchd lft over 2f out: sn rdn and racd awkwardly: no prog fnl 2f* **9/1**

3321 **8** *¾* **Dulcie**[54] 5696 3-8-1 **78** .... AshleyMorgan(5) 1 74
(M H Tompkins) *stdd s: t.k.h: hld up in rr: hdwy on outer 4f out: chsd ldrs and rdn over 2f out: wknd wl over 1f out* **13/2**[3]

1102 **9** *10* **Markington**[11] 6899 6-8-6 **71** ....(b) WilliamCarson(3) 17 55
(P Bowen) *racd in midfield: rdn and no prog over 4f out: swtchd lft to centre 3f out: no prog and wl btn after* **20/1**

4000 **10** *3 ¼* **Judgethemoment (USA)**[13] 6851 4-10-0 **90** ....(p) KFallon 8 70
(Jane Chapple-Hyam) *t.k.h: prom in main gp: pushed along over 4f out: wknd u.p 3f out: wl btn fnl 2f* **12/1**

325 **11** *nk* **Phoenix Flight (IRE)**[13] 6855 4-9-6 **82**..........................(p) JimCrowley 12 62
(H J Evans) *stdd s: t.k.h: hld up in rr: sme hdwy 4f out: no hdwy fnl 3f and nvr a factor* **22/1**
6050 **12** *2* **Bulwark (IRE)**[13] 6851 7-9-10 **86**.......................... StephenDonohoe 5 63
(Ian Williams) *sn niggled along in rr: nvr a factor* **33/1**
522 **13** *2 1/4* **Wicked Daze (IRE)**[41] 6100 6-9-4 **80**..........................(p) NCallan 15 55
(K A Ryan) *t.k.h: hld up in midfield: n.m.r over 3f out: sn rdn: wknd wl over 1f out: eased ins fnl f* **8/1**
2061 **14** *5* **Eseej (USA)**[12] 6878 4-8-11 **78** 6ex.......................... PaulPickard(5) 3 47
(P W Hiatt) *taken down early: sn led: clr over 12f out: hdd and rdn 4f out: sn dropped out: wl bhd fnl 3f* **33/1**
3131 **15** *3 1/4* **Dazinski**[30] 6388 3-8-13 **85**.......................... RHills 14 50
(M H Tompkins) *lw: racd in midfield: rdn 4f out: struggling and lost pl wl over 2f out: wl bhd and eased fnl f* **9/2**[2]

3m 27.31s (-3.49) **Going Correction** -0.025s/f (Good)
WFA 3 from 4yo+ 10lb **15** Ran SP% **124.5**
Speed ratings (Par 107): **107,106,105,104,103 103,102,102,97,95 95,94,93,90,89**
toteswinger: 1&2 £22.00, 1&3 £24.20, 2&3 £60.50. CSF £102.77 CT £2493.76 TOTE £4.30: £1.90, £6.60, £8.60; EX 123.10 TRIFECTA Not won. Place 6: £59.38, Place 5: £32.89..
Owner CGA Racing Partnership 2 **Bred** Stephanie Hanly **Trained** Manton, Wilts

FOCUS
A good staying handicap with the winner getting back to form and the runner-up ratred in line-with his best.

NOTEBOOK
Aaim To Prosper(IRE), without any headgear this time (won twice this year in a visor), took a while to pick up but he was given an inspired ride by the in-form Dettori and got on top in the final strides. Having looked to be going nowhere over 2f out, he ran on when switched to the far rail, which is by no means a bad strip of ground. (op 5-1)
Hawridge King looked the winner when produced with his challenge on the outer inside the final 2f, but he's yet to win beyond 1m6f on the Flat and was just run out of it. (tchd 20-1)
Alnwick was given a positive ride and ran a bit better than of late, but he is a little high in the weights. (op 28-1)
My Mate Max ran okay from a mark 3lb higher (2lb out of handicap) than when winning over 1m7f at Warwick on his previous start. (op 16-1)
Lethal Glaze(IRE) probably wants easier ground. (tchd 14-1)
Perfect Shot(IRE) is much better than he showed as he was continually denied a clear run from around 3f out, when appearing as though he had a lot to offer. (op 10-1)
Dazinski was disappointing off a mark only 5lb higher than when winning at Nottingham on his previous start. Official explanation: jockey said gelding had no more to give (op 6-1)
T/Jkpt: Part won. £7,100.00 to a £1 stake. Pool: £10,000.00. 0.50 winning tickets. T/Plt: £37.20 to a £1 stake. Pool: £68,271.88. 1,338.92 winning tickets. T/Qpdt: £19.60 to a £1 stake. Pool: £5,514.45. 207.90 winning tickets. SP

7136 WOLVERHAMPTON (A.W) (L-H)
Friday, October 30

OFFICIAL GOING: Standard
Wind: Fresh across Weather: Overcast

7152 ARENA LEISURE ALL-WEATHER 20TH ANNIVERSARY H'CAP 1m 141y(P)
6:20 (6:20) (Class 7) (0-50,50) 3-Y-O+ **£2,183** (£644; £322) **Stalls** Low

Form RPR
0-33 **1** **Mighty Mover (IRE)**[30] 6394 7-9-0 **50**.......................... LukeMorris 4 59
(B Palling) *led early: chsd ldr tl led over 2f out: rdn and hung rt fr over 1f out: r.o* **3/1**[2]
0300 **2** *2 1/4* **Bidable**[8] 6967 5-9-0 **50**.......................... NeilChalmers 1 54
(B Palling) *a.p: racd keenly: rdn over 1f out: r.o* **12/1**
0-40 **3** *hd* **Lunar Limelight**[168] 2039 4-8-13 **49**.......................... SebSanders 2 52
(P J Makin) *pushed along in rr early: hdwy into mid-div over 5f out: rdn over 1f out: r.o* **9/1**
00 **4** *1 3/4* **Just Spike**[71] 5179 6-8-13 **49**.......................... CatherineGannon 10 48+
(B P J Baugh) *s.i.s: hld up: hdwy u.p over 1f out: hung lft ins fnl f: nt trble ldrs* **25/1**
-045 **5** *nse* **Headache**[35] 6256 4-9-0 **50**..........................(t) DavidProbert 6 49
(B W Duke) *chsd ldrs: ev ch 2f out: sn rdn: no ex ins fnl f* **9/1**
5404 **6** *nk* **Al Rayanah**[10] 6924 6-8-13 **49**..........................(p) SaleemGolam 3 48
(G Prodromou) *s.i.s: sn prom: rdn over 2f out: styd on* **7/1**[3]
0430 **7** *1 1/2* **Turkish Sultan (IRE)**[178] 1770 6-8-10 **49**..........................(p) MCGeran(3) 13 44
(J M Bradley) *sn pushed along in rr: r.o ins fnl f: nvr nrr* **33/1**
0000 **8** *1 3/4* **Kirstys Lad**[14] 6818 7-8-12 **48**.......................... RobertHavlin 9 39
(M Mullineaux) *mid-div: rdn over 3f out: wknd over 1f out* **16/1**
0560 **9** *4* **Heavenly Saint**[9] 6945 4-9-0 **50**..........................(p) RichardThomas 12 32
(C Roberts) *hld up: n.d* **100/1**
2260 **10** *5* **Carnival Dream**[29] 6415 4-8-9 **50**.......................... SladeO'Hara(5) 5 20
(H A McWilliams) *sn led: rdn and hdd over 2f out: wknd over 1f out* **20/1**
06- **11** *3 1/4* **May Parkin (IRE)**[366] 7074 4-8-7 **50**.......................... TobyAtkinson(7) 11 13
(M Wigham) *trckd ldrs: rdn 3f out: wknd 2f out* **7/4**[1]
406- **12** *11* **Fareeha**[16] 5813 4-8-13 **49**.......................... SJCraine 7 —
(J Mackie) *mid-div: rdn 1/2-way: wknd over 3f out* **66/1**

1m 50.29s (-0.21) **Going Correction** -0.025s/f (Stan) **12** Ran SP% **121.5**
Speed ratings (Par 97): **99,97,96,95,95 94,93,92,88,84 81,71**
toteswinger: 1&2 £8.40, 1&3 £3.90, 2&3 £24.40. CSF £37.92 CT £252.42 TOTE £3.70: £1.30, £3.70, £2.60; EX 39.30.
Owner Bryn Palling **Bred** Humphrey Okeke **Trained** Tredodridge, Vale Of Glamorgan

FOCUS
With a ratings band of 45-50, this had to be a modest event. The placed horses are the best guides.

7153 LADBROKES ALL-WEATHER 20TH ANNIVERSARY H'CAP 1m 141y(P)
6:50 (6:50) (Class 5) (0-70,70) 3-Y-O+ **£3,238** (£963; £481; £240) **Stalls** Low

Form RPR
21-1 **1** **Alqaahir (USA)**[13] 6861 7-9-5 **67**.......................... LiamJones 3 74+
(Lee Smyth, Ire) *chsd ldrs: rdn to ld over 1f out: styd on* **7/2**[2]
-063 **2** *3/4* **Via Mia**[185] 1584 3-9-2 **68**.......................... TomEaves 4 73
(George Baker) *mid-div: rdn 1/2-way: hdwy 2f out: chsd wnr fnl f: r.o* **18/1**
4512 **3** *hd* **Red Suede Shoes**[8] 6977 3-9-1 **70**..........................(p) JamesMillman(3) 5 75
(B R Millman) *hld up: hdwy and n.m.r over 1f out: r.o* **2/1**[1]
1244 **4** *1/2* **Magroom**[9] 6937 5-9-4 **69**.......................... MCGeran(3) 7 72+
(R J Hodges) *sn pushed along in rr: hdwy and nt clr run over 1f out: swtchd rt and r.o ins fnl f: nt rch ldrs* **11/1**
0630 **5** *1/2* **Ella Woodcock (IRE)**[13] 6860 5-8-12 **60**..........................(b) DavidAllan 9 62
(E J Alston) *mid-div: hdwy over 2f out: rdn and edgd rt over 1f out: r.o* **10/1**
6305 **6** *1/2* **Fiefdom (IRE)**[19] 6703 7-9-6 **68**.......................... FrederikTylicki 8 69
(I W McInnes) *hld up: hdwy 2f out: sn rdn: r.o* **20/1**

000 **7** *1/2* **Great Bounder (CAN)**[15] 6807 3-8-3 **58**.......................... MarcHalford(3) 1 58
(J R Best) *chsd ldrs: rdn over 3f out: no ex fnl f* **20/1**
0 **8** *2 1/4* **Illicit**[95] 4378 4-9-8 **70**.......................... JerryO'Dwyer 6 65
(J R Holt) *s.i.s: in rr and pushed along over 3f out: styd on ins fnl f: n.d* **66/1**
0323 **9** *9* **Arashi**[15] 6806 3-9-0 **66**..........................(p) SteveDrowne 10 40
(Lucinda Featherstone) *led: rdn and hdd 2f out: wknd fnl f* **7/1**[3]
2400 **10** *3 1/4* **Fortunate Bid (IRE)**[11] 6908 3-9-3 **69**.......................... TGMcLaughlin 2 36
(Mrs L Stubbs) *chsd ldr tl led 2f out: sn rdn and hdd: edgd lft and wknd sn after* **18/1**
2400 **11** *18* **Superstitious Me (IRE)**[15] 6787 3-8-4 **56** oh1.......................... DavidProbert 11 —
(B Palling) *chsd ldrs: rdn and wknd over 2f out* **14/1**

1m 50.48s (-0.02) **Going Correction** -0.025s/f (Stan)
WFA 3 from 4yo+ 4lb **11** Ran SP% **113.7**
Speed ratings (Par 103): **99,98,98,97,97 96,96,94,86,83 67**
toteswinger: 1&2 £14.70, 1&3 £2.40, 2&3 £11.60. CSF £60.35 CT £156.41 TOTE £4.60: £1.70, £3.40, £1.60; EX 39.90.
Owner Leslie Laverty **Bred** Shadwell Farm LLC **Trained** Dungannon, Co Tyrone

FOCUS
A modest handicap with the runner-up back to his juvenile form and the third close to his recent best.
Magroom Official explanation: jockey said gelding was denied a clear run
Illicit Official explanation: jockey said gelding hung right
Superstitious Me(IRE) Official explanation: jockey said filly lost its action

7154 AT THE RACES ALL-WEATHER 20TH ANNIVERSARY H'CAP 2m 119y(P)
7:20 (7:20) (Class 6) (0-60,60) 3-Y-O+ **£2,388** (£705; £352) **Stalls** Low

Form RPR
1 **He's Cool (IRE)**[36] 4554 4-9-1 **49**..........................(p) TedDurcan 11 61+
(Aidan Anthony Howard, Ire) *a.p: led over 2f out: sn rdn clr: eased towards fin* **10/1**
0633 **2** *5* **Wester Lodge (IRE)**[13] 6859 7-9-3 **51**.......................... LukeMorris 12 56
(J M P Eustace) *mid-div: hdwy 5f out: rdn to chse wnr over 1f out: hung lft fnl f: no imp* **5/1**[2]
6044 **3** *1 1/4* **Squirtle (IRE)**[13] 6859 6-9-4 **52**.......................... KirstyMilczarek 2 55
(W M Brisbourne) *prom: outpcd 3f out: rallied 2f out: edgd lft and no ex fnl f* **7/1**
0200 **4** *1/2* **Colourful Move**[56] 5642 4-9-5 **53**.......................... SteveDrowne 5 56
(P G Murphy) *hld up: hdwy over 2f out: nt rch ldrs* **20/1**
4534 **5** *1* **Pertemps Power**[11] 6457 5-8-12 **49**..........................(t) RussellKennemore(3) 4 51
(B G Powell) *hld up: hdwy over 1f out: nt trble ldrs* **28/1**
/23- **6** *1 1/4* **Watch Out**[22] 661 5-8-12 **46** oh1..........................(t) DavidProbert 9 46
(D Burchell) *hld up: hdwy over 4f out: rdn over 2f out: hung lft and wknd fnl f* **16/1**
4300 **7** *8* **Sir Sandicliffe (IRE)**[13] 6859 5-9-10 **58**.......................... TGMcLaughlin 6 48
(W M Brisbourne) *s.s: bhd: rdn and hung lft over 1f out: n.d* **25/1**
8 *1 1/2* **Annie Go (IRE)**[15] 6599 5-9-12 **60**.......................... JerryO'Dwyer 7 49
(Aidan Anthony Howard, Ire) *s.s: hld up: rdn over 2f out: wknd over 1f out* **13/2**[3]
0031 **9** *1* **Bute Street**[13] 6859 4-8-13 **50**.......................... MCGeran(3) 13 37
(R J Hodges) *sn pushed along to chse ldr: led wl over 2f out: sn rdn and hdd: wknd over 1f out* **5/1**[2]
0350 **10** *13* **Amroth**[18] 6742 3-8-12 **56**..........................(v[1]) TomEaves 8 28
(P D Evans) *hld up: pushed along 7th out: wknd over 3f out* **20/1**
4221 **11** *9* **Park's Prodigy**[3] 7080 5-9-5 **53** 6ex.......................... DanielTudhope 10 14
(G A Harker) *hld up: hdwy 5f out: rdn: hung lft and wknd over 3f out* **7/2**[1]
000 **12** *7* **Our Last Call (IRE)**[121] 3508 3-8-9 **53** ow1..........................(b[1]) SebSanders 1 6
(Sir Mark Prescott) *sn drvn along to ld: hdd wl over 2f out: sn wknd* **16/1**
0/2- **13** *1 3/4* **Power Shared (IRE)**[552] 524 5-9-8 **56**.......................... RobertHavlin 3 7
(P G Murphy) *chsd ldrs tl rdn and wknd over 3f out* **40/1**

3m 42.03s (0.23) **Going Correction** -0.025s/f (Stan)
WFA 3 from 4yo+ 10lb **13** Ran SP% **121.5**
Speed ratings (Par 101): **98,95,95,94,94 93,90,89,88,82 78,75,74**
toteswinger: 1&2 £10.10, 1&3 £22.60, 2&3 £9.30. CSF £56.26 CT £384.32 TOTE £12.10: £3.00, £2.20, £2.50; EX 96.00.
Owner Matthew Mullen **Bred** Eoin And Stephanie Hanly **Trained** Kildalkey, Co Meath

FOCUS
A tight handicap in which the Irish challenger won very easily. The form, rated around the placed horses, looks sound but limited.

7155 TOTE ALL-WEATHER 20TH ANNIVERSARY H'CAP 5f 216y(P)
7:50 (7:52) (Class 4) (0-85,85) 3-Y-O+ **£5,046** (£1,510; £755; £377; £188) **Stalls** Low

Form RPR
3023 **1** **Orpenindeed (IRE)**[27] 6495 6-9-2 **85**..........................(p) AndreaAtzeni(3) 6 96
(M Botti) *trckd ldrs: plld hrd: rdn over 1f out: edgd lft and led wl ins fnl f: r.o* **3/1**[2]
5101 **2** *1 1/4* **Bahamian Lad**[18] 6723 4-9-0 **80**.......................... JerryO'Dwyer 8 87
(R Hollinshead) *chsd ldrs: rdn and ev ch ins fnl f: styd on* **10/1**[3]
2422 **3** *1/2* **Lochan Mor**[8] 6964 3-8-12 **79**.......................... HayleyTurner 4 84
(M L W Bell) *led: hdd over 4f out: led again over 2f out: rdn and edgd rt over 1f out: hdd and unable qck ins fnl f* **13/8**[1]
0044 **4** *hd* **Drawnfromthepast (IRE)**[6] 7026 4-9-4 **84**..........................(t) ShaneKelly 9 89
(J A Osborne) *a.p: rdn and ev ch ins fnl f: styd on same pce* **18/1**
030 **5** *2 1/4* **Blown It (USA)**[17] 6764 3-8-7 **74**.......................... TomEaves 3 72
(I Semple) *prom: rdn over 1f out: styd on same pce fnl f* **12/1**
0004 **6** *hd* **Princess Valerina**[30] 6396 5-8-12 **83**.......................... AndrewHeffernan(5) 2 80
(D Haydn Jones) *dwlt: hld up: racd keenly: rdn over 1f out: hung lft and r.o ins fnl f: nt rch ldrs* **16/1**
5010 **7** *1* **Methaaly (IRE)**[9] 6949 6-8-11 **77**..........................(be) AlanMunro 1 71
(M Mullineaux) *dwlt: hld up: styd on ins fnl f: nvr nrr* **12/1**
3305 **8** *2 1/2* **The Tatling (IRE)**[20] 6666 12-9-1 **84**.......................... JackDean(3) 5 70
(J M Bradley) *hld up: plld hrd: rdn over 1f out: n.d* **20/1**
6100 **9** *1 1/4* **Green Park (IRE)**[11] 6897 6-8-3 **76**..........................(b) NeilFarley(7) 10 58
(D Carroll) *plld hrd and prom: led over 4f out to over 2f out: wknd over 1f out* **25/1**
6-62 **10** *5* **La Brigitte**[88] 4601 3-9-4 **85**..........................(e[1]) FrederikTylicki 7 51
(J A Glover) *hld up in tch: rdn over 2f out: sn wknd* **12/1**

1m 14.26s (-0.74) **Going Correction** -0.025s/f (Stan)
WFA 3 from 4yo+ 1lb **10** Ran SP% **115.0**
Speed ratings (Par 105): **103,101,100,100,97 97,95,92,90,84**
toteswinger: 1&2 £5.60, 1&3 £1.60, 2&3 £3.00. CSF £32.76 CT £63.59 TOTE £4.30: £1.50, £3.00, £1.30; EX 36.40.
Owner Giuliano Manfredini **Bred** A Pereira **Trained** Newmarket, Suffolk

FOCUS
A decent handicap and the winner was back to his best with the third the best guide.

7156 CORAL ALL-WEATHER 20TH ANNIVERSARY NURSERY 5f 20y(P)
8:20 (8:20) (Class 5) (0-75,74) 2-Y-O **£3,238** (£963; £481; £240) **Stalls** Low

Form RPR

2161 **1** **Living It Large (FR)**[7] 6983 2-9-8 **74** 6ex.................. TonyHamilton 6 81
(R F Fisher) *mde all: rdn and edgd rt over 1f out: r.o* **7/2**[1]

0503 **2** *1 1/2* **Vilnius**[24] 6554 2-8-1 **53**.................................. CatherineGannon 1 55
(M R Channon) *prom: rdn over 1f out: chsd wnr ins fnl f: r.o* **11/1**

634 **3** *shd* **Flaxen Lake**[32] 6347 2-9-3 **69**.............................. GrahamGibbons 2 70
(R Hollinshead) *a.p: rdn to chse wnr 2f out: styd on* **8/1**

3313 **4** *3/4* **Night Trade (IRE)**[13] 6841 2-9-4 **73**.................. RussellKennemore(3) 12 72
(Mrs D J Sanderson) *s.i.s: swtchd lft sn after s: hld up: hdwy over 1f out: nt rch ldrs* **6/1**

0006 **5** *2* **Rightcar**[19] 6700 2-8-2 **57**..........................(b) AndreaAtzeni(3) 7 48
(Peter Grayson) *hld up: hung lft and r.o ins fnl f: nrst fin* **50/1**

0030 **6** *3/4* **Sovereign Secure (IRE)**[12] 6882 2-9-7 **73**..................(p) SebSanders 3 62
(Lee Smyth, Ire) *hld up: rdn and hung rt 1f out: nvr nrr* **22/1**

0001 **7** *1* **Wanchai Whisper**[8] 6970 2-8-8 **65** 6ex.................. MartinLane(5) 4 50
(P D Evans) *chsd ldrs: rdn over 1f out: no ex fnl f* **16/1**

021 **8** *nk* **I'Malwaysright (IRE)**[15] 6802 2-9-6 **72**...................... HayleyTurner 5 56
(D R C Elsworth) *s.i.s: hld up: hung rt over 3f out: rdn over 1f out: n.d* **4/1**[2]

603 **9** *1 1/4* **Maldon Prom (IRE)**[81] 4856 2-9-6 **72**........................ JerryO'Dwyer 13 51
(C A Dwyer) *sn outpcd: nvr nrr* **20/1**

2100 **10** *nk* **Koo And The Gang (IRE)**[31] 6354 2-9-4 **70**.................. TomEaves 9 48+
(B Ellison) *chsd wnr 3f: wkng whn hmpd 1f out* **16/1**

0160 **11** *1 3/4* **Monte Mayor One**[22] 6619 2-8-4 **61**.................. AndrewHeffernan(5) 8 33+
(D Haydn Jones) *chsd ldrs: rdn over 1f out: wkng whn hmpd sn after* **33/1**

0601 **12** *7* **Blue Neptune**[9] 6938 2-8-10 **62** 6ex.......................... MartinDwyer 11 9+
(W R Muir) *prom: rdn and wkng whn hmpd 1f out* **11/2**[3]

62.36 secs (0.06) **Going Correction** -0.025s/f (Stan) **12** Ran SP% **117.1**
Speed ratings (Par 95): **98,95,95,94,91 89,88,87,85,85 82,71**
toteswinger: 1&2 £9.20, 1&3 £6.00, 2&3 £17.00. CSF £40.22 CT £295.11 TOTE £4.10: £2.10, £3.40, £2.30; EX 47.40.
Owner Des Johnston **Bred** Sunny Days Limited **Trained** Ulverston, Cumbria

FOCUS
An ordinary nursery.

NOTEBOOK
Living It Large(FR) didn't get home over 7f but won with authority over 6f at Ayr seven days earlier and had no trouble dropping back to the minimum distance. Despite a 6lb penalty he was only 1lb higher than his last winning mark, and this first try on the surface went smoothly. It seems he can switch between distances which opens up options, and the only immediate problem is the Handicapper. (tchd 3-1)
Vilnius, without a win in 13 attempts since landing a seller in April, made the best of the ideal draw. She looks capable of winning off this mark. (op 12-1 tchd 9-1)
Flaxen Lake was in a handicap for the first time and, despite lack of experience, was able to lay up from his good draw. He will be even more streetwise next time.
Night Trade(IRE) ran a cracking race considering he missed the kick and was switched from an outside stall to get to the inside. He did get a good run from the home turn and, despite having made a sharp rise in the ratings from 46 to 73 in his last three outings, he should be hard to beat when the draw is kinder. Official explanation: jockey said filly was slowly away (op 11-1 tchd 12-1 and 11-2)
Rightcar had been raised 7lb for finishing a close sixth of seven in a maiden at Lingfield last time but finished well enough to suggest he might be competitive if tried back at 6f. (op 66-1)
I'Malwaysright(IRE) took a keen hold early and was dropping back a furlong but that wasn't excuse enough for this disappointing effort. He isn't the most straightforward but seems best when right on the pace. (op 9-2)
Blue Neptune was at a big disadvantage from the draw and raced on the outside. He was beaten when badly hampered up the straight, and this effort is best forgotten. Official explanation: jockey said colt suffered interference in the home straight (op 9-2)

7157 ARENA LEISURE ALL-WEATHER 20TH ANNIVERSARY MEDIAN AUCTION MAIDEN STKS 7f 32y(P)
8:50 (8:51) (Class 6) 2-Y-O **£2,729** (£806; £403) **Stalls** Low

Form RPR

1 **Hudoo** 2-8-12 0.. TedDurcan 6 70
(Saeed Bin Suroor) *hld up in tch: rdn and edgd lft over 1f out: r.o to ld wl ins fnl f* **9/4**[1]

50 **2** *hd* **Madame Excelerate**[13] 6842 2-8-12 0........................ TGMcLaughlin 7 70
(W M Brisbourne) *s.i.s: hld up: hdwy over 1f out: rdn to ld wl ins fnl f: sn hdd: r.o* **150/1**

0536 **3** *1 1/2* **Another Magic Man (USA)**[19] 6697 2-9-0 76.............. MarcHalford(3) 1 71
(J R Best) *led: hdd over 5f out: led again over 3f out: rdn and hdd wl ins fnl f: unable qck* **7/1**

0 **4** *shd* **Feeling Fragile (IRE)**[99] 4219 2-9-3 0........................ DavidProbert 3 71
(Pat Eddery) *a.p: chsd ldr 3f out: rdn over 1f out: styd on same pce ins fnl f* **7/1**

4U0 **5** *1* **New Christmas (USA)**[60] 5528 2-9-3 0.................... MartinDwyer 10 69+
(B J Meehan) *hld up: hdwy u.p and edgd lft over 1f out: running on whn nt clr run wl ins fnl f: nt rch ldrs* **14/1**

06 **6** *3* **Chookie Avon**[39] 6154 2-9-3 0.................................. TomEaves 5 61
(I Semple) *sn pushed along in rr: styd on fr over 1f out: n.d* **50/1**

62 **7** *4 1/2* **Suranam**[14] 6826 2-9-3 0.. LiamJones 9 50
(W J Haggas) *hmpd sn after s: hdwy over 5f out: rdn over 1f out: wknd fnl f* **9/2**[3]

3 **8** *9* **Juicy Pear (IRE)**[21] 6638 2-9-3 0.............................. HayleyTurner 4 28
(M L W Bell) *chsd ldrs: rdn over 2f out: wknd over 1f out* **7/2**[2]

0 **9** *1* **Franki J**[20] 6672 2-8-12 0...................................... JerryO'Dwyer 8 20
(D Donovan) *prom: rdn 3f out: wknd 2f out* **14/1**

0000 **10** *7* **Antique Diamond (IRE)**[10] 6922 2-8-12 31.................. NeilChalmers 2 3
(Lucinda Featherstone) *chsd ldr tl led over 5f out: hdd over 3f out: wknd over 2f out* **200/1**

0 **11** *2* **Bona Fortuna**[35] 6254 2-9-3 0................................ SebSanders 12 3
(Sir Mark Prescott) *sn drvn along: a in rr: wknd 3f out* **28/1**

1m 29.74s (0.14) **Going Correction** -0.025s/f (Stan) **11** Ran SP% **116.1**
Speed ratings (Par 93): **98,97,96,95,94 91,86,75,74,66 64**
toteswinger: 1&2 £76.50, 1&3 £4.60, 2&3 £176.80. CSF £421.35 TOTE £3.10: £1.10, £33.30, £1.90; EX 387.40.
Owner Godolphin **Bred** Mount Coote Partnership **Trained** Newmarket, Suffolk

FOCUS
A modest maiden.

NOTEBOOK
Hudoo does not look one of Godolphin's premier league two-year-olds, but he showed a willing enough attitude to buckle down and win on his racecourse debut. He was tapped for pace at halfway and didn't look at home around the bends, so it is hardly surpring that connections will now put him away and campaign him over 1m2f next year. He should stay further than that. (op 7-2)
Madame Excelerate made the form questionable as she had shown nothing on her two previous appearances over this distance and was pushed along from the start but stayed on dourly. Connections will be waiting with apprehension to see what the Handicapper does when a mark is allotted as the third is rated 76.
Another Magic Man(USA) didn't help by taking a keen hold, but this move back to 7f was the right one. He's shown enough to win a race of this calibre when the big yards close down. (op 9-1)
Feeling Fragile(IRE) hadn't run since his debut in July but this was much better. Perhaps the seller entry made by connections was premature. (op 9-1)
New Christmas(USA) was staying on but didn't have much room in the closing stages and was value for a little closer. He is now due a mark and might be better over another furlong. (op 10-1)
Chookie Avon is now due a mark but doesn't look completely straightforward.
Suranam wasn't given a hard time when his chance had gone and is one to look out for in longer races than this when he gets a mark. Official explanation: jockey said gelding did not pick up in home straight (op 4-1 tchd 5-1)
Juicy Pear(IRE) Official explanation: jockey said gelding ran too free

7158 WEATHERBYS ALL-WEATHER 20TH ANNIVERSARY FILLIES' H'CAP 7f 32y(P)
9:20 (9:20) (Class 5) (0-75,75) 3-Y-0+ **£3,238** (£963; £481; £240) **Stalls** Low

Form RPR

5501 **1** **La Gifted**[1] 7129 3-8-4 **61** oh1.............................. CatherineGannon 8 70
(M R Channon) *chsd ldr tl led over 2f out: sn rdn: r.o wl* **4/1**[1]

0060 **2** *2* **Miss Eze**[18] 6731 3-9-3 **74**...................................... HayleyTurner 3 78
(M L W Bell) *broke wl: n.m.r and lost pl 5f out: hdwy u.p over 1f out: nt rch wnr* **4/1**[1]

1546 **3** *nse* **Weet A Surprise**[15] 6801 4-8-6 **68**........................(v) AlexEdwards(7) 4 72
(J W Unett) *a.p: chsd wnr 2f out: sn rdn: styd on* **10/1**[3]

3401 **4** *1* **Beautiful Filly**[20] 6667 3-8-8 **70**..........................(b) MartinLane(5) 5 71
(D M Simcock) *hld up: hdwy over 1f out: sn rdn and hung lft: styd on same pce ins fnl f* **4/1**[1]

4344 **5** *hd* **Bold Ring**[10] 6914 3-8-4 **61** oh1.............................. DavidProbert 2 61
(E J Creighton) *hld up: hdwy over 1f out: styd on same pce ins fnl f* **12/1**

2140 **6** *1 3/4* **Labisa (IRE)**[105] 4072 3-9-1 **72**................................ SteveDrowne 6 68
(H Morrison) *hld up: hdwy over 2f out: rdn: hung lft and wknd fnl f* **4/1**[1]

6050 **7** *5* **Langland Bay**[95] 4375 3-8-5 **62**.............................. MartinDwyer 7 44
(W R Muir) *prom: rdn 1/2-way: wknd wl over 1f out* **33/1**

1300 **8** *nse* **Flying Valentino**[74] 5099 5-9-6 **75**........................ FrederikTylicki 1 57
(Ian Williams) *led: rdn and hdd over 2f out: wknd over 1f out* **7/1**[2]

1m 29.07s (-0.53) **Going Correction** -0.025s/f (Stan)
WFA 3 from 4yo+ 2lb **8** Ran SP% **112.2**
Speed ratings (Par 100): **102,99,99,98,98 96,90,90**
toteswinger: 1&2 £2.30, 1&3 £6.00, 2&3 £10.40. CSF £18.92 CT £146.53 TOTE £3.80: £1.80, £2.10, £2.20; EX 22.70 Place 6: £66.58, Place 5: £19.19..
Owner Patrick and Simon Trant **Bred** Patrick & Simon Trant **Trained** West Ilsley, Berks

FOCUS
With no natural front-runner there was a chance there might have been a false pace, and while it wasn't the strongest it was enough for the winner. The winner repeated her form of the previous day with the runner-up back to her juvenile form.
Bold Ring Official explanation: jockey said filly was denied a clear run
T/Plt: £171.40 to a £1 stake. Pool: £95,441.62. 406.45 winning tickets. T/Qpdt: £40.50 to a £1 stake. Pool: £8,193.13. 149.50 winning tickets. CR

MOULINS-LA-MARCHE (R-H)
Friday, October 30

OFFICIAL GOING: Very soft

7166a PRIX AREAS-MOULINS 7f
1:00 (12:00) 2-Y-O **£6,311** (£2,524; £1,893; £1,262; £631)

RPR

1 **Contrary (IRE)**[39] 6164 2-8-13.................................. RonanThomas —
(E J O'Neill) *broke well, restrained tracking leaders, led 100yds out, easily (61/10)* **61/10**[1]

2 *1* **Compton Effect** 2-8-13.. ASanglard —
(F Brogi, Italy)

3 *2* **Fancy Starlett (FR)** 3-8-5...................................... ALarue(3) —
(O Auchere, France)

4 *1* **Sangh Blue (FR)** 2-8-8 .... —
(D Allard, France)

5 *nk* **Regal Holiday (USA)** 2-9-2 .... —
(F-X De Chevigny, France)

6 *1* **Parisis (FR)**[49] 5850 2-9-2 .... —
(J-M Capitte, France)

7 *3/4* **Piquetera** 2-8-13 .... —
(A Fabre, France)

8 *8* **Lady Roulard (FR)**[15] 2-8-13 .... —
(P Lenogue, France)

9 *3/4* **Exotica (FR)**[10] 2-8-13 ....(b) —
(B Goudot, France)

1m 35.4s (95.40) **9** Ran SP% **14.1**
PARI-MUTUEL (including 1 Euro stake): WIN 7.10; PL 5.60, 6.30, 9.20;DF 44.90.
Owner Ballygallon Stud Limited **Bred** Ballygallon Stud Limited **Trained** Southwell, Notts

6982 AYR (L-H)
Saturday, October 31

OFFICIAL GOING: Soft (heavy in places in the back straight; 3.9)
Home bend dolled out extending all distances by circa 15yards.
Wind: Breezy, half against Weather: Overcast

7167 KELBURNE CONSTRUCTION MAIDEN STKS 7f 50y
12:30 (12:32) (Class 5) 2-Y-O **£3,885** (£1,156; £577; £288) **Stalls** High

Form RPR

5 **1** **Tipperary Boutique (IRE)**[91] 4542 2-8-12 0.................. PaulHanagan 4 75+
(B W Hills) *trckd ldr: led 2f out: drvn out fnl f* **5/4**[1]

2 2 3/4 **Xilerator (IRE)** 2-9-3 0 AdrianTNicholls 6 73
(D Nicholls) *dwlt: t.k.h and led after 1f: hdd 2f out: rallied: one pce fnl f* **13/2[3]**

40 3 8 **Honest Broker (IRE)**[14] 6842 2-9-3 0 GregFairley 5 54
(M Johnston) *chsd ldrs: rdn over 2f out: outpcd wl over 1f out* **10/1**

4 6 **Song Of Parkes** 2-9-12 0 DavidAllan 1 35
(E J Alston) *trckd ldrs: drvn over 2f out: wknd over 1f out* **14/1**

5 5 2 3/4 **Alsufooh (USA)**[14] 6842 2-8-12 0 JoeFanning 9 28
(M Johnston) *hld up in tch: rdn and hung lft over 2f out: sn wknd* **10/3[2]**

55 6 nk **Dies Solis**[30] 6408 2-9-3 0 TonyHamilton 7 32
(I Semple) *hld up: pushed along over 2f out: sn btn* **18/1**

00 7 5 **Acol**[18] 6763 2-9-3 0 AndrewMullen 8 20
(A G Foster) *s.i.s: bhd: drvn 1/2-way: sn struggling* **100/1**

8 7 **Margarets John (IRE)** 2-9-3 0 PJMcDonald 2 4
(G A Swinbank) *s.i.s: bhd and drvn 1/2-way: sn wknd* **7/1**

1m 39.51s (6.11) **Going Correction** +0.775s/f (Yiel) **8** Ran SP% **115.4**
Speed ratings (Par 95): **96,92,83,76,73 73,67,59**
toteswinger: 1&2 £2.00, 1&3 £2.30, 2&3 £4.90. CSF £10.25 TOTE £2.20: £1.20, £1.30, £3.00; EX 10.50.
Owner Noel O'Callaghan **Bred** Ashview Bloodstock Ltd **Trained** Lambourn, Berks

FOCUS
Very testing conditions, especially for these juveniles, and that took its toll in the final two furlongs.

NOTEBOOK
Tipperary Boutique(IRE) was happy to take a lead from the free-going Xilerator, but she began to grind that rival down approaching the furlong pole before asserting. She is a half-sister to useful middle-distance performer Leitmotiv, and she saw this test out well, so it's likely she'll be campaigned over further next term. (op 7-4)
Xilerator(IRE) was a bit too free for his own good in the early stages, probably just through greenness more than anything else, but he travelled well for a long way and pulled a mile clear of the remainder, so this was a very decent debut, and he will take some beating in similar company next time. (op 9-2 tchd 4-1)
Honest Broker(IRE) plugged on from a long way back to edge out Song Of Parkes for third. (tchd 9-1)
Song Of Parkes couldn't pick up for pressure and was caught for third. (op 20-1 tchd 12-1)
Alsufooh(USA) tried to make headway turning for home but she could make no inroads and dropped away tamely. She probably didn't handle the ground so is best forgiven this. (op 11-4 tchd 5-2)

7168 JOHN SMITH'S NURSERY 7f 50y
1:05 (1:07) (Class 5) (0-75,75) 2-Y-O **£3,885** (£1,156; £577; £288) **Stalls** High

Form RPR

045 1 **Starry Mount**[41] 6136 2-8-11 **65** ow2 PhillipMakin 3 73
(A B Haynes) *trckd ldrs: rdn and led over 1f out: edgd lft ins fnl f: kpt on wl* **13/2**

3215 2 2 1/4 **Masked Dance (IRE)**[12] 6906 2-9-7 **75** (p) PaulMulrennan 5 77
(K A Ryan) *led: rdn and hdd over 1f out: rallied: kpt on same pce ins fnl f* **6/1[3]**

0352 3 3/4 **We'll Deal Again**[4] 7088 2-8-4 **65** JamesPSullivan(7) 4 65
(M W Easterby) *t.k.h: prom: rdn and outpcd wl over 1f out: kpt on fnl f: nrst fin* **5/2[1]**

0004 4 9 **Charity Fair**[3] 7114 2-7-10 **53** oh3 ow1 DominicFox(3) 6 31
(A Berry) *bhd: rdn and hdwy on outside 2f out: kpt on fnl f: nvr able to chal* **25/1**

6300 5 1 **Lord's Seat**[68] 5303 2-7-13 **60** oh2 ow8 BillyCray(7) 2 36
(A Berry) *trckd ldrs: drvn 2f out: wknd over 1f out* **80/1**

3234 6 1/2 **Demonstrative (USA)**[13] 6874 2-9-3 **71** JoeFanning 1 45
(M Johnston) *midfield: rdn over 3f out: wknd over 2f out* **4/1[2]**

0545 7 4 1/2 **Lady Lefroy (IRE)**[19] 6721 2-8-4 **58** (b[1]) PaulHanagan 11 21
(R A Fahey) *in tch: drvn over 3f out: wknd over 2f out* **8/1**

0060 8 3/4 **Stanley Bridge**[8] 6982 2-8-0 **54** ow7 ow2 AndrewMullen 10 16
(A Berry) *dwlt: hld up: hdwy and in tch 3f out: sn rdn and wknd* **100/1**

5002 9 4 **Ochilview Warrior (IRE)**[8] 6983 2-8-0 **54** (b) DuranFentiman 9 6
(R Bastiman) *s.i.s: bhd: shortlived effrt ent st: sn wknd* **10/1**

1456 10 11 **Miami Gator (IRE)**[80] 4895 2-8-4 **58** AndrewElliott 7 —
(A P Jarvis) *pressed ldr tl rdn and wknd over 2f out* **18/1**

2416 11 10 **Rescent**[12] 6901 2-8-1 **55** FrancisNorton 8 —
(Mrs R A Carr) *reluctant to enter stalls: bhd: struggling over 3f out: sn btn: eased whn no ch fnl f* **12/1**

1m 39.46s (6.06) **Going Correction** +0.775s/f (Yiel) **11** Ran SP% **115.4**
Speed ratings (Par 95): **96,93,92,82,81 80,75,74,70,57 46**
toteswinger: 1&2 £15.10, 1&3 £15.10, 2&3 £1.90. CSF £44.04 CT £123.59 TOTE £8.40: £2.20, £2.30, £1.90; EX 78.90.
Owner Graham Robinson **Bred** G Robinson **Trained** Limpley Stoke, Bath
■ Stewards' Enquiry : Paul Mulrennan one-day ban: used whip with excessive frequency (Nov 14)
Billy Cray caution: used whip with excessive frequency

FOCUS
Just an ordinary nursery.

NOTEBOOK
Starry Mount, the least exposed runner in the field and making his handicap debut, travelled supremely well in touch with the pace before finding plenty when popped the question to assert from long-time leader Masked Dance in the final furlong. He seemed to appreciate the return to 7f, has started handicap life off a modest mark and has loads of scope for improvement next season, while this run confirms his effectiveness on testing going. (op 7-1 tchd 15-2)
Masked Dance(IRE) was stepping up in trip and he travelled well for a long way, relishing the conditions (as so many by his sire do) before just tiring in the closing stages. It's harsh to conclude that he didn't see the 7f out as he ran very well off what looks a stiff mark, but time may be that 6f is his best trip. (op 11-2 tchd 13-2)
We'll Deal Again closed in on the runner-up in the final half furlong, but he had been hard a work from early in the straight and he just couldn't find the change of gear to land a telling blow. (op 7-2 tchd 4-1)
Charity Fair, a 12-race maiden rated just 52, doing best of the rest, which doesn't say a great deal for the strength of the form. (op 28-1)
Rescent Official explanation: jockey said filly became upset in the stalls

7169 JOHN SMITH'S NO NONSENSE H'CAP 1m
1:40 (1:40) (Class 3) (0-90,88) 3-Y-O+ **£9,714** (£2,890; £1,444; £721) **Stalls** Low

Form RPR

1113 1 **Collateral Damage (IRE)**[13] 6876 6-9-7 **88** (t) DavidAllan 6 99
(T D Easterby) *prom: rdn to ld over 1f out: edgd lft: kpt on gamely fnl f* **11/4[1]**

431 2 1 1/4 **Cool Baranca (GER)**[8] 6987 3-8-4 **74** oh2 FrancisNorton 2 82
(P Monteith) *s.i.s: niggled in last pl after 3f: hdwy over 2f out: pressed wnr over 1f out: one pce wl ins fnl f* **7/1**

1140 3 3 **Moody Tunes**[44] 6016 6-8-8 **80** GaryBartley(5) 5 81
(A P Jarvis) *cl up: rdn and lost pl over 2f out: rallied over 1f out: no imp fnl f* **9/1**

5325 4 1 **Osteopathic Remedy (IRE)**[22] 6633 5-9-5 **86** PhillipMakin 4 85
(M Dods) *hld up in tch: effrt over 2f out: no imp over 1f out* **3/1[2]**

2100 5 3/4 **Faithful Ruler (USA)**[13] 6876 5-9-7 **88** PaulHanagan 3 85
(R A Fahey) *led tl rdn and hdd over 1f out: sn wknd* **5/1**

0030 6 7 **Silver Rime (FR)**[22] 6645 4-9-1 **82** PaulMulrennan 1 63
(Miss L A Perratt) *trckd ldrs: effrt over 2f out: wknd over 1f out* **4/1[3]**

1m 48.43s (4.63) **Going Correction** +0.775s/f (Yiel)
WFA 3 from 4yo+ 3lb **6** Ran SP% **110.8**
Speed ratings (Par 107): **107,105,102,101,101 94**
toteswinger: 1&2 not won, 1&3 £3.50, 2&3 not won. CSF £21.15 TOTE £2.50: £1.60, £4.20; EX 12.60.
Owner Middleham Park Racing Xxv **Bred** Minch Bloodstock And Castletown Stud **Trained** Great Habton, N Yorks

FOCUS
Quite a competitive little handicap on paper. Improvement from the first two in a race rated through the third.

NOTEBOOK
Collateral Damage(IRE), who has been a revelation this term, relished the return to turf having been turned over on Fibresand last time, and he ground out a fifth victory of the season. The 6yo relishes ease in the ground, so conditions were never going to be a problem for him, and although he had never won off a mark this high, he has never been in better form. He stayed on dourly towards the stands side to see off Cool Baranca and post another good performance. (op 3-1)
Cool Baranca(GER) is seen as a long-term hurdling prospect by connections, so this drop back in trip was always going to be a slight concern but she did really well to overcome a sluggish start and work her way into contention towards the far side of the group in the straight. Unexposed and improving, she looks a stout stayer on the level and is one to keep a close eye on back up in trip. (op 15-2 tchd 8-1)
Moody Tunes shaped better than last time but appears in the handicapper's grip for now. (op 16-1)
Osteopathic Remedy(IRE), who was a little keen early as he can often be, is also exactly where the handicapper wants him.

7170 JOHN SMITH'S EXTRA SMOOTH H'CAP 1m 7f
2:15 (2:15) (Class 4) (0-85,75) 3-Y-O+ **£7,352** (£2,201; £1,100; £551; £274; £138) **Stalls** High

Form RPR

-000 1 **Sphinx (FR)**[21] 6676 11-9-6 **67** (b) PaulMulrennan 6 77
(E W Tuer) *hld up in midfield: smooth hdwy over 3f out: led on bit over 1f out: sn rdn: styd on wl fnl f* **9/1**

3621 2 3 1/2 **Bollin Judith**[15] 6822 3-9-1 **71** DavidAllan 2 77
(T D Easterby) *prom: rdn over 3f out: hdwy and ev ch over 1f out: no ch w wnr fnl f* **3/1[1]**

1136 3 4 1/2 **Puy D'Arnac (FR)**[8] 6995 6-10-0 **75** PJMcDonald 8 76
(G A Swinbank) *hld up in midfield: hdwy to chse ldrs over 2f out: sn rdn: edgd lft and outpcd fnl f* **6/1[3]**

1312 4 1/2 **John Forbes**[16] 6803 7-9-9 **75** LanceBetts(5) 5 75
(B Ellison) *prom: drvn over 2f out: outpcd wl over 1f out* **6/1[3]**

2004 5 4 **Bajan Parkes**[14] 6840 6-9-9 **75** (p) GaryBartley(5) 7 70
(E J Alston) *w ldr: led over 4f out to over 1f out: sn wknd* **11/1**

3346 6 nk **Summer Soul (IRE)**[18] 6767 7-9-7 **68** (v) JoeFanning 4 63
(Miss Lucinda V Russell) *trckd ldrs tl hung lft and wknd 2f out* **14/1**

5420 7 1 **Danzatrice**[21] 6676 7-9-6 **67** PaulHanagan 1 61
(C W Thornton) *hld up: outpcd over 5f out: plugged on fnl f: n.d* **10/1**

4062 8 3/4 **Black Or Red (IRE)**[20] 6692 4-9-4 **65** (b) TonyHamilton 3 58
(I A Wood) *hld up: struggling over 3f out: n.d after* **7/2[2]**

6050 9 14 **Forrest Flyer (IRE)**[43] 6053 5-9-2 **63** PhillipMakin 11 39
(I Semple) *led to over 4f out: rdn and wknd over 2f out* **14/1**

630- 10 13 **Asrar**[425] 5559 7-8-2 **56** oh11 JamesPSullivan(7) 9 16
(Miss Lucinda V Russell) *dwlt: bhd: struggling over 5f out: t.o* **100/1**

3m 35.97s (15.57) **Going Correction** +0.775s/f (Yiel)
WFA 3 from 4yo+ 9lb **10** Ran SP% **117.5**
Speed ratings (Par 105): **89,87,84,84,82 82,81,81,73,66**
toteswinger: 1&2 £20.80, 1&3 £9.00, 2&3 £20.80. CSF £36.49 CT £179.79 TOTE £11.10: £1.70, £1.80, £2.00; EX 74.30.
Owner E Tuer **Bred** Martyn Arbib **Trained** Great Smeaton, N Yorks

FOCUS
The return to testing ground brought about a much improved performance from confirmed mudlark Sphinx. The third is the best guide to the form.
Sphinx(FR) Official explanation: trainer said, regarding apparent improvement in form, that the gelding was better suited by the softer ground.
Black Or Red(IRE) Official explanation: trainer had no explanation for the poor form shown

7171 JOHN SMITH'S H'CAP 7f 50y
2:45 (2:45) (Class 4) (0-80,80) 3-Y-O+ **£6,231** (£1,866; £933; £467; £233; £117) **Stalls** High

Form RPR

0040 1 **Keys Of Cyprus**[10] 6946 7-9-1 **74** AdrianTNicholls 5 84
(D Nicholls) *in tch: hdwy over 2f out: sn rdn: led ins fnl f: drvn out* **9/2[2]**

1202 2 3/4 **Grissom (IRE)**[4] 7083 3-8-9 **77** BillyCray(7) 3 85
(A Berry) *cl up: led over 2f out to ins fnl f: kpt on u.p* **5/1[3]**

2042 3 1/2 **Stellite**[8] 6985 9-8-11 **70** DanielTudhope 8 77
(J S Goldie) *hld up: hdwy 2f out: chsd ldrs 1f out: kpt on tl no ex last 50yds* **11/1**

0006 4 1 1/4 **Northern Fling**[12] 6897 5-9-0 **78** GaryBartley(5) 7 81+
(J S Goldie) *hld up: hdwy on outside over 2f out: kpt on fnl f: nrst fin* **9/1**

55-0 5 8 **Zhukhov (IRE)**[10] 6952 6-9-1 **79** BACurtis(5) 9 62
(T G McCourt, Ire) *hld up: drvn along 3f out: no imp over 1f out* **14/1**

2321 6 2 1/4 **Ishiadancer**[8] 6984 4-9-2 **75** DuranFentiman 10 52
(E J Alston) *cl up: led over 3f out to over 2f out: sn rdn and wknd* **3/1[1]**

2262 7 2 1/4 **Leonid Glow**[18] 6764 4-9-2 **75** PhillipMakin 12 46
(M Dods) *hld up: rdn over 2f out: nvr able to chal* **8/1**

000 8 13 **Santiago Atitlan**[14] 5943 7-8-7 **66** (v[1]) TonyHamilton 1 3
(P Monteith) *hld up: struggling 3f out: sn btn* **50/1**

0330 9 5 **Hazelrigg (IRE)**[14] 6846 4-8-13 **72** (p) PaulMulrennan 11 —
(T D Easterby) *cl up: ev ch over 3f out: wknd 2f out* **8/1**

040 10 nk **The Bear**[30] 6413 6-8-7 **66** oh2 ow1 PJMcDonald 2 —
(Miss L A Perratt) *led to over 3f out: sn rdn and struggling* **20/1**

6064 11 15 **Dabbers Ridge (IRE)**[17] 6783 7-8-13 **72** PaulHanagan 4 —
(I W McInnes) *hld up: rdn along over 3f out: sn btn: eased whn no ch fnl f* **16/1**

1m 37.97s (4.57) **Going Correction** +0.775s/f (Yiel)
WFA 3 from 4yo+ 2lb **11** Ran SP% **119.7**
Speed ratings (Par 105): **104,103,102,101,92 89,86,72,66,65 48**
toteswinger: 1&2 £8.40, 1&3 £4.90, 2&3 £26.00. CSF £27.87 CT £237.83 TOTE £5.40: £1.80, £2.20, £2.10; EX 31.50.
Owner The Beasley Gees **Bred** Juddmonte Farms **Trained** Sessay, N Yorks
■ Stewards' Enquiry : Billy Cray caution: used whip with excessive frequency.

FOCUS
They went hard from the start and the field were well strung out from the start. Sound form considering the ground.
Hazelrigg(IRE) Official explanation: jockey said gelding hung right-handed throughout
Dabbers Ridge(IRE) Official explanation: jockey said horse lost its action turn into home straight

7172 SYNERGY CIVIL ENGINEERING LTD H'CAP — 7f 50y
3:20 (3:20) (Class 5) (0-75,74) 3-Y-0+ — £3,885 (£1,156; £577; £288) Stalls High

Form — RPR
1100 **1** **Lordship (IRE)**[10] 6937 5-8-1 **62** .... JakePayne(7) 6 — 76
(A W Carroll) *trckd ldrs: led over 2f out: pushed clr fnl f* **14/1**
00 **2** *5* **Miss Bootylishes**[16] 6790 4-8-13 **67** .... JoeFanning 14 — 68
(A B Haynes) *s.i.s: sn in tch: hdwy to chse wnr over 1f out: r.o fnl f* **16/1**
1616 **3** *1 1/4* **Scrapper Smith (IRE)**[8] 6988 3-8-9 **65** .... PJMcDonald 7 — 63+
(A C Whillans) *bhd tl hdwy over 1f out: kpt on fnl f: nrst fin* **25/1**
3005 **4** *1 1/2* **Celtic Step**[32] 6357 5-9-2 **70** ....(b) PaulHanagan 3 — 64
(P D Niven) *prom: rdn over 2f out: one pce fr over 1f out* **10/1**
6002 **5** *1/2* **Jonny Lesters Hair (IRE)**[8] 6984 4-8-11 **65** .... DavidAllan 13 — 58
(T D Easterby) *trckd ldrs: drvn 3f out: one pce fnl 2f* **11/2**[2]
1130 **6** *2 3/4* **Capone (IRE)**[25] 6579 4-8-13 **70** .... DominicFox(3) 4 — 55
(R Curtis) *hld up in midfield: hdwy 3f out: rdn and outpcd over 1f out* **8/1**[3]
1000 **7** *2* **Golden Penny**[44] 6016 4-9-2 **73** .... NeilBrown(3) 5 — 53
(M Dods) *s.i.s: bhd tl sme late hdwy: nvr on terms* **40/1**
1000 **8** *hd* **Ninth House (USA)**[3] 7125 7-9-3 **71** ....(t) AndrewElliott 1 — 51
(Mrs R A Carr) *t.k.h in midfield: rdn over 2f out: sn outpcd* **11/1**
6001 **9** *6* **Botham (USA)**[8] 6985 5-8-11 **65** .... DanielTudhope 11 — 29
(J S Goldie) *hld up: shortlived effrt over 2f out: btn over 1f out* **10/1**
1651 **10** *2* **Liberty Trail (IRE)**[15] 6824 3-9-2 **72** .... PaulMulrennan 2 — 31
(I Semple) *led to over 2f out: wknd over 1f out* **12/1**
5503 **11** *3/4* **Cara's Request (AUS)**[4] 7083 4-9-6 **74** .... AdrianTNicholls 8 — 31
(D Nicholls) *chsd ldr: rdn and ev ch 3f out: wknd wl over 1f out* **7/2**[1]
4016 **12** *2 1/4* **Finsbury**[18] 6765 6-8-4 **61** .... KellyHarrison(3) 10 — 12
(J S Goldie) *s.i.s: bhd: rdn 3f out: nvr on terms* **14/1**
4410 **13** *1 1/2* **Tiddliwinks**[8] 6997 3-9-0 **70** .... TonyHamilton 9 — 17
(K A Ryan) *midfield: rdn 3f out: sn btn* **14/1**
500 **14** *8* **Misphire**[14] 6847 6-9-1 **69** ....(p) PhillipMakin 12 — —
(M Dods) *dwlt: hld up: rdn over 2f out: nvr on terms* **16/1**

1m 37.84s (4.44) **Going Correction** +0.775s/f (Yiel)
WFA 3 from 4yo+ 2lb — **14** Ran SP% **121.0**
Speed ratings (Par 103): **105,99,97,96,95 92,90,89,83,80 79,77,75,66**
toteswinger: 1&2 £14.10, 1&3 not won, 2&3 not won. CSF £222.14 CT £5598.52 TOTE £12.80: £2.90, £3.80, £11.90; EX 82.30.
Owner Group 1 Racing (1994) Ltd **Bred** John Costello **Trained** Cropthorne, Worcs

FOCUS
Modest handicap form but the pace was strong and it produced an emphatic and improved winner. This was the pick of the four C/D times.
Lordship(IRE) Official explanation: trainer said, regarding apparent improvement in form, that the gelding was better suited by the soft ground.
Liberty Trail(IRE) Official explanation: jockey said gelding had no more to give
Cara's Request(AUS) Official explanation: trainer had no explanation for poor form shown

7173 2009 SCOTTISH POPPY APPEAL H'CAP (DIV I) — 1m 1f 20y
3:55 (3:56) (Class 6) (0-60,60) 3-Y-0+ — £2,266 (£674; £337; £168) Stalls Low

Form — RPR
1 **On The Loose (IRE)**[64] 4683 5-8-10 **53** .... BACurtis(5) 3 — 63
(T G McCourt, Ire) *hld up: gd hdwy 3f out: led over 1f out: hld on wl fnl f* **15/2**[3]
040 **2** *3/4* **Croeso Cusan**[9] 6967 4-8-12 **55** .... SophieDoyle(5) 5 — 63
(J L Spearing) *in tch: stdy hdwy to chse wnr appr fnl f: kpt on ins fnl f* **8/1**
1651 **3** *1 1/4* **Social Rhythm**[30] 6411 5-9-7 **59** .... PJMcDonald 4 — 65+
(A C Whillans) *s.i.s: hld up: hdwy to chse ldrs over 1f out: kpt on same pce ins fnl f* **5/1**[2]
5000 **4** *9* **Natural Rhythm (IRE)**[8] 6999 4-8-13 **51** ....(b) JoeFanning 1 — 38
(Mrs R A Carr) *led: clr over 3f out: hdd over 1f out: sn wknd* **12/1**
6604 **5** *6* **Noche De Reyes**[10] 6950 4-9-2 **54** .... DavidAllan 7 — 28
(E J Alston) *chsd ldrs tl rdn and wknd over 2f out* **14/1**
4005 **6** *2 1/2* **Istiqdaam**[57] 5624 4-9-8 **60** ....(b[1]) PhillipMakin 9 — 29
(M W Easterby) *in tch: stdy hdwy over 3f out: rdn over 2f out: edgd lft and sn wknd* **9/4**[1]
040 **7** *nse* **Jim Martin**[44] 6012 4-8-13 **58** .... JamesPSullivan(7) 13 — 27
(Miss L A Perratt) *hld up: drvn over 3f out: nvr rchd ldrs* **12/1**
606 **8** *20* **Special Cuvee**[86] 4719 3-9-3 **59** .... PaulHanagan 10 — —
(A B Haynes) *towards rr: drvn over 3f out: sn wknd* **12/1**
-400 **9** *3* **Oscar Wild**[14] 5332 7-8-12 **50** .... DanielTudhope 12 — —
(I Semple) *midfield: struggling 3f out: sn btn* **50/1**
0550 **10** *11* **Severio (IRE)**[10] 6950 3-9-4 **60** .... AndrewElliott 2 — —
(A P Jarvis) *chsd ldr tl wknd fr 3f out* **14/1**
00-0 **11** *2* **Kunte Kinteh**[38] 6216 5-9-0 **52** .... AdrianTNicholls 14 — —
(D Nicholls) *missed break: bhd: rdn over 3f out: sn btn* **16/1**
5-00 **12** *4 1/2* **Monaco Mistress (IRE)**[115] 3727 3-8-8 **53** .... KellyHarrison(3) 8 — —
(N Tinkler) *in tch tl rdn and wknd over 2f out* **40/1**
13 *29* **Catcher Of Dreams (IRE)**[396] 6372 3-9-2 **58** .... AndrewMullen 6 — —
(A G Foster) *bhd and sn drvn along: lost tch after 4f: virtually p.u in st* **33/1**

2m 7.15s (8.75) **Going Correction** +0.775s/f (Yiel)
WFA 3 from 4yo+ 4lb — **13** Ran SP% **119.9**
Speed ratings (Par 101): **92,91,90,82,76 74,74,56,54,44 42,38,12**
toteswinger: 1&2 not won, 1&3 £23.70, 2&3 £8.40. CSF £65.90 CT £334.58 TOTE £10.70: £2.70, £4.30, £1.80; EX 69.30.
Owner On The Loose Syndicate **Bred** Mattie Harty **Trained** Stamullen, Co Meath

FOCUS
A poor-quality handicap but a gusty effort from On The Loose who improved on what he had been doing in Ireland. The second and third are rated to their marks.

7174 2009 SCOTTISH POPPY APPEAL H'CAP (DIV II) — 1m 1f 20y
4:25 (4:25) (Class 6) (0-60,60) 3-Y-0+ — £2,266 (£674; £337; £168) Stalls Low

Form — RPR
0233 **1** **Bosamcliff (IRE)**[3] 7127 4-9-2 **59** .... RichardEvans(5) 2 — 69
(P D Evans) *chsd ldrs: led over 2f out: hld on wl fnl f* **3/1**[1]
2545 **2** *1 1/4* **Hawkit (USA)**[8] 6987 8-9-1 **53** .... PaulMulrennan 5 — 60
(P Monteith) *hld up in tch: hdwy 2f out: chsd wnr ins fnl f: hld last 50yds* **6/1**[2]
2-0 **3** *4* **Rue De Cabestan (IRE)**[19] 6749 4-8-12 **55** ....(p) BACurtis(5) 6 — 54
(T G McCourt, Ire) *hld up: hdwy 3f out: ev ch and rdn over 1f out: sn outpcd* **14/1**
0440 **4** *1* **Red Skipper (IRE)**[30] 6411 4-9-4 **56** .... AndrewMullen 7 — 53
(N Wilson) *t.k.h early: cl up: ev ch and rdn over 2f out: no ex over 1f out* **13/2**[3]
0004 **5** *1 3/4* **Wednesdays Boy (IRE)**[49] 5888 6-8-11 **49** ....(p) PaulHanagan 12 — 42
(P D Niven) *bhd: drvn over 3f out: hdwy and hung lft 2f out: kpt on: nvr able to chal* **13/2**[3]
06-4 **6** *1/2* **Seaquel**[16] 6787 3-8-13 **55** .... JoeFanning 10 — 47
(A B Haynes) *midfield: drvn and outpcd over 2f out: n.d after* **16/1**
2020 **7** *1 1/4* **Ulysees (IRE)**[3] 7113 10-8-5 **50** .... SFeeney(7) 8 — 40
(I Semple) *hld up: hdwy on outside over 2f out: no further imp over 1f out* **14/1**
0004 **8** *3 3/4* **Kool Katie**[12] 6900 4-9-3 **55** .... AndrewElliott 1 — 37
(Mrs G S Rees) *midfield: drvn and effrt over 2f out: wknd over 1f out* **9/1**
00-0 **9** *6* **Querido (GER)**[45] 6005 5-9-3 **55** ....(t) VinceSlattery 14 — 24
(M Bradstock) *hld up: drvn over 3f out: nvr on terms* **10/1**
2600 **10** *1 3/4* **Apache Nation (IRE)**[30] 6411 6-9-2 **54** ....(b) PhillipMakin 9 — 19
(M Dods) *trckd ldrs tl rdn and wknd over 2f out* **14/1**
0005 **11** *5* **Glenluji**[8] 6985 4-8-12 **50** .... DanielTudhope 11 — 5
(J S Goldie) *led tl rdn and hdd over 2f out: sn btn* **20/1**
26 **12** *7* **Coolnaharan (IRE)**[27] 6520 9-9-2 **54** .... TonyHamilton 13 — —
(Lee Smyth, Ire) *midfield: drvn over 3f out: wknd over 2f out* **22/1**

2m 8.20s (9.80) **Going Correction** +0.775s/f (Yiel)
WFA 3 from 4yo+ 4lb — **12** Ran SP% **120.0**
Speed ratings (Par 101): **87,85,82,81,79 79,78,75,69,68 63,57**
toteswinger: 1&2 £10.10, 1&3 not won, 2&3 £20.80. CSF £20.20 CT £223.51 TOTE £4.30: £1.90, £2.50, £4.30; EX 17.40 Place 6: £371.19, Place 5: £238.93..
Owner W Clifford **Bred** London Thoroughbred Services Ltd **Trained** Pandy, Monmouths

FOCUS
A weak handicap in which the field finished well strung out. The winner is rated back to her best.
T/Plt: £492.70 to a £1 stake. Pool: £49,040.88. 72.65 winning tickets. T/Qpdt: £230.60 to a £1 stake. Pool: £2,899.33. 9.30 winning tickets. RY

7105 KEMPTON (A.W) (R-H)
Saturday, October 31

OFFICIAL GOING: Standard
Wind: Virtually nil

7175 DON WETHERELL CLAIMING STKS — 6f (P)
4:35 (4:35) (Class 6) 2-Y-0 — £2,047 (£604; £302) Stalls High

Form — RPR
0500 **1** **Little Perisher**[12] 6906 2-8-11 65 .... NCallan 3 — 75
(A P Jarvis) *broke wl: w ldr 1f: styd in 2nd tl led ins fnl 2f: drvn out fnl f* **5/1**[3]
4432 **2** *1* **Chocolate Cookie (IRE)**[28] 6494 2-7-13 65 .... AndreaAtzeni(3) 7 — 63
(J R Boyle) *in rr: pushed along and hdwy ins fnl 2f: styd on fnl f to take 2nd cl home but no ch of rching wnr* **6/4**[1]
0010 **3** *1/2* **Wanchai Whisper**[1] 7156 2-8-2 64 .... CatherineGannon 10 — 62
(P D Evans) *in rr: hdwy 2f out: chsd wnr appr fnl f but no imp and lost 2nd cl home* **3/1**[2]
60 **4** *3* **Bobby's Doll**[15] 6826 2-8-6 0 .... KirstyMilczarek 12 — 57
(T T Clement) *chsd ldrs: rdn over 2f out: wknd appr fnl f* **14/1**
2 **5** *4 1/2* **Ishe A Lord**[107] 4018 2-8-8 0 .... JackDean(3) 1 — 48
(W G M Turner) *sn chsng ldrs: rdn over 2f out: sn btn* **16/1**
4130 **6** *2 1/2* **Arken Lad**[31] 6373 2-8-4 67 ....(e) MartinLane(5) 8 — 39
(D Donovan) *chsd ldrs: styng on one pce whn hmpd over 1f out: nt rcvr* **8/1**
000 **7** *3/4* **Annia (IRE)**[33] 6328 2-8-4 68 .... LukeMorris 11 — 31
(N P Littmoden) *plld hrd: sn led: rdn and hdd ins fnl 2f: hung rt and wknd appr fnl f* **16/1**

1m 13.32s (0.22) **Going Correction** -0.05s/f (Stan) — **7** Ran SP% **111.2**
Speed ratings (Par 93): **96,94,94,90,84 80,79**
toteswinger: 1&2 £3.30, 1&3 £4.00, 2&3 £2.00. CSF £12.21 TOTE £5.90: £3.00, £1.30; EX 15.00.
Owner Christopher Shankland **Bred** Mrs Ann Jarvis **Trained** Middleham Moor, N Yorks

FOCUS
Much depleted field with the non-runners and a claimer, which centred around the first three home who have been largely disappointing after some fairly promising efforts at the beginning of the season.

NOTEBOOK
Little Perisher was always up with the pace and once driven to the front over a furlong out ran on well. Quite highly tried early in the season but he had completely lost his way of late being soundly beaten in nurseries but appreciated this drop in grade and should be capable of repeating this effort. (op 4-1)
Chocolate Cookie(IRE) came wide off the home turn and was closing all the way up the straight but was never going to catch the winner as he had already poached a good lead when striking the front. She had been placed at this level for Richard Hannon the last two times before joining present connections. She should be capable of going one better in a similar contest. (op 2-1)
Wanchai Whisper was another to come from off the pace but could never mount a serious challenge and lost second near the finish. She finished seventh at Wolverhampton the previous night after winning a claimer here nine days ago, so the edge might just have been taken off. (op 7-2 tchd 11-4)
Bobby's Doll has an overall modest profile but shaped with some promise at this level after showing little in a couple of maidens. (op 12-1 tchd 11-1)
Ishe A Lord was second in a seller on debut and again ran to that level but was never a serious threat. (op 12-1 tchd 11-1)
Annia(IRE) Official explanation: jockey said filly hung right-handed

7176 TIMEFORM RADIO H'CAP — 6f (P)
5:05 (5:05) (Class 7) (0-50,50) 3-Y-0+ — £2,047 (£604; £302) Stalls High

Form — RPR
0002 **1** **Sonhador**[24] 6581 3-8-13 **50** .... SaleemGolam 4 — 57
(G Prodromou) *hld up towards rr: gd hdwy over 1f out: drvn and qcknd ins fnl f to ld cl home: jst hld on* **4/1**[2]
2440 **2** *shd* **Dancing Welcome**[40] 6175 3-8-13 **50** ....(b) LukeMorris 8 — 57
(J M Bradley) *wnt lft s: in rr and sn pushed along: hrd rdn and hung bdly lft fr over 1f out: styd on u.p fnl f: fin wl: nt quite get up* **7/2**[1]
305 **3** *nk* **Reigning Monarch (USA)**[71] 5219 6-9-0 **50** ....(b) SamHitchcott 7 — 56
(Miss Z C Davison) *bmpd s: sn chsng ldr: rdn to chal ins fnl 2f: led over 1f out: styd on u.p whn chal ins fnl f: hdd cl home* **7/1**
0000 **4** *3/4* **Ishibee (IRE)**[5] 7051 5-8-9 **48** ....(v) MarcHalford(3) 2 — 52
(J J Bridger) *stdd and taken rt to ins sn after s: in rr tl gd hdwy over 1f out to press ldrs ins fnl f: no ex fnl 50yds* **12/1**

0100 **5** *1* **Equinity**[5] 7069 3-8-8 **50**...(t) SimonPearce(5) 6 50
(J Pearce) *bmpd s: sn chsng ldrs: rdn and ev ch ins fnl f: wknd fnl 50yds* **14/1**

2003 **6** *3 1/2* **Head To Head (IRE)**[24] 6581 5-8-13 **49**...(tp) SteveDrowne 9 38
(A D Brown) *led: rdn over 2f out and kpt slt advantage tl hdd over 1f out: wknd ins fnl f* **9/2[3]**

060- **7** *3 1/4* **High Ridge**[471] 4102 10-9-0 **50**...(b) KevinGhunowa 11 29
(J L Flint) *chsd ldrs: rdn over 2f out: wknd appr fnl f* **16/1**

0-04 **8** *8* **See That Girl**[47] 5954 3-8-6 **50**... AdamCarter(7) 12 3
(B Smart) *s.i.s: a outpcd in rr* **11/2**

0600 **9** *3/4* **Lady Amberlini**[50] 5842 4-9-0 **50**...(p) LPKeniry 10 1
(C R Dore) *in tch: rdn 1/2-way and sn bhd* **12/1**

1m 13.22s (0.12) **Going Correction** -0.05s/f (Stan)
WFA 3 from 4yo+ 1lb **9** Ran SP% **116.2**
Speed ratings (Par 97): **97,96,96,95,94 89,85,74,73**
toteswinger: 1&2 £1.60, 1&3 £5.10, 2&3 £4.60. CSF £18.57 CT £94.86 TOTE £5.40: £2.00, £1.10, £1.70; EX 21.60.

Owner George Prodromou **Bred** Mrs W Miller **Trained** East Harling, Norfolk

■ Stewards' Enquiry : Luke Morris one-day ban: excessive use of the whip (Nov 14)

FOCUS
A tight 45-50 handicap which resulted in a blanket finish. Moderate but sound form.

See That Girl Official explanation: trainer said filly was in season

7177 BETFAIR CASINO MAIDEN AUCTION STKS — 7f (P)
5:35 (5:36) (Class 5) 2-Y-O **£2,590** (£770; £385; £192) **Stalls** High

Form RPR

0 **1** **Totally Ours**[19] 6722 2-8-2 0... AndreaAtzeni(3) 5 76+
(W R Muir) *in rr and pushed along over 4f out: hdwy on ins 3f out: styd on wl to dispute 2nd appr fnl 2: clr ldr appr fnl f: styd on strly to hd fading ldr fnl 30yds: won gng away* **25/1**

32 **2** *1* **Flouncing (IRE)**[19] 6728 2-8-9 0... LiamJones 9 77
(W J Haggas) *led but plld hrd over 2f: c readily clr ins fnl 3f and 5 l ahd over 1f out: fdd ins fnl f and hdd fnl 30yds* **6/5[1]**

2632 **3** *1 3/4* **Baby Dottie**[11] 6912 2-8-4 71... CatherineGannon 7 68
(P M Phelan) *in tch: hdwy 3f out: disputed 2nd over 2f out: styd on fnl f but nvr gng pce of wnr* **3/1[2]**

4 *4 1/2* **Lily In The Pond** 2-8-7 0... LukeMorris 6 59
(Miss Gay Kelleway) *s.i.s: bhd: rdn along and green after s: hdwy over 2f out: styd on fr over 1f out but nvr nr ldng trio* **14/1[3]**

0005 **5** *5* **Show Willing (IRE)**[11] 6912 2-8-0 61 ow1... MartinLane(5) 1 45
(A P Jarvis) *in rr: mod prog fnl f* **25/1**

0225 **6** *4* **Inside Track (IRE)**[19] 6727 2-8-11 80... NCallan 10 41
(B J Meehan) *chsd clr ldr: rdn ins fnl 3f: wknd over 2f out* **3/1[2]**

000 **7** *3/4* **True To Form (IRE)**[8] 7001 2-8-11 0... SebSanders 3 39
(Sir Mark Prescott) *wnt rt s: in tch whn pushed wd and wknd bnd 3f out* **33/1**

0 **8** *1 3/4* **Laid Bare**[10] 6931 2-8-4 0... KirstyMilczarek 2 28
(Mrs P N Dutfield) *chsd ldrs: rdn and wknd over 3f out* **100/1**

00 **9** *1/2* **Tregony Bridge**[11] 6911 2-8-11 0... SteveDrowne 8 33
(M Blanshard) *chsd ldrs tl wknd and edgd lft bnd 3f out* **100/1**

000 **10** *nk* **Barafundle Boy**[20] 6696 2-8-2 53... RyanClark(7) 4 31
(J J Bridger) *squeezed s: a bhd* **100/1**

1m 25.15s (-0.85) **Going Correction** -0.05s/f (Stan) **10** Ran SP% **115.7**
Speed ratings (Par 95): **102,100,98,93,88 83,82,80,80,79**
toteswinger: 1&2 £10.70, 1&3 £12.20, 2&3 £1.90. CSF £54.71 TOTE £27.80: £5.40, £1.10, £1.30; EX 92.90.

Owner Foursome Thoroughbreds **Bred** W Muir And Foursome Thoroughbreds **Trained** Lambourn, Berks

FOCUS
This maiden looked to good opportunity for Flouncing to open her account after a couple of promising efforts but that was not the case as she was caught as the line loomed.

NOTEBOOK
Totally Ours never figured on her debut after missing the break earlier in the month. Again she was untidy leaving the stalls but recovered well enough to sit in the mid-field. She got a dream run around the inside entering the straight and powered home in the final furlong to collar the favourite nearing the finish to win going away. She had clearly benefited from her experience and the way in which she knuckled to her task here suggests there should be plenty more to come. She will now be put away for the winter as she has a lot of maturing to do but connections hold this filly in the highest regard.

Flouncing(IRE) travelled well out in front and looked to have put the race to bed when over four lengths clear in the straight. She had no answers when collared but it will be a surprise if she is not soon off the mark. (op 5-4)

Baby Dottie has a consistent profile and again put up a solid effort in defeat. She never looked as if she would get to Flouncing to mount a challenge and just stuck on at the same pace. (op 5-2 tchd 100-30 and 7-2 in a place)

Lily In The Pond is related to plenty of winners and made a pleasing enough debut. She was always going to struggle to get involved with the front three after missing the break but she will have benefited from this experience and is worth keeping an eye on.

7178 BETFAIR MOBILE H'CAP — 2m (P)
6:05 (6:05) (Class 4) (0-85,78) 3-Y-O **£4,727** (£1,406; £702; £351) **Stalls** High

Form RPR

4411 **1** **Bow To No One (IRE)**[9] 6975 3-9-2 **76**... MartinLane(5) 2 89
(A P Jarvis) *trckd ldrs in 3rd and a travelling wl: qcknd to ld 2f out and sn in command: drvn rt out fnl f* **11/4[2]**

2321 **2** *10* **Samaaha**[40] 6166 3-9-9 **78**... MartinDwyer 3 82
(Saeed Bin Suroor) *trckd ldr: drvn to chal fr over 4f out: slt ld ins fnl 3f: hdd 2f out and sn no ch w wnr: eased ins fnl f* **5/4[1]**

1236 **3** *12* **Strathcal**[78] 4988 3-9-8 **77**... SteveDrowne 4 73
(H Morrison) *led: rdn and kpt slt advantage whn chal fr over 4f out: narrowly hdd ins fnl 3f: wknd over 2f out: eased whn wl btn fnl f* **3/1[3]**

22-4 **4** *20* **Inflammable**[10] 6951 3-9-0 **69**... SebSanders 1 32
(Sir Mark Prescott) *t.k.h: settled in 4th but wl in tch: hdwy to disp 3rd over 4f out: nvr a threat and wknd 3f out: eased whn no ch* **15/2**

3m 29.49s (-0.61) **Going Correction** -0.05s/f (Stan) **4** Ran SP% **107.9**
Speed ratings (Par 103): **99,94,88,78**
CSF £6.60 TOTE £3.50; EX 5.00.

Owner Geoffrey Bishop **Bred** Albert Conneally **Trained** Middleham Moor, N Yorks

FOCUS
All four runners were trying the trip for the first time in this tricky little heat and it was no better than a steady pace pace until leaving the back straight. The winner produced another clear personal best, but there are doubts over the strength of the form as the second and third were both eased.

7179 TIMEFORM BETFAIR RACING CLUB H'CAP (DIV I) — 7f (P)
6:35 (6:36) (Class 6) (0-65,65) 3-Y-O+ **£1,619** (£481; £240; £120) **Stalls** High

Form RPR

0020 **1** **Tudor Prince (IRE)**[19] 6738 5-9-6 **65**... NCallan 7 76
(A W Carroll) *t.k.h: chsd ldrs: led ins fnl 2f: drvn clr fnl f* **4/1[1]**

5446 **2** *2* **Goodbye Cash (IRE)**[15] 6828 5-8-12 **57**... PaulDoe 4 63+
(P D Evans) *hmpd s: in rr and swtchd rt: stl last 2f out: hdwy and nt clr run appr fnl f: rapid hdwy fnl 110yds and fin fast to take 2nd cl home but nvr any ch w wnr* **16/1**

0053 **3** *1 1/2* **The Happy Hammer (IRE)**[22] 6637 3-9-1 **62**... MartinDwyer 1 63
(E V Stanford) *chsd ldr: led over 3f out: rdn and hdd ins fnl 2f: styd chsng wnr but no ch fnl f: lost 2nd cl home* **6/1[3]**

5222 **4** *hd* **Westwood Dawn**[8] 7002 4-8-8 **58**...(v) MartinLane(5) 6 59
(D Shaw) *wnt lft s: towards rr but in tch: hdwy 2f out: styd on fnl f but nvr gng pce to trble ldrs* **6/1[3]**

0200 **5** *1/2* **No Grouse**[8] 6989 9-8-11 **56**... LiamJones 2 56
(E J Alston) *chsd ldrs: rdn and styd on same pce fr over 1f out* **33/1**

4502 **6** *1/2* **Peopleton Brook**[31] 6377 7-9-4 **63**...(t) SteveDrowne 10 61
(B G Powell) *in rr: pushed along and hdwy over 1f out: styd on ins fnl f but nvr gng pce to get into contention: fdd cl home* **11/1**

0600 **7** *nk* **Purus (IRE)**[16] 6790 7-9-5 **64**...(b[1]) SebSanders 8 62
(R A Teal) *in rr: pushed along over 2f out: styd on ins fnl f and gng on cl home but nvr any threat* **5/1[2]**

0526 **8** *1* **Convince (USA)**[44] 6028 8-8-11 **59**... AndreaAtzeni(3) 9 54
(J L Flint) *in tch on ins tl outpcd 4f out: hdwy ins fnl 3f and chsd ldrs 2f out: wknd fnl f* **15/2**

0000 **9** *1 1/4* **Prince De Fortune**[24] 6587 3-8-5 **52**... AdrianMcCarthy 12 42
(Mrs C A Dunnett) *chsd ldrs: rdn over 2f out: wknd fnl f* **50/1**

0465 **10** *2 1/2* **Carmenero (GER)**[19] 6738 6-9-6 **65**... LPKeniry 5 50
(C R Dore) *a towards rr* **17/2**

0440 **11** *3/4* **Jord (IRE)**[16] 6801 5-9-2 **61**...(p) JimCrowley 3 44
(J A Glover) *t.k.h: bhd tl sme prog on outside 3f out: nvr rchd ldrs and sn wknd* **16/1**

-600 **12** *dist* **Lunces Lad (IRE)**[162] 2224 5-9-5 **64**... GeorgeBaker 11 —
(G Brown) *led tl hdd over 3f out: wknd qckly: t.o* **16/1**

1m 25.32s (-0.68) **Going Correction** -0.05s/f (Stan)
WFA 3 from 4yo+ 2lb **12** Ran SP% **118.4**
Speed ratings (Par 101): **101,98,97,96,96 95,95,94,92,89 89,—**
toteswinger: 1&2 £7.60, 1&3 £5.50, 2&3 £13.00. CSF £70.53 CT £392.51 TOTE £6.90: £2.10, £6.40, £2.70; EX 91.90.

Owner Allan Jones **Bred** Edmond And Richard Kent **Trained** Cropthorne, Worcs

FOCUS
A competitive 51-65 handicap but only run at a fair pace.

Goodbye Cash(IRE) ◆ Official explanation: jockey said mare was denied a clear run

7180 TIMEFORM BETFAIR RACING CLUB H'CAP (DIV II) — 7f (P)
7:05 (7:05) (Class 6) (0-65,65) 3-Y-O+ **£1,618** (£481; £240; £60; £60) **Stalls** High

Form RPR

302 **1** **King Of Defence**[20] 6699 3-9-1 **62**... NCallan 10 74+
(M A Jarvis) *s.i.s: hld up towards rr: gd hdwy on ins whn hmpd over 2f out: swtchd lft and rapid hdwy over 1f out: led ins fnl f: edgd lft and sn drvn clr* **11/8[1]**

3200 **2** *1* **Fly By Nelly**[98] 4305 3-9-0 **61**... SteveDrowne 2 67
(H Morrison) *hld up in rr: pushed along and hung rt ins fnl 3f: gd hdwy over 1f out: str run ins fnl f to take 2nd cl home but no ch w wnr* **12/1**

2631 **3** *nk* **Cativo Cavallino**[59] 5576 6-9-2 **64**... NataliaGemelova(3) 7 70
(J E Long) *led: rdn and kpt on whn strly chal fr over 2f out: hdd and outpcd ins fnl f: lost 2nd cl home* **15/2[3]**

4400 **4** *1 3/4* **Crystallize**[29] 6455 3-9-4 **65**... StephenDonohoe 8 65
(A B Haynes) *chsd ldrs: drvn to chal 1f out: outpcd ins fnl f* **20/1**

0200 **4** *dht* **Kings Ace (IRE)**[11] 6914 3-8-6 **58**... MartinLane(5) 1 58
(A P Jarvis) *chsd ldrs: rdn 2f out: outpcd ins fnl f* **25/1**

-656 **6** *2 3/4* **Lindy Hop (IRE)**[20] 6701 3-9-1 **65**... AndreaAtzeni(3) 9 58
(W R Swinburn) *in rr: rdn and hdwy over 2f out: chsd ldrs over 1f out: wknd ins fnl f* **11/2[2]**

4066 **7** *3/4* **Dream Express (IRE)**[19] 6738 4-9-6 **65**...(b) IanMongan 3 57
(P Howling) *swtchd rt s: in rr: rdn: hung rt and hd high over 2f out: sme prog fnl f: nt resolute* **14/1**

0006 **8** *nk* **Dawson Creek (IRE)**[53] 5750 5-8-10 **58**...(p) JackMitchell(3) 4 49
(B Gubby) *chsd ldr: rdn 3f out: btn 2f out* **12/1**

0040 **9** *1/2* **Norcroft**[15] 6828 7-8-12 **57**...(p) AdrianMcCarthy 6 47
(Mrs C A Dunnett) *a in rr* **66/1**

3126 **10** *1* **Idle Power (IRE)**[9] 6964 11-9-6 **65**... PatCosgrave 5 52
(J R Boyle) *chsd ldrs: rdn over 3f out: wknd over 2f out* **8/1**

4050 **11** *1/2* **Pic Up Sticks**[16] 6799 10-8-9 **54**... KirstyMilczarek 11 40
(B G Powell) *stmbld s: chsd ldrs: rdn and edgd rt over 2f out: styd chsng ldrs tl wknd ins fnl f* **20/1**

1m 25.37s (-0.63) **Going Correction** -0.05s/f (Stan)
WFA 3 from 4yo+ 2lb **11** Ran SP% **117.3**
Speed ratings (Par 101): **101,99,99,97,97 94,93,93,92,91 90**
toteswinger: 1&2 £5.60, 1&3 £3.40, 2&3 £7.20. CSF £18.41 CT £98.30 TOTE £2.50: £1.20, £4.90, £2.40; EX 21.70.

Owner Barnett, Manasseh & Partners **Bred** M E Wates **Trained** Newmarket, Suffolk

FOCUS
A modest handicap and sound form based around the third.

7181 BETFAIR MULTIPLES H'CAP — 7f (P)
7:35 (7:35) (Class 4) (0-85,84) 3-Y-O **£4,727** (£1,406; £702; £351) **Stalls** High

Form RPR

1 **Bay Knight (IRE)**[46] 6086 3-8-12 **78**... NCallan 5 86
(W McCreery, Ire) *trckd ldrs: drvn to ld appr fnl f: in command whn hung lft nr fin* **8/1**

6514 **2** *1 1/2* **Arachnophobia (IRE)**[10] 6944 3-9-1 **81**... RobertWinston 6 85
(Pat Eddery) *chsd ldr: drvn to take slt ld ins fnl 2f: hdd appr fnl f: styd on same pce ins fnl f* **7/2[2]**

1065 **3** *1* **Snow Bay**[33] 6348 3-8-5 **78**... AdamCarter(7) 7 79
(B Smart) *led at modest pce: rdn and hdd ins fnl 2f: styd on same pce fnl f* **7/1**

1326 **4** *3/4* **Sunshine Always (IRE)**[17] 6773 3-9-2 **82**... KirstyMilczarek 2 81
(T D McCarthy) *in rr: stl last over 2f out: swtchd rt and styd on thrght fnl f: kpt on cl home but nvr a threat* **4/1[3]**

2311 **5** ½ **Bea Menace (USA)**[7] 7027 3-9-4 84 JimCrowley 1 82
(P F I Cole) *t.k.h early off mod pce: chsd ldrs: pushed along 2f out and styd on same pce fnl f* **11/8**[1]
-000 **6** 15 **Touching (IRE)**[70] 5260 3-9-2 82 SteveDrowne 4 39
(R Hannon) *plld hrd in rr off mod early pce: rdn: hung rt and btn over 2f out* **20/1**
1m 26.49s (0.49) **Going Correction** -0.05s/f (Stan) **6** Ran SP% **112.7**
Speed ratings (Par 103): **95,93,92,91,90 73**
toteswinger: 1&2 £4.80, 1&3 £11.60, 2&3 £6.60. CSF £35.89 TOTE £14.30: £6.80, £2.50; EX 38.40 Place 6: £33.10 Place 5: £20.13.
Owner Iona Equine Syndicate **Bred** Pat Roach **Trained** Maynooth, Co.Kildare
FOCUS
Not much pace on and it was the slowest of the three C&D races. The favourite was disappointing and the runner-up is the best guide.
Touching(IRE) Official explanation: jockey said filly ran too free
T/Plt: £41.00 to a £1 stake. Pool: £50,954.54. 906.09 winning tickets. T/Qpdt: £34.50 to a £1 stake. Pool: £3,228.48. 69.20 winning tickets. ST

7145 NEWMARKET (R-H)
Saturday, October 31

OFFICIAL GOING: Good (good to soft in places)
Stands' side course used.
Wind: Mediuim, half against Weather: Overcast, dull

7182 FINANCIALS AT BET365 E B F MAIDEN FILLIES' STKS (DIV I) 7f
12:20 (12:23) (Class 4) 2-Y-O **£4,857** (£1,445; £722; £360) **Stalls** Low

Form RPR
3 **1** **Revered**[19] 6729 2-9-0 0 KFallon 2 79
(Sir Michael Stoute) *chsd ldrs: pushed along and jnd ldrs 2f out: rdn to ld over 1f out: hld on wl fnl f* **13/8**[1]
2 ½ **Call To Reason (IRE)** 2-9-0 0 EddieAhern 18 78+
(J Noseda) *trckd ldrs: rdn and ev ch over 1f out: pressed wnr thrght fnl f: kpt on wl but a jst hld* **14/1**
0 **3** 1 **Miss Mittagong (USA)**[40] 6163 2-9-0 0 JimCrowley 20 75
(R M Beckett) *racd alone on far rail: chsng ldrs thrght: rdn over 1f out: chsd ldng pair fnl f: no ex fnl 50yds* **20/1**
4 2¼ **Fashion Insider (USA)** 2-9-0 0 MartinDwyer 14 70
(B J Meehan) *chsd ldrs: rdn ent fnl 2f: ev ch whn edgd lft over 1f out: outpcd by ldng trio fnl f* **20/1**
5 hd **Ajool (USA)** 2-9-0 0 RHills 4 69
(B W Hills) *racd in midfield: hdwy to chse ldrs 2f out: rdn and kpt on same pce fr over 1f out* **12/1**
6 2¼ **Consequential** 2-9-0 0 RichardMullen 11 64+
(D M Simcock) *in tch: rdn and carried rt ent fnl 2f: styd on steadily but no imp on ldrs fr over 1f out* **100/1**
7 shd **Countenance Divine** 2-9-0 0 MichaelHills 5 63+
(B W Hills) *chsd ldrs: jnd ldr over 2f out: led wl over 1f out: sn hdd: jst beginning to weaken whn hit in face by rivals whip jst over 1f out: wl hld fnl f* **13/2**[3]
8 ¾ **Peaceful Soul (USA)** 2-9-0 0 ChrisCatlin 1 61
(D R Lanigan) *towards rr: rdn along and no prog over 2f out: rallied and styd on wl fnl f: nt pce to trble ldrs* **33/1**
9 1 **Sunrise Shuffle** 2-9-0 0 WilliamBuick 12 59+
(B W Hills) *s.i.s: hld up towards rr: sme hdwy whn hmpd and pushed lft over 1f out: no imp after* **40/1**
10 ¾ **Vaultage (USA)** 2-9-0 0 RichardHughes 3 57
(E A L Dunlop) *chsd ldrs: rdn ent fnl 2f: sn struggling: wknd over 1f out* **33/1**
11 ¾ **Alice Cullen** 2-9-0 0 ShaneKelly 13 55+
(W R Swinburn) *racd in midfield: rdn and outpcd 3f out: styd on again fr over 1f out: nvr trbld ldrs* **100/1**
12 ½ **Cheerfully** 2-9-0 0 JimmyFortune 8 54+
(J H M Gosden) *s.i.s: towards rr: rdn and effrt whn swvd lft and bmpd rival over 1f out: rn green and no prog after* **8/1**
13 2 **Best Intent** 2-9-0 0 PhilipRobinson 6 49
(M A Jarvis) *chsd ldr tl led 3f out: sn rdn: hdd wl over 1f out: sn wknd* **20/1**
14 3¼ **Tiger Court** 2-9-0 0 SteveDrowne 19 41
(E A L Dunlop) *a towards rr: rdn and struggling 3f out: nvr trbld ldrs* **66/1**
15 ½ **Happy Mood** 2-9-0 0 FergusSweeney 9 40
(G L Moore) *in tch in midfield: rdn wl over 2f out: sn struggling: wl btn fnl f* **100/1**
16 1¼ **Star Of Soho (IRE)** 2-9-0 0 EdwardCreighton 15 36
(E J Creighton) *s.i.s: a bhd* **125/1**
0 **17** 1¼ **Batgirl**[21] 6679 2-9-0 0 MickyFenton 10 33
(John Berry) *led tl 3f out: sn rdn and wkng: hung rt over 2f out: sn wl bhd* **150/1**
18 2 **Profligate (IRE)** 2-9-0 0 AlanMunro 17 28
(W Jarvis) *s.i.s: a bhd* **100/1**
19 15 **Fayre Bella** 2-9-0 0 TPO'Shea 7 —
(J Gallagher) *t.k.h: in tch tl rdn and stuggling 1/2-way: wl bhd fnl 2f* **150/1**
6 **20** ½ **Free Grain**[58] 5604 2-9-0 0 TedDurcan 16 —
(J L Dunlop) *a bhd and nvr gng wl: wl bhd fnl 2f* **11/2**[2]
1m 27.96s (2.56) **Going Correction** +0.15s/f (Good) **20** Ran SP% **122.5**
Speed ratings (Par 94): **91,90,89,86,86 83,83,82,81,80 80,79,77,73,72 71,70,67,50,50**
toteswinger: 1&2 £9.30, 1&3 £21.70, 2&3 £61.90. CSF £23.37 TOTE £2.40: £1.60, £4.40, £6.90; EX 31.60.
Owner K Abdulla **Bred** Juddmonte Farms Ltd **Trained** Newmarket, Suffolk
FOCUS
Following some overnight rain, the ground was eased to good, good to soft in places, with the GoingStick reading 7.3. Apple Charlotte and Sariska won divisions of this maiden last year, while Infallible won one the previous year, so it's a race that can throw up some decent fillies.
NOTEBOOK
Revered had finished third in a soft-ground Salisbury maiden on her debut and was expected to have come on plenty. Her experience got her through, doing the job in workmanlike style, and, given her pedigree, she looks the type who will improve from two to three. (op 5-4)
Call To Reason(IRE), whose dam won a Group 3 over this trip as a juvenile, comes from a stable that can get a newcomer ready. She ran really well and it will be interesting to see how much improvement there is to come from her. (op 16-1)
Miss Mittagong(USA) stayed on the far-side rail and it might prove she was at an advantage there. Still, having been green and well beaten on her debut on the Polytrack, she stepped up considerably for the benefit of that experience. Given her dirt pedigree, a return to the artificial surfaces could well help her get off the mark before the end of the year. (op 25-1)
Fashion Insider(USA) ◆, who cost $460,000, is a half-sister to a couple of high-class dirt performers. A little keen to post and prominent throughout on this debut, she's another who might find a race on Polytrack before the year is out if connections decide to persevere.
Ajool(USA) wasn't knocked about and should benefit from this debut effort. (op 16-1)
Consequential showed ability and looks the type to do better once she's eligible for handicaps.
Countenance Divine, representing the owner of Sariska, ran well for a long way. Quite tall, her pedigree suggests she might not want to go much further than 1m next year. (op 9-1 tchd 6-1)
Cheerfully, the first foal of Light Of Morn, a daughter of Yorkshire Oaks/Prix Vermeille winner My Emma, ran green, but she is bred to make a middle-distance three-year-old and there should be better to come from her next year. (op 9-1)
Free Grain ran all right on her debut in a similar heat at Salisbury but she was in trouble a long way out here and clearly didn't run her race. Official explanation: jockey said filly never travelled (op 7-1 tchd 15-2)

7183 FINANCIALS AT BET365 E B F MAIDEN FILLIES' STKS (DIV II) 7f
12:55 (1:00) (Class 4) 2-Y-O **£4,857** (£1,445; £722; £360) **Stalls** Low

Form RPR
1 **Field Day (IRE)** 2-9-0 0 MartinDwyer 20 78+
(B J Meehan) *in tch in midfield: hdwy and pushed along ent fnl 2f: rdn to chse ldr over 1f out: led ins fnl f: r.o strly* **14/1**
4 **2** 1½ **Scorn (USA)**[19] 6730 2-9-0 0 JimmyFortune 12 74
(J H M Gosden) *chsd ldr tl led ent fnl 3f: rdn and hrd pressed wl over 1f out: hdd ins fnl f: styd on same pce after* **3/1**[2]
3 1½ **Safina** 2-9-0 0 KFallon 3 70+
(Sir Michael Stoute) *hld up wl in tch: hdwy over 2f out: rdn to press ldr over 1f out: drvn and kpt on same pce fnl f* **11/4**[1]
4 ¾ **Perfect Note** 2-9-0 0 LDettori 18 68
(Saeed Bin Suroor) *hld up wl in tch: hdwy over 2f out: chsd ldr 2f out: drvn and ev ch over 1f out: outpcd ent fnl f* **4/1**[3]
5 1 **Madhaaq (IRE)** 2-9-0 0 RHills 14 66
(J L Dunlop) *in tch: pushed along and unable qck 2f out: styd on same pce and no imp fnl f* **16/1**
0 **6** 1¾ **Montelissima (IRE)**[100] 4239 2-9-0 0 TedDurcan 1 62
(E A L Dunlop) *hld up towards rr: rdn and hdwy jst over 2f out: chsd ldrs over 1f out: no imp fnl f* **100/1**
7 1¾ **Flotation (USA)** 2-9-0 0 RobertWinston 15 57+
(B W Hills) *restless in stalls: rrd s and s.i.s: in tch in midfield after 2f out: outpcd and edging rt 2f out: kpt on steadily fnl f* **33/1**
8 nk **Warling (IRE)** 2-9-0 0 EddieAhern 16 56+
(J Noseda) *chsd ldr tl 2f out: sn rdn and struggling: wknd over 1f out* **16/1**
0 **9** ½ **Swish Dish (CAN)**[23] 6616 2-9-0 0 RichardHughes 19 55
(R Hannon) *chsd ldrs tl rdn ent fnl 2f: wknd over 1f out and wl hld fnl f* **33/1**
10 1 **Park View** 2-9-0 0 MichaelHills 2 53
(B W Hills) *stdd s: bhd: pushed along and struggling wl over 2f out: no prog tl styd on past btn horses fnl f: nvr trbld ldrs* **20/1**
00 **11** 2 **Dhan Dhana (IRE)**[5] 7050 2-9-0 0 TonyCulhane 17 48
(W J Haggas) *led tl hdd ent fnl 3f: wknd u.p wl over 1f out: wl btn fnl f* **50/1**
12 hd **Shianda** 2-9-0 0 DaneO'Neill 7 47+
(G L Moore) *s.i.s: sn pushed along in rr: nvr trbld ldrs* **100/1**
0 **13** 1¼ **Jemimaville (IRE)**[75] 5096 2-9-0 0 TravisBlock 8 44
(G C Bravery) *chsd ldrs: rdn over 2f out: wkng whn sltly short of room over 1f out: wl btn fnl f* **150/1**
14 ½ **Acquainted** 2-9-0 0 HayleyTurner 9 43
(M L W Bell) *s.i.s: sn pushed along: hdwy into midfield after 2f: wknd 2f out and wl btn after* **50/1**
15 hd **Perse** 2-9-0 0 AlanMunro 10 42
(W Jarvis) *hld up in tch in midfield: lost pl and bhd over 2f out: wl bhd fr over 1f out* **50/1**
0 **16** 1½ **Dance With Chance (IRE)**[53] 5752 2-9-0 0 ShaneKelly 4 39
(W R Swinburn) *a towards rr: rdn and struggling 3f out: nvr trbld ldrs* **100/1**
17 2 **Alwarqaa** 2-9-0 0 TPO'Shea 5 34
(B W Hills) *s.i.s: a in rr: nvr a factor* **25/1**
6 **18** ½ **Three Times**[10] 6947 2-9-0 0 ChrisCatlin 6 32
(D R Lanigan) *in tch in midfield: pushed along and struggling 3f out: n.d fnl 2f* **100/1**
19 5 **On Her Way** 2-9-0 0 IanMongan 13 20+
(H R A Cecil) *restless in stalls: s.i.s and sn rdn in detached last: rn v green and all over the pl: nvr on terms* **16/1**
0 **20** nk **Ava Doll**[4] 7095 2-8-7 0 DannyBrock(7) 11 19
(J R Jenkins) *in tch in midfield tl lost pl over 3f out: wl bhd fnl 2f* **200/1**
1m 28.05s (2.65) **Going Correction** +0.15s/f (Good) **20** Ran SP% **121.5**
Speed ratings (Par 94): **90,88,86,85,84 82,80,80,79,78 76,76,74,74,73 72,69,69,63,63**
toteswinger: 1&2 £8.30, 1&3 £15.80, 2&3 £5.40. CSF £50.90 TOTE £18.80: £4.00, £1.50, £2.40; EX 79.10.
Owner Ballymacoll Stud **Bred** Ballymacoll Stud Farm Ltd **Trained** Manton, Wilts
FOCUS
Very marginally the slower of the two divisions.
NOTEBOOK
Field Day(IRE) ◆, whose trainer sent out the fourth in the first division and had won a division of this race twice in the previous four years, produced this filly to score first time up. Drawn highest of all, she raced on the outside of the bunch nearest the far-side rail, picked up well from the Dip and saw out her race strongly. A daughter of Cape Cross out of a mare from the high-class family of Grecian Sea and Islington, she took a while to pull up after the line and gave the impression she'll stay at least 1m next year. She is held in some regard and her connections plan to run her in a Guineas trial in the spring. (op 16-1 tchd 18-1)
Scorn(USA) had run with promise at Salisbury on her debut 19 days earlier and showed the benefit of the outing by being up with the pace and posting a solid effort. She can probably find a maiden on the sand if connections keep going with her. (op 4-1)
Safina ◆, the second foal of top-class miler Russian Rhythm, had been delayed in making her debut by niggly problems. Drawn low, unlike those around her at the finish, she shaped with plenty of promise, and the daughter of Pivotal looks the type to do much better at three. (tchd 5-2 and 3-1)
Perfect Note ◆ ended her trainer's impressive winning streak, Bin Suroor having connected with his last eight runners, but she ran a perfectly good race on her debut. A half-sister to Claremont, who won a 1m4f Group 3 in France, out of a mare who won the Prix Vermeille, she's another who is bred to make a better three-year-old. (op 5-2)
Madhaaq(IRE), a half-sister to four winners, showed signs of inexperience but displayed ability and is likely to come on plenty for this first run.
Montelissima(IRE) lost her action on firm ground on her debut but she'd been given plenty of time off since and these conditions clearly suited her better. Her pedigree suggests she'll be a middle-distance filly next year.
Flotation(USA), whose jockey wore her owner's second colours, is a half-sister to three winners and she showed enough to suggest she has a future.

Warling(IRE) wasn't knocked about once she began to tire. She's bred to stay further than her very useful half-brother War Native. (op 20-1)
Park View, who was given a patient ride, ran green and can only do better with this debut experience under her belt. (tchd 22-1)

7184 BET365 08000 322365 ZETLAND CONDITIONS STKS 1m 2f
1:30 (1:30) (Class 2) 2-Y-O

£8,723 (£2,612; £1,306; £653; £326; £163) **Stalls** Low

Form RPR

2104 **1** **Take It To The Max**[56] 5659 2-9-0 97 JimmyFortune 1 95
(G M Moore) *racd keenly: led for 2f: chsd ldr after: rdn to ld again over 2f out: hdd over 1f out: rallied gamely u.str.p to ld again last stride* **9/1**

1 **2** *shd* **Anhar (USA)**[24] 6592 2-9-0 0 LDettori 4 95
(Saeed Bin Suroor) *hld up wl in tch: rdn and effrt ent fnl 2f: drvn to ld and wanting to edge rt over 1f out: hld narrow advantage tl hdd last stride* **7/4**[1]

01 **3** *1* **Ted Spread**[20] 6697 2-9-0 80 JimmyQuinn 2 93
(M H Tompkins) *stdd and dropped in bhd after s: rdn and effrt over 2f out: chsd ldrs and hrd drvn over 1f out: no imp tl styd on fnl 100yds: wnt 3rd nr fin: unable to rch ldrs* **5/1**[3]

120 **4** *nk* **Private Story (USA)**[34] 6319 2-9-0 89 RichardHughes 6 92
(R Hannon) *hld up in last pair: reminder over 4f out: rdn over 2f out: edging rt u.p and chsd ldng pair over 1f out: kpt on but nt pce to chal: lost 3rd nr fin* **3/1**[2]

031 **5** *7* **Natural Law (IRE)**[35] 6291 2-9-0 83 (v[1]) TedDurcan 3 80
(Saeed Bin Suroor) *chsd ldr tl led after 2f: rdn and hdd over 2f out: wknd and wl btn over 1f out* **11/1**

3114 **6** *18* **Mingun Bell (USA)**[28] 6472 2-9-0 93 EddieAhern 5 47
(H R A Cecil) *t.k.h: hld up in tch: rdn and dropped out qckly over 2f out: wl bhd and eaesd fnl f* **13/2**

2m 7.57s (1.77) **Going Correction** +0.15s/f (Good) **6** Ran SP% **109.7**
Speed ratings (Par 101): **98,97,97,96,91 76**
toteswinger: 1&2 £3.90, 1&3 £7.40, 2&3 £1.80. CSF £24.14 TOTE £7.00: £2.20, £2.40; EX 12.20.
Owner Mrs Phillipa Davies **Bred** Whatton Manor Stud **Trained** Middleham Moor, N Yorks

FOCUS
All these runners were trying the trip for the first time, the early pace was not strong and they finished in a bit of a heap, so the suspicion is that this is not strong form.

NOTEBOOK
Take It To The Max had the highest official rating and was also the most experienced runner. He looked as though he might improve for a longer trip at Haydock last time, and although he's by Bahamian Bounty, his dam won over almost 1m7f, so there was the stamina in his pedigree to back up that view. While the runner-up hung and ran green, the winner was far more professional, responding to pressure to edge it on the line, but the bare form suggests he didn't have to improve on his previous best. He should get 1m4f next season. (tchd 8-1)
Anhar(USA) had more to do than when successful in a Nottingham maiden first time up, but he's well bred and was representing a stable in cracking form. He showed his inexperience by hanging right, though, and didn't help Dettori much in the finish. As a son of Kingmambo, quicker ground would have probably suited him, too. (op 5-4 tchd 2-1)
Ted Spread, who won over 1m1f last time, showing stamina to be his strong suit, proved difficult to settle and in the circumstances did well to finish as close as he did. A stronger pace will undoubtedly suit him better. (op 6-1 tchd 9-2)
Private Story(USA) was given a couple of sharp reminders with around five furlongs to run and was one-paced in the closing stages. The ground was probably not to his liking. (op 9-2)
Natural Law(IRE), the Godolphin second string, had a visor on for the first time instead of cheekpieces, and took them along for much of the way. He simply looked to be outclassed. (op 10-1)
Mingun Bell(USA), who had an excuse last time as he lost a front shoe, stopped quickly and presumably something was amiss. Official explanation: jockey said colt ran flat (op 7-1 tchd 15-2)

7185 BET365 BEST ODDS H'CAP 1m
2:05 (2:05) (Class 2) (0-105,105) 3-Y-O+

£11,215 (£3,358; £1,679; £840; £419; £210) **Stalls** Low

Form RPR

2-33 **1** **Secrecy**[19] 6732 3-9-6 **102** LDettori 6 116+
(Saeed Bin Suroor) *taken down early: hld up towards rr: hdwy to trck ldrs and nt clr run ent fnl 2f tl ent fnl f: qcknd through gap to ld 1f out: sn clr: v easily* **7/4**[1]

0003 **2** *5* **Benandonner (USA)**[38] 6217 6-8-13 **92** FrederikTylicki 1 95
(R A Fahey) *in tch: rdn and effrt over 2f out: ev ch and drvn over 1f out: no ch w wnr fnl f but kpt on to go 2nd nr fin* **9/1**

0361 **3** *nk* **Fastnet Storm (IRE)**[16] 6795 3-8-10 **92** MickyFenton 3 94
(T P Tate) *restless in stalls: led: rdn wl over 1f out: hdd 1f out: sn no ch w wnr: lost 2nd nr fin* **9/1**

0666 **4** *1 1/4* **Lucky Dance (BRZ)**[13] 6876 7-8-7 **86** oh4 RichardMullen 4 85
(A G Foster) *chsd ldrs: rdn over 3f out: drvn to chsd ldr over 2f out: ev ch over 1f out: plugged on same pce fnl f* **16/1**

2400 **5** *1/2* **Moynahan (USA)**[13] 6876 4-9-1 **94** AlanMunro 5 92
(P F I Cole) *stdd s: hld up in rr: rdn over 2f out: sme prog u.p and swtchd lft over 1f out: nvr trbld ldrs* **12/1**

4-20 **6** *1/2* **Liberation (IRE)**[199] 1291 3-9-7 **103** TedDurcan 14 100
(Saeed Bin Suroor) *stdd s: hld up in rr: rdn and effrt 2f out: rdn and no prog over 1f out and wl btn fnl f* **15/2**[3]

0105 **7** *4* **Marvo**[16] 6795 5-8-2 **86** oh3 AshleyMorgan(5) 7 74
(M H Tompkins) *awkward leaving stalls and s.i.s: bhd: rdn and nt clr run 2f out: swtchd rt over 1f out: nvr trbld ldrs* **11/1**

/20- **8** *3 3/4* **Miyasaki (CHI)**[20] 7-9-6 **99** (b) EspenSki 13 78
(Rune Haugen, Norway) *w ldr tl rdn over 2f out: sn struggling: wl btn over 1f out* **66/1**

-110 **9** *1* **Infiraad**[136] 3011 3-9-4 **100** RHills 12 77
(B W Hills) *t.k.h: chsd ldrs: rdn ent fnl 2f: sn wknd* **7/1**[2]

0060 **10** *hd* **King Of Rome (IRE)**[35] 6290 4-9-12 **105** (bt[1]) PatCosgrave 11 81
(M F De Kock, South Africa) *in tch: rdn and struggling whn rt over 2f out: wl btn over 1f out* **16/1**

1100 **11** *3 1/4* **Crown Choice**[20] 6702 4-8-10 **89** (t) WilliamBuick 8 58
(W R Swinburn) *hld up towards rr: pushed along 3f out: rdn and no prog ent fnl 2f: wl btn over 1f out* **11/1**

1m 37.87s (-0.73) **Going Correction** +0.15s/f (Good)
WFA 3 from 4yo+ 3lb **11** Ran SP% **118.2**
Speed ratings (Par 109): **109,104,103,102,101 101,97,93,92,92 89**
toteswinger: 1&2 £4.20, 1&3 £2.80, 2&3 £122.70. CSF £18.22 CT £115.72 TOTE £2.40: £1.20, £2.10, £1.60; EX 24.10 Trifecta £74.60 Pool: £514.80 - 5.10 winning units..
Owner Godolphin **Bred** Whatton Manor Stud **Trained** Newmarket, Suffolk

FOCUS
They raced towards the stands' side this time and the first five home occupied the lowest five stalls. The impressive winner looks a potential Group horse and the third is the best guide.

NOTEBOOK
Secrecy ◆ made a mockery of his mark of 102 and quickened up in fine style to stamp himself a Pattern-class performer in the making. Getting plenty of cover off the solid gallop, he travelled strongly into contention and, when asked to go on, put the race to bed in a matter of strides. It wouldn't be surprising were he to win at Group level next year, and he's scheduled to appear at the Dubai carnival. (op 11-4)
Benandonner(USA), down to a mark 2lb lower than when last successful, bounced back to form, running on well up the rail to take second. He is admirably versatile with regard to ground conditions. (op 12-1)
Fastnet Storm(IRE), a progressive sort, was dropping back from 1m2f. Once again he made a bold bid from the front, but a combination of the drop back in trip and a career-high mark found him out. (op 13-2)
Lucky Dance(BRZ), a shock winner of this race last year, was off the same mark this time being 4lb wrong, and ran a sound race. He was under pressure from some way out but, to his credit, kept responding. (op 20-1)
Moynahan(USA), well below his best in his last two starts, stayed on late without being a threat and remains very hard to win with. (tchd 14-1)
Liberation(IRE), in Godolphin's second colours, raced widest of all for a portion of the race and carried his head high when put under pressure. He'd been off the track since the spring, having had respiratory problems, so it wasn't a bad run in the circumstances. (op 8-1)
Infiraad, off the track since finishing down the field in the Jersey Stakes, was weak in the market and proved difficult to settle in the race. As a result, it wasn't a great surprise to see him tire quite badly in the closing stages. (op 4-1 tchd 15-2)

7186 BET365 BEN MARSHALL STKS (LISTED RACE) 1m
2:35 (2:35) (Class 1) 3-Y-O+ **£22,708** (£8,608; £4,308; £2,148; £1,076) **Stalls** Low

Form RPR

11 **1** **Prince Of Dance**[19] 6732 3-8-11 100 RichardKingscote 3 112+
(Tom Dascombe) *taken down early: wnt rt s: plld hrd: chsd ldr: rdn to ld narrowly over 1f out hld on v gamely fnl f* **7/2**[2]

4-50 **2** *hd* **Shaweel**[174] 1917 3-8-11 115 LDettori 2 112
(Saeed Bin Suroor) *trckd ldrs: rdn and ev ch over 1f out: pressed wnr thrght: r.o but a jst hld* **6/4**[1]

5120 **3** *nk* **Bushman**[15] 6812 5-9-0 105 JimCrowley 4 111
(D M Simcock) *hmpd s: hld up in tch in rr: hdwy on outer ent fnl 2f: drvn ent fnl f: ev ch ins fnl f: kpt on* **9/1**

-113 **4** *1 1/2* **City Style (USA)**[175] 1865 3-8-11 109 TedDurcan 1 107
(Saeed Bin Suroor) *hld up in tch in last pair: rdn and effrt over 2f out: hanging rt after: chsd ldng trio fnl f: continued to hang bdly rt and unable to chal* **6/1**[3]

2213 **5** *4 1/2* **Plum Pudding (IRE)**[77] 5024 6-9-0 109 RichardHughes 5 99
(R Hannon) *led: rdn and hdd over 1f out: eased whn btn ins fnl f* **7/2**[2]

1m 39.11s (0.51) **Going Correction** +0.15s/f (Good)
WFA 3 from 5yo+ 3lb **5** Ran SP% **108.7**
Speed ratings (Par 111): **103,102,102,101,96**
CSF £8.98 TOTE £5.10: £2.00, £1.60; EX 17.40.
Owner Five Horses Ltd **Bred** Five Horses Ltd **Trained** Lambourn, Berks
■ Stewards' Enquiry : L Dettori two-day ban: used whip with excessive frequency without giving colt time to respond (Nov 14,16)

FOCUS
This race was won by subsequent Lockinge winner Virtual last year. This year's renewal was muddling though the form makes sense at face value. The form makes sense at face value.

NOTEBOOK
Prince Of Dance could make his mark in Group company next year as he retained his unbeaten record despite pulling hard early. Throwing his head about and eager to go faster, a stronger pace would have undoubtedly seen him in a better light, but he still impressed in digging deep and seeing off his two main rivals close home. A progressive sort, a bit of ease in the ground is essential to him. (tchd 3-1)
Shaweel, off the track since finishing in mid-division in the French 2,000 Guineas, has yet to recapture his two-year-old best. He's entitled to come on for this run, though, and perhaps his connections can find a race for him abroad before the year is out. (op 2-1)
Bushman, at his best with plenty of cut in the ground, could have done with it being even softer. This is his level, though, and it was a solid effort giving weight to the three-year-olds. (op 15-2)
City Style(USA), another returning from a layoff stretching back to the spring, had done all his racing on quicker ground. He didn't handle the track and will no doubt appreciate getting back on a decent surface in Dubai. Official explanation: jockey said gelding lost its action (op 7-1)
Plum Pudding(IRE), a course specialist, looked to be enjoying the run of the race out in front but dropped away tamely once challenged. He'd been off for 77 days, having not been at his best over the summer, and this was not his true form. Official explanation: jockey said gelding had no more to give (op 11-4)

7187 CASINO AT BET365.COM EBF MONTROSE FILLIES' STKS (LISTED RACE) 1m
3:10 (3:11) (Class 1) 2-Y-O

£17,031 (£6,456; £3,231; £1,611; £807; £405) **Stalls** Low

Form RPR

21 **1** **Timepiece**[22] 6628 2-8-12 83 EddieAhern 9 101
(H R A Cecil) *chsd ldrs: pushed into ld 3f out: rdn and hdd over 1f out: hrd drvn ent fnl f: kpt on gamely to ld again wl ins fnl f: all out* **4/1**[2]

523 **2** *nse* **Nurture (IRE)**[34] 6319 2-8-12 0 KFallon 3 101
(R Hannon) *chsd ldrs: pushed along 3f out: rdn and ev ch 2f out: led narrowly over 1f out: hrd drvn fnl f: hdd wl ins fnl f: jst btn* **13/2**

0115 **3** *4 1/2* **Clarietta**[50] 5825 2-8-12 97 TedDurcan 2 91
(J L Dunlop) *hld up in tch: rdn and chsd ldrs over 2f out: drvn and battling for 3rd fr over 1f out: no imp on ldng pair fnl f* **8/1**

3312 **4** *hd* **Marie De Medici (USA)**[11] 6929 2-8-12 104 RHills 14 91
(M Johnston) *awkward leaving stalls: sn rcvrd and led after 1f: hdd and rdn 3f out: styd handy tl wknd u.p 1f out: lost 3rd nr fin* **11/4**[1]

241 **5** *2 1/4* **Flip Flop (IRE)**[25] 6563 2-8-12 75 MichaelHills 7 86
(B W Hills) *led for 1f: styd chsng ldrs: rdn and outpcd ent fnl 2f: plugged on same pce after* **33/1**

3 **6** *1* **Tashzara (IRE)**[24] 6600 2-8-12 0 RobertWinston 1 83
(Christopher Phillips, Ire) *stdd s: hld up in rr: switching rt and hdwy ent fnl 2f: no imp u.p fr over 1f out* **16/1**

1353 **7** *5* **Dark Eyes (IRE)**[28] 6481 2-8-12 81 DaneO'Neill 8 72
(D J Coakley) *t.k.h: hld up in tch in midfield: wnt rt and bmpd rival over 5f out: rdn and struggling 3f out: n.d fnl 2f* **40/1**

31 **8** *nse* **Thrill**[19] 6729 2-8-12 81 JimmyFortune 4 72
(J H M Gosden) *chsd ldrs: rdn and outpcd whn hung rt wl over 2f out: no ch w ldrs fr wl over 1f out* **6/1**[3]

1 **9** *6* **Bint Almatar (USA)**[31] 6389 2-8-12 0 LDettori 6 59+
(Saeed Bin Suroor) *s.i.s: hld up towards rr: hdwy 1/2-way: rdn and struggling over 2f out: wl btn and eased ins fnl f* **10/1**

53 **10** *14* **Yankee Bright (USA)**[18] 6762 2-8-12 0 AlanMunro 12 28
(J G Given) *in tch tl rdn and struggling 3f out: wl bhd fnl 2f: eased fr wl over 1f out* **100/1**

511 **11** *4* **Wild Rose**[28] 6491 2-8-12 83 .... HayleyTurner 10 19
(M L W Bell) *hld up in tch in midfield: rdn and btn over 3f out: wl bhd and eased fr over 1f out* **20/1**

531 **12** *1 1/2* **Cat Hunter**[11] 6911 2-8-12 72 .... JimCrowley 13 16
(Mrs A J Perrett) *hld up in midfield: rdn and struggling 3f out: wl bhd whn eased fr over 1f out* **50/1**

01 **13** *3/4* **Sunarise (IRE)**[11] 6912 2-8-12 82 .... RichardHughes 11 15
(R Hannon) *in tch in midfield: bmpd over 5f out: rdn and btn 3f out: wl bhd and eased fr wl over 1f out* **16/1**

1m 38.98s (0.38) **Going Correction** +0.15s/f (Good) **13** Ran SP% **119.3**
Speed ratings (Par 100): **104,103,99,99,97 96,91,90,84,70 66,65,64**
toteswinger: 1&2 £6.60, 1&3 £6.50, 2&3 £5.70. CSF £28.92 TOTE £4.70: £1.60, £2.80, £2.60; EX 54.10 Trifecta £546.20 Part won. Pool: £738.24 - 0.30 winning units..
Owner K Abdulla **Bred** Juddmonte Farms Ltd **Trained** Newmarket, Suffolk
■ Stewards' Enquiry : Eddie Ahern one-day ban: used whip with excessive frequency (Nov 14)

FOCUS
An interesting Listed event featuring seven last-time-out winners, and form to be positive about.

NOTEBOOK
Timepiece ◆ has a lot to live up to as her trainer won this race with Passage Of Time in 2006 and sent out Midday to finish fourth last year - both went on to take Group 1 honours. Prominent from the outset, she drifted over towards the stands' side from two and a half furlongs out but kept on strongly with the runner-up to finish well clear of the third. Bred to improve with time and distance, she'll surely appear in an Oaks trial next season, and the 33-1 opening show for the Epsom Classic looks a fair price considering her profile, pedigree and connections. It's worth bearing in mind that she doesn't want quick ground, though. (op 7-2 tchd 9-2)
Nurture(IRE), third in the Goffs Million Mile last time out, had Fallon in the saddle this time and, under a strong ride up the stands' side, she came up just short. It was a great effort, though, confirming her improvement since being stepped up in trip, and she has the makings of a smart middle-distance performer next season. (op 9-1 tchd 10-1)
Clarietta, beaten just over four lengths into fourth in the May Hill on her latest start, stayed on well but couldn't live with the first two, and was beaten a similar distance. She looks to have run her race, though, and is probably a fair guide to the level of the form. (tchd 15-2)
Marie De Medici(USA), second in a Group 3 in France last time out, came into the race with the highest official rating and, although it's doubtful she quite ran to that mark, it was another good effort, and it won't be a surprise if she races for Godolphin next year. (op 7-2)
Flip Flop(IRE) came into the race with a mark of just 75, but she was representing a top stable and the step up to 1m looked sure to suit her on pedigree. So it proved, as she posted a career-best performance.
Tashzara(IRE), runner-up in a decent-looking maiden at Navan last time (fourth won a Listed race next time up), showed more than enough to suggest she can win when dropped back in grade.
Official explanation: jockey said filly was unsuited by the good (good to soft places) ground
Thrill is a sister to Infallible, so this trip was possibly too far for her at this stage of her career. There should be better to come from her at three. (op 9-2 tchd 13-2)
Bint Almatar(USA) faced a much stiffer task than when winning at Nottingham on her debut. The ground was a concern for her and she wasn't knocked about once her chance had gone. (op 8-1)
Sunarise(IRE) Official explanation: jockey said filly lost its action

7188 BET365.COM JAMES SEYMOUR STKS (LISTED RACE) 1m 2f
3:45 (3:45) (Class 1) 3-Y-0+
£22,708 (£8,608; £4,308; £2,148; £1,076; £540) **Stalls** Low

Form RPR

1121 **1** **Laaheb**[37] 6234 3-8-12 103 .... RHills 3 116
(M A Jarvis) *chsd ldrs: wnt 2nd over 2f out: rdn to ld over 1f out: kpt on wl u.p fnl f* **3/1[2]**

311 **2** *1* **Prince Siegfried (FR)**[42] 6093 3-9-2 114 .... LDettori 2 118
(Saeed Bin Suroor) *chsd ldr tl led over 3f out: rdn and hdd over 1f out: kpt on trying fnl f but a hld: eased nr fin* **10/11[1]**

5063 **3** *3/4* **Saphira's Fire (IRE)**[14] 6853 4-8-12 112 .... MartinDwyer 4 108
(W R Muir) *t.k.h: hld up in last pair: rdn and hdwy over 2f out: chsd ldng pair over 1f out: kpt on fnl f but nt pce to rch ldng pair* **4/1[3]**

30-0 **4** *4* **Hebridean (IRE)**[15] 6812 4-9-3 110 .... KFallon 1 105
(L M Cumani) *hld up in tch: hdwy to chse ldrs and rdn 3f out: edgd rt u.p and btn over 1f out* **18/1**

230 **5** *3 1/4* **Perks (IRE)**[35] 6290 4-9-3 104 .... JimmyQuinn 5 98
(J L Dunlop) *stdd s: hld up in last pl: clsd over 3f out: rdn and btn 2f out: wl btn fnl f* **16/1**

0060 **6** *1 1/4* **Suits Me**[28] 6506 6-9-3 108 .... MickyFenton 6 96
(T P Tate) *sn pushed into ld: hdd and rdn over 3f out: wknd 2f out: wl btn whn wandered ent fnl f* **25/1**

2m 7.61s (1.81) **Going Correction** +0.15s/f (Good)
WFA 3 from 4yo+ 5lb **6** Ran SP% **112.4**
Speed ratings (Par 111): **98,97,96,93,90 89**
toteswinger: 1&2 £1.10, 1&3 £1.70, 2&3 £1.10. CSF £6.13 TOTE £3.90: £1.80, £1.20; EX 5.90.
Owner Hamdan Al Maktoum **Bred** Darley **Trained** Newmarket, Suffolk

FOCUS
A muddling pace to this Listed event but the first three came clear and the form is worth taking at face value. The progressive winner took another step forward.

NOTEBOOK
Laaheb had the lowest official rating of these, but he has progressed through the handicapping ranks and confirmed himself a rapidly improving three-year-old with success at his first try at Listed level. By Cape Cross out of a mare from the family of Luso, Warrsan and Needle Gun, who all improved with age, he threatens to be even better at four, when success in Group company can be expected. (op 9-2)
Prince Siegfried(FR), who won a similar race at Ayr last time out, likes a bit of juice in the ground, so the overnight rain was no doubt welcome to him. He had no excuse apart from simply bumping into a more progressive rival. (op 4-5 tchd Evens)
Saphira's Fire(IRE), who put up a career-best effort when third in the Group 2 Pride Stakes last time out, was taking on colts for the first time. She wasn't helped by the drop back in distance from 1m4f, but showed enough to suggest she can score at this level again back in fillies' races. (op 5-1)
Hebridean(IRE) ran a lot better than on his debut for this yard 15 days earlier, but remains well below his best, and his rating of 110 clearly flatters him. He could yet improve for being in Cumani's care for longer, though. (op 16-1)
Perks(IRE), who cannot have the ground too soft, hasn't been at his best in his last two starts now. (op 14-1)
Suits Me was unable to put up much of a fight once headed. (tchd 20-1)

7189 POKER AT BET365.COM H'CAP 7f
4:15 (4:16) (Class 4) (0-85,83) 3-Y-0+ **£5,180** (£1,541; £770; £384) **Stalls** Low

Form RPR

223 **1** **Bended Knee**[26] 6551 3-8-8 72 .... FergusSweeney 3 80
(H Candy) *taken down early: swtchd lft s and racd on stands'rail: mde virtually all: rdn over 1f out: jst hld on: all out* **11/1**

2444 **2** *hd* **Jordaura**[16] 6798 3-8-11 75 .... WilliamBuick 5 82
(W R Swinburn) *stdd s: hld up in tch: rdn and effrt over 2f out: drvn to chse wnr over 1f out: clsng fin but nvr quite getting to wnr* **9/1**

41-0 **3** *hd* **Emeebee**[150] 2600 3-8-9 73 .... AlanMunro 15 79+
(W J Musson) *hld up towards rr: rdn and hdwy towards far side ent fnl 2f: disp 2nd ins fnl f: r.o but nvr quite getting to wnr* **16/1**

0140 **4** *1/2* **Perfect Silence**[17] 6776 4-9-1 77 ....(b) EddieAhern 4 83
(C G Cox) *w ldr: grad edgd rt to r nrest far rail: rdn 2f out: kpt on same pce fnl f* **20/1**

4621 **5** *1 1/2* **Misplaced Fortune**[18] 6764 4-9-0 79 ......(v) Louis-PhilippeBeuzelin(3) 16 81
(N Tinkler) *wnt rt s: hld up towards rr: hdwy and n.m.r wl over 1f out: edging lft u.p ent fnl f: kpt on but nt pce to rch ldrs* **10/1**

6100 **6** *nk* **Edgeworth (IRE)**[17] 6773 3-8-13 77 .... KFallon 12 77+
(B G Powell) *taken down early: bhd: short of room and hmpd 3f out: hdwy u.p over 1f out: styd on past btn horses fnl f: gng on at the fin but nvr able to rch ldrs* **16/1**

0112 **7** *shd* **Swift Chap**[5] 7060 3-9-5 83 .... JimmyFortune 6 83
(B R Millman) *chsd ldrs: rdn 3f out: drvn and one pce fr over 1f out* **4/1[1]**

216 **8** *1* **Regeneration (IRE)**[36] 6243 3-9-0 78 .... HayleyTurner 8 75
(M L W Bell) *t.k.h: chsd ldrs: rdn and unable qck ent fnl 2f: hrd drvn and one pce fr over 1f out* **13/2[2]**

1500 **9** *3/4* **Koraleva Tectona (IRE)**[28] 6476 4-9-0 76 .... FrederikTylicki 9 72
(Pat Eddery) *chsd ldrs: rdn over 2f out: drvn and one pce fr over 1f out* **16/1**

5404 **10** *shd* **Seek The Fair Land**[17] 6776 3-8-12 76 .... PatCosgrave 11 71
(J R Boyle) *chsd ldrs: rdn ent fnl 2f: drvn and wknd over 1f out* **20/1**

2314 **11** *1 3/4* **Pegasus Again (USA)**[53] 5746 4-9-5 81 ....(p) MichaelHills 13 72
(T G Mills) *bhd: pushed along ent fnl 2f: sme hdwy over 1f out: nvr trbld ldrs* **9/1**

5020 **12** *2 1/4* **King Columbo (IRE)**[28] 6476 4-8-10 72 .... RobertWinston 1 57
(Miss J Feilden) *chsd ldrs: rdn 3f out: wknd wl over 1f out and btn whn hung rt over 1f out* **16/1**

5160 **13** *2* **Inheritor (IRE)**[52] 5766 3-9-4 82 .... TomEaves 7 61
(B Smart) *t.k.h: chsd ldrs tl wknd u.p wl over 1f out: wl hld fnl f* **18/1**

33 **14** *4 1/2* **Bibury**[44] 6019 3-8-8 72 .... JimmyQuinn 14 39
(David P Myerscough, Ire) *racd in midfield tl lost pl and rdn 3f out: wl bhd fnl f* **7/1[3]**

2000 **15** *8* **Zowington**[21] 6666 7-9-3 82 ....(v) WilliamCarson(3) 2 28
(S C Williams) *bmpd s: a towards rr: wl bhd fr over 1f out* **33/1**

1500 **16** *5* **Brunelleschi**[10] 6944 6-8-8 77 ....(b) JosephineBruning(7) 10 10
(P L Gilligan) *midfield tl dropped to rr and rdn over 3f out: wl bhd fnl 2f* **50/1**

1m 27.02s (1.62) **Going Correction** +0.15s/f (Good)
WFA 3 from 4yo+ 2lb **16** Ran SP% **126.5**
Speed ratings (Par 105): **96,95,95,94,93 92,92,91,90,90 88,86,83,78,69 63**
toteswinger: 1&2 £72.00, 1&3 £72.00, 2&3 £36.00. CSF £106.02 CT £1675.05 TOTE £10.90: £1.80, £2.80, £2.80, £5.20; EX 65.60 Place 6: £23.68, Place 5: £11.81..
Owner Major M G Wyatt **Bred** Dunchurch Lodge Stud Co **Trained** Kingston Warren, Oxon
■ Stewards' Enquiry : Alan Munro one-day ban: used whip with excessive frequency without giving gelding time to respond (Nov 14)

FOCUS
A competitive handicap and a tight finish. Ordinary form for the grade, but fairly sound.
Misplaced Fortune Official explanation: jockey said filly reared at the start
T/Plt: £29.80 to a £1 stake. Pool: £76,342.10. 1,868.23 winning tickets. T/Qpdt: £15.30 to a £1 stake. Pool: £5,160.11. 249.05 winning tickets. SP

7152 WOLVERHAMPTON (A.W) (L-H)
Saturday, October 31

OFFICIAL GOING: Standard
Wind: Light half-behind Weather: Overcast

7190 CLEANEVENT MEDIAN AUCTION MAIDEN STKS 5f 216y(P)
6:50 (6:51) (Class 5) 2-Y-O **£2,914** (£867; £433; £216) **Stalls** Low

Form RPR

2 **1** **Basle**[19] 6722 2-8-12 0 .... JerryO'Dwyer 4 64+
(Miss Gay Kelleway) *mde all: rdn over 1f out: r.o* **1/4[1]**

00 **2** *2* **Valmina**[19] 6737 2-9-3 0 ....(t) RichardKingscote 5 63
(Tom Dascombe) *plld hrd and prom: trckd wnr 1/2-way: rdn and ev ch over 1f out: styd on same pce ins fnl f* **6/1[2]**

00 **3** *2 3/4* **Future Regime (IRE)**[4] 7079 2-8-12 0 .... SJCraine 3 50
(Patrick Morris) *trckd ldrs: rdn over 1f out: no ex fnl f* **40/1**

4 *15* **Little Weed (IRE)** 2-9-3 0 .... DavidProbert 2 —
(B Palling) *s.s: hdwy to join wnr 5f out: rdn 1/2-way: wknd over 1f out* **9/1[3]**

1m 16.85s (1.85) **Going Correction** -0.05s/f (Stan) **4** Ran SP% **106.7**
Speed ratings (Par 95): **85,82,78,58**
CSF £2.09 TOTE £1.30; EX 2.00.
Owner Raymond Tooth **Bred** W H R John And Partners **Trained** Exning, Suffolk

FOCUS
There was no addition to the 3mm of overnight rain prior to racing, and the meeting commenced in cool, dry, largely wind-free conditions. Very modest form, with Basle not needing to run up to her debut level.

NOTEBOOK
Basle faced what looked a straightforward task, but she was workmanlike rather than flashy in victory and needed a few cracks up the straight to make sure. None of her half-siblings to have managed a win have followed up after landing juvenile maidens, but Basle's trainer is hopeful she has the potential to become Group class next season when less weak and backward. (tchd 2-9)
Valmina, nearer last than first in both turf starts previously, was a bit fractious prior to loading and refused to settle over the first couple of furlongs. He still had enough fight left to get to within three parts of a length of the winner just over a furlong out, which doesn't pay the form the greatest compliment even though he may have improved a touch for the switch to Polytrack. Official explanation: jockey said colt ran too free (op 17-2)
Future Regime(IRE), who raced on the inner throughout, dropped out of contention up the straight and looks unlikely to win outside of selling grade. (op 25-1)
Little Weed(IRE), half-brother to two maiden performers for the same yard, gifted his rivals 2l at the start before racing too wastefully once back upsides and fading right away turning in. Even allowing for inexperience, this was not encouraging. (op 8-1 tchd 11-1)

7191 CLEANDOMAIN H'CAP 5f 216y(P)
7:20 (7:20) (Class 5) (0-75,75) 3-Y-0+ **£3,238** (£963; £481; £240) **Stalls** Low

Form RPR

6264 **1** **Onceaponatime (IRE)**[5] 7053 4-8-9 65 .... AlanMunro 1 74
(M D Squance) *a.p: chsd ldr 2f out: led 1f out: rdn and edgd lft ins fnl f: r.o* **7/2[2]**

4100 **2** *1 1/4* **Sutton Veny (IRE)**[47] 5937 3-8-10 67 .... WilliamBuick 8 72
(J R Gask) *sn led: rdn and hdd 1f out: styd on same pce* **14/1**

003 **3** *nk* **Great Charm (IRE)**[13] 6879 4-9-2 72 .... HayleyTurner 3 76+
(M L W Bell) *hld up: hdwy u.p over 1f out: edgd lft ins fnl f: r.o* **11/4[1]**

31P1 **4** 1 3/4 **Gwilym (GER)**[22] 6642 6-8-11 **72**.......................... AndrewHeffernan(5) 2 70
(D Haydn Jones) *chsd ldrs: rdn over 1f out: styd on* **11/4**[1]

0100 **5** *hd* **Dig Deep (IRE)**[43] 6072 7-9-5 **75**.......................... TomEaves 7 73
(J J Quinn) *sn outpcd: r.o ins fnl f: nrst fin* **12/1**

400 **6** 2 3/4 **Resplendent Alpha**[42] 6112 5-9-5 **75**.......................... J-PGuillambert 5 64
(P Howling) *hld up: racd keenly: rdn over 2f out: nt trble ldrs* **14/1**

2000 **7** *nk* **Mey Blossom**[18] 6764 4-8-6 **62**..........................(p) DO'Donohoe 4 50
(R M Whitaker) *chsd ldrs: lost pl over 4f out: n.d after* **10/1**[3]

6000 **8** 5 **Forward Feline (IRE)**[4] 7082 3-8-10 **67**..........................(v[1]) DavidProbert 9 39
(B Palling) *chsd ldr tl rdn 2f out: wknd sn after* **14/1**

1m 13.94s (-1.06) **Going Correction** -0.05s/f (Stan)
WFA 3 from 4yo+ 1lb **8** Ran SP% **112.3**
Speed ratings (Par 103): **105,103,102,100,100 96,96,89**
toteswinger: 1&2 £11.70, 1&3 £1.60, 2&3 £12.60. CSF £48.25 CT £152.04 TOTE £4.50: £1.40, £2.90, £1.40; EX 55.10.
Owner M D Squance **Bred** Dermot O'Rourke **Trained** Newmarket, Suffolk

FOCUS
A moderate handicap, but one run at a generous pace from the start, and the winning time was 2.9 seconds quicker than the opener over the same C&D. Modest form, the winner the best guide.

7192 CLEAN WASTE SOLUTIONS H'CAP 7f 32y(P)
7:50 (7:50) (Class 5) (0-70,70) 3-Y-O+ **£3,238** (£963; £481; £240) **Stalls** Low

Form RPR

0502 **1** **Tourist**[14] 6861 4-9-5 **70**.......................... DaneO'Neill 11 84
(D Shaw) *chsd ldr tl led over 2f out: sn rdn: r.o: edgd lft towards fin* **9/1**

00 **2** 2 **Little Arrows (IRE)**[10] 6957 3-9-3 **70**..........................(p) WilliamBuick 2 78
(W McCreery, Ire) *a.p: rdn to chse wnr over 1f out: hung lft ins fnl f: styd on* **9/2**[2]

5061 **3** 3 1/4 **Fault**[7] 7028 3-9-3 **70**..........................(t) MickyFenton 6 69+
(Stef Liddiard) *hld up: swtchd rt over 1f out: edgd lft and r.o ins fnl f: too much to do* **6/1**[3]

0600 **4** *nk* **Bahamian Kid**[19] 6725 4-9-2 **67**..........................(p) JerryO'Dwyer 4 66
(R Hollinshead) *hld up: hdwy over 2f out: rdn over 1f out: edgd lft and styd on same pce* **14/1**

0650 **5** *hd* **Woolston Ferry (IRE)**[19] 6726 3-8-13 **66**.......................... ChrisCatlin 7 63
(David Pinder) *s.i.s: hld up: hdwy u.p over 1f out: r.o* **14/1**

0560 **6** 1 1/4 **Cornus**[14] 6847 7-9-4 **69**..........................(be) FrederikTylicki 1 64
(J A Glover) *hld up in tch: rdn over 2f out: edgd rt and styd on same pce appr fnl f* **9/1**

4230 **7** 2 **Aussie Blue (IRE)**[31] 6383 5-8-13 **64**.......................... DO'Donohoe 5 60+
(R M Whitaker) *sn outpcd: styng on whn hmpd ins fnl f: n.d* **16/1**

0432 **8** 3 **This Ones For Eddy**[8] 6989 4-9-4 **69**.......................... TonyCulhane 3 51
(J Balding) *chsd ldrs: rdn over 2f out: wknd over 1f out* **11/4**[1]

2352 **9** 1/2 **Whitbarrow (IRE)**[17] 6782 10-9-0 **68**..........................(b) JamesMillman(3) 8 48
(B R Millman) *led: rdn and hdd over 2f out: wknd over 1f out* **16/1**

006 **10** *nk* **Eastern Gift**[19] 6726 4-9-5 **70**.......................... SimonWhitworth 12 49
(Miss Gay Kelleway) *mid-div: rdn over 2f out: sn wknd* **14/1**

0040 **11** 1/2 **Not My Choice (IRE)**[22] 6642 4-9-1 **66**.......................... DavidProbert 10 44
(J Balding) *prom: rdn over 2f out: wknd over 1f out* **28/1**

000 **12** 1/2 **Sendreni (FR)**[35] 6294 5-8-11 **69**..........................(t) TobyAtkinson(7) 9 46
(M Wigham) *s.i.s: hld up: racd keenly: nvr nr to chal* **12/1**

1m 28.18s (-1.42) **Going Correction** -0.05s/f (Stan)
WFA 3 from 4yo+ 2lb **12** Ran SP% **122.0**
Speed ratings (Par 103): **106,103,100,99,99 98,95,92,91,91 90,90**
toteswinger: 1&2 £6.90, 1&3 £11.30, 2&3 £5.00. CSF £50.73 CT £274.76 TOTE £9.80: £2.70, £1.90, £2.60; EX 77.20.
Owner M Shirley **Bred** Juddmonte Farms Ltd **Trained** Danethorpe, Notts

FOCUS
Recent winning form was in short supply here, and several of those involved in the finish were taking advantage of falling marks. The winner was rated back to something like his best with the second to this year's form.
Fault Official explanation: jockey said colt was denied a clear run
Bahamian Kid Official explanation: jockey said gelding hung left in straight
Aussie Blue(IRE) Official explanation: jockey said saddle slipped
Sendreni(FR) Official explanation: jockey said gelding ran too free

7193 CLEAN CONCIERGE MAIDEN AUCTION STKS 1m 141y(P)
8:20 (8:20) (Class 5) 2-Y-O **£3,238** (£963; £481; £240) **Stalls** Low

Form RPR

543 **1** **Crunched**[45] 5981 2-8-12 72.......................... HayleyTurner 2 73
(M L W Bell) *chsd ldr to over 3f out: rdn and ev ch fr over 1f out: r.o to ld towards fin* **2/1**[2]

0322 **2** *nse* **Anaya**[3] 7106 2-8-7 72.......................... ChrisCatlin 3 68
(M R Channon) *led: rdn over 1f out: r.o: hdd towards fin* **13/8**[1]

3204 **3** *shd* **Merchant Of Medici**[11] 6911 2-8-12 70..........................(b[1]) WilliamBuick 4 73
(W R Muir) *prom: chsd ldr over 3f out: rdn and ev ch fr over 1f out: r.o* **4/1**[3]

4 2 1/4 **Mercoliano** 2-8-12 0.......................... JerryO'Dwyer 1 68+
(M Botti) *s.i.s: hld up: shkn up over 2f out: r.o: will improve* **6/1**

1m 50.63s (0.13) **Going Correction** -0.05s/f (Stan) **4** Ran SP% **105.7**
Speed ratings (Par 95): **97,96,96,94**
toteswinger: 1&2 £3.60. CSF £5.38 TOTE £2.90; EX 5.10.
Owner R P B Michaelson **Bred** D J And Mrs Deer **Trained** Newmarket, Suffolk

FOCUS
Just a modest maiden.

NOTEBOOK
Crunched has improved with each run, as befitting a horse connections confirm is still growing. On his toes beforehand, he sat off Anaya's early pace peaceably enough before being threaded up the inner rail turning in and responding splendidly for pressure to hold on close home. Plans remain fluid, but there should still be more to come from him. (op 5-2)
Anaya, edgy in the preliminaries and keenest in the first half of the race, nevertheless sustained her challenge until the very end. It would be churlish to point out this was the second successive race in which she has lost a lead late in the piece, given that the previous occasion was only three nights earlier and this was her first try outside of fillies-only company. She won't be long in gaining compensation. (op 11-8 tchd 7-4)
Merchant Of Medici hasn't gone on as expected after a fair debut, and the lameness to the off-fore that curtailed his summer may have left more of a mark than experiments with different running styles and tonight's first try with headgear can rectify fully. For all that, he still has enough raw ability to win a small winter maiden. (op 7-2)
Mercoliano ◆ was marginally the slowest out of the stalls, but it was his inability to work out what was required under pressure until too late that cost him a closer finish. He will have learned plenty, however, and it should be noted that both of his half-siblings to have raced won second time out, one of them at this venue. (op 13-2 tchd 7-1)

7194 CE RISK, SAFETY & SECURITY H'CAP 1m 1f 103y(P)
8:50 (8:51) (Class 3) (0-90,88) 3-Y-O- **£7,569** (£2,265; £1,132; £566; £282) **Stalls** Low

Form RPR

1035 **1** **Wing Play (IRE)**[24] 6594 4-9-2 **82**..........................(p) ShaneKelly 9 94+
(H Morrison) *hld up: nt clr run and swtchd lft wl over 1f out: hdwy and swtchd rt jst over 1f out: r.o to ld nr fin* **12/1**

51 **2** *hd* **Black Eagle (IRE)**[16] 6794 3-9-2 **86**.......................... TedDurcan 2 98+
(Saeed Bin Suroor) *sn led: rdn over 1f out: edgd rt and hdd nr fin* **6/5**[1]

0420 **3** 3/4 **Stand Guard**[30] 6435 5-8-13 **84**.......................... AndrewHeffernan(5) 3 94
(P Howling) *chsd ldrs: rdn and hung lft ins fnl f: r.o* **25/1**

0024 **4** 1 1/2 **Spinning**[15] 6830 6-9-0 **80**..........................(b) TomEaves 7 87
(T D Barron) *dwlt: sn mid-div: pushed along over 3f out: hdwy over 2f out: rdn and nt clr run ins fnl f: swtchd rt: r.o* **11/1**

0210 **5** 3/4 **Handsome Falcon**[22] 6645 5-9-1 **81**.......................... FrederikTylicki 1 86
(R A Fahey) *t.k.h: trckd ldr to over 6f out: remained handy: rdn over 1f out: no ex ins fnl f* **11/2**[2]

0500 **6** 3/4 **Just Bond (IRE)**[28] 6485 7-8-11 **82**.......................... BMcHugh(5) 12 86+
(G R Oldroyd) *hld up: rdn and r.o ins fnl f: nvr nrr* **33/1**

2000 **7** 3/4 **Ilie Nastase (FR)**[30] 6435 5-9-5 **85**.......................... ChrisCatlin 4 87+
(D M Simcock) *hld up: r.o ins fnl f: nvr trbld ldrs* **20/1**

4055 **8** 1 1/4 **Shavansky**[28] 6480 5-9-5 **88**.......................... JamesMillman(3) 10 88
(B R Millman) *hld up: plld hrd: hdwy over 5f out: rdn and wknd over 1f out* **10/1**[3]

0200 **9** 3/4 **Charlie Cool**[16] 6795 6-9-4 **84**..........................(tp) TGMcLaughlin 5 82
(Mrs R A Carr) *mid-div: rdn over 2f out: wknd over 1f out* **25/1**

-330 **10** 1 1/2 **Avertis**[8] 7000 4-8-13 **79**..........................(t) MickyFenton 8 74
(Stef Liddiard) *t.k.h: prom: trckd ldr over 6f out: rdn and ev ch 2f out: wkng whn hmpd ins fnl f* **25/1**

0000 **11** *nk* **Final Verse**[19] 6733 6-9-0 **80**.......................... WilliamBuick 6 74
(Matthew Salaman) *hld up: plld hrd: sme hdwy over 2f out: sn wknd* **16/1**

1561 **12** *shd* **Brett Vale (IRE)**[16] 6116 3-9-2 **86**.......................... DaneO'Neill 11 80
(P R Hedger) *prom: rdn over 2f out: wknd over 1f out* **50/1**

0211 **13** 21 **Nevada Desert (IRE)**[7] 7014 9-8-12 **78**.......................... DO'Donohoe 13 28
(R M Whitaker) *hld up: plld hrd: hdwy over 6f out: wknd over 2f out* **20/1**

1m 59.83s (-1.87) **Going Correction** -0.05s/f (Stan)
WFA 3 from 4yo+ 4lb **13** Ran SP% **117.8**
Speed ratings (Par 107): **106,105,105,103,103 102,101,100,100,98 98,98,79**
toteswinger: 1&2 £6.50, 1&3 £75.60, 2&3 £12.00. CSF £24.04 CT £381.03 TOTE £17.60: £4.20, £1.40, £6.60; EX 45.10.
Owner Watching Brief **Bred** Churchtown House Stud **Trained** East Ilsley, Berks

FOCUS
The faster of the two races over 1m1f by 1.73 seconds, despite an ordinary looking early pace which saw several competitors pull for their heads. Good handicap form with the winner, better than ever recently on turf, doing well to score from the rear. The third is the best guide to the form.

NOTEBOOK
Wing Play(IRE) came with a searing late run up the inner rail to get up. This was no mean performance, as he may have appreciated a faster-run race and had to change direction twice up the straight to pass tiring rivals. The awkward head carriage of his last two defeats was absent, too. Already 10lb above his previous highest winning mark, however, another career-best will probably be needed to follow up. (op 16-1)
Black Eagle(IRE), an imposing colt, travelled kindly under Ted Durcan and dictated every fraction until the final 25 yards. He looked to have got in lightly on 86 following his simple Nottingham maiden win, but he can't be counted as that unlucky a loser on this handicap debut as Wing Play could have mastered him sooner with a clear passage. It was still a decent effort, and the best may still to be seen of him. (op 11-10 tchd Evens and 5-4)
Stand Guard, a C&D winner off 4lb lower in February, ran as well as he ever has done at this venue, but is a shade more consistent around Kempton.
Spinning, a four-time 1m course winner, ran a near-identical race to last time, finding trouble before running on once switched. Back on his last winning mark, his turn could be near again. (op 9-1)
Handsome Falcon's win on his Polytrack debut earlier in the month came over a furlong shorter, and his refusal to settle this time wrecked his prospects of being able to see out the extra distance effectively. He's better than this. (tchd 7-1)
Shavansky, the Cambridgeshire fifth, pulled hard enough in the early stages that the disadvantage of his poor draw quickly became academic. (op 12-1 tchd 9-1)
Final Verse Official explanation: jockey said gerlding ran too free
Nevada Desert(IRE) Official explanation: jockey said gelding ran flat

7195 CE PROPERTY SERVICES GROUP MAIDEN STKS 1m 1f 103y(P)
9:20 (9:21) (Class 5) 3-Y-O+ **£2,729** (£806; £403) **Stalls** Low

Form RPR

1 **Naseehah (USA)** 3-9-3 0.......................... TedDurcan 9 77+
(Saeed Bin Suroor) *dwlt: hld up: hdwy over 5f out: led over 1f out: r.o wl* **8/15**[1]

3340 **2** 2 **Oriental Cavalier**[26] 6538 3-9-3 68..........................(p) HayleyTurner 12 63
(R Hollinshead) *chsd ldrs: led over 2f out: rdn and hdd over 1f out: styd on same pce ins fnl f* **10/1**[3]

4324 **3** 2 **Insolence (USA)**[10] 6934 3-8-12 71.......................... WilliamBuick 1 56
(Sir Michael Stoute) *prom: rdn over 2f out: styd on same pce appr fnl f* **5/2**[2]

0606 **4** 3 3/4 **Miss Perfectionist**[52] 5775 3-8-12 52.......................... J-PGuillambert 4 46
(P Howling) *hld up: hdwy over 1f out: r.o: nt trble ldrs* **50/1**

0000 **5** 1 1/4 **Vigorosa (IRE)**[15] 6831 3-8-7 40.......................... AndrewHeffernan(5) 6 44
(P Howling) *trckd ldrs: plld hrd: rdn over 2f out: wknd over 1f out* **100/1**

-056 **6** *nk* **Desert Fairy**[10] 6941 3-8-12 46.......................... TomEaves 3 43
(J W Unett) *hld up: rdn over 4f out: n.d* **150/1**

0 **7** 3/4 **Albiera (IRE)**[19] 6741 4-9-2 0.......................... TravisBlock 8 41
(H Morrison) *chsd ldr tl led 3f out: sn rdn and hdd: wknd over 1f out* **66/1**

8 1/2 **Alfies Express**[39] 5-9-7 0.......................... JamesDoyle 2 45
(S Curran) *mid-div: rdn over 3f out: wknd sn after* **200/1**

0300 **9** *nk* **Interchoice Star**[10] 6940 4-9-4 48.......................... RussellKennemore(3) 10 45
(R Hollinshead) *mid-div: effrt over 2f out: sn wknd* **50/1**

0/ **10** 13 **Dawn Storm (IRE)**[848] 3283 4-9-4 0.......................... JamesMillman(3) 5 17
(J L Spearing) *sn pushed along in rr: n.d* **100/1**

050 **11** 14 **Barathea's Acclaim**[23] 6608 3-8-12 50..........................(tp) DaneO'Neill 7 —
(P R Hedger) *sn led: rdn and hdd 3f out: sn wknd* **150/1**

2m 1.56s (-0.14) **Going Correction** -0.05s/f (Stan)
WFA 3 from 4yo+ 4lb **11** Ran SP% **112.1**
Speed ratings (Par 103): **98,96,94,91,90 89,89,88,88,76 64**
toteswinger: 1&2 £1.60, 1&3 £1.70, 2&3 £2.10. CSF £7.08 TOTE £1.70: £1.10, £1.70, £1.10; EX 5.60 Place 6: £24.87 Place 5: £19.19.
Owner Godolphin **Bred** C C Howell & Gainsborough Farm Llc Et Al **Trained** Newmarket, Suffolk

FOCUS
This maiden featured as little strength in depth as a market of 50-1 bar three would indicate, and that trio duly filled the podium places. The race was steadily run and the likes of the fifth and sixth limit the form. The winner is sure to improve on this bare form.
T/Plt: £57.30 to a £1 stake. Pool: £69,784.21. 887.60 winning tickets. T/Qpdt: £20.20 to a £1 stake. Pool: £5,738.42. 210.10 winning tickets. CR

FLEMINGTON (L-H)
Saturday, October 31
OFFICIAL GOING: Good to soft changing to good after the 2.20am

7196a MACKINNON STKS (GROUP 1) 1m 2f
3:05 (3:05) 3-Y-O+
£219,417 (£65,534; £32,767; £16,383; £9,102; £7,282)

RPR
1 **Scenic Shot (AUS)**[7] 7040 7-9-4 ShaneScriven 8 120
(Daniel Morton, Australia) **15/2**[3]
2 *2* **Miss Maren (NZ)**[28] 5-9-0 CraigNewitt 2 112
(Mick Price, Australia) **30/1**
3 *nk* **Viewed (AUS)**[14] 6871 6-9-4 (b) BradRawiller 9 115
(Bart Cummings, Australia) **7/1**[2]
4 *1 1/4* **Racing To Win (AUS)**[21] 7-9-4 (b) HughBowman 6 113
(John O'Shea, Australia) **14/1**
5 *shd* **Master O'Reilly (NZ)**[14] 6871 7-9-4 VladDuric 13 113
(Danny O'Brien, Australia) **20/1**
6 *hd* **Newport (AUS)**[14] 7-9-4 PeterWells 11 112
(Paul Perry, Australia) **100/1**
7 *shd* **Rangirangdoo (NZ)**[7] 5-9-4 (b) CoreyBrown 4 112
(Chris Waller, Australia) **7/4**[1]
8 *shd* **Drumbeats (AUS)**[14] 4-9-2 KerrinMcEvoy 3 110
(Peter Snowden, Australia) **9/1**
9 *1* **Cima De Triomphe (IRE)**[14] 6871 4-9-4 (b) DamienOliver 10 110
(L M Cumani) *racd keenly: led to 2f out: one pce* **14/1**
10 *3/4* **Mandela (NZ)**[241] 8-9-4 MarkZahra 12 108
(Richard Yuill, New Zealand) **50/1**
11 *2* **Sir Slick (NZ)**[21] 8-9-4 MichellePayne 1 104
(Graeme Nicholson, New Zealand) **66/1**
2m 3.46s (123.46) **11 Ran SP% 96.4**

Owner D Morton, E Galante et al **Bred** R & Mrs A Anderson **Trained** Australia

NOTEBOOK
Scenic Shot(AUS) travelled well just off the leader and quickened away inside the final furlong. He has now won 15 of his 54 starts and has earnt his connections over $A2.4 million.
Viewed(AUS), the Caulfield Cup winner, finished strongly under a hand ride on the outside to take third. He had been struck into after 2f and suffered a superficial cut to his off-hind hock, which was bleeding when he returned to weigh in, but he was not lame. This was a great trial for the Melbourne Cup.
Master O'Reilly(NZ), who was drawn widest of all, finished well down the outside and, although on a long losing run, has been prepared with the Melbourne Cup (fourth last year) in mind.
Newport(AUS) stayed on late but was never a threat.
Cima De Triomphe(IRE) needed to win to get into the Melbourne Cup, but he was disappointing, racing keenly in front and dropping away tamely in the closing stages.

7129 LINGFIELD (L-H)
Sunday, November 1
OFFICIAL GOING: Standard
Times suggested the surface was riding on the slow side.
Wind: Very strong behind, strong across from race 4 Weather: Heavy rain, stopping after race 1, and very windy

7197 WATERY LANE H'CAP (DIV I) 1m (P)
12:20 (12:20) (Class 6) (0-55,58) 3-Y-O+ **£1,706** (£503; £252) **Stalls** High

Form RPR
0000 1 **Spinning Ridge (IRE)**[9] 6999 4-8-13 **51** DavidProbert 12 59+
(R A Harris) *hld up in last trio: stdy hdwy fr 3f out: stl plenty to do and switching rt wl over 1f out: chsd ldrs and switching lft 1f out: wnt between horses ins fnl f: r.o wl to ld last strides* **50/1**
0-00 2 *hd* **Josr's Magic (IRE)**[20] 6719 5-9-3 **55** JimCrowley 11 63
(T E Powell) *chsd ldr: rdn to ld jst over 2f out: drvn over 1f out: kpt on wl tl hdd last strides* **14/1**
0000 3 *1 1/4* **Wunder Strike (USA)**[17] 6787 3-8-12 **52** (p) NickyMackay 1 57
(J R Boyle) *in tch in midfield: hdwy to chse ldng pair and rdn jst over 2f out: chsd ldr over 1f out: kpt on same pce ins fnl f* **9/1**
0664 4 *1 1/4* **Mountain Forest (GER)**[18] 6771 3-8-7 **47** TravisBlock 7 49
(H Morrison) *chsd ldrs on outer: rdn over 2f out: one pce and no imp fr over 1f out* **14/1**
5542 5 *4* **Clerical (USA)**[4] 7105 3-8-12 **55** (p) AndreaAtzeni(3) 2 47
(R M H Cowell) *led: rdn and hdd jst over 2f out: wknd u.p over 1f out: no ch fnl f* **10/3**[2]
6006 6 *4* **Harty Boy (USA)**[181] 1746 3-8-12 **55** (t) RobertLButler(3) 5 38
(Jim Best) *hld up in last trio: rdn and effrt wl over 1f out: sme hdwy but nvr trbld ldrs* **7/1**[3]
0-04 7 *2* **Gracie's Games**[18] 6777 3-8-10 **50** FrederikTylicki 8 28
(R J Price) *in tch on outer: rdn and outpcd by ldrs jst over 2f out: no prog fnl 2f* **10/1**
0/06 8 *1/2* **Sir Orpen (IRE)**[26] 6568 6-9-2 **54** RichardHughes 6 36
(J F Panvert) *in tch: pushed along and no hdwy over 2f out: tenderly handled and no ch w ldrs fnl 2f* **12/1**
551 9 *1 1/2* **Confide In Me**[9] 6999 5-9-6 **58** (tp) HayleyTurner 10 31
(G A Butler) *hld up in last trio: rdn and effrt towards inner wl over 1f out: no real hdwy and wl hld whn clipped heels and stmbld jst over 1f out: nvr trbld ldrs* **2/1**[1]
1650 10 *3 3/4* **Kinsman (IRE)**[249] 674 12-8-8 **46** (p) CatherineGannon 4 —
(T D McCarthy) *t.k.h: hld up towards rr: rdn and no prog over 2f out: no ch fnl 2f* **25/1**
6002 11 *2* **Rascal In The Mix (USA)**[16] 6831 3-9-0 **54** DO'Donohoe 3 —
(R M Whitaker) *in tch in midfield on inner: pushed along 5f out: rdn and struggling whn hmpd and dropped to rr over 2f out: wl bhd fnl 2f* **20/1**
-041 12 *2 1/4* **Riviera Red (IRE)**[264] 482 9-8-9 **47** (v) LukeMorris 9 —
(L Montague Hall) *t.k.h: towards rr: rdn wl over 3f out: drvn and wknd 2f out: wl bhd after* **12/1**
1m 39.75s (1.55) **Going Correction** +0.125s/f (Slow)
WFA 3 from 4yo+ 2lb **12 Ran SP% 127.3**
Speed ratings (Par 101): **97,96,95,94,90 86,84,83,82,78 76,74**
toteswingers: 1&2 £57.50, 1&3 £31.20, 2&3 £30.20. CSF £668.81 CT £6841.56 TOTE £69.50: £20.90, £5.20, £3.00; EX 582.80 TRIFECTA Not won..
Owner Robert & Nina Bailey **Bred** Eddie O'Leary **Trained** Earlswood, Monmouths
FOCUS
A moderate but quite open handicap and there was a real surprise result, with the first pair coming from the two outside stalls. Not much got into it and there is a bit of doubt over the form.
Sir Orpen(IRE) Official explanation: jockey said gelding hung left and lost its action

7198 HEVER ROAD CLAIMING STKS 1m 2f (P)
12:50 (12:50) (Class 6) 3-Y-O **£2,047** (£604; £302) **Stalls** Low

Form RPR
3363 1 **Farncombe (IRE)**[17] 6804 3-8-7 **67** HayleyTurner 1 67
(M P Tregoning) *t.k.h: led tl over 8f out: chsd ldr after: rdn to chal wl over 1f out: led jst ins fnl f: styd on wl* **13/8**[2]
0501 2 *3 1/2* **Hector Spectre (IRE)**[10] 6966 3-9-2 **66** PaulDoe 3 69
(P D Evans) *sn bustled along to press ldr: led over 8f out: jnd and rdn jst over 2f out: hdd jst ins fnl f: no ex* **13/2**[3]
0001 3 *5* **Satwa Gold (USA)**[11] 6940 3-9-7 **77** RichardHughes 2 64
(E A L Dunlop) *stdd s: hld up in tch: chsd clr ldng pair and rdn 3f out: no imp and wl btn over 1f out* **5/6**[1]
4000 4 *10* **Quick Single (USA)**[8] 7022 3-8-7 **51** (be) KellyHarrison(3) 4 33
(P S McEntee) *a in rr: rdn along wl over 3f out: sn struggling and wl btn* **33/1**
0000 5 *11* **Day In Dubai**[27] 6551 3-8-4 **45** ow1 MarcHalford(3) 5 8
(J J Bridger) *chsd ldng pair tl 3f out: sn lost tch* **66/1**
2m 7.64s (1.04) **Going Correction** +0.125s/f (Slow) **5 Ran SP% 110.4**
Speed ratings (Par 98): **100,97,93,85,76**
CSF £12.07 TOTE £2.00: £1.10, £2.90; EX 9.30.Francombe was claimed by Ron Harris for £6,000.
Owner Park Walk Racing **Bred** Ballyphilip Stud **Trained** Lambourn, Berks
FOCUS
Modest and unconvincing form which has been rated around the front pair.

7199 ROMAN ROAD MEDIAN AUCTION MAIDEN STKS 1m (P)
1:20 (1:24) (Class 6) 2-Y-O **£2,047** (£604; £302) **Stalls** High

Form RPR
1 **Sowaylm** 2-9-3 0 (t) TedDurcan 11 82+
(Saeed Bin Suroor) *s.i.s: stdy hdwy to chse ldr 5f out: c centre and rdn bnd 2f out: sn ev ch: led ins fnl f: r.o strly* **9/4**[2]
04 2 *2 3/4* **Perceptive**[51] 5839 2-8-12 0 HayleyTurner 12 69
(J R Fanshawe) *prom tl led after 1f and grad crossed to ins rail: rdn and chal 2f out: flashed tail u.p over 1f out: hdd ins fnl f: sn no ch w wnr but hld on for 2nd* **11/1**
042 3 *hd* **Ebony Boom (IRE)**[53] 5770 2-9-3 **75** TPQueally 8 74
(H R A Cecil) *in tch in midfield: hdwy on outer over 3f out: chsd ldrs over 2f out: rdn wl over 1f out: kpt on to press for 2nd nr fin but no ch w wnr* **6/1**[3]
64 4 *1/2* **New Innocence**[96] 4396 2-9-3 0 (t) FrederikTylicki 6 72
(G A Butler) *in tch: rdn to chse ldng pair 2f out: kpt on same pce fr over 1f out* **2/1**[1]
5 *9* **Astral Flower** 2-8-12 0 NCallan 3 48
(Sir Michael Stoute) *chsd ldng pair: rdn jst over 2f out: outpcd by ldrs 2f out: wknd over 1f out* **11/1**
6 *1 1/2* **Mazamorra (USA)** 2-8-9 0 AndreaAtzeni(3) 4 44
(M Botti) *dwlt: in tch in midfield: rdn and struggling 3f out: wl btn after* **25/1**
0 7 *2 1/4* **Empress Leizu (IRE)**[12] 6921 2-8-12 0 TGMcLaughlin 10 39
(E A L Dunlop) *a towards rr and sn pushed along: struggling and wl bhd fr 3f out* **80/1**
50 8 *1 3/4* **Tom Wade (IRE)**[24] 6607 2-9-3 0 PhilipRobinson 5 41
(M A Jarvis) *chsd ldrs: rdn over 4f out: wknd qckly over 2f out and sn wl btn* **20/1**
0 9 *3/4* **Pleasant Way (IRE)**[12] 6920 2-8-12 0 RichardHughes 2 34
(D R Lanigan) *led for 1f: in tch after: rdn wl over 3f out: sn struggling: wl bhd fr over 2f out* **20/1**
0 10 *1* **Jinto**[24] 6607 2-9-3 0 PatCosgrave 9 37
(R M H Cowell) *stdd s: t.k.h: hld up in rr: rdn and no prog over 3f out: sn wl bhd* **25/1**
0 11 *6* **Tumbled Again**[99] 4318 2-8-10 0 TobyAtkinson(7) 1 24
(M E Rimmer) *dwlt: a towards rr: lost tch 3f out* **66/1**
12 *14* **Highland Bridge** 2-9-3 0 DaneO'Neill 7 —
(D R C Elsworth) *v.s.a: rn green and sn pushed along in rr: lost tch 3f out: t.o* **50/1**
1m 38.69s (0.49) **Going Correction** +0.125s/f (Slow) **12 Ran SP% 117.0**
Speed ratings (Par 94): **102,99,99,98,89 88,85,84,83,82 76,62**
toteswingers: 1&2 £10.10, 1&3 £5.30, 2&3 £5.60. CSF £24.27 TOTE £3.20: £1.60, £3.30, £1.30; EX 28.20 Trifecta £187.50 Part won. Pool: £253.50 - 0.65 winning units..
Owner Godolphin **Bred** Darley **Trained** Newmarket, Suffolk
FOCUS
A fair maiden won by a promising colt.
NOTEBOOK
Sowaylm, a half-brother to a 7f 3-y-o winner out of 1,000 Guineas winner Ameerat, took this maiden with ease on his debut. Wearing a tongue tie, he overcame his wide draw to race almost alongside the leader into the first bend, and travelled comfortably to the turn-in. He showed his inexperience by not cornering well into the straight, edging right and carrying the third and fourth wide, but once straightened up he picked up well and ran out a clear-cut winner. On pedigree he might well be happy staying at this trip next season. Saeed Bin Suroor's record with 2-y-os at this track over the last five seasons now reads an impressive 15 winners from 33 runners. (op 5-4)
Perceptive took a big step in the right direction at Wolverhampton last time and this was another improved effort. Handicaps are now open to her but there should be a minor maiden to be won with her on this surface if connections opt to continue down this route. (op 16-1 tchd 20-1)
Ebony Boom(IRE) improved for the step up to 1m1/2f at Epsom last time and saw his race out well here too. There's plenty of stamina in his pedigree and he should be suited by 1m4f next season. (op 11-2 tchd 7-1)
New Innocence, who apparently found the ground too fast at Beverley last time, was fitted with a tongue tie for this AW debut. Perhaps he needed the outing as he hadn't run for three months, but he was very well supported into favouritism, so that's unlikely. Handicaps are now an option for him. (op 7-2 tchd 15-8)
Astral Flower, a half-sister to Feilden Stakes winner Redwood, is bred to do better over further next year. She ran as the market suggested and it was no help that she stuck to the inside in the straight. (op 12-1)

Mazamorra(USA), who cost $120,000, ran green but shaped with ability. She will make her mark in time, perhaps once eligible for handicaps. (tchd 20-1)

7200 WATERY LANE H'CAP (DIV II) 1m (P)
1:55 (1:55) (Class 6) (0-55,55) 3-Y-0+ **£1,706** (£503; £252) **Stalls** High

Form RPR
560 **1** **Final Drive (IRE)**[30] 6440 3-9-1 **55** EdwardCreighton 6 62+
(E J Creighton) *dwlt: pushed along briefly but sn t.k.h and hld up in last trio: stl last jst over 2f out: c v wd st: str run fnl f to ld wl ins fnl f: edgd lft and eased nr fin* **8/1**
0662 **2** ½ **Party In The Park**[4] 7110 4-8-12 **50** PatCosgrave 4 56
(J R Boyle) *chsd ldrs: rdn to chse clr ldr wl over 1f out: sn hrd drvn: pressed ldr wl ins fnl f: nt pce of wnr towards fin* **4/1**[2]
3455 **3** 1 **Russian Angel**[6] 7051 5-8-11 **49** DaneO'Neill 3 53
(Jean-Rene Auvray) *chsd ldng pair: chsd ldr over 3f out: led over 2f out: sn rdn clr: drvn over 1f out: hdd and no ex wl ins fnl f* **11/2**[3]
4561 **4** ½ **Inquisitress**[4] 7110 5-8-13 **54** 6ex MarcHalford(3) 7 56
(J J Bridger) *hld up in last: hdwy on outer over 2f out: chsd ldrs and rdn wl over 1f out: kpt on same pce fnl 100yds* **7/1**
600 **5** ¾ **Toballa**[64] 5435 4-8-8 **46** oh1 (tp) LukeMorris 8 47
(P Leech) *t.k.h: hld up in midfield: rdn and effrt over 2f out: hrd drvn over 1f out: styd on ins fnl f: nvr gng pce to rch ldrs* **25/1**
4054 **6** 1½ **Red Current**[73] 5179 5-8-13 **51** (p) DavidProbert 10 48
(R A Harris) *hld up towards rr: hdwy and n.m.r bnd jst over 2f out: swtchd ins over 1f out: no real imp fnl f* **8/1**
3034 **7** ¾ **Shake On It**[4] 7109 5-9-0 **52** JimCrowley 2 47
(M R Hoad) *chsd ldr tl wl over 1f out: sn hrd drvn: wknd fnl f* **11/4**[1]
00 **8** ¾ **Sufficient Warning**[4] 7109 5-8-10 **55** (b) KierenFox(7) 1 48
(R J Smith) *s.i.s: t.k.h: hld up in tch towards rr: hdwy and swtchd rt 2f out: no prog fr over 1f out* **16/1**
00-0 **9** 3½ **Safaseef (IRE)**[87] 4718 4-8-10 **48** JimmyQuinn 9 33
(K A Morgan) *in tch in midfield: lost pl and bhd 2f out: no ch after* **16/1**
6460 **10** 5 **Lilleput**[104] 4146 4-8-8 **46** oh1 LiamJones 5 19
(E A Wheeler) *s.i.s: hld up in rr: nvr trbld ldrs* **25/1**
5060 **11** 21 **Turn To Dreams**[4] 7127 3-8-8 **55** (v) HollyHall(7) 11 —
(P D Evans) *t.k.h: led tl over 2f out: sn dropped out and wl bhd* **25/1**

1m 39.43s (1.23) **Going Correction** +0.125s/f (Slow)
WFA 3 from 4yo+ 2lb **11** Ran **SP% 120.1**
Speed ratings (Par 101): **98,97,96,96,95 93,93,92,88,83 62**
toteswingers: 1&2 £12.40, 1&3 £6.80, 2&3 £6.70. CSF £39.99 CT £190.50 TOTE £9.70: £2.70, £1.50, £1.90; EX 49.40 Trifecta £181.10 Part won. Pool: £244.77 - 0.45 winning units..
Owner Par 4 Racing **Bred** D Day & B Cantwell **Trained** Mill Hill, London NW7

FOCUS
The quicker of the two divisions by 0.32sec and it looks the more solid form.
Red Current Official explanation: jockey said mare was denied a clear run
Safaseef(IRE) Official explanation: jockey said filly hung right

7201 BET MULTIPLES - BETDAQ H'CAP 1m 5f (P)
2:30 (2:30) (Class 4) (0-85,80) 3-Y-0+ **£5,180** (£1,541; £770; £384) **Stalls** Low

Form RPR
5064 **1** **King Supreme (IRE)**[11] 6936 4-9-3 **72** (b) RichardHughes 1 79
(R Hannon) *led tl over 10f out: chsd ldrs after: rdn along over 4f out: drvn to chse ldr over 2f out: chal 1f out: plugged on to ld towards fin* **7/2**[3]
2405 **2** *hd* **Force Group (IRE)**[11] 6936 5-8-8 **68** (b) AshleyMorgan(5) 3 75
(M H Tompkins) *t.k.h: chsd ldr over 10f out: led gng wl over 3f out: clr over 2f out: rdn wl over 1f out: pressed 1f out: worn down and hdd towards fin* **7/1**
0423 **3** 1 **Ethics Girl (IRE)**[15] 6855 3-8-13 **75** AlanMunro 6 81
(John Berry) *hld up in last pair: hdwy 4f out: chsd ldng pair over 2f out: wanting to hang lft and kpt on same pce fnl f* **3/1**[2]
2162 **4** 15 **Jadalee (IRE)**[21] 6704 6-9-7 **76** (tp) HayleyTurner 2 59
(G A Butler) *chsd ldr tl led over 10f out: hdd and rdn over 3f out: sn wknd: wl btn 2f out* **5/4**[1]
0-05 **5** *nk* **Ragdollianna**[75] 3532 5-9-6 **75** LPKeniry 5 58
(Norma Twomey) *s.i.s: hld up in rr: rdn 5f out: wl bhd fnl 3f* **20/1**
210- **6** 15 **Taaresh (IRE)**[415] 5865 4-9-11 **80** JimmyQuinn 4 40
(K A Morgan) *hld up in tch in last trio: rdn and lost tch qckly over 3f out: t.o* **12/1**

2m 45.8s (-0.20) **Going Correction** +0.125s/f (Slow)
WFA 3 from 4yo+ 7lb **6** Ran **SP% 116.6**
Speed ratings (Par 105): **105,104,104,95,94 85**
toteswingers: 1&2 £6.00, 1&3 £1.60, 2&3 £5.40. CSF £28.27 TOTE £7.40: £2.30, £2.30; EX 16.10.
Owner Brian C Oakley **Bred** Miss Joan Murphy **Trained** East Everleigh, Wilts
■ Stewards' Enquiry : Richard Hughes two-day ban: used whip with excessive frequency (Nov 16-17)

FOCUS
No more than a fair handicap, with the top-weight weighing in 5lb below the ceiling for the race. The pace was reasonable but the favourite's poor showing weakened the race and the winner probably only had to match his recent turf form.
Ethics Girl(IRE) Official explanation: jockey said filly hung left under pressure
Jadalee(IRE) Official explanation: jockey said gelding ran flat

7202 BET PREMIER LEAGUE FOOTBALL - BETDAQ H'CAP 5f (P)
3:05 (3:05) (Class 3) (0-95,100) 3-Y-0+ **£9,066** (£2,697; £1,348; £673) **Stalls** High

Form RPR
3145 **1** **Green Manalishi**[9] 7007 8-9-9 **100** (p) NCallan 5 109+
(K A Ryan) *trckd ldrs gng wl: pushed along and qcknd to ld ins fnl f: sn in command: comf* **10/3**[1]
0001 **2** 1¼ **Fantasy Explorer**[8] 7026 6-8-11 **88** JimmyQuinn 10 93
(J J Quinn) *hld up in tch: rdn and effrt over 1f out: r.o u.p fnl f to go 2nd ins fnl f: nt gng pce to threaten wnr* **7/1**
605 **3** ½ **Toms Laughter**[15] 6843 5-8-12 **89** (b) DavidProbert 7 92
(R A Harris) *dwlt: hld up towards rr: hdwy and rdn over 1f out: n.m.r briefly 1f out: r.o u.p fnl f: nt pce to chal ldr* **15/2**
10-0 **4** *nse* **Cerito**[21] 6694 3-8-8 **85** TPQueally 1 88
(J R Boyle) *s.i.s: bhd: hdwy jst over 1f out: r.o wl ins fnl f: nt rch ldrs* **33/1**
0406 **5** ½ **Macdillon**[23] 6631 3-8-11 **88** FergusSweeney 2 89+
(W S Kittow) *trckd ldrs on inner: swtchd rt and hdwy over 1f out: kpt on u.p fnl f: unable to chal wnr* **8/1**
6100 **6** 1 **Stolt (IRE)**[15] 6843 5-8-3 **85** PaulPickard(5) 8 82
(N Wilson) *pressed ldrs on outer: ev ch and rdn 2f out: stl ev ch tl nt pce of wnr ins fnl f* **20/1**
0404 **7** ¾ **Tabaret**[13] 6897 6-8-9 **86** DO'Donohoe 6 81
(R M Whitaker) *pressed ldr: ev ch and rdn 2f out: led ent fnl f: hdd ins fnl f: wknd fnl 100yds* **11/1**
0141 **8** *hd* **Go Go Green (IRE)**[13] 6902 3-8-9 **86** FrederikTylicki 9 80
(D H Brown) *towards rr: rdn and effrt on outer jst over 2f out: kpt on but nvr gng pce to rch ldrs* **4/1**[2]
5-10 **9** 2½ **Mondovi**[15] 6843 5-8-12 **89** RichardKingscote 4 74
(Tom Dascombe) *a towards rr: rdn and no prog over 2f out: eased whn wl btn ins fnl f* **8/1**
161 **10** ¾ **Crimea (IRE)**[113] 3855 3-8-8 **85** JoeFanning 3 67
(M Johnston) *led narrowly: rdn jst over 2f out: hdd ent fnl f: sn wknd* **11/2**[3]

58.10 secs (-0.70) **Going Correction** +0.125s/f (Slow) **10** Ran **SP% 121.0**
Speed ratings (Par 107): **110,108,107,107,106 104,103,103,99,98**
toteswingers: 1&2 £6.30, 1&3 £6.40, 2&3 £14.30. CSF £28.26 CT £172.23 TOTE £5.00: £2.20, £2.50, £2.70; EX 34.40 Trifecta £280.60 Part won. Pool: £379.30 - 0.20 winning units..
Owner Mrs S McCarthy, J Brennan & J Smith **Bred** E Aldridge **Trained** Hambleton, N Yorks

FOCUS
A decent sprint handicap run at a good pace. Green Manalishi is rated back to his best.

NOTEBOOK
Green Manalishi, although asked to give plenty of weight to his rivals, was taking on a much lower class of opposition than he is used to racing against. Settled in behind the leaders, his biggest problem was getting a gap in the straight, but when it finally came he burst through in fine style, drawing away to win cosily. A return to Listed company beckons. (op 9-2 tchd 5-1)
Fantasy Explorer has recorded his last two wins over 6f but he's perfectly effective over the minimum trip. Drawn in the widest stall, he was on the winner's outside for much of the race and got a cleaner run through in the straight, but he couldn't match that one's turn of foot. (op 8-1)
Toms Laughter, who has been dropped 8lb since his belated reappearance at the end of August, is well handicapped on his best form from last year. Warm beforehand, he ran a sound race, although as a fast-ground lover perhaps the way the track was riding wasn't ideal for him. (op 10-1)
Cerito did best of the four 3-y-os in the line-up. Although well drawn, he was slowest away and trailed the field early. He finished his race off well, though, leaving behind his disappointing reappearance run and showing he can be competitive off his current mark.
Macdillon didn't run badly considering he was stuck near the inside rail for most of the race. He might just need a little help from the handicapper, though. (tchd 9-1)
Stolt(IRE) has tended to struggle once elevated to marks in the mid 80s.
Go Go Green(IRE) lacked the pace to get competitive. (op 9-2)
Crimea(IRE), weak in the betting on his return from a 113-day layoff, was another who was stuck towards the inside throughout and dropped away tamely in the straight. (op 3-1)

7203 STICK HILL H'CAP 6f (P)
3:40 (3:46) (Class 5) (0-70,72) 3-Y-0+ **£2,729** (£806; £403) **Stalls** Low

Form RPR
2502 **1** **Sister Clement (IRE)**[12] 6915 3-9-6 **72** (p) RichardHughes 12 85+
(R Hannon) *sn chsng ldrs: wnt 2nd over 2f out: rdn to ld over 1f out: in command ins fnl f: comf* **5/2**[1]
6313 **2** 1½ **Titus Gent**[16] 6825 4-9-1 **67** DavidProbert 7 73+
(R A Harris) *in tch in midfield: shuffled bk and dropped towards rr 4f out: rdn wl over 1f out: hdwy ent fnl f: r.o wl to go 2nd wl ins fnl f: nvr gng to rch wnr* **6/1**[3]
4360 **3** ½ **Forest Dane**[17] 6791 9-8-8 **60** LukeMorris 4 65
(Mrs N Smith) *t.k.h: chsd ldrs: rdn jst over 2f out: chsd wnr over 1f out: kpt on same pce fnl f* **7/1**
0504 **4** ½ **Kyle (IRE)**[12] 6916 5-8-12 **64** LPKeniry 3 67
(C R Dore) *racd in last trio: rdn and hdwy jst over 1f out: r.o wl fnl f: nvr able to chal* **8/1**
0613 **5** *hd* **Fault**[1] 7192 3-9-4 **70** (t) TPQueally 11 72
(Stef Liddiard) *stdd s: hld up in rr: hdwy on outer 3f out: chsng ldrs whn v wd and lost pl bnd 2f out: rallied and styd on u.p ins fnl f: nvr able to chal* **5/1**[2]
262 **6** *shd* **Louphole**[52] 5805 7-8-12 **64** JimmyQuinn 8 66
(J R Jenkins) *stdd s: t.k.h: hld up in rr: hdwy towards inner jst over 1f out: rn fnl f: nvr trbld ldrs* **8/1**
4000 **7** *hd* **Requisite**[12] 6915 4-9-1 **67** (v) NCallan 10 68
(I A Wood) *in tch: effrt to chse ldrs and rdn ent fnl 2f: one pce and no hdwy over 1f out* **14/1**
0535 **8** 1¼ **Lord Deevert**[144] 2806 4-8-9 **61** SaleemGolam 5 58
(W G M Turner) *led: rdn over 2f out: hdd over 1f out: wknd fnl f* **20/1**
2046 **9** *nk* **Speak The Truth (IRE)**[17] 6798 3-8-13 **65** (p) PatCosgrave 1 61
(J R Boyle) *chsd ldr tl over 2f out: struggling and lost pl 2f out: wl hld fnl f* **14/1**
2263 **10** *nk* **Ghost Dancer**[8] 7023 5-9-3 **69** (p) RichardKingscote 2 64
(J M Bradley) *stdd s: t.k.h and hld up in rr: n.d* **15/2**

1m 12.04s (0.14) **Going Correction** +0.125s/f (Slow) **10** Ran **SP% 124.1**
Speed ratings (Par 103): **104,102,101,100,100 100,100,98,97,97**
toteswingers: 1&2 £4.70, 1&3 £8.30, 2&3 £13.50. CSF £18.91 CT £100.57 TOTE £3.10: £1.50, £2.40, £2.90; EX 21.60 Trifecta £110.50 Pool: £545.31 - 3.65 winning units..
Owner P Byrne **Bred** J Egan, J Corcoran And J Judd **Trained** East Everleigh, Wilts

FOCUS
A modest handicap but straightforward and sound form. Another step forward from the winner.
Ghost Dancer Official explanation: jockey said gelding ran too free

7204 BET MELBOURNE CUP - BETDAQ H'CAP 1m 2f (P)
4:10 (4:11) (Class 5) (0-75,75) 3-Y-0+ **£2,729** (£806; £403) **Stalls** Low

Form RPR
041 **1** **Miss Sophisticat**[13] 6909 3-8-11 **68** (v) JimCrowley 1 76
(W J Knight) *chsd ldr: rdn over 2f out: drvn to ld over 1f out: styd on wl to assert ins fnl f* **9/2**[3]
6261 **2** 1¼ **Cry Alot Boy**[95] 4426 6-9-8 **75** PatCosgrave 3 81
(K A Morgan) *stdd s and s.i.s: t.k.h: hld up wl bhd: gd hdwy on outer over 2f out: drvn to press wnr jst over 1f out: no ex and btn fnl 100yds* **6/1**
1250 **3** *nk* **My Girl Jode**[13] 6910 3-8-4 **61** JimmyQuinn 2 66
(M H Tompkins) *t.k.h: hld up off the pce in midfield: clsd 4f out: c towards centre and effrt wl over 1f out: drvn to chse ldng pair jst ins fnl f: kpt on same pce u.p after* **14/1**
6433 **4** 2 **Merrymadcap (IRE)**[23] 6634 7-9-7 **74** LPKeniry 6 75
(Matthew Salaman) *led: rdn over 2f out: drvn and hdd over 1f out: wknd ins fnl f* **3/1**[2]
315P **5** ½ **Trifti**[163] 2221 8-9-8 **75** DaneO'Neill 5 75
(Miss Jo Crowley) *stdd s: hld up off the pce in midfield: dropped to last 3f out: hdwy u.p on inner over 1f out: kpt on but nvr gng pce to rch ldrs* **11/2**
4304 **6** ¾ **Nassar (IRE)**[15] 6860 6-8-10 **63** (p) SaleemGolam 7 61
(G Prodromou) *s.i.s: rdn along early: racd off the pce in last pair: hdwy into midfield over 3f out: unable qck u.p ent fnl 2f: wl hld fnl f* **8/1**

2502 7 17 **Gross Prophet**[19] 6761 4-9-5 72 HayleyTurner 8 36
(A J Lidderdale) *chsd ldng pair tl drvn and lost pl wl over 2f out: sn lost tch* **11/4**[1]

2m 7.20s (0.60) **Going Correction** +0.125s/f (Slow)
WFA 3 from 4yo+ 4lb **7** Ran SP% **117.3**
Speed ratings (Par 103): **102,101,100,99,98 98,84**
toteswingers: 1&2 £5.10, 1&3 £6.80, 2&3 £6.00. CSF £32.41 CT £352.42 TOTE £5.20: £3.10, £2.00; EX 14.00 Trifecta £286.80 Part won. Pool: £387.57 - 0.45 winning units. Place 6: £813.14, Place 5: £83.30..
Owner Mrs Sheila Mitchell **Bred** Newsells Park Stud Limited **Trained** Patching, W Sussex

FOCUS
There was a ragged start to this handicap and the form looks muddling. The winner probably didn't need to match his latest Windsor win.
T/Plt: £1,025.40 to a £1 stake. Pool: £48,394.99. 34.45 winning tickets. T/Qpdt: £29.00 to a £1 stake. Pool: £8,142.58. 207.10 winning tickets. SP

7046 CAPANNELLE (R-H)
Sunday, November 1

OFFICIAL GOING: Good

7205a PREMIO GUIDO BERARDELLI (GROUP 3) 1m 1f
2:50 (2:58) 2-Y-O **£42,660** (£19,956; £11,233; £5,616)

RPR
1 **Tauman (IRE)**[42] 2-8-11 MDemuro 12 101
(V Caruso, Italy) *a cl up on outside: 5th st: smooth hdwy to ld 2f out: drvn clr over 1f out: r.o wl (2.59/1)* **13/5**[1]
2 1 ½ **Occhio Della Mente (IRE)** 2-8-11 GBietolini 10 98
(R Brogi, Italy) *mid-div: 7th st: hdwy on outside: rdn to chse wnr fr dist: r.o* **48/10**[3]
3 hd **Kidnapping (IRE)** 2-8-11 NPinna 8 98
(S Botti, Italy) *a.p: 3rd st: ev ch 2f out: r.o same pce u.p* **5/1**
4 shd **Martilzo**[49] 2-8-11 URispoli 9 97
(S Botti, Italy) *mid-div: 6th st: rdn and hdwy over 2f out: disp 2nd 1f out: one pce* **69/10**
5 1 ½ **Lord Chaparral (IRE)** 2-8-11 SSulas 5 94
(R Brogi, Italy) *a.p: 4th st: one pce fnl 2f* **48/10**[3]
6 ¾ **Air Crew (USA)**[21] 6716 2-8-11 CFiocchi 2 93
(R Menichetti, Italy) *hld up: last 4f out: hdwy and nt clr run 3f out: swtchd lft: kpt on same pce* **9/2**[2]
7 4 **Borgo Pio (GER)**[49] 2-8-11 SDiana 3 85
(A Candi, Italy) *towards rr to st: outpcd and stl in rr 2f out: sme late prog* **50/1**
8 1 **Collesano (IRE)**[21] 6716 2-8-11 MMonteriso 4 83
(R Biondi, Italy) *led to 2f out* **51/10**
9 hd **Golden Down (USA)**[49] 2-8-11 MEsposito 6 83
(G Fratini, Italy) *mid-div: c wdst in st: nvr in contention* **45/1**
10 1 ½ **Saratoga Black (IRE)** 2-8-11 FBranca 11 80
(Gianluca Bietolini, Italy) *a in rr* **25/1**
11 ½ **Big Creek (IRE)** 2-8-11 DVargiu 7 79
(B Grizzetti, Italy) *pressed ldr: 2nd st: wknd over 2f out* **22/1**
12 ½ **Titus Awarded (IRE)**[98] 2-8-11 GMarcelli 1 78
(G Ligas, Italy) *in rr to st: effrt on rails whn nt clr run over 2f out: swtchd lft: sn struggling* **37/1**

1m 52.7s (-2.00) **12** Ran SP% **141.1**
(including one euro stakes): WIN 3.59; PL 1.73, 2.17, 2.26; DF 12.79.
Owner Scuderia Incolinx **Bred** Azienda Agricola Rosati Colareti Antonio **Trained** Italy

7206a PREMIO C & F.ALOISI (EX PREMIO UMBRIA) (GROUP 3) 6f
3:55 (4:07) 2-Y-O+ **£30,152** (£30,152; £10,570; £2,643; £2,643)

RPR
1 **Thinking Robins (IRE)**[105] 6-9-9 SSulas 11 105
(Alessandro Turco, Italy) *racd wd in middle early: a.p: led over 2f out: drvn over 1f out: hdd ins fnl f: rallied to force dead-heat on line (8.13/1)* **81/10**
1 dht **Morgan Drive (IRE)**[14] 6894 4-9-9 MDemuro 9 105
(M Gasparini, Italy) *a in tch towards outside: cl up whn carried wd 2f out: led ins fnl f: ct on line (2.13/1)* **21/10**[1]
3 1 ½ **Titus Shadow (IRE)**[14] 6894 5-9-12 DVargiu 4 103
(B Grizzetti, Italy) *a.p nr rails: r.o to take 3rd cl home* **12/5**[2]
4 ½ **Remarque (IRE)**[140] 4-9-12 GMarcelli 10 102
(L Riccardi, Italy) *led til hdd over 2f out: kpt on* **5/2**[3]
4 dht **Grenso (ITY)**[29] 2-8-5 URispoli 3 95
(S Botti, Italy) *mid-div: hdwy wl over 1f out: 3rd 1f out: kpt on same pce* **7/2**
6 nk **L'Indiscreta**[14] 6894 4-9-9 CColombi 8 98
(B Grizzetti, Italy) *cl up whn bmpd and wnt sharply rt 2f out: kpt on same pce* **12/5**[2]
7 1 ½ **Ciamarro** 4-9-9 PAragoni 2 93
(Giuseppe Chianese, Italy) *outpcd tl styng on fr over 1 1/2f out* **63/1**
8 hd **Jakor (ITY)**[42] 3-9-9 PConvertino 6 92
(M Marcialis, Italy) *hdwy 1/2-way: cl up whn carried rt 2f out: nt rcvr* **34/1**
9 8 **Xenes**[14] 6894 5-9-9 CFiocchi 7 67
(R Menichetti, Italy) *prom: rdn and hung rt jst over 2f out: sn wknd* **21/1**
10 nse **White Rose (ITY)**[196] 1394 5-9-5 CDemuro 5 62
(Luigi Rosa, Italy) *in tch to 2f out* **60/1**
11 1 ½ **Vallodiadriano (IRE)**[105] 3-9-9 MBelli 1 62
(S Onofrio, Italy) *disp ld on rails tl wkng 2f out* **35/1**

68.20 secs (-2.10) **11** Ran SP% **166.2**
WIN 1.89 (Morgan Drive), 3.60 (Thinking Robins); PL 1.55 (MorganDrive), 2.19 (Thinking Robins), 1.73 (Titus Shadow); DF 17.63.
Owner Razza Montalbano **Bred** Razza Montalbano **Trained** Italy
Owner San Paolo Agri Stud Srl **Bred** Sao Paolo Agricola Stud Srl **Trained** Italy

7128 SAINT-CLOUD (L-H)
Sunday, November 1

OFFICIAL GOING: Very soft

7207a CRITERIUM INTERNATIONAL (GROUP 1) (C&F) 1m
1:00 (1:03) 2-Y-O **£138,689** (£55,485; £27,743; £13,859; £6,942)

RPR
1 **Jan Vermeer (IRE)**[36] 6300 2-9-0 CO'Donoghue 117
(A P O'Brien, Ire) *mde all: led field to stands' side ent st: sn pushed along: rdn clr appr fnl f: drvn out* **10/1**
2 4 **Emerald Commander (IRE)**[57] 5659 2-9-0 LDettori 109
(Saeed Bin Suroor) *disp 4th: 4th st: sn rdn: rchd 2nd 1f out: nvr nr wnr* **5/1**[3]
3 1 ½ **Rosanara (FR)**[28] 6523 2-8-11 C-PLemaire 103
(A De Royer-Dupre, France) *hld up: 6th st: kpt on one pce to take 3rd last strides* **1/1**[1]
4 hd **Midas Touch**[20] 6744 2-9-0 JMurtagh 105
(A P O'Brien, Ire) *disp 2nd: 3rd st: drvn 2f out: kpt on one pce* **9/2**[2]
5 1 ½ **Prizefighting (USA)**[6] 7050 2-9-0 JimmyFortune 102
(J H M Gosden) *trckd wnr: 2nd st: one pce fnl 2f* **15/2**
6 1 ½ **Royal Bench (IRE)**[19] 2-9-0 IMendizabal 99
(Robert Collet, France) *disp 4th: 5th st: sn btn* **25/1**
7 ¾ **Arasin (IRE)**[43] 6133 2-9-0 OPeslier 98
(P Bary, France) *hld up: last st: rdn and btn wl over 1f out* **20/1**

1m 45.6s (-1.90) **7** Ran SP% **114.3**
PARI-MUTUEL: WIN 5.00 (coupled with Midas Touch); PL 10.00, 3.80;SF 188.80.
Owner Michael Tabor **Bred** Shadow Song Syndicate **Trained** Ballydoyle, Co Tipperary

FOCUS
Not the strongest of the juvenile Group 1s but quite a decisive winner.

NOTEBOOK
Jan Vermeer(IRE) had improved from his debut to win his maiden on fast ground at Gowran Park, when he had Midas Touch back in third, so it was perhaps slightly surprising that Johnny Murtagh chose to ride the latter. The son of Montjeu got an uncontested lead and, picking up from the home turn, came away to score without being extended. He was given a quote of 10-1 for next year's Derby and, with plenty of stamina in his pedigree and ground conditions not a problem, he would not be the worst each-way prospect for that race if going on from this.
Emerald Commander(IRE), who was bought by Godolphin after finishing runner-up in the Acomb Stakes and then winning a Listed race at Haydock, had gained both his successes on soft ground. He sat off the pace but could not pick up well enough to trouble the winner, but he beat the rest well enough and could have run into a really smart colt who had everything go his way.
Rosanara(FR), an impressive winner of the Prix Marcel Boussac last time, was another settled off the pace and seemed to be travelling well enough turning in. However, once off the bridle she could not pick up in the ground and only struggled into third place. She can be given another chance on a sounder surface. Her first main target in 2010 will be the Poule d'Essai des Pouliches, and she will probably run before in the Prix de la Grotte.
Midas Touch had a bit to find with the winner on their previous form but he had since won his maiden on soft ground since and was preferred by Murtagh. He appeared to have every chance but could find no more in the last two furlongs.
Prizefighting(USA), who cost $500,000, had made quite an impression when successful on his debut on Polytrack at the beginning of the week. He raced a little keenly in the early stages on this soft ground and paid for it late on. This may have come a bit soon for him and he can be expected to do better next season.

7208a PRIX PERTH (GROUP 3) 1m
1:35 (1:35) 3-Y-O+ **£38,835** (£15,534; £11,650; £7,767; £3,883)

RPR
1 **Zafisio (IRE)**[49] 5924 3-8-11 DBoeuf 10 114
(R Curtis) *a.p on outside: 4th st: drvn to ld over 1f out: r.o wl* **10/1**
2 1 ½ **Border Patrol**[29] 6503 3-9-1 SteveDrowne 4 115
(R Charlton) *hld up bhd ldrs: 6th st: drvn and hdwy wl over 1f out: ev ch over 1f out: kpt on same pce u.p* **7/2**[1]
3 ½ **Racinger (FR)**[29] 6505 6-9-3 DBonilla 11 114
(F Head, France) *racd in mid-div on outside: 9th st: r.o fnl 2f but could nvr rch first two* **6/1**
4 2 ½ **Schutzenjunker (GER)**[21] 6713 4-9-3 YLerner 9 108
(Uwe Ostmann, Germany) *led to over 1f out: one pce* **16/1**
5 1 ½ **Usbeke (GER)**[23] 6657 3-8-11 TThulliez 12 101
(J-P Carvalho, Germany) *mid-div trcking wnr on outside: 7th st: nvr nr to chal* **25/1**
6 ¾ **Murcielago (FR)**[29] 6505 4-9-0 (b) FSpanu 7 100
(T Castanheira, France) *towards rr to st: hdwy wl over 1f out: no ex fr dist* **10/1**
7 hd **Expresso Star (USA)**[149] 2670 4-9-0 JimmyFortune 3 99
(J H M Gosden) *a.p: 2nd st: rdn and btn over 1 1/2f out* **11/2**[3]
8 3 **Kissing The Camera**[17] 6808 3-8-8 TJarnet 2 89
(R Pritchard-Gordon, France) *pressed ldr: 3rd st: sn btn* **33/1**
9 3 **King Of Sydney (USA)**[21] 6718 3-9-3 MGuyon 8 91
(Mario Hofer, Germany) *in rr to st: nvr a factor* **16/1**
10 8 **Danse Grecque (USA)**[29] 6505 4-8-10 OPeslier 5 63
(E Lellouche, France) *cl up: 5th st: sn wknd* **5/1**[2]
11 **Moyenne Corniche**[23] 6658 4-9-0 IMendizabal 1 67
(M L W Bell) *last st: a bhd* **14/1**
12 **Handsome Maestro (IRE)**[29] 6505 3-8-11 SPasquier 6 66
(D Smaga, France) *mid-div: 8th st: sn wknd* **10/1**

1m 45.3s (-2.20)
WFA 3 from 4yo+ 2lb **12** Ran SP% **121.1**
PARI-MUTUEL: WIN 8.20; PL 2.40, 2.10, 1.90; DF 21.10.
Owner H Downs & D Looney **Bred** Airlie Stud And Sir Thomas Pilkington **Trained** Lambourn, Berks

NOTEBOOK
Zafisio(IRE) revelled on this testing ground back where he took a Group 1 race a year ago. He looked in great shape in the paddock, was well placed in the early stages, responded well when asked to challenge for the lead and was never in danger of defeat during the final furlong, eventually winning with something in hand. He will only be campaigned in the future when there is cut in the ground, but when conditions are right, he is a high-class performer over a mile and slightly further. He now heads for the Group 3 Hessen Pokal at Frankfurt on November 14.
Border Patrol didn't act as well on the ground as the winner. Dropped out in the early stages, he came with a progressive late run up the centre of the track and stayed on gamely to hold second place inside the final furlong. He met a soft-ground specialist on this occasion and lost little in defeat.
Racinger(FR), not the easiest of rides, was towards the tail of the field early on, although it wasn't the intention to be better placed. He came with his challenge up the stands' rail and battled on well to the line.

Schutzenjunker(GER) was taken immediately into the lead and stayed at the head of affairs until the furlong marker. He then gradually dropped out of contention but was still game till the line.
Expresso Star(USA), absent since early June, was never far from the leader and was still in contention coming into the straight. He then gradually tired as the race came to an end.
Moyenne Corniche was never seen with a chance of finishing in the frame and was always behind. His jockey felt the colt didn't act on the ground.

7190 WOLVERHAMPTON (A.W) (L-H)
Monday, November 2

OFFICIAL GOING: Standard
Wind: Fresh behind Weather: Cloudy

7209 BET MELBOURNE CUP - BETDAQ MAIDEN STKS — 7f 32y(P)
2:05 (2:07) (Class 5) 2-Y-O — **£3,238** (£963; £481; £240) **Stalls** High

Form / RPR

1 **Elspeth's Boy (USA)** 2-9-3 0 ... DavidProbert 2 — 80+
(J R Best) *chsd ldrs: lost pl over 4f out: edgd rt wl over 3f out: hdwy u.p and swtchd lft over 1f out: r.o to ld wl ins fnl f: sn clr* **33/1**

624 2 *1 ¼* **Music Maestro (IRE)**[23] 6672 2-9-3 75 ... RHills 7 — 77
(B W Hills) *hld up in tch: rdn to ld 1f out: hdd and unable qck wl ins fnl f* **12/1**

3 *2 ½* **Mureb (USA)** 2-9-3 0 ... TedDurcan 8 — 71+
(Saeed Bin Suroor) *dwlt: sn pushed along in rr: hdwy u.p and hung lft over 1f out: styds on to go 3rd nr fin: nt trble ldrs* **5/4**[1]

02 4 *hd* **Tesslam**[30] 6484 2-9-3 0 ... PhilipRobinson 3 — 70
(M A Jarvis) *chsd ldrs: rdn over 2f out: styd on same pce fnl f* **15/8**[2]

4 5 *1 ¾* **Gramercy (IRE)**[30] 6493 2-9-3 0 ... HayleyTurner 9 — 66
(M L W Bell) *sn led: rdn and hdd 1f out: no ex* **8/1**[3]

30 6 *½* **Argaum (IRE)**[20] 6759 2-9-3 0 ... AdamKirby 10 — 65
(W R Swinburn) *hld up: nt clr run over 1f out: sn edgd lft: styd on: nvr nrr* **33/1**

00 7 *11* **Heligoland**[37] 6291 2-8-12 0 ... FergusSweeney 1 — 33
(A G Newcombe) *son pushed along in rr: rdn 1/2-way: wknd over 2f out* **150/1**

02 8 *2 ¼* **Fivefold (USA)**[13] 6911 2-9-3 0 ... J-PGuillambert 5 — 32
(J Akehurst) *chsd ldr: rdn over 2f out: wknd over 1f out* **20/1**

2330 9 *½* **State Fair**[9] 7029 2-9-3 80 ... NCallan 6 — 31
(P F I Cole) *prom: rdn over 2f out: wknd over 1f out* **16/1**

1m 29.37s (-0.23) **Going Correction** +0.15s/f (Slow) — **9** Ran SP% **115.2**
Speed ratings (Par 96): **107,105,102,102,100 99,87,84,84**
toteswingers: 1&2 £20.30, 1&3 £10.90, 2&3 £4.00 CSF £363.12 TOTE £34.00: £6.00, £2.00, £1.50; EX 394.00 TRIFECTA Not won..
Owner D Gorton **Bred** S M D Ltd **Trained** Hucking, Kent

FOCUS
A fair juvenile maiden and the time was very good; 3.04 seconds quicker than the following 2-y-o seller won by the 65-rated Tucker's Law, who carried 8st11lb. The proximity of the runner-up limits the form but it looks worth giving the race a chance.

NOTEBOOK
Elspeth's Boy(USA) ◆ posted a good performance on a debut apparently delayed by the bug that affected John Best's yard earlier in the year. Although dismissed at 33/1, his trainer said this wasn't a surprise, and he is a colt held in high regard. An $11,000 foal and half-brother to a 6f winner and a 1m scorer, he broke well enough, but was soon racing well off the pace and lacked the sharpness of some of these. However, once switched towards the inside in the straight, he picked up well to ultimately win going away. He has some scope and looks a useful type in the making.
Music Maestro(IRE), dropped in trip, looked the winner when taking over around 1f out but had no answer to the winner's late surge. This was a good effort in defeat.
Mureb(USA) ◆, a $500,000 half-brother to six winners, including top-class miler Summoner, winner of Queen Elizabeth Stakes, and Eclipse winner Compton Admiral, was too green to do himself justice. He raced out the back after losing a few lengths at the start and swung wide into the straight. There should be a lot better to come. (op 11-8 tchd Evens)
Tesslam ran well below the form he showed when runner-up at Redcar on his previous start and was disappointing. He was well placed and travelled well, but found little for pressure. There may be more to come now handicaps are an option, but he still doesn't appeal as one to follow. (op 7-4 tchd 9-4)
Gramercy(IRE), a promising fourth over 6f around here on debut, ran like a non-stayer over this extra furlong, even though his pedigree suggested the trip should have been fine. He travelled well, but basically just looks a horse with a lot of speed.
Argaum(IRE) got messed about a bit, receiving a bump leaving the back straight and being short of room over 1f out. He was unsuited by the drop in trip and can do better now handicaps are an option.
Fivefold(USA) Official explanation: jockey said colt hung right
State Fair ran poorly on this Polytrack debut and is regressing. His dam was a multiple sprint winner and perhaps he'll be worth a try over a little shorter. Official explanation: jockey said colt had no more to give (op 14-1)

7210 WOLVERHAMPTON-RACECOURSE.CO.UK (S) STKS — 7f 32y(P)
2:40 (2:40) (Class 6) 2-Y-O — **£2,388** (£705; £352) **Stalls** High

Form / RPR

6652 1 **Tucker's Law**[19] 6775 2-8-11 65 ... FergusSweeney 2 — 57
(B R Millman) *hld up in tch: racd keenly: rdn to ld 1f out: edgd lft: r.o* **5/2**[1]

16 2 *¾* **Push Me (IRE)**[7] 7056 2-8-11 64 ... LiamJones 6 — 57+
(M S Tuck) *prom: stmbld and lost pl wl over 4f out: nt clr run over 1f out: edgd lft and r.o wl ins fnl f: nt rch wnr* **12/1**

600 3 *½* **Lord Victor**[26] 6591 2-8-6 50 ... MartinLane(5) 3 — 54
(A J McCabe) *sn led: rdn and hdd 1f out: sn edgd lft: styd on same pce* **33/1**

400 4 *½* **Taper Jean Girl (IRE)**[39] 6228 2-8-3 66 ... AndreaAtzeni(3) 4 — 48
(M Botti) *chsd ldrs: rdn over 2f out: styd on u.p* **4/1**[2]

0402 5 *½* **Whipperway (IRE)**[6] 7098 2-8-6 66 ... ChrisCatlin 12 — 47
(M R Channon) *sn pushed along in rr: hdwy over 4f out: rdn and ev ch over 1f out: sn edgd lft: no ex ins fnl f* **13/2**[3]

1500 6 *½* **Kapelad Junior (IRE)**[26] 6589 2-9-2 57 ... PaulEddery 10 — 55+
(Pat Eddery) *prom: rdn and nt clr run over 1f out and ins fnl f: styd on same pce* **25/1**

330 7 *¾* **Lord Raglan (IRE)**[46] 6009 2-8-11 70 ... AndrewElliott 1 — 48
(A P Jarvis) *chsd ldrs: rdn 1/2-way: styd on same pce fnl f* **15/2**

042 8 *nse* **Pont D'Avignon**[26] 6586 2-8-6 63 ... FrankieMcDonald 9 — 43
(F J Brennan) *s.i.s: hdwy into mid-div over 5f out: rdn 1/2-way: outpcd 2f: sn hung lft: styd on ins fnl f* **8/1**

0050 9 *hd* **Ellmollell**[38] 6241 2-8-6 54 ... DavidProbert 5 — 43
(S Kirk) *hld up: rdn over 2f out: styd on u.p fnl f: nvr trbld ldrs* **16/1**

5000 10 *½* **Golden Pippin**[61] 5573 2-7-13 52 ... CharlesEddery(7) 8 — 42
(R Hannon) *hld up: rdn 1/2-way: n.d* **28/1**

6 11 *½* **Blast**[17] 6826 2-8-6 0 ... (b) LukeMorris 7 — 40
(J R Gask) *s.i.s: sn pushed along in rr: n.d* **16/1**

3000 12 *3 ¾* **Mary Celest (IRE)**[4] 7139 2-8-6 54 ... (p) JoeFanning 11 — 31
(K A Ryan) *hdwy over 4f out: jnd ldrs 1/2-way: wknd over 1f out* **28/1**

1m 32.41s (2.81) **Going Correction** +0.15s/f (Slow) — **12** Ran SP% **117.9**
Speed ratings (Par 94): **89,88,87,87,86 85,85,84,84,84 83,79**
toteswingers: 1&2 £9.70, 1&3 £17.50, 2&3 £37.20 CSF £32.66 TOTE £3.20: £1.30, £3.80, £5.90; EX 41.60 Trifecta £209.00 Part won. Pool: £282.45 - 0.55 winning units..There was no bid for the winner.
Owner Mrs J Laws **Bred** D R Tucker **Trained** Kentisbeare, Devon

FOCUS
An ordinary 2-y-o seller run in a slow time and the field finished in something of a bunch. The third is an apparent improver but the sixth helps set the level.

NOTEBOOK
Tucker's Law proved well suited by the step up in trip and gained his first success at the 11th attempt. Having been well placed, he won in decent enough style and should be competitive back in handicaps. (op 7-2)
Push Me(IRE), carrying a penalty for her debut success in this grade over the same C&D, was unlucky not to give the winner more of a race as she lost her place when hampered down the back straight and was then denied a clear run over 1f out. Official explanation: jockey said filly was denied a clear run (op 11-1)
Lord Victor, without the blinkers and back up in trip, kept on surprisingly well once headed, but still didn't do enough to warrant support next time. (op 25-1)
Taper Jean Girl(IRE), not for the first time, was a bit keen early and never looked like winning. (op 5-1)
Whipperway(IRE) stayed on from off the pace but was ultimately well held. She might benefit from some headgear to sharpen her up. (op 11-2 tchd 7-1)

7211 ENJOY THE LUCKY 7 GROUP OFFER H'CAP — 1m 141y(P)
3:15 (3:15) (Class 6) (0-65,63) 3-Y-O — **£2,388** (£705; £352) **Stalls** Low

Form / RPR

0006 1 **Fitzolini**[67] 5362 3-8-5 50 ... (p) JimmyQuinn 9 — 53
(A D Brown) *mde all: rdn and hung rt over 1f out: styd on u.p* **25/1**

0153 2 *1* **Why Nee Amy**[13] 6924 3-8-11 56 ... ChrisCatlin 10 — 57
(T Keddy) *hld up: rdn over 3f out: r.o wl ins fnl f: nt rch wnr* **10/1**

0500 3 *½* **Join Up**[4] 7142 3-8-5 50 ow1 ... LiamJones 3 — 50
(W M Brisbourne) *plld hrd: trckd ldrs: rdn over 1f out: styd on same pce ins fnl f* **9/1**[3]

3551 4 *shd* **Vamos (IRE)**[16] 6862 3-9-1 60 ... RobertHavlin 7 — 60
(J R Gask) *hld up: hdwy over 2f out: sn rdn: hung lft fnl f: styd on* **11/4**[1]

0440 5 *nse* **Cause For Applause (IRE)**[33] 6383 3-8-7 52 ... AdrianTNicholls 4 — 52
(R Craggs) *hld up: hdwy over 1f out: sn rdn: r.o* **25/1**

2605 6 *½* **Barbarian**[12] 6951 3-9-4 63 ... GrahamGibbons 6 — 62
(A D Brown) *chsd ldrs: rdn over 1f out: sn hung lft: no ex fnl f* **9/2**[2]

6466 7 *¾* **Herecomethegirls**[25] 6608 3-8-10 55 ... HayleyTurner 8 — 52
(M L W Bell) *s.i.s: hld up: nt clr run over 1f out: r.o ins fnl f: nvr nrr* **10/1**

2055 8 *1 ¼* **Lilly Blue (IRE)**[66] 5384 3-8-13 58 ... PatCosgrave 1 — 52
(R Brotherton) *chsd ldrs: rdn over 2f out: no ex fnl f* **10/1**

4006 9 *4 ½* **Royal Willy (IRE)**[19] 6784 3-9-3 62 ... JoeFanning 5 — 46
(W Jarvis) *prom: chsd wnr over 6f out: rdn over 2f out: wknd fnl f* **11/4**[1]

1m 52.29s (1.79) **Going Correction** +0.15s/f (Slow) — **9** Ran SP% **116.5**
Speed ratings (Par 98): **98,97,96,96,96 96,95,94,90**
toteswingers: 1&2 £8.70, 1&3 £16.80, 2&3 £14.70 CSF £253.79 CT £2443.11 TOTE £21.90: £5.00, £2.70, £2.40; EX 218.60 TRIFECTA Not won..
Owner Mrs Susan Johnson **Bred** Mrs S Johnson **Trained** Yedingham, N Yorks
■ Stewards' Enquiry : Jimmy Quinn caution: careless riding
Pat Cosgrave caution: careless riding.

FOCUS
The pace was steady and this was a moderate handicap.

7212 BET CHAMPIONS LEAGUE FOOTBALL - BETDAQ H'CAP — 1m 4f 50y(P)
3:50 (3:50) (Class 5) (0-70,70) 3-Y-O+ — **£3,885** (£1,156; £577; £288) **Stalls** Low

Form / RPR

0063 1 **Chookie Hamilton**[24] 6636 5-9-10 70 ... TomEaves 4 — 85
(I Semple) *chsd ldrs: rdn to ld 1f out: styd on wl* **7/2**[2]

0-02 2 *1 ¼* **Kazbow (IRE)**[18] 6807 3-9-0 66 ... WilliamBuick 1 — 79
(L M Cumani) *led 2f: chsd ldr tl led again over 2f out: rdn: hung rt and hdd 1f out: styd on same pce* **7/4**[1]

-045 3 *9* **Lilac Moon (GER)**[30] 6490 5-9-6 66 ... RichardKingscote 3 — 65
(Tom Dascombe) *s.i.s: hld up: hdwy u.p over 1f out: wnt 3rd ins fnl f: nvr trbld ldrs* **7/1**

0626 4 *1 ¼* **Moonshine Creek**[17] 6832 7-9-3 63 ... ChrisCatlin 8 — 60
(P W Hiatt) *chsd ldr tl led after 2f: rdn and hdd over 2f out: wknd fnl f* **16/1**

2004 5 *2 ¼* **Augustus John (IRE)**[102] 4235 6-9-9 69 ... PatCosgrave 7 — 62
(R Brotherton) *hld up: hdwy over 2f out: sn rdn: wknd over 1f out* **16/1**

005- 6 *5* **Stage Acclaim (IRE)**[23] 6400 4-9-1 61 ... RobertHavlin 5 — 46
(C J Down) *hld up: rdn over 3f out: wknd over 2f out* **33/1**

0440 7 *4 ½* **Rehabilitation**[34] 6369 4-9-5 65 ... (tp) DavidProbert 6 — 43
(W R Swinburn) *chsd ldrs: rdn over 3f out: wknd 2f out* **4/1**[3]

0000 8 *2 ¼* **Petsas Pleasure**[16] 6861 3-8-10 62 ... FrederikTylicki 2 — 36
(Ollie Pears) *prom: rdn over 2f out: wknd over 1f out* **16/1**

5145 9 *3 ¾* **Trachonitis (IRE)**[22] 6704 5-9-9 69 ... NCallan 9 — 37
(J R Jenkins) *s.s: hld up: hdwy over 3f out: rdn and wknd 2f out* **12/1**

2m 40.61s (-0.49) **Going Correction** +0.15s/f (Slow)
WFA 3 from 4yo+ 6lb — **9** Ran SP% **119.4**
Speed ratings (Par 103): **107,106,100,99,97 94,91,90,87**
toteswingers: 1&2 £2.60, 1&3 £5.20, 2&3 £5.00 CSF £10.41 CT £41.02 TOTE £4.70: £1.70, £1.60, £1.60; EX 12.90 Trifecta £52.90 Pool: £342.18 - 4.70 winning units..
Owner Raeburn Brick Limited **Bred** D And J Raeburn **Trained** Carluke, S Lanarks

FOCUS
A modest handicap run at a steady pace.

7213 SPONSOR A RACE BY CALLING 01902 390000 MEDIAN AUCTION MAIDEN STKS — 5f 20y(P)
4:20 (4:20) (Class 5) 2-Y-O — **£3,885** (£1,156; £577; £288) **Stalls** Low

Form / RPR

445 1 **Tartufo Dolce (IRE)**[30] 6493 2-8-12 72 ... TPQueally 1 — 71
(J G Given) *chsd ldrs: rdn to ld 1f out: jst hld on* **11/2**[3]

5232 2 *hd* **Excellent Thought**[12] 6932 2-8-12 69 ... RHills 2 — 70
(W J Haggas) *broke wl: sn outpcd: hdwy over 1f out: rdn and ev ch ins fnl f: r.o* **6/5**[1]

6 3 *1 ½* **Fair Passion**[11] 6971 2-8-12 0 ... DaneO'Neill 7 — 65
(D Shaw) *chsd ldrs: hung rt 1/2-way: rdnn over 1f out: edgd lft: styd on* **33/1**

4 4 *2* **Mosa Mine**[116] 3762 2-8-12 0 ... PhillipMakin 10 — 58
(D H Brown) *sn led: rdn and hdd over 1f out: no ex ins fnl f* **10/1**

00 **5** 1/2 **Mosqueta**14 6903 2-8-12 0.......... CatherineGannon 3 56
(P D Evans) *sn outpcd: r.o ins fnl f: nvr nrr* **66/1**
3243 **6** 2 **Bronze Beau**14 6903 2-9-3 72.......... TomEaves 5 54
(Mrs L Stubbs) *s.v.s: wl bhd tl r.o ins fnl f: nvr nrr* **6/1**
0 **7** 1 1/4 **Kyoatee Kilt**151 2631 2-9-3 0.......... NCallan 6 49
(P F I Cole) *prom: drvn along 1/2-way: wknd over 1f out* **20/1**
030 **8** 7 **Safari Camp (IRE)**5 7115 2-9-3 64.......... FrederikTylicki 9 24
(A Berry) *mid-div: sn pushed along: wknd over 1f out* **66/1**
0 **9** 2 1/4 **Youcanalwaysdream (IRE)**12 6932 2-8-12 0.......... FergusSweeney 8 11
(K A Ryan) *sn chsng ldr: ev ch over 2f out: rdn and wknd over 1f out* **9/2**[2]

63.29 secs (0.99) **Going Correction** +0.15s/f (Slow) **9** Ran SP% **113.1**
Speed ratings (Par 96): **98,97,95,92,91 88,86,74,71**
toteswingers: 1&2 £12.50, 1&3 £3.30, 2&3 £16.00 CSF £11.95 TOTE £4.50: £2.10, £1.10, £5.30; EX 16.20 Trifecta £272.30 Part won. Pool: £368.08 - 0.90 winning units..
Owner Danethorpe Racing Partnership **Bred** Limestone And Tara Studs **Trained** Willoughton, Lincs

FOCUS
A modest sprint maiden rated around the first two.

NOTEBOOK
Tartufo Dolce(IRE) proved well suited by the drop back to the minimum trip. An official mark of 72 seems fair enough and she should be competitive in handicaps, either this season or next year. (op 5-1 tchd 6-1)
Excellent Thought kept on well for pressure in the straight but was just held. This was a solid run in defeat and a similarly ordinary race should come her way. (op Evens tchd 11-8)
Fair Passion ◆ built on the promise she showed on her debut at Kempton. She has plenty of ability and looks the type to go on improving.
Mosa Mine, off the track since showing ability on her debut in July, displayed plenty of speed. She should come on for this and ought to find a race. (tchd 12-1)
Mosqueta kept on after being outpaced and is of interest now she can switch to handicaps, especially as she should improve over a little further.
Bronze Beau lost his race with a very slow start. Official explanation: jockey said gelding missed the break (op 7-1)
Youcanalwaysdream(IRE) hinted at ability on her debut at Bath, but this was disappointing. (op 13-2)

7214 BET IN-RUNNING - BETDAQ H'CAP — 1m 5f 194y(P)
4:50 (4:51) (Class 6) (0-60,60) 3-Y-0+ — £2,388 (£705; £352) Stalls Low

Form RPR
0125 **1** **Leyte Gulf (USA)**24 6636 6-9-9 59.......... DaneO'Neill 8 66+
(C C Bealby) *hld up: hdwy 2f out: rdn to ld ins fnl f: hung lft: styd on* **10/3**[1]
25/ **2** 3/4 **Day Care**17 6839 8-8-11 52.......... MartinLane(5) 11 58
(R McGlinchey, Ire) *chsd ldrs: led over 1f out: rdn and hdd ins fnl f: styd on* **8/1**
0443 **3** 1 1/2 **Squirtle (IRE)**3 7154 6-9-2 52.......... LukeMorris 6 56
(W M Brisbourne) *hld up: hdwy over 1f out: r.o wl: nt rch ldrs* **11/2**[2]
5233 **4** nk **Tivers Song (USA)**19 6770 5-9-3 53..........(b) PatCosgrave 2 56
(John A Harris) *hld up: hdwy over 6f out: rdn over 1f out: styd on same pce ins fnl f* **8/1**
406- **5** 1/2 **Major Promise**420 5758 4-9-6 56.......... JimmyQuinn 12 59
(Jane Chapple-Hyam) *hld up: plld hrd: hdwy over 2f out: sn rdn: styd on* **16/1**
0635 **6** 1 1/4 **Supernoverre (IRE)**9 7025 3-9-2 60..........(p) IanMongan 1 61
(P Howling) *chsd ldrs: rdn over 1f out: no ex fnl f* **12/1**
0060 **7** 1 1/4 **Paint The Town Red**20 6761 4-9-7 60.......... JackMitchell(3) 13 59
(H J Collingridge) *hld up and bhd: hdwy on outside wl over 1f out: styd on same pce ins fnl f* **18/1**
4044 **8** 2 **Tuppenny Piece**39 6226 3-8-7 58..........(p) KierenFox(7) 5 54
(W R Swinburn) *prom: rdn over 3f out: wknd over 1f out* **12/1**
1010 **9** 3 1/4 **Looks The Business (IRE)**51 5885 8-9-7 57.......... FergusSweeney 4 49
(A B Haynes) *hld up: rdn over 2f out: sn wknd* **16/1**
0-06 **10** 2 **Royal Rainbow**26 5939 5-8-9 48.......... WilliamCarson(3) 3 37
(P W Hiatt) *led: rdn and hdd over 1f out: wknd fnl f* **66/1**
1162 **11** 5 **Sparkaway**21 6742 3-9-2 60.......... ChrisCatlin 9 42
(W J Musson) *hld up in tch: rdn over 2f out: wknd over 1f out* **6/1**[3]
2154 **12** nk **Chichen Daawe**17 6817 3-8-6 50.......... FrederikTylicki 10 32
(B Ellison) *hld up: plld hrd: hdwy to chsd ldr over 10f out: rdn over 2f out: wknd over 1f out* **14/1**

3m 9.04s (3.04) **Going Correction** +0.15s/f (Slow)
WFA 3 from 4yo+ 8lb **12** Ran SP% **115.5**
Speed ratings (Par 101): **97,96,95,95,95 94,93,92,90,89 86,86**
toteswingers: 1&2 £8.30, 1&3 £6.20, 2&3 £9.20 CSF £28.85 CT £142.77 TOTE £4.00: £1.90, £2.80, £2.10; EX 31.10 TRIFECTA Not won. Place 6: £86.18 Place 5: £48.67 .
Owner Robert Jenkinson **Bred** Paradigm Thoroughbred Inc **Trained** Barrowby, Lincs

FOCUS
A moderate handicap.
Chichen Daawe Official explanation: jockey said filly suffered interference in running
T/Plt: £130.10 to a £1 stake. Pool: £62,667.36. 351.49 winning tickets. T/Qpdt: £20.90 to a £1 stake. Pool: £6,316.93. 223.40 winning tickets. CR

7196 FLEMINGTON (L-H)
Tuesday, November 3

OFFICIAL GOING: Good to soft

7215a EMIRATES MELBOURNE CUP (H'CAP) (GROUP 1) — 2m
4:00 (4:02) 3-Y-0+
£1,674,757 (£405,340; £203,883; £106,796; £72,816; £55,825)

RPR
1 **Shocking (AUS)**3 4-8-0..........(b) CoreyBrown 21 115
(Mark Kavanagh, Australia) *in tch in mid-div: 8th st: pushed along to chal 1 1/2f out: led 150yds out: styd on wl fnl stages* **9/1**[3]
2 3/4 **Crime Scene (IRE)**13 6961 6-8-5..........(b1) KerrinMcEvoy 10 118
(Saeed Bin Suroor) *settled in 7th: 6th and gng wl st: chal 2f out: led over 1 1/2f out: narrowly hdd 150yds out: styd on* **40/1**
3 1 1/2 **Mourilyan (IRE)**66 5425 5-8-8.......... GlynSchofield 13 119+
(H J Brown, South Africa) *towards rr of mid-div: drvn and gd hdwy fr 2f out: rdn fnl f and wnt 3rd 100yds out: nrest at fin* **20/1**
4 1 1/2 **Master O'Reilly (NZ)**3 7196 7-8-9.......... VladDuric 15 119+
(Danny O'Brien, Australia) *towards rr: rdn and hdwy down outside fr 2f out: kpt on steadily to go 4th nr fin* **11/1**
5 nk **Harris Tweed (NZ)**17 6871 4-8-4..........(b) CraigNewitt 19 113
(Murray & Bjorn Baker, New Zealand) *hld up: hdwy over 3f out on outside: pressing ldrs 1 1/2f out: 3rd over 1f out: no ex fnl stages* **100/1**
6 hd **Alcopop (AUS)**24 5-8-4.......... DominicTourneur 11 112
(Jake Stephens, Australia) *in tch: effrt and hdwy over 1 1/2f out: disputing 4th 100yds out: no ex fnl stages* **15/4**[1]
7 shd **Viewed (AUS)**3 7196 6-9-2..........(b) BradRawiller 8 124
(Bart Cummings, Australia) *mid-div: bhd appr st: pushed along 2f out: sme hdwy but nvr in chalng position* **11/2**[2]
8 1/2 **C'Est La Guerre (NZ)**17 6871 5-8-10.......... NicholasHall 6 118
(John D Sadler, Australia) *in tch: drvn to chse ldrs ent st: no ex fr over 1f out* **25/1**
9 1/2 **Kibbutz (NZ)**10 5-8-4.......... ChrisSymons 7 111
(Jarrod McLean, Australia) *mid-div: hrd drvn st: kpt on at one pce u.p: nvr able to chal* **66/1**
10 hd **Newport (AUS)**3 7196 7-8-4.......... PeterWells 17 111
(Paul Perry, Australia) *mid-div: dropped bk towards rr appr st: nvr able to chal* **40/1**
11 3/4 **Daffodil (NZ)**17 6871 4-8-2.......... ChrisMunce 20 108
(Kevin Gray, New Zealand) *mid-div: nvr in chalng position* **14/1**
12 hd **Munsef**51 5933 7-8-5.......... ZaxPurton 4 110
(Ian Williams) *in tch in mid-div: shkn up st: no imp* **50/1**
13 1/2 **Gallions Reach (NZ)**6 7-8-3..........(b) DwayneDunn 5 108
(Richard Yuill, New Zealand) *prom in 5th: 4th st: drvn and disputing ld over 1 1/2f out: sn no ex* **200/1**
14 hd **Leica Ding (AUS)**13 6961 5-7-13.......... CraigAWilliams 1 104
(Darren Weir, Australia) *towards rr of mid-div: nvr a factor* **25/1**
15 hd **Ista Kareem (NZ)**10 9-8-6.......... LukeNolen 22 110
(Colin Little, Australia) *racd in rr: n.d* **100/1**
16 1/2 **Allez Wonder (AUS)**17 6871 4-7-13..........(b) MichellePayne 12 104
(Bart Cummings, Australia) *mid-div: drvn on ins early st: n.d* **25/1**
17 nk **Capecover (NZ)**6 7-8-2.......... NoelHarris 18 105
(Alexander Fieldes, New Zealand) *bhd: nvr a factor* **100/1**
18 3 1/2 **Basaltico (IRE)**13 6961 5-8-2.......... DannyNikolic 9 101
(L M Cumani) *bhd: last st: nvr a factor* **25/1**
19 1 1/4 **Zavite (NZ)**17 6871 7-8-5..........(b) MarkZahra 2 103
(Anthony Cummings, Australia) *prom in 4th on ins: 5th and drvn st: one pce fr 2f out* **60/1**
20 nk **Spin Around (AUS)**13 6961 9-8-3.......... MarkDuPlessis 3 101
(Steven Cooper, Australia) *prom: 7th on ins st: sn outpcd* **200/1**
21 3 1/2 **Roman Emperor (NZ)**17 6871 4-8-7..........(b) HughBowman 14 101
(Bart Cummings, Australia) *sn racing in 2nd: pushed along to chal st: disp ld briefly 2f out: sn wknd* **10/1**
22 3 1/2 **Fiumicino (NZ)**17 6871 6-8-10.......... StevenKing 23 —
(Michael, Wayne & John Hawkes, Australia) *racd in 3rd: pushed along ent st: u.p 2f out: wknd* **66/1**
23 30 **Warringah**66 5446 4-8-5.......... DamienOliver 16 —
(Chris Waller, Australia) *sn led: hdd over 1 1/2f out: wknd* **30/1**

3m 23.87s (4.23)
WFA 3 from 4yo+ 9lb **23** Ran SP% **109.3**

Owner Eales Racing Pty Ltd **Bred** Mrs F Fraser **Trained** Australia

NOTEBOOK
Shocking(AUS) backed up his success in the Lexus Handicap just three days earlier in great style. He became just the second horse following Brew's win in 2000 to complete that double and did very well to defy his wide berth. He had stamina to prove, but the race was hardly run to suit the stouter stayers as the early pace was only moderate, and that played into his hands. He got little cover through the contest, but was still well positioned and travelled easily into the home straight. His response once asked to win the race was immediate and he dug deep to repel the runner-up inside the final furlong. He will now be trained specifically for a defence of the race next year.

Crime Scene(IRE) finished only sixth in the Geelong Cup on his prep for this 13 days earlier, but shaped there as though the race would bring him on, and he ran a blinder in first-time blinkers. With a favourable draw, he raced more or less upsides the winner throughout the race and locked horns with that rival nearing the final furlong. He lacked the tactical speed to get on top, but still finished nicely clear in second and he too registered a career-best. It should be noted, however, that the way the race unfolded also meant his stamina wasn't fully tested.

Mourilyan(IRE), in contrast to the first two, recorded his best effort when finishing second in the Goodwood Cup, over this trip on soft ground in July, so he would have enjoyed a more truly-run race. He stayed on with purpose to grab third and would have given the front two more to think about under a more positive ride. Connections will no doubt be eyeing a return for him in 12 months time.

Master O'Reilly(NZ) is a confirmed hold-up performer and was another that got caught out by the lack of real early pace, but he still stayed on to repeat his fourth in the race last year. He helps to provide a benchmark for the form.

Harris Tweed(NZ) travelled sweetly into contention and was upsides the winner nearing the final furlong. He lacked an immediate change of gear, though, and really wants more cut underfoot.

Alcopop(AUS), the ante-post favourite, came into the race off another impressive success and had a decent racing weight. He got a lovely run on the inside from his draw in 12, but his rider (who hadn't even raced at the track prior to the race day) got caught out as he attempted to pull him out for a challenge rounding the final turn. That cost him vital ground and, while he still picked up down the centre of the home straight to have his chance, he eventually flattened out. He also ran freely early on due to the moderate pace on, which would have blunted his finishing effort, and the best of him was not seen here. With that in mind he should be a big player in this in 2010, where another year's experience on his back would make him the one to beat.

Viewed(AUS), well backed, was bidding to give his trainer a remarkable 13th win in the Cup. He was penalised only a kilogram for his Caufield Cup win and ran an eye-catching prep for this when a staying-on third in the Mackinnon three days previously. He was yet another that failed to really shine due to the ordinary early gallop and he finished well, faring best of his trainer's three runners. The suspicion is, even with an end-to-end gallop, that top weight would have still just found him out, though.

Munsef has not looked back since winning a claimer at Chester this season and deserved his chance. He had an ideal trip through the race from his decent draw, but was done with as the tempo got serious and could have done without the ground easing.

Basaltico(IRE) was never seriously in the hunt from off the pace and maintained his trainer's frustrating run since bringing his team down under. He looked to have plenty to find on paper, but has to be considered somewhat disappointing considering he finished one place behind Crime Scene at Geelong.

Warringah was having his first run since being bought out of Sir Michael Stoute's yard specifically for this race. He got an uncontested lead and was responsible for the way the race developed. He eventually dropped right out in the home straight to finish a tailed-off last.

CHOLET (R-H)

Sunday, November 1

OFFICIAL GOING: Heavy

7216a GRAND PRIX DE CHOLET — 6f 165y

1:30 (12:00) 3-Y-O+ **£15,534** (£6,214; £4,660; £3,107; £1,553)

Pos	Btn	Horse	Jockey	RPR
1		**Stop Making Sense**38 7-9-9 (R Pritchard-Gordon, France)	THuet	90
2	1 ½	**Moscow Eight (IRE)**15 6857 3-8-12 (E J O'Neill) *raced in 2nd 2 lengths behind winner, kept under under pressure final 2f but always held*	ABourgeais	76
3	¾	**Johanan (FR)**18 3-9-7 (F-X De Chevigny, France)	LHuart	83
4	6	**Lutece Eria (FR)**19 3-9-6 (C Diard, France)		65
5	15	**Mister Charm (FR)**65 9-9-0 (J-C Rouget, France)		16
6	dist	**Cadeau For Maggi**26 6579 4-9-9 (H-A Pantall, France)		—

1m 28.35s (88.35)
WFA 3 from 4yo+ 1lb — **6** Ran
PARI-MUTUEL (including 1 Euro stake): WIN 3.70; PL 3.10, 4.50;SF 72.20.
Owner Mme A M Springer & R Matossian **Bred** Skymarc Farm Inc & A J O'Reilly **Trained** France

7079 CATTERICK (L-H)

Tuesday, November 3

OFFICIAL GOING: Soft (6.7)
Wind: fresh 1/2 against Weather: mainly fine and sunny, very breezy

7217 SPONSOR A RACE AT CATTERICK RACECOURSE MAIDEN AUCTION STKS — 5f 212y

1:40 (1:40) (Class 6) 2-Y-O **£2,388** (£705; £352) **Stalls** Low

Form	Pos	Btn	Horse	Jockey	RPR
3202	1		**Confessional**11 7001 2-9-2 79 (T D Easterby) *trckd ldrs: t.k.h: led over 1f out: sn pushed clr: eased towards fin* **5/6**1	DavidAllan 4	80+
0225	2	4	**Gower Sophia**18 6827 2-8-4 66 (M Brittain) *led: hung rt and hdd over 1f out: no ch w wnr* **9/4**2	(v) JimmyQuinn 7	53
5640	3	3 ¾	**Hot Rod Mamma (IRE)**43 6169 2-7-11 57 (A Berry) *hld up: hdwy over 4f out: effrt towards centre over 2f out: one pce* **20/1**	BillyCray(7) 1	42
25	4	9	**Briary Mac**7 7079 2-8-4 0 (N Bycroft) *chsd ldrs: drvn over 2f out: lost pl over 1f out* **6/1**3	FrancisNorton 6	15
	5	6	**Bravo Belle (IRE)** 2-8-8 0 ow4 (T H Caldwell) *dwlt: in rr: sme hdwy 3f out: sn wknd* **33/1**	TomEaves 2	—
0	6	shd	**Light Nights (IRE)**66 5417 2-8-8 0 (T D Easterby) *chsd ldrs: sn drvn along: lost pl over 2f out* **40/1**	DuranFentiman 5	—
0606	7	20	**Selina Rio**28 6554 2-8-3 30 ow4 (L A Mullaney) *dwlt: sn detached in last: t.o 3f out* **125/1**	(p) PaulPickard(5) 3	—

1m 17.99s (4.39) **Going Correction** +0.80s/f (Soft) — **7** Ran SP% **110.5**
Speed ratings (Par 94): **102,96,91,79,71 71,44**
toteswingers: 1&2 £1.40, 1&3 £3.80, 2&3 £5.10 CSF £2.60 TOTE £1.80: £1.20, £1.50; EX 3.50.
Owner T G & Mrs M E Holdcroft **Bred** Bearstone Stud **Trained** Great Habton, N Yorks

FOCUS
An uncompetitive maiden and, with the ground soft, the runners were soon strung out. They raced stands' side in the straight and the clear-cut winner is the best guide to the level.

NOTEBOOK
Confessional, the only male in the line up, was a class apart, as his odds suggested, and got off the mark at the 7th attempt. He should be competitive in handicaps off a mark around 80. (op Evens)
Gower Sophia, with a visor re-fitted, went off quickly and had no answer when joined and passed by the winner. She's not proving easy to place and may need to be dropped in grade. (op 5-2 tchd 11-4)
Hot Rod Mamma(IRE) raced further away from stands' rail than the front two and was well held. She'll be better off in low-grade handicaps. (tchd 18-1)
Briary Mac again failed to handle testing ground. She has some ability, judged on her first outing when the ground was quick, and handicaps are now an option. (op 5-1 tchd 7-1)

7218 GO RACING AT DONCASTER THIS SATURDAY NURSERY — 7f

2:10 (2:11) (Class 4) (0-85,82) 2-Y-O **£4,209** (£1,252; £625; £312) **Stalls** Centre

Form	Pos	Btn	Horse	Jockey	RPR
6153	1		**Kumbeshwar**28 6557 2-8-13 79 (P D Evans) *mde virtually all: hld on towards fin* **9/2**2	RichardEvans(5) 3	81
5434	2	nk	**Count Bertoni (IRE)**13 6948 2-8-11 72 (S Gollings) *trckd ldrs: chal 2f out: hung lft and no ex wl ins fnl f* **11/2**3	IanMongan 5	73
2050	3	shd	**Music Of The Moor (IRE)**15 6895 2-8-7 68 (T P Tate) *in rr: hdwy 3f out: edgd rt 2f out: upsides 1f out: no ex cl home* **6/1**	AndrewElliott 7	69
5012	4	7	**Transfixed (IRE)**12 6963 2-9-2 82 (P D Evans) *sn chsng ldrs: wknd over 1f out* **13/2**	AndrewHeffernan(5) 9	65
3005	5	½	**Lord's Seat**3 7168 2-7-5 59 oh9 (A Berry) *in rr: hdwy and jinked lft over 2f out: nvr nr ldrs* **40/1**	MatthewLawson(7) 2	41
3103	6	4 ½	**Baby Judge (IRE)**8 7055 2-7-5 59 oh1 (M C Chapman) *chsd ldrs: swtchd rt over 2f out: wknd over 1f out* **9/1**	CharlotteKerton(7) 4	30
3660	7	9	**Professor John (IRE)**23 6693 2-9-2 77 (M L W Bell) *uns rdr bef s: trckd ldrs: hmpd 2f out: sn wknd and eased* **8/1**	PaulHanagan 1	25
1	8	14	**Cono Zur (FR)**64 5512 2-9-7 82 (M Johnston) *s.i.s: sn detached in last: bhd fnl 4f* **3/1**1	JoeFanning 8	—
5330	9	2 ¾	**Cassidy K**28 6557 2-7-12 59 oh1 (D W Thompson) *sn chsng ldrs: hmpd 2f out: lost pl over 1f out: heavily eased* **25/1**	DuranFentiman 6	—

1m 32.89s (5.89) **Going Correction** +0.80s/f (Soft) — **9** Ran SP% **113.6**
Speed ratings (Par 98): **98,97,97,89,88 83,73,57,54**
toteswingers: 1&2 £4.50, 1&3 £7.00, 2&3 £7.30 CSF £28.92 CT £148.72 TOTE £6.50: £2.60, £1.90, £2.00; EX 36.30.
Owner G E Amey **Bred** G E Amey **Trained** Pandy, Monmouths

FOCUS
An ordinary nursery for the grade and limited form, but competitive enough. They raced stands' side in the straight.

NOTEBOOK
Kumbeshwar benefited from the return to front-running tactics around a speed-favouring track and handled the soft ground well. He looked in trouble when strongly challenged on both sides in the straight, but battled on gamely, so typical of one from the Evans stable. This versatile gelding should remain competitive and there seems no obvious reason why he won't handle Polytrack if connections opt for a winter campaign. (op 6-1)
Count Bertoni(IRE), without the blinkers this time, grabbed the stands' rail in the straight but was inclined to carry his head at a slight angle and didn't look totally comfortable. (op 5-1 tchd 9-2)
Music Of The Moor(IRE) was ridden along a fair way off the pace through the early stages but he stayed on well, three-wide of the stands' rail in the straight. This was a good effort considering the track was favouring speed. (op 10-1)
Transfixed(IRE), a stablemate of the winner, was given a positive enough ride but she dropped away and didn't really handle the soft ground. (op 9-2 tchd 7-1)
Professor John(IRE) dumped his rider before the off and dropped away tamely after showing early speed. (op 11-1)
Cono Zur(FR), off the track since winning a fast-ground maiden at Newcastle in August, didn't go a yard under these vastly different conditions and was detached from the main bunch throughout. He has a low action, so the soft ground was no use to him, and he probably wants further now as well. Fanning reported the colt was never travelling. Official explanation: jockey said colt never travelled (op 5-2)

7219 GO RACING IN YORKSHIRE CLAIMING STKS — 5f

2:40 (2:41) (Class 6) 3-Y-O+ **£2,388** (£705; £352) **Stalls** Low

Form	Pos	Btn	Horse	Jockey	RPR
4350	1		**Northern Bolt**25 6647 4-9-0 75 (D Nicholls) *w ldr: rdn to ld appr fnl f: forged clr last 100yds* **6/4**1	(v) AdrianTNicholls 4	84
-311	2	3	**Absa Lutte (IRE)**8 7053 6-8-5 69 (Miss Gay Kelleway) *rrd s: sn chsng ldrs: kpt on to take 2nd nr fin* **4/1**3	(t) PaulHanagan 3	64
4260	3	½	**Godfrey Street**17 6857 6-8-6 70 (A G Newcombe) *slt ld: hdd appr fnl f: wknd fnl 75yds* **7/2**2	(b) JimmyQuinn 7	63
0600	4	2 ½	**Grimes Faith**7 7086 6-8-5 53 (K A Ryan) *mid-div: kpt on fnl 2f: nvr nr to chal* **20/1**	(p) AmyRyan(5) 8	58
2200	5	2 ½	**King's Sabre**8 7057 3-8-6 58 (R C Guest) *chsd ldrs stands' side: one pce fnl 2f* **25/1**	(p) GrahamGibbons 11	45
2403	6	¾	**Fivefootnumberone (IRE)**17 6857 3-8-3 70 (J J Quinn) *mid-div: kpt on fnl 2f: nvr trbld ldrs* **4/1**3	(v) IJBrennan(7) 10	46
6000	7	9	**Mr Rooney (IRE)**43 6161 6-8-4 39 (A Berry) *dwlt: a in rr: bhd fnl 2f* **100/1**	FrancisNorton 9	8
0300	8	hd	**Elusive Style (IRE)**41 6219 3-7-8 42 (S P Griffiths) *s.s: detached in last: nvr on terms* **150/1**	MatthewLawson(7) 2	4
0400	9	1 ½	**Coconut Moon**41 6221 7-7-11 44 ow1 (A Berry) *towards rr: bhd fnl 2f* **40/1**	BillyCray(7) 6	2
-000	10	10	**Take That**34 6379 4-8-6 34 (S P Griffiths) *swighed rt sn after s: towards rr: sme hdwy over 2f out: sn lost pl* **200/1**	(p) AndrewMullen 1	—

62.50 secs (2.70) **Going Correction** +0.625s/f (Yiel) — **10** Ran SP% **115.4**
Speed ratings (Par 101): **103,98,97,93,89 88,73,73,71,55**
.Absa Lutte was claimed by Patrick Morris for £8000.\n\x\x
Owner Jim Dale **Bred** Mrs C Regalado-Gonzalez **Trained** Sessay, N Yorks

FOCUS
A modest claimer in which they raced stands' side.

7220 BOOK ON-LINE AT CATTERICKBRIDGE.CO.UK H'CAP — 7f

3:10 (3:10) (Class 4) (0-80,83) 3-Y-O+ **£5,180** (£1,541; £770; £384) **Stalls** Centre

Form	Pos	Btn	Horse	Jockey	RPR
1220	1		**Tamasou (IRE)**25 6630 4-8-12 73 (A J McCabe) *w ldrs: led over 2f out: edgd rt over 1f out: hld on wl towards fin* **12/1**	ShaneKelly 11	83
4401	2	1	**Conry (IRE)**7 7083 3-9-0 83 6ex (Patrick Morris) *s.i.s: hdwy and swtchd wd over 1f out: upsides wl ins fnl f: no ex* **5/1**2	TobyAtkinson(7) 7	89+
3531	3	1 ¾	**Kingswinford (IRE)**15 6904 3-8-11 78 (P D Evans) *trckd ldrs: t.k.h: styd on same pce fnl f* **9/1**	AndrewHeffernan(5) 5	80
2022	4	½	**Grissom (IRE)**3 7171 3-9-1 77 (A Berry) *chsd ldrs: effrt on stands' side and almost upsides whn n.m.r over 1f out: styd on same pce* **3/1**1	FrederikTylicki 9	78
1001	5	2 ½	**Lordship (IRE)**3 7172 5-8-0 68 6ex (A W Carroll) *led: hung rt bnd 4f out: hdd over 2f out: wknd fnl f* **6/1**3	JakePayne(7) 8	63
0040	6	5	**Bold Marc (IRE)**12 6976 7-9-4 79 (A P Jarvis) *chsd ldrs: hung lft and lost pl over 2f out: kpt on steadily wout ever threatening to take a hand* **11/1**	AndrewElliott 10	61
5500	7	1	**Borasco (USA)**24 6667 4-9-1 76 (T D Barron) *in rr div: sme hdwy 2f out: nvr on terms* **10/1**	PhillipMakin 6	55
0502	8	1 ¼	**Kashimin (IRE)**11 7000 4-9-1 76 (G A Swinbank) *towards rr: sme hdwy over 2f out: sn wknd* **8/1**	PJMcDonald 4	52
4255	9	4	**Inter Vision (USA)**7 7083 9-9-1 76 (A Dickman) *in rr: brief effrt on outer 2f out: sn wknd* **11/1**	DanielTudhope 3	42
1020	10	7	**Violent Velocity (IRE)**37 6309 6-8-9 77 (J J Quinn) *s.i.s: in rr div on outer: lost pl over 2f out* **16/1**	IJBrennan(7) 13	25
0003	11	3	**Western Art (USA)**48 5982 4-8-4 65 oh13 (Miss Gay Kelleway) *trckd ldrs: lost pl over 2f out* **33/1**	PaulHanagan 2	5
-000	12	14	**Frill A Minute**81 4977 5-8-4 65 oh20 (Miss L C Siddall) *in rr: bhd fnl 3f* **300/1**	(b1) JimmyQuinn 1	—

1m 31.38s (4.38) **Going Correction** +0.80s/f (Soft)
WFA 3 from 4yo+ 1lb — **12** Ran SP% **119.7**
Speed ratings (Par 105): **106,104,102,102,99 93,92,91,86,78 75,59**
toteswingers: 1&2 £12.50, 1&3 £21.80, 2&3 £12.20 CSF £71.69 CT £588.65 TOTE £11.70: £3.40, £2.30, £3.90; EX 100.00.
Owner Brooklands Racing **Bred** Garry Gleeson **Trained** Averham Park, Notts

■ Stewards' Enquiry : Shane Kelly two-day ban: careless riding (Nov 17-18)
Toby Atkinson for two-day ban: careless riding (Nov 17-18)

FOCUS
A fair handicap. Once again they raced stands' side in the straight.

Bold Marc(IRE) Official explanation: jockey said, regarding running and riding, that his orders were to jump off handily and if there was plenty of pace to sit in fourth or fifth, adding that he niggled the gelding along leaving the back straight and it began to hang badly left and he felt no response after turn into straight.

7221 HAMBLETON MAIDEN STKS — 1m 3f 214y
3:40 (3:43) (Class 5) 3-Y-O+ — **£2,914** (£867; £433; £216) **Stalls** Low

Form				RPR
3532	1		**Bruton Street (USA)**[11] 6996 3-9-3 79 RobertHavlin 15 (J H M Gosden) *mde all: qckdn 4f out: drvn over 2f out: sn wnt clr: heavily eased ins fnl f* **9/2**[3]	89+
6624	2	10	**Outrageous Request**[94] 4519 3-9-3 80 FrederikTylicki 10 (Pat Eddery) *hld up in mid-div: hdwy to chse ldr over 3f out: kpt on: no ch w wnr* **5/1**	70
	3	7	**French Hollow**[93] 4-9-9 0 PaulMulrennan 6 (T J Fitzgerald) *s.i.s: hld up: hdwy 4f out: drvn over 2f out: kpt on one pce: tk modest 3rd towards fin* **66/1**	59
6252	4	½	**Cotillion**[27] 6595 3-9-3 77 PaulHanagan 2 (W J Haggas) *t.k.h in mid-div: effrt over 3f out: sn rdn and chsng 1st 2: one pce* **15/8**[1]	58
03	5	13	**Time Book (IRE)**[19] 6794 3-9-3 0 NickyMackay 4 (J H M Gosden) *chsd ldrs: drvn over 3f out: wknd over 1f out* **4/1**[2]	37
4	6	12	**Smarties Party**[159] 2403 6-9-4 0 PAspell 14 (C W Thornton) *in rr: effrt over 3f out: nvr on terms* **100/1**	13
	7	7	**Zafranagar (IRE)**[264] 4-9-9 77 ShaneKelly 1 (A W Carroll) *t.k.h: trckd ldrs: wknd over 2f out: eased ins fnl f* **22/1**	7
60-	8	6	**Tazbar (IRE)**[200] 7174 7-9-9 0 PhillipMakin 8 (K G Reveley) *s.i.s: bhd and racd wd: drvn along 6f out: kpt on fnl 3f: nvr on terms* **12/1**	—
46-	9	6	**Sligo**[543] 1943 4-9-9 87 TomEaves 5 (A J McCabe) *mid-div: drvn 7f out: lost pl 4f out: sn bhd* **14/1**	—
5	10	½	**Owls FC (IRE)**[33] 6425 3-8-7 0 AndrewHeffernan(5) 12 (M C Chapman) *chsd ldrs: rdn 7f out: lost pl over 4f out: sn bhd* **200/1**	—
0-5	11	18	**Dovedon Angel**[129] 3384 3-8-12 0 JerryO'Dwyer 9 (Miss Gay Kelleway) *trckd ldrs: drvn over 4f out: wknd qckly over 3f out* **100/1**	—
53-	12	2 ¼	**Maraased**[545] 1918 4-9-9 0 IanMongan 7 (S Gollings) *trckd ldrs: lost pl over 3f out: bhd whn eased 2f out* **25/1**	—
P	P		**Amber Glow**[38] 6276 5-8-11 0 BillyCray(7) 3 (A Berry) *rrd s: detached in last: t.o after 3f: p.u over 3f out* **300/1**	—

2m 46.86s (7.96) **Going Correction** +0.80s/f (Soft)
WFA 3 from 4yo+ 6lb — **13** Ran SP% **116.5**
Speed ratings (Par 103): **105,98,93,93,84 76,72,68,64,63 51,50,—**
toteswingers: 1&2 £7.90, 1&3 £36.40, 2&3 £56.40 CSF £25.86 TOTE £5.80: £1.80, £1.90, £12.90; EX 33.70.
Owner H R H Princess Haya Of Jordan **Bred** Tracy Farmer **Trained** Newmarket, Suffolk

FOCUS
They finished surprisingly strung out and the beaten distances suggest this is form to treat with caution.
Zafranagar(IRE) Official explanation: jockey said gelding had no more to give
Maraased Official explanation: jockey said gelding was unsuited by the soft ground

7222 NATIONAL HUNT SEASON STARTS ON 2ND DECEMBER H'CAP — 1m 5f 175y
4:10 (4:10) (Class 5) (0-75,70) 3-Y-O+ — **£2,914** (£867; £433; £216) **Stalls** Low

Form				RPR
0445	1		**Royal Trooper (IRE)**[11] 6995 3-9-8 70 FrederikTylicki 1 (J G Given) *led at stdy pce: qckd gallop over 3f out: hotly chal and hld on gamely* **4/1**[2]	78
1564	2	nk	**Soundbyte**[11] 6995 4-9-10 64 JerryO'Dwyer 7 (J Gallagher) *trckd ldrs: jnd wnr over 5f out: no ex wl ins fnl f* **6/1**	71
0051	3	¾	**Beat The Shower**[7] 7085 3-8-8 56 6ex PaulHanagan 8 (P D Niven) *trckd ldrs: t.k.h: effrt on outer over 2f out: kpt on same pce ins fnl f* **4/1**[2]	62
3102	4	1	**No Wonga**[7] 7080 4-9-0 59 AndrewHeffernan(5) 4 (P D Evans) *trckd ldrs: effrt over 2f out: kpt on same pce fnl f* **11/4**[1]	64
3653	5	nk	**Red Wine**[7] 7084 10-9-11 65 PhillipMakin 5 (J A Glover) *t.k.h in rr: hdwy over 2f out: kpt on: nvr able to chal* **9/2**[3]	70
0005	6	6	**River Danube**[7] 7084 6-8-10 50 TomEaves 2 (T J Fitzgerald) *sn chsng ldr: hung lft and outpcd over 2f out: sn lost pl* **20/1**	46
0630	7	8	**Eijaaz (IRE)**[31] 6490 8-9-8 62 DanielTudhope 6 (G A Harker) *hld up towards rr: hdwy over 3f out: rdn to chse ldrs over 1f out: wknd and eased jst ins fnl f* **11/1**	47

3m 23.56s (19.96) **Going Correction** +0.80s/f (Soft)
WFA 3 from 4yo+ 8lb — **7** Ran SP% **112.2**
Speed ratings (Par 103): **74,73,73,72,72 69,64**
toteswingers: 1&2 £4.30, 1&3 £3.70, 2&3 £5.60 CSF £26.72 CT £99.85 TOTE £3.50: £3.00, £3.80; EX 32.70 Place 6: £81.19 Place 5: £73.59.
Owner J Barson **Bred** Western Bloodstock **Trained** Willoughton, Lincs

FOCUS
Throughout the day it had been obvious that those who raced handy were at an advantage, so it was a real surprise Royal Trooper was allowed to dictate a steady pace, whilst several of his rivals raced keenly under restraint. This is form to treat with caution.
T/Plt: £254.50 to a £1 stake. Pool: £48,302.74. 138.50 winning tickets. T/Qpdt: £52.10 to a £1 stake. Pool: £3,732.83. 53.00 winning tickets. WG

7175 KEMPTON (A.W) (R-H)
Tuesday, November 3

OFFICIAL GOING: Standard
Wind: Moderate, across - away from stands Weather: Fine, after heavy rain before racing.

7223 KIA SOUL, SAFE BET H'CAP (DIV I) — 5f (P)
2:20 (2:20) (Class 5) (0-70,75) 3-Y-O+ — **£2,266** (£674; £337; £168) **Stalls** High

Form				RPR
0300	1		**Lord Of The Reins (IRE)**[6] 7123 5-8-13 64 SebSanders 2 (J G Given) *s.i.s: mostly in last trio and racd wd: gd prog jst over 1f out: r.o wl between rivals to ld nr fin despite rdr dropping whip* **15/2**[3]	73+
0-54	2	½	**Irish Music (IRE)**[7] 7100 4-8-4 60 MartinLane(5) 11 (A P Jarvis) *mostly in midfield: hanging over 1f out: prog after to chal ins fnl f: upsides 50yds out: outpcd* **4/1**[2]	67
2352	3	nk	**Femme De Fer**[25] 6635 3-9-4 69 AdamKirby 10 (C G Cox) *rn wd bnd over 3f out: chsd ldrs: prog over 1f out: led ins fnl f: hdd and outpcd nr fin* **2/1**[1]	75+
0005	4	2	**Cape Royal**[10] 7021 9-9-2 67 (bt) KevinGhunowa 4 (J M Bradley) *trckd ldr: led over 1f out: hdd ins fnl f: wknd last 100yds* **20/1**	66
4030	5	½	**Quasi Congaree (GER)**[10] 7028 3-9-2 67 NCallan 7 (I A Wood) *chsd ldng pair: nt qckn over 1f out: sn lost pl: kpt on same pce fnl f* **12/1**	64
0404	6	¾	**Ask Jenny (IRE)**[13] 6939 7-8-1 55 oh1 AndreaAtzeni(3) 9 (Patrick Morris) *s.i.s: mostly in last trio: shkn up over 1f out: kpt on one pce* **10/1**	49
0005	7	½	**Punching**[24] 6669 5-8-9 60 LPKeniry 12 (C R Dore) *awkward bnd over 3f out and lost grnd into midfield: effrt over 1f out: one pce fnl f* **8/1**	53
0300	8	3 ½	**Ten Down**[14] 6916 4-8-5 59 WilliamCarson(3) 6 (M Quinn) *led to over 1f out: wknd rapidly fnl f* **16/1**	39
0000	9	¾	**Asaint Needs Brass (USA)**[20] 6782 3-8-8 59 ow1 SteveDrowne 8 (J R Best) *hld up in rr: shkn up over 1f out: no real prog* **20/1**	36
3305	10	8	**La Capriosa**[6] 7123 3-9-3 68 (p) RobertWinston 1 (J A Glover) *racd wd: chsd ldrs: pushed along 1/2-way: wknd rapidly over 1f out: t.o* **11/1**	16
0006	11	1 ¾	**Stoneacre Pat (IRE)**[213] 1134 4-8-4 55 oh8 (b) FrankieMcDonald 5 (Peter Grayson) *racd wd: in tch to 1/2-way: sn struggling: t.o* **66/1**	—

60.10 secs (-0.40) **Going Correction** 0.0s/f (Stan) — **11** Ran SP% **118.2**
Speed ratings (Par 103): **103,102,101,98,97 96,95,90,88,76 73**
toteswingers: 1&2 £7.60, 1&3 £5.20, 2&3 £3.20 CSF £36.97 CT £85.16 TOTE £8.20: £2.90, £1.60, £1.40; EX 39.70.
Owner Danethorpe Racing Partnership **Bred** C Farrell **Trained** Willoughton, Lincs
■ Stewards' Enquiry : William Carson one-day ban: careless riding (Nov 17)

FOCUS
A modest handicap, but no hanging about with confirmed front-runners Ten Down, Cape Royal and La Capriosa vying for the lead from the off. This was a race of changing fortunes with five different leaders inside the last 2f.

7224 KIA SOUL, SAFE BET H'CAP (DIV II) — 5f (P)
2:50 (2:50) (Class 5) (0-70,71) 3-Y-O+ — **£2,266** (£674; £337; £168) **Stalls** High

Form				RPR
3266	1		**Chandika**[42] 6186 3-8-8 58 (p) LukeMorris 1 (C G Cox) *sn off the pce in abt 5th: drvn 1/2-way: prog over 1f out: r.o fnl f to ld last stride* **12/1**	65
0032	2	hd	**Bookiesindex Boy**[24] 6669 5-9-1 65 RichardHughes 4 (J R Jenkins) *chsd clr ldr: drvn to cl fnl f: led last 75yds: hdd post* **6/1**	72
0030	3	¾	**Embra (IRE)**[11] 6989 4-8-7 57 AlanMunro 2 (T J Etherington) *s.i.s: wl off the pce in last trio: stl only 9th 1f out: rapid prog fnl f: gaining fast at fin* **12/1**	61
1203	4	nk	**Silver Prelude**[25] 6635 8-9-3 67 (t) AdamKirby 5 (S C Williams) *led and spreadeagled field: stl in charge ins fnl f: wknd and hdd last 75yds* **4/1**[2]	70
2040	5	1 ¼	**Cocktail Party (IRE)**[15] 6904 3-7-13 56 oh8 ow2 (t) KierenFox(7) 11 (J W Hills) *s.i.s: hld up in last pair and wl off the pce: prog on inner over 1f out: styd on fnl f: unable to chal* **20/1**	54
2100	6	hd	**Nomoreblondes**[31] 6489 5-9-4 68 (p) TonyCulhane 7 (P T Midgley) *chsd clr ldng trio: tried to cl over 1f out: one pce fnl f* **12/1**	66
0306	7	nk	**Compton Classic**[19] 6799 7-8-12 67 (p) JemmaMarshall(5) 8 (J R Boyle) *off the pce in abt 6th: rdn 2f out: kpt on fnl f: nvr gng pce to threaten* **8/1**	64
5062	8	1	**Come On Buckers (IRE)**[10] 7021 3-8-10 60 (b) EdwardCreighton 10 (E J Creighton) *chsd ldng pair to 1f out: wknd* **11/2**[3]	53
0403	9	1	**Chosen Son (IRE)**[14] 6916 3-8-12 62 WilliamBuick 12 (P J O'Gorman) *s.i.s: hld up in rr: and wl off the pce: shkn up on outer 2f out: no rspnse* **3/1**[1]	51
530U	10	2	**Radiator Rooney (IRE)**[10] 7023 6-8-11 61 SJCraine 3 (Patrick Morris) *stdd s: hld up last: no prog* **25/1**	43

60.34 secs (-0.16) **Going Correction** 0.0s/f (Stan) — **10** Ran SP% **117.5**
Speed ratings (Par 103): **101,100,99,99,97 96,96,94,93,89**
toteswingers: 1&2 £8.30, 1&3 £13.20, 2&3 £14.30 CSF £82.90 CT £650.81 TOTE £15.20: £3.60, £2.00, £3.40; EX 87.40.
Owner B D H & R J H Preston **Bred** Mrs T Brudenell **Trained** Lambourn, Berks
■ Stewards' Enquiry : Luke Morris one-day ban: used whip down shoulder in the forehand (Nov 17)

FOCUS
As with the first division, there were plenty of established trailblazers in this and any race featuring Silver Prelude is almost certain to be run at a frantic pace. Again the strong early tempo played into the hands of a finisher and with the pace eventually collapsing, the winning time was 0.24 seconds slower than division one.

7225 WILLIAM HILL WINTER FESTIVAL - BOOK NOW H'CAP — 1m 2f (P)
3:20 (3:21) (Class 6) (0-65,65) 3-Y-O+ — **£2,047** (£604; £302) **Stalls** High

Form				RPR
0422	1		**Thunderstruck**[11] 6998 4-9-3 60 (p) ChrisCatlin 2 (J A Glover) *chsd ldr: led 1/2-way: drvn 2f out: hrd pressed last 50yds: jst hld on* **4/1**[1]	71
0200	2	shd	**Seventh Hill**[6] 7112 4-9-1 58 NCallan 1 (M Blanshard) *hld up in midfield: prog on inner over 3f out: chsd ldng pair 2f out: drvn to go 2nd ins fnl f and sn chalng: jst pipped* **10/1**	69
0505	3	3	**Pippbrook Gold**[12] 6967 4-9-3 60 PatCosgrave 11 (J R Boyle) *trckd ldng pair: chsd wnr over 3f out: no imp over 1f out: lost 2nd ins fnl f* **6/1**[3]	65
253	4	1 ¼	**Ask The Oracle**[13] 6950 3-9-4 65 TravisBlock 6 (H Morrison) *chsd ldrs: awkward and sltly hmpd bnd 3f out: sn outpcd and rdn: kpt on fr over 1f out* **9/2**[2]	68
54	5	nk	**True Decision**[8] 7052 3-8-11 58 JamesDoyle 4 (S Kirk) *towards rr: rdn and prog on outer 3f out to chse ldrs 2f out: one pce after* **16/1**	60
060	6	4 ½	**Megalala (IRE)**[10] 7036 8-9-3 60 NeilChalmers 8 (J J Bridger) *t.k.h: hld up in 8th: effrt over 2f out: one pce and nvr on terms w ldrs* **9/1**	53
0140	7	¾	**Blue Turk**[6] 7112 4-9-3 60 SJCraine 5 (J R Boyle) *prom on outer: 3rd briefly over 2f out: steadily wknd* **13/2**	51
0060	8	1 ½	**Binnion Bay (IRE)**[6] 7109 8-8-13 56 (b) FrankieMcDonald 7 (J J Bridger) *dwlt: t.k.h and hld up in last trio: effrt 3f out: nvr threatened ldrs* **20/1**	44
/505	9	3 ¾	**Iffy**[26] 6612 8-9-2 59 SteveDrowne 13 (A B Haynes) *dwlt: hld up in last and wl off the pce: modest late prog: nvr a factor* **25/1**	40
0606	10	6	**Inside Story (IRE)**[22] 6720 7-9-4 61 (b) LPKeniry 14 (C R Dore) *a wl in rr: struggling u.p 3f out: bhd after* **16/1**	30

06 **11** ½ **Rock Exhibition**[182] 1778 4-9-5 **62**........................ AdamKirby 10 30
(B W Duke) *led to 1/2-way: sn u.p: lost pl over 3f out: wl bhd over 1f out* **40/1**

0050 **12** 1 ½ **Azharia**[62] 5582 3-8-10 **57** ow1........................ RichardHughes 3 22
(R Hannon) *stdd s: hld up in last trio: no prog* **12/1**

350- **13** ½ **Etain (IRE)**[251] 5833 5-9-0 **57**........................ DavidProbert 9 21
(Mrs Lawney Hill) *t.k.h: trckd ldrs: rdn and lost pl on inner over 3f out: sn bhd* **20/1**

2m 6.53s (-1.47) **Going Correction** 0.0s/f (Stan)
WFA 3 from 4yo+ 4lb **13** Ran SP% **120.2**
Speed ratings (Par 101): **105,104,102,101,101 97,97,95,92,88 87,86,86**
toteswingers: 1&2 £8.10, 1&3 £8.90, 2&3 £22.70 CSF £42.20 CT £242.99 TOTE £3.80: £1.90, £3.50, £2.70; EX 48.80.
Owner Paul J Dixon **Bred** Mrs Yvette Dixon **Trained** Babworth, Notts

FOCUS
A decent-sized field, but this wasn't much of a race and those that raced handily were at an advantage.
Azharia Official explanation: jockey said filly moved poorly throughout

7226 CHRISTMAS PARTY NIGHTS AT KEMPTON PARK H'CAP 1m 2f (P)
3:50 (3:50) (Class 2) (0-100,96) 3-Y-O+
£11,091 (£3,321; £1,660; £831; £414; £208) **Stalls** High

Form RPR

1113 **1** **Bab Al Salam (USA)**[32] 6453 3-9-3 **95**........................ TedDurcan 7 106+
(Saeed Bin Suroor) *trckd ldr 1f: lft in 2nd again 1/2-way: led jst over 2f out: rdn clr over 1f out: readily* **11/8**[1]

0006 **2** 3 ¼ **Waldvogel (IRE)**[37] 6302 5-9-8 **96**........................ WilliamBuick 5 100
(L M Cumani) *hld up in last pair: prog on outer 3f out: drvn to chse wnr jst over 1f out: no imp* **13/2**[3]

0100 **3** 1 **Coeur De Lionne (IRE)**[46] 6060 5-8-13 **87**........................ SteveDrowne 4 89
(E A L Dunlop) *chsd ldrs: nt qckn over 2f out: kpt on one pce fr over 1f out* **14/1**

3210 **4** 2 ½ **Elna Bright**[31] 6470 4-8-13 **87**........................ SebSanders 1 84
(B R Johnson) *t.k.h: hld up in last pair: effrt on inner over 2f out: disp 2nd over 1f out: wknd fnl f* **12/1**

4500 **5** 2 ½ **Sohcahtoa (IRE)**[10] 7035 3-9-3 **95**........................ RichardHughes 6 87
(R Hannon) *led: reminders 4f out: drvn and hdd jst over 2f out: sn btn: eased ins fnl f* **8/1**

0001 **6** 74 **Rock Ascot (URU)**[25] 6633 5-9-7 **95**........................(b) PatCosgrave 3 —
(G L Moore) *in tch tl wknd rapidly 3f out: sn t.o: eased to walk fnl f* **10/1**

0222 **P** **Mafeking (UAE)**[12] 6973 5-8-9 **83**........................ ChrisCatlin 2 —
(M R Hoad) *chsd ldr after 1f tl p.u 1/2-way: dismntd: b.b.v* **7/2**[2]

2m 5.51s (-2.49) **Going Correction** 0.0s/f (Stan)
WFA 3 from 4yo+ 4lb **7** Ran SP% **112.2**
Speed ratings (Par 109): **109,106,105,103,101 42,—**
toteswingers: 1&2 £2.50, 1&3 £4.90, 2&3 £9.40 CSF £10.44 TOTE £1.80: £1.10, £3.70; EX 12.00.
Owner Godolphin **Bred** Darley **Trained** Newmarket, Suffolk

FOCUS
A decent 86-100 handicap, but with Rock Ascot virtually pulled up and Mafeking exiting the race at halfway after bursting a blood-vessel, this wasn't as competitive as it might have been. Even so, the winning time was over a second quicker than the preceding 51-65 handicap.

NOTEBOOK
Bab Al Salam(USA) ◆, a dual winner on Polytrack whose unbeaten record came to a rather disappointing end at Newmarket last month, put that modest effort behind him with a fluent success. Always on the shoulder of the leader, he took it up on reaching the home straight and soon bounded right away. The best of him is probably still to be seen and he should be able to win something rather better. Something at the Dubai Carnival would seem an obvious target for him. (op 7-4 tchd 15-8)
Waldvogel(IRE), unplaced in five outings for current connections since arriving from Germany but who ran better than his finishing position would have suggested at Ascot last time, was down another 2lb here. Held up early, he moved into a challenging position down the outside once into the straight but lacked the speed to get anywhere near the winner. The drop in trip would not have been ideal and he gives the impression that there are races to be won with him back over further. (op 6-1 tchd 11-2)
Coeur De Lionne(IRE), successful in his last three starts at this track more than two years ago and 5lb lower than for the last of those, had twice run poorly since winning at Newmarket in August. He travelled well in midfield and had his chance turning in, but lacked a turn of foot and, like the runner-up, this drop in trip was against him. (op 16-1)
Elna Bright, beaten a long way in his first attempt at the trip at Epsom last month, briefly looked dangerous when trying to squeeze up the inside rail once into the home straight, but his stamina then ran out. A return to shorter is needed. (op 8-1)
Sohcahtoa(IRE), disappointing since finishing a close third in the Kentucky Derby Challenge here back in March, raced keenly in front early. Given reminders to keep his mind on the job half a mile from home, he was a sitting duck for the favourite and once losing the advantage off the final bend his race was over. Official explanation: jockey said gelding hung left throughout (op 14-1)
Rock Ascot(URU) Official explanation: jockey said horse never travelled
Mafeking(UAE) was suddenly pulled up at halfway after bursting a blood-vessel. Official explanation: vet said gelding bled from the nose (op 3-1 tchd 11-4)

7227 KEMPTON.CO.UK H'CAP 6f (P)
4:20 (4:20) (Class 3) (0-95,95) 3-Y-O+
£7,352 (£2,201; £1,100; £551; £274; £138) **Stalls** High

Form RPR

0504 **1** **Fullandby (IRE)**[10] 7015 7-9-3 **94**........................ AlanMunro 3 105
(T J Etherington) *sn detached in last: pushed along after 2f: prog on outer 2f out: drvn and r.o wl to ld last 75yds: sn clr* **10/1**

5621 **2** 1 ¼ **Servoca (CAN)**[11] 6994 3-8-12 **92**........................ AndreaAtzeni(3) 9 99
(Mike Murphy) *wl in rr: rdn and prog towards inner fr 2f out: clsd on ldrs fnl f: styd on but outpcd last 75yds* **11/2**[3]

3400 **3** hd **Ebraam (USA)**[12] 6964 6-9-4 **95**........................ PaulDoe 10 101
(P Howling) *chsd ldr to 2f out: sn hrd rdn: styd on ins fnl f: outpcd last 75yds* **25/1**

-212 **4** nk **Hajoum (IRE)**[10] 7026 3-8-10 **87**........................ TedDurcan 12 92
(Saeed Bin Suroor) *trckd ldng pair on inner: wnt 2nd 2f out: clsd over 1f out: drvn ahd ins fnl f: hdd & wknd last 75yds* **5/2**[1]

4100 **5** ½ **Filligree (IRE)**[33] 6428 4-8-6 **86**........................ WilliamCarson(3) 7 90
(Rae Guest) *chsd ldrs: u.p and nt qckn over 2f out: kpt on again fr over 1f out: nt pce to chal* **20/1**

0040 **6** ½ **Thebes**[18] 6815 4-9-0 **91**........................ GregFairley 11 93
(M Johnston) *led at gd clip: hrd pressed over 1f out: hdd and fdd ins fnl f* **5/1**[2]

6053 **7** 3 ¼ **Toms Laughter**[2] 7202 5-8-12 **89**........................(b) DavidProbert 4 81
(R A Harris) *stdd s: t.k.h and swtchd to inner: effrt fr midfield over 2f out: nt qckn over 1f out: wknd fnl f* **13/2**

1-10 **8** nk **Rulesn'regulations**[10] 7015 3-9-0 **91**........................ WilliamBuick 8 82
(Matthew Salaman) *chsd ldrs: rdn over 2f out: nt qckn and hld over 1f out: wknd fnl f* **13/2**

2046 **9** nse **Viking Spirit**[23] 6694 7-8-10 **87**........................ RobertWinston 2 78
(W R Swinburn) *nvr beyond midfield: hanging u.p fr over 2f out: fdd over 1f out* **16/1**

5056 **10** 19 **Daddy's Gift (IRE)**[51] 5918 3-8-11 **88**........................ RichardHughes 1 18
(R Hannon) *racd wd: a towards rr: wknd over 2f out: t.o* **25/1**

5106 **11** 1 ¼ **Coleorton Choice**[13] 6949 3-8-8 **85**........................(t) ChrisCatlin 6 11
(K A Ryan) *racd wd towards rr: wknd over 2f out: t.o* **33/1**

1m 11.48s (-1.62) **Going Correction** 0.0s/f (Stan) **11** Ran SP% **117.7**
Speed ratings (Par 107): **110,108,108,107,107 106,102,101,101,76 74**
toteswingers: 1&2 £13.20, 1&3 £27.00, 2&3 £23.40 CSF £61.12 CT £1370.25 TOTE £11.90: £3.40, £1.40, £4.70; EX 43.80.
Owner Miss M Greenwood **Bred** Mrs A Haskell Ellis **Trained** Norton, N Yorks

FOCUS
A very competitive sprint handicap run at a strong pace.

NOTEBOOK
Fullandby(IRE) was well handicapped on his best form and had signalled a return to form at Doncaster last time, but he was without a win in over a year and hadn't been proving that consistent this season. He was by no means best away which is usually the case with him and soon found himself in last place, but the strong pace gave him something to aim at and he produced a withering run down the wide outside to hit the front well inside the last furlong. He may turn out again in the Listed Wentworth Stakes over this trip at Doncaster this weekend. (op 8-1)
Servoca(CAN), bought for 60,000gns since winning off 6lb lower for Barry Hills at Doncaster 11 days earlier, was another given plenty to do but he finished well to grab second close to the line and should continue to give his new connections plenty of fun. (op 6-1)
Ebraam(USA), still 3lb above his last winning mark back in February, likes a strong pace to run at but he was ridden more prominently than he usually is. To his great credit he kept on finding more after looking likely to drop away, and there should be an opportunity waiting for him on this surface in the coming weeks. (tchd 22-1)
Hajoum(IRE), lightly raced but 4lb higher than when just beaten on his handicap debut over C&D last month, travelled well behind the leaders and seemed to have timed it right when hitting the front on the inside entering the last furlong, but he didn't get home. He remains relatively unexposed. (op 11-4 tchd 3-1 in a place)
Filligree(IRE), twice disappointing since winning off 1lb lower at Bath in September, was never far away and kept on battling but she does look better suited to turf.
Thebes, mainly below form on turf since winning at Chepstow in July but winner of four of his eight starts on sand including one over C&D, set a serious pace but he may have done a bit too much and had little left once headed entering the final furlong. (op 6-1)
Toms Laughter, gradually returning to form since his belated reappearance in August and a good third over 5f at Lingfield two days earlier, dived for the inside rail after the cutaway and had his chance but he could make no further progress. Perhaps the inside of the track wasn't a help this time. (op 15-2 tchd 6-1)
Rulesn'regulations, still lightly raced and a dual winner on Polytrack, was particularly disappointing at Doncaster last time when finishing a long way behind Fullandby and though he showed up for a long way here, was eased off when his chance had gone. (op 6-1)
Viking Spirit, not very consistent this season and without a win since May of last year, hung when asked to get closer once into the straight and now has questions to answer. (op 14-1)
Coleorton Choice Official explanation: jockey said colt hung left

7228 BOOK YOUR CHRISTMAS PARTY AT KEMPTON MEDIAN AUCTION MAIDEN STKS 1m (P)
4:50 (4:50) (Class 6) 3-5-Y-O
£2,047 (£604; £302) **Stalls** High

Form RPR

0506 **1** **Dark Camellia**[11] 6999 4-9-0 **50**........................(t) RichardHughes 5 64
(H J L Dunlop) *hld up in tch: smooth prog to trck ldng pair 2f out: produced to chal 1f out: cajoled into ld ins fnl f* **7/1**[3]

5-35 **2** ½ **Lucky Score (IRE)**[166] 2206 3-8-12 **67**........................ NCallan 4 63
(Mouse Hamilton-Fairley) *cl up: trckd ldr over 2f out: rdn to ld wl over 1f out: hung lft after: hdd and nt qckn ins fnl f* **6/5**[1]

060 **3** 4 **Very Distinguished**[11] 7004 3-8-12 **48**........................ AlanMunro 1 53
(S Kirk) *s.s: hld up in last: pushed along and effrt over 2f out: plugged on take 3rd last 75yds: no threat* **14/1**

00-2 **4** ¾ **Banda Sea (IRE)**[276] 356 3-9-3 **70**........................(p) FergusSweeney 6 56
(P J Makin) *led: hung lft fr over 2f out: hdd wl over 1f out: wknd tamely* **2/1**[2]

00 **5** 2 ¼ **Rainiers Girl**[71] 5314 3-8-12 **0**........................ TedDurcan 2 46
(R A Teal) *t.k.h: hld up in tch: rdn over 2f out: edgd lft after: no prog* **33/1**

-0 **6** 7 **Bella Fighetta**[19] 6794 3-8-12 **0**........................ JamesDoyle 3 29
(Ms J S Doyle) *chsd ldr to over 2f out: wknd u.p* **66/1**

0- **7** 1 ¼ **Woodland Violet**[386] 6709 3-8-7 **0**........................ MartinLane(5) 7 26
(I A Wood) *chsd ldrs tl wknd over 2f out* **9/1**

1m 40.73s (0.93) **Going Correction** 0.0s/f (Stan)
WFA 3 from 4yo 2lb **7** Ran SP% **112.4**
Speed ratings (Par 101): **95,94,90,89,87 80,79**
toteswingers: 1&2 £2.20, 1&3 £4.80, 2&3 £3.50 CSF £15.34 TOTE £7.40: £2.90, £1.40; EX 19.40.
Owner Barry Marsden **Bred** N C D Horn **Trained** Lambourn, Berks

FOCUS
One colt against six fillies in this very poor maiden and not a race to take a positive view about.
Lucky Score(IRE) Official explanation: jockey said filly hung left from 2f out
Banda Sea(IRE) Official explanation: jockey said colt hyung left throughout
Rainiers Girl Official explanation: jockey said filly hung left

7229 ALL WEATHER "HANDS AND HEELS" APPRENTICE SERIES H'CAP 1m (P)
5:20 (5:20) (Class 5) (0-75,75) 3-Y-O+ **£2,590** (£770; £385; £192) **Stalls** High

Form RPR

3213 **1** **Dinner Date**[8] 7054 7-8-10 **69**........................ TraceyAddey(5) 7 76
(T Keddy) *trckd ldrs: prog 2f out: pushed into narrow ld 1f out: a doing enough to hold on* **11/4**[1]

0000 **2** ½ **Daniel Thomas (IRE)**[8] 7048 7-9-0 **68**........................(p) RyanClark 9 74
(Mrs A L M King) *dwlt: hld up in last trio: prog to chse ldr jst over 2f out: upsides on inner 1f out: a hld last 150yds* **9/1**

0352 **3** ¾ **Support Fund (IRE)**[13] 6937 5-9-0 **68**........................ JosephineBruning 6 72
(Eve Johnson Houghton) *hld up in last trio and racd wd: urged along over 2f out: prog over 1f out: r.o to take 3rd nr fin* **5/1**[2]

5005 **4** nk **Decameron (USA)**[21] 6761 4-9-5 **73**........................ SPRyan 2 76
(R A Harris) *led: pushed along 2f out: hdd 1f out: one pce* **13/2**

1023 **5** 1 ½ **Rock Anthem (IRE)**[8] 7060 5-9-4 **75**........................ BarryAdams(3) 4 75
(Mike Murphy) *hld up and sn in last trio: prog 2f out: wnt 4th 1f out: one pce and no further imp* **7/1**

0065 **6** 4 **Grey Boy (GER)**[13] 6937 8-8-13 **72**........................ GeorgeDowning(5) 1 63
(A W Carroll) *t.k.h: mostly chsd ldr to jst over 2f out: wknd over 1f out* **10/1**

140 **7** *hd* **Focail Eile**[59] 5673 4-9-7 **75**.................... RyanPowell 5 65
(J Ryan) *trckd ldng trio tl wknd fr 2f out* **6/1**[3]
5000 **8** *1 1/4* **Silver Hotspur**[22] 6725 5-9-2 **70**.................... DavidKenny 3 57
(C R Dore) *dwlt: t.k.h in midfield: no prog 2f out: sn wknd* **33/1**
2130 **9** *7* **Diamond Surprise**[14] 6915 3-8-11 **67**.................... KierenFox 8 38
(R J Smith) *t.k.h: trckd ldng pair tl wknd rapidly jst 2f out* **14/1**

1m 39.68s (-0.12) **Going Correction** 0.0s/f (Stan)
WFA 3 from 4yo+ 2lb **9** Ran SP% **112.2**
Speed ratings (Par 103): **100,99,98,98,96 92,92,91,84**
toteswingers: 1&2 £6.00, 1&3 £3.40, 2&3 £12.80 CSF £27.25 CT £115.39 TOTE £2.60: £1.40, £2.90, £2.10; EX 30.20 Place 5: £145.71 Place 5: £113.57 .
Owner Mrs H Keddy **Bred** J M Greetham **Trained** Newmarket, Suffolk
■ Tracey Addey's first winner.

FOCUS
A modest "hands and heels" apprentice handicap in which the winning time was over a second faster than the preceding maiden.
T/Plt: £166.60 to a £1 stake. Pool: £56,347.43. 246.89 winning tickets. T/Qpdt: £29.50 to a £1 stake. Pool: £3,922.48. 98.14 winning tickets. JN

6682 MAISONS-LAFFITTE (R-H)
Tuesday, November 3

OFFICIAL GOING: Holding

7230a PRIX MIESQUE (GROUP 3) (FILLIES) 7f (S)
1:05 (1:09) 2-Y-O **£38,835** (£15,534; £11,650; £7,767; £3,883)

RPR
1 **Lixirova (FR)**[47] 6045 2-8-11 .... GBenoist 7 103
(D Smaga, France) *fast away fr outside draw: sn on rails: mde all: rdn out (nt tched w whip)* **69/10**
2 *2* **Absolute Music (USA)**[22] 6752 2-8-11 .... JamieSpencer 1 98
(R M H Cowell) *trckd wnr on rails: edgd rt and looking for gap 2f out: rdn 1f out: got through ins fnl f: r.o* **93/10**
3 *1/2* **Ercolini (IRE)**[13] 2-8-11 .... JGrosjean 3 97
(F Rodriguez Puertas, Spain) *hld up in rr: hdwy on rails fr over 1f out: kpt on same pce u.p fnl f* **63/10**
4 *3/4* **Wonderfilly (FR)**[22] 6752 2-8-11 .... MGuyon 5 95
(P Demercastel, France) *pressed wnr on outside tl rdn and no ex ins fnl f* **14/1**
5 *1/2* **Heaven's Heart (IRE)**[51] 5927 2-8-11 .... IMendizabal 4 94
(Y De Nicolay, France) *trckd ldrs: outpcd over 1f out: kpt on fnl f: nvr able to chal* **9/5**[1]
6 *1 1/2* **Elisheba (FR)**[20] 2-8-11 .... OPeslier 8 90
(F Doumen, France) *hld up on outside disputing 3rd: rdn and btn 1f out* **11/2**[3]
7 *1/2* **Irish Cat (IRE)**[22] 6752 2-8-11 .... FBlondel 6 89
(Robert Collet, France) *in rr on outside: btn over 1f out* **18/5**[2]

1m 31.8s (3.50) **Going Correction** +0.725s/f (Yiel) **7** Ran SP% **115.6**
Speed ratings: **109,106,106,105,104 103,102**
PARI-MUTUEL: WIN 7.90; PL 2.70, 3.00, 2.60; DF 33.30.
Owner O El Sharif **Bred** J-L Blot **Trained** Lamorlaye, France

NOTEBOOK
Lixirova(FR) revelled in the testing ground. Ridden for the first time in public by the jockey who rides her on the gallops, she produced an outstanding performance. She was smartly into her stride and was never headed, lengthening from the furlong marker was never threatened. She won with plenty in hand and will start next year over course and distance in the Prix Imprudence and could then go either for 1,000 Guineas or the Poule d'Essai des Pouliches. On soft ground, she will always be a force to be reckoned with over distances of around a mile and she should stay further.
Absolute Music(USA) broke well and was soon racing near the stands rail. Tracking the winner virtually throughout, she started to run on from the furlong marker and finished well, but never looked like making it to the head of affairs though she took second place 100 yards from the line. This was a game effort and all her starts in France have earned herblack type. She will be campaigned in Dubai next year.
Ercolini(IRE), not hurried along in the early stages, was always hugging the stands' rail. She started her run from the furlong marker and was staying on well at the end. This was a decent effort from this Spanish-trained filly.
Wonderfilly(FR) raced near the winner for much of the early stages and took a strong hold. She was outpaced when the race quickened up a furlong out and then stayed on at one pace.

7231a CRITERIUM DE MAISONS-LAFFITTE (GROUP 2) 6f (S)
1:35 (1:37) 2-Y-O **£105,146** (£40,582; £19,369; £12,913; £6,456)

RPR
1 **Our Jonathan**[24] 6660 2-9-0 .... JamieSpencer 2 114+
(K A Ryan) *reluctant ldr for 1 1/2f: led again 2f out: pushed clr: r.o wl* **6/4**[1]
2 *1 1/2* **Ascot Glory (IRE)**[28] 2-8-10 .... RMarchelli 1 104
(S Wattel, France) *restrained early: sent on after 1 1/2f: hdd 2f out: kpt on one pce* **10/1**
3 *hd* **Dolled Up (IRE)**[47] 6044 2-8-10 .... OPeslier 3 103
(Robert Collet, France) *hld up in rr: r.o fr over 1 1/2f out: jst missed 2nd* **3/1**[3]
4 *snk* **Melodyman (FR)**[24] 2-9-0 .... SPasquier 4 107
(N Clement, France) *sn pulling v hrd: disp 3rd: rdn and outpcd wl over 1f out: rallied clsng stages* **14/5**[2]
5 *shd* **Noble Alpha (IRE)**[16] 6887 2-9-0 .... MGuyon 6 106
(Mario Hofer, Germany) *hld up disputing 3rd: rdn 1f out: r.o cl home* **48/10**

1m 19.7s (6.30) **Going Correction** +0.725s/f (Yiel) **5** Ran SP% **117.6**
Speed ratings: **87,85,84,84,84**
PARI-MUTUEL: WIN 2.50; PL 1.80, 3.50; SF 17.10.
Owner Dr Marwan Koukash **Bred** W G M Turner **Trained** Hambleton, N Yorks

NOTEBOOK
Our Jonathan won this race with authority, but it was run at a crawl in the early stages. Reluctantly left in the lead after the start, he settled and was then able to tuck in behind another runner who went to the head of affairs. He was always going well, quickened at the furlong marker and dominated the final stages. He was by no means extended and his jockey never needed to use his whip. Has now won four of his six races and he could turn into a very smart three-year-old. He acted well on the very soft ground, but it is difficult to know whether he will stay further as his stamina was not entirely tested on this occasion. His breeding suggests 1m should be within his range, but there are no plans at the moment.
Ascot Glory(IRE)'s jockey took the initiative after a furlong after the start and he led until being tackled by the winner at the furlong marker. He then stayed on bravely to hold off the rest of the field.
Dolled Up(IRE) was held up last in a race with no early pace. He came with a late run up the stands' rail from 300 yards out and finished well if too late, but held on gamely for third place.
Melodyman(FR) pulled enormously in the early stages and this was another unsuited by the way the race was run early on. He finished well in an event which might have had a different order for the places if run again, with half a length covering the four.\n\x\x past the post after the winner.

7232a PRIX DE SEINE-ET-OISE (GROUP 3) 6f (S)
2:05 (2:05) 3-Y-O+ **£38,835** (£15,534; £11,650; £7,767; £3,883)

RPR
1 **Dunkerque (FR)**[31] 6503 4-8-13 .... DBoeuf 13 107
(Mme C Head-Maarek, France) *mid-div on outside: pushed along bef 1/2-way: drvn over 2f out: r.o to ld ins fnl f: drvn out* **22/5**[2]
2 *3/4* **Salut L'Africain (FR)**[5] 4-8-11 ....(p) THuet 1 103
(Robert Collet, France) *mid-div on stands' side of gp: pushed along 1/2-way: drvn fnl 2f: tk 2nd cl home* **57/10**
3 *snk* **Blue Cayenne (FR)**[28] 6579 4-8-8 .... TJarnet 10 99
(Mlle S-V Tarrou, France) *trckd ldr: led dist to ins fnl f: one pce: lost 2nd cl home* **16/1**
4 *snk* **Tiza (SAF)**[86] 4837 7-8-13 ....(p) MGuyon 6 104
(A De Royer-Dupre, France) *in rr on stands' side of field: last 2f out: styd on fr over 1f out: nrest at fin* **17/5**[1]
5 *1 1/2* **Aranel (IRE)**[30] 3-8-11 .... JGrosjean 9 97
(M Delcher-Sanchez, Spain) *towards rr: rdn wl over 2f out: hdwy 2f out: kpt on steadily fnl f* **17/1**
6 *1* **Bluster (FR)**[28] 6579 3-8-11 .... OPeslier 8 94
(Robert Collet, France) *led to appr fnl f: one pce* **57/10**
7 *hd* **Knot In Wood (IRE)**[24] 6661 7-8-13 .... BMcHugh 5 95
(R A Fahey) *prom: 3rd over 2f out: rdn 2f out: wknd appr fnl f* **60/1**
8 *1 1/2* **Advanced**[10] 7019 6-8-11 ....(b) JamieSpencer 7 88
(K A Ryan) *pressed ldr tl rdn and btn 2f out* **14/1**
9 *1 1/2* **Royal Rock**[24] 6661 5-8-13 ....(p) GeorgeBaker 4 85
(C F Wall) *cl up tl rdn and btn wl over 1f out* **26/5**[3]
10 *2* **Emergency**[23] 6717 3-8-8 .... SPasquier 2 74
(D Smaga, France) *mid-div: btn wl over 1f out* **31/5**
11 **Etoile Nocturne (FR)**[65] 5493 5-8-10 ....(p) YLerner 12 76
(W Baltromei, Germany) *a bhd* **33/1**
12 **Peace Camp (USA)**[28] 6579 3-8-8 .... JVictoire 11 74
(A Fabre, France) *mid-div on outside: btn 2f out: eased* **10/1**

1m 15.7s (2.30) **Going Correction** +0.725s/f (Yiel) **12** Ran SP% **132.9**
Speed ratings: **113,112,111,111,109 108,108,106,104,101 101,101**
PARI-MUTUEL: WIN 5.40; PL 2.50, 3.80, 3.80; DF 23.30.
Owner Alec Head **Bred** A & Mme A Head **Trained** Chantilly, France

NOTEBOOK
Dunkerque(FR) was under pressure from start to finish on the wide outside and still had several lengths to make up on the leaders at the furlong marker. Hard ridden, he took the advantage with 50 yards left to run and it was a game performance by this rather laid-back individual. His jockey was suspended for four days for excessive use of the whip and was fined €400. His trainer describes him as a cold character, but one who loves to get his toe in. He was winning his second Group 3 race of the season and he may remain in training as a five-year-old, when he will be raced over distances of around 1m.
Salut L'Africain(FR), racing for the second time in five days and having his 41st start, put up a brave effort. Always well up with the pace, he knuckled down to the task at the furlong pole and was only run out of first place well inside the final furlong. His jockey was \n\x\x fined for excessive use of the whip.
Blue Cayenne(FR) broke well and was in second place at the halfway stage. He made his effort at the furlong marker and kept up the gallop to the line.
Tiza(SAF) was a disappointing favourite considering he was racing on his favourite ground. Held up in the early stages, he did make some late progress on the stands' side. Not the easiest of rides, the seven-year-old appears to have lost his summer form when he won a Group 3 event.
Knot In Wood(IRE) broke well and raced on the stands' side of the pack. Still well there at the furlong marker, his stride began to shorten shortly after.
Advanced, soon up with the leading group, was going nowhere from the furlong pole and gradually dropped out of contention.
Royal Rock was never seen with a chance of finishing in the frame. He was always at the tail of the field and ran well below his best on this occasion.

7223 KEMPTON (A.W) (R-H)
Wednesday, November 4

OFFICIAL GOING: Standard
Wind: Almost nil Weather: Cloudy

7233 CHAMPAGNE LANSON VINTAGE 1998 H'CAP 1m 2f (P)
5:50 (5:51) (Class 4) (0-85,84) 3-Y-O+ **£4,727** (£1,406; £702; £351) **Stalls** High

Form RPR
255 **1** **Tinshu (IRE)**[23] 6740 3-8-10 **76**.................... DaneO'Neill 10 86
(D Haydn Jones) *chsd ldrs: rdn 2f out: r.o to ld fnl 50yds* **14/1**
0050 **2** *3/4* **King Olav (UAE)**[11] 7018 4-9-6 **82**.................... SebSanders 1 90
(A W Carroll) *wd early: sn pressing ldr: rdn to ld over 1f out: hdd and nt qckn fnl 50yds* **16/1**
1004 **3** *1 3/4* **Chapter And Verse (IRE)**[21] 6773 3-8-11 **80**.......... AndreaAtzeni(3) 2 85
(Mike Murphy) *t.k.h towards rr: rdn over 2f out: r.o fr over 1f out: nrst fin* **20/1**
0005 **4** *1/2* **Aurorian (IRE)**[16] 6907 3-8-11 **77**.................... RichardHughes 9 81
(R Hannon) *hld up disputing 5th: rdn and styd on same pce fnl 2f* **6/1**[3]
2120 **5** *3/4* **Veroon (IRE)**[25] 6680 3-8-12 **78**....................(p) AlanMunro 12 80
(J G Given) *first to break: stdd bk disputing 5th: rdn and one pce fnl 2f* **14/1**
6312 **6** *3/4* **Muftarres (IRE)**[22] 6760 4-9-4 **80**....................(t) NCallan 3 81
(G A Butler) *mid-div: effrt and hrd rdn over 1f out: no imp* **10/1**
1201 **7** *hd* **Uncle Fred**[28] 6583 4-9-8 **84**.................... RichardKingscote 7 84+
(P R Chamings) *stdd towards rr s: plld hrd early: stmbld over 8f out: rdn over 2f out: styd on fnl f: nvr nrr* **7/2**[1]
3124 **8** *hd* **Ordoney (IRE)**[16] 6907 4-9-7 **83**.................... WilliamBuick 5 83
(L M Cumani) *sn led: rdn and hdd over 1f out: sn wknd* **4/1**[2]
0531 **9** *1 1/2* **Mister New York (USA)**[9] 7066 4-9-6 **82** 6ex............(b) GeorgeBaker 6 79
(Noel T Chance) *prom: hanging and rdn on home turn: hung rt and wknd over 1f out* **13/2**
0453 **10** *3* **Suzi Spends (IRE)**[27] 6614 4-9-4 **80**.................... JimmyQuinn 11 71
(H J Collingridge) *s.i.s: sn in midfield on rail: rdn and wknd wl over 1f out* **12/1**
/30- **11** *hd* **First To Call**[564] 1473 5-8-13 **75**....................(t) FergusSweeney 4 65
(P J Makin) *rring at s: a bhd* **66/1**

45-0 **12** *5* **Motarjm (USA)**[13] 6973 5-9-0 **76**.......................... SaleemGolam 8 56
(J Pearce) *dwlt: a bhd* **66/1**

2m 5.56s (-2.44) **Going Correction** -0.025s/f (Stan)
WFA 3 from 4yo+ 4lb **12** Ran SP% **113.6**
Speed ratings (Par 105): **108,107,106,105,105 104,104,104,102,100 100,96**
toteswingers: 1&2 £68.80, 1&3 £41.60, 2&3 £8.90 CSF £207.16 CT £4379.84 TOTE £17.90: £4.50, £4.90, £7.20; EX 202.20.
Owner Llewelyn, Runeckles **Bred** Mrs M L Parry & P Steele-Mortimer **Trained** Efail Isaf, Rhondda C Taff

FOCUS
A couple of in-form sorts in a fair handicap but the gallop was only modest and those held up were at a disadvantage. The two market leaders disappointed and the winner raced centre to far side in the straight. Despite that the form makes some sense rated around the first two.
Suzi Spends(IRE) Official explanation: jockey said filly stumbled and was slowly away
First To Call Official explanation: jockey said gelding reared and was slowly away

7234 EUROPEAN BREEDERS' FUND MAIDEN STKS 6f (P)
6:20 (6:21) (Class 5) 2-Y-O **£3,561** (£1,059; £529; £264) **Stalls** High

Form RPR
34 **1** **Forest Crown**[28] 6582 2-8-12 0.......................... SebSanders 2 76
(R M Beckett) *t.k.h towards rr: rdn and hdwy in centre over 1f out: r.o to ld fnl 50yds* **7/1**[3]
53 **2** *1* **Mutafajer**[9] 7050 2-9-3 0.......................... RHills 1 78
(Saeed Bin Suroor) *plld hrd: pressed ldr: slt ld 2f out: hdd and nt qckn fnl 50yds* **8/13**[1]
3 **3** *2 1/4* **Lago Indiano (IRE)**[15] 6913 2-9-3 0.......................... NCallan 8 71
(Mrs A J Perrett) *chsd ldrs: hrd rdn over 1f out: one pce* **9/2**[2]
4 *4* **Key Light (IRE)** 2-8-12 0.......................... MichaelHills 3 54
(J W Hills) *chsd ldrs: rdn over 2f out: wknd over 1f out* **25/1**
020 **5** *1 1/2* **Young Simon**[16] 6903 2-9-3 68.......................... DaneO'Neill 9 55
(G G Margarson) *chsd ldrs: rdn and btn 2f out* **16/1**
00 **6** *1 3/4* **Farmers Dream (IRE)**[9] 7061 2-8-9 0.......................... JackDean(3) 7 45
(J L Spearing) *dwlt: rdn and bhd: effrt whn nt clr run over 2f out: nt pce to chal* **150/1**
7 *1/2* **Welsh Artist** 2-9-3 0.......................... AdamKirby 4 48
(Mrs A J Perrett) *s.s: rdn along and struggling in detached last most of way: passed btn horses* **33/1**
0 **8** *2* **She's My Rock (IRE)**[82] 4980 2-8-12 0.......................... JamesDoyle 5 37
(S Kirk) *in tch tl rdn and wknd over 2f out* **50/1**
5 **9** *3 1/2* **Rose Aurora**[57] 5749 2-8-12 0.......................... RichardHughes 6 27
(M P Tregoning) *led tl wknd 2f out* **20/1**

1m 12.77s (-0.33) **Going Correction** -0.025s/f (Stan) 9 Ran SP% **112.7**
Speed ratings (Par 96): **101,99,96,91,89 87,86,83,79**
toteswingers: 1&2 £1.20, 1&3 £4.10, 2&3 £1.60 CSF £11.09 TOTE £9.00: £1.80, £1.02, £1.50; EX 16.90.
Owner The Eclipse Partnership **Bred** Car Colston Hall Stud **Trained** Whitsbury, Hants
■ Stewards' Enquiry : Seb Sanders caution: used whip with excessive frequency.

FOCUS
A couple of fair sorts in a race lacking much in the way of strength in depth with the third third the best guide to the form. The gallop was ordinary and the principals raced in the centre in the straight.

NOTEBOOK
Forest Crown is a steadily progressive sort who appreciated the step up to this trip and posted a career best. She should prove equally effective over 7f and is the sort to improve again in handicaps. (op 6-1)
Mutafajer, from a yard in tremendous form, had shown enough over course and distance on his previous start to suggest he had strong claims and he ran creditably, especially as he took a good hold. He is capable of picking up a similarly ordinary event but he does need to learn to settle better. (op 4-6)
Lago Indiano(IRE), who had shown promise over this trip on his debut, raced freely early on but otherwise had the run of the race and had few excuses. His pedigree suggests that the step up to 7f should suit better and he is entitled to improve again. (op 4-1 tchd 7-2)
Key Light(IRE) ◆, a daughter of Group 1 winner Eva Luna, was nibbled at in the market and who shaped respectably on this debut. She is entitled to improve for this. (op 33-1)
Young Simon, the most experienced of these, was nibbled at in the market but again had his limitations exposed in this grade on this all-weather debut. He may do better in handicaps but it remains to be seen whether he is as good as his mark suggests. (op 20-1 tchd 14-1)
Farmers Dream(IRE) bettered the form of her two previous runs on turf but, while the switch to handicaps is sure to suit, she will have to show a bit more before she is a solid betting proposition. (op 66-1)

7235 DIGIBET NURSERY 1m (P)
6:50 (6:50) (Class 6) (0-65,65) 2-Y-O **£1,942** (£578; £288; £144) **Stalls** High

Form RPR
3064 **1** **Nave (USA)**[19] 6829 2-9-2 61.......................... GregFairley 10 66
(M Johnston) *hld up in midfield: hrd rdn over 2f out: hdwy in centre over 1f out: styd on to ld nr fin* **3/1**[1]
600 **2** *1/2* **Calypso Star (IRE)**[14] 6930 2-9-5 64.......................... RichardHughes 6 68
(R Hannon) *chsd ldrs: chal 2f out: rdn to ld 1f out: hdd and nt qckn nr fin* **15/2**
0052 **3** *2 3/4* **Until The Man (IRE)**[15] 6923 2-9-2 61..........................(p) PaulDoe 5 59
(R Ingram) *prom: slt ld 2f out tl 1f out: no ex* **7/1**[3]
2660 **4** *1/2* **Starwatch**[23] 6737 2-8-10 62.......................... RyanClark(7) 7 59
(J J Bridger) *cl up: rdn to press ldrs over 1f out: no ex fnl f* **14/1**
5503 **5** *3* **Underworld Dandy**[6] 7139 2-9-3 62.......................... GeorgeBaker 11 52
(P D Evans) *hld up towards rr: gd hdwy on ins fr 2f out: wknd fnl f* **9/2**[2]
500 **6** *nk* **My Red Kite**[111] 4006 2-9-5 64..........................(p) DaneO'Neill 13 53
(G D Blake) *dwlt: sn in midfield: n.m.r over 2f out: shkn up and styd on same pce fr over 1f out* **25/1**
0063 **7** *nse* **Catchanova (IRE)**[41] 6228 2-9-5 64..........................(t) SebSanders 2 53
(Eve Johnson Houghton) *hld up in rr: hrd rdn and sme hdwy over 1f out: nt rch ldrs* **8/1**
0015 **8** *1/2* **Fine Lace (IRE)**[20] 6793 2-9-6 65.......................... AdamKirby 3 53
(D J S Ffrench Davis) *bhd: rdn 3f out: nvr rchd ldrs* **11/1**
6323 **9** *nk* **Glen Lass**[48] 6034 2-8-11 61.......................... SimonPearce(5) 8 49
(J Pearce) *sn last: pushed along and outpcd fr 1/2-way: styd on fnl f* **16/1**
000 **10** *1 1/4* **Astronomer's Dream**[21] 6781 2-9-6 65.......................... LPKeniry 14 50
(E F Vaughan) *prom tl hrd rdn and wknd qckly on ins over 1f out* **12/1**
000 **11** *1 3/4* **Set To Go**[11] 7024 2-9-2 61.......................... SteveDrowne 12 42
(H J L Dunlop) *led tl 2f out: wknd qckly on ins jst over 1f out* **33/1**
306 **12** *8* **Magneto (IRE)**[7] 7120 2-9-2 61.......................... EdwardCreighton 9 24
(E J Creighton) *in rr and rdn early: swtchd outside and pulling hrd in midfield after 2f: rdn 3f out: wknd 2f out* **25/1**

1m 40.9s (1.10) **Going Correction** -0.025s/f (Stan) **12** Ran SP% **117.8**
Speed ratings (Par 94): **93,92,89,89,86 85,85,85,85,83 82,74**
totewingers: 1&2 £6.00, 1&3 £9.70, 2&3 £6.80 CSF £24.67 CT £149.36 TOTE £3.50: £1.40, £2.80, £2.90; EX 35.60.
Owner Anthony Hogarth **Bred** Mineola Farm II Llc Et Al **Trained** Middleham Moor, N Yorks

FOCUS
A modest nursery and one run at no more than a fair early gallop. The first two, who pulled clear in the closing stages, raced in the centre in the straight. The form looks reasonable rated around the first four.

NOTEBOOK
Nave(USA) ◆ proved suited by the step up to this trip and showed a good attitude to justify the market support. A stronger gallop at this trip would have suited and he looks well worth a try over a bit further. He is in good hands and may be able to build on this. (op 9-2)
Calypso Star(IRE) ◆ had shown only modest form at best in maidens but travelled strongly and turned in an improved effort on this nursery debut. He pulled clear of the remainder, has plenty of size and scope and is more than capable of picking up a similar event over this trip or over 7f. (op 7-1)
Until The Man(IRE), who showed improved form on his previous start, had the run of the race and seemed to give it his best shot after enjoying the run of the race on this all-weather debut. He has improved in nurseries since being fitted with cheekpieces and should continue to run well. (op 11-2)
Starwatch's turf form has a patchy look to it but he ran creditably on this all-weather and nursery debut. There is stamina in his pedigree and he may fare better upped to 1m2f and beyond. (tchd 16-1)
Underworld Dandy was not disgraced, but again had his limitations exposed back in handicap company and is likely to remain vulnerable to the more progressive types in this grade. (op 4-1 tchd 5-1)
My Red Kite, returning after a near four-month break, was keen on this nursery and all-weather debut and may be a little better than the bare facts suggest after meeting trouble as the leaders were quickening away. He is not one to write off yet.

7236 DIGIBET CASINO H'CAP 1m (P)
7:20 (7:20) (Class 6) (0-65,65) 3-Y-O+ **£2,047** (£604; £302) **Stalls** High

Form RPR
1100 **1** **Ensnare**[67] 5448 4-9-6 65.......................... StephenDonohoe 5 82+
(Ian Williams) *chsd ldr: led 2f out: rdn clr: eased nr fin* **14/1**
0526 **2** *3 1/2* **Having A Ball**[16] 6908 5-9-6 65.......................... DaneO'Neill 4 71
(P D Cundell) *in tch in 6th: effrt and hrd rdn 2f out: kpt on to take 2nd ins fnl f: no ch w wnr* **8/1**[3]
0005 **3** *nk* **Marmooq**[9] 7065 6-9-2 61.......................... DavidProbert 7 66
(M J Attwater) *bhd: rdn 3f out: styd on wl fnl 2f: nrst fin* **16/1**
-105 **4** *1* **The Mumbo**[21] 6782 3-9-1 62..........................(b) JoeFanning 2 65
(W Jarvis) *prom: rdn over 3f out: wnt 2nd over 1f out: no ex fnl f* **25/1**
0300 **5** *3/4* **Star Strider**[15] 6926 5-8-12 62.......................... KylieManser(5) 1 63
(T Keddy) *plld hrd in rr of midfield: rdn over 2f out: hdwy over 1f out: one pce fnl f* **50/1**
3-05 **6** *2* **Climate (IRE)**[297] 129 10-8-13 58..........................(v) PaulDoe 9 55
(P D Evans) *mid-div: rdn and struggling to hold pl over 2f out: styd on same pce appr fnl f* **50/1**
0030 **7** *hd* **Foxtrot Alpha (IRE)**[23] 6738 3-9-3 64.......................... LukeMorris 11 60
(P Winkworth) *chsd ldrs tl wknd over 1f out* **16/1**
0000 **8** *1/2* **Lopinot (IRE)**[7] 7110 6-9-1 60..........................(v) GeorgeBaker 14 55
(M R Bosley) *mid-div: effrt over 2f out: no ex over 1f out* **8/1**[3]
6002 **9** *nk* **King Of Legend (IRE)**[7] 7109 5-8-11 59.......................... JackMitchell(3) 13 53
(D Morris) *bhd: drvn along over 2f out: sme late hdwy* **9/2**[1]
5045 **10** *2 3/4* **Burnbrake**[7] 7109 4-9-1 60..........................(v) RobertHavlin 10 56+
(L Montague Hall) *prom: disputing 3rd and hld whn swtchd rt and bdly hmpd over 1f out: sn lost pl* **6/1**[2]
2300 **11** *1/2* **Aussie Blue (IRE)**[4] 7192 5-9-5 64.......................... DO'Donohoe 12 51+
(R M Whitaker) *hld up towards rr: effrt and nt clr run over 1f out: n.m.r and eased fnl f* **12/1**
0000 **12** *2 1/2* **Mr Hichens**[16] 6909 4-9-6 65..........................(p) AlanMunro 3 46+
(Karen George) *towards rr: nt clr run over 2f out: hdwy and in tch on far rail whn bdly hmpd over 1f out: nt rcvr and eased* **8/1**[3]
1545 **13** *4 1/2* **Petomic (IRE)**[18] 6862 4-8-11 61.......................... RossAtkinson(5) 6 32
(M Hill) *led and set gd pce: hrd rdn and hdd 2f out: sn wknd* **9/2**[1]
0500 **14** *8* **Langland Bay**[5] 7158 3-9-1 62.......................... RichardHughes 8 14
(W R Muir) *a bhd: rdn and struggling fnl 3f* **33/1**

1m 38.74s (-1.06) **Going Correction** -0.025s/f (Stan)
WFA 3 from 4yo+ 2lb **14** Ran SP% **120.8**
Speed ratings (Par 101): **104,100,100,99,98 96,96,95,95,92 92,89,85,77**
toteswingers: 1&2 £20.70, 1&3 £27.90, 2&3 £38.50 CSF £119.24 CT £1826.24 TOTE £21.50: £6.60, £2.50, £5.10; EX 266.70.
Owner C Owen **Bred** Cheveley Park Stud Ltd **Trained** Portway, Worcs
■ Stewards' Enquiry : Robert Havlin four-day ban: careless riding (Nov 18-21)

FOCUS
Mainly exposed sorts in a modest handicap and the pace was sound and the form looks solid.
Aussie Blue(IRE) Official explanation: jockey said gelding was denied a clear run
Petomic(IRE) Official explanation: jockey said gelding hung right

7237 DIGIBET FLOODLIT STKS (LISTED RACE) 1m 4f (P)
7:50 (7:50) (Class 1) 3-Y-O+ **£22,708** (£8,608; £4,308; £2,148; £1,076) **Stalls** Centre

Form RPR
3561 **1** **Once More Dubai (USA)**[9] 7059 4-9-3 107..........................(bt) AlanMunro 6 109+
(Saeed Bin Suroor) *hld up in 4th: dropped to last over 3f out: swtchd outside and hdwy over 1f out: qcknd to ld ins fnl f: readily* **7/2**[2]
2534 **2** *1 1/2* **Age Of Reason (UAE)**[67] 5446 4-9-3 108.......................... TedDurcan 3 107
(Saeed Bin Suroor) *led and set modest pce: qcknd over 2f out: hrd rdn and hdd ins fnl f: nt qckn* **10/11**[1]
0124 **3** *2 1/4* **Beauchamp Xerxes**[39] 6290 3-8-11 102.......................... RichardHughes 1 103
(G A Butler) *t.k.h and restrained off the pce in last: wnt 4th over 3f out: drvn to press ldr over 1f out: one pce fnl f* **7/2**[2]
505- **4** *2 3/4* **Numide (FR)**[193] 6980 6-9-3 100.......................... GeorgeBaker 7 99
(G L Moore) *plld hrd: settled in cl 3rd: rdn over 2f out: wknd over 1f out* **16/1**
340 **5** *5* **Young Mick**[25] 6662 7-9-3 93..........................(v) DaneO'Neill 2 91
(G G Margarson) *sn chsng ldr: rdn over 2f out: wknd wl over 1f out* **14/1**[3]

2m 36.09s (1.59) **Going Correction** -0.025s/f (Stan)
WFA 3 from 4yo+ 6lb **5** Ran SP% **109.4**
Speed ratings (Par 111): **93,92,90,88,85**
CSF £7.07 TOTE £4.30: £1.90, £1.20; EX 6.50.
Owner Godolphin **Bred** Cashel Stud Inc **Trained** Newmarket, Suffolk

FOCUS
The two previous runnings of this had fallen to multiple Listed winner and Group 2-placed Dansant and subsequent Group 1 scorer Spanish Moon but, while this year's winner is a smart sort, the steady gallop means the bare form of this uncompetitive event is unreliable. The winner raced centre to far side in the straight.

NOTEBOOK
Once More Dubai(USA) settled better than has been the case of late and showed the best turn of foot to win a muddling event on his all-weather debut. He's a smart sort who should prove equally effective in a truly run race over 1m2f and this victory on a synthetic surface will increase his options at next year's Dubai Carnival. (tchd 100-30 and 4-1)
Age Of Reason(UAE), previously unbeaten on Polytrack, looked the yard's first string but, while running creditably after setting a modest gallop, was readily brushed aside in the closing stages by one with a superior turn of foot. He would almost certainly have been better served by making this a truer test of stamina and he should be able to win a race at this level. (op Evens)
Beauchamp Xerxes is a smart sort who was ridden patiently returned to this longer trip but, while far from disgraced in this messy event, left the strong impression he would have been better suited by a much more truly run race around 1m2f. He is worth another chance in similar company. (op 4-1)
Numide(FR) had a bit to find at the weights, but failed to settle and not surprisingly had precious little to offer in the closing stages on this all-weather debut and first run since April. A more end-to-end gallop would have been much more to his liking but he will be of more interest when switched back to hurdles. (op 14-1 tchd 20-1)
Young Mick had plenty to find at the weights and, although he enjoyed the run of the race returned to Polytrack, he had his limitations firmly exposed in this grade. He is much better on turf. (op 10-1)

7238 KIA SOUL, SAFE BET H'CAP — 1m 4f (P)
8:20 (8:21) (Class 5) (0-75,73) 3-Y-O — **£2,590** (£770; £385; £192) **Stalls** Centre

Form — RPR
0444 **1** — **Mannlichen**[17] 6878 3-9-4 **73** .... JoeFanning 3 — 81+
(M Johnston) *settled in 4th: effrt over 2f out: led over 1f out: rdn clr ins fnl f* **13/8**[1]
4321 **2** *2* **Silent Act (USA)**[7] 7112 3-8-13 **68** 6ex .... NCallan 1 — 73+
(Mrs A J Perrett) *t.k.h: hdwy to chse ldr after 2f: led 2f out tl over 1f out: nt qckn ins fnl f* **5/2**[2]
2130 **3** *3 ½* **Key Regard (IRE)**[13] 6975 3-9-2 **71** .... SebSanders 5 — 70
(P F I Cole) *hld up in rr: hdwy to chse ldrs 2f out: hrd rdn: one pce* **12/1**
1004 **4** *3 ½* **Altimatum (USA)**[7] 7126 3-9-1 **70** ....(t) AlanMunro 7 — 64
(P F I Cole) *prom: rdn over 2f out: sn outpcd* **20/1**
-503 **5** *¾* **Capitelli (IRE)**[14] 6934 3-9-2 **71** .... RichardHughes 6 — 63
(R Hannon) *led tl wknd 2f out* **13/2**[3]
0104 **6** *shd* **Sapphire Prince (USA)**[9] 7048 3-9-1 **70** .... SteveDrowne 4 — 62
(J R Best) *towards rr: mod effrt in centre over 2f out: no imp* **12/1**
6054 **7** *4* **Hazy Dancer**[13] 6975 3-9-0 **69** ....(t) HayleyTurner 2 — 55
(M P Tregoning) *settled in 5th: rdn and dropped to rr 3f out: struggling after* **9/1**

2m 33.56s (-0.94) **Going Correction** -0.025s/f (Stan) — 7 Ran SP% **110.1**
Speed ratings (Par 102): **102,100,98,96,95 95,92**
toteswingers: 1&2 £1.70, 1&3 £5.20, 2&3 £5.30 CSF £5.29 TOTE £2.70: £1.50, £1.70; EX 6.40.
Owner Graham Mezzone **Bred** Miss K Rausing **Trained** Middleham Moor, N Yorks

FOCUS
A fair handicap in which the pace was steady until the home straight and this bare form, although rated at face value, also has a slightly shaky look to it. The winner came down the centre in the straight.
Capitelli(IRE) Official explanation: jockey said filly lost its action on final bend

7239 CHAMPAGNE LANSON ROSE BRUT NV H'CAP (DIV I) — 7f (P)
8:50 (8:50) (Class 6) (0-55,61) 3-Y-O+ — **£1,706** (£503; £252) **Stalls** High

Form — RPR
601 **1** — **Final Drive (IRE)**[3] 7200 3-9-12 **61** 6ex .... RichardHughes 5 — 72+
(E J Creighton) *hld up towards rr: rdn and hdwy in centre over 1f out: r.o to ld fnl 75yds: pushed out: comf* **7/2**[2]
0455 **2** *nk* **Headache**[5] 7152 4-9-2 **50** ....(bt[1]) DavidProbert 10 — 58
(B W Duke) *prom: led over 3f out: rdn 2 l ahd 2f out: hdd and nt pce of wnr fnl 75yds* **11/2**[3]
4506 **3** *1 ¾* **Outer Hebrides**[14] 6933 8-9-6 **54** ....(v) LukeMorris 13 — 57
(J M Bradley) *mid-div: rdn over 2f out: styd on to take 3rd nr fin* **16/1**
0344 **4** *¾* **Diane's Choice**[14] 6933 6-9-5 **53** ....(e) AdamKirby 3 — 54
(Miss Gay Kelleway) *bhd: rdn over 2f out: styd on fnl f: nrst fin* **16/1**
0604 **5** *hd* **Mr Rio (IRE)**[7] 7105 4-9-4 **52** .... AlanMunro 1 — 52
(A P Jarvis) *chsd ldrs: rdn over 2f out: one pce appr fnl f* **16/1**
062 **6** *1 ½* **Copperwood**[9] 7051 4-9-2 **50** .... NCallan 9 — 46
(M Blanshard) *chsd ldrs: hrd rdn over 1f out: no ex* **10/3**[1]
5451 **7** *nk* **Cheery Cat (USA)**[9] 7068 5-8-7 **48** ....(p) DavidKenny[(7)] 14 — 44
(J Balding) *prom: nt clr run on ins over 2f out: rallied over 1f out: wknd fnl f* **15/2**
6000 **8** *¾* **Wotatomboy**[19] 6824 3-8-10 **50** .... AmyRyan[(5)] 7 — 43
(R M Whitaker) *mid-div: rdn and no hdwy fnl 2f* **33/1**
0004 **9** *1 ½* **Ishibee (IRE)**[4] 7176 5-9-0 **48** ....(v) JerryO'Dwyer 6 — 38
(J J Bridger) *plld hrd early: mid-div on outer: rdn over 2f out: sn btn* **25/1**
0020 **10** *½* **Ymir**[23] 6720 3-9-6 **55** ....(p) LiamJones 11 — 42
(M J Attwater) *plld hrd early: led tl over 3f out: wknd over 1f out* **14/1**
4050 **11** *¾* **Valentino Swing (IRE)**[205] 1259 6-9-4 **52** .... StephenDonohoe 2 — 38
(Miss T Spearing) *bhd: rdn over 2f out: nvr trbld ldrs* **40/1**
6000 **12** *1 ¾* **Inside Trade (IRE)**[7] 7105 3-9-5 **54** ....(v[1]) DaneO'Neill 12 — 34
(N P Mulholland) *dwlt: hld up towards rr: nt clr run on ins over 2f out: effrt wl over 1f out: sn wknd* **33/1**
0003 **13** *8* **Sign Of The Cross**[6] 7129 5-9-7 **55** .... LPKeniry 8 — 15
(C R Dore) *plld hrd early: in tch tl wknd over 2f out* **10/1**

1m 26.09s (0.09) **Going Correction** -0.025s/f (Stan)
WFA 3 from 4yo+ 1lb — 13 Ran SP% **118.0**
Speed ratings (Par 101): **98,97,95,94,94 92,92,91,89,89 88,86,77**
toteswingers: 1&2 £15.90, 1&3 £19.20, 2&3 £18.90 CSF £21.96 CT £284.18 TOTE £5.60: £2.30, £2.20, £5.50; EX 26.40.
Owner Par 4 Racing **Bred** D Day & B Cantwell **Trained** Mill Hill, London NW7

FOCUS
The first division of a modest handicap but probably sound form. The gallop was reasonable and the winner raced in the centre in the straight.

7240 CHAMPAGNE LANSON ROSE BRUT NV H'CAP (DIV II) — 7f (P)
9:20 (9:20) (Class 6) (0-55,55) 3-Y-O+ — **£1,706** (£503; £252) **Stalls** High

Form — RPR
4402 **1** — **Dancing Welcome**[4] 7176 3-9-1 **50** ....(b) LukeMorris 8 — 57
(J M Bradley) *chsd ldrs: disp ld 2f out: drvn to ld ins fnl f* **11/2**[3]
031 **2** *nk* **Mister Jingles**[25] 6674 6-9-1 **54** .... AmyRyan[(5)] 13 — 60
(R M Whitaker) *chsd ldrs: rdn over 2f out: kpt on to take 2nd nr fin* **7/2**[1]
4061 **3** *½* **Briannsta (IRE)**[34] 6433 7-9-5 **53** ....(b) RichardThomas 5 — 58
(J E Long) *prom on outer: disp ld 2f out tl nt qckn ins fnl f* **16/1**
0020 **4** *nk* **Just Jimmy (IRE)**[13] 6968 4-9-6 **54** .... GeorgeBaker 1 — 58+
(P D Evans) *hld up in rr: rdn and r.o fnl 2f: nrst fin* **6/1**
06-0 **5** *2* **May Parkin (IRE)**[5] 7152 4-9-2 **50** ....(bt[1]) TGMcLaughlin 14 — 48
(M Wigham) *led tl 2f out: no ex 1f out* **16/1**
-000 **6** *¾* **Ejeed (USA)**[126] 3512 4-9-2 **50** ....(p) SamHitchcott 10 — 46
(Miss Z C Davison) *dwlt: t.k.h towards rr on rail: hdwy on ins 2f out: no imp over 1f out* **66/1**
500 **7** *½* **Josiah Bartlett (IRE)**[7] 7110 3-9-1 **50** .... StephenDonohoe 12 — 45
(Ian Williams) *mid-div: hdwy on ins 2f out: no ex over 1f out* **9/2**[2]
3666 **8** *nk* **Running Flush (USA)**[15] 6914 3-9-6 **55** .... NCallan 2 — 49
(J R Gask) *mid-div: rdn and no hdwy fnl 2f* **8/1**
6000 **9** *nk* **Double Valentine**[23] 6720 6-8-11 **48** ....(b[1]) JackMitchell[(3)] 7 — 41
(R Ingram) *bhd: hdwy on ins over 1f out: same pl fnl f* **25/1**
0000 **10** *2* **Joss Stick**[11] 7023 4-9-5 **53** .... JerryO'Dwyer 4 — 41
(J J Bridger) *mid-div: outpcd fnl 2f* **66/1**
-000 **11** *¾* **Roman Maze**[12] 6999 9-9-4 **52** .... ShaneKelly 9 — 38
(W M Brisbourne) *towards rr: rdn over 2f out: nvr trbld ldrs* **33/1**
-000 **12** *6* **Under Fire (IRE)**[13] 6968 6-9-7 **55** .... SebSanders 6 — 25
(A W Carroll) *prom tl wknd 2f out* **14/1**
0605 **13** *6* **Cullybackey (IRE)**[9] 7069 4-9-0 **48** .... PatCosgrave 11 — 2
(J R Boyle) *in tch tl wknd over 2f out* **9/1**
5600 **14** *1 ¾* **Magic Queen (IRE)**[12] 7004 3-9-4 **53** .... AlanMunro 3 — 2
(A P Jarvis) *in tch: wd and lost pl bnd 4f out: sn bhd* **50/1**

1m 26.15s (0.15) **Going Correction** -0.025s/f (Stan)
WFA 3 from 4yo+ 1lb — 14 Ran SP% **121.4**
Speed ratings (Par 101): **98,97,97,96,94 93,93,92,92,90 89,82,75,73**
toteswingers: 1&2 £4.30, 1&3 £9.70, 2&3 £4.00 CSF £24.42 CT £304.21 TOTE £7.40: £2.20, £1.60, £4.50; EX 30.30 Place 6: £213.12 Place 5: £13.01 .
Owner J M Bradley **Bred** The Hon Mrs E J Wills **Trained** Sedbury, Gloucs

FOCUS
Another moderate handicap run at a fair gallop. Those held up failed to get competitive and the principals raced in the centre in the straight. The form looks sound if limited, rated around the placed horses.
Just Jimmy(IRE) Official explanation: jockey said gelding ran too free
Joss Stick Official explanation: jockey said gelding ran too free
T/Plt: £804.60 to a £1 stake. Pool: £80,904.18. 73.40 winning tickets. T/Qpdt: £18.00 to a £1 stake. Pool: £8,975.48. 368.66 winning tickets. LM

7120 NOTTINGHAM (L-H)
Wednesday, November 4
OFFICIAL GOING: Soft changing to heavy after race 7 (3.25)
Inner course used.
Wind: Virtually nil Weather: Fine and dry

7241 PHS ENVIRONMENTALLY FRIENDLY WASHROOM PRODUCTS H'CAP — 5f 13y
12:10 (12:11) (Class 6) (0-55,59) 3-Y-O+ — **£2,047** (£604; £302) **Stalls** High

Form — RPR
000 **1** — **Mission Impossible**[12] 6985 4-8-8 **52** .... AndrewHeffernan[(5)] 13 — 59
(Miss Tracy Waggott) *dwlt: sn chsng ldrs stands' side: rdn along and hdwy over 1f out: drvn ent fnl f: styd on to ld last 75yds* **16/1**
6365 **2** *hd* **Alacity (IRE)**[8] 7081 3-9-2 **55** .... FrancisNorton 12 — 61
(N Bycroft) *cl up stands' side: effrt and led that gp 2f out: rdn over 1f out and ev ch ins fnl f tl drvn and nt qckn nr fin: 2nd of 10 in gp* **10/1**
2401 **3** *nk* **Silk Gallery (USA)**[8] 7081 4-9-6 **59** 6ex ....(t) GrahamGibbons 17 — 64
(E J Alston) *in tch stands' side: hdwy over 1f out: sn rdn and styd on strly ins fnl f: 3rd of 10 in gp* **9/2**[1]
6050 **4** *nk* **Pinball (IRE)**[14] 6933 3-9-2 **55** ....(v) PaulHanagan 15 — 59
(Mrs L Williamson) *wnt r s and in rr stands' side: hdwy over 1f out: sn rdn and styd on strly ins fnl f: 4th of 10 in gp* **33/1**
0062 **5** *shd* **First Swallow**[12] 6989 4-9-1 **54** ....(t) FrederikTylicki 4 — 57
(D H Brown) *prom far side: hdwy to ld that gp and overall ldr 1 1/2f out and sn rdn: drvn ins fnl f: hdd and no ex last 100yds: 1st of 7 in gp* **17/2**
0006 **6** *½* **Commander Wish**[8] 7086 6-8-13 **52** .... NeilChalmers 1 — 54
(Lucinda Featherstone) *towards rr far side: swtchd rt and hdwy 2f out: sn rdn and styd on wl fnl f: nrst fin: 2nd of 7 in gp* **12/1**
465 **7** *shd* **Desert Pride**[14] 6933 4-9-2 **55** ....(v) FergusSweeney 8 — 56
(W S Kittow) *towards rr stands' side: swtchd lft and hdwy 2f out: rdn over 1f out: kpt on ins fnl f: nrst fin: 5th of 10 in gp* **13/2**[2]
2165 **8** *1 ¾* **Captain Royale (IRE)**[12] 6989 4-9-1 **54** ....(p) RobertWinston 5 — 49
(Miss Tracy Waggott) *chsd ldrs far side: rdn along wl over 2f out: wknd ent fnl f: 3rd of 7 in gp* **8/1**[3]
0020 **9** *3* **Windjammer**[38] 6314 5-8-6 **52** ....(b) IJBrennan[(7)] 2 — 36
(L A Mullaney) *overall ldr far side: rdn along 2f out: sn hdd and grad wknd: 4th of 7in gp* **14/1**
5001 **10** *½* **Shannon Golden**[12] 7002 3-9-2 **55** ....(t) AmirQuinn 9 — 37
(S R Bowring) *cl up stands' side: rdn along 2f out: drvn and wknd over 1f out: 6th of 10 in gp* **16/1**
-500 **11** *nk* **El Potro**[146] 2852 7-9-0 **53** .... JerryO'Dwyer 11 — 34
(J R Holt) *chsd ldrs stands' side: rdn along 2f out: sn drvn and wknd: 7th of 10 in gp* **20/1**
560 **12** *½* **Berrymead**[37] 6341 4-8-11 **55** .... AnnStokell[(5)] 16 — 35
(Miss A Stokell) *s.i.s: a in rr stands' side: 8th of 10 in gp* **40/1**
-200 **13** *1* **Tanley**[8] 7086 4-8-13 **52** .... ChrisCatlin 10 — 28
(J F Coupland) *chsd ldrs stands' side: rdn along over 2f out and sn wknd: 9th of 10 in gp* **25/1**
002 **14** *1 ¾* **Bertbrand**[8] 7086 4-9-0 **53** ....(b) GregFairley 7 — 23
(I W McInnes) *chsd ldrs far side: rdn along 2f out: sn wknd: 5th of 7 in gp* **12/1**
-000 **15** *1 ¾* **Wavertree Princess (IRE)**[8] 7100 4-9-0 **53** .... TedDurcan 6 — 16
(C F Wall) *in tch far side: rdn along over 2f out and sn wknd: 6th of 7 in gp* **25/1**
000 **16** *¾* **The Cuckoo**[46] 6118 3-9-2 **55** .... SebSanders 3 — 16
(M Quinn) *prom far side: rdn along 2f out and sn wknd: 7th of 7 in gp* **50/1**
0003 **17** *3* **Deo Valente (IRE)**[12] 7002 4-9-1 **54** ....(bt) DavidProbert 14 — 4
(J M Bradley) *rrd s: sn chsng ldrs stands' side: rdn along 1/2-way and sn wknd: 10th of 10 in gp* **12/1**

63.69 secs (2.69) **Going Correction** +0.25s/f (Good) — 17 Ran SP% **123.5**
Speed ratings (Par 101): **88,87,87,86,86 85,85,82,78,77 76,75,74,71,68 67,62**
toteswingers: 1&2 £10.10, 1&3 £9.30, 2&3 £18.60 CSF £156.71 CT £618.08 TOTE £25.80: £5.50, £3.20, £1.10, £7.30; EX 318.50.
Owner H Conlon **Bred** Rodney Meredith **Trained** Spennymoor, Co Durham
■ Stewards' Enquiry : Andrew Heffernan two-day ban: used whip with excessive frequency (Nov 18-19)

FOCUS
They split into two groups early, with seven runners going far side, but it was the larger bunch towards the stands' side who had the call, providing the first four finishers. The time was poor; a full second slower than the following 0-70 nursery and the form is modest rated around the placed horses.
Berrymead Official explanation: jockey said filly missed the break

7242 AIRFORCE LOW ENERGY HAND DRYER NURSERY 5f 13y
12:40 (12:41) (Class 5) (0-70,68) 2-Y-O **£3,238** (£963; £481; £240) **Stalls High**

Form RPR
5032 **1** **Vilnius**[5] 7156 2-8-6 **53** WilliamBuick 8 56
(M R Channon) *racd stands' side: led that gp 1f: chsd ldrs: styd on wl to ld fnl 75yds* **4/1**[1]
0654 **2** *3/4* **Boogie Waltzer**[61] 5635 2-8-5 **52** ChrisCatlin 5 52
(S C Williams) *racd stands' side: w ldr: led 1f out: hdd and no ex wl ins fnl f* **16/1**
0500 **3** *nk* **Thinking**[12] 6983 2-8-12 **59** (b[1]) DavidAllan 13 58
(T D Easterby) *racd stands' side: chsd ldrs: edgd lft 1f out: styd on: no ex towards fin* **11/1**
5553 **4** *nk* **Jack Luey**[8] 7079 2-8-12 **66** (p) IJBrennan[(7)] 14 64
(L A Mullaney) *racd stands' side: mid-div: sn drvn along: kpt on wl fnl f* **8/1**
0500 **5** *1* **Pavement Games**[20] 6797 2-8-3 **50** ow2 PaulEddery 4 45
(R C Guest) *swtchd rt and racd stands' side: in rr: hdwy over 1f out: styd on ins fnl f* **33/1**
540 **6** *nk* **Diman Waters (IRE)**[20] 6796 2-9-7 **68** GrahamGibbons 7 61
(E J Alston) *hdwy to ld stands' side gp after 1f: hdd 1f out: no ex* **25/1**
5436 **7** *1 1/4* **Cane Cat (IRE)**[16] 6906 2-7-12 **52** JamesPSullivan[(7)] 9 40
(A W Carroll) *racd stands' side: w ldrs: wknd fnl f* **11/2**[3]
0102 **8** *nk* **Dragonessa (IRE)**[28] 6589 2-8-12 **59** DavidProbert 10 46
(B Palling) *racd stands' side: chsd ldrs: fdd fnl f* **5/1**[2]
4040 **9** *1/2* **Pinnacle Lad (IRE)**[16] 6903 2-9-5 **66** FrancisNorton 3 51+
(J L Spearing) *clr ldr ahd of two others on far side: kpt on same pce appr fnl f: 1st of 3 in gp* **14/1**
1050 **10** *hd* **Whispered Times (USA)**[68] 5393 2-9-0 **66** PatrickDonaghy[(5)] 11 50
(P C Haslam) *racd stands' side: in rr: hdwy and hung lft over 1f out: nvr nr ldrs* **22/1**
0020 **11** *1 1/4* **Lairy (IRE)**[36] 6366 2-8-0 **47** JamieMackay 12 27
(M F Harris) *mid-div: drvn over 2f out: lost pl over 1f out* **9/1**
2064 **12** *3/4* **Point To Prove**[13] 6970 2-9-1 **62** (e[1]) JerryO'Dwyer 1 39+
(Miss Amy Weaver) *chsd ldr far side: fdd over 1f out: 2nd of 3 in gp* **14/1**
0065 **13** *1* **Rightcar**[5] 7156 2-8-7 **57** (b) AndreaAtzeni[(3)] 2 31+
(Peter Grayson) *racd far side: chsd two others: edgd rt and wknd over 1f out: last of 3 in gp* **25/1**
000 **14** *10* **Baze Mac**[18] 6841 2-8-0 **48** oh1 ow2 FrankieMcDonald 6 —
(N Bycroft) *racd wd on stands' side: in rr: bhd and eased over 1f out* **100/1**

62.69 secs (1.69) **Going Correction** +0.25s/f (Good) **14** Ran SP% **116.7**
Speed ratings (Par 96): **96,94,94,93,92 91,89,88,88,87 85,84,82,66**
toteswingers: 1&2 £10.10, 1&3 £9.30, 2&3 £18.60 CSF £63.56 CT £673.96 TOTE £3.90: £1.80, £4.20, £3.50; EX 31.50.
Owner P Trant **Bred** P Trant & Mike Channon Bloodstock Limited **Trained** West Ilsley, Berks
■ Stewards' Enquiry : William Buick caution: careless riding.

FOCUS
The winning time was a full second quicker than the earlier 46-55 handicap for older horses, but this still looked a modest nursery. The three runners who raced far side early - Pinnacle Lad, Point To Prove and Rightcar - had no chance with the remainder towards the stands' side. The winner is rated to her recent form.

NOTEBOOK
Vilnius, who looked in good order beforehand, handled the soft ground well and built on her recent second at Wolverhampton. Her only previous win came in a seller but she should remain competitive. (op 5-1)
Boogie Waltzer responded well to a positive ride and had her chance. She should find a race. (op 12-1)
Thinking benefited from the fitting of a blinkers, running well in defeat. He seemed to be bumped slightly early on but it probably didn't make much difference. (op 12-1 tchd 10-1)
Jack Luey, another who looked well, did not run badly and is due to be eased 3lb. (op 7-1)
Pavement Games, carrying 2lb overweight, got going too late having been well back and gave the impression there may be more to come. (op 28-1)
Dragonessa(IRE) was caught a bit wider than ideal. (op 9-2 tchd 4-1)
Baze Mac Official explanation: jockey said filly hung left-handed throughout

7243 PHS DIRECT ONLINE FLU KITS MAIDEN STKS (DIV I) 1m 75y
1:10 (1:11) (Class 4) 2-Y-O **£4,209** (£1,252; £625; £312) **Stalls Low**

Form RPR
1 **Burj Nahar** 2-9-3 0 TedDurcan 5 87+
(Saeed Bin Suroor) *trckd ldr: smooth hdwy to ld 2f out: sn clr: easily* **8/11**[1]
06 **2** *3 3/4* **Molon Labe (IRE)**[22] 6763 2-9-3 0 RobertWinston 8 73
(T P Tate) *led: pushed along 3f out: rdn and hdd 2f out: drvn over 1f out and kpt on: no ch w wnr* **9/1**[3]
3 *4* **Ashbrittle** 2-9-3 0 RichardKingscote 11 64+
(R M Beckett) *in rr and green: pushed along 1/2-way: rdn and hdwy on outer 2f out: styd on wl u.p ins fnl f to take 3rd nr line* **16/1**
4 *1/2* **Head Hunted** 2-9-3 0 PaulHanagan 4 63
(E A L Dunlop) *towards rr: hdwy wl over 2f out: rdn over 1f out: kpt on ins fnl f* **20/1**
2240 **5** *1/2* **Lutine Charlie (IRE)**[27] 6619 2-9-3 81 LukeMorris 16 62
(P Winkworth) *plld hrd: chsd ldrs on outer: rdn along to chse ldng pair 2f out: sn no imp and wknd ins fnl f* **17/2**[2]
6 *1 3/4* **Gay Mirage (GER)** 2-8-12 0 PhilipRobinson 12 53+
(M A Jarvis) *in rr: hdwy 3f out: kpt on fnl 2f: nrst fin* **12/1**
0 **7** *3* **Bollin Julie**[22] 6762 2-8-12 0 DavidAllan 13 47+
(T D Easterby) *towards rr: hdwy 4f out: rdn along wl over 2f out and sn no imp* **150/1**
0 **8** *1 1/4* **Straversjoy**[12] 6992 2-8-12 0 GrahamGibbons 3 44
(R Hollinshead) *chsd ldrs: rdn along over 3f out and grad wknd* **150/1**
9 *1* **Rock The Stars (IRE)** 2-9-3 0 JerryO'Dwyer 15 47
(M G Quinlan) *a in midfield* **66/1**
00 **10** *3* **Ildiko (USA)**[12] 6992 2-8-12 0 SebSanders 14 36
(Sir Mark Prescott) *prom: rdn along over 3f out and sn wknd* **100/1**
0 **11** *2 1/2* **A P Ling**[20] 6792 2-8-9 0 AndreaAtzeni[(3)] 2 30
(C N Kellett) *chsd ldrs: rdn along 3f out: wknd fnl 2f* **250/1**
0 **12** *4 1/2* **Priestley (IRE)**[12] 6990 2-9-3 0 FrederikTylicki 1 26
(J G Given) *in tch: effrt on inner to chse ldrs over 3f out: sn rdn and wknd* **100/1**
13 *4 1/2* **Ticket To Paradise** 2-9-3 0 ChrisCatlin 9 16
(D R Lanigan) *s.i.s: a in rr* **50/1**
14 *3 1/2* **Salvation** 2-8-12 0 HayleyTurner 7 4
(M L W Bell) *midfield whn hmpd and lost pl after 150yds: a bhd after* **10/1**
15 *18* **Welcome Bounty** 2-9-3 0 NCallan 6 —
(D R Lanigan) *s.i.s: a in rr* **25/1**

1m 50.81s (1.21) **Going Correction** +0.25s/f (Good) **15** Ran SP% **116.9**
Speed ratings (Par 98): **103,99,95,94,94 92,89,88,87,84 81,77,72,69,51**
toteswingers: 1&2 £4.20, 1&3 £8.00, 2&3 £15.70 CSF £6.81 TOTE £1.70: £1.10, £2.50, £4.40; EX 8.40.
Owner Godolphin **Bred** Darley **Trained** Newmarket, Suffolk

FOCUS
A mightily impressive performance from Burj Nahar, who made a winning debut in the manner of a smart colt, and the time, 1.83 seconds quicker than the second division, supports the view that he is well above average, especially as he was not ridden out to the line. He is clearly value for more than rated.

NOTEBOOK
Burj Nahar ◆ had been due carry the Godolphin first colours in a similar contest at this track the previous week, only to be withdrawn and a stablemate win the race by 4l, so it was no surprise to see him well backed. Relaxed in the paddock, in the race itself he travelled kindly in a good position and it was clear from some way out he was going best. He was asked to stretch around 2f out, but didn't have to be fully extended and his rider was soon looking round before easing off inside the final 200 yards or so, with this son of Shamardal looking value for more than double the winning margin. He is bred to be pretty smart - his dam is a half-sister to Sea The Stars - and he has the physical scope to progress. It would be no surprise to see him start off in a Derby trial next year. (op 10-11 tchd Evens)
Molon Labe(IRE) seems to be improving with each run. He was probably favoured by setting the pace, considering he had the benefit of previous experience and the ground was testing, but whatever, he clearly has a fair amount of ability. Handicaps are now an option and he should make a nice 3-y-o, possibly over a little further. (op 8-1)
Ashbrittle ◆ made a pleasing start as he was extremely green for much of the way and needed to be driven along well off the pace some way out, before making good late headway. He has already been gelded but, considering he is bred to come into his own over 1m4f-plus next year, he could be quite useful. (op 12-1)
Head Hunted travelled okay a fair way back and kept on gradually for pressure. This was pleasing start and he should get further before long, being a half-brother to dual 1m3f-1m4f winner Dubai Storming. (op 28-1)
Lutine Charlie(IRE), upped significantly in trip, was a doubtful stayer judged on pedigree and he dropped away in the closing stages, having been much too keen early. He was below his official mark of 80. (op 15-2 tchd 10-1)
Gay Mirage(GER) ◆ fared best of the fillies and looks a nice middle-distancing/staying prospect. This half-sister to quite useful dual 1m3f-1m6f winner Amerigo made encouraging headway from a long way off the pace. (op 9-1 tchd 8-1)
Bollin Julie ◆ showed definite signs of ability, making a brief move in the straight before flattening out. She's bred to make quite a nice stayer as she gets older.
Salvation, out of the stable's Lingfield Oaks Trial winner Birdie, took the eye in the paddock but was never going after being bumped early on and was far too green to do herself justice. (op 18-1)

7244 PHS DIRECT ONLINE FLU KITS MAIDEN STKS (DIV II) 1m 75y
1:40 (1:42) (Class 4) 2-Y-O **£4,209** (£1,252; £625; £312) **Stalls Low**

Form RPR
66 **1** **Green Lightning (IRE)**[22] 6759 2-9-3 0 JoeFanning 10 78
(M Johnston) *mde all: sent clr over 1f out: carried hd high: v readily* **9/1**
2 *2 1/4* **Grande Saggio** 2-9-0 0 AndreaAtzeni[(3)] 5 73+
(M Botti) *trckd ldrs: outpcd over 2f out: styd on to take modest 2nd jst ins fnl f: kpt on wl* **4/1**[2]
000 **3** *7* **Mme De Stael**[15] 6920 2-8-12 0 SebSanders 12 53
(Sir Mark Prescott) *chsd ldrs: drvn 3f out: styd on same pce fnl f* **40/1**
60 **4** *1* **Little Oz (IRE)**[12] 6992 2-8-12 0 PaulHanagan 13 51
(E A L Dunlop) *hld up in mid-div on outer: hdwy 3f out: kpt on fnl f* **15/2**
0 **5** *nk* **Sadler's Mark**[20] 6792 2-9-3 0 RobertWinston 2 55+
(T P Tate) *dwlt: hdwy to trck ldr after 1f: wknd fnl f* **11/2**[3]
00 **6** *3/4* **Keenes Royale**[87] 4817 2-8-12 0 (t) PaulMulrennan 14 48+
(P C Haslam) *mid-div: hdwy over 3f out: wknd over 1f out* **50/1**
7 *nk* **Sir Walter Raleigh** 2-9-3 0 NCallan 7 53+
(Sir Michael Stoute) *prom: effrt over 3f out: sn outpcd: kpt on fnl f* **7/2**[1]
8 *hd* **Chink Of Light** 2-9-3 0 WilliamBuick 8 52
(A M Balding) *in rr div: kpt on fnl 3f: nvr on terms* **14/1**
0 **9** *1 1/2* **Catawollow**[9] 7061 2-8-12 0 PaulEddery 9 44
(R C Guest) *chsd ldrs: t.k.h: lost pl 3f out* **100/1**
10 *1/2* **Leader Of The Land (IRE)** 2-9-3 0 TedDurcan 11 48
(D R Lanigan) *in rr-div: sn drvn along: sme hdwy 3f out: nvr a factor* **8/1**
11 *3 1/2* **Admiral Breese** 2-9-3 0 GrahamGibbons 16 40
(R Hollinshead) *chsd ldrs on outer: hung lft and wknd over 1f out* **33/1**
12 *nse* **Othello (IRE)** 2-9-3 0 LPKeniry 6 40
(E F Vaughan) *mid-div: lost pl over 2f out* **66/1**
13 *3 1/2* **Amylyn** 2-8-12 0 JerryO'Dwyer 1 28
(J R Holt) *s.s: a in rr* **150/1**
00 **14** *2 1/2* **Naughty Norris**[42] 6214 2-9-3 0 DanielTudhope 3 27
(R Bastiman) *mid-div: drvn over 3f out: sn wknd* **200/1**
15 *3 1/4* **Chief Of Ten** 2-9-3 0 ChrisCatlin 4 20
(D R Lanigan) *s.i.s: a in rr* **33/1**
16 *10* **Firetail** 2-8-12 0 HayleyTurner 15 —
(M L W Bell) *s.i.s: in rr and sn drvn along: bhd fnl 3f* **8/1**

1m 52.64s (3.04) **Going Correction** +0.25s/f (Good) **16** Ran SP% **122.2**
Speed ratings (Par 98): **94,91,84,83,83 82,82,82,80,80 76,76,73,70,67 57**
toteswingers: 1&2 £8.30, 1&3 £32.70, 2&3 £43.00 CSF £43.86 TOTE £9.00: £2.10, £1.40, £15.50; EX 53.50.
Owner The Green Dot Partnership **Bred** Western Bloodstock **Trained** Middleham Moor, N Yorks

FOCUS
The winning time was 1.83 seconds slower than the smart-looking Burj Nahar recorded in the first division. The third is rated to her earlier form.

NOTEBOOK
Green Lightning(IRE) might be slightly flattered by the manner of this victory, as he had the benefit of previous experience and enjoyed a soft lead on a track favouring those ridden prominently. However, his breeding suggests he'll keep improving as he goes up in trip. (op 6-1)
Grande Saggio, a 120,000gns half-brother to, among others, smart sprinter Barney McGrew, out of a 1m2f winner, was well backed and made a pleasing start. Having been handily placed, he lacked the speed of the winner when that one committed early in the straight, before keeping on. (op 13-2)
Mme De Stael was helped to get third by putting her experience to good use with a positive ride. She might do better in handicaps. (op 16-1)
Little Oz(IRE) travelled okay and plugged on for pressure. Out of a Sadler's Wells mare, she might do better over further and handicaps are now an option. (op 7-1 tchd 13-2)
Sadler's Mark was well supported, but his trainer describes him as big and backward. (op 10-1 tchd 5-1)

Keenes Royale hinted at ability after nearly three months off. She's another who can now switch to handicaps. (op 40-1)
Sir Walter Raleigh, a 120,000gns first foal of a 7f winner, impressed in the paddock and was sent off favourite but he seemed to need the run on this racecourse debut. (op 3-1 tchd 4-1)
Leader Of The Land(IRE) attracted support was but was far too green to ever challenge. (op 16-1 tchd 18-1)
Amylyn Official explanation: jockey said filly was slowly away
Firetail was solid in the market but, like her stablemate in the first division, she was much too inexperienced. (tchd 7-1)

7245 PHS WASHROOM HAND SANITISER RANGE CONDITIONS STKS 1m 75y
2:15 (2:15) (Class 2) 3-Y-O+

£15,577 (£4,665; £2,332; £1,167; £582; £292) **Stalls** Low

Form RPR
3020 **1** **Alexandros**[141] 2990 4-8-10 116 ... TedDurcan 5 114+
(Saeed Bin Suroor) *t.k.h early: trckd ldrs: hdwy 3f out: cl up 2f out: sn led and pushed clr* **6/5**[1]
2135 **2** 2 ½ **Plum Pudding (IRE)**[4] 7186 6-9-4 109 ... SteveDrowne 3 113
(R Hannon) *led: jnd and rdn 2f out: sn hdd and drvn: kpt on u.p ins fnl f: no ch w wnr* **9/1**[3]
1050 **3** ¾ **General Eliott (IRE)**[32] 6480 4-8-10 106 ... (p) NCallan 6 103
(P F I Cole) *in tch: hdwy to chse ldrs 4f out: rdn wl over 2f out: drvn wl over 1f out and kpt on same pce* **18/1**
3-52 **4** ¾ **Young Pretender (FR)**[11] 7019 4-8-10 107 ... DO'Donohoe 2 102
(Saeed Bin Suroor) *plld hrd: chsd ldr: effrt over 2f out and sn rdn: drvn wl over 1f out and kpt on same pce* **2/1**[2]
0000 **5** 2 **Smokey Oakey (IRE)**[32] 6480 5-8-10 99 ... JimmyQuinn 4 97
(M H Tompkins) *trckd ldrs: effrt 3f out: rdn along over 2f out and sn no imp* **9/1**[3]
0-00 **6** 4 **European Dream (IRE)**[11] 5655 6-8-10 90 ... (p) PaulEddery 7 88
(R C Guest) *a in rr: rdn along and outpcd fr 1/2-way* **18/1**
5005 **7** 32 **Pawan (IRE)**[8] 7090 9-8-10 82 ... AnnStokell 1 14
(Miss A Stokell) *sn towards rr: outpcd 1/2-way and sn wl bhd* **150/1**
1m 49.63s (0.03) **Going Correction** +0.25s/f (Good) 7 Ran SP% **110.0**
Speed ratings (Par 109): **109,106,105,105,103 99,67**
CSF £12.08 TOTE £1.90: £1.10, £3.80; EX 9.90.
Owner Godolphin **Bred** Darley **Trained** Newmarket, Suffolk

FOCUS
A decent, classy conditions contest and the pace was reasonable enough. Most of these ended up avoiding the far rail in the straight, racing more towards the centre. The form looks muddling with the winner not needing to run to his best and the runner-up the best guide to the level.

NOTEBOOK
Alexandros ◆ had a problem after losing his action in the Queen Anne and, having been given plenty of time to recover, Simon Crisford felt he would "definitely need the run". The ground was also softer than ideal judged by the way he carried his head a touch awkwardly in the closing stages, so although he was entitled to win, having upwards of 9lb in hand on official figures, this was still a smart performance, the colt looking value for 3l-plus after being eased. He's now likely to be aimed at the Hong Kong Mile and, an improved horse this year (top five RPRs prior to this gained in 2009), with the possibility of even more to come, he should go well. (op 5-6 tchd 4-5)
Plum Pudding(IRE) had no easy task conceding 8lb all round, and this was a good effort in defeat. (op 14-1)
General Eliott(IRE) should not have minded the ground but he was very easy to back and, after racing a bit keenly, he was well held. (op 22-1)
Young Pretender(FR), the winner's stablemate, didn't help himself by racing keenly and headed to the middle of the track later than the front three. He didn't run up to his official mark of 107 and probably wants better ground. (op 3-1)
Smokey Oakey(IRE) had conditions to suit and looked well, but he's on a long losing run. (op 10-1 tchd 11-1)

7246 PHS TREADSMART ENTRANCE MATTING H'CAP 1m 75y
2:50 (2:50) (Class 5) (0-70,70) 3-Y-O **£3,238** (£963; £481; £240) **Stalls** Low

Form RPR
0220 **1** **Amethyst Dawn (IRE)**[19] 6824 3-8-9 61 ... DavidAllan 8 73+
(T D Easterby) *trckd ldr: hdwy to ld over 2f out: clr wl over 1f out: comf* **5/1**[2]
2422 **2** 2 ½ **Iron Out (USA)**[9] 7062 3-8-13 70 ... PaulPickard(5) 12 76+
(R Hollinshead) *midfield: hdwy over 2f out: sn rdn and styd on ins fnl f: nt rch wnr* **6/1**[3]
4202 **3** 1 ¾ **Garter Knight**[7] 7127 3-8-11 63 ... MickyFenton 2 65
(Mrs P Sly) *midfield: hdwy 3f out: swtchd rt and rdn wl over 1f out: kpt on ins fnl f* **9/2**[1]
3005 **4** nk **Dean Iarracht (IRE)**[47] 6052 3-8-2 59 ... AndrewHeffernan(5) 11 60
(Miss Tracy Waggott) *trckd ldrs: hdwy 3f out: rdn along over 2f out: drvn to chse wnr over 1f out: kpt on same pce* **16/1**
0000 **5** 1 **Woteva**[12] 6997 3-8-8 60 ... ChrisCatlin 14 59
(T P Tate) *midfield: effrt 3f out: rdn along over 2f out: styd on ins fnl f: nrst fin* **14/1**
4 **6** 1 ¼ **Soul Sista (IRE)**[15] 6925 3-8-10 62 ... LiamJones 17 58
(J L Spearing) *sn pushed along in rr: hdwy 3f out: swtchd outside and drvn wl over 1f out: kpt on ins fnl f: nrst fin* **12/1**
0000 **7** ½ **Hard Ball**[8] 7094 3-8-4 56 oh3 ... (v[1]) FrancisNorton 13 51
(M Quinn) *chsd ldrs: rdn along 3f out: drvn over 2f out and grad wknd* **33/1**
-100 **8** 1 ¼ **Bob Stock (IRE)**[15] 6925 3-8-10 62 ... TonyCulhane 9 54
(W J Musson) *in rr tl styd on fnl 2f* **14/1**
1343 **9** ¾ **Sairaam (IRE)**[9] 7062 3-8-4 56 oh1 ... DavidProbert 3 46
(C Smith) *towards rr: hdwy and in tch after 2f: chsd ldrs 3f out and sn rdn: drvn 2f out and grad wknd* **16/1**
45 **10** 1 ½ **Lilly Royal (IRE)**[20] 6789 3-8-13 65 ... NeilChalmers 6 52
(B Palling) *dwlt: a in rr* **16/1**
4046 **11** 1 **Richo**[21] 6016 3-8-10 67 ... MarkCoumbe(5) 15 52
(S A Harris) *nvr nr ldrs* **28/1**
4006 **12** ½ **Moon Lightning (IRE)**[5] 7149 3-8-13 65 ... (p) TedDurcan 5 48
(M H Tompkins) *led: rdn along 3f out: hdd over 2f out: sn drvn and wknd* **10/1**
156 **13** 2 ¼ **Flying Silks (IRE)**[62] 5602 3-9-2 68 ... RobertHavlin 10 46
(J R Gask) *in tch: hdwy to chse ldrs 1/2-way: rdn along 3f out and sn wknd* **10/1**
3400 **14** ½ **Group Leader (IRE)**[8] 7101 3-9-2 68 ... RobertWinston 4 45
(J R Jenkins) *chsd ldrs: rdn along 3f out: sn drvn and wknd fnl 2f* **20/1**
0650 **15** ¾ **Madame Jourdain (IRE)**[12] 6988 3-7-11 56 oh11 CharlotteKerton(7) 16 31
(S A Harris) *midfield: plld hrd on outer: rdn along over 3f out and sn wknd* **100/1**
0346 **16** 9 **Safari Guide**[24] 6699 3-9-0 66 ... LukeMorris 1 21
(P Winkworth) *in tch: hdwy on inner to chse ldrs 1/2-way: rdn along over 3f out: sn lost pl and bhd* **16/1**
1m 50.3s (0.70) **Going Correction** +0.25s/f (Good) 16 Ran SP% **124.0**
Speed ratings (Par 102): **106,103,101,101,100 99,98,97,96,95 94,93,91,90,90 81**
toteswingers: 1&2 £4.70, 1&3 £7.50, 2&3 £7.20 CSF £34.43 CT £156.02 TOTE £6.40: £1.90, £1.60, £1.40, £5.20; EX 36.90.
Owner D A West **Bred** W Kane **Trained** Great Habton, N Yorks

FOCUS
A modest handicap run at a steady pace, and they raced up the centre of the track in the straight. It was raining heavily during this race but the first two are rated to something like their best.
Bob Stock(IRE) Official explanation: jockey said, regarding running and riding, that his orders were to drop the gelding out early, get it settled and do his best, adding that it jumped out smartly from the stalls, and although he managed to get cover it ran very free and hung right-handed for most of the race and it was only when it began to tire in the closing stages that he was able to ride it more vigorously through beaten horses.

7247 PHS TREADSMART MATWELL CLEANING H'CAP (DIV I) 1m 2f 50y
3:25 (3:25) (Class 5) (0-75,75) 3-Y-O+ **£2,914** (£867; £433; £216) **Stalls** Low

Form RPR
544- **1** **Take It Easee (IRE)**[9] 7075 4-8-13 68 ... SteveDrowne 2 80
(Mrs Prunella Dobbs, Ire) *hld up in rr: hdwy and nt clr run 3f out: hung rt and led over 1f out: rdn clr: eased towards fin* **12/1**
345- **2** 5 **Jennie Jerome (IRE)**[122] 4-9-3 75 ... JackMitchell(3) 9 77
(C F Wall) *hld up in rr: hdwy 3f out: wnt 2nd 1f out: no ch w wnr* **15/2**[2]
0640 **3** 2 **Highkingofireland**[11] 7020 3-8-1 63 ow1 ... MartinLane(3) 6 61
(A P Jarvis) *trckd ldrs: smooth hdwy to ld 3f out: hdd over 1f out: kpt on same pce* **14/1**
/121 **4** 1 **Bollin Dolly**[16] 6900 6-9-2 71 ... DavidAllan 4 67
(T D Easterby) *prom: drvn over 2f out: one pce* **3/1**[1]
0244 **5** 3 ½ **Eastern Hills**[12] 6985 4-8-11 66 ... FrederikTylicki 10 56
(J S Wainwright) *trckd ldrs: chal over 2f out: wknd over 1f out* **15/2**[2]
-443 **6** 3 **Elk Trail (IRE)**[195] 1478 4-8-11 66 ... MickyFenton 3 50
(Mrs P Sly) *s.s: t.k.h detached in last: kpt on fnl 3f: nvr nr ldrs* **9/1**
6600 **7** 4 ½ **Capeability (IRE)**[12] 6996 3-9-0 73 ... TonyCulhane 11 48
(M R Channon) *in rr: sn pushed along: nvr a factor* **12/1**
212 **8** 2 **Spring Secret**[55] 5791 3-8-9 68 ... DavidProbert 8 40
(B Palling) *chsd ldrs: wknd over 2f out* **8/1**[3]
3130 **9** 7 **King Of The Moors (USA)**[22] 6760 6-9-3 72 ... (b) RobertWinston 12 30
(R C Guest) *led tl 3f out: wknd and eased over 1f out* **12/1**
0300 **10** nse **General Tufto**[7] 7127 4-8-6 61 ... (b) FrancisNorton 5 19
(C Smith) *mid-div: hdwy over 4f out: sn drvn: lost pl over 2f out* **18/1**
6630 **11** ¾ **Arctic Cape**[11] 7036 4-9-4 73 ... (b) ChrisCatlin 13 30
(D E Pipe) *chsd ldrs: pushed along 6f out: fnd nil and lost pl 3f out* **12/1**
5-P0 **12** 11 **Longspur**[42] 6219 5-8-5 67 ... JamesPSullivan(7) 1 3
(M W Easterby) *tubed: prom: drvn 6f out: lost pl over 3f out: sn bhd* **66/1**
2m 16.76s (2.46) **Going Correction** +0.325s/f (Good)
WFA 3 from 4yo+ 4lb 12 Ran SP% **113.8**
Speed ratings (Par 103): **103,99,97,96,93 91,87,86,80,80 79,71**
toteswingers: 1&2 £13.20, 1&3 £32.40, 2&3 £29.40 CSF £95.23 CT £1274.17 TOTE £12.30: £2.90, £2.90, £5.90; EX 63.00.
Owner David M Fitzgerald **Bred** David Fitzgerald **Trained** Dumganstow, Co Wicklow

FOCUS
The ground was changed to an official description of heavy after this race. Although the general theme of the meeting was that prominent racers were favoured, the leaders probably went a bit too quick this time, setting things up for those waited with. The winning time was 0.93 seconds quicker than the second division and the winner produced her best performance with the placed horses setting the level.
Elk Trail(IRE) Official explanation: jockey said gelding was slowly away and hung right

7248 PHS TREADSMART MATWELL CLEANING H'CAP (DIV II) 1m 2f 50y
4:00 (4:00) (Class 5) (0-75,78) 3-Y-O+ **£2,914** (£867; £433; £216) **Stalls** Low

Form RPR
4030 **1** **I'm In The Pink (FR)**[81] 5028 5-9-3 70 ... PaulHanagan 5 80
(P D Evans) *a.p: cl up 4f out: led 3f out: rdn along 2f out: drvn and edgd rt ent fnl f: kpt on wl* **8/1**[3]
4535 **2** 2 **Rio Guru (IRE)**[39] 6286 4-9-1 68 ... TonyCulhane 9 74
(M R Channon) *dwlt and in rr: hdwy on wd outside 4f out: rdn to chse ldrs 2f out: swtchd lft and drvn to chse wnr ent fnl f: sn no imp* **14/1**
0/0- **3** 2 ¼ **Spear Thistle**[242] 4791 7-8-13 66 ... (p) GrahamGibbons 10 68
(C J Mann) *a.p: effrt over 3f out and sn ev ch: rdn wl over 2f out: drvn and one pce appr fnl f* **7/1**[2]
4 4 ½ **Monreale (GER)**[109] 4091 5-9-6 73 ... VinceSlattery 11 66
(G Brown) *hld up: hdwy over 4f out: rdn to chse ldrs over 2f out: drvn to chse wnr over 1f out: wknd ent fnl f* **17/2**
0402 **5** hd **Croeso Cusan**[4] 7173 4-8-6 59 oh4 ... DavidProbert 13 52
(J L Spearing) *midfield: hdwy 4f out: rdn along to chse ldrs over 2f out: sn drvn and no imp fr wl over 1f out* **7/1**[2]
6000 **6** 1 **Agapanthus (GER)**[11] 7014 4-8-13 66 ... (p) JerryO'Dwyer 12 57
(B J Curley) *midfield: hdwy 4f out: rdn to chse ldrs 2f out: sn drvn and wknd* **20/1**
200 **7** shd **Golden Rock (IRE)**[16] 6907 3-8-13 73 ... Louis-PhilippeBeuzelin(3) 8 64
(R Charlton) *chsd ldrs: rdn along over 3f out: drvn over 2f out and grad wknd* **16/1**
6-12 **8** ½ **Dream Of Olwyn (IRE)**[159] 2442 4-9-4 71 ... HayleyTurner 3 61
(J G Given) *trckd ldrs on inner: hdwy 4f out: rdn along 3f out: drvn over 2f out and sn wknd* **4/1**[1]
0000 **9** 2 ¾ **Desert Vision**[11] 7014 5-8-2 62 ... (t) JamesPSullivan(7) 4 47
(M W Easterby) *midfield: effrt and sme hdwy on inner 4f out: rdn along 3f out and sn wknd* **10/1**
411 **10** 4 ½ **Miss Sophisticat**[3] 7204 3-9-2 78 6ex ... (v) AndrewHeffernan(5) 1 54
(W J Knight) *led: rdn along and hdd 3f out: sn wknd* **9/1**
0-00 **11** 6 **Along The Nile**[16] 6900 7-8-12 65 ... TomEaves 2 30
(K G Reveley) *dwlt: a in rr* **100/1**
5063 **12** 5 **Dubburg (USA)**[19] 6832 4-8-8 61 ... ChrisCatlin 6 16
(W J Musson) *a in rr* **8/1**[3]
0153 **13** ¾ **Applaude**[12] 6987 4-9-1 68 ... (b) RobertWinston 7 22
(R C Guest) *in tch: rdn along over 4f out: sn wknd* **14/1**
2m 17.69s (3.39) **Going Correction** +0.425s/f (Yiel)
WFA 3 from 4yo+ 4lb 13 Ran SP% **121.8**
Speed ratings (Par 103): **103,101,99,96,95 95,94,94,92,88 83,79,79**
toteswingers: 1&2 £25.40, 1&3 £10.80, 2&3 £25.70 CSF £117.39 CT £835.03 TOTE £8.30: £3.30, £5.40, £2.20; EX 131.60 Place 6: £87.09 Place 5: £13.08.
Owner B J Mould **Bred** Mme Catherine Auniac **Trained** Pandy, Monmouths

FOCUS
The winning time was 0.93 seconds slower than the first division and not a race to rate too positively with the runner-up the best guide. Once again they raced towards the stands' side in the straight.
Dream Of Olwyn(IRE) Official explanation: jockey said filly had no more to give
Applaude Official explanation: jockey said gelding had no more to give
T/Jkpt: Part won. £14,784.10 to a £1 stake. Pool: £20,822.70. 0.50 winning tickets. T/Plt: £94.00 to a £1 stake. Pool: £35,415.45. 275.03 winning tickets. T/Qpdt: £12.50 to a £1 stake. Pool: £3,590.76. 211.10 winning tickets. JR

7197 LINGFIELD (L-H)
Thursday, November 5

OFFICIAL GOING: Standard
Wind: Moderate, across towards stands Weather: Overcast

7250 SPARKLER APPRENTICE H'CAP — 1m 2f (P)
1:10 (1:10) (Class 6) (0-65,65) 3-Y-O+ — **£2,388** (£705; £352) **Stalls** Low

Form				RPR
3350	1		**Resentful Angel**[60] 5698 4-9-1 **60** ... TobyAtkinson(3) 10 (Pat Eddery) *trckd ldrs: effrt 2f out: rdn to ld over 1f out: hung rt after: a holding on* **11/4**[1]	68+
5052	2	¾	**Vinces**[30] 6566 5-9-9 **65** ... AshleyMorgan 6 (T D McCarthy) *dwlt: hld up in rr and racd wd: prog and wdst of all over 2f out: styd on to chse wnr ins fnl f: carried rt and nt qckn* **4/1**[2]	71
6310	3	¾	**Gifted Heir (IRE)**[15] 6945 5-9-0 **56** ... PaulPickard 3 (A Bailey) *hld up in rr: prog over 2f out: shkn up to dispute 2nd 1f out: nt qckn fnl f* **13/2**[3]	61
0050	4	1	**Sir Haydn**[64] 5577 9-8-4 **51** oh2 ... DannyBrock(5) 14 (J R Jenkins) *dwlt: hld up wl in rr: stl at bk of main gp 2f out: prog over 1f out: kpt on same pce fnl f* **25/1**	54
0100	5	nk	**Kings Topic (USA)**[27] 6640 9-9-9 **65** ... MartinLane 5 (A B Haynes) *hld up in midfield: prog on outer over 2f out: rdn to chse ldrs 1f out: no ex* **20/1**	67
520	6	3¾	**Fleur De'Lion (IRE)**[24] 6742 3-8-7 **56** ow2 ... LeeNewnes(3) 1 (S Kirk) *hld up towards rr on inner: shuffled along fr 2f out: kpt on one pce: nvr nr ldrs* **16/1**	51
0460	7	nk	**Phluke**[8] 7110 8-9-3 **59** ... SimonPearce 8 (Eve Johnson Houghton) *trckd ldrs: cl enough 2f out: nt qckn over 1f out: fdd* **17/2**	53
0-00	8	1¼	**Candilejas**[8] 7112 3-8-7 **58** ... (t) KierenFox(5) 7 (R J Smith) *prog fr midfield to go 3rd over 6f out: effrt to ld over 2f out: hdd & wknd over 1f out* **25/1**	50
3314	9	½	**Location**[7] 7142 3-8-11 **57** ... RichardEvans 2 (P D Evans) *hld up on inner: trapped bhd wall of rivals 2f out: nt clr run wl over 1f out: no ch to rcvr* **8/1**	48+
060	10	2¾	**Rosy Dawn**[22] 6770 4-8-4 **51** oh6 ... RyanClark(5) 9 (J J Bridger) *led to over 4f out: sn u.p: wknd 2f out* **33/1**	36
0-00	11	4½	**Julie Mill (IRE)**[42] 6223 3-8-2 **51** oh6 ... RosieJessop(3) 4 (R A Teal) *trckd ldr: led over 4f out to over 2f out: wknd rapidly* **100/1**	27
6006	12	1½	**Colangnik (USA)**[10] 7065 3-8-9 **60** ... (v[1]) RyanPowell(5) 12 (J R Best) *racd wd: trckd ldrs: effrt over 2f out: wknd rapidly over 1f out* **12/1**	33
00-0	13	1	**Elizabeth's Quest**[18] 6880 4-8-2 **51** oh6 ... (p) KevinLundie(7) 11 (Miss N A Lloyd-Beavis) *dwlt: rdn and losing tch in last 1/2-way: nvr a factor* **100/1**	22
000	14	11	**Innactualfact**[16] 6917 3-8-9 **55** ... (p) RossAtkinson 13 (L A Dace) *s.s: in tch in rr on outer: prog and wd 3f out: wknd rapidly 2f out: t.o* **20/1**	4

2m 6.88s (0.28) **Going Correction** +0.075s/f (Slow)
WFA 3 from 4yo+ 4lb — **14** Ran SP% **117.3**
Speed ratings (Par 101): **101,100,99,99,98 95,95,94,94,91 88,87,86,77**
toteswingers: 1&2 £4.80, 1&3 £5.80, 2&3 £4.60 CSF £11.48 CT £64.91 TOTE £3.70: £2.60, £1.90, £2.00; EX 15.40 Trifecta £114.10 Pool: £154.30 - 1.00 winning units..
Owner P J J Eddery, Mrs John Magnier, M Tabor **Bred** Patrick Eddery Ltd **Trained** Nether Winchendon, Bucks

FOCUS
A moderate handicap run at an ordinary pace, and straightforward form. These apprentices had not ridden more than 50 winners.
Vinces Official explanation: jockey said gelding was slowly away
Innactualfact Official explanation: jockey said filly was slowly away

7251 EASTWELL MANOR NOVICE STKS — 7f (P)
1:45 (1:46) (Class 4) 2-Y-O — **£3,885** (£1,156; £577; £288) **Stalls** Low

Form				RPR
1	1		**Sahara Kingdom (IRE)**[27] 6629 2-9-5 0 ... TedDurcan 2 (Saeed Bin Suroor) *dwlt but sn led: qcknd 2f out: pushed clr over 1f out: easily* **2/9**[1]	93+
3122	2	5	**Ongoodform (IRE)**[10] 7063 2-9-5 89 ... NCallan 1 (P W D'Arcy) *cl up in 3rd: rdn to chse wnr wl over 1f out: sn outpcd* **7/2**[2]	81
	3	1¼	**Slip Sliding Away (IRE)** 2-8-8 0 ... SteveDrowne 4 (J R Best) *dwlt: rn green in last: effrt on outer over 2f out: outpcd wl over 1f out: plugged on* **50/1**	66
1	4	1¼	**Bellini Rose (IRE)**[34] 6443 2-8-9 0 ... RichardKingscote 5 (Tom Dascombe) *mostly chsd wnr to wl over 1f out: wknd* **25/1**[3]	64

1m 26.75s (1.95) **Going Correction** +0.075s/f (Slow) — **4** Ran SP% **109.9**
Speed ratings (Par 98): **91,85,83,82**
CSF £1.39 TOTE £1.10; EX 1.60.
Owner Godolphin **Bred** John O'Connor **Trained** Newmarket, Suffolk

NOTEBOOK
Sahara Kingdom(IRE) ◆ didn't have to be fully extended to thrash an 89-rated rival, and this more than confirmed the promise he showed when winning over C&D on his debut. Sent to the front this time, he settled beautifully for Ted Durcan, going only a modest gallop early on, and once in the straight he extended in quite taking fashion without being seriously asked by his rider, who was instead taking several looks around for dangers. The winner is a horse with a lot of speed but may well get a little bit further and is yet another Godolphin-owned juvenile who looks capable of making it at pattern level as a 3-y-o. It remains to be seen what the plan is, but presumably he'll winter in Dubai, and perhaps his connections will be tempted to aim him at the UAE Triple Crown series considering the Tapeta surface at Meydan is probably not too dissimilar to Polytrack. (op 4-11 tchd 2-5 in places)
Ongoodform(IRE) is well regarded by Paul d'Arcy, who wants to aim him at next year's Free Handicap. He wasn't sure to get this trip on breeding, however, and despite running well, he didn't conclusively prove his stamina. (op 100-30 tchd 3-1 and 4-1)

Slip Sliding Away(IRE) ◆ was a bit buzzy in the preliminaries but this was a nice introduction. Having raced last of the four runners for much of the way after missing the break, he swung wide into the straight and was slightly outpaced before keeping on. This colt, who is out of a triple 6f-1m winner, looks a useful prospect and should be hard to beat if found an ordinary maiden next time. (op 40-1)
Bellini Rose(IRE) is a half-sister to a bumper winner, out of a mare who won over as far as 1m4f, but there's plenty of speed in her pedigree as well and her debut success at this track was gained over 5f. She was a bit too keen over this longer trip and failed to see her race out. (op 16-1)

7252 BETDAQ ON 0870 178 1221 H'CAP — 7f (P)
2:20 (2:20) (Class 3) (0-90,87) 3-Y-O+ — **£7,771** (£2,312; £1,155; £577) **Stalls** Low

Form				RPR
2331	1		**Hellbender (IRE)**[12] 7028 3-8-6 **76** ... LPKeniry 6 (S Kirk) *trckd ldng quartet: effrt 2f out: prog to ld 1f out: drvn out* **11/1**	86+
1362	2	nk	**Autumn Blades (IRE)**[14] 6976 4-8-8 **77** ... (p) DavidProbert 9 (A Bailey) *hld up in 6th: cruising bhd ldrs over 1f out: nt qckn whn asked for effrt 1f out: r.o w awkward hd carriage to take 2nd nr fin* **11/2**[3]	83
1220	3	nk	**Hightime Heroine (IRE)**[27] 6630 3-8-10 **80** ... JamieSpencer 7 (J Noseda) *trckd ldng trio: rdn to chal over 1f out: nt qckn u.p: chsd wnr ins fnl f: hld whn bmpd and lost 2nd nr fin* **9/2**[1]	85
3663	4	½	**Spitfire**[27] 6633 4-9-4 **87** ... FergusSweeney 4 (J R Jenkins) *hld up in 7th: effrt 2f out: styd on u.p fnl f: nt rch ldrs* **11/2**[3]	91
561	5	½	**Ravi River (IRE)**[27] 6630 5-8-11 **80** ... PatCosgrave 8 (J R Boyle) *chsd ldr: rdn to chal over 1f out: nt qckn and lost pls fnl f* **8/1**	82
3200	6	¾	**Fathsta (IRE)**[76] 5206 4-9-1 **87** ... MartinLane(3) 3 (D M Simcock) *taken down early: led to 1f out: edgd rt and wknd* **5/1**[2]	87
0550	7	nk	**Gallantry**[20] 6830 7-9-0 **83** ... IanMongan 10 (P Howling) *hld up in rr: last 2f out: sme prog over 1f out: reminder ins fnl f: kpt on: nvr nr ldrs* **11/1**	83+
0020	8	¾	**Trafalgar Square**[17] 6908 7-8-10 **79** ... HayleyTurner 5 (M J Attwater) *stdd s: hld up in last: rdn and effrt on outer 2f out: nt qckn over 1f out: kpt on* **8/1**	77+
0000	9	1	**Stevie Gee (IRE)**[10] 7060 5-8-13 **82** ... (b) StephenDonohoe 2 (Ian Williams) *chsd ldng pair on inner: rdn wl over 1f out: wknd fnl f* **16/1**	77
1600	10	2½	**Desert Dreamer (IRE)**[7] 7133 8-8-10 **84** ow1 ... RichardEvans(5) 1 (P D Evans) *taken down early: s.s: a in last trio: rdn and no prog over 2f out: wknd over 1f out* **25/1**	72

1m 24.2s (-0.60) **Going Correction** +0.075s/f (Slow)
WFA 3 from 4yo+ 1lb — **10** Ran SP% **114.2**
Speed ratings (Par 107): **106,105,105,104,104 103,102,102,100,98**
toteswingers: 1&2 £4.00, 2&3 £6.80, 1&3 not won. CSF £68.96 CT £314.77 TOTE £9.40: £3.00, £1.80, £1.80; EX 59.90 Trifecta £122.40 Pool: £488.31- 2.95 winning units..
Owner Mike Newbould **Bred** James Lombard **Trained** Upper Lambourn, Berks

FOCUS
A good handicap run at a fair pace. Prominent racers dominated and the runner-up is probably the best guide to the form. The winner is value for extra.

NOTEBOOK
Hellbender(IRE) ◆, 2lb higher than when dead-heating over 6f at Kempton on his previous start, looked set to follow up in decent style when picking up nicely around 1f out, but not for the first time he idled in front and only just held on. He seems to be thriving right now and his style of racing means he should stay ahead of the handicapper. (op 15-2)
Autumn Blades(IRE) was waited with until inside the final furlong, but once again he looked reluctant under pressure. He's simply not a win-only betting proposition. (op 7-1)
Hightime Heroine(IRE) was denied a clear run over C&D last time, but she was always well placed on this occasion and can have few excuses. She was held when short of room in the final strides. (tchd 5-1 in a place)
Spitfire ran on when switched inside around 1f out, but his head was again a bit high and he never looked like doing enough. (tchd 5-1)
Ravi River(IRE) was always well placed, but he proved unable to defy a 4lb higher mark than when winning over C&D on his previous start. (op 6-1)
Fathsta(IRE), off since being reported to have finished distressed at Chester in August when trained by David Nicholls, took them along but got tired in the straight and is entitled to come on for this. (op 8-1)

7253 BET BREEDERS CUP - BETDAQ H'CAP — 6f (P)
2:55 (2:56) (Class 4) (0-80,79) 3-Y-O+ — **£4,857** (£1,445; £722; £360) **Stalls** Low

Form				RPR
6046	1		**Ektimaal**[22] 6776 6-9-2 **77** ... HayleyTurner 10 (E A L Dunlop) *s.i.s: hld up in last pair and wl off the pce: stl only 9th 2f out: gd prog over 1f out: urged along and r.o fnl f to ld last 50yds* **11/2**[3]	86
5001	2	¾	**River Kirov (IRE)**[34] 6458 6-9-4 **79** ... SteveDrowne 5 (M Wigham) *hld up in midfield: effrt on outer wl over 1f out: r.o fnl f: tk 2nd nr fin: nt pce of wnr* **4/1**[2]	86
144	3	hd	**Cecily**[105] 4244 3-9-4 **79** ... (b[1]) SebSanders 12 (Sir Mark Prescott) *sn led at str pce and crossed fr wd draw: drvn over 1f out: hdd and fdd last 50yds* **12/1**	85
6610	4	1¼	**Evelyn May (IRE)**[47] 6118 3-9-3 **78** ... MichaelHills 7 (B W Hills) *prom: chsd ldr 1/2-way: rdn over 1f out: fdd ins fnl f* **8/1**	80
0425	5	1	**Cut The Cackle (IRE)**[45] 6167 3-8-11 **77** ... AshleyMorgan(5) 2 (P Winkworth) *pushed along in 8th early on and off the pce: shuffled along on outer and styd on fr over 1f out: nvr nr ldrs* **11/1**	76
4500	6	shd	**I Confess**[15] 6944 4-8-10 **76** ow1 ... (b) RichardEvans(5) 6 (P D Evans) *chsd ldr to 1/2-way: sn rdn: styd prom tl fdd fnl f* **10/3**[1]	75
1600	7	1¾	**Mutamared (USA)**[12] 7026 9-9-0 **75** ... (t) PatCosgrave 8 (M J Scudamore) *chsd ldrs: rdn over 2f out: nt qckn over 1f out: fdd* **12/1**	68
5106	8	1¼	**Comadoir (IRE)**[45] 6167 3-9-3 **78** ... FergusSweeney 3 (Miss Jo Crowley) *chsd ldrs: rdn 2f out: nt qckn over 1f out: grdually lost pl* **14/1**	67
2016	9	2½	**Dvinsky (USA)**[12] 7026 8-9-1 **76** ... (b) IanMongan 1 (P Howling) *chsd ldrs on inner: rdn over 2f out: grad fdd over 1f out* **8/1**	57
56	10	2¾	**White Shift (IRE)**[30] 6564 3-9-0 **75** ... PaulDoe 4 (P Howling) *a struggling in last trio: bhd fnl 2f* **25/1**	47
16/0	11	4	**Bold Alaska (IRE)**[185] 1731 6-9-3 **78** ... AdamKirby 9 (Peter Grayson) *s.i.s: a in last trio: keeping on but no ch whn lost action 150yds out: virtually p.u* **66/1**	67

1m 11.09s (-0.81) **Going Correction** +0.075s/f (Slow) — **11** Ran SP% **116.4**
Speed ratings (Par 105): **108,107,106,105,103 103,101,99,96,92 87**
toteswingers: 1&2 £8.80, 1&3 £11.40, 2&3 £4.80 CSF £27.45 CT £260.75 TOTE £7.90: £2.10, £1.80, £3.10; EX 49.80 Trifecta £195.00 Pool: £355.80 -1.35 winning units..
Owner The Serendipity Partnership **Bred** Whitsbury Manor Stud **Trained** Newmarket, Suffolk

FOCUS
A competitive sprint handicap and the only race on the card run in a time under standard. The winner's best effort of the year with the second to form.

Bold Alaska(IRE) Official explanation: vet said gelding returned lame

7254 BET EUROPA LEAGUE - BETDAQ MAIDEN STKS — 5f (P)

3:30 (3:31) (Class 5) 3-Y-0+ — **£2,729** (£806; £403) **Stalls High**

Form — RPR

2-00 **1** **Master Lightfoot**[16] 6916 3-9-3 73 ... AdamKirby 2 68+
(W R Swinburn) *led 1f: chsd ldr: lft in ld w decisive advantage wl over 1f out: rdn out* **1/1**[1]

643- **2** *1 ¾* **Ajjaadd (USA)**[364] 7214 3-9-3 76 ... SteveDrowne 9 61+
(T E Powell) *pressed ldrs on wd outside: 3rd whn carried v wd bnd 2f out: rdn to go 2nd jst over 1f out: no imp last 150yds* **4/1**[3]

0 **3** *1 ¼* **Across The Sands**[19] 6856 3-9-3 0 ... FrankieMcDonald 3 57
(C N Kellett) *s.i.s: hld up in 6th: outpcd 2f out: styd on to take 3rd ins fnl f: no threat* **66/1**

-5 **4** *¾* **Spinning Bailiwick**[66] 5541 3-8-12 42 ... FergusSweeney 5 49
(G L Moore) *pressed ldrs: outpcd fr 2f out: kpt on ins fnl f* **16/1**

0555 **5** *3 ¾* **Tightrope (IRE)**[38] 6335 3-9-3 44 ... (b) DavidProbert 7 41
(T D McCarthy) *pressed ldrs to 1/2-way: fdd over 1f out* **20/1**

0305 **6** *shd* **Quasi Congaree (GER)**[2] 7223 3-9-3 67 ... NCallan 8 40
(I A Wood) *led after 1f on outer: a l ahd whn hung bdly rt bnd 2f out: sn hdd: folded tamely* **11/4**[2]

6-00 **7** *4 ½* **Rightcar Dominic**[27] 6641 4-9-3 48 ... LPKeniry 1 24
(Peter Grayson) *pushed along in last trio after 2f: nvr on terms* **33/1**

0 **8** *7* **Riggs (IRE)**[62] 5645 3-9-3 0 ... (b[1]) JamieMackay 4 —
(Peter Grayson) *snatched up sn after s: a in last trio and nvr on terms: t.o* **100/1**

000 **9** *nk* **Dancing Again**[19] 6856 3-8-12 39 ... LiamJones 6 —
(E A Wheeler) *a in last trio and nvr on terms: t.o* **200/1**

58.72 secs (-0.08) **Going Correction** +0.075s/f (Slow) — **9** Ran SP% **113.2**
Speed ratings (Par 103): **103,100,98,97,91 90,83,72,71**
toteswingers: 1&2 £2.20, 1&3 £19.20, 2&3 £26.90 CSF £5.05 TOTE £1.90: £1.10, £1.20, £9.80; EX 6.70 Trifecta £250.20 Pool: £808.16 - 2.39 winning units..
Owner P W Harris & Miss V Palmer **Bred** Bottisham Heath Stud **Trained** Aldbury, Herts

FOCUS
A weak sprint maiden, best rated through the tird and fifth, and it is doubtful if the winner had to run to form.
Quasi Congaree(GER) Official explanation: jockey said colt hung badly right

7255 VINES BMW H'CAP — 2m (P)

4:00 (4:00) (Class 5) (0-70,68) 3-Y-0+ — **£2,590** (£770; £385; £192) **Stalls Low**

Form — RPR

0-40 **1** **Dubai Diva**[9] 7080 3-8-8 **60** ... JackMitchell(3) 5 70+
(C F Wall) *hld up bhd ldrs: decisive prog on outer to ld wl over 2f out and sn kicked 2 l clr: drvn out* **10/1**

643- **2** *1 ¼* **Whaxaar (IRE)**[399] 6421 5-9-1 **55** ... RobertHavlin 9 63+
(R Ingram) *stdd s: hld up in 7th: prog on wd outside over 2f out but sn outpcd: kpt on to take 2nd ins fnl f: clsd but unable to chal* **14/1**

413- **3** *¾* **L'Homme De Nuit (GER)**[235] 7515 5-10-0 **68** ... (tp) GeorgeBaker 8 73
(G L Moore) *s.v.s: hld up in last: prog on wd outside to dispute 2nd 2f out: outpcd and nt qckn: one pce after* **6/1**[3]

013 **4** *nse* **Calculating (IRE)**[90] 4742 5-9-2 **61** ... LeeNewnes(5) 6 66
(M D I Usher) *prom: disp 2nd 6f out: upsides 3f out: sn outpcd: one pce u.p after* **8/1**

6204 **5** *2* **Little Carmela**[25] 6704 5-9-4 **58** ... (p) SaleemGolam 2 62+
(S C Williams) *dwlt: hld up bhd ldrs: gng strly but nowhere to go as ldr wnt clr over 2f out: keeping on one pce whn no room again ins fnl f* **10/1**

124- **6** *9* **Weybridge Light**[46] 6146 4-9-13 **67** ... (b) JamieSpencer 7 59
(Eoin Griffin, Ire) *t.k.h early: prom: disp 2nd 6f out: upsides 3f out: wknd wl over 1f out* **5/1**[2]

0441 **7** *1* **Benozzo Gozzoli**[8] 7124 3-8-3 **52** 6ex ... NickyMackay 1 43
(H Morrison) *led: rdn over 3f out: hdd wl over 2f out: wknd rapidly over 1f out* **11/8**[1]

-006 **8** *25* **Yaldas Girl (USA)**[20] 6831 3-7-11 **49** ... AndreaAtzeni(3) 4 10
(J R Best) *t.k.h: trckd ldr to 6f out: sn pushed along: wknd rapidly 3f out: t.o* **66/1**

3m 26.19s (0.49) **Going Correction** +0.075s/f (Slow)
WFA 3 from 4yo+ 9lb — **8** Ran SP% **110.5**
Speed ratings (Par 103): **101,100,100,99,98 94,93,81**
toteswingers: 1&2 £16.40, 1&3 £9.80, 2&3 £6.20 CSF £126.74 CT £869.99 TOTE £12.90: £3.10, £4.00, £1.40; EX 133.90 Trifecta £473.30 Part won. Pool: £639.71 - 0.10 winning units. Place 6: £49.75 Place 5: £38.24.
Owner Peter Botham **Bred** Darley **Trained** Newmarket, Suffolk

FOCUS
A modest staying handicap run at an ordinary pace. The favourite disappointed but the form is reasonable for the grade.
Little Carmela Official explanation: jockey said mare was denied a clear run
Benozzo Gozzoli Official explanation: jockey said gelding ran too free
T/Plt: £113.30 to a £1 stake. Pool: £60,422.61. 389.10 winning tickets. T/Qpdt: £39.40 to a £1 stake. Pool: £4,808.55. 90.20 winning tickets. JN

7256 - 7257a (Foreign Racing) - See Raceform Interactive

7071 LEOPARDSTOWN (L-H)

Thursday, November 5

OFFICIAL GOING: Heavy

7258a IRISH STALLION FARMS EUROPEAN BREEDERS FUND PREMIER NURSERY H'CAP — 7f

1:05 (1:08) 2-Y-0 — **£21,489** (£6,304; £3,003; £1,023)

RPR

1 **Jamaayel**[32] 6514 2-8-0 77 ... (t) SHJames(7) 4 86
(Kevin Prendergast, Ire) *chsd ldrs: 4th 1/2-way: hdwy in 3rd 2f out: rdn over 1f out: styd on to ld last 150yds: kpt on wl: comf* **6/1**[3]

2 *3 ½* **Blaze Brightly (IRE)**[20] 6835 2-8-10 80 ... FMBerry 1 80
(Mrs John Harrington, Ire) *led and disp: rdn to ld 1 1/2f out: hdd last 150yds: no ex and kpt on same pce* **8/1**

3 *1 ¼* **Intapeace (IRE)**[27] 6652 2-8-11 86 ... DEMullins(5) 2 83
(Francis Ennis, Ire) *sn led and disp: rdn in 2nd 1 1/2f out: no ex ins fnl f and kpt on same pce* **6/1**[3]

4 *shd* **Smoky Cloud (IRE)**[10] 7074 2-7-13 74 oh1 ... BACurtis(5) 9 71
(W McCreery, Ire) *chsd ldrs: 5th 1/2-way: rdn into 4th 2f out: u.p in 5th 1 1/2f out: kpt on same pce fnl f* **9/1**

5 *hd* **Mark Twain (IRE)**[75] 5267 2-8-11 86 ... GFCarroll(5) 11 82
(D M Simcock) *chsd ldrs: 6th 1/2-way: hdwy in 4th 1 1/2f out: rdn and no ex 1f out: kpt on same pce fnl f* **4/1**[1]

6 *½* **Money Trader (IRE)**[18] 6883 2-8-10 80 ... CDHayes 8 75
(J T Gorman, Ire) *hld up towards rr: rdn into 8th 1 1/2f out: kpt on same pce fnl f* **12/1**

7 *1 ¼* **Knight Eagle (IRE)**[27] 6652 2-8-12 82 ... DPMcDonogh 6 74
(Kevin Prendergast, Ire) *mid-div: rdn in 7th 2f out: no imp in 6th 1f out: short of room and eased ins fnl f* **12/1**

8 *nk* **Harry Hunt**[13] 7011 2-8-4 74 oh3 ... (b) DJMoran 3 65
(Cecil Ross, Ire) *mid-div: 7th 1/2-way: rdn in 8th 2f out: 6th 1 1/2f out: no ex in 7th 1f out: kpt on one pce* **25/1**

9 *1 ¾* **Puncher Clynch (IRE)**[18] 6883 2-9-7 91 ... KJManning 7 78
(J S Bolger, Ire) *towards rr for most: nvr a factor* **5/1**[2]

10 *½* **Lil Ella (IRE)**[24] 6745 2-8-1 78 ... LFRoche(7) 12 63
(C Roche, Ire) *mid-div: rdn in 9th and no imp 2f out: kpt on one pce* **6/1**[3]

11 *11* **Cheval Rouge (IRE)**[79] 5140 2-8-1 74 oh3 ... (p) ShaneFoley(3) 10 32
(H Rogers, Ire) *chsd ldrs: 3rd 1/2-way: rdn and wknd 2f out* **16/1**

12 *½* **Dainty Steps (IRE)**[39] 6316 2-8-12 82 ... JAHeffernan 5 39
(John Joseph Murphy, Ire) *in rr of mid-div: rdn and no imp ent st* **25/1**

1m 33.84s (5.14) **Going Correction** +0.825s/f (Soft) — **12** Ran SP% **129.6**
Speed ratings: **103,99,97,97,97 96,95,94,92,92 79,79**
CSF £58.87 CT £252.04 TOTE £13.60: £3.90, £3.00, £2.90; DF 92.50.
Owner Hamdan Al Maktoum **Bred** Shadwell Estate Company Limite **Trained** Friarstown, Co Kildare

FOCUS
This back-end nursery looked an open affair on paper but it produced a facile winner in Jamaayel who pulled clear well inside the final furlong for her second successive win.

NOTEBOOK
Jamaayel had coped well previously on the Polytrack at Dundalk when scoring over a furlong shorter and she saw out this trip well in contrasting underfoot conditions. (op 7/1)
Blaze Brightly(IRE) made a bold bid to get off the mark contesting her first nursery. She had most of her rivals in trouble when she shrugged off third-placed Intapeace early in the straight but the winner was clearly different class when she arrived with her winning surge. On this evidence the runner-up should win a handicap for connections next year. (op 9/1)
Intapeace(IRE) held every chance rounding the home turn after racing prominently from the outset but this testing ground probably cost her in the end. She had shaped well previously on the all-weather at Dundalk and she's likely to return there with a live hope of getting her head in front for the second time. (op 6/1 tchd 13/2)
Smoky Cloud(IRE), a C&D winner on yielding ground last time, performed with credit considering the ground conditions were probably against him.
Mark Twain(IRE) was fancied to follow up his Cork maiden win over a furlong longer since moving from Ballydoyle. He raced close up but he struggled to raise his game when asked a serious question into the straight. He was 9lb higher since his Gowran Park runner-up finish in a similar contest in August and that burden on this extremely testing ground told in the closing stages. (op 11/2)
Money Trader(IRE) had hinted at some ability off this mark in the Birdcatcher. He was held up before making some headway into the straight but he never looked like getting involved at the business end.
Knight Eagle(IRE), stable companion of the winner, didn't enjoy the clearest of runs in the straight.
Puncher Clynch(IRE) was expected to improve on his Birdcatcher midfield finish last time over 6f but he never got involved. (op 4/1)

7263a RAVENS ROCK H'CAP — 1m 4f

3:55 (3:55) 3-Y-0+ — **£13,588** (£3,986; £1,899; £647)

RPR

1 **Casual**[80] 5116 3-9-6 90 ... (b) PJSmullen 2 98+
(D K Weld, Ire) *hld up towards rr: hdwy in 9th 5f out: 5th 3f out: impr to chal 1 1/2f out: led under 1f out: kpt on wl fnl f* **7/1**[3]

2 *1 ¾* **Tarkari (IRE)**[52] 3991 4-8-8 77 ... GFCarroll(5) 5 81
(W P Mullins, Ire) *chsd ldrs early: 8th 1/2-way: hdwy in 6th 2f out: rdn into 3rd 1 1/2f out: kpt on fnl f to 2nd cl home* **7/1**[3]

3 *nk* **Dafarabad (IRE)**[22] 6263 7-9-1 79 ... NGMcCullagh 13 83
(Niall Madden, Ire) *chsd ldrs: 6th 1/2-way: hdwy in 4th 3f out: rdn to ld 1 1/2f out: hdd under 1f out: no ex ins fnl f: lost 2nd cl home* **20/1**

4 *1 ¾* **Silent Decision (USA)**[10] 7078 3-8-12 82 ... (tp) KJManning 8 83
(J S Bolger, Ire) *chsd ldrs: 7th 1/2-way: rdn in 8th 3f out: styd on to 5th 1f out: kpt on same pce fnl f* **7/1**[3]

5 *2* **Concrete And Clay**[10] 7078 5-8-1 68 ... (p) ShaneFoley(3) 11 66
(Charles O'Brien, Ire) *in rr of mid-div: rdn in 11th 3f out: 9th 2f out: kpt on same pce fr over 1f out* **14/1**

6 *4* **Noble Galileo (IRE)**[11] 7043 3-9-9 93 ... FMBerry 12 84
(John M Oxx, Ire) *chsd ldr in 2nd: rdn in 4th 1 1/2f out: no ex 1f out: kpt on same pce fnl f* **6/1**[1]

7 *7* **Tin Town Boy (IRE)**[11] 7043 8-9-0 85 ... (t) DCByrne(7) 7 65
(H Rogers, Ire) *hld up towards rr: hdwy to 7th 2f out: rdn and no imp 1 1/2f out: kpt on same pce* **14/1**

8 *½* **Citizenship**[11] 7043 3-8-8 78 ... (t) JohnEgan 3 57
(Ian Williams) *chsd ldrs: 4th 1/2-way: rdn in 5th 2f out: no ex and kpt on one pce* **8/1**

9 *2 ½* **Loch Long (IRE)**[33] 6502 3-9-7 96 ... DEMullins(5) 4 71
(Tracey Collins, Ire) *led: rdn and hdd 1 1/2f out: no ex and wknd over 1f out* **10/1**

10 *26* **Burning Sky**[15] 6958 4-8-11 75 ... DPMcDonogh 9 9
(Charles O'Brien, Ire) *a towards rr: eased over 1f out: t.o* **16/1**

11 *5* **Miss Fancy Pants**[18] 6885 5-9-8 86 ... (t) KLatham 10 12
(Noel Meade, Ire) *mid-div early: 5th 1/2-way: rdn and wknd 3f out: eased over 1f out: t.o* **13/2**[2]

12 *1 ¾* **Mutadarek**[46] 6146 8-9-6 84 ... (p) CDHayes 1 7
(Ms Joanna Morgan, Ire) *a towards rr: trailing st: eased over 1f out: t.o* **10/1**

13 *½* **Erdiyna (IRE)**[18] 6885 3-9-6 90 ... MJKinane 6 12
(John M Oxx, Ire) *chsd ldrs: 3rd 1/2-way: wknd 3f out: eased over 1f out: t.o* **6/1**[1]

2m 46.44s (11.14) **Going Correction** +0.825s/f (Soft)
WFA 3 from 4yo+ 6lb — **13** Ran SP% **132.7**
Speed ratings: **95,93,93,92,91 88,83,83,81,64 61,59,59**
CSF £61.92 CT £982.99 TOTE £9.20: £1.50, £4.80, £10.60; DF 91.70.
Owner K Abdulla **Bred** Juddmonte Farms **Trained** The Curragh, Co Kildare

FOCUS
The runner-up has been rated back to his best, with the progressive winner and fourth rated as posting personal bests.

NOTEBOOK
Casual handled summer soft ground when she won over a furlong longer at Killarney in July and she coped with these more testing conditions to record her third career win. She was helped in no uncertain terms by Pat Smullen, who produced a power-packed drive to force the daughter of Nayef to get her head in front inside the final furlong. She was tackling this longer trip for the first time and she saw it out well.

Tarkari(IRE) had every chance when they turned for home but the winner pulled out more under pressure inside the final furlong. He showed enough to suggest he can win a similar contest next year when he encounters these favoured underfoot conditions and could well be winning again over jumps before long.
Dafarabad(IRE) ran creditably considering ground conditions were all against him. He held every chance passing the 2f pole but the ground began to take its toll and he soon had no more to offer. He could well be knocking on the door when he goes back on the all-weather at Dundalk, where he won in September. (op 14/1)
Silent Decision(USA) couldn't raise her game in the straight on this ground tackling this longer journey for the third time in her career. She scored here last month over 2f shorter and should be more effective when she encounters a better surface.
Concrete And Clay performed best of the Charles O'Brien pair after staying on from off the pace.
Noble Galileo(IRE) couldn't quicken after holding every chance into the straight. (op 7/1)
Citizenship, who had finished behind Noble Galileo last time on similar ground, was sending out distress signals rounding the home turn. (op 9/1 tchd 10/1)
Loch Long(IRE) led for a long way but dropped away under his big weight. (op 12/1)
Miss Fancy Pants couldn't go on the ground when asked to close. (op 7/1)
Mutadarek failed to cope with this ground.
Erdiyna(IRE) dropped right away when the race began to take shape on the turn for home. (op 11/2 tchd 5/1)
T/Jkpt: Not won. T/Plt: @19.60 Pool of @9,844.00 -375.19 winning units. II

7259 - 7263a (Foreign Racing) - See Raceform Interactive

BORDEAUX LE BOUSCAT (R-H)

Thursday, November 5

OFFICIAL GOING: Heavy

7264a PRIX PHILIPPE DU VIVIER (MAIDEN) (C&G) 1m

11:15 (11:16) 2-Y-O **£6,796** (£2,718; £2,039; £1,359; £680)

RPR

1 **Amagansett (USA)** 2-9-2 IMendizabal 83
(J-C Rouget, France)

2 1 ½ **Nova Med (IRE)** 2-9-2 JGrosjean 80
(Y Durepaire, Spain)

3 hd **Fairly Dancer (FR)** 2-9-2 RCMontenegro 80
(J-L Maroto-Abascal, France)

4 hd **Vermentino (FR)** 2-9-2 79
(M Roussel, France)

5 4 **Ardennes (FR)** 2-9-2 70
(D Henderson, France)

6 2 **Mister Camilau (FR)** 2-9-2 (b) 66
(Mlle A Imaz-Ceca, France)

7 nk **Thyan (FR)** 2-9-2 65
(C Baillet, France)

8 nk **Kalimutxo (FR)** 2-9-2 65
(R Avial Lopez, Spain)

9 1 **Isma'First (FR)** 2-9-2 62
(Mme C Dufreche, France)

10 4 **Chapi Chapo (FR)**[47] 6131 2-9-2 54
(B De Montzey, France)

0 **Escape To Freedom (IRE)**[14] 6979 2-9-2 ABourgeais —
(E J O'Neill) *immediately pushed along: last thrght: t.o fnl 1 1/2f* **80/1**[1]

0 **Sign Of Oasics (IRE)** 2-9-2 —
(F Rohaut, France)

0 **Sunny King (FR)** 2-9-2 —
(T Lemer, France)

1m 45.09s (105.09) **13** Ran SP% **1.2**
PARI-MUTUEL (including 1 Euro stake): WIN 2.30; PL 1.30, 1.40, 2.10;DF 6.00.
Owner J Allen **Bred** J Allen **Trained** Pau, France

7265a PRIX JEAN CRUSE 6f

12:50 (12:49) 3-Y-O+ **£10,680** (£4,272; £3,204; £2,136; £1,068)

RPR

1 **Salpado (FR)**[102] 3-8-13 CNora 96
(R Martin Sanchez, Spain)

2 ¾ **Moscow Eight (IRE)**[4] 7216 3-8-11 ABourgeais 92
(E J O'Neill) *disp 2nd on outside: led under 2f out: hrd rdn over 1f out: hdd and no ex fnl 50yds* **33/10**[1]

3 hd **White Spire (FR)**[56] 4-8-10 F-XBertras 90
(F Rohaut, France)

4 2 ½ **Rubirosa (IRE)**[30] 4-9-4 90
(C Alonso Pena, Spain)

5 1 ½ **Starmendi (FR)**[545] 4-8-8 75
(P Lhoste, Germany)

6 snk **Alta Luna (FR)**[98] 3-9-0 81
(J-C Rouget, France)

7 10 **Sindjil Mountain**[238] 6-8-11 (p) 46
(Mlle C Nicot, France)

1m 21.01s (81.01) **7** Ran SP% **23.3**
PARI-MUTUEL: WIN 7.10; PL 2.90, 2.30; SF 29.50.
Owner Marquesa De Villatoya **Bred** Eric Puerari & Oceanic Bloodstock **Trained** Spain

7087 SOUTHWELL (L-H)

Friday, November 6

OFFICIAL GOING: Standard
Wind: light 1/2 against Weather: dull, light rain last 2 races

7266 BETDAQ.CO.UK MAIDEN STKS 1m (F)

1:00 (1:00) (Class 5) 2-Y-O **£2,914** (£867; £433; £216) **Stalls** Low

Form RPR

20 1 **Judiciary (IRE)**[21] 6810 2-9-3 0 TedDurcan 3 76
(Saeed Bin Suroor) *drvn to sn ld: narrowly hdd appr fnl f: kpt on to ld fnl strides* **5/6**[1]

2656 2 hd **Comradeship (IRE)**[10] 7099 2-9-3 75 (b¹) RobertHavlin 12 76
(J H M Gosden) *trckd ldrs: chal on bit over 2f out: hung lft and slt ld appr fnl f: hdd towards fin* **6/1**[3]

3 8 **Con Artist (IRE)** 2-9-3 0 DO'Donohoe 2 58
(Saeed Bin Suroor) *s.i.s: sn chsng ldrs: one pce whn eased ins fnl f* **8/1**

00 4 9 **Jinto**[5] 7199 2-9-3 0 HayleyTurner 8 39
(R M H Cowell) *t.k.h on outer: outpcd and lost pl over 3f out: no ch after* **33/1**

0 5 ½ **Always Roses**[32] 6533 2-8-12 0 LPKeniry 9 33
(C C Bealby) *chsd ldrs: lost pl over 3f out: no threat after* **150/1**

40 6 shd **Domination**[13] 7034 2-9-3 0 SteveDrowne 4 37
(H Morrison) *in rr and sn drvn along: n.m.r over 3f out: hung lft: nvr a factor* **7/2**[2]

7 4 **Budva** 2-9-3 0 TravisBlock 6 28
(H Morrison) *s.s: sme hdwy over 2f out: nvr nr ldrs* **14/1**

00 8 nk **Bona Fortuna**[7] 7157 2-9-3 0 SebSanders 11 28
(Sir Mark Prescott) *led early: chsd ldrs: lost pl over 3f out* **100/1**

00 9 19 **Tantsor (FR)**[24] 6763 2-8-12 0 PaulPickard(5) 7 —
(P T Midgley) *in rr: sn drvn along: lost pl over 4f out: sn bhd: t.o* **100/1**

0 10 3 ¾ **Red Valerian Two (IRE)**[19] 6874 2-9-3 0 PaulMulrennan 1 —
(P T Midgley) *chsd ldrs: losing pl whn hmpd on ins over43f out: sn bhd: t.o* **150/1**

1m 42.28s (-1.42) **Going Correction** -0.175s/f (Stan) **10** Ran SP% **115.1**
Speed ratings (Par 96): **100,99,91,82,82 82,78,77,58,55**
toteswingers: 1&2 £2.70, 1&3 £2.40, 2&3 £5.60 CSF £6.38 TOTE £1.60: £1.10, £1.70, £1.80; EX 8.60 Trifecta £19.50 Pool: £260.95 - 9.87 winning units..
Owner Godolphin **Bred** Irish National Stud **Trained** Newmarket, Suffolk

FOCUS
A poor maiden, containing plenty of dead wood, in which the front three had pulled right away from their rivals passing the 3f pole. Very few ever got into this and the form looks moderate.

NOTEBOOK
Judiciary(IRE), a disappointing second favourite at Newmarket last time after showing promise on his Newcastle debut, was given a positive ride on this switch to sand. However, he looked to be getting the worse of the argument over the last couple of furlongs and it was only because he was up against a very reluctant rival in the battle to the line that he was able to snatch the race from the fire. He will need to improve plenty if he is to win again, though. (op 11-10 tchd 6-5)
Comradeship(IRE) was making his sand debut in first-time blinkers having not looked progressive on turf, but his half-brother Foolin Myself took very well to this surface at the first time of asking. For most of the home straight it looked like he would collect on his Fibresand debut too, as he was travelling much better than the favourite, but once inside the last furlong he looked reluctant, hung to his right, and basically threw it away. He can't be trusted after this. (op 9-2)
Con Artist(IRE), a 75,000gns 2y-o and half-brother to a couple of winners on the continent, was close enough turning in but he stuck to the inside rail and was soon left well behind by the front pair. He doesn't look one of the stable's best juveniles by any means. (op 6-1 tchd 5-1)
Jinto now gets a nursery mark, although it will need to be a modest one if he is to come close to winning a race. (tchd 28-1)
Domination Official explanation: jockey said colt hung left
Budva missed the break and looked inexperienced, but did show a little ability mid-race. A half-brother to several winners including the top-class Strategic Choice, he will probably do much better over further in due course. (op 16-1)

7267 SOUTHWELL GOLF CLUB JUNIOR MEMBERS NURSERY 1m (F)

1:30 (1:30) (Class 4) (0-85,79) 2-Y-O **£6,152** (£1,830; £914; £456) **Stalls** Low

Form RPR

0403 1 **Tres Coronas (IRE)**[18] 6901 2-9-2 74 (b¹) PhillipMakin 1 83+
(T D Barron) *mde all: rdn over 1f out: styd on wl: eased towards fin* **9/2**[2]

536 2 4 ½ **Cornish Beau (IRE)**[63] 5627 2-8-9 67 JimmyQuinn 2 66
(M H Tompkins) *sn pushed along in rr: hdwy to chse ldrs after 3f: hrd drvn 3f out: kpt on one pce: tk 2nd nr fin* **13/2**[3]

5151 3 nk **Agony And Ecstasy**[25] 6735 2-9-7 79 (p) SebSanders 3 77
(R M Beckett) *chsd wnr: reminders over 3f out: one pce fnl 2f* **9/2**[2]

003 4 9 **High On A Hill (IRE)**[25] 6728 2-8-10 73 LeeNewnes(5) 5 52
(S Kirk) *in rr and sn drvn along: reminders over 4f out: edgd rt over 1f out: sn bhd* **14/1**

1 5 2 ¾ **Tertiary (USA)**[15] 6965 2-9-4 76 TedDurcan 4 48
(Saeed Bin Suroor) *awkward exit fr stalls and lost grnd: sn trcking ldrs: outrpced and hung lft over 2f out: sn btn: eased ins fnl f* **10/11**[1]

1m 42.2s (-1.50) **Going Correction** -0.175s/f (Stan) **5** Ran SP% **108.7**
Speed ratings (Par 98): **100,95,95,86,83**
CSF £29.84 TOTE £7.00: £2.50, £4.00; EX 39.90.
Owner J Cringan & D Pryde **Bred** Denis McDonnell **Trained** Maunby, N Yorks

FOCUS
The pace seemed solid in this and the winning time was fractionally faster than the maiden.

NOTEBOOK
Tres Coronas(IRE), the most experienced in the field and making his sand debut, had blinkers on for the first time and was well backed against the favourite. Sent straight to the front, he saw off his challengers in gritty style and the race was safely in the bag coming to the last furlong. He seemed to relish the surface and looks well worth returning here, but much depends on whether the headgear will work again. (op 7-1 tchd 15-2)
Cornish Beau(IRE), making his sand and nursery debut after showing ability in three turf maidens, had taken a keen hold in his last two starts but he appeared to settle better off the pace here. He moved into contention on the inside rounding the home bend and, although he lacked the pace to get to the winner, kept plugging away to grab second. (op 8-1)
Agony And Ecstasy, 4lb higher than when scraping home over a similar trip in a Windsor nursery last month and with cheekpieces on for the first time, is a dual winner on soft ground and her sire has a decent record with his offspring on Fibresand, so she had lots going for her. However, she had made all in gaining her two victories and the winner denied her that role here. She did her best even after receiving reminders at halfway, but couldn't find a change of gear when it was needed. (tchd 5-1)
High On A Hill(IRE), making his nursery debut after putting up a much-improved effort when third at 100-1 in a soft-ground maiden on turf last month, was off the bridle and going nowhere before halfway. (op 12-1)
Tertiary(USA) was something of an unknown quantity having narrowly won a Brighton maiden on his debut last month. Following a very awkward start, he was soon back in touch but once he came seriously off the bridle passing the 3f pole, the writing was soon on the wall. Official explanation: jockey said colt never travelled (op 8-11)

7268 BET MULTIPLES-BETDAQ CLAIMING STKS 5f (F)

2:00 (2:00) (Class 6) 2-Y-O **£2,047** (£604; £302) **Stalls** High

Form RPR

2011 1 **Angie's Nap (USA)**[10] 7089 2-7-11 61 (p) AndreaAtzeni(3) 5 59+
(P S McEntee) *w ldrs: led appr fnl f: kpt on wl* **11/10**[1]

4000 2 1 **Thewinnatakesitall**[11] 7056 2-7-12 56 ow4 (p) SophieDoyle(5) 3 58
(H J Evans) *sltly hmpd s: sn chsng ldrs: hung lft over 1f out: no ex ins fnl f* **50/1**

0640 3 1 **Point To Prove**[2] 7242 2-8-4 62 (e¹) HayleyTurner 2 56
(Miss Amy Weaver) *swvd rt s: sn w ldrs on outside: rdn over 2f out: kpt on same pce fnl f* **5/1**[3]

4444 4 1 **Yeadon**[34] 6494 2-8-8 66 (b¹) FrederikTylicki 6 56
(R A Fahey) *trckd ldrs: chal over 2f out: rdn over 1f out: sn wknd* **5/2**[2]

050 **5** *1* **The Two G'S**^{29} 6610 2-7-13 62 .... LukeMorris 1 44
(P D Evans) *led tl hdd appr fnl f: wknd ins fnl f* **20/1**

1360 **6** *5* **Watch Chain (IRE)**^{36} 6418 2-8-7 60 .... AshleyMorgan$^{(5)}$ 7 39
(M H Tompkins) *dwlt: outpcd and lost pl over 2f out* **10/1**

60.51 secs (0.81) **Going Correction** 0.0s/f (Stan) **6** Ran SP% **108.7**
Speed ratings (Par 94): **93,91,89,88,86 78**
toteswingers: 1&2 £6.60, 1&3 £1.70, 2&3 £10.30 CSF £46.44 TOTE £2.00: £1.30, £6.70; EX 35.10 Trifecta £189.90 Pool: £385.00 - 1.50 winning units..
Owner Eventmaker Racehorses **Bred** James Millar & Janice Millar **Trained** Newmarket, Suffolk
■ Stewards' Enquiry : Luke Morris caution: used whip down shoulder in the forehand.

FOCUS
A moderate claimer and five of the six runners were in a line across the track a furlong from home.

NOTEBOOK
Angie's Nap(USA), bidding for a course hat-trick after wins here over 5f and 6f, was prominent from the off but looked just about the first beaten when coming off the bridle at halfway. However, with her stamina not in question she forged her way to the front over a furlong from home and saw it out well. She looks well worth persevering with in modest company on this surface. (op 10-11)
Thewinnatakesitall, making her Fibresand debut and trying the minimum trip for the first time on her seventh outing, had cheekpieces on for the first time. Held up off the pace after getting a bump leaving the stalls, she looked a possible winner when produced between rivals over a furlong from home, but she was never quite doing enough. She may be worth a try over an extra furlong back here. (op 33-1)
Point To Prove, runner-up a couple of times on Polytrack and turf, was making a quick return after disappointing in a first-time eyeshield in soft ground at Nottingham two days earlier. He looked dangerous when produced with his effort towards the far side of the field coming to the last furlong, but lacked a decisive turn of foot. (op 13-2 tchd 9-2)
Yeadon, in the frame in all seven previous starts but a beaten favourite four times including once over C&D, had blinkers on for the first time and he ran fast towards the nearside of the leaders for a long way, but again failed to go through with it. He looks one to avoid. (op 7-2 tchd 4-1)
The Two G'S, unplaced in all four of her previous starts, was nonetheless best in on adjusted official ratings and she had shown decent early speed in her races. She was soon bowling along in front here too, but didn't get home and she may be a short runner. (op 16-1)
Watch Chain(IRE), winner of a C&D nursery in August in his only previous try here, was 12lb worse off with runner-up Angie's Nap and he proved very easy to back. Soon in last place, he tried to make his effort closest to the stands' rail but never got into it. (op 13-2 tchd 11-1)

7269 CARLSBERG H'CAP 5f (F)
2:30 (2:30) (Class 4) (0-80,80) 3-Y-O+ **£5,828** (£1,734; £866; £432) **Stalls** High

Form RPR

620 **1** **Lesley's Choice**^{19} 6879 3-9-1 77 ....(v^{1}) FrankieMcDonald 5 93
(R Curtis) *w ldr: led 3f out: styd on strly fnl f* **5/1**^{2}

4521 **2** *2* **Solemn**^{22} 6799 4-8-10 72 ....(b) DavidProbert 3 81
(J M Bradley) *chsd ldrs: kpt on same pce ins fnl f* **11/2**^{3}

0400 **3** *¾* **Argentine (IRE)**^{18} 6897 5-9-0 76 ....(b) SteveDrowne 8 82
(J A McShane) *in rr: hdwy over 3f out: chsng ldrs over 1f out: hung lft: kpt on same pce* **20/1**

2261 **4** *nk* **Feelin Foxy**^{22} 6801 5-9-4 80 .... AlanMunro 10 85
(J G Given) *chsd ldrs: kpt on fnl f* **9/1**

3026 **5** *3¼* **Legal Eagle (IRE)**^{20} 6843 4-9-2 78 .... AdrianTNicholls 4 71
(Paul Green) *chsd ldrs: edgd rt and fdd appr fnl f* **6/1**

0224 **6** *shd* **Figaro Flyer (IRE)**^{28} 6635 6-8-8 70 .... JimmyQuinn 2 63
(P Howling) *chsd ldrs: hung rt and wknd appr fnl f* **4/1**^{1}

6033 **7** *1¾* **Lucky Art (USA)**^{10} 7082 3-8-10 72 .... AndrewElliott 1 59
(Mrs R A Carr) *chsd ldrs: hung rt and wknd over 1f out* **12/1**

-040 **8** *nk* **Priti Fabulous (IRE)**^{149} 2828 4-8-9 78 .... DeclanCannon$^{(7)}$ 6 64
(A J McCabe) *s.i.s: sn outpcd and in rr: kpt on fnl 2f: nvr on terms* **33/1**

-035 **9** *½* **Danum Dancer**^{19} 6877 5-8-4 66 oh4 .... LukeMorris 9 50
(N Bycroft) *sn in rr* **18/1**

0601 **10** *¾* **Colorus (IRE)**^{19} 6877 6-8-5 72 ....(p) PaulPickard$^{(5)}$ 12 53
(W J H Ratcliffe) *dwlt: nvr on terms* **9/1**

1550 **11** *½* **Revue Princess (IRE)**^{10} 7086 4-8-4 66 oh1 ....(b) DuranFentiman 13 45
(T D Easterby) *sn outpcd and in rr* **50/1**

5203 **12** *30* **Tartatartufata**^{10} 7086 7-8-11 73 ....(v) FrederikTylicki 7 —
(J G Given) *had nose stuck between bars in gate: gate bounced bk and hopelessly lft: virtually tk no part: hacked up t.o* **8/1**

58.85 secs (-0.85) **Going Correction** 0.0s/f (Stan) **12** Ran SP% **120.1**
Speed ratings (Par 105): **106,102,101,101,95 95,92,92,91,90 89,41**
toteswingers: 1&2 £7.90, 1&3 £24.10, 2&3 £24.70 CSF £32.53 CT £522.46 TOTE £7.80: £2.60, £1.70, £5.50; EX 53.00 TRIFECTA Not won..
Owner B C Allen **Bred** B C Allen **Trained** Lambourn, Berks

FOCUS
A competitive sprint handicap and yet again the centre of the track was the place to be. The ability to race handily over this straight 5f was also a major asset as usual. Sound form, with a clear personal best from the winner.
Figaro Flyer(IRE) Official explanation: jockey said gelding hung right
Priti Fabulous(IRE) Official explanation: jockey said filly was outpaced early
Tartatartufata Official explanation: jockey said mare got its nose stuck in the left-hand gate causing both gates to open unevenly.

7270 BET BREEDERS CUP-BETDAQ MAIDEN STKS 6f (F)
3:00 (3:00) (Class 5) 3-4-Y-O **£3,070** (£906; £453) **Stalls** Low

Form RPR

0342 **1** **Ponting (IRE)**^{32} 6551 3-9-3 73 .... SebSanders 5 63
(R M Beckett) *mde all: rdn and hung lft 2f out: kpt on* **4/7**^{1}

3350 **2** *1½* **Catchpenny**^{19} 6880 3-8-12 49 ....(p) NCallan 4 53
(K A Ryan) *sn drvn along and in rr: hung rt bnd over 4f out: hdwy over 2f out: hung lft and styd on over 1f out: tk 2nd nr fin* **18/1**

4340 **3** *shd* **Verinco**^{14} 6988 3-9-3 63 ....(p) TomEaves 7 58
(B Smart) *sn chsng ldrs: styd on same pce fnl f* **9/2**^{2}

030 **4** *½* **Sweet Kiss (USA)**^{18} 6904 4-8-12 44 .... LiamJones 11 51
(M J Attwater) *sn in rr: hdwy over 3f out: hung lft and styd on fnl f* **25/1**

0400 **5** *1* **Pocket's Pick (IRE)**^{52} 5968 3-9-3 61 ....(p) GeorgeBaker 1 53
(G L Moore) *dwlt: sn chsng ldrs: one pce fnl 2f* **8/1**^{3}

0000 **6** *7* **Shining Times (IRE)**^{40} 6308 3-8-12 43 .... TonyHamilton 2 25
(P T Midgley) *chsd ldrs: hung lft and lost pl over 2f out* **66/1**

606 **7** *1* **Inthawain**^{40} 6308 3-8-12 57 .... DuranFentiman 9 22
(N Wilson) *in tch: outpcd over 3f out: wknd 2f out* **12/1**

-000 **8** *1¼* **Valentine Bay**^{16} 6950 3-8-12 35 ....(b) MickyFenton 3 18
(M Mullineaux) *in tch: drvn over 3f out: wknd over 2f out* **100/1**

0006 **9** *6* **Dolly No Hair**^{19} 6880 4-9-3 44 ....(bt^{1}) DanielTudhope 8 4
(N Wilson) *sn in rr on outer: bhd fnl 4f* **50/1**

3000 **10** *29* **Beaux Yeux**^{53} 5954 3-8-7 50 .... AnnStokell$^{(5)}$ 6 —
(Miss A Stokell) *s.i.s: sn bhd: reminders over 4f out: sn t.o* **33/1**

1m 16.73s (0.23) **Going Correction** -0.175s/f (Stan) **10** Ran SP% **117.1**
Speed ratings (Par 103): **91,89,88,88,86 77,76,74,66,27**
toteswingers: 1&2 £3.80, 1&3 £3.00, 2&3 £4.70 CSF £13.43 TOTE £1.50: £1.10, £2.20, £1.70; EX 10.80 Trifecta £34.00 Pool: £484.33 - 10.52 winning units..
Owner Mrs Ralph Beckett **Bred** John McEnery **Trained** Whitsbury, Hants

FOCUS
Not a race that will live long in the memory as this lot had managed to avoid winning after 114 attempts between them. The front five pulled clear. Very modest form, and the winner did not need to match her previous Windsor level.
Sweet Kiss(USA) Official explanation: jockey said filly hung left
Pocket's Pick(IRE) Official explanation: jockey said gelding did not handle the bend
Beaux Yeux Official explanation: jockey said filly resented kickback early stages

7271 MEMBERSHIP OF SOUTHWELL GOLF CLUB H'CAP 1m (F)
3:30 (3:30) (Class 4) (0-85,85) 3-Y-O+ **£6,152** (£1,830; £914; £456) **Stalls** Low

Form RPR

3152 **1** **Salerosa (IRE)**^{10} 7092 4-8-6 71 oh2 .... JimmyQuinn 5 82+
(Mrs A Duffield) *t.k.h in rr: hdwy and nt clr run over 2f out: swtchd ins: chal on bit over 1f out: shkn up to ld jst ins fnl f: rdn and r.o* **4/1**^{1}

0145 **2** *1* **Mcconnell (USA)**^{16} 6946 4-9-3 82 .... GeorgeBaker 1 91
(G L Moore) *hld up in rr: hdwy over 3f out: led over 1f out: hdd and no ex ins fnl f* **9/2**^{2}

3300 **3** *3½* **Avertis**^{6} 7194 4-9-0 79 ....(t) MickyFenton 3 80
(Stef Liddiard) *led tl over 1f out: kpt on same pce: snatched modest 3rd nr line* **5/1**^{3}

0150 **4** *hd* **Mount Hadley (USA)**^{36} 6429 5-9-6 85 .... FrederikTylicki 9 85
(G A Butler) *trckd ldrs on outer: rdn over 1f out: fdd ins fnl f* **5/1**^{3}

0015 **5** *7* **Highly Regal (IRE)**^{16} 6944 4-9-4 83 ....(b) LPKeniry 4 67
(R A Teal) *trckd ldrs: effrt over 2f out: hung lft and wknd over 1f out* **13/2**

0003 **6** *½* **Hilbre Court (USA)**^{16} 6946 4-8-6 71 .... HayleyTurner 8 54
(B P J Baugh) *w ldrs on outer: wknd over 1f out* **11/2**

3000 **7** *3* **Salient**^{8} 7133 5-9-1 80 .... LiamJones 6 56
(M J Attwater) *w ldrs: sn drvn along: lost pl over 2f out* **16/1**

4340 **8** *3¼* **Swiss Art (IRE)**^{16} 6946 3-8-5 72 .... AndrewElliott 2 41
(Mrs R A Carr) *s.i.s: sn w ldrs: lost pl 2f out* **25/1**

4660 **9** *29* **Hurlingham**^{28} 6648 5-9-1 80 ....(p) PaulMulrennan 7 —
(M W Easterby) *sn chsng ldrs: hung rt bnd and lost pl over 3f out: sn bhd: t.o* **25/1**

1m 41.22s (-2.48) **Going Correction** -0.175s/f (Stan)
WFA 3 from 4yo+ 2lb **9** Ran SP% **113.8**
Speed ratings (Par 105): **105,104,100,100,93 92,89,86,57**
toteswingers: 1&2 £3.90, 1&3 £6.60, 2&3 £5.70 CSF £21.65 CT £89.86 TOTE £2.90: £1.30, £2.20, £2.10; EX 27.50 Trifecta £21.70 Pool: £335.77 - 11.40 winning units..
Owner David K Barker & Phil White **Bred** Pedro Rosas **Trained** Constable Burton, N Yorks

FOCUS
Despite the field racing closely packed early, they went a decent pace in this and they were well spread out at the finish. The front four pulled clear. The form is rated around the second and third.

7272 ALL WEATHER "HANDS AND HEELS" APPRENTICE SERIES H'CAP 1m 4f (F)
4:00 (4:01) (Class 5) (0-75,75) 3-Y-O+ **£3,238** (£963; £481; £240) **Stalls** Low

Form RPR

0263 **1** **Resplendent Ace (IRE)**^{11} 7048 5-9-3 67 .... LauraPike 2 76
(P Howling) *hld up in rr: stdy hdwy over 4f out: wnt 3rd over 3f out: tk 2nd 2f out: styd on to ld last 75yds* **7/2**^{2}

0060 **2** *2¼* **Stormy Summer**^{84} 5004 4-8-6 61 oh6 ....(b^{1}) TraceyAddey$^{(5)}$ 5 66
(R W Price) *sn trcking ldr: led over 2f out: edgd lft: hdd and no ex wl ins fnl f* **8/1**

-462 **3** *12* **Wing Diva (IRE)**^{10} 7093 4-8-8 61 oh3 .... AdamCarter$^{(3)}$ 8 47
(B Smart) *dwlt: hdwy to ld after 1f: hung bdly rt and hdd over 2f out: sn wknd* **11/4**^{1}

0060 **4** *1½* **Nawamees (IRE)**^{8} 7137 11-8-11 61 oh4 ....(p) HollyHall 4 45
(P D Evans) *sn outpcd and in rr: drvn over 5f out: kpt on to take modest 4th 2f out: nvr on terms* **9/1**

3000 **5** *19* **Wabbraan (USA)**^{148} 2854 4-9-6 70 .... DavidKenny 3 23
(M Hill) *chsd ldrs: drvn over 6f out: wknd over 3f out* **9/2**^{3}

2400 **6** *3½* **Maslak (IRE)**^{31} 6560 5-9-11 75 .... KierenFox 1 23
(P W Hiatt) *led 1f: chsd ldrs: hrd drvn over 4f out: sn lost pl* **5/1**

2565 **7** *11* **Aven Mac (IRE)**^{20} 6840 3-8-0 61 oh16 .... TerenceFury$^{(5)}$ 7 —
(N Bycroft) *in rr: drvn 6f out: t.o 3f out* **40/1**

0 **8** *5* **Vain Boteli (GER)**^{53} 5940 3-9-0 70 .... NSLawes 6 —
(R Ford) *in rr: drvn 6f out: t.o 3f out* **22/1**

2m 38.7s (-2.30) **Going Correction** -0.175s/f (Stan)
WFA 3 from 4yo+ 6lb **8** Ran SP% **111.6**
Speed ratings (Par 103): **100,98,90,89,76 74,67,63**
toteswingers: 1&2 £6.30, 1&3 £2.00, 2&3 £5.90 CSF £29.76 CT £84.47 TOTE £4.30: £2.20, £2.80, £1.02; EX 31.90 TRIFECTA Not won. Place 6: £41.39 Place 5: £30.94.
Owner Paul Howling **Bred** Newlands House Stud **Trained** Newmarket, Suffolk

FOCUS
A modest "hands and heels" apprentice handicap with half the field out of the handicap, but they went a serious pace in this and they finished spread out all over Nottinghamshire. The winner is rated back to something like his best.
T/Plt: £79.50 to a £1 stake. Pool: £49,931.75. 458.27 winning tickets. T/Qpdt: £6.00 to a £1 stake. Pool: £5,269.02. 641.79 winning tickets. WG

7209 WOLVERHAMPTON (A.W) (L-H)
Friday, November 6

OFFICIAL GOING: Standard
Wind: Fresh, half-behind. Weather: Overcast

7273 LADBROKES.COM APPRENTICE H'CAP 5f 216y(P)
5:50 (5:50) (Class 5) (0-70,70) 3-Y-O+ **£3,238** (£963; £481; £240) **Stalls** Low

Form RPR

5463 **1** **Weet A Surprise**^{7} 7158 4-8-10 68 ....(v) AlexEdwards$^{(7)}$ 4 77
(J W Unett) *chsd ldrs: lost pl over 2f out: hdwy over 1f out: edgd lft and r.o to ld wl ins fnl f* **4/1**^{2}

5-5 **2** *½* **Dash Back (USA)**^{20} 6868 4-8-9 65 .... JamesPSullivan$^{(5)}$ 13 72+
(Adrian McGuinness, Ire) *hld up: hdwy over 1f out: r.o wl: nt rch wnr* **22/1**

03 **3** *1* **Sanjay's Choice (IRE)**^{21} 6833 3-9-5 70 .... WilliamCarson 7 74
(T G McCourt, Ire) *chsd ldr tl led over 2f out: edgd rt over 1f out: hdd wl ins fnl f* **9/1**

6524 **4** *¾* **Joyeaux**^{10} 7081 7-8-7 61 .... PaulPickard$^{(3)}$ 11 63+
(Ollie Pears) *s.i.s: last and pushed along 1/2-way: swtchd rt over 1f out: r.o wl ins fnl f: nrst fin* **16/1**

0343 **5** *nk* **Leading Edge (IRE)**^{8} 7138 4-8-7 63 .... IJBrennan$^{(5)}$ 5 64
(M R Channon) *hld up: rdn over 2f out: hdwy over 1f out: styd on same pce ins fnl f* **11/2**^{3}

0030 **6** *shd* **Romantic Queen**[8] 7138 3-8-7 **61**..........................(t) MatthewDavies(3) 9 61
(George Baker) *hld up: hmpd over 4f out: rdn over 2f out: hdwy over 1f out: edgd lft ins fnl f: styd on* **33/1**

1-02 **7** *½* **Frisbee**[9] 7122 5-9-0 **65**.......................... AndreaAtzeni 10 64
(D W Thompson) *mid-div: hdwy u.p over 1f out: styd on same pce fnl f* **10/1**

3132 **8** *nse* **Titus Gent**[5] 7203 4-9-2 **67**.......................... DavidProbert 12 66
(R A Harris) *hld up: rdn 1/2-way: edgd rt over 1f out: nt trble ldrs* **7/2**[1]

0366 **9** *1¼* **Interactive (IRE)**[27] 6670 6-8-9 **63**.......................... MartinLane(3) 3 58
(D Burchell) *led: rdn and hdd over 2f out: no ex fnl f* **16/1**

0020 **10** *1¼* **Loose Caboose (IRE)**[10] 7090 4-9-0 **70**..................(b) TobyAtkinson(5) 1 61
(A J McCabe) *s.s: hld up: rdn over 2f out: n.d* **12/1**

P103 **11** *1½* **Kheley (IRE)**[13] 7021 3-8-13 **67**.......................... DeanHeslop(3) 8 53
(W M Brisbourne) *chsd ldrs: rdn over 2f out: wknd over 1f out* **20/1**

100 **12** *2¾* **Angelo Poliziano**[51] 5978 3-9-5 **70**..........................(b) JackMitchell 2 47
(Mrs A Duffield) *s.s: hdwy over 4f out: rdn and wknd over 1f out* **8/1**

1m 15.23s (0.23) **Going Correction** +0.10s/f (Slow) **12** Ran SP% **119.3**
Speed ratings (Par 103): **102,101,100,99,98 98,97,97,96,94 92,88**
toteswingers: 1&2 £29.30, 1&3 £14.40, 2&3 £35.50. CSF £93.38 CT £768.85 TOTE £5.80: £1.70, £8.50, £3.10; EX 148.90.
Owner J E Price **Bred** Longdon Stud Ltd **Trained** Tedsmore Hall, Shropshire

FOCUS
A good gallop, but the places were dominated by prominent runners and the strong finishers arrived too late. Sound form, with the third probably the best guide.
Titus Gent Official explanation: jockey said gelding never travelled
Loose Caboose(IRE) Official explanation: jockey said filly missed the break

7274 BEST ODDS GUARANTEED AT LADBROKES.COM NURSERY 5f 20y(P)
6:20 (6:20) (Class 4) (0-85,85) 2-Y-O **£5,046** (£1,510; £755; £377; £188) **Stalls** Low

Form RPR

1611 **1** **Living It Large (FR)**[7] 7156 2-9-13 **85** 6ex.......................... TonyHamilton 5 89
(R F Fisher) *sn pushed along to ld: mde rest: rdn and strly pressed fnl f: r.o gamely* **7/2**[2]

621 **2** *hd* **Desert Poppy (IRE)**[30] 6582 2-9-1 **73**.......................... AdamKirby 1 76
(W R Swinburn) *chsd ldrs: rdn to chal fr over 1f out: r.o* **5/2**[1]

6532 **3** *2¼* **Six Wives**[21] 6827 2-9-6 **78**.......................... FrederikTylicki 2 73
(J A Glover) *edgd rt s: hld up: pushed along 1/2-way: r.o u.p fnl f: nt rch ldrs* **15/2**

1022 **4** *½* **Quaker Parrot**[46] 6169 2-9-7 **79**.......................... RichardKingscote 7 72
(Tom Dascombe) *chsd ldrs: rdn 1/2-way: edgd lft fnl f: styd on* **11/2**

1603 **5** *¾* **Micky's Knock Off (IRE)**[9] 7115 2-9-3 **75**.......................... RobertWinston 4 66
(R C Guest) *chsd ldrs: rdn over 1f out: styd on same pce fnl f* **10/1**

1100 **6** *nk* **Italian Tom (IRE)**[21] 6827 2-9-6 **78**.......................... LukeMorris 6 68
(R A Harris) *s.i.s: swtchd lft sn after s: rdn 1/2-way: n.d* **16/1**

2310 **7** *½* **Lewyn**[9] 7115 2-9-2 **74**.......................... FergusSweeney 3 62
(K A Ryan) *hmpd s: hdwy u.p 2f out: edgd rt over 1f out: no ex* **9/2**[3]

62.21 secs (-0.09) **Going Correction** +0.10s/f (Slow) **7** Ran SP% **111.1**
Speed ratings (Par 98): **104,103,100,99,98 97,96**
toteswingers: 1&2 £1.80, 1&3 £3.50, 2&3 £3.40. CSF £11.92 TOTE £4.90: £2.50, £1.20; EX 9.40.
Owner Des Johnston **Bred** Sunny Days Limited **Trained** Ulverston, Cumbria

FOCUS
Three wins in a row for the in-form winner, who is well suited by these tactics.

NOTEBOOK
Living It Large(FR) completed the hat-trick with another game front-running performance. He is enjoying his racing and was able to defy an 11lb higher mark here, so is very much on the upgrade. (op 11-4 tchd 5-2 and 4-1)
Desert Poppy(IRE) made a fine step into handicap company, only just going under after giving the in-form winner a good race. Her mark looks about right, and she should pay her way this winter. (op 9-4 tchd 2-1)
Six Wives has plenty of early speed but was ridden from behind this time. She has had a busy year, running 15 times, but still looks in good heart and can probably make even more impact while able to use her pace. (op 8-1 tchd 7-1)
Quaker Parrot ran a satisfactory first race on sand and would not be out of similar events. Though a winner at this trip, she gets 6f on turf and the way she stayed on suggests that a slightly longer trip would suit. (tchd 7-1)
Micky's Knock Off(IRE) had shown little on his all-weather debut but this suggests he is worth another try on the surface. (op 14-1)
Italian Tom(IRE) has lost his flying September form and is on a stiff mark at present.
Lewyn is more effective ridden prominently, but she could never get a position after being hampered at the start. (op 13-2)

7275 BET AFTER THE OFF AT LADBROKES.COM H'CAP 7f 32y(P)
6:50 (6:50) (Class 6) (0-62,66) 3-Y-0+ **£2,388** (£705; £352) **Stalls** High

Form RPR

5011 **1** **La Gifted**[7] 7158 3-9-5 **66** 6ex.......................... SamHitchcott 2 74
(M R Channon) *chsd ldrs: led over 1f out: sn rdn: edgd rt ins fnl f: styd on u.p* **15/8**[1]

4400 **2** *½* **Jord (IRE)**[6] 7179 5-9-1 **61**.......................... PaulHanagan 10 68
(J A Glover) *sn led: rdn and hdd over 1f out: edgd lft ins fnl f: styd on* **33/1**

3406 **3** *shd* **Guildenstern (IRE)**[11] 7052 7-8-13 **59**.......................... JimmyQuinn 5 66
(P Howling) *hld up: hdwy over 2f out: rdn over 1f out: r.o* **9/1**

4 *shd* **Scopey**[96] 4575 4-9-1 **61**..........................(t) JerryO'Dwyer 12 67
(Gerard Keane, Ire) *hld up: hdwy 2f out: n.m.r ins fnl f: r.o* **20/1**

3006 **5** *1* **Timber Treasure (USA)**[8] 7138 5-9-2 **62**..................(b) FrancisNorton 1 66
(Paul Green) *hld up: hdwy over 2f out: rdn and swtchd rt over 1f out: styd on* **9/2**[2]

6-66 **6** *2½* **Royal Manor**[38] 6362 4-9-2 **62**.......................... RichardKingscote 9 59
(Tom Dascombe) *chsd ldrs: rdn over 2f out: styd on same pce appr fnl f* **12/1**

6020 **7** *4½* **Ever Cheerful**[90] 4791 8-9-2 **62**..........................(p) SteveDrowne 4 47
(A B Haynes) *chsd ldr: rdn 1/2-way: wknd over 1f out* **14/1**

2030 **8** *2¾* **Witchry**[21] 6825 7-9-0 **60**.......................... DaneO'Neill 6 37
(A G Newcombe) *hld up: hdwy over 2f out: rdn and wknd over 1f out* **12/1**

0000 **9** *1* **Weekend Away (IRE)**[8] 7138 3-8-10 **62**.......................... LeeNewnes(5) 8 37
(S Kirk) *hld up: rdn over 2f out: sn wknd* **15/2**[3]

1020 **10** *6* **Royal Challenge**[23] 6782 8-9-0 **60**.......................... FrederikTylicki 11 19
(I W McInnes) *s.i.s: hdwy 6f out: rdn 1/2-way: wknd over 2f out* **20/1**

0452 **11** *3* **Shakespeare's Son**[34] 6492 4-9-0 **60**..........................(v) VinceSlattery 7 10
(H J Evans) *hld up: racd keenly: rdn and wknd over 2f out* **14/1**

1m 29.74s (0.14) **Going Correction** +0.10s/f (Slow)
WFA 3 from 4yo+ 1lb **11** Ran SP% **115.9**
Speed ratings (Par 101): **103,102,102,102,101 98,93,89,88,81 78**
toteswingers: 1&2 £12.50, 1&3 £5.00, 2&3 £28.80. CSF £83.18 CT £468.39 TOTE £2.50: £1.10, £5.90, £2.60; EX 64.50.
Owner Patrick and Simon Trant **Bred** Patrick & Simon Trant **Trained** West Ilsley, Berks

FOCUS
The pace was solid, and there were both prominent runners and hold-up types involved in the finish. Sound but ordinary form, which should work out.

7276 HOTEL & CONFERENCING AT WOLVERHAMPTON MAIDEN STKS 7f 32y(P)
7:20 (7:22) (Class 5) 2-Y-O **£3,238** (£963; £481; £240) **Stalls** High

Form RPR

0 **1** **Sea Of Heartbreak (IRE)**[13] 7029 2-8-12 0.......................... SteveDrowne 8 69
(R Charlton) *trckd ldrs: hmpd over 1f out: rdn to ld ins fnl f: r.o* **11/1**

6 **2** *¾* **Akamon**[16] 6942 2-8-12 0.......................... HayleyTurner 6 67
(E A L Dunlop) *chsd ldrs: rdn over 1f out: sn ev ch: r.o* **8/1**[3]

00 **3** *½* **Moobeyn**[15] 6965 2-9-3 0..........................(p) GeorgeBaker 3 71
(M P Tregoning) *sn drvn along to ld: rdn and hung lft over 1f out: hdd and nt qckn ins fnl f* **14/1**

4 *1¼* **Top Tigress** 2-8-9 0.......................... Louis-PhilippeBeuzelin(3) 9 63
(Sir Michael Stoute) *s.i.s: hld up: hdwy over 2f out: nt clr run over 1f out: swtchd rt ins fnl f: r.o* **10/1**

0 **5** *1* **Harris Tweed**[16] 6943 2-9-3 0.......................... SebSanders 2 65
(Sir Mark Prescott) *hld up: pushed along 3f out: nt clr run over 2f out: r.o ins fnl f: nrst fin* **14/1**

0 **6** *¾* **Egyptology (IRE)**[10] 7099 2-9-3 0.......................... JoeFanning 10 63
(M Johnston) *sn chsng ldr: chal over 2f out: rdn and hung lft over 1f out: no ex fnl f* **11/8**[1]

6 **7** *1* **Layla's Lad (USA)**[14] 7001 2-9-3 0.......................... PaulHanagan 1 61
(R A Fahey) *hld up: rdn over 2f out: edgd lft and r.o ins fnl f: nvr nrr* **3/1**[2]

8 *nse* **Boy The Bell** 2-9-3 0.......................... ShaneKelly 11 61
(J A Osborne) *chsd ldrs: rdn over 1f out: no ex fnl f* **40/1**

9 *25* **Artful Dodger** 2-9-3 0.......................... LukeMorris 7 —
(T R Gretton) *s.i.s: sn pushed along: a in rr: wknd over 2f out* **50/1**

1m 31.97s (2.37) **Going Correction** +0.10s/f (Slow) **9** Ran SP% **113.4**
Speed ratings (Par 96): **90,89,88,87,86 85,84,83,55**
toteswingers: 1&2 £18.10, 1&3 £20.40, 2&3 £25.20. CSF £93.56 TOTE £15.60: £2.80, £2.50, £4.90; EX 75.20.
Owner D G Hardisty Bloodstock **Bred** D G Hardisty Bloodstock **Trained** Beckhampton, Wilts

FOCUS
Just a modest tempo, with the first three near the front all the way.

NOTEBOOK
Sea Of Heartbreak(IRE) found a good turn of foot to clinch it. This Rock Of Gibraltar filly is out of a daughter of Rainbow Quest and, being a half-sister to a 1m3f winner in Germany, looks the sort to progress. (op 17-2)
Akamon showed promise on her debut at Kempton and stepped up on that here. She is good enough to win an all-weather maiden and should stay further as she matures. (op 7-1)
Moobeyn had attracted the comment "ran green" in his two previous races and again he looked clueless when asked to make the running for a change. However, getting more involved in the race this time should have done him a lot of good mentally and this 155,000gns Selkirk half-brother to three winners from 6f to 2m is finally starting to look like a racehorse. Official explanation: jockey said colt ran green (tchd 16-1)
Top Tigress ◆, a half-sister to three-times winner Worth A King's, made a promising debut despite having bad luck in running. Her sire Tiger Hill was a top-class middle distance performer in Germany and she should improve enough to win races, with longer trips likely to suit before long. Official explanation: jockey said filly was denied a clear run (op 7-1)
Harris Tweed, from a prolific family up to 2m, is bred to stay really well and the way he shaped in the last 2f suggests he will improve with racing. However, in doing so he caught the eyes of the stewards and the matter was referred to the BHA in London. Handicaps are now only one race away, and he will be particularly dangerous when he makes the switch, but he could probably win a maiden too. (op 16-1)
Egyptology(IRE), who has failed to get home in two races to date, needs a handicap mark. A drop to 6f or change of tactics is also worth considering. (op 6-4 tchd 13-8)
Layla's Lad(USA) does not seem to be good enough to win a maiden but he has shown enough to suggest he can make more impact when handicapped. (op 9-2)
Artful Dodger Official explanation: jockey said colt lost its action

7277 GREAT OFFERS AT WOLVERHAMPTON-RACECOURSE.CO.UK MAIDEN AUCTION STKS 1m 141y(P)
7:50 (7:51) (Class 5) 2-Y-0 **£3,412** (£1,007; £504) **Stalls** Low

Form RPR

0203 **1** **First In The Queue (IRE)**[16] 6930 2-8-11 **75**.......................... LeeNewnes(5) 7 81
(S Kirk) *pushed along and prom: outpcd over 6f out: hdwy over 2f out: hung lft over 1f out: rdn to ld wl ins fnl f: r.o* **5/1**[3]

05 **2** *1¾* **Ice Diva**[14] 6992 2-8-6 0.......................... JohnEgan 5 67
(P W D'Arcy) *led: hdd 7f out: remained w ldr tl led over 2f out: sn rdn: edgd rt and hdd wl ins fnl f* **2/1**[1]

6 **3** *3* **Red Courtier**[119] 3794 2-9-1 0.......................... PaulHanagan 2 70
(P F I Cole) *trckd ldrs: racd keenly: rdn over 2f out: styd on same pce appr fnl f* **9/4**[2]

30 **4** *½* **Verity Lane (USA)**[28] 6628 2-8-11 0.......................... FrederikTylicki 6 65
(R M H Cowell) *chsd ldr tl led 7f out: rdn and hdd over 2f out: no ex fnl f* **8/1**

40 **5** *13* **Madame Roulin (IRE)**[25] 6727 2-8-8 0.......................... HayleyTurner 1 35
(M L W Bell) *chsd ldrs tl rdn and wknd over 2f out* **16/1**

6 *¾* **Lily Lily** 2-8-6 0.......................... JimmyQuinn 8 31
(K McAuliffe) *s.s: a wl bhd* **40/1**

7 *1¼* **Royal Treasure (IRE)** 2-9-1 0.......................... ShaneKelly 3 37
(J A Osborne) *dwlt: a wl bhd* **50/1**

8 *2* **Rainbow Six** 2-8-12 0.......................... AndreaAtzeni(3) 4 33
(M Botti) *hld up: rdn over 3f out: sn wknd* **8/1**

1m 50.77s (0.27) **Going Correction** +0.10s/f (Slow) **8** Ran SP% **113.3**
Speed ratings (Par 96): **102,100,97,97,85 85,84,82**
toteswingers: 1&2 £1.60, 1&3 £3.40, 2&3 £2.50. CSF £15.12 TOTE £3.80: £1.60, £1.20, £1.20; EX 20.80.
Owner Liam Breslin **Bred** Holborn Trust Co **Trained** Upper Lambourn, Berks

FOCUS
A testing gallop, accentuated by the fact that the three newcomers were slowly away and unable to go the pace, resulting in the runners soon being strung out by 15 to 20 lengths.

NOTEBOOK
First In The Queue(IRE), who had done reasonably well in four turf maidens, made a winning all-weather debut. He stays 1m really well for a juvenile and longer trips should be in order next year. (op 6-1)
Ice Diva, who had shown promise in two races on turf before this, also showed she can make an impact this winter. She could sneak a maiden but is now qualified for handicaps. (tchd 5-2)
Red Courtier looked immature on his only previous outing in July and a few spins on the all-weather should help to toughen him up. On this evidence he might even find a winning opportunity during the winter. (op 5-2 tchd 11-4 and 15-8)
Verity Lane(USA) can do better now she is ready for handicaps, but she showed plenty of pace here and could probably handle a drop to 7f. (op 6-1)

Madame Roulin(IRE)'s trainer has a good opinion of her but feels she may still be on the weak side. Following a second disappointing run here, it is probably worth giving her time to mature. (op 14-1)
Rainbow Six, a Tiger Hill half-brother to the successful middle-distance stayer Excelsior Academy, travelled better than the two other newcomers but will need longer trips. (op 12-1)

7278 STAY AT THE WOLVERHAMPTON HOLIDAY INN MAIDEN STKS 1m 1f 103y(P)
8:20 (8:20) (Class 5) 3-Y-O+ **£2,590** (£770; £385; £192) **Stalls** Low

Form				RPR
2-	1		**La De Two (IRE)**[420] 5857 3-9-3 0 DaneO'Neill 4 (Saeed Bin Suroor) *dwlt: sn prom: chsd ldr over 5f out: led over 4f out: clr fnl 2f: canter* 1/5[1]	81+
0/	2	8	**Warren Bank**[774] 5679 4-9-6 0 GeorgeBaker 13 (Mrs Mary Hambro) *hmpd s: hld up: hdwy 6f out: styd on to go 2nd ins fnl f: no ch w wnr* 66/1	55
40	3	nk	**Summer Affair (IRE)**[15] 6974 4-9-1 0 MatthewDavies(5) 1 (B I Case) *hld up: styd on u.p fr over 1f out: n.d* 20/1	55+
6	4	2	**Spring Fashion (IRE)**[16] 6934 3-8-9 0 AndreaAtzeni(3) 2 (M Botti) *chsd ldrs: lost pl 7f out: rdn and plenty to do over 3f out: hung lft and r.o ins fnl f* 6/1[2]	49+
6	5	hd	**Heathyards Junior**[14] 7004 3-9-3 0 JerryO'Dwyer 11 (R Hollinshead) *prom: rdn to chse wnr over 2f out: wknd fnl f* 14/1[3]	50
	6	nk	**Nyetimber (USA)** 3-9-3 0 ShaneKelly 8 (J A Osborne) *hld up: hdwy over 2f out: n.d* 20/1	49
00	7	1/2	**Deportista**[11] 7057 3-8-5 0 DavidKenny(7) 10 (J A Pickering) *chsd ldrs: rdn over 2f out: wknd over 1f out* 100/1	43
60	8	4	**Broughtons Point**[50] 6029 3-8-12 0 JamieMackay 12 (W J Musson) *hld up: hdwy over 2f out: n.d* 25/1	35
50	9	1	**Lean Burn (USA)**[25] 6741 3-9-3 0 (t) RichardThomas 5 (A G Newcombe) *prom: lost pl over 3f out: n.d after* 20/1	38
00	10	3/4	**Miskin Spirit**[11] 7067 3-8-12 0 (p) NeilChalmers 3 (B Palling) *hld up: rdn over 2f out: n.d* 66/1	31
00-	11	5	**Harley Fern**[395] 6565 3-8-7 0 ow2 MJMurphy(7) 7 (M E Rimmer) *chsd ldrs tl rdn and wknd over 2f out* 100/1	23
0	12	4	**Spiders Tern**[46] 6172 4-9-6 0 KevinGhunowa 6 (J M Bradley) *chsd ldrs: rdn over 4f out: sn lost pl* 100/1	17
0	13	3 1/4	**Seren Arian**[16] 6934 3-8-12 0 DavidProbert 9 (B Palling) *led: hdd over 4f out: rdn and wknd over 2f out* 66/1	6

2m 3.06s (1.36) **Going Correction** +0.10s/f (Slow)
WFA 3 from 4yo 3lb 13 Ran SP% **129.9**
Speed ratings (Par 103): **97,89,89,87,87 87,86,83,82,81 77,73,70**
toteswingers: 1&2 £7.30, 1&3 £3.50, 2&3 £50.90. CSF £52.24 TOTE £1.20: £1.02, £21.30, £4.90; EX 32.10.
Owner Godolphin **Bred** Airlie Stud And Sir Thomas Pilkington **Trained** Newmarket, Suffolk

FOCUS
With the exception of the winner, this looked a very moderate field so it was no surprise that he annihilated them. The pace was ordinary but La De Two injected a turn of foot around the home turn that left the others standing. He did not need to match last year's debut form.
Spring Fashion(IRE) Official explanation: jockey said fiklly hung left-handed throughout

7279 LADBROKESPOKER.COM H'CAP 1m 5f 194y(P)
8:50 (8:51) (Class 4) (0-85,76) 3-Y-O+ **£5,046** (£1,510; £755; £377) **Stalls** Low

Form				RPR
0134	1		**Calculating (IRE)**[1] 7255 5-8-13 61 DavidProbert 1 (M D I Usher) *hld up: tk clsr order 7f out: rdn to ld over 1f out: styd on wl* 13/8[1]	70
1033	2	3 1/4	**Capable Guest (IRE)**[9] 7118 7-9-5 67 TonyCulhane 4 (M R Channon) *hld up: tk clsr order 7f out: rdn and ev ch over 1f out: styd on same pce* 4/1[3]	71
	3	nk	**Baltimore Patriot (IRE)**[27] 4729 6-9-1 63 KevinGhunowa 3 (R Curtis) *chsd clr ldr: lft in ld 7f out: hdd over 5f out: led again 3f out: rdn and hdd over 1f out: styd on same pce* 8/1	67
0610	4	9	**Eseej (USA)**[7] 7151 4-9-9 76 PaulPickard(5) 2 (P W Hiatt) *led: hung rt thrght: rn wd and hdd 7f out: racd wd fr then onwards: led again over 5f out: hdd 3f out: wknd over 1f out* 7/4[2]	67

3m 7.55s (1.55) **Going Correction** +0.10s/f (Slow) 4 Ran SP% **105.6**
Speed ratings (Par 105): **99,97,96,91**
CSF £7.66 TOTE £2.00; EX 3.90.
Owner Brian Rogan **Bred** Darley **Trained** Upper Lambourn, Berks

FOCUS
A weak gallop set by Eseej, who lost his steering and nearly ran off the track at the 7f bend, developed into a sprint from the final turn. Muddling form which may not prove too reliable.
Eseej(USA) Official explanation: jockey said gelding hung badly right and was unsteerable

7280 LADBROKESCASINO.COM H'CAP 5f 20y(P)
9:20 (9:22) (Class 6) (0-60,64) 3-Y-O+ **£2,388** (£705; £352) **Stalls** Low

Form				RPR
0556	1		**Forever's Girl**[35] 6456 3-9-2 **58** PJMcDonald 6 (G R Oldroyd) *hld up: hdwy over 1f out: rdn to ld wl ins fnl f: r.o* 25/1	71
2030	2	1 1/4	**Micky Mac (IRE)**[20] 6846 5-9-1 **57** FrederikTylicki 2 (C J Teague) *chsd ldr tl rdn to ld over 1f out: sn edgd rt: hdd wl ins fnl f* 11/2[2]	66
6030	3	hd	**Style Award**[25] 6739 4-8-12 **59** (p) PaulPickard(5) 1 (W J H Ratcliffe) *a.p: rdn and nt clr run 1f out: styd on* 11/1	70+
0313	4	1	**Decider (USA)**[42] 6251 6-9-2 **58** (p) DavidProbert 7 (R A Harris) *plld hrd and prom: rdn and ev ch over 1f out: edgd lft and no ex ins fnl f* 11/2[2]	62
2401	5	3/4	**Rosie Says No**[10] 7100 4-9-1 **64** 6ex (p) DeclanCannon(7) 3 (A J McCabe) *dwlt: hld up: hdwy over 1f out: r.o: nt rch ldrs* 10/1	65
0530	6	nk	**Monte Major (IRE)**[10] 7100 8-9-3 **59** (v) AdamKirby 10 (D Shaw) *sn outpcd: hdwy over 1f out: r.o* 16/1	59
2505	7	1/2	**Bluebok**[8] 7136 8-9-1 **60** (bt) JackDean(3) 4 (J M Bradley) *led: rdn and hdd over 1f out: sn edgd lft: styng on same pce whn n.m.r wl ins fnl f* 4/1[1]	61+
0463	8	3/4	**Billy Beetroot (USA)**[16] 6933 3-9-1 **57** (p) LukeMorris 9 (R A Harris) *hld up: hdwy 1/2-way: rdn and hung lft over 1f out: styd on same pce* 9/1	53
0000	9	3/4	**Know No Fear**[126] 3562 4-8-8 **57** AmyScott(7) 12 (A J Lidderdale) *s.i.s: hld up: rdn over 1f out: n.d* 33/1	50
0403	10	1 3/4	**Darcy's Pride (IRE)**[36] 6410 5-9-0 **56** (t) TonyHamilton 5 (P T Midgley) *mid-div: rdn over 2f out: wknd over 1f out* 14/1	43
1444	11	nk	**Multahab**[39] 6341 10-9-4 **60** (tp) JimmyQuinn 8 (M Wigham) *hld up in tch: racd keenly and hung rt: wknd over 1f out* 8/1[3]	46
5011	12	hd	**Metal Guru**[35] 6456 5-8-10 **59** (p) DavidKenny(7) 11 (R Hollinshead) *dwlt: a in rr* 8/1[3]	44
2005	13	5	**King's Sabre**[3] 7219 3-9-2 **58** (be) RobertWinston 13 (R C Guest) *hld up: wknd 2f out* 22/1	25

62.21 secs (-0.09) **Going Correction** +0.10s/f (Slow) 13 Ran SP% **124.1**
Speed ratings (Par 101): **104,102,101,100,98 98,97,96,95,92 91,91,83**
toteswingers: 1&2 £26.10, 1&3 £50.20, 2&3 £12.70. CSF £160.62 CT £1647.42 TOTE £36.70: £10.00, £3.00, £3.70; EX 373.60 Place 6 £58.84, Place 5 £14.67..
Owner R C Bond **Bred** R C Bond **Trained** Brawby, N Yorks
■ Stewards' Enquiry : Frederik Tylicki two-day ban: used whip with excessive frequency (Nov 20-21); one-day ban: careless riding (Nov 24)
David Probert caution: careless riding

FOCUS
A modest but competitive sprint, and sound form.
Multahab Official explanation: jockey said gelding hung right
Metal Guru Official explanation: jockey said mare hit its head on stalls and was slowly away
T/Plt: £102.00 to a £1 stake. Pool: £84,204.79. 602.19 winning tickets. T/Qpdt: £12.20 to a £1 stake. Pool: £8,111.48. 491.30 winning tickets. CR

6685 SANTA ANITA (L-H)
Friday, November 6

OFFICIAL GOING: Pro-ride - fast; turf course - firm

7281a BREEDERS' CUP MARATHON (PRO-RIDE) 1m 6f
8:35 (8:37) 3-Y-O+ **£187,500** (£62,500; £34,375; £20,833; £10,417)

			RPR
1		**Man Of Iron (USA)**[21] 6837 3-8-10 JMurtagh 9 (A P O'Brien, Ire) *hld up: 7th 1/2-way: hdwy 3f out: sn edgd out: 3rd st: chal on ins: drvn to take narrow ld 100yds out: all out* 13/2[3]	119
2	nse	**Cloudy's Knight (USA)**[15] 9-9-0 RosemaryBHomeisterJr 4 (Jonathan Sheppard, U.S.A) *hld up in 6th: clsd up rapidly on outside over 4f out: led 3f out to 100yds out: r.o wl* 10/1	115
3	2 1/4	**Mastery**[55] 5861 3-8-10 LDettori 6 (Saeed Bin Suroor) *a cl up: outpcd over 3f out: 2nd st: effrt on outside: one pce fnl f* 7/4[1]	116
4	11 1/2	**Gangbuster (USA)**[55] 4-9-0 KDesormeaux 10 (J Keith Desormeaux, U.S.A) *hld up in rr: 6th and hdwy st: nvr nr first three* 33/1	95
5	1	**Muhannak (IRE)**[40] 6303 5-9-0 RyanMoore 2 (R M Beckett) *disp 2nd to 4f out: cl up to ins fnl 3f: 7th and btn st* 14/1	94
6	8	**Father Time**[55] 5861 3-8-10 EddieAhern 5 (H R A Cecil) *s.i.s and pushed along early: disp 4th at 1/2-way: rdn over 3f out: 8th and btn st* 11/4[2]	87
7	1 1/2	**Eldaafer (USA)**[34] 6574 4-9-0 RBejarano 8 (Diane Alvarado, U.S.A) *bhd fr 1/2-way* 33/1	81
8	1	**Nite Light (USA)**[34] 6574 5-9-0 JRVelazquez 3 (Todd Pletcher, U.S.A) *disp 2nd: clr 2nd over 3f out: 5th and btn st* 8/1	79
9	10 1/4	**Black Astor (USA)**[68] 5-9-0 ASolis 1 (Lisa Lewis, U.S.A) *led to 3f out* 25/1	65
P		**Sir Dave (USA)**[26] 4-9-0 (b) JRosario 7 (Jack Carava, U.S.A) *bhd fr 1/2-way: t.o whn p.u in st* 33/1	—

2m 54.11s (174.11)
WFA 3 from 4yo+ 8lb 10 Ran SP% **115.9**
PARI-MUTUEL (including $2 stakes): WIN 14.80; PL (1-2) 7.20, 7.40; SHOW (1-2-3) 4.40, 4.60, 2.40; SF 120.20.
Owner D Smith, Mrs J Magnier, M Tabor **Bred** Shell Bloodstock **Trained** Ballydoyle, Co Tipperary
■ This was Aidan O'Brien's first Breeders' Cup winner since in 2003, and Johnny Murtagh's first since 2000.

FOCUS
Many punters expected European runners to dominate the second running of the Marathon, encouraged by the success of the unheralded Muhannak on the Pro-Ride 12 months ago, and with the increase in distance from 1m4f believed to put the home team at a disadvantage. However, while Man Or Iron triumphed for Ireland, the well-fancied British-trained pair, Mastery and Father Time, underperformed to varying degrees. They went a decent enough pace and this is smart form.

NOTEBOOK
Man Of Iron(USA) looked shy of this sort of company on turf, but he's a half-brother to Belmont Stakes winners Jazil and Rags To Riches, as well as the smart Japanese colt Casino Drive, and his recent Polytrack efforts at Dundalk offered encouragement. The big question mark was whether he would stay the trip, 3f further than he had ever tried before, but he answered that with a really gutsy effort, displaying the sort of attitude his sire became famous for. He was given a patient ride by Murtagh, sitting last through the early stages, but had moved into third at the top of the straight and ultimately stayed on best after being switched towards the inside. It's clear artificial surfaces suit Man Of Iron best and he has now been sold to race in Dubai, where he should act well on the Tapeta surface at Meydan and is apparently going to be trained by Luca Cumani. It's interesting to note he was the only one of Aidan O'Brien's seven runners at the meeting to use Lasix.
Cloudy's Knight(USA), bidding to become the oldest winner of a Breeders' Cup race, travelled well and put his long stride to good use when making a big move around the final bend to lead at the top of the straight, but despite keeping on, he was run out of it in the final strides. This was a huge effort from the 2007 Canadian International hero and he is set to race on at ten.
Mastery, using Lasix for the first time, ran a good race but was slightly below the form he showed to win the St Leger on his previous outing. He was well enough placed turning in, but lacked the finishing kick of the front pair. His connections hinted afterwards they felt he was a bit flat at the end of a long season.
Gangbuster(USA) had plenty to find in this sort of company and was duly beaten a long way.
Muhannak(IRE) has struggled since winning this race last year, and the extra distance was unlikely to suit judged on pedigree. He was leaned on for much of the way by Nite Light, who seemed to be hanging left, and all things considered, he didn't run too badly.
Father Time, another who used Lasix for the first time, was fancied by many to reverse St Leger form with Mastery, but after recovering well from a sluggish start to be beautifully positioned down the back straight, he came off the bridle fully 4f out and was quickly beaten.

7282a BREEDERS' CUP JUVENILE FILLIES TURF (FILLIES) 1m (T)
9:08 (9:15) 2-Y-O **£375,000** (£125,000; £68,750; £41,667; £20,833)

			RPR
1		**Tapitsfly (USA)**[33] 2-8-10 RAlbarado 10 (Dale Romans, U.S.A) *wl away fr outside draw: 2nd after 1f: led jst ins fnl f: rdn out* 12/1	112
2	1/2	**Rose Catherine (USA)**[26] 2-8-10 JJCastellano 4 (Todd Pletcher, U.S.A) *led to jst ins fnl f: r.o steadily* 10/1	110
3	3 1/4	**House Of Grace (USA)**[22] 2-8-10 MLuzzi 7 (Kenneth McPeek, U.S.A) *hld up: 8th st: r.o ins fnl f to take 3rd 60yds out* 6/1[2]	103+
4	1 1/4	**Hatheer (USA)**[22] 2-8-10 AGarcia 9 (Kiaran McLaughlin, U.S.A) *a cl up: 3rd st: one pce and lost 3rd 60yds out* 16/1	100

5 *nk* **Jungle Tale (USA)**[48] 2-8-10 .... SXBridgmohan 6 99+
(Steven Asmussen, U.S.A) *in rr: last st: drvn and r.o wl fnl f: nrest at fin* **20/1**

6 *nk* **La Nez (USA)**[34] 2-8-10 .... MESmith 5 99
(J Eric Kruljac, U.S.A) *10th at 1/2-way: 9th st: styd on down outside: nvr a factor* **14/1**

7 *nk* **Potosina (USA)**[12] 2-8-10 ....(b) JRVelazquez 1 98
(Mark Shuman, U.S.A) *disp 3rd: 4th st: wknd fr 1f out* **33/1**

8 *1* **Lillie Langtry (IRE)**[34] 6477 2-8-10 .... JMurtagh 8 96
(A P O'Brien, Ire) *racd in 6th to st: one pce* **6/4**[1]

9 *nse* **Smart Seattle (USA)**[22] 2-8-10 .... JRose 3 96+
(H Graham Motion, U.S.A) *cl up: 5th whn sltly hmpd on turn: stl 5th st: wknd fnl f* **10/1**

10 *nse* **Lisa's Kitten (USA)**[13] 2-8-10 .... JRLeparoux 12 96
(Michael J Maker, U.S.A) *a outpcd* **25/1**

11 *1 1/4* **Elusive Galaxy (IRE)**[48] 2-8-10 .... RBejarano 2 93
(B Cecil, U.S.A) *mid-div on ins: 7th st: sn btn* **25/1**

12 *3 1/4* **Junia Tepzia (IRE)**[34] 2-8-10 .... KFallon 11 85
(P Schiergen, Germany) *mid-div on outside: 6th appr st: sn btn* **13/2**[3]

1m 34.25s (0.38) **12** Ran SP% **121.4**
PARI-MUTUEL: WIN 21.60; PL (1-2) 8.60, 6.80; SHOW (1-2-3) 6.00, 5.80,5.00; SF 152.40.
Owner Frank L Jones Jr **Bred** F Jones **Trained** USA

FOCUS
Only the second running of the Juvenile Fillies Turf. The pace was steadied at halfway and it proved very difficult to make up ground, with the front pair filling the first two positions throughout. The third is the best guide to the level.

NOTEBOOK
Tapitsfly(USA) is a terrific mover with a really long stride, and she handled both the quick turf and the tight bends beautifully. She has won on dirt, but it's clear from her action this surface suits best and she's now 2-2 on grass. It's true she was favoured by racing handily, but she did well to get a prominent position from stall ten and is obviously very smart.
Rose Catherine(USA), a wide-margin winner of a 6f maiden on her first turf start last time, set solid-enough fractions over this longer trip, but she was left alone in front for much of the way and managed to get a breather in down the back straight. She kept on well for pressure in the stretch, but was beginning to look held when her rider had his whip accidentally knocked out of his hand by the jockey on the winner inside the final furlong.
House Of Grace(USA), unbeaten in two starts coming into this, emerges with plenty of credit considering she didn't enjoy the clearest of runs around the final bend yet still finished best of those waited with.
Hatheer(USA) was never too far away and didn't seem to have any excuses.
Jungle Tale(USA) was set far too much to do considering how the race unfolded, being held up last of all for much of the way, and she did well to finish so close.
Lillie Langtry(IRE) looked a better filly than Aidan O'Brien's runner-up in this race last year, Heart Shaped, but she underperformed. It turned out she fractured a knee during the race, and while the injury is not career threatening, she is to have a pin inserted.
Smart Seattle(USA) is better than she showed as she lost her place when hampered rounding the final bend and didn't get the clearest of runs in the straight.
Junia Tepzia(IRE), a German-trained filly who had won both her starts in Ireland, was stuck wide throughout from stall 11 and didn't look to handle the track at all.

7283a GREY GOOSE BREEDERS' CUP JUVENILE FILLIES (GRADE 1) (FILLIES) (PRO-RIDE) 1m 110y(D)

9:45 (9:50) 2-Y-O **£750,000** (£250,000; £137,500; £83,333; £41,667)

RPR

1 **She Be Wild (USA)**[28] 6659 2-8-10 .... JRLeparoux 8 115
(Wayne Catalano, U.S.A) *racd in 3rd to st: got through on rail to ld ins fnl f: r.o wl* **8/1**

2 *3/4* **Beautician (USA)**[28] 6659 2-8-10 .... RAlbarado 4 113
(Kenneth McPeek, U.S.A) *disp 4th: 4th st: 3rd 100yds out: rallied to take 2nd last strides* **8/1**

3 *hd* **Blind Luck (USA)**[33] 6531 2-8-10 ....(b) TBaze 3 113
(Jerry Hollendorfer, U.S.A) *disp 4th on outside: clsd up 3f out: c wd and 5th st: r.o down outside to go 2nd ins fnl f: no ex cl home* **7/2**[1]

4 *3/4* **Biofuel (USA)**[27] 2-8-10 .... ERosaDaSilva 12 113+
(Reade Baker, Canada) *in rr: 11th st on outside: hdwy appr fnl f: carried rt ins fnl f: r.o: nrest at fin* **25/1**

5 *hd* **Always A Princess (USA)**[33] 6531 2-8-10 .... GKGomez 11 111
(Bob Baffert, U.S.A) *led tl ins fnl f* **8/1**

6 *nse* **Negligee (USA)**[28] 6659 2-8-10 ....(b) RMaragh 10 111
(John Terranova II, U.S.A) *towards rr: 8th st: swtchd outside: rdn and hung rt ins fnl f: kpt on* **9/2**[2]

7 *3/4* **Zilva (USA)**[28] 6659 2-8-10 .... JRose 1 109
(H Graham Motion, U.S.A) *bhd to fnl turn: hdwy on ins and 6th st: one pce fnl f* **20/1**

8 *2 1/4* **Connie And Michael (USA)**[20] 2-8-10 .... KDesormeaux 6 104
(Kenneth McPeek, U.S.A) *pressed ldr to st: wknd fr 1f out* **6/1**[3]

9 *2* **Ms Vanenzza (USA)**[34] 2-8-10 .... JRoccoJr 2 100
(Juan C Vazquez, U.S.A) *disp 4th on ins to 3f out: 7th and rdn st: sn btn* **40/1**

10 *1* **Bickersons (CAN)**[33] 6531 2-8-10 .... JRosario 5 98
(Kelly Breen, U.S.A) *mid-div to st: sn wknd* **20/1**

11 *2* **Devil May Care (USA)**[27] 6683 2-8-10 .... JRVelazquez 7 93
(Todd Pletcher, U.S.A) *a towards rr* **15/2**

12 *17 3/4* **Champagne D'Oro (USA)**[60] 2-8-10 .... MGarcia 9 54
(Eric J Guillot, U.S.A) *a in rr: wl bhd fnl 3f* **66/1**

1m 43.8s (1.38) **12** Ran SP% **117.1**
PARI-MUTUEL: WIN 16.80; PL 91-2) 9.00, 9.40; SHOW (1-2-3) 5.00, 6.00,3.00; SF 144.40.
Owner Nancy Mazzoni **Bred** M & N Mazzoni **Trained** USA

FOCUS
A high-class juvenile contest run at an average pace.

NOTEBOOK
She Be Wild(USA) enjoyed a good trip for most of the way and was a decisive winner, in the process reversing recent Keenland placings with Negligee. The only concern for her supporters was when she was briefly short of room at the top of the straight, but she soon found a opening against the inside rail and picked up well. She's not that big, so it remains to be seen how she'll progress.
Beautician(USA), fifth last-time out in the same Keenland Grade 1 that today's winner ran second, got shuffled back a bit further back than ideal after being short of room on the first bend according to her rider, but she recovered to have every chance at the top of the straight.
Blind Luck(USA), a clear-cut winner of the key prep for this, the Oak Leaf over C&D, was another bumped about a bit on the first bend, but her rider wasn't using that as an excuse.
Biofuel(USA) was on edge and sweating beforehand, but she still ran a massive race and was unlucky not to go very close. She was dropped in from stall 12, yet still ended up making her move at least six horse-widths wide around the final bend, and when beginning to finish strongly, was badly bumped by Negligee inside the final furlong. Granted a better trip, she might have won.
Always A Princess(USA) went from the front once again, which was a surprise considering she was outstayed by Blind Luck when attempting to make all in the Oak Leaf, and she duly faded in the straight. She might do better under more patient tactics next time, or perhaps she is simply a sprinter.
Negligee(USA), dropped in from stall ten, took a while to pick up turning into the straight and, when asked to switch out from behind runners around 1f out, she struggled to get on the correct lead and hung badly right, bumping a rival in the process. This was disappointing considering she had today's winner and runner-up behind her when landing a Grade 1 last time.
Zilva(USA) was briefly short of room in the straight.
Connie And Michael(USA) was not given anything like a hard ride.

7284a EMIRATES AIRLINE BREEDERS' CUP FILLY & MARE TURF (GRADE 1) 1m 2f (T)

10:23 (10:25) 3-Y-O+ **£750,000** (£250,000; £137,500; £83,333; £41,667)

RPR

1 **Midday**[33] 6525 3-8-8 .... TPQueally 6 119
(H R A Cecil) *racd in 4th: pushed along to go 2nd appr st: drvn to ld on ins 1f out: drvn out* **15/8**[1]

2 *1* **Pure Clan (USA)**[34] 6510 4-8-12 ....(b) GKGomez 5 117+
(Robert E Holthus, U.S.A) *racd in 7th to st: drvn and hdwy fr 1f out: r.o wl on ins: nrest at fin* **11/1**

3 *1 1/4* **Forever Together (USA)**[27] 6689 5-8-12 .... JRLeparoux 2 115+
(Jonathan Sheppard, U.S.A) *last tl ins fnl f: r.o wl down outside to take 3rd last strides* **3/1**[2]

4 *nk* **Visit**[27] 6685 4-8-12 .... JRVelazquez 1 114
(Robert Frankel, U.S.A) *led to 1f out* **10/1**

5 *nse* **Magical Fantasy (USA)**[27] 6685 4-8-12 .... ASolis 4 114
(Patrick Gallagher, U.S.A) *racd in 6th to st: effrt on outside: 4th 1f out: one pce* **9/2**[3]

6 *1* **Maram (USA)**[25] 3-8-8 .... JLezcano 8 112
(Chad C Brown, U.S.A) *racd in 5th to st: sn one pce* **16/1**

7 *1/2* **Rutherienne (USA)**[48] 5-8-12 .... AGarcia 3 111
(Christophe Clement, U.S.A) *racd in 3rd: 4th over 3f out: rdn and 3rd st: no ex ins fnl f* **14/1**

8 *4 1/4* **Dynaforce (USA)**[34] 6510 6-8-12 .... KDesormeaux 7 102
(William Mott, U.S.A) *sn pressing ldr: 3rd st: sn wknd* **14/1**

1m 59.14s (-0.14)
WFA 3 from 4yo+ 4lb **8** Ran SP% **114.6**
PARI-MUTUEL: WIN 6.60; PL (1-2) 4.80, 7.80; SHOW (1-2-3) 3.00, 4.00,2.40; SF 53.60.
Owner K Abdulla **Bred** Juddmonte Farms Ltd **Trained** Newmarket, Suffolk
■ A first Breeders' Cup winner for Henry Cecil, and also for Tom Queally, who was having his first ride at the meeting.

FOCUS
The form of this year's Filly & Mare Turf looks solid if unspectacular, and there was a worthy winner in the shape of Midday, who became the fifth European-trained runner to take this since 2001, but only the third 3-y-o over that same period. The gallop set by Visit, representing the same owner as the winner, increased leaving the back straight and those held up became outpaced. She is rated back to her best with the winner close to form.

NOTEBOOK
Midday was below her best in the Prix de l'Opera last time, but her trainer said he had left something to work on having giving the filly a break after her success in the Nassau, and she returned to top form with a clear-cut victory. She used Lasix for the first time. Having raced in about mid-division against the inside rail early on, she briefly looked in a bit of trouble when driven along for a few strides early in the back straight, but she responded to move on to the heels of the leader and was well placed for when the pace increased. Once this daughter of Oasis Dream found a gap between Visit and the inside rail early in the straight, she was never in any danger. She stays in training and will have any number of options next year, including a repeat bid in this race, to be run at Churchill Downs.
Pure Clan(USA) didn't give her running when last of all in this race 12 months ago, but this was obviously much better and she emerges with a deal of credit considering she was one of those caught out when pace increased, having been set too much to do.
Forever Together(USA), last year's winner, is a confirmed hold-up mare, but even so, she could have sat a little closer to the pace, rather than being held last of all, and she was basically left with far too much ground to make up. Her trainer understandably didn't sound too pleased afterwards. She is now likely to be retired.
Visit filled the same position as she did in this race last year. She doesn't quite get 1m2f.
Magical Fantasy(USA) had won three consecutive Grade 1s coming into this, including when defeating Visit by 1/2l over C&D last time, so a little better could have been expected.
Maram(USA), last year's Juvenile Fillies' Turf winner, never threatened.

7285a SENTIENT JET BREEDERS' CUP FILLY & MARE SPRINT (GRADE 1) (F&M) (PRO-RIDE) 7f

11:02 (11:03) 3-Y-O+ **£375,000** (£125,000; £68,750; £41,667; £20,833)

RPR

1 **Informed Decision (USA)**[27] 4-8-12 ....(b) JRLeparoux 7 121
(Jonathan Sheppard, U.S.A) *broke wl: pressed ldr on outside: led ent st: rdn out* **3/1**[2]

2 *1 1/4* **Ventura (USA)**[47] 5-8-12 .... GKGomez 9 118+
(Robert Frankel, U.S.A) *hld up: 7th st: gd hdwy on outside fr over 1f out: chsd wnr fnl 120yds: r.o same pce* **1/1**[1]

3 *3* **Free Flying Soul (USA)**[25] 4-8-12 .... MESmith 1 109
(Bruce Headley, U.S.A) *led to st: styd on same pce* **33/1**

4 *3/4* **Sara Louise (USA)**[41] 3-8-10 .... LDettori 2 106
(Saeed Bin Suroor) *a cl up on ins: 4th and drvn st: 3rd appr fnl f: one pce* **7/1**[3]

5 *3/4* **Only Green (IRE)**[22] 6808 3-8-10 .... OPeslier 4 104
(F Head, France) *hld up: hdwy over 2f out: 5th st on ins: one pce* **25/1**

6 *1 1/2* **Silver Swallow (USA)**[111] 5-8-12 .... ASolis 5 101
(Bruce Headley, U.S.A) *disp 5th: 6th st: sn drvn: kpt on down outside: nvr a danger* **40/1**

7 *nse* **Evita Argentina (USA)**[63] 3-8-10 .... JRosario 6 100
(John W Sadler, U.S.A) *last to st: brought wd: nvr a factor* **25/1**

8 *nk* **Seventh Street (USA)**[55] 4-8-12 .... RMaragh 8 99
(Saeed Bin Suroor) *cl up on outside: 3rd st: sn wknd* **20/1**

9 *nk* **Game Face (USA)**[55] 4-8-12 .... EPrado 3 99
(Todd Pletcher, U.S.A) *disp 5th to wl over 2f out: 7th and btn st* **11/1**

1m 21.66s (81.66)
WFA 3 from 4yo+ 1lb **9** Ran SP% **113.7**
PARI-MUTUEL: WIN 8.80; PL (1-2) 3.00, 2.60; SHOW (1-2-3) 2.80, 2.20,7.40; SF 15.40.
Owner Augustin Stable **Bred** C Kidder & N Cole **Trained** USA

FOCUS
When Ventura won this race in 2008 the fractions were 22.26 for the first quarter, 44.02 for the half, and 1:07.91 for 6f, resulting in a final time of 1:19.90. Compare those numbers to this year's sectionals: 23.23, 45.95, and 1:09.66, for a closing time of 1:21.66. The proximity of the front-running third also limits the form.

NOTEBOOK
Informed Decision(USA), who had beaten Ventura back in April on the only other occasion they had met, is seemingly the more versatile of pair as she was ideally placed considering how the race unfolded. She's now 7-7 on synthetics and may have won this regardless of the way the second-placed mare was ridden. The plan is for her to stay in training.
Ventura(USA) did not have the race set up for her this time and, throw a wide trip into the mix, and she has actually run a mighty race behind a filly who is top-class in her own right. While she does need to be delivered late to make use of her acceleration, it's not hard to argue she should have been ridden at least slightly closer to the lead this time.
Free Flying Soul(USA) is surely flattered, having set the steady pace.
Sara Louise(USA), trying synthetics for the first time, failed to run to the pick of her dirt form.

7286a BREEDERS' CUP LADIES CLASSIC (GRADE 1) (FILLIES) (PRO-RIDE) 1m 1f (D)

11:45 (11:45) 3-Y-O+ £750,000 (£250,000; £137,500; £83,333; £41,667)

RPR
1 **Life Is Sweet (USA)**27 6688 4-8-12 GKGomez 2 119
(John Shirreffs, U.S.A) *last and well back to over 3f out, still last straight, brought widest, ran on to lead entering final f, ridden clear, ran on well* **9/1**
2 2 ½ **Mushka (USA)**26 4-8-12 (b) KDesormeaux 3 114
(William Mott, U.S.A) *held up, 7th & ridden straight, came wide, kept on under pressure, chased winner final f, no impression* **20/1**
3 1 **Music Note (USA)**34 6508 4-8-12 RMaragh 7 112+
(Saeed Bin Suroor) *closing 5th on outside half-way, 6th straight, headway on inside approaching final f, kept on one pace* **10/3**2
4 2 ¾ **Proviso**26 4-8-12 JRVelazquez 5 106+
(Robert Frankel, U.S.A) *held up in 6th, closed up on inside 5f out, went 2nd well over 3f out, led 1 1/2f out to 1f out, soon weakened* **5/1**3
5 ½ **Rainbow View (USA)**20 6872 3-8-9 JRLeparoux 8 105+
(J H M Gosden) *disputed 3rd, pushed along 3f out, 4th straight, one pace* **7/1**
6 1 ¾ **Cocoa Beach (CHI)**27 6688 5-8-12 RMigliore 6 101+
(Saeed Bin Suroor) *close up early, 6th half-way, 5th straight, weakened 1f out* **8/1**
7 1 ¼ **Lethal Heat (USA)**27 6688 4-8-12 ASolis 4 99+
(Barry Abrams, U.S.A) *raced in 2nd to well over 3f out, 3rd straight, driven & 2nd approaching final f, soon weakened* **20/1**
8 8 ¾ **Careless Jewel (USA)**34 6575 3-8-9 RLandry 1 80+
(Josie Carroll, Canada) *led, went clear starting back straight,headed 1 1/2f out, weakened quickly* **9/4**1

1m 48.58s (-0.32)
WFA 3 from 4yo+ 3lb **8 Ran SP% 113.6**
PARI-MUTUEL: WIN 18.20; PL (1-2) 8.00, 12.80; SHOW (1-2-3) 5.00, 6.40,3.20; SF 171.60.
Owner Mr & Mrs Martin J Wygod **Bred** Mr & Mrs Martin J Wygood **Trained** USA

FOCUS
They covered the first 4f in 45.78, and 6f in 1:09.74, compared with 48.08 and 1.11.08 last year, with Careless Jewel virtually running away with her rider down the back straight. The first two were held up last, and second last respectively, and this is obviously form to treat with caution, although the runner-up is probably the best guide.

NOTEBOOK
Life Is Sweet(USA), representing the same trainer as Zenyatta, who won this in 2008 but was aimed at the Classic itself this time, is undoubtedly hugely flattered as she was best placed considering how the race unfolded. Produced wide with her challenge in the straight, she ran on strongly past a bunch of horses who, with the exception of the runner-up, were tired.
Mushka(USA), like the winner, benefited from the overly strong gallop.
Music Note(USA), runner-up behind Zenyatta in this race last season, looked set to drop away when coming under pressure rounding the final bend, but she eventually responded and was unlucky not to finish closer as she had nowhere to go when picking up at the top of the straight, and had to switch inside. She has now been retired.
Proviso got to the front at the top of the straight, but that was too soon. She stays in training.
Rainbow View(USA) wasn't at her best on this first try on synthetics, but it would be unfair to judge her too harshly considering how the race unfolded. She will remain in the US to be trained by Jonathan Sheppard.
Cocoa Beach(CHI), last year's third, looked a threat turning in, but she had nothing to offer after being squeezed up against the inside rail by her stablemate early in the straight.
Careless Jewel(USA) ruined her chance by refusing to settle and going too fast.

7013 DONCASTER (L-H)

Saturday, November 7

OFFICIAL GOING: Soft

7287 BET TOTEPOOL ON 0800 221 221 APPRENTICE H'CAP 7f

11:55 (11:58) (Class 4) (0-85,85) 3-Y-O+ £6,476 (£1,927; £963; £481) Stalls High

Form RPR
4442 1 **Jordaura**7 7189 3-8-11 76 AndreaAtzeni 10 86+
(W R Swinburn) *wnt lft s: midfield: hdwy wl over 2f out: led wl over 1f out: rdn appr last: drvn and kpt on wl towards fin* **7/1**1
4132 2 hd **Kiwi Bay**10 7125 4-9-5 83 NeilBrown 9 93+
(M Dods) *bmpd s and hld up in rr: hdwy and n.m.r and nt clr run 2f out: swtchd rt over 1f out: sn rdn and styd on to chal ins fnl f: drvn: edgd lft and kpt on* **12/1**
6215 3 2 ¾ **Misplaced Fortune**7 7189 4-9-1 79 Louis-PhilippeBeuzelin 14 81
(N Tinkler) *midfield: hdwy 3f out: rdn to ld briefly 2f out: sn hdd and drvn: wknd ins fnl f* **25/1**
3634 4 shd **The Galloping Shoe**16 6964 4-8-12 76 AndrewMullen 3 78
(A C Whillans) *towards rr: pushed along 1/2-way: hdwy and rdn along 2f out: drvn over 1f out: kpt on ins fnl f: nrst fin* **20/1**
2450 5 ¾ **Happy Anniversary (IRE)**27 6695 3-8-10 80 LeeNewnes(5) 11 80
(Mrs D J Sanderson) *hld up towards rr: hdwy wl over 2f out: effrt and n.m.r wl over 1f out: sn swtchd rt and rdn: kpt on ins fnl f: nrst fin* **16/1**
-202 6 2 **Aspro Mavro (IRE)**10 7126 3-9-0 79 JackMitchell 16 74
(J H M Gosden) *chsd ldrs: hdwy and cl up 3f out: rdn along over 2f out and kpt on same pce* **8/1**3
2633 7 nk **Observatory Star (IRE)**10 7125 6-8-13 80 (bt) PaulPickard(3) 19 74
(T D Easterby) *in tch: rdn along over 2f out: sn drvn and one pce fr over 1f out* **15/2**2
P034 8 1 ¾ **Ocean Transit (IRE)**10 7125 4-9-0 78 RussellKennemore 20 67
(R J Price) *racd wd: chsd ldrs: rdn along over 2f out: drvn and edgd lft over 1f out: kpt on same pce* **16/1**
534 9 ½ **Toto Skyllachy**11 7083 4-9-2 80 JackDean 15 68
(S Gollings) *prom: effrt over 2f out: sn rdn and ev ch tl drvn and wknd appr fnl f* **11/1**
2620 10 1 **Leonid Glow**7 7171 4-8-5 74 IJBrennan(5) 2 59
(M Dods) *stmbld s and towards rr: hdwy and midfield 1/2-way: rdn to chse ldrs 2f out: sn drvn and no imp* **33/1**
5313 11 ½ **Kingswinford (IRE)**4 7220 3-8-10 78 RichardEvans(3) 8 62
(P D Evans) *prom: hdwy to ld 3f out: rdn along and hdd 2f out: sn drvn and grad wknd* **14/1**
0260 12 nk **The Kyllachy Kid**17 6949 3-9-3 85 AshleyMorgan(3) 12 68
(S Gollings) *a towards rr* **33/1**
4000 13 2 ¼ **Boy Blue**11 7083 4-8-7 76 BillyCray(5) 18 53
(P Salmon) *rrd s and bhd tl sme late hdwy* **28/1**
2201 14 5 **Tamasou (IRE)**4 7220 4-8-12 79 6ex MartinLane(3) 7 43
(A J McCabe) *cl up: rdn along over 2f out: sn wknd* **8/1**3
0000 15 ½ **Slugger O'Toole**141 3091 4-9-2 80 WilliamCarson 17 43
(S C Williams) *nvr bttr than midfield* **11/1**
4540 16 ½ **Bid For Gold**11 7083 5-8-6 73 PatrickDonaghy(3) 4 35
(Jedd O'Keeffe) *cl up: rdn along wl over 2f out and sn wknd* **50/1**
0350 17 3 ¼ **Rising Shadow (IRE)**21 6847 8-8-6 73 DeanHeslop(3) 1 26
(A D Brown) *hld up: a towards rr* **16/1**
0200 18 10 **Fishforcompliments**35 6482 5-9-6 84 FrederikTylicki 6 11
(R A Fahey) *in tch: rdn along 3f out: sn wknd* **16/1**
0000 19 ¾ **Glenridding**11 7083 5-8-8 75 (p) AndrewHeffernan(3) 13 —
(J G Given) *cl up: rdn along 3f out and sn wknd* **50/1**
0001 20 1 ½ **Realt Na Mara (IRE)**12 7062 6-8-4 73 RyanPowell(5) 5 —
(H Morrison) *led: hdd 3f out: sn rdn along and wknd* **20/1**

1m 29.27s (2.97) **Going Correction** +0.475s/f (Yiel)
WFA 3 from 4yo+ 1lb **20 Ran SP% 127.7**
Speed ratings (Par 105): **102,101,98,98,97 95,95,93,92,91 90,90,87,82,81 80,77,65,64,63**
toteswingers: 1&2 £30.90, 1&3 £25.60, 2&3 £61.40 CSF £81.45 CT £2022.93 TOTE £8.90: £2.60, £3.30, £5.40, £6.40; EX 103.20 TRIFECTA Not won..
Owner Carl Hodgson **Bred** Pendley Farm **Trained** Aldbury, Herts
■ Stewards' Enquiry : Neil Brown two-day ban: used whip with excessive frequency (Nov 21,24)

FOCUS
An open handicap in which they went 7-1 the field. The form is straightforward with the third a fair guide.

7288 BET TOTEPOOL AT TOTESPORT.COM EBF MAIDEN STKS (DIV I) 6f

12:25 (12:27) (Class 4) 2-Y-O £6,152 (£1,830; £914; £456) Stalls High

Form RPR
622 1 **Adventure Story**12 7061 2-8-12 71 RichardHughes 15 74
(R Hannon) *trckd ldrs: rdn to ld ins fnl f: drvn out* **4/1**2
2 ¾ **Jarrow (IRE)** 2-9-3 0 JoeFanning 16 77
(M Johnston) *chsd ldr tl led over 3f out: rdn over 1f out: edgd lft and hdd ins fnl f: styd on* **3/1**1
3 nse **Hamloola** 2-8-12 0 RHills 3 72
(W J Haggas) *s.i.s: in rr: hdwy and edgd lft over 1f out: r.o wl* **15/2**
0 4 1 **Kings 'n Dreams**30 6616 2-9-3 0 PatCosgrave 2 74
(D K Ivory) *a.p: rdn over 1f out: styd on* **16/1**
3525 5 3 **Could It Be Magic**18 6913 2-9-0 73 (p) JackDean(3) 4 65
(W G M Turner) *chsd ldrs: rdn and ev ch over 1f out: no ex ins fnl f* **6/1**3
0 6 nk **Tell Halaf**8 7145 2-9-3 0 HayleyTurner 12 64
(M L W Bell) *dwlt: hdwy over 2f out: sn rdn: styd on: nt rch ldrs* **25/1**
7 shd **Bear Tobouggie** 2-8-12 0 PJMcDonald 5 58
(G A Swinbank) *sn pushed along in mid-div: hdwy over 1f out: r.o: nt trble ldrs* **16/1**
05 8 shd **Singin' The Blues**23 6797 2-9-3 0 LukeMorris 11 63
(J M P Eustace) *prom: rdn over 1f out: styd on same pce* **20/1**
50 9 ½ **Orchid Wing**12 7058 2-9-3 0 PaulHanagan 10 62
(R A Fahey) *chsd ldrs: rdn over 2f out: ev ch over 1f out: wknd ins fnl f* **7/1**
10 ½ **Red Scintilla** 2-8-12 0 DO'Donohoe 9 55
(N Tinkler) *s.s: outpcd: rdn and hung lft over 1f out: nvr nrr* **66/1**
11 ¾ **Suzhou** 2-8-12 0 RichardKingscote 6 53
(Tom Dascombe) *s.i.s: sn pushed along: a in rr* **16/1**
P0 12 nk **Dovedon Diva**11 7096 2-8-12 0 LPKeniry 8 52
(T Keddy) *hld up: rdn 1/2-way: sme hdwy over 2f out: sn wknd* **150/1**
13 1 ¼ **Gwenllian (IRE)** 2-8-12 0 CatherineGannon 7 48
(J L Hassett, Ire) *mid-div: hdwy 1/2-way: rdn over 2f out: wknd fnl f* **16/1**
14 8 **Best Trip (IRE)** 2-9-3 0 PaulEddery 14 29
(R C Guest) *led: hdd over 3f out: rdn and wknd 2f out* **40/1**
0 15 6 **Singing Scott (IRE)**19 6896 2-9-3 0 DanielTudhope 1 11
(R Bastiman) *sn outpcd and bhd* **33/1**

1m 16.67s (3.07) **Going Correction** +0.475s/f (Yiel) **15 Ran SP% 123.2**
Speed ratings (Par 98): **98,97,96,95,91 91,91,90,90,89 88,88,86,75,67**
toteswingers: 1&2 £1.10, 1&3 £4.80, 2&3 £4.20 CSF £15.67 TOTE £4.90: £2.30, £1.70, £2.70; EX 13.10 Trifecta £23.30 Pool: £177.42 - 5.63 winning units..
Owner Lady Whent **Bred** Raffin Bloodstock **Trained** East Everleigh, Wilts

FOCUS
Previous experience was the difference here,

NOTEBOOK
Adventure Story, although only rated 71, proved good enough to get off the mark at the fourth attempt. She had the rail to help in the closing stages and handled conditions well enough, although whether she really needs the ground this soft is open to question. (op 7-2 tchd 9-2)
Jarrow(IRE) ran a promising race for a stable whose juveniles invariably improve for a run. A half-brother to five winners, including Group-class sprinter Moss Vale, he looks sure to pay his way next season. (op 9-2 tchd 5-1)
Hamloola ◆, who cost 210,000gns, was green and given a very sympathetic ride on her debut. She finished her race off well towards the stands' side under just a hand ride and will have learned plenty from the experience. She certainly looks the one to take from the race. (op 5-1)
Kings 'n Dreams, sent off a big price when down the field on his debut at Newbury, showed the benefit of that run, but he looks more of a handicap type for next year. (op 40-1)
Could It Be Magic, prominent from the off, didn't quite see it out on his first try on soft ground. He has a mark of 73, which probably flatters him also. (op 8-1)

7289 BET TOTEPOOL AT TOTESPORT.COM EBF MAIDEN STKS (DIV II) 6f

1:00 (1:01) (Class 4) 2-Y-O £6,152 (£1,830; £914; £456) Stalls High

Form RPR
42 1 **London Gold**27 6696 2-9-3 0 DaneO'Neill 7 78
(H Candy) *hld up in tch: hdwy on outer over 2f out: rdn to ld jst over 1f out: edgd rt ins fnl f: styd on* **6/4**1
03 2 ½ **Olney Lass**31 6591 2-8-7 0 PaulPickard(5) 6 72
(W J H Ratcliffe) *prom: effrt over 2f out: rdn to ld wl over 1f out: drvn and hdd appr fnl f: kpt on gamely u.p ins fnl f* **11/1**
3 1 ¾ **Esuvia (IRE)** 2-8-12 0 TomEaves 10 66
(B Smart) *in tch: hdwy wl over 2f out: rdn and ev ch over 1f out: drvn and kpt on same pce ins fnl f* **20/1**

60 **4** 2 ¼ **Redden**[15] 6991 2-9-3 0 RHills 9 65
(W J Haggas) *prom: edgd rt 1/2-way: effrt 2f out: sn rdn and ev ch tl drvn: hung lft and wknd appr fnl f* **4/1**[2]
5 ¾ **Dandarrell** 2-8-12 0 BMcHugh(5) 14 62
(Miss J A Camacho) *dwlt and towards rr: hdwy whn hmpd 1/2-way: sn swtchd rt and rdn along: styd on appr fnl f: nrst fin* **28/1**
6 2 **The Gillie** 2-9-3 0 PaulHanagan 5 56
(R A Fahey) *in rr: rdn along 1/2-way: styd on fnl 2f: nrst fin* **7/1**[3]
04 **7** 1 **Classical Piece (USA)**[18] 6912 2-9-3 0 NCallan 11 53
(Mrs D J Sanderson) *cl up on stands' rail: led wl over 2f out: sn rdn: drvn and hdd wl over 1f out: grad wknd* **16/1**
40 **8** nse **Set Back**[19] 6896 2-9-3 0 AdrianTNicholls 2 53
(D Nicholls) *led: rdn along and hdd wl over 2f out: sn drvn and grad wknd* **25/1**
0 **9** 8 **Compton Way**[8] 7145 2-9-3 0 RobertWinston 12 29
(B W Hills) *midfield: rdn along 1/2-way: sn outpcd* **12/1**
10 7 **Bahamian Bolt** 2-8-12 0 LeeNewnes(5) 8 8
(R Bastiman) *dwlt: sn in tch: rdn along whn hmpd 1/2-way: sn wknd* **66/1**
11 1 ¾ **Natalie N G** 2-8-12 0 GregFairley 1 —
(J R Jenkins) *prom: rdn along 1/2-way: wknd over 2f out* **66/1**
0 **12** 4 **Crystal Glass**[15] 6991 2-9-3 0 DavidAllan 13 —
(T D Easterby) *a towards rr: bhd fnl 2f* **50/1**
13 4 ½ **Velle Est Valere** 2-8-12 0 DanielTudhope 3 —
(C J Teague) *dwlt: swtchd wd after 1f: rdn along 1/2-way and sn outpcd* **100/1**
14 94 **Magic Place** 2-9-3 0 RichardHughes 4 —
(R Hannon) *s.i.s and a in rr: hanging lft and lost tch 1/2-way: sn eased: lame* **11/1**

1m 16.44s (2.84) **Going Correction** +0.475s/f (Yiel) **14** Ran SP% **120.7**
Speed ratings (Par 98): **100,99,97,94,93 90,89,88,78,68 66,61,55,—**
toteswingers: 1&2 £7.30, 1&3 £8.20, 2&3 £66.90 CSF £18.68 TOTE £2.50: £1.30, £2.80, £5.70; EX 15.50 Trifecta £247.40 Part won. Pool: £334.43 - 0.30 winning units..
Owner John Simms **Bred** John Simms **Trained** Kingston Warren, Oxon

FOCUS
Marginally the quicker of the two divisions.\n

NOTEBOOK
London Gold had shown more then enough in his first two starts to suggest he could win a race of this nature, including when second to subsequent Group 3 winner Carnaby Street at Goodwood last time, and he stuck his neck out willingly to see off Olney Lass. He should make a nice sprint handicapper next season. (op 2-1 tchd 85-40 in a place)
Olney Lass improved greatly from her debut to her second start, and this was another step forward. Handicaps will give her more options and her pedigree suggests she should be happy enough sticking to this sort of trip. (op 8-1 tchd 12-1)
Esuvia(IRE) ◆, a half-sister to multiple winning sprinter Resplendent Glory, did best of the newcomers. Bred to handle these conditions, she travelled well for a long way and looks sure to improve plenty for the outing. (op 18-1)
Redden, a son of Pivotal, could have been expected to improve for the switch to softer ground, but he was a little disappointing. Perhaps he needs further, and he might get a chance to show it in handicaps. (op 6-1)
Dandarrell ran green but showed signs of ability. (op 25-1)
The Gillie ◆, who's a half-brother to last year's Cheveley Park fourth Adorn and attracted some market support, kept on late and looks the type to do better at three. (op 9-1 tchd 13-2)
Bahamian Bolt Official explanation: trainer said gelding lost its off-fore shoe
Magic Place Official explanation: vet said colt finished lame

7290 BET ON BREEDERS CUP AT TOTESPORT.COM NURSERY 6f

1:35 (1:37) (Class 4) (0-85,85) 2-Y-O **£6,476** (£1,927; £963; £481) **Stalls** High

Form RPR
213 **1** **Dubai Set**[63] 5658 2-9-4 **82** RichardHughes 1 89
(R Hannon) *chsd ldrs: rdn over 2f out: edgd rt ins fnl f: r.o u.p to ld nr fin* **7/1**[2]
122 **2** hd **Gouray Girl (IRE)**[10] 7108 2-9-5 **83** AdamKirby 15 89
(W R Swinburn) *hld up: hdwy and nt clr run over 2f out: led over 1f out: sn rdn: no ex and hdd nr fin* **8/1**[3]
312 **3** 1 ¼ **Felsham**[33] 6550 2-8-9 **73** DaneO'Neill 13 76
(H Candy) *chsd ldrs: rdn to ld briefly over 1f out: edgd lft ins fnl f: styd on same pce* **6/1**[1]
6003 **4** nk **Jack My Boy (IRE)**[30] 6619 2-8-9 **78** RichardEvans(5) 20 80
(P D Evans) *chsd ldrs: rdn over 1f out: hung lft ins fnl f: styd on same pce* **12/1**
2003 **5** ½ **Flaneur**[29] 6643 2-8-12 **76** (b) DavidAllan 16 76
(T D Easterby) *chsd ldrs: rdn over 1f out: styd on same pce fnl f* **8/1**[3]
251 **6** ¾ **Walvis Bay (IRE)**[29] 6646 2-9-6 **84** MickyFenton 11 82
(T P Tate) *prom: rdn over 1f out: styd on same pce fnl f* **9/1**
3241 **7** 1 ¼ **Dusty Spirit**[17] 6932 2-8-7 **74** JackDean(3) 19 68
(W G M Turner) *chsd ldrs: rdn over 2f out: no ex fnl f* **16/1**
21 **8** 1 **Oil Strike**[18] 6913 2-9-2 **85** AshleyMorgan(5) 4 76
(P Winkworth) *chsd ldrs: rdn over 1f out: no ex ins fnl f* **14/1**
6030 **9** 1 ¼ **Maldon Prom (IRE)**[8] 7156 2-8-8 **72** (t) JerryO'Dwyer 12 60
(C A Dwyer) *hld up: effrt over 2f out: no imp fnl f* **66/1**
0201 **10** ¾ **Coolree Star (IRE)**[19] 6905 2-8-11 **75** TonyHamilton 10 60
(J A Glover) *s.s: hdwy over 3f out: rdn and hung rght over 1f out: sn wknd* **25/1**
010 **11** ½ **Bathwick Gold (IRE)**[35] 6486 2-9-1 **79** CatherineGannon 18 63
(P D Evans) *in rr and pushed along: rdn 1/2-way: n.d* **50/1**
2435 **12** 5 **Lava Lamp (GER)**[33] 6534 2-8-11 **75** DanielTudhope 3 44
(G A Harker) *s.i.s: outpcd: nvr nrr* **66/1**
0450 **13** ¾ **Anjomarba (IRE)**[38] 6398 2-8-11 **78** WilliamCarson(3) 9 45
(W G M Turner) *prom: rdn over 2f out: wknd over 1f out* **50/1**
6254 **14** nk **Farmers Wish (IRE)**[10] 7108 2-8-13 **77** NCallan 5 43
(J L Spearing) *led: rdn and hdd over 1f out: wknd ins fnl f* **12/1**
5032 **15** ¾ **Dancing Freddy (IRE)**[10] 7115 2-9-2 **80** FrederikTylicki 6 43
(J G Given) *chsd ldrs: rdn over 1f out: wknd fnl f* **16/1**
2150 **16** 2 **Miss Lesley**[30] 6619 2-9-0 **78** ChrisCatlin 8 35
(D K Ivory) *prom: rdn over 2f out: sn wknd* **33/1**
2130 **17** 1 ¼ **Bridge Valley**[62] 5692 2-9-1 **79** JamieSpencer 2 33
(R Hannon) *s.s: a outpcd* **33/1**
010 **18** ½ **Dormer Fleet**[11] 7097 2-8-11 **75** JimmyFortune 17 27
(J H M Gosden) *hld up: shkn up over 2f out: a in rr* **16/1**
1311 **19** hd **Bossy Kitty**[29] 6643 2-8-13 **77** JoeFanning 7 29
(N Tinkler) *prom: rdn and wknd over 2f out* **16/1**
5130 **20** 2 ¼ **Our Dream Queen**[30] 6619 2-8-4 **68** (t) WilliamBuick 14 13
(B W Hills) *mid-div: rdn over 2f out: sn wknd* **16/1**

1m 15.86s (2.26) **Going Correction** +0.475s/f (Yiel) **20** Ran SP% **127.1**
Speed ratings (Par 98): **103,102,101,100,100 99,97,96,94,93 92,86,85,84,83 80,79,78,78,75**
toteswingers: 1&2 £3.30, 1&3 £7.80, 2&3 £10.10 CSF £60.15 CT £374.77 TOTE £7.40: £2.30, £2.50, £2.50, £2.80; EX 35.20 Trifecta £152.10 Pool: £308.32 - 1.50 winning units..
Owner Malih L Al Basti **Bred** Malih L Al Basti **Trained** East Everleigh, Wilts
■ Stewards' Enquiry : William Carson caution: careless riding

FOCUS
A competitive-looking nursery in which they raced middle to stands' side. The majority of those involved in the finish were drawn high.

NOTEBOOK
Dubai Set was unfavourably drawn in stall one and tracked Farmers Wish up the middle of the track before edging right once taking his measure. This was a lesser handicap than the one he was third in at Haydock when last seen in September, and he's clearly suited by give in the ground, just like his brother Saxford, so he'll be one to keep in mind for when the turf season kicks off again in the spring. (op 17-2)
Gouray Girl(IRE) tracked the pace towards the stands' side and found a fine turn of foot to hit the front a furlong out. It looked a race-winning move, but she idled and was caught close home, and it would seem that she is the type that needs delivering as late as possible. The talent is clearly there, though, and she should find further success if connections decide to keep going with her for a while on the Polytrack. (tchd 13-2)
Felsham, whose trainer was worried that the colt might be over the top, having gone woolly in his coat, ran a sound race in the circumstances, and saw the extra furlong out perfectly well. (op 13-2 tchd 11-2)
Jack My Boy(IRE), who shaped better at Newbury last time, got to race off a 2lb lower mark and had the stands' rail to help. He probably ran to a similar level and helps rate the form. (op 16-1)
Flaneur got to race with some cut in the ground for the first time since winning at Newcastle in July, but he's 9lb higher now and met one or two better treated. (op 10-1)
Walvis Bay(IRE) looked to have plenty on at the weights on his handicap debut but ran with credit. (op 8-1)
Oil Strike ran a bit better than the bare form suggests as he raced more towards the centre while the main action developed stands' side.
Bathwick Gold(IRE) Official explanation: jockey said colt hung left
Bossy Kitty Official explanation: jockey said filly never travelled

7291 TOTESPORTCASINO.COM EBF GILLIES FILLIES' STKS (LISTED RACE) 1m 2f 60y

2:05 (2:07) (Class 1) 3-Y-O+ **£23,704** (£8,964; £4,480; £2,240) **Stalls** Low

Form RPR
1444 **1** **Queen Of Pentacles (IRE)**[22] 6813 3-8-10 97 RichardHughes 10 103
(J Noseda) *midfield: hdwy 3f out: rdn and squeezed through to chal over 1f out: drvn and styd on to ld ins fnl f: kpt on strly* **14/1**
0020 **2** 1 ¾ **Mooakada (IRE)**[22] 6813 3-8-10 99 RobertHavlin 12 100
(J H M Gosden) *hld up towards rr: gd hdwy on outer over 2f out: rdn and edgd lft over 1f out: led ent fnl f: sn drvn and hdd: one pce last 100yds* **20/1**
6302 **3** nk **Copperbeech (IRE)**[12] 7059 3-8-10 96 TedDurcan 8 99
(Saeed Bin Suroor) *trckd ldrs: hdwy over 3f out: swtchd rt and rdn to ld wl over 1f out: drvn and hdd ent fnl f: kpt on same pce* **17/2**
2013 **4** ½ **Les Fazzani (IRE)**[13] 7046 5-9-0 111 PhillipMakin 4 98+
(K A Ryan) *hld up towards rr: hdwy over 3f out: chsd ldrs and n.m.r 2f out: sn swtchd rt and rdn: kpt on same pce ent fnl f* **2/1**[1]
2640 **5** 2 **Syvilla**[69] 5472 4-9-0 90 ChrisCatlin 11 94
(Rae Guest) *hld up in rr: hdwy 3f out: rdn 2f out: styd on appr fnl f: nrst fin* **100/1**
241 **6** 1 ½ **Hidden Brief**[149] 2847 3-8-10 95 PhilipRobinson 5 91
(M A Jarvis) *led: rdn along and hdd 3f out: drvn 2f out: kpt on same pce* **12/1**
1616 **7** 2 ¾ **Cill Rialaig**[14] 7035 4-9-0 93 SteveDrowne 19 86
(H Morrison) *in tch: hdwy on outer over 3f out: rdn to chse ldrs 2f out: sn drvn and no imp appr fnl f* **25/1**
1 **8** ¾ **Rainbow Desert (USA)**[26] 6741 3-8-10 0 DO'Donohoe 6 84+
(Saeed Bin Suroor) *trckd ldrs: effrt 3f out: rdn along over 2f out: sn drvn and wknd wl over 1f out* **12/1**
42 **9** 1 **Perfect Star**[25] 6757 5-9-0 95 AdamKirby 14 82
(C G Cox) *in tch: rdn along 3f out: drvn over 2f out and sn one pce* **25/1**
03 **10** 1 ½ **Misdaqeya**[114] 4020 3-8-10 93 RobertWinston 13 79
(B W Hills) *trckd ldrs: hdwy 3f out: rdn to ld over 2f out: drvn: edgd lft and hdd wl over 1f out: wknd* **40/1**
4000 **11** 2 ¼ **Hollow Green (IRE)**[8] 7148 3-8-10 77 CatherineGannon 3 75
(P D Evans) *a towards rr* **100/1**
0100 **12** shd **It's Dubai Dolly**[49] 6113 3-8-10 75 HayleyTurner 7 74
(A J Lidderdale) *a in rr* **100/1**
-150 **13** 1 ¼ **Short Affair**[69] 5472 4-9-0 92 JamieSpencer 9 72
(L M Cumani) *a towards rr* **25/1**
515 **14** hd **Arwaah (IRE)**[21] 6853 3-8-10 108 RHills 20 71
(M P Tregoning) *cl up: led over 3f out: rdn over 2f out: sn hdd & wknd* **5/1**[2]
40-5 **15** 7 **Arthur's Girl**[97] 4566 4-9-0 99 (t) JimmyFortune 2 57
(J H M Gosden) *a towards rr* **16/1**
2126 **16** ¾ **Plaisterer**[22] 6813 4-9-0 96 JackMitchell 16 56
(C F Wall) *hld up in rr: effrt on outer over 3f out: sn rdn and nvr a factor* **8/1**[3]
610 **17** 1 ½ **Benedicte (IRE)**[22] 6813 3-8-10 93 AndreaAtzeni 18 53
(M Botti) *a towards rr* **66/1**
6255 **18** 17 **Jenny Soba**[11] 7085 6-9-0 54 DaneO'Neill 15 19
(Lucinda Featherstone) *a in rr* **150/1**
121 **19** 18 **Candy Ride (IRE)**[101] 4441 3-8-10 78 PaulHanagan 1 —
(E A L Dunlop) *midfield: hdwy on inner over 3f out: sn rdn and wknd over 2f out* **50/1**

2m 11.87s (0.67) **Going Correction** +0.30s/f (Good)
WFA 3 from 4yo+ 4lb **19** Ran SP% **125.4**
Speed ratings (Par 108): **109,107,107,106,105 104,101,101,100,99 97,97,96,96,90 90,88,75,60**
toteswingers: 1&2 £65.00, 1&3 £34.40, 2&3 £24.20 CSF £277.84 TOTE £16.00: £4.00, £6.10, £3.50; EX 365.10 Trifecta £453.60 Pool: £674.28 - 1.10 winning units..
Owner Normandie Stud Ltd **Bred** Normandie Stud Ltd **Trained** Newmarket, Suffolk

FOCUS
A big field of fillies chasing some valuable black type before the season is out. Ordinary Listed form overall, but sounder than most as the race was well run.

NOTEBOOK
Queen Of Pentacles(IRE) found the necessary improvement to record her first win at Listed level. She'd been fourth in similar company in her last three starts, but she's a daughter of Selkirk out of a Sadler's Wells mare whose two wins came on easy ground, so this softer surface gave hope that she would go closer this time. She didn't get the clearest of runs 2f out but once the gap came she picked up well and saw the trip out strongly.
Mooakada(IRE) began the season as an Oaks possible but has largely struggled. This soft ground brought about improvement from her, though, and this daughter of Montjeu could be the type to improve from three to four. (tchd 22-1)
Copperbeech(IRE) hasn't reached the heights she promised during her juvenile career in France, but she has always shown a liking for a bit of cut in the ground and this was a sound effort for her in-form stable. (op 10-1)

Les Fazzani(IRE), who won this race last year, was the one to beat at the weights and came here on the back of a fine third in an Italian Group 1 last time out. She didn't run to her best, though, was just staying on one-paced at the finish, and perhaps found this race coming too soon after her travels abroad. (tchd 9-4)
Syvilla, given a break since running poorly at Goodwood in August, bounced back to form, staying on without threatening the principals. She has been consistently held at this level since winning her maiden.
Hidden Brief, off the track since winning her maiden in June, had been sent off favourite for the Cheshire Oaks on her previous start. Fresher than most in the field, she raced a touch keenly in front and was there to be shot at in the straight. (op 14-1)
Cill Rialaig probably doesn't need the ground this soft. (op 20-1)
Arwaah(IRE), who didn't run badly in a Group 2 last time out, dropped out tamely after being headed. She is better than this and perhaps conditions were just too testing for her. (op 8-1)
Arthur's Girl
Plaisterer Official explanation: trainer said regarding running that the filly ran flat after a long season

7292 BEST ODDS GUARANTEED AT TOTESPORT.COM WENTWORTH STKS (LISTED RACE) 6f

2:40 (2:46) (Class 1) 3-Y-O+ **£29,630** (£11,205; £5,600; £2,800) **Stalls High**

Form RPR
5041 **1** **Fullandby (IRE)**[4] 7227 7-9-3 94 .... AlanMunro 7 104
(T J Etherington) *hld up: hdwy and nt clr run over 1f out: swtchd lft: r.o u.p to ld nr fin* **9/2**[1]
0211 **2** *hd* **Arthur's Edge**[16] 6964 5-9-3 85 .... LukeMorris 6 103
(B Palling) *chsd ldr: rdn to ld 1f out: r.o: hdd nr fin* **18/1**
0001 **3** *1 ½* **Lovely Thought**[11] 7082 3-8-12 82 ....(b) RHills 2 94
(W J Haggas) *trckd ldrs: racd keenly: rdn over 1f out: styd on same pce ins fnl f: wnt 3rd towards fin* **22/1**
23 **4** *shd* **Prescription**[27] 6702 4-8-12 96 .... SebSanders 8 93
(Sir Mark Prescott) *chsd ldrs: rdn to ld over 1f out: sn hdd: no ex and lost 3rd towards fin* **6/1**[2]
3125 **5** *½* **Able Master (IRE)**[14] 7019 3-9-3 105 .... TomEaves 11 97
(B Smart) *trckd ldrs: hrd rdn fr over 1f out: styd on* **9/2**[1]
30 **6** *2* **Icelandic**[28] 6661 7-9-3 103 ....(t) SJCraine 10 90
(F Sheridan) *hld up: hdwy over 2f out: rdn over 1f out: wknd ins fnl f* **9/2**[1]
0000 **7** *1 ½* **Protector (SAF)**[14] 7019 8-9-3 86 ....(t) RobertHavlin 3 85
(A G Foster) *prom: rdn over 2f out: wknd fnl f* **33/1**
30 **8** *1* **Festoso (IRE)**[28] 6661 4-9-1 100 ....(b) RichardHughes 13 80
(H J L Dunlop) *led: rdn and hdd over 1f out: wknd ins fnl f* **10/1**
5441 **9** *1* **Crystal Moments**[14] 7032 3-8-12 88 .... PaulHanagan 4 74
(E A L Dunlop) *hld up: nt clr run and outpcd over 1f out: n.d after* **16/1**
33-0 **10** *2* **Sir Gerry (USA)**[178] 1989 4-9-3 110 .... SteveDrowne 5 73
(J R Best) *hld up: hdwy over 2f out: nt clr run and wknd over 1f out* **17/2**
3204 **11** *½* **Vanadium**[12] 7051 7-9-3 55 ....(t) AmyScott 12 71?
(A J Lidderdale) *hld up in tch: rdn and wknd over 1f out* **200/1**
115- **12** *6* **Desert Phantom (USA)**[398] 6520 3-9-3 100 .... WilliamBuick 1 52
(D M Simcock) *chsd ldrs: rdn and ev ch over 1f out: wknd fnl f* **8/1**[3]

1m 14.74s (1.14) **Going Correction** +0.475s/f (Yiel) **12 Ran SP% 118.5**
Speed ratings (Par 111): **111,110,108,108,107 105,103,101,100,97 97,89**
toteswingers: 1&2 £31.40, 1&3 £10.40, 2&3 £29.60 CSF £88.90 TOTE £5.80: £1.80, £5.70, £3.60; EX 100.40 TRIFECTA Not won..
Owner Miss M Greenwood **Bred** Mrs A Haskell Ellis **Trained** Norton, N Yorks
■ Stewards' Enquiry : Luke Morris one-day ban: used whip with excessive frequency (Nov 21)

FOCUS
Not a strong Listed race, with doubts about the highest-rated runners in the line-up. The winner probably ran to somewhere near his Kempton win, with the second and third improving on their recent handicap form.

NOTEBOOK
Fullandby(IRE) looked as good as ever when winning a handicap off 94 at Kempton four days earlier but would not normally be considered good enough to win at this level. He had conditions to suit, though, travelled well off the pace, found the gaps to cut through the field inside the final 2f and ran down Arthur's Edge close home. Although a tough campaigner who takes his racing well, he'll be lucky to find a Listed race as weak as this again. He's apparently unlikely to have an all-weather campaign. (op 6-1)
Arthur's Edge, chasing a hat-trick after winning handicaps off 77 and 80, had plenty to prove in this company, even allowing for the fact that it was a weak race for the class. He ran well, though, confirming his progressive profile, and showing his versatility with regard to ground conditions. (tchd 16-1 and 20-1)
Lovely Thought has a rating of just 82 and it was difficult to see her playing a part, but like the first two she came here in top form, and was proven in soft ground. She looks to have run to her best while others disappointed. (tchd 20-1)
Prescription looked one of the more likely winners on paper, with conditions to suit. She ran well for a long way but didn't see her race out as well as some, and perhaps she has had enough for the season. (op 5-1 tchd 9-2 and 13-2)
Able Master(IRE) looked to hold strong claims in this company but this ground was probably softer than he cares for. (op 5-1 tchd 11-2)
Icelandic, who won this race last year, is from a stable that has had a poor season due to problems connected to rape seed oil and a virus, and he was clearly not at the same level this time around. (op 5-1 tchd 4-1)
Sir Gerry(USA) is used to competing at a higher level than this and was best in at the weights, but he hadn't run since May, was debuting for a new stable and was expected to need the run. His trainer is eyeing a Listed race at Lingfield in a fortnight's time. Official explanation: jockey said colt was struck into (op 7-1 tchd 10-1)

7293 TOTESPORT.COM NOVEMBER H'CAP (HERITAGE HANDICAP) 1m 4f

3:15 (3:17) (Class 2) 3-Y-O+
£59,194 (£17,727; £8,863; £4,436; £2,213; £1,111) **Stalls Low**

Form RPR
5150 **1** **Charm School**[35] 6480 4-8-12 98 .... JimmyFortune 14 111+
(J H M Gosden) *hld up in rr: hdwy 3f out: swtchd ins 2f out: swtchd rt and rdn over 1f out: str run ent fnl f: squeezed through to ld last 100yds: styd on strly* **17/2**[3]
032 **2** *1 ¾* **Hillview Boy (IRE)**[14] 7018 5-8-4 90 .... ChrisCatlin 19 100
(J S Goldie) *hld up and bhd: gd hdwy on outer wl over 2f out: rdn over 1f out: str run to chal ent fnl f and ev ch: sn drvn and edgd lft: kpt on same pce last 100yds* **11/1**
043 **3** *2 ½* **Ella**[23] 6795 5-8-4 90 .... JimmyQuinn 9 96
(G A Swinbank) *prom: led over 4f out: rdn clr over 2f out: jnd and drvn ent fnl f: hdd & wknd last 100yds* **8/1**[2]
2306 **4** *2* **Friston Forest (IRE)**[100] 4457 5-9-7 107 .... DO'Donohoe 24 110
(Saeed Bin Suroor) *midfield: hdwy 4f out: rdn along to chse ldrs over 2f out: drvn over 1f out and kpt on same pce* **40/1**
003 **5** *¾* **Salden Licht**[14] 7035 5-8-9 95 .... LukeMorris 18 97
(J M P Eustace) *hld up towards rr: hdwy on outer 4f out: rdn to chse ldrs 2f out: sn drvn and kpt on same pce* **12/1**
3120 **6** *2 ½* **Merchant Of Dubai**[14] 7031 4-8-11 97 .... RobertWinston 21 95
(G A Swinbank) *prom: effrt and cl up 3f out: sn rdn and ev ch tl drvn wl over 1f out and grad wknd* **25/1**
1504 **7** *1 ½* **Conquisto**[49] 6095 4-8-1 87 .... CatherineGannon 25 82
(S Gollings) *midfield: hdwy on outer 4f out: rdn to chse ldrs over 2f out: sn drvn: edgd lft and one pce* **50/1**
-400 **8** *1 ¼* **Highland Legacy**[21] 6851 5-8-0 86 ....(v) HayleyTurner 15 79
(M L W Bell) *towards rr: effrt over 4f out and sn rdn along: drvn over 2f out: kpt on: nvr nr ldrs* **16/1**
3132 **9** *nk* **Tastahil (IRE)**[14] 7031 5-9-11 111 .... RHills 5 104
(B W Hills) *in tch: hdwy 1/2-way: chsd ldrs 4f out: rdn along 3f out: wknd fnl 2f* **12/1**
2142 **10** *1 ½* **Kings Destiny**[28] 6662 3-8-8 100 .... PhilipRobinson 13 90
(M A Jarvis) *t.k.h: prom: hdwy 4f out: effrt to chal 3f out: sn rdn and wknd 2f out* **7/1**[1]
4500 **11** *½* **Ladies Best**[51] 6013 5-8-1 90 ....(p) MartinLane[(3)] 7 80
(B Ellison) *towards rr: sme hdwy fnl 3f: nvr a factor* **50/1**
2602 **12** *1* **Hevelius**[22] 6816 4-8-4 90 .... WilliamBuick 16 78
(W R Swinburn) *hld up in rr: sme hdwy fnl 3f: nvr a factor* **16/1**
0006 **13** *1 ¼* **Magicalmysterytour (IRE)**[14] 7018 6-8-7 93 .... AlanMunro 23 79
(W J Musson) *hld up: a in rr* **25/1**
-261 **14** *nk* **Baila Me (GER)**[9] 7131 4-9-7 107 .... TedDurcan 10 92
(Saeed Bin Suroor) *trckd ldrs: rdn along over 3f out and sn wknd* **10/1**
3210 **15** *1* **Rangefinder**[28] 6662 5-8-4 90 .... JamieSpencer 20 74
(Jane Chapple-Hyam) *in tch: hdwy over 3f out: swtchd ins and rdn over 2f out: sn btn* **33/1**
0014 **16** *½* **Pevensey (IRE)**[28] 6662 7-8-0 93 ....(p) IJBrennan[(7)] 12 76
(J J Quinn) *nvr bttr than midfield* **25/1**
-006 **17** *nse* **Siberian Tiger (IRE)**[28] 6662 4-8-6 97 ....(b) GFCarroll[(5)] 8 80
(A J Martin, Ire) *a in rr* **14/1**
3323 **18** *15* **Safari Sunup (IRE)**[28] 6662 4-8-6 97 .... AshleyMorgan[(5)] 4 56
(P Winkworth) *midfield on inner: rdn along over 4f out: drvn 3f out and sn wknd* **22/1**
46-0 **19** *4 ½* **Sligo**[4] 7221 4-7-8 87 ....(bt[1]) DeclanCannon[(7)] 6 39
(A J McCabe) *led: rdn along and hdd over 4f out: wknd 3f out* **100/1**
16-0 **20** *3 ¼* **First Avenue**[28] 6662 4-8-5 91 ....(p) FergusSweeney 22 38
(G L Moore) *chsd ldrs: rdn along over 3f out and sn wknd* **66/1**
1/10 **21** *1 ¼* **Broomielaw**[49] 6106 5-8-9 95 .... RichardHughes 17 40
(E A L Dunlop) *a bhd* **20/1**
62-3 **22** *23* **Stormy Weather (FR)**[13] 2275 3-8-6 98 .... FrederikTylicki 2 6
(J Howard Johnson) *chsd ldrs: rdn along over 4f out and sn wknd* **10/1**
60R **R** **Tilt**[11] 7091 7-8-2 88 ....(p) PaulHanagan 1 —
(B Ellison) *ref to r: tk no part* **50/1**

2m 35.96s (0.86) **Going Correction** +0.30s/f (Good)
WFA 3 from 4yo+ 6lb **23 Ran SP% 128.9**
Speed ratings (Par 109): **109,107,106,104,104 102,101,100,100,99 99,98,97,97,96 96,96,86,83,81 80,65,—**
toteswingers: 1&2 £29.30, 1&3 £67.60, 2&3 £16.00 CSF £87.51 CT £801.11 TOTE £9.60: £3.20, £2.70, £2.20, £14.10; EX 95.10 Trifecta £922.70 Pool: £18,831.00 - 15.10 winning units..
Owner H R H Princess Haya Of Jordan **Bred** Highclere Stud **Trained** Newmarket, Suffolk

FOCUS
A decent-quality renewal of this heritage handicap, with the top-weight rated 111. The early gallop didn't look overly strong, with a few racing keenly, but the charge for home began soon enough in the straight and the first two came from well off the pace. Solid form considering the ground and late stage of the season, with a pesonal best from the winner.

NOTEBOOK
Charm School has been on the go for a long time having started off the season in the Lincoln in March. Having been steadily stepped up in distance, he impressed in winning over 1m3f at Kempton before catching the eye running on strongly at the end of the John Smith's Stakes at Newbury. The drop back to 1m1f in the Cambridgeshire, and racing on the wrong part of the track was of no help, but he threatened to be much more effective over this new distance, especially with the ground in his favour, and so it proved. He came with a powerful late run towards the far-side rail, quickened up between the runner-up and third, and eventually won easily. He looks the type that could well develop into a Listed-class performer over this sort of trip next season, and there will always be the option of going abroad in search of the right ground. (op 10-1)
Hillview Boy(IRE), runner-up over the C&D last time out, had his ideal ground conditions and looked to have been primed for the race. He finished strongly from off the pace down the centre of the track and was simply unlucky to run into a rival finding improvement for the step up in trip. A big shell of a horse, he can be expected to do better again next year, when races such as the Ebor are likely to be in his trainer's sights. (op 9-1)
Ella was another who looked to have been prepared with this race in mind for some time. A daughter of Flossy, who won this race in 1999, like her dam she's at home in testing ground, but she doesn't help her cause by racing keenly. She was going strongly and took a few lengths out of her field approaching the 2f pole, but then began to tread water and didn't see it out. Had she settled better she'd have undoubtedly lasted home, but she has always been a keen-going sort. Her trainer's keen to try to pick up some black type with her, and she might go to Dortmund for a Group 3 in the next few weeks. (op 10-1)
Friston Forest(IRE), the stable's second string on jockey bookings, had been off the track since July and is at his best over further than this. The ground made it a test, though, together with the pace picking up plenty soon enough in the straight, and he ran a fine race in face of a stiff task at the weights.
Salden Licht, fresher than most having only had three previous outings this term, was trying this trip for the first time having run as though it might suit when third over 1m2f at Newbury a fortnight earlier. He ran well and it's a shame for him that the season has come to an end as he has looked better with each start. (op 14-1 tchd 16-1)
Merchant Of Dubai struggled upped to Group 3 company last time out but returned to form here. He was never too far off the pace, but the handicapper probably just has his measure for the time being.
Conquisto, having his first outing for his new stable, didn't run badly considering he was quite keen and the ground was softer than ideal.
Tastahil(IRE), runner-up in the St Simon Stakes last time out, faced a different test here giving weight all round, and he wasn't up to it. It looked as if he lost his action in the latter stages. (op 14-1)
Kings Destiny looked to hold strong claims on his Ascot effort, but he didn't settle well enough through the early stages and as a result had little to give in the straight. (op 8-1)
Hevelius Official explanation: jockey said gelding was hampered at start
Baila Me(GER), winner of a German Group 1 last autumn and successful in a Listed race on the Polytrack last time out, was tackling a handicap for the first time. She got bumped around a bit going into the first turn and will appreciate returning to Pattern company. Official explanation: jockey said filly had no more to give (op 17-2)

Broomielaw Official explanation: jockey said gelding had no more to give

7294 BIGGER "WIN ONLY" ODDS AT TOTESPORT.COM H'CAP 7f

3:45 (3:50) (Class 2) (0-105,105) 3-Y-O+£25,904 (£7,708; £3,852; £1,924) **Stalls** High

Form RPR

1131 **1** **Collateral Damage (IRE)**[7] 7169 6-8-11 **92**.....................(t) DavidAllan 5 102
(T D Easterby) *racd centre: hld up: rdn over 2f out: swtchd lft and hdwy over 1f out: rdn to ld wl ins fnl f: r.o* **8/1**[3]

0021 **2** ¾ **Mia's Boy**[14] 7019 5-9-5 **105**........................ BMcHugh(5) 14 113
(C A Dwyer) *racd stands' side: swtchd to r centre over 5f out: hld up: hdwy 1/2-way: rdn over 2f out: ev ch ins fnl f: r.o* **11/2**[1]

4010 **3** ½ **Felday**[22] 6815 3-8-8 **90**........................ SteveDrowne 4 96
(H Morrison) *racd centre: chsd ldrs: rdn to ld ins fnl f: sn hdd: styd on* **17/2**

6000 **4** *hd* **Confuchias (IRE)**[15] 6994 5-8-4 **88**........................ AndreaAtzeni(3) 10 94
(Pat Eddery) *racd centre: chsd ldrs: rdn over 2f out: styd on* **16/1**

4403 **5** 1¼ **Webbow (IRE)**[28] 6675 7-8-6 **90**..................... Louis-PhilippeBeuzelin(3) 7 93
(N Tinkler) *racd centre: mid-div: hdwy u.p over 2f out: styd on same pce ins fnl f* **10/1**

U002 **6** 1¾ **Excusez Moi (USA)**[14] 7015 7-8-12 **93**........................ AndrewElliott 12 91
(Mrs R A Carr) *racd centre: chsd ldr: rdn over 2f out: sn edgd rt: hung lft and no ex fnl f* **25/1**

0430 **7** *nk* **Celtic Sultan (IRE)**[28] 6675 5-8-8 **89**........................ MickyFenton 9 87
(T P Tate) *overall ldr in centre: rdn and edgd rt over 1f out: hdd and no ex ins fnl f* **33/1**

432U **8** 1½ **Cyflymder (IRE)**[14] 7019 3-9-2 **98**........................ RichardHughes 16 91
(R Hannon) *racd stands' side: swtchd to r centre over 5f out: chsd ldrs: rdn over 2f out: wknd ins fnl f* **20/1**

130 **9** ¾ **Cobo Bay**[91] 4779 4-8-9 **90**........................(b) NCallan 17 82
(K A Ryan) *racd stands' side: led that gp: rdn and hung lft over 2f out: wknd over 1f out:* **28/1**

4052 **10** ¾ **Dixey**[14] 7032 4-8-9 **90**........................(p) PhilipRobinson 20 80
(M A Jarvis) *racd stands' side: chsd ldrs: rdn and hung lft over 2f out: wknd over 1f out* **16/1**

6064 **11** *hd* **Mister Hardy**[22] 6815 4-8-12 **93**........................ FrederikTylicki 1 82
(R A Fahey) *racd centre: prom: rdn over 2f out: wknd fnl f* **12/1**

4000 **12** ¾ **Garnica (FR)**[14] 7019 6-9-5 **100**........................ AdrianTNicholls 8 87
(D Nicholls) *racd centre: hld up: rdn and hung lft over 1f out: nvr nrr* **33/1**

2602 **13** 1½ **One Way Or Another (AUS)**[35] 6482 6-8-13 **94**....(p) JamieSpencer 15 77
(J R Gask) *racd stands' side: swtchd to r centre over 5f out: hld up: hdwy u.p and hung rt over 1f out: n.d* **13/2**[2]

0004 **14** ½ **Dhaular Dhar (IRE)**[28] 6675 7-8-11 **92**........................ DanielTudhope 19 74
(J S Goldie) *racd stands' side: chsd ldrs: rdn: hung lft and wknd over 2f out* **16/1**

1000 **15** ¾ **The Osteopath (IRE)**[28] 6675 6-8-11 **92**........................ PhillipMakin 13 72
(M Dods) *racd centre: sn pushed along in rr: rdn over 2f out: n.d* **11/1**

1500 **16** *nk* **Zidane**[15] 6994 7-9-3 **98**........................ GeorgeBaker 18 77
(J R Fanshawe) *racd stands' side: hld up: hdwy over 2f out: rdn over 1f out: sn hung lft and wknd* **14/1**

4100 **17** 3½ **Glen Molly (IRE)**[14] 7032 3-8-7 **89**........................ RobertWinston 11 59
(B W Hills) *racd centre: mid-div: sn pushed along: rdn over 2f out: wkng whn hmpd over 1f out* **16/1**

051 **18** 3¼ **Kyllachy Star**[27] 6702 3-8-10 **92**........................ PaulHanagan 2 54
(R A Fahey) *racd centre: hld up: rdn over 2f out: n.d* **16/1**

5300 **19** ½ **Appalachian Trail (IRE)**[14] 7019 8-9-2 **97**........................(b) TomEaves 3 58
(I Semple) *racd centre: mid-div: sn pushed along: rdn and wknd over 2f out* **40/1**

0010 **20** *nse* **Aldermoor (USA)**[15] 6994 3-8-7 **89**........................ SaleemGolam 6 49
(S C Williams) *racd centre: mid-div: rdn over 2f out: sn wknd* **50/1**

1m 27.89s (1.59) **Going Correction** +0.475s/f (Yiel)
WFA 3 from 4yo+ 1lb **20** Ran SP% **133.9**
Speed ratings (Par 109): **109,108,107,107,105 103,103,101,101,100 99,99,97,96,95 95,91,87,87,87**
toteswingers: 1&2 £4.00, 1&3 £10.90, 2&3 £13.40 CSF £51.36 CT £415.59 TOTE £7.40: £2.00, £1.90, £3.60, £6.00; EX 44.30 Trifecta £1113.00 Pool: £2,105.86 - 1.40 winning units. Place 6 £523.64, Place 5 £130.87.
Owner Middleham Park Racing Xxv **Bred** Minch Bloodstock And Castletown Stud **Trained** Great Habton, N Yorks

■ Stewards' Enquiry : B McHugh 7-day ban: used whip with excessive frequency (Nov 21,24-29)
Philip Robinson caution: careless riding.

FOCUS
They went a decent gallop.

NOTEBOOK
Collateral Damage(IRE), whose most recent form has all been over a mile, was well suited by the generous gallop. He came through strongly in the closing stages to take his winning streak on turf to six, and unsurprisingly his connections are now keen to bring him back in March for the Lincoln. (op 10-1)

Mia's Boy, winner of a conditions event over the C&D last time out, is on a mark off which he can run well in handicaps but invariably finds one or two better treated. (op 13-2)

Felday, who had never run on ground this soft before, clearly handled conditions fine. Still relatively lightly raced, he showed he's up to competing off marks in the low 90s. (op 9-1)

Confuchias(IRE) was getting to race on soft ground for the first time since finishing third in the Ayr Gold Cup last year and it brought about a dramatic return to form. Well handicapped on his best efforts, his current stable might be able to find a race for him on Polytrack, as he won a little conditions event on the surface around this time last year. (op 20-1 tchd 22-1)

Webbow(IRE) remains on a long losing run but continues to run well enough that he doesn't get dropped much in the handicap. (tchd 11-1)

Excusez Moi(USA) didn't get home. He's more effective over sprint distances.

Celtic Sultan(IRE) set a fast pace until caught inside the last. (op 28-1)

One Way Or Another(AUS) didn't look at all happy on the ground when asked to pick up. He'll appreciate a return to a quicker surface. (op 12-1)

T/Jkpt: Not won. T/Plt: £791.00 to a £1 stake. Pool: £104,404.35. 96.35 winning tickets. T/Qpdt: £201.80 to a £1 stake. Pool: £7,638.70. 28.00 winning tickets. JR

7295 - 7296a (Foreign Racing) - See Raceform Interactive

7159 DUNDALK (A.W) (L-H)

Saturday, November 7

OFFICIAL GOING: Standard

7297a IRISH STALLION FARMS EUROPEAN BREEDERS FUND FILLIES H'CAP 7f (P)

7:30 (7:33) (60-100,93) 3-Y-O+ **£16,749** (£4,914; £2,341; £797)

RPR

1 **Dotada (IRE)**[17] 6952 4-8-9 74........................ KLatham 3 81+
(Peter Casey, Ire) *towards rr: swtchd to wd outside early st: hdwy 1 1/2f out: led under 1f out: kpt on wl u.p* **12/1**

2 ½ **Invincible Ash (IRE)**[8] 7161 4-9-9 93........................(b) GFCarroll(5) 6 98+
(M Halford, Ire) *hld up: 9th appr st: swtchd to outer 1 1/2f out: 4th under 1f out: 2nd and chal cl home: kpt on wl* **7/1**[3]

3 2 **Tellelle (IRE)**[13] 7042 3-8-7 78........................ BACurtis(5) 8 78
(Liam McAteer, Ire) *hld up towards rr: hdwy on outer early st: 3rd and chal over 1f out: kpt on same pce u.p* **8/1**

4 *nk* **Maybe Grace (IRE)**[8] 7162 3-9-4 84........................(p) FMBerry 1 83
(Mrs John Harrington, Ire) *trckd ldrs on inner: 4th 1/2-way: 2nd and chal st: kpt on same pce fnl f* **6/1**[2]

5 1 **Beauthea (IRE)**[15] 7010 3-8-13 79........................ WMLordan 4 75
(Ms Joanna Morgan, Ire) *in tch: 6th into st: kpt on same pce fr 1 1/2f out* **9/1**

6 ¾ **Keyala (IRE)**[28] 6667 4-8-11 76........................ RMBurke 9 70
(David P Myerscough, Ire) *sn led: strly pressed st: hdd under 1f out: no ex* **20/1**

7 1¾ **Undaunted Affair (IRE)**[14] 7032 3-9-9 89........................ PJSmullen 10 79
(K A Ryan) *mid-div on outer: 9th appr st: prog into 5th and chal 1 1/2f out: no ex fnl f* **5/1**[1]

8 1¼ **Miranda's Girl (IRE)**[15] 7008 4-9-2 88........................(p) PJCarberry(7) 13 74
(Thomas Cleary, Ire) *mid-div: 7th into st: no imp fr under 2f out* **14/1**

9 ¾ **Magic Mornings (IRE)**[15] 7010 3-9-0 83........................(p) ShaneFoley(3) 7 67
(M Halford, Ire) *trckd ldrs: 3rd and chal early st: edgd rt 2f out: sn no ex* **12/1**

10 ¾ **La Mere Germaine (IRE)**[17] 6957 3-9-0 80........................ DPMcDonogh 5 62
(Kevin Prendergast, Ire) *prom: 2nd appr st: wknd fr 2f out* **6/1**[2]

11 1¾ **Mary Josephine (IRE)**[8] 7161 4-9-1 87........................(tp) DCByrne(7) 12 65
(H Rogers, Ire) *v.s.a and bhd: kpt on one pce u.p st* **16/1**

12 2 **Blue Eyed Miss (IRE)**[40] 6351 4-8-5 70........................ CDHayes 2 42
(J T Gorman, Ire) *a towards rr* **16/1**

13 3 **Qeyaada (USA)**[22] 6833 4-9-8 87........................(p) KJManning 14 51
(James M Ryan, Ire) *trckd ldrs: 5th into st: bmpd 2f out: sn no ex: eased fnl f* **6/1**[2]

1m 24.55s (84.55)
WFA 3 from 4yo 1lb **13** Ran SP% **131.7**
CSF £103.31 CT £743.44 TOTE £14.50: £2.60, £2.00, £4.50; DF 106.70.
Owner Stephen Curran **Bred** Denis McDonnell **Trained** Stamullen, Co Meath

NOTEBOOK
Undaunted Affair(IRE), running on Polytrack for the first time, had a difficult draw to overcome and ended up racing wide throughout. (op 7/2)
Miranda's Girl(IRE) Official explanation: jockey said filly had to check early home straight
Qeyaada(USA) Official explanation: vet said filly was struck into

7300a CARLINGFORD STKS (LISTED RACE) 1m 2f 150y(P)

9:00 (9:02) 3-Y-O+ **£26,861** (£7,881; £3,754; £1,279)

RPR

1 **Indiana Gal (IRE)**[15] 7008 4-9-5 99........................(p) FMBerry 11 99+
(Patrick Martin, Ire) *hld up towards rr: last on inner ent st: swtchd rt under 2f out: 8th whn swtchd rt again over 1f out: r.o strly to ld cl home* **13/2**

2 ¾ **Ransomed Bride**[17] 6959 4-9-2 76........................ PJSmullen 1 92
(D K Weld, Ire) *trckd ldrs: 5th 1/2-way: 4th travelling wl appr st: led 2f out: sn strly pressed: kpt on wl u.p: hdd cl home* **12/1**

3 ¾ **Re Barolo (IRE)**[91] 4781 6-9-8........................ JohnEgan 5 97
(M Botti) *in tch: 6th 1/2-way: prog early st: cl 4th over 1f out: kpt on cl home* **11/4**[1]

4 *hd* **Wymering File (IRE)**[22] 6838 4-9-2 88........................ KJManning 10 90
(M J Grassick, Ire) *hld up towards rr: hdwy on outer ent st: 2nd and chal 1 1/2f out: no ex wl ins fnl f* **12/1**

5 ¾ **Carefree Smile (IRE)**[48] 6141 3-8-12 82........................ KLatham 4 90
(D K Weld, Ire) *mid-div: 7th 1/2-way: hdwy ent st: 3rd and chal 1 1/2f out: no ex wl ins fnl f* **14/1**

6 1¼ **Cruel Sea (USA)**[20] 6885 4-9-2 87........................(t) WJLee 8 86
(C F Swan, Ire) *led: rdn and hdd 2f out: no ex fr over 1f out* **20/1**

7 3 **Timoca (IRE)**[15] 7008 4-9-2 86........................(b) CDHayes 7 80
(Edward Lynam, Ire) *cl up in 3rd: effrt early st: sn no ex* **20/1**

8 4½ **Mid Mon Lady (IRE)**[12] 7076 4-9-2 101........................(b) DCByrne 3 71
(H Rogers, Ire) *in rr early: prog on outer 1/2-way: 7th appr st: no imp fr under 2f out* **4/1**[2]

9 4 **Funatfuntasia**[22] 6837 5-9-5 96........................ WMLordan 6 67
(Ms Joanna Morgan, Ire) *hld up in tch: no imp st* **6/1**[3]

10 4½ **Big Robert**[29] 6654 5-9-5 94........................ WJSupple 9 58
(P D Deegan, Ire) *trckd ldrs in 4th: rdn and lost pl appr st: sn wknd* **12/1**

11 *shd* **Windsor Palace (IRE)**[12] 7077 4-9-5 100........................ JAHeffernan 12 58
(A P O'Brien, Ire) *settled in 2nd: rdn 3f out: wknd early st* **4/1**[2]

2m 12.99s (132.99)
WFA 3 from 4yo+ 5lb **11** Ran SP% **133.6**
CSF £93.47 TOTE £9.10: £2.20, £2.20, £2.60; DF 78.90.
Owner T F Brennan **Bred** Holborn Trust Co **Trained** Navan, Co Meath

NOTEBOOK
Re Barolo(IRE) was below his best on his first start since August, but this will have acted as a nice prep for the Listed Churchill Stakes at Lingfield later in the month, in which he was fourth last year. (op 5/2 tchd 3/1)
Windsor Palace(IRE) Official explanation: jockey said colt ran flat

7301 - (Foreign Racing) - See Raceform Interactive

LE CROISE-LAROCHE
Saturday, November 7

OFFICIAL GOING: Heavy

7302a GRAND PRIX DU NORD (LISTED RACE) 1m 2f 110y
4:35 (4:36) 3-Y-0 £26,699 (£10,680; £8,010; £5,340; £2,670)

RPR
1 **Marinous (FR)**46 6198 3-9-2 .... DBonilla 5 100
(F Head, France)
2 nse **Hermoun (FR)**17 3-9-2 .... GBenoist 1 100
(X Nakkachdji, France)
3 1 **Super Kenny (IRE)**26 3-9-2 .... TThulliez 4 98
(N Clement, France)
4 1 1/2 **Savoie (FR)**55 3-8-13 .... FBlondel 10 92
(Y Barberot, France)
5 1 **Verenitsa (FR)**44 6238 3-8-13 .... MBarzalona 8 90
(E Lellouche, France)
6 1 1/2 **Sundown (FR)**17 3-8-13 .... FPrat 7 87
(T Clout, France)
7 nse **Landora (FR)**22 3-8-13 ....(b) RMarchelli 6 87
(A De Royer-Dupre, France)
8 1 1/2 **Konig Bernard (FR)**20 6891 3-9-2 .... DBoeuf 2 87
(W Baltromei, Germany)
9 20 **Cherry Orchard (IRE)**36 3-8-13 .... MGuyon 9 46
(A Fabre, France)
10 4 **Natural Flair (USA)**30 6618 3-8-13 .... JVictoire 11 39
(P W Chapple-Hyam) *bhd: 10th st: nvr a factor* 14/1[1]
11 **Saffron's Son (IRE)**49 6098 3-9-2 ....(b) VivienAmiot 3 42
(R Ducasteele, France)
11 Ran SP% 6.7

PARI-MUTUEL (Including 1 Euro stake): WIN 6.50; PL 2.00, 2.20, 2.50;DF 22.00.
Owner Saeed Nasser Al Romaithi **Bred** D, J & Mlle V Elias De Proenca **Trained** France

6892 SAN SIRO (R-H)
Saturday, November 7

OFFICIAL GOING: Soft

7303a PREMIO CHIUSURA (GROUP 3) 7f
2:45 (3:15) 2-Y-0+ £42,602 (£19,912; £11,204; £5,602)

RPR
1 **Le Big (GER)**13 7044 5-9-6 .... AStarke 8 104
(U Stoltefuss, Germany) *prom: 3rd 1/2-way: r.o to ld over 1f out: pushed out* 14/5[2]
2 3/4 **Rockhorse (IRE)**27 6718 4-9-6 .... DVargiu 5 102
(B Grizzetti, Italy) *in tch: pushed along over 1 1/2f out: r.o fr over 1f out to go 2nd 150yds out: kpt on: nt pce of wnr* 17/5[3]
3 3 **Ekta**48 5-9-3 .... NPinna 7 91
(S Botti, Italy) *mid-div: pushed along over 1 1/2f out: rdn to go 3rd ins fnl f: styd on* 48/1
4 1 1/2 **Magritte (ITY)**27 6717 4-9-3 .... LManiezzi 11 87
(R Menichetti, Italy) *racd in 2nd: ev ch over 1f out: nt pce of ldrs fnl stages but kpt on at one pce* 13/2
5 2 **Steady As A Rock (FR)**202 5-9-3 .... ZVarga 6 81
(S Peto, Hungary) *prom racing alone towards stands' side tl no ex fnl f* 23/10[1]
6 3/4 **Remarque (IRE)**6 7206 4-9-10 ....(b) GMarcelli 10 86
(L Riccardi, Italy) *led in centre to over 1f out: wknd fnl f* 134/10
7 nk **Senlis (IRE)**160 2525 4-9-6 .... FBranca 3 82
(E Botti, Italy) *mid-div: effrt 1 1/2f out: n.d* 91/10
8 3 1/2 **Sensazione World (IRE)**188 4-9-3 .... CColombi 9 69
(B Grizzetti, Italy) *a towards rr* 31/1
9 shd **Alta Fedelta**27 6717 3-9-3 .... MDemuro 2 70
(V Caruso, Italy) *towards rr on stands' side: n.d* 61/10
10 5 **Moriwood (ITY)**174 5-9-6 .... URispoli 4 58
(S Botti, Italy) *towards rr: wl bhd fr over 1f out* 13/1
11 10 **Lukian (GER)** 4-9-6 .... MTellini 1 31
(Werner Glanz, Germany) *bhd: nvr a factor* 90/1

1m 25.6s (-2.60)
WFA 3 from 4yo+ 1lb 11 Ran SP% 137.0
(Including 1 Euro stake): WIN 3.80; PL 1.55, 1.75, 5.67; DF 7.49.
Owner Gestut Wittekindshof **Bred** Gestut Wittekindshof **Trained** In Germany

7281 SANTA ANITA (L-H)
Saturday, November 7

OFFICIAL GOING: Pro-ride - fast; turf course - firm

7304a BREEDERS' CUP JUVENILE TURF (GRADE 2) (C&G) 1m (T)
6:45 (6:47) 2-Y-0 £375,000 (£125,000; £68,750; £41,667; £20,833)

RPR
1 **Pounced (USA)**34 6524 2-8-10 .... LDettori 4 117
(J H M Gosden) *trckd ldr on ins: 3rd st: split rivals to go 2nd 1f out: led 50yds out: r.o wl* 3/1[1]
2 3/4 **Bridgetown (USA)**49 2-8-10 .... RLandry 7 115
(Kenneth McPeek, U.S.A) *set stdy pce: led to 50yds out: no ex* 15/2[3]
3 hd **Interactif (USA)**27 2-8-10 .... KDesormeaux 10 115
(Todd Pletcher, U.S.A) *a.p: 2nd srtraight: lost 2nd 1f out: one pce* 4/1[2]
4 1/2 **Awesome Act (USA)**21 6849 2-8-10 .... RyanMoore 6 114
(J Noseda) *hld up in 7th: 8th and swung wd ent st: styd on wl: nrst fin* 14/1
5 1 **Buzzword**21 6849 2-8-10 .... AhmedAjtebi 11 112
(Saeed Bin Suroor) *hld up on outside: 10th st: styd on wl fnl f* 10/1
6 1/2 **Dean's Kitten (USA)**13 2-8-10 ....(b) RADominguez 12 111
(Michael J Maker, U.S.A) *racd in 10th: 9th st: styd on steadily fnl f* 50/1
7 1 **Gallant Gent (USA)**34 6532 2-8-10 .... JRosario 5 108
(Craig A Lewis, U.S.A) *in tch: 4th st: sn rdn and one pce* 25/1
8 1/2 **Viscount Nelson (USA)**56 5859 2-8-10 .... JMurtagh 2 107+
(A P O'Brien, Ire) *s.s losing 5 l: last to over 3f out: 11th st: nvr a factor* 4/1[2]
9 1 1/4 **Becky's Kitten (USA)**49 2-8-10 .... JRLeparoux 9 104
(Wesley A Ward, U.S.A) *cl up: 3rd st: sn wknd* 18/1
10 1/2 **King Ledley (USA)**41 6317 2-8-10 ....(b) RBejarano 8 103
(Darrin Miller, U.S.A) *cl up: 5th st: sn wknd* 20/1
11 1 1/2 **Zip Quik (USA)**61 2-8-10 .... MESmith 1 100
(Patrick L Biancone, U.S.A) *hld up: 7th st: nvr a factor* 50/1
12 2 **Codoy (USA)**27 2-8-10 .... GKGomez 3 96
(Mark Hubley, U.S.A) *a in rr* 20/1

1m 35.47s (1.60) 12 Ran SP% 115.1
PARI-MUTUEL (including $2 stake): WIN 6.80; PL (1-2) 4.80, 6.60;SHOW (1-2-3) 3.20, 4.20, 3.20; SF 62.00.
Owner Lady Rothschild **Bred** Carwell Equities Ltd **Trained** Newmarket, Suffolk

FOCUS
The two European-trained runners who took part in this race last season finished first and second, and this year's renewal provided further evidence of the edge the juveniles from Europe have over their American rivals on this surface. The winner and fifth set the level, which looks pretty sound.

NOTEBOOK
Pounced(USA), whose trainer sent out Donativum to win this race last year, was considered to be in the same league as him by his trainer and that view was difficult to argue with considering his last-time-out second in the Prix Jean-Luc Lagardere. That effort made him the pick of the European runners, and the way the race was run also played into his hands. The early pace wasn't particularly strong and, from his decent draw, he bagged a handy position tracking the leader on the rail. Bridgetown got first run on him early in the straight, but he quickened up well between horses to edge ahead inside the last and win a shade cosily. It was interesting that Dettori rode him rather than the Godolphin representative Buzzword, and the expectation is that he'll soon be Dubai bound.
Bridgetown(USA), winner of a Grade 3 at Woodbine last time out, broke well from his middle draw and got to the front without too much trouble. Able to set a fairly steady pace and get first run on his rivals in the straight, he was given every possible chance.
Interactif(USA) looked the strongest of the home contingent on paper, having won a couple of Grade 3s on his last two starts, but he was drawn out in stall ten and ended up going three wide into the first turn. He managed to get a position alongside the leader down the back straight, though, and in a race in which it paid to be prominent he was better placed than most turning in. He wasn't beaten far in the end, and that can be put down to his bad trip early on.
Awesome Act(USA), ninth in the Dewhurst last time out, is a keen-going type and the steady early pace didn't help his cause at all. Still with plenty in front of him turning in, he was angled out wide to be brought with his run down the centre of the track, and flew home once straightened up. Things didn't fall kindly this time, and he doesn't help his cause by being difficult to settle, but he is undoubtedly a talented horse, quite capable of landing a big prize when everything falls right.
Buzzword, one place behind Pounced in the Prix Jean-Luc Lagardere and fifth in the Dewhurst since, was drawn one from the outside and faced a difficult task. He raced two or three wide to the turn into the straight, at which point he swung four or five wide. He ran on really well for fifth and this was a perfectly solid effort in the circumstances.
Viscount Nelson(USA) was well drawn but he fell out of the stalls and Johnny Murtagh chose not to rush him up but to let him get into his stride in his own time. Unfortunately, the early pace was on the sedate side and making up ground on the leaders was always going to be difficult. In a detached last going into the first turn and with a wall of horses in front of him entering the straight, he simply never got involved in the race.

7305a BREEDERS' CUP TURF SPRINT 6f 110y
7:23 (7:27) 3-Y-0+ £375,000 (£125,000; £68,750; £41,667; £20,833)

RPR
1 **California Flag (USA)**38 5-9-0 ....(b) JTalamo 3 124+
(Brian Koriner, U.S.A) *mde all: 3l clr 1f out: rdn out* 9/2[1]
2 1 3/4 **Gotta Have Her (USA)**21 5-8-11 .... TBaze 7 114
(Jenine Sahadi, U.S.A) *in rr: n.m.r over 1 1/2f out and whn making gd hdwy 1f out: split rivals to take 2nd 50yds out: nrst fin* 10/1
3 3/4 **Cannonball (USA)**62 4-9-0 .... RADominguez 6 115
(Wesley A Ward, U.S.A) *towards rr: 9th st: styd on wl fnl 1 1/2f* 7/1[3]
4 hd **Delta Storm (USA)**27 8-9-0 ....(b) GKGomez 14 114
(Mike Mitchell, U.S.A) *midfield: 6th st: kpt on fr over 1f out* 20/1
5 1 1/2 **Canadian Ballet (USA)**42 4-8-11 ....(b) AGarcia 10 107
(Linda Rice, U.S.A) *racd in 2nd to 100yds out: wknd* 28/1
6 hd **Silver Timber (USA)**28 6-9-0 .... JRLeparoux 2 109
(Chad C Brown, U.S.A) *racd in 3rd: rdn 1 1/2f out: kpt on at same pce* 12/1
7 nse **Noble Court (USA)**62 5-9-0 .... JRosario 1 109
(John W Sadler, U.S.A) *in rr: 8th st: styd on fnl f* 10/1
8 hd **El Gato Malo (USA)**29 4-9-0 ....(b) DFlores 11 109
(Craig Dollase, U.S.A) *a towards rr* 40/1
9 hd **Get Funky (USA)**38 6-9-0 ....(b) RBejarano 5 108
(John W Sadler, U.S.A) *racd in 4th: 5th st: sn one pce* 16/1
10 3/4 **Square Eddie (CAN)**27 3-8-12 .... LDettori 8 105
(Doug O'Neill, U.S.A) *6th early: 4th st: sn one pce* 20/1
11 1/2 **Diamondrella**28 6689 5-8-11 .... RMaragh 9 101
(Angel Penna Jr, U.S.A) *a towards rr* 11/2[2]
12 2 **Lord Shanakill (USA)**101 4419 3-8-12 .... JimCrowley 4 98
(Richard E Mandella, U.S.A) *midfield: 10th st: nvr nr ldrs* 8/1
13 1 **Desert Code (USA)**38 5-9-0 ....(b) RMigliore 13 96
(David Hofmans, U.S.A) *8th early: 13th and btn st* 16/1
14 3/4 **Strike The Deal (USA)**49 6107 4-9-0 .... KFallon 12 93
(J Noseda) *a in rr* 14/1

1m 11.28s (71.28) 14 Ran SP% 116.9
PARI-MUTUEL: WIN 8.80; PL (1-2) 5.60, 8.80; SHOW (1-2-3) 3.80, 5.60,4.80; SF 77.20.
Owner Hi Card Ranch **Bred** Hi Card Ranch **Trained** USA

FOCUS
The second running of the Turf Sprint, again run on this rather unique track, which features America's only right-hand bend, is downhill early on, and crosses the Pro-Ride surface just before the straight. The pace was steady and the winner had the run of things.

NOTEBOOK
California Flag(USA) went off much too fast when ultimately well beaten in this race last year, but he was rather surprisingly allowed his own way in front this time and clocked 43.09 at the 4f point, compared with 41.81 12 months ago. Once in the straight, he found more to pull clear of his rivals for a thoroughly convincing success, looking value for more than the winning margin, and is a high-class sprinter. It's worth pointing out he had a chip removed from an ankle after last season's defeat. His next race could well be in Hong Kong.
Gotta Have Her(USA), something of a specialist on this track, ran a big race in second considering the modest pace was against her, staying on from a long way back despite not enjoying the clearest of runs in the straight.
Cannonball(USA), who ran twice at Royal Ascot this year, finishing sixth in the King's Stand and runner-up in the Golden Jubilee, did not really have the race run to suit but still performed well after a two-month break. The plan is for him to go to Hong Kong for the Sprint, then on to Australia for the Lightning Stakes, before then going back to Royal Ascot.

Delta Storm(USA) has yet to win in Graded company but this was a solid effort.
Lord Shanakill(USA), a Group 1 winner over 1m in France earlier in the year, offered very little on his US debut after over three months off. He may now be retired.
Strike The Deal(USA) has benefited from the switch to hold-up tactics recently, so the lack of pace was no use to him, but even so, this was disappointing as he made no progress at all in the straight. After the race Jeremy Noseda revealed the colt had "foot trouble" four days earlier.

7306a SENTIENT JET BREEDERS' CUP SPRINT (GRADE 1) (PRO-RIDE) 6f (D)
8:10 (8:13) 3-Y-0+ **£750,000** (£250,000; £137,500; £83,333; £41,667)

RPR
1 **Dancing In Silks (USA)**[35] 4-9-0 .... JRosario 6 121
(Carla Gaines, U.S.A) *racd in 4th: wnt 2nd 1f out: led fnl strides* **25/1**
2 *nse* **Crown Of Thorns (USA)**[27] 4-9-0 .... RBejarano 4 121+
(Richard E Mandella, U.S.A) *racd in 6th: swtchd outside ent st: r.o strly fnl f: jst failed* **14/1**
3 *hd* **Cost Of Freedom (USA)**[27] 6-9-0 .... TBaze 2 120
(John W Sadler, U.S.A) *led tl hdd fnl strides* **20/1**
4 *nse* **Gayego (USA)**[27] 4-9-0 .... GKGomez 5 121+
(Saeed Bin Suroor) *last tl hdwy on ins on home turn: wnt 4th 1f out: squeezed through narrow gap against rail: jst failed* **2/1**[1]
5 *1 1/2* **Zensational (USA)**[62] 3-8-12 .... VEspinoza 1 113
(Bob Baffert, U.S.A) *trckd ldr in 3rd on ins: 4th 1 1/2f out: kpt on u.p* **11/4**[2]
6 *3/4* **Fatal Bullet (USA)**[29] 4-9-0 ....(b) ERosaDaSilva 3 113
(Reade Baker, Canada) *racd in 2nd to 1f out: one pce* **13/2**[3]
7 *nse* **Fleeting Spirit (IRE)**[34] 6522 4-8-11 .... LDettori 9 109
(J Noseda) *racd in 7th: 5th st: edgd rt over 1f out: sn rdn and unable qck* **9/1**
8 *1* **Capt. Candyman Can (USA)**[29] 3-8-12 .... JJCastellano 8 107
(Ian Wilkes, U.S.A) *racd in 8th: nvr a factor* **8/1**
9 *nse* **Join In The Dance (USA)**[35] 3-8-12 .... JRVelazquez 7 107
(Todd Pletcher, U.S.A) *racd in 5th: wknd 2f out* **66/1**

68.14 secs (-0.12) **9** Ran SP% **111.2**
PARI-MUTUEL: WIN 52.60; PL (1-2) 19.20, 13.20; SHOW (1-2-3) 12.00,8.60, 9.20; SF 455.80.
Owner Ken Kinakin **Bred** Ronald Jex **Trained** USA

FOCUS
With several front-runners in the line-up this promised to be strongly run and there was always the chance that it would be set up for a closer.

NOTEBOOK
Dancing In Silks(USA), supplemented at a cost of $180,000, had never previously run in a graded-stakes race but he came here chasing a four-timer and won over the C&D last time out. Taking up a position tracking the three leaders, he enjoyed a nice trip and, once pulled wide early in the straight, picked up well, albeit while edging left, and just got his nose in front close home.
Crown Of Thorns(USA), runner-up to Gayego in the Grade 1 Ancient Title Stakes over this C&D last time, was held up off the pace but saved ground by being on the rail. Switched out wide entering the straight, he came home really strongly but was just denied.
Cost Of Freedom(USA), who has been difficult to keep sound, has been lightly raced this term and was only fourth in the Ancient Title on his previous start. Fast away, he won the battle for the early lead and saved every inch of ground hugging the rail into the straight. He edged off it in the straight, leaving a gap for Gayego, but kept battling away and wasn't beaten far in the four-way photo. He is likely to go to Dubai next year.
Gayego(USA) won a Grade 1 in impressive style over the C&D last time out and this race promised to be run to suit him, but he was a shade disappointing. Held up in last but saving ground on the rail, he nipped up the inside entering the straight and the gap came at the right time for him to challenge between the leader and the rail inside the last. He didn't quicken well enough, though, and despite being only beaten narrowly he didn't even place in the end.
Zensational(USA), winner of three Grade 1 races this year, likes to blaze, but his rider, keen not to get into a speed duel with Cost Of Freedom up front, reined him back going into the first turn and tracked the leader. Switched out entering the straight, he was crossed by the winner a furlong out and finished rather one-paced. A one-dimensional front-runner, his rider should have been more positive on him.
Fatal Bullet(USA), runner-up in this race last year, is another who needs to make the running to be at his best. He couldn't get to the front here, though, and was swamped inside the last.
Fleeting Spirit(IRE), not out of the first two in her four previous starts this season, all in Group 1 company, didn't quite see out the 6 1/2f of the Turf Sprint at this meeting last year, hence the decision to run her in this tougher contest this time around. Drawn worst of all, she had no trouble going the early pace, but was stuck three wide back in the field and it was always going to be difficult for her to land a blow from there.

7307a GREY GOOSE BREEDERS' CUP JUVENILE (GRADE 1) (C&G) (PRO-RIDE) 1m 110y(D)
8:49 (8:52) 2-Y-0 **£750,000** (£250,000; £137,500; £83,333; £41,667)

RPR
1 **Vale Of York (IRE)**[27] 6716 2-8-10 .... AhmedAjtebi 7 116
(Saeed Bin Suroor) *cl up on ins: 3rd st: stl 3rd whn swtchd off rail ins fnl f: str run to ld cl home* **25/1**
2 *hd* **Lookin At Lucky (USA)**[34] 6532 2-8-10 .... GKGomez 13 116
(Bob Baffert, U.S.A) *towards rr: hdwy on outside over 2f out: 7th st: styd on down outside: ev ch cl home: r.o* **3/1**[1]
3 *1/2* **Noble's Promise (USA)**[28] 6690 2-8-10 .... WMartinez 4 115
(Kenneth McPeek, U.S.A) *cl up on outside: led 1 1/2f out: hdd and no ex cl home* **8/1**
4 *hd* **Piscitelli (USA)**[28] 6690 2-8-10 .... KDesormeaux 2 114
(Gregory D Sacco, U.S.A) *sn led: hdd 1 1/2f out: kpt on gamely* **40/1**
5 *1 3/4* **Aikenite (USA)**[28] 6690 2-8-10 .... AGarcia 9 111
(Todd Pletcher, U.S.A) *midfield: 5th st: sn rdn and one pce* **7/1**[3]
6 *nse* **Beethoven (IRE)**[21] 6849 2-8-10 ....(v) RyanMoore 3 111
(A P O'Brien, Ire) *in rr: 9th and swtchd outside ent st: styd on wl: nrst fin* **12/1**
7 *1 1/2* **Radiohead**[36] 6450 2-8-10 .... MartinDwyer 11 107
(B J Meehan) *in rr: 12th st on outside: kpt on fnl 1 1/2f* **14/1**
8 *3/4* **William's Kitten (USA)**[27] 2-8-10 ....(b) RADominguez 12 106
(Michael J Maker, U.S.A) *hld up in last: styd on steadily fnl 2f* **66/1**
9 *1 3/4* **Eskendereya (USA)**[34] 2-8-10 .... JJCastellano 8 102
(Todd Pletcher, U.S.A) *nvr a factor* **12/1**
10 *1 1/2* **Alfred Nobel (IRE)**[35] 6478 2-8-10 .... JMurtagh 1 98
(A P O'Brien, Ire) *midfield: 6th st on ins: wknd ins fnl f* **9/1**
11 *2 1/2* **Pulsion (USA)**[34] 6532 2-8-10 ....(b) MESmith 6 93
(Patrick L Biancone, U.S.A) *cl up to under 2f out* **14/1**
12 *9* **Aspire (USA)**[28] 6684 2-8-10 .... JRLeparoux 10 73
(Eddie Kenneally, U.S.A) *in tch to 2f out* **25/1**
13 *8* **D' Funnybone (USA)**[49] 2-8-10 .... EPrado 5 56
(Richard Dutrow Jr, U.S.A) *racd in 2nd tl wknd under 2f out: eased* **11/2**[2]

1m 43.48s (1.06) **13** Ran SP% **114.3**
PARI-MUTUEL: WIN 63.20; PL (1-2) 24.40, 4.40; SHOW (1-2-3) 12.40,3.00, 4.60; SF 334.80.
Owner Godolphin **Bred** Stock Vale Ltd **Trained** Newmarket, Suffolk
■ A first Breeders' Cup winner for Ahmed Ajtebi.

FOCUS
This looked a quality renewal, but there was a surprise winner and the race is rated conservatively.

NOTEBOOK
Vale Of York(IRE) has improved with every run, but even so he still looked to have something to find at this level and was difficult to fancy on his first start away from the turf. However, he showed good speed to race in a prominent position, travelling well throughout, and after being denied a clear run against the inside rail early in the straight, he picked up smartly once switched inside the final furlong. He's now going to be aimed at the Kentucky Derby, but it has to be doubtful that he will handle dirt. The Triple Crown series on the Tapeta surface at Meydan will surely be on the agenda before then anyway.
Lookin At Lucky(USA) emerges with a deal of credit considering he was stuck wide throughout and also raced further back than ideal, with stall 13 no help at all.
Noble's Promise(USA), who had a couple of today's rivals behind when winning a Grade 1 at Keenland on his previous start, made a big move to lead at the top of the straight but was just run out of it near the line.
Piscitelli(USA) raced with his ears pricked in front for much of the way, really looking to enjoy himself, but he found a few too strong in the straight and was unable to reverse recent placings with Noble's Promise.
Aikenite(USA) came under strong pressure turning into the straight and lacked the pace of some of these, before keeping on.
Beethoven(IRE), the surprise Dewhurst winner, lost his place when badly squeezed on the first bend and could never make up the lost ground. He performed creditably in the circumstances and is not to be underestimated next year.
Radiohead, the Middle Park runner-up, endured a terrible trip from stall 11, racing too far back after losing his place on the first bend and then swinging extremely wide around the turn into the straight.
Alfred Nobel(IRE) seemed to travel quite well, but he carried his head a little high when placed under pressure and didn't pick up.

7308a TVG BREEDERS' CUP MILE (GRADE 1) (TURF) 1m (T)
9:28 (9:34) 3-Y-0+ **£750,000** (£250,000; £137,500; £83,333; £41,667)

RPR
1 **Goldikova (IRE)**[35] 6503 4-8-11 .... OPeslier 11 123+
(F Head, France) *hld up in 10th: 8th st: styd on strly down outside to ld last 50 yds* **13/8**[1]
2 *1/2* **Courageous Cat (USA)**[28] 3-8-11 .... GKGomez 6 122
(William Mott, U.S.A) *racd in 4th: led 1 1/2f out: edgd rt 1f out: hdd and no ex last 50 yds* **33/1**
3 *1* **Justenuffhumor (USA)**[28] 6691 4-9-0 .... AGarcia 10 120
(Kiaran McLaughlin, U.S.A) *hld up in last: gd hdwy two off rail to take 3rd 100 yds out: one pce* **14/1**
4 *hd* **Court Vision (USA)**[28] 6691 4-9-0 ....(b) RAlbarado 1 120
(Richard Dutrow Jr, U.S.A) *hld up in rr: gd hdwy to go 2nd briefly 1f out: one pce* **20/1**
5 *1 3/4* **Delegator**[42] 6271 3-8-11 .... LDettori 4 115
(Saeed Bin Suroor) *racd in 6th: disputing 3rd appr fnl f: one pce* **11/2**[3]
6 *1/2* **Karelian (USA)**[28] 6691 7-9-0 .... RMaragh 5 115
(George R Arnold II, U.S.A) *racd in 5th: swtchd outside ent st: kpt on at one pce* **40/1**
7 *3 3/4* **Ferneley (IRE)**[48] 5-9-0 .... RBejarano 7 106
(B Cecil, U.S.A) *in rr: last st: kpt on down outside but nvr nr ldrs* **28/1**
8 *1 1/2* **Whatsthescript (IRE)**[28] 6686 5-9-0 .... KDesormeaux 2 102
(John W Sadler, U.S.A) *pressed ldrs on outside in 3rd: wknd under 2f out* **33/1**
9 *3/4* **Gladiatorus (USA)**[27] 6718 4-9-0 .... AhmedAjtebi 9 100
(Saeed Bin Suroor) *sn led but a strly pressed: hdd 2f out: wknd under 1 1/2f out* **9/1**
10 *1/2* **Cowboy Cal (USA)**[28] 6686 4-9-0 .... JRVelazquez 3 99
(Todd Pletcher, U.S.A) *pressed ldr tl led narrowly 2f out: hdd 1 1/2f out: wknd* **9/1**
11 *28* **Zacinto**[42] 6271 3-8-11 .... RyanMoore 8 34
(Sir Michael Stoute) *racd in 7th: lost pl 2f out: eased* **9/2**[2]

1m 32.26s (-1.61)
WFA 3 from 4yo+ 2lb **11** Ran SP% **114.9**
PARI-MUTUEL: WIN 4.80; PL (1-2) 4.00, 12.80; SHOW (1-2-3) 2.60, 8.00,8.00; SF 109.20.
Owner Wertheimer & Frere **Bred** Wertheimer Et Frere **Trained** France

FOCUS
With both Cowboy Cal and Gladiatorus keen to make the running there was always the possibility that this race would be run at a frantic gallop if they took each other on up front, and so it proved, with the pair going off miles too fast and setting up for those ridden more patiently. The winning time was 0.21sec outside the record for the race, set by Val Royal at Belmont Park in 2001.

NOTEBOOK
Goldikova(IRE), impressive winner of this race last year and only beaten twice since, on her reappearance and when given a shocking ride in the Prix de la Foret last time, had been weak in the betting since the draw was made because she had been handed the widest stall. However, the way this race was run, it was never an issue as Peslier was able to drop her out towards the tail of the field and never gave up much ground around the turns. When the inevitable happened and the leaders fell in a hole, she finished strongest of all down the outside to win with a bit up her sleeve, confirming herself the world's best miler on turf. Winner of eight of her last ten starts, including seven at the top level, she joins Miesque, Lure and Da Hoss as dual winners of the race, and while the likelihood is that she'll now be retired, the option of returning in a bid for an unprecedented hat-trick was left open by her trainer.
Courageous Cat(USA) looked to face a stiff task in this company but he ran really well in defeat, especially considering he raced closer to the fast early pace than either the winner or the three horses who followed him home. His stamina for further no doubt helped in that regard.
Justenuffhumor(USA), who found the soft ground against him when suffering his first defeat in seven starts on turf last time, bounced back to form with conditions to suit. Dropped out the back from his wide draw early, he trailed the field for most of the way but got a dream run through towards the inside in the straight and seemed to run right up to his best.
Court Vision(USA), winner of the Grade 1 Shadwell Turf Mile on soft ground last time out, stays 1m2f and the way this race was run helped bring his stamina into play. He ran a sound race but will be suited by a return to a longer distance.
Delegator has tended to travel well but not quite get home over a mile at the top level this term and, while this sharp track promised to help him see it out better, the fast early gallop ensured it was actually a real test at the trip. He had his chance entering the straight but again finished tamely, and it's no surprise that his connections plan to race him over shorter next year.
Gladiatorus(USA), so impressive in winning the Dubai Duty Free back in March, was bitterly disappointing in Europe over the summer, but got a nice confidence booster when successful in Italy last time out. This two-turn mile on a speed-favouring track promised to suit him, but he was drawn out wide and had a rival for the lead in the shape of Cowboy Cal. A one-dimensional front-runner, he simply needs to lead to be at his best, but in getting to the front he was forced to go a suicidal early pace. It was no surprise when he, along with the other pacesetters, hit the wall in a major way early in the straight.

Zacinto didn't handle the tight turns well at all and his rider virtually pulled him up after he took a bad step rounding the bend into the straight. He appeared sound on returning, though, and remains an exciting prospect for next season, when he should be a force in the top races over 1m2f.

7309a BREEDERS' CUP DIRT MILE (GRADE 1) (PRO-RIDE) 1m

10:12 (10:17) 3-Y-0+ **£375,000** (£125,000; £68,750; £41,667; £20,833)

RPR

1 **Furthest Land (USA)**42 4-9-0 ....(b) JRLeparoux 2 120
(Michael J Maker, U.S.A) *cl up: wnt 2nd over 1f out: led 70yds out: r.o wl* **16/1**

2 3/4 **Ready's Echo (USA)**34 4-9-0 ....(b) CHBorel 10 118
(Todd Pletcher, U.S.A) *last to over 1 1/2f out: str run down outside fnl f to take 2nd on line* **25/1**

3 hd **Midshipman (USA)**50 3-8-11 .... GKGomez 3 117
(Saeed Bin Suroor) *led to 70yds out: one pce* **4/1**2

4 3/4 **Mastercraftsman (IRE)**36 6467 3-8-11 .... JMurtagh 1 114+
(A P O'Brien, Ire) *racd in 6th: n.m.r over 2f out: 4th st: pressing front two on ins whn n.m.r 100yds out: no ex* **13/8**1

5 1/2 **Mambo Meister (USA)**21 4-9-0 .... MCruz 6 114
(Philip A Gleaves, U.S.A) *racd in 5th: 7th and taken towards outside st: styd on u.p while carried sltly lft fr over 1f out* **25/1**

6 1 3/4 **Neko Bay (USA)**29 6-9-0 .... MESmith 5 110
(John Shirreffs, U.S.A) *prom: 2nd st: one pce fr over 1f out* **20/1**

7 3 3/4 **Mr. Sidney (USA)**28 6691 5-9-0 .... KDesormeaux 8 101
(William Mott, U.S.A) *cl up: cl 4th st: sn wknd* **16/1**

8 nse **Chocolate Candy (USA)**28 6687 3-8-11 .... JRosario 9 100
(Jerry Hollendorfer, U.S.A) *racd in 9th: nvr a factor* **10/1**

9 3/4 **Bullsbay (USA)**63 5-9-0 .... JRose 4 99
(H Graham Motion, U.S.A) *racd in 8th: nvr a factor* **11/2**3

10 1 1/2 **Pyro (USA)**63 4-9-0 .... JRVelazquez 7 96
(Saeed Bin Suroor) *racd in 7th: nvr a factor* **9/1**

1m 35.5s (95.50)
WFA 3 from 4yo+ 2lb **10** Ran SP% **116.8**
PARI-MUTUEL: WIN 44.60; PL (1-2) 18.40, 18.20; SHOW (1-2-3) 9.60,9.40, 4.20; SF 658.20.
Owner Kenneth L & Sarah K Ramsey **Bred** Catherine Wills **Trained** USA

FOCUS
A weak race for the grade and the way it unfolded was unsatisfactory, with the gallop pretty modest, and the best horse in the line-up, Mastercraftsman, finishing out of the places.

NOTEBOOK
Furthest Land(USA) enjoyed a good trip. With Mastercraftsman below form, he found a soft race for the level and this is form to treat with caution.

Ready's Echo(USA) ran a big race to take second considering he sat last of all off the modest pace and, after swinging extremely wide into the straight, received a hefty bump over 1f out.

Midshipman(USA) had only been seen out once since winning the Juvenile here last year, and that was when landing a 6 1/2f contest on the dirt at Belmont. He was allowed a soft lead but was too keen to take advantage.

Mastercraftsman(IRE) compromised his chance with a sluggish start and was trapped against the rail in mid-division for much of the contest. A colt who can't call on an instant turn of foot, the lack of pace in the race didn't help matters and once in the straight he took a while to pick up. By the time he got going he was pointed at a narrow gap towards the inside with less than a furlong to run, but while there looked to be enough room for him to continue his forward move, he basically seemed reluctant to take the opening and became unbalanced.

Mambo Meister(USA)'s rider lodged an objection against Ready's Echo after the pair came close in the straight, but the Stewards were having none of it.

7310a EMIRATES AIRLINE BREEDERS' CUP TURF (GRADE 1) 1m 4f (T)

10:57 (11:02) 3-Y-O£**1,125,000** (£375,000; £206,250; £125,000; £62,500)

RPR

1 **Conduit (IRE)**34 6526 4-9-0 .... RyanMoore 2 123+
(Sir Michael Stoute) *last early: wnt 5th bef 1/2-way: split rivals to go 2nd but lost hind legs momentarily 1 1/2f out: led 50yds out: edgd clr* **10/11**1

2 1/2 **Presious Passion (USA)**27 6-9-0 ....(b) ETrujillo 5 122
(Mary Hartmann, U.S.A) *set fierce pce: sn 10 l clr: 6 l clr 4f out: less than 1 l up 1 1/2f out: hld on gamely tl hdd last 50yds* **8/1**

3 1 1/4 **Dar Re Mi**34 6526 4-8-11 .... LDettori 4 117
(J H M Gosden) *racd in 3rd: bmpd w Conduit whn disputing 2nd on ins on home turn: kpt on at same pce fnl 1 1/2f* **5/1**3

4 1 1/4 **Spanish Moon (USA)**55 5931 5-9-0 .... KFallon 6 118
(Sir Michael Stoute) *racd in 2nd: edgd off rail 2f out: dropped bk to 4th 1 1/2f out: one pce* **4/1**2

5 1 1/4 **Red Rocks (IRE)**41 6303 6-9-0 .... JRLeparoux 3 116
(B J Meehan) *hld up in rr: hdwy on ins to dispute 5th over 1 1/2f out: tk 5th cl home* **22/1**

6 hd **Monzante (USA)**28 6687 5-9-0 .... RBejarano 7 116
(Mike Mitchell, U.S.A) *a in rr* **40/1**

7 6 **Telling (USA)**35 6511 5-9-0 .... JJCastellano 1 106
(Steve Hobby, U.S.A) *racd in 4th: wnt 3rd over 3f out: wknd over 2f out* **25/1**

2m 23.75s (-2.90) **7** Ran SP% **110.8**
PARI-MUTUEL: WIN 3.80; PL (1-2) 3.00, 5.00; SHOW (1-2-3) 2.20, 3.80, 3.00; SF 25.60.
Owner Ballymacoll Stud **Bred** Ballymacoll Stud Farm Ltd **Trained** Newmarket, Suffolk

FOCUS
A race that the Europeans traditionally dominate (eight winners in the previous ten years) and for the second year in succession the prize went to Conduit.

NOTEBOOK
Conduit(IRE) became only the second horse to land a repeat victory in this race, following High Chaparral, who had to share the spoils with Johar when winning for the second time in 2003. Winner of the King George and fourth in the Arc, he undoubtedly set the standard here, but he's a horse who needs a strong pace to be seen at his best, and the presence in the field of the trailblazing Presious Passion was key to his success. That rival ensured that, for the second year running, this race was run to suit, but in fairness to him he saw off Dar Re Mi and Spanish Moon, who both held legitimate form claims, in good style, and he confirmed himself a top-notch performer over this trip. His form figures over 1m4f plus now read 2111141, and he will bid to enhance that record further in the Japan Cup.

Presious Passion(USA)'s modus operandi is to blast off in front, build up a healthy advantage and try to hold on. True to form, he sprinted out of the gates and down the hill, and was some 12 lengths clear passing the winning post for the first time. Given a breather down the back straight, he kicked on again entering the straight and made Conduit pull out all the stops. It was a great effort and a fine ride.

Dar Re Mi, who ran in this race rather than the Filly & Mare Turf because this longer trip is thought to suit her better, had finished a length behind Conduit in the Arc after enjoying the most perfect trip. She was bumped by him turning into the straight here, and may have been slightly intimidated, but she kept on well and again ran right up to her best.

Spanish Moon(USA), who goes well fresh, had been given a break since winning the Prix Foy. He led the chasing pack and, passing the winning post for the first time, had opened up a four-length gap on the rest, although they rejoined him before they entered the back straight. Not quite up to putting up a serious fight in the closing stages, it's possible he needs a bit of cut in the ground to be seen at his best.

Red Rocks(IRE), winner of this race back in 2006, isn't quite up to this class any longer, but he appreciates a good gallop and was keeping on at the finish.

7311a BREEDERS' CUP CLASSIC (GRADE 1) (PRO-RIDE) 1m 2f (D)

11:45 (11:57) 3-Y-£2,083,333 (£694,444; £381,944; £208,333; £104,167)

RPR

1 **Zenyatta (USA)**28 6688 5-8-11 .... MESmith 4 128+
(John Shirreffs, U.S.A) *missed break, behind, headway on inside 2f out, 6th straight, angled to reach outside 1f out, led 70 yards out, ran on well* **10/3**2

2 1 **Gio Ponti (USA)**35 6511 4-9-0 .... RADominguez 7 127
(Christophe Clement, U.S.A) *held up in 9th, headway on inside over 2f out, 4th straight, burst through to lead 1f out, headed and no extra 70 yards out* **14/1**

3 1 1/4 **Twice Over**21 6850 4-9-0 .... TPQueally 5 125
(H R A Cecil) *raced in 7th, 5th straight, soon hard ridden, kept on* **12/1**

4 3/4 **Summer Bird (USA)**35 6512 3-8-10 ....(b) KDesormeaux 3 123
(Tim Ice, U.S.A) *raced in 6th, 3rd straight, soon ridden, kept on at same pace* **15/2**3

5 1 1/2 **Colonel John (USA)**28 6687 4-9-0 .... GKGomez 2 120
(Eoin Harty, U.S.A) *raced in 3rd, 2nd straight, lost 2nd just over 1f out, one pace* **20/1**

6 1 **Richard's Kid (USA)**28 6687 4-9-0 ....(b) ASolis 6 118
(Bob Baffert, U.S.A) *in rear, 8th towards outside straightm switched inside over 1f out, kept on* **12/1**

7 1 **Awesome Gem (USA)**35 6574 6-9-0 ....(b) DFlores 12 116
(Craig Dollase, U.S.A) *raced in 8th, 7th on outside straight, stayed on at one pace* **66/1**

8 3 1/2 **Regal Ransom (USA)**49 3-8-10 .... RMigliore 11 109
(Saeed Bin Suroor) *led to 1f out, weakened* **33/1**

9 3/4 **Mine That Bird (USA)**28 6687 3-8-10 .... CHBorel 1 108
(Bennie L Woolley Jr, U.S.A) *detached in 11th early, last after 4f, progress in inside from over 1 1/2f out but never near leaders* **25/1**

10 6 1/4 **Rip Van Winkle (IRE)**42 6271 3-8-10 .... JMurtagh 10 95
(A P O'Brien, Ire) *moved up to go 2nd after 2f, pushed along over 3f out, weakened over 2f out* **2/1**1

11 2 **Einstein (BRZ)**62 7-9-0 .... JRLeparoux 8 91
(Helen Pitts-Blasi, U.S.A) *raced in 4th, pushed along when hampered over 2f out, not recover* **20/1**

12 9 3/4 **Girolamo (USA)**27 3-8-10 .... AGarcia 9 72
(Saeed Bin Suroor) *close up til weakened 2 1/2f out, eased* **33/1**

2m 0.62s (0.74)
WFA 3 from 4yo+ 4lb **12** Ran SP% **111.0**
PARI-MUTUEL: WIN 7.60; PL (1-2) 5.60, 9.20; SHOW (1-2-3) 3.80, 6.60,7.00; SF 87.40.
Owner Mr & Mrs Jerome S Moss **Bred** Maverick Production Limited **Trained** USA
■ Zenyatta was not only the first filly or mare to win the Classic, but also the first horse to win two different Breeders' Cup races.

FOCUS
No Rachel Alexandra or Sea The Stars unfortunately, but the race still got a brilliant winner in the shape of Zenyatta. Quality Road was withdrawn after giving trouble at the start, delaying the race.

NOTEBOOK
Zenyatta(USA), taking on males for the first time, rather than defend her crown in the ladies' version, this fine, big type extended her unbeaten record to 14 races with an awesome performance. Although a confirmed hold-up performer, it was still alarming to see her so far behind for much of the way. Having raced in last early, she must have been a good ten lengths off the lead down the back straight, and she still only had one behind rounding the final bend. However, at that point she began to make effortless but significant headway, saving ground towards the inside. Once in line for home, she was switched into the clear over 1f out, and there was something inevitable about what followed. Her trademark turn of foot was more irresistible than ever, not least considering the early gallop had been steady, and she totally overwhelmed her rivals, passing five colts in the final 200 yards. What made this performance all the more remarkable was that she never appeared to be totally flat out and crossed the line with her ears pricked, looking a fresh horse on pulling up. It's hard to dispute her rider's claim that he never got to the bottom of her. It's a shame 'Rachel' and Sea The Stars didn't turn up, for not only would their participation have made for an amazing spectacle, but seeing as the winner is the type who simply does enough (only twice won by more than 3l, despite being in a different league to all she's raced against), it's still impossible to know just how good she really is. Whatever the case, her reputation is now greatly enhanced and those who knocked her previous achievements on the grounds that she was simply beating the same fillies time after time, can have no argument. Credit to her connections for not taking the easy route. This performance will live long in the memory and she retires to the paddocks a true great.

Gio Ponti(USA), like the winner, was held up, although not quite so far back, and he enjoyed a ground-saving trip towards the inside around the final bend. He did everything right but still came off second best. There's a chance he will be aimed at next year's Dubai World Cup.

Twice Over, successful in the Champion Stakes on his previous start, ran a fine race on his first try on a synthetic surface, although he was given a very hard ride - Tom Queally appeared to use his whip over 20 times. He swung wider into the straight than the first two, but it didn't seem to cost him.

Summer Bird(USA), the leading 3-y-o colt in America, couldn't quite match his top-class dirt form on this first try on a synthetic surface, but he ran a superb race nonetheless. He's a strong staying galloper, so a modestly run race on a surface conducive to a turn of foot was never going to suit him ideally, and he deserves a deal of credit. He's been invited to the Japan Cup Dirt, but his connections have yet to decide on a plan.

Colonel John(USA) improved slightly on last year's sixth placing but was still well held.

Richard's Kid(USA) kept on from off the pace without mustering the required speed to threaten.

Regal Ransom(USA) is more of a dirt horse.

Mine That Bird(USA), the Kentucky Derby winner, was probably over the top.

Rip Van Winkle(IRE) had won two Group 1s since chasing home Sea The Stars in the Eclipse, including the Queen Elizabeth II Stakes on his latest outing, the same contest Raven's Pass landed en-route to his win in this last year, but he ran poorly in the race that counted most. The modest early gallop allowed him to recover from a slow beginning (by no means the only O'Brien runner who lost ground at the start at this meeting) and he was soon racing in a handy position, but he was beaten before the straight. It's impossible to know whether or not he was troubled by a foot problem that resurfaced in the build up. Johnny Murtagh said afterwards he believes the colt is a miler who needs to be ridden aggressively, to make use of his long stride. The rider also commented that this son of Galileo has had a hard season. He was the only runner in the line-up who didn't use Lasix.

7205 CAPANNELLE (R-H)
Sunday, November 8

OFFICIAL GOING: Heavy

7312a PREMIO RIBOT (GROUP 2) 1m
2:50 (3:11) 3-Y-0+ £73,670 (£34,184; £19,165; £9,583)

RPR
1 **Silver Arrow (ITY)**[176] 4-9-2 .... CFiocchi 3 109
(R Menichetti, Italy) *in rr to st: swtchd off rails 2f out: led 100yds out: r.o wl (15.84/1)* **158/10**
2 3/4 **Sehrezad (IRE)**[28] 6713 4-9-2 .... GBietolini 6 107
(Andreas Lowe, Germany) *6th st: chsd ldr fr over 1 1/2f out: ev ch ins fnl f: one pce* **105/10**
3 1 1/2 **Pressing (IRE)**[66] 5618 6-9-2 .... NCallan 10 104
(M A Jarvis) *a cl up: 4th st: led wl over 1f out: hdd 100yds out: one pce (49/100)* **1/2**[1]
4 4 **Vattene (IRE)**[28] 6717 4-8-13 .... URispoli 2 91
(M Gasparini, Italy) *in rr: 10th st: hdwy over 2f out: drvn and hung lft wl over 1f out: kpt on one pce* **52/1**
5 1 **Abaton**[14] 3-9-1 .... MDemuro 7 93
(V Caruso, Italy) *clsd up after 2f: 3rd st: wknd wl over 1f out* **48/10**[2]
6 4 **Farrel (IRE)**[63] 4-9-2 ....(b) DVargiu 9 83
(B Grizzetti, Italy) *led to wl over 1f out* **36/5**[3]
7 2 1/2 **Johannes Mozart (IRE)**[14] 3-9-1 .... SBasile 4 78
(Elisabetta Bernadini, Italy) *trckd ldr: 2nd st: wknd 2f out* **133/10**
8 1/2 **Project Dane (IRE)**[189] 5-9-2 .... OFancera 5 76
(L Polito, Italy) *a towards rr* **27/1**
9 3 **Zenone (IRE)**[63] 5-9-2 .... CColombi 11 69
(Laura Grizzetti, Italy) *7th st: wknd over 2f out* **136/10**
10 2 **Angel Rock (IRE)**[53] 6002 4-9-2 .... MMonteriso 8 64
(M Grassi, Italy) *last st: a bhd* **33/1**
11 5 **Apro Lunare (IRE)**[183] 1904 3-9-1 .... FBranca 1 54
(Laura Grizzetti, Italy) *5th st: wknd over 2f out* **136/10**

(-99.80)
WFA 3 from 4yo+ 2lb 11 Ran SP% **139.8**
WIN 16.84; PL 2.79, 1.65, 1.17; DF 225.88.
Owner Razza Dell'Olmo **Bred** Agricola Dell'Olmo Srl **Trained** Italy

NOTEBOOK
Pressing(IRE) copes with this sort of ground but he didn't quite get home this time having been sent on inside the final 2f.

7313a PREMIO ROMA AT THE RACES (GROUP 1) 1m 2f
3:25 (3:39) 3-Y-0+ £153,612 (£74,578; £42,728; £21,364)

RPR
1 **Voila Ici (IRE)**[21] 6893 4-9-2 .... MDemuro 9 119
(V Caruso, Italy) *sn pressing ldr: 2nd st: led wl over 3f out: rdn out (1.26/1)* **5/4**[1]
2 1/2 **Turati**[35] 3-9-0 .... MEsposito 1 120
(G Pucciatti, Italy) *mid-div: 7th st: hdwy 3f out: disp 2nd on ins 2f out: r.o steadily but couldn't worry wnr* **91/10**
3 2 **Sant'Antonio (ITY)**[21] 6893 4-9-2 .... URispoli 5 114
(S Botti, Italy) *hld up: 8th st: 6th and hdwy over 1f out: r.o to take 3rd last strides* **51/10**
4 hd **City Leader (IRE)**[22] 6850 4-9-2 ....(b) JamieSpencer 2 114
(B J Meehan) *broke wl: settled disputing 3rd: 3rd st: disp 2nd 2f out: one pce* **22/5**[3]
5 3/4 **Balius (IRE)**[36] 6506 6-9-2 ....(b) TedDurcan 10 112
(Saeed Bin Suroor) *a cl up: 4th st: disp 2nd 2f out: sn rdn and btn* **4/1**[2]
6 12 **Freemusic (IRE)**[28] 6718 5-9-2 .... GMarcelli 4 88
(L Riccardi, Italy) *disp 3rd: 5th st: wknd over 2f out* **91/10**
7 8 **Sri Putra**[50] 6132 3-9-0 .... PhilipRobinson 6 74
(M A Jarvis) *pushed along bef 1/2-way: 6th st: btn over 2f out* **98/10**
8 1/2 **Sottone**[14] 3-9-0 .... DVargiu 8 73
(B Grizzetti, Italy) *9th st: a in rr* **15/1**
9 hd **Galidon (IRE)**[35] 3-9-0 .... MMonteriso 7 73
(R Brogi, Italy) *last most of way* **28/1**
10 1 1/2 **Estejo (GER)**[36] 6506 5-9-2 .... GBietolini 3 68
(R Rohne, Germany) *led to wl over 3f out* **18/1**

2m 10.4s (7.10)
WFA 3 from 4yo+ 4lb 10 Ran SP% **143.4**
WIN 2.26; PL 1.38, 2.19, 2.24; DF 30.98.
Owner Scuderia Incolinx **Bred** Soc Finanza Locale Consulting Srl **Trained** Italy

NOTEBOOK
City Leader(IRE), fifth in the Champion Stakes last time out, had the blinkers on again and ran quite well, but conditions were a lot more testing than he'd ever encountered before.
Balius(IRE) couldn't cope with the very testing ground and was below his best.
Sri Putra, who has done all his winning on good ground, also found these conditions too much of a test.

1395 KREFELD (R-H)
Sunday, November 8

OFFICIAL GOING: Heavy

7314a GROSSER BOMBADIER-VOSSLOCH HERZOG VON RATIBOR-RENNEN (GROUP 3) 1m 110y
1:45 (1:58) 2-Y-0 £29,126 (£9,709; £5,340; £2,913; £1,456)

RPR
1 **Neatico (GER)** 2-8-13 .... AStarke 6 —
(P Schiergen, Germany) *racd in 4th to st: rdn to ld wl over 1f out: drvn out* **9/5**[1]
2 1 3/4 **Cabimas** 2-8-13 .... FilipMinarik 7 —
(P Schiergen, Germany) *racd in 6th: outpcd on turn and last st: hdwy on outside wl over 1f out: chsd wnr fnl f: no imp* **93/10**
3 2 1/2 **Keep Cool** 2-8-13 .... APietsch 5 —
(Andreas Lowe, Germany) *in rr: 7th st: styd on down outside fr wl over 1f out: nrest at fin* **183/10**
4 1/2 **Kite Hunter (IRE)**[21] 6887 2-9-2 .... EPedroza 3 —
(Mario Hofer, Germany) *racd in 5th to st: drvn and disp 3rd 1f out: one pce* **11/5**[2]
5 1 1/4 **Eternal Power**[65] 5652 2-9-2 .... THellier 2 —
(C Von Der Recke, Germany) *led to wl over 1f out: drvn and stl 2nd 1f out: no ex* **26/5**
6 3/4 **Wellmond (GER)** 2-8-13 .... AHelfenbein 8 —
(H Blume, Germany) *a cl up on outside: 2nd st: wknd over 1f out* **136/10**
7 1 1/2 **Nightdance Paolo (GER)**[21] 6887 2-9-2 .... JiriPalik 1 —
(P Schiergen, Germany) *pressed ldr on ins to 1/2-way: 3rd st: btn 2f out* **12/1**
8 hd **Barzini (GER)**[49] 6151 2-8-13 .... DPorcu 4 —
(Uwe Ostmann, Germany) *a in rr: 6th st: sn btn* **19/5**[3]

1m 48.86s (2.26) 8 Ran SP% **133.4**
WIN 28; PL 16, 22, 39; SF 161.
Owner Gestut Ittlingen **Bred** Gestut Hof Ittlingen **Trained** Germany

7264 BORDEAUX LE BOUSCAT (R-H)
Sunday, November 8

OFFICIAL GOING: Very heavy

7315a PRIX DE PAUILLAC 1m 1f 110y
12:45 (12:00) 2-Y-0 £12,621 (£5,049; £3,786; £2,524; £1,262)

RPR
1 **Royal Menantie (FR)** 2-9-2 .... DMorrison —
(J Boisnard, France)
2 shd **Zircjorien (FR)** 2-9-2 .... PSogorb —
(D Guillemin, France)
3 nk **Brampour (IRE)** 2-8-12 .... IMendizabal —
(J-C Rouget, France)
4 4 **Dream Dealer (FR)** 2-8-12 .... —
(F Rohaut, France)
5 snk **Philander**[33] 6578 2-9-2 .... F-XBertras —
(E J O'Neill)
6 4 **Espartaco (SPA)**[21] 2-8-9 .... —
(C Laffon-Parias, France)
7 3 **Thomaraz (FR)** 2-8-9 .... —
(J-L Dubord, France)
8 8 **Mapale (FR)** 2-8-9 .... —
(X-Thomas Demeaulte, France)

2m 17.52s (137.52) 8 Ran
PARI-MUTUEL (Including 1 Euro stake): WIN 7.30; PL 1.40, 1.50, 1.20;DF 51.20.
Owner G Ferron **Bred** G Ferron & J Chailleux **Trained** France

7316a PRIX DE CAUDERAN (MAIDEN) 1m 1f 110y
1:15 (12:00) 2-Y-0 £6,796 (£2,718; £2,039; £1,359; £680)

RPR
1 **Snowbound (FR)** 2-9-2 .... IMendizabal —
(J-C Rouget, France)
2 shd **Issacar (IRE)**[36] 6501 2-9-2 ....(p) JClaudic —
(A De Watrigant, France) *finished 3rd, placed 2nd*
3 3/4 **Sierra Femina (FR)** 2-8-13 .... J-BEyquem —
(J Boisnard, France) *finished 4th, placed 3rd*
4 1/2 **Caunton Beck (FR)**[19] 6928 2-9-2 .... F-XBertras —
(E J O'Neill) *finished 5th, placed 4th*
5 1/2 **Myasun (FR)**[133] 2-9-2 .... OTrigodet —
(C Baillet, France) *finished 2nd, placed 5th*
6 2 **Sarakan (FR)** 2-9-2 .... —
(C Goudrain, France)
7 3/4 **Ocean's Song (FR)**[39] 2-8-13 .... —
(A De Watrigant, France)
8 3/4 **David's Boy (FR)** 2-9-2 .... —
(C Baillet, France)
9 3 **Strategos (FR)** 2-9-2 ....(b) —
(Mlle A Imaz-Ceca, France)
10 10 **Grand Ami (FR)** 2-9-2 .... —
(Mme C Dufreche, France)
0 **Poisson Pilote (FR)**[95] 4686 2-9-2 .... —
(R Litt, France)
0 **Buttermilk (IRE)**[95] 4686 2-9-2 ....(b) —
(T Lemer, France)
0 **Triton Des Places (FR)** 2-9-2 .... —
(F Nicolle, France)
0 **Messiah Noire (FR)** 2-8-13 .... —
(T Lemer, France)

2m 18.34s (138.34) 14 Ran
PARI-MUTUEL: WIN 3.50; PL 1.50, 3.30, 1.90; DF 41.80.
Owner M Schwartz **Bred** Eric Puerari & Oceanic Bloodstock Inc **Trained** Pau, France

7273 WOLVERHAMPTON (A.W) (L-H)
Monday, November 9

OFFICIAL GOING: Standard
Wind: Nil Weather: Overcast

7317 WOLVERHAMPTON HOLIDAY INN MEDIAN AUCTION MAIDEN STKS 5f 216y(P)
2:05 (2:07) (Class 6) 2-Y-0 £2,729 (£806; £403) Stalls Low

Form RPR
45 1 **Gramercy (IRE)**[7] 7209 2-9-3 0 .... JamieSpencer 6 82+
(M L W Bell) *hdwy over 4f out: edgd lft and led jst over 1f out: easily* **6/4**[1]
63 2 2 1/4 **Goddess Of Light (IRE)**[24] 6826 2-8-12 0 .... ShaneKelly 4 67
(Daniel Mark Loughnane, Ire) *led after 1f: pushed along and hdd jst over 1f out: rdn and edgd rt ins fnl f: one pce* **9/1**
3 1 1/2 **Kingsgate Choice (IRE)** 2-9-3 0 .... RobertWinston 8 69+
(J R Best) *s.i.s: hld up towards rr: hdwy and hung lft jst over 2f out: rdn wl over 1f out: hung lft and r.o to take 3rd last strides* **6/1**[3]

423 **4** *shd* **Pan American**[20] 6912 2-9-3 77 FergusSweeney 11 67
(P J Makin) *s.i.s: sn w ldrs: ev ch wl over 1f out: rdn and edgd lft ent fnl f: one pce* **9/2**[2]

55 **5** *1 1/4* **Notte Di Note (IRE)**[24] 6826 2-8-12 0 ChrisCatlin 3 59
(L M Cumani) *led 1f: prom: rdn over 1f out: one pce* **16/1**

6 **6** *2 1/2* **Mint Whip (IRE)**[14] 7058 2-8-12 0 DaneO'Neill 5 51
(R Hannon) *s.i.s: hld up in rr: pushed along over 2f out: rdn over 1f out: nvr nr ldrs* **13/2**

40 **7** *1 1/2* **Second Brook (IRE)**[17] 6991 2-9-3 0 JerryO'Dwyer 10 52+
(R Hollinshead) *hld up in mid-div: rdn over 2f out: wknd wl over 1f out* **50/1**

00 **8** *nk* **Decency (IRE)**[10] 7145 2-8-12 0 JimmyQuinn 7 46
(E A L Dunlop) *hld up in mid-div: hdwy over 3f out: rdn over 2f out: wknd wl over 1f out* **33/1**

46 **9** *1/2* **Kenswick**[14] 7061 2-8-9 0 AndreaAtzeni(3) 1 44
(Pat Eddery) *hld up and bhd: pushed along over 2f out: rdn and short-lived effrt wl over 1f out* **25/1**

00 **10** *3 1/4* **French Fantasy**[11] 7135 2-8-12 0 SteveDrowne 12 35
(H Morrison) *t.k.h towards rr: hung rt thrght: no ch fnl 2f* **33/1**

0 **11** *8* **Petit Belle**[21] 6903 2-8-12 0 LukeMorris 2 11
(N P Littmoden) *hld up in mid-div: rdn over 2f out: sn bhd* **100/1**

12 *9* **Lets Move It** 2-9-3 0 AdamKirby 9 —
(D Shaw) *hld up in tch: lost pl over 3f out: bhd fnl 2f* **100/1**

1m 15.47s (0.47) **Going Correction** -0.025s/f (Stan) **12** Ran SP% **115.4**
Speed ratings (Par 94): **95,92,90,89,88 84,82,82,81,77 66,54**
toteswingers: 1&2 £5.00, 1&3 £5.60, 2&3 £9.20 CSF £14.83 TOTE £2.30: £1.30, £2.20, £2.60; EX 14.60 Trifecta £105.20 Part won. Pool: £142.17 - 0.55 winning units..
Owner M B Hawtin **Bred** Michael Mullins **Trained** Newmarket, Suffolk

FOCUS
A fair maiden and the form looks sure to be at least as good as rated through the fifth and seventh.

NOTEBOOK
Gramercy(IRE) proved well suited by the return to 6f. He looks quite useful but things will be tougher from now on. (op 13-8 tchd 11-8)
Goddess Of Light(IRE), given a positive ride, had her chance but proved no match for the winner. She might find an ordinary maiden, or handicap. (op 8-1 tchd 10-1)
Kingsgate Choice(IRE) ◆, a £60,000 half-brother to 5f-7f winner in Greece out of a fairly useful sprinter, is the one to take from the race. He raced last early after starting slowly, and then when trying to make his move around the final bend he did not face the kickback at all. Once in the straight, after initially taking a while to pick up, he finished well and should be all the better of this experience. (op 11-2)
Pan American proved unsuited by this drop in trip and was well below his official mark of 77. (tchd 4-1)
Notte Di Note(IRE) didn't offer much, but she might do better over further now she can go handicapping.
Decency(IRE) ◆ didn't seem to handle this left-handed track. She's hinted at ability on all three of her starts to date and might be worth a second look if going handicapping next time off a modest mark. Official explanation: jockey said the filly hung right (op 20-1)

7318 TRY BETDAQ FOR AN EXCHANGE MEDIAN AUCTION MAIDEN STKS 1m 4f 50y(P)
2:35 (2:35) (Class 6) 3-5-Y-O **£2,388** (£705; £352) **Stalls** Low

Form RPR

4006 **1** **Order Order**[38] 6439 3-8-11 55 JimmyQuinn 5 56+
(H J L Dunlop) *a.p: shkn up to ld wl over 1f out: r.o wl* **5/2**[2]

00/3 **2** *1 3/4* **Ishismart**[34] 6558 5-9-0 43 AndreaAtzeni(3) 3 52
(R Hollinshead) *hld up: hdwy over 2f out: rdn over 1f out: wnt 2nd wl ins fnl f: nt trble wnr* **15/8**[1]

0566 **3** *1 1/4* **Desert Fairy**[9] 7195 3-8-11 48 TomEaves 9 50
(J W Unett) *hdwy after 3f: wnt 2nd over 7f out: led over 4f out: rdn over 2f out: hdd wl over 1f out: one pce fnl f* **8/1**

0-50 **4** *1/2* **Dovedon Angel**[6] 7221 3-8-11 0 JerryO'Dwyer 4 51+
(Miss Gay Kelleway) *prom: nt clr run on ins and lost pl over 3f out: sn swtchd rt and pushed along: rallied over 2f out: rdn over 1f out: one pce fnl f* **10/1**

0/0 **5** *2* **Dawn Storm (IRE)**[9] 7195 4-9-8 0 AdamKirby 6 51
(J L Spearing) *s.i.s: rn in snatches in rr: rdn 3f out: hdwy on ins wl over 1f out: n.d* **28/1**

635 **6** *2 1/2* **Davana**[17] 7004 3-8-11 48 DaneO'Neill 8 42
(W J H Ratcliffe) *hld up: stdy prog over 3f out: sn pushed along: rdn over 2f out: wknd wl over 1f out* **8/1**

000 **7** *12* **Silvester**[25] 6794 3-9-2 44 ChrisCatlin 1 28
(R M H Cowell) *hld up towards rr: pushed along over 3f out: lost tch over 2f out* **25/1**

6064 **8** *nse* **Meml**[17] 7004 3-8-11 49 GrahamGibbons 7 23
(J D Bethell) *hld up in tch: hdwy over 6f out: rdn and wknd 2f out* **6/1**[3]

5000 **9** *41* **Carnival Fair**[27] 6758 4-9-3 40 (v[1]) LPKeniry 10 —
(S Wynne) *led: hdd over 4f out: wknd over 3f out: t.o fnl 2f* **66/1**

000 **10** *26* **Elevate Bobbob**[22] 6880 3-8-12 23 ow1 SladeO'Hara(5) 2 —
(A Berry) *hld up in mid-div: lost pl over 5f out: rdn over 3f out: sn lost tch: t.o* **150/1**

2m 42.08s (0.98) **Going Correction** -0.025s/f (Stan)
WFA 3 from 4yo+ 6lb **10** Ran SP% **118.4**
Speed ratings (Par 101): **95,93,93,92,91 89,81,81,54,36**
toteswingers: 1&2 £2.90, 1&3 £6.50, 2&3 £6.30 CSF £7.56 TOTE £3.60: £1.70, £1.10, £3.30; EX 11.30 Trifecta £68.80 Pool: £310.75 - 3.34 winning units..
Owner Mrs Harry Dunlop **Bred** Bloomsbury Stud & The Hon Sir David Sieff **Trained** Lambourn, Berks

FOCUS
A really weak maiden run at a moderate gallop and the winner did not have to improve on previous form to score.

7319 ENJOY THE LUCKY 7 GROUP OFFER CLAIMING STKS 7f 32y(P)
3:05 (3:09) (Class 6) 2-Y-O **£2,729** (£806; £403) **Stalls** High

Form RPR

0012 **1** **Shark Man (IRE)**[26] 6774 2-8-7 73 ow1 JackMitchell(3) 1 68
(P J McBride) *led early: a.p: wnt 2nd over 2f out: rdn wl over 1f out: led ins fnl f: jst hld on* **2/1**[1]

000 **2** *shd* **Zachary Boy (IRE)**[110] 4194 2-8-5 50 FrankieMcDonald 8 63+
(B G Powell) *mid-div: outpcd over 2f out: rdn wl over 1f out: sn hung lft: str run ins fnl f: jst failed* **100/1**

0611 **3** *1 1/2* **Vito Volterra (IRE)**[13] 7098 2-8-11 72 PhillipMakin 12 65
(A B Haynes) *sn led: rdn over 1f out: hdd ins fnl f: no ex towards fin* **3/1**[2]

620 **4** *3/4* **Mind Of Her Own**[167] 2358 2-7-13 61 AndrewHeffernan(5) 2 56
(P D Evans) *hld up in tch: pushed along over 3f out: rdn over 2f out: edgd lft over 1f out: kpt on towards fin* **14/1**

0504 **5** *2 3/4* **Mrs Puff (IRE)**[13] 7098 2-8-2 53 LukeMorris 3 48
(P D Evans) *sn mid-div: pushed along over 3f out: rdn over 2f out: no hdwy* **16/1**

4025 **6** *nk* **Whipperway (IRE)**[7] 7210 2-8-2 65 ChrisCatlin 11 47
(M R Channon) *hld up towards rr: pushed along wl over 1f out: n.d* **11/1**

P000 **7** *1/2* **Scintillating (IRE)**[12] 7120 2-8-3 35 (p) PaulEddery 9 47
(R Hollinshead) *hld up towards rr: pushed along 3f out: short-lived effrt on ins wl over 1f out* **100/1**

8 *nk* **Fever Tree** 2-8-6 0 JimmyQuinn 10 49
(P J Makin) *s.i.s: a in rr* **33/1**

6003 **9** *2* **Lord Victor**[7] 7210 2-8-2 50 AndreaAtzeni(3) 5 43
(A J McCabe) *sn chsng ldr: lost 2nd 3f out: sn wknd* **12/1**

066 **10** *2 1/4* **Tamarind Hill (IRE)**[19] 6943 2-8-9 68 (b[1]) SteveDrowne 6 41
(C R Egerton) *a.p: wnt 2nd briefly 3f out: rdn and wknd wl over 1f out* **10/3**[3]

0630 **11** *4 1/2* **Tiger Hawk (USA)**[60] 5786 2-8-5 48 (b) SaleemGolam 7 26
(P D Evans) *s.i.s: towards rr: rdn over 3f out: sn struggling* **50/1**

1m 30.27s (0.67) **Going Correction** -0.025s/f (Stan) **11** Ran SP% **116.9**
Speed ratings (Par 94): **95,94,93,92,89 88,88,87,85,83 77**
.Shark Man was claimed by J. R. Tooth for £8000. Zachary Boy was subject to a friendly claim.\n\x\x
Owner J Burns **Bred** John Grimes **Trained** Newmarket, Suffolk

FOCUS
An ordinary juvenile claimer with the winner rated to recent form and the runner-up an improver.

NOTEBOOK
Shark Man(IRE) gave the impression he would benefit from the return to this trip when runner-up over 6f at Kempton on his previous start, and he duly went one place better, but only just. Carrying 1lb overweight, he looked set to win decisively when taking over from Vito Volterra inside the final furlong, but he would have been passed in another stride, with the runner-up finishing strongly on his outside. He was claimed by Julia Tooth for £8,000. (op 7-4)
Zachary Boy(IRE), dismissed in the betting at odds of 100-1, was ridden along a fair way out and looked to be going nowhere for much of the straight until finally picking up late on. He ran as though he'll get 1m and there might be a small race in him - he's clearly better than his official mark of 50.
Vito Volterra(IRE), who had made all in a couple of turf claimers over this trip on his last two starts, again went from the front and had his chance. He probably ran close to his official mark of 72. (tchd 11-4)
Mind Of Her Own, trying this trip for the first time, offered some encouragement after 167 days and ought to come on for this.
Mrs Puff(IRE) had something find at the weights with a few of these and may need dropping in grade.
Fever Tree was reported to have missed the break. Official explanation: jockey said that the filly missed the break
Tamarind Hill(IRE), fitted with blinkers for the first time and dropped in grade, was quite well backed but he ran poorly. (op 11-2)

7320 BET PREMIER LEAGUE FOOTBALL - BETDAQ NURSERY 7f 32y(P)
3:40 (3:40) (Class 4) (0-80,79) 2-Y-O **£4,533** (£1,348; £674; £336) **Stalls** High

Form RPR

043 **1** **Tewin Wood**[20] 6922 2-8-13 71 RobertWinston 7 74
(A Bailey) *hld up in tch: chal wl over 1f out: sn rdn: led wl ins fnl f: drvn out* **5/1**[2]

360 **2** *1/2* **Opus Dei**[65] 5668 2-8-12 70 FrederikTylicki 9 72
(J A Glover) *sn hld up in mid-div: pushed along over 2f out: rdn and hdwy on ins to ld over 1f out: sn edgd rt: hdd wl ins fnl f: r.o* **12/1**

3100 **3** *nse* **La Pantera**[32] 6619 2-9-5 77 DaneO'Neill 8 79+
(R Hannon) *dwlt: hld up in rr: swtchd rt over 2f out: rdn and hdwy over 1f out: kpt on ins fnl f* **13/2**[3]

4501 **4** *1/2* **Ever So Bold**[32] 6609 2-8-7 68 (b) AndreaAtzeni(3) 12 68
(W R Muir) *hld up in mid-div: rdn and hdwy on outside over 2f out: c v wd st: kpt on towards fin* **8/1**

1435 **5** *1 1/2* **Kylladdie**[69] 5550 2-9-3 75 IanMongan 10 72
(S Gollings) *hld up towards rr: pushed along and hdwy 2f out: sn rdn: nt qckn ins fnl f* **18/1**

1303 **6** *1/2* **Gobama**[23] 6844 2-9-3 75 SebSanders 1 71
(J W Hills) *led over 1f: w ldr: led over 3f out: hung rt bnd over 2f out: rn wd st: rdn and hdd wl over 1f out: fdd ins fnl f* **11/1**

0444 **7** *1* **Master Of Dance (IRE)**[29] 6693 2-9-3 78 PatrickHills(3) 4 74+
(R Hannon) *prom: hmpd and lost pl sn after s: hld up in rr: pushed along 3f out: hdwy on ins wl over 1f out: sn rdn: no imp ins fnl f* **3/1**[1]

0045 **8** *5* **Perfect Ch'l (IRE)**[23] 6844 2-9-5 77 TonyHamilton 2 58
(I A Wood) *w ldr: led over 5f out tl over 3f out: carried wd ent st: wknd over 1f out* **11/1**

3351 **9** *2 3/4* **Dream Number (IRE)**[14] 7056 2-8-12 70 PhillipMakin 3 44+
(W R Muir) *a.p: n.m.r bnd after 1f: led wl over 1f out: sn rdn and hdd: wknd fnl f* **7/1**

5001 **10** *1* **Little Perisher**[9] 7175 2-9-0 77 MatthewDavies(5) 11 49
(A P Jarvis) *hld up and bhd: rdn over 2f out: sn struggling* **33/1**

012 **11** *14* **Stef And Stelio**[19] 6948 2-9-5 77 (b) ShaneKelly 6 14+
(G A Butler) *prom: rdn over 2f out: wknd wl over 1f out: eased fnl f* **9/1**

1m 29.38s (-0.22) **Going Correction** -0.025s/f (Stan) **11** Ran SP% **121.2**
Speed ratings (Par 98): **100,99,99,98,97 96,95,89,86,85 69**
toteswingers: 1&2 £16.30, 1&3 £8.60, 2&3 £24.50 CSF £65.82 CT £402.44 TOTE £4.00: £2.10, £4.70, £2.90; EX 50.50 Trifecta £118.50 Part won. Pool: £160.18 - 0.10 winning units..
Owner The Perle d'Or Partnership **Bred** Perle D'Or Partnership **Trained** Newmarket, Suffolk

FOCUS
A fair nursery run at a strong pace, with Gobama and Perfect Ch'l taking each other on. The form looks reasonable rated around the fourth and fifth.

NOTEBOOK
Tewin Wood, back up in trip on his nursery debut, was plenty keen enough for some of the way but he still found plenty for pressure. He's still quite immature and may keep progressing. (op 11-2 tchd 9-2)
Opus Dei ran an improved race on this step up in trip and switch to handicap company. He had been off for two months and gave the impression he will progress again.
La Pantera, trying 7f for the first time, lost several lengths with a slow start and has to be considered a bit unlucky. (op 6-1)
Ever So Bold, 4lb higher than when winning at Kempton on his previous start, did well to finish close considering he was stuck very wide around the bend into the straight. (op 9-1 tchd 11-1)
Kylladdie, who was stepped up to this trip for the first time, ran as though he might improve for the first run in over two months. (tchd 16-1 and 20-1)
Master Of Dance(IRE) is better than he showed as he lost his place when badly squeezed out between runners early on. (op 7-2 tchd 9-2)

Dream Number(IRE) was reported by the vet to have spread a near-fore plate. Official explanation: vet said filly spread near-fore plate (tchd 13-2)

7321 HOTEL & CONFERENCING AT WOLVERHAMPTON H'CAP 7f 32y(P)

4:10 (4:12) (Class 5) (0-70,71) 3-Y-O+ **£3,238** (£963; £481; £240) **Stalls** High

Form RPR

1230 **1** **Black Dahlia**[18] 6976 4-9-5 **70**........................ FrederikTylicki 1 79
(J A Glover) *prom: stdd into mid-div over 5f out: n.m.r on ins over 3f out: nt clr run over 2f out: hdwy wl over 1f out: sn rdn: led jst over 1f out: drvn out* **3/1**[2]

0 **2** *1 3/4* **Simla Sunset (IRE)**[51] 6111 3-9-1 **67**........................(t) AdamKirby 7 71+
(J R Gask) *hld up: lost pl over 4f out: c wd st: rdn and hdwy fnl f: tk 2nd nr fin* **11/1**

1003 **3** *1/2* **Tangerine Trees**[23] 6846 4-9-5 **70**........................ TomEaves 8 73
(B Smart) *prom: led over 5f out tl wl over 4f out: led over 3f out: rdn and hdd jst over 1f out: no ex and lost 2nd nr fin* **10/1**

6004 **4** *1/2* **Downhill Skier (IRE)**[16] 7023 5-8-12 **63**........................ ShaneKelly 10 65
(W M Brisbourne) *hld up towards rr: hdwy wl over 1f out: rdn and nt qckn ins fnl f* **11/1**

0111 **5** *shd* **La Gifted**[3] 7275 3-8-12 **71** 6ex........................ IJBrennan[(7)] 2 72
(M R Channon) *led over 1f: a.p: chsd ldr 2f out: rdn and edgd rt over 1f out: nt qckn ins fnl f* **11/4**[1]

3056 **6** *1* **Fiefdom (IRE)**[10] 7153 7-9-1 **66**........................ PhillipMakin 4 65+
(I W McInnes) *hld up in rr: rdn and sme hdwy 1f out: kpt on one pce ins fnl f* **8/1**

2326 **7** *1/2* **Stanley Goodspeed**[31] 6637 6-9-0 **65**........................(tp) SebSanders 5 62
(J W Hills) *hld up towards rr: hdwy on ins wl over 1f out: sn rdn: wknd wl ins fnl f* **13/2**[3]

2060 **8** *1/2* **Royal Envoy (IRE)**[14] 7053 6-8-6 **64**........................ AndrewHeffernan[(5)] 3 60
(P Howling) *prom: lost pl over 3f out: rdn 2f out: swtchd lft wl over 1f out: n.d after* **12/1**

2350 **9** *hd* **War And Peace (IRE)**[147] 2980 5-8-12 **70**........................ LewisWalsh[(7)] 6 65
(Jane Chapple-Hyam) *hld up towards rr: hdwy on outside over 2f out: c wd st: wknd over 1f out* **14/1**

606 **10** *2 1/4* **Trimlestown (IRE)**[231] 934 6-8-12 **68**........................(p) RichardEvans[(5)] 9 57
(P D Evans) *t.k.h early: hdwy after 1f: pushed along and wknd over 1f out* **28/1**

0454 **11** *1 1/2* **Eightdaysaweek**[13] 7093 3-8-8 **60**........................ ChrisCatlin 12 45
(A J McCabe) *hdwy over 5f out: pushed along over 3f out: wknd wl over 1f out* **50/1**

415- **12** *1/2* **Starlight Gazer**[378] 7021 6-9-0 **65**........................(vt) RichardThomas 11 49
(J A Geake) *hdwy after 1f: led wl over 4f out tl over 2f out: wknd wl over 1f out* **25/1**

1m 30.39s (0.79) **Going Correction** -0.025s/f (Stan)
WFA 3 from 4yo+ 1lb **12** Ran SP% **125.5**
Speed ratings (Par 103): **94,92,91,90,90 89,89,88,88,85 83,83**
toteswingers: 1&2 £11.30, 1&3 £7.50, 2&3 £22.40 CSF £38.21 CT £313.88 TOTE £4.30: £1.60, £4.00, £2.20; EX 71.20 TRIFECTA Not won..
Owner Paul J Dixon & Brian Morton **Bred** Worksop Manor Stud **Trained** Babworth, Notts

FOCUS
A modest but competitive handicap run at an ordinary pace. The form is rather messy but the first two are rated to form with the third to his latest mark.
Starlight Gazer Official explanation: jockey said gelding hung right on the bend

7322 BET ASIAN H'CAPS - BETDAQ HANDICAP 1m 141y(P)

4:40 (4:40) (Class 4) (0-80,80) 3-Y-O+ **£5,046** (£1,510; £755; £377; £188) **Stalls** Low

Form RPR

0244 **1** **Spinning**[9] 7194 6-9-6 **80**........................(b) PhillipMakin 6 95
(T D Barron) *s.i.s: hld up in rr: pushed along and hdwy wl over 1f out: rdn to ld ent fnl f: sn clr: eased cl home* **2/1**[1]

5260 **2** *6* **Xpres Maite**[19] 6946 6-9-6 **80**........................(b) AmirQuinn 1 81
(S R Bowring) *hld up towards rr: gd hdwy ins fnl f: tk 2nd nr fin: no ch w wnr* **7/1**[3]

0000 **3** *nk* **Ansells Pride (IRE)**[37] 6496 6-8-7 **67**........................ TomEaves 3 68
(B Smart) *led early: a.p: nt clr run over 2f out: n.m.r and lost pl wl over 1f out: kpt on u.p ins fnl f* **25/1**

5414 **4** *shd* **Gaily Noble (IRE)**[11] 7141 3-9-2 **79**........................ FergusSweeney 11 79
(A B Haynes) *sn led: hdd over 7f out: w ldr: led over 3f out: rdn and hdd ent fnl f: sn edgd rt: one pce* **9/1**

5506 **5** *1 1/2* **Justcallmehandsome**[14] 7054 7-8-2 **69**........................(v) AmyScott[(7)] 5 66
(D J S Ffrench Davis) *hld up towards rr: hdwy 4f out: ev ch over 2f out: sn rdn: one pce whn nt clr run ins fnl f* **12/1**

6305 **6** *1/2* **Ella Woodcock (IRE)**[10] 7153 5-8-6 **66** oh7........................ FrancisNorton 7 66+
(E J Alston) *hld up in mid-div: lost pl 3f out: styng on whn nt clr run wl ins fnl f* **20/1**

5026 **7** *2 1/2* **Fazbee (IRE)**[39] 6421 3-8-11 **74**........................ ShaneKelly 4 64
(P W D'Arcy) *hld up in mid-div: bhd whn rdn wl over 1f out* **7/1**[3]

1-11 **8** *1/2* **Alqaahir (USA)**[10] 7153 7-8-11 **71**........................ LiamJones 8 60
(Lee Smyth, Ire) *hld up in rr: stdy prog over 3f out: wknd over 1f out* **5/1**[2]

0110 **9** *2 1/2* **Lujano**[23] 6861 4-8-10 **70**........................ FrederikTylicki 9 53
(Ollie Pears) *hld up in tch: pressed ldng pair over 2f out: rdn and wknd fnl f* **14/1**

00 **10** *2* **Colonel Sherman (USA)**[171] 2237 4-8-6 **66**........................ ChrisCatlin 10 44
(P A Kirby) *led over 7f out tl over 3f out: wknd over 2f out* **20/1**

1m 48.46s (-2.04) **Going Correction** -0.025s/f (Stan)
WFA 3 from 4yo+ 3lb **10** Ran SP% **112.7**
Speed ratings (Par 105): **108,102,102,102,100 100,98,97,95,93**
toteswingers: 1&2 £5.50, 1&3 £14.30, 2&3 £30.10 CSF £14.79 CT £260.59 TOTE £2.90: £1.40, £2.90, £7.30; EX 18.10 Trifecta £434.90 Pool: £675.96 - 1.15 winning units. Place 6: £34.85 Place 5: £23.29 .
Owner Mrs J Hazell **Bred** Cheveley Park Stud **Trained** Maunby, N Yorks
■ Stewards' Enquiry : Fergus Sweeney two-day ban: careless riding (Nov 24-25)

FOCUS
An ordinary handicap for the grade and the winner is rated to his very best course form with the fourth to his recent mark.
Alqaahir(USA) Official explanation: jockey said horse failed to quicken
T/Jkpt: £4,777.60 to a £1 stake. Pool: £103,560.45. 15.39 winning tickets. T/Plt: £64.80 to a £1 stake. Pool: £75,984.62. 855.45 winning tickets. T/Qpdt: £46.70 to a £1 stake. Pool: £5,542.25. 87.80 winning tickets. KH

7233 KEMPTON (A.W) (R-H)

Wednesday, November 11

OFFICIAL GOING: Standard
Wind: Moderate behind Weather: dark, showers later on

7323 GROOMED TO PERFECTION, THE KIA SOUL CONDITIONS STKS 1m 2f (P)

5:50 (5:50) (Class 3) 3-Y-O+
£7,352 (£2,201; £1,100; £551; £274; £138) **Stalls** High

Form RPR

120- **1** **Anmar (USA)**[396] 6648 3-8-9 **97**........................(v[1]) TedDurcan 5 111+
(Saeed Bin Suroor) *trckd ldrs: veered lft home bnd ins fnl 2f: sn qcknd to ld appr fnl f: sn clr: v easily* **7/4**[1]

5522 **2** *5* **Pachattack (USA)**[26] 6813 3-8-4 **101**........................(b) FrancisNorton 8 92+
(G A Butler) *chsd ldr tl bmpd and lost footing bnd ins fnl 2f: dropped bk to 4th: styd on again past wkng rivals fnl f to go 2nd but no ch w v easy wnr* **5/2**[2]

0050 **3** *1 3/4* **Philatelist (USA)**[26] 6816 5-8-13 **99**........................(v) JimCrowley 6 89
(M A Jarvis) *chsd ldrs: hdwy whn bmpd bnd ins fnl 2f: sn rcvrd to ld: hdd appr fnl f and no ch w wnr: wknd and lost 2nd ins fnl f* **15/2**

2000 **4** *3/4* **Russian Sage (SAF)**[26] 6812 5-9-6 **108**........................ MartinDwyer 9 94
(M F De Kock, South Africa) *led: rdn and hdd ins fnl 2f: no ch w wnr and wknd ins fnl f* **3/1**[3]

5 *1 1/2* **Rajamand (FR)**[32] 3-8-9 0........................ LPKeniry 7 84?
(Miss E C Lavelle) *in rr: pushed along 3f out: mod prog fnl f* **50/1**

5240 **6** *shd* **Hallingdal (UAE)**[20] 6973 4-8-1 74........................ RyanClark[(7)] 3 79
(J J Bridger) *s.i.s: in rr: mod prog fnl f* **50/1**

00 **7** *10* **Bravely Fought (IRE)**[25] 6867 4-8-13 0........................ SteveDrowne 2 64
(Sabrina J Harty, Ire) *a towards rr* **14/1**

-563 **8** *9* **Strategic Mover (USA)**[16] 7057 4-8-10 67........................(t) RobertLButler[(3)] 1 46
(P Butler) *a in rr* **33/1**

2m 6.18s (-1.82) **Going Correction** +0.025s/f (Slow)
WFA 3 from 4yo+ 4lb **8** Ran SP% **115.2**
Speed ratings (Par 107): **108,104,102,102,100 100,92,85**
toteswingers: 1&2 £2.10, 1&3 £3.80, 2&3 £4.30 CSF £6.33 TOTE £3.00: £1.10, £1.30, £1.90; EX 7.60.
Owner Godolphin **Bred** Shadwell Farm LLC **Trained** Newmarket, Suffolk

FOCUS
The feature race of the card, this was a decent conditions event, run in a time just 0.18 of a second outside the standard. The pace soon slackened after an early dash. Only the first four ever got into it and the winner and second can be rated better than the bare form. That said, the fifth and sixth were a bit close for comfort at the line.

NOTEBOOK
Anmar(USA) was highly tried at two, finishing second to subsequent Group 1 winner Zafisio in a Listed race before disappointing in an Ascot Group 3. Visored for the first time, he shrugged off an absence of more than a year, getting caught up in scrimmaging turning for home before cutting down the leader with a strong burst. He was then eased down with the race in the bag, value for further. He looks a smart colt and is very likely to head for the Dubai carnival, where the Tapeta surface at Meydan should suit him. (tchd 9-4 in a place and 2-1 in places)
Pachattack(USA), just denied in a Listed race last time, was the worst affected in the incident on the home turn and was knocked back to fourth. She ran on well again past a couple of opponents in the final furlong and would have been closer to the winner but for the incident, although he was eased. This was a promising debut on this surface. (op 9-4 tchd 11-4)
Philatelist(USA) has a respectable record here and he survived a bump to show ahead temporarily in the straight, but could do nothing whatsoever to stem the winner's run. (op 6-1 tchd 9-1)
Russian Sage(SAF), the pick of the paddock, made the running, and could only keep on at the one pace once headed in the straight. This was his best run so far in Britain but he is yet to recapture the form he was showing in Dubai earlier in the year. (op 7-2 tchd 11-4)
Rajamand(FR) ran respectably on this British/Polytrack debut and is now eligible for a handicap mark. He should have more to offer, probably over further.

7324 BOXINGDAYRACES.CO.UK H'CAP 1m 4f (P)

6:20 (6:25) (Class 7) (0-50,50) 3-Y-O **£2,047** (£604; £302) **Stalls** Centre

Form RPR

6-64 **1** **Private Equity (IRE)**[36] 6570 3-8-11 **47**........................ JoeFanning 14 63+
(W Jarvis) *in rr: hdwy on ins over 3f out: swtchd lft to outside wl over 2f out and str run to chse clr ldr over 1f out: styd on to ld fnl 110yds: pushed out* **11/2**[3]

603 **2** *1 1/2* **Very Distinguished**[8] 7228 3-8-12 **48**........................ LPKeniry 6 62
(S Kirk) *in rr tl gd hdwy on outside 3f out: drvn to ld over 2f out and sn 4 l clr: rdn ins fnl f and hdd fnl 110yds: sn outpcd but styd on fr clr 2nd* **10/1**

4000 **3** *8* **Mediterranean Sea (IRE)**[42] 6371 3-9-0 **50**........................ SimonWhitworth 2 51
(J R Jenkins) *racd towards outside: t.k.h and hdwy to trck ldrs 1/2-way: rdn over 2f out: and one pce: styd on again fnl f to go 3rd but nvr any ch* **14/1**

4333 **4** *hd* **Valkyrie (IRE)**[18] 7025 3-8-11 **47**........................ LukeMorris 13 47
(N P Littmoden) *in tch: hdwy 3f out: nvr quite gng pce to rr ldrs and styd on same pce fnl 2f* **4/1**[1]

3240 **5** *2 3/4* **Tesserae**[27] 6788 3-9-0 **50**........................(v[1]) FergusSweeney 4 46
(A B Haynes) *chsd ldr tl led over 4f out: rdn and hdd over 2f out: sn no ch w ldr and wknd fnl f* **14/1**

-200 **6** *4* **Transfered (IRE)**[65] 5734 3-9-0 **50**........................ TedDurcan 12 40
(Lucinda Featherstone) *in rr: pushed along 4f out: hrd rdn over 2f out and little rspnse* **5/1**[2]

3340 **7** *2 1/2* **Soul Singer**[13] 7137 3-8-12 **48**........................ RichardKingscote 9 34
(J G Portman) *chsd ldrs: rdn 3f out: wknd ins fnl 2f* **13/2**

0055 **8** *1* **Free Falling**[50] 6189 3-8-12 **48**........................(tp) WandersonD'Avila 5 32
(A J Lidderdale) *racd on outside thrght and wd into st 3f out: mod prog fnl f* **50/1**

6000 **9** *1 1/4* **Suhailah**[22] 6918 3-8-12 **48**........................(p) LiamJones 11 30
(M J Attwater) *in tch: pushed along 6f out: wknd fr 3f out* **25/1**

6-55 **10** *1* **Beat Faster**[21] 6950 3-9-0 **50**........................ JimCrowley 1 30
(J G Given) *bhd fr 1/2-way* **12/1**

4 **11** *1* **Intimar (IRE)**[82] 5222 3-8-4 **47**........................ KierenFox[(7)] 3 26
(R J Smith) *s.i.s: a in rr* **20/1**

0436 **12** *16* **Moggy (IRE)**[25] 6840 3-8-11 **47**........................ FrancisNorton 8 —
(G A Harker) *chsd ldrs tl wknd qckly 3f out* **9/1**

0060 **13** *25* **Yaldas Girl (USA)**[6] 7255 3-8-13 **49**........................ SteveDrowne 10 —
(J R Best) *led tl hdd over 4f out: sn wknd* **20/1**

2m 36.54s (2.04) **Going Correction** +0.025s/f (Slow) **13** Ran SP% **120.8**
Speed ratings (Par 96): **94,93,87,87,85 83,81,80,79,79 78,67,51**
toteswingers: 1&2 £7.60, 1&3 £20.80, 2&3 £27.90 CSF £57.30 CT £743.87 TOTE £8.00: £2.30, £3.20, £4.80; EX 43.70.
Owner Mrs Susan Davis **Bred** John And Susan Davis **Trained** Newmarket, Suffolk

■ Stewards' Enquiry : Wanderson D'Avila one-day ban: used whip when out of contention (Nov 25)

FOCUS

A banded-class handicap in which just one of the runners had a previous win against their name. Only 3lb separated the field, which consisted entirely of fillies. The pace was strong early on before slowing down in the back straight. The first two came clear and showed above average form for the grade, and the winner could have more to offer.

7325 DIGIBET MEDIAN AUCTION MAIDEN STKS (DIV I) 7f (P)
6:50 (6:56) (Class 5) 2-Y-0 £2,266 (£674; £337; £168) Stalls High

Form RPR
0522 1 **Mass Rally (IRE)**[15] 7096 2-9-3 81 (t) JimmyFortune 2 84+
(J H M Gosden) *hld up towards rr: gd hdwy fr 3f out: qcknd to ld appr fnl f: sn clr: easily* **5/4**[1]

30 2 4 **Juicy Pear (IRE)**[12] 7157 2-9-3 0 J-PGuillambert 13 74
(M L W Bell) *chsd ldrs: drvn and qcknd on ins to take slt advantage ins fnl 2f: hdd appr fnl f and sn no ch w wnr but kpt on wl for 2nd* **20/1**

3352 3 1 1/4 **Warning Song (USA)**[21] 6943 2-9-3 80 JimCrowley 3 71
(Mrs A J Perrett) *chsd ldrs: drvn to chal ins fnl 2f: outpcd ins fnl f* **6/1**[3]

00 4 3 **On Khee**[13] 7135 2-8-12 0 RobertHavlin 10 58
(H Morrison) *chsd ldrs: rdn over 2f out: wknd ins fnl f* **33/1**

5 1 1/4 **Circus Girl (IRE)** 2-8-12 0 RichardKingscote 9 55
(R M Beckett) *s.i.s: sn in tch: rdn to chse ldrs over 2f out: wknd ins fnl f* **11/1**

6 1/2 **Fetching** 2-8-12 0 MichaelHills 12 54
(B W Hills) *v.s.a: bhd: pushed along over 2f out: str run on ins fr over 1f out: fin wl but nvr in contention* **10/1**

7 1 1/2 **Before The War (USA)** 2-9-3 0 DaneO'Neill 14 55
(L M Cumani) *t.k.h: mid-div tl outpcd 1/2-way: kpt on fnl f: nvr a danger* **16/1**

8 3/4 **Ertiyaad** 2-8-12 0 JoeFanning 1 48
(Sir Michael Stoute) *in rr: sme prog fr over 1f out* **14/1**

0 9 1/2 **Othello (IRE)**[7] 7244 2-9-3 0 LPKeniry 5 52
(E F Vaughan) *s.i.s: in rr: sme late prog* **66/1**

10 1/2 **Bella Charlie (IRE)** 2-9-3 0 AdamKirby 4 51
(M G Quinlan) *in rr: sme late prog* **66/1**

04 11 nk **Star Twilight**[111] 4239 2-8-12 0 TedDurcan 7 45
(D R Lanigan) *sn led: hdd ins fnl 2f: wknd over 1f out* **25/1**

12 hd **Tilsworth Glenboy** 2-9-3 0 SimonWhitworth 8 50
(J R Jenkins) *s.i.s: t.k.h: a in rr* **66/1**

3 13 2 3/4 **Slip Sliding Away (IRE)**[6] 7251 2-9-3 0 SteveDrowne 6 43
(J R Best) *wnt lft s: sn chsng ldrs: rdn over 2f out: sn btn* **5/1**[2]

00 14 24 **Optimistic Duke (IRE)**[18] 7034 2-9-3 0 MartinDwyer 11 —
(W R Muir) *rdn fr s to chse ldrs: hung rt on rail and wknd bnd 3f out* **66/1**

1m 27.29s (1.29) **Going Correction** +0.025s/f (Slow) **14** Ran SP% **122.9**
Speed ratings (Par 96): **93,88,87,83,82 81,79,79,78,77 77,77,74,46**
toteswingers: 1&2 £8.40, 1&3 £2.30, 2&3 £18.50 CSF £35.73 TOTE £2.10: £1.30, £4.00, £1.70; EX 28.30.
Owner H R H Princess Haya Of Jordan **Bred** Round Hill Stud **Trained** Newmarket, Suffolk

FOCUS

Probably just a fair maiden.

NOTEBOOK

Mass Rally(IRE) set the standard with a BHA rating of 81 and was equipped with a tongue-tie for the first time. He was not best drawn in stall 2, but that proved no hindrance and he ran out a comfortable winner. The type for handicaps at around this trip now, he had hung left more than once previously but showed no signs of that here. (op 11-8 tchd 6-4)

Juicy Pear(IRE) ran a promising race on his debut at Wolverhampton but disappointed there next time. From a favourable inside draw, he ran on from the cutaway in the straight, but the winner was too strong. (op 18-1)

Warning Song(USA), just 1lb behind the winner on official figures but probably flattered by his mark, ran his race again but his form has an exposed look to it and he is not going to be easy to place. (op 5-1 tchd 9-2)

On Khee ran a creditable race in fourth and looks a likely type for middle-distance handicaps, as befits his pedigree.

Circus Girl(IRE), a half-sister to a couple of winning sprinters, looked woolly in her coat before this debut but she ran respectably and a fillies' maiden could come her way. (tchd 10-1 and 14-1)

Fetching gave problems in the preliminaries and went to post early. She put in an eyecatching performance, missing the kick badly and still last entering the straight before running on steadily against the rail for sixth. Likely to get a bit further, she will know more next time. Official explanation: jockey said filly was slowly away (op 9-1)

Ertiyaad, whose dam was a Listed winner, made late gains and should leave this running behind. (op 12-1 tchd 16-1)

Bella Charlie(IRE) Official explanation: jockey said colt ran too free

Tilsworth Glenboy gave the impression that there is better to come from him in future. (tchd 150-1)

Slip Sliding Away(IRE) showed ability on his debut at Lingfield six days earlier and was well supported here, but this may have come too soon and he faded badly after racing freely early on. Official explanation: jockey said colt ran too free (op 8-1)

7326 DIGIBET MEDIAN AUCTION MAIDEN STKS (DIV II) 7f (P)
7:20 (7:26) (Class 5) 2-Y-0 £2,266 (£674; £337; £168) Stalls High

Form RPR
1 **Next Move (IRE)** 2-9-3 0 TedDurcan 11 79+
(Saeed Bin Suroor) *n.m.r sn after s but styd in tch: trckd ldrs 3f out: drvn and qcknd fr over 1f out: led fnl 75yds: pushed out and won gng away* **3/1**[2]

4 2 3/4 **Hidden Glory**[29] 6754 2-9-3 0 GeorgeBaker 6 77
(Pat Eddery) *sn trcking ldrs: rdn and styd on fr 2f out: ev ch fnl 75yds: outpcd cl home* **7/4**[1]

0633 3 1 **Mawaddah (IRE)**[27] 6792 2-9-0 77 PatrickHills(3) 7 75
(R Hannon) *sn led: rdn over 2f out: kpt slt ld tl hdd fnl 75yds: no ex* **7/1**[3]

0 4 4 **Plenty O'Toole**[15] 7087 2-9-3 0 IanMongan 9 65
(Mrs D J Sanderson) *wnt rt s: in tch: pushed along and hdwy 2f out: nvr quite gng pce to rch ldrs: one pce appr fnl f* **200/1**

5 1/2 **Maid In Heaven (IRE)** 2-8-12 0 AdamKirby 12 58+
(W R Swinburn) *in rr: virtually last 2f out: styd on appr fnl f: fin strly ins fnl f: gng on cl home* **40/1**

0 6 4 1/2 **Baggsy (IRE)**[51] 6163 2-8-12 0 AmirQuinn 2 47
(Miss J Feilden) *in rr: rdn 3f out: styd on fr 2f out but nvr in contention* **100/1**

7 3 1/4 **La Toya J (IRE)** 2-8-12 0 LPKeniry 10 39
(Edgar Byrne) *in rr: sme prog fnl 2f: nvr a factor* **100/1**

8 3 1/4 **Vocabulary** 2-8-12 0 MichaelHills 5 31
(B W Hills) *slowly away: plld hrd in rr 2f: shkn up and sme late prog* **22/1**

0 9 hd **Faited To Pretend (IRE)**[13] 7135 2-8-12 0 J-PGuillambert 4 30
(M L W Bell) *plld hrd in rr tl mid-div 4f out: chsd ldrs 3f out: wknd ins fnl 2f* **20/1**

35 10 1 **Yabtree (IRE)**[21] 6930 2-9-3 0 SteveDrowne 14 33
(R Charlton) *chsd ldrs: rdn over 2f out: wknd wl over 1f out* **10/1**

60 11 2 1/4 **Consult**[16] 7064 2-9-3 0 SebSanders 13 27
(Sir Mark Prescott) *in tch to 1/2-way* **125/1**

12 8 **Abhar (USA)** 2-9-3 0 TonyCulhane 3 7+
(J R Best) *chsd ldrs on outside: hung lft bdly lft and wknd over 2f out* **10/1**

0 13 9 **Krysanthe**[21] 6942 2-8-12 0 RichardThomas 1 —
(J A Geake) *s.i.s: t.k.h and sn chsng ldrs on outside: wknd ins fnl 3f* **200/1**

1m 26.92s (0.92) **Going Correction** +0.025s/f (Slow) **13** Ran SP% **107.4**
Speed ratings (Par 96): **95,94,93,88,87 82,79,75,75,73 71,62,51**
CSF £6.70 TOTE £3.40: £1.40, £1.10, £1.80; EX 7.40.
Owner Godolphin **Bred** Airlie Stud **Trained** Newmarket, Suffolk
■ Marie De Guise was withdrawn after refusing to enter the stalls (13/2, deduct 10p in the £ under R4.)

FOCUS

Division two of the maiden, run in a slightly quicker time than the first and probably of a similar standard, although the fourth does look to hold down the form.

NOTEBOOK

Next Move(IRE) provided Godolphin with yet another 2yo success. A half-brother to Moyglare winner Chelsea Rose, he got on top in the final furlong and won well enough, but it is hard to gauge where he stands in a stable so full of promising juveniles. (op 9-4 tchd 2-1)

Hidden Glory had been a promising fourth on his debut at Leicester and he ran well on this first try on Polytrack, holding every chance but just lacking a finishing kick. His dam is a half-sister to Yorkshire Cup winner Franklins Gardens and a step up in trip may help him. (op 2-1 tchd 13-8)

Mawaddah(IRE), dropped back to 7f for this Polytrack debut, made most of the running and only gave best inside the last. He is a decent guide to the strength of the race. (op 10-1)

Plenty O'Toole showed nothing on his debut on Fibresand and this was a big improvement, but his proximity does seem to hold down the form. (op 80-1)

Maid In Heaven(IRE) ◆ made eyecatching late progress from the rear and this half-sister to several winners will not be letting down the family. (op 33-1)

Vocabulary, out of a sister to smart 1m2f filly Zante, was notably green on this debut and should improve for the experience. Official explanation: jockey said filly was slowly away (op 18-1)

Abhar(USA) Official explanation: jockey said bit slipped through colt's mouth

7327 DIGIBET.COM H'CAP 7f (P)
7:50 (7:53) (Class 5) (0-75,75) 3-Y-0+ £2,590 (£770; £385; £192) Stalls High

Form RPR
001 1 **Arteus**[36] 6562 3-9-3 74 (b[1]) ShaneKelly 10 82
(Jane Chapple-Hyam) *led: rdn and edgd lft 2f out: jnd over 1f out: styd on gamely thrght fnl f* **8/1**

044 2 3/4 **Tuxedo**[20] 6976 4-9-1 71 LukeMorris 12 77
(P W Hiatt) *chsd ldrs: wnt 2nd over 2f out: chal over 1f out: nt get past wnr and one pce ins fnl f* **5/1**[2]

1214 3 1/2 **Millfield (IRE)**[14] 7111 6-9-4 74 GeorgeBaker 11 79
(P R Chamings) *t.k.h: hld up in rr: hdwy 2f out: styd on u.p fnl f but nvr gng pce to rch ldng duo* **9/2**[1]

6001 4 3/4 **Rondeau (GR)**[27] 6790 4-9-1 71 JimCrowley 9 77+
(P R Chamings) *hld up in rr: hdwy to chse ldrs whn nt clr run and swtchd lft over 1f out: kpt on but nvr gng pce to get into contention* **8/1**

4023 5 1 **Chief Exec**[19] 7000 7-9-5 75 (b) AdamKirby 14 75
(J R Gask) *in rr: hdwy on ins over 2f out: chsd ldrs 1f out: one pce ins fnl f* **7/1**

2000 6 3 1/4 **Highland Harvest**[20] 6964 5-8-13 69 RobertHavlin 5 61
(Jamie Poulton) *chsd ldrs: rdn over 2f out: kpt on ins fnl f but nvr a threat* **20/1**

1426 7 1 1/4 **Lucy Brown**[14] 7111 3-9-3 74 SteveDrowne 3 62
(R Hannon) *stdd in rr s: hdwy over 1f out: kpt on but nvr nr ldrs* **20/1**

0000 8 1 1/2 **Resplendent Nova**[20] 6976 7-9-2 72 IanMongan 7 56
(P Howling) *in tch: hdwy to chse ldrs over 2f out: sn rdn: wknd fnl f* **6/1**[3]

5021 9 3/4 **Tourist**[11] 7192 4-9-5 75 DaneO'Neill 6 57
(D Shaw) *chsd ldrs: rdn over 2f out: wknd wl over 1f out* **5/1**[2]

1500 10 6 **Miss Hollybell**[19] 6997 3-9-0 71 FergusSweeney 1 37
(J Gallagher) *rdn over 2f out: a towards rr* **50/1**

0 11 2 1/4 **Obe Gold**[18] 7026 7-9-2 72 (v) J-PGuillambert 4 32
(P Howling) *a towards rr* **16/1**

202- 12 13 **Dakota Hills**[341] 7555 3-9-1 72 RobertWinston 13 —
(J R Best) *chsd wnr tl over 2f out: sn wknd* **12/1**

1m 25.61s (-0.39) **Going Correction** +0.025s/f (Slow)
WFA 3 from 4yo+ 1lb **12** Ran SP% **125.6**
Speed ratings (Par 103): **103,102,101,100,99 95,94,92,91,85 82,67**
toteswingers: 1&2 £13.90, 1&3 £9.60, 2&3 £7.00 CSF £49.65 CT £210.66 TOTE £8.70: £2.50, £2.00, £1.90; EX 66.10.
Owner Norcroft Park Stud **Bred** Norcroft Park Stud **Trained** Newmarket, Suffolk

FOCUS

An ordinary but open handicap. The form looks pretty solid and should stand up, with the second and third fair guides.

Rondeau(GR) Official explanation: jockey said gelding was denied a clear run

7328 DIGIBET SPORTS BETTING H'CAP 2m (P)
8:20 (8:20) (Class 6) (0-65,64) 3-Y-0+ £2,047 (£604; £302) Stalls High

Form RPR
000- 1 **Purely By Chance**[206] 7401 4-8-7 48 (b) SimonPearce(5) 11 55
(J Pearce) *led 1f: styd trckd ldrs: rdn whn pce qcknd 3f out: kpt to ins and chsd chsd ldrs 2f out: drvn to ld ins fnl f: styd on wl* **14/1**

12 2 1 **Eagle Nebula**[49] 6208 5-9-6 59 JackMitchell(3) 1 65
(B R Johnson) *sn chsng ldr: led ins fnl 3f and kpt torwads centre crse: rdn 2f out: hdd ins fnl f: kpt on same pce* **7/1**[3]

2004 3 1 1/2 **Colourful Move**[12] 7154 4-9-3 53 SteveDrowne 9 57
(P G Murphy) *chsd ldrs: rdn 3f out: styd on wl fr 2f out but nvr gng pce to rch ldng duo* **7/2**[1]

050 4 1/2 **Court Princess**[20] 6974 6-9-7 57 DaneO'Neill 8 60
(George Baker) *in tch: hdwy 3f out: styd on fr 2f out but nt rch ldrs* **20/1**

0620 5 1/2 **Black Or Red (IRE)**[11] 7170 4-10-0 64 SebSanders 12 67+
(I A Wood) *t.k.h: hld up in rr: rdn 3f out: hdwy fr 2f out: styd wl fnl f but nt rch ldrs* **4/1**[2]

-000 6 hd **Cape Greko**[14] 7112 7-9-5 58 (v) RussellKennemore(3) 10 61
(B G Powell) *in rr: hdwy on ins fr 3f out: rdn over 2f out: styd on same pce fnl f* **20/1**

0300 7 3/4 **Adage**[13] 5885 6-8-9 45 (bt[1]) FergusSweeney 7 47
(David Pinder) *chsd ldrs: rdn over 3f out: one pce fnl 2f* **33/1**

03 **8** 1 1/4 **Blockley (USA)**[31] 6692 5-9-12 62.....................(vt) StephenDonohoe 13 62
(Ian Williams) *mid-div: pushed along 3f out: hrd rdn over 2f out: mod late prog* **7/2**[1]
2650 **9** 11 **Home**[66] 4951 4-9-4 54.....................(t) LPKeniry 5 41
(C Gordon) *led after 1f: hdd ins fnl 3f: wknd over 2f out* **9/1**
650/ **10** shd **Ede's**[541] 7069 9-8-2 45..................... CharlotteLatham(7) 2 32
(P M Phelan) *a in rr* **33/1**
50/6 **11** 3/4 **Croix Rouge (USA)**[14] 7112 7-9-5 62..................... KierenFox(7) 3 48
(R J Smith) *in rr: pushed along and sme prog over 2f out: nvr in contention and sn dropped away* **8/1**
06-0 **12** 9 **Highland Homestead**[28] 6785 4-9-8 58..................... JimCrowley 4 33
(M R Hoad) *in rr tl rapid hdwy to press ldrs 1/2-way: wknd qckly over 3f out* **16/1**

3m 40.68s (10.58) **Going Correction** +0.025s/f (Slow) 12 Ran SP% **126.0**
Speed ratings (Par 101): **74,73,72,72,72 72,71,71,65,65 65,60**
toteswingers: 1&2 £43.90, 1&3 £20.40, 2&3 £4.40 CSF £110.59 CT £430.45 TOTE £18.50: £4.20, £2.90, £2.00; EX 253.40.
Owner Lady Green **Bred** Lady Jennifer Green **Trained** Newmarket, Suffolk

FOCUS
A moderate stayers' handicap which was run at a steady pace and became a sprint in the straight. The time was 14 seconds above standard and this is muddling form which needs to be treated with caution. The winner probably only had to match her previous sand best.

7329 BISTRO PRICES FROM £37 H'CAP (DIV I) 6f (P)
8:50 (8:52) (Class 6) (0-65,65) 3-Y-0+ **£1,706** (£503; £252) **Stalls** High

Form RPR
0460 **1** **Speak The Truth (IRE)**[10] 7203 3-8-13 65.........(p) MatthewDavies(5) 10 74
(J R Boyle) *hld up towards rr on ins: hdwy over 2f out: str run fnl f to ld nr fin* **12/1**
2543 **2** 1/2 **Lethal**[16] 7053 6-9-1 62..................... JimCrowley 11 69
(M J Scudamore) *led: rdn over 2f out: styd on u.p tl hdd and no ex nr fin* **2/1**[1]
0005 **3** shd **Musical Script (USA)**[16] 7053 6-9-4 65.....................(b) ChrisCatlin 2 72
(Mouse Hamilton-Fairley) *hld up in rr tl hdwy on ins 2f out: chsd ldrs ins fnl f: nt qckn cl home* **15/2**[3]
5201 **4** 1/2 **Loyal Royal (IRE)**[13] 7138 6-8-13 63.....................(b) JackDean(3) 5 68
(J M Bradley) *in rr: hdwy over 1f out: styd on u.p tl n.m.r and swtchd rt nr fin: kpt on* **8/1**
005 **5** 1 **Caledonia Princess**[18] 7028 3-9-3 64.....................(b[1]) TonyCulhane 12 66
(R Curtis) *chsd ldrs: rdn over 2f out: styd wl there tl outpcd ins fnl f* **7/1**[2]
0626 **6** 1 3/4 **Namir (IRE)**[14] 7122 7-8-13 60.....................(vt) VinceSlattery 8 57
(H J Evans) *chsd ldrs: rdn over 2f out: styd wl there tl wknd ins fnl f* **16/1**
020 **7** 1 1/4 **Fromsong (IRE)**[46] 6293 11-8-13 65..................... MarkCoumbe(5) 7 58
(D K Ivory) *in rr: hdwy 2f out: drvn to chse ldrs 1f out: wknd ins fnl f* **16/1**
0400 **8** 1 1/4 **Hart Of Gold**[133] 3505 5-8-12 59.....................(p) LiamJones 6 48
(R A Harris) *in rr: pushed along 2f out: hrd drvn over 1f out and nvr gng pce to be competitive* **16/1**
-240 **9** 2 1/2 **Cape Cobra**[26] 6828 5-8-11 58.....................(b) SteveDrowne 3 39
(H Morrison) *chsd ldrs on outside: wknd ins fnl 2f* **10/1**
2513 **10** 1 **Agnes Love**[70] 5584 3-8-11 61..................... AndreaAtzeni(3) 9 38
(J Akehurst) *chsd ldrs: rdn over 2f out: wknd qckly appr fnl f* **7/1**[2]
2505 **11** 1/2 **Desert Strike**[23] 6904 3-9-4 65.....................(p) JoeFanning 1 41
(P F I Cole) *in rr: sme hdwy 3f out: sn wknd* **20/1**
4500 **12** 1 1/4 **Rio Royale (IRE)**[22] 6916 3-9-2 63..................... AdamKirby 4 35
(Mrs A J Perrett) *chsd ldrs: rdn 3f out: wknd over 2f out* **12/1**

1m 12.83s (-0.27) **Going Correction** +0.025s/f (Slow) 12 Ran SP% **128.1**
Speed ratings (Par 101): **102,101,101,100,99 96,95,93,90,88 88,86**
toteswingers: 1&2 £9.40, 1&3 £23.80, 2&3 £3.70 CSF £39.11 CT £213.78 TOTE £19.20: £3.30, £1.50, £2.60; EX 64.70.
Owner Inside Track Racing Club **Bred** Gerard Mulligan **Trained** Epsom, Surrey

FOCUS
The first division of this modest sprint handicap, run in a similar time to division two. Sound form.
Desert Strike Official explanation: jockey said gelding ran too free

7330 BISTRO PRICES FROM £37 H'CAP (DIV II) 6f (P)
9:20 (9:24) (Class 6) (0-65,65) 3-Y-0+ **£1,706** (£503; £126; £126) **Stalls** High

Form RPR
4500 **1** **Gentle Guru**[22] 6915 5-9-3 64..................... JamesDoyle 2 75
(R T Phillips) *hmpd s: in rr: hdwy on ins whn nt clr run over 2f out: swtchd lft to outer and str run fr over 1f out: led fnl 50yds: won gng away* **20/1**
3603 **2** 1 **Forest Dane**[10] 7203 9-8-13 60..................... LukeMorris 3 68
(Mrs N Smith) *hmpd s: in rr: swtchd lft and hdwy 2f out: drvn and qcknd to ld ins fnl f: hdd and outpcd fnl 50yds* **9/2**[2]
2212 **3** 3 3/4 **The Name Is Frank**[21] 6933 4-8-6 58.....................(t) SimonPearce(5) 8 54
(Mark Gillard) *in rr: stl plenty to do 2f out: styd on fnl f and fin wl: nt trble ldrs* **7/1**[3]
0422 **3** dht **Yanza**[13] 7138 3-9-2 63.....................(b) RobertHavlin 9 59
(J R Gask) *led: rdn over 2f out: hdd ins fnl f: sn btn* **9/2**[2]
0660 **5** nk **Dream Express (IRE)**[11] 7180 4-9-1 62.....................(v[1]) IanMongan 11 57
(P Howling) *plld hrd: in tch: rdn to chse ldrs over 2f out: one pce ins fnl f* **7/2**[1]
1506 **6** 2 1/4 **Diddums**[18] 7028 3-8-11 65..................... CarolineKelly(7) 6 53
(P S McEntee) *in tch: rdn: hdwy and hung rt 1f out: kpt on: nvr in contention* **33/1**
0000 **7** nk **Steel City Boy (IRE)**[14] 7122 6-9-4 65..................... DaneO'Neill 12 52
(D Shaw) *t.k.h: chsd ldrs: rdn over 2f out: wknd over 1f out* **8/1**
4520 **8** 1 **Shakespeare's Son**[5] 7275 4-8-13 60.....................(v) VinceSlattery 7 43
(H J Evans) *t.k.h: chsd ldrs: rdn 3rd appr fnl f* **16/1**
0015 **9** 9 **Charles Darwin (IRE)**[13] 7138 6-9-0 61..................... FrancisNorton 1 16
(M Blanshard) *hmpd s: in tch: chsd ldrs 3f out: wkng whn hmpd over 1f out* **11/1**
0051 **10** 1 3/4 **Athaakeel (IRE)**[22] 6914 3-9-4 65..................... LiamJones 10 14
(R A Harris) *v reluctant to load: sn rdn and a in rr* **10/1**
5026 **11** 4 **Peopleton Brook**[11] 7179 7-9-2 63..................... SteveDrowne 5 —
(B G Powell) *wnt lft s: a towards rr* **10/1**
0000 **12** 1 **Asaint Needs Brass (USA)**[8] 7223 3-8-11 58............ RobertWinston 4 —
(J R Best) *bmpd s: wnt lft: sn chsng ldrs: wknd over 2f out* **33/1**

1m 12.62s (-0.48) **Going Correction** +0.025s/f (Slow) 12 Ran SP% **125.2**
Speed ratings (Par 101): **104,102,97,97,97 94,93,92,80,78 72,71**PL: Yanza £1.10 My Name is Frank £1.10 TRI: Gentle Guru/Forest Dane/Yanza £250.20 GG/FD/The Name is Frank £363.52 toteswingers: 1&2 £24.30, 1&Yanza £13.40, 1&The Name is Frank £5.30, 2&Yanza £2.50, The Name is Frank £2.00 CSF £112.06 TOTE £28.00: £4.90, £1.80; EX27 Owner Trifecta £Richard Phillips Bred R Phillips And Tweenhills Farm And Stud.

FOCUS
Division two was run at a strong pace and the time was slightly quicker than that for division one. The first two, who came clear, both came from the rear, and the form seems sound.
Peopleton Brook Official explanation: jockey said horse hit the stalls and never travelled

T/Plt: £25.60 to a £1 stake. Pool: £84,066.00. 2,391.35 winning tickets. T/Qpdt: £5.10 to a £1 stake. Pool: £6,963.59. 1,008.40 winning tickets. ST

7266 SOUTHWELL (L-H)
Wednesday, November 11

OFFICIAL GOING: Standard
Wind: Virtually nil Weather: Overcast

7331 BETDAQEXTRA.COM MAIDEN AUCTION STKS 5f (F)
1:00 (1:01) (Class 6) 2-Y-0 **£2,047** (£604; £302) **Stalls** High

Form RPR
0022 **1** **Clear Ice (IRE)**[15] 7087 2-8-11 58..................... AndrewMullen 3 67
(D Nicholls) *trckd ldrs: hdwy 1/2-way: led wl over 1f out: rdn ent fnl f: kpt on wl towards fin* **7/2**[2]
04 **2** hd **Kummel Excess (IRE)**[21] 6942 2-8-5 0..................... MatthewDavies(5) 4 65
(George Baker) *trckd ldrs: effrt and swtchd rt over 1f out: hdwy ent fnl f and sn rdn: sn chsng wnr: drvn and kpt on towards fin* **9/1**
6224 **3** 1 1/2 **Dimaire**[21] 6932 2-8-1 66..................... AndreaAtzeni(3) 1 54
(D Haydn Jones) *dwlt and rdn along early: towards rr tl hdwy 1/2-way: effrt on outer and rdn to chse ldrs over 1f out: drvn along ent fnl f and kpt on one pce* **11/8**[1]
3050 **4** 3/4 **Southwark Newshawk**[58] 5950 2-8-4 55..................... AdrianMcCarthy 2 51
(Mrs C A Dunnett) *led: rdn along 2f out: hdd wl over 1f out: sn drvn and one pce ent fnl f* **22/1**
000 **5** 1 3/4 **Lady Brickhouse**[19] 7001 2-8-4 45..................... LukeMorris 7 45
(M D Squance) *towards rr and pushed along 1/2-way: rdn along wl over 1f out: drvn and kpt on ins fnl f: nrst fin* **80/1**
6 hd **Marshal Plat Club** 2-8-4 0.....................(e[1]) DuranFentiman 8 44
(G R Oldroyd) *chsd ldrs: hdwy over 2f out: rdn and ch over 1f out: drvn and wknd ent fnl f* **40/1**
6403 **7** 3/4 **Hot Rod Mamma (IRE)**[8] 7217 2-8-4 57..................... FrancisNorton 6 42
(A Berry) *sn cl up: rdn along over 2f out: drvn wl over 1f out and sn wknd* **18/1**
2252 **8** 2 1/4 **Gower Sophia**[8] 7217 2-8-4 66.....................(v) JimmyQuinn 10 33
(M Brittain) *prom: rdn along over 2f out: drvn wl over 1f out and wknd appr fnl f* **15/2**[3]
00 **9** 1/2 **Dispol Fay (IRE)**[15] 7079 2-8-4 0..................... JoeFanning 11 32
(P T Midgley) *chsd ldrs on outer: rdn along 2f out: sn wknd* **25/1**
10 3/4 **Thatlittlecolt** 2-8-10 0 ow1..................... PhillipMakin 9 35
(D H Brown) *s.i.s: a in rr* **14/1**
0 **11** 5 **Bombay Mist**[200] 1511 2-8-4 0..................... PaulEddery 5 11
(R C Guest) *cl up: rdn along over 2f out: sn wknd and bhd* **100/1**

60.36 secs (0.66) **Going Correction** 0.0s/f (Stan) 11 Ran SP% **110.9**
Speed ratings (Par 94): **94,93,91,90,87 86,85,82,81,80 72**
toteswingers: 1&2 £6.40, 1&3 £2.20, 2&3 £5.90 CSF £30.86 TOTE £6.20: £1.50, £2.40, £1.20; EX 32.90 Trifecta £112.00 Pool: £302.92 - 2.00 winning units..
Owner J P Honeyman **Bred** Mrs Noelle Walsh **Trained** Sessay, N Yorks

FOCUS
A moderate auction maiden in which most were tackling this surface for the first time. The first four came from the four lowest stalls (in the centre of the track).

NOTEBOOK
Clear Ice(IRE), who had been runner-up on his two previous starts on the course. Dropped back to 5f, he was always in the front rank and, once going on well over a furlong out, looked sure to score comfortably. However, in the end he only held on narrowly, but should remain competitive in handicaps over this C&D, although his trainer believes he is better over an extra furlong. (op 3-1)
Kummel Excess(IRE) ◆ was making her debut on this surface, having run twice on Polytrack, and took to it well. She was held up early, but came out of the pack in the closing stages and closed down the winner all the way to the line. She looks progressive and a win should not be long delayed. (tchd 11-1)
Dimaire, the well-backed favourite, shared highest official rating and had been runner-up here two outings previously. However, she missed the break and was given reminders in the first furlong. She got into a challenging position over a furlong out before her effort flattened out. (op 2-1 tchd 5-4)
Southwark Newshawk had not been beaten far in four previous starts here and again ran with credit. She might be able to pick up a seller around here. (op 25-1 tchd 28-1)
Lady Brickhouse ran with promise having been outpaced in the early stages before keeping on late (op 66-1)
Marshal Plat Club, who wore an eyeshield for this debut, showed speed and should be better for the experience.
Gower Sophia has had plenty of chances but had not run well on her previous try here and disappointed again, although her high draw did not help. (op 5-1 tchd 8-1)

7332 BETDAQ POKER CLAIMING STKS 1m 4f (F)
1:30 (1:30) (Class 6) 3-Y-0+ **£2,047** (£604; £302) **Stalls** Low

Form RPR
0662 **1** **Majehar**[49] 6210 7-9-1 63..................... RobertWinston 5 73
(A G Newcombe) *trckd ldrs: smooth hdwy over 4f out: cl up over 2f out: rdn to ld wl over 1f out: kpt on u.p ins fnl f* **5/1**[2]
5022 **2** 1 1/4 **Lost Soldier Three (IRE)**[14] 7118 8-9-9 70..................... AndrewMullen 4 79
(D Nicholls) *trckd ldrs: hdwy over 4f out: led 3f out: rdn over 2f out: drvn and hdd wl over 1f out: kpt on same pce* **7/1**[3]
120 **3** 5 **Boundless Prospect (USA)**[18] 7036 10-8-4 66 AndrewHeffernan(5) 11 57
(P D Evans) *bhd: hdwy over 4f out: rdn along and in tch over 2f out: drvn and kpt on fr over 1f out: tk 3rd nr fin* **5/1**[2]
0051 **4** hd **Charging Indian (IRE)**[21] 6951 3-9-3 69.....................(p) TonyCulhane 7 71
(P T Midgley) *t.k.h: hld up towards rr: hdwy 1/2-way: rdn along to chse ldrs 3f out: drvn wl over 1f out and sn no imp* **7/2**[1]
1530 **5** 4 **Applaude**[7] 7248 4-8-13 68.....................(be) FrancisNorton 3 54
(R C Guest) *t.k.h: cl up untl led after 4f: rdn along and hdd 3f out: sn wknd* **11/1**
5460 **6** nk **Malt Or Mash (USA)**[19] 6995 5-9-13 90..................... DaneO'Neill 9 68
(R Hannon) *hld up in tch: effrt over 4f out: rdn to chse ldrs 3f out: sn drvn and btn* **7/2**[1]
0 **7** 19 **Dancing Ghost (IRE)**[116] 4097 3-8-0 0 ow2............ FrankieMcDonald 6 16
(Jane Chapple-Hyam) *s.i.s and towards rr: sme hdwy 4f out: sn rdn and nvr a factor* **33/1**
1003 **8** 9 **Inconspicuous Miss (USA)**[21] 6940 3-8-3 66 ow4(p) MatthewDavies(5) 8 10
(George Baker) *trckd ldng pair: pushed along on inner over 4f out: rdn over 3f out and sn wknd* **14/1**
-405 **9** 10 **Mceldowney**[159] 2656 7-8-9 48..................... GregFairley 10 —
(M C Chapman) *chsd ldrs: rdn along after 5f: sn lost pl and bhd: t.o fnl 3f* **66/1**

-000 **10** *6* **A One (IRE)**[16] 7062 10-8-4 42 SophieDoyle[(5)] 2 —
(Mrs H J Manners) *led 4f: rdn along and lost pl 1/2-way: t.o fnl 3f* **200/1**
00-0 **11** *2 1/2* **Kabougg**[14] 7126 3-7-9 35 AndreaAtzeni[(3)] 1 —
(A J McCabe) *prom on inner: rdn along 1/2-way: sn lost pl and bhd: t.o fnl 3f* **150/1**

2m 36.7s (-4.30) **Going Correction** -0.25s/f (Stan)
WFA 3 from 4yo+ 6lb **11** Ran SP% **110.9**
Speed ratings (Par 101): **104,103,99,99,97 96,84,78,71,67 65**
toteswingers: 1&2 £4.20, 1&3 £5.50, 2&3 £5.60 CSF £37.13 TOTE £5.80: £1.40, £2.00, £1.80; EX 31.40 Trifecta £64.00 Pool: £294.07 - 3.40 winning units..Majehar was claimed by E. J. O'Neill for £8000.
Owner J R Salter **Bred** Darley **Trained** Yarnscombe, Devon

FOCUS
The usual wide mix of abilities judged on official ratings in this claimer, which looked a fair race for the grade. The form looks pretty sound.
Dancing Ghost(IRE) Official explanation: jockey said filly was slowly away

7333 BETDAQ.CO.UK NURSERY — 6f (F)
2:00 (2:00) (Class 5) (0-70,68) 2-Y-O — **£2,729** (£806; £403) **Stalls** Low

Form — RPR
5062 **1** **Cape Kimberley**[15] 7089 2-9-7 **68** SebSanders 9 — 74
(J G Given) *a.p: cl up 1/2-way: rdn to ld wl over 1f out: drvn clr ent fnl f: kpt on* **9/2**[2]
4444 **2** *2* **Yeadon**[5] 7268 2-9-5 **66** TonyHamilton 8 — 66
(R A Fahey) *towards rr: hdwy over 2f out: swtchd rt and rdn over 1f out: styd on to chse wnr ins fnl f: no imp* **7/1**
6403 **3** *1 1/2* **Admiral Cochrane (IRE)**[28] 6775 2-9-1 **62** JoeFanning 6 — 58
(W Jarvis) *stmbld s and towards rr: t.k.h and hdwy 1/2-way: rdn and in tch whn edgd lft wl over 1f out: swtchd rt ent fnl f and styd on u.p to take 3rd nr fin* **5/1**[3]
0605 **4** *1/2* **Miss Taken (IRE)**[15] 7088 2-8-3 **50** (b) DuranFentiman 2 — 44
(D Carroll) *prom: rdn along over 2f out: drvn over 1f out: sn one pce: lost 3rd nr fin* **22/1**
654 **5** *2* **Maragna (IRE)**[47] 6246 2-7-12 **50** AndrewHeffernan[(5)] 11 — 38
(Paul Green) *chsd ldrs on outer: rdn along over 2f out: drvn wl over 1f out: sn one pce* **20/1**
6004 **6** *1 1/4* **Bookiesindex Girl (IRE)**[15] 7087 2-8-1 **48** LukeMorris 10 — 32
(J R Jenkins) *dwlt: in tch on wd outside: effrt 1/2-way: rdn along over 2f out and sn no hdwy* **16/1**
4000 **7** *1 3/4* **Gold Diamond (USA)**[20] 6963 2-9-0 **61** (b[1]) GregFairley 1 — 40
(M Johnston) *in tch on inner: rdn along 1/2-way: sn drvn and outpcd* **10/1**
5305 **8** *nk* **Amno Dancer (IRE)**[15] 7097 2-9-7 **68** JimmyQuinn 4 — 46
(M H Tompkins) *t.k.h: chsd ldrs: rdn along over 2f out: hld whn n.m.r wl over 1f out: sn wknd* **4/1**[1]
1036 **9** *1 1/4* **Baby Judge (IRE)**[8] 7218 2-8-8 **58** AndreaAtzeni[(3)] 3 — 32
(M C Chapman) *led: rdn along over 2f out: drvn and hdd wl over 1f out: sn wknd* **17/2**
5003 **10** *2* **Pont De Nuit**[27] 6797 2-9-7 **68** DaneO'Neill 7 — 36
(R Hannon) *s.i.s: a in rr* **10/1**
0420 **11** *2 3/4* **Speedyfix**[15] 7088 2-8-3 **50** (tp) FrancisNorton 5 — 10
(Mrs C A Dunnett) *a in rr* **33/1**

1m 15.99s (-0.51) **Going Correction** -0.25s/f (Stan) **11** Ran SP% **114.0**
Speed ratings (Par 96): **93,90,88,87,85 83,81,80,78,76 72**
toteswingers: 1&2 £6.70, 1&3 £4.20, 2&3 £7.50 CSF £33.82 CT £162.08 TOTE £4.40: £2.00, £3.00, £2.10; EX 40.80 Trifecta £106.80 Pool of £359.51 - 249 winning units..
Owner J David Abell **Bred** Heather Raw **Trained** Willoughton, Lincs

FOCUS
A modest nursery but an open betting race. However, it was turned into something of a procession.

NOTEBOOK
Cape Kimberley ◆, runner-up to a subsequent winner over C&D last time, he was given a positive ride by Sanders and committed for home soon after halfway. He quickly established a clear advantage and galloped on all the way to the line, relishing the surface. There look to be more races in him on this evidence, and he may have another run before being gelded and given a break. (tchd 5-1)
Yeadon was settled just off the good early gallop and looked set to trouble the winner turning in, but despite staying on could never reduce the advantage in the closing stages. He handles this surface but also handles Polytrack, so could have a race in him before the year is out. (op 15-2)
Admiral Cochrane(IRE) pitched slightly leaving the stalls which prevented him from getting a decent early position. He ran on steadily in the straight and gave the impression he can do better when things fall right for him. (op 9-2 tchd 4-1)
Miss Taken(IRE) showed up throughout and only faded gradually in the straight. She has raced over various trips but might be worth a try over 5f on this surface. (op 20-1)
Maragna(IRE) was making his handicap debut and trying this surface for the first time. He ran with credit from his outside draw. (op 16-1)
Amno Dancer(IRE) was never far away but was beaten when squeezed out over a furlong from home. (op 9-2)
Baby Judge(IRE) was backed and showed good pace before fading. (op 16-1 tchd 8-1)

7334 HOSPITALITY AT SOUTHWELL RACECOURSE (S) STKS — 1m (F)
2:30 (2:32) (Class 6) 2-Y-O — **£2,047** (£604; £302) **Stalls** Low

Form — RPR
6300 **1** **Tiger Hawk (USA)**[2] 7319 2-8-11 48 (b) StephenDonohoe 10 — 60
(P D Evans) *chsd ldr: led 1/2-way: rdn over 2f out: sn drvn and hung rt over 1f out: kpt on u.p ins fnl f* **40/1**
3000 **2** *2 1/4* **Rainsborough**[16] 7055 2-9-3 64 (p) RobertWinston 13 — 61
(S Curran) *trckd ldrs on outer: hdwy to chse wnr 1/2-way: rdn to chal 2f out: drvn and edgd lft over 1f out: sn one pce* **7/2**[1]
6000 **3** *3 3/4* **Labretella (IRE)**[26] 6819 2-8-6 58 JimmyQuinn 12 — 42
(D W Thompson) *chsd ldng pair: rdn along wl over 2f out: drvn and one pce fr over 1f out* **9/1**
050 **4** *5* **Spirit Land (IRE)**[37] 6544 2-8-6 58 AshleyMorgan[(5)] 5 — 36
(M H Tompkins) *towards rr: hdwy over 3f out: rdn along and in tch over 2f out: sn one pce* **5/1**[2]
4250 **5** *hd* **Dontbugthebunny (USA)**[13] 7139 2-8-7 54 ow6 MarkCoumbe[(5)] 14 — 36
(George Baker) *s.i.s and in rr: hdwy 3f out: rdn and hung bdly lft over 1f out: kpt on ins fnl f: nrst fin* **13/2**[3]
5045 **6** *6* **Mrs Puff (IRE)**[2] 7319 2-8-1 53 AndrewHeffernan[(5)] 4 — 17
(P D Evans) *in tch on inner: rdn along over 3f out: drvn wl over 2f out and nvr nr ldrs* **8/1**
3120 **7** *2 1/2* **Aegean Destiny**[48] 6228 2-8-12 62 LiamJones 1 — 18
(R A Harris) *in tch on inner: effrt and sme hdwy 3f out: sn drvn and n.d* **5/1**[2]
6005 **8** *6* **Lady Cavendish (IRE)**[14] 7120 2-8-6 60 (p) JamieMackay 2 —
(A Bailey) *a bhd* **7/1**
00 **9** *6* **Red Farasi (IRE)**[70] 5583 2-8-12 0 ow1 (p) AdamKirby 9 —
(B W Duke) *in tch: rdn along 1/2-way: sn outpcd* **100/1**
0540 **10** *1 3/4* **Bury St Edmunds**[58] 5938 2-8-12 49 ow1 SebSanders 8 —
(A G Newcombe) *chsd ldrs: rdn along over 3f out and sn wknd* **14/1**
0000 **11** *21* **Annia (IRE)**[11] 7175 2-8-6 64 LukeMorris 11 —
(N P Littmoden) *led: rdn along and hdd 1/2-way: sn wknd and bhd* **25/1**

1m 43.35s (-0.35) **Going Correction** -0.25s/f (Stan) **11** Ran SP% **116.4**
Speed ratings (Par 94): **91,88,85,80,79 73,71,65,59,57 36**
toteswingers: 1&2 £30.40, 1&3 £18.30, 2&3 £33.50 CSF £173.59 TOTE £52.70: £8.00, £1.60, £3.00; EX 346.70 TRIFECTA Not won..The winner was bought in for 7,000 gns.
Owner Mrs I M Folkes **Bred** Sun Valley Farm **Trained** Pandy, Monmouths
■ The 100th winner of the year on the Flat for trainer David Evans.

FOCUS
A test of stamina in this juvenile seller but a lively betting market. The race concerned just two in the straight.

NOTEBOOK
Tiger Hawk(USA) was rated lowest of those with official marks but the switch to Fibresand and drop in grade produced a much-improved effort. Never far away, he went on at halfway and kept galloping in a style typical of runners from his yard to hold off the favourite. He was bought in and might be up to winning a small handicap on this surface. Official explanation: trainer said, regarding apparent improvement in form, that the colt was better suited by the Fibresand
Rainsborough had shown form on turf and Polytrack and, fitted with cheekpieces instead of blinkers, was backed in to favouritism. He ran well from his wide draw and appeared to be going better than the winner turning in, but he could not find any extra in the last furlong and a half. (op 6-1)
Labretella(IRE) was another who was improved by the switch to this surface and drop in grade. She chased the first two into the straight and, although making no impression, held off the rest well enough. (op 7-1 tchd 6-1)
Spirit Land(IRE), another dropping in grade, was held up early before staying on under pressure in the straight. (op 7-1)
Dontbugthebunny(USA) put up his best previous effort on fast turf. He was slowly into his stride and was tailed off at the end of the back straight. However, he did a lot of good work from that point and narrowly failed to grab fourth place. (op 10-1 tchd 11-1)
Aegean Destiny did not seem suited by the surface but was not helped by racing towards the rail throughout. (op 7-2 tchd 11-2)
Lady Cavendish(IRE) handles turf and Polytrack but did not act on this track and was tailed off leaving the back straight. Official explanation: trainer said, regarding runing, that the filly was possibly unsuited by the Fibresand (op 9-2)

7335 PLAY GOLF AT SOUTHWELL GOLF CLUB NURSERY — 1m (F)
3:00 (3:01) (Class 5) (0-70,70) 2-Y-O — **£2,729** (£806; £403) **Stalls** Low

Form — RPR
6562 **1** **Comradeship (IRE)**[5] 7266 2-9-7 **70** (b) RobertHavlin 8 — 75+
(J H M Gosden) *t.k.h: trckd ldrs: hdwy and cl up 2f out: rdn to ld wl over 1f out: carried hd high and drvn ins fnl f: jst hld on* **5/6**[1]
6002 **2** *hd* **Calypso Star (IRE)**[7] 7235 2-9-1 **64** DaneO'Neill 10 — 68
(R Hannon) *trckd ldrs: hdwy 3f out: pushed along over 2f out: rdn to chse wnr over 1f out: styd on and ev ch wl ins fnl f: jst hld* **4/1**[2]
0004 **3** *3 1/4* **As Brave As You (IRE)**[13] 7139 2-8-4 **53** ow1 ChrisCatlin 2 — 50
(B Ellison) *led: pushed along and hdd 1/2-way: cl up and rdn wl over 2f out: sn drvn and kpt same pce appr fnl f* **28/1**
450 **4** *3 1/2* **Sassanian (IRE)**[41] 6424 2-9-0 **63** IvaMilickova 1 — 52
(Jane Chapple-Hyam) *midfield: hdwy 3f out: rdn along and in tch over 2f out: sn drvn and no imp* **50/1**
000 **5** *shd* **Dazakhee**[65] 5728 2-8-8 **57** TonyCulhane 3 — 46
(P T Midgley) *chsd ldrs: rdn along wl over 2f out: sn drvn and kpt on one pce* **50/1**
0020 **6** *nk* **Creevy (IRE)**[22] 6923 2-8-4 **53** SaleemGolam 6 — 41
(S Kirk) *towards rr tl sme late hdwy* **18/1**
5002 **7** *nk* **Power Of Dreams (IRE)**[16] 7055 2-9-5 **68** JimmyQuinn 4 — 56
(M H Tompkins) *towards rr: hdwy over 3f out: rdn to chse ldrs wl over 1f out: sn drvn and no imp* **15/2**[3]
0055 **8** *2 1/4* **Lord's Seat**[8] 7218 2-7-8 **50** MatthewLawson[(7)] 7 — 33
(A Berry) *cl up: led 1/2-way: rdn along 3f out: drvn over 2f out: sn hdd & wknd* **40/1**
0006 **9** *4 1/2* **Desert Aisling (IRE)**[13] 7139 2-7-10 **48** AndreaAtzeni[(3)] 9 — 21
(Edgar Byrne) *a in rr* **16/1**
4160 **10** *2* **Rescent**[11] 7168 2-8-6 **55** AndrewElliott 11 — 24
(Mrs R A Carr) *prom on wd outside: rdn along over 3f out: sn wknd* **50/1**
000 **11** *1 1/4* **Captain Clint (IRE)**[29] 6754 2-7-13 **48** (t) NickyMackay 5 — 14
(M H Tompkins) *midfield: effrt and in tch over 3f out: sn rdn and wknd* **16/1**

1m 42.32s (-1.38) **Going Correction** -0.25s/f (Stan) **11** Ran SP% **115.1**
Speed ratings (Par 96): **96,95,92,89,88 88,88,86,81,79 78**
toteswingers: 1&2 £8.00, 1&3 £2.50, 2&3 £6.10 CSF £3.75 CT £46.36 TOTE £1.70: £1.10, £1.30, £4.40; EX 4.20 Trifecta £57.00 Pool: £537.37 - 6.97 winning units..
Owner H R H Princess Haya Of Jordan **Bred** Middle Park Stud Ltd **Trained** Newmarket, Suffolk

FOCUS
This nursery looked to involve just three according to the market and that proved more or less correct with the first two in the betting battling it out. The time was 1.03secs faster than the preceding seller.

NOTEBOOK
Comradeship(IRE) was slightly surprisingly sent off at odds-on having appeared to throw a race away here when fitted with the blinkers last time. He ran a similar race, travelling keenly but going on strongly 2f out and looking sure to win easily, then folding inside the last, but this time just holding on. It could be that a drop back a furlong might help him, but he does need to settle better. (tchd 8-11 and 10-11 in places)
Calypso Star(IRE), kept close tabs on the favourite throughout and came through in his slipstream. He looked held over a furlong out but responded to pressure as the winner tired and only just failed to catch him. He handles Polytrack as well as this surface, and should pick up a small handicap before the year is out. (op 11-2)
As Brave As You(IRE) had put up a decent effort on his Polytrack debut over further last time and was ridden positively on this first try on Fibresand. He was no match for the principals but kept on for the minor placing. (op 25-1)
Sassanian(IRE), up in trip for this Fibresand debut, ran on from off the pace but never really figured. (op 40-1)
Dazakhee also ran better for the change of surface and longer distance.
Power Of Dreams(IRE) could not build on his second in a Leicester nursery, but that was on fast ground and he seemed to be unsuited by this deeper surface. (op 13-2 tchd 8-1)

Captain Clint(IRE) Official explanation: vet said colt was struck into

7336 BOOK YOUR TICKETS ONLINE AT SOUTHWELL-RACECOURSE.CO.UK H'CAP 1m 6f (F)

3:30 (3:31) (Class 6) (0-60,59) 3-Y-0+ £2,047 (£604; £302) Stalls Low

Form RPR

0000 1 **Stagecoach Emerald**[28] 6785 7-8-3 45..............(b[1]) TobyAtkinson(7) 11 62
(R W Price) *dwlt: in rr whn hmpd after s and sn bhd: stdy hdwy over 4f out: wd st and sn chsng ldrs: rdn to ld over 1f out: clr ent fnl f and kpt on strly* **16/1**

0301 2 7 **Saute**[16] 7049 3-9-1 58.............................. AdamKirby 5 65
(W R Swinburn) *prom: effrt over 3f out: rdn over 2f out: led briefly wl over 1f out: sn drvn and hdd: kpt on: no ch w wnr* **12/1**

5053 3 2 3/4 **They All Laughed**[36] 6559 6-9-9 58.........................(p) ChrisCatlin 3 61
(Mrs Marjorie Fife) *hld up towards rr: stdy hdwy over 5f out: chsd ldrs on outer 3f out: drvn 2f out and kpt on same pce* **7/1**

5243 4 2 3/4 **Penolva (IRE)**[12] 7164 3-8-11 54........................ TonyCulhane 4 54
(P D Deegan, Ire) *prom: led after 3f: rdn along over 3f out: drvn and hdd wl over 1f out: sn wknd* **11/2**[3]

5 4 1/2 **Ionisphere**[45] 3621 4-8-10 45.......................... ShaneKelly 13 38
(W McCreery, Ire) *cl up: rdn along over 3f out: drvn over 2f out and sn wknd* **16/1**

0305 6 2 1/4 **Astroleo**[28] 6785 3-8-4 47............................ NickyMackay 12 37
(M H Tompkins) *in tch: hdwy 4f out: rdn along 3f out: drvn and plodded on fnl 2f: nvr a factor* **5/1**[2]

5054 7 1 1/4 **Dart**[24] 6875 5-9-10 59............................ RobertWinston 8 47
(Mrs S Lamyman) *hld up and bhd: hdwy 3f out: rdn over 2f out: styd on: nvr a factor* **20/1**

0412 8 1 1/4 **Little Sark (IRE)**[14] 7112 4-9-8 57..................... GeorgeBaker 7 44
(P D Evans) *chsd ldrs: rdn along 4f out: drvn 3f out and sn wknd* **7/1**

0530 9 4 1/2 **Special Chapter (IRE)**[75] 5381 4-8-5 45.............. AmyBaker(5) 1 25
(A B Haynes) *chsd ldrs on inner: rdn along over 3f out: drvn wl over 2f out and sn wknd* **80/1**

1 10 22 **He's Cool (IRE)**[12] 7154 4-9-9 58.........................(p) DaneO'Neill 10 7
(Aidan Anthony Howard, Ire) *prom: rdn along over 3f out: drvn wl over 2f out and sn wknd* **5/2**[1]

11 34 **Montiyra (IRE)**[510] 4144 5-9-9 58........................ JimmyQuinn 2 —
(Miss L C Siddall) *trckd ldrs: effrt over 4f out: rdn along over 3f out and sn wknd* **100/1**

5320 12 2 3/4 **Dimashq**[15] 7085 7-8-10 45........................ PhillipMakin 9 —
(P T Midgley) *led 3f: cl up tl rdn along 5f out and sn wknd* **25/1**

4620 13 2 1/4 **Spiritonthemount (USA)**[190] 1767 4-8-9 47........... WilliamCarson(3) 6 —
(P W Hiatt) *a in rr: wl bhd fnl 4f* **33/1**

0-60 14 29 **Sir Jake**[68] 5642 5-8-7 45....................... AndreaAtzeni(3) 14 —
(T T Clement) *a towards rr: wl bhd fnl 4f* **66/1**

3m 5.48s (-2.82) **Going Correction** -0.25s/f (Stan)
WFA 3 from 4yo+ 8lb 14 Ran SP% **120.3**
Speed ratings (Par 101): **98,94,92,90,88 87,86,85,83,70 51,49,48,31**
toteswingers: 1&2 £39.90, 1&3 £36.80, 2&3 £14.30 CSF £185.18 CT £1481.49 TOTE £24.90: £5.90, £2.80, £2.80; EX 602.50 TRIFECTA Not won..
Owner Future Electrical Services Ltd **Bred** T R G Vestey **Trained** Newmarket, Suffolk

FOCUS
A big field for this moderate staying handicap but a race of changing fortunes and in the end a wide-margin winner, who was 2lb wrong but showed a revival in the blinkers. The race was run at a good pace.
He's Cool(IRE) Official explanation: trainer said, regarding running, that the gelding was unsuited by the Fibresand

7337 CALL 01636 814481 TO SPONSOR A RACE H'CAP 6f (F)

4:00 (4:01) (Class 5) (0-75,75) 3-Y-0+ £2,729 (£806; £403) Stalls Low

Form RPR

064 1 **Imprimis Tagula (IRE)**[24] 6879 5-9-3 74..................(v) RobertWinston 4 87
(A Bailey) *chsd ldr: hdwy 1/2-way: effrt to chal 2f out and sn rdn: drvn to ld ent fnl f: edgd lft and kpt on* **3/1**[1]

1005 2 2 **Rio Cobolo (IRE)**[13] 7141 3-8-9 71...................(v) AndrewHeffernan(5) 3 78
(Paul Green) *trckd ldrs: hdwy over 2f out: rdn to chse ldng pair over 1f out: drvn and n.m.r ent fnl f: swtchd rt and kpt on same pce towards fin* **25/1**

3154 3 1 1/4 **Bonnie Prince Blue**[41] 6434 6-9-4 75.......................(b) AndrewMullen 2 78
(D Nicholls) *led: jnd and rdn 2f out: drvn and hdd over 1f out: ev ch tl one pce ins fnl f* **11/2**[2]

0401 4 2 1/4 **Efisio Princess**[30] 6738 6-8-13 70......................... RichardThomas 14 66+
(J E Long) *in tch on outer: wd st: hdwy over 2f out: sn rdn and chsd ldrs over 1f out: no imp* **9/1**

2020 5 3/4 **Residency (IRE)**[65] 5727 3-8-7 64.................................(v[1]) TomEaves 5 57
(B Smart) *in tch: rdn along over 2f out: drvn over 1f out: kpt on ins fnl f* **22/1**

002 6 3/4 **Miss Bootylishes**[11] 7172 4-8-5 67............................ AmyBaker(5) 11 58+
(A B Haynes) *bhd: hdwy on inner 2f out: sn rdn and kpt on ins fnl f: nrst fin* **14/1**

1346 7 hd **Angel Song**[63] 5777 3-9-2 73............................... SebSanders 13 63
(Sir Mark Prescott) *chsd ldrs: hdwy on outer over 2f out: sn rdn and wknd over 1f out* **14/1**

124 8 1/2 **Premier Lad**[198] 1567 3-9-1 72............................... PhillipMakin 8 61
(T D Barron) *midfield: effrt over 2f out and sn rdn: drvn wl over 1f out and no imp appr fnl f* **6/1**[3]

0520 9 1/2 **Swinbrook (USA)**[25] 6857 8-8-8 72.......................(b) JakePayne(7) 12 59
(R A Harris) *racd wd: a towards rr* **12/1**

0000 10 hd **After The Show**[27] 6799 8-8-4 61 oh3........................ NickyMackay 7 48
(Rae Guest) *a towards rr* **18/1**

1000 11 3/4 **Green Park (IRE)**[12] 7155 6-9-3 74............................(b) DNolan 10 58
(D Carroll) *a in rr* **16/1**

006 12 1 1/2 **Resplendent Alpha**[11] 7191 5-9-1 72........................ JimmyQuinn 9 51
(P Howling) *a in rr* **16/1**

2505 13 6 **Kensington (IRE)**[19] 7000 8-9-2 73.................... StephenDonohoe 1 33
(A J McCabe) *chsd ldrs on inner: rdn along over 2f out and sn wknd* **25/1**

0000 14 4 **Requisite**[10] 7203 4-8-10 67..................................(v) TonyHamilton 6 14
(I A Wood) *dwlt: a in rr* **20/1**

1m 14.7s (-1.80) **Going Correction** -0.25s/f (Stan) 14 Ran SP% **119.5**
Speed ratings (Par 103): **102,99,97,94,93 92,92,91,91,90 89,87,79,74**
toteswingers: 1&2 £17.70, 1&3 £4.90, 2&3 £25.00 CSF £92.58 CT £335.82 TOTE £3.80: £1.90, £5.90, £1.90; EX 93.70 TRIFECTA Not won. Place 6: £102.34 Place 5: £81.91.
Owner Middleham Park Racing XLI & Alan Bailey **Bred** Glashare House Stud **Trained** Newmarket, Suffolk
■ Stewards' Enquiry : Andrew Heffernan one-day ban: used whip with excessive frequency (Nov 25)

FOCUS
Plenty with previous experience on the track in this sprint handicap, and in the end a well-backed winner who looks the best guide to the form.
Miss Bootylishes Official explanation: jockey said filly was slowly away
T/Jkpt: Not won. T/Plt: £43.90 to a £1 stake. Pool: £73,048.80. 1,214.04 winning tickets. T/Qpdt: £18.60 to a £1 stake. Pool: £4,336.70. 172.30 winning tickets. JR

7295 DUNDALK (A.W) (L-H)

Wednesday, November 11

OFFICIAL GOING: Standard

7341a DUNDALKSTADIUM.COM H'CAP 6f (P)

7:30 (7:40) 3-Y-0+ £13,588 (£3,986; £1,899; £647)

RPR

1 **Bay Knight (IRE)**[11] 7181 3-8-8 82.............................. KLatham 13 87+
(W McCreery, Ire) *hld up in rr: last ent st: hdwy on outer under 2f out: r.o strly to ld cl home* **14/1**

2 3/4 **Copper Dock (IRE)**[12] 7161 5-8-13 92........................ BACurtis(5) 3 93+
(T G McCourt, Ire) *racd keenly: settled in mid-div: 9th on inner appr st: 5th and hdwy ins fnl f: r.o strly cl home* **9/1**

3 shd **Richelieu**[38] 6517 7-8-4 78.. JohnEgan 8 79
(J J Lambe, Ire) *sn led: strly pressed st: kpt on u.p: hdd cl home* **25/1**

4 1 1/4 **Green Manalishi**[10] 7202 8-9-12 105...........................(p) DEMullins(5) 5 102
(K A Ryan) *trckd ldrs: 4th into st: rdn to chal fr 1 1/2f out: kpt on u.p ins fnl f* **3/1**[1]

5 3/4 **Sioduil (IRE)**[45] 6315 3-9-9 97...............................(p) KJManning 12 91
(J S Bolger, Ire) *hld up: 10th on outer appr st: 6th under 2f out: kpt on same pce fnl f* **13/2**

6 1/2 **Six Of Hearts**[6] 7259 5-9-4 99..............................(b[1]) KMDonoghue(7) 11 92
(Cecil Ross, Ire) *sn prom: 3rd 1/2-way: chal early st: no imp fr over 1f out: one pce* **12/1**

7 nk **Romeo's On Fire (IRE)**[12] 7161 5-9-4 92.......................... JMurtagh 7 84
(G M Lyons, Ire) *hld up in tch: 9th early st: kpt on same pce fnl f* **5/1**[2]

8 nk **Tornadodancer (IRE)**[33] 6649 6-9-3 91.........................(b) PTownend 4 82
(T G McCourt, Ire) *prom on inner: 4th 1/2-way: 5th st: sn no ex* **16/1**

9 3/4 **Samba School (IRE)**[90] 4958 3-7-11 78..................(b) SHJames(7) 10 66
(Kevin Prendergast, Ire) *prom: 2nd 1/2-way: rdn to chal early st: no ex fr over 1f out* **25/1**

10 shd **Mountain Coral (IRE)**[12] 7161 5-9-8 96.................... NGMcCullagh 2 84
(F Oakes, Ire) *hld up towards rr on inner: nt clr run early st: no imp fr 1 1/2f out* **6/1**[3]

11 hd **Soap Wars**[12] 7161 4-9-2 95.....................................(p) GFCarroll(5) 6 82
(M Halford, Ire) *mid-div: 7th 1/2-way: no imp st* **8/1**

12 1 1/4 **Senor Benny (USA)**[12] 7161 10-8-9 83..........................(b) PJSmullen 14 66
(M McDonagh, Ire) *chsd ldrs on outer: 5th and effrt early st: sn no ex and wknd* **20/1**

13 1 1/2 **Hazelwood Ridge (IRE)**[26] 6833 6-8-4 78 oh5................. WMLordan 9 57
(James Bernard McCabe, Ire) *racd keenly: settled in mid-div: 7th 1/2-way: wknd st* **20/1**

14 1 1/2 **Grigorovitch (IRE)**[21] 6952 7-8-1 78 oh3........................ ShaneFoley(3) 1 52
(Liam McAteer, Ire) *a towards rr* **25/1**

1m 11.7s (71.70) 14 Ran SP% **131.7**
CSF £136.68 CT £3215.68 TOTE £27.10: £6.70, £5.20, £20.00; DF 277.10.
Owner Iona Equine Syndicate **Bred** Pat Roach **Trained** Maynooth, Co.Kildare

FOCUS
A typically open Dundalk sprint handicap that has been rated around the runner-up.

NOTEBOOK
Bay Knight(IRE)'s rider was instructed to miss the break due to his bad draw, which he did, but he was still stone last turning into the straight. However, when he was pulled towards the outside and asked to race the response was impressive and he sustained his effort all the way to the line. (op 12/1)
Copper Dock(IRE) ran his usual good race at this track and was ridden almost exactly the same way as when winning here last time. He was probably held up a little bit further back but got the split at the right time inside the last and his rider put his head in front at exactly the right time. Unfortunately, there was one on the wide outside to do him. (op 8/1)
Richelieu was very much on a going day here and showed very good speed to get to the front early. Without traffic issues to worry about he kept finding a bit in front but was just swallowed up close home.
Green Manalishi was just far too free early on and didn't get home having threatened a furlong or so out. Official explanation: jockey said gelding lost a shoe in running (op 3/1 tchd 10/3)
Sioduil(IRE) came with a dangerous looking run on the outside in the straight but her effort just flattened out inside the last. (op 6/1)
Romeo's On Fire(IRE) didn't miss the break on this occasion but ran into his fair share of traffic problems before coming home well.

7342 - 7345a (Foreign Racing) - See Raceform Interactive

TOULOUSE

Wednesday, November 11

OFFICIAL GOING: Very soft

7346a CRITERIUM DU LANGUEDOC (LISTED RACE) 1m

1:05 (1:06) 2-Y-O £26,699 (£10,680; £8,010; £5,340; £2,670)

RPR

1 **Bottega (USA)** 2-8-11 .... DBoeuf 7 98
(M Delcher-Sanchez, Spain)

2 nse **Maroon Machine (IRE)**[25] 6849 2-8-11 .... OPeslier 6 98
(E J O'Neill) *racd in 5th on outside: hdwy to dispute ld 1f out: hdd 50yds out: r.o* **6/4**[1]

3 2 **Xaarienne**[22] 6929 2-8-8 .... MGuyon 2 91
(H-A Pantall, France)

4 nk **La Joie (FR)**[122] 3934 2-8-8 .... MickaelForest 4 90
(J-C Rouget, France)

5 2 **Blue Panis (FR)**[27] 2-8-11 .... TThulliez 1 89
(F Chappet, France)

6 8 **Itri (FR)**[15] 7103 2-8-8 ....(b) THuet 8 68
(M Boutin, France)

7 dist **Rainfall Shadow (IRE)**[102] 2-8-11 .... IMendizabal 5 —
(J-C Rouget, France)

8 8 **Fauchizo (IRE)** 2-8-11 ....(p) DMichaux 3 —
(R Avial Lopez, Spain)

1m 43.53s (0.23) 8 Ran SP% **40.0**
PARI-MUTUEL (including 1 Euro stake): WIN 22.70; PL 3.80, 1.40, 2.60;DF 23.10.

Owner F Sanz Blanco **Bred** Flaxman Holdings Ltd **Trained** Spain

7347a PRIX FILLE DE L'AIR (GROUP 3) (F&M) 1m 2f 110y
2:05 (2:11) 3-Y-0+ **£38,835** (£15,534; £11,650; £7,767; £3,883)

RPR

1 **Synergy (FR)**[80] 5300 4-8-11 .... OPeslier 5 96
(Y Durepaire, Spain) *cl up: 4th st: swtchd lft over 1 1/2f out: led appr fnl f: r.o wl* **61/10**[3]

2 *1 1/2* **Cavaliere (FR)**[41] 6438 3-8-8 .... FBlondel 2 95
(M Cesandri, France) *towards rr early: 5th st: wnt 2nd ins fnl f: nt pce of wnr* **14/1**

3 *nse* **Alpine Snow (IRE)**[14] 7128 3-8-8 .... RMarchelli 10 95
(S Wattel, France) *a.p: 2nd st: bmpd: carried lft and dropped bk to 4th over 1 1/2f out: rallied fnl f: jst missed 2nd* **25/1**

4 *nk* **Take The Hint**[14] 7128 3-8-8 .... SPasquier 8 94
(Mme C Head-Maarek, France) *racd in 2nd tl led 3f out: hdd appr fnl f: one pce* **78/10**

5 *1 1/2* **Karlisse (IRE)**[36] 6577 3-8-8 .... JVictoire 4 92
(H-A Pantall, France) *towards rr: 11th st: kpt on fnl 1 1/2f* **53/1**

6 *nk* **Rainbow Dancing**[14] 7128 4-8-11 .... TJarnet 3 89
(Mlle H Van Zuylen, France) *in rr early: midfield 1/2-way: 8th st: kpt on* **7/2**[1]

7 *3/4* **Lungwa (IRE)**[24] 6891 3-8-8 .... DBonilla 14 90
(E Lellouche, France) *in rr: 12th st: kpt on fnl 1 1/2f: nrst fin* **17/2**

8 *nse* **Lakuta (IRE)**[53] 4-8-11 ....(p) F-XBertras 1 87
(F Rohaut, France) *hld up: 9th st: hrd rdn and disputing 4th 1f out: wknd* **29/1**

9 *1/2* **Audaz**[70] 4-8-11 .... GMasure 12 87
(C Laffon-Parias, France) *last st: nvr a factor* **29/1**

10 *2* **Dubai Rose**[45] 3-8-8 ....(b) MGuyon 9 85
(H-A Pantall, France) *plld hrd and cl up early: 7th st: rdn and unable qck over 1 1/2f out* **30/1**

11 **Saturnine (IRE)**[41] 6438 4-8-11 .... TThulliez 7 83
(N Clement, France) *towards rr: 10th st: nvr a factor* **11/2**[2]

12 **Valletta**[39] 6504 3-8-8 .... DBoeuf 11 85
(H-A Pantall, France) *led to 3f out: wknd 2f out* **21/1**

13 **Annabelle's Charm (IRE)**[31] 6717 4-8-11 .... JamieSpencer 6 83
(L M Cumani) *midfield early racing keenly: restrained towards rr: 13th st: sn rdn and no imp* **11/1**

14 **Pearlescence (USA)**[61] 5851 3-8-8 .... IMendizabal 13 85
(J-C Rouget, France) *racd in 6th: wknd qckly 1 1/2f out: t.o* **9/1**

2m 22.52s (142.52)
WFA 3 from 4yo 4lb **14 Ran SP% 118.7**
PARI-MUTUEL: WIN 7.10; PL 3.00, 4.30, 7.40; DF 60.10.
Owner De La Fuente Stud **Bred** J Stulen **Trained** Spain

NOTEBOOK
Annabelle's Charm(IRE) never got involved having raced keenly early.

7331 SOUTHWELL (L-H)
Thursday, November 12

OFFICIAL GOING: Standard
Wind: Light against Weather: Overcast and dry

7348 BET GRAND SLAM DARTS - BETDAQ H'CAP (DIV I) 7f (F)
12:20 (12:20) (Class 6) (0-60,60) 3-Y-0+ **£1,706** (£503; £252) **Stalls Low**

Form RPR

4000 1 **My Sweet Georgia (IRE)**[29] 6783 3-9-4 **60**........................(b) AdamKirby 7 72
(Stef Liddiard) *chsd ldrs: rdn along 1/2-way: hdwy to chse ldr 2f out: drvn ent fnl f: styd on to ld nr fin* **8/1**

6106 2 *nk* **Young Gladiator (IRE)**[20] 6985 4-9-3 **58**........................(b) TomEaves 4 69
(Miss J A Camacho) *led: rdn clr over 1f out: drvn ins fnl f: wknd and hdd nr fin* **8/1**

6436 3 *3 1/4* **Rockfield Lodge (IRE)**[17] 7051 4-8-11 **52**........................(p) StephenDonohoe 9 54
(Ian Williams) *chsd ldrs: hdwy 2f out and sn rdn: drvn and kpt on same pce ent fnl f* **6/1**[3]

3430 4 *3* **Sairaam (IRE)**[8] 7246 3-8-9 **54**........................ AndreaAtzeni[(3)] 3 48
(C Smith) *towards rr: hdwy wl over 2f out: rdn to chse ldrs over 1f out: sn drvn and no imp* **14/1**

5600 5 *hd* **The City Kid (IRE)**[27] 6828 6-9-1 **56**........................ ChrisCatlin 6 50
(G D Blake) *midfield: swtchd outside and hdwy 2f out: sn rdn and styd on ins fnl f: nrst fin* **12/1**

034 6 *2 1/4* **Mocha Java**[14] 7129 6-8-12 **58**........................(b) RossAtkinson[(5)] 1 46
(Matthew Salaman) *nvr bttr then midfield* **7/1**

5020 7 *3/4* **Kheskianto (IRE)**[17] 7062 3-8-13 **60**........................ AndrewHeffernan[(5)] 14 46
(M C Chapman) *cl up: rdn along wl over 2f out: grad wknd* **22/1**

0400 8 *3 1/2* **Norcroft**[12] 7180 7-9-0 **55**........................(p) AdrianMcCarthy 10 31
(Mrs C A Dunnett) *prom: rdn along over 2f out and sn wknd* **14/1**

312 9 *nk* **Mister Jingles**[8] 7240 6-8-8 **54**........................(v) AmyRyan[(5)] 5 29
(R M Whitaker) *towards rr: rdn along 1/2-way: nvr a factor* **9/2**[1]

00 10 *2 1/4* **Makshoof (IRE)**[92] 4887 5-9-5 **60**........................ PhillipMakin 2 29
(I W McInnes) *chsd ldrs: rdn along 3f out: sn wknd* **50/1**

4155 11 *shd* **Castano**[17] 7062 5-8-13 **57** ow1........................ JamesMillman[(3)] 8 26
(B R Millman) *s.i.s and sn rdn along: a in rr* **5/1**[2]

3306 12 *2 3/4* **Stand In Flames**[17] 7057 4-8-12 **58**........................ MatthewDavies[(5)] 12 20
(George Baker) *a towards rr* **25/1**

1m 28.64s (-1.66) **Going Correction** -0.25s/f (Stan)
WFA 3 from 4yo+ 1lb **12 Ran SP% 115.0**
Speed ratings (Par 101): **99,98,94,91,91 88,87,83,83,80 80,77**
toteswingers: 1&2 £9.20, 1&3 £11.10, 2&3 £6.20 CSF £66.98 CT £419.44 TOTE £12.90: £3.90, £3.00, £2.60; EX 104.50 TRIFECTA Not won..
Owner Higgi's In The Wings **Bred** Epona Bloodstock Ltd **Trained** Great Shefford, Berks

FOCUS
A moderate handicap and, hardly for the first time here, those who raced handily were at a big advantage. Sound form, with the winner back to last winter's form and the runner-up posting a personal best.

Mister Jingles Official explanation: jockey said gelding never travelled

7349 BET GRAND SLAM DARTS - BETDAQ H'CAP (DIV II) 7f (F)
12:50 (12:51) (Class 6) (0-60,59) 3-Y-0+ **£1,706** (£503; £252) **Stalls Low**

Form RPR

0406 1 **Naomh Geileis (USA)**[23] 6926 4-9-4 **58**........................(b) JoeFanning 9 69+
(M Johnston) *in rr and rdn along after 2f: hdwy 1/2-way: effrt on outer to chse ldrs over 1f out: drvn ent fnl f: styd on strly to ld last 100yds* **11/1**

0406 2 *1 1/2* **Elusive Warrior (USA)**[44] 6361 6-9-5 **59**........................(p) RobertWinston 14 66
(A J McCabe) *cl up: rdn along 2f out: drvn over 1f out: kpt on to ld briefly ins fnl f: sn hdd and one pce* **5/1**[2]

5063 3 *1 3/4* **Outer Hebrides**[8] 7239 8-8-9 **54**........................(v) AmyBaker[(5)] 6 57
(J M Bradley) *in tch: hdwy over 2f out: rdn to chse ldrs wl over 1f out: drvn and one-pce fnl f* **7/1**[3]

0620 4 *nk* **Tri Chara (IRE)**[42] 6437 5-9-5 **59**........................(p) GrahamGibbons 3 61
(R Hollinshead) *cl up: led 4f out: rdn clr wl over 1f out: drvn and hdd ins fnl f: wknd* **9/2**[1]

6013 5 *4 1/2* **Cils Blancs (IRE)**[93] 4879 3-9-4 **59**........................ TomEaves 4 49
(B Smart) *dwlt: sn pushed along and hdwy 1/2-way: rdn along and in tch over 2f out: drvn and kpt on same pce fr over 1f out* **9/1**

2003 6 *2* **Top Flight Splash**[15] 7105 3-8-12 **53**........................(v) LiamJones 13 37
(Mrs G S Rees) *chsd ldrs: rdn along wl over 2f out: drvn wl over 1f out and grad wknd* **12/1**

2000 7 *shd* **Rockson (IRE)**[15] 7109 3-8-9 **50**........................ StephenDonohoe 12 34
(Ian Williams) *bhd tl sme late hdwy* **40/1**

2001 8 *2 1/2* **Charlie Delta**[29] 6777 6-9-2 **56**........................(b) LukeMorris 2 33
(R A Harris) *chsd ldrs on inner: rdn along over 2f out: drvn wl over 1f out and grad wknd* **9/1**

0101 9 *hd* **Straight Face (IRE)**[29] 6782 5-9-1 **55**........................(e) J-PGuillambert 10 32
(Miss Gay Kelleway) *dwlt: nvr bttr than midfield* **11/1**

3450 10 *3* **Byron Bay**[27] 6818 7-9-2 **56**........................(v[1]) ChrisCatlin 11 25
(R Johnson) *dwlt: sn chsng ldrs on outer: rdn along over 2f out: sn wknd* **10/1**

11 *3/4* **Catherine (IRE)**[43] 6403 3-8-12 **53**........................ DarryllHolland 5 20
(Mark L Fagan, Ire) *led: rdn along and hdd 3f out: wknd over 2f out* **16/1**

0105 12 *1/2* **Silidan**[225] 1074 6-9-0 **54**........................ AdamKirby 8 19
(Miss M E Rowland) *dwlt: a towards rr* **25/1**

-420 13 *1 1/2* **Michael Collins (IRE)**[44] 6358 3-9-0 **55**........................(p) FrankieMcDonald 7 16
(G J Smith) *midfield: rdn along 3f out and sn wknd* **50/1**

4020 14 *shd* **Hypnotic**[45] 6349 7-9-1 **58**........................ RobertLButler[(3)] 1 19
(Jim Best) *sn rdn along: a towards rr* **20/1**

1m 28.47s (-1.83) **Going Correction** -0.25s/f (Stan)
WFA 3 from 4yo+ 1lb **14 Ran SP% 119.7**
Speed ratings (Par 101): **100,98,96,95,90 88,88,85,85,81 81,80,78,78**
toteswingers: 1&2 £9.20, 1&3 £11.10, 2&3 £6.20 CSF £62.45 CT £433.30 TOTE £15.50: £4.40, £2.20, £2.50; EX 84.10 TRIFECTA Not won..
Owner Mrs Christine E Budden **Bred** Farfellow Farms Ltd **Trained** Middleham Moor, N Yorks

FOCUS
Another moderate handicap, though not dominated as much by the pacesetters as the opener. The winning time was 0.17 seconds faster than the first division. Sound form, the winner running her best race since her 2yo days.

7350 BET INTERNATIONAL RUGBY - BETDAQ CLAIMING STKS 7f (F)
1:20 (1:21) (Class 6) 3-Y-0+ **£2,047** (£604; £302) **Stalls Low**

Form RPR

4466 1 **Ingleby Princess**[20] 6987 5-8-1 48........................ DuranFentiman 5 61
(T D Barron) *in rr: wd st: hdwy 2f out and sn rdn: n.m.r over 1f out: drvn and styd on to chal ins fnl f and sn edgd lft: kpt on to ld last 75yds* **50/1**

3042 2 *1* **Flores Sea (USA)**[159] 2718 5-9-2 78........................(b) PhillipMakin 11 73
(T D Barron) *chsd ldrs on outer: wd st: rdn 2f out: styd on to ld ins fnl f: sn drvn: hdd and no ex last 75yds* **9/4**[1]

3622 3 *1/2* **Autumn Blades (IRE)**[7] 7252 4-9-1 77........................(p) AndrewHeffernan[(5)] 10 76
(A Bailey) *midfield: hdwy to trck ldrs over 2f out: rdn and ch over 1f out: n.m.r ins fnl f: kpt on same pce* **9/2**[2]

1265 4 *1/2* **Carbon Hoofprint**[19] 7027 3-9-7 80........................ FergusSweeney 6 77
(P J Makin) *led: hdd briefly 1/2-way: led again wl over 2f out: rdn wl over 1f out: drvn ent fnl f: sn hdd: edgd lft and one pce* **5/1**[3]

2020 5 *1 3/4* **La Belle Joannie**[50] 6208 4-8-0 53........................ AndreaAtzeni[(3)] 1 53
(S Curran) *in tch on inner: hdwy to chse ldrs over 2f out: sn rdn and kpt on ins fnl f: nrst fin* **28/1**

0020 6 *1 1/4* **Cook's Endeavour (USA)**[27] 6824 3-9-1 69........................ ChrisCatlin 14 63
(K A Ryan) *cl up: led briefly 1/2-way: rdn along and hdd wl over 2f out: drvn and wknd over 1f out* **28/1**

0000 7 *nse* **Final Verse**[12] 7194 6-9-12 76........................(e[1]) LPKeniry 7 72
(Matthew Salaman) *midfield: hdwy over 2f out: sn rdn and kpt on ins fnl f: nrst fin* **8/1**

0015 8 *4 1/2* **Lordship (IRE)**[9] 7220 5-9-5 72........................ JakePayne[(7)] 12 60
(A W Carroll) *prom: rdn along over 2f out and sn wknd* **20/1**

2200 9 *8* **Monte Mayor Eagle**[20] 7002 3-8-0 54........................ JamieMackay 3 14
(D Haydn Jones) *s.i.s: a in rr* **66/1**

0-00 10 *1/2* **Oxbridge**[69] 5633 4-8-6 48........................ LukeMorris 4 17
(J M Bradley) *a towards rr* **200/1**

00 11 *2 3/4* **Pride Of Nation (IRE)**[31] 6732 7-9-0 75........................(p) RobertWinston 13 18
(A J McCabe) *cl up on outer: rdn along wl over 2f out and sn wknd* **8/1**

0640 12 *7* **Dabbers Ridge (IRE)**[12] 7171 7-8-10 63........................(b) TomEaves 2 —
(I W McInnes) *chsd ldrs on inner: rdn along 3f out: sn wknd* **33/1**

4061 P **Lindoro**[40] 6476 4-9-7 88........................ JamieJones[(5)] 8 —
(M G Quinlan) *in tch: sddle slipped and lost pl after 3f and bhd whn p.u over 2f out* **8/1**

1m 28.46s (-1.84) **Going Correction** -0.25s/f (Stan)
WFA 3 from 4yo+ 1lb **13 Ran SP% 117.5**
Speed ratings (Par 101): **100,98,98,97,95 94,94,89,79,79 76,68,—**
toteswingers: 1&2 £25.70, 1&3 £31.60, 2&3 £3.60 CSF £154.01 TOTE £41.50: £10.10, £1.70, £1.60; EX 83.70 Trifecta £103.50 Pool of £418.28 - 2.99 winning units..Carbon Hoofprint was claimed by S. A. Callaghan for £13,000
Owner Dave Scott **Bred** Wheelersland Stud **Trained** Maunby, N Yorks

FOCUS
A fairly competitive claimer on paper and a one-two for the David Barron stable, but the result makes the form seem a bit suspect. The winner is rated to her best with several rivals below form. The main action took place centre-to-stands' side up the home straight and the winning time was 1/100th of a second faster than the second division of the handicap.

Pride Of Nation(IRE) Official explanation: jockey said horse had no more to give

Lindoro Official explanation: jockey said saddle slipped

7351 BET MULTIPLES - BETDAQ MAIDEN AUCTION STKS 7f (F)
1:50 (1:51) (Class 6) 2-Y-O £3,207 (£947; £473) Stalls Low

Form RPR
32 1 **Vegas Palace (IRE)**[22] 6947 2-8-6 0 RichardKingscote 4 83+
(Tom Dascombe) *mde all: rdn clr over 1f out: comf* **8/13**[1]
0 2 5 **Brigadoon**[13] 7146 2-8-9 0 JoeFanning 1 72
(W Jarvis) *hld up in rr: hdwy 1/2-way: rdn to chse wnr 2f out: drvn wl over 1f out and sn no imp* **10/3**[2]
0034 3 1 **Master Leon**[15] 7116 2-8-9 72 TomEaves 3 69
(B Smart) *chsd ldng pair: rdn along 3f out: wknd over 2f out* **5/1**[3]
0 4 5 **Tealing**[24] 6896 2-8-10 0 ow1 PhillipMakin 2 58
(T D Barron) *cl up: rdn along 3f out: sn drvn and wknd 2f out* **20/1**

1m 28.08s (-2.22) **Going Correction** -0.25s/f (Stan) **4** Ran SP% **106.4**
Speed ratings (Par 94): **102,96,95,89**
CSF £2.82 TOTE £1.40; EX 2.90.
Owner The Brian & Ben Partnership **Bred** Michael Downey And Mrs P O'Connor **Trained** Lambourn, Berks

FOCUS
An uncompetitive maiden auction event, but the winning time was significantly faster than all three of the previous races for older horses over the same trip so the form may be stronger than first impressions. Only one of the quartet had previous experience of this surface and it showed.

NOTEBOOK
Vegas Palace(IRE), runner-up in a C&D maiden last month, made just about every yard and though not given much peace by Tealing up her inside for the first half-mile of the contest, that didn't stop her from forging clear of her rivals inside the last 2f and winning with plenty in hand. Things will be tougher from now on, but she is probably still improving and is likely to be kept on the go. (op 4-5 tchd 4-7)
Brigadoon, who showed early speed before finishing unplaced when a 100-1 shot for a Newmarket maiden over this trip last month, missed the break this time and soon found himself last. He did plug on up the home straight to finish second at a respectful distance, but still looked green so may still be capable of better. (op 11-4)
Master Leon, in the frame in a couple of 1m maidens on turf, tracked the leaders on the outside early but couldn't pick up once off the bridle. He is rated 72 which gives some idea of the level of the form, but he remains vulnerable to improvers and may be worth a try in a nursery. (op 4-1 tchd 6-1)
Tealing, tailed off on his Pontefract debut last month, tried to keep tabs on the favourite early but those exertions took their toll once into the home straight. He probably needs more time. (op 33-1 tchd 40-1)

7352 HOSPITALITY PACKAGES AVAILABLE (S) STKS 6f (F)
2:20 (2:21) (Class 6) 2-Y-O £2,047 (£604; £302) Stalls Low

Form RPR
5534 1 **Jack Luey**[8] 7242 2-8-6 63 (p) AndrewHeffernan(5) 3 59
(L A Mullaney) *prom: led 1/2-way: sn rdn and edgd rt 2f out: drvn and hung lft over 1f out: rdr lost iron and hrd rdn ins fnl f: hung rt nr fin: jst hld on* **2/1**[2]
0030 2 nk **Lord Victor**[3] 7319 2-8-11 50 RobertWinston 4 58
(A J McCabe) *cl up: chal over 2f out: rdn whn bmpd wl over 1f out: sn drvn and ev ch whn hmpd ins fnl f: bmpd nr fin* **10/1**
4103 3 2 3/4 **Zelos Dream (IRE)**[21] 6970 2-8-11 64 LukeMorris 8 50
(R A Harris) *in tch: hdwy to chse ldrs 3f out: rdn to chse ldng pair 2f out: drvn and hung lft over 1f out: kpt on same pce* **15/2**[3]
0111 4 5 **Angie's Nap (USA)**[6] 7268 2-8-11 66 (p) ChrisCatlin 1 35
(P S McEntee) *led to 1/2-way: cl up on inner: rdn 2f out: drvn over 1f out and sn wknd* **6/4**[1]
0463 5 shd **Avec Moi**[16] 7089 2-8-6 47 AdrianMcCarthy 2 29
(Mrs C A Dunnett) *chsd ldrs: rdn along 3f out: drvn over 2f out and sn wknd* **20/1**
6060 6 nk **Selina Rio**[9] 7217 2-8-6 30 AndrewMullen 10 29
(L A Mullaney) *towards rr: effrt over 2f out: sn rdn and nvr a factor* **200/1**
2040 7 3/4 **Prettiest Star (IRE)**[27] 6819 2-8-6 45 (p) FergusSweeney 5 26
(K A Ryan) *chsd ldrs: rdn along 1/2-way: sn drvn and outpcd* **14/1**
0200 8 3/4 **Micky's Bird**[48] 6241 2-8-6 54 PaulEddery 6 24
(R C Guest) *a towards rr* **14/1**
4000 9 3/4 **Lady Bucket**[56] 6018 2-8-6 35 JamieMackay 9 22
(Paul Green) *s.i.s: a in rr* **100/1**

1m 16.43s (-0.07) **Going Correction** -0.25s/f (Stan) **9** Ran SP% **113.8**
Speed ratings (Par 94): **90,89,85,79,79 78,77,76,75**
toteswingers: 1&2 £5.50, 1&3 £5.40, 2&3 £8.20 CSF £21.77 TOTE £2.70: £1.10, £3.00, £1.70; EX 21.90 Trifecta £339.60 Part won. Pool of £458.92 - 0.55 winning units..The winner bought in for 9,000gns.
Owner The Jack Partnership **Bred** Miss D A Johnson **Trained** Great Habton, North Yorkshire
■ Stewards' Enquiry : Andrew Heffernan two-day ban: careless riding (Nov 26-27)

FOCUS
This juvenile seller looked to concern only three judged on official ratings beforehand but that was not quite how it worked out.

NOTEBOOK
Jack Luey had a major chance judged on official ratings on this drop in grade but the switch to this surface was an unknown. However, he travelled well up with the pace but, after going on early in the straight, had to pull out all the stops to hold off the runner-up. He did that rival no favours, leaning into him from over 1f out (his rider losing his right iron in the process) and gave the runner-up a bump just before the line, so had to survive a stewards' enquiry. (op 11-4 tchd 3-1)
Lord Victor had run four of his previous races on Polytrack but was encountering this surface for the first time. Dropping a furlong in distance, he was always in the front rank and gave the winner a good fight, despite that rival leaning into him in the closing stages. He can win a similar contest on this surface. (op 12-1)
Zelos Dream(IRE) made her debut here but has since won on fast turf and run well on Polytrack. She chased the leaders throughout but could not keep up in the last quarter-mile. (op 7-1 tchd 8-1)
Angie's Nap(USA) had won her last three races here, including beating the previous day's clear winner Cape Kimberley over C&D. However, after leading early, she was brushed aside soon after halfway and ran as if over the top. (op 5-4)
Avec Moi had been beaten by the favourite here last month and was worse off at the weights. The fact that she finished so close to her old rival this time indicates how far below her best the latter ran. (op 16-1 tchd 22-1)

7353 HOSPITALITY AT SOUTHWELL RACECOURSE MAIDEN STKS 7f (F)
2:50 (2:50) (Class 5) 3-Y-O £5,118 (£1,511; £756) Stalls Low

Form RPR
5- 1 **Cape Quarter (USA)**[378] 7098 3-9-3 0 LiamJones 8 65+
(W J Haggas) *trckd ldrs: hdwy wl over 2f out: led 1 1/2f out: rdn and rn green ent fnl f: kpt on* **5/6**[1]
552 2 1/2 **Tobrata**[22] 6950 3-8-10 65 JohnCavanagh(7) 9 63
(M Brittain) *towards rr: hdwy on wd outside 2f out: rdn to chse wnr ins fnl f: kpt on wl towards fin* **6/1**[3]
055 3 2 1/4 **Luisa Tetrazzini (IRE)**[17] 7067 3-8-12 59 ChrisCatlin 2 52
(K A Ryan) *cl up on inner: rdn along over 2f out: drvn over 1f out: edgd rt and kpt on same pce ins fnl f* **20/1**
6060 4 1 1/2 **Unconsoled**[57] 5983 3-8-12 42 FranciscoDaSilva 7 48
(J Hetherton) *cl up: led 1/2-way: rdn and jnd 2f out: hdd 1 1/2f out: sn drvn: wknd ent fnl f* **80/1**
0040 5 1/2 **Well Of Echoes**[22] 6939 3-8-12 51 (t) RobertWinston 4 47
(A J McCabe) *led: rdn along and hdd 1/2-way: drvn over 2f out: grad wknd* **12/1**
0400 6 nk **Bold Bomber**[51] 6183 3-8-12 42 PaulPickard(5) 10 51
(Paul Green) *in tch: hdwy to chse ldrs 1/2-way: rdn along over 2f out: drvn wl over 1f out and sn no imp* **40/1**
3302 7 6 **Positivity**[25] 6880 3-8-12 50 TomEaves 6 30
(B Smart) *nvr nr ldrs* **14/1**
0326 8 2 **Anagram**[16] 7082 3-8-12 67 (b) PhillipMakin 1 24
(W R Muir) *in tch: effrt and sme hdwy wl over 2f out: sn rdn and wknd* **5/1**[2]
60 9 3/4 **Short Supply (USA)**[66] 5731 3-8-12 0 GrahamGibbons 11 22
(T D Walford) *a in rr: bhd fr 1/2-way* **20/1**
0060 10 2 1/2 **Hold The Star**[28] 6807 3-8-9 56 ow2 AnnStokell(5) 3 18
(Miss A Stokell) *s.i.s: a bhd* **40/1**
00-0 11 23 **Lunar Romance**[27] 6831 3-8-12 45 LukeMorris 5 —
(T J Pitt) *dwlt: a in rr* **80/1**

1m 28.89s (-1.41) **Going Correction** -0.25s/f (Stan) **11** Ran SP% **116.7**
Speed ratings (Par 102): **98,97,94,93,92 92,85,83,82,79 53**
toteswingers: 1&2 £3.50, 1&3 £6.30, 2&3 £8.50 CSF £5.46 TOTE £1.70: £1.10, £1.50, £2.60; EX 7.50 Trifecta £73.70 Pool of £459.18 - 4.61 winning units..
Owner Bernard Kantor **Bred** Wentworth Racing Pty Ltd **Trained** Newmarket, Suffolk

FOCUS
A very moderate 3-y-o maiden and this lot had run 73 times between them without success. The winner was around a stone off the form he showed on his debut a year ago. Perhaps not surprisingly, the winning time was the slowest of the fives races over the trip at the meeting.
Hold The Star Official explanation: jockey said filly suffered interference leaving stalls

7354 HOSPITALITY AT SOUTHWELL RACECOURSE H'CAP 1m 4f (F)
3:20 (3:20) (Class 6) (0-55,55) 3-Y-O+ £2,047 (£604; £302) Stalls Low

Form RPR
0540 1 **Swords**[56] 6025 7-8-13 48 FergusSweeney 6 61+
(R E Peacock) *hld up towards rr: smooth hdwy 5f out and sn trcking ldrs: led 3f out: rdn clr wl over 1f out: drvn ins fnl f and kpt on* **8/1**[3]
2000 2 1 3/4 **Jackie Kiely**[94] 4857 8-9-0 49 (tp) PhillipMakin 7 59+
(R Brotherton) *hld up towards rr: hdwy into midfield 5f out: trckd ldrs wl over 2f out: rdn to chse wnr over 1f out: drvn ins fnl f: no imp towards fin* **11/1**
1046 3 3 **Iguacu**[15] 7127 5-8-11 51 MatthewDavies(5) 9 56
(George Baker) *hld up and bhd: stdy hdwy 5f out: chsd ldrs 3f out: rdn along over 2f out: drvn over 1f out: styd on ins fnl f: nrst fin* **17/2**
0500 4 1 1/4 **Flying Squad (UAE)**[73] 5532 5-9-6 55 (t) AndrewMullen 13 58
(M F Harris) *trckd ldrs: hdwy 1/2-way: led over 4f out: rdn along and hdd 3f out: drvn 2f out and one pce appr fnl f* **11/2**[1]
0504 5 2 1/2 **Sir Haydn**[7] 7250 9-8-7 49 (v) DannyBrock(7) 14 48
(J R Jenkins) *in tch: hdwy to trck ldrs 1/2-way: effrt 4f out: rdn along to chse ldngpair 3f out: drvn over 2f out and grad wknd* **10/1**
-060 6 2 **Royal Rainbow**[10] 7214 5-8-13 48 ChrisCatlin 5 44
(P W Hiatt) *towards rr: pushed along and hdwy over 3f out: rdn 2f out: kpt on appr last: nvr nr ldrs* **25/1**
0-30 7 3 **Bourn Fair**[14] 7143 3-8-11 52 LukeMorris 11 43
(P J McBride) *rrd at s: sn pushed along to chse ldrs: rdn 5f out: drvn over 3f out and plugged on same pce* **12/1**
300 8 3/4 **Tar (IRE)**[14] 7142 5-8-11 51 (v) MarkCoumbe(5) 10 41
(John A Harris) *t.k.h: cl up: effrt 4f out: rdn along over 3f out: sn drvn and wknd over 2f out* **18/1**
00/0 9 2 **Sonic Anthem (USA)**[19] 4893 7-9-3 52 LeeVickers 12 39
(B D Leavy) *hld up in rr: hdwy on outer 1/2-way: chsd ldrs 5f out: sn rdn and wknd over 3f out* **8/1**[3]
4555 10 1 3/4 **Bernabeu (IRE)**[21] 6969 7-9-3 52 PaulDoe 8 36
(S Curran) *prom: led after 4f: rdn along and hdd over 4f out: drvn over 3f out and sn wknd* **13/2**[2]
0000 11 12 **Prince Rhyddarch**[55] 6053 4-9-4 53 PJMcDonald 1 18
(I Semple) *rdn along to ld early: hdd after 4f: rdn along on inner 1/2-way: sn lost pl and bhd fnl 4f* **8/1**[3]
0206 12 67 **Royal Premier (IRE)**[58] 5975 6-9-4 53 (v) DarryllHolland 2 —
(H J Collingridge) *rdn along sn after s and nt hold position: sn towards rr: wl bhd fnl 3f* **25/1**
1506 13 9 **Seminal Moment**[19] 7025 3-9-0 55 J-PGuillambert 4 —
(J G Given) *a towards rr: wl bhd fnl 3f* **12/1**

2m 38.04s (-2.96) **Going Correction** -0.25s/f (Stan)
WFA 3 from 4yo+ 6lb **13** Ran SP% **118.3**
Speed ratings (Par 101): **99,97,95,95,93 92,90,89,88,87 79,34,28**
toteswingers: 1&2 £22.00, 1&3 £11.70, 2&3 £20.50 CSF £92.22 CT £766.61 TOTE £9.40: £2.90, £4.10, £2.60; EX 80.90 TRIFECTA Not won..
Owner R E Peacock **Bred** Mrs A Yearley **Trained** Kyre Park, Worcs

FOCUS
A modest handicap, but a competitive one and the pace was solid with several having a go at leading at various stages. The form looks sound with the third probably the best guide.
Royal Rainbow Official explanation: jockey said gelding did not face the kickback
Seminal Moment Official explanation: jockey said filly lost its action

7355 BOOK ONLINE AT SOUTHWELL-RACECOURSE.CO.UK H'CAP 5f (F)
3:50 (3:51) (Class 5) (0-75,72) 3-Y-O+ £4,921 (£1,464; £731; £365) Stalls High

Form RPR
0200 1 **Bel Cantor**[21] 6964 6-8-13 72 PaulPickard(5) 10 85
(W J H Ratcliffe) *prom: effrt 2f out: rdn to ld ent fnl f: kpt on wl* **9/2**[2]
4540 2 1 1/2 **Restless Genius (IRE)**[29] 6776 4-8-10 64 PJMcDonald 1 71
(B Ellison) *a cl up: rdn wl over 1f out and ev ch tl drvn and nt qckn ins fnl f* **17/2**
2641 3 shd **Onceaponatime (IRE)**[12] 7191 4-9-1 69 LukeMorris 8 76
(M D Squance) *in tch: hdwy 2f out: sn rdn and styd on ins fnl f* **14/1**
0054 4 3/4 **Cape Royal**[9] 7223 9-8-6 67 (bt) RyanClark(7) 12 71
(J M Bradley) *cl up: led after 2f: rdn along wl over 1f out: drvn and edgd rt ent fnl f: sn hdd & wknd* **28/1**
0051 5 hd **Lithaam (IRE)**[14] 7136 5-8-10 67 (p) JackDean(3) 13 71
(J M Bradley) *trckd ldrs: hdwy 2f out: rdn and edgd lft over 1f out: drvn and one pce ins fnl f* **20/1**

5044 **6** *2 ½* **Under Review (IRE)**[20] 6988 3-8-11 **65**........................(b[1]) PhillipMakin 4 60
(T D Barron) *dwlt: hdwy to trck ldrs 1/2-way: swtchd lft and effrt 2f out: sn rdn and hung lft over 1f out: no imp after* **5/2**[1]

3303 **7** *hd* **Musical Bridge**[20] 6988 3-9-0 **68**........................ JoeFanning 7 62
(Mrs L Williamson) *wnt lft s: sn chsng ldrs: rdn along 2f out and grad wknd* **14/1**

6100 **8** *¾* **Guto**[28] 6791 6-9-4 **72**........................ StephenDonohoe 5 63
(W J H Ratcliffe) *led 2f out: cl up tl rdn along 2f out and grad wknd* **16/1**

4030 **9** *hd* **Chosen Son (IRE)**[9] 7224 3-8-8 **62**........................(t) DarryllHolland 2 52
(P J O'Gorman) *prom: rdn along 2f out: sn drvn and wknd over 1f out* **12/1**

4013 **10** *nk* **Silk Gallery (USA)**[8] 7241 4-8-6 **60** ow2........................(t) GrahamGibbons 11 49
(E J Alston) *a towards rr* **12/1**

000 **11** *¾* **Angelo Poliziano**[6] 7273 3-8-13 **70**........................(v) JackMitchell[(3)] 9 57
(Mrs A Duffield) *a towards rr* **20/1**

2030 **12** *½* **Tartatartufata**[6] 7269 7-9-4 **72**........................(v) J-PGuillambert 6 57
(J G Given) *bmpd and dwlt s: a in rr* **16/1**

0200 **13** *¾* **Loose Caboose (IRE)**[6] 7273 4-9-2 **70**........................(p) AndrewMullen 3 52
(A J McCabe) *dwlt: a in rr* **15/2**[3]

0342 **14** *1* **Chosen One (IRE)**[16] 7081 4-8-8 **62**........................ TomEaves 14 41
(B Smart) *racd stands' rail: a in rr* **16/1**

59.37 secs (-0.33) **Going Correction** +0.025s/f (Slow) **14** Ran SP% **128.4**
Speed ratings (Par 103): **103,100,100,99,98 94,94,93,93,92 91,90,89,87**
toteswingers: 1&2 £15.40, 1&3 £26.30, 2&3 £25.10 CSF £44.67 CT £532.14 TOTE £6.70: £2.90, £3.40, £5.70; EX 73.50 TRIFECTA Not won. Place 6: £49.08 Place 5: £16.35.
Owner W J H Ratcliffe **Bred** Henry And Mrs Rosemary Moszkowicz **Trained** Newmarket, Suffolk

FOCUS
A very competitive sprint handicap dominated by those who raced up the centre and as is usually the case over this straight 5f, the ability to lay up proved crucial. The form is sound, with the winner rated in line with this year's turf best.
Under Review(IRE) Official explanation: jockey said gelding hung left
T/Plt: £106.20 to a £1 stake. Pool: £39,656.96. 272.40 winning tickets. T/Qpdt: £8.20 to a £1 stake. Pool: £4,016.94. 358.70 winning tickets. JR

7317 WOLVERHAMPTON (A.W) (L-H)
Thursday, November 12

OFFICIAL GOING: Standard
Wind: Moderate half-behind Weather: Raining after 5.20

7356 BET PREMIER LEAGUE FOOTBALL - BETDAQ H'CAP 7f 32y(P)
4:20 (4:20) (Class 4) (0-85,85) 3-Y-O **£5,180** (£1,541; £770; £384) **Stalls** High

Form RPR

2600 **1** **The Kyllachy Kid**[5] 7287 3-9-4 **85**........................ IanMongan 2 93
(S Gollings) *sn chsng ldr: led over 2f out: rdn wl over 1f out: hld on wl u.p ins fnl f* **16/1**

1406 **2** *¾* **Labisa (IRE)**[13] 7158 3-8-4 **71**........................ JimmyQuinn 11 77+
(H Morrison) *s.i.s: hld up in rr: nt clr run on ins over 2f out: rdn and hdwy over 1f out: hrd rdn and kpt on ins fnl f* **14/1**

1-03 **3** *shd* **Emeebee**[12] 7189 3-8-7 **74**........................ TonyCulhane 4 80
(W J Musson) *a.p: pressed wnr 2f out: rdn over 1f out: kpt on ins fnl f* **9/2**[2]

4040 **4** *shd* **Seek The Fair Land**[12] 7189 3-8-7 **74**........................ ShaneKelly 10 80
(J R Boyle) *hld up in tch: rdn 2f out: kpt on ins fnl f* **11/1**

6025 **5** *1 ¼* **Kersivay**[17] 7057 3-8-5 **72**........................ FrancisNorton 5 74+
(Ollie Pears) *hld up and bhd: nt clr run and swtchd rt wl over 1f out: styd on fnl f: nt rch ldrs* **8/1**

2-16 **6** *shd* **Bawaardi (IRE)**[31] 6731 3-8-6 **73**........................ SaleemGolam 9 75
(R A Fahey) *hld up in mid-div: pushed along over 3f out: hdwy wl over 1f out: rdn and nt qckn ins fnl f* **16/1**

0060 **7** *nk* **Nora Mae (IRE)**[35] 6618 3-8-11 **78**........................ LPKeniry 12 79
(S Kirk) *hld up and bhd: hdwy 2f out: c wd st: rdn over 1f out: kpt on same pce ins fnl f* **25/1**

0320 **8** *6* **Desert Falls**[64] 5774 3-8-8 **78**........................ MichaelJStainton[(3)] 8 63
(R M Whitaker) *t.k.h in tch: pushed along over 2f out: rdn and wknd over 1f out* **20/1**

1031 **9** *3 ½* **Getcarter**[52] 6167 3-8-13 **80**........................ JimmyFortune 1 56
(R Hannon) *hld up in tch: pushed along and lost pl over 2f out: rdn and wknd over 1f out* **5/2**[1]

2523 **10** *1 ¾* **Jewelled**[24] 6909 3-7-11 **71** oh1........................ AmyScott[(7)] 6 42
(J W Hills) *hld up and bhd: hdwy on outside over 3f out: rdn and c wd bnd over 2f out: wknd wl over 1f out* **9/1**

6510 **11** *1* **Liberty Trail (IRE)**[12] 7172 3-8-5 **72**........................ DuranFentiman 3 40
(I Semple) *led: pushed along and hdd over 2f out: sn rdn: wknd over 1f out* **33/1**

512 **12** *17* **Dance And Dance (IRE)**[19] 7027 3-8-11 **85**........................ TobyAtkinson[(7)] 7 7+
(E F Vaughan) *s.i.s and awkward s: sn lost tch: t.o* **13/2**[3]

1m 30.2s (0.60) **Going Correction** +0.175s/f (Slow) **12** Ran SP% **119.5**
Speed ratings (Par 104): **103,102,102,101,100 100,100,93,89,87 86,66**
toteswingers: 1&2 £39.80, 1&3 £18.50, 2&3 £22.50 CSF £218.37 CT £1203.04 TOTE £25.30: £5.40, £5.00, £1.70; EX 249.80.
Owner P J Martin **Bred** Conor J C Parsons & Brian M Parsons **Trained** Scamblesby, Lincs

FOCUS
A very tight handicap on paper but it was steadily run and the form is perhaps not the most solid. The winer ran a length personal best.
Jewelled Official explanation: jockey said filly hung right-handed
Dance And Dance(IRE) Official explanation: jockey said he lost an iron at start

7357 STAY AT THE WOLVERHAMPTON HOLIDAY INN H'CAP 1m 5f 194y(P)
4:50 (4:50) (Class 5) (0-75,72) 3-Y-O+ **£3,238** (£963; £481; £240) **Stalls** Low

Form RPR

401 **1** **Nakoma (IRE)**[30] 6768 7-9-2 **60**........................ DaneO'Neill 5 68+
(B Ellison) *hld up: stdy prog over 4f out: pushed along over 3f out: rdn wl over 1f out: led jst ins fnl f: drvn out* **8/1**

0202 **2** *1 ¼* **Quince (IRE)**[35] 6612 6-9-10 **68**........................(v) SaleemGolam 7 72
(J Pearce) *hld up in rr: pushed along over 3f out: hdwy 2f out: rdn jst over 1f out: styd on to take 2nd nr fin* **15/2**

5425 **3** *hd* **Summer Lodge**[31] 6724 6-10-0 **72**........................ AdamKirby 4 76
(J A Glover) *t.k.h: hld up in tch: wnt 2nd over 3f out: rdn to ld wl over 1f out: hdd jst ins fnl f: no ex and lost 2nd nr fin* **7/2**[2]

4651 **4** *2 ¼* **Bell Island**[32] 6704 5-9-12 **70**........................(v) SebSanders 3 71
(Lady Herries) *sn chsng ldr: led over 4f out: pushed along and hdd wl over 1f out: sn rdn and carried hd sltly high: wknd wl ins fnl f* **6/4**[1]

0332 **5** *6* **Capable Guest (IRE)**[6] 7279 7-9-9 **67**........................ TonyCulhane 6 59
(M R Channon) *led: hdd over 4f out: rdn over 2f out: wknd over 1f out* **9/2**[3]

4310 **6** *6* **Sphere (IRE)**[26] 6845 4-8-12 **56**........................(p) SJCraine 1 40
(J Mackie) *prom: pushed along over 3f out: rdn and wknd over 2f out* **12/1**

00 **7** *50* **Illicit**[13] 7153 4-9-8 **66**........................(t) JerryO'Dwyer 2 —
(J R Holt) *hld up: hrd rdn over 3f out: sn struggling: t.o whn eased fnl 2f* **20/1**

3m 10.42s (4.42) **Going Correction** +0.175s/f (Slow) **7** Ran SP% **115.7**
Speed ratings (Par 103): **94,93,93,91,88 85,56**
toteswingers: 1&2 £12.10, 1&3 £3.40, 2&3 £5.40 CSF £66.04 TOTE £9.20: £3.30, £3.40; EX 71.20.
Owner Racing Management & Training, K & BGM **Bred** John Davison **Trained** Norton, N Yorks

FOCUS
This was slowly run and the form is weak and a bit muddling, with the favourite disappointing. The winner was value for a bit extra.

7358 WOLVERHAMPTON HOSPITALITY - A PLEASURE CLAIMING STKS 5f 216y(P)
5:20 (5:21) (Class 6) 3-Y-O+ **£2,388** (£705; £352) **Stalls** Low

Form RPR

4003 **1** **Ebraam (USA)**[9] 7227 6-9-2 **95**........................ AndrewHeffernan[(5)] 7 103
(P Howling) *w ldrs: led over 4f out: clr whn rdn over 1f out: pushed out fnl f* **1/3**[1]

0302 **2** *8* **Thunder Bay**[17] 7053 4-8-6 **57**........................ JimmyQuinn 5 62
(R A Fahey) *led over 1f: chsd wnr: rdn and btn over 1f out* **7/1**[2]

060 **3** *5* **Trimlestown (IRE)**[3] 7321 6-8-9 **68**........................(v[1]) SamHitchcott 11 49
(P D Evans) *broke wl: stdd and hld up towards rr: pushed along and prog 2f out: wnt 3rd over 1f out: no imp on ldng pair* **12/1**[3]

4 *2 ½* **Rainbow Above You (IRE)**[181] 2062 3-8-4 **52**........(p) FrancisNorton 10 36
(Noel Lawlor, Ire) *hld up in tch: outpcd by ldng pair over 2f out: wknd over 1f out* **66/1**

4200 **5** *shd* **One More Round (USA)**[14] 7129 11-8-1 **55**........(b) KevinLundie[(7)] 12 40
(P D Evans) *hld up in rr: reminder wl over 1f out: nvr nr ldrs* **33/1**

0060 **6** *5* **Mr Funshine**[160] 2682 4-8-6 **47** ow1........................ WilliamCarson[(3)] 4 25
(R J Hodges) *w ldr over 1f: prom tl outpcd over 2f out: rdn wl over 1f out: sn wknd* **150/1**

2450 **7** *nk* **Steel Blue**[42] 6413 9-8-6 **48**........................(p) MichaelJStainton[(3)] 9 24
(R M Whitaker) *hld up in tch: wknd over 2f out* **40/1**

2120 **8** *8* **Equinine (IRE)**[47] 6294 3-8-9 **70**........................ LPKeniry 1 —
(Peter Grayson) *a in rr: rdn and no ch over 1f out* **14/1**

1m 15.06s (0.06) **Going Correction** +0.175s/f (Slow) **8** Ran SP% **109.4**
Speed ratings (Par 101): **106,95,88,85,85 78,78,67**
toteswingers: 1&2 £1.90, 1&3 £2.20, 2&3 £4.10 CSF £2.61 TOTE £1.40: £1.02, £1.60, £2.90; EX 3.50.Ebraam was claimed by M Murphy for £18,000
Owner The Circle Bloodstock I Limited **Bred** Shadwell Farm LLC **Trained** Newmarket, Suffolk

FOCUS
The official ratings and the betting were clear indicators that this would be an uncompetitive claimer and so it proved. Only the front pair showed their form.
Equinine(IRE) Official explanation: jockey said filly never travelled

7359 BET ASIAN H'CAPS - BETDAQ NURSERY 1m 141y(P)
5:50 (5:50) (Class 5) (0-75,74) 2-Y-O **£3,238** (£963; £481; £240) **Stalls** Low

Form RPR

5001 **1** **Nafura**[20] 7003 2-9-7 **74**........................(p) TedDurcan 6 86+
(Saeed Bin Suroor) *hld up in tch: led wl over 1f out: sn edgd lft: shkn up and clr jst ins fnl f: eased cl home* **10/11**[1]

442 **2** *2 ½* **Duty And Destiny (IRE)**[45] 6331 2-9-5 **72**........................ ShaneKelly 8 77
(B J Meehan) *hld up and bhd: hdwy and edgd lft jst over 2f out: rdn over 1f out: wnt 2nd ins fnl f: nt trble wnr* **10/1**

5061 **3** *3* **House Red (IRE)**[17] 7055 2-9-2 **69**........................ RobertWinston 4 67
(B W Hills) *led early: a.p: pushed along to ld over 2f out: hdd wl over 1f out: sn rdn and swtchd rt: sn btn* **8/1**[3]

5450 **4** *shd* **Sounds Of Thunder**[28] 6793 2-8-13 **66**........................ JimmyQuinn 1 64
(H J L Dunlop) *s.i.s: hld up in rr: nt clr run and swtchd rt whn n.m.r jst over 2f out: prog wl over 1f out: sn rdn: kpt on same pce ins fnl f* **12/1**

5362 **5** *5* **If I Were A Boy (IRE)**[20] 7003 2-9-7 **74**........................ GeorgeBaker 5 62
(S Kirk) *sn prom: nt clr run and squeezed through jst over 2f out: rdn and wknd wl over 1f out* **9/2**[2]

0056 **6** *9* **Emma Dora (IRE)**[16] 7097 2-8-1 **57**........................ AndreaAtzeni[(3)] 9 26
(D R C Elsworth) *hld up and bhd: pushed along over 3f out: rdn and hdwy on outside over 2f out: wknd wl over 1f out* **40/1**

2043 **7** *22* **Merchant Of Medici**[12] 7193 2-9-7 **74**........................(b) SebSanders 2 —
(W R Muir) *t.k.h: led over 7f out: pushed along and hdd over 2f out: sn wknd and hmpd on ins: eased whn no ch over 1f out* **12/1**

2560 **8** *2 ¾* **Pastello**[28] 6793 2-9-3 **70**........................ JimmyFortune 3 —
(R Hannon) *led briefly sn after s: chsd ldr: fading whn hmpd over 2f out: sn bhd: eased whn no ch over 1f out* **20/1**

1m 50.59s (0.09) **Going Correction** +0.175s/f (Slow) **8** Ran SP% **113.4**
Speed ratings (Par 96): **106,104,101,101,97 89,69,67**
toteswingers: 1&2 £1.70, 1&3 £3.80, 2&3 £14.10 CSF £11.02 CT £46.52 TOTE £1.80: £1.20, £1.50, £2.50; EX 10.00.
Owner Godolphin **Bred** Darley **Trained** Newmarket, Suffolk

NOTEBOOK
Nafura, whose improvement when winning here 20 days ago was attributed to the surface, plus the application of cheekpieces, was 9lb higher here but won with plenty in hand once her mind had been made up on the home turn. She looks a cut above the winter norm. (tchd evens in places)
Duty And Destiny(IRE) come out of this handicap debut with plenty of credit. Rated 72 and having her first run since finishing second in a fair Bath maiden 45 days earlier, she still showed signs of immaturity but kept on despite the lost cause. There will be much easier tasks than this throughout the winter, particularly if she goes up in distance - her pedigree is all stamina. (op 8-1)
House Red(IRE) had no excuse. This was a better race than he won and over at least a furlong longer. He will be wiser for this first run on Polytrack and despite being 7lb higher for a half-length win 17 days ago, he can still make his mark. (op 11-1)
Sounds Of Thunder did okay on his Polytrack debut and might be worth a try over a bit further. (op 14-1)
If I Were A Boy(IRE) had a 9lb pull with the winner for being beaten four and a half lengths when they met here 20 days ago, but had no chance to exploit it after getting caught behind weakening horses on the home turn and losing a good rails position. This should be forgotten. (op 5-1)

Merchant Of Medici finished well adrift but may have had a slipping saddle. (op 11-1)

7360 GREAT OFFERS AT WOLVERHAMPTON-RACECOURSE.CO.UK H'CAP 1m 1f 103y(P)

6:20 (6:20) (Class 4) (0-85,85) 3-Y-O+ **£5,180** (£1,541; £770; £384) **Stalls** Low

Form RPR

3023 **1** **Snow Dancer (IRE)**[26] 6860 5-7-12 **70** oh2 JamesPSullivan(7) 2 76
(H A McWilliams) *hld up: hdwy over 2f out: pushed along over 1f out: led jst ins fnl f: pushed out* **16/1**

1 **2** 3/4 **Naseehah (USA)**[12] 7195 3-9-3 **85** TedDurcan 6 90+
(Saeed Bin Suroor) *sn chsng ldr: led 2f out: sn rdn: hdd jst ins fnl f: nt qckn towards fin* **8/13**[1]

5430 **3** 2 1/4 **Barliffey (IRE)**[54] 6117 4-8-6 **71** (v) JimmyQuinn 3 71
(D J Coakley) *dwlt: hld up in rr: hdwy wl over 1f out: sn rdn: kpt on to take 3rd wl ins fnl f* **5/1**[2]

24 **4** 2 1/4 **Thunderball**[21] 6973 3-8-12 **80** ChrisCatlin 9 75
(J A Glover) *hld up in tch: jnd ldrs over 2f out: rdn and wknd ins fnl f* **8/1**[3]

5006 **5** 3/4 **Just Bond (IRE)**[12] 7194 7-8-11 **81** SladeO'Hara(5) 5 75
(G R Oldroyd) *hld up: shkn up wl over 1f out: rdn ins fnl f: nvr trbld ldrs* **10/1**

020- **6** 1 1/4 **Wikaala (USA)**[29] 6196 4-8-7 **72** (b) LPKeniry 1 63
(Gordon Elliott, Ire) *led: pushed along and hdd 2f out: rdn over 1f out: wknd ins fnl f* **16/1**

1003 **7** 13 **Becuille (IRE)**[34] 6640 4-8-7 **72** (b) ShaneKelly 4 36
(B J Meehan) *prom tl rdn and wknd 2f out: eased whn no ch fnl f* **16/1**

2m 2.36s (0.66) **Going Correction** +0.175s/f (Slow)
WFA 3 from 4yo+ 3lb 7 Ran SP% **116.4**
Speed ratings (Par 105): **104,103,101,99,98 97,86**
toteswingers: 1&2 £3.00, 1&3 £7.90, 2&3 £2.10 CSF £27.54 CT £65.35 TOTE £13.50: £4.90, £1.10; EX 29.60.
Owner Mrs L Wohlers **Bred** Liam Queally **Trained** Cockerham, Co Durham

FOCUS
A slowly run race and muddling form. A personal best from the winner judged through the third and fifth.

7361 BETDAQ ON 0870 178 1221 MEDIAN AUCTION MAIDEN STKS 1m 1f 103y(P)

6:50 (6:51) (Class 6) 3-4-Y-O **£2,388** (£705; £352) **Stalls** Low

Form RPR

3402 **1** **Oriental Cavalier**[12] 7195 3-9-3 70 (p) GrahamGibbons 3 63
(R Hollinshead) *led early: w ldr: led 6f out: rdn over 2f out: drvn out* **8/11**[1]

0040 **2** 1/2 **Kool Katie**[12] 7174 4-9-1 53 SebSanders 7 57
(Mrs G S Rees) *hld up in tch: wnt 2nd wl over 2f out: chal wl over 1f out: sn rdn: nt qckn ins fnl f* **11/2**[2]

3000 **3** 2 1/4 **Interchoice Star**[12] 7195 4-9-3 48 RussellKennemore(3) 11 57
(R Hollinshead) *hld up towards rr: hdwy over 2f out: wnt 3rd and rdn wl over 1f out: one pce whn edgd rt ins fnl f* **20/1**

0600 **4** 6 **Katie Girl**[37] 6559 3-8-12 40 (p) JimmyQuinn 9 39
(Mrs G S Rees) *hld up in mid-div: hdwy on wd outside over 2f out: rdn and btn over 1f out* **33/1**

3404 **5** 1 1/4 **Mile High Lad (USA)**[16] 7094 3-8-12 68 (p) MatthewDavies(5) 8 42
(George Baker) *hld up towards rr: hdwy whn n.m.r and squeezed through over 2f out: rdn wl over 1f out: wknd ins fnl f* **17/2**

00- **6** 7 **Arch Event**[381] 7026 4-9-1 0 ShaneKelly 6 22
(A W Carroll) *hld up in tch: pushed along whn n.m.r briefly over 2f out: wknd wl over 1f out* **50/1**

500 **7** 3 **Silvertown Boy**[66] 5731 3-8-12 40 (p) SladeO'Hara(5) 10 21
(H A McWilliams) *hld up in tch: pushed along and wknd jst over 2f out* **100/1**

8 1/2 **Beyond Atlow** 4-9-1 0 AndrewHeffernan(5) 5 20
(Lucinda Featherstone) *s.s: towards rr: rdn over 2f out: no rspnse* **40/1**

6-00 **9** hd **Franchesca's Gold**[14] 7129 3-8-12 45 LPKeniry 13 14
(Jane Southcombe) *in rr: rdn and struggling over 2f out* **66/1**

10 6 **Latin Connection (IRE)**[5] 7301 3-9-3 0 SJCraine 4 7
(Lee Smyth, Ire) *prom tl rdn and wknd 2f out* **33/1**

00 **11** nse **Albiera (IRE)**[12] 7195 4-9-1 0 GeorgeBaker 1 2
(H Morrison) *hld up in mid-div: hmpd and lost pl over 2f out: sn bhd* **8/1**[3]

5 **12** 1/2 **Sleepy Dove**[88] 5072 4-9-1 0 PJMcDonald 2 1
(M E Sowersby) *sn led: hdd 6f out: w wnr tl rdn and wknd qckly over 2f out* **50/1**

2m 4.34s (2.64) **Going Correction** +0.175s/f (Slow)
WFA 3 from 4yo 3lb 12 Ran SP% **114.4**
Speed ratings (Par 101): **95,94,92,87,86 79,77,76,76,71 71,70**
toteswingers: 1&2 £2.00, 1&3 £6.30, 2&3 £12.40 CSF £4.04 TOTE £1.70: £1.10, £2.00, £4.40; EX 5.90 Place 6 £71.40, Place 5 £14.85.
Owner The Three R'S **Bred** Mrs Claire Massey **Trained** Upper Longdon, Staffs

FOCUS
A weak maiden. It was slowly run and the form is modest, with the winner not having to match his best.
Albiera(IRE) Official explanation: jockey said filly was denied a clear run
T/Plt: £42.10 to a £1 stake. Pool: £69,035.22. 1,195.77 winning tickets. T/Qpdt: £1.90 to a £1 stake. Pool: £9,758.83. 3,613.64 winning tickets. KH

[7250]LINGFIELD (L-H)

Friday, November 13

OFFICIAL GOING: Standard
Wind: very strong behind in relation to straight Weather: overcast with showers, some heavy

7362 BET GRAND SLAM DARTS - BETDAQ H'CAP (DIV I) 1m (P)

12:35 (12:36) (Class 5) (0-75,75) 3-Y-O+ **£2,388** (£705; £352) **Stalls** High

Form RPR

-002 **1** **Hurakan (IRE)**[23] 6940 3-9-0 **71** J-PGuillambert 7 78+
(P D Evans) *hld up: hdwy over 1f out: rdn and r.o strly ins fnl f: edgd lft: led nr fin* **11/4**[1]

1001 **2** 1/2 **Ensnare**[9] 7236 4-9-2 **71** 6ex StephenDonohoe 1 77+
(Ian Williams) *trckd ldrs: rdn to ld on farside rail ent fnl f: hdd nr fin* **3/1**[2]

5042 **3** nk **El Libertador (USA)**[14] 7149 3-8-11 **68** LiamJones 3 73
(E A Wheeler) *trckd ldrs: rdn over 2f out: ev ch ent fnl f: kpt on* **6/1**

0002 **4** 1 1/4 **Daniel Thomas (IRE)**[10] 7229 7-8-10 **65** (p) JimmyQuinn 10 67
(Mrs A L M King) *dwlt: last: rdn and hdwy ent fnl f: 1f out: kpt on wout threatening* **9/2**[3]

0602 **5** shd **Miss Eze**[14] 7158 3-9-3 **74** JimmyFortune 8 76
(M L W Bell) *trckd ldr: rdn and ev ch ent fnl f: kpt on same pce* **9/1**

5420 **6** 2 1/4 **Murrin (IRE)**[18] 7054 5-9-1 **70** (p) NCallan 5 66
(T G Mills) *s.i.s: in tch: rdn 2f out: one pce fnl f* **7/1**

0054 **7** 1 **Decameron (USA)**[10] 7229 4-9-4 **73** JoeFanning 4 67
(R A Harris) *led: rdn and hdd ent fnl f: fdd* **11/1**

1m 40.42s (2.22) **Going Correction** +0.25s/f (Slow)
WFA 3 from 4yo+ 2lb 7 Ran SP% **115.0**
Speed ratings (Par 103): **98,97,97,95,95 93,92**
toteswingers: 1&2 £2.40, 1&3 £7.00, 2&3 £8.50 CSF £11.41 CT £44.40 TOTE £4.80: £2.50, £1.80; EX 12.60 Trifecta £89.30 Pool: £294.74 - 2.44 winning units..
Owner J L Guillambert **Bred** Newberry Stud Company **Trained** Pandy, Monmouths

FOCUS
A modest handicap run at only a a steady pace. The third is probably the best guide to the form.

7363 BET MULTIPLES - BETDAQ NURSERY 7f (P)

1:05 (1:05) (Class 5) (0-75,75) 2-Y-O **£2,590** (£770; £385; £192) **Stalls** Low

Form RPR

402 **1** **Mirabella (IRE)**[15] 7135 2-9-6 **74** RyanMoore 5 83
(R Hannon) *mde all: hung to stands-side rails ent st: r.o: drvn out* **9/2**[2]

6510 **2** 3 1/4 **Be A Devil**[21] 7003 2-9-4 **72** NCallan 10 73
(W R Muir) *mid-div: rdn over 2f out: hdwy over 1f out: r.o to go 2nd ins fnl f: a being hld by wnr* **12/1**

0401 **3** 3/4 **Whistle Blower**[22] 6963 2-9-2 **70** JimmyFortune 4 69
(J H M Gosden) *trckd wnr: rdn 2f out: kpt on but a being hld by wnr: lost 2nd ins fnl f* **4/1**[1]

61 **4** 1 3/4 **Highland Quaich**[20] 7024 2-9-7 **75** DaneO'Neill 8 70
(D R C Elsworth) *trckd wnr: rdn 2f out: no ex ent fnl f* **11/2**[3]

0023 **5** 3/4 **Edward Whymper**[32] 6736 2-8-11 **65** JimmyQuinn 11 58
(M H Tompkins) *hld up: rdn 3f out: styd on fr over 1f out: nvr trbld ldrs* **11/1**

4300 **6** hd **Orsett Lad (USA)**[51] 6211 2-8-11 **65** RobertWinston 7 57
(J R Best) *hld up: rdn over 2f out: styd on fr over 1f out: nvr trbld ldrs* **33/1**

2323 **7** 1/2 **Pictures (IRE)**[17] 7097 2-9-6 **74** ChrisCatlin 6 65
(L M Cumani) *trckd ldrs: rdn 2f out: fdd ins fnl f* **9/2**[2]

4014 **8** 1 1/2 **Ice Cool Lady (IRE)**[57] 6035 2-9-4 **75** AndreaAtzeni(3) 3 62
(W R Swinburn) *nvr bttr than mid-div* **16/1**

025 **9** 1 1/2 **Posy Fossil (USA)**[37] 6582 2-8-10 **64** SteveDrowne 1 48
(S C Williams) *nvr bttr than mid-div* **14/1**

2605 **10** nk **Crushing (IRE)**[18] 7055 2-8-7 **61** JamesDoyle 13 44
(A J McCabe) *restrained sn after s: a towards rr* **11/1**

2044 **11** nk **Memory And Magic (USA)**[45] 6366 2-9-1 **69** AdamKirby 14 51
(C G Cox) *sn struggling in rr* **14/1**

0566 **12** 2 1/2 **Lofthouse**[37] 6586 2-8-8 **62** SamHitchcott 9 38
(M R Channon) *a towards rr* **50/1**

1m 25.65s (0.85) **Going Correction** +0.25s/f (Slow) 12 Ran SP% **120.2**
Speed ratings (Par 96): **105,101,100,98,97 97,96,95,93,93 92,89**
toteswingers: 1&2 £14.30, 1&3 £4.20, 2&3 £29.70 CSF £58.72 CT £241.05 TOTE £3.50: £2.30, £4.10, £2.00; EX 62.80 Trifecta £125.00 Part won. Pool: £169.02 - 0.90 winning units..
Owner The Royal Ascot Racing Club **Bred** Irish National Stud **Trained** East Everleigh, Wilts

FOCUS
A competitive nursery run at a fair pace and these 2-y-os certainly made full use of the whole width of the track. Those that raced handily held the edge and few ever really got into it.

NOTEBOOK
Mirabella(IRE) ◆ was making her nursery debut after chasing home a useful Godolphin prospect in a C&D maiden last time and utilised the same positive tactics here. Her rider quickened things from the front rounding the home turn and though she hung right over to the stands' rail - which is no bad thing here - she was always holding her rivals. Apparently held in some regard, she is likely to be put away now and there should be more to come from her next year. (op 4-1)
Be A Devil ◆, very disappointing at Wolverhampton last time having won a nursery at the same track off 5lb lower the time before, was never far away and came wide around the bend, but he finished strongly if unable to get anywhere near the winner. This was a return to form and he should be able to win off this mark. (tchd 14-1)
Whistle Blower, making his sand debut and raised 7lb for his victory in a Brighton nursery last month, was weak in the market earlier in the day though he was popular on-course. He had every chance and though he raced closer to the inside rail than the front pair in the home straight, he was far enough away from it for it not to have affected his performance. (op 6-1)
Highland Quaich, making his nursery debut after narrowly winning a Kempton maiden, was always in a good position and had every chance, but he lacked a turn of foot. A return to 1m looks to be in order and he still has scope for improvement. (op 5-1 tchd 9-2)
Edward Whymper ◆, placed in a couple of turf nurseries since a poor effort on his Polytrack debut, pulled very hard early and had a lot of ground to make up starting the turn for home. Wide around the final bend, he finished with a bit of a rattle and looks another that will appreciate a return to further. (op 14-1)
Orsett Lad(USA), dropped 8lb since his poor effort at Kempton last time, plugged on down the home straight but he lacks to scope of some of those in front of him.
Pictures(IRE), placed in all four of her previous starts in maiden and nursery company, was in a good position early and, considering that the other prominent racers all figured in the finish, it was disappointing to see her fade so tamely. (op 5-1)
Memory And Magic(USA) Official explanation: jockey said filly never travelled

7364 BET GRAND SLAM DARTS - BETDAQ H'CAP (DIV II) 1m (P)

1:35 (1:36) (Class 5) (0-75,75) 3-Y-O+ **£2,388** (£705; £352) **Stalls** High

Form RPR

0622 **1** **Spiritual Art**[18] 7065 3-9-0 **71** (p) PaulDoe 5 81
(L A Dace) *racd keenly in midfield: hdwy 2f out: r.o wl to ld ins fnl f: rdn out* **4/1**[1]

0026 **2** 1 1/2 **Shaded Edge**[22] 6976 5-9-0 **69** JamesDoyle 7 75
(D W P Arbuthnot) *cl up: jnd ldrs 2f out: rdn to ld jst ins fnl f: no ex whn hdd sn after* **9/2**[2]

2114 **3** shd **Dichoh**[22] 6967 6-9-6 **75** (v) AdamKirby 3 81
(M Madgwick) *hld up: hdwy to chse ldrs over 1f out: nt clrest of runs ins fnl f: swtchd rt: r.o towards fin* **11/2**

1400 **4** 1 1/4 **Ivory Lace**[32] 6726 8-9-1 **70** JimCrowley 10 73
(S Woodman) *sn restrained in rr: rdn 2f out: styd on fnl f: nrst fin* **16/1**

1044 **5** hd **Pha Mai Blue**[18] 7065 4-8-10 **65** SJCraine 6 67
(J R Boyle) *trckd ldr: led 2f out: sn rdn: hdd jst ins fnl f: fdd* **9/2**[2]

2163 **6** 1 3/4 **Astrodonna**[30] 6780 4-8-12 **72** AshleyMorgan(5) 4 70
(M H Tompkins) *mid-div: hdwy over 1f out: rdn and one pce fnl f* **10/1**

4-00 **7** nk **Straight And Level (CAN)**[256] 733 4-8-11 **66** FergusSweeney 1 63
(Miss Jo Crowley) *trckd ldrs: rdn and hung lft fr 2f out: one pce fnl f* **14/1**

6020 **8** 1 1/4 **Diamond Twister (USA)**[18] 7048 3-8-10 **67** (t) RobertWinston 2 61
(J R Best) *a towards rr* **5/1**[3]

0004 **9** *nk* **Highland River**[32] 6720 3-8-5 **62**........................ ChrisCatlin 9 56
(D R C Elsworth) *led tl 2f out: wknd fnl f* **14/1**

1m 39.12s (0.92) **Going Correction** +0.25s/f (Slow)
WFA 3 from 4yo+ 2lb **9** Ran SP% **116.7**
Speed ratings (Par 103): **105,103,103,102,101 100,99,98,98**
toteswingers: 1&2 £5.70, 1&3 £2.70, 2&3 £6.50 CSF £22.28 CT £100.32 TOTE £6.60: £1.50, £1.70, £2.00; EX 22.00 Trifecta £199.10 Part won. Pool: £269.07 - 0.95 winning units..
Owner Gerry Boyer & Mike Tokarski **Bred** R Haim **Trained** Five Oaks, W Sussex

FOCUS
A more solid gallop in this than in the first division and the winning time was 1.3 seconds faster. The winner produced a personal best, with the runner-up to form.

7365 EUROPEAN BREEDERS' FUND MAIDEN STKS 5f (P)
2:15 (2:15) (Class 5) 2-Y-O **£3,561** (£1,059; £529; £264) **Stalls** High

Form RPR
53 **1** **Memorandum**[23] 6932 2-8-12 0........................ SteveDrowne 6 75
(R Charlton) *chsd ldrs: rdn into narrow advantage jst ins fnl f: kpt on gamely: all out* **5/4**[1]

00 **2** *hd* **Youcanalwaysdream (IRE)**[11] 7213 2-8-12 0........................ NCallan 9 74
(K A Ryan) *mid-div: hdwy 2f out: sn rdn: str chal thrght fnl f: kpt on* **16/1**

56 **3** *shd* **Sakile**[127] 3772 2-8-12 0........................ JimmyFortune 10 74
(P W Chapple-Hyam) *chsd ldr: rdn to ld briefly ent fnl f: edgd sltly lft but remained w ev ch thrght: hld nr fin* **8/1**[3]

4200 **4** *3 ¼* **Bush Master**[30] 6774 2-9-3 72........................ SJCraine 4 67
(J R Boyle) *mid-div: effrt over 1f out: kpt on but nt pce to mount chal* **4/1**[2]

4 **5** *2* **Mosa Mine**[11] 7213 2-8-12 0........................ RobertWinston 8 55
(D H Brown) *led: rdn and hdd ent fnl f: sn squeezed out and fdd* **4/1**[2]

6 *½* **Cosimo de Medici** 2-9-3 0........................ RobertHavlin 5 58
(H Morrison) *s.i.s: sn outpcd: a in rr* **16/1**

0 **7** *3 ¾* **Sweet Pilgrim**[36] 6615 2-8-12 0........................ TPQueally 3 40
(M D I Usher) *chsd ldrs: effrt over 1f out: wknd fnl f* **25/1**

8 *2 ¾* **Avon Castle** 2-8-12 0........................ FergusSweeney 1 30
(G L Moore) *s.i.s: a outpcd in rr* **33/1**

0240 **9** *5* **Papageno**[25] 6903 2-9-3 64........................ JimCrowley 7 17
(J R Jenkins) *sn outpcd in rr* **20/1**

59.00 secs (0.20) **Going Correction** +0.25s/f (Slow) **9** Ran SP% **118.9**
Speed ratings (Par 96): **108,107,107,102,99 98,92,87,79**
toteswingers: 1&2 £9.50, 1&3 £3.80, 2&3 £6.20 CSF £25.44 TOTE £1.90: £1.10, £4.10, £2.30; EX 25.10 Trifecta £223.30 Pool: £531.14 - 1.76 winning units..
Owner K Abdulla **Bred** Juddmonte Farms Ltd **Trained** Beckhampton, Wilts

FOCUS
An ordinary maiden, though a thrilling finish and the front three pulled clear. All bar Sweet Pilgrim gave the inside rail a wide berth throughout.

NOTEBOOK
Memorandum ◆ has shown progressive form in a couple of Bath maidens and having been close to the pace from the start, she showed a commendable attitude to come out best in a three-way battle to the line. She still gives the impression that another furlong wouldn't come amiss and she should be able to hold her own in handicap company. (tchd 7-4)
Youcanalwaysdream(IRE) ◆, who had only beaten a total of two horses in her first two starts and was a long way behind Memorandum in the first of those, had nonetheless shown some ability. Tracking the leaders early, she had every chance a furlong from home and never stopped trying. There should be more to come from her now that she qualifies for nurseries. (op 33-1)
Sakile ◆, making her sand debut and racing for the firs time since a couple of modest efforts on turf in the summer, ran much better here. Having shown good early speed, she looked the likely winner when challenging down the outside once into the straight, but was just run out of it despite trying her hardest. Nurseries are now an option for her and she is worth keeping an eye on. (op 17-2)
Bush Master travelled well behind the leaders, but could only plug on in the home straight when asked for his effort. He has ability and has been placed a few times, but he has had a lot more chances than the front three. (op 3-1)
Mosa Mine, not for the first time, showed smart early speed but didn't get home. She is another that now qualifies for nurseries, but she is starting to look a short runner. (op 6-1)
Cosimo de Medici ◆ cost 70,000gns as a foal but was bought for just 800gns at the sales last month. A half-brother to three winners, he proved clueless early and was soon right out the back, but he made some late progress and, as the stable's youngsters often improve with racing, he is one to keep an eye on.
Avon Castle Official explanation: jockey said filly did not face the kickback

7366 EUROPEAN BREEDERS' FUND FILLIES' H'CAP 1m 2f (P)
2:50 (2:50) (Class 3) (0-90,90) 3-Y-O **£7,641** (£2,273; £1,136; £567) **Stalls** Low

Form RPR
2551 **1** **Tinshu (IRE)**[9] 7233 3-8-10 **82** 6ex........................ DaneO'Neill 2 90
(D Haydn Jones) *trckd ldrs: gd run on ins fnl bnd to ld sn after: swtchd off rails: r.o wl: rdn out* **5/1**[3]

0056 **2** *½* **Badiat Alzaman (IRE)**[58] 6003 3-9-2 **88**........................ GeorgeBaker 6 95+
(D M Simcock) *restrained s: hdwy on outside 2f out: sn rdn: r.o to chse wnr ins fnl f but a being hld* **6/1**

2131 **3** *2 ½* **Poyle Meg**[22] 6973 3-8-8 **80**........................(p) JimCrowley 8 82
(R M Beckett) *hld up in last pair: hdwy on outside over 2f out: rdn to chal over 1f out: kpt on same pce fnl f* **11/4**[1]

1304 **4** *2* **Stan's Cool Cat (IRE)**[48] 6286 3-8-11 **83**........................ NCallan 4 81
(P F I Cole) *trckd ldrs: rdn whn sltly outpcd 2f out: styd on fnl f* **12/1**

3164 **5** *1 ¾* **Critical Path (IRE)**[32] 6740 3-8-4 **76** oh2........................ ChrisCatlin 7 71
(A M Balding) *trckd ldrs: rdn to ld briefly over 1f out: wknd ins fnl f* **5/1**[3]

2500 **6** *2 ¼* **Accede**[15] 7132 3-9-4 **90**........................ TPQueally 5 80
(J G Portman) *pressed ldr after 3f: rdn over 2f out: wknd over 1f out* **16/1**

1056 **7** *1* **Crimson Ribbon (USA)**[15] 7131 3-9-0 **86**........................ JimmyFortune 3 74
(J H M Gosden) *led: rdn and hdd jst over 1f out: sn wknd* **3/1**[2]

2m 7.13s (0.53) **Going Correction** +0.25s/f (Slow) **7** Ran SP% **112.9**
Speed ratings (Par 103): **107,106,104,103,101 99,99**
toteswingers:1&2:£11.50, 2&3:£3.40, 1&3:£3.40 CSF £33.49 CT £97.40 TOTE £7.40: £2.50, £4.20; EX 69.60 Trifecta £185.00 Pool: £475.23 - 1.90 winning units..
Owner Llewelyn, Runeckles **Bred** Mrs M L Parry & P Steele-Mortimer **Trained** Efail Isaf, Rhondda C Taff

FOCUS
A decent fillies' handicap, but they went no pace early and the seven runners were still within a length or so of each other a furlong and a half from home. Despite the modest tempo, the pair that set the early gallop were the last two home. The progressive winner is rated up a further 4lb.

NOTEBOOK
Tinshu(IRE), carrying a 6lb penalty for her Kempton success nine days earlier, travelled well just behind the leaders and took advantage when an inviting gap appeared for her against the inside rail straightening up for home. Crucially she hung out towards the centre of the track once in front and that can only have helped her see her race out. (tchd 9-2 and 11-2)
Badiat Alzaman(IRE), not disgraced in a Yarmouth Listed race when last seen two months ago, was given a typical George Baker waiting ride. Racing beyond 7f for the first time on sand, she finished strongly down the wide outside but the winner had got first run on her. She has yet to conclusively prove that she stays this far, but she probably does get it and it's just a case of getting the timing right with her. (tchd 15-2)
Poyle Meg, raised 4lb for her narrow success at Kempton last month, just had to be niggled along off the pace half a mile from home, but she responded and was rushed four-wide to just about hit the front on the final bend. However, once there she couldn't see her race out. (op 5-2 tchd 3-1 in a place)
Stan's Cool Cat(IRE), a winner over this trip on turf but whose two previous tries on sand have been modest, showed up for a long way but she found very little once off the bridle inside the last 3f.
Critical Path(IRE), 2lb wrong, raced prominently early and had every chance a furlong from home, but she didn't get home. (op 7-1)
Crimson Ribbon(USA) stays further than this, so it was something of a surprise that her rider didn't set a stronger pace early and she was ultimately swamped off the final bend. (tchd 7-2)

7367 BETDAQ.CO.UK MAIDEN STKS 1m 4f (P)
3:25 (3:26) (Class 5) 3-Y-O+ **£2,729** (£806; £403) **Stalls** Low

Form RPR
00 **1** **Red Hot Desert**[22] 6974 3-9-3 0........................ GeorgeBaker 6 67+
(W R Swinburn) *in tch: shkn up to take clsr order 2f out: led over 1f out: styd on wl: rdn out* **12/1**

3-05 **2** *1 ½* **Starburst**[31] 6760 4-9-4 57........................ ChrisCatlin 11 58
(A M Balding) *hld up towards rr: rdn and hdwy fr 2f out: styd on wl fnl f: snatched 2nd nr fin* **11/2**[3]

2223 **3** *shd* **Kinetix**[53] 6166 3-8-12 71........................ JimmyFortune 5 58
(J H M Gosden) *led: rdn whn hung rt and hdd over 1f out: styd on same pce: lost 2nd nr fin* **5/4**[1]

3 **4** *½* **French Hollow**[10] 7221 4-9-9 0........................ NCallan 3 62
(T J Fitzgerald) *mid-div: rdn and hdwy 2f out to chse ldrs: kpt on same pce fnl f* **11/4**[2]

0 **5** *1* **Magistrate (IRE)**[34] 6673 4-9-4 0........................ SimonPearce(5) 10 60
(Andrew Turnell) *trckd ldr: rdn over 2f out: ev ch over 1f out: fdd ins fnl f* **10/1**

6 *1 ½* **Sure Fire (GER)**[25] 4-9-9 0........................ TPQueally 2 58+
(B J Curley) *dwlt: bhd: rdn 2f out: swtchd lft over 1f out: styd on past btn horses fnl f* **6/1**

00 **7** *½* **Supplementary (IRE)**[22] 6974 7-8-11 0........................ RichardRowe(7) 9 52?
(M J Coombe) *trckd ldrs: jnd ldr 7f out: rdn over 2f out: wknd jst over 1f out* **100/1**

00 **8** *1 ¼* **Dance Gdansk (IRE)**[44] 6375 3-9-3 0........................ SteveDrowne 7 55?
(M Blanshard) *mid-div: rdn 2f out: sn wknd* **50/1**

0 **9** *1 ¼* **Alfies Express**[13] 7195 5-9-9 0........................ DaneO'Neill 4 53?
(S Curran) *hld up towards rr: hdwy fr 3f out to chse ldrs 2f out: wknd ent fnl f* **33/1**

00 **10** *8* **Stardust Memories (UAE)**[29] 6794 3-8-12 0........................ RobertHavlin 1 35?
(John Berry) *in tch: rdn over 2f out: wknd over 1f out* **66/1**

0- **11** *33* **Brahms And Mist (FR)**[350] 7473 9-9-2 0........................ BillyCray(7) 8 —
(D J S Ffrench Davis) *a in rr: t.o fnl 2f* **100/1**

2m 37.62s (4.62) **Going Correction** +0.25s/f (Slow)
WFA 3 from 4yo+ 6lb **11** Ran SP% **125.9**
Speed ratings (Par 103): **94,93,92,92,91 90,90,89,88,83 62**
toteswingers:1&2:£7.60, 2&3:£3.90, 1&3:£5.20 CSF £81.06 TOTE £14.70: £2.90, £2.10, £1.10; EX 82.60 Trifecta £484.40 Pool: £752.80 - 1.15 winning units..
Owner Mrs Doreen M Swinburn **Bred** Genesis Green Stud Ltd **Trained** Aldbury, Herts

FOCUS
Not the most competitive of older-horse maidens and the pace was slow, but there were still a couple of eye-catching performances. The form is rated around the runner-up, fourth and fifth.
Brahms And Mist(FR) Official explanation: jockey said gelding never travelled

7368 ASHURST WOOD APPRENTICE H'CAP 1m 5f (P)
3:55 (3:56) (Class 5) (0-70,73) 3-Y-O+ **£2,729** (£806; £403) **Stalls** Low

Form RPR
443 **1** **Moonbeam Dancer (USA)**[46] 6332 3-9-0 **65**........................ DavidKenny 1 71
(D M Simcock) *trckd ldrs: led 2f out: sn rdn: all out to jst hold on* **4/1**[2]

3105 **2** *hd* **Ardmaddy (IRE)**[24] 6918 5-8-5 **56**........................(b) HarryBentley(7) 4 62+
(G L Moore) *hld up in tch: gng easily whn wnr wnr wnt clr ovr 1f out: pshd along to take 3l 2nd ins fnl f: clsd rpdly: too mch to do* **4/1**[2]

2631 **3** *3 ¼* **Resplendent Ace (IRE)**[7] 7272 5-10-1 **73** 6ex........................ LauraPike 5 74
(P Howling) *t.k.h: hld up: sddle slipped after 4f: jnd ldr sn after: ev ch 2f out: sn rdn: one pce* **11/4**[1]

64-0 **4** *hd* **Karashar (IRE)**[18] 7067 4-9-9 **70**........................ NathanAlison(3) 8 71
(Evan Williams) *plld hrd: trcking ldrs: rdn 2f out: sn one pce* **9/1**[3]

050 **5** *3 ¾* **Brave Mave**[73] 5545 4-9-7 **68**........................ RyanClark(3) 7 63
(Jane Chapple-Hyam) *hld up: rdn 2f out: little imp* **14/1**

5561 **6** *2 ¼* **Hucking Hero (IRE)**[15] 7137 4-9-1 **62**........................(p) AlexEdwards(3) 3 54
(J R Boyle) *racd keenly: set stdy pce: hdd 7f out: trckd ldrs: rdn wl over 1f out: sn wknd* **11/4**[1]

00P0 **7** *12* **Mixing**[33] 6704 7-8-12 **56** oh3........................ KierenFox 6 30
(M J Attwater) *t.k.h: trckd ldr: led 7f out tl 2f out: sn wknd* **25/1**

2m 51.34s (5.34) **Going Correction** +0.25s/f (Slow)
WFA 3 from 4yo+ 7lb **7** Ran SP% **113.8**
Speed ratings (Par 103): **93,92,90,90,88 87,79**
toteswingers:1&2:£4.50, 2&3:£2.80, 1&3:£2.90 CSF £20.10 CT £50.12 TOTE £5.20: £2.70, £2.70; EX 22.40 Trifecta £50.20 Pool: £528.50 - 7.78 winning units. Place 6 £47.68, Place 5 £31.21.
Owner Dr Ali Ridha **Bred** Swifty Farms Inc & Darley **Trained** Newmarket, Suffolk

FOCUS
A nonsense of a contest as nothing wanted to lead and a pedestrian gallop meant that most of these pulled their chances away early. The runner-up arguably should have won and the form looks weak and has been rated negatively.

T/Plt: £45.50 to a £1 stake. Pool: £50,546.97. 810.03 winning tickets. T/Qpdt: £11.10 to a £1 stake. Pool: £4,245.70. 280.65 winning tickets. TM

7356 WOLVERHAMPTON (A.W) (L-H)

Friday, November 13

OFFICIAL GOING: Standard

Wind: Strong, half-behind. Weather: Raining

7369 STAY AT THE WOLVERHAMPTON HOLIDAY INN CLASSIFIED STKS (DIV I) 1m 1f 103y(P)

5:50 (5:50) (Class 6) 3-Y-0+ **£1,706** (£503; £252) **Stalls** Low

Form RPR

260 **1** **Coolnaharan (IRE)**[13] 7174 9-9-1 54 ....(p) SebSanders 13 60
(Lee Smyth, Ire) *hld up in rr: stdy prog on outside 4f out: pushed along over 2f out: led wl over 1f out: sn rdn: edgd lft ins fnl f: r.o* **11/1**

000 **2** *1* **Great Bounder (CAN)**[14] 7153 3-8-12 55.......... TonyCulhane 8 58
(J R Best) *hld up in tch: rdn over 2f out: kpt on u.p to take 2nd cl home* **4/1**[1]

-060 **3** *shd* **Aspirational (IRE)**[17] 7085 3-8-12 53.......... LukeMorris 3 58
(B Palling) *sltly hmpd s: hld up towards rr: pushed along over 3f out: hdwy over 2f out: rdn wl over 1f out: styd on ins fnl f* **25/1**

6004 **4** *3/4* **Royal Keva (IRE)**[15] 7143 3-8-12 53..........(b[1]) JimmyQuinn 2 56
(A D Brown) *wnt rt s: led 1f: chsd ldr: led over 2f out: rdn and hdd wl over 1f out: no ex and lost 2 pls cl home* **9/2**[2]

0026 **5** *1 1/2* **Rebel Woman**[16] 7110 3-8-12 54.......... ShaneKelly 7 53
(J A Osborne) *hld up towards rr: hdwy over 2f out: rdn wl over 1f out: kpt on same pce fnl f* **5/1**[3]

6 *1/2* **Tabaahi (IRE)**[117] 4126 4-9-1 54..........(b) PaulHanagan 9 52
(Gordon Elliott, Ire) *hld up in tch: pushed along and outpcd over 2f out: rallied on ins wl over 1f out: sn rdn: no ex ins fnl f* **9/1**

6053 **7** *15* **Jobekani (IRE)**[21] 7004 3-8-12 54.......... TomEaves 1 20
(Mrs L Williamson) *hld up in mid-div: rdn and wknd over 2f out* **12/1**

0/ **8** *9* **Derby Desire (IRE)**[515] 3096 5-8-8 33..........(t) DebraEngland[(7)] 11 —
(D G Duggan) *led after 1f tl over 2f out: wknd wl over 1f out* **40/1**

0006 **9** *3* **Duke Of Normandy (IRE)**[15] 7142 3-8-12 52.......(tp) GrahamGibbons 5 —
(B P J Baugh) *hld up in mid-div: wknd wl over 3f out: eased whn no ch over 1f out* **14/1**

06-0 **10** *8* **Southoffrance (IRE)**[29] 6788 3-8-9 45..........(b) JackDean[(3)] 10 —
(W G M Turner) *wnt rt s: prom tl rdn and wknd over 3f out: eased whn no ch wl over 1f out* **66/1**

0060 **11** *1/2* **Luthien (IRE)**[22] 6967 3-8-12 50..........(p) LiamJones 4 —
(A M Hales) *bmpd s: hld up towards rr: pushed along 4f out: lost tch over 2f out: eased wl over 1f out* **33/1**

0/23 **12** *2* **Insomnitas**[29] 6800 4-9-1 50.......... JerryO'Dwyer 12 —
(Seamus Fahey, Ire) *s.i.s: sn swtchd lft: hld up in rr: t.o fnl 4f* **6/1**

13 *5* **Kathleen Cox (IRE)**[463] 4800 4-9-1 44.......... FrancisNorton 6 —
(Daniel Mark Loughnane, Ire) *prom tl wknd over 6f out: t.o fnl 4f* **33/1**

2m 4.46s (2.76) **Going Correction** +0.125s/f (Slow)
WFA 3 from 4yo+ 3lb **13 Ran SP% 115.5**
Speed ratings (Par 101): **92,91,91,90,89 88,75,67,64,57 57,55,50**
toteswingers: 1&2 £12.40, 1&3 £65.90, 2&3 £26.60. CSF £50.60 TOTE £13.20: £3.60, £1.50, £9.20; EX 82.90.
Owner Pircan Partnership **Bred** Noel Finegan **Trained** Dungannon, Co Tyrone

■ Stewards' Enquiry : Jimmy Quinn caution: used whip with excessive frequency.

FOCUS
A moderate contest run at a steady pace, and the time was 1.82 seconds slower than the second division, won by Sircozy. The form looks fairly sound, if pretty limited.
Insomnitas Official explanation: jockey said gelding never travelled

7370 BET CHELTENHAM OPEN MEETING - BETDAQ H'CAP (DIV I) 5f 216y(P)

6:20 (6:21) (Class 6) (0-55,56) 3-Y-0+ **£2,047** (£604; £302) **Stalls** Low

Form RPR

0035 **1** **Fantasy Fighter (IRE)**[18] 7068 4-8-11 **52**.......... JimmyQuinn 5 61
(J J Quinn) *hld up in mid-div: stdy prog on ins over 2f out: led ins fnl f: drvn out* **15/2**[3]

4046 **2** *1 1/4* **Ask Jenny (IRE)**[10] 7223 7-8-13 **54**.......... ShaneKelly 8 59
(Patrick Morris) *hld up towards rr: hdwy on outside over 2f out: c wd st: rdn and edgd lft ins fnl f: tk 2nd towards fin* **14/1**

443 **3** *1/2* **Kinigi (IRE)**[49] 6252 3-8-9 **55**..........(p) AndrewHeffernan[(5)] 2 58
(R A Harris) *a.p: led wl over 1f out: sn rdn and edgd lft: hdd ins fnl f: nt qckn* **12/1**

0300 **4** *1* **Only A Game (IRE)**[31] 6755 4-9-0 **55**..........(tp) AdamKirby 10 55+
(I W McInnes) *hld up in rr: pushed along and hdwy over 2f out: swtchd rt wl over 1f out: rdn and nt qckn wl ins fnl f* **12/1**

0000 **5** *2 3/4* **Cool Sands (IRE)**[72] 5576 7-9-0 **55**..........(v) SebSanders 1 46
(J G Given) *hld up towards rr: stdy prog on ins over 2f out: n.m.r briefly over 1f out: one pce fnl f* **14/1**

050 **6** *2 1/2* **Greek Secret**[29] 6799 6-9-0 **55**.......... TonyCulhane 6 38
(J O'Reilly) *hld up towards rr: nt clr run on ins over 2f out: hdwy over 1f out: nvr trbld ldrs* **25/1**

0613 **7** *1/2* **Briannsta (IRE)**[9] 7240 7-8-12 **53**..........(b) RichardThomas 7 34
(J E Long) *sn bhd: pushed along over 2f out: c wd st: rdn over 1f out: n.d* **7/2**[1]

-460 **8** *hd* **Lambrini Lace (IRE)**[21] 6989 4-8-11 **52**..........(v[1]) PaulHanagan 12 33
(Mrs L Williamson) *hld up in tch: wkng whn sltly hmpd 1f out* **12/1**

2420 **9** *3 1/2* **Avrilo**[18] 7068 3-8-13 **54**.......... TomEaves 11 24
(M S Saunders) *w ldrs: led over 3f out tl wl over 1f out: sn rdn: wknd fnl f* **16/1**

2450 **10** *1 1/2* **Cardinal**[31] 6755 4-9-0 **55**.......... LiamJones 3 20
(R A Harris) *sn led: hdd over 3f out: wknd over 1f out* **11/1**

0030 **11** *6* **Deo Valente (IRE)**[9] 7241 4-8-13 **54**..........(bt) LukeMorris 4 —
(J M Bradley) *prom: rdn over 3f out: sn wknd* **14/1**

0-02 **12** *3 1/2* **Bountiful Bay**[18] 7069 4-8-11 **52**.......... LPKeniry 13 —
(Matthew Salaman) *prom tl pushed along and wknd wl over 1f out* **14/1**

2005 **13** *7* **One More Round (USA)**[1] 7358 11-8-10 **56** ow1..(b) RichardEvans[(5)] 9 —
(P D Evans) *hld up in rr: pushed along 3f out: sn struggling* **9/2**[2]

1m 16.01s (1.01) **Going Correction** +0.125s/f (Slow) **13 Ran SP% 120.0**
Speed ratings (Par 101): **98,96,95,94,90 87,86,86,81,79 71,67,57**
toteswingers: 1&2 £16.80, 1&3 £11.30, 2&3 £36.00. CSF £108.66 CT £1299.51 TOTE £6.90: £2.40, £4.80, £4.90; EX 68.60.
Owner The Fantasy Fellowship F **Bred** T C Clarke **Trained** Settrington, N Yorks

FOCUS
A competitive sprint handicap for the level, although the time was 0.52 seconds slower than the second division, won by Nacho Libre. Straightforward form, with the winner back to something like her best.

7371 BET CHELTENHAM OPEN MEETING - BETDAQ H'CAP (DIV II) 5f 216y(P)

6:50 (6:51) (Class 6) (0-55,55) 3-Y-0+ **£2,047** (£604; £302) **Stalls** Low

Form RPR

0404 **1** **Nacho Libre**[21] 6984 4-8-13 **54**..........(b) SebSanders 9 67
(M W Easterby) *mde all: rdn over 1f out: drvn out* **5/1**[3]

3500 **2** *2 3/4* **Exceed Elegance (IRE)**[15] 7129 3-9-0 **55**..........(t) JoeFanning 11 59
(D Shaw) *hld up in mid-div: hdwy over 2f out: chsd wnr over 1f out: rdn and no imp fnl f* **25/1**

6530 **3** *1/2* **Sorrel Point**[17] 7100 6-9-0 **55**..........(v) JerryO'Dwyer 13 58
(H J Collingridge) *hld up towards rr: rdn and hdwy on outside over 1f out: kpt on ins fnl f* **40/1**

3020 **4** *2 1/2* **Miss Firefly**[37] 6587 4-8-10 **54**.......... WilliamCarson[(3)] 12 49
(R J Hodges) *s.i.s: hld up towards rr: r.o ins fnl f: tk 4th post* **15/2**

-003 **5** *shd* **Megalo Maniac**[18] 7068 6-9-0 **55**.......... PaulHanagan 7 49
(R A Fahey) *hld up in mid-div: hdwy over 2f out: rdn over 1f out: one pce ins fnl f* **4/1**[1]

6362 **6** *hd* **Welcome Approach**[43] 6433 6-8-13 **54**.......... DarryllHolland 2 48
(J R Weymes) *hld up in tch: swtchd rt over 1f out: rdn and one pce ins fnl f* **9/2**[2]

025 **7** *1 3/4* **Battimoore (IRE)**[43] 6433 3-8-10 **51**.......... ShaneKelly 8 39
(Daniel Mark Loughnane, Ire) *prom tl wknd ins fnl f* **20/1**

5100 **8** *nk* **Best One**[23] 6939 5-8-11 **52**..........(v) LiamJones 5 39
(R A Harris) *s.i.s: hld up towards rr: pushed along and no hdwy fnl 2f* **14/1**

0020 **9** *2* **Bertbrand**[9] 7241 4-9-0 **55**..........(e[1]) TomEaves 1 36
(I W McInnes) *prom tl rdn and wknd ins fnl f* **10/1**

0 **10** *2 1/4* **Catherine (IRE)**[1] 7349 3-8-7 **53**.......... AndrewHeffernan[(5)] 3 26
(Mark L Fagan, Ire) *sn chsng wnr: rdn and lost 2nd over 1f out: wknd ins fnl f* **20/1**

4 **11** *3/4* **Rainbow Above You (IRE)**[1] 7358 3-8-11 **52**..........(p) FrancisNorton 10 23
(Noel Lawlor, Ire) *dwlt: a in rr* **28/1**

164 **12** *hd* **Chantilly Jewel (USA)**[21] 7002 4-9-0 **55**..........(b) GrahamGibbons 6 25
(R M H Cowell) *hld up in mid-div: rdn and wknd over 2f out* **14/1**

0054 **13** *3* **Jilly Why (IRE)**[16] 7123 8-8-9 **55**..........(b) PaulPickard[(5)] 4 16
(Paul Green) *hld up towards rr: pushed along 4f out: struggling over 2f out* **6/1**

1m 15.49s (0.49) **Going Correction** +0.125s/f (Slow) **13 Ran SP% 122.6**
Speed ratings (Par 101): **101,97,96,93,93 92,90,90,87,84 83,83,79**
toteswingers: 1&2 £23.20, 1&3 £41.10, 2&3 £91.90. CSF £134.32 CT £2898.53 TOTE £5.00: £2.30, £8.10, £9.20; EX 138.10.
Owner Tri Nations Racing Syndicate **Bred** Lostford Manor Stud **Trained** Sheriff Hutton, N Yorks

FOCUS
The winning time was 0.52 seconds quicker than the first division. The winner has sipped a long way in the weights and it is hard to know what he is capable of these days. The next two were close to their best.

7372 NEW BROOM CLEANING SERVICES LTD MANCHESTER NURSERY 5f 20y(P)

7:20 (7:21) (Class 5) (0-75,73) 2-Y-0 **£3,238** (£963; £481; £240) **Stalls** Low

Form RPR

002 **1** **Valmina**[13] 7190 2-9-2 **68**..........(t) RichardKingscote 4 73
(Tom Dascombe) *a.p: pushed along over 2f out: rdn wl over 1f out: r.o to ld wl ins fnl f: drvn out* **12/1**

6212 **2** *3/4* **Desert Poppy (IRE)**[7] 7274 2-9-7 **73**.......... AdamKirby 11 75
(W R Swinburn) *chsd ldr tl over 2f out: regained 2nd wl over 1f out: sn led and rdn: edgd rt 1f out: hdd wl ins fnl f: nt qckn* **2/1**[1]

3243 **3** *1/2* **Lucky Mellor**[25] 6905 2-9-7 **73**.......... SebSanders 8 74
(D K Ivory) *a.p: rdn wl over 1f out: edgd lft wl ins fnl f: r.o* **4/1**[2]

0306 **4** *3 1/2* **Sovereign Secure (IRE)**[6] 7295 2-9-4 **70**..........(p) RobertWinston 3 58
(Lee Smyth, Ire) *led: rdn and hdd over 1f out: wknd wl ins fnl f* **9/1**

1015 **5** *3/4* **On The Piste (IRE)**[38] 6555 2-8-8 **65**.......... GaryBartley[(5)] 7 50
(L A Mullaney) *hld up in mid-div: pushed along over 2f out: effrt over 1f out: rdn and no hdwy fnl f* **25/1**

6343 **6** *nk* **Flaxen Lake**[14] 7156 2-9-4 **70**..........(p) GrahamGibbons 6 54
(R Hollinshead) *s.i.s: hld up towards rr: rdn wl over 1f out: late prog on outside: n.d* **11/2**[3]

0103 **7** *1 1/4* **Wanchai Whisper**[13] 7175 2-8-12 **64**.......... PaulHanagan 9 44
(P D Evans) *hld up towards rr: rdn and sme prog 1f out: sn no imp* **20/1**

6536 **8** *1/2* **Ya Boy Sir (IRE)**[21] 6983 2-8-2 **54**.......... DuranFentiman 2 32
(I Semple) *hld up in mid-div: rdn jst over 1f out: sn btn* **16/1**

0004 **9** *1/2* **Satin Princess (IRE)**[38] 6554 2-7-12 **50** oh1.......... JamieMackay 5 26
(A M Hales) *hld up in rr: pushed along wl over 1f out: nvr nr ldrs* **40/1**

3100 **10** *2* **Lewyn**[7] 7274 2-9-7 **73**..........(v[1]) DarryllHolland 12 42
(K A Ryan) *prom: chsd ldr over 2f out tl wl over 1f out: sn rdn and wknd* **16/1**

6010 **11** *1/2* **Blue Neptune**[14] 7156 2-8-12 **64**.......... RyanMoore 10 31
(W R Muir) *hld up in mid-div: wknd wl over 1f out* **8/1**

3052 **12** *1/2* **True Red (IRE)**[23] 6938 2-8-0 **59**.......... RachelKing[(7)] 1 24
(Mrs N S Evans) *a in rr* **20/1**

63.02 secs (0.72) **Going Correction** +0.125s/f (Slow) **12 Ran SP% 125.1**
Speed ratings (Par 96): **99,97,97,91,90 89,87,86,86,82 82,81**
toteswingers: 1&2 £12.50, 1&3 £11.30, 2&3 £1.90. CSF £36.64 CT £124.52 TOTE £16.50: £3.00, £1.50, £1.80; EX 67.80.
Owner Mayden Stud **Bred** Mayden Stud, J A And D S Dewhurst **Trained** Lambourn, Berks

FOCUS
This modest nursery was run in heavy rain and there was also a strong wind.

NOTEBOOK
Valmina, dropped to the minimum trip for the first time on his nursery debut, having been too free in a 6f maiden around here last time, stayed on strongly after losing ground on the leaders when getting outpaced around the turn into the straight. He looks as though he'll improve again when stepped back up in trip. (op 9-1)
Desert Poppy(IRE) managed to get a handy position from her wide draw, but she wandered around once in front in the straight, possibly not facing the poor weather conditions. She's due to go up 4lb and things will be tougher. (op 5-2 tchd 11-4)
Lucky Mellor has now finished in the first four in six of his last seven starts without adding to his maiden success. He lacks a finishing kick and Fibresand looks to suit him best. (op 11-2)
Sovereign Secure(IRE) emerges with some credit after trying to make all. (op 16-1)
On The Piste(IRE) looks ready for a step up to 6f.

Flaxen Lake, with cheekpieces on for the first time, is better than he showed as he raced very wide into the straight. (op 9-2)

7373 BET INTERNATIONAL RUGBY - BETDAQ H'CAP 1m 4f 50y(P)

7:50 (7:50) (Class 4) (0-85,85) 3-Y-O+ **£5,046** (£1,510; £755; £377; £188) **Stalls** Low

Form RPR

0631 **1** **Chookie Hamilton**[11] 7212 5-9-1 **76** 6ex........................ TomEaves 11 87
(I Semple) *hld up towards rr: hdwy over 2f out: rdn over 1f out: led jst ins fnl f: hrd drvn: jst hld on* **8/1**[3]

5214 **2** *nse* **Follow The Flag (IRE)**[31] 6760 5-8-12 **73**..................(p) RobertWinston 2 84
(A J McCabe) *hld up towards rr: hdwy over 2f out: sn rdn: r.o u.p ins fnl f: jst failed* **16/1**

20-6 **3** *6* **Wikaala (USA)**[1] 7360 4-8-11 **72**..................................(b) PaulHanagan 4 73
(Gordon Elliott, Ire) *hld up in mid-div: hdwy over 3f out: ev ch wl over 1f out: rdn and wknd wl ins fnl f* **28/1**

5005 **4** *1 ¾* **Norwegian Dancer (UAE)**[21] 6996 3-9-2 **83**............ GrahamGibbons 9 82
(E S McMahon) *hld up in tch: led over 2f out: rdn wl over 1f out: hdd jst ins fnl f: wknd* **14/1**

0204 **5** *3 ¼* **Daaweitza**[18] 7060 6-9-0 **75**..................................(b) RyanMoore 10 68
(B Ellison) *swtchd lft sn after s: hld up in rr: pushed along 3f out: rdn and sme hdwy over 1f out: nvr nr ldrs* **9/1**

1151 **6** *5* **Rockfella**[23] 6936 3-8-9 **76**.. DarryllHolland 1 61
(D J Coakley) *hld up in mid-div: rdn over 2f out: wknd wl over 1f out* **8/1**[3]

0332 **7** *3 ½* **Tilos Gem (IRE)**[22] 6975 3-8-9 **76**.................................. JoeFanning 7 56
(M Johnston) *chsd ldr: led 5f out tl over 2f out: wknd wl over 1f out* **9/4**[1]

2303 **8** *¾* **Final Victory**[28] 6816 3-9-4 **85**..................................(p) LPKeniry 3 64
(A M Balding) *prom: rdn and n.m.r on ins over 2f out: wknd wl over 1f out* **5/2**[2]

6104 **9** *17* **Eseej (USA)**[7] 7279 4-9-1 **76**.. LukeMorris 5 27
(P W Hiatt) *led: hung rt bnd and reminder over 6f out: hung rt and hdd 5f out: w ldr tl rdn and wknd over 2f out* **11/1**

00 **10** *dist* **Body Gold (ARG)**[29] 6795 6-9-10 **85**............................... AdamKirby 6 —
(P J Makin) *hld up in tch: lost pl over 6f out: t.o whn eased wl over 1f out* **66/1**

2m 40.91s (-0.19) **Going Correction** +0.125s/f (Slow)
WFA 3 from 4yo+ 6lb **10** Ran SP% **117.4**
Speed ratings (Par 105): **105,104,100,99,97 94,91,91,80,—**
toteswingers: 1&2 £11.10, 1&3 £13.60, 2&3 £22.20. CSF £127.85 CT £3379.22 TOTE £9.30: £2.50, £3.10, £4.10; EX 62.70.
Owner Raeburn Brick Limited **Bred** D And J Raeburn **Trained** Carluke, S Lanarks

FOCUS
A fair handicap, but once again the runners were faced with strong winds and persistent rain. The furst two pulled clear and posted personal bests, but there are slight doubts over how literally to take this form.

Eseej(USA) Official explanation: jockey said gelding hung right
Body Gold(ARG) Official explanation: jockey said gelding hung badly left-handed

7374 STAY AT THE WOLVERHAMPTON HOLIDAY INN CLASSIFIED STKS (DIV II) 1m 1f 103y(P)

8:20 (8:20) (Class 6) 3-Y-O+ **£1,706** (£503; £252) **Stalls** Low

Form RPR

0220 **1** **Sircozy (IRE)**[18] 7049 3-8-9 **55**.............................. WilliamCarson(3) 9 67
(S C Williams) *hld up towards rr: pushed along and hdwy over 2f out: rdn wl over 1f out: sn hung lft: r.o wl to ld cl home* **7/2**[1]

0434 **2** *1 ¼* **Bestowed**[21] 6999 4-9-1 **55**.. PaulDoe 10 64
(P D Evans) *led after 1f: clr whn rdn over 1f out: ct cl home* **7/2**[1]

0363 **3** *4 ½* **Mojeerr**[15] 7143 3-8-12 **50**...................................(p) RobertWinston 7 55
(A J McCabe) *hld up in mid-div: hdwy 3f out: rdn to chse ldr wl over 1f out: sn hung lft: lost 2nd and one pce ins fnl f* **8/1**[3]

0002 **4** *¾* **Castle Myth (USA)**[15] 7142 3-8-12 **54**..........................(bt) TomEaves 2 53
(B Ellison) *hld up towards rr: pushed along and hdwy on ins over 2f out: rdn wl over 1f out: no further prog* **5/1**[2]

4660 **5** *4* **Herecomethegirls**[11] 7211 3-8-12 **55**......................... JamieSpencer 5 49+
(M L W Bell) *hld up in mid-div: rdn and hung lft bnd over 2f out: hung lft and eased over 1f out* **5/1**[2]

0030 **6** *½* **Roleplay (IRE)**[55] 6126 4-9-1 **53**..................................(b) LukeMorris 13 44
(J M P Eustace) *prom: chsd ldr over 3f out: sn rdn: lost 2nd over 1f out: wknd ins fnl f* **8/1**[3]

065 **7** *5* **Fairplaytomyself**[46] 6332 4-9-1 **52**.............................. PaulHanagan 6 33
(P W Hiatt) *dwlt: hld up in rr: pushed along over 2f out: nvr nr ldrs* **25/1**

0060 **8** *1* **Marina's Ocean**[17] 7080 5-9-1 **48**..................................(t) AmirQuinn 8 31
(S R Bowring) *hld up in mid-div: hdwy over 5f out: rdn and wknd wl over 1f out* **20/1**

0066 **9** *6* **Harty Boy (USA)**[12] 7197 3-8-9 **55**.........................(t) RobertLButler(3) 3 19
(Jim Best) *hld up in tch: lost pl over 5f out: no ch fnl 4f* **18/1**

6555 **10** *2 ¼* **Chateauneuf (IRE)**[18] 7049 3-8-12 **52**...........................(p) LiamJones 11 14
(W M Brisbourne) *prom: chsd ldr over 7f out: sn pushed along: lost 2nd over 3f out: sn wknd* **18/1**

006 **11** *5* **She's Pivotal (IRE)**[38] 6573 3-8-12 **42**........................... ShaneKelly 4 —
(J A Osborne) *a towards rr* **33/1**

12 *95* **Final Quest (IRE)**[45] 3189 6-9-1 **42**.............................. TonyCulhane 1 —
(P J McKenna, Ire) *led 1f: prom tl wknd over 5f out: t.o fnl 4f* **50/1**

2m 2.64s (0.94) **Going Correction** +0.125s/f (Slow)
WFA 3 from 4yo+ 3lb **12** Ran SP% **124.0**
Speed ratings (Par 101): **100,98,94,94,90 90,85,84,79,77 73,—**
toteswingers: 1&2 £5.10, 1&3 £5.60, 2&3 £13.00. CSF £15.28 TOTE £4.60: £1.80, £2.50, £2.40; EX 23.40.
Owner R Friends Electric **Bred** Allevamento Pian Di Neve Srl **Trained** Newmarket, Suffolk

FOCUS
This was a moderate contest. The time was good compared with division I and the fornt pair have not had many chances, so a fairly positive view has been taken of the form.

Herecomethegirls Official explanation: jockey said filly hung left

7375 BETDAQEXTRA.COM H'CAP 1m 141y(P)

8:50 (8:50) (Class 2) (0-100,100) 3-Y-O+
£11,215 (£3,358; £1,679; £840; £419; £210) **Stalls** Low

Form RPR

4203 **1** **Stand Guard**[13] 7194 5-8-2 **86** oh1........................ AndrewHeffernan(5) 5 96
(P Howling) *hld up in tch: rdn wl over 1f out: led ins fnl f: r.o* **12/1**

0320 **2** *1* **The Fifth Member (IRE)**[20] 7035 5-8-9 **88**........................ SJCraine 7 96
(J R Boyle) *chsd ldr: led jst over 2f out: rdn and hdd jst ins fnl f: nt qckn* **12/1**

120 **3** *1 ¼* **Fanunalter**[47] 6307 3-8-12 **94**.. RyanMoore 1 99+
(M Botti) *hld up towards rr: nt clr run on ins briefly over 2f out: swtchd rt ent st: hdwy over 1f out: rdn and kpt on ins fnl f: tk 3rd nr fin* **7/4**[1]

041- **4** *nk* **Grand Opera (IRE)**[63] 6799 6-8-7 **86** oh2.......................(t) PaulHanagan 6 90
(Gordon Elliott, Ire) *mid-div: hdwy over 2f out: rdn over 1f out: kpt on one pce ins fnl f* **14/1**

2200 **5** *2 ¾* **Wintercast**[20] 7035 4-8-12 **91**.. AdamKirby 2 89
(W R Swinburn) *led: hdd jst over 2f out: rdn over 1f out: wknd ins fnl f* **5/1**[2]

2515 **6** *1* **Fairmile**[25] 4288 7-9-2 **100**.....................................(t) MatthewDavies(5) 8 96
(George Baker) *hld up towards rr: rdn and styd on ins fnl f: n.d* **25/1**

1153 **7** *1 ½* **Flowing Cape (IRE)**[216] 1212 4-9-2 **95**......................... JamieSpencer 11 87
(R Hollinshead) *stdd and swtchd lft sn after s: hld up in rr: rdn and effrt wl over 1f out: nvr nr ldrs* **11/2**[3]

4005 **8** *hd* **Moynahan (USA)**[13] 7185 4-8-13 **92**.............................(b[1]) JoeFanning 10 84
(P F I Cole) *hld up in mid-div: pushed along over 2f out: wknd wl over 1f out* **12/1**

2106 **9** *¾* **Bomber Command (USA)**[28] 6830 6-8-7 **86** oh2...........(v) LiamJones 3 76
(J W Hills) *prom tl rdn and wknd wl over 1f out* **25/1**

4000 **10** *1 ¼* **Red Somerset (USA)**[15] 7133 6-8-8 **90**.................. WilliamCarson(3) 12 77
(R J Hodges) *swtchd lft sn after s: a in rr* **20/1**

023 **11** *¾* **Persian Peril**[26] 6878 5-8-7 **86** oh2.................................. JimmyQuinn 4 71
(G A Swinbank) *hld up in mid-div: rdn and wknd wl over 1f out* **9/1**

3464 **12** *6* **Carcinetto (IRE)**[15] 7132 7-8-11 **95**........................ RichardEvans(5) 9 66
(P D Evans) *prom tl pushed along and wknd over 2f out* **20/1**

1m 49.25s (-1.25) **Going Correction** +0.125s/f (Slow)
WFA 3 from 4yo+ 3lb **12** Ran SP% **125.4**
Speed ratings (Par 109): **110,109,108,107,105 104,103,102,102,101 100,95**
toteswingers: 1&2 £22.90, 1&3 £7.20, 2&3 £8.90. CSF £147.42 CT £383.64 TOTE £13.60: £2.80, £4.90, £1.70; EX 107.20.
Owner The Circle Bloodstock I Limited **Bred** Juddmonte Farms Ltd **Trained** Newmarket, Suffolk

FOCUS
A decent handicap but a steady pace meant those who raced handily were at an advantage. The winner is rated in line with his latest run here and the second to his turf form.

NOTEBOOK
Stand Guard had gained his five previous wins at around 1m2f, but his connections now believe he's best suited by this sort of trip. Well placed considering how the race unfolded, he gained a decisive success. He's a useful type on Polytrack and his main aim is the Lincoln Trial back over this C&D next year. (op 11-1)
The Fifth Member(IRE) was always well positioned and had every chance. This was arguably a career best in defeat. (op 17-2)
Fanunalter ◆ fared best of those to race off the pace, despite having to be switched around 2f out after being denied a clear run, and emerges with plenty of credit. He was considered good enough to contest a Derby trial in Italy earlier in the year, with Dettori aboard, so he might yet be capable of better with this being only his sixth start. (op 15-8 tchd 13-8)
Grand Opera(IRE), an Irish-trained challenger who had won three times over hurdles since last running on the Flat, ran respectably from 2lb out of the handicap after 63 days off. (op 12-1)
Wintercast was allowed an easy lead and can have no excuses. (op 7-1)
Flowing Cape(IRE) was well held after 216 days off and has yet to conclusively prove he stays this sort of trip. (tchd 13-2)

7376 BLACK COUNTRY'S ONLY RACECOURSE MAIDEN STKS 7f 32y(P)

9:20 (9:21) (Class 5) 2-Y-O **£3,238** (£963; £481; £240) **Stalls** High

Form RPR

1 **Bronze Prince** 2-9-3 0...(t) TedDurcan 8 81+
(Saeed Bin Suroor) *chsd ldr: led wl over 1f out: pushed out* **4/7**[1]

2 *1 ½* **Cabal** 2-8-12 0.. RyanMoore 2 72
(Sir Michael Stoute) *a.p: wnt 2nd jst ins fnl f: kpt on one pce* **7/1**[3]

3 *4* **Barq (IRE)** 2-9-3 0.. JamieSpencer 1 68
(Saeed Bin Suroor) *led: pushed along and hdd wl over 1f out: lost 2nd and wknd ins fnl f* **4/1**[2]

4 *2 ¾* **Silken Aunt** 2-8-12 0.. RobertHavlin 7 56
(J A R Toller) *hld up in tch: wknd wl over 1f out* **66/1**

5 *¾* **Monterosso** 2-9-3 0.. JoeFanning 10 59
(M Johnston) *prom: pushed along over 2f out: wknd wl over 1f out* **12/1**

42 **6** *4* **Battle Study (IRE)**[52] 6181 2-9-3 0..........................(p) RobertWinston 6 49
(A J McCabe) *s.i.s: sn hld up in mid-div: hdwy over 4f out: pushed along over 2f out: rdn and wknd wl over 1f out* **25/1**

5 **7** *2 ¾* **Silent Majority (IRE)**[21] 6990 2-9-3 0......................... PaulHanagan 4 42
(E A L Dunlop) *hld up in mid-div: pushed along and wknd over 2f out* **8/1**

8 *¾* **Corr Point (IRE)** 2-9-3 0... ShaneKelly 3 41
(J A Osborne) *dwlt: a in rr* **40/1**

0 **9** *¾* **Desert Recluse (IRE)**[20] 7024 2-9-3 0......................... DarryllHolland 11 39
(Pat Eddery) *s.i.s: a towards rr* **40/1**

5 **10** *½* **Super Yellow**[21] 7001 2-9-3 0...................................... ChrisCatlin 12 38
(J A Osborne) *s.i.s: a in rr* **20/1**

00 **11** *3 ¾* **Priestley (IRE)**[9] 7243 2-9-3 0.................................. SebSanders 5 28
(J G Given) *hld up towards rr: hdwy over 3f out: rdn and wknd 2f out* **100/1**

12 *33* **Whitley Bay (USA)** 2-9-3 0....................................... TonyCulhane 9 —
(J R Best) *dwlt: a in rr: lost tch 4f out: t.o* **66/1**

1m 30.73s (1.13) **Going Correction** +0.125s/f (Slow) **12** Ran SP% **132.4**
Speed ratings (Par 96): **98,96,91,88,87 83,80,79,78,77 73,35**
toteswingers: 1&2 £1.80, 1&3 £2.00, 2&3 £2.90. CSF £6.30 TOTE £1.90: £1.40, £2.10, £1.60; EX 14.60 Place 6 £1,320.81, Place 5 £395.21.
Owner Godolphin **Bred** Coln Valley Stud **Trained** Newmarket, Suffolk

FOCUS
Some powerful connections were represented and this looked a good maiden for the track and time of year.

NOTEBOOK
Bronze Prince ◆, who is a half-brother to a very useful 6f-7f winner, as well as a winner over 1m4f, and out of a successful miler, was quite keen early on but still found enough in the straight to record a cosy debut victory. A colt with quite a big stride, this 220,000gns purchase has the potential to be very useful next year. (op 4-6 tchd 8-11 after early 4-5)
Cabal, a half-sister to Double Act, who has won over this C&D, out of a 1m1f winner, was always well placed and ran on to the line. She should find a similar race. (op 13-2)
Barq(IRE) ◆ knew what was required and took them along early but simply found a couple too good in the straight. He looks to have the speed for sprint trips. (op 6-1 tchd 13-2)
Silken Aunt, a half-sister to a couple of winning sprinters, showed ability on her debut and should be up to finding a race. (op 80-1)
Monterosso, who is out of a 7.5f Group 1 winner in Australia, posted just a modest effort at best but he's from a stable whose newcomers can improve significantly for a run.
Silent Majority(IRE) failed to build on a promising debut and his rider took look a down at his mount around 1f out, presumably to see if something was amiss.

T/Plt: £1,371.10 to a £1 stake. Pool: £90,364.33. 48.11 winning tickets. T/Qpdt: £143.80 to a £1 stake. Pool: £10,960.00. 56.40 winning tickets. KH

7377 - 7383a (Foreign Racing) - See Raceform Interactive

7230 MAISONS-LAFFITTE (R-H)

Friday, November 13

OFFICIAL GOING: Heavy

7384a PRIX DIATOME (C&G) (STRAIGHT) 1m 1f

12:00 (12:00) 2-Y-O **£16,505** (£6,602; £4,951; £3,301; £1,650)

RPR

1 **Anzas (IRE)**[26] 6889 2-8-12 .... P-CBoudot(6) 100
(R Gibson, France)

2 6 **At Least (FR)**[10] 2-8-10 .... SMaillot 80
(Robert Collet, France)

3 ½ **Magic Prospect (FR)**[26] 2-8-13 .... KirstyMilczarek 82
(E J O'Neill) *pressed ldr: led narrowly over 3f out to over 2f out: remained disputing ld tl over 1f out: one pce* **15/1**[1]

4 5 **Blue Alec (FR)** 2-8-10 69
(Mlle S-V Tarrou, France)

5 2½ **Chic Bliss (FR)**[26] 2-8-10 64
(F Doumen, France)

6 5 **J'En Sais Rien (FR)** 2-8-10 54
(P Demercastel, France)

7 15 **Franz Quercus (FR)**[47] 6322 2-8-10 24
(Y De Nicolay, France)

8 20 **Sivola Gambler (FR)** 2-8-10 .... —
(T Trapenard, France)

9 dist **Dear Boy (FR)** 2-8-10 .... —
(T Trapenard, France)

1m 56.6s (1.90) **9** Ran SP% **6.3**
PARI-MUTUEL (including one euro stakes): WIN 1.60; PL 1.10, 1.20,1.90; DF 2.90.
Owner V Bukhtoyarov **Bred** Fares Stables Ltd **Trained** Lamorlaye, France

7385a PRIX DE SAINT-ARNOULT EN YVELINES (CLAIMER) (STRAIGHT) 6f (S)

1:35 (1:35) 3-Y-O **£10,194** (£4,077; £3,058; £2,039; £1,019)

RPR

1 **Caraziyan (FR)**[22] 3-9-1 .... IMendizabal 75
(P Van De Poele, France)

2 ¾ **Dianeva (FR)**[19] 3-8-9 ....(p) AChampenois(8) 75
(M Boutin, France)

3 2½ **Moscow Eight (IRE)**[8] 7265 3-9-1 .... ABourgeais 65
(E J O'Neill) *led gp in middle: ev ch dist: r.o one pce* **7/2**[1]

4 snk **Isi Going (IRE)**[22] 3-8-8 ....(b) 57
(C Von Der Recke, Germany)

5 nse **Ladouce (FR)**[22] 3-9-1 64
(Robert Collet, France)

6 1½ **D'Outremer (FR)**[22] 3-8-8 52
(D Smaga, France)

7 2½ **Italica (FR)**[44] 3-8-2 ....(p)(6) 44
(T Callejo-Solana, Spain)

8 nk **Salut Adrien (FR)**[4] 3-8-11 46
(Robert Collet, France)

9 ¾ **Marechale (FR)**[19] 3-8-8 41
(Mme C Head-Maarek, France)

10 4 **Waringham (GER)**[15] 3-8-8 ....(3) 31
(F-X De Chevigny, France)

0 **Majestic Lady (IRE)**[35] 6641 3-8-11 .... —
(Mlle C Comte, France)

0 **Palmeral (IRE)**[24] 3-9-1 .... —
(Mlle L Beccaert, France)

0 **Good Star (FR)**[22] 3-9-1 .... —
(B Dutruel, France)

0 **Goodnitesleeptight (FR)**[105] 3-8-11 .... DBonilla —
(David Marnane, Ire) *sn in rr on rails: last 1/2-way: t.o* **22/1**[2]

1m 16.04s (2.64) **14** Ran SP% **26.6**
PARI-MUTUEL: WIN 6.00; PL 1.80, 1.90, 1.60; DF 9.70.
Owner J-L Burgat **Bred** Haras De Son Altesse L'Aga Khan Scea **Trained** France

7386a PRIX DE CLAIREFONTAINE EN YVELINES (CLAIMER) (WOMEN PROFESSIONALS) (RIGHT-HANDED) 1m (S)

2:05 (2:05) 3-Y-O **£10,194** (£4,077; £3,058; £2,039; £1,019)

RPR

1 **Dame Anouska (IRE)**[22] 6980 3-8-8 ....(p) KirstyMilczarek 67
(E J O'Neill) *mde most: wnt clr on turn: stl clr 1f out: drvn out to hold late chal* **17/5**[1]

2 nk **Perky (FR)**[24] 3-8-12 .... MarieFlahault 70
(J Morin, France)

3 6 **Present Of Heaven (GER)**[147] 3-9-4 .... StefanieHofer 63
(W Baltromei, Germany)

4 1½ **Light Silver (FR)**[15] 3-8-11 52
(P Bary, France)

5 4 **Dellaside (FR)**[14] 3-8-11 ....(b) 43
(Rod Collet, France)

6 3 **Stay Cool (FR)**[24] 3-9-2 41
(D Smaga, France)

7 1 **Malegria (FR)**[35] 3-8-5 ....(3) 31
(J-P Delaporte, France)

8 2½ **Blessing Belle (IRE)**[185] 1967 3-8-8 25
(Mme G Rarick, France)

9 8 **Barlia (IRE)**[33] 6753 3-8-8 7
(C Laffon-Parias, France)

10 ¾ **Dusk And Dawn (IRE)**[222] 3-8-8 5
(Mlle A Imaz-Ceca, France)

0 **Karta (IRE)**[19] 3-8-8 .... —
(H-A Pantall, France)

0 **Stella Francesca (FR)**[4] 3-8-2 ....(p)(6) —
(C Boutin, France)

1m 45.09s (2.79) **12** Ran SP% **22.7**
PARI-MUTUEL: WIN 4.40; PL 1.90, 2.80, 2.10; DF 25.20.
Owner Frank Cosgrove **Bred** Mrs Brid Cosgrove **Trained** Southwell, Notts

7387a PRIX DE RAMBOUILLET (CLAIMER) (RIGHT-HANDED) 1m 7f

3:10 (3:09) 4-Y-O+ **£8,738** (£3,495; £2,621; £1,748; £874)

RPR

1 **Molitor (FR)**[30] 7-9-1 ....(p) FSpanu 64
(A Spanu, France)

2 snk **Elegant Dancer (FR)**[14] 4-9-1 .... FPanicucci(3) 67
(N Clement, France)

3 6 **Tori Parry (FR)**[14] 6-8-9 .... BRaballand(3) 54
(Y Fouin, France)

5 ¾ **Miss Naline (FR)**[106] 4-8-8 49
(Andreas Lowe, Germany)

6 8 **Tartesos**[14] 4-8-12 ....(p) 43
(P Chatelain, France)

7 15 **Loustone (FR)**[28] 4-8-13 ....(p) 26
(Mlle S Morosi, France)

8 8 **Saalewuste (GER)**[14] 4-9-3 ....(p) 21
(J-P Gallorini, France)

9 20 **L'Auvergnat (IRE)**[12] 7-8-12 ....(b) —
(Mlle C Cardenne, France)

9 20 **Change The World (IRE)**[14] 4-9-4 ....(b) —
(S Wattel, France)

10 dist **High Curragh**[24] 6924 6-9-4 .... KirstyMilczarek —
(E J O'Neill) *mid-div tl wkng appr st: t.o* **41/1**[1]

3m 29.01s (209.01) **10** Ran SP% **2.4**
PARI-MUTUEL: WIN 6.70; PL 2.30, 2.20, 4.00; DF 16.60.
Owner A Cherifi **Bred** Ecurie Haras De Beauvoir **Trained** France

7362 LINGFIELD (L-H)

Saturday, November 14

OFFICIAL GOING: Standard

Wind: strong, behind Weather: dry, very windy

7388 EUROPEAN BREEDERS' FUND MAIDEN STKS (DIV I) 1m (P)

12:00 (12:02) (Class 5) 2-Y-O **£3,412** (£1,007; £504) **Stalls** High

Form RPR

1 **Rumoush (USA)** 2-8-12 0 .... RHills 1 76
(M P Tregoning) *s.i.s: sn pushed along and hdwy to trck ldrs on inner: rdn to chal wl over 1 f out: led ent fnl f: r.o wl* **11/2**[2]

0 2 ½ **Street Entertainer (IRE)**[37] 6620 2-9-3 0 .... NCallan 12 80
(Mrs A J Perrett) *in tch: hdwy to press ldrs over 2 f out: ev ch and carried to centre wl over 1f out: chsd wnr fnl 150yds: kpt on but a hld* **16/1**

022 3 1¾ **Shamir**[16] 7130 2-9-3 80 .... FergusSweeney 3 76
(Miss Jo Crowley) *led: rdn and c centre wl over 1f out: hdd ent fnl f: wknd fnl 100yds* **10/11**[1]

4 5 **Destiny Blue (IRE)** 2-9-3 0 .... JimCrowley 10 65
(J A Osborne) *s.i.s: hld up towards rr: hdwy on inner over 2f out: kpt on steadily fr over 1f out: nvr gng pce to threaten ldrs* **40/1**

4 5 ½ **Boston Blue**[19] 7064 2-9-3 0 .... LPKeniry 11 64
(W J Knight) *in tch towards rr: rdn over 4f out: drvn and outpcd over 3f out: styd on u.p fnl f: nvr trbld ldrs* **13/2**[3]

0 6 1 **Sansili**[17] 7121 2-9-3 0 .... RobertWinston 7 62
(Pat Eddery) *chsd ldr tl ent fnl 2f: sn hmpd and lost grnd: wl btn over 1f out* **66/1**

7 1 **Thundering Home** 2-9-3 0 .... DaneO'Neill 6 60
(E A L Dunlop) *s.i.s: in tch in midfield: rdn along and chsd clr ldrs over 2f out: one pce and no imp after: lost 2 pls ins fnl f* **10/1**

8 6 **Main Spring** 2-8-12 0 .... RyanMoore 2 41
(Sir Michael Stoute) *s.i.s: sn in tch: rdn and wknd wl over 2f out: wl bhd fr over 1f out* **8/1**

0 9 3¼ **Babycakes (IRE)**[22] 6992 2-8-12 0 .... PaulHanagan 8 34
(M L W Bell) *towards rr on outer: rdn and struggling 3f out: sn wl bhd* **25/1**

00 10 9 **Ava Doll**[14] 7183 2-8-5 0 .... DannyBrock(7) 4 14
(J R Jenkins) *a towards rr: lost tch over 3f out* **100/1**

0 11 ½ **Billyonair**[19] 7063 2-9-3 0 .... PaulEddery 9 18
(W De Best-Turner) *chsd ldrs on outer tl over 3f out: sn lost pl: wl bhd fnl 2f* **150/1**

0 12 2 **Chief Of Ten**[10] 7244 2-9-3 0 .... ChrisCatlin 5 14
(D R Lanigan) *s.i.s: a bhd and rn v green: lost tch 3f out* **100/1**

1m 40.93s (2.73) **Going Correction** +0.20s/f (Slow) **12** Ran SP% **117.6**
Speed ratings (Par 96): **94,93,91,86,86 85,84,78,75,66 65,63**
toteswingers:1&2:£25.20, 2&3:£11.10, 1&3:£2.20 CSF £83.56 TOTE £6.10: £1.80, £6.50, £1.02; EX 103.70 TRIFECTA Not won..
Owner Hamdan Al Maktoum **Bred** Shadwell Farm LLC **Trained** Lambourn, Berks

FOCUS

The time was 0.30 seconds quicker than Con Artist recorded in the second division and this could turn out to be a useful maiden. There was certainly a potentially above-average winner.

NOTEBOOK

Rumoush(USA) ◆ is extremely well bred, being a half-sister to this year's 1,000 Guineas winner Ghanaati (won her maiden on Polytrack) and Champion Stakes runner-up Mawatheeq, and she made a successful debut in likeable fashion. She lost a few lengths at the start, showing her inexperience, but soon recovered to race close up. After nipping through towards the inside in the straight, she did not require maximum pressure to assert, and looked to have a bit in hand. She displayed a fluent, fast-ground action and could be quite smart in time. It would be no surprise to see her start off in a Guineas trial next year and she's one to keep in mind. (op 4-1)

Street Entertainer(IRE) ◆ improved significantly on the form he showed on his debut at Newbury and looks a decent sort in the making. His chance wasn't helped when he was carried wide around the final bend by the favourite, but he was basically beaten by a better one on the day. He looks the type to go on improving.

Shamir was the clear form pick after showing plenty in 7f maidens, including around here, but was slightly below form over this longer trip and looked a non-stayer, even allowing for swinging wide off the final bend. (op 6-4)

Destiny Blue(IRE), whose pedigree is a mix of speed and stamina, was soon racing out the back after taking a while to find his stride and basically just looked badly in need of the experience, but he made encouraging late headway under mainly hands-and-heels riding. (op 33-1)

Boston Blue ◆, who has the same owners as the fourth, did not appear to have learned anything from his debut effort over C&D as he was became badly outpaced shortly after halfway and got going only inside the final furlong. He will be interesting if stepped up to middle distances when going handicapping. (tchd 11-2 and 7-1)

Main Spring is a half-sister to smart middle-distance performer Kingdom Of Fire and useful miler Four Winds, but she needed a blanket for stalls entry and showed little on her racecourse debut, dropping away in the straight after running handily. (op 5-1)

7389 TANDRIDGE NURSERY 7f (P)

12:25 (12:28) (Class 6) (0-60,60) 2-Y-O

£1,869 (£559; £279; £140; £69; £35) **Stalls** Low

Form RPR

0000 **1** **Lisahane Bog**[34] 6697 2-9-3 **56**........................(p) DaneO'Neill 3 61
(P R Hedger) *s.i.s: sn in tch in midfield: chsd ldrs and swtchd ins wl over 1f out: drvn over 1f out: led ins fnl f: sn clr* **66/1**

060 **2** *2* **Kingston Acacia**[37] 6617 2-9-7 **60**........................(v[1]) LPKeniry 2 60
(A M Balding) *led: rdn and c centre wl over 1f out: hdd ins fnl f: no ch w wnr after but kpt on for clr 2nd* **9/1**

0600 **3** *1 1/2* **Dutiful**[37] 6609 2-9-3 **56**........................ TedDurcan 6 52
(M R Channon) *chsd ldrs: rdn jst over 2f out: nt qckn and hung lft over 1f out: styd on ins fnl f to go 3rd nr fin* **12/1**

0500 **4** *hd* **D'Urberville**[37] 6609 2-9-7 **60**........................ RobertHavlin 1 56
(J R Jenkins) *hld up wl in tch: effrt and rdn ent fnl 2f: ev ch and drvn ent fnl f: wknd fnl 100yds* **33/1**

635 **5** *shd* **Marjolly (IRE)**[18] 7087 2-9-1 **57**........................ AndreaAtzeni(3) 4 53
(M Botti) *chsd ldr: ev ch and c centre wl over 1f out: stl ev ch tl wknd fnl 150yds* **9/2**[2]

000 **6** *hd* **Dauntsey Park (IRE)**[31] 6772 2-9-7 **60**........................ FergusSweeney 13 55
(Miss Tor Sturgis) *stdd s: hld up in rr: hdwy on wd outside bnd 2f out: edging lft over 1f out: styd on wl fnl f: nvr trbld ldrs* **25/1**

605 **7** *6* **Laureldean Desert**[25] 6922 2-9-7 **60**........................ PaulHanagan 12 40
(R A Fahey) *in tch: rdn and unable qck over 2f out: one pce and no imp on ldrs fr over 1f out* **9/2**[2]

000 **8** *shd* **Baoli**[21] 7029 2-9-5 **58**........................ RyanMoore 9 38
(R Hannon) *in tch in midfield: rdn and nt qckn ent fnl 2f: racd awkwardly u.p and wl btn over 1f out* **4/1**[1]

4305 **9** *1 1/2* **Wigan Lane**[37] 6610 2-9-7 **60**........................ IanMongan 5 36
(P Howling) *in tch in midfield: rdn and no prog ent fnl 2f: wl btn over 1f out* **14/1**

4050 **10** *1/2* **Phoenix Rose (IRE)**[24] 6938 2-9-5 **58**........................ RobertWinston 10 33
(J R Best) *hld up in last trio: rdn over 2f out: nvr on terms* **16/1**

000 **11** *3/4* **Flash For Freedom (USA)**[21] 7024 2-9-3 **56**........................ TonyCulhane 8 29
(J R Best) *s.i.s: sn t.k.h and hld up in last trio: nvr trbld ldrs* **66/1**

046 **12** *4 1/2* **Recette**[65] 5800 2-9-1 **54**........................ ChrisCatlin 7 16
(R Ingram) *chsd ldng pair: rdn and struggling 3f out: wl btn fnl 2f* **14/1**

556 **13** *1/2* **Be Grateful (IRE)**[24] 6932 2-9-2 **55**........................ SteveDrowne 11 15
(H Morrison) *hld up in midfield on outer: rdn and struggling over 2f out: wl btn fnl 2f* **6/1**[3]

1m 27.79s (2.99) **Going Correction** +0.20s/f (Slow) **13 Ran SP% 117.3**
Speed ratings (Par 94): **90,87,86,85,85 85,78,78,76,76 75,70,69**
Swingers:1&2:£21.10, 2&3: not won, 1&3: not won CSF £572.10 CT £7465.35 TOTE £66.60: £20.10, £4.10, £4.50; EX 222.20 TRIFECTA Not won..

Owner P C F Racing Ltd **Bred** J J Whelan **Trained** Dogmersfield, Hampshire

FOCUS

The horses went straight to post for this nursery, with the wind now very strong (behind the runners in the straight), and it was also raining by the time the race got underway. This was a moderate contest.

NOTEBOOK

Lisahane Bog went the shortest way throughout and may have been at an advantage, as he was probably better shielded from the weather than most. Having recovered well from a slow start, this son of Royal Applause enjoyed a good trip, getting a gap when needed in the straight, and ran on well. It remains to be seen if he can defy a higher mark, however. Official explanation: trainer said, regarding apparent improvement in form, that this was the colt's first run in a handicap and seemed to be suited by the Polytrack.

Kingston Acacia, visored for the first time, set out the make all and, while the wind wasn't favourable all the way around, it was at least behind her in the straight. She should win a similar race. (tchd 10-1)

Dutiful is slowly getting the idea and this was his most encouraging effort to date. (op 16-1)

D'Urberville didn't seem to have any excuses. (op 25-1)

Marjolly(IRE) didn't see his race out after looking a big threat turning into the straight, even if he did go a bit wide. He should appreciate a drop back in trip.

Laureldean Desert raced wider than ideal from stall 12 and was never competitive. (op 6-1)

Baoli was sent off favourite for her nursery debut but was always struggling. (op 5-1 tchd 7-2)

7390 EUROPEAN BREEDERS' FUND MAIDEN STKS (DIV II) 1m (P)

1:00 (1:01) (Class 5) 2-Y-O

£3,412 (£1,007; £504) **Stalls** High

Form RPR

3 **1** **Con Artist (IRE)**[8] 7266 2-9-3 0........................ TedDurcan 3 80
(Saeed Bin Suroor) *mde all: rdn over 1f out: styd on wl fnl f* **7/1**[3]

0 **2** *1 3/4* **Fatanah (IRE)**[29] 6810 2-8-12 0........................ RHills 7 71
(M P Tregoning) *chsd wnr thrght: rdn and tried to chal 2f out: one pce and a hld fnl f* **3/1**[2]

2 **3** *3/4* **Whistleinthewind (IRE)**[24] 6931 2-9-3 0........................ GeorgeBaker 5 74
(G L Moore) *hld wl in tch: rdn to chse ldng pair jst over 2f out: hung lft u.p over 1f out: one pce fnl f* **1/1**[1]

0 **4** *1* **Septemberintherain**[155] 2889 2-9-3 0........................ NCallan 1 72
(T G Mills) *s.i.s: in tch towards rr: hdwy to chse ldrs 3f out: 5th and no prog u.p over 1f out: styd on ins fnl f: nt able to rch ldrs* **33/1**

3 **5** *1 1/2* **Penangdouble O One**[19] 7064 2-9-3 0........................(t) JimCrowley 4 69
(R M Beckett) *chsd ldng pair tl over 2f out: sn outpcd by ldng trio: plugged on same pce fr over 1f out* **9/1**

00 **6** *6* **Jennerous Blue**[31] 6772 2-8-9 0........................ JackMitchell(3) 6 50
(D K Ivory) *bhd: rdn and wnt modest 6th wl over 1f out: no real imp and nvr trbld ldrs* **100/1**

7 *8* **Raqeeb (USA)** 2-9-3 0........................ RyanMoore 12 38
(Sir Michael Stoute) *s.i.s: sn swtchd lft: a bhd: lost tch over 2f out* **12/1**

50 **8** *2 3/4* **Ostentation**[38] 6591 2-9-3 0........................ J-PGuillambert 9 32
(M Johnston) *chsd ldrs tl wknd qckly 3f out: sn wl bhd* **25/1**

0 **9** *3/4* **Aintgottaname**[21] 7024 2-8-12 0........................ ShaneKelly 2 25
(M J McGrath) *in tch in midfield: rdn and struggling 3f out: sn wl bhd* **150/1**

0 **10** *6* **Big Hands Lynch (IRE)**[19] 7064 2-9-3 0........................ SJCraine 8 17
(J R Boyle) *a bhd: lost tch 3f out: nvr a factor* **100/1**

0000 **11** *10* **Vadition (IRE)**[33] 6736 2-8-12 42........................ JerryO'Dwyer 11 —
(J J Bridger) *racd in midfield on outer: rdn and wknd over 3f out: wl bhd after: t.o* **200/1**

12 *2 3/4* **Fochabers** 2-9-3 0........................ SteveDrowne 10 —
(R Charlton) *bhd: rdn and lost tch 4f out: t.o fnl 3f* **66/1**

1m 41.23s (3.03) **Going Correction** +0.20s/f (Slow) **12 Ran SP% 116.6**
Speed ratings (Par 96): **92,90,89,88,87 81,73,70,69,63 53,50**
toteswingers:1&2:£4.30, 2&3:£1.10, 1&3:£3.00 CSF £27.46 TOTE £7.00: £2.00, £1.30, £1.10; EX 25.60 Trifecta £62.30 Pool: £441.74 - 5.24 winning units.

Owner Godolphin **Bred** Airlie Stud **Trained** Newmarket, Suffolk

FOCUS

Another race run in a strong wind, which was again behind the runners in the straight. It proved difficult to make up ground from off the pace in this maiden, which was run in a time 0.30 seconds slower than the potentially smart Rumoush recorded in the first division.

NOTEBOOK

Con Artist(IRE) was weak in the market but looks an uncomplicated individual and made all, with the wind helping him in the straight. This was a significant improvement on the form he showed on his debut on Fibresand and he is open to further progress over the winter, but the suspicion at this stage is that he'll have his limitations when stepped up in grade. (op 10-3)

Fatanah(IRE), whose stable won the first division, was always well placed and had her chance. This effort confirmed the promise she showed when running green on her debut at Newmarket, and she should find a similar race. (op 9-2)

Whistleinthewind(IRE) was never too far away but failed to pick up as many may have expected in the straight and has not progressed from his debut. (op 6-4)

Septemberintherain ◆ looks one to take from the race as he seemed much in need of this experience, only his second start and his first since June. A slow beginning didn't help his chance and he took a while to respond when first coming under pressure, before running on in the straight.

Penangdouble O One ran below the form he showed on his debut over C&D and was a bit disappointing. (op 6-1)

7391 DANNY BEST 60TH BIRTHDAY CLAIMING STKS 1m (P)

1:30 (1:31) (Class 6) 2-Y-O

£1,942 (£578; £288; £144) **Stalls** High

Form RPR

005 **1** **Giulietta Da Vinci**[26] 6905 2-8-6 70........................ SimonWhitworth 2 63+
(R Hannon) *hld up in tch in midfield: hdwy to trck ldrs gng wl jst over 1f out: rdn to ld over 1f out: r.o strly: comf* **5/2**[1]

3040 **2** *4 1/2* **Saint Thomas (IRE)**[33] 6736 2-8-12 66........................ JimCrowley 10 59
(J A Osborne) *led: rdn ent fnl 2f: hdd jst over 1f out: no ch w wnr fnl f but kpt on for 2nd* **7/1**

56 **3** *1 1/4* **Tuscan King**[16] 7130 2-9-1 0........................(b[1]) NCallan 9 59
(W R Muir) *in tch: rdn and unable qck jst over 2f out: drvn over 1f out: plugged on to go 3rd ins fnl f: no ch w wnr* **12/1**

03 **4** *3/4* **Better Be Blue (IRE)**[18] 7098 2-8-4 0........................ NickyMackay 7 47
(H J L Dunlop) *chsd ldng pair: rdn to chse ldr wl over 2f out tl wl over 1f out: one pce fnl f* **5/1**[3]

006 **5** *1 1/2* **Chorus Boy**[18] 7098 2-8-8 47........................(b) LPKeniry 3 47
(G G Margarson) *hmpd sn after s: hld up towards rr: rdn and effrt on outer jst over 2f out: no prog tl styd on ins fnl f: nvr trbld ldrs* **25/1**

06 **6** *hd* **Penderyn**[23] 6962 2-8-3 0........................ JimmyQuinn 6 42
(Mrs A J Perrett) *hld up in last trio: rdn and effrt towards inner 2f out: drvn and no prog over 1f out* **10/1**

0600 **7** *1/2* **Petite Mambo**[24] 6930 2-8-13 54........................ PaulEddery 1 51
(W De Best-Turner) *hld up in tch in rr: rdn and sme hdwy on inner wl over 1f out: nvr gng pce to threaten ldrs* **25/1**

0 **8** *1* **Royal Treasure (IRE)**[8] 7277 2-8-8 0........................ ShaneKelly 4 44
(J A Osborne) *hmpd sn after s: bhd: rdn and effrt ent fnl 2f: nvr on terms* **16/1**

9 *6* **One For Joules (IRE)**[19] 7074 2-8-8 0........................ DEMullins(5) 12 35
(John Joseph Hanlon, Ire) *s.i.s: sn in tch and t.k.h: rdn and wknd ent fnl 2f: wl btn fnl f* **4/1**[2]

00 **10** *3* **Set In Ice**[24] 6931 2-8-3 50........................ SimonPearce(5) 8 24
(Mark Gillard) *chsd ldr tl wl over 2f out: sn wknd: wl bhd fnl 2f* **66/1**

000 **11** *15* **Ramayana (IRE)**[38] 6582 2-8-4 52........................ ChrisCatlin 5 —
(M R Channon) *plld hrd: hld up in midfield: rdn and struggling on outer 3f out: wl bhd fnl 2f: t.o* **10/1**

1m 42.92s (4.72) **Going Correction** +0.20s/f (Slow) **11 Ran SP% 118.7**
Speed ratings (Par 94): **84,79,78,77,76 75,75,74,68,65 50**
.Giulietta da Vinci was claimed by N Tinkler for £8,000.\n\x\x

Owner R Hannon **Bred** Mrs J K Powell **Trained** East Everleigh, Wilts

FOCUS

A moderate claimer run in a slow time. Once more, the wind was strong, behind the runners up the straight.

NOTEBOOK

Giulietta Da Vinci, the only previous winner in the line-up, enjoyed a good trip and won well. Tucked away towards the inside in mid-division for much of the way, she found a gap against the rail entering the straight and was too good for this lot. (op 2-1)

Saint Thomas(IRE) took them along early but ultimately proved no match for the winner and would have been 10lb better off with that rival in a handicap. (op 12-1)

Tuscan King, conceding weight all round, ran respectably in first-time blinkers. (op 14-1 tchd 16-1)

Better Be Blue(IRE) seemed to have every chance but ran below her official mark of 69. (tchd 9-2 and 6-1)

Chorus Boy got going too late after being hampered at the start and swinging wide into the straight.

Petite Mambo lost two places after being eased in the final few strides. (tchd 20-1)

Royal Treasure(IRE) Official explanation: jockey said colt suffered interference immediately after start

One For Joules(IRE) was a bit keen to post and likewise in the race. (op 3-1)

Ramayana(IRE) Official explanation: jockey said filly jumped awkwardly leaving stalls

7392 COOLSHOP.CO.UK DERBY H'CAP 1m 2f (P)

2:00 (2:00) (Class 6) (0-60,60) 3-Y-O

£2,047 (£604; £302) **Stalls** Low

Form RPR

006 **1** **Franco Is My Name**[23] 6974 3-9-4 **60**........................ DaneO'Neill 9 75+
(P R Hedger) *hld up in tch in midfield: hdwy to chse clr ldr 3f out: clsd and c wd bnd 2f out: rdn to ld over 1f out: edging lft and rn green ins fnl f: kpt on and a doing enough* **11/1**

5020 **2** *1/2* **Chanrossa (IRE)**[21] 7022 3-9-2 **58**........................ JimCrowley 6 69
(E A L Dunlop) *hld up towards rr: rdn to chse ldrs jst over 2f out: hrd drvn to chse wnr ins fnl f: pressed wnr fnl 75yds: a hld* **12/1**

4233 **3** *2 3/4* **Salybia Bay**[26] 6910 3-9-2 **58**........................ RyanMoore 4 64
(R Hannon) *hld up in tch in midfield: rdn to dispute 2nd 3f out: clsd on ldr 2f out: sn hrd drvn: wknd 1f out* **9/2**[2]

4060 **4** *1* **Fire King**[23] 6968 3-9-1 **57**........................(p) LPKeniry 11 61
(J A Geake) *hld up in tch: rapid hdwy to ld jst over 3f out: sn clr: rdn and reduced advantage 2f out: hdd over 1f out: wknd fnl 150yds* **12/1**

2300 **5** 3 **Dark Ranger**95 4872 3-9-4 **60** NCallan 14 58
(T J Pitt) *hld up in tch towards rr: rdn and hdwy to chse ldr ent fnl 2f: no prog over 1f out: wknd ins fnl f* **9/1**

3245 **6** 1 **Triple Cee (IRE)**21 7022 3-9-3 **59** TedDurcan 2 55
(M R Channon) *hld up in rr: switching rt to wd outside over 2f out: kpt on: nvr trbld ldrs* **11/2**3

0061 **7** 3/4 **Mystic Touch**16 7142 3-9-0 **56** RobertHavlin 10 50
(A B Haynes) *hld up in rr: nt clr run 4f out: rdn and effrt jst over 2f out: kpt on but nvr on terms* **4/1**1

00-0 **8** 3 1/4 **Meirig's Dream (IRE)**33 6742 3-8-13 **55** PaulFitzsimons 3 43
(Miss N A Lloyd-Beavis) *hld up in tch in midfield: lost pl and bhd over 2f out: n.d after* **66/1**

0640 **9** 3 1/2 **Bubses Boy**19 7049 3-8-11 **53** IanMongan 5 34
(P Howling) *chsd ldng pair tl ent fnl 3f: sn struggling u.p: wl btn fnl 2f* **14/1**

5650 **10** shd **Silken Promise (USA)**17 7112 3-9-3 **59** AdamKirby 12 39
(W R Swinburn) *chsd ldrs: rdn and wnt 2nd briefly jst over 3f out: sn outpcd u.p: wl bhd fnl 2f* **14/1**

0060 **11** 7 **Colangnik (USA)**9 7250 3-8-13 **55** (v) RobertWinston 7 21
(J R Best) *dwlt: sn bustled along: towards rr on outer: rdn and no hdwy over 2f out* **14/1**

5030 **12** 3 **Brooksby**17 7110 3-9-1 **57** (b) SteveDrowne 1 17
(L A Dace) *sn rdn along to ld: rdn and hdd jst over 3f out: sn dropped out and bhd* **12/1**

-202 **13** 8 **Litenup (IRE)**161 2709 3-8-13 **55** WandersonD'Avila 8 —
(A J Lidderdale) *chsd ldr tl over 3f out: sn wknd u.p: t.o fnl 2f* **14/1**

2m 7.47s (0.87) **Going Correction** +0.20s/f (Slow) **13** Ran SP% **123.1**
Speed ratings (Par 98): **104,103,101,100,98 97,96,94,91,91 85,83,76**
toteswingers:1&2:£34.40, 2&3:£6.80, 1&3:£28.80 CSF £140.72 CT £693.68 TOTE £16.80: £5.20, £4.60, £2.60; EX 378.30 TRIFECTA Not won..
Owner P C F Racing Ltd **Bred** J J Whelan **Trained** Dogmersfield, Hampshire

FOCUS
A moderate handicap, but the pace was reasonable with Brooksby and Litenup contesting the lead for much of the way. Again, there was a strong wind, behind the runners in the straight.
Franco Is My Name Official explanation: trainer said, regarding apparent improvement in form, that the gelding was a late developer and had matured over time.

7393 BET CHELTENHAM OPEN MEETING - BETDAQ H'CAP 1m 2f (P)
2:30 (2:30) (Class 2) (0-100,103) 3-Y-0+
£11,215 (£3,358; £1,679; £840; £419; £210) **Stalls** Low

Form RPR
512 **1** **Black Eagle (IRE)**14 7194 3-8-9 **88** TedDurcan 7 104+
(Saeed Bin Suroor) *hld up wl in tch: chsd ldr gng wl jst over 2f out: pushed into ld over 1f out: idling and drvn out ins fnl f* **4/6**1

0400 **2** 3/4 **Bound By Honour (SAF)**42 6470 6-9-0 **89** (b) RyanMoore 8 100
(G L Moore) *chsd ldr 9f out tl rdn to ld over 2f out: drvn and hdd over 1f out: kpt on but a hld by wnr fnl f* **5/1**2

2330 **3** 2 1/4 **Can Can Star**26 6907 6-8-2 **82** oh1 AmyBaker(5) 1 89
(A W Carroll) *hld up in last pair: hdwy to chse ldng pair jst over 2f out: rdn and no imp over 1f out* **14/1**

6634 **4** 11 **Spitfire**9 7252 4-8-12 **87** JimCrowley 2 72
(J R Jenkins) *stdd s: hld up in last: c to outer and effrt over 2f out: sn outpcd by ldrs and n.d fnl 2f* **8/1**

1600 **5** 2 **Alpen Glen**77 5419 3-8-11 **90** J-PGuillambert 5 71
(M Johnston) *led tl hdd and rdn over 2f out: sn wknd and wl btn* **7/1**3

0000 **6** 7 **Weald Park (USA)**34 6695 3-8-3 **82** oh2 JimmyQuinn 4 49
(R Hannon) *chsd ldrs: rdn and struggling over 3f out: sn wl btn* **20/1**

3/- **7** 1 1/2 **Our Teddy (IRE)**903 2031 9-8-7 **82** oh14 (p) FrankieMcDonald 6 46
(R Curtis) *t.k.h: hld up wl in tch: rdn and wknd over 2f out: sn wl btn* **66/1**

2m 6.12s (-0.48) **Going Correction** +0.20s/f (Slow)
WFA 3 from 4yo+ 4lb **7** Ran SP% **113.2**
Speed ratings (Par 109): **109,108,106,97,96 90,89**
toteswingers:1&2:£2.40, 2&3:£8.10, 1&3:£2.00 CSF £4.29 CT £22.75 TOTE £1.70: £1.10, £2.60; EX 4.90 Trifecta £43.30 Pool: £630.03 - 10.75 winning units.
Owner Godolphin **Bred** Darley **Trained** Newmarket, Suffolk

FOCUS
A weak race for the grade, but Black Eagle should be capable of leaving the bare form behind in time. The wind remained strong and behind the runners in the straight.

NOTEBOOK
Black Eagle(IRE), waited with this time, still looked immature. Having needed a reminder before the final bend, he then came back on the bridle and looked set to win well but idled once in front, doing only enough. He looks the type to do better off a strong end-to-end gallop. (op 8-13 tchd 8-11 in places)
Bound By Honour(SAF) was always well placed and travelled nicely but was ultimately flattered to finish so close to the winner. (op 7-1 tchd 9-2)
Can Can Star has won four times over C&D but is plenty high enough in the weights and is thoroughly exposed. (op 12-1 tchd 10-1)
Spitfire, a bit keen to post, offered little on his first run beyond 1m. (tchd 9-1)
Alpen Glen dropped away after being allowed an easy lead. (op 15-2 tchd 9-1)

7394 BET INTERNATIONAL RUGBY - BETDAQ CONDITIONS STKS 6f (P)
3:05 (3:05) (Class 3) 3-Y-0+ **£7,771** (£2,312; £1,155; £577) **Stalls** Low

Form RPR
0020 **1** **Global City (IRE)**35 6678 3-8-12 97 (t) TedDurcan 4 102
(Saeed Bin Suroor) *taken down early: raced in midfield: rdn and effrt to chse ldrs 2f out: str chal ins fnl f: r.o wl to ld nr fin* **6/4**1

1532 **2** nk **Son Of The Cat (USA)**34 6694 3-8-12 92 (t) NCallan 3 101
(B Gubby) *chsd ldng trio: pushed along to chal over 1f out: led ins fnl f: edgd rt fnl 100yds: hdd nr fin* **7/2**2

3444 **3** 1 1/4 **Five Star Junior (USA)**60 5973 3-8-12 100 ShaneKelly 8 97
(Mrs L Stubbs) *hld up off the pce in midfield: hdwy ent fnl 2f: c wd and rdn over 1f out: kpt on but no imp fnl 75yds* **4/1**3

2000 **4** 1/2 **Capricorn Run (USA)**49 6270 6-8-12 102 (v) RobertWinston 7 97+
(A J McCabe) *chsd ldng pair tl pressed ldr over 2f out: rdn to ld narrowly 2f out: hdd ins fnl f: one pce whn hmpd fnl 75yds* **13/2**

1306 **5** 1 **Capone (IRE)**14 7172 4-8-12 70 PaulHanagan 9 92
(R Curtis) *hld up wl off the pce in last quartet: hdwy jst over 2f out: rdn over 1f out: kpt on fnl f but nvr gng pce to rch ldrs* **50/1**

3003 **6** 2 3/4 **Exclamation**18 7090 4-8-12 95 JimCrowley 2 83
(B J Meehan) *led: hung rt and hdd bnd 2f out: wknd u.p 1f out* **10/1**

0560 **7** 2 3/4 **Daddy's Gift (IRE)**11 7227 3-8-7 85 SteveDrowne 11 70
(R Hannon) *racd off the pce in midfield: rn wd and lost pl bnd 2f out: no imp and nt pushed ins fnl f* **33/1**

1240 **8** 2 1/4 **Artistic License (IRE)**44 6428 4-8-8 88 ow1 TonyCulhane 6 63
(M R Channon) *s.i.s: sn bustled along: nvr on terms* **16/1**

5066 **9** 3/4 **Diddums**3 7330 3-8-5 65 CarolineKelly(7) 10 65
(P S McEntee) *swtchd lft after s: a bhd* **200/1**

10 1/2 **Tin Cha Woody (USA)**15 7162 4-8-9 75 AndreaAtzeni(3) 1 63
(Daniel Mark Loughnane, Ire) *stdd s: a bhd* **40/1**

6-06 **11** 6 **Beau Jazz**19 7069 8-8-5 38 (p) LauraPike(7) 5 44
(W De Best-Turner) *chsd ldr tl over 2f out: wknd rapidly: wl bhd fnl f* **200/1**

1m 11.36s (-0.54) **Going Correction** +0.20s/f (Slow) **11** Ran SP% **118.9**
Speed ratings (Par 107): **111,110,108,108,106 103,99,96,95,94 86**
toteswingers:1&2:£36.10, 2&2:£42.60, 1&2:£52.90 CSF £6.74 TOTE £2.20: £1.10, £1.90, £1.70; EX 6.40 Trifecta £76.60 Pool: £930.17 - 8.98 winning units.
Owner Godolphin **Bred** Mrs Monica Hackett **Trained** Newmarket, Suffolk

FOCUS
This looked a good conditions contest beforehand, and the time was 0.20 seconds quicker than Doric Lady managed in the following 71-85 handicap, but the proximity of Capone in fifth, officially rated just 70, limits the form. The wind remained very strong, although in the straight it seemed to be slightly more across the runners than behind this time.

NOTEBOOK
Global City(IRE), a winner over C&D on his only previous Polytrack start, was never too far away and responded willingly to strong pressure in the straight to get up near the line. There will be opportunities for him both on the synthetic surface and turf at the Dubai Carnival next year. (op 9-4 tchd 5-2 in places)
Son Of The Cat(USA) ◆ travelled as well as any, but one suspects Neil Callan would like to have had a lead for even longer, and he was just run out of it in the final strides. On this evidence, he could improve for a drop to the minimum trip. (op 3-1)
Five Star Junior(USA), back on Polytrack after two months off, was given a confident ride, racing just behind the winner for much of the way, but, having travelled well, he couldn't find an immediate turn of foot when finally asked for his effort. (op 7-1)
Capricorn Run(USA), who was best off at the weights on his return from a 49-day break, was slightly squeezed out between the front two near the line, and that may have cost him third. (op 9-2)
Capone(IRE) seemed to run above himself but it remains to be seen whether he can repeat this form.
Exclamation, racing left-handed for the first time, was on the wrong lead going into the final bend and didn't handle that turn well. That cost him his chance. Official explanation: jockey said gelding hung right (op 8-1 tchd 7-1)

7395 HOLLOW LANE H'CAP 6f (P)
3:35 (3:35) (Class 4) (0-85,85) 3-Y-0+ **£5,180** (£1,156; £1,156; £384) **Stalls** Low

Form RPR
000 **1** **Doric Lady**23 6964 4-8-9 **76** KirstyMilczarek 7 86
(J A R Toller) *in tch in midfield: hdwy on inner jst over 2f out: chsd ldng pair and swtchd rt jst over 1f out: led ins fnl f: r.o wl* **14/1**

0513 **2** 1 1/2 **Johnstown Lad (IRE)**15 7161 5-8-11 **81** (t) AndreaAtzeni(3) 8 86
(Daniel Mark Loughnane, Ire) *chsd ldng trio: rdn and c centre on bnd jst over 2f out: unable qck and sltly outpcd over 1f out: rallied ins fnl f: nt pce to chal wnr* **7/1**3

6110 **2** dht **Even Bolder**30 6791 6-8-0 **74** ow1 KierenFox(7) 5 79
(E A Wheeler) *hld up in tch: hdwy on inner to ld wl over 1f out: sn rdn: hdd ins fnl f: wknd fnl 50yds* **14/1**

0444 **4** 2 1/2 **Drawnfromthepast (IRE)**15 7155 4-9-2 **83** (t) ShaneKelly 4 80
(J A Osborne) *chsd ldng pair tl rdn to chse ldr wl over 1f out: outpcd ins fnl f* **12/1**

0461 **5** nk **Ektimaal**9 7253 6-9-1 **82** JimCrowley 3 78
(E A L Dunlop) *bhd: rdn and hdwy towards outer jst over 2f out: swtchd rt over 1f out: r.o but nvr any ch* **2/1**1

0-04 **6** 3/4 **Cerito**13 7202 3-9-4 **85** SJCraine 6 79
(J R Boyle) *hld up in tch: nt clr run on bnd jst over 2f out: drvn and effrt over 1f out: plugged on but nvr gng pce to rch ldrs* **10/1**

2521 **7** 1 3/4 **Taurus Twins**17 7122 3-8-9 **76** (b) RobertWinston 9 64
(R J Price) *chsd ldr tl 2f out: sn lost pl u.p: wl hld fnl f* **9/1**

5406 **8** hd **Sunrise Safari (IRE)**22 6994 6-9-4 **85** (v) PaulHanagan 11 73
(R A Fahey) *hld up towards rr on outer: v wd and rdn on bnd jst over 2f out: nvr trbld ldrs* **4/1**2

000 **9** 4 **Ajigolo**103 4598 6-8-11 **78** NCallan 12 53
(N Wilson) *stdd s and dropped in bhd: hld up in tch: nt clr run bnd jst over 2f out: no ch w ldrs after* **14/1**

0052 **10** nk **Little Pete (IRE)**33 6723 4-9-2 **83** (t) LPKeniry 10 57
(I W McInnes) *nvr gng wl: sn bustled along in midfield: lost pl wl over 3f out: n.d after* **16/1**

4116 **11** 1/2 **Billy Red**36 6642 5-8-9 **76** (b) FergusSweeney 2 48
(J R Jenkins) *led tl rdn and hdd wl over 1f out: wknd qckly over 1f out: wl btn fnl f* **14/1**

2103 **12** 3 1/4 **Zebrano**23 6964 3-8-11 **78** ChrisCatlin 1 40
(Miss E C Lavelle) *sn wl outpcd in last: nvr on terms* **10/1**

1m 11.56s (-0.34) **Going Correction** +0.20s/f (Slow) **12** Ran SP% **134.3**
TOTE £20.80: £5.00 TRIFECTA Not won27 Owner.

FOCUS
A fair sprint handicap run at a decent pace thanks to Billy Red, who was pressured up front. The strong wind appeared to be across the runners in the straight.
Billy Red Official explanation: jockey said gelding lost its action in home straight
Zebrano Official explanation: jockey said gelding moved badly throughout
T/Plt: £201.90 to a £1 stake. Pool: £52,448.20. 189.60 winning tickets. T/Qpdt: £6.00 to a £1 stake. Pool: £3,745.53. 457.50 winning tickets. SP

7369 WOLVERHAMPTON (A.W) (L-H)
Saturday, November 14

OFFICIAL GOING: Standard
Wind: Moderate, behind Weather: Fine

7396 EUROPEAN BREEDERS' FUND MAIDEN FILLIES' STKS 7f 32y(P)
5:50 (5:53) (Class 5) 2-Y-0 **£3,885** (£1,156; £577; £288) **Stalls** High

Form RPR
24 **1** **Huroof (IRE)**83 5284 2-9-0 0 (p) TedDurcan 7 75+
(Saeed Bin Suroor) *chsd ldr: led wl over 4f out: rdn wl over 1f out: clr whn edgd rt ins fnl f: comf* **4/7**1

2 6 **Jounce (USA)** 2-9-0 0 RobertHavlin 3 60
(J H M Gosden) *a.p: outpcd by ldng pair over 2f out: pushed along over 1f out: r.o to take 2nd cl home: no ch w wnr* **10/1**3

0 **3** 1/2 **Evening Tale (IRE)**16 7135 2-9-0 0 NickyMackay 4 59
(B J Meehan) *led: hdd wl over 2f out: pushed along and ev ch 2f out: rdn and btn whn edgd lft in bhd wnr over 1f out: lost 2nd cl home* **25/1**

4 3 1/4 **Chicane** 2-9-0 0 LiamJones 8 51
(W J Haggas) *hld up in tch: pushed along and outpcd over 2f out: kpt on to take 4th ins fnl f* **20/1**

5 1 3/4 **Effervesce (IRE)** 2-9-0 0 RyanMoore 11 47
(Sir Michael Stoute) *dwlt: hld up in rr: pushed along wl over 2f out: kpt on fnl f: n.d* **7/2**[2]

04 6 nk **Princess Mandy (IRE)**[18] 7079 2-9-0 0 TomEaves 10 46
(K A Ryan) *hld up towards rr: pushed along wl over 2f out: nvr nr ldrs* **33/1**

04 7 1 1/2 **The Blue Dog (IRE)**[24] 6947 2-8-9 0 MatthewDavies(5) 9 42
(George Baker) *prom: outpcd over 2f out: n.d after* **100/1**

8 1 1/2 **Hovering Hawk (IRE)** 2-9-0 0 DaneO'Neill 1 39
(B W Hills) *s.i.s: sn hld up in mid-div: pushed along and outpcd over 2f out: rdn and wknd over 1f out* **25/1**

5 9 6 **Cheyenne Chant**[24] 6947 2-9-0 0 StephenDonohoe 6 24
(Sir Mark Prescott) *hld up in mid-div: pushed along over 3f out: sn bhd* **50/1**

10 3/4 **Sweet Caroline (IRE)** 2-9-0 0 DarryllHolland 12 22
(B W Hills) *hld up towards rr: no ch fnl 3f* **20/1**

11 7 **Pinewood Polly** 2-8-9 0 MarkCoumbe(5) 5 5
(S A Harris) *s.i.s: a in rr: no ch fnl 3f* **100/1**

1m 30.96s (1.36) **Going Correction** -0.025s/f (Stan) **11** Ran SP% **119.1**
Speed ratings (Par 93): **91,84,83,79,77 77,75,74,67,66 58**
toteswingers:1&2:£2.70, 1&3:£7.70, 2&3:£17.50 CSF £6.60 TOTE £1.70: £1.02, £2.40, £6.20; EX 10.00.

Owner Godolphin **Bred** Shadwell Estate Company Limited **Trained** Newmarket, Suffolk

■ Stewards' Enquiry : Matthew Davies 10-day ban: did not take all reasonable and permissible measures throughout the race (Nov 28-Dec 7)

FOCUS
As the market suggested, this was not a competitive race, and a steady pace left those held up at a disadvantage. The winner edged off the inside rail in the closing stages.

NOTEBOOK
Huroof(IRE), from a yard that remains in tremendous form, was all the rage in the market on the back of two fair turf runs and probably did not have to improve too much to get off the mark in ready fashion in first-time cheekpieces on this all-weather debut. She had the rub of things in a muddling event but may be capable of further progress. (op 4-6 tchd 8-15)

Jounce(USA) ◆, a sister to the yard's very useful Close Alliance, was fairly easy to back but shaped with promise under a hands and heels ride on this racecourse debut to divide a couple of more experienced rivals. The step up to 1m is going to suit and she looks capable of winning a similar event. (op 8-1)

Evening Tale(IRE) was well beaten after racing keenly on her debut but fared a good deal better this time, despite showing a tendency to hang left under pressure. She had the run of the race though, and may continue to look vulnerable in this type of event. Official explanation: jockey said filly hung left

Chicane, a half-sister to Polytrack winner and to smart miler Whazzis and to a couple of other winners up to 1m, was easy to back in the market but showed ability on this racecourse debut. The step up to 1m and beyond should suit and she should win a race. (op 18-1)

Effervesce(IRE), who cost 280,000gns and who has plenty of winners in his pedigree, attracted support and hinted at ability on this racecourse debut after a tardy start. She was not knocked about, is in very good hands and should leave this bare form well behind in due course. (op 10-3 tchd 3-1 and 4-1)

Princess Mandy(IRE), upped in trip for this return to Polytrack, posted her best effort yet. She leaves the impression she will be well suited by the step up to 1m and the step into run-of-the-mill handicap company.

The Blue Dog(IRE) had been soundly beaten on her first two starts and again had her limitations exposed on this Polytrack debut after racing keenly and edging to her left. She was not knocked about but it was something of a surprise that the stewards saw fit to suspend her rider for 10 days under the non-triers' rule. Low-grade handicaps will be the way forward. Official explanation: jockey said, regarding running and riding, that his orders were to ride the filly as he found it and finish as close as he could, adding that it was hanging both ways and running in snatches throughout, he was concerned that if he let it down it would wander even more.

7397 CLEANEVENT (S) STKS — 5f 20y(P)
6:20 (6:20) (Class 6) 3-Y-0+ — £2,047 (£604; £302) Stalls Low

Form RPR

3134 1 **Decider (USA)**[8] 7280 6-9-9 58 (p) LiamJones 4 68
(R A Harris) *hld up in tch: pushed along over 2f out: rdn to ld wl ins fnl f: r.o* **7/1**[3]

0025 2 nk **Grudge**[18] 7086 4-9-3 63 FrancisNorton 11 61
(Ollie Pears) *w ldr: rdn to ld jst over 1f out: hdd wl ins fnl f: kpt on* **8/1**

2200 3 1 **Monsieur Reynard**[24] 6939 4-9-3 55 RichardKingscote 3 57
(J M Bradley) *hld up in mid-div: carried hd high and hdwy wl over 1f out: sn pushed along: kpt on towards fin* **10/1**

1141 4 1 1/2 **Bertie Southstreet**[28] 6857 6-9-9 67 (v) DarryllHolland 7 58
(Karen George) *led: rdn and hdd jst over 1f out: one pce* **2/1**[1]

3022 5 2 1/4 **Thunder Bay**[2] 7358 4-9-9 57 TomEaves 9 50
(R A Fahey) *hld up towards rr: pushed along 3f out: rdn and sme hdwy over 1f out: one pce fnl f* **7/1**[3]

0650 6 6 **Wreningham**[21] 7021 4-9-3 59 (b[1]) StephenDonohoe 6 22
(P Leech) *prom: rdn jst over 2f out: wknd wl over 1f out* **16/1**

00-6 7 2 3/4 **Edge End**[19] 7068 5-8-12 50 RichardEvans(5) 13 12
(P D Evans) *s.i.s: in rr: reminder over 3f out: nvr nr ldrs* **33/1**

8 1/2 **Queen Of Dobbin (IRE)**[129] 3756 3-8-5 50 JamesPSullivan(7) 5 6
(Lee Smyth, Ire) *chsd ldrs: pushed along over 3f out: wknd wl over 2f out* **50/1**

5005 9 nk **Cheshire Rose**[24] 6939 4-8-12 52 (p) AndrewElliott 12 4
(A M Hales) *s.i.s: a in rr* **33/1**

0404 10 1 **Especially Special (IRE)**[21] 7021 3-8-13 65 ow1 AdamKirby 1 2
(Peter Grayson) *chsd ldrs: pushed along over 2f out: rdn and wknd wl over 1f out* **4/1**[2]

6004 U **Grimes Faith**[11] 7219 6-9-4 63 (p) AmyRyan(5) 2 —
(K A Ryan) *towards rr: pushed along whn hit rails and uns rdr over 3f out* **8/1**

61.61 secs (-0.69) **Going Correction** -0.025s/f (Stan) **11** Ran SP% **123.4**
Speed ratings (Par 101): **104,103,101,99,95 86,81,81,80,79** —
toteswingers:1&2:£16.80, 1&3:£17.00, 2&3:£22.50 CSF £64.32 TOTE £11.00: £2.70, £3.00, £3.20; EX 63.10.There was no bid for the winner. Grimes Faith was claimed by R. C. Guest for £6,000.

Owner Robert Bailey **Bred** Green Willow Farms **Trained** Earlswood, Monmouths

FOCUS
A modest seller in which the pace was sound. The winner raced in the centre in the straight.

Especially Special(IRE) Official explanation: jockey said filly hung left-handed

7398 CLEANDOMAIN H'CAP — 5f 20y(P)
6:50 (6:51) (Class 5) (0-70,70) 3-Y-0+ — £3,238 (£963; £481; £240) Stalls Low

Form RPR

0055 1 **Caledonia Princess**[3] 7329 3-8-12 64 (b) TonyCulhane 1 74
(R Curtis) *hld up in rr: stdy hdwy on ins 2f out: rdn to ld wl ins fnl f: r.o* **7/1**[3]

1600 2 3/4 **Perlachy**[16] 7138 5-8-12 64 (v) KirstyMilczarek 5 71
(J R Holt) *a.p: rdn to ld ins fnl f: sn hdd: kpt on* **16/1**

01 3 shd **Fourtowns Flyer (IRE)**[28] 6856 5-9-3 69 (tp) GeorgeBaker 9 76
(Lee Smyth, Ire) *w ldr: led over 3f out: rdn and hdd wl ins fnl f: kpt on* **7/1**[3]

3321 4 1/2 **Lost In Paris (IRE)**[44] 6410 3-8-13 65 (b) DNolan 8 70
(T D Easterby) *a.p: rdn jst over 1f out: kpt on ins fnl f* **9/2**[2]

3600 5 nk **Stash**[17] 7122 3-9-1 67 JerryO'Dwyer 3 71
(R Hollinshead) *hld up in mid-div: hdwy on ins over 2f out: rdn wl over 1f out: kpt on ins fnl f* **10/1**

0515 6 1 **Lithaam (IRE)**[2] 7355 5-9-1 67 (p) RyanMoore 2 67
(J M Bradley) *hld up towards rr: rdn and r.o fnl f: nt rch ldrs* **5/2**[1]

1006 7 hd **Nomoreblondes**[11] 7224 5-9-1 67 (p) PhillipMakin 4 66
(P T Midgley) *hld up in mid-div: hdwy over 2f out: rdn wl over 1f out: one pce fnl f* **25/1**

0544 8 2 1/4 **Cape Royal**[2] 7355 9-8-13 65 (bt) RichardKingscote 6 56
(J M Bradley) *led over 1f: w ldr tl rdn and wknd 1f out* **11/1**

6005 9 1 1/4 **Sands Crooner (IRE)**[17] 7122 6-9-4 70 (v) TomEaves 10 57
(J G Given) *s.i.s: in rr: rdn over 1f out: nvr nr ldrs* **16/1**

3001 10 nk **Lord Of The Reins (IRE)**[11] 7223 5-9-2 68 TPQueally 11 54
(J G Given) *s.i.s: in rr: pushed along over 2f out: rdn jst over 1f out: nvr nr ldrs* **11/1**

1561 11 2 1/2 **Spirit Of Coniston**[18] 7086 6-8-9 66 PaulPickard(5) 13 43
(P T Midgley) *chsd ldrs on outside: lost pl 3f out: bhd fnl 2f* **16/1**

3000 12 shd **Handsome Cross (IRE)**[28] 6857 8-8-13 65 StephenDonohoe 7 41
(W J Musson) *s.i.s: a in rr* **20/1**

0044 13 2 1/2 **First Order**[16] 7136 8-8-10 67 ow1 (v) AnnStokell(5) 12 34
(Miss A Stokell) *prom tl rdn and wknd 2f out* **33/1**

61.05 secs (-1.25) **Going Correction** -0.025s/f (Stan) **13** Ran SP% **126.7**
Speed ratings (Par 103): **109,107,107,106,106 104,104,100,98,98 94,94,90**
toteswingers:1&2:£35.10, 1&3:£13.20, 2&3:£35.40 CSF £118.01 CT £860.70 TOTE £10.50: £2.70, £4.40, £2.80; EX 220.50.

Owner Isla & Colin Cage **Bred** Mrs I M Cage And C J Cage **Trained** Lambourn, Berks

FOCUS
A modest but fairly open handicap in which the pace was sound and the winner raced towards the centre in the straight.

Fourtowns Flyer(IRE) ◆ Official explanation: jockey said gelding pulled up lame
Spirit Of Coniston Official explanation: jockey said gelding hung left throughout
First Order Official explanation: jockey said gelding ran too freely and hung right

7399 GREENHOUS DAF FILLIES' H'CAP — 1m 1f 103y(P)
7:20 (7:20) (Class 5) (0-70,72) 3-Y-0+ — £3,238 (£963; £481; £240) Stalls Low

Form RPR

3243 1 **Insolence (USA)**[14] 7195 3-9-5 70 RyanMoore 1 76
(Sir Michael Stoute) *mde all: qcknd clr 2f out: rdn wl over 1f out: drvn out* **3/1**[1]

6254 2 1 **Chantilly Pearl (USA)**[56] 6124 3-8-13 64 TPQueally 11 68
(J G Given) *hld up towards rr: hdwy over 2f out: rdn over 1f out: tk 2nd wl ins fnl f: nt rch wnr* **8/1**

3056 3 3/4 **Mutually Mine (USA)**[58] 6023 3-8-13 64 JerryO'Dwyer 5 66
(Mrs P Sly) *hld up in tch: rdn and n.m.r briefly over 2f out: sn chsng wnr: no ex and lost 2nd wl ins fnl f* **14/1**

0344 4 shd **Chatanoogachoochoo**[28] 6861 4-8-13 61 JimmyQuinn 2 63
(M Hill) *hld up in tch on ins: nt clr run and swtchd rt over 2f out: rdn over 1f out: kpt on one pce ins fnl f* **11/2**[3]

5 hd **Sally Bawn (IRE)**[22] 7009 4-9-0 62 RobertWinston 7 64
(Gordon Elliott, Ire) *hld up in tch: lost pl 3f out: sn pushed along: rdn 2f out: styd on fnl f: nt rch ldrs* **7/1**

0-40 6 1 **Belle Noverre (IRE)**[22] 7012 5-9-2 69 (p) DEMullins(5) 12 69
(Shaun Harley, Ire) *hld up in rr: pushed along and hdwy wl over 1f out: sn hrd rdn: one pce fnl f* **12/1**

2336 7 1 1/2 **Arcola (IRE)**[56] 6113 3-9-3 68 DarryllHolland 10 64
(D M Simcock) *hld up in rr: nt clr run on ins ent st: rdn over 1f out: no real prog fnl f* **5/1**[2]

0624 8 1 3/4 **Lunar River (FR)**[16] 7134 6-9-6 68 (t) FergusSweeney 13 61
(David Pinder) *hld up towards rr: pushed along wl over 1f out: sn rdn: nvr nr ldrs* **14/1**

05-0 9 1/2 **Chia (IRE)**[30] 6806 6-9-1 63 DaneO'Neill 9 55
(D Haydn Jones) *hld up towards rr: effrt whn nt clr run ent st: rdn over 1f out: n.d* **25/1**

4110 10 12 **Miss Sophisticat**[10] 7248 3-9-7 72 (v) JimCrowley 4 39
(W J Knight) *sn chsng ldr: pushed along over 3f out: lost 2nd jst over 2f out: wknd wl over 1f out: eased whn no ch ins fnl f* **11/2**[3]

1405 11 7 **Coral Shores**[117] 4139 4-9-2 64 (v) ChrisCatlin 8 16
(P W Hiatt) *prom tl wknd wl over 2f out: eased whn no ch over 1f out* **33/1**

0000 12 38 **Millie's Rock (IRE)**[95] 4876 4-9-7 69 PhillipMakin 3 —
(K A Ryan) *t.k.h early: prom tl rdn and wknd 2f out: virtually p.u fnl f* **20/1**

2m 0.86s (-0.84) **Going Correction** -0.025s/f (Stan)
WFA 3 from 4yo+ 3lb **12** Ran SP% **128.6**
Speed ratings (Par 100): **102,101,100,100,100 99,97,96,95,85 79,45**
toteswingers:1&2:£9.00, 1&3:£15.80, 2&3:£25.60 CSF £29.72 CT £312.48 TOTE £3.50: £2.00, £2.80, £3.50; EX 42.40.

Owner Ms Nicola Mahoney **Bred** Fortress Pacific Equine Llc **Trained** Newmarket, Suffolk

FOCUS
Mainly exposed performers in a modest handicap. The winner, who raced in the centre in the straight, was allowed to dictate an ordinary gallop until quickening clear turning for home and this bare form does not look entirely reliable.

Arcola(IRE) Official explanation: jockey said filly was denied a clear run
Millie's Rock(IRE) Official explanation: jockey said filly lost its action

7400 EBF CLEAN WASTE SOLUTIONS MAIDEN STKS — 1m 1f 103y(P)
7:50 (7:52) (Class 5) 2-Y-0 — £3,885 (£1,156; £577; £288) Stalls Low

Form RPR

1 **Powerful Melody (USA)** 2-9-3 0 DaneO'Neill 2 74
(Saeed Bin Suroor) *s.i.s: hld up in rr: pushed along and hdwy over 2f out: rdn to ld wl ins fnl f: r.o* **7/2**[2]

0 2 1/2 **Bowdler's Magic**[17] 7116 2-9-3 0 AndrewElliott 10 73
(M Johnston) *sn led: rdn over 1f out: hdd wl ins fnl f: nt qckn* **25/1**

352 **3** 3/4 **Royal Etiquette (IRE)**[62] 5907 2-9-3 76 JimmyQuinn 13 72
(H J L Dunlop) *wnt rt s: keen early: sn chsng ldr: rdn over 2f out: no ex wl ins fnl f* **4/1**[3]

5 **4** 1 1/2 **Astral Flower**[13] 7199 2-8-12 0 RyanMoore 5 64
(Sir Michael Stoute) *led early: a.p: pushed along 3f out: rdn over 1f out: kpt on same pce* **8/1**

4 **5** 3/4 **Mercoliano**[14] 7193 2-9-0 0 AndreaAtzeni(3) 8 67
(M Botti) *hld up in tch: pushed along over 2f out: rdn wl over 1f out: one pce fnl f* **7/1**

6 2 1/4 **Willing Foe (USA)** 2-9-3 0 TedDurcan 11 63
(Saeed Bin Suroor) *hld up in tch: wknd wl over 2f out* **1/1**[1]

60 **7** hd **Fusenam**[32] 6763 2-9-3 0 PhillipMakin 6 63
(Miss J A Camacho) *hld up in mid-div: pushed along over 2f out: no hdwy* **66/1**

0 **8** 2 1/4 **Katchmore (IRE)**[65] 5787 2-9-3 0 FergusSweeney 4 58
(Jean-Rene Auvray) *hld up in mid-div: hdwy 3f out: wknd wl over 1f out* **100/1**

00 **9** 1/2 **Lis Pendens**[34] 6697 2-9-3 0 GeorgeBaker 9 57
(W R Muir) *dwlt and half-rrd s: a in rr* **33/1**

50 **10** 15 **Gold Party**[68] 5722 2-9-3 0 ChrisCatlin 12 29
(K McAuliffe) *a in rr* **66/1**

0 **11** 105 **Another Character (USA)**[31] 6772 2-9-3 0 FrancisNorton 3 —
(M Blanshard) *a in rr: t.o fnl 3f* **100/1**

6 **12** 4 **Lily Lily**[8] 7277 2-8-12 0 TonyCulhane 7 —
(K McAuliffe) *a in rr: t.o fnl 3f* **100/1**

2m 1.76s (0.06) **Going Correction** -0.025s/f (Stan) 12 Ran SP% **128.6**
Speed ratings (Par 96): **98,97,96,95,94 92,92,90,90,76 —,—**
toteswingers:1&2:£22.50, 1&3:£4.30, 2&3:£21.90 CSF £92.82 TOTE £4.50: £1.50, £6.60, £1.40; EX 108.20.
Owner Godolphin **Bred** B P Walden, P Madden, L Taylor Et Al **Trained** Newmarket, Suffolk

FOCUS
The overall level of this form is only fair, but the winner looks better than the bare result suggests. The pace was ordinary and the winner raced towards the centre in the straight.

NOTEBOOK
Powerful Melody(USA) ◆, who cost $550,000 last year and who holds a Derby entry, was the in-form stable's perceived second string but created a very favourable impression after falling out of the stalls and after running green to win a shade snugly. He should be all the better for this experience and, although this bare form is nothing special, he has plenty of physical scope and appeals strongly as the type to win again. (tchd 3-1)
Bowdler's Magic, too green to do himself justice on his debut, fared a good deal better upped in trip on this all-weather debut, despite being allowed to dictate an ordinary gallop. His stable tends to improve this type and he is sure to win a race on artificial surfaces.
Royal Etiquette(IRE) had shown fair form in two of his three starts up to 1m on turf and looks the best guide to the worth of this form on this all-weather debut and this first run for two months. He should continue to give a good account, though will remain vulnerable to the better types in this grade.
Astral Flower gave problems at the start but proved more tractable in the race and easily bettered the form of her debut over 1m at Lingfield. She is nothing out of the ordinary but may do better when qualified for a handicap mark. (op 15-2)
Mercoliano again hinted at ability up in trip back at this course and who remains open to further progress. He will be of more interest once handicapped.
Willing Foe(USA), who was well supported from a yard in scintillating form, was the disappointment of the race on this racecourse debut. This half-brother to Ribblesdale winner Michita dropped out fairly tamely after enjoying the run of the race and will have to show a fair bit more before he is a solid betting option. (tchd 11-10 after early 5-4)
Lis Pendens Official explanation: jockey said gelding hung left in straight
Lily Lily Official explanation: jockey said filly had a breathing problem

7401 CLEAN CONCIERGE MAIDEN STKS 1m 141y(P)
8:20 (8:21) (Class 5) 3-Y-O+ **£2,590** (£770; £385; £192) **Stalls** Low

Form RPR

333 **1** **Maria Nunziata**[145] 3214 3-8-12 73 TPQueally 5 76+
(J Noseda) *led early: a.p: led jst over 1f out: sn edgd rt: r.o wl* **2/1**[2]

2 4 1/2 **No Mean Trick (USA)** 3-9-3 0 AdamKirby 2 71+
(C G Cox) *hld up in tch: chsd ldr over 2f out: rdn and ev ch wl over 1f out: one pce ins fnl f* **5/4**[1]

3 **3** 1 1/2 **Laureldeans Best (IRE)**[111] 4354 3-8-12 0 PaulHanagan 9 62
(R A Fahey) *hld up: hdwy 2f out: sn pushed along: styd on same pce fnl f: tk 3rd towards fin* **11/4**[3]

4 3/4 **Harry Days (IRE)**[45] 6404 3-8-10 0 MatthewLawson(7) 12 65
(P J Lally, Ire) *sn chsng ldr: led over 2f out: rdn and hdd jst over 1f out: wknd ins fnl f* **33/1**

400 **5** 2 3/4 **Always The Sun**[15] 7150 3-8-7 42 MarkCoumbe(5) 7 54
(P Leech) *hld up in rr: pushed along over 3f out: short-lived effrt wl over 1f out* **66/1**

4- **6** 10 **Mayta Capac (USA)**[465] 4728 3-9-3 0 DarryllHolland 1 36
(D M Simcock) *hld up in mid-div: wknd over 2f out* **12/1**

7 2 1/4 **Nanny Doe (IRE)**[22] 7008 3-8-5 0 (p) JamesPSullivan(7) 6 26
(Lee Smyth, Ire) *sn led: hdd over 2f out: wknd wl over 1f out* **50/1**

0 **8** 1 1/4 **Latin Connection (IRE)**[2] 7361 3-9-3 0 GeorgeBaker 4 28
(Lee Smyth, Ire) *a in rr: rdn and struggling wl over 1f out* **66/1**

1m 50.84s (0.34) **Going Correction** -0.025s/f (Stan)
WFA 3 from 4yo+ 3lb 8 Ran SP% **120.0**
Speed ratings (Par 103): **97,93,91,91,88 79,77,76**
toteswingers:1&2:£1.50, 1&3:£1.40, 2&3:£1.60 CSF £5.15 TOTE £3.20: £1.10, £1.10, £1.40; EX 4.80.
Owner Normandie Stud Ltd **Bred** Normandie Stud Ltd **Trained** Newmarket, Suffolk

FOCUS
An uncompetitive maiden in which the pace was modest and the form is held down by the proximity of the fourth and the 42-rated fifth. The winner, who challenged on the inside turning for home, drifted into the centre late on.

7402 CE RISK, SAFETY & SECURITY H'CAP 2m 119y(P)
8:50 (8:50) (Class 4) (0-85,84) 3-Y-O+ **£5,046** (£1,510; £755; £377; £188) **Stalls** Low

Form RPR

2505 **1** shd **Clear Reef**[70] 5656 5-9-6 79 (p) AndreaAtzeni(3) 2 87
(Jane Chapple-Hyam) *hld up: hdwy 3f out: chal over 1f out: sn carried rt and hit on nse by rival jockey's whip: rdn and r.o ins fnl f: fin 2nd, shd: awrdd r* **4/1**[2]

220 **2** **Wicked Daze (IRE)**[15] 7151 6-10-0 84 TomEaves 6 92
(K A Ryan) *set slow pce: qcknd over 3f out: rdn and edgd rt fr over 1f out: drvn out: fin 1st disqualified and plcd 2nd* **6/1**

1341 **3** 2 3/4 **Calculating (IRE)**[8] 7279 5-8-2 65 TobyAtkinson(7) 3 70
(M D I Usher) *hld up: rdn and hdwy 2f out: styd on one pce ins fnl f* **5/1**[3]

0005 **4** 5 **Wabbraan (USA)**[8] 7272 4-8-4 65 AmyBaker(5) 7 64
(M Hill) *chsd wnr tl over 3f out: wknd over 2f out* **40/1**

3212 **5** nse **Samaaha**[14] 7178 3-8-11 76 TedDurcan 4 75
(Saeed Bin Suroor) *prom: pushed along over 3f out: wknd wl over 1f out* **6/5**[1]

-564 **6** hd **Bentley Brook (IRE)**[261] 687 7-9-7 77 DarryllHolland 9 75
(R Curtis) *hld up in tch: chsd wnr over 3f out tl over 2f out: rdn over 1f out: wknd ins fnl f* **33/1**

000/ **7** 4 **Genari**[2] 4587 6-8-9 65 (bt) RobertWinston 5 59
(Gordon Elliott, Ire) *s.i.s: hld up and bhd: rdn and struggling over 1f out* **8/1**

0500 **8** 1 3/4 **Bulwark (IRE)**[15] 7151 7-9-12 82 StephenDonohoe 8 74
(Ian Williams) *hld up wl in rr: no ch fnl 4f* **16/1**

3m 42.03s (0.23) **Going Correction** -0.025s/f (Stan)
WFA 3 from 4yo+ 9lb 8 Ran SP% **118.8**
Speed ratings (Par 105): **97,98,96,94,94 94,92,91**
toteswingers:1&2:£5.00, 1&3:£3.30, 2&3:£4.70 CSF £29.36 CT £124.18 TOTE £5.50: £1.40, £2.10, £1.30; EX 29.70.
Owner Mrs Jane Chapple-Hyam **Bred** Hesmonds Stud Ltd **Trained** Newmarket, Suffolk
■ Stewards' Enquiry : Tom Eaves three-day ban: careless riding (Nov 28-30)

FOCUS
A fair handicap featuring mainly exposed sorts but another modest gallop and a race in which the market leader disappointed. The first two ended up towards the centre in the straight but the stewards reversed the first two placings after a lengthy enquiry.
Bulwark(IRE) Official explanation: jockey said gelding never travelled

7403 CE PROPERTY SERVICES GROUP H'CAP 1m 141y(P)
9:20 (9:20) (Class 6) (0-60,63) 3-Y-O+ **£2,388** (£705; £352) **Stalls** Low

Form RPR

4221 **1** **Thunderstruck**[11] 7225 4-9-8 63 (p) ChrisCatlin 8 73
(J A Glover) *mde all: rdn wl over 1f out: edgd rt ins fnl f: drvn out* **3/1**[1]

6100 **2** nk **New World Order (IRE)**[25] 6918 5-9-1 59 (t) JackMitchell(3) 5 68
(Edgar Byrne) *w wnr: rdn jst over 2f out: r.o towards fin* **14/1**

-336 **3** 3 **Lord Of The Dance (IRE)**[26] 6910 3-9-2 60 JimmyQuinn 1 62
(J M P Eustace) *a.p: hrd rdn fr jst over 1f out: one pce ins fnl f* **5/1**[2]

5510 **4** 3 1/2 **Confide In Me**[13] 7197 5-9-0 58 AndreaAtzeni(3) 4 52
(G A Butler) *hld up in tch: pushed along and outpcd over 2f out: btn wl over 1f out* **7/1**[3]

2000 **5** 3/4 **Diamond Lass (IRE)**[26] 6900 4-9-1 56 PaulHanagan 9 48
(R A Fahey) *prom tl rdn and wknd over 2f out* **20/1**

1302 **6** 1/2 **Our Kes (IRE)**[25] 6917 7-9-2 57 IanMongan 2 48+
(P Howling) *hld up in rr: nt clr run over 2f out and wl over 1f out: nt clr run and swtchd lft ins fnl f: nvr nrr* **7/1**[3]

1355 **7** 1/2 **Golden Prospect**[29] 6828 5-9-3 58 PaulFitzsimons 10 48
(Miss J R Tooth) *dwlt: hld up in rr: pushed along wl over 1f out: rdn and kpt on fnl f: n.d* **20/1**

-056 **8** 1/2 **Climate (IRE)**[10] 7236 10-8-10 56 RichardEvans(5) 13 45
(P D Evans) *hld up wl in rr: swtchd rt over 2f out and wl over 1f out: rdn ins fnl f: nvr nr ldrs* **33/1**

6046 **9** 3/4 **Island Music (IRE)**[17] 7113 4-9-3 58 (p) TomEaves 7 45
(J J Quinn) *hld up towards rr: pushed along over 3f out: rdn over 2f out: short-lived effrt on ins wl over 1f out* **14/1**

3103 **10** 3 **Gifted Heir (IRE)**[9] 7250 5-9-2 57 RobertWinston 3 37
(A Bailey) *hld up in mid-div: sme prog on ins over 3f out: rdn and wknd 2f out* **3/1**[1]

4050 **11** 12 **Zabeel Tower**[28] 6847 6-9-2 57 (v) PhillipMakin 6 10
(R Allan) *hld up in mid-div: pushed along over 2f out: wknd over 1f out: eased ins fnl f* **16/1**

1300 **12** 11 **Obe Brave**[36] 6637 6-8-13 59 (b[1]) AndrewHeffernan(5) 12 —
(Lee Smyth, Ire) *dwlt: hld up towards rr: stdy prog on outside 6f out: reminders over 3f out: wknd wl over 2f out: eased ins fnl f* **25/1**

1m 49.35s (-1.15) **Going Correction** -0.025s/f (Stan)
WFA 3 from 4yo+ 3lb 12 Ran SP% **127.2**
Speed ratings (Par 101): **104,103,101,97,97 96,96,95,95,92 81,72**
toteswingers:1&2:£9.60, 1&3:£4.70, 2&3:£17.50 CSF £50.81 CT £219.85 TOTE £5.00: £1.80, £4.20, £2.00; EX 60.90 Place 6 £134.67, Place 5 £97.03.
Owner Paul J Dixon **Bred** Mrs Yvette Dixon **Trained** Babworth, Notts
■ Stewards' Enquiry : Jack Mitchell one-day ban: used whip with excessive force (Nov 28)

FOCUS
A modest handicap and an ordinary gallop meant those up with the pace held a big edge. The winner raced in the centre in the straight.
Our Kes(IRE) Official explanation: jockey said mare was denied a clear run
T/Plt: £103.90 to a £1 stake. Pool: £92,182.45. 647.34 winning tickets. T/Qpdt: £19.90 to a £1 stake. Pool: £8,067.05. 299.90 winning tickets. KH

7249 SAINT-CLOUD (L-H)
Saturday, November 14

OFFICIAL GOING: Heavy

7404a CRITERIUM DE SAINT-CLOUD (GROUP 1) (C&F) 1m 2f
1:35 (1:36) 2-Y-O **£138,689** (£55,485; £27,743; £13,859; £6,942)

RPR

1 **Passion For Gold (USA)**[48] 6318 2-9-0 LDettori 9 117+
(Saeed Bin Suroor) *racd in 5th: hdwy arnd outside to ld ent st 2 1/2f out: sn clr: easily* **6/4**[1]

2 6 **Mikhail Glinka (IRE)**[9] 7260 2-9-0 JAHeffernan 4 106
(A P O'Brien, Ire) *racd in 7th: 8th 1 1/2f out: styd on dourly u.str.p to take 2nd fnl 60yds* **13/5**[2]

3 3/4 **Zazou (GER)**[22] 2-9-0 MGuyon 7 105
(Mario Hofer, Germany) *hld up in 8th: hdwy down outside to go 2nd over 1f out: lost 2nd fnl 60yds* **63/10**

4 2 1/2 **Don Carlos (GER)**[19] 7073 2-9-0 JMurtagh 1 100
(A P O'Brien, Ire) *racd in 6th: hdwy towards ins to dispute 2nd under 1 1/2f out: one pce* **13/5**[2]

5 2 1/2 **Kaage (IRE)**[19] 2-9-0 OPeslier 8 96
(F Head, France) *last to under 2f out: nvr a factor* **89/10**

6 2 1/2 **Gardening Leave**[21] 7034 2-9-0 WilliamBuick 6 91
(A M Balding) *cl up: 5th and rdn ent st: sn wknd* **29/1**

7 2 1/2 **Banyan Tree (IRE)**[9] 7260 2-9-0 CO'Donoghue 2 87
(A P O'Brien, Ire) *prom: 2nd over 2f out: wknd over 1f out* **13/5**[2]

8 1 1/2 **Simon De Montfort (IRE)**[20] 2-9-0 MBarzalona 3 84
(A Fabre, France) *racd in 4th: wknd over 2f out* **6/4**[1]

9 5 **Layali Al Andalus**[48] 6318 2-9-0 .... JoeFanning 5 75
(M Johnston) *led to 2 1/2f out: wknd* **17/5**[3]
2m 19.1s (3.10) **Going Correction** +0.625s/f (Yiel) **9** Ran SP% **213.2**
Speed ratings: **112,107,106,104,102 100,98,97,93**
PARI-MUTUEL: WIN 2.50 (coupled with Simon de Montfort); PL 3.20, 2.80,2.40; DF 30.60.
Owner Godolphin **Bred** Mr And Mrs M Roy Jackson **Trained** Newmarket, Suffolk

NOTEBOOK
Passion For Gold(USA), third to St Nicholas Abbey in the Beresford on the back of a Thirsk maiden win, put himself in the Derby picture with a decisive success in this Group 1. Relishing the underfoot conditions, he pulled right away in the closing stages, proving suited by the extra distance, and earnt himself a 20-1 quote for the Epsom Classic in the process. Perhaps more siginificantly, though, he paid a huge compliment to St Nicholas Abbey.
Mikhail Glinka(IRE), successful in a Leopardstown Listed event in testing ground last time out, again showed his liking for these sort of conditions, but the winner was in a different league.
Don Carlos(GER), considered to be still weak by his rider, is expected to do better on a sounder surface.
Gardening Leave, stepping up in grade and distance, didn't run too badly and there should be better to come next year with a winter on his back.
Layali Al Andalus took them along in the early stages but dropped out tamely inside the final 2f. This ground was just too testing for him.

6714 FRANKFURT (L-H)
Saturday, November 14

OFFICIAL GOING: Heavy

7406a HESSEN POKAL (GROUP 3) 1m 2f
2:05 (2:24) 3-Y-0+ **£31,068** (£9,709; £4,854; £2,913)

RPR
1 **Zafisio (IRE)**[13] 7208 3-9-0 .... GrahamGibbons 4 114
(R Curtis) *5th early: wnt 3rd after 4f: 3rd st: hrd rdn to go 2nd over 1f out: persistent chal to ld last 60yds* **12/5**[2]
2 2 **Liang Kay (GER)**[21] 7039 4-9-3 .... YLerner 12 109
(Uwe Ostmann, Germany) *hld up: gd hdwy to ld over 1 1/2f out: strly pressed fr 1f out: worn down and hdd last 60yds* **17/10**[1]
3 4 **Schiller Danon (GER)**[21] 7039 3-8-11 .... APietsch 10 99
(W Hickst, Germany) *hld up: hdwy to go 2nd on ins over 1 1/2f out: lost 2nd and one pce over 1f out* **44/5**
4 7 **Alianthus (GER)**[349] 6-8-13 .... FilipMinarik 1 83
(J Hirschberger, Germany) *led to over 1 1/2f out: one pce* **98/10**
5 1/2 **Court Canibal**[27] 6890 4-9-3 .... GMasure 11 86
(M Delzangles, France) *midfield: kpt on fnl 2f but nvr nr ldrs* **19/2**
6 2 **Adolfina (GER)**[27] 4-8-11 .... KKerekes 3 76
(W Figge, Germany) *midfield: outpcd fnl 2f* **25/1**
7 26 **Themelie Island (IRE)**[34] 6714 4-8-11 .... EPedroza 2 24
(A Trybuhl, Germany) *hld up in last: outpcd by ldrs fr over 2f out* **159/10**
8 2 **Pont Des Arts (FR)**[21] 7039 5-9-1 .... FSpanu 7 24
(A Scharer, Germany) *racd in 2nd: wknd qckly 2f out* **104/10**
9 1 **White Lightning (GER)**[21] 7039 7-8-13 .... JBojko 13 20
(U Stech, Germany) *hld up in 10th: a bhd* **43/1**
10 15 **Duellant (IRE)**[42] 6500 4-8-13 .... AGoritz 6 —
(P Schiergen, Germany) *cl up tl wknd qckly 2f out* **88/1**
11 1/2 **Woy Woy (IRE)**[104] 5-9-1 .... LennartHammer-Hansen 8 —
(L Reuterskiold Snr, Sweden) *hld up: prog arnd outside to press ldrs over 2f out: wknd rapidly* **57/1**
12 2 **Takhir (IRE)**[435] 5686 3-8-9 .... AStarke 9 —
(P Schiergen, Germany) *a in rr* **74/10**[3]
13 1/2 **Little Fighter (GER)**[48] 4-8-13 ....(b) DPorcu 5 —
(J-P Carvalho, Germany) *cl up tl wknd qckly over 2f out* **70/1**
2m 19.65s (11.08)
WFA 3 from 4yo+ 4lb **13** Ran SP% **132.4**
(including 10 Euro stake): WIN 34; PL 12, 12, 15; SF 86.
Owner H Downs & D Looney **Bred** Airlie Stud And Sir Thomas Pilkington **Trained** Lambourn, Berks
■ Graham Gibbons' first pattern-race win.

NOTEBOOK
Zafisio(IRE), who bounced back to winning form in a French Group 3 last time, had no more to do in this company and, with ground conditions to suit, saw the longer trip out in good style.

7103 NANTES (R-H)
Sunday, November 15

OFFICIAL GOING: Very heavy

7409a PRIX DES ESPOIRS (MAIDEN) 1m
1:00 (12:00) 2-Y-0 **£6,796** (£2,718; £2,039; £1,359; £680)

RPR
1 **Hautevesne (FR)** 2-8-13 .... FLefebvre —
(Dominique Sepulchre, France)
2 4 **Carja (FR)** 2-8-8 .... M-BBoudaud —
(S Renaud, France)
3 3 **Best Of Order (IRE)** 2-8-12 .... JAuge —
(E J O'Neill)
4 2 **Serva Padrona (IRE)** 2-8-8 .... —
(H-A Pantall, France)
5 3/4 **Zifron (IRE)**[86] 2-9-2 .... —
(F Caenepeel, France)
6 2 **Sirena (IRE)** 2-8-13 .... —
(H-A Pantall, France)
7 nse **Zinzoline (FR)**[28] 2-8-13 .... —
(C Diard, France)
8 8 **Mascotte Du Maine (FR)** 2-8-8 .... —
(L Godard, France)
9 2 1/2 **Katapulpe (FR)** 2-9-2 ....(p) —
(J Boisnard, France)
1m 46.79s (106.79) **9** Ran
PARI-MUTUEL (Including 1 Euro stake): WIN 7.90; PL 2.00, 3.40, 1.90;DF 49.60.
Owner D Sepulchre **Bred** Scea De Maulepaire **Trained** France

7396 WOLVERHAMPTON (A.W) (L-H)
Monday, November 16

OFFICIAL GOING: Standard
Wind: Moderate behind Weather: Raining 2.00 and 2.30

7410 BET GRAND SLAM DARTS - BETDAQ CLAIMING STKS 5f 216y(P)
2:00 (2:00) (Class 5) 2-Y-0 **£3,238** (£963; £481; £240) **Stalls** Low

Form RPR
044 1 **Sabatini (IRE)**[28] 6896 2-8-6 67 .... FrancisNorton 8 77+
(R Hannon) *hld up in tch: rdn to ld over 1f out: clr ins fnl f: eased towards fin* **9/2**
1250 2 4 1/2 **Gillburg (USA)**[52] 6247 2-9-2 74 ....(b) NCallan 7 73
(K A Ryan) *chsd ldr tl rdn wl over 1f out: kpt on one pce ins fnl f: regained 2nd post* **11/4**[1]
0306 3 shd **Ramamara (IRE)**[21] 7063 2-8-8 77 .... PaulHanagan 1 64
(P D Evans) *led: rdn and hdd over 1f out: one pce: lost 2nd post* **3/1**[2]
6035 4 3/4 **Micky's Knock Off (IRE)**[10] 7274 2-8-3 73 .... BillyCray(7) 6 64
(R C Guest) *hld up and bhd: rdn wl over 1f out: styng on whn swtchd rt wl ins fnl f* **7/1**
0010 5 3/4 **Little Perisher**[7] 7320 2-8-9 77 .... RobertWinston 4 61
(A P Jarvis) *a.p: rdn over 1f out: one pce fnl f* **7/2**[3]
6006 6 1 1/4 **Michaelmas Daisy**[20] 7089 2-8-1 61 .... JimmyQuinn 2 49
(P Howling) *a.p: rdn over 1f out: one pce* **14/1**
25 7 4 **Ishe A Lord**[16] 7175 2-8-6 0 .... SaleemGolam 3 42
(W G M Turner) *hld up and bhd: pushed along over 2f out: sn struggling* **20/1**
8 12 **Halam Bankes**[27] 2-8-6 0 .... LukeMorris 5 —
(W G M Turner) *hld up and bhd: rdn wl over 2f out: sn struggling* **28/1**
1m 14.57s (-0.43) **Going Correction** +0.05s/f (Slow) **8** Ran SP% **119.4**
Speed ratings (Par 96): **104,98,97,96,95 94,88,72**
.Sabatini was claimed by Jeff Pearce for £10,000\n\x\x
Owner Clipper Logistics **Bred** O Bourke **Trained** East Everleigh, Wilts

FOCUS
The winner looks better than this level.

NOTEBOOK
Sabatini(IRE) ◆, despite racing wider than ideal throughout, with stall eight no help, bounded clear in the straight, in the process recording a time 0.82 seconds quicker than the following older-horse maiden. She should be competitive in handicaps. (op 10-3 tchd 3-1 and 5-1)
Gillburg(USA), conceding weight all round on his return from nearly two months off, proved no match whatsoever for the winner but plugged on to nab second. He has a modest strike-rate for one of such ability. (op 6-1)
Ramamara(IRE) was well drawn and led early, so it was disappointing she ran so far below her official mark of 77. (op 7-2)
Micky's Knock Off(IRE) is probably a bit better than he showed as he ended up a bit too far back after being short of room leaving the back straight. (op 5-1 tchd 9-2)
Little Perisher, having his 17th start of the year, ran some way below his official rating of 77. (tchd 4-1)

7411 HOTEL & CONFERENCING AT WOLVERHAMPTON MAIDEN STKS 5f 216y(P)
2:30 (2:31) (Class 5) 3-Y-0+ **£2,729** (£806; £403) **Stalls** Low

Form RPR
00-6 1 **Spice Run**[75] 5572 6-9-3 66 .... AdamKirby 9 74
(Stef Liddiard) *hld up and bhd: hdwy and swtchd rt over 2f out: rdn over 1f out: led wl ins fnl f: r.o* **7/1**[3]
523- 2 1 1/2 **Zegna (IRE)**[384] 7038 3-9-3 0 .... TomEaves 7 69
(B Smart) *sn w ldr: led over 4f out: rdn over 1f out: hdd and nt qckn wl ins fnl f* **3/1**[1]
033 3 2 **Sanjay's Choice (IRE)**[10] 7273 3-9-0 70 ....(p) WilliamCarson(3) 12 63
(T G McCourt, Ire) *w ldrs: rdn and ev ch over 1f out: no ex wl ins fnl f* **3/1**[1]
5204 4 1/2 **Sweet Applause (IRE)**[32] 6801 3-8-12 65 .... NCallan 11 56
(A P Jarvis) *led early: a.p: rdn wl over 1f out: kpt on one pce fnl f* **4/1**[2]
2224 5 1/2 **Westwood Dawn**[16] 7179 4-9-3 57 ....(vt) DaneO'Neill 8 60
(D Shaw) *hld up: hdwy and hung lft over 2f out: rdn and hung lft over 1f out: one pce* **7/1**[3]
0000 6 1 3/4 **Kamanja (UAE)**[188] 1958 3-8-5 53 .... KierenFox(7) 3 49
(M J Attwater) *hld up: rdn over 2f out: sme prog over 1f out: n.d* **50/1**
-040 7 4 **Gracie's Games**[15] 7197 3-8-12 47 .... RobertWinston 1 36
(R J Price) *chsd ldrs: rdn over 2f out: wknd wl over 1f out* **25/1**
00- 8 2 3/4 **Irish Bay (IRE)**[399] 6705 6-8-10 0 .... TobyAtkinson(7) 13 32
(Luke Comer, Ire) *hld up towards rr: pushed along 3f out: c wd st: struggling wl over 1f out* **33/1**
9 3/4 **Espresso Steps (USA)** 3-8-7 0 .... AndrewHeffernan(5) 4 25
(P Howling) *s.i.s: a in rr* **25/1**
03 10 1 1/2 **Across The Sands**[11] 7254 3-9-3 0 .... FrankieMcDonald 6 25
(C N Kellett) *sn led: hdd over 4f out: pushed along over 2f out: rdn and wknd wl over 1f out* **18/1**
11 shd **Isabel's Pet** 3-8-12 0 .... SteveDrowne 2 20
(Karen George) *s.i.s: outpcd* **50/1**
50 12 4 1/2 **Clincher**[30] 6856 3-8-12 0 .... ShaneKelly 5 5
(J A Osborne) *hld up in tch: n.m.r briefly over 3f out: sn wknd* **28/1**
0052 13 8 **Shirley High**[38] 6641 3-8-12 50 .... JimmyQuinn 10 —
(P Howling) *hld up: rdn over 2f out: sn bhd* **33/1**
1m 15.39s (0.39) **Going Correction** +0.05s/f (Slow) **13** Ran SP% **121.2**
Speed ratings (Par 103): **99,97,94,93,93 90,85,81,80,78 78,72,61**
toteswingers:1&2:£6.10, 2&3:£3.20, 1&3:£5.50 CSF £26.88 TOTE £8.80: £2.70, £1.60, £1.70; EX 56.40 Trifecta £177.60 Part won. Pool £240.02 - 0.10 winning units..
Owner Mrs Sally Doyle **Bred** Cheveley Park Stud Ltd **Trained** Great Shefford, Berks

FOCUS
A moderate maiden run in a slower time than the 2yo claimer. The fifth is probably the best guide to the form.
Westwood Dawn Official explanation: jockey said that the gelding hung left

7412 WOLVERHAMPTON-RACECOURSE.CO.UK (S) STKS 7f 32y(P)
3:00 (3:01) (Class 6) 3-Y-0+ **£2,047** (£604; £302) **Stalls** High

Form RPR
3440 1 **Monashee Rock (IRE)**[19] 7110 4-8-10 58 .... LPKeniry 8 71
(Matthew Salaman) *hld up and bhd: hdwy 2f out: hrd rdn to ld ins fnl f: drvn out* **7/1**
5000 2 1/2 **Borasco (USA)**[13] 7220 4-8-10 74 .... PhillipMakin 4 70
(T D Barron) *hld up in tch: rdn to ld over 1f out: hdd ins fnl f: kpt on* **3/1**[1]

000 **3** 2 1/4 **Pride Of Nation (IRE)**[4] 7350 7-8-8 75..................(p) DeclanCannon(7) 2 69
(A J McCabe) *hld up and bhd: hdwy over 2f out: rdn and kpt on to take 3rd nr fin* **9/2**[3]

3520 **4** 3/4 **Whitbarrow (IRE)**[16] 7192 10-8-13 65 ow1............(b) JamesMillman(3) 6 68
(B R Millman) *led early: chsd ldr: led over 3f out: rdn and hdd over 1f out: one pce ins fnl f* **8/1**

/1-6 **5** 1 1/4 **Sir George (IRE)**[34] 6755 4-8-10 68...................... AndrewHeffernan(5) 9 63
(P D Evans) *hld up in mid-div: hdwy over 3f out: rdn wl over 1f out: wknd ins fnl f* **10/3**[2]

3005 **6** 2 1/4 **Star Strider**[12] 7236 5-8-13 60 ow3.............................. KylieManser(5) 12 60
(T Keddy) *s.i.s: hld up and bhd: short-lived effrt on outside over 2f out: rdn and btn whn edgd lft over 1f out* **16/1**

3660 **7** 4 **Interactive (IRE)**[10] 7273 6-9-7 61.................................. VinceSlattery 3 52
(D Burchell) *prom tl wknd over 1f out* **20/1**

8 15 **Astormfromillinois (USA)**[1377] 6-8-10 0............... MatthewDavies(5) 1 6
(George Baker) *sn led: hdd over 3f out: wknd over 2f out* **16/1**

000 **9** 7 **Sendreni (FR)**[16] 7192 5-9-7 67...(t) SteveDrowne 10 —
(M Wigham) *hld up: hdwy over 5f out: wknd 3f out* **10/1**

1m 29.82s (0.22) **Going Correction** +0.05s/f (Slow)
WFA 3 from 4yo+ 1lb **9** Ran SP% **115.5**
Speed ratings (Par 101): **100,99,96,96,94 92,87,70,62**
toteswingers:1&2:£3.60, 2&3:£3.40, 1&3:£5.70 CSF £28.31 TOTE £7.80: £2.40, £1.80, £1.30; EX 22.20 TRIFECTA Not won..There was no bid for the winner
Owner Mrs P G Lewin & D Grieve **Bred** M J Lewin And D Grieve **Trained** Upper Lambourn, Berks

FOCUS
A good seller on paper, but the actual form is not that good with doubts over what the second and third are capable of now. The winner is rated to her turf form.

7413 BETDAQ POKER H'CAP 1m 4f 50y(P)
3:30 (3:30) (Class 5) (0-75,75) 3-Y-O+ **£3,238** (£963; £481; £240) **Stalls** Low

Form RPR

1606 **1** **Lyra's Daemon**[21] 7048 3-8-11 **70**.................................. NCallan 4 79
(W R Muir) *led early: a.p: rdn to ld over 1f out: r.o wl* **8/1**

0311 **2** 2 **Traphalgar (IRE)**[44] 6488 4-9-8 **75**.. DNolan 9 81
(Ollie Pears) *hld up in rr: pushed along and hdwy wl over 1f out: chsd wnr ins fnl f: nt qckn* **8/1**

0045 **3** 2 1/4 **Augustus John (IRE)**[14] 7212 6-8-12 **65**.......................... TomEaves 5 68
(R Brotherton) *hld up in tch: rdn and one pce ins fnl f* **11/2**[2]

/005 **4** 3/4 **Sagredo (USA)**[20] 7091 5-9-8 **75**..................................... GeorgeBaker 3 76
(Jonjo O'Neill) *hld up in rr: hdwy on ins wl over 1f out: sn pushed along: one pce ins fnl f* **16/1**

3230 **5** 1/2 **Arashi**[17] 7153 3-8-0 **64**..(p) AndrewHeffernan(5) 2 65+
(Lucinda Featherstone) *hld up: sddle slipped after 3f: hdwy over 6f out: led 5f out: hdd over 1f out: wknd ins fnl f* **7/1**[3]

4052 **6** 1 3/4 **Force Group (IRE)**[15] 7201 5-8-12 **70**..................(b) AshleyMorgan(5) 1 68+
(M H Tompkins) *hld up: hdwy on ins over 2f out: nt clr run and swtchd rt ins fnl f: nvr trbld ldrs* **85/40**[1]

0061 **7** 1/2 **Order Order**[7] 7318 3-8-2 **61** 6ex....................................... JimmyQuinn 8 58
(H J L Dunlop) *hld up: pushed along over 2f out: c wd st wl over 1f out: sn edgd lft and btn* **11/1**

130 **8** 1 3/4 **Ladies Dancing**[65] 5876 3-9-2 **75**.................................... ShaneKelly 7 69
(J A Osborne) *half-rrd s: hdwy to chse ldr after 2f: lost 2nd over 5f out: rdn 2f out: wknd wl over 1f out* **16/1**

2100 **9** 4 **Heritage Coast (USA)**[21] 7048 4-9-3 **70**.......................... SteveDrowne 6 58
(H Morrison) *sn led: set stdy pce: hdd 5f out: ev ch over 1f out: wknd and eased ins fnl f* **15/2**

2m 41.7s (0.60) **Going Correction** +0.05s/f (Slow)
WFA 3 from 4yo+ 6lb **9** Ran SP% **114.0**
Speed ratings (Par 103): **100,98,96,96,96 94,94,93,90**
toteswingers:1&2:£9.10, 2&3:£9.20, 1&3:£9.30 CSF £69.05 CT £381.96 TOTE £13.10: £3.10, £2.10, £1.60; EX 60.10 Trifecta £133.50 Part won. Pool £180.43 - 0.10 winning units..
Owner M J Caddy **Bred** Horizon Bloodstock Limited **Trained** Lambourn, Berks

FOCUS
An ordinary handicap. The winner built on April's Bath win and the second was close to his recent best. The seventh casts a slight doubt over the form.
Arashi Official explanation: jockey said hat the gelding's saddle slipped

7414 WOLVERHAMPTON-RACECOURSE.CO.UK H'CAP 5f 20y(P)
4:00 (4:01) (Class 3) (0-95,95) 3-Y-O-**£7,569** (£2,265; £1,132; £566; £282) **Stalls** Low

Form RPR

1353 **1** **Gilt Edge Girl**[28] 6902 3-8-8 **85**.. LukeMorris 9 96+
(C G Cox) *a.p: rdn to ld wl ins fnl f: r.o wl* **16/1**

0535 **2** 1 1/2 **Ivory Silk**[28] 6897 4-8-8 **85** ow1......................................(b) SteveDrowne 2 91
(J R Gask) *hld up towards rr: hmpd on ins wl over 3f out: hdwy over 1f out: sn rdn: r.o wl to take 2nd last strides* **5/1**[2]

0012 **3** hd **Fantasy Explorer**[15] 7202 6-8-11 **88**.............................. JimmyQuinn 1 93
(J J Quinn) *a.p on ins: led wl over 1f out: sn edgd rt: rdn and hdd wl ins fnl f: lost 2nd last strides* **15/8**[1]

0231 **4** 1/2 **Orpenindeed (IRE)**[17] 7155 6-8-9 **89**......................(p) AndreaAtzeni(3) 12 92
(M Botti) *a.p: pushed along over 2f out: lost pl wl over 1f out: sn rdn: r.o ins fnl f* **7/1**[3]

0100 **5** shd **Bertoliver**[37] 6666 5-8-4 **81**.. SaleemGolam 11 84
(S C Williams) *s.i.s: hld up towards rr: pushed along and hdwy over 1f out: rdn and kpt on ins fnl f* **28/1**

4360 **6** nse **Doubtful Sound (USA)**[20] 7090 5-9-4 **95**....................(p) GeorgeBaker 4 98
(R Hollinshead) *hld up in rr: hdwy wl over 1f out: sn rdn: kpt on one pce ins fnl f* **14/1**

0530 **7** nk **Toms Laughter**[13] 7227 5-8-12 **89**...................................(b) DaneO'Neill 6 91+
(R A Harris) *s.i.s: hld up in rr: c v wd in st: rdn and hdwy fnl f: nt rch ldrs* **8/1**

1006 **8** 1/2 **Stolt (IRE)**[15] 7202 5-8-2 **84** ow1... PaulPickard(5) 5 84
(N Wilson) *led: pushed along and rn wd ent st: hdd wl over 1f out: lost 2nd and no ex wl ins fnl f* **16/1**

3243 **9** nk **Rebel Duke (IRE)**[48] 6359 5-8-11 **88**.............................. FrancisNorton 10 87
(Ollie Pears) *chsd ldr: hung rt bnd over 2f out: rn wd st: rdn over 1f out: fdd ins fnl f* **12/1**

4040 **10** 1 3/4 **Tabaret**[15] 7202 6-8-8 **85** ow1.. TonyCulhane 3 77
(R M Whitaker) *hld up towards rr: n.m.r wl over 3f out: hdwy wl over 1f out: sn rdn: fdd wl ins fnl f* **10/1**

000 **11** 1 **Canadian Danehill (IRE)**[23] 7015 7-9-1 **92**......................(p) NCallan 13 81
(R M H Cowell) *prom on outside: c wd st: wknd wl over 1f out* **33/1**

102- **12** 2 1/2 **Bosun Breese**[401] 6650 4-8-4 **81** oh1.................................. LiamJones 8 61
(T D Barron) *hld up in mid-div: pushed along and lost pl 2f out: sn bhd* **20/1**

61.22 secs (-1.08) **Going Correction** +0.05s/f (Slow) **12** Ran SP% **121.4**
Speed ratings (Par 107): **110,107,107,106,106 106,105,104,104,101 100,96**
toteswingers:1&2:£17.00, 2&3:£4.40, 1&3:£10.10 CSF £94.55 CT £229.59 TOTE £17.80: £3.30, £2.30, £1.50; EX 159.00 TRIFECTA Not won..
Owner Wood Street Syndicate V & C J Harper **Bred** Whitsbury Manor Stud **Trained** Lambourn, Berks

FOCUS
A good sprint handicap for the grade, which was strongly run. The fom looks sound.

NOTEBOOK
Gilt Edge Girl's improvement looked to have levelled off recently, but that's clearly not the case as she took this competitive contest in clear-cut fashion. It remains to be seen whether she can defy a higher mark. (op 12-1)
Ivory Silk, carrying 1lb overweight, struggled to lay up with the pace, not being helped by getting hampered over 3f out, and got going much too late. (tchd 11-2)
Fantasy Explorer, favourably drawn, looked to be well placed just in behind the lead against the inside rail for much of the way and got a good run through in the straight when several of his rivals went wide off the bend, but he couldn't take advantage. (op 5-2 tchd 11-4 in places)
Orpenindeed(IRE), 4lb higher than when winning over 6f around here on his previous start, ran well considering he was forced wider than ideal into the straight. (op 10-1)
Bertoliver emerges with plenty of credit considering he couldn't dominate, as he likes to, from stall 11. (op 25-1 tchd 33-1)
Doubtful Sound(USA) was not quite at his best and seems to have lost his way a bit recently. (op 12-1)
Toms Laughter ◆ is better than he showed as he lost ground with a slow start and then came very wide into the straight. There's a nice prize to be won with him if things fall right this winter. (tchd 9-1)
Stolt(IRE) Official explanation: jockey said he gelding hung right handed throughout
Rebel Duke(IRE) Official explanation: jockey said the gelding hung right handed

7415 TRY BETDAQ FOR AN EXCHANGE H'CAP 2m 119y(P)
4:30 (4:30) (Class 5) (0-70,64) 3-Y-O+ **£3,238** (£963; £481; £240) **Stalls** Low

Form RPR

-006 **1** **K'Gari (USA)**[18] 7137 3-8-6 **48**..................................(b) PaulHanagan 2 57
(B Ellison) *mde all: set gd pce: rdn over 2f out: c sltly wd st: sn edgd lft: edgd lft wl ins fnl f: styd on* **14/1**

3 **2** 3/4 **Baltimore Patriot (IRE)**[10] 7279 6-10-0 **61**.................... TonyCulhane 3 69
(R Curtis) *hld up and bhd: hdwy 3f out: rdn to chal wl over 1f out: hld whn carried lft wl ins fnl f* **9/1**

4433 **3** 6 **Squirtle (IRE)**[14] 7214 6-9-5 **52**.. LukeMorris 8 55+
(W M Brisbourne) *hld up: hdwy over 5f out: rdn over 2f out: tk 3rd over 1f out: eased whn btn towards fin* **6/1**[3]

-401 **4** 3 3/4 **Dubai Diva**[11] 7255 3-9-7 **63**.. GeorgeBaker 5 59
(C F Wall) *hld up in tch: rdn 2f out: sn wknd* **8/11**[1]

2024 **5** 1 1/4 **Honorable Endeavor**[45] 6445 3-9-2 **58**..........................(p) LPKeniry 4 53
(E F Vaughan) *hld up: hdwy over 5f out: rdn and wknd 2f out* **9/2**[2]

0012 **6** 3 **Ingenue**[33] 6785 3-9-8 **64**..(b) JimmyQuinn 6 55
(P Howling) *chsd wnr: ev ch over 2f out: sn rdn: lost 2nd and wknd wl over 1f out* **16/1**

/000 **7** 54 **Chicamia**[24] 7004 5-8-12 **45**... SJCraine 1 —
(M Mullineaux) *in rr: pushed along over 7f out: t.o fnl 4f* **100/1**

3m 42.56s (0.76) **Going Correction** +0.05s/f (Slow)
WFA 3 from 5yo+ 9lb **7** Ran SP% **113.9**
Speed ratings (Par 103): **100,99,96,95,94 93,67**
toteswingers:1&2:£8.70, 2&3:£4.90, 1&3:£6.20 CSF £126.55 CT £840.95 TOTE £19.20: £5.90, £3.80; EX 143.10 Trifecta £258.20 Pool: £575.76 - 1.65 winning units.
Owner Mrs C L Ellison & C P Lowther **Bred** Jim Ryan And Geraldine Ryan **Trained** Norton, N Yorks
■ Stewards' Enquiry : Paul Hanagan one-day ban: careless riding (Nov 30)

FOCUS
A modest staying handicap in which K'Gari ensured this was a proper stamina test, setting a reasonable pace with the field soon strung out. He more than confimed his recent improvement, with the third looking the best guide.
K'Gari(USA) Official explanation: trainer said, regarding the runnning of the winner, that the gelding was better suited by the increase in trip today

7416 WOLVERHAMPTON RACECOURSE - ALL CONFERENCING NEEDS MET H'CAP (DIV I) 1m 141y(P)
5:00 (5:00) (Class 6) (0-65,65) 3-Y-O+ **£2,047** (£604; £302) **Stalls** Low

Form RPR

0024 **1** **Castle Myth (USA)**[3] 7374 3-8-7 **54**...............................(bt) TomEaves 10 67
(B Ellison) *dwlt: hld up in rr: gd hdwy to ld 1f out: drvn clr wl ins fnl f: r.o wl* **9/2**[3]

3002 **2** 3 1/2 **Bidable**[17] 7152 5-8-8 **52** oh1 ow1.................................. TonyCulhane 6 57
(B Palling) *led after 1f: rdn 2f out: hdd 1f out: kpt on same pce* **12/1**

-352 **3** nk **Lucky Score (IRE)**[13] 7228 3-9-1 **62**.................................... LPKeniry 7 66
(Mouse Hamilton-Fairley) *hld up in tch: rdn and r.o one pce fnl f* **7/2**[2]

2004 **4** 3/4 **Kings Ace (IRE)**[16] 7180 3-8-10 **57**...................................... NCallan 12 60
(A P Jarvis) *hld up in mid-div: rdn over 1f out: styd on ins fnl f* **9/1**

0053 **5** shd **Marmooq**[12] 7236 6-9-2 **60**... AdamKirby 8 62
(M J Attwater) *hld up towards rr: rdn over 2f out: c wd st: styd on ins fnl f: nvr nrr* **9/1**

-331 **6** nk **Mighty Mover (IRE)**[17] 7152 7-8-11 **55**.............................. LukeMorris 3 57
(B Palling) *a.p: hrd rdn wl over 1f out: no ex towards fin* **3/1**[1]

5056 **7** nk **Dr Jameson (IRE)**[18] 6640 3-9-4 **65**..........................(b[1]) PaulHanagan 13 66
(R A Fahey) *sn w ldr: rdn and ev ch wl over 1f out: wknd ins fnl f* **8/1**

0000 **8** 2 3/4 **Kirstys Lad**[17] 7152 7-8-0 **51** oh5....................................... BillyCray(7) 9 46
(M Mullineaux) *hld up in rr: rdn over 3f out: nvr nr ldrs* **33/1**

3060 **9** 4 1/2 **Stand In Flames**[4] 7348 4-8-9 **58**............................. MatthewDavies(5) 2 42
(George Baker) *led early: prom tl rdn and wknd over 1f out* **50/1**

050- **10** 6 **Tax Dodger (IRE)**[163] 2733 3-8-8 **55**..........................(p) JimmyQuinn 1 26
(Liam McAteer, Ire) *hld up in mid-div: reminder 4f out: struggling whn rdn wl over 1f out* **7/1**

000 **11** 75 **Hannicean**[14] 5698 5-9-4 **65**... JackMitchell(3) 11 —
(N B King) *s.v.s: a wl in rr: t.o fnl 5f* **14/1**

1m 49.96s (-0.54) **Going Correction** +0.05s/f (Slow)
WFA 3 from 4yo+ 3lb **11** Ran SP% **128.3**
Speed ratings (Par 101): **104,100,100,99,99 99,99,96,92,87 20**
toteswingers:1&2:£15.00, 2&3:£11.00, 1&3:£6.00 CSF £63.41 CT £220.25 TOTE £5.30: £2.40, £3.90, £2.50; EX 86.40 Trifecta £199.80 Pool £270.10 - 0.55 winning units..
Owner Locketts Legends **Bred** Mr & Mrs Gerald J Stautberg **Trained** Norton, N Yorks

FOCUS
A moderate handicap run in a time 0.69 seconds quicker than second division. A clear personal best from the winner, in a race rated around the next three home.

Kirstys Lad Official explanation: jockey said the gelding was never travelling

7417 WOLVERHAMPTON RACECOURSE - ALL CONFERENCING NEEDS MET H'CAP (DIV II) 1m 141y(P)
5:30 (5:30) (Class 6) (0-65,63) 3-Y-0+ **£2,047** (£604; £302) **Stalls** Low

Form RPR

0204 **1** **Just Jimmy (IRE)**^{12} 7240 4-8-12 **54** PaulDoe 6 61
(P D Evans) *hld up in mid-div: hdwy 2f out: rdn to ld ent fnl f: r.o* **4/1**^{2}

5514 **2** ¾ **Vamos (IRE)**^{14} 7211 3-8-8 **60** (t) LukeKilgarriff$^{(7)}$ 8 65
(J R Gask) *hld up in mid-div: hdwy on outside 2f out: c wd st: led wl over 1f out: sn rdn: hdd ent fnl f: kpt on one pce* **7/2**^{1}

60-4 **3** ½ **Camerooney**^{21} 7062 6-8-7 **49** oh3 TomEaves 13 53
(B Ellison) *hld up in rr: c wd st: rdn and hdwy over 1f out: swtchd lft wl ins fnl f: r.o u.p to take 3rd towards fin* **12/1**

0001 **4** 1 ¼ **Fine Ruler (IRE)**^{19} 7109 5-9-3 **59** GeorgeBaker 4 60
(M R Bosley) *hld up in tch: ev ch wl over 1f out: sn rdn: nt qckn ins fnl f* **9/2**^{3}

00-6 **5** 2 ¾ **Giant Slalom**^{25} 6123 5-9-5 **61** ShaneKelly 5 56
(T G McCourt, Ire) *hld up in mid-div: hdwy over 1f out: sn rdn: no imp fnl f* **10/1**

0000 **6** *shd* **Wotatomboy**^{12} 7239 3-8-4 **49** oh1 FrancisNorton 11 45+
(R M Whitaker) *hld up in rr: pushed along and nt clr run jst over 2f out: rdn over 1f out: r.o ins fnl f: nvr nrr* **33/1**

1550 **7** 2 **Neo's Mate (IRE)**^{30} 6862 3-8-3 **53** AndrewHeffernan$^{(5)}$ 9 43
(Paul Green) *t.k.h: led: hdd over 3f out: rdn 2f out: wknd over 1f out* **14/1**

0025 **8** 1 ½ **Dream Huntress**^{25} 6968 3-9-4 **63** LiamJones 10 49
(J W Hills) *hld up sn in tch: led over 2f out: hdd wl over 1f out: sn wknd* **6/1**

0004 **9** *hd* **Imperium**^{19} 7110 8-8-12 **54** (p) DaneO'Neill 3 40
(Jean-Rene Auvray) *prom on ins: pushed along over 2f out: rdn and wknd over 1f out* **13/2**

/50- **10** *10* **Misterisland (IRE)**^{558} 1918 4-9-0 **56** SJCraine 7 19
(M Mullineaux) *hld up towards rr: rdn and short-lived effrt on ins over 2f out: eased ins fnl f* **50/1**

4000 **11** *32* **Superstitious Me (IRE)**^{17} 7153 3-8-8 **53** LukeMorris 12 —
(B Palling) *sn w ldr: slt ld over 3f out tl over 2f out: sn rdn and wknd: eased whn no ch over 1f out* **25/1**

1m 50.65s (0.15) **Going Correction** +0.05s/f (Slow)
WFA 3 from 4yo+ 3lb **11 Ran SP% 120.2**
Speed ratings (Par 101): **101,100,99,98,96 96,94,93,92,84 55**
toteswingers:1&2:£5.00, 2&3:£12.10, 1&3:£13.80 CSF £18.59 CT £160.70 TOTE £4.20: £1.90, £1.80, £3.20; EX 24.80 Trifecta £173.60 Part won. Pool £234.72 - 0.10 winning units. Place 6 £263.06, Place 5 £171.22.
Owner Richard Edwards **Bred** Richard Edwards And Gwynne Williams **Trained** Pandy, Monmouths

FOCUS
The winning time was 0.69 seconds slower than the first division. Modest form, with the winner and second the most likely guides.
Superstitious Me(IRE) Official explanation: jockey said that the filly ran too free
T/Jkpt: Not won. T/Plt: £466.60 to a £1 stake. Pool: £84,300.00. 131.86 winning tickets. T/Qpdt: £127.10 to a £1 stake. Pool: £5,929.92. 34.50 winning tickets. KH

7348 SOUTHWELL (L-H)
Tuesday, November 17

OFFICIAL GOING: Standard
Wind: Fresh across Weather: Fine and sunny

7418 PLAY AT POKERINVENICE.COM H'CAP (DIV I) 6f (F)
12:20 (12:21) (Class 6) (0-60,60) 3-Y-0+ **£1,706** (£503; £252) **Stalls** Low

Form RPR

5641 **1** **Diamond Blade**^{55} 6221 3-8-12 **54** (p) DNolan 6 65
(T D Easterby) *led: hdd over 4f out: chsd ldr: rdn to ld and hung lft fr over 1f out: r.o* **13/2**^{3}

0005 **2** ¾ **Cool Sands (IRE)**^{4} 7370 7-8-13 **55** (v) J-PGuillambert 5 63
(J G Given) *chsd ldrs: rdn and edgd lft over 1f out: ev ch ins fnl f: r.o* **9/2**^{2}

0633 **3** *shd* **Outer Hebrides**^{5} 7349 8-8-12 **54** (v) RichardKingscote 3 62
(J M Bradley) *prom: rdn over 2f out: r.o* **7/2**^{1}

0350 **4** 2 ¾ **Danum Dancer**^{11} 7269 5-9-4 **60** (b) LeeVickers 4 59
(N Bycroft) *s.i.s: rcvrd to ld over 4f out: rdn and hdd over 1f out: no ex ins fnl f* **8/1**

0400 **5** *shd* **Dickie Le Davoir**^{54} 6233 5-9-0 **56** (be) StephenDonohoe 13 55
(R C Guest) *dwlt: outpcd: hdwy u.p over 1f out: nt rch ldrs* **8/1**

2123 **6** 1 **The Name Is Frank**^{6} 7330 4-8-11 **58** (t) SimonPearce$^{(5)}$ 8 54
(Mark Gillard) *s.s: hdwy u.p over 1f out: n.d* **7/1**

0000 **7** *nk* **Hit The Switch**^{20} 4491 3-7-11 **46** JamesPSullivan$^{(7)}$ 9 41
(Patrick Morris) *mid-div: sn pushed along: rdn over 1f out: nt trble ldrs* **22/1**

4500 **8** 4 ½ **Steel Blue**^{5} 7358 9-8-1 **48** (p) AmyRyan$^{(5)}$ 1 28
(R M Whitaker) *chsd ldrs: rdn over 2f out: wknd over 1f out* **11/1**

6060 **9** 4 **Inthawain**^{11} 7270 3-8-9 **56** ow1 GaryBartley$^{(5)}$ 12 24
(N Wilson) *sn outpcd and bhd* **33/1**

0100 **10** 3 **Sleepy Blue Ocean**^{32} 6824 3-9-4 **60** RobertWinston 11 18
(J Balding) *prom: rdn over 3f out: wknd over 1f out* **20/1**

6000 **11** ¾ **Green Onions**^{67} 5836 3-8-12 **57** RobertLButler$^{(3)}$ 2 13
(A J Lidderdale) *prom: racd keenly: rdn over 2f out: sn wknd* **40/1**

60-0 **12** *33* **High Ridge**^{17} 7176 10-8-2 **47** (p) AndreaAtzeni$^{(3)}$ 14 —
(J L Flint) *sn outpcd and bhd: t.o* **50/1**

1m 15.54s (-0.96) **Going Correction** -0.175s/f (Stan) **12 Ran SP% 113.2**
Speed ratings (Par 101): **99,98,97,94,94 92,92,86,81,77 76,32**
toteswingers:1&2:£6.70, 2&3:£4.50, 1&3:£3.30 CSF £31.95 CT £118.15 TOTE £7.70: £2.70, £1.90, £1.30; EX 35.50 Trifecta £33.20 Pool: £179.12 - 3.99 winning units.
Owner D A West **Bred** Bumble Bloodstock **Trained** Great Habton, N Yorks

FOCUS
A moderate sprint handicap run in a similar time to division II. Sound form for the grade.

7419 BET DUBAI WORLD GOLF - BETDAQ (S) STKS 7f (F)
12:50 (12:53) (Class 6) 2-Y-0 **£2,047** (£604; £302) **Stalls** Low

Form RPR

4004 **1** **Taper Jean Girl (IRE)**^{15} 7210 2-8-4 **63** AndreaAtzeni$^{(3)}$ 7 55+
(M Botti) *chsd ldrs: led over 4f out: rdn over 1f out: styd on* **3/1**^{1}

0046 **2** 1 ¼ **Bookiesindex Girl (IRE)**^{6} 7333 2-8-7 **48** JimmyQuinn 6 52
(J R Jenkins) *led: hdd over 4f out: remained handy: rdn over 2f out: wnt 2nd over 1f out: kpt on* **6/1**

2505 **3** 1 ¼ **Dontbugthebunny (USA)**^{6} 7334 2-8-3 **54** ow1 MatthewDavies$^{(5)}$ 8 50
(George Baker) *mid-div: sn pushed along: reminders 5f out: hdwy u.p 3f out: styd on: nt trble ldrs* **5/1**^{3}

0000 **4** 1 ¾ **Scintillating (IRE)**^{8} 7319 2-8-0 **35** NicolaJackson$^{(7)}$ 12 44
(R Hollinshead) *sn outpcd: hdwy over 2f out: styd on same pce fnl f* **50/1**

0005 **5** 1 ½ **Wedding Dream**^{30} 6874 2-8-7 **38** TomEaves 5 41
(K A Ryan) *chsd ldrs: outpcd over 2f out: rallied over 1f out: styd on* **22/1**

5006 **6** 1 ¾ **Kapelad Junior (IRE)**^{15} 7210 2-9-3 **61** (b^1) PaulEddery 10 46
(Pat Eddery) *chsd ldrs: rdn over 2f out: wknd ins fnl f* **7/2**^{2}

0500 **7** 2 ¼ **Whispered Times (USA)**^{13} 7242 2-9-3 **64** (p) PhillipMakin 4 41
(P C Haslam) *dwlt: outpcd: hdwy u.p 1/2-way: hung lft fr over 2f out: nt run on* **7/2**^{2}

00 **8** *14* **The Love Guru**^{33} 6792 2-8-9 **0** RobertLButler$^{(3)}$ 1 —
(J R Boyle) *hld up: t.o fr 1/2-way* **22/1**

000 **9** 2 ¾ **Brave Ambition (IRE)**^{112} 4396 2-8-12 **40** StephenDonohoe 9 —
(R C Guest) *sn bhd: t.o fr 1/2-way* **66/1**

06 **10** *5* **Light Nights (IRE)**^{14} 7217 2-8-7 **0** PaulHanagan 2 —
(T D Easterby) *sn pushed along in rr: t.o fr 1/2-way* **40/1**

0000 **11** *58* **Ron The Don**^{32} 6819 2-8-5 **20** (b) BillyCray$^{(7)}$ 11 —
(A Berry) *s.i.s: outpcd: t.o fnl 4f* **200/1**

1m 30.41s (0.11) **Going Correction** -0.175s/f (Stan) **11 Ran SP% 115.5**
Speed ratings (Par 94): **92,90,89,87,85 83,80,64,61,56 —**
toteswingers:1&2:£2.70, 2&3:£4.80, 1&3:£5.10 CSF £19.85 TOTE £3.20: £1.20, £2.20, £1.90; EX 18.10 Trifecta £62.50 Pool: £348.17 - 4.12 winning units.The winner was sold to David Chapman for 3,000 guineas
Owner Frontier Racing Group **Bred** Miss J Murphy **Trained** Newmarket, Suffolk

FOCUS
A moderate contest, even by selling standards. The winner was 10lb off her maiden form.

NOTEBOOK
Taper Jean Girl(IRE) proved suited by this switch to Fibresand and responded well to a positive ride. She was entitled to win this, however, being the best off at the weights (would have been 15lb worse off with the runner-up in a handicap), and her connections will do well to find a race this weak next time. (op 13-8)
Bookiesindex Girl(IRE), upped to her furthest trip to date, was always well placed and ran respectably, but she had little chance with the winner on figures. (op 9-1)
Dontbugthebunny(USA), dropped in trip, was never travelling at any stage and, although she eventually plugged on into third, she was below her official mark of 54. (op 6-1 tchd 9-2)
Scintillating(IRE), trying Fibresand for the first time, kept on after getting well behind early, but her apprentice, who was having her first ride in public, seemed to get noticeably tired in the straight.
Kapelad Junior(IRE) was well placed for much of the race, but he stopped quite quickly in the straight. (op 5-1 tchd 11-2)
Whispered Times(USA) was never travelling. (op 9-2 tchd 5-1)

7420 BET IN-RUNNING - BETDAQ MEDIAN AUCTION MAIDEN STKS 7f (F)
1:20 (1:21) (Class 5) 2-Y-0 **£2,590** (£770; £385; £192) **Stalls** Low

Form RPR

4 **1** **Solicitor**^{21} 7095 2-9-3 **0** JoeFanning 7 83+
(M Johnston) *trckd ldrs: led 2f out: shkn up and sn clr: eased ins fnl f* **4/9**^{1}

5 **2** *9* **Dandarrell**^{10} 7289 2-9-3 **0** TomEaves 4 58+
(Miss J A Camacho) *s.i.s: hld up: plld hrd: hdwy u.p and hung lft over 2f out: styd on to go 2nd ins fnl f: no ch w wnr* **9/2**^{2}

0 **3** *1* **Admiral Breese**^{13} 7244 2-9-3 **0** GrahamGibbons 1 55
(R Hollinshead) *led: rdn and hdd 2f out: sn outpcd* **16/1**

6 **4** *nse* **Bubber (IRE)**^{21} 7079 2-8-12 **0** PaulHanagan 8 50
(R A Fahey) *trckd ldr: racd keenly: rdn over 2f out: sn outpcd* **7/1**^{3}

00 **5** 2 ½ **Inshaallah**^{20} 7121 2-9-3 **0** J-PGuillambert 6 49
(J G Given) *chsd ldrs: rdn over 2f out: wknd over 1f out* **33/1**

00 **6** *10* **Crystal Glass**^{10} 7289 2-9-3 **0** DNolan 9 24
(T D Easterby) *sn pushed along and prom: wknd 1/2-way* **66/1**

0 **7** *nk* **Honoured (IRE)**^{39} 6638 2-9-3 **0** StephenDonohoe 2 23
(Sir Mark Prescott) *hld up: lost tch 1/2-way* **14/1**

8 3 ¼ **Pobs Trophy** 2-8-10 **0** BillyCray$^{(7)}$ 3 15
(R C Guest) *s.s: outpcd* **100/1**

00 **9** *1* **Chardonnay Star (IRE)**^{179} 2226 2-8-12 **0** PJMcDonald 5 7
(C J Teague) *mid-div: rdn over 4f out: wknd 1/2-way* **150/1**

1m 29.44s (-0.86) **Going Correction** -0.175s/f (Stan) **9 Ran SP% 118.6**
Speed ratings (Par 96): **97,86,85,85,82 71,70,67,66**
toteswingers:1&2:£1.80, 2&3:£6.90, 1&3:£3.80 CSF £2.97 TOTE £1.40: £1.02, £1.40, £4.20; EX 3.80 Trifecta £26.50 Pool: £499.93 - 13.93 winning units.
Owner Sheikh Hamdan Bin Mohammed Al Maktoum **Bred** Darley **Trained** Middleham Moor, N Yorks

FOCUS
This was a seriously uncompetitive maiden and the winner was in a different league.

NOTEBOOK
Solicitor totally outclassed his rivals, confirming the promise he showed when fourth in a much stronger race over 1m on his debut at Yarmouth. Having tracked the modest pace early, he bounded clear in the straight, despite still looking immature, and Joe Fanning was able to stop riding fully half a furlong out. It would be unwise to get too carried away, as his only credible rival according to the betting was much too keen, and the time was only 0.97 seconds quicker than the earlier juvenile seller, won by a 63-rated filly, but still this son of Halling is obviously quite decent. (tchd 1-2)
Dandarrell raced too freely in behind the pace early on and, although he managed to get up for second, he probably didn't achieve a great deal. This did not represent a step forward from his encouraging debut over 6f on turf.
Admiral Breese was well ridden from the front, being allowed to dictate an ordinary pace, and he travelled well into the straight before fading in the closing stages. His breeding suggests he'll stay further, but he probably needs more time. (op 22-1)
Bubber(IRE), a daughter of the top-class stayer Westerner, is surely going to want middle-distances at the very least before long.

7421 BETDAQ.CO.UK NURSERY 6f (F)
1:50 (1:53) (Class 6) (0-60,64) 2-Y-0 **£2,047** (£604; £302) **Stalls** Low

Form RPR

3466 **1** **Fair Bunny**^{20} 7115 2-9-6 **59** JimmyQuinn 3 67
(A D Brown) *chsd ldrs: rdn to ld over 1f out: edgd rt: r.o* **16/1**

0221 **2** ½ **Clear Ice (IRE)**^{6} 7331 2-9-6 **64** 6ex RichardEvans$^{(5)}$ 5 70
(D Nicholls) *chsd ldrs: swtchd rt over 2f out: sn rdn: edgd lft ins fnl f: r.o* **15/8**^{1}

040 **3** 3 ¼ **Taeping (IRE)**^{32} 6809 2-9-3 **56** RobertWinston 1 52
(R Hollinshead) *chsd ldr: rdn over 2f out: no ex ins fnl f* **5/1**^{3}

6054 **4** *1* **Miss Taken (IRE)**^{6} 7333 2-8-11 **50** (b) DNolan 4 43
(D Carroll) *led: rdn: hung lft and hdd over 1f out: wknd ins fnl f* **9/2**^{2}

5050 **5** ½ **Princess Shamal**^{29} 6905 2-9-5 **58** StephenDonohoe 7 50
(J R Jenkins) *sn pushed along in rr: hdwy u.p over 1f out: nt trble ldrs* **12/1**

06 **6** ½ **Goodison Goal (IRE)**[33] 6802 2-9-4 **57** SJCraine 11 47
(Patrick Morris) *s.i.s: hld up: hdwy u.p over 1f out: n.d* **16/1**

000 **7** 4½ **Bird On The Wire**[24] 7024 2-9-4 **60** (p) JackDean(3) 9 37
(W G M Turner) *hmpd s: sn chsng ldrs: rdn over 2f out: hung lft and wknd over 1f out* **50/1**

3456 **8** 1¼ **Blue Rum (IRE)**[41] 6589 2-9-4 **57** (p) PhillipMakin 2 30
(P C Haslam) *unruly prior to loading: sn drvn along in mid-div: rdn and wknd over 2f out* **5/1**[3]

3406 **9** ½ **Out The Ring (IRE)**[34] 6775 2-9-6 **59** SimonWhitworth 8 31
(Miss Gay Kelleway) *s.i.s and hmpd s: n.d* **14/1**

0000 **10** 4 **Azzez Life**[64] 5950 2-7-13 **45** (be) BillyCray(7) 10 5
(R C Guest) *wnt lft s: sn pushed along in mid-div: wknd 1/2-way: bhd whn hung lft over 1f out* **100/1**

1m 17.04s (0.54) **Going Correction** -0.175s/f (Stan) **10** Ran SP% **115.4**
Speed ratings (Par 94): **89,88,84,82,82 81,75,73,73,67**
toteswingers:1&2:£7.00, 2&3:£3.00, 1&3:£13.70 CSF £45.80 CT £180.11 TOTE £21.10: £4.30, £1.40, £1.80; EX 67.10 TRIFECTA Not won..
Owner Mrs Susan Johnson **Bred** Mrs S Johnson **Trained** Yedingham, N Yorks

FOCUS
A moderate nursery in which the third and fourth set the level with the first two confirming their 5f improvement.

NOTEBOOK
Fair Bunny was not progressing on the turf, but in fairness she had contested a 0-85 on her latest start and this represented a significant drop in grade. She improved for the switch to Fibresand, showing a good attitude under pressure, and may remain competitive. (tchd 14-1 and 20-1)
Clear Ice(IRE), off the mark in a 5f maiden at this track last time, was switched towards the stands' side in the straight but, despite keeping on all the way to the line, he never quite looked like getting there. Stamina wasn't an issue. (tchd 13-8 and 2-1)
Taeping(IRE), who contested some half-decent maidens on turf, ran respectably and might be able to build on this.
Miss Taken(IRE) had the speed to lead but she didn't respond too kindly to pressure and wandered around in the closing stages. (op 15-2)
Blue Rum(IRE), with cheekpieces re-fitted, played up before the start and ran poorly on his Fibresand debut. (op 13-2)
Out The Ring(IRE) was badly squeezed out between rivals on leaving the stalls, but was not given a hard time to try and make up the lost ground. Official explanation: jockey said gelding suffered interference leaving stalls (op 10-1 tchd 16-1)

7422 HOSPITALITY AT SOUTHWELL RACECOURSE (S) STKS 1m (F)
2:20 (2:21) (Class 6) 3-Y-0+ **£2,047** (£604; £302) **Stalls** Low

Form RPR

3400 **1** **Swiss Art (IRE)**[11] 7271 3-9-4 70 (b) JoeFanning 7 71
(Mrs R A Carr) *trckd ldrs: led wl over 1f out: sn shkn up and edgd rt: r.o* **8/1**

603 **2** 1 **Clear Sailing**[31] 6862 6-9-6 65 (p) DNolan 11 69
(Ollie Pears) *chsd ldrs and pushed along early: led 5f out: rdn and hdd wl over 1f out: styd on* **2/1**[1]

0054 **3** 1 **Celtic Step**[17] 7172 5-9-0 68 PaulHanagan 6 60
(P D Niven) *led: hdd 5f out: remained handy: rdn and ev ch over 1f out: styd on same pce ins fnl f* **5/1**[2]

4661 **4** hd **Ingleby Princess**[5] 7350 5-9-1 48 PhillipMakin 10 61
(T D Barron) *hld up: hdwy 1/2-way: rdn over 2f out: styd on* **6/1**[3]

0016 **5** 1 **Ocean Legend (IRE)**[22] 7062 4-9-6 68 LiamJones 4 64
(Miss J Feilden) *s.i.s: hdwy 1/2-way: rdn over 2f out: edgd lft over 1f out: styd on same pce ins fnl f* **9/1**

030 **6** 1 **Capo Regime**[35] 6755 3-9-4 65 (v) IanMongan 9 61
(P Howling) *prom: rdn and ev ch 2f out: no ex fnl f* **20/1**

00 **7** 2¼ **Bermacha**[96] 4938 4-8-9 50 RichardThomas 1 45
(J E Long) *s.i.s: outpcd: r.o ins fnl f: nvr nrr* **100/1**

0405 **8** ½ **Well Of Echoes**[5] 7353 3-8-0 51 (t) DeclanCannon(7) 3 44
(A J McCabe) *mid-div: rdn 1/2-way: hdwy over 1f out: nvr trbld ldrs* **16/1**

545 **9** 1¾ **True Decision**[14] 7225 3-8-13 57 LeeNewnes(5) 2 51
(S Kirk) *sn pushed along in rr: nvr nrr* **12/1**

0205 **10** 2½ **La Belle Joannie**[5] 7350 4-8-9 53 LPKeniry 13 34
(S Curran) *chsd ldrs: rdn over 2f out: wknd over 1f out* **6/1**[3]

3400 **11** 2 **Georgie Bee**[43] 6539 3-8-9 48 ow2 GrahamGibbons 12 32
(T D Walford) *mid-div: rdn 1/2-way: wknd wl over 2f out* **40/1**

4300 **12** 1½ **Turkish Sultan (IRE)**[18] 7152 6-9-0 48 (p) RichardKingscote 14 31
(J M Bradley) *sn outpcd and bhd* **80/1**

1m 42.41s (-1.29) **Going Correction** -0.175s/f (Stan)
WFA 3 from 4yo+ 2lb **12** Ran SP% **122.7**
Speed ratings (Par 101): **99,98,97,96,95 94,92,92,90,87 85,84**
toteswingers:1&2:£5.50, 2&3:£4.20, 1&3:£9.00 CSF £24.75 TOTE £7.50: £2.20, £1.60, £2.00; EX 25.60 Trifecta £51.70 Pool: £303.53 - 4.34 winning units.There was no bid for the winner
Owner Brian Morton **Bred** John Yarr **Trained** Huby, N Yorks

FOCUS
A reasonable seller but it is doubtful if the form can be taken at face value. The winner probably didn't need to match his best form.
Turkish Sultan(IRE) Official explanation: jockey said gelding never travelled

7423 PLAY GOLF AT SOUTHWELL GOLF CLUB H'CAP 1m (F)
2:50 (2:50) (Class 5) (0-70,70) 3-Y-0+ **£2,729** (£806; £403) **Stalls** Low

Form RPR

0000 **1** **Elusive Fame (USA)**[25] 7000 3-9-2 **68** (b) JoeFanning 6 79
(M Johnston) *trckd ldrs: racd keenly: rdn to ld wl ins fnl f: r.o* **8/1**

4222 **2** nk **Iron Out (USA)**[13] 7246 3-9-4 **70** RobertWinston 13 80
(R Hollinshead) *a.p: rdn to ld over 1f out: edgd lft and hdd wl ins fnl f* **6/1**[2]

0036 **3** ¾ **Hilbre Court (USA)**[11] 7271 4-9-6 **70** GrahamGibbons 11 78
(B P J Baugh) *chsd ldrs: rdn and ev ch fr over 1f out: unable qck towards fin* **7/1**[3]

0315 **4** ½ **Business Class (BRZ)**[20] 7113 4-8-13 **63** AndrewMullen 8 70
(D Nicholls) *chsd ldr tl led 3f out: sn rdn and hung lft: hdd over 1f out: styd on same pce ins fnl f* **4/1**[1]

3513 **5** 2¾ **The Grey One (IRE)**[20] 7109 6-9-2 **66** (p) RichardKingscote 7 67
(J M Bradley) *mid-div: rdn over 2f out: styd on fr over 1f out: nt trble ldrs* **15/2**

5130 **6** 1¼ **Ailsa Craig (IRE)**[50] 6337 3-9-2 **68** PJMcDonald 9 66
(E W Tuer) *s.i.s: hld up: hdwy 3f out: styd on same pce appr fnl f* **20/1**

6123 **7** 5 **Waahej**[27] 6951 3-9-0 **66** LPKeniry 4 52
(P W Hiatt) *chsd ldrs: rdn over 2f out: wknd over 1f out* **17/2**

4002 **8** 4 **Jord (IRE)**[11] 7275 5-8-11 **61** PaulHanagan 5 38
(J A Glover) *led 5f: wkng whn n.m.r 2f out* **9/1**

0306 **9** 1 **Binfield (IRE)**[15] 6719 4-8-11 **64** RussellKennemore(3) 14 39
(B G Powell) *mid-div: rdn 1/2-way: wknd over 3f out* **25/1**

060 **10** nk **Eastern Gift**[17] 7192 4-9-4 **68** SimonWhitworth 10 42
(Miss Gay Kelleway) *hld up: hdwy over 3f out: wknd over 2f out* **25/1**

0-00 **11** 2 **Daltaban (FR)**[21] 7084 5-8-12 **62** PhillipMakin 2 32
(P Salmon) *sn pushed along: a in rr: bhd fnl 3f* **66/1**

0505 **12** 4½ **Border Owl (IRE)**[48] 6383 4-8-8 **65** BillyCray(7) 3 24
(P Salmon) *s.i.s: sn drvn along: a in rr: bhd fnl 3f* **9/1**

3- **13** 9 **Desert Mile (IRE)**[22] 7076 6-9-6 **70** TomEaves 12 9
(Ollie Pears) *s.i.s: outpcd* **16/1**

1m 41.15s (-2.55) **Going Correction** -0.175s/f (Stan)
WFA 3 from 4yo+ 2lb **13** Ran SP% **120.0**
Speed ratings (Par 103): **105,104,103,103,100 99,94,90,89,89 87,82,73**
toteswingers:1&2:£7.40, 2&3:£9.70, 1&3:£12.90 CSF £53.40 CT £372.36 TOTE £11.50: £3.30, £2.20, £2.00; EX 55.90 Trifecta £113.90 Part won. Pool £153.94 - 0.44 winning units..
Owner Mark Johnston Racing Ltd **Bred** Summer Wind Farm **Trained** Middleham Moor, N Yorks

FOCUS
A modest but competitive handicap, and sound form with the first four all probably better here than elsewhere.

7424 PLAY AT POKERINVENICE.COM H'CAP (DIV II) 6f (F)
3:20 (3:21) (Class 6) (0-60,60) 3-Y-0+ **£1,706** (£503; £252) **Stalls** Low

Form RPR

0050 **1** **Punching**[14] 7223 5-9-3 **58** LPKeniry 6 78+
(C R Dore) *trckd ldrs: a gng wl: led on bit over 1f out: c clr fnl f: readily* **7/2**[2]

4021 **2** 3 **Dancing Welcome**[13] 7240 3-8-12 **53** (b) RichardKingscote 2 59
(J M Bradley) *sn pushed along in rr: hdwy u.p over 1f out: wnt 2nd wl ins fnl f: no ch w wnr* **10/1**

4041 **3** ½ **Nacho Libre**[4] 7371 4-8-12 **60** 6ex (b) JamesPSullivan(7) 10 64
(M W Easterby) *trckd ldr tl led over 2f out: rdn and hdd over 1f out: styd on same pce fnl f* **3/1**[1]

0035 **4** 2¾ **Megalo Maniac**[4] 7371 6-9-0 **55** (p) PaulHanagan 13 51
(R A Fahey) *hld up in tch: lost pl over 3f out: hdwy over 1f out: nt trble ldrs* **9/2**[3]

5260 **5** 2¼ **Convince (USA)**[17] 7179 8-9-0 **58** (p) AndreaAtzeni(3) 11 46
(J L Flint) *sn outpcd: drvn along 1/2-way: r.o ins fnl f: nrst fin* **13/2**

0050 **6** 1½ **King's Sabre**[11] 7280 3-9-0 **55** (be) J-PGuillambert 8 39
(R C Guest) *led: rdn and hdd over 2f out: hung lft and wknd over 1f out* **66/1**

4063 **7** 1¼ **Guildenstern (IRE)**[11] 7275 7-9-4 **59** JimmyQuinn 9 39
(P Howling) *hld up: shkn up over 2f out: nvr nr to chal* **8/1**

2050 **8** ½ **Tenancy (IRE)**[21] 7086 5-8-3 **49** ow1 DeanHeslop(5) 1 27
(S A Harris) *hld up in tch: rdn over 2f out: wknd over 1f out* **25/1**

5000 **9** 1 **Gower**[42] 6553 5-8-5 **46** KirstyMilczarek 7 21
(R J Price) *chsd ldrs: rdn over 2f out: wknd over 1f out* **40/1**

-002 **10** 5 **White Ledger (IRE)**[74] 5629 10-8-0 **46** (v) AndrewHeffernan(5) 5 5
(R E Peacock) *mid-div: hdwy over 4f out: rdn over 2f out: sn wknd* **40/1**

0000 **11** 3¾ **Greystoke Prince**[32] 6828 4-8-7 **55** (t) CarolineKelly(7) 12 —
(P S McEntee) *s.i.s and n.m.r after s: sn pushed along: hdwy on outside over 3f out: sn wknd* **50/1**

000 **12** 2 **Kelamon**[48] 6377 5-9-1 **56** SaleemGolam 4 —
(S C Williams) *s.i.s: a in rr* **11/1**

1m 15.5s (-1.00) **Going Correction** -0.175s/f (Stan) **12** Ran SP% **119.5**
Speed ratings (Par 101): **99,95,94,90,87 85,84,83,82,75 70,67**
toteswingers:1&2:£10.60, 2&3:£5.60, 1&3:£4.00 CSF £37.17 CT £120.42 TOTE £4.90: £1.90, £3.30, £1.30; EX 39.00 Trifecta £157.90 Part won. Pool £213.43 - 0.54 winning units..
Owner Liam Breslin **Bred** Cheveley Park Stud Ltd **Trained** Cowbit, Lincs

FOCUS
A moderate contest run in an almost identical time to the first division. The winner is clearly better here than elsewhere and the runner-up ran to her recent best.

7425 SOUTHWELL-RACECOURSE.CO.UK H'CAP 1m 4f (F)
3:50 (3:51) (Class 6) (0-60,60) 3-Y-0+ **£2,047** (£604; £302) **Stalls** Low

Form RPR

3600 **1** **Shadows Lengthen**[35] 6768 3-8-10 **52** (b) GrahamGibbons 2 71+
(M W Easterby) *mde all: pushed clr over 2f out: eased towards fin* **11/1**

5401 **2** 3¼ **Swords**[5] 7354 7-8-13 **54** 6ex AndrewHeffernan(5) 7 65
(R E Peacock) *hld up: hdwy over 3f out: rdn to chse wnr over 2f out: no imp* **10/3**[1]

0002 **3** 3¾ **Jackie Kiely**[5] 7354 8-8-13 **49** (tp) PhillipMakin 5 54+
(R Brotherton) *hld up: nt clr run over 3f out: hdwy over 1f out: r.o: nt rch ldrs* **6/1**[3]

0040 **4** 3 **Inch Lodge**[20] 7112 7-9-9 **59** (t) KirstyMilczarek 1 59
(Miss D Mountain) *prom: chsd wnr 3f out: sn rdn: wknd over 1f out* **16/1**

0533 **5** 1¾ **They All Laughed**[6] 7336 6-9-8 **58** (p) PJMcDonald 3 55
(Mrs Marjorie Fife) *chsd wnr tl rdn 3f out: wknd 2f out* **13/2**

0513 **6** 3½ **Beat The Shower**[14] 7222 3-8-13 **55** PaulHanagan 8 46
(P D Niven) *hld up in tch: rdn over 3f out: wknd over 2f out* **4/1**[2]

5440 **7** 7 **Shanavaz**[21] 7084 3-8-6 **48** (p) JimmyQuinn 14 28
(C J Teague) *s.s: hld up: hdwy over 4f out: rdn and wknd over 2f out* **20/1**

1-53 **8** 1 **Stravita**[294] 301 5-9-7 **60** AndreaAtzeni(3) 13 39
(R Hollinshead) *hld up in tch: rdn over 3f out: wknd over 2f out* **8/1**

0054 **9** 9 **Moon Money (IRE)**[24] 7025 3-8-8 **50** StephenDonohoe 11 14
(K A Ryan) *chsd ldrs tl rdn and wknd over 3f out* **9/1**

023- **10** 2¼ **Sleepy Mountain**[344] 7608 5-8-10 **46** oh1 LPKeniry 10 7
(A Middleton) *s.i.s: a in rr* **28/1**

0000 **11** hd **Solo Choice**[19] 7142 3-8-10 **52** (b) SJCraine 6 12
(I W McInnes) *s.i.s: hld up: rdn and wknd wl over 3f out* **40/1**

1300 **12** 4½ **Jordan's Light (USA)**[42] 6558 6-9-8 **58** (v) TomEaves 9 11
(T J Pitt) *hld up: last and rdn 1/2-way: lost tch fnl 4f* **33/1**

-000 **13** 7 **Monaco Mistress (IRE)**[17] 7173 3-8-6 **48** (t) JoeFanning 4 —
(N Tinkler) *prom tl rdn and wknd over 3f out* **100/1**

2m 36.49s (-4.51) **Going Correction** -0.175s/f (Stan)
WFA 3 from 4yo+ 6lb **13** Ran SP% **120.6**
Speed ratings (Par 101): **108,105,103,101,100 97,93,92,86,85 84,81,77**
toteswingers:1&2:£12.30, 2&3:£4.00, 1&3:£16.20 CSF £45.98 CT £250.36 TOTE £13.60: £3.80, £1.70, £2.20; EX 84.10 TRIFECTA Not won. Place 6 £14.60, Place 5 £10.37.
Owner T A F Frost **Bred** London Thoroughbred Services Ltd **Trained** Sheriff Hutton, N Yorks

FOCUS
Not a bad race for the grade and there was much to like about the winner, who was value for extra. The next two were both on fair marks on their best form round here.
T/Jkpt: Not won. T/Plt: £13.90 to a £1 stake. Pool: £63,942.19. 3,351.50 winning tickets. T/Qpdt: £5.50 to a £1 stake. Pool: £4,753.38. 632.30 winning tickets. CR

7323 KEMPTON (A.W) (R-H)

Wednesday, November 18

OFFICIAL GOING: Standard

Wind: Strong across (away from stands) Weather: Dark

7426 BOOK NOW FOR BOXING DAY APPRENTICE CLASSIFIED CLAIMING STKS 1m 2f (P)

6:20 (6:20) (Class 6) 3-Y-O £2,047 (£604; £302) Stalls High

Form RPR

1532 1 **Why Nee Amy**[16] 7211 3-8-12 56 KylieManser(3) 4 62
(T Keddy) *hld up off the pce in 5th: prog 3f out: wnt 3rd 1f out: drvn and stdy on wl between rivals last 75yds to ld fnl strides* **6/1**

2333 2 *hd* **Too Tall**[22] 7101 3-9-9 67 MatthewDavies 2 69
(J R Boyle) *trckd ldrs: wnt 3rd 4f out: rdn to chse ldr over 1f out and sn chalng: nt qckn and jst hld nr fin* **11/8**[1]

5450 3 *shd* **True Decision**[1] 7422 3-8-11 57 LeeNewnes(3) 3 60
(S Kirk) *trckd ldr after 4f: clsd and rdn to ld over 2f out: hrd pressed fnl f: hdd last strides* **7/2**[3]

-060 4 *2 3/4* **Mr Deal**[16] 4744 3-9-0 48 SimonPearce 7 55
(Eve Johnson Houghton) *hld up and last early: prog to 4th 3f out: disp 3rd and cl enough over 1f out: fdd fnl f* **50/1**

3631 5 *9* **Farncombe (IRE)**[17] 7198 3-9-4 67 SPRyan(5) 1 46
(R A Harris) *led at decent pce to over 2f out: wknd rapidly over 1f out* **11/4**[2]

355 6 *4* **Persian Tomcat (IRE)**[20] 7142 3-8-13 49 AmyBaker 5 28
(Miss J Feilden) *a in last pair: rdn and nt on terms fr over 2f out: sn no ch* **10/1**

00-0 7 *16* **Ready To Prime**[21] 7105 3-8-6 39 BarryAdams(5) 6 —
(Mike Murphy) *chsd ldr 4th: rdn and wknd 4f out: t.o* **100/1**

2m 9.39s (1.39) **Going Correction** +0.15s/f (Slow) 7 Ran SP% 117.3
Speed ratings (Par 98): **100,99,99,97,90 87,74**
toteswingers: 1&2 £2.80, 1&3 £4.30, 2&3 £2.10 CSF £15.36 TOTE £7.60: £2.80, £1.20; EX 22.60.
Owner B Neaves **Bred** D E Jenkins **Trained** Newmarket, Suffolk

FOCUS
A modest claimer that produced a thrilling three-way finish. The pace was sound and the winner got back close to his 2yo best.

7427 KIA SOUL, SAFE BET H'CAP 5f (P)

6:50 (6:51) (Class 7) (0-50,50) 3-Y-0+ £2,047 (£604; £302) Stalls High

Form RPR

4000 1 **Elusive Ronnie (IRE)**[75] 5644 3-8-12 48 (b) JackMitchell(3) 6 56+
(R A Teal) *sn in last pair: rdn and n.m.r briefly on inner 2f out: nt clr run over 1f out and twice swtchd lft: 8th ins fnl f: storming run on outer to ld post* **25/1**

0036 2 *nse* **Head To Head (IRE)**[18] 7176 5-9-1 48 (tp) JimmyQuinn 10 56
(A D Brown) *led: drvn to assert over 1f out: over a l clr wl ins fnl f: ct post* **5/1**[3]

2000 3 *1 1/4* **Tanley**[14] 7241 4-9-3 50 TonyCulhane 9 54
(J F Coupland) *chsd ldr: drvn and no imp fnl f: kpt on but lost 2nd nr fin* **11/1**

0405 4 *nse* **Cocktail Party (IRE)**[15] 7224 3-8-10 50 (t) KierenFox(7) 8 53+
(J W Hills) *hld up in midfield on inner: n.m.r over 1f out: prog after: disp 2nd and drvn last 100yds: one pce* **10/1**

62 5 *shd* **Colombard (IRE)**[23] 7068 4-9-3 50 (b) JamieSpencer 7 53
(Patrick Morris) *hld up in rr: prog jst over 1f out: drvn and clsd on ldrs ins fnl f: no ex last 50yds* **11/4**[2]

0066 6 *nk* **Commander Wish**[14] 7241 6-9-3 50 (p) KFallon 12 52+
(Lucinda Featherstone) *awkward s: detached in last: pushed along 2f out: styd on fnl f but nt as fast as wnr and no ch of catching ldrs* **2/1**[1]

-000 7 *3/4* **Oxbridge**[6] 7350 4-9-1 48 LukeMorris 4 47
(J M Bradley) *towards rr: rdn 1/2-way: struggling 2f out: styd on again last 150yds* **22/1**

006 8 *1 1/4* **Andrasta**[22] 7081 4-8-10 50 CharlotteKerton(7) 2 45
(S A Harris) *pressed ldng pair on outer: bmpd along over 1f out: steadily wknd fnl f* **25/1**

2600 9 *1/2* **Like For Like (IRE)**[72] 5716 3-8-13 49 WilliamCarson(3) 3 42
(R J Hodges) *chsd ldrs: no prog over 1f out: fdd fnl f* **12/1**

1-50 10 *hd* **Summer Rose**[22] 7100 4-9-3 50 (v) JimCrowley 1 42
(R M H Cowell) *trapped wd in midfield: lost pl 2f out: no prog fr rr over 1f out* **10/1**

0000 11 *3/4* **Woodcote (IRE)**[28] 6939 7-9-2 49 (v) AdamKirby 11 38
(Peter Grayson) *broke on terms and cl up bhd ldrs: drvn over 1f out: wknd fnl f* **16/1**

61.67 secs (1.17) **Going Correction** +0.15s/f (Slow) 11 Ran SP% 128.8
Speed ratings (Par 97): **96,95,93,93,93 93,92,90,89,88 87**
toteswingers: 1&2 £38.50, 1&3 £95.90, 2&3 £11.30 CSF £156.16 CT £1505.54 TOTE £29.80: £6.00, £1.90, £2.50; EX 225.10.
Owner R J Ryan **Bred** The Ginger Group **Trained** Ashtead, Surrey

FOCUS
A low-grade handicap.The pace was decent but the second and third both raced prominently and only the surprise winner got into it from behind. The runner-up was the best guide to the form.
Cocktail Party(IRE) Official explanation: jockey said filly was denied a clear run
Colombard(IRE) Official explanation: jockey said gelding hung left throughout
Commander Wish Official explanation: jockey said gelding stumbled leaving stalls

7428 DIGIBET H'CAP 1m 2f (P)

7:20 (7:22) (Class 5) (0-75,75) 3-Y-O £2,590 (£770; £385; £192) Stalls High

Form RPR

6140 1 **Best In Class**[77] 5575 3-9-0 71 JimCrowley 6 80
(S C Williams) *stdd s: hld up in last pair: effrt over 2f out: wound up on outer over 1f out: r.o to ld ins fnl f: sn clr: decisively* **12/1**

6000 2 *2 3/4* **Capeability (IRE)**[14] 7247 3-8-12 69 TonyCulhane 5 72
(M R Channon) *t.k.h early: hld up in tch: effrt 2f out: c between rivals to ld 1f out: sn hdd: edgd lft and outpcd* **9/2**[2]

0632 3 *1 3/4* **Via Mia**[19] 7153 3-8-7 69 MatthewDavies(5) 2 69
(George Baker) *chsd ldrs on wd outside: rdn wl over 2f out: effrt to chal and upsides jst over 1f out: one pce* **13/2**

0050 4 *nk* **Wood Fairy**[19] 7149 3-8-5 62 PaulHanagan 4 61
(R A Fahey) *t.k.h: trckd ldrs: rdn to chal and upsides 1f out: fdd tamely* **15/2**

5060 5 *1* **Kings Troop**[63] 5986 3-8-13 70 TPQueally 10 67
(A King) *t.k.h: hld up in rr: effrt and wriggled through on inner to chse ldrs over 1f out: sn rdn and nt qckn: kpt on* **8/1**

6200 6 *1/2* **Levitation (IRE)**[98] 4902 3-9-0 71 IanMongan 3 67
(W S Kittow) *pressed ldrs on outer: rdn over 2f out: chal over 1f out: nt qckn sn after: wknd ins fnl f* **40/1**

0005 7 *1 3/4* **Woteva**[14] 7246 3-8-4 61 oh3 JimmyQuinn 7 54
(T P Tate) *trckd ldr: rdn to ld over 2f out: hdd & wknd 1f out* **25/1**

3113 8 *3 1/2* **Florentia**[32] 6861 3-8-10 67 StephenDonohoe 13 53
(Sir Mark Prescott) *t.k.h: hld up in rr: drvn and no rspnse 2f out: no ch after* **7/2**[1]

0331 9 *nk* **Strong Storm (USA)**[31] 5482 3-8-8 65 (p) SteveDrowne 9 50
(H J Collingridge) *led at mod pce: tried to qckn over 3f out but no rspnse: hdd and lost pl over 2f out* **11/1**

0202 10 *1/2* **In Secret**[28] 6934 3-9-1 72 TedDurcan 12 56
(J L Dunlop) *hld up in last pair: shkn up and no prog over 2f out: sn no ch* **5/1**[3]

22-0 11 *7* **Saharan Royal**[138] 3581 3-8-10 67 FrancisNorton 11 37
(Matthew Salaman) *rring bef stalls opened: t.k.h: trckd ldrs: hanging and wknd wl over 1f out* **25/1**

2m 8.14s (0.14) **Going Correction** +0.15s/f (Slow) 11 Ran SP% 119.4
Speed ratings (Par 102): **105,102,101,101,100 99,98,95,95,95 89**
toteswingers: 1&2 £10.60, 1&3 £13.60, 2&3 £4.30 CSF £65.19 CT £392.41 TOTE £17.70: £4.10, £1.60, £2.20; EX 98.70.
Owner Mrs A Shone **Bred** Michael Clarke **Trained** Newmarket, Suffolk

FOCUS
A fair handicap, involving a last-time-out winner and three who were placed on their latest start. A decent effort from the winner, with the form best rated around the runner-up.

7429 DIGIBET.COM EBF MAIDEN STKS (DIV I) 7f (P)

7:50 (7:53) (Class 4) 2-Y-O £4,209 (£1,252; £625; £312) Stalls High

Form RPR

44 1 **Khanivorous**[168] 2595 2-9-3 0 SJCraine 8 71
(J R Boyle) *chsd ldng pair: pushed along 1/2-way: wnt 2nd over 2f out: hrd rdn to ld over 1f out: grad drew clr* **15/8**[2]

0 2 *3 1/4* **Ana Moutabahi**[23] 7050 2-9-3 0 AdamKirby 6 63
(C G Cox) *led: drvn and hdd over 1f out: grad outpcd* **8/1**[3]

0 3 *1 3/4* **Highland Bridge**[17] 7199 2-9-3 0 LPKeniry 3 59
(D R C Elsworth) *chsd ldr tl nt qckn over 2f out: one pce in 3rd after* **50/1**

4 *3/4* **Freedom Pass (USA)** 2-8-12 0 KirstyMilczarek 10 52
(J A R Toller) *dwlt: sn cl up: nt qckn over 2f out: one pce after* **10/1**

00 5 *1 3/4* **Kyoatee Kilt**[16] 7213 2-9-3 0 JimCrowley 11 52
(P F I Cole) *t.k.h in midfield: effrt on inner over 2f out: sn no prog and btn* **14/1**

00 6 *hd* **Balsha (USA)**[25] 7034 2-8-12 0 SteveDrowne 1 47
(E A L Dunlop) *dwlt: mostly in last trio: nvr a threat: modest late prog* **16/1**

7 *1/2* **Staff Sergeant** 2-9-3 0 JoeFanning 5 51
(M Johnston) *sn trckd ldrs: shkn up over 2f out: rn green and losing grnd fnl 2f* **7/4**[1]

0000 8 *7* **Barafundle Boy**[18] 7177 2-8-10 45 RyanClark(7) 9 33
(J J Bridger) *a in rr: detached in last trio and struggling over 2f out* **100/1**

9 *9* **Far View (IRE)** 2-9-3 0 (t) GeorgeBaker 4 11
(J W Hills) *restless bef gng in stalls and restless in them: s.s: a in last pair: wknd over 2f out: t.o* **10/1**

1m 28.36s (2.36) **Going Correction** +0.15s/f (Slow) 9 Ran SP% 115.9
Speed ratings (Par 98): **92,88,86,85,83 83,82,74,64**
toteswingers: 1&2 £3.20, 1&3 £42.50, 2&3 £46.20 CSF £17.71 TOTE £3.60: £1.50, £2.80, £8.10; EX 29.80.
Owner M Khan X2 **Bred** Christopher J Mason **Trained** Epsom, Surrey

FOCUS
An ordinary maiden. The winner improved but the fifth and eighth temper enthusiasm for the form.

NOTEBOOK
Khanivorous was withdrawn after pricking a foot when due to contest a seller at Southwell 24 hours earlier but he was allowed to take his chance here. He has plenty of winners on the dam's side of his pedigree, is unexposed at this trip and should be capable of progress after just three starts, but the form of this race is only modest and he will need to learn to travel with more fluency. (op 4-1)
Ana Moutabahi was never going the pace when 66-1 ninth in a C&D maiden on debut last month, but he looked more streetwise here and offered some encouragement under a positive ride. (op 9-1)
Highland Bridge, very green when 50-1 tailed off last of 12 in a 1m Lingfield maiden on debut, seemed to get the hang of things late on here and shaped with some promise. (op 33-1)
Freedom Pass(USA) looked inexperienced when pressure was applied but stayed on quite nicely and showed some ability on debut. She was a 32,000gns breeze-up purchase who is out of a sister to 6f Listed winner Irresistible. (op 8-1)
Staff Sergeant was forced wide for most of the way and was never really factor. He is a first foal of a dual middle-distance winner who is a sister to Oaks third Relish The Thought, so should do better with distance and time, but this has to rate as a fairly disappointing first effort by a horse who was sent off as favourite. (op 11-10)

7430 DIGIBET.COM EBF MAIDEN STKS (DIV II) 7f (P)

8:20 (8:21) (Class 4) 2-Y-O £4,209 (£1,252; £625; £312) Stalls High

Form RPR

55 1 **Hypnotized (USA)**[20] 7130 2-9-3 0 JamieSpencer 9 82+
(M L W Bell) *trckd ldrs: effrt over 2f out: drvn to ld over 1f out: sn wl in command* **2/1**[1]

0 2 *2 1/2* **Vaultage (USA)**[18] 7182 2-8-12 0 HayleyTurner 10 68+
(E A L Dunlop) *hld up in rr: gd prog on inner fr 3f out: led 2f out: hrd rdn and hdd over 1f out: one pce* **6/1**

60 3 *1 3/4* **Aktia (IRE)**[29] 6921 2-8-12 0 KFallon 7 63
(L M Cumani) *s.i.s and rousted along early in rr: rdn over 2f out: kpt on to take 3rd ins fnl f* **4/1**[3]

52 4 *3/4* **Libertino (IRE)**[44] 6542 2-9-3 0 MartinDwyer 3 67
(B J Meehan) *trckd ldrs on outer: cl enough over 2f out: grad fdd over 1f out* **3/1**[2]

06 5 *1 1/2* **Egyptology (IRE)**[12] 7276 2-9-3 0 JoeFanning 6 63
(M Johnston) *trckd ldr: led briefly over 2f out: wknd over 1f out* **9/1**

0 6 *2* **Welsh Artist**[14] 7234 2-9-3 0 NCallan 2 58
(Mrs A J Perrett) *in tch on outer: effrt over 2f out: wknd over 1f out* **20/1**

00 7 *2* **Othello (IRE)**[7] 7325 2-9-3 0 GeorgeBaker 8 53+
(E F Vaughan) *stdd s: hld up in last: lot of whip waving fr 2f out but only one reminder 1f out: nvr nr ldrs* **33/1**

0 8 *1 1/2* **Corr Point (IRE)**[5] 7376 2-9-3 0 FrankieMcDonald 1 49
(J A Osborne) *sn led: hdd & wknd over 2f out* **66/1**

9 *9* **Spirit Of Normandy** 2-8-12 0 PaulDoe 5 22
(R Ingram) *s.i.s: t.k.h early: struggling in last trio over 2f out: t.o* **66/1**

10 2 1/2 **Jokers Wild** 2-9-3 0 ... LPKeniry 4 20
(A M Balding) *t.k.h early: hld up in rr: wknd over 2f out: t.o* **25/1**

1m 28.3s (2.30) **Going Correction** +0.15s/f (Slow) **10** Ran SP% **117.2**
Speed ratings (Par 98): **92,89,87,86,84 82,80,78,68,65**
toteswingers: 1&2 £3.70, 1&3 £3.50, 2&3 £5.00 CSF £13.94 TOTE £3.00: £1.20, £2.30, £1.80; EX 14.40.
Owner Ali Saeed **Bred** Rabbah Bloodstock Llc **Trained** Newmarket, Suffolk

FOCUS
A fair maiden. The pace was modest but they finished well strung out. An improved effort from the winner and the fom could be rated a bit higher.

NOTEBOOK
Hypnotized(USA) had solid claims on his fifth-placed efforts in 7f maidens at Leicester and Lingfield last month. He had to negotiate some traffic problems at the two-furlong pole but burst into the lead and showed a good attitude to forge clear. This should be the springboard to better things for the $110,000 brother to quite useful 6f 2-y-o winner Absent Pleasure. (op 5-2 tchd 7-4 and 11-4 in a place)
Vaultage(USA) was the only one to pose any sort of threat to the winner in the final quarter of the race and stepped up significantly on her 33-1 tenth in a 7f Newmarket fillies' maiden on debut last month. The 135,000gns filly is out of a three-time 6f dirt winner at two, and is a half-sister to smart US 1m winner Renda. There should be quite a bit more to come and she could prove most effective on Polytrack. (op 13-2 tchd 7-1 and 8-1 in a place)
Aktia(IRE) took a while to pick up and never really posed a threat. She is well related and still has time on her side but has not really managed to build on her promising debut effort in two subsequent runs. (op 10-3 tchd 9-2)
Libertino(IRE) had decent form claims on his clear second in a 6f Warwick maiden on return from a break last month. He was forced a bit wide but had every chance and his stamina seemed to buckle on this step up to 7f. (tchd 4-1)
Egyptology(IRE) dropped away in the closing stages when a heavily-backed favourite for a 7f Wolverhampton maiden early in the month and put in another tame effort here. He is one to watch until he starts finishing his races with more conviction but he is now qualified for a mark and it would be no surprise if Mark Johnston finds the key to the half-brother to smart 7f-1m4f performer Naheef. (op 8-1)
Othello(IRE) is the sort to do better now he can contest handicaps.

7431 DIGIBET CASINO CONDITIONS STKS 7f (P)
8:50 (8:51) (Class 3) 3-Y-O+
£7,352 (£2,201; £1,100; £551; £274; £138) **Stalls** High

Form RPR
0123 **1** **Khor Dubai (IRE)**[62] 6030 3-8-10 104 ... (v) TedDurcan 9 92+
(Saeed Bin Suroor) *trckd ldng pair: cruised through to ld over 1f out: rdn clr fnl f* **4/7**[1]
4640 **2** 3 1/4 **Carcinetto (IRE)**[5] 7375 7-8-11 95 ... RichardEvans(5) 7 89
(P D Evans) *chsd ldng trio: pushed along bef 1/2-way: rdn over 2f out: styd on fr over 1f out to take 2nd last 75yds* **40/1**
0004 **3** 3/4 **Confuchias (IRE)**[11] 7294 5-8-8 93 ... AndreaAtzeni(3) 8 82
(Pat Eddery) *trckd ldr: chal 2f out and carried lft: chsd wnr fnl f but no ch: lost 2nd last 75yds* **11/2**[2]
4 3/4 **Jaroslaw (SAF)**[382] 6-8-11 97 ... MartinDwyer 4 80+
(D M Simcock) *hld up: hmpd on inner after 1f and restrained to last pair: effrt over 2f out: kpt on after: nvr able to rch ldrs* **22/1**
043 **5** 3/4 **Soccerjackpot (USA)**[96] 4983 5-8-11 94 ... AdamKirby 10 78
(C G Cox) *led: hung lft fr over 2f out: hdd & wknd over 1f out* **7/1**[3]
005 **6** 5 **Always The Sun**[4] 7401 3-8-5 42 ... (p) LukeMorris 2 59?
(P Leech) *nvr bttr than midfield: lft bhd fr over 2f out* **66/1**
0660 **7** 3 **Diddums**[4] 7394 3-8-3 65 ... CarolineKelly(7) 3 56
(P S McEntee) *hld up in 7th: coaxed along and no rspnse over 2f out* **66/1**
5031 **8** nk **Wigram's Turn (USA)**[49] 6374 4-8-11 90 ... JamieSpencer 5 55
(A M Balding) *s.i.s: hld up in last pair: rdn over 2f out: hanging and no prog after* **10/1**
0265 **9** 37 **Iasia (GR)**[33] 6814 3-8-5 90 ... JimmyQuinn 6 —
(Jane Chapple-Hyam) *chsd ldrs 4f: wknd rapidly: t.o* **11/1**

1m 25.41s (-0.59) **Going Correction** +0.15s/f (Slow)
WFA 3 from 4yo+ 1lb **9** Ran SP% **118.7**
Speed ratings (Par 107): **109,105,104,103,102 97,93,93,50**
toteswingers: 1&2 £11.30, 1&3 £1.90, 2&3 £15.20 CSF £42.57 TOTE £1.50: £1.20, £5.40, £1.40; EX 58.60.
Owner Godolphin **Bred** K And Mrs Cullen **Trained** Newmarket, Suffolk
■ Stewards' Enquiry : Caroline Kelly five-day ban: careless riding (Nov 2-6)

FOCUS
A decent conditions event. The pace was solid and the hot favourite hammered his opponents. The form is decent but limited by the sixth, and the winner did not need to be at his best.

NOTEBOOK
Khor Dubai(IRE) finished third behind subsequent US Grade 1 winner Gitano Hernando in a hot conditions event at Wolverhampton in September, form which had also been boosted by the second Mia's Boy finishing runner-up off a mark of 105 in a Doncaster handicap next time. He set a smart standard, cruised alongside the leader at the two furlong pole and shot clear to register his fifth win on his 18th career start. The 104-rated son of Kheleyf has raised his form another notch on Polytrack recently and could be able to make a big impact in Listed or Group 3 company. (tchd 8-15 and 4-6 in a place)
Carcinetto(IRE) never really posed a threat but the prolific winning 7-y-o put in a good effort under a penalty and rebounded from a disappointment in a Wolverhampton handicap last Friday. (op 33-1)
Confuchias(IRE) deserves some credit for a decent effort in a bid for a repeat success in this race. He has gradually worked his way back to form in five starts for his current yard and is down to a very tempting mark of 93 for handicaps. (op 7-1)
Jaroslaw(SAF) caught the eye staying on from an unpromising position on his first run for a new yard after 382 days off. He won four races at 5f-7f in South Africa and ran respectably in Graded company behind J J The Jet Plane. He should be sharper next time and on this evidence the relatively lightly raced 6-y-o could live up to a mark of 97. Official explanation: jockey said gelding suffered interference in running (op 14-1)
Soccerjackpot(USA) gave it a fair shot from the front and was not given a hard time when his chance was gone. (op 6-1)
Iasia(GR) Official explanation: jockey said filly stopped quickly

7432 NORTHAMBER ACER H'CAP 7f (P)
9:20 (9:21) (Class 5) (0-70,70) 3-Y-O+ **£2,590** (£770; £385; £192) **Stalls** High

Form RPR
0460 **1** **Fernando Torres**[74] 5672 3-8-11 62 ... FrancisNorton 3 73
(Matthew Salaman) *chsd ldr: rdn 2f out: sustained chal over 1f out: led last 50yds: jst hld on* **33/1**
0053 **2** hd **Musical Script (USA)**[7] 7329 6-9-1 65 ... (b) JimCrowley 7 75+
(Mouse Hamilton-Fairley) *t.k.h: hld up towards rr: nt clr run 2f out: prog over 1f out: drvn and r.o fnl f: jst failed* **8/1**
0313 **3** 1/2 **Leelu**[23] 7051 3-8-6 57 ... HayleyTurner 10 66
(D W P Arbuthnot) *led at decent pce: drvn fr 2f out: clung on wl tl hdd last 50yds* **9/2**[2]
0030 **4** 1 1/2 **Lord Fidelio (IRE)**[159] 2879 3-9-2 67 ... LPKeniry 9 72
(A M Balding) *hld up bhd ldrs: effrt over 2f out: drvn to chse ldng pair over 1f out: one pce fnl f* **25/1**
6313 **5** nk **Cativo Cavallino**[18] 7180 6-8-11 64 ... NataliaGemelova(3) 2 68
(J E Long) *chsd ldng trio: wl on terms on outer 2f out: one pce fr over 1f out* **16/1**
6135 **6** 1/2 **Fault**[17] 7203 3-9-5 70 ... (t) AdamKirby 5 72
(Stef Liddiard) *hld up in last pair: rdn and effrt over 2f out: styd on fr over 1f out: nvr rchd ldrs* **11/2**[3]
4462 **7** 2 **Goodbye Cash (IRE)**[18] 7179 5-8-8 58 ... PaulDoe 4 55
(P D Evans) *hld up in rr: rdn wl over 2f out and no prog: modest late hdwy* **13/2**
3021 **8** hd **King Of Defence**[18] 7180 3-9-1 66 ... NCallan 1 63
(M A Jarvis) *wnt lft s: t.k.h in midfield on outer: plld out and asked for effrt 2f out: fnd nil* **13/8**[1]
6505 **9** 3/4 **Woolston Ferry (IRE)**[18] 7192 3-8-11 65 ... JackMitchell(3) 8 59
(David Pinder) *hld up towards rr on inner: prog over 2f out: chsng ldrs over 1f out: wknd fnl f* **16/1**
0-63 **10** 1 **Freeing**[64] 5971 3-8-4 55 oh2 ... KirstyMilczarek 11 47
(J A R Toller) *cl up on inner: stl chsng ldrs over 1f out: sn wknd* **28/1**
6030 **11** hd **One Cool Kitty**[46] 6492 3-8-6 57 ... (t) LiamJones 6 48
(M G Quinlan) *v s.i.s: hld up in detached last: rdn 3f out: nvr a factor* **66/1**
2014 **12** 3/4 **Loyal Royal (IRE)**[7] 7329 6-8-13 63 ... (b) DavidProbert 12 52
(J M Bradley) *mostly in midfield on inner: pushed along 1/2-way: u.p whn nt clr run and swtchd lft over 1f out: wknd* **9/1**

1m 26.27s (0.27) **Going Correction** +0.15s/f (Slow)
WFA 3 from 5yo+ 1lb **12** Ran SP% **129.6**
Speed ratings (Par 103): **104,103,103,101,101 100,98,98,97,96 95,94**
toteswingers: 1&2 £67.30, 1&3 £13.70, 2&3 £12.10 CSF £295.49 CT £1471.77 TOTE £24.60: £8.10, £2.80, £2.00; EX 382.30 Place 6: £92.21 Place 5: £47.84.
Owner Mrs C C Regalado-Gonzalez **Bred** Mrs C Regalado-Gonzalez **Trained** Upper Lambourn, Berks

FOCUS
A competitive handicap, involving a number of 3-y-os and some in-form older horses. The pace was fair and there was a very tight finish. Sound form, the winner stepping up on his debut for the yard and on Polytrack.
T/Plt: £200.00 to a £1 stake. Pool: £85,199.63. 310.97 winning tickets. T/Qpdt: £28.80 to a £1 stake. Pool: £7,711.00. 197.90 winning tickets. JN

7388 LINGFIELD (L-H)
Wednesday, November 18

OFFICIAL GOING: Standard
Wind: Strong, behind Weather: Overcast

7433 BET MULTIPLES - BETDAQ H'CAP (DIV I) 1m (P)
12:00 (12:00) (Class 6) (0-55,55) 3-Y-O+ **£1,637** (£483; £241) **Stalls** High

Form RPR
0003 **1** **Wunder Strike (USA)**[17] 7197 3-8-12 53 ... (p) NickyMackay 9 60
(J R Boyle) *hld up in midfield: hdwy 3f out: led wl over 1f out: drvn out* **9/2**[1]
0200 **2** 1/2 **Ymir**[14] 7239 3-8-13 54 ... JimCrowley 7 60
(M J Attwater) *led over 2f: led over 2f out tl wl over 1f out: hrd rdn: kpt on wl* **6/1**[3]
0546 **3** 1 1/2 **Red Current**[17] 7200 5-8-11 50 ... DavidProbert 2 53
(R A Harris) *chsd ldrs: effrt 2f out: hrd rdn and nt qckn fnl f* **10/1**
0-40 **4** 1/2 **Achromatic**[198] 1746 3-9-0 55 ... AdamKirby 12 56
(W R Swinburn) *towards rr: dropped to last 4f out: hrd rdn over 2f out: rallied to chse ldrs 1f out: styd on same pce* **5/1**[2]
0-05 **5** 1 **Mount Usher**[232] 515 7-9-2 55 ... SteveDrowne 10 54+
(Miss Diana Weeden) *hld up towards rr: effrt and wd st: styd on wl fnl f: nrst fin* **50/1**
5614 **6** 1/2 **Inquisitress**[17] 7200 5-8-13 52 ... LukeMorris 6 50
(J J Bridger) *in tch: lost pl 3f out: rallied to chse ldrs over 1f out: hrd rdn: one pce* **15/2**
1600 **7** 1 1/2 **The Graig**[142] 3470 5-9-2 55 ... (t) JerryO'Dwyer 3 49
(J R Holt) *chsd ldrs tl hrd rdn and wknd over 1f out* **33/1**
0006 **8** 1 3/4 **Ardent Prince**[20] 7129 6-8-11 50 ... RobertWinston 8 40
(A J McCabe) *t.k.h in midfield: rdn and hung lft over 1f out: no imp* **15/2**
-000 **9** 3/4 **Candilejas**[13] 7250 3-8-7 55 ... (p) KierenFox(7) 11 43
(R J Smith) *towards rr: hrd rdn 3f out: mod effrt 2f out: sn wknd* **12/1**
0040 **10** 3/4 **My Flame**[21] 7105 4-9-1 54 ... KFallon 1 40
(J R Jenkins) *w ldr: led over 5f out tl wknd over 2f out* **12/1**
0002 **11** 4 1/2 **Cavalry Guard (USA)**[20] 7129 5-8-6 50 ... AmyBaker(5) 5 26
(T D McCarthy) *chsd ldrs: rdn over 3f out: wknd 2f out* **8/1**
000 **12** 4 **Sufficient Warning**[17] 7200 5-8-9 51 ... JackMitchell(3) 4 17
(R J Smith) *last and reminders after 2f: sme hdwy on outer 3f out: wkng whn rn v wd bnd 2f out* **20/1**

1m 39.34s (1.14) **Going Correction** +0.10s/f (Slow)
WFA 3 from 4yo+ 2lb **12** Ran SP% **117.9**
Speed ratings (Par 101): **98,97,96,95,94 94,92,90,90,89 84,80**
toteswingers: 1&2 £9.90, 1&3 £11.50, 2&3 £16.00 CSF £30.33 CT £263.27 TOTE £5.70: £1.90, £1.80, £3.10; EX 50.00 TRIFECTA Not won..
Owner Mrs B Powell B Walsh P Hughes C Murphy **Bred** Mike Abraham **Trained** Epsom, Surrey

FOCUS
A moderate handicap run in a strong wind that was behind the runners in the straight. It was not strong run although the time was slightly quicker than division II. The winner did not need to match his early-season best.

7434 BET ASIAN H'CAPS - BETDAQ NURSERY 1m (P)
12:30 (12:30) (Class 4) (0-85,81) 2-Y-O **£3,885** (£1,156; £577; £288) **Stalls** High

Form RPR
12 **1** **Diam Queen (GER)**[34] 6805 2-9-7 81 ... KFallon 9 85
(L M Cumani) *led 2f: pressed ldr: drvn to ld again ins fnl f: styd on* **7/2**[1]
0641 **2** 1/2 **Nave (USA)**[14] 7235 2-8-6 66 ... JoeFanning 4 69
(M Johnston) *w ldr: led after 2f and set sedate pce: hrd rdn and hdd ins fnl f: kpt on* **9/2**[2]
3625 **3** 2 1/2 **If I Were A Boy (IRE)**[6] 7359 2-9-0 74 ... RyanMoore 1 71
(S Kirk) *prom: rdn over 2f out: one pce appr fnl f* **5/1**[3]
0402 **4** hd **Wild Rockette**[37] 6736 2-9-1 75 ... MartinDwyer 2 72
(B J Meehan) *hld up towards rr: hdwy on ins ent st: hrd rdn over 1f out: one pce* **7/1**

041 **5** 1 1/2 **Come On Safari (IRE)**[104] 4699 2-9-3 **77** JimCrowley 5 71
(P Winkworth) *hld up in rr: hdwy and shkn up over 1f out: no imp* **8/1**
330 **6** 2 3/4 **Exceedthewildman**[41] 6616 2-8-11 **71** LukeMorris 7 59
(J S Moore) *in tch: stdd in rr after 2f: drvn along over 2f out: nt pce to chal* **6/1**
4450 **7** 2 3/4 **Flipping**[26] 6993 2-9-3 **77** IanMongan 3 59
(W S Kittow) *prom: hrd rdn 2f out: sn wknd* **16/1**
61 **8** *nk* **Miss Starlight**[60] 6125 2-9-7 **81** EdwardCreighton 8 62
(P J McBride) *mid-div: drvn along over 3f out: wd and wknd bnd 2f out* **15/2**
0510 **9** 6 **Danger Mulally**[108] 4565 2-9-0 **74** LPKeniry 6 42
(A M Balding) *in tch tl wd and wknd bnd 2f out* **40/1**

1m 39.29s (1.09) **Going Correction** +0.10s/f (Slow) **9** Ran SP% **115.1**
Speed ratings (Par 98): **98,97,95,94,93 90,87,87,81**
toteswingers: 1&2 £2.80, 1&3 £4.70, 2&3 £7.80 CSF £19.06 CT £78.11 TOTE £3.70: £1.50, £1.40, £1.90; EX 9.40 Trifecta £21.40 Pool: £256.80 - 8.80 winning units..
Owner Jaber Abdullah **Bred** The Kingwood Partnership **Trained** Newmarket, Suffolk

FOCUS
This looked quite a competitive contest beforehand but few were ever involved. The wind was again strong, behind runners up the straight.

NOTEBOOK
Diam Queen(GER) ◆, off the mark on her debut before looking slightly unlucky when runner-up in a Wolverhampton nursery last time, gained a straightforward success. Always close up, the only worry for her supporters was when she didn't seem to handle the sharp turn into the straight all that well, but she was soon on an even keel and was able to reel in the early leader. She still looks quite immature and her breeding suggests she will improve when upped to middle-distances next year. (tchd 4-1)
Nave(USA), 5lb higher than when winning a weaker nursery at Kempton on his previous start, was allowed his own way in front and produced a career best in defeat. (op 5-1)
If I Were A Boy(IRE) didn't run badly but he hasn't progressed as expected since running second behind a useful filly two starts back. (tchd 4-1)
Wild Rockette didn't build on her recent second at Windsor and basically found this tougher. (op 13-2 tchd 8-1)
Come On Safari(IRE) had not been seen since winning a 7f maiden at Folkestone in August. Having raced further back than ideal, he had to wait for a gap rounding the final bend and, after briefly looking as though he might pick up, he got tired, giving the impression the run was needed. (tchd 9-1)
Exceedthewildman failed to improve for the step up in trip on his nursery debut. (op 15-2)
Miss Starlight ran nowhere near the form she showed when winning her maiden at Wolverhampton two months earlier and may have gone over the top. (tchd 8-1)

7435 ASHURST WOOD CLAIMING STKS 7f (P)
1:00 (1:00) (Class 6) 2-Y-O **£1,978** (£584; £292) **Stalls** Low

Form RPR
4322 **1** **Chocolate Cookie (IRE)**[18] 7175 2-7-12 65 NickyMackay 3 66
(J R Boyle) *hld up disputing 4th: effrt 2f out: drvn to ld fnl 100yds* **5/1**[3]
6000 **2** 3/4 **Kirsty's Boy (IRE)**[60] 6104 2-8-6 80 LPKeniry 2 72
(J S Moore) *disp ld 1f: prom: drvn to ld over 1f out: hdd and nt qckn fnl 100yds* **16/1**
3063 **3** 1/2 **Ramamara (IRE)**[2] 7410 2-8-3 77 LukeMorris 7 68
(P D Evans) *hld up in rr: hrd rdn 2f out: hdwy and hung bdly rt fr over 1f out: r.o: nrst fin* **3/1**[2]
0660 **4** 3/4 **Tamarind Hill (IRE)**[9] 7319 2-8-3 68 JoeFanning 5 66
(C R Egerton) *in tch: pushed along after 2f: effrt and hung lft over 1f out: styd on same pce* **9/1**
0146 **5** 1/2 **Royal Box**[67] 5853 2-8-3 72 SimonWhitworth 8 65
(R Hannon) *in rr: pushed along over 4f out: styng on u.p whn carried rt fnl f: nt pce to chal* **5/2**[1]
2256 **6** 3/4 **Inside Track (IRE)**[18] 7177 2-8-11 77 (b[1]) MartinDwyer 4 71
(B J Meehan) *led after 1f: hrd rdn and hdd over 1f out: wknd ins fnl f* **11/2**
1500 **7** *nk* **Miss Lesley**[11] 7290 2-8-3 75 AdrianMcCarthy 1 62
(D K Ivory) *disp ld 1f: prom: rdn over 2f out: wknd over 1f out* **6/1**

1m 25.37s (0.57) **Going Correction** +0.10s/f (Slow) **7** Ran SP% **115.8**
Speed ratings (Par 94): **100,99,98,97,97 96,95**
toteswingers: 1&2 £9.50, 1&3 £2.50, 2&3 £13.60 CSF £76.78 TOTE £5.90: £1.80, £5.70; EX 69.10 Trifecta £171.80 Part won. Pool: £232.26 - 0.54 winning units..The winner was claimed by Miss M. E. Rowland for £7,000. Royal Box was claimed by Mr T. R. Pearson for £7,000.
Owner Mrs Pippa Boyle **Bred** Peter Doyle **Trained** Epsom, Surrey

FOCUS
A moderate juvenile claimer.

NOTEBOOK
Chocolate Cookie(IRE), back up in trip, was always travelling best and found enough for pressure in the straight to gain her first success at the ninth attempt. She was claimed for £7,000 and should remain competitive at this sort of level. (op 11-2 tchd 9-2)
Kirsty's Boy(IRE), trying his furthest trip to date after two months off, was always well placed and had his chance, but he didn't run up to his official mark of 80 considering he would have been 7lb worse off with the winner in a handicap. He's entitled to be sharper next time.
Ramamara(IRE), disappointing over 6f at Wolverhampton two days earlier, took an age to pick up and, although she finally got going late, she still underperformed. (op 5-2)
Tamarind Hill(IRE), without the blinkers this time, didn't run a bad race was still comfortably held. (op 14-1)
Royal Box, dropped in grade on his return from a 67-day break, was never really travelling and took far too long to get going after coming wide into the straight. He will now join Alan McCabe. (op 9-4 tchd 11-4 and 3-1 in places)
Inside Track(IRE) didn't improve for first-time blinkers. (op 12-1)

7436 EUROPEAN BREEDERS' FUND MAIDEN STKS 6f (P)
1:30 (1:32) (Class 5) 2-Y-O **£3,561** (£1,059; £529; £264) **Stalls** Low

Form RPR
2 **1** **Jarrow (IRE)**[11] 7288 2-9-3 0 JoeFanning 2 81+
(M Johnston) *mde all: pushed clr over 1f out: comf* **2/5**[1]
6 **2** 4 1/2 **Picnic Party**[42] 6591 2-8-12 0 RyanMoore 5 63
(J Noseda) *pressed wnr: wd st: sn outpcd* **11/4**[2]
3 1/2 **Prince Of Sorrento** 2-9-3 0 J-PGuillambert 6 66
(J Akehurst) *stdd s: hld up in 4th: pushed along over 4f out: styd on same pce fnl 2f* **100/1**
6 **4** *hd* **Richboy**[100] 4851 2-9-3 0 IanMongan 8 65
(Mrs L J Mongan) *in tch in 5th: rdn to dispute 2nd over 1f out: one pce* **100/1**
5 5 **Final Turn** 2-9-3 0 HayleyTurner 3 50
(H Candy) *prom tl wknd over 1f out* **14/1**[3]
00 **6** 1 1/2 **She's My Rock (IRE)**[14] 7234 2-8-7 0 LeeNewnes(5) 4 41
(S Kirk) *stdd s: hld up in rr: pushed along over 2f out: nvr trbld ldrs* **66/1**
7 1 **One Cool Slash (IRE)** 2-8-12 0 FrankieMcDonald 1 38
(M J McGrath) *s.i.s: rn green and pushed along towards rr: n.d* **100/1**
8 *15* **Torres Del Paine** 2-8-12 0 GabrielHannon(5) 9 —
(J C Fox) *missed break and lost 10 l: pushed along and a wl bhd* **100/1**

1m 12.19s (0.29) **Going Correction** +0.10s/f (Slow) **8** Ran SP% **110.2**
Speed ratings (Par 96): **102,96,95,95,88 86,85,65**
toteswingers: 1&2 £1.02, 1&3 £13.20, 2&3 £21.70 CSF £1.55 TOTE £1.40: £1.02, £1.10, £12.90; EX 1.70 Trifecta £15.00 Pool: £312.52 - 15.32 winning units..
Owner Sheikh Hamdan Bin Mohammed Al Maktoum **Bred** Derek Veitch **Trained** Middleham Moor, N Yorks

FOCUS
An uncompetitive maiden - they went 66/1 bar three and the second favourite was a bit disappointing.

NOTEBOOK
Jarrow(IRE) had little to beat and he ran out a wide-margin winner, confirming the promise he showed runner-up on his debut at Doncaster. He's likely to find things tougher from now on, but is evidently quite useful and should keep progressing. (op 4-9 tchd 1-2 in a place)
Picnic Party failed to pick up after going wide into the straight and didn't really build on the form she showed on her debut at Nottingham. (op 3-1)
Prince Of Sorrento, who is out of a moderate 6f-7f winner, looked green under pressure but kept on and showed ability.
Richboy didn't run badly after over three months off and should find his level once handicapped. (tchd 80-1)
Final Turn is bred to make a high-class sprinter, being by Nunthorpe winner Kyllachy out of a mare who was runner-up in that same race, but he made a disappointing debut. (tchd 12-1 and 16-1)
One Cool Slash(IRE) Official explanation: jockey said filly ran green
Torres Del Paine Official explanation: jockey said colt was slowly away

7437 CLAUDE DUVAL'S 40 YEARS IN THE SUN H'CAP 7f (P)
2:00 (2:00) (Class 4) (0-85,81) 3-Y-0+ **£4,727** (£1,406; £702; £351) **Stalls** Low

Form RPR
1152 **1** **King's Colour**[21] 7111 4-9-2 **78** LPKeniry 2 90
(B R Johnson) *chsd ldr: rdn 2f out: led over 1f out: drvn out* **11/2**[3]
0006 **2** 1 1/2 **Southandwest (IRE)**[81] 5448 5-9-1 **77** RyanMoore 4 85
(J S Moore) *prom: drvn to chse wnr 1f out: kpt on same pce* **9/2**[2]
6223 **3** 1 **Autumn Blades (IRE)**[6] 7350 4-9-2 **78** (p) DavidProbert 3 83
(A Bailey) *dwlt: sn in midfield: rdn to chse ldrs over 1f out: one pce* **4/1**[1]
5500 **4** 3/4 **Gallantry**[13] 7252 7-9-5 **81** PaulDoe 11 84
(P Howling) *hld up towards rr: hdwy on ins ent st: drvn to chse ldrs 1f out: kpt on* **15/2**
5006 **5** *nk* **I Confess**[13] 7253 4-8-5 **74** (b) KevinLundie(7) 8 76
(P D Evans) *led: rdn 3 l ahd over 3f out: hdd over 1f out: sn btn* **11/2**[3]
0200 **6** 3/4 **Trafalgar Square**[13] 7252 7-9-2 **78** JimCrowley 1 78
(M J Attwater) *dwlt: sn in tch in 5th: hrd rdn over 1f out: no ex fnl f* **12/1**
5615 **7** 1/2 **Ravi River (IRE)**[13] 7252 5-8-10 **79** JamesPSullivan(7) 5 78
(J R Boyle) *chsd ldrs tl outpcd fnl 2f* **10/1**
6000 **8** 1 **Desert Dreamer (IRE)**[13] 7252 8-8-13 **80** RichardEvans(5) 6 76
(P D Evans) *sn stdd in rr: rdn over 2f out: nvr trbld ldrs* **33/1**
0004 **9** 1/2 **Alfresco**[40] 6630 5-9-4 **80** (b) TonyCulhane 9 75
(J R Best) *t.k.h: hld up in midfield on outer: cajoled along over 1f out: no rspnse* **8/1**
2500 **10** 2 **Harlech Castle**[25] 7026 4-9-1 **77** SJCraine 10 66
(J R Boyle) *a last: rdn over 2f out: n.d after* **20/1**

1m 24.29s (-0.51) **Going Correction** +0.10s/f (Slow) **10** Ran SP% **116.3**
Speed ratings (Par 105): **106,104,103,102,101 101,100,99,98,96**
toteswingers: 1&2 £8.20, 1&3 £3.40, 2&3 £4.50 CSF £30.41 CT £103.92 TOTE £5.40: £1.80, £2.20, £1.60; EX 35.50 Trifecta £74.60 Pool: £292.37 - 2.90 winning units..
Owner Tann Racing **Bred** Cheveley Park Stud Ltd **Trained** Ashtead, Surrey
■ Stewards' Enquiry : S J Craine one-day ban: used whip when out of contention (Dec 2)

FOCUS
A fair handicap, but the pace was ordinary until increasing at about halfway and it paid to race handy. The wind remained strong, although it seemed to be more across the runners in the straight this time. The form looks sound and the winner is generally progressive.

7438 BET MULTIPLES - BETDAQ H'CAP (DIV II) 1m (P)
2:30 (2:31) (Class 6) (0-55,55) 3-Y-0+ **£1,637** (£483; £241) **Stalls** High

Form RPR
/31- **1** **Holyfield Warrior (IRE)**[454] 542 5-8-8 **54** KierenFox(7) 12 63
(R J Smith) *hld up in midfield: hdwy in centre over 1f out: hrd rdn: styd on to ld fnl 50yds* **25/1**
0001 **2** *nk* **Spinning Ridge (IRE)**[17] 7197 4-9-2 **55** DavidProbert 1 63
(R A Harris) *chsd ldrs: drvn to ld over 1f out: hdd and nt qckn fnl 50yds* **8/1**
6340 **3** 3/4 **Djalalabad (FR)**[23] 7051 5-8-11 **50** (tp) HayleyTurner 10 56
(Mrs C A Dunnett) *patiently rdn in rr: cajoled along and hdwy in centre over 1f out: wnt 3rd ins fnl f: hld fnl 50yds* **14/1**
3444 **4** 1 1/2 **Diane's Choice**[14] 7239 6-8-13 **52** (e) AdamKirby 2 54
(Miss Gay Kelleway) *mid-div: rdn to chse ldrs 1f out: styd on same pce* **12/1**
2040 **5** 1 1/4 **Vanadium**[11] 7292 7-8-9 **55** (t) AmyScott(7) 7 54
(A J Lidderdale) *towards rr on outer: hdwy to press ldrs 3f out: hrd rdn and no ex jst over 1f out* **6/1**[2]
0061 **6** *hd* **Fitzolini**[16] 7211 3-8-12 **53** (p) JimmyQuinn 8 52
(A D Brown) *led: hrd rdn and hdd over 1f out: wknd fnl f* **8/1**
-002 **7** *nk* **Marjury Daw (IRE)**[20] 7143 3-8-13 **54** TPQueally 5 52
(J G Given) *towards rr: rdn over 2f out: modest effrt over 1f out: no imp* **15/2**
6622 **8** 1/2 **Party In The Park**[17] 7200 4-8-12 **51** SJCraine 11 48
(J R Boyle) *in tch in 5th: rdn over 2f out: sn outpcd* **5/1**[1]
330- **9** 3/4 **Tallest Peak (USA)**[354] 7500 4-9-0 **53** TedDurcan 3 50+
(M G Quinlan) *bhd: rdn over 3f out: sme hdwy on ins ent st: nvr able to chal* **9/1**
4105 **10** 5 **Copper King**[28] 6945 5-8-12 **51** KFallon 9 40+
(Miss Tor Sturgis) *chsd ldr: disp ld 3f out tl over 1f out: wknd rapidly ins fnl f: eased* **7/1**[3]
040 **11** 3 **Denices Desert**[28] 6934 3-8-9 **50** (b[1]) RyanMoore 4 26
(M Botti) *in tch in 6th tl wknd over 2f out* **17/2**
3000 **12** 6 **Jiggalong**[21] 7109 3-9-0 **55** PaulDoe 6 17
(Jim Best) *prom tl wknd qckly over 2f out* **16/1**

1m 39.72s (1.52) **Going Correction** +0.10s/f (Slow)
WFA 3 from 4yo+ 2lb **12** Ran SP% **122.1**
Speed ratings (Par 101): **96,95,94,93,92 92,91,91,90,85 82,76**
toteswingers: 1&2 £11.80, 1&3 £44.00, 2&3 £18.60 CSF £219.51 CT £2978.74 TOTE £26.00: £7.00, £3.40, £3.40; EX 223.90 TRIFECTA Not won..
Owner AJ Syndicate **Bred** A Malone **Trained** Epsom, Surrey
■ Jack Smith's first winner since returning from training in Spain.

FOCUS
A moderate contest run in a time 0.38 seconds slower than the first division, which was won by Wunder Strike. Like in the first leg of this handicap, there was a strong wind behind the runners in the straight. Modest form with the surprise winner up 7lb.

7439 BET PREMIER LEAGUE FOOTBALL - BETDAQ MAIDEN STKS 1m 2f (P)
3:00 (3:03) (Class 5) 3-Y-0+ **£2,729** (£806; £403) **Stalls** Low

Form RPR

1 **Royaaty (IRE)** 3-9-3 .... TedDurcan 6 84+
(Saeed Bin Suroor) *t.k.h early: pressed ldr: drvn along over 3f out: disp ld over 2f out and drew clr w runner-up: slt ld 1f out: all out* **5/2**[2]

222 2 *shd* **Troopingthecolour**[34] 6794 3-9-3 80 .... (t) RyanMoore 9 83
(J H M Gosden) *prom: disp ld over 2f out and drew clr w wnr: kpt on up fnl f: jst hld* **8/15**[1]

0-00 3 *13* **December**[152] 3117 3-9-3 .... TPQueally 8 57
(Mrs C A Dunnett) *hld up towards rr: sme hdwy and rdn 3f out: wnt modest 3rd 1f out* **50/1**

4 *1* **Spinning Well (IRE)**[150] 3199 3-8-12 76 .... (t) JimCrowley 4 50
(R M Beckett) *in tch in 5th: rdn 3f out: nt pce of first 2* **8/1**[3]

000 5 *nk* **Set Em Up Mo**[28] 6941 3-8-5 42 .... (v) KierenFox(7) 5 49
(M J Attwater) *sn led: hdd and qckly outpcd by ldng pair over 2f out* **100/1**

0005 6 *1 ½* **Vigorosa (IRE)**[18] 7195 3-8-12 49 .... (p) PaulDoe 7 46
(P Howling) *bhd: drvn along and sme hdwy into midfield 3f out: no imp* **125/1**

7 *2* **New Couture (IRE)** 3-8-12 .... AlanMunro 2 42
(P W Chapple-Hyam) *chsd ldrs: rdn over 3f out: wknd over 2f out* **28/1**

8 *shd* **Cotswold Village (AUS)** 3-8-2 .... FrankieMcDonald 10 32
(M R Bosley) *s.s: in rr of main gp: rdn over 3f out: n.d* **150/1**

0 9 *10* **Northern Genes (AUS)**[53] 6287 3-8-7 .... HayleyTurner 3 17
(M R Bosley) *t.k.h: bhd: pushed along over 4f out: no ch fnl 3f* **100/1**

2m 7.23s (0.63) **Going Correction** +0.10s/f (Slow) **9 Ran SP% 113.8**
Speed ratings (Par 103): **101,100,90,89,89 88,86,86,78**
toteswingers: 1&2 £1.40, 1&3 £9.00, 2&3 £6.10 CSF £4.12 TOTE £3.20: £1.30, £1.02, £5.40; EX 4.70 Trifecta £56.90 Pool: £713.67 - 9.27 winning units..
Owner Godolphin **Bred** Gainsborough Stud Management Ltd **Trained** Newmarket, Suffolk

FOCUS
This only concerned two of the nine-strong field, but that pair are useful using the runner-up's official rating of 80 as a guide. It was steadily run but the form is rated at face value around the runner-up.

7440 THREE BRIDGES AMATEUR RIDERS' H'CAP 1m 4f (P)
3:30 (3:31) (Class 5) (0-70,67) 3-Y-0+ **£2,637** (£811; £405) **Stalls** Low

Form RPR

6264 1 **Moonshine Creek**[16] 7212 7-10-7 60 .... MrSWalker 13 67
(P W Hiatt) *plld hrd: prom: led 7f out: hrd rdn fr over 1f out: all out* **4/1**[2]

2041 2 *hd* **Extremely So**[29] 6919 3-9-9 57 .... MrPCollington(3) 11 64
(P J McBride) *t.k.h: in tch: wnt 2nd 6f out: drvn along fnl 3f: styd on fnl f: clsng at fin* **9/1**

232 3 *½* **Debdene Bank (IRE)**[62] 6025 6-10-0 60 .... MissCBlakey(7) 12 66
(Mrs Mary Hambro) *s.s: hld up in rr of midfield: hdwy on outer 3f out: r.o fnl f: clsng at fin* **6/1**[3]

1052 4 *hd* **Ardmaddy (IRE)**[5] 7368 5-10-0 56 .... (b) MrJoshuaMoore(3) 2 62
(G L Moore) *chsd ldrs: hrd rdn and sltly outpcd 3f out: kpt on fr over 1f out* **6/4**[1]

-516 5 *4* **Venir Rouge**[131] 3814 5-10-7 67 .... MrDKembrey(7) 8 66
(Matthew Salaman) *hld up towards rr: effrt and wd st: shkn up and styd on fnl 2f: nvr nrr* **14/1**

0400 6 *nk* **Director's Chair**[26] 4932 4-10-5 63 .... MrRBirkett(5) 5 62
(Miss J Feilden) *dwlt: disp ld 5f: prom tl outpcd fnl 3f* **66/1**

0000 7 *1 ¼* **Corlough Mountain**[50] 6369 5-9-9 53 oh5 .... MissMBryant(5) 3 50
(P Butler) *mid-div: lost pl 7f out: sme hdwy over 1f out: unable to chal* **40/1**

0420 8 *8* **Rudry World (IRE)**[25] 7036 6-9-13 57 .... MissMMullineaux(5) 7 41
(M Mullineaux) *towards rr: hrd rdn 4f out: n.d* **20/1**

4400 9 *1 ¼* **Artreju (GER)**[28] 6945 6-9-7 53 oh3 .... (p) MissKLoftus(7) 10 35
(P Butler) *hld up in midfield: hdwy into 3rd 3f out: sn wknd* **40/1**

0443 10 *2* **Smooth As Silk (IRE)**[42] 6584 4-9-13 57 .... (p) MrJakeGreenall(5) 4 36
(C R Egerton) *disp ld 5f: prom tl wknd 3f out* **6/1**[3]

0350 11 *1 ¼* **Captain Imperial (IRE)**[32] 6861 3-10-1 65 .... MissRBastiman(5) 1 42
(R Bastiman) *a bhd* **18/1**

5630 12 *8* **Strategic Mover (USA)**[7] 7323 4-10-11 67 .... (t) MissZoeLilly(3) 6 31
(P Butler) *in tch tl wknd 4f out* **40/1**

0600 13 *10* **Binnion Bay (IRE)**[15] 7225 8-9-7 53 .... (b) MrsNParry(7) 9 1
(J J Bridger) *reluctant to s and lost 20 l: a t.o* **33/1**

2m 34.67s (1.67) **Going Correction** +0.10s/f (Slow)
WFA 3 from 4yo+ 6lb **13 Ran SP% 127.0**
Speed ratings (Par 103): **98,97,97,97,94 94,93,88,87,86 85,80,73**
toteswingers: 1&2 £8.70, 1&3 £3.40, 2&3 £8.30 CSF £40.19 CT £225.03 TOTE £5.30: £2.30, £3.00, £2.10; EX 56.50 Trifecta £254.50 Part won. Pool: £343.98 - 0.60 winning units. Place 6: £201.89 Place 5: £91.59.
Owner P W Hiatt **Bred** Lawrence Shepherd **Trained** Hook Norton, Oxon

FOCUS
These riders varied in ability and this is form to treat with caution, although it reads sound enough rated through the second and third. Those who raced handy were at an advantage.
Binnion Bay(IRE) Official explanation: jockey said gelding was slowly away
T/Jkpt: £29,239.30 to a £1 stake. Pool: £41,182.16. 1.00 winning ticket. T/Plt: £132.30 to a £1 stake. Pool: £65,519.34. 361.52 winning tickets. T/Qpdt: £30.00 to a £1 stake. Pool: £6,073.74. 149.80 winning tickets. LM

7441 - 7449a (Foreign Racing) - See Raceform Interactive

7426 KEMPTON (A.W) (R-H)
Thursday, November 19

OFFICIAL GOING: Standard
Wind: Moderate across Weather: Dusk, getting dark, dry

7450 EUROPEAN BREEDERS' FUND MAIDEN FILLIES' STKS (DIV I) 1m (P)
4:00 (4:01) (Class 5) 2-Y-0 **£3,238** (£963; £481; £240) **Stalls** High

Form RPR

1 **Aviate** 2-9-0 0 .... TPQueally 5 76+
(H R A Cecil) *hld up in rr: stdy hdwy on outside 3f out: qcknd smartly fr 2f out to cl on 3l ldr over 1f out: led ins fnl f: easily* **7/4**[1]

2 *1* **Clairvoyance (IRE)** 2-9-0 0 .... NickyMackay 7 74
(J H M Gosden) *chsd ldrs: led over 2f out and pushed 3l clr over 1f out: hdd ins fnl f and sn outpcd by wnr* **6/1**

00 3 *1* **Contredanse (IRE)**[47] 6477 2-9-0 0 .... MartinDwyer 6 72
(B J Meehan) *chsd ldrs: pushed along 2f out: styd on strly thrght fnl f but nt quite pce of ldng duo* **5/1**[3]

0 4 *nk* **Fantastic Cuix (FR)**[27] 6992 2-9-0 0 .... KFallon 1 71
(L M Cumani) *s.i.s: sn chsng ldrs and wnt 2nd over 3f out: pushed along 2f out: styd on fnl f but nvr a threat to ldng duo* **9/2**[2]

5 *½* **Ship's Biscuit** 2-9-0 0 .... RyanMoore 2 70
(Sir Michael Stoute) *in rr: pushed along 3f out: styd on fr 2f out and r.o strly to cl on ldrs fnl f: gng on cl home* **7/1**

40 6 *1* **Love Action (IRE)**[132] 3810 2-8-11 0 .... PatrickHills(3) 12 68
(R Hannon) *in tch tl outpcd and lost position over 4f out: rdn and hdwy ins fnl 2f: styd on fnl f: fin wl* **9/1**

0 7 *1 ¾* **Mater Mater**[162] 2825 2-9-0 0 .... SJCraine 4 64
(M J Scudamore) *led after 1f tl hdd over 2f out: fdd ins fnl f* **66/1**

00 8 *6* **Belle Park**[29] 6932 2-9-0 0 .... TGMcLaughlin 3 51
(Karen George) *chsd ldrs tl wknd over 1f out* **66/1**

9 *½* **Pursestrings** 2-9-0 0 .... SteveDrowne 8 50
(R Charlton) *slowly away: in rr: racd on outside: mod prog appr fnl f* **12/1**

05 10 *8* **Always Roses**[13] 7266 2-9-0 0 .... LPKeniry 13 32
(C C Bealby) *led 1f: chsd ldrs tl wknd over 2f out* **33/1**

00 11 *¾* **Empress Leizu (IRE)**[18] 7199 2-9-0 0 .... JimCrowley 14 31
(E A L Dunlop) *trcking ldrs whn hmpd on rail ins fnl 2f and lost position: nvr a danger after* **50/1**

6 12 *2 ¾* **Hubble Space**[26] 7024 2-8-11 0 .... AndreaAtzeni(3) 9 25
(M Botti) *chsd ldrs unitl wknd ins fnl 3f* **14/1**

13 *3* **Suzybee** 2-9-0 0 .... IanMongan 11 18
(M R Hoad) *s.i.s: in rr: no ch whn hung bdly lft ins fnl 2f* **50/1**

1m 42.11s (2.31) **Going Correction** +0.10s/f (Slow) **13 Ran SP% 132.2**
Speed ratings (Par 93): **92,91,90,89,89 88,86,80,79,71 71,68,65**
toteswingers: 1&2 £1.90, 1&3 £4.50, 2&3 £7.50 CSF £14.02 TOTE £2.60: £1.20, £2.20, £1.90; EX 21.30.
Owner K Abdulla **Bred** Juddmonte Farms Ltd **Trained** Newmarket, Suffolk

FOCUS
The winning time was 0.56secs slower than the second division, won by Eleanora Duse, but that's misleading as they went a steadier pace in this contest and this looked a decent fillies' maiden.

NOTEBOOK
Aviate ◆ made an impressive debut. After starting slowly, she was set a lot to do considering the pace was steady, and by the time Queally got after her 2f out, the runner-up had kicked into a clear lead. However, she displayed a taking change of pace under only hands-and-heels riding to make up the required ground, and this performance was all the more meritorious considering she was noticeably green in the closing stages. She's a sister to Group-race winner Early March and looks a Pattern-class filly in the making. (op 11-4 tchd 3-1 and 10-3 in a place)
Clairvoyance(IRE) ◆, an £80,000 first foal of a 7f-1m winner who was Group placed at three, made a pleasing start. Always nicely enough placed, she looked as though she would be hard to peg back when clear around 2f from the finish, but she came up against an above-average type. She should have no trouble winning a similar race. (op 7-1 tchd 9-2)
Contredanse(IRE) ◆ confirmed the ability she showed behind Lillie Langtry in a sales race at Newmarket on her previous start. She looks a slow learner who is progressing with racing. (op 4-1)
Fantastic Cuix(FR) ◆, who was reported to have banged her head on the stalls first time out, lost ground at the start from the worst draw. However, being a middle-distance stayer in the making, Fallon was keen to get her into a prominent position and there was much to like about the way she kept on in the straight considering she obviously had to use up energy from an early stage. She should make a nice 3-y-o. (tchd 4-1)
Ship's Biscuit ◆, a half-sister to Park Hill winner Hi Calypso and smart middle-distance/stayer Warringah, started slowly and ran green, but she finished strongly. She is well regarded by her owner, who said she has had some hold ups and is really a filly for next year. (op 5-1)
Love Action(IRE) came under pressure a fair way out but kept on in the straight. She was entitled to need this after 132 days off and handicaps are now an option. (op 15-2)
Pursestrings, who was unsurprisingly reported by Steve Drowne to have started slowly, displayed an ungainly action in the straight. Official explanation: jockey said filly was slowly away (op 16-1)

7451 EUROPEAN BREEDERS' FUND MAIDEN FILLIES' STKS (DIV II) 1m (P)
4:30 (4:31) (Class 5) 2-Y-0 **£3,238** (£963; £481; £240) **Stalls** High

Form RPR

60 1 **Eleanora Duse (IRE)**[44] 6567 2-9-0 0 .... RyanMoore 8 78
(Sir Michael Stoute) *trckd ldr: led over 2f out: drvn clr over 1f out: styd on strly thrght fnl f* **6/4**[1]

3 2 *3 ¾* **Inner Angel**[22] 7106 2-8-11 0 .... AndreaAtzeni(3) 5 70
(M Botti) *chsd ldrs: rdn and styd on wl fnl f to take 2nd cl home but nvr any ch w wnr* **11/4**[2]

6 3 *hd* **Leaving Alone (USA)**[38] 6729 2-9-0 0 .... SteveDrowne 12 70
(R Hannon) *led tl hdd over 2f out: styd chsng wnr but sn no ch: lost 2nd cl home* **3/1**[3]

4 *hd* **Elvira Madigan** 2-9-0 0 .... LPKeniry 14 69
(A M Balding) *s.i.s: towards rr tl hdwy and plld lft to outside over 2f out: hung lft and green but styd on wl fr over 1f out and ins fnl f: gng on cl home but nvr a threat to wnr* **12/1**

5 *2 ½* **Western Pearl** 2-9-0 0 .... JimCrowley 2 64
(W J Knight) *s.i.s: bhd: pushed along and hdwy over 2f out: styd on fnl f but nvr any threat* **25/1**

00 6 *2 ¼* **Lady Hetherington**[36] 6781 2-9-0 0 .... IanMongan 13 59
(Jamie Poulton) *chsd ldrs: rdn over 2f out: wknd fnl f* **50/1**

5305 7 *½* **Two Kisses (IRE)**[83] 5379 2-9-0 68 .... KFallon 9 58
(B G Powell) *chsd ldrs: rdn over 2f out: wknd qckly ins fnl f* **16/1**

00 8 *½* **Celebrian**[21] 7135 2-9-0 0 .... (t) AdamKirby 11 56
(W R Swinburn) *mid-div: shkn up 3f out: styd on fr over 1f out but nvr any threat* **33/1**

00 9 *3* **Sparkling Crown**[110] 4542 2-8-7 0 .... RyanPowell(7) 7 50
(J Ryan) *chsd ldrs: rdn over 2f out: sn btn* **66/1**

10 *14* **Blue Glove (IRE)** 2-9-0 0 .... ShaneKelly 10 19
(J A Osborne) *a towards rr* **66/1**

11 *3 ¼* **Morning View (USA)** 2-9-0 0 .... NickyMackay 3 12
(J H M Gosden) *s.i.s: sn mid-div: rdn 3f out: sn btn* **12/1**

0 12 *2* **Firetail**[15] 7244 2-9-0 0 .... HayleyTurner 6 8
(M L W Bell) *a in rr* **25/1**

13 *9* **Mena Rl** 2-9-0 0 .... TGMcLaughlin 1 —
(Karen George) *s.i.s: a in rr* **66/1**

1m 41.55s (1.75) **Going Correction** +0.10s/f (Slow) **13 Ran SP% 130.0**
Speed ratings (Par 93): **95,91,91,91,88 86,85,85,82,68 65,63,54**
toteswingers: 1&2 £2.40, 1&3 £3.00, 2&3 £3.10 CSF £5.97 TOTE £2.40: £1.20, £1.30, £1.80; EX 8.10.
Owner Ballymacoll Stud **Bred** Ballymacoll Stud Farm Ltd **Trained** Newmarket, Suffolk

FOCUS
A time 0.56secs quicker than the smart-looking Aviate recorded in the first division is misleading, because they went a steady pace in that contest.

NOTEBOOK

Eleanora Duse(IRE) was reported to have never been travelling when a beaten favourite in a good Leicester maiden last time, but she had previously shown ability on her debut over 7f around here. The return to Polytrack, as well as the step up in trip, obviously suited and she responded well to a positive ride. Her breeding suggests she may improve for a further rise in distance next year, but she still has to prove herself on turf. (tchd 13-8 and 7-4 in places)

Inner Angel, third over C&D on her debut, took a while to pick up in the straight but she still ran well, especially as she was wider than ideal for most of the way. She's by Motivator, out of a 1m4f winner, so should improve when upped in trip. (op 3-1)

Leaving Alone(USA) failed to prove her stamina on this step up from 7f, matching strides with the winner for much of the way before fading in the last furlong. (tchd 10-3)

Elvira Madigan, a half-sister to modest winning stayer (including on this track) Isabelonabicycle, missed the break and was never really travelling, but she gradually got the idea. There should be better to come as she learns what's required and goes up in trip. (op 14-1)

Western Pearl ◆, a 21,000gns purchase, is yet another bred to want further, being a half-sister to fairly useful 1m6f-2m winner Penang Princess, out of a prolific 1m2f-1m5f scorer, and this was a pleasing start. She was never seen with a chance after losing ground the start but finished well.

7452 WILLIAM HILL WINTER FESTIVAL - BOOK NOW MEDIAN AUCTION MAIDEN STKS — 1m (P)

5:00 (5:00) (Class 5) 3-Y-O — **£2,590** (£770; £385; £192) **Stalls** High

Form — RPR

4024 **1** **Penzena**[129] 3921 3-8-12 66 ... LPKeniry 9 75
(A M Balding) *mde all: pushed clr 2f out: kpt on strly fr over 1f out: unchal* **3/1**[3]

2 *4* **Mainstay** 3-8-12 0 ... RyanMoore 8 66+
(J H M Gosden) *s.i.s: pushed along and hdwy fr 3f out: wnt 3rd over 2f out and sn drvn to cl on 2nd: fnlly tk 2nd nr fin but nvr any ch w wnr* **11/8**[1]

0225 **3** *½* **Piccolo Mondo**[28] 6977 3-9-3 72 ... JimCrowley 7 70
(P Winkworth) *chsd ldrs: wnt 2nd 3f out: nvr any ch w wnr fr over 2f out: styd on one pce and lost 2nd nr fin* **2/1**[2]

55 **4** *6* **West Kirk**[30] 6924 3-9-3 0 ... JoeFanning 3 56+
(W Jarvis) *in tch tl lost position on bnd 3f out: kpt on again fnl 2f wout ev looking any threat* **9/2**

0-0 **5** *6* **Woodland Violet**[16] 7228 3-8-12 0 ... NCallan 6 37
(I A Wood) *in rr: rdn over 3f out: sme prog wl over 2f out but nvr any threat: wknd sn after* **50/1**

3405 **6** *5* **Commandingpresence (USA)**[22] 7105 3-8-5 50 ... RyanClark(7) 1 26
(J J Bridger) *s.i.s: in rr and wd into st 3f out: nvr in contention* **25/1**

4060 **7** *8* **Wicklewood**[30] 6919 3-9-3 43 ... (p) TGMcLaughlin 2 12
(Mrs C A Dunnett) *chsd ldrs wnt 2nd over 4f out tl wknd qckly 3f out* **66/1**

-000 **8** *2 ¼* **Julie Mill (IRE)**[14] 7250 3-8-12 40 ... LukeMorris 5 —
(R A Teal) *chsd ldrs unitl wknd rapidly 3f out* **50/1**

1m 39.9s (0.10) **Going Correction** +0.10s/f (Slow) **8** Ran SP% **127.9**
Speed ratings (Par 102): **103,99,98,92,86 81,73,71**
toteswingers: 1&2 £1.80, 1&3 £1.90, 2&3 £1.30 CSF £8.55 TOTE £5.90: £1.50, £1.10, £1.10; EX 12.80.

Owner Spiers, Taylor, Taylor **Bred** D P And Mrs J A Martin **Trained** Kingsclere, Hants

FOCUS

A modest maiden rated around the winner and third.

7453 COLIN BARRON MEMORIAL NURSERY — 6f (P)

5:30 (5:31) (Class 5) (0-75,75) 2-Y-O — **£2,590** (£770; £385; £192) **Stalls** High

Form — RPR

0601 **1** **Imjin River (IRE)**[23] 7088 2-8-13 **72** ... AshleyMorgan(5) 8 79
(M H Tompkins) *hld up trcking ldrs: drvn to ld jst ins fnl f: pushed out* **13/2**

2010 **2** *¾* **Coolree Star (IRE)**[12] 7290 2-9-7 **75** ... JimCrowley 7 80
(J A Glover) *led 1f: styd trcking ldr: led again wl over 2f out: narrowly hdd jst ins fnl f: kpt on but nt gng pce of wnr* **9/1**

2322 **3** *½* **Excellent Thought**[17] 7213 2-9-3 **71** ... RyanMoore 9 74
(W J Haggas) *in rr: hdwy on ins 2f out and drvn to chal 1f out: no ex u.p ins fnl f* **9/4**[1]

1006 **4** *nk* **Italian Tom (IRE)**[13] 7274 2-9-6 **74** ... LukeMorris 3 76
(R A Harris) *hld up towards rr but in tch: hdwy and swtchd lft ins fnl 2f: styd on wl fnl f: gng on cl home* **14/1**

0621 **5** *¾* **Cape Kimberley**[8] 7333 2-9-6 **74** 6ex ... TPQueally 5 74
(J G Given) *in rr: pushed along 2f out: hdwy appr fnl f: kpt on cl home* **11/2**[3]

6015 **6** *½* **North Shadow**[29] 6948 2-8-7 **61** ... (p) JimmyQuinn 4 60
(A D Brown) *in tch: pushed along and one pce 3f out: sme prog 2f out: nvr rchd ldrs and styd on same pce* **9/1**

4200 **7** *3* **Speedyfix**[8] 7333 2-7-12 **52** oh2 ... (tp) AdrianMcCarthy 6 42
(Mrs C A Dunnett) *in rr: hdwy to chse ldrs 2 out: wknd fnl f* **25/1**

4456 **8** *3 ½* **Mellifera**[62] 6071 2-9-4 **72** ... AdamKirby 11 51
(W R Swinburn) *in tch: hdwy on ins to chse ldrs 2f out: wknd qckly fnl f* **3/1**[2]

0030 **9** *5* **Ballyvonane (USA)**[24] 7063 2-8-0 **54** oh2 ow2 ... (b) FrankieMcDonald 2 18
(L A Dace) *led after 1f: hdd wl over 2f out: wknd qckly over 1f out* **33/1**

0040 **10** *13* **Satin Princess (IRE)**[6] 7372 2-7-9 **52** oh3 ... AndreaAtzeni(3) 1 —
(A M Hales) *chsd ldrs on outside: wknd over 2f out* **50/1**

1m 13.44s (0.34) **Going Correction** +0.10s/f (Slow) **10** Ran SP% **119.9**
Speed ratings (Par 96): **101,100,99,98,97 97,93,88,81,64**
toteswingers: 1&2 £12.20, 1&3 £4.00, 2&3 £5.10 CSF £64.20 CT £165.13 TOTE £9.40: £1.90, £3.20, £1.30; EX 94.60.

Owner Roalco Limited **Bred** Glending Bloodstock **Trained** Newmarket, Suffolk

FOCUS

A fair, competitive nursery.

NOTEBOOK

Imjin River(IRE) ◆, successful off a 7lb lower mark on his nursery debut on Fibresand at Southwell, did well to follow up under these vastly different conditions. He travelled well before finding plenty for pressure, and looks up to completing the hat-trick. (op 11-2)

Coolree Star(IRE), who was a bit keen to post, showed good speed and, although no match for the winner, kept on to the line. This was a respectable effort under top weight. (op 10-1 tchd 8-1)

Excellent Thought, a beaten favourite on three of her five starts, including the last twice, again came up short. She was up a furlong in trip, but still struggled to get a decent position and never looked like doing enough. (op 7-4)

Italian Tom(IRE) ◆ could never get a decent position, with stall three a disadvantage, and ended up a little too far back. The way he stayed on after having to switch inside the final 2f, being short of room, suggests he'll be worth another try over this trip. (op 12-1)

Cape Kimberley ◆, who was carrying a penalty for a recent win on Fibresand, displayed a significant knee action and struggled to handle this quicker surface. It's to his credit he finished so well and he'll be of interest if going back to Southwell. (op 5-1)

Mellifera has now finished weakly on her last two starts and she looks best watched for the time being. (op 9-2)

7454 BOXINGDAYRACES.CO.UK H'CAP — 6f (P)

6:00 (6:01) (Class 3) (0-95,93) 3-Y-O+
£7,352 (£2,201; £1,100; £551; £274; £138) **Stalls** High

Form — RPR

0043 **1** **Earlsmedic**[26] 7026 4-8-2 **80** ... (e1) AndreaAtzeni(3) 7 90
(S C Williams) *chsd ldrs: rdn 2f out: led wl over 1f out: hdd jst ins fnl f: styd w ldr and led again fnl 20yds: all out* **6/1**[3]

0123 **2** *½* **Fantasy Explorer**[3] 7414 6-8-13 **88** ... RyanMoore 8 96
(J J Quinn) *hld up in tch: hdwy 2f out: chal over 1f out and led jst ins fnl f: sn jnd by wnr: hdd and no ex fnl 20yds* **9/4**[1]

0000 **3** *2* **Shifting Star (IRE)**[132] 3818 4-9-4 **93** ... (t) AdamKirby 4 95
(W R Swinburn) *in rr: hdwy 2f out: styd on wl fnl f but nvr gng pce to get to ldng duo* **5/1**[2]

6023 **4** *shd* **Ray Of Joy**[26] 7027 3-8-9 **84** ... JimmyQuinn 10 85
(J R Jenkins) *in rr tl rapid hdwy on ins to chse ldrs fr 2f out: wknd wl ins fnl f* **7/1**

2002 **5** *¾* **Beckermet (IRE)**[21] 7133 7-8-13 **88** ... NCallan 1 87
(R F Fisher) *sn led: rdn over 2f out: hdd wl over 1f out: wknd ins fnl f* **5/1**[2]

4036 **6** *2 ¼* **Beat The Bell**[21] 7133 4-8-13 **88** ... ShaneKelly 9 80
(J A Osborne) *chsd ldrs: rdn over 2f out: wknd fnl f* **16/1**

0046 **7** *¾* **Princess Valerina**[20] 7155 5-8-7 **82** ... FrankieMcDonald 2 71
(D Haydn Jones) *s.i.s: in rr: sme hdwy on outside 3f out: nvr gng pce to get into contention* **33/1**

0012 **8** *6* **River Kirov (IRE)**[14] 7253 6-8-5 **80** ... MartinDwyer 6 50
(M Wigham) *stdd s: sn in tch: wknd fr 3f out* **15/2**

0610 **9** *7* **Sundae**[27] 6994 5-8-9 **87** ... (b1) JackMitchell(3) 5 35
(C F Wall) *chsd ldr tl rdn: hung rt and sn btn wl over 2f out* **10/1**

1m 12.51s (-0.59) **Going Correction** +0.10s/f (Slow) **9** Ran SP% **120.6**
Speed ratings (Par 107): **107,106,103,103,102 99,98,90,81**
toteswingers: 1&2 £4.50, 1&3 £9.00, 2&3 £3.10 CSF £20.86 CT £75.70 TOTE £8.10: £2.70, £1.10, £1.80; EX 33.70.

Owner Mad Man Plus One **Bred** W N Greig **Trained** Newmarket, Suffolk

FOCUS

A good sprint handicap in which the winner reversed recent form with the second. The pair set the level on their previous form.

NOTEBOOK

Earlsmedic was 5lb better off with Fantasy Explorer than when beaten over 2l by that rival over C&D last time and was able to reverse form. He carried his head high under pressure and looked held when strongly challenged by his old rival at the furlong pole, but he proved surprisingly determined. The eyeshields, replacing his usual visor, clearly helped. (op 8-1)

Fantasy Explorer looked sure to win when produced with a strong challenge around 1f out but he couldn't see off Earlsmedic. Still, he ran right up to form in defeat. (op 15-8)

Shifting Star(IRE) has yet to produce his very best form on Polytrack, but this was by no means a bad effort after 132 days off. (op 6-1)

Ray Of Joy couldn't sustain her run after making a big move from well off the pace. (op 11-2)

Beckermet(IRE) ◆ had to use up energy to lead from stall one and was a bit free as well. He remains of interest this winter. (op 7-1 tchd 15-2)

River Kirov(IRE) was reported to have run too free. Official explanation: jockey said gelding ran too free (op 7-1)

Sundae, fitted with blinkers for the first time, was keen early on but looked to be hanging in the straight and stopped very quickly. (op 14-1)

7455 TRY OUR NEW BISTRO MENU CLAIMING STKS — 1m 4f (P)

6:30 (6:31) (Class 6) 3-Y-O — **£2,047** (£604; £302) **Stalls** Centre

Form — RPR

0013 **1** **Satwa Gold (USA)**[18] 7198 3-9-2 75 ... KFallon 5 74
(E A L Dunlop) *hld up in rr: rdn and hdwy to 3f out as ldr remained 12 l clr: drvn to go 2nd over 2f out and swept past tired ldr wl over 1f out: sn clr: easily* **5/4**[1]

206 **2** *4 ½* **Fleur De'Lion (IRE)**[14] 7250 3-8-4 54 ... DavidProbert 4 55
(S Kirk) *chsd ldrs and wnt 2nd bhd 12 l clr over 3f out: dropped bk to 3rd wl over 2f out: styd on past tired ldr jst ins fnl f to take 2nd but nvr any ch w wnr* **7/1**[3]

0035 **3** *8* **The Dial House**[29] 6940 3-9-2 72 ... ShaneKelly 7 54
(J A Osborne) *led: sn clr: 12 l ahd over 3f out: rdn and wknd fr 2f out: hdd wl over 1f out and sn no ch: led 2nd jst ins fnl f* **5/2**[2]

0300 **4** *2* **Flirty (IRE)**[30] 6919 3-7-9 42 ... NoelGarbutt(7) 2 37
(Rae Guest) *chsd ldr ldr tl over 3f out: no ch after* **25/1**

6 **5** *nse* **Nyetimber (USA)**[13] 7278 3-9-0 0 ... TPQueally 3 49
(J A Osborne) *in rr tl mod prog fnl 2f* **14/1**

000- **6** *14* **Baby Is Here (IRE)**[402] 6696 3-7-10 48 ... BillyCray(7) 1 16
(D J S Ffrench Davis) *a in rr* **33/1**

4045 **7** *20* **Mile High Lad (USA)**[7] 7361 3-8-5 68 ... (v1) MatthewDavies(5) 6 —
(George Baker) *chsd ldrs tl wknd 4f out* **7/1**[3]

2m 36.37s (1.87) **Going Correction** +0.10s/f (Slow) **7** Ran SP% **111.5**
Speed ratings (Par 98): **97,94,88,87,87 77,64**
toteswingers: 1&2 £1.30, 1&3 £1.60, 2&3 £3.40 CSF £10.26 TOTE £1.80: £1.10, £2.50; EX 6.50.

Owner The Lamprell Partnership **Bred** B P Walden, L Taylor Et Al **Trained** Newmarket, Suffolk

FOCUS

An uncompetitive claimer and a muddling race withe the runner-up probably the best guide to the form.

7456 BOOK NOW FOR BOXING DAY H'CAP — 1m (P)

7:00 (7:01) (Class 5) (0-75,75) 3-Y-O — **£2,590** (£770; £385; £192) **Stalls** High

Form — RPR

5123 **1** **Red Suede Shoes**[20] 7153 3-8-13 **73** ... (p) JamesMillman(3) 1 82
(B R Millman) *in rr tl gd hdwy over 2f out: led wl over 1f out: pushed out* **7/2**[2]

6431 **2** *¾* **Bennelong**[29] 6950 3-9-4 **75** ... RyanMoore 3 81
(G L Moore) *in rr: hdwy over 2f out: nt clr run and swtchd lft to outer wl over 1f out: styd on to go 2nd jst ins fnl f but a hld by wnr* **7/2**[2]

3060 **3** *2 ½* **Yellow Printer**[24] 7065 3-8-11 **68** ... LPKeniry 4 68
(F J Brennan) *in rr: rdn over 3f out: styd on wl fr over 1f out to take 3rd cl home but nvr a threat to ldng duo* **25/1**

0404 **4** *½* **Seek The Fair Land**[7] 7356 3-9-3 **74** ... SJCraine 9 73
(J R Boyle) *disp ld untl led on ins over 3f out: drvn along over 2f out: hdd wl over 1f out: wknd ins fnl f and lost 3rd nr fin* **3/1**[1]

0423 **5** *5* **El Libertador (USA)**[6] 7362 3-8-11 **68** ... LiamJones 6 56
(E A Wheeler) *chsd ldrs: rdn over 2f out: sn btn* **7/1**

1054 **6** *6* **The Mumbo**[15] 7236 3-8-4 **61** ... (b) JoeFanning 2 35
(W Jarvis) *chsd ldrs: rdn: hmpd and wknd over 2f out* **10/1**

0410 7 8 **Moojeh (IRE)**[40] 6667 3-9-1 **75** AndreaAtzeni(3) 7 30
(M Botti) *s.i.s: in rr: hdwy on ins to chse ldrs 3f out: sn wknd* **5/1**[3]
1046 8 3 **Sapphire Prince (USA)**[15] 7238 3-8-9 **66** RobertWinston 5 15
(J R Best) *disp ld tl slt advantage 4f out: hdd and wd over 3f out: sn wknd* **14/1**
0-24 9 ½ **Banda Sea (IRE)**[16] 7228 3-8-9 **66** (b[1]) SteveDrowne 8 13
(P J Makin) *disp ld over 4f: wd and wknd sn after* **16/1**
1m 39.42s (-0.38) **Going Correction** +0.10s/f (Slow) **9** Ran SP% **124.1**
Speed ratings (Par 102): **105,104,101,101,96 90,82,79,78**
toteswingers: 1&2 £4.20, 1&3 £14.30, 2&3 £19.00 CSF £17.66 CT £277.13 TOTE £5.00: £2.00, £1.50, £7.60; EX 21.60 Place 6: £4.86, Place 5: £3.16..
Owner Essex Racing Club **Bred** Mrs M Campbell-Andenaes **Trained** Kentisbeare, Devon
■ Stewards' Enquiry : S J Craine one-day ban: used whip with excessive force (Dec 3)
FOCUS
An ordinary handicap in which the leaders seemed to go off too fast and the first three finishers raced in the last three places through the early stages. The runner-up is rated back to his juvenile form with the winner progressive.
Seek The Fair Land ◆ Official explanation: jockey said gelding hung left
Banda Sea(IRE) Official explanation: jockey said colt hung left
T/Plt: £5.00 to a £1 stake. Pool: £61,557.27. 8,833.82 winning tickets. T/Qpdt: £3.00 to a £1 stake. Pool: £8,053.04. 1,941.80 winning tickets. ST

1043 FONTAINEBLEAU
Thursday, November 19
OFFICIAL GOING: Very soft

7458a PRIX CONTESSINA (LISTED RACE) 6f
2:10 (2:10) 3-Y-0+ **£25,243** (£10,097; £7,573; £5,049; £2,524)

RPR
1 **Blue Cayenne (FR)**[16] 7232 4-8-13 TJarnet 6 106
(Mlle S-V Tarrou, France)
2 1½ **Salut L'Africain (FR)**[16] 7232 4-9-2 (p) THuet 5 104
(Robert Collet, France)
3 ¾ **Bluster (FR)**[16] 7232 3-9-2 IMendizabal 1 102
(Robert Collet, France)
4 1½ **La Sylvia (IRE)**[76] 5651 4-8-13 JAuge 2 94
(E J O'Neill) *racd in last: pushed along 1/2-way: rdn 1 1/2f out: wnt 4th fnl f: nvr a threat* **10/1**[1]
5 2 **Tiza (SAF)**[16] 7232 7-9-7 (p) DBoeuf 7 96
(A De Royer-Dupre, France)
6 1½ **Johanan (FR)**[18] 7216 3-8-12 SPasquier 4 82
(F-X De Chevigny, France)
7 ¾ **Bella Platina (GER)**[46] 6605 5-8-13 FilipMinarik 3 80
(U Stoltefuss, Germany)
1m 10.7s (70.70) **7** Ran SP% **9.1**
PARI-MUTUEL (Including 1 Euro stake): WIN 5.30; PL 2.10, 1.90; SF 16.80.
Owner Ecurie Haras de Quetieville **Bred** Haras De Grandcamp Earl **Trained** France

7410 WOLVERHAMPTON (A.W) (L-H)
Friday, November 20
OFFICIAL GOING: Standard
Wind: Nil Weather: Fine

7459 LADBROKESPOKER.COM MAIDEN STKS (DIV I) 7f 32y(P)
5:50 (5:52) (Class 5) 3-4-Y-0 **£2,388** (£705; £352) **Stalls** High

Form RPR
02 1 **Simla Sunset (IRE)**[11] 7321 3-8-12 67 (t) AdamKirby 6 71
(J R Gask) *hld up in mid-div: stdy hdwy 4f out: pushed along wl over 1f out: hrd rdn to ld wl ins fnl f: r.o* **5/2**[2]
2 hd **Tejime** 3-9-3 0 NickyMackay 2 75
(J H M Gosden) *a.p: led over 2f out: rdn and hdd wl ins fnl f: kpt on* **15/2**[3]
2-4 3 1½ **Light Sleeper**[153] 3155 3-9-3 0 DarryllHolland 10 71
(P W Chapple-Hyam) *hld up in rr: hdwy on outside 4f out: pushed along over 2f out: rdn and nt qckn ins fnl f* **8/11**[1]
0600 4 7 **Hold The Star**[8] 7353 3-8-10 56 ow3 AnnStokell(5) 4 51
(Miss A Stokell) *hld up in mid-div: sme hdwy on ins whn n.m.r briefly over 2f out: tk 4th over 1f out: no ch w ldng trio* **100/1**
00 5 ½ **Old Firm**[74] 5727 3-9-3 0 JimmyQuinn 11 51
(D A Nolan) *hld up in mid-div: hung lft and rdn over 3f out: short-lived effrt over 2f out* **200/1**
0 6 nk **Quiet Mountain (IRE)**[211] 1476 4-9-4 0 TomEaves 1 50
(Ollie Pears) *hld up in rr: pushed along over 2f out: nvr nr ldrs* **40/1**
0 7 2¼ **Wacato King (IRE)**[25] 7067 3-9-3 0 LPKeniry 5 44
(R A Farrant) *led early: sn lost pl and bhd: pushed along over 3f out: n.d after* **80/1**
000 8 18 **Miskin Spirit**[14] 7278 3-8-12 48 (b[1]) DavidProbert 7 —
(B Palling) *sn led: rdn and hdd over 2f out: wknd qckly wl over 1f out* **80/1**
0330 9 11 **Charlie Allnut**[233] 1057 4-9-4 45 (b) JoeFanning 3 —
(S Wynne) *prom tl wknd 4f out: eased whn no ch wl over 1f out* **33/1**
/40- 10 13 **Proud Linus (USA)**[519] 3155 4-9-4 0 RobertWinston 12 —
(J Ryan) *sn prom: chsd ldr over 5f out tl jst over 3f out: wknd and eased over 2f out: t.o* **14/1**
1m 29.86s (0.26) **Going Correction** +0.05s/f (Slow)
WFA 3 from 4yo 1lb **10** Ran SP% **114.2**
Speed ratings (Par 103): **100,99,98,90,89 89,86,66,53,38**
toteswingers:1&2 £2.80, 2&3 £1.90, 1&3 £1.10 CSF £20.12 TOTE £3.40: £1.10, £1.70, £1.10; EX 17.50.
Owner The Simla Sunset Partnership **Bred** Mrs Joan Murphy **Trained** Sutton Veny, Wilts
■ Stewards' Enquiry : Adam Kirby one-day ban: used whip above shoulder (Dec 4)
FOCUS
This ordinary maiden was run at a brisk early pace and the form looks solid with the three market leaders coming clear. The form is modest rated through the winner.
Tejime ◆ Official explanation: jockey said gelding hung left
Charlie Allnut Official explanation: trainer said gelding broke a blood vessel
Proud Linus(USA) Official explanation: jockey said gelding lost its action and had a breathing problem

7460 BEST ODDS GUARANTEED AT LADBROKES.COM APPRENTICE H'CAP (DIV I) 5f 216y(P)
6:20 (6:20) (Class 6) (0-52,52) 3-Y-0+ **£2,047** (£604; £302) **Stalls** Low

Form RPR
2600 1 **Carnival Dream**[21] 7152 4-8-6 47 AdamCarter(3) 12 58
(H A McWilliams) *t.k.h in mid-div: rdn and hdwy over 1f out: led ins fnl f: r.o wl* **20/1**
0400 2 2¼ **Tag Team (IRE)**[144] 3465 8-8-8 46 oh1 (p) KierenFox 5 50
(John A Harris) *s.i.s: towards rr: pushed along over 3f out: hdwy on ins over 2f out: sn rdn: led 1f out: hdd ins fnl f: no ex* **22/1**
0000 3 ¾ **Gower**[3] 7424 5-8-8 46 (p) JohnCavanagh 9 48
(R J Price) *chsd ldrs: chal over 2f out: sn rdn: carried wd ent st: styng on whn edgd lft wl ins fnl f* **16/1**
655 4 1 **Ride A White Swan**[161] 2879 4-8-7 50 ow4 LeeTopliss(5) 7 48
(D Shaw) *s.i.s: hld up in rr: rdn and hdwy 1f out: kpt on ins fnl f* **6/1**[3]
0506 5 1¾ **Sir Loin**[62] 6119 8-8-3 46 oh1 (v) NoraLooby(5) 4 39
(P Burgoyne) *t.k.h: led: rn wd ent st: hdd 1f out: wknd ins fnl f* **22/1**
0640 6 ¾ **All You Need (IRE)**[30] 6945 5-9-0 52 (p) DavidKenny 2 42
(R Hollinshead) *hld up: sn in tch: pushed along 2f out: ev ch 1f out: wknd wl ins fnl f* **7/2**[1]
0021 7 hd **Sonhador**[20] 7176 3-8-11 52 RyanClark(3) 10 42
(G Prodromou) *hld up in tch: rdn and c v wd st: wknd over 1f out* **4/1**[2]
0300 8 hd **Le Reve Royal**[127] 4004 3-8-13 51 RyanPowell 6 40
(G R Oldroyd) *hld up towards rr: pushed along over 2f out: nvr nr ldrs* **25/1**
4450 9 1½ **Dubai To Barnsley**[41] 6674 4-8-3 48 SFeeney(7) 3 32
(D A Nolan) *a in rr* **8/1**
0-60 10 1 **Edge End**[6] 7397 5-8-12 50 (v) HollyHall 1 31
(P D Evans) *t.k.h: w ldr: rdn and wknd 1f out* **7/1**
0431 11 5 **Boundless Applause**[64] 6038 3-8-11 49 MatthewLawson 13 14
(I A Wood) *prom: rdn over 2f out: wknd wl over 1f out* **7/1**
1m 15.75s (0.75) **Going Correction** +0.05s/f (Slow) **11** Ran SP% **115.8**
Speed ratings (Par 101): **97,94,93,91,89 88,88,87,85,84 77**
toteswingers:1&2 £105.30, 2&3 £53.00, 1&3 £78.40. CSF £374.44 CT £7106.34 TOTE £17.30: £4.20, £3.60, £6.20; EX 437.90.
Owner J D Riches **Bred** Jon Horley, Bishopwood And Trickledown **Trained** Cockerham, Co Durham
FOCUS
A handicap confined to apprentice riders who had yet to ride more than ten winners and it was a seller in all but name. There was a solid early pace on, but it was a messy looking race and the majority of riders showed their inexperience in the home straight. The form is best rated through the winner but looks dubious.
Sir Loin Official explanation: jockey said gelding hung right
Boundless Applause Official explanation: jockey said filly ran too free

7461 LADBROKES.COM H'CAP 1m 5f 194y(P)
6:50 (6:52) (Class 5) (0-70,70) 3-Y-0+ **£3,238** (£963; £481; £240) **Stalls** Low

Form RPR
-641 1 **Private Equity (IRE)**[9] 7324 3-8-3 53 6ex JoeFanning 8 60+
(W Jarvis) *hld up in mid-div: hdwy over 2f out: led over 1f out: rdn ins fnl f: styd on* **7/2**[2]
1251 2 1¼ **Leyte Gulf (USA)**[18] 7214 6-9-7 63 LPKeniry 9 69
(C C Bealby) *hld up towards rr: stdy prog on outside over 3f out: n.m.r briefly ins fnl f: rdn to take 2nd towards fin* **3/1**[1]
24-6 3 ½ **Weybridge Light**[15] 7255 4-9-9 65 (b) AdamKirby 5 70
(Eoin Griffin, Ire) *sn led: hdd after 2f: chsd ldr: led 3f out: rdn and hdd over 1f out: edgd rt ins fnl f: nt qckn* **9/1**
0600 4 1¼ **Paint The Town Red**[18] 7214 4-8-13 58 JackMitchell(3) 11 61
(H J Collingridge) *hld up in rr: c v wd st: rdn and hdwy over 1f out: styd on same pce ins fnl f* **10/1**
0600 5 2 **Jezza**[31] 6918 3-8-1 51 oh2 JamieMackay 3 52+
(Karen George) *a.p: ev ch wl over 1f out: rdn and nt qckn whn hmpd wl ins fnl f* **80/1**
2304 6 1¼ **Drawn Gold**[23] 7124 5-9-4 60 GrahamGibbons 1 63+
(R Hollinshead) *hld up in mid-div: pushed along over 2f out: hdwy wl over 1f out: hrd rdn and nt qckn whn hmpd ins fnl f* **8/1**
4431 7 nse **Moonbeam Dancer (USA)**[7] 7368 3-8-8 65 LauraPike(7) 13 64+
(D M Simcock) *hld up in mid-div: lost pl 4f out: rdn and styng on whn hmpd jst ins fnl f: n.d* **13/2**[3]
136 8 nse **Sheila's Castle**[10] 6704 5-9-5 64 RussellKennemore(3) 12 63+
(S Regan) *hld up in mid-div: pushed along and lost pl over 2f out: rdn wl over 1f out: nt clr run jst ins fnl f: sme late prog* **33/1**
2006 9 2¼ **Transfered (IRE)**[9] 7324 3-7-11 52 oh1 ow1 AndrewHeffernan(5) 2 47
(Lucinda Featherstone) *hld up in tch: rdn over 2f out: wkng whn hung rt and bmpd jst ins fnl f* **40/1**
4-04 10 nk **Karashar (IRE)**[7] 7368 4-10-0 70 GeorgeBaker 4 65
(Evan Williams) *hld up in rr: rdn and hdwy over 1f out: wknd ins fnl f* **8/1**
524/ 11 hd **City Hustler (USA)**[150] 1855 4-9-12 68 RobertWinston 10 63
(Adrian McGuinness, Ire) *led early: prom tl rdn and wknd over 1f out* **20/1**
2550 12 2¼ **Jenny Soba**[13] 7291 6-8-12 54 DarryllHolland 7 46
(Lucinda Featherstone) *s.i.s: hld up in rr: pushed along over 3f out: short-lived effrt on ins wl over 1f out* **25/1**
1100 13 4½ **Shanafarahan (IRE)**[194] 1319 4-9-8 64 JimmyQuinn 6 49
(K A Morgan) *t.k.h: led after 2f: hdd 3f out: wknd 2f out* **20/1**
3m 4.90s (-1.10) **Going Correction** +0.05s/f (Slow)
WFA 3 from 4yo+ 8lb **13** Ran SP% **121.9**
Speed ratings (Par 103): **105,104,104,103,102 101,101,101,100,99 99,98,95**
toteswingers:1&2 £3.50, 2&3 £13.50, 1&3 £8.20. CSF £13.49 CT £90.11 TOTE £5.20: £2.20, £1.90, £1.10; EX 13.50.
Owner Mrs Susan Davis **Bred** John And Susan Davis **Trained** Newmarket, Suffolk
FOCUS
This moderate staying handicap had an open look about it. It was run at an uneven pace and things got tight for the principals inside the final furlong, but the form still looks sound.

7462 BEST ODDS GUARANTEED AT LADBROKES.COM APPRENTICE H'CAP (DIV II) 5f 216y(P)
7:20 (7:21) (Class 6) (0-52,52) 3-Y-0+ **£2,047** (£604; £302) **Stalls** Low

Form RPR
0/5 1 **Diamond Fire (IRE)**[34] 6866 5-8-11 49 (bt) SPRyan 4 57
(Adrian McGuinness, Ire) *hld up towards rr: hdwy on outside over 2f out: rdn fnl f: led last strides* **5/2**[1]

625 2 hd **Colombard (IRE)**[2] 7427 4-8-12 **50**....(b) RichardRowe 9 57
(Patrick Morris) *a.p: rdn wl over 1f out: led jst ins fnl f: edgd lft towards fin: hdd last strides* **9/1**

4510 3 3/4 **Cheery Cat (USA)**[16] 7239 5-8-12 **50**....(p) DavidKenny 5 55
(J Balding) *hld up in mid-div: pushed along over 2f out: swtchd rt over 1f out: rdn and r.o ins fnl f: tk 3rd nr fin* **11/2**

4552 4 1/2 **Headache**[16] 7239 4-9-0 **52**....(bt) MatthewLawson 13 55
(B W Duke) *a.p: led wl over 2f out: sn rdn: hdd jst ins fnl f: no ex towards fin* **5/1**[3]

600 5 nk **Berrymead**[16] 7241 4-8-8 **46** oh1.... LauraPike 10 48
(Miss A Stokell) *hld up in mid-div: pushed along and hdwy 3f out: rdn over 1f out: one pce* **25/1**

0300 6 1/2 **Easy Wonder (GER)**[150] 3242 4-8-9 **47**....(b) HollyHall 6 47
(I A Wood) *hld up in rr: rdn wl over 1f out: r.o fnl f: nrst fin* **33/1**

0040 7 2 **Sandy Par**[23] 7107 4-8-5 **46** oh1....(p) RyanClark(3) 8 40
(J M Bradley) *sn prom: rdn 2f out: wknd fnl f* **20/1**

0560 8 3/4 **Kina Jazz**[29] 6968 3-8-10 **48**....(v[1]) RyanPowell 12 40
(J Ryan) *led over 3f: rdn and ev ch over 1f out: wknd ins fnl f* **20/1**

020 9 1 1/4 **Bountiful Bay**[7] 7370 4-8-7 **52**.... HeatherCork(7) 11 40
(Matthew Salaman) *t.k.h in tch: pushed along over 2f out: rdn and wknd wl over 1f out* **33/1**

0000 10 nk **Roman Maze**[16] 7240 9-8-12 **50**.... KierenFox 1 37
(W M Brisbourne) *hld up in rr: rdn wl over 1f out: no rspnse* **14/1**

0564 11 1 **North South Divide (IRE)**[25] 7068 5-8-1 **46**.... MEPower(7) 7 29
(K A Ryan) *a towards rr* **7/2**[2]

0-0 12 2 **Neat 'n Tidy**[90] 4266 5-8-8 **46** oh1.... JosephineBruning 3 23
(A E Jones) *a towards rr* **100/1**

1m 15.71s (0.71) **Going Correction** +0.05s/f (Slow) **12** Ran SP% **119.8**
Speed ratings (Par 101): **97,96,95,95,94 94,91,90,88,88 86,84**
toteswingers:1&2 £5.50, 2&3 £4.80, 1&3 £5.80. CSF £24.01 CT £118.96 TOTE £2.70: £1.60, £2.80, £2.70; EX 27.00.
Owner Adrian McGuinness **Bred** M Ommer **Trained** Lusk, Co Dublin
■ Stewards' Enquiry : S P Ryan one-day ban: used whip with excessive frequency (Dec 4)

FOCUS
The second division of the apprentice handicap and another very weak affair. As with the first division there was a solid early pace on and inexperience was advertised by the majority of riders. The placed horses are rated close to their previous Lingfield form.
Roman Maze Official explanation: jockey said gelding was hampered going into first bend

7463 BET AFTER THE OFF AT LADBROKES.COM MAIDEN AUCTION STKS 7f 32y(P)
7:50 (7:51) (Class 6) 2-Y-O £2,729 (£806; £403) Stalls High

Form RPR
40 1 **Sidney Melbourne (USA)**[46] 6544 2-8-11 0.... SteveDrowne 8 67
(J R Best) *hld up in mid-div: hdwy over 3f out: rdn wl over 1f out: led ins fnl f: edgd lft: r.o* **3/1**[2]

2 1 **Wishformore (IRE)** 2-7-13 0.... SophieDoyle(5) 1 58
(J S Moore) *hld up in mid-div: hdwy on ins wl over 1f out: kpt on to take 2nd wl ins fnl f* **16/1**

00 3 3/4 **Infinity World**[83] 5439 2-8-4 0.... JimmyQuinn 4 56
(G R Oldroyd) *a.p: led wl over 1f out: rdn and hdd ins fnl f: nt qckn* **10/1**

4 1/2 **Playboy Blues (IRE)** 2-8-11 0.... DarryllHolland 3 62
(P W Chapple-Hyam) *hld up in tch: rdn and nt qckn ins fnl f* **9/2**[3]

5 4 **Peckforton Castle** 2-8-9 0.... SJCraine 11 50
(Patrick Morris) *s.s: sn swtchd lft: hld up in rr: pushed along and sme prog over 2f out: rdn whn swtchd rt jst over 1f out: no imp fnl f* **20/1**

04 6 shd **Feeling Fragile (IRE)**[21] 7157 2-8-9 0.... RobertWinston 7 50
(Pat Eddery) *t.k.h: chsd ldr after 1f: ev ch 2f out: rdn wl over 1f out: wknd ins fnl f* **6/4**[1]

000 7 9 **Sisters Warning**[23] 7106 2-8-4 39.... LiamJones 2 23
(J Ryan) *led: hdd wl over 1f out: sn rdn and wknd* **80/1**

00 8 3 1/4 **Dubara Reef (IRE)**[55] 6285 2-8-8 0.... AndrewHeffernan(5) 6 24
(Paul Green) *sn pushed along: a in rr* **50/1**

4000 9 7 **Tagula Pearl (IRE)**[137] 3686 2-8-6 49....(b[1]) PaulHanagan 10 —
(I W McInnes) *in rr: pushed along over 3f out: sn struggling* **25/1**

1m 30.57s (0.97) **Going Correction** +0.05s/f (Slow) **9** Ran SP% **110.0**
Speed ratings (Par 94): **96,94,94,93,88 88,78,74,66**
toteswingers:1&2 £9.90, 2&3 £5.70, 1&3 £16.70. CSF £42.70 TOTE £4.40: £1.50, £4.10, £2.30; EX 44.00.
Owner Mrs A M Riney **Bred** Sun Valley Farm & Jeffrey Johnson **Trained** Hucking, Kent

FOCUS
This was an ordinary juvenile maiden and the first four came clear.

NOTEBOOK
Sidney Melbourne(USA) is bred to go on an artificial surface and got off the mark at the third time of asking on this AW debut. He took time to hit top gear in the home straight, but he was always going to get on top from the furlong marker and looks the sort that could improve again for another furlong. (op 7-2)
Wishformore(IRE) is related to winners at around this trip and posted a pleasing debut effort. She too took time to get the hang of things when under pressure, but will no doubt improve for this initial experience and will hold good claims on her next outing. (op 14-1)
Infinity World was stepping back up in trip on this return from an 83-day break. She could offer no more inside the final furlong after travelling nicely just off the early leaders, but has now improved with each of her three starts to date and now qualifies for nurseries. On this evidence, though, it may be that a drop back to 6f is best. (op 12-1)
Playboy Blues(IRE) looked to be starting off over a suitable trip on pedigree and turned in a pleasing introduction. He was another that travelled nicely just off the pace and is entitled go come on for the experience, so could take some beating next time out. (op 7-2 tchd 10-3)
Peckforton Castle would have found this sharp enough according to his breeding, so he looked to face an impossible task when falling out of the stalls. The penny dropped from 2f out, however, and he finished encouragingly to grab fifth place. The step up to 1m should prove more up his street and he looks to have a future. (op 16-1)
Feeling Fragile(IRE) set the standard on his fourth over C&D 21 days previously, but he gave himself little chance of lasting home this time by refusing to settle. Official explanation: jockey said gelding ran too free (op 13-8 tchd 7-4)

7464 LADBROKESPOKER.COM MAIDEN STKS (DIV II) 7f 32y(P)
8:20 (8:22) (Class 5) 3-4-Y-O £2,388 (£705; £352) Stalls High

Form RPR
0-4 1 **First Service (IRE)**[25] 7067 3-9-3 0.... SteveDrowne 4 68+
(R Charlton) *hld up in mid-div: hdwy over 2f out: rdn to ld ins fnl f: readily* **11/10**[1]

2 1 1/4 **Watch Amigo (IRE)** 3-9-3 0.... AdamKirby 11 60+
(W R Swinburn) *s.i.s: hld up in rr: c wd st: hdwy over 1f out: edgd lft fnl f: r.o to take 2nd last strides* **4/1**[2]

0553 3 hd **Luisa Tetrazzini (IRE)**[8] 7353 3-8-12 59.... JoeFanning 6 55
(K A Ryan) *led over 3f: led over 2f out: edgd rt over 1f out: rdn and hdd ins fnl f: no ex and lost 2nd last strides* **9/2**[3]

0 4 5 **King's Miracle (IRE)**[215] 1379 3-8-12 0.... LPKeniry 7 41
(J R Gask) *hld up in rr: sme prog over 2f out: rdn and kpt on to take 4th wl ins fnl f* **7/1**

0-60 5 3/4 **Govenor Eliott (IRE)**[35] 6818 4-9-4 45.... PaulHanagan 2 44
(A J Lockwood) *prom: rdn to chse ldr briefly wl over 1f out: wknd ins fnl f* **25/1**

-06 6 1 3/4 **Bella Fighetta**[17] 7228 3-8-7 0.... SophieDoyle(5) 10 34
(Ms J S Doyle) *hld up in mid-div: rdn wl over 1f out: no hdwy* **50/1**

4000 7 1 1/4 **Son Of Monsieur**[114] 4434 3-9-3 51.... PJMcDonald 5 36
(G R Oldroyd) *a towards rr* **40/1**

5000 8 nk **Silvertown Boy**[8] 7361 3-8-12 40....(p) SladeO'Hara(5) 9 35
(H A McWilliams) *sn chsng ldr: led over 3f out: rdn and hdd over 2f out: wknd over 1f out* **66/1**

0- 9 12 **Lady Trish**[371] 7311 3-8-12 0.... RobertWinston 8 —
(C A Dwyer) *hld up in tch: pushed along and wknd wl over 1f out* **16/1**

000/ 10 14 **Charlie Oxo**[772] 6105 4-9-4 37.... J-PGuillambert 3 —
(B P J Baugh) *hld up in tch: lost pl 4f out: bhd fnl 3f* **66/1**

1m 30.22s (0.62) **Going Correction** +0.05s/f (Slow)
WFA 3 from 4yo 1lb **10** Ran SP% **115.4**
Speed ratings (Par 103): **98,96,96,90,89 87,86,86,72,56**
toteswingers:1&2 £2.10, 2&3 £1.60, 1&3 £3.40. CSF £5.31 TOTE £1.80: £1.20, £1.50, £1.60; EX 6.80.
Owner John Livock **Bred** Barnane Stud **Trained** Beckhampton, Wilts

FOCUS
This second division of the maiden for older horses was run at a solid pace and it was another race that saw the first three finish clear of the remainder. Not easy form to assess but the winner could prove interesting in handicaps.
Son Of Monsieur Official explanation: jockey said gelding was denied a clear run

7465 WEATHERBYS PRINTING H'CAP 1m 4f 50y(P)
8:50 (8:51) (Class 2) (0-100,100) 3-Y-O+
£12,462 (£3,732; £1,866; £934; £466; £234) Stalls Low

Form RPR
1206 1 **Merchant Of Dubai**[13] 7293 4-9-4 **96**.... RobertWinston 4 103
(G A Swinbank) *led 2f: chsd ldr: rdn jst over 2f out: led wl ins fnl f: r.o* **11/4**[2]

4240 2 nk **Dance The Star (USA)**[35] 6816 4-8-5 **86** oh1.... MartinLane(3) 10 95+
(D M Simcock) *hld up in mid-div: hdwy over 2f out: rdn whn hmpd over 1f out: r.o to take 2nd post: unlucky* **7/1**

0300 3 shd **Laterly (IRE)**[62] 6106 4-8-11 **89**.... DarryllHolland 3 96
(S Gollings) *chsd ldr: led after 2f: rdn wl over 1f out: hdd wl ins fnl f: kpt on* **6/1**

3512 4 1/2 **Trip The Light**[24] 7091 4-8-8 **86**....(v) PaulHanagan 9 92
(R A Fahey) *hld up in tch: rdn 2f out: edgd lft and bmpd over 1f out: kpt on ins fnl f* **5/2**[1]

0RR 5 3/4 **Tilt**[13] 7293 7-8-10 **88**.... TomEaves 5 93
(B Ellison) *hld up in mid-div: pushed along over 2f out: rdn and hdwy over 1f out: n.m.r jst ins fnl f: nt qckn* **16/1**

/100 6 2 1/2 **Broomielaw**[13] 7293 5-9-2 **94**.... HayleyTurner 2 95
(E A L Dunlop) *hld up in tch: rdn jst over 1f out: fdd towards fin* **9/2**[3]

5156 7 1/2 **Fairmile**[7] 7375 7-9-3 **100**....(t) MatthewDavies(5) 6 100
(George Baker) *hld up towards rr: pushed along and effrt over 2f out: wknd fnl f* **16/1**

6000 8 3/4 **Paktolos (FR)**[133] 3797 6-8-5 **88**.... MarkCoumbe(5) 7 87
(John A Harris) *s.i.s: hld up in rr: pushed along over 2f out: rdn wl over 1f out: no rspnse* **40/1**

001 9 12 **Scamperdale**[128] 3977 7-8-2 **87**.... KierenFox(7) 8 67
(B P J Baugh) *hld up towards rr: short-lived effrt on outside over 2f out: eased whn btn towards fin* **20/1**

2m 37.46s (-3.64) **Going Correction** +0.05s/f (Slow) **9** Ran SP% **119.2**
Speed ratings (Par 109): **114,113,113,113,112 111,110,110,102**
toteswingers:1&2 £5.10, 2&3 £5.20, 1&3 £8.20. CSF £23.38 CT £109.40 TOTE £4.00: £1.50, £2.10, £2.10; EX 24.80.
Owner Highland Racing 2 **Bred** A Smith **Trained** Melsonby, N Yorks

FOCUS
A decent handicap, run at a sound pace. The first four were closely covered at the finish and the proximity of the third and fifth limits the form.

NOTEBOOK
Merchant Of Dubai was 1lb lower than when coming sixth in the November Handicap on his previous outing and got back to winning ways under strong handling. He was never far away and knuckled down gamely when asked for maximum effort. He has now scored on both his outings on the AW and is a very likeable performer. He could go hurdling at some stage this winter. (op 3-1 tchd 7-2)
Dance The Star(USA) ◆ has to rate as unlucky. Back on his preferred surface, he was given a decent ride to attain cover from the outside stall, and responded strongly when asked for an effort around 2f out. It looked as though he was coming with a winning run before he got hampered late on and the fact he was coming right back at the winner near the finish backs up that opinion. He fully deserves compensation and is one to look out for next time, despite the fact he will go up for this. (op 13-2 tchd 6-1 and 8-1)
Laterly(IRE) was making his AW debut for new connections. He got out in front after 2f and kept on gamely once headed, but just looked to pay for running with the choke out through the early parts on this return to 1m4f. (op 7-1 tchd 11-2)
Trip The Light, with the visor back on, had every chance and ran another solid race in defeat, so helps to give the form a good look. He ideally wants a proper test at this shorter trip, though. (op 7-2)
Tilt jumped off without fuss on this return to Polytrack, but is another that really wants an end-to-end gallop over this distance. (op 20-1)
Broomielaw proved very easy to back on this AW debut and still had stamina for this trip to prove. He was ridden as though it wasn't a problem, but was done with at the furlong pole and looked a clear non-stayer. (op 3-1)

7466 LADBROKESCASINO.COM H'CAP 1m 1f 103y(P)
9:20 (9:24) (Class 7) (0-50,50) 3-Y-O+ £2,047 (£604; £302) Stalls Low

Form RPR
0022 1 **Bidable**[4] 7416 5-8-12 **50**.... TonyCulhane 4 62
(B Palling) *a.p: wnt 2nd over 6f out: led over 2f out: 3l clr whn rdn over 1f out: r.o wl* **4/1**[2]

4553 2 3 1/4 **Russian Angel**[19] 7200 5-8-10 **48**.... LPKeniry 3 54
(Jean-Rene Auvray) *led 1f: hld up in tch: rdn to chse wnr wl over 1f out: no imp* **10/1**

2500 3 3/4 **Libre**[22] 7142 9-8-11 **49**.... JerryO'Dwyer 7 53
(F Jordan) *hld up in rr: pushed along and hdwy 2f out: nt clr run and swtchd lft ins fnl f: kpt on* **33/1**

0053 **4** ¾ **Spanish Cross (IRE)**[24] 7094 4-8-11 **49** LiamJones 2 51
(G Prodromou) *hld up in mid-div: pushed along and hdwy 2f out: rdn over 1f out: one pce ins fnl f* **12/1**

3000 **5** ¾ **Turkish Sultan (IRE)**[3] 7422 6-8-10 **48** (p) DavidProbert 1 49
(J M Bradley) *hld up in rr: prog on ins over 3f out: rdn over 2f out: one pce ins fnl f* **20/1**

0565 **6** 3 ¼ **Black Stocking**[22] 7143 4-8-12 **50** AdamKirby 9 44
(Rae Guest) *led briefly after 1f: a.p: rdn over 3f out: wknd ins fnl f* **20/1**

4556 **7** 1 ¼ **Casablanca Minx (IRE)**[22] 7143 6-8-4 **49** ow3 (v) DavidKenny(7) 11 40
(A G Juckes) *s.i.s: hld up in rr: pushed along over 3f out: nvr nr ldrs* **28/1**

6460 **8** ½ **Ruwain**[151] 3215 5-8-7 **48** AndreaAtzeni(3) 12 38
(P J McBride) *led 8f out tl over 2f out: rdn and wknd over 1f out* **12/1**

0-43 **9** ¾ **Camerooney**[4] 7417 6-8-8 **46** TomEaves 6 35
(B Ellison) *hld up towards rr: pushed along over 3f out: sn struggling* **3/1**[1]

10/0 **10** hd **Blue Cross Boy (USA)**[2] 7443 4-8-11 **49** (b) RobertWinston 8 37
(Adrian McGuinness, Ire) *hld up towards rr: pushed along 3f out: no ch fnl 2f* **9/2**[3]

3600 **11** 1 **Castlecarra (IRE)**[24] 7086 4-8-9 **47** (t) FranciscoDaSilva 10 33
(J Hetherton) *hld up in mid-div: rdn and wknd over 2f out* **22/1**

-403 **12** 19 **Lunar Limelight**[21] 7152 4-8-10 **48** SteveDrowne 13 —
(P J Makin) *sn prom: pushed along and wknd over 2f out* **9/1**

000/ **13** 89 **Impure Thoughts**[692] 7264 4-8-8 **46** SamHitchcott 5 —
(D W Thompson) *uns rdr and bolted to s: hld up in mid-div: lost pl over 5f out: t.o fnl 4f* **100/1**

2m 0.87s (-0.83) **Going Correction** +0.05s/f (Slow) 13 Ran SP% **118.9**
Speed ratings (Par 97): **105,102,101,100,100 97,96,95,95,94 93,77,—**
toteswingers:1&2 £5.70, 2&3 £20.10, 1&3 £26.00. CSF £39.10 CT £1168.96 TOTE £5.50: £2.20, £3.70, £7.60; EX 38.50 Place 6: £178.86 Place 5: £155.34 .
Owner Flying Eight Partnership **Bred** W D Hodge **Trained** Tredodridge, Vale Of Glamorgan

FOCUS
A dire handicap but an improved effot from the winner. The form looks sound enough if moderate.
Camerooney Official explanation: jockey said gelding ran flat
T/Plt: £583.20 to a £1 stake. Pool: £97,515.23. 122.05 winning tickets. T/Qpdt: £13.90 to a £1 stake. Pool: £9,734.14. 515.50 winning tickets. KH

7467 - 7473a (Foreign Racing) - See Raceform Interactive

7450
KEMPTON (A.W) (R-H)
Saturday, November 21

OFFICIAL GOING: Standard
Wind: Fairly strong, half-behind. Weather: Raining

7474 KEMPTON.CO.UK CLAIMING STKS 1m 2f (P)
4:00 (4:02) (Class 6) 2-Y-O **£2,047** (£604; £302) **Stalls** High

Form RPR

2441 **1** **Mary Helen**[23] 7139 2-8-8 58 ShaneKelly 2 54
(W M Brisbourne) *hld up in tch in midfield: n.m.r and swtchd lft over 1f out: rdn and qcknd to chal ins fnl f: led fnl 75yds: r.o wl* **9/2**[2]

0402 **2** hd **Saint Thomas (IRE)**[7] 7391 2-8-13 65 JimCrowley 5 59
(J A Osborne) *dwlt: sn rcvrd and chsd ldrs: drvn and ev ch over 1f out: edgd rt and led 1f out: hdd fnl 75yds: nt qckn* **8/1**

0150 **3** ¾ **Fine Lace (IRE)**[17] 7235 2-8-10 63 LPKeniry 3 55
(D J S Ffrench Davis) *sn rdn to chse ldrs: drvn to ld wl over 1f out: hdd 1f out: no ex last 50yds* **5/1**[3]

5035 **4** 3 ½ **Underworld Dandy**[17] 7235 2-8-6 63 AndrewHeffernan(5) 9 49
(P D Evans) *hld up in midfield: effrt towards inner and rdn over 1f out: edgd lft and nt pce of ldrs ins fnl f* **9/2**[2]

6000 **5** hd **Blinka Me**[65] 6034 2-8-8 53 (b[1]) AshleyMorgan(5) 12 51
(M H Tompkins) *stdd and wnt lft s: hld up last: pushed along over 2f out: hdwy and swtchd rt over 1f out: styd on but nt pce to chal* **16/1**

0060 **6** 1 ½ **Expensive Legacy**[31] 6930 2-8-7 49 JimmyQuinn 1 42
(H J L Dunlop) *in tch midfield: rdn and effrt over 1f out: sn no imp* **25/1**

042 **7** shd **Alfalevva**[23] 7139 2-8-13 62 TonyCulhane 13 48
(M R Channon) *w ldr tl led over 7f out: drvn and hdd wl over 1f out: wknd ent fnl f* **4/1**[1]

060 **8** nk **Mactrac**[92] 5212 2-8-10 45 PatrickHills(3) 4 48
(R Hannon) *t.k.h: chsd ldrs: rdn and unable qck over 1f out: wknd ent fnl f* **25/1**

3230 **9** ½ **Glen Lass**[17] 7235 2-8-2 61 (p) SimonPearce(5) 7 41
(J Pearce) *towards rr: rdn and effrt wl over 1f out: styd on fnl f: n.d* **10/1**

0 **10** 4 ½ **Develop U**[24] 7120 2-8-8 0 ow1 JackDean(3) 10 37
(W G M Turner) *s.i.s and hmpd s: a towards rr: effrt and rdn outer over 2f out: sn struggling* **66/1**

3001 **11** 2 **Tiger Hawk (USA)**[10] 7334 2-8-13 62 (b) PaulDoe 8 35
(P D Evans) *led to over 7f out: chsd ldr after tl wknd u.p over 1f out: eased ins fnl f* **6/1**

0050 **12** ½ **Lady Cavendish (IRE)**[10] 7334 2-8-2 58 (p) MartinLane(3) 6 26
(A Bailey) *hmpd s: a bhd: rdn and shortlived effrt on inner over 1f out: wl bhd fnl f* **14/1**

2m 10.52s (2.52) **Going Correction** +0.025s/f (Slow) 12 Ran SP% **129.3**
Speed ratings (Par 94): **90,89,89,86,86 85,85,84,84,80 79,78**
toteswingers: 1&2 £6.30, 1&3 £6.90, 2&3 £13.80 CSF £43.93 TOTE £6.00: £2.50, £2.60, £2.30; EX 34.80.Saint Thomas was claimed by P. Riley for £8,000.
Owner P Mort & Mark Brisbourne **Bred** World Racing Network **Trained** Great Ness, Shropshire

FOCUS
An open looking claimer run at a modest pace. The field quickened leaving the back straight.

NOTEBOOK
Mary Helen had been performing creditably in nurseries off a mark in the 50s and followed up a recent success in similar grade in good fashion. Sat just off the pace, she had to be switched out for a sustained run in the home straight to catch the runner-up towards the finish. She appreciated the step up in trip last time and, once again, seemed to enjoy this further step up. She will be now aimed at a similar contest at Wolverhampton in December.
Saint Thomas(IRE) was always to the fore but, after taking it up entering the final furlong, he was collared towards the finish, despite not stopping. He had looked regressive as the season progressed, but shaped well dropped to this grade last time and ought to be capable of going one better in similar company.
Fine Lace(IRE) landed a nursery off a mark of 59 in October at Wolverhampton and after a couple of modest efforts, although she had her reasons, this was a step back in the right direction. She chased the leaders until taking over hitting the 2f marker and kept on challenging when headed entering the distance.
Underworld Dandy travelled well in mid-division and looked as though he would be a big danger as he moved up turning in, but he could only keep on at the same pace.
Blinka Me was held up off the modest pace and struggled when the pace quickened, but he stayed on well enough in the straight without ever threatening to get involved.

Tiger Hawk(USA) Official explanation: jockey said colt had no more to give

7475 BOXINGDAYRACES.CO.UK H'CAP 1m 2f (P)
4:30 (4:32) (Class 5) (0-75,75) 3-Y-O+ **£2,590** (£770; £385; £192) **Stalls** High

Form RPR

3241 **1** **Free Tussy (ARG)**[23] 7134 5-9-6 **73** (bt) GeorgeBaker 6 84+
(G L Moore) *t.k.h: hld up in midfield: effrt to chse ldr over 1f out: led jst ins fnl f: r.o strly: rdn out* **11/2**

4334 **2** 2 **Merrymadcap (IRE)**[20] 7204 7-9-5 **72** LPKeniry 11 79
(Matthew Salaman) *led 2f: chsd ldr after tl rdn to ld again over 1f out: hdd jst ins fnl f: one pce* **9/1**

4633 **3** 1 ¾ **Jeer (IRE)**[58] 6236 5-9-3 **70** (b[1]) PhillipMakin 10 74+
(M W Easterby) *chsd ldrs: rdn wl over 1f out: chsd clr ldng pair ins fnl f: kpt on* **9/4**[1]

45-2 **4** hd **Jennie Jerome (IRE)**[17] 7247 4-9-5 **75** JackMitchell(3) 1 78
(C F Wall) *stdd s and dropped in bhd: rdn and effrt on wd outside 2f out: r.o to press for 3rd nr fin: nvr trbld ldrs* **4/1**[2]

6313 **5** 1 ½ **Resplendent Ace (IRE)**[8] 7368 5-9-6 **73** IanMongan 8 73
(P Howling) *hld up in last trio: rdn and hdwy over 1f out: r.o ins fnl f: nvr threatened ldrs* **11/1**

0526 **6** nse **Force Group (IRE)**[5] 7413 5-8-12 **70** (b) AshleyMorgan(5) 3 70
(M H Tompkins) *racd keenly: led 8f out tl rdn and hdd over 1f out: wknd ent fnl f* **8/1**

1-06 **7** ¾ **Maria Di Scozia**[28] 7020 4-9-8 **75** (t) SteveDrowne 7 74
(P W Chapple-Hyam) *dwlt: sn rcvrd and in tch: rdn and unable qck wl over 1f out: one pce after* **16/1**

0210 **8** shd **Naheell**[25] 7101 3-8-4 **68** CharlotteKerton(7) 4 66
(G Prodromou) *in tch in midfield: rdn and struggling over 2f out: styd on ins fnl f: nvr gng pce to trble ldrs* **33/1**

6061 **9** ½ **Spring Goddess (IRE)**[32] 6924 8-9-0 **70** MartinLane(3) 2 67
(A P Jarvis) *stdd s and dropped in bhd: rdn 2f out: drvn and no prog over 1f out* **16/1**

4520 **10** ¾ **Northern Spy (USA)**[41] 6695 5-9-6 **73** HayleyTurner 9 69
(S Dow) *t.k.h: chsd ldrs tl lost pl ent fnl 2f: no ch w ldrs fr over 1f out* **5/1**[3]

460- **11** ¾ **Given A Choice (IRE)**[414] 6450 7-8-10 **68** (p) SimonPearce(5) 12 62
(J Pearce) *dwlt: sn midfield: effrt u.p on inner over 2f out: no prog fr over 1f out* **20/1**

0020 **12** shd **King Of Legend (IRE)**[17] 7236 5-8-8 **61** PaulDoe 5 55
(D Morris) *dwlt: t.k.h: hld up towards rr: rdn and unable qck ent fnl 2f: n.d* **25/1**

2m 7.46s (-0.54) **Going Correction** +0.025s/f (Slow)
WFA 3 from 4yo+ 4lb 12 Ran SP% **135.6**
Speed ratings (Par 103): **103,101,100,99,98 98,98,97,97,96 96,96**
toteswingers: 1&2 £9.20, 1&3 £5.30, 2&3 £9.10 CSF £61.55 CT £152.12 TOTE £5.60: £2.00, £3.20, £1.30; EX 46.90.
Owner T Bowley **Bred** Antonio Carlos Iguacel Et Al **Trained** Lower Beeding, W Sussex
■ Stewards' Enquiry : Charlotte Kerton seven-day ban: used whip with excessive frequency without giving colt time to respond (Dec 5-11)

FOCUS
A modest but competitive looking 61-75 handicap run at a fair pace.

7476 BOOK NOW FOR WILLIAM HILL WINTER FESTIVAL H'CAP 1m 4f (P)
5:00 (5:01) (Class 5) (0-75,75) 3-Y-O **£2,590** (£770; £385; £192) **Stalls** Centre

Form RPR

5613 **1** **Ebony Eyes**[52] 6376 3-9-4 **72** JimCrowley 1 85+
(W J Knight) *chsd ldrs: rdn to go 2nd 2f out: led 1f out: in command fnl 100yds: eased towards fin* **13/2**[3]

-022 **2** 1 ½ **Kazbow (IRE)**[19] 7212 3-9-2 **70** KFallon 5 77
(L M Cumani) *led: rdn over 2f out: drvn and hdd 1f out: one pce and comf hld after* **4/6**[1]

2363 **3** 1 ½ **Strathcal**[21] 7178 3-9-7 **75** SteveDrowne 2 79
(H Morrison) *sn chsng ldr: drvn and unable qck jst over 2f out: one pce after* **15/2**

3461 **4** nk **Drum Dragon**[35] 6840 3-8-13 **72** AshleyMorgan(5) 8 76
(M H Tompkins) *hld up in midfield: shkn up 3f out: rdn jst over 2f out: one pce after* **6/1**[2]

1303 **5** 1 **Key Regard (IRE)**[17] 7238 3-9-2 **70** ShaneKelly 3 72
(P F I Cole) *stdd s: hld up in rr: rdn and effrt over 2f out: no imp* **20/1**

1632 **6** 4 ½ **Broughtons Paradis (IRE)**[33] 6910 3-8-9 **63** TonyCulhane 4 58
(W J Musson) *stdd s: hld up in rr: struggling over 3f out: n.d* **10/1**

3360 **7** ¾ **Arcola (IRE)**[7] 7399 3-8-6 **67** JosephineBruning(7) 6 61
(D M Simcock) *chsd ldng pair: pushed along over 3f out: wknd 2f out* **12/1**

0001 **8** 4 ½ **Admirable Duque (IRE)**[37] 6807 3-8-10 **71** (p) TobyAtkinson(7) 7 58
(D J S Ffrench Davis) *t.k.h: hld up in rr: last fr 1/2-way: lost tch over 3f out* **7/1**

2m 34.44s (-0.06) **Going Correction** +0.025s/f (Slow) 8 Ran SP% **133.4**
Speed ratings (Par 102): **101,100,99,98,98 95,94,91**
toteswingers: 1&2 £2.60, 1&3 £5.10, 2&3 £3.40 CSF £13.29 CT £43.07 TOTE £8.60: £1.80, £1.20, £1.80; EX 17.70.
Owner D G Hardisty Bloodstock **Bred** D G Hardisty Bloodstock **Trained** Patching, W Sussex

FOCUS
A fairly competitive looking handicap run at a modest pace.
Admirable Duque(IRE) Official explanation: jockey said gelding had a breathing problem

7477 GROOMED TO PERFECTION, THE KIA SOUL MAIDEN AUCTION STKS 6f (P)
5:30 (5:33) (Class 5) 2-Y-O **£2,590** (£770; £385; £192) **Stalls** High

Form RPR

0 **1** **Pittodrie Star (IRE)**[22] 7146 2-8-13 0 LPKeniry 10 76
(A M Balding) *dwlt off pce in midfield: swtchd lft and rdn jst over 2f out: drvn to chse ldr ins fnl f: r.o u.str.p to ld nr fin* **5/4**[1]

0666 **2** hd **Hill Of Miller (IRE)**[54] 6328 2-8-13 72 MartinDwyer 11 75
(Rae Guest) *hld up wl off the pce in rr of main gp: gd hdwy on inner jst over 2f out: led ent fnl f: edgd lft: kpt on wl: hdd nr fin* **9/2**[2]

0506 **3** 7 **Light The Way**[32] 6911 2-8-11 60 (bt[1]) TPQueally 9 52
(P J Makin) *led: clr after 2f: rdn ent fnl 2f: hdd ent fnl f: sn btn but hld on for modest 3rd* **9/1**

604 **4** 1 ½ **Bobby's Doll**[21] 7175 2-7-11 58 NatashaEaton(7) 7 41
(T T Clement) *prom in main gp: rdn and clsd on ldr 2f out: plugged on same pce fnl f* **16/1**

5 shd **Neduardo** 2-8-13 0 AdrianMcCarthy 8 49
(P W Chapple-Hyam) *hld up in rr of main gp: pushed along over 2f out: styd on steadily fr over 1f out: nvr trbld ldrs* **11/2**[3]

6 **6** ¾ **Weimarland (IRE)**[25] 7087 2-9-3 0 ShaneKelly 2 51
(J A Osborne) *chsd clr ldr: rdn jst over 2f out: clsd on ldr but hung rt over 1f out: wknd fnl f* **33/1**

00 **7** 1¾ **Tenga Venga**[86] 5371 2-9-1 0 AdamKirby 4 44
(P S McEntee) *racd off the pce in midfield: pushed along over 3f out: rdn and kpt on one pce fnl 2f* **50/1**

8 *nk* **Torran Sound** 2-9-3 0 HayleyTurner 5 45
(J M P Eustace) *s.i.s: wl bhd tl styd on and edgd rt ins fnl f: n.d* **16/1**

9 *hd* **Not In The Clock (USA)** 2-8-13 0 SteveDrowne 3 40
(J R Best) *v.s.a: sn wl outpcd in rr* **8/1**

6060 **10** 1¼ **Casanova Kid**[33] 6903 2-9-1 51 EdwardCreighton 6 38
(E J Creighton) *prom in main gp tl rdn over 2f out: wknd ent fnl 2f* **8/1**

0 **11** *11* **Thatlittlecolt**[10] 7331 2-8-11 0 ow2 PhillipMakin 1 1
(D H Brown) *wnt lft s: a wl bhd: t.o* **25/1**

1m 13.33s (0.23) **Going Correction** +0.025s/f (Slow) **11** Ran SP% **130.7**
Speed ratings (Par 96): **99,98,89,87,87 86,83,83,83,81 66**
toteswingers: 1&2 £2.40, 1&3 £4.10, 2&3 £9.50 CSF £7.86 TOTE £2.30: £1.30, £1.50, £2.30; EX 10.40.
Owner Evan M Sutherland **Bred** Gary O'Reilly **Trained** Kingsclere, Hants
■ Stewards' Enquiry : L P Keniry caution: used whip without giving colt time to respond.

FOCUS
The first two came clear in a maiden lacking strength in depth.

NOTEBOOK
Pittodrie Star(IRE), who was heavily backed, is related to a stack of middle-distance winners and had obviously progressed since his debut, in which he was far from disgraced. He had to be switched off the rails over 2f out to begin his effort before being hard ridden to bear down on the leaders. He kept on strongly to catch the leader in the shadow of the post. This was only a modest affair but he showed a good attitude when set about his task and has plenty of scope for further improvement, especially when upped back up in trip. (op 3-1 tchd 6-5)
Hill Of Miller(IRE) was a shade unlucky, for he looked as though he had stolen the race when taking the lead only to get mugged near the finish. He is an inconsistent performer but this was one of his better efforts. (tchd 4-1)
Light The Way broke well and set a good pace in first-time blinkers, but he was in trouble after his early exertions and was a spent force when headed over a furlong out. Although he hung on for third, he sets a modest standard. (op 10-1 tchd 8-1)
Bobby's Doll chased the leader until over a furlong out and is another exposed as modest. (op 14-1)
Neduardo could never land a blow from his midfield position. Official explanation: jockey said colt suffered interference shortly after start (op 10-3 tchd 6-1 in places)
Weimarland(IRE) ran on to challenge for fourth entering the final furlong before fading in the final 100yds.

7478 RACING UK H'CAP 6f (P)
6:00 (6:01) (Class 4) (0-80,86) 3-Y-0+ **£4,727** (£1,406; £702; £351) **Stalls** High

Form RPR

0431 **1** **Earlsmedic**[2] 7454 4-9-3 86 6ex (e) RyanClark(7) 4 97
(S C Williams) *chsd ldng pair: swtchd lft and rdn over 2f out: led 2f out: kpt on wl fnl f* **11/4**[1]

3065 **2** ¾ **Capone (IRE)**[7] 7394 4-9-4 80 HayleyTurner 9 89
(R Curtis) *stdd and sltly hmpd after s: hld up in rr: hdwy and rdn 2f out: drvn and chsd wnr ins fnl f: no imp* **4/1**[2]

5000 **3** 1¼ **Harlech Castle**[3] 7437 4-9-1 77 (b) ShaneKelly 12 82
(J R Boyle) *sn rdn along to chse ldr: ev ch 2f out: drvn and outpcd by wnr ent fnl f* **12/1**

0305 **4** ¾ **Blown It (USA)**[22] 7155 3-8-11 73 PhillipMakin 5 75
(I Semple) *hld up towards rr: effrt and rdn over 1f out: r.o fnl f: nt rch ldrs* **20/1**

1550 **5** *shd* **Brierty (IRE)**[82] 5523 3-9-4 80 DNolan 11 82
(D Carroll) *chsd ldrs: rdn and effrt on inner jst over 2f out: one pce fnl f* **20/1**

0331 **6** *hd* **Perfect Act**[32] 6915 4-8-10 72 TPQueally 3 73
(C G Cox) *stdd and dropped in bhd s: effrt and hanging rt over 1f out: styd on fnl f: nvr trbld ldrs* **7/1**

1435 **7** ½ **Ursula (IRE)**[24] 7111 3-9-3 79 JimCrowley 2 79
(R M Beckett) *chsd ldrs: rdn and unable qckn over 2f out: one pce fnl 2f* **13/2**

0120 **8** *1* **River Kirov (IRE)**[2] 7454 6-9-4 80 SteveDrowne 10 76
(M Wigham) *stdd s: hld up in midfield: rdn and unable qckn 2f out: one pce* **11/2**[3]

5246 **9** 1½ **Brandywell Boy (IRE)**[24] 7123 6-8-9 71 RichardThomas 7 63
(D J S Ffrench Davis) *chsd ldrs: pushed along after 2f: struggling u.p over 2f out: one pce after* **20/1**

1P14 **10** *nk* **Gwilym (GER)**[21] 7191 6-8-10 72 MartinDwyer 6 63
(D Haydn Jones) *led tl rdn and hdd 2f out: wknd ent fnl f* **16/1**

0000 **11** *3* **Ajigolo**[7] 7395 6-8-12 74 (b[1]) DarryllHolland 8 55
(N Wilson) *s.i.s: bhd: hdwy on inner over 2f out: no hdwy over 1f out* **12/1**

560 **12** *13* **White Shift (IRE)**[16] 7253 3-8-11 73 J-PGuillambert 1 12
(P Howling) *racd in midfield on outer: rdn and wknd over 2f out: wl bhd and eased ins fnl f* **66/1**

1m 12.1s (-1.00) **Going Correction** +0.025s/f (Slow) **12** Ran SP% **124.9**
Speed ratings (Par 105): **107,106,104,103,103 102,102,100,98,98 94,77**
toteswingers: 1&2 £4.50, 1&3 £11.60, 2&3 £10.00 CSF £13.43 CT £121.23 TOTE £3.80: £1.40, £2.00, £4.40; EX 22.50.
Owner Mad Man Plus One **Bred** W N Greig **Trained** Newmarket, Suffolk

FOCUS
They went a decent pace here.

7479 TRY OUR NEW BISTRO MENU H'CAP (DIV I) 7f (P)
6:30 (6:30) (Class 6) (0-65,65) 3-Y-0+ **£1,706** (£503; £252) **Stalls** High

Form RPR

3321 **1** **Kuanyao (IRE)**[41] 6701 3-9-4 65 SteveDrowne 1 71
(P J Makin) *mde all and grad crossed to rail: rdn over 2f out: kpt on wl* **5/1**[2]

4620 **2** ½ **Goodbye Cash (IRE)**[3] 7432 5-8-12 58 PaulDoe 4 63
(P D Evans) *chsd ldrs: wnt 2nd 1/2-way: rdn to chal 2f out: one pce fnl f* **8/1**

2635 **3** *nk* **Art Market (CAN)**[24] 7110 6-8-11 57 (p) JamieSpencer 5 61
(Miss Jo Crowley) *chsd wnr tl 1/2-way: styd on same pce u.p fnl 2f* **11/2**[3]

006 **4** *hd* **Dajen**[26] 7067 3-8-12 62 MartinLane(3) 6 66
(D M Simcock) *stdd s: in rr: rdn 3f out: hdwy over 1f out: r.o: nvr rchd ldrs* **22/1**

4-05 **5** 1½ **Sydneysider**[58] 6223 4-9-3 63 ShaneKelly 10 63
(Eve Johnson Houghton) *bhd: rdn over 3f out: hdwy on inner over 1f out: r.o: nvr trbld ldrs* **16/1**

0044 **6** 1½ **Kings Ace (IRE)**[5] 7416 3-8-10 57 JimCrowley 8 53
(A P Jarvis) *hld up towards rr: rdn and effrt over 2f out: kpt on but nvr gng pce to trble ldrs* **15/2**

0533 **7** 3¾ **The Happy Hammer (IRE)**[21] 7179 3-9-0 61 MartinDwyer 9 46
(E V Stanford) *t.k.h: wl in tch: rdn and unable qckn over 2f out: wknd over 1f out* **11/2**[3]

0445 **8** ½ **Pha Mai Blue**[8] 7364 4-8-13 64 MatthewDavies(5) 11 48
(J R Boyle) *t.k.h: hld up in rr: effrt ent fnl 2f: nt clr run over 1f out: nvr trbld ldrs* **9/2**[1]

0021 **9** 2¼ **Hereford Boy**[26] 7052 5-9-0 65 (p) LeeNewnes(5) 12 43
(D K Ivory) *t.k.h: in tch tl stdd towards rr after 2f: rdn over 2f out: no real prog* **9/2**[1]

1460 **10** ¾ **Jeremiah (IRE)**[26] 7057 3-9-2 63 TPQueally 2 39
(J G Portman) *racd in midfield: hdwy to chse ldrs 1/2-way: wknd u.p over 1f out* **22/1**

1m 26.5s (0.50) **Going Correction** +0.025s/f (Slow)
WFA 3 from 4yo+ 1lb **10** Ran SP% **121.3**
Speed ratings (Par 101): **98,97,97,96,95 93,89,88,86,85**
toteswingers:1&2:£10.20, 2&3:£12.70, 1&3:£8.20 CSF £46.68 CT £194.51 TOTE £5.70: £1.60, £2.50, £2.40; EX 62.20.
Owner D M Ahier **Bred** Newlands House Stud **Trained** Ogbourne Maisey, Wilts

FOCUS
Division one of this modest handicap, but run at a fair pace.

7480 TRY OUR NEW BISTRO MENU H'CAP (DIV II) 7f (P)
7:00 (7:01) (Class 6) (0-65,65) 3-Y-0+ **£1,706** (£503; £252) **Stalls** High

Form RPR

0056 **1** **Istiqdaam**[21] 7173 4-8-12 57 (b) PhillipMakin 7 74
(M W Easterby) *trckd ldrs: rdn to go 2nd 2f out: led over 1f out: drew wl clr fnl f* **5/2**[1]

1201 **2** 3¾ **Connor's Choice**[36] 6828 4-9-0 64 SimonPearce(5) 4 70
(Andrew Turnell) *led: rdn 2f out: hdd over 1f out: no ch w wnr after* **15/2**

3260 **3** 1¼ **Stanley Goodspeed**[12] 7321 6-9-4 63 (tp) HayleyTurner 10 66
(J W Hills) *chsd ldrs: rdn and racd awkwardly jst over 2f out: one pce and wl hld after* **9/2**[2]

2-56 **4** 1½ **Cross Section (USA)**[156] 3071 3-9-5 65 (p) JamieSpencer 2 64
(E F Vaughan) *hld up in midfield: edgd out lft and effrt ent fnl 2f: no imp* **12/1**

0044 **5** *nse* **Downhill Skier (IRE)**[12] 7321 5-9-3 62 TGMcLaughlin 6 61
(W M Brisbourne) *t.k.h in midfield: rdn and effrt over 2f out: one pce* **5/1**[3]

4004 **6** *1* **Crystallize**[21] 7180 3-9-4 64 StephenDonohoe 5 60
(A B Haynes) *hld up in rr: sme hdwy u.p over 1f out: n.d* **8/1**

4040 **7** *nse* **Imperial Skylight**[26] 7052 3-8-9 55 SamHitchcott 11 51
(M R Channon) *in tch in midfield: effrt u.p to chse ldrs over 1f out: wknd fnl f* **16/1**

3550 **8** ½ **Golden Prospect**[7] 7403 5-8-12 57 PaulFitzsimons 8 52
(Miss J R Tooth) *s.i.s: a towards rr* **14/1**

1000 **9** 1½ **Bob Stock (IRE)**[17] 7246 3-9-2 62 TonyCulhane 9 53
(W J Musson) *hld up in rr: n.d* **10/1**

3200 **10** *hd* **Jonnie Skull (IRE)**[54] 6339 3-9-1 61 (vt) TPQueally 1 51
(P S McEntee) *chsd ldr tl 2f out: sn wknd u.p* **12/1**

0340 **11** *shd* **Shake On It**[20] 7200 5-8-7 52 JimmyQuinn 3 42
(M R Hoad) *s.i.s: a bhd* **10/1**

1m 25.79s (-0.21) **Going Correction** +0.025s/f (Slow)
WFA 3 from 4yo+ 1lb **11** Ran SP% **132.4**
Speed ratings (Par 101): **102,97,96,94,94 93,93,92,91,90 90**
toteswingers:1&2:£9.40, 2&3:£11.80, 1&3:£3.90 CSF £25.26 CT £90.94 TOTE £4.90: £2.10, £1.90, £2.10; EX 52.50.
Owner Two Old Pals **Bred** Cheveley Park Stud Ltd **Trained** Sheriff Hutton, N Yorks

FOCUS
Division two of the 51-60 handicap which was run at a similar pace to the first but in a slightly quicker time.
Bob Stock(IRE) Official explanation: jockey said gelding hung badly right

7481 CHRISTMAS PARTY NIGHTS AT KEMPTON H'CAP 1m (P)
7:30 (7:30) (Class 5) (0-70,70) 3-Y-0+ **£2,590** (£770; £385; £192) **Stalls** High

Form RPR

0000 **1** **Mr Hichens**[17] 7236 4-9-3 65 (p) DarryllHolland 8 74
(Karen George) *towards rr: hdwy over 2f out: chal ent 1f out: led ins fnl f: pushed out* **3/1**[1]

3363 **2** ¾ **Lord Of The Dance (IRE)**[7] 7403 3-8-9 59 (b[1]) HayleyTurner 6 66
(J M P Eustace) *chsd ldr: led gng wl over 2f out: rdn over 1f out: hdd and no ex ins fnl f* **3/1**[1]

0024 **3** *1* **Daniel Thomas (IRE)**[8] 7362 7-8-13 68 (p) RyanClark(7) 3 73
(Mrs A L M King) *stdd s: hld up bhd: hdwy whn nt clr run and swtchd lft over 1f out: r.o to go 3rd nr fin: nt rch ldrs* **11/1**

0550 **4** *nk* **Spiritofthewest (IRE)**[37] 6798 3-9-6 70 PhillipMakin 11 74
(D H Brown) *t.k.h: chsd ldrs: rdn and unable qckn 2f out: drvn and one pce fr over 1f out* **13/2**[3]

2004 **5** 1½ **Divinatore**[131] 3922 3-8-12 62 MartinDwyer 9 63
(D Haydn Jones) *bhd: rdn along over 3f out: hdwy ent fnl f: styd on: nt rch ldrs* **16/1**

0566 **6** *1* **Fiefdom (IRE)**[12] 7321 7-9-2 64 JimCrowley 1 62
(I W McInnes) *stdd s: hld up bhd: kpt on u.p fnl f: nvr trbld ldrs* **16/1**

6566 **7** 1½ **Lindy Hop (IRE)**[21] 7180 3-8-13 63 AdamKirby 4 58
(W R Swinburn) *t.k.h: chsd ldrs: rdn and unable qckn over 2f out: one pce after* **12/1**

5262 **8** 3¾ **Having A Ball**[17] 7236 5-9-3 65 SimonWhitworth 2 51
(P D Cundell) *hld up in midfield on outer: hdwy to chse ldrs 1/2-way: wknd u.p over 2f out* **15/2**

5061 **9** 3¾ **Dark Camellia**[18] 7228 4-8-12 60 (t) JimmyQuinn 10 37
(H J L Dunlop) *hld up in midfield: rdn and effrt on inner 2f out: wknd over 1f out* **14/1**

412- **10** 2¾ **Le Chiffre (IRE)**[408] 6598 7-9-5 67 (p) StephenDonohoe 7 37
(Miss Sheena West) *led tl rdn and hdd over 2f out: wknd qckly over 1f out* **6/1**[2]

1m 40.52s (0.72) **Going Correction** +0.025s/f (Slow)
WFA 3 from 4yo+ 2lb **10** Ran SP% **123.8**
Speed ratings (Par 103): **97,96,95,94,93 92,90,87,83,80**
toteswingers:1&2:£3.00, 2&3:£9.30, 1&3:£9.70 CSF £11.95 CT £91.34 TOTE £4.30: £1.90, £1.40, £5.10; EX 14.80 Place 6 £51.07, Place 5 £13.23.
Owner Adam Richard Wilson **Bred** C A Green **Trained** Higher Eastington, Devon

FOCUS
An open 56-70 handicap run at just an average pace.
T/Plt: £96.20 to a £1 stake. Pool: £57,084.58. 432.82 winning tickets. T/Qpdt: £18.50 to a £1 stake. Pool: £3,775.60. 151.00 winning tickets. SP

7433 LINGFIELD (L-H)

Saturday, November 21

OFFICIAL GOING: Standard

Wind: Brisk, half-behind. Weather: Overcast

7482 BETDAQ ON 0870 178 1221 (S) STKS — 1m (P)

12:00 (12:01) (Class 6) 2-Y-O — **£1,978** (£584; £292) **Stalls** High

Form RPR

0256 **1** **Whipperway (IRE)**[12] 7319 2-8-6 55 ....(v[1]) SamHitchcott 7 56
(M R Channon) *wl in tch: prog on outer over 2f out: drvn to cl over 1f out: narrow ld last 100yds: hld on* **7/1**

0002 **2** *shd* **Rainsborough**[10] 7334 2-9-2 64 ....(p) RobertWinston 8 66
(S Curran) *sn trckd ldng pair on outer: effrt to ld 2f out: drvn over 1f out: hdd last 100yds: kpt on wl: jst hld* **11/2**[3]

00 **3** *3/4* **Abigails Angel**[30] 6965 2-8-6 0 .... FrankieMcDonald 11 54
(B R Johnson) *stdd s: hld up wl in rr: nt clr run wl over 2f out: prog after: drvn and stl only 6th 1f out: styd on to take 3rd last 75yds* **100/1**

0620 **4** *2 1/4* **Bubbly Braveheart (IRE)**[37] 6793 2-8-11 64 ....(b) SteveDrowne 3 54
(A Bailey) *led: rdn and hdd 2f out: tried to press ldr after: wknd ins fnl f* **5/2**[1]

1200 **5** *1/2* **Aegean Destiny**[10] 7334 2-8-11 59 .... LiamJones 9 53
(R A Harris) *stdd s: dropped to inner and hld up in rr: prog 2f out: nt clr run briefly over 1f out: tried to cl on ldrs fnl f: fdd last 100yds* **12/1**

0504 **6** *1 1/2* **Spirit Land (IRE)**[10] 7334 2-8-6 55 .... AshleyMorgan(5) 1 50
(M H Tompkins) *cl up on inner: effrt 2f out: cl enough over 1f out: wknd ins fnl f* **20/1**

0060 **7** *6* **Knockback (IRE)**[40] 6736 2-8-11 51 .... JimCrowley 5 37
(P R Chamings) *towards rr on outer: prog over 3f out: rdn over 2f out: hanging and wknd over 1f out* **33/1**

03 **8** *hd* **Indigo Ink**[24] 7120 2-8-6 0 .... HayleyTurner 4 31
(Miss Amy Weaver) *t.k.h: trckd ldr to over 2f out: sn wknd* **7/2**[2]

5636 **9** *shd* **Mind The Monarch**[80] 5583 2-8-7 54 ow1 .... LPKeniry 10 32
(R A Teal) *chsd ldrs: u.p and lost pl fr 3f out: sn no ch* **16/1**

60 **10** *3 1/2* **No One Likes Us**[24] 7120 2-8-12 0 ow1 .... AdamKirby 12 29
(S Curran) *reluctant to enter stalls: rel to r and wl bhd: tk fierce hold and difficult to steer: nvr a factor* **20/1**

6204 **11** *2 3/4* **Mind Of Her Own**[12] 7319 2-8-1 60 .... AndrewHeffernan(5) 2 17
(P D Evans) *chsd ldrs to 1/2-way: sn wknd* **8/1**

1m 40.43s (2.23) **Going Correction** +0.125s/f (Slow) **11 Ran SP% 116.8**

Speed ratings (Par 94): **93,92,92,89,89 87,81,81,81,78 75**

toteswingers:1&2 £9.30, 2&3 £43.10, 1&3£82.30 CSF £43.13 TOTE £8.10: £2.70, £1.70, £17.20; EX 47.20 TRIFECTA Not won..There was no bid for the winner.

Owner Jon and Julia Aisbitt **Bred** Mesnil Investments Ltd And Deerpark Stud **Trained** West Ilsley, Berks

■ Stewards' Enquiry : Robert Winston caution: used whip with excessive frequency.

FOCUS

A moderate contest featuring only two previous winners.

NOTEBOOK

Whipperway(IRE) never built on the promise of her first two starts back in July, but the return to a mile in this lowly company, coupled with a visor to sharpen her up, did the trick. She'd looked lazy in her last two starts and responded well to the application of headgear, staying on well down the outside to edge ahead close home. (op 8-1)

Rainsborough, one of two who had won a race before, was kicked on turning into the straight and took a bit of passing. He's a consistent sort at this level. (op 9-2 tchd 6-1 & 13-2 in places)

Abigails Angel, beaten a long way in her first two starts in maiden company, shaped a lot better in this grade. She really got motoring in the straight and, as one of the least exposed in the field, at least has some potential for improvement.

Bubbly Braveheart(IRE), one of the best in at the weights, tried to make all but was a sitting duck turning into the straight. Two of his three best efforts have come when held up. (tchd 9-4 and 11-4 in places)

Aegean Destiny, who was again disappointing, didn't look to be helping her rider much in the closing stages. (tchd 14-1)

Indigo Ink failed to settle through the early part of the race and gave herself little chance of seeing out the trip. (op 4-1)

No One Likes Us Official explanation: jockey said gelding was slowly away, very keen and hung right

7483 BET INTERNATIONAL RUGBY - BETDAQ H'CAP (DIV I) — 6f (P)

12:25 (12:26) (Class 6) (0-60,64) 3-Y-0+ — **£1,637** (£483; £241) **Stalls** Low

Form RPR

0462 **1** **Ask Jenny (IRE)**[8] 7370 7-8-12 54 .... JamieSpencer 10 62
(Patrick Morris) *stdd s: hld up in last: stl there over 1f out: taken to wd outside and drvn fnl f: storming run last 150yds to ld post* **11/1**

4005 **2** *hd* **Pocket's Pick (IRE)**[15] 7270 3-9-2 58 .... RyanMoore 6 65
(G L Moore) *towards rr: drvn and prog on wd outside over 2f out: sustained chal fnl f: led nr fin: hdd post* **8/1**[2]

0501 **3** *nk* **Punching**[4] 7424 5-9-8 64 6ex .... LPKeniry 5 70
(C R Dore) *trckd ldrs gng strly: nt clr run over 1f out and swtchd lft: drvn to ld jst ins fnl f: hdd nr fin* **11/4**[1]

0000 **4** *1/2* **After The Show**[10] 7337 8-9-1 57 .... EddieAhern 7 62
(Rae Guest) *hld up: progres into midfield 1/2-way: cl enough whn rdn and nt qckn over 1f out: styd on wl last 150yds but nvr quite pce to chal* **10/1**

5350 **5** *hd* **Lord Deevert**[20] 7203 4-9-1 60 .... JackDean(3) 4 64
(W G M Turner) *pressed ldr on inner: drvn to ld wl over 1f out: hdd jst ins fnl f: kpt on wl but lost pls nr fin* **17/2**[3]

0504 **6** *nk* **Pinball (IRE)**[17] 7241 3-8-13 55 ....(v) RobertWinston 3 58
(Mrs L Williamson) *dwlt: hld up in rr: prog over 2f out: chsng ldrs whn hmpd over 1f out: tried to chal fnl f: one pce last 100yds* **25/1**

6130 **7** *1 1/2* **Briannsta (IRE)**[8] 7370 7-8-12 54 .... RichardThomas 9 52
(J E Long) *mostly in last pair: rdn over 2f out: styd on fr over 1f out: nt pce to trble ldrs* **14/1**

4000 **8** *3/4* **Cosmic Destiny (IRE)**[37] 6791 7-9-2 58 .... TPQueally 1 54
(E F Vaughan) *wl in tch on inner: trckd ldrs 2f out: effrt to chal 1f out and virtually upsides: wknd last 100yds* **16/1**

0303 **9** *1/2* **Embra (IRE)**[18] 7224 4-9-1 57 .... GregFairley 2 51
(T J Etherington) *hmpd after 1f: snatched up and lost pl: effrt 2f out: cl up whn nt clr run over 1f out: steadily lost pl fnl f* **8/1**[2]

4000 **10** *3/4* **Golden Dixie (USA)**[23] 7138 10-9-1 57 ....(p) DavidProbert 8 49
(R A Harris) *a towards rr: struggling in last pair 2f out* **14/1**

1341 **11** *1 3/4* **Decider (USA)**[7] 7397 6-9-7 63 ....(p) LiamJones 11 49
(R A Harris) *wl away fr wd draw: led to wl over 1f out: eased whn wkng ins fnl f* **8/1**[2]

321 **12** *1/2* **Malapropism**[26] 7069 9-9-0 56 .... SamHitchcott 12 41
(M R Channon) *drvn to go prom fr wdst draw: u.p over 2f out: sn lost pl and btn* **12/1**

1m 12.95s (1.05) **Going Correction** +0.125s/f (Slow) **12 Ran SP% 118.7**

Speed ratings (Par 101): **98,97,97,96,96 96,94,93,92,91 89,88**

toteswingers:1&2:£14.90, 2&3:£5.70, 1&3:£4.90 CSF £96.40 CT £319.53 TOTE £8.10: £2.60, £3.20, £1.20; EX 129.20 TRIFECTA Not won..

Owner W J Crosbie **Bred** Mrs J Costelloe **Trained** Tarporley, Cheshire

FOCUS

There was a good pace on here and it played into the hands of a closer.

Punching Official explanation: vet said gelding had been struck into

Lord Deevert Official explanation: jockey said gelding hung right

Golden Dixie(USA) Official explanation: jockey said gelding hung right

7484 BET INTERNATIONAL RUGBY - BETDAQ H'CAP (DIV II) — 6f (P)

12:50 (12:53) (Class 6) (0-60,63) 3-Y-0+ — **£1,637** (£483; £241) **Stalls** Low

Form RPR

0351 **1** **Fantasy Fighter (IRE)**[8] 7370 4-8-13 55 .... JimmyQuinn 5 67
(J J Quinn) *trckd ldrs gng strly: effrt over 1f out: rdn to ld last 150yds: flashed tail but styd on: jst hld on* **3/1**[2]

0001 **2** *hd* **Elusive Ronnie (IRE)**[3] 7427 3-8-9 54 6ex ....(b) JackMitchell(3) 12 65
(R A Teal) *hld up in last and wl off the pce: stl last wl over 1f out: storming run fnl f: needed two more strides* **9/1**[3]

6032 **3** *2 3/4* **Forest Dane**[10] 7330 9-9-7 63 .... GeorgeBaker 2 66
(Mrs N Smith) *trckd ldrs: effrt 2f out: chal and upsides ent fnl f: outpcd* **5/2**[1]

00 **4** *1/2* **Makshoof (IRE)**[9] 7348 5-9-0 56 ....(p) JimCrowley 8 57
(I W McInnes) *blindfold late off: hld up in last trio: pushed along and no real prog over 1f out: shkn up and styd on last 150yds: nvr nr ldrs* **20/1**

0306 **5** *shd* **Romantic Queen**[15] 7273 3-8-13 60 ....(t) MatthewDavies(5) 4 61+
(George Baker) *bmpd after 150yds: in tch on inner: effrt over 1f out but hanging: clsng on ldrs whn short of room ins fnl f: nt rcvr* **16/1**

4000 **6** *3/4* **Hart Of Gold**[10] 7329 5-9-0 56 ....(p) LiamJones 11 54
(R A Harris) *hld up in last trio: effrt on outer 2f out: no real imp fnl f* **12/1**

0005 **7** *hd* **Grand Palace (IRE)**[28] 7023 6-9-2 58 ....(v) VinceSlattery 6 56
(H J Evans) *pressed ldr: led on inner over 1f out: hdd & wknd last 150yds* **16/1**

0500 **8** *3/4* **Fortina's Boy (USA)**[49] 6492 3-9-2 58 .... AdamKirby 10 53
(W R Swinburn) *mde most: hdd over 1f out: btn whn n.m.r ins fnl f and eased* **12/1**

30U0 **9** *3/4* **Radiator Rooney (IRE)**[18] 7224 6-9-1 57 .... SJCraine 1 50
(Patrick Morris) *hmpd after 150yds but stl cl up bhd ldrs: effrt on inner 2 out: nt qckn over 1f out: fdd* **40/1**

5306 **10** *2* **Monte Major (IRE)**[15] 7280 8-9-0 59 ....(v) MartinLane(3) 9 45
(D Shaw) *drvn in midfield bef 1/2-way: a struggling to stay in tch after* **16/1**

0304 **11** *1 1/2* **Sweet Kiss (USA)**[15] 7270 4-8-11 53 .... NCallan 7 35
(M J Attwater) *bmpd after 150yds: chsd ldrs: rdn over 2f out: wknd over 1f out* **20/1**

1m 13.09s (1.19) **Going Correction** +0.125s/f (Slow) **11 Ran SP% 108.6**

Speed ratings (Par 101): **97,96,93,92,92 91,91,90,89,86 84**

toteswingers:1&2:£5.00, 2&3:£4.40, 1&3:£1.60 CSF £25.55 CT £65.82 TOTE £4.20: £1.60, £2.80, £1.20; EX 23.80 Trifecta £21.20 Pool: £155.05 -5.40 winning units.

Owner The Fantasy Fellowship F **Bred** T C Clarke **Trained** Settrington, N Yorks

■ Accroostheuniverse (10/1) was withdrawn (broke out of stalls). R4 applies, deduct 5p in the £.

■ Stewards' Enquiry : Vince Slattery three-day ban: careless riding (Dec 5-7)

FOCUS

Marginally the slower of the two divisions.

7485 EBF XMAS GIFTS FROM CHRISTIANCHOICEONLINE.COM MAIDEN STKS — 5f (P)

1:25 (1:27) (Class 5) 2-Y-O — **£3,885** (£1,156; £577; £288) **Stalls** High

Form RPR

563 **1** **Sakile**[8] 7365 2-8-12 68 .... JamieSpencer 4 77
(P W Chapple-Hyam) *mde all: drvn and hrd pressed fnl f: hld on wl* **3/1**[2]

002 **2** *hd* **Youcanalwaysdream (IRE)**[8] 7365 2-8-12 68 .... NCallan 2 76+
(K A Ryan) *trckd ldng pair: effrt on inner 2f out but no room and hmpd: wnt 2nd over 1f out: persistent chal fnl f: didn't find enough* **10/3**[3]

243 **3** *2 3/4* **Zubova**[110] 4603 2-8-12 77 .... RyanMoore 9 66
(R Hannon) *sn w wnr: rdn 2f out: nt qckn and lost 2nd over 1f out: one pce after* **5/4**[1]

30 **4** *8* **Slip Sliding Away (IRE)**[10] 7325 2-9-3 0 .... SteveDrowne 3 43
(J R Best) *dwlt: hld up in last pair: outpcd after 2f out: rdn and kpt on to take v modest 4th ins fnl f* **15/2**

0 **5** *1 3/4* **Wild Heather**[78] 5638 2-8-12 0 .... JerryO'Dwyer 5 31
(J R Holt) *chsd ldrs: outpcd after 2f: n.d after: lost v modest 4th ins fnl f* **66/1**

6 *1* **Ruler's Honour (IRE)** 2-9-3 0 .... GregFairley 6 33
(T J Etherington) *reluctant to enter stalls: s.s: mostly in last pair and wl outpcd bef 1/2-way* **33/1**

0 **7** *8* **Lets Move It**[12] 7317 2-9-3 0 .... AdamKirby 1 4
(D Shaw) *sn pushed along: outpcd after 2f: wknd 2f out* **66/1**

0 **8** *9* **Stoneacre Joe (IRE)**[50] 6443 2-9-3 0 .... LPKeniry 8 —
(Peter Grayson) *chsd ldrs: outpcd after 2f: wknd 2f out: t.o* **66/1**

59.40 secs (0.60) **Going Correction** +0.125s/f (Slow) **8 Ran SP% 111.7**

Speed ratings (Par 96): **100,99,95,82,79 78,65,50**

toteswingers:1&2:£2.50, 2&3:£1.80, 1&3:£1.50 CSF £12.65 TOTE £4.00: £1.30, £1.40, £1.20; EX 11.90 Trifecta £21.40 Pool: £676.42 - 23.34 winning units.

Owner C G P Wyatt **Bred** Charlie Wyatt **Trained** Newmarket, Suffolk

FOCUS

A modest maiden and a three-horse race from some way out.

NOTEBOOK

Sakile finished a short head behind Youcanalwaysdream when the pair filled the places in a similar heat here last time. Once again there was little between them, but the verdict went the way of Peter Chapple-Hyam's filly on this occasion. On the evidence of what we've seen so far, the minimum trip seems to be as far as she wants to go for the time being. (op 5-2 tchd 9-4)

Youcanalwaysdream(IRE) showed major improvement to go close last time out and looks to have run to a similar level here, just failing to confirm form with Sakile. Nevertheless, she once again showed enough to suggest a similarly modest maiden can come her way this winter. (tchd 3-1 and 7-2)

Zubova had the worst of the draw and had been off the track since August, but she was given a positive ride and tried to dispute it with the winner out in front. She struggled to match her pace, though, and looks sure to benefit from a return to 6f. (op 11-8 tchd 6-4 and 6-5)

Slip Sliding Away(IRE), down 2f in distance, was ridden patiently before staying on. He's now eligible for a mark and will be of far more interest in handicaps. (op 8-1 tchd 10-1)

Ruler's Honour(IRE) Official explanation: jockey said gelding ran green

7486 LINGFIELD PARK OWNERS CLUB LAUNCHES TODAY H'CAP 7f (P)

1:55 (1:55) (Class 2) (0-100,95) 3-Y-O+ **£11,527** (£3,430; £1,714; £856) **Stalls** Low

Form RPR

2104 **1** **Elna Bright**[18] 7226 4-8-10 **86** KFallon 4 99
(B R Johnson) *hld up in 5th and last of those in tch: prog and nt clr run briefly wl over 1f out: sn chsd ldr: clsd readily to ld last 100yds: sn clr* **8/1**

41 **2** 1 ½ **Jonny Mudball**[26] 7067 3-8-12 **89** RichardKingscote 8 98
(Tom Dascombe) *led at str pce and spreadeagled field: over 2 l up 2f out: hdd and no ex last 100yds* **5/2**[1]

2062 **3** 2 ½ **Everymanforhimself (IRE)**[42] 6675 5-9-5 **95** (v) JamieSpencer 7 97
(K A Ryan) *s.i.s: wl off the pce in 7th: rdn over 2f out: styd on wl to take 3rd nr fin: no ch* **4/1**[2]

2006 **4** 1 ¾ **Fathsta (IRE)**[16] 7252 4-8-9 **85** EddieAhern 1 82
(D M Simcock) *taken down early: chsd ldr: rdn over 2f out: fdd and lost 2nd over 1f out* **9/2**[3]

6402 **5** 1 **Carcinetto (IRE)**[3] 7431 7-8-13 **94** RichardEvans(5) 6 89
(P D Evans) *chsd ldng trio: rdn wl over 2f out: lost tch wl over 1f out: no ch after* **14/1**

3311 **6** 1 ½ **Hellbender (IRE)**[16] 7252 3-8-4 **81** oh3 MartinDwyer 5 72
(S Kirk) *sn pushed along in 6th: nvr on terms w ldrs: no imp over 1f out* **11/1**

0040 **7** ½ **Orchard Supreme**[43] 6633 6-9-0 **90** RyanMoore 3 79
(R Hannon) *settled in 8th and wl off the pce: shkn up 2f out: no real prog and nvr nr ldrs* **8/1**

530 **8** 3 ½ **Flowing Cape (IRE)**[8] 7375 4-9-5 **95** RobertWinston 2 75
(R Hollinshead) *chsd ldng pair: rdn wl over 2f out: wknd wl over 1f out* **8/1**

5000 **9** 11 **Jet D'Eau (FR)**[28] 7032 3-9-1 **92** (b) GeorgeBaker 9 42
(G L Moore) *stdd s: hld up in last and wl off the pce: rdn 1/2-way: no prog: eased over 1f out: t.o* **25/1**

1m 23.79s (-1.01) **Going Correction** +0.125s/f (Slow)
WFA 3 from 4yo+ 1lb **9** Ran SP% **118.9**
Speed ratings (Par 109): **110,108,105,103,102 100,100,96,83**
toteswingers:1&2:£6.80, 2&3:£2.70, 1&3:£6.10 CSF £29.24 CT £95.47 TOTE £11.20: £2.40, £1.40, £2.00; EX 41.30 Trifecta £318.10 Part won. Pool £429.95 - 0.65 winning units..
Owner Peter Crate **Bred** D R Tucker **Trained** Ashtead, Surrey

FOCUS

They were well strung out from an early stage in this handicap as Jonny Mudball took them along at a real good gallop.

NOTEBOOK

Elna Bright stays further than this and appreciated the way the race was run. Only 2lb higher than when successful at Ascot in September, he's done well since joining his current stable in August, and is likely to remain fairly handicapped on his best form even after being reassessed for this win. (op 9-1 tchd 10-1)

Jonny Mudball, who made all to win a maiden over the C&D last time out, attempted to repeat the trick on his handicap debut. It was a brave effort and, although he found one too good for him on the day, he clearly has the ability to win a similar race off his current mark. (op 11-4)

Everymanforhimself(IRE) struggled with the early gallop but found them coming back to him in the latter stages. He finished well for third and, although he's done all his winning over sprint distances, clearly stays this trip well these days. Official explanation: jockey said gelding never travelled (op 3-1 tchd 9-2)

Fathsta(IRE) raced keenly through the early stages, eager to lead. He's dropped back to his last winning mark, but will have to settle better if he's to take advantage. Official explanation: jockey said gelding hung right (op 10-1)

Carcinetto(IRE) is being kept busy. Her current mark leaves little room for error. (op 12-1 tchd 16-1)

Flowing Cape(IRE) paid for trying to keep up with the trail-blazing leader. (op 13-2)

Jet D'Eau(FR) Official explanation: jockey said filly had no more to give

7487 EUROPEAN BREEDERS' FUND FILLIES' H'CAP 1m (P)

2:30 (2:30) (Class 4) (0-85,83) 3-Y-O+ **£4,727** (£1,406; £702; £351) **Stalls** High

Form RPR

5653 **1** **My Best Bet**[29] 6997 3-8-13 **76** TPQueally 7 82
(Stef Liddiard) *hld up in last pair: prog 2f out to chse ldr jst over 1f out: rdn to ld last 100yds: won gng away* **15/2**[3]

0600 **2** 1 **Nora Mae (IRE)**[9] 7356 3-8-13 **76** RyanMoore 4 80
(S Kirk) *led 3f: trckd ldr: led again over 1f out: edgd rt and hdd last 100yds: one pce* **11/4**[1]

5600 **3** 1 ¼ **Daddy's Gift (IRE)**[7] 7394 3-9-6 **83** SteveDrowne 6 84
(R Hannon) *hld up last: effrt 2f out: rdn and prog to take 3rd ins fnl f: nvr able to chal* **14/1**

6221 **4** nk **Spiritual Art**[8] 7364 3-8-12 **75** (p) PaulDoe 3 75
(L A Dace) *s.i.s: sn cl up: rdn over 2f out: tried to cl on ldrs 1f out: kpt on same pce* **11/4**[1]

0111 **5** 4 ½ **Ocean Countess (IRE)**[30] 6968 3-8-1 **67** AndreaAtzeni(3) 1 56
(Miss J Feilden) *trckd ldrs on inner: pushed along 3f out: no imp over 1f out: wknd* **8/1**

3523 **6** 1 ½ **Support Fund (IRE)**[18] 7229 5-8-7 **68** EddieAhern 5 53
(Eve Johnson Houghton) *s.i.s: sn cl up: lost pl 2f out: wknd fnl f* **9/2**[2]

4014 **7** ¾ **Beautiful Filly**[22] 7158 3-8-4 **70** (b) MartinLane(3) 2 54
(D M Simcock) *trckd ldr: led 5f out to over 1f out: wknd rapidly* **8/1**

1m 39.23s (1.03) **Going Correction** +0.125s/f (Slow)
WFA 3 from 5yo 2lb **7** Ran SP% **112.2**
Speed ratings (Par 102): **99,98,96,96,91 90,89**
toteswingers:1&2:£4.50, 2&3:£7.70, 1&3:£10.50 CSF £27.32 TOTE £7.80: £3.60, £1.60; EX 34.20.
Owner Mrs Stef Liddiard **Bred** Phil Jen Racing **Trained** Great Shefford, Berks

FOCUS

They went no more than a fair pace here and were well bunched turning in.

7488 BETDAQ GOLDEN ROSE STKS (LISTED RACE) 6f (P)

3:05 (3:07) (Class 1) 3-Y-O+

£22,708 (£8,608; £4,308; £2,148; £1,076; £540) **Stalls** Low

Form RPR

1100 **1** **Jaconet (USA)**[56] 6283 4-8-11 102 (b) PhillipMakin 6 107
(T D Barron) *fast away: mde all but nt at breakneck pce: kicked on over 2f out: maintained gallop to fin: unchal* **6/1**[2]

0031 **2** 2 ¼ **Ebraam (USA)**[9] 7358 6-9-2 95 MartinDwyer 2 105
(Mike Murphy) *t.k.h early: chsd wnr: rdn and no imp fr 2f out: kpt on to hold on for 2nd* **20/1**

-663 **3** ¾ **Himalya (IRE)**[22] 7150 3-9-2 104 RyanMoore 4 102
(J Noseda) *hld up in 9th: prog fr 2f out: styd on wl to take 3rd last 50yds: no ch* **9/1**

5322 **4** ¾ **Son Of The Cat (USA)**[7] 7394 3-9-2 92 (t) DarrylHolland 1 100
(B Gubby) *sn in midfield: effrt on inner 2f out: kpt on fr over 1f out: n.d* **9/1**

5201 **5** ½ **Arganil (USA)**[29] 7007 4-9-4 108 NCallan 5 100
(K A Ryan) *t.k.h early: chsd wnr: rdn and no imp fr 2f out: fdd fnl f* **4/1**[1]

34 **6** shd **Prescription**[14] 7292 4-8-11 96 StephenDonohoe 7 93+
(Sir Mark Prescott) *dwlt: hld up in last trio: plenty to do whn nt clr run over 2f out: prog over 1f out: kpt on: no ch* **7/1**[3]

3-00 **7** ½ **Sir Gerry (USA)**[14] 7292 4-9-2 107 RobertWinston 8 96
(J R Best) *n.m.r after 2f: chsd ldrs: rdn over 2f out: no prog over 1f out: fdd* **10/1**

0411 **8** 1 ½ **Fullandby (IRE)**[14] 7292 7-9-4 99 GregFairley 3 94+
(T J Etherington) *blindfold late off and dwlt: pushed along in last: no ch after pce qcknd over 2f out: modest late prog* **8/1**

6001 **9** ½ **Rowe Park**[25] 7090 6-9-2 104 SteveDrowne 11 90+
(Mrs L C Jewell) *dwlt: hld up in last pair: no ch after pce qcknd over 2f out: prog on outer and looked to have pl ch ent fnl f: wknd last 100yds* **20/1**

5103 **10** 1 ½ **Ceremonial Jade (UAE)**[204] 1640 6-9-4 105 (t) KFallon 10 87
(M Botti) *hld up in 8th on outer: struggling after pce qcknd over 2f out: no prog after* **9/1**

-246 **11** ¾ **Turn On The Style**[25] 7090 7-9-2 103 (b) EddieAhern 9 83
(J Balding) *hld up in midfield: rdn and no prog 2f out: wknd jst over 1f out* **12/1**

4514 **12** 6 **Green Manalishi**[10] 7341 8-9-2 105 (p) JamieSpencer 12 64
(K A Ryan) *t.k.h: chsd ldng trio: rdn over 2f out: wknd wl over 1f out* **8/1**

1m 10.46s (-1.44) **Going Correction** +0.125s/f (Slow) course record**12** Ran SP% **125.3**
Speed ratings (Par 111): **114,111,110,109,108 108,107,105,104,102 101,93**
toteswingers:1&2:£5.70, 2&3:£3.50, 1&3:£5.80 CSF £126.41 TOTE £9.30: £3.00, £9.30, £3.00; EX 225.80 TRIFECTA Not won..
Owner R G Toes **Bred** Team Block **Trained** Maunby, N Yorks

FOCUS

A competitive Listed event on paper, with nine of the 12 runners separated by just 6lb on adjusted official ratings, but the winner dominated throughout.

NOTEBOOK

Jaconet(USA), who was one of the best in at the weights, didn't let the rest get a look in, making every yard for an eased-down success. Dangerous when allowed an uncontested lead, she's only beaten once in five starts on Polytrack and is more than a stone better on this surface than on turf. (op 5-1 tchd 7-1)

Ebraam(USA), picked up for £18,000 after bolting up in a claimer at Wolverhampton last time out, got a big chunk of that purchase price back for his new connections with a fine effort up in class. He was always well placed tracking the leader in a race dominated by her, though. (tchd 25-1)

Himalya(IRE), who again was ponied to the start, had plenty to do entering the straight, but he stayed on well between horses in the closing stages. He hasn't fulfilled the potential of his injury-curtailed juvenile career, but retains ability and remains relatively unexposed. (op 12-1 tchd 8-1)

Son Of The Cat(USA) has been performing at a consistent level since the summer and this was another solid effort. He might not be that easy to place any longer off his current mark, but he helps set the level of this form. (tchd 10-1)

Arganil(USA), a winner at this level at Dundalk last time, has won six of his nine starts over the minimum trip but just one of his seven starts over further. (op 5-1 tchd 6-1)

Prescription, steadily progressive this term, didn't enjoy the smoothest of passages through the race but finished quite well and left the impression she's capable of better. (op 15-2 tchd 8-1 and 13-2)

Sir Gerry(USA), who was entitled to need the run at Doncaster following a six-month absence, also had the excuse of being struck into that day. Running on Polytrack for the first time, he didn't run badly, although clearly remains well below his best. (op 14-1)

Fullandby(IRE) broke awkwardly from the stalls and struggled to get competitive.

Ceremonial Jade(UAE) got stuck racing wide from stall ten. (op 17-2 tchd 8-1)

Green Manalishi did too much too soon trying to overcome his outside stall. (op 17-2)

7489 BETDAQ CHURCHILL STKS (LISTED RACE) 1m 2f (P)

3:40 (3:41) (Class 1) 3-Y-O+

£22,708 (£8,608; £4,308; £2,148; £1,076; £540) **Stalls** Low

Form RPR

1303 **1** **Tranquil Tiger**[82] 5508 5-9-4 112 (b) TPQueally 1 108
(H R A Cecil) *hld up in 5th: prog to 2nd over 3f out: decisive move to ld over 2f out: drvn and edgd rt fnl f but wl in command* **11/2**[3]

1212 **2** 3 **Presvis**[188] 2117 5-9-10 120 KFallon 7 108
(L M Cumani) *dwlt: hld up in last gp and wl off the pce: pushed along 3f out: prog fr 2f out: styd on fnl f to take 2nd last strides* **4/5**[1]

0606 **3** nk **Suits Me**[21] 7188 6-9-2 106 DarryllHolland 4 99
(T P Tate) *chsd clr ldr to over 3f out: kpt on u.p fr over 2f out to chse wnr ins fnl f: no imp: lost 2nd last strides* **10/1**

0421 **4** ¾ **Beauchamp Viceroy**[26] 7054 5-9-2 82 (b) JerryO'Dwyer 6 98
(G A Butler) *led at str pce and sn spreadeagled field: hdd over 2f out: grad fdd over 1f out* **25/1**

1352 **5** ½ **Plum Pudding (IRE)**[17] 7245 6-9-2 109 RyanMoore 8 97
(R Hannon) *hld up in rr gp and wl off the pce: rdn 3f out: styd on fnl 2f: nrst fin but no ch* **5/1**[2]

5511 **6** 1 **Tinshu (IRE)**[8] 7366 3-8-7 81 MartinDwyer 2 90
(D Haydn Jones) *disp 3rd bhd clr ldrs to over 3f out: kpt on in chsers to over 1f out: fdd* **18/1**

6664 **7** 13 **Lucky Dance (BRZ)**[21] 7185 7-9-2 82 RobertWinston 5 69
(A G Foster) *disp 3rd bhd clr ldrs: rdn over 3f out: wknd over 2f out: t.o* **50/1**

0503 **8** 2 ¾ **General Eliott (IRE)**[17] 7245 4-9-2 105 (p) NCallan 9 63
(P F I Cole) *hld up in rr gp and wl off the pce: u.p in last 3f out: t.o* **20/1**

1243 **9** nk **Beauchamp Xerxes**[17] 7237 3-8-12 101 (t) JamieSpencer 3 63
(G A Butler) *dwlt: hld up in rr gp and wl off the pce: struggling u.p wl over 2f out: t.o* **10/1**

2m 4.67s (-1.93) **Going Correction** +0.125s/f (Slow)
WFA 3 from 4yo+ 4lb **9** Ran SP% **121.6**
Speed ratings (Par 111): **112,109,109,108,108 107,97,94,94**
totewingers:1&2:£2.10, 2&3:£5.30, 1&3:£7.70. CSF £10.67 TOTE £6.20: £1.70, £1.20, £2.30; EX 12.20 Trifecta £178.90 Pool: £1,407.73 - 5.82 winning units. Place 6 £24.38, Place 5 £4.72.
Owner K Abdulla **Bred** Juddmonte Farms Ltd **Trained** Newmarket, Suffolk

NOTEBOOK

Tranquil Tiger, who only had 2lb to find with Presvis at these weights based on official figures, made full use of his edge in fitness over him, quickening away approaching the turn into the straight and building a healthy advantage that the favourite was unable to bridge. This is his level - his form figures in Listed company now read 51412121131, while in Group races they read an uninspiring 804557 - and he seems to go well fresh, so it was to his benefit that he'd been given a bit of a break since his last outing at Epsom. He looks the sort that could pay his way out in Dubai early next year. (op 5-1 tchd 4-1)

Presvis, although officially best in at the weights despite his penalty, hadn't run since May, was fully entitled to need the outing and his connections had made it clear that this race was very much a prep for next month's Hong Kong Cup. Despite that, he was expected by many to outclass his opposition on a track which plays to his strengths. Held up towards the back, he was within striking distance of the winner running down the hill, but got outpaced when that rival quickened to the front and, although he stayed on under a considerate ride, the winner was long gone. His trainer said he was pleased enough and the plan remains to fly out to Hong Kong next, followed by a campaign in Dubai, and a return to Hong Kong and Singapore in the spring. He's a genuine Group 1 performer with a smart turn of foot at his best and, despite this slight reverse, should still be a major contender out in the Far East, although his connections will no doubt be hoping for plenty of pace and luck in running for this confirmed hold-up horse. (tchd Evens and 11-10 in a place)
Suits Me, whose last win came in a three-runner Listed race over this C&D in February, couldn't match the winner's turn of pace rounding the turn into the straight but kept battling away. He would have preferred to have made the running, but had to settle for tracking Beauchamp Viceroy. (op 12-1)
Beauchamp Viceroy was representing Gerard Butler, successful trainer in this race five times in the previous ten years. Carrying the owner's second colours, he set a good gallop out in front and, having been caught, didn't collapse in a heap. It was a fine effort on this big step up in class and, while his performance does put something of a question mark on the overall value of the form, it didn't look to be a fluke. (op 40-1)
Plum Pudding(IRE) normally likes to cut out the running, but he was ridden patiently this time in an attempt to help him get the longer trip. He was keeping on at the finish, but whether he really wants to go this far is open to question. (op 15-2)
Tinshu(IRE) came here chasing a hat-trick, but this was a big step up in class from the handicaps she'd won earlier this month. (op 22-1 tchd 16-1)
General Eliott(IRE) Official explanation: jockey said gelding hung right
Beauchamp Xerxes, brother of Beauchamp Viceroy, was the better fancied of the two but, having been held up out the back, he was disappointingly unable to make up ground in the closing stages. The tongue tie he wore for the first time here hints at issues with his breathing. (op 12-1)
T/Plt: £42.80 to a £1 stake. Pool: £48,099.88. 818.69 winning tickets. T/Qpdt: £6.10 to a £1 stake. Pool: £4,190.30. 504.80 winning tickets. JN

7459 WOLVERHAMPTON (A.W) (L-H)

Saturday, November 21

OFFICIAL GOING: Standard

Wind: Moderate, half-behind Weather: Heavy rain ceased before racing

7490 OVER 50 INSTANT GAMES AT TOTESPORTGAMES.COM H'CAP (DIV I) 1m 4f 50y(P)

6:15 (6:15) (Class 6) (0-65,65) 3-Y-0+ **£2,047** (£604; £302) **Stalls** Low

Form RPR

6001 **1** **Shadows Lengthen**[4] 7425 3-8-9 **58** 6ex................(b) GrahamGibbons 2 69
(M W Easterby) *racd keenly: wnt 2nd over 8f out: led over 4f out: rdn ins fnl f: r.o* **13/8**[1]

000 **2** *1 ¼* **Bull Market (IRE)**[38] 6780 6-9-8 **65**.................................... LiamJones 1 74
(M S Tuck) *hld up in tch: chsd wnr jst over 3f out: rdn and nt qckn ins fnl f* **11/2**[2]

4003 **3** *4* **Kames Park (IRE)**[32] 6917 7-8-13 **56**................................ JoeFanning 8 59
(R C Guest) *s.i.s: sn hld up in mid-div: smooth prog 3f out: shkn up over 1f out: one pce* **12/1**

2305 **4** *hd* **Arashi**[5] 7413 3-9-1 **64**...(p) DavidProbert 3 66
(Lucinda Featherstone) *hld up towards rr: pushed along and hdwy over 2f out: rdn wl over 1f out: one pce fnl f* **11/2**[2]

0600 **5** *2 ¾* **Rare Coincidence**[30] 6767 8-9-2 **59**..............................(tp) EddieAhern 6 57
(R F Fisher) *led after 1f: hdd over 4f out: rdn over 2f out: wknd wl over 1f out* **28/1**

011 **6** *7* **Nakoma (IRE)**[9] 7357 7-9-6 **63**... TomEaves 12 50
(B Ellison) *hld up in tch: pushed along and wknd over 2f out* **15/2**[3]

5616 **7** *5* **Hucking Hero (IRE)**[8] 7368 4-9-3 **60**.............................(p) SJCraine 9 39
(J R Boyle) *hld up in rr: rdn over 2f out: sn struggling* **14/1**

5420 **8** *7* **Piper's Song (IRE)**[45] 5947 6-8-11 **54**........................... PaulHanagan 7 21
(Patrick Morris) *hld up towards rr: rdn and struggling over 2f out* **22/1**

0001 **9** *7* **Zaif (IRE)**[13] 6969 6-8-10 **60**.......................................(p) BillyCray(7) 5 16
(D J S Ffrench Davis) *a in rr: lost tch 5f out: eased wl over 1f out* **22/1**

0/32 **10** *2 ¼* **Ishismart**[10] 7318 5-8-5 **51** oh1...................................... AndreaAtzeni(3) 4 4
(R Hollinshead) *led 1f: prom tl rdn and wknd over 3f out: eased wl over 1f out* **14/1**

2m 39.91s (-1.19) **Going Correction** -0.025s/f (Stan)
WFA 3 from 4yo+ 6lb **10** Ran SP% **113.8**
Speed ratings (Par 101): **102,101,98,98,96 91,88,83,79,77**
toteswingers: 1&2 £1.50, 1&3 £8.40, 2&3 £18.20 CSF £9.68 CT £78.20 TOTE £2.50: £1.30, £1.70, £3.40; EX 12.30.
Owner T A F Frost **Bred** London Thoroughbred Services Ltd **Trained** Sheriff Hutton, N Yorks

FOCUS
Plenty of rain fell at the track before racing but the final time coupled with the ordinary gallop suggests the surface was as the official. A couple of in-form performers in a modest handicap and the winner came down the centre in the straight.
Zaif(IRE) Official explanation: jockey said gelding never travelled

7491 TOTESPORTBINGO.COM MAIDEN STKS 1m 141y(P)

6:45 (6:57) (Class 5) 2-Y-0 **£3,238** (£963; £481; £240) **Stalls** Low

Form RPR

02 **1** **Bowdler's Magic**[7] 7400 2-9-3 0... JoeFanning 6 73
(M Johnston) *mde all: pushed along over 1f out: rdn ins fnl f: r.o wl* **11/4**[2]

5 **2** *2* **Oriental Scot**[29] 6991 2-9-3 0.. LiamJones 2 69
(W Jarvis) *hld up in tch: pushed along over 2f out: rdn to chse wnr 1f out: no imp* **13/8**[1]

0 **3** *1 ¼* **Bonded (IRE)**[28] 7034 2-9-3 0.. EddieAhern 13 66
(B J Meehan) *hld up in mid-div: pushed along over 2f out: hdwy on ins wl over 1f out: swtchd rt ent fnl f: kpt on* **20/1**

0 **4** *6* **Rainbow Six**[15] 7277 2-9-0 0.................................... AndreaAtzeni(3) 3 54
(M Botti) *chsd wnr tl over 6f out: prom: wnt 2nd again over 2f out: rdn wl over 1f out: wknd ins fnl f* **40/1**

5 *½* **Fairy Flight (USA)** 2-8-12 0.. PaulHanagan 9 48
(W J Knight) *s.i.s: hld up in rr: pushed along and sme hdwy over 2f out: nvr nr ldrs* **22/1**

20 **6** *½* **Jamarjo (IRE)**[77] 5674 2-9-3 0.. TomEaves 7 51
(S Gollings) *prom: pushed along over 3f out: wknd wl over 1f out* **25/1**

50 **7** *nse* **Cheyenne Chant**[7] 7396 2-8-5 0.................................... RosieJessop(7) 11 46
(Sir Mark Prescott) *prom: chsd wnr over 6f out tl pushed along over 2f out: wknd wl over 1f out* **100/1**

8 *4 ½* **Senate** 2-9-3 0.. NickyMackay 5 42
(J H M Gosden) *dwlt: a in rr* **7/2**[3]

4 **9** *1* **Jazz Age (IRE)**[31] 6931 2-8-10 0............................... JonathanHinch(7) 4 40
(J A Glover) *s.i.s whn rdr sltly late removing blindfold: hld up in rr: pushed along 3f out: no ch fnl 2f* **7/1**

10 *1 ¼* **Minimusic** 2-8-12 0.. NeilChalmers 8 32
(B Palling) *hld up in mid-div: pushed along over 3f out: sn bhd* **100/1**

11 *16* **Riccoche (IRE)** 2-8-12 0... FrancisNorton 12 —
(J H M Gosden) *s.i.s: a in rr: rdn and lost tch 3f out* **16/1**

1m 52.02s (1.52) **Going Correction** -0.025s/f (Stan) **11** Ran SP% **122.7**
Speed ratings (Par 96): **92,90,89,83,83 82,82,78,77,76 62**
.A P Ling was withdrawn. Price at time of withdrawal was 100-1. Rule 4 does not apply.\n\x\x Kingston Folly was withdrawn. Price at time of withdrawal was 66-1. Rule 4 does not apply.
Owner Paul Dean **Bred** Miss K Rausing **Trained** Middleham Moor, N Yorks

FOCUS
A race delayed nearly 15 minutes. An ordinary gallop to this uncompetitive event but the first three pulled clear. The winner edged towards the inside rail in the closing stages.

NOTEBOOK
Bowdler's Magic ◆ fully confirmed the improvement shown over a furlong further when second to a potentially very useful sort at this course a week ago and responded well to pressure. He won't be inconvenienced by the return to further and appeals as the type to win in handicap company on Polytrack. (op 6-4 tchd 10-3)
Oriental Scot ◆, a colt with plenty of size and scope, still looked a bit green (both in the preliminaries and in the race) but fully confirmed debut promise on this first run on an artificial surface and up in trip after attracting plenty of support. He's the type to progress further and is sure to pick up an ordinary event. (op 5-2)
Bonded(IRE) had not shown much on his debut in soft ground but fared a good deal better on this all-weather debut. He pulled clear of the remainder and is capable of picking up a run-of-the-mill event around this trip in due course. (op 40-1)
Rainbow Six fared a good deal better than he had done over course and distance earlier in the month. He is in good hands and he'll be of much more interest once he is qualified for a handicap mark.
Fairy Flight(USA), a half-sister to an Italian Listed winner, fared the best of the newcomers and should come on a fair bit for this initial experience. (op 20-1 tchd 25-1)
Jamarjo(IRE), gelded since disappointing on his previous start, was not totally disgraced on this all-weather debut but is likely to continue to look vulnerable in this type of event. (op 20-1)
Cheyenne Chant posted her best effort yet and is one to keep an eye on in handicaps next year.

7492 TOTESPORTGAMES.COM CLAIMING STKS 1m 141y(P)

7:15 (7:20) (Class 6) 3-Y-0+ **£2,729** (£806; £403) **Stalls** Low

Form RPR

3000 **1** **Appalachian Trail (IRE)**[14] 7294 8-9-1 95.....................(b) TomEaves 13 71
(I Semple) *hld up towards rr: hdwy wl over 1f out: pushed along to ld ins fnl f: r.o wl* **7/2**[2]

0000 **2** *1 ¼* **Red Somerset (USA)**[8] 7375 6-9-6 87....................... WilliamCarson(3) 5 76
(R J Hodges) *a.p: rdn to chse ldr briefly wl over 1f out: kpt on to re-take 2nd wl ins fnl f* **8/1**[3]

0032 **3** *2 ½* **Benandonner (USA)**[21] 7185 6-9-9 92.......................... PaulHanagan 1 71
(R A Fahey) *led early: hld up in tch: pushed along over 2f out: rdn and sltly outpcd wl over 1f out: styd on to take 3rd last strides* **5/4**[1]

4560 **4** *nk* **Harting Hill**[31] 6940 4-8-10 47....................................... KirstyMilczarek 8 57
(M P Tregoning) *sn led: rdn wl over 1f out: hdd ins fnl f: sn btn* **50/1**

2041 **5** *1* **Just Jimmy (IRE)**[5] 7417 4-8-12 54.................................... SJCraine 3 57
(P D Evans) *hld up in mid-div: hdwy on ins wl over 1f out: sn rdn: btn 1f out* **12/1**

00/0 **6** *½* **Remark (IRE)**[39] 6758 5-8-3 42...........................(t) JamesPSullivan(7) 12 54
(M W Easterby) *hld up towards rr: rdn wl over 1f out: styd on u.p ins fnl f* **100/1**

4142 **7** *nk* **Bee Stinger**[74] 5750 7-8-8 73.............................. RussellKennemore(3) 9 54
(B G Powell) *hld up in mid-div: pushed along on outside over 2f out: c wd and lost pl ent st: rdn wl over 1f out: n.d after* **16/1**

5305 **8** *shd* **Applaude**[10] 7332 4-8-6 62..(be) BillyCray(7) 7 56
(R C Guest) *prom: hung rt bnd over 2f out: rn wd ent st: c to stands' rail 1f out: rdn and wknd fnl f* **20/1**

0003 **9** *¾* **Pride Of Nation (IRE)**[5] 7412 7-8-5 72.................(p) DeclanCannon(7) 4 53
(A J McCabe) *hld up in mid-div: pushed along over 2f out: rdn wl over 1f out: sn wknd* **22/1**

0100 **10** *nse* **White Deer (USA)**[43] 6645 5-8-13 75........................(tp) FrancisNorton 2 54
(G A Harker) *a towards rr* **8/1**[3]

2600 **11** *½* **Foxtrot Bravo (IRE)**[24] 7110 3-8-9 56.................... RichardKingscote 10 52
(Miss S L Davison) *sn w ldr: rdn and ev ch over 2f out: wknd wl over 1f out* **40/1**

/00- **12** *9* **Ireland Dancer (IRE)**[478] 4054 5-8-10 47.......................... LiamJones 6 29
(John Berry) *a in rr: eased whn no ch over 1f out* **100/1**

1m 50.38s (-0.12) **Going Correction** -0.025s/f (Stan)
WFA 3 from 4yo+ 3lb **12** Ran SP% **118.0**
Speed ratings (Par 101): **99,97,95,95,94 94,93,93,93,93 92,84**
toteswingers:1&2:£5.10, 2&3:£5.30, 1&3:£2.10 CSF £29.44 TOTE £5.20: £1.90, £2.00, £1.10; EX 37.30.There was no bid for the winner
Owner G L S Partnership **Bred** Swettenham Stud **Trained** Carluke, S Lanarks
■ Stewards' Enquiry : Kirsty Milczarek three-day ban: careless riding (Dec 5-7)

FOCUS
A wide range of ability on display but a moderate gallop and the proximity of the fourth, fifth and sixth means this bare form is unreliable. The winner came down the centre in the straight.
Applaude Official explanation: jockey said gelding hung right
Foxtrot Bravo(IRE) Official explanation: jockey said gelding lost its action

7493 TOTESPORTCASINO.COM CLAIMING STKS 1m 141y(P)

7:45 (7:45) (Class 6) 2-Y-0 **£2,729** (£806; £403) **Stalls** Low

Form RPR

563 **1** **Tuscan King**[7] 7391 2-8-9 59..(b) FrancisNorton 4 68
(W R Muir) *chsd ldr: rdn to ld over 1f out: sn clr: r.o wl* **7/1**[3]

000 **2** *7* **Land Of Plenty (IRE)**[68] 5942 2-7-10 35........................ AndreaAtzeni(3) 5 43
(E A L Dunlop) *hld up in last: rdn 3f out: hdwy on ins wl over 1f out: tk 2nd wl ins fnl f: no ch w wnr* **25/1**

066 **3** *1 ¼* **Chookie Avon**[22] 7157 2-8-9 66... TomEaves 2 51
(I Semple) *led: rdn 2f out: hdd over 1f out: sn btn: lost 2nd wl ins fnl f* **9/4**[2]

051 **4** *2 ¼* **Giulietta Da Vinci**[7] 7391 2-8-1 70........................... KellyHarrison(3) 3 41
(N Tinkler) *prom: rdn over 2f out: wknd wl over 1f out* **8/11**[1]

1m 50.4s (-0.10) **Going Correction** -0.025s/f (Stan) **4** Ran SP% **105.0**
Speed ratings (Par 94): **99,92,91,89**
.Tuscan King was claimed by Paul Howling for £10,000\n\x\x
Owner M J Caddy **Bred** Horizon Bloodstock Limited **Trained** Lambourn, Berks

FOCUS
A most uncompetitive claimer and one that took a good deal less winning than seemed likely with the two market leaders disappointing. The pace was moderate and the winner raced towards the inside rail in the straight.

NOTEBOOK

Tuscan King, behind Giulietta Da Vinci last time, took advantage of the below-par runs of the two market leaders and did not have to improve to beat a 35-rated rival with plenty in hand. Races don't come much weaker than this one, though, and he will not be an obvious one to follow up. He now joins Paul Howling. (op 11-2)

Land Of Plenty(IRE), having her first run for new connections, was not disgraced in the face of a very stiff task on this all-weather debut in a race where the two market leaders failed to give their running. She shapes as though she will stay further still but her short term future lies in low-grade handicaps. (op 20-1)

Chookie Avon had shown modest form on turf and on Polytrack and looked to have claims in this company over a trip that should have suited but he proved disappointing after enjoying an easy lead. Like many from the yard he does not look entirely straightforward and he has something to prove at present. (tchd 2-1)

Giulietta Da Vinci was the pick of the weights in this uncompetitive event but proved a big disappointment on this first run for new connections and the vet reported she finished lame on her near fore. Given she had won two of her previous seven races, she may be worth another chance in this company. Official explanation: jockey said filly ran flat; vet said filly returned lame off-fore

7494 £10 FREE PLAY AT TOTESPORTBINGO.COM NURSERY 7f 32y(P)

8:15 (8:15) (Class 4) (0-85,83) 2-Y-O £5,046 (£1,510; £755; £377; £188) Stalls High

Form RPR

5221 **1** **Mass Rally (IRE)**[10] 7325 2-9-7 83 (t) NickyMackay 3 89
(J H M Gosden) *hld up in rr: hdwy on ins to ld jst over 1f out: shkn up ins fnl f: r.o wl* **11/10**[1]

0224 **2** 2 **Quaker Parrot**[15] 7274 2-9-3 79 RichardKingscote 2 80
(Tom Dascombe) *led early: chsd ldr: led wl over 1f out: sn rdn and hdd: nt qckn fnl f* **8/1**

4355 **3** 2 1/4 **Kylladdie**[12] 7320 2-8-12 74 TomEaves 6 70
(S Gollings) *hld up: pushed along and effrt wl over 1f out: sn rdn: kpt on same pce fnl f* **22/1**

403 **4** 1 **Honest Broker (IRE)**[21] 7167 2-8-3 65 JoeFanning 5 58
(M Johnston) *hld up in tch: pushed along 3f out: rdn and btn jst over 1f out* **16/1**

0124 **5** 3/4 **Transfixed (IRE)**[18] 7218 2-9-1 82 RichardEvans(5) 1 73
(P D Evans) *sn led: rdn over 2f out: hdd wl over 1f out: wknd ins fnl f* **25/1**

0431 **6** hd **Tewin Wood**[12] 7320 2-8-12 74 RobertWinston 8 65
(A Bailey) *sn prom: rdn wl over 1f out: sn wknd* **7/2**[2]

3602 **7** shd **Opus Dei**[12] 7320 2-8-9 71 (b1) PaulHanagan 7 62
(J A Glover) *hld up: hmpd sn after s: pushed along over 2f out: c wd st: rdn and btn jst over 1f out* **5/1**[3]

1m 29.45s (-0.15) **Going Correction** -0.025s/f (Stan) 7 Ran SP% **111.7**
Speed ratings (Par 98): **99,96,94,93,92 91,91**
toteswingers:1&2:£2.00, 2&3:£13.30, 1&3:£11.40 CSF £10.35 CT £117.26 TOTE £1.80: £1.30, £3.40; EX 10.70.

Owner H R H Princess Haya Of Jordan **Bred** Round Hill Stud **Trained** Newmarket, Suffolk

FOCUS

A fair handicap in which the gallop was an ordinary one. The winner raced against the inside rail in the straight.

NOTEBOOK

Mass Rally(IRE) ◆, again fitted with a tongue-tie, is a progressive individual who turned in his best effort to win a shade snugly and to justify the market support on this nursery debut. This strong traveller should stay 1m, is open to further improvement and appeals as the type to win more races. (op 5-4 tchd Evens)

Quaker Parrot is a consistent sort who had the run of the race and looked to give it her best shot on only this second all-weather start and on this first attempt beyond sprint distances (did not fail through lack of stamina). She's a good guide to the worth of this form and should continue to give it a good account.

Kylladdie ran creditably to reverse recent course and distance placings with Tewin Wood but, although a stronger overall test of stamina would have suited, he doesn't have too much in hand of his current rating. (tchd 20-1)

Honest Broker(IRE), who reportedly wasn't suited by testing ground at Ayr on his previous start, was not totally disgraced on this all-weather and handicap debut but he'll have to show a fair bit more before he is a solid betting proposition. (tchd 14-1)

Transfixed(IRE) has won five times from 22 starts on turf but was below the pick of her efforts on that surface on this all-weather debut after being allowed to do her own thing in front. She will do well to win a competitive Polytrack handicap from this mark. Official explanation: jockey said filly hung right (op 22-1)

Tewin Wood, a recent course-and-distance winner, again raced with the choke out and failed to build on that effort from this 3lb higher mark. He may do better but will have to settle better if he is to progress. Official explanation: jockey said gelding hung right (tchd 4-1)

7495 OVER 50 INSTANT GAMES AT TOTESPORTGAMES.COM H'CAP (DIV II) 1m 4f 50y(P)

8:45 (8:45) (Class 6) (0-65,64) 3-Y-O+ £2,047 (£604; £302) Stalls Low

Form RPR

0000 **1** **Desert Vision**[17] 7248 5-9-4 60 (b1) RobertWinston 10 71
(M W Easterby) *hld up in rr: pushed along and hdwy on outside over 2f out: c wd st: edgd lft and led over 1f out: rdn and narrowly hdd wl ins fnl f: edgd lft: led last strides* **7/2**[2]

2305 **2** hd **Prince Charlemagne (IRE)**[32] 6917 6-9-2 58 GeorgeBaker 6 69
(G L Moore) *hld up towards rr: stdy hdwy over 3f out: rdn and chal over 1f out: slt ld wl ins fnl f: carried lft and hdd last strides* **3/1**[1]

2100 **3** 3 3/4 **Astronomical (IRE)**[24] 7127 7-9-8 64 (p) GrahamGibbons 3 69
(R Hollinshead) *led after 1f: rdn and hdd over 1f out: wknd wl ins fnl f* **6/1**

403 **4** 4 **Summer Affair (IRE)**[15] 7278 4-9-3 59 EddieAhern 7 58
(B I Case) *hld up in rr: c wd st: rdn and sme prog over 1f out: nvr nr ldrs* **5/1**[3]

00 **5** 1 1/4 **Active Asset (IRE)**[33] 6900 7-9-7 63 PaulHanagan 4 60
(J A Glover) *hld up in mid-div: pushed along over 3f out: rdn 2f out: wknd over 1f out* **16/1**

403 **6** 1 1/4 **Little Richard (IRE)**[240] 972 10-9-3 59 (p) KirstyMilczarek 2 54
(M Wellings) *prom: rdn 2f out: wknd wl over 1f out* **6/1**

3406 **7** 1 3/4 **Fine Tolerance**[37] 6788 3-8-4 52 JoeFanning 5 44
(Miss S L Davison) *t.k.h: led 1f: led over 8f out tl over 2f out: rdn and wknd over 1f out* **25/1**

066 **8** 3/4 **Turbo Shandy**[7] 5242 6-8-10 52 FrancisNorton 11 43
(D Burchell) *s.s: t.k.h in rr: rdn and short-lived effrt on ins wl over 1f out* **33/1**

0430 **9** 1 1/2 **Strike Force**[23] 7143 5-8-12 54 (p) TomEaves 8 42
(Miss J Feilden) *hld up in mid-div: hdwy 5f out: wkng whn n.m.r wl over 1f out* **17/2**

6050 **10** 9 **Addiena**[114] 4473 5-9-4 60 NeilChalmers 9 34
(B Palling) *prom tl pushed along and wknd over 2f out* **40/1**

0 **11** 40 **Montiyra (IRE)**[10] 7336 5-8-13 55 SJCraine 1 —
(Miss L C Siddall) *a towards rr: t.o fnl 3f* **66/1**

2m 40.54s (-0.56) **Going Correction** -0.025s/f (Stan)
WFA 3 from 4yo+ 6lb 11 Ran SP% **119.6**
Speed ratings (Par 101): **100,99,97,94,93 93,91,91,90,84 57**
toteswingers:1&2:£2.90, 2&3:£5.10, 1&3:£4.50 CSF £14.31 CT £62.07 TOTE £4.20: £1.20, £1.30, £2.90; EX 15.00.

Owner A Black,R Edmonds,J Holdroyd,J Quickfall **Bred** Gainsborough Stud Management Ltd **Trained** Sheriff Hutton, N Yorks

■ Stewards' Enquiry : Robert Winston caution: careless riding.

FOCUS

The second division of a modest handicap. The pace was an ordinary one and the first two, who raced towards the centre, pulled clear in the straight.

Strike Force Official explanation: jockey said gelding was struck into

Addiena Official explanation: jockey said mare hung right in the home straight

Montiyra(IRE) Official explanation: jockey said gelding hung left

7496 100% NEW PLAYER BONUS AT TOTESPORTCASINO.COM H'CAP 5f 216y(P)

9:15 (9:17) (Class 5) (0-75,77) 3-Y-O+ £3,238 (£963; £481; £240) Stalls Low

Form RPR

6002 **1** **Perlachy**[7] 7398 5-8-7 64 (v) KirstyMilczarek 12 73
(J R Holt) *hld up towards rr: hdwy on outside 2f out: c wd st: rdn and edgd lft ins fnl f: r.o* **12/1**

2001 **2** nk **Bel Cantor**[9] 7355 6-9-1 77 PaulPickard(5) 4 85
(W J H Ratcliffe) *a.p on ins: rdn to ld jst over 1f out: hdd ins fnl f: r.o* **6/1**[3]

6004 **3** hd **Bahamian Kid**[21] 7192 4-8-9 66 (v1) JerryO'Dwyer 7 73
(R Hollinshead) *hld up and sn bhd: hdwy 2f out: rdn and kpt on ins fnl f* **12/1**

5-52 **4** hd **Dash Back (USA)**[15] 7273 4-8-11 68 GrahamGibbons 10 75
(Adrian McGuinness, Ire) *hld up in rr: pushed along wl over 1f out: r.o ins fnl f: nrst fin* **8/1**

6210 **5** nk **Gap Princess (IRE)**[85] 5406 5-8-12 69 FrancisNorton 6 75
(G A Harker) *a.p: kpt on towards fin* **33/1**

5100 **6** 1 1/2 **Liberty Trail (IRE)**[9] 7356 3-8-12 69 TomEaves 11 70
(I Semple) *led early: chsd ldr tl rdn wl over 1f out: one pce ins fnl f* **33/1**

0510 **7** 1 **Speedy Guru**[29] 6997 3-8-8 72 AmyScott(7) 9 70+
(H Candy) *hld up and sn wl in rr: c wd st: rdn and edgd lft wl over 1f out: r.o ins fnl f: nvr nrr* **28/1**

6413 **8** nk **Onceaponatime (IRE)**[9] 7355 4-8-12 69 RichardKingscote 3 66
(M D Squance) *hld up in mid-div on ins: hdwy wl over 1f out: rdn and one pce fnl f* **10/3**[1]

1002 **9** 1/2 **Sutton Veny (IRE)**[21] 7191 3-8-8 68 AndreaAtzeni(3) 1 63
(J R Gask) *sn led: rdn and hdd jst over 1f out: wknd wl ins fnl f* **8/1**

4535 **10** 1 1/4 **Bo McGinty (IRE)**[149] 3295 8-9-2 73 (v) PaulHanagan 2 69+
(R A Fahey) *hld up in rr: pushed along wl over 1f out: no imp whn nt clr run and eased wl ins fnl f* **14/1**

0201 **11** 3 1/4 **Tudor Prince (IRE)**[21] 7179 5-8-13 70 EddieAhern 8 51+
(A W Carroll) *hld up in tch: hmpd 2f out: sn wknd* **7/2**[2]

6600 **12** 13 **Interactive (IRE)**[5] 7412 6-8-1 61 (v1) KellyHarrison(3) 5 —
(D Burchell) *prom tl wknd wl over 1f out: eased whn no ch ins fnl f* **20/1**

1m 14.63s (-0.37) **Going Correction** -0.025s/f (Stan) 12 Ran SP% **118.0**
Speed ratings (Par 103): **101,100,100,100,99 97,96,95,95,93 89,71**
toteswingers: 1&2 £32.00, 1&3 £18.40, 2&3 £11.70 CSF £78.59 CT £901.43 TOTE £17.70: £3.90, £2.80, £4.50; EX 51.50 Place 6 £36.77, Place 5 £24.45.

Owner Mrs N Macauley **Bred** J James **Trained** Peckleton, Leics

FOCUS

A fair handicap run at a decent gallop. The winner hung towards the far rail in the closing stages and several finished in a heap.

Bahamian Kid Official explanation: jockey said gelding hung left

Tudor Prince(IRE) Official explanation: jockey said gelding was denied a clear run

T/Plt: £42.90 to a £1 stake. Pool: £81,088.94. 1,376.83 winning tickets. T/Qpdt: £46.10 to a £1 stake. Pool: £5,163.30. 82.80 winning tickets. KH

KYOTO (R-H)

Sunday, November 22

OFFICIAL GOING: Firm

7498a MILE CHAMPIONSHIP (GRADE 1) 1m

6:40 (6:40) 3-Y-O+ £799,187 (£316,029; £196,378; £115,092; £76,728)

RPR

1 **Company (JPN)**[21] 8-9-0 NYokoyama 4 123+
(H Otonashi, Japan)

2 1 1/4 **Meiner Falke (JPN)**[29] 4-9-0 RWada 13 119
(K Kayano, Japan)

3 nk **Sahpresa (USA)**[50] 6479 4-8-9 OPeslier 15 114
(Rod Collet, France)

4 nse **Captain Thule (JPN)**[21] 4-9-0 YKawada 9 119
(Hideyuki Mori, Japan)

5 3/4 **Absolute (JPN)**[29] 5-9-0 KatsuharuTanaka 7 117
(Y Munakata, Japan)

6 nk **Smile Jack (JPN)**[21] 4-9-0 KoseiMiura 5 116
(S Kobiyama, Japan)

7 nse **Hikaru Ozora (JPN)**[70] 5-9-0 CSoumillon 12 116
(Y Ikee, Japan)

8 1/2 **Fifth Petal (JPN)**[22] 3-8-11 C-PLemaire 8 114
(Y Kato, Japan)

9 nse **Live Concert (IRE)**[29] 5-9-0 YIwata 17 115
(T Shirai, Japan)

10 nk **Eva's Request (IRE)**[28] 7046 4-8-9 AlanMunro 1 109
(M R Channon) *in tch on ins tl no ex fr over 1f out* **32/1**[1]

11 nk **Zarema (JPN)**[29] 5-8-9 HUchida 11 108
(H Otonashi, Japan)

12 nse **San Carlo (JPN)**[29] 3-8-11 YYoshida 16 112
(Y Okubo, Japan)

13 nk **Toreno Jubilee (JPN)**[22] 6-9-0 ASuborics 2 113
(H Fujiwara, Japan)

14 1 1/2 **Strong Garuda (JPN)**[29] 3-8-11 YFukunaga 14 108
(T Kubota, Japan)

15 1/2 **Fine Grain (JPN)**[22] 6-9-0 HMiyuki 6 108
(H Nagahama, Japan)

16 1/2 **Suzuka Causeway (JPN)**[22] 5-9-0 HGoto 10 107
(M Hashida, Japan)

17 *1* **Sandalphon (JPN)**49 6-9-0 .... HShii 18 105
(Masahiro Matsunaga, Japan)
18 *1 3/4* **Maruka Shenck (JPN)**29 6-9-0 .... YShibayama 3 100
(H Kawachi, Japan)
1m 33.2s (93.20)
WFA 3 from 4yo+ 2lb **18** Ran SP% **3.0**
(Including Y100 stake): WIN 230; PL 120, 690, 290; DF 6,690.
Owner Hideko Kondo **Bred** H Kondo **Trained** Japan

NOTEBOOK
Sahpresa(USA), winner of the Sun Chariot last time, ran with plenty of credit against the males on ground that was in her favour.
Eva's Request(IRE) had a tough task on this drop back in trip and faded after showing up early. The ground was fast enough for her.

7418 **SOUTHWELL** (L-H)
Tuesday, November 24
OFFICIAL GOING: Standard
Wind: Light across Weather: Cloudy and dry

7499 BET CHAMPIONS LEAGUE FOOTBALL - BETDAQ AMATEUR RIDERS' H'CAP (DIV I) 1m (F)
12:00 (12:00) (Class 6) (0-60,60) 3-Y-0+ **£1,648** (£507; £253) **Stalls** Low

Form RPR
0000 **1** **Hit The Switch**7 7418 3-9-7 **46** .... MrJBanks(5) 14 61
(Patrick Morris) *swtchd rt sn after s and bhd: pushed along 1/2-way: gd hdwy on outer 3f out: led 2f out: sn rdn clr and styd on strly* **33/1**
0000 **2** *8* **Boy Dancer (IRE)**38 6840 6-9-11 **46** oh1 ....(p) MrTRDavid(3) 2 42
(J J Quinn) *towards rr: hdwy 3f out: swtchd rt and rdn wl over 1f out: styd on but no ch w wnr* **50/1**
3000 **3** *1* **General Tufto**20 7247 4-10-12 **58** ....(b) MissEJJones 13 52+
(C Smith) *towards rr: hdwy over 2f out and sn rdn: styng on whn nt clr run and swtchd lft over 1f out: kpt on ins fnl f: nrst fin* **9/2**2
5426 **4** *1/2* **Bajan Pride**203 1777 5-10-7 **58** .... MissPhillipaTutty(5) 6 51
(R A Fahey) *led: rdn along and hdd 2f out: drvn and edgd rt over 1f out: one pce* **16/1**
6644 **5** *3/4* **Mountain Forest (GER)**23 7197 3-9-13 **47** .... MissSBrotherton 8 38
(H Morrison) *trckd ldrs: hdwy 3f out: sn cl up and ev ch tl rdn 2f out and grad wknd* **7/1**3
3632 **6** *2 1/2* **Lord Of The Dance (IRE)**3 7481 3-10-4 **59** ....(b) MrDJEustace(7) 1 44
(J M P Eustace) *pushed along early and sn trcking ldrs on inner: smooth hdwy 3f out and sn cl up: rdn and ev ch tl drvn: edgd lft and wknd over 1f out* **3/1**1
1340 **7** *2 1/4* **Elliwan**6 2233 4-10-6 **55** ....(bt) MissJCoward(3) 5 35
(M W Easterby) *cl up: rdn along wl over 2f out and grad wknd* **9/1**
-003 **8** *1 3/4* **Miss Jabba (IRE)**40 6787 3-9-7 **46** oh1 .... MrRBirkett(5) 9 22
(Miss J Feilden) *chsd ldrs: rdn along 1/2-way: sn wknd* **9/1**
3633 **9** *1/2* **Mojeerr**11 7374 3-9-9 **50** ....(p) MissNVorster(7) 11 25
(A J McCabe) *cl up on outer: rdn along 3f out: sn drvn and wknd* **12/1**
3000 **10** *1 1/4* **Tar (IRE)**12 7354 5-10-0 **51** ow3 ....(v) MissABevan(5) 7 23
(John A Harris) *cl up: rdn along 3f out and sn wknd* **8/1**
0460 **11** *26* **Westport**27 7113 6-10-2 **53** ....(p) MissRBastiman(5) 4 —
(R Bastiman) *a bhd: t.o fnl 3f* **28/1**
4660 **12** *7* **Ten Pole Tudor**38 6862 4-10-6 **52** ....(p) MrSDobson 12 —
(R A Harris) *v.s.a and a t.o* **18/1**
1m 42.8s (-0.90) **Going Correction** -0.175s/f (Stan)
WFA 3 from 4yo+ 2lb **12** Ran SP% **114.0**
Speed ratings (Par 101): **97,89,88,87,86 84,82,80,79,78 52,45**
toteswingers:1&2:£89.90, 2&3:£32.50, 1&3:£32.10 CSF £1100.88 CT £8668.66 TOTE £32.00: £9.70, £10.00, £2.00; EX 624.80 TRIFECTA Not won..
Owner Rob Lloyd Racing Limited **Bred** Mrs M T Dawson **Trained** Tarporley, Cheshire
FOCUS
A typically open handicap for amateur riders. The winner is rated to his 3-y-o best for now.
General Tufto ◆ Official explanation: jockey said gelding was denied a clear run

7500 BET CHAMPIONS LEAGUE FOOTBALL - BETDAQ AMATEUR RIDERS' H'CAP (DIV II) 1m (F)
12:30 (12:30) (Class 6) (0-60,60) 3-Y-0+ **£1,648** (£507; £253) **Stalls** Low

Form RPR
5035 **1** **Prince Golan (IRE)**45 6668 5-10-6 **56** .... MrMPrice(5) 5 64
(R J Price) *bhd: swtchd wd and hdwy on outer 3f out: rdn 2f out: styd on wl u.p ent fnl f: led nr line* **16/1**
002 **2** *hd* **Great Bounder (CAN)**11 7369 3-10-8 **55** .... MrSWalker 3 62
(J R Best) *led: rdn along and hdd 2f out: drvn wl over 1f out: rallied wl u.p toregain ld last 30yds: hdd nr line* **4/1**2
0044 **3** *hd* **Royal Keva (IRE)**11 7369 3-10-4 **54** ....(b) MrTRDavid(3) 13 61
(A D Brown) *dwlt and towards rr: hdwy 3f out: rdn to chse ldrs wl over 1f out: sn drvn and styd on wl to have ev ch wl ins fnl f: no ex towards fin* **11/2**
240 **4** *1/2* **Almahaza (IRE)**59 6288 5-10-9 **59** .... MrJeremiahMcGrath(5) 11 65+
(A J Chamberlain) *towards rr: gd hdwy on outer over 3f out: led 2f out and sn rdn clr: hung bdly lft appr fnl f and sn drvn: wknd hdd last 30yds* **7/2**1
0241 **5** *1/2* **Castle Myth (USA)**8 7416 3-10-13 **60** 6ex ....(bt) MissLEllison 1 65
(B Ellison) *dwlt and towards rr: hdwy wl over 2f out: rdn wl over 1f out: styd on ins fibnal f: nrst fin* **7/1**
0-00 **6** *6* **Silk Star (IRE)**155 3228 3-9-7 **45** .... MrJBanks(5) 6 36
(Patrick Morris) *chsd ldrs: hdwy 3f out: rdn over 2f out and kpt on same pce* **40/1**
4500 **7** *nk* **Sparky Vixen**189 2155 5-10-0 **45** .... MissADeniel 9 35
(C J Teague) *chsd ldrs: rdn along 3f out: sn drvn and grad wknd* **50/1**
0/06 **8** *1/2* **Remark (IRE)**3 7492 5-9-9 **45** ....(t) MissJoannaMason(5) 12 34
(M W Easterby) *chsd ldrs: rdn along wl over 2f out: drvn wl over out and grad wknd* **5/1**3
4000 **9** *1/2* **Bernix**63 6183 7-9-7 **45** ....(p) MissLWilson(7) 2 33
(N Tinkler) *dwlt: sn pushed along to chse ldrs on inner: rdn 3f out and wkng whn n.m.r wl over 1f out* **50/1**
5040 **10** *3/4* **Komreyev Star**36 6909 7-10-3 **48** .... MrSDobson 14 34
(R E Peacock) *midfield: hdwy on outer to trck ldrs 3f out: rdn over 2f out: sn drvn and wknd* **20/1**
4330 **11** *1 1/2* **Silly Gilly (IRE)**63 6183 5-10-7 **57** .... MissVBarr(5) 7 40
(R E Barr) *cl up: rdn along 3f out: sn drvn and wknd* **14/1**
0000 **12** *3 3/4* **Rockson (IRE)**12 7349 3-9-8 **48** .... MrJHodson(7) 4 22
(Ian Williams) *chsd ldrs towards inner: rdn along 3f out: wkng whn n.m.r wl over 1f out* **40/1**
0000 **13** *1/2* **Just Call Me Dave (USA)**54 6432 3-9-8 **46** .... MrRJKirk(5) 10 19
(Paul Green) *a bhd* **66/1**
0000 **14** *8* **The Wily Woodcock**74 5842 5-9-12 **50** .... MissAAnderson(7) 8 5
(T Wall) *s.i.s: a bhd* **125/1**
1m 44.22s (0.52) **Going Correction** -0.175s/f (Stan)
WFA 3 from 5yo+ 2lb **14** Ran SP% **115.2**
Speed ratings (Par 101): **90,89,89,89,88 82,82,81,81,80 79,75,74,66**
toteswingers:1&2:£11.10, 2&3:£6.30, 1&3:£13.20 CSF £72.89 CT £414.59 TOTE £14.50: £3.80, £2.20, £2.80; EX 71.20 TRIFECTA Not won..
Owner R J Price **Bred** K Molloy **Trained** Ullingswick, H'fords
■ Stewards' Enquiry : Mr S Walker two-day ban: used whip with excessive frequency (tbn)
FOCUS
The second division of the handicap for amateur riders was another wide-open heat. The form is rated around the placed horses.

7501 BET IN-RUNNING - BETDAQ CLAIMING STKS 7f (F)
1:00 (1:04) (Class 6) 2-Y-O **£2,047** (£604; £302) **Stalls** Low

Form RPR
04 **1** **Tealing**12 7351 2-8-11 0 .... PhillipMakin 12 63+
(T D Barron) *towards rr: gd hdwy over 2f out: swtchd lft and rdn to ld 1/2f out: drvn out* **12/1**
0544 **2** *2* **Miss Taken (IRE)**7 7421 2-8-8 49 ....(b) GrahamGibbons 5 55
(D Carroll) *in tch: smooth hdwy to trck ldrs 3f out: n.m.r and swtchd rt wl over 1f out: rdn to chse wnr ent fnl f: kpt on* **25/1**
0003 **3** *2 3/4* **Labretella (IRE)**13 7334 2-8-9 55 ow1 .... SteveDrowne 2 49
(D W Thompson) *cl up on inner: effrt 3f out: rdn over 2f out and ev ch: drvn over 1f out and one pce ent fnl f* **33/1**
4430 **4** *3/4* **Izuizorizuain't (IRE)**29 7055 2-8-6 56 ....(b1) JoeFanning 11 44
(K A Ryan) *towards rr: hdwy wl over 2f out: swtchd wd and rdn over 1f out: kpt on ins fnl f: nt rch ldrs* **12/1**
2212 **5** *nk* **Clear Ice (IRE)**7 7421 2-9-5 65 .... AndrewMullen 8 57
(D Nicholls) *led: rdn along 3f out: drvn 2f out: hdd over 1f out: edgd rt and wknd ent fnl f* **11/4**2
0065 **6** *4* **Chorus Boy**10 7391 2-8-3 47 ....(b) ChrisCatlin 9 31
(G G Margarson) *chsd ldrs: rdn along 3f out: drvn and wknd over 2f out* **16/1**
0302 **7** *3/4* **Lord Victor**12 7352 2-8-11 64 ....(p) RobertWinston 3 37
(A J McCabe) *cl up: rdn along 3f out: drvn over 2f out and sn wknd* **5/1**3
2000 **8** *1/2* **Micky's Bird**12 7352 2-8-4 50 ow2 .... PaulEddery 7 28
(R C Guest) *in tch: hdwy to chse ldrs 3f out: drvn over 2f out and sn wknd* **66/1**
0041 **9** *5* **Taper Jean Girl (IRE)**7 7419 2-8-6 63 .... AndrewElliott 10 18
(Mrs R A Carr) *chsd ldrs on outer: rdn along wl over 2f out and sn wknd* **5/2**1
034 **10** *2 1/2* **Better Be Blue (IRE)**10 7391 2-8-0 55 ow2 .... JimmyQuinn 4 —
(H J L Dunlop) *a in rr* **6/1**
000 **11** *3 3/4* **The Frying Pan (IRE)**43 6735 2-7-12 38 ....(b) DavidProbert 1 —
(Dr J D Scargill) *s.i.s: a bhd* **100/1**
0606 **12** *17* **Selina Rio**12 7352 2-8-2 40 .... DuranFentiman 6 —
(L A Mullaney) *a in rr* **200/1**
1m 30.37s (0.07) **Going Correction** -0.175s/f (Stan) **12** Ran SP% **117.2**
Speed ratings (Par 94): **92,89,86,85,85 80,79,79,73,70 66,47**
toteswingers:1&2:£11.10, 2&3:£17.60, 1&3:£28.90 CSF £276.23 TOTE £13.10: £4.30, £5.10, £7.80; EX 157.80 Trifecta £309.30 Part won. Pool £418.08 - 0.45 winning units..Tealing was claimed by R. C. Guest for £6,000
Owner Harrowgate Bloodstock Ltd **Bred** Alan A Wright **Trained** Maunby, N Yorks
FOCUS
An ordinary claimer.
NOTEBOOK
Tealing came good at the third time of asking and completed the task readily. He finished last of four in a maiden over C&D 12 days earlier, but ran better than his finishing position implied and the switch to more patient tactics paid off. This was obviously a marked drop in class, but he could have a little more to offer at a slightly higher level as he has few miles on the clock. (op 7-1)
Miss Taken(IRE) travelled sweetly into contention, but hit a flat spot when asked for an effort and it isn't hard to see why she wears headgear. She got the longer trip, though, and looks worth persevering with in this class. (op 20-1)
Labretella(IRE) helped cut out the early running and wasn't disgraced, but probably needs to return to an extra furlong to be most effective. (op 20-1)
Izuizorizuain't(IRE) took time to hit top gear after making up her ground from off the pace, but this was better from her in first-time blinkers. (op 9-1)
Clear Ice(IRE) showed decent early pace, but the positive tactics over this longer trip found him out. (op 3-1 tchd 5-2)
Lord Victor, in first-time cheekpieces, was another that had too much use made of him on this step back up in distance. (op 6-1)
Taper Jean Girl(IRE) was forced wide throughout and ran well below par on this debut for new connections. She was later reported to have run flat. Official explanation: jockey said filly ran flat (op 3-1 tchd 7-2)
Better Be Blue(IRE) Official explanation: jockey said filly never travelled
The Frying Pan(IRE) Official explanation: jockey said filly never travelled

7502 VISIT NOTTINGHAMSHIRE NOVICE STKS 1m (F)
1:30 (1:31) (Class 5) 2-Y-O **£2,590** (£770; £385; £192) **Stalls** Low

Form RPR
1 **Nazreef** 2-8-8 0 .... RobertWinston 3 75+
(H Morrison) *mdeall: shkn up and edgd rt 2f out: sn rdn clr and kpt on wl* **6/1**
2 *3 3/4* **Mighty Mambo** 2-8-8 0 .... ShaneKelly 2 66
(Jane Chapple-Hyam) *trckd ldng pair: hdwy to chse wnr whn n.m.r 2f out: sn rdn and rn green: styd on appr fnl f* **11/4**3
0 **3** *4* **Budva**18 7266 2-8-12 0 .... SteveDrowne 4 62
(H Morrison) *cl up: effrt 3f out: rdn over 2f out: sn drvn and kpt on same pce* **5/2**2
4 *3/4* **Whitby (IRE)** 2-8-3 0 .... JimmyQuinn 6 51
(M W Easterby) *dwlt and rn green: swtchd ins and trckd ldrs 1/2-way: effrt over 2f out: sn rdn and green: hld whn wknd over 1f out* **9/4**1
306 **5** *5* **Rock Of Eire**67 6065 2-8-12 58 .... EdwardCreighton 5 49
(E J Creighton) *chsd ldrs: rdn along 3f out: hung lft and wknd over 2f out* **10/1**
6 *9* **Ever A Gent** 2-8-1 0 .... JamesPSullivan(7) 1 25
(M W Easterby) *dwlt: green and a in rr: outpcd and bhd fr wl over 2f out* **18/1**
1m 42.78s (-0.92) **Going Correction** -0.175s/f (Stan) **6** Ran SP% **114.6**
Speed ratings (Par 96): **97,93,89,88,83 74**
toteswingers:1&2:£2.80, 2&3:£1.40, 1&3:£2.80 CSF £23.43 TOTE £6.90: £2.80, £1.60; EX 23.40.
Owner Deborah Collett & M J Watson **Bred** M J Watson **Trained** East Ilsley, Berks

FOCUS
A moderate novice event.

NOTEBOOK
Nazreef, who is related to numerous winners over this distance, hails from a yard that does well at this venue. He made just about all and came right away from his rivals when asked to seal the race nearing the final furlong. It will be interesting to see how the Handicapper rates this. (op 9-2 tchd 4-1)

Mighty Mambo, a half-brother to AW winner Keenes Day among others, moved nicely through the race but hit a flat spot just as the winner kicked for home. He kept on to finish a clear second-best and should learn plenty for the initial experience. (tchd 5-2 and 3-1)

Budva looked the first string from his stable on jockey bookings and the market spoke in his favour. He couldn't go with his winning stable companion from 2f out, but stayed on to better his debut effort here and is entitled to go forward again for the experience. (op 3-1 tchd 10-3)

Whitby(IRE) missed the break and then ran keenly when asked to get into a prominent position. She paid for those exertions from 2f out, but ought to learn from this debut outing and is bred to appreciate a stiffer test in due course. (op 7-2)

Rock Of Eire set the standard with an official mark of 58, but he obviously ran well below that level on this return from a 67-day break. He was beaten before stamina for the extra distance became an issue. (op 8-1 tchd 11-1)

Ever A Gent was the other Mick Easterby runner and he too missed the break. He proved distinctly green thereafter and showed little, but has scope so could be the type to improve as he matures. (op 12-1)

7503 BOOK YOUR TICKETS ONLINE AT SOUTHWELL-RACECOURSE.CO.UK H'CAP 5f (F)
2:00 (2:01) (Class 6) (0-58,58) 3-Y-O+ **£2,047** (£604; £302) **Stalls** High

Form RPR

0625 **1** **First Swallow**[20] 7241 4-8-13 **54**.......................(t) PhillipMakin 9 65
(D H Brown) *mde all: rdn wl over 1f out: drvn ins fnl f and kpt on wl* **17/2**

3030 **2** *1* **Embra (IRE)**[3] 7483 4-8-13 **57**.......................MartinLane(3) 10 64
(T J Etherington) *dwlt and sn rdn along towards rr: hdwy 2f out: drvn and kpt on wl fnl f* **7/1**[3]

0000 **3** *½* **Sherjawy (IRE)**[54] 6422 5-8-11 **52**.......................(p) SamHitchcott 7 58
(Miss Z C Davison) *cl up: effrt 2f out: sn rdn and ev ch tl drvn and nt qckn wl ins fnl f* **12/1**

4005 **4** *hd* **Dickie Le Davoir**[7] 7418 5-9-1 **56**.......................(be) J-PGuillambert 1 61
(R C Guest) *sn rdn along towards rr: hdwy on wd outside 2f out: cl up and ev ch over 1f out: sn rdn and no ex ins fnl f* **5/1**[1]

4433 **5** *1 ¼* **Kinigi (IRE)**[11] 7370 3-8-8 **54**.......................(p) AndrewHeffernan(5) 4 54
(R A Harris) *chsd ldrs: hdwy 2f out: rdn and ev ch over 1f out: drvn ins fnl f: wknd towards fin* **6/1**[2]

0000 **6** *hd* **Golden Dixie (USA)**[3] 7483 10-9-2 **57**.......................LukeMorris 5 57
(R A Harris) *towards rr: hdwy 2f out: sn rdn and kpt on ins fnl f: nrst fin* **7/1**[3]

0225 **7** *nse* **Thunder Bay**[10] 7397 4-9-1 **56**.......................PaulHanagan 12 55
(R A Fahey) *hld up: hdwy 2f out: sn rdn and edgd lft over 1f out: nvr nr ldrs* **12/1**

6020 **8** *nk* **Ursus**[28] 7081 4-8-13 **54**.......................(p) SJCraine 3 52
(C R Wilson) *cl up: rdn along 2f out: sn drvn and wknd* **14/1**

0130 **9** *¾* **Silk Gallery (USA)**[12] 7355 4-9-2 **57**.......................(t) GrahamGibbons 13 53
(E J Alston) *in tch: rdn along and outpcd 1/2-way: kpt on ins fnl f: nrst fin* **11/1**

2400 **10** *hd* **Cape Cobra**[13] 7329 5-9-1 **56**.......................ShaneKelly 6 51
(H Morrison) *swtchd lft after 1f: a towards rr* **9/1**

0300 **11** *3* **Monte Cassino (IRE)**[36] 6902 4-9-2 **57**.......................TGMcLaughlin 11 41
(J O'Reilly) *chsd ldrs: rdn along 1/2-way: sn wknd* **28/1**

3/0P **12** *4 ½* **Glencairn Star**[118] 4436 8-9-0 **55**.......................ChrisCatlin 8 23
(F Watson) *a in rr: bhd fr 1/2-way* **50/1**

5200 **13** *2* **Shakespeare's Son**[13] 7330 4-9-3 **58**.......................(v) VinceSlattery 14 19
(H J Evans) *s.i.s: a bhd* **33/1**

00-0 **14** *1* **Count Cougar (USA)**[299] 326 9-8-11 **55**.......................MichaelJStainton(3) 2 12
(S P Griffiths) *cl up: rdn along 1/2-way: sn wknd* **33/1**

58.74 secs (-0.96) **Going Correction** -0.175s/f (Stan) **14** Ran SP% **118.2**
Speed ratings (Par 101): **100,98,97,97,95 94,94,94,93,92 88,80,77,76**
toteswingers:1&2:£9.90, 2&3:£6.50, 1&3:£4.30 CSF £63.64 CT £722.30 TOTE £8.60: £2.40, £3.10, £3.50; EX 71.90 Trifecta £131.90 Part won. Pool £178.25 - 0.45 winning units..
Owner The Secret Seven Partnership **Bred** A K Smeaton **Trained** Maltby, S Yorks

FOCUS
A low draw is so often a big advantage over this straight 5f, but that wasn't the case here with the early pace more towards the middle and stall nine beat stall ten. The runner-up is rated in line with his all-weather best.

7504 CALL 01636 814481 TO SPONSOR A RACE MAIDEN STKS 1m 4f (F)
2:30 (2:30) (Class 5) 3-Y-O+ **£2,729** (£806; £403) **Stalls** Low

Form RPR

035 **1** **Time Book (IRE)**[21] 7221 3-9-3 75.......................NickyMackay 5 77
(J H M Gosden) *trckd ldrs: effrt over 3f out and sn pushed along: rdn wl over 2f out: hrd rdn to chal over 1f out: drvn and edgd rt wl ins fnl f: led on line* **11/10**[1]

5-40 **2** *nse* **Lava Steps (USA)**[57] 6338 3-9-3 60.......................TonyCulhane 8 77
(P T Midgley) *trckd ldrs: hdwy on outer 1/2-way: led 5f out: rdn 3f out: drvn 2f out: kpt on u.p ins fnl f tl pushed rt and hdd nr line* **10/1**

2-44 **3** *10* **Inflammable**[24] 7178 3-8-12 66.......................StephenDonohoe 9 56
(Sir Mark Prescott) *led after 1f: pushed along and hdd 5f out: rdn over 3f out: drvn over 2f out: plugged on same pce* **11/4**[2]

0600 **4** *hd* **Dream In Blue**[38] 6840 4-9-9 68.......................(p) ChrisCatlin 10 61
(J A Glover) *prom: rdn along 4f out: drvn over 2f out: kpt on same pce* **25/1**

0-00 **5** *18* **Martha's Girl (USA)**[218] 1397 3-8-12 58.......................DNolan 1 27
(D Carroll) *chsd ldrs: rdn along 5f out: drvn 4f out and sn outpcd* **66/1**

4000 **6** *¾* **Gulnaz**[28] 7085 4-9-4 37.......................PJMcDonald 11 26
(C J Teague) *dwlt: sn pushed along to chse ldrs: cl up and rdn 1/2-way: drvn over 4f out and sn outpcd* **66/1**

5 **7** *17* **Bluegrass Lion (USA)**[71] 5939 3-8-12 0.......................AndrewHeffernan(5) 6 —
(Paul Green) *towards rr: rdn along 1/2-way: sn bhd* **16/1**

0 **8** *6* **Firsaan (IRE)**[222] 1308 3-9-3 55.......................LeeVickers 3 —
(J R Norton) *a bhd: t.o fnl 4f* **66/1**

0/2 **9** *24* **Warren Bank**[18] 7278 4-9-9 0.......................GeorgeBaker 7 —
(Mrs Mary Hambro) *a in rr: t.o fnl 3f* **5/1**[3]

/ **10** *4* **Princess Shirl**[1d] 5-9-4 0.......................JimmyQuinn 2 —
(A D Brown) *a bhd: t.o fnl 4f* **66/1**

/0-0 **11** *102* **Northerner (IRE)**[121] 4350 6-9-9 44.......................TGMcLaughlin 4 —
(J O'Reilly) *led 1f: cl up tl rdn along and lost pl over 6f out: sn bhd: t.o fnl 4f* **150/1**

2m 37.37s (-3.63) **Going Correction** -0.175s/f (Stan)
WFA 3 from 4yo+ 6lb **11** Ran SP% **116.4**
Speed ratings (Par 103): **105,104,98,98,86 85,74,70,54,51** —
toteswingers:1&2:£5.50, 2&3:£5.10, 1&3:£2.40 CSF £13.54 TOTE £1.70: £1.20, £3.50, £1.10; EX 14.60 Trifecta £74.60 Pool £352.92 - 3.50 winning units..
Owner George Strawbridge **Bred** Denis McDonnell **Trained** Newmarket, Suffolk
■ Stewards' Enquiry : Nicky Mackay caution: careless riding; seven-day ban: used whip with excessive frequency down shoulder in the forehand without giving colt time to respond (Dec 8-14)

FOCUS
A weak maiden rated around the winner but could be a few pounds out either way.
Warren Bank Official explanation: jockey said gelding had no more to give

7505 BETDAQ THE BETTING EXCHANGE H'CAP 1m 4f (F)
3:00 (3:00) (Class 5) (0-70,70) 3-Y-O+ **£2,729** (£806; £403) **Stalls** Low

Form RPR

2331 **1** **Bosamcliff (IRE)**[24] 7174 4-8-11 **64**.......................RichardEvans(5) 10 73
(P D Evans) *hld up towards rr: hdwy on wd outside over 3f out: rdn 2f out: styd on strly ins fnl f: led nr fin* **16/1**

0222 **2** *hd* **Lost Soldier Three (IRE)**[13] 7332 8-9-8 **70**.......................AndrewMullen 8 78
(D Nicholls) *sn pushed along in midfield: hdwy over 3f out: chsd ldrs over 2f out: n.m.r and swtchd lft ent fnl f: sn drvn to chal and ev ch tl no ex nr fin* **11/4**[1]

0204 **3** *shd* **Benedict Spirit (IRE)**[20] 6855 4-9-8 **70**.......................(p) DavidProbert 13 78
(D Burchell) *trckd ldrs: hdwy over 3f out: led over 2f out and sn rdn: edgd rt and drvn ent fnl f: hdd and no ex nr fin* **6/1**[3]

6535 **4** *10* **Red Wine**[21] 7222 10-8-8 **56** oh3.......................ChrisCatlin 7 48
(J A Glover) *prom: led over 3f out: rdn and hdd over 2f out: sn drvn and wknd over 1f out* **8/1**

0514 **5** *8* **Charging Indian (IRE)**[13] 7332 3-9-1 **69**.......................(p) TonyCulhane 6 48
(P T Midgley) *s.i.s and sn pushed along in rr: hdwy over 4f out: rdn over 3f out: plugged on: nvr a factor* **15/2**

220- **6** *shd* **Pegasus Prince (USA)**[11] 4046 5-9-1 **63**.......................TomEaves 5 42
(J Wade) *chsd ldrs: rdn along 4f out: drvn 3f out and grad wknd* **9/1**

00-0 **7** *2 ½* **Sir Kyffin's Folly**[85] 5503 4-9-0 **62**.......................SteveDrowne 11 37
(J A Geake) *a in rr* **100/1**

0602 **8** *2 ¼* **Stormy Summer**[18] 7272 4-9-0 **62**.......................(b) JackMitchell 1 33
(R W Price) *trckd ldrs on inner: hdwy over 4f out: effrt and cl up 3f out: sn rdn: hung 2f out and sn wknd* **5/1**[2]

505 **9** *3* **Brave Mave**[11] 7368 4-9-4 **66**.......................JoeFanning 3 33
(Jane Chapple-Hyam) *in tch: rdn along over 4f out and sn wknd* **8/1**

00 **10** *1 ½* **Colonel Sherman (USA)**[15] 7322 4-9-2 **64**.......................LeeVickers 2 28
(P A Kirby) *cl up: rdn along 4f out: drvn over 3f out and sn wknd* **40/1**

002- **11** *½* **Mt Desert**[430] 6115 7-8-13 **61**.......................TonyHamilton 4 24
(E W Tuer) *led: rdn along and hdd over 3f out: sn wknd* **20/1**

-340 **12** *7* **Black Falcon (IRE)**[301] 302 9-8-8 **56** oh3.......................NickyMackay 9 8
(John A Harris) *a in rr: bhd fnl 3f* **80/1**

2m 36.26s (-4.74) **Going Correction** -0.175s/f (Stan)
WFA 3 from 4yo+ 6lb **12** Ran SP% **116.9**
Speed ratings (Par 103): **108,107,107,101,95 95,94,92,90,89 89,84**
toteswingers:1&2:£4.80, 2&3:£4.80, 1&3:£14.00 CSF £58.02 CT £305.48 TOTE £18.10: £4.90, £1.20, £2.50; EX 46.30 TRIFECTA Not won.
Owner W Clifford **Bred** London Thoroughbred Services Ltd **Trained** Pandy, Monmouths

FOCUS
Despite the withdrawal this was still a competitive handicap for the grade. There was a fair pace on and the first three pulled clear in a driving finish with the third the best guide.
Black Falcon(IRE) Official explanation: jockey said gelding hung left

7506 HOSPITALITY AT SOUTHWELL RACECOURSE H'CAP 6f (F)
3:30 (3:31) (Class 5) (0-75,75) 3-Y-O+ **£2,729** (£806; £403) **Stalls** Low

Form RPR

0033 **1** **Great Charm (IRE)**[24] 7191 4-9-1 **72**.......................ShaneKelly 8 81
(E J Alston) *trckd ldrs: hdwy 1/2-way: effrt and edgd lft 2f out: rdn to ld over 1f out: kpt on wl towards fin* **4/1**[1]

1005 **2** *¾* **Dig Deep (IRE)**[24] 7191 7-9-1 **72**.......................PaulHanagan 6 79
(J J Quinn) *in tch: hdwy on inner 2f out: rdn over 1f out and ev ch tl drvn and nt qckn wl ins fnl f* **12/1**

006 **3** *1 ¼* **Kipchak (IRE)**[43] 6739 4-8-8 **65**.......................(p) LPKeniry 4 68
(C R Dore) *prom: hdwy to chse ldr 1/2-way: rdn 2f out and ev ch tl drvn and one pce ins fnl f* **20/1**

0005 **4** *½* **Mozayada (USA)**[28] 7092 5-9-1 **72**.......................RobertWinston 3 73
(M Brittain) *trckd ldrs: hdwy wl over 2f out: rdn over 1f out and sn ev ch tl drvn and one pce ins fnl f* **20/1**

6310 **5** *nk* **Elusive Hawk (IRE)**[33] 6964 5-9-4 **75**.......................JerryO'Dwyer 9 75+
(B J Curley) *dwlt and towards rr: hdwy on wd outside over 2f out: rdn to chse ldrs over 1f out: edgd lft and one pce ins fnl f* **9/2**[2]

4061 **6** *nk* **Naomh Geileis (USA)**[12] 7349 4-8-7 **64**.......................(b) JoeFanning 2 63+
(M Johnston) *dwlt and towards rr: hdwy 2f out: rdn and kpt on ins fnl f: nrst fin* **7/1**

0100 **7** *shd* **He's A Humbug (IRE)**[100] 5073 5-8-12 **69** ow1.......................TGMcLaughlin 7 68
(J O'Reilly) *towards rr: hdwy over 2f out: swtchd lft and rdn wl over 1f out: kpt on ins fnl f* **80/1**

1240 **8** *1 ¼* **Premier Lad**[13] 7337 3-9-0 **71**.......................PhillipMakin 10 66
(T D Barron) *hld up towards rr: hdwy over 2f out: rdn to chse ldrs whn n.m.r over 1f out: sn no imp* **6/1**[3]

0600 **9** *1 ½* **Royal Envoy (IRE)**[15] 7321 6-8-0 **62**.......................AndrewHeffernan(5) 5 52
(P Howling) *prom: rdn along over 2f out: drvn and edgd rt wl over 1f out: sn wknd* **16/1**

0052 **10** *hd* **Rio Cobolo (IRE)**[13] 7337 3-9-1 **72**.......................(v) ChrisCatlin 1 62
(Paul Green) *midfield on inner: rdn along over 2f out and no hdwy* **10/1**

0033 **11** *¾* **Tangerine Trees**[15] 7321 4-8-13 **70**.......................TomEaves 12 57
(B Smart) *chsd ldrs on outer: rdn along over 2f out: sn wknd* **9/1**

0330 **12** *2 ½* **Lucky Art (USA)**[18] 7269 3-8-13 **70**.......................AndrewElliott 11 49
(Mrs R A Carr) *led and sn clr: rdn over 2f out: hung lft and drvn wl over 1f out: sn hdd & wknd* **28/1**

0003 **13** *11* **A Big Sky Brewing (USA)**[54] 6437 5-8-2 **64**.......................DeanHeslop(5) 13 8
(T D Barron) *dwlt: sn rdn along in rr: bhd fr 1/2-way* **16/1**

1m 14.99s (-1.51) **Going Correction** -0.175s/f (Stan) **13** Ran SP% **117.7**
Speed ratings (Par 103): **103,102,100,99,99 98,98,97,95,94 93,90,75**
toteswingers:1&2:£12.10, 2&3:£47.70, 1&3:£25.60 CSF £49.29 CT £863.36 TOTE £3.60: £1.70, £3.70, £3.50; EX 63.10 TRIFECTA Not won. .
Owner Mr & Mrs G Middlebrook **Bred** G And Mrs Middlebrook **Trained** Longton, Lancs

FOCUS
This modest sprint handicap was another race that looked wide-open and there was any amount of chances from 2f out. The winner bult on recent efforts while the runner-up ran his best race of the year.
T/Jkpt: Not won. T/Plt: £1,004.70 to a £1 stake. Pool: £51,079.58. 37.11 winning tickets. T/Qpdt: £140.00 to a £1 stake. Pool: £5,054.90. 26.70 winning tickets. JR

6927 ANGERS (R-H)
Tuesday, November 24

OFFICIAL GOING: Heavy

7507a PRIX GEOFFROY DE LA CELLE (MAIDEN) (C&G) 1m 2f
12:55 (12:58) 2-Y-O £6,796 (£2,718; £2,039; £1,359; £680)

RPR
1 **Flight Tune (FR)** 2-9-2 FVeron —
(H-A Pantall, France)
2 ¾ **Curro Perote (FR)**[27] 2-9-2 JLermyte —
(L A Urbano-Grajales, France)
3 6 **Kazzene (USA)**[46] 2-9-2 (p) CNora —
(F Chappet, France)
4 1 ½ **Apollo Blues (IRE)**[37] 2-9-2 JAuge —
(E J O'Neill) *led or disp ld: 2nd and pushed along st: styd on at one pce tl no ex fr over 1f out* **9/1**[1]
5 3 **Malakhan (FR)** 2-9-2 —
(G Henrot, France)
6 2 **A Tout Coeur (FR)** 2-9-2 (b) —
(Dominique Sepulchre, France)
7 5 **Puerto De Baune (FR)** 2-9-2 —
(C Plisson, France)
8 3 **Polyfonico (FR)** 2-9-2 —
(Y Barberot, France)
9 nk **Lockland (FR)** 2-9-2 —
(C Morineau, France)
10 2 **Two Minds (FR)** 2-9-2 —
(T Cambefort,)
0 **Novy Nick (FR)**[58] 6322 2-9-2 (p) —
(C Diard, France)
0 **Pride Du Clos (FR)** 2-9-2 —
(L Godard, France)
0 **Quatz Seanium (FR)** 2-9-2 —
(Mme C Herisson, France)

2m 14.26s (134.26) **13** Ran SP% **10.0**
PARI-MUTUEL (Including 1 Euro stake): WIN 4.70; PL 1.60, 1.20, 2.00;DF 6.20.
Owner P Baudouin **Bred** Rene Wattinne **Trained** France

7474 KEMPTON (A.W) (R-H)
Wednesday, November 25

OFFICIAL GOING: Standard
Wind: Moderate, half behind Weather: Dark

7510 GROOMED TO PERFECTION, THE KIA SOUL MEDIAN AUCTION MAIDEN STKS 5f (P)
6:20 (6:24) (Class 6) 3-5-Y-O £2,047 (£604; £302) Stalls High

Form RPR
-54 1 **Spinning Bailiwick**[20] 7254 3-8-12 50 TPQueally 1 71
(G L Moore) *mde all: drew rt away fnl 2f: rdn out* **7/2**[2]
2245 2 6 **Westwood Dawn**[9] 7411 4-9-3 57 (vt) DaneO'Neill 2 54
(D Shaw) *chsd ldng trio: rdn 2f out: styd on to take 2nd last 100yds: no ch* **7/4**[1]
0300 3 1 **Chosen Son (IRE)**[13] 7355 3-9-3 60 (t) DarrylHolland 5 51
(P J O'Gorman) *t.k.h: hld up in 6th: pushed along and no prog 2f out: kpt on fnl f to take 3rd last 75yds* **7/4**[1]
0520 4 ¾ **Shirley High**[9] 7411 3-8-12 50 PaulDoe 3 43
(P Howling) *disp 2nd pl to over 1f out: fdd ins fnl f* **16/1**
0400 5 ½ **Sandy Par**[5] 7462 4-9-3 45 (p) LukeMorris 6 46
(J M Bradley) *uns rdr and rn off for abt a m bef r: mostly chsd wnr: lft bhd fr 2f out: wknd and lost pl last 100yds* **8/1**[3]
0000 6 5 **Badtanman**[45] 6699 3-9-3 41 LPKeniry 4 28
(Peter Grayson) *dwlt: mostly last and a outpcd* **33/1**
0000 7 1 ½ **Mrs Medley**[47] 6641 3-8-12 32 AdamKirby 7 18
(D Shaw) *rdn in 5th pl 1/2-way: wknd wl over 1f out* **80/1**

59.91 secs (-0.59) **Going Correction** -0.075s/f (Stan) **7** Ran SP% **116.1**
Speed ratings (Par 101): **101,91,89,88,87 79,77**
toteswingers:1&2:£1.40, 2&3:£1.50, 1&3:£1.40 CSF £10.39 TOTE £5.30: £2.10, £1.40; EX 11.00.
Owner Dr Ian R Shenkin **Bred** Mrs M Shenkin **Trained** Lower Beeding, W Sussex
■ Stewards' Enquiry : Adam Kirby caution: used whip without giving filly time to respond

FOCUS
An extremely weak maiden. The winner was a big improver with the runner-up probably the best guide.

7511 BOXINGDAYRACES.CO.UK H'CAP 5f (P)
6:50 (6:50) (Class 4) (0-85,84) 3-Y-O+ £4,727 (£1,406; £702; £351) Stalls High

Form RPR
6201 1 **Lesley's Choice**[19] 7269 3-9-3 83 (v) FrankieMcDonald 11 92
(R Curtis) *mde all: urged along and over 1l clr 1f out: styd on wl enough* **7/2**[1]
5330 2 nk **Excellent Show**[47] 6647 3-8-11 77 TomEaves 9 85
(B Smart) *nt wl away and bustled up into midfield: effrt over 1f out: styd on to take 2nd ins fnl f: clsng on wnr fin* **8/1**
1012 3 ½ **Bahamian Lad**[26] 7155 4-9-1 81 JerryO'Dwyer 10 87
(R Hollinshead) *chsd ldng pair: rdn over 1f out: kpt on to dispute 2nd ins fnl f: nt qckn after* **15/2**
443 4 nk **Cecily**[20] 7253 3-9-0 80 (b) SebSanders 5 85
(Sir Mark Prescott) *hld up in 10th: rdn over 1f out: gd prog ent fnl f: dispute3d 2nd 100yds out: no ex* **8/1**
3050 5 ½ **The Tatling (IRE)**[26] 7155 12-8-13 82 JackDean(3) 8 85
(J M Bradley) *mostly in midfield: effrt and eased to over 1f out: styd on fnl f: nrst fin but nvr able to threaten* **16/1**
2614 6 ¾ **Feelin Foxy**[19] 7269 5-9-0 80 TPQueally 7 80
(J G Given) *pressed wnr: nt qckn and hld over 1f out: lost pls last 100yds* **8/1**
1102 7 1 **Even Bolder**[11] 7395 6-8-2 75 KierenFox(7) 4 72+
(E A Wheeler) *towards rr on outer: nt clr run wl over 1f out and little ch after: styd on fnl 100yds* **9/2**[2]
0400 8 ½ **Priti Fabulous (IRE)**[19] 7269 4-8-3 76 DeclanCannon(7) 6 71
(A J McCabe) *s.s: last tl styd on u.p fnl f: no ch* **50/1**
-046 9 1 ¼ **Cerito**[11] 7395 3-8-13 84 MatthewDavies(5) 12 75
(J R Boyle) *chsd ldng pair: no prog over 1f out: wknd rapidly fnl f* **7/1**[3]
1600 10 hd **Baunagain (IRE)**[82] 5646 4-9-2 82 NCallan 1 72
(P W Chapple-Hyam) *racd wd in midfield: lost grnd bnd over 2f out: nvr on terms w ldrs after* **20/1**
1145 11 3 ½ **Harry Up**[142] 3694 8-8-13 79 (p) SJCraine 3 56
(M J Scudamore) *unable to ld: chsd ldrs on outer: u.p 1/2-way: wknd over 1f out* **20/1**

59.69 secs (-0.81) **Going Correction** -0.075s/f (Stan) **11** Ran SP% **115.4**
Speed ratings (Par 105): **103,102,101,101,100 99,97,96,94,94 88**
toteswingers:1&2:£10.50, 2&3:£21.90, 1&3:£3.20 CSF £30.22 CT £170.42 TOTE £4.90: £1.70, £3.20, £2.20; EX 46.80.
Owner B C Allen **Bred** B C Allen **Trained** Lambourn, Berks

FOCUS
A tight handicap and the form looks sound with the placed horses to form.

7512 DIGIBET H'CAP 1m 2f (P)
7:20 (7:21) (Class 5) (0-70,68) 3-Y-O+ £2,590 (£770; £385; £192) Stalls High

Form RPR
245 1 **Crazy Chris**[35] 6934 4-9-8 68 DavidProbert 5 83
(B Palling) *cl up on inner: chsd ldr wl over 1f out: upsides fnl f: won on the nod post* **14/1**
2211 2 shd **Thunderstruck**[11] 7403 4-9-8 68 (p) ChrisCatlin 4 83
(J A Glover) *led and nt seriously pressed tl 3f out whn pushed along briefly: kicked on 2f out: jnd fnl f: battled on wl: btn on the nod* **7/2**[2]
5135 3 6 **The Grey One (IRE)**[8] 7423 6-9-6 66 (p) LukeMorris 12 69
(J M Bradley) *t.k.h: wl in tch: rdn over 2f out: kpt on to take 3rd ins fnl f: no ch ldng pair* **11/1**
6146 4 1 ¾ **Inquisitress**[7] 7433 5-8-5 54 oh2 MarcHalford(3) 3 53
(J J Bridger) *hld up in last trio: prog to 8th 3f out: effrt on outer wl over 1f out: disp 3rd fnl f: no ex* **33/1**
5012 5 ¾ **Hector Spectre (IRE)**[24] 7198 3-9-2 66 PaulDoe 9 64
(P D Evans) *mostly chsd ldr: drvn to chal 3f out: btn off 2f out: wknd jst over 1f out* **14/1**
3026 6 ½ **Our Kes (IRE)**[11] 7403 7-8-11 57 IanMongan 6 54+
(P Howling) *stdd s: hld up in last pair: prog but only 10th over 2f out: styd on u.p: no ch* **25/1**
2542 7 1 ¼ **Chantilly Pearl (USA)**[11] 7399 3-9-2 66 TPQueally 13 60
(J G Given) *hld up towards rr: dropped to last trio 4f out and pushed along: styd on fr over 1f out: no ch* **10/1**
0522 8 nk **Vinces**[20] 7250 5-9-7 67 GeorgeBaker 2 60
(T D McCarthy) *t.k.h in midfield: no prog over 2f out: wl btn over 1f out* **8/1**[3]
0113 9 6 **Giant Sequoia (USA)**[28] 7112 5-9-8 68 (t) JamieSpencer 8 49
(Jane Chapple-Hyam) *prom: tried to chal 3f out but sn under heavy press: wknd 2f out* **2/1**[1]
-000 10 ¾ **Alfie Tupper (IRE)**[138] 3811 6-9-7 67 SJCraine 10 47
(J R Boyle) *wl in tch in midfield tl wknd u.p wl over 2f out* **25/1**
0060 11 8 **Sonny Parkin**[30] 7065 7-8-9 60 (v) SimonPearce(5) 7 24
(J Pearce) *stdd s: hld up in last pair: wknd 3f out: bhd after* **50/1**
0563 12 1 ¼ **Mutually Mine (USA)**[11] 7399 3-9-0 64 JerryO'Dwyer 11 25
(Mrs P Sly) *towards rr: u.p and struggling 3f out: sn bhd* **10/1**
000 13 11 **Illicit**[13] 7357 4-9-3 63 (tp) KirstyMilczarek 1 —
(J R Holt) *s.i.s: chsd ldrs on wd outside tl wknd over 3f out: t.o* **66/1**

2m 6.15s (-1.85) **Going Correction** -0.075s/f (Stan)
WFA 3 from 4yo+ 4lb **13** Ran SP% **120.6**
Speed ratings (Par 103): **104,103,99,97,97 96,95,95,90,90 83,82,73**
toteswingers:1&2:£14.40, 2&3:£8.60, 1&3:£34.20 CSF £60.75 CT £580.51 TOTE £16.90: £4.40, £1.70, £3.60; EX 74.40.
Owner E R Griffiths **Bred** E R Griffiths **Trained** Tredodridge, Vale Of Glamorgan

FOCUS
All bar one of these (the winner) were thoroughly exposed, and the third sets the level.

7513 DIGIBET.COM NURSERY (DIV I) 7f (P)
7:50 (7:51) (Class 6) (0-65,65) 2-Y-O £1,706 (£503; £252) Stalls High

Form RPR
0001 1 **Lisahane Bog**[11] 7389 2-9-4 62 (p) DaneO'Neill 10 65+
(P R Hedger) *s.i.s and scrubbed along early in last trio: eased to outer and prog 2f out: shkn up and r.o to ld last 100yds: quite decisively* **4/1**[2]
0235 2 ¾ **Edward Whymper**[12] 7363 2-9-2 65 AshleyMorgan(5) 9 66
(M H Tompkins) *hld up towards rr on inner: prog over 2f out: chal and upsides 1f out: kpt on one pce last 100yds* **7/2**[1]
0640 3 shd **Valkov**[72] 5935 2-9-5 63 RichardKingscote 8 64
(Tom Dascombe) *chsd ldng pair: rdn over 2f out: styd on to ld over 1f out: sn jnd: hdd and one pce last 100yds* **11/1**
6604 4 2 ¼ **Starwatch**[21] 7235 2-8-13 60 MarcHalford(3) 7 55
(J J Bridger) *chsd ldr: upsides wl over 1f out: wknd ent fnl f* **8/1**
000 5 1 **Novillero**[48] 6616 2-8-4 48 FrankieMcDonald 5 41
(J C Fox) *mostly in midfield: rdn over 2f out: tried to cl over 1f out: no imp and fading fnl f* **25/1**
0206 6 2 ¼ **Creevy (IRE)**[14] 7335 2-8-6 50 DavidProbert 6 37
(S Kirk) *cl up: rdn over 2f out: nt qckn over 1f out: wknd fnl f* **5/1**[3]
060 7 1 ¾ **Joe Rua (USA)**[28] 7121 2-8-9 53 (v[1]) JerryO'Dwyer 1 36
(J Ryan) *hld up in last trio: rdn and effrt on outer over 2f out: no imp on ldrs* **25/1**
0600 8 1 ½ **Knockback (IRE)**[4] 7482 2-8-7 51 LPKeniry 11 30
(P R Chamings) *mde most to over 1f out: wknd rapidly* **25/1**
3006 9 1 **Orsett Lad (USA)**[12] 7363 2-9-4 62 RobertWinston 4 39
(J R Best) *stdd s: t.k.h and hld up last: shkn up 3f out: no rspnse* **9/1**
600 10 2 ¾ **Motty's Gift**[93] 5311 2-8-11 55 AdamKirby 3 25
(W R Swinburn) *chsd ldrs: u.p 1/2-way: sn lost pl and btn* **5/1**[3]
5606 11 2 **Pursuit Of Gold**[37] 6905 2-9-0 58 SteveDrowne 2 23
(J R Best) *nvr beyond midfield: pushed along and dropped to last trio 3f out: sn btn* **20/1**

1m 26.63s (0.63) **Going Correction** -0.075s/f (Stan) **11** Ran SP% **121.3**
Speed ratings (Par 94): **93,92,92,89,88 85,83,82,80,77 75**
toteswingers:1&2:£4.40, 2&3:£13.70, 1&3:£20.00 CSF £18.05 CT £127.59 TOTE £5.40: £1.80, £2.00, £3.20; EX 23.60.
Owner P C F Racing Ltd **Bred** J J Whelan **Trained** Dogmersfield, Hampshire

■ Stewards' Enquiry : Ashley Morgan three-day ban: used whip with excessive frequency (Dec 9-11)

FOCUS

A tricky nursery but won with plenty of authority.

NOTEBOOK

Lisahane Bog ◆ is progressive and proved there was no fluke about his 66-1 handicap debut win off 56 at Lingfield 11 days earlier and won this off 62. Once again he was given time to find his stride and was value for more than the winning distance. He has a stout bottom line and gives the distinct impression he'll get further than this. The Handicapper might have trouble holding him next time. (op 5-1)

Edward Whymper ran up to his best over what seems his ideal distance. There's nothing wrong with his mark and he was just unlucky to bump into an improver. (op 9-2)

Valkov, 2lb lower than when making a disappointing handicap debut 72 days ago, was much better here on her second Polytrack appearance and she can certainly win one of these. She had the winner behind her in at Warwick in August, but that was on his debut. (op 12-1)

Starwatch didn't have the pace to make a difference and the 2lb drop was not enough. His right trip seems something of a mystery.

Novillero was off 48 for his handicap debut and showed enough to win a poor race. He'll be sharper for this first run in 48 days. (op 28-1)

Creevy(IRE) seemed better suited by this surface than over 1m at Southwell last time off a 3lb lower mark, but she might need the extra furlong. (op 8-1)

Joe Rua(USA) did well enough from a poor draw on this handicap debut and had to come wide. He should be capable off this mark when the stalls position is kinder.

Motty's Gift, upped a furlong for this handicap debut, went out too quickly for the extra distance to be a factor. (op 7-2 tchd 11-2)

7514 DIGIBET.COM NURSERY (DIV II) 7f (P)

8:20 (8:20) (Class 6) (0-65,65) 2-Y-O £1,706 (£503; £252) Stalls High

Form RPR

636 **1** **Blue Lyric**[40] 6821 2-9-5 **63**........................ KFallon 2 78+
(L M Cumani) *hld up in last pair: sltly hmpd wl over 2f out: gd prog sn after: led over 1f out: shkn up and readily drew clr* **11/4**[1]

4033 **2** *3 ¾* **Admiral Cochrane (IRE)**[14] 7333 2-9-4 **62**.................... RobertHavlin 8 65
(W Jarvis) *trckd ldrs gng wl: moved up to ld briefly wl over 1f out: clr of rest but vain chse of wnr fnl f* **11/4**[1]

6504 **3** *5* **Captain Cool (IRE)**[34] 6963 2-8-7 **51**.................... EddieAhern 6 43+
(R Hannon) *pushed along in rr after 2f: effrt whn nt clr run over 2f out and momentum checked: kpt on fr over 1f out to take modest 3rd last 75yds* **6/1**[3]

4635 **4** *1 ¾* **Avec Moi**[13] 7352 2-8-3 **47**.................... AdrianMcCarthy 3 33
(Mrs C A Dunnett) *towards rr: pushed along bef 1/2-way: prog and in tch 2f out: sn outpcd: disp modest 3rd fnl f* **50/1**

0300 **5** *hd* **Ballyvonane (USA)**[6] 7453 2-8-6 **50**....................(b) LukeMorris 4 35
(L A Dace) *racd on outer: pressed ldng pair: reminder 1/2-way: led over 2f out to wl over 1f out: wknd: lost 3rd last 75yds* **25/1**

000 **6** *7* **Feel The Magic (IRE)**[32] 7024 2-8-9 **53**.................... LPKeniry 10 21
(S Kirk) *in tch in midfield: trbld passage on inner fr 3f out to 2f out: brief effrt u.p wl over 1f out: sn wknd rapidly* **20/1**

4330 **7** *2 ¼* **Ba Jetstream**[30] 7055 2-8-9 **53**.................... JerryO'Dwyer 1 15
(F Jordan) *hld up in last: effrt on outer over 2f out: sme prog but easily outpcd over 1f out: wknd rapidly sn after* **66/1**

3503 **8** *6* **Spinning Spirit (IRE)**[29] 7088 2-9-7 **65**.................... TPQueally 7 12
(J G Given) *pressed ldr at str pce to wl over 2f out: sn wknd* **7/2**[2]

0500 **9** *5* **Phoenix Rose (IRE)**[11] 7389 2-8-11 **55**.................... RobertWinston 11 —
(J R Best) *chsd ldrs but nvr gng easily: u.p and trying to cl whn rdr dropped whip over 2f out: wknd rapidly over 1f out* **25/1**

2040 **10** *1 ¼* **Mind Of Her Own**[4] 7482 2-8-11 **60**....................(v[1]) RichardEvans(5) 9 —
(P D Evans) *tanked along in front at str pce: hdd & wknd over 2f out: eased and sn wl bhd* **16/1**

1m 26.11s (0.11) **Going Correction** -0.075s/f (Stan) 10 Ran SP% 111.6
Speed ratings (Par 94): **96,91,86,84,83 75,73,66,60,59**
toteswingers:1&2:£4.50, 2&3:£3.70, 1&3:£5.20 CSF £9.14 CT £39.85 TOTE £3.10: £1.50, £1.80, £2.10; EX 13.00.
Owner Fittocks Stud & Andrew Bengough **Bred** Cavendish Bloodstock **Trained** Newmarket, Suffolk

FOCUS

The second division of the nursery looked more open on paper than the first but was won with plenty of authority in a time 0.50sec faster

NOTEBOOK

Blue Lyric ◆, a handicap debutante, scored in a fast er time than that taken in the first leg, and it was all the more creditable as her jockey was able to relax in the closing stages. She was ridden with plenty of confidence, dropped out from a poor draw, and although she was beaten over a mile on her previous start 40 days earlier at Redcar, that wouldn't seem a problem on this evidence. Fallon considered she was extremely well suited by the surface and while the Handicapper will administer a severe hike from this lenient 63, she will take some holding next time. (op 5-2 tchd 3-1)

Admiral Cochrane(IRE) was unfortunate to come up against an above-average and unexposed winner. He was off the same mark of 62 that saw him finish third over 6f at Southwell 14 days earlier and he stays this trip, but not as well as the winner. He was well clear of the third so will go up, but has the right attitude. (op 3-1 tchd 5-2)

Captain Cool(IRE) style of running makes him a chancy betting prospect. He needs things to fall his way coming from off the pace and will be sharper for this first run in 34 days. He started off a mark of 60 and is now 51. (op 9-2)

Ballyvonane(USA) ran better than his last two appeances but the step up of a furlong didn't look the right one. (op 20-1)

Ba Jetstream was held up on this Polytrack debut but dropped away late on as if something was amiss.

Spinning Spirit(IRE) had been beaten over a mile, then when dropped back to 6f last time. On this evidence 7f isn't right either so his trip is a mystery. (tchd 10-3 and 4-1)

Mind Of Her Own Official explanation: jockey said filly lost its action

7515 DIGIBET CASINO H'CAP 2m (P)

8:50 (8:50) (Class 4) (0-85,86) 3-Y-0+ £4,727 (£1,406; £702; £351) Stalls High

Form RPR

4310 **1** **Moonbeam Dancer (USA)**[5] 7461 3-8-1 **67**.................... NickyMackay 2 73
(D M Simcock) *stdd s: hld up in last pair: rdn wl over 2f out: prog on outer to ld over 1f out: sn wl in command* **4/1**[3]

1-00 **2** *2 ¾* **Viper**[39] 6851 7-10-1 **86**........................ HayleyTurner 1 89
(R Hollinshead) *content to trck stdy pce: effrt to ld jst over 2f out: hdd and outpcd over 1f out* **11/2**

5052 **3** *4 ½* **Clear Reef**[11] 7402 5-9-8 **82**....................(p) AndreaAtzeni(3) 3 80
(Jane Chapple-Hyam) *hld up last: tk clsr order 6f out: wnt 3rd over 3f out: rdn and nt qckn over 2f out: nvr gng pce* **2/1**[2]

1235 **4** *1* **Mission Control (IRE)**[24] 899 4-9-3 **74**.................... SJCraine 5 70
(Tim Vaughan) *trckd ldng pair: in trble as sn as pce lifted 4f out: dropped to last and wl btn jst over 2f out* **7/4**[1]

6160 **5** *3 ¼* **Hucking Hero (IRE)**[4] 7490 4-8-6 **66** oh6.............(v[1]) RobertLButler(3) 4 59
(J R Boyle) *t.k.h: led at v stdy pce: kicked on 4f out: hdd jst over 2f out: sn wknd* **20/1**

3m 34.73s (4.63) **Going Correction** -0.075s/f (Stan)
WFA 3 from 4yo+ 9lb 5 Ran SP% **109.8**
Speed ratings (Par 105): **85,83,81,80,79**
CSF £24.25 TOTE £4.70: £2.50, £2.90; EX 11.00.
Owner Dr Ali Ridha **Bred** Swifty Farms Inc & Darley **Trained** Newmarket, Suffolk

FOCUS

There wasn't much pace early in this fair staying handicap and the form is limited by the proximity of the fifth.

Mission Control(IRE) Official explanation: trainer's rep said, regarding running, that the gelding was unsuited by the slow early pace.

7516 TRY OUR NEW BISTRO MENU H'CAP 7f (P)

9:20 (9:21) (Class 4) (0-80,84) 3-Y-0+ £4,727 (£1,406; £702; £351) Stalls High

Form RPR

2301 **1** **Black Dahlia**[16] 7321 4-9-2 **75**........................ ChrisCatlin 9 93
(J A Glover) *hld up in 9th: smooth prog on outer 2f out: cruised by u.p rivals jst over 1f out: sn wl clr: impressive* **14/1**

1521 **2** *6* **King's Colour**[7] 7437 4-9-11 **84** 6ex.................... LPKeniry 6 86
(B R Johnson) *hld up in 8th: prog on inner over 2f out: drvn to dispute ld over 1f out: sn lft bhd by wnr* **13/8**[1]

0000 **3** *½* **Resplendent Nova**[14] 7327 7-8-9 **68**........................ PaulDoe 5 69
(P Howling) *hld up in last pair: rdn on outer over 2f out: styd on fr over 1f out to take 3rd last stride* **16/1**

0245 **4** *nse* **Space Station**[36] 6915 3-8-9 **69**........................ TonyCulhane 3 70
(S Dow) *w ldng pair on outer: wnt 2nd wl over 2f out: nt qckn over 1f out: outpcd sn after* **14/1**

0044 **5** *¾* **Esteem Machine (USA)**[37] 6904 5-9-4 **77**.................... LukeMorris 10 75
(R A Teal) *dwlt: hld up in last pair: effrt on inner 2f out: kpt on u.p to press plcd horses ins fnl f* **7/1**[3]

5130 **6** *nse* **Learo Dochais (USA)**[88] 5448 3-8-12 **72**.................... NCallan 1 70
(M A Jarvis) *trckd ldrs: effrt over 2f out: nt qckn over 1f out: kpt on same pce* **14/1**

5233 **7** *½* **Defector (IRE)**[28] 7111 3-8-11 **71**.................... MartinDwyer 7 68
(W R Muir) *mde most to jst over 1f out: wknd* **9/2**[2]

0653 **8** *2* **Snow Bay**[25] 7181 3-9-3 **77**........................ TomEaves 8 69
(B Smart) *t.k.h: trckd ldrs: drvn and cl up over 2f out: nt qckn over 1f out: wknd fnl f* **16/1**

321- **9** *4 ½* **Fen Spirit (IRE)**[384] 7207 3-9-5 **79**.................... RobertHavlin 2 58
(J H M Gosden) *s.i.s: plld hrd early and sn trckd ldrs: wknd 2f out* **15/2**

0020 **10** *6* **Bobs Dreamflight**[65] 6167 3-9-1 **75**.................... DaneO'Neill 4 38
(D K Ivory) *t.k.h: pressed ldr to wl over 2f out: wknd rapidly* **33/1**

1m 24.56s (-1.44) **Going Correction** -0.075s/f (Stan)
WFA 3 from 4yo+ 1lb 10 Ran SP% **115.2**
Speed ratings (Par 105): **105,98,97,97,96 96,96,93,88,81**
toteswingers:1&2:£3.40, 2&3:£9.90, 1&3:£13.00 CSF £36.66 CT £385.23 TOTE £12.10: £2.30, £1.50, £3.40; EX 53.20 Place 6 £154.68, Place 5 £82.72 .
Owner Paul J Dixon & Brian Morton **Bred** Worksop Manor Stud **Trained** Babworth, Notts

FOCUS

A fair handicap run at a sound gallop and best rated around the placed horses.

Esteem Machine(USA) Official explanation: jockey said gelding missed the break

T/Plt: £129.90 to a £1 stake. Pool: £81,355.42. 457.06 winning tickets. T/Qpdt: £28.00 to a £1 stake. Pool: £6,336.70. 167.00 winning tickets. JN

7482 LINGFIELD (L-H)

Wednesday, November 25

OFFICIAL GOING: Standard

Wind: Strong, half behind Weather: Mainly fine, heavy shower race 6, cloudy race 8

7517 ALL WEATHER "HANDS AND HEELS" APPRENTICE H'CAP (DIV I) 7f (P)

12:00 (12:00) (Class 6) (0-58,58) 3-Y-0+ £1,637 (£483; £241) Stalls Low

Form RPR

0000 **1** **Dynamo Dave (USA)**[64] 6186 4-8-3 **46** oh1.............(b) RachelKing(3) 11 54
(M D I Usher) *hld up in midfield: rdn and hdwy over 1f out: r.o to ld nr fin* **25/1**

01 **2** *¾* **Bollywood Style**[285] 531 4-9-2 **56**........................ RyanPowell 8 62
(J R Best) *hld up in midfield: rdn and hdwy over 1f out: slt ld ins fnl f: hdd nr fin* **8/1**

5524 **3** *¾* **Headache**[5] 7462 4-8-12 **52**....................(bt) MatthewLawson 1 56
(B W Duke) *led: rdn over 1f out: hdd and nt qckn ins fnl f* **5/1**[2]

-002 **4** *shd* **Josr's Magic (IRE)**[24] 7197 5-9-1 **58**.................... AdamCarter(3) 9 62
(T E Powell) *chsd ldrs: rdn to chal ins fnl f: kpt on same pce* **4/1**[1]

056 **5** *nk* **Always The Sun**[7] 7431 3-8-9 **50**....................(p) LauraPike 4 53
(P Leech) *chsd ldrs: rdn 2f out: kpt on same pce fnl f* **10/1**

0265 **6** *1 ½* **Rebel Woman**[12] 7369 3-8-9 **53**.................... NathanAlison(3) 14 52
(J A Osborne) *s.i.s: bhd tl pushed along and r.o appr fnl f: nrst fin* **12/1**

6333 **7** *nk* **Outer Hebrides**[8] 7418 8-8-13 **53**....................(v) RyanClark 6 51
(J M Bradley) *in tch: effrt on ins over 2f out: one pce* **5/1**[2]

0000 **8** *nk* **Greystoke Prince**[8] 7424 4-8-10 **55**....................(t) CarolineKelly(5) 7 52
(P S McEntee) *hld up towards rr: pushed along and styd on appr fnl f: nvr nrr* **66/1**

0003 **9** *2* **Batchworth Blaise**[56] 6399 6-8-6 **46** oh1.................... RichardRowe 3 38
(E A Wheeler) *s.s: bhd: sme hdwy over 1f out: no further prog* **20/1**

0000 **10** *2* **Lady Dinsdale (IRE)**[56] 6390 3-8-2 **46** oh1.............. TraceyAddey(3) 10 32
(T Keddy) *prom 5f* **100/1**

6000 **11** *1 ¼* **Metropolitan Chief**[102] 5020 5-8-3 **46** oh1.............(b) AlexEdwards(3) 12 29
(P Burgoyne) *prom tl wknd qckly over 1f out* **40/1**

0610 **12** *¾* **Mystic Touch**[11] 7392 3-9-1 **56**........................ DavidKenny 13 37
(A B Haynes) *sn rdn along towards rr* **7/1**[3]

3300 **13** *1 ½* **Golden Square**[21] 802 7-8-1 **46** oh1.............. GeorgeDowning(5) 5 23
(A W Carroll) *sn outpcd and bhd* **12/1**

005 **14** *10* **Torquemada (IRE)**[27] 7129 8-8-8 **48**....................(tp) KierenFox 2 —
(M J Attwater) *chsd ldrs over 5f: wknd qckly* **20/1**

1m 25.6s (0.80) **Going Correction** +0.15s/f (Slow)
WFA 3 from 4yo+ 1lb 14 Ran SP% **119.7**
Speed ratings (Par 101): **101,100,99,99,98 97,96,96,94,91 90,89,87,76**
toteswingers:1&2:£42.00, 2&3:£7.20, 1&3:£37.90 CSF £202.64 CT £1217.05 TOTE £25.80: £7.00, £5.10, £1.40; EX 242.30 TRIFECTA Not won..
Owner R H Brookes **Bred** Barry Weisbord And Margaret Santulli **Trained** Upper Lambourn, Berks

■ Stewards' Enquiry : Tracey Addey 3-day ban: careless riding (Dec 9-11)

FOCUS
Exposed performers in a moderate handicap, which was run at a reasonable gallop and the form looks sound. The principals came down the centre in the straight.
Headache Official explanation: jockey said gelding hung right in straight
Batchworth Blaise Official explanation: jockey said gelding was slowly away

7518 ARDINGLY H'CAP (DIV I) — 6f (P)
12:30 (12:30) (Class 5) (0-70,70) 3-Y-0+ — £2,388 (£705; £352) Stalls Low

Form — RPR
00- **1** **Partner (IRE)**[18] 7296 3-8-11 **63**..........(b) JamieSpencer 11 — 76+
(David Marnane, Ire) *hld up in rr: rdn and gd hdwy in centre over 1f out: led ins fnl f: sn clr* **4/1**[2]
1320 **2** 2 ½ **Titus Gent**[19] 7273 4-9-2 **68**.......... DavidProbert 4 — 73
(R A Harris) *pressed ldr: led wl over 1f out tl ins fnl f: nt pce of wnr* **8/1**
3620 **3** ½ **Yankee Storm**[34] 6976 4-9-2 **68**.......... KFallon 10 — 71
(H J Collingridge) *bhd: rdn and hdwy over 1f out: styd on to take 3rd ins fnl f* **9/2**[3]
5440 **4** ¾ **Mambo Spirit (IRE)**[160] 3065 5-9-3 **69**.......... TPQueally 2 — 70+
(Stef Liddiard) *t.k.h: chsd ldrs: hrd rdn 1f out: one pce* **2/1**[1]
1220 **5** ½ **Suhayl Star (IRE)**[169] 2799 5-8-12 **64**.......... LukeMorris 7 — 63
(P Burgoyne) *t.k.h: chsd ldrs: hrd rdn 1f out: no ex* **14/1**
5003 **6** ¾ **Cheap Thrills**[32] 7028 3-9-4 **70**.......... ShaneKelly 6 — 67
(J A Osborne) *led tl wl over 1f out: wknd fnl f* **16/1**
5130 **7** ½ **Agnes Love**[14] 7329 3-8-5 **60**.......... AndreaAtzeni(3) 9 — 55
(J Akehurst) *mid-div: hrd rdn 2f out: no imp* **20/1**
514 **8** ½ **Todber**[27] 7138 4-9-4 **70**..........(v) HayleyTurner 5 — 64
(M P Tregoning) *hld up towards rr: rdn over 1f out: nt trble ldrs* **9/1**
02-0 **9** ½ **Dakota Hills**[14] 7327 3-9-3 **69**.......... RobertWinston 8 — 61
(J R Best) *pressed ldrs tl wknd over 1f out* **33/1**
5000 **10** 2 **Miss Hollybell**[14] 7327 3-9-1 **67**.......... ChrisCatlin 1 — 53
(J Gallagher) *a in rr: rdn and lost tch over 2f out* **40/1**
400- **11** ½ **Doctor Hilary**[376] 7315 7-9-4 **70**..........(v) RobertHavlin 3 — 54
(A B Haynes) *in tch tl wknd over 1f out* **66/1**

1m 12.67s (0.77) **Going Correction** +0.15s/f (Slow) 11 Ran SP% **116.8**
Speed ratings (Par 103): **100,96,96,95,94 93,92,92,91,88 88**
toteswingers:1&2:£5.00, 2&3:£8.10, 1&3:£5.10 CSF £34.45 CT £152.71 TOTE £4.90: £1.30, £3.10, £2.30; EX 39.40 TRIFECTA Not won..
Owner Philip Lloyd/Mrs Melanie Marnane **Bred** Miss Joan Murphy **Trained** Bansha, Co Tipperary

FOCUS
A modest handicap that was run at an ordinary gallop for a race over 6f but the form looks sound enough overall. The winner came down the centre in the straight.
Mambo Spirit(IRE) Official explanation: jockey said gelding ran too free early
Miss Hollybell Official explanation: jockey said filly hung right

7519 ARDINGLY H'CAP (DIV II) — 6f (P)
1:00 (1:04) (Class 5) (0-70,70) 3-Y-0+ — £2,388 (£705; £352) Stalls Low

Form — RPR
2654 **1** **Billberry**[36] 6915 4-9-1 **67**..........(t) AdamKirby 9 — 77
(S C Williams) *hld up in midfield: rdn and hdwy over 1f out: led ins fnl f: all out* **11/4**[2]
1632 **2** ½ **Make My Dream**[28] 7123 6-9-3 **69**.......... JimCrowley 6 — 77
(J Gallagher) *led after 1f: hrd rdn and hdd ins fnl f: kpt on* **10/1**
221 **3** *shd* **Wake Up Call**[28] 7107 3-9-4 **70**.......... JackMitchell 5 — 78
(C F Wall) *led 1f: prom: hrd rdn and chal fnl f: r.o* **6/5**[1]
0532 **4** 3 ½ **Musical Script (USA)**[7] 7432 6-9-0 **66**..........(b) NCallan 7 — 63
(Mouse Hamilton-Fairley) *dwlt: bhd: hdwy whn gap clsd ent st: wnt 4th ins fnl f: nt pce to chal* **5/1**[3]
/55- **5** 1 ¼ **Desert Dust**[348] 7644 6-8-1 **56** oh11.......... AndreaAtzeni(3) 10 — 49
(H J Collingridge) *t.k.h: w ldrs tl hrd rdn and wknd jst over 1f out* **100/1**
2246 **6** 1 ½ **Figaro Flyer (IRE)**[19] 7269 6-9-3 **69**.......... IanMongan 2 — 57
(P Howling) *t.k.h towards rr: n.m.r on rail and dropped to last 3f out: sme hdwy over 1f out: n.d* **25/1**
5001 **7** *nse* **Gentle Guru**[14] 7330 5-9-4 **70**.......... SteveDrowne 11 — 58
(R T Phillips) *towards rr: effrt on outer 2f out: sn outpcd* **18/1**
6600 **8** ½ **Diddums**[7] 7431 3-8-4 **63**.......... CarolineKelly(7) 4 — 49
(P S McEntee) *in tch tl wknd 2f out* **40/1**
200 **9** 10 **Swinbrook (USA)**[14] 7337 8-9-4 **70**..........(v) LiamJones 1 — 24
(R A Harris) *chsd ldrs: drvn along over 3f out: sn wknd: towards rr and btn whn hmpd over 2f out* **20/1**

1m 12.05s (0.15) **Going Correction** +0.15s/f (Slow) 9 Ran SP% **115.2**
Speed ratings (Par 103): **105,104,104,99,97 95,95,95,81**
toteswingers:1&2:£3.60, 2&3:£4.00, 1&3:£2.70 CSF £28.39 CT £48.08 TOTE £4.20: £1.50, £1.70, £1.10; EX 32.40 Trifecta £119.80 Pool: £518.08 - 3.20 winning units..
Owner Essex Racing Club (Billberry) **Bred** G Deacon **Trained** Newmarket, Suffolk

FOCUS
Another ordinary handicap and, as in the first division, the early gallop was just an ordinary one. The first three, who pulled clear, came down the centre in the straight and the form looks solid with the runner-up a sound guide.
Musical Script(USA) Official explanation: jockey said gelding was denied a clear run

7520 BET CHAMPIONS LEAGUE FOOTBALL - BETDAQ CLAIMING STKS — 7f (P)
1:30 (1:31) (Class 6) 3-Y-0+ — £1,978 (£584; £292) Stalls Low

Form — RPR
3601 **1** **Aeroplane**[69] 6024 6-9-6 101.......... JamieSpencer 7 — 90+
(Ian Williams) *hld up in 2nd last: smooth hdwy in centre over 1f out: led on bit ins fnl f: hrd hld* **1/5**[1]
4401 **2** ½ **Monashee Rock (IRE)**[9] 7412 4-8-7 58.......... LPKeniry 8 — 65
(Matthew Salaman) *in tch in 4th: drvn to dispute ld over 1f out: hdd ins fnl f: no ch w cantering wnr* **9/1**[3]
6001 **3** 1 ¼ **Rioliina (IRE)**[30] 7057 3-8-9 75.......... FrankieMcDonald 6 — 65
(J G Portman) *chsd ldr: rdn to dispute ld over 1f out: hdd ins fnl f and nt pce of cantering wnr ins fnl f* **8/1**[2]
0200 **4** 1 **Ever Cheerful**[19] 7275 8-8-7 61..........(p) GillianDawson(7) 5 — 66
(A B Haynes) *sn led: hrd rdn and hdd over 1f out: one pce* **20/1**
0000 **5** 5 **Double Valentine**[21] 7240 6-8-5 46..........(b) KirstyMilczarek 1 — 43
(R Ingram) *in tch in 5th: hrd rdn and btn over 1f out* **50/1**
500 **6** 3 ¼ **Bluebird Chariot**[79] 5717 6-8-10 42.......... RobertWinston 2 — 40?
(J M Bradley) *s.i.s: a bhd: drvn along and struggling 3f out* **50/1**
5565 **7** ½ **Incy Wincy**[239] 1046 3-8-9 42..........(p) LukeMorris 3 — 38?
(J M Bradley) *chsd ldrs: rdn 3f out: wknd 2f out* **50/1**
60RL **R** **Flawed Genius**[59] 6312 4-9-6 82..........(tp) NCallan 4 — —
(K A Ryan) *ref to r again* **10/1**

1m 25.84s (1.04) **Going Correction** +0.15s/f (Slow)
WFA 3 from 4yo+ 1lb 8 Ran SP% **124.2**
Speed ratings (Par 101): **100,99,98,96,91 87,86,—**
toteswingers:1&2:£2.10, 2&3:£3.10, 1&3:£2.20 CSF £3.67 TOTE £1.20: £1.02, £2.10, £2.40; EX 4.00 Trifecta £17.10 Pool: £683.45 - 29.52 winning units..Aeroplane was claimed by P. D. Evans £15,000
Owner Dr Marwan Koukash **Bred** C R Mason **Trained** Portway, Worcs

FOCUS
A most uncompetitive claimer in which the well-backed short-priced favourite, who came down the centre in the straight, won with any amount in hand. The gallop was soon reasonable and although the form is muddling, the fourth looks the best guide.

7521 ALL WEATHER "HANDS AND HEELS" APPRENTICE H'CAP (DIV II) — 7f (P)
2:00 (2:02) (Class 6) (0-58,57) 3-Y-0+ — £1,637 (£483; £241) Stalls Low

Form — RPR
0212 **1** **Dancing Welcome**[8] 7424 3-8-13 **53**..........(b) RyanClark 7 — 65
(J M Bradley) *chsd ldrs: led over 1f out: rdn out* **5/2**[1]
6005 **2** 2 ¼ **Divine Force**[36] 6926 3-9-2 **56**.......... SPRyan 11 — 61
(M Wigham) *stdd s and s.i.s: plld hrd in rr: n.m.r after 2f: hdwy 3f out: chsd wnr over 1f out: kpt on same pce* **4/1**[2]
0010 **3** 3 ½ **Charlie Delta**[13] 7349 6-9-0 **56**..........(b) JakePayne(3) 13 — 50+
(R A Harris) *s.s: sn in midfield: in tch whn bdly hmpd on rail over 3f out: rallied over 1f out: styd on to take 3rd ins fnl f* **8/1**[3]
346 **4** ¾ **Mocha Java**[13] 7348 6-8-13 **57**..........(b) HeatherCork(5) 6 — 48
(Matthew Salaman) *plld hrd: prom: led 4f out tl wd and hdd ent st: no ex* **8/1**[3]
0006 **5** ½ **Kamanja (UAE)**[9] 7411 3-8-13 **53**.......... KierenFox 5 — 43
(M J Attwater) *towards rr: rdn over 2f out: styd on fr over 1f out* **16/1**
400 **6** *nk* **Womaniser (IRE)**[27] 7143 5-8-7 **49**..........(b[1]) TraceyAddey(3) 2 — 38
(T Keddy) *chsd ldrs: outpcd fnl 2f* **14/1**
0060 **7** ½ **Ardent Prince**[7] 7433 6-8-11 **50**.......... RichardRowe 4 — 37
(A J McCabe) *disp ld 3f: led briefly ent st: wknd over 1f out* **8/1**[3]
3300 **8** ¾ **Talamahana**[30] 7069 4-8-8 **47**..........(v) DavidKenny 3 — 32
(A B Haynes) *hld up in midfield: effrt over 2f out: no imp over 1f out* **40/1**
000- **9** 5 **Macademy Royal (USA)**[491] 4285 6-8-1 **45**..........(t) LindseyWhite(5) 9 — 14
(Miss N A Lloyd-Beavis) *hld up in rr on outer: sme late hdwy* **50/1**
5000 **10** 1 ½ **El Potro**[21] 7241 7-8-3 **45**.......... NoelGarbutt(3) 8 — 9
(J R Holt) *sn in midfield: wd and wknd ent st* **16/1**
005 **11** ¾ **Toballa**[24] 7200 4-8-6 **45**..........(t) MatthewLawson 12 — 7
(P Leech) *disp ld 3f: rdn and wknd over 2f out* **14/1**
00-6 **12** 1 **Arch Event**[13] 7361 4-8-6 **45**.......... RyanPowell 10 — 3
(A W Carroll) *a bhd* **33/1**
0050 **13** 22 **One More Round (USA)**[12] 7370 11-8-9 **53**..........(b) KevinLundie(5) 1 — —
(P D Evans) *chsd ldrs over 4f: wknd qckly* **16/1**

1m 25.63s (0.83) **Going Correction** +0.15s/f (Slow)
WFA 3 from 4yo+ 1lb 13 Ran SP% **120.2**
Speed ratings (Par 101): **101,98,94,93,93 92,92,91,85,83 82,81,56**
toteswingers:1&2:£3.30, 2&3:£7.60, 1&3:£5.60 CSF £11.55 CT £74.18 TOTE £3.00: £1.50, £1.90, £3.20; EX 10.30 Trifecta £29.00 Pool: £180.62 - 4.61 winning units..
Owner J M Bradley **Bred** The Hon Mrs E J Wills **Trained** Sedbury, Gloucs
■ Stewards' Enquiry : Tracey Addey three-day ban: careless riding (Dec 9-11)

FOCUS
Few in-form sorts in a moderate handicap. The gallop was an ordinary one and the winner raced centre to far side in the straight. The first two pulled clear and the runner-up is rated to his best form for his current trainer.
Charlie Delta Official explanation: jockey said gelding suffered interference 3f out
Kamanja(UAE) Official explanation: jockey said filly suffered interference in running

7522 EUROPEAN BREEDERS' FUND MAIDEN STKS — 1m (P)
2:35 (2:37) (Class 5) 2-Y-0 — £3,561 (£1,059; £529; £264) Stalls High

Form — RPR
23 **1** **Whistleinthewind (IRE)**[11] 7390 2-9-3.......... GeorgeBaker 11 — 81+
(G L Moore) *disp ld: led 2f out: rdn clr over 1f out: readily* **2/1**[2]
2 2 ½ **Rock My World (IRE)** 2-8-12.......... NCallan 10 — 70
(M A Jarvis) *prom: rdn to chse wnr 1f out: one pce* **9/1**[3]
3 1 **Valid Reason** 2-9-3.......... KFallon 8 — 72+
(Mrs A J Perrett) *in tch in 5th: rdn 3f out: r.o fnl f: should improve* **9/1**[3]
02 **4** 2 ¼ **Street Entertainer (IRE)**[11] 7388 2-9-3.......... JimCrowley 3 — 67
(Mrs A J Perrett) *disp ld tl 2f out: hrd rdn and wknd over 1f out* **6/5**[1]
5 1 **Lady Of Akita (USA)** 2-8-12.......... RobertHavlin 2 — 60
(J H M Gosden) *mid-div: rdn and sltly outpcd over 3f out: styd on same pce appr fnl f* **18/1**
0 **6** 1 ½ **Goldtrek (USA)**[48] 6620 2-8-12.......... SteveDrowne 7 — 57
(R Charlton) *t.k.h in midfield: rdn and no hdwy fnl 2f* **40/1**
7 1 ¼ **Sasheen** 2-8-12.......... SJCraine 1 — 54
(J R Boyle) *chsd ldrs tl wknd over 1f out* **100/1**
0 **8** 6 **Leader Of The Land (IRE)**[21] 7244 2-9-3.......... ChrisCatlin 6 — 46
(D R Lanigan) *bhd: rdn over 4f out: nvr trbld ldrs* **33/1**
9 ¾ **Lucky Quay (IRE)** 2-9-3.......... AdamKirby 5 — 44
(W R Swinburn) *towards rr: shkn up 3f out: n.d* **33/1**
00 **10** 2 ¼ **Honoured (IRE)**[8] 7420 2-9-3.......... StephenDonohoe 4 — 39+
(Sir Mark Prescott) *towards rr: rdn over 3f out: sn bhd* **100/1**
11 4 **Bonamassa** 2-9-3.......... PaulDoe 12 — 31
(M J Attwater) *t.k.h in midfield on outer: wknd over 3f out* **100/1**
0 **12** 4 ½ **Pilannski**[78] 5741 2-8-12.......... LPKeniry 9 — 16
(R A Teal) *rdn 4f out: a bhd* **100/1**

1m 39.22s (1.02) **Going Correction** +0.15s/f (Slow) 12 Ran SP% **116.3**
Speed ratings (Par 96): **100,97,96,94,93 91,90,84,83,81 77,73**
toteswingers:1&2:£3.40, 2&3:£6.70, 1&3:£3.90 CSF £19.45 TOTE £3.00: £1.40, £1.80, £2.40; EX 26.20 Trifecta £95.60 Pool: £471.84 - 3.65 winning units..
Owner R A Green **Bred** Mervyn Stewkesbury **Trained** Lower Beeding, W Sussex

FOCUS
With the market leader disappointing, this did not take as much winning as seemed likely. The gallop was an ordinary one in driving rain and the winner edged towards the inside rail in the closing stages.

NOTEBOOK
Whistleinthewind(IRE) ◆ took advantage of the below par performance of the favourite and probably did not have to improve too much to get off the mark at the third attempt. Although he again showed a tendency to lug left, he is in good hands and has the physical scope to progress in handicaps. (op 7-4 tchd 9-4)
Rock My World(IRE) ◆, a half-sister to 7f scorer Narvik and a couple of middle distance winners, was relatively easy to back but showed a fair level of ability on her racecourse debut. She should have no problems with 1m2f and appeals as the sort to win a race on this surface. (tchd 8-1 and 10-1)

Valid Reason, a half-brother to the useful Truism, was also easy to back but shaped with degree of promise under a hands and heels ride on this racecourse debut. He should be all the better for this experience and should be able to pick up a minor event. (op 11-1)
Street Entertainer(IRE), who had shown improved form over C&D on his previous start, was the disappointment of the race. He failed to get home, despite having the run of the race. It is too soon to write him off but he's not one to back at skinny odds in this type of event. (op 6-4 tchd 11-10 and 13-8 in places)
Lady Of Akita(USA), loaded wearing a stalls blanket, has a couple of very smart performers in her pedigree but she showed only modest form on this debut. She is entitled to improve for the run and ordinary handicaps may provide her best chance of success. (op 14-1)
Goldtrek(USA), who hails from a yard that has been among the winners, ran better than on her debut in a decent Newbury maiden and she should be seen to better effect once handicapped.
Bonamassa Official explanation: jockey said colt hung left

7523 BET MULTIPLES - BETDAQ H'CAP 1m (P)
3:10 (3:10) (Class 4) (0-85,85) 3-Y-O+ **£4,727** (£1,406; £702; £351) **Stalls** High

Form RPR
113 **1** **Mr Willis**[228] 1214 3-8-13 **78** SteveDrowne 7 89+
(J R Best) *bhd: hung lft and gd hdwy towards stands' side over 1f out: led ent fnl f: rdn out* **4/1**[2]
5150 **2** *1 1/2* **Tiger Dream**[33] 6986 4-8-3 **71** (p) AmyRyan(5) 9 79
(K A Ryan) *chsd ldrs: hmpd and swtchd lft over 1f out: rallied to take 2nd ins fnl f* **16/1**
5120 **3** *1 1/4* **Dance And Dance (IRE)**[13] 7356 3-9-3 **85** MartinLane(3) 11 89
(E F Vaughan) *t.k.h in rr of midfield: rdn and hdwy over 1f out: styd on fnl f* **8/1**
4625 **4** *1/2* **Quick Release (IRE)**[34] 6973 4-8-8 **74** AndreaAtzeni(3) 2 77
(D M Simcock) *t.k.h: in tch in 5th: drvn to chal 1f out: one pce* **7/1**
40 **5** *hd* **L'Hirondelle (IRE)**[65] 6168 5-9-5 **82** PaulDoe 8 84
(M J Attwater) *led: hung rt and hdd ent fnl f: no ex* **10/1**
0656 **6** *1 1/4* **Grey Boy (GER)**[22] 7229 8-8-1 **71** GeorgeDowning(7) 5 70
(A W Carroll) *t.k.h towards rr: hdwy on ins to press ldrs 1f out: no ex fnl f* **25/1**
4414 **7** *3/4* **Hawaana (IRE)**[30] 7054 4-9-2 **79** KFallon 3 77
(Miss Gay Kelleway) *bhd: effrt into midfield ent st: no imp fnl f* **5/1**[3]
0155 **8** *2* **Highly Regal (IRE)**[19] 7271 4-9-5 **82** (b) LPKeniry 6 75
(R A Teal) *prom: drvn to chal over 1f out: wknd ins fnl f* **10/1**
-353 **9** *8* **December Draw (IRE)**[156] 3220 3-9-3 **82** JimCrowley 4 56
(W J Knight) *towards rr: rdn over 2f out: sn lost tch* **3/1**[1]
044- **10** *1/2* **Meydan Dubai (IRE)**[464] 5140 4-8-8 **71** RobertWinston 1 43
(J R Best) *prom tl wknd qckly over 1f out* **20/1**
1m 38.42s (0.22) **Going Correction** +0.15s/f (Slow)
WFA 3 from 4yo+ 2lb 10 Ran SP% **118.0**
Speed ratings (Par 105): **104,102,101,100,100 99,98,96,88,88**
toteswingers:1&2:£15.40, 2&3:£29.70, 1&3:£8.40 CSF £66.68 CT £392.42 TOTE £5.80: £1.50, £4.60, £3.30; EX 75.60 Trifecta £286.60 Part won. Pool: £387.41 - 0.45 winning units..
Owner Miss Sara Furnival **Bred** John Best **Trained** Hucking, Kent

FOCUS
A decent handicap in which the market leader disappointed. The moderate early gallop increased approaching the straight and the winner edged into the centre late on. the form is rated around the placed horses with the winner looking sure to do better.
L'Hirondelle(IRE) Official explanation: jockey said gelding hung right

7524 BETDAQ.CO.UK H'CAP 1m 2f (P)
3:45 (3:45) (Class 6) (0-65,65) 3-Y-O+ **£1,978** (£584; £292) **Stalls** Low

Form RPR
0535 **1** **Marmooq**[9] 7416 6-9-3 **60** LukeMorris 7 69
(M J Attwater) *covered up in midfield: hrd rdn and hdwy over 1f out: r.o to ld last stride* **16/1**
0202 **2** *hd* **Chanrossa (IRE)**[11] 7392 3-8-13 **60** (p) JimCrowley 8 69
(E A L Dunlop) *prom: drvn to ld over 1f out: kpt on u.p: ct last stride* **10/1**
3501 **3** *1* **Resentful Angel**[20] 7250 4-9-0 **64** TobyAtkinson(7) 4 71+
(Pat Eddery) *chsd ldrs early: stdd in rr after 3f: pushed along over 3f out: rdn and styd on wl fnl 2f: gng on at fin* **4/1**[1]
2002 **4** *shd* **Seventh Hill**[22] 7225 4-9-3 **60** NCallan 1 67
(M Blanshard) *in tch in 7th: drvn to chse ldrs over 1f out: kpt on* **8/1**
0200 **5** *nk* **Diamond Twister (USA)**[12] 7364 3-9-4 **65** (t) RobertWinston 10 71
(J R Best) *t.k.h: chsd ldrs: hrd rdn over 1f out: kpt on same pce* **10/1**
4432 **6** *1 3/4* **Solo River**[56] 6394 4-9-7 **64** ChrisCatlin 9 67
(P J Makin) *led tl over 1f out: no ex fnl f* **7/1**[3]
-010 **7** *1/2* **Kashmina**[13] 5365 4-9-8 **65** StephenDonohoe 6 67
(Miss Sheena West) *hld up and bhd: shkn up and styd on appr fnl f: nvr nrr* **12/1**
1236 **8** *1/2* **Siena Star (IRE)**[178] 2516 11-9-7 **64** TPQueally 14 65
(Stef Liddiard) *wd early: sn rdn up to press ldr: wknd over 1f out* **11/1**
-055 **9** *1 1/4* **Mount Usher**[7] 7433 7-8-12 **55** SteveDrowne 2 53
(Miss Diana Weeden) *t.k.h towards rr: effrt into midfield ent st: hrd rdn: no imp* **16/1**
10 *shd* **San Marco (GER)**[70] 5735 7-9-0 **60** RobertLButler(3) 5 58
(P Butler) *mid-div: hrd rdn over 1f out: no imp* **150/1**
1005 **11** *1/2* **Kings Topic (USA)**[20] 7250 9-9-7 **64** (p) DaneO'Neill 13 61
(A B Haynes) *prom tl rdn and wknd over 1f out* **20/1**
0030 **12** *3 1/4* **Inconspicuous Miss (USA)**[14] 7332 3-8-11 **63** (tp) MatthewDavies(5) 3 54
(George Baker) *towards rr: rdn and hmpd ent st: n.d* **50/1**
0000 **13** *16* **Old Romney**[110] 4759 5-9-8 **65** KFallon 11 24
(P Howling) *s.s: towards rr: wkng whn rn wd bnd 2f out* **6/1**[2]
2503 **14** *2* **My Girl Jode**[24] 7204 3-8-10 **62** AshleyMorgan(5) 12 17
(M H Tompkins) *t.k.h: in tch in 6th on outer: wd and wknd bnd 2f out* **10/1**
2m 8.82s (2.22) **Going Correction** +0.15s/f (Slow)
WFA 3 from 4yo+ 4lb 14 Ran SP% **120.3**
Speed ratings (Par 101): **97,96,96,95,95 94,93,93,92,92 92,89,76,75**
toteswingers:1&2:£26.00, 2&3:£7.00, 1&3:£23.00 CSF £165.87 CT £776.07 TOTE £18.10: £4.30, £3.50, £1.60; EX 231.60 Trifecta £253.50 Part won. Pool: £342.60 - 0.45 winning units. Place 6 £26.19, Place5 £7.06..
Owner The Attwater Partnership **Bred** Matthews Breeding And Racing Ltd **Trained** Epsom, Surrey

FOCUS
A modest handicap run at just a moderate gallop. The principals came down the centre in the straight and the form looks reasonable with the runner-up and fourth close to sound recent efforts.
San Marco(GER) Official explanation: vet said gelding returned lame
Old Romney Official explanation: jockey said, regarding running and riding, that his orders were to settle the gelding in the early stages, to make the best of his way home and finish as close as he could, adding that, having ridden it on previous occasions, he felt that it was not moving as well as usual on the way to post and it would not settle in the early stages as planned, started to make his effort 3 1/2f out, at this stage there was little reponse and felt in the straight it had nothing more to give.
T/Jkpt: Not won. T/Plt: £26.50 to a £1 stake. Pool: £52,842.87. 1,451.90 winning tickets. T/Qpdt: £3.30 to a £1 stake. Pool: £5,037.70. 1,124.10 winning tickets. LM

7529 - 7532a (Foreign Racing) - See Raceform Interactive

7510 KEMPTON (A.W) (R-H)
Thursday, November 26

OFFICIAL GOING: Standard
Wind: virtually nil Weather: dry

7533 WIN A CAR AT KEMPTON.CO.UK MEDIAN AUCTION MAIDEN STKS 6f (P)
4:00 (4:03) (Class 6) 3-5-Y-O **£2,047** (£604; £302) **Stalls** High

Form RPR
4 **1** **The Wee Chief (IRE)**[124] 4324 3-9-3 0 RichardSmith 6 69+
(J C Fox) *chsd ldr: pushed into ld ent fnl 2f: rn green over 1f out tl rdn clr ins fnl f: comf* **4/1**[2]
-542 **2** *3 1/4* **Irish Music (IRE)**[23] 7223 4-9-3 62 TPQueally 8 59
(A P Jarvis) *led: rdn and hdd ent fnl 2f: v one pce u.p and btn fnl 150yds* **2/5**[1]
554 **3** *4* **Ride A White Swan**[6] 7460 4-9-0 46 MartinLane(3) 7 46
(D Shaw) *taken down early: a disputing 3rd pl: rdn and outpcd by ldng pair over 2f out: drvn and wl hld fr over 1f out* **15/2**[3]
0000 **4** *nse* **Oxbridge**[8] 7427 4-9-3 46 (p) LukeMorris 4 46
(J M Bradley) *a disputing 3rd pl: rdn and nt qckn over 2f out: drvn and no ch fr over 1f out* **33/1**
-066 **5** *1* **Bella Fighetta**[6] 7464 3-8-7 0 (b[1]) SophieDoyle(5) 1 38
(Ms J S Doyle) *a bhd: rdn and struggling over 2f out: no ch fnl 2f* **33/1**
6050 **6** *7* **Cullybackey (IRE)**[22] 7240 4-8-7 46 (b[1]) JemmaMarshall(5) 5 15
(J R Boyle) *bmpd sn after s: alway bhd: lost tch over 2f out* **20/1**
7 *1 3/4* **Lunaticus** 3-8-12 0 PaulDoe 2 10
(M J Attwater) *s.i.s: t.k.h and rn green in rr thrght* **33/1**
1m 12.75s (-0.35) **Going Correction** -0.05s/f (Stan) 7 Ran SP% **116.8**
Speed ratings (Par 101): **100,95,90,90,88 79,77**
toteswingers:1&2:£1.30, 2&3:£1.90, 1&3:£1.80 CSF £6.09 TOTE £4.40: £1.40, £1.40; EX 7.90.
Owner Rick Kavanagh & Johnny Lonergan **Bred** Dermot Kilmartin **Trained** Collingbourne Ducis, Wilts

FOCUS
A low-grade and uncompetitive maiden run at an ordinary gallop and one in which the market leader disappointed. The winner raced centre to far side in the straight. The winner built on her fair debut with the third and fourth the best guides.

7534 GROOMED TO PERFECTION, KIA SOUL CLAIMING STKS (DIV I) 6f (P)
4:30 (4:30) (Class 6) 3-Y-O+ **£1,706** (£503; £252) **Stalls** High

Form RPR
610 **1** **Misaro (GER)**[35] 6972 8-9-7 77 (v) DavidProbert 9 74
(R A Harris) *mde all: rdn ent fnl 2f: hrd pressed ent fnl f: styd on wl to assert fnl 100yds* **7/2**[2]
1324 **2** *1* **Total Impact**[59] 6329 6-9-3 85 TonyHamilton 10 67
(R A Fahey) *hld up wl in tch: hdwy to trck wnr wl over 1f out: rdn to chal ent fnl f: sn drvn and nt qckn: btn fnl 100yds* **10/11**[1]
0500 **3** *nk* **Valentino Swing (IRE)**[22] 7239 6-8-9 50 HayleyTurner 7 58
(Miss T Spearing) *stdd s: hld up in rr: hdwy jst over 2f out: nt clr run and swtchd lft over 1f out: hdwy to chse ldng pair ins fnl f: no imp fnl 75yds* **40/1**
0260 **4** *1 1/2* **Peopleton Brook**[15] 7330 7-8-13 61 (t) SteveDrowne 4 57
(B G Powell) *hld up towards rr: hdwy on inner jst over 2f out: wnt 3rd and nt clr run briefly ent fnl f: one pce after* **20/1**
6045 **5** *1 1/4* **Mr Rio (IRE)**[22] 7239 4-8-8 52 BNeto(5) 6 53
(A P Jarvis) *chsd ldrs: rdn and unable qck 2f out: plugged on same pce fr over 1f out* **33/1**
3302 **6** *nk* **Piazza San Pietro**[31] 7057 3-9-3 68 SebSanders 3 59+
(A B Haynes) *chsd ldrs: rdn and effrt to chse ldng pair over 1f out tl 1f out: wknd ins fnl f* **13/2**
0040 **7** *2 3/4* **Tadlil**[61] 6293 7-8-13 45 LukeMorris 5 43
(J M Bradley) *in tch in midfield: rdn and unable qck over 2f out: wl btn over 1f out* **50/1**
60 **8** *3/4* **Brazilian Brush (IRE)**[118] 4479 4-8-6 44 (t) RyanClark(7) 1 41
(J M Bradley) *chsd wnr tl 2f out: sn wknd u.p* **66/1**
0436 **9** *7* **All About You (IRE)**[33] 7027 3-9-11 76 J-PGuillambert 2 30
(P Howling) *s.i.s: sn pushed along and nvr gng wl in rr thrght* **11/2**[3]
1m 12.31s (-0.79) **Going Correction** -0.05s/f (Stan) 9 Ran SP% **116.9**
Speed ratings (Par 101): **103,101,101,99,97 97,93,92,83**
toteswingers:1&2:£2.00, 2&3:£15.90, 1&3:£29.00 CSF £6.92 TOTE £6.00: £1.50, £1.10, £9.50; EX 8.90.
Owner Messrs Criddle Davies Dawson & Villa **Bred** Wilhelm Fasching **Trained** Earlswood, Monmouths

FOCUS
A couple of fair sorts but the proximity of 50-rated third and 52-rated fifth showed this bare form is ordinary. The winner did not need to match his Wolverhampton win two starts ago. The pace was fair (nearly half a second quicker than the opening maiden) and the winner raced in the centre in the straight.
All About You(IRE) Official explanation: trainer said, having been dropped back to 6f, colt was outpaced.

7535 GROOMED TO PERFECTION, KIA SOUL CLAIMING STKS (DIV II) 6f (P)
5:00 (5:01) (Class 6) 3-Y-O+ **£1,706** (£503; £252) **Stalls** High

Form RPR
5432 **1** **Lethal**[15] 7329 6-8-13 63 JimCrowley 4 71
(M J Scudamore) *mde all: rdn 2 l clr 2f out: styd on wl fnl f* **11/10**[1]
1444 **2** *1 3/4* **Desperate Dan**[40] 6857 8-8-13 72 (v) TPQueally 7 65
(A B Haynes) *mounted on crse: take down early: hld up in rr: hdwy jst over 2f out: shkn up to chse wnr over 1f out: no imp under hands and heels riding fnl f* **11/4**[2]
00 **3** *2* **Obe Gold**[15] 7327 7-9-3 69 J-PGuillambert 3 63
(P Howling) *chsd ldrs: wnt 2nd 3f out: drvn and nt qckn 2f out: lost 2nd over 1f out and one pce after* **6/1**[3]
053 **4** *2 1/2* **Reigning Monarch (USA)**[26] 7176 6-8-10 50 (p) SamHitchcott 9 48
(Miss Z C Davison) *bustled along leaving stalls: in tch in midfield: rdn and unable qck over 2f out: no prog fr over 1f out* **10/1**
450 **5** *2 3/4* **Deckchair**[29] 6442 3-8-0 48 (v) FrankieMcDonald 1 29
(S Curran) *s.i.s: bhd: effrt and rdn on outer over 2f out: no imp and nvr trbld ldrs* **20/1**
0606 **6** *1 1/4* **Mr Funshine**[14] 7358 4-9-4 46 WilliamCarson(3) 10 46
(R J Hodges) *chsd wnr tl 3f out: wknd u.p over 1f out: fdd fnl f* **33/1**
0010 **7** *1/2* **Sam's Cross (IRE)**[33] 7023 4-8-12 63 MarcHalford(3) 6 39
(J J Bridger) *a bhd: rdn and no rspnse over 2f out* **9/1**

000 8 1 1/2 **Hayley's Girl**[40] 6856 3-8-0 44 AmyBaker(5) 2 24
(S W James) *sn nudged along: chsd ldrs tl wknd jst over 2f out* 66/1

1m 12.36s (-0.74) **Going Correction** -0.05s/f (Stan) 8 Ran SP% **116.9**

Speed ratings (Par 101): **102,99,97,93,90 88,87,85**

toteswingers:1&2:£1.10, 2&3:£2.80, 1&3:£2.20 CSF £4.26 TOTE £2.00: £1.10, £1.20, £1.80; EX 4.40.

Owner A S Reid **Bred** A S Reid **Trained** Bromsash, Herefordshire

FOCUS

An ordinary claimer run at a reasonable gallop and in a slightly slower time to division one. The principals raced in the centre in the straight. The winner is the best guide to the form.

Sam's Cross(IRE) Official explanation: jockey said gelding hung left in straight

7536 WILLIAM HILL WINTER FESTIVAL - BOOK NOW NURSERY 6f (P)

5:30 (5:30) (Class 4) (0-90,90) 2-Y-O £3,885 (£1,156; £577; £288) **Stalls** High

Form RPR

0104 1 **Yer Woman (IRE)**[52] 6541 2-8-13 82 RichardHughes 7 89+
(R Hannon) *stdd s: hld up in rr: hdwy to trck ldrs on bit waiting for gap over 1f out: swtchd lft and wnt between horses 1f out: cruised into ld ins fnl f: sn nudged clr: easily* 9/2[3]

220 2 1 3/4 **Going French (IRE)**[118] 4488 2-8-1 70 FrankieMcDonald 3 70
(R Curtis) *t.k.h: chsd ldrs: rdn and effrt wl over 1f out: kpt on to chse wnr ins fnl f: no ch w wnr* 12/1

6011 3 1/2 **Imjin River (IRE)**[7] 7453 2-8-4 78 6ex AshleyMorgan(5) 6 77
(M H Tompkins) *stdd s: t.k.h and hld up wl in tch: hdwy between horses and rdn to ld 1f out: sn hdd by wnr and brushed aside* 7/4[1]

6111 4 2 **Living It Large (FR)**[20] 7274 2-9-7 90 TonyHamilton 2 83
(R F Fisher) *led narrowly: rdn ent fnl 2f: hdd 1f out: sn outpcd* 11/4[2]

010 5 1/2 **Interlace**[40] 6844 2-8-11 80 (b[1]) SebSanders 1 71
(Sir Mark Prescott) *racd wd: a towards rr: rdn 4f out: plugged on same pce and no imp fnl 3f* 8/1

0200 6 1 1/4 **Kings Of Leo**[29] 7108 2-8-9 78 SJCraine 8 65
(J R Boyle) *t.k.h: in tch: effrt on inner and rdn jst over 2f out: wknd over 1f out* 25/1

5323 7 2 1/4 **Six Wives**[20] 7274 2-8-7 76 ChrisCatlin 4 57
(J A Glover) *w ldr: ev ch and rdn wl over 1f out: wknd ent fnl f* 15/2

1m 12.58s (-0.52) **Going Correction** -0.05s/f (Stan) 7 Ran SP% **115.6**

Speed ratings (Par 98): **101,98,98,95,94 93,90**

toteswingers:1&2:£6.90, 2&3:£4.30, 1&3:£3.50 CSF £55.35 CT £128.58 TOTE £5.00: £2.10, £7.30; EX 70.60.

Owner Mrs R McArdle **Bred** Mrs Clodagh McStay **Trained** East Everleigh, Wilts

FOCUS

A couple of in-form sorts in a useful nursery. The pace was fair (though slower than both divisions of the claimer) and the winner made her ground in the centre in the straight. Solid form, and the winner can rate higher on this surface.

NOTEBOOK

Yer Woman(IRE) hadn't been at her best on turf on her last two starts but she posted a career best under a typically confident ride to score in convincing fashion on her all-weather debut. She isn't the biggest around but she certainly has an engine and it will be interesting to see if this can be built on next year. (op 11-2 tchd 4-1)

Going French(IRE) had not been at her best on his nursery debut on his previous start in late July but fared much better on this Polytrack debut. He shaped as though the return to 7f would suit and should be able to win a race in a lesser grade of handicap. (op 14-1)

Imjin River(IRE), unbeaten in two previous starts on artificial surfaces, had the run of the race and ran creditably under his penalty. He will be 2lb lower in future and is lightly raced enough to be open to a bit of further progress. (tchd 2-1 in places)

Living It Large(FR) has developed into a very useful performer but he was harried for the lead throughout and was found out returned to 6f from this 5lb higher mark. He's high in the weights now but will be of more interest back over 5f when it looks like he can dominate. (op 3-1 tchd 9-4)

Interlace had disappointed on her nursery debut on turf last time but, although faring better back on Polytrack, did not look the easiest of rides in the first time blinkers. The return to 7f may help but she has little margin for error from her mark. (op 7-1)

Kings Of Leo was again below her best for her current stable and, although the step back to 5f may suit better, she is going to have to show a fair bit more before she is a solid betting proposition. (op 20-1)

7537 EUROPEAN BREEDERS' FUND MAIDEN STKS (DIV I) 7f (P)

6:00 (6:01) (Class 5) 2-Y-O £3,238 (£963; £481; £240) **Stalls** High

Form RPR

1 **Bramshaw (USA)** 2-9-3 0 NCallan 9 72
(Mrs A J Perrett) *t.k.h: hld up wl in tch: swtchd lft: rdn and unable qck over 2f out: rallied over 1f out: pressed wnr ins fnl f: led fnl 50yds: r.o wl* 8/1[3]

50 2 1/2 **Count Of Anjou (USA)**[33] 7034 2-9-3 0 RichardHughes 4 71
(R Hannon) *chsd ldrs: wnt 2nd 4f out: ev ch and rdn 2f out: led over 1f out: drvn 1f out: hdd and no ex fnl 50yds* 8/11[1]

3 2 1/4 **Red Gulch** 2-9-3 0 KFallon 1 65
(E A L Dunlop) *s.i.s: sn in tch and t.k.h: effrt to join ldrs over 2f out: sn hdd but stl ev ch tl wknd jst ins fnl f* 8/1[3]

04 4 1 3/4 **Kings 'n Dreams**[19] 7288 2-9-3 0 TPQueally 6 61
(D K Ivory) *t.k.h: led: rdn and pressed over 2f out: hdd over 1f out: wknd ent fnl f* 11/2[2]

5 1/2 **Prince Yarraman (IRE)** 2-9-3 0 MichaelHills 8 60+
(J A Osborne) *s.i.s: bhd: rdn and hdwy wl over 1f out: kpt on steadily fnl f: nvr gng pce to rch ldrs* 50/1

5 6 shd **Bondage (IRE)**[30] 7096 2-9-3 0 HayleyTurner 5 60
(J R Fanshawe) *t.k.h: wl in tch tl dropped to lst trio over 4f out: rdn over 2f out: styd on but nvr gng pce to rch ldrs* 10/1

2004 7 1 1/2 **Bush Master**[13] 7365 2-9-3 72 SJCraine 7 56
(J R Boyle) *t.k.h: chsd ldr tl 4f out: wknd u.p wl over 1f out* 14/1

8 2 1/2 **Blue Again** 2-8-12 0 AdamKirby 10 45
(W R Swinburn) *in tch: rdn and effrt on inner ent fnl 2f: rn green and wknd qckly over 1f out* 20/1

9 nse **Tiger Star** 2-9-3 0 (b[1]) LukeMorris 2 49+
(J M P Eustace) *stdd and swtchd rt s: sn plld hrd and in tch: barging match w rival 6f out: wknd u.p ent fnl 2f* 33/1

10 14 **Southern Breeze** 2-9-3 0 GeorgeBaker 3 14
(S Kirk) *s.i.s and sn swtchd rt: a wl bhd* 20/1

1m 27.2s (1.20) **Going Correction** -0.05s/f (Stan) 10 Ran SP% **125.7**

Speed ratings (Par 96): **91,90,87,85,85 85,83,80,80,64**

toteswingers:1&2:£2.50, 2&3:£2.50, 1&3:£6.60 CSF £14.87 TOTE £11.10: £2.00, £1.10, £2.70; EX 23.10.

Owner Paul & Clare Cuttill, Brenda Karn-Smith **Bred** T/C Stable **Trained** Pulborough, W Sussex

FOCUS

This looked a fair maiden but one in which the early gallop was only moderate. The winner came down the centre in the closing stages.

NOTEBOOK

Bramshaw(USA) ◆, who cost $130,000 and is a half-brother to a high-class Canadian juvenile, has reportedly been slow to come to hand and was noticeably green but created a very good impression on this racecourse debut. He'll be well suited by the step up to 1m and has the size and scope to progress into a very useful sort at least next year. He will reportedly be put away for the winter. (tchd 9-1)

Count Of Anjou(USA) attracted plenty of support and turned in his best effort on this all-weather debut after racing keenly in a moderately run race. Although he lacks the scope of the winner, he should be able to make amends in ordinary maiden or handicap company if settling better. (op 10-11)

Red Gulch ◆, the first foal of a 7f winner, was easy to back but shaped pleasingly on this racecourse debut after racing on the outside throughout. He should be all the better for this experience and is sure to win a race. (op 7-1)

Kings 'n Dreams, who had the run of the race on this all-weather debut, failed to build on the form shown in a soft-ground maiden at Doncaster but again showed ability. Ordinary handicaps will be the way forward for him. (op 9-2)

Prince Yarraman(IRE), who has winners in his pedigree, showed ability without being knocked about on this racecourse debut. He is entitled to come on for this initial experience and should be able to pick up an ordinary event in due course.

Bondage(IRE) again showed ability at an ordinary level on his all-weather debut and once again left the impression that he would not be seen to best effect until going over middle distances in handicaps next year. (op 12-1)

7538 EUROPEAN BREEDERS' FUND MAIDEN STKS (DIV II) 7f (P)

6:30 (6:30) (Class 5) 2-Y-O £3,238 (£963; £481; £240) **Stalls** High

Form RPR

1 **Too Putra (IRE)** 2-9-3 0 SteveDrowne 2 73+
(R Charlton) *chsd ldrs: rdn and effrt ent fnl 2f: ev ch whn rdn jst over 1f out: wnt between horses to ld fnl 75yds: kpt on wl* 5/2[1]

04 2 hd **Plenty O'Toole**[15] 7326 2-9-3 0 TPQueally 8 69+
(Mrs D J Sanderson) *stdd s: hld up in tch: effrt ent fnl 2f: rdn to chal over 1f out: drvn ahd jst ins fnl f: hdd fnl 100yds: kpt on but a hld* 3/1[2]

06 3 3/4 **Welsh Artist**[8] 7430 2-9-3 0 NCallan 3 67
(Mrs A J Perrett) *chsd ldr: led jst over 2f out: sn rdn: drvn and hdd jst ins fnl f: one pce after* 10/1

64 4 3/4 **Richboy**[8] 7436 2-9-3 0 IanMongan 4 65
(Mrs L J Mongan) *led: rdn and hdd jst over 2f out: stl ev ch tl wknd u.p fnl 150yds* 5/1[3]

0 5 1 1/2 **Tilsworth Glenboy**[15] 7325 2-9-3 0 SimonWhitworth 10 62
(J R Jenkins) *chsd ldng pair: swtchd ins and effrt ent fnl 2f: pressed ldrs and drvn over 1f out: wknd fnl f* 33/1

0 6 1 1/4 **Bella Charlie (IRE)**[15] 7325 2-9-3 0 AdamKirby 9 61+
(M G Quinlan) *t.k.h: hld up in tch: swtchd ins and effrt jst over 2f out: no hdwy over 1f out* 7/1

7 3 3/4 **Ring Of Fire** 2-9-3 0 LiamJones 5 49
(J L Spearing) *s.i.s: sn bustled along: a bhd* 20/1

00 8 1 1/2 **Corr Point (IRE)**[8] 7430 2-9-3 0 FrankieMcDonald 7 45
(J A Osborne) *t.k.h: hld up in last trio: n.d* 25/1

9 1 1/4 **Compton Park** 2-9-3 0 JimCrowley 6 42
(W J Knight) *s.i.s: bhd: rdn and rn green over 2f out: n.d* 15/2

1m 28.45s (2.45) **Going Correction** -0.05s/f (Stan) 9 Ran SP% **115.1**

Speed ratings (Par 96): **84,83,82,82,80 78,74,72,71**

toteswingers:1&2:£3.20, 2&3:£4.40, 1&3:£4.00 CSF £9.75 TOTE £3.10: £1.30, £1.30, £2.80; EX 11.40.

Owner H R H Sultan Ahmad Shah **Bred** Lynch Bages Ltd **Trained** Beckhampton, Wilts

FOCUS

The weaker of the divisions and a steady early gallop (over a second slower than the first division) saw several finish in a heap. The first two raced in the centre. The fourth and fifth are the best guides and the winner has more to offer.

NOTEBOOK

Too Putra(IRE) ◆, a 100,000gns yearling who is closely related to Listed placed Imoya and to a useful middle distance winner, responded well to pressure to justify the market support on this racecourse debut. He'll be suited by further and a stronger gallop and it won't surprise to see him leave this bare form well behind in due course. (op 7-2)

Plenty O'Toole is a steadily progressive sort who turned in his best effort in this ordinary contest. While vulnerable to the better types in this grade, he is bred to stay further and should be able to pick up a small event. (tchd 11-4)

Welsh Artist had the rub of this moderately run race and turned in his best effort. While he may be a shade flattered given the way things panned out he looks the type that could progress a little in ordinary handicaps. (op 8-1)

Richboy had the run of the race and confirmed the bit of promise shown on his previous start. He is likely to remain vulnerable against the more progressive types in this grade. (op 7-2)

Tilsworth Glenboy also had the run of the race and left his debut form behind but it will be a surprise if he is able to win in this grade.

Bella Charlie(IRE) ◆ caught the eye without being at all knocked about on only this second outing. He was still green and he's definitely one to take into handicaps over 1m, especially if the market speaks in his favour. (op 8-1)

Corr Point(IRE) Official explanation: jockey said colt hung right throughout

7539 BOXINGDAYRACES.CO.UK H'CAP 1m 4f (P)

7:00 (7:00) (Class 4) (0-80,79) 3-Y-O+ £4,727 (£1,406; £702; £351) **Stalls** Centre

Form RPR

1200 1 **Mildoura (FR)**[28] 7131 4-9-8 79 IanMongan 8 89
(Mrs L J Mongan) *dwlt: hdwy to chse ldng pair 10f out: wnt 2nd 8f out: rdn to chal over 2f out: carried lft over 1f out: led ins fnl f: styd on wl* 10/1

4441 2 1 1/4 **Mannlichen**[22] 7238 3-9-1 78 GregFairley 4 86
(M Johnston) *grad crossed over to ld after 1f: rdn 2f out: sn edgd lft u.p: hdd ins fnl f: no ex* 4/5[1]

301- 3 1 **Green Wadi**[393] 3362 4-9-4 75 GeorgeBaker 9 81
(G L Moore) *chsd ldng trio: rdn to chse ldng trio and swtchd rt wl over 1f out: kpt on same pce u.p after* 10/1

4020 4 3 **Saloon (USA)**[34] 6995 5-9-4 75 (p) EddieAhern 7 77
(Jane Chapple-Hyam) *hld up towards rr: hdwy and rdn over 2f out: swtchd rt and hld hd awkwardly over 1f out: kpt edging rt and no imp after* 7/1

6061 5 5 **Lyra's Daemon**[10] 7413 3-8-13 76 6ex MartinDwyer 10 70
(W R Muir) *led for 1f: chsd ldr after tl 8f out: rdn over 3f out: wknd u.p 2f out* 6/1[3]

4614 6 1/2 **Drum Dragon**[5] 7476 3-8-4 72 AshleyMorgan(5) 11 65
(M H Tompkins) *in tch in midfield: rdn and unable qck over 2f out: wl btn fr over 1f out* 9/2[2]

30-0 7 4 **First To Call**[22] 7233 5-9-1 72 (t) SebSanders 1 58
(P J Makin) *hld up in last trio: rdn and effrt wl over 2f out: no prog and n.d* 20/1

2406 **8** *hd* **Hallingdal (UAE)**[15] 7323 4-9-1 **75**................................ MarcHalford(3) 6 61
(J J Bridger) *stdd s: hld up in last pair: rdn and effrt on inner ent fnl 2f: no prog and n.d* **25/1**

5-00 **9** *14* **Motarjm (USA)**[22] 7233 5-9-1 **72**................................ SaleemGolam 2 36
(J Pearce) *in tch in midfield: rdn ent fnl 3f: sn btn and wl bhd* **50/1**

6-50 **10** *53* **Cupid's Glory**[56] 6435 7-9-8 **79**................................ FergusSweeney 3 —
(G L Moore) *stdd s: hld up in last: rdn and struggling over 3f out: lost tch over 2f out: eased fnl f: t.o* **40/1**

2m 31.23s (-3.27) **Going Correction** -0.05s/f (Stan)
WFA 3 from 4yo+ 6lb **10** Ran SP% **131.7**
Speed ratings (Par 105): **108,107,106,104,101 100,98,98,88,53**
toteswingers:1&2:£5.60, 2&3:£6.10, 1&3:£10.70 CSF £20.46 CT £103.22 TOTE £9.30: £2.60, £1.20, £4.10; EX 46.10.
Owner Mrs P J Sheen **Bred** H H The Aga Khan's Studs Sc **Trained** Epsom, Surrey

FOCUS
A fair handicap in which the ordinary gallop suited the prominent racers. The winner came down the centre in the straight. The winner is rated to her turf best and the form looks sound.

7540 PANORAMIC BAR & RESTAURANT H'CAP 1m (P)
7:30 (7:30) (Class 4) (0-85,85) 3-Y-O **£4,727** (£1,406; £702; £351) **Stalls** High

Form RPR

3201 **1** **Big Bay (USA)**[29] 7126 3-9-4 **85**................................ NCallan 1 96+
(Jane Chapple-Hyam) *chsd ldng trio: rdn to chal jst over 2f out: led wl over 1f out: styd on wl to forge clr fnl 100yds* **5/2[2]**

0043 **2** *1 ¾* **Chapter And Verse (IRE)**[22] 7233 3-8-10 **80**............ AndreaAtzeni(3) 6 87
(Mike Murphy) *stdd s: hld up in last pair: hdwy on outer 4f out: rdn to chal over 1f out: drvn and nt pce of wnr fnl 150yds* **7/2[3]**

4312 **3** *1 ½* **Bennelong**[7] 7456 3-8-8 **75**................................ PaulDoe 5 78+
(G L Moore) *stdd s: hld up in rr: hdwy over 4f out: nt clr run 2f out: tl rdn and effrt jst over 1f out: wnt 3rd ins fnl f: no imp fnl 100yds* **7/4[1]**

3264 **4** *1 ¼* **Sunshine Always (IRE)**[26] 7181 3-9-0 **81**................ KirstyMilczarek 2 81
(T D McCarthy) *hld up in tch in last trio: swtchd lft and effrt wl over 1f out: one pce and wl hld fnl f* **15/2**

6002 **5** *4* **Nora Mae (IRE)**[5] 7487 3-8-9 **76**................................ LPKeniry 7 67
(S Kirk) *led: rdn and hrd pressed jst over 2f out: hdd wl over 1f out: wknd qckly over 1f out* **8/1**

3044 **6** *2* **Stan's Cool Cat (IRE)**[13] 7366 3-8-13 **80**..................(b) EddieAhern 3 66
(P F I Cole) *chsd ldr tl jst over 2f out: lost pl qckly over 1f out and sn wl btn* **16/1**

1m 39.19s (-0.61) **Going Correction** -0.05s/f (Stan) **6** Ran SP% **115.9**
Speed ratings (Par 104): **101,99,97,96,92 90**
toteswingers:1&2:£2.40, 2&3:£1.90, 1&3:£1.80 CSF £12.20 TOTE £3.70: £1.80, £3.00; EX 14.10 Place 6 £11.11, Place 5 £10.27 .
Owner Jane Chapple-Hyam & Mrs B J Hirst **Bred** Hermitage Farm Llc **Trained** Newmarket, Suffolk

FOCUS
A fair handicap run at just a moderate gallop. The winner continued the trend of racing in the centre in the straight. An improved effort from the winner, with the runner-up the best guide.
T/Plt: £24.30 to a £1 stake. Pool: £51,839.28. 1,553.59 winning tickets. T/Qpdt: £17.30 to a £1 stake. Pool: £5,736.50. 244.70 winning tickets. SP

7548 - (Foreign Racing) - See Raceform Interactive

7517 LINGFIELD (L-H)
Friday, November 27

OFFICIAL GOING: Standard
Wind: fresh, across Weather: dry, breezy

7549 HINDLEAP WALK (S) STKS 1m 4f (P)
12:50 (12:50) (Class 6) 3-Y-O+ **£1,978** (£584; £292) **Stalls** Low

Form RPR

00 **1** **Doubnov (FR)**[48] 6665 6-9-6 80................................(p) JamieSpencer 12 70+
(Ian Williams) *stdd s: t.k.h: hld up in midfield: hdwy to chse ldrs over 2f out: rdn and qcknd to ld ent fnl 2f: sn clr and in n.d after* **4/1[1]**

1420 **2** *3 ¾* **Bee Stinger**[6] 7492 7-9-11 73................................ SebSanders 15 67+
(B G Powell) *stdd s: hld up wl in rr: hdwy over 2f out: hmpd bnd 2f out: styd on u.p fr over 1f out: wnt 2nd towards fin: no ch w wnr* **9/2[2]**

0040 **3** *1* **Dream Of Fortune (IRE)**[36] 6973 5-9-6 73................(t) JamieJones(5) 3 66
(M G Quinlan) *stdd s: hld up towards rr: hdwy into midfield 1/2-way: swtchd rt and hdwy over 2f out: edgd lft bnd 2f out: kpt on to go 3rd nr fin: no ch w wnr* **9/2[2]**

0006 **4** *½* **Cape Greko**[16] 7328 7-9-3 56..........................(v) RussellKennemore(3) 14 60
(B G Powell) *s.i.s: chsd ldrs 8f out: rdn to chse ldr wl over 2f out: nt pce of wnr 2f out: chsd wnr wl over 1f out: no imp: lost 2 pls towards fin* **7/1[3]**

5550 **5** *2* **Bernabeu (IRE)**[15] 7354 7-9-6 49................................ EmmettStack 5 57
(S Curran) *chsd ldr tl 10f out: styd prom tl unable qck u.p over 2f out: one pce after* **20/1**

0604 **6** *1 ¼* **Nawamees (IRE)**[21] 7272 11-9-6 54.....................(p) RichardEvans(5) 16 60
(P D Evans) *chsd ldr 10f out tl led over 3f out: rdn and hdd ent fnl 2f: sn outpcd by wnr: wknd over 1f out* **16/1**

4002 **7** *¾* **Fantasy Ride**[29] 7137 7-9-1 52................................ SimonPearce(5) 6 58+
(J Pearce) *stdd s: hld up bhd: hdwy and rdn over 2f out: swtchd rt over 1f out: styd on but nvr trbld ldrs* **10/1**

6005 **8** *¾* **Musashi (IRE)**[17] 3919 4-9-6 50................................(b[1]) IanMongan 8 52
(Mrs L J Mongan) *s.i.s: sn pushed up into midfield: struggling u.p over 3f out: wl btn fnl 2f* **9/1**

6450 **9** *3 ¼* **Turner's Touch**[36] 6969 7-9-6 47................................(b) AmirQuinn 2 47
(G L Moore) *stdd s: hld up in rr: effrt and rdn over 2f out: nt clr run bnd 2f out: nvr trbld ldrs* **20/1**

300 **10** *shd* **Felicia**[37] 6941 4-8-12 44................................ NataliaGemelova(3) 1 42
(J E Long) *in tch on outer: rdn wl over 2f out: sn struggling: wl btn over 1f out* **66/1**

00 **11** *6* **Alfies Express**[14] 7367 5-9-6 0................................ DaneO'Neill 4 37
(S Curran) *a towards rr: rdn on outer over 3f out: sn wl btn* **33/1**

0060 **12** *1* **Dalrymple (IRE)**[25] 6788 3-9-5 45................................(t) AdamKirby 7 41
(M Madgwick) *a in rr: rdn and no rspnse over 4f out: sn wl bhd* **100/1**

/000 **13** *5* **Lady Romanov (IRE)**[15] 5028 6-8-12 48................... RobertLButler(3) 10 23
(P Butler) *a bhd: rdn and toiling bdly 4f out: sn wl bhd* **100/1**

/50- **14** *1* **Bond Cruz**[15] 2456 6-8-13 37................................ TraceyAddey(7) 11 26
(T Keddy) *chsd ldrs tl lost pl qckly over 3f out: wl bhd fr over 2f out* **125/1**

23-0 **15** *1 ¼* **Sleepy Mountain**[10] 7425 5-9-6 45................................ LPKeniry 9 24
(A Middleton) *led after 1f: rdn and hdd over 3f out: sn drvn and lost pl: wl bhd and eased ins fnl f* **14/1**

2m 32.27s (-0.73) **Going Correction** 0.0s/f (Stan)
WFA 3 from 4yo+ 6lb **15** Ran SP% **117.2**
Speed ratings (Par 101): **102,99,98,98,97 96,95,95,93,93 89,88,85,84,83**
toteswingers:1&2:£4.80, 2&3:£5.20, 1&3:£11.10 CSF £19.62 TOTE £6.30: £2.80, £2.60, £2.80; EX 5.10 TRIFECTA Pool: £275.09 - 4.23 winning units..The winner was bought in for 12,000 guineas
Owner Dr Marwan Koukash **Bred** Daniel Valley Masson Et Al **Trained** Portway, Worcs
■ Stewards' Enquiry : Dane O'Neill caution: used whip when out of contention.

FOCUS
A reasonable seller. The first three are above avaerage for the grade but the fourth and fifth are the more likely guides to the form. Prominent racers appeared favoured.
Fantasy Ride Official explanation: jockey said gelding was denied a clear run

7550 GALLEONS LAP MAIDEN STKS 1m 2f (P)
1:20 (1:20) (Class 5) 3-Y-O **£2,729** (£806; £403) **Stalls** Low

Form RPR

2222 **1** **Troopingthecolour**[9] 7439 3-9-3 80................................(t) JimmyFortune 5 86
(J H M Gosden) *chsd ldr tl led 5f out: rdn over 2f out: drew wl clr ent fnl f: comf* **1/4[1]**

2020 **2** *8* **In Secret**[9] 7428 3-8-12 72................................ EddieAhern 2 65
(J L Dunlop) *dwlt: trckd ldng pair tl wnt 2nd over 4f out: rdn over 2f out: btn over 1f out* **12/1[3]**

2244 **3** *1 ¼* **Shakalaka (IRE)**[10] 6209 3-9-3 78................................(p) GeorgeBaker 4 68
(G L Moore) *hld up wl in tch in last pl: wnt 3rd over 4f out: rdn: hung lft and btn over 1f out* **9/2[2]**

00 **4** *26* **Northern Genes (AUS)**[9] 7439 3-8-7 0................... FrankieMcDonald 3 6
(M R Bosley) *sn led: hdd and rdn 5f out: sn dropped to last: lost tch over 2f out: t.o* **100/1**

2m 5.89s (-0.71) **Going Correction** 0.0s/f (Stan) **4** Ran SP% **106.9**
Speed ratings (Par 102): **102,95,94,73**
CSF £4.04 TOTE £1.10; EX 3.90.
Owner H R H Princess Haya Of Jordan **Bred** Meon Valley Stud **Trained** Newmarket, Suffolk

FOCUS
A simple opportunity for the winner, who sets the level. It is unlikely that he had to improve, with doubts over the next two.

7551 EDEN BROOK NURSERY 7f (P)
1:55 (1:55) (Class 5) (0-75,74) 2-Y-O **£2,590** (£770; £385; £192) **Stalls** Low

Form RPR

3306 **1** **Exceedthewildman**[9] 7434 2-8-13 **71**......................(p) SophieDoyle(5) 8 73
(J S Moore) *t.k.h: sn chsng ldr: led ent fnl 2f: rdn wl over 1f out: hld on wl fnl f* **7/1**

020 **2** *nk* **Fivefold (USA)**[25] 7209 2-9-7 **74**................................ J-PGuillambert 9 75
(J Akehurst) *t.k.h: in tch in midfield on outer: hdwy to press wnr 2f out: unable qck and a jst hld fnl f* **10/1**

5255 **3** *1 ¼* **Could It Be Magic**[20] 7288 2-9-1 **71**......................(p) JackDean(3) 2 69+
(W G M Turner) *t.k.h: in tch tl hmpd twice and lost pl over 5f out: swtchd rt and bmpd rival wl over 1f out: r.o u.p fnl f to go 3rd towards fin: nt rch ldrs* **16/1**

5014 **4** *½* **Ever So Bold**[18] 7320 2-9-1 **68**................................(b) MartinDwyer 4 65
(W R Muir) *t.k.h: in tch: rdn ent fnl 2f: chsd ldng pair 1f out: sn no imp: lost 2nd towards fin* **5/2[1]**

0010 **5** *½* **So Surreal (IRE)**[30] 7108 2-9-4 **71**..........................(b) GeorgeBaker 7 66
(G L Moore) *in tch: rdn and effrt on outer 2f out: kpt on same pce fnl f* **5/1[3]**

500 **6** *hd* **Ostentation**[13] 7390 2-8-5 **58**................................ GregFairley 3 53+
(M Johnston) *dwlt: in tch towards rr on inner: effrt and rdn over 1f out: kpt on but nvr gng pce to rch ldrs* **8/1**

5600 **7** *1* **Pastello**[15] 7359 2-9-0 **67**................................ JimmyFortune 1 59
(R Hannon) *t.k.h: chsd ldrs: rdn 2f out: wknd ins fnl f* **20/1**

4063 **8** *½* **Cuthbert (IRE)**[60] 6334 2-9-0 **67**................................(b[1]) EddieAhern 5 58+
(W Jarvis) *dwlt: hld up wl in tch in last: effrt and rdn whn hmpd wl over 1f out: no prog after* **8/1**

2502 **9** *8* **Gillburg (USA)**[11] 7410 2-9-7 **74**................................ JamieSpencer 6 45+
(K A Ryan) *led: rdn over 2f out: hdd ent fnl 2f: wknd qckly u.p jst over 1f out* **4/1[2]**

1m 26.19s (1.39) **Going Correction** 0.0s/f (Stan) **9** Ran SP% **119.7**
Speed ratings (Par 96): **92,91,90,89,89 88,87,87,78**
toteswingers:1&2:£20.00, 2&3:£21.30, 1&3:£18.60 CSF £76.95 CT £1101.44 TOTE £8.60: £2.30, £4.60, £5.50; EX 129.70 TRIFECTA Not won..
Owner E Moore & J S Moore **Bred** Horizon Bloodstock Limited **Trained** Upper Lambourn, Berks
■ Stewards' Enquiry : Jack Dean one-day ban: careless riding (Dec 11)
Sophie Doyle three-day ban: careless riding (Dec 11-13)

FOCUS
They went a steady pace, resulting in a time 1.51 seconds slower than the following juvenile conditions contest, and it paid to race handy. The form is ordinary but sound.

NOTEBOOK
Exceedthewildman proved suited by the drop back from 1m, as well as the fitting of cheekpieces, and was given a well-judged ride considering the lack of pace in the race. He was a bit keen on the pace early, but showed a good attitude when strongly challenged in the straight. There might be a bit more to come. (op 15-2 tchd 13-2)
Fivefold(USA) ◆ did very well to finish so close considering he raced very keenly early on when stuck out wide with no cover. He can surely win a similar race if settling better, and a stronger pace will probably help. (op 12-1 tchd 16-1)
Could It Be Magic ◆ lost his place when hampered early on and, with the steady pace was against him, he took an age to pick up in the straight. He eventually finished strongly and may yet do better.
Ever So Bold, 4lb higher than when winning at Kempton two starts back, didn't help himself by racing keenly and is another who would have preferred a stronger pace. (op 10-3 tchd 7-2)
So Surreal(IRE) did not improve for the step up in trip. (op 4-1 tchd 7-2)
Ostentation ◆ lost his race with a slow start and can be given another chance. (op 11-1 tchd 12-1)
Gillburg(USA) was pressured by the winner up front, but even so he was able to set just a modest pace and it was disappointing he dropped away so tamely. (tchd 5-1)

7552 JACKSBRIDGE CONDITIONS STKS 7f (P)
2:30 (2:30) (Class 3) 2-Y-O **£7,641** (£2,273; £1,136; £567) **Stalls** Low

Form RPR

1245 **1** **Transfixed (IRE)**[6] 7494 2-8-9 82................................ PaulDoe 1 74
(P D Evans) *chsd ldng pair: swtchd ins and rdn wl 1f out: ev ch ent fnl f: led fnl 100yds: kpt on wl* **11/1[3]**

4440 **2** *nse* **Master Of Dance (IRE)**[18] 7320 2-9-3 78 .... JimmyFortune 3 82
(R Hannon) *chsd ldng trio: rdn and effrt wl over 1f out: led jst ins fnl f: hdd fnl 100yds: kpt on but a jst hld* **7/1[2]**

21 **3** *2 ¾* **Jarrow (IRE)**[9] 7436 2-9-3 0 .... GregFairley 4 75+
(M Johnston) *led: rdn wl over 1f out: edgd rt u.p over 1f out: hdd jst ins fnl f: sn btn* **1/4[1]**

0633 **4** *3* **Ramamara (IRE)**[9] 7435 2-8-9 77 .... JamieSpencer 5 60+
(P D Evans) *chsd ldr: ev ch and rdn ent fnl 2f: wkng whn short of room ent fnl f: wl hld after* **16/1**

00 **5** *22* **During The War (USA)**[53] 6544 2-9-0 0 .... ShaneKelly 2 10+
(C A Dwyer) *awkward leaving stalls and v.s.a: a detached in last: lost tch over 2f out* **50/1**

1m 24.68s (-0.12) **Going Correction** 0.0s/f (Stan) **5** Ran SP% **108.7**
Speed ratings (Par 100): **100,99,96,93,68**
CSF £73.47 TOTE £5.30: £12.50, £9.40; EX 52.80.
Owner Mrs I M Folkes **Bred** Rathasker Stud **Trained** Pandy, Monmouths

FOCUS
The leaders went off much too fast and the form is worth treating with some caution. The winner did not need to match her recent best and the runner-up is rated to his best earlier form.

NOTEBOOK
Transfixed(IRE), already having her 24th start, had the race set up for her and showed a good attitude to gain her sixth success. However, she may not have had to run up to her very best considering she had 7lb in hand over the runner-up. (op 10-1 tchd 12-1)
Master Of Dance(IRE) benefited from a couple of his rivals going off too fast and only just failed to get up. (op 13-2 tchd 6-1)
Jarrow(IRE) got an ill-judged ride from Fairley, going off too fast. He is a half-brother to, among others, high-class sprinter Moss Vale, so he'll probably appreciate a drop back in trip. (op 3-10 tchd 1-3 in places)
Ramamara(IRE), who had the same chance as the winner strictly on official figures, also went off much faster than ideal. (op 12-1)

7553 NEW CHAPEL H'CAP 6f (P)
3:05 (3:05) (Class 4) (0-85,82) 3-Y-O+ **£4,727** (£1,406; £702; £351) **Stalls** Low

Form RPR
2460 **1** **Brandywell Boy (IRE)**[6] 7478 6-8-0 71 .... BillyCray(7) 9 79
(D J S Ffrench Davis) *chsd ldrs: sn niggled along: rdn ent fnl 2f: chsd ldr over 1f out: led ins fnl f: hld on gamely* **28/1**

1160 **2** *hd* **Billy Red**[13] 7395 5-8-11 75 ....(b) FergusSweeney 2 82
(J R Jenkins) *led for 1f: chsd ldr after tl led again and edgd rt u.p over 1f out: hdd ins fnl f: edgd lft and rallied fnl 50yds: jst hld* **14/1**

0652 **3** *¾* **Capone (IRE)**[6] 7478 4-9-2 80 .... HayleyTurner 7 85+
(R Curtis) *stdd and swtchd lft after s: hld up in last pair: hdwy on inner and rdn over 1f out: chsd ldrs ins fnl f: edgd rt fnl 100yds: nt rch ldrs* **11/8[1]**

0260 **4** *2* **Fazbee (IRE)**[18] 7322 3-8-7 71 ....(p) LiamJones 8 69
(P W D'Arcy) *restless in stalls: hld up in rr: sltly hmpd wl over 1f out: r.o wl fnl f: nvr trbld ldrs* **14/1**

5132 **5** *hd* **Johnstown Lad (IRE)**[13] 7395 5-9-4 82 ....(t) ShaneKelly 4 80
(Daniel Mark Loughnane, Ire) *hld up in tch: effrt and nt clr run over 1f out: sn swtchd lft and squeezed between horses: no imp ins fnl f* **5/2[2]**

0510 **6** *nk* **Lucky Leigh**[39] 6902 3-8-11 75 .... SamHitchcott 5 72
(M R Channon) *t.k.h: hld up towards rr: rdn and hung lft over 1f out: kpt on but nvr gng pce to threaten ldrs* **20/1**

0050 **7** *¾* **Pawan (IRE)**[23] 7245 9-8-13 82 .... AnnStokell(5) 1 76
(Miss A Stokell) *in tch: rdn ent 2f out: no prog u.p over 1f out: wl hld fnl f* **28/1**

1200 **8** *nk* **River Kirov (IRE)**[6] 7478 6-9-2 80 .... SebSanders 3 73
(M Wigham) *t.k.h: in tch: rdn and unable qck wl over 1f out: n.d fnl f* **7/1[3]**

166 **9** *2 ¼* **For Life (IRE)**[108] 4870 7-8-6 73 .... NataliaGemelova(3) 6 59
(J E Long) *taken down early: racd keenly: chsd ldr tl led after 1f: hdd over 1f out: wknd fnl f* **14/1**

1m 11.2s (-0.70) **Going Correction** 0.0s/f (Stan) **9** Ran SP% **114.8**
Speed ratings (Par 105): **104,103,102,100,99 99,98,98,95**
toteswingers:1&2:£18.50, 2&3:£8.60, 1&3:£15.70 CSF £357.00 CT £913.97 TOTE £36.10: £7.30, £4.00, £1.20; EX 261.50 TRIFECTA Not won..
Owner P B Gallagher **Bred** Mountarmstrong Stud **Trained** Lambourn, Berks

FOCUS
A fair sprint handicap and another race that looked to favour front runners. The winner's best run for about three years.

7554 HORLEY H'CAP 5f (P)
3:35 (3:35) (Class 5) (0-70,70) 3-Y-O+ **£2,729** (£806; £403) **Stalls** High

Form RPR
5212 **1** **Edith's Boy (IRE)**[43] 6791 3-8-12 64 .... HayleyTurner 5 75
(S Dow) *mde all: rdn and edgd rt over 1f out: styd on wl fnl f* **10/1**

2 *1 ¼* **Ability N Delivery**[41] 6863 4-9-0 66 ....(p) JimmyFortune 8 73
(Michael J Browne, Ire) *sn chsng wnr: rdn wl over 1f out: drvn and styd on same pce ins fnl f* **3/1[1]**

3523 **3** *½* **Femme De Fer**[24] 7223 3-9-4 70 .... AdamKirby 4 75+
(C G Cox) *stdd s: hld up towards rr: rdn and hdwy over 1f out: r.o wl ins fnl f to go 3rd nr fin: nt rch ldrs* **5/1[3]**

4315 **4** *nk* **Littlemisssunshine (IRE)**[90] 5421 4-9-2 68 ....(p) LPKeniry 6 72
(J S Moore) *chsd ldrs: rdn wl over 1f out: kpt on same pce u.p fr over 1f out: lost 3rd nr fin* **33/1**

5156 **5** *shd* **Lithaam (IRE)**[13] 7398 5-8-7 66 ....(p) RyanClark(7) 2 70+
(J M Bradley) *s.i.s: bhd: swtchd ins and hdwy over 1f out: r.o wl ins fnl f: nt rch ldrs* **16/1**

6322 **6** *1 ½* **Make My Dream**[2] 7519 6-9-3 69 .... MartinDwyer 10 67
(J Gallagher) *towards rr: rdn and effrt on outer bnd 2f out: styd on fnl f but nvr gng pce to rch ldrs* **7/2[2]**

0551 **7** *nk* **Caledonia Princess**[13] 7398 3-9-1 67 ....(b) TonyCulhane 3 64
(R Curtis) *s.i.s: bhd: rdn wl over 1f out: nvr trbld ldrs* **13/2**

5440 **8** *2 ½* **Cape Royal**[13] 7398 9-8-12 64 ....(bt) DavidProbert 7 52
(J M Bradley) *chsd ldrs: struggling u.p ent fnl 2f: wl hld fnl f* **25/1**

2034 **9** *¾* **Silver Prelude**[24] 7224 8-9-1 67 ....(t) GeorgeBaker 9 52
(S C Williams) *in tch in midfield on outer: rdn and wknd over 1f out* **8/1**

0322 **10** *1* **Bookiesindex Boy**[24] 7224 5-9-1 67 .... EddieAhern 1 49
(J R Jenkins) *chsd ldrs: effrt on inner and rdn 2f out: wknd ent fnl f* **20/1**

58.02 secs (-0.78) **Going Correction** 0.0s/f (Stan) **10** Ran SP% **114.9**
Speed ratings (Par 103): **106,104,103,102,102 100,99,95,94,92**
toteswingers:1&2:£5.50, 2&3:£4.60, 1&3:£9.90 CSF £38.63 CT £170.85 TOTE £11.30: £3.00, £1.60, £2.00; EX 57.40 Trifecta £327.30 Pool: £464.54 - 1.05 winning units. Place 6 £243.70, Place 5 £163.2..
Owner A Lindsay **Bred** C Grehan **Trained** Epsom, Surrey

FOCUS
The time was very quick for the class of race, being less than a second outside the track record. It was another race where the leaders didn't come back though. The fourth looks the key guide to the form.

7490 WOLVERHAMPTON (A.W) (L-H)
Friday, November 27

OFFICIAL GOING: Standard
Wind: Nil Weather: Fine

7555 EVENTMASTERS.CO.UK CORPORATE HOSPITALITY H'CAP (DIV I) 5f 216y(P)
6:20 (6:20) (Class 6) (0-65,65) 3-Y-O+ **£2,047** (£604; £302) **Stalls** Low

Form RPR
3435 **1** **Leading Edge (IRE)**[21] 7273 4-9-1 62 .... ChrisCatlin 12 74
(M R Channon) *outpcd in rr: hdwy over 1f out: hrd rdn to ld wl ins fnl f: r.o* **12/1**

0000 **2** *¾* **Sea Rover (IRE)**[45] 6765 5-9-2 63 .... TomEaves 7 73
(M Brittain) *a.p: rdn to ld jst over 1f out: hdd wl ins fnl f* **9/1**

0052 **3** *nk* **Cool Sands (IRE)**[10] 7418 7-8-6 53 ....(v) FrancisNorton 6 62
(J G Given) *chsd ldrs: sn pushed along: rdn to chal and edgd lft ins fnl f: nt qckn cl home* **8/1**

0400 **4** *3 ½* **Not My Choice (IRE)**[27] 7192 4-9-3 64 ....(t) LukeMorris 8 62
(J Balding) *sn w ldr: rdn to ld briefly over 1f out: wknd wl ins fnl f* **16/1**

5244 **5** *2 ½* **Joyeaux**[21] 7273 7-9-0 61 .... PaulHanagan 9 51
(Ollie Pears) *mid-div: hdwy wl over 1f out: rdn and wknd ins fnl f* **6/1**

0054 **6** *hd* **Dickie Le Davoir**[3] 7503 5-8-9 56 ....(be) J-PGuillambert 2 45
(R C Guest) *s.i.s: in rr: pushed along over 3f out: swtchd rt over 1f out: nvr nr ldrs* **11/2[3]**

5500 **7** *¾* **Neo's Mate (IRE)**[11] 7417 3-8-3 53 .... AndreaAtzeni(3) 3 40
(Paul Green) *s.i.s: in rr: pushed along over 3f out: rdn over 2f out: c wd st: n.d* **22/1**

/0-6 **8** *1* **Granakey (IRE)**[51] 6581 6-8-4 51 oh2 .... SaleemGolam 4 35
(Ian Williams) *hld up in tch: pushed along 3f out: sn wknd* **33/1**

3421 **9** *1 ½* **Ponting (IRE)**[21] 7270 3-9-4 65 ....(p) JimCrowley 5 44
(R M Beckett) *sn w ldrs: led 2f out: rdn and hdd over 1f out: wknd ins fnl f* **4/1[1]**

0302 **10** *2* **Micky Mac (IRE)**[21] 7280 5-8-11 58 .... RobertWinston 1 30
(C J Teague) *led: pushed along and hdd 2f out: wknd fnl f* **9/2[2]**

0 **11** *5* **Queen Of Dobbin (IRE)**[13] 7397 3-7-11 51 oh1(p) JamesPSullivan(7) 10 7
(Lee Smyth, Ire) *mid-div: pushed along over 2f out: wknd wl over 1f out* **100/1**

1m 13.96s (-1.04) **Going Correction** -0.05s/f (Stan) **11** Ran SP% **110.8**
Speed ratings (Par 101): **104,103,102,97,94 94,93,92,90,87 80**
toteswingers: 1&2 £9.50, 1&3 £18.60, 2&3 £26.40 CSF £107.01 CT £901.55 TOTE £10.60: £3.40, £2.80, £2.40; EX 104.60.
Owner M Channon **Bred** Rathasker Stud **Trained** West Ilsley, Berks

FOCUS
An open, if modest, sprint handicap contested by several in-form horses that had run well here lately, in addition to others that looked potentially well treated on some not too distant runs. The pace was good and none of the trio that disputed it managed to hang on for a place. A stronger race than division II, with the first three clear.

7556 EVENTMASTERS.CO.UK CORPORATE HOSPITALITY MEDIAN AUCTION MAIDEN STKS 5f 216y(P)
6:50 (6:53) (Class 5) 2-Y-O **£2,729** (£806; £403) **Stalls** Low

Form RPR
3 **1** **Kingsgate Choice (IRE)**[18] 7317 2-9-3 0 .... RobertWinston 7 76+
(J R Best) *plld hrd: a.p: pushed along to ld jst over 1f out: rdn ins fnl f: r.o* **5/4[1]**

3 **2** *¾* **Esuvia (IRE)**[20] 7289 2-8-12 0 .... TomEaves 9 68
(B Smart) *a.p: rdn over 1f out: r.o ins fnl f* **13/8[2]**

0 **3** *1 ¾* **Boy The Bell**[21] 7276 2-9-3 0 .... ShaneKelly 6 68
(J A Osborne) *hld up in tch: rdn and r.o one pce fnl f* **9/1[3]**

4 *½* **Spirit Of Love (IRE)** 2-8-10 0 .... TobyAtkinson(7) 3 66
(M Wigham) *sn bhd: pushed along over 2f out: hdwy wl over 1f out: sn hung lft: r.o to take 4th cl home* **28/1**

0 **5** *2 ¼* **Exearti**[135] 3987 2-8-12 0 .... SebSanders 5 55
(A J McCabe) *w ldr: led over 3f out: rdn and hdd jst over 1f out: wknd wl ins fnl f* **10/1**

0 **6** *3 ½* **Bertie Buckle (IRE)**[43] 6802 2-9-3 0 .... LukeMorris 13 49
(J R Gask) *hld up: swtchd lft after s: pushed along over 3f out: short-lived effrt over 2f out* **66/1**

7 *2 ¼* **Darling Buds** 2-8-12 0 .... NCallan 10 37
(K A Ryan) *s.s: sn wl in tch: rdn over 1f out: nvr nr ldrs* **28/1**

8 *¾* **Major Monty (IRE)** 2-9-3 0 .... RichardKingscote 2 40
(Tom Dascombe) *led: hdd over 3f out: pushed along over 2f out: rdn and wknd over 1f out* **12/1**

0 **9** *¾* **Young George**[52] 6556 2-9-0 0 .... KellyHarrison(3) 8 38
(C W Fairhurst) *t.k.h: w ldrs: pushed along and ev ch over 2f out: wkng whn hung lft over 1f out* **100/1**

0 **10** *2 ¼* **Special Betty**[35] 7001 2-8-12 0 .... ChrisCatlin 1 26
(D Haydn Jones) *sn bhd* **100/1**

00 **11** *2 ¾* **Petit Belle**[18] 7317 2-8-5 0 .... HollyHall(7) 4 18
(N P Littmoden) *sn bhd* **125/1**

12 *34* **Zando's Pearl** 2-8-9 0 .... RussellKennemore(3) 11 —
(C J Price) *s.i.s: sn t.o* **100/1**

13 *20* **Missprint** 2-8-12 0 .... GrahamGibbons 12 —
(B P J Baugh) *s.s: a t.o* **100/1**

1m 15.2s (0.20) **Going Correction** -0.05s/f (Stan) **13** Ran SP% **122.5**
Speed ratings (Par 96): **96,95,92,92,89 84,81,80,79,76 72,27,—**
toteswingers: 1&2 £1.30, 1&3 £3.50, 2&3 £5.90 CSF £3.41 TOTE £2.30: £1.30, £1.10, £2.50; EX 4.00.
Owner John Mayne **Bred** Michael Staunton **Trained** Hucking, Kent

FOCUS
A fair maiden, nothing more, and one in which the market leaders, as expected, came to the fore. The pace was sound and the form makes sense.

NOTEBOOK
Kingsgate Choice(IRE) had shown a fair amount of promise first time out and confirmed that while still looking some way from the finished article. He tended to race very freely early on and then ran around a bit once in front, but his rider didn't need to get unduly serious with him and he appeals as one that will do well in nurseries if allowed to take his chance. He'll stay further, but this trip looks fine for now. (tchd 11-8 in places)
Esuvia(IRE) didn't improve for her debut and doesn't look to possess the scope of the winner. Nonetheless, she showed a good attitude after travelling the least well of the first three turning for home, and kept on in a manner that suggests she will stay further. (op 2-1)

Boy The Bell seemed to benefit from the drop back in trip and caught the eye travelling well turning in only to get messed about a bit at the top of the straight. He wasn't unlucky in any sense, but might well have a bit more to give. (tchd 12-1)
Spirit Of Love(IRE) ◆ was a big eye-catcher and promises to step up on this, either sooner or later. He was noticeably green in the straight, but over a trip that is almost certainly a bare minimum for him even now finished with quite a flourish from midfield under his young claimer. His trainer gets very few juveniles to work with, and it may not be until he goes into handicaps that the best is seen of him. (op 22-1)
Exearti stepped up on her debut to fare best of the three that cut out the pace and might well improve seeing as it was her first run for five months since moving stables. (tchd 7-1)
Bertie Buckle(IRE) was another to improve on his first run and might yet have a future at a modest level over further once handicapped.
Darling Buds missed the break badly but made late headway to finish in mid-division and ought to be a fair bit sharper next time. (op 20-1)
Major Monty(IRE) shaped with only a glimmer of promise and is clearly one of the stable's lesser lights. (op 14-1 tchd 10-1)

7557 LARKSHILL ENGINEERING MAIDEN STKS — 1m 5f 194y(P)
7:20 (7:22) (Class 5) 3-Y-O+ — **£2,729** (£806; £403) **Stalls** Low

Form				RPR
4	**1**		**King Red**[226] 1286 5-9-11 0 RichardKingscote 2 (Tom Dascombe) *hld up in tch: pushed along and wnt 2nd 2f out: rdn over 1f out: led ins fnl f: edgd rt nr fin: styd on* **3/1**[2]	67
-443	**2**	*1*	**Inflammable**[3] 7504 3-8-12 66 SebSanders 5 (Sir Mark Prescott) *hld up in tch: led wl over 2f out: rdn wl over 1f out: hdd ins fnl f: nt qckn* **5/2**[1]	60
46	**3**	*3 ¾*	**Smarties Party**[24] 7221 6-9-6 0 TomEaves 4 (C W Thornton) *sn hld up in mid-div: pushed along and hdwy 2f out: hrd rdn over 1f out: one pce* **14/1**	55
65	**4**	*3 ¼*	**Nyetimber (USA)**[8] 7455 3-9-3 0 ShaneKelly 8 (J A Osborne) *hld up towards rr: pushed along and hdwy over 2f out: rdn over 1f out: no imp* **25/1**	55
5503	**5**	*1 ¾*	**Pure Crystal**[11] 7049 3-8-12 51 JerryO'Dwyer 9 (M G Quinlan) *a.p: chsd ldr 6f out tl pushed along 3f out: rdn and wknd 2f out* **6/1**	48
4400	**6**	*1 ½*	**Shanavaz**[10] 7425 3-8-12 48 (p) PaulHanagan 1 (C J Teague) *s.i.s: hld up in rr: pushed along over 2f out: rdn wl over 1f out: nvr nr ldrs* **22/1**	46
64	**7**	*½*	**Spring Fashion (IRE)**[21] 7278 3-8-9 0 AndreaAtzeni(3) 7 (M Botti) *led early: chsd ldr to 6f out: pushed along over 3f out: wknd over 2f out* **7/2**[3]	45
0060	**8**	*2 ¼*	**Transfered (IRE)**[7] 7461 3-8-12 47 NCallan 6 (Lucinda Featherstone) *sn led: hdd wl over 2f out: rdn and wknd wl over 1f out* **14/1**	42
0	**9**	*6*	**Beyonda Dream**[88] 5531 3-8-12 0 NeilChalmers 3 (Lucinda Featherstone) *hld up in mid-div: pushed along over 5f out: rdn and bhd 4f out* **100/1**	34
0-00	**10**	*2 ¾*	**Kabougg**[16] 7332 3-8-12 30 RobertWinston 12 (A J McCabe) *hld up in rr: pushed along over 3f out: short-lived effrt over 2f out* **100/1**	30
	11	*22*	**Heronway (IRE)**[11] 7-9-8 0 RobertLButler(3) 11 (W J Greatrex) *hld up in mid-div: rdn and hung bdly rt 3f out: sn bhd: t.o* **66/1**	4
P00	**12**	*118*	**The Coach**[70] 6073 3-8-12 0 MarkCoumbe(5) 10 (T Wall) *a towards rr: t.o fnl 5f* **200/1**	—

3m 7.43s (1.43) **Going Correction** -0.05s/f (Stan)
WFA 3 from 5yo+ 8lb — 12 Ran SP% **115.6**
Speed ratings (Par 103): **93,92,90,88,87 86,86,85,81,80 67,—**
toteswingers: 1&2 £3.00, 1&3 £11.40, 2&3 £12.90 CSF £10.21 TOTE £3.50: £1.60, £1.30, £3.80; EX 15.00.
Owner John Reed **Bred** A Smith **Trained** Lambourn, Berks

FOCUS
A weak maiden run at something of a stop-start gallop. The bare form is limited byt the winner can do better.

7558 PHOSTERS H'CAP — 7f 32y(P)
7:50 (7:51) (Class 3) (0-90,90) 3-Y-O+ **£7,569** (£2,265; £1,132; £566; £282) **Stalls** High

Form				RPR
2220	**1**		**Caprio (IRE)**[30] 7111 4-8-7 78 NickyMackay 11 (J R Boyle) *hld up in rr: sn swtchd lft: c v wd st: str run and edgd lft ins fnl f: r.o to ld towards fin* **33/1**	87
1600	**2**	*¾*	**Inheritor (IRE)**[27] 7189 3-8-9 81 TomEaves 3 (B Smart) *a.p: led wl over 1f out: sn rdn: hdd towards fin* **22/1**	88
0062	**3**	*shd*	**Southandwest (IRE)**[9] 7437 5-8-6 77 LPKeniry 5 (J S Moore) *hld up in mid-div: pushed along over 3f out: hdwy on ins 2f out: rdn and r.o ins fnl f* **10/3**[2]	84
3216	**4**	*1*	**Ishiadancer**[27] 7171 4-8-2 76 oh1 KellyHarrison(3) 1 (E J Alston) *led: rdn and hdd wl over 1f out: no ex ins fnl f* **10/1**	80
6001	**5**	*¾*	**The Kyllachy Kid**[15] 7356 3-9-1 87 IanMongan 2 (S Gollings) *s.i.s: hld up in rr: pushed along over 2f out: rdn and r.o ins fnl f: nrst fin* **8/1**	89
2001	**6**	*½*	**Carnivore**[85] 5601 7-8-2 78 DeanHeslop(5) 4 (T D Barron) *hld up towards rr: hmpd on ins over 2f out: rdn and hdwy over 1f out: one pce ins fnl f* **14/1**	79
4615	**7**	*¾*	**Ektimaal**[13] 7395 6-8-11 82 HayleyTurner 12 (E A L Dunlop) *s.i.s: hld up in rr: rdn and hdwy 1f out: sn no imp* **15/2**[3]	81
1112	**8**	*nk*	**Street Power (USA)**[84] 5646 4-9-3 88 SteveDrowne 7 (J R Gask) *s.i.s: hld up towards rr: hdwy on outside over 2f out: c wd st: rdn wl over 1f out: edgd lft ins fnl f: sn btn* **11/4**[1]	86
4100	**9**	*2 ¼*	**Malcheek (IRE)**[31] 7083 7-8-9 80 GrahamGibbons 9 (T D Easterby) *t.k.h in tch: pushed along over 2f out: rdn and wknd over 1f out* **25/1**	72
2000	**10**	*nk*	**Fishforcompliments**[20] 7287 5-8-10 81 TonyHamilton 10 (R A Fahey) *prom: ev ch over 2f out: rdn and wknd 1f out* **20/1**	72
0025	**11**	*½*	**Beckermet (IRE)**[8] 7454 7-9-3 88 NCallan 8 (R F Fisher) *chsd ldr after 1f tl wl over 2f out: rdn and wknd wl over 1f out* **9/1**	78

1m 27.6s (-2.00) **Going Correction** -0.05s/f (Stan)
WFA 3 from 4yo+ 1lb — 11 Ran SP% **114.3**
Speed ratings (Par 107): **109,108,108,106,106 105,104,104,101,101 100**
toteswingers: 1&2 £140.00, 1&3 £26.50, 2&3 £19.80 CSF £585.89 CT £3125.94 TOTE £33.60: £6.20, £6.10, £1.40; EX 175.80.
Owner M Khan X2 **Bred** P Rabbitte **Trained** Epsom, Surrey

FOCUS
A useful handicap, though one that despite the presence of several known pacesetters wasn't run at quite the breakneck gallop that seemed likely. The form looks sound, with the winner back to his best.

NOTEBOOK
Caprio(IRE) recorded just the third win of his career and in much stronger grade as well than he usually contests, but there seemed no fluke about it as he ran on strongly to put his stamp on the race late coming widest of all. He is usually thereabouts on this surface, and his win capped a good spell for his rider who is starting to get a few more rides again after a quiet year.
Inheritor(IRE) ran a fine race trying this surface for the first time and can usually be relied upon to give his running. (op 25-1)
Southandwest(IRE) might have finished a clear second had he not met trouble on the home turn, he perhaps didn't put as much into his finishing effort as seemed likely. He might be worth a try in headgear. (op 4-1 tchd 3-1)
Ishiadancer ran well under a competent front running ride from just out of the handicap in much higher grade than usual. She still looks to be improving and is worth looking out for when dropped slightly in class. (op 12-1 tchd 14-1)
The Kyllachy Kid ran well considering the opposition was tougher than last time and his new yard clearly have him in fine fettle. (op 9-1)
Carnivore was just about to begin his run when forced to check. (op 12-1)
Street Power(USA) didn't see his race out and left the impression that now he is this high in the weights. (op 9-4 tchd 3-1)
Beckermet(IRE) extended his modest run of efforts at this trip and is another that will also be better off reverting to sprinting. (op 12-1)

7559 EVENTMASTERS.CO.UK CORPORATE HOSPITALITY NURSERY — 5f 20y(P)
8:20 (8:20) (Class 6) (0-60,60) 2-Y-O — **£2,729** (£806; £403) **Stalls** Low

Form				RPR
0321	**1**		**Vilnius**[23] 7242 2-9-3 56 ChrisCatlin 8 (M R Channon) *chsd ldrs: hrd rdn to ld wl ins fnl f: drvn out* **11/4**[1]	59
4060	**2**	*nk*	**Out The Ring (IRE)**[10] 7421 2-9-1 59 KylieManser(5) 12 (Miss Gay Kelleway) *hmpd s: sn swtchd lft: hld up in rr: swtchd rt to outside wl over 1f out: hdwy ent fnl f: sn rdn: r.o to take 2nd last strides* **25/1**	61+
5066	**3**	*hd*	**Caol Ila (IRE)**[37] 6938 2-9-1 54 TPQueally 9 (J G Given) *a.p: rdn and ev ch over 1f out: kpt on ins fnl f* **8/1**	55
6403	**4**	*¾*	**Point To Prove**[21] 7268 2-9-6 59 (e) HayleyTurner 3 (Miss Amy Weaver) *chsd ldrs: rdn to ld 1f out: hdd wl ins fnl f: nt qckn* **5/1**[3]	58
003	**5**	*¾*	**Future Regime (IRE)**[27] 7190 2-9-3 56 SJCraine 4 (Patrick Morris) *towards rr: pushed along 3f out: swtchd lft and hdwy on ins whn nt clr run 1f out: swtchd rt ins fnl f: r.o* **12/1**	57+
0650	**6**	*nk*	**Rightcar**[23] 7242 2-9-2 55 (b) AdamKirby 7 (Peter Grayson) *hld up in mid-div: hdwy whn nt clr run and swtchd lft jst over 1f out: rdn and nt qckn ins fnl f* **33/1**	52+
0000	**7**	*nse*	**Annia (IRE)**[16] 7334 2-9-4 57 (t) LukeMorris 6 (N P Littmoden) *led: rdn 2f out: hdd 1f out: one pce* **50/1**	52
0002	**8**	*½*	**Thewinnatakesitall**[21] 7268 2-9-4 60 (p) KellyHarrison(3) 5 (H J Evans) *chsd ldrs: pushed along over 1f out: nt qckn ins fnl f* **16/1**	53
6050	**9**	*1*	**Crushing (IRE)**[14] 7363 2-9-5 58 (p) RobertWinston 1 (A J McCabe) *hld up in rr: pushed along over 2f out: c v wd st: nvr trbld ldrs* **9/2**[2]	47
0630	**10**	*2*	**Duke Of Rainford**[74] 5950 2-9-1 54 PaulHanagan 11 (M Herrington) *fly-jmpd s: sn mid-div: rdn and btn over 1f out* **16/1**	36
505	**11**	*¾*	**The Two G'S**[21] 7268 2-8-13 57 RichardEvans(5) 2 (P D Evans) *a towards rr* **25/1**	36
0520	**12**	*nk*	**True Red (IRE)**[14] 7372 2-8-12 58 RachelKing(7) 13 (Mrs N S Evans) *prom tl wknd wl over 1f out* **25/1**	36
000	**13**	*3 ¾*	**Clayton Flick (IRE)**[67] 6154 2-8-9 53 (v[1]) AmyBaker(5) 10 (A B Haynes) *mid-div: pushed along over 2f out: rdn and wknd wl over 1f out* **7/1**	18

63.10 secs (0.80) **Going Correction** -0.05s/f (Stan) — 13 Ran SP% **121.0**
Speed ratings (Par 94): **91,90,90,89,87 87,87,86,84,81 80,79,73**
toteswingers: 1&2 £27.90, 1&3 £7.10, 2&3 £22.50 CSF £85.89 CT £510.62 TOTE £2.80: £1.30, £8.90, £3.10; EX 115.80.
Owner P Trant **Bred** P Trant & Mike Channon Bloodstock Limited **Trained** West Ilsley, Berks

FOCUS
Few that could be seriously fancied in a weakish nursery contested largely by exposed sorts, though the pace at least was good and hard-luck stories were few and far between. Selling-class form, rated around the principals.

NOTEBOOK
Vilnius is a tough cookie and made it two wins in succession with another game display to get the best of a bunch finish. She can't go up much in the weights for this, and as she has already proved herself in higher grade may not have stopped winning yet. (op 3-1)
Out The Ring(IRE) flashed home from a poor position and ran as if he will appreciate a return to further. His current mark looks a fair one and he can continue to be competitive in similar events. (op 20-1)
Caol Ila(IRE) showed her last nursery running to be all wrong with a solid effort up with the pace all the way and 5f looks to be her trip for now. (op 13-2)
Point To Prove reversed latest Southwell form with Thewinnatakesitall and ran another solid race while leaving the impression a return to a bit further may suit. (op 15-2)
Future Regime(IRE) missed the break and then found his path blocked on more than one occasion before staying on He's worth another chance off this mark in similar grade, perhaps back at 6f. (tchd 14-1)
Rightcar was another that didn't get the best of runs, though couldn't be considered unlucky. (op 25-1)
Annia(IRE) showed much more than recently dropped back sharply in trip and tried in a tongue tie. (op 40-1)
Crushing(IRE) found things happening all too quickly back at the minimum trip. (op 5-1 tchd 11-2)
Clayton Flick(IRE), a morning gamble, once again dropped away tamely despite another drop in trip and isn't one to be making many excuses for. (op 6-1 tchd 8-1)

7560 BROADWAY H'CAP — 1m 141y(P)
8:50 (8:50) (Class 2) (0-100,95) 3-Y-O+
£11,215 (£3,358; £1,679; £840; £419; £210) **Stalls** Low

Form				RPR
2441	**1**		**Spinning**[18] 7322 6-8-13 89 (b) PhillipMakin 2 (T D Barron) *s.i.s: hld up in rr: pushed along and hdwy 2f out: c wd st: rdn and edgd lft ins fnl f: sn led: r.o* **3/1**[1]	97
0432	**2**	*1*	**Chapter And Verse (IRE)**[1] 7540 3-7-13 81 oh1 AndreaAtzeni(3) 7 (Mike Murphy) *hld up in rr: prog on outside 3f out: edgd lft and led jst over 1f out: sn rdn: hdd wl ins fnl f* **7/1**	87
3022	**3**	*4*	**Gala Casino Star (IRE)**[29] 6795 4-8-13 89 PaulHanagan 3 (R A Fahey) *hld up in tch: pushed along over 3f out: sn lost pl: rdn wl over 1f out: rallied to take 3rd wl ins fnl f* **6/1**	86
6020	**4**	*¾*	**One Way Or Another (AUS)**[20] 7294 6-9-2 92 SteveDrowne 1 (J R Gask) *hld up: hdwy 3f out: rdn wl over 1f out: wknd ins fnl f* **4/1**[2]	87
20	**5**	*2*	**Perfect Star**[20] 7291 5-9-5 95 AdamKirby 4 (C G Cox) *prom: rdn jst over 2f out: wknd wl over 1f out* **4/1**[2]	85

4144 **6** 1 1/2 **Gaily Noble (IRE)**[18] 7322 3-7-11 **81** oh3 AmyBaker(5) 6 68
(A B Haynes) *w ldr: led 6f out: rdn jst over 2f out: hdd over 1f out: wknd ins fnl f* **20/1**

3202 **7** 2 **The Fifth Member (IRE)**[14] 7375 5-8-13 **89** SJCraine 5 71
(J R Boyle) *led: hdd 6f out: chsd ldr tl rdn wl over 1f out: wknd fnl f* **5/1**[3]

1m 47.93s (-2.57) **Going Correction** -0.05s/f (Stan)
WFA 3 from 4yo+ 3lb 7 Ran SP% **113.2**
Speed ratings (Par 109): **109,108,104,103,102 100,99**
toteswingers: 1&2 £7.20, 1&3 £2.30, 2&3 £9.00 CSF £23.84 TOTE £3.30: £1.80, £4.50; EX 27.90.
Owner Mrs J Hazell **Bred** Cheveley Park Stud **Trained** Maunby, N Yorks

FOCUS
A weak affair for the grade and one that was run at a steady pace until the last half mile, and it doesn't look form to be going overboard about. The winner enhanced his excellent C/D record, and a personal best too from the runner-up.

NOTEBOOK
Spinning is in the form of his life right now and defied a mark 9lb higher than last time and 6lb higher than he has ever raced off before. The tactical nature of the race probably didn't suit him ideally and he wasn't able to assert until late having been caught flat-footed when the pace increased, but he was still comfortably on top passing the line. The Lincoln Trial here in the spring could well be a long-term objective, but that will demand a fair bit more improvement still. (tchd 10-3)
Chapter And Verse(IRE) ran a good race for the second day running but once again left the impression that he will be suited by a return to further suit and, carrying his head rather high, might helped by cheekpieces. (op 13-2)
Gala Casino Star(IRE) was patently unsuited by the steady gallop at this trip and only got going again late after losing his place, but his win record isn't one to be bragging about and the jury is still out as to whether this surface suits as well as turf. (op 8-1)
One Way Or Another(AUS) is none too consistent and produced a tame response after seemingly going well on the home turn; he might not be one to be making too many excuses for. (op 9-2)
Perfect Star was disappointing seeing as she has been campaigned in much better grade during this year. (op 5-1 tchd 11-2)
Gaily Noble(IRE) doesn't seem the force of old after dropping away weakly despite having had the run of the race from the front. (op 18-1 tchd 22-1)
The Fifth Member(IRE) was also better placed than most as the race developed and this has to rate a disappointing effort. (op 4-1 tchd 7-2)

7561 EVENTMASTERS.CO.UK CORPORATE HOSPITALITY H'CAP (DIV II) 5f 216y(P)
9:20 (9:22) (Class 6) (0-65,65) 3-Y-0+ **£2,047** (£604; £302) **Stalls** Low

Form RPR

3626 **1** **Welcome Approach**[14] 7371 6-8-6 **53** LukeMorris 10 60
(J R Weymes) *hld up in rr: pushed along over 2f out: hdwy wl over 1f out: sn swtchd lft: led ins fnl f: rdn and r.o* **16/1**

000 **2** 3/4 **Josiah Bartlett (IRE)**[23] 7240 3-8-4 **51** oh3 HayleyTurner 9 56
(Ian Williams) *hld up in rr: n.m.r on ins briefly over 3f out: hdwy over 1f out: rdn and r.o to take 2nd last strides* **9/1**

0020 **3** hd **Jord (IRE)**[10] 7423 5-9-0 **61** ChrisCatlin 2 65
(J A Glover) *a.p: pushed along over 1f out: rdn and ev ch ins fnl f: kpt on* **9/1**

252 **4** hd **Colombard (IRE)**[7] 7462 4-8-4 **51** oh1 (v) PaulHanagan 7 54
(Patrick Morris) *hld up in tch: rdn whn bmpd jst over 1f out: kpt on* **9/2**[3]

5402 **5** 3/4 **Restless Genius (IRE)**[15] 7355 4-9-0 **64** MartinLane(3) 6 72+
(B Ellison) *hld up towards rr: pushed along whn swtchd lft over 1f out: sn nt clr run: rdn and r.o ins fnl f: nrst fin* **9/4**[1]

063 **6** shd **Kipchak (IRE)**[3] 7506 4-9-4 **65** (p) LPKeniry 1 66
(C R Dore) *t.k.h: prom: chsd ldr wl over 3f out: rdn and ev ch 1f out: nt qckn* **4/1**[2]

0036 **7** 1 1/4 **Top Flight Splash**[15] 7349 3-8-5 **52** (v) LiamJones 11 49
(Mrs G S Rees) *in rr: pushed along over 3f out: c v wd st: late prog: n.d* **20/1**

2010 **8** 1 1/4 **Mandhooma**[103] 5065 3-8-13 **60** ow2 PhillipMakin 8 53
(P W Hiatt) *led early: prom: rdn 2f out: wknd 1f out* **20/1**

004U **9** 3/4 **Grimes Faith**[13] 7397 6-9-2 **63** (p) J-PGuillambert 5 53+
(R C Guest) *hld up in mid-div: prog on ins whn nt clr run over 2f out: rdn whn nt clr run jst ins fnl f: nt rcvr* **28/1**

000 **10** nse **Lujiana**[91] 5396 4-8-4 **51** oh3 FrancisNorton 12 41
(M Brittain) *hld up in mid-div: pushed along over 2f out: wknd wl over 1f out* **33/1**

3210 **11** nk **Malapropism**[6] 7483 9-8-4 **56** MatthewDavies(5) 4 45
(M R Channon) *sn led: rdn and hdd ins fnl f: sn wknd* **10/1**

1m 14.44s (-0.56) **Going Correction** -0.05s/f (Stan) 11 Ran SP% **119.8**
Speed ratings (Par 101): **101,100,99,99,98 98,96,95,94,93 93**
toteswingers: 1&2 £20.40, 1&3 £21.70, 2&3 £10.50 CSF £147.07 CT £1423.46 TOTE £20.50: £2.30, £3.20, £2.40; EX 292.40 Place 6: £206.43, Place 5: £24.86..
Owner T A Scothern **Bred** P Wyatt And Ranby Hall **Trained** Middleham Moor, N Yorks

FOCUS
A competitive finale run at the expectedly strong pace that rather teed things up for those produced from behind. The time was still a bit slower than the first division and the time is ordinary for the grade.
T/Plt: £88.20 to a £1 stake. Pool: £104,506.87. 864.03 winning tickets. T/Qpdt: £20.40 to a £1 stake. Pool: £9,310.85. 336.90 winning tickets. KH

7457 FONTAINEBLEAU
Friday, November 27

OFFICIAL GOING: Very soft

7569a PRIX BELLE DE NUIT (LISTED RACE) (F&M) 1m 4f 110y
1:40 (1:42) 3-Y-0+ **£25,243** (£10,097; £7,573; £5,049; £2,524)

RPR

1 **Wysiwyg Lucky (FR)**[13] 6-8-13 GBenoist 14 93
(J-L Gay, France)

2 3/4 **Lunduv (IRE)**[26] 4-8-13 SMaillot 8 92
(C Von Der Recke, Germany)

3 nse **Bella Ida (FR)**[86] 5586 5-8-13 YLerner 5 92
(J E Hammond, France)

4 3/4 **Greylady (FR)**[76] 5896 3-8-8 IMendizabal 12 93
(J-C Rouget, France)

5 1 1/2 **La Tournesol (GER)**[26] 4-8-13 GMasure 7 89
(P Schiergen, Germany)

6 snk **Majura (GER)**[26] 4-8-13 MGuyon 2 88
(A Fabre, France)

7 1 **Tangaspeed (FR)**[13] 7405 4-8-13 THuet 13 87
(R Laplanche, France)

8 1 1/2 **Folle Allure (FR)**[57] 6438 4-8-13 FBlondel 6 85
(J-C Rouget, France)

9 2 **Excellent Girl**[36] 6978 3-8-12 (p) P-CBoudot 4 88
(Y De Nicolay, France)

10 1 1/2 **Deliberate**[37] 3-8-8 SPasquier 18 81
(A Fabre, France)

0 **Teeky**[28] 7148 3-8-8 RobertHavlin 9 —
(J H M Gosden) *in tch on outside: 5th 1/2-way: pushed along over 3f out: 9th st: sn btn* **11/1**[1]

0 **One Clever Cat (IRE)**[30] 7128 3-8-12 FPrat 16 —
(T Clout, France)

0 **Terre Du Vent (FR)**[30] 7128 3-8-12 J-BEyquem 10 —
(Y De Nicolay, France)

0 **Andrea (GER)**[30] 7128 3-8-12 MBarzalona 11 —
(F Head, France)

0 **Landora (FR)**[20] 7302 3-8-8 (p) TThulliez 3 —
(A De Royer-Dupre, France)

0 **Rainbow Muhtatir (FR)**[69] 4-8-13 RMarchelli 1 —
(M Rolland, France)

0 **Isla Canela (USA)**[18] 3-8-8 DBoeuf 15 —
(A De Royer-Dupre, France)

2m 49.6s (169.60)
WFA 3 from 4yo+ 6lb 17 Ran SP% **8.3**
PARI-MUTUEL (Including 1 Euro stake): WIN 7.30; PL 2.80, 19.40, 9.30;DF 199.40.
Owner Mme N Petit-Levi **Bred** Mlle Nadine Petit **Trained** France

NOTEBOOK
Teeky, the winner of a Newmarket handicap last time, probably found the ground against her on this step up in grade.

7549 LINGFIELD (L-H)
Saturday, November 28

OFFICIAL GOING: Standard
Wind: fresh, across Weather: bright and breezy

7570 BET HENNESSY GOLD CUP - BETDAQ NURSERY 5f (P)
12:05 (12:05) (Class 5) (0-70,73) 2-Y-0 **£2,590** (£770; £385; £192) **Stalls** High

Form RPR

632 **1** **Goddess Of Light (IRE)**[19] 7317 2-9-4 **67** ShaneKelly 1 73
(Daniel Mark Loughnane, Ire) *trckd ldrs: rdn to chse ldr wl over 1f out: edgd rt u.p over 1f out: led jst ins fnl f: r.o wl* **9/1**

1030 **2** 1 3/4 **Wanchai Whisper**[15] 7372 2-8-11 **60** PaulDoe 3 60
(P D Evans) *hld up in tch in last pair: rdn and hdwy on inner 2f out: pressed ldrs ent fnl f: no ex fnl 75yds* **25/1**

0100 **3** 3/4 **Blue Neptune**[15] 7372 2-9-0 **63** MartinDwyer 8 60
(W R Muir) *led: rdn 2f out: drvn ent fnl f: hdd jst ins fnl f: one pce after* **12/1**

042 **4** nk **Kummel Excess (IRE)**[17] 7331 2-9-0 **63** TonyCulhane 5 59
(George Baker) *in tch on outer: rdn and unable qck bnd 2f out: kpt on same pce fr over 1f out* **12/1**

531 **5** nk **Memorandum**[15] 7365 2-9-10 **73** SteveDrowne 7 68
(R Charlton) *chsd ldr after 1f: rdn ent fnl 2f: unable qck and lost pl wl over 1f out: edgd lft and plugged on same pce after* **2/1**[1]

6542 **6** 3/4 **Boogie Waltzer**[24] 7242 2-8-1 **53** AndreaAtzeni(3) 2 45
(S C Williams) *chsd ldr over 1f out: lost pl but stl wl in tch over 3f out: one pce u.p fnl 2f* **5/2**[2]

3211 **7** 4 1/2 **Vilnius**[1] 7559 2-8-13 **62** 6ex ChrisCatlin 4 38
(M R Channon) *s.i.s: a bhd* **4/1**[3]

58.42 secs (-0.38) **Going Correction** -0.10s/f (Stan) 2y crse rec 7 Ran SP% **111.1**
Speed ratings (Par 96): **99,96,95,94,94 92,85**
toteswingers:1&2:£14.60, 2&3:£26.10, 1&3:£13.00 CSF £171.23 CT £2600.14 TOTE £9.10: £3.00, £9.70; EX 125.50 TRIFECTA Not won..
Owner M V Kirby **Bred** Mr & Mrs K Downey **Trained** Trim, Co Meath

FOCUS
An ordinary nursery in which they all kept well away from the inside rail in the home straight. The form looks sound enough rated around the first two.

NOTEBOOK
Goddess Of Light(IRE) ◆, who was making her nursery debut after making the frame in a couple of Wolverhampton maidens, was racing over the minimum trip for the first time since her racecourse debut and it obviously suited. Content to track the pace this time, she found plenty when pulled out for her effort, hitting the front half a furlong from home and winning going away. There should be more to come on this surface. (op 13-2)
Wanchai Whisper, much more exposed than the winner with this being her 11th outing, had gained her two wins in selling and claiming company, but a 4lb drop in the weights brought about an improved effort. Settled off the pace, she got a nice run through on the inside of the field rounding the home bend and had every chance 1f out but couldn't match the winner for finishing speed. (op 33-1)
Blue Neptune showed bright speed from the outside stall and wasn't overhauled until inside the last furlong. This return to forcing tactics saw a better performance following two poor efforts at Wolverhampton. (op 16-1 tchd 20-1)
Kummel Excess(IRE), lightly raced and progressive coming into this, was trapped out wide throughout and although she stayed on up the home straight, she lacked a decisive turn of foot. She may need a slightly stiffer test than this.
Memorandum, noticeably weak in the market beforehand, was handy from the start but never looked that happy and didn't find much off the bridle. She had looked in need of 6f before this, but wouldn't have won this race at any trip. (op 11-8 tchd 9-4 in a place)
Boogie Waltzer attracted substantial market support, but she was under pressure passing the 2f pole and could never get back into the contest. She has already shown enough to suggest she can win a race. (op 5-1)
Vilnius, bidding for a hat-trick and making a quick reappearance under a 6lb penalty for her narrow win at Wolverhampton the previous evening, barely went a yard and the obvious conclusion is that this came too quick. (op 7-2)

7571 BET INTERNATIONAL RUGBY - BETDAQ MAIDEN STKS 6f (P)
12:35 (12:38) (Class 5) 2-Y-0 **£3,238** (£963; £481; £240) **Stalls** Low

Form RPR

1 **Tenacestream (CAN)** 2-9-3 0 RobertWinston 3 79+
(J R Best) *chsd ldng pair: wnt 2nd and rdn ent fnl 2f: led ent fnl f: r.o wl* **5/1**[2]

2 3/4 **Passion Overflow (USA)** 2-8-12 0 TPQueally 6 72+
(J Noseda) *in tch: chsd ldrs: clsd over 2f out: rdn and ev ch over 1f out: kpt on but nt quite pce of wnr ins fnl f* **9/2**[1]

05 **3** *2 ½* **The Strig**[37] 6971 2-9-0 0 .... WilliamCarson(3) 10 69
(S C Williams) *chsd ldr tl led over 2f out: rdn and hrd pressed 2f out: hdd ent fnl f: nt pce of ldng pair but kpt on for clr 3rd* **5/1**[2]

0 **4** *3 ¼* **Torres Del Paine**[10] 7436 2-9-3 0 .... MartinDwyer 5 60
(J C Fox) *s.i.s: racd off the pce in midfield: rdn wl over 2f out: hdwy to go modest 4th over 1f out: nvr trbld ldrs* **100/1**

6 **5** *2 ¼* **Cosimo de Medici**[15] 7365 2-9-3 0 .... SteveDrowne 8 53
(H Morrison) *racd off the pce in midfield: dropped to last trio and rdn along wl over 3f out: kpt on fr over 1f out: nvr trbld ldrs* **8/1**[3]

0 **6** *½* **Abhar (USA)**[17] 7326 2-9-3 0 .... TonyCulhane 1 51
(J R Best) *rrd as stalls opened and slowly away: bhd in last pair: pushed along over 3f out: styd on past btn horses fr over 1f out: nvr on terms* **10/1**

7 *2 ½* **Saharia (IRE)** 2-9-3 0 .... ShaneKelly 12 44
(J Noseda) *s.i.s: sn rdn along and in midfield: no prog fr wl over 2f out* **8/1**[3]

8 *1 ¼* **Purple Gallery (IRE)** 2-9-3 0 .... KFallon 9 40+
(J S Moore) *hung rt thrght: chsd ldrs tl lost pl and rn v wd bnd 2f out: wl btn after* **9/2**[1]

9 *2* **Ming Master (FR)** 2-9-3 0 .... LiamJones 11 34
(W J Haggas) *s.i.s: a wl bhd* **16/1**

0 **10** *½* **South African Gold (USA)**[138] 3920 2-9-3 0 .... LukeMorris 2 33
(J M P Eustace) *hld up off the pce in midfield: lost pl and bhd wl over 2f out: no ch whn swtchd rt over 1f out* **20/1**

0 **11** *3 ½* **Torran Sound**[7] 7477 2-9-3 0 .... HayleyTurner 4 22
(J M P Eustace) *racd off the pce in midfield: struggling and rdn over 2f out: wl bhd fnl 2f* **33/1**

0 **12** *9* **Jokers Wild**[10] 7430 2-9-3 0 .... LPKeniry 7 —
(A M Balding) *led tl over 2f out: wknd qckly: wl bhd and eased ins fnl f* **40/1**

1m 11.44s (-0.46) **Going Correction** -0.10s/f (Stan) 2y crse rec **12** Ran SP% **118.0**
Speed ratings (Par 96): **99,98,94,90,87 86,83,81,79,78 73,61**
toteswingers:1&2:£7.30, 2&3:£27.60, 1&3:£18.60 CSF £26.80 TOTE £4.60: £1.10, £3.00, £2.60; EX 32.90 Trifecta £82.70 Part won. Pool: £111.79 - 0.45 winning units..

Owner Kent Bloodstock **Bred** William D Graham **Trained** Hucking, Kent

FOCUS

An ordinary maiden and, with the seven who held previous experience never having made the frame, it was little surprise the first two home were newcomers. The third looks the best guide to the level.

NOTEBOOK

Tenacestream(CAN) ◆, a $115,000 colt related to some decent performers in Canada on the dam's side, was popular in the market and the support proved right. He was always in a good position and, making his effort up the favoured centre of the track, battled on well to score. Connections thought he may just need it, so there should be more to come from him on this surface and he may be given one more run before being put away. (op 15-2 tchd 9-2)

Passion Overflow(USA) ◆ was weak in the market beforehand. A half-sister to four speedy winners, including the high-class Ocean Ridge, she travelled into the race smoothly and had every chance but found the winner too strong. She shouldn't take long in going one better. (op 11-4)

The Strig, who was stepping up a furlong, was always up with the pace and kept on but couldn't match the front two inside the last furlong. Admittedly, he did hold the advantage in experience over the front pair but was clear of the others and now has the option of nurseries. (op 15-2 tchd 9-1)

Torres Del Paine stayed on from the middle of the field over the last couple of furlongs and certainly stepped up a huge amount from his debut. He is another likely to come into his own once handicapped.

Cosimo de Medici ◆, despite moving up a furlong from his debut, was struggling to go the pace from the start and stayed on only when it was too late. He remains one to be interested in once handicapped, possibly when stepped up again in trip. (op 6-1 tchd 11-2)

Abhar(USA), a stable companion of the winner, had the bit slip though his mouth on debut. Out the back early, he was another noting doing all his best work late and is probably capable of better back over further. (op 14-1 tchd 8-1)

Purple Gallery(IRE), a $100,000 half-brother to a couple of Polytrack winners, was up there early but seemed to hesitate at around halfway and then became virtually unrideable. Official explanation: jockey said colt hung badly right (op 6-1 tchd 7-1 in a place)

7572 BET PREMIER LEAGUE FOOTBALL - BETDAQ H'CAP 6f (P)

1:10 (1:13) (Class 7) (0-50,58) 3-Y-O+ **£2,047** (£604; £302) **Stalls** Low

Form RPR

-541 **1** **Spinning Bailiwick**[3] 7510 3-9-5 **56** 6ex .... GeorgeBaker 4 74+
(G L Moore) *in tch: chsd ldr over 2f out: rdn to ld over 1f out: drew wl clr fnl f: easily* **4/5**[1]

0012 **2** *4 ½* **Elusive Ronnie (IRE)**[7] 7484 3-9-0 **58** .... (b) TobyAtkinson(7) 1 60
(R A Teal) *stdd s: hld up bhd: stl 8th 2f out: hdwy on inner over 1f out: rn to go 2nd nr fin: no ch w wnr* **5/1**[2]

4056 **3** *½* **Commandingpresence (USA)**[9] 7452 3-8-9 **49** .... MarcHalford(3) 9 49
(J J Bridger) *chsd ldrs: lost pl over 3f out: rdn over 2f out: no ch w wnr fnl f but plugged on to go 3rd last strides* **25/1**

0362 **4** *hd* **Head To Head (IRE)**[10] 7427 5-8-13 **50** .... (tp) DarryllHolland 8 49
(A D Brown) *led: rdn ent fnl 2f: hdd over 1f out: no ch w wnr ins fnl f: lost 2 pls nr fin* **8/1**[3]

4310 **5** *1* **Boundless Applause**[8] 7460 3-8-12 **49** .... NCallan 5 45
(I A Wood) *in tch in midfield: rdn and effrt on inner jst over 2f out: chsd ldng pair over 1f out: no prog and wknd ins fnl f* **14/1**

0250 **6** *½* **Battimoore (IRE)**[15] 7371 3-8-13 **50** .... ShaneKelly 7 45
(I W McInnes) *stdd s: in tch towards rr: rdn 4f out: nvr trbld ldrs* **16/1**

0330 **7** *1 ½* **Tricky Trev (USA)**[31] 4643 3-8-13 **50** ow1 .... (t) AdamKirby 10 40
(S Curran) *chsd ldr tl over 2f out: lost pl u.p bnd 2f out: wl btn fnl f* **20/1**

0265 **8** *4 ½* **Native Dame (IRE)**[128] 4240 3-8-13 **50** .... (bt) LPKeniry 2 25
(Edgar Byrne) *a towards rr: lost tch over 2f out: wl bhd and eased ins fnl f* **16/1**

1005 **9** *2 ¼* **Equinity**[28] 7176 3-8-7 **49** .... (t) SimonPearce(5) 6 17
(J Pearce) *reluctant to go to post: hung rt thrght: reminders bnd 4f out: lost pl and rn wd bnd 2f out: wl bhd after* **20/1**

1m 11.47s (-0.43) **Going Correction** -0.10s/f (Stan) **9** Ran SP% **115.1**
Speed ratings (Par 97): **98,92,91,91,89 89,87,81,78**
toteswingers:1&2:£2.10, 2&3:£21.10, 1&3:£4.60 CSF £4.64 CT £54.45 TOTE £1.90: £1.10, £1.70, £5.90; EX 4.60 Trifecta £39.40 Pool: £520.64 - 9.77 winning units..

Owner Dr Ian R Shenkin **Bred** Mrs M Shenkin **Trained** Lower Beeding, W Sussex

■ Stewards' Enquiry : Darryll Holland one-day ban: failed to keep straight from stalls (Dec 12)

FOCUS

Rock-bottom stuff and ultimately a one-horse race. The third to her recent best sets the standard.

7573 MARSH GREEN H'CAP 1m 5f (P)

1:45 (1:45) (Class 3) (0-90,87) 3-Y-O+

£7,477 (£2,239; £1,119; £560; £279; £140) **Stalls** Low

Form RPR

1 **1** **King's Salute (USA)**[37] 6974 3-8-11 **82** .... GregFairley 3 97+
(M Johnston) *w ldrs for 1f: chsd ldng pair after until wnt 2nd over 2f out: rdn to ld over 1f out: styd on strly and drew clr fnl f* **5/2**[1]

1003 **2** *2 ½* **Coeur De Lionne (IRE)**[25] 7226 5-9-8 **86** .... SteveDrowne 4 92
(E A L Dunlop) *t.k.h: hld up in tch: rdn and effrt on outer bnd 2f out: chsd wnr ins fnl f: kpt on but no ch w wnr* **13/2**[3]

0364 **3** *½* **Evident Pride (USA)**[33] 7066 6-9-6 **84** .... KFallon 7 89
(B R Johnson) *stdd and swtchd lft after s: hld up in last: hdwy and rdn over 2f out: chalng for 2nd jst ins fnl f: kpt on but no ch w wnr* **13/2**[3]

201 **4** *3 ½* **Wicked Daze (IRE)**[14] 7402 6-9-4 **87** .... AmyRyan(5) 6 87
(K A Ryan) *pushed along leaing stalls and sn led: hdd over 10f out: chsd ldr after tl led again 3f out: rdn and 2 l clr 2f out: hdd over 1f out: wknd qckly ins fnl f* **15/2**

6311 **5** *8* **Chookie Hamilton**[15] 7373 5-9-4 **82** .... PJMcDonald 2 70
(I Semple) *hld up in tch: rdn and unable qck ent fnl 2f: wknd u.p over 1f out* **13/2**[3]

03-2 **6** *6* **Basalt (IRE)**[12] 7005 5-9-0 **78** .... PaulHanagan 5 57
(T J Pitt) *pushed along leaving stalls and chsd ldr tl led over 10f out: slowed pce and hdd 5f out: sn lost pl and rdn: last and struggling 3f out* **7/1**

5040 **7** *2 ¾* **Conquisto**[21] 7293 4-9-7 **85** .... IanMongan 1 60
(S Gollings) *t.k.h: hld up in last pair: hdwy on outer to ld 5f out: hdd and rdn 3f out: wknd qckly 2f out and sn bhd* **9/2**[2]

2m 42.84s (-3.16) **Going Correction** -0.10s/f (Stan) course record
WFA 3 from 4yo+ 7lb **7** Ran SP% **111.0**
Speed ratings (Par 107): **105,103,103,101,96 92,90**
toteswingers:1&2:£7.30, 2&3:£8.10, 1&3:£8.10 CSF £17.88 TOTE £2.80: £1.80, £3.10; EX 14.70.

Owner Sheikh Hamdan Bin Mohammed Al Maktoum **Bred** Darley **Trained** Middleham Moor, N Yorks

FOCUS

A decent staying handicap, but spoiled to a degree by a stop-start gallop. The placed horses set the level.

NOTEBOOK

King's Salute(USA) ◆ was much the least exposed and was having his first start in a handicap after making a successful debut for the yard in a Kempton maiden last month, the form of which has since been boosted. Never far off the pace, he had a bit of ground to make up starting the final turn but powered into the lead 1f from home and soon put daylight between himself and his rivals. He is likely to keep on progressing and could be a nice middle-distance handicapper in the making. (op 2-1 tchd 11-4 in places)

Coeur De Lionne(IRE), back up to a more suitable trip though he has yet to win beyond 1m4f, made an effort from off the pace off the final bend and finished well, but the winner had gone well beyond recall. A more end-to-end gallop may have suited him better. (tchd 6-1 and 7-1)

Evident Pride(USA), minus the visor and trying this trip for the first time, is now 4lb lower than when successful here at the start of the year. Switched off out the back early, he tried to get into the race in the home straight but was never doing enough. (op 5-1)

Wicked Daze(IRE), raised 3lb after losing the race in the stewards' room at Wolverhampton a fortnight earlier, took a keen hold early and his rider was content to get a lead after a couple of furlongs. Back in front approaching the home bend, he tried to steal the race and poached a couple of lengths but the winner was soon looming alongside and he had little left. (op 8-1 tchd 7-1)

Chookie Hamilton, bidding for a hat-trick off a 6lb higher mark and racing at this track for the first time, came off the bridle rounding the home bend but found nothing. He is very much a Wolverhampton specialist. (op 11-2)

Basalt(IRE), back on the Flat after a moderate performance over hurdles, was in front after a couple of furlongs but lost the advantage passing the 5f pole and was soon on the retreat. (op 12-1)

7574 JACKSBRIDGE H'CAP 1m 2f (P)

2:15 (2:17) (Class 2) (0-100,95) 3-Y-O+

£11,215 (£3,358; £1,679; £840; £419; £210) **Stalls** Low

Form RPR

4002 **1** **Bound By Honour (SAF)**[14] 7393 6-9-4 **91** .... (b) GeorgeBaker 6 101+
(G L Moore) *in tch tl hdwy to join ldr over 5f out: led gng wl over 2f out: edgd rt fr over 1f out: in command fnl f: eased towards fin* **11/4**[1]

1460 **2** *1* **The Cayterers**[56] 6480 7-8-12 **90** .... SimonPearce(5) 1 96
(A W Carroll) *dwlt: hld up in tch in last trio: hdwy wl over 1f out: chsd wnr 1f out: hung rt fnl f: kpt on but no threat to wnr* **10/1**

0351 **3** *¾* **Wing Play (IRE)**[28] 7194 4-9-0 **87** .... (p) ShaneKelly 11 94+
(H Morrison) *hld up in tch in last trio: wd and rdn bnd 2f out: hdwy ent fnl f: r.o wl: nt rch ldrs* **3/1**[2]

1005 **4** *1 ¾* **Faithful Ruler (USA)**[28] 7169 5-8-13 **86** .... PaulHanagan 10 90+
(R A Fahey) *hld up in tch in last trio: effrt and rdn ent fnl 2f: nt clr run over 1f out tl swtchd lft jst ins fnl f: r.o: nvr able to chal* **16/1**

2450 **5** *hd* **Sgt Schultz (IRE)**[168] 2932 6-9-7 **94** .... LPKeniry 2 95
(J S Moore) *t.k.h: trckd ldrs: rdn and effrt ent fnl 2f: kpt on same pce u.p fnl f* **20/1**

5240 **6** *2* **Baylini**[177] 2641 5-8-12 **90** .... SophieDoyle(5) 8 87
(Ms J S Doyle) *t.k.h: chsd ldrs: rdn ent fnl f: plugged on same pce fr over 1f out* **20/1**

0026 **7** *½* **Mohathab (IRE)**[80] 5772 4-8-8 **81** oh2 .... MartinDwyer 5 77
(Tim Vaughan) *chsd ldrs: rdn and lost pl over 3f out: rallied u.p over 1f out: no prog fnl f* **33/1**

2031 **8** *½* **Stand Guard**[15] 7375 5-8-11 **89** .... AndrewHeffernan(5) 9 84
(P Howling) *t.k.h: rdn and unable qck ent fnl 2f: n.d fnl f* **11/2**

1514 **9** *hd* **Splinter Cell (USA)**[36] 6996 3-8-13 **90** .... KFallon 3 84
(M Botti) *sn led on inner: jnd over 5f out: rdn and hdd over 2f out: wknd jst over 1f out* **4/1**[3]

2m 5.27s (-1.33) **Going Correction** -0.10s/f (Stan)
WFA 3 from 4yo+ 4lb **9** Ran SP% **114.5**
Speed ratings (Par 109): **101,100,99,98,98 96,96,95,95**
toteswingers:1&2:£9.80, 2&3:£9.50, 1&3:£2.70 CSF £29.53 CT £87.02 TOTE £3.70: £1.70, £2.90, £1.50; EX 33.80 Trifecta £60.10 Pool: £278.17 - 4.04 winning units..

Owner Blue Diamond Racing **Bred** Waterford Stud **Trained** Lower Beeding, W Sussex

FOCUS

A quality handicap on paper, but the early pace was modest and it developed into a sprint. The runner-up is the best guide to the form.

NOTEBOOK

Bound By Honour(SAF) was 2lb higher than when runner-up on his Polytrack debut over C&D a fortnight earlier, his best effort since arriving in Britain. He was always in a good position in a steadily run race and, having grabbed the lead on his own starting the turn for home, kept on finding enough to keep his rivals at bay. The form may not be totally reliable, but he remains unexposed on the surface. (tchd 5-2 and 3-1)

The Cayterers was having his first run beyond 7f on sand but is a winner over this trip on turf. Having his first start since finishing eighth in the Cambridgeshire, he missed the break and found himself out the back of the field in a moderately run race. He got a nice run against the inside rounding the home bend and did his best to get to the winner, but could not. (op 8-1)

Wing Play(IRE), raised 5lb for his Wolverhampton success last month, gave himself even more to do after missing the break and had the whole field in front of him turning for home. Unlike the runner-up, he had to make his effort widest off the home bend but, not for the first time, his head carriage was unappealing and he was never doing enough. (tchd 11-4 and 10-3)

Faithful Ruler(USA) ◆, 12lb higher than for his last win on sand at Wolverhampton in March, has still conclusively to prove his stamina for the trip, so the modest early gallop would have been a help, but he managed to get himself into all sorts of trouble when trying to get a run over 1f from home and by the time he got through it was far too late. He can be rated much closer. Official explanation: jockey said gelding was denied a clear run

Sgt Schultz(IRE) has won over this trip on the slower surface at Great Leighs, but his six wins here have all come over 1m4f. He didn't run badly under the circumstances, if lacking the required turn of foot in a steadily run race over an inadequate trip, but was entitled to need this first start outing since June. (tchd 25-1)

Baylini, returning from a similar layoff, was keen enough in a handy position so she too should come on for it, but is putting together a lengthy losing run. (op 25-1)

Stand Guard, raised 3lb for his Wolverhampton success, did his chances little good by pulling too hard early. (op 13-2 tchd 9-2)

Splinter Cell(USA) was disappointing, given that he had the run of the race out in front in a steadily run race yet still dropped tamely away. (op 5-1)

7575 FORD MANOR H'CAP 1m (P)

2:50 (2:55) (Class 5) (0-75,75) 3-Y-O+ £2,590 (£770; £385; £192) Stalls High

Form RPR

0000 1 **Final Verse**[16] 7350 6-9-4 73 (e) LPKeniry 10 87
(Matthew Salaman) *t.k.h: hld up in midfield: hdwy over 2f out: rdn to chse clr ldr 1f out: r.o wl to ld nr fin* **15/2**[3]

4100 2 *nk* **Tiddliwinks**[28] 7172 3-8-13 70 NCallan 4 83
(K A Ryan) *t.k.h: trckd ldrs: hdwy to chse ldr jst over 2f out: led over 1f out: 3 l clr 1f out: tired and edgd lft ins fnl f: hdd nr fin* **16/1**

14 3 2 ¾ **Silver Guest**[36] 7000 4-9-6 75 ChrisCatlin 1 81
(M R Channon) *dwlt: sn pushed up into midfield: rdn and effrt jst over 2f out: chsd ldng pair ins fnl f: kpt on but nvr able to chal* **10/1**

0065 4 1 ¼ **I Confess**[10] 7437 4-8-13 73 (b) RichardEvans(5) 2 76
(P D Evans) *chsd ldr tl over 5f out: styd chsng ldrs: rdn and unable qck jst over 2f out: rallied over 1f out: no imp fnl f* **6/1**[2]

2143 5 ½ **Millfield (IRE)**[17] 7327 6-9-5 74 GeorgeBaker 8 76+
(P R Chamings) *taken down early: stdd s: t.k.h: hld up in rr: hdwy over 1f out: swtchd lft and r.o fnl f: nvr trbld ldrs* **15/2**[3]

1143 6 *hd* **Dichoh**[15] 7364 6-9-6 75 (v) AdamKirby 11 77+
(M Madgwick) *stdd s: hld up in rr: rdn and effrt wl over 1f out: styd on but nvr trbld ldrs* **6/1**[2]

4250 7 *nse* **Isphahan**[70] 6117 6-9-6 75 (v) DavidProbert 6 77
(A M Balding) *in tch in midfield on outer: rdn and unable qck over 2f out: no ch w ldrs fnl 2f* **11/2**[1]

0243 8 ½ **Daniel Thomas (IRE)**[7] 7481 7-8-13 68 (p) HayleyTurner 7 68
(Mrs A L M King) *v.s.a: bhd: sme hdwy 5f out: rdn and effrt over 2f out: kpt on but n.d* **8/1**

5065 9 3 ¾ **Justcallmehandsome**[19] 7322 7-8-5 67 (v) BillyCray(7) 5 58
(D J S Ffrench Davis) *chsd ldrs: wnt 2nd over 5f out: led wl over 2f out: rdn ent fnl 2f: hdd over 1f out: sn outpcd by wnr: wknd fnl f* **25/1**

0001 10 3 ¾ **Elusive Fame (USA)**[11] 7423 3-9-0 71 (b) GregFairley 3 53
(M Johnston) *led tl wl over 2f out: wknd qckly jst over 2f out: sn wl bhd* **9/1**

4004 11 3 **Ivory Lace**[15] 7364 8-9-0 69 JimCrowley 12 44
(S Woodman) *a in rr: n.d* **25/1**

6-50 12 ½ **Northern Tour**[218] 1489 3-9-4 75 MartinDwyer 9 49
(P F I Cole) *a towards rr: rdn and struggling 3f out: wl bhd fnl 2f* **14/1**

1m 36.44s (-1.76) **Going Correction** -0.10s/f (Stan)
WFA 3 from 4yo+ 2lb **12 Ran SP% 117.9**
Speed ratings (Par 103): **104,103,100,99,99 99,98,98,94,90 87,87**
toteswingers:1&2:£27.40, 2&3:£15.40, 1&3:£16.60 CSF £120.61 CT £1215.69 TOTE £9.50: £3.80, £3.50, £2.60; EX 192.60.
Owner Mrs N L Young **Bred** A Christodoulou **Trained** Upper Lambourn, Berks

FOCUS
An ordinary handicap run at just a modest early pace. The third is rated to his recent best.

7576 CROWHURST MAIDEN STKS 1m (P)

3:20 (3:24) (Class 5) 3-Y-O £2,590 (£770; £385; £192) Stalls High

Form RPR

0234 1 **Mustakmil (IRE)**[77] 5858 3-9-3 74 HayleyTurner 3 76+
(S Dow) *hld up in tch: hdwy to press ldrs on inner jst over 2f out: led ent fnl f: r.o strly: readily* **13/8**[2]

2 3 ¼ **Peponi** 3-9-3 0 NCallan 1 68
(P J Makin) *dwlt: sn in tch: chsd ldr 4f out: led over 2f out: rdn and hrd pressed 2f out: hdd ent fnl f: nt pce of wnr fnl f* **8/1**[3]

322 3 1 ¼ **Passkey**[68] 6158 3-8-12 77 SebSanders 9 60
(Sir Mark Prescott) *dwlt and pushed along early: in tch on outer: chsd ldng pair over 2f out: rdn 2f out: flashed tail u.p over 1f out: btn jst ins fnl f* **1/1**[1]

00 4 2 ¼ **Big Sur**[33] 7067 3-9-3 0 LPKeniry 5 60+
(T Keddy) *stdd s: hld up bhd: hdwy over 2f out: styd on steadily but nvr any threat to ldrs* **66/1**

-005 5 8 **Cativo**[31] 7107 3-8-12 45 ow3 (t) JamesMillman(3) 10 39
(B R Millman) *t.k.h: led after 1f tl rdn and hdd over 2f out: sn wknd* **33/1**

0 6 6 **Espresso Steps (USA)**[12] 7411 3-8-7 0 AndrewHeffernan(5) 8 21
(P Howling) *t.k.h: chsd ldrs: rdn and wknd over 2f out: sn wl bhd* **66/1**

7 7 **Madame McManus** 3-8-12 0 PaulDoe 7 4
(P D Evans) *led early: sn hdd: lost pl and rdn over 4f out: lost tch wl over 2f out* **25/1**

0450 8 9 **Mile High Lad (USA)**[9] 7455 3-9-3 55 (tp) GeorgeBaker 2 —
(George Baker) *s.i.s: nvr gng wl in rr: lost tch 3f out* **14/1**

005 9 16 **Iron Master**[153] 3432 3-9-0 48 MarcHalford(3) 6 —
(J J Bridger) *chsd ldr after 1f tl 4f out: sn lost pl u.p: t.o fr wl over 1f out* **66/1**

1m 38.08s (-0.12) **Going Correction** -0.10s/f (Stan) **9 Ran SP% 117.1**
Speed ratings (Par 102): **96,92,91,89,81 75,68,59,43**
toteswingers:1&2:£2.30, 2&3:£1.90, 1&3:£1.10 CSF £14.59 TOTE £2.50: £1.10, £2.50, £1.02; EX 19.80 Trifecta £31.50 Place 6 £665.17, Place 5 £26.60.
Owner Simon Caunce **Bred** Shadwell Estate Company Limited **Trained** Epsom, Surrey

FOCUS
An uncompetitive maiden with which to end the card and few could be given much of a chance. Despite a three-way battle for the early lead, the winning time was 1.64 seconds slower than the preceding handicap and the winner is probably the best guide to the form.
T/Plt: £582.80 to a £1 stake. Pool: £45,768.89. 57.32 winning tickets. T/Qpdt: £30.90 to a £1 stake. Pool: £5,725.50. 137.10 winning tickets. SP

7555 WOLVERHAMPTON (A.W) (L-H)

Saturday, November 28

OFFICIAL GOING: Standard changing to standard to fast after race 1 (5.50)
Wind: Light half against Weather: Raining 6.50 onwards

7577 CLEANEVENT H'CAP 5f 216y(P)

5:50 (5:50) (Class 5) (0-75,75) 3-Y-O+ £3,238 (£963; £481; £240) Stalls Low

Form RPR

0210 1 **Tourist**[17] 7327 4-9-4 75 DaneO'Neill 12 88
(D Shaw) *hld up in mid-div: hdwy on outside wl over 1f out: sn rdn: led and edgd lft ins fnl f: r.o wl* **11/1**

0021 2 2 ¾ **Perlachy**[7] 7496 5-8-9 66 (v) KirstyMilczarek 7 70
(J R Holt) *a.p: rdn wl over 1f out: ev ch ins fnl f: nt qckn* **7/2**[1]

0255 3 ½ **Kersivay**[16] 7356 3-9-0 71 FrancisNorton 9 74
(Ollie Pears) *hld up in rr: pushed along and hdwy fnl f: r.o to take 3rd last stride* **4/1**[2]

2000 4 *hd* **Loose Caboose (IRE)**[16] 7355 4-8-11 68 (b) RobertWinston 8 70
(A J McCabe) *sn led: rdn over 1f out: hdd ins fnl f: sn edgd lft: no ex* **33/1**

4130 5 *nse* **Onceaponatime (IRE)**[7] 7496 4-8-12 69 LukeMorris 3 71+
(M D Squance) *hld up in mid-div: rdn and hdwy 1f out: carried sltly lft whn styng on u.p wl ins fnl f* **11/2**

0000 6 ¾ **Green Park (IRE)**[17] 7337 6-9-1 72 (b) DNolan 10 71+
(D Carroll) *hld up and bhd: pushed along wl over 1f out: nt clr run and swtchd rt ins fnl f: r.o* **16/1**

0300 7 1 ¼ **Tartatartufata**[16] 7355 7-8-13 70 (v) J-PGuillambert 2 65
(J G Given) *led early: prom: rdn over 1f out: fdd wl ins fnl f* **33/1**

4601 8 1 ¼ **Speak The Truth (IRE)**[17] 7329 3-8-11 68 (p) SJCraine 5 59
(J R Boyle) *hld up in tch: pushed along over 2f out: rdn over 1f out: one pce whn hmpd ins fnl f* **7/1**

0043 9 6 **Bahamian Kid**[7] 7496 4-8-9 66 (b[1]) JerryO'Dwyer 1 38
(R Hollinshead) *hld up in mid-div on ins: rdn 2f out: wknd fnl f* **9/2**[3]

1000 10 1 **Guto**[16] 7355 6-8-11 71 KellyHarrison(3) 6 40
(W J H Ratcliffe) *sn chsng ldr: rdn and lost 2nd 2f out: sn wknd* **28/1**

0001 11 1 ¼ **My Sweet Georgia (IRE)**[16] 7348 3-8-9 66 (p) PaulHanagan 4 31
(Stef Liddiard) *outpcd: sn wl in rr: no ch whn hung rt over 1f out* **20/1**

1m 13.42s (-1.58) **Going Correction** -0.075s/f (Stan) **11 Ran SP% 116.6**
Speed ratings (Par 103): **107,103,102,102,102 101,99,98,90,88 87**
toteswingers:1&2:£7.40, 2&3:£2.80, 1&3:£9.00 CSF £47.03 CT £182.83 TOTE £12.10: £3.00, £1.50, £2.20; EX 59.20.
Owner M Shirley **Bred** Juddmonte Farms Ltd **Trained** Danethorpe, Notts

FOCUS
A modest handicap but a decisive winner in a decent time and the form looks pretty sound.

7578 WOLVERHAMPTON-RACECOURSE.CO.UK CLAIMING STKS 1m 5f 194y(P)

6:20 (6:20) (Class 6) 3-Y-O+ £2,914 (£867; £324; £324) Stalls Low

Form RPR

3035 1 **Key Regard (IRE)**[7] 7476 3-8-13 68 ShaneKelly 7 70
(P F I Cole) *s.i.s: hld up in rr: gd hdwy to ld 6f out: pushed along and qcknd clr 2f out: rdn and edgd rt ins fnl f: drvn out* **7/1**[3]

2 1 ½ **Naxox (FR)**[14] 8-9-7 0 TonyCulhane 5 68
(George Baker) *hld up in rr: pushed along and prog 2f out: rdn over 1f out: styd on to take 2nd ins fnl f: nt trble wnr* **40/1**

0464 3 *nk* **Easterly Breeze (IRE)**[31] 7112 5-8-4 61 (bt) AlexEdwards(7) 10 58
(Mrs L J Young) *a.p: shkn up wl over 1f out: styd on same pce ins fnl f* **10/1**

524 3 *dht* **Zuwaar**[63] 6280 4-9-7 69 (tp) EddieAhern 9 68
(Ian Williams) *a.p: rdn wl over 1f out: styd on one pce ins fnl f* **2/1**[1]

2022 5 ½ **Quince (IRE)**[16] 7357 6-9-1 68 (v) SimonPearce(5) 6 66
(J Pearce) *hld up in mid-div: hdwy over 5f out: rdn wl over 1f out: styd on one pce ins fnl f* **9/2**[2]

02-3 6 7 **Acropolis (IRE)**[89] 8-9-3 75 RobertWinston 4 53
(Mrs J L Le Brocq, Jersey) *hld up in mid-div: pushed along and hdwy 3f out: wknd over 1f out* **12/1**

4-16 7 ¾ **Market Watcher (USA)**[42] 6859 8-8-8 55 MartinLane(3) 3 46
(Seamus Fahey, Ire) *hld up in tch: rdn and wknd over 2f out* **14/1**

63/5 8 1 **Carr Hall (IRE)**[89] 5540 6-9-7 48 EmmettStack 1 55?
(Mrs J L Le Brocq, Jersey) *plld hrd in tch: lost pl and n.m.r briefly on ins over 3f out: hung rt bnd over 2f out: sn bhd* **20/1**

5 9 1 **Davids City (IRE)**[30] 7137 5-8-11 0 PJMcDonald 2 43
(G A Harker) *s.i.s: t.k.h in mid-div: lost pl on ins over 6f out: bhd fnl 4f* **33/1**

0/0- 10 13 **The Chip Chopman (IRE)**[41] 4866 7-8-11 44 LiamJones 11 25
(R A Harris) *hld up in rr: pushed along 4f out: sn struggling* **100/1**

41/ 11 ¾ **Carlesimo (IRE)**[57] 3365 11-9-3 79 PaulHanagan 8 30
(Noel Meade, Ire) *led: hdd 6f out: pushed along over 3f out: wknd wl over 2f out* **9/2**[2]

3m 7.88s (1.88) **Going Correction** -0.075s/f (Stan)
WFA 3 from 4yo+ 8lb **11 Ran SP% 116.8**
Speed ratings (Par 101): **91,90,89,89,89 85,85,84,84,76 76**
PL: Zuwaar £0.70 Easterly Breeze £1.20. toteswingers Key Regard & Naxox:£24.50, KR&Z:£2.60, KR&EB:£5.90, N&Z: £6.10, N&EB:£19.40. CSF £261.11 TOTE £8.20: £2.20, £8.10; EX 217.30.
Owner Jared Sullivan **Bred** D G Iceton **Trained** Whatcombe, Oxon

FOCUS
The usual mixed bunch in this claimer and the early pace was moderate. The winner is rated to his recent best with the runner-up to his old French Flat form, but the form behind is a bit messy.

7579 CLEANDOMAIN H'CAP — 7f 32y(P)
6:50 (6:50) (Class 6) (0-55,57) 3-Y-O+ — **£2,388** (£705; £352) **Stalls High**

Form — RPR
-600 **1** **Philmack Dot Com**[30] 7129 3-8-13 **55**.........................(t) JerryO'Dwyer 6 63
(D Donovan) *mde all: rdn wl over 1f out: drvn out* **25/1**
0012 **2** *hd* **Spinning Ridge (IRE)**[10] 7438 4-9-2 **57**............................. LiamJones 1 64
(R A Harris) *a.p: chsd wnr 2f out: rdn and sustained chal fnl f: r.o* **7/2**[1]
6005 **3** *2 ½* **The City Kid (IRE)**[16] 7348 6-8-13 **54**............................. DaneO'Neill 10 54
(G D Blake) *hld up in tch: pushed along over 2f out: rdn wl over 1f out: kpt on same pce fnl f* **8/1**[3]
0003 **4** *nse* **Interchoice Star**[16] 7361 4-8-10 **54**.................(p) RussellKennemore(3) 9 54
(R Hollinshead) *hld up in mid-div: sme prog over 2f out: swtchd rt over 1f out: sn rdn: kpt on ins fnl f* **9/1**
0000 **5** *½* **Romantic Verse**[52] 6588 4-8-11 **55**...................(bt) MichaelJStainton(3) 4 54
(S Curran) *t.k.h: a.p: pushed along over 2f out: rdn wl over 1f out: kpt on one pce fnl f* **16/1**
-000 **6** *¾* **Chosen Forever**[111] 4823 4-8-13 **54**................................ PJMcDonald 2 51+
(G R Oldroyd) *hld up towards rr: pushed along over 1f out: swtchd rt jst over 1f out: kpt on ins fnl f* **11/2**[2]
/0-5 **7** *3 ½* **King's Jester (IRE)**[58] 6415 7-8-13 **54**...................(tp) RobertWinston 12 41
(Lee Smyth, Ire) *sn prom: chsd ldr after 1f tl rdn 2f out: wknd over 1f out* **12/1**
2050 **8** *1* **Silca Meydan**[79] 5791 3-8-12 **54**....................................... DavidProbert 5 39
(R J Price) *hld up towards rr: rdn on ins over 2f out: nvr nr ldrs* **10/1**
3502 **9** *3* **Catchpenny**[22] 7270 3-8-13 **55**..(p) PhillipMakin 8 31
(K A Ryan) *hld up in rr: pushed along and c wd st: sn struggling* **9/1**
0354 **10** *1 ½* **Megalo Maniac**[11] 7424 6-8-13 **54**..............................(v) PaulHanagan 11 26
(R A Fahey) *hld up in mid-div: pushed along over 2f out: rdn and wknd wl over 1f out* **9/1**
0506 **11** *2 ¾* **Greek Secret**[15] 7370 6-9-0 **55**... TonyCulhane 3 20
(J O'Reilly) *a in rr* **8/1**[3]
6001 **12** *½* **Carnival Dream**[8] 7460 4-8-6 **54**............................... JamesPSullivan(7) 7 18
(H A McWilliams) *t.k.h: prom: stmbld over 4f out: lost pl over 3f out: bhd fnl 2f* **11/1**

1m 29.03s (-0.57) **Going Correction** -0.075s/f (Stan)
WFA 3 from 4yo+ 1lb — 12 Ran SP% **124.7**
Speed ratings (Par 101): **100,99,96,96,96 95,91,90,86,85 82,81**
toteswingers:1&2:£23.30, 2&3:£7.10, 1&3:£53.90 CSF £116.58 CT £813.28 TOTE £28.90: £7.70, £1.60, £3.00; EX 403.00.
Owner Philip Mclaughlin **Bred** Mrs T A Foreman **Trained** Newmarket, Suffolk
■ Stewards' Enquiry : Robert Winston four-day ban: careless riding (Dec 12-15)

FOCUS
A very moderate handicap but pretty competitive and a surprise result. The form does not look strong with the placed horses the best guide.
Philmack Dot Com Official explanation: trainer said, regarding apparent improvement in form, that on the gelding's last run the saddle slipped, when it looked as if it may run into a place.

7580 PLAY AT POKERINVENICE.COM MAIDEN STKS — 7f 32y(P)
7:20 (7:21) (Class 5) 2-Y-O — **£3,238** (£963; £481; £240) **Stalls High**

Form — RPR
022 **1** **Robust Wish (USA)**[45] 6772 2-9-3 79..........................(b[1]) EddieAhern 7 78+
(B J Meehan) *a.p: shkn up to ld wl over 1f out: drew clr fnl f: comf* **8/11**[1]
00 **2** *5* **Seamster**[137] 3957 2-9-3 0.. GregFairley 2 66
(M Johnston) *led: hdd wl over 1f out: sn rdn and btn* **10/1**
3 *1 ¾* **Riviera Chic (USA)** 2-8-12 0.. AdamKirby 10 56+
(R M Beckett) *hld up in rr: hdwy over 2f out: tk 3rd jst ins fnl f: kpt on* **25/1**
0 **4** *2* **Pomeroy**[70] 6108 2-9-3 0.. RichardKingscote 9 57
(Tom Dascombe) *a.p: rdn over 2f out: wknd wl over 1f out* **12/1**
0 **5** *hd* **Before The War (USA)**[17] 7325 2-9-3 0................................ KFallon 1 56
(L M Cumani) *hld up in mid-div: pushed along over 3f out: swtchd rt over 1f out: sme prog towards fin* **7/1**[3]
6455 **6** *1* **Bubbly Bellini (IRE)**[133] 4081 2-9-3 74........................ RobertWinston 3 54
(A Bailey) *chsd ldr: ev ch over 2f out: lost 2nd wl over 1f out: sn hung lft and wknd* **33/1**
7 *½* **My Grand Duke (USA)** 2-9-3 0....................................... ShaneKelly 5 52
(J A Osborne) *hld up in mid-div: pushed along over 2f out: nvr nr ldrs* **50/1**
20 **8** *½* **Stefanki (IRE)**[36] 6991 2-9-3 0.. TonyCulhane 6 54+
(R Curtis) *s.i.s: hld up in rr: pushed along over 2f out: swtchd lft over 1f out: n.d* **20/1**
9 *1 ¾* **Right Grand** 2-9-3 0... LiamJones 4 47
(W J Haggas) *s.i.s and wnt lft s: pushed along and c wd st: a in rr* **9/2**[2]
10 *6* **Luminosa** 2-8-9 0.. AndreaAtzeni(3) 8 27
(D Donovan) *hld up in mid-div: pushed along over 2f out: sn bhd* **66/1**

1m 28.96s (-0.64) **Going Correction** -0.075s/f (Stan) — 10 Ran SP% **120.4**
Speed ratings (Par 96): **100,94,92,90,89 88,88,87,85,78**
toteswingers:1&2:£3.60, 2&3:£35.60, 1&3:£11.30 CSF £9.13 TOTE £1.80: £1.10, £3.20, £3.00; EX 9.00.
Owner Thomas Conway **Bred** Dinwiddie Farm **Trained** Manton, Wilts

FOCUS
An uncompetitive maiden and an easy winner who is rated to his pre-race mark.

NOTEBOOK
Robust Wish(USA), rated 79 having finished runner-up in his two previous starts, looked to have been found a good opportunity and so it proved. Fitted with blinkers for the first time, once he struck the front early in the straight the race was over. He should remain competitive in handicaps on this surface. (op 4-5)
Seamster, having his first try on the AW following a break, was always in the front rank but had no answer when challenged by the winner. He at least qualifies for handicaps now and should not be badly treated. (op 8-1)
Riviera Chic(USA) ◆, a $60,000 yearling, made an encouraging debut, staying on late and should be better for the experience.
Pomeroy improved on his debut effort, which was over two months previously, keeping on under pressure. (op 16-1)
Before The War(USA) also improved but looks the sort to do better in handicaps in time. (op 6-1 tchd 15-2)
Bubbly Bellini(IRE) Official explanation: jockey said gelding hung badly left
Stefanki(IRE) Official explanation: jockey said colt was denied a clear run
Right Grand is out of a 1m4f winner and was always behind after a slow start. He will know more next time. (op 11-2 tchd 7-1)

7581 CLEAN WASTE SOLUTIONS (S) STKS — 1m 141y(P)
7:50 (7:52) (Class 6) 3-Y-O+ — **£2,388** (£705; £352) **Stalls Low**

Form — RPR
6600 **1** **Ten Pole Tudor**[4] 7499 4-9-0 52..................................(p) LiamJones 6 60
(R A Harris) *hld up and bhd: hdwy over 3f out: led over 2f out: edgd rt over 1f out: sn rdn: drvn out* **25/1**
0030 **2** *2 ¼* **Pride Of Nation (IRE)**[7] 7492 7-9-0 68......................(p) RobertWinston 1 55
(A J McCabe) *a.p: rdn to chse wnr over 1f out: edgd rt: no imp* **9/4**[1]
6356 **3** *½* **Davana**[19] 7318 3-8-3 47.. KellyHarrison(3) 4 49
(W J H Ratcliffe) *led: hdd over 5f out: pushed along over 3f out: lost pl over 2f out: rallied u.p over 1f out: tk 3rd ins fnl f* **16/1**
0650 **4** *1 ¼* **Fairplaytomyself**[15] 7374 4-8-2 49.................................. TobyAtkinson(7) 9 46
(P W Hiatt) *hld up in rr: pushed along and hdwy over 1f out: nvr trbld ldrs* **25/1**
200/ **5** *½* **Flighty Fellow (IRE)**[104] 9-9-5 65.................................(b) EmmettStack 5 55
(Mrs J L Le Brocq, Jersey) *hld up and bhd: rdn and sme hdwy wl over 1f out: kpt on ins fnl f* **16/1**
0600 **6** *8* **Brer Rabbit**[44] 6806 3-8-8 65... MartinLane(3) 7 31
(Seamus Fahey, Ire) *hld up in mid-div: hdwy over 6f out: rdn and wknd wl over 1f out* **16/1**
2010 **7** *1 ¾* **Pianoforte (USA)**[42] 6862 7-9-5 55........................(b) GrahamGibbons 10 32
(E J Alston) *prom: led over 5f out tl over 3f out: led wl over 2f out: sn hdd: eased whn btn ins fnl f* **5/1**[3]
0306 **8** *1* **Nuit Sombre (IRE)**[42] 6846 9-9-0 55...............................(p) PJMcDonald 8 25
(G A Harker) *a.p: led over 3f out tl wl over 2f out: sn rdn: wknd wl over 1f out* **12/1**
-000 **9** *1 ½* **Zain (IRE)**[82] 5730 5-9-0 44...(t) J-PGuillambert 13 22
(J G Given) *hld up in rr: pushed along over 3f out: sn struggling* **25/1**
5400 **10** *shd* **General Feeling (IRE)**[166] 2965 8-9-5 68......................... PaulHanagan 2 26
(Ollie Pears) *hld up in tch: lost pl over 5f out: bhd fnl 3f* **7/2**[2]
030 **11** *1* **Gifted Heir (IRE)**[14] 7403 5-8-7 57............................. NatashaEaton(7) 11 19
(A Bailey) *hld up in mid-div: hdwy 6f out: lost pl over 3f out: bhd fnl 2f* **7/1**

1m 50.99s (0.49) **Going Correction** -0.075s/f (Stan)
WFA 3 from 4yo+ 3lb — 11 Ran SP% **119.0**
Speed ratings (Par 101): **94,92,91,90,90 82,81,80,79,79 78**
toteswingers: 1&2 £12.60, 1&3 £42.10, 2&3 £6.90 CSF £80.56 TOTE £25.20: £6.00, £1.40, £3.70; EX 147.20.There was no bid for the winner.
Owner Mrs Jan Adams **Bred** Rockdown Investments **Trained** Earlswood, Monmouths

FOCUS
A surprise result in this seller and the form looks muddling.
Pianoforte(USA) Official explanation: jockey said gelding had no more to give

7582 CLEAN CONCIERGE MAIDEN STKS — 5f 20y(P)
8:20 (8:23) (Class 5) 2-Y-O — **£3,238** (£963; £481; £240) **Stalls Low**

Form — RPR
0022 **1** **Youcanalwaysdream (IRE)**[7] 7485 2-8-12 72.................... PhillipMakin 8 80+
(K A Ryan) *a gng wl: led wl over 1f out: pushed clr ins fnl f: easily* **11/8**[1]
2 **2** *5* **Liberty Lady (IRE)**[66] 6207 2-8-9 0............................ AndreaAtzeni(3) 6 60
(D Donovan) *hld up: pushed along over 3f out: rdn wl over 1f out: r.o to take 2nd cl home: no ch w wnr* **6/1**[3]
620 **3** *¾* **Suranam**[29] 7157 2-9-3 75.. KFallon 3 62
(W J Haggas) *s.i.s: t.k.h: sn prom: rdn and edgd lft over 1f out: one pce* **7/4**[2]
60 **4** *1 ¾* **Layla's Lad (USA)**[22] 7276 2-9-3 0.................................. PaulHanagan 5 56
(R A Fahey) *outpcd in rr: c wd st: sme late prog: nrst fin* **12/1**
66 **5** *hd* **Weimarland (IRE)**[7] 7477 2-9-3 0..................................... ShaneKelly 1 55
(J A Osborne) *s.i.s: sn prom: wknd wl over 1f out* **28/1**
0 **6** *¾* **Gibraltar Lass (USA)**[38] 6942 2-8-12 0.......................... DarryllHolland 4 48
(H J Collingridge) *prom: pushed along over 2f out: rdn and wknd over 1f out* **20/1**
00 **7** *1 ¾* **Lets Move It**[7] 7485 2-9-3 0...(v[1]) AdamKirby 2 46
(D Shaw) *led: hdd over 2f out: wknd wl over 1f out* **100/1**
00 **8** *11* **Redoubtable Grace**[73] 5977 2-9-3 0................................ LukeMorris 9 7
(Mrs R A Carr) *bhd: hung rt over 3f out: sn struggling* **66/1**

62.17 secs (-0.13) **Going Correction** -0.075s/f (Stan) — 8 Ran SP% **111.1**
Speed ratings (Par 96): **98,90,88,86,85 84,81,64**
toteswingers: 1&2 £2.90, 1&3 £1.02, 2&3 £2.00 CSF £9.45 TOTE £2.40: £1.10, £1.60, £1.10; EX 8.20.
Owner Mrs T Marnane **Bred** Glenlogan Park Stud **Trained** Hambleton, N Yorks

FOCUS
A fair maiden and a clear-cut winner, who is rated close to previous form with those behind helping set the level.

NOTEBOOK
Youcanalwaysdream(IRE), runner-up at Lingfield on her two previous starts, got a good tow into the race and, leading over a furlong out won this pretty easily. She looks capable of winning again on this surface but is already rated 72, so is going to have to step up to win handicaps, but at least her confidence will be high now. (op 6-4 tchd 13-8)
Liberty Lady(IRE), who ran well in a decent race on her debut, had been off for two months since and she took time to get going before staying on late. The outing should bring her on. (op 9-2 tchd 4-1)
Suranam, dropping in trip, was given every chance up with the pace but lacked an extra gear in the straight. (op 2-1 tchd 13-8)
Layla's Lad(USA), another dropping back to the minimum, could not go the early pace but was staying on and a return to 6f should help. He now qualifies for a handicap mark. Official explanation: jockey said colt resented kickback (tchd 14-1)
Weimarland(IRE) got a good lead and slipped through on the inside to dispute the lead turning in. However, he was soon passed by the winner and faded in the last furlong. (tchd 25-1 and 33-1)

7583 CE RISK, SAFETY & SECURITY H'CAP — 1m 1f 103y(P)
8:50 (8:51) (Class 4) (0-85,84) 3-Y-O+ **£5,046** (£1,510; £755; £377; £188) **Stalls Low**

Form — RPR
0065 **1** **Just Bond (IRE)**[16] 7360 7-9-2 **79**.................................... PJMcDonald 1 86
(G R Oldroyd) *led early: a.p: wnt 2nd wl over 1f out: shkn up to ld wl ins fnl f: rdn and r.o* **8/1**
220P **2** *½* **Brouhaha**[43] 6830 5-9-7 **84**... RichardKingscote 7 90
(Tom Dascombe) *sn led: hdd over 7f out: chsd ldr: led over 2f out: rdn wl over 1f out: hdd wl ins fnl f: r.o* **8/1**
4233 **3** *1 ½* **Ethics Girl (IRE)**[27] 7201 3-8-9 **75**............................... DarryllHolland 2 78
(John Berry) *t.k.h: prom: stdd and lost pl after 2f: pushed along and hdwy over 2f out: rdn wl over 1f out: kpt on one pce fnl f* **6/1**[3]
0100 **4** *hd* **Agilete**[43] 6830 7-9-0 **82**... SimonPearce(5) 3 84
(J Pearce) *hld up: hdwy wl over 1f out: nt qckn ins fnl f* **25/1**

0231 **5** 1 1/4 **Snow Dancer (IRE)**[16] 7360 5-8-5 **75**........................ JamesPSullivan(7) 8 75
(H A McWilliams) *hld up: c wd st: rdn jst over 1f out: nvr able to chal* **8/1**

2000 **6** nk **Charlie Cool**[28] 7194 6-9-4 **81**..(b[1]) LukeMorris 5 80
(Mrs R A Carr) *n.m.r sn after s: hld up in last: rdn wl over 1f out: kpt on ins fnl f: nvr trbld ldrs* **11/2**[2]

2142 **7** 2 1/4 **Follow The Flag (IRE)**[15] 7373 5-9-2 **79**...................(p) RobertWinston 6 73
(A J McCabe) *bmpd sn after s: t.k.h: sn prom: led over 6f out: pushed along and hdd over 2f out: sn wknd* **13/2**

0402 **8** 3 **Laurie Grove (IRE)**[30] 7141 3-9-2 **82**.. KFallon 4 70
(T G Mills) *t.k.h early: hld up in tch: ev ch over 2f out: rdn wl over 1f out: sn wknd: eased wl ins fnl f* **15/8**[1]

2m 0.80s (-0.90) **Going Correction** -0.075s/f (Stan)
WFA 3 from 5yo+ 3lb **8** Ran SP% **115.0**
Speed ratings (Par 105): **101,100,99,99,97 97,95,93**
toteswingers: 1&2 £8.20, 1&3 £10.80, 2&3 £12.20 CSF £69.69 CT £412.53 TOTE £9.80: £2.60, £3.10, £2.40; EX 60.50.
Owner R C Bond **Bred** Schwindibode Ag **Trained** Brawby, N Yorks

FOCUS
A fair handicap and another win for a course specialist. The runner-up is probably the best guide to the form.
Laurie Grove(IRE) Official explanation: trainer had no explanation for the poor form shown

7584 CE PROPERTY SERVICES GROUP NURSERY 7f 32y(P)
9:20 (9:20) (Class 6) (0-60,57) 2-Y-O **£2,388** (£705; £352) **Stalls** High

Form RPR

6003 **1** **Dutiful**[14] 7389 2-9-5 **55**.. KFallon 1 61+
(M R Channon) *hld up: hdwy on ins over 2f out: chsd ldr over 1f out: sn rdn: r.o to ld towards fin* **3/1**[2]

650 **2** 1 **Knightfire (IRE)**[176] 2649 2-9-0 **50**.. AdamKirby 4 54
(W R Swinburn) *led: clr wl over 1f out: rdn ins fnl f: ct towards fin* **15/2**

046 **3** 2 1/2 **Princess Mandy (IRE)**[14] 7396 2-9-5 **55**........................... PhillipMakin 7 52
(K A Ryan) *hld up in rr: n.m.r wl over 1f out: swtchd lft and hdwy on ins jst over 1f out: rdn and one pce ins fnl f* **9/4**[1]

2005 **4** 1 3/4 **Aegean Destiny**[7] 7482 2-9-7 **57**... LiamJones 6 50
(R A Harris) *hld up: pushed along on outside over 2f out: c wd st: edgd lft fr over 1f out: rdn and kpt on to take 4th cl home* **12/1**

6044 **5** 1 **Bobby's Doll**[7] 7477 2-8-12 **55**.................................... NatashaEaton(7) 3 46
(T T Clement) *prom: chsd ldr over 4f out to 2f out: rdn and edgd lft over 1f out: wknd ins fnl f* **28/1**

0403 **6** 2 **Taeping (IRE)**[11] 7421 2-9-6 **56**.. DavidProbert 8 42
(R Hollinshead) *hld up: hdwy 3f out: pushed along and wknd wl over 1f out* **8/1**

066 **7** 1 3/4 **Goodison Goal (IRE)**[11] 7421 2-9-5 **55**.................................. SJCraine 2 37
(Patrick Morris) *chsd ldr tl over 4f out: regained 2nd 2f out: wknd over 1f out* **16/1**

5442 **8** 9 **Miss Taken (IRE)**[4] 7501 2-8-11 **47**.......................................(b) DNolan 5 6
(D Carroll) *hld up in tch: pushed along and lost pl over 2f out: sn bhd* **4/1**[3]

1m 29.83s (0.23) **Going Correction** -0.075s/f (Stan) **8** Ran SP% **115.7**
Speed ratings (Par 94): **95,93,91,89,87 85,83,73**
toteswingers: 1&2 £3.50, 1&3 £4.10, 2&3 £4.80 CSF £26.04 CT £59.54 TOTE £4.30: £1.70, £2.10, £1.60; EX 10.10 Place 6: £16.67 Place 5: £9.18.
Owner Wood Street Syndicate II **Bred** J Repard **Trained** West Ilsley, Berks

FOCUS
A moderate nursery but a good finish and the form looks sound enough.

NOTEBOOK
Dutiful, eased in the market as a result of support for the third, put up an improved effort last time and built on that. He looked as if he might not be able to reel in the leader early in the straight but found extra as that rival weakened and cut him down near the finish. He can go on from this. (op 5-2)
Knightfire(IRE), who played up in the paddock beforehand, had been gelded since his last start and was making his handicap debut. He made the running then kicked clear off the turn and looked like holding on, but ran out of petrol late on. This was an improvement and he can gain compensation, possibly back at 6f. (op 11-2 tchd 8-1)
Princess Mandy(IRE) was backed into favouritism but never looked like winning. She was held up and, rather than make her run around the outside on the turn, switched inside and only kept on late without really threatening. (op 9-2)
Aegean Destiny was a market drifter and was held up before staying on in the straight. (tchd 14-1)
Bobby's Doll ran reasonably well before weakening in the straight, not helped by her rider dropping his whip. She might need to drop to selling company. (op 33-1)
Miss Taken(IRE), runner-up at Southwell earlier in the week, ran no sort of race and her rider looked down in the straight as if something was amiss. Official explanation: jockey said filly ran too keen (tchd 7-2)
T/Plt: £22.20 to a £1 stake. Pool: £107,160.39. 3,521.46 winning tickets. T/Qpdt: £9.60 to a £1 stake. Pool: £7,796.22. 600.60 winning tickets. KH

7533 KEMPTON (A.W) (R-H)
Sunday, November 29

OFFICIAL GOING: Standard
Wind: Strong, half behind Weather: Grim with frequent heavy downpours

7585 EUROPEAN BREEDERS' FUND MAIDEN FILLIES' STKS 6f (P)
2:10 (2:11) (Class 5) 2-Y-O **£3,561** (£1,059; £529; £264) **Stalls** High

Form RPR

4 **1** **Key Light (IRE)**[25] 7234 2-9-0 0.. KFallon 3 74+
(J W Hills) *sn trckd ldr: sustained chal fr 2f out: narrow ld fnl f: hld on* **15/2**[3]

2433 **2** hd **Zubova**[8] 7485 2-9-0 73... RichardHughes 9 73
(R Hannon) *led at stdy pce: pressed over 2f out: narrowly hdd fnl f: kpt on wl but a jst hld* **5/4**[1]

5524 **3** 2 **Caramelita**[34] 7061 2-9-0 68.. JimCrowley 11 67
(J R Jenkins) *chsd ldng pair: effrt on inner 2f out: kpt on but no imp fr over 1f out* **8/1**

4 nk **Elation (IRE)** 2-9-0 0... GregFairley 7 66+
(M Johnston) *dwlt: rn green in last pair: taken to wd outside over 3f out: prog fr 2f out: kpt on fnl f: nvr rchd ldrs* **7/4**[2]

3 **5** nk **Thistlestar (USA)**[72] 6047 2-9-0 0..................................... PaulHanagan 6 65+
(R A Fahey) *chsd ldrs: wnt 4th and hrd rdn 2f out: nt qckn and no imp: keeping on nr fin* **8/1**

0 **6** 1 1/4 **Avon Castle**[16] 7365 2-9-0 0.. FergusSweeney 12 61
(G L Moore) *dwlt: towards rr on inner: effrt over 2f out: shkn up and kpt on one pce fr over 1f out* **50/1**

7 1 1/4 **Singingintherain (IRE)** 2-9-0 0... NCallan 5 58
(T G Mills) *hld up in rr: quick move on outer to chse ldrs over 3f out: lost pl over 2f out: plugged on u.p* **20/1**

8 1 **Sweet Avon** 2-9-0 0... AdamKirby 1 56+
(Matthew Salaman) *dwlt and wnt lft s: rn green in detached last: nudged along and kpt on takingly fnl 2f: bttr for experience* **50/1**

00 **9** shd **Billie Jean**[30] 7145 2-9-0 0... MichaelHills 2 54
(B W Hills) *t.k.h: prom on outer: rdn over 2f out: grad wknd* **16/1**

10 1 1/4 **Hanbelation (USA)** 2-9-0 0.. LPKeniry 4 51
(E F Vaughan) *t.k.h early: hld up bhd ldrs: lost pl and struggling in rr over 2f out* **20/1**

00 **11** 3 1/4 **Wannabee (IRE)**[49] 6696 2-8-7 0.................................. RyanClark(7) 8 41
(J J Bridger) *dwlt: nvr beyond midfield: dropped to rr over 2f out: sn wknd* **100/1**

1m 13.65s (0.55) **Going Correction** 0.0s/f (Stan) **11** Ran SP% **135.1**
Speed ratings (Par 93): **96,95,93,92,92 90,88,87,87,85 81**
toteswingers: 1&2 £4.30, 1&3 £8.70, 2&3 £3.10 CSF £19.44 TOTE £8.80: £2.20, £1.20, £2.00; EX 27.90.
Owner Mrs P De W Johnson **Bred** Castlemartin Stud And Skymarc Farm **Trained** Upper Lambourn, Berks

FOCUS
A bitterly-cold, overcast afternoon. Heavy morning rain had no effect on the Polytrack and the going remained Standard. There was a stiff following breeze down the home straight. An ordinary EBF maiden fillies' event, run at a modest pace into a headwind early on and those with previous experience contested the finish. The placed horses set the level of the form.

NOTEBOOK
Key Light(IRE), whose yard's runners usually come on for their first run, had the benefit of a previous spin here on November 4th, when fourth to Forest Crown. The daughter of Group 1 winner Eva Luna has plenty of speed in her pedigree and was always up with the pace. She got the better of a protracted duel under a well-judged ride and won a shade cosily in the end. She may get a bit further on this evidence and will be put away for next year.

Zubova disappointed previously when dropped back to 5f on this surface here, having shaped well in her three previous runs over 6f on turf. Well-backed, she made most of the running and only just failed, showing a willing attitude. She shouldn't be too hard to place in handicap company and can gain compensation sooner rather than later. (op 7-4 tchd 15-8 and 2-1 in a place)

Caramelita, rated 5lb inferior to the runner-up, appeared to run to that mark. Well-drawn, she hugged the inside rail and simply found a couple too good, her run flattening out late on. This was her fifth run and she always seems to run her race. She can pick up a small race or two on this evidence, though handicapping will be her game. (op 10-1)

Elation(IRE) ◆, the first foal of the stable's top-class Attraction, spoiled her chance by breaking slowly and had to come wide off the bend. She made significant headway despite running green and will certainly come on for the experience. This was a highly pleasing debut and she clearly has plenty of ability. (op 5-2)

Thistlestar(USA) had just one start coming into this, a pleasing debut when third at Ayr (both the winner and runner-up had gone close again subsequently). She had learned plenty from that and ran well within herself on her Polytrack debut, staying on quite nicely towards the finish. There is more to come from her. (op 13-2)

Avon Castle did better than her debut effort, but was well beaten in the end. She looks modest, though will improve with racing.

7586 FRED WILLIAMS 60TH BIRTHDAY H'CAP (DIV I) 1m (P)
2:45 (2:45) (Class 6) (0-65,65) 3-Y-O+ **£1,706** (£503; £252) **Stalls** High

Form RPR

0210 **1** **Hereford Boy**[8] 7479 5-9-6 **65**.......................................(p) JamieSpencer 2 72
(D K Ivory) *stdd s fr wd draw and hld up in last pair: prog on outer 2f out: r.o to ld jst ins fnl f: a holding on* **10/1**

-666 **2** 1/2 **Royal Manor**[23] 7275 4-8-10 **60**.................................... RossAtkinson(5) 1 66
(Tom Dascombe) *stdd s and dropped in fr wd draw: t.k.h and hld up in last pair early: prog fr 3f out: brought to chal 1f out: pressed wnr after: a hld* **12/1**

0306 **3** 1 **Stark Contrast (USA)**[158] 3258 5-7-13 **51** oh2.............. RachelKing(7) 6 55
(M D I Usher) *trckd ldrs: prog on outer to ld narrowly 2f out: pushed along and hdd jst ins fnl f: one pce* **33/1**

0014 **4** nk **Fine Ruler (IRE)**[13] 7417 5-8-13 **58**.................................... JimCrowley 3 61+
(M R Bosley) *hld up in rr: effrt over 2f out: prog over 1f out: r.o fnl f and nrly snatched 3rd* **6/1**[3]

5104 **5** 1/2 **Confide In Me**[15] 7403 5-8-12 **57**...............................(tp) RichardHughes 7 59+
(G A Butler) *hld up in midfield: nt clr run as r unfolded 2f out: prog over 1f out: r.o fnl f: no hope of catching ldrs* **4/1**[1]

1464 **6** 1/2 **Inquisitress**[4] 7512 5-8-4 **52**.. MarcHalford(3) 10 53
(J J Bridger) *trckd ldrs: upsides gng wl 2f out: stl w ldr 1f out u.p: nt qckn and lost pl fnl 100yds* **15/2**

000 **7** 1 1/2 **Efficiency**[87] 5616 3-9-3 **64**... NCallan 11 61
(M Blanshard) *hld up on inner towards rr: prog to chse ldrs over 1f out: kpt on same pce and no imp after* **12/1**

-000 **8** 3/4 **Straight And Level (CAN)**[16] 7364 4-9-5 **64**.............. FergusSweeney 4 59
(Miss Jo Crowley) *pressed ldr's stdy pce: upsides 2f out: stl cl enough jst over 1f out: wknd* **8/1**

6000 **9** 3/4 **Rock Art (IRE)**[86] 5628 3-8-10 **57** ow1........................(p) DarryllHolland 13 51
(Karen George) *hld up in rr: rdn 2f out: no prog tl styd on ins fnl f: no ch* **25/1**

6000 **10** 1 1/2 **Purus (IRE)**[29] 7179 7-9-3 **62**..(b) LukeMorris 12 52
(R A Teal) *t.k.h early: pressed ldrs: effrt on inner 2f out and upsides: sn rdn and fnd nil: wknd* **5/1**[2]

0000 **11** 4 1/2 **Grey Gurkha**[46] 5983 8-8-6 **51** oh6..............................(p) GregFairley 14 31
(I W McInnes) *slowest away: hld up and mostly in last trio: pushed along and no prog 2f out* **66/1**

6300 **12** 1/2 **Strategic Mover (USA)**[11] 7440 4-9-1 **63**..............(vt[1]) RobertLButler(3) 5 42
(P Butler) *pressed ldrs: upsides 2f out: sn wknd tamely* **50/1**

1306 **13** 2 1/2 **Playful Asset (IRE)**[85] 5679 3-8-11 **58**.................................... KFallon 8 31
(P Howling) *led at stdy pce to 2f out: wknd rapidly* **8/1**

1m 41.69s (1.89) **Going Correction** 0.0s/f (Stan)
WFA 3 from 4yo+ 2lb **13** Ran SP% **119.7**
Speed ratings (Par 101): **90,89,88,88,87 87,85,84,84,82 78,77,75**
toteswingers: 1&2 £15.90, 1&3 £42.80, 2&3 £47.00 CSF £121.24 CT £3789.33 TOTE £8.30: £2.40, £4.80, £7.70; EX 108.70.
Owner Recycled Products Limited **Bred** Mrs L R Burrage **Trained** Radlett, Herts

FOCUS
A poor but open-looking handicap run in a rainstorm and the pace was muddling, with the confirmed front-runner Rock Art surprisingly held up in mid-pack early on. The race turned into a 3f sprint and although there were few excuses, the form may not work out.

7587 FRED WILLIAMS 60TH BIRTHDAY H'CAP (DIV II) 1m (P)
3:15 (3:17) (Class 6) (0-65,65) 3-Y-0+ £1,706 (£503; £252) Stalls High

Form RPR
2224 1 **French Art**[32] 7113 4-9-4 62 (p) KFallon 3 71
(N Tinkler) *hld up early: moved into midfield on outer 5f out: prog over 2f out: led wl over 1f out: drifted rt but in command fnl f* 11/4[1]
1003 2 1 1/4 **Bavarica**[60] 6392 7-8-13 64 AdamBeschizza(7) 12 70
(Miss J Feilden) *dwlt: hld up in rr: stdy prog on inner fr 2f out: pushed along and r.o to chse wnr last 100yds: no imp* 20/1
4601 3 shd **Fernando Torres**[11] 7432 3-9-5 65 FrancisNorton 11 71+
(Matthew Salaman) *trckd ldng pair: looking for room fr over 2f out: styd on same pce fnl f whn in the clr* 11/4[1]
2002 4 3/4 **Ymir**[11] 7433 3-8-11 57 JimCrowley 5 61
(M J Attwater) *pressed ldr: led briefly 2f out: nt qckn over 1f out: hld whn nt clr run ins fnl f: lost pl sn after* 8/1[2]
434- 5 hd **Kenton Street**[34] 7075 4-9-5 63 JamieSpencer 2 67
(Michael J Browne, Ire) *hld up in rr: rdn and hanging fr over 2f out to over 1f out: styd on ins fnl f: nrst fin* 11/1
0000 6 1/2 **Lopinot (IRE)**[25] 7236 6-9-0 58 (v) FergusSweeney 10 61
(M R Bosley) *hld up in last: stdy prog on inner fr 2f out: nudged along in midfield 1f out: reminders and kpt on ins fnl f: nvr nr ldrs* 20/1
4000 7 1/2 **Action Girl**[101] 5195 4-8-13 57 (p) NCallan 13 58
(R M H Cowell) *mostly in midfield: effrt whn nt clr run wl over 1f out: kpt on same pce after* 33/1
5666 8 1 **Fiefdom (IRE)**[8] 7481 7-9-4 62 PaulHanagan 7 61
(I W McInnes) *wl in tch: chsd ldng trio over 3f out: cl enough 2f out: nt qckn over 1f out: fdd fnl f* 11/1
46 9 4 1/2 **Soul Sista (IRE)**[25] 7246 3-9-0 60 AdamKirby 6 49
(J L Spearing) *hld up in rr: struggling over 2f out: sn no ch* 14/1
6605 10 1/2 **Dream Express (IRE)**[18] 7330 4-9-2 60 (v) IanMongan 8 48
(P Howling) *racd freely: led at decent pce: hdd 2f out: wkng whn hmpd jst over 1f out* 14/1
0604 11 3/4 **Fire King**[15] 7392 3-8-9 55 (p) SteveDrowne 4 41
(J A Geake) *nvr beyond midfield: u.p 3f out: sn btn* 10/1[3]
5005 12 25 **Second To Nun (IRE)**[52] 5905 3-8-8 54 LPKeniry 1 —
(Jean-Rene Auvray) *prom to 1/2-way: wknd rapidly: t.o* 50/1

1m 39.53s (-0.27) **Going Correction** 0.0s/f (Stan)
WFA 3 from 4yo+ 2lb **12** Ran SP% **118.0**
Speed ratings (Par 101): **101,99,99,98,98 98,97,96,92,91 90,65**
toteswingers: 1&2 £17.50, 1&3 £3.00, 2&3 £14.00 CSF £68.36 CT £169.68 TOTE £3.40: £1.60, £5.20, £1.30; EX 47.40.
Owner Nicolas Patsalides **Bred** Newsells Park Stud Limited **Trained** Langton, N Yorks
■ Stewards' Enquiry : K Fallon one-day ban: careless riding (Dec 13)

FOCUS
This division was was run at a much truer pace.
Kenton Street Official explanation: jockey said gelding hung right final 2f

7588 HYDE STKS (LISTED RACE) 1m (P)
3:45 (3:46) (Class 1) 3-Y-0+

£22,708 (£8,608; £4,308; £2,148; £1,076; £540) Stalls High

Form RPR
4166 1 **Without A Prayer (IRE)**[108] 4949 4-9-4 109 JimCrowley 7 116
(R M Beckett) *w.w in midfield: prog on outer over 2f out: led wl over 1f out: shkn up and in command fnl f: r.o wl* 7/2[2]
063 2 3 **Re Barolo (IRE)**[22] 7300 6-9-2 104 KFallon 10 107
(M Botti) *n.m.r on inner and lost pl over 6f out: midfield after: prog on inner over 2f out: chal wl over 1f out: chsd wnr after: styd on wl but no imp* 9/2[3]
0001 3 6 **Appalachian Trail (IRE)**[8] 7492 8-9-2 95 (b) PaulHanagan 4 93
(I Semple) *settled in 8th rdn 3f out and struggling: prog over 1f out: styd on fnl f to snatch 3rd nr fin* 25/1
0523 4 shd **Shampagne**[67] 6222 3-9-0 97 JamieSpencer 8 93
(P F I Cole) *cl up bhd ldrs: rdn over 2f out: sn lost pl: plugged on* 13/2
1420 5 2 1/4 **Sarah Park (IRE)**[31] 7132 4-8-11 93 MartinDwyer 3 83
(B J Meehan) *cl up bhd ldrs: pushed along over 3f out: lost pl over 2f out: tried to renew effrt over 1f out: no ch* 25/1
013- 6 1 1/2 **Dunelight (IRE)**[488] 4506 6-9-2 0 (v) AdamKirby 5 84
(C G Cox) *led at str pce: jnd over 5f out: hdd wll over 1f out: steadily wknd* 3/1[1]
3525 7 6 **Plum Pudding (IRE)**[8] 7489 6-9-2 109 RichardHughes 1 71
(R Hannon) *racd wd of rivals 1st 2f: jnd ldr over 5f out to over 2f out: sn wknd* 3/1[1]
0006 8 3/4 **Ejeed (USA)**[25] 7240 4-9-2 49 (p) SamHitchcott 6 69?
(Miss Z C Davison) *dwlt: a in last trio: struggling sn after 1/2-way* 100/1
-220 9 3 1/4 **Ada River**[64] 6267 4-8-11 100 NCallan 2 56
(A M Balding) *prom on outer to 1/2-way: struggling 3f out: sn bhd* 15/2
0004 10 12 **Quick Single (USA)**[13] 7198 3-9-0 48 CarolineKelly 9 34
(P S McEntee) *last and tailing off 1/2-way* 100/1

1m 36.89s (-2.91) **Going Correction** 0.0s/f (Stan)
WFA 3 from 4yo+ 2lb **10** Ran SP% **125.2**
Speed ratings (Par 111): **114,111,105,104,102 101,95,94,91,79**
toteswingers: 1&2 £4.80, 1&3 £18.30, 2&3 £19.20 CSF £20.95 TOTE £4.90: £1.80, £1.80, £4.40; EX 27.10.
Owner McDonagh Murphy And Nixon **Bred** Brownstown Stud **Trained** Whitsbury, Hants

FOCUS
A cracking Listed race run at a breakneck pace and just outside the 1m course record.

NOTEBOOK
Without A Prayer(IRE) seems to be getting quicker with age. He travelled the best of all throughout and was sixth entering the turn in, alongside the subsequent runner-up, but came with a sweeping run up the centre of the track and soon put matters to rest. This was a superb effort conceding weight all round and, though he has decent form over 1m2f, connections will keep him at 1m because they believe the Tapeta surface at Meydan will play to his strengths over the winter. That seems a sound plan. (op 5-1)
Re Barolo(IRE) had proven form on this surface and was aided by the fast pace. He made his run at the same time as the winner, taking the inner rail, which may have been a shade slower. He was well beaten in the end, but the pair drew well clear. He will continue to pay his way in the best AW races this winter. (op 3-1)
Appalachian Trail(IRE) had dropped into a claimer to win last time. That had obviously helped his confidence and he ran a cracker. He seems to have found his best form after a lean spell and should pay his way, but he was beaten a long way. (tchd 33-1)
Shampagne had no excuses. She has not managed to get her head in front this year, but ran another solid race in defeat and continues to pay for her consistency. (op 6-1 tchd 7-1)
Sarah Park(IRE) ran another game race in defeat, but in truth she looked out of her depth against this opposition. She is consistent on this surface.
Dunelight(IRE) was making his first appearance since finishing third to Paco Boy in the Group 2 Lennox Stakes at Goodwood in July and he was plenty fresh enough for his first run in 488 days. He travelled well, but a shade too quickly at the head of affairs, a pace accentuated by the proximity of Plum Pudding who took him on approaching the turn. He was making his AW debut, but handled the surface well enough and will come on a lot for it. (op 9-2)
Plum Pudding(IRE) has been nothing but consistent this term, but has disappointed for his rider in the past. The Bunbury Cup winner has been on the go for a while, though, and looks in need of a break on this showing. (op 7-2 tchd 5-1)

7589 WILD FLOWER STKS (LISTED RACE) 1m 4f (P)
4:15 (4:15) (Class 1) 3-Y-0+

£22,708 (£8,608; £4,308; £2,148; £1,076; £540) Stalls Centre

Form RPR
0134 1 **Les Fazzani (IRE)**[22] 7291 5-9-1 111 JamieSpencer 7 107
(K A Ryan) *mde all at decent pce: shkn up over 2f out: styd on strly fr over 1f out and nvr seriously threatened* 15/8[1]
0202 2 1 **Mooakada (IRE)**[22] 7291 3-8-9 99 RobertHavlin 5 105
(J H M Gosden) *hld up in 7th: prog 3f out: disp 2nd on outer fr 2f out: kpt on wl but no real imp on wnr* 9/2[3]
0633 3 nk **Saphira's Fire (IRE)**[29] 7188 4-9-1 111 MartinDwyer 8 105
(W R Muir) *hld up in 6th: prog on inner 3f out: disp 2nd 2f out: kpt on wl but no real imp on wnr fnl f* 11/4[2]
5222 4 1 1/2 **Pachattack (USA)**[18] 7323 3-8-9 98 (p) RichardHughes 4 103
(G A Butler) *chsd wnr 3f and again 3f out to 2f out: kpt on same pce after* 6/1
0136 5 6 **Dakiyah (IRE)**[27] 4212 5-9-1 80 (p) IanMongan 1 93
(Mrs L J Mongan) *hld up last: drvn over 2f out: sn outpcd by ldrs and no ch* 50/1
0-04 6 1 3/4 **Hebridean (IRE)**[29] 7188 4-9-6 107 KFallon 6 95
(L M Cumani) *t.k.h: hld up in 6th: prog to 4th 5f out: rdn and carried wd bnd 3f out: sn wknd* 9/1
5544 7 7 **Princess Taylor**[31] 7131 5-9-1 98 (t) DarryllHolland 2 79
(M Botti) *chsd wnr after 3f: c wd bnd 3f out and wknd u.p* 12/1
2000 8 19 **Jonnie Skull (IRE)**[8] 7480 3-9-0 59 (t) CarolineKelly 3 54
(P S McEntee) *chsd ldng trio to 5f out: sn wknd: t.o* 100/1

2m 30.72s (-3.78) **Going Correction** 0.0s/f (Stan)
WFA 3 from 4yo+ 6lb **8** Ran SP% **114.6**
Speed ratings (Par 111): **112,111,111,110,106 104,100,87**
toteswingers: 1&2 £3.00, 1&3 £2.10, 2&3 £3.20 CSF £10.78 TOTE £2.80: £1.30, £1.70, £1.10; EX 12.40.
Owner Dr Marwan Koukash **Bred** J Erhardt And Mrs J Schonwalder **Trained** Hambleton, N Yorks

FOCUS
The pace was again quicker than standard for this well-contested Listed 1m4f event.

NOTEBOOK
Les Fazzani(IRE) made every yard of the running. She loves soft ground and stamina is her forte, so Spencer set out to make it a true test and judged it to perfection. She never saw another horse and after her rider had given her a breather down the back straight, she had plenty to spare when the runner-up made a vain attempt to reel her in. This was her first success on the AW and she deserves a step up into Group company. (tchd 2-1)
Mooakada(IRE) has not won since making her debut in a Newmarket maiden, but having twice gone second to earn valuable black type in two Listed races, she again found one too good. This was her first attempt on the AW and she handled it well, running on gamely in defeat without ever looking like nailing the winner. She has the ability to win a decent prize next year and the suspicion is she would be better suited by a strongly-run 1m2f, rather than this trip. (op 11-2)
Saphira's Fire(IRE) is clearly well regarded, having been campaigned in Group 1 company. The drop in class on her previous two runs appeared to have restored her confidence and she again ran a fine race, despite being a bit keen early on, which did not help her cause at the business end. She may prefer a shorter trip. (tchd 9-4)
Pachattack(USA) ran well in cheekpieces, but the jury is out on whether she gets this trip. She handled the surface, but her run flattened out. (op 7-1)
Dakiyah(IRE) was facing a stiff task, having won on the surface off a mark of 78. She is not in this class.
Hebridean(IRE) was keen early on and after looming large off the final bend, his exertions took their toll. (op 8-1)
Princess Taylor Official explanation: jockey said mare hung right in straight

7590 WIN A KIA SOUL AT KEMPTON.CO.UK MEDIAN AUCTION MAIDEN STKS 1m 4f (P)
4:45 (4:45) (Class 5) 3-5-Y-0 £2,590 (£770; £385; £192) Stalls Centre

Form RPR
0222 1 **Kazbow (IRE)**[8] 7476 3-9-3 72 KFallon 1 70
(L M Cumani) *sn led: drew clr wl over 2f out: rdn and looked briefly threatened 2f out: styd on wl* 2/5[1]
-052 2 4 1/2 **Starburst**[16] 7367 4-9-4 60 GeorgeBaker 2 58
(A M Balding) *hld up last: smooth prog on outer to go 2nd over 2f out and briefly threatened sn after: rdn and nt qckn over 1f out* 7/1[3]
04 3 4 1/2 **Alpha Vega (IRE)**[38] 6974 3-8-12 0 (v) EddieAhern 3 51
(J R Fanshawe) *trckd wnr: rdn and fnd nil wl over 2f out: sn lost 2nd: jst hld on for modest 3rd* 4/1[2]
0 4 nse **Dovedon Earl**[64] 6287 3-9-3 0 LPKeniry 6 56
(T Keddy) *settled in 4th: outpcd whn spooked over 2f out and lost further grnd: duelled for modest 3rd fr over 1f out* 66/1
000 5 9 **Bengers Lass (USA)**[39] 6934 3-8-12 0 (t) TonyCulhane 7 36
(R Curtis) *in tch tl lft bhd fr over 3f out* 66/1
0000 6 16 **Suhailah**[18] 7324 3-8-12 45 (v[1]) JimCrowley 4 11
(M J Attwater) *chsd ldng pair to 3f out: wknd rapidly: t.o* 50/1

2m 34.39s (-0.11) **Going Correction** 0.0s/f (Stan)
WFA 3 from 4yo 6lb **6** Ran SP% **108.9**
Speed ratings (Par 103): **100,97,94,93,87 77**
toteswingers: 1&2 £1.30, 1&3 £1.10, 2&3 £1.60 CSF £3.54 TOTE £1.40: £1.70, £1.30; EX 2.90.
Owner Bruce Corman **Bred** Airlie Stud **Trained** Newmarket, Suffolk

FOCUS
A very modest median auction maiden run at a steady pace, and it didn't take a lot of winning.

7591 WILLIAM HILL WINTER FESTIVAL - BOOK NOW H'CAP (DIV I) 7f (P)
5:15 (5:16) (Class 6) (0-60,60) 3-Y-0+ £1,619 (£481; £240; £120) Stalls High

Form RPR
626 1 **Copperwood**[25] 7239 4-8-11 52 NCallan 2 67
(M Blanshard) *hld up in 8th: nt clr run on inner briefly over 2f out: sn prog to go 2nd: clsd to ld ent fnl f: sn in command* 15/2[3]
1440 2 1 1/2 **Dr Wintringham (IRE)**[60] 6399 3-9-3 59 DarryllHolland 5 70
(Karen George) *towards rr: 9th and rdn 1/2-way: prog u.p fr 2f out: styd on wl to take 2nd last 50yds: no ch to chal* 16/1

2121 **3** 1 1/2 **Dancing Welcome**[4] 7521 3-8-5 **54**.....(b) RyanClark(7) 1 61
(J M Bradley) *chsd ldrs: rdn over 3f out: prog on outer over 2f out: kpt on one pce fnl f: tk 3rd post* **9/2**[1]

3133 **4** *shd* **Leelu**[11] 7432 3-9-1 **57**..... EddieAhern 7 64
(D W P Arbuthnot) *led: drew 3 l clr 1/2-way: drvn over 2f out: hdd ent fnl f: wknd last 75yds* **9/2**[1]

6400 **5** 1 1/2 **Dabbers Ridge (IRE)**[17] 7350 7-9-4 **59**..... JimCrowley 6 62
(I W McInnes) *mostly in midfield: rdn in 7th 1/2-way: struggling and no prog after tl styd on fnl f: nrst fin* **25/1**

0002 **6** *nse* **Josiah Bartlett (IRE)**[2] 7561 3-8-6 **48**.....(v) SaleemGolam 10 50
(Ian Williams) *chsd ldrs: rdn to try to cl fr wl over 2f out: one pce and no real imp* **8/1**

5243 **7** *nk* **Headache**[4] 7517 4-8-4 **52**.....(bt) MatthewLawson(7) 9 54
(B W Duke) *disp 2nd to 2f out: wknd fnl f* **5/1**[2]

0610 **8** 3/4 **Dark Camellia**[8] 7481 4-9-5 **60**.....(t) RichardHughes 8 60
(H J L Dunlop) *dwlt and stdd s: hld up in last: nudged along to improve over 2f out: cajoled along and kpt on fnl f: nvr any ch* **16/1**

5500 **9** 1 1/4 **Golden Prospect**[8] 7480 5-9-0 **55**..... PaulFitzsimons 4 51
(Miss J R Tooth) *hld up wl in rr: rdn 3f out: limited prog and n.d* **25/1**

0000 **10** 1/2 **Know No Fear**[23] 7280 4-8-7 **55**..... AmyScott(7) 14 50
(A J Lidderdale) *disp 2nd: rdn 1/2-way: wknd 2f out* **25/1**

0004 **11** 3/4 **Athboy Auction**[32] 7107 4-8-7 **48**.....(t) JerryO'Dwyer 3 41
(H J Collingridge) *dwlt and sltly hmpd s: mostly in last pair: struggling fr 3f out* **50/1**

0000 **12** 7 **Lady Dinsdale (IRE)**[4] 7517 3-8-4 **46** oh1..... FrankieMcDonald 12 20
(T Keddy) *a in rr: rdn 1/2-way: struggling after* **50/1**

0001 **13** 2 **Dynamo Dave (USA)**[4] 7517 4-7-12 **46** oh1.....(b) RachelKing(7) 13 15
(M D I Usher) *disp 2nd to over 2f out: shkn up and sn wknd: eased* **8/1**

1m 25.13s (-0.87) **Going Correction** 0.0s/f (Stan)
WFA 3 from 4yo+ 1lb **13** Ran SP% **114.2**
Speed ratings (Par 101): **104,102,100,100,98 98,98,97,96,95 94,86,84**
toteswingers: 1&2 £18.20, 1&3 £9.20, 2&3 £16.80 CSF £108.12 CT £459.46 TOTE £8.70: £2.70, £4.50, £1.60; EX 134.70.
Owner Mrs Rosemary K Wilkerson **Bred** Hertford Offset Press **Trained** Upper Lambourn, Berks

FOCUS
Desperate prize-money for a competitive, if low-grade handicap, run at a strong pace.
Dark Camellia Official explanation: jockey said, regarding running and riding, that he agreed with the trainer that he would ride the filly in the same way as when winning on November 3rd, adding that on that occasion he managed to coax it to get its head in front, and, if put under pressure, does not respond; trainer confirmed, adding that it had beemn difficult to win with, and if it ran again it would be over a mile.

7592 WILLIAM HILL WINTER FESTIVAL - BOOK NOW H'CAP (DIV II) 7f (P)
5:45 (5:45) (Class 6) (0-60,59) 3-Y-0+ **£1,619** (£481; £240; £120) **Stalls High**

Form RPR

0056 **1** **Star Strider**[13] 7412 5-9-0 **59**..... KylieManser(5) 9 67
(T Keddy) *t.k.h: hld up but sn in 6th: smooth prog over 2f out: led over 1f out: shkn up and sn clr* **11/2**

3000 **2** 2 1/4 **Talamahana**[4] 7521 4-8-2 **47**.....(v) AmyBaker(5) 7 49
(A B Haynes) *w ldr: led 1/2-way: drvn and hdd over 1f out: sn no ch w wnr: jst hld on for 2nd* **20/1**

0000 **3** *nse* **Metropolitan Chief**[4] 7517 5-8-5 **45**..... LukeMorris 12 47
(P Burgoyne) *awkward s: t.k.h: hld up in last: gng easily on outer 3f out: prog after but sn rdn: kpt on fnl f and nrly tk 2nd* **12/1**

3006 **4** 1 1/4 **Sovereignty (JPN)**[32] 7109 7-8-12 **57**..... SophieDoyle(5) 5 56
(D K Ivory) *hld up towards rr: rdn and prog over 2f out: kpt on fr over 1f out: one pce ins fnl f* **5/1**[3]

2 **5** 1/2 **Nativity**[32] 7107 3-8-11 **55**..... JackDean(3) 10 52
(J L Spearing) *wl in rr: rdn wl over 2f out: prog u.p over 1f out: one pce fnl f* **4/1**[2]

6000 **6** 4 **Bahamian Bliss**[73] 6028 4-8-12 **52**..... SteveDrowne 11 38
(J A R Toller) *trckd ldrs: rdn and no qckn over 2f out: wknd fnl f* **7/1**

000 **7** 5 **Kilmun**[44] 6823 3-8-4 **45**..... FrancisNorton 1 18
(K A Ryan) *pressed ldng pair: upsides wl over 1f out: wknd rapidly* **10/1**

0405 **8** *nk* **Vanadium**[11] 7438 7-9-1 **55**.....(tp) KFallon 6 27
(A J Lidderdale) *t.k.h early: chsd ldrs: rdn and nt qckn wl over 2f out: sn wknd* **7/2**[1]

-000 **9** 2 **Rightcar Dominic**[24] 7254 4-8-7 **47**.....(b[1]) LPKeniry 14 14
(Peter Grayson) *led to 1/2-way: wknd rapidly fnl 2f* **28/1**

0460 **10** *nk* **Keibla Spirit**[60] 6377 3-9-2 **57**..... RobertHavlin 13 23
(R Ingram) *u.p towards rr bef 1/2-way: sn struggling and no ch* **22/1**

0000 **11** 2 **Time For Old Time**[34] 7052 3-8-1 **45**..... AndreaAtzeni(3) 2 6
(I A Wood) *drvn in rr after 3f: nvr a factor after* **25/1**

1m 26.03s (0.03) **Going Correction** 0.0s/f (Stan)
WFA 3 from 4yo+ 1lb **11** Ran SP% **120.0**
Speed ratings (Par 101): **99,96,96,94,94 89,84,83,81,81 78**
toteswingers: 1&2 £16.80, 1&3 £19.30, 2&3 £46.50 CSF £115.14 CT £1279.55 TOTE £6.40: £1.90, £5.90, £3.60; EX 167.80 Place 6 £111.04, Place 5 £63.27..
Owner A C Maylam **Bred** Snailwell Stud Co Ltd **Trained** Newmarket, Suffolk

FOCUS
The second division of the 0-65 handicap was run at a slower pace than the first division.
T/Jkpt: Not won. T/Plt: £53.50 to a £1 stake. Pool: £67,734.36. 924.10 winning tickets. T/Qpdt: £4.30 to a £1 stake. Pool: £5,639.64. 963.80 winning tickets. JN

TOKYO (L-H)
Sunday, November 29

OFFICIAL GOING: Firm

7593a JAPAN CUP (GRADE 1) (TURF) 1m 4f
6:20 (6:21) 3-Y-0+

£1,947,855 (£775,754; £487,624; £291,568; £191,821; £134,275)

RPR

1 **Vodka (JPN)**[28] 5-8-10..... C-PLemaire 5 118
(Katsuhiko Sumii, Japan) *a wl plcd: 5th st: led appr fnl f: two l up 150yds out: drvn out and jst hld on* **13/5**[1]

2 *nse* **Oken Bruce Lee (JPN)**[28] 4-9-0..... HUchida 10 122
(H Otonashi, Japan) *hld up in rr: last and brought wdst st: str run on outside fnl 2f: jst failed* **37/10**[2]

3 1 1/2 **Red Desire (JPN)**[42] 3-8-5..... HShii 6 117
(Mikio Matsunaga, Japan) *mid-div: towards ins ent st: edgd rt 2f out: gd hdwy over 1f out: tk 3rd 100yds out: styd on steadily* **43/5**

4 1 1/4 **Conduit (IRE)**[22] 7310 4-9-0..... RyanMoore 16 118
(Sir Michael Stoute) *hld up: 12th 5f out: 9th st: drvn and styng on over 1f out: kpt on same pce fnl f* **39/10**[3]

5 1 1/4 **Air Shady (JPN)**[28] 8-9-0..... HGoto 3 116
(M Ito, Japan) *hld up towards rr: styd on ins and nt clr run over 2f out: styd on fnl 2f: nvr nr to chal* **44/1**

6 1/2 **Eishin Deputy (JPN)**[28] 7-9-0..... KTosaki 4 115
(A Nomoto, Japan) *first to show: settled in 3rd: 2nd st: ev ch wl over 1f out: wknd fnl f* **38/1**

7 1/2 **Just As Well (USA)**[43] 6873 6-9-0..... JRLeparoux 7 114
(Jonathan Sheppard, U.S.A) *mid-div: 13th 5f out: swtchd out over 2f out: kpt on steadily: nvr nr to chal* **46/1**

8 *nse* **Meiner Kitz (JPN)**[49] 6-9-0.....(b) MMatsuoka 8 114
(S Kunieda, Japan) *in rr to st: sme prog on outside fnl 2f: nvr a factor* **31/1**

9 1 1/2 **Reach The Crown (JPN)**[35] 3-8-10..... YTake 9 114
(K Hashiguchi, Japan) *led after 2f to appr fnl f* **76/10**

10 2 **Never Bouchon (JPN)**[210] 6-9-0..... HKitamura 2 108
(M Ito, Japan) *racd in 6th: 8th st: btn over 2f out* **144/1**

11 *nk* **Scintillo**[42] 6890 4-9-0..... GMosse 12 108
(R Hannon) *racd in 7th to st: drvn and disp 4th wl over 1f out: sn wknd* **114/1**

12 3 1/2 **Cosmo Bulk (JPN)**[28] 8-9-0..... FIgarashi 17 102
(K Tabe, Japan) *hld up: a towards rr* **123/1**

13 1/2 **Screen Hero (JPN)**[28] 5-9-0..... MDemuro 18 101
(Y Shikato, Japan) *mid-div: hdwy and 6th st: rdn and btn wl over 1f out* **13/2**

14 1/2 **Interpatation (USA)**[57] 6511 7-9-0..... DCohen 15 101
(Robert Barbara, U.S.A) *a towards rr* **89/1**

14 *dht* **Inti Raimi (JPN)**[15] 7-9-0..... CSoumillon 14 101
(S Sasaki, Japan) *racd in 8th tl wkng appr st* **123/1**

16 5 **Asakusa Kings (JPN)**[28] 5-9-0..... YIwata 1 93
(R Okubo, Japan) *led 2f: trckd ldr to 3f out: 3rd st: btn 2f out* **43/1**

17 1/2 **Marsh Side (USA)**[43] 6873 6-9-0..... JJCastellano 11 92
(Neil Drysdale, U.S.A) *10th 5f out: rdn ent st: bhd fnl 2f* **32/1**

18 6 **Yamanin Kingly (JPN)**[28] 4-9-0..... YShibayama 13 82
(H Kawachi, Japan) *prom: 4th st: wknd over 2f out* **70/1**

2m 22.4s (-3.10)
WFA 3 from 4yo+ 6lb **18** Ran SP% **125.9**
(including 100 yen stakes): WIN 360; PL 140, 160, 260; DF 1020; SF2020.
Owner Y Tanimizu **Bred** Country Bokujo **Trained** Japan

NOTEBOOK
Vodka(JPN), having been in the frame in this on her two previous tries, just lasted home over what his her maximum trip and recorded her seventh Group 1 victory. She came back with blood running from her nose, and might now be retired.
Conduit(IRE), who won the last two runnings of the Breeders' Cup Turf, ran a creditable race but was being pushed along turning in and could not find an extra gear in the straight. He has been sold and will be retired to stud in Japan now.
Scintillo had a stiff task in this company and appeared to run his race without being good enough.

7577 WOLVERHAMPTON (A.W) (L-H)
Monday, November 30

OFFICIAL GOING: Standard
Wind: Moderate across Weather: Sunny and cold

7594 STAY AT THE WOLVERHAMPTON HOLIDAY INN H'CAP (FOR AMATEUR RIDERS) 1m 5f 194y(P)
2:10 (2:10) (Class 6) (0-65,63) 3-Y-0+ **£2,307** (£709; £354) **Stalls Low**

Form RPR

3052 **1** **Prince Charlemagne (IRE)**[9] 7495 6-10-7 **61**..... MrRBirkett(5) 1 75+
(G L Moore) *hmpd s: hld up towards rr: smooth hdwy over 2f out: rdn to ld over 1f out: sn edgd rt: rdn out* **7/1**[2]

0453 **2** 2 1/4 **Augustus John (IRE)**[14] 7413 6-10-11 **63**..... MrTRDavid(3) 4 73
(R Brotherton) *hmpd s: hld up in rr: stdy prog over 3f out: rdn over 1f out: chsd wnr ins fnl f: no imp* **7/1**[2]

3046 **3** 3 3/4 **Drawn Gold**[10] 7461 5-10-5 **59**..... MrStephenHarrison(5) 9 64
(R Hollinshead) *led 1f: a.p: pushed along to ld over 2f out: rdn and hdd over 1f out: one pce fnl f* **8/1**[3]

32 **4** 1 **Baltimore Patriot (IRE)**[14] 7415 6-10-7 **63**..... MissCBoxall(7) 5 67
(R Curtis) *hld up in rr: hdwy wl over 1f out: sn pushed along: one pce fnl f* **7/1**[2]

-406 **5** 1 **Dark Energy**[30] 6025 5-10-5 **57**.....(t) MrRMahon(3) 8 59
(M J Scudamore) *prom: rdn and wknd over 1f out* **14/1**

2323 **6** 1 3/4 **Debdene Bank (IRE)**[12] 7440 6-10-5 **61**..... MissCBlakey(7) 11 61
(Mrs Mary Hambro) *hld up in mid-div: lost pl over 4f out: short-lived effrt on ins over 1f out* **6/1**[1]

036 **7** 3 **Little Richard (IRE)**[9] 7495 10-10-4 **58**.....(p) MrLRPayter(5) 12 54
(M Wellings) *hld up in tch: pushed along on outside over 2f out: rdn and wknd wl over 1f out* **28/1**

-300 **8** 2 3/4 **Dreams Jewel**[36] 4332 9-10-8 **57**..... MissIsabelTompsett 3 49
(C Roberts) *s.i.s: hld up towards rr: hdwy 9f out: pushed along over 5f out: rdn and wknd over 2f out* **8/1**[3]

6005 **9** 3 **Rare Coincidence**[9] 7490 8-10-6 **55**.....(tp) MrSWalker 10 43
(R F Fisher) *led after 1f tl over 5f out: led over 3f out: pushed along and hdd over 2f out: wknd wl over 1f out* **8/1**[3]

2022 **10** 10 **Barodine**[100] 5246 6-9-13 **55**..... MrPPrince(7) 7 29
(R J Hodges) *t.k.h: prom: led over 5f out tl over 3f out: wknd 2f out* **8/1**[3]

2334 **11** 12 **Tivers Song (USA)**[28] 7214 5-9-13 **53**.....(b) MissABevan(5) 13 10
(John A Harris) *hld up in mid-div: pushed along and wknd over 2f out* **16/1**

3500 **12** 24 **Captain Imperial (IRE)**[12] 7440 3-10-0 **62**..... MissRBastiman(5) 6 —
(R Bastiman) *hld up in mid-div: pushed along and lost pl over 5f out: sn bhd: t.o fnl 3f* **25/1**

3m 7.91s (1.91) **Going Correction** +0.15s/f (Slow)
WFA 3 from 5yo+ 8lb **12** Ran SP% **116.1**
Speed ratings (Par 101): **100,98,96,96,95 94,92,91,89,83 76,63**
toteswingers: 1&2 £7.70, 1&3 £19.10, 2&3 £15.00 CSF £54.17 CT £402.62 TOTE £6.50: £1.60, £2.70, £2.70; EX 38.10 Trifecta £88.10 Part won. Pool: £119.16 - 0.20 winning units..
Owner A Grinter **Bred** Michael O'Mahony **Trained** Lower Beeding, W Sussex
■ Stewards' Enquiry : Mr S Walker one-day ban: failed to rkeep straight from stalls (TBC)
Mr Stephen Harrison one-day ban: failed to rkeep straight from stalls (TBC)

FOCUS
A moderate amateur riders' handicap. It was well run and the form is sound.

7595 BETDAQ THE BETTING EXCHANGE H'CAP (DIV I) 5f 20y(P)
2:40 (2:40) (Class 6) (0-65,64) 3-Y-0+ £2,047 (£604; £302) Stalls Low

Form RPR
0252 **1** **Grudge**[16] 7397 4-9-2 62 (e[1]) FrancisNorton 7 71
(Ollie Pears) *led: hdd jst over 2f out: sn pushed along: led 1f out: rdn out* 13/2

3410 **2** 1 **Decider (USA)**[9] 7483 6-9-3 63 (p) TonyCulhane 11 68
(R A Harris) *chsd ldr: led jst over 2f out: pushed along and hdd 1f out: sn rdn: nt qckn* 5/1[2]

0U00 **3** ¾ **Radiator Rooney (IRE)**[9] 7484 6-8-9 55 (v) SJCraine 6 58+
(Patrick Morris) *s.i.s: in rr: hdwy whn carried sltly lft jst ins fnl f: r.o* 25/1

5050 **4** 1 **Bluebok**[24] 7280 8-8-12 58 (bt) LukeMorris 4 57
(J M Bradley) *hld up in mid-div: hdwy on ins over 2f out: sn pushed along: rdn over 1f out: one pce* 10/1

0200 **5** nse **Fromsong (IRE)**[19] 7329 11-8-12 63 MarkCoumbe(5) 1 62
(D K Ivory) *a.p: pushed along over 2f out: rdn and kpt on same pce ins fnl f* 11/2[3]

5002 **6** ½ **Exceed Elegance (IRE)**[17] 7371 3-8-6 55 (t) MartinLane(3) 8 52
(D Shaw) *hld up towards rr: rdn wl over 1f out: hdwy whn swtchd lft jst ins fnl f: one pce* 8/1

0506 **7** ¾ **King's Sabre**[13] 7424 3-8-7 53 (be) PaulEddery 5 47
(R C Guest) *hld up in mid-div: pushed along over 2f out: rdn and btn wl over 1f out* 18/1

0002 **8** ½ **Sea Rover (IRE)**[3] 7555 5-9-3 63 RobertWinston 12 56
(M Brittain) *hld up in tch: pushed along on outside and hung rt bnd over 2f out: rdn wl over 1f out: wknd ins fnl f* 7/2[1]

0006 **9** ½ **Almaty Express**[32] 7136 7-9-4 64 (b) DarryllHolland 2 55
(J R Weymes) *chsd ldrs: pushed along over 2f out: wknd wl over 1f out* 8/1

041 **10** nse **Tongalooma**[52] 6641 3-8-10 56 PJMcDonald 13 47
(James Moffatt) *hld up towards rr: rdn over 1f out: no rspnse* 16/1

40-0 **11** 3¾ **Proud Linus (USA)**[10] 7459 4-9-0 60 (t) ChrisCatlin 3 37
(J Ryan) *s.i.s: a in rr* 16/1

62.29 secs (-0.01) **Going Correction** +0.15s/f (Slow) 11 Ran SP% **119.8**
Speed ratings (Par 101): **106,104,103,101,101 100,99,98,97,97 91**
toteswingers: 1&2 £4.40, 1&3 £10.90, 2&3 £5.00 CSF £39.80 CT £776.78 TOTE £5.90: £2.20, £2.00, £7.10; EX 29.30 TRIFECTA Not won..
Owner K C West **Bred** D H Brailsford **Trained** Norton, N Yorks
■ Stewards' Enquiry : Martin Lane one-day ban: careless riding (Dec 14)

FOCUS
A moderate sprint handicap run in a time 0.29 seconds slower than the second division. The front pair were always 1-2 and are rated to their marks.
Proud Linus(USA) Official explanation: jockey said that the gelding was unbalanced throughout

7596 WOLVERHAMPTON-RACECOURSE.CO.UK (S) STKS 7f 32y(P)
3:10 (3:10) (Class 6) 3-Y-0+ £2,047 (£604; £302) Stalls High

Form RPR
1-65 **1** **Sir George (IRE)**[14] 7412 4-9-4 65 PaulDoe 8 65
(P D Evans) *hld up in mid-div: hdwy over 3f out: pushed along over 2f out: led wl over 1f out: edgd rt ins fnl f: drvn out* 8/1[3]

003 **2** 1¼ **Obe Gold**[4] 7535 7-9-10 69 (v) J-PGuillambert 7 68
(P Howling) *hld up in mid-div: rdn and hdwy jst over 1f out: r.o to take 2nd last stride* 20/1

6150 **3** shd **Ravi River (IRE)**[12] 7437 5-9-10 78 SJCraine 3 67
(J R Boyle) *hld up in tch: ev ch wl over 1f out: rdn and nt qckn ins fnl f: lost 2nd last stride* 8/11[1]

0000 **4** 1 **Smalljohn**[59] 6455 3-9-3 66 (v) GregFairley 2 59
(B Smart) *led: rdn and hdd wl over 1f out: no ex ins fnl f* 11/1

0103 **5** 1¼ **Charlie Delta**[5] 7521 6-9-10 56 (b) TonyCulhane 11 61
(R A Harris) *swtchd lft sn after s: hld up in rr: pushed along over 2f out: hdwy wl over 1f out: rdn and one pce fnl f* 20/1

0203 **6** 2½ **Jord (IRE)**[3] 7561 5-9-5 61 ChrisCatlin 6 50
(J A Glover) *chsd ldr tl pushed along wl over 1f out: wknd fnl f* 13/2[2]

3-0 **7** 2 **Desert Mile (IRE)**[13] 7423 6-8-13 68 PJMcDonald 1 38
(Ollie Pears) *s.i.s: hld up towards rr: pushed along over 2f out: nvr nr ldrs* 10/1

4015 **8** 4½ **Rosie Says No**[24] 7280 4-9-5 63 (p) RobertWinston 5 32
(A J McCabe) *hld up in mid-div: wknd wl over 1f out* 14/1

0000 **9** 1½ **Sendreni (FR)**[14] 7412 5-9-10 63 SteveDrowne 4 33
(M Wigham) *prom tl rdn and wknd wl over 1f out* 33/1

00 **10** 9 **Spiders Tern**[24] 7278 4-9-4 0 LukeMorris 10 3
(J M Bradley) *in rr: pushed along over 3f out: sn struggling* 100/1

0 **11** 6 **Madame McManus**[2] 7576 3-8-12 0 StephenDonohoe 12 —
(P D Evans) *a in rr* 100/1

00 **12** 45 **Seren Arian**[24] 7278 3-8-12 0 NeilChalmers 9 —
(B Palling) *prom tl wknd over 3f out: t.o fnl 2f* 100/1

1m 30.11s (0.51) **Going Correction** +0.15s/f (Slow)
WFA 3 from 4yo+ 1lb 12 Ran SP% **121.9**
Speed ratings (Par 101): **103,101,101,100,98 96,93,88,86,76 69,18**
toteswingers: 1&2 £14.50, 1&3 £4.10, 2&3 £9.70 CSF £161.01 TOTE £7.50: £2.80, £5.80, £1.10; EX 141.50 Trifecta £176.60 Part won. Pool: £238.71 - 0.95 winning units..There was no bid for the winner. Ravi River was claimed by Diamond Racing Ltd for £6000.
Owner Diamond Racing Ltd **Bred** Bernard Colclough **Trained** Pandy, Monmouths

FOCUS
A fair seller despite the poor run of the favourite. The winner built on his C/D latest with the fifth looking the best guide.
Seren Arian Official explanation: jockey said that the filly hung right handed throughout

7597 BETDAQEXTRA.COM NURSERY 1m 141y(P)
3:40 (3:41) (Class 6) (0-65,65) 2-Y-0 £2,914 (£867; £433; £216) Stalls Low

Form RPR
4504 **1** **Sounds Of Thunder**[18] 7359 2-9-7 65 EddieAhern 5 70+
(H J L Dunlop) *hld up in mid-div: hdwy 2f out: swtchd lft wl over 1f out: rdn to ld ent fnl f: rdn out* 7/2[1]

6204 **2** 1½ **Bubbly Braveheart (IRE)**[9] 7482 2-9-4 62 (p) RobertWinston 7 64
(A Bailey) *hld up in rr: rdn over 2f out: kpt on to take 2nd nr fin* 4/1[2]

006 **3** nk **She's My Rock (IRE)**[12] 7436 2-8-8 52 LPKeniry 4 53
(S Kirk) *sn chsng ldr: led 2f out: rdn and hdd ent fnl f: no ex and lost 2nd nr fin* 10/1

006 **4** 1¼ **Jennerous Blue**[16] 7390 2-8-8 52 JackMitchell 10 51
(D K Ivory) *in rr: pushed along over 3f out: c wd st: rdn and hdwy over 1f out: kpt on ins fnl f* 11/1

005 **5** 3 **Kyoatee Kilt**[12] 7429 2-9-2 60 DarryllHolland 13 53+
(P F I Cole) *hld up in rr: pushed along over 2f out: rdn and hdwy 1f out: edgd lft ins fnl f: nvr trbld ldrs* 14/1

0043 **6** ½ **As Brave As You (IRE)**[19] 7335 2-8-5 52 MartinLane(3) 8 43
(B Ellison) *s.i.s: sn hld up in mid-div: pushed along over 3f out: hdwy 1f out: n.d* 8/1

000 **7** 1¼ **Heligoland**[28] 7209 2-8-8 52 FergusSweeney 11 41
(A G Newcombe) *hld up in rr: short-lived effrt wl over 1f out* 33/1

0010 **8** 1 **Tiger Hawk (USA)**[9] 7474 2-9-4 62 (b) StephenDonohoe 3 49
(P D Evans) *hld up in tch: rdn over 2f out: wknd over 1f out* 22/1

400 **9** 1¾ **Second Brook (IRE)**[21] 7317 2-9-4 62 ChrisCatlin 1 45
(R Hollinshead) *led 1f: prom: pushed along over 3f out: wknd 2f out* 20/1

040 **10** ¾ **Always De One**[45] 6821 2-9-1 59 GregFairley 12 40
(M Johnston) *s.i.s: hld up towards rr: pushed along over 3f out: no ch whn swtchd rt ins fnl f* 13/2[3]

2150 **11** 5 **Alphacino**[88] 5595 2-9-6 64 (p) KFallon 9 35
(P C Haslam) *t.k.h in mid-div: short-lived effrt over 2f out* 12/1

0156 **12** 6 **North Shadow**[11] 7453 2-8-10 59 DeanHeslop(5) 2 17
(A D Brown) *t.k.h: led after 1f: rdn and hdd 2f out: wknd over 1f out* 15/2

1m 53.29s (2.79) **Going Correction** +0.15s/f (Slow) 12 Ran SP% **122.3**
Speed ratings (Par 94): **93,91,91,90,87 87,86,85,83,82 78,73**
toteswingers: 1&2 £9.60, 1&3 £3.70, 2&3 £10.20 CSF £17.28 CT £132.52 TOTE £4.80: £1.70, £1.70, £4.30; EX 17.70 Trifecta £102.80 Pool: £189.08 - 1.36 winning units..
Owner Lady Mary Manton & Dr Fred Mosselmans **Bred** Southill Stud **Trained** Lambourn, Berks

FOCUS
A moderate nursery, but the form looks sound enough and the winner has more to offer.

NOTEBOOK
Sounds Of Thunder didn't get the best of runs when fourth in a better race over C&D on her previous start, but she enjoyed a much smoother passage this time and was a clear-cut winner. A rise in the weights will force her back up in class. (tchd 4-1)
Bubbly Braveheart(IRE), a beaten favourite in selling company last time, had cheekpieces replacing blinkers and ran better. He might win a minor race. (op 15-2)
She's My Rock(IRE), upped in trip on her nursery debut, was always well placed and had her chance. This well-bred filly is still finding her way and can make her mark. (op 8-1)
Jennerous Blue did well to get so closer after coming under pressure out the back down the back straight, and then swung much wider than ideal into the straight. On this evidence, she's going to want a staying trip in time. (op 12-1)
Kyoatee Kilt was no sure thing to stay this trip on breeding, but he didn't run badly considering he raced further back than ideal.

7598 TRY BETDAQ FOR AN EXCHANGE H'CAP 2m 119y(P)
4:10 (4:10) (Class 5) (0-75,75) 3-Y-0+ £3,885 (£1,156; £433; £433) Stalls Low

Form RPR
5646 **1** **Bentley Brook (IRE)**[16] 7402 7-10-0 75 TonyCulhane 4 80
(R Curtis) *hld up in tch: wnt 2nd over 3f out: rdn jst over 2f out: led wl ins fnl f: drvn out* 22/1

6312 **2** nk **Follow The Dream**[79] 5885 6-8-10 57 DarryllHolland 1 62+
(Karen George) *hld up towards rr: swtchd rt over 2f out: c wd st: rdn and hdwy whn edgd lft over 1f out: ev ch wl ins fnl f: styd on* 13/8[1]

2045 **3** nse **Daaweitza**[17] 7373 6-9-11 72 DaneO'Neill 3 77
(B Ellison) *hld up in rr: hdwy over 2f out: rdn wl over 1f out: ev ch wl ins fnl f: styd on* 7/1[2]

5243 **3** dht **Zuwaar**[2] 7578 4-9-8 69 (tp) EddieAhern 7 74
(Ian Williams) *chsd ldr: led 5f out: rdn wl over 1f out: hdd wl ins fnl f: styd on* 13/8[1]

5420 **5** 4½ **Abstract Folly (IRE)**[34] 7084 7-8-12 59 SebSanders 2 59
(J D Bethell) *prom: pushed along over 3f out: rdn over 1f out: wknd wl ins fnl f* 8/1[3]

0P0- **6** 6 **Command Marshal (FR)**[11] 5199 6-9-6 67 SJCraine 6 59
(M J Scudamore) *hld up towards rr: hdwy over 3f out: rdn over 2f out: wknd wl over 1f out* 14/1

220/ **7** 30 **Dan Buoy (FR)**[247] 3963 6-9-0 61 (p) J-PGuillambert 5 17
(R C Guest) *led: hdd 5f out: wknd over 3f out: t.o fnl 2f* 20/1

3m 46.28s (4.48) **Going Correction** +0.15s/f (Slow) 7 Ran SP% **115.6**
Speed ratings (Par 103): **95,94,94,94,92 89,75**
toteswingers: 1&2 £5.40, 1&Daaweitza £5.40, 1&Zuwaar £2.70, 2&Daaweitza £1.70, 2&Zuwaar £0.70 CSF £59.71 TOTE £18.80: £6.20, £1.60; EX 65.20 TRIFECTA Not won..
Owner John Wardle **Bred** Christopher Maye **Trained** Lambourn, Berks
■ Stewards' Enquiry : Eddie Ahern caution: careless riding

FOCUS
They went a steady pace and the first four finished in a bunch. Muddling form.

7599 ENJOY THE LUCKY 7 GROUP OFFER H'CAP (DIV I) 1m 1f 103y(P)
4:40 (4:41) (Class 6) (0-55,58) 3-Y-0+ £2,047 (£604; £302) Stalls Low

Form RPR
5004 **1** **Head First**[45] 6831 3-8-9 52 DavidProbert 1 57+
(W Jarvis) *hld up in tch on ins: rdn jst over 1f out: sltly hmpd ins fnl f: r.o to ld last strides* 16/1

0616 **2** hd **Fitzolini**[12] 7438 3-8-10 53 (p) DarryllHolland 6 58
(A D Brown) *led after 1f: rdn over 1f out: edgd rt ins fnl f: hdd last strides* 16/1

6045 **3** ¾ **Noche De Reyes**[30] 7173 4-8-12 52 EddieAhern 4 55
(E J Alston) *led 1f: a.p: rdn over 1f out: ev ch ins fnl f: kpt on* 40/1

0000 **4** ½ **King Of Rhythm (IRE)**[148] 3653 6-9-1 55 KFallon 9 57
(D Carroll) *hld up towards rr: stdy prog 3f out: rdn 1f out: kpt on towards fin* 12/1

6352 **5** ½ **Carragold**[75] 5983 3-8-12 55 RobertWinston 7 56+
(M Brittain) *s.i.s: hld up in mid-div: pushed along over 5f out: rdn over 2f out: nt clr run wl over 1f out: styd on ins fnl f* 9/1

0000 **6** 1¾ **Kirstys Lad**[14] 7416 7-8-6 46 GregFairley 11 43
(M Mullineaux) *hld up in rr: effrt on wd outside over 2f out: c v wd st: rdn over 1f out: one pce fnl f* 25/1

0044 **7** ¾ **King Of Connacht**[38] 6998 6-9-1 55 (p) KirstyMilczarek 3 51
(M Wellings) *hld up in tch: pushed along 2f out: rdn over 1f out: one pce ins fnl f* 10/1

4222 **8** ¾ **Herbert Crescent**[38] 6999 4-9-0 54 SebSanders 8 48
(Ollie Pears) *s.i.s: hld up in rr: rdn and short-lived effrt over 1f out* 7/2[2]

0402 **9** ¾ **Kool Katie**[18] 7361 4-8-13 53 TonyCulhane 2 46
(Mrs G S Rees) *hld up in tch: hmpd briefly wl over 1f out: wknd ins fnl f* 17/2[3]

6064 **10** 1¼ **Miss Perfectionist**[30] 7195 3-8-9 52 J-PGuillambert 12 42
(P Howling) *hld up in rr: swtchd lft to ins sn after s: pushed along over 3f out: rdn and short-lived effrt on ins over 1f out* 3/1[1]

6001 **11** 2¾ **Ten Pole Tudor**[2] 7581 4-8-11 58 6ex (p) JakePayne(7) 5 42
(R A Harris) *hld up towards rr: n.m.r on ins over 3f out: swtchd rt to outside over 2f out: c v wd st: n.d* 12/1

4405 **12** ½ **Cause For Applause (IRE)**[28] 7211 3-8-8 **51**.................. ChrisCatlin 10 34
(R Craggs) *prom: wnt 2nd 7f out: ev ch over 2f out: wknd over 1f out* **25/1**

30-0 **13** ½ **Tallest Peak (USA)**[12] 7438 4-8-11 **51**.......................... JerryO'Dwyer 13 33
(M G Quinlan) *hld up in tch on outside: rdn and wknd over 2f out* **28/1**

2m 3.28s (1.58) **Going Correction** +0.15s/f (Slow)
WFA 3 from 4yo+ 3lb **13** Ran SP% **117.6**
Speed ratings (Par 101): **98,97,97,96,96 94,94,93,92,91 89,88,88**
toteswingers: 1&2 £32.00, 1&3 £62.80, 2&3 £41.40 CSF £235.32 CT £9625.83 TOTE £18.30: £4.80, £4.10, £11.60; EX 232.60 TRIFECTA Not won..
Owner Mrs Jo Reffo **Bred** Amethyst Stud **Trained** Newmarket, Suffolk

FOCUS
The pace seemed to slow before the straight and there was a bit of a messy finish to this moderate handicap, but the winning time was still 0.29 seconds quicker than the second division. It was a weak race and the form is hard to view positively.
King Of Connacht Official explanation: jockey said at the gelding ran flat
Miss Perfectionist Official explanation: jockey said that the filly moved poorly throughout

7600 ENJOY THE LUCKY 7 GROUP OFFER H'CAP (DIV II) 1m 1f 103y(P)
5:10 (5:11) (Class 6) (0-55,55) 3-Y-O+ **£2,047** (£604; £302) **Stalls** Low

Form RPR
0000 **1** **Royal Society**[38] 6987 3-8-11 **54** ow1................................ DaneO'Neill 11 61
(R A Farrant) *s.i.s: hld up towards rr: hdwy 2f out: c wd st: rdn fnl f: r.o to ld last strides* **14/1**

550 **2** *hd* **Kielty's Folly**[149] 3637 5-8-9 **49** ow2................................. TonyCulhane 3 56
(B P J Baugh) *hld up in tch: pushed along whn carried rt over 1f out: led ins fnl f: rdn and hdd last strides* **14/1**

0003 **3** 1 ¼ **Hi Spec (IRE)**[33] 7110 6-8-3 **46**..................................(p) AndreaAtzeni(3) 1 50
(Miss M E Rowland) *a.p: led wl over 1f out: sn edgd rt: rdn and hdd ins fnl f: no ex towards fin* **12/1**

4304 **4** ¾ **Sairaam (IRE)**[18] 7348 3-8-9 **52**.................................. KirstyMilczarek 12 55
(C Smith) *hld up in rr: c wd st: swtchd lft and nt clr run briefly over 1f out: r.o ins fnl f: nrst fin* **12/1**

0100 **5** ½ **Pianoforte (USA)**[2] 7581 7-9-1 **55**..........................(b) GrahamGibbons 5 57
(E J Alston) *hld up in tch on ins: rdn over 1f out: nt qckn ins fnl f* **7/1**[3]

00 **6** *hd* **Plenilune (IRE)**[34] 7093 4-8-12 **52**................................ RobertWinston 9 53
(M Brittain) *a.p: ev ch over 2f out: rdn over 1f out: fdd ins fnl f* **22/1**

4646 **7** *nse* **Stoic Leader (IRE)**[112] 4861 9-8-12 **52**............................ ChrisCatlin 10 53
(R F Fisher) *hld up towards rr: pushed along and hdwy over 1f out: rdn ins fnl f: hld whn nt clr run cl home* **25/1**

-000 **8** *nse* **Da Bomber (IRE)**[168] 2968 4-8-12 **52**........................ FergusSweeney 6 53
(J W Unett) *hmpd s: hld up in rr: hdwy on ins over 1f out: nt qckn ins fnl f* **50/1**

0340 **9** 1 **Rowan Lodge (IRE)**[38] 6987 7-8-12 **52**........................(b) PJMcDonald 7 52+
(Ollie Pears) *hld up towards rr: pushed along and sme prog 1f out: hld whn nt clr run wl ins fnl f* **9/1**

5003 **10** 2 ¼ **Libre**[10] 7466 9-8-8 **48**... JerryO'Dwyer 13 42
(F Jordan) *hld up in tch: pushed along on outside over 2f out: c v wd st: rdn and wknd wl over 1f out* **16/1**

0560 **11** 5 **Climate (IRE)**[16] 7403 10-8-10 **55** ow1.......................... RichardEvans(5) 8 39
(P D Evans) *hld up in mid-div: pushed along 2f out: sn bhd* **8/1**

3316 **12** 1 ¼ **Mighty Mover (IRE)**[14] 7416 7-9-1 **55**............................... LukeMorris 2 36
(B Palling) *led: rdn and hdd wl over 1f out: sn wknd* **7/2**[1]

0020 **13** 5 **Marjury Daw (IRE)**[12] 7438 3-8-11 **54**.......................... J-PGuillambert 4 25
(J G Given) *w ldr: ev ch over 2f out: wkng whn hmpd over 1f out: eased ins fnl f* **4/1**[2]

2m 3.57s (1.87) **Going Correction** +0.15s/f (Slow)
WFA 3 from 4yo+ 3lb **13** Ran SP% **120.6**
Speed ratings (Par 101): **97,96,95,95,94 94,94,94,93,91 87,85,81**
toteswingers: 1&2 £42.60, 1&3 £35.80, 2&3 £25.50 CSF £194.27 CT £2428.05 TOTE £15.50: £4.90, £5.20, £4.00; EX 275.60 Trifecta £108.00 Not won..
Owner M Sawers **Bred** Gainsborough Stud Management Ltd **Trained** East Garston, Berks
■ Stewards' Enquiry : Andrea Atzeni two-day ban: careless riding (Dec 14, 15)

FOCUS
They went a steady pace and the time was 0.29 seconds slower than the first division. Similarly weak form, rated through the third and fourth.
Da Bomber(IRE) Official explanation: jockey said that the gelding was denied a clear run
Rowan Lodge(IRE) Official explanation: jockey said that the gelding was denied a clear run
Climate(IRE) Official explanation: jockey said the gelding felt wrong in the closing stages
Marjury Daw(IRE) Official explanation: jockey said that the filly suffered interference in running

7601 BETDAQ THE BETTING EXCHANGE H'CAP (DIV II) 5f 20y(P)
5:40 (5:41) (Class 6) (0-65,63) 3-Y-O+ **£2,047** (£604; £302) **Stalls** Low

Form RPR
5561 **1** **Forever's Girl**[24] 7280 3-9-4 **63**.. PJMcDonald 3 76
(G R Oldroyd) *hld up and bhd: hdwy over 1f out: rdn to ld wl ins fnl f: r.o* **7/2**[1]

2003 **2** *nk* **Monsieur Reynard**[16] 7397 4-8-10 **55**............................... LukeMorris 5 66
(J M Bradley) *led early: chsd ldr: carried hd high and rdn to ld briefly ins fnl f: r.o* **7/2**[1]

0110 **3** 1 ¾ **Metal Guru**[24] 7280 5-8-11 **59**............................(p) RussellKennemore(3) 9 64
(R Hollinshead) *a.p: pushed along over 2f out: rdn jst over 1f out: kpt on to take 3rd post* **8/1**[3]

0422 **4** *nse* **Cayman Fox**[32] 7136 4-8-10 **62**............................(e) MatthewLawson(7) 11 67
(James Moffatt) *sn led: 3 l clr whn rdn over 1f out: hdd ins fnl f: no ex* **5/1**[2]

030 **5** 1 ¼ **Across The Sands**[14] 7411 3-8-10 **55**............................ FrankieMcDonald 7 56
(C N Kellett) *hld up in mid-div: hung lft bnd over 2f out: rdn and sme prog 1f out: hld whn hit on hd by rival jockey's whip wl ins fnl f* **22/1**

2000 **6** 1 **Shakespeare's Son**[6] 7503 4-8-13 **58**.......................... VinceSlattery 10 55
(H J Evans) *bhd: shkn up over 3f out: rdn wl over 1f out: kpt on ins fnl f* **33/1**

4223 **7** ½ **Yanza**[19] 7330 3-8-11 **63**...(b) LukeKilgarriff(7) 2 58
(J R Gask) *prom: hrd rdn wl over 1f out: wknd ins fnl f* **5/1**[2]

3000 **8** 1 ¾ **Monte Cassino (IRE)**[6] 7503 4-8-12 **57**......................... TonyCulhane 4 46
(J O'Reilly) *outpcd: a in rr* **20/1**

0000 **9** 1 ¼ **Steel City Boy (IRE)**[19] 7330 6-9-4 **63**............................ DaneO'Neill 8 47
(D Shaw) *hld up in mid-div: pushed along over 2f out: c wd st: rdn and wknd over 1f out* **16/1**

2022 **10** 2 ½ **Rocket Ruby**[133] 4137 3-8-6 **54**...................................... MartinLane(3) 6 29
(D Shaw) *hld up in mid-div: pushed along on ins over 2f out: wknd over 1f out* **20/1**

0430 **11** 11 **Northern Empire (IRE)**[96] 5341 6-9-2 **61**....................(p) JerryO'Dwyer 12 —
(F Jordan) *s.i.s: sn swtchd lft and outpcd: no ch whn hung rt ins fnl f* **25/1**

62.00 secs (-0.30) **Going Correction** +0.15s/f (Slow) **11** Ran SP% **115.4**
Speed ratings (Par 101): **108,107,104,104,102 101,100,97,95,91 73**
toteswingers: 1&2 £6.20, 1&3 £8.00, 2&3 £8.80 CSF £13.57 CT £91.73 TOTE £5.70: £1.60, £1.60, £2.10; EX 21.50 Trifecta £108.00 Pool of £490.45 - 3.36 winning units. Place 6: £805.85 Place 5: £275.47 .
Owner R C Bond **Bred** R C Bond **Trained** Brawby, N Yorks

FOCUS
This was wel run and the winning time was 0.29 seconds quicker than the first division. Sound form, with the winner stepping up on his recent course win. The next three all made the frame in a C/D handicap in October (race 6456).
Monte Cassino(IRE) Official explanation: jockey said that the gelding was hampered on leaving the stalls
Northern Empire(IRE) Official explanation: jockey said that the gelding hung right
T/Jkpt: Not won. T/Plt: £775.40 to a £1 stake. Pool: £93,850.93. 88.35 winning tickets. T/Qpdt: £50.70 to a £1 stake. Pool: £7,162.30. 104.50 winning tickets. KH

7570 LINGFIELD (L-H)
Tuesday, December 1

OFFICIAL GOING: Standard
Wind: Almost nil Weather: Fine and crisp

7602 PAM ELLIOTT'S BIRTHDAY SURPRISE H'CAP (DIV I) 6f (P)
12:30 (12:32) (Class 6) (0-60,60) 3-Y-O+ **£1,637** (£483; £241) **Stalls** Low

Form RPR
0052 **1** **Divine Force**[6] 7521 3-9-0 **56**....................................... SimonWhitworth 9 68
(M Wigham) *reluctant to go nr stalls: dwlt: hld up in last trio: looking for run fr over 2f out: prog over 1f out: r.o to ld last 100yds: sn clr* **11/2**[2]

0425 **2** 2 ½ **Green Velvet**[63] 6362 4-9-4 **60**... SebSanders 4 64
(P J Makin) *pressed ldr: led over 1f out: styd on: hdd and outpcd last 100yds* **8/1**

3330 **3** 2 **Outer Hebrides**[6] 7517 8-8-12 **54**..................................(v) DavidProbert 1 52
(J M Bradley) *chsd ldng pair on inner: rdn 2f out: nt qckn over 1f out: kpt on fnl f* **13/2**[3]

524 **4** 1 **Colombard (IRE)**[4] 7561 4-8-10 **52**.............................. JamieSpencer 10 46
(Patrick Morris) *spd fr wd draw to ld and cross to rail: hdd over 1f out: fdd* **4/1**[1]

0050 **5** ¾ **Grand Palace (IRE)**[10] 7484 6-8-13 **55**.....................(v) FergusSweeney 3 47
(H J Evans) *hld up in last trio on inner: pushed along and sme prog over 1f out: no ch whn nt clr run ins fnl f: nvr nr ldrs* **12/1**

0006 **6** 2 **Hart Of Gold**[10] 7484 5-8-12 **54**......................................(p) LukeMorris 2 40
(R A Harris) *t.k.h: trckd ldng pair: rdn over 2f out: wknd fnl f* **11/1**

1300 **7** ½ **Briannsta (IRE)**[10] 7483 7-8-11 **53**.............................(b) SamHitchcott 5 37
(J E Long) *struggling to hold pl after 2f: dropped to rr over 2f out: plugged on fnl f* **20/1**

-412 **8** ½ **Waterloo Dock**[244] 1076 4-9-4 **60**.................................... MartinDwyer 11 42
(M Quinn) *chsd ldrs: rdn over 2f out: wknd over 1f out* **7/1**

0004 **9** *nk* **After The Show**[10] 7483 8-9-1 **57**..............................(p) EddieAhern 7 38
(Rae Guest) *racd on outer: chsd ldrs: u.p fr 1/2-way: wknd over 1f out* **7/1**

3065 **10** *nk* **Romantic Queen**[10] 7484 3-9-4 **60**..............................(t) DaneO'Neill 6 40
(George Baker) *dwlt: in last trio: effrt on wd outside whn nt clr run wl over 1f out: no prog* **8/1**

1m 11.25s (-0.65) **Going Correction** -0.05s/f (Stan) **10** Ran SP% **116.7**
Speed ratings (Par 101): **102,98,96,94,93 91,90,89,89,88**
toteswingers: 1&2 £5.60, 1&3 £7.30, 2&3 £6.40 CSF £49.07 CT £300.00 TOTE £5.40: £2.30, £2.60, £2.60; EX 30.10 Trifecta £221.70 Part won. Pool: £299.70 - 0.56 winning units..
Owner R J Lorenz **Bred** Capt J H Wilson **Trained** Newmarket, Suffolk

FOCUS
A moderate race, run in a near identical time to the second division. The form is rated around the runner-up, with a personal best from the winner.
Colombard(IRE) Official explanation: jockey said gelding hung left
Briannsta(IRE) Official explanation: vet said gelding was struck into right-fore
Romantic Queen Official explanation: jockey said filly missed the break

7603 BET ON TONIGHT'S FOOTBALL AT TOTESPORT.COM H'CAP 1m (P)
1:00 (1:00) (Class 4) (0-80,84) 3-Y-O+ **£4,727** (£1,406; £702; £351) **Stalls** High

Form RPR
1131 **1** **Mr Willis**[6] 7523 3-9-8 **84** 6ex.. SteveDrowne 6 93+
(J R Best) *hld up in 5th: pushed along whn pce lifted over 3f out: prog on outer 2f out: rdn to ld 1f out: styd on wl* **1/1**[1]

3140 **2** 1 **Pegasus Again (USA)**[31] 7189 4-9-5 **80**......................(p) MichaelHills 5 87
(T G Mills) *pressed ldr: led wl over 2f out: drvn and hdd 1f out: tried to rally but readily hld fnl 100yds* **10/1**

1231 **3** 1 ½ **Red Suede Shoes**[12] 7456 3-8-13 **78**.....................(p) JamesMillman(3) 8 81
(B R Millman) *trckd ldng pairon outer: effrt to chse ldr over 2f out to over 1f out: styd on same pce* **10/3**[2]

6254 **4** *hd* **Quick Release (IRE)**[6] 7523 4-8-10 **74**........................... MartinLane(3) 3 77
(D M Simcock) *chsd ldng trio: pushed along over 3f out: nt qckn over 2f out: styd on again fr over 1f out* **8/1**[3]

2006 **5** 1 ½ **Trafalgar Square**[13] 7437 7-9-2 **77**..................................... JimCrowley 2 76
(M J Attwater) *hld up in 7th and off the pce: effrt over 2f out: rdn over 1f out: one pce and no imp* **28/1**

0445 **6** *nk* **Esteem Machine (USA)**[6] 7516 5-9-2 **77**......................... JamieSpencer 1 76
(R A Teal) *s.s: hld up in last and wl off the pce: quick move wl over 1f out: nvr rchd ldrs and effrt petered out fnl 100yds* **25/1**

0040 **7** 1 ¾ **Alfresco**[13] 7437 5-9-3 **78**...(b) RobertWinston 7 72
(J R Best) *dwlt and stdd s: hld up in 6th: lost pl and last over 2f out: taken to outer and shuffled along: nvr in the r* **14/1**

3003 **8** 2 **Avertis**[25] 7271 4-9-2 **77**..(tp) ChrisCatlin 4 67
(Stef Liddiard) *racd freely: led at mod tempo: upped the pce over 3f out: hdd wl over 2f out: sn lost pl and btn* **16/1**

1m 38.1s (-0.10) **Going Correction** -0.05s/f (Stan)
WFA 3 from 4yo+ 1lb **8** Ran SP% **113.1**
Speed ratings (Par 105): **98,97,95,95,93 93,91,89**
toteswingers: 1&2 £3.80, 1&3 £1.80, 2&3 £3.70 CSF £12.14 CT £25.41 TOTE £1.90: £1.20, £1.90, £1.30; EX 12.40 Trifecta £16.50 Pool: £333.31 - 14.91 winning units..
Owner Miss Sara Furnival **Bred** John Best **Trained** Hucking, Kent

FOCUS
A fair handicap, but the pace was steady until just after halfway, resulting in a time 0.07 seconds slower than the following 0-75 nursery. The form is rated around the second to the fourth.

7604 BEST ODDS AT TOTESPORT.COM NURSERY 1m (P)
1:30 (1:30) (Class 5) (0-75,73) 2-Y-0 **£2,729** (£806; £403) **Stalls** High

Form RPR
4U05 **1** **New Christmas (USA)**[32] 7157 2-9-6 **72**.......................... EddieAhern 4 76
(B J Meehan) *trckd ldng pair: wnt 2nd wl over 2f out: rdn to ld wl over 1f out: kpt on wl enough fnl f* **3/1**[2]
2352 **2** ½ **Edward Whymper**[6] 7513 2-8-12 **64**.............................. DarryllHolland 6 67
(M H Tompkins) *hld up: trbld passage early in rr: rdn fr 3f out: prog wl over 1f out: chsd wnr last 100yds: clsd but a hld* **9/4**[1]
330 **3** 1¼ **Kathindi (IRE)**[114] 4825 2-9-1 **67**.......................... LukeMorris 1 67
(J S Moore) *chsd ldrs: effrt over 2f out: drvn to dispute 2nd 1f out: one pce after* **11/1**
4131 **4** nk **Al Khimiya (IRE)**[50] 6721 2-9-2 **68**........................ JimCrowley 8 67
(S Woodman) *chsd ldrs: prog to go 3rd over 2f out: drvn to dispute 2nd 1f out: nt qckn after* **15/2**
6253 **5** 2¾ **If I Were A Boy (IRE)**[13] 7434 2-9-2 **73**.....................(p) LeeNewnes(5) 3 66
(S Kirk) *pushed along to hold pl in midfield 4f out: struggling over 2f out: in rr and nt clr run wl over 1f out: kpt on last 150yds* **4/1**[3]
000 **6** ½ **Roybuoy**[36] 7050 2-7-12 **50** oh2.................................(b[1]) NickyMackay 5 42
(H J L Dunlop) *led after 2f to wl over 1f out: wknd fnl f* **28/1**
5100 **7** nk **Danger Mulally**[13] 7434 2-9-4 **70**.................................(t) LPKeniry 9 62
(A M Balding) *racd wd: hld up: gng bttr than most 3f out: rdn and nt qckn 2f out: no prog after* **14/1**
0400 **8** nk **Mnarani (IRE)**[101] 5274 2-8-11 **68**.......................... SophieDoyle(5) 2 59
(J S Moore) *led 2f: pressed ldr to wl over 2f out: grad wknd on inner over 1f out* **14/1**
0000 **9** 6 **Flash For Freedom (USA)**[17] 7389 2-7-11 **52**........... AndreaAtzeni(3) 7 30
(J R Best) *hld up in last pair: struggling over 2f out: sn bhd* **50/1**

1m 38.03s (-0.17) **Going Correction** -0.05s/f (Stan) **9** Ran SP% **114.6**
Speed ratings (Par 96): **98,97,96,95,93 92,92,92,86**
toteswingers: 1&2 £2.10, 1&3 £5.10, 2&3 £6.30 CSF £10.07 CT £63.16 TOTE £4.40: £1.50, £1.40, £2.50; EX 12.60 Trifecta £47.70 Pool: £260.58 - 4.04 winning units..
Owner Jaber Abdullah **Bred** Eithne Hamilton **Trained** Manton, Wilts

FOCUS
A fair nursery in which the winner showed the anticipated improvement.

NOTEBOOK
New Christmas(USA) improved for the step up in trip on this switch to nursery company. He's obviously progressive and the follow up cannot be ruled out. (op 4-1)
Edward Whymper raced further back than ideal and was messed about a bit early on, but he didn't really help himself, not travelling well enough to gain a better position. He took a while to get organised in the straight and it's probably no coincidence his three siblings to have run have all sported headgear at some stage. (op 5-2 tchd 11-4)
Kathindi(IRE), making his nursery debut, ran respectably on this step up in trip and is entitled to be fitter next time, having been off for 114 days. (op 12-1)
Al Khimiya(IRE), claimed by these connections after winning at Kempton on her previous start, found this tougher but still ran respectably. (op 7-1 tchd 13-2)
If I Were A Boy(IRE) took an age to respond to pressure and was already looking held when short of room over 1f out. She eventually ran on, but is just not progressing and some more severe headgear might be worth a try. (op 3-1 tchd 9-2)

7605 BIGGER "WIN ONLY" ODDSL AT TOTESPORT.COM CLAIMING STKS 5f (P)
2:00 (2:06) (Class 6) 3-Y-0+ **£1,978** (£584; £292) **Stalls** High

Form RPR
0100 **1** **Glamorous Spirit (IRE)**[101] 5247 3-9-0 87.......................... ChrisCatlin 3 91
(R A Harris) *mde all: rdn over 1f out: hld on wl fnl f* **4/1**[2]
0312 **2** nk **Ebraam (USA)**[10] 7488 6-8-12 97.................................. BarryAdams(7) 6 95
(Mike Murphy) *s.i.s: hld up: last tl prog on outer 1/2-way: wnt 2nd jst over 1f out: tried to chal fnl f: nt qckn last 100yds* **4/9**[1]
0505 **3** ¾ **The Tatling (IRE)**[6] 7511 12-8-9 82 ow1.......................... JackDean(3) 5 85
(J M Bradley) *mostly in 6th tl prog 2f out: disp 2nd over 1f out: kpt on same pce fnl f* **9/2**[3]
4040 **4** 3¾ **Especially Special (IRE)**[17] 7397 3-8-1 61............ FrankieMcDonald 4 61
(Peter Grayson) *chsd ldrs: lost pl wl over 1f out: n.d fnl f* **66/1**
000- **5** 2¼ **Miesko (USA)**[91] 5555 4-8-1 62..............................(b[1]) AndreaAtzeni(3) 7 55
(M G Quinlan) *hld up: wd bnd 2f out: hanging and wknd* **33/1**
0000 **6** 2¼ **Gleaming Spirit (IRE)**[33] 7136 5-8-4 43..................(v) KirstyMilczarek 8 47
(Peter Grayson) *chsd wnr to over 1f out: wknd rapidly* **100/1**

57.98 secs (-0.82) **Going Correction** -0.05s/f (Stan) **6** Ran SP% **112.9**
Speed ratings (Par 101): **104,103,102,96,92 89**
toteswingers: 1&2 £1.50, 1&3 £1.30, 2&3 £1.30 CSF £6.34 TOTE £4.90: £1.70, £1.20; EX 6.60 Trifecta £23.70 Pool: £641.45 - 19.98 winning units..Ebraam was claimed by S Curran for £20,000.
Owner Robert Bailey **Bred** Carlo Soria **Trained** Earlswood, Monmouths

FOCUS
A good claimer in which the form trio came clear. The time was modest and the winner looks the best guide.
Ebraam(USA) Official explanation: jockey said gelding missed the break

7606 PAM ELLIOTT'S BIRTHDAY SURPRISE H'CAP (DIV II) 6f (P)
2:30 (2:32) (Class 6) (0-60,60) 3-Y-0+ **£1,637** (£483; £241) **Stalls** Low

Form RPR
4621 **1** **Ask Jenny (IRE)**[10] 7483 7-9-1 **57**.............................. JamieSpencer 5 65
(Patrick Morris) *hld up in last trio: plenty to do whn prog 2f out: cajoled along to cl 1f out: styd on fnl f to ld last strides* **3/1**[1]
3505 **2** hd **Lord Deevert**[10] 7483 4-9-1 **60**.................................(p) JackDean(3) 7 67
(W G M Turner) *chsd ldr: chal 2f out: led over 1f out: kpt on wl fnl f: hdd last strides* **11/2**[3]
04 **3** 1½ **Makshoof (IRE)**[10] 7484 5-8-13 **55**..............................(p) JimCrowley 4 57
(I W McInnes) *hld up in abt 6th and gng wl: prog on inner 2f out: chsd ldrs over 1f out but nt qckn: kpt on last 100yds* **11/1**
0052 **4** nse **Pocket's Pick (IRE)**[10] 7483 3-9-4 **60**.......................... GeorgeBaker 2 62
(G L Moore) *trckd ldng pair gng wl: effrt over 1f out: edgd rt and nt qckn fnl f* **9/2**[2]
3410 **5** nk **Thoughtsofstardom**[64] 6341 6-8-5 **54**...................... CarolineKelly(7) 3 55
(P S McEntee) *led at str pce: hdd over 1f out: wknd last 100yds* **33/1**
012 **6** ¾ **Bollywood Style**[6] 7517 4-9-0 **56**.............................. RobertWinston 11 55
(J R Best) *chsd ldrs on outer: rdn whn v wd bnd 2f out and lost grnd: kpt on again fnl f* **9/2**[2]
0122 **7** ¾ **Elusive Ronnie (IRE)**[3] 7572 3-8-9 **58**....................(b) TobyAtkinson(7) 1 54
(R A Teal) *dwlt: hld up in last and wl off the pce: prog on inner over 1f out: kpt on but n.d* **6/1**
0300 **8** 1½ **Triumphant Welcome**[41] 6933 4-8-10 **52**.................. FergusSweeney 12 43
(H J Evans) *t.k.h: hld up in abt 8th: nt clr run wl over 1f out: no ch after: one pce* **18/1**
0500 **9** nk **One More Round (USA)**[6] 7521 11-8-11 **53**............(b) J-PGuillambert 9 44
(P D Evans) *dwlt: hld up in last trio and wl off the pce: nvr a factor but plugged on fr over 1f out on inner* **25/1**
4000 **10** 7 **Truly Divine**[210] 1777 4-8-10 **52**.............................. JerryO'Dwyer 6 20
(C A Dwyer) *dwlt: rousted along to chse ldrs: u.p over 2f out: wknd wl over 1f out* **28/1**
4630 **11** 2½ **Billy Beetroot (USA)**[25] 7280 3-8-13 **55**.....................(p) LukeMorris 10 15
(R A Harris) *chsd ldrs but sn rdn to hold pl: wknd wl over 1f out* **8/1**

1m 11.26s (-0.64) **Going Correction** -0.05s/f (Stan) **11** Ran SP% **126.0**
Speed ratings (Par 101): **102,101,99,99,99 98,97,95,94,85 82**
toteswingers: 1&2 £8.60, 1&3 £7.40, 2&3 £10.50 CSF £20.83 CT £169.80 TOTE £4.60: £2.00, £2.30, £3.40; EX 35.70 Trifecta £382.10 Part won. Pool: £516.44 - 0.56 winning units..
Owner W J Crosbie **Bred** Mrs J Costelloe **Trained** Tarporley, Cheshire

FOCUS
The winning time was almost identical to the first division. The winner confirmed recent C/D placing with the second and fourth, with the runner-up a fair guide to this form.
Pocket's Pick(IRE) Official explanation: jockey said gelding hung right throughout

7607 WOUND HEALING CENTRE H'CAP 1m 2f (P)
3:00 (3:00) (Class 4) (0-80,80) 3-Y-0+ **£4,727** (£1,406; £702; £351) **Stalls** Low

Form RPR
3035 **1** **Black N Brew (USA)**[48] 6778 3-8-10 **72**...................... RobertWinston 4 77
(J R Best) *t.k.h: trckd ldrs: shkn up wl over 2f out: effrt on outer over 1f out: drvn and styd on fnl f to ld last strides* **8/1**
5556 **2** hd **Basra (IRE)**[107] 5062 6-9-6 **79**.............................. JamieSpencer 6 84
(Miss Jo Crowley) *hld up in last pair: clsd on ldrs 2f out: gng easily and brought to chal 1f out: led ins fnl f: fnd nil in front and hdd last strides* **11/2**[3]
0021 **3** hd **Hurakan (IRE)**[18] 7362 3-8-12 **74**.......................... J-PGuillambert 5 79
(P D Evans) *hld up in tch: cl up and pushed along over 2f out: effrt on inner over 1f out: chal and upsides ins fnl f: nt qckn nr fin* **5/4**[1]
3303 **4** shd **Can Can Star**[17] 7393 6-9-0 **80**.............................. DebraEngland(7) 7 84
(A W Carroll) *stdd s: hld up in last pair: effrt on wd outside over 2f out: lost grnd bnd sn after: r.o again fnl f: jst hld* **5/2**[2]
6252 **5** hd **Addwaitya**[12] 6900 4-9-5 **78**.....................................(p) IanMongan 8 82
(Mrs L J Mongan) *led after 1f tl after 3f: trckd ldr: drvn to chal 2f out: led 1f out: hdd ins fnl f: nt qckn* **11/1**
2612 **6** 1¾ **Cry Alot Boy**[30] 7204 6-9-4 **77**.............................. TonyCulhane 3 78
(K A Morgan) *stdd s: hld up tl prog to ld after 3f and injected pce: breather over 3f out: kicked on over 2f out: hanging and hdd 1f out: folded* **8/1**
6030 **7** 6 **Theonebox (USA)**[154] 3481 4-9-4 **77**.......................... ChrisCatlin 2 66
(N P Moore) *t.k.h: led 1f: trckd ldrs after tl wknd over 1f out* **40/1**

2m 8.22s (1.62) **Going Correction** -0.05s/f (Stan)
WFA 3 from 4yo+ 3lb **7** Ran SP% **121.4**
Speed ratings (Par 105): **91,90,90,90,90 89,84**
toteswingers: 1&2 £7.70, 1&3 £5.20, 2&3 £3.90 CSF £54.45 CT £93.46 TOTE £10.20: £3.60, £3.40; EX 61.80 Trifecta £272.20 Pool: £503.97 - 1.37 winning units..
Owner Martin Long **Bred** Ponder Hill Inc **Trained** Hucking, Kent

FOCUS
Form to treat with real caution as the pace was steady and there was a bunch finish. A small personal best from the winner but it is hard to treat this form positively.

7608 BET LIVE IN PLAY AT TOTESPORT.COM AMATEUR RIDERS' H'CAP 2m (P)
3:30 (3:30) (Class 6) (0-60,59) 3-Y-0+ **£1,911** (£588; £294) **Stalls** Low

Form RPR
0504 **1** **Court Princess**[20] 7328 6-10-13 **56**.......................... MissSBrotherton 10 68
(George Baker) *hld up in midfield: stdy prog over 3f out to trck ldr over 2f out: led wl over 1f out: shkn up and styd on wl* **11/2**
00/6 **2** 2 **Isle De Maurice**[48] 6785 7-10-9 **55**..................(b) MrJoshuaMoore(3) 12 64
(G L Moore) *hld up wl in rr: stdy prog over 3f out: chsd wnr over 1f out: styd on but no real imp* **3/1**[2]
0412 **3** 4½ **Extremely So**[13] 7440 3-10-5 **59**.............................. MrPCollington(3) 3 63
(P J McBride) *hld up in midfield on inner: no room and eased to outer 3f out: sn rdn and prog: kpt on to take 3rd ins fnl f: no ch ldng pair* **9/2**[3]
3000 **4** 8 **Adage**[20] 7328 6-9-13 **45**.....................................(bt) MrTRDavid(3) 7 39
(David Pinder) *dwlt: hld up in rr: rapid prog on wd outside over 4f out to ld over 3f out: hdd & wknd wl over 1f out* **20/1**
000 **5** 4½ **Dance Gdansk (IRE)**[18] 7367 3-9-13 **55**.................. MrJSherwood(5) 9 44
(M Blanshard) *trckd ldrs: prog to chal over 3f out: nt go w ldrs over 2f out: wknd over 1f out* **33/1**
P00/ **6** 2¼ **Wee Ziggy**[22] 4499 6-9-11 **45**.............................. MissMMullineaux(5) 11 31
(M Mullineaux) *awkward s: hld up in last: prog on wd outside fr 3f out to chse ldrs over 2f out: sn outpcd and btn* **66/1**
4100 **7** ½ **Trempari**[51] 6692 6-10-3 **51**.................................(b) MissSLWatson(5) 4 37
(Mike Murphy) *led at decent pce to 7f out: lost pl qckly 3f out: no ch after: uns rdr after fin* **16/1**
0064 **8** nk **Cape Greko**[4] 7549 7-10-8 **56**........................(v) MrJeremiahMcGrath(5) 6 41
(B G Powell) *prom: cl up bhd ldrs 3f out: sn wknd* **11/1**
2045 **9** 1¼ **Little Carmela**[26] 7255 5-11-0 **57**.............................(p) MrSWalker 5 41
(S C Williams) *hld up in midfield on inner: pushed along 5f out: lost pl and struggling over 3f out: sn n.d* **5/2**[1]
0000 **10** 1¼ **Lady Romanov (IRE)**[4] 7549 6-10-2 **48**....................(v) MissZoeLilly(3) 8 30
(P Butler) *lost tch in last after 6f: no ch after: plugged on fnl f* **80/1**
/00- **11** 10 **Sovereign Spirit (IRE)**[29] 7-10-5 **55**............................(t) MrCBevan(7) 14 25
(C Gordon) *racd v wd most of way: chsd ldr after 3f tl 9f out: sn dropped to rr: last 3f out* **40/1**
0600 **12** 1½ **Cragganmore Creek**[48] 6785 6-9-11 **45**........................(v) MrBMMorris(5) 2 14
(D Morris) *ldng trio: led 7f out and increased already decent pce: hdd & wknd rapidly over 3f out* **22/1**
0000 **13** 10 **Corlough Mountain**[13] 7440 5-10-0 **48**.......................... MissMBryant(5) 13 5
(P Butler) *a towards rr: wd and losing tch over 4f out: sn wl bhd* **25/1**

3m 24.49s (-1.21) **Going Correction** -0.05s/f (Stan)
WFA 3 from 5yo+ 8lb **13** Ran SP% **122.4**
Speed ratings (Par 101): **101,100,97,93,91 90,90,89,89,88 83,82,77**
toteswingers: 1&2 £6.40, 1&3 £4.20, 2&3 £4.50 CSF £21.44 CT £83.76 TOTE £6.70: £2.20, £1.80, £1.70; EX 30.80 Trifecta £121.30 Pool: £434.70 - 2.65 winning units. Place 6: £65.64 Place 5: £20.61.
Owner Derek & Cheryl Holder **Bred** Mrs C R Holder **Trained** Moreton Morrell, Warwicks
■ Stewards' Enquiry : Mr Jeremiah McGrath one-day ban: used whip when out of contention (tbn)

FOCUS
This moderate contest was dominated by horses who were partnered by arguably some of the better amateurs in the race. The pace was solid and the form looks sound for the grade. The winner produced a clear personal best.
T/Jkpt: £24,866.80 to a £1 stake. Pool: £35,023.80. 0.50 winning tickets. T/Plt: £90.00 to a £1 stake. Pool: £59,312.89. 480.90 winning tickets. T/Qpdt: £19.40 to a £1 stake. Pool: £4,866.65. 185.20 winning tickets. JN

7585 KEMPTON (A.W) (R-H)
Wednesday, December 2

OFFICIAL GOING: Standard
Wind: Light, half behind Weather: Raining 1st 2 races; dry remainder

7609 BOXINGDAYRACES.CO.UK ALL WEATHER "HANDS AND HEELS" APPRENTICE SERIES H'CAP — 1m (P)
6:50 (6:50) (Class 7) (0-50,51) 3-Y-O+ **£2,047** (£604; £302) **Stalls** High

Form / RPR

05 **1** **Topcroft**[91] 5574 3-8-10 **50**................(v[1]) LeeTopliss(3) 8 69
(D Shaw) *chsd clr ldr and clr of rest after 3f: rdn to cl 2f out: led over 1f out: sn clr* **11/4**[1]

5003 **2** *6* **Join Up**[30] 7211 3-8-12 **49**................ KierenFox 6 52
(W M Brisbourne) *prom in chsng gp: wnt modest 4th over 3f out and 3rd 2f out: styd on fnl f to take 2nd nr fin: sddle slipped* **8/1**

0000 **3** *shd* **Tamino (IRE)**[81] 5883 6-8-6 **47**................ Julie-AnneCumine(5) 14 50
(P Howling) *blasted off in front and spreadeagled field: c bk to wnr fr 2f out: hdd over 1f out but stl clr of rest: wknd and lost 2nd nr fin* **33/1**

0060 **4** *nk* **Ejeed (USA)**[3] 7588 4-8-13 **49**................(p) RichardRowe 5 51
(Miss Z C Davison) *hld up in rr: prog fr 4f out to go prom in chsng gp 3f out: kpt on fnl 2f: nrly snatched 3rd* **5/1**[3]

0001 **5** *5* **Hit The Switch**[8] 7499 3-9-0 **51** 6ex................ RyanClark 10 39
(Patrick Morris) *prom in chsng gp but nvr on terms: pushed along and struggling over 3f out: plugged on fr over 1f out* **7/2**[2]

5463 **6** *2 ½* **Red Current**[14] 7433 5-9-0 **50**................ SPRyan 1 31
(R A Harris) *hld up in rr and racd wd: prog 4f out to go prom in chsng gp 3f out: no hdwy fnl 2f* **14/1**

4006 **7** *½* **Womaniser (IRE)**[7] 7521 5-8-10 **49**................(b) TraceyAddey(3) 11 29
(T Keddy) *s.s: wl in rr and off the pce: pushed along and prog into midfield over 2f out: no hdwy after and no ch* **14/1**

000 **8** *1* **H Harrison (IRE)**[56] 6587 9-9-0 **50**................ AdamCarter 9 27
(I W McInnes) *chsd clr ldng pair: no imp 3f out: wknd and lost pls fr 2f out* **33/1**

000 **9** *½* **Deportista**[26] 7278 3-8-11 **48**................ DavidKenny 7 24
(J A Pickering) *chsd clr ldng trio to over 3f out: steadily wknd* **28/1**

0600 **10** *½* **Rock Tech**[119] 4667 4-8-11 **50**................ DannyBrock(3) 12 25
(J R Jenkins) *dwlt: wl in rr and off the pce: in last pair 3f out: plugged on* **66/1**

00-0 **11** *5* **Nightstrike (IRE)**[34] 7129 6-8-6 **47**................ AdamBeschizza(5) 4 8
(Luke Comer, Ire) *s.v.s and lost at least ten l: ct up rr of field after 3f: nvr a factor after* **12/1**

5400 **12** *½* **Weet In Nerja**[21] 4279 3-8-12 **49**................(p) AlexEdwards 3 9
(J W Unett) *hld up in rr: v wd bnd 3f out: struggling and no ch after* **40/1**

3600 **13** *9* **Jaq's Sister**[171] 2950 3-8-13 **50**................(b) MatthewLawson 2 —
(M Blanshard) *a wl in rr: no ch over 2f out: t.o* **50/1**

1630 **14** *6* **Stargazy**[296] 473 5-9-0 **50**................(tp) HollyHall 13 —
(A J Lidderdale) *plld hrd: hld up in midfield and wl off the pce: wknd 3f out: t.o* **16/1**

1m 39.15s (-0.65) **Going Correction** +0.05s/f (Slow)
WFA 3 from 4yo+ 1lb **14** Ran SP% **118.8**
Speed ratings (Par 97): **105,99,98,98,93 91,90,89,89,88 83,83,74,68**
toteswingers: 1&2 £8.30, 1&3 £27.50, 2&3 £61.10 CSF £23.43 CT £622.40 TOTE £3.50: £1.80, £3.40, £8.40; EX 26.20.
Owner Mrs V Franklin & Partners **Bred** Mrs C A Dunnett **Trained** Danethorpe, Notts
■ Stewards' Enquiry : Julie-Anne Cumine seven-day ban: used whip in a hands and heels race (Dec 16, 18, Jan 1, 4, 6, 6-8)

FOCUS
An uncompetitive contest in which these apprentices were not allowed to use their whips, but the race was notable for a significant gamble on Topcroft, who had been available at 20-1 in the morning and was also very solid on the exchanges. He was much improved, in a race rated around the runner-up.
Topcroft ◆ Official explanation: trainer said, regarding apparent improvement in form, that this was the gelding's first run for him.
Join Up Official explanation: jockey said saddle slipped
Stargazy Official explanation: jockey said gelding ran too free

7610 DIGIBET.COM MEDIAN AUCTION MAIDEN STKS — 7f (P)
7:20 (7:20) (Class 5) 3-5-Y-O **£2,590** (£770; £385; £192) **Stalls** High

Form / RPR

0304 **1** **Lord Fidelio (IRE)**[14] 7432 3-9-3 66................ LPKeniry 4 61+
(A M Balding) *hld up in tch: lost pl sltly over 2f out: rdn and decisive prog over 1f out: edgd rt but led last 100yds: sn in command* **2/1**[2]

6326 **2** *1* **Lord Of The Dance (IRE)**[8] 7499 3-9-3 60................(v[1]) LukeMorris 7 58
(J M P Eustace) *dwlt: sn cl up on inner: rdn and effrt to chal 2f out: led briefly ins fnl f: outpcd last 100yds* **7/1**[3]

6060 **3** *1* **Charlie Smirke (USA)**[175] 2809 3-9-3 61................ GeorgeBaker 10 56
(G L Moore) *t.k.h early: w ldr: led 3f out: drvn 2f out: hdd and one pce ins fnl f* **25/1**

0600 **4** *2 ½* **Wicklewood**[13] 7452 3-9-3 42................(b[1]) AdrianMcCarthy 9 49?
(Mrs C A Dunnett) *t.k.h: trckd ldrs: nt qckn 2f out: sn outpcd* **66/1**

2-43 **5** *½* **Light Sleeper**[12] 7459 3-9-3 75................ RichardHughes 6 48
(P W Chapple-Hyam) *pressed ldng pair: pushed along and lost pl sltly over 2f out: cl enough wl over 1f out: rdn and nt qckn: btn after* **1/1**[1]

25 **6** *1 ¼* **Nativity**[3] 7592 3-8-9 55................ JackDean(3) 1 39
(J L Spearing) *hld up in rr: prog on outer wl over 2f out: looked dangerous over 1f out: wknd fnl f* **16/1**

7 *shd* **Sir Tom** 4-9-0 0................ MarcHalford(3) 2 44
(J J Bridger) *dwlt: mostly in last trio: outpcd fr 2f out* **80/1**

-055 **8** *1 ¾* **Sydneysider**[11] 7479 4-9-3 61................ ShaneKelly 5 39
(Eve Johnson Houghton) *hld up: mostly in last trio: outpcd fr 2f out* **14/1**

0-0 **9** *10* **Lady Trish**[12] 7464 3-8-6 0 ow1................ GerardGalligan(7) 8 8
(C A Dwyer) *led at mod pce: sddle slipped and hdd 3f out: sn dropped out* **66/1**

1m 27.31s (1.31) **Going Correction** +0.05s/f (Slow) **9** Ran SP% **116.4**
Speed ratings (Par 103): **94,92,91,88,88 86,86,84,73**
toteswingers: 1&2 £2.10, 1&3 £8.30, 2&3 £5.50 CSF £16.32 TOTE £2.80: £1.30, £2.00, £7.00; EX 14.50.
Owner J B Munz **Bred** G S A Bloodstock Ptl Ltd **Trained** Kingsclere, Hants

FOCUS
A weak maiden run at a steady pace, and the time was slow compared to the two other 7f races on the card. The winner did not need to match his latest handicap form.
Lady Trish Official explanation: jockey said saddle slipped

7611 DIGIBET NURSERY — 7f (P)
7:50 (7:50) (Class 4) (0-85,81) 2-Y-O **£3,885** (£1,156; £577; £288) **Stalls** High

Form / RPR

6361 **1** **Blue Lyric**[7] 7514 2-8-9 **69** 6ex................ KFallon 1 79+
(L M Cumani) *trckd ldng trio: pushed along and effrt 2f out: rdn and r.o to ld last 150yds: in command after* **10/11**[1]

4402 **2** *1* **Master Of Dance (IRE)**[5] 7552 2-9-4 **78**................ RichardHughes 2 83+
(R Hannon) *stdd s: hld up last: pushed along over 1f out: stl last ent fnl f: rdn and r.o to take 2nd fnl 50yds: no ch to chal* **4/1**[2]

5102 **3** *1 ¼* **Be A Devil**[19] 7363 2-8-13 **73**................ MartinDwyer 4 73
(W R Muir) *trckd ldng pair: effrt on inner to ld narrowly 2f out: hdd and outpcd last 150yds* **11/1**

3241 **4** *hd* **Edgewater (IRE)**[58] 6534 2-9-7 **81**................ DaneO'Neill 3 81
(J Akehurst) *w ldr: upsides 2f out: one pce fnl f* **10/1**[3]

01 **5** *1 ½* **Pittodrie Star (IRE)**[11] 7477 2-9-3 **77**................ LPKeniry 5 73
(A M Balding) *led narrowly at mod pce: shkn up and hdd 2f out: wknd fnl f* **4/1**[2]

1m 26.29s (0.29) **Going Correction** +0.05s/f (Slow) **5** Ran SP% **109.8**
Speed ratings (Par 98): **100,98,97,97,95**
CSF £4.82 TOTE £1.80: £1.40, £1.70; EX 4.10.
Owner Fittocks Stud & Andrew Bengough **Bred** Cavendish Bloodstock **Trained** Newmarket, Suffolk

FOCUS
There were just five runners, but the first two finishers were officially well in. The form looks reliable, rated through the third.

NOTEBOOK
Blue Lyric ◆ was 6lb ahead of the handicapper under the penalty she picked up for her recent success in a similar event over this C&D and she followed up with something to spare. She's not that big, but still looks to a bit weak and could well keep progressing. (op Evens tchd 11-10)
Master Of Dance(IRE) was 7lb well in following his recent second in a conditions contest at Lingfield, although he did have the race set up for him on that occasion. Again ridden patiently, it needs pointing out the winner very much got first run on him, and he was doing all his best work late on. Even so, he'll probably struggle off his new mark. (op 5-1 tchd 7-2)
Be A Devil might be able to win a lesser race. (op 10-1 tchd 9-1)
Edgewater(IRE), bought by these connections for 24,000gns after winning a 6f nursery winner off a 5lb lower mark for Brian Meehan, was comfortably held but is entitled to come on for this first run in nearly two months. (op 9-1 tchd 11-1)
Pittodrie Star(IRE) failed to build on his recent win in a 6f course maiden, dropping away after being ridden much handier this time. (op 7-2)

7612 DIGIBET CASINO H'CAP — 1m 4f (P)
8:20 (8:20) (Class 4) (0-85,81) 3-Y-O **£4,727** (£1,406; £702; £351) **Stalls** Centre

Form / RPR

10 **1** **Tripitaka**[55] 6613 3-9-0 **77**................ NCallan 5 84+
(M A Jarvis) *mde all: set stdy pce to 4f out: rdn 2 l clr over 1f out: edgd lft but in n.d fnl f* **5/1**

5610 **2** *1 ½* **Brett Vale (IRE)**[32] 7194 3-9-4 **81**................ DaneO'Neill 4 84
(P R Hedger) *hld up in last: rdn and prog over 1f out: edging lft but styd on to take 2nd ins fnl f: no imp on wnr* **9/2**

2210 **3** *1 ¼* **Rocky's Pride (IRE)**[44] 6907 3-9-1 **78**................ GeorgeBaker 1 79
(G L Moore) *trckd wnr: pushed along wl over 2f out: no imp over 1f out: lost 2nd ins fnl f* **11/4**[2]

5 **4** *4 ½* **Rajamand (FR)**[21] 7323 3-9-3 **80**................ LPKeniry 2 74
(Miss E C Lavelle) *t.k.h: trckd ldng pair: pushed along and no rspnse 3f out: rdn and wknd over 1f out* **10/3**[3]

0131 **5** *8* **Satwa Gold (USA)**[13] 7455 3-9-0 **77**................ KFallon 3 58
(E A L Dunlop) *t.k.h: hld up in 3rd: rdn and nt qckn over 2f out: wknd over 1f out: eased ins fnl f* **9/4**[1]

2m 39.1s (4.60) **Going Correction** +0.05s/f (Slow) **5** Ran SP% **115.4**
Speed ratings (Par 104): **86,85,84,81,75**
CSF £27.42 TOTE £5.30: £1.80, £1.90; EX 22.70.
Owner The Tripitaka Partnership **Bred** Genesis Green Stud Ltd **Trained** Newmarket, Suffolk

FOCUS
Only the winner and third-placed finisher settled through the early stages in this slowly run race (time over eight seconds above standard) and the form needs treating with caution. That said the winner was the least exposed and it could be worth taking the form at something like face value.
Satwa Gold(USA) Official explanation: jockey ssid colt hung right

7613 KIA SOUL H'CAP — 6f (P)
8:50 (8:50) (Class 4) (0-85,85) 3-Y-O+ **£4,727** (£1,406; £702; £351) **Stalls** High

Form / RPR

6003 **1** **Daddy's Gift (IRE)**[11] 7487 3-9-2 **83**................ RichardHughes 12 91
(R Hannon) *trckd ldrs on inner: prog 2f out: drvn ahd jst ins fnl f: hld on* **15/2**[3]

0064 **2** *½* **Fathsta (IRE)**[11] 7486 4-9-2 **83**................ EddieAhern 11 96+
(D M Simcock) *hld up in midfield: nt clr run over 2f out: trying to cl and rn into wall of rivals over 1f out: 8th and swtchd lft ent fnl f: r.o wl to take 2nd nr fin* **2/1**[1]

0520 **3** *½* **Little Pete (IRE)**[18] 7395 4-9-1 **82**................ LPKeniry 9 87
(I W McInnes) *wl in tch: in midfield: prog fr 2f out: nt qckn but kpt on to chse wnr wl ins fnl f: a hld and lost 2nd nr fin* **20/1**

4005 **4** *½* **Thunderous Mood (USA)**[39] 7026 3-8-11 **78**................(bt) JamieSpencer 3 81
(P F I Cole) *hld up in rr: taken to outer over 2f out: drvn and prog wl over 1f out but hanging rt: disp 2nd ins fnl f and looked dangerous: nt sustain effrt* **11/1**

0160 **5** *nk* **Dvinsky (USA)**[27] 7253 8-8-8 **75**................(b) PaulDoe 7 77
(P Howling) *led: kpt on wl fr 2f out: hdd jst ins fnl f: wknd last 75yds* **16/1**

5352 **6** *nk* **Ivory Silk**[16] 7414 4-9-4 **85**................ ChrisCatlin 4 86
(J R Gask) *hld up in rr: pushed along over 2f out: no real prog and stl only 10th jst over 1f out: rdn and r.o fnl f: gaining at fin* **15/2**[3]

0460 **7** *2* **Princess Valerina**[13] 7454 5-8-13 **80**................ FrankieMcDonald 8 78+
(D Haydn Jones) *dwlt: hld up in last trio: nt clr run over 2f out: pushed along and only 11th ent fnl f: nt clr run again sn after: r.o fnl 100yds* **33/1**

0003 **8** *1 ¼* **Harlech Castle**[11] 7478 4-8-9 **76**................(b) NickyMackay 1 67
(J R Boyle) *gd spd fr wdst draw to press ldng pair: wknd wl over 1f out* **16/1**

5505 **9** *1 ¼* **Brierty (IRE)**[11] 7478 3-8-12 **79**................ KFallon 6 66
(D Carroll) *restless stalls: nvr beyond midfield: no prog 2f out: fdd* **10/1**

0366 **10** *¾* **Beat The Bell**[13] 7454 4-9-4 **85**................(p) ShaneKelly 2 70
(J A Osborne) *chsd ldrs: rdn over 2f out: grad wknd fr over 1f out* **20/1**

The Form Book, Raceform Ltd, Compton, RG20 6NL

434 **11** ¾ **Cecily**[7] 7511 3-8-13 **80**..(b) SebSanders 5 62
(Sir Mark Prescott) *w ldr tl wknd rapidly over 1f out* **8/1**

5650 **12** 6 **Pearly Wey**[60] 6482 6-9-3 **84**.................................. AdamKirby 10 47
(I W McInnes) *jockey v late in removing blindfold in stalls: mostly in last and nvr able to rcvr: brief effrt over 2f out: sn wknd* **6/1**[2]

1m 11.42s (-1.68) **Going Correction** +0.05s/f (Slow) **12** Ran SP% **123.9**
Speed ratings (Par 105): **113,112,111,111,110 110,107,105,104,103 102,94**
toteswingers: 1&2 £4.00, 1&3 £18.50, 2&3 £11.60 CSF £23.26 CT £278.57 TOTE £7.20: £2.90, £1.70, £6.50; EX 17.60.
Owner Charlee & Hollie Allan **Bred** Vincent Dunne **Trained** East Everleigh, Wilts

FOCUS
A competitive sprint handicap run in a time only 0.31 seconds outside the track record. Solid form overall, although the runner-up was unlucky.
Thunderous Mood(USA) Official explanation: jockey said colt hung right
Harlech Castle ◆ Official explanation: jockey said gelding had no more to give
Beat The Bell Official explanation: jockey said gelding lost its action
Pearly Wey Official explanation: jockey said gelding missed the break

7614 TRY OUR NEW BISTRO MENU CLASSIFIED STKS 7f (P)
9:20 (9:21) (Class 6) 3-Y-O+ **£2,047** (£604; £302) **Stalls** High

Form RPR

5604 **1** **Harting Hill**[11] 7492 4-9-0 54.................................. GeorgeBaker 11 62+
(M P Tregoning) *sn trckd ldng pair on inner: swtchd lft over 2f out: carried lft after: rdn and styd on to ld over 1f out: wl in command fnl f* **9/4**[1]

0020 **2** 1 ½ **Cavalry Guard (USA)**[14] 7433 5-8-9 50..................(b) AmyBaker(5) 14 58
(T D McCarthy) *hld up in midfield on inner: prog fr 2f out: styd on to take 2nd ins fnl f: unable to chal* **16/1**

6660 **3** 1 ¾ **Running Flush (USA)**[28] 7240 3-9-0 54......................(b[1]) LukeMorris 9 53
(J R Gask) *t.k.h early: trckd ldrs on inner: rdn fr 3f out: effrt 2f out: kpt on to take 3rd wl ins fnl f* **6/1**

2506 **4** ½ **Battimoore (IRE)**[4] 7572 3-9-0 50.................................. AdamKirby 7 52
(I W McInnes) *hld up in last pair: prog and swtchd to inner 2f out: styd on to take 4th nr fin: nvr nrr* **33/1**

0400 **5** 1 **My Flame**[14] 7433 4-9-0 52..(b[1]) NCallan 3 49
(J R Jenkins) *sn pressed ldr: chal 2f out: hung bdly lft after: upsides over 1f out: wknd* **25/1**

0065 **6** 1 ¼ **Kamanja (UAE)**[7] 7521 3-8-7 52.................................. KierenFox(7) 12 46
(M J Attwater) *hld up in last pair: prog 2f out: rdn over 1f out: kpt on: nvr nr ldrs* **14/1**

5425 **7** *shd* **Clerical (USA)**[31] 7197 3-9-0 55.................................(v[1]) JimCrowley 4 46
(R M H Cowell) *wl in tch: effrt and rdn over 2f out: no prog over 1f out: one pce after* **13/2**

0060 **8** *nk* **Turfwolke (GER)**[104] 5195 4-9-0 53.......................... FergusSweeney 8 45
(Mrs H S Main) *led: edgd lft 2f out: hdd & wknd over 1f out* **11/2**[3]

0055 **9** 2 ¼ **Cativo**[4] 7576 3-8-11 45..(t) JamesMillman(3) 10 39
(B R Millman) *t.k.h: hld up wl in rr: struggling and no prog over 2f out: n.d after* **25/1**

0056 **10** ½ **Madhal**[40] 7002 3-8-11 52......................................(e[1]) RobertLButler(3) 1 37
(Matthew Salaman) *plld hrd: racd wd: in tch to over 2f out: sn btn* **25/1**

022 **11** 5 **Great Bounder (CAN)**[8] 7500 3-9-0 55.......................... RobertWinston 5 24
(J R Best) *racd v wd: prom: lost grnd bnd 4f out to 3f out: sn btn* **3/1**[2]

06-0 **12** 2 ¾ **Tagula Minx (IRE)**[40] 7004 3-9-0 51.......................... SaleemGolam 6 16
(J Pearce) *chsd ldrs to 2f out: wknd u.str.p* **33/1**

50-0 **13** 2 ¼ **Misterisland (IRE)**[16] 7417 4-9-0 54........................(be[1]) EddieAhern 2 10
(M Mullineaux) *racd wd: chsd ldrs: lost grnd bnd fr 4f out: wknd 3f out* **66/1**

1m 26.26s (0.26) **Going Correction** +0.05s/f (Slow) **13** Ran SP% **130.2**
Speed ratings (Par 101): **100,98,96,95,94 93,93,92,90,89 83,80,78**
toteswingers: 1&2 £9.90, 1&3 £5.50, 2&3 £15.00 CSF £42.91 TOTE £3.40: £1.40, £6.20, £3.00; EX 57.30 Place 6: £168.20 Place 5: £65.86 .
Owner Miss S Sharp **Bred** Stanley J Sharp **Trained** Lambourn, Berks
■ Stewards' Enquiry : George Baker one-day ban: careless riding (Dec 16)

FOCUS
A very moderate contest but the form looks sound, with a clear personal best from the winner.
Kamanja(UAE) Official explanation: jockey said filly suffered interference in running
Cativo Official explanation: jockey said filly was struck into
T/Plt: £151.50 to a £1 stake. Pool: £106,964.58. 515.30 winning tickets. T/Qpdt: £22.90 to a £1 stake. Pool: £8,000.74. 258.40 winning tickets. JN

7594 WOLVERHAMPTON (A.W) (L-H)
Thursday, December 3

OFFICIAL GOING: Standard
Wind: Light half behind Weather: Fine

7615 TOTEPLACEPOT WIN WITHOUT BACKING A WINNER APPRENTICE H'CAP 1m 141y(P)
3:45 (3:45) (Class 5) (60-92,70) 3-Y-O+ **£2,590** (£770; £385; £192) **Stalls** Low

Form RPR

0650 **1** **Justcallmehandsome**[5] 7575 7-8-13 **67**.........................(v) BillyCray(5) 2 78+
(D J S Ffrench Davis) *chsd ldng pair: led wl over 2f out: sn clr: eased towards fin* **4/1**[3]

3056 **2** 2 ½ **Ella Woodcock (IRE)**[24] 7322 5-8-13 **62**.......................... KellyHarrison 8 66+
(E J Alston) *hld up and bhd: hdwy 2f out: squeezed through jst over 1f out: wnt 2nd jst ins fnl f: no ch w wnr* **7/2**[2]

2415 **3** 3 **Castle Myth (USA)**[9] 7500 3-8-3 **61**..........................(bt) AdamCarter(7) 4 58+
(B Ellison) *hld up in rr: pushed along and hdwy whn nt clr run wl over 1f out: swtchd lft ent fnl f: kpt on to take 3rd ins fnl f* **11/4**[1]

0000 **4** 1 ¾ **Son Of Monsieur**[13] 7464 3-8-0 **56** oh8.......................... RyanPowell(5) 5 49
(G R Oldroyd) *hld up: hdwy over 2f out: chsd wnr over 1f out tl rdn jst ins fnl f: one pce* **66/1**

0010 **5** 2 ¾ **Shannon Golden**[29] 7241 3-8-8 **59**......................(t) RussellKennemore 3 46
(S R Bowring) *hld up: pushed along and hdwy over 2f out: swtchd lft wl over 1f out: sn rdn: no further prog* **22/1**

6323 **6** *nse* **Via Mia**[15] 7428 3-9-4 **69**.. AndreaAtzeni 6 56
(George Baker) *hld up: pushed along and hdwy on outside over 2f out: rdn wl over 1f out: wknd ins fnl f* **11/4**[1]

1300 **7** *nk* **King Of The Moors (USA)**[29] 7247 6-9-4 **70**............(b) JamieJones(3) 1 56
(R C Guest) *led: hdd over 6f out: w ldr: led wl over 3f out tl wl over 2f out: wkng whn bmpd jst over 1f out* **16/1**

4006 **8** 11 **Bold Bomber**[21] 7353 3-7-12 **56** oh6.......................... JordanLDodd(7) 9 17
(Paul Green) *stdd s: sn swtchd lft: hld up wl in rr: rdn over 2f out: no rspnse* **50/1**

6200 **9** 2 ½ **Echo Dancer**[37] 7093 3-8-12 **66**.................................. MartinLane(3) 11 21
(T Wall) *sn chsng ldrs: pushed along over 3f out: wkng whn hmpd wl over 1f out* **22/1**

000- **10** 28 **Blushing Dreamer (IRE)**[376] 7425 3-8-0 **56** oh11.......... RyanClark(5) 7 —
(Miss N A Lloyd-Beavis) *t.k.h: sn w ldr: led over 6f out tl wl over 3f out: wknd qckly over 2f out: t.o* **100/1**

1m 49.54s (-0.96) **Going Correction** -0.075s/f (Stan)
WFA 3 from 5yo+ 2lb **10** Ran SP% **114.6**
Speed ratings (Par 103): **101,98,96,94,92 92,91,82,79,54**
toteswingers:1&2:£4.40, 2&3:£3.40, 1&3:£3.60 CSF £17.27 CT £45.07 TOTE £5.10: £1.70, £1.60, £1.90; EX 19.60.
Owner Mrs J E Taylor **Bred** Mrs J E Taylor **Trained** Lambourn, Berks

FOCUS
An ordinary contest run at a decent clip and won very easily by course specialist. The runner-up sets the level.
Blushing Dreamer(IRE) Official explanation: jockey said filly ran too free

7616 STAY AT THE WOLVERHAMPTON HOLIDAY INN (S) STKS 1m 141y(P)
4:15 (4:15) (Class 6) 2-Y-O **£2,047** (£604; £302) **Stalls** Low

Form RPR

2042 **1** **Bubbly Braveheart (IRE)**[3] 7597 2-8-12 62..........(p) RobertWinston 12 64+
(A Bailey) *a.p: led 2f out: rdn over 1f out: drvn out* **6/5**[1]

2300 **2** *nk* **Glen Lass**[12] 7474 2-8-7 57..(b[1]) SaleemGolam 8 58
(J Pearce) *hld up towards rr: rdn over 2f out: hdwy wl over 1f out: wnt 2nd ins fnl f: r.o* **20/1**

0 **3** 2 ¼ **Grams And Ounces**[41] 6990 2-8-12 0.......................... JerryO'Dwyer 2 59
(Miss Amy Weaver) *hld up towards rr: pushed along and hdwy over 2f out: sn rdn: kpt on same pce fnl f* **9/1**

0100 **4** 9 **Tiger Hawk (USA)**[3] 7597 2-8-12 62..................(b) AndrewHeffernan(5) 1 45
(P D Evans) *mde most: hdd 3f out: rdn wl over 1f out: wknd fnl f* **11/1**

00 **5** *nk* **Develop U**[12] 7474 2-8-9 0.. JackDean(3) 5 39
(W G M Turner) *hld up towards rr: pushed along over 2f out: sme prog over 1f out: n.d* **100/1**

0006 **6** 2 **Feel The Magic (IRE)**[8] 7514 2-8-7 53.......................... LPKeniry 13 30
(S Kirk) *hld up towards rr: hdwy 5f out: pushed along and wknd wl over 1f out* **40/1**

00 **7** 4 **Franki J**[34] 7157 2-8-7 0.. DavidProbert 7 22
(D Donovan) *w ldr: led 3f out to 2f out: wknd over 1f out* **9/2**[2]

5000 **8** 3 ¾ **Elie Shore**[45] 6895 2-8-4 60..(v) MartinLane(3) 9 14
(P C Haslam) *hld up in mid-div: rdn and short-lived effrt on ins over 2f out* **33/1**

4304 **9** 2 ¾ **Izuizorizuain't (IRE)**[9] 7501 2-8-7 56..........................(b) PaulHanagan 10 8
(K A Ryan) *t.k.h: hdwy over 6f out: wknd over 2f out* **10/1**

00 **10** 8 **Master Of Song**[38] 7058 2-8-12 0..........................(b[1]) AmirQuinn 11 —
(S R Bowring) *s.s: hld up in rr: hdwy over 5f out: rdn and wknd wl over 2f out* **66/1**

300 **11** 1 ¾ **Cotton Top (IRE)**[47] 6842 2-8-7 62.......................... ChrisCatlin 6 —
(M R Channon) *prom tl pushed along and wknd 4f out* **6/1**[3]

04 **12** 40 **Charmaxjoanne**[97] 5393 2-8-2 0.......................... PatrickDonaghy(5) 4 —
(P C Haslam) *a towards rr: pushed along over 3f out: eased whn no ch wl over 1f out* **50/1**

1m 50.49s (-0.01) **Going Correction** -0.075s/f (Stan) **12** Ran SP% **119.9**
Speed ratings (Par 94): **97,96,94,86,86 84,81,77,75,68 66,31**
toteswingers:1&2:£8.50, 2&3:£24.70, 1&3:£8.10 CSF £34.72 TOTE £1.90: £1.10, £4.20, £2.80; EX 32.20.There was no bid for the winner.
Owner The Champagne Club **Bred** Albert Conneally **Trained** Newmarket, Suffolk

FOCUS
A moderate seller rated through the exposed runner-up to her best.

NOTEBOOK
Bubbly Braveheart(IRE), second in a C&D handicap off 62 last time out, set the standard on this drop in class. His rider did well to overcome the outside stall and get him into a prominent position early, and it was fairly straightforward from there. The form looks solid enough for the level and on what we've seen already he should remain competitive back in handicap company. (op 6-4 tchd 11-10)
Glen Lass took a while to get into top gear but, not for the first time, finished her race off really well. The positive effect of cheekpieces wore off pretty quickly, and it remains to be seen whether the blinkers go the same way. (op 16-1)
Grams And Ounces was always towards the rear on his debut in a Doncaster maiden, but this was a much easier assignment and he ran well despite being on and off the bridle for much of the way. Open to further improvement, he should be able to find a similar race. (op 10-1 tchd 14-1)
Tiger Hawk(USA), whose only win to date came at Southwell, has a style of running and pedigree that is far more suited to Fibresand. He'll be something to bet on when returning to that track. (op 16-1)
Izuizorizuain't(IRE)'s rider reported that the filly hung right. Official explanation: jockey said filly hung right (op 8-1 tchd 11-1)
Master Of Song Official explanation: jockey said gelding hung right
Cotton Top(IRE) looked favoured by the weights judged by her official rating, but her previous three outings had seen a lesser effort each time. She lacks size and was weak in the market beforehand. She dropped right out before the turn out of the back straight. (op 5-1)

7617 TOTESWINGER THREE WAYS TO WIN H'CAP 7f 32y(P)
4:45 (4:45) (Class 4) (0-85,81) 3-Y-O+ **£5,046** (£1,510; £755; £377; £188) **Stalls** High

Form RPR

011 **1** **Arteus**[22] 7327 3-9-1 **77**..(b) ShaneKelly 4 89+
(Jane Chapple-Hyam) *mde all: rdn and edgd sltly rt jst over 1f out: r.o wl* **5/1**[3]

2233 **2** 2 ¼ **Autumn Blades (IRE)**[15] 7437 4-9-1 **77**.......................(p) DavidProbert 7 83
(A Bailey) *hld up in tch: kpt on to take 2nd wl ins fnl f: nt trble wnr* **7/1**

2101 **3** ¾ **Tourist**[5] 7577 4-9-5 **81** 6ex.. DaneO'Neill 5 85
(D Shaw) *chsd wnr: rdn jst over 1f out: no ex and lost 2nd ins fnl f* **11/4**[1]

0235 **4** 1 **Chief Exec**[22] 7327 7-8-13 **75**..(b) AdamKirby 3 76
(J R Gask) *hld up in rr: pushed along over 2f out: swtchd rt and c wd st: hdwy 1f out: r.o ins fnl f: nvr nrr* **8/1**

340 **5** 3 ½ **Toto Skyllachy**[26] 7287 4-9-3 **79**.. IanMongan 2 71
(S Gollings) *hld up: pushed along jst over 2f out: rdn over 1f out: no hdwy* **9/2**[2]

3116 **6** ¾ **Hellbender (IRE)**[12] 7486 3-8-11 **78**.......................... LeeNewnes(5) 8 68
(S Kirk) *prom: rdn 2f out: edgd rt and wknd 1f out* **8/1**

5004 **7** 2 **Gallantry**[15] 7437 7-8-13 **80**.......................... AndrewHeffernan(5) 1 64
(P Howling) *s.i.s: sn hld up in tch: rdn over 2f out: sn wknd* **8/1**

0056 **8** ½ **Dancing Maite**[46] 6879 4-9-1 **77**.. AmirQuinn 6 60
(S R Bowring) *hld up towards rr: rdn and sme prog on outside 2f out: c wd st: wknd over 1f out* **25/1**

5020 **9** 6 **Kashimin (IRE)**[30] 7220 4-9-0 **76**..............................(b) RobertWinston 9 43
(G A Swinbank) *t.k.h: sme prog on outside over 3f out: pushed along and wknd 2f out* **16/1**

1m 28.05s (-1.55) **Going Correction** -0.075s/f (Stan) **9** Ran SP% **117.1**
Speed ratings (Par 105): **105,102,101,100,96 95,93,92,85**
toteswingers:1&2:£6.10, 2&3:£5.10, 1&3:£3.80 CSF £40.38 CT £115.88 TOTE £4.70: £1.90, £2.40, £1.70; EX 23.60.
Owner Norcroft Park Stud **Bred** Norcroft Park Stud **Trained** Newmarket, Suffolk

FOCUS
Not a bad handicap, and it was one of the two progressive 3-y-os who came out on top. The runner-up is the best guide to the level.
Kashimin(IRE) Official explanation: jockey said gelding ran too free

7618 TOTEEXACTA THE BETTER VALUE FORECAST MAIDEN STKS 5f 216y(P)
5:15 (5:16) (Class 5) 2-Y-O **£2,590** (£770; £385; £192) **Stalls** Low

Form RPR

2 **1** **Wellmarked (IRE)**[115] 4856 2-9-3 0.................................. EddieAhern 5 76+
(John A Quinn, Ire) *chsd ldr: rdn wl over 1f out: led jst ins fnl f: r.o* **1/2**[1]

2 ¾ **Katy's Secret** 2-8-12 0.. LPKeniry 3 66
(W Jarvis) *s.i.s: sn hld up in tch: rdn jst over 1f out: tk 2nd ins fnl f: kpt on* **12/1**

0 **3** 3 ¼ **Sparking**[166] 3152 2-8-12 0... JimmyQuinn 7 56
(Mrs G S Rees) *hld up: hdwy on ins wl over 1f out: sn pushed along: one pce ins fnl f* **33/1**

00 **4** 1 ½ **Special Betty**[6] 7556 2-8-12 0.. AdamKirby 4 52
(D Haydn Jones) *led: rdn over 1f out: hdd jst ins fnl f: sn wknd* **66/1**

0424 **5** nk **Brinscall**[47] 6842 2-8-12 70.. PaulHanagan 1 51
(R A Fahey) *prom: rdn wl over 1f out: wknd ins fnl f* **10/3**[2]

6 4 ½ **Court Drinking (USA)** 2-9-3 0................................... RobertWinston 8 42
(J R Best) *s.i.s: pushed along over 3f out: a in rr* **7/1**[3]

7 1 ¼ **Paint By Numbers** 2-9-3 0.. ChrisCatlin 6 38
(J A Glover) *s.i.s: a in rr* **20/1**

8 hd **Burning Thread (IRE)** 2-9-0 0................................. MartinLane(3) 9 38
(T J Etherington) *s.i.s: pushed along over 3f out: a in rr* **20/1**

1m 15.24s (0.24) **Going Correction** -0.075s/f (Stan) **8** Ran SP% **123.9**
Speed ratings (Par 96): **95,94,89,87,87 81,79,79**
toteswingers:1&2:£2.80, 2&3:£33.40, 1&3:£8.10 CSF £9.18 TOTE £1.50: £1.02, £3.80, £9.90; EX 10.10.
Owner Charles McGrath **Bred** Charlie McGrath **Trained** Blackmiller Hill, Co. Kildare

FOCUS
A weak maiden won by the well-backed odds-on favourite, who can rate higher, with the third and fourth possibly flattered.

NOTEBOOK
Wellmarked(IRE), runner-up on his debut here back in August, he ran without the tongue-tie this time but it didn't seem to make any difference and he won cosily enough. His future lies in the hands of the assessor, but a mark in the low-70s looks likely, and he should be a player in handicaps with improvement to come. (op 8-13 tchd 4-5 in a place)
Katy's Secret, whose dam won a couple of juvenile sprints on the Fibresand, is bred to be speedy, but her stable isn't known for getting them revved up first time. This was a promising debut and she can only improve. (op 11-1)
Sparking, off the track since finishing last on her debut in June, is a half-sister to six winners. She was keeping on at the finish and will make more appeal in handicaps after one more run.
Special Betty, behind throughout in her first two starts, broke best of all this time and made much of the running. She clearly has more ability than had previously been suggested, and she can go the handicap route now.
Brinscall looked to hold solid claims on paper but her rider was always niggling along on her and she was one-paced in the straight. (op 3-1 tchd 7-2)
Court Drinking(USA), who has a dirt sprinter's pedigree, was slowest away and ran green. He'll come on for the experience. His rider reported that he missed the break and ran green. Official explanation: jockey said colt missed the break and ran green (op 9-1)

7619 CLEANEVENT NURSERY 5f 216y(P)
5:45 (5:45) (Class 6) (0-65,65) 2-Y-O **£2,388** (£705; £352) **Stalls** Low

Form RPR

0332 **1** **Admiral Cochrane (IRE)**[8] 7514 2-9-4 **62**...................... RobertHavlin 1 70+
(W Jarvis) *hld up and bhd: hdwy whn nt clr run wl over 1f out: rdn to ld wl ins fnl f: r.o* **1/1**[1]

4360 **2** ¾ **Cane Cat (IRE)**[29] 7242 2-8-6 **50**................................ FrancisNorton 3 54
(A W Carroll) *hld up in mid-div: hdwy on ins wl over 1f out: led jst over 1f out: sn edgd rt: rdn and hdd wl ins fnl f: nt qckn* **10/1**

304 **3** 1 ¾ **Slip Sliding Away (IRE)**[12] 7485 2-9-6 **64**.................... SteveDrowne 7 63
(J R Best) *hld up towards rr: pushed along 3f out: hdwy over 1f out: rdn and kpt on to take 3rd wl ins fnl f* **6/1**[2]

6506 **4** ¾ **Rightcar**[6] 7559 2-8-11 **55**.. LPKeniry 6 51
(Peter Grayson) *hld up in rr: hdwy on ins whn n.m.r briefly jst over 1f out: rdn and nt qckn ins fnl f* **33/1**

6545 **5** 2 ¼ **Maragna (IRE)**[22] 7333 2-8-0 **49** ow1................ AndrewHeffernan(5) 4 39
(Paul Green) *hld up in mid-div: rdn wl over 1f out: kpt on same pce fnl f* **28/1**

4661 **6** ¾ **Fair Bunny**[16] 7421 2-9-7 **65**.. JimmyQuinn 10 52
(A D Brown) *prom: pushed along and edgd lft jst over 1f out: rdn and wknd ins fnl f* **9/1**

020 **7** nk **Sixties Rock**[51] 6754 2-9-3 **61**... EddieAhern 2 47
(J A Glover) *s.i.s: in rr: pushed along over 1f out: kpt on fnl f: n.d* **13/2**[3]

0400 **8** nk **Mind Of Her Own**[8] 7514 2-8-11 **60**........................ RichardEvans(5) 11 45
(P D Evans) *sn led: rdn and hdd over 1f out: wknd ins fnl f* **66/1**

0500 **9** 1 ½ **Crushing (IRE)**[6] 7559 2-9-0 **58**............................(p) GrahamGibbons 8 39
(A J McCabe) *hld up in mid-div: pushed along over 2f out: c wd st: rdn and wknd wl over 1f out* **14/1**

4036 **10** ½ **Taeping (IRE)**[5] 7584 2-8-12 **56**............................(p) RobertWinston 9 35
(R Hollinshead) *led early: prom: btn whn nt clr run over 1f out* **22/1**

340 **11** ½ **Bitter Honey**[48] 6826 2-9-5 **63**...................................... PaulHanagan 5 41
(Mrs G S Rees) *prom: pushed along whn bmpd wl over 1f out: rdn and wknd ins fnl f* **40/1**

040 **12** 2 ¼ **Star Twilight**[22] 7325 2-9-4 **62**.....................................(t) ChrisCatlin 12 33
(D R Lanigan) *w ldr: ev ch over 2f out: rdn and edgd lft wl over 1f out: sn wknd* **14/1**

1m 15.28s (0.28) **Going Correction** -0.075s/f (Stan) **12** Ran SP% **124.7**
Speed ratings (Par 94): **95,94,91,90,87 86,86,85,83,83 82,79**
toteswingers:1&2:£6.20, 2&3:£8.20, 1&3:£3.50 CSF £12.44 CT £49.10 TOTE £1.90: £1.30, £2.20, £1.70; EX 15.60.
Owner Dr J Walker **Bred** E Landi **Trained** Newmarket, Suffolk

FOCUS
An ordinary nursery featuring only one previous winner. The form is rated around those in the frame behind the winner.

NOTEBOOK
Admiral Cochrane(IRE) bumped into one last time out at Kempton, but that form had been given a big boost the previous day when the winner went in again off a 6lb higher mark. That suggested that this colt, whose mark remained unchanged, was well handicapped, and he was sent off a well-supported even-money favourite, having been as big as 15-8 in the morning. Things didn't go entirely smoothly in the race, as he missed the break and was behind a wall of horses turning in, but the gap came for him on the inside and he quickened up well once in the clear. He looks up to defying a penalty on this evidence. (op 11-8 tchd 10-11)
Cane Cat(IRE), drawn low like the winner, raced in front of him on the inside for much of the way. She hung right approaching the furlong pole, though, which presented Admiral Cochrane with the gap he needed. She kept on well enough for second but has a fairly exposed profile. (op 9-1)
Slip Sliding Away(IRE), who was a little free to post, didn't break particularly well so was rushed up to make up lost ground, then reined back before being vigorously pushed along. He stayed on well through beaten horses and shaped as though capable of better. (op 9-2)
Rightcar, dropped out and ridden patiently over this longer trip, seemed to stay all right, but he's another who looks pretty exposed now.
Fair Bunny found the combination of a 6lb higher mark, a quicker surface and an outside draw too much to overcome. (op 10-1)
Sixties Rock raced too freely in maiden company and was given a ride here that suggested the priority was to teach him to settle. (op 10-1)

7620 TOTEPOOL A BETTER WAY TO BET H'CAP 1m 1f 103y(P)
6:15 (6:15) (Class 4) (0-85,80) 3-Y-O **£5,046** (£1,510; £755; £377; £188) **Stalls** Low

Form RPR

2222 **1** **Iron Out (USA)**[16] 7423 3-8-9 **71**.................................. RobertWinston 1 79
(R Hollinshead) *a.p on ins: pushed along and swtchd rt ent st: rdn to ld wl ins fnl f: r.o* **15/2**

4021 **2** 1 ¼ **Oriental Cavalier**[21] 7361 3-8-8 **70**.......................(p) GrahamGibbons 2 76
(R Hollinshead) *led: rdn and edgd rt over 1f out: hdd wl ins fnl f: nt qckn* **11/2**[3]

0333 **3** hd **Andhaar**[63] 6420 3-9-4 **80**... IanMongan 3 85
(S Gollings) *a.p: jnd ldr and edgd lft jst over 2f out: rdn wl over 1f out: ev ch ins fnl f: nt qckn* **8/1**

1300 **4** 7 **Ladies Dancing**[17] 7413 3-8-10 **72**................................ ShaneKelly 7 63
(J A Osborne) *sn w ldr: n.m.r briefly jst over 2f out: sn wknd* **40/1**

0002 **5** nk **Capeability (IRE)**[15] 7428 3-8-9 **71**.............................. TonyCulhane 6 61
(M R Channon) *hld up in last: prog on outside over 2f out: c wd st: wknd wl over 1f out* **5/1**[2]

6 1 **Scrupulous**[107] 5139 3-8-10 **72**............................. RichardKingscote 5 60
(Tom Dascombe) *stdd s: t.k.h: pushed along jst over 2f out: sn struggling* **22/1**

041- **7** 1 **Prohibition (IRE)**[393] 7200 3-9-4 **80**............................ JamieSpencer 4 66
(W J Haggas) *t.k.h: stdy prog over 3f out: rdn 2f out: edgd lft and wknd wl over 1f out* **4/6**[1]

2m 0.77s (-0.93) **Going Correction** -0.075s/f (Stan) **7** Ran SP% **121.7**
Speed ratings (Par 104): **101,99,99,93,93 92,91**
toteswingers:1&2:£3.50, 2&3:£2.80, 1&3:£3.70 CSF £51.30 TOTE £8.40: £3.00, £2.60; EX 27.50 Place 6 £31.30, Place 5 £20.68.
Owner John L Marriott **Bred** Leslie Hagan **Trained** Upper Longdon, Staffs

FOCUS
There wasn't much pace on here and it paid to race handily. The runner-up to his best looks the guide to the form for now.
Scrupulous Official explanation: jockey said filly ran too free
Prohibition(IRE) Official explanation: trainer's rep said colt ran too free
T/Plt: £29.40 to a £1 stake. Pool: £72,624.90. 1,798.83 winning tickets. T/Qpdt: £10.10 to a £1 stake. Pool: £8,983.17. 653.56 winning tickets. KH

6978 DEAUVILLE (R-H)
Thursday, December 3

OFFICIAL GOING: Standard

7621a PRIX LUTHIER (LISTED RACE) (ALL-WEATHER) 7f 110y
1:25 (1:28) 3-Y-O+ **£25,243** (£10,097; £7,573; £5,049; £2,524)

RPR

1 **Dalghar (FR)**[35] 3-8-11 .... J-BEyquem 16 —
(A De Royer-Dupre, France)

2 1 ½ **Rockette (FR)**[29] 4-8-8 .... MaximeFoulon 11 —
(Y De Nicolay, France)

3 hd **Desertar (FR)**[77] 3-8-11 .... GBenoist 9 —
(P Demercastel, France)

4 1 ½ **Kachgai (IRE)**[61] 6505 6-9-1 .... P-CBoudot 5 —
(Y De Nicolay, France)

5 ¾ **Polarix**[55] 6657 3-8-11 .... FVeron 12 —
(H-A Pantall, France)

6 1 ½ **Red Dune (IRE)**[46] 6886 4-8-8 .... F-XBertras 7 —
(M A Jarvis) *mid-div: 10th st: outpcd 2f out: swtchd outside over 1f out: r.o ins fnl f: n.d* **15/1**[1]

7 hd **Stop Making Sense**[32] 7216 7-8-11 .... JAuge 15 —
(R Pritchard-Gordon, France)

8 shd **Violon Sacre (USA)**[73] 6176 4-9-1 .... FBlondel 10 —
(J-C Rouget, France)

9 hd **Sokar (FR)**[37] 3-8-11 .... MAndrouin 8 —
(J Boisnard, France)

10 1 ½ **Kfar Yona (FR)**[23] 6-8-11 .... RMarchelli 2 —
(A Bonin, France)

11 **Belliflore (FR)**[394] 7187 5-8-8 .... MSautjeau 6 —
(Y Fouin, France)

12 **Salut L'Africain (FR)**[14] 7458 4-9-1 ....(p) THuet 3 —
(Robert Collet, France)

13 **Slickly Royal (FR)**[70] 5-8-11 ....(p) SMaillot 1 —
(P Demercastel, France)

14 **Take D'Or (FR)**[209] 1858 3-8-11 .... RonanThomas 14 —
(J Boisnard, France)

15 **Surpressa (FR)**[44] 3-8-8 .... SRuis 4 —
(Y De Nicolay, France)

1m 29.0s (89.00) **15** Ran SP% **6.3**
PARI-MUTUEL: WIN 3.10; PL 2.10, 7.70, 12.30; DF 56.90.
Owner H H Aga Khan **Bred** H H The Aga Khan's Studs S C **Trained** Chantilly, France

NOTEBOOK
Red Dune(IRE) was making her AW debut and took a while to get going before staying on late.

7602 LINGFIELD (L-H)

Friday, December 4

OFFICIAL GOING: Standard

Wind: fairly modest, across Weather: bright, chilly

7622 FRED & RON GIBSON MEMORIAL MAIDEN FILLIES' STKS (DIV I) 1m (P)

12:10 (12:11) (Class 5) 2-Y-O £2,388 (£705; £352) Stalls High

Form RPR

5 **1** **Fairy Flight (USA)**[13] 7491 2-9-0 0 JimCrowley 11 76
(W J Knight) *broke wl: w ldr tl over 4f out: styd chsng ldrs: rdn to chse ldr and edgd rt bnd 2f out: led jst ins fnl f: kpt on wl* **14/1**

63 **2** ½ **Leaving Alone (USA)**[15] 7451 2-9-0 0 RichardHughes 1 75
(R Hannon) *led at stdy gallop tl hdd over 4f out: chsd ldr after: rdn ent fnl 2f: ev ch jst ins fnl f: unable qck fnl 75yds* **4/1**[3]

4 **3** ¾ **Elvira Madigan**[15] 7451 2-9-0 0 LPKeniry 4 73
(A M Balding) *chsd ldrs: effrt on outer to chse ldng pair 3f out: racd awkwardly bnd 2f out: drvn and nt qckn fr over 1f out* **9/4**[1]

3222 **4** 2½ **Anaya**[34] 7193 2-9-0 69 KFallon 6 68
(M R Channon) *chsd ldrs tl hdwy to ld and qcknd pce over 4f out: rdn jst over 2f out: hdd jst ins fnl f: wknd fnl 75yds* **7/2**[2]

2535 **5** nk **If I Were A Boy (IRE)**[3] 7604 2-8-9 73 LeeNewnes(5) 5 67
(S Kirk) *s.i.s: sn in tch: rdn and hdwy to chse ldrs 3f out: unable qck u.p ent fnl 2f: kpt on same pce after* **8/1**

06 **6** 1¼ **Goldtrek (USA)**[9] 7522 2-9-0 0 SteveDrowne 10 64
(R Charlton) *stdd after s: hld up in tch in rr: rdn 2f out: kpt on ins fnl f: nvr trbld ldrs* **20/1**

7 1 **Al Shababiya (IRE)** 2-9-0 0 FergusSweeney 9 62+
(D M Simcock) *in tch towards rr: pushed along over 4f out: kpt on fnl f: nvr trbld ldrs* **25/1**

8 nse **Magic Spirit** 2-9-0 0 LukeMorris 3 62
(J S Moore) *s.i.s: in tch towards rr: pushed along after 1f: swtchd rt and rdn over 2f out: nvr gng pce to threaten ldrs* **66/1**

4 **9** ¾ **Lily In The Pond**[34] 7177 2-9-0 0 JerryO'Dwyer 2 60
(Miss Gay Kelleway) *chsd ldrs: rdn and struggling over 2f out: wknd over 1f out* **14/1**

10 ½ **Tallulah Mai** 2-9-0 0 SaleemGolam 7 59
(Matthew Salaman) *s.i.s: in tch in rr: rdn and no prog over 2f out: n.d* **50/1**

11 ¾ **Mushagak (IRE)** 2-9-0 0 EddieAhern 8 58
(E A L Dunlop) *s.i.s: sn in tch in midfield on outer: rdn and lost pl 3f out: n.d fnl 2f* **16/1**

1m 39.3s (1.10) **Going Correction** -0.05s/f (Stan) **11** Ran SP% **115.4**

Speed ratings (Par 93): **92,91,90,88,87 86,85,85,84,84 83**

toteswinger:1&2:£13.80, 2&3:£2.80, 1&3:£10.00 CSF £65.96 TOTE £18.00: £4.50, £1.70, £1.50; EX 99.10 TRIFECTA Part won. Pool: £220.66 - 0.55 winning units..

Owner Bluehills Racing Limited **Bred** Lynch Bages & Samac **Trained** Patching, W Sussex

FOCUS

This was a modest fillies' maiden, run at an ordinary pace. The form still looks straightforward enough with the fourth setting the level.

NOTEBOOK

Fairy Flight(USA) showed the clear benefit of her debut experience last month and got off the mark at the second attempt. She got across early from her outside stall and her rider deserves credit for not panicking as she was passed for the lead around the halfway stage. She stuck her head down gamely when asked to win the race and is entitled to go forward again for the experience. (op 11-1)

Leaving Alone(USA) saw out the trip better than had been the case at Kempton last time out, mainly due to having Hughes back on and being ridden more patiently. She really ought to find an opening during the winter and now qualifies for a mark. (op 10-3 tchd 3-1)

Elvira Madigan, who motored home behind Leaving Alone on debut at Kempton last time, was well backed to reverse that form. She broke a lot better here, but lost ground coming wide off the home bend and ultimately still proved too green to do herself full justice. This scopey filly certainly has a future and, while she now has to prove she is not as temperamental as some of her relatives, her next run should reveal more. (op 3-1)

Anaya, who came into this rated 69 and having finished second on her last three runs. She injected some much-needed pace into the race at halfway, but was a sitting duck for the principals from the furlong pole. She sets the standard. (tchd 4-1)

If I Were A Boy(IRE), easy to back, wasn't disgraced yet couldn't improve on her previous fifth over C&D five days earlier. (op 13-2)

7623 TOTEPOOL A BETTER WAY TO BET CLAIMING STKS 1m 2f (P)

12:40 (12:40) (Class 6) 3-Y-O+ £1,978 (£584; £292) Stalls Low

Form RPR

0063 **1** **Full Toss**[76] 6114 3-9-5 85 RichardHughes 8 82
(R Hannon) *hld up in last pl: hdwy over 2f out: chsd ldrs and swtchd ins over 1f out: drvn to chse ldr jst over 1f out: led fnl 100yds: hld on wl* **4/6**[1]

3112 **2** hd **Traphalgar (IRE)**[18] 7413 4-9-8 77 KFallon 5 82
(Ollie Pears) *t.k.h: stdd towards rr 9f out: hdwy to chse ldng trio and rdn over 2f out: drvn and edgd lft u.p fnl f: str chal fnl 100yds: hld nr fin* **5/2**[2]

0403 **3** 1½ **Dream Of Fortune (IRE)**[7] 7549 5-8-11 73 ow2 (t) JamieJones(5) 6 73
(M G Quinlan) *dwlt: hld up towards rr: hdwy trck ldrs 3f out: led on inner 2f out: drvn over 1f out: hdd fnl 100yds: keeping on same pce and btn whn short of room wl ins fnl f* **10/1**[3]

/00- **4** 3½ **Painted Sky**[191] 2155 6-9-2 70 EddieAhern 4 66
(R A Fahey) *chsd ldrs: sltly hmpd over 9f out: hdwy over 3f out: ev ch jst over 2f out: wknd fnl f* **20/1**

-003 **5** 4 **Awatuki (IRE)**[43] 6966 6-9-4 78 SJCraine 3 60
(J R Boyle) *chsd ldrs: wnt 2nd 4f out: led 3f out: rdn and hdd 2f out: wknd qckly over 1f out* **10/1**[3]

0050 **6** 2¼ **Kings Topic (USA)**[9] 7524 9-8-7 64 (p) AmyBaker(5) 7 50
(A B Haynes) *in tch on outer: sltly hmpd over 9f out: rdn over 3f out: wknd over press over 2f out: wl bhd over 1f out* **20/1**

6400 **7** 7 **Boffin**[85] 5790 4-8-3 46 (p) SimonPearce(5) 1 32
(Eve Johnson Houghton) *led tl hung rt and hdd over 9f out: chsd ldr after tl 4f out: sn struggling u.p: wl bhd fnl 2f* **66/1**

4000 **8** 12 **Artreju (GER)**[16] 7440 6-8-11 49 (v[1]) RobertLButler(3) 2 14
(P Butler) *dwlt: sn pushed up to go handy: led over 9f out: hdd and drvn 3f out: sn dropped out: t.o* **66/1**

2m 5.42s (-1.18) **Going Correction** -0.05s/f (Stan)

WFA 3 from 4yo+ 3lb **8** Ran SP% **119.3**

Speed ratings (Par 101): **102,101,100,97,94 92,87,77**

toteswinger:1&2:£1.10, 2&3:£3.90, 1&3:£3.20 CSF £2.55 TOTE £1.50: £1.02, £1.20, £2.40; EX 2.80 Trifecta £13.90 Part won. Pool: £489.12 - 26.01 winning units.Full Toss was claimed by P. D. Evans for £12,000. Traphalgar was claimed by P. D. Evans for £12,000

Owner R Hannon **Bred** The Queen **Trained** East Everleigh, Wilts

■ Stewards' Enquiry : K Fallon two day ban: careless riding (Dec 18-20)

FOCUS

A fair claimer but the form is muddling, with the winner not needing to run to this year's form to beat the placed horses, who are rated close to their marks.

7624 FRED & RON GIBSON MEMORIAL MAIDEN FILLIES' STKS (DIV II) 1m (P)

1:15 (1:17) (Class 5) 2-Y-O £2,388 (£705; £352) Stalls High

Form RPR

30 **1** **Gifted Apakay (USA)**[45] 6912 2-9-0 0 KFallon 4 75
(E A L Dunlop) *dwlt and pushed along early: in tch: rdn to chse ldrs ent fnl 2f: swtchd ins over 1f out: r.o wl u.p to ld towards fin* **14/1**[3]

4 **2** nk **Fashion Insider (USA)**[34] 7182 2-9-0 0 MartinDwyer 5 74
(B J Meehan) *chsd ldr tl led jst over 2f out: sn hrd pressed and drvn over 1f out: kpt on tl hdd and no ex towards fin* **30/100**[1]

0 **3** ¾ **Sasheen**[9] 7522 2-9-0 0 SJCraine 6 72
(J R Boyle) *chsd ldrs: upsides ldr ent fnl 2f: rdn over 1f out: unable qck ins fnl f* **33/1**

0 **4** 7 **Pursestrings**[15] 7450 2-9-0 0 SteveDrowne 2 57
(R Charlton) *dwlt: sn pushed along and in tch: chsd ldrs and rdn over 2f out: outpcd wl over 1f out: wnt modest 4th and edgd lft jst over 1f out* **25/1**

5 **5** 1¾ **Qaraqum (USA)**[37] 7106 2-9-0 0 DarryllHolland 7 53
(D J Coakley) *t.k.h: hld up in tch: rdn and effrt over 2f out: outpcd by ldrs jst over 2f out: no ch fr wl over 1f out* **16/1**

6 1 **Chief Wren (USA)** 2-9-0 0 LPKeniry 1 51
(E F Vaughan) *restless stalls: in tch in midfield on inner: pushed along and outpcd over 2f out: no ch fnl 2f* **33/1**

00 **7** 2½ **Mater Mater**[15] 7450 2-9-0 0 JimCrowley 3 45
(M J Scudamore) *led: hdd jst over 2f out: wknd qckly over 1f out* **25/1**

0 **8** ½ **Jinksy Minx**[167] 3160 2-9-0 0 SamHitchcott 9 44
(Miss Suzy Smith) *stdd after s: a bhd: struggling wl over 2f out: no ch fnl 2f* **100/1**

9 3¾ **Concorde Kiss (USA)** 2-9-0 0 RichardHughes 10 36
(S Kirk) *towards rr on outer: rdn over 4f out: lost tch over 3f out* **25/1**

10 ½ **Kleio** 2-9-0 0 EddieAhern 8 35
(H R A Cecil) *stdd after s: a bhd: lost tch over 3f out* **11/2**[2]

00 **11** 1½ **Aintgottaname**[20] 7390 2-9-0 0 FrankieMcDonald 11 32
(M J McGrath) *in tch on outer: rdn and struggling ent fnl 3f: wl bhd fnl 2f* **100/1**

1m 39.05s (0.85) **Going Correction** -0.05s/f (Stan) **11** Ran SP% **124.3**

Speed ratings (Par 93): **93,92,91,84,83 82,79,79,75,74 73**

toteswinger:1&2:£3.70, 2&3:£9.80, 1&3:£53.50 CSF £19.15 TOTE £12.20: £3.50, £1.02, £9.90; EX 39.10 Trifecta £447.80 Part won. Pool: £605.23 - 0.45 winning units..

Owner V I Araci **Bred** R D Hubbard **Trained** Newmarket, Suffolk

FOCUS

The second division of the fillies' maiden was run at a fair pace and the first three came well clear. The winning time was nearly half a second quicker than the first and the form looks solid enough.

NOTEBOOK

Gifted Apakay(USA) bounced right back to form and showed a gutsy attitude to come out on top. She flopped on her second outing here 45 days previously, but that clearly wasn't her true running and this return to the extra furlong is no doubt what she wanted. The best of her has likely still to be seen so it will be interesting to see what mark she is allotted. (op 12-1)

Fashion Insider(USA) looked to have outstanding claims if able to build on the promise of her Newmarket debut. She broke well and tracked the early leader, but she didn't look that comfortable nearing the top of the home straight as her rider asked her for an effort. She took time to master Sasheen and having done so at the furlong pole, her stride began to shorten. The winner mugged her at the business end and, while there was nothing wrong with her attitude, she obviously ran well below expectations. It may well be that this track was not for her and it is too soon to be writing her off. (op 4-7 tchd 4-6 in places)

Sasheen ◆ showed herself to be progressive with a much-improved effort in defeat and, clear of the rest at the finish, should soon be winning.

Pursestrings raced more professionally than she did on debut at Kempton 15 days earlier and looks the type to improve again for the experience. (op 16-1)

Qaraqum(USA) still showed signs of inexperience on this step up in trip and will be more interesting when qualifying for a mark after her next assignment.

7625 TOTESWINGER THREE WAYS TO WIN NURSERY 6f (P)

1:50 (1:51) (Class 4) (0-85,83) 2-Y-O £3,885 (£1,156; £577; £288) Stalls Low

Form RPR

0441 **1** **Sabatini (IRE)**[18] 7410 2-9-5 75 SaleemGolam 7 79
(J Pearce) *swtchd lft after s: bhd: rdn over 2f out: hdwy u.p 1f out: r.o wl to ld fnl 50yds* **11/4**[1]

0021 **2** ½ **Valmina**[21] 7372 2-9-2 72 (t) RichardKingscote 4 74+
(Tom Dascombe) *stdd after s: t.k.h: hld up in tch in last trio: edgd out rt and hdwy over 1f out: hung lft u.p ev ch fnl 100yds: kpt on* **4/1**[3]

6334 **3** ¾ **Ramamara (IRE)**[7] 7552 2-8-12 73 AndrewHeffernan(5) 5 73
(P D Evans) *led: rdn clr wl over 1f out: drvn ent fnl f: hdd and no ex fnl 50yds* **18/1**

3043 **4** 1¼ **Slip Sliding Away (IRE)**[1] 7619 2-8-8 64 SteveDrowne 2 60
(J R Best) *sn niggled along in last trio: rdn over 2f out: keeping on whn nt clr run and swtchd rt jst ins fnl f: styd on but nvr gng pce to threaten ldrs* **12/1**

2451 **5** ¾ **Transfixed (IRE)**[7] 7552 2-9-8 83 6ex RichardEvans(5) 3 77
(P D Evans) *t.k.h: chsd ldrs: rdn to dispute 2nd ent fnl 2f: no imp over 1f out: plugged on same pce after* **8/1**

3442 **6** 1¾ **Maoi Chinn Tire (IRE)**[57] 6609 2-8-11 67 (p) LPKeniry 1 56
(J S Moore) *t.k.h: chsd ldr on inner: rdn and nt pce of wnr wl over 1f out: wknd ins fnl f* **4/1**[3]

0102 **7** 1¾ **Coolree Star (IRE)**[15] 7453 2-9-7 77 JimCrowley 6 61
(J A Glover) *taken down early: sn chsng ldrs on outer: rdn and wknd bnd 2f out: sn bhd* **10/3**[2]

1m 11.25s (-0.65) **Going Correction** -0.05s/f (Stan) 2y crse rec **7** Ran SP% **113.8**

Speed ratings (Par 98): **102,101,100,98,97 95,93**

toteswinger:1&2:£2.80, 2&3:£9.70, 1&3:£8.10 CSF £13.89 TOTE £3.70: £2.00, £2.50; EX 18.20.

Owner A Watford **Bred** O Bourke **Trained** Newmarket, Suffolk

■ Stewards' Enquiry : Richard Kingscote two-day ban: careless riding (Dec 18-19)

FOCUS

A competitive nursery, run at a strong pace. The runner-up was slightly unlucky but the third stepped up on previous efforts.

NOTEBOOK

Sabatini(IRE) made a winning debut for her new connections and followed up her claiming success at Wolverhampton 18 days previously. She got a little outpaced round the home turn and took time to pick up when asked for maximum effort in the home straight, but the strong early pace ultimately played right into her hands. Her rider got stuck into her inside the closing stages and, while she may lack scope, she certainly gives her all. (op 3-1 tchd 10-3 and 7-2 in places)

Valmina, off the mark at Wolverhampton last time, proved easy to back on this step back up in trip. She was also suited by the way the race was run and, only losing out narrowly, this rates another improved effort. Official explanation: jockey said colt hung left (op 7-2 tchd 9-2)
Ramamara(IRE) failed to get revenge on the winner, but still reversed last-time-out form with Transfixed over this shorter trip and deserves credit considering she did so much early on. (op 20-1 tchd 16-1)
Slip Sliding Away(IRE) was keeping on towards the finish and posted an improved effort to that of his third at Wolverhampton the previous night. Perhaps another furlong would be more in his favour. (op 8-1)
Transfixed(IRE) ran a brave race under her penalty and is really most effective over 7f. (op 6-1)
Maoi Chinn Tire(IRE) was well backed on this drop back in trip. He proved free despite the strong early pace, though, and was cooked from the furlong marker. (op 13-2)
Coolree Star(IRE), another that got well backed, paid for chasing the early pace and ran well below his previous level. (op 9-2 tchd 3-1)

7626 BLACKBERRY LANE H'CAP — 1m (P)
2:25 (2:25) (Class 3) (0-95,95) 3-Y-0+ **£7,641** (£2,273; £1,136; £567) **Stalls** High

Form RPR
1505 **1** **Falcativ**[125] 4541 4-8-11 **87** JerryO'Dwyer 3 95+
(M Botti) *hld up in tch in midfield: gng wl whn shuffled bk towards rr jst over 2f out: rdn and hdwy between horses 1f out: r.o wl under hands and heels ins fnl f to ld nr fin* **9/2**[2]
2455 **2** *nk* **Den's Gift (IRE)**[87] 5746 5-8-6 **82** (b) LukeMorris 5 90
(C G Cox) *chsd ldr tl led 3f out: rdn clr wl over 1f out: kpt on u.p tl worn down and hdd nr fin* **6/1**[3]
0003 **3** *¾* **Glow Star (SAF)**[36] 7133 5-8-11 **87** FergusSweeney 10 93
(G L Moore) *stdd after s: t.k.h: hld up in tch in rr: effrt on outer over 2f out: carried sltly rt jst ins fnl f: edgd rt after but kpt on wl* **10/3**[1]
05 **4** *shd* **L'Hirondelle (IRE)**[9] 7523 5-8-6 **82** MartinDwyer 4 88
(M J Attwater) *t.k.h: chsd ldrs: rdn and unable qck 2f out: edgd rt u.p fr jst over 1f out: kpt on fnl f* **11/1**
4140 **5** *1* **Hawaana (IRE)**[9] 7523 4-8-2 **81** oh2 KellyHarrison(3) 7 84
(Miss Gay Kelleway) *stdd s: hld up in tch in rr: rdn and hdwy ent 2f out: swtchd rt wl over 1f out: styd on fnl f: n.m.r nr fin* **10/1**
0400 **6** *hd* **Orchard Supreme**[13] 7486 6-8-12 **88** RichardHughes 8 91
(R Hannon) *hld up in tch in rr: hdwy over 2f out: 3rd and rdn ent fnl f: no imp fnl 150yds* **7/1**
4025 **7** *5* **Carcinetto (IRE)**[13] 7486 7-9-0 **95** RichardEvans(5) 1 87
(P D Evans) *led tl 3f out: lost pl u.p over 2f out: wknd over 1f out* **33/1**
4600 **8** *1 ¼* **Samarinda (USA)**[78] 6019 6-9-3 **93** SJCraine 9 82
(Mrs P Sly) *racd in midfield: struggling and rdn over 2f out: no threat to ldrs fnl 2f* **16/1**
0002 **9** *1* **Red Somerset (USA)**[13] 7492 6-8-8 **87** WilliamCarson(3) 2 73
(R J Hodges) *dwlt: sn pushed up to chse ldrs after 1f: rdn and wkng whn n.m.r and hmpd wl over 1f out: n.d after* **14/1**
6344 **10** *2 ¼* **Spitfire**[20] 7393 4-8-10 **86** (v[1]) JimCrowley 6 67
(J R Jenkins) *t.k.h: hld up in tch: hdwy to chse ldrs over 2f out: wknd qckly over 1f out* **13/2**

1m 36.05s (-2.15) **Going Correction** -0.05s/f (Stan) course record **10** Ran SP% **114.3**
Speed ratings (Par 107): **108,107,106,106,105 105,100,99,98,96**
toteswinger:1&2:£8.40, 2&3:£8.40, 1&3:£7.80 CSF £31.01 CT £102.89 TOTE £4.50: £1.90, £2.40, £1.80; EX 35.50 Trifecta £293.90 Part won. Pool: £397.19 - 0.80 winning units..
Owner Dioscuri Srl **Bred** Az Agr Francesca **Trained** Newmarket, Suffolk

FOCUS
A good handicap, run at a solid pace and the form looks sound, with the four immediately behind the winner close to their marks.

NOTEBOOK
Falcativ, returning from a 125-day break, made a winning start for his new connections with a last-gasp success. He hugged the inner all the way round, but momentarily had to wait before making his challenge when finding a little trouble off the home bend. Once he got organised from the furlong marker, he ate up the ground and eventually won with something to spare. This was a marked drop in trip and the generous pace helped on that front. There should really be more improvement back over 1m2f and there should be more opportunities for him here this winter, but a rise back up the weights will make things tougher. (op 7-1)
Den's Gift(IRE), easy to back, has to be considered unfortunate. He wasn't left alone in the lead and went off hard enough. His response when asked to go clear was immediate and he looked to have stolen a march on his rivals, but failed to sustain his effort as the winner hit top gear. He certainly deserves compensation. (op 5-1)
Glow Star(SAF) was back up in trip and again ridden with restraint. He was never in with a serious chance and lost ground by being carried wide in the home straight, but likely ran close to his previous level. (op 3-1 tchd 11-4 and 7-2 in places)
L'Hirondelle(IRE), another to drift wide after the home turn, took time to settle just off the pace and lacked a turn of foot when asked for his effort. He wasn't suited by being unable to dominate, though, so wasn't disgraced by any means. (op 10-1 tchd 12-1)
Hawaana(IRE), 2lb out of the weights, stayed on steadily from off the pace and ran a little better than his finishing position indicates. This was more like it from him and a drop back down in class can see him back to winning ways. (op 16-1)

7627 TOTEEXACTA THE BETTER VALUE FORECAST H'CAP — 7f (P)
3:00 (3:02) (Class 5) (0-75,75) 3-Y-0+ **£2,729** (£806; £403) **Stalls** Low

Form RPR
4044 **1** **Seek The Fair Land**[15] 7456 3-8-13 **73** WilliamCarson(3) 1 83
(J R Boyle) *chsd ldng pair: effrt to ld on inner bnd 2f out: hrd pressed ent fnl f: hld on gamely u.p* **8/1**
0014 **2** *hd* **Rondeau (GR)**[23] 7327 4-9-0 **71** JimCrowley 8 81
(P R Chamings) *stdd s: hld up wl in rr: hdwy on outer jst over 2f out: str run u.p jst over 1f out: r.o wl to press wnr cl home: nt quite get to wnr* **9/2**[2]
43 **3** *nk* **Silver Guest**[6] 7575 4-9-4 **75** KFallon 3 84
(M R Channon) *t.k.h: hld up in midfield: hdwy over 2f out: swtchd ins and chsd wnr over 1f out: drvn and str chal ent fnl f: unable qck and a jst hld after: lost 2nd nr fin* **11/4**[1]
4062 **4** *2* **Labisa (IRE)**[22] 7356 3-9-0 **71** SteveDrowne 9 75
(H Morrison) *hld up wl off the pce in rr: rdn and hdwy over 2f out: chsd ldng pair and drvn ent fnl f: no ex and no imp fnl 150yds* **8/1**
2330 **5** *3 ¼* **Defector (IRE)**[9] 7516 3-9-0 **71** RichardHughes 11 66
(W R Muir) *stdd after s: hld up wl bhd in last pl: hdwy over 2f out: kpt on: nvr trbld ldrs* **12/1**
0654 **6** *nk* **I Confess**[6] 7575 4-8-11 **73** (b) RichardEvans(5) 7 67
(P D Evans) *chsd ldr tl over 2f out: sn unable qck u.p: wknd ent fnl f* **9/2**[2]
2205 **7** *3* **Suhayl Star (IRE)**[9] 7518 5-8-7 **64** LukeMorris 5 50
(P Burgoyne) *chsd ldrs: effrt and ev ch 2f out: rdn wl over 1f out: sn wknd* **25/1**
0100 **8** *5* **Hazytoo**[169] 3057 5-9-0 **71** FergusSweeney 2 43
(P J Makin) *racd keenly: led tl hdd and rdn 2f out: wknd qckly over 1f out* **33/1**
0262 **9** *2 ¼* **Shaded Edge**[21] 7364 5-8-12 **69** MartinDwyer 4 35
(D W P Arbuthnot) *nvr gng wl in rr: n.d* **15/2**[3]
0500 **10** *2 ¼* **Tidal Force (USA)**[128] 4425 3-7-12 **62** (be) DeclanCannon(7) 10 22
(A J McCabe) *in tch in midfield: rdn and struggling wl over 2f out: wl btn fnl 2f* **66/1**
-200 **11** *13* **Trading Nation (USA)**[176] 2849 3-9-1 **72** SaleemGolam 6 —
(P W Hiatt) *t.k.h: hld up in midfield: rdn and struggling over 3f out: sn wl btn: eased ins fnl f* **20/1**

1m 22.76s (-2.04) **Going Correction** -0.05s/f (Stan) course record **11** Ran SP% **117.8**
Speed ratings (Par 103): **109,108,108,106,102 102,98,92,90,87 72**
toteswinger:1&2:£13.40, 2&3:£5.90, 1&3:£9.10 CSF £42.35 CT £128.26 TOTE £11.70: £3.30, £1.80, £1.70; EX 55.10 Trifecta £154.80 Pool: £650.69 - 3.11 winning units.
Owner Chris Watkins And David N Reynolds **Bred** Raimon Bloodstock **Trained** Epsom, Surrey

FOCUS
An open handicap, run at a solid pace and sound form.

7628 BET BRISTISH WITH TOTEPOOL H'CAP — 1m 4f (P)
3:30 (3:30) (Class 4) (0-85,78) 3-Y-0+ **£4,727** (£1,406; £702; £351) **Stalls** Low

Form RPR
0054 **1** **Aurorian (IRE)**[30] 7233 3-9-1 **77** RichardHughes 3 83
(R Hannon) *led tl over 8f out: chsd ldr after tl 3f out: stl wl in tch: rdn and hdwy on inner to chse ldr again ent fnl f: r.o wl to ld nr fin* **5/2**[2]
4412 **2** *½* **Mannlichen**[8] 7539 3-9-2 **78** GregFairley 5 83
(M Johnston) *chsd ldr tl led over 8f out: rdn ent fnl 2f: hrd pressed ins fnl f: hdd and no ex nr fin* **8/11**[1]
1 **3** *2* **Gunslinger (FR)**[15] 6595 4-9-7 **78** KFallon 4 80
(M J Scudamore) *hld up in last pair: rdn and effrt on outer bnd 2f out: no imp tl styd on u.p ins fnl f to go 3rd fnl 100yds: nt pce to chal ldrs* **7/1**[3]
0404 **4** *½* **Inch Lodge**[17] 7425 7-8-4 **64** oh8 (t) WilliamCarson(3) 2 65
(Miss D Mountain) *stdd s: hld up in last pair: hdwy on outer to press ldr over 2f out: unable qck u.p wl over 1f out: one pce after* **25/1**
14 **5** *1 ¼* **Slip**[32] 4450 4-9-4 **75** SJCraine 1 74
(Tim Vaughan) *trckd ldng pair: wnt 2nd briefly 3f out: rdn and unable qck over 1f out: no imp and btn ins fnl f* **16/1**

2m 35.31s (2.31) **Going Correction** -0.05s/f (Stan)
WFA 3 from 4yo+ 5lb **5** Ran SP% **108.7**
Speed ratings (Par 105): **90,89,88,88,87**
CSF £4.57 TOTE £3.40: £1.60, £1.10; EX 7.30 Place 6 £4.84, Place 5 £3.09.
Owner Martin Mitchell **Bred** Richard Moses Bloodstock **Trained** East Everleigh, Wilts

FOCUS
An interesting little handicap. Unsurprisingly it proved a tactical affair, but the two market leaders still fought out the finish. The time was slow and the form is muddling.
T/Jkpt: Not won. T/Plt: £10.30 to a £1 stake. Pool: £49,469.22. 3,486.67 winning tickets. T/Qpdt: £5.80 to a £1 stake. Pool: £4,533.76. 575.40 winning tickets. SP

7615 WOLVERHAMPTON (A.W) (L-H)
Friday, December 4

OFFICIAL GOING: Standard
Wind: Nil Weather: Raining

7629 CLEANDOMAIN MAIDEN STKS — 5f 20y(P)
6:50 (6:51) (Class 5) 3-Y-0+ **£2,729** (£806; £403) **Stalls** Low

Form RPR
1 **Norse Warrior (USA)**[27] 7299 3-9-3 73 (v[1]) LPKeniry 2 68
(David P Myerscough, Ire) *wnt rt s: a.p: hrd rdn over 1f out: r.o u.p to ld cl home* **9/2**
0220 **2** *½* **Rocket Ruby**[4] 7601 3-8-12 54 DaneO'Neill 6 61
(D Shaw) *led: rdn over 1f out: hdd cl home* **4/1**[3]
5533 **3** *4* **Luisa Tetrazzini (IRE)**[14] 7464 3-8-12 59 ChrisCatlin 4 47
(K A Ryan) *wnt lft s: hld up in mid-div: pushed along over 2f out: hdwy wl over 1f out: sn rdn: edgd rt over 1f out: sn rdn to take 3rd wl ins fnl f* **5/2**[2]
0305 **4** *3 ¼* **Across The Sands**[4] 7601 3-9-3 55 FrankieMcDonald 3 40
(C N Kellett) *n.m.r and bmpd after s: t.k.h: prom: hung lft thrght: rdn over 1f out: wknd fnl f* **9/4**[1]
5204 **5** *1 ¾* **Shirley High**[9] 7510 3-8-12 50 JimmyQuinn 9 29
(P Howling) *chsd ldrs: rdn over 1f out: wknd fnl f* **16/1**
0000 **6** *½* **Rightcar Dominic**[5] 7592 4-9-3 47 (b) PaulHanagan 5 32
(Peter Grayson) *hmpd sn after s: in rr: pushed along over 2f out: rdn over 1f out: nvr nr ldrs* **25/1**
0665 **7** *shd* **Bella Fighetta**[8] 7533 3-8-7 43 (p) SophieDoyle(5) 8 27
(Ms J S Doyle) *outpcd: a in rr* **33/1**
050- **8** *3 ¾* **Myriola**[357] 7644 4-8-9 0 MartinLane(3) 10 13
(D Shaw) *t.k.h: sn in rr* **66/1**
306U **9** *5* **Paddy Jack**[38] 7086 4-9-3 44 (be) LukeMorris 13 —
(J R Weymes) *prom tl rdn and wknd wl over 1f out* **40/1**

62.06 secs (-0.24) **Going Correction** +0.025s/f (Slow) **9** Ran SP% **114.1**
Speed ratings (Par 103): **102,101,94,89,86 86,85,79,71**
toteswingers: 1&2 £4.00, 1&3 £2.80, 2&3 £1.80 CSF £21.85 TOTE £6.50: £1.70, £1.50, £1.50; EX 27.00.
Owner Goldmine Racing Limited **Bred** Connie Huy & Edward E Huy **Trained** Newbridge, Co Kildare

FOCUS
A moderate sprint maiden and, although the form is not totally convincing, it is worth giving it a chance.
Across The Sands Official explanation: jockey said colt hung left-handed throughout
Rightcar Dominic Official explanation: jockey said colt was hampered on leaving stalls

7630 BET TOTEPOOL AT TOTESPORT.COM MAIDEN FILLIES' STKS — 7f 32y(P)
7:20 (7:20) (Class 5) 2-Y-0 **£3,885** (£1,156; £577; £288) **Stalls** High

Form RPR
5 **1** **Lady Of Akita (USA)**[9] 7522 2-9-0 0 NickyMackay 5 76+
(J H M Gosden) *chsd ldr: led over 2f out: rdn jst over 1f out: r.o* **5/6**[1]
00 **2** *1 ¼* **Kai Mook**[53] 6730 2-9-0 0 SteveDrowne 9 73
(R Ingram) *sn hld up in tch: pushed along and ev ch over 2f out: rdn wl over 1f out: kpt on ins fnl f* **16/1**
0 **3** *6* **Fareham Town**[77] 6069 2-9-0 0 LPKeniry 7 58
(S Kirk) *a.p: rdn and wknd over 1f out* **66/1**
4 **4** *2* **Silken Aunt**[21] 7376 2-9-0 0 KirstyMilczarek 6 54
(J A R Toller) *led: hdd over 2f out: sn n.m.r briefly on ins: wknd over 1f out* **11/4**[2]
00 **5** *nse* **A P Ling**[30] 7243 2-9-0 0 FrankieMcDonald 1 54+
(C N Kellett) *hld up in tch: hung rt on ins and n.m.r bnd over 2f out: sn wknd* **100/1**
040 **6** *10* **The Blue Dog (IRE)**[20] 7396 2-9-0 0 TonyCulhane 3 29
(George Baker) *sn outpcd: lost tch 4f out* **33/1**

7 1¾ **Seeking Rio** 2-9-9 0 .... LeeNewnes(5) 8 24
(R J Hodges) *s.i.s: hld up: hdwy over 5f out: pushed along over 3f out: wknd over 2f out* **40/1**

8 2¼ **Charles Bear** 2-9-0 0 .... GrahamGibbons 2 19
(E S McMahon) *s.v.s: sme prog 5f out: wknd wl over 1f out* **12/1**

9 1¼ **Belgooree** 2-9-0 0 .... PaulHanagan 4 16
(J G Given) *s.i.s: plld hrd: sme prog over 5f out: wknd 2f out* **11/2[3]**

1m 30.99s (1.39) **Going Correction** +0.025s/f (Slow) 9 Ran SP% **118.0**
Speed ratings (Par 93): **93,91,84,82,82 70,68,66,64**
toteswingers: 1&2 £3.50, 1&3 £12.70, 2&3 £37.80 CSF £18.13 TOTE £1.90: £1.10, £3.30, £13.60; EX 12.90.
Owner Catesby W Clay **Bred** Runnymede Farm Inc Et Al **Trained** Newmarket, Suffolk

FOCUS
More modest fare and tricky to pin down, although the first two were clear.

NOTEBOOK
Lady Of Akita(USA), who shaped well on debut, stepped up to get off the mark at the second attempt. John Gosden's filly tracked pacesetter Silken Aunt before going on turning for home and kicking clear. She had to be kept up to her work in the closing stages to hold off the challenge of Kai Mook, but she did so despite still looking green. This clearly is not strong form, but she still has plenty of maturing to do and is clearly going the right way. (op 4-5 tchd 8-11 and Evens)
Kai Mook ◆ posted easily her best effort to date. The only one to make a race of it with the winner, she will be interesting in similar company next time.
Fareham Town took a huge step forward from her debut, travelling eyecatchingly well in behind the pace before lacking a bit of toe at the business end.
Silken Aunt dropped away rather tamely having cut out the running and didn't build on her promising debut, so she has questions to answer now. (op 3-1 tchd 5-2)

7631 BET TOTEPOOL ON 0800 221 221 CLASSIFIED CLAIMING STKS 1m 141y(P)
7:50 (7:50) (Class 5) 3-Y-0+ £3,238 (£963; £481; £240) Stalls Low

Form RPR

032 1 **Clear Sailing**[17] 7422 6-8-4 65 ....(p) FrancisNorton 11 74
(Ollie Pears) *racd keenly: a.p: wnt 2nd over 4f out: led jst over 2f out: rdn wl over 1f out: drvn out* **3/1[1]**

4-46 2 1¼ **Fujin Dancer (FR)**[190] 2392 4-8-1 70 .... TimothyAyres(7) 7 75
(R A Fahey) *hld up: hdwy on outside over 2f out: chsd wnr fnl f: rdn and kpt on same pce* **8/1**

0543 3 2¼ **Celtic Step**[17] 7422 5-8-2 65 .... PaulHanagan 10 64
(P D Niven) *hld up in tch: hrd rdn over 2f out: one pce fnl f* **8/1**

0302 4 3½ **Pride Of Nation (IRE)**[6] 7581 7-8-8 68 ....(p) RobertWinston 1 62
(A J McCabe) *hld up in tch: pushed along and wknd over 1f out* **7/1**

0302 5 2 **My Mate Mal**[41] 6342 5-8-4 64 .... ChrisCatlin 2 53
(B Ellison) *led: hdd over 6f out: chsd ldr tl over 4f out: pushed along over 3f out: rdn wl over 1f out: sn wknd* **7/2[2]**

0165 6 3½ **Ocean Legend (IRE)**[17] 7422 4-8-4 66 .... LukeMorris 5 45
(Miss J Feilden) *hld up in rr: pushed along over 3f out: rdn wl over 1f out: sn edgd lft and btn* **9/2[3]**

0000 7 ¾ **Jojesse**[39] 7052 5-8-3 42 ow1 ....(b) SimonWhitworth 3 42
(W Storey) *hld up: rdn over 2f out: sn bhd* **100/1**

4001 8 1¾ **Swiss Art (IRE)**[17] 7422 3-8-2 70 ....(t) JimmyQuinn 8 39
(Mrs R A Carr) *hmpd sn after s: hld up in rr: pushed along over 3f out: rdn wl over 1f out: sn struggling* **5/1**

0200 9 1½ **Transmission (IRE)**[48] 6862 4-8-12 61 ....(v[1]) GregFairley 4 44
(B Smart) *w ldr: led over 6f out tl jst over 2f out: sn rdn: wknd wl over 1f out* **33/1**

1m 48.88s (-1.62) **Going Correction** +0.025s/f (Slow)
WFA 3 from 4yo+ 2lb 9 Ran SP% **120.7**
Speed ratings (Par 103): **108,106,104,101,100 96,96,94,93**
toteswingers: 1&2 £8.10, 1&3 £7.20, 2&3 £7.00 CSF £29.34 TOTE £4.60: £1.70, £2.50, £3.10; EX 42.50.Fujin Dancer claimed by Mr K. A. Ryan for £8,000. Swiss Art claimed by Mrs J. B. Pye for £6,000.
Owner We-Know Partnership **Bred** Juddmonte Farms Ltd **Trained** Norton, N Yorks

FOCUS
A good gallop to this claimer, but it concerned only two in the final furlong. The form looks sound rated around the first pair.
Swiss Art(IRE) Official explanation: jockey said gelding never travelled

7632 JMC SURFACING - M&A DOOCEY APPRENTICE H'CAP 1m 1f 103y(P)
8:20 (8:20) (Class 6) (0-65,65) 3-Y-0+ £2,072 (£616; £308; £153) Stalls Low

Form RPR

5013 1 **Resentful Angel**[9] 7524 4-9-6 64 .... TobyAtkinson 2 74+
(Pat Eddery) *hld up in tch: n.m.r over 2f out: rdn over 1f out: led ins fnl f: r.o* **7/4[1]**

1353 2 ¾ **The Grey One (IRE)**[9] 7512 6-9-4 65 ....(p) RyanClark(3) 12 74
(J M Bradley) *stdd s: hld up in rr: hdwy over 2f out: chal ins fnl f: nt qckn* **6/1[3]**

0054 3 3½ **Dean Iarracht (IRE)**[30] 7246 3-8-7 58 .... AlexEdwards(5) 1 59
(Miss Tracy Waggott) *w ldr: led 3f out: rdn wl over 1f out: hdd ins fnl f: wknd towards fin* **10/1**

5565 4 ½ **Hucking Heat (IRE)**[50] 6806 5-9-4 62 ....(p) LeeNewnes 9 62
(R Hollinshead) *hld up towards rr: hdwy on outside over 2f out: ev ch 1f out: wknd wl ins fnl f* **10/1**

3523 5 nse **Lucky Score (IRE)**[18] 7416 3-8-13 62 .... RyanPowell(3) 4 62
(Mouse Hamilton-Fairley) *prom on ins: wnt 2nd wl over 1f out: ev ch ins fnl f: sn wknd* **8/1**

2601 6 5 **Coolnaharan (IRE)**[21] 7369 9-8-13 57 ....(p) JamesPSullivan 7 47
(Lee Smyth, Ire) *hld up towards rr: hdwy over 3f out: chsd ldr over 2f out tl wl over 1f out: sn wknd* **14/1**

1530 7 2¼ **Make Amends (IRE)**[87] 5740 4-8-13 60 .... KierenFox(3) 10 45
(R J Hodges) *hld up in tch: ev ch over 2f out: sn rdn: wknd wl over 1f out* **40/1**

0324 8 shd **Lady Florence**[19] 7057 4-9-5 63 .... ByronMoorcroft 6 48
(A B Coogan) *w ldr to 4f out: wkng whn hmpd over 2f out* **28/1**

500- 9 13 **Impressionist Art (USA)**[14] 7471 3-8-12 61 .... DavidKenny(3) 11 18
(Patrick J Flynn, Ire) *hld up towards rr: prog on outside over 3f out: wknd over 2f out* **7/2[2]**

010/ 10 4½ **Thistimesforgood (IRE)**[38] 6520 6-8-5 52 ....(b) MatthewLawson(3) 8 —
(Paul Stafford, Ire) *prom: led over 4f out to 3f out: wknd over 2f out* **25/1**

2m 1.39s (-0.31) **Going Correction** +0.025s/f (Slow)
WFA 3 from 4yo+ 2lb 10 Ran SP% **118.6**
Speed ratings (Par 101): **102,101,98,97,97 93,91,91,79,75**
toteswingers: 1&2 £3.80, 1&3 £8.00, 2&3 £8.90 CSF £12.61 CT £84.07 TOTE £3.20: £1.50, £2.00, £3.00; EX 16.30.
Owner P J J Eddery, Mrs John Magnier, M Tabor **Bred** Patrick Eddery Ltd **Trained** Nether Winchendon, Bucks

FOCUS
A very messy race despite the sound gallop. The placed horses set the level.
Lady Florence Official explanation: jockey said filly was hampered when weakening round final bend

7633 BEST ODDS GUARANTEED AT TOTESPORT.COM H'CAP 1m 141y(P)
8:50 (8:50) (Class 4) (0-85,85) 3-Y-0+ £5,046 (£1,510; £755; £377; £188) Stalls Low

Form RPR

2-14 1 **Plush**[281] 694 6-9-0 79 .... RossAtkinson(5) 3 86+
(Tom Dascombe) *stdd s: hld up in last: pushed along and c wd st: swtchd lft and hdwy over 1f out: rdn to ld cl home* **11/1**

2010 2 nk **Tamasou (IRE)**[27] 7287 4-9-3 77 .... ShaneKelly 1 83
(A J McCabe) *led: hrd rdn and hdd cl home* **4/1[2]**

0651 3 ½ **Just Bond (IRE)**[6] 7583 7-9-11 85 6ex .... PJMcDonald 2 90
(G R Oldroyd) *a.p: pushed along to chal ins fnl f: sn rdn: nt qckn nr fin* **6/1[3]**

1165 4 1½ **Arizona John (IRE)**[37] 7125 4-9-4 78 .... SJCraine 4 80
(J Mackie) *a.p: rdn wl over 1f out: nt clr run and swtchd rt ins fnl f: nt qckn* **8/1**

0623 5 2¾ **Southandwest (IRE)**[7] 7558 5-9-4 78 .... LPKeniry 7 73
(J S Moore) *hld up: hdwy 3f out: sn pushed along: wkng whn nt clr run and swtchd lft jst ins fnl f* **4/1[2]**

0012 6 2½ **Ensnare**[21] 7362 4-9-0 74 .... KFallon 5 63
(Ian Williams) *a.p: wnt 2nd over 6f out: chal over 2f out: rdn over 1f out: wknd ins fnl f* **13/8[1]**

0000 7 6 **Ninth House (USA)**[34] 7172 7-8-13 73 ....(b) LukeMorris 6 49
(Mrs R A Carr) *half-rrd s: hld up: pushed along 3f out: rdn and bhd fnl 2f* **28/1**

1m 50.52s (0.02) **Going Correction** +0.025s/f (Slow) 7 Ran SP% **115.3**
Speed ratings (Par 105): **100,99,99,97,95 93,87**
toteswingers: 1&2 £11.80, 1&3 £9.00, 2&3 £4.50 CSF £55.05 CT £293.55 TOTE £11.10: £4.50, £2.00; EX 53.50.
Owner John Reed **Bred** Cheveley Park Stud Ltd **Trained** Lambourn, Berks

FOCUS
A decent handicap, but a steady pace and bit of a bunch finish, so the form looks muddling. The third and fourth set the level.
Ensnare Official explanation: jockey said gelding moved poorly throughout

7634 TEXT YOUR TOTESPORT BET TO 60021 H'CAP 5f 20y(P)
9:20 (9:21) (Class 5) (0-75,75) 3-Y-0+ £3,238 (£963; £481; £240) Stalls Low

Form RPR

12-0 1 **Anne Of Kiev (IRE)**[50] 6801 4-9-4 75 ....(t) LukeMorris 4 84
(J R Gask) *hld up towards rr: swtchd rt 2f out: rdn and hdwy over 1f out: r.o wl u.p ins fnl f: edgd lft and led last strides* **14/1**

6010 2 ½ **Colorus (IRE)**[28] 7269 6-8-10 72 ....(p) PaulPickard(5) 1 79
(W J H Ratcliffe) *led: rdn jst over 1f out: hdd last strides* **16/1**

0212 3 nk **Perlachy**[6] 7577 5-8-9 66 ....(v) KirstyMilczarek 12 72
(J R Holt) *hld up in tch: pushed along 2f out: rdn jst over 1f out: kpt on towards fin* **13/2**

-001 4 hd **Master Lightfoot**[29] 7254 3-9-2 73 .... ShaneKelly 2 78
(W R Swinburn) *a.p: kpt on towards fin* **9/2[1]**

5106 5 ½ **Lucky Leigh**[7] 7553 3-9-4 75 .... KFallon 9 78
(M R Channon) *a.p: ev ch over 1f out: rdn and nt qckn cl home* **12/1**

4224 6 ¾ **Cayman Fox**[4] 7601 4-7-12 62 ....(e) MatthewLawson(7) 5 63+
(James Moffatt) *s.i.s: plld hrd early in rr: nt clr run 2f out: hdwy on ins wl over 1f out: nvr able to chal* **5/1[2]**

3511 7 ½ **Fantasy Fighter (IRE)**[13] 7484 4-8-4 61 oh1 .... JimmyQuinn 13 60+
(J J Quinn) *hld up in rr: c wd st: r.o fnl f: nrst fin* **9/1**

5510 8 shd **Caledonia Princess**[7] 7554 3-8-10 67 .... TonyCulhane 3 66
(R Curtis) *hld up in mid-div: pushed along and hdwy on ins jst over 2f out: one pce fnl f* **6/1[3]**

4003 9 1½ **Argentine (IRE)**[28] 7269 5-9-4 75 ....(b) SteveDrowne 8 68
(J A McShane) *hld up in tch: nt clr run and lost pl 2f out: n.d after* **7/1**

5350 10 ½ **Bo McGinty (IRE)**[13] 7496 8-8-6 70 ....(v) MarzenaJeziorek(7) 7 61
(R A Fahey) *hld up towards rr: rdn whn bmpd over 2f out: nvr trbld ldrs* **33/1**

50-4 11 6 **Parc Aux Boules**[14] 7467 8-8-11 68 ....(t) GrahamGibbons 6 38
(Paul Stafford, Ire) *hld up in mid-div: pushed along over 2f out: wknd wl over 1f out* **40/1**

0030 12 1¾ **Love You Louis**[45] 6916 3-8-13 70 ....(b) PaulHanagan 10 34
(J R Jenkins) *s.i.s: t.k.h: sn mid-div on outside: c wd st: wknd wl over 1f out* **33/1**

06 13 1¾ **Keyala (IRE)**[14] 7467 4-9-1 72 .... LPKeniry 11 29
(David P Myerscough, Ire) *prom tl wknd wl over 1f out* **16/1**

61.99 secs (-0.31) **Going Correction** +0.025s/f (Slow) 13 Ran SP% **119.4**
Speed ratings (Par 103): **103,102,101,101,100 99,98,98,96,95 85,82,80**
toteswingers: 1&2 £39.40, 1&3 £27.40, 2&3 £28.20 CSF £216.77 CT £1650.25 TOTE £18.90: £5.20, £4.90, £2.50; EX 359.80 Place 6: £243.99 Place 5: £156.21.
Owner Horses First Racing Limited **Bred** Deerfield Farm **Trained** Sutton Veny, Wilts

FOCUS
A bunch finish to this sprint handicap but the form appears sound enough rated around the placed horses.
Cayman Fox ◆ Official explanation: jockey said filly was denied a clear run
T/Plt: £229.20 to a £1 stake. Pool: £123,777.82. 394.19 winning tickets. T/Qpdt: £98.80 to a £1 stake. Pool: £10,328.28. 77.30 winning tickets. KH

7499 SOUTHWELL (L-H)
Saturday, December 5

OFFICIAL GOING: Standard
Wind: Light across Weather: Sunny and dry

7635 LIANNE DAVIS H'CAP (DIV I) 1m 6f (F)
11:50 (11:50) (Class 6) (0-60,60) 3-Y-0+ £1,619 (£481; £240; £120) Stalls Low

Form RPR

0000 1 **Merrion Tiger (IRE)**[28] 6767 4-9-1 50 .... GregFairley 6 69
(A G Foster) *cl up: led over 4f out: jnd and rdn 3f out: drvn 2f out: styd on wl appr fnl f* **8/1**

5200 2 7 **Altos Reales**[100] 5377 5-8-13 48 ow1 .... SebSanders 10 57
(M J Scudamore) *hld up in tch: hdwy to trck ldrs 6f out: effrt to chal 3f out: sn rdn and ev ch tl drvn wl over 1f out and kpt on same pce* **12/1**

0023 3 2½ **Jackie Kiely**[18] 7425 8-9-2 51 ....(tp) PhillipMakin 8 57
(R Brotherton) *trckd ldrs: hdwy 4f out: rdn to chse ldng pair wl over 2f out: drvn and no imp fr wl over 1f out* **3/1[1]**

0001 4 2¼ **Stagecoach Emerald**[24] 7336 7-8-10 52 ....(b) TobyAtkinson(7) 1 54
(R W Price) *in rr and pushed along after 4f: lost tch and rdn along 6f out: hdwy over 3f out: wd st and kpt on u.p fnl 2f: nt rch ldrs* **5/1[3]**

4012 **5** *2½* **Swords**[18] 7425 7-9-8 **57**.. FergusSweeney 4 56
(R E Peacock) *trckd ldrs: hdwy 4f out: rdn along 3f out: drvn over 2f out and no imp* **9/2**[2]

0056 **6** *5* **River Danube**[32] 7222 6-8-11 **46** oh1..............................(t) PaulHanagan 9 38
(T J Fitzgerald) *hld up towards rr: hdwy 6f out: rdn to chse ldrs over 3f out: sn wknd* **40/1**

0245 **7** *8* **Honorable Endeavor**[19] 7415 3-9-0 **56**..............................(v) LPKeniry 7 37
(E F Vaughan) *led: pushed along and hdd 1/2-way: rdn and lost pl over 5f out: sn in rr* **7/1**

0350 **8** *2* **Russian Invader (IRE)**[127] 2163 5-9-4 **60**....................(be) JRoberts(7) 3 38
(R C Guest) *trckd ldng pair: hdwy to ld 1/2-way: pushed along 5f out: hdd over 4f out: sn rdn and wknd* **33/1**

0/60 **9** *9* **Arctic Wings (IRE)**[13] 1609 5-8-13 **55**.................. GeorgeDowning(7) 11 20
(A W Carroll) *a in rr: rdn along over 6f out: sn outpcd and bhd* **13/2**

3m 8.76s (0.46) **Going Correction** -0.125s/f (Stan)
WFA 3 from 4yo+ 7lb **9** Ran SP% **109.9**
Speed ratings (Par 101): **93,89,87,86,84 82,77,76,71**
toteswingers: 1&2 £16.40, 1&3 £11.20, 2&3 £15.70 CSF £90.94 CT £328.76 TOTE £8.90: £3.00, £4.10, £1.40; EX 112.30 TRIFECTA Not won..
Owner A G Foster **Bred** Denis Fehan **Trained** Haddington, East Lothian

FOCUS
A moderate staying handicap with some Fibresand stalwarts. The early pace was only fair and the runner-up to this year's form is the best guide.
Merrion Tiger(IRE) Official explanation: trainer said, regarding apparent improvement of form, that the gelding benefited from a return to the Fibresand.

7636 BET BRITISH WITH TOTEPOOL NURSERY 5f (F)
12:20 (12:20) (Class 4) (0-85,75) 2-Y-O **£4,533** (£1,348; £674; £336) **Stalls** High

Form RPR

4034 **1** **Point To Prove**[8] 7559 2-8-2 **59**................................(e) AndreaAtzeni(3) 7 64
(Miss Amy Weaver) *trckd ldrs: rdn along and outpcd 1/2-way: hdwy over 1f out: styd on wl u.p ins fnl f to ld last 50yds* **7/1**

2433 **2** *¾* **Lucky Mellor**[22] 7372 2-9-5 **73**..(b) SebSanders 5 75
(D K Ivory) *trckd ldrs: hdwy to chal wl over 1f out: rdn to ld ent fnl f: sn drvn and edgd lft: hdd and nt qckn last 50yds* **9/4**[1]

3230 **3** *1½* **Six Wives**[9] 7536 2-9-7 **75**... ChrisCatlin 6 72
(J A Glover) *dwlt: hdwy to ld after 2f: rdn along wl over 1f out and sn jnd: drvn and hdd ent fnl f: one pce* **16/1**

0532 **4** *1½* **Olympic Ceremony**[39] 7079 2-9-3 **71**................................ PaulHanagan 3 63
(R A Fahey) *cl up: rdn along over 2f out: drvn wl over 1f out and sn one pce* **7/2**[2]

4451 **5** *nk* **Tartufo Dolce (IRE)**[33] 7213 2-9-4 **72**.................................. TomEaves 4 62
(J G Given) *dwlt: pushed along and n.m.r after 2f: sn swtchd lft and rdn: styd on u.p on outer ins fnl f: nrst fin* **13/2**

1114 **6** *1½* **Angie's Nap (USA)**[23] 7352 2-8-12 **66**.......................(p) RobertWinston 1 51
(P S McEntee) *led 2f: cl up tl rdn along 2f out and sn wknd* **8/1**

0354 **7** *nk* **Micky's Knock Off (IRE)**[19] 7410 2-9-2 **70**................. J-PGuillambert 2 54
(R C Guest) *dwlt: sn pushed along to chse ldrs: rdn 1/2-way and sn outpcd* **9/2**[3]

60.37 secs (0.67) **Going Correction** -0.075s/f (Stan) **7** Ran SP% **114.0**
Speed ratings (Par 98): **91,89,87,85,84 82,81**
toteswingers: 1&2 £4.60, 1&3 £9.20, 2&3 £4.10 CSF £23.03 TOTE £9.60: £4.10, £1.50; EX 33.10.
Owner Michael Bringloe **Bred** Limestone And Tara Studs **Trained** Newmarket, Suffolk

FOCUS
A fair nursery and no hanging about. The usual bias towards those who race up the centre of the track over this straight 5f was well and truly blown apart. The form looks solid rated around the first two, if somewhat limited.

NOTEBOOK
Point To Prove had yet to win after 12 attempts, but he was 8lb better off with Angie's Nap for a two-length beating over course and distance last month. He broke well enough, but then seemed to get outpaced and had plenty of ground to make up at halfway. Despite switching to the stands' rail, which is normally a graveyard on this sprint track, he put in a sustained effort to hit the front close home and the performance may be a bit better than it looked. He heads to the Doncaster Sales. (op 8-1 tchd 13-2)
Lucky Mellor, proven under these conditions, had the blinkers back on and usually races up with the pace, but on this occasion he was unable to take a prominent early position. He did work his way to the front entering the last furlong and looked likely to win, but the winner mugged him close to the line. (op 5-2 tchd 2-1 and 11-4 in places)
Six Wives, a dual winner on Polytrack, was making her Fibresand debut but she possesses plenty of early speed, which is an asset over this 5f track, and she had every chance until entering the last furlong. She remains 4lb above her latest winning mark. (op 11-1)
Olympic Ceremony, often placed but yet to win after nine attempts and trying sand for the first time, showed up for a long way but could never land an effective blow and would probably appreciate a return to 6f. (op 7-1)
Tartufo Dolce(IRE), making her nursery debut and trying Fibresand for the first time following her Wolverhampton maiden success, was never getting there in time towards the centre of the track and will probably appreciate a return to Polytrack. (op 7-2 tchd 7-1)
Angie's Nap(USA), very disappointing in a seller here last time but successful three times on this surface including twice over this trip, was very weak in the market. She broke well enough out in the centre of the track, but had lost the advantage before halfway, then carried her head to one side, and was soon struggling. She looks to have gone off the boil. (op 15-2 tchd 7-1 and 9-1)

7637 TOTESWINGER THREE WAYS TO WIN MAIDEN AUCTION STKS 5f (F)
12:50 (12:51) (Class 6) 2-Y-O **£1,942** (£578; £288; £144) **Stalls** High

Form RPR

000 **1** **R Woody**[79] 6026 2-8-11 **53**.. SteveDrowne 4 72
(Mrs L C Jewell) *prom: cl up 1/2-way: rdn to ld wl over 1f out: clr ins fnl f: kpt on wl* **100/1**

0300 **2** *3* **Maldon Prom (IRE)**[28] 7290 2-8-13 **68**......................(v[1]) DarryllHolland 8 64
(C A Dwyer) *dwlt: sn cl up: rdn along and ev ch 2f out: drvn over 1f out: kpt on same pce u.p ins fnl f* **5/1**[3]

02 **3** *nk* **Brigadoon**[23] 7351 2-8-9 0... KFallon 1 59
(W Jarvis) *chsd ldrs towards outer: rdn along 1/2-way: hdwy wl over 1f out: drvn and one pce ent fnl f* **5/4**[1]

202 **4** *nk* **Going French (IRE)**[9] 7536 2-8-9 **71**................................ TonyCulhane 7 58
(R Curtis) *sn led: rdn along over 2f out: hdd wl over 1f out and sn drvn: wknd ent fnl f* **13/8**[2]

0 **5** *2¾* **Major Monty (IRE)**[8] 7556 2-8-13 0................................ RichardSmith 5 52
(Tom Dascombe) *in tch: rdn along and outpcd 1/2-way: styd on appr fnl f: nvr a factor* **20/1**

300 **6** *6* **Safari Camp (IRE)**[33] 7213 2-8-11 **55**...................... StephenDonohoe 6 28
(A Berry) *sn outpcd and bhd fr 1/2-way* **100/1**

000 **7** *1¼* **Dispol Fay (IRE)**[24] 7331 2-8-4 **41**....................................... PaulHanagan 2 17
(P T Midgley) *wnt rt s: cl up: rdn along 1/2-way: wknd fnl 2f* **100/1**

8 *3* **Adam De Beaulieu (USA)** 2-9-1 0...............................(t) PhillipMakin 3 17
(P C Haslam) *s.i.s and wnt bdly lft s: a bhd* **16/1**

59.26 secs (-0.44) **Going Correction** -0.075s/f (Stan) **8** Ran SP% **112.8**
Speed ratings (Par 94): **100,95,94,94,89 80,78,73**
toteswingers: 1&2 £4.60, 1&3 £27.10, 2&3 £2.00 CSF £527.46 TOTE £112.20: £8.20, £1.50, £1.10; EX 394.50 TRIFECTA Not won..
Owner Quintessential Thoroughbreds Solar Syn **Bred** R, D And M Close **Trained** Sutton Valence, Kent

FOCUS
An uncompetitive maiden in which they bet 16-1 bar three, but it resulted in a complete boil-over for punters. The runner-up sets the level. Again the nearside of the track seemed the place to be and the winning time was 1.11 seconds faster than the nursery.

NOTEBOOK
R Woody, officially rated just 53, had yet to show ability in three previous starts and had started at 100-1 in each of them. It was a similar story here, but he travelled particularly well behind the leaders and having taken it up passing the 2f pole, gradually forged clear. There seemed no fluke about it and he obviously relished the switch to Fibresand, but just as significantly he had apparently been gelded since his last run. Official explanation: trainer said, regarding apparent improvement in form, that it had benefited from being gelded.
Maldon Prom(IRE), who hasn't seemed to be progressing, had a visor on for the first time. Up with the pace from the off, he could do nothing about the winner and merely plugged on up the stands' rail to hold on to second. This was a little better, but he still didn't achieve that much. (op 4-1)
Brigadoon, who had shown ability in two starts over 7f, the latest of them here, didn't seem suited by the drop to the minimum trip, as he struggled to go the pace up the centre of the track. He did plug on, but it was very laboured. (op 11-8 tchd 13-8)
Going French(IRE), placed in six of his seven starts including once over course and distance, helped share the early pace, but he didn't find a lot off the bridle passing the 2f pole. Official explanation: jockey said colt became upset in the stalls (op 15-8 tchd 11-8)
Major Monty(IRE), who showed early speed before fading over an extra furlong at Wolverhampton on his debut, struggled to lay up here and though he did stay on a little bit he never looked like figuring. (op 16-1)
Safari Camp(IRE) Official explanation: jockey said colt moved poorly

7638 EUROPEAN BREEDERS' FUND MAIDEN STKS 1m (F)
1:20 (1:23) (Class 5) 2-Y-O **£4,094** (£1,209; £604) **Stalls** Low

Form RPR

1 **Doctor Zhivago** 2-9-3 0.. GregFairley 8 76+
(M Johnston) *in tch and sn pushed along: rdn and outpcd 1/2-way: hdwy to chse ldrs 3f out: chsd ldr over 1f out: styd on strly ent fnl f: led last 100yds* **3/1**[2]

0343 **2** *2* **Master Leon**[23] 7351 2-9-3 **70**...(v[1]) TomEaves 11 70
(B Smart) *led: rdn clr 2f out: drvn ent fnl f: hdd and one pce last 100yds* **6/1**[3]

0033 **3** *6* **Labretella (IRE)**[11] 7501 2-8-12 **51**.................................. JimmyQuinn 7 52
(D W Thompson) *trckd ldrs: hdwy 3f out: rdn along 2f out: sn drvn and kpt on same pce* **12/1**

4 *shd* **Dynamic Idol (USA)** 2-9-3 0.. PaulHanagan 12 57
(M A Magnusson) *prom on outer: rdn along 3f out: drvn 2f out and sn one pce* **11/8**[1]

4 **5** *8* **Whitby (IRE)**[11] 7502 2-8-5 0................................. JamesPSullivan(7) 9 34
(M W Easterby) *v.s.a and bhd: hdwy wl over 2f out: swtchd rt over 1f out: kpt on ins fnl f: nt rch ldrs* **12/1**

6 **6** *1* **Ever A Gent**[11] 7502 2-8-12 0.. BMcHugh(5) 3 37
(M W Easterby) *towards rr: hdwy over 2f out: styd on appr fnl f: nt rch ldrs* **100/1**

03 **7** *½* **Budva**[11] 7502 2-9-3 0... SteveDrowne 1 36
(H Morrison) *in rr tl styd on fnl 2f: nvr a factor* **10/1**

8 *nk* **Mon Mon (IRE)** 2-8-12 0... PJMcDonald 10 30
(G A Swinbank) *trckd ldrs: effrt 3f out: rdn along over 2f out and grad wknd* **28/1**

00 **9** *1* **Cordiality**[59] 6593 2-9-3 0... RobertHavlin 2 33
(P G Murphy) *a towards rr* **50/1**

00 **10** *1¼* **Straversjoy**[31] 7243 2-8-12 0.. GrahamGibbons 5 25
(R Hollinshead) *s.i.s and bhd: hdwy to chse ldrs 1/2-way: rdn along 3f out and sn wknd* **33/1**

00 **11** *28* **Catawollow**[31] 7244 2-8-12 0... PaulEddery 13 —
(R C Guest) *chsd ldrs on wd outside: rdn along bef 1/2-way and sn wknd* **66/1**

1m 43.19s (-0.51) **Going Correction** -0.125s/f (Stan) **11** Ran SP% **116.7**
Speed ratings (Par 96): **97,95,89,88,80 79,79,79,78,76 48**
toteswingers: 1&2 £7.50, 1&3 £20.80, 2&3 £3.80 CSF £20.55 TOTE £3.50: £1.10, £2.10, £3.10; EX 23.00 Trifecta £66.00 Pool: £402.62 - 4.51 winning units..
Owner Sheikh Hamdan Bin Mohammed Al Maktoum **Bred** Meon Valley Stud **Trained** Middleham Moor, N Yorks

FOCUS
A few in this field had made the frame at the track, but most of them look more long-term prospects. They went a fair pace, though, and few ever got into it. The runner-up is rated to form and it looks pretty solid.

NOTEBOOK
Doctor Zhivago ◆, a 150,000gns half-brother to three winners including the smart Alkaadhem, looked green in the early stages as, although he was fairly handy, he was having to be nudged along to keep in touch well before halfway. He got stronger as the race progressed, however, and kept on to hit the front well inside the last furlong. He should get further on breeding and looks to have a future. (tchd 11-4 and 10-3)
Master Leon, who was starting to look exposed, had a visor on for the first time and it seemed to make a difference. Soon in front, he had poached a useful lead turning for home and it seemed he would take some catching. He kept plugging away and maintained the margin over the rest of the field, but the winner proved a different proposition. He can win if the headgear works again and may be worth a try in a nursery off a mark of 70. (op 11-2)
Labretella(IRE) attracted each-way support and was handy throughout, but she had been placed in a claimer here the last twice and is rated just 51. (op 20-1)
Dynamic Idol(USA), a $250,000 half-brother to the high-class Nasheej, was all the rage in the market but despite racing handily early, he had to be given some sharp reminders when hanging on the home bend and could only plug on. He is worth another chance to prove himself better than this, but he will need to in order to start justifying his purchase price. (op 13-8 tchd 7-4)
Whitby(IRE) gave her rivals a start and trailed the field for much of the way, but she did make some late progress. A beaten favourite here on her debut, she does have ability and looks one for handicaps in due course. Official explanation: jockey said filly hung left leaving stalls and clipped heels 4f out (tchd 14-1)

7639 TOTEEXACTA THE BETTER VALUE FORECAST H'CAP 6f (F)
1:50 (1:50) (Class 2) (0-100,101) 3-Y£0+,354 (£3,398; £1,699; £849; £423) **Stalls** Low

Form RPR

0103 **1** **Felday**[28] 7294 3-8-8 **90**... SteveDrowne 7 97
(H Morrison) *hdwy on outer over 2f out: rdn to chal over 1f out: drvn ins fnl f and styd on to ld last 100yds* **13/8**[1]

5311 2 ½ **Ingleby Arch (USA)**45 6949 6-8-11 93 PhillipMakin 2 98
(T D Barron) *led 2f: cl up tl led again 2f out and sn rdn: drvn ent fnl f: hdd and nt qckn last 100yds* 11/4[2]

1602 3 ½ **Indian Skipper (IRE)**53 6755 4-7-13 86 oh13 (be) BillyCray(5) 4 89?
(R C Guest) *dwlt and in rr: hdwy over 2f out: swtchd lft and rdn to chse ldng pair over 1f out: drvn and no ex last 100yds* 33/1

0043 4 3½ **Confuchias (IRE)**17 7431 5-8-11 93 (p) RobertWinston 5 85
(Pat Eddery) *cl up: led after 2f: rdn along and hdd 2f out: sn drvn and grad wknd* 5/1[3]

300 5 2 **Flowing Cape (IRE)**14 7486 4-8-10 92 DarryllHolland 6 78
(R Hollinshead) *trckd ldng pair: swtchd lft and rdn over 2f out: drvn and wknd over 1f out* 6/1

1161 6 hd **Esprit De Midas**200 2148 3-8-6 88 ChrisCatlin 1 73
(K A Ryan) *trckd ldrs on inner: effrt 1/2-way: rdn along over 2f out and outpcd fr wl over 1f out* 9/1

1m 14.69s (-1.81) **Going Correction** -0.125s/f (Stan) 6 Ran SP% **108.7**
Speed ratings (Par 109): **107,106,105,101,98 98**
toteswingers: 1&2 £1.40, 1&3 £9.30, 2&3 £4.60 CSF £5.80 CT £80.15 TOTE £2.00: £2.00, £2.10; EX 9.20 Trifecta £132.60 Pool: £286.91 - 1.60 winning units..
Owner Exors Of The Late Mrs R C A Hammond **Bred** Rockwell Bloodstock **Trained** East Ilsley, Berks

FOCUS
A decent sprint handicap despite the small field and there was no hanging about. There are doubts over the form but the first two are pretty solid and set the standard.

NOTEBOOK
Felday ◆, in good form on turf in recent months, was on sand for the first time but represented a yard whose runners are always to be feared here and he attracted market support. His best previous form had come over 7f, so the strong pace was very much in his favour and having been handy on the outside from the off, he responded well to pressure to get up near the line. Highly regarded by connections, there should be plenty more where this came from. (op 15-8)
Ingleby Arch(USA), bidding for a hat-trick off a 5lb higher mark and 6-10 over course and distance, tried to make most of the running and he did his best under pressure, but came up against an unexposed rival. He will always have to be considered here, but is on a stiff mark now. (op 5-2)
Indian Skipper(IRE), making his Fibresand debut and beaten in a seller last time, seemed to have it all to do from 13lb wrong, so this was a remarkable effort considering he was outpaced in a detached last in the early stages, yet put in a sterling late effort once switched inside. The problem for him is what the Handicapper will make of this performance. (op 40-1 tchd 50-1)
Confuchias(IRE), who had seemed to be running back into form following his belated return for his new yard, was trying this surface for the first time with the aid of cheekpieces. He helped force the early pace, but was keen enough and didn't get home. (op 6-1)
Flowing Cape(IRE), back down to probably his ideal trip, had never raced on Fibresand before and failed to pick up sufficiently when asked for his effort. (op 7-1)
Esprit De Midas, a three-time winner over 7f here in February, was having his first start since winning over this trip off 9lb lower on turf in May. Off the bridle on the inside passing halfway, he could never land a blow and while he was entitled to need this, it remains to be seen how well handicapped he is now. (op 11-2)

7640 TOTEPOOL A BETTER WAY TO BET H'CAP 1m 3f (F)
2:20 (2:22) (Class 3) (0-95,93) 3-Y-O+
£7,477 (£2,239; £1,119; £560; £279; £140) Stalls Low

Form RPR
0121 1 **Lucky Punt**39 7091 3-8-9 84 FergusSweeney 5 99+
(B G Powell) *trckd ldr: led 7f out: rdn over 2f out: sn clr: styd on wl* 11/8[1]

0662 2 5 **Dunaskin (IRE)**7 6875 9-8-9 80 oh4 ow1 (e1) TomEaves 2 86
(B Ellison) *trckd ldrs: rdn along 4f out: styd on u.p to chse wnr 2f out: sn drvn and no imp* 8/1

0/23 3 2½ **Prince Picasso**13 6250 6-8-8 79 oh3 PaulHanagan 3 81
(R A Fahey) *led: hdd 7f out: rdn along and outpcd over 4f out: styd on u.p fnl 2f* 11/2

0000 4 1¼ **Paktolos (FR)**15 7465 6-8-9 85 (b) MarkCoumbe(5) 1 85
(John A Harris) *s.i.s and hld up in rr: effrt and sme hdwy over 3f out: sn rdn and n.d* 20/1

52-4 5 6 **Luberon**262 864 6-9-8 93 KFallon 7 83
(M Johnston) *hld up in tch: hdwy 1/2-way: cl up 4f out: rdn along wl over 2f out: rdr dropped whip 2f out and grad wknd* 4/1[2]

1233 6 7 **River Ardeche**28 3000 4-8-3 79 PatrickDonaghy(5) 6 57
(P C Haslam) *trckd ldrs: chsd wnr 1/2-way: rdn along over 4f out: drvn over 3f out and sn wknd* 5/1[3]

2m 24.85s (-3.15) **Going Correction** -0.125s/f (Stan)
WFA 3 from 4yo+ 4lb 6 Ran SP% **110.0**
Speed ratings (Par 107): **106,102,100,99,95 90**
toteswingers: 1&2 £3.70, 1&3 £1.70, 2&3 £6.10 CSF £12.56 TOTE £2.00: £1.20, £3.50; EX 11.60.
Owner I S Smith **Bred** S A Douch **Trained** Upper Lambourn, Berks

FOCUS
A good middle-distance handicap and the presence of some established front-runners might have been expected to result in a strongly run race, but the tactics were changed on a few of them, so the shape of the race was a little different. The form is probably not that strong for the class, although the winner is on the upgrade.

NOTEBOOK
Lucky Punt, winner of four of his five starts here this year including once over this trip, had a 5lb higher mark to overcome but having taken over in front after half a mile or so, he gradually beat off his rivals one by one and was clear passing the 2f pole. He stays 1m6f well, so is pretty versatile and is a credit to connections. (op 5-4 tchd Evens and 6-4)
Dunaskin(IRE), in good form over hurdles in recent months, hasn't won on the Flat since June 2007 but he did run well over three furlongs further here in October. Sporting a first-time eyeshield and a springer in the market, he used to be a trailblazer but was held up on this occasion. He had to be given some reminders before exiting the back straight, but did respond and stayed on once into the straight. (op 16-1)
Prince Picasso, without a win on the level since July 2006 but running well on the Flat and over hurdles for his new yard of late, was trying this surface for the first time. In front early, he seemed likely to drop away after losing the advantage after half a mile but rallied to snatch third, albeit a long way behind the winner. (op 8-1)
Paktolos(FR), well beaten on his debut for the yard last month, was another trying this surface for the first time but after breaking very slowly he never made much of an impression. (op 16-1 tchd 25-1)
Luberon, yet another making his Fibresand debut on this first start since March, is another that usually forces it but after tanking along behind the leaders early, he wasn't asked to bid for the lead until reaching the home bend. He already seemed to be getting the worst of it when his rider lost his whip over 2f from home, but he looked very much in need of the run in any case, so should come on plenty. (op 3-1 tchd 9-2)
River Ardeche, successful in his only previous try on this surface when making all over an extra furlong, didn't try to lead this time and the writing was on the wall when he came off the bridle 5f from home. (tchd 9-2)

7641 BELVOIR LETTINGS H'CAP 1m 3f (F)
2:50 (2:50) (Class 5) (0-75,75) 3-Y-O+ £2,590 (£770; £385; £192) Stalls Low

Form RPR
0011 1 **Shadows Lengthen**14 7490 3-8-1 65 (b) JamesPSullivan(7) 3 84+
(M W Easterby) *mde all: set sound pce: clr fnl 2f: easily* 11/8[1]

0351 2 9 **Onemoreandstay**226 1478 4-9-0 67 RobertWinston 1 69
(M D Squance) *trckd ldrs: hdwy 4f out: chsd wnr 3f out and sn rdn: drvn and no imp fnl 2f* 8/1

4050 3 1¼ **Coral Shores**21 7399 4-8-9 62 (v) ChrisCatlin 4 62
(P W Hiatt) *trckd ldng pair: effrt to chse wnr over 4f out: rdn along 3f out: sn drvn andkpt on same pce fnl 2f* 22/1

2043 4 4½ **Benedict Spirit (IRE)**11 7505 4-9-8 75 (p) DavidProbert 5 67
(D Burchell) *hld up in rr: hdwy over 3f out: rdn along wl over 2f out and n.d* 2/1[2]

3311 5 11 **Bosamcliff (IRE)**11 7505 4-8-12 70 RichardEvans(5) 2 44
(P D Evans) *chsd wnr: rdn along over 4f out and sn wknd* 4/1[3]

2m 25.03s (-2.97) **Going Correction** -0.125s/f (Stan)
WFA 3 from 4yo 4lb 5 Ran SP% **110.9**
Speed ratings (Par 103): **105,98,97,94,86**
toteswingers: 1&2 £17.80 CSF £12.67 TOTE £2.20: £1.20, £1.70; EX 8.40.
Owner T A F Frost **Bred** London Thoroughbred Services Ltd **Trained** Sheriff Hutton, N Yorks

FOCUS
A weaker handicap than the preceding contest over the same trip, but competitive nonetheless with four of the five runners already successful at this track this year and the winning time was only 0.18 seconds slower. It proved to be a remarkably uneventful race, however, with the winner oprogressive and the second the guide to the form.
Bosamcliff(IRE) Official explanation: trainer's rep had no explanation for the poor form shown

7642 LIANNE DAVIS H'CAP (DIV II) 1m 6f (F)
3:25 (3:27) (Class 6) (0-60,58) 3-Y-O+ £1,619 (£481; £240; £120) Stalls Low

Form RPR
3012 1 **Saute**24 7336 3-9-4 58 AdamKirby 5 72
(W R Swinburn) *trckd ldr: led 1/2-way: jnd and rdn 3f out: drvn and edgd rt wl over 1f out: styd on wl fnl f* 7/2[2]

0540 2 4 **Dart**24 7336 5-9-9 56 RobertWinston 10 64
(Mrs S Lamyman) *trckd ldrs: cl up 1/2-way: chsd wnr 6f out: rdn to chal 3f out: drvn and swtchd lft wl over 1f out: kpt on same pce* 12/1

0043 3 8 **Colourful Move**24 7328 4-9-6 53 SteveDrowne 8 50
(P G Murphy) *towards rr: hdwy over 5f out: rdn to chse ldrs 3f out: drvn over 2f out and plugged on same pce* 7/2[2]

0600 4 ½ **Muntami (IRE)**19 7124 8-8-12 45 (v) StephenDonohoe 2 41
(John A Harris) *trckd ldrs on inner: pushed along and outpcd 5f out: rdn 4f out: drvn and hdwy 3f out: kpt on same pce fnl 2f* 66/1

-530 5 1¼ **Stravita**18 7425 5-9-4 58 (p) DavidKenny(7) 9 52
(R Hollinshead) *in tch: effrt 4f out: rdn along 3f out: drvn over 2f out and plugged on same pce* 14/1

/00- 6 1½ **Birthday Star (IRE)**19 7688 7-8-12 45 (p) DavidProbert 6 37
(Mrs L C Jewell) *hld up towards rr: pushed along over 5f out: rdn and hdwy 3f out: drvn and plugged on same pce fnl 2f: nvr a factor* 50/1

160 7 3 **Dazzling Begum**49 6859 4-9-3 50 (p) RobertHavlin 7 38
(J Pearce) *hld up in rr: hdwy over 4f out: rdn along 3f out: drvn over 2f out: nvr gng pce* 6/1[3]

5354 8 3¼ **Red Wine**11 7505 10-9-5 52 (p) ChrisCatlin 1 35
(J A Glover) *hld up and bhd: sme hdwy over 4f out: sn rdn along and nvr a factor* 9/1

06-5 9 7 **Major Promise**33 7214 4-9-9 56 JimmyQuinn 3 30
(Jane Chapple-Hyam) *t.k.h: chsd ldrs: effrt 4f out: rdn along over 3f out: drvn and wknd over 2f out* 3/1[1]

-005 10 67 **Martha's Girl (USA)**11 7504 3-9-1 55 GrahamGibbons 4 —
(D Carroll) *led: hdd 1/2-way: rdn along 5f out and sn wknd: bhd fnl 3f* 50/1

5060 11 dist **Seminal Moment**23 7354 3-8-13 53 SebSanders 11 —
(J G Given) *towards rr: hdwy on outer to join ldrs after 6f: rdn along 5f out: sn wknd and bhd fnl 3f* 18/1

3m 5.77s (-2.53) **Going Correction** -0.125s/f (Stan)
WFA 3 from 4yo+ 7lb 11 Ran SP% **118.8**
Speed ratings (Par 101): **102,99,95,94,94 93,91,89,85,—,—**
CSF £45.41 CT £160.01 TOTE £5.50: £1.90, £3.60, £1.90; EX 43.00 TRIFECTA Not won. Place 6: £33.28 Place 5: £13.19.
Owner The Lucky Few **Bred** Azienda Agricola Rosati Colarieti **Trained** Aldbury, Herts

FOCUS
Like the first division a modest handicap, but they went a much better gallop in this and the winning time was almost three seconds faster than division one. Again it paid to race close to the pace and the front pair had the contest to themselves over the last 3f. The winner is progressive and the form could be rated higher on the runner-up's old form.
Major Promise Official explanation: jockey said gelding ran too free
Martha's Girl(USA) Official explanation: jockey said filly stopped quickly
Seminal Moment Official explanation: jockey said filly stopped quickly and lost its action
T/Plt: £31.10 to a £1 stake. Pool: £42,073.57. 984.51 winning tickets. T/Qpdt: £5.90 to a £1 stake. Pool: £3,807.51. 477.01 winning tickets. JR

7629 WOLVERHAMPTON (A.W) (L-H)
Saturday, December 5

OFFICIAL GOING: Standard
Wind: Fresh behind Weather: Raining

7643 BEST ODDS GUARANTEED AT TOTESPORT.COM H'CAP 7f 32y(P)
5:50 (5:50) (Class 5) (0-70,70) 3-Y-O+ £3,238 (£963; £481; £240) Stalls High

Form RPR
-524 1 **Dash Back (USA)**14 7496 4-9-2 68 GrahamGibbons 4 83
(Adrian McGuinness, Ire) *a.p: rdn to chse ldr wl over 1f out: sn swtchd rt: r.o u.p to ld wl ins fnl f: eased nr fin* 7/2[3]

0561 2 nk **Istiqdaam**14 7480 4-8-13 65 (b) PhillipMakin 2 79
(M W Easterby) *led: hdd over 5f out: chsd ldr tl led again over 2f out: rdn over 1f out: hdd wl ins fnl f* 11/10[1]

0 3 3¾ **Tin Cha Woody (USA)**21 7394 4-9-1 70 AndreaAtzeni(3) 3 74
(Daniel Mark Loughnane, Ire) *sn prom: rdn 1/2-way: styd on same pce fnl f* 8/1

0000 **4** 1 ¾ **Sadeek**[49] 6846 5-9-2 **68** .... TomEaves 11 67
(B Smart) *dwlt: hdwy over 5f out: rdn over 2f out: styng on same pce whn hung lft fr over 1f out* **33/1**

5050 **5** 1 ¼ **Kensington (IRE)**[24] 7337 8-8-10 **69** .... (p) DeclanCannon(7) 7 65
(A J McCabe) *trckd ldr: plld hrd: led over 5f out: hdd over 2f out: wknd fnl f* **28/1**

0600 **6** ½ **Eastern Gift**[18] 7423 4-9-0 **66** .... SimonWhitworth 6 60
(Miss Gay Kelleway) *hld up: wnt wdst of all turning for home: reminder over 1f out: hung lft ins fnl f: nvr nrr* **33/1**

5000 **7** nk **Electric Warrior (IRE)**[45] 6946 6-9-4 **70** .... LPKeniry 5 64
(C R Dore) *prom: hmpd over 6f out: rdn and wknd over 1f out* **40/1**

1000 **8** ½ **He's A Humbug (IRE)**[11] 7506 5-9-1 **67** .... DarryllHolland 10 59
(J O'Reilly) *hld up: rdn over 2f out: n.d* **28/1**

0010 **9** 3 ¼ **My Sweet Georgia (IRE)**[7] 7577 3-9-0 **66** .... (p) AdamKirby 1 49
(Stef Liddiard) *hld up: a in rr: rdn over 2f out: wknd fnl f* **20/1**

0000 **10** 1 ½ **Silver Hotspur**[32] 7229 5-8-9 **66** .... SimonPearce(5) 9 45
(C R Dore) *s.s: a bhd* **50/1**

1115 **11** 18 **La Gifted**[26] 7321 3-9-4 **70** .... KFallon 12 —
(M R Channon) *chsd ldrs: rdn over 2f out: wknd over 1f out: eased* **3/1**[2]

1m 29.16s (-0.44) **Going Correction** +0.05s/f (Slow) **11** Ran SP% **127.9**
Speed ratings (Par 103): **104,103,99,97,95 95,95,94,90,89 68**
toteswinger:1&2:£2.10, 2&3:£4.90, 1&3:£5.50 CSF £7.98 CT £31.89 TOTE £3.60: £1.60, £1.30, £2.40; EX 11.70.
Owner Edward Battersby **Bred** March Thoroughbreds **Trained** Lusk, Co Dublin

FOCUS
A modest contest but straightforward form rated around the first two and it could rate a little higher.
La Gifted Official explanation: jockey said filly finished lame

7644 OVER 50 INSTANT GAMES AT TOTESPORTGAMES.COM MAIDEN STKS 7f 32y(P)
6:20 (6:20) (Class 5) 2-Y-O **£3,238** (£963; £481; £240) **Stalls** High

Form RPR
0 **1** **Saharia (IRE)**[7] 7571 2-9-3 0 .... ShaneKelly 5 80+
(J Noseda) *chsd ldrs: pushedc along and hung lft over 1f out: shkn up to ld wl ins fnl f: r.o* **9/1**[3]

2 ½ **Barreq (USA)** 2-9-3 0 .... TomEaves 4 79
(B Smart) *dwlt: hdwy over 5f out: pushed along over 2f out: rdn and hung lft over 1f out: r.o to go 2nd nr fin* **33/1**

3 hd **High Constable** 2-9-3 0 .... SteveDrowne 7 78
(R Charlton) *a.p: chsd ldr 3f out: led over 1f out: hdd wl ins fnl f: lost 2nd nr fin* **1/2**[1]

0 **4** 2 **Ming Master (FR)**[7] 7571 2-9-3 0 .... TonyCulhane 1 73
(W J Haggas) *s.i.s: hld up: hdwy 2f out: rdn and edgd lft over 1f out: nt rch ldrs* **50/1**

3432 **5** 3 ¾ **James Barrymore**[68] 6334 2-9-3 72 .... KFallon 2 64
(R Hannon) *led early: chsd ldr tl led 1/2-way: rdn and hdd over 1f out: no ex fnl f* **5/2**[2]

6 7 **Fusaichi Flyer (USA)** 2-9-3 0 .... ChrisCatlin 6 47
(R Charlton) *s.s: hld up: sme hdwy 2f out: sn wknd* **33/1**

000 **7** 4 **Set In Ice**[21] 7391 2-9-3 50 .... NeilChalmers 3 37
(Mark Gillard) *s.i.s: pushed along and rcvrd to ld over 6f out: hdd 1/2-way: rdn and wknd over 2f out* **200/1**

1m 30.67s (1.07) **Going Correction** +0.05s/f (Slow) **7** Ran SP% **113.6**
Speed ratings (Par 96): **95,94,94,91,87 79,75**
toteswinger:1&2:£4.90, 2&3:£4.40, 1&3:£1.10 CSF £175.22 TOTE £12.70: £3.10, £5.40; EX 79.50.
Owner Timeform Betfair Racing Club Ltd **Bred** Woodcote Stud Ltd **Trained** Newmarket, Suffolk

FOCUS
This looked a fair maiden and is best rated around the fifth and seventh.

NOTEBOOK
Saharia(IRE) showed little on his debut over 6f at Lingfield, but that race may well prove to be better than it looked at the time. Clearly suited by this step up in trip, he travelled well throughout and responded to pressure when nipping through towards the inside in the straight to ultimately win with something to spare. He looks potentially useful, but perhaps even more interesting for the future is his stablemate Passion Overflow, who also made his debut in that aforementioned Lingfield maiden and, having been sent off at a shorter price than this one, finished a pleasing second. (op 7-1 tchd 10-1)
Barreq(USA), a 48,000gns half-brother to a couple of winners in the US, did well to finish so close considering he started slowly and basically looked in need of the experience. (op 28-1 tchd 25-1)
High Constable, a half-brother to Group 1 winner Right Approach, was strongly supported to make a winning debut but, having travelled as well as anything into the straight, he didn't see his race out. This colt, who was fitted with front bandages, probably ran into a couple of fair types, but even so better was clearly expected. (op 10-11 tchd 4-9)
Ming Master(FR) improved on the form he showed when behind today's winner on debut at Lingfield. He still looked immature, and while he might be able to find a weak maiden, he'll probably be seen at his best when sent into handicaps. (op 40-1)
James Barrymore ruined his chance by pulling hard down the back straight. He's out of a Royal Applause mare and has to be worth a try over a sprint trip on this evidence. (op 15-8 tchd 10-3)

7645 STAY AT THE WOLVERHAMPTON HOLIDAY INN (S) STKS 5f 216y(P)
6:50 (6:51) (Class 6) 3-Y-O+ **£2,047** (£604; £302) **Stalls** Low

Form RPR
0005 **1** **Bentley**[56] 6674 5-9-0 48 .... SebSanders 8 65
(J G Given) *sn pushed along in rr: hdwy over 1f out: rdn to ld wl ins fnl f: r.o* **16/1**

1414 **2** 1 **Bertie Southstreet**[21] 7397 6-9-6 67 .... (v) DarryllHolland 6 68
(Karen George) *led: rdn over 1f out: hdd and unable qck wl ins fnl f* **4/1**[2]

5204 **3** ¾ **Whitbarrow (IRE)**[19] 7412 10-8-11 65 .... (b) JamesMillman(3) 10 60
(B R Millman) *mid-div: hdwy over 2f out: sn rdn: edgd lft 1f out: styd on* **7/1**

0150 **4** hd **Rosie Says No**[5] 7596 4-8-8 63 .... (p) DeclanCannon(7) 4 60
(A J McCabe) *s.s: hdwy over 4f out: rdn to chse ldr over 1f out: no ex towards fin* **16/1**

3500 **5** ¾ **War And Peace (IRE)**[26] 7321 5-8-7 68 .... LewisWalsh(7) 9 57
(Jane Chapple-Hyam) *prom: pushed along 1/2-way: edgd rt 1f out: styd on* **9/2**[3]

0030 **6** 1 **Imperial House**[42] 7027 3-9-6 65 .... (b[1]) TonyCulhane 5 65+
(R A Harris) *s.s: outpcd: hmpd 1f out: r.o towards fin: nt rch ldrs* **12/1**

0003 **7** 4 **Tanley**[17] 7427 4-9-0 50 .... (b[1]) ChrisCatlin 13 41
(J F Coupland) *prom: lost pl 5f out: rdn 1/2-way: n.d after* **40/1**

4300 **8** 1 ¼ **Miss Pusey Street**[92] 5629 3-8-9 49 .... PaulDoe 2 32
(P D Evans) *chsd ldr tl over 4f out: rdn 1/2-way: wknd over 1f out* **33/1**

2250 **9** 1 ½ **Thunder Bay**[11] 7503 4-9-6 54 .... PaulHanagan 1 38
(R A Fahey) *prom: outpcd 1/2-way: nt clr run and swtchd rt over 2f out: rdn and wknd over 1f out* **9/1**

6300 **10** ½ **Billy Beetroot (USA)**[4] 7606 3-9-6 55 .... (b) LukeMorris 3 36
(R A Harris) *prom: chsd ldr over 4f out tl rdn wl over 1f out: wknd fnl f* **20/1**

5000 **11** hd **One More Round (USA)**[4] 7606 11-8-13 50 .... (b) HollyHall(7) 11 36
(P D Evans) *sn outpcd* **66/1**

061P **12** 7 **Lindoro**[23] 7350 4-9-1 88 .... JamieJones(5) 12 13
(M G Quinlan) *s.s: a outpcd and bhd* **7/2**[1]

1m 15.41s (0.41) **Going Correction** +0.05s/f (Slow) **12** Ran SP% **114.0**
Speed ratings (Par 101): **99,97,96,96,95 94,88,87,85,84 84,74**
toteswinger:1&2:£8.20, 2&3:£5.90, 1&3:£12.00 CSF £73.81 TOTE £17.40: £5.50, £2.20, £3.10; EX 94.50.There was no bid for the winner. Bertie Southstreet was claimed by J. O'Reilly £6,000
Owner Danethorpe Racing Partnership **Bred** Paul Blows And Jenny Hall **Trained** Willoughton, Lincs
■ Stewards' Enquiry : Declan Cannon one-day ban: used whip with excessive frequency (Dec 19)

FOCUS
A modest seller and probably not form to be positive about.
Lindoro Official explanation: jockey said gelding never travelled

7646 £10 FREE PLAY AT TOTESPORTBINGO.COM H'CAP 5f 20y(P)
7:20 (7:20) (Class 4) (0-85,85) 3-Y-O+ **£5,046** (£1,510; £755; £377; £188) **Stalls** Low

Form RPR
0006 **1** **Green Park (IRE)**[7] 7577 6-8-4 **71** .... (b) JimmyQuinn 5 82
(D Carroll) *s.i.s and hmpd sn after s: hld up: hdwy to chse clr ldr over 1f out: rdn ins fnl f: hung rt and r.o to ld post* **8/1**

4541 **2** shd **Nickel Silver**[38] 7123 4-8-10 **77** .... (v[1]) TomEaves 2 88
(B Smart) *led: clr 1/2-way: rdn over 1f out: hdd post* **5/2**[1]

101 **3** 3 ¾ **Misaro (GER)**[9] 7534 8-8-10 **77** .... (b) DavidProbert 1 74
(R A Harris) *chsd ldr 1f: remained handy: rdn over 1f out: styd on same pce fnl f* **5/1**[3]

1325 **4** shd **Johnstown Lad (IRE)**[8] 7553 5-9-1 **82** .... (t) ShaneKelly 8 79
(Daniel Mark Loughnane, Ire) *chsd ldrs: rdn over 1f out: styd on* **7/1**

-104 **5** nk **Mrs Penny (AUS)**[273] 785 5-9-4 **85** .... (p) AdamKirby 6 81+
(J R Gask) *edgd lft s: hld up: swtchd rt over 1f out: r.o ins fnl f: nt rch ldrs* **11/4**[2]

6360 **6** 1 **Chjimes (IRE)**[44] 6972 5-8-10 **77** .... LPKeniry 7 69
(C R Dore) *chsd ldrs: rdn and hung lft over 1f out: no ex fnl f* **8/1**

7 1 ¾ **Lilly Be (IRE)**[50] 6833 6-8-6 **73** .... (b) ChrisCatlin 9 59
(Paul Magnier, Ire) *chsd ldr 4f out: pushed along and outpcd 1/2-way: sn rdn: wknd ins fnl f* **25/1**

1450 **8** 1 **Harry Up**[10] 7511 8-8-10 **77** .... (p) SJCraine 3 59
(M J Scudamore) *s.i.s: hld up: effrt over 1f out: n.m.r and wknd fnl f* **16/1**

61.75 secs (-0.55) **Going Correction** +0.05s/f (Slow) **8** Ran SP% **116.4**
Speed ratings (Par 105): **106,105,99,99,99 97,94,93**
toteswinger:1&2:£4.20, 2&3:£3.20, 1&3:£8.60 CSF £28.92 CT £112.61 TOTE £10.70: £2.70, £1.40, £1.50; EX 35.20.
Owner G A Fixings Ltd **Bred** James Burns And A Moynan **Trained** Sledmere, E Yorks

FOCUS
A fair sprint handicap run at a good pace and the form makes sense at face value.

7647 CLEAN WASTE SOLUTIONS CLAIMING STKS 1m 4f 50y(P)
7:50 (7:50) (Class 6) 3-Y-O+ **£2,729** (£806; £403) **Stalls** Low

Form RPR
4202 **1** **Bee Stinger**[8] 7549 7-8-10 68 .... KFallon 7 71
(B G Powell) *hld up: plld hrd: hdwy 3f out: chsd ldr 2f out: shkn up to ld over 1f out: edgd lft ins fnl f: styd on wl* **15/8**[1]

2-36 **2** 3 ¾ **Acropolis (IRE)**[7] 7578 8-9-0 70 .... StephenDonohoe 8 69
(B G Powell) *chsd ldr tl led 4f out: rdn and hdd over 1f out: styd on same pce* **8/1**

0000 **3** 2 ¼ **Midnight Bay**[41] 4279 3-8-0 47 .... AndrewHeffernan(5) 6 61?
(P D Evans) *trckd ldrs: plld hrd early: rdn over 2f out: no ex fnl f* **50/1**

612- **4** 1 **Chocolate Caramel (USA)**[497] 4439 7-9-10 82 .... PaulHanagan 1 74
(R A Fahey) *sn led: hdd 4f out: rdn over 2f out: wknd fnl f* **9/4**[2]

-000 **5** 1 **Anfield Road**[26] 7036 4-9-2 70 .... (p) LPKeniry 4 64
(L Corcoran) *dwlt: hld up: rdn and edgd lft over 3f out: outpcd fr over 2f out* **10/1**

6-16 **6** 12 **Red Expresso (IRE)**[39] 7093 4-8-9 63 .... KellyHarrison(3) 3 41
(Ollie Pears) *hld up in tch: rdn over 4f out: hmpd and wknd over 3f out* **10/3**[3]

2m 41.78s (0.68) **Going Correction** +0.05s/f (Slow)
WFA 3 from 4yo+ 5lb **6** Ran SP% **110.8**
Speed ratings (Par 101): **99,96,95,94,93 85**
toteswinger:1&2:£2.40, 2&3:£26.20, 1&3:£13.30 CSF £16.72 TOTE £2.40: £1.30, £3.60; EX 17.70.
Owner Ms Heather Dalton **Bred** Templeton Stud **Trained** Upper Lambourn, Berks

FOCUS
An uncompetitive claimer - the third-placed finisher was rated just 47 - and the they went a steady gallop through the first few furlongs. The form is not the most reliable with the first two setting the level.
Midnight Bay Official explanation: jockey said gelding hung left final 2f

7648 ENJOY THE LUCKY 7 GROUP OFFER MAIDEN STKS 1m 4f 50y(P)
8:20 (8:20) (Class 5) 3-Y-O+ **£2,729** (£806; £403) **Stalls** Low

Form RPR
4432 **1** **Inflammable**[8] 7557 3-8-12 65 .... SebSanders 12 66
(Sir Mark Prescott) *stdd s: hld up: hdwy over 2f out: swept through on outside to ld over 1f out: hrd rdn ins fnl f: all out* **5/2**[1]

34 **2** hd **French Hollow**[22] 7367 4-9-8 0 .... PhillipMakin 10 71
(T J Fitzgerald) *hld up: hdwy over 2f out: rdn to chse ldr and edgd rt over 1f out: styd on* **10/1**

33 **3** 7 **Laureldeans Best (IRE)**[21] 7401 3-8-12 0 .... PaulHanagan 5 58+
(R A Fahey) *hld up: hdwy over 4f out: cl up and gng okay whn nt clr run over 1f out: sn swtchd rt: hung lft and styd on same pce fnl f* **4/1**[2]

0 **4** nk **New Couture (IRE)**[17] 7439 3-8-12 0 .... AdrianMcCarthy 7 54
(P W Chapple-Hyam) *mid-div: hdwy over 4f out: rdn over 2f out: wknd fnl f* **20/1**

5663 **5** 2 ½ **Desert Fairy**[26] 7318 3-8-12 48 .... TomEaves 3 50
(J W Unett) *trckd ldrs: plld hrd: led over 2f out: rdn and hdd over 1f out: edgd lft: wknd fnl f* **25/1**

24/0 **6** ½ **City Hustler (USA)**[15] 7461 4-9-8 65 .... AdamKirby 2 54
(Adrian McGuinness, Ire) *chsd ldrs: led over 6f out: rdn and hdd over 2f out: hmpd and wknd over 1f out* **15/2**[3]

332- **7** 5 **The Last Bottle (IRE)**[428] 6447 4-9-8 58 .... GrahamGibbons 9 46
(W M Brisbourne) *prom: rdn over 2f out: wknd over 1f out* **12/1**

6 **8** 1 ¾ **Lastroseofsummer (IRE)**[38] 7126 3-8-12 0 .... ChrisCatlin 8 38
(Rae Guest) *plld hrd and prom: pushed along and lost pl over 7f out: rdn and wknd over 3f out* **8/1**

0 **9** *12* **Beyond Atlow**[23] 7361 4-9-3 0 AndrewHeffernan(5) 1 24
(Lucinda Featherstone) *mid-div: hdwy 1/2-way: rdn over 3f out: wknd 2f out* **100/1**
00 **10** *hd* **Beyonda Dream**[8] 7557 3-8-12 0 NeilChalmers 4 19
(Lucinda Featherstone) *led: hung rt bnd 7f out: hdd sn after: wknd 3f out* **200/1**
11 *3/4* **Misty Kit**[51] 4-9-3 0 ShaneKelly 6 18
(W M Brisbourne) *s.i.s: hld up and a in rr: wknd 4f out* **50/1**
5- **12** *dist* **Gheed (IRE)**[490] 4651 4-9-3 0 JimmyQuinn 11 —
(K A Morgan) *mid-div: plld hrd: hdwy to trckd ldr over 9f out: rdn and wknd over 5f out: sn t.o: virtually p.u fnl 4f* **4/1**[2]

2m 42.22s (1.12) **Going Correction** +0.05s/f (Slow)
WFA 3 from 4yo 5lb **12** Ran SP% **120.3**
Speed ratings (Par 103): **98,97,93,93,91 91,87,86,78,78 77,—**
toteswinger:1&2:£7.40, 2&3:£7.80, 1&3:£2.60 CSF £28.80 TOTE £4.10: £2.00, £2.30, £1.90; EX 23.60.
Owner Cheveley Park Stud **Bred** Cheveley Park Stud Ltd **Trained** Newmarket, Suffolk
■ Stewards' Enquiry : Seb Sanders one-day ban: used whip with excessive freaquency (Dec 19)

FOCUS
A modest maiden and the early pace was steady. The winner is rated to this year's form backed up by the fifth.
Gheed(IRE) Official explanation: jockey said filly finished distressed

7649 WOLVERHAMPTON-RACECOURSE.CO.UK H'CAP 2m 119y(P)
8:50 (8:50) (Class 6) (0-65,63) 3-Y-O+ **£2,388** (£705; £352) **Stalls** Low

Form RPR
6205 **1** **Black Or Red (IRE)**[24] 7328 4-10-0 **63** GeorgeBaker 4 79+
(I A Wood) *hld up: hdwy over 3f out: led over 2f out: sn rdn clr: hung lft 1f out: eased fnl 1/2 f* **9/2**[2]
030 **2** *7* **Blockley (USA)**[24] 7328 5-9-11 **60** (vt) StephenDonohoe 1 64
(Ian Williams) *sn pushed along in rr: hdwy over 4f out: edgd lft over 3f out: rdn to chse wnr over 1f out: hung lft and no imp* **7/1**
0/05 **3** *3/4* **Dawn Storm (IRE)**[26] 7318 4-9-1 **50** (p) AdamKirby 8 53
(J L Spearing) *hld up: hdwy u.p 3f out: styd on same pce fnl 2f* **22/1**
4333 **4** *nk* **Squirtle (IRE)**[19] 7415 6-9-1 **50** LukeMorris 2 53
(W M Brisbourne) *mid-div: pushed along 7f out: rdn over 4f out: outpcd over 3f out: styd on appr fnl f* **13/2**[3]
-233 **5** *2 1/4* **Diktatorship (IRE)**[23] 1533 6-9-1 **50** SJCraine 10 50
(Jennie Candlish) *prom: wnt 3rd 1/2-way: led wl over 2f out: sn hdd: wknd fnl f* **16/1**
00-1 **6** *3 1/4* **Purely By Chance**[24] 7328 4-8-12 **52** (b) SimonPearce(5) 12 48
(J Pearce) *chsd ldrs: wnt 2nd over 10f out to over 6f out: sn rdn: hmpd and wknd over 3f out* **13/2**[3]
6405 **7** *4 1/2* **Bold Adventure**[43] 7005 5-9-11 **60** TonyCulhane 3 51
(W J Musson) *hld up: pushed along on outside over 2f out: n.d* **7/1**
0061 **8** *3/4* **K'Gari (USA)**[19] 7415 3-8-9 **52** (b) PaulHanagan 9 42
(B Ellison) *sn rdn to ld: hdd wl over 2f out: wknd over 1f out* **3/1**[1]
00/3 **9** *14* **Catskill**[30] 6147 7-9-3 **52** (b) GrahamGibbons 7 25
(Adrian McGuinness, Ire) *prom: chsd ldr 6f out to over 3f out: rdn and wknd over 2f out* **16/1**
0005 **10** *36* **Dance Gdansk (IRE)**[4] 7608 3-8-12 **55** SteveDrowne 11 —
(M Blanshard) *mid-div: hdwy over 5f out: wknd 3f out* **20/1**
335/ **11** *81* **Acuzio**[827] 4994 8-9-8 **57** LPKeniry 6 —
(S Wynne) *chsd ldr 6f: sn rdn: lost pl 8f out: t.o fnl 7f* **33/1**

3m 42.44s (0.64) **Going Correction** +0.05s/f (Slow)
WFA 3 from 4yo+ 8lb **11** Ran SP% **118.7**
Speed ratings (Par 101): **100,96,96,96,95 93,91,91,84,67 29**
toteswinger:1&2:£7.70, 2&3:£47.10, 1&3:£20.90 CSF £35.47 CT £633.69 TOTE £5.40: £1.90, £2.80, £6.30; EX 38.60.
Owner Graham Bradbury **Bred** Dr John Hollowood And Aiden Murphy **Trained** Upper Lambourn, Berks

FOCUS
A weak race, but the winner hacked up. The pace was good, before slowing slightly at about halfway. The placed horses set the standard.
Acuzio Official explanation: jockey said gelding stopped quickly

7650 100% NEW PLAYER BONUS AT TOTESPORTCASINO.COM H'CAP 1m 141y(P)
9:20 (9:20) (Class 6) (0-60,60) 3-Y-O+ **£2,388** (£705; £352) **Stalls** Low

Form RPR
0415 **1** **Just Jimmy (IRE)**[14] 7492 4-9-2 **56** PaulDoe 2 64
(P D Evans) *chsd ldrs: rdn to ld ins fnl f: jst hld on* **5/1**
5000 **2** *hd* **Golden Prospect**[6] 7591 5-9-1 **55** (b[1]) PaulFitzsimons 5 63
(Miss J R Tooth) *s.i.s: hld up: plld hrd: hdwy over 1f out: rdn and ev ch ins fnl f: r.o* **18/1**
0000 **3** *nk* **Bob Stock (IRE)**[14] 7480 3-9-3 **59** TonyCulhane 1 66
(W J Musson) *hld up: hdwy over 2f out: rdn and hung lft over 1f out: r.o* **4/1**[2]
1165 **4** *2* **Bickersten**[15] 7471 3-9-3 **59** (p) GeorgeBaker 7 61
(C Moore, Ire) *chsd ldr tl led over 3f out: rdn and hdd ins fnl f: no ex* **7/2**[1]
4264 **5** *nse* **Bajan Pride**[11] 7499 5-8-10 **57** LeeTopliss(7) 13 59
(R A Fahey) *s.i.s: hld up: hdwy over 3f out: rdn to chse ldr over 2f out: no ex fnl f* **16/1**
6662 **6** *1 1/4* **Royal Manor**[6] 7586 4-9-1 **60** RossAtkinson(5) 11 59
(Tom Dascombe) *s.i.s: hld up and bhd: hdwy and hung lft over 1f out: nt rch ldrs* **9/2**[3]
1260 **7** *3 1/4* **Alfredtheordinary**[247] 1080 4-9-5 **59** SamHitchcott 8 51
(M R Channon) *hld up: hdwy over 3f out: rdn and wknd over 1f out* **25/1**
0050 **8** *4* **Woteva**[17] 7428 3-9-0 **56** ChrisCatlin 4 39
(T P Tate) *led: hdd over 3f out: rdn and wknd over 1f out* **14/1**
0221 **9** *1/2* **Bidable**[15] 7466 5-9-2 **56** NeilChalmers 12 37
(B Palling) *chsd ldrs: pushed along 3f out: wknd 2f out* **15/2**
3000 **10** *4 1/2* **Jul's Lad (IRE)**[151] 3718 3-9-2 **58** GrahamGibbons 9 29
(D Carroll) *chsd ldrs: rdn: hung lft and wknd 3f out* **13/2**

1m 50.11s (-0.39) **Going Correction** +0.05s/f (Slow)
WFA 3 from 4yo+ 2lb **10** Ran SP% **123.8**
Speed ratings (Par 101): **103,102,102,100,100 99,96,93,92,88**
toteswinger:1&2:£9.40, 2&3:£21.70, 1&3:£7.60 CSF £95.84 CT £339.34 TOTE £5.50: £1.90, £5.60, £2.20; EX 140.30 Place 6 £325.67, Place 5 £239.40.
Owner Richard Edwards **Bred** Richard Edwards And Gwynne Williams **Trained** Pandy, Monmouths
■ Stewards' Enquiry : Paul Fitzsimons seven-day ban: used whip with excessive frequency down shoulder in the forehand (Dec 19-22, Dec 26-28)
Paul Doe one-day ban: used whip with excessive frequency (Dec 19)

FOCUS
A moderate handicap run at a good pace and the form looks sound.
Jul's Lad(IRE) Official explanation: jockey said gelding hung left
T/Plt: £147.00 to a £1 stake. Pool: £103,386.75. 513.41 winning tickets. T/Qpdt: £5.00 to a £1 stake. Pool: £10,422.19. 1,542.16 winning tickets. CR

7622 LINGFIELD (L-H)
Sunday, December 6

OFFICIAL GOING: Standard
Wind: Fresh, across Weather: dry and brightening after heavy morning rain

7651 EDDIE MILLS 80TH BIRTHDAY H'CAP (DIV I) 5f (P)
12:00 (12:00) (Class 6) (0-60,70) 3-Y-O+ **£2,047** (£604; £302) **Stalls** High

Form RPR
5411 **1** **Spinning Bailiwick**[8] 7572 3-10-0 **70** GeorgeBaker 10 76+
(G L Moore) *chsd ldrs on outer: drvn and unable qck over 1f out: hdwy u.p fnl 100yds: r.o wl to ld last strides* **2/1**[1]
0323 **2** *nk* **Jolly Ranch**[46] 6939 3-8-9 **54** MartinLane(3) 3 59
(A G Newcombe) *led: rdn wl over 1f out: wandered jst ins fnl f: hung rt fnl 150yds: hdd last strides* **8/1**
1000 **3** *1/2* **Best One**[23] 7371 5-8-9 **51** (b) ChrisCatlin 1 54
(R A Harris) *dwlt: sn chsng ldrs on inner: effrt u.p over 1f out: str chal ins fnl f: unable qck fnl 75yds* **20/1**
5046 **4** *1/2* **Pinball (IRE)**[15] 7483 3-8-10 **55** (v) KellyHarrison(3) 4 56
(Mrs L Williamson) *restless stalls: stdd s: t.k.h: hld up in tch in rr: rdn and effrt on inner over 1f out: kpt on but nvr quite pce to rch ldrs* **10/1**
0032 **5** *hd* **Monsieur Reynard**[6] 7601 4-8-13 **55** LukeMorris 5 56
(J M Bradley) *t.k.h: trckd ldrs: rdn and effrt whn nt clr run and swtchd rt jst ins fnl f: keeping on same pce whn nt clr run and hmpd ins fnl f: unable to chal* **5/2**[2]
5561 **6** *hd* **Spoof Master (IRE)**[46] 6939 5-9-0 **56** LPKeniry 9 56
(C R Dore) *pressed ldr: rdn and ev ch 2f out: drvn and unable qck over 1f out: keeping on same pce whn short of room and eased nr fin* **16/1**
0666 **7** *nk* **Commander Wish**[18] 7427 6-8-7 **49** (p) KFallon 6 48
(Lucinda Featherstone) *s.i.s: in tch in rr on outer: rdn wl over 2f out: kpt on u.p ins fnl f: nvr gng pce to trble ldrs* **5/1**[3]
-400 **8** *1/2* **Winterbourne**[58] 6641 3-8-5 **47** JimmyQuinn 8 44
(M Blanshard) *dwlt: sn bustled along: in tch in last trio: unable qck u.p ent fnl 2f: kpt on same pce after* **50/1**

58.68 secs (-0.12) **Going Correction** -0.05s/f (Stan) **8** Ran SP% **111.4**
Speed ratings (Par 101): **98,97,96,95,95 95,94,94**
toteswinger:1&2:£3.80, 2&3:£19.60, 1&3:£7.70 CSF £17.76 CT £237.36 TOTE £2.80: £1.10, £1.70, £3.60; EX 14.50 Trifecta £224.50 Part won. Pool: £303.43 - 0.90 winning units..
Owner Dr Ian R Shenkin **Bred** Mrs M Shenkin **Trained** Lower Beeding, W Sussex
■ Stewards' Enquiry : Martin Lane three-day ban: careless riding (Dec 20-22)

FOCUS
An ordinary sprint handicap and a bit of a bunch finish.

7652 BEST ODDS GUARANTEED AT TOTESPORT.COM APPRENTICE H'CAP (DIV I) 1m (P)
12:30 (12:30) (Class 6) (0-55,54) 3-Y-O+ **£2,047** (£604; £302) **Stalls** High

Form RPR
0032 **1** **Join Up**[4] 7609 3-8-13 **49** RossAtkinson 11 56
(W M Brisbourne) *t.k.h: hld up in rr: sltly hmpd 6f out: gd hdwy on outer 3f out: chsd clr ldr jst over 2f out: rdn to ld ins fnl f: sn in command and pushed out after* **4/1**[1]
6540 **2** *1 1/4* **Louisiade (IRE)**[80] 6038 8-8-7 **45** (p) BillyCray(3) 8 49
(R C Guest) *broke v fast: led for 1f: chsd ldr after: clsd qckly to ld again wl over 2f out: sn clr: rdn 2f out: hdd ins fnl f: sn btn* **12/1**
0005 **3** *2 3/4* **Turkish Sultan (IRE)**[16] 7466 6-8-6 **46** (p) RyanClark(5) 2 43
(J M Bradley) *racd off the pce in midfield: rdn and effrt over 2f out: chsd clr ldng pair wl over 1f out: kpt on but nvr gng pce to rch ldng pair* **9/1**
3400 **4** *1* **Shake On It**[15] 7480 5-9-1 **50** JamieJones 9 48
(M R Hoad) *stdd s: hld up in rr: hdwy and nt clr run jst over 2f out: wnt modest 4th and edgd rt wl over 1f out: kpt on but nvr trbld ldrs* **13/2**[3]
6000 **5** *6* **Foxtrot Bravo (IRE)**[15] 7492 3-8-13 **54** BarryAdams(5) 6 35
(Miss S L Davison) *chsd ldrs: rdn and struggling jst over 2f out: wl hld whn short of room over 1f out: no ch after* **14/1**
0565 **6** *3/4* **Always The Sun**[11] 7517 3-8-12 **53** (p) LauraPike(5) 7 32
(P Leech) *a bhd: pushed along over 3f out: sme hdwy over 2f out: nvr trbld ldrs* **11/2**[2]
3403 **7** *3 1/2* **Djalalabad (FR)**[18] 7438 5-9-1 **50** (tp) SimonPearce 10 20
(Mrs C A Dunnett) *taken down early: stdd s: hld up in rr: hdwy and nt clr run jst over 2f out: nvr trbld ldrs* **11/2**[2]
330 **8** *4* **Baba Ghanoush**[165] 3269 7-8-5 **45** (v) KierenFox(5) 1 6
(M J Attwater) *chsd ldrs: struggling u.p over 2f out: no ch fr wl over 1f out* **20/1**
6640 **9** *5* **Superior Duchess**[67] 6375 4-8-4 **46** LewisWalsh(7) 5 —
(Jane Chapple-Hyam) *t.k.h: hld up off the pce in midfield: swtchd rt 6f out: struggling wl over 2f out: wl btn fnl 2f* **8/1**
0-05 **10** *5* **Woodland Violet**[17] 7452 3-8-9 **45** AshleyMorgan 4 —
(I A Wood) *racd off the pce in midfield tl lost pl and rdn over 4f out: wl bhd fnl 2f* **50/1**
0000 **11** *20* **Green Onions**[19] 7418 3-9-0 **53** (be) AmyScott(3) 3 —
(A J Lidderdale) *taken down early: racd freely: led after 1f: sn clr: hdd wl over 2f out: sn fdd: wl bhd fr over 1f out: t.o and eased fnl f* **33/1**
0-56 **12** *7* **Countrywide Jaime (IRE)**[309] 358 3-8-9 **48** TobyAtkinson(3) 12 —
(M Wigham) *t.k.h: hld up off the pce in midfield: lost pl u.p 4f out: t.o* **16/1**

1m 37.87s (-0.33) **Going Correction** -0.05s/f (Stan)
WFA 3 from 4yo+ 1lb **12** Ran SP% **115.1**
Speed ratings (Par 101): **99,97,95,94,88 87,83,79,74,69 49,42**
toteswinger:1&2:£8.60, 2&3:£15.80, 1&3:£6.20 CSF £50.63 CT £413.10 TOTE £4.70: £1.60, £4.70, £3.00; EX 32.40 TRIFECTA Not won..
Owner P R Kirk **Bred** A Reid **Trained** Great Ness, Shropshire

FOCUS
Green Onions ensured a good gallop here, going off far too fast for his own good in front, and the race was set up nicely for a closer. The time was almost a second quicker than the second division.

7653 BEST ODDS GUARANTEED AT TOTESPORT.COM APPRENTICE H'CAP (DIV II) 1m (P)
1:00 (1:00) (Class 6) (0-55,53) 3-Y-O+ **£2,047** (£604; £302) **Stalls** High

Form RPR
0030 **1** **Batchworth Blaise**[11] 7517 6-8-6 **45** RichardRowe(5) 10 53
(E A Wheeler) *stdd s and dropped in in bhd: hdwy on outer over 3f out: chsd ldr wl over 1f out: led ent fnl f: rdn out* **10/1**
6220 **2** *3/4* **Party In The Park**[18] 7438 4-8-12 **51** NathanAlison(5) 6 57+
(J R Boyle) *hld up in rr: hdwy into modest 6th over 1f out: r.o wl fnl f: wnt 2nd towards fin: nt rch ldr* **5/1**[2]

364 **3** ½ **Prince Valentine**[45] 6966 8-8-4 **45**............................(p) HarryBentley(7) 1 50
(G L Moore) *chsd ldrs: wnt 2nd over 2f out: unable qck u.p over 1f out: 3rd and one pce whn short of room and swtchd rt ins fnl f: kpt on* **10/1**

0400 **4** 1 **Imperial Skylight**[15] 7480 3-9-4 **53**........................ AndrewHeffernan 9 55
(M R Channon) *chsd ldr for 1f: chsd ldrs after tl led over 2f out: drvn wl over 1f out: hdd ent fnl f: wknd and lost 2 pls towards fin* **5/1**[2]

005 **5** 1¼ **Rainiers Girl**[33] 7228 3-8-7 **47**.. KierenFox(5) 11 46
(R A Teal) *chsd ldrs: lost pl and rdn 3f out: edgd lft and hdwy over 2f out: kpt on u.p fnl f but nvr gng pce to rch ldrs* **20/1**

3063 **6** 1¼ **Stark Contrast (USA)**[7] 7586 5-8-12 **49**......................... LeeNewnes(3) 8 45
(M D I Usher) *in tch on outer: hdwy to chse ldrs 3f out: rdn and unable qck ent fnl 2f: wknd jst ins fnl f* **11/4**[1]

6-50 **7** ½ **Parkview Love (USA)**[85] 5888 8-8-13 **47**........................ SimonPearce 4 42
(A G Newcombe) *hld up in rr: hmpd on inner wl over 2f out: hdwy and barging match w rival 2f out: kpt on but nvr able to chal* **8/1**

5650 **8** ½ **Incy Wincy**[11] 7520 3-8-5 **45**..(p) RyanClark(5) 3 39
(J M Bradley) *a towards rr: plugged on u.p fnl 2f: nvr trbld ldrs* **33/1**

6504 **9** 9 **Fairplaytomyself**[8] 7581 4-8-10 **47**............................ TobyAtkinson(3) 2 19
(P W Hiatt) *chsd ldr after 1f tl over 2f out: wkng whn wd bnd 2f out: sn bhd* **7/1**[3]

0030 **10** 3½ **Miss Jabba (IRE)**[12] 7499 3-8-3 **45**...................(b1) AdamBeschizza(7) 12 9
(Miss J Feilden) *sn rdn along to ld: hdd over 2f out: sn wknd: wl btn whn barging match w rival 2f out* **10/1**

1m 38.85s (0.65) **Going Correction** -0.05s/f (Stan)
WFA 3 from 4yo+ 1lb **10** Ran SP% **118.6**
Speed ratings (Par 101): **94,93,92,91,90 89,88,88,79,75**
toteswinger:1&2:£12.10, 2&3:£4.80, 1&3:£13.80 CSF £60.46 CT £538.57 TOTE £12.30: £2.90, £2.10, £2.40; EX 76.40 Trifecta £86.80 Part won. Pool: £117.39 - 0.45 winning units..

Owner Astrod TA Austin Stroud & Co **Bred** Mrs D Price **Trained** Whitchurch-on-Thames, Oxon

■ Stewards' Enquiry : Adam Beschizza caution: used whip when out of contention.

FOCUS
The slower of the two divisions by 0.98sec.

Party In The Park Official explanation: jockey said gelding was denied a clear run

Rainiers Girl Official explanation: jockey said filly hung left

7654 BIGGER "WIN ONLY" ODDS AT TOTESPORT.COM NURSERY 7f (P)
1:30 (1:31) (Class 5) (0-75,76) 2-Y-O **£3,238** (£963; £481; £240) **Stalls** Low

Form RPR

0011 **1** **Lisahane Bog**[11] 7513 2-8-12 **66**......................................(p) DaneO'Neill 4 69
(P R Hedger) *dwlt: sn niggled along in last trio: wd and rdn 3f out: hdwy u.p over 1f out: edgd lft u.p but r.o strly fnl f to ld wl ins fnl f* **9/2**[1]

1023 **2** nk **Be A Devil**[4] 7611 2-9-5 **73**.. MartinDwyer 10 75
(W R Muir) *hld up in tch in rr: gd hdwy and edging lft jst over 1f out: drvn to ld fnl 100yds: hdd wl ins fnl f: kpt on* **13/2**[3]

0202 **3** nk **Fivefold (USA)**[9] 7551 2-9-8 **76**..................................... J-PGuillambert 9 77
(J Akehurst) *chsd ldr tl rdn to ld ent fnl 2f: edgd rt u.p ins fnl f: hdd fnl 100yds: kpt on same pce after* **8/1**

3061 **4** 2 **Exceedthewildman**[9] 7551 2-9-1 **74**.........................(p) SophieDoyle(5) 7 70
(J S Moore) *in tch: effrt to chse ldng pair 2f out: rdn and unable qck over 1f out: sltly hmpd and swtchd lft ins fnl f: kpt on same pce* **6/1**[2]

000 **5** 1 **The Love Guru**[19] 7419 2-7-12 **52** oh2........................(b) NickyMackay 11 46
(J R Boyle) *led and crossed over to rail: rdn and hdd 2f out: one pce u.p fr over 1f out* **40/1**

3050 **6** 1 **Two Kisses (IRE)**[17] 7451 2-8-11 **65**........................ StephenDonohoe 8 56
(B G Powell) *chsd ldrs: rdn and unable qck wl over 1f out: drvn and one pce fr over 1f out* **40/1**

2553 **7** 1 **Could It Be Magic**[9] 7551 2-9-0 **71**..............................(p) JackDean(3) 3 60
(W G M Turner) *t.k.h: hld up in tch in midfield: rdn and no prog wl over 1f out* **16/1**

6231 **8** 1¼ **Rezwaan**[52] 6793 2-9-4 **72**.. ShaneKelly 2 58
(M J McGrath) *chsd ldrs on inner: rdn and unable qck ent fnl 2f: n.d fnl f* **8/1**

0031 **9** nk **Dutiful**[8] 7584 2-8-8 **62**.. KFallon 6 47
(M R Channon) *stdd s: hld up in rr: rdn and effrt wl over 1f out: no real prog* **9/2**[1]

4316 **10** 2½ **Tewin Wood**[15] 7494 2-9-5 **73**.. SteveDrowne 1 52
(A Bailey) *hld up in tch in midfield: rdn and no prog over 1f out: wl hld fnl f* **7/1**

504 **11** 5 **Ermyntrude**[39] 7106 2-8-1 **55**... JimmyQuinn 5 21
(P M Phelan) *restless stalls: in tch: rdn 3f out: sn struggling: bhd wl over 1f out* **16/1**

1m 24.65s (-0.15) **Going Correction** -0.05s/f (Stan) **11** Ran SP% **115.3**
Speed ratings (Par 96): **98,97,97,95,93 92,91,90,89,86 81**
toteswinger:1&2:£5.50, 2&3:£9.30, 1&3:£5.20 CSF £32.66 CT £228.67 TOTE £5.50: £1.90, £2.90, £2.80; EX 25.20 Trifecta £152.80 Part won. Pool: £206.59 - 0.50 winning units..

Owner P C F Racing Ltd **Bred** J J Whelan **Trained** Dogmersfield, Hampshire

FOCUS
A competitive handicap featuring a number of in-form and improving juveniles. The form looks sound and the winner progressive.

NOTEBOOK
Lisahane Bog was held up off the pace and brought with his challenge widest of all entering the straight. He tended to hang under pressure but the momentum was with him in the closing stages and he got up close home to complete the hat-trick. His style of running means he doesn't win by too far, and for that reason there's every chance he can remain one step of the handicapper. (op 4-1 tchd 5-1)

Be A Devil found a passage between horses in the straight having been held up for a late run. He was arguably disadvantaged by challenging more towards the inside late on, while the first two were wider out, and so this was a sound effort. (op 7-1 tchd 11-2)

Fivefold(USA), prominent throughout and a bit keen early, had no excuses. He reversed course and distance form with Exceedthewildman, who beat him by a neck last time, on 6lb better terms. (tchd 15-2 and 9-1 in places)

Exceedthewildman was a little disappointing as he travelled well to the entrance to the straight but found little once in line for home. (op 15-2)

The Love Guru, 2lb wrong at the weights on his handicap debut, had plenty of use made of him early to cross over from the outside stall and make the running. This was a big step up on his efforts in maiden company and he could be interesting in a similar contest when handed a better draw. (op 66-1)

Dutiful, 7lb higher than when successful at Wolverhampton, missed the break and never got involved from off the pace. (op 5-1)

7655 BET ON TODAY'S FOOTBALL AT TOTESPORT.COM MAIDEN AUCTION STKS 6f (P)
2:00 (2:01) (Class 6) 2-Y-O **£2,729** (£806; £403) **Stalls** Low

Form RPR

4234 **1** **Pan American**[27] 7317 2-8-10 **75**................................. FergusSweeney 4 73
(P J Makin) *t.k.h: chsd ldr tl led gng wl 2f out: rdn over 1f out: styd on wl fnl f* **15/8**[1]

4556 **2** ¾ **Bubbly Bellini (IRE)**[8] 7580 2-8-3 **70**......................... TobyAtkinson(7) 5 71
(A Bailey) *wnt rt s: sn niggled along in last pair: swtchd ins and hdwy u.p over 1f out: chsd wnr ins fnl f: no imp fnl 50yds* **9/2**[3]

00 **3** ¾ **Ermyn Express**[39] 7106 2-8-4 0... JimmyQuinn 1 63
(P M Phelan) *led: rdn and hdd 2f out: kpt on same pce u.p fnl f* **50/1**

6662 **4** 1½ **Hill Of Miller (IRE)**[15] 7477 2-8-12 **76**............................ MartinDwyer 2 66
(Rae Guest) *t.k.h: trckd ldrs: rdn and effrt ent fnl 2f: styd on same pce u.p fnl f* **5/2**[2]

0 **5** 2½ **Not In The Clock (USA)**[15] 7477 2-8-11 0.................... SteveDrowne 7 58
(J R Best) *s.i.s: a bhd: nvr trbld ldrs* **8/1**

0040 **6** nk **Bush Master**[10] 7537 2-8-13 **70**... SJCraine 3 59
(J R Boyle) *akward leaving stalls: sn chsng ldrs: rdn and unable qck ent fnl 2f: drvn and btn over 1f out* **7/1**

1m 12.3s (0.40) **Going Correction** -0.05s/f (Stan) **6** Ran SP% **107.1**
Speed ratings (Par 94): **95,94,93,91,87 87**
toteswinger:1&2:£2.40, 2&3:£10.40, 1&3:£8.20 CSF £9.59 TOTE £2.50: £1.30, £2.40; EX 12.90.

Owner D R Tucker **Bred** D R Tucker **Trained** Ogbourne Maisey, Wilts

FOCUS
A modest maiden but despite the small field a number could be given a chance. It has been rated around the runner-up.

NOTEBOOK
Pan American got the job done in professional fashion and probably didn't have to improve on his best previous form to score. Sent on turning into the straight, he made use of his 7f stamina, and a return to that trip in handicap company shouldn't pose a problem. (tchd 2-1)

Bubbly Bellini(IRE) ran a better race than at Wolverhampton last time when returning from an absence, although making her challenge nearest the inside rail was probably no help. (tchd 5-1)

Ermyn Express took them along for much of the race but was fairly easily brushed aside by the winner. This was still by far her best run to date, though, on her first try over 6f, and handicaps will now be an option. (op 40-1)

Hill Of Miller(IRE), an inconsistent sort, was keen early and struggled to pick up in the straight. (op 9-4 tchd 2-1)

Not In The Clock(USA) Official explanation: jockey said colt was slowly away

7656 BET LIVE IN PLAY AT TOTESPORT.COM H'CAP 6f (P)
2:30 (2:32) (Class 4) (0-80,80) 3-Y-O+ **£5,180** (£1,541; £770; £384) **Stalls** Low

Form RPR

641 **1** **Imprimis Tagula (IRE)**[25] 7337 5-8-13 **80**..................(v) LeeNewnes(5) 5 91
(A Bailey) *restless stalls: hld up wl in tch: hdwy to chse ldrs and rdn over 1f out: led ins fnl f: r.o wl to assert fnl 75yds* **9/2**[1]

1602 **2** 1¾ **Billy Red**[9] 7553 5-9-1 **77**..(b) FergusSweeney 6 82
(J R Jenkins) *chsd ldrs: wnt 2nd over 2f out: rdn over 1f out: pressed wnr ins fnl f: no ex and btn fnl 75yds* **8/1**

0125 **3** 1¼ **Poppanan (USA)**[47] 6916 3-8-10 **72**................................. TonyCulhane 8 73
(S Dow) *s.i.s and short of room sn after s: hdwy into midfield over 3f out: swtchd rt jst over 2f out: kpt on wl u.p fnl f: wnt 3rd last stride* **6/1**

1605 **4** shd **Dvinsky (USA)**[4] 7613 8-8-13 **75**...(b) PaulDoe 4 76
(P Howling) *sn bustled along to press ldr: led over 2f out: drvn over 1f out: hdd ins fnl f: wknd fnl 100yds* **8/1**

21-0 **5** 1½ **Fen Spirit (IRE)**[11] 7516 3-9-3 **79**.................................... RobertHavlin 11 75
(J H M Gosden) *stdd and short of room sn after s: a towards rr: looking for run towards outer over 2f out: drvn over 1f out: kpt on but nvr able to chal ldrs* **9/1**

1060 **6** nk **Comadoir (IRE)**[31] 7253 3-9-0 **76**....................................... IanMongan 10 71
(Miss Jo Crowley) *towards rr: hdwy into midfield and rdn ent fnl 2f: one pce and no hdwy fr over 1f out* **16/1**

1013 **7** nk **Misaro (GER)**[1] 7646 8-9-1 **77**.......................................(b) DavidProbert 9 71
(R A Harris) *a towards rr: hmpd jst over 2f out: c wd st: kpt on but nvr gng pce to threaten ldrs* **11/2**[3]

6000 **8** ½ **Mutamared (USA)**[31] 7253 9-8-10 **72**................................(t) SJCraine 12 64
(M J Scudamore) *hld up towards rr on outer: effrt on outer jst over 2f out: nvr trbld ldrs* **16/1**

1020 **9** ¾ **Even Bolder**[11] 7511 6-8-6 **75**.. KierenFox(7) 7 65
(E A Wheeler) *trckd ldrs: nt clr run and shuffled bk bnd jst over 2f out: rdn and unable qck wl over 1f out: wknd fnl f* **5/1**[2]

1660 **10** 15 **For Life (IRE)**[9] 7553 7-8-7 **72**............................ NataliaGemelova(3) 3 14
(J E Long) *sn bustled along to ld: hdd over 2f out: wknd qckly over 1f out: wl btn and eased ins fnl f* **20/1**

1m 10.84s (-1.06) **Going Correction** -0.05s/f (Stan) **10** Ran SP% **113.3**
Speed ratings (Par 105): **105,102,101,100,98 98,98,97,96,76**
toteswinger:1&2:£8.00, 2&3:£4.90, 1&3:£3.80 CSF £39.18 CT £215.49 TOTE £6.00: £2.00, £1.90, £1.90; EX 45.00 Trifecta £127.00 Part won. Pool: £171.75 - 0.95 winning units..Bobs Dreamflight was withdrawn. Price at time of withdrawal was 20-1. Rule 4 does not apply.

Owner Middleham Park Racing XLI & Alan Bailey **Bred** Glashare House Stud **Trained** Newmarket, Suffolk

FOCUS
This sprint handicap had an open look to it, but in the event very few got involved.

Even Bolder Official explanation: jockey said gelding was denied a clear run

For Life(IRE) Official explanation: jockey said gelding never travelled

7657 EDDIE MILLS 80TH BIRTHDAY H'CAP (DIV II) 5f (P)
3:00 (3:01) (Class 6) (0-60,60) 3-Y-O+ **£2,047** (£604; £302) **Stalls** High

Form RPR

0000 **1** **Triskaidekaphobia**[78] 6119 6-8-4 **46**..................(t) WandersonD'Avila 3 55
(Miss J R Tooth) *mde all: clr ent 2f out: edgd rt and wkng ins fnl f: a jst gng to hold on* **33/1**

4105 **2** ½ **Thoughtsofstardom**[5] 7606 6-8-9 **54**......................... KellyHarrison(3) 7 61
(P S McEntee) *chsd ldrs: 3rd and rdn over 1f out chsd wnr fnl 100yds: kpt on but nvr quite getting to wnr* **7/2**[2]

U003 **3** 1 **Radiator Rooney (IRE)**[6] 7595 6-8-13 **55**........................(v) SJCraine 1 59
(Patrick Morris) *hld up in midfield: shkn up and effrt towards inner over 1f out: rdn and styd on fnl f: wnt 3rd on post* **6/1**

0504 **4** shd **Bluebok**[6] 7595 8-9-2 **58**...(bt) LukeMorris 6 61
(J M Bradley) *chsd ldrs: rdn to chse clr ldr wl over 1f out: kpt on but nvr looked looked like chalng wnr: lost 2 pls fnl 100yds* **4/1**[3]

0000 **5** *nse* **Handsome Cross (IRE)**[22] 7398 8-9-4 **60**..........(v[1]) StephenDonohoe 2 63
(W J Musson) *dwlt: racd in midfield: rdn and effrt 2f out: kpt on u.p fnl f but nvr gng pce to rch ldr* **8/1**

1236 **6** *½* **The Name Is Frank**[19] 7418 4-8-13 **55**..........(t) KFallon 4 56
(Mark Gillard) *s.i.s: bhd: rdn and effrt ent fnl 2f: hdwy on inner fnl f: kpt on wl but nvr gng pce to rch ldrs* **11/4**[1]

0000 **7** *1 ½* **Cosmic Destiny (IRE)**[15] 7483 7-8-11 **56**.......... MartinLane(3) 8 52
(E F Vaughan) *stdd s: hld up towards rr: rdn and effrt over 1f out: nvr gng pce to rch ldrs* **10/1**

2100 **8** *hd* **Malapropism**[9] 7561 9-8-13 **55**.......... ChrisCatlin 10 50
(M R Channon) *chsd ldr: rdn and outpcd jst over 2f out: lost 2nd wl over 1f out: wknd fnl f* **20/1**

0060 **9** *3 ½* **Stoneacre Pat (IRE)**[33] 7223 4-8-5 **47**..........(b) FrankieMcDonald 5 30
(Peter Grayson) *v.s.a: a bhd* **40/1**

58.48 secs (-0.32) **Going Correction** -0.05s/f (Stan) **9** Ran SP% **113.5**
Speed ratings (Par 101): **100,99,97,97,97 96,94,93,88**
toteswinger:1&2:£30.80, 2&3:£3.40, 1&3:£31.30 CSF £141.23 CT £815.65 TOTE £35.00: £9.10, £1.50, £2.20; EX 145.60 TRIFECTA Not won..
Owner Raymond Tooth And Steve Gilbey **Bred** K Bowen **Trained** Upper Lambourn, Berks

FOCUS
The quicker of the two divisions by 0.2sec.
Stoneacre Pat(IRE) Official explanation: jockey said colt was slowly away and hung badly right

7658 GODSTONE H'CAP — 1m 4f (P)
3:30 (3:33) (Class 7) (0-50,50) 3-Y-O+ **£2,047** (£604; £302) **Stalls** Low

Form RPR

0344 **1** **Mr Plod**[34] 6770 4-8-13 **50**.......... SJCraine 6 65+
(M J Scudamore) *stdd s: hld up in rr: stl plenty to do over 2f out: hdwy 2f out: pushed along and gd hdwy to ld fnl 100yds: sn clr: comf* **11/4**[1]

0205 **2** *1 ¾* **Russian Music (USA)**[81] 5983 4-8-12 **49**.......... StephenDonohoe 11 56
(Ian Williams) *hld up in tch in midfield: rdn and effrt to chse ldrs 2f out: ev ch briefly ins fnl f: sn brushed aside by wnr: kpt on* **13/2**[2]

4060 **3** *1* **Fine Tolerance**[15] 7495 3-8-7 **49**.......... DavidProbert 12 54
(Miss S L Davison) *s.i.s: r.o snatches: bhd: rdn 5f out: gd hdwy on outer over 3f out: chsd ldrs over 2f out: ev ch briefly ins fnl f: nt pce of wnr fnl 100yds* **20/1**

3/50 **4** *1* **Carr Hall (IRE)**[8] 7578 6-8-10 **50**.......... PatrickHills(3) 13 54
(B G Powell) *t.k.h: hld up towards rr: hdwy on outer to chse ldr over 5f out: led 3f out: rdn clr 2f out: drvn over 1f out: hdd fnl 100yds: wknd* **7/1**[3]

4500 **5** *1 ¾* **Turner's Touch**[9] 7549 7-8-10 **47**..........(b) AmirQuinn 3 48
(G L Moore) *bustled along leaving stalls: sn in tch: pushed along over 3f out: kpt on same pce fnl 2f* **14/1**

000- **6** *¾* **Three Thieves (UAE)**[359] 2832 6-8-10 **47**.......... SteveDrowne 1 47+
(Jim Best) *in tch: rdn and nt clr run and shuffled bk jst over 2f out: swtchd rt and drvn 2f out: kpt on but nvr able to rch ldrs* **8/1**

5500 **7** *2 ¾* **Jenny Soba**[16] 7461 6-8-13 **50**.......... KFallon 9 45
(Lucinda Featherstone) *s.i.s and pushed along early: bhd: rdn and effrt over 2f out: c wd bnd 2f out: plugged on u.p: nvr trbld ldrs* **9/1**

0000 **8** *1 ¼* **Lyrical Intent**[43] 7022 3-8-7 **49**.......... JimmyQuinn 4 42
(P Howling) *towards rr: rdn wl over 2f out: plugged on steadily fnl 2f: nvr trbld ldrs* **16/1**

0000 **9** *4* **Desert Hawk**[38] 7137 8-8-9 **46**.......... LukeMorris 2 33
(W M Brisbourne) *hld up in midfield: rdn and struggling wl over 3f out: nvr trbld ldrs* **33/1**

-006 **10** *nk* **Berrynarbor**[87] 5790 4-8-11 **48**.......... FergusSweeney 5 35
(A G Newcombe) *in tch in midfield whn n.m.r bnd 9f out: towards rr after: hdwy and rdn 3f out: chsd ldrs and drvn 2f out: wknd qckly over 1f out* **20/1**

5045 **11** *½* **Sir Haydn**[24] 7354 9-8-5 **49**.......... DannyBrock(7) 10 35
(J R Jenkins) *chsd ldrs: wnt 3rd over 3f out: nt clr run and shuffled bk bnd jst over 2f out: no ch after* **14/1**

-300 **12** *¾* **Bourn Fair**[24] 7354 3-8-8 **50**.......... ChrisCatlin 8 35
(P J McBride) *in tch: pushed along over 4f out: lost pl and rdn over 2f out: wl btn fnl 2f* **14/1**

000 **13** *18* **Albiera (IRE)**[24] 7361 4-8-9 **46**.......... ShaneKelly 14 2
(H Morrison) *chsd ldr tl over 5f out: lost pl and last 3f out: sn lost tch: eased ins fnl f: t.o* **25/1**

0660 **14** *3* **Harty Boy (USA)**[23] 7374 3-8-7 **49**..........(b[1]) MartinDwyer 7 —
(Jim Best) *sn pushed up into ld: hdd 3f out: wknd qckly over 2f out: eased fr over 1f out: t.o* **16/1**

2m 31.88s (-1.12) **Going Correction** -0.05s/f (Stan)
WFA 3 from 4yo+ 5lb **14** Ran SP% **121.7**
Speed ratings (Par 97): **101,99,99,98,97 96,95,94,91,91 90,90,78,76**
toteswinger:1&2:£3.00, 2&3:£38.40, 1&3:£20.30 CSF £18.17 CT £309.23 TOTE £3.30: £1.80, £1.80, £8.60; EX 20.20 TRIFECTA Not won. Place 6 £119.25, Place 5 £53.18..
Owner A S Reid **Bred** A S Reid **Trained** Bromsash, Herefordshire

FOCUS
An ordinary handicap.
Desert Hawk Official explanation: jockey said gelding missed the break
Sir Haydn Official explanation: jockey said gelding was denied a clear run
T/Plt: £54.20 to a £1 stake. Pool: £48,371.75. 651.10 winning tickets. T/Qpdt: £10.80 to a £1 stake. Pool: £5,107.70. 349.60 winning tickets. SP

7659 - 7743a (Foreign Racing) - See Raceform Interactive

7651 LINGFIELD (L-H)
Monday, December 7

OFFICIAL GOING: Standard
Wind: strong, behind Weather: raining, windy

7660 TEXT YOUR TOTESPORT BET TO 60021 H'CAP (DIV I) — 1m 2f (P)
12:30 (12:30) (Class 6) (0-52,52) 3-Y-O+ **£1,637** (£483; £241) **Stalls** Low

Form RPR

6000 **1** **Binnion Bay (IRE)**[19] 7440 8-8-11 **50**..........(b) MarcHalford(3) 2 56
(J J Bridger) *t.k.h: hld up in midfield: rdn and effrt 2f out: swtchd lft and gd hdwy jst ins fnl f: r.o wl to ld nr fin* **12/1**

3000 **2** *½* **Felicia**[10] 7549 4-8-10 **46** oh1.......... SamHitchcott 8 51
(J E Long) *in tch: rdn to chse ldr wl over 1f out: drvn to ld over 1f out: kpt on wl tl hdd and no ex nr fin* **12/1**

-504 **3** *1 ¼* **Dovedon Angel**[28] 7318 3-8-12 **51**.......... JerryO'Dwyer 10 54
(Miss Gay Kelleway) *t.k.h: hld up wl in tch towards rr: hdwy towards outer 3f out: pressed ldrs and drvn 2f out: kpt on same pce ins fnl f* **15/2**

0000 **4** *hd* **Greystoke Prince**[12] 7517 4-8-9 **52**..........(t) CarolineKelly(7) 12 54
(P S McEntee) *t.k.h: hld up wl in tch in last: plld out and gd hdwy on outer wl over 3f out: pressed ldrs and wd bnd 2f out: kpt on same pce fnl f* **20/1**

0604 **5** *1 ¼* **Mr Deal**[19] 7426 3-8-6 **50**.......... SimonPearce(5) 5 50
(Eve Johnson Houghton) *hld up in tch in rr: rdn and hdwy over 1f out: styd on wl fnl f: nvr rchd ldrs* **9/2**[2]

-050 **6** *1* **Woodland Violet**[1] 7652 3-8-4 **46** oh1.......... MartinLane(3) 11 44
(I A Wood) *chsd ldr tl rdn to ld 2f out: hdd over 1f out: wknd ins fnl f* **50/1**

4636 **7** *nk* **Red Current**[5] 7609 5-9-0 **50**..........(b[1]) LukeMorris 6 47
(R A Harris) *t.k.h: chsd ldrs: drvn and unable qck over 1f out: one pce fnl f* **4/1**[1]

6-46 **8** *2 ½* **Seaquel**[37] 7174 3-8-8 **52**.......... AmyBaker(5) 1 44
(A B Haynes) *in tch in midfield on inner: shuffled bk and lost pl over 2f out: rdn and no prog 2f out* **9/2**[2]

-005 **9** *1* **My Jeanie (IRE)**[68] 6394 5-8-10 **46**.......... RichardSmith 7 36
(J C Fox) *t.k.h: led tl rdn and hdd 2f out: wknd over 1f out* **13/2**[3]

0550 **10** *5* **Free Falling**[26] 7324 3-8-7 **46** oh1..........(tp) WandersonD'Avila 13 26
(A J Lidderdale) *hld up in tch towards rr: struggling and rdn over 3f out: wl btn fnl 2f* **66/1**

600 **11** *1 ½* **Broughtons Point**[31] 7278 3-8-8 **47**.......... TonyCulhane 9 24
(W J Musson) *chsd ldrs tl wknd u.p over 2f out: wl btn fnl f* **8/1**

2m 9.16s (2.56) **Going Correction** +0.125s/f (Slow)
WFA 3 from 4yo+ 3lb **11** Ran SP% **116.2**
Speed ratings (Par 101): **94,93,92,92,91 90,90,88,87,83 82**
toteswingers: 1&2 £23.00, 1&3 £11.30, 2&3 £24.40 CSF £143.10 CT £1157.75 TOTE £12.00: £3.50, £3.60, £2.40; EX 200.80 TRIFECTA Not won..
Owner J J Bridger **Bred** Fieldspring Ltd **Trained** Liphook, Hants
■ Stewards' Enquiry : Luke Morris caution: careless riding

FOCUS
A moderate handicap and the pace was steady, resulting in a time 1.57 seconds slower than the second division. The form is a bit muddling as a consequence, rated around the second and third.

7661 "NIGHT AT THE OSCARS CHRISTMAS PARTIES" (S) STKS — 6f (P)
1:00 (1:01) (Class 6) 2-Y-O **£1,978** (£584; £292) **Stalls** Low

Form RPR

6113 **1** **Vito Volterra (IRE)**[28] 7319 2-9-2 70.......... TonyCulhane 11 69
(A B Haynes) *mde all: rdn wl over 1f out: styd on wl fnl f* **5/2**[1]

6604 **2** *1 ¼* **Tamarind Hill (IRE)**[19] 7435 2-8-11 69..........(b) SteveDrowne 8 60
(C R Egerton) *chsd ldrs: wnt 2nd 4f out: drvn and tried to chal over 1f out: no imp on wnr after: jst hld on for 2nd* **9/2**[3]

1033 **3** *shd* **Zelos Dream (IRE)**[25] 7352 2-8-11 63.......... LukeMorris 2 60
(R A Harris) *in tch on inner: drvn to chse ldng pair over 1f out: kpt on same pce fnl f* **7/1**

5000 **4** *nse* **Miss Lesley**[19] 7435 2-8-11 73..........(b[1]) AdrianMcCarthy 5 60
(D K Ivory) *t.k.h: hld up in midfield: hdwy 2f out: hmpd and swtchd rt over 1f out: rdn and r.o wl ins fnl f* **11/2**

4560 **5** *1 ¾* **Miami Gator (IRE)**[37] 7168 2-9-2 54.......... JimCrowley 3 61+
(J R Weymes) *t.k.h: chsd ldrs tl hmpd and lost pl 5f out: towards rr and nt clr run 2f out: swtchd rt 1f out: r.o fnl f: nt rch ldrs* **16/1**

040 **6** *½* **Moonlight Serenade**[196] 2319 2-7-13 60.......... KierenFox(7) 12 48
(W G M Turner) *wnt bdly rt s and s.i.s: bhd: hdwy over 2f out: hanging lft and swtchd rt over 1f out: r.o fnl f: nt rch ldrs* **66/1**

0602 **7** *nk* **Out The Ring (IRE)**[10] 7559 2-8-11 61.......... KFallon 1 52
(Miss Gay Kelleway) *chsd ldrs: rdn and unable qck ent fnl 2f: one pce u.p after* **3/1**[2]

8 *1 ¼* **Jonny No Eyebrows** 2-8-8 0.......... MartinLane(3) 4 48
(I A Wood) *s.i.s: sn in tch in midfield: lost pl and rdn wl over 2f out: rallied and hdwy on inner over 1f out: no imp fnl f* **20/1**

000 **9** *nse* **Belle Park**[18] 7450 2-8-1 55.......... SimonPearce(5) 6 43
(Karen George) *bhd: rdn and styd on fnl f: nvr trbld ldrs* **66/1**

06 **10** *¾* **Graceandgratitude**[46] 6970 2-8-3 0.......... WilliamCarson(3) 9 41
(S C Williams) *t.k.h: chsd wnr tl 4f out: wknd u.p 2f out* **33/1**

250 **11** *1 ½* **Ishe A Lord**[21] 7410 2-8-10 54 ow2.......... JackDean(3) 10 44
(W G M Turner) *a towards rr: rdn and hanging rt bnd 2f out: nvr trbld ldrs* **20/1**

0000 **12** *½* **Argyll**[42] 7055 2-8-11 52.......... SaleemGolam 7 40
(J Pearce) *chsd ldrs: rdn over 2f out: wknd u.p over 1f out* **10/1**

1m 13.03s (1.13) **Going Correction** +0.125s/f (Slow) **12** Ran SP% **130.1**
Speed ratings (Par 94): **97,95,95,95,92 92,91,90,90,89 87,86**
toteswingers: 1&2 £2.40, 1&3 £4.10, 2&3 £7.70 CSF £14.93 TOTE £3.00: £1.70, £1.70, £2.80; EX 10.90 Trifecta £61.40 Pool: £190.96 - 2.30 winning units..The winner was bought in for 9,600gns. Miss Lesley was subject to a friendly claim.
Owner Ms J Loylert **Bred** O McElroy **Trained** Limpley Stoke, Bath

FOCUS
A reasonable seller, but those who raced handy seemed to be at an advantage. The third and fifth anchor the level.

NOTEBOOK
Vito Volterra(IRE) had the speed to get an uncontested lead on this drop in trip and stayed on well to gain his third win from just six starts. He was bought in for 9,600gns at the subsequent auction and is obviously a good type for this sort of level. (op 11-4 tchd 9-4)
Tamarind Hill(IRE) did well to finish so close, considering he lost ground when short of room at the first bend and used up plenty of energy to recover into a prominent position. (tchd 11-2)
Zelos Dream(IRE) raced against the inside rail throughout, although the way the track has been riding in recent days suggests that might not have been the disadvantage that is often the case. (op 9-1 tchd 10-1)
Miss Lesley ◆, the best off at the weights, was possibly an unlucky loser. Having been hampered at the first bend, she lost her place and ended up racing keenly in first-time blinkers. She seemed to be going okay turning into the straight, but her rider took an age to get serious and she was left with too much to do once switched into clear over 1f out. (op 5-1)
Miami Gator(IRE) probably would have finished a little closer granted a better trip. (op 20-1)
Moonlight Serenade was reported to have hung badly right. Official explanation: jockey said filly hung right in the straight
Out The Ring(IRE) tracked the winner for much of the way, but found nothing for pressure and couldn't justify market support. (op 9-2 tchd 6-1and 13-2 in a place)
Belle Park was reported to have hung right. Official explanation: jockey said filly hung right

7662 LINGFIELDPARK.CO.UK CLAIMING STKS — 7f (P)
1:30 (1:32) (Class 6) 3-Y-O+ **£1,978** (£584; £292) **Stalls** Low

Form RPR

0323 **1** **Benandonner (USA)**[16] 7492 6-9-0 90.......... BMcHugh(5) 4 79
(R A Fahey) *anticipated s and broke sltly early: in tch: rdn and effrt over 1f out: r.o u.p to ld fnl 75yds: r.o wl* **2/1**[1]

0000 **2** *½* **Desert Dreamer (IRE)**[19] 7437 8-9-1 77.......... PaulDoe 10 73
(P D Evans) *taken down early: stdd s: hld up in rr: hdwy on outer over 1f out: r.o wl to press wnr fnl 50yds: no imp after* **14/1**

0130 **3** *½* **Trade Centre**[42] 7054 4-9-0 72.......... NCallan 11 71
(W R Muir) *t.k.h: chsd ldrs: rdn to chal ent fnl 2f: led wl over 1f out: hdd and no ex fnl 75yds* **8/1**

4012 **4** 1¾ **Monashee Rock (IRE)**[12] 7520 4-8-7 65................................ LPKeniry 8 59
(Matthew Salaman) *hld up in last pair: nt clr run wl over 2f out: swtchd rt and hdwy over 1f out: chsd ldng trio ins fnl f: no imp fnl 75yds* **12/1**

0200 **5** ¾ **Bolodenka (IRE)**[25] 6732 7-9-5 88................................(t) TonyHamilton 5 69
(R A Fahey) *in tch: rdn and effrt over 1f out: kpt on u.p fnl f: nvr gng pce to rch ldrs* **9/2**[2]

0200 **6** ¾ **Secret Witness**[54] 6776 3-9-2 76................................(b[1]) TonyCulhane 2 64
(R A Harris) *trckd ldrs: rdn to chse ldrs over 1f out: drvn and one pce fnl f* **12/1**

0060 **7** ¾ **Womaniser (IRE)**[5] 7609 5-8-12 48...........................(b) SaleemGolam 1 58
(T Keddy) *dwlt: in tch in midfield: rdn and lost pl over 2f out: rallied and hdwy u.p over 1f out: no prog fnl f* **100/1**

5200 **8** *hd* **Northern Spy (USA)**[16] 7475 5-9-5 72.............................. DaneO'Neill 6 64
(S Dow) *chsd ldr: rdn and ev ch 2f out: wknd u.p ins fnl f* **15/2**[3]

062 **9** ½ **Geezers Colours**[57] 6703 4-9-2 78.............................. JimCrowley 12 60
(J R Weymes) *in tch in midfield on outer: rdn and one pce fr wl over 1f out* **14/1**

2000 **10** *1* **River Kirov (IRE)**[10] 7553 6-9-0 78................................ SteveDrowne 7 55
(M Wigham) *stdd after s: t.k.h: hld up in tch towards rr: effrt and rdn over 1f out: sn hanging lft and no real prog* **9/1**

0013 **11** *2* **Rioliina (IRE)**[12] 7520 3-8-9 71................................ FrankieMcDonald 3 45
(J G Portman) *led: hrd pressed and rdn ent fnl 2f: hdd wl over 1f out: wknd qckly fnl f* **25/1**

2004 **12** 3¼ **Ever Cheerful**[12] 7520 8-8-8 62...................................(p) AmyBaker(5) 9 40
(A B Haynes) *pressed ldrs tl wknd ent fnl 2f: bhd fnl f* **33/1**

1m 24.81s (0.01) **Going Correction** +0.125s/f (Slow) **12** Ran SP% **120.9**
Speed ratings (Par 101): **104,103,102,100,100 99,98,98,97,96 94,90**
toteswingers: 1&2 £9.30, 1&3 £6.00, 2&3 £30.40 CSF £33.87 TOTE £2.80: £1.20, £4.90, £3.50; EX 52.80 Trifecta £227.10 Part won. Pool : £306.90 - 0.55 winning units..Benandonner was claimed by Mike Murphy for £15,000.
Owner J C Parsons & Sinead Parsons **Bred** Gainsborough Farm Llc **Trained** Musley Bank, N Yorks

FOCUS
A fair claimer run at a decent pace. They finished in a bit of a heap and the seventh devalues the form.
River Kirov(IRE) Official explanation: jockey said gelding hung left

7663 BET TOTEPOOL AT TOTESPORT.COM MEDIAN AUCTION MAIDEN STKS 1m (P)
2:00 (2:02) (Class 6) 2-Y-O **£1,978** (£584; £292) **Stalls** High

Form RPR

42 **1** **Hidden Glory**[26] 7326 2-9-3 0.............................. RobertWinston 8 77+
(Pat Eddery) *chsd ldrs: hdwy to challeneg 2f out: rdn to ld over 1f out: drew clr fnl f: comf* **1/3**[1]

2 *3* **Spice Fair** 2-8-12 0.............................. LeeNewnes(5) 2 67
(M D I Usher) *in tch: stmbld over 5f out: rdn ent fnl 2f: kpt on fnl f to go 2n fnl 75yds: nt pce to threaten wnr* **66/1**

0 **3** ½ **Thundering Home**[23] 7388 2-9-3 0.............................. DaneO'Neill 12 66+
(E A L Dunlop) *s.i.s: t.k.h: sn in tch on outer: rdn and effrt ent fnl 2f: pressing for 2nd ent fnl f: kpt on to go 3rd nr fin: no threat to wnr* **6/1**[2]

0 **4** *nk* **Fochabers**[23] 7390 2-9-3 0.............................. GeorgeBaker 3 65
(R Charlton) *broke wl: set stdy gallop: rdn and qcknd over 2f out: hdd over 1f out: nt pce of wnr fnl f: lost 2 pls fnl 75yds* **33/1**

5 2½ **Kingston Folly** 2-9-3 0.............................. NCallan 10 60
(A B Haynes) *chsd ldrs: rdn ent fnl 2f: outpcd jst over 1f out: wl hld fnl f* **25/1**

0 **6** 1¼ **Fever Tree**[28] 7319 2-8-12 0.............................. SteveDrowne 11 52
(P J Makin) *t.k.h: hld up in tch in midfield: rdn and outpcd ent fnl 2f: wl hld after* **25/1**

7 ½ **That's Showbiz** 2-9-3 0.............................. ShaneKelly 6 56
(W J Knight) *chsd ldr tl jst over 2f out: sn wknd* **20/1**

8 2¼ **Lucky Breeze (IRE)** 2-8-12 0.............................. JimCrowley 1 46
(W J Knight) *v.s.a: hld up in rr on outer: struggling over 2f out* **12/1**[3]

00 **9** *3* **Big Hands Lynch (IRE)**[23] 7390 2-9-0 0.................. RobertLButler(3) 5 44
(J R Boyle) *hld up in last trio: rdn and struggling over 2f out: no ch fnl 2f* **66/1**

0 **10** ½ **Scarlet Ridge**[82] 5984 2-8-12 0.............................. JackMitchell 9 38
(D K Ivory) *s.i.s: hld up in last trio: struggling over 2f out* **66/1**

11 ¾ **Monyati** 2-9-0 0.............................. MartinLane(3) 7 42
(D M Simcock) *s.i.s: in tch in midfield tl wknd over 2f out: wl btn over 1f out* **12/1**[3]

1m 44.69s (6.49) **Going Correction** +0.125s/f (Slow) **11** Ran SP% **124.6**
Speed ratings (Par 94): **72,69,68,68,65 64,63,61,58,58 57**
toteswingers: 1&2 £16.70, 1&3 £2.10, 2&3 £33.00 CSF £61.24 TOTE £1.40: £1.02, £21.10, £1.50; EX 34.40 Trifecta £265.10 Part won. Pool : £358.35 - 0.90 winning units..
Owner Pat Eddery Racing (Reel Buddy) **Bred** P Balding **Trained** Nether Winchendon, Bucks

FOCUS
A weak maiden run at a very steady pace. The winner probably did not need to improve but is capable of doing so.

NOTEBOOK
Hidden Glory was a beaten favourite in a 7f maiden at Kempton on his previous start, but this was much easier. He's likely to face stiffer competition next time, but has some size about him and should make a useful handicapper. (op 4-9 tchd 1-2)
Spice Fair, a half-brother to 1m selling winner Pambo, out of a 1m3f scorer in Italy, hit a flat spot when first coming under pressure but ran on quite nicely in the straight and evidently has ability.
Thundering Home, who unseated his rider when on edge down at the start, was much too keen early on in the race itself. He should do better off a stronger pace, probably when handicapped. (op 11-2)
Fochabers stepped up on the form he showed over C&D on his debut is another who's probably more of a handicap type.
Kingston Folly, already gelded, didn't run too badly considering he was very keen to post ahead of this debut. (tchd 33-1)

7664 BEST ODDS GUARANTEED AT TOTESPORT.COM H'CAP 1m (P)
2:30 (2:31) (Class 5) (0-75,75) 3-Y-O+ **£2,729** (£806; £403) **Stalls** High

Form RPR

5004 **1** **Young Dottie**[49] 6910 3-8-13 70.............................. IanMongan 2 79
(P M Phelan) *stdd after s: hld up in midfield: effrt and rdn over 2f out: drvn to chse ldrs over 1f out: chal ins fnl f: r.o wl to ld towards fin* **6/1**

0-00 **2** *nk* **Mister Green (FR)**[173] 3028 3-9-1 72.............................. NCallan 11 80
(K McAuliffe) *hld up in tch in midfield: hdwy to chse ldrs over 2f out: drvn to ld ins fnl f: hdd and no ex towards fin* **25/1**

0040 **3** *2* **Prince Of Thebes (IRE)**[42] 7054 8-9-1 71.............................. JimCrowley 5 74
(M J Attwater) *sn pushed along to chse ldr: rdn and chal over 1f out: no ex and btn fnl 100yds* **10/1**

1436 **4** ¾ **Dichoh**[9] 7575 6-9-5 75..................................(v) GeorgeBaker 7 77
(M Madgwick) *chsd ldrs: rdn and effrt to press ldrs wl over 1f out: keeping on same pce and btn whn n.m.r ins fnl f* **5/1**[3]

0241 **5** ½ **Penzena**[18] 7452 3-9-1 72.............................. LPKeniry 10 73
(A M Balding) *led: rdn wl over 1f out: hdd ins fnl f: wknd fnl 75yds* **5/2**[1]

5236 **6** 2¾ **Support Fund (IRE)**[16] 7487 5-8-11 67.............................. ShaneKelly 4 61
(Eve Johnson Houghton) *hld up bhd: effrt and rdn bnd 2f out: kpt on: nvr trbld ldrs* **20/1**

0000 **7** *nk* **Alfie Tupper (IRE)**[12] 7512 6-8-8 64.............................. SteveDrowne 6 58
(J R Boyle) *stdd after s: hld up in rr: rdn ent fnl 2f: nvr threatened ldrs* **16/1**

2100 **8** 1¾ **Naheell**[16] 7475 3-8-10 67.............................. SaleemGolam 9 56
(G Prodromou) *dwlt: a towards rr: nvr trbld ldrs* **16/1**

4450 **9** ¾ **Pha Mai Blue**[16] 7479 4-8-7 63.............................. NickyMackay 1 51
(J R Boyle) *a towards rr: nvr trbld ldrs* **12/1**

0001 **10** ¾ **Mr Hichens**[16] 7481 4-8-13 69..................................(v) DarryllHolland 3 55
(Karen George) *in tch: rdn and nt qckn jst over 2f out: wl btn over 1f out* **9/2**[2]

12-0 **11** *32* **Le Chiffre (IRE)**[16] 7481 7-8-7 66...........................(p) RobertLButler(3) 8 —
(Miss Sheena West) *chsd ldrs tl lost pl qckly over 2f out: wl bhd and eased ins fnl f: t.o* **16/1**

1m 37.37s (-0.83) **Going Correction** +0.125s/f (Slow)
WFA 3 from 4yo+ 1lb **11** Ran SP% **120.7**
Speed ratings (Par 103): **109,108,106,105,105 102,102,100,99,99 67**
toteswingers: 1&2 £40.10, 1&3 £14.90, 2&3 £26.50 CSF £147.50 CT £1514.11 TOTE £6.90: £2.10, £9.80, £4.40; EX 239.20 TRIFECTA Not won..
Owner Tony Smith **Bred** Tony J Smith **Trained** Epsom, Surrey

FOCUS
An ordinary handicap run at an even pace. The winner produced a personal best and the form is rated around the third.
Pha Mai Blue Official explanation: jockey said gelding hung left

7665 BIGGER "WIN ONLY" ODDS AT TOTESPORT.COM H'CAP 1m 4f (P)
3:00 (3:00) (Class 5) (0-70,69) 3-Y-O **£2,729** (£806; £403) **Stalls** Low

Form RPR

2201 **1** **Sircozy (IRE)**[24] 7374 3-8-4 58.............................. WilliamCarson(3) 8 62+
(S C Williams) *dropped in bhd after s: c wd st: stl plenty to do and rdn over 1f out: r.o wl to ld fnl 100yds: sn in command: comf* **7/2**[2]

5604 **2** *2* **Taste The Wine (IRE)**[63] 6543 3-8-10 61.............................. LukeMorris 6 62
(J S Moore) *chsd ldrs: wnt 2nd over 8f out: rdn and ev ch wl over 1f out: led ins fnl f: sn hdd and nt pce of wnr* **11/1**

6531 **3** *nse* **Quinsman**[66] 6440 3-9-1 66.............................. LPKeniry 2 67
(J S Moore) *in tch: effrt and rdn 2f out: hdwy between horses ins fnl f: pressing for 2nd fnl 50yds: no ch w wnr* **9/2**

0504 **4** *1* **Wood Fairy**[19] 7428 3-8-10 61.............................. TonyHamilton 5 60
(R A Fahey) *t.k.h: hld up in tch: swtchd ins and effrt wl over 1f out: ev ch briefly ins fnl f: nt pce of wnr fnl 100yds* **12/1**

-003 **5** 1½ **December**[19] 7439 3-8-13 64.............................. NCallan 3 61
(Mrs C A Dunnett) *led: hung rt: c centre and rdn wl over 1f out: hdd ins fnl f: wknd fnl 75yds* **16/1**

001 **6** *nk* **Red Hot Desert**[24] 7367 3-9-4 69.............................. GeorgeBaker 1 65
(W R Swinburn) *t.k.h: chsd ldr tl over 8f out: styd handy: rdn and effrt jst over 2f out: kpt on same pce ins fnl f* **4/1**[3]

2534 **7** *4* **Ask The Oracle**[34] 7225 3-8-13 64.............................. SteveDrowne 4 54
(H Morrison) *in tch: rdn and effrt over 2f out: outpcd wl over 1f out: n.d fnl f* **5/2**[1]

6315 **8** *8* **Farncombe (IRE)**[19] 7426 3-9-0 65.............................. TonyCulhane 7 42
(R A Harris) *t.k.h: hld up in tch: dropped to last and rdn wl over 2f out: lost tch over 1f out* **14/1**

2m 33.44s (0.44) **Going Correction** +0.125s/f (Slow) **8** Ran SP% **117.6**
Speed ratings (Par 102): **103,101,101,100,99 97,97,91**
toteswingers: 1&2 £11.20, 1&3 £4.80, 2&3 £11.10 CSF £42.22 CT £178.14 TOTE £3.30: £1.60, £4.10, £1.80; EX 35.90 Trifecta £237.00 Part won. Pool : £320.39 - 0.81 winning units..
Owner R Friends Electric **Bred** Allevamento Pian Di Neve Srl **Trained** Newmarket, Suffolk

FOCUS
They went a steady pace through the early stages and the form is a bit muddling. Just a modest contest.
December Official explanation: jockey said gelding hung left

7666 TEXT YOUR TOTESPORT BET TO 60021 H'CAP (DIV II) 1m 2f (P)
3:30 (3:30) (Class 6) (0-52,52) 3-Y-O+ **£1,637** (£483; £241) **Stalls** Low

Form RPR

4030 **1** **Lunar Limelight**[17] 7466 4-8-12 48.............................. JimCrowley 8 57
(P J Makin) *t.k.h: hld up in tch towards rr: hdwy over 2f out: drvn to chse ldrs over 1f out: led fnl 100yds: r.o wl* **9/1**

463 **2** ¾ **Iguacu**[25] 7354 5-9-0 50.............................. DaneO'Neill 5 58
(George Baker) *in tch: rdn and hdwy to join ldr 2f out: drvn to ld ins fnl f: sn hdd and unable qck fnl 100yds* **3/1**[1]

4646 **3** 2¾ **Inquisitress**[8] 7586 5-8-13 52.............................. MarcHalford(3) 12 54
(J J Bridger) *stdd and dropped in bhd after s: hdwy ent fnl 2f: r.o fnl f to go 3rd nr fin: nvr gng to rch ldrs* **7/1**

5035 **4** *nk* **Sestet**[75] 6208 4-9-2 52.............................. NCallan 9 53
(S Dow) *t.k.h: led at stdy pce: rdn and hdd 2f out: outpcd ent fnl f: lost 3rd nr fin* **5/1**[3]

0200 **5** ½ **Fitzwarren**[40] 7113 8-8-10 46 oh1...............................(tp) DarryllHolland 3 46
(A D Brown) *hld up towards rr: rdn and unable qck over 2f out: hdwy u.p in fnl f: styd on but nvr gng pce to threaten ldrs* **16/1**

6445 **6** *1* **Mountain Forest (GER)**[13] 7499 3-8-8 47 ow1........... SteveDrowne 10 45
(H Morrison) *chsd ldrs wnt 2nd 9f out tl jst over 2f out: outpcd u.p over 1f out: wl hld fnl f* **4/1**[2]

0540 **7** *hd* **Mid Valley**[35] 4388 6-8-10 46 oh1.............................. TonyCulhane 1 44
(J R Jenkins) *stdd s: hld up in rr: rdn and effrt on outer 2f out: nvr trbld ldrs* **14/1**

0000 **8** ½ **Mister Frosty (IRE)**[147] 3923 3-8-11 50.............................. SaleemGolam 4 47
(G Prodromou) *t.k.h: chsd ldrs: rdn and unable qck jst over 2f out: wknd u.p over 1f out* **25/1**

0600 **9** 1¾ **Tiffany Lady**[48] 6917 3-8-0 46 oh1.............................. RachelKing(7) 6 40
(M D I Usher) *in tch in midfield tl rdn and btn jst over 2f out* **50/1**

000 **10** 3¾ **Supplementary (IRE)**[24] 7367 7-8-8 51.............................. RichardRowe(7) 2 37
(M J Coombe) *hld up in rr: struggling u.p over 2f out: wl btn fnl 2f* **20/1**

0056 **11** *1* **Vigorosa (IRE)**[19] 7439 3-8-10 49...................................(p) PaulDoe 7 33
(P Howling) *chsd ldrs tl wknd u.p over 2f out* **16/1**

5000 **12** *25* **Choosy Floosy**[46] 6969 3-8-13 **52**.............................. RobertWinston 11 —
(Pat Eddery) *dwlt: sn pushed up to chse ldrs: rdn 3f out: sn struggling: eased ins fnl f: t.o* **14/1**

2m 7.59s (0.99) **Going Correction** +0.125s/f (Slow)
WFA 3 from 4yo+ 3lb **12** Ran SP% **119.8**
Speed ratings (Par 101): **101,100,98,97,97 96,96,96,94,91 91,71**
toteswingers: 1&2 £7.10, 1&3 £12.60, 2&3 £7.60 CSF £35.77 CT £207.48 TOTE £11.20: £2.70, £1.20, £3.10; EX 40.50 Trifecta £203.80 Part won. Pool : £375.42 - 0.20 winning units. Place 6: £335.57 Place 5: £46.31.
Owner Mrs Jacqueline McColl **Bred** Angmering Park Stud **Trained** Ogbourne Maisey, Wilts
■ Stewards' Enquiry : Richard Rowe one-day ban: used whip when out of contention (Dec 21)

FOCUS
The winning time was 1.57 seconds quicker than the first division and the form is sound, if very moderate.
Fitzwarren Official explanation: jockey said gelding ran too freely
T/Plt: £458.80 to a £1 stake. Pool: £46,293.85. 73.65 winning tickets. T/Qpdt: £34.30 to a £1 stake. Pool: £5,606.25. 120.60 winning tickets. SP

7643 WOLVERHAMPTON (A.W) (L-H)
Monday, December 7

OFFICIAL GOING: Standard
Wind: Moderate behind Weather: Fine

7667 BET BRITISH WITH TOTEPOOL AMATEUR RIDERS' H'CAP (DIV I) 1m 1f 103y(P)
2:10 (2:11) (Class 5) (0-75,77) 3-Y-0+ **£2,810** (£871; £435; £217) **Stalls** Low

Form RPR
2221 **1** **Iron Out (USA)**[4] 7620 3-10-12 **77** 6ex................ MrStephenHarrison(5) 5 85
(R Hollinshead) *a.p: led jst over 2f out: drvn out and hld on ins fnl f* **11/4**[2]
0032 **2** *nk* **Bavarica**[8] 7587 7-10-3 **64**.. MrRBirkett(3) 3 71
(Miss J Feilden) *hld up towards rr: hdwy on ins over 2f out: chal over 1f out: kpt on* **10/1**
1230 **3** *2 1/4* **Waahej**[20] 7423 3-10-5 **65**.. MrSWalker 10 67
(P W Hiatt) *s.i.s: hld up: hdwy over 3f out: rdn wl over 1f out: one pce fnl f* **11/2**
2112 **4** *nk* **Thunderstruck**[12] 7512 4-11-0 **72**..................................(p) MrSDobson 1 74
(J A Glover) *hd down whn stalls opened: t.k.h and stmbld sn after s: sn in tch: led over 4f out: edgd rt and hdd jst over 2f out: sn rdn: one pce fnl f* **2/1**[1]
4/06 **5** *2* **City Hustler (USA)**[2] 7648 4-10-2 **65**.......................... MrMGriffiths(5) 9 62
(Adrian McGuinness, Ire) *hld up in rr: stdy prog on outside over 3f out: rdn over 2f out: c wd st: wknd wl over 1f out* **20/1**
6333 **6** *1/2* **Jeer (IRE)**[16] 7475 5-10-12 **70**...(t) MrOGreenall 7 66
(M W Easterby) *led: hdd 6f out: wknd over 3f out* **5/1**[3]
0000 **7** *6* **Mr Fantozzi (IRE)**[143] 4060 4-9-7 **58**.............................. MrESullivan(7) 4 42
(D Donovan) *s.i.s: hld up and bhd: pushed along over 2f out: sn struggling* **66/1**
0000 **8** *21* **Western Roots**[108] 5211 8-9-9 **58** oh1......................(p) MissMBryant(5) 6 —
(P Butler) *prom: led 6f out tl over 4f out: wknd wl over 2f out* **80/1**
5630 **9** *24* **Mutually Mine (USA)**[12] 7512 3-10-3 **63**...................... MissGAndrews 2 —
(Mrs P Sly) *hld up: wl bhd fnl 3f: t.o* **16/1**

2m 2.51s (0.81) **Going Correction** +0.025s/f (Slow)
WFA 3 from 4yo+ 2lb **9** Ran SP% **114.5**
Speed ratings (Par 103): **97,96,94,94,92 92,86,68,46**
toteswingers: 1&2 £7.90, 1&3 £3.50, 2&3 £7.90 CSF £29.43 CT £141.40 TOTE £3.40: £1.40, £2.80, £1.30; EX 31.70.
Owner John L Marriott **Bred** Leslie Hagan **Trained** Upper Longdon, Staffs

FOCUS
The winning time was almost 2secs slower than the second division, but the form still looks straightforward enough judged around the winner and third.

7668 BET BRITISH WITH TOTEPOOL AMATEUR RIDERS' H'CAP (DIV II) 1m 1f 103y(P)
2:40 (2:40) (Class 5) (0-75,75) 3-Y-0+ **£2,810** (£871; £435; £217) **Stalls** Low

Form RPR
0001 **1** **Desert Vision**[16] 7495 5-10-3 **64**..................................(vt1) MrOGreenall 3 75
(M W Easterby) *led early: a.p: chsd clr ldr over 2f out: rdn to ld ins fnl f: r.o wl* **5/4**[1]
3135 **2** *1 3/4* **Resplendent Ace (IRE)**[16] 7475 5-10-5 **71**...................... MrJBanks(5) 6 78
(P Howling) *hld up in rr: hdwy over 2f out: rdn 1f out: tk 2nd ins fnl f: nt trble wnr* **12/1**
1130 **3** *2 1/4* **Florentia**[19] 7428 3-9-13 **67**.. MrBMMorris(5) 5 70
(Sir Mark Prescott) *hld up: hdwy 3f out: rdn and one pce fnl f* **11/2**[2]
3054 **4** *1 1/4* **Arashi**[16] 7490 3-9-8 **62**..(p) MrJPFeatherstone(5) 1 62
(Lucinda Featherstone) *hld up: rdn over 2f out: edgd lft wl over 1f out: kpt on to take 4th cl home* **13/2**
6454 **5** *7* **Dudley Docker (IRE)**[44] 4916 7-9-13 **67**......................(b) MrJPearce(7) 8 50
(D C O'Brien) *dwlt: hld up in rr: pushed along wl over 1f out: nvr nr ldrs: fin 6th: plcd 5th* **25/1**
00 **6** *6* **Colonel Sherman (USA)**[13] 7505 4-9-7 **61**.................. MrATBrook(7) 4 32
(P A Kirby) *sn led: hdd over 5f out: chsd ldr tl pushed along over 2f out: sn wknd: fin 7th: plcd 6th* **16/1**
0351 **7** *14* **Prince Golan (IRE)**[13] 7500 5-9-11 **61** oh3........................ MrMPrice(3) 7 —
(R J Price) *s.i.s: in rr: pushed along over 3f out: sn struggling: fin 8th: plcd 7th* **8/1**
3000 **8** *4 1/2* **Strategic Mover (USA)**[8] 7586 4-9-11 **63**...............(v) MissMBryant(5) 10 —
(P Butler) *t.k.h: prom tl wknd qckly wl over 2f out: fin 9th: plcd 8th* **66/1**
0000 **9** *6* **Artreju (GER)**[3] 7623 6-9-7 **61** oh12.............................. MissKLoftus(7) 2 —
(P Butler) *s.i.s: in rr: reminder 4f out: sn lost tch: fin 10th: plcd 9th* **100/1**
0434 **D** *3/4* **Benedict Spirit (IRE)**[2] 7641 4-11-0 **75**...........(p) MissIsabelTompsett 9 73+
(D Burchell) *sn w ldr: led over 5f out: clr over 3f out: rdn over 2f out: hdd ins fnl f: wknd: fin 5th: disq: rdr failed to draw correct weight* **6/1**[3]

2m 0.73s (-0.97) **Going Correction** +0.025s/f (Slow)
WFA 3 from 4yo+ 2lb **10** Ran SP% **118.5**
Speed ratings (Par 103): **105,103,101,100,93 88,75,71,66,99**
toteswingers: 1&2 £5.70, 1&3 £5.70, 2&3 £3.90 CSF £18.87 CT £66.50 TOTE £2.40: £1.20, £2.00, £2.10; EX 16.20.
Owner A Black,R Edmonds,J Holdroyd,J Quickfall **Bred** Gainsborough Stud Management Ltd **Trained** Sheriff Hutton, N Yorks
■ Stewards' Enquiry : Miss Isabel Tompsett three-day ban: failed to draw the correct weight when weighing in(tbn)

FOCUS
This second division of the handicap for amateur riders was run at a much stronger early pace. The placed horses set the level.

7669 TOTEPOOL RACING'S BIGGEST SUPPORTER CLAIMING STKS 1m 141y(P)
3:10 (3:10) (Class 6) 2-Y-0 **£2,729** (£806; £403) **Stalls** Low

Form RPR
000 **1** **Empress Leizu (IRE)**[18] 7450 2-7-11 50...................... AndreaAtzeni(3) 1 52+
(E A L Dunlop) *mde all: pushed along over 2f out: rdn and edgd lft over 1f out: hung rt ins fnl f: drvn out* **14/1**
4500 **2** *1 3/4* **Flipping**[19] 7434 2-8-8 76 ow1.. FergusSweeney 7 57+
(W S Kittow) *a.p: pushed along 2f out: rdn and kpt on same pce ins fnl f* **6/4**[1]
2566 **3** *3/4* **Inside Track (IRE)**[19] 7435 2-8-5 75.............................(b) MartinDwyer 5 52+
(B J Meehan) *t.k.h: chsd wnr: rdn and edgd lft wl over 1f out: lost 2nd and no ex wl ins fnl f* **5/2**[2]
60 **4** *1 1/2* **Hubble Space**[18] 7450 2-8-12 0.. JimmyQuinn 8 56
(M Botti) *t.k.h and bhd: pushed along wl over 1f out: r.o ins fnl f: tk 4th last strides* **28/1**
0354 **5** *1/2* **Underworld Dandy**[16] 7474 2-8-0 62.................(v) AndrewHeffernan(5) 9 48
(P D Evans) *hld up towards rr: rdn and hdwy over 1f out: one pce ins fnl f* **15/2**
0000 **6** *1/2* **Clayton Flick (IRE)**[10] 7559 2-8-5 50............................... DavidProbert 4 47
(A B Haynes) *stdd s: hld up in rr: hdwy on ins 2f out: one pce fnl f* **33/1**
0500 **7** *1/2* **Ellmollell**[35] 7210 2-8-0 52.. JamieMackay 6 41
(S Kirk) *hld up: rdn over 1f out: nvr nr to chal* **33/1**
1465 **8** *1 1/4* **Royal Box**[19] 7435 2-8-13 70...(b1) ChrisCatlin 3 51
(A J McCabe) *prom: rdn over 2f out: wknd ins fnl f* **5/1**[3]
00U **9** *11* **Typical Female**[39] 7139 2-8-1 0.. BillyCray(5) 2 21
(A B Haynes) *a in rr* **125/1**

1m 56.23s (5.73) **Going Correction** +0.025s/f (Slow) **9** Ran SP% **113.8**
Speed ratings (Par 94): **75,73,72,71,71 70,70,69,59**
.Empress Leizu was claimed by A. W. Carroll for £5,000. Flipping was subject to a friendly claim. Underworld Dandy was claimed by John E. Mills for £5,000.\n\x\x
Owner Mrs Janice Quy **Bred** Lynn Lodge Stud **Trained** Newmarket, Suffolk
■ Stewards' Enquiry : Andrea Atzeni trainer's rep said, regarding the apparent improvement in form shown, filly seemed to benefit from a change to front-running tactics

FOCUS
A typically moderate juvenile claimer. The winner is among those who limit the form, but she may be capable of a bit better.

NOTEBOOK
Empress Leizu(IRE) made all to open her account at the fourth time of asking. She had shown little in maiden company coming into this, but was better than the bare form of her latest effort at Kempton and the switch to front-running obviously suited. She did get a freebie out in front, but there was something to like about her attitude when kicked for home off the final bend. She also ran green late in the day, so could progress again for the experience. (op 20-1 tchd 12-1)
Flipping had every chance and returned to form on this debut in a claimer, but didn't really convince with his stamina for the distance. A drop back to 7f in this grade could well see him go one better again. (tchd 7-4)
Inside Track(IRE) was officially best in at the weights on this step back up a furlong. He had his chance, but didn't look straightforward under pressure and is evidently flattered by a mark of 75. (op 11-4 tchd 9-4)
Hubble Space, one place behind the winner at Kempton last time out, was never a serious player yet this was still a step in the right direction. She showed her inexperience so could go forward for the run, and a stronger pace over this trip is what she wants. (tchd 33-1)
Underworld Dandy kept on from off the pace and was another that would have benefited from a more truly run race, as he took a keen hold through the race. (op 6-1)

7670 WOLVERHAMPTON-RACECOURSE.CO.UK (S) STKS 1m 4f 50y(P)
3:40 (3:41) (Class 6) 3-Y-0+ **£2,047** (£604; £302) **Stalls** Low

Form RPR
1533 **1** **Ghufa (IRE)**[39] 7137 5-9-8 64.. EddieAhern 6 65
(George Baker) *hld up in mid-div: smooth prog to chse ldr 3f out: rdn over 1f out: led ins fnl f: drvn out* **4/5**[1]
600- **2** *3/4* **Shandelight (IRE)**[418] 6728 5-8-13 0.................................... TomEaves 2 55
(Miss J A Camacho) *led 1f: chsd ldr: led over 3f out: rdn wl over 1f out: hdd ins fnl f: nt qckn* **25/1**
0020 **3** *2* **Fantasy Ride**[10] 7549 7-9-4 52................................. StephenDonohoe 12 57
(J Pearce) *hld up in rr: stdy hdwy over 3f out: pushed along wl over 1f out: rdn and kpt on same pce ins fnl f* **6/1**[3]
2405 **4** *4 1/2* **Tesserae**[26] 7324 3-8-8 48.. FergusSweeney 5 44
(A B Haynes) *hld up in tch: rdn over 2f out: wknd fnl f* **22/1**
5560 **5** *2 1/4* **Casablanca Minx (IRE)**[17] 7466 6-8-10 45...............(b) DavidKenny(7) 4 45
(A G Juckes) *hld up towards rr: pushed along over 2f out: rdn and hdwy wl over 1f out: nvr nr ldrs* **33/1**
6004 **6** *2 1/2* **Dream In Blue**[13] 7504 4-9-4 65..(p) ChrisCatlin 9 42
(J A Glover) *hld up in tch: rdn over 2f out: wknd wl over 1f out* **11/2**[2]
0640 **7** *5* **Markadam**[62] 6559 3-8-13 47... JimmyQuinn 3 34
(Miss S E Hall) *hld up towards rr: pushed along over 3f out: rdn over 2f out: n.d* **25/1**
50 **8** *2 1/2* **Davids City (IRE)**[9] 7578 5-9-4 0...................................... PJMcDonald 7 30
(G A Harker) *hld up in mid-div: rdn over 3f out: bhd fnl 2f* **12/1**
0000 **9** *8* **Desert Hawk**[1] 7658 8-9-1 46................................... MatthewLawson(7) 10 21
(W M Brisbourne) *stmbld s whn rdr had trble removing blindfold: pushed along and rcvrd to ld after 1f: hdd over 3f out: rdn and wknd over 2f out* **50/1**
0 **10** *11* **Misty Kit**[2] 7648 4-8-8 0.. PaulPickard(5) 1 —
(W M Brisbourne) *in rr: pushed along and struggling over 3f out* **100/1**
6300 **11** *1* **York Cliff**[108] 5210 11-9-4 45....................................... GrahamGibbons 11 —
(W M Brisbourne) *a towards rr: pushed along and struggling over 3f out* **66/1**
0-60 **12** *23* **Rising Force (IRE)**[39] 5577 6-9-4 55..............................(b) LiamJones 8 —
(J L Spearing) *hld up towards rr: hdwy over 5f out: wknd over 2f out* **28/1**

2m 39.94s (-1.16) **Going Correction** +0.025s/f (Slow)
WFA 3 from 4yo+ 5lb **12** Ran SP% **115.8**
Speed ratings (Par 101): **104,103,102,99,97 96,92,91,85,78 77,62**
toteswingers: 1&2 £7.40, 1&3 £3.10, 2&3 £18.30 TOTE £1.70: £1.10, £6.20, £1.80; EX 29.40.There was no bid for the winner.
Owner Miss Camilla Jenks **Bred** Shadwell Estate Company Limited **Trained** Moreton Morrell, Warwicks

FOCUS
A weak seller but the form is sound, best judged around the winner.

7671 CLEAN CONCIERGE MAIDEN STKS 1m 141y(P)
4:10 (4:10) (Class 5) 3-Y-0+ £2,729 (£806; £403) Stalls Low

Form RPR
65 1 **Heathyards Junior**[31] 7278 3-9-3 0 .... GrahamGibbons 12 68
(R Hollinshead) *hld up towards rr: hdwy wl over 1f out: sn rdn: r.o to ld towards fin* **12/1**
-564 2 ½ **Cross Section (USA)**[16] 7480 3-8-12 63 .... EddieAhern 5 62
(E F Vaughan) *hld up in tch: rdn over 1f out: ev ch wl ins fnl f: kpt on* **11/4**[1]
522 3 1¼ **Tobrata**[25] 7353 3-9-3 65 .... TomEaves 11 64
(M Brittain) *sn led: rdn over 1f out: hdd ins fnl f: nt qckn* **9/2**[3]
2006 4 nse **Levitation (IRE)**[19] 7428 3-8-12 68 .... FergusSweeney 13 59
(W S Kittow) *sn chsng ldr: chal over 2f out: sn rdn: nt qckn ins fnl f* **7/2**[2]
0 5 nk **Mutajaaser (USA)**[136] 4276 4-9-5 0 .... JimmyQuinn 3 63
(K A Morgan) *led early: a.p: rdn wl over 1f out: led ins fnl f: hdd and no ex towards fin* **6/1**
044 6 1½ **Altimatum (USA)**[33] 7238 3-9-3 67 ....(b) ChrisCatlin 6 60
(P F I Cole) *t.k.h in tch: rdn over 1f out: fdd ins fnl f* **9/2**[3]
6004 7 2¼ **Hold The Star**[17] 7459 3-8-10 57 ow3 .... AnnStokell(5) 10 53
(Miss A Stokell) *hld up in mid-div: effrt on outside over 2f out: c wd st: rdn wl over 1f out: wknd ins fnl f* **40/1**
0 8 ¾ **Lily Wood**[40] 7126 3-8-7 0 .... MarkCoumbe(5) 1 48
(J W Unett) *towards rr: pushed along over 3f out: rdn over 1f out: n.d* **100/1**
9 1½ **Turning Circle** 3-9-0 0 .... MichaelJStainton(3) 7 49
(M Brittain) *hld up in mid-div: pushed along on ins over 2f out: sme prog wl over 1f out: wknd ins fnl f* **33/1**
10 4 **Lady Champagne**[48] 3-8-12 0 .... AmirQuinn 4 35
(Miss J Feilden) *hld up towards rr: pushed along on ins over 2f out: no rspnse* **100/1**
11 shd **Auntie Craik**[55] 5-9-0 0 .... SJCraine 8 35
(S Gollings) *hld up in mid-div: pushed along over 3f out: rdn and wknd wl over 1f out* **100/1**
12 ½ **Lily Eva** 3-8-12 0 .... DavidProbert 9 34
(D Donovan) *a in rr* **28/1**
13 18 **La Preciosa**[22] 4-9-0 0 .... PJMcDonald 2 —
(I W McInnes) *s.i.s: a in rr: lost tch 4f out* **100/1**

1m 50.51s (0.01) **Going Correction** +0.025s/f (Slow)
WFA 3 from 4yo+ 2lb 13 Ran SP% **120.0**
Speed ratings (Par 103): **100,99,98,98,98 96,94,94,92,89 89,88,72**
toteswingers: 1&2 £7.70, 1&3 £8.80, 2&3 £3.30 CSF £44.57 TOTE £15.80: £4.00, £1.60, £1.70; EX 58.80.
Owner L A Morgan **Bred** L A Morgan **Trained** Upper Longdon, Staffs

FOCUS
A moderate maiden. It was steadily run and this is not form to be too positive about, with the third looking the best guide.
Hold The Star Official explanation: jockey said filly had no more to give

7672 TOTEPOOL OUR PROFITS STAY IN RACING H'CAP 1m 141y(P)
4:40 (4:41) (Class 5) (0-75,73) 3-Y-0+ £3,238 (£963; £481; £240) Stalls Low

Form RPR
4356 1 **African Cheetah**[49] 6900 3-9-3 72 .... AdamKirby 2 84+
(R Hollinshead) *hld up: rdn and hdwy over 1f out: hrd rdn to ld nr fin* **7/2**[2]
0003 2 nk **Ansells Pride (IRE)**[28] 7322 6-8-13 66 .... TomEaves 5 73
(B Smart) *led: rdn over 1f out: hdd nr fin* **8/1**
-166 3 shd **Bawaardi (IRE)**[25] 7356 3-8-10 72 .... LeeTopliss(7) 7 79
(R A Fahey) *hld up in rr: rdn over 1f out: r.o ins fnl f* **6/1**[3]
0005 4 1¾ **Hyde Lea Flyer**[51] 6861 4-8-12 65 .... GrahamGibbons 4 68+
(E S McMahon) *t.k.h: prom: chsd ldr 4f out: ev ch over 2f out: rdn wl over 1f out: lost 2nd and no ex ins fnl f* **5/2**[1]
3000 5 1¾ **Fandango Boy**[11] 7542 8-9-6 73 .... EddieAhern 1 72
(J P Broderick, Ire) *hld up in tch: rdn wl over 1f out: wknd ins fnl f* **7/2**[2]
-110 6 1 **Alqaahir (USA)**[28] 7322 7-9-4 71 .... LiamJones 3 68
(Lee Smyth, Ire) *hld up: pushed along and effrt over 2f out: wknd 1f out* **10/1**
2106 7 21 **Secret Hero**[49] 6909 3-8-6 68 .... JamesPSullivan(7) 6 16
(Lee Smyth, Ire) *prom tl wknd over 3f out: t.o fnl 2f* **20/1**

1m 50.02s (-0.48) **Going Correction** +0.025s/f (Slow)
WFA 3 from 4yo+ 2lb 7 Ran SP% **112.3**
Speed ratings (Par 103): **103,102,102,101,99 98,79**
toteswingers: 1&2 £4.10, 1&3 £4.80, 2&3 £8.50 CSF £29.65 TOTE £4.70: £2.80, £2.10; EX 29.70.
Owner Ray Robinson **Bred** Sheikh Abdulla Bin Isa Al-Khalifa **Trained** Upper Longdon, Staffs

FOCUS
A fair handicap for the class, run at an uneven tempo. The form is rated around the runner-up.

7673 BET TOTEPOOL TO SUPPORT YOUR SPORT H'CAP 5f 216y(P)
5:10 (5:11) (Class 5) (0-70,74) 3-Y-0+ £3,238 (£963; £481; £240) Stalls Low

Form RPR
2105 1 **Gap Princess (IRE)**[16] 7496 5-9-3 69 .... ChrisCatlin 1 79
(G A Harker) *hld up in mid-div: hdwy on ins wl over 1f out: rdn to ld ent fnl f: drvn out* **11/2**[2]
3406 2 nk **Espy**[44] 7023 4-8-12 64 .... PJMcDonald 4 73
(I W McInnes) *s.i.s: hld up in rr: hdwy on ins wl over 1f out: rdn ins fnl f: r.o* **14/1**
1305 3 1¼ **Onceaponatime (IRE)**[9] 7577 4-9-2 68 .... JimmyQuinn 11 73+
(M D Squance) *hld up: sn bhd: pushed along over 2f out: c wd st: r.o ins fnl f: tk 3rd nr fin* **8/1**
5241 4 ½ **Dash Back (USA)**[2] 7643 4-9-8 74 6ex .... EddieAhern 8 77+
(Adrian McGuinness, Ire) *s.i.s: sn hld up in mid-div: rdn and hdwy jst over 1f out: nt qckn ins fnl f* **2/1**[1]
5265 5 ½ **Charles Parnell (IRE)**[58] 6670 6-8-11 66 .... MichaelJStainton(3) 6 68
(S P Griffiths) *t.k.h: led 1f: prom: rdn jst over 1f out: one pce* **28/1**
3202 6 1¼ **Titus Gent**[12] 7518 4-9-2 68 .... DavidProbert 10 66
(R A Harris) *led after 1f: rdn and hdd wl over 1f out: fdd wl ins fnl f* **13/2**
6005 7 hd **Stash**[23] 7398 3-9-0 66 .... GrahamGibbons 3 63
(R Hollinshead) *prom: pushed along over 1f out: rdn and one pce fnl f* **6/1**[3]
4025 8 nk **Restless Genius (IRE)**[10] 7561 4-8-12 64 .... TomEaves 12 60
(B Ellison) *hld up in tch: rdn over 1f out: wknd ins fnl f* **6/1**[3]
600 9 hd **White Shift (IRE)**[16] 7478 3-8-11 70 .... KierenFox(7) 2 66
(P Howling) *hld up towards rr: pushed along over 2f out: rdn wl over 1f out: nvr trbld ldrs* **33/1**
00-0 10 ¾ **Doctor Hilary**[12] 7518 7-8-13 65 ....(v) StephenDonohoe 9 58
(A B Haynes) *sn chsng ldr: rdn to ld wl over 1f out: hdd ent fnl f: wknd towards fin* **50/1**

1m 14.23s (-0.77) **Going Correction** +0.025s/f (Slow) 10 Ran SP% **116.8**
Speed ratings (Par 103): **106,105,103,103,102 100,100,100,100,99**
CSF £77.36 CT £633.03 TOTE £7.10: £2.40, £2.50, £2.60; EX 115.40 Place 6: £35.11 Place 5: £10.61.
Owner Brian Morton **Bred** D Veitch And Musagd Abo Salim **Trained** Thirkleby, N Yorks

FOCUS
This open handicap was run at a sound pace which suited the closers. The runner-up is the best guide to the form.
T/Jkpt: Not won. T/Plt: £60.40 to a £1 stake. Pool: £67,439.12. 814.95 winning tickets. T/Qpdt: £12.60 to a £1 stake. Pool: £5,699.40. 333.60 winning tickets. KH

7635 SOUTHWELL (L-H)
Tuesday, December 8

OFFICIAL GOING: Standard
Wind: Light across Weather: Fine and sunny

7674 BEST ODDS GUARANTEED AT TOTESPORT.COM NURSERY 5f (F)
12:00 (12:00) (Class 5) (0-75,74) 2-Y-0 £2,729 (£806; £403) Stalls High

Form RPR
0064 1 **Italian Tom (IRE)**[19] 7453 2-9-7 74 .... LiamJones 5 80
(R A Harris) *chsd ldrs: rdn 1/2-way: led over 1f out: hung lft ins fnl f: drvn out* **2/1**[2]
500 2 1½ **Orchid Wing**[31] 7288 2-9-0 67 .... TonyHamilton 3 68
(R A Fahey) *s.i.s: sn pushed along and prom: jnd ldrs over 3f out: rdn and ev ch over 1f out: styd on same pce ins fnl f* **15/8**[1]
5243 3 1 **Caramelita**[9] 7585 2-9-1 68 .... FergusSweeney 4 65
(J R Jenkins) *w ldr tl led over 3f out: rdn and hdd over 1f out: no ex ins fnl f* **11/4**[3]
0360 4 6 **Baby Judge (IRE)**[27] 7333 2-8-1 59 ow4 .... AndrewHeffernan(5) 6 34
(M C Chapman) *led: rdn and hdd over 3f out: edgd lft and wknd over 1f out* **12/1**
0000 5 8 **Nidamar**[70] 6354 2-8-0 53 oh6 ow2 .... FrankieMcDonald 8 —
(Mrs R A Carr) *chsd ldrs: rdn over 3f out: wknd 2f out* **100/1**
000 6 1½ **Redoubtable Grace**[10] 7582 2-8-0 53 oh6 ow2 .... JimmyQuinn 2 —
(Mrs R A Carr) *chsd ldrs: rdn over 3f out: wknd 1/2-way* **25/1**

59.87 secs (0.17) **Going Correction** -0.075s/f (Stan) 6 Ran SP% **107.3**
Speed ratings (Par 96): **95,92,91,81,68 66**
toteswinger:1&2:£1.60, 2&3:£1.20, 1&3:£1.60 CSF £5.54 CT £7.16 TOTE £3.10: £1.50, £1.50; EX 5.70 Trifecta £9.90 Pool: £185.88 - 13.96 winning units..
Owner S & A Mares **Bred** Tom Radley **Trained** Earlswood, Monmouths

FOCUS
A weak nursery and few were ever involved, the first three finishing clear. The form has a solid look to it.

NOTEBOOK
Italian Tom(IRE) had sufficient speed to cope with the drop back in distance and handled the surface well at the first attempt. He might be worth another try over 6f on Polytrack at some point, but when racing on Fibresand this may well prove to be his trip. (op 13-8)
Orchid Wing ◆ is struggling to justify his price tag (68,000gns earlier in the year) but this wasn't a bad effort, as he showed plenty of speed after missing the break. He handled this surface okay, but he looks all speed and Polytrack may suit even better. (op 2-1 tchd 9-4 and 7-4)
Caramelita didn't see her race out after showing loads of pace. She'll be worth a try over this distance on Polytrack. (op 3-1 tchd 5-2)
Baby Judge(IRE) carried 4lb overweight and was soon beaten. (op 14-1 tchd 16-1)

7675 BET ON TONIGHT'S FOOTBALL AT TOTESPORT.COM H'CAP 1m 6f (F)
12:30 (12:30) (Class 5) (0-75,81) 3-Y-0+ £2,729 (£806; £403) Stalls Low

Form RPR
3122 1 **Follow The Dream**[8] 7598 6-8-10 57 .... DarrylHolland 6 67
(Karen George) *hld up in tch: chsd ldr 5f out: led wl over 3f out: rdn and edgd lft over 1f out: styd on wl* **11/4**[2]
0204 2 2½ **Saloon (USA)**[12] 7539 5-9-9 73 ....(p) AndreaAtzeni(3) 2 79
(Jane Chapple-Hyam) *chsd ldrs: rdn over 3f out: sn outpcd: rallied and edgd lft over 1f out: n.m.r and wnt 2nd nr fin* **7/2**[3]
2512 3 hd **Leyte Gulf (USA)**[18] 7461 6-9-3 64 .... DaneO'Neill 4 70
(C C Bealby) *slowly into sride: hld up: racd keenly: hdwy over 4f out: chsd wnr over 3f out: rdn and hung lft fr over 1f out: styd on same pce fnl f: lost 2nd nr fin* **7/4**[1]
6461 4 11 **Bentley Brook (IRE)**[8] 7598 7-10-6 81 6ex .... TonyCulhane 3 71
(R Curtis) *trckd ldr: racd keenly: led 6f out: rdn and hdd wl over 3f out: wknd 2f out* **6/1**
1355 5 10 **Victory Quest (IRE)**[232] 1399 9-9-11 72 ....(v) RobertWinston 5 48
(Mrs S Lamyman) *led 8f: rdn over 4f out: sn wknd* **10/1**

3m 11.05s (2.75) **Going Correction** -0.225s/f (Stan) 5 Ran SP% **108.6**
Speed ratings (Par 103): **83,81,81,75,69**
toteswinger: 1&2 £7.20. CSF £12.14 TOTE £3.00: £1.70, £2.40; EX 12.00.
Owner Eastington Racing Club **Bred** Miss Karen George **Trained** Higher Eastington, Devon
■ Stewards' Enquiry : Dane O'Neill caution: careless riding.

FOCUS
An interesting handicap, despite the small field, but the pace was steady for most of the way. Interestingly, all of the runners avoided the inside rail until the straight. The form makes sense at face value.

7676 BET ON LIVE SPORT AT TOTESPORT.COM H'CAP 5f (F)
1:00 (1:00) (Class 3) (0-95,90) 3-Y-0+ £7,771 (£2,312; £1,155; £577) Stalls High

Form RPR
2011 1 **Lesley's Choice**[13] 7511 3-9-1 87 ....(b) FrankieMcDonald 2 97
(R Curtis) *w ldr tl led over 3f out: rdn over 1f out: r.o* **2/1**[1]
0340 2 ¾ **Equuleus Pictor**[45] 7015 5-8-11 86 .... JackDean(3) 8 93
(J L Spearing) *led: hdd over 3f out: rdn over 1f out: r.o* **16/1**
0102 3 hd **Colorus (IRE)**[4] 7634 6-8-0 77 oh4 ow1 ....(p) PaulPickard(5) 1 84
(W J H Ratcliffe) *chsd ldrs: rdn 1/2-way: r.o* **15/2**[3]
0012 4 1½ **Bel Cantor**[17] 7496 6-8-3 78 .... KellyHarrison(3) 3 79
(W J H Ratcliffe) *chsd ldrs: rdn 1/2-way: styd on* **17/2**
2430 5 nk **Rebel Duke (IRE)**[22] 7414 5-9-1 87 .... TonyHamilton 4 87
(Ollie Pears) *mid-div: hdwy 1/2-way: rdn over 1f out: styd on same pce ins fnl f: b.b.v* **9/4**[2]
000 6 ¾ **Canadian Danehill (IRE)**[22] 7414 7-9-4 90 ....(p) DarrylHolland 7 87
(R M H Cowell) *s.i.s: outpcd: r.o ins fnl f: nrst fin* **20/1**
0500 7 ¾ **Pawan (IRE)**[11] 7553 9-8-9 86 ow6 .... AnnStokell(5) 5 81
(Miss A Stokell) *s.i.s: sn pushed along in rr: kpt on ins fnl f: nvr trbld ldrs* **25/1**

-100 **8** *nk* **Mondovi**[37] 7202 5-8-11 **88** .... RossAtkinson(5) 9 82
(Tom Dascombe) *chsd ldrs: rdn and edgd lft over 1f out: styd on same pce* **22/1**

6000 **9** *½* **Baunagain (IRE)**[13] 7511 4-8-8 **80** .... AdrianMcCarthy 10 72
(P W Chapple-Hyam) *mid-div: rdn and hung lft over 1f out: n.d* **33/1**

5300 **10** *2¾* **Toms Laughter**[22] 7414 5-9-2 **88** ....(b) LiamJones 6 70
(R A Harris) *s.i.s: a outpcd* **12/1**

58.38 secs (-1.32) **Going Correction** -0.075s/f (Stan) **10** Ran SP% **115.9**
Speed ratings (Par 107): **107,105,105,103,102 101,100,99,98,94**
toteswinger:1&2:£5.50, 2&3:£10.30, 1&3:£2.50 CSF £32.64 CT £208.68 TOTE £2.70: £1.20, £5.10, £1.90; EX 52.30 Trifecta £263.60 Part won. Pool: £356.29 - 0.45 winning units..
Owner B C Allen **Bred** B C Allen **Trained** Lambourn, Berks
■ Stewards' Enquiry : Frankie McDonald Once one got to his girths, he pulled out more. His confidence is sky-high at the moment.-Frankie McDonald, trainer

FOCUS
A good sprint handicap, but those ridden prominently up the middle of the track were favoured. A personal best from the winener, with the second to his turf form.

NOTEBOOK
Lesley's Choice, who had blinkers on in place of a visor, defied a 4lb higher mark than when winning at Kempton on his previous start with a game effort to complete the hat-trick. His style of racing was well suited to the way this straight track was riding, but even so, he's better than ever and, versatile with regards surface, could well go in again. (op 5-2)
Equuleus Pictor, having only his second start on an artificial surface, and his first on Fibresand, showed good speed throughout and ran well. Further opportunities could be limited this winter as he is considered best on a straight track (not a well-balanced horse according to his trainer), but he'll be worthy of respect if brought back to Southwell.
Colorus(IRE) ran very well considering he was 4lb out of the handicap and also carried 1lb overweight. (op 8-1 tchd 17-2)
Bel Cantor, a stablemate of the third, ran well off a mark 6lb higher than when winning over C&D two starts back. (op 7-1 tchd 9-1)
Rebel Duke(IRE), not for the first time, attracted plenty of money beforehand, but he was reported to have bled from the nose. Official explanation: trainer said gelding bled from the nose (tchd 11-4 in places)
Canadian Danehill(IRE) lost his race with a slow start and can do better. (op 16-1)
Pawan(IRE), racing for the 150th time, had little chance with Ann Stokell aboard putting up 6lb overweight. (op 28-1 tchd 33-1)
Toms Laughter ◆ started slowly again (his trainer said beforehand that is becoming an issue) and didn't face the kickback. Things haven't gone his way lately, but he'll probably have more chance of getting away with missing the break back on Polytrack and, nicely handicapped, he remains one to be interested in. (op 10-1)

7677 BET IN-PLAY AT TOTESPORT.COM H'CAP 1m 3f (F)
1:30 (1:31) (Class 6) (0-65,71) 3-Y-O+ £2,047 (£604; £302) Stalls Low

Form RPR

0111 **1** **Shadows Lengthen**[3] 7641 3-9-1 **71** 6ex........(b) JamesPSullivan(7) 7 86+
(M W Easterby) *mde all: shkn up over 1f out: readily* **30/100**[1]

203 **2** *2* **Boundless Prospect (USA)**[27] 7332 10-8-12 **62** AndrewHeffernan(5) 2 71
(P D Evans) *hld up: hdwy over 3f out: rdn to chse wnr fnl f: no imp* **9/1**[2]

0003 **3** *3¾* **General Tufto**[14] 7499 4-8-13 **58**........(b) KirstyMilczarek 6 61
(C Smith) *trckd ldrs: wnt 2nd over 3f out: rdn 2f out: no ex fnl f* **10/1**[3]

5165 **4** *1* **Venir Rouge**[20] 7440 5-9-6 **65**........ LPKeniry 4 66
(Matthew Salaman) *chsd wnr tl rdn over 3f out: styd on same pce fnl 2f* **14/1**

4540 **5** *nk* **Eightdaysaweek**[29] 7321 3-8-8 **57**........(p) ChrisCatlin 10 57
(A J McCabe) *in rr and sn pushed along: hdwy over 6f out: rdn over 3f out: styd on same pce fnl 2f* **16/1**

0446 **6** *shd* **Bicksta**[58] 6705 3-8-0 **52** oh2 ow1........ KellyHarrison(3) 11 52
(P T Midgley) *mid-div: rdn over 3f out: edgd lft and styd on same pce fnl 2f* **33/1**

3400 **7** *15* **Black Falcon (IRE)**[14] 7505 9-8-6 **51**........ FrankieMcDonald 9 26
(John A Harris) *prom: rdn over 3f out: sn wknd: hung lft 2f out* **100/1**

/56- **8** *6* **April The Second**[608] 1266 5-8-3 **51** oh1........ AndreaAtzeni(3) 8 16
(R J Price) *prom: rdn over 5f out: wknd over 4f out* **33/1**

-200 **9** *1¾* **St Savarin (FR)**[224] 584 8-9-6 **65**........ VinceSlattery 5 27
(M S Tuck) *chsd ldrs: rdn 1/2-way: sn lost pl: bhd fnl 4f* **100/1**

0452 **10** *1½* **Moscow Oznick**[56] 6758 4-9-1 **60**........ DavidProbert 3 19
(D Donovan) *s.i.s: hld up: rdn over 4f out: sn lost tch* **16/1**

0000 **11** *1* **Rock Art (IRE)**[9] 7586 3-8-9 **58** ow2........(p) DarryllHolland 1 15
(Karen George) *hld up: swtchd wd 1/2-way: rdn over 4f out: wknd sn after* **40/1**

2m 23.49s (-4.51) **Going Correction** -0.225s/f (Stan)
WFA 3 from 4yo+ 4lb **11** Ran SP% **124.7**
Speed ratings (Par 101): **107,105,102,102,101 101,90,86,85,84 83**
toteswinger:1&2:£3.20, 2&3:£4.30, 1&3:£2.70 CSF £4.34 CT £16.11 TOTE £1.30: £1.10, £1.80, £1.90; EX 5.20 Trifecta £23.20 Pool: £402.87 - 12.82 winning units..
Owner T A F Frost **Bred** London Thoroughbred Services Ltd **Trained** Sheriff Hutton, N Yorks
■ Stewards' Enquiry : Andrew Heffernan two-day ban: used whip with excessive frequency (Dec 22, 26)

FOCUS
A weak race in which the winner stood out under his penalty and won with something in hand. The form is rated around the runner-up.
Black Falcon(IRE) Official explanation: jockey said gelding hung left

7678 BOOK YOUR TICKETS ON LINE AT SOUTHWELL-RACECOURSE.CO.UK H'CAP 7f (F)
2:00 (2:00) (Class 6) (0-60,60) 3-Y-O+ £2,047 (£604; £302) Stalls Low

Form RPR

0000 **1** **Jonnie Skull (IRE)**[9] 7589 3-9-3 **59**........(vt) RobertWinston 1 69
(P S McEntee) *led: rdn and hdd ins fnl f: rallied to ld nr fin* **10/1**

5065 **2** *hd* **Zeffirelli**[121] 4812 4-8-7 **52**........ AndreaAtzeni(3) 7 62
(M Quinn) *a.p: chsd wnr 2f out: led and hung lft ins fnl f: outbattled and hdd nr fin* **12/1**

0015 **3** *3¼* **Hit The Switch**[6] 7609 3-9-0 **56**........ SJCraine 2 57
(Patrick Morris) *trckd ldrs: rdn over 1f out: no ex fnl f* **9/2**[2]

6614 **4** *nk* **Ingleby Princess**[21] 7422 5-9-2 **58**........ PhillipMakin 9 58+
(T D Barron) *hld up: hdwy u.p over 1f out: nt rch ldrs* **11/4**[1]

006 **5** *2½* **Plenilune (IRE)**[8] 7600 4-8-10 **52**........ TomEaves 13 45
(M Brittain) *chsd ldrs: outpcd 1/2-way: hrd rdn and styd on appr fnl f* **10/1**

0053 **6** *¾* **The City Kid (IRE)**[10] 7579 6-8-12 **54** ow1........ DaneO'Neill 4 45
(G D Blake) *hmpd s: sn pushed along in rr: hdwy 1/2-way: rdn and hung lft over 1f out: wknd ins fnl f* **5/1**[3]

0604 **7** *¾* **Unconsoled**[26] 7353 3-8-8 **50**........ FranciscoDaSilva 10 39
(J Hetherton) *sn chsng wnr: rdn over 1f out: wknd fnl f* **16/1**

0200 **8** *4½* **Kheskianto (IRE)**[26] 7348 3-9-2 **58**........ GeorgeBaker 8 35
(M C Chapman) *mid-div: pushed along over 4f out: rdn over 2f out: n.d* **10/1**

1000 **9** *1¼* **Artesium**[46] 7002 3-8-11 **53**........ LPKeniry 6 27
(Patrick Morris) *s.i.s: hld up: n.d* **28/1**

0000 **10** *nse* **Dhhamaan (IRE)**[76] 6221 4-8-11 **53**........(b) KirstyMilczarek 14 27
(Mrs R A Carr) *s.s: hdwy 1/2-way: wknd over 2f out* **28/1**

000- **11** *1* **Saving Grace**[426] 6580 3-8-11 **53**........ GrahamGibbons 11 24
(E J Alston) *s.i.s: sn prom: lost pl 4f out: wknd 1/2-way* **16/1**

0050 **12** *1¼* **Dark Velvet (IRE)**[42] 7082 3-8-8 **50**........ ShaneKelly 5 18
(E J Alston) *s.i.s: sn pushed along: a in rr* **50/1**

0 **13** *½* **Riverside**[83] 5982 4-8-8 **50**........ JimmyQuinn 12 16
(M Brittain) *s.i.s: a in rr* **66/1**

3040 **14** *2¼* **Circle Dance (IRE)**[116] 5008 4-9-4 **60**........(p) AdamKirby 3 20
(Miss M E Rowland) *chsd ldrs: rdn 1/2-way: wknd over 2f out: eased over 1f out* **25/1**

1m 27.65s (-2.65) **Going Correction** -0.225s/f (Stan) **14** Ran SP% **122.4**
Speed ratings (Par 101): **106,105,102,101,98 98,97,92,90,90 89,87,87,84**
toteswinger:1&2:£23.40, 2&3:£14.40, 1&3:£11.90 CSF £120.87 CT £643.95 TOTE £14.80: £3.60, £3.60, £2.60; EX 121.90 TRIFECTA Not won..
Owner Mrs Rebecca McEntee **Bred** Canice Farrell Jnr **Trained** Newmarket, Suffolk

FOCUS
This was the only race on the card in which the time dipped under standard and the front pair probably posted good efforts in the context of the grade. Both produced personal bests, with the form rated around the runner-up.
Dhhamaan(IRE) Official explanation: jockey said gelding anticipated start and was slow away
Dark Velvet(IRE) Official explanation: jockey said filly never travelled

7679 MEMBERSHIP AT SOUTHWELL GOLF CLUB CLASSIFIED CLAIMING STKS 6f (F)
2:30 (2:31) (Class 6) 3-Y-O+ £2,047 (£604; £302) Stalls Low

Form RPR

0036 **1** **Cheap Thrills**[13] 7518 3-8-7 68........ ShaneKelly 9 69
(J A Osborne) *led: hdd over 4f out: chsd ldr tl led again over 2f out: hdd over 1f out: rallied u.p to ld ins fnl f: r.o* **9/2**[1]

3464 **2** *nk* **Mocha Java**[13] 7521 6-8-3 56 ow1........(b) ChrisCatlin 10 64
(Matthew Salaman) *s.i.s: sn pushed along: hdwy over 3f out: rdn over 2f out: r.o* **10/1**[3]

0306 **3** *nk* **Capo Regime**[21] 7422 3-8-3 62........(v) KirstyMilczarek 2 63
(P Howling) *s.i.s and hmpd s: sn prom: rdn and swtchd lft over 1f out: r.o* **8/1**[2]

0004 **4** *½* **Loose Caboose (IRE)**[10] 7577 4-8-11 67........(b) RobertWinston 11 69
(A J McCabe) *chsd ldrs: rdn to ld over 1f out: hdd ins fnl f: unable qck towards fin* **8/1**[2]

0002 **5** *½* **Borasco (USA)**[22] 7412 4-8-3 70........ DeanHeslop(5) 5 65
(T D Barron) *sn pushed along in rr: rdn over 1f out: hung lft and r.o ins fnl f: nt rch ldrs* **9/2**[1]

5005 **6** *nk* **War And Peace (IRE)**[3] 7645 5-8-0 68........ LewisWalsh(7) 3 64
(Jane Chapple-Hyam) *s.i.s and hmpd s: bhd: hdwy over 1f out: eased last few strides* **9/2**[1]

0002 **7** *nk* **Mango Music**[50] 6904 6-8-4 60........ AndreaAtzeni(3) 8 62
(M Quinn) *chsd ldrs: rdn over 2f out: styd on* **10/1**[3]

2000 **8** *3½* **Swinbrook (USA)**[13] 7519 8-8-4 67........(v) LiamJones 7 48
(R A Harris) *sn pushed along in rr: rdn over 1f out: n.d* **10/1**[3]

0040 **9** *½* **Angaric (IRE)**[85] 5955 6-8-7 59........ TomEaves 4 49
(B Smart) *prom: drvn along over 4f out: outpcd fr 1/2-way* **22/1**

4444 **10** *nk* **Diane's Choice**[20] 7438 6-8-2 51........(e) DavidProbert 6 43
(Miss Gay Kelleway) *mid-div: rdn 1/2-way: wknd over 2f out* **18/1**

0600 **11** *10* **Inthawain**[21] 7418 3-8-2 53........ JimmyQuinn 1 11
(N Wilson) *w ldr tl led over 4f out: rdn and hdd over 2f out: wknd over 1f out* **66/1**

1m 15.52s (-0.98) **Going Correction** -0.225s/f (Stan) **11** Ran SP% **115.1**
Speed ratings (Par 101): **97,96,96,95,94 94,94,89,88,88 75**
toteswinger:1&2:£10.20, 2&3:£14.20, 1&3:£8.80 CSF £49.86 TOTE £4.60: £2.00, £3.00, £3.60; EX 55.10 Trifecta £204.20 Part won. Pool: £275.98 - 0.40 winning units..
Owner Mr And Mrs Christopher Wright **Bred** Stratford Place Stud **Trained** Upper Lambourn, Berks
■ Stewards' Enquiry : Chris Catlin five-day ban: used whip with excessive frequency, down shoulder in the forehand (Dec 22, 26-29)
Kirsty Milczarek five-day ban: used whip with excessive frequency (Dec 22, 26-29)

FOCUS
A competitive claimer, but the time was slower than both divisions of the 46-60 handicap and the form is modest. It is a bit muddling too, with the first seven in a heap.

7680 HOSPITALITY AT SOUTHWELL RACECOURSE H'CAP (DIV I) 6f (F)
3:00 (3:01) (Class 6) (0-60,60) 3-Y-O+ £1,706 (£503; £252) Stalls Low

Form RPR

3504 **1** **Danum Dancer**[21] 7418 5-9-1 **57**........(b) LeeVickers 9 68
(N Bycroft) *a.p: chsd ldr over 4f out: rdn and edgd rt over 1f out: led ins fnl f: r.o wl* **7/1**[3]

3004 **2** *1½* **Only A Game (IRE)**[25] 7370 4-8-13 **55** ow1........(tp) AdamKirby 12 61
(I W McInnes) *hld up in tch: gng wl over 1f out: rdn and ev ch ins fnl f: sn hung rt and nt run on* **25/1**

0523 **3** *2* **Cool Sands (IRE)**[11] 7555 7-8-13 **55**........(v) J-PGuillambert 7 55
(J G Given) *dwlt: outpcd: hdwy over 1f out: sn hrd rdn: styd on same pce ins fnl f* **4/1**[2]

6251 **4** *hd* **First Swallow**[14] 7503 4-9-3 **59**........(t) PhillipMakin 6 58
(D H Brown) *led: rdn and edgd rt over 1f out: hdd and no ex ins fnl f* **4/1**[2]

0006 **5** *½* **Golden Dixie (USA)**[14] 7503 10-8-13 **55**........ LiamJones 2 53
(R A Harris) *wnt rt s: sn prom: edgd rt: bmpd and lost pl over 4f out: hdwy over 2f out: sn rdn: no ex ins fnl f* **25/1**

600 **6** *¾* **Brazilian Brush (IRE)**[12] 7534 4-8-4 **46** oh1........(tp) LukeMorris 8 41
(J M Bradley) *chsd ldrs: rdn over 2f out: styd on same pce fnl f* **33/1**

55-5 **7** *nk* **Desert Dust**[13] 7519 6-8-1 **46** oh1........ AndreaAtzeni(3) 1 40
(H J Collingridge) *trckd ldrs: rdn over 1f out: no ex fnl f* **12/1**

0026 **8** *1¼* **Josiah Bartlett (IRE)**[9] 7591 3-8-10 **52**........ ShaneKelly 5 42
(Ian Williams) *s.i.s and hmpd s: sn pushed along in rr: n.d* **11/1**

000 **9** *½* **Fulford**[116] 4998 4-8-4 **46**........ JimmyQuinn 11 35
(M Brittain) *chsd ldrs: rdn over 2f out: wknd over 1f out* **33/1**

6204 **10** *1* **Tri Chara (IRE)**[26] 7349 5-8-9 **58**........(p) DavidKenny(7) 10 43
(R Hollinshead) *dwlt: hdwy over 3f out: rdn over 2f out: wknd over 1f out* **3/1**[1]

0000 **11** *1½* **Forrest Star**[122] 4772 4-8-4 **46** oh1........ GregFairley 3 27
(M Johnston) *hmpd s: hld up: rdn over 2f out: n.d* **11/1**

2300 **12** *½* **Music Box Express**[145] 4023 5-8-13 **60**........ MatthewDavies(5) 4 39
(George Baker) *s.i.s: sn mid-div: hmpd and lost pl over 4f out: n.d after* **22/1**

1m 15.3s (-1.20) **Going Correction** -0.225s/f (Stan) **12** Ran SP% **119.8**
Speed ratings (Par 101): **99,97,94,94,93 92,92,90,89,88 86,85**
toteswinger:1&2:£29.50, 2&3:£12.10, 1&3:£9.70 CSF £176.95 CT £808.47 TOTE £10.90: £2.90, £5.30, £1.40; EX 98.60 Trifecta £378.10 Pool: £510.95 - 1.00 winning units..

Owner G Hart, B Abbott, R McGrane, K Senior **Bred** Barton Stud **Trained** Brandsby, N Yorks

FOCUS

The time was 0.21 seconds slower than the second division. The form looks sound, rated through the runner-up.

7681 HOSPITALITY AT SOUTHWELL RACECOURSE H'CAP (DIV II) 6f (F)

3:30 (3:30) (Class 6) (0-60,60) 3-Y-0+ **£1,706** (£503; £252) **Stalls** Low

Form RPR

6411 **1** **Diamond Blade**[21] 7418 3-9-1 **57**............(p) DNolan 1 71+
(T D Easterby) *half-rrd s: sn rcvrd to ld: rdn over 1f out: r.o: eased nr fin* **6/4**[1]

0400 **2** 1 1/4 **Tadlil**[12] 7534 7-8-4 **46** oh1............(v) LukeMorris 2 56
(J M Bradley) *chsd wnr: rdn and hung lft fr over 1f out: styd on* **16/1**

4335 **3** 1 1/2 **Kinigi (IRE)**[14] 7503 3-8-8 **55**............(p) AndrewHeffernan(5) 5 60
(R A Harris) *sn pushed along in rr: hdwy u.p over 1f out: nt rch ldrs* **10/1**

3355 **4** nk **Nabeeda**[213] 1889 4-8-12 **54**............ RobertWinston 3 58
(M Brittain) *chsd ldrs: rdn over 2f out: nt clr run over 1f out: styd on same pce* **6/1**[2]

0044 **5** 2 **Hollow Jo**[83] 5989 9-9-4 **60**............ FergusSweeney 4 58
(J R Jenkins) *mid-div: hdwy over 2f out: sn rdn: no imp fnl f* **14/1**

4002 **6** 1 3/4 **Tag Team (IRE)**[18] 7460 8-8-4 **46**............ ChrisCatlin 11 38
(John A Harris) *chsd ldrs: rdn over 2f out: wknd over 1f out* **22/1**

0003 **7** 1/2 **Gower**[18] 7460 5-8-4 **46** oh1............(p) DavidProbert 7 37
(R J Price) *sn pushed along in rr: rdn over 2f out: n.d* **16/1**

0546 **8** 3 **Dickie Le Davoir**[11] 7555 5-9-0 **56**............(be) J-PGuillambert 8 46
(R C Guest) *dwlt and hmpd s: outpcd: nt clr run over 2f out: swtchd lft over 1f out: sn rdn: eased ins fnl f* **6/1**[2]

0002 **9** 2 3/4 **Dancing Wave**[49] 6926 3-9-3 **59**............ GeorgeBaker 10 31
(M C Chapman) *chsd ldrs tl rdn and wknd over 2f out* **13/2**[3]

-605 **10** nk **Govenor Eliott (IRE)**[18] 7464 4-8-10 **52**............ TomEaves 6 23
(A J Lockwood) *s.i.s: outpcd* **25/1**

6000 **11** 8 **Castlecarra (IRE)**[18] 7466 4-8-4 **46** oh1............(bt[1]) FranciscoDaSilva 9 —
(J Hetherton) *s.i.s and hmpd s: hdwy and hung rt fr over 4f out: wknd over 2f out* **40/1**

1m 15.09s (-1.41) **Going Correction** -0.225s/f (Stan) **11** Ran SP% **120.1**

Speed ratings (Par 101): **100,98,96,95,93 90,90,86,82,82 71**

toteswinger:1&2:£8.70, 2&3:£18.40, 1&3:£5.90 CSF £29.64 CT £192.49 TOTE £2.50: £1.40, £3.90, £2.90; EX 37.90 Trifecta £207.30 Part won. Pool: £280.17 - 0.55 winning units. Place 6 £42.15, Place 5 £33.98 .

Owner D A West **Bred** Bumble Bloodstock **Trained** Great Habton, N Yorks

FOCUS

The quicker of the two divisions by 0.21 seconds. The winner is progressing and the third is a decent yardstick.

T/Jkpt: Part won. £10,905.70 to a £1 stake. Pool: £15,360.19. 0.50 winning tickets. T/Plt: £125.30 to a £1 stake. Pool: £47,558.30. 277.02 winning tickets. T/Qpdt: £45.80 to a £1 stake. Pool: £4,694.30. 75.70 winning tickets. CR

7609 KEMPTON (A.W) (R-H)

Wednesday, December 9

OFFICIAL GOING: Standard

Wind: Almost nil Weather: Dark

7682 WIN A CAR AT KEMPTON.CO.UK H'CAP 5f (P)

6:20 (6:20) (Class 5) (0-75,75) 3-Y-0+ **£2,590** (£770; £385; £192) **Stalls** High

Form RPR

0010 **1** **Lord Of The Reins (IRE)**[25] 7398 5-8-11 **68**............ JimCrowley 10 80+
(J G Given) *hld up in midfield on inner: eased off rail 2f out: rdn and prog over 1f out: r.o between rivals fnl f to ld last 50yds* **9/2**[2]

1565 **2** 1/2 **Lithaam (IRE)**[12] 7554 5-8-2 **66**............(p) RyanClark(7) 11 76
(J M Bradley) *chsd ldrs: wnt 3rd 2f out: urged along on outer over 1f out: led last 150yds: hdd and outpcd fnl 50yds* **6/1**[3]

2005 **3** 1 3/4 **Fromsong (IRE)**[9] 7595 11-8-6 **63**............(p) MartinDwyer 7 67
(D K Ivory) *chsd ldr: rdn over 1f out: clsd grad fnl f but sn hdd and outpcd by ldng pair* **8/1**

0340 **4** 1/2 **Silver Prelude**[12] 7554 8-8-8 **65**............(t) ChrisCatlin 5 67
(S C Williams) *led and sn crossed to rail: drvn over 1f out: hdd & wknd last 150yds* **12/1**

6211 **5** 2 **Ask Jenny (IRE)**[8] 7606 7-8-1 **63** 6ex............ AndrewHeffernan(5) 6 58
(Patrick Morris) *mostly in midfield: pushed along 2f out: no real imp on ldrs u.p fnl f* **10/1**

4000 **6** hd **Priti Fabulous (IRE)**[14] 7511 4-8-11 **75**............ DeclanCannon(7) 9 69
(A J McCabe) *blindfold late off and slowest away: hld up in last pair: effrt on inner over 1f out: kpt on but nvr involved* **33/1**

4300 **7** hd **Northern Empire (IRE)**[9] 7601 6-8-4 **61**............(p) JimmyQuinn 8 55
(F Jordan) *hld up in last pair: effrt over 1f out: shkn up and kpt on: nvr involved* **25/1**

3-11 **8** 1 3/4 **Barnezet (GR)**[277] 784 3-8-11 **73**............ SimonPearce(5) 2 60
(J Pearce) *racd wd: chsd ldng pair to 2f out: sn lost pl and btn* **20/1**

3220 **9** 2 **Bookiesindex Boy**[12] 7554 5-8-9 **66**............ FrancisNorton 3 46
(J R Jenkins) *racd wd: hld up in midfield: lost grnd bnd 2f out: shuffled along and no prog after: nvr nr ldrs* **12/1**

4404 **10** 3 3/4 **Mambo Spirit (IRE)**[14] 7518 5-8-11 **68**............ AdamKirby 12 35
(Stef Liddiard) *chsd ldng pair to 2f out: wknd rapidly* **7/4**[1]

59.49 secs (-1.01) **Going Correction** -0.10s/f (Stan) **10** Ran SP% **116.0**

Speed ratings (Par 103): **104,103,100,99,96 96,95,92,89,83**

toteswinger:1&2:£5.50, 2&3:£13.40, 1&3:£10.00 CSF £30.65 CT £210.21 TOTE £6.90: £1.90, £2.70, £1.60; EX 24.90.

Owner Danethorpe Racing Partnership **Bred** C Farrell **Trained** Willoughton, Lincs

FOCUS

A competitive sprint handicap with a strong pace guaranteed. Plenty of confirmed front runners helped to record a time just below RPR standard. Good form for the grade from the first two.

Mambo Spirit(IRE) Official explanation: trainer had no explanation for the poor form shown

7683 DIGIBET MAIDEN AUCTION STKS 1m 2f (P)

6:50 (6:50) (Class 5) 2-Y-0 **£2,590** (£770; £385; £192) **Stalls** High

Form RPR

63 **1** **Red Courtier**[33] 7277 2-8-13 0............ GregFairley 3 80
(P F I Cole) *pushed up to ld: mde all: nt less than 3 l clr fr 1/2-way: wl ahd over 1f out: rdn out* **5/1**[3]

05 **2** 6 **Cast Of Stars (IRE)**[59] 6697 2-9-0 0............ JimCrowley 7 70
(R M Beckett) *chsd ldng pair: rdn and nt qckn over 2f out: plugged on to take 2nd jst over 1f out: no ch w wnr* **13/8**[2]

543 **3** 2 3/4 **Ipswich Lad**[62] 6607 2-9-0 74............(v[1]) LPKeniry 8 65
(A M Balding) *chsd wnr: str reminders over 3f out: no imp after: one pce and lost 2nd jst over 1f out* **6/4**[1]

066 **4** 4 1/2 **Creevy (IRE)**[14] 7513 2-8-5 48............ MartinDwyer 1 48
(S Kirk) *hld up in 5th: pushed along to go 4th 4f out: shkn up and no imp wl over 1f out: wknd nr fin* **20/1**

055 **5** 1 3/4 **Kyoatee Kilt**[9] 7597 2-9-0 60............ DarryllHolland 2 54
(P F I Cole) *t.k.h: hld up in rr: wl bhd whn asked for effrt 3f out: rchd poor 5th wl over 1f out: plugged on* **16/1**

004 **6** 13 **The Great Husk (IRE)**[99] 5543 2-8-4 52............ SophieDoyle(5) 4 26
(J S Moore) *t.k.h: hld up: hanging lft bnd over 3f out: sn wl bhd* **33/1**

00 **7** 11 **Sisters Warning**[19] 7463 2-8-4 35............ KirstyMilczarek 6 1
(J Ryan) *chsd ldng trio to 4f out: sn wknd: t.o* **50/1**

000 **8** 23 **Sparkling Crown**[20] 7451 2-7-11 52............ RyanPowell(7) 5 —
(J Ryan) *in tch to 4f out: sn wknd and wl t.o* **33/1**

2m 6.32s (-1.68) **Going Correction** -0.10s/f (Stan) **8** Ran SP% **113.2**

Speed ratings (Par 96): **102,97,95,91,90 79,70,52**

toteswinger:1&2:£2.10, 2&3:£1.02, 1&3:£4.50 CSF £13.04 TOTE £5.50: £1.40, £1.20, £1.10; EX 14.70.

Owner C Shiacolas **Bred** Pegasus Racing Ltd **Trained** Whatcombe, Oxon

FOCUS

A two-year-old 1m 2f maiden where, on paper, only three could be considered seriously beforehand. The winner impressed and the next two help with the level. The first five finished clear.

NOTEBOOK

Red Courtier made virtually all. The forceful tactics employed seemed to play to his strengths and, after taking up the running soon after a furlong, he stayed on strongly to draw clear in the straight. He did little wrong and evidently relished the step up in trip, but there has to be question marks over what he has beat. (op 9-2)

Cast Of Stars(IRE) probably had the best form on offer and was well-supported, but he looks one-paced and could have a better time in handicaps as a three-year-old. (op 7-4 tchd 6-4 and 15-8 in a place)

Ipswich Lad was equipped with a first-time visor and had shown some ability in his three runs but, after chasing the winner for much of the way, found little in the straight and does not look one to rely upon. (tchd 13-8)

Creevy(IRE) is exposed as very moderate.

Kyoatee Kilt Official explanation: jockey said colt ran too freely

Sparkling Crown Official explanation: vet said filly returned lame on near-fore

7684 DIGIBET.COM H'CAP 1m 2f (P)

7:20 (7:21) (Class 4) (0-85,85) 3-Y-0+ **£4,727** (£1,406; £702; £351) **Stalls** High

Form RPR

1313 **1** **Poyle Meg**[26] 7366 3-8-13 **80**............(p) JimCrowley 7 89
(R M Beckett) *trckd ldng trio: wnt 3rd over 2f out: rdn to chse ldr over 1f out: clsd and drvn ahd last 50yds* **8/1**

222P **2** hd **Mafeking (UAE)**[36] 7226 5-9-5 **83**............ ChrisCatlin 9 92
(M R Hoad) *led at str pce: breather 1/2-way: kicked on again over 2f out: over a l clr 1f out: drvn and hdd last 50yds: kpt on wl* **10/1**

5602 **3** 3/4 **Indy Driver**[44] 7054 4-8-13 **77**............(p) FrancisNorton 11 84+
(Matthew Salaman) *hld up in 7th: effrt whn forced wd bnd 2f out: prog over 1f out: styd on to take 3rd ins fnl f: nvr quite able to chal* **4/1**[1]

1405 **4** nk **Hawaana (IRE)**[5] 7626 4-8-12 **79**............ KellyHarrison(3) 5 85
(Miss Gay Kelleway) *hld up in last pair: gd prog on inner 2f out: clsd on ldrs 1f out: n.m.r and one pce fnl 100yds* **12/1**

0213 **5** 1 3/4 **Hurakan (IRE)**[8] 7607 3-8-7 **74**............ PaulDoe 3 77+
(P D Evans) *hld up in 9th: u.p and dropped to last trio 3f out: prog over 1f out: styd on wl to take 5th nr fin* **6/1**[2]

3530 **6** 1/2 **December Draw (IRE)**[14] 7523 3-9-1 **82**............(p) ShaneKelly 8 84
(W J Knight) *chsd ldr: rdn over 2f out: nt qckn over 1f out and hld: wknd ins fnl f* **16/1**

2131 **7** shd **Dinner Date**[36] 7229 7-8-7 **71**............ LPKeniry 10 73
(T Keddy) *trckd ldng quartet: effrt over 2f out: drvn over 1f out: no imp after: fdd fnl 100yds* **10/1**

210- **8** 1 1/2 **Princess Lomi (IRE)**[75] 6263 4-8-7 **71**............ LukeMorris 4 70
(Andrew Heffernan, Ire) *mostly in same pl: rdn on inner 2f out: stl in tch but no imp over 1f out: fdd* **25/1**

0010 **9** hd **Scamperdale**[19] 7465 7-9-7 **85**............ RichardHughes 2 85+
(B P J Baugh) *hld up in rr: prog 2f out: kpt on over 1f out: no ch whn short of room nr fin* **25/1**

5352 **10** 1 **Rio Guru (IRE)**[35] 7248 4-9-2 **80**............ TonyCulhane 1 76
(M R Channon) *sn last and nt gng wl: drvn over 3f out: stl last over 1f out: modest prog fnl f* **25/1**

2525 **11** 1 1/2 **Addwaitya**[8] 7607 4-9-0 **78**............(p) IanMongan 12 71
(Mrs L J Mongan) *racd wd: hld up in 6th: rdn wl over 2f out: wdst of all bnd 2f out: sn wknd* **22/1**

1401 **12** 2 3/4 **Best In Class**[21] 7428 3-8-11 **78**............ DaneO'Neill 6 66
(S C Williams) *stdd s: hld up in 11th and racd wd: rdn 3f out: wd bnd 2f out and struggling: sn wknd* **7/1**[3]

01-3 **13** 3 **Green Wadi**[13] 7539 4-8-11 **75**............ FergusSweeney 13 57
(G L Moore) *trckd ldng pair tl wknd rapidly over 2f out* **6/1**[2]

2m 5.35s (-2.65) **Going Correction** -0.10s/f (Stan) **13** Ran SP% **119.8**

WFA 3 from 4yo+ 3lb

Speed ratings (Par 105): **106,105,105,105,103 103,103,101,101,100 99,97,95**

toteswinger:1&2:£13.90, 2&3:£8.00, 1&3:£7.20 CSF £81.42 CT £365.13 TOTE £7.50: £2.00, £3.50, £2.30; EX 80.00.

Owner Cecil Wiggins **Bred** Miss Alison Wiggins **Trained** Whitsbury, Hants

FOCUS

A very competitive 71-85 handicap with plenty holding claims, run at a good pace. Sound form, with the runner-up probably the best guide.

Scamperdale Official explanation: jockey said gelding was denied a clear run

7685 DIGIBET CASINO NURSERY 1m (P)

7:50 (7:50) (Class 4) (0-85,85) 2-Y-0 **£3,885** (£1,156; £577; £288) **Stalls** High

Form RPR

1000 **1** **Danger Mulally**[8] 7604 2-8-6 **70**............(t) DavidProbert 5 73
(A M Balding) *chsd ldrs: rdn to go 3rd 2f out: clsd grad on outer fr over 1f out: led nr fin and hld on* **20/1**

6412 **2** shd **Nave (USA)**[21] 7434 2-8-6 **70**............ GregFairley 2 73
(M Johnston) *s.i.s: in last pair tl effrt on wd over 2f out: prog u.p over 1f out: styd on to chal nr fin: jst pipped* **5/2**[2]

51 **3** hd **Huygens**[166] 3344 2-9-4 **82**............ DarryllHolland 3 85
(D J Coakley) *trckd ldr after 3f: pushed into narrow ld 2f out: hrd rdn over 1f out: kpt on but hdd last strides* **7/1**

2023 **4** 3/4 **Fivefold (USA)**[3] 7654 2-8-12 **76**............ J-PGuillambert 1 77
(J Akehurst) *led at decent pce: shkn up and hdd narrowly 2f out: styd pressing ldr tl no ex last 100yds* **11/2**[3]

441 **5** 1 1/2 **Khanivorous**[21] 7429 2-9-0 **78** ... SJCraine 6 76
(J R Boyle) *chsd ldrs: pushed along fr 1/2-way: effrt u.p over 2f out: one pce fr over 1f out* **7/1**
4022 **6** 3/4 **Master Of Dance (IRE)**[7] 7611 2-9-7 **85** ... RichardHughes 7 81
(R Hannon) *stdd s: hld up last: shkn up over 2f out: one pce and no imp whn rdn over 1f out* **7/4**[1]
0600 **7** 17 **Joe Rua (USA)**[14] 7513 2-7-8 **62** oh14 ow3 ...(v) RyanPowell(7) 4 24
(J Ryan) *chsd ldr 3f: wknd rapidly over 2f out: t.o* **40/1**
1m 39.0s (-0.80) **Going Correction** -0.10s/f (Stan) 7 Ran SP% **112.5**
Speed ratings (Par 98): **100,99,99,98,97 96,79**
toteswinger:1&2:£6.70, 2&3:£4.50, 1&3:£11.20 CSF £67.65 TOTE £22.70: £10.60, £1.50; EX 94.30.
Owner John Dwyer **Bred** D Robb **Trained** Kingsclere, Hants
■ Stewards' Enquiry : David Probert four-day ban: used whip with excessive frequency without giving gelding time to respond (Dec 26-29)

FOCUS
A decent nursery despite the small field, run at just a fair pace until quickening up entering the straight, resulting in a blanket finish. The fourth looks the best guide to the form.

NOTEBOOK
Danger Mulally had cut little ice in nurseries since landing a Folkestone maiden and was well held by the runner-up on their previous meeting. This was a much better performance. Always up with the pace, he came with a strong run in the straight and narrowly got the verdict in a very tight finish. Clearly he has come on for his two runs since his break, meeting trouble in running last time, and it would be disappointing if he cannot build upon this. (tchd 25-1)
Nave(USA) can be considered slightly unlucky, as he missed the break and that probably cost him the race. He is progressing well and sets a good standard. He should gain some quick compensation. (tchd 11-4)
Huygens was returning from a break of 166 days and ran with plenty of credit. He took a narrow advantage inside the final furlong only to go down narrowly, but he looks one with plenty of potential and should come on for this. (op 5-1)
Fivefold(USA) has been in good heart of late and tried to make all. But, after quickening well entering the straight, he had little more to give when headed towards the finish. (tchd 6-1 in places)
Khanivorous ran a sound enough race but could never land a blow. His mark looks to be anchoring him. (op 13-2 tchd 11-4)
Master Of Dance(IRE) was keen enough in rear but, when closing on the leaders and asked for his effort, failed to find the required pace to land a blow. (op 5-2 tchd 11-4 in places)

7686 GROOMED TO PERFECTION, THE KIA SOUL MAIDEN STKS 6f (P)
8:20 (8:20) (Class 5) 3-Y-O+ **£2,590** (£770; £385; £192) **Stalls** High

Form RPR
23-2 **1** **Zegna (IRE)**[23] 7411 3-9-3 70 ... TomEaves 6 78
(B Smart) *t.k.h: trckd ldng pair: produced to ld jst over 1f out: sn rdn clr* **7/4**[1]
43-2 **2** 3 1/2 **Ajjaadd (USA)**[34] 7254 3-9-3 72 ... SteveDrowne 5 67
(T E Powell) *led: shkn up and hdd jst over 1f out: no answer to wnr and wl btn fnl f* **7/4**[1]
054 **3** 1 1/2 **Suzi's Dancer**[62] 6611 3-8-12 55 ... JackMitchell 3 57
(H J Collingridge) *wnt lft s: t.k.h: hld up last: awkward bnd 4f out and trying to hang lft fr over 2f out: plugged on to take 3rd nr fin* **14/1**[3]
2340 **4** nk **Major Lawrence (IRE)**[44] 7067 3-9-3 72 ... RichardHughes 4 61
(J Noseda) *trckd ldr: rdn and nt qckn over 2f out: wknd over 1f out: lost 3rd nr fin* **11/4**[2]
000 **5** 4 1/2 **Clever Omneya (USA)**[42] 7107 3-8-9 44 ... MartinLane(3) 2 42
(J R Jenkins) *chsd ldng trio: rdn over 2f out: wknd wl over 1f out* **50/1**
0000 **6** 3 3/4 **Lady Dinsdale (IRE)**[10] 7591 3-8-12 37 ...(b[1]) LPKeniry 8 30
(T Keddy) *settled in 5th: cl enough 2f out: sn wknd rapidly* **66/1**
1m 11.91s (-1.19) **Going Correction** -0.10s/f (Stan) 6 Ran SP% **109.5**
Speed ratings (Par 103): **103,98,96,95,89 84**
toteswinger:1&2:£1.20, 2&3:£1.30, 1&3:£3.60 CSF £4.75 TOTE £2.90: £1.30, £1.80; EX 5.80.
Owner Clipper Logistics **Bred** Castlefarm Stud **Trained** Hambleton, N Yorks

FOCUS
A modest sprint maiden run at a decent pace. The winner is rated back to his 2yo form and may do better.

7687 BISTRO PRICES FROM £37 H'CAP (DIV I) 1m 4f (P)
8:50 (8:52) (Class 6) (0-55,56) 3-Y-O+ **£1,706** (£503; £252) **Stalls** Centre

Form RPR
0033 **1** **Kames Park (IRE)**[18] 7490 7-9-3 **54** ... JimCrowley 2 62
(R C Guest) *stdd s: hld up in last: smooth prog on inner over 2f out: cajoled along and styd on to ld last 100yds* **9/2**[3]
5 **2** 3/4 **Sovento (GER)**[53] 6845 5-9-1 **52** ... HayleyTurner 8 59
(Shaun Harley, Ire) *plld hrd: hld up bhd ldrs: nt clr run briefly over 2f out: effrt to ld over 1f out: drvn and hdd last 100yds: kpt on* **7/1**
6005 **3** 3 **Jezza**[19] 7461 3-8-7 **49** ... JamieMackay 6 51
(Karen George) *trckd ldr 4f and again 3f out: led over 2f out to over 1f out: nt qckn* **8/1**
0203 **4** hd **Fantasy Ride**[2] 7670 7-8-10 **52** ... SimonPearce(5) 10 56+
(J Pearce) *hld up in rr: effrt whn rn into trble over 2f out: sme prog over 1f out: r.o nr fin and nrly snatched 3rd* **4/1**[2]
6025 **5** 1/2 **Noah Jameel**[74] 6288 7-9-4 **55** ... FergusSweeney 9 56
(A G Newcombe) *hld up in midfield: smooth prog over 3f out: brought to chal and upsides over 2f out to over 1f out: wknd tamely fnl f* **3/1**[1]
5-00 **6** 1 3/4 **Time To Play**[50] 6925 4-9-4 **55** ... AdamKirby 1 53
(T T Clement) *hld up in rr: in trble whn pce lifted over 4f out: shkn up and kpt on fnl 2f: nvr rchd ldrs* **50/1**
500 **7** 5 **Michael Laskey**[218] 1771 3-8-10 **55** ... JamesMillman(3) 5 45
(B R Millman) *t.k.h: hld up in midfield: asked for effrt and hung rt over 2f out: fnd nil and wknd over 1f out* **14/1**
0645 **8** 9 **Flying Gazebo (IRE)**[100] 5503 3-8-12 **54** ... LukeMorris 7 30
(J S Moore) *t.k.h: hld up in tch: rdn on and off fr 1/2-way: struggling whn hmpd over 2f out: no ch after* **8/1**
640 **9** 3 1/2 **Spring Fashion (IRE)**[12] 7557 3-8-10 **52** ... JerryO'Dwyer 4 22
(M Botti) *trckd ldr after 4f to 3f out: losing pl whn hmpd over 2f out: wknd* **10/1**
0000 **10** 17 **Innactualfact**[34] 7250 3-8-10 **52** ...(b[1]) PaulDoe 3 —
(L A Dace) *dwlt: sn led and racd freely: slow pce for 4f: upped tempo fr 5f out: hdd and wnt out like a light over 2f out* **33/1**
2m 34.1s (-0.40) **Going Correction** -0.10s/f (Stan)
WFA 3 from 4yo+ 5lb 10 Ran SP% **118.6**
Speed ratings (Par 101): **97,96,94,94,94 92,89,83,81,69**
toteswinger:1&2:£12.00, 2&3:£14.60, 1&3:£5.00 CSF £36.78 CT £248.27 TOTE £4.30: £1.70, £2.40, £2.40; EX 31.50.
Owner Future Racing (Notts) Limited **Bred** Pat Beirne **Trained** Stainforth, S Yorks

FOCUS
A poor 46-55 handicap. It was run slightly quicker than the second division but was arguably the weaker race, with the winner the best guide to the form.
Michael Laskey Official explanation: jockey said gelding hung right
Spring Fashion(IRE) Official explanation: jockey said filly hung left

7688 BISTRO PRICES FROM £37 H'CAP (DIV II) 1m 4f (P)
9:20 (9:23) (Class 6) (0-55,59) 3-Y-O+ **£1,706** (£503; £252) **Stalls** Centre

Form RPR
4632 **1** **Iguacu**[2] 7666 5-8-8 **50** ... MatthewDavies(5) 4 58+
(George Baker) *tk hold early: hld up in last: taken to outer over 2f out: hanging and prog to go 2nd 1f out: styd on wl to last fnl strides* **7/2**[2]
6500 **2** nk **Silken Promise (USA)**[25] 7392 3-8-13 **55** ...(p) AdamKirby 12 62
(W R Swinburn) *led and set varied pce: kicked on over 2f out: 2 l clr over 1f out and looked like holding on: collared fnl strides* **20/1**
0-00 **3** nk **Meirig's Dream (IRE)**[25] 7392 3-8-8 **50** ... PaulFitzsimons 10 57
(Miss N A Lloyd-Beavis) *plld hrd early: prom: chsd ldr over 1f out but no imp: clsd w wnr fnl f but a jst outpcd* **33/1**
400 **4** 2 3/4 **Kickahead (USA)**[39] 3735 7-9-0 **51** ...(t) StephenDonohoe 9 54+
(Ian Williams) *hld up in last: looking for room fr over 2f out: sme prog over 1f out: kpt on to take 4th wl ins fnl f: no ch* **5/2**[1]
5500 **5** 1 3/4 **Peintre D'Argent (IRE)**[41] 7143 3-8-9 **51** ... JimCrowley 11 51
(W J Knight) *cl up: wnt 2nd on inner over 2f out to over 1f out: wknd fnl f* **10/1**
00-6 **6** 1/2 **Three Thieves (UAE)**[3] 7658 6-8-10 **47** ... SteveDrowne 3 46
(Jim Best) *in tch: lost pl and struggling whn pce lifted wl over 2f out: plugged on again fnl f* **13/2**
0220 **7** 2 **Barodine**[9] 7594 6-9-4 **55** ... GeorgeBaker 2 51
(R J Hodges) *trckd ldrs: hanging and nt qckn over 2f out: sn lost pl: wl btn whn checked over 1f out* **8/1**
0001 **8** hd **Royal Society**[9] 7600 3-9-3 **59** 6ex ... DaneO'Neill 6 54
(R A Farrant) *hld up towards rr: sing pulling fr 1/2-way: effrt over 2f out: one pce and nvr on terms* **4/1**[3]
2020 **9** 1 1/2 **Litenup (IRE)**[25] 7392 3-8-12 **54** ...(t) WandersonD'Avila 1 47
(A J Lidderdale) *t.k.h: trckd ldr to over 2f out: sn btn* **33/1**
0P00 **10** 4 **Mixing**[26] 7368 7-8-8 **52** ... KierenFox(7) 5 39
(M J Attwater) *sn restrained to rr: effrt on outer over 3f out: lost pl qckly 2f out* **33/1**
0040 **11** 2 **Imperium**[23] 7417 8-9-2 **53** ... LPKeniry 7 36
(Jean-Rene Auvray) *hld up in midfield: sed pulling 1/2-way: trapped on inner and dropped to rr 3f out: sn wknd* **14/1**
2m 35.08s (0.58) **Going Correction** -0.10s/f (Stan)
WFA 3 from 4yo+ 5lb 11 Ran SP% **124.6**
Speed ratings (Par 101): **94,93,93,91,90 90,88,88,87,85 83**
toteswinger:1&2:£12.90, 2&3:£46.10, 1&3:£31.90 CSF £79.08 CT £1999.89 TOTE £5.60: £1.40, £5.00, £9.60; EX 107.80 Place 6 £53.64, Place 5 £22.37 .
Owner Derek & Cheryl Holder **Bred** Cheveley Park Stud Ltd **Trained** Moreton Morrell, Warwicks

FOCUS
The second division of the low-grade 46-55 handicap and marginally the slower of the two. The runner-up, who set a muddling pace, is the best guide to the form.
Barodine Official explanation: jockey sasld gelding hung right
T/Plt: £94.60 to a £1 stake. Pool: £90,220.56. 696.09 winning tickets. T/Qpdt: £21.90 to a £1 stake. Pool: £8,355.51. 281.21 winning tickets. JN

7660 LINGFIELD (L-H)
Wednesday, December 9

OFFICIAL GOING: Standard
Wind: medium, half behind Weather: overcast, dry

7689 LINGFIELDPARK.CO.UK (S) STKS 5f (P)
12:30 (12:30) (Class 6) 3-Y-O+ **£1,978** (£584; £292) **Stalls** High

Form RPR
6060 **1** **Buy On The Red**[83] 6010 8-9-4 67 ... KFallon 3 70
(D Nicholls) *sn chsng ldr: led over 2f out: rdn ent fnl 2f: kpt on wl fnl f* **4/1**[2]
4102 **2** hd **Decider (USA)**[9] 7595 6-9-4 63 ...(p) LiamJones 6 69
(R A Harris) *trckd ldrs: effrt towards inner over 1f out: chsd wnr 1f out: kpt on wl but nvr quite getting to wnr* **8/1**
2005 **3** 1/2 **Sir Edwin Landseer (USA)**[48] 6972 9-8-12 82 ...(v) FergusSweeney 8 61
(G L Moore) *trckd ldrs: rdn and nt qckn over 1f out: r.o ins fnl f: nt rch ldng pair* **15/8**[1]
5244 **4** 2 1/2 **Colombard (IRE)**[8] 7602 4-8-12 52 ...(v) RichardHughes 7 52
(Patrick Morris) *s.i.s: sn niggled along in rr: hdwy u.p fnl f: nvr trbld ldrs* **10/1**
1000 **5** 1 1/2 **The Magic Blanket (IRE)**[169] 3252 4-9-4 62 ... AdamKirby 4 53
(Stef Liddiard) *sn pushed up to ld: hdd over 2f out: rdn 2f out: wknd ent fnl f* **15/2**[3]
0060 **6** 3/4 **Meikle Barfil**[81] 6119 7-9-4 44 ...(tp) LukeMorris 5 50
(J M Bradley) *dwlt: hld up in tch: effrt and rdn wl over 1f out: no prog and wl hld after* **66/1**
/000 **7** nk **Tan Bonita (USA)**[56] 6777 4-8-2 48 ow2 ... KierenFox(7) 10 40
(R J Smith) *a towards rr: rdn and struggling ent fnl 2f: no imp u.p over 1f out* **50/1**
5000 **8** 2 **Nordic Light (USA)**[90] 5788 5-8-12 38 ...(b) DavidProbert 2 36
(J M Bradley) *in tch whn hmpd bnd 4f out: sn rdn along: wknd over 1f out* **100/1**
0000 **9** 8 **Hayley's Girl**[13] 7535 3-8-2 40 ...(b) AmyBaker(5) 1 2
(S W James) *in tch whn bdly hmpd and lost pl bnd 4f out: bhd and no ch after* **80/1**
58.66 secs (-0.14) **Going Correction** +0.05s/f (Slow) 9 Ran SP% **92.4**
Speed ratings (Par 101): **103,102,101,97,95 94,93,90,77**
toteswinger:1&2:£3.40, 2&3:£2.00, 1&3:£3.90 CSF £21.56 TOTE £4.70: £1.80, £2.20, £1.10; EX 12.30 TRIFECTA Part won. Pool: £42.29 - 0.40 winning units..There was no bid for the winner.
Owner R Haim **Bred** J Gittins And Capt J H Wilson **Trained** Sessay, N Yorks
■ Desperate Dan (7/2) was withdrawn after being kicked in the paddock. R4 applies, deduct 20p in the £.

FOCUS
Although the favourite ran well below his rating, the form looks solid enough for the level rated around the runner-up.
Hayley's Girl Official explanation: jockey said filly suffered interference in running

7690 HARTFIELD CLAIMING STKS 7f (P)
1:00 (1:00) (Class 6) 2-Y-O **£1,978** (£584; £292) **Stalls** Low

Form RPR
0002 **1** **Kirsty's Boy (IRE)**[21] 7435 2-9-0 76 ... LPKeniry 6 73
(J S Moore) *sn chsng ldr: rdn over 2f out: drvn to ld over 1f out: hld on wl fnl f* **4/1**[2]

4332 **2** *hd* **Zubova**[10] 7585 2-8-11 73.. RichardHughes 3 70
(R Hannon) *hld up in last trio: hdwy to trck ldrs over 2f out: rdn and effrt over 1f out: kpt wanting to hang lft: evenually r.o fnl 100yds: wnt 2nd last stride* **4/6**[1]

5663 **3** *nse* **Inside Track (IRE)**[2] 7669 2-8-9 75.............................(b) MartinDwyer 5 67
(B J Meehan) *sn led: rdn ent fnl 2f: hdd over 1f out: kpt on same pce u.p fnl f: lost 2nd on post* **13/2**[3]

4500 **4** *2 ¾* **Anjomarba (IRE)**[32] 7290 2-8-8 75.............................. JackDean(3) 2 63
(W G M Turner) *chsd ldrs: rdn ent fnl 2f: outpcd over 1f out: keeping on same pce and hld whn swtchd rt ins fnl f* **12/1**

0630 **5** *2* **Cuthbert (IRE)**[12] 7551 2-9-2 65...............................(b) J-PGuillambert 1 63
(W Jarvis) *rdn along after s: racd in last trio: rdn and nt qckn jst over 2f out: kpt on same pce fnl 2f* **20/1**

030 **6** *11* **Indigo Ink**[18] 7482 2-8-4 58.. AndreaAtzeni(3) 7 26
(Miss Amy Weaver) *in tch in last trio: rdn and struggling over 2f out: wl btn fnl 2f* **33/1**

0000 **7** *3 ¼* **New York Lights (IRE)**[58] 6736 2-7-11 48.................. RachelKing(7) 4 15
(M D I Usher) *taken down early: stdd s: t.k.h: in tch: lost pl qckly over 2f out sn bhd* **100/1**

1m 25.03s (0.23) **Going Correction** +0.05s/f (Slow) 7 Ran SP% **109.7**
Speed ratings (Par 94): **100,99,99,96,94 81,78**
toteswinger:1&2:£1.60, 2&3:£2.10, 1&3:£2.00 CSF £6.45 TOTE £4.00: £2.00, £1.10; EX 8.30.Inside Track was claimed by P T Midgley for £3,000.
Owner F J Stephens **Bred** Edmond Kent **Trained** Upper Lambourn, Berks

FOCUS
A fair claimer but a rather messy race. The winner is rated to his recent best.

NOTEBOOK
Kirsty's Boy(IRE) didn't have to improve on his second in a similar affair here last time to win, and he was aided by the fact that Inside Track was on his inner, stuck on the rail, while the favourite showed no interest in going past. He remains opposable if returning to handicap company. (op 5-1 tchd 11-2 and 7-2)
Zubova has failed to win in six starts now, despite being sent off at 5-4 or shorter in four of those races. This drop in class promised to give her her best chance yet, but she hung in behind the winner when brought to challenge and clearly didn't fancy it much. (tchd 4-5)
Inside Track(IRE), officially best in at the weights, scraped paint the whole way round and, although he kept battling away, he was always at a bit of a disadvantage. (op 11-2 tchd 5-1)
Anjomarba(IRE) was struggling from the turn in and will be suited by a drop back in distance. (tchd 14-1)

7691 BEST ODDS GUARANTEED AT TOTESPORT.COM (S) STKS 7f (P)
1:30 (1:30) (Class 6) 3-Y-0+ **£1,978** (£584; £292) **Stalls** Low

Form RPR
1303 **1** **Trade Centre**[2] 7662 4-9-4 72.. MartinDwyer 11 72
(W R Muir) *in tch in midfield: hdwy on outer 3f out: chsd ldr over 2f out: rdn to ld ent fnl f: kpt on wl* **10/11**[1]

0004 **2** *½* **Smalljohn**[9] 7596 3-8-12 66...(v) TomEaves 6 65
(B Smart) *sn led: rdn ent fnl 2f: hdd ent fnl f: kpt on* **15/2**[3]

0301 **3** *2 ¾* **Batchworth Blaise**[3] 7653 6-8-5 44.......................... RichardRowe(7) 2 57
(E A Wheeler) *stdd s: hld up bhd: hdwy over 1f out: kpt on fnl f to snatch 3rd on post: nvr trbld ldrs* **20/1**

0032 **4** *nse* **Obe Gold**[9] 7596 7-9-4 67...(v) J-PGuillambert 5 63
(P Howling) *chsd ldrs: rdn and unable qck jst over 2f out: disputing 3rd and btn ent fnl f: kpt on same pce* **4/1**[2]

603 **5** *hd* **Trimlestown (IRE)**[27] 7358 6-8-12 65...............................(p) PaulDoe 8 57
(P D Evans) *t.k.h: hld up in midfield: rdn and effrt jst over 2f out: disputing 3rd and btn ent fnl f: kpt on same pce* **8/1**

1035 **6** *1* **Charlie Delta**[9] 7596 6-9-4 55..(b) LiamJones 3 60
(R A Harris) *hld up in last trio: rdn whn nt clr run bnd 2f out: drvn and hdwy over 1f out: no imp fnl f* **16/1**

0064 **7** *nk* **Sovereignty (JPN)**[10] 7592 7-8-13 57............................ SophieDoyle(5) 1 59
(D K Ivory) *taken down early: t.k.h: hld up in last pair: effrt on wd outside bnd 2f out: kpt on fnl f: nvr trbld ldrs* **25/1**

4600 **8** *1 ½* **Keibla Spirit**[10] 7592 3-8-7 57.. RobertHavlin 9 44
(R Ingram) *chsd ldrs tl lost pl and wd bnd 2f out: sn wl btn* **66/1**

4120 **9** *1 ¾* **Waterloo Dock**[8] 7602 4-9-4 60.. ChrisCatlin 4 50
(M Quinn) *led: sn hdd: chsd ldr after tl over 2f out: wknd and bhd over 1f out* **14/1**

1m 24.79s (-0.01) **Going Correction** +0.05s/f (Slow) 9 Ran SP% **117.9**
Speed ratings (Par 101): **102,101,98,98,98 96,96,94,92**
toteswinger:1&2:£2.40, 2&3:£6.70, 1&3:£12.80 CSF £8.59 TOTE £2.50: £1.30, £1.90, £4.20; EX 8.20 Trifecta £57.60 Pool: £214.84 - 2.76 winning units.The winner was sold to N McLoughlin for 9,200gns
Owner K Mercer,C Edginton,S Jones,M Dawson **Bred** Usk Valley Stud **Trained** Lambourn, Berks

FOCUS
An ordinary seller. The winner only had to run to his recent level.

7692 BET ON TONIGHT'S FOOTBALL AT TOTESPORT.COM H'CAP 7f (P)
2:00 (2:00) (Class 4) (0-85,82) 3-Y-0+ **£4,981** (£1,470; £735) **Stalls** Low

Form RPR
1002 **1** **Tiddliwinks**[11] 7575 3-8-11 75.. RichardHughes 4 89+
(K A Ryan) *broke wl: led for 1f: chsd ldr: upsides gng much the best jst over 2f out: led over 1f out: pushed along and asserted jst ins fnl f: eased nr fin: easily* **7/4**[1]

210 **2** *1* **King Of Defence**[21] 7432 3-8-4 68 oh2.............................. ChrisCatlin 7 73
(M A Jarvis) *stdd after s: hld up in last: rdn and hdwy ent fnl f: wnt 2nd fnl 100yds: no ch w wnr* **11/2**[3]

2465 **3** *½* **Totally Focussed (IRE)**[268] 850 4-9-0 78.................... HayleyTurner 1 82
(S Dow) *hld up in last pair: effrt and rdn on inner wl over 1f out: kpt on same pce ins fnl f* **8/1**

0000 **4** *1 ¾* **Timeteam (IRE)**[154] 3747 3-9-4 82................................ RobertWinston 2 81
(A Bailey) *t.k.h: hld up in tch: hdwy to press ldrs ent fnl 2f: outpcd over 1f out: wknd ins fnl f* **12/1**

4306 **5** *½* **Hustle (IRE)**[47] 7000 4-9-0 78.. JerryO'Dwyer 8 76
(Miss Gay Kelleway) *led after 1f and set stdy gallop: jnd over 2f out: rdn 2f out: hdd over 1f out: wknd ins fnl f* **12/1**

6541 **6** *¾* **Billberry**[14] 7519 4-8-2 69...(t) AndreaAtzeni(3) 5 65
(S C Williams) *t.k.h: chsd ldrs: lost pl and rdn jst over 2f out: one pce and edgd lft fnl f* **2/1**[2]

1m 25.65s (0.85) **Going Correction** +0.05s/f (Slow) 6 Ran SP% **111.6**
Speed ratings (Par 105): **97,95,95,93,92 91**
toteswinger:1&2:£1.90, 2&3:£5.40, 1&3:£3.00 CSF £11.65 CT £57.49 TOTE £2.40: £2.00, £3.40; EX 12.80 Trifecta £40.60 Pool: £286.06 -5.21 winning units.
Owner Guy Reed **Bred** Guy Reed **Trained** Hambleton, N Yorks

FOCUS
They went fairly steady early here and it turned into a bit of a sprint. The form is not the most solid but the progressive winner appeared to win with plenty in hand.

7693 BET ON LIVE SPORT AT TOTESPORT.COM APPRENTICE H'CAP 1m (P)
2:30 (2:30) (Class 6) (0-62,68) 3-Y-0+ **£1,978** (£584; £292) **Stalls** High

Form RPR
0031 **1** **Wunder Strike (USA)**[21] 7433 3-8-11 57....................(p) MatthewDavies 1 67
(J R Boyle) *chsd ldrs: rdn and effrt jst over 2f out: led ent fnl f: fnd ex and asserted fnl 75yds* **8/1**

0004 **2** *1 ¼* **Greystoke Prince**[2] 7660 4-8-0 52...........................(t) CarolineKelly(7) 4 59
(P S McEntee) *t.k.h: hld up in rr: hdwy on inner jst over 2f out: nt clr run briefly over 1f out: sn swtchd rt and hdwy: chal jst ins fnl f: edgd lft and no ex fnl 100yds* **14/1**

0250 **3** *½* **Dream Huntress**[23] 7417 3-9-1 61................................ PaulPickard 2 67+
(J W Hills) *hld up bhd: effrt and hdwy on outer bnd 2f out: r.o fnl f: nt rch ldng pair* **20/1**

2241 **4** *3* **French Art**[10] 7587 4-9-6 68 6ex...................................(p) LeeNewnes(3) 6 67
(N Tinkler) *chsd ldrs on outer: hdwy to join ldrs and rdn jst over 2f out: wknd ent fnl f* **2/1**[1]

0- **5** *½* **Law Of The Jungle (IRE)**[81] 6127 3-9-1 61.............. RossAtkinson 12 59
(Tom Dascombe) *awkward leaving stalls and flashing tail sn after s: bhd: rdn over 3f out: drvn and kpt on fr over 1f out: nvr gng pce to trble ldrs* **8/1**

0024 **6** *nse* **Ymir**[10] 7587 3-8-6 57.. KierenFox(5) 10 55
(M J Attwater) *t.k.h: chsd ldr tl led jst over 2f out: hdd ent fnl f: wknd qckly fnl 150yds* **9/2**[2]

0060 **7** *1 ¼* **Dawson Creek (IRE)**[39] 7180 5-8-5 55......................(b[1]) RyanClark(5) 5 50
(B Gubby) *chsd ldrs: rdn over 2f out: struggling 2f out and wl hld after* **16/1**

0024 **8** *½* **Josr's Magic (IRE)**[14] 7517 5-8-9 59............................ AdamCarter(5) 7 53
(T E Powell) *led tl jst over 2f out: stl pressing ldrs tl wknd qckly jst ins fnl f* **5/1**[3]

6400 **9** *10* **Give Us A Song (USA)**[120] 4872 3-9-0 60...................... SophieDoyle 3 31
(J S Moore) *t.k.h: hld up wl in tch: lost pl wl over 2f out: wl btn over 1f out* **50/1**

0060 **U** **Very Well Red**[65] 6545 6-8-8 56.................................. TobyAtkinson(3) 9 —
(P W Hiatt) *emerged fr stalls wout the rdr* **10/1**

1m 37.55s (-0.65) **Going Correction** +0.05s/f (Slow)
WFA 3 from 4yo+ 1lb 10 Ran SP% **118.8**
Speed ratings (Par 101): **105,103,103,100,99 99,98,97,87,—**
toteswinger:1&2:£2.70, 2&3:£6.40, 1&3:£2.80 CSF £115.44 CT £1433.35 TOTE £10.90: £2.60, £4.80, £4.30; EX 193.60 Trifecta £157.20 Part won. Pool: £212.47 - 0.40 winning units..
Owner Mrs B Powell B Walsh P Hughes C Murphy **Bred** Mike Abraham **Trained** Epsom, Surrey

FOCUS
A modest handicap, but it was well run and the form is probably sound. The race is rated around the winner.
Very Well Red Official explanation: jockey said mare anticipated start, putting its head down, causing him to become unbalanced and left in the rigging.

7694 BET IN-PLAY AT TOTESPORT.COM MEDIAN AUCTION MAIDEN STKS 1m 2f (P)
3:00 (3:01) (Class 6) 3-5-Y-0 **£1,978** (£584; £292) **Stalls** Low

Form RPR
4625 **1** **Pyrus Time (IRE)**[65] 6537 3-9-4 68................................ LukeMorris 3 72
(J S Moore) *hld up in tch: trckd ldrs over 2f out: pushed into ld ins fnl f: eased nr fin* **6/4**[1]

2 *1* **I Am The Man** 4-9-7 0.. JackMitchell 6 70
(B J McMath) *s.i.s: hld up in last trio: hdwy over 2f out: chal on inner jst over 1f out: chsd wnr fnl 100yds: no imp* **11/1**

3 *1* **Look Officer (USA)**[80] 6142 3-8-13 68.................... RichardKingscote 7 63
(Tom Dascombe) *led: rdn ent fnl 2f: hrd drvn over 1f out: hdd ins fnl f: v one pce* **9/4**[2]

4 *4 ½* **On Terms (USA)** 3-8-13 0.. HayleyTurner 4 54
(S Dow) *w ldr tl over 2f out: outpcd by ldng trio over 1f out* **8/1**

4-6 **5** *7* **Mayta Capac (USA)**[25] 7401 3-9-1 0................................ MartinLane(3) 8 45
(D M Simcock) *t.k.h: hld up wl in tch: rdn and unable to quicen jst over 2f out: wknd qckly wl over 1f out* **7/1**[3]

0 **6** *2* **Blue Celeste**[49] 6934 3-8-13 0.. SteveDrowne 9 36
(R T Phillips) *dwlt: a towards rr: rdn and toiling 4f out: sn lost tch* **20/1**

0000 **7** *½* **Silvester**[30] 7318 3-9-4 42...(p) JimCrowley 2 40
(R M H Cowell) *in tch in midfield: rdn and qckly lost tch 3f out* **50/1**

0- **8** *5* **Sinchiroka (FR)**[418] 6789 3-9-1 0................................ RobertLButler(3) 5 30
(R J Smith) *s.i.s: a bhd: lost tch over 4f out* **16/1**

2m 8.89s (2.29) **Going Correction** +0.05s/f (Slow)
WFA 3 from 4yo 3lb 8 Ran SP% **115.3**
Speed ratings (Par 101): **92,91,90,86,81 79,79,75**
toteswinger:1&2:£2.70, 2&3:£6.40, 1&3:£2.80 CSF £19.92 TOTE £2.40: £1.10, £3.40, £1.10; EX 17.10 TRIFECTA Pool: £195.91 - 2.71 winning units.
Owner J Wells & A Wright **Bred** Miss Nadja Humphreys **Trained** Upper Lambourn, Berks

FOCUS
A weak maiden run at a steady early gallop. Muddling form, rated around the winner.

7695 MARSH GREEN H'CAP 1m 4f (P)
3:30 (3:30) (Class 5) (0-70,68) 3-Y-0+ **£2,729** (£806; £403) **Stalls** Low

Form RPR
0016 **1** **Chalice Welcome**[22] 6218 6-9-6 67................................ JackMitchell 1 75
(N B King) *stdd s: hld up towards rr: hdwy towards inner wl over 1f out: chsd ldrs and drvn ent fnl f: led ins fnl f: r.o wl* **25/1**

2641 **2** *¾* **Moonshine Creek**[21] 7440 7-9-2 63................................ ChrisCatlin 14 70
(P W Hiatt) *led over 10f out: rdn ent fnl 2f: hdd and no ex ins fnl f* **11/1**

0125 **3** *½* **Hector Spectre (IRE)**[3] 7512 3-8-13 65............................ PaulDoe 5 71
(P D Evans) *chsd ldrs: rdn to chse ldng pair jst over 2f out: chsd ldr 1f out: kpt on same pce fnl f* **33/1**

0521 **4** *1* **Prince Charlemagne (IRE)**[9] 7594 6-9-6 67 6ex........... GeorgeBaker 8 72
(G L Moore) *stdd s: hld up towards rr: hdwy into midfield over 5f out: chsd ldrs and drvn over 1f out: kpt on ins fnl f: nvr gng pce to rch ldrs* **7/2**[2]

122 **5** *1* **Eagle Nebula**[28] 7328 5-9-0 61.. KFallon 7 64
(B R Johnson) *chsd ldr: rdn over 2f out: drvn over 1f out: lost 2nd 1f out: one pce fnl f* **9/2**[3]

2133 **6** *hd* **Where's Susie**[22] 5642 4-9-1 62................................ RobertHavlin 10 65+
(M Madgwick) *in tch in midfield: rdn wl over 1f out: kpt on fnl f: nvr gng pce to rch ldrs* **16/1**

4065 **7** *½* **Dark Energy**[9] 7594 5-8-10 57...(t) SJCraine 13 59
(M J Scudamore) *chsd ldrs tl rdn and lost plae over 2f out: kpt on again ins fnl f: nt pce to rch ldrs* **16/1**

6514 **8** *hd* **Bell Island**[27] [7357] 5-9-7 **68**......(v) RichardHughes 12 70
(Lady Herries) *chsd ldng pair tl rdn and unable qck ent fnl 2f: one pce and btn over 1f out* **5/2**[1]
0450 **9** *nk* **Little Carmela**[8] [7608] 5-8-10 **57**......(v[1]) SaleemGolam 11 58
(S C Williams) *in tch: rdn and struggling 3f out: one pce and no ch w ldrs fnl 2f* **16/1**
2022 **10** *nse* **Chanrossa (IRE)**[14] [7524] 3-8-10 **62**......(p) JimCrowley 6 63
(E A L Dunlop) *hld up in tch in rr: rdn and effrt jst over 2f out: no real prog* **8/1**
0405 **11** *½* **Star Choice**[132] [4449] 4-8-9 **61**...... SimonPearce(5) 2 61
(J Pearce) *chsd ldrs early: sn settled in midfield: pushed along over 3f out: no prog fnl 2f* **25/1**
130 **12** *1* **Ross Moor**[100] [5532] 7-9-0 **64**...... AndreaAtzeni(3) 9 63
(Mike Murphy) *stdd s: hld up in tch in rr: effrt on outer jst over 2f out: no prog fr wl over 1f out* **40/1**
4004 **13** *1* **Magnitude**[10] [5124] 4-9-2 **63**...... AdamKirby 3 60
(M E Rimmer) *hld up in last pair: pushed along over 8f out: rdn and no rspnse over 2f out* **50/1**

2m 33.59s (0.59) **Going Correction** +0.05s/f (Slow)
WFA 3 from 4yo+ 5lb **13** Ran SP% **121.1**
Speed ratings (Par 103): **100,99,99,98,97 97,97,97,97,97 96,96,95**
toteswinger:1&2:£40.50, 2&3:£66.70, 1&3:£91.90 CSF £271.08 CT £8806.96 TOTE £48.70: £8.80, £3.50, £9.30; EX 194.70 TRIFECTA Not won. Place 6 £27.52, Place 5 £21.30.
Owner The Dyball Partnership **Bred** The Dyball Partnership **Trained** Newmarket, Suffolk

FOCUS
An ordinary handicap but the form looks sound. A personal best from the winner.
Magnitude Official explanation: jockey said gelding made a noise
T/Plt: £20.00 to a £1 stake. Pool: £44,231.97. 1,610.16 winning tickets. T/Qpdt: £14.20 to a £1 stake. Pool: £3,233.86. 167.90 winning tickets. SP

7621 DEAUVILLE (R-H)
Wednesday, December 9

OFFICIAL GOING: Standard

7696a PRIX DE LA PLAGE (H'CAP) 6f 110y
11:20 (11:25) 3-Y-O **£9,709** (£3,883; £2,913; £1,942; £971)

RPR
1 **Allez Bailey (FR)**[30] 3-8-3 ...... AlexisBadel —
(D De Watrigant, France)
2 *2 ½* **Amico Fritz (GER)**[50] 3-8-10 ...... MGuyon —
(H-A Pantall, France)
3 *nk* **Moscow Eight (IRE)**[26] [7385] 3-8-12 ...... JAuge —
(E J O'Neill) *restrained in 14th: swtchd outside 1 1/2f out: styd on wl: nrst fin* **27/1**[1]
4 *nk* **Pink Candie (FR)**[96] 3-9-2 ...... —
(Y De Nicolay, France)
5 *snk* **Caraziyan (FR)**[26] [7385] 3-8-7 ...... —
(P Van De Poele, France)
6 *shd* **Chelgui (FR)**[48] 3-9-0 ...... —
(C Baillet, France)
7 *snk* **Nexcity (FR)**[78] 3-8-6 ...... —
(Mlle V Dissaux, France)
8 *shd* **Caerleon Wind (IRE)**[48] 3-9-7 ...... —
(Mlle V Dissaux, France)
9 *hd* **Collimateur (FR)**[66] [6606] 3-8-7 ...... —
(A Lamotte D'Argy, France)
10 *¾* **Helipad (FR)**[30] 3-8-11 ...... —
(F-X De Chevigny, France)
0 **Olga D'Or (USA)**[66] [6606] 3-8-11 ...... —
(R Gibson, France)
0 **Ladouce (FR)**[26] [7385] 3-8-7 ...... —
(Robert Collet, France)
0 **Flyingwithbebe (USA)**[15] [7509] 3-9-0 ......(b) —
(T Doumen, France)
0 **Azagra (IRE)**[48] 3-8-7 ...... —
(T Lemer, France)
0 **Good Star (FR)**[26] [7385] 3-8-4 ...... —
(B Dutruel, France)
0 **Betica** 3-8-13 ...... —
(Y Durepaire, Spain)

1m 20.5s (80.50) **16** Ran SP% **3.6**
PARI-MUTUEL (including 1 Euro stake): WIN 21.20; PL 6.40, 2.90, 7.10;DF 62.40.
Owner G R Bailey Ltd **Bred** J Hernon & J Ince **Trained** France

NOTEBOOK
Moscow Eight(IRE) finished well on this return to Polytrack and the extra half-furlong seemed to suit. He might be worth a try over 7f.

7697a PRIX PETITE ETOILE (LISTED RACE) (FILLIES) 1m 1f 110y
12:55 (12:55) 3-Y-O **£26,699** (£10,680; £8,010; £5,340; £2,670)

RPR
1 **Savoie (FR)**[20] [7457] 3-8-11 ...... DBonilla 14 —
(Y Barberot, France)
2 *¾* **Lake Palace**[20] [7457] 3-8-11 ...... J-BEyquem 11 —
(N Clement, France)
3 *nk* **Hidden Brief**[32] [7291] 3-8-11 ...... JamieSpencer 18 —
(M A Jarvis) *pushed up fr outside draw to ld: rdn over 2f out: hdd appr fnl f: rallied and ev ch 100yds out: fin 4th, ¾l, 1l, nk: plcd 3rd* **19/1**[1]
4 *nk* **Sahabah (USA)**[49] 3-8-11 ...... YLerner 15 —
(J E Hammond, France) *fin 5th: plcd 4th*
5 *shd* **Cool And Composed (USA)**[35] [7249] 3-8-11 ...... F-XBertras 5 —
(F Rohaut, France) *fin 6th: plcd 5th*
6 *1* **Karlisse (IRE)**[28] [7347] 3-8-11 ...... MGuyon 4 —
(H-A Pantall, France) *fin 3rd, ¾l & 1l: disqualified and plcd 6th*
7 *hd* **The Only Key**[52] 3-8-11 ...... FilipMinarik 17 —
(P Schiergen, Germany)
8 *nk* **Volver (IRE)**[45] 3-8-11 ...... FBlondel 10 —
(J-C Rouget, France)
9 *1* **Isaonor (FR)**[35] [7249] 3-8-11 ...... SRuis 16 —
(Y Fouin, France)
10 *nk* **Black Rose (FR)**[45] 3-8-11 ...... THuet 13 —
(F Chappet, France)
0 **Entre Deux Eaux (FR)**[45] [7044] 3-9-0 ...... GBenoist 9 —
(Robert Collet, France)
0 **Singing Machine (USA)**[45] 3-8-11 ...... RMarchelli 2 —
(M Delzangles, France)
0 **Symba's Dream (USA)**[88] [5897] 3-8-11 ...... MickaelForest 12 —
(J-C Rouget, France)
0 **Becomes You**[45] 3-8-11 ...... MSautjeau 6 —
(M Delzangles, France)
0 **Russiana (IRE)**[20] [7457] 3-8-11 ...... MBarzalona 1 —
(A Fabre, France)
0 **All Annalena (IRE)**[59] [6714] 3-8-11 ...... HGrewe 8 —
(Andreas Lowe, Germany)
0 **Liberty Chery**[20] [7457] 3-8-11 ...... FSpanu 7 —
(J E Hammond, France)
0 **Guerande (IRE)**[15] [7509] 3-8-11 ...... TJarnet 3 —
(A De Royer-Dupre, France)

2m 0.60s (120.60) **18** Ran SP% **5.0**
PARI-MUTUEL: WIN 12.80; PL 3.90, 2.90, 5.70; DF 49.70.
Owner P Bellaiche **Bred** Alec & Mme Ghislaine Head **Trained** France

NOTEBOOK
Hidden Brief was having his first try on this surface but has been held at this level before. She was promoted a place after the third was demoted to sixth and as a result earns black type.

7682 KEMPTON (A.W) (R-H)
Thursday, December 10

OFFICIAL GOING: Standard
Wind: Virtually nil

7698 BOXINGDAYRACES.CO.UK CLAIMING STKS 5f (P)
4:00 (4:00) (Class 6) 2-Y-O **£2,047** (£604; £302) **Stalls** High

Form RPR
0302 **1** **Wanchai Whisper**[12] [7570] 2-8-6 61...... PaulDoe 7 58
(P D Evans) *s.i.s: in rr tl gd hdwy over 1f out: drvn and qcknd to ld fnl 100yds: edgd lft but styd on strly* **13/8**[1]
6360 **2** *nk* **Mind The Monarch**[19] [7482] 2-8-2 52...... LukeMorris 9 53
(R A Teal) *chsd ldrs: rdn to go 2nd 2f out: kpt on to chse wnr fnl 30yds: styd on cl home but a hld* **9/1**
1003 **3** *1 ¾* **Blue Neptune**[12] [7570] 2-8-12 62...... AndreaAtzeni(3) 6 60
(W R Muir) *sn led: rdn ins fnl 2f: hdd fnl 100yds: wknd into 3rd fnl 30yds* **3/1**[2]
2006 **4** *hd* **Kings Of Leo**[14] [7536] 2-8-13 73...... SJCraine 4 57
(J R Boyle) *t.k.h early: chsd ldrs: rdn over 1f out: styd on fnl f but nvr gng pce to chal* **4/1**[3]
0200 **5** *1 ¼* **Lairy (IRE)**[36] [7242] 2-8-7 45...... JamieMackay 8 46
(M F Harris) *in tch: trckd ldrs on ins over 1f out: sn rdn and kpt on same pce* **33/1**
060 **6** *nk* **Graceandgratitude**[3] [7661] 2-7-13 0 ow1...... AndrewHeffernan(5) 2 42
(S C Williams) *in rr tl sme prog fnl f* **16/1**
665 **7** *1* **Weimarland (IRE)**[12] [7582] 2-8-8 62...... ShaneKelly 5 43
(J A Osborne) *s.i.s: in rr: sme hdwy whn n.m.r over 1f out: nvr in contention* **14/1**
05 **8** *4* **Wild Heather**[19] [7485] 2-8-4 0...... KirstyMilczarek 3 24
(J R Holt) *chsd ldrs on outside: hung lft and wknd wl over 1f out* **33/1**
5063 **9** *3* **Light The Way**[19] [7477] 2-9-2 59......(bt) FergusSweeney 1 26
(P J Makin) *chsd wnr tl wknd 2f out* **10/1**

60.52 secs (0.02) **Going Correction** -0.15s/f (Stan) **9** Ran SP% **120.6**
Speed ratings (Par 94): **93,92,89,89,87 86,85,78,74**
toteswinger:1&2:£3.70, 2&3:£5.80, 1&3:£3.50 CSF £18.91 TOTE £1.80: £1.10, £2.40, £1.50; EX 25.30.
Owner M&R Refurbishments Ltd **Bred** Mike Smith **Trained** Pandy, Monmouths

FOCUS
A modest claimer but the race might produce one or two winners at a similar level.

NOTEBOOK
Wanchai Whisper raced off the pace after a sluggish start but she picked up well once getting a gap in the straight. She probably only had to run up to something like her current mark considering she had 5lb in hand over the runner-up, and 8lb over the third-placed finisher. (op 7-4 tchd 2-1)
Mind The Monarch had sufficient speed to cope with this drop back from 1m and had her chance. (op 12-1 tchd 8-1)
Blue Neptune looked set to take a bit of catching when sent clear early in the straight but he couldn't sustain his run. This was a respectable effort considering he had something to find with the front two at the weights. (op 4-1 tchd 11-4)
Kings Of Leo had upwards of 5lb in hand at the weights, but she was a bit free early and failed to pick up in the straight. A disappointing performance. (op 3-1)
Lairy(IRE) ran respectably, but he's rated only 45 and limits the form.
Graceandgratitude, carrying a pound overweight, started slowly from an unfavourable draw and was outpaced early on, but she responded to pressure in the straight and is not totally without hope. (op 14-1)
Weimarland(IRE) raced out the back after missing the break and was blocked in his run when trying to make ground in the straight. He can be given another chance. Official explanation: jockey said colt was denied a clear run (tchd 12-1)

7699 TRY OUR NEW BISTRO MENU H'CAP 1m 2f (P)
4:30 (4:30) (Class 5) (0-70,70) 3-Y-O+ **£2,590** (£770; £385; £192) **Stalls** High

Form RPR
1130 **1** **Giant Sequoia (USA)**[15] [7512] 5-9-7 **68**......(t) EddieAhern 14 82+
(Jane Chapple-Hyam) *hld up in tch: hdwy on outside over 2f out: str run to ld appr fnl f: pushed clr: comf* **5/1**[3]
0131 **2** *2 ¾* **Resentful Angel**[6] [7632] 4-9-5 **66**...... DarryllHolland 11 72
(Pat Eddery) *in rr tl hdwy 3f out: rdn and styd on fr over 1f out: r.o to take 2nd last stride but no ch w wnr* **9/4**[1]
5351 **3** *shd* **Marmooq**[15] [7524] 6-9-2 **63**...... LukeMorris 10 68
(M J Attwater) *chsd ldrs: rdn to take slt advantage wl over 1f out: hdd appr fnl f and no ch w wnr ins: lost 2nd last stride* **8/1**
3532 **4** *¾* **The Grey One (IRE)**[6] [7632] 6-8-11 **65**......(p) RyanClark(7) 2 69
(J M Bradley) *awkward stalls and bhd: rdn and hdwy on outside fr 2f out: styd on wl fnl f but nvr gng pce to get into contention* **9/2**[2]
0045 **5** *½* **Divinatore**[19] [7481] 3-8-11 **61**...... ChrisCatlin 13 64
(D Haydn Jones) *chsd ldrs: rdn 3f out: styd on same pce fnl 2f* **16/1**
2360 **6** *hd* **Siena Star (IRE)**[15] [7524] 11-9-1 **62**...... AdamKirby 5 64
(Stef Liddiard) *chsd ldr: rdn over 3f out: led jst ins fnl 2f: hdd wl over 1f out: wknd fnl f* **25/1**

-600 **7** ¾ **Shannersburg (IRE)**[50] 6937 4-9-7 **68**..............(t) GregFairley 8 69
(D E Pipe) *in tch: rdn and lost position over 3f out: rdn and sme prog again fr over 1f out but nvr a threat* **33/1**

3000 **8** *hd* **Aflaam (IRE)**[45] 7048 4-9-1 **67**.............. AndrewHeffernan(5) 3 68
(R A Harris) *in rr tl hdwy 3f out: styng on to chse ldrs whn edgd rt over 1f out: nvr a threat and wknd ins fnl f* **16/1**

2213 **9** *nk* **Squad**[65] 6566 3-9-6 **70**.............. HayleyTurner 9 70+
(S Dow) *in rr: pushed along and plenty to do over 2f out: sme prog ins fnl f* **8/1**

44-0 **10** 2¼ **Meydan Dubai (IRE)**[15] 7523 4-9-4 **68**.............. MarcHalford(3) 4 63
(J R Best) *a towards rr* **25/1**

6000 **11** 2¾ **Criterion**[190] 2614 4-9-7 **68**.............. StephenDonohoe 12 58
(Ian Williams) *in rr tl hdwy on ins fr 2f out: in tch whn hmpd over 1f out and sn bhd* **33/1**

0353 **12** 6 **The Dial House**[21] 7455 3-9-6 **70**.............. ShaneKelly 7 48
(J A Osborne) *chsd ldrs tl led ins fnl 5f: hdd ins fnl 2f: sn btn* **25/1**

0453 **13** ¾ **Lilac Moon (GER)**[38] 7212 5-9-3 **64**.............. RichardKingscote 1 40
(Tom Dascombe) *sn led: hdd ins fnl 5f: wknd qckly 2f out* **10/1**

2m 6.17s (-1.83) **Going Correction** -0.15s/f (Stan)
WFA 3 from 4yo+ 3lb **13** Ran SP% **126.1**
Speed ratings (Par 103): **101,98,98,98,97 97,96,96,96,94 92,87,87**
toteswinger:1&2:£4.70, 2&3:£7.70, 1&3:£12.00 CSF £16.55 CT £93.28 TOTE £6.80: £2.10, £1.20, £2.60; EX 15.80.
Owner Mrs Jane Chapple-Hyam **Bred** Strategy Bloodstock **Trained** Newmarket, Suffolk
■ Stewards' Enquiry : Andrew Heffernan three-day ban: careless riding (Dec 26-28)

FOCUS
A fair handicap for the grade. The winner confirmed the merit of his October Lingfield win. The pace increased noticeably at about halfway.
Giant Sequoia(USA) ◆ Official explanation: trainer said, regarding apparent improvement in form, that some of the other horses in heryard were running below par.

7700 WIN A CAR AT KEMPTON.CO.UK MEDIAN AUCTION MAIDEN STKS — 7f (P)
5:00 (5:01) (Class 6) 2-Y-O **£2,914** (£867; £433; £216) **Stalls** High

Form RPR

3 **1** **Prince Of Sorrento**[22] 7436 2-9-3 0.............. J-PGuillambert 10 73+
(J Akehurst) *sn trcking ldrs: rdn and styd on to chse ldr over 1f out: kpt on u.p to ld fnl 75yds: styd on strly* **9/4**[1]

046 **2** ½ **Feeling Fragile (IRE)**[20] 7463 2-9-3 74.............. DarryllHolland 11 72
(Pat Eddery) *led: rdn and styd on 2f out: hdd and outpcd fnl 75yds* **11/2**[3]

0 **3** 3 **La Toya J (IRE)**[29] 7326 2-8-12 0.............. DaneO'Neill 4 60
(R Curtis) *towards rr tl hdwy over 2f out: pushed along and qcknd ins fnl f: styd on wl to take 3rd cl home but no ch w ldng duo* **25/1**

4 ½ **Lou Bear (IRE)** 2-9-3 0.............. AdamKirby 5 63+
(J Akehurst) *sltly hmpd s and bhd: stdy hdwy between horses over 1f out: fin wl but nvr a threat* **25/1**

04 **5** *shd* **St Ignatius**[47] 7024 2-9-3 0.............. JimCrowley 9 63
(R M Beckett) *disp 2nd tl chsd ldr over 2f out: sn no imp: wknd ins fnl f* **9/2**[2]

6 *nk* **Red Yarn** 2-8-12 0.............. LPKeniry 1 57+
(G L Moore) *green and in rr tl pushed along and hdwy over 2f out: drvn and styd on wl fnl f but nvr a threat* **20/1**

5 **7** ¾ **Ambrogina**[202] 2226 2-8-9 0.............. AndreaAtzeni(3) 7 55
(M Botti) *in tch: rdn and one pce on outside 3f out: kpt on again fr over 1f out but nvr in contention* **9/2**[2]

0 **8** 2 **Erebus (IRE)**[59] 6737 2-9-3 0.............. EddieAhern 6 55
(S Kirk) *wnt lft s: chsd ldrs: rdn over 2f out and sn one pce: wknd over 1f out* **7/1**

9 ¾ **Explorator (IRE)** 2-8-12 0.............. MatthewDavies(5) 14 54
(George Baker) *chsd ldrs: rdn 2f out: wknd appr fnl f* **20/1**

00 **10** 1¼ **Philippa Jane**[43] 7106 2-8-12 0.............. LukeMorris 13 45
(P Winkworth) *in tch: t.k.h: rdn over 2f out: wknd appr fnl f* **50/1**

060 **11** 2 **Pie Poudre**[59] 6737 2-9-3 0.............. TomEaves 3 45
(R Brotherton) *s.i.s: rn green on outside and a in rr* **50/1**

0 **12** 17 **Hovering Hawk (IRE)**[26] 7396 2-8-12 0.............. MichaelHills 2 —
(B W Hills) *a towards rr* **14/1**

1m 25.91s (-0.09) **Going Correction** -0.15s/f (Stan) **12** Ran SP% **122.8**
Speed ratings (Par 94): **94,93,90,89,89 88,88,85,84,83 81,61**
toteswinger:1&2:£3.90, 2&3:£31.10, 1&3:£19.30 CSF £13.95 TOTE £2.80: £1.30, £2.30, £7.40; EX 18.80.
Owner Mrs Pam Akhurst **Bred** Mrs P Akhurst **Trained** Epsom, Surrey

FOCUS
This looked a modest maiden but the form is straightforward. There could be more to come from the winner.

NOTEBOOK
Prince Of Sorrento, who ran green on his debut over 6f at Lingfield, showed improved form over this longer trip. He might struggle next time if the handicapper takes this literally. (op 11-4 tchd 15-8)
Feeling Fragile(IRE), reported to have raced too freely at Wolverhampton last time, was again much too keen, this time in front, and that he was still able to finish second probably highlights the lack of strength in depth in the race. (op 9-2 tchd 13-2)
La Toya J(IRE) improved on her debut but still looked immature and should do better again.
Lou Bear(IRE), a stablemate of the winner, stayed on from a long way back to fare best of the newcomers and there should be plenty of improvement to come. Official explanation: jockey said colt ran green
St Ignatius ◆ now has the option of switching to handicaps and his sprint pedigree means he'll be interesting if dropped in trip. (op 10-3 tchd 5-1)
Red Yarn, a half-sister to useful 7f winner South Cape, wasn't going at all well early on, needing to be driven along to try and keep touch, but she eventually responded and stuck on well against the inside rail in the straight to finish much closer than had appeared likely at one stage. (op 16-1)

7701 WILLIAM HILL WINTER FESTIVAL - BOOK NOW H'CAP — 2m (P)
5:30 (5:33) (Class 4) (0-85,85) 3-Y-O+ **£4,727** (£1,406; £702; £351) **Stalls** High

Form RPR

6102 **1** **Brett Vale (IRE)**[8] 7612 3-9-0 **81**.............. DaneO'Neill 6 91
(P R Hedger) *hld up in rr: stdy hdwy 2f out: qcknd to ld fnl 120yds: comf* **5/1**[3]

3101 **2** 2¾ **Moonbeam Dancer (USA)**[15] 7515 3-8-1 **71**.............. AndreaAtzeni(3) 8 77
(D M Simcock) *hld up in rr: hdwy over 2f out: rdn and styd on to chal ins fnl f tl easily outpcd by wnr fnl 120yds* **7/4**[1]

014 **3** *nk* **Wicked Daze (IRE)**[12] 7573 6-9-12 **85**.............. TomEaves 5 91
(K A Ryan) *led 1f: styd trcking ldrs: rdn to ld again over 1f out tl hdd and easily outpcd by wnr fnl 120yds* **7/2**[2]

0-00 **4** ¾ **First To Call**[14] 7539 5-8-10 **69**.............. FergusSweeney 3 74
(P J Makin) *in rr tl hdwy on outside 3f out: chsd ldrs 2f out: rdn to chal 1f out: outpcd fnl 120yds* **25/1**

-002 **5** 5 **Viper**[15] 7515 7-9-12 **85**.............. HayleyTurner 2 84
(R Hollinshead) *led: pushed along over 2f out and one pce: hdd over 1f out and sn wknd* **11/2**

-0 **6** 4 **Lesoto Diamond (IRE)**[15] 7531 7-9-7 **80**.............. EddieAhern 7 74
(P A Fahy, Ire) *chsd ldrs: rdn and effrt on ins 2f out: nvr quite upsides and wknd appr fnl f* **15/2**

320- **7** 3 **Estate**[241] 5934 7-8-11 **70**.............. GregFairley 4 61
(D E Pipe) *chsd ldrs: rdn over 3f out: wknd over 2f out* **10/1**

4-63 **8** ¾ **Weybridge Light**[20] 7461 4-8-7 **66** oh2..............(v[1]) ChrisCatlin 1 56
(Eoin Griffin, Ire) *chsd ldr after 2f: rdn over 3f out: wknd over 2f out* **8/1**

3m 26.86s (-3.24) **Going Correction** -0.15s/f (Stan)
WFA 3 from 4yo+ 8lb **8** Ran SP% **126.5**
Speed ratings (Par 105): **102,100,100,100,97 95,94,93**
toteswinger:1&2:£3.00, 2&3:£2.60, 1&3:£4.30 CSF £15.88 CT £37.43 TOTE £6.10: £1.70, £1.20, £1.40; EX 20.40.
Owner P C F Racing Ltd **Bred** Mrs O Murtagh **Trained** Dogmersfield, Hampshire

FOCUS
A fair staying handicap run at a reasonable pace. The winner looks back to his best with the next two close to form.

7702 BISTRO PRICES FROM £37 H'CAP — 6f (P)
6:00 (6:00) (Class 4) (0-85,84) 3-Y-O+ **£4,727** (£1,406; £702; £351) **Stalls** High

Form RPR

0642 **1** **Fathsta (IRE)**[8] 7613 4-9-3 **83**.............. EddieAhern 3 94+
(D M Simcock) *hmpd s: bhd tl hdwy 2f out: rdn to ld fnl 110yds: readily* **5/6**[1]

0123 **2** 1¾ **Bahamian Lad**[15] 7511 4-9-2 **82**.............. JerryO'Dwyer 1 87
(R Hollinshead) *wnt rt s: trckd ldr tl slt ld fr ins fnl 2f: hdd and readily outpcd by wnr fnl 110yds* **10/1**[3]

0100 **3** *shd* **Methaaly (IRE)**[41] 7155 6-8-11 **77**..............(be) GregFairley 10 82
(M Mullineaux) *s.i.s: bhd: hdwy over 1f out: styd on strly thrght fnl f to press for 2nd last strides but no ch w wnr* **25/1**

1005 **4** 1 **Bertoliver**[24] 7414 5-9-0 **80**.............. DaneO'Neill 4 81
(S C Williams) *hmpd s and behind: hdwy on outside over 1f out: kpt on fnl f but nvr gng pce to chal* **10/1**[3]

0000 **5** *hd* **Fishforcompliments**[13] 7558 5-8-13 **79**.............. TonyHamilton 8 80
(R A Fahey) *led tl narrowly hdd ins fnl 2f: styd wl there tl no xtra fnl 50yds* **16/1**

6054 **6** *nk* **Dvinsky (USA)**[4] 7656 8-8-9 **75**..............(b) PaulDoe 2 75
(P Howling) *pushed rt and rdn s: chsd ldrs tl no ex fnl 50yds* **20/1**

5203 **7** 1½ **Little Pete (IRE)**[8] 7613 4-9-2 **82**.............. LPKeniry 7 77
(I W McInnes) *chsd ldrs: rdn 2f out: wknd ins fnl f* **8/1**[2]

0234 **8** *hd* **Ray Of Joy**[21] 7454 3-9-3 **83**.............. JimmyQuinn 6 77
(J R Jenkins) *chsd ldrs: rdn over 2f out: wknd ins fnl f* **8/1**[2]

0000 **9** 3¾ **Mogok Ruby**[47] 7026 5-8-10 **76**.............. LukeMorris 5 58
(L Montague Hall) *racd on outside: a towards rr* **33/1**

6500 **10** 3¼ **Pearly Wey**[8] 7613 6-9-4 **84**.............. AdamKirby 9 56
(I W McInnes) *in tch on ins tl wknd qckly over 2f out* **16/1**

1m 11.49s (-1.61) **Going Correction** -0.15s/f (Stan) **10** Ran SP% **118.3**
Speed ratings (Par 105): **104,101,101,100,99 99,97,97,92,87**
toteswinger:1&2:£2.30, 2&3:£29.80, 1&3:£10.80 CSF £10.02 CT £133.34 TOTE £1.70: £1.10, £2.40, £7.90; EX 11.50.
Owner Dr Marwan Koukash **Bred** Brian Miller **Trained** Newmarket, Suffolk

FOCUS
A fair sprint handicap. The comfortable winner atoned for last week's luckless run and the form is rated around the runner-up.
Methaaly(IRE) Official explanation: jockey said gelding was slowly away

7703 CHRISTMAS PARTY NIGHTS AT KEMPTON PARK APPRENTICE H'CAP — 6f (P)
6:30 (6:31) (Class 7) (0-50,56) 3-Y-O+ **£2,047** (£604; £302) **Stalls** High

Form RPR

051 **1** **Topcroft**[8] 7609 3-9-1 **56** 6ex..............(v) LeeTopliss(5) 11 73
(D Shaw) *towards rr: pushed along and hdwy over 2f out: str run to ld jst ins fnl f: forged clr fnl 100yds: readily* **1/1**[1]

-060 **2** 5 **Place The Duchess**[54] 6856 3-8-8 **49**..............(t) NathanAlison(5) 8 50
(A J Lidderdale) *s.i.s: chsd ldrs 1/2-way: styd on to take 2nd cl home but nvr any ch w wnr* **40/1**

4054 **3** 1 **Cocktail Party (IRE)**[22] 7427 3-9-0 **50**..............(t) AmyScott 10 48
(J W Hills) *chsd ldrs: led over 2f out: hdd jst ins fnl f: sn no ch w wnr: hung lft and lost 2nd cl home* **12/1**

0534 **4** *nk* **Reigning Monarch (USA)**[14] 7535 6-8-11 **50**.........(p) RichardRowe(3) 1 47
(Miss Z C Davison) *in rr tl hdwy fr 2f out: styd on wl fnl f but nvr any threat* **12/1**

0005 **5** 1¼ **Dontuwishitwereso**[107] 5326 3-9-0 **50**.............. TobyAtkinson 3 44
(P W D'Arcy) *slowly away: in rr tl hdwy over 2f out: styng on but nt a threat whn hmpd cl home* **11/2**[3]

0563 **6** 1¼ **Commandingpresence (USA)**[12] 7572 3-8-10 **49**.............. SPRyan(3) 2 38
(J J Bridger) *towards rr: pushed along 1/2-way: styd on same pce fr over 1f out* **25/1**

0300 **7** ½ **Deo Valente (IRE)**[27] 7370 4-8-11 **50**..............(bt) RyanClark(3) 6 37
(J M Bradley) *led 2f: styd chsng ldrs: pushed along and one pce 2f out: wknd fnl f* **20/1**

3040 **8** ½ **Sweet Kiss (USA)**[19] 7484 4-8-11 **50**.............. KierenFox(3) 12 36
(M J Attwater) *led after 2f: hdd over 2f out: wknd over 1f out* **22/1**

-500 **9** 1¼ **Summer Rose**[22] 7427 4-8-10 **49**..............(v) RyanPowell(3) 5 31
(R M H Cowell) *in tch over 3f* **25/1**

5103 **10** 1 **Cheery Cat (USA)**[20] 7462 5-8-11 **50**..............(p) DavidKenny(3) 4 28
(J Balding) *in tch on outside over 3f* **9/2**[2]

2650 **11** ¾ **Native Dame (IRE)**[12] 7572 3-8-13 **49**..............(bt) DeclanCannon 9 25
(Edgar Byrne) *a in rr* **33/1**

1m 12.5s (-0.60) **Going Correction** -0.15s/f (Stan) **11** Ran SP% **121.1**
Speed ratings (Par 97): **98,91,90,89,87 86,85,84,83,81 80**
toteswinger:1&2:£21.90, 2&3:£125.60, 1&3:£5.70 CSF £70.25 CT £354.61 TOTE £2.00: £1.10, £13.80, £2.90; EX 98.10 Place 6 £7.16, Place 5 £5.22.
Owner Mrs V Franklin & Partners **Bred** Mrs C A Dunnett **Trained** Danethorpe, Notts

FOCUS
This moderate contest was all about Topcroft, who is significantly better than the level.
Dontuwishitwereso Official explanation: jockey said gelding suffered interference at start
T/Plt: £5.00 to a £1 stake. Pool: £76,384.71. 11,064.91 winning tickets. T/Qpdt: £3.40 to a £1 stake. Pool: £8,930.38. 1,927.90 winning tickets. ST

7696 DEAUVILLE (R-H)

Thursday, December 10

OFFICIAL GOING: Standard

7704a PRIX LYPHARD (LISTED RACE) (ALL-WEATHER) 1m 1f 110y

12:55 (12:56) 3-Y-0+ **£26,699** (£10,680; £8,010; £5,340; £2,670)

RPR

1 **Sky Crusader**[96] 5662 7-8-12 .... THuet 17 —
(M Nigge, France) **22/5**[1]

2 2 **Eire**[44] 7102 5-8-9 .... HGrewe 9 —
(M Nigge, France)

3 1/2 **Fleur Enchantee (FR)**[19] 7497 5-8-9 .... (p) DBonilla 5 —
(P Van De Poele, France)

4 nk **Magic Eye (IRE)**[39] 4-8-12 .... APietsch 18 —
(Andreas Lowe, Germany)

5 1 1/2 **Willywell (FR)**[26] 7408 7-9-2 .... YFournand 13 —
(J-P Gauvin, France)

6 hd **Philatelist (USA)**[29] 7323 5-8-12 .... (b) JAuge 11 —
(M A Jarvis) *mid-div: 8th and pushed along st: rdn over 1f out: styd on at one pce: nvr trbld ldrs* **68/1**[2]

7 hd **Risquillo (FR)**[256] 3-8-11 .... SRuis 7 —
(A Sanchez, Spain)

8 1 1/2 **Burn The Breeze (IRE)**[68] 6504 4-8-9 .... RonanThomas 16 —
(Mlle H Van Zuylen, France)

9 hd **Pallodio (IRE)**[59] 4-8-12 .... YLerner 12 —
(J E Hammond, France)

10 2 1/2 **Bigzam**[70] 6438 4-8-9 .... FVeron 4 —
(E Leenders, France)

0 **Forthe Millionkiss (GER)**[30] 5-8-12 .... GBenoist 14 —
(Uwe Ostmann, Germany)

0 **Indian Daffodil (IRE)**[271] 846 4-8-12 .... MGuyon 3 —
(S Wattel, France)

0 **Time For Gold (FR)**[30] 4-8-12 .... (p) AlexisBadel 6 —
(Mme M Bollack-Badel, France)

0 **For Joy**[58] 4-8-9 .... J-BEyquem 10 —
(A De Royer-Dupre, France)

0 **Il Divo (GER)**[103] 5461 4-9-2 .... EPedroza 1 —
(A Wohler, Germany)

0 **Arlanda (GER)**[481] 5115 8-8-9 .... ABonnefoy 8 —
(Katja Gernreich, Germany)

0 **Audaz**[29] 7347 4-8-9 .... GMasure 2 —
(C Laffon-Parias, France)

0 **Darjani (IRE)**[69] 3 8 11 .... TJarnet 15 —
(Mlle S-V Tarrou, France)

1m 57.1s (117.10)
WFA 3 from 4yo+ 2lb **18** Ran SP% **20.0**
PARI-MUTUEL (including one euro stakes): WIN 5.40; PL 2.10, 6.10,2.50; DF 57.60.
Owner G Augustin-Normand **Bred** M V S And Mrs Aram **Trained** France

NOTEBOOK
Philatelist(USA) is well suited by this surface but put up something of a below-par effort, the second time he has failed to run to form on two trips abroad this year.

7674 SOUTHWELL (L-H)

Friday, December 11

OFFICIAL GOING: Standard

Wind: Nil Weather: Overcast and misty

7705 EUROPEAN BREEDERS' FUND MAIDEN STKS 7f (F)

11:30 (11:30) (Class 5) 2-Y-O **£3,753** (£1,108; £554) **Stalls** Low

Form RPR

0 1 **Right Grand**[13] 7580 2-9-3 0 .... LiamJones 4 77+
(W J Haggas) *chsd ldrs on inner: pushed along 1/2-way: rdn to ld wl over 2f out: clr appr fnl f and styd on strly* **9/4**[1]

5 2 6 **Prince Yarraman (IRE)**[15] 7537 2-9-3 0 .... ShaneKelly 5 60
(J A Osborne) *trckd ldrs on outer: effrt to chse wnr over 2f out: rdn and hung lft over 1f out: sn drvn and one pce* **5/2**[2]

45 3 2 **Whitby (IRE)**[6] 7638 2-8-5 0 .... JamesPSullivan(7) 2 50
(M W Easterby) *hld up: hdwy on inner over 2f out: kpt on appr fnl f: nrst fin* **7/1**[3]

000 4 4 **Tenga Venga**[20] 7477 2-9-3 50 .... JerryO'Dwyer 1 45
(P S McEntee) *led: rdn along 1/2-way: hdd wl over 2f out: wkng whn n.m.r and swtchd rt over 1f out* **22/1**

3 5 nse **Always Dixie (IRE)**[252] 1097 2-8-12 0 .... GregFairley 6 40
(M Johnston) *in rr: rdn along 1/2-way: sn rdn along and nvr a factor* **9/4**[1]

66 6 2 **Ever A Gent**[6] 7638 2-9-3 0 .... PhillipMakin 3 40
(M W Easterby) *chsd ldrs: rdn along 3f out: sn wknd* **50/1**

1m 27.97s (-2.33) **Going Correction** -0.45s/f (Stan) **6** Ran SP% **108.9**
Speed ratings (Par 96): **95,88,85,81,81 78**
toteswinger:1&2:£1.90, 2&3:£6.90, 1&3:£5.20 CSF £7.68 TOTE £3.00: £1.60, £2.60; EX 7.80 Trifecta £25.90 Pool: £112.49 - 3.21 winning units..
Owner Clipper Logistics **Bred** G R Bailey Ltd **Trained** Newmarket, Suffolk

FOCUS
This race was run in heavy mist, which severely restricted viewing. The form looks modest but looks reliable through the horses in the frame.

NOTEBOOK
Right Grand ◆ stepped up significantly on his debut effort at Wolverhampton and was a convincing winner. He probably didn't beat a great deal, but is a nice-looking colt and looks the type to keep progressing. (op 5-2)
Prince Yarraman(IRE) probably didn't improve much, if at all, on the form he showed first time up. Official explanation: jockey said colt hung badly left up the straight (op 11-4)
Whitby(IRE) didn't improve for the drop in trip and the way she kept on suggests she may do better over further when handicapped. (tchd 8-1)
Tenga Venga looks very moderate and probably needs dropping in grade. (op 25-1)
Always Dixie(IRE) ran to only a moderate level first time up over 5f at Musselburgh in April and hadn't been seen since. Under these vastly different conditions, she was soon struggling to keep touch as the race began to get interesting and offered little. (op 2-1)

7706 BET TOTEPOOL TO SUPPORT YOUR SPORT (S) STKS 1m (F)

12:00 (12:00) (Class 6) 2-Y-O **£1,942** (£578; £288; £144) **Stalls** Low

Form RPR

1004 1 **Tiger Hawk (USA)**[8] 7616 2-8-11 62 .... (b) RichardEvans(5) 3 63
(P D Evans) *cl up: led 3f out: rdn clr over 1f out: hung rt ins fnl f: kpt on* **4/1**[2]

60 2 1/2 **Lily Lily**[27] 7400 2-8-6 0 .... (b[1]) ChrisCatlin 5 52
(K McAuliffe) *s.i.s and sn rdn along in rr: hdwy on outer 3f out: wd stand rdn over 2f out: edgd lft and styd on u.p ins fnl f: no ex towards fin* **50/1**

0462 3 3 **Bookiesindex Girl (IRE)**[24] 7419 2-8-6 51 .... JimmyQuinn 2 45
(J R Jenkins) *led: pushed along and hdd 3f out: sn rdn: drvn wl over 1f out and kpt on same pce* **6/1**[3]

0410 4 2 3/4 **Taper Jean Girl (IRE)**[17] 7501 2-8-8 58 .... AndreaAtzeni(3) 8 44
(Mrs R A Carr) *chsd ldng pair: rdn along over 2f out: drvn over 1f out: kpt on same pce* **8/1**

0022 5 1 1/4 **Rainsborough**[20] 7482 2-9-2 64 .... (p) RobertWinston 7 47
(S Curran) *dwlt: sn trcking ldrs: effrt on outer 3f out: rdn along over 2f out: drvn over 1f out and no imp* **5/4**[1]

0004 6 7 **Scintillating (IRE)**[24] 7419 2-8-8 46 ow2 .... GrahamGibbons 1 23
(R Hollinshead) *chsd ldrs: rdn along 3f out: drvn over 2f out and sn wknd* **12/1**

5000 7 2 **Ellmollell**[4] 7669 2-8-6 52 .... DavidProbert 9 17
(S Kirk) *towards rr: rdn and hdwy over 3f out: sn drvn and wknd over 2f out* **9/1**

0000 8 1 3/4 **Micky's Bird**[17] 7501 2-8-6 44 .... PaulEddery 6 13
(R C Guest) *dwlt: a towards rr* **40/1**

0000 9 nk **The Frying Pan (IRE)**[17] 7501 2-8-6 38 .... (b) FrankieMcDonald 4 12
(Dr J D Scargill) *a towards rr* **100/1**

1m 42.17s (-1.53) **Going Correction** -0.45s/f (Stan) **9** Ran SP% **112.9**
Speed ratings (Par 94): **89,88,85,82,81 74,72,70,70**
toteswinger:1&2:£8.60, 2&3:£22.00, 1&3:£1.80 CSF £168.65 TOTE £5.50: £2.60, £1.50, £4.30; EX 82.00 TRIFECTA Not won..There was no bid for the winner.
Owner Freddie Ingram **Bred** Sun Valley Farm **Trained** Pandy, Monmouths

FOCUS
An uncompetitive seller, but the form is solid and average for the grade.

NOTEBOOK
Tiger Hawk(USA) landed a similar event over this trip on his only previous try on Fibresand and he was a ready winner on his return to a surface that clearly suits. In future, he'll be opposable back on Polytrack, but worthy of respect around here. (op 3-1)
Lily Lily, reported to have a breathing problem at Wolverhampton last time, improved for the fitting of blinkers, but she looked hard work. Having missed the break, she was one of the first to come under pressure, before finally staying on in the straight. (op 80-1)
Bookiesindex Girl(IRE), up in trip, reversed recent course form with Taper Jean Girl but was well held by the front two. (op 13-2)
Taper Jean Girl(IRE) has lost her way in two runs since winning a 7f seller around here. (op 13-2)
Rainsborough was proven on this surface and came into the race in form, but having travelled well, he found very little for pressure. This was disappointing. (op 13-8)

7707 TOTEPOOL OUR PROFITS STAY IN RACING NURSERY 6f (F)

12:30 (12:30) (Class 5) (0-75,72) 2-Y-O **£2,729** (£806; £403) **Stalls** Low

Form RPR

2125 1 **Clear Ice (IRE)**[17] 7501 2-9-3 **68** .... AndrewMullen 4 74
(D Nicholls) *chsd ldr: hdwy over 2f out: rdn to chal wl over 1f out: led appr fnl f: styd on* **3/1**[2]

0212 2 1 3/4 **Valmina**[7] 7625 2-9-7 **72** .... (t) RichardKingscote 2 73+
(Tom Dascombe) *led: rdn along 2f out: drvn and edgd rt over 1f out: hdd appr fnl f and kpt on same pce* **7/4**[1]

5001 3 4 **Athwaab**[98] 5636 2-9-3 **68** .... TonyCulhane 7 57
(M G Quinlan) *chsd ldrs on outer: hdwy 3f out: rdn and edgd lft wl over 1f out: sn one pce* **7/2**[3]

4000 4 hd **Mind Of Her Own**[8] 7619 2-8-3 **57** .... KellyHarrison(3) 8 45
(P D Evans) *towards in rr: wd st: hdwy on outer over 2f out: rdn wl over 1f out: kpt on ins fnl f: nrst fin* **16/1**

5050 5 4 1/2 **The Two G'S**[14] 7559 2-7-12 **54** ow1 .... AndrewHeffernan(5) 6 29
(P D Evans) *dwlt: hdwy 1/2-way: chsd ldrs wl over 2f out and sn rdn: drvn and one pce fr wl over 1f out* **25/1**

6616 6 3 **Fair Bunny**[8] 7619 2-9-0 **65** .... JimmyQuinn 3 31
(A D Brown) *chsd ldrs on inner: rdn along 3f out and sn wknd* **9/2**

0005 7 10 **Nidamar**[3] 7674 2-8-0 **51** oh4 ow2 .... FrankieMcDonald 5 —
(Mrs R A Carr) *chsd ldrs: rdn and hung rt 1/2-way: sn wknd and bhd* **100/1**

1m 14.86s (-1.64) **Going Correction** -0.45s/f (Stan) **7** Ran SP% **112.5**
Speed ratings (Par 96): **92,89,84,84,78 74,60**
toteswinger:1&2:£1.10, 2&3:£1.90, 1&3:£8.00 CSF £8.37 CT £17.50 TOTE £3.60: £1.80, £1.80; EX 4.50 Trifecta £29.50 Pool: £242.39 - 6.07 winning units..
Owner J P Honeyman **Bred** Mrs Noelle Walsh **Trained** Sessay, N Yorks

FOCUS
A modest nursery run in a time 0.30 seconds slower than the following juvenile maiden won by Esuvia. Fair form from the first two, who pulled away.

NOTEBOOK
Clear Ice(IRE) was a ready winner on this drop in trip, despite being intimidated by the drifting runner-up. His form figures over 5f-6f on Fibresand read 22121 and he should remain competitive around here. (tchd 5-2 and 10-3)
Valmina, reported to have hung left at Lingfield on his previous start, edged right in the straight this time, and that compromised his chance. He's holding his form well but is perhaps not entirely straightforward. Official explanation: jockey said saddle slipped (op 6-4 tchd 11-8 and 2-1)
Athwaab, bought out of Ed Dunlop's yard for 12,000gns after winning a nursery over this trip off a 1lb lower mark in September, did not seem fully effective on this slower surface, but she's entitled to come on for the run fitness-wise. (op 4-1 tchd 9-2)
Mind Of Her Own made no impression on her first Fibresand start and is due to be dropped 2lb. (op 20-1 tchd 28-1)
Fair Bunny was very disappointing considering she had today's winner behind when successful over C&D off a 6lb lower mark on her penultimate start. (op 11-2)

7708 BET BRITISH WITH TOTEPOOL MEDIAN AUCTION MAIDEN STKS 6f (F)

1:05 (1:05) (Class 6) 2-Y-O **£2,047** (£604; £302) **Stalls** Low

Form RPR

32 1 **Esuvia (IRE)**[14] 7556 2-8-12 0 .... TomEaves 7 71
(B Smart) *cl up: effrt wl over 2f out and sn led: rdn over 1f out: kpt on* **6/5**[1]

03 **2** 2 3/4 **Boy The Bell**[14] 7556 2-9-3 0.. ShaneKelly 1 68
(J A Osborne) *chsd ldng pair on inner: rdn along 2f out: drvn and sltly outpcd over 1f out: kpt on u.p ins fnl f* **7/1**[3]

05 **3** *nk* **Exearti**[14] 7556 2-8-12 0.. RobertWinston 6 62
(A J McCabe) *chsd ldrs: hdwy over 2f out: rdn over 1f out: chsd wnr ins fnl f: drvn: edgd lft and lost 2nd towards fin* **14/1**

3436 **4** *1* **Flaxen Lake**[28] 7372 2-9-3 70.. GrahamGibbons 2 64
(R Hollinshead) *led: rdn along 3f out: hdd over 2f out: drvn and one pce ent fnl f* **9/1**

344 **5** 2 3/4 **Major Maximus**[56] 6826 2-9-3 72.. DaneO'Neill 3 56
(George Baker) *dwlt and sn pushed along: swtchd outside and rdn 1/2-way: drvn over 2f out and n.d* **11/4**[2]

0 **6** *9* **Darling Buds**[14] 7556 2-8-12 0.. PhillipMakin 5 24
(K A Ryan) *dwlt and sn swtchd to outer: rdn along 1/2-way: sn outpcd and bhd* **12/1**

1m 14.56s (-1.94) **Going Correction** -0.45s/f (Stan) **6** Ran SP% **109.0**
Speed ratings (Par 94): **94,90,89,88,84 72**
toteswinger:1&2:£2.50, 2&3:£2.60, 1&3:£5.90 CSF £9.56 TOTE £1.70: £1.60, £2.40; EX 6.10.
Owner Ceffyl Racing **Bred** Round Hill Stud **Trained** Hambleton, N Yorks

FOCUS
A very modest maiden, but the time was 0.30 seconds quicker than the 68-rated Clear Ice recorded in the earlier nursery. The winner posted slightly improved form.

NOTEBOOK
Esuvia(IRE), in front straightening for home, readily came clear inside the final quarter-mile. Runner-up to a fair prospect at Wolverhampton last time, she had earlier placed in a soft-ground maiden at Doncaster and this surface looked to bring out the best in her. It will be interesting to see what mark she is given by Handicapper. (op 11-8 tchd 11-10)
Boy The Bell, just a length behind the winner at Wolverhampton, again stayed on in a manner to suggest he wants a step back up in trip. His dam was a winner on this surface and a small race should come his way at some stage. (op 5-1)
Exearti had run in the same Wolverhampton maiden contested by the front pair, finishing fifth, and she will find easier opportunities now qualified for a handicap mark.
Flaxen Lake has an official rating of 70 but he's exposed now. He was going without the cheekpieces this time but didn't appear to see out the sixth furlong. (op 11-2 tchd 10-1)
Major Maximus, trying this surface for the first time, never recovered from a sluggish start. (op 4-1)

7709 TOTEPOOL RACING'S BIGGEST SUPPORTER H'CAP (DIV I) 5f (F)
1:40 (1:40) (Class 6) (0-55,55) 3-Y-O+ **£1,706** (£503; £252) **Stalls** High

Form RPR

1052 **1** **Thoughtsofstardom**[5] 7657 6-8-11 54........................ KellyHarrison(3) 1 67
(P S McEntee) *cl up on outer: hdwy to chse ldr 2f out: rdn to chal over 1f out: edgd lft ins fnl f: styd on to ld last 100yds* **3/1**[1]

3624 **2** 1 1/2 **Head To Head (IRE)**[13] 7572 5-8-10 50........................(bt) JimmyQuinn 9 58
(A D Brown) *led: rdn along wl over 1f out: drvn ins fnl f: hdd and no ex last 100yds* **17/2**

5056 **3** *2* **Handsinthemist (IRE)**[142] 4192 4-8-5 50.................... PaulPickard(5) 11 51+
(P T Midgley) *chsd ldr: rdn along 2f out: drvn over 1f out: kpt on same pce* **8/1**

0500 **4** *shd* **Tenancy (IRE)**[24] 7424 5-8-3 48 ow2............................ DeanHeslop(5) 2 48
(S A Harris) *prom: rdn along wl over 1f out: drvn and one pce ent fnl f* **20/1**

3530 **5** *1* **Albero Di Giuda (IRE)**[181] 2921 4-9-0 54............................(t) SJCraine 3 51
(F Sheridan) *chsd ldrs: rdn along 2f out: sn drvn and no imp fnl f* **7/1**

0065 **6** 2 1/2 **Golden Dixie (USA)**[3] 7680 10-9-1 55............................(p) LiamJones 5 43
(R A Harris) *midfield: hdwy 2f out: sn rdn and no imp fnl f* **11/2**[3]

5-50 **7** *hd* **Desert Dust**[3] 7680 6-8-3 46 oh1............................(p) AndreaAtzeni(3) 8 33
(H J Collingridge) *towards rr: swtchd lft and hdwy wl over 1f out: sn rdn and kpt on ins fnl f* **5/1**[2]

0000 **8** *1* **Woodcote (IRE)**[23] 7427 7-8-6 46 oh1......................(v) KirstyMilczarek 7 30
(Peter Grayson) *s.i.s: sme hdwy 2f out: sn swtchd lft and rdn over 1f out: sn btn* **40/1**

000- **9** *nk* **Steel Mask (IRE)**[374] 7528 4-8-9 49 ow2........................(t) RobertWinston 10 31
(M Brittain) *s.i.s: a in rr* **25/1**

0200 **10** 2 1/4 **Ursus**[17] 7503 4-8-12 52..(p) PhillipMakin 12 26
(C R Wilson) *a towards rr* **12/1**

5060 **11** 1 1/4 **King's Sabre**[11] 7595 3-8-13 53..(be) J-PGuillambert 4 23
(R C Guest) *a towards rr* **8/1**

6600 **12** 1/2 **Singapore Girl**[143] 4174 3-7-13 46 oh1........................ RyanPowell(7) 6 14
(G R Oldroyd) *s.i.s: a in rr* **66/1**

58.59 secs (-1.11) **Going Correction** -0.15s/f (Stan) **12** Ran SP% **122.5**
Speed ratings (Par 101): **102,99,96,96,94 90,90,88,88,84 82,81**
toteswinger:1&2:£2.00, 2&3:£5.00, 1&3:£4.00 CSF £29.36 CT £195.54 TOTE £4.30: £2.00, £2.80, £1.80; EX 14.70 Trifecta £20.80 Pool: £130.99 - 4.64 winning units..
Owner Eventmaker Racehorses **Bred** B Bargh **Trained** Newmarket, Suffolk

FOCUS
A moderate sprint handicap run in a time 0.33 seconds quicker than the second division. As usual over this C&D, it paid to race handy. The winner's best run since this time last year.
Woodcote(IRE) Official explanation: jockey said gelding hung right
Steel Mask(IRE) Official explanation: jockey said colt missed the break and resented the kick-back.
Singapore Girl Official explanation: jockey said filly was slowly away

7710 TOTEPOOL RACING'S BIGGEST SUPPORTER H'CAP (DIV II) 5f (F)
2:15 (2:15) (Class 6) (0-55,55) 3-Y-O+ **£1,706** (£503; £252) **Stalls** High

Form RPR

0003 **1** **Best One**[5] 7651 5-8-11 51..(b) ChrisCatlin 1 61
(R A Harris) *cl up in centre: led over 2f out: rdn over 1f out: drvn ins fnl f and kpt on wl towards fin* **11/4**[2]

0003 **2** 1 1/4 **Sherjawy (IRE)**[17] 7503 5-8-12 52............................(p) SamHitchcott 4 57
(Miss Z C Davison) *racd in centre led: rdn along and hdd over 2f out: sn drvn and sltly outpcd: kpt on u.p ins fnl f* **7/2**[3]

6066 **3** *2* **Mr Funshine**[15] 7535 4-8-6 46.. JimmyQuinn 5 44
(R J Hodges) *chsd ldrs: rdn along 2f out: drvn over 1f out: kpt on same pce ins fnl f* **14/1**

3554 **4** *nse* **Nabeeda**[3] 7681 4-9-0 54.. RobertWinston 3 52+
(M Brittain) *towards rr: hdwy 2f out: rdn over 1f out: styd on ins fnl f: nrst fin* **5/2**[1]

6005 **5** *hd* **Berrymead**[21] 7462 4-8-9 54 oh1 ow8............................ AnnStokell(5) 12 51+
(Miss A Stokell) *rrd s and in rr: hdwy 2f out: sn rdn and kpt on ins fnl f: nrst fin* **33/1**

0505 **6** *shd* **Admiral Bond (IRE)**[66] 6553 4-8-10 50........................(p) PJMcDonald 2 47
(G R Oldroyd) *chsd ldrs on outer: rdn along 2f out: drvn over 1f out: kpt on same pce* **13/2**

0030 **7** 2 1/4 **Tanley**[6] 7645 4-8-10 50.. TonyCulhane 10 38
(J F Coupland) *racd towards stands' rail: cl up: rdn along 2f out and ev ch tl drvn and wknd appr fnl f* **16/1**

640 **8** *2* **Chantilly Jewel (USA)**[28] 7371 4-8-13 53................(v) GrahamGibbons 8 34
(R M H Cowell) *chsd ldrs: rdn along 2f out: grad wknd* **22/1**

6000 **9** *6* **Bold Rose**[132] 4536 3-8-10 55..(p) LeeNewnes(5) 6 15
(M D I Usher) *dwlt: a towards rr* **25/1**

0000 **10** 1/2 **Mrs Medley**[16] 7510 3-8-3 46 oh1.. KellyHarrison(3) 9 4
(D Shaw) *dwlt: a in rr* **100/1**

0-0U **11** 1 3/4 **Egyptian Lord**[158] 3678 6-8-6 46 oh1............................(b) KirstyMilczarek 7 —
(Peter Grayson) *chsd ldrs: rdn along 2f out: sn wknd* **40/1**

58.92 secs (-0.78) **Going Correction** -0.15s/f (Stan) **11** Ran SP% **117.9**
Speed ratings (Par 101): **100,98,94,94,94 94,90,87,77,77 74**
toteswinger:1&2:£3.10, 2&3:£23.40, 1&3:£12.40 CSF £12.20 CT £114.62 TOTE £4.20: £1.60, £1.90, £4.10; EX 16.10 Trifecta £137.60 Part won. Pool: £186.08 - 0.45 winning units..
Owner The Govin Partnership **Bred** Darley **Trained** Earlswood, Monmouths
■ Stewards' Enquiry : Sam Hitchcott six-day ban: used whip with excessive force (December 26-31)\n\x\x

FOCUS
The pace horses dominated as usual, and this was a weak race, with the time 0.33 seconds slower than the first division. The winner was up a length on his previous best.
Berrymead Official explanation: jockey said filly reared leaving stalls

7711 SOUTHWELL-RACECOURSE.CO.UK H'CAP 1m (F)
2:50 (2:51) (Class 5) (0-75,75) 3-Y-O+ **£2,729** (£806; £403) **Stalls** Low

Form RPR

1521 **1** **Salerosa (IRE)**[35] 7271 4-9-5 75.. JimmyQuinn 4 86
(Mrs A Duffield) *hld up in tch: hdwy on inner 2f out: rdn to chal ins fnl f: sn edgd rt: drvn and styd on wl to ld last 75yds* **2/1**[1]

0054 **2** *nk* **Mozayada (USA)**[17] 7506 5-9-2 72................................ RobertWinston 2 82
(M Brittain) *slt ld: rdn along 2f out: sn hdd and cl up tl led again over 1f out: drvn ins fnl f: hdd and no ex last 75yds* **10/1**

0010 **3** 1 1/4 **Elusive Fame (USA)**[13] 7575 3-9-0 71............................(b) GregFairley 8 78
(M Johnston) *trckd ldrs on outer: hdwy 3f out: rdn 2f out: drvn over 1f out: kpt on same pce ins fnl f* **7/2**[2]

6023 **4** 1 1/4 **Indian Skipper (IRE)**[6] 7639 4-9-3 73............................(be) ChrisCatlin 3 77
(R C Guest) *hld up in tch: hdwy to chse ldrs over 3f out: rdn over 2f out: drvn over 1f out: kpt on same pce* **5/1**

5050 **5** *nse* **Border Owl (IRE)**[24] 7423 4-8-1 62................................ PaulPickard(5) 9 66
(P Salmon) *cl up: rdn to ld briefly wl over 1f out: drvn and hdd over 1f out: wknd ent fnl f* **20/1**

0000 **6** 1 1/4 **Silver Hotspur**[6] 7643 5-8-10 66.. LiamJones 7 67
(C R Dore) *dwlt: hdwy wl over 2f out: sn rdn and no imp ins fnl f* **14/1**

0363 **7** 3/4 **Hilbre Court (USA)**[24] 7423 4-9-0 70............................ GrahamGibbons 6 69
(B P J Baugh) *prom: rdn along 1/2-way: drvn wl over 2f out and sn btn* **9/2**[3]

0000 **8** 3 1/4 **Golden Penny**[41] 7172 4-9-2 72.. PhillipMakin 1 64
(M Dods) *chsd ldrs: rdn along 3f out: sn drvn and wknd over 2f out* **25/1**

600- **9** *30* **Mezuzah**[15] 1327 9-8-7 63.. SamHitchcott 5 —
(Miss J E Foster) *sn rdn along: a in rr: bhd fnl 2f* **50/1**

1m 40.5s (-3.20) **Going Correction** -0.45s/f (Stan)
WFA 3 from 4yo+ 1lb **9** Ran SP% **116.7**
Speed ratings (Par 103): **98,97,96,95,95 93,93,89,59**
toteswinger:1&2:£1.60, 2&3:£5.50, 1&3:£3.50 CSF £23.41 CT £68.04 TOTE £2.90: £1.50, £3.80, £1.40; EX 26.90 Trifecta £50.30 Pool: £297.11 - 4.37 winning units.
Owner David K Barker & Phil White **Bred** Pedro Rosas **Trained** Constable Burton, N Yorks

FOCUS
A good handicap for the grade and another personal best from the winner. The third is the best guide.

7712 MEMBERSHIP AT SOUTHWELL GOLF CLUB APPRENTICE H'CAP 1m 4f (F)
3:25 (3:25) (Class 6) (0-65,77) 3-Y-O+ **£2,047** (£604; £302) **Stalls** Low

Form RPR

1111 **1** **Shadows Lengthen**[3] 7677 3-10-2 77 12ex.........(b) JamesPSullivan(5) 4 84+
(M W Easterby) *mde all: shkn up wl over 1f out: rdn ins fnl f and kpt on* **4/9**[1]

6020 **2** *nk* **Stormy Summer**[17] 7505 4-9-4 60............................(b) TobyAtkinson(5) 3 66
(R W Price) *t.k.h: trckd ldrs: hdwy to chse wnr 4f out: rdn to chal 2f out: ev ch tl drvn and no ex ins fnl f* **6/1**[2]

0000 **3** *11* **Dado Mush**[73] 6358 6-9-6 57..(p) WilliamCarson 5 45
(T T Clement) *chsd ldng pair: rdn along 4f out and sn outpcd: drvn and kpt on fnl 2f: no ch w ldng pair* **28/1**

1465 **4** *nk* **Astrolibra**[25] 7093 5-9-6 60.. SimonPearce(3) 1 48
(M H Tompkins) *hld up: effrt 4f out: sn rdn and nvr a factor* **7/1**[3]

654 **5** *10* **Nyetimber (USA)**[14] 7557 3-8-13 58................................ MartinLane(3) 2 30
(J A Osborne) *a in rr* **12/1**

-000 **6** 1/2 **Daltaban (FR)**[24] 7423 5-9-0 56............................(v) DavidKenny(5) 6 27
(P Salmon) *chsd wnr: rdn along 5f out: drvn over 3f out and sn wknd* **66/1**

2m 36.44s (-4.56) **Going Correction** -0.45s/f (Stan)
WFA 3 from 4yo+ 5lb **6** Ran SP% **108.7**
Speed ratings (Par 101): **97,96,89,89,82 82**
toteswinger:1&2:£1.60, 2&3:£5.50, 1&3:£3.50 CSF £3.26 TOTE £1.50: £1.10, £2.10; EX 3.10 Place 6 £41.20, Place 5 £22.87.
Owner T A F Frost **Bred** London Thoroughbred Services Ltd **Trained** Sheriff Hutton, N Yorks

FOCUS
This was a moderate contest, officially described as being open to horses rated 51-65, although the winner is far better than that. The first two finished clear.
T/Plt: £18.80 to a £1 stake. Pool: £33,325.07. 1,292.81 winning tickets. T/Qpdt: £3.00 to a £1 stake. Pool: £3,896.00. 933.55 winning tickets. JR

7667 WOLVERHAMPTON (A.W) (L-H)
Friday, December 11

OFFICIAL GOING: Standard
Wind: Nil Weather: Fine

7713 BET TOTEPOOL AT TOTESPORT.COM CLAIMING STKS 5f 216y(P)
5:50 (5:50) (Class 6) 2-Y-O **£2,729** (£806; £403) **Stalls** Low

Form RPR

5562 **1** **Bubbly Bellini (IRE)**[5] 7655 2-8-2 70............................ AndreaAtzeni(3) 2 69
(A Bailey) *hld up: pushed along over 2f out: hdwy wl over 1f out: sn rdn and edgd lft: r.o to ld last strides* **15/8**[2]

3343 **2** *nk* **Ramamara (IRE)**[7] 7625 2-7-13 72........................ AndrewHeffernan(5) 5 68
(P D Evans) *w ldr: led over 3f out: 3 l clr whn hrd rdn over 1f out: ct last strides* **5/4**[1]

5004 **3** 1½ **Anjomarba (IRE)**[2] 7690 2-7-13 75........................ RyanClark[(7)] 6 65
(W G M Turner) *hld up: rdn on outside over 2f out: r.o to take 3rd wl ins fnl f* **15/2**[3]

3020 **4** 1¼ **Lord Victor**[17] 7501 2-8-3 64........................ FrancisNorton 3 58
(A J McCabe) *led: hdd over 3f out: rdn wl over 1f out: one pce fnl f* **14/1**

400 **5** ¾ **Bitter Honey**[8] 7619 2-8-0 65 ow2........................ JimmyQuinn 1 53
(Mrs G S Rees) *hld up in tch: rdn over 1f out: one pce* **40/1**

0333 **6** 1 **Zelos Dream (IRE)**[4] 7661 2-8-2 63........................ LiamJones 4 52
(R A Harris) *prom: chsd ldr 3f out tl rdn over 1f out: wknd ins fnl f* **15/2**[3]

0000 **7** 27 **Tagula Pearl (IRE)**[21] 7463 2-8-0 47 ow2................ FrankieMcDonald 7 —
(I W McInnes) *outpcd: t.o fnl 4f* **100/1**

1m 15.6s (0.60) **Going Correction** -0.025s/f (Stan) **7** Ran SP% **112.9**
Speed ratings (Par 94): **95,94,92,90,89 88,52**
toteswingers: 1&2 £1.20, 1&3 £1.80, 2&3 £2.40 CSF £4.43 TOTE £2.90: £1.20, £1.90; EX 5.40.
Owner The Champagne Club **Bred** J P Hand **Trained** Newmarket, Suffolk

■ Stewards' Enquiry : Andrew Heffernan two-day ban: used wip with excessive frequency (Dec 30-31)

FOCUS
A couple of fair sorts in an ordinary claimer, rated around the front two. The gallop was reasonable and the winner hung towards the far rail in the straight.

NOTEBOOK
Bubbly Bellini(IRE) doesn't look the easiest of rides but justified the market support to get off the mark in this lesser grade. He looks a bit better than the bare form, may appreciate the return to 7f and is lightly raced enough to be open to a bit more improvement. (op 5-2)
Ramamara(IRE), a free-going type, is a typically tough sort from this yard who had the the run of the race and performed creditably returned to this grade. She is a good guide to this form and should continue to give a good account away from progressive sorts. (op 11-8)
Anjomarba(IRE), who had a good chance at the weights, was easy to back beforehand and, although not disgraced, she did not look the most straightforward and left the impression that the return to 7f would suit. (op 9-2)
Lord Victor has not been the most reliable but was not disgraced in the face of a stiffish task with the cheekpieces left off. However, it remains to be seen whether this will be built on next time. (op 16-1)
Bitter Honey, who had a bit to find dropped to this grade for the first time, carried 2lb of overweight but it made little difference to the result. All her best efforts have been on easy and in testing ground on turf and she may be of more interest at Southwell. (op 33-1)

7714 LAURA GLENDINING BIRTHDAY PARTY MEDIAN AUCTION MAIDEN STKS 5f 20y(P)
6:20 (6:21) (Class 6) 3-5-Y-O **£2,729** (£806; £403) **Stalls** Low

Form RPR

0525 **1** **Brynfa Boy**[166] 3428 3-9-3 57........................ TonyCulhane 10 71
(P W D'Arcy) *hld up in tch: led jst over 1f out: rdn and edgd lft ins fnl f: r.o* **3/1**[3]

2 ¾ **American Light**[56] 6833 3-9-0 0........................ MartinLane[(3)] 1 68
(D M Simcock) *led 1f: a.p: rdn over 1f out: kpt on ins fnl f* **5/4**[1]

2202 **3** 1¾ **Rocket Ruby**[7] 7629 3-8-12 54........................ DaneO'Neill 6 57
(D Shaw) *led after 1f: rdn and hdd jst over 1f out: no ex ins fnl f* **11/4**[2]

4005 **4** 4½ **Sandy Par**[16] 7510 4-8-10 44........................(b) RyanClark[(7)] 3 46
(J M Bradley) *trckd ldrs: rdn and wknd over 1f out* **25/1**

50-0 **5** shd **Myriola**[7] 7629 4-8-9 44........................ KellyHarrison[(3)] 4 40
(D Shaw) *bmpd sn after s: hld up and bhd: swtchd rt ent st: sn rdn: nvr trbld ldrs* **66/1**

600 **6** 5 **Sunshine Ellie**[249] 1157 3-8-12 42........................ GrahamGibbons 5 22
(D Shaw) *wnt lft sn after s: bhd: pushed along over 2f out: sn struggling* **50/1**

0-00 **7** shd **Misterisland (IRE)**[9] 7614 4-9-3 54........................(be) GregFairley 9 27
(M Mullineaux) *s.i.s: outpcd* **66/1**

6650 **8** 6 **Frisky Queen (IRE)**[71] 6410 3-8-12 0........................(p) TPQueally 7 —
(T G McCourt, Ire) *hld up in tch: pushed along over 3f out: wknd over 2f out* **40/1**

2045 **9** 1½ **Shirley High**[7] 7629 3-8-12 49........................ PaulDoe 8 —
(P Howling) *w ldrs: ev ch over 2f out: pushed along and wknd wl over 1f out* **40/1**

62.37 secs (0.07) **Going Correction** -0.025s/f (Stan) **9** Ran SP% **109.8**
Speed ratings (Par 101): **98,96,94,86,86 78,78,68,66**
toteswingers: 1&2 £1.40, 1&3 £1.90, 2&3 £1.30 CSF £6.48 TOTE £4.70: £1.40, £1.30, £1.10; EX 9.50.Oxbridge was withdrawn. Price at time of withdrawal 20/1. Rule 4 does not apply.
Owner The Golf Oil Partnership **Bred** David And Mrs Vicki Fleet **Trained** Newmarket, Suffolk

FOCUS
A modest and low-grade maiden. The pace was sound and the first three in the market pulled clear of the rest. The winner ended up just off the inside rail in the closing stages. He posted a personal best and the form is rated around the second and the fifth.

7715 BET LIVE IN-PLAY AT TOTESPORT.COM H'CAP (DIV I) 7f 32y(P)
6:50 (6:52) (Class 6) (0-65,65) 3-Y-0+ **£2,388** (£705; £352) **Stalls** High

Form RPR

5612 **1** **Istiqdaam**[6] 7643 4-9-4 65........................(b) PhillipMakin 2 79
(M W Easterby) *a.p: pushed along and wnt 2nd 2f out: rdn to ld jst over 1f out: r.o wl* **4/5**[1]

0500 **2** 3½ **Striker Torres (IRE)**[49] 6997 3-9-2 63........................(v[1]) TomEaves 5 68
(B Smart) *led: rdn and hung lft over 1f out: carried hd awkwardly and sn hdd: kpt on same pce* **20/1**

0642 **3** hd **Just Timmy Marcus**[63] 6637 3-9-3 64........................ GrahamGibbons 6 68
(B P J Baugh) *chsd ldr after 1f tl rdn 2f out: edgd lft wl ins fnl f: kpt on one pce* **7/1**[3]

0046 **4** ¾ **Crystallize**[20] 7480 3-9-1 62........................ StephenDonohoe 4 64
(A B Haynes) *hld up in tch: rdn wl over 1f out: one pce whn nt clr run and swtchd rt wl ins fnl f* **25/1**

000/ **5** ½ **All Of Me (IRE)**[94] 5757 5-9-1 62........................(tp) TPQueally 7 63
(Paul W Flynn, Ire) *hld up towards rr: rdn over 2f out: styd on ins fnl f* **11/1**

0000 **6** ½ **Diapason (IRE)**[71] 6421 3-9-2 63........................ RichardKingscote 10 62
(Tom Dascombe) *stdd sn after s: t.k.h: hdwy on outside over 5f out: rdn over 2f out: one pce* **33/1**

1213 **7** ½ **Dancing Welcome**[12] 7591 3-8-4 58........................(b) RyanClark[(7)] 3 56
(J M Bradley) *hld up towards rr: pushed along over 2f out: prog on ins fnl f: n.d* **13/2**[2]

02-4 **8** 2½ **Luckydolly (IRE)**[15] 7543 3-8-13 60........................ DaneO'Neill 9 51
(F Costello, Ire) *hld up in tch: wknd 2f out* **33/1**

9 ¾ **Lady Rockfield (IRE)**[15] 7541 3-9-4 65........................(b) EddieAhern 1 54
(M J Grassick, Ire) *s.i.s: hld up towards rr: stdy prog on ins over 3f out: rdn over 1f out: wknd ins fnl f* **14/1**

5003 **10** 2¾ **Valentino Swing (IRE)**[15] 7534 6-8-10 57........................ HayleyTurner 11 39
(Miss T Spearing) *a in rr* **50/1**

1m 29.31s (-0.29) **Going Correction** -0.025s/f (Stan) **10** Ran SP% **112.8**
Speed ratings (Par 101): **100,96,95,94,94 93,93,90,89,86**
toteswingers: 1&2 £8.10, 1&3 £1.60, 2&3 £19.10 CSF £24.02 CT £71.45 TOTE £1.90: £1.40, £4.70, £1.90; EX 29.40.
Owner Two Old Pals **Bred** Cheveley Park Stud Ltd **Trained** Sheriff Hutton, N Yorks

FOCUS
A modest handicap in which the one progressive performer ran out a decisive winner. The pace was only ordinary and those held up were at a disadvantage. The winner raced towards the far rail in the straight.

7716 BET LIVE IN-PLAY AT TOTESPORT.COM H'CAP (DIV II) 7f 32y(P)
7:20 (7:21) (Class 6) (0-65,65) 3-Y-0+ **£2,388** (£705; £352) **Stalls** High

Form RPR

636 **1** **Kipchak (IRE)**[14] 7561 4-9-4 65........................(p) TPQueally 5 75
(C R Dore) *sn led: rdn over 1f out: drvn out* **7/1**[3]

000F **2** 2¼ **Seldom (IRE)**[56] 6824 3-9-3 64........................ JimmyQuinn 10 68
(M Brittain) *hld up in tch: rdn over 1f out: r.o to take 2nd post* **40/1**

0122 **3** shd **Spinning Ridge (IRE)**[13] 7579 4-8-13 60........................(p) LiamJones 2 64
(R A Harris) *led early: a.p: chsd wnr 2f out: rdn over 1f out: nt qckn ins fnl f: lost 2nd post* **8/1**

0124 **4** 1¼ **Monashee Rock (IRE)**[4] 7662 4-9-4 65........................ LPKeniry 11 66
(Matthew Salaman) *hld up towards rr: pushed along over 2f out: hdwy over 1f out: rdn and no ex towards fin* **6/1**[2]

6202 **5** ½ **Goodbye Cash (IRE)**[20] 7479 5-8-12 59........................ PaulDoe 9 58
(P D Evans) *hld up towards rr: c wd st: rdn and hdwy over 1f out: one pce ins fnl f* **14/1**

0140 **6** 1¼ **Loyal Royal (IRE)**[23] 7432 6-8-9 63........................(b) RyanClark[(7)] 3 59
(J M Bradley) *s.i.s: hld up in rr: rdn and hdwy on ins wl over 1f out: no imp fnl f* **16/1**

2603 **7** hd **Stanley Goodspeed**[20] 7480 6-9-1 62........................(bt[1]) EddieAhern 4 62+
(J W Hills) *hld up in mid-div: nt clr run wl over 1f out: nvr trbld ldrs* **4/1**[1]

126 **8** 1¾ **Bollywood Style**[10] 7606 4-8-10 57........................ RobertWinston 7 48
(J R Best) *hld up in mid-div: pushed along and hdwy over 2f out: sn rdn: wknd ins fnl f* **16/1**

4 **9** 1¼ **Scopey**[15] 7542 4-9-0 61........................(t) DaneO'Neill 1 48
(Gerard Keane, Ire) *hld up in mid-div on ins: hdwy 2f out: rdn over 1f out: wknd ins fnl f* **4/1**[1]

2002 **10** nk **Fly By Nelly**[41] 7180 3-9-1 62........................ SteveDrowne 6 48
(H Morrison) *hld up: sn mid-div: pushed along over 3f out: sn bhd* **9/1**

6050 **11** 4 **Dream Express (IRE)**[12] 7587 4-8-13 60........................ KirstyMilczarek 12 36
(P Howling) *hld up and bhd: c v wd st: pushed along wl over 1f out: sn struggling* **33/1**

0625 **12** 6 **Yakama (IRE)**[206] 2166 4-8-10 57 ow1........................ DarryllHolland 8 16
(Mrs C A Dunnett) *sn chsng ldr: pushed along and lost 2nd 2f out: wknd qckly over 1f out* **25/1**

1m 28.73s (-0.87) **Going Correction** -0.025s/f (Stan) **12** Ran SP% **115.6**
Speed ratings (Par 101): **103,100,100,98,98 96,96,94,93,92 88,81**
toteswingers: 1&2 £54.10, 1&3 £9.60, 2&3 £69.40 CSF £259.38 CT £2298.24 TOTE £9.40: £2.90, £15.30, £1.80; EX 247.70.
Owner Liam Breslin **Bred** Miss Mary Davidson & Mrs Steffi Von Schilcher **Trained** Cowbit, Lincs

FOCUS
Exposed performers in a modest handicap. Although the pace was fair, those held up couldn't get competitive and the winner raced in the centre in the straight. The time was quicker than division one and the winner was close to his spring form.

7717 BEST ODDS AT TOTESPORT.COM CONDITIONS STKS 1m 141y(P)
7:50 (7:51) (Class 3) 2-Y-O **£7,758** (£2,454; £1,321) **Stalls** Low

Form RPR

1100 **1** **Mister Angry (IRE)**[49] 6993 2-9-3 85........................ GregFairley 2 84
(M Johnston) *chsd ldr: led 2f out: rdn and hung rt ins fnl f: r.o* **5/6**[1]

6 **2** 2½ **Consequential**[41] 7182 2-8-9 0........................ HayleyTurner 1 71
(D M Simcock) *hld up: rdn to chse wnr over 1f out: nt qckn ins fnl f* **2/1**[2]

1340 **3** 6 **Tukitinyasok (IRE)**[104] 5433 2-9-0 85........................ TonyHamilton 6 63
(R F Fisher) *led: rdn and hdd 2f out: wknd ins fnl f* **3/1**[3]

P **Early Dart** 2-8-12 0 ow6........................ GrahamGibbons 3 —
(A Berry) *reluctant to go to post: s.i.s: bucked and kicked sn after s: qckly p.u* **50/1**

1m 50.44s (-0.06) **Going Correction** -0.025s/f (Stan) **4** Ran SP% **114.8**
Speed ratings (Par 100): **99,96,91,—**
CSF £3.10 TOTE £2.20; EX 2.70.
Owner The Originals **Bred** Darley **Trained** Middleham Moor, N Yorks

FOCUS
A couple of useful performers but an uncompetitive race and a disappointing turnout for the money on offer. The gallop was a moderate one and the winner veered into the centre in the straight. He has scope to do better next year.

NOTEBOOK
Mister Angry(IRE) had been well beaten in nurseries on his last two starts but probably did not have to better his previous form to maintain his unbeaten record at this course in this uncompetitive event, despite diving to his right in closing stages. He's a strong sort with scope and he may be able to build on this next year. (op 4-5 tchd 10-11 in places after early Evens in places)
Consequential, had shown ability on her debut at Newmarket and confirmed that promise when chasing home a useful sort at a respectable distance after attracting market support. A stiffer test of stamina over this trip would have suited and she looks capable of winning in ordinary maiden company. (op 3-1)
Tukitinyasok(IRE) had shown useful form on turf but dropped away tamely once headed on this all-weather debut and was the disappointment of the race. He was beaten before stamina became an issue and he will be hard to place on this evidence on Polytrack. (op 5-2 tchd 10-3)
Early Dart looked to face a very stiff task on this racecourse debut but gave problems before the start and displayed a very mulish attitude leaving the stalls. She is one to steer well clear of.

7718 VAROL LUBRICANTS H'CAP (DIV I) 1m 1f 103y(P)
8:20 (8:20) (Class 6) (0-60,60) 3-Y-0+ **£2,047** (£604; £302) **Stalls** Low

Form RPR

6016 **1** **Coolnaharan (IRE)**[7] 7632 9-8-10 57........................(p) JamesPSullivan[(7)] 10 66
(Lee Smyth, Ire) *hld up in rr: hdwy on outside 2f out: c wd st: rdn to ld wl ins fnl f: r.o* **16/1**

31-1 **2** shd **Holyfield Warrior (IRE)**[23] 7438 5-8-10 57........................ KierenFox[(7)] 11 65
(R J Smith) *hld up in rr: hdwy on ins wl over 1f out: sn rdn: ev ch ins fnl f: r.o* **5/1**[2]

0006 **3** 1¼ **Kirstys Lad**[11] 7599 7-8-6 46........................ GregFairley 4 51
(M Mullineaux) *led after 1f: edgd rt over 1f out: sn rdn: hdd wl ins fnl f: nt qckn* **14/1**

0000 4 hd **Ryker (IRE)**[44] 7110 3-9-1 57 .... EddieAhern 5 62
(J W Hills) *hld up towards rr: swtchd rt over 1f out: rdn and r.o ins fnl f: nrst fin* 11/1

330 5 shd **Corrib (IRE)**[50] 6969 6-8-6 46 oh1 .... DavidProbert 9 51
(B Palling) *hld up in rr: pushed along over 1f out: rdn and r.o ins fnl f: nrst fin* 8/1[3]

5000 6 1 **John Potts**[228] 1556 4-8-9 49 .... GrahamGibbons 7 52
(B P J Baugh) *hld up in mid-div on ins: pushed along and hdwy over 1f out: rdn and nt qckn ins fnl f* 16/1

0053 7 1 1/4 **Turkish Sultan (IRE)**[5] 7652 6-7-13 46 .... (p) RyanClark(7) 12 46
(J M Bradley) *t.k.h: sn prom: rdn over 2f out: fdd towards fin* 12/1

5-00 8 hd **Chia (IRE)**[27] 7399 6-9-6 60 .... DaneO'Neill 6 60
(D Haydn Jones) *hld up towards rr: pushed along and sme prog 1f out: sn rdn: no imp* 10/1

6460 9 nk **Stoic Leader (IRE)**[11] 7600 9-8-12 52 .... TonyHamilton 3 51
(R F Fisher) *sn hld up in mid-div: pushed along over 2f out: rdn jst over 1f out: sn btn* 10/1

00-0 10 hd **Northgate Lodge (USA)**[99] 5599 4-8-6 46 oh1 .... JimmyQuinn 13 45
(M Brittain) *sn prom: chsd ldr over 7f out tl rdn wl over 1f out: wknd ins fnl f* 50/1

2-3 11 1 3/4 **Magners Hill (IRE)**[33] 2618 5-9-2 56 .... LPKeniry 8 56+
(Gerard Keane, Ire) *sn hld up in mid-div: pushed along whn nt clr run over 1f out: n.d after* 10/1

0010 12 1 **Ten Pole Tudor**[11] 7599 4-9-4 58 .... (p) LiamJones 2 51
(R A Harris) *prom tl wknd ins fnl f* 16/1

-404 13 15 **Achromatic**[23] 7433 3-8-13 55 .... AdamKirby 1 16
(W R Swinburn) *led 1f: prom: rdn over 2f out: wknd over 1f out: eased ins fnl f* 7/2[1]

2m 2.36s (0.66) **Going Correction** -0.025s/f (Stan)
WFA 3 from 4yo+ 2lb 13 Ran SP% 119.6
Speed ratings (Par 101): **96,95,94,94,94 93,92,92,92,91 90,89,76**
toteswingers: 1&2 £10.80, 1&3 £36.80, 2&3 £18.20 CSF £94.21 CT £1174.14 TOTE £16.50: £5.30, £1.90, £3.50; EX 119.50.
Owner Pircan Partnership **Bred** Noel Finegan **Trained** Dungannon, Co Tyrone

FOCUS
A moderate handicap in which the gallop was a moderate one and the time was slower than division one. The winner raced in the centre in the straight and the form is sound enough.

7719 VAROL LUBRICANTS H'CAP (DIV II) 1m 1f 103y(P)
8:50 (8:50) (Class 6) (0-60,59) 3-Y-0+ £2,047 (£604; £302) Stalls Low

Form RPR

0440 1 **King Of Connacht**[11] 7599 6-9-2 55 .... (v[1]) AdamKirby 9 64
(M Wellings) *hld up towards rr: stdy hdwy over 2f out: rdn to ld ins fnl f: r.o* 7/1[2]

6650 2 1/2 **Grey Command (USA)**[79] 6218 4-8-11 50 .... JimmyQuinn 5 58
(M Brittain) *a.p: swtchd rt jst over 2f out: led over 1f out: rdn and hdd ins fnl f: kpt on* 15/2[3]

3 3 **Grove View Star**[15] 7544 4-9-3 56 .... SJCraine 13 58
(Patrick Morris) *hld up towards rr: hdwy 2f out: rdn and kpt on to take 3rd wl ins fnl f* 12/1

00-4 4 1/2 **Feeling (IRE)**[15] 5873 5-8-6 45 .... DavidProbert 7 46
(D Burchell) *prom: rdn whn sltly hmpd jst over 2f out: one pce fnl f* 14/1

6 5 1 3/4 **Tabaahi (IRE)**[6] 7369 4-9-0 53 .... (b) ShaneKelly 1 50
(Gordon Elliott, Ire) *a.p: pushed along to ld 2f out: rdn and hdd over 1f out: wknd ins fnl f* 15/2[3]

600 6 1/2 **Bobering**[239] 1314 9-8-3 45 .... KellyHarrison(3) 11 41
(B P J Baugh) *hld up towards rr: prog on ins 2f out: wknd ins fnl f* 40/1

7 hd **Lady Mickataine (USA)**[15] 7544 3-9-4 59 .... EddieAhern 6 54
(M J Grassick, Ire) *hld up in mid-div: lost pl over 2f out: n.d after* 22/1

4005 8 nk **Dabbers Ridge (IRE)**[12] 7591 7-9-6 59 .... DaneO'Neill 3 54
(I W McInnes) *hld up in mid-div: hdwy on ins over 2f out: ev ch wl over 1f out: sn rdn: wknd ins fnl f* 8/1

6500 9 2 3/4 **Incy Wincy**[5] 7653 3-8-4 45 .... (b[1]) LiamJones 10 34
(J M Bradley) *hld up in rr: pushed along wl over 2f out: no rspnse* 50/1

0033 10 1 1/4 **Hi Spec (IRE)**[11] 7600 6-8-4 46 .... (p) AndreaAtzeni(3) 4 32
(Miss M E Rowland) *hld up in mid-div: hdwy 2f out: c wd st: rdn and wknd over 1f out* 8/1

0 11 11 **Stage Dream (IRE)**[43] 7142 4-8-3 49 .... (p) JamesPSullivan(7) 12 12
(Lee Smyth, Ire) *hld up in mid-div: pushed along on outside over 2f out: c v wd st: sn bhd* 50/1

6001 12 5 **Philmack Dot Com**[13] 7579 3-9-4 59 .... (t) JerryO'Dwyer 2 12
(D Donovan) *led: pushed along over 3f out: rdn and hdd 2f out: wknd over 1f out* 11/4[1]

300 13 8 **Gifted Heir (IRE)**[13] 7581 5-9-2 55 .... (p) RobertWinston 8 —
(A Bailey) *prom: pushed along and wknd over 2f out: eased wl over 1f out* 14/1

2m 1.55s (-0.15) **Going Correction** -0.025s/f (Stan)
WFA 3 from 4yo+ 2lb 13 Ran SP% 116.7
Speed ratings (Par 101): **99,98,95,95,93 93,93,93,90,89 79,75,68**
toteswingers: 1&2 £6.00, 1&3 £14.70, 2&3 £16.20 CSF £55.61 CT £619.42 TOTE £6.00: £2.90, £3.40, £2.90; EX 66.60.
Owner Ann Lindsay,Francis Lindsay,Jim O'Connor **Bred** B Burrough **Trained** Six Ashes, Shropshire

FOCUS
A moderate handicap run at a reasonable gallop. The winner raced centre to far side in the straight and the first two pulled clear. Straightforward form, with the winner back to his best.

7720 TEXT YOUR TOTESPORT BET TO 60021 H'CAP 1m 4f 50y(P)
9:20 (9:20) (Class 2) (0-100,97) 3-Y-0+
£11,215 (£3,358; £1,679; £840; £419; £210) Stalls Low

Form RPR

56-0 1 **Dirar (IRE)**[21] 7472 4-8-11 87 .... EddieAhern 6 96
(Gordon Elliott, Ire) *hld up: hdwy over 5f out: led over 2f out: clr whn edgd rt over 1f out: pushed out* 5/2[1]

5310 2 1 3/4 **Mister New York (USA)**[37] 7233 4-8-7 83 oh1 .... (b) HayleyTurner 5 89
(Noel T Chance) *hld up in rr: pushed along and hdwy 2f out: c wd st: rdn to chse wnr and edgd lft ent fnl f: nt qckn* 28/1

2402 3 2 **Dance The Star (USA)**[21] 7465 4-8-10 89 .... MartinLane(3) 3 92
(D M Simcock) *hld up: pushed along and hdwy 2f out: rdn wl over 1f out: one pce whn sltly hmpd ins fnl f* 7/2[3]

1430 4 6 **Nanton (USA)**[55] 6851 7-9-7 97 .... GeorgeBaker 1 90
(J S Goldie) *hld up in tch: pushed along and wnt 2nd wl over 1f out: wknd fnl f* 3/1[2]

003 5 7 **Laterly (IRE)**[21] 7465 4-9-1 91 .... DarryllHolland 8 73
(S Gollings) *chsd ldr after 2f: pushed along to ld over 3f out: hdd over 2f out: wknd wl over 1f out* 12/1

0032 6 6 **Coeur De Lionne (IRE)**[13] 7573 5-8-11 87 .... SteveDrowne 4 60
(E A L Dunlop) *hld up in tch: pushed along over 2f out: wknd wl over 1f out* 9/2

4505 7 15 **Sgt Schultz (IRE)**[13] 7574 6-9-3 93 .... LPKeniry 9 42
(J S Moore) *hld up towards rr: rdn 3f out: sn struggling* 20/1

6005 8 4 1/2 **Alpen Glen**[27] 7393 3-8-6 87 .... GregFairley 7 28
(M Johnston) *led over 10f out tl over 3f out: wknd qckly wl over 2f out* 16/1

5000 9 43 **Ladies Best**[13] 7293 5-8-12 88 .... TomEaves 2 —
(B Ellison) *led over 1f: prom: hung lft and lost pl over 5f out: t.o fnl 4f* 22/1

2m 35.85s (-5.25) **Going Correction** -0.025s/f (Stan)
WFA 3 from 4yo+ 5lb 9 Ran SP% 120.1
Speed ratings (Par 109): **116,114,113,109,104 100,90,87,59**
toteswingers: 1&2 £10.20, 1&3 £10.90, 2&3 £5.00 CSF £81.80 CT £255.08 TOTE £5.40: £2.40, £3.40, £2.00; EX 114.10 Place 6: £57.60 Place 5: £46.28 .
Owner Mick White **Bred** Hh The Aga Khans Studs Sc **Trained** Capranny, Co. Meath

FOCUS
A valuable handicap in which the gallop was sound and the winner raced in the centre in the straight. The first three finished clear and this is solid form.

NOTEBOOK
Dirar(IRE) ◆ was well backed throughout the day and this strong traveller ran as well as he ever has done on the Flat to win with a bit in hand over what is probably his optimum distance. Life will be tougher after reassessment but he may be capable of better on Polytrack. He also progressed into a useful hurdler in summer and will be interesting back in that sphere when the ground isn't testing. (op 7-2)
Mister New York(USA) proved suited by the return to 1m4f and was not far off his best in this valuable handicap, despite showing a tendency to drift left in the straight. He is fairly unexposed over this trip and, although vulnerable to the more progressive sorts from this mark, there may be a bit more to come. (tchd 25-1)
Dance The Star(USA), who looked unlucky over course and distance last time, was beaten with no apparent excuses this time. Although he has not won for over a year, he's a reliable type on Polytrack who pulled clear of the rest and should continue to give a good account on this surface. (tchd 4-1)
Nanton(USA), who thrived on turf in autumn, is currently on a lower all-weather mark than turf, but is still 14lb higher than his last all-weather run and failed to translate that recent improvement back to sand. He only raced once on sand last winter and it won't be a surprise if he is put away now. (tchd 7-2)
Laterly(IRE) was closely matched with Dance The Star on a previous course and distance run but was a fair way below that level after helping to force a generous pace. His form has been patchy since his last win but he will always be seen to best effect when allowed an uncontested lead. His rider reported he hung left. (op 11-1)
Coeur De Lionne(IRE) had run up to his best at Lingfield last time but, although he got a decent gallop this time, he turned in a laboured effort on his first start at this course and proved disappointing. He is probably worth another chance. (op 5-1 tchd 4-1)
Alpen Glen, back up in trip, helped to force a generous pace but dropped out as though something was amiss once headed. She looks one to have reservations about at present. (op 10-1)
T/Plt: £22.10 to a £1 stake. Pool: £107,168.57. 3,535.03 winning tickets. T/Qpdt: £18.50 to a £1 stake. Pool: £8,189.20. 327.40 winning tickets. KH

7705 SOUTHWELL (L-H)
Saturday, December 12

OFFICIAL GOING: Standard
Wind: Virtually nil Weather: Fine and dry

7721 EUROPEAN BREEDERS' FUND MAIDEN STKS 1m (F)
11:35 (11:35) (Class 5) 2-Y-0 £3,885 (£1,156; £577; £288) Stalls Low

Form RPR

1 **Sweet Child O'Mine** 2-8-12 0 .... FrancisNorton 5 69+
(R C Guest) *dwlt and in rr: hdwy over 3f out: chsd ldrs 2f out and sn rdn: styd on ent fnl f to ld last 100yds* 100/1

3432 2 1 1/4 **Master Leon**[7] 7638 2-9-3 70 .... (v) TomEaves 1 69
(B Smart) *led: rdn along over 2f out: drvn over 1f out: hdd and no ex last 100yds* 11/4[2]

6 3 3 **Claddagh**[89] 5951 2-9-3 0 .... JoeFanning 3 62
(M Johnston) *chsd ldr: rdn along over 2f out: drvn and edgd lft over 1f out: sn one pce* 7/2[3]

00 4 1 1/2 **Leader Of The Land (IRE)**[17] 7522 2-9-3 0 .... LPKeniry 6 59
(D R Lanigan) *in rr: hdwy over 2f out: rdn appr last: sn no imp* 20/1

52 5 5 **Oriental Scot**[21] 7491 2-9-3 0 .... RobertHavlin 2 48
(W Jarvis) *trckd ldng pair: hdwy 3f out: rdn along over 2f out: drvn wl over 1f out and sn wknd* 1/1[1]

0 6 20 **My Grand Duke (USA)**[14] 7580 2-9-3 0 .... ShaneKelly 4 4
(J A Osborne) *chsd ldrs: rdn along 3f out: sn wknd and heavily eased over 1f out* 22/1

1m 40.9s (-2.80) **Going Correction** -0.325s/f (Stan) 6 Ran SP% 109.0
Speed ratings (Par 96): **101,99,96,95,90 70**
toteswingers: 1&2 £6.70, 1&3 £8.90, 2&3 £1.60 CSF £336.19 TOTE £25.00: £17.50, £1.70; EX 91.20.
Owner EERC **Bred** A Reid **Trained** Stainforth, S Yorks

FOCUS
An ordinary-looking maiden in which two horses were subject to jockey changes. The only filly in the race made a successful start and the runner-up sets the level.

NOTEBOOK
Sweet Child O'Mine, the first foal of a dam who was placed over sprint distances, and ridden by Norton in place of Paul Eddery, belied her odds by winning in good style. The further she went the better she looked, and presumably, despite the lack of interest she attracted at the sales, can be expected to improve for this experience. (op 40-1)
Master Leon, with an official mark of 70, had run on the Fibresand twice previously and the visor he wore last time was retained. He went off in front again before being worn down inside the final furlong. (op 5-2)
Claddagh, absent since running at Redcar in mid-September, is a half-brother to a smart filly Bahia Breeze but is not showing anywhere near the same ability as his relation. (tchd 10-3 and 4-1)
Leader Of The Land(IRE) had been well beaten in two previous starts but hinted at a little better in this, staying on well in the latter stages. (op 25-1)
Oriental Scot, a brother to Mannlichen, who is currently doing well on Polytrack, tracked the leader in the early stages before finding little off the home bend. A big sort, he may still need time to strengthen up. (op 5-4)

My Grand Duke(USA) Official explanation: jockey said colt had no more to give

7722 BET TOTEPOOL AT TOTESPORT.COM NURSERY 1m (F)
12:05 (12:05) (Class 6) (0-65,65) 2-Y-O **£2,047** (£604; £302) **Stalls** Low

Form RPR

0055 **1** **Wedding Dream**[25] 7419 2-8-1 **45** FrancisNorton 8 56
(K A Ryan) *cl up on inner: led 3f out: rdn along 2f out: edgd lft and swished tail over 1f out: sn drvn: clr whn hung bdly rt ins fnl f: kpt on* **20/1**

041 **2** *6* **Tealing**[18] 7501 2-9-2 **60** GrahamGibbons 10 58
(R C Guest) *led: pushed along and hdd 3f out: rdn over 2f out: sn drvn and ev ch tl wknd appr fnl f* **9/2**[3]

4034 **3** *hd* **Honest Broker (IRE)**[21] 7494 2-9-4 **62** JoeFanning 1 59
(M Johnston) *midfield: hdwy 1/2-way: rdn along 3f out: drvn to chse ldng pair wl over 1f out: kpt on same pce ins fnl f* **7/2**[2]

4000 **4** *3* **Second Brook (IRE)**[12] 7597 2-9-0 **58** AdamKirby 2 49
(R Hollinshead) *towards rr: hdwy over 2f out: sn rdn and kpt on ins fnl f: nvr nr ldrs* **10/1**

162 **5** *2* **Push Me (IRE)**[40] 7210 2-9-7 **65** EddieAhern 5 51
(John A Quinn, Ire) *trckd ldrs: hdwy 3f out: rdn along over 2f our: sn drvn and btn* **15/8**[1]

0005 **6** *6* **Man In The Mirror (IRE)**[46] 7098 2-8-11 **55** (v) JerryO'Dwyer 9 28
(P L Gilligan) *chsd ldrs on outer: rdn along wl over 2f out: sn edgd lft and wknd* **16/1**

0063 **7** *3 3/4* **She's My Rock (IRE)**[12] 7597 2-8-9 **53** LPKeniry 4 18
(S Kirk) *prom: pused along after 3f: sn lost pl and bhd* **6/1**

0565 **8** *1/2* **Vittachi**[54] 6901 2-8-3 **47** (b[1]) JimmyQuinn 6 11
(J D Bethell) *s.i.s: a bhd* **16/1**

0000 **9** *4* **Woodenitbenice**[113] 5224 2-8-1 **45** JamieMackay 7 —
(D Shaw) *a in rr* **100/1**

3300 **10** *2 1/4* **Ba Jetstream**[17] 7514 2-8-6 **50** AndrewElliott 3 —
(F Jordan) *chsd ldrs: rdden along 1/2-way: sn drvn and wknd* **66/1**

1m 40.78s (-2.92) **Going Correction** -0.325s/f (Stan) **10** Ran SP% **117.6**
Speed ratings (Par 94): **101,95,94,91,89 83,80,79,75,73**
toteswingers: 1&2 £9.80, 1&3 £14.40, 2&3 £4.80 CSF £107.99 CT £412.04 TOTE £20.60: £5.10, £1.60, £2.00; EX 63.00 Trifecta £133.40 Part won. Pool: £180.33 - 0.20 winning units..
Owner J H Henderson **Bred** Lofts Hall Stud **Trained** Hambleton, N Yorks

FOCUS
Most of these came into this contest in form, so the form should be sound for the level despite the long-priced winner, with the third the best guide.

NOTEBOOK
Wedding Dream, running in her first handicap, produced her best effort last time in a 7f seller and progressed again from that run with a clear-cut success, despite showing signs of temperament inside the final furlong. Official explanation: trainer's rep said, regarding apparent improvement in form, that the filly had improved and benefited from a step up in trip. (tchd 18-1)
Tealing, also running in a handicap for the first time and having his first run for Richard Guest, broke quickly from a wide draw and duelled with the winner from the start. He did not get home as well as Wedding Dream, and the step up in trip may have stretched him. (op 7-2 tchd 5-1)
Honest Broker(IRE) took a while to find his stride by stayed on strongly. He shapes like a horse that needs a good test.
Second Brook(IRE) was really struggling in the first couple of furlongs but passed plenty of his rivals up the home straight. (op 16-1)
Push Me(IRE), having his first start for this trainer, was prominent from the off and looked to be travelling well rounding the final bend. However, he found little off the bridle and may not have stayed 1m on this surface. (op 2-1 tchd 5-2 in places)
Man In The Mirror(IRE) took a lot of pushing and dropped away up the home straight. (op 20-1)
She's My Rock(IRE) raced prominently on the run to the bend but was soon ridden along and posed little threat under pressure. (op 11-2)

7723 BET ON TODAY'S FOOTBALL AT TOTESPORT.COM (S) STKS 1m (F)
12:40 (12:40) (Class 6) 3-Y-0+ **£2,047** (£604; £302) **Stalls** Low

Form RPR

0100 **1** **Ten Pole Tudor**[1] 7718 4-9-7 57 (p) LiamJones 3 62
(R A Harris) *s.i.s: sn in tch on outer: hdwy 3f out: rdn over 2f out: drvn and edgd lft over 1f out: styd on to ld ins fnl f: hld on wl towards fin* **18/1**

5433 **2** *hd* **Celtic Step**[8] 7631 5-9-1 62 TomEaves 4 56
(P D Niven) *towards rr: hdwy wl over 2f out: rdn to chse ldrs over 1f out: drvn and put hd in air ent fnl f: sn ev ch tl hung rt and no ex nrfin* **2/1**[2]

3563 **3** *3/4* **Davana**[14] 7581 3-8-6 47 KellyHarrison(3) 2 49
(W J H Ratcliffe) *chsd ldrs: rdn along over 2f out: drvn wl over 1f out: styd on ins fnl f: ev ch whn n.m.r and one pce towards fin* **20/1**

0001 **4** *nk* **Jonnie Skull (IRE)**[4] 7678 3-9-6 59 (vt) JerryO'Dwyer 7 59+
(P S McEntee) *cl up: led wl over 2f out: rdn wl over 1f out: drvn ent fnl f: sn hdd andwkng whn n.m.r towards fin* **15/8**[1]

/000 **5** *6* **Tango Step (IRE)**[44] 7136 9-9-1 43 (p) DNolan 5 40
(D Carroll) *chsd ldrs: rdn along 3f out: drvn over 2f out and sn no imp* **50/1**

3362 **6** *18* **United Nations**[270] 858 8-9-2 74 (b) GaryBartley(5) 1 4
(N Wilson) *sn led: rdn along over 3f out: hdd wl over 2f out and sn wknd* **3/1**[3]

0- **7** *12* **Fiveonthreeforjd**[448] 6114 4-8-10 0 PaulPickard(5) 6 —
(W J H Ratcliffe) *a towards rr* **25/1**

0000 **8** *12* **Chinese Profit**[23] 5544 4-9-1 45 AdamKirby 8 —
(G C Bravery) *dwlt: sn prom: rdn along over 3f out and sn wknd* **50/1**

1m 41.85s (-1.85) **Going Correction** -0.325s/f (Stan)
WFA 3 from 4yo+ 1lb **8** Ran SP% **110.9**
Speed ratings (Par 101): **96,95,95,94,88 70,58,46**
toteswingers: 1&2 £5.40, 1&3 £9.70, 2&3 £4.30 CSF £51.22 TOTE £15.80: £4.40, £1.10, £2.30; EX 40.70 TRIFECTA Not won..There was no bid for the winner.
Owner Mrs Jan Adams **Bred** Rockdown Investments **Trained** Earlswood, Monmouths

FOCUS
A competitive seller. The race changed shape dramatically up the home straight. The third sets the standard with the winner a slight improver.
Ten Pole Tudor Official explanation: trainer's rep said, regarding apparent improvement in form, that the gelding appeared to benefit from a true-run race and drop in class to a seller.
Chinese Profit Official explanation: vet said gelding bled from the nose

7724 BET ON LIVE SPORT AT TOTESPORT.COM H'CAP 1m 4f (F)
1:10 (1:10) (Class 5) (0-75,83) 3-Y-0+ **£2,729** (£806; £403) **Stalls** Low

Form RPR

4556 **1** **Profit's Reality (IRE)**[155] 3797 7-9-7 **75** AdamKirby 4 83+
(M J Attwater) *trckd ldrs: chsd ldr after 4f: led 3f out: rdn 2f out: drvn and styd on wl ins fnl f* **4/1**[3]

4006 **2** *1 1/4* **Maslak (IRE)**[36] 7272 5-9-5 **73** ChrisCatlin 7 78
(P W Hiatt) *led: rdn along and hdd 3f out: drvn over 2f out: kpt on u.p* **12/1**

0453 **3** *3/4* **Daaweitza**[12] 7598 6-9-4 **72** (v[1]) DaneO'Neill 3 76
(B Ellison) *hld up in rr: hdwy on inner wl over 2f out: rdn wl over 1f out: drvn to chse ldng pair ent fnl f: kpt on* **11/4**[2]

3401 **4** *2 1/2* **Ibrox (IRE)**[46] 7093 4-9-5 **73** (p) GrahamGibbons 2 73
(A D Brown) *trckd ldrs: effrt 3f out and sn rdn: drvn and kpt on same pce fnl 2f* **5/2**[1]

10-0 **5** *1* **Princess Lomi (IRE)**[3] 7684 4-9-3 **71** GregFairley 6 69
(Andrew Heffernan, Ire) *trckd ldrs: rdn along over 3f out: drvn over 2f out and sn one pce* **6/1**

2 **6** *41* **Naxox (FR)**[14] 7578 8-9-1 **69** TonyCulhane 1 2
(George Baker) *cl up: rdn along over 4f out: sn lost pl and bhd fnl 2f* **15/2**

2m 36.83s (-4.17) **Going Correction** -0.325s/f (Stan)
WFA 3 from 4yo+ 5lb **6** Ran SP% **109.0**
Speed ratings (Par 103): **100,99,98,97,96** —
toteswingers: 1&2 £6.80, 1&3 £2.60, 2&3 £7.00 CSF £43.36 TOTE £5.20: £2.10, £6.90; EX 36.20.
Owner Roger Milner & Charles Bamford **Bred** Michael Munnelly **Trained** Epsom, Surrey

FOCUS
This looked a decent race, but it was weakened when the multiple winner Shadows Lengthen, who had won the previous day, was taken out during the morning with a self certificate. The form is best rated through the third.

7725 BET IN PLAY AT TOTESPORT.COM MAIDEN STKS 1m 4f (F)
1:45 (1:45) (Class 5) 3-4-Y-0 **£3,412** (£1,007; £504) **Stalls** Low

Form RPR

-402 **1** **Lava Steps (USA)**[18] 7504 3-9-3 70 TonyCulhane 6 73+
(P T Midgley) *trckd ldr: cl up 4f out: led wl over 2f out: sn rdn and hdd wl over 1f out: drvn and rallied to regain ld ins fnl f: kpt on gamely* **4/7**[1]

0202 **2** *3/4* **In Secret**[15] 7550 3-8-12 69 EddieAhern 7 67
(J L Dunlop) *t.k.h: trckd ldng pair: hdwy 3f out: led wl over 1f out and sn rdn: drvn and hdd ins fnl f: no ex last 75yds* **5/2**[2]

6 **3** *2 1/2* **Sure Fire (GER)**[29] 7367 4-9-8 0 TPQueally 2 68
(B J Curley) *led: rdn along 4f out: hdd wl over 2f out: sn drvn and kpt on same pce* **7/1**[3]

00 **4** *27* **Aquapark**[57] 6823 3-9-3 0 JimmyQuinn 5 25
(R Craggs) *chsd ldrs: rdn along 1/2-way: sn lost pl and outpcd fnl 3f* **50/1**

5 *10* **Frankie Falco**[31] 3-9-3 0 AdamKirby 4 9
(G Fierro) *dwlt and in rr: sme hdwy and in tch 5f out: rdn along and wknd wl over 3f out* **66/1**

2m 39.57s (-1.43) **Going Correction** -0.325s/f (Stan)
WFA 3 from 4yo 5lb **5** Ran SP% **108.2**
Speed ratings (Par 103): **91,90,88,70,64**
toteswingers: 1&2 £2.40, 1&3 not won, 2&3 not won CSF £2.13 TOTE £1.50: £1.10, £1.30; EX 2.00.
Owner Townville C C Racing Club **Bred** Mr & Mrs G Middlebrook **Trained** Westow, N Yorks

FOCUS
A weak maiden best rated through the winner.

7726 DINE IN THE PANTRY RESTAURANT H'CAP (DIV I) 7f (F)
2:20 (2:20) (Class 6) (0-55,55) 3-Y-0+ **£1,104** (£1,104; £252) **Stalls** Low

Form RPR

2430 **1** **Headache**[13] 7591 4-8-13 **52** (bt) DaneO'Neill 3 60
(B W Duke) *slt ld on inner: rdn along over 2f out: drvn over 1f out: edgd rt ins fnl f: kpt on: jnd on line* **11/4**[1]

2605 **1** *dht* **Convince (USA)**[25] 7424 8-8-11 **55** (p) RossAtkinson(5) 5 63
(J L Flint) *towards rr: hdwy on inner 3f out: swtchd markedly rt to outer rail over 2f out and sn rdn: str run ent fnl f: jnd ldr on line* **9/1**

3353 **3** *1 3/4* **Kinigi (IRE)**[4] 7681 3-8-11 **55** (p) AndrewHeffernan(5) 2 58
(R A Harris) *chsd ldrs: hdwy 2f out: rdn to chse ldr ent fnl f: sn drvn and kpt on same pce* **7/2**[2]

1010 **4** *3/4* **Straight Face (IRE)**[30] 7349 5-8-13 **55** (p) KellyHarrison(3) 4 56
(Miss Gay Kelleway) *hld up and bhd: hdwy on wd outside over 2f out: rdn and styng on whn swtchd lft ent fnl f: fin wl* **11/1**

4363 **5** *1 1/4* **Rockfield Lodge (IRE)**[30] 7348 4-8-12 **51** (v[1]) StephenDonohoe 6 49
(Ian Williams) *cl up: rdn and ev ch 2f out tl drvn and wknd ent fnl f* **4/1**[3]

-430 **6** *1* **Camerooney**[22] 7466 6-8-7 **49** ow1 (e[1]) MartinLane(3) 12 44
(B Ellison) *in tch on outer: rdn along whn hmpd over 2f out: sn drvn and kpt on appr fnl f: nrst fin* **10/1**

6000 **7** *1/2* **Angle Of Attack (IRE)**[120] 5008 4-8-11 **50** GrahamGibbons 11 44
(A D Brown) *cl up: rdn along wl over 2f out: sn drvn and wknd wl over 1f out* **20/1**

4050 **8** *1/2* **Cause For Applause (IRE)**[12] 7599 3-8-11 **50** ChrisCatlin 9 42
(R Craggs) *chsd ldrs: rdn along over 2f out: sn drvn and one pce* **14/1**

050 **9** *11* **Distant Dreamer (USA)**[88] 5965 3-8-7 **46** oh1 LiamJones 7 9
(Rae Guest) *a in rr* **50/1**

0-00 **10** *hd* **Safaseef (IRE)**[41] 7200 4-8-7 **46** (v[1]) JimmyQuinn 10 8
(K A Morgan) *a in rr* **28/1**

0600 **11** *nk* **Marina's Ocean**[29] 7374 5-8-11 **50** ow3 (t) AmirQuinn 8 11
(S R Bowring) *chsd ldrs: rdn along 1/2-way: sn wknd* **25/1**

1m 27.83s (-2.47) **Going Correction** -0.325s/f (Stan) **11** Ran SP% **117.0**
Speed ratings (Par 101): **101,101,99,98,96 95,95,94,81,81 81**WIN: Convince £4.80, Headache £1.30 PL:Convince £2.70, Headache £1.40 Kinigi £2.40; EX: C/H £13.70 H/C £24.40; CSF: £13.45; TRICAST: C/H/Kingi £52.42 H/C/K£44.26 toteswingers: Convince&3 £11.20, C/Headache £6.20, H&3 £4.10, £27Owner Brendan W Duke Racing Trifecta £Bred Bearstone Stud Trained.
Owner M Matthews (Mid-Glamorgan) **Bred** Juddmonte Farms Inc **Trained** Kenfig Hill, Bridgend

FOCUS
Most of the field are in-and-out performers, so there is no guarantee this form will work out. The form looks sound with the third rated close to his best.

7727 DINE IN THE PANTRY RESTAURANT H'CAP (DIV II) 7f (F)
2:55 (2:56) (Class 6) (0-55,55) 3-Y-0+ **£1,706** (£503; £252) **Stalls** Low

Form RPR

0000 **1** **Hard Ball**[38] 7246 3-8-9 **48** (v) FrancisNorton 11 57
(M Quinn) *trckd ldrs: hdwy 3f out: chal over 2f out: rdn to ld over 1f out: drvn and edgd lft ins fnl f: kpt on wl towards fin* **8/1**

0443 **2** *1 1/2* **Royal Keva (IRE)**[18] 7500 3-9-2 **55** (b) GrahamGibbons 9 60
(A D Brown) *prom: effrt and cl up wl over 2f out: sn rdn and ev ch tl drvn and one pce ins fnl f* **11/4**[1]

3020 **3** *1/2* **Positivity**[30] 7353 3-8-11 **50** (p) TomEaves 1 54
(B Smart) *slt ld on inner: rdn along over 2f out: sn drvn and hdd over 1f out: kpt on same pce ins fnl f* **16/1**

060 **4** *1 1/4* **Special Cuvee**[42] 7173 3-9-2 **55** (v) RobertHavlin 3 56
(A B Haynes) *dwlt and sn pushed along in rr: rdn along 3f out: hdwy on outer 2f out: sn drvn and hung lft ent fnl f: kpt on: nrst fin* **5/1**[3]

5402 **5** *1 ¼* **Louisiade (IRE)**[6] 7652 8-8-7 **46** oh1................(p) ChrisCatlin 6 43
(R C Guest) *towards rr: effrt and rdn along 1/2-way: drvn over 2f out: n.m.r over 1f out: plugged on ins fnl f* **7/2**[2]

0200 **6** *nk* **Bertbrand**[29] 7371 4-9-0 **53**................ SJCraine 4 49
(I W McInnes) *cl up: rdn along over 3f out: drvn 2f out and grad wknd* **16/1**

3044 **7** *shd* **Sairaam (IRE)**[12] 7600 3-8-12 **51**................ KirstyMilczarek 5 47
(C Smith) *t.k.h in midfield: effrt 3f out and sme hdwy wl over 2f out: sn rdn and n.d* **6/1**

0360 **8** *2 ¾* **Top Flight Splash**[15] 7561 3-8-12 **51**................(v) LiamJones 7 44
(Mrs G S Rees) *chsd ldrs: rdn along 3f out: drvn 2f out: wkng whn n.m.r over 1f out* **9/1**

0050 **9** *4* **Toballa**[17] 7521 4-8-7 **46** oh1................(tp) JimmyQuinn 10 24
(P Leech) *dwlt: a towards rr* **20/1**

543 **10** *nk* **Ride A White Swan**[16] 7533 4-8-7 **46**................ JamieMackay 2 23
(D Shaw) *t.k.h: chsd ldrs on inner: rdn 3f out: sn wknd* **20/1**

-500 **11** *22* **Iron Max (IRE)**[192] 2593 3-8-4 **48**................ RossAtkinson(5) 8 —
(Tom Dascombe) *a towards rr: rdn along and rn wd st: bhd after* **16/1**

1m 28.0s (-2.30) **Going Correction** -0.325s/f (Stan) **11** Ran SP% **128.1**
Speed ratings (Par 101): **100,98,97,96,94 94,94,91,86,86 61**
toteswingers: 1&2 £7.30, 1&3 £13.20, 2&3 £5.70 CSF £33.09 CT £368.25 TOTE £16.90: £3.20, £1.60, £3.50; EX 44.70 TRIFECTA Not won..
Owner Henry, Blake, Newby, Hesketh & Caypon **Bred** Hascombe And Valiant Studs **Trained** Newmarket, Suffolk
■ A 19,088/1 treble from just three rides for Franny Norton.
■ Stewards' Enquiry : Robert Havlin caution: careless riding.

FOCUS
The early pace appeared to be modest, which meant the three towards the front turning in fought out the finish. However, the winning time was fairly good and the form looks sound enough for the grade with the runner-up the best guide.

7728 SOUTHWELL-RACECOURSE.CO.UK H'CAP — 1m (F)
3:30 (3:31) (Class 6) (0-65,64) 3-Y-0+ **£2,047** (£604; £302) **Stalls** Low

Form RPR

0033 **1** **General Tufto**[4] 7677 4-8-13 **58**................(b) KirstyMilczarek 3 71
(C Smith) *trckd ldrs: smooth hdwy 3f out: led 2f out: clr whn edgd lft ent fnl f: kpt on strly* **13/8**[1]

4623 **2** *4 ½* **Wing Diva (IRE)**[36] 7272 4-8-13 **58**................ TomEaves 2 61
(B Smart) *prom: led over 3f out: rdn and hdd 2f out: drvn and hung rt appr last: one pce* **5/1**[2]

0616 **3** *nk* **Naomh Geileis (USA)**[18] 7506 4-9-5 **64**................(b) JoeFanning 7 66
(M Johnston) *in rr: hdwy wl over 2f out: rdn to chse ldng pair wl over 1f out: sn drvn and kpt on same pce* **13/8**[1]

51- **4** *6* **Greek Theatre (USA)**[389] 7088 4-9-5 **64**................ JerryO'Dwyer 1 52
(P S McEntee) *chsd ldrs on inner: rdn along wl over 2f out: sn outpcd* **11/1**[3]

15-0 **5** *2 ¼* **Starlight Gazer**[33] 7321 6-9-4 **63**................(vt) RobertHavlin 4 46
(J A Geake) *a towards rr* **18/1**

0400 **6** *hd* **Komreyev Star**[18] 7500 7-8-5 **50** oh4................(p) JimmyQuinn 8 33
(R E Peacock) *led: rdn along and hdd over 3f out: sn wknd* **33/1**

0400 **7** *1 ½* **Kingsmaite**[100] 5612 8-9-4 **63**................(b) AmirQuinn 6 42
(S R Bowring) *chsd ldrs on outer: rdn along 3f out and sn wknd* **22/1**

430 **8** *3 ¾* **If You Knew Suzy**[204] 2246 4-8-12 **60**................ KellyHarrison(3) 5 30
(R E Barr) *prom: rdn along over 3f out: sn wknd* **16/1**

1m 40.12s (-3.58) **Going Correction** -0.325s/f (Stan) **8** Ran SP% **119.6**
Speed ratings (Par 101): **104,99,99,93,90 90,89,85**
toteswingers: 1&2 £2.50, 1&3 £1.60, 2&3 £2.70 CSF £11.25 CT £15.33 TOTE £2.40: £1.40, £1.70, £1.20; EX 10.30 Trifecta £34.30 Pool: £565.82 - 12.20 winning units. Place 6: £132.47, Place 5: £44.51.
Owner Phil Martin & Trev Sleath **Bred** Hascombe And Valiant Studs **Trained** Temple Bruer, Lincs

FOCUS
A very one-sided affair as soon as Kirsty Milczarek let General Tufto lengthen clear. The form is rated at a face value with the first three close to their marks.
T/Plt: £151.40 to a £1 stake. Pool: £38,358.36. 184.94 winning tickets. T/Qpdt: £16.90 to a £1 stake. Pool: £3,511.90. 153.10 winning tickets. JR

7713 WOLVERHAMPTON (A.W) (L-H)
Saturday, December 12

OFFICIAL GOING: Standard
Wind: Nil Weather: Fine

7729 BEST ODDS AT TOTESPORT.COM H'CAP — 7f 32y(P)
6:20 (6:20) (Class 5) (0-70,70) 3-Y-0+ **£2,520** (£2,520; £577; £288) **Stalls** High

Form RPR

3211 **1** **Kuanyao (IRE)**[21] 7479 3-9-2 **68**................ SteveDrowne 2 76
(P J Makin) *mde all: rdn and edgd rt ins fnl f: drvn out: jnd post* **11/4**[1]

0000 **1** *dht* **Forward Feline (IRE)**[42] 7191 3-8-10 **62**................ DavidProbert 5 70
(B Palling) *hld up: hdwy over 2f out: swtchd rt ent st: rdn wl over 1f out: all out to join ldr post* **33/1**

3305 **3** *1* **Defector (IRE)**[8] 7627 3-9-4 **70**................ GeorgeBaker 1 75
(W R Muir) *hld up in tch on ins: wnt 2nd wl over 1f out: sn rdn: kpt on ins fnl f* **9/2**[3]

-651 **4** *hd* **Sir George (IRE)**[12] 7596 4-8-13 **65**................ PaulDoe 3 69
(P D Evans) *hld up in tch: pushed along 2f out: rdn 1f out: kpt on* **3/1**[2]

2025 **5** *1 ¼* **Goodbye Cash (IRE)**[1] 7716 5-8-2 **59**................ AndrewHeffernan(5) 7 60
(P D Evans) *hld up in mid-div: pushed along over 2f out: rdn and hdwy 1f out: kpt on one pce* **14/1**

2655 **6** *1 ½* **Charles Parnell (IRE)**[5] 7673 6-8-11 **66**................ MichaelJStainton(3) 6 63
(S P Griffiths) *hld up: nt clr run on ins over 2f out: sn pushed along: hdwy over 1f out: rdn and one pce fnl f* **14/1**

00/5 **7** *1 ¼* **All Of Me (IRE)**[1] 7715 5-8-10 **62**................(tp) SJCraine 9 56
(Paul W Flynn, Ire) *s.i.s: hld up in rr: hdwy 2f out: rdn over 1f out: no imp fnl f* **40/1**

0030 **8** *1 ¼* **A Big Sky Brewing (USA)**[18] 7506 5-8-7 **64**................(b) DeanHeslop(5) 12 54
(T D Barron) *t.k.h: sn prom on outside: pushed along over 2f out: c wd st: wkng whn edgd lft over 1f out* **14/1**

6253 **9** *nk* **Cabernet Sauvignon**[28] 6128 3-9-0 **66**................(t) ShaneKelly 11 55+
(Gordon Elliott, Ire) *hld up in mid-div: lost pl and nt clr run over 2f out: c wd st: rdn and edgd lft 1f out: n.d* **33/1**

2221 **10** *¾* **Steel Stockholder**[50] 6997 3-8-13 **65**................ JimmyQuinn 4 52
(M Brittain) *chsd joint wnr: ev ch over 2f out: pushed along and lost 2nd wl over 1f out: sn wknd* **8/1**

0000 **11** *5* **Electric Warrior (IRE)**[7] 7643 6-9-1 **67**................ LPKeniry 10 41
(C R Dore) *hld up and bhd: c v wd st: rdn jst over 1f out: sn struggling* **33/1**

12 *6* **Refuse To Sell (IRE)**[157] 3755 4-9-4 **70**................ ChrisCatlin 8 28
(F Costello, Ire) *hld up in tch: pushed along and wknd wl over 1f out* **20/1**

1m 29.09s (-0.51) **Going Correction** +0.075s/f (Slow) **12** Ran SP% **117.0**
Speed ratings (Par 103): **105,105,103,103,102 100,99,97,97,96 90,83**WIN: Kuanyao 1.60, Forward Feline 23.60. PLACES: K 1.70, FF 10.70, Defector 1.50. CSF: K & FF £52.93, FF & K £58.33, TRICAST: K, FF & D 201.90, FF, K & D 254.85.EXACTA: K & FF £162.70, FF & K £90.80 toteswingers: K & FF £22.70. K & D £4.10, FF & D £26.50.27 CSF £Owner CT £D M Ahier TOTE £Bred: £Newlands House Stud, £Trained, £Ogbourne Maisey, Wilts.
Owner Derek And Jean Clee **Bred** D D And Mrs Jean P Clee **Trained** Tredodridge, Vale Of Glamorgan

FOCUS
Several of these went into the race in reasonably good form, and the judge was unable to split the first two. The third and fourth are rated close to recent marks and set the level.

7730 MAJESTICARE'S LUXURY MAIDEN STKS — 7f 32y(P)
6:50 (6:50) (Class 5) 3-Y-0+ **£2,729** (£806; £403) **Stalls** High

Form RPR

2 **1** **Watch Amigo (IRE)**[22] 7464 3-9-3 0................ AdamKirby 1 74+
(W R Swinburn) *hld up and bhd: hdwy over 3f out: pushed along and wnt 2nd wl over 1f out: rdn to ld and edgd lft ins fnl f: r.o* **5/2**[2]

2 *1* **Midnight Strider (IRE)** 3-9-3 0................ RichardKingscote 4 71+
(Tom Dascombe) *sn wl in rr: pushed along over 4f out: sme hdwy over 2f out: swtchd rt wl over 1f out: r.o wl ins fnl f: nt rch wnr* **17/2**

2 **3** *2 ½* **Tejime**[22] 7459 3-9-3 0................ RobertHavlin 6 64
(J H M Gosden) *led: rdn over 1f out: hdd ins fnl f: no ex* **13/8**[1]

0040 **4** *½* **Hold The Star**[5] 7671 3-8-8 **54** ow1................ AnnStokell(5) 2 59
(Miss A Stokell) *broke wl: sn lost pl: hld up: pushed along and sme prog over 2f out: rdn over 1f out: one pce* **66/1**

2-40 **5** *1* **Luckydolly (IRE)**[1] 7715 3-8-12 60................ ChrisCatlin 7 55
(F Costello, Ire) *in rr: sme prog on outside over 2f out: rdn wl over 1f out: no imp fnl f* **16/1**

06- **6** *3 ¼* **Bravalto**[399] 7240 3-9-3 0................ TomEaves 5 52
(B Smart) *chsd ldrs: rdn 4f out: wknd 2f out* **20/1**

3223 **7** *5* **Passkey**[14] 7576 3-8-12 75................(b[1]) StephenDonohoe 9 33
(Sir Mark Prescott) *sn chsng ldr: pushed along 3f out: rdn and lost 2nd wl over 1f out: wknd ent fnl f* **4/1**[3]

0 **8** *12* **Nanny Doe (IRE)**[28] 7401 3-8-12 0................(b[1]) DJMoran 8 —
(Lee Smyth, Ire) *plld hrd: prom tl pushed along and wknd 3f out* **100/1**

06 **9** *3* **Espresso Steps (USA)**[14] 7576 3-8-7 0................ AndrewHeffernan(5) 3 —
(P Howling) *hld up in mid-div: pushed along and struggling over 3f out: sn bhd* **100/1**

1m 29.69s (0.09) **Going Correction** +0.075s/f (Slow) **9** Ran SP% **111.3**
Speed ratings (Par 103): **102,100,98,97,96 92,86,73,69**
toteswingers: 1&2 £5.40, 1&3 £1.50, 2&3 £3.60 CSF £22.09 TOTE £4.00: £1.40, £2.80, £1.10; EX 30.60.
Owner Ian Harris & Tim Halpin **Bred** Thurso Limited **Trained** Aldbury, Herts

FOCUS
A decent gallop set the race up for the winner but a couple in behin can do better, although the form is limited by the proximity of the fourth.
Tejime Official explanation: jockey said gelding ran too freely

7731 OVER 50 INSTANT GAMES AT TOTESPORTGAMES.COM CLAIMING STKS — 1m 1f 103y(P)
7:20 (7:20) (Class 5) 2-Y-0 **£3,885** (£1,156; £577; £288) **Stalls** Low

Form RPR

3002 **1** **Glen Lass**[9] 7616 2-8-3 58 ow1................(b) ChrisCatlin 10 59
(J Pearce) *hld up in rr: pushed along over 3f out: hdwy on ins over 2f out: swtchd rt ent st: rdn to ld wl ins fnl f: r.o* **11/1**

4411 **2** *1* **Mary Helen**[21] 7474 2-8-10 61................ ShaneKelly 8 64
(W M Brisbourne) *hld up: hdwy on outside over 3f out: pushed along to ld over 1f out: rdn and hdd wl ins fnl f: nt qckn* **6/1**[3]

5631 **3** *5* **Tuscan King**[21] 7493 2-9-1 64................(b) J-PGuillambert 5 60
(P Howling) *a.p: wnt 2nd over 4f out: pushed along to ld jst over 2f out: rdn and hdd over 1f out: wknd wl ins fnl f* **5/1**[2]

504 **4** *½* **Sassanian (IRE)**[31] 7335 2-8-11 60................ IvaMilickova 7 55
(Jane Chapple-Hyam) *prom: chsd ldr over 6f out tl over 4f out: pushed along and lost pl over 3f out: styd on ins fnl f* **20/1**

0002 **5** *nk* **Land Of Plenty (IRE)**[21] 7493 2-7-11 41................ AndreaAtzeni(3) 6 43+
(E A L Dunlop) *hld up: hdwy on outside whn edgd lft and bmpd over 3f out: rdn wl over 2f out: sn wknd* **22/1**

0421 **6** *3 ¼* **Bubbly Braveheart (IRE)**[9] 7616 2-8-9 64................ EddieAhern 3 54+
(A Bailey) *hld up: bdly hmpd over 3f out: sn bhd: c v wd st: n.d after* **11/8**[1]

4 **7** *1 ¾* **Premium Charge**[60] 6756 2-8-7 0................(b[1]) JerryO'Dwyer 4 47+
(C A Dwyer) *s.i.s: hdwy on ins whn nt clr run 7f out: bdly hmpd over 3f out: sn bhd* **14/1**

8 *nk* **Tough Regime (IRE)**[15] 7564 2-8-4 0................(t) HayleyTurner 2 37
(Niall Moran, Ire) *led 1f: prom tl pushed along and wknd wl over 1f out* **13/2**

5400 **9** *12* **Bury St Edmunds**[31] 7334 2-8-5 48................ DavidProbert 9 19+
(A G Newcombe) *led after 1f: rdn and hdd jst over 2f out: wknd wl over 1f out* **66/1**

2m 4.00s (2.30) **Going Correction** +0.075s/f (Slow) **9** Ran SP% **112.0**
Speed ratings (Par 96): **92,91,86,86,85 83,81,81,70**
toteswingers: 1&2 £4.70, 1&3 £12.10, 2&3 £3.30 CSF £71.18 TOTE £11.50: £2.10, £1.80, £1.70; EX 58.50.
Owner Ian Bishop **Bred** Limestone And Tara Studs **Trained** Newmarket, Suffolk
■ Stewards' Enquiry : Andrea Atzeni three-day ban: careless riding (Dec 26-28)

FOCUS
A rough race, with interference around the first bend, and an absolute scrum towards the end of the back straight which effectively ended the chances of Bubbly Braveheart and Premium Charge. The early pace was poor, which was probably part of the problem and the form is anchored by the proximity of the fifth.

NOTEBOOK
Glen Lass, who bypassed all the trouble, swooped late to win even though the weak pace would not have been ideal for the hold-up running style she adopted here. This was her first win at the tenth attempt, but the return to a longer distance was a big help. (op 8-1)
Mary Helen has been doing well in claimers and this was a solid run in defeat. Only beaten by a rival who is largely unexposed at this trip, she came out of the race with credit and is one to consider again in similar company. (op 11-2 tchd 5-1 and 7-1)
Tuscan King did well considering this was a tougher race than the one he won here last time, but he is probably better at a slightly shorter trip anyway. (op 9-2 tchd 4-1)
Sassanian(IRE) has shown only minor ability and has yet to come close to living up to his £54,000 price tag. (op 22-1)

Land Of Plenty(IRE), like several others, suffered a bump, but it was self-inflicted and it cost her rider a suspension. She is modest and was lucky to find such a poor race when finishing second on her previous outing (op 25-1)
Bubbly Braveheart(IRE)'s attempt to maintain his recent improvement in fortune was hindered by the scrimmaging between the 3f and 4f poles. (op 7-4)
Premium Charge was hampered twice and eventually squeezed out of the contest. Highly tried in his only previous race, on turf, he is worth monitoring. (op 12-1 tchd 16-1)
Tough Regime(IRE), who showed promise over the Dundalk 7f last time, probably needs to be dropped back in trip. (op 15-2 tchd 8-1)

7732 RAYTON ELECTRICAL WHOLESALE LTD H'CAP (DIV I) 1m 4f 50y(P)
7:50 (7:50) (Class 6) (0-60,60) 3-Y-O+ **£2,047** (£604; £302) **Stalls** Low

Form RPR
600 **1** **Dazzling Begum**[7] 7642 4-9-8 **48**.......... RobertHavlin 1 56
(J Pearce) *led 1f: a.p: led wl over 1f out: rdn and edgd rt ins fnl f: drvn out* **10/1**
2 *1 1/2* **Mad Existence (IRE)**[16] 7544 5-8-6 **48**..........(b) SMGorey(3) 4 54
(Mrs Valerie Keatley, Ire) *a.p: pushed along over 2f out: rdn wl over 1f out: chsd wnr fnl f: nt qckn* **4/1**[1]
3 *3 1/4* **Torina (IRE)**[65] 6625 4-9-7 **60**.......... EddieAhern 7 61+
(M J Grassick, Ire) *hld up: pushed along and hung lft fr over 2f out: rdn and styd on to take 3rd wl ins fnl f* **4/1**[1]
0360 **4** *2 1/2* **Little Richard (IRE)**[12] 7594 10-9-2 **55**..........(p) AdamKirby 12 52
(M Wellings) *wnt lft s: set slow pce after 1f: hdd 8f out: prom: rdn 2f out: wknd ins fnl f* **9/2**[2]
1000 **5** *1 1/4* **Shanafarahan (IRE)**[22] 7461 4-9-7 **60**.......... JimmyQuinn 10 55
(K A Morgan) *t.k.h towards rr: gd hdwy to ld 8f out: rdn and hdd wl over 1f out: wknd ins fnl f* **14/1**
0000 **6** *3 1/4* **Action Girl**[13] 7587 4-9-3 **56**..........(p) HayleyTurner 2 46
(R M H Cowell) *hld up: rdn over 2f out: no hdwy* **8/1**
3525 **7** *2* **Carragold**[12] 7599 3-8-11 **55**.......... TomEaves 3 41
(M Brittain) *hld up towards rr: pushed along 7f out: struggling 3f out* **5/1**[3]
65 **8** *3/4* **Tabaahi (IRE)**[1] 7719 4-9-0 **53**..........(b) SJCraine 8 38
(Gordon Elliott, Ire) *hld up in tch: pushed along and wknd 2f out* **16/1**
0000 **9** *3 1/2* **Jojesse**[6] 7631 5-8-7 **46** oh1..........(b) SimonWhitworth 5 26
(W Storey) *hld up in rr: prog on outside over 3f out: wknd wl over 1f out* **50/1**
-000 **10** *13* **Warrior Nation (FR)**[47] 7065 3-9-2 **60**.......... DavidProbert 11 19
(A J Chamberlain) *swtchd lft sn after s: hld up in rr: pushed along wl over 2f out: sn struggling* **40/1**
11 *14* **Patriot Jack (IRE)**[15] 3646 4-8-7 **46** oh1..........(v[1]) ChrisCatlin 9 —
(T G McCourt, Ire) *a towards rr: lost tch over 5f out* **33/1**
2m 42.41s (1.31) **Going Correction** +0.075s/f (Slow)
WFA 3 from 4yo+ 5lb **11** Ran SP% **114.9**
Speed ratings (Par 101): **98,97,94,93,92 90,88,88,86,77 68**
toteswingers: 1&2 £8.80, 1&3 £17.30, 2&3 £4.60 CSF £48.13 CT £189.04 TOTE £10.10: £2.50, £1.50, £2.30; EX 60.90.
Owner Macniler Racing Partnership **Bred** Ian Bryant **Trained** Newmarket, Suffolk
FOCUS
The pace was woeful for the first 3f, and Shanafarahan's attempt to force a better tempo after that merely set the race up for others. The form is a bit muddling rated around the first three.
Warrior Nation(FR) Official explanation: jockey said gelding hung left

7733 RAYTON ELECTRICAL WHOLESALE LTD H'CAP (DIV II) 1m 4f 50y(P)
8:20 (8:20) (Class 6) (0-60,60) 3-Y-O+ **£2,047** (£604; £302) **Stalls** Low

Form RPR
2002 **1** **Altos Reales**[7] 7635 5-8-8 **47**.......... HayleyTurner 6 53+
(M J Scudamore) *hld up: swtchd rt and hdwy 2f out: hung lft fr over 1f out: led towards fin: r.o* **4/1**[2]
6-50 **2** *1* **Major Promise**[7] 7642 4-9-2 **55**.......... ShaneKelly 10 59
(Jane Chapple-Hyam) *t.k.h: prom: led over 8f out: 4 l clr whn pushed along wl over 1f out: rdn fnl f: hdd towards fin* **8/1**
005 **3** *1 1/4* **Active Asset (IRE)**[21] 7495 7-9-7 **60**.......... ChrisCatlin 3 62
(J A Glover) *hld up towards rr: hdwy on ins 2f out: rdn jst over 1f out: tk 3rd cl home* **8/1**
0603 **4** *shd* **Aspirational (IRE)**[29] 7369 3-8-11 **55**.......... DavidProbert 4 57
(B Palling) *led over 3f: prom: hit rail over 3f out: sn pushed along: rdn 2f out: no ex and lost 3rd cl home* **11/2**[3]
1-00 **5** *1* **Sunny Spells**[47] 7048 4-9-7 **60**.......... SaleemGolam 1 60
(S C Williams) *a.p: pushed along over 3f out: rdn wl over 1f out: styd on one pce fnl f* **11/8**[1]
/000 **6** *4* **Silent Lucidity (IRE)**[56] 6845 5-8-9 **48**.......... TomEaves 8 42
(P D Niven) *hld up in tch: pushed along over 3f out: rdn over 2f out: wknd over 1f out* **18/1**
0000 **7** *17* **Intavac Boy**[46] 7085 8-8-7 **46** oh1..........(p) JimmyQuinn 2 13
(S P Griffiths) *hld up in rr: pushed along over 3f out: rdn and struggling wl over 1f out* **66/1**
0000 **8** *3 1/2* **Treetops Hotel (IRE)**[57] 6817 10-8-7 **46** oh1.......... AndrewElliott 5 7
(L R James) *hld up towards rr: lost tch 3f out* **66/1**
2-30 **9** *11* **Magners Hill (IRE)**[1] 7718 5-9-3 **56**.......... LPKeniry 11 —
(Gerard Keane, Ire) *prom: rdn over 3f out: wknd 2f out* **20/1**
2m 40.86s (-0.24) **Going Correction** +0.075s/f (Slow)
WFA 3 from 4yo+ 5lb **9** Ran SP% **112.7**
Speed ratings (Par 101): **103,102,101,101,100 98,86,84,77**
toteswingers: 1&2 £6.50, 1&3 £5.70, 2&3 £8.30 CSF £34.19 CT £240.07 TOTE £5.00: £1.60, £2.40, £2.30; EX 32.20.
Owner F K Jennings **Bred** Goldford Stud And P E Clinton **Trained** Bromsash, Herefordshire
FOCUS
A solid gallop played into the hands of the winner but the form looks sound if limited.
Aspirational(IRE) Official explanation: jockey said gelding hung left

7734 £10 FREE PLAY AT TOTESPORTBINGO.COM H'CAP 1m 141y(P)
8:50 (8:50) (Class 4) (0-85,85) 3-Y-O+ **£5,046** (£1,510; £755; £377; £188) **Stalls** Low

Form RPR
6002 **1** **Inheritor (IRE)**[15] 7558 3-9-1 **82**.......... TomEaves 4 91
(B Smart) *led early: a.p: led over 1f out: sn rdn: edgd lft ins fnl f: drvn out* **9/4**[1]
3034 **2** *1* **Can Can Star**[11] 7607 6-9-3 **82**.......... ShaneKelly 1 88
(A W Carroll) *hld up: hdwy whn nt clr run and swtchd rt over 1f out: rdn and r.o ins fnl f: nt rch wnr* **10/3**[3]
150 **3** *1* **Laafet**[51] 6973 4-8-7 **72**.......... JimmyQuinn 3 76
(K A Morgan) *s.i.s: hld up in last: pushed along over 2f out: rdn and r.o to take 3rd ins fnl f* **9/1**
6513 **4** *1 3/4* **Just Bond (IRE)**[8] 7633 7-9-6 **85**.......... PJMcDonald 7 85
(G R Oldroyd) *hld up: hdwy over 3f out: rdn over 1f out: one pce* **3/1**[2]
0422 **5** *3* **Flores Sea (USA)**[30] 7350 5-8-12 **77**..........(b) PhillipMakin 5 70
(T D Barron) *sn led: rdn and hdd jst over 2f out: wknd ins fnl f* **11/2**
0260 **6** *1* **Mohathab (IRE)**[14] 7574 4-8-13 **78**..........(v[1]) SJCraine 6 69
(Tim Vaughan) *prom: wnt 2nd 7f out: jnd ldr over 4f out: led jst over 2f out: hdd over 1f out: sn rdn: wknd ins fnl f* **11/1**
1m 50.24s (-0.26) **Going Correction** +0.075s/f (Slow)
WFA 3 from 4yo+ 2lb **6** Ran SP% **112.6**
Speed ratings (Par 105): **104,103,102,100,98 97**
toteswingers: 1&2 £2.60, 1&3 £5.20, 2&3 £6.40 CSF £10.08 TOTE £3.10: £2.00, £1.90; EX 8.20.
Owner Richard Page **Bred** Dominic O'Neill And Julie White **Trained** Hambleton, N Yorks
FOCUS
They went quick, but the hectic pace did neither of the front-runners any good and they eventually filled the last two places. The placed horses set the standard.

7735 100% NEW PLAYER BONUS AT TOTESPORTCASINO.COM H'CAP 5f 216y(P)
9:20 (9:22) (Class 5) (0-75,74) 3-Y-O+ **£3,885** (£1,156; £577; £288) **Stalls** Low

Form RPR
010 **1** **Sarah's Art (IRE)**[106] 5404 6-9-2 **72**..........(t) AdamKirby 7 80
(Stef Liddiard) *in rr: pushed along over 3f out: hdwy over 1f out: str run and rdn to ld cl home* **17/2**
5110 **2** *1/2* **Fantasy Fighter (IRE)**[8] 7634 4-8-4 **60**.......... JimmyQuinn 4 66+
(J J Quinn) *s.i.s: hld up and bhd: swtchd rt and hdwy on outside 1f out: edgd lft ins fnl f: rdn and flashed tail towards fin: r.o to take 2nd post* **9/2**[3]
0413 **3** *shd* **Nacho Libre**[25] 7424 4-8-5 **61**..........(b) ChrisCatlin 6 67
(M W Easterby) *led over 1f: a.p: rdn wl over 1f out: led briefly wl ins fnl f: lost 2nd post* **5/2**[1]
3053 **4** *3/4* **Onceaponatime (IRE)**[5] 7673 4-8-12 **68**.......... JerryO'Dwyer 1 72
(M D Squance) *hld up: hdwy on ins to ld over 1f out: rdn and hdd wl ins fnl f* **11/4**[2]
3000 **5** *nk* **Elijah Pepper (USA)**[72] 6413 4-8-2 **63**.......... DeanHeslop(5) 8 66
(T D Barron) *sn w ldr: led over 4f out: rdn and hdd over 1f out: no ex wl ins fnl f* **10/1**
000 **6** *1 3/4* **Obe Brave**[16] 7543 6-8-4 **60**..........(b) DJMoran 2 57
(Lee Smyth, Ire) *a.p: rdn wl over 1f out: wknd ins fnl f* **16/1**
4650 **7** *1/2* **Carmenero (GER)**[42] 7179 6-8-1 **62**.......... SimonPearce(5) 5 57
(C R Dore) *hld up and bhd: pushed along over 2f out: c wd st: rdn whn hmpd wl over 1f out: n.d* **25/1**
0502 **8** *1/2* **Mandarin Spirit (IRE)**[45] 7119 9-8-13 **69**..........(b) PhillipMakin 3 63
(Miss L A Perratt) *hld up: hdwy over 2f out: sn pushed along: btn whn bmpd 1f out* **16/1**
0030 **9** *3 1/2* **Argentine (IRE)**[8] 7634 5-9-4 **74**..........(b) TomEaves 9 57
(J A McShane) *s.i.s: t.k.h: hdwy 4f out: wkng whn nt clr run 1f out* **16/1**
1m 14.32s (-0.68) **Going Correction** +0.075s/f (Slow) **9** Ran SP% **114.5**
Speed ratings (Par 103): **107,106,106,105,104 102,101,101,96**
toteswingers: 1&2 £5.10, 1&3 £4.30, 2&3 £2.80 CSF £46.15 CT £124.40 TOTE £9.40: £2.70, £1.70, £1.80; EX 56.20 Place 6: £51.83, Place 5: £26.35..
Owner ownaracehorse.co.uk (Shefford) **Bred** Newtownbarry House Stud **Trained** Great Shefford, Berks
FOCUS
A good sprint pace enabled the winner to get up from last place and the form looks solid rated around the placed horses to their marks.
T/Plt: £42.90 to a £1 stake. Pool: £105,768.16. 1,796.71 winning tickets. T/Qpdt: £19.20 to a £1 stake. Pool: £7,696.60. 295.20 winning tickets. KH

7698 KEMPTON (A.W) (R-H)
Sunday, December 13

OFFICIAL GOING: Standard
Wind: light, half against Weather: overcast, chilly

7736 BETFAIR MOBILE MAIDEN STKS 6f (P)
2:25 (2:26) (Class 5) 2-Y-O **£3,238** (£963; £481; £240) **Stalls** Low

Form RPR
2 **1** **Passion Overflow (USA)**[15] 7571 2-8-12 0.......... ShaneKelly 7 67+
(J Noseda) *dwlt and short of room sn after s: hld up in midfield: hdwy and rdn jst over 2f out: chal over 1f out: led jst ins fnl f: r.o wl u.p* **4/7**[1]
04 **2** *1 1/4* **Torres Del Paine**[15] 7571 2-9-3 0.......... MartinDwyer 9 66
(J C Fox) *led: rdn ent fnl 2f: hdd jst ins fnl f: kpt on same pce after* **22/1**
3 *nk* **Victory Ide Say (IRE)** 2-9-3 0.......... AdrianMcCarthy 1 67+
(P W Chapple-Hyam) *stdd s and dropped in bhd: hdwy and swtchd rt ent fnl f: r.o wl to go 3rd towards fin: nt rch ldrs* **40/1**
0 **4** *3/4* **Rathbawn Girl (IRE)**[68] 6563 2-8-12 0.......... JimmyQuinn 3 58
(Miss J Feilden) *s.i.s: hld up towards rr: hdwy towards inner jst over 2f out: edgd out lft over 1f out: chsd ldng trio ent fnl f: kpt on* **66/1**
5 *nk* **Clifton Bridge** 2-9-3 0.......... JimCrowley 10 62
(R M Beckett) *in tch in midfield: gd hdwy on inner ent fnl 2f: chsd ldng pair u.p over 1f out: one pce after: lost 2 pls fnl 100yds* **15/2**[2]
22 **6** *1 1/2* **Liberty Lady (IRE)**[15] 7582 2-8-12 0.......... DavidProbert 4 52
(D Donovan) *in tch in midfield on outer: rdn and effrt jst over 2f out: styd on one pce u.p fr over 1f out* **15/2**[2]
65 **7** *hd* **Cosimo de Medici**[15] 7571 2-9-3 0.......... SteveDrowne 6 57
(H Morrison) *s.i.s: towards rr: hdwy and nt clr run briefly wl over 1f out: plugged on same pce after* **12/1**[3]
8 *1/2* **Millden** 2-9-3 0..........(b[1]) DaneO'Neill 5 55
(H Candy) *s.i.s and sn pushed along towards rr: lost pl over 2f out: swtchd lft and rallied over 1f out: no imp fnl f* **16/1**
06 **9** *2* **Bertie Buckle (IRE)**[16] 7556 2-9-3 0.......... AdamKirby 12 49
(J R Gask) *chsd ldrs tl wknd u.p over 1f out* **50/1**
0 **10** *1 1/4* **Go Blue Chip**[195] 2533 2-9-3 0.......... FrankieMcDonald 8 47
(H Candy) *chsng ldrs: hanging lft and pushed along bnd over 4f out: lost pl jst over 2f out: no ch after* **40/1**
0 **11** *9* **Akubra (IRE)**[94] 5808 2-8-12 0.......... LPKeniry 2 14
(Norma Twomey) *pressed ldr tl over 2f out: sn struggling and btn whn n.m.r wl over 1f out: edgd lft and no ch after* **100/1**
1m 13.29s (0.19) **Going Correction** -0.025s/f (Stan) **11** Ran SP% **114.4**
Speed ratings (Par 96): **97,95,94,93,93 91,91,90,87,86 74**
toteswingers: 1&2 £3.50, 1&3 £11.20, 2&3 £29.10 CSF £21.98 TOTE £1.60: £1.02, £4.20, £11.70; EX 13.40.
Owner D Brennan **Bred** Swettenham Stud **Trained** Newmarket, Suffolk
FOCUS
Probably just a modest maiden. The winning time was very moderate and the winner did not need to match her debut effort.

NOTEBOOK
Passion Overflow(USA) had two of her rivals today behind her when creating a good impression at Lingfield on her first run and did not have to reproduce that effort to gain success. She was not quickly away and took a while to get to the front before grinding out victory. (tchd 8-13 and 4-6 in places)
Torres Del Paine wasn't beaten far when starting at 100/1 last time at Lingfield behind Passion Overflow, and proved that effort was not a fluke with another sound performance. A similar contest can be won with her. (op 20-1)
Victory Ide Say(IRE), who did not have a good draw, was undoubtedly the eyecatcher. Held up at the rear, he finished strongly and will surely be difficult to beat next time.
Rathbawn Girl(IRE) was seen travelling well 2f from home and stayed on nicely for pressure. She was not beaten too far and has ability. (op 80-1)
Clifton Bridge, a half-brother to a sprint winner, shaped nicely on his first outing and kept on up the inside rail after being switched there at the cut-away. (op 17-2 tchd 7-1)
Liberty Lady(IRE) was never far away but could not quicken in the latter stages. (op 8-1)
Millden is a half-brother to plenty of winners, including the top-class sprinter Kyllachy, but had blinkers fitted for his racecourse debut. He was not quickly away and showed signs of greenness under pressure, but did just enough to make him of some interest next time. (tchd 14-1)
Go Blue Chip Official explanation: jockey said gelding hung left throughout

7737 BETFAIR FRONT ROOM CLAIMING STKS 1m 4f (P)
2:55 (2:55) (Class 6) 3-Y-O £2,047 (£604; £302) Stalls Centre

Form RPR
2062 **1** **Fleur De'Lion (IRE)**[24] 7455 3-8-7 57 DavidProbert 2 62
(S Kirk) *hld up in last pl: rdn and qcknd on outer to ld 2f out: r.o wl and a holding runner-up after* **8/1**
2443 **2** ¾ **Shakalaka (IRE)**[16] 7550 3-9-6 76 (be[1]) GeorgeBaker 3 73
(G L Moore) *t.k.h early: hld up in tch: effrt to chal 2f out: chsd wnr and edgd lft after: kpt on but a hld* **2/1**[2]
5-42 **3** 3 **Leulahleulahlay**[29] 4599 3-8-13 75 (p) ShaneKelly 1 61
(Evan Williams) *sn chsng ldr: rdn over 3f out: drvn and outpcd jst over 2f out: plugged on same pce fnl f* **4/1**[3]
1253 **4** 1 ½ **Hector Spectre (IRE)**[4] 7695 3-8-13 65 PaulDoe 5 59
(P D Evans) *led at stdy gallop: hdd and rdn 2f out: outpcd by ldng pair over 1f out: lost 3rd ins fnl f* **6/4**[1]
556 **5** 22 **Persian Tomcat (IRE)**[25] 7426 3-8-9 47 (p) JimmyQuinn 4 19
(Miss J Feilden) *dwlt: sn chsng ldng pair: rdn 3f out: lost tch over 2f out* **40/1**

2m 35.06s (0.56) **Going Correction** -0.025s/f (Stan) **5** Ran SP% **106.9**
Speed ratings (Par 98): **97,96,94,93,78**
CSF £22.92 TOTE £8.90: £5.50, £3.50; EX 28.80.
Owner Mrs John Lee **Bred** Paget Bloodstock **Trained** Upper Lambourn, Berks

FOCUS
The pace was fairly modest as one would have expected in a small field, and only two mattered inside the final 2f.

7738 BETFAIR POKER H'CAP (DIV I) 6f (P)
3:25 (3:26) (Class 5) (0-70,70) 3-Y-O+ £2,266 (£674; £337; £168) Stalls Low

Form RPR
12 **1** **Absa Lutte (IRE)**[40] 7219 6-9-3 69 (t) SJCraine 6 78+
(Patrick Morris) *trckd ldrs: cruised upsides ldrs on bit 2f out: led jst over 1f out: rdn ins fnl f: a doing enough to hold runner-up* **11/2**[3]
0060 **2** nk **Resplendent Alpha**[32] 7337 5-9-3 69 JimmyQuinn 9 77
(P Howling) *stdd s: t.k.h: hld up towards rr: hdwy and swtchd lft over 1f out: chsd wnr ins fnl f: r.o but a being hld by wnr* **9/1**
3420 **3** 1 ¼ **Chosen One (IRE)**[31] 7355 4-8-10 62 TomEaves 4 66
(B Smart) *bmpd s: racd in midfield: rdn and effrt over 2f out: styd on u.p fnl f to go 3rd nr fin: nvr threatened wnr* **12/1**
1030 **4** ½ **Kheley (IRE)**[37] 7273 3-8-12 64 LiamJones 12 66
(W M Brisbourne) *in tch in midfield: rdn and effrt jst over 2f out: styd on to chse wnr briefly ins fnl f: no imp and lost 2 pls after* **16/1**
0300 **5** nk **Love You Louis**[9] 7634 3-9-1 67 ShaneKelly 8 70+
(J R Jenkins) *chsd ldr for 2f: short of room and lost pl wl over 1f out: swtchd lft and rallied u.p over 1f out: sltly hmpd ins fnl f: kpt on same pce* **33/1**
4321 **6** 1 ¾ **Lethal**[17] 7535 6-9-1 67 JimCrowley 7 63
(M J Scudamore) *led tl rdn and hdd jst over 2f out: led again over 1f out: sn hdd: wknd ins fnl f* **7/2**[1]
6203 **7** hd **Yankee Storm**[18] 7518 4-9-1 67 ChrisCatlin 1 62+
(H J Collingridge) *stdd s: hld up in last pair: plld out and effrt 2f out: styd on fnl f but nvr gng pce to rch ldrs* **13/2**
5100 **8** 1 ¼ **Speedy Guru**[22] 7496 3-9-4 70 DaneO'Neill 5 61
(H Candy) *dwlt and short of room sn after s: sn pushed along in rr: drvn and kpt on same pce fnl f 2f* **12/1**
6000 **9** ½ **White Shift (IRE)**[6] 7673 3-9-4 70 IanMongan 2 60
(P Howling) *hld up in last pair: rdn and effrt ent fnl 2f: nvr trbld ldrs* **50/1**
4014 **10** ½ **Efisio Princess**[32] 7337 6-9-0 69 NataliaGemelova(3) 11 57
(J E Long) *racd in midfield: rdn and unable qck over 2f out: n.d fr over 1f out* **11/1**
41 **11** 3 ½ **The Wee Chief (IRE)**[17] 7533 3-9-3 69 RichardSmith 3 46
(J C Fox) *racd keenly: chsd ldr 4f out: led over 2f out: rdn and rn green 2f out: hdd over 1f out: wknd qckly ent fnl f* **4/1**[2]

1m 11.99s (-1.11) **Going Correction** -0.025s/f (Stan) **11** Ran SP% **115.4**
Speed ratings (Par 103): **106,105,103,103,102 100,100,98,97,97 92**
toteswingers: 1&2 £7.40, 1&3 £17.10, 2&3 £26.70 CSF £53.26 CT £581.88 TOTE £7.10: £1.90, £3.00, £4.20; EX 55.40.
Owner D & D Coatings Ltd **Bred** Ian Amond **Trained** Tarporley, Cheshire

FOCUS
The two favourites disputed a strong pace and failed to get home.
The Wee Chief(IRE) Official explanation: jockey said gelding ran too freely

7739 BETFAIR POKER H'CAP (DIV II) 6f (P)
3:55 (3:55) (Class 5) (0-70,70) 3-Y-O+ £2,266 (£674; £337; £168) Stalls Low

Form RPR
0020 **1** **Sutton Veny (IRE)**[22] 7496 3-9-1 67 AdamKirby 9 75
(J R Gask) *mde virtually all: rdn and 2 l clr over 1f out: reduced advantage fnl 100yds but a gng to hold on* **16/1**
2454 **2** nk **Space Station**[18] 7516 3-9-3 69 TonyCulhane 8 76
(S Dow) *in tch: rdn and effrt jst over 2f out: chsd wnr 1f out: kpt on u.p but nvr quite gng to rch wnr* **3/1**[1]
5020 **3** 1 ¼ **Jack Rackham**[73] 6413 5-9-4 70 (v) TomEaves 10 73
(B Smart) *t.k.h: in tch: rdn ent fnl 2f: pressing for 2nd 1f out: kpt on same pce after* **14/1**
0323 **4** nk **Forest Dane**[22] 7484 9-8-10 62 StephenDonohoe 6 64+
(Mrs N Smith) *stdd s: hld up bhd: effrt and rdn on outer over 1f out: r.o ins fnl f: nt rch ldrs* **10/1**
6010 **5** hd **Speak The Truth (IRE)**[15] 7577 3-8-11 68 (p) MatthewDavies(5) 11 69
(J R Boyle) *stdd s: hld up towards rr: effrt towards inner 2f out: kpt on same pce u.p fnl f* **9/1**
2604 **6** nk **Fazbee (IRE)**[16] 7553 3-9-4 70 (v) ShaneKelly 12 70
(P W D'Arcy) *hld up in tch in midfield: swtchd rt and hdwy over 1f out: no imp u.p ins fnl f* **7/1**[3]
451 **7** nse **Another Try (IRE)**[54] 6926 4-8-12 64 JimmyQuinn 5 64
(A P Jarvis) *chsd ldrs: rdn and unable qck jst over 2f out: kpt on same pce u.p fr over 1f out* **7/1**[3]
3226 **8** 1 ¼ **Make My Dream**[16] 7554 6-9-3 69 JimCrowley 3 65
(J Gallagher) *w wnr tl unable qck u.p 2f out: one pce and no threat to ldrs fnl f* **8/1**
0010 **9** ½ **Gentle Guru**[18] 7519 5-9-3 69 SteveDrowne 7 64
(R T Phillips) *mounted on crse and taken down early: hld up in tch in rr: rdn and effrt over 1f out: no real prog: nt clr run fnl 75yds* **14/1**
5324 **10** nse **Musical Script (USA)**[18] 7519 6-9-1 67 (b) ChrisCatlin 2 62
(Mouse Hamilton-Fairley) *stdd and dropped in bhd after s: swtchd ins and effrt 2f out: no real prog and nvr trbld ldrs* **11/2**[2]
2466 **11** ½ **Figaro Flyer (IRE)**[18] 7519 6-9-1 67 IanMongan 1 60
(P Howling) *dropped in after s: rdn and effrt over 1f out: no prog: nt clr run and eased fnl 75yds* **33/1**

1m 12.07s (-1.03) **Going Correction** -0.025s/f (Stan) **11** Ran SP% **117.7**
Speed ratings (Par 103): **105,104,102,102,102 101,101,100,99,99 98**
toteswingers: 1&2 £13.80, 1&3 £32.90, 2&3 £13.10 CSF £63.81 CT £712.83 TOTE £16.10: £5.70, £1.60, £3.50; EX 70.30.
Owner The Sutton Veny Syndicate **Bred** Rathbarry Stud **Trained** Sutton Veny, Wilts

FOCUS
The second division of this sprint handicap was run in a time only slightly slower than the preceding one.

7740 BETFAIR RACING MULTIPLES H'CAP 1m 4f (P)
4:25 (4:25) (Class 6) (0-60,58) 3-Y-O £2,047 (£604; £302) Stalls Centre

Form RPR
0000 **1** **Jiggalong**[25] 7438 3-8-11 51 PaulDoe 7 55
(Jim Best) *stdd s: t.k.h early: hld up in rr: rdn and hdwy ent fnl 2f: drvn to ld fnl 100yds: r.o wl* **20/1**
-460 **2** 1 **Seaquel**[6] 7660 3-8-7 52 AmyBaker(5) 5 54
(A B Haynes) *led at stdy gallop tl over 10f out: chsd ldrs after: rdn 3f out: rdr dropped whip over 2f out: sn outpcd by ldrs: rallied ins fnl f: kpt on to snatch 2nd on post* **25/1**
4456 **3** nse **Mountain Forest (GER)**[6] 7666 3-8-6 46 JimmyQuinn 2 48
(H Morrison) *chsd ldr tl led over 10f out: rdn and fnd ex whn chal over 2f out: drvn and hdd fnl 100yds: no ex: lost 2nd on post* **6/1**[3]
3060 **4** 1 ¾ **Playful Asset (IRE)**[14] 7586 3-9-2 56 TonyCulhane 3 56
(P Howling) *stdd s: hld up in tch in last pl: hdwy on inner jst over 2f out: chsd ldrs and drvn over 1f out: no imp fnl f* **28/1**
6411 **5** 2 ¼ **Private Equity (IRE)**[23] 7461 3-9-3 57 JoeFanning 6 53
(W Jarvis) *t.k.h early: chsd ldrs: wnt 2nd 8f out: rdn to chal over 2f out: drvn and unable qck 2f out: wknd 1f out* **4/5**[1]
6 4 ½ **Mackintosh (IRE)**[32] 7345 3-8-12 52 SJCraine 8 41
(Patrick Morris) *stdd s: t.k.h early: hld up in tch: rdn and wknd over 2f out* **14/1**
032 **7** 3 ¾ **Very Distinguished**[32] 7324 3-9-1 55 LPKeniry 1 38
(S Kirk) *stdd s: t.k.h early: hld up in tch in midfield: rdn and btn over 2f out* **7/2**[2]

2m 37.01s (2.51) **Going Correction** -0.025s/f (Stan) **7** Ran SP% **110.8**
Speed ratings (Par 98): **90,89,89,88,86 83,81**
toteswingers: 1&2 £15.60, 1&3 £5.90, 2&3 £8.90 CSF £351.09 CT £3218.86 TOTE £19.20: £6.50, £8.70; EX 223.10.
Owner M&R Refurbishments Ltd **Bred** Norcroft Park Stud **Trained** Lewes, E Sussex

FOCUS
There was no pace on in the early stages in this handicap, and the winning time was slower than the five-runner claimer earlier on the card, which tells you everything about the value of this form.
Jiggalong Official explanation: trainer had no explanation for the apparent improvement in form.
Private Equity(IRE) Official explanation: jockey said filly was unsuited by the slow early pace

7741 TOTE U.S. ON BETFAIR H'CAP 7f (P)
4:55 (4:55) (Class 4) (0-80,86) 3-Y-O+ £4,727 (£1,406; £702; £351) Stalls Low

Form RPR
0441 **1** **Seek The Fair Land**[9] 7627 3-8-10 75 WilliamCarson(3) 10 91
(J R Boyle) *hld up in midfield: hdwy over 2f out: pushed into ld over 1f out: rdn clr fnl f: comf* **11/8**[1]
411 **2** 4 **Imprimis Tagula (IRE)**[7] 7656 5-9-5 86 6ex (v) LeeNewnes(5) 8 93+
(A Bailey) *hld up wl bhd: nt clr run on inner over 2f out: swtchd lft wl over 1f out: gd hdwy jst over 1f out: chsd wnr fnl 150yds: no imp* **11/2**[2]
6546 **3** ¾ **I Confess**[9] 7627 4-8-10 72 (v) PaulDoe 3 74
(P D Evans) *chsd ldr for 1f: chsd ldrs after: n.m.r over 2f out: sn rdn: chsd clr wnr briefly 1f out: kpt on same pce fnl f* **16/1**
0003 **4** hd **Resplendent Nova**[18] 7516 7-8-6 68 JimmyQuinn 7 69
(P Howling) *stdd and dropped in bhd after s: hld up wl bhd: plld to outer and rdn wl over 1f out: r.o fnl f to press for 3rd nr fin: no ch w wnr* **14/1**
3065 **5** ½ **Hustle (IRE)**[4] 7692 4-9-2 78 SteveDrowne 1 78
(Miss Gay Kelleway) *stdd and dropped in bhd after s: wl off the pce in rr: hdwy 3f out: in tch whn hung rt: nt clr run and swtchd lft jst over 1f out: kpt on fnl f: no ch w wnr* **20/1**
2644 **6** ¾ **Sunshine Always (IRE)**[17] 7540 3-9-4 80 JimCrowley 11 78
(T D McCarthy) *stdd s: hld up wl bhd in last pl: rdn and effrt on inner 2f out: kpt on but nvr able to chal* **11/2**[2]
6566 **7** 3 ¼ **Grey Boy (GER)**[18] 7523 8-8-1 70 GeorgeDowning(7) 9 59
(A W Carroll) *hld up wl off the pce in rr: nvr trbld ldrs* **20/1**
3316 **8** 1 **Perfect Act**[22] 7478 4-8-10 72 IanMongan 2 59
(C G Cox) *t.k.h: chsd ldrs: effrt to chse ldr over 2f out: drvn and nt pce of wnr over 1f out: wknd fnl f* **16/1**
0025 **9** ¾ **Nora Mae (IRE)**[17] 7540 3-9-1 77 LPKeniry 5 61
(S Kirk) *racd off the pce in midfield: rdn and unable qck over 2f out: wl btn fnl f* **33/1**
0030 **10** shd **Avertis**[12] 7603 4-8-13 75 (bt[1]) AdamKirby 12 59
(Stef Liddiard) *led and sn clr: rdn and hdd over 1f out: sn edgd rt and wknd* **15/2**[3]
4-20 **11** 5 **Final Salute**[47] 7082 3-8-11 73 (v) TomEaves 4 44
(B Smart) *dwlt: sn t.k.h: hdwy to chse ldr after 1f tl over 2f out: edgd rt and u.p sn after: wknd wl over 1f out* **33/1**

1m 23.65s (-2.35) **Going Correction** -0.025s/f (Stan) **11** Ran SP% **118.5**
Speed ratings (Par 105): **112,107,106,106,105 104,101,100,99,99 93**
toteswingers: 1&2 £3.90, 1&3 £9.70, 2&3 £11.80 CSF £8.33 CT £85.15 TOTE £2.50: £1.40, £1.90, £3.90; EX 13.20.
Owner Chris Watkins And David N Reynolds **Bred** Raimon Bloodstock **Trained** Epsom, Surrey

FOCUS
Some fairly in-form horses squared off against each other in this, and the time was a course record, so the form ought to be sound.
Hustle(IRE) Official explanation: jockey said gelding hung right

7742 WATCH U.S. RACING ON BETFAIR H'CAP — 1m (P)
5:25 (5:25) (Class 5) (0-70,70) 3-Y-O — **£2,590** (£770; £385; £192) **Stalls** Low

Form — RPR

0311 **1** **Wunder Strike (USA)**[4] 7693 3-8-5 **57**............................(p) JoeFanning 5 66
(J R Boyle) *trckd ldrs: rdn to chal and edgd rt over 1f out: led ins fnl f: kpt on wl* **15/8**[2]

0603 **2** ¾ **Charlie Smirke (USA)**[11] 7610 3-8-7 **59**.......................... ShaneKelly 8 66
(G L Moore) *chsd ldrs: rdn and unable qck whn n.m.r and swtchd lft jst over 1f out: rallied u.p ins fnl f to go 2nd nr fin* **16/1**

6013 **3** *nk* **Fernando Torres**[14] 7587 3-9-0 **66**................................ FrancisNorton 9 72
(Matthew Salaman) *led: rdn ent fnl 2f: hdd ins fnl f: kpt on same pce after* **13/8**[1]

3005 **4** *nk* **Dark Ranger**[29] 7392 3-8-6 **58**.. RobertHavlin 4 64
(T J Pitt) *t.k.h early: stdd towards rr after 1f: plld out and rdn jst over 2f out: styd on u.p fnl f: nt pce to rch ldrs* **25/1**

5235 **5** *nk* **Lucky Score (IRE)**[9] 7632 3-8-9 **61**..............................(p) ChrisCatlin 7 66
(Mouse Hamilton-Fairley) *chsd ldr: ev ch and rdn whn n.m.r jst over 1f out: one pce fnl f* **5/1**[3]

1115 **6** 3½ **Ocean Countess (IRE)**[22] 7487 3-8-12 **64**...................... JimmyQuinn 3 61
(Miss J Feilden) *dwlt and bustled along early: effrt and rdn on inner 2f out: wknd jst ins fnl f* **14/1**

0460 **7** ½ **Sapphire Prince (USA)**[24] 7456 3-8-13 **65**.................... SteveDrowne 2 60
(J R Best) *hld up in rr: rdn and no real prog over 2f out: nvr trbld ldrs* **25/1**

0546 **8** *1* **Grand Honour (IRE)**[141] 4304 3-9-4 **70**.......................... IanMongan 10 63
(P Howling) *stdd s: hld up in rr: rdn and effrt jst over 2f out: no real prog and nvr trbld ldrs* **18/1**

1m 40.23s (0.43) **Going Correction** -0.025s/f (Stan) **8** Ran SP% **115.0**
Speed ratings (Par 102): **96,95,94,94,94 90,90,89**
toteswingers: 1&2 £7.80, 1&3 £1.20, 2&3 £5.90 CSF £31.85 CT £56.33 TOTE £2.40: £1.20, £2.70, £1.10; EX 19.40 Place 6: £1332.13 Place 5: £895.89.
Owner Mrs B Powell B Walsh P Hughes C Murphy **Bred** Mike Abraham **Trained** Epsom, Surrey

FOCUS
An ordinary handicap run at a modest pace.
T/Plt: £5,980.50 to a £1 stake. Pool: £77,010.11. 9.40 winning tickets. T/Qpdt: £1,208.30 to a £1 stake. Pool: £5,552.10. 3.40 winning tickets. SP

[1553] SHA TIN (R-H)
Sunday, December 13

OFFICIAL GOING: Good

7744a CATHAY PACIFIC HONG KONG VASE (GROUP 1) — 1m 4f
6:00 (6:03) 3-Y-0+
£716,338 (£276,481; £125,673; £71,813; £41,293; £25,135)

RPR

1 **Daryakana (FR)**[71] 6504 3-8-6 ow1....................................... GMosse 3 115+
(A De Royer-Dupre, France) *hld up in last: 12th st: str run down outside to ld last strides* **57/10**[3]

2 *shd* **Spanish Moon (USA)**[36] 7310 5-9-0 .... RyanMoore 5 117
(Sir Michael Stoute) *a cl up: 4th st: split rivals to ld 1f out: hdd last strides* **17/10**[1]

3 *nk* **Kasbah Bliss (FR)**[70] 6527 7-9-0 .... TThulliez 4 117
(F Doumen, France) *racd in 8th: swtchd lft over 1 1/2f out: styd on strly fnl f to take 3rd on line* **44/1**

4 *shd* **Jaguar Mail (JPN)**[35] 5-9-0 ....(b) CSoumillon 1 117
(N Hori, Japan) *towards rr early: wnt 6th bef 1/2-way: 5th st: ev ch 1f out: kpt on at one pce* **10/1**

5 ½ **Cirrus Des Aigles (FR)**[56] 6890 3-8-9 .... FBlondel 10 116
(Mme C Barande-Barbe, France) *cl up on outside: 3rd st: led narrowly 2f out to 1f out: one pce* **17/2**

6 1¼ **Viva Pataca**[28] 7-9-0 .... DarrenBeadman 13 114
(J Moore, Hong Kong) *towards rr: 6th st on outside: ev ch 1 1/2f out to 1f out: one pce* **89/10**

7 ½ **Thumbs Up (NZ)**[28] 5-9-0 ....(b) BrettPrebble 12 113
(C S Shum, Hong Kong) *in rr: 9th and swtchd outside ent st: styd on but nvr a factor* **84/10**

8 ½ **Jamesina (AUS)**[28] 6-9-0 .... JeffLloyd 8 112
(D Ferraris, Hong Kong) *in rr: 11th st: nvr a factor* **61/1**

9 *1* **Buccellati**[57] 6873 5-9-0 ....(v) WilliamBuick 9 111
(A M Balding) *hld up towards rr: 10th st on ins: swtchd lft over 1 1/2f out: sn rdn and one pce* **40/1**

10 *1* **Youmzain (IRE)**[70] 6526 6-9-0 ....(v) KFallon 7 109
(M R Channon) *midfield: chsng ldrs on ins whn hmpd over 1 1/2f out: no ch after* **22/5**[2]

11 4½ **Packing Winner (NZ)**[28] 7-9-0 .... BrettDoyle 6 102
(L Ho, Hong Kong) *led: jnd 4f out: hdd 2f out: wknd* **29/1**

12 1½ **Jackpot Delight (NZ)**[28] 6-9-0 .... JamesWinks 11 100
(C Fownes, Hong Kong) *prom on outside: disp ld 4f out to 2f out: sn wknd* **100/1**

13 *dist* **Black Mamba (NZ)**[49] 6-8-10 .... ODoleuze 2 —
(John W Sadler, U.S.A) *racd in 3rd: pushed along 4f out: wknd 3f out* **66/1**

2m 27.51s (-0.69)
WFA 3 from 5yo+ 5lb **13** Ran SP% **122.9**
(including $HK10 stakes): WIN 67.00; PL 24.50, 13.00, 106.50; DF 96.00.
Owner H H Aga Khan **Bred** H H The Aga Khan's Studs S C **Trained** Chantilly, France

FOCUS
Seven of the last eight winners of this valuable contest had been trained either in the United Kingdom or France, which strongly suggested that the home team had plenty on to keep the prize in the Far East. Hong Kong-based Packing Winner took up pacemaking duties and set an ordinary-looking early gallop, but it was very clear from an early stage in the home straight that a runner from Europe was going to claim the Vase again.

NOTEBOOK
Daryakana(FR) completed what has been a meteoric rise to Group 1 success in a relatively short space of time. Unraced until July of this year, and not tried in Listed company until her third outing, she impressed when taking the Group 2 Prix Royallieu last time with a good turn of foot. Held up here and quite some way behind, she looked to have plenty on as she turned in to the straight wide of the field, but the burst of acceleration she showed at Longchamp clicked in again and she edged out the runner-up in the shadows of the post. A 3-y-o filly did win this in 2003 and her trainer/owner had a similar type in Shamdala run fourth behind Ouija Board in this race in 2005, but with so much hopefully still to come, this was surely a better performance than when Vallee Enchantee won. If there was betting already for the event, one would imagine that she would head the market for the Arc, which looks her obvious target next season if staying in training.

Spanish Moon(USA)is lightly raced for a horse of his age and clearly enjoys racing abroad while banned in the United Kingdom. Ryan Moore had been bullish all week about his mount's chances in this and the partnership almost claimed the prize. It was bad luck on his connections to be denied so close to the line but there should be more to come from him next year. He reportedly heads to Dubai in the spring.\n

Kasbah Bliss(FR) was a fascinating contender when considering that only a few months ago he was being heralded as a possible leading Champion Hurdle prospect after once again showing excellent form on the Flat. His trainer, who had tasted victory in Hong Kong with Jim And Tonic in the past, had told everyone that would listen all week that his horse was not going to be disgraced, although he appeared to have negatives to overcome, and he was proved completely right. It will be interesting to see how he is campaigned next year as, if the ground came up soft, he would enter Arc calculations, using the winner and runner-up as markers.

Jaguar Mail(JPN) produced a good effort in this race last year under Michael Kinane, and although he had not won after, most of his subsequent runs suggested that he was as good as he showed last season. Fitted with blinkers, he moved his way to the head of affairs at the right stage but was unable to lengthen once there.

Cirrus Des Aigles(FR) took a while to reveal his best form but was most progressive towards the end of the French Flat season, collecting an ordinary Group 2 contest at Longchamp on his 14th outing of the season. He took his form to a new level in this, as he rallied well after leading briefly about a furlong out.

Viva Pataca has captured the hearts and minds of the residents of Hong Kong over the years, but it was difficult to get away from the fact that he often finds the best from other countries too tough to handle when they come to his turf. It was a similar story again and he does not have the excuses that he did when finding little room in the race last season.

Thumbs Up(NZ) is a very consistent performer in Hong Kong and regularly duels with the best over a range of trips. Fitted with blinkers for the first time, he came with his challenge up the home straight but could not get on terms.

Jamesina(AUS) landed a hat-trick last season, which saw him take a Group 3 handicap on the final of those three wins. He had flown home on his last outing and did the same again after being held up.

Buccellati had appeared to show a bit of attitude last time in Canada when running well, although the ground may have been a bit firm there, but never made much impression in this.

Youmzain(IRE) is a talented individual and it was hard to find many negatives about his chance in this, even allowing for his modest win record, as trip and going appear to be no problem. He was staying on quite well towards the inside when completely stopped by the weakening front-runner. It's fair to say he looked unlucky not to be involved in the finish despite coming on-and-off the bridle at various stages of the race.

7745a CATHAY PACIFIC HONG KONG SPRINT (GROUP 1) — 6f
6:40 (6:42) 3-Y-0+
£614,004 (£236,984; £107,720; £61,041; £35,907; £21,544)

RPR

1 **Sacred Kingdom (AUS)**[21] 6-9-0 .... BrettPrebble 7 118
(P F Yiu, Hong Kong) *racd in 5th: 6th st: wnt 2nd over 1f out: led 120yds out: r.o wl* **31/20**[1]

2 ½ **One World (AUS)**[21] 5-9-0 .... DarrenBeadman 12 116
(J Moore, Hong Kong) *hld up in rr: last st: str run down outside fnl 1 1/2f: nrest at fin* **9/1**

3 *nk* **Joy And Fun (NZ)**[21] 6-9-0 .... BrettDoyle 6 115
(D Cruz, Hong Kong) *s.i.s: hld up: 8th st: switching lft whn momentarily short of room over 1 1/2f out: styd on wl fnl f* **20/1**

4 ¾ **Green Birdie (NZ)**[273] 6-9-0 .... ODoleuze 5 113
(C Fownes, Hong Kong) *hld up: 9th st: kpt on down outside fnl 1 1/2f* **13/1**

5 *shd* **California Flag (USA)**[36] 7305 5-9-0 ....(b) JTalamo 4 112
(Brian Koriner, U.S.A) *led after 100yds: hdd after 1f: led again on ins after 2f: two l clr 1 1/2f out: hdd 120yds out: one pce* **10/1**

6 1¼ **Total Gallery (IRE)**[70] 6522 3-9-0 .... JMurtagh 2 108
(J S Moore) *led briefly early then racd in 3rd: wnt 2nd over 1 1/2f out: lost 2nd over 1f out: one pce* **28/1**

7 ½ **Apache Cat (AUS)**[36] 7-9-0 ....(b) DamienOliver 9 107
(Greg Eurell, Australia) *in rr: 11th st: nvr a factor* **12/1**

8 *hd* **All Silent (AUS)**[36] 6-9-0 ....(b) NicholasHall 14 106
(Grahame Begg, Australia) *in rr: 12th st: keeping on towards ins whn swtchd sharply rt 1f out: nvr nr ldrs* **4/1**[2]

9 *nse* **Inspiration (AUS)**[21] 6-9-0 .... JamesWinks 11 106
(J Moore, Hong Kong) *in rr: 13th st: nvr a factor* **34/1**

10 *hd* **Cannonball (USA)**[36] 7305 4-9-0 .... RADominguez 1 105
(Wesley A Ward, U.S.A) *racd in 4th: 5th st: sn rdn and one pce* **34/1**

11 1¾ **Borderlescott**[70] 6522 7-9-0 .... NCallan 8 100
(R Bastiman) *hld up: 10th and rdn ent st: unable qck* **83/1**

12 2¼ **War Artist (AUS)**[70] 6522 6-9-0 .... OPeslier 10 92
(J M P Eustace) *6th early: 4th st on outside: wknd over 1 1/2f out* **42/1**

13 ½ **Laurel Guerreiro (JPN)**[70] 5-9-0 .... SFujita 13 91
(Mitsugi Kon, Japan) *rushed up on outside to ld after 1f: hdd after 2f: 2nd st: wknd over 1 1/2f out* **40/1**

14 6¼ **Scenic Blast (AUS)**[70] 5-9-0 .... StevenArnold 3 71
(Daniel Morton, Australia) *hld up: 7th st on ins: sn btn and eased* **83/10**[3]

69.16 secs (69.16) **14** Ran SP% **123.8**
WIN 25.50; PL 13.50, 27.00, 48.50; DF 144.50.
Owner Sin Kang Yuk **Bred** Mrs N F Calvert & Estate Of The Late A M Calvert **Trained** Hong Kong

FOCUS
This looked like one of the best sprints of recent years beforehand, with a truly top-class international line up - between them this lot had won 16 Grade or Group 1 contests in seven different countries. There was, however, a noticeable absentee in the shape of C&D trial winner Happy Zero, who instead contested the Mile (finished runner-up), and a strong challenge from the overseas runners failed to materialise, with the locals, as per-usual, totally dominant. This was a ninth win in the race for Hong Kong from only 11 renewals, and the prize has now stayed at home seven years on the bounce. All things considered, the bare form is not as strong as it might have been. The pace was solid.

NOTEBOOK
Sacred Kingdom(AUS) repeated his success of 2007, and he did so with far more authority than the official margin suggests. It's true he was 2l behind Happy Zero last time, but he was conceding 5lb, and in any case, the run clearly brought him. In the absence of his old rival, he did enough for a strong case to be made for him being described as the best turf sprinter in the world. Travelling powerfully in a good position, just better than mid-division, he produced a change of pace that his rivals simply couldn't match when asked to go inside the final 400m. He looked set to win by open lengths when in front around 100m from the finish, but he idled noticeably, allowing the chasing pack to close the gap.

One World(AUS) ran a terrific race from an unfavourable draw, but even so, he's slightly flattered to finish so close to the winner. His lack of tactical speed was his undoing, as he was last of all at the top of the straight, but his finishing kick was most impressive as he covered the final 400m over half a second quicker than any of his rivals, albeit Sacred Kingdom was idling.

Joy And Fun(NZ) didn't help himself with a slow start but he displayed good mid-race speed to recover to a point, and was tracking the winner early in the straight. Once getting a gap, he lacked that one's burst of acceleration, but still finished well. He seems like a lazy type (usually wears headgear) but if he can apply himself better early on, he can win a Group 1 sprint.

Green Birdie(NZ) was bumped by Joy And Fun in the straight but it made no difference. This was a good effort from last year's runner-up considering he had been off since March with an injury to his hoof.

California Flag(USA) was unable to dominate like he did when winning the Breeders' Cup Turf Sprint, and he also hung right under pressure in the straight, so it's to his credit he managed to finish so close. He's a horse with a serious amount of talent, but his racing style is currently too one dimensional.

Total Gallery(IRE), the Prix de l'Abbaye winner, had the stats against him as European runners have a poor record in this, and so too do 3-y-os. As such, this was a noteworthy performance from Stan Moore's colt, who ran a nice race to easily fare the best of the British trio, and with the physical scope to go on improving, he looks the real deal. He could go to Dubai next year for the Golden Shaheen, which will be run on Tapeta on Meydan, and Singapore is also apparently an option.

Apache Cat(AUS), last year's third, was well held this time. He returned lame on his near-fore and had lost an off-hind plate.

All Silent(AUS) was below the form he showed when winning a Group 1 (Apache Cat fourth) in Australia last time, but the widest draw gave him little chance and this performance is easily excused.

Inspiration(AUS), last season's shock winner, made no show, but the signs were ominous when he scoped badly after running a poor race in the trial.

Borderlescott is better over 5f, but even so, he found this company a bit hot.

War Artist(AUS) was well beaten after racing wide without any cover for most of the way.

Laurel Guerreiro(JPN), well held in this 12 months ago, had made all in the Sprinters Stakes in Japan on his latest start, but he used up too much energy getting to the front this time after starting sluggishly from an outside gate.

Scenic Blast(AUS) was awesome when winning the King's Stand at Royal Ascot earlier in the year, but he's a horse with problems now. Having swallowed his tongue in the July Cup, he then returned with thumps after contesting the Sprinters Stakes, and this time he bled from both nostrils. He had also been forced to miss his intended prep for this with a bruised heel.

7746a CATHAY PACIFIC HONG KONG MILE (GROUP 1) 1m
7:50 (7:50) 3-Y-0+

£818,671 (£315,978; £124,362; £81,688; £47,576; £28,725)

			RPR
1		**Good Ba Ba (USA)**[21] 7-9-0 ... ODoleuze 9 (D Cruz, Hong Kong) *hld up in rr: 12th on outside st: str run to go 4th 100yds out: r.o wl to ld cl home* **53/20**[2]	121
2	½	**Happy Zero (AUS)**[21] 5-9-0 ... DarrenBeadman 11 (J Moore, Hong Kong) *hld up towards rr: 11th st: styd on wl down outside to press ldrs 50yds out: r.o* **9/10**[1]	120
3	hd	**Fellowship (NZ)**[21] 7-9-0 ... ZacPurton 1 (P O'Sullivan, Hong Kong) *racd in 4th: wnt 3rd over 1 1/2f out: ev ch 100yds out: led briefly 50yds out: sn hdd and no ex* **12/1**[3]	120
4	nk	**Egyptian Ra (NZ)**[21] 8-9-0 ... FCoetzee 14 (A S Cruz, Hong Kong) *sn led: jnd 1 1/2f out: rallied to regain ld 1f out: hdd 50yds out: lost 3rd on line* **18/1**	119
5	¾	**Ferneley (IRE)**[36] 7308 5-9-0 ... KFallon 4 (B Cecil, U.S.A) *hld up towards rr: 8th towards ins 1f out: kpt on wl* **70/1**	117
6	shd	**Confront**[72] 6448 4-9-0 ... RyanMoore 12 (Sir Michael Stoute) *hld up in rr: 13th st: kpt on wl fnl f: nrest at fin* **33/1**	117
7	1 ¼	**Alexandros**[39] 7245 4-9-0 ... LDettori 7 (Saeed Bin Suroor) *racd in 5th: rdn and one pce fr over 1 1/2f out* **21/1**	114
8	nk	**Able One (NZ)**[21] 7-9-0 ... BrettPrebble 3 (J Moore, Hong Kong) *led briefly early then racd in 2nd: disp ld 1 1/2f out to 1f out: wknd* **16/1**	113
9	nse	**Sweet Hearth (USA)**[71] 6503 3-8-9 ... GMosse 13 (A De Royer-Dupre, France) *hld up in last: kpt on steadily down outside fnl 2f: nt rch ldrs* **25/1**	109
10	shd	**Gris De Gris (IRE)**[29] 7408 5-9-0 ... TThulliez 2 (A De Royer-Dupre, France) *midfield: disputing 5th on ins st: n.m.r against rail but unable qck fr 1 1/2f out* **75/1**	113
11	nk	**Sight Winner (NZ)**[21] 6-9-0 ... DWhyte 5 (J Size, Hong Kong) *racd in 3rd tl over 1 1/2f out: one pce* **21/1**	112
12	shd	**Duff (IRE)**[70] 6530 6-9-0 ... FMBerry 6 (Edward Lynam, Ire) *hld up: in tight quarters chsng ldrs 2f out: swtchd ins over 1 1/2f out: sn hrd rdn and one pce* **100/1**	112
13	2 ¼	**Racing To Win (AUS)**[43] 7196 7-9-0 ...(b) HughBowman 10 (John O'Shea, Australia) *midfield: disputing 5th on outside ent st: sn rdn and one pce* **30/1**	107
14	dist	**Pressing (IRE)**[35] 7312 6-9-0 ... NCallan 8 (M A Jarvis) *racd in 6th on outside: lost pl ent st: wknd over 1 1/2f out* **65/1**	—

1m 34.6s (-0.10)
WFA 3 from 4yo+ 1lb **14** Ran SP% **123.2**
WIN 36.50; PL 13.00, 12.50, 23.50; DF 34.50.
Owner John Yuen Se Kit **Bred** Haras Santa Maria De Araras **Trained** Hong Kong

FOCUS
As the odds suggested, two of these stood out on form beforehand, and although not quite as dominant as expected, with there being something of a bunch finish, they still came to the fore.

NOTEBOOK
Good Ba Ba(USA), attempting to add to his previous victories in the race and become the first horse to win at this meeting three times, was the proven star, whereas Happy Zero was the pretender, having looked every inch a top notcher in the making when, bizarrely enough, winning the trial for the sprint over 6f. As it turned out, it was the defending champion who prevailed to create a little bit of history, and this special racehorse did so in typical style. Held up as usual, he still had at least 6l to find 400m out, and for a brief second or two it seemed as though he was struggling to make up the required ground, but soon enough he produced his trademark change of pace to get out of trouble. He winner has moved stables this year, but his preparation was almost identical to last season and he confirmed that, at the age of seven, he retains all of his ability. His rider, who was aboard for the 2007 victory but jocked off last season, thinks the gelding may benefit from a step up to 1m2f, and that was certainly the visual impression. With that in mind, hopefully he'll be considered for something like the Dubai World Cup next year - his style of racing should be suited to synthetics - because he has nothing left to prove on his own territory.
Happy Zero(AUS) had the first three finishers from this year's Hong Kong Sprint behind him when impressively winning the trial for that race, so although he ran a blinder on this step up in trip, he still met with defeat, and his connections must be thinking 'what if…?'. The reason for him being rerouted to this race was because his rider felt he could not have gone any quicker through the early stages last time, and he certainly seemed well suited by this distance. He did everything right, only to be picked off by the past master, and this effort confirms him to be a genuinely high-class gelding.
Fellowship(NZ), who won the trial when getting 5lb from, among others, Good Ba Ba, seemed to have every chance and ran well.
Egyptian Ra(NZ), a confirmed front-runner, was always going to struggle to see his race out after having to use up energy from a wide draw. It was the same story last year.
Ferneley(IRE), the US-trained challenger, kept on from well off the pace but simply lacked the speed of some of these.
Confront\n\x\x 's time for the final section was quicker than all bar the winner, and it's clear Sir Michael Stoute's runner was doing his best work late on after getting behind. His connections think he might want 1m2f now and he's expected to be on his travels again at some stage.
Alexandros had every chance but simply wasn't up to this level.
Able One(NZ), last year's runner-up, didn't feature at the finish this time having been close up for most of the journey.
Sweet Hearth(USA), ridden positively when runner-up in the Prix de la Foret on her previous start, was never seen with a chance after being dropped in from her wide draw.
Gris De Gris(IRE) was struck on the nose by a rival jockey's whip 300m out but he was held at the time.
Duff(IRE) ran well for a long way but his stamina seemed to give out late on.
Racing To Win(AUS) lost an off-hind plate and sustained a cut to his off-hind.
Pressing(IRE) was well beaten in this race for the second year in succession. He lost an off-hind plate.

7747a CATHAY PACIFIC HONG KONG CUP (GROUP 1) 1m 2f
8:30 (8:30) 3-Y-0+

£1,023,339 (£394,973; £179,533; £102,334; £59,246; £35,907)

			RPR
1		**Vision D'Etat (FR)**[70] 6526 4-9-0 ... OPeslier 7 (E Libaud, France) *racd in 6th: hdwy to ld appr fnl f: drvn out* **61/10**[3]	124
2	¾	**Collection (IRE)**[28] 4-9-0 ... DarrenBeadman 10 (J Moore, Hong Kong) *hld up in 7th: briefly n.m.r and swtchd ins over 1 1/2f out: wnt 2nd jst ins fnl f: r.o but a hld* **9/10**[1]	122
3	2 ½	**Presvis**[22] 7489 5-9-0 ... KFallon 9 (L M Cumani) *last early: 9th st: hrd rdn over 1 1/2f out: styd on between horses to take 3rd 50yds out* **5/2**[2]	117
4	nk	**Ashalanda (FR)**[57] 6853 3-8-7 ... GMosse 2 (A De Royer-Dupre, France) *disp 3rd: 4th st: wnt 2nd towards ins over 1 1/2f out: lost 2nd appr fnl f: lost 3rd 50yds out* **12/1**	112
5	¾	**Eagle Mountain**[21] 5-9-0 ... KShea 1 (M F De Kock, South Africa) *racd in 5th: kpt on steadily fnl 1 1/2f* **18/1**	115
6	shd	**Starlish (IRE)**[47] 7102 4-9-0 ... ACrastus 5 (E Lellouche, France) *hld up in 8th: styd on down outside fnl 1 1/2f but nvr nr ldrs* **90/1**	115
7	¾	**Special Days (NZ)**[21] 6-9-0 ... CraigAWilliams 8 (J Size, Hong Kong) *last st: a in rr* **83/1**	113
8	1 ¼	**Mr Medici (IRE)**[28] 4-9-0 ... LDettori 6 (L Ho, Hong Kong) *disp 3rd: 3rd st: rdn and one pce fr over 1 1/2f out* **12/1**	111
9	nk	**Eyshal (IRE)**[28] 5-9-0 ...(b) WCMarwing 4 (J Moore, Hong Kong) *disp ld early: racd in 2nd: disp ld again 2 1/2f out: led under 2f out to appr fnl f: wknd* **62/1**	110
10	2 ¾	**Queen Spumante (JPN)**[28] 5-8-10 ... HTanaka 3 (S Kojima, Japan) *briefly rdn along to ld: set str pce: jnd 2 1/2f out: hdd under 2f out: wknd* **34/1**	101

2m 1.86s (0.46)
WFA 3 from 4yo+ 3lb **10** Ran SP% **122.7**
WIN 70.50; PL 18.50, 11.00, 13.00; DF 83.00.
Owner Jacques Detre **Bred** Gaetan Gilles **Trained** France

FOCUS
A strong field lined up for this very valuable prize.

NOTEBOOK
Vision D'Etat(FR), despite an injury scare the previous day, showed exactly why is one of the best 1m2f turf horses in the world. Only beaten once at trips from 1m1f to 1m2f in nine starts, it was clear on turning in that he was going to be difficult to beat, and he readily held the runner-up. His rider reported afterwards that his mount had been a bit lazy at times during the contest, and he did not want to get to the front too early in case he decided to stop. The good news for racing fans is that he is set to stay in training and will possibly be aimed towards Dubai in the spring. He could quite easily be good enough to hold a leading chance in the Dubai World Cup.
Collection(IRE), whom locals got stuck into backing, was 2/2 over the C&D, and he ran well without quite looking in the class of the winner, even allowing for the blocked passage he had to endure over 300m out. He seems the right horse to take over from the now ageing Viva Pataca as the horse to beat in Hong Kong. He would also demand plenty of respect if making an appearance in Dubai.
Presvis quickly developed into a Group 1 performer after a fairly successful spell in Dubai, and claimed the scalp of Viva Pataca in April at this course before being slightly unlucky at Kranji. It was difficult to get that excited about his reappearance effort at Lingfield after a summer break despite staying on and giving weight away, and although he made some late ground in this, his run came all too late and it was another slightly laboured effort. He gives the impression that 1m4f could now be his optimum distance, and races such as the Japan Cup or Hong Kong Vase may be more suitable targets next winter. However, the trainer reported afterwards that his horse heads to Dubai, where a rematch with the winner in the Dubai World Cup is a possibility.
Ashalanda(FR) was possibly the most interesting runner in the line-up, as this was only her fifth career-outing. She had a few traffic problems in the home straight but was beaten on merit. That said, she should be a major force in domestic mares and fillies' races next season.
Eagle Mountain, a decisive winner of this race last season but absent after due to injury, did not show much on his recent comeback, where he was well over his ideal racing weight, but was not completely disgraced here. He still needs to find more to get back into the winner's enclosure, however.

Starlish(IRE) had been progressing at the end of the French Flat season and ran a cracker against some tough opponents, although one got the impression that he was finding the ground a bit too firm for him under pressure.
Special Days(NZ), a three-time winner in handicap company last season, had shown no obvious promise in his two most recent runs, so this effort was much the best he had done for a while.
Mr Medici(IRE) was a smart sort in Ireland for Kevin Prendergast before moving to new connections. A consistent sort in Hong Kong, he seemed to run up to expectations without being good enough.
Eyshal(IRE) had not shown anything that suggested he should be winning a race of this nature and predictably weakened quickly in the latter stages after sitting just behind the leader early.
Queen Spumante(JPN), as predicted, went off in front after being rousted to get there, and set a fair pace, without going as far clear as she did last time in her home country. She was a big disappointment considering she took a decent Group 1 on her previous start, and was easily beaten off rounding the home bend.

7729 WOLVERHAMPTON (A.W) (L-H)
Monday, December 14

OFFICIAL GOING: Standard
Wind: Almost nil Weather: Fine

7748 TOTEPLACEPOT WIN WITHOUT BACKING A WINNER MAIDEN AUCTION STKS 5f 20y(P)
2:15 (2:16) (Class 5) 2-Y-O £2,914 (£867; £433; £216) Stalls Low

Form				RPR
0424	1		**Kummel Excess (IRE)**[16] 7570 2-8-6 63 MatthewDavies(5) 2 (George Baker) *a.p: jnd ldrs over 2f out: rdn over 1f out: led ins fnl f: r.o* **2/1**[2]	64
2243	2	½	**Dimaire**[33] 7331 2-8-4 62 FrankieMcDonald 1 (D Haydn Jones) *wnt rt s: chsd ldrs: ev ch whn pushed along over 2f out: outpcd and rdn over 1f out: rallied to take 2nd nr fin* **7/4**[1]	55
5426	3	½	**Boogie Waltzer**[16] 7570 2-8-4 53 ChrisCatlin 3 (S C Williams) *led: rdn and hdd ins fnl f: nt qckn and lost 2nd nr fin* **8/1**	53
520	4	1¼	**Gower Sophia**[33] 7331 2-8-4 60 (v) JimmyQuinn 4 (M Brittain) *hld up: hrd rdn and effrt over 1f out: one pce fnl f* **7/2**[3]	49
6020	5	1¼	**Out The Ring (IRE)**[7] 7661 2-8-10 61 (p) KellyHarrison(3) 5 (Miss Gay Kelleway) *hld up in last: rdn wl over 1f out: no hdwy* **11/1**	53

63.15 secs (0.85) **Going Correction** +0.05s/f (Slow) 5 Ran SP% **111.4**
Speed ratings (Par 96): **95,94,93,91,89**
CSF £6.00 TOTE £2.60: £1.10, £2.10; EX 8.60.
Owner Mrs V P Baker & Partners **Bred** John Donegan **Trained** Moreton Morrell, Warwicks

FOCUS
A very moderate maiden and selling form in all but name. The form is sound enough.

NOTEBOOK
Kummel Excess(IRE) gained her first success at the fifth attempt in straightforward fashion, despite being 6lb wrong at the weights with the runner-up. She should be competitive in minor handicap company. (op 5-2)
Dimaire lacked the speed of the winner and kept on too late. She probably didn't run up to her official mark and is proving hard to win with. (op 9-4 tchd 5-2)
Boogie Waltzer had her chance in an uncontested lead, but she had a bit to find with the first two finishers at the weights. (op 6-1)
Gower Sophia ran some way below her official rating of 60 and is now 0-12. She looks one to avoid. (op 10-3 tchd 3-1)
Out The Ring(IRE) was easy to back and offered nothing. (op 8-1 tchd 12-1)

7749 FREE HORSE RACING TIPS AT BIGTIPS.CO.UK (S) STKS 5f 216y(P)
2:50 (2:50) (Class 6) 2-Y-O £2,388 (£705; £352) Stalls Low

Form				RPR
0	1		**Magenta Strait**[94] 5835 2-8-7 0 ChrisCatlin 2 (R Hollinshead) *hld up and bhd: hdwy whn nt clr run wl over 1f out: sn swtchd rt: rdn and r.o wl to ld cl home* **20/1**[3]	60+
5621	2	hd	**Bubbly Bellini (IRE)**[3] 7713 2-8-12 70 (p) LeeNewnes(5) 9 (A Bailey) *hld up in mid-div: rdn and hdwy on outside 2f out: r.o u.p towards fin* **5/6**[1]	69
6042	3	1	**Tamarind Hill (IRE)**[7] 7661 2-8-12 69 (b) SteveDrowne 10 (C R Egerton) *a.p: led wl over 1f out: sn rdn: hdd cl home* **4/1**[2]	61
0406	4	2½	**Moonlight Serenade**[7] 7661 2-8-0 60 KierenFox(7) 11 (W G M Turner) *hld up and bhd: rdn on outside over 2f out: hdwy 1f out: kpt on to take 4th towards fin* **33/1**	49
0066	5	1¼	**Feel The Magic (IRE)**[11] 7616 2-8-7 48 LPKeniry 13 (S Kirk) *a.p: rdn jst over 1f out: wknd wl ins fnl f* **40/1**	45
050	6	1	**Wild Heather**[4] 7698 2-8-7 0 GregFairley 4 (J R Holt) *led over 2f: led jst over 2f out: rdn and hdd jst over 1f out: wknd wl ins fnl f* **100/1**	42
6036	7	¾	**Raine Supreme**[104] 5543 2-8-8 54 ow1 GrahamGibbons 8 (E S McMahon) *prom: pushed along wl over 1f out: sn briefly n.m.r: wknd ins fnl f* **22/1**	42
0	8	hd	**Seeking Rio**[10] 7630 2-8-7 0 JimmyQuinn 7 (R J Hodges) *s.s: in rr: rdn wl over 1f out: nvr nr ldrs* **100/1**	39
0004	9	½	**Mind Of Her Own**[3] 7707 2-8-0 55 KevinLundie(7) 1 (P D Evans) *in rr: rdn on ins 2f out: sme prog over 1f out: nvr nr ldrs* **20/1**[3]	38
3602	10	1¾	**Cane Cat (IRE)**[11] 7619 2-8-7 54 FrancisNorton 3 (A W Carroll) *prom on ins pushed along over 2f out: rdn over 1f out: wknd fnl f* **4/1**[2]	32
0	11	8	**Kidnap (IRE)**[52] 7001 2-8-12 0 JerryO'Dwyer 12 (M G Quinlan) *chsd ldrs on outside: led over 3f out: rdn and hdd jst over 2f out: wkng whn sltly hmpd wl over 1f out* **100/1**	13
	12	23	**Makarthy** 2-8-12 0 TomEaves 6 (H A McWilliams) *s.v.s: a wl in rr* **66/1**	—
0	L		**Jonny No Eyebrows**[7] 7661 2-8-12 0 PaulDoe 5 (I A Wood) *ref to r: tk no part* **33/1**	—

1m 15.91s (0.91) **Going Correction** +0.05s/f (Slow) 13 Ran SP% **121.2**
Speed ratings (Par 94): **95,94,93,90,88 87,86,85,85,82 72,41,—**
toteswinger:1&2:£7.70, 2&3:£3.00, 1&3:£8.40 CSF £36.14 TOTE £19.10: £4.40, £1.10, £1.90; EX 56.90 Trifecta £228.10 Pool: £631.97 - 2.05 winning units..There was no bid for the winner. Bubbly Bellini was claimed by George Baker for £6,000
Owner M Johnson **Bred** R Hollinshead And M Johnson **Trained** Upper Longdon, Staffs

FOCUS
Average selling form which should prove reliable. The form is rated around the second.

NOTEBOOK
Magenta Strait stepped up significantly on the form she showed in a C&D claimer on her debut three months earlier, overcoming trouble in-running to win. Having raced well off the pace, she had nowhere to go around the bend into the straight, and the second and third-placed finishers had very much got first run by the time she was switched into the clear just over a furlong out. Although entitled to be sharper next time, she lacks scope.
Bubbly Bellini(IRE), bidding to follow up a recent C&D claiming success, came off the bridle a fair way out when challenging wide into the straight and, although he eventually responded, the winner finished that bit faster. He will now join George Baker, having been claimed. (op 11-10 tchd 5-4and 11-8 in places)
Tamarind Hill(IRE) showed good speed throughout and, having looked the winner for much of the straight and still been in front 1/2f out, he was matched at 1.01, but he lost two places in the final strides. He probably has the pace for 5f. (op 3-1)
Moonlight Serenade, reported to have hung right last time, lost ground when going widest of all into the straight, not looking comfortable around the bend, but she made some late headway. (tchd 40-1)
Cane Cat(IRE) was nowhere near the form she showed when runner-up in a C&D nursery off a mark of 50 on her previous start. (op 9-2 tchd 7-2)

7750 TOTESWINGER THREE WAYS TO WIN H'CAP (DIV I) 1m 5f 194y(P)
3:20 (3:22) (Class 6) (0-55,56) 3-Y-O+ £2,047 (£604; £302) Stalls Low

Form				RPR
3334	1		**Squirtle (IRE)**[9] 7649 6-8-11 48 LukeMorris 11 (W M Brisbourne) *hld up towards rr: pushed along 4f out: rdn and hdwy 2f out: edgd lft and led wl ins fnl f: styd on* **5/1**[2]	57
4500	2	hd	**Little Carmela**[5] 7695 5-9-4 55 (v) SaleemGolam 7 (S C Williams) *hld up in tch: pushed along to ld over 1f out: sn rdn: hdd wl ins fnl f: nt qckn* **8/1**	63
0606	3	1½	**Royal Rainbow**[28] 7354 5-8-9 46 oh1 ChrisCatlin 3 (P W Hiatt) *hld up in rr: stdy prog 2f out: rdn and nt qckn ins fnl f* **25/1**	52
/504	4	2	**Carr Hall (IRE)**[8] 7658 6-8-13 50 VinceSlattery 2 (B G Powell) *s.s: hld up in rr: hdwy on ins wl over 1f out: sn rdn: one pce ins fnl f* **10/1**	53
0433	5	3	**Colourful Move**[9] 7642 4-9-0 51 SteveDrowne 13 (P G Murphy) *led after 1f: hdd over 3f out: rdn over 2f out: wknd fnl f* **7/1**[3]	50
2335	6	hd	**Diktatorship (IRE)**[9] 7649 6-8-11 48 SJCraine 6 (Jennie Candlish) *prom tl rdn and wknd over 1f out* **7/1**[3]	47
6321	7	nk	**Iguacu**[5] 7688 5-9-0 56 6ex MatthewDavies(5) 4 (George Baker) *s.i.s: t.k.h in rr: stdy prog 6f out: led over 3f out: rdn and hdd over 1f out: wknd ins fnl f* **2/1**[1]	54
5605	8	nse	**Casablanca Minx (IRE)**[7] 7670 6-8-9 46 oh1 (b) GrahamGibbons 10 (A G Juckes) *hld up in rr: stdy hdwy on outside over 3f out: rdn and wknd wl over 1f out* **28/1**	44
2200	9	1	**Barodine**[5] 7688 6-9-2 53 GeorgeBaker 9 (R J Hodges) *hld up in tch: rdn over 1f out: wknd fnl f* **12/1**	50
0-16	10	2	**Purely By Chance**[9] 7649 4-8-9 51 (b) SimonPearce(5) 12 (J Pearce) *led 1f: prom tl wknd over 3f out* **16/1**	45
-000	11	20	**Spruzzo**[28] 1363 3-8-2 49 KellyHarrison(3) 1 (C W Thornton) *hld up in tch on ins: lost pl 5f out: bhd fnl 4f: t.o fnl 2f* **40/1**	15

3m 7.35s (1.35) **Going Correction** +0.05s/f (Slow)
WFA 3 from 4yo+ 7lb 11 Ran SP% **118.5**
Speed ratings (Par 101): **98,97,97,95,94 94,93,93,93,92 80**
toteswinger:1&2:£7.70, 2&3:£30.40, 1&3:£18.30 CSF £44.23 CT £920.05 TOTE £6.20: £2.00, £2.50, £6.40; EX 43.50 TRIFECTA Not won..
Owner J Jones Racing Ltd **Bred** Ballygallon Stud Limited **Trained** Great Ness, Shropshire

FOCUS
A moderate handicap run in a time 2.73 seconds slower than the second division. The form is a bit muddling but the winner is rated in line with her recent runs here.

7751 TOTESWINGER THREE WAYS TO WIN H'CAP (DIV II) 1m 5f 194y(P)
3:50 (3:50) (Class 6) (0-55,55) 3-Y-O+ £2,047 (£604; £302) Stalls Low

Form				RPR
2052	1		**Russian Music (USA)**[8] 7658 4-8-12 49 StephenDonohoe 13 (Ian Williams) *hld up towards rr: rdn and hdwy on outside over 2f out: styd on wl u.p to ld last strides* **15/8**[1]	60+
0300	2	nk	**Bright Sparky (GER)**[17] 6559 6-8-2 46 oh1 (bt) JamesPSullivan(7) 9 (M W Easterby) *hld up in rr: stdy prog on outside over 3f out: wnt 2nd over 2f out: rdn wl over 1f out: led ins fnl f: hdd last strides* **12/1**	56
6500	3	2	**Home**[18] 7328 4-9-0 51 (vt[1]) AdamKirby 10 (C Gordon) *chsd ldr: led 3f out: rdn wl over 1f out: hdd ins fnl f: no ex* **13/2**[2]	58
0005	4	4½	**Duneen Dream (USA)**[61] 6770 4-8-4 48 RachelKing(7) 5 (Mrs N S Evans) *prom: rdn and n.m.r 2f out: wknd fnl f* **33/1**	49
5000	5	½	**Jenny Soba**[8] 7658 6-8-8 50 AndrewHeffernan(5) 4 (Lucinda Featherstone) *hld up in mid-div: rdn over 2f out: no hdwy* **25/1**	50
5305	6	¾	**Stravita**[9] 7642 5-9-4 55 (p) GrahamGibbons 7 (R Hollinshead) *hld up towards rr: swtchd rt ent st: styd on fnl f: n.d* **7/1**[3]	54
3000	7	1¾	**Sir Sandicliffe (IRE)**[45] 7154 5-9-4 55 (p) ShaneKelly 3 (W M Brisbourne) *s.i.s: hld up in rr: pushed along over 2f out: c v wd st: nvr nr ldrs* **9/1**	52
0004	8	2½	**Adage**[13] 7608 6-8-9 46 oh1 (bt) FergusSweeney 11 (David Pinder) *hld up in tch: rdn and wknd wl over 1f out* **17/2**	39
6400	9	2	**Markadam**[7] 7670 3-8-3 47 (p) JimmyQuinn 2 (Miss S E Hall) *s.i.s: t.k.h: sn in mid-div: pushed along over 3f out: nt clr run on ins over 2f out: n.d after* **20/1**	38
00	10	nk	**A Chailin Mo Chroi (IRE)**[59] 6831 4-8-9 46 oh1 (p) LPKeniry 8 (Aidan Anthony Howard, Ire) *hld up in tch: pushed along and wknd over 2f out* **50/1**	36
0050	11	nk	**Rare Coincidence**[14] 7594 8-9-1 52 (tp) ChrisCatlin 1 (R F Fisher) *led: hdd 3f out: wknd wl over 1f out* **9/1**	42
/0-	12	4½	**Hawksbury Heights**[12] 4848 7-8-10 47 oh1 ow1 TonyCulhane 12 (J J Lambe, Ire) *hld up in mid-div: pushed along over 3f out: sn bhd* **16/1**	30
000	13	nk	**Beyonda Dream**[9] 7648 3-8-2 46 oh1 (p) FrankieMcDonald 6 (Lucinda Featherstone) *hld up in rr: no ch whn rdn wl over 1f out* **66/1**	29

3m 4.62s (-1.38) **Going Correction** +0.05s/f (Slow)
WFA 3 from 4yo+ 7lb 13 Ran SP% **119.7**
Speed ratings (Par 101): **105,104,103,101,100 100,99,97,96,96 96,93,93**
toteswinger:1&2:£5.90, 2&3:£11.10, 1&3:£5.80 CSF £24.89 CT £128.26 TOTE £2.30: £1.40, £3.40, £1.80; EX 33.70 Trifecta £77.40 Part won. Pool: £104.69 - 0.45 winning units..
Owner R J Turton **Bred** Denis O'Flynn **Trained** Portway, Worcs

FOCUS
The time was 2.73 seconds quicker than the first division and this should be reliable form for the level. The winner progressed again and the second ran to form.

7752 WOLVERHAMPTON HOLIDAY INN ALL WEATHER "HANDS AND HEELS" APPRENTICE SERIES H'CAP 1m 1f 103y(P)
4:20 (4:20) (Class 5) (0-75,72) 3-Y-O+ £3,885 (£1,156; £577; £288) Stalls Low

Form				RPR
0562	1		**Ella Woodcock (IRE)**[11] 7615 5-9-0 63 KierenFox 5 (E J Alston) *hld up and bhd: hdwy 2f out: swtchd rt 1f out: r.o to ld towards fin* **6/1**[3]	71

0011 2 ½ **Desert Vision**7 7668 5-9-5 71 6ex....(vt) LeeTopliss(3) 2 78
(M W Easterby) *a.p: led over 3f out: pushed along over 2f out: hdd towards fin* **1/1**1
0322 3 1 **Bavarica**7 7667 7-8-11 65.... AdamBeschizza(5) 7 70
(Miss J Feilden) *hld up: hdwy whn nt clr run briefly wl over 1f out: swtchd lft jst ins fnl f: r.o to take 3rd towards fin* **9/1**
0212 4 1¾ **Oriental Cavalier**11 7620 3-9-7 72....(p) DavidKenny 3 73
(R Hollinshead) *in tch: sn pushed along: one pce ins fnl f* **7/2**2
2430 5 ½ **Daniel Thomas (IRE)**16 7575 7-9-4 67....(v1) RyanClark 4 67
(Mrs A L M King) *s.i.s: sn hld up in tch: pushed along and ev ch wl over 1f out: no ex wl ins fnl f* **20/1**
2303 6 3 **Waahej**7 7667 3-9-0 65.... JohnCavanagh 1 59
(P W Hiatt) *led 1f: prom on ins: pushed along and wknd wl over 1f out* **8/1**
3435 7 2¼ **Formidable Guest**220 1834 5-8-12 66.... SophieSilvester(5) 8 55
(J Pearce) *hld up and bhd: stdy prog on outside 5f out: c wd st: wknd wl over 1f out* **25/1**
3025 8 shd **My Mate Mal**10 7631 5-9-0 63.... AdamCarter 6 52
(B Ellison) *led after 1f: hdd over 3f out: pushed along and wknd wl over 1f out* **20/1**
0040 9 2 **Highland River**31 7364 3-8-9 60.... AlexEdwards 10 45
(A Sadik) *prom tl wknd 2f out* **40/1**
03 10 5 **Tin Cha Woody (USA)**9 7643 4-9-6 69....(t) MatthewLawson 9 43
(Daniel Mark Loughnane, Ire) *hld up in rr: pushed along 3f out: sn struggling* **25/1**

2m 1.08s (-0.62) **Going Correction** +0.05s/f (Slow)
WFA 3 from 4yo+ 2lb **10** Ran SP% **127.3**
Speed ratings (Par 103): **104,103,102,101,100 98,96,95,94,89**
toteswinger:1&2:£3.60, 2&3:£4.40, 1&3:£6.50 CSF £12.84 CT £61.50 TOTE £8.60: £2.20, £1.10, £1.80; EX 20.10 Trifecta £97.30 Pool: £460.50 - 3.50 winning units.
Owner Derrick Mossop **Bred** Pippa Hackett **Trained** Longton, Lancs

FOCUS
A modest handicap and these apprentices were not allowed to use their whips. The pace seemed to be fair and the form looks sound.

7753 TOTEEXACTA BETTER VALUE FORECAST MEDIAN AUCTION MAIDEN STKS 1m 141y(P)
4:50 (4:50) (Class 5) 3-5-Y-O **£2,729** (£806; £403) **Stalls** Low

Form RPR
1 **Woolfall Sovereign (IRE)** 3-9-3 0.... TPQueally 4 63+
(G G Margarson) *hld up towards rr: pushed along and hdwy over 2f out: led jst over 1f out: rdn out* **7/2**2
6056 2 ½ **Barbarian**17 7211 3-9-3 61....(v1) GrahamGibbons 9 62
(A D Brown) *prom: pushed along and outpcd over 2f out: sn rdn: rallied over 1f out: kpt on u.p ins fnl f* **7/2**2
5223 3 2½ **Tobrata**7 7671 3-9-3 65.... TomEaves 11 56
(M Brittain) *hld up in tch: wnt 2nd 3f out: rdn and ev ch over 1f out: no ex ins fnl f* **13/8**1
0000 4 1¼ **Deportista**12 7609 3-8-10 45 ow1.... RussellKennemore(3) 12 49
(J A Pickering) *hld up in tch: rdn 2f out: one pce ins fnl f* **100/1**
06 5 nk **Quiet Mountain (IRE)**24 7459 4-9-5 0.... PJMcDonald 8 58+
(Ollie Pears) *hld up towards rr: pushed along and n.m.r over 2f out: styd on fnl f: nrst fin* **25/1**
00 6 1 **Lily Wood**7 7671 3-8-7 0.... MarkCoumbe(5) 5 45
(J W Unett) *hld up in mid-div: pushed along over 3f out: rdn and edgd lft over 1f out: kpt on fnl f* **33/1**
0000 7 1¾ **Chicamia**28 7415 5-9-0 40....(be1) GregFairley 2 41
(M Mullineaux) *prom tl wknd 3f out* **66/1**
4000 8 ¾ **Boffin**10 7623 4-9-0 45....(p) SimonPearce(5) 3 45
(Eve Johnson Houghton) *hld up in rr: pushed along over 2f out: rdn and sme hdwy on ins wl over 1f out: n.d* **50/1**
9 3¼ **Clarity Of Passion**18 7548 4-9-0 0.... ShaneKelly 10 32
(James Halpin, Ire) *hld up in mid-div: hdwy on outside over 6f out: led over 3f out: pushed along and 3 l clr 2f out: rdn and hdd jst over 1f out: wknd qckly ins fnl f* **66/1**
6004 10 9 **Katie Girl**32 7361 3-8-12 40....(p) JimmyQuinn 1 11
(Mrs G S Rees) *led: hdd over 3f out: wknd 2f out* **14/1**
11 2½ **American Champ (IRE)** 3-9-3 0.... SJCraine 6 11
(Patrick Morris) *s.i.s: rdn wl over 1f out: a in rr* **40/1**
12 1¾ **Owner Occupier**17 7563 4-9-5 55.... JerryO'Dwyer 13 7
(Miss Susan A Finn, Ire) *prom: w ldr over 6f out tl pushed along over 3f out: wknd wl over 2f out* **7/1**3
00 13 20 **Madame McManus**14 7596 3-8-12 0....(v1) PaulDoe 7 —
(P D Evans) *towards rr: pushed along over 3f out: eased whn no ch wl over 1f out* **100/1**

1m 51.9s (1.40) **Going Correction** +0.05s/f (Slow)
WFA 3 from 4yo+ 2lb **13** Ran SP% **117.9**
Speed ratings (Par 103): **95,94,92,91,90 90,88,87,84,76 74,73,55**
toteswinger:1&2:£4.20, 2&3:£3.50, 1&3:£3.60 CSF £15.24 TOTE £5.00: £1.80, £1.80, £1.30; EX 33.30 Trifecta £60.90 Pool: £453.30 - 5.50 winning units.
Owner Woolfall Manor Stud **Bred** Saud Bin Saad **Trained** Newmarket, Suffolk

FOCUS
The time was significantly slower than both divisions of the 46-55 handicap and this was a very weak maiden. The form is rated around the runner-up and the favourite was below par, but the winner can do better.

7754 TOTETRIFECTA WIN BIG MONEY TODAY H'CAP (DIV I) 1m 141y(P)
5:20 (5:20) (Class 6) (0-55,55) 3-Y-O+ **£2,047** (£604; £302) **Stalls** Low

Form RPR
0301 1 **Lunar Limelight**7 7666 4-9-2 54 6ex.... JimCrowley 10 67+
(P J Makin) *hld up in rr: nt clr run over 2f out: swtchd rt to outside ent st: hdwy over 1f out: r.o wl u.p to ld post* **7/1**3
2202 2 shd **Party In The Park**8 7653 4-8-8 51.... MatthewDavies(5) 7 62
(J R Boyle) *hld up in tch: rdn wl over 1f out: led wl ins fnl f: hdd post* **9/2**2
0006 3 1¾ **Chosen Forever**16 7579 4-9-1 53.... PJMcDonald 11 60
(G R Oldroyd) *hld up towards rr: rdn and hdwy over 1f out: r.o to take 3rd last strides* **20/1**
0034 4 nk **Interchoice Star**16 7579 4-8-12 53.... RussellKennemore(3) 13 59
(R Hollinshead) *hld up towards rr: hdwy on outside over 2f out: rdn wl over 1f out: ev ch 1f out: nt qckn* **16/1**
4342 4 dht **Bestowed**31 7374 4-9-3 55.... PaulDoe 8 61
(P D Evans) *hld up in tch: led over 2f out: rdn wl over 1f out: hdd and no ex wl ins fnl f* **13/8**1
0550 6 3¾ **Mount Usher**19 7524 7-9-1 53.... SteveDrowne 5 50
(Miss Diana Weeden) *hld up in mid-div: hdwy wl over 1f out: sn rdn: wknd ins fnl f* **18/1**

4600 7 1¼ **Stoic Leader (IRE)**3 7718 9-8-12 50.... TonyHamilton 9 45
(R F Fisher) *hld up in mid-div: pushed along over 2f out: rdn and wknd wl over 1f out* **16/1**
00-0 8 hd **Saving Grace**6 7678 3-8-13 53.... GrahamGibbons 2 47
(E J Alston) *pushed along over 7f out: a towards rr* **40/1**
065 9 4½ **Plenilune (IRE)**6 7678 4-8-12 50.... TomEaves 3 34
(M Brittain) *chsd ldrs tl wknd over 3f out* **8/1**
0000 10 nk **Dhhamaan (IRE)**6 7678 4-9-1 53.... KirstyMilczarek 1 36
(Mrs R A Carr) *led early: prom tl rdn and wknd wl over 1f out* **40/1**
3060 11 9 **Nuit Sombre (IRE)**16 7581 9-9-1 53....(v) ChrisCatlin 6 15
(G A Harker) *sn led: pushed along and hdd over 2f out: wknd over 1f out* **40/1**
6/ 12 9 **San Giustino (IRE)**24 7473 7-9-1 53....(t) StephenDonohoe 12 —
(B P Galvin, Ire) *a in rr: eased whn no ch over 2f out* **66/1**
0000 13 ¾ **Da Bomber (IRE)**14 7600 4-9-0 52.... FergusSweeney 4 —
(J W Unett) *prom: wnt 2nd 6f out: ev ch 3f out: rdn and wknd wl over 1f out: eased fnl f* **12/1**

1m 49.85s (-0.65) **Going Correction** +0.05s/f (Slow)
WFA 3 from 4yo+ 2lb **13** Ran SP% **118.2**
Speed ratings (Par 101): **104,103,102,102,102 98,97,97,93,93 85,77,76**
toteswinger:1&2:£2.90, 2&3:£11.80, 1&3:£12.00 CSF £36.46 CT £610.21 TOTE £8.60: £2.30, £1.80, £5.90; EX 20.20 Trifecta £212.20 Pool: £410.12 - 1.43 winning units.
Owner Mrs Jacqueline McColl **Bred** Angmering Park Stud **Trained** Ogbourne Maisey, Wilts

FOCUS
A strongly run affair and the quickest of the three races over the trip, including being 1.07 seconds faster than the second division. Sound form, the winner a bit beter than the bare figure.

7755 TOTETRIFECTA WIN BIG MONEY TODAY H'CAP (DIV II) 1m 141y(P)
5:50 (5:51) (Class 6) (0-55,55) 3-Y-O+ **£2,047** (£604; £302) **Stalls** Low

Form RPR
5600 1 **Climate (IRE)**14 7600 10-9-0 52....(p) PaulDoe 2 61
(P D Evans) *broke wl: led early: hld up in mid-div: hdwy on ins to ld jst over 1f out: r.o wl* **16/1**
4040 2 2½ **Achromatic**3 7718 3-9-1 55....(v) AdamKirby 10 58
(W R Swinburn) *hld up in rr: hdwy on ins over 1f out: rdn and r.o fnl f: nt trble wnr* **12/1**
0004 3 shd **King Of Rhythm (IRE)**14 7599 6-9-3 55....(p) DNolan 1 58
(D Carroll) *hld up in mid-div: hdwy wl over 1f out: rdn and r.o one pce fnl f* **9/2**3
0041 4 nk **Head First**14 7599 3-9-1 55.... DavidProbert 5 59+
(W Jarvis) *hld up towards rr: rdn over 2f out: nt clr run and swtchd rt over 1f out: r.o wl towards fin* **3/1**1
502 5 hd **Kielty's Folly**14 7600 5-8-13 51.... TonyCulhane 13 53
(B P J Baugh) *hld up towards rr: hdwy on outside 2f out: c v wd st: rdn and kpt on ins fnl f* **7/1**
6162 6 hd **Fitzolini**14 7599 3-9-1 55....(v) JimmyQuinn 4 56
(A D Brown) *led 7f out tl over 5f out: w ldr: led 2f out: rdn and hdd over 1f out: one pce fnl f* **4/1**2
3400 7 shd **Rowan Lodge (IRE)**14 7600 7-8-12 50....(b) PJMcDonald 9 51
(Ollie Pears) *hld up in mid-div: hdwy 3f out: rdn jst over 1f out: one pce* **11/1**
6000 8 nk **The Graig**26 7433 5-9-2 54....(t) JerryO'Dwyer 3 54
(J R Holt) *a.p on ins: rdn to ld briefly over 1f out: lost 2nd and fdd towards fin* **25/1**
0500 9 1 **Silca Meydan**16 7579 3-8-11 51.... ShaneKelly 6 49
(R J Price) *hld up in mid-div: pushed along over 2f out: rdn and no real prog fnl f* **20/1**
0-50 10 nk **King's Jester (IRE)**16 7579 7-8-7 52....(b) JamesPSullivan(7) 7 49
(Lee Smyth, Ire) *hld up in rr: pushed along on wd outside bnd over 2f out: c v wd st: rdn over 1f out: no rspnse* **33/1**
6065 11 shd **Sion Hill (IRE)**52 6999 8-8-12 53....(p) KellyHarrison(3) 12 50
(John A Harris) *prom: led over 5f out to 2f out: rdn over 1f out: wknd ins fnl f* **14/1**
0-60 12 nse **Mid Wicket (USA)**133 4606 3-9-1 55.... JimCrowley 11 52
(Mouse Hamilton-Fairley) *sn led: hdd 7f out: prom tl rdn and wknd over 1f out* **33/1**
00 13 1 **Wacato King (IRE)**24 7459 3-8-13 53....(t) LPKeniry 8 48
(R A Farrant) *hld up in tch: pushed along and wknd 2f out* **25/1**

1m 50.92s (0.42) **Going Correction** +0.05s/f (Slow)
WFA 3 from 5yo+ 2lb **13** Ran SP% **122.6**
Speed ratings (Par 101): **100,97,97,97,97 97,96,96,95,95 95,95,94**
toteswinger:1&2:£65.70, 2&3:£16.10, 1&3:£30.30 CSF £186.65 CT £1046.85 TOTE £25.50: £6.10, £2.40, £2.00; EX 300.40 TRIFECTA Not won. Place 6 £10.02, Place 5 £8.15. .
Owner J E Abbey **Bred** Mrs A Naughton **Trained** Pandy, Monmouths

FOCUS
They finished in a heap behind the clear-cut winner, owing to a steady early pace, and the time was 1.07 seconds slower than the first division. The form is rated around the winner, with the second, fourth and sixth all close to their recent running here.
T/Jkpt: Not won. T/Plt: £8.80 to a £1 stake. Pool: £83,817.53. 6,916.71 winning tickets. T/Qpdt: £5.40 to a £1 stake. Pool: £6,554.80. 882.50 winning tickets. KH

7721 SOUTHWELL (L-H)
Tuesday, December 15

OFFICIAL GOING: Standard
Wind: Light across Weather: Overcast

7756 BEST ODDS GUARANTEED AT TOTESPORT.COM (S) STKS 7f (F)
12:10 (12:10) (Class 6) 2-Y-O **£2,047** (£604; £302) **Stalls** Low

Form RPR
0204 1 **Lord Victor**4 7713 2-8-11 64.... ShaneKelly 3 63
(A J McCabe) *mde all: shkn up over 2f out: rdn clr fr over 1f out* **5/2**2
0006 2 4½ **Clayton Flick (IRE)**8 7669 2-8-4 50.... GillianDawson(7) 5 52
(A B Haynes) *trckd ldrs: plld hrd: rdn to chse wnr over 1f out: styd on same pce* **28/1**
4420 3 ¾ **Miss Taken (IRE)**17 7584 2-8-6 47....(b) JimmyQuinn 1 45
(D Carroll) *chsd ldrs: pushed along over 4f out: rdn over 2f out: styd on same pce appr fnl f* **9/2**
504 4 ½ **City Gossip (IRE)**48 7120 2-8-3 65.... MartinLane(3) 4 44
(M G Quinlan) *dwlt: sn pushed along in rr: rdn and hung lft fr over 2f out: nt run on* **9/4**1
0514 5 ½ **Giulietta Da Vinci**24 7493 2-8-11 70.... J-PGuillambert 6 47
(N Tinkler) *chsd ldrs: pushed along 1/2-way: rdn over 2f out: sn outpcd* **4/1**3

4104 6 7 **Taper Jean Girl (IRE)**[4] 7706 2-8-11 58 LukeMorris 2 30
(Mrs R A Carr) *w wnr tl rdn over 2f out: wknd over 1f out* **10/1**

1m 29.89s (-0.41) **Going Correction** -0.175s/f (Stan) 6 Ran SP% **110.1**
Speed ratings (Par 94): **95,89,89,88,87 79**
toteswingers: 1&2 £9.10, 1&3 £2.20, 2&3 £13.10 CSF £53.14 TOTE £3.40: £2.00, £11.50; EX 40.50.There was no bid for the winner.
Owner Khalifa Dasmal **Bred** Ellis Stud Partnership **Trained** Averham Park, Notts

FOCUS
An ordinary seller. The winner is fractionally better than this grade and the second produced a personal best too.

NOTEBOOK
Lord Victor was able to dominate, as he likes to, and ran on strongly in the straight to record his first win at the ninth attempt. He probably didn't achieve a great deal considering he had 14lb in hand over the runner-up at the weights and this is his level. (op 11-4 tchd 9-4)
Clayton Flick(IRE), buzzed up early and quite keen, made no impression on the winner under his inexperienced apprentice. (op 50-1)
Miss Taken(IRE) was well below the form she showed when ahead of today's winner in C&D claimer on her penultimate start. (op 6-1)
City Gossip(IRE) was immediately behind after starting slowly and never travelled with much enthusiasm. (op 11-4)
Giulietta Da Vinci, reported to have finished lame last time, was again well below form. (op 5-2)

7757 PLAY GOLF BEFORE RACING AT SOUTHWELL NURSERY 6f (F)
12:40 (12:48) (Class 6) (0-60,56) 2-Y-O **£2,047** (£604; £302) **Stalls** Low

Form RPR
0005 1 **The Love Guru**[9] 7654 2-9-1 50 (b) NickyMackay 9 59+
(J R Boyle) *led: hdd briefly over 1f out: rdn clr ins fnl f* **10/1**
5360 2 3 ½ **Ya Boy Sir (IRE)**[32] 7372 2-9-3 52 DarryllHolland 10 51
(N Wilson) *chsd wnr: rdn to ld briefly and hung lft fr over 1f out: styd on same pce fnl f* **11/2**[2]
6355 3 1 ½ **Marjolly (IRE)**[31] 7389 2-9-7 56 (p) JimmyQuinn 2 50+
(M Botti) *s.i.s: hld up: hdwy over 2f out: rdn over 1f out: no ex fnl f* **6/4**[1]
6306 4 ½ **Nabrina (IRE)**[49] 7088 2-8-10 52 JohnCavanagh(7) 5 45
(M Brittain) *prom: racd keenly: rdn over 2f out: styd on same pce appr fnl f* **17/2**
2005 5 ½ **Lairy (IRE)**[5] 7698 2-8-10 45 JamieMackay 1 36
(M F Harris) *chsd ldrs: rdn over 2f out: hung lft and styd on same pce appr fnl f* **11/1**
0505 6 ¾ **The Two G'S**[4] 7707 2-8-13 53 (p) AndrewHeffernan(5) 4 42
(P D Evans) *hld up: rdn over 2f out: nt trble ldrs* **25/1**
0040 7 1 **Mind Of Her Own**[1] 7749 2-9-1 55 RichardEvans(5) 6 41
(P D Evans) *hld up: hdwy over 2f out: rdn rdn: hung lft fnl f: nt trble ldrs* **12/1**
000 8 ½ **Master Of Song**[12] 7616 2-8-10 45 (b) StephenDonohoe 3 29
(S R Bowring) *hld up: bhd and pushed along 4f out: styd on towards fin: nvr nrr* **66/1**
0665 9 1 **Feel The Magic (IRE)**[1] 7749 2-8-13 48 ShaneKelly 8 29
(S Kirk) *chsd ldrs: rdn and edgd rt over 2f out: wknd fnl f* **16/1**
5064 10 ½ **Rightcar**[12] 7619 2-9-4 53 TPQueally 7 33
(Peter Grayson) *s.s: sn pushed along in rr: sme hdwy u.p over 2f out: sn wknd* **15/2**[3]

1m 16.88s (0.38) **Going Correction** -0.175s/f (Stan) 10 Ran SP% **114.0**
Speed ratings (Par 94): **90,85,83,82,82 81,79,79,77,77**
toteswingers: 1&2 £5.90, 1&3 £4.10, 2&3 £3.10 CSF £62.69 CT £131.94 TOTE £9.60: £2.10, £1.90, £1.50; EX 78.10 Trifecta £167.80 Part won. Pool of £226.78 - 0.20 winning units..
Owner M Khan X2 **Bred** Ambersham Stud **Trained** Epsom, Surrey
■ Stewards' Enquiry : Shane Kelly cautiion: careless riding

FOCUS
A moderate nursery and, just as in the opener, it proved difficult to make up ground. Low-grade but sound form, rated around the second and fourth, with a big step up from the winner.

NOTEBOOK
The Love Guru showed good speed to make the running on this drop back to his shortest trip to date and was game when strongly challenged in the straight to eventually draw away. It seems the way the track was riding put him at an advantage, but even so, he can probably win again, especially on this surface. Official explanation: the trainer's representative said, regarding the running of the gelding, that the horse appreciated the drop from seven furlongs and wearing blinkers (op 7-1)
Ya Boy Sir(IRE) was always handily placed and had his chance. (op 9-2)
Marjolly(IRE), well backed, emerges with plenty of credit considering not only did he fare best of those who raced off the pace, having missed the break, but he also raced towards the inside for much of the way, which probably wasn't ideal. (op 9-4 tchd 11-8)
Nabrina(IRE) plugged on without threatening and is now 0-8. (op 10-1 tchd 11-1)
Lairy(IRE) is still looking for a first win. He didn't improve for the switch to Fibresand. (tchd 10-1)
Master Of Song beat a couple of rivals despite running loose beforehand and getting behind in the race itself. (op 40-1)

7758 BIGGER "WIN ONLY" ODDS AT TOTESPORT.COM H'CAP 5f (F)
1:10 (1:13) (Class 4) (0-85,82) 3-Y-O+ **£4,857** (£1,445; £722; £360) **Stalls** High

Form RPR
5412 1 **Nickel Silver**[10] 7646 4-9-3 81 (v) TomEaves 12 94
(B Smart) *mde all: shkn up over 1f out: drvn out* **9/1**
1023 2 ¾ **Colorus (IRE)**[7] 7676 6-8-4 73 (p) PaulPickard(5) 5 83
(W J H Ratcliffe) *a.p: chsd wnr over 3f out: rdn over 1f out: r.o* **10/3**[1]
5000 3 1 ½ **Pawan (IRE)**[7] 7676 9-8-11 80 (b) AnnStokell(5) 13 85
(Miss A Stokell) *sn pushed along towards rr: hdwy u.p over 1f out: edgd lft ins fnl f: r.o: nt rch ldrs* **33/1**
0060 4 1 **Stolt (IRE)**[29] 7414 5-9-4 82 (p) DarryllHolland 7 83
(N Wilson) *chsd ldrs: rdn over 1f out: styd on same pce* **14/1**
3500 5 ¾ **Bo McGinty (IRE)**[11] 7634 8-7-11 68 oh1 (v) TimothyAyres(7) 10 66+
(R A Fahey) *hld up: nt clr run 1f out: swtchd rt and r.o ins fnl f: nt trble ldrs* **33/1**
600 6 ½ **Ingleby Star (IRE)**[48] 7119 4-8-6 70 (p) JimmyQuinn 8 67
(N Wilson) *edgd rt s: chsd ldrs: rdn 1/2-way: styd on same pce fnl f* **40/1**
0124 7 ½ **Bel Cantor**[7] 7676 6-8-11 78 KellyHarrison(3) 1 73
(W J H Ratcliffe) *prom: rdn 1/2-way: wknd ins fnl f* **7/2**[2]
0044 8 hd **Loose Caboose (IRE)**[7] 7679 4-7-11 68 oh1 (b) DeclanCannon(7) 4 62
(A J McCabe) *sn drvn along in rr: nvr nrr* **12/1**
6066 9 2 ¼ **Flash McGahon (IRE)**[88] 6051 5-9-2 80 AndrewMullen 3 66
(D Nicholls) *dwlt: sn bhd and pushed along: nvr nrr* **11/1**
2603 10 ¾ **Godfrey Street**[42] 7219 6-8-2 71 oh1 ow3 (b) AndrewHeffernan(5) 6 54
(A G Newcombe) *chsd ldrs: rdn 1/2-way: wknd over 1f out* **22/1**
3130 11 ½ **Steelcut**[67] 6632 5-8-6 70 JoeFanning 14 51
(M J Scudamore) *chsd ldrs: rdn 1/2-way: wknd over 1f out* **20/1**
3105 12 ¾ **Elusive Hawk (IRE)**[21] 7506 5-8-11 75 TPQueally 11 54
(B J Curley) *rrd s: wl bhd: rdn over 1f out: mod late prog* **12/1**
5053 13 1 ¼ **The Tatling (IRE)**[14] 7605 12-9-1 82 JackDean(3) 2 56
(J M Bradley) *chsd ldrs: pushed along 1/2-way: wknd over 1f out* **12/1**
0035 14 5 **Calmdownmate (IRE)**[141] 4374 4-8-8 72 LukeMorris 9 28
(Mrs R A Carr) *hmpd sn after s: pushed along in rr: lost tch fnl 3f* **15/2**[3]

59.93 secs (0.23) **Going Correction** +0.175s/f (Slow) 14 Ran SP% **122.6**
Speed ratings (Par 105): **105,103,101,99,98 97,97,96,93,91 91,89,87,79**
toteswingers: 1&2 £2.40, 1&3 £4.50, 2&3 £5.90 CSF £37.37 CT £1006.26 TOTE £6.60: £2.40, £2.00, £5.50; EX 30.30 Trifecta £278.90 Part won. Pool of £376.98 - 0.55 winning units..
Owner M Barber **Bred** Mrs Sheila White **Trained** Hambleton, N Yorks
■ Stewards' Enquiry : Paul Pickard three-day ban: used whip with excessive frequency (29 -31 Dec(

FOCUS
A fair handicap won well by Nickel Silver who produced a clear personal best.

7759 BET ON TONIGHT'S FOOTBALL AT TOTESPORT.COM H'CAP 1m (F)
1:40 (1:41) (Class 4) (0-85,85) 3-Y-O+ **£4,857** (£1,445; £722; £360) **Stalls** Low

Form RPR
6530 1 **Snow Bay**[20] 7516 3-8-10 76 GregFairley 9 87
(B Smart) *chsd ldrs: pushed along and hung rt over 3f out: sn rdn: led ins fnl f: r.o* **10/1**
6601 2 nk **Miss Glitters (IRE)**[49] 7092 4-9-1 80 SteveDrowne 5 90
(H Morrison) *sn pushed along and prom: rdn to ld over 1f out: hdd ins fnl f: r.o* **3/1**[2]
3256 3 2 ¼ **Ours (IRE)**[48] 7125 6-8-9 74 ow1 (p) DarryllHolland 10 79
(John A Harris) *mid-div: pushed along 1/2-way: hdwy over 2f out: rdn and edgd lft fr over 1f out: r.o* **10/1**
0020 4 hd **Hits Only Jude (IRE)**[73] 6495 6-8-12 77 DNolan 4 82
(D Carroll) *hld up: hdwy over 1f out: sn rdn: r.o* **16/1**
0102 5 1 **Tamasou (IRE)**[11] 7633 4-8-13 78 ShaneKelly 1 80
(A J McCabe) *chsd ldr: rdn and ev ch over 1f out: no ex ins fnl f* **13/2**[3]
0103 6 1 ½ **Elusive Fame (USA)**[4] 7711 3-8-5 71 (b) JoeFanning 8 70
(M Johnston) *trckd ldrs: rdn over 2f out: no ex fnl f* **5/2**[1]
5504 7 nk **Spiritofthewest (IRE)**[24] 7481 3-8-4 70 oh1 AndrewMullen 3 68
(D H Brown) *led: rdn over 2f out: hdd over 1f out: wknd ins fnl f* **14/1**
1446 8 3 ¼ **Gaily Noble (IRE)**[18] 7560 3-8-12 78 FergusSweeney 7 69
(A B Haynes) *hld up: effrt over 2f out: wknd over 1f out* **12/1**
2602 9 nse **Xpres Maite**[36] 7322 6-9-1 80 (b) AmirQuinn 6 71
(S R Bowring) *sn pushed along in rr: bhd and rdn 1/2-way: nvr nrr* **7/1**
6 10 17 **Lastkingofscotland (IRE)**[15] 6143 3-9-5 85 PaulDoe 11 36
(G C Bravery) *dwlt: outpcd* **33/1**
0300 11 ½ **Theonebox (USA)**[14] 7607 4-8-10 75 StephenDonohoe 2 25
(N P Moore) *sn pushed along and prom: rdn over 3f out: wknd 2f out* **66/1**

1m 41.1s (-2.60) **Going Correction** -0.175s/f (Stan)
WFA 3 from 4yo+ 1lb 11 Ran SP% **122.3**
Speed ratings (Par 105): **106,105,103,103,102 100,100,97,97,80 79**
toteswingers: 1&2 £12.70, 1&3 £18.70, 2&3 £8.30 CSF £41.73 CT £328.88 TOTE £13.40: £3.70, £2.20, £1.70; EX 76.50 TRIFECTA Not won..
Owner Pinnacle Bahamian Bounty Partnership **Bred** West Dereham Abbey Stud **Trained** Hambleton, N Yorks

FOCUS
A fair handicap. The first two pulled clear with a personal best from Snow Bay to beat the progressive Miss Glitters.

7760 BET LIVE IN PLAY AT TOTESPORT.COM H'CAP 2m (F)
2:10 (2:10) (Class 5) (0-75,73) 3-Y-O+ **£2,729** (£806; £403) **Stalls** Low

Form RPR
3413 1 **Calculating (IRE)**[31] 7402 5-9-0 64 LeeNewnes(5) 6 74
(M D I Usher) *hld up: hdwy over 2f out: rdn to ld and hung rt fr over 1f out: styd on wl* **4/1**[2]
2222 2 3 ½ **Lost Soldier Three (IRE)**[21] 7505 8-10-0 73 AndrewMullen 7 79
(D Nicholls) *trckd ldrs: racd keenly: wnt 2nd over 3f out: rdn and ev ch over 1f out: styd on same pce ins fnl f* **15/8**[1]
1352 3 1 ¼ **Resplendent Ace (IRE)**[8] 7668 5-9-12 71 IanMongan 3 76
(P Howling) *hld up: hdwy over 3f out: rdn over 2f out: nt clr run and swtchd lft ins fnl f: no ex* **7/1**
2433 4 2 **Zuwaar**[15] 7598 4-9-10 69 (tp) JoeFanning 4 71
(Ian Williams) *led: rdn over 2f out: hung rt fr over 1f out: wknd ins fnl f* **9/2**[3]
3555 5 ½ **Victory Quest (IRE)**[7] 7675 9-9-8 72 (v) AndrewHeffernan(5) 1 74
(Mrs S Lamyman) *prom: rdn over 3f out: styd on same pce fnl 2f* **28/1**
-020 6 2 ½ **Three Boars**[27] 7124 7-9-1 60 (b) DarryllHolland 2 59
(S Gollings) *pushed along early: hld up: tk clsr order 6f out: rdn over 4f out: outpcd fnl 3f* **16/1**
4014 7 17 **Dubai Diva**[29] 7415 3-8-8 61 TomEaves 5 39
(C F Wall) *racd keenly: trckd ldr tl rdn over 3f out: wknd over 2f out* **9/2**[3]

3m 43.23s (-2.27) **Going Correction** -0.175s/f (Stan)
WFA 3 from 4yo+ 8lb 7 Ran SP% **113.0**
Speed ratings (Par 103): **98,96,95,94,94 93,84**
toteswingers: 1&2 £9.60, 1&3 £7.70, 2&3 £6.00 CSF £11.64 TOTE £4.40: £2.40, £2.10; EX 15.50.
Owner Brian Rogan **Bred** Darley **Trained** Upper Lambourn, Berks

FOCUS
A fair handicap, but the pace was steady until increasing down the back straight. The winner is rated in line with this year's form.

7761 HOSPITALITY AT SOUTHWELL RACECOURSE (S) STKS 1m 3f (F)
2:40 (2:40) (Class 6) 3-Y-O+ **£2,047** (£604; £302) **Stalls** Low

Form RPR
0046 1 **Dream In Blue**[8] 7670 4-8-12 65 (p) SimonPearce(5) 9 66
(J A Glover) *hld up: rdn over 4f out: hdwy u.p to ld and hung lft fr over 1f out: clr ins fnl f* **8/1**
/05- 2 3 ¾ **Jazrawy**[644] 847 7-9-3 60 ShaneKelly 6 60
(A J McCabe) *hld up in tch: rdn over 2f out: chsd wnr fnl f: styd on same pce* **11/1**
0250 3 nk **My Mate Mal**[1] 7752 5-9-9 63 TomEaves 1 65
(B Ellison) *led: pushed along over 3f out: rdn and hdd over 1f out: styd on same pce fnl f* **6/1**[3]
2330 4 ½ **Mustajed**[127] 4855 8-9-6 74 JamesMillman(3) 8 64
(B R Millman) *hld up: hdwy u.p over 1f out: nt trble ldrs* **2/1**[1]
-362 5 hd **Acropolis (IRE)**[10] 7647 8-9-3 65 VinceSlattery 7 58
(B G Powell) *pushed along early: rdn and hung lft fr over 4f out: styd on same pce appr fnl f* **9/2**[2]
0000 6 6 **Bernix**[21] 7500 7-9-3 43 (p) J-PGuillambert 2 51
(N Tinkler) *chsd ldr: pushed along over 4f out: rdn and wknd over 1f out: eased ins fnl f* **100/1**

2656 **7** 1 ½ **Friends Hope**[225] 8-8-12 72 .... FrankieMcDonald 4 40
(R Curtis) *chsd ldrs: bmpd after 1f: rdn over 2f out: wknd over 1f out* **2/1**[1]
5300 **8** 7 **Special Chapter (IRE)**[34] 7336 4-8-7 41 .... AmyBaker(5) 5 28
(A B Haynes) *chsd ldrs: rdn over 5f out: wknd 3f out* **50/1**
2/5- **9** hd **Marsam (IRE)**[52] 47 6-9-3 69 .... (b[1]) JerryO'Dwyer 3 33
(M G Quinlan) *s.i.s: hld up: rdn over 5f out: lost tch fr over 3f out* **20/1**
2m 26.26s (-1.74) **Going Correction** -0.175s/f (Stan) **9 Ran SP% 126.3**
Speed ratings (Par 101): **99,96,96,95,95 91,90,85,84**
toteswingers: 1&2 £9.60, 1&3 £7.70, 2&3 £6.00 CSF £97.31 TOTE £9.10: £2.40, £3.40, £1.70; EX 106.00 Trifecta £266.50 Part won. Pool of £360.17 - 0.10 winning units..There was no bid for the winner.
Owner Paul J Dixon & Brian Morton **Bred** Shutford Stud **Trained** Babworth, Notts

FOCUS
An ordinary seller. It was well run but the form is a bit suspect. It has been rated around the winner.

7762 BOOK YOUR TICKETS AT SOUTHWELL-RACECOURSE.CO.UK H'CAP 7f (F)
3:10 (3:11) (Class 6) (0-65,71) 3-Y-O+ **£2,047** (£604; £302) **Stalls** Low

Form RPR
2043 **1** **Whitbarrow (IRE)**[10] 7645 10-8-13 **63** .... (b) JamesMillman(3) 9 73
(B R Millman) *w ldr tl led 1/2-way: rdn over 1f out: styd on wl* **9/1**
4062 **2** 1 ¾ **Elusive Warrior (USA)**[33] 7349 6-9-0 **61** .... (p) ShaneKelly 10 66
(A J McCabe) *led to 1/2-way: chsd wnr thereafter: rdn over 1f out: styd on* **7/1**[3]
6361 **3** 1 ½ **Kipchak (IRE)**[4] 7716 4-9-10 **71** 6ex .... (p) TPQueally 13 72
(C R Dore) *wnt lft s: chsd ldrs: rdn over 2f out: sn hung lft: styd on u.p* **9/2**[1]
026 **4** 1 **Miss Bootylishes**[34] 7337 4-8-13 **65** .... AmyBaker(5) 6 64
(A B Haynes) *mid-div: hdwy 2f out: r.o: nt rch ldrs* **20/1**
6163 **5** 1 ¾ **Naomh Geileis (USA)**[3] 7728 4-9-3 **64** .... (b) JoeFanning 1 58
(M Johnston) *sn pushed along and prom: rdn over 2f out: styd on same pce appr fnl f* **5/1**[2]
3210 **6** 2 ¼ **Gracie's Gift (IRE)**[201] 2418 7-8-10 **57** .... GrahamGibbons 11 45+
(R C Guest) *hmpd s: sn chsng ldrs: rdn over 2f out: wknd over 1f out* **15/2**
6000 **7** shd **Avoir Choisi (IRE)**[53] 6984 3-9-4 **65** .... DarryllHolland 4 52
(N Wilson) *sn pushed along in rr: hung lft and rdn over 1f out: n.d* **16/1**
5041 **8** ½ **Danum Dancer**[7] 7680 5-9-2 **63** 6ex .... (b) LeeVickers 5 49+
(N Bycroft) *s.s: sme hdwy over 1f out: eased ins fnl f* **7/1**[3]
3-00 **9** nk **Desert Mile (IRE)**[15] 7596 6-9-3 **64** .... PJMcDonald 7 49
(Ollie Pears) *s.i.s: a in rr: no ch whn nt clr run wl over 1f out* **50/1**
0630 **10** 2 ¼ **Guildenstern (IRE)**[28] 7424 7-8-12 **59** .... JimmyQuinn 8 38
(P Howling) *hld up: shkn up over 2f out: nvr on terms* **20/1**
3063 **11** 2 ¼ **Capo Regime**[7] 7679 3-9-1 **62** .... (v) KirstyMilczarek 3 35
(P Howling) *prom: racd keenly: rdn 1/2-way: wknd over 2f out* **17/2**
035 **12** 15 **Trimlestown (IRE)**[6] 7691 6-8-13 **65** .... (v) RichardEvans(5) 2 —
(P D Evans) *prom: rdn 1/2-way: sn wknd* **28/1**
3403 **13** 5 **Verinco**[39] 7270 3-9-1 **62** .... (p) TomEaves 12 —
(B Smart) *hmpd s: sn prom: rdn and wknd over 2f out* **12/1**
1m 28.73s (-1.57) **Going Correction** -0.175s/f (Stan) **13 Ran SP% 120.6**
Speed ratings (Par 101): **101,99,97,96,94 91,91,90,90,87 85,68,62**
toteswingers: 1&2 £6.70, 1&3 £8.80, 2&3 £4.80 CSF £68.23 CT £267.04 TOTE £11.70: £3.00, £2.30, £2.30; EX 87.60 TRIFECTA Not won. Place 6: £201.22 Place 5: £67.25.
Owner Mrs H Brain **Bred** James Burns And A Moynan **Trained** Kentisbeare, Devon

FOCUS
The first three were in the front three throughout, continuing the theme of pace horses being at an advantage in races at up to 1m on this card. The winner is rated back to his early-season form.
T/Plt: £873.90 to a £1 stake. Pool: £48,846.04. 40.80 winning tickets. T/Qpdt: £121.30 to a £1 stake. Pool: £6,427.90. 39.20 winning tickets. CR

7736 KEMPTON (A.W) (R-H)
Wednesday, December 16

OFFICIAL GOING: Standard
Wind: Light, half behind Weather: Steady rain, cold

7763 EUROPEAN BREEDERS' FUND MAIDEN STKS (DIV I) 1m (P)
5:50 (5:50) (Class 5) 2-Y-O **£3,885** (£1,156; £577; £288) **Stalls** High

Form RPR
1 **Gracious Melange** 2-8-12 0 .... KFallon 1 76+
(M Botti) *trckd ldng trio: pushed along over 3f out: prog on outer 2f out: shkn up to ld 1f out: sn in command* **12/1**
0 **2** 2 **Tiger Star**[20] 7537 2-9-3 0 .... LukeMorris 7 76
(J M P Eustace) *awkward s: in last trio tl prog on inner over 2f out: drvn and styd on wl ins fnl f: tk 2nd fnl strides* **22/1**
43 **3** hd **Elvira Madigan**[12] 7622 2-8-12 0 .... LPKeniry 9 71
(A M Balding) *led: rdn 2f out: hdd 1f out: sn hld by wnr: lost 2nd last strides* **11/4**[2]
04 **4** 1 ¼ **Ming Master (FR)**[11] 7644 2-9-3 0 .... TonyCulhane 5 73
(W J Haggas) *sn in 5th: pushed along over 3f out: no prog whn shkn up over 2f out: styd on ins fnl f: snatched 4th on post* **6/1**
03 **5** shd **Sasheen**[12] 7624 2-8-12 0 .... SJCraine 10 68
(J R Boyle) *trckd ldng pair: wnt 2nd 2f out to over 1f out: fdd fnl f* **5/2**[1]
56 **6** 6 **Bondage (IRE)**[20] 7537 2-9-3 0 .... HayleyTurner 4 60
(J R Fanshawe) *settled in 6th: pushed along over 3f out: hanging and no prog over 2f out: wknd over 1f out* **9/1**
536 **7** 2 ¼ **Love Delta (USA)**[100] 5728 2-9-3 75 .... JoeFanning 3 55
(M Johnston) *chsd ldr to 2f out: wknd rapidly* **7/2**[3]
8 3 ¼ **Colonel Henry** 2-9-3 0 .... PaulDoe 8 48
(S Dow) *s.v.s: mostly in last and nvr on terms* **50/1**
0 **9** 12 **Bonamassa**[21] 7522 2-9-3 0 .... JimCrowley 2 21
(M J Attwater) *a in last trio: t.o* **100/1**
1m 39.21s (-0.59) **Going Correction** 0.0s/f (Stan) **9 Ran SP% 116.7**
Speed ratings (Par 96): **102,100,99,98,98 92,90,86,74**
toteswinger:1&2:£15.20, 2&3:£11.60, 1&3:£6.80 CSF £226.14 TOTE £10.40: £3.50, £4.00, £1.10; EX 225.20.
Owner Mrs R J Jacobs **Bred** Newsells Park Stud **Trained** Newmarket, Suffolk

FOCUS
A reasonable maiden run at a fair pace. The time was 1.41 seconds above standard.

NOTEBOOK
Gracious Melange was weak in the market but got a good position just behind the pace and swept to the front at the furlong marker to win in good style on debut. The £58,000 daughter of Medicean has plenty of winners at 7f-1m4f on the dam's side of her pedigree and looks a nice prospect. (op 11-1 tchd 10-1)

Tiger Star caught the eye staying on strongly against the far rail and improved significantly on his debut effort in blinkers over 7f here last month. He could be capable of better at this trip, or over further, and is out of a well-related mare who has produced the useful Rapscallion and the smart/quirky Orcadian. (op 20-1 tchd 16-1)

Elvira Madigan set the standard and gave it a good shot from the front but was just outgunned in the closing stages. Some of her close relatives have looked temperamental but she looks a willing customer and adds some solidity to the form. (op 5-2 tchd 7-2)

Ming Master(FR) was nudged along some way out but stayed on steadily and has confirmed the promise of his 50-1 fourth in a Wolverhampton maiden this month. He still has a bit to learn but could be the type to do well in handicaps at 1m-1m2f. (tchd 11-2)

Sasheen had decent form claims on her third at 33-1 in a 1m Lingfield maiden this month. She was well backed and got an ideal position just behind the leaders but did not find as much as expected and could only plug on. (op 7-2)

Love Delta(USA) raced keenly near the pace and was beaten halfway up the straight. He has been disappointing in three runs since a promising debut at Goodwood in August and needs to learn to settle better. (tchd 3-1)

7764 EUROPEAN BREEDERS' FUND MAIDEN STKS (DIV II) 1m (P)
6:20 (6:22) (Class 5) 2-Y-O **£3,885** (£1,156; £577; £288) **Stalls** High

Form RPR
3 **1** **Valid Reason**[21] 7522 2-9-3 0 .... JimCrowley 8 78+
(Mrs A J Perrett) *pushed up to ld after 1f: mde rest: rdn and edgd lft over 2f out: hrd pressed and edgd lft again fnl f: kpt on wl* **8/13**[1]
2 ¾ **Balducci** 2-9-3 0 .... LPKeniry 1 76+
(A M Balding) *dwlt: rn green early and pushed along in last trio: taken to outer and prog over 2f out: wnt 2nd over 1f out and sn chalng: pressed wnr 100yds out: green again and hld after* **8/1**
03 **3** 2 ¼ **Bonded (IRE)**[25] 7491 2-9-3 0 .... EddieAhern 6 71
(B J Meehan) *trckd ldng pair: hd high and nt qckn u.p over 2f out: styd on again fnl f* **11/2**[3]
4 2 ¾ **Capricornus (USA)** 2-9-3 0 .... JoeFanning 4 65
(M Johnston) *led 1f: chsd wnr: rdn over 2f out: lost 2nd over 1f out: fdd* **4/1**[2]
40 **5** 4 **Jazz Age (IRE)**[25] 7491 2-9-3 0 .... ChrisCatlin 7 57
(J A Glover) *fastest away but restrained into last trio: pushed along and modest prog over 2f out: nvr nr ldrs* **33/1**
00 **6** nk **New Den**[188] 2844 2-9-3 0 .... SJCraine 2 56
(J R Boyle) *mostly in same pl: rdn 3f out: no real prog* **33/1**
7 1 ¼ **Double Fortune** 2-8-12 0 .... RobertHavlin 5 48
(Jamie Poulton) *chsd ldng trio to over 2f out: lost pl qckly* **100/1**
8 nk **Your Lad** 2-9-3 0 .... JackMitchell 3 52
(C F Wall) *s.i.s: mostly in last trio: brief effrt over 2f out: sn btn* **20/1**
0 **9** 4 ½ **Ring Of Fire**[20] 7538 2-9-3 0 .... LiamJones 9 43
(J L Spearing) *chsd ldrs: rdn 3f out: wknd 2f out* **66/1**
1m 40.82s (1.02) **Going Correction** 0.0s/f (Stan) **9 Ran SP% 121.5**
Speed ratings (Par 96): **94,93,91,88,84 83,82,82,77**
toteswinger:1&2:£3.50, 2&3:£4.20, 1&3:£2.80 CSF £6.87 TOTE £1.60: £1.10, £2.70, £1.30; EX 11.60.Highland Cadett was withdrawn price at time of withdrawal 50/1. Rule 4 does not apply.
Owner K Abdulla **Bred** Juddmonte Farms Ltd **Trained** Pulborough, W Sussex

FOCUS
A fair maiden won in tenacious style by the hot favourite and there was plenty of promise from a couple of newcomers.

NOTEBOOK
Valid Reason set the target for the others to aim at on his third of 12 in a fair 1m Lingfield maiden on debut last month. He had to work hard under a forcing ride to see off a persistent late challenger but pulled out more when needed and looks a co-operative type. His half-brother Truism is an improving miler, who was second off 87 in October, and he could develop a similarly progressive profile. (tchd 4-6)

Balducci ran a huge race on debut. He missed the break and was a bit keen early on but produced a power-packed finish off the steady pace to give the favourite a major scare. He should have learned a lot from this initial experience and is a brother to two useful Polytrack winners and a half-brother to two other winners. (op 16-1)

Bonded(IRE) carried his head at an awkward angle but responded well to pressure when switched out wide. The half-brother to top-class 2-y-o Flashy Wings is not entirely streetwise and may have a quirk or two, but he seems to be quietly progressing and is now qualified for a mark. (tchd 13-2)

Capricornus(USA) showed up well for a long way on his debut and should know more next time. He cost $65,000 as a yearling and has a decent US pedigree and a scopey physique. (op 5-1)

Jazz Age(IRE) showed some ability when blinkered for John Gosden on debut but failed to build on that for his new trainer last month and was well held again here.

Highland Cadett gave trouble at the start and refused to enter the stalls.

7765 DIGIBET MEDIAN AUCTION MAIDEN STKS 1m 3f (P)
6:50 (6:51) (Class 6) 3-5-Y-O **£2,047** (£604; £302) **Stalls** High

Form RPR
0630 **1** **Champagne Fizz (IRE)**[57] 6918 3-8-12 55 .... DaneO'Neill 4 59
(Miss Jo Crowley) *hld up in last but cl up: prog on outer to ld 2f out: rdn and styd on wl* **9/2**[3]
5043 **2** 2 **Dovedon Angel**[9] 7660 3-8-12 51 .... JerryO'Dwyer 5 56
(Miss Gay Kelleway) *hld up in midfield and cl up: prog to chse ldng pair over 1f out: hanging and nt qckn: kpt on to take 2nd nr fin* **4/1**[2]
0004 **3** nk **Ryker (IRE)**[5] 7718 3-9-3 57 .... EddieAhern 6 60
(J W Hills) *trckd ldng pair: looking for gap fr 3f out which appeared jst over 2f out: nt qckn w wnr: chsng after and hld: lost 2nd nr fin* **15/8**[1]
4 1 ¾ **Danderek**[11] 3-8-12 0 .... BMcHugh(5) 8 57+
(R A Fahey) *hld up in rr but in cl tch: outpcd jst over 2f out and swtchd to outer: signs of greenness but kpt on fnl f* **9/2**[3]
4060 **5** 3 **Haling Park (UAE)**[13] 6787 3-8-12 48 .... DavidProbert 1 47
(G L Moore) *wl in tch: rdn and nt qckn jst over 2f out: fdd* **8/1**
-000 **6** 2 ½ **Franchesca's Gold**[34] 7361 3-8-12 45 .... LPKeniry 3 43
(Jane Southcombe) *w ldr: led 3f out to 2f out: wknd* **50/1**
40 **7** 13 **Intimar (IRE)**[35] 7324 3-8-12 45 .... HayleyTurner 2 21
(R J Smith) *led at mod pce to 3f out: wknd rapidly 2f out: t.o* **25/1**
2m 22.95s (1.05) **Going Correction** 0.0s/f (Stan)
WFA 3 from 4yo 4lb **7 Ran SP% 108.1**
Speed ratings (Par 101): **96,94,94,93,90 89,79**
toteswinger:1&2:£3.20, 2&3:£2.50, 1&3:£1.90 CSF £20.15 TOTE £7.10: £3.10, £2.50; EX 14.80.
Owner Mrs Liz Nelson **Bred** Mrs R I Nelson **Trained** Whitcombe, Dorset

FOCUS
An ordinary maiden auction and muddling form, despite the first three being rated close to their marks.

7766 DIGIBET CASINO H'CAP (DIV I) 1m 3f (P)
7:20 (7:20) (Class 6) (0-60,60) 3-Y-O+ £1,706 (£503; £252) Stalls High

Form RPR
4050 **1** **Tyrana (GER)**[56] 6945 6-9-0 **52**.................. StephenDonohoe 11 64
(Ian Williams) *trckd ldng pair: wnt 2nd over 3f out: rdn to cl fr 2f out: styd on wl to edge ahd ins fnl f* **11/4**[1]
5002 **2** *¾* **Silken Promise (USA)**[7] 7688 3-8-13 **55**..........(p) AdamKirby 2 66
(W R Swinburn) *set stdy pce: kicked on 2f out: hrd rdn and worn down ins fnl f* **4/1**[3]
0000 **3** *4* **Mister Frosty (IRE)**[9] 7666 3-8-8 **50**.................. SaleemGolam 6 54
(G Prodromou) *trckd ldrs: wnt 3rd 3f out: rdn and outpcd by ldng pair over 2f out: kpt on wl but no imp* **20/1**
0450 **4** *4* **Sir Haydn**[10] 7658 9-8-4 **49**..................(v) DannyBrock(7) 4 46
(J R Jenkins) *stdd s: t.k.h in rr: prog on outer to go prom 4f out: chsd ldng trio over 2f out: no imp* **20/1**
0266 **5** *shd* **Our Kes (IRE)**[21] 7512 7-9-5 **57**.................. IanMongan 7 54+
(P Howling) *hld up in last pair: effrt on inner 3f out: sme prog to take 5th 2f out but ldrs already wl gone: no imp* **9/2**
0/60 **6** *2* **Croix Rouge (USA)**[35] 7328 7-9-1 **60**.................. KierenFox(7) 1 54
(R J Smith) *hld up in last pair: taken to wd outside bnd 3f out: limited prog fnl 2f but nvr any ch* **9/1**
0/20 **7** *1* **Warren Bank**[22] 7504 4-9-7 **59**.................. HayleyTurner 3 51
(Mrs Mary Hambro) *t.k.h in midfield: outpcd and shkn up over 2f out: nvr on terms after* **33/1**
P000 **8** *shd* **Mixing**[7] 7688 7-8-9 **52**.................. JemmaMarshall(5) 5 44
(M J Attwater) *hld up towards rr: easily outpcd fr over 2f out* **33/1**
3 **9** *shd* **Grove View Star**[5] 7719 4-9-4 **56**..................(t) SJCraine 8 48
(Patrick Morris) *awkward s: hld up in last trio: gng easily whn nt clr run over 2f out: swtchd ins and rn into trble again: lost all ch after* **7/2**[2]
000/ **10** *1 ¾* **Immaculate Red**[27] 3752 6-8-8 **46** oh1.................. LukeMorris 10 35
(C Roberts) *trckd ldrs tl wknd u.p over 2f out* **80/1**
000/ **11** *4 ½* **Zizou (IRE)**[465] 630 6-8-8 **46** oh1.................. KirstyMilczarek 9 27
(S Curran) *chsd ldr to over 3f out: wknd rapidly* **25/1**

2m 22.43s (0.53) **Going Correction** 0.0s/f (Stan)
WFA 3 from 4yo+ 4lb **11 Ran SP% 117.6**
Speed ratings (Par 101): **98,97,94,91,91 90,89,89,89,87 84**
toteswinger:1&2:£3.90, 2&3:£8.30, 1&3:£19.60 CSF £12.58 CT £183.47 TOTE £4.00: £2.10, £1.60, £3.80; EX 17.20.
Owner T Bhoot **Bred** Gestut Brummerhof **Trained** Portway, Worcs

FOCUS
An ordinary handicap run at a steady pace, but the first two pulled a long way clear. One was well backed and the other went close on her previous start, so the form could work out.

7767 DIGIBET CASINO H'CAP (DIV II) 1m 3f (P)
7:50 (7:50) (Class 6) (0-60,59) 3-Y-O+ £1,706 (£503; £252) Stalls High

Form RPR
0-30 **1** **Winning Show**[16] 1463 5-9-0 **51**..................(t) LPKeniry 7 60
(C Gordon) *hld up in rr: dived to inner and prog 2f out: drvn to ld narrowly ins fnl f: hld on* **16/1**
000 **2** *shd* **Under Fire (IRE)**[42] 7240 6-9-1 **52**.................. ShaneKelly 8 61
(A W Carroll) *led at decent clip: rdn over 2f out: pressed on all sides over 1f out: hrd rdn and hdd ins fnl f: kpt on wl: jst foiled* **16/1**
4044 **3** *nk* **Inch Lodge**[12] 7628 7-9-5 **59**..................(t) WilliamCarson(3) 3 67
(Miss D Mountain) *dwlt: hld up in last trio: prog on wd outside 3f out: drvn to cl on ldrs 2f out: wnt 3rd ins fnl f: gaining at fin* **4/1**[2]
6000 **4** *1 ¼* **Rock Tech**[14] 7609 4-8-2 **46**.................. DannyBrock(7) 9 52
(J R Jenkins) *mostly chsd ldr to 2f out: styd cl up: one pce fnl f* **100/1**
0003 **5** *2* **Midnight Bay**[11] 7647 3-8-7 **53**.................. AndrewHeffernan(5) 2 55
(P D Evans) *trckd ldrs: rdn to chal over 2f out: cl enough over 1f out: wknd fnl f* **16/1**
0000 **6** *½* **Lyrical Intent**[10] 7658 3-8-8 **49**.................. JimmyQuinn 5 51
(P Howling) *trckd ldrs: tried to chal over 2f out: nt qckn and nt clr run over 1f out: fdd* **25/1**
3441 **7** *2* **Mr Plod**[10] 7658 4-9-5 **56** 6ex.................. SJCraine 6 54
(M J Scudamore) *hld up in midfield gng wl: angled off rail looking for run over 2f out: no rspnse whn rdn 2f out* **4/6**[1]
3100 **8** *3 ½* **Hatch A Plan (IRE)**[136] 4563 8-9-6 **57**.................. JimCrowley 1 49
(Mouse Hamilton-Fairley) *blindfold late off and dwlt: hld up last: rdn over 2f out: sn lft bhd by ldrs* **22/1**
9 *shd* **Andaman Sunset**[226] 1728 4-9-4 **55**..................(tp) RobertWinston 10 47
(J L Spearing) *trckd ldrs: tried to chal over 2f out: wknd rapidly over 1f out* **13/2**[3]
2060 **10** *13* **Royal Premier (IRE)**[34] 7354 6-8-13 **50**..................(v) JerryO'Dwyer 4 20
(H J Collingridge) *reminders in midfield after 2f: nvr gng wl after: in tch to over 2f out: eased whn no ch* **50/1**

2m 21.67s (-0.23) **Going Correction** 0.0s/f (Stan)
WFA 3 from 4yo+ 4lb **10 Ran SP% 122.1**
Speed ratings (Par 101): **100,99,99,98,97 96,95,92,92,83**
toteswinger:1&2:£29.50, 2&3:£16.00, 1&3:£11.10 CSF £239.83 CT £1235.96 TOTE £20.10: £3.30, £3.50, £1.60; EX 156.80.
Owner Roger Alwen **Bred** Sir Gordon Brunton **Trained** Morestead, Hants

FOCUS
A modest handicap run at a sedate pace but stillf aster than the other two races over the trip. The form is rated around the placed horses.

7768 DIGIBET SUNBURY STKS (LISTED RACE) 7f (P)
8:20 (8:21) (Class 1) 3-Y-O+
£22,708 (£8,608; £4,308; £2,148; £1,076; £540) Stalls High

Form RPR
202 **1** **Dohasa (IRE)**[73] 6530 4-9-2 **109**.................. EJMcNamara 6 109
(G M Lyons, Ire) *t.k.h: hld up in 5th: shkn up on outer 2f out: clsd over 1f out: drvn and styd on wl to ld last strides* **6/5**[1]
13-6 **2** *hd* **Dunelight (IRE)**[17] 7588 6-9-2 **109**..................(v) AdamKirby 11 108
(C G Cox) *trckd ldr: led 3f out: drvn and pressed over 1f out: styd on wl: hdd last strides* **5/1**[2]
1030 **3** *½* **Ceremonial Jade (UAE)**[25] 7488 6-9-4 **105**..................(t) KFallon 10 109
(M Botti) *trckd ldng trio: wnt 2nd over 2f out: drvn to chal over 1f out: upsides ins fnl f: no ex last 75yds* **7/1**[3]
6633 **4** *nk* **Himalya (IRE)**[25] 7488 3-9-2 **100**.................. ShaneKelly 8 106
(J Noseda) *hld up in midfield: effrt over 2f out: hanging but prog over 1f out: styd on fnl f: nrst fin* **7/1**[3]
3011 **5** *1 ¼* **Black Dahlia**[21] 7516 4-8-11 **89**.................. ChrisCatlin 7 98
(J A Glover) *hld up in rr: rdn over 2f out: sme prog over 1f out: styd on fnl f: nvr able to chal* **14/1**
6011 **6** *1 ¾* **Aeroplane**[21] 7520 6-9-2 **100**.................. RichardEvans 12 98
(P D Evans) *hld up in midfield: prog on inner over 2f out: chsd ldrs over 1f out: fdd fnl f* **8/1**
-000 **7** *nk* **Sir Gerry (USA)**[25] 7488 4-9-2 **100**.................. SteveDrowne 2 97
(J R Best) *t.k.h: hld up towards rr: rdn and nt qckn over 2f out: sn btn* **20/1**
0250 **8** *nk* **Carcinetto (IRE)**[12] 7626 7-8-11 **93**.................. StephenDonohoe 5 92
(P D Evans) *led to 3f out: steadily wknd* **40/1**
0004 **9** *8* **Capricorn Run (USA)**[32] 7394 6-9-2 **101**..................(v) RobertWinston 3 75
(A J McCabe) *chsd ldng pair to 3f out: wknd rapidly* **20/1**
0000 **10** *1* **Know No Fear**[17] 7591 4-9-2 **52**.................. AmyScott 9 72
(A J Lidderdale) *rrd s: a in last pair: lost tch 1/2-way* **200/1**
6300 **11** *10* **Stargazy**[14] 7609 5-9-2 **48**.................. KylieManser 1 45
(A J Lidderdale) *plld hrd early: hld up: wknd 3f out: t.o* **200/1**

1m 24.39s (-1.61) **Going Correction** 0.0s/f (Stan) **11 Ran SP% 117.9**
Speed ratings (Par 111): **109,108,108,107,106 104,104,103,94,93 82**
toteswinger: 1&2 £2.80, 2&3 £7.70 1&3 £2.60 CSF £6.87 TOTE £2.40: £1.10, £2.20, £2.50; EX 8.30.
Owner Sean Jones **Bred** Eamon D Delaney **Trained** Dunsany, Co. Meath

FOCUS
Seven of the runners held an official rating between 100 and 109 in this Listed event. The pace was decent and there was an exciting finish.The time was 0.21 seconds under standard and the form looks solid.

NOTEBOOK
Dohasa(IRE) was just foiled in a bid for a hat-trick when second in a Group 3 over an extended 7f at Tipperary in October. He had strong claims if reproducing that form and found a sustained run out wide to mow down the leader in the closing stages and improve his record on AW tracks to 2111. The Bold Fact gelding has taken his form to a new high this year and this win should be a good stepping stone to another spell at the Dubai Carnival, where he was third in two handicaps and a Group 3 in February. (op 13-8)
Dunelight(IRE) is a five-time 1m winner and put in a very brave bid under a positive ride against some 7f specialists, particularly as he was taken on by Carcinetto in the early stages. This second run back from a long break proves that all of his ability is intact and he could take some catching if allowed an easier lead in a similar 7f/1m Listed event next time. (op 9-2)
Ceremonial Jade(UAE), just under 2l third in this race last year, got a bit closer to target this time and emerges with plenty of credit on his second run back from six months off. He was a Listed winner at Wolverhampton in March and has an excellent record of 7-20 on AW tracks, so should remain a serious force at this level. (op 13-2 tchd 15-2)
Himalya(IRE) wanted to hang a bit to the right in the closing stages but ran a big race stepped up to 7f. He hasn't quite fulfilled the promise of his injury-curtailed juvenile career but has had just seven outings and this was a second consecutive step back in the right direction. (op 6-1)
Black Dahlia was impressive when completing a handicap double off a mark of 75 over C&D last month. She took a huge hike in grade against some proven Listed performers but stayed on strongly after being denied a run and seems to be improving fast. (tchd 12-1)
Aeroplane coasted to success in a pair of 7f claimers the last twice. He had some much stiffer competition to deal with here but put in a respectable effort and probably ran close to his official mark of 100. (op 10-1 tchd 12-1 in places)

7769 KIA MOTORS, SAFE BET H'CAP 1m (P)
8:50 (8:50) (Class 4) (0-85,85) 3-Y-O £4,727 (£1,406; £702; £351) Stalls High

Form RPR
2341 **1** **Mustakmil (IRE)**[18] 7576 3-8-8 **75**.................. HayleyTurner 10 83
(S Dow) *trckd ldng pair: wnt 2nd on inner jst over 1f out: shkn up to ld over 1f out: nrly jnd last 100yds: battled on wl* **10/3**[2]
1663 **2** *hd* **Bawaardi (IRE)**[9] 7672 3-8-5 **72**.................. JimmyQuinn 6 80
(R A Fahey) *trckd ldrs: lost pl sltly over 2f out: prog wl over 1f out: r.o to press wnr ins fnl f and looked likely wnr: nt qckn* **9/2**[3]
6531 **3** *1* **My Best Bet**[25] 7487 3-9-0 **81**.................. AdamKirby 3 87
(Stef Liddiard) *dropped in fr wd draw and hld up last: smooth prog 2f out: checked sltly 1f out but sn 3rd: pushed along and no imp on ldng pair* **10/1**
2313 **4** *1* **Red Suede Shoes**[15] 7603 3-8-8 **78**..................(p) JamesMillman(3) 8 81
(B R Millman) *hld up in 6th on inner: prog 2f out: tried to cl on ldrs 1f out: nt qckn and no imp fnl f* **3/1**[1]
3123 **5** *1 ½* **Bennelong**[20] 7540 3-8-11 **78**.................. PaulDoe 7 78
(G L Moore) *stdd s: t.k.h in 7th: pushed along and sme prog on outer 2f out: shkn up and nvr nr ldrs after* **9/2**[3]
3-1 **6** *1 ¼* **Alsahil (USA)**[252] 1176 3-8-13 **80**.................. JimCrowley 1 77
(Micky Hammond) *led: kicked on over 3f out: hdd & wknd over 1f out* **10/1**
130 **7** *2* **Life's Challenge (USA)**[56] 6946 3-8-13 **80**.................. GregFairley 5 72
(M Johnston) *chsd ldr: pushed along over 3f out: lost pl jst over 2f out: wknd* **10/1**
-000 **8** *8* **Take The Micky**[196] 2600 3-8-6 **73** ow1.................. JackMitchell 4 47
(C F Wall) *racd wd: t.k.h: trckd ldrs tl wknd 2f out* **25/1**

1m 38.95s (-0.85) **Going Correction** 0.0s/f (Stan) **8 Ran SP% 115.6**
Speed ratings (Par 104): **104,103,102,101,100 99,97,89**
toteswinger:1&2:£4.90,2&3:£5.10 1&3:£4.70 CSF £19.00 CT £135.94 TOTE £4.60: £1.80, £2.40, £2.70; EX 33.90.
Owner Simon Caunce **Bred** Shadwell Estate Company Limited **Trained** Epsom, Surrey

FOCUS
A decent handicap, involving three last-time-out winners. The pace was solid, there was a thrilling finish and the form looks sound enough rated around the fourth and fifth to previous course form.

7770 BOXINGDAYRACES.CO.UK CLASSIFIED STKS 6f (P)
9:20 (9:20) (Class 6) 3-Y-O+ £2,047 (£604; £302) Stalls High

Form RPR
0220 **1** **Kingsgate Castle**[55] 6967 4-9-0 55..................(b) LukeMorris 10 61
(Miss Gay Kelleway) *hld up in 6th: prog wl over 2f out: edgd lft fr 2f out but r.o to ld 1f out: drvn out* **3/1**[1]
56 **2** *1 ¼* **Nativity**[14] 7610 3-8-11 52.................. JackDean(3) 11 57
(J L Spearing) *hld up towards rr: prog over 2f out: r.o to take 2nd ins fnl f: no real imp on wnr and hung bdly lft last 75yds* **7/2**[2]
0006 **3** *2 ½* **Shakespeare's Son**[16] 7601 4-8-9 55.................. SimonPearce(5) 8 49
(H J Evans) *trckd ldng pair: effrt to ld over 1f out: hdd 1f out: fdd* **4/1**[3]
0000 **4** *hd* **Black Draft**[187] 2880 7-8-9 33.................. SophieDoyle(5) 2 48
(B Forsey) *hld up in towards rr: hanging on outer over 2f out: prog over 1f out: pushed along and styd on on fnl f: nrly snatched 3rd* **100/1**
3000 **5** *1 ¾* **Miss Pusey Street**[11] 7645 3-9-0 49..................(v[1]) PaulDoe 12 43
(P D Evans) *led to over 1f out: wknd fnl f* **8/1**
0210 **6** *½* **Sonhador**[26] 7460 3-9-0 52..................(b) SaleemGolam 5 41
(G Prodromou) *t.k.h: trckd ldr to over 1f out: wknd* **11/2**

-000 **7** *1 ½* **Safaseef (IRE)**[4] 7726 4-9-0 46 ....(v) JimmyQuinn 6 36
(K A Morgan) *hld up in last pair: effrt on inner over 2f out: no prog over 1f out* **25/1**

0003 **8** *2 ½* **Metropolitan Chief**[17] 7592 5-9-0 43 .... JackMitchell 4 28
(P Burgoyne) *awkward s: mostly in last pair: effrt over 2f out: sn no prog* **11/1**

0400 **9** *5* **Sweet Kiss (USA)**[6] 7703 4-9-0 50 ....(b) JimCrowley 3 12
(M J Attwater) *t.k.h: prom on outer: lost pl sn after 1/2-way: wknd* **16/1**

0000 **10** *5* **Green Onions**[10] 7652 3-8-11 53 ....(be) RobertLButler(3) 7 —
(A J Lidderdale) *prom tl lost pl sn after 1/2-way: wknd* **33/1**

1m 11.91s (-1.19) **Going Correction** 0.0s/f (Stan) **10** Ran SP% **115.7**
Speed ratings (Par 101): **107,105,102,101,99 98,96,93,86,80**
toteswinger: 1&2 £3.70, 2&3 £4.30 1&3 £3.90 CSF £13.22 TOTE £4.30: £1.30, £1.80, £1.60; EX 16.80 Place 6 £77.22, Place 5 £25.16.
Owner Miss Gay Kelleway **Bred** Broughton Bloodstock **Trained** Exning, Suffolk

FOCUS
A modest race in which the runners had managed just five wins between them in a total of 192 starts. The form is best rated around the first two.
T/Plt: £67.30 to a £1 stake. Pool: £85,978.90. 931.93 winning tickets. T/Qpdt: £25.80 to a £1 stake. Pool: £7,386.60. 211.80 winning tickets. JN

7689 LINGFIELD (L-H)
Wednesday, December 16

OFFICIAL GOING: Standard
Wind: Moderate, half behind Weather: Overcast, occasional light snow flurries

7771 BEST ODDS GUARANTEED AT TOTESPORT.COM H'CAP (DIV I) 6f (P)
12:00 (12:01) (Class 6) (0-55,59) 3-Y-0+ **£1,637** (£483; £241) **Stalls** Low

Form RPR

0042 **1** **Only A Game (IRE)**[8] 7680 4-8-13 **54** ....(tp) AdamKirby 11 61
(I W McInnes) *towards rr: wd st: hdwy in centre over 1f out: led jst ins fnl f: rdn out* **3/1**[1]

2366 **2** *¾* **The Name Is Frank**[10] 7657 4-9-0 **55** ....(t) EddieAhern 5 59
(Mark Gillard) *dwlt: mid-div: hdwy to press ldrs 3f out: kpt on fnl f* **4/1**[2]

0400 **3** *shd* **Stormburst (IRE)**[51] 7068 5-8-6 **47** .... DavidProbert 1 51
(A J Chamberlain) *s.s: towards rr: gd hdwy over 1f out: pressed ldrs fnl f: kpt on* **33/1**

2444 **4** *¾* **Colombard (IRE)**[7] 7689 4-8-11 **52** ....(b) SJCraine 10 54
(Patrick Morris) *mid-div on outer: hdwy 3f out: pressed ldrs over 1f out: nt qckn fnl f* **13/2**

200 **5** *hd* **Bountiful Bay**[26] 7462 4-8-10 **51** ....(t) LPKeniry 2 52
(Matthew Salaman) *trckd ldrs: effrt and swtchd lft over 1f out: hrd rdn and one pce ins fnl f* **25/1**

0521 **6** *¾* **Thoughtsofstardom**[5] 7709 6-9-1 **59** 6ex .... KellyHarrison(3) 6 58+
(P S McEntee) *plld hrd: trckd ldrs: n.m.r and lost pl 2f out: shkn up and nt clr run over 1f out: styd on same pce* **9/2**[3]

5636 **7** *nse* **Commandingpresence (USA)**[6] 7703 3-8-5 **49** .... MarcHalford(3) 12 47
(J J Bridger) *wnt rt s: sn prom: led 4f out tl hdd & wknd jst ins fnl f* **16/1**

0204 **8** *½* **Miss Firefly**[33] 7371 4-8-9 **53** .... WilliamCarson(3) 3 53+
(R J Hodges) *t.k.h: sn stdd towards rr: promising hdwy on rail whn bdly hmpd over 1f out: nt rcvr* **8/1**

0535 **9** *1* **Nawaaff**[70] 6581 4-8-7 **48** .... ShaneKelly 8 42
(M Quinn) *dwlt: sn led: hdd 4f out: w ldrs tl wknd 1f out* **14/1**

3006 **10** *hd* **Easy Wonder (GER)**[26] 7462 4-8-7 **48** ow1 ....(b) PaulDoe 7 41
(I A Wood) *dwlt: outpcd and bhd: rdn 2f out: n.d* **20/1**

0-00 **11** *9* **Lady Trish**[14] 7610 3-8-9 **50** .... SteveDrowne 9 14
(C A Dwyer) *prom over 3f: sn lost pl* **33/1**

1m 12.06s (0.16) **Going Correction** -0.125s/f (Stan) **11** Ran SP% **114.7**
Speed ratings (Par 101): **93,92,91,90,90 89,89,88,87,87 75**
toteswinger: 1&2 £4.00, 1&3 £23.70, 2&3 £28.60 CSF £13.51 CT £321.15 TOTE £4.60: £1.50, £2.10, £9.50; EX 17.50 TRIFECTA Not won..
Owner Hall Farm Racing **Bred** Maggie And Eric Hemming **Trained** Catwick, E Yorks
■ Stewards' Enquiry : L P Keniry two-day ban: careless riding (Dec 30-31)

FOCUS
Following an overnight frost the track appeared to ride slightly faster than usual. This was a low-grade sprint, and very moderate form. The time was 1.25 seconds sloer than division two. The winner ran to his latest Southwell form and the third limits the form a little.

7772 EUROPEAN BREEDERS' FUND MAIDEN FILLIES' STKS 7f (P)
12:30 (12:32) (Class 5) 2-Y-0 **£3,561** (£1,059; £529; £264) **Stalls** Low

Form RPR

4 **1** **Elation (IRE)**[17] 7585 2-9-0 0 .... JoeFanning 8 80+
(M Johnston) *mde all: rdn clr over 1f out: comf* **8/11**[1]

0030 **2** *4 ½* **Freddie's Girl (USA)**[117] 5212 2-9-0 64 .... AdamKirby 7 66
(Stef Liddiard) *trckd ldrs: rdn to join wnr 2f out: wd st: sn outpcd* **22/1**

0 **3** *1* **Mnasikia (USA)**[54] 7001 2-9-0 0 .... KFallon 10 63
(L M Cumani) *mid-div: rdn over 2f out: styd on to take 3rd ins fnl f* **20/1**

0 **4** *¾* **Singingintherain (IRE)**[17] 7585 2-9-0 0 .... NCallan 3 61
(T G Mills) *chsd ldrs: rdn over 2f out: hung rt over 1f out: one pce* **12/1**[3]

632 **5** *1 ¼* **Leaving Alone (USA)**[12] 7622 2-9-0 72 .... SteveDrowne 9 58
(R Hannon) *chsd wnr: outpcd over 2f out: sn btn* **9/4**[2]

0505 **6** *3 ½* **Princess Shamal**[29] 7421 2-9-0 55 .... JimCrowley 5 50
(J R Jenkins) *dwlt: hld up towards rr: shkn up 2f out: nvr able to chal* **50/1**

7 *2 ¼* **Sunley Spinalonga** 2-9-0 0 .... DaneO'Neill 4 44
(D R C Elsworth) *s.s: rn green and bhd: rdn 3f out: styng on at fin* **20/1**

8 *nk* **Miss Polly Plum** 2-9-0 0 .... JerryO'Dwyer 6 43
(C A Dwyer) *dwlt: off the pce in rr of midfield: pushed along 2f out: nvr trbld ldrs* **50/1**

9 *nk* **Chichi (IRE)** 2-8-11 0 .... PatrickHills(3) 2 42
(R Hannon) *s.s: hld up towards rr: pushed along over 2f out: nvr nr ldrs* **40/1**

0 **10** *5* **Blue Glove (IRE)**[27] 7451 2-9-0 0 .... ShaneKelly 1 30
(J A Osborne) *dwlt: sn in tch in 5th: rdn 4f out: wknd 3f out* **66/1**

1m 24.72s (-0.08) **Going Correction** -0.125s/f (Stan) **10** Ran SP% **118.1**
Speed ratings (Par 93): **95,89,88,87,86 82,79,79,79,73**
toteswinger: 1&2 £7.20, 1&3 £5.70, 2&3 £20.90 CSF £25.62 TOTE £1.90: £1.10, £4.80, £4.10; EX 28.90 Trifecta £157.80 Part won. Pool of £213.30 - 0.95 winning units..
Owner Duke Of Roxburghe **Bred** Floors Farming **Trained** Middleham Moor, N Yorks

FOCUS
An ordinary fillies' maiden lacking strength in depth, but an easy winner in Elation.

NOTEBOOK
Elation(IRE) missed the break quite badly on her debut over 6f at Kempton, but there was no repeat and she was away smartly to lead. Able to set just a steady pace, she came right away in the final furlong. Reported to have fractured a pastern in the spring, she can certainly build on this fairly modest bare form and looks an interesting prospect for turf next year. (op 10-11)
Freddie's Girl(USA), off the track since August, had been held in four previous runs over shorter and has an official rating of 64. After racing a shade keenly, she was about to challenge the winner when she ran wide off the home turn and she was soon left trailing, although she did keep going well enough for second. (op 20-1)
Mnasikia(USA) improved on what she had shown over a furlong less on her Wolverhampton debut, staying on past a couple of rivals in the latter stages. (op 16-1)
Singingintherain(IRE) was under three lengths behind Elation when the pair of them made their debuts at Kempton. This half-sister to smart sprinter Danehill Destiny may not have appreciated today's longer trip. (op 11-1)
Leaving Alone(USA) is rated 72 after placed efforts over a mile on her last two runs. Down in trip, she was slightly hampered in fourth place entering the straight and was one-paced from there. (op 2-1 tchd 15-8)
Sunley Spinalonga, a half-sister to a couple of AW winners, showed a bit of promise for the future. She missed the break and looked clueless in rear, but ran on late as she started to find her feet. (op 22-1)

7773 E B F ALFIE JEEVES 70TH BIRTHDAY MAIDEN STKS (C&G) 7f (P)
1:00 (1:01) (Class 5) 2-Y-0 **£3,561** (£1,059; £529; £264) **Stalls** Low

Form RPR

0323 **1** **Licence To Till (USA)**[108] 5467 2-9-0 72 .... JoeFanning 6 85+
(M Johnston) *mde all: pushed clr over 1f out: edgd rt: easily* **7/4**[1]

40 **2** *8* **Christmas Coming**[63] 6772 2-9-0 0 .... DaneO'Neill 9 63
(D R C Elsworth) *sn in tch in 4th: effrt 2f out: kpt on take 2nd 1f out: no ch w wnr* **5/1**[3]

500 **3** *1 ½* **Gold Party**[32] 7400 2-9-0 58 ....(t[1]) KFallon 2 59
(K McAuliffe) *t.k.h: chsd wnr 2f: prom tl outpcd over 1f out* **33/1**

4 *nse* **Calculus Affair (IRE)** 2-9-0 0 .... TPQueally 3 59+
(J Noseda) *s.s: towards rr: shkn up and r.o fr over 1f out: should improve* **10/3**[2]

065 **5** *hd* **Brave Ghurka**[57] 6911 2-9-0 70 .... DavidProbert 10 58
(S Kirk) *towards rr: hdwy on outer over 2f out: no ex over 1f out* **11/1**

0006 **6** *nse* **Roybuoy**[15] 7604 2-9-0 46 ....(b) JimmyQuinn 5 58
(H J L Dunlop) *prom: chsd wnr 5f out: hrd rdn over 1f out: sn wknd* **100/1**

0 **7** *nk* **Purple Gallery (IRE)**[18] 7571 2-9-0 0 .... LPKeniry 1 57
(J S Moore) *in tch on rail: rdn 2f out: no imp over 1f out* **8/1**

8 *1 ¾* **Seek The Cash (USA)** 2-9-0 0 .... ShaneKelly 4 53
(M Quinn) *in tch in 5th: outpcd 2f out: sn btn* **20/1**

0 **9** *shd* **Rock The Stars (IRE)**[42] 7243 2-9-0 0 .... NCallan 7 53
(M G Quinlan) *in rr of midfield: rdn 3f out: nvr trbld ldrs* **16/1**

10 *1 ½* **Maxijack (IRE)** 2-9-0 0 .... SJCraine 11 49
(G Brown) *s.s: pushed along in rr: struggling fnl 3f* **100/1**

11 *nse* **Brave Enough (USA)** 2-9-0 0 .... EddieAhern 12 49
(M A Magnusson) *s.i.s: rdn 3f out: a bhd* **16/1**

1m 23.98s (-0.82) **Going Correction** -0.125s/f (Stan) 2y crse rec **11** Ran SP% **117.0**
Speed ratings (Par 96): **99,89,88,88,87 87,87,85,85,83 83**
toteswinger: 1&2 £9.00, 1&3 £14.80, 2&3 £26.10 CSF £10.27 TOTE £2.60: £1.40, £2.00, £4.50; EX 11.20 Trifecta £169.10 Pool of £244.53 - 1.07 winning units.
Owner The Vine Accord **Bred** John Hettinger **Trained** Middleham Moor, N Yorks

FOCUS
This maiden was run during a snowstorm. The winning time was three-quarters of a second quicker than the earlier fillies' race. Licence To Till impressed but the depth of this form is certainly questionable. The form is rated at face value.

NOTEBOOK
Licence To Till(USA) ◆ slammed some limited opposition. The colt had been placed in three turf maidens, but was tackling an extra 2f after a 108-day break. He had been rather keen in previous races but did not show that trait over the longer trip here, quickly out to lead before bounding away in the final furlong for a very impressive success. He is out of a mare who has produced five good winners on dirt and was high-class on that surface herself, and he looks potentially smart on artificial tracks. It would not surprise if the offers were to come in from the USA. (op 15-8 tchd 13-8 and 2-1 in a place)
Christmas Coming had no chance with the winner but looks worth returning to a mile and is now eligible for handicaps. (tchd 9-2 and 11-2)
Gold Party is officially rated 58, which limits the form somewhat, but he seemed to improve for the headgear and stayed on up the rail having been keen early on.
Calculus Affair(IRE) missed the break but ran on nicely late on and would have been third in another stride. A brother to the useful sprinter Bond City, who is well at home on Polytrack, he is the second-best prospect in this field. His rider confirmed that he had run green. Official explanation: jockey said colt ran green (op 7-2 tchd 9-2)
Brave Ghurka is more experienced than most of these and he ran respectably, but is still proving something of a weak finisher. (op 15-2 tchd 12-1)
Roybuoy is rated just 46 but ran creditably and was still clinging on to third spot inside the final furlong. (op 80-1)
Purple Gallery(IRE) had failed to handle the home bend when starting favourite for his debut here, but he railed better this time and would have been a little closer had he not been tightened up entering the final furlong. (op 10-1)
Seek The Cash(USA)a $70,000 half-brother to several winners in the US, did not show a great deal on this debut. (op 25-1 tchd 33-1)
Brave Enough(USA), a $120,000 buy, was coltish in the preliminaries and always at the back of the field. (op 11-1 tchd 20-1)

7774 BEST ODDS GUARANTEED AT TOTESPORT.COM H'CAP (DIV II) 6f (P)
1:35 (1:35) (Class 6) (0-55,55) 3-Y-0+ **£1,637** (£483; £241) **Stalls** Low

Form RPR

0003 **1** **Tamino (IRE)**[14] 7609 6-8-6 **47** .... JimmyQuinn 9 58
(P Howling) *mde all: rdn over 2f out: hld on wl u.p fnl f* **4/1**[1]

0505 **2** *1* **Grand Palace (IRE)**[15] 7602 6-8-13 **54** ow1 ....(v) AdamKirby 2 61
(H J Evans) *prom: wnt 2nd ent st: hrd rdn and edgd lft 1f out: kpt on: a hld* **11/2**[2]

0033 **3** *hd* **Radiator Rooney (IRE)**[10] 7657 6-9-0 **55** ....(v) SJCraine 1 62
(Patrick Morris) *in tch disputing 5th: rdn to chse ldrs over 1f out: r.o fnl f* **8/1**

660 **4** *½* **Davids Mark**[76] 6433 9-8-9 **50** .... SimonWhitworth 8 55
(J R Jenkins) *hld up towards rr: gd hdwy to chse ldrs 1f out: nt qckn wl ins fnl f* **28/1**

0042 **5** *¾* **Greystoke Prince**[7] 7693 4-8-4 **52** ....(t) CarolineKelly(7) 4 55+
(P S McEntee) *hld up in rr: pushed along and hdwy over 1f out: styd on fnl f* **6/1**[3]

0660 **6** *1 ½* **Dicey Affair**[55] 6967 3-8-7 **48** ....(t) FergusSweeney 7 46
(G L Moore) *dwlt: bhd: rdn and wd st: r.o fnl f: nrst fin* **14/1**

0005 **7** *shd* **Romantic Verse**[18] 7579 4-8-10 **54** ....(b) MichaelJStainton(3) 5 52
(S Curran) *dwlt: in rr of midfield: drvn along and wd st: no imp* **16/1**

043 **8** *¾* **Makshoof (IRE)**[15] 7606 5-9-0 **55** ....(p) JimCrowley 10 50
(I W McInnes) *s.s: in last pair: rdn 2f out: nvr trbld ldrs* **4/1**[1]

3105 **9** *hd* **Boundless Applause**[18] 7572 3-8-7 **48** ow1 ....(p) PaulDoe 12 43
(I A Wood) *pressed wnr tl ent st: sn wknd* **16/1**

3000 **10** ½ **Briannsta (IRE)**[15] 7602 7-8-11 **52**..............................(b) SamHitchcott 6 45
(J E Long) *chsd ldrs: rdn over 2f out: wknd ent st* **11/1**

5555 **11** 3¼ **Tightrope (IRE)**[41] 7254 3-8-7 **48**..............................(b) DavidProbert 3 31
(T D McCarthy) *disp 5th tl outpcd 2f out* **22/1**

1m 10.81s (-1.09) **Going Correction** -0.125s/f (Stan) 11 Ran SP% **115.3**
Speed ratings (Par 101): **102,100,100,99,98 96,96,95,95,94 90**
toteswinger: 1&2 £8.50, 1&3 £2.80, 2&3 £8.00 CSF £24.85 CT £170.06 TOTE £4.20: £1.20, £2.10, £3.00; EX 26.70 Trifecta £117.30 Part won. Pool of £156.58 - 0.45 winning units..
Owner Paul Howling **Bred** Century Bloodstock **Trained** Newmarket, Suffolk

FOCUS
This moderate handicap was run at a good pace and was over a second quicker than division one. The form is sound with the winner back to something like last year's best.
Boundless Applause Official explanation: jockey said filly hung left

7775 BIGGER "WIN ONLY" ODDS AT TOTESPORT.COM H'CAP 1m 2f (P)
2:10 (2:10) (Class 4) (0-85,83) 3-Y-0+ **£4,727** (£1,406; £702; £351) **Stalls** Low

Form RPR

064 **1** **Confidentiality (IRE)**[21] 7528 5-9-1 **79**.............................. NickyMackay 4 87
(M Wigham) *chsd ldrs: effrt over 2f out: pressed ldr ins fnl f: led fnl stride* **12/1**

22P2 **2** *shd* **Mafeking (UAE)**[7] 7684 5-9-5 **83**.............................. ChrisCatlin 3 91
(M R Hoad) *led: wnt 6 l clr 5f out: rdn 2f out: kpt on fnl f: ct fnl stride* **9/2**[1]

1122 **3** *1* **Traphalgar (IRE)**[12] 7623 4-8-13 **77**.............................. J-PGuillambert 9 83
(P D Evans) *in rr of midfield: rdn and hdwy over 1f out: chsd ldrs ent fnl f: kpt on* **5/1**[2]

4060 **4** 1¼ **Hallingdal (UAE)**[20] 7539 4-8-5 **72**.............................. MarcHalford(3) 1 76
(J J Bridger) *chsd ldrs: wnt 2nd over 2f out: one pce fnl f* **40/1**

4530 **5** ¾ **Suzi Spends (IRE)**[42] 7233 4-9-2 **80**.............................. JimmyQuinn 6 82
(H J Collingridge) *dwlt: sn in midfield: rdn and hdwy 2f out: chsd ldrs over 1f out: no ex ins fnl f* **16/1**

/233 **6** 1¾ **Prince Picasso**[11] 7640 6-8-6 **75**.............................. BMcHugh(5) 2 74
(R A Fahey) *chsd ldr tl over 2f out: wknd over 1f out* **8/1**[3]

0001 **7** ½ **Final Verse**[18] 7575 6-9-1 **79**..............................(e) LPKeniry 10 77+
(Matthew Salaman) *plld hrd: restrained towards rr: promising hdwy on rail ent st: sn wknd* **9/2**[1]

6126 **8** *8* **Cry Alot Boy**[15] 7607 6-8-13 **77**.............................. TonyCulhane 8 59+
(K A Morgan) *s.s: plld hrd in rr: sme hdwy on outer 4f out: wknd 3f out* **20/1**

2211 **9** ½ **Iron Out (USA)**[9] 7667 3-9-1 **82** 6ex.............................. RobertWinston 5 63
(R Hollinshead) *prom tl wknd over 2f out* **8/1**[3]

0035 **10** *6* **Awatuki (IRE)**[12] 7623 6-8-8 **75**.............................. RobertLButler(3) 11 44
(J R Boyle) *rrd s and missed break: a bhd: rdn and no ch fnl 3f* **50/1**

4362 **11** *17* **Sharpazmax (IRE)**[70] 6583 5-8-13 **77**.............................. SteveDrowne 7 12
(P J Makin) *in tch in 5th: wknd 3f out: eased whn no ch over 1f out* **5/1**[2]

2m 3.63s (-2.97) **Going Correction** -0.125s/f (Stan)
WFA 3 from 4yo+ 3lb 11 Ran SP% **114.7**
Speed ratings (Par 105): **106,105,105,104,103 102,101,95,94,90 76**
toteswinger:1&2:£5.70, 2&3:£4.60, 1&3:£5.70 CSF £62.64 CT £309.56 TOTE £12.10: £3.30, £1.80, £2.30; EX 49.50 TRIFECTA Pool of £297.23 - 1.35 winning units.
Owner J M Cullinan **Bred** Kevin Foley **Trained** Newmarket, Suffolk

FOCUS
An open and competitive handicap. The runner-up set his own pace and he looks the best guide to the form. The winner returned to something like her best.
Iron Out(USA) Official explanation: jockey said gelding ran flat
Sharpazmax(IRE) Official explanation: vet said gelding was distressed

7776 BET LIVE IN PLAY AT TOTESPORT.COM CLASSIFIED CLAIMING STKS 1m 2f (P)
2:45 (2:45) (Class 6) 3-Y-0+ **£1,978** (£584; £292) **Stalls** Low

Form RPR

2300 **1** **Atacama Sunrise**[47] 7149 3-8-6 63.............................. SaleemGolam 10 71
(J Pearce) *hld up towards rr: rdn and hdwy ent st: pressed ldr fnl f: drvn to ld fnl 50yds* **33/1**

-462 **2** ½ **Fujin Dancer (FR)**[12] 7631 4-8-13 68.............................. NCallan 9 74
(K A Ryan) *led 3f: pressed ldr: led jst over 1f out: kpt on u.p fnl f: hdd fnl 50yds* **2/1**[2]

4033 **3** 1¾ **Dream Of Fortune (IRE)**[12] 7623 5-8-10 69..............................(t) JamieJones(5) 8 73
(M G Quinlan) *dwlt: towards rr: rdn 3f out: wd st: chsd ldng pair 1f out: kpt on* **15/2**[3]

3530 **4** 1¼ **The Dial House**[6] 7699 3-8-10 70..............................(t) ShaneKelly 12 68
(J A Osborne) *stdd s: hld up in rr: rdn and hdwy over 1f out: styd on fnl f* **16/1**

1210 **5** *1* **Rapid City**[195] 1785 6-8-13 69..............................(p) FergusSweeney 11 66
(G L Moore) *hld up in rr: rdn and wd st: hdwy over 1f out: styd on: nt pce to chal* **11/1**

2021 **6** 1¾ **Bee Stinger**[11] 7647 7-8-5 68.............................. LiamJones 5 55
(P R Hedger) *in tch in 5th: rdn 3f out: sn btn* **15/8**[1]

6606 **7** 1¼ **Realism (FR)**[19] 6878 9-8-5 70..............................(vt) ChrisCatlin 2 52
(M W Easterby) *in tch on rail in 6th: outpcd over 2f out: sn btn* **11/1**

4000 **8** *hd* **General Feeling (IRE)**[18] 7581 8-8-3 66.............................. HayleyTurner 3 50
(Ollie Pears) *mid-div: outpcd over 2f out: sn struggling in rr: modest hdwy at fin* **20/1**

0000 **9** ½ **Western Roots**[9] 7667 8-8-8 57.............................. RobertLButler(3) 1 57
(P Butler) *prom: hrd rdn over 2f out: wknd over 1f out* **100/1**

2-00 **10** 1¼ **Saharan Royal**[28] 7428 3-8-2 64.............................. LukeMorris 4 48
(Matthew Salaman) *chsd ldrs tl hrd rdn and wknd over 1f out* **33/1**

300 **P** **Ross Moor**[7] 7695 7-8-6 64..............................(p) AndreaAtzeni(3) 6 —
(Mike Murphy) *prom: led 7f out: jst hdd whn broke knee and p.u 1f out: dead* **20/1**

2m 4.22s (-2.38) **Going Correction** -0.125s/f (Stan)
WFA 3 from 4yo+ 3lb 11 Ran SP% **118.8**
Speed ratings (Par 101): **104,103,102,101,100 99,98,97,97,96** —
CSF £96.36 TOTE £41.80: £10.40, £1.60, £2.50; EX 221.60 TRIFECTA Not won..Rapid City was claimed by P. D. Evans for £10,000
Owner Jim Furlong **Bred** J R Furlong **Trained** Newmarket, Suffolk

FOCUS
A reasonable 0-70 claimer run at what appeared to be a steady pace. The form seems sound at face value with the first three close to their marks.
Bee Stinger Official explanation: jockey said gelding never travelled

7777 BET ON TONIGHT'S FOOTBALL AT TOTESPORT.COM APPRENTICE H'CAP 1m 4f (P)
3:20 (3:20) (Class 5) (0-75,74) 3-Y-0+ **£2,729** (£806; £403) **Stalls** Low

Form RPR

2011 **1** **Sircozy (IRE)**[9] 7665 3-8-10 **64** 6ex.............................. WilliamCarson 1 72+
(S C Williams) *hld up in 2nd last: effrt and wd st: tk a while to pick up: hrd rdn and styd on wl fnl f: led fnl strides* **1/1**[1]

0062 **2** *hd* **Maslak (IRE)**[4] 7724 5-9-5 **73**.............................. TobyAtkinson(5) 7 78
(P W Hiatt) *prom: led 5f out: rdn 4 l clr over 2f out: hrd rdn fnl f: ct fnl strides* **13/2**[2]

3336 **3** 1¼ **Jeer (IRE)**[9] 7667 5-9-2 **70**..............................(bt) JamesPSullivan(5) 2 73
(M W Easterby) *t.k.h: led 3f: restrained to 3rd: wnt 3 l 2nd over 1f out: styd on same pce* **8/1**

6042 **4** *shd* **Taste The Wine (IRE)**[9] 7665 3-8-4 **61**.............................. SophieDoyle(3) 3 64+
(J S Moore) *chsd ldrs: lost pl over 3f out: rallied 1f out: kpt on* **7/1**[3]

0100 **5** *hd* **Kashmina**[21] 7524 4-9-1 **64**.............................. RussellKennemore 4 67
(Miss Sheena West) *hld up in last: rdn over 2f out: r.o fr over 1f out: nt rch ldrs* **20/1**

0351 **6** *3* **Black N Brew (USA)**[15] 7607 3-9-6 **74**.............................. MarcHalford 6 72
(J R Best) *hld up in 6th: rdn over 2f out: no imp* **12/1**

5220 **7** 1¼ **Vinces**[21] 7512 5-9-3 **66**.............................. DavidProbert 5 62
(T D McCarthy) *dwlt: hld up in 5th: disp 2nd 3f out: wknd over 1f out* **8/1**

0225 **8** *10* **Quince (IRE)**[18] 7578 6-9-2 **68**..............................(v) SimonPearce(3) 8 48
(J Pearce) *chsd ldrs: led after 3f tl 5f out: rdn 3f out: sn wknd* **12/1**

2m 32.17s (-0.83) **Going Correction** -0.125s/f (Stan)
WFA 3 from 4yo+ 5lb 8 Ran SP% **118.2**
Speed ratings (Par 103): **97,96,96,95,95 93,93,86**
toteswinger: 1&2 £2.50, 1&3 £4.10, 2&3 £5.50 CSF £8.43 CT £36.16 TOTE £2.00: £1.30, £2.10, £2.40; EX 7.30 Trifecta £32.90 Pool of £513.85 - 11.53 winning units. Place 6 £28.09, Place 5 £15.76.
Owner R Friends Electric **Bred** Allevamento Pian Di Neve Srl **Trained** Newmarket, Suffolk

FOCUS
An ordinary apprentice handicap that was steadily run and produced a rather muddling race, with several of them racing keenly. The form will probably not work out literally, but Sircozy is better than the bare form and could do better again.
T/Plt: £48.00 to a £1 stake. Pool: £50,946.89. 773.28 winning tickets. T/Qpdt: £12.60 to a £1 stake. Pool: £4,972.34. 289.80 winning tickets. LM

7756 SOUTHWELL (L-H)
Thursday, December 17

OFFICIAL GOING: Standard
Wind: Fresh across Weather: Bright and dry

7778 TEXT YOUR TOTESPORT BET TO 60021 NURSERY 5f (F)
12:30 (12:30) (Class 6) (0-60,60) 2-Y-O **£2,047** (£604; £302) **Stalls** High

Form RPR

000 **1** **Billie Jean**[18] 7585 2-9-2 **55**.............................. MichaelHills 10 67+
(B W Hills) *trckd ldrs: hdwy to ld wl over 1f out: rdn ins fnl f and kpt on wl* **8/1**

0000 **2** *2* **Turf Time**[72] 6554 2-8-6 **45**.............................. ChrisCatlin 6 48
(J A Glover) *t.k.h: trckd ldrs: swtchd rt and effrt 2f out: rdn to chse wnr over 1f out: drvn and kpt on ins fnl f* **9/1**

000 **3** 2½ **Lets Move It**[19] 7582 2-8-11 **50**..............................(v) GrahamGibbons 8 44
(D Shaw) *cl up: led 1/2-way: rdn along and hdd wl over 1f out: sn drvn and kpt on same pce* **14/1**

0663 **4** 3½ **Caol Ila (IRE)**[20] 7559 2-9-3 **56**.............................. TPQueally 4 37
(J G Given) *dwlt and wnt lft s: in tch: rdn along and hdwy to chse ldrs 2f out: sn drvn and one pce appr fnl f* **11/4**[2]

0020 **5** *2* **Thewinnatakesitall**[20] 7559 2-9-0 **60**..............................(p) DavidKenny(7) 9 34
(H J Evans) *t.k.h: hld up towards rr: hdwy and hung lft 2f out: sn rdn and kpt on ins fnl f: nt rch ldrs* **14/1**

5200 **6** *nse* **True Red (IRE)**[20] 7559 2-8-9 **55**.............................. RachelKing(7) 3 29
(Mrs N S Evans) *cl up: rdn along 2f out and ev ch tl drvn over 1f out and grad wknd* **12/1**

6300 **7** *1* **Duke Of Rainford**[20] 7559 2-8-13 **52**.............................. TonyCulhane 5 22
(M Herrington) *led: pushed along and hdd 1/2-way: rdn along wl over 1f out and sn wknd* **15/2**[3]

0000 **8** 1¾ **Annia (IRE)**[20] 7559 2-9-2 **55**..............................(t) LukeMorris 12 19
(N P Littmoden) *chsd ldrs: rdn along after 2f and sn wknd* **25/1**

000 **9** *1* **Rightcar Marian**[71] 6582 2-8-6 **45**.............................. KirstyMilczarek 2 6
(Peter Grayson) *chsd ldrs: rdn along 1/2-way: sn wknd* **50/1**

0360 **10** *11* **Taeping (IRE)**[14] 7619 2-8-11 **50**.............................. RobertWinston 1 —
(R Hollinshead) *s.i.s and sn pushed along in rr: rdn after 1 1/2f out: a outpcd and bhd whn eased over 1f out* **9/4**[1]

60.86 secs (1.16) **Going Correction** +0.10s/f (Slow) 10 Ran SP% **117.1**
Speed ratings (Par 94): **94,90,86,81,78 77,76,73,71,54**
toteswingers: 1&2 £16.20, 1&3 £14.70, 2&3 £26.60 CSF £78.13 CT £997.27 TOTE £9.80: £2.90, £2.70, £4.50; EX 139.20 TRIFECTA Not won..
Owner Phil Cunningham **Bred** G Flannery Developments **Trained** Lambourn, Berks

FOCUS
A run-of-the-mill nursery, run at a decent pace and the form is best rated through the runner-up to his mark.

NOTEBOOK
Billie Jean was making her handicap and Fibresand debuts. A half-sister to dual 2000 Guineas winner Cockney Rebel, this will have done her paddock value no harm and she should have no problem following up in the coming weeks. She should also have little difficulty staying further in due course. Official explanation: trainer's rep said, regarding apparent improvement in form, that ther filly had been suited by the step back to 5f and the Fibresand track. (op 11-2)
Turf Time raced keenly on his first start in 72 days and going one better shortly should be well within his grasp at this time of year. Time may prove he was unlucky to run in to an above-average winner for this grade. (op 11-1)
Lets Move It, lightly raced, pulled well clear of the rest and, on the evidence of this, can lose his maiden tag in the not-too-distant future. (op 12-1 tchd 10-1)
Caol Ila(IRE), easy to back beforehand, was awkward at the start and never troubled the leaders. (op 5-2 tchd 9-4)
Duke Of Rainford Official explanation: jockey said gelding missed the break and never travelled
Rightcar Marian Official explanation: jockey said filly hung right

Taeping(IRE) also fluffed his lines at the start and could never get competitive. (op 3-1)

7779 BEST ODDS GUARANTEED AT TOTESPORT.COM H'CAP 1m 4f (F)
1:00 (1:00) (Class 5) (0-70,70) 3-Y-0+ **£2,729** (£806; £403) **Stalls** Low

Form RPR
2032 **1** **Boundless Prospect (USA)**[9] 7677 10-8-8 **62**.... AndrewHeffernan(5) 6 72
(P D Evans) *sn pushed along in rr and rn in snatches: hdwy 5f out: rdn along 4f out: drvn and hdwy to chse ldng pair over 2f out: styd on u.p to ld last 100yds* **5/2**[1]
6412 **2** *2 3/4* **Moonshine Creek**[8] 7695 7-8-13 **62**.... ChrisCatlin 4 67
(P W Hiatt) *cl up: effrt to ld briefly 3f out: sn rdn and hdd: drvn to ld again over 1f out: hdd and no ex last 100yds* **3/1**[3]
3512 **3** *1 1/2* **Onemoreandstay**[12] 7641 4-9-4 **67**....(p) RobertWinston 5 70
(M D Squance) *hld up in tch: hdwy on outer to chal 3f out: sn led and swtchd wd to stands' rail: rdn wl over 1f out: drvn: edgd lft and hdd appr last: one pce* **11/4**[2]
4 *11* **Academy Gigsnreels (USA)**[27] 7473 4-8-12 **61**....(t) LPKeniry 1 46
(Seamus Fahey, Ire) *led: rdn along over 4f out: drvn and hdd 3f out: sn wknd* **12/1**
2104 **5** *1/2* **Crimson Mitre**[107] 5545 4-9-6 **69**.... LukeMorris 2 54
(J Jay) *cl up: effrt 4f out: rdn along 3f out and sn wknd* **4/1**
6000 **6** *3 1/2* **La Columbina**[65] 6758 4-9-7 **70**.... AdamKirby 3 49
(H J Evans) *trckd ldrs: rdn along over 4f out: drvn over 3f out and sn outpcd* **40/1**

2m 38.05s (-2.95) **Going Correction** -0.325s/f (Stan) **6** Ran SP% **110.4**
Speed ratings (Par 103): **96,94,93,85,85 83**
toteswingers: 1&2 £2.30, 1&3 £2.50, 2&3 £1.60 CSF £9.96 TOTE £2.80: £1.50, £2.70; EX 11.80.
Owner Diamond Racing Ltd **Bred** Mrs Edgar Scott Jr & Mrs Lawrence Macelree **Trained** Pandy, Monmouths

FOCUS
A 56-70 handicap run at an even pace with the winner and third rated close to previous course form.

7780 BIGGER "WIN ONLY" ODDS AT TOTESPORT.COM MAIDEN STKS 1m 3f (F)
1:30 (1:31) (Class 5) 3-Y-0+ **£2,729** (£806; £403) **Stalls** Low

Form RPR
1 **Abayaan** 3-9-3 0.... ShaneKelly 6 71+
(Jane Chapple-Hyam) *trckd ldrs: pushed along 1/2-way: hdwy on outer over 4f out: chsd ldr over 2f out: rdn to ld 1 1/2f out: kpt on ins fnl f* **3/1**[3]
6242 **2** *nk* **Outrageous Request**[44] 7221 3-9-3 77.... DarryllHolland 3 70
(Pat Eddery) *cl up on inner: rdn along to ld over 3f out: hdd 1 1/2f out and sn drvn: kpt on u.p ins fnl f* **11/8**[1]
60- **3** *9* **Hydrant**[23] 5468 3-9-3 0.... GregFairley 9 55
(P Salmon) *chsd ldrs: hdwy and cl up 4f out: rdn along 3f out: drvn and one pce fnl 2f* **50/1**
-036 **4** *7* **All Guns Firing (IRE)**[146] 4280 3-9-3 74.... DNolan 2 43
(D Carroll) *chsd ldrs: rdn along and outpcd over 4f out: wd st and drvn along: n.d* **8/1**
0/24 **5** *4 1/2* **Etruscan (IRE)**[54] 7036 4-9-7 75.... ChrisCatlin 7 35
(C Gordon) *trckd ldrs: rdn along 4f out: drvn 3f out: outpcd fr over 2f out* **15/8**[2]
4466 **6** *9* **Bicksta**[9] 7677 3-8-12 49....(v) TonyCulhane 4 15
(P T Midgley) *led: rdn along 4f out: hdd over 3f out: sn drvn and wknd* **25/1**
50 **7** *24* **Owls FC (IRE)**[14] 7221 3-8-12 0.... AmirQuinn 8 —
(M C Chapman) *s.i.s and a in rr: bhd fr 1/2-way* **100/1**
0 **8** *97* **La Preciosa**[10] 7671 4-8-13 0....(p) KellyHarrison(3) 1 —
(I W McInnes) *a in rr: bhd fr 1/2-way: t.o fnl 3f* **100/1**

2m 24.85s (-3.15) **Going Correction** -0.325s/f (Stan)
WFA 3 from 4yo+ 4lb **8** Ran SP% **120.8**
Speed ratings (Par 103): **98,97,91,86,82 76,58,—**
toteswingers: 1&2 £2.40, 1&3 £9.10, 2&3 £8.10 CSF £8.02 TOTE £3.90: £1.50, £1.20, £3.80; EX 11.00 Trifecta £78.80 Pool: £312.10 - 2.93 winning units..
Owner Mrs Jane Chapple-Hyam **Bred** Belgrave Bloodstock & Sphere Bloodstock **Trained** Newmarket, Suffolk

FOCUS
A maiden lacking strength in depth. It was run at a very sound pace, though, and the first two pulled clear. The runner-up sets the standard.

7781 BET ON TONIGHT'S FOOTBALL AT TOTESPORT.COM MAIDEN AUCTION STKS 7f (F)
2:00 (2:00) (Class 6) 2-Y-0 **£2,047** (£604; £302) **Stalls** Low

Form RPR
6633 **1** **Inside Track (IRE)**[8] 7690 2-8-13 75....(b) TonyCulhane 1 69
(P T Midgley) *trckd ldrs: hdwy over 2f out: sn swtchd rt and rdn: drvn over 1f out: kpt on u.p to ld last 100yds* **4/5**[1]
5044 **2** *1 1/4* **City Gossip (IRE)**[2] 7756 2-8-5 65.... KirstyMilczarek 3 58
(M G Quinlan) *cl up on inner: led 1/2-way: rdn along wl over 1f out: drvn ent fnl f: hddand one pce last 100yds* **5/1**[3]
03 **3** *5* **Admiral Breese**[30] 7420 2-8-10 0.... GrahamGibbons 4 51
(R Hollinshead) *cl up: rdn along over 2f out: ev ch tl drvn and one pce fr over 1f out* **13/8**[2]
0004 **4** *1* **Tenga Venga**[6] 7705 2-9-2 50....(p) AdamKirby 2 54
(P S McEntee) *cl up on outer: rdn along 3f out: drvn over 2f out and sn wknd* **14/1**

1m 29.23s (-1.07) **Going Correction** -0.325s/f (Stan) **4** Ran SP% **117.0**
Speed ratings (Par 94): **93,91,85,84**
CSF £5.88 TOTE £1.40; EX 4.60.
Owner P T Midgley **Bred** Round Hill Stud **Trained** Westow, N Yorks

FOCUS
A very poor maiden fought out by two that have been plying their trade in claimers and sellers. Not form to be with.

NOTEBOOK
Inside Track(IRE), beaten in claimers on his three previous starts, was having his first race for this yard. Happy to take a lead, it took all of his rider's strength to force him ahead in the closing stages. Likely to be suited by 1m plus, he will struggle in handicap company from a mark of 75 and the plan is to return here for a seller on New Year's Day. (op 10-11 tchd 6-5 and 5-4 in places)
City Gossip(IRE), fourth in a selling race here two days earlier, went on at halfway and went down fighting. Her official mark of 65 flatters her. (tchd 9-2 and 6-1)
Admiral Breese, having his third start, made this a true test but he showed his inexperience by hanging in behind the runner-up. This at least opens up the nursery route. (op 15-8 after early 9-4 in a place)
Tenga Venga, rated just 50, was quite keen racing on the outer. Driven once in line for home, he carried his head at an awkward angle and was soon shaken off. (tchd 12-1)

7782 BOOK YOUR TICKETS AT SOUTHWELL-RACECOURSE.CO.UK CLAIMING STKS 1m (F)
2:30 (2:30) (Class 6) 3-4-Y-0 **£2,047** (£604; £302) **Stalls** Low

Form RPR
1452 **1** **Mcconnell (USA)**[41] 7271 4-9-4 83.... GeorgeBaker 7 85
(G L Moore) *trckd ldrs: effrt and n.m.r 2f out: rdn over 1f out: styd on to ld ins fnl f* **4/9**[1]
2000 **2** *1 3/4* **Transmission (IRE)**[13] 7631 4-8-8 58.... TomEaves 8 71
(B Smart) *cl up on outer: hdwy to ld 2f out: rdn wl over 1f out: drvn and edgd lft ent fnl f: sn hdd and one pce* **10/1**[3]
0560 **3** *1 3/4* **Dr Jameson (IRE)**[31] 7416 3-8-3 63....(v1) FrankieMcDonald 6 63
(R A Fahey) *cl up: led 3f out: rdn and hdd 2f out: sn drvn and kpt on same pce* **8/1**[2]
1001 **4** *2* **Ten Pole Tudor**[5] 7723 4-8-6 57....(p) LiamJones 4 60
(R A Harris) *dwlt: midfield and rdn along 1/2-way: wd st: hdwy 2f out: sn drvn and no imp appr fnl f* **16/1**
0010 **5** *6* **Swiss Art (IRE)**[13] 7631 3-8-13 70....(b) ChrisCatlin 9 55
(R Hollinshead) *towards rr: hdwy over 2f out: sn rdn along and no imp fr over 1f out* **8/1**[2]
2220 **6** *nk* **Herbert Crescent**[17] 7599 4-8-4 53....(e1) FrancisNorton 5 44
(Ollie Pears) *cl up: rdn along 3f out: drvn 2f out and grad wknd* **16/1**
0000 **7** *4 1/2* **Golden Penny**[6] 7711 4-9-4 72....(b1) PhillipMakin 1 48
(M Dods) *led: rdn along and hdd 3f out: sn drvn and wknd* **16/1**
5060 **8** *16* **Princess Zhukova (IRE)**[303] 574 4-7-13 43.... LukeMorris 10 —
(M Wellings) *a in rr* **100/1**
6006 **9** *hd* **Brer Rabbit**[19] 7581 3-7-12 60.... NickyMackay 3 —
(Seamus Fahey, Ire) *dwlt: sn chsng ldrs on inner: rdn along after 3f and sn wknd* **33/1**
0050 **10** *hd* **Martha's Girl (USA)**[12] 7642 3-8-12 52....(v1) DNolan 2 5
(D Carroll) *prom: rdn along 1/2-way: sn wknd* **100/1**

1m 40.58s (-3.12) **Going Correction** -0.325s/f (Stan)
WFA 3 from 4yo 1lb **10** Ran SP% **123.1**
Speed ratings (Par 101): **102,100,98,96,90 90,85,69,69,69**
.McConnell was claimed by B. D. Haynes for £12000\n\x\x
Owner Joe McCarthy **Bred** Hall Et Al Farm **Trained** Lower Beeding, W Sussex

FOCUS
A-run-of-the-mill claimer, run at a strong pace with the third and fourth rated close to recent Polytrack marks..
Transmission(IRE) Official explanation: caution: careless riding.

7783 COME RACING TOMORROW H'CAP 1m (F)
3:00 (3:01) (Class 5) (0-75,75) 3-Y-0+ **£1,767** (£1,767; £403) **Stalls** Low

Form RPR
0300 **1** **Avertis**[4] 7741 4-9-5 **75**....(t) AdamKirby 5 83
(Stef Liddiard) *trckd ldrs: hdwy on outer 3f out and sn rdn: drvn over 1f out: edgd lft and kpt on to ld wl ins fnl f: jnd nr line* **5/2**[2]
3630 **1** *dht* **Hilbre Court (USA)**[6] 7711 4-9-0 **70**....(p) GrahamGibbons 2 78
(B P J Baugh) *cl up: led 3f out: rdn and hdd 2f out: cl up and drvn over 1f out: kpt ongamely u.p ins fnl f to join ldr on line* **10/3**[3]
0542 **3** *1/2* **Mozayada (USA)**[6] 7711 5-9-2 **72**.... RobertWinston 4 79
(M Brittain) *cl up: led 2f out and sn rdn: drvn over 1f out: hdd ins fnl f: n.m.r and no ex last 50yds* **5/4**[1]
0660 **4** *3 1/4* **West End Lad**[52] 7062 6-8-13 **69** ow2....(b) PhillipMakin 3 69
(S R Bowring) *dwlt: sn chsng ldrs: rdn along 3f out: drvn 2f out and kpt on same pce* **15/2**
3000 **5** *10* **King Of The Moors (USA)**[14] 7615 6-8-12 **68**....(b) FrancisNorton 1 44
(R C Guest) *led: rdn along and hdd 3f out: sn wknd* **11/1**

1m 41.06s (-2.64) **Going Correction** -0.325s/f (Stan)
WFA 3 from 4yo+ 1lb **5** Ran SP% **116.2**
Speed ratings (Par 103): **100,100,99,96,86**
WIN: Avertis £1.70 Hilbre Court £1.40 PL: A £1.70, HC £1.60 EX: A/HC £6.20 HC/A £5.70 CSF: A/HC £5.89 HC/A £6.37 toteswingers: Avertis& Hilbre Court £4.00.
Owner Mrs Sally Doyle **Bred** Mrs Sally Doyle **Trained** Great Shefford, Berks
Owner Saddle Up Racing **Bred** Richard Nip & Omar Trevino **Trained** Audley, Staffs

FOCUS
A tight 67-75 handicap run at a strong pace and each of the first three traded at odds-on at some stage on the exchanges. The first two are rated to previous course marks with the third 3lb off.

7784 HOSPITALITY AT SOUTHWELL RACECOURSE H'CAP 1m (F)
3:30 (3:31) (Class 6) (0-60,64) 3-Y-0+ **£2,047** (£604; £302) **Stalls** Low

Form RPR
511 **1** **Topcroft**[7] 7703 3-8-11 **60**....(v) LeeTopliss(7) 8 74
(D Shaw) *towards rr: smooth hdwy to trck ldrs 1/2-way: effrt on outer to ld 2f out: rdn and hung bdly lft over 1f out: drvn ins fnl f and kpt on wl towards fin* **6/4**[1]
404 **2** *3/4* **Almahaza (IRE)**[23] 7500 5-9-4 **59**.... DavidProbert 2 72
(A J Chamberlain) *midfield: gd hdwy on inner 3f out: rdn wl over 1f out and ev ch tl drvn ins fnl f and no ex towards fin* **9/2**[3]
604 **3** *1* **Special Cuvee**[5] 7727 3-8-13 **55**....(v) RobertHavlin 6 65
(A B Haynes) *in tch: hdwy on outer over 2f out: rdn wl over 1f out: drvn to chse ldng pair over 1f out: kpt on u.p ins fnl f* **10/1**
0650 **4** *4* **Plenilune (IRE)**[3] 7754 4-8-10 **51** ow1.... RobertWinston 7 52
(M Brittain) *prom: hdwy to ld briefly over 2f out: sn rdn and hdd: drvn and one pce appr fnl f* **25/1**
2645 **5** *3/4* **Bajan Pride**[12] 7650 5-8-8 **56**.... FrazerWilliams(7) 9 55
(R A Fahey) *in rr and rdn along 1/2-way: styd on fnl 2f: n.d* **14/1**
4006 **6** *shd* **Komreyev Star**[5] 7728 7-8-5 **46**.... GregFairley 13 45
(R E Peacock) *cl up: rdn along over 3f out: drvn 2f out and kpt on same pce* **66/1**
0331 **7** *2 3/4* **General Tufto**[5] 7728 4-9-9 **64** 6ex....(b) KirstyMilczarek 1 57
(C Smith) *trckd ldrs on inner: hdwy 3f out: rdn and ev ch 2f out: sn drvn and wknd over 1f out* **9/4**[2]
0000 **8** *2* **Jul's Lad (IRE)**[12] 7650 3-9-0 **56**....(b) DNolan 14 44
(D Carroll) *sn led: rdn along over 3f out: hdd over 2f out and sn wknd* **33/1**
-500 **9** *1 1/2* **Parkview Love (USA)**[11] 7653 8-8-6 **47**....(b) LukeMorris 3 32
(A G Newcombe) *nvr nr ldrs* **33/1**
060U **10** *1 1/2* **Very Well Red**[8] 7693 6-9-1 **56**.... DarryllHolland 10 37
(P W Hiatt) *prom: rdn along bef 1/2-way: sn lost pl and bhd* **12/1**
1223 **11** *13* **Spinning Ridge (IRE)**[6] 7716 4-9-5 **60**....(p) LiamJones 11 11
(R A Harris) *midfield on outer: rdn along 1/2-way and sn bhd* **16/1**

0003 **12** ½ **Dado Mush**[6] 7712 6-8-13 **57**....................(p) WilliamCarson(3) 5 7
(T T Clement) *bhd fr 1/2-way* **40/1**

1m 40.86s (-2.84) **Going Correction** -0.325s/f (Stan)
WFA 3 from 4yo+ 1lb **12** Ran SP% **131.9**
Speed ratings (Par 101): **101,100,99,95,94 94,91,89,88,86 73,73**
toteswingers: 1&2 £5.20, 1&3 £6.80, 2&3 £8.60 CSF £59.78 CT £59.78 TOTE £3.30: £1.90, £2.00, £3.80; EX 19.10 Trifecta £60.30 Pool: £475.22 - 5.83 winning units. Place 6: £68.62 Place 5: £8.95 .
Owner Mrs V Franklin & Partners **Bred** Mrs C A Dunnett **Trained** Sproxton, Leics

FOCUS
A 46-64 handicap and again a strong pace. The form looks good for the grade.
Jul's Lad(IRE) Official explanation: jockey said gelding hung left
T/Plt: £96.60 to a £1 stake. Pool: £39,805.96. 300.77 winning tickets. T/Qpdt: £13.20 to a £1 stake. Pool: £3,451.89. 192.90 winning tickets. JR

7748

WOLVERHAMPTON (A.W) (L-H)

Thursday, December 17

OFFICIAL GOING: Standard
Wind: Fresh against Weather: Cloudy with sunny periods

7785 BET LIVE IN PLAY AT TOTESPORT.COM H'CAP 1m 5f 194y(P)
4:00 (4:02) (Class 5) (0-75,75) 3-Y-0+ **£3,238** (£963; £481; £240) **Stalls** Low

Form RPR
41 **1** **King Red**[20] 7557 5-9-11 **72**.................... RichardKingscote 13 80+
(Tom Dascombe) *hld up: hdwy and hung lft fr over 3f out: led wl over 1f out: drvn out* **2/1**[1]

4532 **2** ¾ **Augustus John (IRE)**[17] 7594 6-9-4 **65**.................... HayleyTurner 12 70
(R Brotherton) *hld up: hdwy over 2f out: rdn to chse wnr and hung lft fnl f: r.o* **7/1**

3640 **3** 1¼ **Tropical Blue**[130] 4822 3-9-6 **74**.................... SJCraine 11 79+
(Jennie Candlish) *hld up: hdwy: hung lft and nt clr run over 1f out: r.o: wnt 3rd nr fin: nt rch ldrs* **40/1**

5 **4** hd **Sally Bawn (IRE)**[12] 7399 4-9-1 **62**.................... DPMcDonogh 6 65
(Gordon Elliott, Ire) *prom: rdn over 2f out: styd on same pce ins fnl f* **6/1**[3]

/53- **5** 1¼ **Accompanist**[20] 7568 6-9-6 **67**....................(p) EddieAhern 5 68
(T G McCourt, Ire) *chsd ldrs: rdn over 2f out: styd on same pce fnl f* **16/1**

0054 **6** 1¼ **Wabbraan (USA)**[33] 7402 4-8-6 **58**.................... AmyBaker(5) 8 57
(M Hill) *led 1f: chsd ldr to over 8f out: remained handy: led again over 2f out: rdn and hdd wl over 1f out: no ex ins fnl f* **20/1**

116 **7** nk **Nakoma (IRE)**[26] 7490 7-9-1 **62**.................... DaneO'Neill 7 61
(B Ellison) *prom: rdn over 2f out: styd on same pce appr fnl f* **12/1**

5214 **8** ¾ **Prince Charlemagne (IRE)**[8] 7695 6-9-6 **67**.................... FergusSweeney 9 65
(G L Moore) *hld up: hdwy and nt clr run over 1f out: nvr trbld ldrs* **5/1**[2]

4050 **9** 10 **Bold Adventure**[12] 7649 5-8-10 **57**.................... StephenDonohoe 4 41
(W J Musson) *s.i.s: hld up: bhd fnl 4f* **14/1**

110- **10** 5 **Pocket Too**[16] 3942 6-10-0 **75**....................(p) KFallon 10 52
(Matthew Salaman) *prom: chsd ldr over 8f out: rdn and ev ch over 2f out: wknd over 1f out* **8/1**

1360 **11** 1½ **Sheila's Castle**[27] 7461 5-8-11 **61**.................... RussellKennemore(3) 3 36
(S Regan) *led after 1f: rdn and hdd over 2f out: sn wknd* **16/1**

12 2 **Stalingrad (IRE)**[21] 7545 4-9-4 **68**.................... EJMcNamara(3) 2 40
(Thomas Cleary, Ire) *hld up in tch: rdn over 3f out: wknd over 2f out* **66/1**

3m 5.43s (-0.57) **Going Correction** +0.025s/f (Slow)
WFA 3 from 4yo+ 7lb **12** Ran SP% **122.7**
Speed ratings (Par 103): **102,101,100,100,100 99,99,98,93,90 89,88**
toteswingers: 1&2 £4.60, 1&3 £21.30, 2&3 £41.70 CSF £16.51 CT £448.27 TOTE £2.80: £1.50, £2.50, £12.70; EX 21.60.
Owner John Reed **Bred** A Smith **Trained** Lambourn, Berks
■ Stewards' Enquiry : D P McDonogh one-day ban: used whip with excessive frequency (Dec 31)

FOCUS
Although they didn't appear to go that fast early, the principals came from off the pace. The runner-up is a fair guide with the third better than his finishing position due to interference.

7786 £10 FREE PLAY AT TOTESPORTBINGO.COM NURSERY 5f 216y(P)
4:30 (4:30) (Class 4) (0-90,89) 2-Y-0 **£4,533** (£1,348; £674; £336) **Stalls** Low

Form RPR
3002 **1** **Maldon Prom (IRE)**[12] 7637 2-7-11 **68**.................... AndreaAtzeni(3) 1 73
(C A Dwyer) *mde all: rdn over 1f out: styd on wl* **8/1**[3]

4411 **2** 1½ **Sabatini (IRE)**[13] 7625 2-8-11 **79**.................... SaleemGolam 5 79
(J Pearce) *s.i.s: racd keenly and sn prom: rdn and nt clr run over 1f out: r.o to go 2nd post: nt trble wnr* **10/11**[1]

4515 **3** nse **Transfixed (IRE)**[13] 7625 2-8-5 **78**.................... AndrewHeffernan(5) 6 78
(P D Evans) *trckd wnr: racd keenly: rdn and hung lft over 1f out: styd on: lost 2nd post* **8/1**[3]

3553 **4** ¾ **Kylladdie**[26] 7494 2-8-4 **72**.................... HayleyTurner 2 70
(S Gollings) *chsd ldrs: rdn and edgd rt over 1f out: kpt on* **9/4**[2]

6624 **5** 1¼ **Hill Of Miller (IRE)**[11] 7655 2-8-6 **74**.................... MartinDwyer 4 68
(Rae Guest) *hld up: plld hrd: rdn over 1f out: no imp fnl f* **8/1**[3]

1m 15.45s (0.45) **Going Correction** +0.025s/f (Slow) **5** Ran SP% **116.5**
Speed ratings (Par 98): **98,96,95,94,93**
toteswingers: 1&2 £8.20 1&3 not won, 2&3 not won. CSF £17.04 TOTE £8.90: £5.80, £1.10; EX 27.20.
Owner The Super Four **Bred** Michael McGlynn **Trained** Burrough Green, Cambs

FOCUS
Not a bad nursery but a bit of a tactical affair. The form is rated around the placed horses.

NOTEBOOK
Maldon Prom(IRE) had excuses for his last three defeats - trip too short twice and soft ground on the other occasion - but whose third in a C&D maiden before that gave him sound prospects off a mark of 68. Fast away from stall one, he took them along at an ordinary gallop before drifting to the centre of the track in the straight and staying on well for a cosy success. There should be more to come from him, although his trainer plans to give him a little break now and bring him back in February. (tchd 9-1)
Sabatini(IRE) wasn't alone in wanting the leader to set a stronger pace. Her run was blocked when Transfixed crossed in front of her approaching the furlong pole, but she finished well once switched to the outside. She remains in good form despite this defeat. (op Evens tchd 6-5)
Transfixed(IRE) ran well considering her best distance is probably 7f, but she was well placed, racing alongside the winner, in a race not run to suit the hold-up horses. (op 6-1)
Kylladdie didn't find the return to 6f proving the answer and he probably just needs more help from the Handicapper. (op 11-4)
Hill Of Miller(IRE), who also looks high enough in the weights, refused to settle through the early stages of the race and gave himself little chance of playing a part in the finish. (op 9-1)

7787 H HARRISON HAPPY RETIREMENT H'CAP 7f 32y(P)
5:00 (5:01) (Class 7) (0-50,50) 3-Y-0+ **£1,706** (£503; £252) **Stalls** High

Form RPR
0-00 **1** **Tallest Peak (USA)**[17] 7599 4-9-2 **49**....................(b[1]) GeorgeBaker 9 63
(M G Quinlan) *hld up in tch: led wl over 1f out: sn rdn clr: eased nr fin* **7/2**[2]

5000 **2** 4 **Neo's Mate (IRE)**[20] 7555 3-8-12 **50**.................... AndrewHeffernan(5) 8 53+
(Paul Green) *hld up: hdwy u.p on outside wl over 1f out: hung lft ins fnl f: wnt 2nd post: no ch w wnr* **20/1**

4050 **3** hd **Well Of Echoes**[30] 7422 3-9-2 **49**....................(tp) AndrewMullen 12 51
(A J McCabe) *chsd ldrs: led over 2f out: rdn and hdd wl over 1f out: styd on same pce fnl f: lost 2nd post* **25/1**

2443 **4** 2 **Short Cut**[91] 6039 3-9-3 **50**....................(t) StephenDonohoe 3 47
(Ian Williams) *chsd ldrs: rdn over 2f out: styd on same pce appr fnl f* **7/4**[1]

0055 **5** 1½ **Dontuwishitwereso**[7] 7703 3-9-3 **50**.................... TonyCulhane 4 43
(P W D'Arcy) *hld up: hdwy u.p over 1f out: nt trble ldrs* **7/1**

4030 **6** nk **Djalalabad (FR)**[11] 7652 5-9-3 **50**....................(tp) HayleyTurner 5 42
(Mrs C A Dunnett) *s.i.s: hld up: nt clr run over 1f out: swtchd lft: styd on: nvr rchd ldrs* **9/2**[3]

6004 **7** 2 **Wicklewood**[15] 7610 3-9-3 **50**....................(b) AdrianMcCarthy 2 37
(Mrs C A Dunnett) *prom: n.m.r and lost pl 6f out: rallied over 4f out: rdn 1/2-way: wknd over 1f out* **20/1**

6360 **8** 2¼ **Red Current**[10] 7660 5-9-3 **50**....................(b) KevinGhunowa 6 31
(R A Harris) *hld up: pushed along 1/2-way: sme hdwy over 2f out: wknd wl over 1f out* **14/1**

5064 **9** 2½ **Battimoore (IRE)**[15] 7614 3-9-3 **50**.................... DaneO'Neill 7 24
(I W McInnes) *hld up: hdwy over 2f out: rdn and wknd wl over 1f out* **14/1**

000 **10** 4½ **H Harrison (IRE)**[15] 7609 9-9-3 **50**....................(p) AndrewElliott 11 12
(I W McInnes) *chsd ldr: rdn and ev ch over 2f out: wknd wl over 1f out: eased* **33/1**

0560 **11** ½ **Madhal**[15] 7614 3-9-3 **50**.................... LPKeniry 10 10
(Matthew Salaman) *led: rdn and hdd over 2f out: wknd over 1f out* **20/1**

0500 **12** 5 **Dark Velvet (IRE)**[9] 7678 3-9-3 **50**....................(p) SteveDrowne 1 —
(E J Alston) *pushed along early: chsd ldrs: wknd 1/2-way* **50/1**

1m 29.35s (-0.25) **Going Correction** +0.025s/f (Slow) **12** Ran SP% **125.6**
Speed ratings (Par 97): **102,97,97,94,93 92,90,88,85,80 79,73**
toteswingers: 1&2 £14.60, 1&3 £25.10, 2&3 £62.60 CSF £80.73 CT £1576.17 TOTE £4.60: £1.50, £5.40, £9.70; EX 127.70.
Owner The Chicken On A Chain Partnership **Bred** Barnett Enterprises **Trained** Newmarket, Suffolk

FOCUS
A very tight handicap, with each of the runners rated 49 or 50. The winner recorded a personal best in the blinkers with the third setting the level.

7788 OVER 50 INSTANT GAMES AT TOTESPORTGAMES.COM CLAIMING STKS 1m 141y(P)
5:30 (5:30) (Class 6) 2-Y-0 **£2,729** (£806; £403) **Stalls** Low

Form RPR
0021 **1** **Glen Lass**[5] 7731 2-8-3 58 ow1....................(b) ChrisCatlin 6 58+
(J Pearce) *trckd ldrs: edgd lft 7f out: led over 1f out: rdn and r.o wl* **9/4**[1]

0600 **2** 4½ **Pie Poudre**[7] 7700 2-8-11 0.................... SJCraine 3 57
(R Brotherton) *hld up: hmpd 7f out: hdwy on outside 2f out: rdn and hung lft fnl f: styd on same pce* **25/1**

6313 **3** ½ **Tuscan King**[5] 7731 2-9-3 64....................(b) J-PGuillambert 8 62
(P Howling) *chsd ldr 2f: remained handy: rdn over 1f out: styd on same pce fnl f* **4/1**[3]

5650 **4** ¾ **Vittachi**[5] 7722 2-8-7 47....................(b) JimmyQuinn 10 50
(J D Bethell) *hld up: racd keenly: hdwy to chse wnr over 6f out: rdn and hung lft over 1f out: styd on same pce* **33/1**

5000 **5** hd **Crushing (IRE)**[14] 7619 2-8-11 53.................... SteveDrowne 9 54
(A J McCabe) *led: rdn and hdd over 1f out: no ex* **25/1**

664 **6** 1¾ **Creevy (IRE)**[8] 7683 2-8-2 48.................... JamieMackay 7 41
(S Kirk) *prom: rdn over 2f out: wknd over 1f out* **16/1**

4325 **7** 1 **James Barrymore**[12] 7644 2-8-11 69.................... EddieAhern 5 58+
(R Hannon) *trckd ldrs: racd keenly: hmpd 7f out: sn lost pl: hdwy over 2f out: rdn and hung lft over 1f out: sn wknd and eased* **5/2**[2]

0054 **8** hd **Aegean Destiny**[19] 7584 2-8-1 54 ow2.................... AndrewHeffernan(5) 4 42
(R A Harris) *s.i.s: hld up: rdn over 3f out: wknd wl over 1f out* **10/1**

00 **9** 3½ **Twoellies**[175] 3310 2-8-10 0.................... FrancisNorton 1 39
(Ollie Pears) *hld up: plld hrd: rdn 1/2-way: wknd over 2f out* **50/1**

604 **10** ¾ **Hubble Space**[10] 7669 2-8-5 0.................... AndreaAtzeni(3) 2 35
(M Botti) *chsd ldrs: lost pl over 6f out: wknd 3f out* **11/2**

1m 51.78s (1.28) **Going Correction** +0.025s/f (Slow) **10** Ran SP% **122.3**
Speed ratings (Par 94): **95,91,90,89,89 88,87,87,83,83**
toteswingers: 1&2 £30.60, 1&3 £2.00, 2&3 £29.40 CSF £67.62 TOTE £2.50: £1.10, £10.20, £2.20; EX 95.50.Glen Lass was subject to a friendly claim.
Owner Ian Bishop **Bred** Limestone And Tara Studs **Trained** Newmarket, Suffolk

FOCUS
A modest claimer with the winner setting the level.

NOTEBOOK
Glen Lass, though her rider was putting up 1lb overweight, was one of the best in at the weights, travelled kindly through the race and stayed on strongly in the straight. Although the bare form of this contest is ordinary, she's at the top of her game and might be worth trying back in handicap company. (op 15-8 tchd 5-2)
Pie Poudre, dropping into a claimer for the first time having cut little ice in maiden company, did quite well as he was keen to post and badly hampered going into the first bend. He circled the field into the straight and stayed on well, hinting at better to come. (op 66-1 tchd 80-1)
Tuscan King, beaten six lengths by Glen Lass over a furlong further here last time, didn't get much closer despite the drop back to this distance promising to suit. (op 5-1 tchd 11-2)
Vittachi was slow to break and towards the rear early but he pulled his way into second rounding the first turn. He paid for that early effort later on. (op 50-1)
Crushing(IRE), trying a longer trip, made the running and didn't get home. (tchd 20-1)
James Barrymore, best in at the weights but weak on Betfair on this drop in class, got hampered going into the first bend and was heavily restrained. He then got into a bumping match with Aegean Destiny inside the final furlong and his jockey stopped riding. (op 3-1)

7789 100% NEW PLAYER BONUS AT TOTESPORTCASINO.COM H'CAP 1m 1f 103y(P)
6:00 (6:00) (Class 2) (0-100,98) 3-Y-0+
£11,215 (£3,358; £1,679; £840; £419; £210) **Stalls** Low

Form RPR
5140 **1** **Splinter Cell (USA)**[19] 7574 3-8-7 **90**.................... AndreaAtzeni(3) 6 99
(M Botti) *hld up: hdwy over 2f out: rdn to ld and bmpd 1f out: sn edgd lft: r.o* **12/1**

1311 **2** *1 ½* **Mr Willis**[16] 7603 3-8-10 **90** .... SteveDrowne 1 96
(J R Best) *chsd ldrs: rdn and ev ch whn hung rt 1f out: styd on same pce ins fnl f* **13/2**

0062 **3** *shd* **Waldvogel (IRE)**[44] 7226 5-9-4 **96** .... DaneO'Neill 9 102
(L M Cumani) *hld up: hdwy over 1f out: sn rdn: r.o* **5/1**[3]

0631 **4** *hd* **Full Toss**[13] 7623 3-8-2 **85** .... KellyHarrison(3) 2 91
(P D Evans) *hld up: hdwy 2f out: rdn over 1f out: styd on same pce ins fnl f* **11/1**

0054 **5** *1 ¼* **Faithful Ruler (USA)**[19] 7574 5-8-8 **86** .... TonyHamilton 11 89
(R A Fahey) *sn pushed along in last pl: nt clr run over 2f out: hdwy over 1f out: sn rdn: nt qckn wl ins fnl f* **16/1**

0021 **6** *¾* **Bound By Honour (SAF)**[19] 7574 6-9-4 **96** .... (b) GeorgeBaker 5 97
(G L Moore) *prom: rdn over 2f out: edgd lft over 1f out: styd on same pce* **7/2**[2]

41-4 **7** *1* **Grand Opera (IRE)**[22] 7530 6-8-13 **91** .... (p) DPMcDonogh 8 90
(Gordon Elliott, Ire) *chsd ldrs: rdn on outside over 2f out: hung lft and wknd ins fnl f* **3/1**[1]

20P2 **8** *hd* **Brouhaha**[19] 7583 5-8-8 **86** .... RichardKingscote 3 85
(Tom Dascombe) *led: hdd 7f out: chsd ldr tl led again over 4f out: rdn and hdd 1f out: wknd wl ins fnl f* **14/1**

0020 **9** *12* **Red Somerset (USA)**[13] 7626 6-8-6 **84** .... JimmyQuinn 7 58
(R J Hodges) *s.i.s: hdwy 7f out: rdn and wknd over 1f out* **33/1**

035 **10** *13* **Laterly (IRE)**[6] 7720 4-8-13 **91** .... IanMongan 10 37
(S Gollings) *chsd ldrs: led 7f out: hdd over 4f out: rdn and wknd over 2f out* **8/1**

2m 0.11s (-1.59) **Going Correction** +0.025s/f (Slow)
WFA 3 from 4yo+ 2lb **10** Ran SP% **119.8**
Speed ratings (Par 109): **108,106,106,106,105 104,103,103,92,81**
toteswingers: 1&2 £17.70, 1&3 £11.90, 2&3 £5.00 CSF £90.30 CT £450.58 TOTE £13.30: £3.20, £2.70, £1.80; EX 155.20.

Owner Op - Center **Bred** Old Carhue Stud **Trained** Newmarket, Suffolk

FOCUS
A competitive handicap and pretty straightforward form.

NOTEBOOK
Splinter Cell(USA) had to make his own running at Lingfield last time but he's much happier when held up off the pace. This race was run to suit and he stayed on strongly to score. He needs cut on turf but is also effective on this surface and, looking further ahead, could be the type to aim at the Rosebery Stakes at Kempton towards the end of March. (op 20-1)

Mr Willis ran well as he raced closer to the decent gallop than those who finished around him at the finish. The longer trip itself didn't find him out and he's capable of winning again despite having been put up 6lb for his last success. (op 11-2 tchd 7-1)

Waldvogel(IRE) raced towards the outside throughout and swung widest into the straight. He took a while to hit top gear and this trip looked on the short side for him. (op 9-2 tchd 7-2)

Full Toss, winner of a claimer at Lingfield last time, was having his first start for David Evans and ran well, although he probably still needs a little help from the Handicapper. (op 14-1)

Faithful Ruler(USA), dropped in last from the widest draw, found things opening up for him on the inside in the straight and he stayed on quite well. The race was run to suit him, though. (op 20-1)

Bound By Honour(SAF), 5lb higher for his Lingfield win, was a little disappointing, although he was never that far off the decent early gallop. (op 3-1 tchd 4-1)

Grand Opera(IRE), who went without the tongue tie he wore in his last two starts, including when successful at Dundalk, didn't live up to market expectations. Perhaps the tongue tie will be back on next time. (op 7-2 tchd 4-1)

7790 £1000 IN FREE BETS AT BIGTIPS.CO.UK MEDIAN AUCTION MAIDEN STKS 1m 4f 50y(P)
6:30 (6:30) (Class 6) 3-5-Y-O **£2,047** (£604; £302) **Stalls** Low

Form RPR

0522 **1** **Starburst**[18] 7590 4-9-3 59 .... GeorgeBaker 8 67+
(A M Balding) *hld up: hdwy over 2f out: led on bit over 1f out: sn rdn clr: eased wl ins fnl f* **10/3**[2]

53-0 **2** *3 ¾* **Maraased**[44] 7221 4-9-8 0 .... IanMongan 4 64
(S Gollings) *chsd ldrs: rdn and ev ch fr over 2f out tl hung fr lft over 1f out: styd on same pce* **7/1**[3]

4520 **3** *3 ½* **Moscow Oznick**[9] 7677 4-9-8 60 .... (p) DavidProbert 2 62+
(D Donovan) *hld up: hdwy over 4f out: led 3f out: rdn and hdd whn hmpd over 1f out: no ex* **16/1**

3444 **4** *7* **Chatanoogachoochoo**[33] 7399 4-9-3 61 .... JimmyQuinn 5 42
(M Hill) *plld hrd and prom: hmpd after 1f: rdn over 2f out: wknd over 1f oute* **8/1**

5 *5* **Kalimanka (FR)**[21] 7548 3-8-9 70 .... (tp) ShaneFoley(3) 1 34
(M Halford, Ire) *hld up: hdwy over 3f out: rdn over 2f out: sn wknd* **3/1**[1]

0544 **6** *16* **Arashi**[10] 7668 3-9-3 62 .... (p) SteveDrowne 6 14
(Lucinda Featherstone) *chsd ldrs: hmpd after 1f: rdn and wknd over 2f out: t.o* **10/3**[2]

03 **7** *¾* **Venture Capitalist**[15] 5123 3-9-3 61 .... DaneO'Neill 9 12
(B Ellison) *s.i.s: sn pushed along in rr: rdn over 3f out: wknd over 2f out: t.o* **10/1**

8 *6* **Wheresmeneckstrap (IRE)**[91] 6041 4-9-8 0 .... EddieAhern 3 3
(T G McCourt, Ire) *s.i.s: plld hrd and sn trcking ldr: led over 5f out: hdd 3f out: sn rdn and wknd: t.o* **33/1**

000- **9** *83* **Charlie Green (IRE)**[172] 7446 4-9-3 37 .... (v) AndrewHeffernan(5) 7 —
(Paul Green) *led: hdd over 5f out: rdn and wknd wl over 3f out: t.o* **100/1**

2m 40.87s (-0.23) **Going Correction** +0.025s/f (Slow)
WFA 3 from 4yo 5lb **9** Ran SP% **113.7**
Speed ratings (Par 101): **101,98,96,91,88 77,77,73,17**
toteswingers: 1&2 £5.60, 1&3 £7.60, 2&3 £12.50 CSF £26.48 TOTE £4.30: £1.20, £1.80, £3.10; EX 25.80 Place 6: £219.12 Place 5: £98.65 .

Owner Holistic Racing Ltd **Bred** Winterbeck Manor Stud **Trained** Kingsclere, Hants

■ Stewards' Enquiry : David Probert caution: careless riding.

FOCUS
Ordinary maiden form best rated through the third.

Maraased Official explanation: jockey said gelding ran green closing stages

Chatanoogachoochoo Official explanation: jockey said filly ran too free early stages

Arashi Official explanation: jockey said saddle slipped

T/Plt: £263.40 to a £1 stake. Pool: £75,489.86. 209.17 winning tickets. T/Qpdt: £175.80 to a £1 stake. Pool: £7,580.16. 31.90 winning tickets. CR

7778 SOUTHWELL (L-H)
Friday, December 18

OFFICIAL GOING: Standard to slow
Wind: Fresh half behind Weather: Bright, dry and cold

7791 TOTEPLACEPOT WIN WITHOUT BACKING A WINNER NURSERY 7f (F)
11:55 (11:57) (Class 6) (0-65,65) 2-Y-O **£2,047** (£604; £302) **Stalls** Low

Form RPR

0412 **1** **Tealing**[6] 7722 2-9-2 **60** .... PhillipMakin 9 68
(R C Guest) *in tch: hdwy on outer over 2f out: rdn wl over 1f out: styd on strly ent fnl f to ld last 100yds* **7/2**[2]

6502 **2** *2* **Knightfire (IRE)**[20] 7584 2-8-11 **55** .... JoeFanning 10 58
(W R Swinburn) *prom: smooth hdwy to ld over 2f out: rdn over 1f out: hung rt ins fnl f: hdd and one pce last 100yds* **9/2**[3]

4203 **3** *1 ¼* **Miss Taken (IRE)**[3] 7756 2-7-10 **47** .... NeilFarley(7) 1 47
(D Carroll) *led: rdn along and hdd over 2f out: drvn over 1f out: kpt on same pce* **14/1**

1625 **4** *½* **Push Me (IRE)**[6] 7722 2-9-7 **65** .... RobertWinston 2 64
(A J McCabe) *trckd ldrs: hdwy 3f out: rdn along 2f out: drvn and one pce fr over 1f out* **15/2**

604 **5** *1 ¼* **Layla's Lad (USA)**[20] 7582 2-9-7 **65** .... TonyHamilton 6 61
(R A Fahey) *chsd ldrs: rdn along over 2f out: sn no imp* **5/2**[1]

0200 **6** *¾* **Sixties Rock**[15] 7619 2-8-10 **59** .... RossAtkinson(5) 8 53
(J A Glover) *a towards rr* **11/1**

0041 **7** *6* **Tiger Hawk (USA)**[7] 7706 2-9-2 **65** 6ex .... (b) RichardEvans(5) 3 44
(P D Evans) *s.i.s: sn in tch on inner: rdn along 1/2-way and sn wknd* **7/1**

3604 **8** *nk* **Baby Judge (IRE)**[10] 7674 2-8-4 **55** .... DavidKenny(7) 4 33
(M C Chapman) *prom: rdn along 3f out and sn wknd* **33/1**

1600 **9** *2 ¼* **Rescent**[37] 7335 2-8-1 **52** .... MatthewLawson(7) 7 24
(Mrs R A Carr) *a in rr* **66/1**

1m 31.71s (1.41) **Going Correction** +0.125s/f (Slow) **9** Ran SP% **112.7**
Speed ratings (Par 94): **96,93,92,91,90 89,82,82,79**
toteswinger:1&2:£3.60, 2&3:£5.10, 1&3:£7.10 CSF £19.08 CT £192.08 TOTE £4.00: £1.60, £2.20, £3.00; EX 17.90 Trifecta £96.60 Part won. Pool: £130.61 - 0.50 winning units..

Owner Future Racing (Notts) Limited **Bred** Alan A Wright **Trained** Stainforth, S Yorks

FOCUS
This was just a moderate nursery but the winner goes well here and the runner-up and fourth set the level.

NOTEBOOK
Tealing got behind early on but that didn't seem to affect his chance and he stayed on strongly in the straight, taking his course record to 2-4. He can win again around here this winter. (op 9-2)

Knightfire(IRE), 5lb higher than when runner-up in a similar event on Polytrack last time, seemed to handle the Fibresand well at the first attempt and, having been well placed throughout, can have few excuses. (op 5-1)

Miss Taken(IRE), ridden by an inexperienced apprentice, showed plenty of speed but stuck towards the inside for most of the way, which is rarely ideal at this track. (op 10-1)

Push Me(IRE), just as when a beaten favourite over 1m around here on her previous start, travelled well but found little, and the drop in trip didn't have the desired effect. Perhaps she'll appreciate a return to Polytrack. (op 10-1)

Layla's Lad(USA), reported to have resented the kickback on Polytrack last time, was stepped back in trip for this first try on Fibresand, but he came under strong pressure before the straight and made no progress. (op 9-4 tchd 11-4 and 3-1 in places)

Tiger Hawk(USA) was a winner on his two previous starts on Fibresand, but both of those victories came over 1m in selling company and he was never seen with a chance this time after starting slowly. Official explanation: jockey said colt was slowly away (op 9-2)

7792 ARCHER ELECTRICAL FILLIES' MEDIAN AUCTION MAIDEN STKS 1m (F)
12:25 (12:26) (Class 5) 2-Y-O **£2,729** (£806; £403) **Stalls** Low

Form RPR

602 **1** **Lily Lily**[7] 7706 2-9-0 0 .... (b) JoeFanning 2 62
(K McAuliffe) *dwlt: sn cl up on inner: led 1/2-way: rdn along 2f out and sn jnd: drvn over 1f out: styd on gamely u.p ins fnl f* **8/1**[3]

50 **2** *hd* **Ambrogina**[8] 7700 2-9-0 0 .... TomEaves 5 62
(M Botti) *trckd ldrs: hdwy over 2f out: effrt to chal over 1f out: sn rdn to dispute ld and ev ch tl drvn ins fnl f and nt qckn nr fin* **4/1**[2]

3 *2 ¼* **Privy Speech (IRE)** 2-9-0 0 .... RobertWinston 7 57
(Rae Guest) *chsd ldrs towards outer: hdwy 2f out: sn rdn and ev ch tl drvn and kpt on same ent fnl f* **8/1**[3]

035 **4** *shd* **Puteri (IRE)**[121] 5165 2-9-0 67 .... TonyCulhane 8 57
(M A Jarvis) *trckd ldrs: smooth hdwy 3f out: chal 2f out: sn rdn and ev ch tl drvn and one pce ent fnl f* **8/11**[1]

00 **5** *4* **Little Meadow (IRE)**[132] 4790 2-9-0 0 .... TonyHamilton 6 48
(Miss J Feilden) *prom on outer: rdn along 3f out: drvn 2f out and ev ch tl wknd appr fnl f* **100/1**

066 **6** *6* **Penderyn**[34] 7391 2-8-9 46 .... PaulPickard(5) 1 35
(C Smith) *in tch on inner: rdn along 3f out: wknd 2f out* **33/1**

7 *½* **Que Belle (IRE)** 2-8-9 0 .... RossAtkinson(5) 3 34
(Tom Dascombe) *green and sn rdn along in rr: a outpcd* **12/1**

0333 **8** *nk* **Labretella (IRE)**[13] 7638 2-9-0 54 .... SteveDrowne 4 33
(D W Thompson) *led to 1/2-way: cl up: rdn along over 2f out: drvn and wknd wl over 1f out* **10/1**

1m 45.52s (1.82) **Going Correction** +0.125s/f (Slow) **8** Ran SP% **120.8**
Speed ratings (Par 93): **95,94,92,92,88 82,81,81**
toteswinger:1&2:£4.70, 2&3:£4.90, 1&3:£6.30 CSF £42.35 TOTE £8.10: £2.00, £1.70, £3.30; EX 46.00 Trifecta £138.90 Pool: £354.93 - 1.89 winning units.

Owner K W J McAuliffe **Bred** Dr Celia Marr **Trained** Fernham, Oxon

FOCUS
A moderate fillies' maiden, but some of these are open to improvement. The form is rated at around plating level.

NOTEBOOK
Lily Lily ruined her winning chance with a slow start when runner-up over C&D on her previous outing but, although again missing the break, she was able to recover into a good position in a share of the lead this time, and that made the difference. However, seeing as she has already been beaten in a seller, and has been reported to have a breathing problem in the past, she doesn't appeal as worth following.

Ambrogina ◆ travelled nicely in behind the leaders for much of the way and looked the winner when still going well early in the straight but, despite keeping on, she couldn't quite get up. This isn't form to get carried away with, but she has some size about her and gives the impression she'll improve again. (op 11-2)

Privy Speech(IRE), who cost 15,000gns the last time she went through a public auction, is a half-sister to former high-class US juvenile filly Brusque, and fairly useful Critical Acclaim, while her dam won two minor races on dirt in the States. She travelled okay for some of the way and should improve enough to make her mark. (op 17-2 tchd 9-1)

Puteri(IRE) failed to improve for the switch to Fibresand on her return from four months off and her official mark of 67 looks stiff enough. (after early 10-11 in places)
Que Belle(IRE) cost 40,000gns as a foal, but fetched only 2,000euros as a yearling. After starting slowly, she was pushed along in a detached last for much of the way, looking to be struggling through a lack of experience as well as having to face a wall of kickback, but she made some minor progress late on, hinting at ability. (op 10-1)
Labretella(IRE) Official explanation: jockey said filly had no more to give

7793 TOTEEXACTA THE BETTER VALUE FORECAST NURSERY 5f (F)
1:00 (1:00) (Class 4) (0-85,80) 2-Y-O **£6,152** (£1,830; £914; £456) **Stalls High**

Form RPR
4332 **1** **Lucky Mellor**[13] 7636 2-9-7 **74**....................(b) NCallan 8 84
(D K Ivory) *trckd ldr: hdwy on bit wl over 1f out: shkn up to ld jst ins fnl f: sn rdn and hung lft: kpt on* **6/4**[1]
2303 **2** *3* **Six Wives**[13] 7636 2-9-6 **73**.................... ChrisCatlin 6 72
(J A Glover) *led: jnd and rdn along over 1f out: drvn and hdd jst ins fnl f: kpt on same pce* **7/1**[3]
0013 **3** *shd* **Athwaab**[7] 7707 2-9-1 **68**.................... TonyCulhane 9 67
(M G Quinlan) *chsd ldrs: rdn along 2f out: drvn and sltly outpcd over 1f out: kpt on ins fnl f* **7/1**[3]
0641 **4** *4* **Italian Tom (IRE)**[10] 7674 2-9-13 **80** 6ex.................... LiamJones 3 64
(R A Harris) *swtchd lft after s and sn cl up: rdn along 1/2-way: drvn wl over 1f out and sn wknd* **2/1**[2]
1146 **5** *3/4* **Angie's Nap (USA)**[13] 7636 2-8-12 **65**....................(p) RobertWinston 1 47
(P S McEntee) *cl up: rdn along 1/2-way and sn wknd* **16/1**
3600 **6** *10* **Taeping (IRE)**[1] 7778 2-7-12 **51** oh1.................... DavidProbert 7 —
(R Hollinshead) *sn rdn along and a outpcd in rr* **10/1**
60.58 secs (0.88) **Going Correction** +0.125s/f (Slow) **6** Ran SP% **113.3**
Speed ratings (Par 98): **97,92,92,85,84 68**
toteswinger:1&2:£2.30, 2&3:£3.60, 1&3:£4.00 CSF £12.86 CT £55.54 TOTE £2.00: £1.50, £3.00; EX 8.40 Trifecta £13.60 Pool: £349.69 - 18.89 winning units.
Owner L M Baker **Bred** Mr And Mrs L Baker **Trained** Radlett, Herts

FOCUS
An ordinary nursery for the class and there are doubts about the form with a few below their best; however the winner can be given a chance to confirm this effort.

NOTEBOOK
Lucky Mellor had no bother in confirming recent C&D form with Six Wives, finding plenty for pressure having travelled ominously well when getting a good lead off his old rival. He's yet to finish out of the first two in four starts on this surface. (tchd 7-4)
Six Wives showed plenty of speed but didn't quite see her race out and her two wins to date have been gained on the quicker Polytrack surface. (op 6-1 tchd 11-2)
Athwaab again failed to prove herself as effective on Fibresand as she is on Polytrack, although this drop in trip may not have suited. (op 10-1)
Italian Tom(IRE), carrying a penalty for a win over C&D the previous week, didn't help himself with a sluggish start and was in trouble by about halfway. A disappointing effort. (op 9-4 tchd 15-8)
Angie's Nap(USA) has won three times on this surface, but she again carried her head to one side and was one of the first beaten. Perhaps she has had enough for the time being. (tchd 14-1)

7794 TOTEPOOL A BETTER WAY TO BET H'CAP 1m 3f (F)
1:35 (1:35) (Class 5) (0-70,68) 3-Y-O **£2,729** (£806; £403) **Stalls Low**

Form RPR
0043 **1** **Through The Forest (USA)**[79] 6371 3-8-4 **54** oh1.......... ChrisCatlin 6 56
(W R Swinburn) *trckd ldrs: hdwy on outer 4f out: rdn along 3f out: drvn: edgd lft and sltly outpcd over 1f out: styd on u.str driving ins fnl f to ld last 75yds* **11/4**[1]
0003 **2** *1/2* **Mister Frosty (IRE)**[2] 7766 3-7-11 **54** oh4.......... CharlotteKerton(7) 7 55
(G Prodromou) *cl up: led 7f out: rdn along 3f out: drvn and hdd 1 1/2f out: rallied wl u.p and ev ch ins fnl f tl no ex towards fin* **14/1**
5405 **3** *hd* **Eightdaysaweek**[10] 7677 3-8-0 **57**....................(p) DeclanCannon(7) 1 58
(A J McCabe) *trckd ldrs: hdwy to chse ldr 3f out: rdn to take slt ld 1 1/2f out: drvn ent fnl f: sn edgd rt: hdd and no ex last 75yds* **9/2**[3]
5145 **4** *8* **Charging Indian (IRE)**[24] 7505 3-9-3 **67**....................(p) TonyCulhane 5 54
(P T Midgley) *in rr and sn pushed along: sme hdwy over 4f out: sn rdn along and nvr a factor* **11/4**[1]
3004 **5** *5* **Ladies Dancing**[15] 7620 3-9-4 **68**.................... SteveDrowne 3 47
(J A Osborne) *cl up: led after 2f: hdd 7f out: cl up tl rdn along 3f out and wknd fnl 2f* **7/1**
6 *7* **Phantasy Rock (IRE)**[30] 7449 3-8-11 **61**.................... FrancisNorton 2 28
(W P Mullins, Ire) *led 2f: prom tl rdn along 4f out and sn wknd* **4/1**[2]
2m 28.98s (0.98) **Going Correction** +0.125s/f (Slow) **6** Ran SP% **110.7**
Speed ratings (Par 102): **101,100,100,94,91 85**
toteswinger:1&2:£7.00, 2&3:£8.10, 1&3:£3.10 CSF £38.00 TOTE £3.20: £1.80, £4.30; EX 28.60.
Owner Mrs Doreen M Swinburn **Bred** Mike G Rutherford **Trained** Aldbury, Herts
■ Stewards' Enquiry : Charlotte Kerton nine-day ban: used whip with excessive frequency in incorrect place without giving gelding time to respond (Jan 1-9)

FOCUS
A moderate middle-distance handicap run at a muddling pace and best rated through the third.
Phantasy Rock(IRE) Official explanation: jockey said filly did not face the kickback

7795 TOTESWINGER THREE WAYS TO WIN CLAIMING STKS 6f (F)
2:05 (2:09) (Class 6) 3-Y-O+ **£2,047** (£604; £302) **Stalls Low**

Form RPR
4210 **1** **Ponting (IRE)**[21] 7555 3-8-5 62.................... PaulPickard(5) 3 67
(P T Midgley) *mde all: rdn 2f out: drvn over 1f out: kpt on gamely ins fnl f* **10/1**
0434 **2** *nk* **Confuchias (IRE)**[13] 7639 5-9-3 90.................... RobertWinston 11 73
(Pat Eddery) *bmpd s and in rr: hdwy over 2f out: switrchd rt and rdn over 1f out: drvn and styd on ins fnl f: jst hld* **10/11**[1]
3242 **3** *3/4* **Total Impact**[22] 7534 6-8-10 82.................... TonyHamilton 1 64
(R A Fahey) *trckd ldrs on inner: hdwy 1/2-way: swtchd rt and rdn to chal wl over 1f out: ev ch tl drvn and no ex wl ins fnl f* **9/2**[2]
0026 **4** *1/2* **Tag Team (IRE)**[10] 7681 8-8-7 46....................(p) DavidProbert 6 59
(John A Harris) *chsd ldrs: hdwy over 2f out: sn rdn and ev ch tl drvn and wknd wl ins fnl f* **80/1**
2006 **5** *3* **Secret Witness**[11] 7662 3-9-0 76....................(b) LiamJones 10 56
(R A Harris) *hmpd s and bhd: hdwy on inner over 2f out: sn rdn: styd on ins fnl f: nrst fin* **17/2**[3]
2036 **6** *3/4* **Jord (IRE)**[18] 7596 5-8-3 61 ow1.................... ChrisCatlin 8 43
(J A Glover) *chsd ldrs on outer: rdn along over 2f out: drvn wl over 1f out and grad wknd* **10/1**
5606 **7** *1* **Cornus**[48] 7192 7-8-11 68 ow1.................... PhillipMakin 2 48
(J A Glover) *dwlt: sn chsng ldrs: rdn along over 2f out: grad wknd* **22/1**
0060 **8** *1 1/2* **Kannon**[52] 7080 4-7-10 45 ow1....................(p) DeclanCannon(7) 12 35
(A J McCabe) *a towards rr* **80/1**
0100 **9** *1 1/4* **Mandhooma**[21] 7561 3-8-7 58.................... LukeMorris 5 35
(P W Hiatt) *cl up: rdn along 1/2-way: sn wknd* **40/1**
5510 **10** *3/4* **Cape Of Storms**[247] 1285 6-8-9 64....................(b) TomEaves 7 35
(R Brotherton) *t.k.h: chsd ldrs on outer: rdn along over 2f out: drvn over 1f out and sn wknd* **16/1**
1m 16.96s (0.46) **Going Correction** +0.125s/f (Slow) **10** Ran SP% **114.4**
Speed ratings (Par 101): **101,100,99,98,94 93,92,90,88,87**
toteswinger:1&2:£4.70, 2&3:£2.60, 1&3:£4.80 CSF £18.87 TOTE £11.50: £2.80, £1.10, £1.50; EX 31.80 Trifecta £99.10 Pool: £580.15 - 4.33 winning units.Confuchias was claimed by Horses First Racing Limited £15,000
Owner A Taylor Jnr **Bred** John McEnery **Trained** Westow, N Yorks
■ Stewards' Enquiry : Paul Pickard four-day ban: used whip with excessive frequency in incorrect place (Jan 1-4)

FOCUS
This looked a good claimer beforehand, but both the winner and the fourth limit the form.
Confuchias(IRE) Official explanation: jockey said horse stumbled leaving stalls
Secret Witness Official explanation: jockey said gelding was hampered leaving stalls

7796 ANGLING PUBLICATIONS CLASSIFIED STKS 7f (F)
2:40 (2:40) (Class 6) 3-Y-O+ **£1,942** (£578; £288; £144) **Stalls Low**

Form RPR
0043 **1** **King Of Rhythm (IRE)**[4] 7755 6-9-0 55....................(b[1]) DNolan 13 62
(D Carroll) *hld up in tch: smooth hdwy 2f out: swtchd rt and chsd ldr over 1f out: rdn and qcknd to ld ins fnl f: styd on* **6/1**
0600 **2** *1 3/4* **King's Sabre**[7] 7709 3-8-9 50....................(be) BillyCray(5) 9 57
(R C Guest) *chsd ldrs: hdwy 3f out: rdn to ld 1 1/2f out: drvn ent fnl f: sn hdd and kpt on same pce* **25/1**
6330 **3** *1 3/4* **Mojeerr**[24] 7499 3-8-7 48....................(p) DeclanCannon(7) 6 53
(A J McCabe) *dwlt and towards rr: gd hdwy on inner over 2f out: sn rdn and styd on wl fnl f: nrst fin* **16/1**
600 **4** *1* **Jenny's Pride (IRE)**[73] 6570 3-9-0 52.................... DavidProbert 10 50
(John A Harris) *towards rr: hdwy 2f out: sn rdn and kpt on ins fnl f: nrst fin* **28/1**
0000 **5** *hd* **Artesium**[10] 7678 3-9-0 53.................... SJCraine 5 49
(Patrick Morris) *midfield: hdwy to chse ldrs over 2f out: swtchd rt and rdn wl over 1f out: sn drvn and one pce* **20/1**
0652 **6** *1* **Zeffirelli**[10] 7678 4-9-0 52.................... NCallan 2 47
(M Quinn) *cl up: rdn along wl over 2f out: drvn wl over 1f out and grad wknd* **5/4**[1]
4301 **7** *1/2* **Headache**[6] 7726 4-8-13 52....................(bt) MatthewLawson(7) 1 51
(B W Duke) *led: rdn along and hdd 3f out: sn rdn and led again 2f out: drvn and hdd1 1/2f out: sn hung rt and wknd* **7/2**[2]
0-0 **8** *5* **Eyesore**[111] 5442 3-8-9 15.................... DeanHeslop(5) 7 32
(S A Harris) *cl up: led 3f out: rdn and hdd 2f out: grad wknd* **250/1**
0000 **9** *1 1/4* **Elevate Bobbob**[39] 7318 3-8-9 20....................(v[1]) MarkCoumbe(5) 4 29
(A Berry) *dwlt: sn chsng ldrs: rdn along over 3f out and sn wknd* **250/1**
0-00 **10** *4 1/2* **Obvious**[101] 5744 3-8-9 55.................... PaulPickard(5) 3 16
(Miss J Feilden) *prom: rdn along bef 1/2-way and sn wknd* **22/1**
6603 **11** *1 1/4* **Running Flush (USA)**[16] 7614 3-9-0 52....................(b) LukeMorris 14 13
(J R Gask) *a towards rr* **11/2**[3]
0000 **12** *3 3/4* **Kilmun**[19] 7592 3-8-9 41....................(b[1]) AmyRyan(5) 11 3
(K A Ryan) *in tch: rdn along wl over 2f out and sn wknd* **33/1**
560 **13** *1* **Camomile**[63] 6823 3-8-9 41.................... AndrewHeffernan(5) 12 —
(Miss Tracy Waggott) *a in rr* **50/1**
1m 31.56s (1.26) **Going Correction** +0.125s/f (Slow) **13** Ran SP% **124.3**
Speed ratings (Par 101): **97,95,93,91,91 90,89,84,82,77 76,71,70**
toteswinger:1&2:£27.90, 2&3:£46.30, 1&3:£15.40 CSF £151.65 TOTE £8.20: £1.90, £7.00, £3.50; EX 104.70 Trifecta £333.00 Part won. Pool: £450.101 - 0.10 winning units..
Owner Miss C King **Bred** Illuminatus Investments **Trained** Sledmere, E Yorks

FOCUS
A weak race and tricky form to pin down, with the third and fourth the best guides.
King's Sabre Official explanation: jockey said gelding ran too freely
Headache Official explanation: jockey said gelding hung right

7797 HOSPITALITY AT SOUTHWELL RACECOURSE H'CAP 1m (F)
3:15 (3:15) (Class 6) (0-65,65) 3-Y-O **£2,047** (£604; £302) **Stalls Low**

Form RPR
0153 **1** **Hit The Switch**[10] 7678 3-8-9 **56**.................... SJCraine 6 63
(Patrick Morris) *trckd ldrs: hdwy 3f out: chsd ldr 2f out: rdn to chal ent fnl f: styd on u.p to ld last 50yds* **2/1**[1]
0014 **2** *nk* **Jonnie Skull (IRE)**[6] 7723 3-9-4 **65** 6ex....................(vt) DNolan 5 71
(P S McEntee) *cl up: led over 3f out: rdn along wl over 1f out: drvn ins fnl f: edgd rt: hdd and no ex last 75yds* **3/1**[2]
0100 **3** *5* **My Sweet Georgia (IRE)**[13] 7643 3-9-4 **65**....................(b) VinceSlattery 4 60
(Stef Liddiard) *trckd ldrs: rdn along over 2f out: drvn over 1f out: sn one pce* **10/3**[3]
5333 **4** *3/4* **Luisa Tetrazzini (IRE)**[14] 7629 3-8-7 **59**....................(p) MarkCoumbe(5) 7 52
(John A Harris) *hld up: hdwy wl over 2f out: rdn to chse ldrs wl over 1f out: sn drvn and one pce appr fnl f* **9/1**
2000 **5** *4 1/2* **Kheskianto (IRE)**[10] 7678 3-8-8 **58**.................... RobertLButler(3) 9 41
(M C Chapman) *in rr: hdwy on inner 3f out: rdn to chse ldrs 2f out: sn drvn and wknd* **33/1**
5660 **6** *3 1/2* **Lindy Hop (IRE)**[27] 7481 3-8-13 **60**.................... TonyCulhane 3 35
(K A Ryan) *chsd ldrs: rdn along over 2f out: sn drvn and wknd wl over 1f out* **8/1**
0004 **7** *shd* **Amber Sunset**[68] 6699 3-8-11 **65**.................... CharlotteKerton(7) 2 39
(J Jay) *led: hdd over 3f out and sn wknd* **10/1**
000 **8** *6* **Hohrod**[126] 5010 3-8-4 **51** oh3.................... FrankieMcDonald 8 12
(John A Harris) *a in rr* **40/1**
1m 44.16s (0.46) **Going Correction** +0.125s/f (Slow) **8** Ran SP% **117.0**
Speed ratings (Par 98): **102,101,96,95,91 87,87,81**
toteswinger:1&2:£2.30, 2&3:£3.20, 1&3:£3.40 CSF £8.37 CT £18.64 TOTE £2.80: £1.30, £1.40, £1.60; EX 8.00 Trifecta £17.40 Pool: £665.41 - 28.22 winning units. Place 6 £213.56, Place 5 £100.94.
Owner Rob Lloyd Racing Limited **Bred** Mrs M T Dawson **Trained** Tarporley, Cheshire
■ Stewards' Enquiry : Charlotte Kerton nine-day ban: used whip with excessive frequency (Jan 1-9)

FOCUS
An ordinary race for the grade and modest form.
T/Plt: £143.30 to a £1 stake. Pool: £59,307.06. 302.08 winning tickets. T/Qpdt: £18.90 to a £1 stake. Pool: £6,500.90. 253.60 winning tickets. JR

7785 WOLVERHAMPTON (A.W) (L-H)

Friday, December 18

OFFICIAL GOING: Standard to slow changing to standard after race 1 (6.20)

Wind: Almost nil Weather: Fine and cold

7798 GMS GROUP H'CAP (DIV I) 1m 1f 103y(P)

6:20 (6:20) (Class 6) (0-65,71) 3-Y-0+ **£2,047** (£604; £302) **Stalls** Low

Form RPR

0112 **1** **Desert Vision**[4] 7752 5-9-13 **71** 6ex....................(vt) PhillipMakin 5 82+
(M W Easterby) *hld up in mid-div: hdwy on ins 2f out: led jst over 1f out: rdn clr ins fnl f: r.o wl* **15/8**[1]

6/ **2** *3* **Matjar (IRE)**[21] 7563 6-9-2 **60**.................................... LPKeniry 11 65
(Joseph Quinn, Ire) *hld up towards rr: hdwy on outside wl over 1f out: sn rdn: edgd lft ins fnl f: r.o to take 2nd towards fin: nt trbld wnr* **14/1**

0424 **3** *1 ½* **Networker**[203] 2459 6-9-6 **64**.................................... DaneO'Neill 1 66
(P J McBride) *led: rdn and hdd jst over 1f out: one pce and lost 2nd towards fin* **33/1**

4 *nk* **Spring Hawk (IRE)**[28] 7471 3-8-6 **55**.......................... WilliamCarson(3) 4 56
(T G McCourt, Ire) *hld up in mid-div on ins: rdn 2f out: hdwy over 1f out: kpt on same pce fnl f* **8/1**[3]

5621 **5** *nk* **Ella Woodcock (IRE)**[4] 7752 5-9-2 **63**......................... KellyHarrison(3) 7 64
(E J Alston) *hld up in mid-div: pushed along and swtchd rt wl over 1f out: sltly hmpd ins fnl f: nvr nr to chal* **9/4**[2]

4401 **6** *shd* **King Of Connacht**[7] 7719 6-9-1 **59** 6ex..............................(v) AdamKirby 2 59
(M Wellings) *hld up in tch on ins: rdn ins fnl f: one pce* **11/1**

0063 **7** *½* **Kirstys Lad**[7] 7718 7-8-0 **51** oh6.................................... DeclanCannon(7) 3 50
(M Mullineaux) *chsd ldr: ev ch over 2f out: rdn over 1f out: fdd ins fnl f* **40/1**

00-0 **8** *1 ½* **Coughlans Locke (IRE)**[118] 5268 6-9-0 **58**....................(b) ShaneKelly 8 54
(Kieran P Cotter, Ire) *stdd s: sn swtchd lft to ins: hld up towards rr: short-lived effrt on ins wl over 1f out* **12/1**

2236 **9** *1 ¼* **Mullitovermaurice**[295] 689 3-9-5 **65**.............................. J-PGuillambert 6 59
(J G Given) *hld up in mid-div: lost pl 5f out: pushed along 2f out: no rspnse* **25/1**

0561 **10** *½* **Star Strider**[19] 7592 5-8-13 **62**...................................... KylieManser(5) 12 55
(T Keddy) *hld up in rr: stdy prog on outside 4f out: rdn wl over 1f out: wknd fnl f* **25/1**

4423 **11** *15* **Follow The Sun (IRE)**[52] 7080 5-8-9 **56**..................(p) EJMcNamara(3) 9 17
(Ronald O'Leary, Ire) *hld up in tch: pushed along and wknd qckly wl over 2f out* **20/1**

2m 0.28s (-1.42) **Going Correction** 0.0s/f (Stan)
WFA 3 from 5yo+ 2lb **11** Ran SP% **117.2**
Speed ratings (Par 101): **106,103,102,101,101 101,100,99,98,98 84**
toteswingers: 1&2 £8.10, 1&3 £11.10, 2&3 £29.00 CSF £27.14 CT £664.77 TOTE £2.90: £1.10, £4.20, £7.90; EX 35.30.
Owner A Black,R Edmonds,J Holdroyd,J Quickfall **Bred** Gainsborough Stud Management Ltd **Trained** Sheriff Hutton, N Yorks
■ Stewards' Enquiry : L P Keniry caution: careless riding.

FOCUS
Several recent winners and a few other in-form types in an ordinary handicap. The gallop was a good one and the form looks pretty decent rated around the second and fourth. There was plenty of kickback but the official time prompted the clerk of the course to change the going from "standard to slow" to "standard".
Matjar(IRE) Official explanation: jockey said gelding hung left-handed
Coughlans Locke(IRE) Official explanation: jockey said gelding suffered interference at 2f mark
Star Strider Official explanation: jockey said gelding ran too free

7799 BEST ODDS GUARANTEED AT TOTESPORT.COM MEDIAN AUCTION MAIDEN FILLIES' STKS 5f 216y(P)

6:50 (6:51) (Class 5) 2-Y-0 **£2,729** (£806; £403) **Stalls** Low

Form RPR

0506 **1** **Two Kisses (IRE)**[12] 7654 2-9-0 65.......................... StephenDonohoe 6 64
(B G Powell) *a.p: pushed along over 2f out: rdn wl over 1f out: led towards fin: r.o* **14/1**

06 **2** *nk* **Avon Castle**[19] 7585 2-9-0 0.................................... FergusSweeney 1 63
(G L Moore) *a.p on ins: led wl over 1f out: sn edgd rt: rdn fnl f: hdd towards fin* **8/1**[3]

4200 **3** *nse* **Emma Jean Lass (IRE)**[73] 6563 2-9-0 65.......................... PaulDoe 7 63
(P D Evans) *hld up in mid-div: rdn and hdwy wl over 1f out: nt clr run and swtchd rt 1f out: r.o towards fin* **9/2**[2]

0 **4** *2 ¼* **Charles Bear**[14] 7630 2-9-0 0.................................... GrahamGibbons 11 56
(E S McMahon) *hld up and bhd: pushed along and hdwy over 1f out: rdn fnl f: no ex towards fin* **50/1**

06 **5** *nk* **Darling Buds**[7] 7708 2-9-0 0.................................... TomEaves 3 55
(K A Ryan) *hld up in mid-div on ins: hdwy wl over 1f out: rdn and one pce fnl f* **33/1**

003 **6** *1* **Infinity World**[28] 7463 2-9-0 59.................................... PhillipMakin 10 52
(G R Oldroyd) *broke wl: sn stdd into mid-div: c v wd st: rdn over 1f out: nvr trbld ldrs* **10/1**

64 **7** *nk* **Bubber (IRE)**[31] 7420 2-9-0 0.................................... TonyHamilton 9 51
(R A Fahey) *sn bhd: pushed along wl over 1f out: sme late prog: n.d* **25/1**

2 **8** *½* **Katy's Secret**[15] 7618 2-9-0 0.................................... LPKeniry 4 50
(W Jarvis) *sn chsng ldr: ev ch wl over 1f out: sn rdn: wknd ins fnl f* **10/11**[1]

560 **9** *1* **Hathaway (IRE)**[74] 6544 2-9-0 53.................................... ShaneKelly 12 47
(W M Brisbourne) *a bhd* **50/1**

004 **10** *4* **Special Betty**[15] 7618 2-9-0 58.................................... AdamKirby 5 35
(D Haydn Jones) *led: rdn and hdd wl over 1f out: wknd fnl f* **33/1**

11 *½* **Bibiana Bay** 2-8-9 0.................................... MatthewDavies(5) 8 33
(B I Case) *s.i.s: outpcd* **80/1**

03 **12** *2 ½* **Fareham Town**[14] 7630 2-9-0 0.................................... EddieAhern 13 26
(S Kirk) *hld up in mid-div: rdn and wknd wl over 1f out* **14/1**

1m 15.86s (0.86) **Going Correction** 0.0s/f (Stan) **12** Ran SP% **119.0**
Speed ratings (Par 93): **94,93,93,90,90 88,88,87,86,81 80,77**
toteswingers: 1&2 £12.00, 1&3 £12.00, 2&3 £6.90 CSF £115.12 TOTE £15.60: £4.90, £3.00, £2.30; EX 100.10.
Owner Brian McNamee & Jeff Mould **Bred** Jim Cockburn **Trained** Upper Lambourn, Berks

FOCUS
A modest maiden lacking strength and one that took less winning than seemed likely with the market leader disappointing. The gallop was reasonable and the first three (two of whom were rated 65) came down the centre in the straight.

NOTEBOOK
Two Kisses(IRE) has had more chances than the majority but she appreciated the step back to this trip and showed a good attitude to get off the mark at the ninth attempt. However, this was not a strong race and she would not look an obvious one to follow up. (op 17-2 tchd 16-1)
Avon Castle is a steadily progressive individual who had the run of the race and posted her best effort yet. She is now eligible for a mark and she should be able to win an ordinary handicap on this surface. (tchd 15-2)
Emma Jean Lass(IRE), absent since early October, ran creditably on this first run for her new and in-form stable. This was only her second start on Polytrack and, while vulnerable to an improver in this grade, she should be able to pick up a modest event. (op 5-1 tchd 11-2)
Charles Bear had been soundly beaten after a slow start at this course on her debut but fared a good deal better, despite racing keenly early on. Modest handicaps over a bit further will be the way forward in due course. (tchd 40-1)
Darling Buds bettered the form of her two previous outings on artificial surfaces and will be suited by the switch to run-of-the-mill handicaps. She is in good hands and may be capable of a little better. (op 40-1)
Bubber(IRE) ◆ again showed ability at a very ordinary level over a trip that looked on the sharp side and is one to keep an eye on. The step up to 1m will suit and it'll be a surprise if she is not able to win a race. (op 28-1)
Katy's Secret raced with the choke out in the early stages and failed by some way to confirm debut promise. While too soon to write off, she will be one to watch rather than punt on next time. (op 6-5 tchd 5-4)

7800 £10 FREE PLAY AT TOTESPORTBINGO.COM MAIDEN STKS 7f 32y(P)

7:20 (7:22) (Class 5) 2-Y-0 **£3,238** (£963; £481; £240) **Stalls** High

Form RPR

4 **1** **Playboy Blues (IRE)**[28] 7463 2-9-3 0.......................... DarrylHolland 2 73
(P W Chapple-Hyam) *t.k.h: hdwy to ld over 4f out: rdn over 1f out: r.o wl* **7/2**[2]

6 **2** *1 ¼* **Fusaichi Flyer (USA)**[13] 7644 2-9-3 0.......................... SteveDrowne 5 70+
(R Charlton) *s.i.s: in rr: pushed along and hdwy over 1f out: wnt 2nd wl ins fnl f: nt trble wnr* **33/1**

2 **3** *nk* **Barreq (USA)**[13] 7644 2-9-3 0.................................... TomEaves 9 69
(B Smart) *led over 1f: a.p: pushed along over 2f out: rdn over 1f out: kpt on ins fnl f* **4/5**[1]

02 **4** *½* **Ana Moutabahi**[30] 7429 2-9-3 0.................................... AdamKirby 11 68
(C G Cox) *t.k.h: led over 5f out tl over 4f out: prom: rdn and nt qckn ins fnl f* **9/1**[3]

35 **5** *¾* **Thistlestar (USA)**[19] 7585 2-8-12 0.......................... TonyHamilton 12 61
(R A Fahey) *hld up in mid-div: rdn wl over 1f out: kpt on same pce ins fnl f* **12/1**

04 **6** *½* **Pomeroy**[20] 7580 2-9-3 0.................................... RichardSmith 1 65
(Tom Dascombe) *hld up in mid-div: pushed along and hdwy over 1f out: fdd towards fin* **11/1**

35 **7** *¾* **Always Dixie (IRE)**[7] 7705 2-8-12 0.......................... JoeFanning 8 58
(M Johnston) *prom: chsd wnr over 3f out tl rdn wl over 1f out: wknd ins fnl f* **25/1**

8 *5* **Royal Torbo (ISR)** 2-8-12 0.................................... MatthewDavies(5) 4 51
(George Baker) *dwlt: pushed along 4f out: a in rr* **100/1**

9 *2* **Belles Beau** 2-8-12 0.................................... GrahamGibbons 10 41
(R Hollinshead) *s.i.s: a in rr* **33/1**

10 *1 ¼* **French Wind** 2-9-0 0.................................... MartinLane(3) 7 43
(Pat Eddery) *s.i.s: a bhd* **40/1**

1m 30.84s (1.24) **Going Correction** 0.0s/f (Stan) **10** Ran SP% **117.0**
Speed ratings (Par 96): **92,90,90,89,88 88,87,81,79,77**
toteswingers: 1&2 £17.40, 1&3 £1.10, 2&3 £8.40 CSF £116.45 TOTE £4.70: £1.60, £8.20, £1.02; EX 108.80.
Owner Playboy Kennels **Bred** Islanmore Stud **Trained** Newmarket, Suffolk

FOCUS
Not the strongest of maidens but a couple of interesting performances for the future. The gallop was only fair and the winner raced centre to far side in the straight.

NOTEBOOK
Playboy Blues(IRE) had shown ability at a modest level on his debut but stepped up on that level after being allowed to set his own pace from halfway. Although the market leader was a shade disappointing, he's entitled to improve again and it will be interesting to see what sort of mark he is allotted for handicaps. (op 3-1)
Fusaichi Flyer(USA) ◆ turned in a much-improved effort on this second start without being unduly knocked about to fare the best of those held up and he was the eyecatcher. He'll stay 1m, is open to further progress and appeals as the type to win a race on this surface. (op 40-1)
Barreq(USA) attracted plenty of support in what looked an uncompetitive event but failed to build on the form he showed over course and distance on his debut after racing keenly early on. However, he still looked green and left the impression a stiffer test of stamina would have suited. He is worth another chance. (op 5-6 tchd 10-11 in places)
Ana Moutabahi travelled strongly for a long way and probably ran to a similar level as he did on his previous start at Kempton. He is now eligible for a mark and should be able to improve in ordinary handicaps. (op 12-1 tchd 14-1)
Thistlestar(USA) was far from disgraced and was not knocked about from his double figure draw. She is in very good hands and should be better suited by the step up to 1m. She should be able to pick up a small event. (tchd 14-1)
Pomeroy was nibbled at in the market and again showed ability at an ordinary level. His record is one of steady improvement and the step into modest handicaps should see him in a better light. (op 14-1)

7801 OVER 50 INSTANT GAMES AT TOTESPORTGAMES.COM H'CAP 7f 32y(P)

7:50 (7:52) (Class 4) (0-85,85) 3-Y-0+ **£5,046** (£1,510; £755; £377; £188) **Stalls** High

Form RPR

2332 **1** **Autumn Blades (IRE)**[15] 7617 4-8-10 **77**....................(p) DavidProbert 8 84
(A Bailey) *hld up in mid-div: hdwy 2f out: rdn wl over 1f out: edgd lft ent fnl f: led towards fin: jst hld on* **13/2**[2]

0002 **2** *nse* **Desert Dreamer (IRE)**[11] 7662 8-8-10 **77**.......................... PaulDoe 6 84
(P D Evans) *s.i.s: in rr: pushed along 3f out: rdn and hdwy 1f out: r.o wl u.p towards fin: jst failed* **16/1**

1013 **3** *1* **Tourist**[15] 7617 4-9-1 **82**.................................... DaneO'Neill 1 86
(D Shaw) *hld up in mid-div: hdwy on ins over 1f out: nt clr run and swtchd rt ins fnl f: kpt on* **11/4**[1]

2354 **4** *nk* **Chief Exec**[15] 7617 7-8-7 **74**....................................(b) LukeMorris 11 77
(J R Gask) *swtchd lft sn after s: hld up in rr: pushed along over 3f out: gd hdwy fnl f: kpt on* **8/1**[3]

0111 **5** *¾* **Arteus**[15] 7617 3-9-1 **82**....................................(b) ShaneKelly 5 83
(Jane Chapple-Hyam) *led: rdn jst over 1f out: hdd and no ex towards fin* **11/4**[1]

1503 **6** *nk* **Ravi River (IRE)**[18] 7596 5-8-10 **77**.......................... J-PGuillambert 7 77
(P D Evans) *hld up and bhd: pushed along over 3f out: swtchd lft over 1f out: rdn and r.o ins fnl f: nt rch ldrs* **14/1**

2164 **7** *¾* **Ishiadancer**[21] 7558 4-8-5 **75**.................................... KellyHarrison(3) 4 73
(E J Alston) *sn chsng ldr: rdn and lost 2nd over 1f out: fdd wl ins fnl f* **8/1**[3]

0040 **8** *1* **Gallantry**[15] 7617 7-8-6 **78**.................................... AndrewHeffernan(5) 9 74
(P Howling) *hld up in tch: pushed along over 2f out: btn whn nt clr run ins fnl f* **25/1**

0-00 **9** 1 1/4 **Miranda's Girl (IRE)**[21] 7565 4-9-1 **85**......................(p) EJMcNamara(3) 3 77
(Thomas Cleary, Ire) *prom: rdn over 1f out: nt qckn whn nt clr run ins fnl f* **14/1**

5050 **10** 1 3/4 **Brierty (IRE)**[16] 7613 3-8-10 **77**......................(v[1]) DNolan 10 65
(D Carroll) *hld up towards rr: rdn over 2f out: sn struggling* **20/1**

1m 28.22s (-1.38) **Going Correction** 0.0s/f (Stan) **10** Ran SP% **116.7**
Speed ratings (Par 105): **107,106,105,105,104 104,103,102,100,98**
toteswingers: 1&2 £16.80, 1&3 £4.30, 2&3 £11.80 CSF £104.36 CT £360.17 TOTE £6.70: £2.30, £4.00, £1.30; EX 57.80.
Owner John Stocker **Bred** Dr D Crone & P Lafarge & P Johnston **Trained** Newmarket, Suffolk
■ Stewards' Enquiry : Dane O'Neill one-day ban: careless riding (Jan 1)

FOCUS
A decent handicap in which the sound pace was against the prominent racers. The first two came down the centre in the straight and the form looks sound with the winner, third and fourth running close to previous course form relative to each other.

7802 INTERIOR HARDWARE H'CAP — 1m 141y(P)
8:20 (8:21) (Class 7) (0-50,60) 3-Y-0+ **£1,706** (£503; £252) **Stalls** Low

Form RPR
4004 **1** **Shake On It**[12] 7652 5-8-9 **52** ow2......................JamieJones(5) 9 59+
(M R Hoad) *hld up in rr: stdy prog 2f out: led on bit wl ins fnl f: cleverly* **15/2**[3]

0030 **2** 3/4 **Libre**[18] 7600 9-8-10 **48**......................JoeFanning 3 53
(F Jordan) *a.p: shkn up to ld 1f out: pushed along and hdd wl ins fnl f: nt qckn* **10/1**

600 **3** 1 1/4 **Ardent Prince**[23] 7521 6-8-3 **48**......................DeclanCannon(7) 7 51
(A J McCabe) *hld up in mid-div: hdwy wl over 1f out: sn rdn: nt qckn ins fnl f* **14/1**

6635 **4** 2 **Desert Fairy**[13] 7648 3-8-10 **50**......................TomEaves 8 48
(J W Unett) *hld up in tch: n.m.r and lost pl over 2f out: c wd st: rdn and swtchd lft over 1f out: swtchd rt and rallied wl ins fnl f: nt rch ldrs* **22/1**

-0R0 **5** nk **Kirkie (USA)**[32] 918 4-8-12 **50** ow2......................AdamKirby 11 47
(T J Pitt) *hld up towards rr: stdy hdwy 2f out: rdn over 1f out: one pce whn edgd lft ins fnl f* **66/1**

-001 **6** 1/2 **Tallest Peak (USA)**[1] 7787 4-8-11 **49**......................(b) DarryllHolland 13 45
(M G Quinlan) *hld up in rr: pushed along on outside wl over 2f out: c wd st: swtchd lft wl over 1f out: kpt on ins fnl f: nvr trbld ldrs* **13/8**[1]

0500 **7** hd **Anduril**[182] 3092 8-8-10 **48**......................DNolan 12 44
(D Carroll) *hdwy to chse ldr over 6f out: pushed along over 2f out: lost 2nd wl over 1f out: rdn and wknd wl ins fnl f* **66/1**

5532 **8** 2 **Russian Angel**[28] 7466 5-8-10 **48**......................LPKeniry 4 39
(Jean-Rene Auvray) *led 7f out: rdn and hdd 1f out: wknd ins fnl f* **10/3**[2]

4600 **9** 7 **Lambrini Lace (IRE)**[35] 7370 4-8-12 **50**......................(p) TonyHamilton 2 25
(Mrs L Williamson) *led over 1f: prom: rdn jst over 2f out: wknd over 1f out* **16/1**

0030 **10** nk **Western Art (USA)**[45] 7220 4-8-12 **50**......................LukeMorris 1 24
(Miss Gay Kelleway) *hld up in mid-div: rdn and wknd 2f out* **14/1**

3000 **11** 19 **Bourn Fair**[12] 7658 3-8-10 **50**......................(t) DaneO'Neill 10 —
(P J McBride) *hdwy over 6f out: pushed along and wknd over 2f out: eased whn no ch over 1f out* **16/1**

1m 50.98s (0.48) **Going Correction** 0.0s/f (Stan)
WFA 3 from 4yo+ 2lb **11** Ran SP% **114.5**
Speed ratings (Par 97): **97,96,95,93,93 92,92,90,84,84 67**
toteswingers: 1&2 £16.90, 1&3 £11.90, 2&3 £32.40 CSF £76.83 CT £1020.01 TOTE £9.90: £2.90, £3.60, £2.50; EX 96.30.
Owner Mrs L Bangs **Bred** Car Colston Hall Stud **Trained** Lewes, E Sussex

FOCUS
Few in-form sorts in a moderate handicap and, with the two market leaders disappointing, this took less winning than seemed likely. The pace was reasonable and the first three, who finished clear, came down the centre in the straight. The form is rated around the placed horses to recent marks.

7803 GMS GROUP H'CAP (DIV II) — 1m 1f 103y(P)
8:50 (8:50) (Class 6) (0-65,65) 3-Y-0+ **£2,047** (£604; £302) **Stalls** Low

Form RPR
3424 **1** **Bestowed**[4] 7754 4-8-6 **55**......................(v[1]) AndrewHeffernan(5) 2 61
(P D Evans) *plld hrd in tch: rdn and rdr lost whip ins fnl f: r.o to ld nr fin* **7/4**[1]

6006 **2** 1/2 **Eastern Gift**[13] 7643 4-9-6 **64**......................(p) GeorgeBaker 7 69
(Miss Gay Kelleway) *hld up and bhd: hdwy wl over 1f out: rdn to ld ins fnl f: hdd nr fin* **3/1**[2]

1-4 **3** 3/4 **Rambling Dancer (IRE)**[21] 7563 5-9-1 **62**......................SMGorey(3) 5 65
(Mrs Valerie Keatley, Ire) *t.k.h: hld up and bhd: smooth prog on ins over 2f out: led on bit wl over 1f out: sn edgd rt: hdd ins fnl f: rdn and nt qckn* **15/2**

5-00 **4** 3 1/4 **Pachakutek (USA)**[235] 1573 3-9-5 **65**......................MartinDwyer 1 62
(L M Cumani) *led after 1f: rdn and hdd wl over 1f out: wknd ins fnl f* **15/2**

305 **5** 1/2 **Corrib (IRE)**[7] 7718 6-8-7 **51** oh6......................DavidProbert 4 47
(B Palling) *hld up: pushed along over 2f out: n.m.r and stmbld ent st: sn swtchd lft and rdn: no hdwy fnl f* **14/1**

00/5 **6** 8 **Flighty Fellow (IRE)**[20] 7581 9-9-2 **60**......................(b) VinceSlattery 6 39
(B G Powell) *prom tl rdn and wknd wl over 1f out* **6/1**[3]

554 **7** 1/2 **West Kirk**[29] 7452 3-9-4 **64**......................JoeFanning 3 42
(W Jarvis) *led 1f: chsd ldr: ev ch over 2f out: rdn and wknd over 1f out* **6/1**[3]

2m 2.65s (0.95) **Going Correction** 0.0s/f (Stan)
WFA 3 from 4yo+ 2lb **7** Ran SP% **120.1**
Speed ratings (Par 101): **95,94,93,91,90 83,83**
toteswingers: 1&2 £3.10, 1&3 £3.10, 2&3 £5.00 CSF £6.41 CT £25.87 TOTE £2.80: £1.70, £2.40; EX 8.00.
Owner Diamond Racing Ltd **Bred** Mrs A M Jenkins And E D Kessly **Trained** Pandy, Monmouths

FOCUS
A modest handicap but a slow pace resulted in a time nearly 2.5 secs slower than the opening handicap over the same trip and this bare form does not look reliable. The winner raced in the centre in the straight and did not need to run to his previous course mark to score, with the placed horses setting the level.

7804 100% NEW PLAYER BONUS AT TOTESPORTCASINO.COM NURSERY — 1m 141y(P)
9:20 (9:20) (Class 4) (0-85,76) 2-Y-0 **£4,533** (£1,348; £674; £336) **Stalls** Low

Form RPR
U051 **1** **New Christmas (USA)**[17] 7604 2-9-7 **76**......................EddieAhern 1 84+
(B J Meehan) *hld up: wnt 2nd over 2f out: chal over 1f out: hrd rdn to ld wl ins fnl f: r.o* **13/8**[1]

0232 **2** nk **Be A Devil**[12] 7654 2-9-4 **73**......................MartinDwyer 5 80+
(W R Muir) *hld up: hdwy on ins 2f out: swtchd rt ent st: pushed along to ld over 1f out: rdn and hdd wl ins fnl f: kpt on* **2/1**[2]

5130 **3** 10 **Epic (IRE)**[56] 7003 2-9-6 **75**......................JoeFanning 6 61
(M Johnston) *led: rdn and hdd over 1f out: wknd fnl f* **9/2**[3]

6440 **4** 4 **Ant Music (IRE)**[161] 3821 2-8-12 **67**......................LPKeniry 2 45
(J S Moore) *chsd ldr tl over 2f out: sn rdn: wknd wl over 1f out* **9/1**

1503 **5** 3 3/4 **Fine Lace (IRE)**[27] 7474 2-8-2 **62**......................BillyCray(5) 3 32
(D J S Ffrench Davis) *hld up: pushed along over 3f out: short-lived effrt on outside over 2f out* **8/1**

1m 50.78s (0.28) **Going Correction** 0.0s/f (Stan) **5** Ran SP% **110.7**
Speed ratings (Par 98): **98,97,88,85,81**
toteswingers: 1&2 £5.30 CSF £5.21 TOTE £2.60: £1.50, £1.60; EX 4.30 Place 6: £84.24 Place 5: £39.58 .
Owner Jaber Abdullah **Bred** Eithne Hamilton **Trained** Manton, Wilts
■ Stewards' Enquiry : Eddie Ahern one-day ban: used whip in incorrect place (Jan 1)

FOCUS
A fair handicap in which the two market leaders, who raced in the centre in the straight, pulled a long way clear of the remainder. The pace was reasonable and the form could rate higher but their previous profiles suggest it is form worth treating with a little caution.

NOTEBOOK
New Christmas(USA) ◆, loaded with a stalls blanket, seems much better at the start than in his early days and he showed himself to be a progressive sort who also has the right attitude. This beating of a reliable yardstick, with the pair clear, represented a career best and he may well be capable of further progress. (tchd 15-8)
Be A Devil, bandaged all round, is a reliable sort who ran as well as he ever has done returned to this longer trip. He was a long way clear of the remainder and, although he'll be up in the weights for this, he remains capable of winning again on Polytrack. (tchd 9-4)
Epic(IRE), having his first run since being gelded, was proven over this course and distance but was again disappointing after a short break after being allowed his own way in front. He will have to show a fair bit more before he is a solid betting proposition. (tchd 5-1)
Ant Music(IRE) was nibbled at in the market on this all-weather debut but fared no better than on his first run in nursery company on turf upped in trip. This first run since the summer (and first since being gelded) may have been needed but he has plenty to prove at present. (op 11-1)
Fine Lace(IRE) faced a tougher task than in a Kempton claimer on his previous start but ran poorly all the same. She has something to prove.
T/Plt: £271.90 to a £1 stake. Pool: £112,742.05. 302.69 winning tickets. T/Qpdt: £27.40 to a £1 stake. Pool: £10,964.42. 296.10 winning tickets. KH

7771 LINGFIELD (L-H)
Saturday, December 19

OFFICIAL GOING: Standard
Wind: Modest, against Weather: Bright, very cold

7805 BET ON TODAY'S FOOTBALL AT TOTESPORT.COM CLAIMING STKS — 6f (P)
12:20 (12:26) (Class 6) 2-Y-0 **£1,978** (£584; £292) **Stalls** Low

Form RPR
0004 **1** **Miss Lesley**[12] 7661 2-8-11 **70**......................(b) MartinDwyer 4 70
(D K Ivory) *mde all: rdn 2f out: hld on wl fnl f* **6/1**[3]

3322 **2** nk **Zubova**[10] 7690 2-8-9 **72** ow1......................EddieAhern 3 67
(R Hannon) *hld up in tch in rr: hdwy on inner wl over 1f out: chsd wnr ent fnl f: nt qckn and a hld after* **7/4**[1]

0043 **3** 1/2 **Anjomarba (IRE)**[8] 7713 2-8-5 **72**......................(p) WilliamCarson(3) 5 65
(W G M Turner) *chsd ldng pair: rdn and unable qck wl over 1f out: rallied ins fnl f: r.o but nt quite pce to rch ldng pair* **14/1**

3432 **4** 3/4 **Ramamara (IRE)**[8] 7713 2-8-9 **73**......................StephenDonohoe 2 65
(P D Evans) *awkward leaving stalls and s.i.s: bhd: gd hdwy on inner ent fnl f: chsng ldrs whn nt clr run and swtchd rt fnl 100yds: kpt on but nvr able to chal* **10/3**[2]

3602 **5** 1 3/4 **Mind The Monarch**[9] 7698 2-8-5 **54**......................LukeMorris 7 54
(R A Teal) *in tch in last trio: niggled along 4f out: no prog u.p 2f out tl kpt on fnl 150yds: nvr able to chal* **40/1**

4442 **6** nk **Yeadon**[38] 7333 2-8-10 **66**......................TonyHamilton 1 58
(R A Fahey) *chsd ldrs: rdn to chse wnr wl over 1f out tl ent fnl f: wknd ins fnl f* **17/2**

0423 **7** 1 1/4 **Tamarind Hill (IRE)**[5] 7749 2-8-9 **68**......................(p) SteveDrowne 8 53
(C R Egerton) *in tch in midfield: hdwy on outer 3f out: racd awkwardly bnd and rdn jst over 2f out: no prog fr over 1f out* **14/1**

1251 **8** 2 1/4 **Clear Ice (IRE)**[8] 7707 2-9-4 **73**......................AndrewMullen 6 56
(D Nicholls) *restless stalls: chsd wnr tl wl over 1f out: sn wknd u.p* **6/1**[3]

1m 11.74s (-0.16) **Going Correction** -0.125s/f (Stan) **8** Ran SP% **114.3**
Speed ratings (Par 94): **96,95,94,93,91 91,89,86**
toteswinger: 1&2: £4.80, 2&3: £19.00, 1&3: £4.00 CSF £16.92 TOTE £7.60: £1.80, £1.20, £4.40; EX 22.20 Trifecta £217.90 Pool £350.43 - 1.19 winning units..Zubova was claimed by M. J. Attwater for £7,000.
Owner Mrs L A Ivory **Bred** Richard Kent **Trained** Radlett, Herts

FOCUS
A competitive claimer, although the proximity of the 54-rated Mind The Monarch limits the form, so not a race to be with.

NOTEBOOK
Miss Lesley arguably should have won on her previous start when given an unsatisfactory ride in a C&D seller (finished two places behind Tamarind Hill) and her performance this time seems to support that view. With Dwyer taking over in the saddle, she responded well to uncomplicated tactics and, despite having been a little free in front, battled on well when strongly challenged. (op 8-1)
Zubova, who carried 1lb overweight, nipped through against the inside rail in the straight and had her chance, but the winner proved more willing. Still a maiden, she has now been a beaten favourite on five of her seven starts. She will join Michael Attwater, having been claimed for £7,000. (op 2-1 tchd 9-4 in a place)
Anjomarba(IRE) ran okay without improving for the fitting of cheekpieces and she seems to be regressing. (tchd 12-1)
Ramamara(IRE) was unlucky not to finish closer, as she was left with a lot to do after missing the break and was blocked in her run when keeping on in the straight. (op 3-1 tchd 11-4 and 7-2)
Clear Ice(IRE), trying Polytrack for the first time, dropped away tamely after displaying speed and was well below the form he showed when winning a nursery on Fibresand off a mark of 68 on his previous start. (op 5-1 tchd 13-2)

7806 CWB CONTROLS NOVICE STKS — 7f (P)
12:50 (1:01) (Class 5) 2-Y-0 **£3,885** (£1,156; £577; £288) **Stalls** Low

Form RPR
002 **1** **Kai Mook**[15] 7630 2-8-8 **70** ow1......................SteveDrowne 6 75
(R Ingram) *sn led: mde rest: rdn and wnt 2 l clr over 1f out: kpt on wl u.p fnl f* **13/2**[3]

1135 **2** 1 **Stargaze (IRE)**[91] 6105 2-9-10 **103**......................RobertWinston 2 88
(A Bailey) *chsd ldrs: rdn and effrt to press ldrs ent fnl 2f: chsd wnr jst over 1f out: kpt on u.p but nvr getting to wnr* **4/7**[1]

0614 **3** 3 3/4 **Exceedthewildman**[13] 7654 2-9-2 74........(p) LPKeniry 3 71
(J S Moore) *chsd wnr: upsides and rdn ent fnl 2f: btn jst over 1f out: wknd ins fnl f* **5/1**[2]

4 1/2 **Minortransgression (USA)** 2-8-12 0........ FergusSweeney 7 66+
(G L Moore) *s.i.s: hld up in last pl: rdn 2f out: rn green and outpcd over 1f out: kpt on fnl f but nvr a threat to ldrs* **20/1**

5 2 1/2 **American Agent (USA)** 2-8-12 0........ MartinDwyer 4 60
(P F I Cole) *hld up in tch in last pair: rdn and effrt ent fnl 2f: outpcd over 1f out: wl hld fnl f* **8/1**

0 **6** 6 **One Cool Slash (IRE)**[31] 7436 2-8-7 0........ FrankieMcDonald 1 40
(M J McGrath) *chsd ldrs: rdn and struggling wl over 2f out: bhd fr over 1f out* **100/1**

1m 24.03s (-0.77) **Going Correction** -0.125s/f (Stan) 6 Ran SP% **110.5**
Speed ratings (Par 96): **99,97,93,93,90 83**
toteswinger: 1&2: £1.50, 2&3: £3.00, 1&3: £1.20 CSF £10.41 TOTE £7.30: £2.40, £1.10; EX 13.30.
Owner Miss L McIntosh **Bred** Miss Lois McIntosh **Trained** Epsom, Surrey

FOCUS
The favourite was below form and, using the 74-rated third as a guide, this looked an ordinary novice event. The winner, third and sixth help set the level.

NOTEBOOK
Kai Mook had 17lb (including 1lb overweight) to find with Stargaze, but she was able to take advantage of that one's below-par showing. Given a really positive ride, she kicked clear off the final bend and stayed on well for a decisive success. Although flattered by the bare result, she's clearly a little better than her rating of 70 suggests. (op 11-2 tchd 7-1)
Stargaze(IRE) ran well below form on his first start since leaving Andrew Balding and after a three-month break. This performance was particularly disappointing considering he shaped as though in need of 7f when fifth in the Mill Reef on his final start for his previous yard. (op 8-13 tchd 4-6)
Exceedthewildman, successful off a mark of 71 at the course last month, had it all to do at the weights and was left behind from over 1f out, having travelled nicely into the straight. (op 13-2)
Minortransgression(USA), a £24,000 purchase, was closing in on the third as they crossed the line and will find easier opportunities in maiden company. A scopey gelding, this was a promising start and he should learn a good deal from the outing. (op 16-1)
American Agent(USA), a half-brother to some winners on dirt in the US, showed only limited potential but may improve with time. (tchd 17-2)

7807 WILLIAM LENNOX 87TH BIRTHDAY H'CAP (DIV I) 5f (P)
1:25 (1:35) (Class 5) (0-70,70) 3-Y-O+ **£2,388** (£705; £352) **Stalls** High

Form RPR
0053 **1** **Fromsong (IRE)**[10] 7682 11-8-9 61........(p) MartinDwyer 3 72
(D K Ivory) *taken down early: chsd ldr: hmpd bnd 4f out: rdn to chal over 1f out: drvn ahd fnl 100yds: r.o* **6/1**

5652 **2** 1/2 **Lithaam (IRE)**[10] 7682 5-8-9 68........(p) RyanClark(7) 1 77
(J M Bradley) *chsd ldrs: effrt and rdn on inner over 1f out: drvn to ld jst ins fnl f: hdd fnl 100yds: unable qck after* **5/1**[3]

5044 **3** 1 1/4 **Kyle (IRE)**[48] 7203 5-8-11 63........ LPKeniry 4 68
(C R Dore) *chsd ldrs: rdn and unable qck over 1f out: kpt on again ins fnl f: wnt 3rd fnl 75yds* **12/1**

1022 **4** nk **Decider (USA)**[10] 7689 6-8-12 64........(p) LiamJones 10 67+
(R A Harris) *taken down early: racd in midfield on outer: rdn wl over 1f out: r.o ins fnl f: nt rch ldrs* **8/1**

5005 **5** shd **Bo McGinty (IRE)**[4] 7758 8-9-1 67........(v) TonyHamilton 5 70
(R A Fahey) *in tch whn hmpd and lost pl after 1f: rdn and hdwy over 1f out: kpt on u.p ins fnl f: nt threaten ldrs* **4/1**[2]

3000 **6** 1 **Ten Down**[46] 7223 4-8-2 57........ AndreaAtzeni(3) 9 56
(M Quinn) *broke wl to ld and grad crossed to rail: rdn over 1f out: drvn and hdd jst ins fnl f: wknd fnl 100yds* **16/1**

0000 **7** 1/2 **Steel City Boy (IRE)**[19] 7601 6-8-5 60........ MartinLane(3) 7 58
(D Shaw) *taken down early: anticipated s and awkward leaving stalls: a in rr: rdn 2f out: keeping on but no ch whn nt clr run and eased fnl 50yds* **25/1**

2126 **8** 1/2 **The Geester**[215] 2130 5-8-7 59........(b) ChrisCatlin 6 55
(Stef Liddiard) *hmpd s and s.i.s: a towards rr: rdn and no real prog fnl 2f* **7/1**

5233 **9** 2 3/4 **Femme De Fer**[22] 7554 3-9-4 70........ AdamKirby 8 56
(C G Cox) *taken down early: racd keenly: prom tl 2f out: sn wknd: bhd fnl f* **3/1**[1]

57.87 secs (-0.93) **Going Correction** -0.125s/f (Stan) 9 Ran SP% **117.0**
Speed ratings (Par 103): **102,101,99,98,98 96,96,95,90**
toteswinger: 1&2: £4.60, 2&3: £10.20, 1&3: £7.10 CSF £36.55 CT £285.86 TOTE £8.10: £2.70, £2.10, £2.40; EX 35.20 Trifecta £301.40 Part won. Pool £407.43 - 0.84 winning units..
Owner Dean Ivory **Bred** Mrs Teresa Bergin **Trained** Radlett, Herts

FOCUS
The winning time was 0.33 seconds quicker than the second division and the form looks solid for the grade rated around the winner and third.

7808 WILLIAM LENNOX 87TH BIRTHDAY H'CAP (DIV II) 5f (P)
2:00 (2:07) (Class 5) (0-70,69) 3-Y-O+ **£2,388** (£705; £352) **Stalls** High

Form RPR
5216 **1** **Thoughtsofstardom**[3] 7771 6-8-7 58........ ChrisCatlin 6 67
(P S McEntee) *broke wl and led early: sn stdd to chse ldrs: hdwy and swtchd rt over 1f out: rdn to ld fnl 100yds: r.o wl* **2/1**[1]

0601 **2** 1/2 **Buy On The Red**[10] 7689 8-9-2 67........ AndrewMullen 2 74
(D Nicholls) *sn chsng ldr: clsd over 2f out: drvn over 1f out: ev ch ins fnl f: kpt on* **7/1**[3]

3154 **3** nk **Littlemisssunshine (IRE)**[22] 7554 4-9-3 68........(p) LPKeniry 4 74
(J S Moore) *dwlt: towards rr: rdn and effrt jst over 2f out: nt clr run briefly and swtchd lft over 1f out: r.o wl fnl f: nt quite rch ldng pair* **8/1**

0040 **4** 1/2 **After The Show**[18] 7602 8-8-6 57........ MartinDwyer 5 61
(Rae Guest) *towards rr: rdn wl over 1f out: swtchd rt jst ins fnl f: r.o wl fnl 100yds: nt rch ldrs* **14/1**

4400 **5** 1/2 **Cape Royal**[22] 7554 9-8-11 62........(bt) KevinGhunowa 1 64
(J M Bradley) *sn led: rdn over 1f out: hdd fnl 100yds: wknd towards fin* **22/1**

6664 **6** 1/2 **Raimond Ridge (IRE)**[56] 7028 3-8-12 63........ LukeMorris 7 64
(J Jay) *dwlt: bhd: effrt on outer bnd 2f out: hung lft over 1f out: nt clr run ins fnl f: kpt on but nvr able to chal* **8/1**

2604 **7** 1/2 **Peopleton Brook**[23] 7534 7-8-9 60........(t) SteveDrowne 3 59
(B G Powell) *towards rr: hdwy u.p on inner wl over 1f out: no imp ins fnl f* **16/1**

2121 **8** 1 1/2 **Edith's Boy (IRE)**[22] 7554 3-9-4 69........ HayleyTurner 9 62
(S Dow) *s.i.s: racd on outer: hdwy to chse ldrs 3f out: rdn ent fnl 2f: wknd fnl f* **11/4**[2]

0404 **9** 2 1/2 **Especially Special (IRE)**[18] 7605 3-8-10 61........ FrankieMcDonald 8 45
(Peter Grayson) *chsd ldrs: rdn and unable qck jst over 2f out: btn whn sltly hmpd over 1f out* **50/1**

58.20 secs (-0.60) **Going Correction** -0.125s/f (Stan) 9 Ran SP% **113.6**
Speed ratings (Par 103): **99,98,97,96,96 95,94,92,88**
toteswinger: 1&2: £5.50, 2&3: £6.90, 1&3: £5.90 CSF £16.36 CT £91.71 TOTE £3.40: £1.60, £2.10, £2.20; EX 17.80 Trifecta £57.10 Pool £710.59 - 9.20 winning units..
Owner Eventmaker Racehorses **Bred** B Bargh **Trained** Newmarket, Suffolk

FOCUS
A modest sprint run in a time 0.33 seconds slower than the first division. The form looks sound enough rated around the first three.

7809 BET LIVE IN PLAY AT TOTESPORT.COM QUEBEC STKS (LISTED RACE) 1m 2f (P)
2:30 (2:43) (Class 1) 3-Y-O+
£22,708 (£8,608; £4,308; £2,148; £1,076; £540) **Stalls** Low

Form RPR
3031 **1** **Tranquil Tiger**[28] 7489 5-9-5 112........(b) TPQueally 1 112
(H R A Cecil) *t.k.h: chsd ldr: gng much the best 2f out: shkn up to chal over 1f out: pushed along ins fnl f: led last strides* **5/6**[1]

6063 **2** shd **Suits Me**[28] 7489 6-9-3 105........ DarryllHolland 6 110
(T P Tate) *sn pushed up to ld: rdn over 1f out: clr w wnr fnl f: flashed tail ins fnl f: hdd last strides* **8/1**[3]

65-0 **3** 2 3/4 **Settigano (IRE)**[29] 7470 6-9-3 100........(p) JAHeffernan 3 104
(Michael Joseph Fitzgerald, Ire) *hld up wl in tch in last pair: rdn and effrt ent fnl 2f: hanging lft over 1f out: chsd ldng pair fnl f: no imp* **12/1**

6333 **4** 1 1/4 **Saphira's Fire (IRE)**[20] 7589 4-8-12 110........ MartinDwyer 7 97
(W R Muir) *disp 2nd pl tl jst over 2f out: outpcd u.p over 1f out: no ch w ldng pair fnl f* **5/2**[2]

5250 **5** 1/2 **Plum Pudding (IRE)**[20] 7588 6-9-3 108........ DaneO'Neill 2 101
(R Hannon) *hld up wl in tch in last pair: effrt on inner 2f out: kpt on same pce* **16/1**

0/41 **6** 11 **Sky Crusader**[9] 7704 7-9-5 102........ SteveDrowne 8 81
(M Nigge, France) *dwlt: niggled along early: in tch tl rdn and dropped to last over 2f out: wl btn over 1f out: eased ins fnl f* **10/1**

2m 2.01s (-4.59) **Going Correction** -0.125s/f (Stan) course record 6 Ran SP% **116.9**
Speed ratings (Par 111): **113,112,110,109,109 100**
toteswinger: 1&2: £2.70, 2&3: £3.30, 1&3: £8.10 CSF £9.25 TOTE £2.10: £1.20, £3.10; EX 7.00 Trifecta £29.10 Pool £1,321.85 - 33.55 winning units..
Owner K Abdulla **Bred** Juddmonte Farms Ltd **Trained** Newmarket, Suffolk

FOCUS
A disappointing turnout numerically - two non-runners didn't help - but this was still a decent enough race for the grade. The pace was good and the final time was fast. The placed horses are the best guides to the level.

NOTEBOOK
Tranquil Tiger, who defeated Presvis in a similar event over C&D on his first start on Polytrack, narrowly followed up. He looked set to win convincingly when travelling strongly around the turn into the straight, but the runner-up is a tough sort, and he really had to battle to get by that rival. He also made his move towards the inside rail, which isn't always the best place to be at this track. It's no surprise that he may well be aimed at the Winter Derby. (op 10-11 tchd Evens and 11-10 in places)
Suits Me wasn't able to dominate, as he likes to, when well held behind today's winner around here on his previous start, but he had his own way up front this time and was a different proposition. He unshipped his rider beforehand, but that didn't compromise his chance and this was a game effort in defeat. (tchd 10-1)
Settigano(IRE), successful over 1m at Dundalk on his previous start, didn't seem to fail through a lack of stamina; he simply ran into two smart types. He hung left in the straight, but still kept on and this was a solid effort in defeat. (op 25-1)
Saphira's Fire(IRE) shaped as though worth another try at this trip when third over 1m4f at Kempton on her previous start, but she failed to run up to her best and proved to be a bit disappointing. (op 100-30)
Plum Pudding(IRE) is at his best when dominating over 7f-1m. (op 14-1)

7810 BEST ODDS GUARANTEED AT TOTESPORT.COM CONDITIONS STKS 1m (P)
3:05 (3:14) (Class 3) 3-Y-O+ **£7,641** (£2,273; £1,136; £567) **Stalls** High

Form RPR
4 **1** **Jaroslaw (SAF)**[31] 7431 6-8-12 97........ MartinDwyer 6 78+
(D M Simcock) *hld up in tch in last pair: rdn and effrt on outer wl over 1f out: chsd ldr ins fnl f: r.o wl u.p to ld towards fin* **5/2**[1]

2010 **2** nk **Ace Of Hearts**[168] 3639 10-8-12 99........ JackMitchell 3 77
(C F Wall) *reluctant and eventually led to s: trckd ldrs: rdn to chal jst over 2f out: led wl over 1f out: kpt on wl u.p tl hdd towards fin* **5/2**[1]

5030 **3** 1 3/4 **General Eliott (IRE)**[28] 7489 4-8-12 102........ TPQueally 4 73
(P F I Cole) *led tl 5f out: chsd ldr after tl ent fnl 2f: chsd ldr again over 1f out tl ins fnl f: one pce after* **5/2**[1]

6640 **4** nk **Lucky Dance (BRZ)**[28] 7489 7-8-12 81........ RobertHavlin 2 72
(A G Foster) *restless in stalls: trckd ldrs: rdn and unable qck over 2f out: rallied ins fnl f: kpt on to press for 3rd nr fin* **14/1**[3]

3024 **5** 1/2 **Pride Of Nation (IRE)**[15] 7631 7-8-5 61........(p) DeclanCannon(7) 5 71
(A J McCabe) *dwlt: sn pushed along and hdwy to press ldr after 1f: led 5f out tl wl over 1f out: drvn and one pce fr over 1f out* **80/1**

6 3/4 **Drogba (ARG)**[552] 4-8-12 95........(v[1]) JerryO'Dwyer 1 69
(M Botti) *in tch in last pair: rdn and unable qck ent fnl 2f: one pce and no prog after* **9/2**[2]

1m 36.06s (-2.14) **Going Correction** -0.125s/f (Stan) course record 6 Ran SP% **111.8**
Speed ratings (Par 107): **105,104,102,102,102 101**
toteswinger: 1&2: £2.40, 2&3: £1.20, 1&3: £1.80. CSF £8.88 TOTE £3.70: £2.00, £1.80; EX 10.70.
Owner H M K Al Mehairi **Bred** Oldlands Stud **Trained** Newmarket, Suffolk

FOCUS
The pace seemed reasonable enough, and the time wasn't bad, but the form is muddling and the proximity of the 61-rated Pride Of Nation, and to a lesser extent the 81-rated Lucky Dance, suggests the bare form is ordinary for the level.

NOTEBOOK
Jaroslaw(SAF), ex-South African, confirmed the promise he showed on his British debut over 7f at Kempton. He had never previously won over a trip this far, but as it turned out, he needed just about every yard of the distance and may even stay 1m2f. The plan is for him to head to Dubai for the 2010 Carnival. (tchd 3-1)
Ace Of Hearts, who had to be led to the start, shaped well after 168 days off, only just failing to hang on after leading early in the straight. (op 3-1 tchd 2-1)
General Eliott(IRE) was taken on up front by Pride Of Nation, which can't have helped his chance, and he looked hard work under pressure. Just like last time, he was reported to have hung right. (op 9-4 tchd 11-4)
Lucky Dance(BRZ) had plenty to find with a few of these at the weights, so while he ran well, this is muddling form. (tchd 12-1 and 16-1)

Pride Of Nation(IRE) was quite decent on his day, but he has been beaten in selling and claiming company recently and limits the form. (tchd 66-1)
Drogba(ARG) was a Listed and Grade 3 winner in Peru in 2008, but he had been off since June of that year. He's apparently only been with Marco Botti for a month and ran as though in need of the outing. (op 11-2 tchd 13-2)

7811 BIGGER "WIN ONLY" ODDS AT TOTESPORT.COM H'CAP — 1m 4f (P)
3:35 (3:41) (Class 4) (0-85,86) 3-Y-0+ — £4,727 (£1,406; £702; £351) Stalls Low

Form — RPR

2001 **1** **Mildoura (FR)**[23] 7539 4-9-6 **84** ... IanMongan 7 — 91
(Mrs L J Mongan) *t.k.h: chsd ldr over 10f out: led 4f out: rdn 3 l clr 3f out: kpt on wl u.p fnl f* **15/2**

0004 **2** 1 1/4 **Paktolos (FR)**[14] 7640 6-9-4 **82** ...(p) FergusSweeney 9 — 87
(John A Harris) *stdd s and dropped in bhd: hdwy on outer over 2f out: edgd lft over 1f out: chsd wnr ins fnl f: kpt on but nvr gng to rch wnr* **20/1**

1021 **3** 3/4 **Brett Vale (IRE)**[9] 7701 3-9-3 **86** ... DaneO'Neill 1 — 90+
(P R Hedger) *stdd s: hld up in last trio: effrt on inner and nt clr run ent fnl 2f: swtchd rt and nt clr run again wl over 1f out: hdwy u.p over 1f out: chsd ldrs ins fnl f: kpt on* **5/1**[2]

3102 **4** 2 3/4 **Mister New York (USA)**[8] 7720 4-9-7 **85** ...(b) GeorgeBaker 2 — 84
(Noel T Chance) *stdd and dropped in bhd after s: hld up bhd: rdn and no rspnse over 2f out: swtchd to outer 2f out: hdwy and edging lft ent fnl f: styd on: nvr trbld ldrs* **11/4**[1]

1420 **5** shd **Follow The Flag (IRE)**[21] 7583 5-9-0 **78** ...(p) TPQueally 8 — 77
(A J McCabe) *stdd after s: t.k.h: hld up in midfield: rdn and effrt over 3f out: chsd clr wnr over 1f out: one pce and lost 2 pls ins fnl f* **20/1**

3643 **6** 1 **Evident Pride (USA)**[21] 7573 6-9-6 **84** ... AdamKirby 4 — 82
(B R Johnson) *hld up in midfield: rdn and unable qck over 2f out: short of room and shuffled bk over 1f out: kpt on fnl f: nvr able to chal* **11/2**[3]

2135 **7** 1/2 **Hurakan (IRE)**[10] 7684 3-8-3 **75** ... KellyHarrison(3) 3 — 72
(P D Evans) *t.k.h: chsd ldrs: rdn and unable qck over 2f out: one pce and no ch w wnr fnl 2f* **11/2**[3]

0615 **8** 4 **Lyra's Daemon**[23] 7539 3-8-7 **76** ... MartinDwyer 6 — 66
(W R Muir) *t.k.h: sn led: hdd 4f out: sn outpcd by wnr: lost 2nd and wknd over 2f out: wl btn over 1f out* **12/1**

001 **9** nk **Doubnov (FR)**[22] 7549 6-9-2 **80** ...(p) EddieAhern 5 — 70
(Ian Williams) *t.k.h: chsd ldrs: rdn to chse clr wnr over 2f out: no imp: lost 2nd over 1f out: sn wknd* **8/1**

2m 31.38s (-1.62) **Going Correction** -0.125s/f (Stan)
WFA 3 from 4yo+ 5lb — **9** Ran SP% **114.2**
Speed ratings (Par 105): **100,99,98,96,96 96,95,93,92**
toteswinger: 1&2: £16.40, 2&3: £6.80, 1&3: £37.60. CSF £140.00 CT £814.44 TOTE £9.20: £1.90, £5.30, £2.00; EX 144.40 TRIFECTA Not won. Place 6 £19.85, Place 5 £10.67..
Owner Mrs P J Sheen **Bred** H H The Aga Khan's Studs Sc **Trained** Epsom, Surrey

FOCUS
A fair handicap run at a steady pace through the early stages and rated through the runnerup to his recent best.
T/Plt: £21.80 to a £1 stake. Pool: £76,906.71. 2,567.19 winning tickets. T/Qpdt: £10.20 to a £1 stake. Pool: £8,694.39. 629.04 winning tickets. SP

7798 WOLVERHAMPTON (A.W) (L-H)
Saturday, December 19

OFFICIAL GOING: Standard
Wind: Almost nil Weather: Fine and cold

7812 £32 FREE AT 32RED.COM H'CAP — 1m 141y(P)
1:20 (1:20) (Class 4) (0-87,85) 3-Y-0+ — £4,731 (£1,416; £708; £354) Stalls Low

Form — RPR

2544 **1** **Quick Release (IRE)**[18] 7603 4-8-8 73 ... NickyMackay 4 — 79
(D M Simcock) *dwlt: hld up in last: pushed along and hdwy 2f out: chal over 1f out: rdn fnl f: led towards fin* **9/2**[3]

6632 **2** nk **Bawaardi (IRE)**[3] 7769 3-8-7 74 ... JimmyQuinn 5 — 79
(R A Fahey) *hld up in 3rd: wnt 2nd 2f out: led jst over 1f out: rdn and hdd towards fin* **10/11**[1]

6501 **3** 7 **Justcallmehandsome**[16] 7615 7-8-4 74 ...(v) BillyCray(5) 1 — 63
(D J S Ffrench Davis) *led 1f: chsd ldr: led over 3f out: rdn and hdd jst over 1f out: wknd fnl f* **5/2**[2]

2005 **4** 4 **Bolodenka (IRE)**[12] 7662 7-9-1 85 ... BMcHugh(5) 2 — 65
(R A Fahey) *led after 1f: hdd over 3f out: pushed along and wknd wl over 1f out* **9/1**

1m 50.88s (0.38) **Going Correction** +0.075s/f (Slow)
WFA 3 from 4yo+ 2lb — **4** Ran SP% **109.1**
Speed ratings (Par 105): **101,100,94,90**
CSF £9.27 TOTE £6.90; EX 7.70.
Owner Tick Tock Partnership **Bred** Mrs C Regalado-Gonzalez **Trained** Newmarket, Suffolk

FOCUS
Despite the small field there was a good pace on and the winner came from last to first. However, the form looks muddling and the winner to his recent best is probably the best guide.

7813 32RED.COM H'CAP — 7f 32y(P)
1:55 (1:55) (Class 6) (0-68,66) 3-Y-0+ — £2,047 (£604; £302) Stalls High

Form — RPR

5002 **1** **Striker Torres (IRE)**[8] 7715 3-9-1 63 ...(v) TomEaves 7 — 73
(B Smart) *sn led: rdn over 1f out: edgd lft ins fnl f: drvn out* **15/2**

4510 **2** 1/2 **Another Try (IRE)**[6] 7739 4-9-2 64 ... JimCrowley 8 — 73
(A P Jarvis) *led early: t.k.h: chsd ldr: rdn over 1f out: kpt on towards fin* **5/1**[3]

0324 **3** 3/4 **Obe Gold**[10] 7691 7-9-4 66 ... J-PGuillambert 5 — 73
(P Howling) *chsd ldrs: rdn over 1f out: kpt on towards fin* **8/1**

6423 **4** 1 3/4 **Just Timmy Marcus**[8] 7715 3-9-2 64 ...(p) GrahamGibbons 1 — 66
(B P J Baugh) *hld up in mid-div: hdwy on ins 2f out: rdn over 1f out: one pce ins fnl f* **10/3**[1]

0025 **5** 2 **Borasco (USA)**[11] 7679 4-9-3 65 ... PhillipMakin 6 — 62+
(T D Barron) *hld up in rr: c wd st: r.o ins fnl f: nrst fin* **9/2**[2]

0000 **6** 1 1/4 **Electric Warrior (IRE)**[7] 7729 6-8-12 65 ... BMcHugh(5) 11 — 58
(C R Dore) *prom: pushed along over 2f out: rdn and wknd wl over 1f out* **22/1**

006 **7** 2 **Obe Brave**[7] 7735 6-8-11 59 ...(b) DJMoran 9 — 47
(Lee Smyth, Ire) *hld up in tch: pushed along over 2f out: wknd wl over 1f out* **16/1**

0002 **8** 1/2 **Golden Prospect**[14] 7650 5-8-10 58 ...(b) WandersonD'Avila 3 — 44
(Miss J R Tooth) *s.i.s: t.k.h in rr on ins: short-lived effrt over 2f out* **13/2**

0400 **9** 1/2 **Highland River**[5] 7752 3-8-5 60 ... AlexEdwards(7) 10 — 45
(A Sadik) *hld up: stdy prog over 5f out: lost pl over 3f out: pushed along over 2f out: sn bhd* **40/1**

1426 **10** 3 **Vogarth**[9] 6925 5-8-7 62 ...(b) DavidKenny(7) 4 — 39
(M C Chapman) *hld up towards rr: rdn and struggling over 2f out* **50/1**

0500 **11** 22 **Whatyouwoodwishfor (USA)**[136] 4664 3-8-10 65 ... LeeTopliss(7) 12 — —
(R A Fahey) *prom tl wknd over 3f out* **20/1**

1m 28.8s (-0.80) **Going Correction** +0.075s/f (Slow) — **11** Ran SP% **113.5**
Speed ratings (Par 101): **107,106,105,103,101 99,97,97,96,93 67**
toteswinger: 1&2: £12.70, 2&3: £9.50, 1&3: £9.20 CSF £41.37 CT £308.04 TOTE £4.30: £1.90, £1.90, £3.00; EX 53.90.
Owner R C Bond **Bred** T Stack & Lynchbages Ltd **Trained** Hambleton, N Yorks
■ Stewards' Enquiry : Wanderson D'Avila caution: careless riding.

FOCUS
The first three home were in the front trio throughout and the form looks sound rated around the first three with the fourth just below his best.

7814 BET AT 32REDBET.COM H'CAP — 1m 141y(P)
2:25 (2:27) (Class 7) (0-50,53) 3-Y-0+ — £1,364 (£403; £201) Stalls Low

Form — RPR

025 **1** **Kielty's Folly**[5] 7755 5-9-2 50 ... TonyCulhane 13 — 59
(B P J Baugh) *hld up in rr: swtchd rt and stdy prog over 2f out: c wd st: swtchd rt over 1f out: rdn to ld wl ins fnl f: r.o* **4/1**[1]

5040 **2** 3/4 **Fairplaytomyself**[13] 7653 4-8-4 45 ... TobyAtkinson(7) 3 — 52
(P W Hiatt) *s.i.s: hld up in rr: pushed along and hdwy on outside 3f out: c wd st: rdn over 1f out: led ins fnl f: sn hdd: nt qckn* **16/1**

0630 **3** 3/4 **Kirstys Lad**[1] 7798 7-8-12 46 ... GregFairley 7 — 51
(M Mullineaux) *sn chsng ldr: rdn and ev ch over 1f out: nt qckn wl ins fnl f* **5/1**[2]

0006 **4** 1 **Lyrical Intent**[3] 7767 3-8-10 46 ... J-PGuillambert 8 — 49
(P Howling) *hld up in mid-div: pushed along and hdwy 2f out: rdn over 1f out: one pce fnl f* **8/1**

5633 **5** 1/2 **Davana**[7] 7723 3-8-6 47 ... PaulPickard(5) 9 — 49
(W J H Ratcliffe) *prom: pushed along over 3f out: rdn wl over 1f out: one pce fnl f* **13/2**[3]

0031 **6** 1/2 **Tamino (IRE)**[3] 7774 6-9-5 53 6ex ... JimmyQuinn 6 — 54
(P Howling) *sn led: rdn over 1f out: hdd ins fnl f: no ex* **4/1**[1]

0260 **7** 2 **Josiah Bartlett (IRE)**[11] 7680 3-9-0 50 ... TomEaves 11 — 46
(Ian Williams) *hld up towards rr: pushed along wl over 1f out: kpt on fnl f: n.d* **10/1**

0000 **8** 2 1/2 **Boffin**[5] 7753 4-8-11 45 ...(p) FrancisNorton 5 — 36
(Eve Johnson Houghton) *hld up in mid-div: pushed along whn n.m.r briefly over 2f out: wknd over 1f out* **16/1**

3000 **9** 1 3/4 **Le Reve Royal**[29] 7460 3-8-6 49 ... RyanPowell(7) 4 — 35
(G R Oldroyd) *hld up in tch: rdn and wknd over 1f out* **50/1**

0656 **10** 1/2 **Kamanja (UAE)**[17] 7614 3-8-13 49 ...(p) JimCrowley 10 — 34
(M J Attwater) *hld up towards rr: rdn over 1f out: no rspnse* **8/1**

0060 **11** 5 **Easy Wonder (GER)**[3] 7771 4-8-13 47 ...(b) GrahamGibbons 2 — 21
(I A Wood) *hld up in mid-div: pushed along on ins over 2f out: wknd wl over 1f out* **25/1**

400 **12** 9 **Gracie's Games**[33] 7411 3-8-6 47 ... AndrewHeffernan(5) 1 — —
(R J Price) *prom on ins tl pushed along and wknd over 3f out* **33/1**

1m 51.03s (0.53) **Going Correction** +0.075s/f (Slow)
WFA 3 from 4yo+ 2lb — **12** Ran SP% **121.8**
Speed ratings (Par 97): **100,99,98,97,97 96,95,92,91,90 86,78**
toteswinger: 1&2: £30.50, 2&3: £3.90, 1&3: £16.60 CSF £71.98 CT £340.43 TOTE £4.80: £2.00, £6.30, £2.80; EX 73.40.
Owner Saddle Up Racing **Bred** Stanneylands Livery **Trained** Audley, Staffs

FOCUS
A poor handicap but the form looks sound rated around the third, fourth and fifth to their recent marks.

7815 32RED CASINO H'CAP (DIV I) — 5f 216y(P)
3:00 (3:00) (Class 6) (0-63,63) 3-Y-0+ — £1,706 (£503; £252) Stalls Low

Form — RPR

6261 **1** **Welcome Approach**[22] 7561 6-8-11 56 ... JimmyQuinn 12 — 64
(J R Weymes) *hld up and bhd: hdwy on ins wl over 1f out: pushed along to ld ins fnl f: r.o* **6/1**[3]

2106 **2** 3/4 **Gracie's Gift (IRE)**[4] 7762 7-8-7 57 ... BillyCray(5) 4 — 62
(R C Guest) *in rr: pushed along wl over 3f out: rdn and hdwy over 1f out: edgd rt ins fnl f: r.o to take 2nd last strides* **9/2**[1]

4056 **3** shd **Don Pele (IRE)**[99] 5836 7-9-1 60 ...(p) TonyCulhane 5 — 65
(R A Harris) *led after 1f: edgd rt over 1f out: rdn and hdd ins fnl f: nt qckn and lost 2nd last strides* **6/1**[3]

0205 **4** nk **Residency (IRE)**[38] 7337 3-9-3 62 ...(p) TomEaves 10 — 66
(B Smart) *a.p: rdn over 1f out: kpt on ins fnl f* **8/1**

2115 **5** 1 **Ask Jenny (IRE)**[10] 7682 7-9-2 61 ... SJCraine 6 — 62
(Patrick Morris) *hld up and bhd: hdwy wl over 1f out: rdn and one pce fnl f* **11/2**[2]

0300 **6** 3/4 **Tanley**[8] 7710 4-8-1 51 oh3 ... AndrewHeffernan(5) 1 — 49
(J F Coupland) *led 1f: prom: rdn wl over 1f out: wknd ins fnl f* **33/1**

340 **7** 3/4 **Where's Reiley (USA)**[143] 4436 3-9-4 63 ... PhillipMakin 2 — 59
(T D Barron) *hld up and bhd: pushed along and short-lived effrt 2f out* **13/2**

0020 **8** nk **White Ledger (IRE)**[32] 7424 10-8-7 52 oh5 ow1 ... GregFairley 7 — 47
(R E Peacock) *s.i.s: hld up in rr: rdn and swtchd lft over 1f out: nvr trbld ldrs* **33/1**

0410 **9** 5 **Villaruz (IRE)**[173] 3464 3-9-1 60 ... GrahamGibbons 8 — 39
(J W Unett) *prom: rdn over 2f out: wknd wl over 1f out* **15/2**

200/ **10** 6 **Descargo**[973] 1151 5-7-13 51 oh1 ... RyanPowell(7) 9 — 11
(C R Dore) *hld up in tch: hung rt and rn wd ent st: sn wknd* **33/1**

0050 **11** 3 1/4 **Romantic Verse**[3] 7774 4-8-2 54 ...(b) MarzenaJeziorek(7) 11 — 3
(S Curran) *prom on outside: pushed along and wknd over 2f out* **11/1**

1m 15.3s (0.30) **Going Correction** +0.075s/f (Slow) — **11** Ran SP% **115.5**
Speed ratings (Par 101): **101,100,99,99,98 97,96,95,89,81 76**
toteswinger: 1&2: £3.70, 2&3: £9.70, 1&3: £10.80 CSF £31.98 CT £169.76 TOTE £5.20: £2.00, £2.10, £2.50; EX 26.30.
Owner T A Scothern **Bred** P Wyatt And Ranby Hall **Trained** Middleham Moor, N Yorks

FOCUS
A low-grade sprint handicap run at a good pace. The winner is rated back to his best with the placed horses close to their marks.

7816 32REDPOKER.COM MAIDEN FILLIES STKS 1m 141y(P)
3:30 (3:32) (Class 5) 2-Y-O £2,590 (£770; £385; £192) Stalls Low

Form RPR
5355 1 **If I Were A Boy (IRE)**[15] 7622 2-9-0 70.....(p) DavidProbert 1 77+
(S Kirk) *led early: chsd ldr: led jst over 2f out: clr whn rdn over 1f out: r.o wl* 5/2[2]
0 2 5 **Al Shababiya (IRE)**[15] 7622 2-9-0 0..... NickyMackay 2 67
(D M Simcock) *a.p: rdn over 2f out: tk 2nd ins fnl f: no ch w wnr* 9/2[3]
3 3 1 3/4 **Riviera Chic (USA)**[21] 7580 2-9-0 0..... JimCrowley 8 63
(R M Beckett) *hld up in mid-div: hdwy 3f out: sn pushed along: one pce fnl 2f* 11/8[1]
0 4 3 **Tough Regime (IRE)**[7] 7731 2-9-0 0.....(t) DJMoran 5 57
(Niall Moran, Ire) *sn led: rdn and hdd jst over 2f out: sn btn: wknd ins fnl f* 25/1
0 5 3/4 **Concorde Kiss (USA)**[15] 7624 2-8-9 0..... LeeNewnes(5) 7 55+
(S Kirk) *hld up in mid-div: sme prog over 2f out: rdn and btn over 1f out* 50/1
0406 6 8 **The Blue Dog (IRE)**[15] 7630 2-9-0 0..... TonyCulhane 10 38
(George Baker) *hld up in rr: pushed along over 3f out: sn struggling* 40/1
7 nk **Silkenveil (IRE)** 2-8-9 0..... BMcHugh(5) 3 38
(R A Fahey) *hld up in rr: rdn 3f out: sn struggling* 7/1
0600 8 14 **Crystal Bridge**[63] 6858 2-8-7 30.....(p) DavidKenny(7) 4 8
(Mrs L Williamson) *prom tl pushed along and wknd wl over 2f out* 100/1
9 6 **Swain's Quest (USA)** 2-8-9 0..... AndrewHeffernan(5) 6 —
(Eve Johnson Houghton) *s.i.s: sn hld up in mid-div: pushed along over 3f out: sn struggling* 25/1
10 43 **Halfway There** 2-9-0 0..... J-PGuillambert 11 —
(J G Given) *rn green and rel to r: sn t.o* 25/1

1m 52.23s (1.73) **Going Correction** +0.075s/f (Slow) **10** Ran SP% **118.3**
Speed ratings (Par 96): **95,90,89,86,85 78,78,65,60,22**
toteswinger: 1&2: £2.30, 2&3: £1.10, 1&3: £2.60 CSF £13.39 TOTE £3.20: £1.10, £1.30, £1.40; EX 12.40.
Owner Miss A Jones **Bred** Kilco Builders **Trained** Upper Lambourn, Berks

FOCUS
An ordinary maiden best rated through the easy winner.

NOTEBOOK
If I Were A Boy(IRE) is thoroughly exposed and set just a modest standard but she still proved miles too good for her rivals. It's doubtful she improved on her previous best here, but this easy win should do her confidence some good. (op 11-4)
Al Shababiya(IRE), who was expected to appreciate this slightly longer trip, tracked the winner for a long way but got outpaced on the turn into the straight. She probably wants further still. (op 13-2 tchd 4-1)
Riviera Chic(USA) got trapped out wide for much of the race and hung left in the straight. She needs one more run for a mark. (op 6-5 tchd 13-8)
Tough Regime(IRE) weakened badly in the straight after making much of the running. A drop back to 7f, the trip over which she ran her best race in Ireland, might help her. (op 20-1)
Concorde Kiss(USA), stablemate of the winner, is a half-sister to a number of winners including Grade 1 winner Sarafan. She improved on her debut effort but still looks moderate.

7817 32RED.COM CLAIMING STKS 1m 1f 103y(P)
4:00 (4:00) (Class 6) 3-Y-O+ £2,047 (£604; £302) Stalls Low

Form RPR
5331 1 **Ghufa (IRE)**[12] 7670 5-8-13 64..... MatthewDavies(5) 1 70
(George Baker) *hld up towards rr: stdy hdwy over 2f out: pushed along wl over 1f out: rdn to ld ins fnl f: drvn out* 5/2[1]
0014 2 hd **Ten Pole Tudor**[2] 7782 4-8-12 61.....(p) TonyCulhane 12 63
(R A Harris) *hld up towards rr: hdwy on outside over 2f out: rdn fnl f: r.o wl towards fin* 9/2[3]
6 3 2 **Mackintosh (IRE)**[6] 7740 3-8-4 52.....(b[1]) SaleemGolam 9 53
(Patrick Morris) *s.i.s: sn swtchd lft: sn hld up in mid-div: hdwy on ins whn nt clr run over 2f out: sn swtchd rt: rdn and nt qckn wl ins fnl f* 33/1
-500 4 1 3/4 **Northern Tour**[21] 7575 3-8-11 72.....(t) DTDaSilva(7) 4 63
(P F I Cole) *a.p: wnt 2nd 2f out: sn rdn: wknd ins fnl f* 10/1
40/ 5 nk **Back To Paris (IRE)**[832] 2587 7-8-1 75..... PaulPickard(5) 7 49
(Paul Murphy) *chsd ldr: led 3f out: rdn wl over 1f out: hdd ins fnl f: wknd towards fin* 8/1
00-4 6 1 1/2 **Painted Sky**[15] 7623 6-8-9 67..... LeeTopliss(7) 2 56
(R A Fahey) *hld up in mid-div on ins: nt clr run over 2f out: swtchd rt and rdn wl over 1f out: no hdwy fnl f* 4/1[2]
00-6 7 3 1/4 **Finnegans Rainbow**[19] 5936 7-7-13 35.....(b) RachelKing(7) 8 39
(M C Chapman) *hld up in tch: rdn whn n.m.r 2f out: sn wknd* 150/1
6- 8 1 3/4 **Jack Rio (IRE)**[23] 7547 4-8-11 56.....(p) DJMoran 13 40
(Niall Moran, Ire) *hld up towards rr: pushed along and hdwy on outside 3f out: wknd wl over 1f out* 33/1
3050 9 8 **Applaude**[10] 7492 4-8-5 60.....(be) BillyCray(5) 10 22
(R C Guest) *a in rr: pushed along and struggling over 3f out* 12/1
0000 10 1 **Days Of Thunder (IRE)**[89] 6172 4-9-2 30..... LeeVickers 5 26
(B R Summers) *hld up in mid-div: rdn and wknd over 2f out* 200/1
0446 11 3/4 **Kings Ace (IRE)**[28] 7479 3-8-10 55..... JimCrowley 3 21
(A P Jarvis) *led: hdd 3f out: wknd wl over 1f out* 6/1

2m 2.83s (1.13) **Going Correction** +0.075s/f (Slow)
WFA 3 from 4yo+ 2lb **11** Ran SP% **116.0**
Speed ratings (Par 101): **97,96,95,93,93 91,89,87,80,79 78**
toteswinger: 1&2: £3.70, 2&3: £27.30, 1&3: £26.80 CSF £13.30 TOTE £4.10: £1.20, £1.50, £9.60; EX 15.30.
Owner Miss Camilla Jenks **Bred** Shadwell Estate Company Limited **Trained** Moreton Morrell, Warwicks

FOCUS
A fairly competitive claimer with the winner back to his old form and the runner-up to his recent best.
Applaude Official explanation: jockey said gelding hung right and felt wrong behind

7818 32RED BEST CASINO SINCE 2003 H'CAP 1m 1f 103y(P)
4:30 (4:30) (Class 6) (0-55,54) 3-Y-O+ £2,047 (£604; £302) Stalls Low

Form RPR
0063 1 **Chosen Forever**[5] 7754 4-9-4 53..... JimmyQuinn 8 65+
(G R Oldroyd) *hld up in mid-div: stdy prog on outside 3f out: pushed along to ld jst over 1f out: r.o wl* 3/1[1]
0321 2 2 1/4 **Join Up**[13] 7652 3-8-10 52..... RossAtkinson(5) 7 59
(W M Brisbourne) *hld up towards rr: pushed along and hdwy on outside 2f out: c wd st: rdn and edgd lft jst over 1f out: chsd wnr ins fnl f: no imp* 7/2[2]
0006 3 2 **John Potts**[8] 7718 4-9-0 49..... GrahamGibbons 3 52
(B P J Baugh) *hld up towards rr: stdy prog whn nt clr run ent st: rdn and r.o to take 3rd cl home* 12/1
-500 4 hd **King's Jester (IRE)**[5] 7755 7-9-3 52.....(b) DJMoran 6 54
(Lee Smyth, Ire) *hld up in mid-div on ins: hdwy wl over 1f out: sn hrd rdn: one pce fnl f* 33/1
0600 5 nk **Turn To Dreams**[2] 7200 3-8-8 50.....(v) AndrewHeffernan(5) 9 52
(P D Evans) *hld up in mid-div: pushed along over 2f out: rdn over 1f out: kpt on one pce ins fnl f* 50/1
0000 6 2 1/4 **Rockson (IRE)**[25] 7500 3-8-8 45.....(v[1]) GregFairley 1 42
(Ian Williams) *prom: rdn over 1f out: wknd ins fnl f* 16/1
0004 7 nk **Deportista**[5] 7753 3-8-8 45..... FrancisNorton 13 41
(J A Pickering) *led: rdn and hdd 2f out: wknd ins fnl f* 20/1
0530 8 nk **Jobekani (IRE)**[36] 7369 3-9-2 53.....(p) TomEaves 11 49
(Mrs L Williamson) *hld up in tch: pushed along to ld 2f out: rdn and hdd over 1f out: wknd ins fnl f* 28/1
5000 9 3 1/4 **Michael Laskey**[10] 7687 3-8-12 52..... JamesMillman(3) 5 41
(B R Millman) *hld up towards rr: pushed along over 2f out: no rspnse* 14/1
0004 10 3 1/2 **Son Of Monsieur**[16] 7615 3-8-5 49..... RyanPowell(7) 10 31
(G R Oldroyd) *sn w ldr: ev ch over 2f out: wknd wl over 1f out* 16/1
6-00 11 11 **Tagula Minx (IRE)**[17] 7614 3-8-11 48..... SaleemGolam 12 6
(J Pearce) *stdd s: sn swtchd lft: hld up towards rr: rdn over 2f out: no rspnse* 33/1
0640 12 7 **Miss Perfectionist**[19] 7599 3-9-1 52..... J-PGuillambert 2 —
(P Howling) *prom tl wknd over 2f out: eased whn no ch wl over 1f out* 10/1
043 13 11 **Special Cuvee**[2] 7784 3-9-3 54.....(v) TonyCulhane 4 —
(A B Haynes) *s.i.s: a in rr: pushed along and struggling over 3f out* 4/1[3]

2m 1.88s (0.18) **Going Correction** +0.075s/f (Slow)
WFA 3 from 4yo+ 2lb **13** Ran SP% **118.5**
Speed ratings (Par 101): **102,100,98,98,97 95,95,95,92,89 79,73,63**
toteswinger: 1&2: £4.80, 2&3: £9.60, 1&3: £5.90 CSF £12.23 CT £111.01 TOTE £4.50: £1.50, £1.20, £4.10; EX 15.70.
Owner R C Bond **Bred** R C Bond **Trained** Brawby, N Yorks

FOCUS
A moderate handicap and fair form for the grade with the principals in good form and the third getting back to last winter's level.
Special Cuvee Official explanation: jockey said gelding never travelled

7819 32RED CASINO H'CAP (DIV II) 5f 216y(P)
5:00 (5:02) (Class 6) (0-63,63) 3-Y-O+ £1,706 (£503; £252) Stalls Low

Form RPR
0356 1 **Charlie Delta**[10] 7691 6-8-11 56.....(b) TonyCulhane 5 65
(R A Harris) *hld up and bhd: hdwy on outside 2f out: c wd st: rdn to ld 1f out: drvn out* 9/2[3]
440 2 1 3/4 **First Order**[35] 7398 8-8-13 63.....(v) AnnStokell(5) 8 66
(Miss A Stokell) *t.k.h in tch: nt clr run and swtchd rt 2f out: rdn wl over 1f out: edgd lft ins fnl f: nt qckn* 12/1
4444 3 hd **Colombard (IRE)**[3] 7771 4-8-6 51.....(v) DJMoran 10 53
(Patrick Morris) *hld up in rr: c wd st: rdn and hdwy fnl f: r.o* 5/1
0051 4 3/4 **Bentley**[14] 7645 5-9-1 60..... JimCrowley 3 60
(J G Given) *sn pushed along and bhd: hdwy wl over 1f out: rdn and kpt on ins fnl f* 4/1[2]
0000 5 1/2 **El Potro**[24] 7521 7-8-6 51 oh6..... NickyMackay 6 49
(J R Holt) *hld up: hdwy over 3f out: rdn and ev ch over 1f out: one pce ins fnl f* 40/1
0060 6 2 1/2 **Almaty Express**[19] 7595 7-9-2 61.....(b) JimmyQuinn 7 51
(J R Weymes) *a.p: pushed along and ev ch over 1f out: rdn and wknd wl ins fnl f* 10/1
3000 7 1/2 **Music Box Express**[11] 7680 5-8-9 59..... MatthewDavies(5) 12 48
(George Baker) *led: rdn and hdd 1f out: wknd ins fnl f* 16/1
5422 8 2 **Irish Music (IRE)**[23] 7533 4-9-3 62..... FrancisNorton 4 44
(A P Jarvis) *broke wl: sn hld up in mid-div: hdwy on ins wl over 1f out: rdn ent fnl f: eased whn btn towards fin* 5/2[1]
-000 9 1 1/4 **Misterisland (IRE)**[8] 7714 4-8-1 51 oh5.....(be) BillyCray(5) 1 29
(M Mullineaux) *sn outpcd* 66/1
2230 10 3/4 **Yanza**[19] 7601 3-9-2 61.....(b) GregFairley 11 37
(J R Gask) *prom tl wknd wl over 1f out* 6/1

1m 15.13s (0.13) **Going Correction** +0.075s/f (Slow) **10** Ran SP% **124.3**
Speed ratings (Par 101): **102,99,99,98,97 94,93,91,89,88**
toteswinger: 1&2: £12.30, 2&3: £6.00, 1&3: £22.00 CSF £61.46 CT £289.67 TOTE £6.00: £1.30, £3.40, £1.80; EX 72.80 Place 6 £116.73, Place 5 £13.66..
Owner Robert & Nina Bailey **Bred** P K Gardner **Trained** Earlswood, Monmouths

FOCUS
The leaders went quick here and the race was set up for the closers. The placed horses are rated close to recent efforts, although the proximity of the fifth limits the form.
T/Plt: £104.60 to a £1 stake. Pool: £92,015.42. 642.15 winning tickets. T/Qpdt: £5.30 to a £1 stake. Pool: £8,482.91. 1,172.68 winning tickets. KH

7704 DEAUVILLE (R-H)
Saturday, December 19

OFFICIAL GOING: Standard

7820a PRIX DE PRAIL (C&G) (ALL-WEATHER) 7f 110y
10:20 (10:22) 3-Y-O £10,194 (£4,077; £3,058; £2,039; £1,019)

RPR
1 **Jacdan (FR)**[40] 3-8-12..... SRuis —
(J Rossi, France)
2 1/2 **Moscow Eight (IRE)**[10] 7696 3-9-2..... JAuge —
(E J O'Neill) *prom: 4th st: hdwy fr 1f out: pressing ldr 100yds out: styd on* 4/1[1]
3 3 **Mistaken Identity (FR)**[35] 3-9-2..... TThulliez —
(P Bary, France)
4 3 **Film Set (USA)**[128] 4954 3-9-2..... —
(F Vermeulen, France)
5 nk **Le Roc (FR)**[40] 3-9-2.....(p) —
(C Boutin, France)
6 10 **Mariston (GER)**[85] 3-8-12..... —
(W Baltromei, Germany)
7 8 **Monsieur Bob (FR)** 3-8-12..... —
(R Laplanche, France)

8 *8* **Valmont Du Pecos (FR)** 3-8-12 ....(p) —
(S Morineau, France)
1m 29.8s (89.80) 8 Ran SP% 20.0
PARI-MUTUEL (Including 1 Euro stake): WIN 4.40; PL 1.20, 1.20, 1.20;DF 7.00.
Owner G Lheritier **Bred** Ecurie Du Sud & Idatzi Co **Trained** France

7821a PRIX DE LA BRECHE AU DIABLE (FEMALE PROFESSIONAL JOCKEYS) (ALL-WEATHER) 1m 1f 110y
1:50 (1:49) 4-Y-0+ **£9,223** (£3,689; £2,767; £1,845; £922)

RPR
1 **Winterwind (IRE)** 4-8-11 ....(p) NoemiHerren —
(Frau Carmen Bocksai, Germany)
2 *nse* **Beetuna (IRE)**[91] 4-9-2 ....(b) CelineHerissondeBeauvoir —
(X-Thomas Demeaulte, France)
3 *2* **Voxna (FR)**[45] 5-8-10 .... NadegeOuakli —
(Robert Collet, France)
4 *1* **Sina (GER)**[16] 4-9-1 .... —
(S Smrczek, Germany)
5 *nk* **Rafale Bere (FR)**[48] 4-9-1 ....(p) —
(D Prod'Homme, France)
6 *snk* **Kersimon (FR)**[62] 6-9-4 .... —
(Mlle B Joly, France)
7 *2* **Lasse (GER)**[80] 6-9-2 .... —
(P Vovcenko, Germany)
8 *1* **Fire Sale (ARG)**[45] 4-8-8 .... —
(A De Royer-Dupre, France)
9 *1 ½* **Four Dancers (GER)**[83] 6323 4-9-4 .... —
(Frau E Mader, Germany)
10 *1* **Indian Saphir (FR)** 4-8-11 .... —
(R Lecomte, France)
0 **Ilie Nastase (FR)**[49] 7194 5-8-11 ....(p) KirstyMilczarek —
(E J O'Neill) *towards rr on outside: 9th 1/2-way: 6th and pushed along st: sn no ex* **68/10**[1]
0 **Grillonnie (FR)** 4-8-8 .... —
(X-L Le Stang, France)
1m 58.4s (118.40) 12 Ran SP% 12.8
PARI-MUTUEL: WIN 23.10; PL 4.40, 2.60, 1.80; DF 73.90.
Owner Frau Carmen Bocksai **Bred** Denis & Teresa Bergin **Trained** Germany

7822a PRIX CASINO BARRIERE DE DEAUVILLE (GENTLEMEN RIDERS CLAIMER) (ALL-WEATHER) 7f 110y
2:55 (2:56) 4-Y-0+ **£7,767** (£3,107; £2,330; £1,553; £777)

RPR
1 **Tuning Mozart**[16] 6-10-13 .... MrArthurHoyeau —
(S Wattel, France)
2 *shd* **Star Godess (FR)**[412] 5-10-2 .... MrJ-PBoisgontier —
(J De Roualle, France)
3 *1* **Florentiner (GER)**[57] 6-10-12 .... MrFGuy —
(A Trybuhl, Germany)
4 *snk* **Vestris (IRE)**[184] 4-10-8 ....(p) —
(J-M Beguigne, France)
5 *¾* **Tuaoi (USA)**[39] 4-11-2 .... —
(J Morin, France)
6 *hd* **Esposito**[250] 7-10-5 .... —
(Frau E Mader, Germany)
6 *dht* **Dubai Queen (IRE)**[111] 4-10-8 ....(p) —
(P Demercastel, France)
8 *1 ½* **Zariyan (FR)**[112] 5464 6-10-12 .... —
(Mlle C Nicot, France)
9 *¾* **Berina (FR)**[51] 4-10-2 ....(b) —
(U Suter, France)
10 **Troom Girl (FR)** 4-10-2 .... —
(N Leenders, France)
0 **High Curragh**[36] 7387 6-10-8 ....(p) MrSWalker —
(E J O'Neill) *sn racing in cl 2nd: plld hrd early: disputing ld ent st: wknd fr 1 1/2f out* **100/1**[1]
0 **Gunpowder (IRE)**[39] 5-10-8 ....(p) —
(Mme I T Oakes-Cottin, France)
0 **Chikablue (FR)**[51] 4-10-5 ....(b) —
(H De Waele, Belgium)
0 **La Marea (FR)**[70] 4-10-5 .... —
(F Danloux, France)
1m 29.6s (89.60) 14 Ran SP% 1.0
PARI-MUTUEL: WIN 6.80; PL 2.00, 2.10, 1.70; DF 33.40.
Owner L Haegel **Bred** Haras De Borgeauville **Trained** France

7763 KEMPTON (A.W) (R-H)
Sunday, December 20

OFFICIAL GOING: Standard
Wind: Virtually nil Weather: Sunny

7823 WILLIAM HILL KING GEORGE VI BETTING - 0800 44 40 40 H'CAP 1m 2f (P)
2:15 (2:16) (Class 5) (0-75,75) 3-Y-0+ **£2,590** (£770; £385; £192) **Stalls High**

Form RPR
0333 1 **Dream Of Fortune (IRE)**[4] 7776 5-8-10 **69**....(t) JamieJones(5) 4 79
(M G Quinlan) *s.i.s: hld up in rr: stdy hdwy on outside over 2f out: chsd ldr over 1f out: drvn to ld fnl 120yds: styd on wl u.p* **10/1**
0604 2 *1* **Hallingdal (UAE)**[4] 7775 4-9-1 **72**.... MarcHalford(3) 9 80
(J J Bridger) *in rr tl hdwy on outside fr 2f out: styd on u.p fnl f to take 2nd last strides but nt rch wnr* **10/1**
1124 3 *hd* **Thunderstruck**[13] 7667 4-9-4 **72**....(p) ChrisCatlin 1 80
(J A Glover) *led after 3f: rdn over 2f out: hdd and outpcd fnl 120yds: lost 2nd last strides* **9/4**[1]
1350 4 *5* **Hurakan (IRE)**[1] 7811 3-9-4 **75**.... J-PGuillambert 12 73
(P D Evans) *broke wl: stdd towards rr: rdn along 3f out: styd on fnl 2f but nvr any threat to ldrs* **4/1**[2]
5324 5 *1 ¾* **The Grey One (IRE)**[10] 7699 6-8-12 **66**....(p) KevinGhunowa 8 60
(J M Bradley) *in rr: rdn and hdwy to chse ldrs 2f out: nvr on terms and wknd fnl f* **8/1**[3]
15P5 6 *1 ¾* **Trifti**[49] 7204 8-9-6 **74**.... DaneO'Neill 2 65
(Miss Jo Crowley) *s.i.s: in rr: rdn over 2f out: mod prog fnl f* **33/1**
7 *nk* **Oxford City (IRE)**[55] 7075 5-9-0 **68**....(t) LukeMorris 14 58
(P M Phelan) *chsd ldrs: rdn 3f out: sn lost pl: nvr any threat after* **12/1**
0403 8 *1 ¼* **Prince Of Thebes (IRE)**[13] 7664 8-9-2 **70**.... JimCrowley 6 58
(M J Attwater) *chsd ldrs: rdn 3f out: wknd fr 2f out* **10/1**
0016 9 *5* **Red Hot Desert**[13] 7665 3-8-11 **68**.... EddieAhern 10 46
(W R Swinburn) *led 1f: styd chsng ldrs and wnt 2nd 4f out: rdn 2f out: wknd over 1f out* **12/1**
2400 10 *3* **Cossack Prince**[96] 5964 4-9-2 **70**.... IanMongan 13 42
(Mrs L J Mongan) *led after 1f tl hdd after 3f: wknd 3f out* **16/1**
10-6 11 *9* **Taaresh (IRE)**[49] 7201 4-9-7 **75**.... JimmyQuinn 3 29
(K A Morgan) *chsd ldrs: rdn 3f out: wknd qckly over 2f out* **33/1**
2m 5.13s (-2.87) **Going Correction** -0.125s/f (Stan)
WFA 3 from 4yo+ 3lb 11 Ran SP% 116.3
Speed ratings (Par 103): **106,105,105,101,99 98,98,97,93,90 83**
toteswingers: 1&2 £12.50, 1&3 £4.70, 2&3 £7.30 CSF £104.77 CT £303.40 TOTE £12.50: £2.80, £3.70, £1.50; EX 101.60.
Owner Norman Jones Snr **Bred** Newborough Stud **Trained** Newmarket, Suffolk

FOCUS
The early lead was disputed and, although Thunderstruck eventually overcame his poor draw to get to the front rounding the turn into the back straight, he'd used up a fair amount of energy to do so, and the race eventually fell to a closer.
Taaresh(IRE) Official explanation: jockey said colt stopped quickly

7824 ALL BOXING DAY BETTING @ WILLIAMHILL.COM NURSERY 7f (P)
2:45 (2:46) (Class 5) (0-75,76) 2-Y-0 **£2,590** (£770; £385; £192) **Stalls High**

Form RPR
1314 1 **Al Khimiya (IRE)**[19] 7604 2-9-0 **68**.... JimCrowley 3 74
(S Woodman) *in rr: pushed lft wl over 1f out: rapid hdwy ins fnl f to ld cl home* **6/1**[3]
0250 2 *nk* **Fazza**[62] 6896 2-8-11 **65**.... DavidProbert 7 70
(D W P Arbuthnot) *n.m.r sn after s: in rr: hdwy whn pushed lft over 1f out: hdwy appr fnl f: led ins fnl f: hdd cl home* **25/1**
3321 3 *½* **Admiral Cochrane (IRE)**[17] 7619 2-9-1 **69**.... RobertHavlin 8 73
(W Jarvis) *n.m.r after s: towards rr and n.m.r whn pushed lft wl over 1f out: rapid hdwy fnl f to chal wl ins fnl f: no ex cl home* **3/1**[1]
6044 4 *2 ¾* **Starwatch**[25] 7513 2-8-4 **61** ow1.... MarcHalford(3) 11 58
(J J Bridger) *chsd ldrs: drvn to chal jst ins fnl f: wknd cl home* **14/1**
0021 5 *½* **Kai Mook**[1] 7806 2-9-8 **76** 6ex.... KirstyMilczarek 4 72+
(R Ingram) *wnt rt sn after s: led: rdn and edgd lft wl over 1f out: hdd & wknd ins fnl f* **5/1**[2]
614 6 *nk* **Highland Quaich**[37] 7363 2-9-2 **75**.... KylieManser(5) 5 70
(D R C Elsworth) *s.i.s: in rr: rdn and hung rt wl over 1f out: drvn to chse ldrs 1f out: wknd ins fnl f* **8/1**
030 7 *4* **May Chorus (IRE)**[51] 7145 2-8-11 **65**.... SJCraine 10 50
(J R Boyle) *in tch: pushed lft and rdn wl over 1f out: sme prog fnl f* **16/1**
253 8 *1* **Tiradito (USA)**[211] 2280 2-9-3 **74**.... AndreaAtzeni(3) 13 57
(M Botti) *in rr: hdwy 2 out: chsd ldrs over 1f out: wknd ins fnl f* **13/2**
4324 9 *½* **Ramamara (IRE)**[1] 7805 2-9-0 **73**.... RichardEvans(5) 2 54
(P D Evans) *chsd ldrs: rdn and pushed rt wl over 1f out: sn wknd* **14/1**
0225 10 *¾* **Rainsborough**[9] 7706 2-8-10 **64**.... ShaneKelly 6 44
(S Curran) *chsd ldrs over 4f* **16/1**
0655 11 *6* **Brave Ghurka**[4] 7773 2-9-2 **70**.... GeorgeBaker 12 35
(S Kirk) *keeen hold: chsd ldrs: ev ch 2f out: wknd qckly* **14/1**
1m 25.56s (-0.44) **Going Correction** -0.125s/f (Stan) 11 Ran SP% 116.0
Speed ratings (Par 96): **97,96,96,92,92 92,87,86,85,84 78**
toteswingers: 1&2 £29.80, 1&3 £5.00, 2&3 £13.60 CSF £141.68 CT £547.34 TOTE £6.80: £1.70, £6.10, £1.90; EX 209.30.
Owner Al Khimiya Partnership **Bred** Plantation Stud **Trained** East Lavant, W Sussex

FOCUS
The leaders went off too quick here and the principals came from off the pace. The race is rated around the runner-up and fourth.

NOTEBOOK
Al Khimiya(IRE) has tended to race more prominently in the past but she was wisely dropped in from her low draw this time and, in a race run to suit the hold-up horses, came through with a strong late finish to retain her unbeaten record at this track. The likelihood is that there's a bit more to come from her. (op 8-1)
Fazza, returning from a two-month break and stepping up in distance, had no trouble staying the trip in what was a strongly run race. An unexposed sort open to further improvement, he can cope with a little rise in the weights. (op 20-1)
Admiral Cochrane(IRE), 7lb higher and stepping back up to 7f, was short of room on the turn in and was denied a clear run early in the straight. It wasn't a bad effort in the circumstances but the winner showed that bit more zip at the finish. (op 2-1)
Starwatch didn't run badly, although he benefited from a high draw and a good trip. (op 33-1)
Kai Mook, a winner at Lingfield the previous day, had too much use made of her early to get to the lead and she paid the price in the closing stages. (op 11-2)
Highland Quaich, keen and stuck towards the outside throughout, was one of the first to kick for home in the straight and inevitably got tired. He did a bit better than the bare form suggests. (op 9-1)

7825 WILLIAM HILL KING GEORGE VI @ WILLIAMHILL.COM MAIDEN AUCTION STKS 1m (P)
3:15 (3:15) (Class 6) 2-Y-0 **£2,047** (£604; £302) **Stalls High**

Form RPR
0 1 **Shoot The Pot (IRE)**[69] 6728 2-8-10 0.... JimCrowley 5 69+
(R M Beckett) *trckd ldrs: pushed along over 2f out and one pce: hdwy u.p appr fnl f: str run ins fnl f to ld cl home* **15/2**
52 2 *½* **Prince Yarraman (IRE)**[9] 7705 2-8-10 0.... ShaneKelly 4 68
(J A Osborne) *in rr: shkn up and hdwy over 2f out: str run fnl f: edgd lft and led fnl 100yds: hdd cl home* **7/2**[2]
03 3 *¾* **Grams And Ounces**[17] 7616 2-8-12 0.... JerryO'Dwyer 8 68
(Miss Amy Weaver) *chsd ldr: rdn to ld wl over 1f out: hdd fnl 100yds: wknd cl home* **12/1**
003 4 *3 ¼* **Ermyn Express**[14] 7655 2-8-4 67.... JimmyQuinn 9 53
(P M Phelan) *led tl hdd wl over 1f out: wknd ins fnl f* **7/1**
2224 5 *8* **Anaya**[16] 7622 2-8-7 67.... ChrisCatlin 7 38
(M R Channon) *sn in tch: chsd ldrs 1/2-way: wknd qckly 2f out* **6/4**[1]
6 *hd* **Gra Adhmhar (IRE)** 2-8-9 0.... EddieAhern 2 40
(D J Coakley) *racd towards outside: bhd fr 1/2-way* **11/2**[3]
0 7 *2 ½* **Suzybee**[31] 7450 2-8-4 0.... FrankieMcDonald 1 29
(M R Hoad) *plld hrd: stdd in rr after 1f out and styd there* **100/1**
0 8 *9* **Paint By Numbers**[17] 7618 2-8-9 0.... MartinDwyer 10 15
(J A Glover) *s.i.s: a in rr* **40/1**
1m 39.91s (0.11) **Going Correction** -0.125s/f (Stan) 8 Ran SP% 113.0
Speed ratings (Par 94): **94,93,92,89,81 81,78,69**
toteswingers: 1&2 £4.70, 1&3 £9.20, 2&3 £3.70 CSF £33.10 TOTE £10.40: £2.60, £1.30, £2.80; EX 47.90.
Owner Des Anderson & Richard Morecombe **Bred** Michael Dalton **Trained** Whitsbury, Hants

FOCUS
No more than a modest maiden and the form looks weak with the third having been beaten in a seller previously.

NOTEBOOK
Shoot The Pot(IRE) didn't show a great deal on his debut in soft ground at Salisbury two months earlier, but he'd clearly learnt from that experience and his sire has a good record with his runners on Polytrack. He took a while to get on top, but he's out of a Kahyasi mare and the chances are that he'll get further than this in time. (op 9-1)

Prince Yarraman(IRE) ran on well towards the inside only to be grabbed close home by the winner. Despite his sprinting pedigree the step up to 1m suited him. Of some concern, however, is that for the second race in succession he was reported to have hung left. Official explanation: jockey said colt hung left (op 4-1 tchd 9-2)

Grams And Ounces ran well in a seller last time but this required more. Judged by the improvement he showed here he's going the right way, and handicaps now become an option.

Ermyn Express was given every chance from the front but just didn't see out the trip as well as the first three. Despite being a half-sister to a 1m6f winner it looks as if a mile stretches her stamina at the moment.

Anaya has been a little frustrating but on this occasion she was beaten with over 2f to run and patently failed to run up to her previous form. (op 5-4 tchd 6-5 in places)

Gra Adhmhar(IRE) was not without his supporters on his debut but he had a poor draw to overcome, ended up racing wide and was struggling from the turn in. He might be capable of better. (op 7-1)

7826 WILLIAM HILL WINTER FESTIVAL - BOXINGDAYRACES.COM MAIDEN STKS 1m (P)
3:45 (3:46) (Class 5) 3-4-Y-0 **£2,590** (£770; £385; £192) **Stalls** High

Form RPR
0 **1** **Erinjay (IRE)**[288] 784 3-8-10 0 TobyAtkinson(7) 8 75
(M Wigham) *trckd ldrs: pushed along to ld 1f out: sn clr: comf* **20/1**

6032 **2** 3 1/2 **Charlie Smirke (USA)**[7] 7742 3-9-3 59 GeorgeBaker 9 67
(G L Moore) *chsd ldrs: led over 2f out: rdn and hdd 1f out: sn outpcd by wnr but styd on wl for 2nd* **9/2**[3]

2 **3** 2 **No Mean Trick (USA)**[36] 7401 3-9-3 0 AdamKirby 1 62
(C G Cox) *chsd ldrs: rdn and kpt on fnl 2f: styd on ins fnl f but nt trble ldng duo* **2/1**[1]

5642 **4** nk **Cross Section (USA)**[13] 7671 3-8-12 62 EddieAhern 11 56
(E F Vaughan) *in tch: rdn and hdwy fr 2f out: chsd ldrs fnl f: kpt on same pce* **7/2**[2]

5 **5** 1 1/2 **Silken Sands (IRE)**[69] 6741 3-8-13 0 ow1 IanMongan 5 54
(C G Cox) *chsd ldrs: rdn over 2f out: styd on same pce fr over 1f out* **12/1**

0604 **6** hd **Ejeed (USA)**[18] 7609 4-9-4 49 (p) SamHitchcott 3 57
(Miss Z C Davison) *in rr: rdn and hdwy over 2f out: styd on fnl f but nvr a threat* **25/1**

7 3/4 **Melting Bob (USA)** 3-8-12 0 ShaneKelly 13 51
(Dr J D Scargill) *s.i.s: in rr: rapid hdwy and green over 1f out: fin wl: gng on cl home* **25/1**

0 **8** 1 **Katie The Hatter (IRE)**[55] 7067 3-8-12 0 JimCrowley 6 48
(Mike Murphy) *mid-div: pushed along and one pce fr over 2f out* **5/1**

0200 **9** 2 1/4 **Litenup (IRE)**[11] 7688 3-8-12 52 (t) WandersonD'Avila 7 43
(A J Lidderdale) *led tl hdd over 2f out: wknd wl over 1f out* **33/1**

5-0 **10** nk **Gheed (IRE)**[15] 7648 4-8-13 0 (t) JimmyQuinn 14 42
(K A Morgan) *in tch over 5f* **40/1**

04 **11** 2 3/4 **King's Miracle (IRE)**[30] 7464 3-8-12 0 MartinDwyer 4 35
(J R Gask) *plld hrd: stdd in rr and nvr in contention* **33/1**

12 1 1/4 **Puitin**[78] 4-9-4 0 LPKeniry 2 37
(M Madgwick) *s.i.s: a in rr* **80/1**

0 **13** 1/2 **Sir Tom**[18] 7610 4-9-1 0 MarcHalford(3) 10 36
(J J Bridger) *a in rr* **80/1**

U **14** 6 **Gospel Spirit**[188] 2981 4-9-4 0 SimonWhitworth 12 22
(J R Jenkins) *a in rr* **100/1**

1m 39.52s (-0.28) **Going Correction** -0.125s/f (Stan)
WFA 3 from 4yo 1lb **14** Ran SP% **122.3**
Speed ratings (Par 103): **96,92,90,90,88 88,87,86,84,84 81,80,79,73**
toteswingers: 1&2 £20.20, 1&3 £15.90, 2&3 £3.10 CSF £103.84 TOTE £30.30: £6.30, £1.50, £1.30; EX 165.60.
Owner Seyhan Osman & Robert Kibble **Bred** Bill Benson **Trained** Newmarket, Suffolk

FOCUS
A weak maiden - the sixth-placed finisher Ejeed was rated just 49 - and it proved difficult to make up significant amounts of ground.

7827 WILLIAM HILL KING GEORGE VI TICKETS - 01932 782292 H'CAP 1m (P)
4:15 (4:16) (Class 2) (0-100,100) 3-Y-0+
£11,091 (£3,321; £1,660; £831; £414; £208) **Stalls** High

Form RPR
5051 **1** **Falcativ**[16] 7626 4-8-10 91 JerryO'Dwyer 8 102
(M Botti) *hld up: gd hdwy fr 2f out: slt ld fnl 120yds: shkn up and responded wl whn chal fnl 50yds: readily* **3/1**[1]

0116 **2** 3/4 **Aeroplane**[4] 7768 6-9-0 100 (p) RichardEvans(5) 13 109
(P D Evans) *hld up in rr: hdwy on bit and squeezed through ins fnl f to press wnr fnl 50yds but readily hld* **10/1**

4411 **3** 3/4 **Spinning**[23] 7560 6-9-0 95 (b) PhillipMakin 2 103
(T D Barron) *slowly away: bhd: rdn over 2f out: stl last over 1f out: str run ins fnl f: fin strly but nt rch ldng duo* **14/1**

3231 **4** 1 **Benandonner (USA)**[13] 7662 6-8-9 90 MartinDwyer 12 95
(Mike Murphy) *broke wl: stdd but wl in tch: w ldrs: hdwy and rdn over 2f out: wnt 3rd over 1f out: styd on same pce fnl f* **9/1**

513 **5** shd **Bravo Echo**[100] 5832 3-8-4 86 DavidProbert 11 91
(M J Attwater) *chsd ldr: slt ld appr fnl 3f: kpt slt advantage tl hdd fnl 120yds: wknd nr fin* **11/1**

0105 **6** nk **Grand Vizier (IRE)**[128] 4983 5-8-8 89 ow1 EddieAhern 6 93
(C F Wall) *chsd ldrs: rdn over 2f out: styd on same pce ins fnl f* **10/1**

-342 **7** nk **Nezami (IRE)**[225] 1861 4-8-6 90 AndreaAtzeni(3) 10 94
(J Akehurst) *in rr: hdwy on ins fr 3f out: chsd ldrs and rdn 2f out: kpt on same pce ins fnl f* **8/1**

1120 **8** nk **The Scorching Wind (IRE)**[86] 6243 3-8-4 86 (t) ChrisCatlin 9 89
(S C Williams) *t.k.h: in rr: hdwy on outside but u.str.p appr fnl f: kpt on cl home but nvr in contention* **7/1**[3]

0310 **9** shd **Stand Guard**[22] 7574 5-8-3 89 AndrewHeffernan(5) 3 92
(P Howling) *in rr: pushed along over 2f out: styd on ins fnl f but nvr gng pce to get into contention* **14/1**

1041 **10** 1/2 **Elna Bright**[29] 7486 4-8-9 90 DaneO'Neill 4 92
(B R Johnson) *in tch and rdn over 2f out: nvr in contention* **5/1**[2]

11 3/4 **Winter Fever (SAF)**[296] 5-8-6 87 LukeMorris 7 87
(J M P Eustace) *sn led: hdd appr fnl 3f: styd pressing ldr tl wknd jst ins fnl f* **50/1**

1m 37.59s (-2.21) **Going Correction** -0.125s/f (Stan)
WFA 3 from 4yo+ 1lb **11** Ran SP% **117.1**
Speed ratings (Par 109): **106,105,104,103,103 103,102,102,102,101 101**
toteswingers: 1&2 £9.30, 1&3 £5.30, 2&3 £12.20 CSF £33.81 CT £374.45 TOTE £4.00: £1.40, £3.20, £4.00; EX 39.40 Trifecta £526.49 - 0.50 winning units..
Owner Dioscuri Srl **Bred** Az Agr Francesca **Trained** Newmarket, Suffolk

FOCUS
A decent handicap run at a good pace.

NOTEBOOK
Falcativ ◆, a winner over this trip at Lingfield on his first start since leaving Luca Cumani, defied a 4lb higher mark to follow up. Having travelled well, he proved far more responsive to pressure than the runner-up and is a horse very much on the up. He cost these connections only 8,000gns and was clearly a shrewd purchase.

Aeroplane's only previous try over this trip came in the 2006 St James's Palace Stakes, but he didn't fail through a lack of stamina this time, he simply seemed reluctant to go by the winner when finally coming off the bridle, having been given a fine hold-up ride. Still, strictly on the figures, this was a smart effort in defeat. (op 12-1)

Spinning, who was bidding for a hat-trick following wins at Wolverhampton, was up a further 6lb. Having started slowly as usual, he was being driven along in last place before the straight, but he eventually responded and finished strongly, proving he's still competitive off his new mark. (op 11-1)

Benandonner(USA) didn't have to be at his best to win a claimer for Richard Fahey on his previous start, after which he joined these connections for £15,000, and this was better. He fared best of those who raced on the pace and emerges with credit. (op 14-1)

Bravo Echo, bought out of John Gosden's yard for 48,000gns since he was last seen in September, ran well on his debut for new connections, although he did look to be hanging right under pressure in the straight. Whatever, though, being quite a sizeable colt, he's entitled to come on for this fitness-wise. (op 12-1)

Grand Vizier(IRE) is entitled to improve for this first run in over four months. (op 9-1)

Nezami(IRE) can also be expected to come on for the outing, having been off for 225 days. (op 10-1)

The Scorching Wind(IRE) ◆, returning from nearly three months off, had little chance after being asked to race much wider than ideal pretty much throughout, and he can certainly be given another chance. (op 13-2)

Elna Bright, 4lb higher than when winning over 7f at Lingfield, dropped out tamely in the straight after being stuck wide. (op 4-1)

7828 ENJOY BOXING DAY @ WILLIAMHILL.COM H'CAP 6f (P)
4:45 (4:46) (Class 5) (0-75,75) 3-Y-0+ **£2,590** (£770; £385; £192) **Stalls** High

Form RPR
3160 **1** **Perfect Act**[7] 7741 4-9-1 72 LukeMorris 8 84
(C G Cox) *in rr tl stdy hdwy over 1f out: drvn and qcknd to ld jst ins fnl f: pushed clr: comf* **13/2**

1035 **2** 2 **New Leyf (IRE)**[147] 4338 3-9-1 72 LPKeniry 3 81+
(J R Gask) *stdd and swtchd rt s: gd hdwy fr 2f out: stayin on whn bdly hmpd 1f out: kpt on again fnl 100yds and tk 2nd last strides but no ch w wnr* **25/1**

4111 **3** hd **Spinning Bailiwick**[14] 7651 3-9-3 74 GeorgeBaker 4 79
(G L Moore) *chsd ldr: rdn to chal 1f out: chsd wnr ins fnl f but a readily hld: lost 2nd last strides* **6/1**[3]

0602 **4** 3/4 **Resplendent Alpha**[7] 7738 5-8-12 69 JimmyQuinn 2 72
(P Howling) *in rr: hdwy over 2f out: rdn and styd on to chse ldrs ins fnl f: one pce nr fin* **15/2**

0624 **5** nk **Labisa (IRE)**[16] 7627 3-9-0 71 SteveDrowne 10 73
(H Morrison) *chsd ldrs: drvn to chal 1f out: kpt on same pce ins fnl f* **5/1**[2]

3240 **6** 1 1/4 **Musical Script (USA)**[7] 7739 6-8-10 67 (b) MartinDwyer 12 65
(Mouse Hamilton-Fairley) *s.i.s: t.k.h and sn trcking ldrs: rdn 2f out: wknd fnl 120yds* **9/2**[1]

000 **7** nk **Westwood**[108] 5612 4-8-11 68 DaneO'Neill 11 65
(D Haydn Jones) *led tl hdd & wknd jst ins fnl f* **33/1**

1401 **8** 1/2 **Lujeanie**[134] 4787 3-9-4 75 (p) JimCrowley 1 70
(D K Ivory) *stdd and swtchd rt s: outpcd* **12/1**

0014 **9** 3/4 **Master Lightfoot**[16] 7634 3-9-2 73 AdamKirby 9 66
(W R Swinburn) *chsd ldrs: rdn 3f out: wknd fr 2f out* **5/1**[2]

2400 **10** 2 3/4 **Premier Lad**[26] 7506 3-8-12 69 PhillipMakin 7 53
(T D Barron) *in tch tl dropped in rr over 2f out* **14/1**

4351 **11** 3 **Leading Edge (IRE)**[23] 7555 4-8-10 67 ChrisCatlin 5 41
(M R Channon) *a towards rr on outside* **20/1**

1m 11.83s (-1.27) **Going Correction** -0.125s/f (Stan) **11** Ran SP% **116.8**
Speed ratings (Par 103): **103,100,100,99,98 97,96,95,94,91 87**
toteswingers: 1&2 £32.80, 1&3 £5.00, 2&3 £18.10 CSF £159.32 CT £1026.83 TOTE £8.90: £2.30, £7.00, £1.80; EX 350.90 Placen 6: £178.41 Place 5: £91.42.
Owner Dr Bridget Drew & E E Dedman **Bred** Howard Barton Stud **Trained** Lambourn, Berks
■ Stewards' Enquiry : Luke Morris two-day ban: careless riding (Jan 3-4)

FOCUS
A fair sprint handicap run at a reasonable pace.
T/Jkpt: Not won. T/Plt: £81.30 to a £1 stake. Pool: £128,246.43. 1,151.17 winning tickets. T/Qpdt: £21.50 to a £1 stake. Pool: £8,956.70. 307 winning tickets. ST

7823 KEMPTON (A.W) (R-H)
Monday, December 21

OFFICIAL GOING: Standard
Wind: Moderate, across towards stands Weather: Mixture of rain, sleet and sloppy snow, cold

7829 KEMPTON.CO.UK MEDIAN AUCTION MAIDEN STKS 7f (P)
2:00 (2:00) (Class 6) 3-5-Y-0 **£2,047** (£604; £302) **Stalls** High

Form RPR
1 **Celtic Sovereign (IRE)** 3-9-3 0 JerryO'Dwyer 4 68
(M G Quinlan) *slowest away: hld up in last trio: gd prog 2f out: c through rivals over 1f out: edgd lft but led ins fnl f: pushed out: readily* **20/1**

2 **2** 1 1/2 **Peponi**[23] 7576 3-9-3 0 NCallan 11 64
(P J Makin) *sltly awkward s: sn trckd ldr: led over 2f out: drifted lft after: hdd u.p ins fnl f: kpt on* **6/5**[1]

4 **3** 1 1/2 **Perfect Secret**[233] 1671 3-8-12 0 LPKeniry 1 55
(A M Balding) *hld up in last trio: prog over 2f out: to chal wl over 1f out: sn rdn and nt qckn: one pce* **9/2**[3]

0020 **4** shd **Fly By Nelly**[10] 7716 3-8-12 62 SteveDrowne 2 55
(H Morrison) *hld up bhd ldrs: pushed along and nt qckn over 2f out: kpt on fr over 1f out: nrly snatched 3rd* **17/2**

0400 **5** *hd* **Peninsular War**[54] 7119 3-9-3 67 TonyHamilton 8 59
(R A Fahey) *t.k.h early: trckd ldrs: effrt on inner to try to chal wl over 1f out: rdn and nt qckn* **33/1**

2355 **6** *2 ½* **Lucky Score (IRE)**[8] 7742 3-8-12 61 (p) ChrisCatlin 6 47
(Mouse Hamilton-Fairley) *chsd ldng pair: grad lost pl fr over 2f out* **8/1**

0550 **7** *½* **Cativo**[19] 7614 3-8-12 45 ow3 (t) JamesMillman(3) 3 49
(B R Millman) *mde most to over 2f out: grad fdd u.p* **66/1**

8 *2 ½* **Cheveyo (IRE)**[26] 7528 3-9-0 74 EJMcNamara(3) 5 44
(Patrick Morris) *in tch on outer: rdn wl over 2f out: no prog wl over 1f out: btn after: fdd* **4/1**[2]

0000 **9** *16* **Mrs Medley**[10] 7710 3-8-12 32 DaneO'Neill 7 —
(D Shaw) *plld hrd: hld up in last trio: wknd 3f out: t.o* **250/1**

0 **10** *9* **Lunaticus**[25] 7533 3-8-12 0 JimCrowley 9 —
(M J Attwater) *rdn to stay in tch 1/2-way: sn bhd: t.o* **66/1**

1m 25.59s (-0.41) **Going Correction** -0.05s/f (Stan) **10** Ran SP% **116.4**
Speed ratings (Par 101): **100,98,96,96,96 93,92,89,71,61**
toteswinger:1&2:£7.00, 2&3:£2.60, 1&3:£7.50 CSF £44.05 TOTE £16.90: £5.00, £1.20, £1.80; EX 63.50.
Owner Burns Farm Racing **Bred** Burns Farm Stud **Trained** Newmarket, Suffolk

FOCUS
An ordinary maiden and, with the time 0.95 seconds slower than 72-rated Moojeh, a 3-y-o filly, recorded in the following handicap, this is not form to get carried away with. A decent start by the winner all the same.

7830 DIGIBET H'CAP 7f (P)
2:30 (2:31) (Class 5) (0-75,75) 3-Y-O+ **£3,238** (£963; £481; £240) **Stalls** High

Form RPR

4100 **1** **Moojeh (IRE)**[32] 7456 3-9-1 72 JerryO'Dwyer 6 79
(M Botti) *dwlt: hld up in last trio: prog fr 2f out: got through rivals fnl f to ld last 100yds: styd on best* **20/1**

31-0 **2** *¾* **Monsieur Fillioux (USA)**[132] 4871 3-9-3 74 HayleyTurner 9 79
(J R Fanshawe) *hld up towards rr: effrt over 2f out: prog u.p over 1f out: got through rivals to chal last 150yds: jst outpcd* **25/1**

0505 **3** *hd* **Kensington (IRE)**[16] 7643 8-8-3 67 (p) DeclanCannon(7) 12 71
(A J McCabe) *t.k.h early: trckd ldng pair: effrt over 2f out: drvn and kpt on to chal over 1f out: ev ch ins fnl f: nt qckn* **25/1**

2101 **4** *nk* **Hereford Boy**[22] 7586 5-8-10 67 (p) RobertHavlin 3 71
(D K Ivory) *hld up in last trio: taken to wd outside and effrt over 2f out: prog over 1f out: styd on fnl f but nvr quite pce to chal* **9/1**

5463 **5** *¾* **I Confess**[8] 7741 4-9-1 72 (v) PaulDoe 10 74
(P D Evans) *mde most: jnd over 2f out: hdd and fdd ins fnl f* **4/1**[2]

0546 **6** *nse* **Dvinsky (USA)**[11] 7702 8-9-2 73 (b) DaneO'Neill 7 74
(P Howling) *pressed ldr: upsides fr over 2f out tl ins fnl f: fdd last 75yds* **7/1**

021 **7** *shd* **Simla Sunset (IRE)**[31] 7459 3-9-0 71 (t) LPKeniry 14 72
(J R Gask) *trckd ldrs on inner: gng strly over 2f out: drvn to chal over 1f out: ev ch ins fnl f: fdd* **15/2**

0004 **8** *1 ¼* **Sadeek**[16] 7643 5-8-9 66 TomEaves 11 64
(B Smart) *trckd ldng pair: pushed along wl over 2f out: nt qckn and hld wl over 1f out: kpt on* **6/1**[3]

6200 **9** *hd* **Cut And Thrust (IRE)**[76] 6562 3-9-1 72 (p) ChrisCatlin 5 69
(M Wellings) *trckd ldrs: shkn up and no imp 2f out: lost pl over 1f out: no prog after* **25/1**

0142 **10** *1 ¼* **Rondeau (GR)**[17] 7627 4-9-1 72 JimCrowley 1 66
(P R Chamings) *s.s: plld hrd early in last: wd bnds 4f out and again 3f out where looked ill at ease: a struggling after* **11/4**[1]

11 *½* **The Mouse Carroll (IRE)**[52] 7160 5-8-8 65 FrankieMcDonald 13 58
(B R Johnson) *in tch on inner: shkn up over 2f out: dropped to last pair and btn over 1f out* **50/1**

1m 24.64s (-1.36) **Going Correction** -0.05s/f (Stan) **11** Ran SP% **113.5**
Speed ratings (Par 103): **105,104,103,103,102 102,102,101,100,99 98**
toteswinger:1&2:£23.80, 2&3:£41.70, 1&3:£52.80 CSF £402.48 CT £12045.46 TOTE £25.10: £6.40, £6.20, £6.40; EX 153.40.
Owner Can Artam **Bred** Shadwell Estate Company Limited **Trained** Newmarket, Suffolk
■ Stewards' Enquiry : Declan Cannon three-day ban: used whip with excessive frequency in incorrect place (Jan 4-6)

FOCUS
An ordinary handicap and, despite the pace appearing strong (backed up by a fair time), nine of these were covered by only about 2l with a furlong to run. The fifth is one of the most likely guides to the form.
Dvinsky(USA) Official explanation: jockey said gelding missed the break

7831 DIGIBET.COM H'CAP 1m 4f (P)
3:05 (3:07) (Class 5) (0-75,75) 3-Y-O **£3,238** (£722; £722; £240) **Stalls** Centre

Form RPR

5313 **1** **Quinsman**[14] 7665 3-8-9 66 LPKeniry 9 72
(J S Moore) *hld up in 5th: smooth prog to trck ldrs over 2f out: hrd rdn to chal over 1f out: carried lft but led last 75yds: jst hld on* **7/2**[2]

0424 **2** *shd* **Taste The Wine (IRE)**[5] 7777 3-8-4 61 LukeMorris 4 67
(J S Moore) *trckd ldng trio: smooth prog to ld over 2f out: sn kicked on but limited rspnse: hrd drvn and edgd lft fr over 1f out: hdd last 75yds: kpt on* **4/1**[3]

0111 **2** *dht* **Sircozy (IRE)**[5] 7777 3-8-5 65 WilliamCarson(3) 3 71
(S C Williams) *hld up in 6th: pushed along wl over 2f out: hrd rdn to cl on ldng pair over 1f out: carried lft and nrly upsides ins fnl f: jst hld* **10/11**[1]

0621 **4** *2 ½* **Fleur De'Lion (IRE)**[8] 7737 3-8-6 63 6ex DavidProbert 6 65
(S Kirk) *hld up in last pair: effrt to chse ldng trio wl over 1f out: kpt on but no real imp after* **16/1**

6326 **5** *7* **Broughtons Paradis (IRE)**[30] 7476 3-8-4 61 ChrisCatlin 5 52
(W J Musson) *hld up in last pair: pushed along over 2f out whn nt on terms: modest 5th jst over 1f out: nvr nr ldrs* **10/1**

0035 **6** *3 ¼* **December**[14] 7665 3-8-5 62 AdrianMcCarthy 8 48
(Mrs C A Dunnett) *led to over 2f out: sn wknd* **12/1**

0 **7** *½* **Mallorey**[103] 5782 3-8-1 61 oh1 AndreaAtzeni(3) 2 46
(A M Hales) *chsd ldr to 3f out: sn lost pl and btn* **33/1**

2-10 **8** *1 ¼* **Choral Festival**[137] 4709 3-9-1 75 MarcHalford(3) 7 58
(J J Bridger) *chsd ldng pair to over 3f out: wknd over 2f out* **20/1**

2m 35.25s (0.75) **Going Correction** -0.05s/f (Stan) **8** Ran SP% **125.0**
Speed ratings (Par 102): **95,94,94,93,88 86,86,85**
Place: Sarcozy £1.10, Taste The Wine £1.70; EX: QM/SR £4.80, QM/TW £10.90 CSF: QM/SR £3.90, QM/TW £9.96, TRI: QM/SR/TW £7.12, QM/TW/SR £11.69 toteswinger: QM&SR £2.50, TW&SR £2.70, QM&TW £3.40 TOTE £5.60: £2.20.
Owner Donald M Kerr **Bred** Mr & Mrs G Middlebrook **Trained** Upper Lambourn, Berks

FOCUS
A fair handicap which was steadily run and there was a tight finish, with little between three old rivals. The winner, weighted to reverse Lingfield form with the favourite, produced a 3lb personal best.

December Official explanation: jockey said gelding hung left

7832 DIGIBET CASINO H'CAP 6f (P)
3:35 (3:36) (Class 4) (0-85,82) 3-Y-O+ **£5,180** (£1,541; £770; £384) **Stalls** High

Form RPR

6523 **1** **Capone (IRE)**[24] 7553 4-9-4 82 HayleyTurner 10 95+
(R Curtis) *hld up in 6th: prog over 2f out: effrt to ld over 1f out: pushed out and won decisively* **11/4**[1]

0500 **2** *¾* **Vhujon (IRE)**[70] 6723 4-9-0 78 PaulDoe 3 89
(P D Evans) *dropped in fr wd draw and hld up in 8th: darted to ins rail and gd prog jst over 2f out: w wnr over 1f out: styd on wl but readily hld* **10/1**

0005 **3** *2 ¾* **Fishforcompliments**[11] 7702 5-8-13 77 TonyHamilton 7 79
(R A Fahey) *trckd ldng trio: rdn over 2f out and nt qckn: kpt on fr over 1f out to take 3rd last 100yds* **8/1**

0130 **4** *¾* **Misaro (GER)**[15] 7656 8-8-11 75 (b) DavidProbert 8 74
(R A Harris) *racd freely: led at gd pce: hdd over 1f out: fdd* **15/2**

6150 **5** *shd* **Ektimaal**[24] 7558 6-9-3 81 EddieAhern 4 80
(E A L Dunlop) *hld up in 7th: shkn up on outer wl over 2f out: sme prog wl over 1f out: one pce after* **7/1**[3]

5416 **5** *dht* **Billberry**[12] 7692 4-8-5 69 (t) ChrisCatlin 2 68
(S C Williams) *hld up in last: rdn wl over 2f out: styd on fr over 1f out: clsng on plcd horses fin* **8/1**

4601 **7** *shd* **Brandywell Boy (IRE)**[24] 7553 6-8-5 74 BillyCray(5) 12 73
(D J S Ffrench Davis) *chsd ldng pair: rdn over 2f out: lost pl and fdd over 1f out* **12/1**

52-4 **8** *¾* **Vintage (IRE)**[207] 2396 5-9-2 80 DaneO'Neill 6 76
(J Akehurst) *hld up in 5th: shkn up and no rspnse jst over 2f out: grad lost pl* **9/2**[2]

1-05 **9** *¾* **Fen Spirit (IRE)**[15] 7656 3-8-13 77 RobertHavlin 9 71
(J H M Gosden) *chsd ldr: rdn over 2f out: cl enough over 1f out: sn wknd* **10/1**

1m 11.31s (-1.79) **Going Correction** -0.05s/f (Stan) **9** Ran SP% **117.2**
Speed ratings (Par 105): **109,108,104,103,103 103,103,102,101**
totewinger:1&2:£7.30, 2&3:£18.00, 1&3:£6.10 CSF £31.99 CT £200.34 TOTE £4.20: £1.60, £4.80, £3.00; EX 32.70 TRIFECTA Not won..
Owner Brooklands Racing **Bred** S J Macdonald **Trained** Lambourn, Berks

FOCUS
A fair sprint handicap run at a fast pace, and the time was only 0.19 seconds outside the track record. As a result, those held up were at an advantage. The winner confirmed his recent improvement.

7833 WEATHERBYS PRINTING H'CAP 7f (P)
4:05 (4:07) (Class 4) (0-85,83) 3-Y-O+ **£5,180** (£1,541; £770; £384) **Stalls** High

Form RPR

054 **1** **L'Hirondelle (IRE)**[17] 7626 5-9-4 82 PaulDoe 4 89
(M J Attwater) *w ldr: narrow ld 1/2-way: hrd pressed over 1f out: battled on gamely fnl f* **7/1**[3]

4411 **2** *shd* **Seek The Fair Land**[8] 7741 3-9-0 81 6ex WilliamCarson(3) 1 88
(J R Boyle) *t.k.h: trckd ldng pair: moved up to chal fr 2f out: upsides fnl f: a jst being denied* **8/11**[1]

0000 **3** *1 ½* **Baunagain (IRE)**[13] 7676 4-8-13 77 AdrianMcCarthy 7 80
(P W Chapple-Hyam) *wnt lft s: t.k.h: hld up in 6th: effrt over 2f out: kpt on same pce fr over 1f out: nvr able to chal* **33/1**

3321 **4** *nse* **Autumn Blades (IRE)**[3] 7801 4-9-5 83 6ex (p) DavidProbert 8 86
(A Bailey) *hld up in 5th: effrt over 2f out: rdn to chse ldng pair over 1f out: kpt on same pce* **7/2**[2]

0016 **5** *1* **Carnivore**[24] 7558 7-9-0 78 HayleyTurner 5 78
(T D Barron) *dwlt and bmpd s: hld up in detached last: urged along fr over 2f out: styd on fr over 1f out but nvr gng pce to pose a threat* **9/1**

6-40 **6** *3 ¼* **Durgan**[200] 2638 3-8-9 72 ow1 SteveDrowne 2 64
(Mrs L C Jewell) *plld hrd early: hld up in 4th: shuffled along fr 2f out: lost pl and btn sn after* **50/1**

4020 **7** *¾* **Laurie Grove (IRE)**[23] 7583 3-9-4 82 NCallan 3 71
(T G Mills) *led to 1/2-way: wknd 2f out* **12/1**

1m 25.67s (-0.33) **Going Correction** -0.05s/f (Stan) **7** Ran SP% **115.2**
Speed ratings (Par 105): **99,98,97,97,95 92,91**
toteswinger:1&2:£2.30, 2&3:£8.10, 1&3:£9.30 CSF £12.77 CT £162.87 TOTE £7.20: £3.00, £1.60; EX 14.70.
Owner Canisbay Bloodstock **Bred** Gainsborough Stud Management Ltd **Trained** Epsom, Surrey

FOCUS
A noticeably steady pace resulted in the time being the slowest of three races 7f on the card, despite this contest being much the best. As such, it proved difficult to make up ground. There was a bunhc finish and the winner probably did not have to improve.

7834 BISTRO PRICES FROM £37 H'CAP (DIV I) 6f (P)
4:35 (4:36) (Class 6) (0-55,61) 3-Y-O+ **£1,706** (£503; £252) **Stalls** High

Form RPR

0030 **1** **Valentino Swing (IRE)**[10] 7715 6-9-0 55 JackDean(3) 8 64
(Miss T Spearing) *hld up towards rr: prog over 2f out: burst through rivals to ld over 1f out: in command after: drvn out* **12/1**

2201 **2** *¾* **Kingsgate Castle**[5] 7770 4-9-4 61 6ex (b) KylieManser(5) 10 68
(Miss Gay Kelleway) *hld up in last trio: looking for run fr 2f out: gd prog ent fnl f: bmpd along and r.o to take 2nd nr fin* **4/1**[2]

0656 **3** *nk* **Golden Dixie (USA)**[10] 7709 10-9-1 53 LukeMorris 9 59
(R A Harris) *trckd ldrs: drvn to chal 2f out: nt qckn over 1f out: hrd rdn to chse wnr after: lost 2nd nr fin* **8/1**

0000 **4** *nse* **Strategic Mover (USA)**[14] 7668 4-9-0 55 (vt) RobertLButler(3) 12 61
(P Butler) *dwlt: hld up in last: gd prog on inner over 2f out: chsng ldrs over 1f out: styd on ins fnl f and nrly snatched 3rd* **33/1**

0001 **5** *1 ¼* **Straboe (USA)**[137] 4718 3-8-13 51 TomEaves 4 53
(S C Williams) *trckd ldr 3f: styd prom: led gng easily 2f out: hdd over 1f out: fnd nil over 1f out* **3/1**[1]

0640 **6** *¾* **Sovereignty (JPN)**[12] 7691 7-9-3 55 (p) SteveDrowne 6 54
(D K Ivory) *t.k.h: hld up towards rr: shkn up over 2f out: kpt on one pce fr over 1f out and nvr on terms w ldrs* **5/1**[3]

0066 **7** *½* **Hart Of Gold**[20] 7602 5-9-0 52 (b) LiamJones 5 50+
(R A Harris) *t.k.h: hld up in midfield: dropped to rr whn n.m.r and snatched up jst over 1f out: no ch after: kpt on* **12/1**

0464 **8** *½* **Pinball (IRE)**[15] 7651 3-9-2 54 (v) HayleyTurner 3 50
(Mrs L Williamson) *trckd ldrs on outer: cl enough and rdn on wd outside 2f out: sn fdd* **12/1**

0000 **9** *1* **Monte Cassino (IRE)**[21] 7601 4-9-2 54 TonyCulhane 7 47
(J O'Reilly) *mde most to 2f out: sn lost pl and btn* **25/1**

3540 **10** ½ **Megalo Maniac**[23] 7579 6-9-0 **52**..............................(v) TonyHamilton 11 43
(R A Fahey) *chsd ldrs: rdn and nt qckn 2f out: stl wl in tch ent fnl f: wknd rapidly* **12/1**

0455 **11** 4 **Mr Rio (IRE)**[25] 7534 4-9-0 **52**.............................. DaneO'Neill 2 31
(A P Jarvis) *racd freely fr wdst draw and jnd ldr 1/2-way: wknd over 2f out* **11/1**

1m 12.39s (-0.71) **Going Correction** -0.05s/f (Stan) **11** Ran SP% **118.7**
Speed ratings (Par 101): **102,101,100,100,98 97,97,96,95,94 89**
toteswinger:1&2:£11.80, 2&3:£8.20, 1&3:£17.20 CSF £60.12 CT £418.71 TOTE £17.80: £4.30, £1.80, £2.90; EX 83.50.
Owner D J Oseman **Bred** Sean P Bourke **Trained** Alcester, Warwicks

FOCUS
A moderate sprint handicap run at a good pace and in the samer time as division II. Sound form.

7835 BISTRO PRICES FROM £37 H'CAP (DIV II) 6f (P)
5:05 (5:05) (Class 6) (0-55,55) 3-Y-0+ **£1,706** (£503; £252) **Stalls** High

Form RPR

0032 **1** **Sherjawy (IRE)**[10] 7710 5-9-0 **52**..............................(p) SamHitchcott 1 62+
(Miss Z C Davison) *fast away fr wdst draw: pressed ldr: led 2f out: rdn and kpt on wl to hold off rivals fnl f* **16/1**

5233 **2** ¾ **Cool Sands (IRE)**[13] 7680 7-9-3 **55**..............................(v) J-PGuillambert 10 63
(J G Given) *trckd ldng trio: effrt over 2f out: rdn to chse wnr over 1f out: styd on but a hld* **9/2**[2]

2010 **3** ¾ **Fuzzy Cat**[62] 6926 3-9-1 **53**.............................. HayleyTurner 9 58
(T D Barron) *stdd s: hld up in last trio: prog on inner and plenty of room fr over 2f out: styd on fnl f to take 3rd nr fin* **10/3**[1]

3533 **4** nk **Kinigi (IRE)**[9] 7726 3-8-12 **55**..............................(p) AndrewHeffernan(5) 5 59
(R A Harris) *awkward s: hld up in last trio: shkn up on outer over 2f out: gd prog fr jst over 1f out: nrst fin* **14/1**

562 **5** hd **Nativity**[5] 7770 3-8-11 **52**.............................. JackDean(3) 7 56
(J L Spearing) *hld up in midfield: prog to chse ldng pair over 1f out: rdn and fnd nil after: lost 2 pls nr fin* **11/2**

5060 **6** ¾ **Greek Secret**[23] 7579 6-9-0 **52**..............................(b) TonyCulhane 12 53
(J O'Reilly) *plld hrd in abt 5th: shkn up 2f out: kpt on same pce but no real imp on ldrs* **25/1**

0333 **7** ½ **Radiator Rooney (IRE)**[5] 7774 6-9-0 **55**..............................(b) EJMcNamara(3) 4 55
(Patrick Morris) *hld up towards rr on outer: prog over 2f out: cl enough and shkn up over 1f out: effrt fizzled out* **5/1**[3]

604 **8** ½ **Davids Mark**[5] 7774 9-8-12 **50**.............................. SimonWhitworth 6 51+
(J R Jenkins) *hld up in midfield: effrt over 2f out: trying to cl whn nowhere to go and snatched up ent fnl f: no ch after* **16/1**

3662 **9** ¾ **The Name Is Frank**[5] 7771 4-9-1 **53**..............................(t) EddieAhern 3 49
(Mark Gillard) *hld up in 6th: lost pl sn after 1/2-way but gng wl enough: shkn up briefly over 1f out: nvr nr ldrs after* **13/2**

026 **10** ½ **Exceed Elegance (IRE)**[21] 7595 3-9-3 **55**..............................(t) TomEaves 8 49
(D Shaw) *dwlt: hld up in last: taken fr inner to wd outside in home st: stl last 1f out: pushed along and keeping on at fin* **16/1**

1000 **11** 1¼ **Malapropism**[15] 7657 9-8-11 **54**.............................. MatthewDavies(5) 2 44
(M R Channon) *fast away fr wd draw: led to 2f out: wknd over 1f out* **40/1**

2005 **12** 2¾ **Bountiful Bay**[5] 7771 4-8-13 **51**..............................(t) LPKeniry 11 32
(Matthew Salaman) *mostly chsd ldng pair to 2f out: wknd rapidly fnl f* **12/1**

1m 12.39s (-0.71) **Going Correction** -0.05s/f (Stan) **12** Ran SP% **124.9**
Speed ratings (Par 101): **102,101,100,99,99 98,97,97,96,95 93,90**
toteswinger:1&2:£8.50, 2&3:£6.50, 1&3:£17.10 CSF £91.29 CT £314.95 TOTE £15.20: £3.80, £2.20, £2.00; EX 72.20 Place 6 £369.47, Place 5 £243.88.
Owner Charlie's Starrs **Bred** Darley **Trained** Hammerwood, E Sussex

FOCUS
Another moderate handicap. The time was identical to the first division and the form is similarly sound. The winner is rated to form at face value despite the worst draw.
T/Jkpt: Not won. T/Plt: £288.70 to a £1 stake. Pool: £99,901.74. 252.55 winning tickets. T/Qpdt: £5.80 to a £1 stake. Pool: £9,174.80. 1,168.39 winning tickets. JN

7791 SOUTHWELL (L-H)
Tuesday, December 22

OFFICIAL GOING: Standard to slow
Wind: Light half behind Weather: Bright and dry

7836 EUROPEAN BREEDERS' FUND MAIDEN STKS 7f (F)
12:25 (12:25) (Class 5) 2-Y-0 **£3,753** (£1,108; £554) **Stalls** Low

Form RPR

1 **Secretive** 2-9-3 0.............................. JoeFanning 5 77+
(M Johnston) *led 2f: sn rdn along and rn green 1/2-way: hdwy 2f out: led over 1f out: kpt on wl fnl f* **8/11**[1]

2 3 **Golden Tiger** 2-9-3 0.............................. PhillipMakin 4 69
(T P Tate) *trckd ldng pair: hdwy 3f out: rdn to chse wnr appr fnl f: sn no imp* **5/1**[3]

053 **3** 7 **Exearti**[11] 7708 2-8-5 62.............................. DeclanCannon(7) 9 46
(A J McCabe) *cl up: led after 2f: pushed along and qcknd clr wl over 2f out: rdn over 1f out: sn hdd & wknd* **4/1**[2]

4 10 **Blades Harmony** 2-9-3 0.............................. GrahamGibbons 7 26
(E S McMahon) *in tch: hdwy on outer to chse ldrs 3f out: rdn along over 2f out and sn outpcd* **17/2**

5 13 **Last Of The Ravens** 2-8-7 0.............................. MarkCoumbe(5) 1 —
(J F Coupland) *s.i.s: rn green and a bhd* **50/1**

6 6 **Clifton Kid (IRE)** 2-8-12 0.............................. BillyCray(5) 2 —
(R C Guest) *dwlt: a towards rr: outpcd and bhd fnl 3f* **33/1**

1m 33.42s (3.12) **Going Correction** +0.175s/f (Slow) **6** Ran SP% **110.0**
Speed ratings (Par 96): **89,85,77,66,51 44**
toteswinger:1&2:£1.70, 2&3:£1.70, 1&3:£1.80 CSF £4.58 TOTE £1.90: £1.20, £1.90; EX 5.40 Trifecta £13.70 Pool £244.20 - 13.13 winning units..
Owner Sheikh Hamdan Bin Mohammed Al Maktoum **Bred** T A Scothern **Trained** Middleham Moor, N Yorks

FOCUS
The track was worked overnight with temperatures getting down to -4C and the surface was described as riding standard to slow. This was an uncompetitive maiden, in which the 62-rated third probably didn't run up to her mark and so the race has been rated cautiously.

NOTEBOOK
Secretive, who was well backed, is a 60,000gns half-brother to, among others, smart sprinter Mystical Land. He looked in trouble when coming under pressure around the bend into the straight, but the leader dropped away and he stayed on well enough, despite hanging to his left. This performance couldn't be described as impressive, but the impression is that he's well regarded and there should be better to come. (op 4-5 tchd 4-6)
Golden Tiger's sales price dropped to just £2,600 earlier this year, the lowest amount he fetched from three public auctions. A half-brother to Night Kiss, a dual winner over 7f, he travelled okay to a point but ran on at only the one pace in the straight and this probably represents modest form. (op 7-1 tchd 9-2)
Exearti looked set to take a bit of catching when going strongly in the lead around the turn into the straight, but this was her first run beyond 6f and her stamina soon gave out. (tchd 7-2)
Blades Harmony ended up being beaten a long way, but this run wasn't without some promise as, having been very slowly away, he recovered into a challenging position, before simply getting tired. He's nicely enough bred, being a £30,000 half-brother to a 5f winner, out of a multiple sprinter scorer, and better can be expected. (op 6-1)

7837 BET TOTEPOOL TO SUPPORT YOUR SPORT H'CAP 7f (F)
12:55 (12:56) (Class 2) (0-100,103) 3-Y-0+ **£16,241** (£4,795; £2,399) **Stalls** Low

Form RPR

4112 **1** **Imprimis Tagula (IRE)**[9] 7741 5-7-11 **86** oh1........(v) DeclanCannon(7) 4 104
(A Bailey) *trckd ldrs: hdwy 1/2-way: led wl over 2f out: rdn clr over 1f out: styd on strly* **5/1**[3]

3112 **2** 9 **Ingleby Arch (USA)**[17] 7639 6-8-11 **93**.............................. PhillipMakin 7 87
(T D Barron) *chsd ldrs: hdwy over 2f out: rdn to chse wnr wl over 1f out: sn drvn and no imp* **7/2**[2]

0042 **3** 2¼ **Nightjar (USA)**[62] 6949 4-8-13 **95**.............................. NCallan 9 83
(K A Ryan) *dwlt: in tch on outer: hdwy 3f out: rdn along 2f out: sn drvn and kpt on same pce* **9/4**[1]

2024 **4** 4 **Eisteddfod**[124] 5196 8-9-7 **103**.............................. GeorgeBaker 5 80
(P F I Cole) *in tch: effrt and hdwy 3f out: sn rdn and kpt on same pce fnl 2f* **17/2**

0234 **5** ¾ **Indian Skipper (IRE)**[11] 7711 4-8-1 **88** oh1 ow2..........(be) BillyCray(5) 2 63
(R C Guest) *s.i.s and bhd: rdn along 1/2-way: hdwy on inner over 2f out: nvr nr ldrs* **28/1**

3005 **6** 4½ **Flowing Cape (IRE)**[17] 7639 4-8-3 **90**..............................(p) PaulPickard(5) 6 53
(R Hollinshead) *cl up: led 3f out: sn rdn and hdd: drvn and wknd 2f out* **12/1**

1000 **7** 2½ **My Gacho (IRE)**[73] 6678 7-8-8 **90**..............................(v) J-PGuillambert 8 46
(M Johnston) *hld up towards rr: sme hdwy wl over 2f out: sn rdn and btn* **14/1**

5301 **8** 1¾ **Snow Bay**[7] 7759 3-8-4 **82** 6ex..............................(v[1]) GregFairley 3 37
(B Smart) *t.k.h: led: rdn along and hdd 3f out: sn wknd* **6/1**

0013 **9** 13 **Appalachian Trail (IRE)**[23] 7588 8-8-10 **92**.............................. TomEaves 1 8
(N Wilson) *a towards rr: bhd and eased fnl 2f* **12/1**

1m 29.65s (-0.65) **Going Correction** +0.175s/f (Slow) **9** Ran SP% **120.0**
Speed ratings (Par 109): **110,99,97,92,91 86,83,81,66**
toteswinger:1&2:£6.90, 2&3:£3.00, 1&3:£3.80 CSF £23.87 CT £51.30 TOTE £6.60: £2.10, £1.40, £1.30; EX 25.20 Trifecta £44.20 Pool £496.21 - 8.30 winning units..
Owner Middleham Park Racing XLI & Alan Bailey **Bred** Glashare House Stud **Trained** Newmarket, Suffolk

FOCUS
Decent prizemoney looked to have attracted a good line-up, and a competitive race was expected, but the winner turned it into a procession. He produced a personal best but this is probably not form to go overboard about.

NOTEBOOK
Imprimis Tagula(IRE) ◆ absolutely bolted up. A regular in claimers not that long ago, for a while he didn't look an obvious improver, but he had disproved that theory with career-best RPRs on his last two starts, and he took another significant step forward with a taking display. It's true the deep conditions probably exaggerated the winning margin somewhat, but still, his recent profile means it's tempting to believe he is genuinely progressing into a very useful type on artificial surfaces and, while he faces a significant rise in the weights, on this evidence he'll at least be worthy of a rating somewhere in the mid-90s. Also he's already proven his versatility with regards trip and surface, and he could bid to defy a penalty back on Polytrack at Wolverhampton on Monday. Incidentally, the winner paid a nice compliment to Seek The Fair Land, who was unlucky at Kempton the previous day, and is the only horse to have beaten Imprimis Tagula on that one's last four starts. (op 7-2)
Ingleby Arch(USA) has only ever won over 6f, so this longer trip on a surface riding on the slow side couldn't have been considered ideal beforehand, but he ran well behind the improving winner. (op 5-1 tchd 10-3)
Nightjar(USA), sold out of Mark Johnston's yard for 25,000gns since he was last seen in October, was bidding to enhance a fine track record, including 3-3 over C&D, but while he ran creditably enough off a career-high mark, this did look a somewhat laboured effort. He has won on Fibresand described as standard to slow in the past, but racing wide throughout probably didn't help, and he's entitled to be sharper next time, so he could yet pick up a nice prize this winter. (op 5-2 tchd 11-4 in places)
Eisteddfod surprisingly had the blinkers removed for this first try on Fibresand, with all its kickback, and he failed to run to form. (op 8-1 tchd 9-1)
Indian Skipper(IRE) was soon driven along in a detached last after missing the break, and he looked set to stay there, so credit to Billy Cray, who put up 2lb overweight, for keeping at the gelding. Official explanation: jockey said gelding was never travelling
Snow Bay, 6lb higher than when winning over 1m around here on his previous start, was a bit free in first-time blinkers (didn't wear headgear last time) and dropped away in the straight. (op 15-2)

7838 TOTEPOOL OUR PROFITS STAY IN RACING H'CAP (DIV I) 5f (F)
1:25 (1:25) (Class 6) (0-60,64) 3-Y-0+ **£1,706** (£503; £252) **Stalls** High

Form RPR

0663 **1** **Mr Funshine**[11] 7710 4-8-4 **46** oh1.............................. HayleyTurner 9 56
(D Shaw) *trckd ldrs: hdwy whn hmpd over 1f out: rdn: squeezed through and edgd lft ent fnl f: drvn to ld last 75yds* **14/1**

2514 **2** hd **First Swallow**[14] 7680 4-9-3 **59**..............................(t) PhillipMakin 10 68
(D H Brown) *trckd ldrs: smooth hdwy to go cl up 1/2-way: rdn to ld and hung lft over 1f out: drvn and edgd lft ins fnl f: hdd and nt qckn last 75yds* **3/1**[1]

1504 **3** 2¼ **Rosie Says No**[17] 7645 4-8-11 **60**..............................(p) DeclanCannon(7) 4 61
(A J McCabe) *dwlt and squeezed out s: swtchd lft after 2f: hdwy on inner 2f out: sn rdn and kpt on ins fnl f: nrst fin* **14/1**

2161 **4** ½ **Thoughtsofstardom**[3] 7808 6-9-5 **64** 6ex.............................. KellyHarrison(3) 3 63
(P S McEntee) *prom: effrt 2f out: sn rdn and ev ch tl drvn and one pce ent fnl f* **4/1**[2]

0031 **5** nse **Best One**[11] 7710 5-8-13 **55**..............................(b) KevinGhunowa 6 54
(R A Harris) *led: rdn along 2f out: drvn and hdd over 1f out: grad wknd* **4/1**[2]

5056 **6** nk **Admiral Bond (IRE)**[11] 7710 4-8-3 **50** ow2..............................(p) PaulPickard(5) 5 48
(G R Oldroyd) *bhd and rdn along 1/2-way: styd on appr fnl f: nrst fin* **8/1**[3]

0000 **7** 1¾ **Ronnie Howe**[90] 6221 5-8-4 **46** oh1..............................(bt) LukeMorris 11 38
(S R Bowring) *dwlt and sn swtchd lft: hdwy 1/2-way: rdn along wl over 2f out: drvn and kpt on same pce ins fnl f* **33/1**

3054 **8** shd **Across The Sands**[18] 7629 3-8-11 **53**.............................. FrankieMcDonald 8 51+
(C N Kellett) *cl up: rdn 2f out: drvn and hld whn n.m.r and hmpd ent fnl f* **10/1**

0020 **9** *2* **Dancing Wave**[14] 7681 3-9-0 **59** RobertLButler(3) 2 43
(M C Chapman) *chsd ldrs: rdn along over 2f out: sn wknd* **20/1**

005 **10** *1 1/2* **Miss Pusey Street**[6] 7770 3-8-9 **51** ow2 (v) J-PGuillambert 1 30
(P D Evans) *cl up: rdn along 2f out: sn drvn and wknd* **14/1**

2500 **11** *2* **Fasliyanne (IRE)**[60] 6988 3-9-4 **60** (b) NCallan 12 31
(K A Ryan) *in tch towards outer: rdn along 1/2-way: sn wknd* **25/1**

-0U0 **12** *10* **Egyptian Lord**[11] 7710 6-8-4 **46** oh1 (b) GregFairley 7 —
(Peter Grayson) *cl up: rdn along 1/2-way: sn wknd* **66/1**

3000 **13** *9* **Northern Empire (IRE)**[13] 7682 6-9-2 **58** (p) JimmyQuinn 13 —
(F Jordan) *racd stands' rail: bhd fr 1/2-way* **20/1**

61.10 secs (1.40) **Going Correction** +0.275s/f (Slow) **13 Ran SP% 123.0**
Speed ratings (Par 101): **99,98,95,94,94 93,90,90,87,85 81,65,51**
toteswinger:1&2:£9.60, 2&3:£16.90, 1&3:£23.20 CSF £54.24 CT £650.33 TOTE £16.10: £4.50, £1.70, £5.60; EX 85.70 Trifecta £179.60 Part won. Pool £242.82 - 0.20 winning units..
Owner Unity Farm Holiday Centre Ltd **Bred** Unity Farm Holiday Centre Ltd **Trained** Sproxton, Leics

FOCUS
The winning time was 0.40 seconds slower than the second division but the form seems sound enough.
Across The Sands Official explanation: jockey said the colt hung very badly left

7839 TOTEPOOL OUR PROFITS STAY IN RACING H'CAP (DIV II) 5f (F)
1:55 (1:55) (Class 6) (0-60,60) 3-Y-0+ **£1,706** (£503; £252) **Stalls** High

Form RPR

0524 **1** **Pocket's Pick (IRE)**[21] 7606 3-9-4 **60** GeorgeBaker 4 72
(G L Moore) *in tch: smooth hdwy to trck ldrs 1/2-way: rdn to ld over 1f out: drvn and edgd rt ins fnl f: kpt on* **7/2**[2]

1103 **2** *1 1/2* **Metal Guru**[22] 7601 5-9-0 **59** (p) RussellKennemore(3) 10 66
(R Hollinshead) *trckd ldrs: led over 2f out: rdn and hdd over 1f out: swtchd lft and drvn ins fnl f: kpt on same pce* **15/2**[3]

6400 **3** *1/2* **Divertimenti (IRE)**[63] 6918 5-8-11 **53** ow1 (b) PhillipMakin 6 58
(S R Bowring) *in tch: hdwy 2f out: sn rdn and styd on to chse ldng pair ins fnl f: sn drvn and no imp* **17/2**

0445 **4** *1 3/4* **Hollow Jo**[14] 7681 9-9-4 **60** (v) ShaneKelly 1 59
(J R Jenkins) *wnt rt s: chsd ldrs on wd outside: rdn along 2f out: kpt on same pce appr fnl f* **8/1**

0030 **5** *hd* **Gower**[14] 7681 5-7-11 **46** oh1 (p) RachelKing(7) 3 44
(R J Price) *chsd ldrs: rdn along 2f out: sn drvn and kpt on same pce* **16/1**

-500 **6** *1/2* **Desert Dust**[11] 7709 6-8-1 **46** oh1 AndreaAtzeni(3) 5 42
(H J Collingridge) *chsd ldrs: rdn along 2f out: sn one pce* **8/1**

5616 **7** *2* **Spoof Master (IRE)**[16] 7651 5-9-0 **56** LPKeniry 11 45
(C R Dore) *cl up: rdn along 1/2-way: sn drvn and grad wknd* **11/1**

0055 **8** *1 1/4* **Berrymead**[11] 7710 4-8-9 **56** ow8 AnnStokell(5) 13 41
(Miss A Stokell) *rrd at s: a towards rr* **20/1**

0563 **9** *1* **Don Pele (IRE)**[3] 7815 7-9-4 **60** (p) TonyCulhane 2 41
(R A Harris) *dwlt and hmpd s: a in rr* **11/4**[1]

0-05 **10** *1 3/4* **Myriola**[11] 7714 4-8-4 **46** oh1 HayleyTurner 7 21
(D Shaw) *chsd ldrs: rdn along bef 1/2-way and sn wknd* **40/1**

6530 **11** *7* **Dodaa (USA)**[239] 1564 6-8-5 **54** ShirleyTeasdale(7) 9 4
(N Wilson) *led: rdn along 1/2-way: sn hdd & wknd* **33/1**

60.70 secs (1.00) **Going Correction** +0.275s/f (Slow) **11 Ran SP% 117.8**
Speed ratings (Par 101): **103,100,99,97,96 95,92,90,89,86 75**
toteswinger:1&2:£5.10, 2&3:£13.20, 1&3:£10.40 CSF £29.46 CT £212.78 TOTE £5.00: £1.70, £2.60, £3.60; EX 34.10 Trifecta £248.90 Part won. Pool £336.37 - 0.44 winning units..
Owner David & Jane George **Bred** John Cullinan **Trained** Lower Beeding, W Sussex

FOCUS
The pace was middle to stands' side, but the result suggests there was no major draw bias. This was a moderate handicap, although the time was 0.40 seconds quicker than the first division.
Hollow Jo Official explanation: jockey said the gelding hung right leaving the stalls
Berrymead Official explanation: jockey said he filly reared leaving the stalls
Don Pele(IRE) Official explanation: jockey said t the gelding attempted to anticipate the start but in so doing became unbalanced leaving the stalls, missed the break and was never travelling thereafter

7840 BET BRITISH WITH TOTEPOOL H'CAP 1m 4f (F)
2:25 (2:26) (Class 6) (0-60,60) 3-Y-0+ **£2,047** (£604; £302) **Stalls** Low

Form RPR

-005 **1** **Sunny Spells**[10] 7733 4-9-4 **58** WilliamCarson(3) 8 73
(S C Williams) *hld up in rr: hdwy 5f out: jnd ldrs over 3f out: rdn to chal over 2f out: drvn over 1f out: fnd ex u.p wl ins fnl f to ld nr fin* **7/1**

0233 **2** *nk* **Jackie Kiely**[17] 7635 8-8-12 **49** (tp) PhillipMakin 3 64
(R Brotherton) *hld up in tch: hdwy over 4f out: cl up 3f out: rdn to ld over 2f out: drvn over 1f out: edgd rt u.str.p ins fnl f: hdd and no ex nr fin* **5/1**[2]

1-12 **3** *8* **Holyfield Warrior (IRE)**[11] 7718 5-9-2 **60** KierenFox(7) 7 62
(R J Smith) *hld up towards rr: hdwy 1/2-way: led over 4f out: rdn along 3f out: hdd and drvn over 2f out: kpt on same pce* **12/1**

0001 **4** *8* **Jiggalong**[9] 7740 3-8-12 **57** 6ex RobertLButler(3) 14 46
(Jim Best) *stdd and swtchd lft s: hld up in rr: hdwy over 4f out: rdn to chse ldrs wl over 2f out: sn drvn and plugged on same pce* **25/1**

3500 **5** *8* **Russian Invader (IRE)**[13] 7635 5-9-1 **57** (be) BillyCray(5) 9 33
(R C Guest) *bhd: hdwy 4f out: sn rdn along and wd st: drvn 2f out and plugged on: nvr nr ldrs* **50/1**

3056 **6** *2* **Stravita**[8] 7751 5-9-4 **55** (p) GrahamGibbons 11 28
(R Hollinshead) *trckd ldrs: pushed along over 3f out: rdn wl over 2f out and sn outpcd* **6/1**[3]

3240 **7** *12* **Lady Florence**[18] 7632 4-9-9 **60** LPKeniry 5 14
(A B Coogan) *led 2f: prom tl rdn along 4f out: drvn over 3f out and sn wknd* **33/1**

0021 **8** *3 3/4* **Altos Reales**[10] 7733 5-8-13 **50** HayleyTurner 12 —
(M J Scudamore) *sn rdn along in rr: nvr a factor* **10/3**[1]

56-0 **9** *2 1/4* **April The Second**[14] 7677 5-8-10 **50** AndreaAtzeni(3) 10 —
(R J Price) *a towards rr* **40/1**

000 **10** *nk* **Colonel Sherman (USA)**[15] 7668 4-9-6 **57** LeeVickers 6 —
(P A Kirby) *chsd ldrs: rdn along over 4f out: sn wknd* **66/1**

05-2 **11** *17* **Jazrawy**[7] 7761 7-9-9 **60** ShaneKelly 2 —
(A J McCabe) *cl up: led briefly 1/2-way: rdn along and hdd 4f out: sn wknd* **14/1**

0-00 **12** *14* **Sir Kyffin's Folly**[28] 7505 4-9-8 **59** RichardThomas 1 —
(J A Geake) *a towards rr* **100/1**

0352 **13** *1* **Oke Bay**[161] 3954 3-8-13 **55** (v) JimCrowley 13 —
(R M Beckett) *prom: led after 2f: rdn along and hdd 1/2-way: sn wknd* **13/2**

2042 **14** *3 3/4* **Mekong Miss**[198] 2742 3-9-1 **57** LukeMorris 4 —
(J Jay) *chsd ldrs: rdn along over 5f out: sn wknd* **7/1**

2m 41.91s (0.91) **Going Correction** +0.175s/f (Slow)
WFA 3 from 4yo+ 5lb **14 Ran SP% 120.4**
Speed ratings (Par 101): **103,102,97,92,86 85,77,74,73,73 61,52,51,49**
toteswinger:1&2:£6.80, 2&3:£28.90, 1&3:£12.50 CSF £40.26 CT £422.99 TOTE £9.30: £2.50, £2.10, £4.60; EX 55.60 Trifecta £271.20 Pool £458.27 - 1.25 winning units..
Owner W E Enticknap **Bred** Whitsbury Manor Stud **Trained** Newmarket, Suffolk

FOCUS
The pace was much too fast in this moderate handicap, particularly with the surface riding deep. Unsurprisingly, those held up early on completely dominated, and they finished well strung out. The first two were clear.
Jazrawy Official explanation: jockey said the gelding ran flat
Sir Kyffin's Folly Official explanation: jockey said that the filly was never travelling
Mekong Miss Official explanation: trainer said that the filly was in season

7841 TOTEPOOL RACING'S BIGGEST SUPPORTER H'CAP 1m 3f (F)
2:55 (2:55) (Class 4) (0-85,85) 3-Y-0+ **£4,857** (£1,445; £722; £360) **Stalls** Low

Form RPR

6314 **1** **Full Toss**[5] 7789 3-9-8 **85** J-PGuillambert 5 92
(P D Evans) *hld up: hdwy to trck ldng pair over 4f out: rdn to chse ldr 3f out: drvn to chal on inner appr fnl f: styd on u.str driving to ld last 100yds* **4/1**[2]

5561 **2** *1/2* **Profit's Reality (IRE)**[10] 7724 7-9-5 **78** AdamKirby 3 84
(M J Attwater) *prom early: trckd ldr after 3f: led over 4f out: pushed clr 3f out: rdn wl over 1f out: drvn and jnd appr fnl f: sn edgd lft: hdd and no ex last 100yds* **5/4**[1]

-006 **3** *12* **Such Optimism**[130] 5009 3-9-7 **84** JimCrowley 1 70
(R M Beckett) *led 1f: trckd ldng pair: rdn along and wd st: sn drvn and plugged on same pce* **15/2**

-060 **4** *6* **Maria Di Scozia**[31] 7475 4-8-13 **72** (t) NCallan 6 48
(P W Chapple-Hyam) *led after 1f: rdn along and hdd over 4f out: sn drvn and wknd 3f out* **11/2**[3]

13 **5** *1 1/2* **Gunslinger (FR)**[18] 7628 4-9-5 **78** SJCraine 4 51
(M J Scudamore) *hld up in rr: effrt and sme hdwy 4f out: rdn along over 3f out and nvr a factor* **4/1**[2]

2m 29.06s (1.06) **Going Correction** +0.175s/f (Slow)
WFA 3 from 4yo+ 4lb **5 Ran SP% 111.6**
Speed ratings (Par 105): **103,102,93,89,88**
toteswinger:1&2:£4.00 CSF £9.67 TOTE £4.80: £2.30, £1.10; EX 9.10.
Owner J L Guillambert **Bred** The Queen **Trained** Pandy, Monmouths

FOCUS
A fair handicap run at an ordinary pace. The winner is rated in line with his 3yo best and the runner-up to his latest win here, the pair clear.

7842 SOUTHWELL GOLF CLUB H'CAP 1m 6f (F)
3:25 (3:29) (Class 6) (0-65,65) 3-Y-0+ **£2,047** (£604; £302) **Stalls** Low

Form RPR

5402 **1** **Dart**[17] 7642 5-9-4 **55** AndrewMullen 9 68
(Mrs S Lamyman) *hld up in midfield: stdy hdwy 5f out: trckd ldrs 4f out: rdn to chal wl over 2f out: drvn to ld over 1f out: styd on wl towards fin* **3/1**[2]

0001 **2** *2 1/2* **Merrion Tiger (IRE)**[17] 7635 4-9-8 **59** GregFairley 12 68
(A G Foster) *prom: hdwy to ld over 4f out: rdn along wl ovedr 2f out: drvn and hdd over 1f out: kpt on same pce ins fnl f* **5/2**[1]

/053 **3** *1/2* **Dawn Storm (IRE)**[17] 7649 4-8-8 **48** (b[1]) KellyHarrison(3) 13 56
(J L Spearing) *trckd ldrs: hdwy over 4f out: cl up 3f out: rdn and ev ch over 2f out: sn drvn and one pce appr fnl f* **10/1**

5335 **4** *13* **They All Laughed**[35] 7425 6-9-3 **54** PhillipMakin 4 44
(Mrs Marjorie Fife) *stmbld s and rdr lost iron: hld up in rr: hdwy 4f out: rdn along to chse ldrs over 2f out: sn drvn and no imp* **3/1**[2]

001 **5** *3 1/4* **Dazzling Begum**[10] 7732 4-9-2 **53** RobertHavlin 8 39
(J Pearce) *trckd ldrs: effrt 4f out: rdn along over 3f out: drvn wl over 2f out and sn btn* **12/1**

5500 **6** *5* **Free Falling**[15] 7660 3-8-2 **46** oh1 (tp) JimmyQuinn 11 25
(A J Lidderdale) *in tch: effrt and chsd ldrs 1/2-way: rdn along over 4f out and grad wknd* **40/1**

3/2- **7** *6* **Drizzi (IRE)**[343] 3328 8-9-6 **60** (tp) RobertLButler(3) 1 30
(Jim Best) *hld up in rr: hdwy 4f out: rdn along and in tch 3f out: sn drvn and btn* **33/1**

000/ **8** *5* **Mustakhlas (USA)**[311] 7172 8-8-9 **46** oh1 GrahamGibbons 14 9
(B P J Baugh) *led 2f: chsd ldrs tl rdn and wknd over 4f out* **66/1**

3004 **9** *44* **Flirty (IRE)**[33] 7455 3-7-13 **46** oh1 AndreaAtzeni(3) 6 —
(Rae Guest) *a in rr: bhd fnl 3f* **33/1**

0202 **10** *7* **Stormy Summer**[11] 7712 4-9-7 **65** (b) TobyAtkinson(7) 2 —
(R W Price) *cl up: led after 2f: rdn along and hdd over 4f out: sn wknd* **17/2**[3]

11 *3* **Games (IRE)**[19] 5534 8-8-9 **46** oh1 (p) FrankieMcDonald 5 —
(C N Kellett) *a in rr: lost tch 1/2-way: sn t.o* **100/1**

3m 10.14s (1.84) **Going Correction** +0.175s/f (Slow)
WFA 3 from 4yo+ 7lb **11 Ran SP% 116.7**
Speed ratings (Par 101): **101,99,99,91,90 87,83,80,55,51 50**
toteswinger:1&2:£3.50, 2&3:£4.60, 1&3:£5.80 CSF £10.52 CT £65.44 TOTE £4.50: £1.70, £1.40, £2.60; EX 12.30 Trifecta £138.00 Pool £835.78 - 4.48 winning units. Place 6 £41.11, Place 5 £30.15.
Owner Mrs S Lamyman **Bred** St Clare Hall Stud **Trained** Ruckland, Lincs

FOCUS
A moderate handicap. It was soundly run and the first three finished well clear. The first two look on good marks but it is probably best not to take this form too literally.
Stormy Summer Official explanation: jockey said that the gelding lost its action
T/Jkpt: Not won. T/Plt: £30.40 to a £1 stake. Pool: £143,096.00. 3,435.31 winning tickets. T/Qpdt: £17.70 to a £1 stake. Pool: £12,501.57. 520.08 winning tickets. JR

7812 WOLVERHAMPTON (A.W) (L-H)
Saturday, December 26

OFFICIAL GOING: Standard
Wind: Light half behind Weather: Sunny

7843 BET TOTEPOOL AT TOTESPORT.COM MAIDEN STKS 5f 20y(P)
1:45 (1:45) (Class 5) 2-Y-0 **£3,885** (£1,156; £577; £288) **Stalls** Low

Form RPR

5 **1** **Clifton Bridge**[13] 7736 2-9-3 **0** RichardKingscote 5 79
(R M Beckett) *led: narrowly hdd 3f out: led 2f out: rdn jst ins fnl f: drvn out* **6/1**[3]

2 1 1/4 **Praesepe** 2-8-12 0 LiamJones 4 69+
(W J Haggas) *mid-div: pushed along over 3f out: hdwy wl over 1f out: r.o to take 2nd ins fnl f: nt trble wnr* **10/11**[1]

2303 3 2 **Texas Queen**[64] 7001 2-8-12 72 TonyCulhane 9 62
(M R Channon) *w wnr: slt ld 3f out to 2f out: rdn over 1f out: no ex and lost 2nd ins fnl f* **3/1**[2]

5 4 3 1/4 **American Agent (USA)**[7] 7806 2-9-3 0 MartinDwyer 1 55
(P F I Cole) *prom tl rdn and wknd 1f out* **10/1**

0035 5 nse **Future Regime (IRE)**[29] 7559 2-8-12 56 ShaneKelly 2 50
(Patrick Morris) *s.i.s: in rr: pushed along over 3f out: rdn wl over 1f out: styng on whn edgd lft ins fnl f: n.d* **25/1**

5 6 3 **Final Turn**[38] 7436 2-9-3 0 FrankieMcDonald 7 44
(H Candy) *hld up towards rr: pushed along and hdwy over 2f out: wknd over 1f out* **12/1**

0000 7 4 **Rightcar Marian**[9] 7778 2-8-12 40 TomEaves 8 25
(Peter Grayson) *hld up in rr: sme prog on ins over 2f out: rdn and wknd fnl f* **100/1**

0506 8 6 **Wild Heather**[12] 7749 2-8-12 49 GregFairley 6 3
(J R Holt) *bhd fnl 3f* **100/1**

9 2 3/4 **Aurora Lights** 2-8-5 0 LeeTopliss(7) 3 —
(R A Fahey) *chsd ldrs: pushed along over 3f out: hung rt bnd over 2f out: sn wknd* **20/1**

63.08 secs (0.78) **Going Correction** +0.10s/f (Slow) 9 Ran SP% **119.0**
Speed ratings (Par 96): **97,95,91,86,86 81,75,65,61**
toteswingers: 1&2 £6.00, 1&3 £2.40, 2&3 £2.00 CSF £12.05 TOTE £7.20: £2.20, £1.10, £1.20; EX 16.30 Trifecta £54.30 Pool: £293.71 - 4 winning units..
Owner Landmark Racing Limited **Bred** D K Ivory **Trained** Whitsbury, Hants

FOCUS
An ordinary juvenile maiden.

NOTEBOOK
Clifton Bridge improved on the form he showed on his debut over 6f at Kempton with a straightforward victory, finding plenty for pressure having travelled just about best early on. He should make a fair handicapper. (op 4-1)
Praesepe ◆ is a sister to high-class sprinter Enticing, out of the really smart juvenile Superstar Leo. She ended up too far back after losing her place when slightly short of room at the first bend, and was always struggling thereafter, but she ran on nicely in the straight without being given a hard time. Better can be expected. (op 7-4)
Texas Queen showed plenty of speed from her wide draw on this drop in trip and had her chance, but she wasn't good enough. She's not progressing. (op 11-4)
American Agent(USA) dropped away disappointingly in the straight and seemed to run below the form he showed over 7f on his debut. (op 9-1 tchd 8-1)
Future Regime(IRE) again started slowly and soon needed stern remainders to take an interest. She made some late progress, but was never seen with a chance and looks in need of both a longer trip and headgear. (op 20-1)

7844 CE RISK, SAFETY & SECURITY NOVICE STKS 1m 141y(P)
2:15 (2:16) (Class 5) 2-Y-O £3,885 (£1,156; £577; £288) Stalls Low

Form RPR

1 **Dubai Bounty** 2-8-3 0 NickyMackay 5 66+
(G A Butler) *hld up: prog on outside over 2f out: pushed along wl over 1f out: rdn to ld wl ins fnl f: r.o* **11/4**[3]

0 2 nk **Lovers Causeway (USA)**[104] 5907 2-8-12 0 GregFairley 2 74
(M Johnston) *bmpd s: sn led: rdn wl over 1f out: hdd wl ins fnl f: kpt on* **15/8**[1]

1 3 1 **Sweet Child O'Mine**[14] 7721 2-9-0 69 TomEaves 1 74
(R C Guest) *wnt rt s: led early: chsd ldr: ev ch over 2f out: rdn over 1f out: nt qckn wl ins fnl f* **2/1**[2]

0 4 6 **Yorksters Prince (IRE)**[71] 6810 2-8-12 0 JimmyQuinn 3 59
(M G Quinlan) *hld up: rdn jst over 2f out: btn wl over 1f out* **13/2**

1m 52.42s (1.92) **Going Correction** +0.10s/f (Slow) 4 Ran SP% **108.1**
Speed ratings (Par 96): **95,94,93,88**
CSF £8.17 TOTE £3.90; EX 12.40.
Owner The Distaff 2 Partnership **Bred** A S Denniff **Trained** Newmarket, Suffolk

FOCUS
In the absence of Awesome Act, who would have been long odds-on, this was an open novice event and the form looks fair.

NOTEBOOK
Dubai Bounty, a 50,000gns first foal of a quite useful dual 5f winner, travelled nicely for much of the way before picking up well for pressure. She looked a little green in the latter stages, so there should be improvement forthcoming. (op 3-1 tchd 5-2)
Lovers Causeway(USA) ◆ is a big colt with a long stride and, allowed to dominate, he stepped up significantly on the form he showed on his only previous start around three months earlier. There was plenty to like about the way he stuck on when headed and there should be more to come. (op 9-4 tchd 11-4)
Sweet Child O'Mine found this tougher than the Fibresand maiden she won on debut, when 100-1. (op 5-4)
Yorksters Prince(IRE) didn't show much on his return from over two months off and an entry in a claimer next week suggests he's not up to much. (op 12-1 tchd 11-2)

7845 BIGTIPS.CO.UK FOR FREE BETS AND TIPS CLAIMING STKS 7f 32y(P)
2:50 (2:50) (Class 6) 3-Y-O+ £2,729 (£806; £403) Stalls High

Form RPR

0200 1 **Red Somerset (USA)**[9] 7789 6-9-5 82 GeorgeBaker 9 80
(R J Hodges) *hld up in mid-div: pushed along over 2f out: rdn and hdwy on outside whn swtchd rt over 1f out: led wl ins fnl f: r.o* **3/1**[2]

0430 2 1 1/2 **Bahamian Kid**[28] 7577 4-9-5 66 (v) AdamKirby 8 76
(R Hollinshead) *hld up towards rr: swtchd lft and hdwy on ins 2f out: rdn and ev ch wl ins fnl f: nt qckn* **14/1**

20 3 shd **Geezers Colours**[19] 7662 4-8-11 75 AndrewElliott 2 68
(J R Weymes) *a.p: led over 2f out: rdn wl over 1f out: hdd ins fnl f: nt qckn towards fin* **12/1**[3]

3031 4 shd **Trade Centre**[17] 7691 4-8-6 72 MatthewDavies(5) 7 67
(George Baker) *a.p: rdn to ld ins fnl f: sn hdd: nt qckn* **11/4**[1]

4004 5 4 1/2 **Imperial Skylight**[20] 7653 3-8-7 52 (v) NickyMackay 6 51
(M R Channon) *prom: lost pl bnd after 1f: hdwy over 2f out: rdn wl over 1f out: wknd ins fnl f* **25/1**

0022 6 5 **Desert Dreamer (IRE)**[8] 7801 8-9-0 79 RichardEvans(5) 10 50
(P D Evans) *n.m.r s: hld up in rr: pushed along over 3f out: rdn over 1f out: nvr nr ldrs* **3/1**[2]

0540 7 7 **Decameron (USA)**[43] 7362 4-9-5 71 (p) GregFairley 3 31
(R A Harris) *led: pushed along and hdd over 2f out: rdn and wknd wl over 1f out* **12/1**[3]

4642 8 3 1/4 **Mocha Java**[18] 7679 6-8-5 59 (b) KevinGhunowa 11 8
(Matthew Salaman) *chsd ldr after 1f tl pushed along over 2f out: wknd wl over 1f out* **16/1**

0255 9 nk **Goodbye Cash (IRE)**[14] 7729 5-7-7 59 KevinLundie(7) 12 2
(P D Evans) *prom tl rdn and wknd 3f out* **16/1**

4000 10 20 **Give Us A Song (USA)**[17] 7693 3-8-5 57 (p) LukeMorris 4 —
(J S Moore) *s.i.s: sn hld up in mid-div: rdn over 3f out: bhd fnl 2f* **50/1**

1m 29.61s (0.01) **Going Correction** +0.10s/f (Slow) 10 Ran SP% **116.3**
Speed ratings (Par 101): **103,101,101,101,95 90,82,78,78,55**
toteswingers: 1&2 £7.70, 1&3 £9.40, 2&3 £28.20 CSF £44.57 TOTE £3.90: £1.50, £4.00, £3.70; EX 47.10 TRIFECTA Not won..Trade Centre was claimed by Mr R. A. Harris for £8,000.
Owner R J Hodges **Bred** Haras D'Etreham **Trained** Charlton Mackrell, Somerset

FOCUS
A good claimer, although the leaders seemed to go off a bit too fast.

7846 BET TOTEPOOL ON 0800 221 221 NURSERY 7f 32y(P)
3:20 (3:21) (Class 4) (0-85,83) 2-Y-O £5,677 (£1,699; £849; £424; £211) Stalls High

Form RPR

21 1 **Wellmarked (IRE)**[23] 7618 2-9-2 78 ShaneKelly 7 87
(John A Quinn, Ire) *hld up and bhd: hdwy on outside 2f out: led over 1f out: sn rdn: edgd rt cl home: drvn out* **9/2**[2]

0005 2 2 1/2 **Itsthursdayalready**[117] 5526 2-8-10 72 J-PGuillambert 4 75
(J G Given) *hld up and bhd: rdn and r.o to take 2nd towards fin: nt trble wnr* **20/1**

3231 3 1 1/4 **Licence To Till (USA)**[10] 7773 2-9-7 83 GregFairley 6 83
(M Johnston) *chsd ldr: led wl over 1f out: sn hdd and rdn: no ex and lost 2nd towards fin* **10/11**[1]

0434 4 3/4 **Slip Sliding Away (IRE)**[22] 7625 2-7-8 63 RyanPowell(7) 5 61
(J R Best) *hld up in tch: rdn 2f out: nt clr run wl over 1f out: one pce fnl f* **8/1**

3030 5 2 1/2 **Craicattack (IRE)**[82] 6541 2-9-0 76 LukeMorris 3 68
(J S Moore) *hld up in tch: rdn wl over 1f out: wknd ins fnl f* **25/1**

5153 6 1 3/4 **Transfixed (IRE)**[9] 7786 2-8-12 79 RichardEvans(5) 1 67
(P D Evans) *prom: pushed along over 2f out: rdn and wknd wl over 1f out* **12/1**

2242 7 7 **Quaker Parrot**[35] 7494 2-9-4 80 RichardKingscote 2 60
(Tom Dascombe) *led: rdn and hdd wl over 1f out: wknd and eased ins fnl f* **5/1**[3]

1m 30.01s (0.41) **Going Correction** +0.10s/f (Slow) 7 Ran SP% **114.6**
Speed ratings (Par 98): **101,98,96,95,93 91,83**
toteswingers: 1&2 £11.30, 1&3 £2.00, 2&3 £4.60 CSF £81.05 TOTE £6.70: £2.90, £5.40; EX 123.30.
Owner Charles McGrath **Bred** Charlie McGrath **Trained** Blackmiller Hill, Co. Kildare

FOCUS
A fair nursery.

NOTEBOOK
Wellmarked(IRE), successful in a 6f maiden around here on his previous start, followed up with a useful performance. A progressive sort, he's clearly one to keep onside. (op 8-1)
Itsthursdayalready was trying his furthest trip to date after nearly four months off and ran encouragingly behind the improving winner, who got first run. (op 16-1)
Licence To Till(USA) won a maiden by 8l at Lingfield last time, but this much tougher as he was 11lb higher than when running third on his only previous start in a nursery. Although a beaten favourite, this was a creditable enough effort considering he fared best of those to race on the pace. (op Evens tchd 11-10)
Slip Sliding Away(IRE) was short of room at the top of the straight, but he was by no means unlucky. (op 6-1)
Craicattack(IRE) failed to prove his stamina, but he might come on for this having been off for 82 days. (tchd 33-1)
Quaker Parrot seemed to go off plenty quick enough, but even so she was still very disappointing. (op 11-2 tchd 9-2)

7847 BIGGER "WIN ONLY" ODDS AT TOTESPORT.COM H'CAP 1m 4f 50y(P)
3:55 (3:55) (Class 5) (0-75,72) 3-Y-O+ £3,784 (£1,132; £566; £283; £141) Stalls Low

Form RPR

0331 1 **Kames Park (IRE)**[17] 7687 7-8-7 60 BillyCray(5) 9 66
(R C Guest) *dwlt: hld up in rr: c wd st: hdwy wl over 1f out: carried hd high and led ins fnl f: drvn out* **5/1**[3]

3604 2 nk **Little Richard (IRE)**[14] 7732 10-8-7 55 oh2 (p) LiamJones 7 61
(M Wellings) *hld up: pushed along over 2f out: hdwy wl over 1f out: rdn and sustained chal ins fnl f: kpt on* **8/1**

/010 3 3/4 **Mexican Bob**[44] 5530 6-9-1 63 AdamKirby 2 67
(C E Longsdon) *hld up in tch: rdn and ev ch ins fnl f: nt qckn* **5/1**[3]

2124 4 hd **Oriental Cavalier**[12] 7752 3-9-5 72 (p) GrahamGibbons 6 76
(R Hollinshead) *hld up in tch: rdn to ld wl over 1f out: hdd ins fnl f: nt qckn* **4/1**[2]

0612 5 2 3/4 **Barbirolli**[64] 5210 7-8-7 55 LukeMorris 8 55
(W B Stone) *hld up: pushed along and hdwy on ins wl over 1f out: sn rdn: wknd ins fnl f* **20/1**

1654 6 2 1/2 **Venir Rouge**[18] 7677 5-9-1 63 KevinGhunowa 5 59
(Matthew Salaman) *chsd ldr: rdn and ev ch wl over 1f out: wknd ent fnl f* **11/4**[1]

0053 7 13 **Active Asset (IRE)**[14] 7733 7-8-11 59 MartinDwyer 4 34
(J A Glover) *led: pushed along and hdd wl over 1f out: sn rdn and wknd* **5/1**[3]

2m 42.65s (1.55) **Going Correction** +0.10s/f (Slow)
WFA 3 from 5yo+ 5lb 7 Ran SP% **112.5**
Speed ratings (Par 103): **98,97,97,97,95 93,85**
toteswingers: 1&2 £6.80, 1&3 £3.90, 2&3 £5.40 CSF £41.86 CT £207.74 TOTE £4.90: £3.00, £2.70; EX 47.00 Trifecta £291.00 Pool: £393.36 - 1 winning unit..
Owner Future Racing (Notts) Limited **Bred** Pat Beirne **Trained** Stainforth, S Yorks

FOCUS
The pace seemed honest enough, but the runners were still well bunched at the top of the straight and this was an ordinary handicap.

7848 BEST ODDS GUARANTEED AT TOTESPORT.COM H'CAP 1m 1f 103y(P)
4:25 (4:25) (Class 4) (0-85,85) 3-Y-O+ £6,308 (£1,888; £944; £472; £235) Stalls Low

Form RPR

0100 1 **Scamperdale**[17] 7684 7-9-2 83 TonyCulhane 1 92
(B P J Baugh) *led early: hld up in tch: rdn over 1f out: led ins fnl f: drvn out* **9/1**

0641 2 nk **Confidentiality (IRE)**[10] 7775 5-9-2 83 NickyMackay 3 91
(M Wigham) *hld up in mid-div: pushed along and hdwy wl over 1f out: rdn and r.o wl to take 2nd nr fin* **6/1**

2110 3 nk **Iron Out (USA)**[10] 7775 3-8-7 81 PaulPickard(5) 4 89
(R Hollinshead) *sn chsng ldr: ev ch over 2f out: sn rdn: kpt on towards fin* **10/1**

0405 4 1/2 **Supercast (IRE)**[61] 7048 6-8-4 71 oh1 LukeMorris 7 78
(N J Vaughan) *sn led: rdn wl over 1f out: hdd ins fnl f: no ex cl home* **16/1**

-141 **5** *1 1/2* **Plush**[22] 7633 6-8-10 **82** .... RossAtkinson(5) 8 86
(Tom Dascombe) *s.i.s: hld up in rr: pushed along wl over 2f out: rdn wl over 1f out: r.o ins fnl f: nrst fin* **7/2**[1]
2315 **6** *shd* **Snow Dancer (IRE)**[28] 7583 5-8-8 **75** .... TomEaves 12 78
(H A McWilliams) *sn hld up in tch: pushed along over 2f out: rdn and wknd 1f out* **18/1**
6023 **7** *1* **Indy Driver**[17] 7684 4-8-11 **78** ....(p) MartinDwyer 2 79
(Matthew Salaman) *hld up in mid-div: pushed along and sme prog wl over 1f out: rdn and fdd ins fnl f* **4/1**[2]
5134 **8** *1/2* **Just Bond (IRE)**[14] 7734 7-9-4 **85** .... JimmyQuinn 13 85
(G R Oldroyd) *hld up towards rr: rdn over 1f out: nvr nr ldrs* **10/1**
1223 **9** *1 1/4* **Traphalgar (IRE)**[10] 7775 4-8-10 **77** .... J-PGuillambert 10 75
(P D Evans) *hld up towards rr: pushed along wl over 1f out: no rspnse* **9/2**[3]
0054 **10** *1* **Bolodenka (IRE)**[7] 7812 7-8-10 **82** ....(t) BMcHugh(5) 9 77
(R A Fahey) *hld up towards rr: pushed along over 2f out: rdn wl over 1f out: no rspnse* **18/1**

2m 3.77s (2.07) **Going Correction** +0.10s/f (Slow)
WFA 3 from 4yo+ 2lb **10** Ran SP% **119.3**
Speed ratings (Par 105): **94,93,93,93,91 91,90,90,89,88**
toteswingers: 1&2 £14.10, 1&3 £15.00, 2&3 £15.70 CSF £63.62 CT £560.46 TOTE £10.00: £2.90, £2.20, £3.50; EX 47.90 Trifecta £514.20 Pool: £514.20 - 1.10 winning units. Place 6 £237.07, Place 5 £237.31.
Owner Saddle Up Racing **Bred** Mrs J A Prescott **Trained** Audley, Staffs

FOCUS
A fair handicap, but they went just an ordinary gallop.
T/Plt: £5,812.60 to a £1 stake. Pool: £66,885.73. 8.40 winning tickets. T/Qpdt: £1,327.00 to a £1 stake. Pool: £4,841.80. 4841.80 winning tickets. KH

7836 SOUTHWELL (L-H)
Sunday, December 27

OFFICIAL GOING: Standard to slow
Wind: Fresh half behind Weather: Ovecast

7849 BET TOTEPOOL ON ALL UK RACING NURSERY 6f (F)
12:10 (12:11) (Class 5) (0-75,70) 2-Y-O **£2,729** (£806; £403) **Stalls** Low

Form RPR
3606 **1** **Flow Chart (IRE)**[87] 6409 2-9-0 **63** ....(b) PhillipMakin 7 70
(T D Barron) *in rr: gd hdwy on outer over 2f out: rdn to chse ldr wl over 1f out: chal appr fnl f: styd on to ld ins fnl f: sn edgd lft and kpt on* **11/4**[1]
0051 **2** *1 3/4* **The Love Guru**[12] 7757 2-8-11 **60** ....(b) NickyMackay 5 62
(J R Boyle) *cl up: led 1/2-way: rdn clr 2f out: jnd and drvn over 1f out: hdd ins fnl f and kpt on same pce* **11/4**[1]
2041 **3** *2 3/4* **Lord Victor**[12] 7756 2-9-1 **64** .... ShaneKelly 2 58
(A J McCabe) *led to 1/2-way: cl up: rdn along wl over 2f out: drvn wl over 1f out and kpt on same pce* **4/1**[2]
0005 **4** *1 1/2* **Lady Brickhouse**[46] 7331 2-8-0 **51** oh1 ow2 .... LukeMorris 3 38
(M D Squance) *trckd ldrs: hdwy 3f out: rdn over 2f out: sn drvn and kpt on same pce* **14/1**
0640 **5** *9* **Rightcar**[12] 7757 2-8-4 **53** .... FrankieMcDonald 6 15
(Peter Grayson) *half rrd s: t.k.h and in tch: rdn along over 3f out: drvn over 2f out and sn wknd* **33/1**
2031 **6** *3/4* **Silver Linnet (IRE)**[82] 6555 2-9-7 **70** .... AdamKirby 4 30
(M G Quinlan) *hld up in tch: effrt 3f out: sn rdn and outpcd fnl 2f* **9/2**[3]
2003 **7** *13* **Emma Jean Lass (IRE)**[9] 7799 2-9-2 **65** .... J-PGuillambert 1 —
(P D Evans) *chsd ldrs: rdn along 3f out: drvn over 2f out and sn wknd* **10/1**

1m 18.18s (1.68) **Going Correction** +0.125s/f (Slow) **7** Ran SP% **110.2**
Speed ratings (Par 96): **93,90,87,85,73 72,54**
toteswingers: 1&2 £2.40, 1&3 £3.40, 2&3 £1.50. CSF £9.55 TOTE £3.90: £2.10, £2.00; EX 11.40.
Owner J Starbuck **Bred** John Starbuck **Trained** Maunby, N Yorks
■ Stewards' Enquiry : Luke Morris caution: use of whip

FOCUS
The track was riding slow according to the winning jockey in the first and the time was nearly four seconds above standard. Decent nursery form for the modest grade.

NOTEBOOK
Flow Chart(IRE), for whom there was market support, rewarded his backers with what was in the end a fairly cosy win, coming from last place to run down the leader inside the last. The return of blinkers following a break seemed to help, and he handled the surface well at his first attempt. This looks his optimum trip for now. (op 9-2)
The Love Guru went up 10lb after his win over course and distance earlier this month. In front by halfway, he tried hard but was put in his place in the final furlong. (op 9-4)
Lord Victor's recent win here came in a 7f seller. Driven from the stalls to lead in an attempt to replicate his winning tactics, he was soon headed and he could not race on with the first two in the straight. (op 5-1)
Lady Brickhouse, who was 3lb wrong all told, again showed a hint of ability. (op 16-1)
Silver Linnet(IRE), 10lb higher than when winning a 5f Catterick nursery on her final outing for Tim Easterby, had the blinkers left off and was always in rear up in trip on this Fibresand debut. (op 4-1 tchd 5-1)
Emma Jean Lass(IRE) weakened quickly under pressure in the straight on her second start for this yard and first try on the surface. (op 6-1)

7850 BET TOTEPOOL ON ALL IRISH RACING (S) STKS 5f (F)
12:40 (12:40) (Class 6) 2-Y-O **£2,047** (£604; £302) **Stalls** High

Form RPR
6212 **1** **Bubbly Bellini (IRE)**[13] 7749 2-8-12 75 ....(p) MatthewDavies(5) 1 76
(George Baker) *cl up: led over 3f out: rdn and hung lft over 1f out: drvn ins fnl f: kpt on* **2/1**[2]
0120 **2** *1* **Star Promise**[72] 6827 2-8-7 76 .... DeanHeslop(5) 4 67
(T D Barron) *cl up: pushed along 1/2-way: sn rdn: drvn to chse wnr ent fnl f: kpt on same pce* **1/1**[1]
4230 **3** *3 1/2* **Tamarind Hill (IRE)**[8] 7805 2-8-12 67 ....(b) RobertWinston 2 55
(A J McCabe) *sn led: hdd over 3f out: rdn over 2f out: drvn wl over 1f out and kpt on same pce* **7/2**[3]
00 **4** *46* **Stoneacre Joe (IRE)**[36] 7485 2-8-12 0 .... LPKeniry 3 —
(Peter Grayson) *cl up: rdn along bef 1/2-way and sn wknd* **50/1**

60.08 secs (0.38) **Going Correction** 0.0s/f (Stan) **4** Ran SP% **107.5**
Speed ratings (Par 94): **96,94,88,—**
CSF £4.37 TOTE £3.10; EX 4.50.The winner was bought in for 4,750gns.
Owner Mrs C E S Baker **Bred** J P Hand **Trained** Moreton Morrell, Warwicks

FOCUS
An ordinary seller but a clear personal best from the winner.

NOTEBOOK
Bubbly Bellini(IRE) made a winning debut for George Baker, having been claimed from Alan Bailey after a narrow defeat in this grade at Wolverhampton. He made most of the running and stayed on well despite hanging a little to his left under pressure. A return to 6f will not bother him. (op 9-4)
Star Promise, the winner of a C&D maiden three starts back and dropped in grade here, was the one to beat on these terms. She chased the winner hard through the final furlong but could never quite get to grips with him. (tchd 11-10)
Tamarind Hill(IRE), previously with Charles Egerton, was left behind by the first two from the furlong pole. He was further behind today's winner than he had been at Wolverhampton on the same terms over 6f two starts back. (tchd 10-3)
Stoneacre Joe(IRE) has now finished a tailed-off last on all three starts. (op 40-1)

7851 SHERWOOD MARQUEES H'CAP 1m 3f (F)
1:10 (1:10) (Class 5) (0-75,79) 3-Y-O+ **£2,729** (£806; £403) **Stalls** Low

Form RPR
1450 **1** **Trachonitis (IRE)**[55] 7212 5-8-12 **67** .... ShaneKelly 2 76
(J R Jenkins) *hld up in rr: stdy hdwy over 4f out: trckd ldrs 3f out: smooth hdwy to chal over 1f out: led on bit ins fnl f 100yds: cheekily* **9/1**
1121 **2** *1/2* **Desert Vision**[9] 7798 5-9-10 **79** ....(vt) PhillipMakin 8 87
(M W Easterby) *hld up in tch: smooth hdwy over 4f out: led over 2f out: rdn over 1f out: jnd and drvn ent fnl f: hdd last 100yds* **2/1**[1]
0461 **3** *7* **Dream In Blue**[12] 7761 4-8-10 **65** ....(p) RobertWinston 3 61
(J A Glover) *chsd ldng pair: hdwy 3f out: rdn along over 2f out: drvn wl over 1f out: sn wknd* **7/1**
1040 **4** *2 3/4* **Eseej (USA)**[44] 7373 4-9-3 **72** .... LukeMorris 5 63
(P W Hiatt) *led: hung rt and pushed along bnd over 4f out: rdn over 3f out: hdd over 2f out: sn drvn and wknd wl over 1f out* **10/3**[2]
0032 **5** *1 1/4* **Mister Frosty (IRE)**[9] 7794 3-7-9 **61** oh9 .... CharlotteKerton(7) 7 50
(G Prodromou) *chsd ldr: rdn along 3f out: drvn 2f out and grad wknd* **11/1**
3523 **6** *25* **Resplendent Ace (IRE)**[12] 7760 5-9-3 **72** .... J-PGuillambert 6 19
(P Howling) *chsd ldrs: rdn along over 4f out and sn wknd* **4/1**[3]
0500 **7** *15* **Applaude**[8] 7817 4-8-1 **61** oh3 ....(be) BillyCray(5) 1 —
(R C Guest) *a in rr: rdn along and detached bef 1/2-way: t.o fnl 3f* **25/1**
1600 **8** *3 3/4* **Monfils Monfils (USA)**[25] 6769 7-8-5 **63** .... KellyHarrison(3) 4 —
(R E Barr) *chsd ldrs: rdn along and lost pl 5f out: sn bhd and t.o fnl 3f* **33/1**

2m 27.13s (-0.87) **Going Correction** +0.125s/f (Slow)
WFA 3 from 4yo+ 4lb **8** Ran SP% **114.0**
Speed ratings (Par 103): **108,107,102,100,99 81,70,67**
toteswingers: 1&2 £4.20, 1&3 £9.40, 2&3 £3.30. CSF £27.29 CT £135.69 TOTE £14.30: £2.80, £1.30, £2.70; EX 50.30 TRIFECTA Not won..
Owner Mr & Mrs C Schwick **Bred** D H W Dobson **Trained** Royston, Herts

FOCUS
A modest handicap, the pace was sound and it produced an easy winner. The first two finished clear and should pay to follow in the short term.
Trachonitis(IRE) ◆ Official explanation: trainer's representativen said, regarding the apparent improvement of form, that the gelding had benefited from a break, return to the Fibresand surface and today's strong pace
Resplendent Ace(IRE) Official explanation: jockey said the gelding was unsuited by the slow surface
Applaude Official explanation: jockey said the gelding was wrong behind

7852 BET ON TODAY'S FOOTBALL AT TOTESPORT.COM CLAIMING STKS 5f (F)
1:40 (1:41) (Class 6) 3-Y-O+ **£2,047** (£604; £302) **Stalls** High

Form RPR
2423 **1** **Total Impact**[9] 7795 6-8-9 77 .... TonyHamilton 4 79
(R A Fahey) *cl up: rdn wl over 1f out: styd on to ld jst ins fnl f: drvn out* **2/1**[1]
2521 **2** *1* **Grudge**[27] 7595 4-8-8 65 ....(e) TomEaves 10 74
(Ollie Pears) *led: rdn 2f out: drvn and jnd over 1f out: hdd jst ins fnl f: kpt on* **8/1**
3000 **3** *2 1/4* **Tartatartufata**[29] 7577 7-8-4 68 ....(v) LukeMorris 3 62
(J G Given) *chsd ldrs: hdwy 2f out: rdn wl over 1f out: kpt on ins fnl f: nrst fin* **12/1**
6030 **4** *1 1/4* **Godfrey Street**[12] 7758 6-8-0 65 ....(p) KellyHarrison(3) 7 57
(A G Newcombe) *chsd ldrs: rdn along 2f out: drvn over 1f out and kpt on same pce* **14/1**
0440 **5** *1/2* **Loose Caboose (IRE)**[12] 7758 4-8-9 65 ow1 ....(be) ShaneKelly 1 61
(A J McCabe) *cl up on outer: rdn along 1/2-way: drvn wl over 1f out: wknd appr fnl f* **15/2**[3]
1032 **6** *2 1/4* **Metal Guru**[5] 7839 5-7-9 59 ow2 ....(p) MatthewLawson(7) 6 46
(R Hollinshead) *wnt lft s: sn rdn along in rr: nvr a factor* **5/1**[2]
2300 **7** *1/2* **Yanza**[8] 7819 3-7-12 58 ....(b) AdrianMcCarthy 11 40
(J R Gask) *chsd ldrs: rdn along over 2f out: sn drvn and wknd* **16/1**
5043 **8** *2 1/2* **Rosie Says No**[5] 7838 4-7-12 60 ....(p) NickyMackay 8 31
(A J McCabe) *dwlt and hmpd s: sn rdn along and a in rr* **9/1**
04U0 **9** *5* **Grimes Faith**[30] 7561 6-8-1 61 ow3 ....(p) BillyCray(5) 9 21
(R C Guest) *wnt lft s: a in rr* **8/1**

59.95 secs (0.25) **Going Correction** 0.0s/f (Stan) **9** Ran SP% **114.2**
Speed ratings (Par 101): **98,96,92,90,90 86,85,81,73**
toteswingers: 1&2 £3.60, 1&3 £7.20, 2&3 £8.70. CSF £18.31 TOTE £3.10: £1.50, £2.90, £2.30; EX 22.40 Trifecta £147.00 Pool: £329.90 - 1.66 winning units..Total Impact claimed by Mr C. R. Dore for £8,000.
Owner The Wakey Exiles **Bred** C A Cyzer **Trained** Musley Bank, N Yorks

FOCUS
An ordinary claimer. As usual over the 5f here those who raced prominently proved hard to peg back.
Loose Caboose(IRE) Official explanation: jockey said the filly hung right-handed throughout
Grimes Faith Official explanation: the jockey said that the gelding suffered interference at the start

7853 BET LIVE IN PLAY AT TOTESPORT.COM MAIDEN STKS 6f (F)
2:15 (2:15) (Class 5) 3-Y-O+ **£2,729** (£806; £403) **Stalls** Low

Form RPR
1 **Poet's Place (USA)** 4-9-3 0 .... PhillipMakin 5 76
(T D Barron) *hld up: hdwy 1/2-way: led 2f out: sn clr: comf* **13/2**[2]
2 *4* **Bandstand** 3-9-3 0 .... TomEaves 4 63
(B Smart) *towards rr on inner: swtchd rt and hdwy over 2f out: rdn to chse wnr ins fnl f: sn drvn and no imp* **13/2**[2]
0602 **3** *3 3/4* **Place The Duchess**[17] 7703 3-8-5 49 ....(t) NathanAlison(7) 6 46
(A J Lidderdale) *prom: led 1/2-way: rdn and hdd 2f out: sn drvn and kpt on same pce* **16/1**[3]
30 **4** *shd* **Montego Breeze**[60] 7126 3-8-12 0 .... RobertWinston 2 46
(John A Harris) *cl up: rdn along 1/2-way: drvn 2f out and grad wknd* **25/1**

030 **5** 2 **Manana Manana**222 2154 3-9-3 63 AdamKirby 7 44
(J Balding) *in rr: hdwy on outer 2f out: rdn and keeping on whn hung lft over 1f out: nvr nr ldrs* **25/1**
300 **6** hd **If You Knew Suzy**15 7728 4-8-9 58 KellyHarrison(3) 8 39
(R E Barr) *chsd ldrs on outer: rdn along wl over 2f out: sn drvn and wknd* **20/1**
23 **7** 1 3/4 **Tejime**15 7730 3-9-3 0 NickyMackay 3 38
(J H M Gosden) *t.k.h: trckd ldrs on inner: effrt and n.m.r 1/2-way: swtchd rt and rdn to chse ldrs 2f out: sn drvn and btn* **4/7**1
65 **8** 11 **Freya's Flight (IRE)**200 2805 3-8-12 0 TonyHamilton 1 —
(K A Ryan) *sn led on inner: hdd and rdn along 1/2-way: sn wknd* **20/1**
1m 16.77s (0.27) **Going Correction** +0.125s/f (Slow) **8** Ran SP% **113.4**
Speed ratings (Par 103): **103,97,92,92,89 89,87,72**
toteswingers: 1&2 £3.20, 1&3 £11.40, 2&3 £8.50. CSF £43.32 TOTE £10.70: £2.20, £1.40, £2.40; EX 22.30 Trifecta £143.70 Pool: £438.98 - 2.26 winning units..
Owner Mrs Elaine Russell **Bred** Burning Daylight Farms **Trained** Maunby, N Yorks
FOCUS
Bryan Smart and David Barron have both been responsible for recent winners of this maiden and the pair's representatives dominated. It is usually won by a horse with previous experience but the first two this time were debutants.
Manana Manana Official explanation: jockey said that the gelding hung badly left from 3 furlongs out
Tejime Official explanation: jockey said gelding had no more to give; vet said gelding was suffering from a contagious skin disease

7854 MEMBERSHIP AT SOUTHWELL GOLF CLUB H'CAP 1m (F)
2:50 (2:50) (Class 5) (0-75,79) 3-Y-0+ **£2,729** (£806; £403) **Stalls** Low

Form RPR
2563 **1** **Ours (IRE)**12 7759 6-8-12 73 (p) BMcHugh(5) 11 85
(John A Harris) *s.i.s and bhd: rdn along over 3f out: hdwy over 2f out: rdn to chal over 1f out: led jst ins fnl f: sn edgd lft and drvn out* **6/1**3
6301 **2** 2 1/4 **Hilbre Court (USA)**10 7783 4-9-4 74 (p) RobertWinston 4 81
(B P J Baugh) *chsd ldrs: hdwy to chse ldr 3f out: rdn 2f out: drvn to chal and led briefly 1f out: sn hdd and one pce* **9/1**
1036 **3** 2 1/2 **Elusive Fame (USA)**12 7759 3-9-1 72 (b) GregFairley 2 73
(M Johnston) *cl up: led after 2f: rdn along 2f out: drvn and hdd 1f out: wknd ins fnl f* **11/2**2
0000 **4** 2 3/4 **Criterion**17 7699 4-8-9 65 ow1 ShaneKelly 5 60
(Ian Williams) *towards rr: hdwy and rdn along over 2f out: drvn and kpt on appr fnl f: nvr nrr* **12/1**
0032 **5** 1 3/4 **Ansells Pride (IRE)**20 7672 6-8-12 68 TomEaves 1 59
(B Smart) *led 2f: cl up tl rdn along over 2f out and grad wknd* **5/1**1
0-24 **6** 1 1/4 **Moonlight Man**229 1962 8-9-4 74 (tp) LPKeniry 8 62
(C R Dore) *prom: rdn along wl over 2f out: drvn over 1f out and grad wknd* **33/1**
3310 **7** 2 1/4 **General Tufto**10 7784 4-8-6 67 (b) PaulPickard(5) 6 50
(C Smith) *sn outpcd and pushed along: a in rr* **12/1**
4225 **8** 2 1/2 **Flores Sea (USA)**15 7734 5-9-5 75 (b) PhillipMakin 7 52
(T D Barron) *dwlt: hdwy on outer and in tch after 2f: rdn along 3f out: sltly hmpd and swtchd rt 2f out: sn drvn and wknd* **11/2**2
3001 **9** 18 **Avertis**10 7783 4-9-9 79 (t) AdamKirby 3 15
(Stef Liddiard) *chsd ldrs on inner: rdn along over 3f out: sn wknd* **6/1**3
0006 **10** 25 **Silver Hotspur**16 7711 5-8-8 64 NickyMackay 10 —
(C R Dore) *a in rr: bhd fr 1/2-way: heavily eased fnl 2f* **7/1**
1m 44.24s (0.54) **Going Correction** +0.125s/f (Slow)
WFA 3 from 4yo+ 1lb **10** Ran SP% **116.8**
Speed ratings (Par 103): **102,99,97,94,92 91,89,86,68,43**
toteswingers: 1&2 £10.50, 1&3 £6.30, 2&3 £9.30. CSF £59.04 CT £322.21 TOTE £6.60: £2.00, £2.70, £2.50; EX 51.80 TRIFECTA Not won..
Owner Peter Smith P C Coaches Limited **Bred** David John Brown **Trained** Eastwell, Leics
FOCUS
A wide-open handicap in which the leaders went off very hard.
Silver Hotspur Official explanation: jockey said the gelding dwelt in the stalls and was slowly away

7855 STAVELEY MINERS WELFARE F.C. H'CAP 1m (F)
3:25 (3:25) (Class 6) (0-60,66) 3-Y-0+ **£2,047** (£604; £302) **Stalls** Low

Form RPR
4000 **1** **Hint Of Honey**186 3281 3-8-5 47 LukeMorris 8 57
(A G Newcombe) *dwlt: hdwy and in tch 1/2-way: rdn to chse ldrs over 2f out: swtchd rt and drvn to chal over 1f out: styd on to ld ins fnl f: r.o* **40/1**
5500 **2** 1 1/4 **Trans Sonic**203 2746 6-9-3 58 FranciscoDaSilva 11 65
(J Hetherton) *cl up: effrt 3f out: rdn to ld over 1f out: drvn and edgd rt ent fnl f: sn hdd: kpt on* **16/1**
423- **3** 2 1/2 **Pendragon (USA)**533 3954 6-8-9 55 PaulPickard(5) 2 56
(B Ellison) *in rr and rdn along 1/2-way: hdwy on inner over 2f out: kpt on u.p appr fnl f: nrst fin* **10/1**
0002 **4** 1 **Transmission (IRE)**10 7782 4-9-4 66 AdamCarter(7) 6 65
(B Smart) *cl up: led after 2f: rdn along over 2f out: drvn and hdd over 1f out: wknd fnl f* **3/1**2
3000 **5** 1/2 **Provost**89 6361 5-9-5 60 PhillipMakin 12 58
(M W Easterby) *s.i.s and bhd: hdwy on inner over 3f out: swtchd rt 2f out: kpt on u.p appr fnl f: nrst fin* **16/1**
1531 **6** 1/2 **Hit The Switch**9 7797 3-9-3 59 SJCraine 1 56
(Patrick Morris) *midfield: hdwy to chse ldrs 1/2-way: rdn along wl over 2f out: drvn wl over 1f out: sn one pce* **5/2**1
4000 **7** 3/4 **Highland River**8 7813 3-9-1 57 ShaneKelly 5 52
(A Sadik) *chsd ldrs: rdn along 3f out: sn drvn and no hdwy* **25/1**
0000 **8** 2 3/4 **Mr Fantozzi (IRE)**20 7667 4-9-0 55 (tp) AdamKirby 3 44
(D Donovan) *led 2f: cl up on inner: rdn along wl over 2f out: sn drvn and wknd* **10/1**
4306 **9** 1 **Camerooney**15 7726 6-8-9 50 ow2 (e) TomEaves 10 36
(B Ellison) *t.k.h: chsd ldrs tl lost pl 1/2-way: drvn and plugged on fnl 2f: nvr a factor* **9/1**3
4025 **10** 13 **Louisiade (IRE)**15 7727 8-8-0 46 oh1 (p) BillyCray(5) 13 3
(R C Guest) *chsd ldrs on outer tl lost pl 1/2-way: sn bhd* **12/1**
0000 **11** 8 **Forrest Star**19 7680 4-8-5 43 oh1 GregFairley 14 —
(M Johnston) *chsd ldrs on outer: rdn along and lost pl 1/2-way: sn bhd* **16/1**
-050 **12** 23 **Classic Blue (IRE)**166 3949 5-8-11 52 SaleemGolam 4 —
(Ian Williams) *a outpcd in rr: bhd fnl 3f* **10/1**
1m 44.64s (0.94) **Going Correction** +0.125s/f (Slow)
WFA 3 from 4yo+ 1lb **12** Ran SP% **122.5**
Speed ratings (Par 101): **100,98,96,95,94 94,93,90,89,76 68,45**
toteswingers: 1&2 £80.60, 1&3 £44.20, 2&3 £26.10. CSF £596.69 CT £6844.58 TOTE £34.40: £11.70, £6.70, £3.30; EX 421.40 TRIFECTA Not won. Place 6: £148.94 Place 5: £97.56..
Owner A G Newcombe **Bred** P A Mason **Trained** Yarnscombe, Devon

The Form Book, Raceform Ltd, Compton, RG20 6NL

FOCUS
A low-grade handicap dominated by horses returning from breaks.
T/Plt: £271.40 to a £1 stake. Pool: £66,067.47. 177.65 winning tickets. T/Qpdt: £88.80 to a £1 stake. Pool: £5,981.30. 49.80 winning tickets. JR

7843 WOLVERHAMPTON (A.W) (L-H)
Monday, December 28

OFFICIAL GOING: Standard
Wind: Nil Weather: Fine and cold

7856 BET TOTEPOOL ON ALL UK RACING H'CAP (DIV I) 1m 1f 103y(P)
1:35 (1:36) (Class 6) (0-60,60) 3-Y-0+ **£1,706** (£503; £252) **Stalls** Low

Form RPR
300 **1** **Make Amends (IRE)**24 7632 4-9-4 58 GeorgeBaker 8 65
(R J Hodges) *hld up in tch: led over 1f out: sn rdn: drvn out* **28/1**
3212 **2** nk **Join Up**9 7818 3-8-5 52 RossAtkinson(5) 2 58
(W M Brisbourne) *hld up: sn mid-div: pushed along over 2f out: hdwy wl over 1f out: rdn and ev ch wl ins fnl f: kpt on* **9/2**2
4241 **3** nk **Bestowed**10 7803 4-8-13 58 (v) DeanHeslop(5) 11 63
(P D Evans) *hld up in mid-div: rdn and hdwy on outside wl over 1f out: kpt on ins fnl f* **3/1**1
0414 **4** 1/2 **Head First**14 7755 3-8-13 55 HayleyTurner 5 59
(W Jarvis) *a.p: rdn over 1f out: nt qckn ins fnl f* **5/1**3
2230 **5** nk **Spinning Ridge (IRE)**11 7784 4-9-6 60 LiamJones 9 64
(R A Harris) *hld up towards rr: pushed along and hdwy over 1f out: nt qckn ins fnl f* **16/1**
4016 **6** nk **King Of Connacht**10 7798 6-9-5 59 (v) AdamKirby 7 62
(M Wellings) *hld up towards rr: hdwy wl over 1f out: rdn and nt qckn ins fnl f* **17/2**
6060 **7** 1/2 **Inside Story (IRE)**55 7225 7-9-4 58 (b) LPKeniry 13 60
(C R Dore) *hld up in rr: pushed along whn swtchd rt jst over 1f out: kpt on ins fnl f: nvr nrr* **22/1**
-000 **8** 1/2 **Chia (IRE)**17 7718 6-9-4 58 (p) FrankieMcDonald 4 59
(D Haydn Jones) *hld up in tch: nt clr run on ins over 2f out: nt clr run wl over 1f out: styng on whn nt clr run wl ins fnl f* **10/1**
0440 **9** nk **Sairaam (IRE)**16 7727 3-8-3 50 PaulPickard(5) 10 50
(C Smith) *hld up in rr: pushed along on outside over 2f out: sme late prog* **10/1**
320 **10** 9 **Very Distinguished**15 7740 3-8-12 54 RobertWinston 1 35
(S Kirk) *led: hdd 7f out: chsd ldr: rdn and ev ch over 2f out: wknd 1f out* **16/1**
0010 **11** 1/2 **Royal Society**19 7688 3-9-0 56 DaneO'Neill 6 36
(R A Farrant) *prom: led 7f out: rdn and hdd wl over 1f out: sn edgd lft: wknd fnl f* **10/1**
0636 **12** 1 3/4 **Stark Contrast (USA)**22 7653 5-8-3 50 RachelKing(7) 3 27
(M D I Usher) *t.k.h: prom: pushed along whn hmpd on ins jst over 1f out: nt rcvr* **16/1**
2m 3.74s (2.04) **Going Correction** +0.175s/f (Slow)
WFA 3 from 4yo+ 2lb **12** Ran SP% **123.1**
Speed ratings (Par 101): **97,96,96,96,95 95,95,94,94,86 85,84**
toteswinger:1&2:£20.20, 2&3:£3.80, 1&3:£21.90 CSF £155.86 CT £510.16 TOTE £25.20: £5.90, £2.20, £1.90; EX 193.10 TRIFECTA Not won..
Owner Miss R Dobson **Bred** Moyglare Stud Farm Ltd **Trained** Charlton Mackrell, Somerset
■ Stewards' Enquiry : Dane O'Neill two-day ban: careless riding (11-12 Jan)
FOCUS
A moderate handicap but a few in-form sorts and, although the gallop was reasonable, the time was on the slow side. The winner came down the centre in the straight.
Chia(IRE) ◆ Official explanation: jockey said that the mare was denied a clear run

7857 BET TOTEPOOL ON ALL UK RACING H'CAP (DIV II) 1m 1f 103y(P)
2:05 (2:06) (Class 6) (0-60,60) 3-Y-0+ **£1,706** (£503; £252) **Stalls** Low

Form RPR
0631 **1** **Chosen Forever**9 7818 4-9-4 58 JimmyQuinn 7 71
(G R Oldroyd) *sn chsng ldr: led 3f out: hrd rdn over 1f out: r.o wl* **5/4**1
1530 **2** 4 **Guiseppe Verdi (USA)**96 6210 5-9-6 60 DaneO'Neill 4 65
(Miss Tor Sturgis) *hld up in mid-div: pushed along and hdwy over 3f out: rdn over 2f out: wnt 2nd wl ins fnl f: nt trble wnr* **17/2**3
0-5 **3** nk **Law Of The Jungle (IRE)**19 7693 3-8-13 60 (p) RossAtkinson(5) 1 64
(Tom Dascombe) *led: rdn and hdd 3f out: one pce: lost 2nd wl ins fnl f* **9/1**
63 **4** 1/2 **Mackintosh (IRE)**9 7817 3-8-10 52 (b) SJCraine 8 55
(Patrick Morris) *s.i.s: hld up towards rr: stdy prog over 2f out: edgd lft 1f out: one pce* **20/1**
0255 **5** shd **Noah Jameel**19 7687 7-9-0 54 SteveDrowne 3 57
(A G Newcombe) *hld up in mid-div: pushed along on ins 3f out: rdn and hdwy wl over 1f out: one pce ins fnl f* **9/1**
0302 **6** 1/2 **Libre**10 7802 9-8-8 48 JoeFanning 12 50
(F Jordan) *hld up in rr: pushed along over 2f out: hdwy whn nt clr run and swtchd lft ins fnl f: kpt on* **20/1**
4153 **7** 1 **Castle Myth (USA)**25 7615 3-9-4 60 (bt) TomEaves 13 60
(B Ellison) *hld up in rr: pushed along over 3f out: rdn over 1f out: styng on whn swtchd rt wl ins fnl f: n.d* **6/1**2
6001 **8** 2 **Climate (IRE)**14 7755 10-9-3 57 (p) PaulDoe 10 52
(P D Evans) *hld up towards rr: pushed along on ins over 2f out: rdn jst over 1f out: nvr nr ldrs* **20/1**
2456 **9** 3/4 **Triple Cee (IRE)**44 7392 3-9-2 58 TonyCulhane 9 52
(M R Channon) *prom: pushed along over 6f out: rdn over 2f out: btn whn sltly hmpd ins fnl f* **20/1**
0063 **10** 2 3/4 **John Potts**9 7818 4-8-9 49 ow2 GrahamGibbons 5 37
(B P J Baugh) *hld up in mid-div: pushed along on outside over 2f out: c wd st: wknd over 1f out* **12/1**
2130 **11** 8 **Lady Longcroft**286 857 4-9-4 58 RobertWinston 2 29
(J Pearce) *t.k.h: prom: pushed along over 2f out: rdn and wknd over 1f out* **14/1**
-305 **12** 7 **Helpmeronda**326 403 3-8-10 52 LiamJones 6 9
(W M Brisbourne) *hld up towards rr: pushed along 4f out: no ch fnl 2f* **66/1**
2m 3.59s (1.89) **Going Correction** +0.175s/f (Slow)
WFA 3 from 4yo+ 2lb **12** Ran SP% **124.2**
Speed ratings (Par 101): **98,94,94,93,93 93,92,90,89,87 80,74**
toteswinger:1&2:£5.60, 2&3:£15.40, 1&3:£6.50 CSF £11.93 CT £76.45 TOTE £2.50: £1.30, £3.10, £3.10; EX 16.90 Trifecta £88.90 Part won. Pool: £120.25 - 0.90 winning units..
Owner R C Bond **Bred** R C Bond **Trained** Brawby, N Yorks

FOCUS
Division two of an ordinary handicap but, although the overall time was quicker than the first leg, this race was run at a steady pace and those held up were at a disadvantage. The winner came down the centre in the straight.
Libre Official explanation: jockey said that the gelding was denied a clear run
Lady Longcroft Official explanation: jockey said that the filly ran too free

7858 FUNKY ERIC STEVENS 70TH BIRTHDAY APPRENTICE (S) STKS 1m 141y(P)
2:40 (2:41) (Class 6) 3-Y-0+ **£2,047** (£604; £302) **Stalls** Low

Form RPR
4305 **1** **Daniel Thomas (IRE)**[14] 7752 7-8-13 66........................(v) RyanClark(3) 4 76
(Mrs A L M King) *hld up: hdwy on outside to ld 2f out: clr whn rdn over 1f out: r.o wl* **9/4**[1]
0142 **2** *12* **Ten Pole Tudor**[9] 7817 4-9-3 61........................(p) JakePayne(5) 6 54
(R A Harris) *hld up in tch: led over 5f out to 2f out: sn rdn: no ch w wnr* **11/2**[3]
0245 **3** *hd* **Pride Of Nation (IRE)**[9] 7810 7-9-2 66........................(p) DeclanCannon 2 48
(A J McCabe) *hld up: lost pl on ins over 6f out: hdwy on ins over 2f out: rdn wl over 1f out: one pce* **3/1**[2]
6/0- **4** *1 ¼* **Crimson Flame (IRE)**[656] 862 6-8-13 40............ MatthewLawson(3) 3 45
(M S Tuck) *prom: lost pl over 5f out: bhd 3f out: styd on to take 4th wl ins fnl f* **10/1**
0105 **5** *hd* **Swiss Art (IRE)**[11] 7782 3-9-6 68........................ RosieJessop 7 51
(R Hollinshead) *stdd s: hdwy over 5f out: rdn over 2f out: wknd wl over 1f out* **11/1**
0344 **6** *10* **Interchoice Star**[14] 7754 4-8-9 53........................ NicolaJackson(7) 8 22
(R Hollinshead) *t.k.h in rr: hdwy over 5f out: ev ch over 2f out: wknd wl over 1f out* **6/1**
0000 **7** *2 ½* **Misterisland (IRE)**[9] 7819 4-8-11 44........................(be) RachelKing(5) 5 16
(M Mullineaux) *prom: rdn over 2f out: wknd over 1f out* **100/1**
0006 **8** *38* **Electric Warrior (IRE)**[9] 7813 6-9-8 62........................ TobyAtkinson 1 —
(C R Dore) *led: hdd over 5f out: wkng whn hmpd on ins over 3f out: eased whn no ch wl over 1f out* **8/1**

1m 51.13s (0.63) **Going Correction** +0.175s/f (Slow)
WFA 3 from 4yo+ 2lb 8 Ran SP% **115.0**
Speed ratings (Par 101): **104,93,93,92,91 82,80,46**
toteswinger:1&2:£3.50, 2&3:£3.60, 1&3:£2.40 CSF £15.23 TOTE £3.30: £1.70, £1.50, £1.90; EX 14.80 TRIFECTA Pool: £403.42 - 4.45 winning units..The winner was bought in for 6,500gns. Ten Pole Tudor was claimed by J Harris for £6,000
Owner George Martin **Bred** Lawn Stud **Trained** Wilmcote, Warwicks
■ Stewards' Enquiry : Declan Cannon three-day ban: careless riding (11-13 Jan(

FOCUS
Exposed performers in a modest seller. The gallop was ordinary and the easy winner was another to come down the centre in the straight.

7859 BET TOTEPOOL ON TODAY'S IRISH RACING MAIDEN STKS 7f 32y(P)
3:15 (3:16) (Class 5) 2-Y-0 **£3,238** (£963; £481; £240) **Stalls** High

Form RPR
4 **1** **Capricornus (USA)**[12] 7764 2-9-3 0........................ JoeFanning 10 72
(M Johnston) *mde all: rdn fnl f: r.o* **13/8**[1]
03 **2** *½* **Mnasikia (USA)**[12] 7772 2-8-12 0........................ DaneO'Neill 11 66
(L M Cumani) *sn chsng wnr: ev ch over 2f out: rdn over 1f out: kpt on towards fin* **13/2**
3 *½* **Brave Decision** 2-9-3 0........................ ShaneKelly 8 70
(A J McCabe) *hld up towards rr: hdwy wl over 1f out: rdn fnl f: r.o to take 3rd cl home* **25/1**
00 **4** *½* **South African Gold (USA)**[30] 7571 2-9-3 0........................ LukeMorris 6 69
(J M P Eustace) *hld up in tch: pushed along over 3f out: hrd rdn over 2f out: kpt on ins fnl f* **50/1**
0 **5** *1 ½* **Brave Enough (USA)**[12] 7773 2-9-3 0........................ AdamKirby 5 65
(M A Magnusson) *hld up towards rr: pushed along over 1f out: r.o ins fnl f: nt rch ldrs* **33/1**
00 **6** *nk* **Erebus (IRE)**[18] 7700 2-9-3 0........................ LPKeniry 3 64
(S Kirk) *hld up in mid-div on ins: swtchd rt 2f out: sme prog over 1f out: sn rdn: one pce ins fnl f* **16/1**
62 **7** *¾* **Fusaichi Flyer (USA)**[10] 7800 2-9-3 0........................ SteveDrowne 12 62
(R Charlton) *prom: rdn over 1f out: sn btn* **5/2**[2]
00 **8** *¾* **Monograph**[81] 6616 2-9-3 0........................ GeorgeBaker 9 61
(J W Hills) *hld up in mid-div: hdwy over 2f out: rdn wl over 1f out: wknd ins fnl f* **9/2**[3]
9 *1 ¼* **Celestial Girl** 2-8-12 0........................ RobertHavlin 4 53+
(H Morrison) *dwlt: towards rr: pushed along and short-lived effrt on outside over 2f out* **11/1**
10 *9* **All Right Now** 2-8-12 0........................ LeeNewnes(5) 2 35
(S Kirk) *s.s: a in rr* **25/1**
00 **11** *8* **Seeking Rio**[14] 7749 2-8-12 0........................ JimmyQuinn 7 11
(R J Hodges) *prom on ins: wknd 2f out* **100/1**
12 *14* **Dunfishin (IRE)** 2-9-3 0........................ VinceSlattery 1 —
(M S Tuck) *s.s: a in rr* **50/1**

1m 31.5s (1.90) **Going Correction** +0.175s/f (Slow) 12 Ran SP% **127.9**
Speed ratings (Par 96): **96,95,94,94,92 92,91,90,89,78 69,53**
toteswinger:1&2:£3.80, 2&3:£17.20, 1&3:£14.70 CSF £13.77 TOTE £3.30: £1.60, £1.90, £6.00; EX 15.60 Trifecta £330.80 Pool: £527.65 - 1.18 winning units..
Owner Sheikh Hamdan Bin Mohammed Al Maktoum **Bred** Dr White Jr Et Al **Trained** Middleham Moor, N Yorks

FOCUS
No more than a fair maiden and, with the second favourite performing below expectations, one that took less winning than seemed likely. The gallop was an ordinary one and they finished up rather compressed. The winner, who raced up the centre in the straight, improved by a few lengths on his debut effort.

NOTEBOOK
Capricornus(USA), who had shown ability on his debut, had the run of the race and fully confirmed that promise. He showed a decent attitude, should have no problems with 1m and appeals as the type to progress again. (tchd 15-8)
Mnasikia(USA) is a steadily progressive sort who was well placed given the way the race panned out and turned in her best effort yet. Stepping into ordinary handicaps and moving up to 1m should bring about further improvement and she looks sure to win a race. (op 5-1 tchd 7-1)
Brave Decision, who is related to AW winners over a variety of distances, shaped with a degree of promise to fare best of those held up on this racecourse debut. He should have no problems with 1m and can be expected to step up on this level next time. (op 28-1)
South African Gold(USA) had been soundly beaten on both previous starts but shaped much better over this longer trip after being well placed in a moderately run race. He may be a shade flattered by the way things unfolded but might do better granted an even stiffer stamina test in handicaps.
Brave Enough(USA) was not unduly knocked about and will be of more interest in ordinary handicaps in due course.
Erebus(IRE) bettered the form of his two previous starts and is another from this race that should be seen to better effect in ordinary handicaps.
Fusaichi Flyer(USA) failed to build on his previous C&D run and was the disappointment of the race. However, a more truly run race over a bit further might suit him better and he's not one to write off yet. (op 9-4 tchd 2-1 and 11-4)
Monograph, well beaten at big odds in much better maiden company on turf, was backed from 25-1 into single-figure odds for this AW debut but still looked green when asked for an effort and was not able to land a blow. However, he has a bit of scope and may do better in handicaps. (op 25-1)
Celestial Girl, out of a half-sister to Oaks winner Lady Carla, should be all the better for this debut experience. (op 12-1 tchd 10-1)

7860 BET ON TODAY'S FOOTBALL AT TOTESPORT.COM H'CAP (DIV I) 7f 32y(P)
3:45 (3:45) (Class 6) (0-65,65) 3-Y-0+ **£1,706** (£503; £252) **Stalls** High

Form RPR
4151 **1** **Just Jimmy (IRE)**[23] 7650 4-8-13 **60**........................ PaulDoe 10 67
(P D Evans) *hld up in mid-div: rdn and hdwy wl over 1f out: led wl ins fnl f: drvn out* **5/1**[3]
310 **2** *hd* **Rubenstar (IRE)**[255] 1320 6-9-4 **65**........................ SJCraine 7 71
(Patrick Morris) *hld up in rr: hdwy 1f out: pushed along and r.o wl to take 2nd cl home: nt rch wnr* **14/1**
4234 **3** *½* **Just Timmy Marcus**[9] 7813 3-9-3 **64**........................ TonyCulhane 6 69
(B P J Baugh) *a.p: edgd lft and rdn over 1f out: edgd lft ins fnl f: kpt on* **4/1**[1]
040 **4** *1 ½* **Haasem (USA)**[246] 1539 6-8-12 **59**........................ SimonWhitworth 9 60
(J R Jenkins) *hld up towards rr: prog on outside over 3f out: c wd st: rdn wl over 1f out: kpt on same pce fnl f* **25/1**
0062 **5** *shd* **Eastern Gift**[10] 7803 4-9-4 **65**........................(v[1]) GeorgeBaker 5 66
(Miss Gay Kelleway) *hld up in tch on ins: rdn to ld jst over 1f out: hdd wl ins fnl f: no ex* **9/2**[2]
0220 **6** *1* **Great Bounder (CAN)**[26] 7614 3-8-4 **56**........................ AmyBaker(5) 8 54
(A B Haynes) *chsd ldr after 1f: pushed along and lost 2nd 2f out: sn rdn: hld whn hmpd wl ins fnl f* **20/1**
1554 **7** *nk* **Smirfys Systems**[269] 1103 10-9-2 **63**........................ GrahamGibbons 4 60
(E S McMahon) *led: rdn and hdd jst over 1f out: wknd towards fin* **5/1**[3]
060 **8** *1* **Obe Brave**[9] 7813 6-8-5 **57**........................ JamesPSullivan(5) 1 51
(Lee Smyth, Ire) *hld up towards rr: pushed along jst over 2f out: no rspnse* **8/1**
2130 **9** *2* **Dancing Welcome**[17] 7715 3-8-11 **58**........................(b) LukeMorris 3 47
(J M Bradley) *in rr: hrd rdn and struggling over 2f out* **9/2**[2]

1m 30.73s (1.13) **Going Correction** +0.175s/f (Slow) 9 Ran SP% **116.1**
Speed ratings (Par 101): **100,99,99,97,97 96,95,94,92**
toteswinger:1&2:£11.00, 2&3:£11.40, 1&3:£2.60 CSF £71.90 CT £309.61 TOTE £4.70: £2.40, £3.50, £1.90; EX 70.80 Trifecta £308.30 Pool: £416.67 - 1.00 winning units..
Owner Richard Edwards **Bred** Richard Edwards And Gwynne Williams **Trained** Pandy, Monmouths

FOCUS
A modest handicap run at just an ordinary gallop. The winner continued the trend of racing towards the centre in the straight.
Just Timmy Marcus Official explanation: caution: careless riding

7861 BET ON TODAY'S FOOTBALL AT TOTESPORT.COM H'CAP (DIV II) 7f 32y(P)
4:15 (4:15) (Class 6) (0-65,65) 3-Y-0+ **£1,706** (£503; £252) **Stalls** High

Form RPR
0006 **1** **Diapason (IRE)**[17] 7715 3-9-0 **61**........................ RichardKingscote 3 72
(Tom Dascombe) *hld up and bhd: hdwy 2f out: hrd rdn to ld ins fnl f: r.o wl* **3/1**[2]
6514 **2** *3 ½* **Sir George (IRE)**[16] 7729 4-8-13 **65**........................ DeanHeslop(5) 7 67
(P D Evans) *a.p: rdn to ld wl over 1f out: sn hdd: styng on one pce whn edgd lft wl ins fnl f: tk 2nd post* **5/2**[1]
000- **3** *nse* **Double Bill (USA)**[434] 6864 5-8-13 **60**........................ JosedeSouza 1 61
(P F I Cole) *led early: a.p: led jst over 1f out: rdn and hdd ins fnl f: no ex: lost 2nd post* **11/1**
6300 **4** *1 ¼* **Guildenstern (IRE)**[13] 7762 7-8-10 **57**........................ JimmyQuinn 4 55
(P Howling) *hld up in mid-div: pushed along and prog over 2f out: rdn and one pce fnl f* **5/1**[3]
0040 **5** *½* **Amber Sunset**[10] 7797 3-9-2 **63**........................ LukeMorris 5 60
(J Jay) *sn led: rdn and hdd wl over 1f out: wkng whn sltly hmpd wl ins fnl f* **20/1**
0020 **6** *2 ½* **Golden Prospect**[9] 7813 5-8-11 **58**........................(b) WandersonD'Avila 2 48
(Miss J R Tooth) *hld up in rr: sme prog on ins over 2f out: rdn and wknd over 1f out* **9/1**
5610 **7** *nse* **Star Strider**[10] 7798 5-8-13 **65** ow3........................ KylieManser(5) 8 55
(T Keddy) *dwlt: hld up in rr: c wd st: rdn and struggling whn edgd lft over 1f out* **8/1**
0010 **8** *16* **Manchestermaverick (USA)**[117] 5569 4-8-9 **56**.........(t) SteveDrowne 9 3
(Dr J R J Naylor) *hld up in tch: wknd over 3f out* **20/1**
3440 **9** *½* **Riflessione**[104] 5968 3-9-4 **65**........................(p) LiamJones 10 10
(R A Harris) *t.k.h: hdwy on outside over 5f out: wknd over 2f out* **14/1**

1m 30.25s (0.65) **Going Correction** +0.175s/f (Slow) 9 Ran SP% **115.9**
Speed ratings (Par 101): **103,99,98,97,96 94,94,75,75**
toteswinger:1&2:£2.70, 2&3:£9.60, 1&3:£9.90 CSF £10.98 CT £68.57 TOTE £4.00: £1.80, £1.50, £4.20; EX 13.00 Trifecta £78.50 Pool: £687.00 - 6.48 winning units..
Owner John Brown **Bred** Miss Alice Fitzgerald **Trained** Lambourn, Berks

FOCUS
Another modest handicap but a moderate gallop in which several failed to settle. The winner raced centre to far side in the straight.

7862 BET LIVE IN PLAY AT TOTESPORT.COM H'CAP 5f 216y(P)
4:45 (4:45) (Class 2) (0-100,101) 3-Y-0+
£11,215 (£3,358; £1,679; £840; £419; £210) **Stalls** Low

Form RPR
1121 **1** **Imprimis Tagula (IRE)**[6] 7837 5-8-3 **92** 6ex........(v) DeclanCannon(7) 11 102
(A Bailey) *t.k.h: a.p: pushed along 3f out: rdn wl over 1f out: led wl ins fnl f: r.o* **9/2**[2]
3122 **2** *hd* **Ebraam (USA)**[27] 7605 6-9-1 **97**........................(t) RobertWinston 12 106
(S Curran) *hld up in tch: hmpd over 2f out: rdn over 1f out: r.o ins fnl f* **6/1**[3]
0400 **3** *½* **Matsunosuke**[65] 7015 7-9-5 **101**........................ TonyCulhane 2 108
(A B Coogan) *stdd s: hld up in rr: pushed along and hdwy on ins jst over 1f out: r.o* **18/1**
0056 **4** *nse* **Flowing Cape (IRE)**[6] 7837 4-8-3 **90**........................(t) PaulPickard(5) 10 97
(R Hollinshead) *led: hdd 3f out: pushed along to ld 2f out: hdd wl ins fnl f* **14/1**
4311 **5** *¾* **Earlsmedic**[37] 7478 4-8-1 **90**........................(e) RyanClark(7) 1 95
(S C Williams) *hld up towards rr: hdwy 1f out: kpt on ins fnl f* **10/3**[1]

5231 **6** *nk* **Capone (IRE)**[7] 7832 4-8-6 **88** 6ex................................ HayleyTurner 9 92
(R Curtis) *hld up towards rr: pushed along wl over 1f out: rdn whn swtchd rt ins fnl f: nrst fin* **10/3**[1]

4443 **7** *1 ½* **Five Star Junior (USA)**[44] 7394 3-9-4 **100**........................ ShaneKelly 5 99
(Mrs L Stubbs) *hld up in tch on ins: n.m.r and squeezed through over 2f out: rdn and one pce ins fnl f* **17/2**

1045 **8** *2 ½* **Mrs Penny (AUS)**[23] 7646 5-8-4 **86** oh2........................(b[1]) LukeMorris 3 77
(J R Gask) *s.i.s: t.k.h towards rr: effrt on outside 2f out: c wd st: rdn and wknd over 1f out* **17/2**

3000 **9** *5* **Toms Laughter**[20] 7676 5-8-5 **87**.....................................(b) LiamJones 7 62
(R A Harris) *s.i.s: t.k.h: hdwy after 1f: led 3f out to 2f out: rdn over 1f out: wknd ins fnl f* **20/1**

6400 **10** *3 ¾* **Smokey Ryder**[142] 4771 3-8-10 **92**.............................. KevinGhunowa 6 55
(R A Harris) *w ldr tl pushed along 3f out: wknd wl over 1f out* **50/1**

1m 14.42s (-0.58) **Going Correction** +0.175s/f (Slow) **10** Ran SP% **118.3**
Speed ratings (Par 109): **110,109,109,109,108 107,105,102,95,90**
toteswinger:1&2:£5.00, 2&3:£22.10, 1&3:£21.50 CSF £32.26 CT £455.74 TOTE £5.00: £1.60, £2.80, £5.80; EX 23.30 Trifecta £202.40 Pool: £727.88 - 2.66 winning units..

Owner Middleham Park Racing XLI & Alan Bailey **Bred** Glashare House Stud **Trained** Newmarket, Suffolk

FOCUS
A decent handicap featuring several in-form sorts but the early gallop was less than frenetic and those up with the pace held the edge. The winner and second came down the centre in the straight.

NOTEBOOK
Imprimis Tagula(IRE) is thriving at present and followed up his wide-margin Fibresand 7f win with a battling display back in trip under his penalty. Life will be tougher after reassessment but he is a very useful sort who may have further improvement in him on artificial surfaces. (op 4-1)

Ebraam(USA), fitted with a first-time tongue tie on this first run for connections, ran right up to his best from his double-figure draw and may well have won had he not suffered interference turning for home. He has little margin for error from this mark so a further rise will leave him vulnerable to the more progressive or better handicapped types, but he should continue to go well in this type of race. (op 8-1 tchd 5-1)

Matsunosuke, who thrived on Polytrack earlier this year, may not be in that sort of form but he can be rated a bit better than the bare result as he fared best of those held up on this first run for two months. He will always be seen to best effect in strongly run races. (op 16-1 tchd 20-1)

Flowing Cape(IRE) ◆ had the run of the race but was far from disgraced back over sprint distances in the first-time tongue tie. This surface suits him better than Fibresand and he's steadily slipping back to a decent mark. He'll be of interest back over 7f. (op 11-1)

Earlsmedic had been unbeaten in two starts over this trip at Kempton in an eyeshield and he ran well after being ridden with a bit more patience from his inside draw this time. He remains at the top of his game and should continue to go well on Polytrack. (op 4-1 tchd 9-2)

Capone(IRE) turned in a career-best effort on his previous start but failed to build on that under his penalty in a race run at just an ordinary early pace. His style of racing means an end-to-end gallop will always show him in his most favourable light and he is worth another chance. (op 7-2)

Five Star Junior(USA) is a reliable type who shaped as though this first run after a short break was just needed. He was not knocked about but is another with little room for manoeuvre from his current mark. Official explanation: two-day ban:careless riding (11-12 Jan) (tchd 10-1)

7863 CE PROPERTY SERVICES GROUP MAIDEN STKS 1m 141y(P)
5:15 (5:15) (Class 5) 3-Y-0+ **£2,729** (£806; £403) **Stalls** Low

Form RPR

0064 **1** **Levitation (IRE)**[21] 7671 3-8-12 65.................................. IanMongan 12 71
(W S Kittow) *sn led: pushed along over 2f out: rdn over 1f out: clr fnl f: r.o wl* **5/1**[2]

2 **2** *5* **Midnight Strider (IRE)**[16] 7730 3-9-3 0.................. RichardKingscote 1 65
(Tom Dascombe) *prom on ins: pushed along and lost pl over 3f out: rdn over 1f out: styd on to take 2nd wl ins fnl f: no ch w wnr* **4/6**[1]

3404 **3** *½* **Major Lawrence (IRE)**[19] 7686 3-9-3 68.......................... ShaneKelly 10 63
(J Noseda) *hld up towards rr: pushed along over 2f out: rdn wl over 1f out: styd on wl ins fnl f: tk 3rd cl home* **13/2**[3]

0562 **4** *1 ½* **Barbarian**[14] 7753 3-9-3 62.....................................(v) GrahamGibbons 5 60
(A D Brown) *led early: a.p: rdn jst over 2f out: edgd lft 1f out: one pce* **7/1**

6606 **5** *shd* **Lindy Hop (IRE)**[10] 7797 3-8-12 58...................................... TomEaves 7 55
(K A Ryan) *chsd wnr 7f out: rdn over 2f out: no imp: lost 2nd wl ins fnl f* **25/1**

0404 **6** *4 ½* **Hold The Star**[16] 7730 3-8-7 55.. AnnStokell(5) 2 44
(Miss A Stokell) *hld up in tch: rdn over 1f out: wknd ins fnl f* **25/1**

0-60 **7** *7* **Arch Event**[33] 7521 4-9-0 32.. SteveDrowne 3 28
(A W Carroll) *hld up in mid-div: pushed along and struggling over 3f out* **200/1**

00 **8** *shd* **Latin Connection (IRE)**[44] 7401 3-9-3 0......................... LiamJones 6 33
(Lee Smyth, Ire) *hld up in mid-div: pushed along 3f out: sn wknd* **100/1**

9 *13* **Morning Spring**[18] 4-9-0 0... AdamKirby 4 —
(D Shaw) *s.s: a wl in rr* **100/1**

10 *¾* **Barony (IRE)** 3-8-12 0.. JamesPSullivan(5) 9 —
(Lee Smyth, Ire) *s.s: a wl in rr* **50/1**

030 **11** *9* **Venture Capitalist**[11] 7790 3-9-3 59................................ DaneO'Neill 11 —
(B Ellison) *pushed along and reminder sn after s: hdwy over 6f out: wknd over 3f out: eased whn no ch wl over 1f out* **20/1**

1m 51.45s (0.95) **Going Correction** +0.175s/f (Slow)
WFA 3 from 4yo+ 2lb **11** Ran SP% **119.4**
Speed ratings (Par 103): **102,97,97,95,95 91,85,85,73,73 65**
toteswinger:1&2:£2.30, 2&3:£2.90, 1&3:£5.90 CSF £8.51 TOTE £6.80: £1.80, £1.20, £1.90; EX 12.90 Trifecta £99.70 Pool: £889.35 - 6.60 winning units. Place 6 £14.08, Place 5 £6.80.

Owner Philip Gibbs **Bred** The Hon Mrs R Pease **Trained** Blackborough, Devon

■ Stewards' Enquiry : James P Sullivan ten-day ban: in breach of Rule 59.4 (11-20 Jan)

FOCUS
A modest and uncompetitive maiden and one that took less winning than seemed likely, with the market leader disappointing. The gallop was only fair and the winner came down the centre.

Midnight Strider(IRE) Official explanation: jockey said that the colt hung right

Morning Spring Official explanation: jockey said that the filly hung left

Barony(IRE) Official explanation: jockey said that his instructions were to to jump out and settle in mid-division, get some cover and to do his best. He added that the gelding was slowly away and therefore he was not able to comply with the instructions. He further stated that he made every effort throughout the race to get back on terms but was mindful that on this, the gelding's, racecourse debut, he did not want to be too hard on his mount. Trainer confirmed the instructions and felt that the gelding's performance was compromised by his slow start, adding that the gelding has proved troublesome in the stalls at home. The Trainer said he was satisfied with his rider's efforts.

T/Plt: £11.10 to a £1 stake. Pool: £72,535.74. 4,730.08 winning tickets. T/Qpdt: £5.00 to a £1 stake. Pool: £5,430.20. 790.50 winning tickets. KH

7849 SOUTHWELL (L-H)
Tuesday, December 29

OFFICIAL GOING: Standard to slow
Wind: Light across Weather: Overcast turning to light rain prior to race 5

7864 BET TOTEPOOL ON ALL UK RACING MAIDEN STKS 6f (F)
12:15 (12:15) (Class 5) 2-Y-0 **£2,590** (£770; £385; £192) **Stalls** Low

Form RPR

0533 **1** **Exearti**[7] 7836 2-8-12 62.. RobertWinston 5 69
(A J McCabe) *mde all: rdn over 1f out: hung rt ins fnl f: styd on u.p* **17/2**

3222 **2** *1 ¼* **Zubova**[10] 7805 2-8-12 72...(t) ShaneKelly 6 65
(M J Attwater) *s.i.s: sn chsng wnr: rdn over 1f out: nt clr run ins fnl f: styd on* **11/4**[2]

3 *2* **Paintball (IRE)** 2-9-3 0.. MartinDwyer 3 64
(W R Muir) *hld up in tch: pushed along 1/2-way: hdwy over 2f out: rdn over 1f out: styd on same pce fnl f* **3/1**[3]

4 *1 ½* **Duellist** 2-9-3 0... JoeFanning 4 60
(M Johnston) *sn chsng ldrs: rdn over 2f out: hung lft over 1f out: no ex fnl f* **13/8**[1]

04 **5** *7* **Rathbawn Girl (IRE)**[16] 7736 2-8-12 0.............................. JimmyQuinn 2 34
(Miss J Feilden) *chsd ldrs: rdn over 2f out: sn wknd* **14/1**

06 **6** *5* **Bella Charlie (IRE)**[33] 7538 2-9-3 0.................................. AdamKirby 1 24
(M G Quinlan) *in rr: swtchd rt over 4f out: lost tch 1/2-way* **25/1**

5 **7** *nk* **Last Of The Ravens**[7] 7836 2-8-10 0 ow3................. MarkCoumbe(5) 7 21
(J F Coupland) *chsd ldrs tl rdn and wknd 1/2-way* **200/1**

1m 19.41s (2.91) **Going Correction** +0.225s/f (Slow) **7** Ran SP% **111.3**
Speed ratings (Par 96): **89,87,84,82,73 66,66**
toteswinger:1&2:£2.10, 2&3:£11.80, 1&3:£5.70 CSF £30.40 TOTE £9.10: £4.20, £2.00; EX 25.70.

Owner A J McCabe **Bred** P A Mason **Trained** Averham Park, Notts

FOCUS
A very modest maiden fought out by the two with most experience, and given their limitations going into the race, not form that makes much appeal as worth following. The first two held those positions throughout and the winner almost certainly showed improvement.

NOTEBOOK
Exearti had finished legless over 7f here last time and was starting to come to the end of his tether towards the finish here, but had enough to hold on. He will have to go into handicaps now and, for all his mark doesn't look particularly lenient, his prominent racing style will make him a tough opponent, at least round here. (op 10-1 tchd 8-1)

Zubova didn't appear to do much wrong on this occasion on her first start for her new yard and on this surface, and simply ran into a better rival on the day, but her current BHA rating flatters her. (op 3-1 tchd 10-3 in a place)

Paintball(IRE) attracted some support in the morning but never really threatened to land a blow after a slowish start. He plugged on willingly enough in the straight, showing a rather pounding action, and if he is typical of newcomers from his yard he will step up on this next time. (op 4-1 tchd 11-4)

Duellist, for whom there was no great market confidence, is a half-brother to the Middle Park winner Lujain and the UAE Oaks winner Satin Kiss among other good horses. Nevertheless, this debut effort has to be rated as disappointing. He was close enough if good enough turning in, but lacked any sort of change of gear and tended to carry his head awkwardly. (op 11-8 tchd 15-8)

Rathbawn Girl(IRE) showed little trying this surface for the first time but is at least now eligible for handicaps. (op 12-1 tchd 11-1 and 16-1)

Bella Charlie(IRE) was always struggling back in trip and seemed to resent the kickback. Official explanation: that the colt was unsuited by the kickback (op 20-1)

7865 BET TOTEPOOL ON TODAY'S IRISH RACING MAIDEN STKS 1m (F)
12:45 (12:45) (Class 5) 2-Y-0 **£2,590** (£770; £385; £192) **Stalls** Low

Form RPR

03 **1** **Thundering Home**[22] 7663 2-9-3 0................................ HayleyTurner 9 72+
(E A L Dunlop) *s.i.s: hld up: hdwy over 3f out: rdn and hung lft over 1f out: hung rt and styd on u.p to ld wl ins fnl f: eased nr fin* **4/1**[3]

5003 **2** *1* **Gold Party**[13] 7773 2-9-3 62.......................................(t) RobertWinston 2 70
(K McAuliffe) *pushed along to ld after 1f: rdn over 1f out: hdd and unable qck wl ins fnl f* **8/1**

522 **3** *4 ½* **Prince Yarraman (IRE)**[9] 7825 2-9-3 0......................... ShaneKelly 6 60
(J A Osborne) *trckd ldrs: racd keenly: rdn over 3f out: wknd ins fnl f* **9/4**[1]

63 **4** *2 ¼* **Claddagh**[17] 7721 2-9-3 0.. JoeFanning 10 55
(M Johnston) *led 1f: chsd ldr tl rdn over 2f out: wknd fnl f* **3/1**[2]

04 **5** *11* **Fochabers**[22] 7663 2-9-3 0.. SteveDrowne 7 31
(R Charlton) *sn pushed along and prom: rdn and lost pl 5f out: out: wknd over 3f out* **13/2**

6 *hd* **Sternian** 2-8-5 0... LauraPike(7) 3 26
(M E Rimmer) *s.i.s: sn pushed along in rr: sme hdwy over 3f out: sn wknd* **150/1**

006 **7** *5* **New Den**[13] 7764 2-9-3 65.. SJCraine 5 20
(J R Boyle) *sn pushed along to chse ldrs: rdn and wknd 3f out* **25/1**

0044 **8** *3 ½* **Tenga Venga**[12] 7781 2-9-3 55.......................................(p) AdamKirby 8 12
(P S McEntee) *sn pushed along to chse ldrs: rdn and wknd 3f out* **50/1**

06 **9** *3 ¾* **My Grand Duke (USA)**[17] 7721 2-9-3 0................... FrankieMcDonald 4 —
(J A Osborne) *hld up: rdn and wknd over 3f out* **80/1**

05 **10** *29* **Concorde Kiss (USA)**[10] 7816 2-8-7 0......................... LeeNewnes(5) 1 —
(S Kirk) *sn pushed along in rr: lost tch 1/2-way: t.o* **33/1**

1m 46.49s (2.79) **Going Correction** +0.225s/f (Slow) **10** Ran SP% **110.9**
Speed ratings (Par 96): **95,94,89,87,76 76,71,67,63,34**
toteswinger:1&2:£6.80, 2&3:£5.20, 1&3:£1.80 CSF £32.26 TOTE £4.20: £1.90, £2.20, £1.10; EX 45.30 Trifecta £146.00 Pool: £375.02 - 1.90 winning units..

Owner Salem Suhail **Bred** Rabbah Bloodstock Limited **Trained** Newmarket, Suffolk

FOCUS
No more than a fair maiden and, despite the pace looking just an ordinary one, the field was already strung out turning for home and conditions ensured it was still a test of stamina at the trip. The form could rate higher and the runner-up looks the key.

NOTEBOOK
Thundering Home has an action that suggests he should be suited by a testing surface and, despite drifting left then right, stayed on stoutly to win a touch readily. He's by Storming Home and this effort, as well as his last, suggests that further will suit once he goes into handicaps. (op 5-1)

Gold Party seems to have improved in this headgear combination and saw his race out well enough despite a tendency to look around him in front. This was his first run on the surface and it seemed to suit him well. (tchd 9-1)

Prince Yarraman(IRE) travelled well to the straight, but looked one-paced after that and didn't finish his race with the same zest as the front two. He's clearly only modest, but shapes as though he will be suited by a return to Polytrack. (tchd 5-2)

Claddagh had every chance but couldn't sustain his run and, unless he needs dropping back in trip, looks rather limited. (op 11-4 tchd 5-2)

Fochabers had finished just behind the winner at Lingfield, but seemed all at sea on this different surface and only began to stay on when the race was over. He looks like he might want a trip, and is the sort to do better back on a faster surface in handicaps. (op 6-1 tchd 7-1)
Sternian showed a glimmer of ability after a slow start without ever threatening, and ought to improve for the experience.

7866 BET TOTEPOOL AT TOTESPORT.COM H'CAP 5f (F)

1:20 (1:20) (Class 3) (0-95,91) 3-Y-O+

£7,477 (£2,239; £1,119; £560; £279; £140) **Stalls** High

Form RPR

543- **1** **Fitz Flyer (IRE)**[433] 6894 3-9-4 **91** .... PhillipMakin 7 100
(D H Brown) *chsd ldrs: rdn 1/2-way: r.o u.p to ld post* **8/1**

4305 **2** *nse* **Rebel Duke (IRE)**[21] 7676 5-8-8 **86** .... BMcHugh(5) 5 95
(Ollie Pears) *a.p: chsd ldr over 3f out: rdn to ld ins fnl f: edgd rt: hdd post* **7/2**[1]

3402 **3** *1* **Equuleus Pictor**[21] 7676 5-8-10 **86** .... JackDean(3) 3 91
(J L Spearing) *led: rdn and hung rt over 1f out: hdd ins fnl f: unable qck towards fin* **7/2**[1]

0133 **4** *1 1/4* **Tourist**[11] 7801 4-8-9 **82** .... RobertWinston 8 83
(D Shaw) *s.i.s and n.m.r after s: sn pushed along in rr: hdwy and swtchd lft over 1f out: rdn and no imp ins fnl f* **7/1**

0003 **5** *2 3/4* **Pawan (IRE)**[14] 7758 9-8-5 **83** ow3 .... (b) AnnStokell(5) 1 74
(Miss A Stokell) *s.i.s: sn drvn along in rr: n.d* **12/1**

006 **6** *1* **Canadian Danehill (IRE)**[21] 7676 7-9-1 **88** .... (p) GrahamGibbons 4 75
(R M H Cowell) *chsd ldrs: rdn 3f out: sn lost pl: in rr whn edgd rt over 1f out* **12/1**

0232 **7** *1/2* **Colorus (IRE)**[14] 7758 6-8-1 **77** .... (p) KellyHarrison(3) 6 63
(W J H Ratcliffe) *chsd ldr to over 3f out: rdn 1/2-way: wknd over 1f out* **13/2**[3]

0000 **8** *3 1/2* **Peak District (IRE)**[108] 5860 5-8-9 **87** .... AmyRyan(5) 2 60
(K A Ryan) *s.i.s: sn pushed along in rr: nvr on terms* **5/1**[2]

59.73 secs (0.03) **Going Correction** +0.20s/f (Slow) **8** Ran SP% **113.4**
Speed ratings (Par 107): **107,106,105,103,98 97,96,90**
toteswinger:1&2:£14.20, 2&3:£6.20, 1&3:£6.30 CSF £35.54 CT £116.96 TOTE £9.90: £2.90, £2.30, £1.50; EX 74.60 Trifecta £221.70 Pool: £458.54 - 1.53 winning units..
Owner Ron Hull **Bred** Colin Kennedy **Trained** Maltby, S Yorks

FOCUS
An open affair and a dress rehearsal for the big sprint over the same trip here on New Year's Day, with seven of these engaged in that race. It produced a tight finish, much as the ratings suggested it might.

NOTEBOOK
Fitz Flyer(IRE) produced a cracking performance on his first start since October 2008 to defy top weight and win his first race in the process, staying on strongly nearest the rail to get the verdict on the nod. He has always been well regarded and is clearly useful, though whether he would be able to reproduce this level of form turned out again after a break of just three days (and for which he gets a 6lb penalty) given his long absence, is a moot point. (op 7-1 tchd 13-2)
Rebel Duke(IRE) was just denied reverting to more usual tactics for him, having been held up last time, and must have good prospects if turned out again later in the week given his good record here. (op 4-1 tchd 9-2)
Equuleus Pictor ran right up to his recent C&D form without seeming to have any excuses, and is another likley to turn up here on Friday. (op 5-2)
Tourist acquitted himself with credit considering he was dropping back to 5f and trying this surface for the first time. He didn't quite have the pace to challenge, though, and left the impression that he will be happier back at 6f. (op 8-1 tchd 6-1)
Pawan(IRE) never threatened while kept more towards the inside rail than the others. (op 16-1 tchd 18-1)
Canadian Danehill(IRE) ran a moody race before consenting to run on late and isn't in top form right now.
Colorus(IRE) ran moderately for no apparent reason. (op 8-1 tchd 6-1)
Peak District(IRE) hadn't been in top form when last seen in the autumn and, despite this being a drop in grade, ran poorly and was beaten a long way out. Perhaps this isn't his surface, but he's becoming frustrating. (op 13-2)

7867 BET TOTEPOOL ON 0800 221 221 H'CAP 1m 6f (F)

1:55 (1:55) (Class 4) (0-85,91) 3-Y-O+

£4,984 (£1,492; £746; £373; £186; £93) **Stalls** Low

Form RPR

0523 **1** **Clear Reef**[34] 7515 5-10-0 **80** .... (p) ShaneKelly 3 88
(Jane Chapple-Hyam) *hld up: hdwy over 3f out: swtchd lft over 2f out: shkn up to ld over 1f out: styd on wl* **12/1**

2422 **2** *2* **Outrageous Request**[12] 7780 3-8-11 **77** .... TobyAtkinson(7) 10 82
(Pat Eddery) *plld hrd and prom: rdn to ld over 1f out: sn hdd: hung rt ins fnl f: styd on same pce* **11/4**[2]

0051 **3** *1 3/4* **Sunny Spells**[7] 7840 4-8-9 **64** 6ex .... WilliamCarson(3) 5 67
(S C Williams) *hld up: hdwy over 3f out: rdn over 1f out: edgd lft: styd on* **5/2**[1]

3141 **4** *3 1/4* **Full Toss**[7] 7841 3-10-4 **91** 6ex .... J-PGuillambert 11 89
(P D Evans) *trckd ldrs: plld hrd: rdn over 3f out: ev ch 2f out: no ex fnl f* **7/1**

0510 **5** *1/2* **Bushy Dell (IRE)**[81] 6636 4-8-11 **68** .... AmyBaker(5) 6 66
(Miss J Feilden) *led 2f: chsd ldr tl pushed along to ld over 3f out: rdn and hdd over 1f out: no ex fnl f* **40/1**

6622 **6** *6* **Dunaskin (IRE)**[24] 7640 9-9-12 **78** .... (e) TomEaves 1 67
(B Ellison) *chsd ldr tl led after 2f: rdn and hdd over 3f out: wknd over 1f out* **14/1**

4131 **7** *1* **Calculating (IRE)**[14] 7760 5-8-11 **68** .... LeeNewnes(5) 9 56
(M D I Usher) *s.i.s: hld up: rdn over 4f out: sn wknd* **9/2**[3]

12-4 **8** *19* **Chocolate Caramel (USA)**[24] 7647 7-9-11 **77** .... TonyHamilton 8 38
(R A Fahey) *hld up: hdwy 1/2-way: rdn and wknd over 3f out: t.o* **18/1**

4614 **9** *20* **Bentley Brook (IRE)**[21] 7675 7-9-8 **74** .... TonyCulhane 4 7
(R Curtis) *hld up: a in rr: rdn and wknd wl over 3f out: t.o* **28/1**

1-00 **10** *39* **Tenjack King**[168] 3941 4-9-7 **73** .... LPKeniry 2 —
(Joss Saville) *mid-div: pushed along over 8f out: wknd 6f out: t.o* **100/1**

5555 **11** *dist* **Victory Quest (IRE)**[14] 7760 9-9-1 **67** .... (v) RobertWinston 7 —
(Mrs S Lamyman) *chsd ldrs tl rdn and wknd 4f out: eased fnl 3f: t.o* **16/1**

3m 10.41s (2.11) **Going Correction** +0.225s/f (Slow)
WFA 3 from 4yo+ 7lb **11** Ran SP% **118.3**
Speed ratings (Par 105): **102,100,99,98,97 94,93,82,71,49** —
toteswinger:1&2:£9.10, 2&3:£3.30, 1&3:£11.70 CSF £45.00 CT £113.16 TOTE £13.30: £2.80, £1.50, £1.80; EX 76.50 Trifecta £105.00 Pool: £503.88 - 3.55 winning units..
Owner Mrs Jane Chapple-Hyam **Bred** Hesmonds Stud Ltd **Trained** Newmarket, Suffolk

FOCUS
Just an ordinary gallop to this fair staying event, though the two leaders still paid in the end for going for home too soon and those ridden with more patience came through late. There were enough in-form horses well held here to think that this is good form.

Victory Quest(IRE) Official explanation: jockey said that the gelding stopped very quickly

7868 BEST ODDS GUARANTEED AT TOTESPORT.COM CLAIMING STKS 7f (F)

2:30 (2:31) (Class 5) 2-Y-O **£2,729** (£806; £403) **Stalls** Low

Form RPR

0413 **1** **Lord Victor**[2] 7849 2-8-10 64 .... ShaneKelly 3 66
(A J McCabe) *mde virtually all: rdn over 1f out: edgd rt ins fnl f: styd on u.p* **9/4**[2]

2121 **2** *nk* **Bubbly Bellini (IRE)**[2] 7850 2-8-8 75 .... (p) MatthewDavies(5) 4 68
(George Baker) *hld up in tch: chsd wnr 2f out: sn rdn: hung rt and rdrs whip broke ins fnl f: styd on u.p* **5/6**[1]

1465 **3** *6* **Angie's Nap (USA)**[11] 7793 2-8-2 63 .... (p) LukeMorris 6 42
(P S McEntee) *sn chsng wnr: rdn 1/2-way: wknd fnl f* **10/1**

4064 **4** *5* **Moonlight Serenade**[15] 7749 2-7-13 57 .... KierenFox(7) 2 34
(W G M Turner) *plld hrd and prominen trdn over 2f out: wknd over 1f out* **25/1**

2033 **5** *1* **Miss Taken (IRE)**[11] 7791 2-7-9 47 .... NeilFarley(7) 1 27
(D Carroll) *chsd ldrs: rdn over 2f out: sn hung lft: wknd over 1f out* **9/1**[3]

00 **6** *23* **Thatlittlecolt**[38] 7477 2-8-13 0 .... (p) PhillipMakin 5 —
(D H Brown) *in rr and rdn over 4f out: sn lost tch: t.o* **40/1**

1m 31.34s (1.04) **Going Correction** +0.225s/f (Slow) **6** Ran SP% **110.7**
Speed ratings (Par 96): **103,102,95,90,88 62**
totewinger:1&2:£1.10, 2&3:£2.40, 1&3:£4.50 CSF £4.32 TOTE £3.30: £1.60, £1.20; EX 5.00.
Owner Khalifa Dasmal **Bred** Ellis Stud Partnership **Trained** Averham Park, Notts

FOCUS
A weakish claimer run at an ordinary gallop with the proven stayer just prevailing in a tight finish. The form is rated around the winner and the second was 8lb off his recent selling win here.

NOTEBOOK
Lord Victor had scored under this rider in similar fashion here two runs back and just outstayed the favourite after getting first run in the straight. He's going to be a formidable opponent here into the new year kept to this grade, but will struggle in handicaps if the assessor takes this beating of a below-par 75-rated animal literally. (op 3-1)
Bubbly Bellini(IRE) had finished well held in both previous runs at 7f, but saw the trip out well here, albeit in a race that wasn't truly run. That said, he wasn't quite at his best and, given the company he has been keeping, looks rather flattered by his official rating. (tchd 10-11)
Angie's Nap(USA) was a bit disappointing considering how the race panned out as she has winning form at sprint trips. She isn't at her best right now. (op 15-2)
Moonlight Serenade didn't have much of a chance at the weights and didn't figure once the race began in earnest. Official explanation: jockey said that the filly hung right (op 20-1)
Thatlittlecolt was reluctant to enter the stalls and was soon labouring despite the headgear and drop in grade. (op 33-1)

7869 BET ON TONIGHT'S FOOTBALL AT TOTESPORT.COM H'CAP 6f (F)

3:05 (3:05) (Class 7) (0-50,50) 3-Y-O+ **£1,942** (£578; £288; £144) **Stalls** Low

Form RPR

0000 **1** **Angle Of Attack (IRE)**[17] 7726 4-8-11 **48** .... (v[1]) GrahamGibbons 7 64
(A D Brown) *mde all: rdn over 1f out: edgd rt ins fnl f: drvn out* **12/1**

0264 **2** *3 1/2* **Tag Team (IRE)**[11] 7795 8-8-7 **49** ow1 .... (p) MarkCoumbe(5) 4 54
(John A Harris) *a.p: rdn to chse wnr 2f out: styd on same pce ins fnl f* **7/1**

4002 **3** *1 3/4* **Tadlil**[21] 7681 7-8-11 **48** .... (v) LukeMorris 8 47
(J M Bradley) *chsd ldrs: rdn over 2f out: styd on same pce fnl f* **5/1**[2]

0555 **4** *1 1/2* **Dontuwishitwereso**[12] 7787 3-8-11 **48** .... (e) TonyCulhane 13 42
(P W D'Arcy) *s.i.s: in rr: styd on u.p fr over 1f out: wnt 4th cl home: nvr nrr* **6/1**[3]

5004 **5** *hd* **Tenancy (IRE)**[18] 7709 5-8-4 **46** .... DeanHeslop(5) 5 40
(S A Harris) *chsd wnr tl rdn 2f out: wknd fnl f* **16/1**

4003 **6** *1/2* **Stormburst (IRE)**[13] 7771 5-8-10 **47** .... SteveDrowne 6 39
(A J Chamberlain) *mid-div: hdwy 1/2-way: sn rdn: wknd fnl f* **16/1**

3000 **7** *3/4* **Triumphant Welcome**[28] 7606 4-8-13 **50** .... (b[1]) FergusSweeney 9 40
(H J Evans) *hld up: hdwy 1/2-way: rdn and hung lft over 1f out: wknd fnl f* **7/1**

0203 **8** *3* **Positivity**[17] 7727 3-8-13 **50** .... (p) TomEaves 3 30
(B Smart) *s.i.s: sn pushed along in rr: rdn over 2f out: nvr on terms* **4/1**[1]

6023 **9** *2* **Place The Duchess**[2] 7853 3-8-5 **49** .... (t) NathanAlison(7) 12 23
(A J Lidderdale) *s.i.s: a in rr* **10/1**

0040 **10** *2 1/2* **Divine White**[85] 6551 6-8-8 **45** .... (b[1]) JimmyQuinn 10 11
(G P Enright) *prom: rdn 1/2-way: wknd 2f out* **33/1**

0006 **11** *3 3/4* **Rightcar Dominic**[25] 7629 4-8-8 **45** .... (b) LPKeniry 1 —
(Peter Grayson) *s.i.s: a in rr* **100/1**

0005 **12** *7* **El Potro**[10] 7819 7-8-8 **45** .... NickyMackay 11 —
(J R Holt) *mid-div: pushed along 1/2-way: sn wknd* **14/1**

6000 **13** *5* **Lambrini Lace (IRE)**[11] 7802 4-8-10 **47** .... (p) TonyHamilton 14 —
(Mrs L Williamson) *mid-div: racd on outside: pushed along and wknd 1/2-way* **25/1**

1m 17.63s (1.13) **Going Correction** +0.225s/f (Slow) **13** Ran SP% **118.9**
Speed ratings (Par 97): **101,96,94,92,91 91,90,86,83,80 75,65,59**
toteswinger:1&2:£18.10, 2&3:£4.40, 1&3:£16.50 CSF £92.13 CT £483.60 TOTE £19.30: £4.60, £3.30, £2.10; EX 163.00 Trifecta £213.90 Pool: £312.18 - 1.08 winning units..
Owner S Pedersen **Bred** Travel Spot Girl Partnership **Trained** Yedingham, N Yorks

FOCUS
A bottom-grade handicap run at a decent gallop but, as is so often the case here, little got into the race from off the pace.

7870 BET LIVE IN PLAY AT TOTESPORT.COM H'CAP 6f (F)

3:35 (3:35) (Class 5) (0-75,75) 3-Y-O+ **£2,590** (£770; £385; £192) **Stalls** Low

Form RPR

0030 **1** **Harlech Castle**[27] 7613 4-9-4 **75** .... (b) SJCraine 7 86
(J R Boyle) *a.p: pushed along over 3f out: nt clr run and swtchd lft 2f out: led over 1f out: shkn up and styd on wl* **6/1**[3]

0534 **2** *3/4* **Onceaponatime (IRE)**[17] 7735 4-8-11 **68** .... LukeMorris 10 77
(M D Squance) *hld up: hdwy 1/2-way: rdn and ev ch fr over 1f out: unable qck towards fin* **4/1**[1]

0100 **3** *3* **Gentle Guru**[16] 7739 5-8-10 **67** .... SteveDrowne 13 66
(R T Phillips) *sn outpcd: hdwy u.p over 1f out: r.o: nt rch ldrs* **25/1**

0361 **4** *1/2* **Cheap Thrills**[21] 7679 3-8-11 **68** .... ShaneKelly 2 66
(J A Osborne) *led: hdd over 4f out: remained w ldr tl led again over 2f out: rdn: hung rt and hdd over 1f out: no ex fnl f* **10/1**

0055 **5** *2* **Bo McGinty (IRE)**[10] 7807 8-8-8 **65** .... (v) MartinDwyer 4 56
(R A Fahey) *chsd ldrs: rdn and ev ch over 2f out: styd on same pce appr fnl f* **8/1**

0250 **6** *3/4* **Restless Genius (IRE)**[22] 7673 4-8-4 **64** .... MartinLane(3) 6 53
(B Ellison) *s.i.s: hld up: hdwy 1/2-way: rdn over 2f out: sn btn* **8/1**

0443 **7** *hd* **Kyle (IRE)**[10] 7807 5-8-6 **63** .... SimonWhitworth 8 51
(C R Dore) *hld up: hdwy 1/2-way: rdn and nt clr run wl over 1f out: wknd fnl f* **16/1**

2132 **8** nse **Madison Belle**[242] 1652 3-9-2 **73** AndrewElliott 9 61
(J R Weymes) *chsd ldrs: rdn 1/2-way: nt clr run over 1f out: wknd fnl f* **20/1**

0410 **9** 2 1/4 **Danum Dancer**[14] 7762 5-8-6 **63** (b) JimmyQuinn 3 44
(N Bycroft) *s.i.s: hdwy to ld over 4f out: rdn and hdd over 2f out: wknd over 1f out* **11/2**[2]

-200 **10** 1 1/2 **Final Salute**[16] 7741 3-8-13 **70** (v) TomEaves 11 46
(B Smart) *s.i.s: sn pushed along and a in rr* **12/1**

6030 **11** hd **Stanley Goodspeed**[18] 7716 6-8-4 **61** (bt) LiamJones 5 37
(J W Hills) *s.i.s and hmpd s: a in rr* **12/1**

1635 **12** 8 **Naomh Geileis (USA)**[14] 7762 4-8-6 **63** (b) JoeFanning 1 13
(M Johnston) *s.i.s: sn pushed along and a in rr* **8/1**

1m 17.47s (0.97) **Going Correction** +0.225s/f (Slow) 12 Ran SP% **122.0**
Speed ratings (Par 103): **102,101,97,96,93 92,92,92,89,87 87,76**
toteswinger:1&2:£6.30, 2&3:£34.00, 1&3:£36.20 CSF £31.13 CT £583.63 TOTE £6.30: £2.40, £1.90, £8.30; EX 41.50 Trifecta £417.80 Part won. Pool: £564.61 - 0.90 winning units. Place 6 £29.95, Place 5 £7.71.
Owner Elite Racing Club **Bred** Elite Racing Club **Trained** Epsom, Surrey

FOCUS
A decent handicap run at a strong pace and probably good form for the grade.
Madison Belle Official explanation: jockey said that the filly hung left
T/Plt: £26.10 to a £1 stake. Pool: £70,463.23. 1,965.48 winning tickets. T/Qpdt: £6.30 to a £1 stake. Pool: £8,371.30. 982.10 winning tickets. CR

7829 KEMPTON (A.W) (R-H)
Wednesday, December 30

OFFICIAL GOING: Standard
Wind: Moderate, half against Weather: Raining, cold

7871 CITY & SUBURBAN PARKING NURSERY 5f (P)
6:50 (6:50) (Class 5) (0-75,75) 2-Y-O **£2,590** (£770; £385; £192) **Stalls High**

Form RPR
3021 **1** **Wanchai Whisper**[20] 7698 2-8-7 **61** PaulDoe 5 70
(P D Evans) *slowest away: sn in 8th: gd prog over 1f out and weaved through: led ins fnl f: sn clr* **6/1**[2]

0133 **2** 2 **Athwaab**[12] 7793 2-8-13 **67** TonyCulhane 9 69
(M G Quinlan) *dwlt: t.k.h and hld up in midfield: prog on inner over 1f out: rdn and styd on to take 2nd nr fin* **7/1**

0064 **3** nk **Kings Of Leo**[20] 7698 2-8-9 **68** MatthewDavies(5) 10 69
(J R Boyle) *mde most: edgd lft fr over 1f out: hdd and outpcd ins fnl f: lost 2nd nr fin* **5/1**[1]

0001 **4** nse **R Woody**[25] 7637 2-9-5 **73** SteveDrowne 7 74
(Mrs L C Jewell) *chsd ldng pair: cl up whn checked jst over 1f out: styd on nr fin but no ch* **8/1**

0041 **5** 1 3/4 **Miss Lesley**[11] 7805 2-9-7 **75** (b) MartinDwyer 3 69
(D K Ivory) *chsd ldng pair on outer: rdn and nt qckn over 1f out: fdd fnl f* **13/2**[3]

0033 **6** shd **Blue Neptune**[20] 7698 2-8-8 **62** HayleyTurner 11 56
(W R Muir) *w ldr: stl upsides 1f out: wknd* **5/1**[1]

6245 **7** 1/2 **Hill Of Miller (IRE)**[13] 7786 2-8-13 **70** WilliamCarson(3) 8 62
(Rae Guest) *dwlt: mostly in midfield: in tch tl fdd over 1f out* **7/1**

3032 **8** 6 **Six Wives**[12] 7793 2-9-5 **73** ChrisCatlin 6 43
(J A Glover) *pushed along on outer in midfield: no prog over 1f out: wknd rapidly fnl f* **5/1**[1]

0040 **9** 6 **Special Betty**[12] 7799 2-8-2 **56** FrankieMcDonald 1 5
(D Haydn Jones) *dwlt: outpcd after 2f and wl bhd after* **66/1**

0003 **10** 10 **Lets Move It**[13] 7778 2-7-12 **52** oh2 (v) JamieMackay 4 —
(D Shaw) *wl bhd after 2f: t.o* **33/1**

59.94 secs (-0.56) **Going Correction** +0.05s/f (Slow) 10 Ran SP% **118.2**
Speed ratings (Par 96): **106,102,102,102,99 99,98,88,79,63**
toteswinger:1&2:£7.20, 2&3:£12.80, 1&3:£8.90 CSF £48.32 CT £233.59 TOTE £7.30: £2.30, £2.50, £2.30; EX 34.70.
Owner M&R Refurbishments Ltd **Bred** Mike Smith **Trained** Pandy, Monmouths

FOCUS
A tight nursery run at a fast pace. A pesonal best from the winner.

NOTEBOOK
Wanchai Whisper appreciated the good gallop and came from off the speed. Her previous three wins had come in selling/claiming grade and this was a career-best effort. She won with authority, off the same rating as when successful 20 days earlier and, although well beaten off 69 earlier in the year, she is clearly a different proposition now. (op 13-2)
Athwaab did well on her return to Polytrack and five furlongs but she was never quite going the pace on this faster surface. She might be more effective over another furlong. (op 6-1)
Kings Of Leo and Blue Neptune had finished just behind the winner here last time but they were hustling each other on the pace and did too much running early. In the circumstances, Kings Of Leo comes out of this with a degree of credit. (op 10-1)
R Woody looks progressive but his debut win last time came on the slower Southwell surface over this distance. On Polytrack, he surely needs a sixth furlong. (op 15-2)
Miss Lesley wasn't helped by a moderate draw and had to use her speed to cope with the fast early pace. Her two wins have been over 6f, the latest in a claimer, and she may need to return to that grade and distance. (op 7-1)
Blue Neptune was clearly feeling the effects of the hard tussle with Kings Of Leo in the closing stages. (op 9-2 tchd 4-1)
Hill Of Miller(IRE) is not an easy ride. He might be worth another try at this distance, as his recent form has been over 6f, but his record is now 0-11.
Six Wives could never get on the pace and went out very tamely. (op 6-1)

7872 CITY & SUBURBAN PARKING H'CAP 5f (P)
7:20 (7:20) (Class 4) (0-85,80) 3-Y-O+ **£4,727** (£1,406; £702; £351) **Stalls High**

Form RPR
3302 **1** **Excellent Show**[35] 7511 3-9-3 **79** TomEaves 3 87
(B Smart) *w ldr: rdn over 1f out: edgd ahd ins fnl f: hld on* **10/3**[2]

0530 **2** nk **The Tatling (IRE)**[15] 7758 12-9-1 **80** JackDean(3) 6 87
(J M Bradley) *trckd ldng pair: effrt over 1f out: intimidated fnl f but kpt trying: grabbed 2nd on post* **16/1**

0054 **3** hd **Bertoliver**[20] 7702 5-9-0 **79** WilliamCarson(3) 7 85
(S C Williams) *mde most on inner: tried to kick on over 1f out: worn down ins fnl f: lost 2nd post* **7/4**[1]

1543 **4** 1/2 **Littlemisssunshine (IRE)**[11] 7808 4-8-6 **68** (p) LukeMorris 5 72
(J S Moore) *trckd ldng pair: drvn to chal 1f out: nt qckn and a jst hld* **5/1**[3]

3606 **5** 1/2 **Chjimes (IRE)**[25] 7646 5-8-13 **75** FergusSweeney 4 78
(C R Dore) *trckd ldng quartet: shkn up and nt qckn over 1f out: drvn and kpt on fnl f: nvr quite able to chal* **16/1**

0006 **6** hd **Priti Fabulous (IRE)**[21] 7682 4-8-4 **73** DeclanCannon(7) 8 75
(A J McCabe) *v awkward s: mostly in last trio: rdn on inner over 1f out: clsd grad fnl f wout threatening* **25/1**

0101 **7** 1 3/4 **Lord Of The Reins (IRE)**[21] 7682 5-8-13 **75** JimCrowley 1 71
(J G Given) *s.i.s: hld up in last trio: rdn and nt qckn wl over 1f out: no prog after* **5/1**[3]

1 **8** 1 3/4 **Norse Warrior (USA)**[26] 7629 3-8-11 **73** (v) FrankieMcDonald 2 62
(Peter Grayson) *s.i.s: struggling in last after 2f: n.d* **20/1**

59.70 secs (-0.80) **Going Correction** +0.05s/f (Slow) 8 Ran SP% **113.1**
Speed ratings (Par 105): **108,107,107,106,105 105,102,99**
toteswinger:1&2:£6.40, 2&3:£5.80, 1&3:£2.50 CSF £52.33 CT £120.71 TOTE £4.00: £1.20, £3.90, £1.30; EX 43.30.
Owner A Turton, P Langford & S Brown **Bred** Bearstone Stud And T Herbert Jackson **Trained** Hambleton, N Yorks

FOCUS
A cautionary note as this was run only 0.24sec faster than the earlier nursery.

7873 DIGIBET H'CAP 2m (P)
7:50 (7:50) (Class 5) (0-75,75) 3-Y-O+ **£2,590** (£770; £385; £192) **Stalls High**

Form RPR
-500 **1** **Dani's Girl (IRE)**[32] 6470 6-9-7 **75** KierenFox(7) 6 80
(P M Phelan) *stdd s: t.k.h and hld up in last pair: pushed along and prog over 3f out: wnt 3rd over 2f out: edgd lft but rdn to ld over 1f out: v readily* **4/1**[2]

-003 **2** 1 3/4 **Meirig's Dream (IRE)**[21] 7688 3-8-8 **63** oh5 ow7 PaulFitzsimons 2 66
(Miss N A Lloyd-Beavis) *trckd ldrs: wnt 2nd over 3f out: rdn to ld jst over 2f out: hdd u.p over 1f out: no ch w wnr after* **28/1**

6200 **3** 1 1/4 **Spiritonthemount (USA)**[49] 7336 4-8-6 **56** oh11 (b) WilliamCarson(3) 5 57
(P W Hiatt) *t.k.h: sn prom: led 5f out and kicked on sn after: hdd jst over 2f out: one pce* **50/1**

0524 **4** 2 1/4 **Ardmaddy (IRE)**[42] 7440 5-8-9 **56** (b) FergusSweeney 9 54
(G L Moore) *hld up towards rr: prog to go 3rd over 3f out to over 2f out: one pce u.p after* **4/1**[2]

-423 **5** 7 **Leulahleulahlay**[17] 7737 3-9-5 **74** ShaneKelly 3 64
(Evan Williams) *led: drvn 7f out: hdd 5f out: sn btn* **14/1**

P0-6 **6** shd **Command Marshal (FR)**[30] 7598 6-9-2 **63** SJCraine 4 53
(M J Scudamore) *trckd ldr to 1/2-way: rdn 4f out: steadily wknd* **16/1**

1005 **7** 8 **Kashmina**[14] 7777 4-8-13 **63** RobertLButler(3) 1 43
(Miss Sheena West) *hld up in rr: pushed along over 4f out: struggling u.p over 2f out: wknd* **16/1**

5041 **8** 11 **Court Princess**[29] 7608 6-9-0 **61** DaneO'Neill 7 28
(George Baker) *t.k.h early: prom: chsd ldr 5f out to over 3f out: wknd u.p: t.o* **2/1**[1]

43-2 **9** 25 **Whaxaar (IRE)**[55] 7255 5-8-9 **56** oh1 RobertHavlin 8 —
(R Ingram) *stdd s: t.k.h: hld up in last pair: rdn and no prog over 3f out: wknd: t.o* **11/2**[3]

3m 34.09s (3.99) **Going Correction** +0.05s/f (Slow)
WFA 3 from 4yo+ 8lb 9 Ran SP% **112.6**
Speed ratings (Par 103): **92,91,90,89,85 85,81,76,63**
toteswinger:1&2:£10.50, 2&3:£50.90, 1&3:£34.30 CSF £100.90 CT £4715.29 TOTE £4.50: £1.50, £6.90, £6.10; EX 156.10.
Owner Clive Craig **Bred** R S Bennett **Trained** Epsom, Surrey

7874 DIGIBET.COM CLAIMING STKS 1m (P)
8:20 (8:20) (Class 6) 2-Y-O **£2,047** (£604; £302) **Stalls High**

Form RPR
0211 **1** **Glen Lass**[13] 7788 2-8-8 58 (b) ChrisCatlin 4 71
(J Pearce) *rn in snatches early: mostly in 3rd: chal over 2f out: chsd ldr after: kpt on u.p to ld ins fnl f* **4/1**[3]

0021 **2** 1 1/4 **Kirsty's Boy (IRE)**[21] 7690 2-8-9 76 LukeMorris 1 69
(J S Moore) *trckd ldr: hanging lft bnd 4f out to 3f out: pushed into ld over 2f out: edgd lft u.p and hdd ins fnl f: nt qckn* **10/11**[1]

3445 **3** 2 3/4 **Major Maximus**[19] 7708 2-8-5 70 MartinDwyer 5 59
(George Baker) *hld up last: pushed into 3rd 2f out: rdn and fnd nil over 1f out* **2/1**[2]

00 **4** 14 **Blue Glove (IRE)**[14] 7772 2-8-0 0 ow2 FrankieMcDonald 2 23
(J A Osborne) *rdn to ld: hdd & wknd over 2f out: t.o* **33/1**

1m 42.63s (2.83) **Going Correction** +0.05s/f (Slow) 4 Ran SP% **108.7**
Speed ratings (Par 94): **87,85,83,69**
CSF £8.24 TOTE £4.00; EX 5.80.
Owner Ian Bishop **Bred** Limestone And Tara Studs **Trained** Newmarket, Suffolk

FOCUS
The winner built on recent efforts to complete a hat-trick, but the form is rated a shade negatively.

NOTEBOOK
Glen Lass was 17lb behind the winner on adjusted official figures but she's on a roll at present, completing a hat-trick, having previously won over an extended 1m1f and a mile at Wolverhampton. A bit further certainly helps her. (tchd 7-2)
Kirsty's Boy(IRE) had the best of this modest event on adjusted official ratings but hung his chance away from four furlongs out. He had gone the other way round at Lingfield on his last two outings and this was the first time he had raced right handed. Due to his deviation it is impossible to say if he stayed a mile at this first attempt. (op 11-10 tchd 5-4)
Major Maximus is clearly saving his ability and connections are clearly searching for answers to bring it out. This was his first attempt in a claimer, having run over various trips recently. (op 7-4)
Blue Glove(IRE) doesn't look much good and might not try too hard.

7875 DIGIBET CASINO H'CAP 6f (P)
8:50 (8:50) (Class 4) (0-85,88) 3-Y-O+ **£4,727** (£1,406; £702; £351) **Stalls High**

Form RPR
4010 **1** **Lujeanie**[10] 7828 3-8-10 **75** (p) JimCrowley 8 86
(D K Ivory) *sltly hmpd s: t.k.h: hld up in 6th: quick move on inner to ld wl over 1f out: rdn and styd on wl* **15/2**[3]

5002 **2** 1 **Vhujon (IRE)**[9] 7832 4-8-13 **78** PaulDoe 4 86
(P D Evans) *hld up in 7th: rdn and prog fr 2f out to go 2nd 1f out: styd on but no real imp on wnr* **7/2**[2]

5466 **3** 2 1/4 **Dvinsky (USA)**[9] 7830 8-8-8 **73** (b) ShaneKelly 5 74
(P Howling) *pressed ldr: upsides 2f out: nt qckn u.p and sn outpcd: kpt on to snatch 3rd post* **10/1**

1232 **4** shd **Bahamian Lad**[20] 7702 4-9-3 **82** JerryO'Dwyer 9 82
(R Hollinshead) *wnt lft s: led to wl over 1f out: nt qckn: fdd fnl f: lost 3rd post* **7/2**[2]

1003 **5** 1 1/2 **Methaaly (IRE)**[20] 7702 6-8-12 **77** (be) GregFairley 1 72
(M Mullineaux) *chsd ldrs on outer: shkn up and nt qckn 2f out: grad wknd* **16/1**

4600 **6** *shd* **Princess Valerina**[28] 7613 5-9-0 **79** .... FrankieMcDonald 3 74
(D Haydn Jones) *s.s: hld up in 8th: taken to wd outside over 1f out: shuffled along and kpt on: nvr nr ldrs* **33/1**
2340 **7** *nk* **Ray Of Joy**[20] 7702 3-9-3 **82** .... JimmyQuinn 7 76
(J R Jenkins) *hmpd s: chsd ldng pair: chal and upsides 2f out: nt qckn over 1f out: wknd fnl f* **10/1**
6000 **8** *1* **Gone Hunting**[200] 2934 3-9-4 **83** .... (t) SaleemGolam 2 74
(J Pearce) *s.v.s: detached in last: reminder over 1f out and ins fnl f: nvr on terms* **33/1**
3-21 **9** *1* **Zegna (IRE)**[21] 7686 3-8-11 **76** .... TomEaves 6 64
(B Smart) *hmpd s: plld hrd bhd ldrs: wknd over 1f out* **5/2**[1]
1m 12.53s (-0.57) **Going Correction** +0.05s/f (Slow) **9** Ran SP% **114.7**
Speed ratings (Par 105): **105,103,100,100,98 98,98,96,95**
toteswinger:1&2:£12.40, 2&3:£11.40, 1&3:£12.40 CSF £33.71 CT £264.36 TOTE £8.90: £2.40, £2.00, £3.50; EX 36.80.
Owner K T Ivory **Bred** K T Ivory **Trained** Radlett, Herts

7876 HAPPY NEW YEAR TO ALL OUR CUSTOMERS H'CAP 7f (P)
9:20 (9:20) (Class 5) (0-70,70) 3-Y-O+ **£2,590** (£770; £385; £192) **Stalls** High

Form RPR
3053 **1** **Defector (IRE)**[18] 7729 3-9-4 **70** .... MartinDwyer 13 79
(W R Muir) *hld up bhd ldrs: gng strly 2f out: effrt over 1f out: r.o to ld ent fnl f: rdn clr* **13/2**[3]
0133 **2** *1 1/4* **Fernando Torres**[17] 7742 3-9-0 **66** .... (p) RobertWinston 9 72
(Matthew Salaman) *trckd ldng pair: effrt over 2f out: rdn to ld over 1f out: hdd and one pce ent fnl f* **4/1**[1]
1406 **3** *1/2* **Loyal Royal (IRE)**[19] 7716 6-8-7 **62** .... (b) JackDean(3) 10 67
(J M Bradley) *hld up in midfield on inner: prog over 2f out: chal over 1f out: nt qckn fnl f* **14/1**
034 **4** *hd* **Resplendent Nova**[17] 7741 7-9-1 **67** .... JimmyQuinn 2 71
(P Howling) *dropped in fr wd draw and off the pce in last pair: gd prog on inner over 2f out: looked dangerous 1f out: no ex* **6/1**[2]
4542 **5** *2* **Space Station**[17] 7739 3-9-4 **70** .... TonyCulhane 4 69
(S Dow) *racd wd in midfield: effrt u.p on wd outside 2f out: kpt on same pce and n.d* **7/1**
3613 **6** *1/2* **Kipchak (IRE)**[15] 7762 4-9-4 **70** .... (p) FergusSweeney 7 67
(C R Dore) *t.k.h early: pressed ldr: led over 2f out to over 1f out: wknd fnl f* **7/1**
0514 **7** *nse* **Bentley**[11] 7819 5-8-8 **60** ow1 .... JimCrowley 5 57
(J G Given) *pushed along in 9th after 3f: effrt u.p over 2f out: plugged on one pce* **20/1**
4500 **8** *1 3/4* **Pha Mai Blue**[23] 7664 4-8-9 **61** .... NickyMackay 6 54
(J R Boyle) *hld up in 10th: pushed along and keeping on whn stuck bhd rivals 1f out: shuffled along and no ch after* **33/1**
5053 **9** *1/2* **Kensington (IRE)**[9] 7830 8-8-8 **67** .... (p) DeclanCannon(7) 3 58
(A J McCabe) *trckd ldng pair: lost pl and rdn 2f out: struggling after* **14/1**
102 **10** *2 1/2* **King Of Defence**[21] 7692 3-9-2 **68** .... ChrisCatlin 8 52
(M A Jarvis) *hld up in midfield: gng wl enough over 2f out: sn rdn and nt qckn: wknd over 1f out* **4/1**[1]
5460 **11** *9* **Grand Honour (IRE)**[17] 7742 3-9-3 **69** .... PaulDoe 1 29
(P Howling) *dwlt and wnt lft s: dropped in bhd fr wd draw and wl off the pce in last: nvr nr ldrs: eased fnl f* **40/1**
010 **12** *2 1/2* **Whodunit (UAE)**[301] 760 5-8-5 **57** .... (b) SaleemGolam 12 10
(P W Hiatt) *led to over 2f out: wknd rapidly: t.o* **33/1**
1m 25.6s (-0.40) **Going Correction** +0.05s/f (Slow) **12** Ran SP% **119.0**
Speed ratings (Par 103): **104,102,102,101,99 98,98,96,96,93 83,80**
toteswinger:1&2:£6.60, 2&3:£10.90, 1&3:£30.20 CSF £31.57 CT £291.60 TOTE £9.20: £2.80, £1.70, £4.50; EX 35.60 Place 6 £609.06, Place 5 £232.03.
Owner David Knox & Partners **Bred** Grenane House Stud, Steve Hillen & Sean Graham **Trained** Lambourn, Berks

FOCUS
A tight handicap.
T/Plt: £1842.70 to a £1 stake. Pool: £121038.67. 47.95 winning tickets. T/Qpdt: £391.50 to a £1 stake. Pool: £8888.90. 16.80 winning tickets. JN

7805 LINGFIELD (L-H)
Wednesday, December 30
OFFICIAL GOING: Standard
Wind: very modest, across Weather: overcast, showers

7877 JEFF FIELDEN'S 60TH BIRTHDAY H'CAP (DIV I) 7f (P)
12:20 (12:21) (Class 6) (0-52,52) 3-Y-O+ **£1,637** (£483; £241) **Stalls** Low

Form RPR
13 **1** **Orangeleg**[134] 5121 3-8-11 **52** .... WilliamCarson(3) 3 64
(S C Williams) *hld up towards rr: hdwy on outer 3f out: rdn and wanting to edge lft over 1f out: str run to ld ins fnl f: sn in command* **9/4**[1]
0660 **2** *2 1/4* **Hart Of Gold**[9] 7834 5-9-0 **52** .... (p) LiamJones 12 58
(R A Harris) *t.k.h: chsd ldrs tl hdwy to ld 5f out: rdn wl over 1f out: hdd and nt pce of wnr ins fnl f: kpt on to hold 2nd* **18/1**
0010 **3** *1/2* **Dynamo Dave (USA)**[31] 7591 4-8-4 **49** .... (b) RachelKing(7) 1 54
(M D I Usher) *hld up in midfield: wd and lost pl bnd ent fnl 2f: bhd and pushed along wl over 1f out: r.o wl under hands and heels riding fnl f: nt rch ldrs* **22/1**
6606 **4** *nk* **Dicey Affair**[14] 7774 3-8-9 **47** .... (t) FergusSweeney 5 51
(G L Moore) *broke wl: sn stdd to trck ldrs: rdn and effrt ent fnl 2f: swtchd rt ins fnl f: kpt on one pce* **14/1**
6003 **5** *1/2* **Ardent Prince**[12] 7802 6-8-2 **47** .... DeclanCannon(7) 10 50
(A J McCabe) *awkward leaving stalls: sn wl in tch: rdn to chse ldng trio ent fnl 2f: kpt on one pce u.p fr over 1f out* **12/1**
0536 **6** *nk* **The City Kid (IRE)**[22] 7678 6-9-0 **52** .... (p) DaneO'Neill 11 54
(G D Blake) *t.k.h: led tl 5f out: chsd ldr over 2f out: rdn to chse ldr again wl over 1f out tl ent fnl f: wknd fnl 100yds* **8/1**[3]
2600 **7** *nk* **Josiah Bartlett (IRE)**[11] 7814 3-8-10 **48** .... HayleyTurner 9 49
(Ian Williams) *hld up in rr: rdn and effrt wl over 1f out: swtchd rt ent fnl f: styd on but nvr gng to rch ldrs* **6/1**[2]
0005 **8** *6* **Artesium**[12] 7796 3-8-12 **50** .... SJCraine 2 35
(Patrick Morris) *hld up in last trio: rdn and effrt wl over 1f out: no rspnse and n.d* **9/1**
5305 **9** *hd* **Albero Di Giuda (IRE)**[19] 7709 4-9-0 **52** .... (t) RobertWinston 14 36
(F Sheridan) *t.k.h: chsd ldng pair tl wnt 2nd over 2f out tl wl over 1f out: wknd qckly fnl f* **25/1**
0064 **10** *1 1/4* **Minnola**[81] 6674 4-8-11 **49** .... MartinDwyer 4 30
(Rae Guest) *a in rr: niggled along 4f out: rdn and no prog fr over 2f out* **10/1**
640 **11** *7* **North South Divide (IRE)**[40] 7462 5-8-8 **46** .... ChrisCatlin 8 8
(K A Ryan) *in tch: rdn and struggling 3f out: bhd fnl 2f* **6/1**[2]
1m 25.31s (0.51) **Going Correction** +0.075s/f (Slow) **11** Ran SP% **117.4**
Speed ratings (Par 101): **100,97,96,96,95 95,95,88,88,86 78**
toteswinger:1&2:£9.60, 2&3:£23.20, 1&3:£7.30 CSF £48.64 CT £737.21 TOTE £3.00: £1.30, £5.50, £4.10; EX 52.60 Trifecta £363.00 Part won. Pool: £490.61 - 0.50 winning units..
Owner K Harrison, J Allen **Bred** Baroness Bloodstock & Redmyre Bloodstock **Trained** Newmarket, Suffolk

FOCUS
There wasn't much pace on early here and a few were plenty keen enough through the early stages.

7878 BET ON TONIGHT'S FOOTBALL AT TOTESPORT.COM NURSERY 6f (P)
12:50 (12:50) (Class 4) (0-85,81) 2-Y-O **£3,885** (£1,156; £577; £288) **Stalls** Low

Form RPR
2414 **1** **Edgewater (IRE)**[28] 7611 2-9-7 **81** .... DaneO'Neill 6 84
(J Akehurst) *hld up in last: plld out and effrt u.p to press ldr over 1f out: led 1f out: r.o wl* **9/1**[3]
1536 **2** *1* **Transfixed (IRE)**[4] 7846 2-9-5 **79** .... PaulDoe 2 79
(P D Evans) *led: rdn ent fnl 2f: hdd 1f out: kpt on same pce after* **16/1**
5315 **3** *1/2* **Memorandum**[32] 7570 2-8-13 **73** .... SteveDrowne 3 72
(R Charlton) *chsd ldr: ev ch whn hung rt bnd 2f out: sn lost 2nd: kpt on same pce fnl f* **5/1**[2]
1 **4** *nk* **Tenacestream (CAN)**[32] 7571 2-9-3 **77** .... RobertWinston 4 75+
(J R Best) *racd in 3rd: rdn whn racd awkwardly and dropped to last bnd 2f out: sn detached and no prog tl kpt on again ins fnl f* **30/100**[1]
1m 12.61s (0.71) **Going Correction** +0.075s/f (Slow) **4** Ran SP% **109.5**
Speed ratings (Par 98): **98,96,96,95**
toteswinger: 1&2:£13.80 CSF £78.37 TOTE £8.40; EX 37.70.
Owner One More Bid Partnership **Bred** R Ahamad & P Scott **Trained** Epsom, Surrey

FOCUS
A decent nursery. The winner showed a bit of improvement to beat the tough runner-up.

NOTEBOOK
Edgewater(IRE), who had run respectably for these connections on his first outing for them at Kempton last time, showed a decent turn of foot entering the final furlong, which got him to the front at the right time. The drop back to 6f suited, and he looks the type to win again given similar conditions. (op 6-1)
Transfixed(IRE) was by a long way the most experienced runner in the race, as she'd been solidly on the go since April. Tough and consistent, she responded well to pressure after leading and battled all the way to the line. (op 12-1 tchd 10-1)
Memorandum was disappointing on her handicap debut last time and arguably again in this. She appeared to have every chance over a 1f out but her effort off the bridle was minimal and she finished at the one pace. The step up in trip did not help. (op 10-3)
Tenacestream(CAN), a big sort, was well backed to follow up his debut success over C&D. Evidently well regarded by the stable, as his trainer had an eye on a $1m Grade 1 in Canada or the Jersey Stakes at Royal Ascot in 2010, he gave the impression that he was still green (he jumped something on passing the winning post) and was not helped by coming a little wide off the final bend. Not beaten far, he is better than his last-place position suggests. (op 4-6)

7879 TEXT YOUR TOTESPORT BET TO 60021 (S) STKS 6f (P)
1:20 (1:20) (Class 6) 3-Y-O+ **£1,978** (£584; £292) **Stalls** Low

Form RPR
3243 **1** **Obe Gold**[11] 7813 7-9-6 **66** .... J-PGuillambert 2 63
(P Howling) *mde all: rdn wl over 1f out: kpt on wl and a holding runner-up fnl f* **9/4**[2]
0050 **2** *1/2* **Equinity**[32] 7572 3-9-1 **47** .... (t) SaleemGolam 4 56
(J Pearce) *in tch: rdn and effrt on inner over 1f out: pressed wnr thrght fnl f: kpt on but a hld* **40/1**
6040 **3** *nk* **Peopleton Brook**[11] 7808 7-9-0 **58** .... (t) SteveDrowne 9 54
(B G Powell) *hld up in tch in last pair: plld out and rdn over 1f out: r.o ins fnl f: nt quite rch ldng pair* **14/1**
3561 **4** *3/4* **Charlie Delta**[11] 7819 6-9-6 **61** .... (b) TonyCulhane 5 58
(R A Harris) *pressed wnr: rdn ent fnl 2f: unable qck u.p over 1f out: kpt on one pce fnl f* **6/1**[3]
0053 **5** *1 3/4* **Sir Edwin Landseer (USA)**[21] 7689 9-9-0 **79** .... (v) GeorgeBaker 8 46
(G L Moore) *taken down early: hld up in tch: hdwy on outer to chse ldng pair jst over 2f out: rdn 2f out: fnd nil and btn ent fnl f* **11/10**[1]
0100 **6** *21* **Sam's Cross (IRE)**[34] 7535 4-9-3 **62** .... MarcHalford(3) 6 —
(J J Bridger) *chsd ldrs tl rdn and lost pl over 2f out: wl bhd fnl f* **14/1**
1m 13.17s (1.27) **Going Correction** +0.075s/f (Slow) **6** Ran SP% **108.4**
Speed ratings (Par 101): **94,93,92,91,89 61**
toteswinger:1&2:£7.30, 2&3:£11.80, 1&3:£3.20 CSF £59.52 TOTE £3.10: £1.70, £7.20; EX 64.60 Trifecta £395.40 Part won. Pool: £534.34 - 0.95 winning units..There was no bid for the winner
Owner Paul Howling **Bred** Mrs M Mason **Trained** Newmarket, Suffolk

7880 JEFF FIELDEN'S 60TH BIRTHDAY H'CAP (DIV II) 7f (P)
1:55 (1:56) (Class 6) (0-52,52) 3-Y-O+ **£1,637** (£483; £241) **Stalls** Low

Form RPR
0000 **1** **Bold Rose**[19] 7710 3-8-9 **52** .... (p) LeeNewnes(5) 9 61
(M D I Usher) *s.i.s: bhd and sn rdn along: stl plenty to do and wd bnd 2f out: hdwy ent fnl f: r.o wl to ld nr fin* **50/1**
0316 **2** *1/2* **Tamino (IRE)**[11] 7814 6-8-13 **51** .... JimmyQuinn 1 59
(P Howling) *chsd ldng pair: clsd jst over 2f out: rdn to ld over 1f out: drvn ins fnl f: hdd and no ex nr fin* **9/2**[1]
0202 **3** *1 1/4* **Cavalry Guard (USA)**[28] 7614 5-8-9 **52** .... (b) AmyBaker(5) 4 57
(T D McCarthy) *wl off the pce in midfield: hdwy on outer over 2f out: rdn along wl over 1f out: styd on wl to go 3rd nr fin* **13/2**[2]
0600 **4** *1/2* **Easy Wonder (GER)**[11] 7814 4-8-5 **46** oh1 .... (b) MartinLane(3) 6 49
(I A Wood) *s.i.s: bhd: rdn over 2f out: hdwy towards inner u.p jst over 1f out: styd on fnl f: nt rch ldrs* **25/1**
4440 **5** *hd* **Diane's Choice**[22] 7679 6-8-12 **50** .... LukeMorris 3 53
(Miss Gay Kelleway) *racd wl off the pce in midfield: rdn and effrt over 2f out: hdwy over 1f out: chsd ldr ins fnl f: no imp and wknd fnl 100yds* **8/1**
0045 **6** *3/4* **Imperial Skylight**[4] 7845 3-9-0 **52** .... (v) ChrisCatlin 13 53
(M R Channon) *racd wl off the pce in midfield: hdwy over 2f out: edgd lft u.p and plugged on steadily fnl f: nvr gng to rch ldrs* **8/1**
0503 **7** *nk* **Well Of Echoes**[13] 7787 3-8-11 **49** .... (tp) AndrewMullen 10 49
(A J McCabe) *taken down early: chsd ldng trio: drvn over 2f out: in tch over 1f out: kpt on same pce fnl f* **9/2**[1]

00 **8** *2* **Bishopbriggs (USA)**[226] 2130 4-9-0 **52**.............................. AdamKirby 8 47
(M G Quinlan) *chsd ldr: rdn to ld over 2f out: hdd over 1f out: wknd ins fnl f* **12/1**

643 **9** *nk* **Prince Valentine**[24] 7653 8-8-8 **46**..........................(p) FergusSweeney 12 40
(G L Moore) *a wl off the pce in rr: rdn and effrt wl over 1f out: nvr trbld ldrs* **7/1**[3]

6463 **10** *5* **Inquisitress**[23] 7666 5-8-9 **50**............................ MarcHalford(3) 11 30
(J J Bridger) *wl bhd in last pair: rdn and effrt 2f out: nvr on terms* **7/1**[3]

0000 **11** *2 ½* **Truly Divine**[29] 7606 4-8-11 **49**...................................(v[1]) SteveDrowne 7 22
(C A Dwyer) *led at fast gallop: hdd and rdn over 2f out: wknd qckly over 1f out* **33/1**

-000 **12** *44* **Forever Changes**[303] 727 4-8-10 **48**........................... RobertWinston 5 —
(L Montague Hall) *chsd ldrs tl struggling u.p over 3f out: wl bhd and heavily eased fr wl over 1f out* **25/1**

1m 25.01s (0.21) **Going Correction** +0.075s/f (Slow) **12** Ran SP% **117.2**
Speed ratings (Par 101): **101,100,99,98,98 97,97,94,94,88 85,35**
toteswinger:1&2:£23.40, 2&3:£3.80, 1&3:£36.30 CSF £255.83 CT £1717.77 TOTE £40.10: £8.90, £1.30, £2.40; EX 144.80 Trifecta £352.20 Pool: £642.70 - 1.35 winning units.
Owner Ushers Court **Bred** J And Mrs Bowtell **Trained** Upper Lambourn, Berks

FOCUS
Truly Divine took them along at a really fast pace here and the race was set up for a closer. It was run in a time 0.3sec faster than the first division.

7881 BEST ODDS GUARANTEED AT TOTESPORT.COM CLAIMING STKS 1m 2f (P)
2:30 (2:31) (Class 6) 3-4-Y-O **£1,978** (£584; £292) **Stalls** Low

Form RPR

2103 **1** **Rocky's Pride (IRE)**[28] 7612 3-9-0 **77**............................ GeorgeBaker 3 81
(G L Moore) *chsd ldr tl led over 2f out: rdn wl over 1f out: in command whn jinked rt ins fnl f: comf* **4/5**[1]

2534 **2** *1 ½* **Hector Spectre (IRE)**[13] 7737 3-8-5 **64**........................(v) JimmyQuinn 2 69
(P D Evans) *trckd ldng pair: swtchd rt off of rail over 2f out: rdn to chse wnr wl over 1f out: swtchd rt ins fnl f: no imp after and hld whn nt clr run wl ins fnl f* **9/2**[3]

0200 **3** *1 ½* **Laurie Grove (IRE)**[9] 7833 3-9-5 **82**............................(p) JoeFanning 4 80
(T G Mills) *t.k.h: hld up in tch: effrt and rdn over 1f out: nt qckn and one pce after* **5/2**[2]

6560 **4** *8* **Kamanja (UAE)**[11] 7814 3-7-13 **46**................................ NickyMackay 5 44
(M J Attwater) *hld up in tch in last: rdn and effrt ent fnl 2f: sn outpcd and wl btn* **33/1**

/04- **5** *3 ¼* **Rock Me (IRE)**[31] 4990 4-8-12 **37**................................ DaneO'Neill 1 48
(Mrs Lawney Hill) *led tl rdn and hdd over 2f out: sn wknd* **33/1**

2m 8.10s (1.50) **Going Correction** +0.075s/f (Slow)
WFA 3 from 4yo 3lb **5** Ran SP% **108.2**
Speed ratings (Par 101): **97,95,94,88,85**
CSF £4.67 TOTE £1.80: £1.10, £2.30; EX 4.40.Rocky's Pride was claimed by A. B. Haynes for £15,000.
Owner Mrs M Findlay **Bred** London Thoroughbred Services Ltd **Trained** Lower Beeding, W Sussex

FOCUS
With two of these running off official marks under 50, only three of the field made any sort of appeal.

7882 ZENDRILL SCAFFOLDING MAIDEN STKS 1m 2f (P)
3:05 (3:06) (Class 5) 3-Y-O **£2,729** (£806; £403) **Stalls** Low

Form RPR

4432 **1** **Shakalaka (IRE)**[17] 7737 3-9-3 **75**...............................(be) GeorgeBaker 9 78
(G L Moore) *stdd and dropped in bhd after s: hdwy to trck ldrs but buried in bhd over 2f out: gap opened and pushed into ld jst ins fnl f: cruised clr: easily* **5/2**[2]

0220 **2** *4 ½* **Chanrossa (IRE)**[21] 7695 3-8-12 **61**................................(p) JimCrowley 4 64
(E A L Dunlop) *chsd ldrs: wnt 2nd 3f out: rdn to ld over 1f out: sn drvn: hdd jst ins fnl f: no ch w wnr but kpt on for 2nd* **7/2**[3]

40-0 **3** *1* **Big Nige (IRE)**[194] 3115 3-9-3 **64**.................................. SaleemGolam 6 67
(J Pearce) *racd in mid-div: hdwy to chse ldrs over 2f out: rdn and ev ch over 1f out: nvr gng pce of wnr ins fnl f* **20/1**

2000 **4** *4* **Litenup (IRE)**[10] 7826 3-8-12 **52**.............................(t) WandersonD'Avila 5 54
(A J Lidderdale) *led: clr 7f out: rdn ent fnl 2f: hdd wl over 1f out: wknd fnl f* **33/1**

5 *4* **Zerzura** 3-9-3 0.. JimmyQuinn 7 51
(H R A Cecil) *in tch in midfield: rn green and bustled along at times: hdwy to chse ldrs over 2f out: rdn and wknd over 1f out: wl btn fnl f* **11/8**[1]

04 **6** *10* **New Couture (IRE)**[25] 7648 3-8-12 0........................... AdrianMcCarthy 8 26
(P W Chapple-Hyam) *chsd ldrs: rdn over 2f out: wknd 2f out and sn wl btn* **9/1**

0005 **7** *3* **Set Em Up Mo**[42] 7439 3-8-5 **49**..................................(v) KierenFox(7) 3 20
(M J Attwater) *chsd ldr tl 3f out: sn wknd u.p: wl bhd fnl 2f* **66/1**

8 *4* **Sacco D'Oro**[25] 3-8-12 0..(be[1]) GregFairley 1 12
(M Mullineaux) *s.i.s: a bhd: rdn and struggling 4f out wl bhd fnl 2f* **66/1**

0 **9** *1 ¾* **Lily Eva**[23] 7671 3-8-12 0... ChrisCatlin 2 9
(D Donovan) *stdd after s: hld up in last trio: rdn 4f out: sn struggling: wl bhd fnl 2f* **40/1**

2m 4.71s (-1.89) **Going Correction** +0.075s/f (Slow) **9** Ran SP% **116.0**
Speed ratings (Par 102): **110,106,105,102,99 91,88,85,84**
toteswinger:1&2:£2.60, 2&3:£10.80, 1&3:£8.20 CSF £11.24 TOTE £3.50: £1.40, £1.90, £3.30; EX 9.50 Trifecta £62.70 Pool: £907.69 - 10.71 winning units.
Owner Graham Gillespie **Bred** Swordlestown Stud **Trained** Lower Beeding, W Sussex

FOCUS
A modest maiden when considering the calibre of horse taking part, but it produced another fantastic riding performance from George Baker.

7883 BET LIVE IN PLAY AT TOTESPORT.COM H'CAP 1m (P)
3:35 (3:35) (Class 4) (0-85,83) 3-Y-O+ **£4,727** (£1,406; £702; £351) **Stalls** High

Form RPR

1402 **1** **Pegasus Again (USA)**[29] 7603 4-9-4 **82**........................... JoeFanning 8 93
(T G Mills) *sn led: mde rest: rdn wl over 1f out: styd on wl fnl f* **6/1**[3]

4552 **2** *1* **Den's Gift (IRE)**[26] 7626 5-9-5 **83**...............................(b) AdamKirby 7 92
(C G Cox) *led briefly early: chsd wnr after: rdn 2f out: kpt on u.p but a hld by wnr after* **5/2**[1]

6235 **3** *½* **Southandwest (IRE)**[26] 7633 5-9-0 **78**............................ JimmyQuinn 3 86
(J S Moore) *t.k.h: chsd ldng pair: rdn and effrt 2f out: pressing for 2nd fnl f: kpt on* **12/1**

5036 **4** *1* **Ravi River (IRE)**[12] 7801 5-8-12 **76**.......................... J-PGuillambert 5 81
(P D Evans) *hld up in last pair: hdwy on outer jst over 1f out: r.o wl ins fnl f: wnt 4th nr fin: nt rch ldrs* **8/1**

0400 **5** *½* **Gallantry**[12] 7801 7-8-12 **76**... PaulDoe 2 80
(P Howling) *hld up in tch in midfield: hmpd and lost pl jst over 2f out: hdwy on inner over 1f out: kpt on but nt able to rch ldrs: edgd rt nr fin* **16/1**

2214 **6** *½* **Spiritual Art**[39] 7487 3-8-10 **75**................................(p) JimCrowley 9 77
(L A Dace) *t.k.h: hld up in midfield on outer: rdn to chse ldng trio ent fnl 2f: kpt on same pce fr over 1f out* **12/1**

0010 **7** *¾* **Final Verse**[14] 7775 6-9-1 **79**.....................................(e) RobertWinston 1 80
(Matthew Salaman) *stdd s: hld up in mid-div on inner: rdn and hdwy 2f out: kpt on same pce and hld whn nt clr run and eased towards fin* **7/2**[2]

4653 **8** *1 ½* **Totally Focussed (IRE)**[21] 7692 4-8-13 **77**.................... HayleyTurner 6 75
(S Dow) *stdd and dropped in bhd after s: nt clr run jst over 2f out tl 2f out: rdn and effrt over 1f out: nt clr run and eased ins fnl f: n.d* **6/1**[3]

3410 **9** *7* **Head Down**[44] 5574 3-8-11 **76**...................................... SteveDrowne 4 56
(Mrs L C Jewell) *chsd ldng trio: rdn and unable qck over 2f out: bhd fr over 1f out* **33/1**

1m 37.52s (-0.68) **Going Correction** +0.075s/f (Slow)
WFA 3 from 4yo+ 1lb **9** Ran SP% **114.7**
Speed ratings (Par 105): **106,105,104,103,103 102,101,100,93**
toteswinger:1&2:£3.20, 2&3:£5.10, 1&3:£11.80 CSF £21.22 CT £175.33 TOTE £6.30: £1.80, £1.10, £3.90; EX 13.30 Trifecta £140.90 Pool: £805.94 - 4.23 winning units. Place 6 £479.04, Place 5 £192.99.
Owner T G Mills **Bred** Stonestreet Mares Llc **Trained** Headley, Surrey

FOCUS
Not a bad handicap, and it looked to be run at a sound gallop, but the first three were in those positions almost throughout.
T/Jkpt: Not won. T/Plt: £257.20 to a £1 stake. Pool: £83,692.84. 237.53 winning tickets. T/Qpdt: £10.60 to a £1 stake. Pool: £8,152.54. 564.57 winning tickets. SP

7877 LINGFIELD (L-H)
Thursday, December 31

OFFICIAL GOING: Standard
Wind: Fresh, half against Weather: cloudy, chilly

7884 VIEW OUR 2010 FIXTURES AT LINGFIELDPARK.CO.UK NURSERY (DIV I) 7f (P)
12:00 (12:00) (Class 6) (0-60,60) 2-Y-O **£1,637** (£483; £241) **Stalls** Low

Form RPR

5605 **1** **Miami Gator (IRE)**[24] 7661 2-9-5 **58**........................... AndrewElliott 9 64+
(J R Weymes) *t.k.h: chsd ldrs: rdn 4f out: pressed ldr ent fnl 2f: led over 1f out: styd on wl fnl f* **11/2**[3]

6405 **2** *1 ¼* **Rightcar**[4] 7849 2-9-0 **53**... AdamKirby 10 54
(Peter Grayson) *towards rr: rdn over 2f out: plld out and drvn over 1f out: r.o wl fnl f to go 2nd nr fin: nt rch wnr* **33/1**

660 **3** *½* **Goodison Goal (IRE)**[33] 7584 2-8-12 **51**.......................... SJCraine 7 51
(Patrick Morris) *chsd ldrs: shkn up 2f out: drvn over 1f out: chsd wnr ins fnl f: one pce after and lost 2nd nr fin* **14/1**

6025 **4** *hd* **Mind The Monarch**[12] 7805 2-9-4 **57**............................ LukeMorris 3 56
(R A Teal) *in tch in midfield: effrt ent fnl 2f: chsd ldrs and drvn ent fnl f: kpt on but no imp on wnr ins fnl f: swtchd rt fnl 50yds* **6/1**

060 **5** *1 ½* **Sonny G (IRE)**[83] 6629 2-9-0 **53**............................... RobertWinston 6 49
(J R Best) *plld hrd: hld up trcking ldrs: swtchd out off ins rail jst over 2f out: chsd ldng pair and drvn ent fnl f: no ex and btn fnl 100yds* **9/2**[2]

5004 **6** *hd* **D'Urberville**[47] 7389 2-9-6 **59**.................................... ShaneKelly 1 54
(J R Jenkins) *stdd after s: hld up in tch in midfield: hmpd after 1f: effrt but hanging lft over 1f out: plld out rt 1f out: kpt on but nvr gng pce to chal ldrs* **4/1**[1]

6650 **7** *nk* **Feel The Magic (IRE)**[16] 7757 2-8-9 **48**........................ DavidProbert 4 42
(S Kirk) *led for 1f: chsd ldr tl led again over 2f out: rdn and hdd over 1f out: wknd ins fnl f* **16/1**

2110 **8** *1 ¾* **Vilnius**[33] 7570 2-9-6 **59**... ChrisCatlin 8 49
(M R Channon) *t.k.h early: hld up towards rr: rdn and struggling over 2f out: nvr trbld ldrs* **7/1**

0600 **9** *2 ½* **Mactrac**[40] 7474 2-8-12 **54**.. PatrickHills(3) 5 38
(R Hannon) *midfield early tl dashed up to ld after 1f: sn clr: hdd over 2f out: wknd qckly over 1f out* **10/1**

005 **10** *6* **Delta Sky (IRE)**[142] 4869 2-9-7 **60**............................ JerryO'Dwyer 2 29
(Miss Amy Weaver) *hld up in last trio: rdn and struggling 3f out: wl bhd fnl 2f* **9/1**

1m 26.32s (1.52) **Going Correction** +0.075s/f (Slow) **10** Ran SP% **114.9**
Speed ratings (Par 94): **94,92,92,91,90 89,89,87,84,77**
toteswinger: 1&2 £22.40, 1&3 £24.30, 2&3 £41.80 CSF £162.05 CT £1635.30 TOTE £6.70: £2.50, £6.80, £4.50; EX 85.90 TRIFECTA Not won..
Owner Mrs Elaine M Burke **Bred** Newlands House Stud **Trained** Middleham Moor, N Yorks

FOCUS
A low-grade contest. The winner built on previous promise and the second was back to his best.

NOTEBOOK
Miami Gator(IRE), raised 4lb after an unlucky fifth on his AW debut here, raced up with the pace throughout. After taking charge once in line for home he was always doing more than enough. His small stable has enjoyed a fruitful end to the year. (op 13-2 tchd 7-1)
Rightcar, worst drawn, is a maiden after 15 previous attempts. Soon struggling in the rear, he found an extra gear coming to the final furlong and finished with a flourish. Stamina was not a problem and on this showing he will be even better suited by a mile. (op 40-1)
Goodison Goal(IRE), dropped 6lb since her nursery debut two outings ago, ran easily her best race so far on her sixth career start. (op 12-1)
Mind The Monarch, a mover on the morning line, was tackling 7f for the first time and was 9lb lower than her previous try in handicap company. (tchd 13-2)
Sonny G(IRE), making his handicap bow, pulled far too hard on the heels of the leaders. He will need to learn to settle if he is to progress. (op 4-1)
D'Urberville was trapped on the inner with nowhere to go once in line for home. Pulled wide, he kept on but his chance had gone. (tchd 7-2 and 9-2)

7885 OVER 50 INSTANT GAMES AT TOTESPORTGAMES.COM MEDIAN AUCTION MAIDEN STKS (DIV I) 7f (P)
12:30 (12:30) (Class 6) 2-Y-O **£1,637** (£483; £241) **Stalls** Low

Form RPR

6305 **1** **Cuthbert (IRE)**[22] 7690 2-9-3 **65**............................... JoeFanning 6 73+
(W Jarvis) *mde all: rdn clr over 1f out: wl clr ins fnl f: eased towards fin* **7/1**[3]

00 **2** *2 ¼* **Katchmore (IRE)**[47] 7400 2-9-3 0.................................. JimCrowley 7 62
(Jean-Rene Auvray) *sn bustled up to chse wnr: rdn ent fnl 2f: nt pce of wnr over 1f out: clsd on eased wnr towards fin* **15/2**

6 **3** *nk* **Red Yarn**[21] 7700 2-8-12 0....................................... FergusSweeney 4 57
(G L Moore) *chsd ldng pair: rdn and nt pce of wnr over 1f out: kpt on pressing for 2nd but no ch w wnr* **3/1**[1]

4 **4** *3 1/4* **Jodawes (USA)** 2-9-3 0 SteveDrowne 8 54
(J R Best) *chsd ldng trio: rdn ent fnl 2f: hanging lft and outpcd over 1f out: wl hld fnl f* **8/1**

03 **5** *3/4* **La Toya J (IRE)**[21] 7700 2-8-12 0 TonyCulhane 5 47
(R Curtis) *hld up in rr: hdwy into midfield whn nt clr run ent fnl 2f: rdn and no prog whn carried lft 1f out* **3/1**[1]

2 **6** *nk* **Spice Fair**[24] 7663 2-8-12 0 LeeNewnes(5) 1 51
(M D I Usher) *hmpd s: wl bhd: hdwy on outer 3f out: in tch and rdn whn rn wd bnd 2f out: no hdwy and wl hld fr over 1f out* **9/2**[2]

0 **7** *6* **Chichi (IRE)**[15] 7772 2-8-12 0 DaneO'Neill 9 31
(R Hannon) *racd in midfield: lost pl and rdn jst over 2f out: sn wl btn* **25/1**

00 **8** *shd* **Desert Recluse (IRE)**[48] 7376 2-9-3 0 RobertWinston 3 36
(Pat Eddery) *wnt lft s: a bhd: flashing tail fr over 4f out* **28/1**

0 **9** *2 1/2* **Maxijack (IRE)**[15] 7773 2-9-3 0 SJCraine 2 29
(G Brown) *s.i.s and hmpd sn after s: a bhd: lost tch 3f out* **80/1**

1m 25.15s (0.35) **Going Correction** +0.075s/f (Slow) **9** Ran SP% **112.1**
Speed ratings (Par 94): **101,98,98,94,93 93,86,86,83**
toteswinger:1&2 £8.50, 1&3 £4.30, 2&3 £6.10 CSF £55.24 TOTE £8.90: £2.20, £2.40, £1.30; EX 44.90 Trifecta £52.00 Pool: £351.46 - 5.00 winning units..
Owner The Square Mile Syndicate **Bred** Gerard Callanan **Trained** Newmarket, Suffolk

FOCUS
A very modest maiden, but the winner impressed and was value for further. The form has been rated positively.

NOTEBOOK
Cuthbert(IRE) was having his ninth career start but only his third try on the all-weather. Given an excellent ride from the front, he quickened clear once in line for home and was able to take things easily near the end. The blinkers he wore on his last two starts were dispensed with here and he can surely hold his own in modest handicap company. (tchd 8-1)
Katchmore(IRE), who came in for market support, was dropping back in trip. He kept tabs on the winner but in the end proved no match. This third outing at least opens up the handicap route for him. (op 11-1 tchd 7-1)
Red Yarn, three places and about a length behind La Toya J on her debut at Kempton three weeks earlier, turned the tables without ever threatening to get in a blow.
Jodawes(USA) made a satisfactory debut but will need to improve a good deal for it if he is to get off the mark, at least in the short term. His jockey said he hung left and the vet reported that the colt had suffered a mouth injury. (op 10-1)
La Toya J(IRE) had to be checked for a few strides 2f from home but, once in the clear, she was unable to make any impression. (op 7-2 tchd 11-4)
Spice Fair, runner-up first time over a mile here, was drawn one and was hampered by the errant Desert Recluse soon after the start. Brought widest of all, she showed an ungainly action. She should do better given a fair bit more time. (op 10-3)

7886 OVER 50 INSTANT GAMES AT TOTESPORTGAMES.COM MEDIAN AUCTION MAIDEN STKS (DIV II) 7f (P)
1:00 (1:09) (Class 6) 2-Y-O **£1,637** (£483; £241) **Stalls** Low

Form RPR

2502 **1** **Fazza**[11] 7824 2-9-3 65 DavidProbert 5 72
(D W P Arbuthnot) *in rr of main gp: niggled along 4f out: swtchd to outer and hdwy over 2f out: chsd clr wnr jst over 1f out: str run to ld fnl 50yds* **10/3**[2]

0523 **2** *1 3/4* **Until The Man (IRE)**[57] 7235 2-9-3 61 (p) PaulDoe 3 68
(R Ingram) *led: rdn clr 2f out: 4 l clr 1f out: drvn ins fnl f: hdd fnl 50yds* **20/1**

3303 **3** *4 1/2* **Kathindi (IRE)**[30] 7604 2-9-3 67 LukeMorris 2 56
(J S Moore) *rdn leaving stalls: sn in tch in main gp: rdn along over 3f out: kpt on u.p to go modest 3rd ins fnl f: no ch w ldrs* **9/1**

0 **4** *1/2* **Explorator (IRE)**[21] 7700 2-8-12 0 MatthewDavies(5) 10 55
(George Baker) *in rr of main gp: rdn 4f out: styd on u.p to press for modest 3rd ins fnl f: nvr trbld ldrs* **100/1**

4 **5** *3 1/2* **Calculus Affair (IRE)**[15] 7773 2-9-3 0 ShaneKelly 1 46
(J Noseda) *chsd ldng pair on inner: rdn and nt qckn ent fnl 2f: drvn and wl btn over 1f out* **13/8**[1]

062 **6** *1 3/4* **Avon Castle**[13] 7799 2-8-12 65 FergusSweeney 8 37
(G L Moore) *uns rdr and got loose bef s: in tch in main gp on outer: rdn and unable qck jst over 2f out: no ch fr over 1f out* **14/1**

4 **7** *1/2* **Lou Bear (IRE)**[21] 7700 2-9-3 0 AdamKirby 7 41
(J Akehurst) *chsd ldr: rdn and wl outpcd over 2f out: lost 2nd jst over 1f out: fdd fnl f* **5/1**[3]

40 **8** *1 3/4* **Lily In The Pond**[27] 7622 2-8-12 0 JimCrowley 9 31
(Miss Gay Kelleway) *stdd and swtchd lft after s: a in rr* **40/1**

05 **9** *6* **Not In The Clock (USA)**[25] 7655 2-9-3 0 SteveDrowne 6 21
(J R Best) *s.i.s and rdn along early: in tch in main gp after 1f: rdn and lost pl qckly jst over 2f out: wl bhd over 1f out* **7/1**

10 *21* **Sparkle Park** 2-8-12 0 MartinDwyer 4 —
(B J Meehan) *s.i.s: v green and sn wl detached in last: t.o fr 1/2-way* **25/1**

1m 25.01s (0.21) **Going Correction** +0.075s/f (Slow) **10** Ran SP% **119.0**
Speed ratings (Par 94): **101,99,93,93,89 87,86,84,77,53**
toteswinger: 1&2 £8.20, 1&3 £5.40, 2&3 £6.40 CSF £71.75 TOTE £4.30: £1.50, £3.10, £2.10; EX 56.30 Trifecta £373.40 Pool: £504.67 - 0.45 winning units..
Owner Nursery End Syndicate **Bred** D R Tucker **Trained** Compton, Berks

FOCUS
Part two was another modest maiden and the picture changed dramatically late on. The standard is set around the runner-up and fourth.

NOTEBOOK
Fazza, rated 67 and runner-up in a nursery at Kempton after a two-month break, went in pursuit of the clear leader a furlong out. He showed a good turn of foot to overhaul him and was right on top at the line. He can surely give a good account of himself returned to handicap company. (tchd 5-2 and 7-2)
Until The Man(IRE), rated 61, is much improved since being fitted with cheekpieces. He looked to have stolen it when quickening clear off the home turn but in the end was readily put in his place by the winner. His trainer reckons he has been a slow learner. (op 16-1)
Kathindi(IRE), having his second outing after a four-month break, looks to lack a couple of gears and will be suited by a return to a mile. (op 10-1 tchd 12-1)
Explorator(IRE) improved on his debut effort and there should be even better to come, but it may not be until he tackles handicap company that he shows his true potential.
Calculus Affair(IRE), on edge beforehand, raced keenly but he seemed to check and drop back after a furlong or so. This may be best overlooked after a promising show on his debut here two weeks earlier. Shane Kelly reported that the colt lost his action in the early stages. (tchd 7-4)
Avon Castle gave problems at the start. She unseated her rider, ran loose and crashed through a rail. She took her chance but, racing wide, tired markedly in the final furlong. Whether she should have been allowed to take her chance is a moot point. (op 12-1 tchd 16-1)
Lou Bear(IRE) did not improve at all on his debut effort at Kempton three weeks earlier. He is quite well thought of and this may be best overlooked. (op 9-2)
Not In The Clock(USA), a springer in the market, never looked like justifying the support. (op 33-1)

7887 VIEW OUR 2010 FIXTURES AT LINGFIELDPARK.CO.UK NURSERY (DIV II) 7f (P)
1:30 (1:34) (Class 6) (0-60,60) 2-Y-O **£1,637** (£483; £241) **Stalls** Low

Form RPR

4623 **1** **Bookiesindex Girl (IRE)**[20] 7706 2-8-12 **51** ShaneKelly 7 54
(J R Jenkins) *mde all: rdn and drew clr wl over 1f out: edgd rt u.p but styd on wl fnl f* **11/1**

5043 **2** *1 1/4* **Captain Cool (IRE)**[36] 7514 2-8-11 **50** DaneO'Neill 2 50
(R Hannon) *chsd ldrs: rdn to chse clr wnr over 1f out: kpt on same pce ins fnl f* **11/2**[2]

0644 **3** *1 1/4* **Moonlight Serenade**[2] 7868 2-9-1 **57** JackDean(3) 3 54
(W G M Turner) *v awkward leaving stalls and slowly away: sn pushed up to get in tch: hdwy and swtchd rt wl over 1f out: flashed tail u.p but kpt on to go 3rd ins fnl f: nvr threatened ldrs* **16/1**

0630 **4** *1/2* **She's My Rock (IRE)**[19] 7722 2-9-0 **53** DavidProbert 8 49
(S Kirk) *sn rdn along: in tch: chsd ldng trio u.p 2f out: plugged on same pce fr over 1f out* **4/1**[1]

000 **5** *4 1/2* **Franki J**[28] 7616 2-9-2 **55** ChrisCatlin 5 39
(D Donovan) *in tch: effrt to chse ldrs 2f out: rdn and no rspnse over 1f out: wl hld fnl f* **10/1**

0060 **6** *hd* **Orsett Lad (USA)**[36] 7513 2-9-7 **60** RobertWinston 1 44
(J R Best) *chsd wnr on inner: rdn and unable qck ent fnl 2f: lost 2nd over 1f out: wknd ent fnl f* **15/2**

0066 **7** *8* **Roybuoy**[15] 7773 2-9-3 **56** (b) SteveDrowne 6 20
(H J L Dunlop) *in tch: rdn and btn ent fnl 2f: sn bhd* **6/1**[3]

350 **8** *1* **Always Dixie (IRE)**[13] 7800 2-9-6 **59** JoeFanning 4 20
(M Johnston) *s.i.s: sn rdn: nvr gng and a bhd* **7/1**

0000 **9** *1/2* **New York Lights (IRE)**[22] 7690 2-8-0 **46** (be1) RachelKing(7) 10 6
(M D I Usher) *in tch on outer: lost pl over 2f out: sn wl btn* **33/1**

0555 **10** *4* **Kyoatee Kilt**[22] 7683 2-9-5 **58** (b1) JimCrowley 9 8
(P F I Cole) *chsd ldrs tl lost pl qckly jst over 2f out: sn bhd* **13/2**

1m 26.09s (1.29) **Going Correction** +0.075s/f (Slow) **10** Ran SP% **113.5**
Speed ratings (Par 94): **95,93,92,91,86 86,77,75,75,70**
toteswinger: 1&2 £5.50, 1&3 £15.00, 2&3 £10.20 CSF £68.51 CT £990.82 TOTE £11.50: £2.80, £1.70, £3.90; EX 46.50 Trifecta £296.30 Pool: £400.47 - 1.00 winning units..
Owner Bookmakers Index Ltd **Bred** Michael Woodlock And Seamus Kennedy **Trained** Royston, Herts

FOCUS
Part two was another low-grade nursery and again it paid to race up with the pace. A personal best from the winner to beat the exposed runner-up, and not form to be with.

NOTEBOOK
Bookiesindex Girl(IRE) was the second winner to record an all-the-way success. Well beaten in two previous nursery starts, she had been placed in selling company on her two most recent outings. She quickened clear off the home turn and never looked in any real danger. (op 12-1)
Captain Cool(IRE), down 10lb since his nursery bow, was in pursuit of the winner throughout. (op 5-1 tchd 9-2)
Moonlight Serenade, making her handicap debut, made a tardy start and looked to carry her head to one side. She made up a deal of ground once in line for home despite flashing her tail and would have snatched second spot with a bit further to go. (op 14-1 tchd 12-1)
She's My Rock(IRE), happy to be back on Polytrack, was hard at work in midfield at halfway. She looks to lack pace and needs a return to a mile. (op 5-1)
Franki J, well beaten in selling company on her previous starts, never entered the argument on her nursery bow. (op 11-1)
Orsett Lad(USA), who started life in nurseries from a stone higher mark, matched strides with Captain Cool in pursuit of the winner but he dropped right away in the final furlong. He seems to be going the wrong way. (op 11-1 tchd 12-1)

7888 MARRIOTT HOTEL OPENING SPRING 2010 (S) STKS 1m 4f (P)
2:00 (2:04) (Class 6) 3-Y-O+ **£1,978** (£584; £292) **Stalls** Low

Form RPR

6000 **1** **Shannersburg (IRE)**[21] 7699 4-9-4 66 (bt) ChrisCatlin 5 66
(D E Pipe) *hld up in rr: stdy hdwy 1/2-way: chsd clr ldr and rdn over 2f out: led over 1f out: sn clr: rdn out* **4/1**[2]

3311 **2** *5* **Ghufa (IRE)**[12] 7817 5-9-3 68 MatthewDavies(5) 9 62
(George Baker) *stdd s: hld up wl bhd: hdwy 6f out: rdn to chse ldng pair ent fnl 2f: chsd clr wnr 1f out: no imp after* **6/4**[1]

0604 **3** *3/4* **Playful Asset (IRE)**[18] 7740 3-8-12 55 TonyCulhane 10 56
(P Howling) *stdd s: hld up wl in rr: hdwy on outer 5f out: rdn 3f out: wnt modest 4th over 1f out: plugged on to go 3rd ins fnl f: nvr rchd ldrs* **25/1**

2034 **4** *2 1/4* **Fantasy Ride**[22] 7687 7-9-4 52 SaleemGolam 11 53
(J Pearce) *hld up towards rr: hdwy into modest 7th ent fnl 2f: kpt on fnl f: nvr trbld ldrs* **14/1**

5044 **5** *1 1/2* **Carr Hall (IRE)**[17] 7750 6-9-8 48 VinceSlattery 6 55
(B G Powell) *racd in main gp: hmpd bnd 4f out and sn swtchd rt and rdn: plugged on same pce fnl 2f: nvr trbld ldrs* **20/1**

3625 **6** *2 3/4* **Acropolis (IRE)**[16] 7761 8-9-4 60 (v) StephenDonohoe 13 46
(B G Powell) *sn pressing ldr: led 10f out: clr 8f out: 10 l clr 4f out: rdn and nt look keen jst over 2f out: hdd over 1f out: sn btn: wknd fnl f* **5/1**[3]

0- **7** *2 3/4* **Maverick's Magic**[478] 5778 3-8-10 0 JackDean(3) 14 42
(W G M Turner) *racd wl off the pce in midfield: pushed along 1/2-way: rdn and no prog fr over 3f out* **100/1**

3224 **8** *3 3/4* **King's Majesty (IRE)**[59] 1178 7-9-4 64 RobertWinston 1 36
(A M Hales) *prom in main gp: chsd clr ldr 4f out tl over 2f out: wknd u.p 2f out* **13/2**

0035 **9** *1/2* **Midnight Bay**[14] 7767 3-8-13 52 PaulDoe 8 35
(P D Evans) *prom in main gp: rdn over 3f out: wnt modest 3rd briefly over 2f out: no prog and wl btn wl over 1f out* **33/1**

5400 **10** *1/2* **Mid Valley**[24] 7666 6-9-4 40 (v) ShaneKelly 3 34
(J R Jenkins) *hld up towards rr: hdwy into midfield 8f out: rdn and and no prog 3f out: wl btn fnl 2f* **40/1**

6000 **11** *21* **Bright Wire (IRE)**[124] 5430 3-8-13 45 FrankieMcDonald 2 1
(M Madgwick) *a towards rr: bhd and rdn 5f out: t.o over 2f out* **100/1**

12 *8* **Blushing Soul (USA)**[23] 1901 3-8-6 72 (p) HarryBentley(7) 4 —
(L A Dace) *led tl 10f out: chsd ldr clr of remainder 8f out tl 4f out: sn dropped out: t.o over 2f out* **33/1**

13 *2* **Blakeneys Pet (IRE)**[14] 3-8-5 0 WilliamCarson(3) 12 —
(W G M Turner) *prom in main gp: rdn 4f out: sn struggling: wl bhd and eased fr wl over 1f out* **66/1**

The Form Book, Raceform Ltd, Compton, RG20 6NL

400- **14** *20* **Bollywood (IRE)**[297] 7676 6-9-1 47............................(b) MarcHalford(3) 7 —
(J J Bridger) *prom in main gp early: steadily lost pl: wl t.o fnl 3f* **100/1**

2m 33.17s (0.17) **Going Correction** +0.075s/f (Slow)
WFA 3 from 4yo+ 5lb **14** Ran SP% **118.1**
Speed ratings (Par 101): **102,98,98,96,95 93,92,89,89,88 74,69,68,54**
toteswinger: 1&2 £3.70, 1&3 £17.30, 2&3 £8.30 CSF £9.38 TOTE £5.70: £2.20, £1.30, £3.40; EX 13.70 Trifecta £372.60 Part won. Pool: £503.60 - 0.60 winning units..The winner was bought in for 7,200gns. Ghufa was claimed by Jeff Pearce for £6,000.
Owner Mrs S J Brookhouse **Bred** Dermot Cantillon And Fiona Craig **Trained** Nicholashayne, Devon

FOCUS
Plenty of deadwood in this seller, which was run at a furious pace thanks to the very positive tactics adopted by Acropolis.

7889 100% NEW PLAYER BONUS AT TOTESPORTCASINO.COM H'CAP 5f (P)
2:30 (2:33) (Class 6) (0-55,55) 3-Y-O+ **£1,978** (£584; £292) **Stalls** High

Form RPR
0606 **1** **Greek Secret**[10] 7835 6-8-12 **52**.....................................(b) TonyCulhane 3 62
(J O'Reilly) *hld up in tch: hdwy to chse ldrs 2f out: rdn to ld ins fnl f: r.o wl* **16/1**

5052 **2** *1* **Grand Palace (IRE)**[15] 7774 6-9-1 **55**..............................(v) AdamKirby 5 61
(H J Evans) *sn in rr and rdn along: hdwy over 1f out: styng on whn nt clr run and swtchd rt ins fnl f: r.o to go 2nd towards fin: unable to chal wnr* **9/2**[2]

0063 **3** *3/4* **Shakespeare's Son**[15] 7770 4-8-12 **52**.............................. JimCrowley 8 55
(H J Evans) *hld up in last pair: hdwy wl over 1f out: rdn and r.o wl fr over 1f out: pressing for 2nd fnl 100yds: nt rch wnr* **12/1**

0315 **4** *nk* **Best One**[9] 7838 5-9-1 **55**..(b) KevinGhunowa 1 57
(R A Harris) *chsd ldr: drvn over 1f out: ev ch ins fnl f: no ex and lost 2 pls fnl 75yds* **9/2**[2]

3330 **5** *3/4* **Radiator Rooney (IRE)**[10] 7835 6-9-1 **55**....................(b) GeorgeBaker 4 55
(Patrick Morris) *s.i.s and stmbld sn after s: hld up wl in tch on inner: trying to go between horses fr over 1f out: squeezed out and hmpd ins fnl f: nvr able to chal* **5/2**[1]

2106 **6** *1/2* **Sonhador**[15] 7770 3-8-12 **52**... SaleemGolam 7 50
(G Prodromou) *hld up in tch towards rr: rdn and effrt over 1f out: kpt on but nt pce to chal* **20/1**

2023 **7** *1/2* **Rocket Ruby**[20] 7714 3-9-0 **54**.. DaneO'Neill 2 50
(D Shaw) *led: rdn wl over 1f out: hdd ins fnl f: wknd towards fin* **5/1**[3]

0000 **8** *12* **Malapropism**[10] 7835 9-8-9 **54**..............................(v) MatthewDavies(5) 10 7
(M R Channon) *pressed ldrs on outer tl jst over 2f out: sn bhd* **33/1**

4443 **9** *3 3/4* **Colombard (IRE)**[12] 7819 4-8-11 **51**..............................(b) ChrisCatlin 6 —
(Patrick Morris) *chsd ldrs tl jst over 2f out: sn struggling and bhd* **8/1**

59.53 secs (0.73) **Going Correction** +0.075s/f (Slow) **9** Ran SP% **114.0**
Speed ratings (Par 101): **97,95,94,93,92 91,90,71,65**
toteswinger: 1&2 £12.60, 1&3 £19.10, 2&3 £8.90 CSF £85.42 CT £913.86 TOTE £15.90: £3.80, £2.10, £3.10; EX 86.90 Trifecta £47.90 Pool: £676.49 - 10.45 winning units..
Owner The Boot & Shoe Ackworth Partnership **Bred** James Clark **Trained** Doncaster, S Yorks

FOCUS
A low-grade 51-55 sprint handicap and the pace was strong.

7890 BEST ODDS GUARANTEED AT TOTESPORT.COM H'CAP 6f (P)
3:00 (3:01) (Class 6) (0-60,66) 3-Y-O+ **£1,978** (£438; £438) **Stalls** Low

Form RPR
0005 **1** **Handsome Cross (IRE)**[25] 7657 8-9-3 **59**.............(v) StephenDonohoe 9 66
(W J Musson) *plld hrd early: hld up in tch: hdwy 2f out: r.o u.p fnl f to ld last stride* **10/1**

4454 **2** *hd* **Hollow Jo**[9] 7839 9-9-4 **60**...(v) FergusSweeney 12 66
(J R Jenkins) *chsd ldrs: hdwy over 2f out: rdn and ev ch jst over 1f out: led ins fnl f: hdd last stride* **8/1**[3]

0301 **2** *dht* **Valentino Swing (IRE)**[10] 7834 6-9-2 **61** 6ex.................... JackDean(3) 3 67
(Miss T Spearing) *t.k.h: hld up in tch towards rr: rdn and effrt 2f out: r.o wl u.p ins fnl f: nt quite rch wnr* **12/1**

5630 **4** *1* **Don Pele (IRE)**[9] 7839 7-9-4 **60**...................................(p) TonyCulhane 10 63
(R A Harris) *chsd ldng pair: wnt 2nd 1/2-way: ev ch and drvn over 1f out: unable qck fnl 100yds* **10/1**

3234 **5** *1/2* **Forest Dane**[18] 7739 9-9-4 **60**... LukeMorris 4 62
(Mrs N Smith) *t.k.h: hld up wl in tch: rdn and effrt over 1f out: kpt on same pce fnl f* **3/1**[2]

1500 **6** *hd* **Hatman Jack (IRE)**[72] 6914 3-8-13 **58**............... RussellKennemore(3) 6 59
(B G Powell) *led: rdn 2f out: kpt on wl tl hdd ins fnl f: no ex fnl 100yds* **14/1**

5241 **7** *nk* **Pocket's Pick (IRE)**[9] 7839 3-9-10 **66** 6ex........................ GeorgeBaker 5 66
(G L Moore) *stdd s: t.k.h: hld up in last pair: hanging rt and wd and rdn bnd wl over 1f out: no hdwy tl r.o wl ins fnl f: nt rch ldrs* **9/4**[1]

000 **8** *3/4* **Trip Switch**[97] 6252 3-8-11 **60**.................................. CharlotteKerton(7) 8 58
(G Prodromou) *chsd ldr tl 1/2-way: lost pl jst over 2f out: rdn along and no prog fr over 1f out* **66/1**

1220 **9** *nk* **Elusive Ronnie (IRE)**[30] 7606 3-8-9 **58**...................(b) TobyAtkinson(7) 1 55
(R A Teal) *in tch: shuffled bk and lost pl jst over 2f out: kpt on same pce fr over 1f out* **12/1**

6000 **10** *1 1/2* **Diddums**[36] 7519 3-8-11 **60**.. CarolineKelly(7) 2 52
(P S McEntee) *in tch in midfield on inner: rdn and no prog over 1f out: wl hld fnl f* **25/1**

420 **11** *5* **Crystal B Good (USA)**[146] 4748 3-9-2 **58**................. RobertWinston 11 34
(J R Best) *stdd after s: t.k.h: hld up in rr: struggling u.p 2f out: n.d* **28/1**

0000 **12** *nse* **Northern Empire (IRE)**[9] 7838 6-9-2 **58**.........................(p) ChrisCatlin 7 34
(F Jordan) *stdd after s: hld up in rr: rdn and no rspnse ent fnl 2f* **28/1**

1m 12.89s (0.99) **Going Correction** +0.075s/f (Slow) **12** Ran SP% **119.3**
Speed ratings (Par 101): **96,95,95,94,93 93,93,92,91,89 83,82**PL: Valentino Swing £3.40, Hollow Jo £2.80; EX: HC-VS £72.30, HC-HJ, £45.90; CSF: HC-VS £60.06, HC-HJ £42.62; TRICAST: HC-VS-HJ £515.60, HC-HJ-VS £498.49; toteswinger: 1&2 (VS) £24.90, 1&2 (HJ) £25.20, 2&3 £17.20 TOTE £14.90: £4.00 Trifecta £27 Owner McHugh & Partners II.

FOCUS
A modest 58-66 sprint handicap with a blanket covering half a dozen horses inside the last.

7891 £10 FREE PLAY AT TOTESPORTBINGO.COM H'CAP 7f (P)
3:30 (3:30) (Class 4) (0-80,80) 3-Y-O+ **£4,727** (£1,406; £702; £351) **Stalls** Low

Form RPR
3214 **1** **Autumn Blades (IRE)**[10] 7833 4-9-4 **80**.......................(p) DavidProbert 4 88
(A Bailey) *racd in last trio: niggled along 4f out: rdn and effrt jst over 2f out: hdwy to chse ldr jst ins fnl f: racd awkwardly but kpt on to ld towards fin* **4/1**[2]

2620 **2** *nk* **Shaded Edge**[27] 7627 5-8-6 **68**... MartinDwyer 6 75
(D W P Arbuthnot) *chsd ldr: rdn to ld 2f out: kpt on wl tl hdd and no ex towards fin* **10/1**

0226 **3** *1 1/2* **Desert Dreamer (IRE)**[5] 7845 8-9-3 **79**.................................. PaulDoe 3 82
(P D Evans) *taken down early: t.k.h: hld up in last pair: rdn jst over 2f out: r.o one pce u.p ins fnl f* **12/1**

6446 **4** *nk* **Sunshine Always (IRE)**[18] 7741 3-9-2 **78**........................ JimCrowley 2 80
(T D McCarthy) *trckd ldrs on inner: plld out and rdn over 1f out: kpt on u.p fnl f* **9/2**[3]

1253 **5** *1 1/4* **Poppanan (USA)**[25] 7656 3-8-9 **71**................................. TonyCulhane 8 70
(S Dow) *stdd s: t.k.h: hld up in last: hdwy and rdn over 1f out: no imp ins fnl f* **9/4**[1]

0003 **6** *1/2* **Baunagain (IRE)**[10] 7833 4-9-1 **77**............................. AdrianMcCarthy 7 75
(P W Chapple-Hyam) *plld hrd: hld up in tch: rdn and effrt jst over 2f out: kpt on same pce fnl f* **15/2**

1306 **7** *2 1/4* **Learo Dochais (USA)**[36] 7516 3-8-8 **70**............................. ChrisCatlin 1 62
(M A Jarvis) *led tl 2f out: wknd fnl f* **8/1**

5060 **8** *2* **Lastroarofdtiger (USA)**[142] 4870 3-8-11 **73**.................. AndrewElliott 5 59
(J R Weymes) *chsd ldrs: rdn over 2f out: wknd over 1f out* **33/1**

1m 25.34s (0.54) **Going Correction** +0.075s/f (Slow) **8** Ran SP% **111.6**
Speed ratings (Par 105): **99,98,96,96,95 94,92,89**
toteswinger: 1&2 £6.40, 1&3 £5.60, 2&3 £7.20 CSF £40.68 CT £427.90 TOTE £5.90: £1.60, £2.50, £3.10; EX 45.60 Trifecta £225.20 Pool: £849.32 - 2.79 winning units. Place 6 £559.21, Place 5 £132.36.
Owner John Stocker **Bred** Dr D Crone & P Lafarge & P Johnston **Trained** Newmarket, Suffolk

FOCUS
A competitive 68-80 handicap to wind up Lingfield's racing year.
T/Plt: £551.30 to a £1 stake. Pool: £75,627.87. 100.13 winning tickets. T/Qpdt: £33.60 to a £1 stake. Pool: £10,547.70. 231.70 winning tickets. SP

INDEX TO MEETINGS FLAT 2009

† Abandoned
* All-Weather
(M) Mixed meeting

INDEX TO FLAT RACING

Horses are shown in alphabetical order; the trainer's name follows the name of the horse. The figures to the right are current master ratings for all-weather and turf; the all-weather rating is preceded by the letter 'a'. Underneath the horse's name is its age, colour and sex in abbreviated format e.g. 6 b g indicates the horse is six-years-old, bay in colour, and a gelding. The descriptive details are followed by the race numbers of the races in which it has taken part in chronological order; a superscript figure indicates its finishing position in that race (brackets indicate it was the winner of the race).

Admirable Duchess *D J S Ffrench Davis* 69
2 gr f Compton Place—Smart Hostess (Most Welcome))
3858[5] ◆ 4323[3] 4711[4] 5899[5] ◆ 6418[7]

Admirable Duque (IRE) *D J S Ffrench Davis* a76 76
3 b g Selkirk(USA) —Stunning (USA) (Nureyev (USA))
1408[3] (1747) 2084[7] 2208[7] 3697[5] 4325[8] 4911[9] 4988[11] 5593[8] *6613[8]* *(6807)* *7476[8]*

Admiral (IRE) *S Parr* 39
8 b g Alhaarth(IRE) —Coast Is Clear (IRE) (Rainbow Quest (USA))
1473[4] 1665[8] 1826[8] 2262[10] 2592[7] 3023[10]

Admiral Arry *J M Bradley* a30 14
4 ch g Compton Admiral—Loreto Rose (Lahib (USA))
1047[9] 1784[12] 2537[6]

Admiral Bond (IRE) *G R Oldroyd* a69 69
4 ch g Titus Livius(FR) —Where's Charlotte (Sure Blade (USA))
15[2] *269[5]* *431[5]* *681[2]* *794[5]* 4823[17] *5610[8]* *6119[5]* *6251[9]* 6553[5] *7710[6]* 7838[6]

Admiral Breese *R Hollinshead* a55 40
2 b g Halling(USA) —Covet (Polish Precedent (USA))
7244[11] *7420[3]* *7781[3]*

Admiral Cochrane (IRE) *W Jarvis* a73 64
2 b c Noverre(USA) —Michelle Hicks (Ballad Rock)
4515[6] 4906[4] 5934[9] *6775[3]* *7333[3]* *7514[2]* *(7619)* *7824[3]*

Admiral Dundas (IRE) *W Jarvis* a84 90
4 b g Noverre(USA) —Brandish (Warning)
1722[8] 2894[2] 3752[9] 4315[7] 4957[6] 5510[4] (6137) *6435[5]* 6733[6] 7014[8]

Admiral Of The Dee (IRE) *Patrick Morris* 28
3 b g Catcher In The Rye(IRE) —Grandmette (IRE) (Grand Lodge (USA))
3237[6]

Admiral Sandhoe (USA) *Mrs A J Perrett* a70 75
3 ch g Diesis—Dancing Sea (USA) (Storm Cat (USA))
1574[9] 1895[2] *2600[10]* 2849[11] *4202[4]* 4700[6] 5429[19]

Admirals Way *C N Kellett* a61 65
4 ch g Observatory(USA) —Dockage (CAN) (Riverman (USA))
420[8] *471[4]* *666[7]* *(803)* *895[4]* *1080[13]*

Admire The View (IRE) *D R Lanigan* 90
2 ch f Dubawi(IRE) —Miss Honorine (IRE) (Highest Honor (FR))
3858[7] ◆ (4278) ◆ 4795[10]

Adnams *C F Wall* a47 66
3 b g Nayef(USA) —Bedford Joy (GER) (Big Shuffle (USA))
3168[5] 3549[5] 4145[7] ◆ 4744[6] ◆ *5782[13]*

Adolfina (GER) *W Figge* 104
4 b m Sholokhov(IRE) —Akilinda (FR) (Monsun (GER))
5461a[7] 6152a[2] 7406a[6]

Adoring (IRE) *W J Haggas* 82
3 b f One Cool Cat(USA) —Refined (IRE) (Statoblest)
(2298) 4317[5] 5030[6]

Adorn *J Noseda* a86 104
3 b f Kyllachy—Red Tiara (USA) (Mr Prospector (USA))
2271[5] ◆ 2928[9] 4516[9] 5069[9]

Adozen Dreams *N Bycroft* a54 61
3 b f Monsieur Bond(IRE) —Chicago Bond (USA) (Real Quiet (USA))
1469[8] 4343[7] 4596[11] 5254[15] 5468[7] 5983[8] 6488[7]

A Dream Come True *D K Ivory* a68 64
4 b m Where Or When(IRE) —Katy Ivory (IRE) (Night Shift (USA))
4389[7] 4745[9] *5195[10]*

Advanced *K A Ryan* a96 109
6 b g Night Shift(USA) —Wonderful World (GER) (Dashing Blade)
1018[2] (1398) 2259[3] 3141[6] 4523[20] 4796[4] 5039[3] 6091[8] (6270) 6530a[4] 7019[4] 7232a[8]

Adventure Story *R Hannon* 74
2 ch f Bold Edge—Birthday Venture (Soviet Star (USA))
6616[6] 6903[2] 7061[2] (7288)

Adversane *A J Lidderdale* a32 39
5 ch g Alhaarth(IRE) —Cragreen (Green Desert (USA))
623[8] *790[11]* *871[11]*

Advertise *A M Balding* 71
3 br g Passing Glance—Averami (Averti (IRE))
2638[6] 3375[5] 3790[2] 5804[4] 6111[10] 6790[4]

Advertisement (USA) *J Noseda* a72 81
2 bb c Mr Greeley(USA) —Banner (USA) (A.P. Indy (USA))
4336[4] *4790[3]*

Advice (USA) *Todd Pletcher* a110 98
3 bb c Chapel Royal(USA) —Word O' Wisdom (USA) (Hennessy (USA))
1688a[13]

Advisor (FR) *M L W Bell* 85
3 gr g Anabaa(USA) —Armilina (FR) (Linamix (FR))
1257[5] (1574) 2174[6] 2884[4] 4008[4] 4518[2] 4709[6]

Aegean (USA) *Wesley A Ward* a100 71
2 b f Northern Afleet(USA) —Apt To Star (USA) (Aptitude (USA))
3086[9]

Aegean Dancer *B Smart* a105 102
7 b g Piccolo—Aegean Flame (Anshan)
1278[2] 4135[7] 5132[17] (Dead)

Aegean Destiny *R A Harris* a60 65
2 b f Beat Hollow—Starlist (Observatory (USA))
1810[6] 2563[7] 4689[3] (5543) 5868[2] *6228[10]* *7334[7]* *7482[5]* *7584[4]* *7788[8]*

Aegean King *M Wigham* a50 55
3 b g Falbrav(IRE) —Aegean Dream (IRE) (Royal Academy (USA))
1317[6] 1617[6] 2157[5] 3611[3]

Aegean Pride *A Berry* a62 62
4 b m Sakhee(USA) —Aegean Dream (IRE) (Royal Academy (USA))
179[6] *290[8]* *626[7]* 1228[8] 1734[9] 2812[14]

Aegean Prince *P Howling* a86 86
5 b g Dr Fong(USA) —Dizzydaisy (Sharpo)
1635[2] *2146[6]* 2706[12] *3734[10]* 4098[7] *6636[10]*

Aegean Rose *M Blanshard* a52 23
4 br m Superior Premium—Lady Sabina (Bairn (USA))
80[7] *731[4]* *949[8]* 1254[13] *1463[11]* *1967[13]*

Aegean Shadow *M Wigham* a43 65
3 ch f Sakhee(USA) —Noble View (USA) (Distant View (USA))
(4199) *5806[7]*

Aerodynamic (IRE) *Pat Eddery* 78
2 b c Oratorio(IRE) —Willowbridge (IRE) (Entrepreneur)
(2853) 3138[6]

Aeroplane *P D Evans* a109 97
6 b h Danehill Dancer(IRE) —Anita At Dawn (IRE) (Anita's Prince)
(73) *123[4]* *291[3]* *781[3]* *916[6]* 1861[12] *(6024)* *(7520)* *7768[6]* *7827[2]*

Aestival *Sir Mark Prescott* a44 29
3 b g Falbrav(IRE) —Summer Night (Nashwan (USA))
6910[16]

Aetos *M P Tregoning* 61
2 b c Royal Applause—Hagwah (USA) (Dancing Brave (USA))
4410[4]

Affaire De Famille (FR) *Mme C Dufreche*
2 b f Charge D'Affaires—Tordesillas (FR) (Astair (FR))
6325a[3]

Affirmable *J W Hills* 55
2 b f Doyen(IRE) —Bella Bellisimo (IRE) (Alzao (USA))
5000[6]

Affirmatively *A W Carroll* a69 52
4 b m Diktat—Circlet (Lion Cavern (USA))
111[10] *395[11]* *474[4]* *727[3]* *895[2]* *1134[7]* 1970[13] 2712[3] 2913[9] 3591[5] 4023[9] *4204[9]*

Affluent *R Charlton* a81 94
3 b f Oasis Dream—Valencia (Kenmare (FR))
1078[2] ◆ 1486[3] (2140) ◆ 3145[5] 4099[5] 5245[4]

Aflaam (IRE) *R A Harris* a72 86
4 br g Dubai Destination(USA) —Arjuzah (IRE) (Ahonoora)
1433[12] 2050[7] 2665[4] *3928[9]* 4501[5] 4852[3] 5441[15] *6725[10]* *7048[11]* *7699[8]*

African Art (USA) *B J Meehan* a71 89
3 ch c Johannesburg(USA) —Perovskia (USA) (Stravinsky (USA))
(1508) ◆ 2004[4] 3144[8] 6429[5] 6535[3] *7027[8]*

African Cheetah *R Hollinshead* a84 80
3 ch c Pivotal—Miss Queen (USA) (Miswaki (USA))
1015[3] ◆ 1252[6] 1461[3] (1739) 5997[4] 6190[4] ◆ 6385[3] 6560[5] 6900[6] ◆ *(7672)*

African Rose *Mme C Head-Maarek* 116
4 ch m Observatory(USA) —New Orchid (USA) (Quest For Fame)
2523a[4] 3819[6] 4837a[11]

Africa's Star (IRE) *M Dods* a59 67
3 br f Johannesburg(USA) —Grable (IRE) (Sadler's Wells (USA))
2365[8] 3003[3] 3611[12] 3853[4] 4596[8] 5621[8]

After The Show *Rae Guest* a69 78
8 b g Royal Applause—Tango Teaser (Shareef Dancer (USA))
165[2] *645[3]* 1776[7] 2228[10] *2596[8]* 6799[8] *7337[10]* *7483[4]* *7602[9]* *7808[4]*

Afton View (IRE) *S Parr* a64 64
4 gr g Clodovil(IRE) —Moonlight Partner (IRE) (Red Sunset)
174[5] *222[6]* *294[8]* *347[2]* *487[2]* *565[7]* *792[11]*

Again (IRE) *David Wachman* 114
3 b f Danehill Dancer(IRE) —Cumbres (FR) (Kahyasi)
(2304a) 3088[7] 5686a[3] 6525a[7]

Against The Rules *J A R Toller* a45 55
3 b g Diktat—Bella Bellisimo (IRE) (Alzao (USA))
5574[8]

Agapanthus (GER) *B J Curley* a75 88
4 b g Tiger Hill(IRE) —Astilbe (GER) (Monsun (GER))
(1261) 3361[6] 4426[8] 6761[8] 7014[11] 7248[6]

Ageebah *C E Brittain* a68 63
3 b f Acclamation—Flag (Selkirk (USA))
397[2] ◆ *(586)* *782[5]*

Agent Archie (USA) *J R Best* 70
2 b c Smart Strike(CAN) —Dans La Ville (CHI) (Winning (USA))
5966[6] (6200)

Agent Boo *E S McMahon* a59 65
2 b c Monsieur Bond(IRE) —Silca Boo (Efisio)
1277[10] 1764[5] *2128[6]* *3925[3]* *4371[8]* (5358) *6345[6]*

Agente Parmigiano (IRE) *G A Butler* a97 91
3 ch c Captain Rio—Kama's Wheel (Magic Ring (IRE))
863[8] *1118[4]* 1828[3] 2674[6] 3375[4] 3839[5] *5092[4]* 5766[3] 6815[17]

Agente Romano (USA) *G A Butler* a72 72
4 br h Street Cry(IRE) —Dixie Bay (USA) (Dixieland Band (USA))
1945[6] 2172[5] 2497[10] 3169[2] 3521[5] 4021[2]

Agent Stone (IRE) *D Nicholls* 74
3 ch g Night Shift(USA) —Just One Smile (IRE) (Desert Prince (IRE))
1061[9] (1662) 2028[6]

Age Of Aquarius (IRE) *A P O'Brien* a83 118
3 b c Galileo(IRE) —Clara Bow (FR) (Top Ville)
(1872) 2705[7] 3970a[2]

Age Of Couture *M Jarvis* 50
3 ch f Hold That Tiger(USA) —Three Wishes (Sadler's Wells (USA))
2664[7]

Age Of Reason (UAE) *Saeed Bin Suroor* a107 113
4 b g Halling(USA) —Time Changes (USA) (Danzig (USA))
185a[3] (338a) 2955a[2] 3397[5] 5023[3] 5446[4] *7237[2]*

Aggbag *Miss M E Rowland* a60 60
5 b g Fath(USA) —Emaura (Dominion)
130[5] *277[4]* *473[3]* *748[2]* *984[2]* 1243[4] *1438[11]* 1883[4] 2473[12] (3077) 3322[2] 3730[3] *4376[3]* 5229[8] 6256[8]

Agglestone Rock *P A Kirby* a67 71
4 b g Josr Algarhoud(IRE) —Royalty (IRE) (Fairy King (USA))
333[3] *(485)* 2237[14] 3760[7] 7084[2]

Aggravation *D R C Elsworth* a72 78
7 b g Sure Blade(USA) —Confection (Formidable (USA))
1633[3] *1833[3]* 2245[8] 2977[5] 3112[11] 3525[3] 4060[6] 6547[8]

Agilete *J Pearce* a84 87
7 b g Piccolo—Ingerence (FR) (Akarad (FR))
(254) *353[2]* *(571)* *(1042)* 1261[4] *2824[10]* 3151[2] (4437) (4710) 4737[3] 5266[8] (6002) 6594[8] *6830[11]* *7583[4]*

Agnes Love *J Akehurst* a64 27
3 gr f Piccolo—Erracht (Emarati (USA))
3162[8] 3663[6] *4204[2]* *4978[5]* *(5164)* *5584[3]* *7329[10]* *7518[7]*

Agony And Ecstasy *R M Beckett* a77 78
2 ch f Captain Rio—Agony Aunt (Formidable (USA))
2175[6] 3785[5] (4534) *6211[5]* (6735) *7267[3]*

Agricultural *Mrs L B Normile* 30
3 b c Daylami(IRE) —Rustic (IRE) (Grand Lodge (USA))
3680[6] 4014[7]

Ahla Wasahl *D M Simcock* a105 101
3 br f Dubai Destination(USA) —In Full Cry (USA) (Seattle Slew (USA))
1599[2] 2057[5] 3320[7] 5260[4] (6267) *7132[2]*

Ahlawy (IRE) *F Sheridan* a96 83
6 gr g Green Desert(USA) —On Call (Alleged (USA))
(105) *(220)* *330[3]* *(981)* *(1107)* *2597[10]* 3374[6] 4450[2] 5186[2]

Ahmedy (IRE) *J J Quinn* a77 34
6 b g Polish Precedent(USA) —Nawaji (USA) (Trempolino (USA))
(6498) 7020[8]

Ahwahnee *R M Beckett* a43
2 ch f Compton Place—Tahara (IRE) (Caerleon (USA))
6971[7]

Aiboa (IRE) *L A Urbano-Grajales* 107
3 ch f King Charlemagne(USA) —Spirit of Hope (IRE) (Danehill Dancer (IRE))
3908a[3] 4637a[5] 5495a[5]

Aikenite (USA) *Todd Pletcher* a111
2 b c Yes It's True(USA) —Silverlado (USA) (Saint Ballado (CAN))
7307a[5]

Ailsa Carmel (IRE) *M R Channon* 76
2 b f Antonius Pius(USA) —Dancing Duchess (IRE) (Danehill Dancer (IRE))
2034[3] 2354[6] (2735) (2963) 3311[2] 3430[4]

Ailsa Craig (IRE) *E W Tuer* a66 72
3 b f Chevalier(IRE) —Sharplaw Destiny (IRE) (Petardia)
1743[6] 2776[3] 2879[2] 3381[2] 4266[5] (5063) 5602[3] 6337[9] *7423[6]*

Ailton (GER) *G Raveneau* 96
5 b g Fly To The Stars—Aznavour (GER) (Lagunas)
1555a[7] 7102a[4]

Aimeeskeepingfaith *M R Channon* a49 50
2 b f Beckett(IRE) —Keeping The Faith (IRE) (Ajraas (USA))
5605[17] 5800[7] *6069[10]*

Aim To Achieve (IRE) *B W Hills* a70 78
3 b f Galileo(IRE) —Sabander Bay (USA) (Lear Fan (USA))
2937[4] *(3297)* 4095[3]

Aine (IRE) *T Stack* 102
4 ch m Danehill Dancer(IRE) —Antinnaz (IRE) (Thatching)
1374a[4] 2271[7] 2644a[7] 5491a[5]

Aine's Delight (IRE) *Andrew Turnell* a17 67
3 b f King's Best(USA) —Gentle Thoughts (Darshaan)
1844[7] 2515[9] (3426) 4305[4] 5179[13] 6394[4] (6910)

Ainia *D M Simcock* a52 81
4 b m Alhaarth(IRE) —Vayavaig (Damister (USA))
2317[2] (3060) 4088[6] 4566[6] 5472[7] 6886a[10]

Ain Jalout (IRE) *M Phelan* a61 61
3 bb g Catcher In The Rye(IRE) —Classic Motive (ITY) (Love The Groom (USA))
4392a[7]

Aintgottaname *M J McGrath* a32
2 b f Trade Fair—Emouna (Cadeaux Genereux)
7024[12] *7390[9]* *7624[11]*

Ainthegorgeous *P T Midgley* 30
2 b c Dr Fong(USA) —Free Spirit (IRE) (Caerleon (USA))
4396[12] 4888[9] 5519[10]

Ain't Talkin' *M J Attwater* a53 49
3 ch c Zaha(CAN) —Royal Ivy (Mujtahid (USA))
(267)

Aintwogrand (IRE) *M R Channon* a40 53
2 b f Acclamation—Rebel Clan (IRE) (Tagula (IRE))
2906[8] 3101[5] 4011[6] 4384[5] *4747[5]*

Air Bag (FR) *Mme C Barande-Barbe* a77 81
5 b m Poliglote—Avrilana (FR) (Deep Roots)
4335a[5]

Air Chief Marshal (IRE) *A P O'Brien* 110
2 b c Danehill Dancer(IRE) —Hawala (IRE) (Warning)
2286a[3] 2993[11] 3895a[6] 4359a[2] 5486a[2] 5892a[4] 6317a[5] 7072a[4]

Air Crew (USA) *R Menichetti* 101
2 b c Pollard's Vision(USA) —Crystal Bull (USA) (Holy Bull (USA))
3185a[3] 6716a[7] 7205a[6]

Airforce (GER) *W Hickst* 95
3 b f Big Shuffle(USA) —Alzara (GER) (Air Express (IRE))
1240a[7] 5651a[9]

Air Lion (USA) *R M H Cowell* a59
3 b g Lion Heart(USA) —Swigert (USA) (Fusaichi Pegasus (USA))
602[2] *686[3]* *4174[6]*

Air Maze *Sir Mark Prescott* a75 76
3 b f Dansili—Begueule (FR) (Bering)
251[2] ◆ *564[2]* *(678)* (4224) 4569[3] 5593[2] *6027[3]* 6560[8]

Air Ransom (ITY) *V Caruso* 95
3 b g Blu Air Force(IRE) —Blu Ransom (IRE) (Fasliyev (USA))
6894a[5]

Air Shady (JPN) *M Ito* 121
8 ch h Sunday Silence(USA) —Air Deja Vu (JPN) (Northern Taste (CAN))
7593a[5]

Aisy (IRE) *T Stack* 64
2 b f Oasis Dream—Granny Kelly (USA) (Irish River (FR))
2286a[9]

Aizavoski (IRE) *E Lellouche* 113
3 b c Monsun(GER) —Arlesienne (IRE) (Alzao (USA))
5930a[3] 6502a[3]

Ajaan *H R A Cecil* 108
5 br h Machiavellian(USA) —Alakananda (Hernando (FR))
1790[2] 3390[7] 5609[4] 6851[5]

Ajara (IRE) *N J Vaughan* a69
3 b f Elusive City(USA) —My-Lorraine (IRE) (Mac's Imp (USA))
276[7]

Ajara Boy *Tom Dascombe* a16 36
2 ch c Avonbridge—Cultural Role (Night Shift (USA))
3571[8] 6231[6] *6443[6]* *6858[9]*

Ajdaad (USA) *J E Hammond* 77
2 b c Horse Chestnut(SAF) —Hasene (FR) (Akarad (FR))
6578a[4]

Ajhar (USA) *M P Tregoning* a107 106
5 b g Diesis—Min Alhawa (USA) (Riverman (USA))
1004[7] (5004)

Ajigolo *N Wilson* a55 99
6 ch g Piccolo—Ajig Dancer (Niniski (USA))
1018[20] 1278[11] 1676[8] 2059[10] 2707[11] 3706[13] 3877[12] 4598[11] *7395[9]* *7478[11]* (Dead)

Ajjaadd (USA) *T E Powell* a78 67
3 b g Elusive Quality(USA) —Millstream (USA) (Dayjur (USA))
7254[2] *7686[2]*

Ajool (USA) *B W Hills* 69
2 ch f Aljabr(USA) —Tamgeed (USA) (Woodman (USA))
7182[5]

Akabar *R M Beckett* 51
3 b g Piccolo—Fredora (Inchinor)
2250[9] 3460[4] 4324[6] 4905[10]

Akamon *E A L Dunlop* a67
2 ch f Monsun(GER) —Akanta (GER) (Wolfhound (USA))
6942[6] *7276[2]*

Akash (IRE) *K M Prendergast* a36 36
9 b g Dr Devious(IRE) —Akilara (IRE) (Kahyasi)
107[7] *300[12]*

Akbabend *M Johnston* a87 89
3 b g Refuse To Bend(IRE) —Akdariya (IRE) (Shirley Heights)
1101[2] 2104[13] 4715[5] 4974[2] ◆ *(6855)* *7066[3]*

Akdarena *J S Bolger* 93
2 b f Hernando(FR) —Akdariya (IRE) (Shirley Heights)
6708a[3]

Akhenaten *M R Channon* a93 98
3 b c High Chaparral(IRE) —Lady Adnil (IRE) (Stravinsky (USA))
(764) *863[12]* 1326[7] 1679[6] 2279[2] 2469[2] 2673[4] 2934[8] 3747[12] 4459[3] 5206[3] (5766) 6270[25]

Akiem (IRE) *Andreas Lowe* 100
4 b g Kutub(IRE) —Anacapri (FR) (Anabaa (USA))
1143a[5]

Akmal *J L Dunlop* 109
3 ch g Selkirk(USA) —Ayun (USA) (Swain (IRE))
1087[2] 1349[3] (2181) (2545) 3280[2] (3827) 4420[5] (5230) (6036) (6854)

Akram (IRE) *Jonjo O'Neill* 63
7 b g Night Shift(USA) —Akdariya (IRE) (Shirley Heights)
4321[9] 6369[5]

Aktia (IRE) *L M Cumani* a63 68
2 b f Danehill Dancer(IRE) —La Gandilie (FR) (Highest Honor (FR))
6284[6] ◆ 6921[7] *7430[3]*

Akton City (FR) *J-P Delaporte* a71 79
2 b c Sagacity(FR) —Tanea (FR) (Exit To Nowhere (USA))
5713a[6]

Akua'Ba (IRE) *J S Bolger* a90 101
5 b m Sadler's Wells(USA) —Ghana (IRE) (Lahib (USA))
340a[9] 416a[8] 609a[10]

Akubra (IRE) *Norma Twomey* a26
2 b f One Cool Cat(USA) —Dreaming Waters (Groom Dancer (USA))
5808[10] *7736[11]*

Akula (IRE) *M H Tompkins* 66
2 ch c Soviet Star(USA) —Danielli (IRE) (Danehill (USA))
3957[3] 4524[11] 6066[13]

Alacity (IRE) *N Bycroft* 61
3 b f Elusive City(USA) —Minamala (IRE) (Desert King (IRE))
1922[3] 3876[6] 4505[4] 5405[9] 5624[6] 6553[3] 6823[6] 7081[5] 7241[2]

Al Adham *Saeed Bin Suroor* 54
2 b c Dansili—Miss Meggy (Pivotal)
4233[6] 4595[8]

Alainmaar (FR) *M A Jarvis* 110
3 b g Johar(USA) —Lady Elgar (IRE) (Sadler's Wells (USA))
5435[2] ◆ (6022) ◆ (6453) ◆

Alaivan (IRE) *John M Oxx* 112 3 b g Kalanisi(IRE) —Alaya (IRE) (Ela-Mana-Mou) 2306a^{2} (3700a)

Alaiyma (IRE) *John M Oxx* a95 98 3 b f Refuse To Bend(IRE) —Alasana (IRE) (Darshaan) (6867a)

Alanbrooke *M Johnston* 106 3 gr c Hernando(FR) —Alouette (Darshaan) 2038^{2} ◆ 2715^{6} ◆ 3069^{8} (3587) ◆ (3793) 4260^{2} 4767^{6} 5230^{2} 5656^{3} 6115^{2} 6851^{16} 7117^{3}

Alan Devonshire *M H Tompkins* 99 4 br g Mtoto—Missed Again (High Top) 2500^{10} 3014^{25} 3586^{10} 4526^{11} 6024^{12} 6596^{8} 6924^{12} 7057^{7}

Alandi (IRE) *John M Oxx* 118 4 b h Galileo(IRE) —Aliya (IRE) (Darshaan) (1546a) 2425a^{2} 3413a^{2} 4033a^{5} (5891a) (6527a)

Alannah (IRE) *Mrs P N Dutfield* a38 43 4 b m Alhaarth(IRE) —Aljeeza (Halling (USA)) 4220^{8} 5381^{4} 6758^{11}

Alarazi (IRE) *T G Mills* a99 110 5 b g Spectrum(IRE) —Alaya (IRE) (Ela-Mana-Mou) 1004^{5} 1352^{10} 2398^{3} 3089^{11} 4794^{3}

Alazeyab (USA) *M A Jarvis* 106 3 b c El Prado(IRE) —Itnab (Green Desert (USA)) 1678^{5} 2077^{8} (3399) 3873^{10} 4455^{12} 5200^{2} 5863^{4} 6480^{17}

Al Azy (IRE) *D M Simcock* a61 66 4 b h Nayef(USA) —Nasheed (USA) (Riverman (USA)) 546^{5} 733^{10} 969^{10} 1154^{3} 1767^{7} (2172) 2609^{8} (3552)

Albaasha (IRE) *Sir Michael Stoute* a61 68 3 ch c Lemon Drop Kid(USA) —Cozy Maria (USA) (Cozzene (USA)) 1874^{5} 2104^{5} 2667^{2} 3300^{5} 3674^{6}

Albacocca *Sir Mark Prescott* a47 35 2 gr f With Approval(CAN) —Ballymac Girl (Niniski (USA)) 5839^{7} 5984^{8} 6284^{9}

Albaher *J L Dunlop* 79 3 b c Oasis Dream—Dance Sequence (USA) (Mr Prospector (USA)) 1487^{4} 5832^{10} 6243^{12} 6680^{16}

Albaqaa *R A Fahey* a95 100 4 ch g Medicean—Basbousate Nadia (Wolfhound (USA)) 1003^{5} 1172^{3} 1986^{4} 2933^{2} 3873^{3}

Al Barq (IRE) *Miss D Mountain* 46 2 ch f Traditionally(USA) —Prayer (IRE) (Rainbow Quest (USA)) 4497^{9} 4915^{7} 5519^{15}

Albaseet (IRE) *M P Tregoning* a75 70 3 b g Desert Style(IRE) —Double Eight (IRE) (Common Grounds) 5110^{3}

Al Batal (FR) *W Baltromei* a69 80 3 b c Trempolino(USA) —Today (IRE) (Royal Academy (USA)) 5783a^{4}

Albeed *J L Dunlop* 60 2 b f Tiger Hill(IRE) —Ayun (USA) (Swain (IRE)) 4542^{13} 6363^{9} 6992^{10}

Albero Di Giuda (IRE) *F Sheridan* a57 27 4 b m Clodovil(IRE) —All Away (IRE) (Glow (USA)) 349^{4} 557^{6} 777^{8} 919^{3} 1038^{5} 2682^{3} 2921^{10} 7709^{5} 7877^{9}

Albertine Rose *W R Muir* a72 87 3 gr f Namid—Barathiki (Barathea (IRE)) 2928^{8} 4069^{11} 4601^{9}

Alberts Story (USA) *R A Fahey* a62 61 5 b g Tale Of The Cat(USA) —Hazino (USA) (Hazaam (USA)) 193^{4} 368^{3} 493^{7}

Albertus Maximus (USA) *Kiaran McLaughlin* a121 5 b h Albert The Great(USA) —Chasethewildwind (USA) (Forty Niner (USA)) 1013a^{6}

Albiera (IRE) *H Morrison* a41 7 4 b m Xaar—Madam Waajib (IRE) (Waajib) 6741^{12} 7195^{7} 7361^{11} 7658^{13}

Albisola (IRE) *Robert Collet* 116 4 b m Montjeu(IRE) —Mahalia (IRE) (Danehill (USA)) 1597a^{3} 2428a^{7} 4365a^{0}

Alcalde *M Johnston* 95 3 b g Hernando(FR) —Alexandrine (IRE) (Nashwan (USA)) 4518^{7} 5034^{2} 5230^{13} 5828^{10} (6546) 6795^{6} 7018^{3}

Alcopop (AUS) *Jake Stephens* 115 5 b g Jeune—Iota Of Luck (AUS) (Blevic (AUS)) 7215a^{6}

Aldaado (IRE) *M Dods* 78 3 b g Alhaarth(IRE) —Zobaida (IRE) (Green Desert (USA)) 1308^{14} 1739^{4} 1950^{3} (2370) (3480) 3608^{5} 4741^{3} 6680^{17}

Al Dafa (USA) *Saeed Bin Suroor* 65 2 ch c Kingmambo(USA) —Crimson Conquest (USA) (Diesis) 5017^{4} 5966^{7}

Alderbed *George Baker* a44 46 3 b g Bahri(USA) —Tanasie (Cadeaux Genereux) 2772^{6} 3054^{6}

Aldermoor (USA) *S C Williams* 98 3 b g Tale Of The Cat(USA) —Notting Hill (BRZ) (Jules (USA)) 1296^{4} 2016^{8} 2279^{7} 4330^{14} 5032^{10} 5695^{14} (6482) 6994^{16} 7294^{20}

Aldiruos (IRE) *A W Carroll* a59 9 ch g Bigstone(IRE) —Ball Cat (FR) (Cricket Ball (USA)) 72^{5} 485^{9}

Aldorable *R A Teal* a19 59 2 ch f Starcraft(NZ) —Aldora (Magic Ring (IRE)) 3507^{9} 5800^{4} 6424^{4} 6775^{11}

Aldoussa (FR) *Mme M Bollack-Badel* 73 3 b f Numerous(USA) —Advalor (FR) (Synefos (USA)) 5462a^{7}

Aleagueoftheirown (IRE) *David Wachman* 101 5 b m Danehill Dancer(IRE) —Golden Coral (USA) (Slew O'Gold (USA)) 2644a^{9} 3516a^{10}

Aleatricis *J J Quinn* a31 88 4 bg g Kingmambo(USA) —Alba Stella (Nashwan (USA)) 1473^{2} 1886^{2} (2249) 3146^{4} 3850^{3} 6115^{9}

Aleqa *C F Wall* 2 b f Oasis Dream—Vanishing Point (USA) (Caller I.D. (USA)) 6615^{14}

Aleron (IRE) *J J Quinn* a14 69 11 b g Sadler's Wells(USA) —High Hawk (Shirley Heights) 1058^{7} 1767^{2} 2262^{5} 5554^{3}

Alessano *G L Moore* a73 86 7 ch g Hernando(FR) —Alessandra (Generous (IRE)) 4212^{5} 4793^{10} 5781^{5} 6734^{P}

Aleutian *F Nass* a105 91 9 gr g Zafonic(USA) —Baked Alaska (Green Desert (USA)) 523a^{7} 698a^{14}

Alexander Family (IRE) *E F Vaughan* a66 57 3 b f Danetime(IRE) —Villa Nova (IRE) (Petardia) (214) 542^{5}

Alexander Gulch (USA) *K A Ryan* a85 83 3 b g Thunder Gulch(USA) —Lovely Later (USA) (Green Dancer (USA)) 532^{2} 755^{2} 1019^{5}

Alexander Guru *M Blanshard* a69 65 5 ch g Ishiguru(USA) —Superspring (Superlative) 253^{8} 512^{7} 577^{5}

Alexander Loyalty (IRE) *E F Vaughan* a43 64 3 b f Invincible Spirit(IRE) —Nassma (IRE) (Sadler's Wells (USA)) 1077^{7} 2160^{12} 2827^{8} 3427^{5}

Alexander Youth (IRE) *David Wachman* a84 94 3 ch f Exceed And Excel(AUS) —Wolf Cleugh (IRE) (Last Tycoon) 3516a^{9} 5921a^{3}

Alexandros *Saeed Bin Suroor* 119 4 ch h Kingmambo(USA) —Arlette (IRE) (King Of Kings (IRE)) (265a) (436a) ◆ 1011a^{3} 1553a^{7} 2076^{2} 2990^{8} (7245) ◆ 7746a^{7}

Alfalasteeni *Ian Williams* 22 2 ch g Kyllachy—Mrs Nash (Night Shift (USA)) 2196^{8} 2484^{8} 4075^{6} 4547^{9}

Alfalevva *M R Channon* a57 46 2 b g Piccolo—Evanesce (Lujain (USA)) 4424^{10} 4851^{9} 5119^{6} 6334^{8} 6721^{4} 7139^{2} 7474^{7}

Alfathaa *W J Haggas* 105 4 b g Nayef(USA) —Arctic Char (Polar Falcon (USA)) 3014^{5} ◆ 3639^{5} ◆ 4404^{5} 5200^{6} 5794^{6} 6307^{2} 6480^{13}

Alfie Flits *G A Swinbank* a96 104 7 b g Machiavellian(USA) —Elhilmeya (IRE) (Unfuwain (USA)) 4781^{8}

Alfie Lee (IRE) *D A Nolan* a3 50 12 ch g Case Law—Nordic Living (IRE) (Nordico (USA)) 3109^{5} 3445^{11}

Alfies Express *S Curran* a53 5 br g My Best Valentine—Ali Rose (Cigar) 7195^{8} 7367^{9} 7549^{11}

Alfie Tupper (IRE) *J R Boyle* a78 67 6 ch g Soviet Star(USA) —Walnut Lady (Forzando) 2407^{10} 3024^{12} 3811^{10} 7512^{10} 7664^{7}

Alfonso The Wise (IRE) *J Noseda* 44 2 b c Galileo(IRE) —Dalawara (IRE) (Top Ville) 6620^{10}

Alfred Nobel (IRE) *A P O'Brien* a98 113 2 b c Danehill Dancer(IRE) —Glinting Desert (IRE) (Desert Prince (IRE)) (3436a) (4359a) 5892a^{6} 6478^{5} 7307a^{10}

Alfredtheordinary *M R Channon* a65 58 4 b g Hunting Lion(IRE) —Solmorin (Fraam) 320^{10} (749) 867^{2} 898^{6} 1080^{9} 7650^{7}

Alfresco *J R Best* a91 83 5 b g Mtoto—Maureena (IRE) (Grand Lodge (USA)) 910^{6} 1116^{3} ◆ 1213^{5} (2326) 2549^{2} 2929^{10} 4461^{20} 5404^{12} 5646^{10} 5914^{9} 6630^{4} 7437^{9} 7603^{7}

Alf Tupper *Adrian McGuinness* a73 53 6 b g Atraf—Silvery (Petong) 105^{4} (256)

Al Ghazal (USA) *Saeed Bin Suroor* 100 2 b c Motivator—Mansfield Park (Green Desert (USA)) 3692^{3} (4908) (6569) 7017^{8}

Al Gillani (IRE) *J R Boyle* a92 61 4 b g Monashee Mountain(USA) —Whisper Dawn (IRE) (Fasliyev (USA)) (954) ◆ 1321^{8} 3795^{6} 4870^{2}

Alhabeeb (IRE) *Kevin Prendergast* a91 99 4 b g Alhaarth(IRE) —Elfaslah (IRE) (Green Desert (USA)) 2305a^{5}

Alhaque (USA) *W J Haggas* a70 83 3 ch g Galileo(IRE) —Safeen (USA) (Storm Cat (USA)) 1088^{3} 2002^{8} 5531^{6} 6225^{2} 6417^{2}

Alhena (IRE) *K A Ryan* 54 2 b f Alhaarth(IRE) —Mail Boat (Formidable (USA)) 5949^{7} 6284^{11}

Alianthus (GER) *J Hirschberger* 90 6 b h Hernando(FR) —Allure (GER) (Konigsstuhl (GER)) 7406a^{4}

Alicante *Sir Mark Prescott* 78 3 gr f Pivotal—Alba Stella (Nashwan (USA)) 1626^{5} (4039) (4178) 4506^{10} 5912^{6}

Alice Alleyne (IRE) *Sir Michael Stoute* a77 77 2 b f Oasis Dream—Vas Y Carla (USA) (Gone West (USA)) 5638^{2} 5969^{2} (6436)

Alice Cullen *W R Swinburn* 55 2 b f Bertolini(USA) —Albavilla (Spectrum (IRE)) 7182^{11}

Alice De La Vis (FR) *J De Roualle* a83 97 3 ch f Bahhare(USA) —Buckwood (Saumarez) 4394a^{5} 4971a^{8}

Alimarr (IRE) *S Parr* a60 53 3 ch f Noverre(USA) —Tiger Desert (GER) (Desert King (IRE)) 358^{5} 520^{9} 560^{5} 684^{6}

Alinghi (IRE) *R Hannon* a60 2 b f Oratorio(IRE) —The Stick (Singspiel (IRE)) 6942^{5}

Alis Aquilae (IRE) *T J Etherington* 63 3 b g Captain Rio—Garnock Academy (USA) (Royal Academy (USA)) 1840^{5} 3003^{10}

Alittlemoreflair *J Pearce* a62 48 3 ch f Grape Tree Road—Native Flair (Be My Native (USA)) 440^{7} 570^{4} 779^{5} 953^{10} 1070^{3} 1954^{12} 2866^{8} 3511^{7} 4498^{3} 5579^{7} 6037^{5}

Aliybee (IRE) *E J O'Neill* a56 3 b f Barathea(IRE) —Aliyshan (IRE) (Darshaan) 138^{10}

Aliyfa (IRE) *John M Oxx* a94 104 3 b f Spinning World(USA) —Aliya (IRE) (Darshaan) 4033a^{3} 4510a^{4} (5539a)

Al Jaadl *W Jarvis* 61 2 b f Shamardal(USA) —Three Wishes (Sadler's Wells (USA)) 6567^{5}

Al Jathaab (USA) *M Wigham* a66 4 gr g Aljabr(USA) —Al Ihsas (IRE) (Danehill (USA)) 386^{7} 658^{5} 800^{3}

Al Joza *C E Brittain* a64 61 2 b f Dubawi(IRE) —Avila (Ajdal (USA)) 3733^{4} 6062^{8} 6477^{14}

Alkhafif *E A L Dunlop* a32 93 3 b g Royal Applause—My First Romance (Danehill (USA)) 3298^{8} 5766^{9}

Al Khaleej (IRE) *E A L Dunlop* a107 112 5 b g Sakhee(USA) —Mood Swings (IRE) (Shirley Heights) 4330^{8} ◆ 4796^{9}

Al Khali (USA) *William Mott* a84 110 3 b c Medaglia D'Oro(USA) —Maya (USA) (Capote (USA)) 6511a^{5}

Alkhataaf (USA) *J L Dunlop* 43 2 b c Green Desert(USA) —Elrafa Ah (USA) (Storm Cat (USA)) 6054^{13}

Al Khawarezmi *M Johnston* 36 2 b c Shamardal(USA) —Mrs Ting (USA) (Lyphard (USA)) 4515^{12} 6754^{14}

Al Khimiya (IRE) *S Woodman* a74 70 2 b f Van Nistelrooy(USA) —Golden Flyer (FR) (Machiavellian (USA)) 2631^{8} 2997^{2} 3344^{3} ◆ 3786^{6} 5841^{4} (6228) 6431^{3} (6721) 7604^{4} (7824)

All About You (IRE) *P Howling* a74 86 3 b g Mind Games—Expectation (IRE) (Night Shift (USA)) 1879^{3} 2674^{9} 2926^{4} 4902^{5} 5333^{10} 6111^{4} 6537^{3} 7027^{6} 7534^{9}

Allanit (GER) *B J Curley* a72 103 5 b g Tiger Hill(IRE) —Astilbe (GER) (Monsun (GER)) 156^{7} 550^{8} 798^{12} 5227^{9}

Allannah Abu *Sir Mark Prescott* a51 2 b f Dubawi(IRE) —Alexandrine (IRE) (Nashwan (USA)) 6164^{12} 6781^{11} 7135^{11}

All Annalena (IRE) *Andreas Lowe* 101 3 b f Dubai Destination(USA) —Alla Prima (IRE) (In The Wings) 1914a^{4} 2757a^{6} 4583a^{7} 6714a^{6} 7697a^{0}

Allegoria (IRE) *V Valiani* 100 4 b m Spectrum(IRE) —Alignment (IRE) (Alzao (USA)) 6715a^{2} 7046a^{9}

Allexes (IRE) *J R Boyle* a45 57 3 bb f Exceed And Excel(AUS) —Lizanne (USA) (Theatrical (IRE)) 2679^{7} 3815^{7} 5007^{12} 5090^{8} 5581^{9} 6289^{10}

Allez Bailey (FR) *D De Watrigant* 35 3 b g Orpen(USA) —Herba Buena (FR) (Fabulous Dancer (USA)) (7696a)

Allez Frank (GER) *A E Jones* a57 59 8 b g Macanal(USA) —Agua Clara (GER) (Roi Dagobert) 4263^{3}

Allez Wonder (AUS) *Bart Cummings* 109 4 b m Redoute's Choice(AUS) —Luna Tudor (AUS) (Military Plume (NZ)) 6871a^{8} 7215a^{16}

Allformary *B Smart* a64 78 3 b f Tobougg(IRE) —Bollin Rita (Rambo Dancer (CAN)) 1509^{3} 2073^{7} 2786^{11} 4171^{5} 4658^{5} (5672) 6052^{2} 6357^{9} 6847 7

All For You (IRE) *M Botti* a68 75 3 b f High Chaparral(IRE) —Quatre Saisons (FR) (Homme De Loi (IRE)) 2433^{7} 2857^{2} (3387) 3789^{3} 4452^{5} 5677^{9} 6455^{3}

All Guns Firing (IRE) *D Carroll* a65 78 3 b g High Chaparral(IRE) —Lili Cup (FR) (Fabulous Dancer (USA)) 2930^{11} ◆ 3587^{3} 4280^{6} 7780^{4}

Allied Powers (IRE) *M L W Bell* a70 113 4 b h Invincible Spirit(IRE) —Always Friendly (High Line) 1460^{7} (2031) 2410^{11} 4329^{2} 5539a^{3} 5685a^{2} 6873a^{7}

All In The Red (IRE) *A Crook* a73 75 4 ch g Redback—Light-Flight (IRE) (Brief Truce (USA)) (515) (545) 765^{3} 1014^{7} (1192) 1479^{8} 1779^{5} 1990^{7} 2200^{2} ◆ 2724^{7} 2818^{3} 3266^{14} 3911^{8} 4351^{7} 4434^{3}

All I Want *Andreas Lowe* 84 2 ch f King's Best(USA) —All Prima (IRE) (In The Wings) 7045a^{5}

All Moving Parts (USA) *J S Wainwright* 58 2 bb g Forest Camp(USA) —Smooth Player (USA) (Bertrando (USA)) 5439^{8} 6009^{9} 6593^{6} 6923^{6}

All Of Me (IRE) *Paul W Flynn* a63 46 5 b g Xaar—Silk Point (IRE) (Barathea (IRE)) 7715^{5} 7729^{7}

Alloro *A Kirtley* a23 51 5 ch g Auction House(USA) —Minette (Bishop Of Cashel) 61^{10} 174^{7}

All Right Now *S Kirk* a35 2 b c Night Shift(USA) —Cookie Cutter (IRE) (Fasliyev (USA)) 7859^{10}

All Silent (AUS) *Grahame Begg* 117 6 b g Belong To Me(USA) —Lisheenowen (AUS) (Semipalatinsk (USA)) 7745a^{8}

All Spin (IRE) *A P Jarvis* a65 69 3 ch g Spinning World(USA) —Mad Annie (USA) (Anabaa (USA)) 2355^{6} 3009^{4} 3299^{3} ◆ 3845^{4} 4712^{7} 5517^{F}

All The Aces (IRE) *M A Jarvis* a113 114 4 b g Spartacus(IRE) —Lili Cup (FR) (Fabulous Dancer (USA)) 2075^{2} ◆ (3397) 3781^{5} 5662^{2} ◆ 5891a^{5} 7031^{6}

All The Nines (IRE) *Mrs D J Sanderson* a72 86 3 b f Elusive City(USA) —Sagaing (Machiavellian (USA)) 1491^{6} (1563) (2028) (2438) 3001^{5} 3453^{6} 3956^{14} 4507^{8}

All The Winds (GER) *T Mundry* 89 4 ch h Samum(GER) —All Our Luck (GER) (Spectrum (IRE)) 6658a^{9}

Allybar (IRE) *C Laffon-Parias* 110 3 ch c King's Best(USA) —Irika (USA) (Irish River (FR)) 1979a^{3} 3230a^{2} 4367a^{6} 5084a^{3} 6132a^{3}

All You Need (IRE) *R Hollinshead* a67 58 5 b g Iron Mask(USA) —Choice Pickings (IRE) (Among Men (USA)) 277^{8} 452^{5} (574) 675^{8} 1475^{16} 1781^{6} (2534) 2812^{5} 3490^{12} 4508^{6} 6433^{4} 6945^{12} 7460^{6}

Almadaa *E A L Dunlop* a68 38 2 b c Exceed And Excel(AUS) —Masaader (USA) (Wild Again (USA)) 2017^{9} 2631^{3} 5368^{4} 6643^{12}

Almahaza (IRE) *A J Chamberlain* a72 56 5 b g Alzao(USA) —Morna's Moment (USA) (Timeless Moment (USA)) 221^{9} (608) ◆ 733^{8} (979) 1589^{4} 1936^{12} 2746^{2} 4373^{4} 6288^{11} 7500^{4} 7784^{2}

Almail (USA) *F Head* 101 3 b c Swain(IRE) —Khassah (Green Desert (USA)) 2951a^{3}

Almajd (IRE) *M Al Muhairi* a69 98 4 b h Marju(IRE) —Irish Valley (USA) (Irish River (FR)) 696a^{4}

Almamia *Sir Mark Prescott* a47 68 4 b m Hernando(FR) —Alborada (Alzao (USA)) 178^{6}

Almatlaie (USA) *J W Unett* a33 35 3 b f Elusive Quality(USA) —Hachiyah (IRE) (Generous (IRE)) 4860^{6} 5882^{12}

Almaty Express *J R Weymes* a86 58 7 b g Almaty(IRE) —Express Girl (Sylvan Express) 170^{5} 654^{7} (971) (1494) 2397^{9} 2770^{9} 3212^{10} 3938^{10} 6253^{9} 6459^{8} 6669^{9} 7136^{6} 7595^{9} 7819 6

Almazar *J L Dunlop* a57 55 3 b g Green Desert(USA) —Zaqrah (USA) (Silver Hawk (USA)) 1746^{5} 2417^{5}

Almiqdaad *M A Jarvis* 105 3 b c Haafhd—Etizaaz (USA) (Diesis) 4760^{5} 5262^{11} (6106) ◆ 6480^{11}

Almoradi (IRE) *A De Royer-Dupre* a96 101 3 b c Barathea(IRE) —Alamouna (IRE) (Indian Ridge) 6132a^{7}

Almora Guru *W M Brisbourne* a52 60 5 b m Ishiguru(USA) —Princess Almora (Pivotal) 247^{9} 513^{13} 569^{5} 760^{5} 933^{4} 1037^{4}

Al Morhij (KSA) *B Resaque* a77 5 b h Race Leader(USA) —Sweet Honey (USA) (Pine Bluff (USA)) 1008a^{12}

Almost Married (IRE) *J S Goldie* a54 65 5 b g Indian Ridge—Shining Hour (USA) (Red Ransom (USA)) 2158^{9} 4772^{10} 6413^{14}

Almowj *G H Jones* a41 38 6 b g Fasliyev(USA) —Tiriana (Common Grounds) 1578^{13} 2317^{8} 4220^{7}

Al Mugtareb (IRE) *M Johnston* a70 73 3 b c Acclamation—Billie Bailey (USA) (Mister Baileys) (1062) 1561^{8} 2028^{2} 2393^{5} 3316^{11} 3804^{5} 4316^{7} 5340^{8}

Al Muheer (IRE) *C E Brittain* a104 110 4 b h Diktat—Dominion Rose (USA) (Spinning World (USA)) 331^{4} 445^{6} (636) (778) 916^{3} 1212^{7} 1640^{5} 2470^{5} 3091^{2} 3818^{18} (4297) 5024^{9} 6270^{27}

Al Mukaala (IRE) *B N Pollock* a57 67
3 ch g Cadeaux Genereux—Crescent Moon (Mr Prospector (USA))
808[9]

Almuktahem *Sir Michael Stoute* a88 86
3 b c Green Desert(USA) —Nasanice (IRE) (Nashwan (USA))
2081[5] 2664[4] 3238[2] (3984) 4715[3] 5209[12] *5648[3]*

Al Munadel (FR) *C Boutin* 72
2 ch c Russian Blue(IRE) —Pegmatite (USA) (Fusaichi Pegasus (USA))
6960a[0]

Almuntaser (IRE) *Ian Williams* 57
2 b g Celtic Swing—Fire Reply (IRE) (Royal Academy (USA))
2979[4] 3572[7] 4075[5] 6247[10] 6590[5] 6905[8]

Almutaham (USA) *J L Dunlop* 52
2 bb c Dynaformer(USA) —Forest Lady (USA) (Woodman (USA))
4258[9] 5499[11]

Almutawaazin *M P Tregoning*
3 b g Nayef(USA) —Crown Water (USA) (Chief's Crown (USA))
1350[11] 1809[8]

Alnadana (IRE) *A De Royer-Dupre* 112
4 gr m Danehill Dancer(IRE) —Alnamara (FR) (Linamix (FR))
1029a[2] 1658a[5] 2703[2] (4113a) 6479[7]

Al Naouwee (USA) *B Smart* a61 80
2 bb c Forest Camp(USA) —Dancehall Deelites (CAN) (Afternoon Deelites (USA))
4939[3] 5440[2] *6254[4]* 7016[10]

Alnitak (USA) *B Olsen* 97
8 br h Nureyev(USA) —Very True (USA) (Proud Truth (USA))
4585a[8] 5302a[9] 5933a[6]

Alnwick *P D Cundell* a83 83
5 b g Kylian(USA) —Cebwob (Rock City)
233[3] 1215[7] 1435[2] 1732[4] 1863[4] 3073[8] *3737[4]*
4092[2] 4417[5] *(5094)* 5346[3] 5917[7] 7005[4] 7151[3]

Aloe (IRE) *V Caruso* 87
3 ch f Fantastic Light(USA) —River Hill (ITY) (Danehill (USA))
3186a[14]

Alone He Stands (IRE) *J C Hayden* a86 91
9 b g Flying Spur(AUS) —Millennium Tale (FR) (Distant Relative)
2289a[7]

Along The Nile *K G Reveley* 53
7 b g Desert Prince(IRE) —Golden Fortune (Forzando)
6490[11] 6900[12] 7248[11]

Alotago (IRE) *D Nicholls* a19 46
2 ch f Tagula(IRE) —Batool (USA) (Bahri (USA))
4888[11] 5417[6] 6011[7] *6639[11]*

A Lot Of Red (IRE) *P J O'Gorman* 49
3 b c Barathea(IRE) —A Lot Of Kir (IRE) (Selkirk (USA))
3168[9] 3460[6] 4199[13] 5747[14] 6112[10] 6365[5]
6390[13]

Alpacco (IRE) *F Reuterskiold* a91 105
7 b g Desert King(IRE) —Albertville (GER) (Top Ville)
2587a[4]

Alpacina (GER) *H Blume* 66
2 b f Dashing Blade—Al Shuua (Lomitas)
6892a[11]

Alpen Glen *M Johnston* a71 97
3 ch f Halling(USA) —Anne D'Autriche (IRE) (Rainbow Quest (USA))
(2877) (3333) ◆ 3586[6] 4455[11] 5419[10] *7393[5]*
7720[8]

Alpes Maritimes *G L Moore* a92 63
5 b g Danehill Dancer(IRE) —Miss Riviera (Kris)
271[10] 550[5] 648[5] 1750[6] *1962[3] 3024[8]*

Alphacino *P C Haslam* a46 66
2 b g Hunting Lion(IRE) —Fading Away (Fraam)
1044[4] *1158[3]* 2319[2] 2541[5] 2861[5] 3605[4] 4188[2]
(4503) 4931[5] 5595[15] *7597[11]*

Alpha Tauri (USA) *H R A Cecil* a51 77
3 b c Aldebaran(USA) —Seven Moons (JPN) (Sunday Silence (USA))
1250[2] 1852[7] 3764[13] 4786[15]

Alpha Vega (IRE) *J R Fanshawe* a65 49
3 b f Marju(IRE) —Szabo (IRE) (Anabaa (USA))
2165[9] *6974[4] 7590[3]*

Alpina (FR) *J-V Toux* 59
3 gr f Pinmix(FR) —Very Very Nice (IRE) (Soviet Star (USA))
6606a[7]

Alpine Rose (FR) *A De Royer-Dupre* 116
4 gr m Linamix(FR) —Fragrant Hill (Shirley Heights)
(2428a) 3443a[2] (5300a) 6525a[4] 6850[13]

Alpine Snow (IRE) *S Wattel* a79 98
3 gr f Verglas(IRE) —Altruiste (USA) (Diesis)
(2989a) 7128a[10] 7347a[3]

Alqaahir (USA) *Lee Smyth* a74 76
7 b h Swain(IRE) —Crafty Example (USA) (Crafty Prospector (USA))
(6861) (7153) 7322[8] 7672[6]

Alqaffay (IRE) *J H M Gosden* a76 79
4 b h King's Best(USA) —Spirit Of Tara (IRE) (Sadler's Wells (USA))
3425[2] 3707[3] 4822[3] 5215[2] 5773[2]

Al Qasi (IRE) *P W Chapple-Hyam* a85 114
6 b h Elnadim(USA) —Delisha (Salse (USA))
3398[6] 3881a[4] 5657[11] 6848[9]

Al Qeddaaf (IRE) *W J Haggas* a84 83
3 b g Alhaarth(IRE) —Just Special (Cadeaux Genereux)
2250[5] (2863) ◆ 3115[8] *6209[7] 6973[3]*

Alrafid (IRE) *G L Moore* a63
10 ch g Halling(USA) —Ginger Tree (USA) (Dayjur (USA))
161[2] 302[4] 393[5]

Alrasm (IRE) *M A Jarvis* 92
2 b g Acclamation—New Deal (Rainbow Quest (USA))
2037[2] ◆ (2467) 2993[9] 5198[12] 6993[2]

Al Rayanah *G Prodromou* a60 60
6 b m Almushtarak(IRE) —Desert Bloom (FR) (Last Tycoon)
1741[2] 3077[6] 4060[8] *4376[5]* 4667[4] 5111[10] 6924[4]
7152[6]

Alrescha (IRE) *B Dutruel* 33
3 b f Marju(IRE) —Reve D'Iman (FR) (Highest Honor (FR))
4130a[10]

Al Sabaheya *C E Brittain* a81 85
3 b f Kheleyf(USA) —Baalbek (Barathea (IRE))
1001[9] 1702[5] 2209[2] 2703[7] 3102[5] 3843[5] 4540[8]
5591[4] *5810[6]* 6190[8] 6562[3] *6778[3]*

Alsace Lorraine (IRE) *J R Fanshawe* 96
4 b m Giant's Causeway(USA) —Mer De Corail (IRE) (Sadler's Wells (USA))
(1256) (2665) ◆ 3843[2] (4422) 5472[4] 6267[2]

Alsadaa (USA) *Mrs L J Mongan* a82 77
6 b g Kingmambo(USA) —Aljawza (USA) (Riverman (USA))
585[6] 5802[11]

Alsahil (USA) *Micky Hammond* a77 78
3 ch c Diesis—Tayibah (IRE) (Sadler's Wells (USA))
(1176) *7769[6]*

Alseraaj (USA) *Ian Williams* a53 71
4 ch m El Prado(IRE) —Barzah (IRE) (Darshaan)
256[10] 4931[1] 1122[3]

Al Shababiya (IRE) *D M Simcock* a67
2 b f Dubawi(IRE) —Multaka (USA) (Gone West (USA))
7622[7] 7816[2]

Alshahbaa (IRE) *Kevin Prendergast* 94
2 b f Alhaarth(IRE) —Adaala (USA) (Sahm (USA))
(2302a) 4028a[2] 4726a[6] 7072a[9]

Al Shemali *M bin Shafya* 113
5 ch h Medicean—Bathilde (IRE) (Generous (IRE))
263a[3] 338a[7] ◆

Alsufooh (USA) *M Johnston* 56
2 ch f Haafhd—Dufoof (USA) (Kingmambo (USA))
6842[5] 7167[5]

Alta Fedelta *V Caruso* 103
3 b f Oasis Dream—Infiel (Luge)
1659a[4] 6717a[8] 7303a[9]

Alta Luna (FR) *J-C Rouget* 90
3 b f Fasliyev(USA) —Lunatoria (IRE) (Vettori (IRE))
7265a[6]

Altarma (IRE) *A & G Botti* 54
3 b f Rock Of Gibraltar(IRE) —Ma Bouche (IRE) (Shirley Heights)
2310a[18]

Alternative Choice (USA) *N P Littmoden* a62
3 b g Grand Slam(USA) —Northern Fleet (USA) (Afleet (CAN))
663[5] 1036[2]

Althabea *Ian Williams* 46
2 b c Avonbridge—Mandolin (IRE) (Sabrehill (USA))
3715[12] 4018[6] 5527[11] 6589[10] 6906[11]

Altilhar (USA) *G L Moore* a83 83
6 b g Dynaformer(USA) —Al Desima (Emperor Jones (USA))
511[4]

Altimatum (USA) *P F I Cole* a64 74
3 ch c Rahy(USA) —Aldiza (USA) (Storm Cat (USA))
3660[2] 4246[7] *6977[8]* 7126[4] *7238[4] 7671[6]*

Alto Singer (IRE) *L A Dace* a36 61
4 b m Alhaarth(IRE) —Sonatina (Distant Relative)
3571[0] 5131[2]

Altos Reales *M J Scudamore* a57 48
5 b m Mark Of Esteem(IRE) —Karsiyaka (IRE) (Kahyasi)
353[7] 541[7] 669[7] 2233[5] *4170[2]* 4944[8] *5377[7]*
7635[2] (7733) 7840[8]

Alubari *W R Swinburn* a51
2 b c Tiger Hill(IRE) —Why So Silent (Mill Reef (USA))
7050[6]

Alucica *D Shaw* a62 50
6 b m Celtic Swing—Acicula (IRE) (Night Shift (USA))
397 60[3] 387[5] 494[12]

Alvee (IRE) *J R Fanshawe* a63 62
4 br m Key Of Luck(USA) —Alleluia (Caerleon (USA))
4388[7] 5530[7] *6025[7]*

Alwaary (USA) *J H M Gosden* a75 120
3 b c Dynaformer(USA) —Tabrir (IRE) (Unfuwain (USA))
1872[4] (2176) 3781[2] ◆ 4298[4] 5134[6]

Alwarqaa *B W Hills* 34
2 b f Oasis Dream—Al Sifaat (Unfuwain (USA))
7183[17]

Al Wasef (USA) *J S Goldie* 73
4 b g Danzig(USA) —Widady (USA) (Gone West (USA))
1737[9] 2071[11] 2589[5] 3093[3] 3448[11] 3857[6]

Always A Princess (USA) *Bob Baffert* a111
2 ch f Leroidesanimaux(BRZ) —Gabriellina Giof (Ashkalani (IRE))
7283a[5]

Always Beautiful (USA) *David Wachman* a88 97
4 b m Kingmambo(USA) —Diali (USA) (Dayjur (USA))
2960a[P] (Dead)

Always Best *R Allan* a59 55
5 b g Best Of The Bests(IRE) —Come To The Point (Pursuit Of Love)
2448[3] 2592[4] 3068[12] 4462[P] 5162[6] 5732[9]

Always Be True (IRE) *David Wachman* 88
3 b f Danehill Dancer(IRE) —Doctrine (Barathea (IRE))
2304a[8] 3894a[5] 4923a[11] 5490a[22]

Always Bold (IRE) *D McCain Jnr* a93 94
4 ch g King's Best(USA) —Tarakana (USA) (Shahrastani (USA))
2994[8] ◆ 3728[2] 4417[7] 4769[3]

Always Certain (USA) *P G Murphy* a68 70
4 ch g Giant's Causeway(USA) —Mining Missharriet (USA) (Mining (USA))
59[6] 161[5] 743[6]

Always Dazzling *M Johnston* 62
2 ch f Cadeaux Genereux—Woodlass (USA) (Woodman (USA))
3910[2]

Always De One *M Johnston* a40 57
2 b f Fruits Of Love(USA) —Yes Virginia (USA) (Roanoke (USA))
5980[10] 6484[4] 6821[7] *7597[10]*

Always Dixie (IRE) *M Johnston* a58 50
2 b f Lucky Story(USA) —Jerre Jo Glanville (USA) (Skywalker (USA))
1097[3] *7705[5] 7800[7] 7887[8]*

Always Engaged *J R Norton* a24
4 b m Compton Place—Good Standing (USA) (Distant View (USA))
36[8] 380[6]

Always Roses *C C Bealby* a33 30
2 ch f Generous(IRE) —Arcady (Slip Anchor)
6533[7] *7266[5] 7450[10]*

Always The Sun *P Leech* a59 50
3 b f Intikhab(USA) —Dane Dancing (IRE) (Danehill (USA))
383[10] 2630[U] 3245[5] 4155[4] 4718[12] 7150[8]
7401[5] 7431[6] 7517[5] 7652[6]

Alyarf (USA) *B W Hills* 109
3 b c Dixie Union(USA) —Tabheej (IRE) (Mujtahid (USA))
1300[4] (2278)

Alyazwa *Joseph Quinn* a72 76
3 ch g Selkirk(USA) —Rose Croix (USA) (Chief's Crown (USA))
4392a[12]

Alyseve *Mrs C A Dunnett* a19 33
4 b m Averti(IRE) —Leen (Distant Relative)
1662[11] 1940[11] 2268[6] 2913[8] 3245[6]

Al Zaeem *Miss D Mountain* a47 49
2 b c Mujahid(USA) —Tycho's Star (Mystiko (USA))
4757[10] 5319[5] *6431[11]*

Al Zir (USA) *Saeed Bin Suroor* 109
2 b c Medaglia D'Oro(USA) —Bayou Plans (USA) (Bayou Hebert (USA))
(4756) (5827) 7017[3] ◆

Amagansett (USA) *J-C Rouget* 83
2 b c Fusaichi Pegasus(USA) —Wonder Woman (USA) (Storm Cat (USA))
(7264a)

Amanda Carter *R A Fahey* 92
5 b m Tobougg(IRE) —Al Guswa (Shernazar)
1613[3] ◆ 2031[8] 3189[5] 3333[4] 4597[7] 5170[6]
5696[6] (6095) 6412[5] 7018[5]

Amanjena *A M Balding* a86 95
4 b m Beat Hollow—Placement (Kris)
2697[6] 3333[5] 6003[9] 6239[9]

Amarama (IRE) *David P Myerscough* 96
4 br m Fraam—Amarapura (FR) (Common Grounds)
5490a[19]

Amarillo Slim (IRE) *S Curran* a37 13
5 b g Danehill Dancer(IRE) —Jungle Story (IRE) (Alzao (USA))
2634[12]

Amarna (USA) *M bin Shafya* a104 100
5 bb g Danzig(USA) —Mysterial (USA) (Alleged (USA))
771a[13]

Amary (IRE) *C E Brittain* 81
2 b f Acclamation—Amistad (GER) (Winged Love (IRE))
(2401) 3782[2] 6090[12] 6447[6]

Amatara (IRE) *B G Powell* a30 38
3 b f Indian Haven—Mother's Hope (IRE) (Idris (IRE))
598[7] 964[7] 1183[7]

Amazing Blue Sky *Mrs R A Carr* a63 77
3 b g Barathea(IRE) —Azure Lake (USA) (Lac Ouimet (USA))
759[11] 808[3] 883[3] 964[2] 1063[6] *1441[2]* 2236[7]
2370[11] *2742[5]* 2790[2] 3018[9] 3454[7] 3636[2] 3684[3]
(4004) (4230) 4401[3] (4715)

Amazing King (IRE) *P A Kirby* a68 74
5 b g King Charlemagne(USA) —Kraemer (USA) (Lyphard (USA))
2263[8] 2573[6] (4156) 4529[2] 4755[2] 6768[12]

Amazing Memories (IRE) *John A Harris* 16
3 b c Barathea(IRE) —Early Memory (USA) (Devil's Bag (USA))
6573[8]

Amazing Tiger (GER) *M Johnston* a85 73
3 b c Tiger Hill(IRE) —Allure (GER) (Konigsstuhl (GER))
998[5] (3061) ◆ *5781[9]* 6474[6] *6778[2]* 6846[12]

Amazing Valour (IRE) *P Bowen*
7 b g Sinndar(IRE) —Flabbergasted (IRE) (Sadler's Wells (USA))
4168[10]

Ambassador (GER) *T Mundry* a97 110
5 b h Acatenango(GER) —After Eight Blues (CAN) (Bold Ruckus (USA))
1143a[2] 1549a[4] (2309a) 3441a[10] 4128a[5] 5461a[5]
6324a[8] 7039a[7]

Amber Glow *A Berry*
5 ch m Tumbleweed Ridge—Sweet Victoria (IRE) (Mukaddamah (USA))
6276[P] 7221[P]

Amber Moon *Miss A Stokell* a60 49
4 ch m Singspiel(IRE) —Merewood (USA) (Woodman (USA))
104[2] 175[2] 290[4] 405[3] 674[3] (760) (792)
897[5] 979[6] 1254[11] 1566[5] *1743[9]* 2768[8] *3717[9]*

Amber Ridge *B P J Baugh* a41 56
4 b g Tumbleweed Ridge—Amber Brown (Thowra (FR))
608[9] 775[9] 970[6] 1556[11] 1773[3] 2125[8] 2473[2]
3112[2] 3800[8] 4389[9] 4938[8] 5179[10]

Amber Sunset *J Jay* a64 78
3 b f Monsieur Bond(IRE) —Quantum Lady (Mujadil (USA))
3804[9] 4540[13] 5349[8] *5677[7] 6455[9] 6699[4] 7797[7]*
7861[5]

Ambitious Choice (IRE) *Muredach Kelly* a24 43
3 b f Choisir(AUS) —Alexander Ambition (IRE) (Entrepreneur)
5941[7]

Ambrogina *M Botti* a62 47
2 b f Osorio(GER) —Oh Bej Oh Bej (IRE) (Distinctly North (USA))
2226[5] *7700[7] 7792[2]* ◆

Ambrose Princess (IRE) *M J Scudamore* a60 63
4 b m Chevalier(IRE) —Mark One (Mark Of Esteem (IRE))
4168[2] (4301)

Ameeq (USA) *Dr R D P Newland* a75 78
7 bb g Silver Hawk(USA) —Haniya (IRE) (Caerleon (USA))
549[11] 591[5] 3721[8] 4742[2] 5068[3]

Ameer (IRE) *Saeed Bin Suroor* 100
2 b c Monsun(GER) —Ailette (Second Set (IRE))
(5400) ◆ (6057) 6656a[3]

Amenable (IRE) *D Nicholls* a77 35
2 b g Bertolini(USA) —Graceful Air (IRE) (Danzero (AUS))
5596[11] 6009[13] *(6356)*

Americain (USA) *A Fabre* 109
4 br h Dynaformer(USA) —America (IRE) (Arazi (USA))
1552a[4] (2118a)

American Agent (USA) *P F I Cole* a60
2 b c Eavesdropper(USA) —Storm Season (USA) (Storm Cat (USA))
7806[5] 7843[4]

American Champ (IRE) *Patrick Morris* a11
3 b g Pyrus(USA) —Sandy Fitzgerald (IRE) (Last Tycoon)
7753[11]

American Light *D M Simcock* a76 71
3 b g Statue Of Liberty(USA) —Break Of Dawn (USA) (Mt. Livermore (USA))
7714[2]

American Nizzy (FR) *Y De Nicolay* 100
2 b f American Post—Quietude (USA) (Woodman (USA))
3967a[2] 5279a[3] 6045a[4] 6523a[6] 6929a[5]

American Spin *L A Dace* a82 82
5 ch g Groom Dancer(USA) —Sea Vixen (Machiavellian (USA))
(58) 428[2] ◆ *549[4]* 2177[8] 3143[5] *3737[7]*

Amerigo (IRE) *M A Jarvis* 102
4 gr g Daylami(IRE) —Geminiani (IRE) (King Of Kings (IRE))
1790[5] 2486[7] 3143[3] 3642[6] 5481[2]

Ames Souer (IRE) *P D Evans* a44 34
6 b m Fayruz—Taispeain (IRE) (Petorius)
56[6]

Amethyst Dawn (IRE) *T D Easterby* 76
3 gr f Act One—A L'Aube (IRE) (Selkirk (USA))
1280[7] 1559[5] 1882[8] 2571[5] 3687[2] 4280[3] 5011[5]
5732[7] 6182[2] 6383[2] ◆ 6824[9] (7246)

Am I Blue *H J L Dunlop* a48 65
3 b f Dubai Destination(USA) —Seal Indigo (IRE) (Glenstal (USA))
1092[4] ◆ *1532[10]* 2881[8] 4744[10] *5679[7]* 6188[2]
6543[5]

Amical Risks (FR) *W J Musson* a65 51
5 bl g Take Risks(FR) —Miss High (FR) (Concorde Jr (USA))
4382[4] 4893[11] 7085[3]

Amico Fritz (GER) *H-A Pantall* a80 77
3 b c Fasliyev(USA) —Arctic Appeal (IRE) (Ahonoora)
7696a[2]

Amico Mio (FR) *J-M Beguigne* 97
3 br c Best Of The Bests(IRE) —Maid Of Kashmir (IRE) (Dancing Brave (USA))
2951a[5] 5711a[4] 6502a[6]

A Mind Of Her Own (IRE) *David Wachman* 90
2 ch f Danehill Dancer(IRE) —Gilded Vanity (IRE) (Indian Ridge)
1993a[3] 2557a[3] 6319a[14]

Amir Pasha (UAE) *Micky Hammond* a58 58
4 br g Halling(USA) —Clarinda (IRE) (Lomond (USA))
1102[3] 1242[11] 3617[8]

Amitola (IRE) *T D Barron* 89
2 ch f Choisir(AUS) —Emly Express (IRE) (High Estate)
(6408) 7147[5]

Amjad *S G West* 37
12 ch g Cadeaux Genereux—Babita (Habitat)
2656[7]

Amneris (FR) *A Blanpin* 46
3 ch f Septieme Ciel(USA) —Miss Balines (FR) (Grape Tree Road)
5784a[10]

Amno Dancer (IRE) *M H Tompkins* a61 74
2 b g Namid—Special Dancer (Shareef Dancer (USA))
2631[6] 3017[5] 3546[3] 5596[8] 7097[5] *7333[8]*

Amosite *J R Jenkins* a66 73
3 b f Central Park(IRE) —Waterline Dancer (IRE) (Danehill Dancer (IRE))
162[4] 1196[9] (1359) 2005[3] 3118[7] 4231[5] 4712[3]
4952[7]

Amouretta *T T Clement* a40 24
4 b m Daylami(IRE) —Allumette (Rainbow Quest (USA))
6188[13]

Amoureuse *I W McInnes* 32
2 b f Needwood Blade—Good Health (Magic Ring (IRE))
1358[9] 1764[9] 2089[12] *2575[10]*

Amour Propre *H Candy* 119
3 ch c Paris House—Miss Prim (Case Law)
(1676) ◆ 2991[10] 5233[5]

Amour Sacre (FR) *Robert Collet*
2 b c Equerry(USA) —Erdijiya (IRE) (Kahyasi)
6979a[0]

Amron Hill *R Hollinshead* a52 35
6 b g Polar Prince(IRE) —Maradata (IRE) (Shardari)
148[3] 300[3]

Amroth *P D Evans* a28 56
3 b f Rock Of Gibraltar(IRE) —Gwen John (USA) (Peintre Celebre (USA))
2074[7] 5939[4] 6276[5] 6742[7] 7154[10]

Amtaar *C E Brittain* a67 53
2 b f Nayef(USA) —Emerald Fire (Pivotal)
3249[14] 3979[3] 4869[2] 6181[4]

Amuseur (FR) *P Lefevre*
3 b c Equerry(USA) —Sainte Grace (FR) (Akarad (FR))
5784a[0]

Amwell Brave *J R Jenkins* a62 53
8 b g Pyramus(USA) —Passage Creeping (IRE) (Persian Bold)
116[3] (169) 448[3] 546[7] 1463[5] 2634[4] 3714[5] 5246[8] 6204[11]

Amwell House *J R Jenkins* a53 52
4 gr g Auction House(USA) —Amwell Star (USA) (Silver Buck (USA))
61[8] 247[4] 482[3] 598[8] 802[11]

Amylyn *J R Holt* 28
2 b f Starcraft(NZ) —Skirt Around (Deploy)
7244[13]

Ana Americana (FR) *P Demercastel* 101
3 b f American Post—Ana Marie (FR) (Anabaa (USA))
1550a[5] 2119a[3] 2952a[10]

Anacot Steel (IRE) *Patrick Morris* 17
4 ch g Danehill Dancer(IRE) —Paper Moon (IRE) (Lake Coniston (IRE))
2229[9] 4347[12]

Anacreon (IRE) *J H M Gosden* a76 57
3 b g Dansili—Anbella (FR) (Common Grounds)
869[2] (1120) 1291[17] 4148[11]

Anagram *W R Muir* a65 47
3 b f Efisio—Saint Ann (USA) (Geiger Counter (USA))
5717[9] 5882[3] 6430[2] 7082[6] 7353[8]

Anak Nakal (USA) *Nicholas Zito* a111
4 bb h Victory Gallop(CAN) —Misk (USA) (Quiet American (USA))
1013a[14]

Ana Moutabahi *C G Cox* a68
2 b c Anabaa(USA) —Runaway Venus (USA) (Runaway Groom (CAN))
7050[9] 7429[2] 7800[4]

Ananda Kanda (USA) *B Ellison* a56 75
2 b f Hero's Tribute(USA) —Roja (USA) (L'Enjoleur (CAN))
1275[11] (2226) 3978[8] 4306[4] 5324[5] 6011[6]

Anani (USA) *S Seemar* a101 78
9 ch g Miswaki(USA) —Mystery Rays (USA) (Nijinsky (CAN))
527a[13]

Anasy (USA) *T Keddy* a39
3 b f Gone West(USA) —Blue Moon (FR) (Lomitas)
5193[7] 5789[9] 6831[7]

Anaverna (IRE) *D K Weld* 79
2 b f Galileo(IRE) —Agnetha (GER) (Big Shuffle (USA))
6316a[11]

Anaxis (FR) *C Laffon-Parias* 63
2 ch c Muhtathir—Monadis (USA) (Miswaki (USA))
4807a[8]

Anaya *M R Channon* a71 71
2 b f Tobougg(IRE) —Nacho Venture (FR) (Rainbow Quest (USA))
5498[13] 5741[7] 6284[3] 6762[2] 7106[2] 7193[2] 7622[4] 7825[5]

Anchorage Boy (USA) *Miss Amy Weaver* 56
2 b g Southern Image(USA) —Alaskan Winter (USA) (Gulch (USA))
3395[10] 4152[13] 4666[5]

Ancien Regime (IRE) *Saeed Bin Suroor* a97 113
4 b g King's Best(USA) —Sadalsud (IRE) (Shaadi (USA))
3388[2] 3819[13] 4516[3] (5196) 5434[10] 6661[19]

Ancient Cross *M W Easterby* a73 83
5 b g Machiavellian(USA) —Magna Graecia (IRE) (Warning)
1060[6] 1480[3] 1737[4] 2133[2] 2235[4] 2998[3] 4592[5] 4887[2] 5423[4] 5730[3] (5948) 6175[2] (6846) ◆

Ancient Lights *H R A Cecil* a100 89
4 b h High Chaparral(IRE) —Fascinating Hill (FR) (Danehill (USA))
1642[3] ◆

Ancient Oak *H A McWilliams*
2 ch c Compton Place—Dolce Piccata (Piccolo)
5957[8] 6246[6]

Anco Marzio *A De Royer-Dupre* 98
3 b c American Post—Atlantic Blue (USA) (Nureyev (USA))
2755a[7]

Andaman Sunset *J L Spearing* a77 74
4 b h Red Ransom(USA) —Miss Amanpuri (Alzao (USA))
550[9] 660[10] 798[13] 1042[13] 1728[13] 7767[9]

And A Partridge *J A Osborne* a53 20
3 ch g Compton Place—Dunloe (IRE) (Shaadi (USA))
1130[5] 1811[13] 2487[5]

Andean Margin (IRE) *M W Easterby* a75 72
3 b g Giant's Causeway(USA) —Spiritual Air (Royal Applause)
74[2] 122[2] 317[2] 2406[3] 4841[8] 5418[8] 6178[13] 6804[7]

Andhaar *S Gollings* a85 81
3 b g Bahri(USA) —Deraasaat (Nashwan (USA))
1428[3] 2170[2] (3384) 4008[7] 5255[3] 5876[3] 6420[3] 7620[3]

Andina (IRE) *J W Hills* 72
2 ch f Singspiel(IRE) —Fragrant Oasis (USA) (Rahy (USA))
2494[3]

Andorn (GER) *P A Kirby* a59 84
5 b h Monsun(GER) —Anthyllis (GER) (Lycius (USA))
1243[18] 1530[3] 2569[2] 2898[10] 3499[3] 3809[5] 4600[6] (6310) 6845[6]

Andrasta *S A Harris* a45 61
4 b m Bertolini(USA) —Real Popcorn (IRE) (Jareer (USA))
738[5] 1628[7] 1689[7] (2032) 2225[9] 2436[9] 2625[9] 3021[6] 3153[4] 4016[4] 4136[5] (4778) 5073[5] 5309[5] 5911[6] 6010[19] 6553[8] 7081[6] 7427[8]

Andraste (USA) *N Clement* 59
3 u f — (Diesis)
6753a[7]

Andrea (GER) *F Head* 100
3 ch f Dashing Blade—Annouche (GER) (Unfuwain (USA))
2874a[2] 3604a[8] 4583a[3] 7128a[9] 7569a[0]

Andrea Palladio (IRE) *David Wachman* 81
3 b c Danehill Dancer(IRE) —Coralita (IRE) (Night Shift (USA))
3435a[18]

Andrei Roublev (USA) *D Windrif* 77
8 b g Woodman(USA) —Albertine (FR) (Irish River (FR))
5204a[3]

Anduril *D Carroll* a52 57
8 ch g Kris—Attribute (Warning)
7[8] 78[5] 221[10] 3092[10] 7802[7]

Anessia *Tom Dascombe* a55 55
3 b f Fantastic Light(USA) —Lamarque (IRE) (Nureyev (USA))
3384[4] 4066[5] 4519[11] 5988[11]

Anfield Road *L Corcoran* a74 75
4 ch g Dr Fong(USA) —Mackenzie's Friend (Selkirk (USA))
72[7] 428[8] 7036[7] 7647[5]

Anfield Star (IRE) *Patrick Morris* a36 59
3 b g Celtic Swing—Shenkara (IRE) (Night Shift (USA))
5645[6] 6213[13] 7002[7]

Angaric (IRE) *B Smart* a69 78
6 ch g Pivotal—Grannys Reluctance (IRE) (Anita's Prince)
303[9] 1456[3] (1650) 2156[8] 2453[8] 2658[7] 5343[4] 5955[12] 7679[9]

Ange Doree (FR) *Frau Carmen Bocksai*
3 ch f Sinyar(IRE) —Ariola (GER) (Acatenango (GER))
6980a[0]

Angela Jones *D K Ivory*
2 ch f Cape Town(IRE) —Full English (Perugino (USA))
4384[14] 4912[9]

Ange Fontenaille (FR) *Mlle A Voraz*
4 gr m Ange Gabriel(FR) —Diane Fontenaille (FR) (Tel Quel (FR))
5089a[0]

Angelena Ballerina (IRE) *A Bailey* a69 80
2 ch f Indian Haven—Nom Francais (First Trump)
1802[4] ◆ 2047[2] 2372[4] 2765[2] 3396[7] 6009[6] 6436[5] 6563[6] 6858[2]

Angelica's Art (IRE) *B J Meehan* 55
3 b f Marju(IRE) —Flatter (IRE) (Barathea (IRE))
1302[8] 1843[7] 2192[7] 3776[7] 4650[13]

Angel Of Fashion (IRE) *B W Hills* a62 77
2 b f Invincible Spirit(IRE) —Vanitycase (IRE) (Editor's Note (USA))
1323[10] 1742[2] 1968[4] 2354[5] 3271[6] (4017) 4539[9] 5692[11] (6169) 6541[6]

Angelofthenorth *C J Teague* 53
7 b m Tomba—Dark Kristal (IRE) (Gorytus (USA))
1558[11] 2158[6] 2451[7] 3678[4] 3909[3] 4192[5] 4467[2] 4754[3] 5008[8]

Angelo Poliziano *Mrs A Duffield* a74 74
3 ch g Medicean—Helen Sharp (Pivotal)
1250[8] 1400[4] 1895[8] 2336[7] 3125[6] (3229) 3464[4] 3828[5] 4136[4] 4343[4] (4653) 4899[7] 5978[8] 7273[12] 7355[11]

Angel Rock (IRE) *M Grassi* a86 89
4 b h Rock Of Gibraltar(IRE) —Nomothetis (IRE) (Law Society (USA))
1357[9] (2197) 2933[5] 4779[5] 6002[10] 7312a[10]

Angels And Demons (IRE) *R C Guest* a5 35
3 b f Golan(IRE) —I Want You Now (IRE) (Nicolotte)
3712[8] 4196[8] 4354[8] 5947[5] 6310[8]

Angelsbemine *J R Norton* a10 30
3 b f Almaty(IRE) —Undercover Girl (IRE) (Barathea (IRE))
41[8]

Angel Song *Sir Mark Prescott* a70 65
3 b f Dansili—Something Blue (Petong)
(227) 562[3] 5340[4] 5777[6] 7337[7]

Angel's Pursuit (IRE) *R Hannon* a87 106
2 ch c Pastoral Pursuits—Midnight Angel (Machiavellian (USA))
(2295) ◆ 2995[8] 3583[3] ◆ 3779[6] 4221[2] 5057a[2] 5661[7] (5763) 6105[2] ◆ 6486[7]

Angels Story (IRE) *J S Bolger* 96
4 b m Galileo(IRE) —Love Excelling (FR) (Polish Precedent (USA))
5689a[9]

Angel Voices (IRE) *K R Burke* a73 72
6 b m Tagula(IRE) —Lithe Spirit (IRE) (Dancing Dissident (USA))
57[2] 475[6] 651[6] 861[10] 1528[11]

Angie's Nap (USA) *P S McEntee* a67 60
2 ch f Lion Heart(USA) —Magick Top (USA) (Topsider (USA))
1810[7] 2135[7] 2457[2] 3709[7] 3742[8] 4153[6] 5372[2] 5776[10] (6354) (7089) (7268) 7352[4] 7636[6] 7793[5] 7868[3]

Angle Of Attack (IRE) *A D Brown* a71 83
4 b g Acclamation—Travel Spot Girl (Primo Dominie)
1334[7] 1768[7] 1951[9] 2225[13] 2745[6] 3445[12] 4436[16] 5008[16] 7726[7] (7869)

Anglezarke (IRE) *T D Easterby* 107
3 br f Acclamation—Welsh Mist (Damister (USA))
(2016) 2481[2] 2991[3] 3638[6]

Angolaner (GER) *H Blume* 94
2 b c Golan(IRE) —Anna Thea (IRE) (Turfkonig (GER))
6887a[5]

Angus Newz *M Quinn* a79 100
6 ch m Compton Place—Hickleton Lady (IRE) (Kala Shikari)
1325[13] 1582[4] 1791[3] 2102[5] 2271[8] 3434a[4] 3784[9] 3848[5] 4059[4] 4559[7] 4885[3] 5546[3] 5973[3] 6020[5] 6428[6] 6843[11]

Anhar (USA) *Saeed Bin Suroor* 95
2 bb c Kingmambo(USA) —Because (IRE) (Sadler's Wells (USA))
(6592) ◆ 7184[2]

Anice Stellato (IRE) *R M Beckett* 93
3 br f Dalakhani(IRE) —Summer Spice (IRE) (Key Of Luck (USA))
1871[5] 3047[10] 5321[2] (6113) 6419[5]

Animator *C Grant* a78 75
4 b g Act One—Robsart (IRE) (Robellino (USA))
1845[7] 2200[12]

Anita's Luck (IRE) *B Palling* 66
2 b g Key Of Luck(USA) —Anita's Contessa (IRE) (Anita's Prince)
1083[4]

Anitra's Dance *P Howling* a22 32
2 b f Tobougg(IRE) —Dancemma (Emarati (USA))
2825[8] 3356[7] 3925[8]

Anjella (GER) *J Hirschberger* 96
3 ch f Monsun(GER) —Attilia (GER) (Tiger Hill (IRE))
1914a[6] 2757a[8] 4583a[12]

Anjomarba (IRE) *W G M Turner* a68 80
2 b f Tillerman—Golden Charm (IRE) (Common Grounds)
1044[8] 1195[3] 1396[2] 1933[4] 2175[5] (2414) (2541) (2896) 3579[7] 4165[4] 4850[5] 6398[7] 7290[13] 7690[4] 7713[3] 7805[3]

Anmar (USA) *Saeed Bin Suroor* a111 99
3 ch c Rahy(USA) —Ranin (Unfuwain (USA))
(7323)

Annabelle's Charm (IRE) *L M Cumani* a77 99
4 ch m Indian Ridge—Kylemore (IRE) (Sadler's Wells (USA))
(120) 361[5] 1261[3] (1621) 2150[2] 2639[4] (5064) 6267[13] 6717a[2] 7347a[13]

Annacaboe (IRE) *Mrs L C Jewell*
2 b f Footstepsinthesand—Alexandria (IRE) (Irish River (FR))
4906[7]

Annambo *Andrew Reid* a66 63
9 ch g In The Wings—Anna Matrushka (Mill Reef (USA))
1815[7] 2172[3] 2552[6] 3563[7] 3923[4] 5246[3] 5680[2] 6025[10] (6226)

Annan Rock (IRE) *W J Musson* a41 37
3 b g Statue Of Liberty(USA) —My Enigma (Rainbow Quest (USA))
3718[10] 4083[6] 4381[10]

Anna's Boy *A Berry* 42
2 ch g Reel Buddy(USA) —Simianna (Bluegrass Prince (IRE))
4075[8] 5157[6] 6381[3]

Ann Birkett *Miss J Feilden* 33
3 ch f Beat Hollow—Blue Gentian (USA) (Known Fact (USA))
3549[8]

Annelko *A B Haynes* 21
2 b c Sulamani(IRE) —Creeking (Persian Bold)
6931[9]

Anne Of Kiev (IRE) *J R Gask* a87 68
4 b m Oasis Dream—Top Flight Queen (Mark Of Esteem (IRE))
6801[9] (7634) ◆

Annes Rocket (IRE) *J C Fox* a67 62
4 b h Fasliyev(USA) —Aguilas Perla (IRE) (Indian Ridge)
344[10] 512[9] 874[6] 1074[6] 1535[2] (1741) (2223) 2806[U] 3662[8] 4321[10] 4697[8] 5429[2] 5842[7] 6213[10] 6399[4] (6587) 7051[11]

Annes Sound (IRE) *Patrick Morris* a43 50
3 gr f Mull Of Kintyre(USA) —Striking Sound (USA) (Rubiano (USA))
1793[9] 2627[9] 4224[12] 4944[13] 5872[10]

Annia (IRE) *N P Littmoden* a66 74
2 b f Antonius Pius(USA) —Floosie (IRE) (Night Shift (USA))
4989[8] 5611[9] 6328[9] 7175[7] 7334[11] 7559[7] 7778[8]

Annia Galeria (IRE) *C A Dwyer* a52 58
2 b f Antonius Pius(USA) —Jay Gee (IRE) (Second Set (IRE))
(4018) 4153[3] 4868[10] 5310[5] 5776[7] 5950[13]

Annibale Caro *J S Goldie* a58 79
7 b g Mtoto—Isabella Gonzaga (Rock Hopper)
2315[7] 2666[9] 2815[10] 5334[12]

Annie Go (IRE) *Aidan Anthony Howard* a49 63
5 b m Golan(IRE) —Simple Annie (Simply Great (FR))
7154[8]

Annosh (TUR) *Y Simsek* 106
6 b m Nashwan(USA) —Anam (Persian Bold)
5619a[4]

Anonimo Veneziano *V Caruso* 97
3 b c Compton Place—Supercharger (Zamindar (USA))
1393a[10] 1905a[4]

Another Bottle (IRE) *Mrs S Leech* a64 80
8 b g Cape Cross(IRE) —Aster Aweke (IRE) (Alzao (USA))
1213[9] 1433[10] 1621[5] 2040[4] 2493[14]

Another Character (USA) *M Blanshard*
2 bb c Giant's Causeway(USA) —Mambo Halo (USA) (Southern Halo (USA))
6772[13] 7400[11]

Another Decree *M Dods* a44 69
4 b g Diktat—Akhira (Emperor Jones (USA))
1246[6] 3354[11] 3655[5] 4995[3] 5601[8] 6103[3] 6349[7] 6840[9]

Another Echo *W Storey* 22
3 b f Bahamian Bounty—Blue Nile (IRE) (Bluebird (USA))
5513[11]

Another Genepi (USA) *E J Creighton* a71 68
6 br m Stravinsky(USA) —Dawn Aurora (USA) (Night Shift (USA))
179[4] 886[8]

Another Grand (IRE) *Mrs R A Carr* a39 39
2 b g Statue Of Liberty(USA) —Fallacy (Selkirk (USA))
2231[9] 2467[F] 2575[6] 2996[8]

Another Luke (IRE) *T J Etherington* a46 48
3 b c Captain Rio—Belalzao (IRE) (Alzao (USA))
1926[18] 2154[8] 3611[10] 4133[8] 6823[15]

Another Magic Man (USA) *J R Best* a71 71
2 bb c Chief Seattle(USA) —Georgia Anna (USA) (Stutz Blackhawk (USA))
3344[9] 5191[5] 5966[3] 6697[6] 7157[3]

Another Socket *E S McMahon* a72 74
4 b m Overbury(IRE) —Elsocko (Swing Easy (USA))
956[7] 1038[2]

Another Sold *A Berry* 14
2 ch f Auction House(USA) —Countrywide Girl (IRE) (Catrail (USA))
1764[11] 2339[12] 3370[6]

Another True Story *Z Koplik* a58 67
5 b h Piccolo—Lost In Lucca (Inchinor)
6522a[16]

Another Try (IRE) *A P Jarvis* a73 70
4 b g Spinning World(USA) —Mad Annie (USA) (Anabaa (USA))
1074[8] 1606[12] (2134) (2920) 3401[6] 3732[3] 5188[4] 5675[5] (6926) 7739[7] 7813[2]

Ans Bach *D Selvaratnam* a106 97
6 b g Green Desert(USA) —Bezzaaf (Machiavellian (USA))
433a[11] 637a[9]

Ansells Pride (IRE) *B Smart* a73 91
6 b g King Charlemagne(USA) —Accounting (Sillery (USA))
1593[7] 1684[8] 4400[11] 4779[10] 5598[10] 6496[8] 7322[3] 7672[2] 7854[5]

An Tadh (IRE) *G M Lyons* a104 97
6 b g Halling(USA) —Tithcar (Cadeaux Genereux)
1791[7]

Antara (GER) *R Dzubasz* 115
3 b f Platini(GER) —Auenpracht (GER) (General Assembly (USA))
(6500a)

Antara Rose (GER) *W Hefter*
3 ch f Pentire—Antigua (GER) (Protektor (GER))
5783a[0]

Antarctic Desert (IRE) *K A Ryan* 71
2 b g Green Desert(USA) —Arctic Silk (Selkirk (USA))
5669[4] 6009[14] 6231[2]

Anthemion (IRE) *Mrs J C McGregor* a48 55
12 ch g Night Shift(USA) —New Sensitive (Wattlefield)
3481[7] 3683[9]

Anthology *B Smart* 87
3 b c Haafhd—Annapurna (IRE) (Brief Truce (USA))
1307[5] 2281[7] 2571[3]

Antigua Sunrise (IRE) *R A Fahey* 82
3 b f Noverre(USA) —Staff Approved (Teenoso (USA))
1098[3] 1470[3] (2060) (2371) (3069) 3827[5] 4328[3] 5037[4] 6138[7]

Antillia *C F Wall* a76 53
4 b m Red Ransom(USA) —Milly Of The Vally (Caerleon (USA))
219[11] 631[3]

Antinori (IRE) *W R Swinburn* a92 103
3 b g Fasliyev(USA) —Albavilla (Spectrum (IRE))
1284[2] ◆ 1489[3] (2210) 2935[3] 5262[2] ◆ 6106[8]

Antipodean (UAE) *P T Midgley* a50 47
3 ch g Halling(USA) —Anka Britannia (USA) (Irish River (FR))
151[3] 306[6] 621[6] 1629[3] 1953[8] 2790[12] 3192[6] 4818[8] 5465[9] 6184[15]

Antique Diamond (IRE) *Lucinda Featherstone* a3 33
2 b f Chineur(FR) —Flash And Dazzle (IRE) (Bertolini (USA))
1866[11] 2604[9] 3337[8] 6389[8] 6922[9] 7157[10]

Ant Music (IRE) *J S Moore* a61 66
2 b g Antonius Pius(USA) —Day Is Dawning (IRE) (Green Forest (USA))
1290[6] 2033[4] 2997[4] 3821[8] 7804[4]

Antoella (IRE) *Ian Williams* a40 55
2 gr f Antonius Pius(USA) —Bella Estella (GER) (Sternkoenig (IRE))
5129[8] 6363[6] 6912[8]

Antoniola (IRE) *T D Easterby* 83
2 b g Antonius Pius(USA) —Balliamo (IRE) (Royal Academy (USA))
3310[2] 6009[3] 6484[3] (6993)

Antonius Moris (IRE) *Tom Dascombe* 85
2 b c Antonius Pius(USA) —Suaad (IRE) (Fools Holme (USA))
(1891) 2547[4] 2995[20] 3807[3] 4063[2] 4525[8] 5853[4] 6397[4]

Antonius Park (IRE) *Rodger Sweeney* a61 10
2 b f Antonius Pius(USA) —Special Park (USA) (Trempolino (USA))
4590[10]

Anwilka (FR) *P Bary* a65
2 gr f Nombre Premier—Matakana (FR) (Green Tune (USA))
4970a[4]

Any Day (IRE) *R M Beckett* a67 70
2 b f Kheleyf(USA) —Daylight Ahead (IRE) (Tenby)
1119[6] 1637[2] 2383[3] 3006[6] (3742) 3993[3] 4850[3] 5899[3] 6827[7]

Any Given Moment (IRE) *D M Simcock* a51 56
3 b g Alhaarth(IRE) —Shastri (USA) (Alleged (USA))
1963[9] 2416[11] 3168[6] 4722[5] 5382[3] 5990[10]

Any Secrets *Karen George* a31 16
3 b g Compton Place—Anyhow (IRE) (Distant Relative)
2318[13] 3228[10] 4303[9] 5614[13] 6611[12]

Anzas (IRE) *R Gibson* 100
2 b c Anabaa(USA) —Lake Baino (Highest Honor (FR))
5280a[3] 6889a[5] (7384a)

A One (IRE) *Mrs H J Manners* a43 55
10 b g Alzao(USA) —Anita's Contessa (IRE) (Anita's Prince)
4321^{11} 5936^{7} 7062^{10} *7332^{10}*

Apache Cat (AUS) *Greg Eurell* 121
7 ch g Lion Cavern(USA) —Tennessee Blaze (AUS) (Whiskey Road (USA))
7745a^{7}

Apache Dawn *A Sadik* a79 51
5 ch g Pursuit Of Love—Taza (Persian Bold)
100^{5} 588^{4} 983^{7} 3258^{5} 3631^{3} 3943^{9} *4170^{10}*

Apache Fort *T Keddy* a78 75
6 b g Desert Prince(IRE) —Apogee (Shirley Heights)
319^{7} 660^{3} 750^{3} 894^{6} 1073^{4} 1287^{11} 1966^{10} 2684^{2} 3114^{6} 4602^{4} 5680^{7} 5885^{5} 6457^{11}

Apache Kid (IRE) *B R Millman* 57
2 b c Antonius Pius(USA) —She's The Tops (Shernazar)
5785^{8} 6200^{5}

Apache Moon *R Curtis* a19
3 ch g Monsieur Bond(IRE) —Mighty Squaw (Indian Ridge)
963^{7}

Apache Nation (IRE) *M Dods* a42 63
6 b g Fruits Of Love(USA) —Rachel Green (IRE) (Case Law)
1612^{11} 2532^{4} 3070^{2} 3653^{6} 5364^{8} 6411^{12} *7174^{10}*

Apache Ridge (IRE) *K A Ryan* 76
3 ch g Indian Ridge—Seraphina (IRE) (Pips Pride)
1592^{6} (1831) 2336^{2}

Apex *M Hill* a74 58
8 ch g Efisio—Royal Loft (Homing)
3274^{7} 3801^{8} *5663^{5} 6168^{7}* 6365^{7}

Aphrodisia *Ian Williams* a73 82
5 b m Sakhee(USA) —Aegean Dream (IRE) (Royal Academy (USA))
(60) 354^{3} 798^{8} 952^{5} (1348) 1826^{4} 3627^{5} ◆

Aphrodite's Rock *Miss Gay Kelleway* 69
3 ch f Falbrav(IRE) —Comtesse Noire (CAN) (Woodman (USA))
1825^{6} ◆ 2179^{8} 3278^{5} 4704^{2} 4943^{7}

A P Ling *C N Kellett* a54 31
2 b f Antonius Pius(USA) —Spain (Polar Falcon (USA))
6792^{9} 7243^{11} *7630^{5}*

A Pocketful Of Rye (IRE) *J A Osborne* a68 66
2 b f Acclamation—Rye (IRE) (Charnwood Forest (IRE))
3733^{5} 6274^{2} *6628^{6} 7003^{10}*

Apollo Blues (IRE) *E J O'Neill* 58
2 ch c Starcraft(NZ) —Blue Sirocco (Bluebird (USA))
6576a^{DSQ} 7507a^{4}

Apollo Shark (IRE) *J Howard Johnson* 77
4 ch g Spartacus(IRE) —Shot Of Redemption (Shirley Heights)
1737^{8} 2312^{6} 2998^{6} (4504) 5409^{12}

Apollo Star (GER) *Ms C Erichsen* 117
7 ch g Devil River Peek(USA) —Arwina (GER) (Windwurf (GER))
436a^{8}

Apostle Of Rome (IRE) *Tom Dascombe* a59 59
2 b g Oratorio(IRE) —Novelette (Darshaan)
3589^{4} 4048^{14} 4825^{6} *6639^{6}*

Apotheosis *W R Swinburn* a71 73
4 ch g Dr Fong(USA) —Carradale (Pursuit Of Love)
386^{5} 580^{7} (813) 1192^{4} 2039^{2} *2923^{9}* 4378^{3} 5035^{6} *6288^{3}*

Appalachian Trail (IRE) *N Wilson* a93 113
8 b g Indian Ridge—Karinski (USA) (Palace Music (USA))
1865^{8} 4077^{3} 4352^{5} 5529^{5} 6094^{3} 6675^{11} 7019^{12} 7294^{19} *(7492) 7588^{3} 7837^{9}*

Appeal To Reason (USA) *J R Best*
2 b c Successful Appeal(USA) —Grand Mirage (USA) (Southern Halo (USA))
6561^{6} 6754^{16}

Appel Au Maitre (FR) *Wido Neuroth* 117
5 ch h Starborough—Rotina (FR) (Crystal Glitters (USA))
(2587a) 4128a^{3} 5302a^{2} 5933a^{3}

Appelouse *D W Thompson* a64 19
4 b m Zaha(CAN) —Appelone (Emperor Jones (USA))
564^{4} 820^{5} 3467^{5} 3929^{5} (4376) 5364^{12} *6074^{11}*

Appia Nova (FR) *G Botti* 42
2 b c Kingsalsa(USA) —Ardalina (FR) (Sillery (USA))
6928a^{8}

Applaude *R C Guest* a68 80
4 b g Royal Applause—Flossy (Efisio)
2073^{12} 2392^{7} 2817^{3} 3705^{5} 4350^{7} (4740) *5327^{2}* 5698^{12} (6012) 6248^{5} 6987^{3} 7248^{13} *7332^{5} 7492^{8} 7817^{9} 7851^{7}*

Applause (IRE) *J Noseda* a79 98
3 b f Danehill Dancer(IRE) —Sniffle (IRE) (Shernazar)
(3696) (4433) 6267^{6} 6480^{4}

Apple Charlotte *H R A Cecil* a99 108
3 b f Royal Applause—Maid Of Camelot (Caerleon (USA))
(1599) (2036) 2846^{2} *7132^{3}*

Applesnap (IRE) *Miss Amy Weaver* a73 76
4 b m Clodovil(IRE) —Apple Brandy (USA) (Cox's Ridge (USA))
1403^{10} 2168^{7} 2539^{5} 2806^{9} *3269^{4}* 3581^{7} 4721^{8}

Apprimus (IRE) *S Botti* 103
3 b c Trans Island—Athlumney Dancer (Shareef Dancer (USA))
1904a^{4} 6153a^{5}

Apres Ski (IRE) *J F Coupland* a50 52
6 b g Orpen(USA) —Miss Kinabalu (Shirley Heights)
3174^{7}

April Fool *J A Geake* a76 79
5 ch g Pivotal—Palace Affair (Pursuit Of Love)
1833^{6} 2125^{5} (2518) 2977^{9} (3258) 3812^{6} 3996^{7} 4641^{14} *5780^{11}*

April Lady (IRE) *A Berry* a32 22
3 b f Tagula(IRE) —Dusty Diamond (IRE) (Royal Abjar (USA))
36^{7} 286^{7} 364^{7} 2343^{9} 2394^{7}

April's Daughter *B R Millman* 57
4 b m Kyllachy—April Stock (Beveled (USA))
2246^{11} 3217^{3} 3919^{8} 4220^{4} 4640^{10}

April The Second *R J Price* a16 56
5 b g Tomba—Little Kenny (Warning)
7677^{8} 7840^{9}

Apro Lunare (IRE) *Laura Grizzetti* 100
3 b c Orpen(USA) —My Filly (FR) (Last Tycoon)
1393a^{8} 1904a^{8} 7312a^{11}

Apurna *John A Harris* 22
4 ch m Rock Of Gibraltar(IRE) —Dance Lesson (In The Wings)
6595^{10}

Aqlaam *W J Haggas* 125
4 b h Oasis Dream—Bourbonella (Rainbow Quest (USA))
2076^{10} 2990^{3} (3841) 5086a^{2} (5710a) 6271^{4}

Aqmaar *E Charpy* a95 95
5 b h Green Desert(USA) —Hureya (USA) (Woodman (USA))
439a^{7}

Aquapark *R Craggs* a25
3 b g Shinko Forest(IRE) —Waterpark (Namaqualand (USA))
5599^{13} 6823^{17} *7725^{4}*

Aquarian Dancer *Jedd O'Keeffe* a48 49
4 b m Mujahid(USA) —Admonish (Warning)
748^{5} 3451^{8} 4034^{7} 6219^{8}

Aquarian Spirit *R A Fahey* 83
2 b g Fantastic Light(USA) —Notable Lady (IRE) (Victory Note (USA))
3494^{3} 3971^{3} (4308) 4931^{2} 5515^{3} 6088^{2}

Aquarius Star (IRE) *Pat Eddery* 72
2 ch f Danehill Dancer(IRE) —Easter Heroine (IRE) (Exactly Sharp (USA))
4396^{2} 4817^{5}

Aqua Vitae (IRE) *Saeed Bin Suroor* 51
2 ch f Camacho—Baileys Cream (Mister Baileys)
5800^{5}

Aqwaal (IRE) *E A L Dunlop* 104
3 b c Red Ransom(USA) —Mubkera (IRE) (Nashwan (USA))
(1489) (2077) 3087^{5} 3780^{6} (Dead)

Aqwaas (USA) *Sir Michael Stoute* a65 77
3 ch f Diesis—Jinaan (USA) (Mr Prospector (USA))
2433^{2} (3237)

Arabian Flame (IRE) *M R Channon* 81
3 b g King's Best(USA) —Frappe (IRE) (Inchinor)
1355^{4}

Arabian Gleam *J Noseda* a89 119
5 b h Kyllachy—Gleam Of Light (IRE) (Danehill (USA))
2483^{3} 2990^{7} 5862^{3} (6848)

Arabian Jewel *D M Simcock* 36
2 b f Kheleyf(USA) —Lady Liesel (Bin Ajwaad (IRE))
2490^{11}

Arabian Mirage *B J Meehan* a86 85
3 b f Oasis Dream—Bathilde (IRE) (Generous (IRE))
1293^{4} 3016^{16} 3746^{12}

Arabian Moonlight *E F Vaughan* a5 57
3 b f Barathea(IRE) —Ludynosa (USA) (Cadeaux Genereux)
1406^{13} 2633^{5} *3300^{7}*

Arabian Pearl (IRE) *P W Chapple-Hyam* a70 79
3 b f Refuse To Bend(IRE) —Intercede (Pursuit Of Love)
1329^{8} 1843^{2} (2375) 2967^{2} 3537^{4} *6374^{8} 6776^{8}*

Arabian Pride *D M Simcock* 80
2 b g Cadeaux Genereux—Noble Peregrine (Lomond (USA))
2231^{3} 2676^{2} 3311^{4} 4497^{2} (5029) 5521^{5} 6063^{5}

Arabian Silk (IRE) *D M Simcock* a51 54
3 b f Barathea(IRE) —Anthyllis (IRE) (Night Shift (USA))
201^{8} 548^{7} 4004^{13} 5873^{2} *6917^{11}* 6969^{6}

Arabian Spirit *E A L Dunlop* a96 97
4 b g Oasis Dream—Royal Flame (IRE) (Royal Academy (USA))
879^{4} 1352^{2} 1861^{11} 2412^{11} *3988^{5}* 4310^{11} 6092^{8} *6374^{6} 6830^{10}*

Arabian Sun *C P Morlock* a61 61
5 b g Singspiel(IRE) —Bright Halo (IRE) (Bigstone (IRE))
2127^{11} *3275^{7}*

Arab League (IRE) *R J Price* 69
4 b g Dubai Destination(USA) —Johnny And Clyde (USA) (Sky Classic (CAN))
2318^{6} 2975^{2} ◆ 3533^{2} 4263^{2} 4951^{2} (5720) 5962^{3} (6622) 7124^{3}

Arachnophobia (IRE) *Pat Eddery* a86 77
3 b g Redback—La Mata (IRE) (Danehill Dancer (IRE))
936^{3} (1155) 1434^{3} 2578^{2} 3028^{8} *(3982)* 4494^{6} *4984^{5} (6212) 6944^{4}* 7181^{2}

Aranel (IRE) *M Delcher-Sanchez* 97
3 ch c Hawk Wing(USA) —Antinnaz (IRE) (Thatching)
3011^{8} 7232a^{5}

Arapaho Miss (AUS) *Pat Carey* 101
5 b f Danehill Dancer(IRE) —Happy Heart (FR) (Exit To Nowhere (USA))
6961a^{14}

Arashi *Lucinda Featherstone* a71 63
3 b g Fantastic Light(USA) —Arriving (Most Welcome)
2170^{6} 2446^{6} 4022^{2} 4813^{4} 5366^{9} *6031^{3} 6349^{2} 6806^{3} 7153^{9} 7413^{5} 7490^{4} 7668^{4}* 7790^{6}

Arasin (IRE) *P Bary* 106
2 ch c Footstepsinthesand—Arazena (USA) (Woodman (USA))
4073a^{3} 6133a^{2} 7207a^{7}

Arcadia's Angle (USA) *P Bary* a82 109
4 bb h Aldebaran(USA) —Diane's Birthday (USA) (With Approval (CAN))
1029a^{5} 1658a^{6}

Arcano (IRE) *B J Meehan* 116
2 b c Oasis Dream—Tariysha (IRE) (Daylami (IRE))
(2844) ◆ (3779) (5299a)

Arc De Triomphe (GER) *F Vermeulen* 99
7 b h Big Shuffle(USA) —Alepha (Celestial Storm (USA))
3202a^{5}

Arch *A M Crow* 27
6 ch g Arkadian Hero(USA) —Loriner's Lass (Saddlers' Hall (IRE))
2943^{13}

Archers Road (IRE) *M R Channon* 97
2 b g Titus Livius(FR) —Somoushe (IRE) (Black Minnaloushe (USA))
994^{2} (1083) (1126) 1598^{2} 1788^{2} 2136^{2} (2260) 2714^{5} 3805^{3} 4089^{3} 4407^{3} 5174^{6} 5822^{5} 6049^{4} 6677^{11} 7016^{4}

Arch Event *A W Carroll* a28
4 ch m Umistim—Arch Angel (IRE) (Archway (IRE))
7361^{6} 7521^{12} 7863^{7}

Archie Rice (USA) *W Jarvis* a79 91
3 b g Arch(USA) —Gold Bowl (USA) (Seeking The Gold (USA))
2049^{8} 2674^{8} 3816^{10} 5432^{5} ◆ 5832^{9} *6702^{10}*

Archimboldo (USA) *T Wall* a64 62
6 ch g Woodman(USA) —Awesome Strike (USA) (Theatrical (IRE))
148^{7} 249^{7}

Archipenko (USA) *M F De Kock* 122
5 b h Kingmambo(USA) —Bound (USA) (Nijinsky (CAN))
(702a) ◆ 1011a^{6} 1554a^{6}

Archissime (FR) *Y Barberot* a72 69
3 b c Arch(USA) —Nobilissime (Halling (USA))
7037a^{5}

Architrave *Sir Mark Prescott* a72 68
2 ch g Hernando(FR) —White Palace (Shirley Heights)
5787^{8} 5951^{5} ◆ 6235^{3} *6805^{3}*

Archived (IRE) *Are Hyldmo* 90
4 b h Millkom—La Fija (USA) (Dixieland Band (USA))
5302a^{15}

Arch Rebel (USA) *Noel Meade* a95 107
8 b g Arch(USA) —Sheba's Step (USA) (Alysheba (USA))
5685a^{5} 6093^{3}

Arch Walker (IRE) *Jedd O'Keeffe*
2 ch g Choisir(AUS) —Clunie (Inchinor)
1610^{9}

Arcola (IRE) *D M Simcock* a72 74
3 ch f Nayef(USA) —Ashbilya (USA) (Nureyev (USA))
2433^{8} 3209^{8} (3661) 3949^{2} *5168^{3}* 5567^{3} 6113^{6} *7399^{7} 7476^{7}*

Arctic (IRE) *Tracey Collins* 111
2 gr c Shamardal(USA) —Shawanni (Shareef Dancer (USA))
(4357a) (5486a) 6450^{5}

Arctic Cape *D E Pipe* 81
4 b g Cape Cross(IRE) —Arctic Air (Polar Falcon (USA))
1401^{6} (1830) 2103^{6} 2894^{6} 3378^{3} 7036^{9} 7247^{11}

Arctic Cosmos (USA) *J H M Gosden* a72 68
2 b c North Light(IRE) —Fifth Avenue Doll (USA) (Marquetry (USA))
6607^{4} 6821^{4}

Arctic Destiny (IRE) *K R Burke* 49
2 b c Trans Island—Partytime (IRE) (Tagula (IRE))
1623^{6} 2231^{11} 2778^{5} 3263^{5}

Arctic Freedom (USA) *E A L Dunlop* a67 71
3 b f War Chant(USA) —Polar Bird (Thatching)
1250^{5} 2300^{12} *2685^{6}* 3009^{6} 3476^{4} 3708^{7}

Arctic Wings (IRE) *A W Carroll* a55 75
5 b g In The Wings—Arctic Hunt (IRE) (Bering)
142^{6} 1609^{12} 7635^{9}

Ardennes (FR) *D Henderson* 70
2 b c Della Francesca(USA) —Mud Band (USA) (Dixieland Band (USA))
7264a^{5}

Ardent Prince *A J McCabe* a65 60
6 b g Polar Prince(IRE) —Anthem Flight (USA) (Fly So Free (USA))
105^{9} (221) 272^{2} 353^{10} (395) 580^{3} 657^{11} 844^{11} 898^{12} 5229^{10} 5683^{9} 5842^{9} 7129^{6} ◆ 7433^{8} 7521^{7} 7802^{3} 7877^{5}

Ardistan (IRE) *C Roche* 72
5 b g Selkirk(USA) —Asmara (USA) (Lear Fan (USA))
1376a^{8}

Ardmaddy (IRE) *G L Moore* a62 57
5 b g Generous(IRE) —Yazmin (IRE) (Green Desert (USA))
213^{3} (534) 6584^{9} 6918^{5} 7368^{2} 7440^{4} 7873^{4}

Ard Na Greine (IRE) *J S Bolger* a84 103
3 b c Galileo(IRE) —Alfaguara (USA) (Red Ransom (USA))
258a^{16}

Are Can (USA) *J S Wainwright* 55
3 bb c Arch(USA) —Golden Show (USA) (Theatrical (IRE))
3120^{11} 4819^{13}

Areeda (IRE) *C E Brittain* 66
2 b f Refuse To Bend(IRE) —Raindancing (IRE) (Tirol)
2711^{5} 3820^{6}

Areeg (IRE) *W Jarvis* 40
2 b f Doyen(IRE) —Total Aloof (Groom Dancer (USA))
5284^{10} 6363^{11}

Ares Choix *P C Haslam* 92
3 b f Choisir(AUS) —Ares Vallis (IRE) (Caerleon (USA))
5069^{12}

Arfinnit (IRE) *Mrs A L M King* a66 63
8 b g College Chapel—Tidal Reach (USA) (Kris S (USA))
44^{2} 111^{8} 294^{11} 1784^{5} 3242^{7}

Arganil (USA) *K A Ryan* a110 109
4 ch g Langfuhr(CAN) —Sherona (USA) (Mr Greeley (USA))
(821) ◆ *(911)* ◆ 1989^{14} 2272^{4} 3388^{5} 5654^{2} ◆ 6091^{13} *(7007a) 7488^{5}*

Argaum (IRE) *W R Swinburn* a71 64
2 ch c Medicean—Poppy Carew (IRE) (Danehill (USA))
6162^{3} 6759^{7} *7209^{6}*

Argent Avia *M Brittain* 44
3 gr f Silver Patriarch(IRE) —Mountain Bird (Superlative)
4550^{9} 5259^{7} 5731^{9}

Argentine (IRE) *J A McShane* a82 84
5 b g Fasliyev(USA) —Teller (ARG) (Southern Halo (USA))
198^{4} 367^{3} 675^{5} (794) 976^{4} 1310^{4} 1695^{3} (2625) (2812) (2966) 3111^{2} 3295^{3} (3483) ◆ 3681^{8} 3855^{4} 4134^{10} 6897^{9} 7269^{3} 7634^{9} 7735^{9}

Argun River (IRE) *R Gibson* 73
2 b c Oasis Dream—Apperella (Rainbow Quest (USA))
6927a^{2}

Argyll *J Pearce* a43 57
2 b c Xaar—Vitesse (IRE) (Royal Academy (USA))
3402^{8} 4093^{8} 5000^{7} *5369^{10}* 5715^{11} 6215^{11} 7055^{13} *7661^{12}*

Aria Di Festa (IRE) *B Grizzetti* 103
3 b f Orpen(USA) —Alarme Belle (Warning)
1659a^{2} 2521a^{3} 4971a^{11}

Ariadnes Filly (IRE) *Mrs A J Perrett* a63 62
3 b f Xaar—Christaleni (Zilzal (USA))
1703^{5} 2122^{9} *2827^{13}*

Ariel Bender *Peter Grayson* 46
2 gr g Needwood Blade—Wandering Stranger (Petong)
2027^{5} 2484^{9} 2778^{7} 3478^{7} 3807^{6} 4076^{6} 4327^{12}

Arikinui *K R Burke* a55 38
4 b m Noverre(USA) —Off The Blocks (Salse (USA))
290^{3} 657^{13}

Arizona John (IRE) *J Mackie* a80 86
4 b g Rahy(USA) —Preseli (IRE) (Caerleon (USA))
1100^{8} 1507^{6} 1766^{9} 2257^{5} 2938^{13} (3541) 3558^{3} 5003^{3} (5441) (6004) 6485^{6} 7125^{5} ◆ *7633^{4}*

Arjemis *C R Wilson* 60
3 b f Hunting Lion(IRE) —Kungfu Kerry (Celtic Swing)
3036^{15} 3611^{9} 4276^{4} 4653^{5} 4942^{2} (5338) 6103^{13}

Arkellion *P D Evans* 48
2 b g Mark Of Esteem(IRE) —Lovellian (Machiavellian (USA))
2430^{9} 4557^{5} 4946^{11} 5967^{12}

Arken Lad *D Donovan* a58 63
2 b g Arakan(USA) —Object Of Vertu (FR) (Kendor (FR))
2414^{P} 2997^{11} *3719^{4}* (4384) 4757^{3} *6373^{7} 7175^{6}*

Arlanda (GER) *Katja Gernreich*
8 br m Lando(GER) —Artemis (GER) (Lagunas)
7704a^{0}

Arlene Phillips *R Hannon* a48 52
3 ch f Groom Dancer(USA) —Careful Dancer (Gorytus (USA))
1671^{7} *1967^{3}* 2380^{4} 3217^{9} 5011^{9} (5873) *6446^{6} 6918^{13}*

Arlequin *J D Bethell* 77
2 b c Rock Of Gibraltar(IRE) —Fairy Dance (IRE) (Zafonic (USA))
4847^{8} 5793^{7} (6382) ◆ 6993^{10}

Armada (NZ) *J Size* 115
8 ch g Towkay(AUS) —Dance In Time (NZ) (Red Tempo (NZ))
1553a^{9}

Armour *M J Grassick* a77 72
2 b c Azamour(IRE) —Tenable (Polish Precedent (USA))
(6026)

Armure *A De Royer-Dupre* a94 108
4 gr m Dalakhani(IRE) —Bombazine (IRE) (Generous (IRE))
(5058a) 5929a^{7} 6527a^{7}

Army Scout (USA) *J-C Rouget* a75
2 b c Giant's Causeway(USA) —Volga (IRE) (Caerleon (USA))
6979a^{3}

Arnie Guru *M J Attwater* 56
2 ch g Ishiguru(USA) —Who Goes There (Wolfhound (USA))
4699^{9} 5722^{4}

Aromatic *J H M Gosden* a89 82
3 b f Medicean—Red Garland (Selkirk (USA))
(2006) *(2384)* 2796^{5} 4328^{9} 5996^{4}

Around Me (IRE) *Robert Collet* 85
2 b f Johannesburg(USA) —Moon Flower (IRE) (Sadler's Wells (USA))
3648a^{7}

Aroundthebay *H J L Dunlop* a86 84
3 b f Diktat—Bayleaf (Efisio)
(852) 2079^{16} (2761) 3320^{6} 3641^{9} *5104^{9} 5665^{11} 7132^{9}*

Arqaam *Doug Watson* a99 108
5 b h Machiavellian(USA) —Khams-Alhawas (IRE) (Marju (IRE))
338a^{6} 419a^{4} *612a^{4} 773a^{10}*

Arrabiata *C N Kellett* a51 35
4 b m Piccolo—Paperweight (In The Wings)
37^{9}

Arrieta (IRE) *Y Durepaire* a69 76
2 ch c Captain Rio—St Bride's Bay (Caerleon (USA))
6960a^{6}

Arriva La Diva *J J Quinn* 57
3 ch f Needwood Blade—Hillside Girl (IRE) (Tagula (IRE))
3036^{14} 3352^{10} 3853^{2} (4137) 4777^{2} 4999^{3} 5626^{7}

Arrivederla (IRE) *H J L Dunlop* a63 85
3 b f Acclamation—Alwiyda (USA) (Trempolino (USA))
1066^{3} ◆ (1837) (2198) 2696^{4}

Arrogance *G L Moore* a64 63
3 b g Josr Algarhoud(IRE) —Rise 'n Shine (Night Shift (USA))
1428^{5} 1670^{4} 2479^{9}

Arry's Orse *B Smart* 69
2 b c Exceed And Excel(AUS) —Georgianna (IRE) (Petardia)
5234[5]

Arson Squad (USA) *Richard Dutrow Jr* a115 108
6 bb g Brahms(USA) —Majestic Fire (USA) (Green Dancer (USA))
1013a[11]

Art Connoisseur (IRE) *M L W Bell* 120
3 b c Lucky Story(USA) —Withorwithoutyou (IRE) (Danehill (USA))
1292[7] (3140) 3819[12] 5233[15] 5657[12] 6304[11]

Art Deco (IRE) *C R Egerton* a103 115
6 ch h Peintre Celebre(USA) —Sometime (IRE) (Royal Academy (USA))
2398[5]

Art Discovery (IRE) *M H Tompkins* a53 36
3 br g Indian Haven—Lady Cinders (IRE) (Dance Of Life (USA))
64[2] 4177[7] 6788[10]

Artesium *Patrick Morris* a59 48
3 ch g Haafhd—Multicolour (Rainbow Quest (USA))
3336[11] 4589[5] 4749[7] 5582[7] (5644) 6213[11] 6719[10] 7002[11] 7678[9] 7796[5] 7877[8]

Arteus *Jane Chapple-Hyam* a89 79
3 b g Fantastic Light(USA) —Enchanted (Magic Ring (IRE))
1837[2] 2198[13] 2917[2] 3566[4] (4981) 5575[12] 6178[12] (6562) (7327) (7617) 7801[5] ◆

Arte Viva (USA) *G A Butler* a77 46
2 ch f Giant's Causeway(USA) —Helsinka (FR) (Pennekamp (USA))
5639[2] ◆ 6436[4] 6920[14]

Art Excellence *S A Callaghan* a73 82
2 b c Noverre(USA) —Her Ladyship (Polish Precedent (USA))
6214[6] (6607) 7030[11]

Art Exhibition (IRE) *B R Millman* a68 46
4 ch g Captain Rio—Miss Dilletante (Primo Dominie)
1654[5] 2163[9]

Artful Dodger *T R Gretton*
2 b c Josr Algarhoud(IRE) —Artistic Belle (IRE) (Orpen (USA))
7276[9]

Art Fund (USA) *G L Moore* a65 50
3 b g Speightstown(USA) —Kew Garden (USA) (Seattle Slew (USA))
159[6] 200[6] 345[5]

Art Gallery *D W Thompson* a42 41
5 ch g Indian Ridge—Party Doll (Be My Guest (USA))
302[13] 3617[7] 4617[3] 5307[7] 6559[9]

Arthur's Edge *B Palling* a82 103
5 b g Diktat—Bright Edge (Danehill Dancer (IRE))
2144[7] 2977[7] (3801) 4293[3] 4641[10] 5182[5] 5884[9] 6201[2] (6694) (6964) 7292[2]

Arthur's Girl *J H M Gosden* a86 104
4 b m Hernando(FR) —Maid Of Camelot (Caerleon (USA))
4566[5] 7291[15]

Artica (GER) *T Mundry* 46
2 br f Pentire—Astica (GER) (Surumu (GER))
7045a[9]

Article Rare (USA) *E Lellouche* 105
3 gr f El Prado(IRE) —Action Francaise (USA) (Nureyev (USA))
1237a[6] 2119a[2] 5298a[2] 6525a[8]

Artimino *I Mohammed* a105 106
5 b g Medicean—Palatial (Green Desert (USA))
335a[9] ◆ 413a[9] 638a[9] 770a[6]

Artistic License (IRE) *M R Channon* a94 94
4 b m Chevalier(IRE) —Alexander Eliott (IRE) (Night Shift (USA))
543[2] 714[3] 852[4] 1094[2] 1197[7] 1418[6] 1806[4] (1965) 2102[9] 2334[4] (2911) 3164[3] 3453[3] 4273[7] 4485[9] (5471) 5901[2] 6020[4] 6428[8] 7394[8]

Art Jewel (IRE) *S A Callaghan* a67 64
2 b f Bertolini(USA) —Ma N'Ieme Biche (USA) (Key To The Kingdom (USA))
(1637) 1927[3] 2054[11] 3719[2]

Art Machine (USA) *Sir Mark Prescott* a67 49
2 ch f Sky Mesa(USA) —Grazia (Sharpo)
5639[4] 6069[6] 6334[6]

Art Man *G L Moore* a92 75
6 b g Dansili—Persuasion (Batshoof)
124[6] 283[6] 724[9] 850[4] ◆ 1382[3] (1966) 3273[3]

Art Market (CAN) *Miss Jo Crowley* a66 68
6 ch g Giant's Causeway(USA) —Fantasy Lake (USA) (Salt Lake (USA))
1606[8] 2598[2] 4791[2] 5813[6] 6783[3] 7110[5] 7479[3]

Art Of War (SAF) *M F De Kock* a106
5 b g Kahal—Cariad (SAF) (Northern Guest (USA))
184a[8] 334a[5] 435a[2] (523a) 698a[2] 773a[3] 1008a[10]

Artreju (GER) *P Butler* a68 76
6 ch g Perugino(USA) —Art Of Easter (GER) (Dashing Blade)
42[4] 569[8] 733[11] 1314[4] 1785[7] 2675[8] 2851[2] 3421[5] 4269[10] 4563[8] 4698[4] 5211[4] 6369[10] 6945[9] 7440[9] 7623[8] 7668[9]

Art Scholar (IRE) *G L Moore* 90
2 b c Pyrus(USA) —Marigold (FR) (Marju (IRE))
(5379) 5721[2] 6104[9]

Arts Guild (USA) *W J Musson* a81 83
4 b g Theatrical(IRE) —Gilded Edge (Cadeaux Genereux)
5127[2]

Artsu *M Dods* a67 83
4 b g Bahamian Bounty—War Shanty (Warrshan (USA))
1685[8] 2071[4] 2770[2] 3149[2] 3491[4] 4069[8] 4899[3] 5978[6] ◆ 6434[9]

Art Summer *D M Simcock* 64
2 ch f Compton Place—Karminskey Park (Sabrehill (USA))
3849[4] 4302[3] 5380[2] 5800[3] 6443[P] (Dead)

Art Value *M Wigham* a65 55
4 ch g Barathea(IRE) —Empty Purse (Pennine Walk)
969[2] 1589[9] 2222[4] 2609[5] 3171[5] 3561[2] 4156[10] 4640[12]

Arty Crafty (USA) *Sir Mark Prescott* a82 68
3 b f Arch(USA) —Princess Kris (Kris)
(5775) (6156) (6289) 6376[2] (6445) 7131[8]

Arwaah (IRE) *M P Tregoning* 106
3 b f Dalakhani(IRE) —Sahool (Unfuwain (USA))
1599[5] ◆ (4991) ◆ 6853[5] 7291[14]

Aryacoddinme (IRE) *G A Harker*
2 b c Pyrus(USA) —Rainbow Pet (IRE) (Spectrum (IRE))
1450[9] 2541[7]

Asaab (IRE) *C E Brittain* 54
2 b f Refuse To Bend(IRE) —Shalev (GER) (Java Gold (USA))
3187[6] 4047[11]

Asaba *S Kirk*
2 b f Desert Style(IRE) —Hoh Hedsor (Singspiel (IRE))
3534[9]

Asaint Needs Brass (USA) *J R Best* a81 83
3 bb g Lion Hearted(USA) —British Columbia (Selkirk (USA))
5197[6] 5646[11] 6167[11] 6632[10] 6782[10] 7223[9] 7330[12]

Asakusa *H R A Cecil* a48 43
3 b f Royal Applause—Kiss And Don'Tell (USA) (Rahy (USA))
1198[10] 1532[7] 2169[9] 2744[8]

Asakusa Kings (JPN) *R Okubo* 121
5 b h White Muzzle—Croupier Star (JPN) (Sunday Silence (USA))
7593a[16]

Asateer (IRE) *B W Hills* 87
3 b g Alhaarth(IRE) —Catatonic (Zafonic (USA))
1291[8] 1793[6] 5010[3] 5348[2]

As Brave As You (IRE) *B Ellison* a51 39
2 b g Hawk Wing(USA) —Scanno's Choice (IRE) (Pennine Walk)
2258[10] 2610[7] 3170[7] 5358[8] 7139[4] 7335[3] 7597[6]

Ascendant *Sir Mark Prescott* a85 96
3 ch g Medicean—Ascendancy (Sadler's Wells (USA))
(4974) ◆ 5666[4] (5961) (6313)

Ascot And Co (IRE) *S Wattel* a72 63
2 b f Xaar—Batilde (IRE) (Victory Piper (USA))
6501a[10] 6960a[5]

Ascot Glory (IRE) *S Wattel* a82 104
2 b f Kheleyf(USA) —Lake Victoria (IRE) (Lake Coniston (IRE))
3667a[7] 7231a[2]

As De Trebol (USA) *G Arizkorreta Elosegui* 92
3 gr c Tapit(USA) —Adelphi (USA) (Danzig (USA))
2513a[2] 3908a[9] 5709a[8]

Ashaaq *F Head* 108
3 b c Anabaa(USA) —Al Ishq (FR) (Nureyev (USA))
7102a[5]

Ashalanda (FR) *A De Royer-Dupre* 115
3 gr f Linamix(FR) —Ashaninka (USA) (Woodman (USA))
(3442a) 6153a[2] (6853) 7747a[4]

Ashbrittle *R M Beckett* 64
2 b g Rainbow Quest(USA) —Caesarea (GER) (Generous (IRE))
7243[3] ◆

Ashes Summer (IRE) *P R Webber* a58 65
3 b f Rock Of Gibraltar(IRE) —Time Ahead (Spectrum (IRE))
5718[4] 6166[5]

Ashka (IRE) *G M Lyons* a95 77
4 b m Catcher In The Rye(IRE) —Road Harbour (USA) (Rodrigo De Triano (USA))
5689a[14]

Ashkalara *H S Howe* 60
2 b f Footstepsinthesand—Asheyana (IRE) (Soviet Star (USA))
2175[10] 4226[7] 4945[3] 6055[9]

Ashmolian (IRE) *Miss Z C Davison* a56 55
6 b g Grand Lodge(USA) —Animatrice (USA) (Alleged (USA))
301[5] 378[3] 546[8]

Ashram (IRE) *Saeed Bin Suroor* a108 113
3 ch g Indian Haven—Tara's Girl (IRE) (Fayruz)
1675[13] 2411[2] 3011[3] 4052[2] 4521[9] (5313) (6058) 6848[5]

Asian Power (IRE) *P J O'Gorman* a77 76
4 ch g Bertolini(USA) —Cynara (Imp Society (USA))
167[9] 243[5]

Asian Tale (IRE) *P D Evans* a70 73
3 br f Namid—Literary (Woodman (USA))
672[4] 924[8] 1744[5] 2300[18]

Asian Tiger (GER) *P Schiergen* 81
3 b c Tiger Hill(IRE) —Asuma (GER) (Surumu (GER))
1718a[7]

Asiatic Boy (ARG) *Kiaran McLaughlin* a119 121
6 b h Not For Sale(ARG) —S. S. Asiatic (USA) (Polish Navy (USA))
417a[3] (773a) ◆ 1013a[12] 6512a[7]

Ask *Sir Michael Stoute* 124
6 b h Sadler's Wells(USA) —Request (Rainbow Quest (USA))
(2056) (2670) 4298[3] (7047a)

Askabad Maybe (FR) *C Plisson*
2 u f (FR) — (FR) (Kaldoun (FR))
6576a[6]

Askar Tau (FR) *M P Tregoning* a106 115
4 b g Montjeu(IRE) —Autriche (IRE) (Acatenango (GER))
4457[8] (5171) (5824) 6527a[5] 7047a[6]

Ask Dan (IRE) *M Dods* a59 66
3 b g Refuse To Bend(IRE) —Bush Cat (USA) (Kingmambo (USA))
1725[4] 1926[10] 2154[10] 3108[5] 3305[5] (3614) 4013[6] 4279[11] 4348[5] (4528) 4897[7] 5306[4] 5621[2] 6414[4] 6985[7]

Ask Frank (IRE) *G A Swinbank* 97
2 b g Hawk Wing(USA) —Riva Royale (Royal Applause)
3147[3] (3613)

Ask Jack (USA) *Joseph G Murphy* a89 98
5 ch g Mt. Livermore(USA) —Moll (USA) (Criminal Type (USA))
4574a[2] 5490a[24]

Ask Jenny (IRE) *Patrick Morris* a65 64
7 b m Marju(IRE) —Waltzing Matilda (Mujtahid (USA))
582[4] 832[12] 861[3] 1182[7] 1241[4] 1360[7] 1970[3] 2124[2] 2316[4] 2418[5] 2712[4] 2811[8] 3239[4] 3471[9] 6939[4] 7223[6] 7370[2] ◆ (7483) (7606) 7682[5] 7815[5]

Ask The Oracle *H Morrison* a68
3 ch g Where Or When(IRE) —Delphic Way (Warning)
1490[2] ◆ 6608[5] 6950[3] 7225[4] 7665[7]

Asmodea *B G Powell* a58 46
4 b m Dr Fong(USA) —Latina (IRE) (King's Theatre (IRE))
130[6] 385[9]

Asoraya (IRE) *F-X De Chevigny* a69 62
2 gr f American Post—Alminieh (FR) (Highest Honor (FR))
6960a[2]

Aspectoflove (IRE) *John M Oxx* a85 108
3 b f Danetime(IRE) —Rose Vibert (Caerleon (USA))
6267[10]

Aspectus (IRE) *T Mundry* 112
6 ch h Spectrum(IRE) —Anna Thea (IRE) (Turfkonig (GER))
(2113a) 3416a[8] 4582a[2] 5563a[4] 6718a[9]

Aspendale (IRE) *D Carroll* 27
4 b g Docksider(USA) —Ambria (ITY) (Final Straw)
2404[11]

Aspen Darlin (IRE) *A Bailey* 109
3 b f Indian Haven—Manuka Magic (IRE) (Key Of Luck (USA))
1698[P]

Aspirational (IRE) *B Palling* a58 49
3 ch g Rainbow Quest(USA) —Londonnetdotcom (IRE) (Night Shift (USA))
1771[11] 2323[6] 7085[10] 7369[3] 7733[4]

Aspire (USA) *Eddie Kenneally* a109
2 b c Tale Of The Cat(USA) —Mamselle Nanette (USA) (Southern Halo (USA))
7307a[12]

Aspro Mavro (IRE) *J H M Gosden* a77 77
3 b c Spartacus(IRE) —Alexia Reveuse (IRE) (Dr Devious (IRE))
5614[2] 6223[7] 7126[2] 7287[6]

Asraab (IRE) *Saeed Bin Suroor* 82
2 b c Oasis Dream—Alexander Queen (IRE) (King's Best (USA))
(7145)

Asrar *Miss Lucinda V Russell* 38
7 b m King's Theatre(IRE) —Zandaka (FR) (Doyoun)
7170[10]

Assabiyya (IRE) *Saeed Bin Suroor* 86
3 b f Cape Cross(IRE) —Coretta (IRE) (Caerleon (USA))
(4606) 5285[2] 6286[6]

Assahab (GER) *U Stech* 96
6 ch h Lando(GER) —Akasha (GER) (Dashing Blade)
3416a[10] 4364a[7] 5461a[10] 6500a[10]

Assail *H Morrison* a83 6
3 b g Bertolini(USA) —Roofer (IRE) (Barathea (IRE))
306[3] 2981[12] (3980) 4649[3] 5570[4]

Assam (GER) *Carmen Bocskai* a75 35
7 b h Big Shuffle(USA) —Arbarine (GER) (Aspros (GER))
464a[7] 652a[6]

Assent (IRE) *B R Millman* a68 67
3 b f Kheleyf(USA) —Villafranca (IRE) (In The Wings)
986[2] 1588[6] 2160[4] 2321[4]

Asserting *J A McShane* 61
3 b f Reset(AUS) —Appelone (Emperor Jones (USA))
1831[2] 2154[7] (2593) 2964[5]

Asset (IRE) *Saeed Bin Suroor* a105 119
6 b g Marju(IRE) —Snow Peak (Arazi (USA))
259a[4] (434a) 611a[8] (1513) 2483[4] 3141[2] 4837a[9] 5474[2] 5657[6] 6304[6] 6848[6]

As Speed (FR) *P Khozian* a76
2 b f Keltos(FR) —Assaranxa (FR) (Linamix (FR))
5240a[6]

Astarta (IRE) *P F I Cole* a67 66
2 b f Green Desert(USA) —Broken Romance (IRE) (Ela-Mana-Mou)
2034[6] 2490[5] 3733[3]

Asterllini (IRE) *C E Brittain* 51
2 b f Refuse To Bend(IRE) —Alithini (IRE) (Darshaan)
6066[10]

Aston Boy *M Blanshard* a48 50
4 ch g Dr Fong(USA) —Hectic Tina (Hector Protector (USA))
117[7] 1156[5]

Astonishment (IRE) *S Kirk* a76 96
2 b c Desert Style(IRE) —Lucky Norwegian (IRE) (Almutawakel)
2771[10] 3344[2] 3786[4] 4152[2] (4646) 5265[2] (5913) 6305[5] 6619[4] 6898[4]

Aston Lad *Micky Hammond* 49
8 b g Bijou D'Inde—Fishki (Niniski (USA))
2233[12]

Astormfromillinois (USA) *George Baker* a6
6 ch g Illinois Storm(USA) —Sweetannieannie (USA) (Marquetry (USA))
7412[8]

Astral Flower *Sir Michael Stoute* a64
2 b f Kalanisi(IRE) —Arum Lily (USA) (Woodman (USA))
7199[5] 7400[4]

Astroangel *M H Tompkins* a69 60
5 b m Groom Dancer(USA) —Nutmeg (IRE) (Lake Coniston (IRE))
2458[7] 3007[4] 3490[3] 3946[2] 4697[10] 5111[5] 5479[4] 6845[10]

Astrobrava *M H Tompkins* a53 55
3 ch f Falbrav(IRE) —Nutmeg (IRE) (Lake Coniston (IRE))
1954[5] 2380[5] 3610[3] 4642[6] 5328[9]

Astrodiva *M H Tompkins* a48 77
3 b f Where Or When(IRE) —Astromancer (USA) (Silver Hawk (USA))
1269[2] ◆ 2723[2] 3022[2] 3827[3] 4480[3] 5205[3] 5987[4] 6766[2]

Astrodonna *M H Tompkins* a75 78
4 ch m Carnival Dancer—Mega (IRE) (Petardia)
1256[2] 1633[6] 1964[3] 2539[10] 3165[4] 3624[6] 4179[2] (4916) 5190[6] 6780[3] 7364[6]

Astroleo *M H Tompkins* a54 54
3 ch g Groom Dancer(USA) —Astrolove (IRE) (Bigstone (IRE))
2742[3] 3561[3] (3954) 4470[7] 5483[3] 5990[12] 6785[5] 7336[6]

Astrolibra *M H Tompkins* a65 61
5 b m Sakhee(USA) —Optimistic (Reprimand)
1881[4] 1961[7] 2221[5] 3074[3] 3475[4] 3949[8] (5377) 5593[4] 5962[6] 7093[5] 7712[4]

Astromoon *M H Tompkins* 59
2 b f Beat Hollow—Astromancer (USA) (Silver Hawk (USA))
6062[11] 7095[6]

Astronomer's Dream *E F Vaughan* a58 57
2 ch f Galileo(IRE) —Danehill's Dream (IRE) (Danehill (USA))
4055[11] 4542[9] 6781[8] 7235[10]

Astronomical (IRE) *R Hollinshead* a69 71
7 b g Mister Baileys—Charm The Stars (Roi Danzig (USA))
3151[5] 3563[2] 4229[9] 4658[11] 5423[2] 5698[7] 6017[2] (6392) 6760[10] 7127[9] 7495[3]

Astrophysical Jet *E S McMahon* 89
2 b f Dubawi(IRE) —Common Knowledge (Rainbow Quest (USA))
(5129) 6090[3] 6852[5]

Astrovenus *M H Tompkins* 49
2 ch f Tobougg(IRE) —Astrolove (IRE) (Bigstone (IRE))
5478[9] 7096[7]

Aswaaq (IRE) *J L Dunlop* 65
3 b f Peintre Celebre(USA) —Hureya (USA) (Woodman (USA))
5435[5]

As You Like It (IRE) *John Joseph Murphy* a53 55
2 b f Footstepsinthesand—Callanish (Inchinor)
6820[5] 6841[5]

Atabaas Allure (FR) *M Johnston* a82 85
3 b f Alhaarth(IRE) —Atabaa (FR) (Anabaa (USA))
1613[5] 2208[6] 2874a[7] 3941[3] 4422[8] 5037[7]

Atacama Crossing (IRE) *B W Hills* 77
2 b c Footstepsinthesand—Endure (IRE) (Green Desert (USA))
1867[2] (2358) 4758[9] 5762[11]

Atacama Sunrise *J Pearce* a71 70
3 b f Desert Sun—Top Of The Morning (Keen)
1092[5] 1260[4] 1573[6] 2152[7] 2858[11] (3551) 5229[2] 5479[3] 5791[12] 7149[9] (7776)

At A Great Rate (USA) *H R A Cecil* 79
3 b f Arch(USA) —Glia (USA) (A.P. Indy (USA))
(1362) 2189[4] 2607[4] 4050[6] 4799[3] 5189[5]

Atakora (IRE) *Mrs A J Perrett* a59 62
2 b f King's Best(USA) —Orinoco (IRE) (Darshaan)
5604[9] 6163[8] 6416[6]

Atalia (GER) *Mario Hofer* 97
4 ch m Sholokhov(IRE) —Anna Kalinka (GER) (Lion Cavern (USA))
1394a[15]

Atasari (IRE) *J S Bolger* 109
2 b f Whipper(USA) —Azra (IRE) (Danehill (USA))
2286a[12] 5895a[5] 6708a[2] 6852[2]

Ateeb *M Johnston* a61 69
3 b g Red Ransom(USA) —Design Perfection (USA) (Diesis)
1087[5]

Athaakeel (IRE) *R A Harris* a66 6
3 b f Almutawakel—Asaafeer (USA) (Dayjur (USA))
2151[9] (2683) 5612[9] 6170[9] 6252[5] (6914) 7330[10]

Athania (IRE) *A P Jarvis* a76 69
3 ch f Fath(USA) —Xania (Mujtahid (USA))
1068[4] 1808[6] 2198[10] 2827[3] 3281[6] (3804) 4262[11] 4642[5] 6052[10]

Athboy Auction *H J Collingridge* a46 57
4 b m Auction House(USA) —Thabeh (Shareef Dancer (USA))
355[9] 1634[8] 2455[4] 2921[3] 3381[7] 4880[7] 6005[8] 7107[4] 7591[11]

Atheer Dubai (IRE) *E F Vaughan* a73 57
4 b h Dubai Destination(USA) —Atheer (USA) (Lear Fan (USA))
499[2] 710[5] 2382[3]

Athenian Garden (USA) *H R A Cecil* a67 59
2 b f Royal Academy(USA) —Webee (USA) (Kingmambo (USA))
6436[6] 6965[4]

Atherton (IRE) *J G Given* a44
2 b c Cadeaux Genereux—Bibi Karam (IRE) (Persian Bold)
6026[9] 6356[10] 6796[9]

Athlone (IRE) *L M Cumani* 98
5 b m Montjeu(IRE) —Almi Ad (USA) (Silver Hawk (USA))
2482[8] 2974[6]

Athwaab *M G Quinlan* a70 64
2 b f Cadeaux Genereux—Ahdaaf (USA) (Bahri (USA))
2919[5] 3271[9] 4537[7] (5636) ◆ 7707[3] 7793[3] 7871[2]

Atlaal (USA) *M A Jarvis* 83
2 ch c Speightstown(USA) —Deputy Maiden (USA) (Deputy Minister (CAN))
4336[2] 5129[4] (6246)

Atlantic Beach *J Hetherton* 76
4 ch g Kyllachy—Amused (Prince Sabo)
1885[4] ◆ 2276[3] ◆ 2628[2] 3001[4] 3855[6] 4783[8]

Atlantic Dancer (GER) *A Schennach* a34 86
6 b g Starborough—Arousal (GER) (Goofalik (USA))
464a[11]

Atlantic Gamble (IRE) *K R Burke* a66 60
9 b g Darnay—Full Traceability (IRE) (Ron's Victory (USA))
81[11]

Atlantic King (FR) *F Vermeulen* a67 52
5 gr g Balleroy(USA) —Atlantica (FR) (Arctic Tern (USA))
5301a[5]

Atlantic Mist (FR) *Y De Nicolay*
2 b c Muhtathir—Beg Meil (FR) (Tel Quel (FR))
6979a[0]

Atlantic Sport (USA) *M R Channon* 111
4 b h Machiavellian(USA) —Shy Lady (FR) (Kaldoun (FR))
1346[4] 2076[7] 2483[5] 3388[6]

Atlantic Story (USA) *M W Easterby* a115 96
7 bb g Stormy Atlantic(USA) —Story Book Girl (USA) (Siberian Express (USA))
206[4] 916[11] 1365[3] 3172[3] 3567[6] 3877[4] 4598[5] 5257[3] 5799[3] 6283[3]

Atlantic Wave (USA) *R Tugusev* 70
4 ch h Stormy Atlantic(USA) —Million Questions (USA) (Olympio (USA))
6522a[15]

Atlantis Star *Saeed Bin Suroor* 99
2 b c Cape Cross(IRE) —Ladeena (IRE) (Dubai Millennium)
(4659) 5250[2] 5743[3] 6478[17]

Atlas Silk *P Bary* a77 90
3 b f Dansili—Marani (Ashkalani (IRE))
2754a[6]

At Least (FR) *Robert Collet* 85
2 b c Miesque's Son(USA) —Rendorina (FR) (Kendor (FR))
6578a[5] 7384a[2]

Atomic Rain (USA) *Kelly Breen* a107
3 b c Smart Strike(CAN) —Paradise Pond (USA) (Cox's Ridge (USA))
1688a[16]

Atomic Twister *P F I Cole* 34
2 b f Dubawi(IRE) —Lauren (GER) (Lightning (FR))
2793[10] 2978[10]

A Touch Of Luck *T D Easterby* 39
2 b g Lucky Story(USA) —Optimise (IRE) (Danehill (USA))
1275[8] 1735[4] 2231[12]

A Tout Coeur (FR) *Dominique Sepulchre*
2 b g Limnos(JPN) —Entouka (FR) (Bluebird (USA))
7507a[6]

Attainable *Mrs A J Perrett* a68 37
3 bb f Kalanisi(IRE) —Balleta (USA) (Lyphard (USA))
5314[3] 6975[6]

Attorney General (IRE) *C Gordon* 42
10 b g Sadler's Wells(USA) —Her Ladyship (Polish Precedent (USA))
7036[12]

Aturo (FR) *C Sprengel* 101
5 br h Big Shuffle(USA) —Avanti Adda (GER) (Law Society (USA))
2097a[6] 7044a[10]

At Wits End *J A R Toller* a75
3 b g Orpen(USA) —Pagan Princess (Mujtahid (USA))
5614[4] 6073[4] (6673)

Auburn Place *E F Vaughan* a16
2 ch f Compton Place—Barboukh (Night Shift (USA))
7106[9]

Auction Belle *R Curtis* a36 48
4 b m Auction House(USA) —Island Colony (USA) (Pleasant Colony (USA))
11[5] 90[7] 249[6]

Audacity Of Hope *P J McBride* 101
2 b c Red Ransom(USA) —Aliena (IRE) (Grand Lodge (USA))
2000[3] (2610) 4758[2] 5261[8] (5762) (6063) 6426[4] 7030[3]

Audaz *C Laffon-Parias* 97
4 br m Oasis Dream—Albahaca (USA) (Green Dancer (USA))
4365a[8] 7347a[9] 7704a[0]

Audemar (IRE) *E F Vaughan* a90 71
3 ch c Exceed And Excel(AUS) —Bathe In Light (USA) (Sunshine Forever (USA))
2148[6] 4649[4] (4984) 5432[10] 5665[4] 6168[4] (6614) 6773[3]

Audrinna (IRE) *M G Quinlan* 50
2 b f Oratorio(IRE) —Zvezda (USA) (Nureyev (USA))
2047[11] 3626[2]

Augusta Gold (USA) *N P Littmoden* a68 68
3 b c Medaglia D'Oro(USA) —Golden Gorse (USA) (His Majesty (USA))
662[5] 883[2] 978[2]

August Days (IRE) *J Pearce* a46 56
3 ch f Noverre(USA) —Vitesse (IRE) (Royal Academy (USA))
1095[6] 1359[12] 2534[8] 3005[8] 3257[14] 4196[6] 5367[7]

August Gale (USA) *M W Easterby* a83 66
4 b g Storm Cat(USA) —Lady Bonanza (USA) (Seeking The Gold (USA))
1039[12]

Augustus John (IRE) *R Brotherton* a78 73
6 gr g Danehill(USA) —Rizerie (FR) (Highest Honor (FR))
90[3] 178[3] 342[2] 528[2] (735) 860[3] 1069[2] 1435[7] 3814[7] 4128[5] 7413[3] 7594[2] 7785[2]

Augustusthestrong (USA) *A P O'Brien* a99 89
3 bb c A.P. Indy(USA) —Fire The Groom (USA) (Blushing Groom (FR))
6467a[3]

Auld Arty (FR) *T G Mills* a77 72
3 bb g Dansili—Provisoire (USA) (Gone West (USA))
127[2] (315) 672[3] 1033[6] 2010[11] 2786[12] 3476[7] 5283[7]

Aultcharn (FR) *B J Meehan* 71
2 b c Kyllachy—Nuit Sans Fin (FR) (Lead On Time (USA))
6615[10] 7029[6]

Aumale (FR) *H-A Pantall* 57
3 u f — (Shining Steel)
6753a[9]

Auntie Craik *S Gollings* a35
5 b m Cotation—Mrs Poppyford (Mistertopogigo (IRE))
7671[11]

Auntie Mame *D J Coakley* a68 70
5 b m Diktat—Mother Molly (USA) (Irish River (FR))
1785[3] (2517)

Aunt Nicola *M L W Bell* a71 82
3 b f Reel Buddy(USA) —Night Gypsy (Mind Games)
1677[4] 2102[7] 2886[8] 3789[6] 4198[8] 5007[2] 5471[3]

Aunty Betty (IRE) *M S Tuck* 20
2 b f Camacho—Jina (IRE) (Petardia)
4851[7]

Aura *H J L Dunlop* a39 47
4 b m Barathea(IRE) —Finger Of Light (Green Desert (USA))
90[8]

Aura Of Calm (IRE) *Ronald O'Leary* a43 63
7 ch g Grand Lodge(USA) —Perils Of Joy (IRE) (Rainbow Quest (USA))
2264[P] 2969[8] 3035[7]

Aureate *B Ellison* a95 90
5 ch g Jade Robbery(USA) —Anne D'Autriche (IRE) (Rainbow Quest (USA))
82[3] (325) 1458[10] 1826[6] (2129) 2743[2] (3223) 3266[12] 5622[3] 6095[8] 7137[4]

Aurora Lights *R A Fahey*
2 ch f Fantastic Light(USA) —Sweet Revival (Claude Monet (USA))
7843[9]

Aurora Sky (IRE) *J Akehurst* a70 75
3 gr f Hawk Wing(USA) —To The Skies (USA) (Sky Classic (CAN))
2179[4] 2849[4] 4010[2] 4700[5] 5169[10] 5591[5]

Aurorian (IRE) *R Hannon* a87 88
3 b g Fantastic Light(USA) —Aurelia (Rainbow Quest (USA))
1326[6] 2077[5] 2701[6] 3049[27] 3780[11] 4520[9] 6907[5] 7233[4] (7628)

Ausonius *L M Cumani* a62 46
3 b g Kyllachy—Baileys Silver (USA) (Marlin (USA))
5965[7] 6339[14] 6784[U] 7022[2]

Aussie Blue (IRE) *R M Whitaker* a60 69
5 b g Bahamian Bounty—Luanshya (First Trump)
1194[7] 1332[13] 1955[9] 2245[10] 2532[2] (2791) 3124[5] 3568[2] 4046[9] 4435[6] 4887[4] 5441[2] 6023[3] 6383[7] 7192[7] 7236[11]

Aussie Pearl (FR) *C Boillot* 55
3 b f Leadership—Bangwelu (Emperor Jones (USA))
6682a[0]

Australia Day (IRE) *P R Webber* a98 106
6 gr g Key Of Luck(USA) —Atalina (FR) (Linamix (FR))
284[5] (2891) 3586[3] 4404[10] 5794[4] 6302[2]

Authentic *L M Cumani* 49
4 ch g Pivotal—Red Passion (USA) (Seeking The Gold (USA))
6094[12]

Autocracy *W J Haggas* a71 55
2 b c Green Desert(USA) —Imperial Bailiwick (IRE) (Imperial Frontier (USA))
4243[7] 4546[3] 6802[3]

Autumn Blades (IRE) *A Bailey* a88 83
4 ch g Daggers Drawn(USA) —September Tide (IRE) (Thatching)
282[4] 457[7] 730[2] (806) 922[3] 1089[2] 1436[3] 2050[4] 2086[12] 2695[11] 3265[11] 3924[3] 4181[3] 4386[4] 4871[3] 5404[8] 6024[3] (6336) 6726[3] 6924[6] 6976[2] 7252[2] 7350[3] 7437[3] 7617[2] (7801) 7833[4] (7891)

Autumn Charm *Lucinda Featherstone* a46 44
4 ch m Reel Buddy(USA) —Eurolink Cafe (Grand Lodge (USA))
116[7] 169[8] 300[9] 341[10] 2975[8] 3862[11] 4170[7] 4617[4] 5327[6]

Autumn Harvest *A J McCabe* 78
5 b g Beat Hollow—Welsh Autumn (Tenby)
1681[6] (2090) 2315[4] 2698[6]

Autumn Morning (IRE) *P D Evans* a60 49
3 b f Danetime(IRE) —Soviet Maid (IRE) (Soviet Star (USA))
77[5] 134[5] 287[7] 450[2] 479[5] 741[4] 776[7] 2149[4] 2515[10] 3209[9] 3257[4] 3502[6]

Ava Doll *J R Jenkins* a14 19
2 b f Statue Of Liberty(USA) —Foolish Gift (FR) (Barathea (IRE))
7095[11] 7183[20] 7388[10]

A Valley Away (IRE) *Jane Chapple-Hyam* a46
5 ch m City On A Hill(USA) —Sharkiyah (IRE) (Polish Precedent (USA))
1[4] 116[8]

Avanguardia (GER) *D Prod'Homme* a81 100
4 b m Choisir(AUS) —Anthurium (GER) (Hector Protector (USA))
4335a[6]

Ava's World (IRE) *Peter Grayson* a63 33
5 b m Desert Prince(IRE) —Taibhseach (USA) (Secreto (USA))
3775[6] 4012[4] 4621[6]

Ave *Sir Michael Stoute* a88 109
3 b f Danehill Dancer(IRE) —Anna Amalia (IRE) (In The Wings)
1679[3] (3870) 4287[2] ◆ (4903) (6298a) 6853[8]

Avec Moi *Mrs C A Dunnett* a48 48
2 b f Reset(AUS) —Pardon Moi (First Trump)
1188[7] 1630[4] 2383[11] 2919[8] 3742[5] 4176[10] 4383[8] 4912[4] 5950[11] 6169[11] 6355[4] 6796[6] 7089[3] 7352[5] 7514[4]

Aven Mac (IRE) *N Bycroft* 48
3 ch f Indian Haven—Anamara (IRE) (Fairy King (USA))
3942[5] 4284[11] 4819[8] 5549[2] 6177[5] 6766[6] 6840[5] 7272[7]

Avenuesnalleyways (IRE) *R M Beckett* a73
2 b c Bertolini(USA) —Princess Mood (GER) (Muhtarram (USA))
5311[7]

Averoo *M D Squance* a61 71
4 br g Averti(IRE) —Roo (Rudimentary (USA))
880[7] 1258[15] 2088[12] 2418[13] 2864[9] 4998[2] (5443) 6039[2] (6568) 6828[4] 7062[11]

Averroes (IRE) *C G Cox* 86
2 ch c Galileo(IRE) —Shapely (USA) (Alleged (USA))
4985[4] (5499) 6133a[5]

Avertis *Stef Liddiard* a84 84
4 b g Averti(IRE) —Double Stake (USA) (Kokand (USA))
5745[3] 6357[3] ◆ 7000[7] 7194[10] 7271[3] 7603[8] 7741[10] (7783) 7854[9]

Avertitop *J Gallagher* a68 62
4 b g Averti(IRE) —Lucayan Belle (Cadeaux Genereux)
1047[10]

Avertor *R Charlton* 86
3 b g Oasis Dream—Avessia (Averti (IRE))
2250[2] (2700) 3362[4]

Avertuoso *B Smart* a77 85
5 b g Averti(IRE) —First Musical (First Trump)
3497[8] 4141[8] 4662[5] 5148[14] 5421[2] 7119[6]

Avery *R J Hodges* a18 62
5 gr g Averti(IRE) —Bandanna (Bandmaster (USA))
104[12]

Aviate *H R A Cecil* a76
2 b f Dansili—Emplane (USA) (Irish River (FR))
(7450) ◆

Aviso (GER) *B J Curley* a76 97
5 b g Tertullian(USA) —Akasma (GER) (Windwurf (GER))
124[7] 490[10] 850[6] 999[17] 4502[10]

Avitus *Micky Hammond* 64
3 gr g Monsieur Bond(IRE) —Top (Shirley Heights)
1522[3] 1925[2] 2371[7] 3454[9] 6236[2]

Avoca Dancer (IRE) *Karen George* a69 65
6 ch m Compton Place—Kashra (IRE) (Dancing Dissident (USA))
14[13] 166[7] 305[3] 487[4] 646[5] 853[7] 1421[7] 2184[3] (2921) 3224[4] 3732[7] 4082[7] 4533[10] 5019[6] 5502[5] 6213[5] ◆ 7052[5]

Avoir Choisi (IRE) *N Wilson* a74 68
3 ch g Choisir(AUS) —Dolara (IRE) (Dolphin Street (FR))
115[2] (230) 1331[3] 2578[10] 3115[9] 3734[6] 6052[12] 6640[7] 6984[8] 7762[7]

Avon Called *W M Brisbourne*
2 b f Avonbridge—Bahawir Pour (USA) (Green Dancer (USA))
6461[9]

Avon Castle *G L Moore* a63
2 b f Avonbridge—Castellina (USA) (Danzig Connection (USA))
7365[8] 7585[6] 7799[2] 7886[6]

Avoncreek *B P J Baugh* a45 58
5 b g Tipsy Creek(USA) —Avondale Girl (IRE) (Case Law)
1558[8] 1846[6] 2812[8] 3851[14] 4225[14] 5150[6] 6039[5] 6216[7]

Avongate *R Hannon* a33 78
2 b g Avonbridge—Palacegate Episode (IRE) (Drumalis)
2533[11] 4219[7] (4568) 6247[11] 7108[10]

Avon Grounds *J M Bradley* a5 58
2 b c Avonbridge—Good Grounds (USA) (Alleged (USA))
3500[9] 6214[9] 6364[6] 6938[10]

Avon Krystal *R Hannon* a47 23
2 b f Avonbridge—Kryssa (Kris)
4147[11] 4626[4] 5638[7] 5868[7]

Avon Lady *J R Fanshawe* 69
2 b f Avonbridge—Delightful Rhythm (USA) (Diesis)
5722[6] (6786)

Avonlini *B P J Baugh* a22 42
3 b f Bertolini(USA) —Avondale Girl (IRE) (Case Law)
3590[6] 3859[10] 4805[7] 5614[11]

Avon River *R Hannon* a72 82
2 ch c Avonbridge—Night Kiss (FR) (Night Shift (USA))
1577[7] (1726) 2702[9] (3340) 4565[7] 4901[3] 5265[9] 5742[7]

Avon Rock *J W Hills* 55
2 b g Avonbridge—Big Pink (IRE) (Bigstone (IRE))
6054[11] 6615[7] 6962[7]

Avonrose *M Johnston* 87
2 b f Avonbridge—Loveleaves (Polar Falcon (USA))
1920[8] (2360) 2957a[5] 3528[2] ◆ 4049[6] 5347[2] 5797[11] 6486[15]

Avontuur (FR) *Mrs R A Carr* a66 75
7 ch g Kabool—Ipoh (FR) (Funambule (USA))
975[8] 1655[8] 2531[10] (2686) 3021[3] 3488[2] 3612[2] 3730[7] 4015[4] 4134[4] 4285[6] 4657[8] 5391[4] (5516) 5597[2] 5960[7] 6764[3] 6984[11]

Avonvalley *M S Saunders* a76 73
2 b f Avonbridge—Piper's Ash (USA) (Royal Academy (USA))
1090[3] ◆ 1577[2] 1933[2] (2348) 2995[18] 4221[3] 4989[9] 5241[4]

A Votre Sante (GER) *W Baltromei* 48
3 ch f Samum(GER) —Auenspiel (GER) (Big Shuffle (USA))
5784a[8]

Avow (USA) *J S Moore* a66 70
2 b g Mingun(USA) —Knoosh (USA) (Storm Bird (CAN))
2771[8] 3138[12] 4080[3] 4488[12] 4915[5] 5583[3] 5935[7] 6122[2] 6292[2]

Avrilo *M S Saunders* a58 58
3 ch f Piccolo—Arctic High (Polar Falcon (USA))
964[3] 1270[7] 1982[8] 2562[4] 2654[2] 3281[8] 4051[6] 4223[2] 4483[2] 4829[4] 5383[3] 5645[2] 6856[4] 6939[2] 7068[7] 7370[9]

Await The Dawn (USA) *A P O'Brien* 93
2 b c Giant's Causeway(USA) —Valentine Band (USA) (Dixieland Band (USA))
5859[7]

Awaken *Miss Tracy Waggott* 47
8 b m Zafonic(USA) —Dawna (Polish Precedent (USA))
1472[8] 2965[8] 3314[3] 3545[4] 4804[8] 4944[9]

Awani *E F Vaughan* a47 44
3 b f Sakhee(USA) —Hatton Gardens (Auction Ring (USA))
4867[3] 5328[8] 6375[6]

Award Ceremony (IRE) *D K Weld* a63 99
4 b g Green Desert(USA) —Ripple Of Pride (IRE) (Sadler's Wells (USA))
2289a[6]

Awaseef (USA) *J H M Gosden* a72
2 ch f Haafhd—Emtyazat (Gone West (USA))
5639[3] 5984[2]

Awatuki (IRE) *J R Boyle* a87 61
6 b g Distant Music(USA) —Itkan (IRE) (Marju (IRE))
4378[10] 4957[7] 6966[3] 7623[5] 7775[10]

Awe *Mrs N S Evans* 35
5 b g Muhtarram(USA) —Fleet Of Light (Spectrum (IRE))
3207[12]

Awesome Act (USA) *J Noseda* a81 114
2 ch c Awesome Again(CAN) —Houdini's Honey (USA) (Mr Prospector (USA))
4756[2] 5400[2] 5664[3] (6416) ◆ 6849[9] 7304a[4]

Awesome Gem (USA) *Craig Dollase* a116 114
6 ch g Awesome Again(CAN) —Piano (USA) (Pentelicus (USA))
7311a[7]

Awesome Surprise (USA) *J Noseda* a72 75
3 b f Awesome Again(CAN) —Native Roots (IRE) (Indian Ridge)
3168[4] 4854[2] 5394[3] (5840)

Awinnersgame (IRE) *J Noseda* 108
3 b g Kyllachy—Polish Descent (IRE) (Danehill (USA))
1292[2] 2035[3] 2485[5] 3011[9] (5973) 6661[13]

A Wish For You *D K Ivory* a70 68
4 ch m Tumbleweed Ridge—Peperonata (IRE) (Cyrano De Bergerac)
108[11]

Awsaal *J L Dunlop* 61
2 b c Nayef(USA) —Design Perfection (USA) (Diesis)
7146[11]

Awzaan *M Johnston* 119
2 br c Alhaarth(IRE) —Nufoos (Zafonic (USA))
(3017) (3782) ◆ (6105) ◆ (6450)

Axinit (GER) *E J Creighton* a30 3
9 gr g Linamix(FR) —Assia (IRE) (Royal Academy (USA))
6210[12]

Axiom *L M Cumani* a85 109
5 ch h Pivotal—Exhibitor (USA) (Royal Academy (USA))
2412[2] 3014[6] (4423) 5249[4] 6270[2]

Aye Aye Digby (IRE) *H Candy* 98
4 b g Captain Rio—Jane Digby (IRE) (Magical Strike (USA))
1197[3] (1668) ◆ 2078[2] 2707[6] (4273) 4784[4] 5424[4] 6089[25] 6694[3] 6994[12]

Aypeeyes (IRE) *A King* a84 86
5 b g King Charlemagne(USA) —Habaza (IRE) (Shernazar)
82[4] 549[6] (1578)

Ayrpassionata *I Semple* 36
4 ch m Where Or When(IRE) —Least Said (USA) (Trempolino (USA))
3022[5]

Ay Tay Tate (IRE) *D Shaw* a50 68
3 b g Catcher In The Rye(IRE) —Vintage Belle (IRE) (Waajib)
1361[10] 4660[7] 5225[11] 5624[12] 6804[6] 7004[8]

Ayun Tara (FR) *X Nakkachdji* 104
2 gr f Martaline—Annee De La Femme (IRE) (Common Grounds)
(5713a) (6501a) 6929a[2]

Azaday (IRE) *C F Wall* 54
2 b f Azamour(IRE) —Generous Lady (Generous (IRE))
5741[12] 6759[10] 6992[17]

Azagra (IRE) *T Lemer* 73
3 b f Elusive City(USA) —Souvenir Souvenir (Highest Honor (FR))
7696a[0]

Azharia *R Hannon* a61 53
3 b f Oasis Dream—Presto Vento (Air Express (IRE))
810[3] 951[5] 1174[4] 1588[13] 2913[7] 3580[12] 4749[5] 5582[9] 7225[12]

Azif *Miss Gay Kelleway* 73
2 ch f Where Or When(IRE) —Dance Away (Pivotal)
1298[5] ◆ (1569) 2054[5] 2372[15] 2995[17] 4539[16] 5445[5] 6185[8]

Aziz (IRE) *Miss D Mountain* a36 49
3 b c Catcher In The Rye(IRE) —Imposition (UAE) (Be My Guest (USA))
1747[10]

Azizi *W J Haggas* a73 99
2 b c Haafhd—Harayir (USA) (Gulch (USA))
3546[4] (4201) (4651) 5433[2] (5864) ◆ 6664[4]

Azlak (USA) *C E Brittain* 58
2 ch c Shamardal(USA) —Nasaieb (IRE) (Fairy King (USA))
4080[7] 4314[13] 4953[6] 5864[6]

Azmeel *J H M Gosden* 101
2 b c Azamour(IRE) —Best Side (IRE) (King's Best (USA))
(4439) ◆ (5022) 6319a[12]

Azure Mist *M H Tompkins* a71 73
4 ch m Bahamian Bounty—Inquirendo (USA) (Roberto (USA))
2769[3] 3021[2] 5188[7] 5525[3] 5723[3] 6846[8] (6925)

Azygous *M W Easterby* a70 69
6 ch g Foxhound(USA) —Flag (Selkirk (USA))
4399[11] 5073[9]

Azzez Life *R C Guest* a5 38
2 br g Avonbridge—Glascoed (Adbass (USA))
4349[8] 5129[9] 5519[11] 5950[15] 7421[10]

Baahama (IRE) *A Fabre* 103
2 b f Anabaa(USA) —Silver Rain (FR) (Rainbow Quest (USA))
6045a[2] 6523a[8]

Baaher (USA) *J S Goldie* a71 62
5 b g War Chant(USA) —Raajiya (USA) (Gulch (USA))
5359[2] 5734[9] 6053[8] 6767[8]

Baan (USA) *H J Collingridge* a72 70
6 ch g Diesis—Madaen (USA) (Nureyev (USA))
142[3] 333[2] 591[2] 723[4] 3073[3] 3721[6] (4388) (4848) 5410[4] 5696[5] 6432[7] 6899[3] 7084[9]

Baariq *P W Chapple-Hyam* a74 82
3 b g Royal Applause—Second Of May (Lion Cavern (USA))
1679[7] 4056[8] 4386[7] 6348[8] 6780[5]

Baba Ghanoush *M J Attwater* a47 11
7 ch m Zaha(CAN) —Vrennan (Suave Dancer (USA))
56[3] 153[8] 2471[2] 513[8] 661[7] 802[3] 867[3] 3269[8] 7652[8]

Babajaga (IRE) *J M P Eustace* a29
2 ch f Night Shift(USA) —Art Fair (Alzao (USA))
3744[7] 4176[13]

Bab Al Salam (USA) *Saeed Bin Suroor* a106 99
3 b c Seeking The Gold(USA) —Encandiladora (ARG) (Equalize (USA))
(5221) (5648) (5904) 6453[3] (7226) ◆

Bab Al Shams (IRE) *Saeed Bin Suroor* 76
2 br c Cape Cross(IRE) —Shimna (Mr Prospector (USA))
6033[2] 6478[16]

Bab At The Bowster (IRE) *W J Haggas* 83
2 b f Footstepsinthesand—Charmingly (USA) (King Of Kings (IRE))
4257[3] (4693) 5265[7] (5853) (6481)

Babayigit (TUR) *O Yenihayat* a89
5 b h Royal Abjar(USA) —Prima Facie (Primo Dominie)
5587a[9]

Babel *M Wigham* a68 72
4 b m Xaar—Day Star (Dayjur (USA))
269[8] 467[7] 896[6]

Babilu *A G Newcombe* a74 65
4 ch m Lomitas—Creeking (Persian Bold)
2040[3] 2898[8] 3527[4] (4264)

Babycakes (IRE) *M L W Bell* a34 45
2 b f Marju(IRE) —Dark Rosaleen (IRE) (Darshaan)
6992[16] 7388[9]

Baby Dottie *P M Phelan* a72 69
2 ch f Dr Fong(USA) —Auntie Dot Com (Tagula (IRE))
3745[2] 4825[2] 6241[6] 6582[3] 6912[2] 7177[3]

Baby Is Here (IRE) *D J S Ffrench Davis* a21 46
3 br f Namid—Attymon Lill (IRE) (Marju (IRE))
7455[6]

Baby Josr *I A Wood* a63 59
3 br g Josr Algarhoud(IRE) —Bella Helena (Balidar)
(831) 986[3] 1574[5] 2417[4] 2863[10] 3741[7] 4749[2] 5582[8] 5791[9] 6224[7]

Baby Judge (IRE) *M C Chapman* a58 58
2 ch g Captain Rio—Darling Clementine (Lion Cavern (USA))
2147[7] 2978[13] 3317[4] 3606[10] 3918[5] 4173[5] 4370[8] 5253[8] 5372[6] 5552[6] 5938[3] (6035) 6923[8] 7055[3] 7218[6] 7333[9] 7674[4] 7791[8]

Babylonian *M Johnston* 70
2 b f Shamardal(USA) —Evil Empire (GER) (Acatenango (GER))
2503[3] 2699[2] 3820[5]

Baby Queen (IRE) *B P J Baugh* a40 68
3 b f Royal Applause—Kissing Time (Lugana Beach)
655[11] 758[5] 1173[7] 1359[9] (2162) (2654) 3118[8] 3704[6] 4829[9]

Baby Rock *C F Wall* 72
4 b g Selkirk(USA) —Vanishing Point (USA) (Caller I.D. (USA))
1248[11] 1890[12] 5406[3]

Baby's Memory (FR) *P Vovcenko*
5 b m Garuda(IRE) —Baby Sitting (FR) (Son Of Silver)
5301a[0]

Baby Strange *D Shaw* a94 105
5 gr g Superior Premium—The Manx Touch (IRE) (Petardia)
1321[4] 1699[13] (2405) 2941[6] 3141[17] 4037[10] 4423[11] 5104[4] 5615[8] 6359[11] 6723[3] 6944[10]

Bacarrita (FR) *L A Urbano-Grajales* a80 80
4 b m Marathon(USA) —Congostena (IRE) (Dr Devious (IRE))
5464a[3]

Back In The Red (IRE) *R A Harris* a79 69
5 ch g Redback—Fureur De Vivre (IRE) (Bluebird (USA))
(146) (304) 422[3] (518) 606[4] 757[7] 965[5] 3261[7] 3713[10]

Backlash *A W Carroll* a48 41
8 b m Fraam—Mezza Luna (Distant Relative)
117[5] 248[10] 469[13] 601[10]

Back On *G C Bravery* a22 46
2 b c Reset(AUS) —Teal Flower (Pivotal)
2295[4] 2595[7] 3167[12]

Back To Paris (IRE) *Paul Murphy* a49 99
7 b g Lil's Boy(USA) —Alisco (IRE) (Shalford (IRE))
7817[5]

Baddam *Ian Williams* 97
7 b g Mujahid(USA) —Aude La Belle (FR) (Ela-Mana-Mou)
1601[3] 2994[15] 4417[19] 5171[4] 5346[2] 6115[7]

Badge *R Charlton* 70
3 b g Acclamation—Be My Wish (Be My Chief (USA))
1419[6] 2070[3]

Badge Of Honour *M Johnston* a76
3 ch g Storming Home—Loch Katrine (Selkirk (USA))
201[2] ◆ 529[2] (658) (840)

Badiat Alzaman (IRE) *D M Simcock* a95 90
3 b f Zamindar(USA) —Fair Weather (IRE) (Marju (IRE))
1491[2] (1745) 2703[5] 3016[15] 5175[7] 5472[5] 6003[6] 7366[2]

Bad Mistone (FR) *H-A Pantall* 81
2 b c Bad As I Wanna Be(IRE) —Miss Bahamas (FR) (Shining Steel)
5117a[2]

Bad Moon Rising *J Akehurst* a57 51
4 ch g Piccolo—Janette Parkes (Pursuit Of Love)
131[2] 802[9]

Ba Dreamflight *H Morrison* a59 58
4 b g Noverre(USA) —Aunt Tate (Tate Gallery (USA))
213[8] 368[7] 2516[3] 2983[9] 3631[7] 3943[5] 5015[6] 5873[5]

Badtanman *Peter Grayson* a47 41
3 ch c Primo Valentino(IRE) —Pearls (Mon Tresor)
624[6] 758[4] 1157[3] 1311[7] 1529[3] 1644[7] 2394[4] 3063[5] 3853[6] 4137[6] 5105[8] 5336[8] 6161[11] 6699[9] 7510[6]

Bagamoyo *J R Fanshawe* a91 86
2 b c Acclamation—Queen Of Silk (IRE) (Brief Truce (USA))
(4515) 5038[3] 5769[2] 6585[2]

Bagber *P Monteith* a82 77
3 b g Diktat—Torcross (Vettori (IRE))
944[3] 1362[3] 1931[4] 2232[2] 2892[2] 3869[4] 4650[3] (5314) (6395) 6986[4]

Baggsy (IRE) *Miss J Feilden* a55
2 b f Statue Of Liberty(USA) —Nisibis (In The Wings)
6163[9] 7326[6]

Ba Globetrotter *M R Channon* a51 52
3 ch g Needwood Blade—Generous Share (Cadeaux Genereux)
1270[6] 1982[3] 2651[4] 2918[6] 3305[9] 3651[3]

Bagmati (FR) *M Droueche*
3 b g Freedom Cry—Melgarde (FR) (Garde Royale)
7037a[0]

Bahama Baileys *C A Dwyer* 51
4 ch g Bahamian Bounty—Baileys Silver (USA) (Marlin (USA))
4183[12] 5911[9] 6335[10] 6924[9] 7094[10]

Bahama Bay (GER) *A Fabre* 93
3 b f Dansili—Borgia (GER) (Acatenango (GER))
2754a[4]

Bahamarama (IRE) *R A Harris* a56 50
4 ch m Bahamian Bounty—Cole Slaw (Absalom)
487[11] 756[7] 895[9]

Bahamian Babe *M L W Bell* a78 93
3 ch f Bahamian Bounty—Baby Bunting (Wolfhound (USA))
1582[5] 2502[10] (2915) 3166[7] 4099[4] 5203[12] 6428[9]

Bahamian Ballad *J D Bethell* a49 54
4 ch m Bahamian Bounty—Record Time (Clantime)
2316[2] 2966[4] 3562[8] 4281[9] 4929[4] 5396[9] 6380[9]

Bahamian Ballet *E S McMahon* a83 86
7 ch g Bahamian Bounty—Plie (Superlative)
1518[2] ◆ 1685[7] 2359[3] 2840[5] 3422[2] 4141[5] 5148[10]

Bahamian Bay *M Brittain* a53 17
7 b m Bahamian Bounty—Moly (Inchinor)
62[9] 175[3] 327[10]

Bahamian Bliss *J A R Toller* a67 37
4 b m Bahamian Bounty—Fragrance (Mtoto)
1587[4] 2088[13] 3591[6] 4203[8] 5225[12] 6028[9] 7592[6]

Bahamian Bolt *R Bastiman* 8
2 ch g Bahamian Bounty—Feeling Blue (Missed Flight)
7289[10]

Bahamian Box *T Larriviere*
2 b c Bahamian Bounty—Bible Box (IRE) (Bin Ajwaad (IRE))
5850a[3]

Bahamian Ceilidh *B N Pollock* a65 76
3 ch f Bahamian Bounty—Crofters Ceilidh (Scottish Reel)
1272[4] 1618[3] 1985[3] 2386[3] 3304[5] 3926[7] 5345[10] 5612[12] 5900[8] 6362[8] 6570[13]

Bahamian Kid *R Hollinshead* a76 76
4 b g Bahamian Bounty—Barachois Princess (USA) (Barachois (CAN))
1775[9] (3075) 3331[13] 4019[6] 6250[11] 6725[11] 7192[4] 7496[3] 7577[9] 7845[2]

Bahamian Lad *R Hollinshead* a87 76
4 b g Bahamian Bounty—Danehill Princess (IRE) (Danehill (USA))
362[9] (691) (780) 901[6] 1313[5] 3164[7] 3529[3] 4507[9] 5916[5] (6120) 6434[10] (6723) 7155[2] 7511[3] 7702[2] 7875[4]

Bahamian Mouse (IRE) *Andrew Turnell* 33
3 ch f Bahamian Bounty—Minnina (IRE) (In The Wings)
4947[5] 5789[10]

Bahamian Music (IRE) *R A Fahey* a78 81
2 b f Bahamian Bounty—Strings (Unfuwain (USA))
2997[3] (4307) (4858) 5797[4] 6305[10]

Bahamian Reward (IRE) *W J Burke* 69
3 b g Bahamian Bounty—Classic Fan (USA) (Lear Fan (USA))
4392a[15]

Bahamian Sun (IRE) *Tom Dascombe*
2 ch g Bahamian Bounty—Firesteed (IRE) (Common Grounds)
4515[14] 5787[13]

Bahati (IRE) *J G Portman* 82
2 ch f Intikhab(USA) —Dawn Chorus (IRE) (Mukaddamah (USA))
(2494) 4245[7] 4539[4] ◆ 5797[6]

Baheeya *C E Brittain* 58
3 ch f Almutawakel—My American Beauty (Wolfhound (USA))
9981[0] 2179[7]

Bahiano (IRE) *C E Brittain* a89 81
8 ch g Barathea(IRE) —Trystero (Shareef Dancer (USA))
910[5] 1067[7] 2243[7]

Bahkov (IRE) *Andrew Turnell* a59 63
3 ch g Bahamian Bounty—Petrikov (IRE) (In The Wings)
1350[5] 1704[4] 2320[11] 3463[6] 3939[4] 4905[3] 5384[6] 6251[6]

Bahrain Storm (IRE) *Patrick J Flynn* a91 100
6 b g Bahhare(USA) —Dance Up A Storm (USA) (Storm Bird (CAN))
6851[8]

Bahraj (USA) *M Johnston* 67
2 bb f Key Of Luck(USA) —Alattrah (USA) (Shadeed (USA))
3910[4] 4463[6] 4928[4] (6557) ◆

Baibars (USA) *G A Butler* a53
2 bb c Gone West(USA) —Mombasa (USA) (Dynaformer (USA))
6943[8]

Baie Aux Anges (FR) *T Doumen*
4 b m Ange Gabriel(FR) —Sally's Cry (FR) (Freedom Cry)
5301a[0]

Baila Me (GER) *Saeed Bin Suroor* a106 110
4 b m Samum(GER) —Bandeira (GER) (Law Society (USA))
6093[2] ◆ 6853[6] (7131) ◆ 7293[14]

Baileys Cacao (IRE) *R Hannon* 104
3 b f Invincible Spirit(IRE) —Baileys Cream (Mister Baileys)
1353[12] 1873[2] 2278[5] 2703[4]

Baileys Red *J G Given* a48 48
3 b g Diktat—Red Ryding Hood (Wolfhound (USA))
2461[12] 3157[9]

Baileys Vision *M Johnston* 68
2 b f Kyllachy—Southern Psychic (USA) (Alwasmi (USA))
1968[2] 2388[2] 3086[14] 4035[4] 5369[12] 6035[5] 6844[4] 7079[7]

Bailieborough (IRE) *B Ellison* a64 62
10 b g Charnwood Forest(IRE) —Sherannda (USA) (Trempolino (USA))
25[5] 221[2] 353[6] 1014[14] 1131[8]

Baizically (IRE) *G A Swinbank* a94 76
6 ch g Galileo(IRE) —Baize (Efisio)
1690[12] 2200[5] (2629) (2720) 3107[2] 3266[7] 3679[6]

Bajan Parkes *E J Alston* 91
6 bb g Zafonic(USA) —My Melody Parkes (Teenoso (USA))
3573[4] 4561[9] (5308) 5961[2] 6281[7] 6681[16] 6840[4] 7170[5]

Bajan Pride *R A Fahey* a67 71
5 b g Selkirk(USA) —Spry (Suave Dancer (USA))
384[6] 580[6] 656[5] 981[4] 1276[2] 1777[6] 7499[4] 7650[5] 7784[5]

Bajan Tryst (USA) *K A Ryan* a79 87
3 bb g Speightstown(USA) —Garden Secrets (USA) (Time For A Change (USA))
(947) ◆ 1727[7] 2279[13] (3688) 4338[11] 5203[7] 5523[2] 5799[13]

Ba Jetstream *F Jordan* a15 52
2 b g Monsieur Bond(IRE) —Merch Rhyd-Y-Grug (Sabrehill (USA))
2547[6] 2771[11] 3203[4] 3547[3] 4188[3] 7055[14] 7514[7] 7722[10]

Bakoulele (FR) *C Scandella*
2 b c Okawango(USA) —Fountain Of Joy (IRE) (King's Theatre (IRE))
5850a[6]

Balaagha (USA) *M A Jarvis* 100
3 b f Mr Greeley(USA) —Echo Echo Echo (USA) (Eastern Echo (USA))
1302[2] (1825) 3102[2] 3746[2] 4259[2] 5064[6] 6267[U]

Balais Folly (FR) *D Haydn Jones* a47 53
4 ch g Act One—Bhima (Polar Falcon (USA))
6660[9] 6782[7] 7109[11]

Balata *B R Millman* a76 83
4 b g Averti(IRE) —Manila Selection (USA) (Manila (USA))
157[3] 457[10] 2713[2] 3211[6] 4019[4] 4607[14] 4871[5] (5544) 5884[6] (6187) 6645[2]

Balcarce Nov (ARG) *T P Tate* a55 110
4 b h Romanov(IRE) —Rosada Fitz (ARG) (Fitzcarraldo (ARG))
524a[2] 769a[4] 1009a[10] 4077[4] (4779) 5232[5] 5863[2] 6270[16] 6812[8]

Baldemar *R A Fahey* 95
4 b g Namid—Keen Melody (USA) (Sharpen Up)
1018[14] 1278[12] 1849[11] (2707) 3389[9] 5695[11] (6050) 6270[17] 6675[7] 6994[8]

Balducci *A M Balding* a76
2 b c Dansili—Miss Meltemi (IRE) (Miswaki Tern (USA))
7764[2]

Balerno *Mrs L J Mongan* a57 58
10 b g Machiavellian(USA) —Balabina (USA) (Nijinsky (CAN))
23[2] 210[8] 294[7] 496[8] 587[7]

Balfour House *D Burchell* a1 20
6 b g Wizard King—Tymeera (Timeless Times (USA))
5124[10] 5630[9]

Balierus (GER) *Saeed Bin Suroor* 64
2 b c Singspiel(IRE) —Brighella (GER) (Lomitas)
6423[6] 6982[7]

Baligha *G A Swinbank* a52 52
4 ch m Alhaarth(IRE) —Najmat Jumairah (USA) (Mr Prospector (USA))
786[7] 1101[5] 2030[8] 2268[5]

Balilla (ITY) *Laura Grizzetti* 93
4 b m Northern Flagship(USA) —Flower Show (Royal Academy (USA))
6715a[9]

Balius (IRE) *Saeed Bin Suroor* a120 120
6 b h Mujahid(USA) —Akhla (USA) (Nashwan (USA))
(774a) ◆ 1011a[13] 2117a[7] (5587a) 6506a[11] 7313a[5]

Baliyana (IRE) *John M Oxx* 104
3 gr f Dalakhani(IRE) —Balanka (IRE) (Alzao (USA))
(1911a) 3088[10]

Ballachulish *H Candy* 56
2 b g Kyllachy—Romantic Drama (IRE) (Primo Dominie)
3317[5] 4243[6] 4825[7] 5256[12] 6328[7]

Ballade De La Mer *A G Foster* a44 51
3 b f Ishiguru(USA) —Riviere Rouge (Forzando)
2790[11] 4039[2] 4755[4] 5359[9] 7118[5]

Ballantrae (IRE) *M L W Bell* 92
3 b f Diktat—Badawi (USA) (Diesis)
5005[6]

Ballantynes (IRE) *F & S Brogi* 83
4 b m Imperial Ballet(IRE) —Glamour Stock (USA) (Marfa (USA))
1043a[8]

Ballarina *E J Alston* 49
3 b f Compton Place—Miss Uluwatu (IRE) (Night Shift (USA))
2157[6] 2394[6]

Ballet Dancer (IRE) *M A Jarvis* a69 74
3 b f Refuse To Bend(IRE) —Showlady (USA) (Theatrical (IRE))
(1532) 2008[3] 3026[4] 4008[8] 4720[7]

Ballinteni *M G Quinlan* a89 100
7 b g Machiavellian(USA) —Silabteni (USA) (Nureyev (USA))
1216[7] 1433[7] 1750[3] 2639[3] 3431[9] 6210[4] 6239[5] 6812[11]

Ballivor (IRE) *W T Farrell* a76 88
6 b g Marju(IRE) —Delphinus (Soviet Star (USA))
5490a[20]

Ballodair (IRE) *R A Fahey* 80
2 b g Antonius Pius(USA) —Vision Of Dreams (Efisio)
2853[2] (3487) ◆ 4035[2] 4525[10] 5136[8] 6247[8]

Ballyalla *R Hannon* a17 82
3 b f Mind Games—Molly Brown (Rudimentary (USA))
1860[5] 2674[14] 2948[5] 3537[7] 4902[4] 5285[3] 6583[8]

Ballycommon (USA) *K A Ryan* 47
2 b g Roman Ruler(USA) —Seth's Choice (USA) (Rahy (USA))
3910[5]

Ballycroy Boy (IRE) *Miss M E Rowland* a71 12
4 b g Captain Rio—Royal Baldini (USA) (Green Dancer (USA))
304[3] 489[3] (619) 886[2] ◆ 975[2] 1480[4] 2235[12]

Ballyvonane (USA) *L A Dace* a46 44
2 b c Strong Hope(USA) —Wild Light (USA) (Tabasco Cat (USA))
1749[4] 2328[10] 5778[10] 6610[3] 7063[7] 7453[9] 7514[5]

Balnagore *J L Dunlop* a79 74
5 bb g Tobougg(IRE) —Bogus Mix (IRE) (Linamix (FR))
(1604) 2039[8] 2923[10] 3977[2] (4644) 5667[7] 6244[3] 6724[6]

Balsha (USA) *E A L Dunlop* a47 52
2 ch f Mr Greeley(USA) —Carefree Cheetah (USA) (Trempolino (USA))
6062[13] 7034[13] 7429[6]

Balthazaar's Gift (IRE) *C G Cox* a56 119
6 b h Xaar—Thats Your Opinion (Last Tycoon)
257a[9] 418a[3] (638a) 1010a[11] 3398[3] 3846[2] 4406[2] (5024) 5710a[7] 6503a[5]

Baltic Ben (USA) *Eve Johnson Houghton* 60
2 b g Johannesburg(USA) —Baltic Dip (IRE) (Benny The Dip (USA))
6393[9] 6728[11]

Baltimore Clipper (USA) *P F I Cole* a72 79
2 b c Mizzen Mast(USA) —Resounding Grace (USA) (Thunder Gulch (USA))
3395[6] 3716[2] 5428[2] 5864[2] 6728[5]

Baltimore Jack (IRE) *T D Walford* a64 76
5 b g Night Shift(USA) —Itsibitsi (IRE) (Brief Truce (USA))
1244[3] 2529[9] 3070[5] (4804) 5438[3] (6017) ◆ (6218) 6490[3] 7014[10]

Baltimore Patriot (IRE) *R Curtis* a69 63
6 b g Tiger Hill(IRE) —Berenice (Groom Dancer (USA))
7279[3] 7415[2] 7594[4] ◆

Balwearie (IRE) *Miss L A Perratt* 63
8 b g Sesaro(USA) —Eight Mile Rock (Dominion)
3911[S]

Balzarine *M Blanshard* a48 37
3 ch f Auction House(USA) —Worsted (Whittingham (IRE))
3278[9] 5010[5] 5348[7] 5751[6] 6170[8]

Bamboo Ere (JPN) *A Adachi* a107 107
6 ch h Afleet(CAN) —Rainbow Wood (Rainbow Quest (USA))
1010a[4]

Banana Republic (IRE) *P F I Cole* a75 71
2 ch c Danehill Dancer(IRE) —Elite Guest (IRE) (Be My Guest (USA))
4048[7] 5371[2] 6548[7]

Banco Busto (IRE) *H S Howe* a13 37
2 b f Chineur(FR) —Banco Solo (Distant Relative)
6164[14] 6567[10]

Bandama (IRE) *Mrs A J Perrett* a74 96
6 b g Green Desert(USA) —Orinoco (IRE) (Darshaan)
2003[5] 2706[13] (6612)

Bandanaman (IRE) *G A Swinbank* a43 76
3 b g Danehill Dancer(IRE) —Band Of Angels (IRE) (Alzao (USA))
1466[10] 1925[8] 2662[5]

Banda Sea (IRE) *P J Makin* a68 61
3 b c Tagula(IRE) —Non Ultra (USA) (Peintre Celebre (USA))
356[2] 7228[4] 7456[9]

Bandear (IRE) *C E Brittain* a31 63
2 b f Royal Applause—Royals Special (IRE) (Caerleon (USA))
3468[5] 4239[3] 4946[3] 5589[12] 6035[3] 6418[11]
Bandeau Charmer *C N Kellett*
6 b m Band On The Run—Fair Enchantress (Enchantment I)
3951[6]
Bandstand *B Smart* a63
3 b g Royal Applause—Incise (Dr Fong (USA))
7853[2]
Ban Garda (IRE) *J S Moore* a73 54
3 b f Daggers Drawn(USA) —Lifeguard (IRE) (Desert Prince (IRE))
4854[6]
Banged Up Abroad (IRE) *M G Quinlan*
2 b c Royal Applause—Annette Vallon (IRE) (Efisio)
5778[11]
Bankable (IRE) *G L Moore* 121
5 b h Medicean—Dance To The Top (Sadler's Wells (USA))
(642a) ◆ 1011a[5] 2117a[3] 5447[2] (5995)
Bank Guard (IRE) *Rod Collet* 95
4 ch g Peintre Celebre(USA) —Blue Cloud (IRE) (Nashwan (USA))
3045a[9]
Banknote *A M Balding* a102 103
7 b h Zafonic(USA) —Brand (Shareef Dancer (USA))
340a[10] 615a[6]
Banks And Braes *R Hannon* 72
2 b c Red Ransom(USA) —Bonnie Doon (IRE) (Grand Lodge (USA))
5006[3] 5251[5] 5879[4] 6736[7]
Bannaby (FR) *M Delcher-Sanchez* 115
6 ch h Dyhim Diamond(IRE) —Trelakari (FR) (Lashkari)
2118a[3] 3969a[6]
Bantu *J H M Gosden* a66 1
4 bb m Cape Cross(IRE) —Lalindi (IRE) (Cadeaux Genereux)
2877[10] 3508[8] 5718[11]
Banyan Tree (IRE) *A P O'Brien* 92
2 b c Danehill Dancer(IRE) —User Friendly (Slip Anchor)
7404a[7]
Baoli *R Hannon* a38 55
2 b f Dansili—Thorntoun Piccolo (Groom Dancer (USA))
2175[12] 6109[9] 7029[9] 7389[8]
Barack (IRE) *Francis Ennis* a89 94
3 b c Pyrus(USA) —Morna's Fan (FR) (Lear Fan (USA))
5490a[5]
Baraconti (IRE) *R A Fahey* a59 67
2 b g Barathea(IRE) —Continuous (IRE) (Darshaan)
6214[5] 6672[10]
Barafundle Boy *J J Bridger* a33 40
2 b g Deportivo—Barawin (FR) (Fijar Tango (FR))
5749[11] 6108[15] 6696[9] 7177[10] 7429[8]
Baralaka *Sir Mark Prescott* a67
2 ch g Barathea(IRE) —Shakalaka Baby (Nashwan (USA))
5571[10] 5778[5] ◆ 6629[7]
Barastar *J R Boyle* 57
2 b g Sampower Star—Barachois Princess (USA) (Barachois (CAN))
2771[7] 3584[10] 3767[5]
Barataria *R Bastiman* a78 76
7 ch g Barathea(IRE) —Aethra (USA) (Trempolino (USA))
362[3] 683[2] 807[6] 1479[2] 2274[10] 3264[9] (4389) 5441[16] 6023[15] 6987[8]
Barathea's Acclaim *P R Hedger* a48
3 b f Acclamation—Missbarathea (IRE) (Barathea (IRE))
5572[12] 6029[5] 6608[7] 7195[11]
Barawin (IRE) *K R Burke* a81 79
4 ch m Hawk Wing(USA) —Cosabawn (IRE) (Barathea (IRE))
84[4] 226[9]
Barbarian *A D Brown* a71 73
3 b g Noverre(USA) —Love In The Mist (USA) (Silver Hawk (USA))
829[2] 1574[2] 2209[9] 2685[5] 3358[2] 5731[6] 6052[11] 6951[5] 7211[6] 7753[2] 7863[4]
Barbaricus (AUS) *Danny O'Brien* 114
5 gr g Lion Hunter(AUS) —Light Of Erin (AUS) (Palace Music (USA))
527a[3] ◆ 703a[9]
Barbecue Eddie (USA) *Doug Watson* a108
5 bb g Stormy Atlantic(USA) —The Green Owl (USA) (Carson City (USA))
264a[9] 770a[8]
Barbee (IRE) *E A L Dunlop* a59 75
3 ch f Night Shift(USA) —Barbizou (FR) (Selkirk (USA))
1743[7] 2827[7]
Barbegal (USA) *A Fabre* 99
2 ch c Elusive Quality(USA) —Sunlit Silence (USA) (Trempolino (USA))
(5088a) 5708a[5]
Barbeito *M D Squance* a40 38
3 b f Zaha(CAN) —Tinta (Robellino (USA))
2577[6] 3005[12]
Barbirolli *W B Stone* a60 59
7 b g Machiavellian(USA) —Blushing Barada (USA) (Blushing Groom (FR))
935[6] (1200) 1463[8] (1938) 1974[4] 2222[6] 2634[3] 2971[6] 3023[3] 3247[3] 3594[4] 3974[5] 4193[9] 4640[6] (4927) 5210[2] 7847[5]
Bar Blu (IRE) *G A Swinbank*
4 b m Mull Of Kintyre(USA) —Ruwy (Soviet Star (USA))
3862[13]
Barcode *R Hannon* a53 57
3 b f Tobougg(IRE) —Truly Madly Deeply (Most Welcome)
77[2] 759[9] 943[8]

Bari Bay *J W Mullins* a51 53
3 b f Bahri(USA) —Sea Nymph (IRE) (Spectrum (IRE))
1066[11] 1250[7] 1967[10] 2487[2] 2772[4] 4735[3] 5579[4] 5812[5]
Bariolo (FR) *Noel T Chance* a66 72
5 b g Priolo(USA) —La Bardane (FR) (Marignan (USA))
559[6] 734[7]
Barlaman (USA) *Saeed Bin Suroor* a74
2 ch c Langfuhr(CAN) —Party Circuit (USA) (Kingmambo (USA))
5311[4] 5571[3] 6026[2] 6347[3] 6802[2]
Barley Bree (IRE) *Mrs A Duffield* 40
4 ch m Danehill Dancer(IRE) —Aunty Mary (Common Grounds)
3003[7] 3611[13] 4467[6] 4929[13]
Barlia (IRE) *C Laffon-Parias* 63
3 b f Montjeu(IRE) —Suite Royale (USA) (Diesis)
6753a[4] 7386a[9]
Barliffey (IRE) *D J Coakley* a78 78
4 b g Bahri(USA) —Kildare Lady (IRE) (Indian Ridge)
2641[4] 3526[2] 4247[5] 5003[4] 5914[3] 6117[8] 7360[3]
Barndeh (IRE) *Lee Smyth* a56 53
6 b g Marju(IRE) —Sweetest Thing (IRE) (Prince Rupert (FR))
2390[4] 4861[9]
Barnes Bridge *M J Attwater*
4 ch g Zaha(CAN) —Mo Stopher (Sharpo)
3984[9] 4205[11]
Barney McGrew (IRE) *M Dods* a101 112
6 b g Mark Of Esteem(IRE) —Success Story (Sharrood (USA))
1018[5] 2941[2] 3389[2] 4037[11] 4330[2] 4523[21] (5132) 5860[15] 6091[2]
Barnezet (GR) *J Pearce* a76 68
3 b f Invincible Spirit(IRE) —Le Meridien (IRE) (Magical Wonder (USA))
(34) (784) 7682[8]
Barodine *R J Hodges* a61 59
6 ch g Barathea(IRE) —Granted (FR) (Cadeaux Genereux)
105[5] 187[4] 346[11] 500[5] 711[2] (775) 1042[6] 1153[4] 1538[5] 2400[5] 2764[4] 3077[3] 3470[3] 3927[2] 4263[7] 4735[2] 5246[2] 7594[10] 7688[7] 7750[9]
Baron De'L (IRE) *Edward P Harty* a78 104
6 ch g In The Wings—Lightstorm (IRE) (Darshaan)
1546a[4] 3089[10]
Barongo (IRE) *U Suter* 114
4 ch g Distant Music(USA) —Blazing Soul (IRE) (Common Grounds)
2522a[4] 5932a[8]
Baron Otto (IRE) *W J Haggas* a49 73
3 b g Anabaa(USA) —Marie Laurencin (Peintre Celebre (USA))
2282[5] 2681[4] 3009[12]
Baronovici (IRE) *D W Barker* 59
4 b g Namid—Allegrina (IRE) (Barathea (IRE))
1057[5] 1243[3] 1650[6] 1924[7]
Barons Spy (IRE) *R J Price* a84 93
8 b g Danzero(AUS) —Princess Accord (USA) (D'Accord (USA))
1894[8] 2059[4] 2241[5] 2976[7] (3318) 3802[2] 4353[3] 5206[9] 5529[4] 5695[4] 5959[6] 6540[6]
Barony (IRE) *Lee Smyth*
3 ch g Swift Gulliver(IRE) —Musical Flyer (IRE) (Prince Of Birds (USA))
7863[10]
Barouda (FR) *J-M Beguigne* 105
2 ch f My Risk(FR) —Baroudia (FR) (Kaldoun) (6929a)
Barq (IRE) *Saeed Bin Suroor* a68
2 br c Green Desert(USA) —Zaeema (Zafonic (USA))
7376[3] ◆
Barraland *J S Goldie* a67 77
4 b g Compton Place—Dance Land (IRE) (Nordance (USA))
2717[11] 3149[9]
Barreq (USA) *B Smart* a79
2 b c Proud Citizen(USA) —The Wrong Face (USA) (Marlin (USA))
7644[2] 7800[3]
Barricado (FR) *E J O'Neill* a74 87
4 b g Anabaa(USA) —Aube D'Irlande (FR) (Selkirk (USA))
1766[2] 1964[5] (2402) 3045a[5] 3419a[4] 4335a[8] (5464a)
Barshiba (IRE) *D R C Elsworth* a84 114
5 ch m Barathea(IRE) —Dashiba (Dashing Blade)
1301[4] 1697[3] 3139[5] (3619) (4094) 4522[4] 5201[4] 6850[7]
Barter *L M Cumani* 57
3 ch f Daylami(IRE) —Souk (IRE) (Ahonoora)
1844[8] 2178[9] 2763[7]
Bartica (IRE) *R Hannon* a70 62
3 b c Tagula(IRE) —More Risk (IRE) (Fayruz)
397[7] (547) 1429[2]
Barton Chancer *W G M Turner* a32
2 b f Dubai Destination(USA) —Lloc (Absalom)
1147[9] 1637[5] 2457[6]
Barton Sands (IRE) *Andrew Reid* a63 43
12 b g Tenby—Hetty Green (Bay Express)
320[5] 711[8] 1589[8] 2182[11]
Barwell Bridge *S Kirk* a92 96
3 b g Red Ransom(USA) —Sentimental Value (USA) (Diesis)
101[2] 138[2] (209) 1707[2] (1992) 3051[3] 4420[13] 4767[4] 5230[10] 6165[4] 6302[7]
Barynya *Sir Michael Stoute* 76
3 ch f Pivotal—Russian Rhythm (USA) (Kingmambo (USA))
1327[3] ◆ 1844[3] 3876[2]
Barzan (IRE) *Tom Dascombe* 84
2 ch c Danehill Dancer(IRE) —Le Montrachet (Nashwan (USA))
2033[3] (2218) 2702[5] 3967a[7] 6478[20]
Barzini (GER) *Uwe Ostmann* 97
2 b c Lando(GER) —Bella Flora (GER) (Slip Anchor)
6151a[2] 7314a[8]

Basalt (IRE) *T J Pitt* a84 86
5 b g Rock Of Gibraltar(IRE) —Sniffle (IRE) (Shernazar)
7005[2] 7573[6]
Basaltico (IRE) *L M Cumani* 113
5 b h Shantou(USA) —Sfilza (Indian Ridge)
263a[13] 437a[7] 699a[3] 4484[6] 5023[8] 5248[4] 5609[2] 6961a[7] 7215a[18]
Bashkirov *Luke Comer* a98 114
4 ch h Galileo(IRE) —Tina Heights (Shirley Heights)
4412a[16] 5891a[7]
Baskerville *Mrs L Williamson* a66 69
6 b g Foxhound(USA) —Miss Up N Go (Gorytus (USA))
4561[8]
Basle *Miss Gay Kelleway* a73
2 b f Trade Fair—Gibaltarik (IRE) (Jareer (USA))
6722[2] (7190)
Basque Beauty *W J Haggas* 96
4 b m Nayef(USA) —River Cara (USA) (Irish River (FR))
1860[11] 3116[13]
Basra (IRE) *Miss Jo Crowley* a88 88
6 b g Soviet Star(USA) —Azra (IRE) (Danehill (USA))
(163) 550[2] 893[4] 1750[5] 2641[5] 3578[5] 5062[6] 7607[2]
Bassel (FR) *H-A Pantall* 104
4 b h Daliapour(IRE) —Bint El Hawa (FR) (River Mist (USA))
5932a[6] 6527a[P]
Bassinet (USA) *J A R Toller* a83 80
5 b m Stravinsky(USA) —Berceau (USA) (Alleged (USA))
156[5] (726) 915[8] 1319[7] 1966[2] 2475[10] 3169[8] 6634[7]
Batchworth Blaise *E A Wheeler* a60 60
6 b g Little Jim—Batchworth Dancer (Ballacashtal (CAN))
114[6] 234[7] 1535[13] 1710[4] 1876[8] 2330[5] 4305[11] 5120[11] 5429[14] 6399[3] 7517[9] (7653) 7691[3]
Bateau Bleu *P C Haslam* a59 62
2 b g Auction House(USA) —Fresh Look (IRE) (Alzao (USA))
1277[9] 2099[7] 2997[10] (6391) 6639[4]
Bateleur *M R Channon* a57 74
5 b g Fraam—Search Party (Rainbow Quest (USA))
646[6] 854[6] 946[2] 1076[5] 1558[13] 1846[2] 2202[2] 2418[6] (2564) 2680[2] 2920[3] 3208[3] (3261) 3866[2] 3995[4] 4607[11] 5020[4] 5065[5] 5525[8] 5955[14]
Batgirl *John Berry* 33
2 ch f Mark Of Esteem(IRE) —Serriera (FR) (Highest Honor (FR))
6679[10] 7182[17]
Bathwick Gino *P D Evans* a55 55
2 b g Alamshar(IRE) —Rockstine (IRE) (Ballad Rock)
1249[6] 1783[4] 2861[7] 4912[6] 5224[4] 5613[5] 5835[5] 6345[9]
Bathwick Gold (IRE) *P D Evans* 73
2 b c Noverre(USA) —Taalluf (USA) (Hansel (USA))
4900[11] (5934) 6486[22] 7290[11]
Bathwick Man *D E Pipe* a52 57
4 b g Mark Of Esteem(IRE) —Local Abbey (IRE) (Primo Dominie)
4625[3] 5812[2] 5885[9]
Bathwick Pursuit *P D Evans* a54 37
3 b g Pursuit Of Love—Society Rose (Saddlers' Hall (IRE))
2074[10] 2543[5] 3303[6] 3473[5] 3919[14]
Bathwick Xaara *J G Portman* a60 69
2 br f Xaar—Anapola (GER) (Polish Precedent (USA))
2494[4] 3248[4] 3576[3] 4539[15] 5166[6] 6169[6] 6775[8]
Battimoore (IRE) *I W McInnes* a52 52
3 b f Beckett(IRE) —Silver Spoon (IRE) (College Chapel)
3449[8] 4131[2] 6433[5] 7371[7] 7572[6] 7614[4] 7787[9]
Battle *H Morrison* a61 74
3 gr g Compton Place—Molly Moon (IRE) (Primo Dominie)
1196[4] ◆ 1814[10] 4483[3] (5383) 6387[4]
Battlecat *A Fabre* 84
2 b c Tiger Hill(IRE) —Applecross (Glint Of Gold)
6507a[4]
Battle Honour *H Candy* 58
2 b g Mark Of Esteem(IRE) —Proserpine (Robellino (USA))
7146[14]
Battlemaiden (IRE) *Saeed Bin Suroor* a74 75
2 br f Shamardal(USA) —Kirk (Selkirk (USA))
4257[6] 4792[4] 5478[2] 5808[2] 6418[6]
Battle Paint (USA) *J H M Gosden* a106 100
5 b h Tale Of The Cat(USA) —Black Speck (USA) (Arch (USA))
1006[3] 5232[11]
Battle Planner (USA) *I Semple* a84 86
3 b c War Chant(USA) —The Administrator (USA) (Afleet (CAN))
2210[5] 3564[2] 5334[13] 5979[3] 6671[4]
Battle Royal (IRE) *B Smart* 62
3 b c Refuse To Bend(IRE) —Style Of Life (USA) (The Minstrel (CAN))
4277[4] 4660[4] 5544[4] 6411[11]
Battle Study (IRE) *A J McCabe* a49 66
2 bb g Fath(USA) —Osprey Point (IRE) (Entrepreneur)
5408[4] 6181[2] 7376[6]
Battling Lil (IRE) *J L Spearing* a50 56
5 b m Daggers Drawn(USA) —Salva (Grand Lodge (USA))
211[7]
Baunagain (IRE) *P W Chapple-Hyam* a81 92
4 b g No Excuse Needed—Manuka Honey (Mystiko (USA))
3164[2] (3787) 4500[6] 5104[12] 5646[7] 7511[10] 7676[9] 7833[3] 7891[6]

Bavarian Nordic (USA) *Mrs A Duffield* a86 81
4 b g Barathea(IRE) —Dubai Diamond (Octagonal (NZ))
3034[5] 3761[5] 4003[6] 4229[5] ◆ 4597[3] 5375[4] 5622[2] 6648[7]
Bavarica *Miss J Feilden* a72 71
7 b m Dansili—Blue Gentian (USA) (Known Fact (USA))
(28) 132[3] 171[2] 285[3] 344[9] 470[5] (651) 830[6] 948[3] 1179[3] 1834[7] 2244[10] 2675[2] 2764[3] 3322[5] 3777[3] (4269) 4658[10] 5910[7] 6392[3] 7587[2] 7667[2] 7752[3]
Bawaardi (IRE) *R A Fahey* a80 76
3 b g Acclamation—Global Trend (Bluebird (USA))
(5965) 6731[6] 7356[6] 7672[3] 7769[2] 7812[2]
Bawadi (USA) *Saeed Bin Suroor* a88 87
3 bb c Medaglia D'Oro(USA) —Chartreuse (CAN) (Danzatore (CAN))
(4979) 5315[4] 6239[8]
Bawdsey Bank *John A Harris* 21
3 b g Tipsy Creek(USA) —Busy (IRE) (In The Wings)
6573[7] 7126[10]
Bayberry King (USA) *Mrs A M Thorpe* a47 52
6 b g Lear Fan(USA) —Myrtle (Batshoof)
131[12]
Baybshambles (IRE) *R E Barr* 77
5 b g Compton Admiral—Payvashooz (Ballacashtal (CAN))
1768[9] 1951[2] ◆ 2363[5] 3065[5] 3304[2] (3607) 3828[8] 4283[8] 4399[4] 4891[7] 6489[12]
Baycat (IRE) *J G Portman* 92
3 b g One Cool Cat(USA) —Greta D'Argent (IRE) (Great Commotion (USA))
1324[11] 1869[8] 2329[10]
Bay Knight (IRE) *W McCreery* a87 81
3 b c Johannesburg(USA) —Sabeline (IRE) (Caerleon (USA))
(7181) (7341a)
Baylini *Ms J S Doyle* a97 90
5 gr m Bertolini(USA) —Bay Of Plenty (FR) (Octagonal (NZ))
124[2] 284[3] 445[3] 724[11] 864[2] 913[9] 1003[4] 1696[9] 1859[5] 2239[2] 2407[4] 2641[8] 7574[6]
Bazart *B J Llewellyn* a76 83
7 b g Highest Honor(FR) —Summer Exhibition (Royal Academy (USA))
3423[6]
Baze Mac *N Bycroft* 29
2 b f Needwood Blade—Miss Maisey (IRE) (Entrepreneur)
4844[10] 5519[14] 6841[12] 7242[14]
Bazergan (IRE) *C E Brittain* a96 94
4 b g Machiavellian(USA) —Lunda (IRE) (Soviet Star (USA))
724[3] 801[5] 1003[9] 1458[11] 1673[5] 2468[3] (4930) 5262[6] 5794[5] 6106[12]
Bazsharani *P D Evans* a46 67
2 bl f Auction House(USA) —Ewenny (Warrshan (USA))
2778[4] 3370[2] 3500[5] 5282[6] 5583[7] 5899[7] 6590[12]
Beach Boy (IRE) *S Wynne* a26 30
2 ch c Pearl Of Love(IRE) —Mermaid Beach (Slew O'Gold (USA))
2575[11] 3226[10] 3468[9] 4018[8]
Beach Bunny (IRE) *Kevin Prendergast* a70 110
4 b m High Chaparral(IRE) —Miss Hawai (FR) (Peintre Celebre (USA))
1913a[3] 2285a[2] 3412a[2] 4253a[4] 4609a[7] 6298a[4]
Beacon Lodge (IRE) *C G Cox* 117
4 b h Clodovil(IRE) —Royal House (FR) (Royal Academy (USA))
996[7] (1865) 2483[2] (2953a) 4419[6] 5426[3] 6505a[5]
Be A Devil *W R Muir* a80 33
2 ch c Dubai Destination(USA) —Devil's Imp (IRE) (Cadeaux Genereux)
2979[9] 3226[6] 6254[5] (6829) 7003[11] 7363[2] ◆ 7611[3] 7654[2] 7804[2]
Bea Menace (USA) *P F I Cole* a90 83
3 b f Mizzen Mast(USA) —Questonia (Rainbow Quest (USA))
2079[15] 2498[2] 2632[5] 2879[7] 3630[5] (4240) 4700[2] 4940[3] (6537) (7027) 7181[5]
Bear Tobouggie *G A Swinbank* 58
2 b f Tobougg(IRE) —Brave Bear (Bold Edge)
7288[7]
Beat Baby (IRE) *J Howard Johnson* 65
2 ch g Johannesburg(USA) —Najiya (Nashwan (USA))
3875[9] 5234[7]
Beat Companion *P Howling* a69 59
3 ch c Beat Hollow—Comanche Companion (Commanche Run)
2395[7] 4057[9] 4789[4]
Beat Faster *J G Given* a53 48
3 b f Beat Hollow—Supersonic (Shirley Heights)
6390[5] 6950[5] 7324[10]
Beat Seven *Miss Gay Kelleway* 102
3 ch f Beat Hollow—Twenty Seven (IRE) (Efisio)
2846[7] 3016[7] 3641[5]
Beat Surrender (FR) *G M Lyons* a90 96
2 b c Bertolini(USA) —Waking Redhead (USA) (Miswaki (USA))
5133[8] 5486a[4]
Beat The Bell *J A Osborne* a98 75
4 b g Beat All(USA) —Bella Beguine (Komaite (USA))
86[5] 5959[4] 6278[11] 6631[3] 7133[6] 7454[6] 7613[10]
Beat The Devil *T R George* 57
3 ch g Nayef(USA) —Proud Titania (IRE) (Fairy King (USA))
4798[5]
Beat The Odds *F Sheridan* a41 88
5 b g Beat Hollow—Biodotis (Warning)
825[4]
Beat The Rush *Miss J A Camacho* 74
2 b g Tobougg(IRE) —Rush Hour (IRE) (Night Shift (USA))
4308[2] 4993[5] 5407[6] (6901)
Beat The Shower *P D Niven* a46 62
3 b g Beat Hollow—Crimson Shower (Dowsing (USA))
4276[6] 4505[10] 4838[7] 5952[5] (7085) 7222[3] 7425[6]

Beaubahhare (FR) *J-P Delaporte* 69
4 b g Bahhare(USA) —Offense Vive (USA) (Sharpen Up)
5204a[4]

Beaubrav *P W D'Arcy* a69 63
3 b g Falbrav(IRE) —Wavy Up (IRE) (Brustolon)
1183[2] 2204[4] 2809[2] 2982[6] 4157[3] 4734[2] 5286[5]

Beau Brummell (NZ) *D Hill* 94
5 ch g My Halo(ARG) —Lady In Blue (NZ) (Crested Wave (USA))
2116a[10]

Beauchamp Unique *E J Cooper* 21
6 b m Compton Admiral—Beauchamp Jade (Kalaglow)
3223[10] 3291[10] 4344[10]

Beauchamp Viceroy *G A Butler* a98 84
5 ch g Compton Admiral—Compton Astoria (USA) (Lion Cavern (USA))
915[5] 1642[6] 2193[6] 3301[4] (3717) 5025[9] 5375[6] 5887[8] 6024[4] 6495[2] (7054) 7489[4]

Beauchamp Viking *S C Burrough* a45 42
5 b g Compton Admiral—Beauchamp Jade (Kalaglow)
2330[15] 2516[5] 2912[10]

Beauchamp Wizard *G A Butler* a77 73
4 b h Compton Admiral—Compton Astoria (USA) (Lion Cavern (USA))
5473[5] ◆ 6212[14] 6454[2]

Beauchamp Wonder *G A Butler* a61 71
4 b m Compton Admiral—Beauchamp Jade (Kalaglow)
3617[2] 4053[3]

Beauchamp Xenia *H Candy* a58 69
3 b f Compton Admiral—Beauchamp Jade (Kalaglow)
1573[7] 2051[5] 5093[3] 5430[6]

Beauchamp Xerxes *G A Butler* a103 104
3 ch c Compton Admiral—Compton Astoria (USA) (Lion Cavern (USA))
1297[4] 1793[4] 2176[2] 3087[12] 3751[8] (4854) 6110[2] 6290[4] 7237[3] 7489[9]

Beauchamp Xiara *H Candy* a69 71
3 b f Compton Admiral—Beauchamp Buzz (High Top)
2006[4] 6166[2] 6698[8]

Beauchamp Yeoman *H Candy* 40
2 b g Compton Admiral—One Way Street (Habitat)
7146[17]

Beauchamp Yorker *H Candy* 85
2 ch c Compton Admiral—Compton Astoria (USA) (Lion Cavern (USA))
(6108)

Beau Fighter *C F Wall* a50 80
4 b g Tobougg(IRE) —Belle De Jour (Exit To Nowhere (USA))
(2039) 2678[6] 4737[4] 7020[3]

Beau Jazz *W De Best-Turner* a44 31
8 br g Merdon Melody—Ichor (Primo Dominie)
3211[12] 7069[6] 7394[11]

Beaumont Boy *J A McShane* 54
5 b g Foxhound(USA) —Play The Game (Mummy's Game)
2155[4] 2594[3] 2718[6] 2816[4] 2965[3] 3105[8]

Beaumont Princess (IRE) *G A Swinbank* 7
3 b f Elusive City(USA) —Pantera Piceno (IRE) (College Chapel)
2439[8]

Beaumont's Party (IRE) *R Hannon* a70 69
2 b c High Chaparral(IRE) —Miss Champagne (FR) (Bering)
6109[6] 6627[4] 7145[5] ◆

Beauthea (IRE) *Ms Joanna Morgan* a75 83
3 b f Barathea(IRE) —Beau Cheval (IRE) (Spectrum (IRE))
1024a[11] 2304a[12] 7297a[5]

Beautician (USA) *Kenneth McPeek* a113
2 gr f Dehere(USA) —Caroni (USA) (Rubiano (USA))
7283a[2]

Beautiful Breeze (IRE) *M Johnston* 81
3 ch g Tobougg(IRE) —Khayrat (IRE) (Polar Falcon (USA))
1471[4] (1895) 2638[8] 3144[5] (3504)

Beautiful Filly *D M Simcock* a73 62
3 b f Oasis Dream—Royal Alchemist (USA) (Royal Academy (USA))
(1379) 2079[18] 2632[7] 3272[2] 3989[7] 5090[3] 5810[4] 6333[7] (6667) 7158[4] 7487[7]

Beautiful Lady (IRE) *P F I Cole* a67 74
4 b m Peintre Celebre(USA) —Puteri Wentworth (Sadler's Wells (USA))
2040[5] 2123[7]

Beauty O' Gwaun (IRE) *Christophe Clement* 105
3 b f Rainbow Quest(USA) —Angel Of The Gwaun (IRE) (Sadler's Wells (USA))
(1996a) 3896a[10] 4609a[3] 6510a[7]

Beaux Yeux *Miss A Stokell* a55 39
3 b f Cadeaux Genereux—Cloud Hill (Danehill (USA))
36[5] 227[3] 602[3] 796[4] 920[3] 5145[7] 5624[11] 5954[8] 7270[10]

Beaver Patrol (IRE) *Eve Johnson Houghton* a109 109
7 ch g Tagula(IRE) —Erne Project (IRE) (Project Manager)
418a[7] 637a[8] (696a) 996[9] 1513[4] 1861[22] 3141[19] 3818[16] 4523[17] 5039[16] 5874[9]

Bebenine (IRE) *Patrick Morris* a63 61
2 b f Antonius Pius(USA) —Lady Fonic (Zafonic (USA))
1312[4] 1521[4] 1802[7] 2147[6]

Bebopalula (IRE) *B W Hills* 69
2 gr f Galileo(IRE) —Pearl Bright (FR) (Kaldoun (FR))
6992[6]

Becausewecan (USA) *M Johnston* a87 94
3 b g Giant's Causeway(USA) —Belle Sultane (USA) (Seattle Slew (USA))
1056[2] ◆ (3359) 3618[6] 4420[3] ◆ 4520[4] 5315[2] (6816)

Beckenham's Secret *A W Carroll* a46 52
5 b g Foxhound(USA) —Berliese (IRE) (High Estate)
23[8] 42[5] 131[3] 2471[0] 482[7] 587[5] 1784[7] 2333[9] 2609[3] 2912[7]

Beckermet (IRE) *R F Fisher* a93 114
7 b g Second Empire(IRE) —Razida (IRE) (Last Tycoon)
781[7] 4559[5] 5232[9] 5434[7] 5878[8] 6135[2] 6304[13] 6675[13] 7133[2] ◆ 7454[5] ◆ 7558[11]

Becky Quick (IRE) *Bruce Hellier*
4 b m Fantastic Light(USA) —Private Bluff (USA) (Pine Bluff (USA))
3155[7] 3712[10] 5163[7]

Becky's Kitten (USA) *Wesley A Ward* a58 104
2 bb c Kitten's Joy(USA) —Caterette (USA) (Cozzene (USA))
7304a[9]

Becomes You *M Delzangles* a89 102
3 ch f Lomitas—Joyeuse Entree (Kendor (FR))
1550a[6] 7697a[0]

Becqu Adoree (FR) *Mme G Lecomte* 110
3 b f Nombre Premier—L'Etoile La Lune (IRE) (Groom Dancer (USA))
2754a[3] 5929a[6]

Becuille (IRE) *B J Meehan* a76 73
4 b m Redback—Danz Danz (Efisio)
830[5] 1042[7] (1133) 1834[3] 2351[7] 3070[8] (3960) 4992[9] 6346[7] 6640[3] 7360[7]

Bedarra Boy *D W P Arbuthnot* a49 52
3 ch g Needwood Blade—Roonah Quay (IRE) (Soviet Lad (USA))
1585[8] 2795[14] 3472[6] 3985[3] 4650[8] 5286[7] 6188[3]

Bedawina (FR) *Mme P Alexanian* 64
3 b f Bedawin(FR) —Lonesome Dove (FR) (Petit Loup (USA))
6753a[8]

Bed Fellow (IRE) *P Monteith* a65 70
5 b g Trans Island—Moonlight Partner (IRE) (Red Sunset)
1883[10] 3023[5] 4755[3] 5294[5] 5944[2] 6312[7] 7113[2]

Bedloe's Island (IRE) *N Bycroft* a34 74
4 b g Statue Of Liberty(USA) —Scenaria (IRE) (Scenic)
(3125) ◆ 4620[4] 4891[2] ◆ 5148[3] 6220[2]

Bedouin Blue (IRE) *A J Lidderdale* a71 66
6 b g Desert Style(IRE) —Society Fair (FR) (Always Fair (USA))
622[7] 745[3] 836[8] 972[7]

Bedouin Style (IRE) *Mrs A M Thorpe*
3 b g Desert Style(IRE) —Samaritan Woman (IRE) (Priolo (USA))
2323[13]

Bees River (IRE) *A P Jarvis* a63 71
3 b f Acclamation—Notley Park (Wolfhound (USA))
1095[3] 1311[5] 1583[5] 2010[14] 2654[4] 2973[8] 3663[3] 4942[9] 5341[4] 6379[8]

Bee Sting *Mrs L Williamson* a96 93
5 b g Selkirk(USA) —Desert Lynx (IRE) (Green Desert (USA))
1798[12]

Bee Stinger *P R Hedger* a81 89
7 b g Almaty(IRE) —Nest Egg (Prince Sabo)
791[0] 283[9] 392[4] 507[4] (841) 1035[4] 5750[2] 7492[7] 7549[2] (7647) 7776[6]

Beethoven (IRE) *A P O'Brien* a111 118
2 b c Oratorio(IRE) —Queen Titi (IRE) (Sadler's Wells (USA))
2017[3] 3138[4] 3895a[3] 4359a[5] 5892a[3] 6317a[4] 6524a[6] (6849) 7307a[6]

Beetuna (IRE) *X-Thomas Demeaulte* a82 77
4 b g Statue Of Liberty(USA) —High Atlas (Shirley Heights)
7821a[2]

Be Fair (USA) *D Wayne Lukas* a104
3 bb f Exchange Rate(USA) —Go Donna Go (USA) (Wild Again (USA))
1763a[4]

Before The War (USA) *L M Cumani* a56
2 ch c El Corredor(USA) —Adrenalin Running (USA) (A.P. Indy (USA))
7325[7] 7580[5]

Before You Go (IRE) *E Charpy* a96 74
6 b g Sadler's Wells(USA) —Here On Earth (USA) (Mr Prospector (USA))
185a[12] 338a[10] 644a[10]

Befortyfour *M A Jarvis* a102 109
4 b g Kyllachy—Ivania (First Trump)
4059[5]

Be Grateful (IRE) *H Morrison* a49 54
2 bb f Efisio—Dwingeloo (IRE) (Dancing Dissident (USA))
5829[5] ◆ 6347[5] 6932[6] 7389[13]

Beguiler *H-A Pantall* a68 70
3 b f Refuse To Bend(IRE) —Most Charming (FR) (Darshaan)
4130a[4] 6606a[4]

Beheshtam (FR) *A De Royer-Dupre* 117
3 ch c Peintre Celebre(USA) —Behkara (IRE) (Kris)
2756a[4] 3970a[6] 5930a[2] 6526a[12]

Behind Blue Eyes *Karen George* 46
3 b g Kyllachy—Mamoura (IRE) (Lomond (USA))
296[13] 1423[7] 1579[10]

Behkabad (FR) *J-C Rouget* 108
2 b c Cape Cross(IRE) —Behkara (IRE) (Kris) (6133a)

Be Invincible (IRE) *B W Hills* 83
2 b c Invincible Spirit(IRE) —Lupulina (CAN) (Saratoga Six (USA))
(1404) 2247[3] 7013[8]

Be Kind *Karen George* a41 45
3 b f Generous(IRE) —Aquavita (Kalaglow)
4854[7] 5314[6] 6225[8] 6859[7]

Belango (GER) *F Willenbrock* 86
3 ch c Tertullian(USA) —Brighella (GER) (Lomitas)
6891a[8]

Belated Silver (IRE) *Tom Dascombe* a74 72
3 rg g Clodovil(IRE) —Premier Place (USA) (Out Of Place (USA))
1033[4] 1331[4] 1656[3] 2198[6] (3225) 3577[3]

Bel Cantor *W J H Ratcliffe* a85 95
6 b h Largesse—Palmstead Belle (IRE) (Wolfhound (USA))
1018[15] 1398[6] 1663[10] 2203[8] 2570[3] 2938[9] (3512) 3738[9] 4353[11] 4598[4] 4853[2] 5167[11] 5257[7] 5404[7] 5856[2] 6050[21] 6279[2] 6540[8] 6964[12] (7355) 7496[2] 7676[4] 7758[7]

Belgooree *J G Given* a16
2 b f Haafhd—Ziggy Zaggy (Diktat)
7630[9]

Belinsky (IRE) *S A Callaghan* a71 69
2 b c Compton Place—Westwood (FR) (Anabaa (USA))
2979[3] 3402[6] 4370[3] 5325[4] (5583)

Bella Charlie (IRE) *M G Quinlan* a61
2 b c Pyrus(USA) —Beseeching (IRE) (Hamas (IRE))
7325[10] 7538[6] ◆ 7864[6]

Bella Fighetta *Ms J S Doyle* a38 11
3 b f Bertolini(USA) —My Girl (Mon Tresor)
6794[11] 7228[6] 7464[6] 7533[5] 7629[7]

Bellaharry (IRE) *Matthew Salaman* a24 37
2 b f Lucky Story(USA) —Saharan Song (IRE) (Singspiel (IRE))
5498[11] 6122[6] 7120[13]

Bella Ida (FR) *J E Hammond* 92
5 b m Hernando(FR) —Bayourida (USA) (Slew O'Gold (USA))
7569a[3]

Bella Medici *P G Murphy* a60 68
4 ch m Medicean—Missouri (Charnwood Forest (IRE))
502[7]

Bella Platina (GER) *U Stoltefuss* 97
5 ch m Platini(GER) —Burgberg Lady (Fleetwood (IRE))
5651a[2] (6605a) 7458a[7]

Bella Rowena *A M Balding* 70
3 b f Kyllachy—Luxurious (USA) (Lyphard (USA))
1825[8] 3387[11]

Bellaside (IRE) *E Leon Penate* 79
2 b f Le Vie Dei Colori—Brockton Saga (IRE) (Perugino (USA))
4584a[5]

Bella Swan *W R Swinburn* 88
2 ch f Leporello(IRE) —Lydia Maria (Dancing Brave (USA))
2047[3] 2914[2] (3820) 5427[5] 6447[4]

Belle Amie (IRE) *C Boutin* a58 60
2 ch f Consolidator(USA) —Lexa (FR) (Sanglamore (USA))
6501a[12]

Belle Bellino (FR) *R M Beckett* 64
4 b m Robellino(USA) —Hoh Chi Min (Efisio)
1091[6] 1591[14]

Belle Chose (IRE) *John Joseph Murphy* a62 67
3 b f Selkirk(USA) —Shimaal (Sadler's Wells (USA))
3896a[9]

Belle Des Airs (IRE) *R M Beckett* 90
3 ch f Dr Fong(USA) —Belle Reine (King Of Kings (IRE))
2079[4] ◆ 2886[2] 4198[2] 4761[5] 5005[3] (5774) 5918[2]

Belle Epoch *J-C Rouget* 92
3 b f Sadler's Wells(USA) —Solaia (USA) (Miswaki (USA))
2989a[6]

Belle Eponine *E J O'Neill* a54 59
2 b f Fraam—Red Ryding Hood (Wolfhound (USA))
1764[6] 2360[8] (3119) 4371[7] 6325a[7] 6960a[11]

Belle Et Celebre (FR) *A De Royer-Dupre* 110
4 b m Peintre Celebre(USA) —Rotina (FR) (Crystal Glitters (USA))
846a[11]

Belle Noverre (IRE) *Shaun Harley* a79 76
5 b m Noverre(USA) —Belle Etoile (FR) (Lead On Time (USA))
5126[4] 6846[7] 7399[6]

Belle Park *Karen George* a54 33
2 b f Hamairi(IRE) —Cape Siren (Warning)
6207[9] 6932[7] 7450[8] 7661[9]

Belles Beau *R Hollinshead* a41
2 b f Fraam—Victory Flip (IRE) (Victory Note (USA))
7800[9]

Belle's Ridge *Timothy Doyle* a77 98
5 ch h Tumbleweed Ridge—Alton Belle (Blakeney)
4412a[10] 5490a[9] 6867a[12]

Belle Syrienne (GER) *P Schiergen* 100
3 b f Golan(IRE) —Bela-M (IRE) (Ela-Mana-Mou) (2874a)

Belle Zorro *M L W Bell* a52
2 br f Dr Fong(USA) —Special Beat (Bustino)
5984[11] 6291[7] 6627[10]

Belliflore (FR) *Y Fouin* a77 110
5 gr m Verglas(IRE) —Truffle (IRE) (Ezzoud (IRE))
7621a[11]

Bellini Rose (IRE) *Tom Dascombe* a65
2 b f Bertolini(USA) —Prospectress (USA) (Mining (USA))
(6443) 7251[4]

Bell Island *Lady Herries* a83 83
5 b g Dansili—Thermal Spring (Zafonic (USA))
392[8] (631) (894) 1435[5] 2497[4] 2931[4] ◆ 3169[6] 5740[5] (6704) 7357[4] 7695[8]

Bellomi (IRE) *A G Juckes* a75 94
4 gr g Lemon Drop Kid(USA) —Reina Blanca (Darshaan)
1894[10] 2149[9]

Bellona (FR) *D Allard* 30
2 b f Enrique—Belle Muse (FR) (Courtroom (FR))
3934a[6]

Bell's Ocean (USA) *J Ryan* a67 72
2 b f Proud Citizen(USA) —Golden Train (USA) (Slew O'Gold (USA))
1810[2] 2047[5] (2238) 3086[15] 3821[6] 4539[12] 4850[7] 5635[3] 5967[3] ◆ 6227[5] 6643[9] 6905[7]

Belondine (FR) *Y De Nicolay* 74
3 gr f Kendor(FR) —Michellisa (Indian Ridge)
4810a[3]

Below Zero (IRE) *M Johnston* 93
2 b c Shamardal(USA) —Chilly Start (IRE) (Caerleon (USA))
2388[3] (2649)

Beltanus (GER) *F Willenbrock* 106
5 ch h Tertullian(USA) —Brighella (GER) (Lomitas)
2953a[8]

Bemboka *R Pritchard-Gordon* 58
2 ch f Haafhd—Stella Nova (FR) (Bering)
1482a[3]

Be My Gallery (FR) *J-P Gallorini*
2 b c Gallery Of Zurich(IRE) —Swiss Native (IRE) (Be My Native (USA))
3935a[0]

Ben *P G Murphy* a64 58
4 b g Bertolini(USA) —Bold Byzantium (Bold Arrangement)
99[8] 245[8] 474[7] 1038[11]

Benadalid (FR) *C Laffon-Parias* 68
2 b c Green Tune(USA) —Agapimou (IRE) (Spectrum (IRE))
5713a[0]

Benandonner (USA) *Mike Murphy* a102 103
6 ch g Giant's Causeway(USA) —Cape Verdi (IRE) (Caerleon (USA))
781[4] 997[11] 1212[2] 1352[13] (2612) 3391[4] 3818[11] 4486[14] 5522[9] 6217[3] 7185[2] 7492[3] (7662) 7827[4]

Benayoun *B J Llewellyn* a57 44
5 b g Inchinor—Sosumi (Be My Chief (USA))
2609[6]

Ben Bacchus (IRE) *P W Hiatt* a57 39
7 b g Bahhare(USA) —Bodfaridistinction (IRE) (Distinctly North (USA))
(248) 342[5] 448[5] 528[7] 669[6] 2040[7] 2222[10] 2337[3] 3382[6] 3594[6]

Benbaun (IRE) *K A Ryan* 120
8 b g Stravinsky(USA) —Escape To Victory (Salse (USA))
1374a[8] 1919a[2] 2523a[3] (3434a) 5233[2] 5928a[4] 6522a[4]

Ben Chorley *D R Lanigan* a23 98
5 gr g Inchinor—Arantxa (Sharpo)
3312[5] 3873[18]

Bencoolen (IRE) *D Nicholls* a52 99
4 b g Daylami(IRE) —Jakarta (IRE) (Machiavellian (USA))
1170[2] 1460[13] 1684[3] 1986[10] 2669[7] 4409[17] (4526) 4768[3] 6480[31]

Bended Knee *H Candy* 80
3 b f Refuse To Bend(IRE) —Flavian (Catrail (USA))
5242[2] 5789[2] 6551[3] (7189)

Benedicte (IRE) *M Botti* 91
3 b f Galileo(IRE) —Rachelle (IRE) (Mark Of Esteem (IRE))
4991[6] (6276) 6813[10] 7291[17]

Benedict Spirit (IRE) *D Burchell* a78 75
4 b g Invincible Spirit(IRE) —Kathy Caerleon (IRE) (Caerleon (USA))
(65) 142[5] 687[3] 822[2] 923[2] 1177[2] 1721[2] 2200[7] 2499[2] 6460[8] 6855[4] 7505[3] ◆ 7641[4] 7668[DSQ]

Benetti (IRE) *M Madgwick* 43
3 ch g Kheleyf(USA) —Assigh Lady (IRE) (Great Commotion (USA))
2009[11] 2651[8]

Benfleet Boy *B G Powell* a54 79
5 gr g Fasliyev(USA) —Nicely (IRE) (Bustino)
6060[2] 7036[8]

Bengal Tiger *A M Balding* a85 61
3 ch g Tagula(IRE) —Floriana (Selkirk (USA))
2082[7] 4246[6] 5314[2] (5987)

Bengers Lass (USA) *R Curtis* a36 1
3 ch f Orientate(USA) —Wiedniu (USA) (Danzig Connection (USA))
6287[9] 6741[14] 6934[14] 7590[5]

Benhego *G L Moore* a92 76
4 ch g Act One—Sadaka (USA) (Kingmambo (USA))
(511) ◆ (723) 1007[4]

Benitez Bond *G R Oldroyd* a58 39
4 ch g Bahamian Bounty—Triple Tricks (IRE) (Royal Academy (USA))
2789[9] 4376[2] 4656[6] 5103[7] 5617[6]

Benllech *D M Simcock* a101 99
5 b g Lujain(USA) —Four Legs Good (IRE) (Be My Guest (USA))
433a[10] 637a[4] ◆ 916[7] 1006[8] 2474[7] 3122[2] 3318[2]

Bennelong *G L Moore* a81 82
3 b g Bahamian Bounty—Bundle Up (USA) (Miner's Mark (USA))
1355[5] 1963[2] 2600[6] 2885[4] 3319[3] (6950) 7456[2] 7540[3] 7769[5]

Bennie Blue (SAF) *M F De Kock* a95 95
7 ch h Rich Man's Gold(USA) —Biloxi Blue (SAF) (Al Mufti (USA))
262a[6] 337a[4]

Benny The Bear *James Moffatt* 62
2 ch g Rambling Bear—Mitchelland (Namaqualand (USA))
4652[3] 5157[4]

Benozzo Gozzoli *H Morrison* a51 62
3 ch g Medicean—Star Precision (Shavian)
1516 306[8] 828[4] 1050[7] 2143[13] 3942[7] 5630[7] 5872[4] 6785[4] (7124) 7255[7]

Benrish (IRE) *B Smart* 73
2 b c Refuse To Bend(IRE) —Miss Trish (IRE) (Danetime (IRE))
3147[2] 4132[2]

Ben's Dream (IRE) *A M Balding* a48 73
3 br g Kyllachy—Kelso Magic (USA) (Distant View (USA))
1068[5] 1419[5] 2010[7] 2888[4] (3592) 4148[4] 4494[7] 6230[10] 6739[3]

Bentesina (GER) *Leo J Temple* a68 84
7 b m Waky Nao—Bellinda (GER) (Peking Opera (IRE))
1376a[10]

Bentley *J G Given* a69 62
5 b g Piccolo—April Lee (Superpower)
1244[9] 2145[10] 2722[6] 3490[9] 3972[7] 4654[8] 6674[5] (7645) 7819[4] 7876[7]

Bentley Brook (IRE) *R Curtis* a85 51
7 ch g Singspiel(IRE) —Gay Bentley (USA) (Riverman (USA))
82[5] 511[6] 687[4] 7402[6] (7598) 7675[4] 7867[9]

Benwilt Barney (IRE) *John C McConnell* 82
2 b c Trans Island—Image Of Truce (IRE) (Brief Truce (USA))
5274a[3]

Beran (TUR) *M H Esin* a106
6 b h West By West(USA) —Best Of All (IRE) (Try My Best (USA))
5587a[4]

Berathan (TUR) *I Gulbudak* a108
3 ch f Unaccounted For(USA) —Iclal (IRE) (Prince Of Birds (USA))
5587a[3]

Berberi *A G Newcombe*
3 ch c Bertolini(USA) —Bird Of Prey (IRE) (Last Tycoon)
1508[11]

Berbice (IRE) *S Donohoe* a93 95
4 gr g Acclamation—Pearl Bright (FR) (Kaldoun (FR))
2203[5] 5031[6] 5565[2] 6370[2] (6976) 7054[5]

Bere Davis (FR) *M A Barnes* a61 80
4 gr g Verglas(IRE) —Zerelda (Exhibitioner)
1048[2] 1246[3] 1722[3] (1887) 2313[7] 2565[5] 2998[4] 3504[2] 3801[6] 3996[8] 4641[9] 5409[3] 6015[10] 6365[4] 6545[5] 6987[4]

Beresford Lady *A D Brown* a47 48
5 b m Presidium—Coney Hills (Beverley Boy)
80[6]

Berg Bahn (IRE) *G M Lyons* 84
2 b f Big Bad Bob(IRE) —Ski For Me (IRE) (Barathea (IRE))
6708a[4]

Bergonzi (IRE) *J Howard Johnson* a78 81
5 ch g Indian Ridge—Lady Windley (Baillamont (USA))
1059[5] 1721[6] 2315[3] 2815[7] (3728) 4619[2] 5235[6] 6822[5]

Berina (FR) *U Suter* 65
4 b m Count On Me(FR) —Hollyhead (FR) (Green Tune (USA))
7822a[9]

Bering De Lauriere (FR) *B G Powell* a37
6 ch g Evening World(FR) —Shenedova (FR) (Hellios (USA))
393[11] 516[4]

Berkalani (IRE) *P D Evans* 12
3 b f Ashkalani(IRE) —Berkeley Hall (Saddlers' Hall (IRE))
5628[10] 6934[11]

Berling (IRE) *J L Dunlop* 72
2 gr c Montjeu(IRE) —Danaskaya (IRE) (Danehill (USA))
5002[6] 5879[5] 6697[3]

Bermacha *J E Long* a63 69
4 ch m Bertolini(USA) —Machaera (Machiavellian (USA))
1495[11] 2746[5] 3949[12] 4938[12] 7422[7]

Bermondsey Bob (IRE) *J L Spearing* a14 72
3 b g Trans Island—Tread Softly (IRE) (Roi Danzig (USA))
1686[8] 2010[16] 3159[9] 3427[12] 4304[4] 4643[5] (5633) 6340[5] 6739[9]

Bermondsey Girl *C F Wall* a67 73
3 b f Bertolini(USA) —Upend (Main Reef)
2080[5] 2885[9] 3566[6] ◆ (4304) 6070[7] 6437[11] 6925[3]

Bermuda Rye (IRE) *M bin Shafya* a74 106
4 b h Cape Cross(IRE) —Alleluia Tree (IRE) (Royal Academy (USA))
6384a[6] ◆ 697a[10]

Bernabeu (IRE) *S Curran* a64 54
7 b g Mark Of Esteem(IRE) —Snow Ballet (IRE) (Sadler's Wells (USA))
18[5] 248[2] 584[4] 838[4] 4857[5] 6025[5] 6969[5] 7354[10] 7549[5]

Bernie The Bolt (IRE) *A M Balding* a50 102
3 br g Milan—Chaparral Lady (IRE) (Broken Hearted)
1931[5] 2323[3] 2881[3] 3793[3] (4743) 5230[3] (6115)

Bernix *N Tinkler* a51 32
7 gr g Linamix(FR) —Bernique (USA) (Affirmed (USA))
2068[15] 2608[13] 3710[4] 4170[11] 4932[12] 6183[9] 7500[9] 7761[6]

Berraksu (TUR) *H Ergin* 107
4 b m Sri Pekan(USA) —Ozlemcan (TUR) (Palace Pageant (USA))
5588a[4]

Berriedale *Mrs A Duffield* a14 54
3 ch f Fraam—Carradale (Pursuit Of Love)
1168[5] 1441[10] (1724) 2838[6] 3454[4] 4529[8] 4755[7]

Berrymead *Miss A Stokell* a51 61
4 br m Killer Instinct—Mill End Quest (King's Signet (USA))
62[10] 222[7] 574[6] 682[7] 791[9] 1091[3] 1248[8] 1695[7] 1985[6] 2546[8] (2811) 3246[5] 3477[6] 3945[4] 4452[9] 4736[5] 6160[6] 6341[7] 7241[12] 7462[5] 7710[5] 7839[8]

Berrynarbor *A G Newcombe* a35 57
4 b m Tobougg(IRE) —River Art (USA) (Irish River (FR))
4857[8] 5381[9] 5790[6] 7658[10]

Bertbrand *I W McInnes* a69 75
4 b g Bertolini(USA) —Mi Amor (IRE) (Alzao (USA))
2130[2] 2579[10] 2745[10] 3227[5] (3465) 3720[4] 3926[8] 5678[11] 6335[8] 7086[2] 7241[14] 7371[9] 7727[6]

Bertie Bacon *W G M Turner*
3 b g Bertolini(USA) —Streaky (IRE) (Danetime (IRE))
5367[13]

Bertie Black *N Tinkler*
2 b g Bertolini(USA) —Bella Chica (IRE) (Bigstone (IRE))
2100[8]

Bertie Boo *G J Smith* 52
4 b g Where Or When(IRE) —Lucy Boo (Singspiel (IRE))
1777[9]

Bertie Buckle (IRE) *J R Gask* a49
2 b g Bertolini(USA) —Buckle (IRE) (Common Grounds)
6802[10] 7556[6] 7736[9]

Bertie's Best *F Doumen* 88
2 ch f King's Best(USA) —Just Wood (FR) (Highest Honor (FR))
(2694a) 5708a[7]

Bertie's Birthday (IRE) *Jonjo O'Neill* 44
3 b f Elnadim(USA) —Goldfinch (Zilzal (USA))
1972[6] 2496[12]

Bertie Smalls *M H Tompkins* a55 51
3 b g Xaar—Largo (IRE) (Selkirk (USA))
1363[14] 2772[7] 3005[3]

Bertie Southstreet *Karen George* a73 78
6 bb g Bertolini(USA) —Salvezza (IRE) (Superpower)
96[3] 167[6] 355[8] 1587[5] (3345) 3459[3] 3917[9] 4203[5] 4479[7] (5225) (5612) 6670[4] (6857) 7397[4] 7645[2]

Bertie Vista *T D Easterby* a59 66
4 b g Bertolini(USA) —Off Camera (Efisio)
1332[16] 1563[5] 1723[7] 2361[4] 3224[3] 3730[4] 4887[5] 5225[5] 6414[9] 6823[3]

Bertoliver *S C Williams* a85 101
5 b g Bertolini(USA) —Calcavella (Pursuit Of Love)
1457[8] 1836[7] 2227[8] 2782[3] 3372[2] 4232[2] 4567[8] (5247) 5654[14] 6666[10] 7414[5] 7702[4] 7872[3]

Bert's Memory *Jennie Candlish* a55 55
5 b m Bertolini(USA) —Meg's Memory (IRE) (Superlative)
3798[2] 4193[4] 4625[7] 5548[5] 6097[9]

Bespoke Boy *Mrs N S Evans* a61 70
4 b g Acclamation—Milly Fleur (Primo Dominie)
132[4] 362[10] 969[7] 3206[7] 3798[6] 4263[9]

Bessie Lou (IRE) *K A Ryan* a53 73
3 b f Montjeu(IRE) —Almond Mousse (FR) (Exit To Nowhere (USA))
2446[2] ◆ 3379[6] 4562[7] 5295[7] 5858[8] 6052[8] 6807[6]

Best Bidder (USA) *Patrick Morris* a41 72
3 bb f Mr Greeley(USA) —Party Stripes (USA) (Candy Stripes (USA))
826[9] 1361[11] 1580[8] 1954[7] 2152[9] 3482[9]

Best In Class *S C Williams* a80 71
3 gr g Best Of The Bests(IRE) —Third Party (Terimon)
121[2] (599) 1574[4] 1928[14] 2432[11] 3427[6] (4202) 5169[4] 5575[11] (7428) 7684[12]

Best Intent *M A Jarvis* 49
2 ch f King's Best(USA) —Hydro Calido (USA) (Nureyev (USA))
7182[13]

Best Joking (GER) *W Hefter* 102
4 ch m Big Shuffle(USA) —Bergwelt (GER) (Solarstern (FR))
2097a[8] 3202a[9] 4637a[0] 5651a[7] (6499a)

Best Of Order (IRE) *E J O'Neill*
2 ch c Pivotal—Groom Order (Groom Dancer (USA))
7409a[3]

Best One *R A Harris* a77 85
5 ch g Best Of The Bests(IRE) —Nasaieb (IRE) (Fairy King (USA))
1418[9] 1836[5] 2219[10] 2520[7] 2908[3] 3246[6] 3720[8] 4204[6] 5125[14] 5184[10] 5501[8] 5911[5] (6581) 6674[7] 6939[7] 7371[8] 7651[3] (7710) 7838[5] 7889[4]

Bestowed *P D Evans* a64 58
4 b g Kyllachy—Granted (FR) (Cadeaux Genereux)
1407[14] 1848[7] 1888[4] 2458[15] 2859[10] 3919[9] 4402[12] 5549[4] 6172[3] 6999[4] 7374[2] 7754[4] (7803) 7856[3]

Best Prospect (IRE) *M Dods* a87 94
7 b g Orpen(USA) —Bright Prospect (USA) (Miswaki (USA))
563[4] 1593[12] 1986[9] 2933[13] 3393[3] 4003[10] 4471[2] 5334[5]

Best Shot *B W Hills*
3 b f Xaar—Xaymara (USA) (Sanglamore (USA))
1605[12]

Best Show (IRE) *Mrs A J Perrett* 59
2 b c King's Best(USA) —Showering (Danehill (USA))
5401[6] 5722[P]

Best Trip (IRE) *R C Guest* 29
2 b g Whipper(USA) —Tereed Elhawa (Cadeaux Genereux)
7288[14]

Best Tune *J Noseda* a54 53
3 b f King's Best(USA) —Silver Rhapsody (USA) (Silver Hawk (USA))
2240[4] 2738[4] 3508[6]

Besty *B Smart* 71
2 ch g Compton Place—Petrovna (IRE) (Petardia)
5668[11] 5977[4] 6231[3] 6983[8] (7115)

Beta Leo (USA) *P Bary* 92
2 b f A.P. Indy(USA) —Denebola (USA) (Storm Cat (USA))
5085a[4] 6045a[7]

Bethrah (IRE) *D K Weld* 84
2 br f Marju(IRE) —Reve D'Iman (FR) (Highest Honor (FR))
6317a[10]

Betica *Y Durepaire*
3 ch f Noverre(USA) —Miss Twinkletoes (IRE) (Zafonic (USA))
7696a[0]

Bet Noir (IRE) *A W Carroll* a62 64
4 b m King's Best(USA) —Ivowen (USA) (Theatrical (IRE))
449[10] 483[4] 674[7] 802[7] 1210[8]

Betony (USA) *M L W Bell* a37 67
3 b f Elusive Quality(USA) —Cala (FR) (Desert Prince (IRE))
2142[9] 4180[2] 5193[6]

Betoula *Mrs A L M King* a38
3 ch f Bertolini(USA) —Pab's Choice (Telsmoss)
5716[12]

Betsy The Best *R Bastiman* a4 12
3 ch f Best Of The Bests(IRE) —Dusty's Darling (Doyoun)
5[4]

Betteras Bertie *M Brittain* a63 72
6 gr g Paris House—Suffolk Girl (Statoblest)
7[2] 63[3] 362[5] 565[3] (2473) 2791[7] (3457) 4663[14] 6023[8] 6236[7] 6946[9]

Better Be Blue (IRE) *H J L Dunlop* a47 65
2 b f Big Bad Bob(IRE) —Ginger Lily (IRE) (Lucky Guest)
6819[13] 7098[3] 7391[4] 7501[10]

Better In Time (USA) *Jane Chapple-Hyam* a65 60
3 b f City Place(USA) —Ineda Doll (USA) (Langfuhr (CAN))
1406[10] 3693[12]

Bettys Touch *K G Reveley* 33
4 b m Lujain(USA) —Fadaki Hawaki (USA) (Vice Regent (CAN))
5727[5] 6380[8] 6553[14]

Betws Y Coed (IRE) *A Bailey* a53 49
3 br f Indian Haven—Tommys Queen (IRE) (Ali-Royal (IRE))
77[6] 136[7] 296[5] 363[5] 383[5]

Bewdley *R E Peacock* a39 58
4 b m Best Of The Bests(IRE) —Garota De Ipanema (FR) (Al Nasr (FR))
150[10] 401[7] 775[10] 1131[11]

Bewitched (IRE) *Charles O'Brien* a80 78
2 gr f Dansili—Abbatiale (FR) (Kaldoun (FR))
1993a[7]

Beyonda Dream *Lucinda Featherstone* a34
3 b f And Beyond(IRE) —Richenda (Mister Baileys)
5531[14] 7557[9] 7648[10] 7751[13]

Beyond Atlow *Lucinda Featherstone* a24
4 ch g And Beyond(IRE) —Argostoli (Marju (IRE))
7361[8] 7648[9]

Beyond Desire *M A Jarvis* 103
2 b f Invincible Spirit(IRE) —Compradore (Mujtahid (USA))
(4421) ◆ 5199[2] 6090[4]

Beyond The City (USA) *R Hannon* a54 59
2 b c Elusive Quality(USA) —Whats Doin (USA) (Relaunch (USA))
3584[11] 4638[7] 5793[9] 6373[6] 6938[9]

Bhaylana (USA) *N Clement* a78 71
2 b f Doneraile Court(USA) —Lady Lyra (USA) (Storm Creek (USA))
5956a[6]

Bianca Capello *J R Fanshawe* a52 46
4 b m Medicean—Totom (Mtoto)
290[5] 1974[9]

Biancarosa (IRE) *B Grizzetti* 98
2 b f Dalakhani(IRE) —Rosa Di Brema (ITY) (Lomitas)
6892a[7]

Biarritz (FR) *H Steinmetz* 64
3 gr f Kendor(FR) —Boylene (FR) (Le Balafre (FR))
5783a[9]

Biarritz (SAF) *M F De Kock* 109
6 b h Count Dubois—Corlia's Bid (AUS) (Polish Patriot (USA))
260a[3] ◆ 436a[2] 702a[8] 774a[9]

Biased *M Delzangles* 95
3 ch f Haafhd—Pas D'Heure (IRE) (Arazi (USA))
7128a[13]

Bibiana Bay *B I Case* a33
2 b f Leporello(IRE) —Polisonne (Polish Precedent (USA))
7799[11]

Bibury *David P Myerscough* a78 78
3 b f Royal Applause—Dahlia's Krissy (USA) (Kris S (USA))
5810[3] 6019[3] 7189[14]

Bickersons (CAN) *Kelly Breen* a105
2 b f Silver Deputy(CAN) —Dancehall Floozy (USA) (Paramount Jet (USA))
7283a[10]

Bickersten *C Moore* a73 21
3 ch g Piccolo—Niseem (USA) (Hennessy (USA))
(394) (829) 1331[6] 2092[5] 7650[4]

Bicksta *P T Midgley* a52 54
3 b f Haafhd—Premiere Dance (IRE) (Loup Solitaire (USA))
1327[12] 1825[11] 2240[3] 2942[11] 5015[10] 5567[4] 5983[4] 6705[6] 7677[6] 7780[6]

Bidable *B Palling* a62 57
5 b m Auction House(USA) —Dubitable (Formidable I (USA))
216[8] 868[7] 5502[3] 5791[10] 6967[7] 7152[2] 7416[2] (7466) 7650[9]

Bid Art (IRE) *Jamie Snowden* a65 65
4 b g Hawk Wing(USA) —Crystal Theatre (IRE) (King's Theatre (IRE))
285[14] 320[11] 494[14]

Bideeya (USA) *C E Brittain* a36 62
2 bb f Dubawi(IRE) —Menhoubah (USA) (Dixieland Band (USA))
3332[2] 3810[13] 4603[6] 6609[12]

Bid For Glory *H J Collingridge* a73 98
5 ch h Auction House(USA) —Woodland Steps (Bold Owl)
3378[7] 4716[6] 5190[12] 5886[2] ◆ 6074[3] 6640[10]

Bid For Gold *Jedd O'Keeffe* a36 78
5 b g Auction House(USA) —Gold And Blue (IRE) (Bluebird (USA))
1169[17] 2133[10] 2312[7] 2769[2] (3021) (3612) 4072[4] 5597[5] 6765[4] 7083[15] 7287[16]

Bienheureux *Miss Gay Kelleway* a61 68
8 b g Bien Bien(USA) —Rochea (Rock City)
65[3] 147[3] 301[6] 1537[3]

Bigalo's Star (IRE) *L A Mullaney* a40 71
3 b g Xaar—Toi Toi (IRE) (In The Wings)
2060[12] 6098[7] 6840[11]

Big Apple Boy (IRE) *Jedd O'Keeffe* 94
3 b c Statue Of Liberty(USA) —Go For Grace (IRE) (Shalford (IRE))
1559[4] 2092[2] 2406[6] 3144[4] (3455) 3747[18]

Big Audio (IRE) *R Hannon* 103
2 b c Oratorio(IRE) —Tarbela (IRE) (Grand Lodge (USA))
2187[4] ◆ 2467[2] (3138) 3817[7] 4418[4] (5214)

Big Bay (USA) *Jane Chapple-Hyam* a96 87
3 b c Horse Chestnut(SAF) —Takipy (USA) (Persian Bold)
1297[3] 1730[3] ◆ 2415[2] 3049[16] (7126) (7540) ◆

Big Boom *M Quinn* a45 72
4 ch g Cadeaux Genereux—Kastaway (Distant Relative)
175[5] 2864[2] 4183[2] (4428) 4668[4]

Big Bound (USA) *J H M Gosden* a80 103
3 b c Grand Slam(USA) —Golden Cat (USA) (Storm Cat (USA))
(1034) ◆ 1485[2] 1822[5] 2277[3] 3050[11] (4020) 4405[7] 6327a[8]

Big Buzz (IRE) *Mrs L Stubbs*
2 b g Redback—Aphra Benn (IRE) (In The Wings)
4705[9]

Big City Man (USA) *J Barton* a124
4 ch h Northern Afleet(USA) —Mini Appeal (USA) (Valid Appeal (USA))
(264a) 770a[2] (1010a)

Big Creek (IRE) *B Grizzetti* 79
2 b c Galileo(IRE) —Baranja (USA) (St Jovite (USA))
7205a[11]

Big Drama (USA) *David Fawkes* a112
3 bb c Montbrook(USA) —Riveting Drama (USA) (Notebook (USA))
2098a[5]

Bigfanofthat (IRE) *M D Squance* a48 64
4 b g Rock Of Gibraltar(IRE) —Miss Salsa (USA) (Unbridled (USA))
721[5] 1258[3] 1634[9] 2864[6] 3732[9] 4667[10]

Big Hands Lynch (IRE) *J R Boyle* a44
2 b c Hawkeye(IRE) —Mrs Kanning (Distant View (USA))
7064[11] 7390[10] 7663[9]

Big Nige (IRE) *J Pearce* a68 55
3 br g Mull Of Kintyre(USA) —Queen's Quest (Rainbow Quest (USA))
3115[14] 7882[3]

Big Noise *Dr J D Scargill* a96 99
5 b h Lake Coniston(IRE) —Mitsubishi Video (IRE) (Doulab (USA))
(3628) 4796[5] ◆ 5826[5] 6270[12] ◆ 6815[9]

Big Robert *P D Deegan* a105 104
5 b h Medicean—Top Flight Queen (Mark Of Esteem (IRE))
262a[3] 419a[5] 640a[8] 864[3] 1003[11] 6467a[7] 7300a[10]

Big Slick (IRE) *M Brittain* a36 62
4 ch h Rossini(USA) —Why Worry Now (IRE) (College Chapel)
1480[8] 2722[3] 3730[11]

Big Sur *T Keddy* a60
3 ch g Selkirk(USA) —Bombazine (IRE) (Generous (IRE))
6430[8] 7067[12] 7576[4]

Big Talk *S Kirk* 40
2 b c Selkirk(USA) —Common Request (USA) (Lear Fan (USA))
5627[9] 6697[10] 7029[14]

Big Tower (IRE) *Giuseppe Chianese* 84
3 ch c American Post—Margi (FR) (General Holme (USA))
1393a[12]

Big Wave Bay (IRE) *A P Jarvis* 58
2 b c Alamshar(IRE) —Lady Pahia (IRE) (Pivotal)
4258[6] 5407[4] 6046[7]

Big Whitfield *M Dods* a51 57
3 b g Tobougg(IRE) —Natalie Jay (Ballacashtal (CAN))
3120[5] 6673[8] 7126[5]

Bigzam *E Leenders* a86 91
4 b m Zamindar(USA) —Intrum Morshaan (IRE) (Darshaan)
6438a[6] 7704a[10]

Bijou Dan *G M Moore* a49 71
8 ch g Bijou D'Inde—Cal Norma's Lady (IRE) (Lyphard's Special (USA))
1058[3] 1242[9] (1767) 2194[8] 2969[5] (3499) 3728[5]

Bikini Babe (IRE) *M Johnston* 98
2 b f Montjeu(IRE) —Zeiting (IRE) (Zieten (USA))
2401[7] (2889) 3138[9] 4245[3] 4795[9] 6316a[2]

Bilash *R Hollinshead* 68
2 rg c Choisir(AUS) —Goldeva (Makbul)
3452[3] 5129[5] 5763[8] 6018[7]

Bilboa *J M Bradley* a57 60
4 b g Averti(IRE) —Anita Marie (IRE) (Anita's Prince)
1617[12] 2122[8] 2534[11] 3632[8] 4479[14] 5716[9]

Billberry *S C Williams* a77 69
4 gr g Diktat—Elderberry (Bin Ajwaad (IRE))
2400[3] 3211[2] 3512[7] 4181[4] 4502[7] 5031[3] 5723[2] 6294[6] 6726[5] 6915[4] ◆ (7519) 7692[6] 7832[5]

Billich *S W Hall* a91 84
6 ch h Observatory(USA) —Pomponette (USA) (Rahy (USA))
4857[10]

Billie Jean *B W Hills* a67 38
2 b f Bertolini(USA) —Factice (USA) (Known Fact (USA))
1810[12] 7145[11] 7585[9] (7778)

Billionaire Boy (IRE) *Patrick Morris*
2 b c Acclamation—Shalwell (IRE) (Shalford (IRE))
6381[5]

Billy Beetroot (USA) *R A Harris* a65 67
3 b g Rossini(USA) —Grazia (Sharpo)
1095[2] 1190[3] 1271[2] 1424[2] 1617[3] 1949[3] 2355[2] (2740) (2759) 3176[4] 3193[8] 3464[2] 3580[7] 4082[15] 5383[7] 5500[4] 5809[6] 6933[5] 7280[8] 7606[11] 7645[10]

Billy Bowmore *P A Kirby* a58 63
4 b g Bahamian Bounty—Shaieef (IRE) (Shareef Dancer (USA))
823[11] 979[13] 2366[13] 2805[6] 3031[6]

Billy Cadiz *N Tinkler* a14 29
4 b g Zilzal(USA) —Faraway Moon (Distant Relative)
3764[12] 4225[17] 6847[14]

Billy Dane (IRE) *F P Murtagh* a77 96
5 b g Fayruz—Lomalou (IRE) (Lightning Dealer)
(1507) (1952) 2197[10] 2787[6] 3335[7] 3872[7] 4592[2] 4779[2] 5522[2] 6094[2] 6675[16]

Billy Hot Rocks (IRE) *Miss Gay Kelleway* a64 63
4 b g Intikhab(USA) —Rock Abbey (IRE) (College Chapel)
118[10] 380[5] 811[9] 1057[9]

Billyonair *W De Best-Turner* a18
2 ch g Auction House(USA) —Westmead Tango (Pursuit Of Love)
7063[8] 7388[11]

Billy Red *J R Jenkins* a82 73
5 ch g Dr Fong(USA) —Liberty Bound (Primo Dominie)
(167) 281[6] 1197[12] 1468[10] 1540[2] 1957[2] 2472[9] 2929[11] (3246) 3775[2] 4733[6] 5374[10] 5836[4] (6028) (6444) 6426[6] 7395[11] 7553[2] ◆ 7656[2]

Billy's Bid *I W McInnes* 32
2 b f Kyllachy—Bajan Blue (Lycius (USA))
1396[7] 3232[5] 4001[9]

Billy Simmonds *Miss J Feilden* a26
4 b g Man Among Men(IRE) —Lizzie Simmonds (IRE) (Common Grounds)
5572[13] 6022[9]

Billy Smart (IRE) *A J Lidderdale* a41 58
3 ch c Exceed And Excel(AUS) —Amber Tide (IRE) (Pursuit Of Love)
1363[5] 2091[11] 2577[4] 3946[9] 4010[7] 5873[7]

Billy The Gas *N Tinkler*
4 b g Dr Fong(USA) —Hawayah (IRE) (Shareef Dancer (USA))
4022[7]

Bilyboy (FR) *J-L Pelletan* a65 78
2 b c Rashbag—Dajariya (IRE) (Tenby)
6979a[8]

Binanti *P R Chamings* a69 97
9 b g Bin Ajwaad(IRE) —Princess Rosananti (IRE) (Shareef Dancer (USA))
2241[6] 2828[10] 3469[12]

Bin End *M L W Bell* 89
3 b g King's Best(USA) —Overboard (IRE) (Rainbow Quest (USA))
(1087) ◆ 1992[4] ◆ 2189[2]

Binfield (IRE) *B G Powell* a77 72
4 b m Officer(USA) —Identify (IRE) (Persian Bold)
651[3] 878[8] 1020[6] 1417[2] 1860[10] 2212[4] 2910[7] 3736[11] 5791[3] 6547[9] 6719[6] ◆ 7423[9]

Biniou (IRE) *R M H Cowell* a101 111
6 b g Mozart(IRE) —Cap Coz (IRE) (Indian Ridge)
(2094) (4099) 4523[9] (4885)

Binnion Bay (IRE) *J J Bridger* a61 57
8 b g Fasliyev(USA) —Literary (Woodman (USA))
321[6] (496) 661[3] 874[7] 1710[3] 2330[7] 2675[10] 2851[3] 2924[8] 3158[2] 4149[8] 4321[7] 4563[13] 5019[7] 5473[6] 7109[7] 7225[8] 7440[13] (7660)

Bin Shamardal (IRE) *B W Hills* 59
2 ch c Shamardal(USA) —Lonely Ahead (USA) (Rahy (USA))
4524[9]

Bintalaleumydarlin (IRE) *M Johnston* 53
2 b f Refuse To Bend(IRE) —Silly Game (IRE) (Bigstone (IRE))
4847[7] 5290[4] 5505[10] 6319a[19] 6895[6]

Bint Almatar (USA) *Saeed Bin Suroor* 71
2 b f Kingmambo(USA) —Firth Of Lorne (IRE) (Danehill (USA))
(6389) ◆ 7187[9]

Bintalwaadi *E A L Dunlop* 66
2 b f Barathea(IRE) —Al Durrah (USA) (Darshaan)
4468[2]

Bint Doyen *C E Brittain* 79
2 br f Doyen(IRE) —Zonda (Fabulous Dancer (USA))
(6561) ◆ 6852[11]

Biofuel (USA) *Reade Baker* a113 84
3 b f Stormin Fever(USA) —Ms Cornstalk (USA) (Indian Charlie (USA))
7283a[4]

Birbone (FR) *Saeed Bin Suroor* a95 101
4 b g Sendawar(IRE) —Labour Of Love (USA) (Silver Deputy (CAN))
2398[6]

Birdinthehand (FR) *H R A Cecil* a67 73
3 b f Nayef(USA) —Bird In The Sky (CAN) (Sky Classic (CAN))
1780[3] 2538[2] 3432[2]

Bird On The Wire *W G M Turner* a55
2 gr f Compton Place—Pomponette (USA) (Rahy (USA))
6069[7] 6722[7] 7024[11] 7421[7]

Birkside *Miss L A Perratt* a92 94
6 ch g Spinning World(USA) —Bright Hope (IRE) (Danehill (USA))
1826[5] 1990[8] (2437) 2815[11] 3266[6] 3854[2] 4038[4] 4288[7] (4874) 5943[5] 6310[3] 6498[5] 7118[6]

Birthday Star (IRE) *Mrs L C Jewell* a48 58
7 b g Desert King(IRE) —White Paper (IRE) (Marignan (USA))
7642[6]

Bishaara (IRE) *J H M Gosden* a64
3 b f Alhaarth(IRE) —Majmu (USA) (Al Nasr (FR))
849[6]

Bishopbriggs (USA) *M G Quinlan* a74 69
4 ch g Victory Gallop(CAN) —Inny River (USA) (Seattle Slew (USA))
235[9] 387[11] 590[10] 861[11] 2130[12] 7880[8]

Bishop Rock (USA) *M H Tompkins* a61 60
3 b c Vicar(USA) —Rhumba Rage (USA) (Nureyev (USA))
529[5] 2567[12] 3099[11]

Bitter Honey *Mrs G S Rees* a53 62
2 b f Reset(AUS) —Piccolo Cativo (Komaite (USA))
2226[4] 2778[8] 4075[3] 4493[4] 6826[9] 7619[11] 7713[5]

Bitter Man (IRE) *M R Channon* 71
2 b c Azamour(IRE) —Savieres (IRE) (Sadler's Wells (USA))
2889[3]

Bivouac (UAE) *G A Swinbank* a60 69
5 b g Jade Robbery(USA) —Tentpole (USA) (Rainbow Quest (USA))
1436[8] 2666[6] 3098[5] 3863[8] 4402[4] 4932[6] 5364[10] 5953[10]

Black Astor (USA) *Lisa Lewis* a65 111
5 b g Black Minnaloushe(USA) —Bagasse (USA) (Sunshine Forever (USA))
7281a[9]

Black Attack (IRE) *Paul Green* a50 74
3 br g Invincible Spirit(IRE) —Mughetta (Prince Sabo)
568[7]

Black Baccara *P S McEntee* 65
2 b f Superior Premium—Areish (IRE) (Keen)
(1044)

Black Bear Island (IRE) *A P O'Brien* 113
3 b c Sadler's Wells(USA) —Kasora (IRE) (Darshaan)
1239a[3] (2014) 2705[10] 3087[3] 3970a[7]

Black Beauty *M G Quinlan* a59 56
6 br g Diktat—Euridice (IRE) (Woodman (USA))
1014[9]

Black Cloud *G P Enright* a26 45
6 gr g Cloudings(IRE) —Dutch Czarina (Prince Sabo)
3275[10] 3774[7]

Black Crystal (USA) *Robert Collet* 93
3 b f Elusive Quality(USA) —Watership Crystal (IRE) (Sadler's Wells (USA))
1657a[5]

Black Daddy *R Hannon* a40 56
2 b g Night Shift(USA) —Sareb (FR) (Indian Ridge)
1005[6] 1188[8] 5505[7] 5938[7] 6589[3]

Black Dahlia *J A Glover* a98 80
4 br m Dansili—South Rock (Rock City)
932[3] 1020[5] 1348[7] 2246[4] 2573[3] 2768[4] 3267[6] 4003[11] 4619[7] 6023[5] (6174) ◆ 6365[2] 6725[3] 6976[10] (7321) (7516) ◆ 7768[5]

Black Draft *B Forsey* a48 12
7 bb g Josr Algarhoud(IRE) —Tilia (Primo Dominie)
513[11] 921[11] 2630[7] 2880[13] 7770[4]

Black Eagle (IRE) *Saeed Bin Suroor* a104 91
3 b c Cape Cross(IRE) —Shimna (Mr Prospector (USA))
6539[5] ◆ (6794) ◆ 7194[2] (7393)

Black Emblem (JPN) *S Kojima* 113
4 br m War Emblem(USA) —Vin De Noir (JPN) (Hector Protector (USA))
643a[P]

Black Falcon (IRE) *John A Harris* a68 62
9 ch g In The Wings—Muwasim (USA) (Meadowlake (USA))
40[3] 147[4] 302[11] 7505[12] 7677[7]

Black Jacari (IRE) *A King* 89
4 b g Black Sam Bellamy(IRE) —Amalia (IRE) (Danehill (USA))
4212[3]

Black Law (FR) *R Rohne* 70
3 b c Classic Law—La Grinta (FR) (Le Balafre (FR))
(5784a)

Black Mamba (NZ) *John W Sadler* 113
6 b m Black Minnaloushe(USA) —Sneetch (NZ) (Grosvenor (NZ))
7744a[13]

Black Mambazo (IRE) *L Riccardi* 116
4 b h Statue Of Liberty(USA) —Rich Gift (Cadeaux Genereux)
434a[5] 1905a[2] 2523a[2] 6522a[5]

Black Moma (IRE) *J R Boyle* a36 69
5 b m Averti(IRE) —Sareb (FR) (Indian Ridge)
1619[7] 2130[13] 4702[4] 5008[6] 5156[6]

Black N Brew (USA) *J R Best* a77 76
3 b g Milwaukee Brew(USA) —Natural Glow (USA) (Siphon (BRZ))
164[2] 389[2] 962[3] 1930[9] 6562[3] 6778[5] (7607) 7777[6]

Black Nun *S Wynne* a61 49
3 b f Fasliyev(USA) —Roxy (Rock City)
1937[6] 3466[8] 3923[10] 4065[6]

Black Or Red (IRE) *I A Wood* a79 71
4 b g Cape Cross(IRE) —Gentle Thoughts (Darshaan)
1936[7] 2127[2] (4168) 4551[2] 5094[4] 5625[8] 6432[6] 6692[2] 7170[8] 7328[5] (7649)

Black Piranha (AUS) *Con Karakatsanis* 119
6 br g Clang(AUS) —Jazztrack (AUS) (Distinctly North (USA))
7040a[9]

Black Quartz (FR) *A P O'Brien* 100
2 b c Danehill Dancer(IRE) —Mirina (FR) (Pursuit Of Love)
2302a[4]

Black Rain *M Wigham* a82 79
4 b g Desert Prince(IRE) —Antigua (Selkirk (USA))
1357[8] 3840[7] 4759[8] 5448[10] 6174[7] (6832) ◆ 6900[7]

Black River Falls (USA) *I Semple* a48 58
3 b g Fusaichi Pegasus(USA) —La Lorgnette (CAN) (Val De L'Orne (FR))
1562[4] 2030[7] 3294[4] 4079[10] 5470[3] ◆ 5838[10] 6139[7]

Black Rock Lake (IRE) *T G McCourt* a41 64
3 gr f Daylami(IRE) —God Speed (IRE) (Be My Guest (USA))
6075[8]

Black Rose (FR) *F Chappet* 101
3 b f Sagacity(FR) —Black Dahlia (FR) (Sanglamore (USA))
3668a[5] 4334a[3] 5298a[5] 6238a[3] 7697a[10]

Black Salix (USA) *Mrs P Sly* 50
3 br f More Than Ready(USA) —Woodman's Dancer (USA) (Woodman (USA))
3859[9] 4179[7] 5111[9] 6390[14]

Black Sapphire *Miss Amy Weaver* 61
2 b f Motivator—Esquiline (USA) (Gone West (USA))
4055[5] 4557[8] 5428[12]

Black Seventeen (USA) *Brian Koriner* a117 104
5 ch h Is It True(USA) —Fuzzy Navel (USA) (Strike The Anvil (USA))
1010a[6]

Black Snowflake (USA) *Saeed Bin Suroor* 97
2 b c Elusive Quality(USA) —Black Escort (USA) (Southern Halo (USA))
3113[2] (3571) (4488) 5214[3] 5659[3] 6133a[4] 6898[5]

Black Spirit (USA) *C G Cox* 101
2 b c Black Minnaloushe(USA) —L'Extra Honor (USA) (Hero's Honor (USA))
(3794) 5261[4] 6268[9]

Black Stocking *Rae Guest* a44 56
4 br m Dansili—Mariette (Blushing Scribe (USA))
1941[6] 5747[10] 5965[5] 6771[6] 7143[5] 7466[6]

Blackstone Vegas *J Howard Johnson* 66
3 ch g Nayef(USA) —Waqood (USA) (Riverman (USA))
1829[7] 2627[2]

Blacktoft (USA) *Evan Williams* a81 80
6 bb g Theatrical(IRE) —Black Truffle (USA) (Mt. Livermore (USA))
29[3] 143[4] (452) (483) (577) 693[3]

Black Tor Figarro (IRE) *B W Duke* a55 67
4 b g Rock Of Gibraltar(IRE) —Will Be Blue (IRE) (Darshaan)
341[12] 668[5]

Blackwater Fort (USA) *J Gallagher* a32 62
3 bb g Doneraile Court(USA) —Clearwater (USA) (Seeking The Gold (USA))
1956[4] 2377[7] 2810[4] 3476[8] 4791[14]

Blackwell Nation (IRE) *Adrian McGuinness* a68 58
3 b f Kheleyf(USA) —No Tippling (IRE) (Unblest)
3651[2] 4137[4]

Blade Of Class *P D Evans* a7
2 b f Needwood Blade—Top Of The Class (IRE) (Rudimentary (USA))
2128[11]

Blade Of Glory *A J McCabe* a44 33
2 ch f Needwood Blade—Jewel (IRE) (Cyrano De Bergerac)
2765[8] 3226[8] 5106[6] 5519[13] 5811[8]

Blades Harmony *E S McMahon* a26
2 b g Needwood Blade—Yabint El Sham (Sizzling Melody)
7836[4]

Blades Princess *E S McMahon* a72 91
3 ch f Needwood Blade—Breezy Palms (Tragic Role (USA))
1582[16] 2443[11] 4849[6] 5149[8] 5830[8] 6669[6]

Blaise Tower *G L Moore* a78 82
3 ch g Fantastic Light(USA) —Blaise Castle (USA) (Irish River (FR))
(74) 209[4] 2432[7] 2884[3] 4520[12]

Blakeneys Pet (IRE) *W G M Turner*
3 b f Celtic Swing—Kathryn's Pet (Blakeney)
7888[13]

Blakeshall Diamond *A J Chamberlain* a67 47
4 gr m Piccolo—Hi Hoh (IRE) (Fayruz)
2682[12] 2811[7] 4778[7] 5125[10] 5480[6] 5525[5] 5911[7]

Blakeshall Quest *R Brotherton* a56 15
9 b m Piccolo—Corniche Quest (IRE) (Salt Dome (USA))
95[8] 367[4] 487[5] 675[9] 2134[4] 2579[2] 2745[4]

Blakey's Boy *J L Dunlop* 86
2 b g Hawk Wing(USA) —Divine Grace (IRE) (Definite Article)
(3867) 5022[3] 6664[8]

Blandford Flyer *M J Gingell* a45 23
6 b g Soviet Star(USA) —Vento Del Oreno (FR) (Lando (GER))
3011[3]

Blank Cheque (SAF) *H J Brown*
6 ch g Rich Man's Gold(USA) —Kenmare Belle (AUS) (Kenmare (FR))
414a[14]

Blas Ceoil (USA) *J S Bolger* a94 95
3 br f Mr Greeley(USA) —Extraterrestral (USA) (Storm Bird (CAN))
1376a[5]

Blast *J R Gask* a58 59
2 ch f Avonbridge—Pain Perdu (IRE) (Waajib)
6826[6] 7210[11]

Blastie *T D Walford* 48
4 b g Josr Algarhoud(IRE) —Passerella (FR) (Brustolon)
1888[7] 4505[13] 4805[4] 5423[11] 5953[8]

Blaze Brightly (IRE) *Mrs John Harrington* a84 80
2 b f Big Bad Bob(IRE) —Kristal's Paradise (IRE) (Bluebird (USA))
7258a[2]

Blazing Buck *A W Carroll* 74
3 ch g Fraam—Anapola (GER) (Polish Precedent (USA))
1105[6] 3588[10] 4196[7] 4934[4] 5790[5]

Blazing Heights *J S Goldie* a61 76
6 b g Compton Place—Harrken Heights (IRE) (Belmez (USA))
1685[4] ◆ 2225[10] 2717[12] 3111[5] 3681[7] 3909[6] 4467[7] 4778[4] 4877[3] 5411[9] 5946[8] 6010[16] 6314[9] 6410[12] 6989[14] 7086[12]

Blessed Luck (IRE) *S Botti* 102
2 b f Rock Of Gibraltar(IRE) —Pinky Mouse (IRE) (Machiavellian (USA))
(6892a)

Blessed Place *D J S Ffrench Davis* a68 71
9 ch g Compton Place—Cathedra (So Blessed)
2202[13] 2549[9] 2799[8] 3422[9] 3720[9] 3917[5] 4051[2] (4283) 4662[3] 4907[10]

Blessing Belle (IRE) *Mme G Rarick* a52 57
3 ch f Traditionally(USA) —Kind Of Loving (Diesis)
(1691) 1967[5] 7386a[8]

Bleue Doloise (FR) *A Bonin* a55 86
5 br m Marchand De Sable(USA) —Ramonda (FR) (Fabulous Dancer (USA))
3045a[8]

Blind Luck (USA) *Jerry Hollendorfer* a114
2 ch f Pollard's Vision(USA) —Lucky One (USA) (Best Of Luck (USA))
7283a[3]

Blinka Me *M H Tompkins* a51 47
2 b c Tiger Hill(IRE) —Easy To Love (USA) (Diesis)
2860[6] 3395[11] 4385[9] 6034[8] 7474[5]

Blissful Moment (USA) *Sir Michael Stoute* 76
2 bb c Dynaformer(USA) —Arabian Spell (IRE) (Desert Prince (IRE))
6423[4] ◆

Blitzed *G L Moore* 66
2 b g Fantastic Light(USA) —Broken Peace (USA) (Devil's Bag (USA))
7146[6]

Blizzard Blues (USA) *H R A Cecil* 98
3 ch c Mr Greeley(USA) —Blush Damask (USA) (Green Dancer (USA))
(3751) 6644[3]

Blockley (USA) *Ian Williams* a73 70
5 b g Johannesburg(USA) —Saintly Manner (USA) (St Jovite (USA))
(18) 126[7] 692[2] (809) (983) 1273[2] ◆ 1732[3] 4269[6] 4563[11] 5444[8] 6692[3] 7328[8] 7649[2]

Block Party *R Charlton* a85 86
3 b c Dansili—Mylania (Midyan (USA))
2662[4] 3624[2] ◆ (4381) 4902[3] 6111[7] 6614[2] 6773[11]

Blow Hole (USA) *Paul Mason* a77 67
4 ch g Mr Greeley(USA) —Nevis (USA) (Cox's Ridge (USA))
3461[8] 4083[7]

Blown It (USA) *I Semple* a78 82
3 bb g More Than Ready(USA) —Short Shadow (USA) (Out Of Place (USA))
1828[4] 2393[3] 3096[4] 3681[5] 4134[12] (4776) ◆ 5405[7] 6489[3] 6764[14] 7155[5] 7478[4]

Blow Up (IRE) *R Menichetti* 99
2 ch c Daggers Drawn—Miss Buffy (Polar Falcon (USA))
6716a[6]

Blow Your Mind *Karen McLintock* 64
3 b c Mind Games—Ashkernazy (IRE) (Salt Dome (USA))
3484[9] 4653[6] 5396[12] 6161[6]

Blue Again *W R Swinburn* a45
2 b f Leporello(IRE) —Forever Blue (Spectrum (IRE))
7537[8]

Blue Alec (FR) *Mlle S-V Tarrou* 69
2 b c Russian Blue(IRE) —Attendrie (IRE) (Miner's Mark (USA))
7384a[4]

Blue And Gold (FR) *Mlle S-V Tarrou* a92 98
3 ch f Spinning World(USA) —Blue Story (FR) (Gold Away (IRE))
5495a[4] 6579a[14]

Blue Angel (IRE) *R Hannon* a75 102
2 b f Oratorio(IRE) —Blue Cloud (IRE) (Nashwan (USA))
(3507) 4272[2] 4795[7] 5427[4] 6269[6]

Blue Avon *R A Fahey* 57
2 b f Avonbridge—Blue Nile (IRE) (Bluebird (USA))
3571[6] 4278[11] 4652[2] 5938[13]

Blue Bajan (IRE) *Andrew Turnell* a108 113
7 b g Montjeu(IRE) —Gentle Thoughts (Darshaan)
2056[2] 5854[4] 6854[4]

Bluebaru *L R James* 28
3 b g Bahamian Bounty—Gina Of Hithermoor (Reprimand)
1335[13]

Bluebell Ridge (IRE) *D W P Arbuthnot* a70 44
4 b m Distant Music(USA) —Miss Indigo (Indian Ridge)
103[7] (299)

Bluebird Chariot *J M Bradley* a40 40
6 b g Bluebird(USA) —Boadicea's Chariot (Commanche Run)
4238[5] 5634[12] 5717[8] 7520[6]

Blue Black Jack (IRE) *A & G Botti* 101
3 b c Sakhee(USA) —Blue Melody (ITY) (Bluebird (USA))
1904a[6]

Bluebok *J M Bradley* a75 67
8 ch g Indian Ridge—Blue Sirocco (Bluebird (USA))
15[9] 96[6] 165[3] 349[3] 582[5] 645[4] 956[2] (1134) 1182[2] 1540[3] 1877[5] 2180[9] 2596[3] 2801[5] 3252[6] 3304[15] (4204) 4978[3] 5184[5] 5411[6] 5792[2] 6205[5] 7021[8] 7136[5] 7280[7] 7595[4] 7657[4]

Blue Bond *P T Midgley* a46 38
2 ch g Monsieur Bond(IRE) —Azula (Bluebird (USA))
1083[8] 1158[4] 1364[6] 2896[14] 3494[6] 3958[7] 4173[6] 4858[9]

Blue Cayenne (FR) *Mlle S-V Tarrou* a73 106
4 b m Anabaa Blue—Nakiya (FR) (Kendor (FR))
3908a[6] 5495a[6] 6579a[4] 7232a[3] (7458a)

Blue Celeste *R T Phillips* a36 13
3 b f Sakhee(USA) —Ellie Ardensky (Slip Anchor)
6934[10] 7694[6]

Blue Charm *I W McInnes* a82 73
5 b g Averti(IRE) —Exotic Forest (Dominion)
9[2] 31[3] 106[3] 606[2] 806[3] 1169[4] (1612) 2245[12] 2261[6] 3234[4] 3637[11] 4144[3] 4400[12]

Blue Coral (IRE) *T Satra* 99
5 b h Grand Lodge(USA) —Pharmacist (IRE) (Machiavellian (USA))
6718a[6]

Bluecrop Boy *D J S Ffrench Davis* a57 44
5 b g Zaha(CAN) —Pearl Dawn (IRE) (Jareer (USA))
5885[6]

Blue Cross Boy (USA) *Adrian McGuinness* a54 60
4 gr g Sunday Break(JPN) —Introducer (USA) (Cozzene (USA))
6410[9] 7466[10]

Blue Dagger (IRE) *P C Haslam* 66
3 ch g Daggers Drawn(USA) —Sports Post Lady (IRE) (M Double M (USA))
4279[17]

Blue Dynasty (USA) *Mrs A J Perrett* a68 67
3 b g Dynaformer(USA) —Saudia (USA) (Gone West (USA))
2540[6] 3593[6]

Blue Emirate *P C Haslam* 28
2 b g Dubai Destination(USA) —Dorinda Gray (IRE) (Dockside (USA))
2784[3] 3494[7] 5519[12]

Blue Exit (USA) *Jerry Hollendorfer* a106 102
4 b h Pulpit(USA) —Black Speck (USA) (Arch (USA))
789a[P]

Blue Eyed Miss (IRE) *J T Gorman* a58 57
4 b m Statue Of Liberty(USA) —Classic Jenny (IRE) (Green Desert (USA))
7297a[12]

Blue Fang (IRE) *T Clout* a61 52
4 gr h Clodovil(IRE) —Eelaf (IRE) (Marju (IRE))
5301a[3]

Bluefields (FR) *E Leray* 100
8 br g Anabaa(USA) —Providenc Mill (FR) (French Stress (USA))
5932a[7] 6527a[9]

Blue Glove (IRE) *J A Osborne* a30
2 b f Bertolini(USA) —Red Shoe (Selkirk (USA))
7451[10] 7772[10] 7874[4]

Bluegrass Lion (USA) *Paul Green* 50
3 bb g Volponi(USA) —Exactly Dixie (USA) (Dixie Brass (USA))
5939[5] *7504[7]*

Blue Hills *P W Hiatt* a71 63
8 br g Vettori(IRE) —Slow Jazz (USA) (Chief's Crown (USA))
38[5] (301) 402[2] 604[4] 692[6] 735[9] 1442[4] 1936[13]

Blue Jack *W R Muir* a84 102
4 b g Cadeaux Genereux—Fairy Flight (IRE) (Fairy King (USA))
1094[3] 1418[2] ◆ 1699[15] 2326[6] (2637) 2946[5] (3694) 4135[8] (4461) (5263) 5654[11] 6091[18]

Bluejain *Miss Gay Kelleway* a87 73
4 b g Lujain(USA) —Belle Of The Blues (IRE) (Blues Traveller (IRE))
199[P] (Dead)

Blue Jet (USA) *R M Whitaker* a59 61
5 b g Black Minnaloushe(USA) —Clickety Click (USA) (Sovereign Dancer (USA))
1242[12] 1765[6] 2344[3] 2785[2] *3714[11]* 5359[12] 5600[7] 6102[3] 6559[6]

Blue Ksar (FR) *E Charpy* 109
6 b h Anabaa(USA) —Delicieuse Lady (Trempolino (USA))
436a[3] 614a[3] 774a[8]

Blue Lyric *L M Cumani* a79 59
2 b f Refuse To Bend(IRE) —Powder Blue (Daylami (IRE))
5478[6] *6026[3]* 6821[6] *(7514)* ◆ *(7611)* ◆

Blue Maiden *P J McBride* 104
2 b f Medicean—Bluebelle (Generous (IRE))
3248[2] (4318) 4795[2] 6447[5]

Blue Monday *R Charlton* a104 119
8 b g Darshaan—Lunda (IRE) (Soviet Star (USA))
4090[4] 5059a[4]

Blue Neptune *W R Muir* a64 34
2 ch c Compton Place—Centre Court (Second Set (IRE))
3263[10] 5829[6] *6347[7] (6938) 7156[12] 7372[11] 7570[3] 7698[3] 7871[6]*

Blue Noodles *P D Evans* a72 72
3 b g Reset(AUS) —Gleam Of Light (IRE) (Danehill (USA))
797[7] 1062[3] 1452[3] 1686[5] (2234) 2660[5] 2970[2] 3342[3] 3729[6] 4425[2] 4812[3] (5628) *(6070)* 6790[2]

Blue Nymph *R M Beckett* a93 82
3 ch f Selkirk(USA) —Blue Icon (Peintre Celebre (USA))
3508[2] 3951[2] 4687[2] *(6225) (6875)*

Blue Panis (FR) *F Chappet* 91
2 b c Panis(USA) —Rhapsody In Blue (FR) (Bering)
3667a[8] 4584a[4] 5416a[3] 6326a[5] 7346a[5]

Blue Rum (IRE) *P C Haslam* a30 51
2 b g Pyrus(USA) —Secret Combe (IRE) (Mujadil (USA))
1364[3] 1624[4] 2100[5] 6589[6] *7421[8]*

Blues And Rock (ARG) *M F De Kock* a98
4 br h Casual Meeting(ARG) —Free Many (ARG) (Freelancer (USA))
258a[4] 526a[5]

Blue Savanna *H Le S Vautier* a51 51
9 ch g Bluegrass Prince(IRE) —Dusk In Daytona (Beveled (USA))
5540a[9]

Blues Jazz *Miss Gay Kelleway* a49
3 b g Josr Algarhoud(IRE) —Belle Of The Blues (IRE) (Blues Traveller (IRE))
6223[8]

Blue Sky Basin *Saeed Bin Suroor* a105 108
4 b g Desert Prince(IRE) —Kimba (USA) (Kris S (USA))
413a[10] ◆ *521a[8]* ◆ 637a[3] ◆ 1861[14]

Blue Sky Thinking (IRE) *K R Burke* a72 89
10 b g Danehill Dancer(IRE) —Lauretta Blue (IRE) (Bluebird (USA))
12[10] 105[10]

Blues Minor (IRE) *M Mullineaux* a72 68
4 b g Acclamation—Narbayda (IRE) (Kahyasi)
3469[11] 3924[11] 4710[17] *5683[10]*

Blue Sparkle (IRE) *Mrs A J Perrett* 67
2 b f Acclamation—Westlife (IRE) (Mind Games)
2676[3] 5096[9] 5604[3]

Blue Spartan (IRE) *B J Meehan* 82
4 gr g Spartacus(IRE) —Bridelina (FR) (Linamix (FR))
1603[12]

Blue Spinnaker (IRE) *M W Easterby* 91
10 b g Bluebird(USA) —Suedoise (Kris)
1593[11] 1952[9] 2374[6] 2894[7] 3656[8] 4400[9] 4881[6] 5673[11] 6900[11]

Blue Tango (IRE) *Mrs A J Perrett* a73 71
3 ch c Noverre(USA) —It Takes Two (IRE) (Alzao (USA))
595[4] 840[8] 1408[10] 3575[7] *3954[3]* 4442[8] *(6075) 6342[11] 6584[6]* 6910[10]

Blue Tomato *Miss L A Perratt* a88 93
8 b g Orpen(USA) —Ocean Grove (IRE) (Fairy King (USA))
349[2] 422[2] 510[2] 690[2] (739) 756[3] (973) 1104[3] 1227[7] 1849[5] 1924[2] 2185[3] (2451) (2717) 2814[9] 3678[2] (4036) 4464[4] 4753[11] 6051[8]

Blue Turk *J R Boyle* a64 59
4 b g Where Or When(IRE) —Pearly River (Elegant Air)
4533[2] 4916[7] *(6288) 6588[4] 7112[10] 7225[7]*

Blue Warrior (IRE) *J R Best*
4 b g Touch Of The Blues(FR) —Warrior Wings (Indian Ridge)
3161[11]

Blue Zephyr *W R Muir* a62
2 br c Pastoral Pursuits—Pippa's Dancer (IRE) (Desert Style (IRE))
1119[5]

Bluie *D Nicholls* 79
2 b g Ishiguru(USA) —Flying Highest (Spectrum (IRE))
1764[8] 2099[4] 2896[3] (3572) (4525) (4895) 5658[4] 6048[4]

Blushing (IRE) *B J Meehan* 61
2 b f Fasliyev(USA) —Danseuse Du Bois (USA) (Woodman (USA))
3256[5] 3534[4] *5368[12]*

Blushing Bertie *J W Unett* a39
3 b g Bertolini(USA) —Blushing Sunrise (USA) (Cox's Ridge (USA))
3228[7]

Blushing Dreamer (IRE) *Miss N A Lloyd-Beavis* a23
3 ch f Frenchmans Bay(FR) —Second Dream (IRE) (Second Set (IRE))
7615[10]

Blushing Heart *G M Moore* a50 61
5 b m Observatory(USA) —Navarazi (Arazi (USA))
147[5] 368[12]

Blushing Hilary (IRE) *Mrs S J Humphrey* a58 65
6 ch m City On A Hill(USA) —Trinida (Jaazeiro (USA))
248[8] (Dead)

Blushing Maid *H S Howe* a63 67
3 br f Namid—Music Maid (IRE) (Inzar (USA))
1985[4] 2520[6] *2632[6]* 2913[8] 3995[6] *4748[11]* 4950[6] *5809[8]* 6362[10]

Blushing Soul (USA) *L A Dace* a70
3 ch g Perfect Soul(IRE) —Kalimenta (USA) (Rahy (USA))
7888[12]

Bluster (FR) *Robert Collet* 107
3 b c Indian Rocket—Tell Me Why (FR) (Distant Relative)
1043a[4] 5928a[3] 6579a[3] 7232a[6] 7458a[3]

Blythe Knight (IRE) *J J Quinn* a99 117
9 ch g Selkirk(USA) —Blushing Barada (USA) (Blushing Groom (FR))
815[2] 997[7] 1346[6] 2015[5] 3639[14] 4404[14]

Board Meeting (IRE) *E Lellouche* 111
3 b f Anabaa(USA) —Bright Moon (USA) (Alysheba (USA))
1657a[2] 2952a[5] (4578a) 5929a[3] 6525a[2]

Bobal Girl *M D Squance* a53 44
4 ch m Tobougg(IRE) —Al Guswa (Shernazar)
43[12]

Bobbie Soxer (IRE) *J L Dunlop* a77 83
3 br f Pivotal—Fantasy Girl (IRE) (Marju (IRE))
1434[2] 1814[2] (2336) ◆ 2611[4] 3453[8] 4338[9] 5130[2] 5901[4] ◆ *6723[7]*

Bobble Rock (IRE) *J R Best* a27 53
3 ch c Rock Of Gibraltar(IRE) —Torosay Spring (First Trump)
3773[3] 4180[6] 4786[12] 5479[12] *6213[12] 6371[11]*

Bobby Charles *Dr J D Scargill* a87 63
8 ch g Polish Precedent(USA) —Dina Line (USA) (Diesis)
4054[7]

Bobby McGee *Jedd O'Keeffe* 43
2 b f Captain Rio—Al Kahina (Mark Of Esteem (IRE))
6408[6]

Bobbyscot (IRE) *P D Deegan* a65 97
2 b c Alhaarth(IRE) —Sogno Verde (IRE) (Green Desert (USA))
6318a[5]

Bobby's Doll *T T Clement* a57 48
2 ch f Needwood Blade—Nine To Five (Imp Society (USA))
6424[6] *6826[7]* 7175[4] 7477[4] *7584[5]*

Bobeachway (IRE) *M Dods* 51
3 b g Chevalier(IRE) —Miss Barcelona (IRE) (Mac's Imp (USA))
1508[7] 1888[8] 2105[5]

Bobering *B P J Baugh* a43 43
9 b g Bob's Return(IRE) —Ring The Rafters (Batshoof)
132[7] 254[9] 537[6] 775[8] 1314[10] 7719[6]

Bob Goes Electric (IRE) *J R Best* 39
2 br c Camacho—Gracious Gretclo (Common Grounds)
1669[8]

Bobs Dreamflight *D K Ivory* a81 72
3 b g Royal Applause—Millybaa (USA) (Anabaa (USA))
109[2] 1486[10] 1814[7] 2849[9] 3342[2] *6167[8] 7516[10]*

Bobski (IRE) *Miss Gay Kelleway* a91 82
7 b g Victory Note(USA) —Vivid Impression (Cure The Blues (USA))
223[6] 357[4] 452[3] 504[3] 569[2] 959[9] 1194[2] 1539[3]

Bobs Pride (IRE) *D K Weld* a96 98
7 b g Marju(IRE) —Vyatka (Lion Cavern (USA))
4412a[3]

Bob Stock (IRE) *W J Musson* a66 67
3 b g Dubai Destination(USA) —Red Rita (IRE) (Kefaah (USA))
1746[2] 2048[8] 6925[7] 7246[8] *7480[9] 7650[3]*

Bob's Your Uncle *J G Portman* a61 61
6 br g Zilzal(USA) —Bob's Princess (Bob's Return (IRE))
1537[8] 2429[3] *3029[10]* 3774[6] 5246[9]

Body Gold (ARG) *P J Makin* 19
6 b g Body Glove(ARG) —Aurifera (ARG) (Climber (USA))
6302[11] 6795[14] *7373[10]*

Boffin *Eve Johnson Houghton* a50 60
4 b g Kalanisi(IRE) —Phi Beta Kappa (USA) (Diesis)
1931[9] *2922[4]* 3538[6] 4987[4] 5381[10] 5790[12] *7623[7] 7753[8] 7814[8]*

Boga (IRE) *R J Hodges* a46 61
2 b f Invincible Spirit(IRE) —Miznapp (Pennekamp (USA))
1637[4] (1783) 2041[3] 2325[4] 2907[5] 4901[11] *5310[9]*

Bogside Theatre (IRE) *G M Moore* a32 99
5 b m Fruits Of Love(USA) —Royal Jubilee (IRE) (King's Theatre (IRE))
1519[8] 2031[9] 6095[7] *7091[4]*

Bogula (IRE) *Mrs A Duffield* 61
3 b f Tagula(IRE) —Bobbydazzle (Rock Hopper)
2364[4] 2613[4] 3120[10] 6017[4] 6183[13] 6766[10]

Bohobe (IRE) *Rae Guest* a63 65
4 b m Noverre(USA) —Green Life (Green Desert (USA))
1421[2] *2134[7]* (2799) 3505[7] (4154) 4536[11] 5504[8]

Boho Chic *George Baker* a59 69
3 b f Kyllachy—Summer Lightning (IRE) (Tamure (IRE))
4791[8] 5576[11] (5716) 5900[6] (6340) *6825[11] 6914[2]*

Bois Joli (IRE) *M Botti* a81 78
4 b m Orpen(USA) —Claba Di San Jore (IRE) (Barathea (IRE))
456[3]

Bojangles Andrews *B G Powell* 51
2 b c Avonbridge—Polished Up (Polish Precedent (USA))
4314[17] 4851[4] 5431[10] 6589[17] 7056[8]

Bolanderi (USA) *Andrew Turnell* a51 80
4 ch g Seeking The Gold(USA) —Lilium (Nashwan (USA))
468[3] 2857[3] 3472[3] 4150[3] 4855[4] 5244[5] (5548) 5869[2]

Bolckow *J T Stimpson* a59 59
6 b g Marju(IRE) —Stamatina (Warning)
5377[9]

Bold Account (IRE) *Garry Moss* a66 66
3 bb g Bold Fact(USA) —Generate (Generous (IRE))
229[11] 365[4] 1157[10] 1652[5] 2355[11] *2581[3]* 3031[10] *4172[9]* 4621[9]

Bold Adventure *W J Musson* a72 69
5 ch g Arkadian Hero(USA) —Impatiente (USA) (Vaguely Noble)
(627) 732[2] (835) ◆ *983[2] 1609[6] 1936[6]* 2445[4] *6457[12] 7005[5] 7649[7] 7785[9]*

Bold Alaska (IRE) *Peter Grayson* a67 85
6 b g Cape Cross(IRE) —Dramatic Entry (IRE) (Persian Bold)
1731[10] 7253[11]

Bold Argument (IRE) *Mrs P N Dutfield* a56 74
6 ch g Shinko Forest(IRE) —Ivory Bride (Domynsky)
1320[9] 1572[10] 2202[3] (2549) 2637[10] 3422[10] 4167[7] 5065[10] 5608[8]

Bold Bomber *Paul Green* a51 51
3 b c Kyllachy—Latina (IRE) (King's Theatre (IRE))
1064[8] 1308[7] 1926[8] 2918[7] 3651[10] 4594[4] 5145[9] 6183[11] *7353[6] 7615[8]*

Bold Cross (IRE) *E G Bevan* a75 87
6 b g Cape Cross(IRE) —Machikane Akaiito (IRE) (Persian Bold)
(1775) *2144[6]* 2274[6] 2495[2] (2842) 2976[3] (3378) 3628[4] 4409[8] 4641[4] 5062[2] 5349[9] 5510[5] *5887[7]*

Bold Diktator *R M Whitaker* a83 68
7 b g Diktat—Madam Bold (Never So Bold)
3457[3] 3863[14] *6861[13]*

Bold Diva *A W Carroll* a65 50
4 ch m Bold Edge—Trina's Pet (Efisio)
13[5] 44[5] 118[8] 355[2] 496[4] 646[3] 749[4] 830[3] 1039[4] 1413[6] 1655[2] 2134[3]

Bold Hawk *Mrs C A Dunnett* a44 50
3 b g Mujahid(USA) —Girl Next Door (Local Suitor (USA))
1840[14] 3010[12] 3632[11] *3743[7]*

Bold Haze *Miss S E Hall* 14
7 ch g Bold Edge—Melody Park (Music Boy)
1924[17]

Bold Indian (IRE) *M E Sowersby* a71 66
5 b g Indian Danehill(IRE) —Desert Gift (Green Desert (USA))
215[5] 353[9] 2626[5] 3110[6] ◆ 3448[3] 4034[5] 4897[2] 5465[3] 5953[2] 6219[2] 6488[3]

Boldinor *M R Bosley* a57 67
6 b g Inchinor—Rambold (Rambo Dancer (CAN))
2124[8] 2353[9] 3407[10] 4023[5] 4238[3] 4732[4] 5018[3] 5501[3] 5566[2] 6038[6] 6335[7]

Bold Marc (IRE) *A P Jarvis* a76 86
7 b g Bold Fact(USA) —Zara's Birthday (IRE) (Waajib)
1365[7] 1682[2] 2274[4] 2402[4] *2824[3]* 3265[3] (3496) 4333[9] 4560[10] *6294[4] 6976[11]* 7220[6]

Bold Minstrel (IRE) *M Quinn* a45 84
7 br g Bold Fact(USA) —Ponda Rosa (IRE) (Case Law)
474[10]

Bold Ring *E J Creighton* a64 62
3 ch f Bold Edge—Floppie Disk (Magic Ring (IRE))
753[2] 826[7] 1084[8] 1253[10] 1469[6] 1772[11] (1969) 2365[4] 2602[6] 2776[12] (3859) 4237[3] 4990[6] *5105[4] 5584[2] 5809[7]* 6120[4] 6362[3] 6492[4] 6914[4] 7158[5]

Bold Rose *M D I Usher* a62 67
3 ch f Bold Edge—Bowden Rose (Dashing Blade)
45[5] 229[8] (379) 804[8] (1772) 2160[15] 2321[10] 2776[6] 3917[10] 4061[7] 4536[14] *7710[9] (7880)*

Bold Tie *R Hannon* 75
3 ch g Bold Edge—Level Pegging (IRE) (Common Grounds)
2562[5]

Bolivia (GER) *W Hickst* 106
3 ch f Monsun(GER) —Be My Lady (GER) (Be My Guest (USA))
2524a[2] 3670a[13] 4583a[9]

Bollin Andrew *T D Easterby* 46
2 b c Bollin Eric—Bollin Roberta (Bob's Return (IRE))
4993[12] 5669[9] 5951[8]

Bollin Dolly *T D Easterby* 74
6 ch m Bien Bien(USA) —Bollin Roberta (Bob's Return (IRE))
(4822) 6490[2] (6900) 7247[4]

Bollin Felix *T D Easterby* 98
5 br g Generous(IRE) —Bollin Magdalene (Teenoso (USA))
1519[5] 2055[5] 2486[2] 2895[4]

Bollin Franny *J E Long* a58 44
5 br g Bertolini(USA) —Bollin Ann (Anshan)
46[5] 832[9] 946[3] 1076[6] 1970[14] *2184[5] 2745[11]* 4082[8] 5020[6] 6038[10]

Bollin Freddie *A J Lockwood* a51 59
5 ch g Golden Snake(USA) —Bollin Roberta (Bob's Return (IRE))
2233[9] (2803)

Bollin Greta *T D Easterby* 76
4 bb m Mtoto—Bollin Zola (Alzao (USA))
1366[4] 1648[4] 2445[5] 3035[3] (3563)

Bollin Jasmine *T D Easterby*
2 b f Silver Patriarch(IRE) —Bollin Zola (Alzao (USA))
6214[11]

Bollin Judith *T D Easterby* a53 77
3 b f Bollin Eric—Bollin Nellie (Rock Hopper)
1282[4] 1724[3] (2340) 3575[3] 4506[3] 5131[6] 5952[2] (6822) 7170[2]

Bollin Julie *T D Easterby* 47
2 b f Bollin Eric—Bollin Nellie (Rock Hopper)
6762[10] 7243[7] ◆

Bollin Rachel *T D Easterby* 18
2 gr f Silver Patriarch(IRE) —Bollin Ann (Anshan)
3170[8]

Bollywood (IRE) *J J Bridger* a22 51
6 ch g Indian Rocket—La Fille De Cirque (Cadeaux Genereux)
7888[14]

Bollywood Style *J R Best* a63
4 b m Josr Algarhoud(IRE) —Dane Dancing (IRE) (Danehill (USA))
25[4] 114[2] 321[8] (531) 7517[2] 7606[6] 7716[8]

Bolodenka (IRE) *R A Fahey* a86 101
7 b g Soviet Star(USA) —My-Lorraine (IRE) (Mac's Imp (USA))
783[10] 997[17] 4779[8] 5206[10] 5551[2] ◆ 6094[8] 6732[12] *7662[5] 7812[4] 7848[10]*

Bolshoi King (IRE) *B J Meehan* 34
3 b g Fasliyev(USA) —Nawaji (USA) (Trempolino (USA))
2856[11] 3345[6] 3459[10]

Boltcity (FR) *J-C Rouget* 99
2 b c Elusive City(USA) —Combloux (USA) (Southern Halo (USA))
4579a[4] 5416a[2]

Bolton Hall (IRE) *W K Goldsworthy* a47 50
7 b g Imperial Ballet(IRE) —Muneera (USA) (Green Dancer (USA))
449[6] 627[6] 3503[8] 3997[4] 4168[7] 5444[4] 5873[8]

Bombadero (IRE) *J L Dunlop* 67
2 b c Sadler's Wells(USA) —Fantasy Girl (IRE) (Marju (IRE))
6617[14] 7034[4]

Bombardier Wells *C J Down* a74 69
4 b g Red Ransom(USA) —Bow River Gold (Rainbow Quest (USA))
(500)

Bombay Mist *R C Guest* a11
2 b f Rambling Bear—Paris Mist (Paris House)
1511[9] *7331[11]*

Bomber Brown (IRE) *P W Chapple-Hyam* a78 79
3 b g Pyrus(USA) —Secret Of Gold (IRE) (Peintre Celebre (USA))
201[7] 343[3] 2338[4] 3549[2] (4151) 4716[3] *6209[5]* 6420[4] 6680[12]

Bomber Command (USA) *J W Hills* a99 82
6 b g Stravinsky(USA) —Parish Manor (USA) (Waquoit (USA))
879[5] 1212[13] 1603[10] 1861[24] 3796[9] *3988[6]* 4293[12] *4983[2] (5640) 6168[10] 6830[6] 7375[9]*

Bombie Boy *K W Hogg*
4 b g Tobougg(IRE) —Waraqa (USA) (Red Ransom (USA))
3022[6]

Bombina *P W Chapple-Hyam* 78
3 b f Lomitas—Firebelly (Nicolotte)
(2001) 2858[2] 3763[4] 4198[3] 4720[5]

Bom Boms (IRE) *Tom Dascombe* a20
2 b c Fayruz—Mechilie (Belmez (USA))
6347[11] 6638[10]

Bo McGinty (IRE) *R A Fahey* a80 89
8 ch g Fayruz—Georges Park Lady (IRE) (Tirol)
67[6] 270[4] 382[3] 424[5] 451[4] 690[3] 870[2] 985[2] 1278[4] 1334[4] 1685[6] 2071[9] 2591[4] 2782[5] 3236[3] 3295[5] 7496[10] 7634[10] 7758[5] 7807[5] 7870[5]

Bona Fortuna *Sir Mark Prescott* a51
2 ch g Mark Of Esteem(IRE) —Time Honoured (Sadler's Wells (USA))
6254[7] ◆ *7157[11] 7266[8]*

Bonamassa *M J Attwater* a31
2 b c Sulamani(IRE) —Anastasia Venture (Lion Cavern (USA))
7522[11] 7763[9]

Bonasera (IRE) *A Berry* 32
2 b f Kheleyf(USA) —Jumlah (Unfuwain (USA))
2655[5] 3495[6] 5330[6] 5728[11] 6820[8] *7088[10]*

Bondage (IRE) *J R Fanshawe* a60 57
2 b g Whipper(USA) —Shamah (Unfuwain (USA))
7096[5] *7537[6] 7763[6]*

Bond Casino *G R Oldroyd* a63 54
5 b m Kyllachy—Songsheet (Dominion)
38[10] 790[10]

Bond City (IRE) *G R Oldroyd* a94 102
7 b g Trans Island—Where's Charlotte (Sure Blade (USA))
2059[7] 2405[5] 3318[5] 3567[7] *3928[2]* 4330[17] 4485[6] 4598[8] *5104[3]* 5363[12] *5615[10]* 6050[11] 6645[14] *6949[7]* 7083[11]

Bond Cruz *T Keddy* a26 22
6 b g King's Best(USA) —Arabis (Arazi (USA))
7549[14]

Bonded (IRE) *B J Meehan* a71 51
2 b c Oasis Dream—Lovealoch (IRE) (Lomond (USA))
7034[12] *7491[3] 7764[3]*

Bond Fastrac *G R Oldroyd* a53 93
2 b c Monsieur Bond(IRE) —Kanisfluh (Pivotal)
3226[5] (4430) 5136[2] 5763[5]

Bond Together *P D Evans* a50 48
2 ch g Monsieur Bond(IRE) —My Bonus (Cyrano De Bergerac)
994[10] *1158[2] 1934[3]* 2896[9] 4153[5]

Bonfire Knight *J J Quinn* a71 80
2 b c Red Ransom(USA) —Attune (Singspiel (IRE))
3468[2] ◆ 4067[3] (4618) 5198[9] 5515[2] ◆

Bon Grain (FR) *J J Napoli* 108
4 b h Muhtathir—Such Is Life (FR) (Akarad (FR))
3085a[3] 6506a[7]

Bonheurs Art (IRE) *B W Hills* 76
2 b f Acclamation—Anneliina (Cadeaux Genereux)
4421[4] ◆ 4851[2] 5431[5] 6905[2]

Bonne *Miss J R Tooth* a52 68
4 b m Namid—Jouet (Reprimand)
3722[8] 4154[7] 4285[8] 4380[10] 4536[13]

Bonnet O'Bonnie *J Mackie* a55 10
5 br m Makbul—Parkside Prospect (Piccolo)
810[2] 1781[10] 3972[9]

Bonnie Bea *B I Case* a49 5
3 b f Royal Applause—Boojum (Mujtahid (USA))
6029[4] 6741[13]

Bonnie Brae *G G Margarson* a61 67
2 b f Mujahid(USA) —Skara Brae (Inchinor)
6607[7] 6962[2]

Bonnie Charlie *R Hannon* a76 109
3 ch c Intikhab(USA) —Scottish Exile (IRE) (Ashkalani (IRE))
3298[5] 4052[6] 5032[7] 5766[4] 6240[4] 6661[4] 6815[2]

Bonnie Prince Blue *D Nicholls* a80 83
6 ch g Tipsy Creek(USA) —Heart So Blue (Dilum (USA))
1832[2] 2267[4] 2938[15] 4285[15] 4620[3] (5343) 5623[5] 6434[4] 7337[3]

Bon Spiel *L M Cumani* a105 92
5 b h Singspiel(IRE) —L'Affaire Monique (Machiavellian (USA))
338a[5] 640a[7] 1004[8] 4781[14] 5880[5] 6795[11]

Bonus (IRE) *G A Butler* a115 96
9 b g Cadeaux Genereux—Khamseh (Thatching)
73[2] 123[3] 458[3] 636[4] 781[6] (Dead)

Bonzo *P Howling* a54 21
4 b g Where Or When(IRE) —Making Memories (IRE) (Alzao (USA))
169[12]

Boo *J W Unett* a77 61
7 b g Namaqualand(USA) —Violet (IRE) (Mukaddamah (USA))
693[5] 5503[6] 6460[11] 7127[4]

Boogie Dancer *H S Howe* a62 68
5 b m Tobougg(IRE) —Bolero (Rainbow Quest (USA))
115[7]

Boogie Diva *M Botti* 78
2 b f Tobougg(IRE) —Distant Diva (Distant Relative)
4817[3] 5397[2] 6055[7] 6567[3]

Boogie Waltzer *S C Williams* a53 52
2 b f Tobougg(IRE) —Upping The Tempo (Dunbeath (USA))
3767[7] 4239[6] 4427[5] 5635[4] 7242[2] 7570[6] 7748[3]

Bookend *D Smaga* a90 89
5 b g Dansili—Roupala (USA) (Vaguely Noble)
(5281a)

Bookiebasher Babe (IRE) *M Quinn* a74 72
4 b m Orpen(USA) —Jay Gee (IRE) (Second Set (IRE))
60[6] 176[4] 344[12] 617[6] 1530[4] (1566) (1778) 2212[7] 3060[5] 4060[2] 4179[11] 4759[5] 6346[10] 6703[8]

Bookiesindex Boy *J R Jenkins* a79 65
5 bb g Piccolo—United Passion (Emarati (USA))
83[5] 165[7] 971[6] 1591[11] 2758[13] 3860[13] 5629[3] 6669[2] 7224[2] 7554[10] 7682[9]

Bookiesindex Girl (IRE) *J R Jenkins* a54 45
2 b f Rakti—Distant Valley (Distant Relative)
1841[8] 2860[10] 3709[6] 5635[8] 6061[10] 7087[4] 7333[6] 7419[2] 7706[3] (7887)

Book Of Music (IRE) *S Seemar* a54 98
6 b g Sadler's Wells(USA) —Novelette (Darshaan)
185a[9] 437a[11] 640a[4] 699a[7]

Book Of Truth (USA) *D M Simcock* a31 57
2 bb c Truluck(USA) —Elise's Notebook (USA) (Notebook (USA))
4209[8] 4534[10] 4646[9] 5868[8]

Bootleg *D Nicholls* 14
3 b g Bahamian Bounty—Asbo (Abou Zouz (USA))
1831[7]

Boquito (IRE) *Miss Amy Weaver* a77 62
2 b c Rahy(USA) —Fantasia Girl (IRE) (Caerleon (USA))
2430[8] 4424[4] 5006[8] (5573) (6211) ◆ 6373[3] 7003[5]

Borasco (USA) *T D Barron* a83 91
4 ch m Stormy Atlantic(USA) —Seek (USA) (Devil's Bag (USA))
491[5] ◆ 2045[5] 2402[10] 6667[11] 7220[7] 7412[2] 7679[5] 7813[5]

Border Artist *J Pearce* a59 54
10 ch g Selkirk(USA) —Aunt Tate (Tate Gallery (USA))
1958[5]

Borderlescott *R Bastiman* a105 121
7 b g Compton Place—Jeewan (Touching Wood (USA))
1676[3] 2272[2] 2991[5] (3848) 4456[4] (5233) 6522a[6] 7745a[11]

Border Owl (IRE) *P Salmon* a85 81
4 b g Selkirk(USA) —Nightbird (IRE) (Night Shift (USA))
1886[9] 2274[5] 2542[3] 2891[13] 3496[5] 6023[13] 6383[5] 7423[12] 7711[5]

Border Patrol *R Charlton* 115
3 b c Selkirk(USA) —Ffestiniog (IRE) (Efisio)
(1350) ◆ (2035) (2411) (5924a) 6503a[9] 7208a[2]

Border Tale *James Moffatt* a44 59
9 b g Selkirk(USA) —Likely Story (IRE) (Night Shift (USA))
566[9] 679[8] 2044[2] 2448[2] 3291[2] 4193[3] 5734[11]

Borehan *D Selvaratnam* a85 40
6 b g Agnes World(USA) —Crime Ofthecentury (Pharly (FR))
336a[11]

Borgo Pio (GER) *A Candi* 85
2 b c Barathea(IRE) —Be Crafty (USA) (Crafty Prospector (USA))
7205a[7]

Born A Dancer (IRE) *J W Hills* 54
2 b f Danehill Dancer(IRE) —Born Beautiful (USA) (Silver Deputy (CAN))
5026[8] 6241[22]

Born Romantic *H J L Dunlop* a22 44
3 b f High Chaparral(IRE) —Maid For Romance (Pursuit Of Love)
2074[9] 3025[11]

Born To Be King (USA) *A P O'Brien* 103
3 b c Storm Cat(USA) —Quarter Moon (IRE) (Sadler's Wells (USA))
1022a[3] 1917a[11] 2729a[6] 2992[9]

Born Tobouggie (GER) *H R A Cecil* a106 103
4 b m Tobougg(IRE) —Braissim (Dancing Brave (USA))
(1210) ◆ 1667[3]

Born To Perform *G A Swinbank* 55
4 b g Theatrical(IRE) —My Hansel (USA) (Hansel (USA))
2943[8] 3294[5] 4347[5] 5289[11]

Born West (USA) *N B King* a62 71
5 b g Gone West(USA) —Admirer (USA) (Private Terms (USA))
449[9] 627[3] 732[8] 1154[11]

Borodin (FR) *B Barbier* 64
2 b c Ocean Of Wisdom(USA) —Mystina (FR) (Noblequest (FR))
4368a[7] 4073a[8]

Borodinsky *R E Barr* a42 52
8 b g Magic Ring(IRE) —Valldemosa (Music Boy)
2816[6] 3174[10] 3539[6]

Borouj (IRE) *Joss Saville* a61 61
7 ch g Unfuwain(USA) —Amanah (USA) (Mr Prospector (USA))
554[9] 603[9]

Borromeo (USA) *M Johnston* 64
3 ch g Mr Greeley(USA) —Luxury On The Lake (USA) (Salt Lake (USA))
2446[9] 2640[6] 3056[3] 3260[2]

Bosamcliff (IRE) *P D Evans* a73 69
4 b m Daylami(IRE) —L'Animee (Green Tune (USA))
4950[5] 5449[6] 5791[4] 6218[7] 6909[2] 6967[3] 7127[3] (7174) (7505) 7641[5]

Boscage (USA) *M Johnston* a97 74
4 b g Forestry(USA) —Prospinsky (USA) (Mr Prospector (USA))
(731) (858) 1093[4] 1352[22]

Bosphorus Queen (IRE) *P D Deegan* 82
2 b f Sri Pekan(USA) —Turunc (IRE) (Danehill Dancer (IRE))
3514a[3]

Boss Hog *P T Midgley* a73 55
4 b g Key Of Luck(USA) —Dania (GER) (Night Shift (USA))
289[2] (425) 617[5] 793[3] 868[10] 1123[12] 1438[5] 2133[9] 3539[5] 3730[12] 4140[5] 4466[8] 4887[8] 5147[5] 5465[6] 5982[4] 6358[2] 7051[10]

Boss's Destination *G A Swinbank* 65
2 b g Dubai Destination(USA) —Blushing Sunrise (USA) (Cox's Ridge (USA))
4342[5] 4847[5]

Bossy Kitty *N Tinkler* 77
2 ch f Avonbridge—Between The Sticks (Pharly (FR))
1275[7] 1802[5] 2069[9] 2435[7] 3032[3] 3606[4] 4327[2] 4782[5] 5136[11] (5553) 5992[3] (6409) (6643) 7290[19]

Boston Blue *W J Knight* a66
2 b g Halling(USA) —City Of Gold (IRE) (Sadler's Wells (USA))
7064[4] 7388[5] ◆

Boston Lodge *F Nass* a74 83
9 ch g Grand Lodge(USA) —Ffestiniog (IRE) (Efisio)
182a[8] 334a[9] 609a[8]

Bosun Breese *T D Barron* a61 89
4 b g Bahamian Bounty—Nellie Melba (Hurricane Sky (AUS))
7414[12]

Botanist *Sir Michael Stoute* 82
2 b c Selkirk(USA) —Red Camellia (Polar Falcon (USA))
4986[8] ◆ 5993[2] (6759) ◆

Botham (USA) *J S Goldie* a58 71
5 bb g Cryptoclearance(USA) —Oval (USA) (Kris S (USA))
2158[10] (2441) 2812[2] 3092[9] 3655[6] (4016) 4772[7] (4894) 5150[2] 5516[6] 6157[10] 6411[7] (6985) 7172[9]

Both Ends Burning (IRE) *J S Wainwright* 31
2 ch f Choisir(AUS) —Giadamar (IRE) (Be My Guest (USA))
4430[10] 4817[15]

Bothwell Castle (IRE) *P C Haslam* a41 57
2 b g Captain Rio—Majesty's Nurse (Indian King (USA))
2231[8] 2788[3] 2996[4] 6590[9] 6639[7]

Bothy *R M Beckett* 91
3 ch g Pivotal—Villa Carlotta (Rainbow Quest (USA))
(1461) 2029[6] 6795[4] ◆

Botley Bell *M R Channon* a52 59
2 b f Imperial Dancer—Curbridge Bell (Fraam)
2914[7] 3507[7] 3858[6] 4153[7] 4384[10]

Bottega (USA) *M Delcher-Sanchez* 98
2 ch c Mineshaft(USA) —Sun Is Up (JPN) (Sunday Silence (USA))
(7346a)

Bouggie Daize *C G Cox* 70
3 b f Tobougg(IRE) —Milly's Lass (Mind Games)
2845[8] 4326[9]

Bould Mover *R Curtis* a51 105
2 b c Kyllachy—Maugwenna (Danehill (USA))
1005[4] 1044[3] (3058) (3559) ◆ 4407[5] 4487[9] 5822[2] 6660[4]

Boule Masquee *David P Myerscough* a69 83
5 ch m Compton Place—Burqa (Nashwan (USA))
6120[5]

Boum Des Aigles (FR) *Mme C Barande-Barbe* 68
2 b f Slickly(FR) —Bali Boom (FR) (Jeune Homme (USA))
5117a[3]

Bound By Honour (SAF) *G L Moore* a101 101
6 b g Rambo Dancer(CAN) —Child Of Grace (SAF) (Only A Pound)
265a[4] ◆ 415a[10] 613a[8] 703a[5] 5137[12] 5880[4] 6106[9] 6470[8] 7393[2] (7574) 7789[6]

Bound For Stardom *W S Kittow* 2
2 b f Royal Applause—Liberty Bound (Primo Dominie)
5379[8]

Boundless Applause *I A Wood* a45 54
3 b f Royal Applause—Liberty Bound (Primo Dominie)
2651[7] 3031[3] 3632[7] 5018[4] 5500[3] (6038) 7460[11] 7572[5] 7774[9]

Boundless Prospect (USA) *P D Evans* a74 71
10 b g Boundary(USA) —Cape (USA) (Mr Prospector (USA))
12[3] (237) 406[2] (744) 6012[2] 7036[10] 7332[3] 7677[2] (7779)

Bountiful Bay *Matthew Salaman* a63 51
4 b m Bahamian Bounty—My Preference (Reference Point)
3407[11] 7069[2] 7370[12] 7462[9] 7771[5] 7835[12]

Bounty Box *C F Wall* 100
3 b f Bahamian Bounty—Bible Box (IRE) (Bin Ajwaad (IRE))
2774[3] (4096) (5032) ◆ 6428[2] 6814[6]

Bounty Quest *Doug Watson* a92 100
7 b g Fasliyev(USA) —Just Dreams (Salse (USA))
336a[3] 414a[4]

Bounty Reef *P D Evans* a33 56
3 b f Bahamian Bounty—Shaieef (IRE) (Shareef Dancer (USA))
2357[10] 2950[7] 3334[5] 3588[6] 4224[7] 4642[9] 5628[4] 6369[14]

Bourbon Highball (IRE) *P C Haslam* a25 61
4 b g Catcher In The Rye(IRE) —Be Exciting (IRE) (Be My Guest (USA))
107[9]

Bourne *L M Cumani* a78 72
3 gr g Linamix(FR) —L'Affaire Monique (Machiavellian (USA))
2082[4] 2640[11] 5531[4] 6613[4]

Bourn Fair *P J McBride* a53 31
3 ch f Systematic—Astelia (Sabrehill (USA))
6831[3] ◆ 7143[8] 7354[7] 7658[12] 7802[11]

Bourse (IRE) *A G Foster* a68 71
4 b g Dubai Destination(USA) —Quarter Note (USA) (Danehill (USA))
220[7] 238[4] 1100[6] 1332[5] 1646[5] 2237[13] 2626[8] 3653[11] 4313[4] 4465[5] 4944[5] 5294[8] 5947[6]

Bouvardia *H R A Cecil* 101
3 b f Oasis Dream—Arabesque (Zafonic (USA))
1272[2] ◆ (1879) (2279) 5069[2]

Bow Beaver (USA) *J Howard Johnson* 79
2 b c Vindication(USA) —Miss Carolina (USA) (Unbridled (USA))
(2526) 4939[2] 6134[7]

Bowder Stone (IRE) *E J Alston* 86
4 b g Rock Of Gibraltar(IRE) —Ghita (IRE) (Zilzal (USA))
999[19] 1826[7]

Bowdler's Magic *M Johnston* a73 44
2 b c Hernando(FR) —Slew The Moon (ARG) (Kitwood (USA))
7116[7] 7400[2] (7491) ◆

Bowmaker *M Johnston* a79
2 b g Dubawi(IRE) —Viola Da Braccio (IRE) (Vettori (IRE))
(7087)

Bowsers Beau *M P Tregoning* a65 52
3 br g Sakhee(USA) —Shawahid (USA) (A.P. Indy (USA))
5215[4] 6608[4] 6941[2]

Bow To No One (IRE) *A P Jarvis* a89 69
3 b f Refuse To Bend(IRE) —Deadly Buzz (IRE) (Darshaan)
2847[5] 3297[4] 4022[3] 4569[11] 4994[4] 6139[4] (6538) ◆ (6975) ◆ (7178)

Box Office *M Johnston* 86
3 b c Storming Home—Dream Ticket (USA) (Danzig (USA))
1559[6]

Boy Blue *P Salmon* a51 87
4 b h Observatory(USA) —Rowan Flower (IRE) (Ashkalani (IRE))
1170[5] 1507[3] 2073[4] 2780[7] 3391[3] 4549[4] 5333[11] 6357[7] 7083[10] 7287[13]

Boycott (IRE) *J H M Gosden* a62 61
2 b g Refuse To Bend(IRE) —Withorwithoutyou (IRE) (Danehill (USA))
3167[9] 4314[16] 5251[7] 5589[10] 5985[4] 6609[3]

Boy Dancer (IRE) *J J Quinn* a46 65
6 ch g Danehill Dancer(IRE) —Mary Gabry (IRE) (Kris)
2314[10] 2804[9] 3653[12] 4435[14] 5294[13] 5423[13] 6840[10] 7499[2]

Boy Racer (IRE) *C J Teague* a67 67
4 br g Singspiel(IRE) —Gombay Girl (USA) (Woodman (USA))
4432[10] 7118[7]

Boytard (FR) *F Belmont* 71
4 b h Tot Ou Tard(IRE) —Ballerina Girl (FR) (Moscow Ballet (USA))
6658a[10]

Boy The Bell *J A Osborne* a68
2 b g Choisir(AUS) —Bella Beguine (Komaite (USA))
7276[8] 7556[3] 7708[2]

Boz *L M Cumani* a99 97
5 gr h Grand Lodge(USA) —Dali's Grey (Linamix (FR))
1696[3] 2085[4] 3142[11] 5170[14]

Braddock (IRE) *S Donohoe* a73 70
6 b g Pivotal—Sedna (FR) (Bering)
1376a[3] 7023[2] 7053[6]

Bradford (IRE) *K R Burke* a47 72
2 b c Pyrus(USA) —Lypharden (IRE) (Lyphard's Special (USA))
2388[4] 2721[2] 3468[4] 4152[6]

Brads House (IRE) *J G M O'Shea* 37
7 b g Rossini(USA) —Gold Stamp (Golden Act (USA))
5028[9] 6021[9]

Brad's Luck (IRE) *M Blanshard* a55 62
3 ch g Lucky Story(USA) —Seymour (IRE) (Eagle Eyed (USA))
2230[4] 2779[4] 3279[9] 4004[9] 4744[11] 5838[9] 6497[12] 6785[8] 6859[2]

Brae Hill (IRE) *M L W Bell* a74 97
3 b g Fath(USA) —Auriga (Belmez (USA))
2049[7] (3375) 4459[7] 5615[7] 6278[2]

Braggadocio *P Winkworth*
2 br g Fraam—Brangane (IRE) (Anita's Prince)
3744[9]

Brahms And Mist (FR) *D J S Ffrench Davis* a8
9 b g River Mist(USA) —Strabit (Stradavinsky)
7367[11]

Braille *T D Walford* 71
4 b g Bahamian Bounty—Branston Gem (So Factual (USA))
1518[11] 2770[14] 4399[11] 4620[12]

Bramalea *B W Duke* a73 72
4 b m Whitmore's Conn(USA) —Aster (IRE) (Danehill (USA))
1133[3] 1415[3] 1604[9] 1983[2] 2183[3] 2379[2] 2650[4] 4053[2] 4269[8] 4744[4] 5195[11] 5593[3] 5964[3] (6126) 6498[4]

Brambleberry *Tom Dascombe* a86 62
4 b f Cape Cross(IRE) —Miss Satamixa (FR) (Linamix (FR))
(3210) ◆ 3583[8] 4558[5] (4746) 5194[5] 6179[5]

Brampour (IRE) *J-C Rouget*
2 b c Daylami(IRE) —Brusca (USA) (Grindstone (USA))
7315a[3]

Bramshaw (USA) *Mrs A J Perrett* a72
2 rg c Langfuhr(CAN) —Milagra (USA) (Maria's Mon (USA))
(7537) ◆

Bramshill Lady (IRE) *Pat Eddery* 65
2 rg f Verglas(IRE) —Jinx Johnson (IRE) (Desert King (IRE))
2135[4] 2547[5] 5153[7] 7055[7]

Branaanx (USA) *K A Ryan* 48
2 b c Red Ransom(USA) —Shady Reflection (USA) (Sultry Song (USA))
6990[8]

Branderburgo (IRE) *M Botti* 89
2 b c High Chaparral(IRE) —Farhad (Red Ransom (USA))
2467[6] 3584[3] ◆ 4006[5] 5970[3] 6923[7]

Brandy Butter *A M Balding* a54 54
3 ch g Domedriver(IRE) —Brand (Shareef Dancer (USA))
2395[9] 3384[6] 4205[7] 6375[5] 6935[4]

Brandywell Boy (IRE) *D J S Ffrench Davis* a79 74
6 b g Danetime(IRE) —Alexander Eliott (IRE) (Night Shift (USA))
212[8] 510[3] (589) 870[3] 954[7] 1150[8] 1468[8] 1877[7] 2180[4] 2460[2] 2929[7] (3252) 3422[3] 3860[6] 3998[4] 4604[11] 4907[4] 5323[5] 5608[2] 5911[2] (6205) 6422[5] 6916[2] 6972[4] 7123[6] 7478[9] (7553) 7832[7]

Brannagh (USA) *J Noseda* a76 74
2 ch c Hennessy(USA) —Green Room (USA) (Theatrical (IRE))
6424[3] 7130[3] ◆

Brasingaman Eric *Mrs G S Rees* a51 43
2 b c Bollin Eric—Serene Pearl (IRE) (Night Shift (USA))
3152[4] 3571[4] 3716[6]

Brasingaman Hifive *Mrs G S Rees* a74 84
4 b m High Estate—Our Miss Florence (Carlitin)
1507[9] 2274[3] 3154[5] 4560[3] 5441[12] 5887[6] 7125[9]

Brass Damask (USA) *P Schiergen* 94
4 b m Lemon Drop Kid(USA) —Blush Damask (USA) (Green Dancer (USA))
5651a[10]

Brassini *B R Millman* a68 96
4 gr g Bertolini(USA) —Silver Spell (Aragon)
1212[14] 1663[8] 2050[3] 2434[5] (2927) 3335[10]

Bravalto *B Smart* a52 59
3 b c Falbrav(IRE) —Bunty Boo (Noalto)
7730[6]

Brave Ambition (IRE) *R C Guest* a32 22
2 b g Spartacus(IRE) —I Want You Now (IRE) (Nicolotte)
2575[8] 2996[10] 4396[10] 7419[9]

Brave Beat *H J L Dunlop* a38 43
3 b g Beat Hollow—Be Brave (FR) (Green Forest (USA))
1286[7] 2323[8] 2930[15] 3593[8]

Brave Bugsy (IRE) *A M Balding* a60 66
6 b g Mujadil(USA) —Advancing (IRE) (Ela-Mana-Mou)
2127[5] 2519[2] 3029[6] (3997)

Brave Dealer *R Charlton* 63
3 ch g Falbrav(IRE) —Sharp Terms (Kris)
2074[8] 2930[6] ◆ 3703[7]

Brave Decision *A J McCabe* a70
2 gr g With Approval(CAN) —Brave Vanessa (USA) (Private Account (USA))
7859[3]

Brave Enough (USA) *M A Magnusson* a65
2 b c Yes It's True(USA) —Courageous (USA) (Kingmambo (USA))
7773[11] 7859[5]

Brave Falcon (IRE) *Leo J Temple* a91 94
5 b g Fasliyev(USA) —Don't Care (IRE) (Nordico (USA))
1374a[7] 3898a[6]

Brave Ghurka *S Kirk* a59 67
2 b g Bahamian Bounty—Wondrous Maid (GER) (Mondrian I (GER))
3867[9] 6737[6] 6911[5] 7773[5] 7824[11]

Braveheart Move (IRE) *Sir Mark Prescott* a78 98
3 b g Cape Cross(IRE) —Token Gesture (IRE) (Alzao (USA))
(1792) ◆ 4420[12] (5067) 5230[8] (6138)

Brave Knave (IRE) *B De Haan* 43
4 b h Averti(IRE) —Recall (IRE) (Revoque (IRE))
3432[6]

Bravely (IRE) *T D Easterby* 81
5 b g Rock Of Gibraltar(IRE) —Raghida (IRE) (Nordico (USA))
1060[3] 1333[4] 2235[2] 2402[2] 2938[8] 3172[6] 3825[13] (4311) 4662[11] 5516[4] 5768[11] 6489[14] 6897[2] 7123[8]

Bravely Fought (IRE) *Sabrina J Harty* a98 96
4 b g Indian Ridge—Amazing Tale (Shareef Dancer (USA))
4404[7] 6867a[11] 7323[7]

Brave Mave *Jane Chapple-Hyam* a83 74
4 gr m Daylami(IRE) —Baalbek (Barathea (IRE))
299[7] 5034[5] 5545[8] 7368[5] 7505[9]

Brave Optimist (IRE) *Paul Green* a23 36
4 b m Diktat—Maine Lobster (USA) (Woodman (USA))
556[6]

Brave Prospector *P W Chapple-Hyam* 110
4 b h Oasis Dream—Simply Times (USA) (Dodge (USA))
3141[14] 4523[7] 5132[16] (5826) 6091[25] 6661[3] ◆

Brave Tin Soldier (USA) *M F De Kock* a109 106
5 b h Storm Cat(USA) —Bless (USA) (Mr Prospector (USA))
183a[2] 335a[4] 639a[8] 702a[4] 1008a[5]

Brave Victory (USA) *Nicholas Zito* a100
3 b c Lion Heart(USA) —I'm In Celebration (USA) (Copelan (USA))
2734a[7]

Bravo Belle (IRE) *T H Caldwell*
2 b f Bertolini(USA) —Dazilyn Lady (USA) (Zilzal (USA))
7217[5]

Bravo Blue (IRE) *T H Caldwell* 6
2 b f Mark Of Esteem(IRE) —Fantazia (Zafonic (USA))
6245[9] 6756[6] 6991[11]

Bravo Bravo *Eve Johnson Houghton*
2 b g Sadler's Wells(USA) —Top Table (Shirley Heights)
5831[9]

Bravo Echo *M J Attwater* a91 94
3 b c Oasis Dream—Bold Empress (USA) (Diesis)
2072[11] 2638[3] 3163[5] (4095) 5832[3] 7827[5]

Brazilian Brush (IRE) *J M Bradley* a68 74
4 ch g Captain Rio—Ejder (IRE) (Indian Ridge)
235[12] 461[8] 739[9] 956[6] 2180[14] 2534[9] 3632[6] 4479[8] 7534[8] 7680[6]

Brazilian Star (IRE) *Y De Nicolay* a87 69
4 b g Galileo(IRE) —Braziliz (USA) (Kingmambo (USA))
5281a[7]

Breach Of Peace (USA) *R Charlton* a54 67
3 b f Royal Academy(USA) —Hasardeuse (USA) (Distant View (USA))
1066[8] 1406[6] 2001[6] 2567[5]

Breadstick *H Morrison* a67 71
3 br f Diktat—Poilane (Kris)
1670[2] 2206[10] 3209[6] 5016[4] 5628[6]

Breakevie (IRE) *R A Fahey* 50
3 b f Mull Of Kintyre(USA) —Skehana (IRE) (Mukaddamah (USA))
1662[4] 2154[9]

Breakheart (IRE) *A M Balding* 74
2 b g Sakhee(USA) —Exorcet (FR) (Selkirk (USA))
6754[11] 6930[2]

Breathless Kiss (USA) *K A Ryan* 71
2 b f Roman Ruler(USA) —Crusading Miss Cox (USA) (Crusader Sword (USA))
(3762) 5521[6]

Breeze Of The Air *M R Channon* 55
2 ch c Compton Place—Dixieanna (Night Shift (USA))
2649[6] 3920[6] 4194[5]

Breizh Touch (FR) *J Boisnard* 72
2 b f Country Reel(USA) —Roncha (FR) (Kaldoun (FR))
(6576a)

Brenda Duke *J G Portman* a52 43
2 ch f Bachelor Duke(USA) —Fiina (Most Welcome)
6586[11] 7120[8]

Brenin Taran *D M Simcock* a87 93
3 gr g Lujain(USA) —Silver Chime (Robellino (USA))
(1368) 1486[7] 2016[6] 3166[4] 3806[4] 5032[9] 5777[2] 5902[2] 6240[7]

Brer Rabbit *Seamus Fahey* a69 56
3 b f Invincible Spirit(IRE) —Red Rabbit (Suave Dancer (USA))
586[2] (741) 962[8] 1315[8] 6031[6] 6547[11] 6806[8] 7581[6] 7782[9]

Brett Vale (IRE) *P R Hedger* a91 91
3 br g Sinndar(IRE) —Pinta (IRE) (Ahonoora)
236[11] 3645 ◆ 552[5] 663[7] ◆ (2709) ◆ (2809) 2865[2] (4910) 5223[5] 5648[6] (6116) 7194[12] 7612[2] (7701) 7811[3] ◆

Briannsta (IRE) *J E Long* a58 59
7 b g Bluebird(USA) —Nacote (IRE) (Mtoto)
23[6] 661[4] 811[7] 854[3] 4732[5] 5018[2] 5283[4] 6039[7] 6340[6] (6433) 7240[3] 7370[7] 7483[7] 7602[7] 7774[10]

Briary Mac *N Bycroft* 68
2 b f Royal Applause—Red May (IRE) (Persian Bold)
6820[2] 7079[5] 7217[4]

Brick Red *A M Balding* a78 84
2 ch g Dubawi(IRE) —Duchcov (Caerleon (USA))
4986[8] (5311) 5762[6] 6693[2]

Bricks And Porter (IRE) *T G McCourt* a65 67
9 b g College Chapel—Camassina (IRE) (Taufan (USA))
2290a[8] 5680[9] 6126[10]

Bridal Dance (IRE) *T Stack* a39 59
3 b f Danehill Dancer(IRE) —Feather Bride (IRE) (Groom Dancer (USA))
4392a[13]

Brideview *Edgar Byrne* a58 15
3 ch f Kyllachy—Dolce Piccata (Piccolo)
2654[9] 3176[11]

Bridge Note (USA) *J Noseda* a44 28
3 b f Stravinsky(USA) —Myrtle (Batshoof)
1563[7] 1840[12]

Bridge Of Fermoy (IRE) *D C O'Brien* a76 60
4 b g Danetime(IRE) —Banco Solo (Distant Relative)
97[5] 224[9] 355[6] 545[5] 657[9] 2923[13] 3158[6] 6917[13]

Bridge Of Gold (USA) *M A Magnusson* a78 100
3 b c Giant's Causeway(USA) —Lady Doc (USA) (Doc's Leader (USA))
(1355) ◆ 2411[4] 3298[4]

Bridgetown (USA) *Kenneth McPeek* 115
2 ch c Speightstown(USA) —Ellesmere (USA) (Tabasco Cat (USA))
7304a[2]

Bridge Valley *R Hannon* 78
2 ch g Avonbridge—Go Between (Daggers Drawn (USA))
2771[4] 3403[5] 3785[3] 4265[2] (4906) 5445[3] 5692[8] 7290[17]

Bridgewater Boys *T J Pitt* a76 72
8 b g Atraf—Dunloe (IRE) (Shaadi (USA))
84[2] 219[3] ◆ 333[4] 393[6] (528) 712[2] (805) 935[3] 1000[12] 1099[2] 1366[2] 1533[9] 1692[2] 2018[11] 2499[9] 2656[6] 5377[12] 6097[10]

Brief Candle *W R Swinburn* a77 83
3 b f Diktat—Bright Hope (IRE) (Danehill (USA))
2281[5] 2925[8] 5448[5] 6243[16]

Brief Encounter (IRE) *A M Balding* a105 103
3 br g Pyrus(USA) —Just One Look (Barathea (IRE))
1324[6] (1987) 3049[9] (3816) 4521[6] 5313[2] 5863[5] 6480[21]

Brief Look *H R A Cecil* a94 90
3 b f Sadler's Wells(USA) —Half Glance (Danehill (USA))
2847[2] ◆ 4838[2] (5093) (5649) 6113[3] 6734[9]

Brierty (IRE) *D Carroll* a82 83
3 b f Statue Of Liberty(USA) —Bridelina (FR) (Linamix (FR))
2072[7] 2544[2] 2999[6] 4096[4] (4289) 4820[5] 5130[5] 5523[9] 7478[5] 7613[9] 7801[10]

Briery Blaze *T Wall* a54 58
6 b m Dansili—Sabonis (USA) (The Minstrel (CAN))
292[10] 349[5] 567[11]

Briery Lane (IRE) *J M Bradley* a54 56
8 ch g Tagula(IRE) —Branston Berry (IRE) (Mukaddamah (USA))
173[7] 294[6] 474[9] 575[7] 2759[7] 3673[6]

Brigadoon *W Jarvis* a72 63
2 b c Compton Place—Briggsmaid (Elegant Air)
7146[8] 7351[2] 7637[3]

Bright Falcon *J Balding* a57 73
4 ch g Hawk Wing(USA) —Cream Tease (Pursuit Of Love)
519[8] 1242[15] 1399[10] 1475[11] 1690[7] 2473[11] 2626[9] (3031) 4998[8] 6005[12]

Bright Halo (BRZ) *J De Roualle* a47 78
5 b m Spring Halo(ARG) —Bright Blue (BRZ) (Bright Again (USA))
261a[7]

Bright Sparky (GER) *M W Easterby* a56 54
6 ch g Dashing Blade—Braissim (Dancing Brave (USA))
(377) 623[11] 4402[10] 4806[3] 5554[11] 6559[7] 7751[2]

Bright Wire (IRE) *M Madgwick* a45 44
3 b g Elusive City(USA) —Alinga (IRE) (King's Theatre (IRE))
1071[4] 1420[7] 1967[11] 2635[6] 3303[8] 4480[10] 5430[14] 7888[11]

Brilliana *D R Lanigan* a75 89
3 b f Danehill Dancer(IRE) —Streak Of Silver (USA) (Dynaformer (USA))
2848[3] ◆ 3456[2] 4085[5] (5061) 5771[2]

Bring It On Home *G L Moore* a57 69
5 b g Beat Hollow—Dernier Cri (Slip Anchor)
603[2]

Bring Sweets (IRE) *B Ellison* 43
2 b g Firebreak—Missperon (IRE) (Orpen (USA))
1623[9] 1847[6] 2526[6] 7055[9]

Brink *T J Pitt* a47 64
2 b f Powerscourt—Fonage (Zafonic (USA))
6461[5] 6842[3] 7114[2]

Brinscall *R A Fahey* a51 70
2 b f Lucky Story(USA) —Happy Lady (FR) (Cadeaux Genereux)
1396[5] 2195[3] 2699[6] 4931[7] 6009[4] 6378[2] 6842[4] 7618[5]

Brisant (GER) *R Suerland* 111
7 br g Goofalik(USA) —Beresina (Surumu (GER))
3493a[3]

Brisbane (IRE) *J H M Gosden* 70
2 b g Kheleyf(USA) —Waroonga (IRE) (Brief Truce (USA))
2037[4] 2413[2] 2940[7]

Bristol Delauriere (FR) *Miss N A Lloyd-Beavis* a19
5 b g Epistolaire(IRE) —Shenedova (FR) (Hellios (USA))
6225[11]

British Luck (SPA) *Y Durepaire*
2 ch c British Open(CHI) —Lucky Filly (FR) (First Trump)
6325a[10]

Broad Cairn *R Charlton* a91 94
3 b g Green Desert(USA) —Celtic Cross (Selkirk (USA))
2080[3] (2446) 2926[7] (4210) 4909[3] (5349) 5766[8] 6702[4]

Broad Town Girl *W S Coltherd* a36
6 b m Woodborough(USA) —Fortunes Course (IRE) (Crash Course)
3023[11]

Brockfield *M Brittain* 62
3 ch c Falbrav(IRE) —Irish Light (USA) (Irish River (FR))
2572[4] 2937[11] 3690[5] 4660[5]

Broctune Papa Gio *K G Reveley* 23
2 b g Tobougg(IRE) —Fairlie (Halling (USA))
6821[16]

Brody's Boy *G L Moore*
2 ch c Tumbleweed Ridge—Raffelina (USA) (Carson City (USA))
7145[16]

Broken In Light (FR) *T Larriviere* a97 105
3 b c Divine Light(JPN) —Broken Innate (IRE) (Broken Hearted)
1238a[5] 2755a[6] 3649a[4] 6891a[4]

Broken Kitten (FR) *T Larriviere* 95
2 b f Martaline—Broken Innate (IRE) (Broken Hearted)
5279a[8] 6080a[2]

Bromhead (USA) *Mrs C A Dunnett* a73 60
3 ch g Johannesburg(USA) —Caramel Queen (NZ) (Turbulent Dancer (USA))
98[5] (343) 662[4] 776[4] 1429[4] 1958[11] 3274[8] 3960[5] 4157[8] 5479[7] 5972[8] 6497[9] 6758[8] 6919[3] 7094[9]

Bronte's Hope *M P Tregoning* a58 56
5 ch m Gorse—General Jane (Be My Chief (USA))
1421[3]

Bronze Beau *Mrs L Stubbs* a54 69
2 ch g Compton Place—Bella Cantata (Singspiel (IRE))
1005[5] 1275[4] 1735[2] 2069[7] 2435[5] 4844[2] 5337[3] 5596[2] 6409[4] 6903[3] 7213[6]

Bronze Cannon (USA) *J H M Gosden* a112 122
4 bb h Lemon Drop Kid(USA) —Victoria Cross (IRE) (Mark Of Esteem (IRE))
913[3] 1004[3] (1674) (3139) 4369a[4] 6324a[7]

Bronze Prince *Saeed Bin Suroor* a81
2 b c Oasis Dream—Sweet Pea (Persian Bold)
(7376) ◆

Brooklands Bay (IRE) *J R Weymes* a68
2 b g Pyrus(USA) —Brooklands Time (IRE) (Danetime (IRE))
(6858)

Brooklyn Spirit *C G Cox* 73
3 ch g Cadeaux Genereux—Serengeti Bride (USA) (Lion Cavern (USA))
(2930) 5876[9] 6420[8]

Brooksby *L A Dace* a73 68
3 b f Diktat—Lovely Lyca (Night Shift (USA))
1284[6] 2796[12] 3030[5] 3358[6] 4005[3] 4322[2] 4791[4] 5016[2] 5511[4] 5806[5] 6570[11] 6782[3] 7110[11] 7392[12]

Broomfield Buddy *D W Barker*
3 b f Reel Buddy(USA) —Tancred Arms (Clantime)
1451[8]

Broomielaw *E A L Dunlop* a95 105
5 ch g Rock Of Gibraltar(IRE) —Peony (Lion Cavern (USA))
(4541) 6106[11] 7293[21] 7465[6]

Brootommitty (IRE) *I Semple* 36
2 b f Azamour(IRE) —Polyandry (IRE) (Pennekamp (USA))
5330[4]

Brother Barry (USA) *G A Swinbank* a64 65
4 bb g Forestry(USA) —Saratoga Sugar (USA) (Gone West (USA))
1777[4] 1889[3] 2316[14]

Brother Cha (IRE) *M G Quinlan* 82
3 ch c Indian Ridge—Sun On The Sea (IRE) (Bering)
1295[7] (5181)

Broughton Beck (IRE) *R F Fisher* a58
3 ch g Distant Music(USA) —Mauras Pride (IRE) (Cadeaux Genereux)
529[6] 659[4]

Broughtons Day *W J Musson* 50
2 b g Mujahid(USA) —Rainy Day Song (Persian Bold)
5029[6]

Broughtons Flight (IRE) *W J Musson* a67 67
4 ch m Hawk Wing(USA) —Aldburgh (Bluebird (USA))
132[2] 193[3] 320[9]

Broughtons Paradis (IRE) *W J Musson* a61 68
3 b f Royal Applause—Amankila (IRE) (Revoque (IRE))
2489[2] 2950[3] 4545[2] (4722) ◆ 6075[6] 6742[3] 6910[2] 7476[6] 7831[5]

Broughtons Point *W J Musson* a43 41
3 b f Falbrav(IRE) —Glowing Reference (Reference Point)
5482[6] 6029[7] 7278[8] 7660[11]

Broughtons Silk *W J Musson* a51 60
4 b m Medicean—Soviet Cry (Soviet Star (USA))
2856[10] 3467[7] 3929[11] 4179[9] (4667) 4916[6] 5484[5] 6256[6] 6945[8]

Brouhaha *Tom Dascombe* a90 85
5 b g Bahhare(USA) —Top Of The Morning (Keen)
(217) (558) (656) 713[8] (798) 1003[10] (1316) 1603[17] 2597[6] 3301[2] 3695[4] 4064[7] 4957[2] 6059[2] 6435[7] 6830[P] 7583[2] 7789[8]

Brown Lentic (IRE) *Miss J Feilden* a51 41
3 b c Invincible Spirit(IRE) —Indienne (IRE) (Indian Ridge)
(316) 481[5] 889[5] 1157[8] 1529[9]

Bruges (IRE) *A Al Raihe* a73 94
4 b h Marju(IRE) —Liege (IRE) (Night Shift (USA))
260a[7] 334a[11] 415a[2] 616a[10] 697a[12]

Brunelleschi *P L Gilligan* a81 86
6 ch g Bertolini(USA) —Petrovna (IRE) (Petardia)
(728) (880) (1403) 2088[10] 2799[2] 5167[12] (5404) 6112[5] 6666[15] 6944[11] 7189[16]

Brunette (IRE) *R Hannon* a75 60
2 br f Camacho—Hidden Agenda (FR) (Machiavellian (USA))
2490[10] 3027[2] 3507[2] 4705[4] 5213[9] 6067[7] 6391[10]

Brunston *R Charlton* 92
3 gr g High Chaparral(IRE) —Molly Mello (GER) (Big Shuffle (USA))
1176[2] (1707) 2038[5] (2189) 3051[9] 3618[4]

Brushing *M H Tompkins* 71
3 ch f Medicean—Seasonal Blossom (IRE) (Fairy King (USA))
(4913) 6015[6]

Brut *D W Barker* a58 76
7 b g Mind Games—Champenoise (Forzando)
1096[8] 1227[11] 1456[5] 1921[6] 2158[8] 2657[3] 3020[5]

Bruton Street (USA) *J H M Gosden* 89
3 bb g Dynaformer(USA) —Fit For A Queen (USA) (Fit To Fight (USA))
1151[3] 1573[4] 3636[3] ◆ 4270[5] 6595[3] 6996[2] (7221)

Bryman (FR) *C Aubert* 67
3 gr g Linamix(FR) —Brusca (USA) (Grindstone (USA))
5784a[3]

Brynfa Boy *P W D'Arcy* a71 62
3 b g Namid—Funny Girl (IRE) (Darshaan)
1662[8] 1840[7] 2162[9] 3010[5] 3118[2] 3428[5] (7714)

Buachaill Dona (IRE) *D Nicholls* a101 110
6 b g Namid—Serious Contender (IRE) (Tenby)
259a[8] 611a[10] (1608) 1868[6] 2502[12] 3351[2] 4523[13] 4766[2] 5132[15] 5860[12] 6180[6]

Buail Isteach (IRE) *E J Creighton* a44 47
4 b m Acclamation—Its All Eurs (IRE) (Barathea (IRE))
251[7] 663[6] 874[11] 1940[5] 2361[8] 3671[8] 3946[7]

Bubbelas *J J Quinn* 71
2 b f Pastoral Pursuits—Arctic High (Polar Falcon (USA))
2258[8] (2765) 3702[5] 3971[6] 4975[7] 6169[4]

Bubber (IRE) *R A Fahey* a51 42
2 b f Westerner—Bubble N Squeak (IRE) (Catrail (USA))
7079[6] 7420[4] 7799[7] ◆

Bubble Zack (FR) *D Prod'Homme* 76
2 ch c Muhtathir—Bubble Back (FR) (Grand Lodge (USA))
6501a[5]

Bubbly Bellini (IRE) *George Baker* a76 73
2 b g Mull Of Kintyre(USA) —Gwapa (IRE) (Imperial Frontier (USA))
2087[6] 2887[4] 3167[5] 4081[5] 7580[6] 7655[2] (7713) 7749[2] (7850) 7868[2]

Bubbly Braveheart (IRE) *A Bailey* a65 67
2 b g Cape Cross(IRE) —Infinity (FR) (Bering)
2383[12] 2889[5] 3584[6] 4758[7] 5399[6] 6639[2] 6793[9] 7482[4] 7597[2] (7616) 7731[6]

Bubses Boy *P Howling* a60 61
3 ch g Needwood Blade—Welcome Home (Most Welcome)
1050[3] ◆ 1441[9] 2489[4] 2982[9] 4157[4] (4669) 5131[5] 5782[10] 5988[6] 6538[4] 7049[11] 7392[9]

Buccellati *A M Balding* 118
5 ch h Soviet Star(USA) —Susi Wong (IRE) (Selkirk (USA))
1526[3] (1823) 2670[8] 5931a[4] 6873a[3] 7744a[9]

Bucintoro (IRE) *C Theodorakis* a26 107
5 b h Galileo(IRE) —Dear Girl (IRE) (Fairy King (USA))
419a[10] 612a[11]

Buck Cannon (IRE) *P M Phelan* a52
4 b g High Chaparral(IRE) —Folgore (USA) (Irish River (FR))
61[9]

Bucked Off (SAF) *T P Tate* a97 94
5 b g Casey Tibbs(IRE) —See Me Fly (SAF) (Caesour (USA))
261a[6] 415a[4] 644a[5] 5170[13] 6013[4] 6307[4] 6665[7]

Buckie Boy (IRE) *J S Goldie* a86 78
3 b g Bahri(USA) —Woodren (USA) (Woodman (USA))
1874[4] 2640[2] 2981[4] 3549[3] 4789[5] 5987[2] (6375) 6704[3] 7117[8]

Buckie Massa *J S O Arthur* a79 80
5 ch g Best Of The Bests(IRE) —Up On Points (Royal Academy (USA))
5540a[3]

Buckle Up *D K Ivory* a44 42
3 ch g Primo Valentino(IRE) —Ambitious (Ardkinglass)
390[5] ◆ 753[9] 2122[10] 2744[6] 3005[10] 3862[6] 4196[4] 4425[9]

Budai (GER) *A Trybuhl* 93
3 b c Dai Jin—Bejaria (GER) (Konigsstuhl (GER))
2560a[6]

Buddhist Monk *Ian Williams* a79 94
4 b g Dr Fong(USA) —Circle Of Light (Anshan)
999[6] ◆ 1274[3] 1826[3] 2283[3] 2501[5] 3390[12] 4770[9] 5235[15] (5568) (5936) 6172[2] (6248)

Buddy Holly *Pat Eddery* a87 84
4 b g Reel Buddy(USA) —Night Symphonie (Cloudings (IRE))
1779[3] 2249[4] 2773[3] (3024) 3361[4] 3461[9] 4426[6] 5640[9] 6204[2] 6724[11]

Buddy Marvellous (IRE) *R A Harris* a34 55
3 ch g Redback—La Paola (IRE) (Common Grounds)
159[9] 308[10]

Buds Dilemma *S Gollings* a45 50
5 b m Anabaa(USA) —Lady Thynn (FR) (Crystal Glitters (USA))
175[4] 802[13]

Budva *H Morrison* a62
2 b c Kylian(USA) —Danlu (USA) (Danzig (USA))
7266[7] 7502[3] 7638[7]

Buffett *L M Cumani* a66 66
2 b c Bertolini(USA) —Batik (IRE) (Peintre Celebre (USA))
5109[6] 5505[5] 5867[5] 6211[4]

Bugaku *Sir Michael Stoute* a96 91
4 b g Montjeu(IRE) —Bryony Brind (IRE) (Kris)
(2211) ◆ 2597[3] 4091[9] 4794[6] 5641[4] 5823[8] 6681[15]

Bugsy's Boy *George Baker* a73 77
5 b g Double Trigger(IRE) —Bugsy's Sister (Aragon)
6622[2]

Bulberry Hill *R W Price* a46 45
8 b g Makbul—Hurtleberry (IRE) (Tirol)
301[10] 1439[6]

Bulella *Garry Moss* a61 48
3 b f Makbul—Bella Tutrice (IRE) (Woodborough (USA))
41[3]

Bullet Duck (IRE) *Tom Dascombe* 27
2 bg f Redback—Helibel (IRE) (Pivotal)
6245[11] 6591[13]

Bullet Man (USA) *L M Cumani* a87 94
4 br g Mr Greeley(USA) —Silk Tapestry (USA) (Tank's Prospect (USA))
1274[6] 1593[6] (2239) 3189[2] 3822[15] 5437[9]

Bullet Train *H R A Cecil* 77
2 b c Sadler's Wells(USA) —Kind (IRE) (Danehill (USA))
(7099) ◆

Bullish Cash (NZ) *A S Cruz* 104
7 b g Howbaddouwantit(USA) —La Mafia (NZ) (Phizam (NZ))
1554a^{10}

Bull Market (IRE) *M S Tuck* a76 84
6 b g Danehill(USA) —Paper Moon (IRE) (Lake Coniston (IRE))
238^{3} 713^{9} 5593^{9} 6258^{9} 6780^{8} 7490^{2}

Bullsbay (USA) *H Graham Motion* a124
5 b h Tiznow(USA) —The Hess Express (USA) (Lord Carson (USA))
7309a^{9}

Bulwark (IRE) *Ian Williams* a74 108
7 b g Montjeu(IRE) —Bulaxie (Bustino)
2409^{6} 3143^{6} 3874^{7} 4769^{5} 6851^{21} 7151^{12} 7402^{8}

Bumble Rose (IRE) *A G Foster* 41
6 b m Kornado—Bukowina (GER) (Windwurf (GER))
1231^{7} 1739^{6} 2030^{9} 2594^{5} 3023^{8}

Bundle Up *J L Flint* a57 53
6 b m Diktat—Bundle (Cadeaux Genereux)
669^{9} 3950^{6} 6859^{10}

Bungie *Jennie Candlish* a48 35
5 gr g Forzando—Sweet Whisper (Petong)
133^{8}

Bun Oir (USA) *R Hannon* 61
2 bb c Seeking The Gold(USA) —Fraulein (Acatenango (GER))
3823^{8} 4314^{10} 5400^{9} 6735^{7}

Bun Penny *G M Moore* 36
3 ch f Bertolini(USA) —Mint Royale (IRE) (Cadeaux Genereux)
2375^{9} 2970^{10}

Bureaucrat *P J Hobbs* 96
7 b g Machiavellian(USA) —Lajna (Be My Guest (USA))
2706^{7} 4408^{10} 4988^{8}

Burgau Royal *M R Channon* 74
2 b c Noverre(USA) —Regal Ransom (IRE) (Anabaa (USA))
4377^{4} 5017^{2} 5445^{2}

Burgundy Ice (USA) *Saeed Bin Suroor* a96 87
3 rg f Storm Cat(USA) —Cara Rafaela (USA) (Quiet American (USA))
4211^{2} 5175^{10} 6311^{3} (6773) 6946^{2}

Burj Nahar *Saeed Bin Suroor* 87
2 b c Shamardal(USA) —Melikah (IRE) (Lammtarra (USA))
(7243) ◆

Burlada *C Laffon-Parias* 83
3 b f Selkirk(USA) —Well Known (Sadler's Wells (USA))
5784a^{0}

Burma Rock (IRE) *L M Cumani* a87 79
3 b g Danehill Dancer(IRE) —Burmese Princess (USA) (King Of Kings (IRE))
2795^{3} 3812^{4} ◆ 5349^{5} 6250^{4} ◆ 6673^{2} (7048)

Burnbank (IRE) *J M Jefferson* a72 75
6 ch g Danehill Dancer(IRE) —Roseau (Nashwan (USA))
559^{P}

Burnbrake *L Montague Hall* a71 73
4 b g Mujahid(USA) —Duena (Grand Lodge (USA))
318^{6} 597^{5} 2039^{12} 6719^{4} 7109^{5} 7236^{10}

Burnett (IRE) *Saeed Bin Suroor* 85
2 b c Dynaformer(USA) —Secret Garden (IRE) (Danehill (USA))
(6763) ◆ 7030^{13}

Burning Incense (IRE) *M Dods* a82 91
6 b g Namid—Night Scent (IRE) (Scenic)
5148^{12} 5697^{12} 6495^{6} 6765^{11}

Burning Sky *Charles O'Brien* a68 78
4 b g Rainbow Quest(USA) —Flamingo Queen (GER) (Surumu (GER))
7263a^{10}

Burning Thread (IRE) *T J Etherington* a38
2 b g Captain Rio—Desert Rose (Green Desert (USA))
7618^{8}

Burns Night *M Johnston* a77 83
3 ch c Selkirk(USA) —Night Frolic (Night Shift (USA))
2664^{6} (3238) 3608^{3} ◆ 3812^{2} 4143^{4} 4641^{11} 5510^{7} 6257^{5} 6907^{7}

Burnt Cream *B Smart* 62
2 b f Exceed And Excel(AUS) —Basbousate Nadia (Wolfhound (USA))
2089^{4} ◆ 6179^{4}

Burn The Breeze (IRE) *Mlle H Van Zuylen* a91 108
4 b m Beat Hollow—Madiyla (Darshaan)
4365a^{2} 6504a^{6} 7704a^{8}

Burnwynd Boy *D Nicholls* 106
4 b g Tobougg(IRE) —Cadeau Speciale (Cadeaux Genereux)
2570^{9} 3172^{8} 4273^{9} 4485^{22} 5001^{9} 6050^{3} 6135^{8}

Burtondale Boy (IRE) *P T Midgley* 39
2 b g Shinko Forest(IRE) —Irish Moss (USA) (Irish River (FR))
994^{12} 1920^{9} 5253^{13} 5596^{9} 6354^{10} 6555^{10}

Bury St Edmunds *A G Newcombe* a19 52
2 ch c Zafeen(FR) —Naivety (Machiavellian (USA))
3867^{10} 4689^{5} 5319^{4} 5938^{14} 7334^{10} 7731^{9}

Bury Treasure (IRE) *Miss Gay Kelleway* a69 59
4 ch g Choisir(AUS) —Future Treasure (Habitat)
171^{8} 362^{11}

Burza *J Mackie* a63 76
3 ch f Bold Edge—Welcome Star (IRE) (Most Welcome)
(716) 1937^{5} ◆ 2300^{9} ◆ 2607^{3} (3251) 4050^{5} 5009^{7} 5475^{3} 5940^{11}

Buscador (USA) *W M Brisbourne* a69 50
10 ch g Crafty Prospector(USA) —Fairway Flag (USA) (Fairway Phantom (USA))
105^{2} 194^{10} 253^{5} 448^{4} 735^{7} 836^{3} 1409^{5} 1533^{5}

Bushman *D M Simcock* a82 111
5 gr g Maria's Mon(USA) —Housa Dancer (FR) (Fabulous Dancer (USA))
1526^{7} 1799^{6} 2476^{7} 4002^{5} (4543) 5655^{2} ◆ 6812^{9} 7186^{3}

Bush Master *J R Boyle* a70 67
2 b g Hunting Lion(IRE) —Patandon Girl (IRE) (Night Shift (USA))
1404^{13} 3865^{10} 4201^{2} 4851^{3} 5218^{2} 5564^{6} 6247^{4} 6443^{2} 6550^{8} 6774^{8} 7365^{4} 7537^{7} 7655^{6}

Bushranger (IRE) *David Wachman* a102 119
3 b c Danetime(IRE) —Danz Danz (Efisio)
2287a^{4} 3140^{11} 5657^{9}

Bush Tucker (IRE) *P Winkworth* a73 85
2 b c Choisir(AUS) —Queen's Victory (Mujadil (USA))
3918^{2} 4537^{2} (5060) 5769^{3}

Bushveld (IRE) *M Johnston* a85 26
3 b c Cape Cross(IRE) —Gold Sunrise (USA) (Forty Niner (USA))
209^{2} 312^{2}

Bushy Dell (IRE) *Miss J Feilden* a76 91
4 br m King Charlemagne(USA) —Nisibis (In The Wings)
1966^{8} 2322^{5} 3721^{5} 4498^{8} 5446^{5} (6258) 6636^{8} 7867^{5}

Business As Usual *M A Jarvis* a87 80
2 b c Invincible Spirit(IRE) —Lesgor (USA) (Irish River (FR))
(6000) ◆ 6779^{2} ◆

Business Class (BRZ) *D Nicholls* a73 64
4 b g Thignon Lafre(BRZ) —Dioner (BRZ) (Rotioner (BRZ))
1054^{3} 1769^{3} 2235^{14} 4140^{8} 4435^{9} 6101^{3} (6358) ◆ 7113^{5} 7423^{4}

Businessman *M Johnston* 83
2 b c Acclamation—Venus Rising (Observatory (USA))
(5234) 5521^{P}

Bussell Along (IRE) *M L W Bell* a47 52
3 b f Mujadil(USA) —Waaedah (USA) (Halling (USA))
1620^{11} 1940^{3} 3685^{4} 4177^{3}

Bustan (IRE) *G C Bravery* a73 86
10 b g Darshaan—Dazzlingly Radiant (Try My Best (USA))
1524^{3} 1952^{11} 2641^{9} 4211^{11} 4502^{8} 5003^{9} 5367^{10}

Bustard Bay (IRE) *J G Given* 56
2 b g Footstepsinthesand—Toy Show (IRE) (Danehill (USA))
3634^{5} 4194^{7} 4618^{5} 5595^{10} 6590^{7}

Buster Hyvonen (IRE) *J R Fanshawe* a101 89
7 b g Dansili—Serotina (IRE) (Mtoto)
801^{7} 1007^{8}

Butch And Sundance *B J Meehan* 88
2 b g Captain Rio—Be My Wish (Be My Chief (USA))
3692^{9} (4176) 4565^{6} 4901^{2} 5198^{13} 6088^{3} 6993^{19}

Bute Street *R J Hodges* a53 34
4 b g Superior Premium—Hard To Follow (Dilum (USA))
5061^{8} 5617^{7} 6025^{3} (6859) 7154^{9}

Butstillitmoves (IRE) *J H M Gosden* a55
3 b f Galileo(IRE) —Deuxieme (IRE) (Second Empire (IRE))
876^{6}

Butterfly Flip (FR) *J-P Perruchot* a28 43
5 b m Cardoun(FR) —Barisha (FR) (Baryshnikov (AUS))
4335a^{11}

Butterfly Lady *A Wohler* a72 93
3 b f Royal Dragon(USA) —Ballet Ruse (Rainbow Quest (USA))
1240a^{4}

Buttermilk (IRE) *T Lerner* 15
2 ch c Muhtathir—Margie Queen (GER) (Sternkoenig (IRE))
4686a^{10} 7316a^{0}

Buxton *R Ingram* a79 86
5 b g Auction House(USA) —Dam Certain (IRE) (Damister (USA))
1197^{2} 1572^{8} 2188^{15} 2980^{13} 4009^{7} 4914^{6} 5288^{4} 5370^{3} 5753^{8} 5991^{5} 6614^{10}

Buy On The Red *D Nicholls* a78 78
8 b g Komaite(USA) —Red Rosein (Red Sunset)
1244^{8} 1343^{2} 1694^{3} 1951^{7} (3304) 3612^{U} 3681^{6} 4620^{7} 4899^{6} 6010^{9} (7689) 7808^{2}

Buzz Bird *T D Barron* 51
2 b f Danbird(AUS) —Ashtaroute (USA) (Holy Bull (USA))
4278^{8} 4817^{8} 5253^{10} 6215^{6}

Buzzword *Saeed Bin Suroor* 115
2 b c Pivotal—Bustling (Danehill (USA))
3403^{2} (3920) 4487^{2} 5261^{2} (5708a) 6524a^{3} 6849^{5} 7304a^{5}

By Command *J W Hills* a62 96
4 b g Red Ransom(USA) —Rafha (Kris)
1812^{7} 2407^{5} 2773^{4} 3206^{6} 3761^{3} 4207^{4} 4714^{10} 4824^{8} 5559^{3} 6074^{7} 6395^{4} 6940^{4}

Bygone Age (IRE) *D K Weld* 87
2 b g Whipper(USA) —Twiggy's Sister (IRE) (Flying Spur (AUS))
2302a^{5}

By Request *Sir Mark Prescott* 60
3 b f Giant's Causeway(USA) —Approach (Darshaan)
5520^{8} 5718^{6}

Byron Bay *R Johnson* a64 73
7 b g My Best Valentine—Candarela (Damister (USA))
1442^{8} 2044^{11} 2233^{14} (2746) 3070^{11} 3353^{7} 4171^{2} 4313^{3} 4656^{4} 6358^{5} 6813^{6} 7349^{10}

By The Sea (IRE) *M P Sunderland* a48 49
4 b m Monashee Mountain(USA) —Sesame Heights (IRE) (High Estate)
7143^{13}

By The Wind (IRE) *T J Etherington* a21
3 b g Iron Mask(USA) —Macha Rua (IRE) (Eagle Eyed (USA))
686^{7} 947^{7} 4860^{12}

Byword *A Fabre* 110
3 ch c Peintre Celebre(USA) —Binche (USA) (Woodman (USA))
5084a^{4} 6132a^{4}

Byzantine *A P O'Brien* 86
3 b c Sadler's Wells(USA) —Miss Satamixa (FR) (Linamix (FR))
2729a^{8} 3438a^{10}

Cabal *Sir Michael Stoute* a72
2 b f Kyllachy—Secret Flame (Machiavellian (USA))
7376^{2}

Cabaret (IRE) *A P O'Brien* 106
2 b f Galileo(IRE) —Witch Of Fife (USA) (Lear Fan (USA))
(4028a) 6523a^{11}

Cabernet Sauvignon *Gordon Elliott* a75 75
3 br g Dansili—Halcyon Daze (Halling (USA))
1252^{8} 1882^{6} 2572^{2} 3238^{5} 3660^{3} 7729^{9}

Cabimas *P Schiergen* 100
2 bb c King's Best(USA) —Casanga (IRE) (Rainbow Quest (USA))
7314a^{2}

Cabopino (IRE) *K R Burke* a53 37
4 ch m Captain Rio—Fey Rouge (IRE) (Fayruz)
222^{9} 367^{5}

Cacao Bey (FR) *P Chevillard*
2 b c Nuclear Freeze(USA) —Marliny (FR) (Marignan (USA))
4807a^{0}

Cactus Curtsey *J R Fanshawe* a48 53
3 b f Royal Applause—Prairie Flower (IRE) (Zieten (USA))
3569^{3} 4057^{10} 4337^{5} 5225^{7} 5403^{9}

Cactus King *P M Phelan* a81 87
6 b g Green Desert(USA) —Apache Star (Arazi (USA))
266^{5} 878^{7} 1177^{3} 1962^{6} 2708^{9}

Cadeau For Maggi *H-A Pantall* 106
4 ch h Cadeaux Genereux—Maggi For Margaret (Shavian)
4637a^{3} 6579a^{8} 7216a^{6}

Cadeaux Fax *B R Millman* a72 66
4 ch g Largesse—Facsimile (Superlative)
3501^{5} 4322^{7} 4812^{4} 4938^{2} 5179^{12} (5502) 5634^{3} 6339^{2} (6588) 6909^{5}

Cadley Road (IRE) *R Hannon* 95
2 b c Elusive City(USA) —Rouge Noir (USA) (Saint Ballado (CAN))
3522^{3} (4209) ◆ 5085a^{2} 6319a^{6} 7030^{6}

Cadouble (FR) *G Chaignon*
6 b g Cadoudal(FR) —Pampa Girl (FR) (Pampabird)
5074a^{P}

Cadre (IRE) *J H M Gosden* a87 104
4 b g King's Best(USA) —Desert Frolic (IRE) (Persian Bold)
1116^{11} (1942) ◆ 2412^{6} 3014^{18} 4543^{4} 5995^{3} 6270^{26}

Caerlaverock (IRE) *G A Swinbank* 85
4 br g Statue Of Liberty(USA) —Daziyra (IRE) (Doyoun)
1562^{5} (1693) 2249^{3} 2698^{3} 2895^{8}

Caerleon Wind (IRE) *Mlle V Dissaux* a87 95
3 b c Ransom O'War(USA) —Caerosa (Caerleon (USA))
7696a^{8}

Caerus (USA) *W J Knight* a71 64
3 b c Greatness(USA) —Bellewood (USA) (Alydar (USA))
1380^{8} 1662^{6} 2300^{6} 3115^{11} 3672^{3}

Cafe Fiore (IRE) *T J Pitt* a50 42
3 b f Clodovil(IRE) —Carpet Lover (IRE) (Fayruz)
91^{8}

Cafe Greco *P J Makin* a70 73
2 b g Red Ransom(USA) —Mocca (IRE) (Sri Pekan (USA))
3420^{2} 3867^{4} 4790^{7} 5841^{5} 6211^{11} 6735^{4}

Cake (IRE) *R Hannon* a90 98
4 b m Acclamation—Carpet Lady (IRE) (Night Shift (USA))
1325^{10} (1672) 2191^{2} 2704^{10} 3360^{5} 3582^{11} 5132^{14} 5871^{7}

Cake Stand *J A R Toller* a52 55
3 b g Haafhd—Galette (Caerleon (USA))
1422^{9} 2082^{5} 2863^{13} 5647^{5} 5998^{15} 6771^{P}

Cakilhan (TUR) *G Gungor* 100
3 b f Native Procida(TUR) —Ravive (St Jovite (USA))
5619a^{7}

Calabaza *M J Attwater* a44 62
7 ch g Zaha(CAN) —Mo Stopher (Sharpo)
1421^{9} 3917^{11}

Calahonda *P W D'Arcy* a87 86
3 ch f Haafhd—Californie (IRE) (Rainbow Quest (USA))
1353^{13} 2299^{5} 3028^{6} 3738^{7} 4228^{9} 5090^{4} (5329)

Calaloo (IRE) *C R Egerton* a81 82
3 b g Dansili—Maraami (Selkirk (USA))
1751^{7} 2138^{3} 2829^{3} 3466^{4} 5532^{5} 5834^{2} 6059^{5} 6613^{10} 6936^{14}

Calatrava Cape (IRE) *J L Dunlop* 73
2 bb f Cape Cross(IRE) —Pershaan (IRE) (Darshaan)
3810^{5} 4460^{10} 5284^{7} 5742^{6} ◆ 6232^{2}

Calbuco (FR) *Mme E Holmey* a93 95
5 b g Kendor(FR) —Pennegale (IRE) (Pennekamp (USA))
1043a^{7}

Calculating (IRE) *M D I Usher* a78 84
5 b g Machiavellian(USA) —Zaheemah (USA) (El Prado (IRE))
72^{6} 233^{4} 325^{4} 459^{7} 511^{5} 692^{4} 809^{2} (860) 1426^{U} 1936^{3} 2163^{3} 2429^{9} 3029^{4} 3510^{2} 3737^{3} 4092^{7} (4449) 4742^{3} 7255^{4} (7279) 7402^{3} (7760) 7867^{7}

Calculus Affair (IRE) *J Noseda* a59
2 b c Trans Island—Where's Charlotte (Sure Blade (USA))
7773^{4} 7886^{5}

Caldercruix (USA) *T P Tate* 67
2 ch c Rahy(USA) —Al Theraab (USA) (Roberto (USA))
5512^{8} 6679^{7} 6990^{3}

Caldermud (IRE) *J R Best* a52 67
2 ch c Chineur(FR) —Dalal (Cadeaux Genereux)
4825^{5} 5778^{8}

Calders *A Berry*
2 b f Monsieur Bond(IRE) —Delicious (Dominion)
3937^{12} 4187^{7} 4800^{11}

Caledonia Princess *R Curtis* a74 74
3 b f Kyllachy—Granuaile O'Malley (IRE) (Mark Of Esteem (IRE))
1296^{8} 2079^{12} 2826^{6} 6361^{12} 6738^{9} 7028^{5} 7329^{5} (7398) 7554^{7} 7634^{8}

California Bright (IRE) *J G Given* 56
3 ch f Rock Of Gibraltar(IRE) —Woodyousmileforme (USA) (Woodman (USA))
1611^{13} 2659^{3}

California Flag (USA) *Brian Koriner* 124
5 rg g Avenue Of Flags(USA) —Ultrafleet (USA) (Afleet (CAN))
(7305a) 7745a^{5}

Calissee (FR) *J De Roualle* a82 101
5 b m Ocean Of Wisdom(USA) —Calyx (FR) (Irish River (FR))
4365a^{0} 5058a^{5}

Calle Vistamar *S Wynne*
2 ch f Stage Pass—Champagne Bubbleigh Vii (Damsire Unregistered)
5835^{9} 6122^{P}

Calley Ho *Mrs L Stubbs* a70 66
3 b g Kyllachy—Lucayan Belle (Cadeaux Genereux)
3342^{8} 3862^{14}

Call For Liberty (IRE) *B Smart* a75 60
4 b h Statue Of Liberty(USA) —Give A Whistle (IRE) (Mujadil (USA))
1493^{10} 2269^{5}

Calligrapher (USA) *M A Jarvis* a67 85
3 ch g Rahy(USA) —Calista (Caerleon (USA))
2279^{12} 2821^{6}

Calling Birds (IRE) *Karen George* a49 39
3 b f Royal Applause—Jezyah (USA) (Chief's Crown (USA))
849^{12} 943^{5} 1578^{9} 2220^{7} 3984^{6} 4084^{11}

Calling Victory (FR) *M Botti* a66 49
3 b f Vettori(IRE) —Calling Card (Bering)
658^{2} 833^{2} 1260^{6} 2246^{10} 2709^{11}

Callisto Moon *R Curtis* a69 88
5 b g Mujahid(USA) —Nursling (IRE) (Kahyasi)
459^{4} 604^{5} (2931) (3059) 3346^{5} (4212) (5903) 7117^{7}

Callis Wood *Ollie Pears* 35
3 br f Shinko Forest(IRE) —Meltonby (Sayf El Arab (USA))
1625^{9} 2105^{10}

Call It On (IRE) *M H Tompkins* 91
3 ch g Raise A Grand(IRE) —Birthday Present (Cadeaux Genereux)
1992^{9} ◆ 2248^{3} 2935^{5} 3644^{3} ◆ 4827^{2} 6114^{6} 6740^{3} 6996^{8}

Call Me Al (IRE) *J J Lambe* a73 60
4 b g Alhaarth(IRE) —Takarna (IRE) (Mark Of Esteem (IRE))
627^{8} 2441^{13}

Call Me Alice (USA) *David Wachman* a77 95
3 b f Johannesburg(USA) —Charming Girl (USA) (L'Emigrant (USA))
2555a^{4}

Call Me Courageous (IRE) *R A Harris* a15 54
3 ch g Captain Rio—Golden Concorde (Super Concorde (USA))
1746^{14} 2515^{12} 3471^{7} 3673^{4} 4155^{2} 4643^{13} 5326^{9} 5628^{12}

Call Me Kitty (FR) *U Suter* a76 81
4 b m Marchand De Sable(USA) —Fifty Niner (FR) (Fijar Tango (FR))
4335a^{7}

Call Me Rosy (IRE) *B Smart* a60 46
5 ch m Shinko Forest(IRE) —Fanciful (IRE) (Mujtahid (USA))
1769^{5} 2366^{8} 3484^{10}

Call Of Duty (IRE) *Mrs Dianne Sayer* a75 62
4 br g Storming Home—Blushing Barada (USA) (Blushing Groom (FR))
2043^{10} 2531^{11} 3070^{7} 3615^{6} 3943^{7} 4462^{4} 4898^{2} 4972^{4} 5625^{10} 6184^{9}

Call Of Ktulu (IRE) *J S Wainwright* 32
4 b g Noverre(USA) —Yankee Dancer (Groom Dancer (USA))
1888^{12} 2404^{12} 3558^{11}

Call Of The Kings *R A Teal* a32 55
2 b g Acclamation—Surrey Down (USA) (Forest Wildcat (USA))
2676^{4} 6629^{11}

Call To Arms (IRE) *M Johnston* 78
2 br g Shamardal(USA) —Requesting (Rainbow Quest (USA))
3487^{2} ◆ 4738^{3} 5958^{2}

Call To Reason (IRE) *J Noseda* 78
2 ch f Pivotal—Venturi (Danehill Dancer (IRE))
7182^{2}

Calm And Serene (USA) *Rae Guest* 47
2 b f Quiet American(USA) —Charm Away (USA) (Silver Charm (USA))
6592^{9} 6786^{7}

Calm Bay (IRE) *H Rogers* a86 78
3 b g Medecis—Queen Sigi (IRE) (Fairy King (USA))
1375a^{5} 7007a^{10}

Calmdownmate (IRE) *Mrs R A Carr* a80 85
4 b g Danehill Dancer(IRE) —Lady Digby (IRE) (Petorius)
(89) 326^{2} 400^{7} (561) 1309^{16} (1776) 2770^{13} 3377^{8} 3956^{3} 4374^{5} 7758^{14}

Calming Influence (IRE) *Saeed Bin Suroor* 109
4 b h King's Best(USA) —Idilic Calm (IRE) (Indian Ridge)
260a^{2} 413a^{2} 697a^{4}

Calm Storm (IRE) *J Noseda* a63 33
2 b c Whipper(USA) —Dark Hyacinth (IRE) (Darshaan)
5000[12] 5368[6] 5571[6] 5985[12] 6735[12]

Calrissian (GER) *F Reuterskiold* a99 109
5 ch g Efisio—Centaine (Royal Academy (USA))
3650a[7] 6503a[8]

Caltire (GER) *M G Quinlan* a66 65
4 b g Pentire—Caluna (SWI) (Lagunas)
342[6] 423[6] 872[8]

Calvados Blues (FR) *A Fabre* 112
3 ch c Lando(GER) —Persian Belle (Machiavellian (USA))
1145a[6] (1858a) 2756a[5] 3669a[4] 5710a[6] 6327a[6]

Calvero (FR) *Robert Collet* a63 75
2 b c Sabiango(GER) —La Bastoche (IRE) (Kaldoun (FR))
2694a[4] 3935a[0]

Calypso Bay (IRE) *J Noseda* a56 85
3 b c Galileo(IRE) —Poule De Luxe (IRE) (Cadeaux Genereux)
1289[3] 1793[7] 2488[6]

Calypso Girl (IRE) *P D Evans* a65 76
3 gr f Verglas(IRE) —Clochette (IRE) (Namaqualand (USA))
2300[15] 2355[5] 2776[7] 2920[5] 4237[7] 4829[8] 5362[7] 5501[14] 5716[8]

Calypso Prince *M D I Usher* a42 54
3 ch g Lucky Story(USA) —Eleonora D'Arborea (Prince Sabo)
214[11] 328[11] 506[9]

Calypso Star (IRE) *R Hannon* a68 47
2 ch c Exceed And Excel(AUS) —Reematna (Sabrehill (USA))
2037[6] 6781[9] 6930[9] 7235[2] ◆ 7335[2]

Calzaghe (IRE) *Jim Best* a72 75
5 ch g Galileo(IRE) —Novelette (Darshaan)
237[5] 423[3] 559[4] 836[11] 935[4] 1200[7] ◆ (1378) 1537[5]

Camacho Flyer (IRE) *P T Midgley* a27 69
2 b g Camacho—Despondent (IRE) (Broken Hearted)
1083[7] 1304[9] 2258[7] 2467[13] 3446[4] 3952[5] (5337) 5945[7] 6179[6] 6841[10]

Cambuslang (IRE) *I Semple* 59
2 b c Chevalier(IRE) —Zafine (Zafonic (USA))
1645[5] 2027[3] 3652[3] 4306[8] 4895[7] 6134[9]

Came Back (IRE) *Miss A Stokell* a99 63
6 ch g Bertolini(USA) —Distant Decree (USA) (Distant View (USA))
68[6] 86[4] 382[5] 756[5] 901[8] 1565[8]

Camelot Queen *W S Kittow* a37 27
4 gr m Baryshnikov(AUS) —Guarded Expression (Siberian Express (USA))
386[11] 626[6] 849[13] 1703[11]

Camera Shy (IRE) *K A Morgan* a57 59
5 ch g Pivotal—Shy Danceuse (FR) (Groom Dancer (USA))
2420[3] (3004) (3308)

Camerooney *B Ellison* a61 49
6 b g Sugarfoot—Enkindle (Relkino)
7062[4] 7417[3] 7466[9] 7726[6] 7855[9]

Camill (IRE) *P Kalas* 106
5 b g Monsun(GER) —Classic Light (IRE) (Classic Secret (USA))
6153a[4] 6890a[9]

Camilla Knight (IRE) *W R Swinburn* a34 29
3 ch f Night Shift(USA) —Koukla Mou (Keen)
4981[9] 5747[11]

Camille's Secret (FR) *R Gibson* 65
3 b f Oasis Dream—Maid Of Dawkins (IRE) (Kendor (FR))
4810a[4]

Camomile *Miss Tracy Waggott* 26
3 b f Xaar—Pretty Davis (USA) (Trempolino (USA))
3975[5] 4531[6] 6823[10] 7796[13]

Campaigner *J W Hills* a38 52
2 b c Dansili—Rosapenna (IRE) (Spectrum (IRE))
1866[13] 2839[7] 4439[9] 4856[6] 5635[7] 5913[7] 6586[12]

Campanaca (FR) *C Boutin* a78 62
2 b f Prince Kirk(FR) —Green Maid (USA) (Green Dancer (USA))
6960a[7]

Campanologist (USA) *Saeed Bin Suroor* a102 119
4 b h Kingmambo(USA) —Ring Of Music (Sadler's Wells (USA))
2410[6] 3139[2] 3781[8] 4780[2] (5447) 6056[3] 6303[2] 6850[9]

Campbells Lad *A Berry* a60 33
8 b g Mind Games—T O O Mamma'S (IRE) (Classic Secret (USA))
2264[7]

Campli (IRE) *B Ellison* a76 76
7 b g Zafonic(USA) —Sept A Neuf (Be My Guest (USA))
767[2] 939[5] 1228[2] 1343[7] (1493) 1766[3] 2313[6] 3264[4]

Camps Bay (USA) *Mrs A J Perrett* 106
5 b g Cozzene(USA) —Seewillo (USA) (Pleasant Colony (USA))
2471[4] 4408[8] 5173[19] 5909[7] 6483[4] 6816[4] 7018[13]

Canadian Ballet (USA) *Linda Rice* a68 107
4 ch m City Zip(USA) —Canadian Flagship (USA) (Northern Flagship (USA))
7305a[5]

Canadian Danehill (IRE) *R M H Cowell* a87 99
7 b g Indian Danehill(IRE) —San Jovita (CAN) (St Jovite (USA))
67[3] 270[8] 451[2] 539[3] 821[6] 985[3] (2053) 2637[2] 2946[6] (3582) (3784) 4135[13] 5263[11] 7015[19] 7414[11] 7676[6] 7866[6]

Canary Girl *G Prodromou* a19 35
6 br m Primo Valentino(IRE) —Cumbrian Concerto (Petong)
1958[6] 3076[10] 7062[12]

Can Can Star *A W Carroll* a89 86
6 br h Lend A Hand—Carrie Can Can (Green Tune (USA))
21[4] 202[3] (285) (392) 648[4] 879[3] 999[5] ◆ 1213[4] 1750[4] 2150[4] 2666[8] 3024[6] (3864) 4426[5] 4605[3] 5062[4] 5448[2] 5781[3] 6470[3] 6907[11] 7393[3] 7607[4] 7734[2]

Candilejas *R J Smith* a63 44
3 br f Diktat—Nacho Venture (FR) (Rainbow Quest (USA))
6908[9] 7112[11] 7250[8] 7433[9]

Candle *T R George* a89 96
6 br m Dansili—Celia Brady (Last Tycoon)
3510[7] 4408[11] 4840[10]

Candleshoe (IRE) *R Hannon* 69
2 b f Danehill Dancer(IRE) —Keepers Dawn (IRE) (Alzao (USA))
4147[4] ◆ 4460[7] 5096[5]

Candy Anchor (FR) *R E Peacock* a48 47
10 b m Slip Anchor—Kandavu (Safawan)
2337[F]

Candyfloss Girl *H J L Dunlop* a65 64
2 b f Intikhab(USA) —Annatalia (Pivotal)
3248[10] 3534[8] 4219[6] 4647[3] (5310) 5635[5] 6227[3] 6481[7] 7033[11]

Candy Gift (ARG) *T Clout* 114
6 ch h Candy Stripes(USA) —Sly Sarah (USA) (On The Sly (USA))
1762a[4] 5297a[3] 5932a[5]

Candy Ride (IRE) *E A L Dunlop* 80
3 ch f Pivotal—Mia Mambo (USA) (Affirmed (USA))
1327[5] 2139[2] (2856) 3408[2] (4441) 7291[19]

Candy Rose *M P Tregoning* a58 63
4 b m Tobougg(IRE) —Cottage Maid (Inchinor)
4645[8] 4992[6] 5723[4] 6213[9] 6940[6]

Cane Cat (IRE) *A W Carroll* a54 59
2 bb f One Cool Cat(USA) —Seven Wonders (USA) (Rahy (USA))
1344[5] 1782[6] 2348[4] 2919[9] 3978[6] 5344[5] 6343[4] 6590[3] 6906[6] 7242[7] 7619[2] 7749[10]

Canford Cliffs (IRE) *R Hannon* 118
2 b c Tagula(IRE) —Mrs Marsh (Marju (IRE))
(2033) ◆ (2993) ◆ 5299a[3]

Canmoss (USA) *A Bonin* a70 70
3 ch c Maria's Mon(USA) —Dance For Free (CAN) (Fly So Free (USA))
1614[2] 1747[5] 1842[6] 6682a[8]

Cannonball (USA) *Wesley A Ward* a81 121
4 bb g Catienus(USA) —No Deadline (USA) (Skywalker (USA))
2991[6] 3140[2] 7305a[3] 7745a[10]

Canongate *Miss E C Lavelle* a84 92
5 gr g Highest Honor(FR) —Tremiere (FR) (Anabaa (USA))
4315[8] 4957[9]

Cansili Star *M A Jarvis* 81
2 b g Dansili—Canis Star (Wolfhound (USA))
3546[2] ◆ 4041[4] 4900[5] 5913[2] 6561[4]

Cantabilly (IRE) *R J Hodges* a67 69
6 b g Distant Music(USA) —Cantaloupe (Priolo (USA))
361[9] 500[6] 679[4] 835[5]

Canton Road *P F I Cole* a59 64
3 b g Galileo(IRE) —Welsh Diva (Selkirk (USA))
3056[2] 4205[6] 4987[7] 5327[3] 5679[12]

Canucatcher (IRE) *T D Walford* a37 32
3 b f Catcher In The Rye(IRE) —Never Zal (Zilzal (USA))
883[4]

Canwinn (IRE) *M R Channon* a77 102
3 b c Refuse To Bend(IRE) —Born To Glamour (Ajdal (USA))
1118[6] 1459[6] 2273[8] 3049[10] 3816[4] ◆ 4433[3] 5070[7] 5670[2]

Canyon Ranch *L M Cumani* 71
3 b c Danehill Dancer(IRE) —Model Queen (USA) (Kingmambo (USA))
2282[4] 2937[8] 3690[2]

Caoba *V R A Dartnall* 68
5 b m Hernando(FR) —Seeker (Rainbow Quest (USA))
(2163) 2429[7]

Caol Ila (IRE) *J G Given* a55 52
2 b f Invincible Spirit(IRE) —Pink Cashmere (IRE) (Polar Falcon (USA))
5611[5] 5949[9] 6347[6] 6938[6] 7559[3] 7778[4]

Capablanca (AUS) *D Baertschiger* 104
8 br g Scenic—Ahava (AUS) (Southern Appeal (USA))
2116a[5]

Capable Guest (IRE) *M R Channon* a91 94
7 bb g Cape Cross(IRE) —Alexander Confranc (IRE) (Magical Wonder (USA))
766[4] 2669[9] 2933[7] 3189[6] 3797[4] 4091[5] 4696[7] 4988[5] 5252[7] 5781[6] 6204[3] (6385) 6584[7] 7036[3] 7118[3] 7279[2] 7357[5]

Capacity (IRE) *M Johnston* 75
2 b c Cape Cross(IRE) —Carry On Katie (USA) (Fasliyev (USA))
2533[4] 2936[5] 4075[2] 4558[2]

Capania (IRE) *E G Bevan* a61 57
5 br m Cape Cross(IRE) —Gentle Papoose (Commanche Run)
473[12]

Capeability (IRE) *M R Channon* a77 91
3 b g Cape Cross(IRE) —Mennetou (IRE) (Entrepreneur)
280[2] ◆ 786[2] 1291[6] 6022[6] 6539[7] 6996[11] 7247[7] 7428[2] 7620[5]

Cape Amber (IRE) *R M Beckett* 111
4 b m Cape Cross(IRE) —Maramba (Rainbow Quest (USA))
4903[5]

Cape Blanco (IRE) *A P O'Brien* 108
2 ch c Galileo(IRE) —Laurel Delight (Presidium)
(4250a) (5275a)

Cape Cobra *H Morrison* a60 60
5 ch g Inchinor—Cape Merino (Clantime)
5211[2] 6637[4] 6828[9] 7329[9] 7503[10]

Cape Colony *R Hannon* a86 84
4 gr h Cape Town(IRE) —Lucky Princess (Bijou D'Inde)
585[7] 761[7] 1184[6] 1432[5] (2698) 2931[10] 3273[4]

Capecover (NZ) *Alexander Fieldes* 108
7 b g Cape Cross(IRE) —Set Up (NZ) (Zabeel (NZ))
7215a[17]

Cape Dancer (IRE) *J S Wainwright* a45 46
5 b m Cape Cross(IRE) —Yankee Dancer (Groom Dancer (USA))
2723[6]

Cape D'Or (IRE) *R Hannon* 74
2 b c Cape Cross(IRE) —Sombreffe (Polish Precedent (USA))
3113[5] 3376[3]

Cape Express (IRE) *M A Jarvis* a102 94
4 b g Cape Cross(IRE) —Lilissa (IRE) (Doyoun)
(82) 1003[3] 2031[6] 5004[4]

Capefly *P W Chapple-Hyam* a71 71
4 b m Cape Cross(IRE) —Patacake Patacake (USA) (Bahri (USA))
167[3] 281[8]

Cape Greko *B G Powell* a61 58
7 ro g Loup Sauvage(USA) —Onefortheditch (USA) (With Approval (CAN))
1356[11] 6761[12] 7112[7] 7328[6] 7549[4] 7608[8]

Cape Hawk (IRE) *R Hannon* a104 97
5 b g Cape Cross(IRE) —Hawksbill Special (IRE) (Taufan (USA))
1209[7] 1527[10] 2193[3] 2480[4] 3431[6] 3796[7] 4526[4] 4852[2] 5746[7] 5914[5] (6695)

Cape Kimberley *J G Given* a74 47
2 b g Arakan(USA) —Etoile Volant (USA) (Silver Hawk (USA))
4839[4] 5325[5] 5728[10] 6355[6] 7089[2] (7333) ◆ 7453[5] ◆

Cape Marien (IRE) *D R Lanigan* a84 68
3 b f Cape Cross(IRE) —Marienbad (FR) (Darshaan)
1488[10] (3432) 4178[13] 5988[2] (6457) (6584) ◆ 7005[3]

Cape Melody *H Morrison* a39 79
3 b f Piccolo—Cape Charlotte (Mon Tresor)
951[13] 1173[2] 1703[2] 2205[4] (2879) 3537[6] 4167[2] 5264[5] 5968[4] 6964[10]

Cape Of Luck (IRE) *P M Phelan* a76 81
6 b g Cape Cross(IRE) —Fledgling (Efisio)
546[4] 813[3] 871[7] 1415[7] 1807[4] 2244[11]

Cape Of Storms *R Brotherton* a68 60
6 b g Cape Cross(IRE) —Lloc (Absalom)
13[6] 95[4] 222[4] 303[5] (487) 607[3] 811[5] 886[5] (975) 1285[8] 7795[10]

Cape Quarter (USA) *W J Haggas* a78
3 b g Elusive Quality(USA) —June Moon (IRE) (Sadler's Wells (USA))
(7353)

Capercaillie (USA) *M Johnston* 90
2 ch f Elusive Quality(USA) —Silent Eskimo (USA) (Eskimo (USA))
(2449) (2714) ◆ 3015[4] ◆ 3748[4] 6677[8]

Cape Roberto (IRE) *John Berry* a56 56
4 b g Cape Cross(IRE) —Kalwada (USA) (Roberto (USA))
7094[11]

Cape Rock *W J Knight* a76 87
4 b g Cape Cross(IRE) —Wildwood Flower (Distant Relative)
(2880) 3795[2] 4501[3] 5182[3]

Cape Royal *J M Bradley* a73 84
9 b g Prince Sabo—Indigo (Primo Dominie)
2219[8] 2840[6] 2946[3] ◆ 3162[2] 3386[3] 3623[7] 3998[3] 4268[2] 4469[2] 4607[10] 5156[5] (5323) 5830[2] 5919[2] 6253[7] 6489[9] 6669[7] 6791[10] 7021[5] 7223[4] 7355[4] 7398[8] 7554[8] 7808 5

Cape Tribulation *J M Jefferson* 91
5 b g Hernando(FR) —Gay Fantastic (Ela-Mana-Mou)
2486[13] 7018[14]

Cape Vale (IRE) *D Nicholls* 93
4 b g Cape Cross(IRE) —Wolf Cleugh (IRE) (Last Tycoon)
1227[8] 2093[4] 2707[8] 3491[5] 3497[2] (4167) 4507[2] (5960) 6089[21] 6843[2] 7015[12]

Caphe Sabrina (FR) *J-Y Beaurain*
4 br m Canyon Creek(IRE) —Onphee (FR) (The Wonder (FR))
5204a[0]

Capistrano *Paul Mason* a54 54
6 b g Efisio—Washita (Valiyar)
857[4] 1439[12]

Capitaine Courage (IRE) *F Doumen* 108
4 ch g Bering—Four Green (FR) (Green Tune (USA))
(6658a) 7102a[2]

Capital Attraction (USA) *H R A Cecil* 68
2 ch c Speightstown(USA) —Cecilia's Crown (USA) (Chief's Crown (USA))
6759[4]

Capitalise (IRE) *Miss Gay Kelleway* a63 65
6 b g City On A Hill(USA) —Prime Interest (IRE) (Kings Lake (USA))
126[10] 333[7] 534[8] 679[5] 835[4]

Capitelli (IRE) *R Hannon* a70 81
3 b f Cape Cross(IRE) —Dear Girl (IRE) (Fairy King (USA))
2008[5] 2356[7] 6934[3] 7238[5]

Capo Malfatano (IRE) *R Brogi* 64
3 b c High Chaparral(IRE) —Toy Show (IRE) (Danehill (USA))
1392a[12] 1904a[18]

Capone (IRE) *R Curtis* a95 79
4 b g Daggers Drawn(USA) —Order Of The Day (USA) (Dayjur (USA))
3339[8] 3730[6] (4225) ◆ (4668) 4783[3] 6579a[9] 7172[6] 7394[5] 7478[2] 7553[3] ◆ (7832) 7862[6]

Capo Regime *P Howling* a76 68
3 ch g Captain Rio—Ashtree Belle (Up And At 'Em)
1190[11] (1652) 3225[12] 3502[3] 4056[7] 4275[5] 4956[5] 6243[17] 6442[3] 6755[7] 7422[6] 7679[3] 7762[11]

Cappagh Strand (USA) *David P Myerscough* a67 61
3 b f Grand Slam(USA) —Quiet Eclipse (USA) (Quiet American (USA))
5747[3] 6029[3]

Capped For Victory (USA) *W Storey* a48 54
8 b g Red Ransom(USA) —Nazoo (IRE) (Nijinsky (CAN))
7[6] 1131[10]

Capricorn Run (USA) *A J McCabe* a106 106
6 bb g Elusive Quality(USA) —Cercida (USA) (Copelan (USA))
30[3] 206[8] 291[4] (388) 538[3] (635) 783[13] 916[8] 1018[7] 1124[3] 1560[6] 1640[2] 2470[7] 2707[16] 6270[13] 7394[4] 7768[9]

Capricornus (USA) *M Johnston* a72
2 ch c Rahy(USA) —Silent Partner (USA) (Capote (USA))
7764[4] (7859)

Caprio (IRE) *J R Boyle* a87 86
4 ch g Captain Rio—Disarm (IRE) (Bahamian Bounty)
94[2] (543) 680[2] 806[2] 866[3] 922[2] 1436[5] (1806) 2203[3] 2396[7] 3771[5] 4005[2] 4386[2] 5120[2] 7111[7] (7558)

Cap St Jean (IRE) *R Hollinshead* a73 66
5 b g Cape Cross(IRE) —Karminiya (IRE) (Primo Dominie)
37[2] 223[2] 489[4] (715) 793[2] 933[6] (1438) 2576[7]

Captain Blake (IRE) *P D Evans* a21 38
2 bb g Captain Rio—Green Flower (USA) (Fappiano (USA))
1119[7] 1275[10] 4933[10] 5627[7] 5868[6] 6215[17]

Captain Bluebird (IRE) *D Donovan* a37 61
2 ch c Captain Rio—Dolly Blue (IRE) (Pennekamp (USA))
3744[5] 4093[10] 4564[4]

Captain Bradz (USA) *P T Midgley* a31
3 ch c Diesis—Garden Rose (IRE) (Caerleon (USA))
5[2] 92[6] 273[9]

Captain Brilliance (USA) *J Noseda* 108
4 ch h Officer(USA) —Bloomin Genius (USA) (Beau Genius (CAN))
(3116) ◆ 3818[2] ◆ 4297[15] 5200[16] 6448[6] 7019[3]

Captain Carey *M S Saunders* a79 91
3 b g Fraam—Brigadiers Bird (IRE) (Mujadil (USA))
936[7] (966) (1095) 1272[6] 2140[2] 2443[5] ◆ (2774) 5245[5]

Captain Cash *T D Easterby* 36
2 ch g Kyllachy—Fission (Efisio)
2568[7] 3310[12] 5407[9]

Captain Cavendish (IRE) *A Bailey* a59
3 b g Captain Rio—Fahan (IRE) (Sri Pekan (USA))
366[6] 1492[11] 2141[8] 2417[15] 2681[8] 5403[12]

Captain Clint (IRE) *M H Tompkins* a14 47
2 b g Captain Rio—Lake Poopo (IRE) (Persian Heights)
5109[7] 5401[13] 6754[12] 7335[11]

Captain Cool (IRE) *R Hannon* a50 50
2 ch g Captain Rio—Aiaie (Zafonic (USA))
1290[5] 1404[10] 2324[7] 4931[6] 5320[5] 5715[8] 6963[4] 7514[3] 7887[2]

Captain Dancer (IRE) *B W Hills* a5 77
3 ch g Danehill Dancer(IRE) —Rain Flower (IRE) (Indian Ridge)
1656[8] 6731[5] 6997[6]

Captain Dunne (IRE) *T D Easterby* a101 105
4 b g Captain Rio—Queen Bodicea (IRE) (Revoque (IRE))
1560[9] 2094[2] 2704[2] 3351[14] 4135[16] 4766[6] 5132[5] 5654[6] 5860[3] (6180) 6678[7]

Captain Ellis (USA) *A P Jarvis* a33 85
3 b g Five Star Day(USA) —Adventure (USA) (Unbridled's Song (USA))
3155[3] (3531) 3839[9] 5375[13]

Captain Flack *J A R Toller* a61 54
3 ch g Lucky Story(USA) —Au Contraire (Groom Dancer (USA))
2488[10] (3157) 3861[7] 4857[3] 5483[4]

Captain Flasheart (IRE) *S C Williams* a73 81
3 ch g Captain Rio—Catfoot Lane (Batshoof)
208[5] 1317[5] 4535[8] 5295[3] (5806) (5998)

Captain Gerrard (IRE) *B Smart* 113
4 b h Oasis Dream—Delphinus (Soviet Star (USA))
1989[13] 2272[7] 2481[10] 2991[4] 3434a[8] 3638[10] 3848[2] 5233[13] 5765[6] 6107[7] 6427[11] 6678[17] 7015[6]

Captain Hook *Daniel Mark Loughnane* a34 65
5 b g Rock Of Gibraltar(IRE) —Biloxi (Caerleon (USA))
219[8]

Captain Imperial (IRE) *R Bastiman* a68 73
3 b g Captain Rio—Imperialist (IRE) (Imperial Frontier (USA))
2767[7] 3687[P] 4229[P] 4518[8] 4846[3] 5621[5] 6861[8] 7440[11] 7594[12]

Captain Jacksparra (IRE) *K A Ryan* a88 91
5 b g Danehill(USA) —Push A Venture (Shirley Heights)
1016[18] 1229[2] 1436[9] 1649[7] 2576[10] 2965[2] 3501[3] (4083) 4560[12] 5107[7] 5779[5]

Captain Kallis (IRE) *D J S Ffrench Davis* a64 64
3 ch g Captain Rio—Alicedale (USA) (Trempolino (USA))
1567[3] 1772[2] 1969[5] 2478[5] 4374[10] 4428[3] 4664[8] 5632[7]

Captain Macarry (IRE) *B Smart* a96 96
4 ch g Captain Rio—Grannys Reluctance (IRE) (Anita's Prince)
9[4] 404[4] (625) 1016[6] 1229[8] (1723) 1952[3] 2695[8] 3560[5] (4592) 4996[2] (5884) 6270[14] (6944)

Captain Mainwaring *N P Littmoden* a61 66
4 b g Auction House(USA) —Shalyah (IRE) (Shalford (IRE))
534[3] 734[9] 871[8] 2294[9] 3004[5] 4156[12]

Captain Oats (IRE) *Mrs P Ford* a54 54
6 b g Bahhare(USA) —Adarika (Kings Lake (USA))
2608[6] 2971[11] 3631[4] 4602[6] 4938[4] 5720[2]

Captain Peachey *B R Millman* 36
3 b c Pursuit Of Love—Dekelsmary (Komaite (USA))
1252[11] 1704[10] 2080[8] 2603[6] 4023[11] 4690[7]

Captain Ramius (IRE) *S A Callaghan* a100 87
3 b c Kheleyf(USA) —Princess Mood (GER) (Muhtarram (USA))
1211[7] 2278[6]

Captainrisk (IRE) *Mrs C A Dunnett* a76 76
3 b g Captain Rio—Helderberg (USA) (Diesis)
239[2] 397[3] (629) 924[3] 1895[5] 3156[2] 4914[5]

Captain Royale (IRE) *Miss Tracy Waggott* a61 60
4 ch g Captain Rio—Paix Royale (Royal Academy (USA))
1276^{16} *1655^{7}* 1734^{12} *2579^{9}* 4225^{5} 4654^{4} 4823^{6} 5159^{2} (6161) 6410^{6} 6989^{5} 7241^{8}

Captain Sachin (IRE) *T J Etherington*
2 b g Captain Rio—Belalzao (IRE) (Alzao (USA))
1661^{P}

Captain Scooby *R M Whitaker* 75
3 b g Captain Rio—Scooby Dooby Do (Atraf)
1305^{3} 1686^{3} 2227^{4} 3033^{3} 3856^{4} 4227^{5} (5148) 5335^{6} 5978^{11} 6798^{9}

Captains Dilemma (IRE) *P D Deegan* a58 76
2 ch c Captain Rio—Meas (IRE) (Mark Of Esteem (IRE))
5895a^{7}

Captain Sirus (FR) *P Butler* a44
6 b g Fly To The Stars—Zudika (IRE) (Ezzoud (IRE))
1876^{11}

Captain's Lover (SAF) *Todd Pletcher* a71 109
5 b m Captain Al(SAF) —Sunshine Lover (SAF) (Badger Land (USA))
6508a^{4}

Captain's Paradise (IRE) *Sir Mark Prescott* a35 42
2 b f Rock Of Gibraltar(IRE) —Minnie Habit (Habitat)
3226^{7} 4278^{7}

Captain Teddo *R Ingram* a5 14
3 ch c Auction House(USA) —Charlottevalentina (IRE) (Perugino (USA))
4786^{14} *5572^{14}* 5900^{11}

Captain Thule (JPN) *Hideyuki Mori* 119
4 b h Agnes Tachyon(JPN) —Air Thule (JPN) (Tony Bin)
7498a^{4}

Captain Walcot *R Hannon* a59 55
3 b g Fantastic Light(USA) —Princess Minnie (Mistertopogigo (IRE))
205^{5} *287^{6}*

Captain Webb *Saeed Bin Suroor* 103
4 br h Storming Home—Criquette (Shirley Heights)
262a^{2} 419a^{3} 616a^{4}

Capt. Candyman Can (USA) *Ian Wilkes* a123
3 b g Candy Ride(ARG) —Stormy Way (USA) (Storm Creek (USA))
7306a^{8}

Capucci *J J Quinn* a88 87
4 b g King's Best(USA) —Design Perfection (USA) (Diesis)
1123^{6} 1507^{5} 2612^{3} 2822^{6} *3469^{2}* 4598^{6} 5361^{5} 5598^{8} 6178^{4} *(6495)* 6846^{5}

Capulet Monteque (IRE) *T Stack* a72 87
2 b f Camacho—Family At War (USA) (Explodent (USA))
3895a^{5} *5452a^{9}* 6317a^{17}

Caracal *M Johnston* 61
2 b c Dubai Destination(USA) —Desert Lynx (IRE) (Green Desert (USA))
3785^{7} 4307^{4}

Caracciola (GER) *B W Hills* 109
12 b g Lando(GER) —Capitolina (FR) (Empery (USA))
(2501) (3143) 4457^{4}

Caramelita *J R Jenkins* a67 71
2 b f Deportivo—Apple Of My Eye (Fraam)
4826^{5} 5969^{5} 6563^{2} 7061^{4} *7585^{3}* *7674^{3}*

Caranbola *M Brittain* 91
3 br f Lucky Story(USA) —Ladywell Blaise (IRE) (Turtle Island (IRE))
1368^{6} 2102^{6} 2611^{7} 3688^{7} 4227^{9} 4494^{10} 4997^{3} 5405^{5} 5978^{2} 6159^{7}

Cara's Request (AUS) *D Nicholls* a55 82
4 gr g Urgent Request(IRE) —Carahill (AUS) (Danehill (USA))
2197^{7} 3055^{5} 5031^{5} 6645^{19} 7083^{3} 7172^{11}

Caravan Of Dreams (IRE) *M A Jarvis* a69 63
3 b f Anabaa(USA) —Smart 'n Noble (USA) (Smarten (USA))
317^{5}

Caraziyan (FR) *P Van De Poele* a70 75
3 b c Slickly(FR) —Carlitta (USA) (Olympio (USA))
(7385a) *7696a^{5}*

Carbon Hoofprint *P J Makin* a80 86
3 b g Green Tune(USA) —Salome's Attack (Anabaa (USA))
201^{3} ◆ *944^{2}* 1176^{3} 1928^{6} 2845^{2} 3115^{2} (4691) 5243^{2} 5914^{6} *7027^{5}* *7350^{4}*

Carbon Print (USA) *P R Webber* 61
4 ch g Johannesburg(USA) —Caithness (USA) (Roberto (USA))
2981^{7} 3425^{8} 4054^{4} 4745^{5} 5484^{7}

Carcinetto (IRE) *P D Evans* a94 102
7 b m Danetime(IRE) —Dolphin Stamp (IRE) (Dolphin Street (FR))
351^{5} *579^{5}* *1006^{7}* (1094) 1251^{3} 1365^{2} 1513^{3} 1582^{14} 1791^{8} 1880^{2} 2102^{4} (2536) 2948^{6} 3141^{23} 3846^{9} 4559^{4} 5069^{6} (5249) 5474^{7} 5798^{10} 5855^{3} 6428^{4} 6487^{6} 7132^{4} 7375^{12} 7431^{2} 7486^{5} 7626^{7} 7768^{8}

Car City (ITY) *L Riccardi* 73
2 b c Elusive City(USA) —Hiragana (Arazi (USA))
3185a^{5}

Cardenio (USA) *J R Gask* a31 48
3 bb f Proud Citizen(USA) —Divine Diva (USA) (Theatrical (IRE))
3161^{9} 3813^{7} 4324^{9} *5647^{11}* *6771^{7}*

Cardinal *R A Harris* a57 62
4 ch h Pivotal—Fictitious (Machiavellian (USA))
1380^{9} 1703^{8} 3175^{5} 4105^{2} 4533^{4} 5633^{5} 6755^{10} *7370^{10}*

Cardinal James (IRE) *Miss Tor Sturgis* a51
5 br g Bishop Of Cashel—Dilwara (IRE) (Lashkari)
670^{5}

Cardio Dancer (TUR) *Y Simsek* 91
6 b h Alhaarth(IRE) —Miss Salsa Dancer (Salse (USA))
5619a^{9}

Cardossi *M L W Bell* 40
2 ch f Dr Fong(USA) —English Harbour (Sabrehill (USA))
6921^{12}

Carefree Smile (IRE) *D K Weld* a90 81
3 b f Invincible Spirit(IRE) —Frippet (IRE) (Ela-Mana-Mou)
7300a^{5}

Careless Jewel (USA) *Josie Carroll* a121
3 rg f Tapit(USA) —Sweet And Careless (USA) (Hennessy (USA))
7286a^{8}

Cariad Coch *Mrs L Stubbs* a37 33
2 b f Reset(AUS) —Silly Mid-On (Midyan (USA))
1097^{5} *1653^{9}* 2226^{7} *5226^{7}* *6343^{10}*

Caribbean Coral *A B Haynes* a73 87
10 ch g Brief Truce(USA) —Caribbean Star (Soviet Star (USA))
83^{3} *165^{4}* *589^{7}* 1259^{12} 1784^{2} 2137^{2} 2349^{4} 2456^{3} 2759^{3} (2908) (3242) 3345^{2} 3477^{7} 5125^{2} 5900^{4} 6160^{3} 6341^{6}

Caribou Island *Saeed Bin Suroor* 62
2 b c Dansili—Lake Nipigon (Selkirk (USA))
4638^{5}

Carioca (IRE) *M Botti* 71
2 br f Rakti—Cidaris (IRE) (Persian Bold)
4001^{4} 4792^{6}

Carja (FR) *S Renaud*
2 b f Califet(FR) —Arja (FR) (Welkin (CAN))
7409a^{2}

Carlcol Girl *Mrs C A Dunnett* a9 45
2 b f Where Or When(IRE) —Capstick (JPN) (Machiavellian (USA))
4152^{9} 4385^{12} *5106^{8}* 6033^{5} 6735^{13} 7097^{8}

Carlesimo (IRE) *Noel Meade* a30 83
11 bb g Erins Isle—Diamond Display (IRE) (Shardari)
7578^{11}

Carleton *W J Musson* a80 96
4 b g Hunting Lion(IRE) —Canadian Capers (Ballacashtal (CAN))
1572^{5} ◆ 2071^{10} 2549^{6} 2980^{4} *3469^{4}* ◆ *3928^{3}*

Carlitos Spirit (IRE) *B R Millman* a81 87
5 ch g Redback—Negria (IRE) (Al Hareb (USA))
866^{5} 1016^{18} 1524^{7} 1876^{5} 2491^{3} (3159) 3357^{8} 3801^{5} *5095^{6}* *5640^{5}* *6212^{7}*

Carlton Mac *N Bycroft* a44 58
4 ch g Timeless Times(USA) —Julie's Gift (Presidium)
3068^{11} (4617) 4927^{8} 5625^{9} 6177^{6}

Carlton Scroop (FR) *J Jay* a67 64
6 ch g Priolo(USA) —Elms Schooldays (Emarati (USA))
(117) *346^{3}* *546^{2}* *627^{2}* *816^{U}* *(871)*

Carmela Maria *M E Sowersby* a68 64
4 b m Medicean—Carmela Owen (Owington)
1261^{10} *1834^{8}* 2762^{2} 2975^{3} 3217^{5} 3475^{5} 4053^{5} 4704^{6} 5484^{2} *5679^{2}* 6097^{6}

Carmenero (GER) *C R Dore* a78 80
6 b g Barathea(IRE) —Claire Fraser (USA) (Gone West (USA))
2185^{6} 2736^{4} *3211^{4}* 4005^{5} (4732) *5107^{10}* 5418^{10} *5991^{4}* *6444^{6}* 6738^{5} *7179^{10}* *7735^{7}*

Carmen's Boy (FR) *C Baillet* 72
2 b c One Cool Cat(USA) —Anchusa (IRE) (Nashwan (USA))
4686a^{3}

Carnaby Street (IRE) *R Hannon* 102
2 b c Le Vie Dei Colori—Prodigal Daughter (Alhaarth (IRE))
3500^{8} 4377^{2} 4900^{7} 5198^{2} 5795^{9} (6696) (7030)

Carnacki (USA) *J Noseda* a24
2 b c Ghostzapper(USA) —Guana (FR) (Sillery (USA))
5807^{14}

Carnaval Court (IRE) *A M Balding* a57 60
2 b f Saffron Walden(FR) —Bellagio Princess (Kris)
4257^{8} 4933^{4} 5498^{7} *5985^{9}* 6366^{8} *6721^{2}*

Carnival Dream *H A McWilliams* a58 56
4 b m Carnival Dancer—Reach The Wind (USA) (Relaunch (USA))
473^{9} *760^{8}* 1243^{13} 2527^{4} 2965^{7} 3061^{3} 3490^{11} 4821^{4} 4995^{2} 5304^{2} 5514^{6} 6415^{7} *7152^{10}* *(7460)* 7579^{12}

Carnival Fair *S Wynne* 45
4 b m Carnival Dancer—Testament (Darshaan)
1128^{9} 1231^{5} 1562^{8} 2473^{13} 6758^{14} *7318^{9}*

Carnival Time (IRE) *C G Cox* 28
2 ch g Captain Rio—Latest (IRE) (Bob Back (USA))
3692^{13} 4933^{9}

Carnivore *T D Barron* a81 84
7 ch g Zafonic(USA) —Ermine (IRE) (Cadeaux Genereux)
218^{8} *(536)* *1065^{6}* 1734^{2} 2402^{9} 3264^{16} (5601) *7558^{6}* *7833^{5}*

Caro Jina (FR) *A Trybuhl* 99
3 gr f Dai Jin—Caronment (Environment Friend) (3520a) 5563a^{5} 6713a^{8}

Carole Os (IRE) *S W Hall* a27 39
4 b m Catcher In The Rye(IRE) —Kuda Chantik (IRE) (Lashkari)
7251^{0}

Carousel Lady (FR) *Dominique Sepulchre* a76 48
3 b f Bachelor Duke(USA) —Carousel Girl (USA) (Gulch (USA))
4810a^{10}

Carpe Diem *R A Fahey* a48 59
4 b g Stravinsky(USA) —Spare That Tree (AUS) (Woodman (USA))
1955^{4} 2441^{9} 2804^{2} 2968^{3} 3448^{7} *3710^{6}* 4588^{16} 4845^{4} 5549^{10} 5982^{8}

Carragold *M Brittain* a56 58
3 b c Diktat—Shadow Roll (IRE) (Mark Of Esteem (IRE))
2574^{4} 3036^{6} 3237^{3} 4656^{5} 5983^{2} *7599^{5}* *7732^{7}*

Carrazara (IRE) *Edgar Byrne* a40 29
3 b f Namid—Carrozzina (Vettori (IRE))
391^{6} 1329^{14} 1745^{7} 2162^{14} 3174^{9}

Carr Hall (IRE) *B G Powell* a55 58
6 b g Rossini(USA) —Pidgeon Bay (IRE) (Perugino (USA))
5540a^{5} *7578^{8}* *7658^{4}* *7750^{4}* *7888^{5}*

Carries Lass *J A Osborne* 42
2 br f Auction House(USA) —Carranita (IRE) (Anita's Prince)
2354^{9} 2514^{6} 2978^{6} 3626^{7}

Carry On Cleo *A Berry* a60 56
4 ch m First Trump—Classy Cleo (IRE) (Mujadil (USA))
275^{7} *427^{7}* *537^{9}* *581^{6}*

Carsington *Lucinda Featherstone* 40
5 ch m And Beyond(IRE) —Nutmeg Point (Nashwan (USA))
2447^{7}

Carson's Spirit (USA) *J R Gask* a73 71
5 ch g Carson City(USA) —Pascarina (FR) (Exit To Nowhere (USA))
3577^{8}

Carte Diamond (USA) *B Ellison* a103 108
8 ch g Theatrical(IRE) —Liteup My Life (USA) (Green Dancer (USA))
1017^{6} *1383^{3}* 1790^{15} 3390^{14} 3826^{9} *7091^{3}*

Carte D'Oro (IRE) *R M Beckett* 59
3 b f Medaglia D'Oro(USA) —Prospectress (USA) (Mining (USA))
1092^{7} 2848^{5} 3279^{5} 4904^{9} 5568^{4}

Carter *W M Brisbourne* a62 63
3 b g Reset(AUS) —Cameo Role (GER) (Acatenango (GER))
1509^{7} 3018^{4} (3336) 4562^{11} 5331^{5} 6139^{6} *7022^{6}* *7049^{2}*

Cartoon *M A Jarvis* 79
3 br f Danehill Dancer(IRE) —Elfin Laughter (Alzao (USA))
(1406)

Cartoonist (IRE) *M Mullineaux* a18 55
6 ch g Fruits Of Love(USA) —Verusa (IRE) (Petorius)
213^{11}

Carved Emerald *D R C Elsworth* a86 84
4 b m Pivotal—Emerald Peace (IRE) (Green Desert (USA))
1268a^{6} *6374^{9}* *6723^{5}* *7026^{7}*

Carygali (IRE) *John Joseph Murphy* 66
3 b f Catcher In The Rye(IRE) —Gas Light (IRE) (Victory Note (USA))
4392a^{4}

Casa Battlo (FR) *Robert Collet* 67
2 b c Green Tune(USA) —Victoria Royale (FR) (Garde Royale)
4807a^{9}

Casablanca Minx (IRE) *A G Juckes* a61 56
6 br m Desert Story(IRE) —Conspire (IRE) (Turtle Island (IRE))
78^{6} *469^{8}* *(567)* *790^{7}* 2294^{8} 2634^{7} 3215^{4} 3631^{2} 4156^{4} 4735^{5} 4927^{5} *7143^{6}* *7466^{7}* 7670^{5} 7750^{8}

Casanova Kid *E J Creighton* a38 41
2 b c Pastoral Pursuits—Dust (Green Desert (USA))
5180^{6} *5368^{10}* 5749^{6} 6903^{8} *7477^{10}*

Cascata (IRE) *L M Cumani* a73 88
3 b f Montjeu(IRE) —Leaping Water (Sure Blade (USA))
1315^{4} 2796^{6} 5037^{2} ◆ 6113^{4}

Casewick Star *P W D'Arcy*
2 ch f Reset(AUS) —Be My Tinker (Be My Chief (USA))
4383^{10}

Casey's Rebel (IRE) *M G Quinlan* 32
2 b f Antonius Pius(USA) —Agent Scully (IRE) (Simply Great (FR))
4468^{4} 4757^{9} 5543^{10}

Cashelgar (IRE) *A De Royer-Dupre* 119
3 b c Anabaa(USA) —Tropical Barth (IRE) (Peintre Celebre (USA))
3050^{2} ◆ 4367a^{4}

Cash In The Attic *M R Channon* a52 58
3 b f Auction House(USA) —Aziz Presenting (IRE) (Charnwood Forest (IRE))
296^{2} *363^{6}* *649^{7}* *707^{4}* 3108^{4} 3473^{6} 3541^{5} 4425^{13}

Cashleen (USA) *K A Ryan* a31 67
3 ch f Lemon Drop Kid(USA) —Radu Cool (USA) (Carnivalay (USA))
1315^{10} 2299^{7} 2607^{10} 3316^{9} 3859^{5} 4940^{6}

Cash On (IRE) *Karen George* a71 28
7 ch g Spectrum(IRE) —Lady Lucre (IRE) (Last Tycoon)
836^{5} *894^{4}* *1069^{8}* 2182^{16}

Cash Queen Anna (IRE) *B W Hills* 79
2 b f Dr Fong(USA) —Cashel Queen (USA) (Kingmambo (USA))
4047^{3} 4817^{2} 5505^{2} (6214) 6481^{2}

Casilda (IRE) *A M Balding* a96 101
4 b m Cape Cross(IRE) —Koniya (IRE) (Doyoun)
1216^{3} 1697^{2} 5447^{8} 6093^{6}

Casino Drive (USA) *Kazuo Fujisawa* a118
4 ch h Mineshaft(USA) —Better Than Honour (USA) (Deputy Minister (CAN))
1013a^{8}

Casino Night *F P Murtagh* a52 80
4 ch m Night Shift(USA) —Come Fly With Me (Bluebird (USA))
688^{5} *823^{9}* 1123^{2} 1229^{9} 1507^{11} 1646^{7} 2261^{4} 2531^{8} 3060^{3} 3293^{4} 4040^{2} 4345^{3} (4532) 5160^{4} 5361^{4} 6016^{7} 6385^{6} 6648^{14}

Cassidy K *D W Thompson* 55
2 ch f Zafeen(FR) —Alizar (IRE) (Rahy (USA))
1680^{3} 2100^{2} 2401^{5} 2996^{3} 3605^{3} 6557^{8} 7218^{9}

Cassique Lady (IRE) *Mrs L Wadham* a85 103
4 b m Langfuhr(CAN) —Palacoona (FR) (Last Tycoon)
1667^{7} 2482^{3} (2974) 4458^{2} 5796^{8}

Castaneous (IRE) *P J Rothwell* a66 51
5 b g Lahib(USA) —Witchy Native (IRE) (Be My Native (USA))
(240)

Castano *B R Millman* a69 74
5 br g Makbul—Royal Orchid (IRE) (Shalford (IRE))
2137^{3} 2353^{3} 2794^{6} 3283^{8} *3983^{4}* 4428^{12} 5788^{4} *(6251)* 6596^{5} 7062^{5} *7348^{11}*

Castellina *E J Creighton* a55 96
5 ch m Medicean—Protectorate (Hector Protector (USA))
1770^{2} *1962^{8}* 2785^{8} *6668^{11}*

Caster Sugar (USA) *R Hannon* a56 84
3 b f Cozzene(USA) —Only Royale (IRE) (Caerleon (USA))
2321^{3} ◆ 2539^{7} *2827^{4}* 3209^{5} (3581) (4010) 4441^{6} 5101^{2} (5567) (6420)

Casting Couch (IRE) *B W Hills* a48 68
3 b f Royal Applause—Mcqueenie (IRE) (Danehill (USA))
1302^{4} 2795^{11} 5181^{3} 5789^{8}

Castle Bar Sling (USA) *T J O'Mara* a80 92
4 b h Diesis—Lady Of The Woods (USA) (Woodman (USA))
4412a^{8} 4574a^{4}

Castlebury (IRE) *G A Swinbank* 71
4 b g Spartacus(IRE) —La Vie En Rouge (IRE) (College Chapel)
1612^{4} 1830^{5} 2245^{7} 2722^{4} 3354^{7} (4351) 4528^{4} 4821^{5}

Castlecarra (IRE) *J Hetherton* a33 46
4 b g Mull Of Kintyre(USA) —Sketch Pad (Warning)
5422^{3} 5599^{6} 5727^{7} 7086^{11} *7466^{11}* *7681^{11}*

Castlefish (IRE) *D Burchell* 33
5 b g Carrowkeel(IRE) —Haven Island (IRE) (Revoque (IRE))
5242^{8} 5632^{13}

Castle Myth (USA) *B Ellison* a67 54
3 bb g Johannesburg(USA) —Castlemania (CAN) (Bold Ruckus (USA))
1098^{9} *2131^{10}* *2681^{3}* 4279^{8} 4562^{12} 5331^{8} 5730^{10} *7142^{2}* *7374^{4}* *(7416)* ◆ *7500^{5}* *7615^{3}* 7857^{7}

Castles In The Air *R A Fahey* a95 97
4 b g Oasis Dream—Dance Parade (USA) (Gone West (USA))
1309^{7} (1832) 2938^{6} 3339^{2} 3752^{7} (4293) 4796^{8} *5615^{2}* 5826^{2} 6270^{8}

Cast Of Stars (IRE) *R M Beckett* a70 68
2 b g Nayef(USA) —Scarpe Rosse (IRE) (Sadler's Wells (USA))
5499^{7} 6697^{5} *7683^{2}*

Casual *D K Weld* 98
3 b f Nayef(USA) —Costa Rica (IRE) (Sadler's Wells (USA))
(7263a)

Casual Conquest (IRE) *D K Weld* 123
4 b g Hernando(FR) —Lady Luck (IRE) (Kris)
1674^{2} (2303a) 4253a^{3} (5076a) 5688a^{7}

Casual Garcia *Sir Mark Prescott* a56 80
4 gr g Hernando(FR) —Frosty Welcome (USA) (With Approval (CAN))
1863^{11} 3986^{6} 4417^{18} 5068^{4} 5339^{7} 5917^{6}

Catai *P Monteith* a34
5 b h Mark Of Esteem(IRE) —China (Royal Academy (USA))
566^{8}

Catalan Bay (AUS) *J R Gask* a82 81
5 b m Rock Of Gibraltar(IRE) —Kim Angel (AUS) (Serheed (USA))
281^{2} *680^{4}* 3153^{2} 3866^{8} 4386^{5} 5182^{4} 6020^{6}

Catalina Sunrise (USA) *L M Cumani* a56
3 ch f Malibu Moon(USA) —Jealous Forum (USA) (Open Forum (USA))
3297^{10}

Catawollow *R C Guest* 44
2 b f Beat Hollow—Catalonia (IRE) (Catrail (USA))
7061^{7} 7244^{9} *7638^{11}*

Catbells (IRE) *A Bailey* 75
2 ch f Rakti—Moonbi Ridge (IRE) (Definite Article)
4706^{2} 5208^{5} 6009^{8} 6090^{6} 6481^{11}

Catchanova (IRE) *Eve Johnson Houghton* a65 58
2 b c Catcher In The Rye(IRE) —Head For The Stars (IRE) (Head For Heights)
3692^{15} 4478^{9} 5212^{6} *6228^{3}* *7235^{7}*

Catcher Of Dreams (IRE) *A G Foster* a62 45
3 b c Catcher In The Rye(IRE) —No Islands (Lomond (USA))
7173^{13}

Catch Key (IRE) *T D Easterby* 51
3 b f Key Of Luck(USA) —Catch Me (Rudimentary (USA))
1683^{6} 1950^{4} 2375^{8} 3610^{4}

Catchmeifyoucan (FR) *C G Cox* a61 60
3 b g Marju(IRE) —Catch Us (FR) (Selkirk (USA))
2551^{11} 3751^{12} *6287^{6}* 6910^{12}

Catchpenny *K A Ryan* a53 47
3 b f Piccolo—Noble Penny (Pennekamp (USA))
5304^{3} 5727^{3} *6344^{5}* *6880^{7}* *7270^{2}* *7579^{9}*

Catch Roy (IRE) *Daniel Mark Loughnane* 60
3 b g Catcher In The Rye(IRE) —Top Of Jumbo (IRE) (Fayruz)
5184^{16}

Catch Wind (USA) *S Botti* 95
3 ch f Mr Greeley(USA) —Busy Windsong (USA) (Clever Trick (USA))
3186a^{2}

Categorical *K G Reveley* a69 70
6 b g Diktat—Zibet (Kris)
1242^{7}

Cate Washington *Mrs L Williamson* a33 25
6 b m Superior Premium—Willisa (Polar Falcon (USA))
198^{9} *475^{7}* *666^{13}* 1556^{10} 2517^{9}

Catherine (IRE) *Mark L Fagan* a49 55
3 ch f Modigliani(USA) —Jillians Pride (IRE) (Persian Mews)
7349^{11} *7371^{10}*

Catherines Call (IRE) *D Donovan* a50
2 b f Captain Rio—It's Academic (Royal Academy (USA))
5638^{6}

Cat Hunter *Mrs A J Perrett* a65 64
2 b f One Cool Cat(USA) —Eoz (IRE) (Sadler's Wells (USA))
5368^{5} 6544^{3} *(6911)* 7187^{12}

Cativo *B R Millman* a49 36
3 b f Deportivo—Catriona (Bustino)
1745^{8} 4097^{10} *7107^{5}* *7576^{5}* *7614^{9}* *7829^{7}*

Cativo Cavallino *J E Long* a78 81
6 ch g Bertolini(USA) —Sea Isle (Selkirk (USA))
1121^{5} *2382^{4}* *2598^{3}* 3866^{3} 4082^{2} *4791^{6}* 5019^{3} *(5576)* *7180^{3}* *7432^{5}*

Cat Junior (USA) *B J Meehan* a89 117
4 bb h Storm Cat(USA) —Luna Wells (IRE) (Sadler's Wells (USA))
1008a^{13} 5196^{3} 5474^{3} 5862^{2} 6503a^{4}

Cats Fun (AUS) *Jarrod McLean* 104
7 b g Catbird(AUS) —She's Zeel (NZ) (Zabeel (NZ))
6961a^{8}

Cat Six (USA) *T Wall* a26 21
5 b m Tale Of The Cat(USA) —Hurricane Warning (USA) (Thunder Gulch (USA))
3503^{11} 4373^{10}

Catskill *Adrian McGuinness* a25 58
7 ch g Inchinor—Manhattan Sunset (USA) (El Gran Senor (USA))
3654^{3} 7649^{9}

Caucus *J L Dunlop* 70
2 b c Cape Cross(IRE) —Maid To Perfection (Sadler's Wells (USA))
3867^{8} 4985^{10} 5542^{4}

Caudillo (GER) *Dr A Bolte* 113
6 b h Acatenango(GER) —Corsita (Top Ville)
1552a^{6} 2216a^{4} 6521a^{4}

Caught In Paradise (IRE) *D W Thompson* 59
4 b g Catcher In The Rye(IRE) —Paradis (Bijou D'Inde)
61^{11}

Caught On Camera *M L W Bell* a59 58
3 b f Red Ransom(USA) —Colorsnap (Shirley Heights)
2709^{13} 3741^{4} 4545^{9} 4944^{3}

Caunton Beck (FR) *E J O'Neill* 77
2 b c Captain Rio—La Menorquina (USA) (Woodman (USA))
6131a^{5} 6501a^{13} 6928a^{2} 7316a^{4}

Causa Proxima (FR) *A De Royer-Dupre* 96
3 b f Kendor(FR) —Rotina (FR) (Crystal Glitters (USA))
4394a^{9}

Cause (USA) *Myung Kwon Cho* a104
4 ch h Giant's Causeway(USA) —Awwaliya (Distant Relative)
789a^{11}

Cause For Applause (IRE) *R Craggs* a56 42
3 b f Royal Applause—Polyandry (IRE) (Pennekamp (USA))
(5) 228^{7} 808^{4} 964^{4} 6383^{8} 7211^{5} 7599^{12} 7726^{8}

Causeway Coast (USA) *P W Chapple-Hyam* 36
2 bb f Giant's Causeway(USA) —Manda Island (USA) (Dynaformer (USA))
6992^{19}

Causeway King (USA) *A King* a62 68
3 ch g Giant's Causeway(USA) —A P Petal (USA) (A.P. Indy (USA))
3980^{7} 4650^{5} 5286^{11}

Caustic Wit (IRE) *M S Saunders* a68 67
11 b g Cadeaux Genereux—Baldemosa (FR) (Lead On Time (USA))
2137^{6} 2224^{5} (2353) 2564^{5} 2799^{7} 2908^{4} 3208^{9} 4428^{11} 5065^{9}

Cavaliere (FR) *M Cesandri* 95
3 b f Traditionally(USA) —Lavandou (Sadler's Wells (USA))
6438a^{3} 7347a^{2}

Cavalry Guard (USA) *T D McCarthy* a58 57
5 ch g Officer(USA) —Leeward City (USA) (Carson City (USA))
23^{4} 210^{6} 395^{4} 666^{3} 749^{3} 961^{7} 1641^{5} 1883^{2} 2921^{8} 3401^{8} 3863^{11} 6945^{11} 7129^{2} 7433^{11} 7614^{2} 7880^{3}

Cavalryman *A Fabre* 125
3 b c Halling(USA) —Silversword (FR) (Highest Honor (FR))
1979a^{2} (3970a) (5930a) 6526a^{3}

Cavan Girl *Michael Mulvany* 64
2 b f Xaar—Golden Way (IRE) (Cadeaux Genereux)
5274a^{7}

Cavendish *J M P Eustace* a69 77
5 b g Pursuit Of Love—Bathwick Babe (IRE) (Sri Pekan (USA))
6258^{10}

Cavendish Road (IRE) *W R Muir* a74 72
3 b g Bachelor Duke(USA) —Gronchi Rosa (IRE) (Nashwan (USA))
(1620) 1746^{16} 2797^{4} (3476) 4240^{3} (5121) 5869^{8} 6337^{3} 7065^{3}

Cave Of The Giant (IRE) *T D McCarthy* 49
7 b g Giant's Causeway(USA) —Maroussie (FR) (Saumarez)
3423^{5}

Caviar *R Hannon* a58 69
2 gr f Thunder Gulch(USA) —Cozzene'Saffair (USA) (Black Tie Affair)
2699^{3} 3187^{8} 3733^{6}

Cavitie *Andrew Reid* a55 55
3 b g Teofilio(IRE) —Kirriemuir (Lochnager)
1465^{6} 1840^{10} 2265^{2} 2581^{2} 3010^{6} 6777^{8}

Cawdor (IRE) *H Candy* a74 83
3 b g Kyllachy—Dim Ots (Alhijaz)
1419^{2} 1814^{3} 2888^{2} 3163^{10} 5506^{9} (6798)

Cayman Fox *James Moffatt* a77 64
4 ch m Cayman Kai(IRE) —Kalarram (Muhtarram (USA))
1768^{13} 2451^{5} (3020) 3479^{2} 4189^{3} 5518^{5} 5610^{2} 6010^{15} 6456^{4} 6801^{2} 7136^{2} 7601^{4} 7634^{6} ◆

Cayman Sky *R Hannon* a65 69
3 b g Fantastic Light(USA) —Comme Ca (Cyrano De Bergerac)
914^{6} 1416^{4} 1570^{3} 1930^{6} 2479^{4} 2881^{2} 3222^{9} 4744^{9} 6210^{3} 6742^{8} 6941^{3} 7049^{4}

Cayo Costa (IRE) *A J McCabe*
2 ch f Kheleyf(USA) —Tropical Paradise (USA) (Manila (USA))
7120^{15}

Cecil's Gift *W G M Turner* a23 40
2 b f Act One—Poyle Jenny (Piccolo)
2978^{9} 3203^{5} 3709^{10}

Cecily *Sir Mark Prescott* a85 79
3 b f Oasis Dream—Odette (Pursuit Of Love)
109^{3} 288^{5} 509^{4} 685^{6} 814^{3} 1068^{2} 1180^{4} (1414) 1727^{4} 4244^{4} 7253^{3} ◆ 7511^{4} 7613^{11}

Cecily Parsley *H Morrison* a6 49
3 b f Fantastic Light(USA) —Salim Toto (Mtoto)
3538^{5} 4480^{7} 5061^{6} 6445^{9}

Cecina Marina *Mrs K Walton* a20 52
6 b m Sugarfoot—Chasetown Cailin (Suave Dancer (USA))
1651^{8} 2656^{3} 3171^{12} 3927^{12} 5161^{2} 6183^{8} 6369^{8} 6840^{3} 7080^{5}

Ceedwell *E Libaud* 90
2 ch f Exceed And Excel(AUS) —Muja Farewell (Mujtahid (USA))
(2311) (2655) 3015^{3} 3748^{6} 5739a^{5}

Ceilidh House *R M Beckett* 80
2 ch f Selkirk(USA) —Villa Carlotta (Rainbow Quest (USA))
(6593) ◆

Celebra (FR) *C Laffon-Parias* 102
3 ch f Peintre Celebre(USA) —Thearena (USA) (Seattle Slew (USA))
1550a^{2} 2521a^{7} 2952a^{11}

Celebrian *W R Swinburn* a56 8
2 b f Fasliyev(USA) —Triplemoon (USA) (Trempolino (USA))
6729^{14} 7135^{9} 7451^{8}

Celebrissime (IRE) *F Head* 110
4 ch h Peintre Celebre(USA) —Ring Beaune (USA) (Bering)
2120a^{4} 2953a^{7}

Celebrity Choice (IRE) *E Libaud* 55
2 b c Choisir(AUS) —Femme Celebre (IRE) (Peintre Celebre (USA))
6322a^{7}

Celendine *G A Swinbank* 58
2 b f Oratorio(IRE) —Affaire D'Amour (Hernando (FR))
6154^{7}

Celesta (HUN) *S Szuna*
5 ch m Overseas Transfer(IRE) —Country Weave (USA) (Mujtahid (USA))
465a^{8}

Celestial Dream (IRE) *A M Balding* a69 65
3 b f Oasis Dream—Lochangel (Night Shift (USA))
1956^{2} (2386) 2654^{3}

Celestial Girl *H Morrison* a53
2 b f Dubai Destination(USA) —Brightest Star (Unfuwain (USA))
7859^{9}

Celestial Tryst *G M Moore* 74
2 b f Tobougg(IRE) —Celestial Welcome (Most Welcome)
3263^{8} (4226) 5280a^{6} 6693^{9}

Celimene (IRE) *C Lerner* 115
3 b f Dr Fong(USA) —Lunassa (FR) (Groom Dancer (USA))
(1267a) 2952a^{4} 4583a^{13} (7128a)

Cellarmaster (IRE) *Mark Gillard* a43
8 ch g Alhaarth(IRE) —Cheeky Weeky (Cadeaux Genereux)
190^{9}

Celtic Carisma *K G Reveley* 51
7 b m Celtic Swing—Kathryn's Pet (Blakeney)
2044^{6} 2344^{8} 2725^{2} 5068^{6} 5734^{4}

Celtic Change (IRE) *M Dods* a73 87
5 br g Celtic Swing—Changi (IRE) (Lear Fan (USA))
1100^{2} 1646^{8} 2894^{11} 3264^{6} (3624) (4400) 5040^{6} 5598^{2} 6014^{8} 6485^{10}

Celtic Charlie (FR) *P M Phelan* a34 19
4 ch h Until Sundown(USA) —India Regalona (USA) (Dehere (USA))
6770^{11}

Celtic Commitment *R Hannon* a67 67
3 gr c Mull Of Kintyre(USA) —Grey Again (Unfuwain (USA))
2315

Celtic Dane (IRE) *Kevin Prendergast* a80 104
5 b g Danetime(IRE) —Quelle Celtique (FR) (Tel Quel (FR))
4412a^{15}

Celticello (IRE) *P D Evans* a74 83
7 bb g Celtic Swing—Viola Royale (IRE) (Royal Academy (USA))
584^{7}

Celtic Gold (USA) *Andrew Turnell* a71 73
5 b g Elusive Quality(USA) —Fortune (IRE) (Night Shift (USA))
(102) 285^{6} 497^{5} 1287^{6} 1514^{2}

Celtic Lass *M A Jarvis* a44 39
3 b f Celtic Swing—Nsx (Roi Danzig (USA))
3025^{6} 4145^{12}

Celtic Lynn (IRE) *M Dods* 83
4 br m Celtic Swing—Sheryl Lynn (Miller's Mate)
(1737) 2402^{5} 3353^{5} 4228^{3} 4896^{6} 5697^{14}

Celtic Ransom *J W Hills* a36 58
2 b c Red Ransom(USA) —Welsh Valley (USA) (Irish River (FR))
6109^{10} 6616^{8} 7050^{11}

Celtic Rebel (IRE) *S A Callaghan* a58 46
3 b g Bahri(USA) —Farjah (IRE) (Charnwood Forest (IRE))
673^{4} 804^{U} 1455^{8}

Celtic Sovereign (IRE) *M G Quinlan* a68
3 b g Celtic Swing—Penny Ha'Penny (Bishop Of Cashel)
(7829)

Celtic Spirit (IRE) *G L Moore* a100 78
6 ch g Pivotal—Cavernista (Lion Cavern (USA))
33^{5} 1458^{13}

Celtic Step *P D Niven* a67 84
5 br g Selkirk(USA) —Inchiri (Sadler's Wells (USA))
2894^{12} 4104^{3} 4333^{14} 4548^{11} 6357^{5} 7172^{4} 7422^{3} 7631^{3} 7723^{2}

Celtic Sultan (IRE) *T P Tate* 108
5 b g Celtic Swing—Farjah (IRE) (Charnwood Forest (IRE))
1560^{7} 1821^{8} (2266) 2470^{2} 3091^{19} 3567^{2} 3846^{8} 4423^{8} 5249^{8} 5826^{7} 6278^{4} ◆ 6482^{3} 6675^{14} 7294^{7}

Cent Cheveux Blanc (GER) *W Hickst* 92
3 ch f Pentire—Centaine (Royal Academy (USA))
6886a^{7}

Centenary (IRE) *M W Easterby* a48 49
5 b g Traditionally(USA) —Catherinofaragon (USA) (Chief's Crown (USA))
2725^{9} 3171^{8}

Centenerola (USA) *D Shaw* a38 85
4 b m Century City(IRE) —Lady Angharad (IRE) (Tenby)
39^{8}

Centennial (IRE) *J H M Gosden* 114
4 gr h Dalakhani(IRE) —Lurina (IRE) (Lure (USA))
1351^{2} 2056^{6} 3048^{7} 4457^{7} 5932a^{10}

Centeo (SPA) *Mlle A De Clerck* a71 84
4 b h Wagon Master(FR) —Red White And Blue (Zafonic (USA))
5089a^{7}

Centigrade (IRE) *W J Haggas* 89
2 gr g Verglas(IRE) —American Queen (FR) (Fairy King (USA))
4093^{4} ◆ (5527) (6088) ◆

Centime *B J Meehan* 51
2 b f Royal Applause—Argent Du Bois (USA) (Silver Hawk (USA))
6729^{11} 6992^{15}

Centurio *R Charlton* 78
2 b c Pivotal—Grain Of Gold (Mr Prospector (USA))
5993^{3} ◆ 6617^{2}

Ceodora (GER) *W Baltromei* 93
4 b m Efisio—Caerosa (Caerleon (USA))
6499a^{5}

Cereal Killer (IRE) *R Hannon* 71
2 br c Xaar—Snap Crackle Pop (IRE) (Statoblest)
5829^{9} 6108^{13} 6696^{4}

Ceremonial Jade (UAE) *M Botti* a112 62
6 b g Jade Robbery(USA) —Talah (Danehill (USA))
633^{5} (781) 1124^{10} 1640^{3} 7488^{10} 7768^{3}

Cerito *J R Boyle* a88 91
3 ch g Bahamian Bounty—Pascali (Compton Place)
6694^{14} 7202^{4} 7395^{6} 7511^{9}

Certain Justice (USA) *Stef Liddiard* a72 76
11 gr g Lit De Justice(USA) —Pure Misk (Rainbow Quest (USA))
94^{8}

Certifiable *Miss Z C Davison* a54 37
8 b g Deploy—Gentle Irony (Mazilier (USA))
211^{8}

Cesare *J R Fanshawe* a99 123
8 b g Machiavellian(USA) —Tromond (Lomond (USA))
2990^{2} 3841^{5} 4543^{3} 5426^{5} 6030^{4}

C'Est La Guerre (NZ) *John D Sadler* 119
5 b g Shinko King(IRE) —La Magnifique (NZ) (Kampala)
6871a^{15} 7215a^{8}

Chabal (IRE) *J S Bolger* 116
2 b c Galileo(IRE) —Vagary (IRE) (Zafonic (USA))
5892a^{2} ◆ 6849^{10}

Chachamaidee (IRE) *H R A Cecil* 93
2 b f Footstepsinthesand—Canterbury Lace (USA) (Danehill (USA))
(2711) 3086^{3} 4795^{6} 5199^{5}

Chadwell Spring (IRE) *Miss J Feilden* a68 74
3 b f Statue Of Liberty(USA) —Cresalin (Coquelin (USA))
1531^{3} 1937^{12} 2320^{9} 3009^{3} 3387^{6} (3741) 4720^{6} 5195^{13} (5803) 6023^{4} 6474^{7}

Chain Of Events *B W Hills* 73
2 ch g Nayef(USA) —Ermine (IRE) (Cadeaux Genereux)
4048^{3} 5793^{8}

Chain Of Office *W J Haggas* 72
2 ch f Mark Of Esteem(IRE) —Lady Mayor (Kris)
5397^{6} ◆ (5906) 6923^{11}

Chairman Pat (USA) *Tom Dascombe* a65 70
2 ch c Proud Citizen(USA) —Sejm's Lunar Star (USA) (Sejm (USA))
2792^{7} ◆ 3270^{5} 4080^{2} 4693^{5} 5213^{8} 5913^{6} 6793^{7}

Chakacha (FR) *D Prod'Homme* a83 86
3 b f Victory Note(USA) —Vodka (FR) (Ali-Royal (IRE))
5462a^{6} (6222a)

Chalentina *J E Long* a52 59
6 b m Primo Valentino(IRE) —Chantilly Myth (Sri Pekan (USA))
23^{3} 308^{4} 666^{5} 844^{12} 853^{10}

Chalice Welcome *N B King* a78 74
6 b g Most Welcome—Blue Peru (IRE) (Perugino (USA))
(193) 275^{2} 320^{6} 1728^{2} ◆ (1961) 2244^{9} 2419^{12} 5365^{8} (5975) 6218^{6} (7695)

Chalk Hill Blue *Eve Johnson Houghton* a54 62
3 b f Reset(AUS) —Golubitsa (IRE) (Bluebird (USA))
1363^{11} 2489^{6} 3209^{12} 3919^{10} 4224^{11}

Challenging (UAE) *M W Easterby* 53
3 b f Halling(USA) —Small Change (IRE) (Danzig (USA))
2370^{10} 3610^{7}

Chamir (FR) *C Martens* a59 55
3 gr g Charming Groom(FR) —Sheer Drop (FR) (Kenmare (FR))
6606a^{0}

Champagne All Day *S P Griffiths* 8
3 ch g Timeless Times(USA) —Miss Ceylon (Brief Truce (USA))
6823^{13}

Champagne Cocktail (IRE) *R J Price* a51
8 b g Dushyantor(USA) —Kunuz (Ela-Mana-Mou)
2580^{3} 3029^{13}

Champagne D'Oro (USA) *Eric J Guillot* a96
2 b f Medaglia D'Oro(USA) —Champagne Glow (USA) (Saratoga Six (USA))
7283a^{12}

Champagne Fizz (IRE) *Miss Jo Crowley* a60 67
3 gr f King Charlemagne(USA) —Silver Moon (Environment Friend)
3815^{6} 4305^{8} 4904^{6} 6445^{3} 6918^{10} (7765)

Champagne Future *W R Swinburn* 86
3 b f Compton Place—Jade Pet (Petong)
1174^{3} (1419) ◆ 2058^{2} ◆

Champagnelifestyle *B W Hills* 85
2 b f Montjeu(IRE) —White Rose (GER) (Platini (GER))
(4055) 6852^{10}

Champagne Shadow (IRE) *J Pearce* a67 71
8 b g Kahyasi—Moet (IRE) (Mac's Imp (USA))
168^{4} 3382^{3}

Champagne Style (USA) *B J Meehan* a82 100
2 ch c Lion Heart(USA) —Statute (USA) (Verzy (CAN))
4908^{2} ◆ 5580^{2} (6811)

Champain Sands (IRE) *E J Alston* a61 71
10 b g Green Desert(USA) —Grecian Bride (IRE) (Groom Dancer (USA))
1332^{9} 1401^{2} 1887^{4} 2313^{2} (2542) 2968^{8} 3264^{7} 4019^{8} 4663^{7} 5243^{7} 5418^{11}

Champion Girl (IRE) *D Haydn Jones* a40 65
3 b f Captain Rio—Sea Of Serenity (USA) (Conquistador Cielo (USA))
2321^{12} 2685^{10} 4535^{4} 5228^{7} 5628^{8}

Champs Elysees *Robert Frankel* a117 121
6 b h Danehill(USA) —Hasili (IRE) (Kahyasi)
789a^{2} (6873a)

Chandika *C G Cox* a65 65
3 b f Exceed And Excel(AUS) —Jitterbug (IRE) (Marju (IRE))
2205^{7} 2496^{6} 4324^{5} 4829^{3} 5219^{2} 5383^{6} 6186^{6} (7224)

Chandrayaan *E A L Dunlop* a66 62
2 ch g Bertolini(USA) —Muffled (USA) (Mizaaya)
4152^{7} 4534^{8} 5106^{5} 5674^{8} 5967^{4} (6343) 6609^{8}

Change Alley (USA) *A Al Raihe* a104 83
4 b h Elusive Quality(USA) —Fortune (IRE) (Night Shift (USA))
(336a) 434a^{7} 525a^{3} 770a^{5} 1010a^{10}

Change The World (IRE) *S Wattel* a75 112
4 b h Sakhee(USA) —Mrs Seek (Unfuwain (USA))
5089a^{4} 7387a^{9}

Changingoftheguard (IRE) *A P O'Brien* 117
3 b c Montjeu(IRE) —Miletrian (IRE) (Marju (IRE))
1793^{2} 5173^{2} ◆ 5861^{6}

Changing Skies (IRE) *B J Meehan* 111
4 b m Sadler's Wells(USA) —Magnificient Style (USA) (Silver Hawk (USA))
2013^{4}

Changing The Guard *R A Fahey* a84 91
3 b g King's Best(USA) —Our Queen Of Kings (Arazi (USA))
(85) 288^{2} 432^{2} (782) ◆ 1001^{3} 1471^{2} 2270^{5} (2935) 3780^{5} ◆ 4455^{10}

Channel Crossing *S Wynne* a42 73
7 b g Deploy—Wave Dancer (Dance In Time (CAN))
2332^{9} 2537^{4} 3308^{3} 4021^{8} 5962^{7} 6969^{11}

Chanrossa (IRE) *E A L Dunlop* a69 62
3 b f Galileo(IRE) —Palacoona (FR) (Last Tycoon)
2211^{5} 2848^{6} 3462^{8} 4498^{5} 5782^{5} 5988^{8} 6440^{2} 7022^{10} 7392^{2} 7524^{2} 7695^{10} 7882^{2}

Chantilly Creme (USA) *R Gibson* 100
2 b f Johannesburg(USA) —Creme De La Creme (FR) (Vettori (IRE))
3015^{5} 3667a^{2} (4584a) 5279a^{12} 6269^{7}

Chantilly Dancer (IRE) *M Quinn* a47 58
3 b f Danehill Dancer(IRE) —Antiguan Jane (Shirley Heights)
228^{5} 383^{6} 649^{6} 943^{9} 1270^{4} 2169^{5} 2461^{4} (3005) 4918^{6} 6001^{5}

Chantilly Jewel (USA) *R M H Cowell* a56 60
4 b m Century City(IRE) —Betty's Star (USA) (Pentelicus (USA))
381^{8} 626^{9} 810^{4} 1055^{5} 1379^{5} 2455^{5} 3125^{2} 3591^{7} 3959^{4} 4182^{7} (5645) 6939^{6} 7002^{4} 7371^{12} 7710^{8}

Chantilly Lace (IRE) *Reginald Roberts* a77 89
3 b f Celtic Swing—Civic Duty (IRE) (Definite Article)
5689a^{19}

Chantilly Passion (FR) *B Storey*
8 b g Double Trigger(IRE) —Chantilly Fashion (FR) (Northern Fashion (USA))
3314^{9}

Chantilly Pearl (USA) *J G Given* a68 69
3 bb f Smart Strike(CAN) —Cataballerina (USA) (Tabasco Cat (USA))
2001^{8} 2967^{4} 3545^{6} 4994^{2} 5258^{5} 6124^{4} 7399^{2} 7512^{7}

Chantilly Tiffany *E A L Dunlop* a98 108
5 ch m Pivotal—Gaily Royal (IRE) (Royal Academy (USA))
1873^{10} 2285a^{7} 3012^{4} 3516a^{11} 5313^{3} 6272^{4} 7044a^{6}

Chaperno (USA) *Saeed Bin Suroor* a95 97
2 bb c More Than Ready(USA) —Timeless Forest (USA) (Forestry (USA))
2839^{2} ◆ 3392^{2} (3875) 4418^{8} 4826^{3} 5661^{6} 6398^{2} (7063)

Chapi Chapo (FR) *B De Montzey* 65
2 b c Diableneyev(USA) —My Sweet (FR) (Zafonic (USA))
6131a^{7} 7264a^{10}

Chapter (IRE) *Mrs A L M King* a46 52
7 ch g Sinndar(IRE) —Web Of Intrigue (Machiavellian (USA))
1463^{9} 1770^{10}

Chapter And Verse (IRE) *Mike Murphy* a88 85
3 gr g One Cool Cat(USA) —Beautiful Hill (IRE) (Danehill (USA))
(1168) 3808^{4} 4315^{6} (5040) 5598^{9} 5832^{8} 6773^{4} 7233^{3} 7540^{2} 7560^{2}

Chardonnay *G A Swinbank* a74 63
2 br f Piccolo—Icy (Mind Games)
5949^{3} (6638)

Chardonnay Star (IRE) *C J Teague* a7 8
2 b f Bertolini(USA) —Coup De Coeur (IRE) (Kahyasi)
2089^{11} 2226^{8} 7420^{9}

Charger *J Noseda* 76
3 b g Rock Of Gibraltar(IRE) —Ruthless Rose (USA) (Conquistador Cielo (USA))
3117^{4} ◆ 3751^{7} 5744^{4} 6595^{7} (6789)

Charging Indian (IRE) *P T Midgley* a78 74
3 b g Chevalier(IRE) —Kathy Tolfa (IRE) (Sri Pekan (USA))
1214[8] 2248[7] 3592[8] 6015[11] 6370[10] 6768[5] (6951) 7332[4] 7505[5] 7794[4]

Charismatic Lady *Jane Chapple-Hyam* 65
3 ch f Bertolini(USA) —Norcroft Lady (Mujtahid (USA))
1843[6] 2170[5] 3545[3] 4068[8] 4669[5] 6339[10] 6537[7] 6924[14]

Charitable Man (USA) *Kiaran McLaughlin* a113
3 bb c Lemon Drop Kid(USA) —Charitabledonation (USA) (Saint Ballado (CAN))
1225a[7] 2734a[4]

Charity Belle (USA) *J H M Gosden* 106
3 b f Empire Maker(USA) —Sweet Charity (USA) (A.P. Indy (USA))
(2403) 2846[4] 4166[2] (5298a) 6504a[5] 6853[9]

Charity Fair *A Berry* 49
2 ch f Bahamian Bounty—Be Most Welcome (Most Welcome)
1827[6] 2311[9] 3446[5] 3686[10] 4306[7] 4803[6] 5207[8] 5358[3] 6099[8] 6215[12] 6983[7] 7114[4] 7168[4]

Charles Bear *E S McMahon* a56
2 br f Needwood Blade—Zamyatina (IRE) (Danehill Dancer (IRE))
7630[8] 7799[4]

Charles Darwin (IRE) *M Blanshard* a68 86
6 ch g Tagula(IRE) —Seymour (IRE) (Eagle Eyed (USA))
843[4] 954[6] 1510[8] 2276[15] 2799[6] 3159[3] 3800[9] 4533[12] 5020[7] (5836) 7138[5] 7330[9]

Charles Parnell (IRE) *S P Griffiths* a89 81
6 b g Elnadim(USA) —Titania (Fairy King (USA))
68[2] 2770[11] 3354[9] 3956[5] 4372[7] 5147[3] 5406[5] 5676[2] 6458[6] 6670[5] 7673[5] 7729[6]

Charleston *R Rowe* a49
8 ch g Pursuit Of Love—Discomatic (USA) (Roberto (USA))
168[8] 3931[0] 750[6]

Charlevoix (IRE) *C F Wall* a74 78
4 b m King Charlemagne(USA) —Cayman Sound (Turtle Island (IRE))
1256[5] (1633) ◆ 2243[4] 3076[7]

Charlie Allnut *S Wynne* a50 58
4 b g Desert Style(IRE) —Queen Of Africa (USA) (Peintre Celebre (USA))
473[11] 575[11] 748[3] 811[3] 1057[8] 7459[9]

Charlie Be (IRE) *Mrs P N Dutfield* a47 44
4 ch g King Charlemagne(USA) —Miriana (IRE) (Bluebird (USA))
4220[9] 5120[8]

Charlie Bear *Miss Z C Davison* a51 46
8 ch h Bahamian Bounty—Abi (Chief's Crown (USA))
8[14] 341[11] 377[4] 541[9] 885[6] 1200[10]

Charlie Cool *Mrs R A Carr* a82 101
6 ch h Rainbow Quest(USA) —Tigwa (Cadeaux Genereux)
183a[8] 415a[7] (644a) 3399[4] 4352[6] 4781[9] 5200[11] 5694[2] 6239[7] 6795[8] 7194[9] 7583[6]

Charlie Delta *R A Harris* a65 78
6 b g Pennekamp(USA) —Papita (IRE) (Law Society (USA))
1775[11] 2224[9] 3057[6] 3505[11] 5184[12] 5502[4] 5634[2] 5905[7] 6175[7] (6777) 7349[8] 7521[3] 7596[5] 7691[6] (7819) 7879[4]

Charlie Farnsbarns (IRE) *B J Meehan* 116
5 b g Cape Cross(IRE) —Lafleur (IRE) (Grand Lodge (USA))
1011a[12] 1526[5] 1859[4] 2327[3] 3404[5] 5655[6] (6110) 6812[4]

Charlie Green (IRE) *Paul Green* a33 35
4 b g Traditionally(USA) —Saninka (IRE) (Doyoun)
7790[9]

Charlie Oxo *B P J Baugh* 27
4 br g Puissance—Aegean Mist (Prince Sabo)
7464[10]

Charlies Island (SAF) *H J Brown* a61 62
6 b g Lizard Island(AUS) —Lady Camilla (SAF) (Jallad (USA))
336a[10] 414a[11] 637a[10]

Charlie Smirke (USA) *G L Moore* a68 62
3 b g Gulch(USA) —Two Altazano (USA) (Manzotti (USA))
1034[6] 1932[10] 2380[6] 2809[7] 7610[3] 7742[2] 7826[2]

Charlie Tipple *T D Easterby* 90
5 b g Diktat—Swing Of The Tide (Sri Pekan (USA))
1246[2] 1684[5] 2101[7] 3154[2] 3312[9] 3872[14] 5361[7] 6485[3] 7060[5]

Charlie Tokyo (IRE) *R A Fahey* a99 91
6 b g Trans Island—Ellistown Lady (IRE) (Red Sunset)
2055[9] 2468[5] 2781[3] 2932[8] 3705[3] (4815) 5694[4] 6013[8] 6648[8] 6986[2]

Charlietoo *E G Bevan* a53 67
3 b g King Charlemagne(USA) —Ticcatoo (IRE) (Dolphin Street (FR))
1084[2] 1492[7] 2142[8] 2917[7] 4937[14] 5610[7]

Charlotte Grey *P J McBride* a64 64
5 gr m Wizard King—Great Intent (Aragon)
(62) (150) 401[2] 607[7]

Charlotte Ki (FR) *M Boutin* a67 78
3 ch f Sin Kiang(FR) —Autarcie (FR) (Ski Chief (USA))
5118a[9]

Charlotte Point (USA) *P F I Cole* a88 89
3 b f Distorted Humor(USA) —Skygusty (USA) (Skywalker (USA))
1466[2] (1808) (2607) 3400[2] 3981[3] 5175[12] 5986[8] 6907[15]

Charlottesometimes (USA) *D M Simcock* a48 48
2 bb f Dehere(USA) —Alexander Charlote (IRE) (Titus Livius (FR))
3715[6] 3944[4] 4379[6]

Charmaxjoanne *P C Haslam* 49
2 ch f Lucky Story(USA) —Dance Of The Swans (IRE) (Try My Best (USA))
4928[8] 5393[4] 7616[12]

Charmel's Lad *W R Swinburn* a62 64
4 ch g Compton Place—Fittonia (FR) (Ashkalani (IRE))
114[10] 304[4] 619[5] 934[5]

Charminamix (IRE) *A J Martin* a93 91
6 gr g Linamix(FR) —Cheeky Charm (USA) (Nureyev (USA))
4404[8] 5137[6]

Charming Escort *T T Clement* a62 45
5 ch g Rossini(USA) —Iktizawa (Entrepreneur)
25[6] 118[7]

Charm School *J H M Gosden* a99 111
4 b g Dubai Destination(USA) —Eve (Rainbow Quest (USA))
997[8] ◆ 1352[7] 1631[4] 2671[5] (5641) 6106[5] ◆ 6480[10] (7293)

Charpoy Cobra *J A R Toller* a61 64
2 b f Mark Of Esteem(IRE) —Duena (Grand Lodge (USA))
5398[7] 5984[6] 6441[3] 6923[10]

Chartist *B P J Baugh* a76 93
4 ch g Choisir(AUS) —Sareb (FR) (Indian Ridge)
1089[5] 1229[4] ◆ 1663[12] 2658[8] 2897[13] 3065[12] 6596[13]

Chasca (IRE) *Mrs A J Perrett* a69 72
3 b f Namid—Daganya (IRE) (Danehill Dancer (IRE))
(842) 1032[4] (1618) 5264[9] 5525[6] 6028[5] 6739[10]

Chase End *J M P Eustace* a45
3 ch f Arkadian Hero(USA) —Sestina (FR) (Bering)
127[6] 236[9]

Chasing Amy *M G Quinlan* a61 57
3 b f Namid—Inspiring (IRE) (Anabaa (USA))
2602[10] 3010[13] 3718[8] 4981[8] 5644[6] 6344[9]

Chasing Stars *Mme C Head-Maarek* 99
4 ch m Observatory(USA) —Post Modern (USA) (Nureyev (USA))
1873[9] 2513a[4]

Chasse Croise (FR) *J Bertran De Balanda* a65 67
3 gr g Kendor(FR) —Veiled Wings (FR) (Priolo (USA))
5278a[7]

Chatanoogachoochoo *M Hill* a65 69
4 ch m Piccolo—Taza (Persian Bold)
2493[9] 3800[2] ◆ 4266[6] 4482[4] 5063[9] 5473[3] 6166[4] 6861[4] 7399[4] 7790[4]

Chat De La Burg (USA) *J R Best* a76 76
2 ch c Johannesburg(USA) —Catsuit (USA) (Sir Cat (USA))
6424[2] (6971) ◆

Chat De Soie (IRE) *J S Moore* a39 61
2 b f Barathea(IRE) —Margay (IRE) (Marju (IRE))
4314[15] 5153[5] 5417[4] 5985[14] 6200[4]

Chateauneuf (IRE) *W M Brisbourne* a54 56
3 b f Marju(IRE) —Night Eyes (IRE) (Night Shift (USA))
2885[6] 3921[6] 4472[5] 5775[5] 7049[5] 7374[10]

Chateau Zara *C G Cox* a48
2 b f Zaha(CAN) —Glensara (Petoski)
7024[9]

Chatterszaha *C Drew* a64 54
3 ch f Zaha(CAN) —Chatter's Princess (Cadeaux Genereux)
5326[13] 5881[9] 6611[8] 7100[13]

Chaussini *J A R Toller* 76
2 b f Dubawi(IRE) —Miss Chaussini (IRE) (Rossini (USA))
5478[8] 5969[3] 6809[2] 7147[12]

Chausson Dore (IRE) *A De Royer-Dupre* 100
3 b f Hawk Wing(USA) —Don't Worry Me (IRE) (Dancing Dissident (USA))
1919a[6] 3892a[7]

Cheam Forever (USA) *R Charlton* a69 80
3 b g Exchange Rate(USA) —Many Charms (USA) (St Jovite (USA))
1075[3] 2010[12] 2578[11] (3708) (4642) 5243[3] 5803[3] (6365) 6545[4]

Cheap Street *J G Portman* a59 73
5 ch g Compton Place—Anneliina (Cadeaux Genereux)
155[10] 4082[14] 4905[2] 5502[6] 5634[5]

Cheap Thrills *J A Osborne* a75 77
3 ch f Bertolini(USA) —Licence To Thrill (Wolfhound (USA))
(162) 313[3] 1973[2] ◆ (2300) 2661[3] 3537[8] 5677[5] 6212[9] 6642[13] 7028[3] ◆ 7518[6] (7679) 7870[4]

Checklow (USA) *J Noseda* a94 98
4 b g Street Cry(IRE) —Comstock Queen (USA) (Silver Hawk (USA))
1209[2] ◆ 1433[5] 1986[2] 2342[9] 2933[14] 6665[11]

Check The Anchor (IRE) *N Tinkler* 43
2 ch g Observatory(USA) —Fleet River (USA) (Riverman (USA))
5439[11] 5951[10] 6214[10]

Check Up (IRE) *J L Flint* a40 62
8 b g Frimaire—Melons Lady (IRE) (The Noble Player (USA))
444[9]

Ched (USA) *F-X De Chevigny* 67
2 b c Belong To Me(USA) —Cape (USA) (Mr Prospector (USA))
6928a[5]

Cheeky Crumpet *A Berry* 10
3 b f Mind Games—Woore Lass (IRE) (Persian Bold)
1174[12] 1335[15]

Cheerfully *J H M Gosden* 54
2 br f Sadler's Wells(USA) —Light Of Morn (Daylami (IRE))
7182[12]

Cheers Big Ears (IRE) *J R Best* a56 54
3 br c Kheleyf(USA) —Grey Galava (Generous (IRE))
6255[6] 6573[4] 6823[12] 7069[3]

Cheers For Thea (IRE) *T D Easterby* a76 62
4 gr m Distant Music(USA) —Popiplu (USA) (Cozzene (USA))
1279[9] 1472[2] 1881[3] 2246[5] 2803[3] 4068[4] 4593[4] 5103[3] (5683) 6023[7] (6349) ◆

Cheery Cat (USA) *J Balding* a56 68
5 bb g Catienus(USA) —Olinka (USA) (Wolfhound (USA))
811[8] 1244[4] 1475[7] 1889[7] 3070[15] 3683[5] 4998[4] 5998[5] (7068) 7239[7] 7462[3] 7703[10]

Cheetah *L M Cumani* 78
2 b f Tiger Hill(IRE) —Kassiyra (IRE) (Kendor (FR))
5906[2] ◆ 6992[3]

Cheetah Beetah *H S Howe* a6 25
3 ch f Compton Place—Scylla (Rock City)
4691[7] 4982[7] 5500[6]

Chef De Camp (FR) *M R Hoad* a21
6 gr g Smadoun(FR) —Jolie Cheftaine (FR) (Chef De Clan (FR))
119[6]

Chelgui (FR) *C Baillet* a78 87
3 ch f Indian Rocket—Qui Es Tu (IRE) (Desert King (IRE))
7696a[6]

Chelsea Morning (USA) *B W Hills* 72
2 ch f Giant's Causeway(USA) —Binya (GER) (Royal Solo (IRE))
3810[3]

Chenin (IRE) *Peter Grayson* a41
3 b f Statue Of Liberty(USA) —Baltic Beach (IRE) (Polish Precedent (USA))
842[9] 1077[8] 2157[11] 3229[8] 4174[9] 5105[6] 5645[5]

Cherie Bibie (FR) *C Lerner* 80
2 b f Statue Of Liberty(USA) —Ozalid (FR) (Rudimentary (USA))
5927a[7]

Cherish The Moment (IRE) *B W Hills* 75
3 b c Galileo(IRE) —Belleclaire (IRE) (Bigstone (IRE))
1087[3] 1611[9] 4599[7] 5322[2] 5578[3] 6698[4]

Cherries On Top (IRE) *D Nicholls* a42 36
4 ch g Elnadim(USA) —Easy Going (Hamas (IRE))
1769[RR]

Cherri Fosfate *D Carroll* a74 74
5 b g Mujahid(USA) —Compradore (Mujtahid (USA))
2542[5] 2998[10]

Cherry Bee *M Johnston* 72
2 gr f Acclamation—Norfolk Lavender (CAN) (Ascot Knight (CAN))
2568[2] 2893[4] 3337[2] 4895[3] (5320)

Cherry Belle (IRE) *P D Evans* a46 58
3 b f Red Ransom(USA) —Pondicherry (USA) (Sir Wimborne (USA))
2950[11] 3336[12] 3588[8] 6172[6]

Cherry Orchard (IRE) *A Fabre* 93
3 b f King's Best(USA) —Epping (Charnwood Forest (IRE))
7302a[9]

Cherry Plum *A M Balding* a46
3 ch f Medicean—Putuna (Generous (IRE))
386[9] 695[4]

Chesapeake Bay *J J Lambe* a68 69
4 b g High Chaparral(IRE) —Coyote (Indian Ridge)
2440[6]

Cheshire Lady (IRE) *W M Brisbourne* 43
2 b f Marju(IRE) —Kiris World (Distant Relative)
2778[6] 3633[10]

Cheshire Prince *W M Brisbourne* 97
5 br g Desert Prince(IRE) —Bundle Up (USA) (Miner's Mark (USA))
(1798) 2342[15] 2932[15] 4091[2] 4315[2] 4781[13] 5248[6] 5437[10] 6100[7] 6546[6]

Cheshire Rose *A M Hales* a67 69
4 ch m Bertolini(USA) —Merch Rhyd-Y-Grug (Sabrehill (USA))
326[5] 518[6] 1041[2] 1310[12] 2046[6] 4536[3] 4886[3] 5374[5] 6205[8] 6456[11] 6939[5] 7397[9]

Cheval Rouge (IRE) *H Rogers* a53 70
2 ch f Tagula(IRE) —Izibi (FR) (Saint Cyrien (FR))
7258a[11]

Cheveton *R J Price* a106 103
5 ch g Most Welcome—Attribute (Warning)
(1052) 1325[5] 1647[2] 2012[3] 3351[10] 3844[3] 4330[12] 4766[5] 5039[17] (5654) 6678[2] 7015[10]

Cheveyo (IRE) *Patrick Morris* a73 68
3 br g Celtic Swing—La Catalane (IRE) (Marju (IRE))
7829[8]

Cheviot (USA) *M A Jarvis* a75 90
3 b g Rahy(USA) —Camlet (Green Desert (USA))
1305[2] 1705[3] 3375[2]

Cheyenne Chant *Sir Mark Prescott* a46
2 ch f Singspiel(IRE) —Apache Song (USA) (Dynaformer (USA))
6947[5] 7396[9] 7491[7]

Cheyenne Red (IRE) *M Dods* a57 71
3 br g Namid—Red Leggings (Shareef Dancer (USA))
1563[4] 2070[4] 2250[4] ◆ 3003[2] ◆ 3856[3] 4343[2] (4531) 4777[3] 5335[4] (6140) 6798[2]

Cheyrac (FR) *X Nakkachdji* 98
3 gr f Smadoun(FR) —One Way (FR) (Exit To Nowhere (USA))
6657a[4]

Chi (TUR) *A Ozgen* 100
3 ch f Unaccounted For(USA) —Agas Joy (TUR) (Agam (FR))
5588a[6]

Chia (IRE) *D Haydn Jones* a60 66
6 ch m Ashkalani(IRE) —Motley (Rainbow Quest (USA))
6806[7] 7399[9] 7718[8] 7856[8] ◆

Chiberta King *A M Balding* 97
3 b g King's Best(USA) —Glam Rock (Nashwan (USA))
(1408) (2084) ◆ 3051[2] 4420[7] 4767[2] 5870[2] 6302[9]

Chicago Cop (IRE) *D Nicholls* a15 83
3 b g Fasliyev(USA) —Sassari (IRE) (Darshaan)
1214[12]

Chicamia *M Mullineaux* a41 27
5 b m Kyllachy—Inflation (Primo Dominie)
4932[11] 6817[8] 7004[10] 7415[7] 7753[7]

Chicane *W J Haggas* a51
2 b f Motivator—Wosaita (Generous (IRE))
7396[4]

Chic Bliss (FR) *F Doumen* 64
2 b c High Yield(USA) —Marital Bliss (FR) (Double Bed (FR))
7384a[5]

Chicha Morada (USA) *D M Simcock* a57
2 b f Tale Of The Cat(USA) —Unbridled Charmer (USA) (Unbridled (USA))
3979[6]

Chichen Daawe *B Ellison* a32 55
3 b f Daawe(USA) —Chichen Itza (Shareef Dancer (USA))
1474[5] 3036[5] 3352[5] 3942[3] 4819[7] 4943[2] (5872) 6183[5] 6817[4] 7214[12]

Chichi (IRE) *R Hannon* a42
2 ch f Tomba—Chiffon (Polish Precedent (USA))
7772[9] 7885[7]

Chichina (USA) *M Johnston* a39 46
2 b f Afleet Alex(USA) —St Aye (USA) (Nureyev (USA))
6009[19] 6544[11] 6858[7]

Chicita Banana *George Baker* a65 68
3 b f Danehill Dancer(IRE) —Night Frolic (Night Shift (USA))
994[7] (1090) 1330[2] 2054[9] 3086[13] 5166[3] 5526[3] 6227[7]

Chicken Momo *A Lund* a70 98
3 b g Pyrus(USA) —Italian Affair (Fumo Di Londra (IRE))
5302a[4]

Chicora (USA) *J H M Gosden* a66 66
3 b f Congaree(USA) —Old Money (AUS) (Old Spice (AUS))
1302[5] 1963[3] 2178[6] 2633[3] 2942[10] 5222[2]

Chic Shanique (USA) *Tom Dascombe* a57 59
3 bb f Dynaformer(USA) —Toll Order (USA) (Loup Sauvage (USA))
1355[8] 1834[11] 2802[2] 3383[5] 4156[9]

Chief Editor *M A Jarvis* a99 118
5 b g Tomba—Princess Zara (Reprimand)
(1325) ◆ 1676[F] (Dead)

Chief Exec *J R Gask* a81 54
7 br g Zafonic(USA) —Shot At Love (IRE) (Last Tycoon)
1258[10] 2185[11] (3722) 3983[2] 4305[6] 5107[4] 5780[9] 6072[2] 7000[3] 7327[5] 7617[4] 7801[4]

Chief Lone Eagle (USA) *A P O'Brien* a100 104
3 ch c Giant's Causeway(USA) —Legend Maker (IRE) (Sadler's Wells (USA))
1755a[2] 2306a[11] 4253a[6] 6867a[10]

Chief Of Ten *D R Lanigan* a14 20
2 ch c Doyen(IRE) —Fudge (Polar Falcon (USA))
7244[15] 7388[12]

Chief Red Cloud (USA) *A P Jarvis* a72 65
3 bb g Cherokee Run(USA) —Pertuisane (Zamindar (USA))
2805[4] (3302) 3980[4] 4741[4] 5612[3] 6070[5] 6437[10]

Chief Wild Cat (IRE) *C Moore* a42 68
3 b g One Cool Cat(USA) —Soft (USA) (Lear Fan (USA))
236[8]

Chief Wren (USA) *E F Vaughan* a51
2 b f Elusive Quality(USA) —Sea Gift (USA) (A.P. Indy (USA))
7624[6]

Chifah *P D Evans* a36 45
2 b f Choisir(AUS) —Danifah (IRE) (Perugino (USA))
1304[10] 1653[6] 2319[6]

Chiff Chaff *C R Dore* a57 62
5 b m Mtoto—Hen Harrier (Polar Falcon (USA))
983[3] 1058[8] 1154[10] 4388[10]

Chikablue (FR) *H De Waele* 74
4 b h Until Sundown(USA) —Chic Marie (FR) (In Fijar (USA))
7822a[0]

Chikorita (IRE) *L Riccardi* 93
2 gr f Verglas(IRE) —Just One Smile (IRE) (Desert Prince (IRE))
6892a[6]

Child Of Our Time (IRE) *P W Chapple-Hyam* 61
2 b f Oratorio(IRE) —Shariyfa (FR) (Zayyani)
6567[8] 6921[8]

Chilean Fizz *Mrs A Duffield* 47
2 b f Domedriver(IRE) —Alter Ego (Alzao (USA))
3187[14] 3726[5] 4463[4] 5337[8]

Chill Out Charley *J J Bridger*
2 b g Cyrano De Bergerac—We're Joken (Statoblest)
3072[8] 3403[9]

Chilly Filly (IRE) *M Johnston* a69 73
3 b f Montjeu(IRE) —Chill Seeking (USA) (Theatrical (IRE))
957[2] (1349)

Chimbonda *S Parr* a63 67
3 ch c Dr Fong(USA) —Ambonnay (Ashkalani (IRE))
655[13] 736[2] 804[9] 889[4] 966[5] 1190[8] 1455[6] 1691[8] 1949[5] 3020[9]

China Bay *P M Phelan* a42 7
2 b f Reset(AUS) —Kathryn Janeway (IRE) (In The Wings)
1312[6] 2741[5] 2978[12] 7106[6]

China Lily (USA) *Saeed Bin Suroor* a45 53
2 bb f Street Cry(IRE) —Lil Lisa Can (USA) (Lil's Lad (USA))
5980[6] 6436[11]

Chinchon (IRE) *C Laffon-Parias* 115
4 b h Marju(IRE) —Jarama (IRE) (Hector Protector (USA))
846a[3] 1554a[4] 2522a[2] (6327a)

Chincoteague (IRE) *B J Meehan* 66
3 b f Daylami(IRE) —Blue Water (USA) (Bering)
5718[3] 6332[2]

Chinese Democracy (USA) *P F I Cole* a45 49
2 b f Proud Citizen(USA) —Double's Lass (USA) (Mr. Leader (USA))
1742[6] 2490[8] 2907[4] 6938[5]

Chinese Evergreen (FR) *F Rohaut* 78
3 b f Dyhim Diamond(IRE) —Trelakari (FR) (Lashkari)
2989a[8]

Chinese Mandarin (USA) *E Van Doorn* a93 100
6 ch h Kingmambo(USA) —Rose Gypsy (Green Desert (USA))
4585a[2]

Chinese Profit *G C Bravery* a40 56
4 b g Acclamation—Tancholo (So Factual (USA))
1940[2] 2458[14] 3735[13] 4538[11] 5544[12] 7723[8]

Chinese White (IRE) *D K Weld* 116
4 gr m Dalakhani(IRE) —Chiang Mai (IRE) (Sadler's Wells (USA))
1996a[3] (4923a) (5487a) (5890a) 7046a[10]

Chink Of Light *A M Balding* 52
2 ch c Dr Fong(USA) —Isle Of Flame (Shirley Heights)
7244[8]

Chinoise (IRE) *P M Phelan* 48
2 b f Chineur(FR) —Grey Pursuit (IRE) (Pursuit Of Love)
2978[5] 3979[12]

Chintz (IRE) *David Wachman* 107
3 b f Danehill Dancer(IRE) —Gold Dodger (USA) (Slew O'Gold (USA))
1024a[9] 2304a[5] 3088[9] 3882a[6] 5487a[4] 5924a[7]

Chin Wag (IRE) *J S Goldie* a76 69
5 b g Iron Mask(USA) —Sweet Chat (IRE) (Common Grounds)
3094[3] 3653[8] 4133[5] 4552[13] 4775[6] 5513[10]

Chip N Pin *T D Easterby* 46
5 b m Erhaab(USA) —Vallauris (Faustus (USA))
3499[11]

Chipolini (IRE) *D Carroll* 59
3 b g Bertolini(USA) —Chimere (FR) (Soviet Lad (USA))
1247[8] 1949[9] 2577[11] 3031[5] 3562[14]

Chips O'Toole (IRE) *B J Meehan* a83 88
2 b c Fasliyev(USA) —Miss Megs (IRE) (Croco Rouge (IRE))
4219[3] 4564[2] 5180[3] 5526[7] (6418) 6841[2] 7108[6] 7150[4]

Chirkova (USA) *A P O'Brien* 90
3 b f Sadler's Wells(USA) —Fanny Cerrito (USA) (Gulch (USA))
2306a[10] 3896a[8] 5689a[7] 6298a[9]

Chjimes (IRE) *C R Dore* a92 79
5 b g Fath(USA) —Radiance (IRE) (Thatching)
(270) 442[3] (632) (754) 985[4] 3212[6] 4069[10] 4387[6] 4891[14] 5197[3] 6253[6] 6459[3] 6632[6] 6972[8] 7646[6] 7872[5]

Choc'A'Moca (IRE) *I W McInnes* 34
2 b g Camacho—Dear Catch (IRE) (Bluebird (USA))
1277[13] 5674[9] 7079[10]

Chock A Block (IRE) *Saeed Bin Suroor* 110
3 gr c Dalakhani(IRE) —Choc Ice (IRE) (Kahyasi)
2176[5] 5764[3] (6452) 7031[7]

Chocolate Candy (USA) *Jerry Hollendorfer* a115
3 b c Candy Ride(ARG) —Crownette (USA) (Seattle Slew (USA))
1688a[5] 2734a[9] 6687a[5] 7309a[8]

Chocolate Caramel (USA) *R A Fahey* a74 89
7 b g Storm Creek(USA) —Sandhill (BRZ) (Baynoun)
7647[4] 7867[8]

Chocolate Cookie (IRE) *J R Boyle* a66 72
2 b f Desert Style(IRE) —Back At De Front (IRE) (Cape Cross (IRE))
3865[3] 4089[8] ◆ 4379[3] 5153[4] 5379[4] 5811[3] 6494[2] 7175[2] (7435)

Chocolat Noir (FR) *J Boisnard* 57
3 b c Hawk Wing(USA) —Fille Dansante (IRE) (Dancing Dissident (USA))
2293a[9]

Chocolicious (IRE) *B Smart* a65 71
3 bb f Captain Rio—Queenfisher (Scottish Reel)
403[4] (1084) 1492[3] (1628) 1832[3] (2355)

Choctaw Nation *J J Lambe* 66
5 b g Sadler's Wells(USA) —Space Quest (Rainbow Quest (USA))
4600[3]

Choice *Sir Michael Stoute* 67
2 b f Azamour(IRE) —Poise (IRE) (Rainbow Quest (USA))
6921[6]

Choir Solo *J H M Gosden* 38
2 b f Medicean—Choirgirl (Unfuwain (USA))
6921[13]

Choiseau (IRE) *Pat Eddery* a80 91
4 b g Choisir(AUS) —Little Linnet (Be My Guest (USA))
3956[4] ◆ 4501[2]

Choisharp (IRE) *M Botti* a62 74
3 b c Choisir(AUS) —Ballea Queen (IRE) (College Chapel)
1563[6] 2005[4] 2603[2] 3010[3] 3676[2] 4718[3] (5480)

Chookie Avon *I Semple* a61 62
2 ch g Avonbridge—Lady Of Windsor (IRE) (Woods Of Windsor (USA))
5728[8] 6154[6] 7157[6] 7493[3]

Chookie Hamilton *I Semple* a85 79
5 ch g Compton Place—Lady Of Windsor (IRE) (Woods Of Windsor (USA))
65[2] ◆ 219[4] 1125[10] (1692) (2315) (3095) 4038[2] 4619[5] 5334[11] 5837[8] 6138[6] 6636[3] (7212) ◆ (7373) 7573[5]

Chookie Heiton (IRE) *I Semple* a65 68
11 br g Fumo Di Londra(IRE) —Royal Wolff (Prince Tenderfoot (USA))
87[5] 352[9] 1695[6] 2438[7] 2964[14]

Choose Me (IRE) *Kevin Prendergast* a83 102
3 ch f Choisir(AUS) —Hecuba (Hector Protector (USA))
1756a[6] 4923a[5] 5490a[4] 6298a[2]

Choosy Floosy *Pat Eddery* a29 47
3 b f Lend A Hand—In The Stocks (Reprimand)
5222[5] 5614[9] 6390[7] 6969[8] 7666[12]

Chopastair (FR) *T Lemer* a108 111
8 b g Astair(FR) —Very Sol (FR) (Solicitor (FR))
1029a[8] 4113a[4] 6657a[8]

Chorale D'Anges (FR) *M Houdoin* a79 86
3 b f Ange Gabriel(FR) —Radio Mesnil (FR) (Nashamaa)
3417a[2]

Choral Festival *J J Bridger* a75 74
3 b f Pivotal—Choirgirl (Unfuwain (USA))
(3951) 4709[7] 7831[8]

Choral Service *W J Haggas* 71
3 ch g Pivotal—Choir Mistress (Chief Singer)
2165[8] ◆ 2415[4] 3321[3]

Choree (IRE) *T D Easterby* 34
3 ch f Choisir(AUS) —Reem Al Fala (Green Desert (USA))
1852[6] 2268[4] 3003[9]

Choreography *Jim Best* a48 86
6 ch g Medicean—Stark Ballet (USA) (Nureyev (USA))
1668[7] 1836[11] 2188[14] 2434[10] 3659[6] 4733[8] 5124[6] 5288[5] (5565) 6337[7] 6562[9]

Chorus Boy *G G Margarson* a47 40
2 ch c Kyllachy—Dame Jude (Dilum (USA))
5318[7] 6809[10] 7098[6] 7391[5] 7501[6]

Chosen Forever *G R Oldroyd* a71 66
4 b g Choisir(AUS) —Forever Bond (Danetime (IRE))
2312[15] 4171[10] 4823[15] 7579[6] 7754[3] (7818) (7857)

Chosen One (IRE) *B Smart* a66 68
4 ch g Choisir(AUS) —Copious (IRE) (Generous (IRE))
2071[8] 2852[10] 4225[9] 4620[10] 6010[3] 6799[4] ◆ 7081[2] 7355[14] 7738[3]

Chosen Son (IRE) *P J O'Gorman* a69
3 bb g Kheleyf(USA) —Choice Pickings (IRE) (Among Men (USA))
3506[7] 3989[8] 5164[7] 5813[4] 6726[12] 6916[3] 7224[9] 7355[9] 7510[3]

Chris's Jem *J R Jenkins* a60 58
3 b f Makbul—Royal Orchid (IRE) (Shalford (IRE))
664[10] 1045[2] (1617) 4244[5] 4514[7] 5164[6] 5724[5] 6377[8]

Christina Rossetti *J H M Gosden* a66 64
3 b f Falbrav(IRE) —First Exhibit (Machiavellian (USA))
949[3] ◆ 1302[7]

Christmascametwice *J A Osborne* a60
3 b f Monsieur Bond(IRE) —My Poppet (Midyan (USA))
729[3] 842[6] 1129[7] 1982[13]

Christmas Carnival *B J Meehan* a79 71
2 ch c Cadeaux Genereux—Ellebanna (Tina's Pet)
6108[5] 6672[3]

Christmas Coming *D R C Elsworth* a70
2 b c Cape Cross(IRE) —Aunty Rose (IRE) (Caerleon (USA))
6372[4] ◆ 6772[7] 7773[2]

Christophers Quest *Miss N A Lloyd-Beavis* a69 67
4 b g Forzando—Kaprisky (IRE) (Red Sunset)
6399[11] 6908[12]

Christopher Wren (USA) *J R Best* a59 73
2 ch c D'Wildcat(USA) —Ashley's Coy (USA) (Country Pine (USA))
4201[3] 5312[11] 6416[3] (6736)

Chushka *B Smart* 60
2 ch f Pivotal—Ravine (Indian Ridge)
4430[4] 5949[4]

Ciamarro *Giuseppe Chianese* 93
4 ch h Captain Rio—Celine Leroy (ITY) (Inchinor)
7206a[7]

Cian Rooney (IRE) *Mrs A Duffield* 74
2 b g Camacho—Exponent (USA) (Exbourne (USA))
2311[10] 3937[4] ◆ (4349) 4803[9]

Ciara Eile (IRE) *D Carroll* a17 54
9 b m Victory Note(USA) —Graceful Resign (Most Welcome)
2068[4] 2344[11]

Ciel Rouge (FR) *J-C Rouget* 103
3 b f Red Ransom(USA) —Raisonnable (Common Grounds)
2521a[4] 3892a[5]

Cigalas *Mrs J C McGregor* 80
4 ch g Selkirk(USA) —Langoustine (AUS) (Danehill (USA))
1100[9] 1229[10] 1646[9] 2391[4] 3094[5] 3656[10] 5601[9] 6157[8]

Cihangir (IRE) *D K Weld* a73 86
4 br g Fasliyev(USA) —Toujours Irish (USA) (Irish River (FR))
3898a[13] 4360a[11]

Cilium (IRE) *Andrew Oliver* a80 89
3 b f War Chant(USA) —Venturi (Danehill Dancer (IRE))
5487a[5] 5798[8] 6467a[9]

Cill Rialaig *H Morrison* a82 96
4 gr m Environment Friend—Pang Valley Girl (Rock Hopper)
1088[4] 1430[3] 1809[3] (2796) 3578[2] (5510) 6106[6] ◆ (6665) 7035[6] 7291[7]

Cils Blancs (IRE) *B Smart* a49 63
3 b f Barathea(IRE) —Immortelle (Arazi (USA))
1508[6] 2446[10] (4550) 4879[3] 7349[5]

Cima De Triomphe (IRE) *L M Cumani* 119
4 gr h Galileo(IRE) —Sopran Londa (IRE) (Danehill (USA))
1551a[6] (2410) 3640[4] 4809a[4] 6871a[13] 7196a[9]

Cindy Incidentally *Miss Gay Kelleway* a47 43
3 ch f Shinko Forest(IRE) —Bayrami (Emarati (USA))
286[6] 624[4] 889[10] 2162[15] 2603[7] 3498[3] 3975[2] 4643[6] 5624[P] 6255[9]

Cinematic (IRE) *J R Boyle* a77 82
6 b g Bahhare(USA) —Eastern Star (IRE) (Sri Pekan (USA))
507[2] 597[9] 1192[14] 1604[5]

Cinnamon Tart (IRE) *John Joseph Murphy* 53
2 b f Intikhab(USA) —Bint Alhaarth (IRE) (Alhaarth (IRE))
1993a[9] 2286a[11]

Cipher *M Johnston* 84
3 b g Reset(AUS) —Subtle Charm (Machiavellian (USA))
2343[8] (2789) ◆ 3394[3]

Circle Dance (IRE) *Miss M E Rowland* a71 74
4 bb g Namid—Rivana (Green Desert (USA))
85[2] 208[3] 286[3] 400[6] 655[5] (758) 2359[7] 2596[7] 3057[5] 3562[7] 3713[11] 4183[3] 4225[3] 4552[7] 4823[4] 5008[14] 7678[14]

Circuit Dancer (IRE) *D Nicholls* a73 76
9 b g Mujadil(USA) —Trysinger (IRE) (Try My Best (USA))
1096[7] 1768[5] ◆ 2472[8] 2852[6] 3484[5]

Circumvent *P F I Cole* a95 106
2 ch g Tobougg(IRE) —Seren Devious (Dr Devious (IRE))
(5325) ◆ 5664[2] (6173) ◆ (6656a) 6889a[2]

Circus Clown (IRE) *P Monteith* 60
4 b g Vettori(IRE) —Comic (IRE) (Be My Chief (USA))
6156[6]

Circus Girl (IRE) *R M Beckett* a55
2 ch f Bertolini(USA) —Blew Her Top (USA) (Blushing John (USA))
7325[5]

Cirrus Des Aigles (FR) *Mme C Barande-Barbe* a101 116
3 b g Even Top(IRE) —Taille De Guepe (FR) (Septieme Ciel (USA))
(6132a) (6890a) 7744a[5]

Citizenship *Ian Williams* a73 81
3 b g Beat Hollow—Three More (USA) (Sanglamore (USA))
276[6] (450) ◆ 1086[5] 1792[5] (2152) ◆ 2715[4] 4045[4] 4520[2] 4709[2] 6680[6] 7263a[8]

Citrus Star (USA) *C F Wall* 102
2 b g Broken Vow(USA) —Twist A Lime (USA) (Copelan (USA))
5129[2] (6018) (6550) 7016[3]

City Dancer (IRE) *A Berry* a89 99
3 b f Elusive City(USA) —Calypso Dancer (FR) (Celtic Swing)
1647[3] 1824[3] 2016[4] 2716[5] ◆ 2928[6] 3145[2] 4559[3] 5069[8] 5420[8] 6135[6]

City For Conquest (IRE) *John A Harris* a57 56
6 b m City On A Hill(USA) —Northern Life (IRE) (Distinctly North (USA))
305[6] 1456[4] 2134[5] 2539[6] 2913[5] 3381[6] 3938[9] 4225[16]

City Gossip (IRE) *M G Quinlan* a64 51
2 b f Shinko Forest(IRE) —Lady At War (Warning)
6069[5] 6493[10] 7120[4] 7756[4] 7781[2]

City Hustler (USA) *Adrian McGuinness* a63 43
4 b g Century City(IRE) —French Buster (USA) (Housebuster (USA))
7461[11] 7648[6] 7667[5]

City Leader (IRE) *B J Meehan* 118
4 gr h Fasliyev(USA) —Kanmary (FR) (Kenmare (FR))
6056[4] 6506a[10] 6850[5] 7313a[4]

City Line (IRE) *John Joseph Murphy* 60
2 b c Antonius Pius(USA) —Indian Myth (USA) (Lear Fan (USA))
5543[15]

City Of Rome (IRE) *R Hannon* 52
2 b c Elusive City(USA) —Marain (IRE) (Marju (IRE))
3584[12] 4265[5] 4946[10] 5715[14]

City Of The Kings (IRE) *G A Harker* a83 101
4 b g Cape Cross(IRE) —Prima Volta (Primo Dominie)
2612[2] (3067) (3872) 4768[10] 5522[15] 6249[8] 6675[18] 7060[9]

City Queen (URU) *O Mohammed* a1 42
4 ch m Decisive(ARG) —Cousy (USA) (State Dinner (USA))
524a[11]

Cityscape *R Charlton* 112
3 ch c Selkirk(USA) —Tantina (USA) (Distant View (USA))
1354[2] 1675[14]

City Stable (IRE) *M Wigham* a86 77
4 b g Machiavellian(USA) —Rainbow City (IRE) (Rainbow Quest (USA))
787[7] 977[3] 1586[6] 2708[6] 3114[7] 4235[9]

City Style (USA) *Saeed Bin Suroor* 108
3 ch g City Zip(USA) —Brattothecore (CAN) (Katahaula County (CAN))
(524a) (769a) ◆ 1865[3] 7186[4]

City Vaults Girl (IRE) *R A Fahey* 69
2 b f Oratorio(IRE) —Uriah (GER) (Acatenango (GER))
3187[3] ◆ 3686[3] 4226[5] 6382[4] 6923[3]

City Well *Mrs L J Young* a73
6 b g Sadler's Wells(USA) —City Dance (USA) (Seattle Slew (USA))
5837[10] 6432[13]

Claddagh *M Johnston* a62 49
2 b g Dubai Destination(USA) —Ring Of Love (Magic Ring (IRE))
5951[6] 7721[3] 7865[4]

Claimant (IRE) *Miss J R Tooth* 46
2 b g Acclamation—Between The Winds (USA) (Diesis)
4048[12] 4286[8]

Clairvoyance (IRE) *J H M Gosden* a74
2 b f Shamardal(USA) —Crystal View (IRE) (Imperial Ballet (IRE))
7450[2] ◆

Clanachy *A G Foster* 37
3 b f Kyllachy—Antonia's Dream (Clantime)
3680[7] 4505[9] 5394[7] 5946[10] 6308[4]

Clan Piper *J H M Gosden* 45
2 b c Exceed And Excel(AUS) —Song Of Skye (Warning)
1323[12] 2167[4] 5006[9]

Clare Glen (IRE) *Lee Smyth* a65 65
3 b f Sakhee(USA) —Desert Grouse (USA) (Gulch (USA))
4287[8] 5520[4] 6124[11]

Claremont (IRE) *A Fabre* 113
3 b c Sadler's Wells(USA) —Mezzo Soprano (USA) (Darshaan)
1761a[3] (2951a) 5930a[4] 6502a[4]

Clarietta *J L Dunlop* 98
2 bb f Shamardal(USA) —Claxon (Caerleon (USA))
3249[7] (4001) (4758) 5825[5] 7187[3]

Clarissa Directa *C Sprengel* 84
3 f Big Shuffle(USA) —Capua (GER) (Platini (GER))
2757a[10]

Clarity Of Passion *James Halpin* a33
4 br m Zamindar(USA) —Millazure (USA) (Dayjur (USA))
7753[9]

Clash City Rocker *G A Swinbank* 25
3 bl g Needwood Blade—Wandering Stranger (Petong)
4276[10]

Clashnacree (IRE) *T Stack* 84
2 bb c Footstepsinthesand—Miss Moore (IRE) (Tagula (IRE))
2995[15]

Clasp *Doug Watson* a101 98
7 ch g Singspiel(IRE) —Embrace Me (Nashwan (USA))
337a[7] (612a)

Class Attraction (IRE) *J E Hammond* a83 98
5 b m Act One—She's All Class (USA) (Rahy (USA))
5472[10]

Classically (IRE) *R Charlton* a73 84
3 b g Indian Haven—Specifically (USA) (Sky Classic (CAN))
998[3] ◆ 1291[16] 2930[10] 4058[8] 5614[3] (6608) 6977[4]

Classical Piece (USA) *Mrs D J Sanderson* a69 53
2 b g Brahms(USA) —Nueva (USA) (Jade Hunter (USA))
6372[11] 6912[4] 7289[7]

Classical Rhythm (IRE) *J R Boyle* a60 68
4 ch g Traditionally(USA) —Golden Angel (USA) (Slew O'Gold (USA))
1415[6] 1581[4] 2183[6] 2580[10] 3919[11] 4007[7] 4300[9] 4437[4] 4640[2] 5152[3] 5444[9]

Classical World (USA) *T Christensen* 93
4 gr h El Prado(IRE) —Tethkar (Machiavellian (USA))
4585a[5]

Classic Blade (IRE) *Doug Watson* a74 107
3 b c Daggers Drawn(USA) —Queen Bodicea (IRE) (Revoque (IRE))
258a[9] 769a[12]

Classic Blue (IRE) *Ian Williams* a60 43
5 b m Tagula(IRE) —Palace Blue (IRE) (Dara Monarch)
3077[9] 3631[5] 3949[7] 7855[12]

Classic Colori (IRE) *Tom Dascombe* 89
2 b c Le Vie Dei Colori—Beryl (Bering)
(3692) 7030[8]

Classic Contours (USA) *J J Quinn* 77
3 b g Najran(USA) —What's Up Kittycat (USA) (Tabasco Cat (USA))
1098[8] 1470[5] (1829) (1954) 2371[2] 2667[3] 3371[4] 3861[3] 5291[4] 5952[4]

Classic Dancer *Jane Chapple-Hyam* a9
4 b m Groom Dancer(USA) —Versatility (Teenoso (USA))
4617[9]

Classic Descent *P J Makin* a85 90
4 b g Auction House(USA) —Polish Descent (IRE) (Danehill (USA))
2050[9] 3030[6] 6815[14] 6944[9]

Classic Hero (GER) *H Hiller* a76
2 b c Konigstiger(GER) —Classic Queen (GER) (Greinton)
6979a[2]

Classic Legend *B J Meehan* a93 90
4 b m Galileo(IRE) —Lady Lahar (Fraam)
1860[7] 2480[8] 2999[5] (3573) 4166[6]

Classic Port (FR) *J R Best* a103 100
5 gr h Slickly(FR) —Portella (GER) (Protektor (GER))
3282[6]

Classic Punch (IRE) *D R C Elsworth* 111
6 b g Mozart(IRE) —Rum Cay (USA) (Our Native (USA))
437a[13] 616a[2] 772a[13] (1523) 3397[3] 4340[13] 5004[2] 5446[3] 6452[4]

Classic Summer (GER) *M Trybuhl* a74 87
3 ch f Pentire—Classic Queen (GER) (Greinton)
1240a[4] 1914a[10] 5118a[3]

Classic Vintage (USA) *Mrs A J Perrett* 103
3 b c El Prado(IRE) —Cellars Shiraz (USA) (Kissin Kris (USA))
1489[6] 2275[7] (3280) 3822[3] (4420) 5230[6] 5425[4] 6662[8]

Class Is Class (IRE) *Sir Michael Stoute* 103
3 b g Montjeu(IRE) —Hector's Girl (Hector Protector (USA))
(2416) 3780[3] ◆ 5170[2] 6106[4] ◆ 6662[12]

Classlin *J S Goldie* 49
2 b f Bertolini(USA) —Class Wan (Safawan)
4774[7] 5693[5] 6090[11] 6409[8]

Clayton Flick (IRE) *A B Haynes* a52 45
2 b c Kheleyf(USA) —Mambodorga (USA) (Kingmambo (USA))
5312[13] 5722[9] 6154[8] 7559[13] 7669[6] 7756[2]

Clear Hand *B R Millman* a52 50
3 b g Lend A Hand—Miss Maisey (IRE) (Entrepreneur)
2709[10] 3241[8] 4061[6] 4324[8] 4643[4] 4937[3] 5632[12] 6170[10]

Clear Ice (IRE) *D Nicholls* a74 56
2 gr g Verglas(IRE) —Mynu Girl (IRE) (Charnwood Forest (IRE))
2388[5] 2963[5] 3572[4] 3937[8] 4803[11] 6096[8] 6355[2] 7087[2] (7331) 7421[2] 7501[5] (7707) 7805[8]

Clearing House *R W Price* a55
4 ch g Zamindar(USA) —Easy Option (IRE) (Prince Sabo)
1478[10] 5813[10] 6587[14]

Clear Reef *Jane Chapple-Hyam* a88 88
5 b h Hernando(FR) —Trinity Reef (Bustino)
82[6] 142[2] 226[5] 952[4] ◆ 1184[5] 1432[3] (2194) 2486[15] 3822[9] 4098[2] 4544[5] 4793[7] 5656[5] (7402) 7515[3] (7867)

Clear Sailing *Ollie Pears* a80 82
6 b g Selkirk(USA) —Welsh Autumn (Tenby)
12[2] (171) 515[2] 617[2] 765[4] 1314[6] 6012[10] 6862[3] 7422[2] (7631)

Cleaver *Lady Herries* a82 86
8 ch g Kris—Much Too Risky (Bustino)
1356[3] 2177[2] 2895[3] 4092[6] 6995[12]

Clegan (FR) *J Bertran De Balanda* 62
2 b c Martaline—Maissa (FR) (Lost World (IRE))
6501a[14]

Cleisthenes (USA) *W J Haggas* 87
3 b g Pleasantly Perfect(USA) —Do The Mambo (USA) (Kingmambo (USA))
(1956) ◆

Clerical (USA) *R M H Cowell* a59 47
3 b g Yes It's True(USA) —Clerical Etoile (ARG) (The Watcher (USA))
3506[3] 4718[9] 5164[5] 5480[5] 5809[4] 7105[2] 7197[5] 7614[7]

Clerk's Choice (IRE) *W Jarvis* a74 90
3 b g Bachelor Duke(USA) —Credit Crunch (IRE) (Caerleon (USA))
2072[3] 2356[3] (2925) 3780[12] 5209[2] 6002[4] 6571[3]

Cleveland *R Hollinshead* a71 57
7 b g Pennekamp(USA) —Clerio (Soviet Star (USA))
401[6] 619[2]

Clever Molly (IRE) *E J Alston* a46 57
2 b f Mull Of Kintyre(USA) —Mother Molly (USA) (Irish River (FR))
3032[9] 3613[5] 4011[2] 4590[6] 4844[4] 5596[3] 6009[12] 6355[7]

Clever Omneya (USA) *J R Jenkins* a42 36
3 ch f Toccet(USA) —Clever Empress (Crafty Prospector (USA))
4199[9] 4860[10] 7107[7] 7686[5]

Clientele (USA) *M Johnston* a87 88
3 bb g Mr Greeley(USA) —Pracer (USA) (Lyphard (USA))
4014[4] ◆ (4354) 4852[7] 5349[2] 5887[4] 6092[10] 6830[P]

Cliffy's Future (USA) *Darrin Miller* a95 87
3 br c The Cliff's Edge(USA) —Future Act (USA) (Known Fact (USA))
1225a[11]

Clifton Bridge *R M Beckett* a79
2 b g Avonbridge—Ambitious (Ardkinglass)
7736[5] (7843)

Clifton Dancer *Tom Dascombe* 98
4 b m Fraam—Crofters Ceilidh (Scottish Reel)
180a[3] 416a[9] 3091[27] 4423[12]

Clifton Encore (USA) *Tom Dascombe* 4
2 b f War Chant(USA) —Theatrical Pause (USA) (Theatrical (IRE))
6932[10]

Clifton Kid (IRE) *R C Guest*
2 b g Danbird(AUS) —Flossytoo (Royal Applause)
7836[6]

Climate (IRE) *P D Evans* a63 36
10 ch g Catrail(USA) —Burishki (Chilibang)
105[8] 129[5] 7236[6] 7403[8] 7600[11] (7755) 7857[8]

Clincher *J A Osborne* a26 39
3 b f Royal Applause—Clincher Club (Polish Patriot (USA))
6551[5] 6856[9] 7411[12]

Clinging Vine (USA) *R Hannon* a61
3 bb f Fusaichi Pegasus(USA) —Nemea (USA) (The Minstrel (CAN))
201[9]

Clipperdown (IRE) *E J Creighton* a69 66
8 b g Green Desert(USA) —Maroussie (FR) (Saumarez)
1621[7] 1962[2] 2708[3] 2923[2] 3552[3] 3675[7] 4745[8] 4992[7] 5367[2] 5750[5] 6668[8]

Clippity Clop (IRE) *J A Osborne* a70 58
3 b g Clodovil(IRE) —Son Chou (Cyrano De Bergerac)
(855) 1416[9] 2605[8] 3985[4] 5791[6] 6031[7] 6807[8]

Clockmaker (IRE) *J H M Gosden* 86
3 b c Danetime(IRE) —Lady Ingabelle (IRE) (Catrail (USA))
1355[2]

Clopf (IRE) *Andrew Heffernan* a74 83
8 b g Dr Massini(IRE) —Chroma (IRE) (Supreme Leader)
2994[13]

Close Alliance (USA) *J H M Gosden* a94 97
3 b c Gone West(USA) —Shoogle (USA) (A.P. Indy (USA))
863[7] ◆ 1300[6] 1678[4]

Cloudesley (IRE) *A M Balding* a71 74
3 b g Trans Island—Decatur (Deploy)
503[6] 2048[2] 2236[2] 2925[3] ◆ 3279[6] 6223[2] 6549[6] 6761[6]

Cloudor (FR) *P Demercastel* 73
7 b g Kendor(FR) —Glaoutchka (FR) (Glaieul (USA))
(5204a)

Cloud's End *W J Haggas* a73 68
2 b f Dubawi(IRE) —Kangra Valley (Indian Ridge)
6386[3] ◆ (6722) ◆

Cloudy City (USA) *M Johnston* 70
2 bb g Giant's Causeway(USA) —Mambo Slew (USA) (Kingmambo (USA))
4439[6] 4953[4] 5428[3]

Cloudy's Knight (USA) *Jonathan Sheppard* a115 112
9 ch g Lord Avie(USA) —Cloudy Spot (USA) (Solar City (USA))
7281a[2]

Cloudy Start *H R A Cecil* a108 108
3 b c Oasis Dream—Set Fair (USA) (Alleged (USA))
1324[9] 1631[3] (2674) (3298) ◆ 3783[2] 4486[7] 5855[4]

Clovis *Andrew Turnell* a73 71
4 b g Kingmambo(USA) —Darling Flame (USA) (Capote (USA))
(468) 733[5] ◆ 798[5] 1178[6] 1287[10] 1785[8] 3259[2] 3811[6] 4300[10] (5381) 6210[6]

Clowance *R Charlton* 114
4 b m Montjeu(IRE) —Freni (GER) (Sternkoenig (IRE))
5891a[2] 7047a[4]

Clowance House *R Charlton* 94
3 ch g Galileo(IRE) —Corsican Sunset (USA) (Thunder Gulch (USA))
1328[3] (1708) 2084[3] 3090[7] 4248[3] 5870[6]

Club Tahiti *R Charlton* 90
3 b f Hernando(FR) —Freni (GER) (Sternkoenig (IRE))
2846[8] 4088[4] ◆ 4422[3]

Clueless *G A Charlton* a33 90
7 b g Royal Applause—Pure (Slip Anchor)
923[6]

Clumber Place *R C Guest* a64 69
3 ch f Compton Place—Inquirendo (USA) (Roberto (USA))
1001[10] 1471[6] 1882[11] 2164[6] 5295[9] (5941)

Clumber Pursuits *S A Harris* 4
2 ch f Pastoral Pursuits—Inquirendo (USA) (Roberto (USA))
5109[9] 5439[12]

Cluny *J R Fanshawe* a35 62
3 b f Celtic Swing—Muschana (Deploy)
1622[3] 2170[4] 5726[4] 6742[14] 7049[10]

C'Mon You Irons (IRE) *M R Hoad* a73 85
4 b g Orpen(USA) —Laissez Faire (IRE) (Tagula (IRE))
97[2] 266[4] 314[4] 721[4] 2326[7] 2920[2] (3407) (3691) (4072) 4353[7] 5424[16] 6564[5]

Cnocan Gold (IRE) *D K Weld* 89
3 b f Danehill Dancer(IRE) —Gold Script (FR) (Script Ohio (USA))
2555a[5] 6707a[10]

Cnoc Moy (IRE) *O Sherwood* a80 86
5 b g Mull Of Kintyre(USA) —Ewar Sunrise (Shavian)
459[5]

Coastal Path *A Fabre* 119
5 b h Halling(USA) —Coraline (Sadler's Wells (USA))
1762a[2] 2118a[7]

Cobo Bay *K A Ryan* a83 103
4 b g Primo Valentino(IRE) —Fisher Island (IRE) (Sri Pekan (USA))
997[12] 1352[12] 2671[9] 3067[4] 3656[2] ◆ (4064) 4310[3] 4779[7] 7294[9]

Cobos *Ms E L McWilliam* a64 53
3 b f Royal Applause—Darya (USA) (Gulch (USA))
2091[5] 3217[8] 3474[6] 3980[14]

Cockney Class (USA) *B J Meehan* 75
2 rg c Speightstown(USA) —Snappy Little Cat (USA) (Tactical Cat (USA))
3794[3] 4499[3]

Cockney Colonel (USA) *E J Creighton* 18
2 bb g Dixie Union(USA) —Kristina's Wish (USA) (Smart Strike (CAN))
3918[9] 4153[9]

Cocktail Party (IRE) *J W Hills* a55 62
3 b f Acclamation—Irish Moss (USA) (Irish River (FR))
2160[16] 2776[10] 4179[14] 5145[11] 5500[2] 5629[11] 5911[4] 6904[13] 7224[5] 7427[4] 7703[3]

Cocoa Beach (CHI) *Saeed Bin Suroor* a121 118
5 bb m Doneraile Court(USA) —Visionera (CHI) (Edgy Diplomat (USA))
7286a[6]

Coco L'Escargot *J R Jenkins* a41 56
5 b m Slip Anchor—Dafne (Nashwan (USA))
58[6]

Coconino (IRE) *C Boutin* 68
2 b f Okawango(USA) —Cancalaise (IRE) (Entrepreneur)
5117a[4]

Coconut Moon *A Berry* a77 72
7 b m Bahamian Bounty—Lunar Ridge (Indian Ridge)
1768[12] 2158[11] 2682[10] 3002[12] 3445[7] 3657[U] 3938[11] 4281[4] 4552[13] 4772[4] 6160[7] 6221[12] 7219[9]

Coconut Shy *G Prodromou* a72 89
3 b f Bahamian Bounty—Lets Be Fair (Efisio)
3953[4] 4372[3]

Coda Agency *D W P Arbuthnot* a71 55
6 b g Agnes World(USA) —The Frog Lady (IRE) (Al Hareb (USA))
112[8] (3029) 3737[8] 5642[10]

Co Dependent (USA) *J A Osborne* a68 39
3 ch c Cozzene(USA) —Glowing Breeze (USA) (Southern Halo (USA))
295[7] 586[3] 716[2]

Codoy (USA) *Mark Hubley* a85 102
2 b c Bernstein(USA) —Puype's Dream (USA) (Kris S (USA))
7304a[12]

Coeur Brule (FR) *Edgar Byrne* a47 41
3 b g Polish Summer—Sally's Cry (FR) (Freedom Cry)
5215[7] 5990[9]

Coeur Courageux (FR) *M D Squance* a76 39
7 b g Xaar—Linoise (FR) (Caerwent)
844[9] 1153[12] 1258[14]

Coeur De Lionne (IRE) *E A L Dunlop* a93 84
5 b g Invincible Spirit(IRE) —Lionne (Darshaan)
3034[6] 4003[8] (4544) 5671[14] 6060[7] 7226[3] 7573[2] 7720[6]

Cognac Boy (USA) *A B Haynes* a63 57
3 bb g Hennessy(USA) —City Sleeper (USA) (Carson City (USA))
74[5] (159) 345[4] 649[5] 827[4] 2009[10] 2744[10] 3225[11] 3473[2] 3946[4] 5283[3] 5502[13]

Coiled Spring *Mrs A J Perrett* 82
3 b g Observatory(USA) —Balmy (Zafonic (USA))
1579[3] 2090[4]

Coill Glas (IRE) *W J Haggas* a57
4 b g Green Desert(USA) —Forest Express (AUS) (Kaaptive Edition (NZ))
80[3]

Coin From Heaven (IRE) *R A Fahey* 86
2 b f Invincible Spirit(IRE) —Capital Gain (FR) (Bluebird (USA))
6245[3] (6820) 7147[7]

Coin Of The Realm (IRE) *G L Moore* a78 93
4 b g Galileo(IRE) —Common Knowledge (Rainbow Quest (USA))
1458[4] (2706) 5170[12] 6662[17]

Cojo (IRE) *B J Meehan* a47 76
2 b f Rock Of Gibraltar(IRE) —Love Excelling (FR) (Polish Precedent (USA))
5969[6] 6730[2] 7140[5]

Colangnik (USA) *J R Best* a72 52
3 b f Sky Classic(CAN) —Rainbow Strike (USA) (Smart Strike (CAN))
4569[13] 5915[12] 6289[6] 6376[10] 6784[7] 7065[6] 7250[12] 7392[11]

Cold Mountain (IRE) *J W Mullins* 51
7 b g Inchinor—Streak Of Silver (USA) (Dynaformer (USA))
4935[3]

Cold Quest (USA) *Miss L A Perratt* a86 97
5 b g Seeking The Gold(USA) —Polaire (IRE) (Polish Patriot (USA))
4781[15] 5137[17] 5551[12] 6137[6] 6312[6] 6984[12]

Cold Turkey *G L Moore* a93 98
9 bb g Polar Falcon(USA) —South Rock (Rock City)
271[12] 549[10] 648[6] 847[6] ◆ 1184[8] 1435[3]

Coleorton Choice *K A Ryan* a74 87
3 ch c Choisir(AUS) —Tayovullin (IRE) (Shalford (IRE))
1368[2] 1517[4] 1869[5] (2393) 2934[15] 6949[6] 7227[11]

Coleorton Dancer *K A Ryan* a81 74
7 ch g Danehill Dancer(IRE) —Tayovullin (IRE) (Shalford (IRE))
2312[8] 2852[12]

Colepeper *M Johnston* 90
2 b c Cape Cross(IRE) —Autumn Wealth (IRE) (Cadeaux Genereux)
5157[2] ◆ 5669[7] (6096) ◆ 6643[5]

Colin Staite *R Brotherton* 21
3 b g Superior Premium—Downclose Duchess (King's Signet (USA))
92[8]

Collateral Damage (IRE) *T D Easterby* a92 102
6 b g Orpen(USA) —Jay Gee (IRE) (Second Set (IRE))
1123[4] 1524[2] 2612[7] 2894[10] 3265[10] 3941[5] 4663[3] 5040[4] (5333) (5598) (6016) (6485) 6876[3] (7169) (7294)

Collection (IRE) *J Moore* 122
4 b g Peintre Celebre(USA) —Lasting Chance (USA) (American Chance (USA))
1553a[5] 7747a[2]

College Land Boy *A Kirtley* 47
5 b g Cois Na Tine(IRE) —Welcome Lu (Most Welcome)
6184[12]

College Scholar (GER) *Liam McAteer* a48 83
5 ch g Dr Fong(USA) —Colina (GER) (Caerleon (USA))
1375a[6]

Collesano (IRE) *R Biondi* 98
2 ch c Pearl Of Love(IRE) —Mother's Hope (IRE) (Idris (IRE))
6716a[10] 7205a[8]

Collimateur (FR) *A Lamotte D'Argy* 73
3 b g Victory Note(USA) —Helen's Gamble (IRE) (Spectacular Bid (USA))
6606a[5] 7696a[9]

Collingwood (IRE) *T M Walsh* a71 65
7 br g Machiavellian(USA) —Almaaseh (IRE) (Dancing Brave (USA))
20[3]

Collow (GER) *M Weiss* 104
9 b g Lando(GER) —Conga (Robellino (USA))
466a[2] 653a[2]

Colombard (IRE) *Patrick Morris* a65 57
4 b g Almutawakel—Searching Star (Rainbow Quest (USA))
1244[12] 1285[10] 1846[4] 2223[5] 2686[10] 3241[6] 4665[4] 4748[3] 5443[6] 5883[6] 7068[2] 7427[5] 7462[2] 7561[4] 7602[4] 7689[4] 7771[4] 7819[3] 7889[9]

Colonel Carter (IRE) *B J Meehan* 80
2 br c Danehill Dancer(IRE) —Pina Colada (Sabrehill (USA))
6109[3] 6592[4]

Colonel Flay *Mrs P N Dutfield* a71 79
5 ch g Danehill Dancer(IRE) —Bobbie Dee (Blakeney)
(1878) 2931[5] 3423[2] 4951[3] 5217[3] 6060[5] 7066[5]

Colonel Henry *S Dow* a48
2 br g Imperial Dancer—Spark Of Life (Rainbows For Life (CAN))
7763[8]

Colonel John (USA) *Eoin Harty* a124 114
4 b h Tiznow(USA) —Sweet Damsel (USA) (Turkoman (USA))
6687a[2] 7311a[5]

Colonel Mak *D H Brown* 91
2 br g Makbul—Colonel's Daughter (Colonel Collins (USA))
2663[9] 2940[3] (3292) ◆ 3702[2] (4035) 4272[3] 5038[4] 5763[3] 6105[6] 7016[5]

Colonel Munro (IRE) *D Nicholls* a29
2 b c Azamour(IRE) —Zooming (IRE) (Indian Ridge)
6431[13]

Colonel Sherman (USA) *P A Kirby* a74 54
4 bb h Mr Greeley(USA) —Spankin 'n Fannin (USA) (Lear Fan (USA))
(100) 285[2] 497[3] 1283[3] 1690[14] 2237[10] 7322[10] 7505[10] 7668[6] 7840[10]

Colonial (IRE) *A Fabre* 106
2 b c Cape Cross(IRE) —Elizabeth Bay (USA) (Mr Prospector (USA))
(3967a) 5708a[6]

Colony (IRE) *Saeed Bin Suroor* 99
4 b h Statue Of Liberty(USA) —Funoon (IRE) (Kris)
262a[7] 613a[5]

Colorus (IRE) *W J H Ratcliffe* a84 77
6 b g Night Shift(USA) —Duck Over (Warning)
89[8] 243[8] 326[3] 400[4] 645[6] 742[2] (818) 1310[8] 1565[2] 1776[5] (3917) 4283[9] 5323[8] 5856[7] (5974) 6205[10] 6422[6] 6791[11] (6877) 7269[10] 7634[2] 7676[3] 7758[2] 7866[7]

Colourful Move *P G Murphy* a67 63
4 b h Rainbow Quest(USA) —Flit (USA) (Lyphard (USA))
40[4] 190[3] (1609) 1892[4] 2429[11] 3275[2] 4168[8] 5642[8] 7154[4] 7328[3] 7642[3] 7750[5]

Colour Of Money *S A Callaghan* a65 46
4 b h Kyllachy—Euridice (IRE) (Woodman (USA))
(874) 1039[5] 2400[4] 2686[8]

Coloursoftheglen (IRE) *Tom Dascombe* a75 83
2 ch c Le Vie Dei Colori—Gertie Laurie (Lomond (USA))
2196[2] ◆ 3160[2] (3468) 4271[2] 4488[5]

Colour Trooper (IRE) *P Winkworth* a67 75
4 ch g Traditionally(USA) —Viola Royale (IRE) (Royal Academy (USA))
1581[5] 2183[5] 2552[9] 3811[12]

Comadoir (IRE) *Miss Jo Crowley* a81 77
3 ch c Medecis—Hymn Of The Dawn (USA) (Phone Trick (USA))
(188) 509[3] 709[4] 1068[11] 1434[6] 3159[5] (3989) 5370[10] 6167[6] 7253[8] 7656[6]

Combat Dance (GER) *A Cascio* 102
5 b h Alzao(USA) —Corgetta (Hernando (FR))
1903a[7]

Come And Go (UAE) *G A Swinbank* 81
3 b g Halling(USA) —Woven Silk (USA) (Danzig (USA))
1987[9] 2341[5] 2696[5] 3144[6] 3688[2] 4044[7] 4820[2] 5340[7]

Come April *P R Webber* a79 67
5 b m Singspiel(IRE) —So Admirable (Suave Dancer (USA))
6204[10] 6900[14]

Comedie Francaise *J Bertran De Balanda*
3 u f — (Shining Steel)
6753a[0]

Comedy Act *Sir Mark Prescott* a41 50
2 b g Motivator—Comic (IRE) (Be My Chief (USA))
3052[5] 3522[9] 4790[8]

Comedy Hall (USA) *M Johnston* a78 93
2 b c Valid Expectations(USA) —Comedy At The Met (USA) (Metfield (USA))
4093[5] 5325[2] ◆ (5620) 6048[7] (6541)

Comeintothespace (IRE) *R A Farrant* a57 43
7 b g Tagula(IRE) —Playa Del Sol (IRE) (Alzao (USA))
444[4] ◆ 581[9] 750[5] 918[12] 1378[11] 1770[6] 2222[11] 2442[7] 3269[7]

Come On Buckers (IRE) *E J Creighton* a62 62
3 ch g Fath(USA) —Deerussa (IRE) (Jareer (USA))
736[11] 1958[5] 3464[3] 3673[2] 3859[11] 4372[6] 4425[6] 4719[10] 5316[2] 5647[4] (5809) 6458[5] 6492[7] 6916[6] 7021[2] 7224[8]

Come On Safari (IRE) *P Winkworth* a71 80
2 b g Antonius Pius(USA) —Calypso Dancer (FR) (Celtic Swing)
3692[8] 4219[4] (4699) 7434[5]

Come On Toby *Miss Amy Weaver* a21 30
3 b g Piccolo—Fleeting Moon (Fleetwood (IRE))
839[10]

Coming Back *J H M Gosden* a77 87
3 ch f Fantastic Light(USA) —Return (USA) (Sadler's Wells (USA))
(876) 2008[2] 3251[5]

Commanche Raider (IRE) *M Dods* 73
2 b g Tale Of The Cat(USA) —Alsharq (IRE) (Machiavellian (USA))
2153[4] (6556) ◆

Commander Wish *Lucinda Featherstone* a52 80
6 ch g Arkadian Hero(USA) —Flighty Dancer (Pivotal)
2770[3] 3164[11] 3607[7] 4141[10] 4907[12] 5073[7] 5420[10] 5830[6] 6233[8] 6433[7] 6926[8] 7086[6] 7241[6] 7427[6] 7651[7]

Commandingpresence (USA) *J J Bridger* a69 55
3 bb f Thunder Gulch(USA) —Sehra (USA) (Silver Hawk (USA))
121[7] 356[3] 586[8] 829[7] 960[7] 1253[8] 1584[6] 1811[7] 2220[8] 5647[6] 5965[3] 6344[4] 7052[8] 7105[5] 7452[6] 7572[3] 7703[6] 7771[7]

Command Marshal (FR) *M J Scudamore* a59 79
6 b g Commands(AUS) —Marsakara (IRE) (Turtle Island (IRE))
7598[6] 7873[6]

Commando Scott (IRE) *I W McInnes* a72 73
8 b g Danetime(IRE) —Faye (Monsanto (FR))
1649[10] 2059[12] 2695[10] 3265[13] 3722[2] ◆ 4072[5] 4663[5] 4859[4] 5673[7]

Comme Un Accord (FR) *Mme C Vergne & D Sicaud* 60
2 b c Konig Shuffle(GER) —Miss Rangoon (FR) (Rangoon (FR))
4073a[7]

Commissionaire *J H M Gosden* 80
2 b c Medicean—Appointed One (USA) (Danzig (USA))
(7095) ◆

Common Diva *A J McCabe* a77 77
3 ch f Auction House(USA) —Vida (IRE) (Wolfhound (USA))
136[3] (239) 332[4] (479) 586[7] (776) 1155[3] 1315[6] 1559[2] 2057[6] 2248[5] 2607[5] 6462[3] 6667[9]

Company (JPN) *H Otonashi* 127
8 b h Miracle Admire(JPN) —Brilliant Very (JPN) (Northern Taste (CAN))
(7498a)

Compatriote (FR) *M Houdoin*
2 b c Kaldounevees(FR) —Cospicua (IRE) (High Estate)
5014a[10]

Competitor *J Akehurst* a67 39
8 b g Danzero(AUS) —Ceanothus (IRE) (Bluebird (USA))
171[6] 528[5] 588[5]

Complete Frontline (GER) *K R Burke* a60 57
4 ch g Tertullian(USA) —Carola Rouge (Arazi (USA))
1332[17] 2155[7]

Completion (NZ) *Brendan Woodman* 15
7 b g Zabeel(NZ) —Royal Magic (NZ) (Lord Ballina (AUS))
6961a[17]

Comprimario (IRE) *J L Dunlop* 9
3 b g Montjeu(IRE) —Soubrette (USA) (Opening Verse (USA))
1708[6]

Compton Blue *R Hannon* a52 78
3 b c Compton Place—Blue Goddess (IRE) (Blues Traveller (IRE))
1772[12] 2852[4] 3299[6] (4714) 5169[7] 5429[10] 6243[10] 6547[2] (6908)

Compton Charlie *J G Portman* a52 64
5 b g Compton Place—Tell Tale Fox (Tel Quel (FR))
1200[12] 2634[14] 3503[13]

Compton Classic *J R Boyle* a74 67
7 b g Compton Place—Ayr Classic (Local Suitor (USA))
27[8] 166[2] 243[7] 486[3] 590[2] 691[2] 861[8] 880[2] (1285) 1468[4] 4203[11] 4479[2] 4886[7] 5608[3] 5989[7] 6799[6] 7224[7]

Compton Effect *F Brogi*
2 ch f Compton Place—Guntakal (IRE) (Night Shift (USA))
7166a[2]

Compton Falcon *H Candy* a64 73
5 ch g Peintre Celebre(USA) —Lesgor (USA) (Irish River (FR))
18[3] 5577[13]

Compton Ford *M Dods* a57 68
3 ch g Compton Place—Coffee Time (IRE) (Efisio)
1064[3] (1455) 1644[2] 2394[5] 2454[4] 3063[6] 3355[8] 3926[4] 4596[5]

Compton Lad *D A Nolan* a11 37
6 b g Compton Place—Kintara (Cyrano De Bergerac)
2157[14]

Compton Park *W J Knight* a42
2 ch c Compton Place—Corps De Ballet (IRE) (Fasliyev (USA))
7538[9]

Compton Rose *H Candy* 69
4 ch m Compton Place—Benjarong (Sharpo)
1360[8] 1787[14] 2202[12] 5501[11] 5792[10]

Compton's Eleven *M R Channon* a88 90
8 gr g Compton Place—Princess Tara (Prince Sabo)
282[5] 446[2] 486[2] 1333[8] 1682[7] 1894[5] 2188[13] 2491[8] 2565[4] 2976[6] 3401[5] 3655[2] 4009[5] 4236[7] 4657[2] 4914[8] 5429[6] 5804[7] 6568[5] 6985[3]

Comptonspirit *B P J Baugh* a66 73
5 ch m Compton Place—Croeso Cynnes (Most Welcome)
1103[7] 1241[2] 1518[10] 1877[4] 2225[5] 2625[6] 2913[3] 3591[4] 4355[8] 5073[3] 5323[5] 6038[2] 6379[4]

Compton Way *B W Hills* 40
2 b c Compton Place—Never Away (Royal Applause)
7145[13] 7289[9]

Comrade Cotton *J Ryan* a65 62
5 b g Royal Applause—Cutpurse Moll (Green Desert (USA))
3957 961[4] 1074[7] 1079[4] 1259[9] 1883[3] 1961[3] 2244[2] (2337) 2608[7] 2824[7]

Comradeship (IRE) *J H M Gosden* a76 80
2 ch c Dubawi(IRE) —Friendlier (Zafonic (USA))
5002[7] 5499[2] 5907[6] 6593[5] 7099[6] 7266[2] (7335)

Con Artist (IRE) *Saeed Bin Suroor* a80
2 b c Invincible Spirit(IRE) —Hoodwink (IRE) (Selkirk (USA))
7266[3] (7390)

Conclave (IRE) *Adrian Sexton* a30 61
5 b m Key Of Luck(USA) —Dathuil (IRE) (Royal Academy (USA))
6271[0]

Conclusive *R M Beckett* a56 50
3 b g Selkirk(USA) —Never A Doubt (Night Shift (USA))
1185[8] 1295[14] 2797[15] 3302[5]

Concorde Kiss (USA) *S Kirk* a55
2 b f Harlan's Holiday(USA) —Saraa Ree (USA) (Caro)
7624[9] 7816 [5] 7865[10]

Concrete And Clay *Charles O'Brien* a6 66
5 ch g Medicean—Daralaka (IRE) (The Minstrel (CAN))
7263a[5]

Conduit (IRE) *Sir Michael Stoute* a79 127
4 ch h Dalakhani(IRE) —Well Head (IRE) (Sadler's Wells (USA))
2410[2] ◆ 3640[3] (4298) 6526a[4] (7310a) 7593a[4]

Confessional *T D Easterby* a75 80
2 b g Dubawi(IRE) —Golden Nun (Bishop Of Cashel)
2444[8] 3606[12] 5552[3] 5957[2] 6486[14] 7001[2] (7217)

Confide In Me *G A Butler* a63 66
5 b g Medicean—Confidante (USA) (Dayjur (USA))
2458[2] (2764) 2859[2] 3653[4] 3980[5] 4300[8] 4645[6] 5229[5] 6005[5] (6999) 7197[9] 7403[4] 7586[5]

Confidentiality (IRE) *M Wigham* a91 81
5 b m Desert Style(IRE) —Confidential (Generous (IRE))
(271) 354[5] 915[7] 1348[6] 2384[4] (7775) 7848[2]

Confront *Sir Michael Stoute* a95 119
4 b g Nayef(USA) —Contiguous (USA) (Danzig (USA))
(1673) ◆ 2668[2] 3585[4] 3841[2] 4949[2] (5232) (5655) (6448) ◆ 7746a[6]

Confuchias (IRE) *Pat Eddery* a109 107
5 b h Cape Cross(IRE) —Schust Madame (IRE) (Second Set (IRE))
257a[8] 433a[6] 637a[5] 696a[6] 6282[11] 6678[15] 6994[15] 7294[4] 7431[3] 7639[4] 7795[2]

Confucius Fortune (IRE) *J R Boyle* a80 48
2 gr g Verglas(IRE) —Duck Over (Warning)
4377[8] (6372)

Coniston Wood *M W Easterby* a46 45
3 b f Needwood Blade—Litewska (IRE) (Mujadil (USA))
968[5] 1247[11]

Conjecture *R Bastiman* a46 68
7 b g Danzig(USA) —Golden Opinion (USA) (Slew O'Gold (USA))
1456[2] 1694[5] 2202[6] 2660[9] 3657[4] 4191[6] 4823[7] 5443[15]

Connie And Michael (USA) *Kenneth McPeek* a104
2 b f Roman Ruler(USA) —Detect (USA) (Devil's Bag (USA))
7283a[8]

Conniption (IRE) *B J Meehan* 94
2 b f Danehill Dancer(IRE) —Showbiz (IRE) (Sadler's Wells (USA))
(4047) 5606[5] 6090[5] 7147[4]

Connor's Choice *Andrew Turnell* a70 69
4 b g Bertolini(USA) —Susan's Dowry (Efisio)
3283[10] (5018) 5633[2] 6377[11] (6828) 7480[2]

Conny Nobel (IRE) *C Roberts* a51 56
5 gr g Marju(IRE) —Beauharnaise (FR) (Linamix (FR))
566[3]

Cono Zur (FR) *M Johnston* 79
2 b c Anabaa(USA) —Alaskan Idol (USA) (Carson City (USA))
(5512) 7218[8]

Conquest (IRE) *M bin Shafya* a112 114
5 b g Invincible Spirit(IRE) —Aguinaga (IRE) (Machiavellian (USA))
259a[7] 335a[16] 418a[10]

Conquisto *S Gollings* a60 96
4 ch g Hernando(FR) —Seal Indigo (IRE) (Glenstal (USA))
2249[5] (3564) 4770[5] 5656[9] 6095[4] 7293[7] 7573[7]

Conry (IRE) *Patrick Morris* a80 89
3 ch g Captain Rio—Altizaf (Zafonic (USA))
(5340) 5774[4] 6212[4] 6614[7] (7083) 7220[2]

Consequence *A Dickman* 42
3 gr g Paris House—Scrutinize (IRE) (Selkirk (USA))
4277[11] 4805[6]

Consequential *D M Simcock* a71 64
2 b f Pivotal—Thirteen Tricks (USA) (Grand Slam (USA))
7182[6] 7717[2]

Consider Yourself (USA) *M L W Bell* 64
2 rg f Afleet Alex(USA) —Champagne Royale (USA) (French Deputy (USA))
5398[9] 6062[7]

Constant Cheers (IRE) *W R Swinburn* a78 86
6 b g Royal Applause—Juno Marlowe (IRE) (Danehill (USA))
1621[4] 3024[5] (3766) 5062[5] 5772[4] 5875[5]

Constant Contact *A M Balding* 89
2 b c Passing Glance—Floriana (Selkirk (USA))
3786[8] 5119[5] (5505) 6471[2]

Constant Lover (IRE) *Robert Collet* 87
2 b c King's Best(USA) —Nipping (IRE) (Night Shift (USA))
3648a[6]

Consult *Sir Mark Prescott* a33
2 ch g Dr Fong(USA) —Merle (Selkirk (USA))
6874[6] 7064[10] 7326[11]

Contat (GER) *P Vovcenko* 109
6 br h Diktat—Conga (Robellino (USA))
(2097a) 2513a[12] 3650a[4] (4363a) 5493a[6] 7044a[7]

Contemplate *Dr J D Scargill* a28 59
3 ch f Compton Place—Billie Blue (Ballad Rock)
820[6] 1269[14] 5998[11] 6573[2] 6925[11]

Contest (IRE) *C Theodorakis* a115 111
5 b h Danehill Dancer(IRE) —Mala Mala (IRE) (Brief Truce (USA))
(123) ◆ 259a[10] 434a[6] 611a[5] ◆ 700a[4] 1043a[2] 1919a[7] 3202a[3] 3908a[7] 4637a[9] 5495a[2] 5709a[7] 6579a[11]

Conti Di Luna (FR) *Mlle B Renk* 97
3 b f Anabaa Blue—Continental Kid (IRE) (Exit To Nowhere (USA))
4334a[6]

Contract Caterer (IRE) *Pat Eddery* 86
2 b c Azamour(IRE) —Nawaji (USA) (Trempolino (USA))
2196[4] ◆ 3052[2] (3494) 4488[4] (5742)

Contrada *J A B Old* a59 70
4 b g Medicean—Trounce (Barathea (IRE))
1073[8]

Contrary (IRE) *E J O'Neill* a53
2 ch f Mark Of Esteem(IRE) —Crystal Gaze (IRE) (Rainbow Quest (USA))
6164[9] (7166a)

Contredanse (IRE) *B J Meehan* a72 71
2 br f Danehill Dancer(IRE) —Ahdaab (USA) (Rahy (USA))
6108[8] 6477[8] 7450[3] ◆

Convallaria (FR) *C F Wall* a67 40
6 b m Cape Cross(IRE) —Scarlet Davis (FR) (Ti King (FR))
387[2] 725[7] 1320[4] 2598[5] 3224[9] 3983[11]

Converti *H J Manners* a57 56
5 b g Averti(IRE) —Conquestadora (Hernando (FR))
3788[5] 4092[10]

Convince (USA) *J L Flint* a63 67
8 ch g Mt. Livermore(USA) —Conical (Zafonic (USA))
104[3] (308) 496[3] (746) 853[4] (2381) 2880[5] 3401[2] 4225[13] 4333[5] 5632[2] 6028[6] 7179[8] 7424[5] (7726)

Convitezza *M E Sowersby* 29
3 b f Domedriver(IRE) —Condoleezza (USA) (Cozzene (USA))
5071[6] 5520[12] 6022[5] 6539[6] 6824[11] 6997[14]

Convivial Spirit *E F Vaughan* a72 64
5 b g Lake Coniston(IRE) —Ruby Princess (IRE) (Mac's Imp (USA))
357[8]

Convocation (IRE) *Mme M Bollack-Badel* 63
2 b f Bertolini(USA) —Indaba (IRE) (Indian Ridge)
5713a[7] 6751a[0]

Cookie Galore *J A Glover* a48 53
2 ch f Monsieur Bond(IRE) —Ginger Cookie (Bold Edge)
5596[6] 5934[8] 6356[4] 6797[8] 6938[3]

Cook's Endeavour (USA) *K A Ryan* a66 81
3 b g Gone West(USA) —Weekend In London (USA) (Belong To Me (USA))
1307[9] 2072[8] 4019[3] 4494[3] 4802[7] 5340[9] 5677[11] 5999[2] 6821[3] 7350[6]

Cool And Composed (USA) *F Rohaut* a77 99
3 ch f Buddha(USA) —Fire And Shade (USA) (Shadeed (USA))
7697a[5]

Cool Art (IRE) *J S Wainwright* a80 71
3 b g One Cool Cat(USA) —Fee Faw Fum (IRE) (Great Commotion (USA))
1033[7] 1434[7] 1584[4] 2028[7] 2393[6] 3428[6] 3953[7] 5584[10] 6442[4] 6926[14] 6989[11]

Cool Baranca (GER) *P Monteith* 82
3 b f Beat Hollow—Cool Storm (IRE) (Rainbow Quest (USA))
5731[4] 6158[3] (6987) 7169[2]

Cool Contest (IRE) *R Brogi* 94
2 b f One Cool Cat(USA) —Love Contest (IRE) (Love The Groom (USA))
(2586a)

Coolcullen Times (IRE) *J S Bolger* a83 92
3 b c Rock Of Gibraltar(IRE) —Key To Coolcullen (IRE) (Royal Academy (USA))
(2290a)

Cool Ebony *P J Makin* a67 83
6 br g Erhaab(USA) —Monawara (IRE) (Namaqualand (USA))
2186[8] 3076[5] 4149[6] (4824)

Coole Dodger (IRE) *B Ellison* a52 75
4 ch g Where Or When(IRE) —Shining High (Shirley Heights)
2103[7] 2527[7] 3558[6] 3983[12] 4402[6] 4816[3] 4932[3] 6358[10]

Coolella (IRE) *J R Weymes* a44 53
2 gr f Verglas(IRE) —Tianella (GER) (Acatenango (GER))
4067[7] 4590[3] 4839[6] 5358[7] 6125[6]

Cool Fashion (IRE) *Ollie Pears* a46 43
4 b m Orpen(USA) —Fun Fashion (IRE) (Polish Patriot (USA))
1921[9] 2529[10]

Cool Hand Jake *P J Makin* a87 65
3 b g Storming Home—Monawara (IRE) (Namaqualand (USA))
(115) 1193[6] (2685) (3274) 4649[8] 5575[3] 6209[10]

Cool Judgement (IRE) *M A Jarvis* 101
4 b g Peintre Celebre(USA) —Sadinga (IRE) (Sadler's Wells (USA))
1709[2]

Cool Kitten (IRE) *W J Knight* 49
2 b f One Cool Cat(USA) —Zoom Lens (IRE) (Caerleon (USA))
2490[7] 3249[12] 6786[6]

Cool Libby (IRE) *A B Haynes* a30 50
3 br f One Cool Cat(USA) —Cosabawn (IRE) (Barathea (IRE))
2446[14] 3257[6] 4177[10] 5540a[8]

Cool Madam *D Flood* a29 13
3 b f Ishiguru(USA) —Face The Judge (USA) (Benny The Dip (USA))
127[7] 429[5] 796[7] 1578[11]

Coolminx (IRE) *R A Fahey* 91
2 b f One Cool Cat(USA) —Greta D'Argent (IRE) (Great Commotion (USA))
(5693) (6179) 6677[2]

Coolnaharan (IRE) *Lee Smyth* a66 58
9 b g Blues Traveller(IRE) —Alma Assembly (General Assembly (USA))
5790[2] 6126[6] 7174[12] (7369) 7632[6] (7718)

Coolree Star (IRE) *J A Glover* a80 73
2 ch g Kheleyf(USA) —Amount (Salse (USA))
3918[10] (4153) 4525[5] 5635[9] 6247[2] 6643[8] (6905) 7290[10] 7453[2] 7625[7]

Cool Sands (IRE) *J G Given* a78 56
7 b g Trans Island—Shalerina (USA) (Shalford (IRE))
1311 2133[5] 2964[12] 3956[13] 4374[9] 4843[9] 5576[10] 7370[5] 7418[2] 7555[3] 7680[3] 7835[2]

Cool Sonata (IRE) *M Brittain* a36 42
3 b f One Cool Cat(USA) —Sonatina (Distant Relative)
228[9]

Cool Strike (UAE) *A M Balding* a67 93
3 b g Halling(USA) —Velour (Mtoto)
1928[10] 2479[2] (2909) ◆ 3371[3] (3822) 4408[5]

Cool Valentine *A M Balding* a78 82
2 b c One Cool Cat(USA) —Miss Mirasol (Sheikh Albadou)
2383[2] 3767[4] 4478[6] (5265) ◆ 5742[4] 6373[4]

Cooper Island Kid (USA) *P W D'Arcy* a48 61
3 bb g Arch(USA) —Raven Quiver (USA) (Old Trieste (USA))
1408[14] 3710[7] 4178[9] 4470[9]

Cooperman *P T Midgley* 40
3 b g Sulamani(IRE) —Minibule (FR) (Funambule (USA))
998[9] 1127[4] 1611[10] 2667[7] 3976[11]

Coordinated Cut (IRE) *P W Chapple-Hyam* 93
2 b c Montjeu(IRE) —Apache Star (Arazi (USA))
(5793) 7017[10]

Copperbeech (IRE) *Saeed Bin Suroor* a101 105
3 b f Red Ransom(USA) —Aynthia (USA) (Zafonic (USA))
2190[6] 6290[3] 6813[7] 7059[2] 7291[3]

Copper Dock (IRE) *T G McCourt* a100 86
5 b g Docksider(USA) —Sundown (Polish Precedent (USA))
2502[13] 4135[10] 6283[8] 7341a[2]

Copper King *Miss Tor Sturgis* a60 44
5 ch g Ishiguru(USA) —Dorissio (IRE) (Efisio)
71[10] 749[7] 792[5] 1039[9] 1655[4] (2924) 3980[12] 6945[5] 7438[10]

Copper Penny *D R Lanigan* 52
2 b f Dansili—Makara (Lion Cavern (USA))
4792[11]

Copper Sovereign *Jamie Poulton* a18 18
7 ch g Compton Place—Lady Kitty (Petong)
4786[13] 5747[13] 6703[9]

Copper State (USA) *Steven Asmussen* a103
5 b m Jump Start(USA) —Orrefor (USA) (Our Native (USA))
6508a[3]

Copperwood *M Blanshard* a67 56
4 ch g Bahamian Bounty—Sophielu (Rudimentary (USA))
192[3] 395[6] 513[3] 1495[7] 2459[6] 7051[2] 7239[6] (7591)

Coralamber (IRE) *Garry Moss* a34 33
2 gr f Monsieur Bond(IRE) —Silver Sun (Green Desert (USA))
2201[7] 2541[6] 2575[7] 3495[5]

Coral Point (IRE) *S Curran* a36 53
3 ch g Hawkeye(IRE) —Green Crystal (Green Dancer (USA))
2772[5]

Coral Shores *P W Hiatt* a62 69
4 b m Carnival Dancer—Leading Role (Cadeaux Genereux)
176[6] 285[8] 324[4] 813[5] 857[5] 1378[5] 1537[4] (1974) 2222[3] 2517[3] (2975) 3244[4] 3739[7] 4139[5] 7399[11] 7641[3]

Corcovada (IRE) *Edward P Harty* 95
2 ch f Captain Rio—Misty Mountain (IRE) (Namaqualand (USA))
2286a[7] 6316a[3]

Cordell (IRE) *R Ingram* a98 70
4 b g Fasliyev(USA) —Urgele (FR) (Zafonic (USA))
1209[5] ◆ 1352[23] 2083[9] 2434[14] 2891[11] 4438[6] (4731) 5190[10] 6476[12] 6633[7] 6702[13] 6924[13]

Cordiality *P G Murphy* a53 56
2 b g Kingsalsa(USA) —Peace (Sadler's Wells (USA))
6291[10] 6593[7] 7638[9]

Cordoba *Sir Michael Stoute* a76
3 b f Oasis Dream—Spanish Sun (USA) (El Prado (IRE))
(3508)

Cordoba (GER) *H Steinmetz* a83 87
3 b f Tiger Hill(IRE) —Chato's Girl (GER) (Chato (USA))
2874a[6]

Core Element (IRE) *Adrian Sexton* a53 67
2 b f Consolidator(USA) —Millstream (USA) (Dayjur (USA))
3086[20]

Coriante (FR) *C Boutin* 85
2 b f Indian Rocket—Camibas (FR) (Solicitor (FR))
3648a[4]

Corioliss (IRE) *R Menichetti* 97
3 gr c Verglas(IRE) —Queen's Ransom (IRE) (Last Tycoon)
2114a[2]

Corking (IRE) *J L Flint* a46 59
4 b m Montjeu(IRE) —Scanno's Choice (IRE) (Pennine Walk)
38[7] 735[10] (2127) 2519[7]

Corleone (FR) *D Windrif* 69
7 gr g Saint Preuil(FR) —Isis Du Berlais (FR) (Cadoudal (FR))
5074a[0]

Corlough Mountain *P Butler* a55 66
5 ch g Inchinor—Two Step (Mujtahid (USA))
(213) 341[6] (566) 735[6] 1537[12] 1710[10] 4698[7] 6369[12] 7440[7] 7608[13]

Cornakill (USA) *Kevin Prendergast* 87
2 b f Stormin Fever(USA) —It's Heidi's Dance (USA) (Green Dancer (USA))
6316a[9] 6708a[6]

Cornish Baroness *R Hannon*
2 b f Reset(AUS) —Milady Lillie (IRE) (Distinctly North (USA))
5547[13]

Cornish Beau (IRE) *M H Tompkins* a66 68
2 ch c Pearl Of Love(IRE) —Marimar (IRE) (Grand Lodge (USA))
4152[5] 5153[3] 5627[6] 7267[2]

Cornish Castle (USA) *T D Walford* 76
3 ch g Mizzen Mast(USA) —Rouwaki (USA) (Miswaki (USA))
998[7] (1193) (1361) 1626[4] 2571[7] 3489[4]

Cornus *J A Glover* a80 83
7 ch g Inchinor—Demerger (USA) (Distant View (USA))
191[10] (297) (486) 576[5] 680[3] 780[7] 834[6] 1016[8] 1089[3] (1369) 1682[12] 1864[4] 2093[8] 2695[6] 4501[7] 5107[8] 5697[5] 5960[6] 6847 [13] 7192[6] 7795[7]

Corola (FR) *W Walton*
2 b f Coroner(IRE) —Sete Cidades (FR) (Astair (FR))
6325a[9]

Coronado's Gold (USA) *B Ellison* a40 63
8 ch g Coronado's Quest(USA) —Debit My Account (USA) (Classic Account (USA))
1058[12] 1125[8] 1767[10] 2263[3]

Coronaria *W J Haggas*
2 b f Starcraft(NZ) —Anthos (GER) (Big Shuffle (USA))
4331[8]

Coronata (ITY) *M Innocenti* 93
3 b f Guys And Dolls—Corona Ferrea (Sri Pekan (USA))
4394a[6]

Coronelli (FR) *C Lerner* a73 72
3 ch c Numerous(USA) —Les Yeux Mauves (FR) (Tot Ou Tard (IRE))
4581a[5]

Corporal Maddox *H R A Cecil* 104
2 b c Royal Applause—Noble View (USA) (Distant View (USA))
1188[4] (2027) (2702) 3667a[3] 4418[3] 5172[6] (6663) 7016[6]

Corrib (IRE) *B Palling* a60 53
6 b m Lahib(USA) —Montana Miss (IRE) (Earl Of Barking (IRE))
493[6] 1651[4] 1980[7] 2912[4] 3503[4] 3949[3] 5872[3] 6969[12] 7718[5] 7803[5]

Corriolanus (GER) *A M Balding* a67 73
9 b g Zamindar(USA) —Caesarea (GER) (Generous (IRE))
119[3] 285[10] 497[6] 1578[4] (2040)

Corr Point (IRE) *J A Osborne* a49
2 b c Azamour(IRE) —Naazeq (Nashwan (USA))
7376[8] 7430[8] 7538[8]

Corrybrough *H Candy* a86 114
4 ch h Kyllachy—Calamanco (Clantime)
5196[5] 5657[7] (Dead)

Corsica (IRE) *M Johnston* 79
2 b c Cape Cross(IRE) —Cedar Sea (IRE) (Persian Bold)
4713[2] 5407[5] 5831[5] (6982)

Corton Charlemagne (IRE) *Rae Guest* a63 77
3 b f King Charlemagne(USA) —Teller (ARG) (Southern Halo (USA))
1588[9] 1969[2] 4454[5] (4829) (4999) 5264[3] (5724) 6118[5] 6387[5]

Corum (IRE) *Mrs K Waldron* a89 73
6 b g Galileo(IRE) —Vallee Des Reves (USA) (Kingmambo (USA))
3788[9]

Cosimo *Sir Michael Stoute* a69 72
3 ch g Medicean—Flight Soundly (IRE) (Caerleon (USA))
1515[5] 2138[4] 3307[2] 3636[5]

Cosimo de Medici *H Morrison* a58
2 b g Medicean—Wish (Danehill (USA))
7365[6] ◆ 7571[5] ◆ 7736[7]

Cosmea *A King* a51 86
4 b m Compton Place—St James's Antigua (IRE) (Law Society (USA))
(2641) 3213[4] 4903[8] 5912[3] 6060[4]

Cosmic *T D Easterby* 44
3 b g Nayef(USA) —Urania (Most Welcome)
1245[8] 1522[7]

Cosmic Destiny (IRE) *E F Vaughan* a78 76
7 b m Soviet Star(USA) —Cruelle (USA) (Irish River (FR))
243[10] 270[7] 843[8] 1540[5] 2180[5] 2219[3] 2492[3] 3162[5] 3246[4] 5125[8] 5323[4] 6118[10] 6341[8] 6791[7] 7483[8] 7657[7]

Cosmic Orbit *K R Burke* 56
2 b c Royal Applause—Susquehanna Days (USA) (Chief's Crown (USA))
3170[5] 4308[5]

Cosmic Sun *R A Fahey* 102
3 b g Helissio(FR) —Cosmic Case (Casteddu)
1992[10] 2715[9] (3051) 3618[3] (3826) 4420[4] ◆ 5230[4] 5823[3]

Cosmo Bulk (JPN) *K Tabe* 112
8 b h Zagreb(USA) —Iseno Tosho (JPN) (Tosho Boy (JPN))
7593a[12]

Cosmopolitan *J H M Gosden* 96
4 ch m Cadeaux Genereux—Parisian Elegance (Zilzal (USA))
(2679) (3165) 3749[8] (4088) 4489[13] 6267[15]

Cossack Prince *Mrs L J Mongan* a78 73
4 b g Dubai Destination(USA) —Danemere (IRE) (Danehill (USA))
202[10] (584) 726[7] (1807) 2331[2] 3421[4] 3521[8] 5964[7] 7823[10]

Cost Of Freedom (USA) *John W Sadler* a121
6 bb g Cee's Tizzy(USA) —Freedom Dance (USA) (Moscow Ballet (USA))
7306a[3]

Cote D'Argent *L Lungo* 68
6 b g Lujain(USA) —In The Groove (Night Shift (USA))
1738[3] 2068[8] 2725[4] 3095[2]

Cotillion *W J Haggas* 81
3 b g Sadler's Wells(USA) —Riberac (Efisio)
2074[2] ◆ 3117[6] 4270[2] 4599[5] 6595[2] 7221[4]

Cotswolds *M Johnston* 82
4 br g Green Desert(USA) —Valley Of Gold (FR) (Shirley Heights)
(1769) ◆ 2257[7] 2639[5] 3055[3] (3560)

Cotswold Village (AUS) *M R Bosley* a32
3 b f Hawk Wing(USA) —Scenic Bold Dancer (AUS) (Scenic)
7439[8]

Cottam Breeze *J S Wainwright* a19 29
4 b m Diktat—Flower Breeze (USA) (Rahy (USA))
2805[7]

Cottonfields (USA) *Mrs H S Main* a52 57
3 rg g Maria's Mon(USA) —Known Romance (USA) (Known Fact (USA))
2081[7] 4606[7] 4979[5]

Cottonmouth (IRE) *S Botti* 107
5 b m Noverre(USA) —Nafzira (IRE) (Darshaan)
(6715a) 7046a[14]

Cotton Top (IRE) *M R Channon* a59 68
2 b f Fath(USA) —Common Cause (Polish Patriot (USA))
6363[3] 6638[7] 6842[9] 7616[11]

Coughlans Locke (IRE) *Kieran P Cotter* a54 62
6 b g All My Dreams(IRE) —Inniu (IRE) (Tirol)
2390[8] 7798[8]

Could It Be Magic *W G M Turner* a69 72
2 b c Dubai Destination(USA) —Lomapamar (Nashwan (USA))
994[6] 4163[3] 4396[5] 4933[2] 6913[5] 7288[5] 7551[3] ◆ 7654[7]

Councellor (FR) *Stef Liddiard* a97 79
7 b g Gilded Time(USA) —Sudden Storm Bird (USA) (Storm Bird (CAN))
(6) 291[2] 458[5] 635[4] 778[8] 1603[7] 2188[6] 2434[2] 2883[10]

Count Bertoni (IRE) *S Gollings* a60 73
2 b c Bertolini(USA) —Queen Sceptre (IRE) (Fairy King (USA))
2231[2] 2663[6] 3652[5] 6047[4] 6679[3] 6948[4] 7218[2]

Count Ceprano (IRE) *C R Dore* a88 89
5 b g Desert Prince(IRE) —Camerlata (Common Grounds)
20[4] ◆ 128[2] 197[2] 212[6] 446[4] 538[6] 691[6] 2086[13] 2326[8] 2828[9] 3234[5] 3637[3] 3863[7] 4181[7] 4548[6] 4816[7] 5329[12] 5998[13]

Count Cougar (USA) *S P Griffiths* a41 19
9 b g Sir Cat(USA) —Gold Script (USA) (Seeking The Gold (USA))
326[11] 7503[14]

Countdown *R A Fahey* a89 88
7 ch g Pivotal—Quiz Time (Efisio)
1699[16] 2050[5] 2828[8] 3116[11] 5697[16]

Countenance *W J Haggas* a68 65
3 ch g Medicean—Glamorous (Sanglamore (USA))
1087[7] 2105[3] 2710[4] 4004[7] 6784[9]

Countenance Divine *B W Hills* 63
2 ch f Pivotal—Sundari (IRE) (Danehill (USA))
7182[7]

Counterbid (IRE) *C Laffon-Parias* a65 82
3 b c Rainbow Quest(USA) —Brooklyn Gleam (FR) (Caerleon (USA))
6682a[0] 7037a[8]

Countess Comet (IRE) *R M Beckett* 57
2 b f Medicean—Countess Sybil (IRE) (Dr Devious (IRE))
6792[4]

Countess Zara (IRE) *A M Balding* a52 70
3 b f Xaar—Lochridge (Indian Ridge)
1588[11] 2431[5] 2797[5] 3281[4]

Count John (IRE) *J T Gorman* 103
3 b c Intikhab(USA) —Triton Dance (IRE) (Hector Protector (USA))
1755a[3]

Count Lucien *J H M Gosden* 70
3 b c Danehill Dancer(IRE) —Paquita (IRE) (Sadler's Wells (USA))
2211[4] ◆ 2930[7] 4246[5]

Count Of Anjou (USA) *R Hannon* a71 65
2 bb c Lion Heart(USA) —Woodmaven (USA) (Woodman (USA))
6615[5] ◆ 7034[9] 7537[2]

Count Of Tuscany (USA) *Mrs A J Perrett* a78 77
3 b c Arch(USA) —Corsini (Machiavellian (USA))
4798[2] 5744[3] (6941)

Count On Guest *G G Margarson* 63
3 ch g Fantastic Light(USA) —Countess Guest (IRE) (Spectrum (IRE))
1260[5] 1570[11] 2170[7] 3427[8] 4241[7] 4719[2] 5121[8] 5403[8] 5972[9]

Count Paris (USA) *M Johnston* a74 75
3 ch c Pivotal—Dearly (Rahy (USA))
1068[10] 1434[4]

Countrycraft *Miss S E Hall* 32
2 b g Pastoral Pursuits—Turn Back (Pivotal)
3606[9]

Country Love (FR) *David Marnane* a84 75
2 b f Country Reel(USA) —White Love (FR) (Northern Crystal)
5057a[8] 5240a[3]

Countrymans Dream *J R Weymes* 35
2 b g Mark Of Esteem(IRE) —Lateralle (IRE) (Unfuwain (USA))
1764[12] 2526[5] 2963[7] 4931[10] 6215[14]

Country Princess (FR) *R M Beckett* 57
2 b f Country Reel(USA) —Millefiori (USA) (Machiavellian (USA))
1090[9] 1810[4] 2047[10]

Country Road (IRE) *P W Chapple-Hyam* a68 74
3 b c Montjeu(IRE) —Souffle (Zafonic (USA))
4519[9] 5531[3] 6794[6] 6974[5]

Countrystyle Lass (IRE) *P Winkworth* a43 43
3 b f Kheleyf(USA) —Davis Rock (Rock City)
3696[11] 4381[4] 4854[8] 5647[7] 6339[15]

Countrywide City (IRE) *Jane Southcombe* a64 75
3 b g Elusive City(USA) —Handy Station (IRE) (Desert Style (IRE))
1705[9] 2520[9] 3428[8]

Countrywide Comet (IRE) *P Howling* a47 60
4 b g Desert Style(IRE) —Darzao (IRE) (Alzao (USA))
97[11] 215[10] 515[7] 581[4] 674[11] 802[8]

Countrywide Ice (IRE) *K A Ryan* 50
2 gr g Verglas(IRE) —Samaritan Woman (IRE) (Priolo (USA))
1623[8] 2128[13] 2339[10] 3952[7] 4076[4] 4739[8] 5303[5] 5519[17]

Countrywide Jaime (IRE) *M Wigham* a33
3 b f Danetime(IRE) —Naraina (IRE) (Desert Story (IRE))
85[5] 358[6] 7652[12]

Countrywide Sun *A C Whillans* 17
7 b g Benny The Dip(USA) —Sundae Girl (USA) (Green Dancer (USA))
2159[8]

Count Trevisio (IRE) *J R Gask* a85 71
6 b g Danehill(USA) —Stylish (Anshan)
73[6] 232[8] 453[3] ◆ 761[6] 1107[4] 1316[5] 2495[7]

Coup De Torchon (FR) *J A Osborne* a26 56
4 b m Namid—Tashtiyana (IRE) (Doyoun)
4305[16]

Courageous (IRE) *B Smart* 99
3 ch c Refuse To Bend(IRE) —Bella Bella (IRE) (Sri Pekan (USA))
1292[8] 2278[3] 2500[8] 4352[9] 7019[9]

Courageous Cat (USA) *William Mott* 122
3 b c Storm Cat(USA) —Tranquility Lake (USA) (Rahy (USA))
7308a[2]

Courchevel (IRE) *Robert Collet* 95
2 b f Whipper(USA) —Choc Ice (IRE) (Kahyasi)
4577a[2] 5279a[5]

Course De Diamante (IRE) *D R Lanigan* 68
3 b f Galileo(IRE) —Desert Bluebell (Kalaglow)
1844[9] 2192[6] 2847[4] 3462[5]

Court Canibal *M Delzangles* 107
4 b h Montjeu(IRE) —Pas D'Heure (IRE) (Arazi (USA))
(846a) 1144a[8] 6890a[4] 7406a[5]

Court Drinking (USA) *J R Best* a42
2 ch c Alke(USA) —Royal Forum (USA) (Open Forum (USA))
7618[6]

Court Gown (IRE) *E S McMahon* 77
2 b f Zafeen(FR) —Silk Law (IRE) (Barathea (IRE))
4226[2] ◆ (5440)

Court Masterpiece *J J Quinn* a100 108
9 b h Polish Precedent(USA) —Easy Option (IRE) (Prince Sabo)
2500[3] 3398[5] 4486[10] 5232[12] 5694[3] 6312[4]

Court Princess *George Baker* a68 35
6 b m Mtoto—Fairfields Cone (Celtic Cone)
5718[10] 6225[5] 6974[7] 7328[4] (7608) 7873[8]

Court Vision (USA) *Richard Dutrow Jr* a110 120
4 bb h Gulch(USA) —Weekend Storm (USA) (Storm Bird (CAN))
789a[7] 7308a[4]

Court Wing (IRE) *George Baker* 21
3 b f Hawk Wing(USA) —Nicely (IRE) (Bustino)
1185[13] 1844[11] 2192[9]

Cousin Charlie *S Kirk* a66 31
3 b g Choisir(AUS) —Michelle Ma Belle (IRE) (Shareef Dancer (USA))
160[8]

Cover Drive (USA) *Christian Wroe* a74 61
6 b br g Giant's Causeway(USA) —Woodland Orchid (IRE) (Woodman (USA))
59[9] 244[6]

Cover Story (FR) *E Libaud*
2 b f Okawango(USA) —Julia's Dance (IRE) (Alhaarth (IRE))
5014a[2]

Covert Ambition *Saeed Bin Suroor* a111 110
4 ch h Singspiel(IRE) —Super Tassa (IRE) (Lahib (USA))
(2597) 3585[2] ◆ 4090[2] 5609[6]

Covert Mission *P D Evans* a66 61
6 b m Overbury(IRE) —Peg's Permission (Ra Nova)
6832[5] 7085[4]

Cowboy Cal (USA) *Todd Pletcher* a114 118
4 bb h Giant's Causeway(USA) —Texas Tammy (USA) (Seeking The Gold (USA))
789a[8] 7308a[10]

Coyote Creek *E F Vaughan* 91
5 b g Zilzal(USA) —High Barn (Shirley Heights)
1274[7] 2040[2] 2898[9]

Cozy Tiger (USA) *W J Musson* a76 70
4 gr g Hold That Tiger(USA) —Cozelia (USA) (Cozzene (USA))
310[6]

Crackdown (IRE) *M Johnston* 107
3 b c Refuse To Bend(IRE) —Whitefoot (Be My Chief (USA))
(1307) 3049[18] 3639[2] ◆ 3816[2] 4297[12] 4486[17]

Crackentorp *R M Beckett* a91 99
4 b g Generous(IRE) —Raspberry Sauce (Niniski (USA))
2475[2] ◆ 3142[9] 6546[2]

Cracking Lass (IRE) *R A Fahey* 77
2 b f Whipper(USA) —Lady From Limerick (IRE) (Rainbows For Life (CAN))
4515[9] 5234[8] (5669) 6064[5] 6477[7]

Cragganmore Creek *D Morris* a53 46
6 b g Tipsy Creek(USA) —Polish Abbey (Polish Precedent (USA))
378[2] 567[5] 790[2] 918[4] 1442[7] 2244[6] 2419[9] 3552[6] 4170[9] 6785[11] 7608[12]

Crag Path *D R C Elsworth* a59 50
3 b f Celtic Swing—Juvenilia (IRE) (Masterclass (USA))
280[4] 1034[3] 1198[9] 1531[7]

Craicattack (IRE) *J S Moore* a68 76
2 ch g Arakan(USA) —Jack-N-Jilly (IRE) (Anita's Prince)
2792[10] 2996[2] (3240) 3559[6] 4639[3] 5274a[8] 6104[3] 6541[7] 7846[5]

Craighall *D M Simcock* 62
2 b f Dubawi(IRE) —Craigmill (Slip Anchor)
6992[8]

Craigstown *E Charpy* a66 94
4 b g Cape Cross(IRE) —Craigmill (Slip Anchor)
262a[12]

Cranworth Blaze *A G Newcombe* a49 46
5 b m Diktat—Julietta Mia (USA) (Woodman (USA))
1921[8] 2157[10] 3569[7] 5406[11] 6966[10]

Crazy Bold (GER) *A W Carroll* a34 44
6 ch g Erminius(GER) —Crazy Love (GER) (Presto)
1651[5] 4880[5]

Crazy Chris *B Palling* a83 70
4 b m Ishiguru(USA) —Ellopassoff (Librate)
5751[2] 6276[4] 6934[5] (7512)

Crazy Colours *Jane Chapple-Hyam* a63
3 ch g Dalakhani(IRE) —Eternity Ring (Alzao (USA))
115[4] ◆ 295[6]

Creachadoir (IRE) *Saeed Bin Suroor* 124
5 b h King's Best(USA) —Sadima (IRE) (Sadler's Wells (USA))
1011a[15]

Creative (IRE) *M H Tompkins* a57 63
4 b g Acclamation—Pride Of Pendle (Grey Desire)
1259[5] 1465[2] 1695[2] 2134[9] 2456[6] 2759[4] 3020[2] 3109[4]

Credential *John A Harris* a58 58
7 b g Dansili—Sabria (USA) (Miswaki (USA))
2420[8] 3004[4] 3552[2] (4170) 4403[7] 4880[6]

Credit Swap *M Wigham* a84 98
4 b g Diktat—Locharia (Wolfhound (USA))
780[8] 892[5] 1197[8] 1619[4] 2491[2] 2828[7] 3116[5] (3812) (4262) (4502) 6117[2] 6307[3]

Creese *H R A Cecil* 80
2 b f Halling(USA) —Why Dubai (USA) (Kris S (USA))
(5284)

Creevy (IRE) *S Kirk* a54 56
2 b f Trans Island—Kilbride Lass (IRE) (Lahib (USA))
3249[10] 3715[5] 5498[10] 5935[9] 6367[2] 6923[9] 7335[6] 7513[6] 7683[4] 7788[6]

Creshendo *R M Beckett* a55 71
3 b g Kyllachy—Dry Wit (IRE) (Desert Prince (IRE))
1068[9] 1584[8] 1982[5] 2349[10]

Cridda Boy *A G Newcombe* 28
3 ch g Mark Of Esteem(IRE) —Second Affair (IRE) (Pursuit Of Love)
1508[9] 2074[11] 2795[17]

Crimea (IRE) *M Johnston* a67 90
3 b g Kheleyf(USA) —Russian Countess (USA) (Nureyev (USA))
(3003) ◆ 3491[6] (3855) 7202[10]

Crime Scene (IRE) *Saeed Bin Suroor* a93 118
6 b g Royal Applause—Crime (USA) (Gulch (USA))
(185a) 338a[11] 613a[2] 2677[6] (4090) 4484[9] 6961a[6] 7215a[2]

Crime Writer (USA) *M Johnston* 80
3 b g Elusive Quality(USA) —Larrocha (IRE) (Sadler's Wells (USA))
2439[3] 2805[2] (3093) 3567[8] 4009[3] 4210[6] 4597[10]

Crimson Fern (IRE) *M S Saunders* a96 102
5 ch m Titus Livius(FR) —Crimada (IRE) (Mukaddamah (USA))
911[5] ◆ 1325[9] 1582[2] 2191[6] 2704[P]

Crimson Flame (IRE) *M S Tuck* a45 73
6 b g Celtic Swing—Wish List (IRE) (Mujadil (USA))
7858[4]

Crimson Mist *J J Quinn* a23 39
3 b g Red Ransom(USA) —Lavinia Fontana (IRE) (Sharpo)
3036[10] 3712[6] 4277[10]

Crimson Mitre *J Jay* a79 68
4 b h Bishop Of Cashel—Pink Champagne (Cosmonaut)
1478[4] 2068[13] 2601[9] 3714[2] (4373) 4840[9] 5545[4] 7779[5]

Crimson Ribbon (USA) *J H M Gosden* a90 85
3 b f Lemon Drop Kid(USA) —Victoria Cross (IRE) (Mark Of Esteem (IRE))
1532[3] ◆ (2051) 6003[10] 6618[5] 7131[6] 7366[7]

Cripsey Brook *K G Reveley* 68
11 ch g Lycius(USA) —Duwon (IRE) (Polish Precedent (USA))
1402[8] 2068[6] 2334[5] 2944[4] 3171[3] 3544[4] 4350[11] 4806[11] 4927[7] 5600[6] 6768[11]

Cristal Island (IRE) *Thomas Mullins* a79 93
3 ch f Trans Island—Cristalita (IRE) (Entrepreneur)
4923a[10]

Criterion *Ian Williams* a78 81
4 b g Dr Fong(USA) —Film Script (Unfuwain (USA))
459[6] 1356[10] 2018[8] 2614[7] 7699[11] 7854[4] ◆

Critical Moment (USA) *B W Hills* 96
2 b c Aptitude(USA) —Rouwaki (USA) (Miswaki (USA))
5400[3] ◆ (6109) 7030[5]

Critical Path (IRE) *A M Balding* a72 79
3 b f Noverre(USA) —Elemental (Rudimentary (USA))
1605[4] ◆ 2433[3] (4234) ◆ 5997[6] 6740[4] 7366[5]

Criticism *Thomas Albertrani* a104 108
5 b m Machiavellian(USA) —Innuendo (IRE) (Caerleon (USA))
6510a[2]

Criticize (USA) *R Charlton* a57 71
3 b g Mizzen Mast(USA) —Euphonize (USA) (Seattle Slew (USA))
2081[2] ◆ 4936[4] 5751[4]

Crocodile Bay (IRE) *John A Harris* a81 93
6 b g Spectrum(IRE) —Shenkara (IRE) (Night Shift (USA))
35[2] 152[2] 304[5] 747[8] 1259[4] 1480[9] 1723[6] 3055[8] 3558[8] 4375[4] 4887[10]

Crocus Rose *H J L Dunlop* a79 82
3 b f Royal Applause—Crodelle (IRE) (Formidable (USA))
2847[6] 3508[5] 4229[3] ◆ 4491[2] (5217) 5666[3] (6995)

Croeso Cusan *J L Spearing* 67
4 b m Diktat—Croeso Croeso (Most Welcome)
1773[11] 2125[6] 2859[12] 5630[4] 6967[8] 7173[2] 7248[5]

Croeso Ynol *J L Spearing* 41
3 ch f Medicean—Croeso Croeso (Most Welcome)
3460[7] ◆ 4164[9] 5181[4] 5501[6] 6005[6]

Croft Bridge *M Dods* a26 48
2 ch g Avonbridge—Aahgowangowan (IRE) (Tagula (IRE))
4844[7] 5292[5] 5519[7] 6494[10]

Croi Mo Ri (IRE) *Daniel Miley* a85 97
4 b g Monashee Mountain(USA) —Wide Meadow (Zafonic (USA))
5141a[13]

Croisultan (IRE) *Liam McAteer* a83 100
3 ch c Refuse To Bend(IRE) —Zoudie (Ezzoud (IRE))
1543a[2] 2673[9] 3898a[10] 5079a[4]

Croix Madame (FR) *F Doumen* 70
2 b f Forestier(FR) —She Runs (FR) (Sheyrann)
6578a[6] 6928a[4]

Croix Rouge (USA) *R J Smith* a67 70
7 b g Chester House(USA) —Rougeur (USA) (Blushing Groom (FR))
7112[6] 7328[11] 7766[6]

Cronkyvoddy *Mrs A Malzard* 49
8 b g Groom Dancer(USA) —Miss Pout (Kris)
4587a[5] 5540a[10]

Cronsa (GER) *S Botti* 101
2 b f Martino Alonso(IRE) —Croa (IRE) (Alzao (USA))
6892a[3]

Crooked Throw (IRE) *C F Swan* a89 96
10 bb g Anshan—Mary's View (IRE) (Phardante (FR))
2289a[9]

Croon *Andrew Turnell* a13 47
7 b g Sinndar(IRE) —Shy Minstrel (USA) (The Minstrel (CAN))
2552[8] 6584[14]

Crooner (IRE) *A Al Raihe* a84 82
6 b g Titus Livius(FR) —John's Ballad (IRE) (Ballad Rock)
770a[9]

Crosby Jemma *M E Sowersby* 48
5 ch m Lomitas—Gino's Spirits (Perugino (USA))
221[13]

Crossbow Creek *M G Rimell* a89 88
11 b g Lugana Beach—Roxy River (Ardross)
1215[6] 2146[7] 3266[13] 4602[5] (6244) 6734[5]

Crossharbour *A Fabre* 119
5 b h Zamindar(USA) —Docklands (USA) (Theatrical (IRE))
(5059a) 5931a[3]

Crossing *William J Fitzpatrick* a97 86
8 b m Cape Cross(IRE) —Piney River (Pharly (FR))
4253a[8] 4923a[7]

Cross Key (IRE) *R A Fahey* 56
2 b f Trans Island—Cayman Sunrise (IRE) (Peintre Celebre (USA))
4100[4] 4595[4] 5146[5]

Cross Of Lorraine (IRE) *J Wade* a72 69
6 b g Pivotal—My-Lorraine (IRE) (Mac's Imp (USA))
1695[11] 2852[9] 3070[10] 3234[6] 4435[11] 4887[7] 5332[11] 5465[4]

Cross Reef *R A Harris* a64 46
4 b m Cape Cross(IRE) —Mureefa (USA) (Bahri (USA))
890[7] 1407[11] *1532[6]* 1773[8] 2517[8] *2746[9] 3470[8]* 4266[9] 5965[8]

Cross Section (USA) *E F Vaughan* a71 57
3 bb f Cape Cross(IRE) —Demure (Machiavellian (USA))
2664[5] 3071[6] *7480[4] 7671[2] 7826[4]*

Cross The Boss (IRE) *P C Haslam* 4
2 b g Cape Cross(IRE) —Lady Salsa (IRE) (Gone West (USA))
6991[12]

Cross The Line (IRE) *A P Jarvis* a88 71
7 b g Cape Cross(IRE) —Baalbek (Barathea (IRE))
878[2] 1067[3]

Crowded House *B J Meehan* a94 120
3 ch c Rainbow Quest(USA) —Wiener Wald (USA) (Woodman (USA))
2014[8] 2705[6]

Crowfoot (IRE) *A P O'Brien* a91 89
3 b c Sadler's Wells(USA) —Grecian Bride (IRE) (Groom Dancer (USA))
1145a[7]

Crown (IRE) *R Hannon* 88
2 b f Royal Applause—Bolivia (USA) (Distant View (USA))
1090[5] 1298[7] (1749) (1927) 3015[8] 3748[5] 4245[5] 5208[4] 6447[8]

Crown Affair (IRE) *J W Hills* a58 37
3 b f Royal Applause—Alyousufeya (IRE) (Kingmambo (USA))
251[4] 547[4] 839[9] 3741[14] *5016[10]*

Crown Choice *W R Swinburn* a97 78
4 b g King's Best(USA) —Belle Allemande (CAN) (Royal Academy (USA))
(1185) ◆ *(1607)* 5874[7] ◆ *6702[8]* 7185[11]

Crown Of Thorns (USA) *Richard E Mandella* a121
4 b h Repent(USA) —Crowning Touch (USA) (Thunder Gulch (USA))
7306a[2]

Croy (IRE) *S Parr*
4 b m Elnadim(USA) —Flower Fairy (FR) (Fairy King (USA))
227[9] 488[5]

Cruciform (IRE) *D Nicholls* 31
3 bb g Cape Cross(IRE) —Tshusick (Dancing Brave (USA))
5394[10]

Cruel Sea (USA) *C F Swan* a86 87
4 gr m Mizzen Mast(USA) —Storm Dove (USA) (Storm Bird (CAN))
5689a[2] *7300a[6]*

Cruikadyke *P F I Cole* a72 93
3 b c Kyllachy—Shoshone (Be My Chief (USA))
1484[6] 2273[10] 2855[8] 3307[3] 4008[6] (4322) *4649[12]* 5999[7]

Cruise Control *R J Price* a47 20
3 b g Piccolo—Urban Dancer (IRE) (Generous (IRE))
236[6] 2165[12] 4267[7] 4937[15] *5614[10] 6255[11]*

Cruise Director *Ian Williams* a62 89
9 b g Zilzal(USA) —Briggsmaid (Elegant Air)
393[7] 712[3] 743[4]

Crunched *M L W Bell* a73 73
2 b c Dubai Destination(USA) —Amica (Averti (IRE))
4811[5] 5428[4] 5981[3] *(7193)*

Crush (IRE) *D M Simcock* a25
3 b c Kheleyf(USA) —Premier Amour (Salmon Leap (USA))
1108[6]

Crushing (IRE) *A J McCabe* a54 67
2 b g Kheleyf(USA) —Filmgame (IRE) (Be My Guest (USA))
2568[4] 3064[2] 3606[6] 6247[7] 7055[5] *7363[10] 7559[9] 7619[9] 7788[5]*

Crux *R E Barr* a40 58
7 b g Pivotal—Penny Dip (Cadeaux Genereux)
1243[15] 1769[6] 2441[6] 2718[3] 3070[3] 3490[P]

Cry Alot Boy *K A Morgan* a81 79
6 ch g Spinning World(USA) —Intellectuelle (Caerleon (USA))
1380[6] 2199[2] 2416[6] 2843[2] 3864[6] (4426) *7204[2] 7607[6] 7775[8]*

Cry For The Moon (USA) *Mrs A J Perrett* 84
3 b g Street Cry(IRE) —Kafaf (USA) (Zilzal (USA))
(1614) 2208[3] 3276[3] 4248[4] 5216[7] 5876[6] 6368[5]

Crying Aloud (USA) *J T Gorman* a93 75
4 b m Street Cry(IRE) —Angelic Deed (USA) (Alydeed (CAN))
1376a[12]

Cry Of Freedom (USA) *M Johnston* a77 99
3 b c Street Cry(IRE) —Tustarta (USA) (Trempolino (USA))
1118[5] 1291[18]

Cry Of Truth (IRE) *D W Barker* 50
3 b f Danetime(IRE) —Clandolly (IRE) (Burslem)
1451[6] 1683[8] 1852[4] 2593[7]

Cry Presto (USA) *S T Nolan* a46 44
5 b g Street Cry(IRE) —Sabaah Elfull (Kris)
6859[5]

Crystal B Good (USA) *J R Best* a41 58
3 bb f Successful Appeal(USA) —Unbridled Run (USA) (Unbridled (USA))
552[6] 1379[7] 1838[4] 2431[9] 3161[4] 3625[2] *4748[10] 7890[11]*

Crystal Bridge *Mrs L Williamson* a28 23
2 b f Avonbridge—Heaven-Liegh-Grey (Grey Desire)
3633[8] 3849[6] 4398[7] *6858[8] 7816[8]*

Crystal Capella *Sir Michael Stoute* a75 116
4 b m Cape Cross(IRE) —Crystal Star (Mark Of Esteem (IRE))
(2013) 6525a[5] 6853[2] ◆

Crystal Crown (IRE) *B G Powell* a60 9
5 b g Grand Lodge(USA) —Top Crystal (IRE) (Sadler's Wells (USA))
2243[9]

Crystal Feather *E F Vaughan* a59 66
3 ch f Monsieur Bond(IRE) —Prince's Feather (IRE) (Cadeaux Genereux)
963[3] 1476[3] 1967[6] (2143) 2461[6] (4721) 5524[3]

Crystal Gal (IRE) *Kevin Prendergast* 89
2 b f Galileo(IRE) —Park Crystal (IRE) (Danehill (USA))
6319a[7] 6708a[5]

Crystal Gale (IRE) *W J Knight* 71
2 gr f Verglas(IRE) —Mango Groove (IRE) (Unfuwain (USA))
2490[3] ◆ 2793[7] 4001[3] 5002[3] 5627[5]

Crystal Glass *T D Easterby* a24
2 b g Exceed And Excel(AUS) —Cumbrian Crystal (Mind Games)
6991[13] 7289[12] *7420[6]*

Crystallize *A B Haynes* a65 69
3 b g Bertolini(USA) —Adamas (IRE) (Fairy King (USA))
1036[7] 1253[6] 1620[5] *(2141)* (2417) 3075[4] 3243[4] 6140[7] *6455[8] 7180[4] 7480[6] 7715[4]*

Crystal Merit (FR) *R Lecomte* 87
3 b f Enrique—Luminescence (FR) (Signe Divin (USA))
3417a[8]

Crystal Moments *E A L Dunlop* a91 93
3 b f Haafhd—Celestial Choir (Celestial Storm (USA))
1639[2] 2469[7] 3145[10] 4096[2] 5471[5] 6155[4] *6631[4]* (7032) 7292[9]

Crystal Prince *C E Longsdon* a68 76
5 b g Marju(IRE) —Crystal Ring (IRE) (Kris)
2983[15]

Crystal Reign (IRE) *Mrs J L Le Brocq* a71 74
4 b g Noverre(USA) —Crystal Springs (IRE) (Kahyasi)
(4587a)

Crystany (IRE) *E A L Dunlop* a94 98
4 b m Green Desert(USA) —Crystal Music (USA) (Nureyev (USA))
1394a[8] 1880[5] 2886[6]

Cuccinello (IRE) *K W Hogg* 10
6 b m Makbul—Costa Verde (King Of Spain)
2718[8]

Cuckoo Rock (IRE) *J G Portman* 32
2 b g Refuse To Bend(IRE) —Ringmoor Down (Pivotal)
4209[11] 5787[12]

Cuis Ghaire (IRE) *J S Bolger* 112
3 b f Galileo(IRE) —Scribonia (IRE) (Danehill (USA))
1698[2] 2304a[15] 6848[7]

Cullybackey (IRE) *J R Boyle* a41 52
4 ch m Golan(IRE) —Leitrim Lodge (IRE) (Classic Music (USA))
1955[12] 2390[6] 3023[7] *7069[5] 7240[13] 7533[6]*

Cultivar *B W Hills* 71
2 b c Xaar—New Orchid (USA) (Quest For Fame)
4985[3] 5542[6]

Cultured Pride (IRE) *R Hannon* 77
2 ch f King's Best(USA) —Cultured Pearl (IRE) (Lammtarra (USA))
2494[14] (3101) 3842[5] 4758[5] 5742[3] 6241[27]

Cumana Bay *R Hannon* a82 89
3 b f Dansili—Mayaro Bay (Robellino (USA))
960[2] 1808[2] (2498) 3220[2] (3400) 3746[6] 4326[5] 5099[2] 5432[9] *7133[5]*

Cumbrian Gold (USA) *B Smart* a41
3 ch g Gilded Time(USA) —Brackenber (USA) (Lycius (USA))
383[9]

Cumbrian Knight (IRE) *J M Jefferson* a67 53
11 b g Presenting—Crashrun (Crash Course)
8[12] 301[11]

Cumulus Nimbus *R Hannon* 85
2 ch c Muhtathir—Supreme Talent (Desert King (IRE))
(4080) 5088a[2] 5261[7] 5994[3] 6756[3]

Cunning Plan (IRE) *P W Chapple-Hyam* 50
2 ch c Bachelor Duke(USA) —Madamaa (IRE) (Alzao (USA))
6416[7] 6922[6]

Cup Cake (FR) *Mme Pia Brandt* 60
2 ch f Bahhare(USA) —Territorial (Selkirk (USA))
4577a[9]

Cupid's Glory *G L Moore* a88 83
7 b g Pursuit Of Love—Doctor's Glory (USA) (Elmaamul (USA))
1666[5] *6435[13] 7539[10]*

Curacao *Mrs A J Perrett* a78 83
3 br g Sakhee(USA) —Bourbonella (Rainbow Quest (USA))
1464[2] 1643[3] 2189[5] (3869) (4325) 4911[3] *5376[4]* 6388[3]

Curlew (IRE) *M Johnston* 30
3 b g Cape Cross(IRE) —Billbill (USA) (Storm Cat (USA))
3485[7]

Curro Perote (FR) *L A Urbano-Grajales* 66
2 gr c Smadoun(FR) —First Choice (FR) (Exit To Nowhere (USA))
7507a[2]

Curtain Call (FR) *L M Cumani* 115
4 b h Sadler's Wells(USA) —Apsara (FR) (Darshaan)
(1758a) 2120a[6] 3443a[4] 4329[4] 5076a[2] *5662[P]* (Dead)

Curtains *S Dow* 89
2 b f Dubawi(IRE) —Voile (IRE) (Barathea (IRE))
1534[3] 1782[3] 2490[2] 2735[DSQ] 3086[5] 3396[4]

Custody (IRE) *Sir Michael Stoute* a85 73
3 b g Fusaichi Pegasus(USA) —Shahtoush (IRE) (Alzao (USA))
5531[5] 5744[6] *6225[3]* 6595[9]

Cut And Thrust (IRE) *M Wellings* a78 62
3 b g Haafhd—Ego (Green Desert (USA))
(158) ◆ *4649[6] 5169[2] 5575[8]* 6562[7] *7830[9]*

Cute Ass (IRE) *K R Burke* 94
4 b m Fath(USA) —John's Ballad (IRE) (Ballad Rock)
2591[2]

Cuthbert (IRE) *W Jarvis* a73 66
2 ch c Bertolini(USA) —Tequise (IRE) (Victory Note (USA))
3240[3] 3767[2] 4080[4] 4884[12] 5589[6] 6334[3] *7551[8] 7690[5] (7885)*

Cutlass Bay (UAE) *A Fabre* 114
3 b c Halling(USA) —Dunnes River (USA) (Danzig (USA))
(1979a)

Cuts Both Ways (USA) *P F I Cole* a31 53
2 b g Johannesburg(USA) —Wise Investor (USA) (Belong To Me (USA))
4701[4] *5191[10]* 5499[14] 7056[3]

Cut The Cackle (IRE) *P Winkworth* a81 84
3 b f Danetime(IRE) —Alexander Anapolis (IRE) (Spectrum (IRE))
1486[6] *1965[2]* 2882[6] 4148[9] 4712[4] 5471[2] *6167[5] 7253[5]*

Cwmni *B Palling* a50 53
3 b f Auction House(USA) —Sontime (Son Pardo)
345[6] 492[4] 662[8] 2009[4] 2876[10] 3632[12] (4479) 5501[9] 5633[8]

Cwm Rhondda (USA) *P W Chapple-Hyam* a16 79
4 b m Gulch(USA) —Frayne (USA) (Red Ransom (USA))
1606[13] 1883[5] (2171) (2420) 3114[4] (3550) 5037[5] 6003[11]

Cyan Eyed *Tom Dascombe* a65 54
2 b f Orpen(USA) —Morale (Bluebird (USA))
5605[10] 6241[18] *6970[2]*

Cyber Space *B J McMath* a52 32
5 b g Medicean—Coyaima (GER) (Night Shift (USA))
1963[10] 2142[10] 3549[9] *4538[4]*

Cyborg *D R C Elsworth* a84 84
5 ch g Halling(USA) —Ciboure (Norwick (USA))
1571[4] ◆ 1990[5] 2798[3] 3521[3] (3814) 4092[5] 4661[3] 5402[5] *6724[4]*

Cyflymder (IRE) *R Hannon* a83 99
3 b g Mujadil(USA) —Nashwan Star (IRE) (Nashwan (USA))
(1033) 1214[7] 1803[4] (2638) (3163) (3643) 4708[2] 5025[4] 5529[3] 5855[2] 7019[U] 7294[8]

Cyfrwys (IRE) *B Palling* a52 52
8 b m Foxhound(USA) —Divine Elegance (IRE) (College Chapel)
513[6] 587[11] 933[7] 1775[8] 2352[15]

Cygnet *L M Cumani* 90
3 b c Dansili—Ballet Princess (Muhtarram (USA))
6002[2]

Cygnet Committee (IRE) *J S Wainwright* 55
2 gr f Kheleyf(USA) —Forest Light (IRE) (Rainbow Quest (USA))
2089[9] 3119[7] 3547[8] 4138[5] 4800[4] 5393[3] 5519[4] 5976[13] 6589[7] 6819[6] 7098[11]

Cyril The Squirrel *Karen George* a51
5 b g Cyrano De Bergerac—All Done (Northern State (USA))
1728[11]

Cyrnea (FR) *C Boutin* 61
3 b f Solon(GER) —Kallistea (FR) (Sicyos (USA))
6980a[F]

Daasij (IRE) *D K Weld* a42 92
4 b g Dalakhani(IRE) —Alyakkh (IRE) (Sadler's Wells (USA))
2305a[6]

Daaweitza *B Ellison* a77 94
6 ch g Daawe(USA) —Chichen Itza (Shareef Dancer (USA))
999[18] 1123[8] 1343[8] 1524[6] 2257[3] ◆ 2402[8] 3124[2] 3264[2] 3615[4] 4285[13] 4353[5] 4560[8] (5438) 5598[5] *6435[8]* 6485[2] 6795[7] 7060[4] *7373[5]* 7598[3] 7724[3]

Dabbers Ridge (IRE) *I W McInnes* a83 93
7 b h Indian Ridge—Much Commended (Most Welcome)
778[7] 995[11] 1649[4] 2045[7] *2576[8]* (3174) *3467[3]* (3539) 5944[6] 6217[11] *6703[6] 6783[4]* 7171[11] *7350[12] 7591[5]* 7719[8]

Da Bomber (IRE) *J W Unett* a53 58
4 b g Tagula(IRE) —Talahari (IRE) (Roi Danzig (USA))
2229[11] 2446[11] 2968[9] *7600[8] 7754[13]*

Daddy Cool *W G M Turner* a37 82
5 b g Kyllachy—Addicted To Love (Touching Wood (USA))
967

Daddy's Gift (IRE) *R Hannon* a91 84
3 b f Trans Island—Lady Corduff (IRE) (Titus Livius (FR))
852[2] (1002) 1324[16] 1705[7] 2299[3] 2886[5] 3347[10] 5774[5] 5918[6] *7227[10] 7394[7] 7487[3] (7613)*

Dado Mush *T T Clement* a50 42
6 b g Almushtarak(IRE) —Princess Of Spain (King Of Spain)
5329[11] 5791[8] *6074[10] 6358[9] 7712[3] 7784[12]*

Dafarabad (IRE) *Niall Madden* a76 83
7 b g Cape Cross(IRE) —Daftara (IRE) (Caerleon (USA))
7263a[3]

Dafeef *Saeed Bin Suroor* 87
2 b c Medicean—Almahab (USA) (Danzig (USA))
4900[2] (5431)

Daffodil (NZ) *Kevin Gray* 108
4 b m No Excuse Needed—Spring (NZ) (O'Reilly (NZ))
6871a[4] ◆ 7215a[11]

Daft Lad *L A Mullaney* 54
2 bb c Danbird(AUS) —Stolen Melody (Robellino (USA))
1719[8] 2069[8] *3709[13]* 3937[11] 4889[7] 5519[16]

Daggerman *R Curtis* a55 36
4 ch g Daggers Drawn(USA) —Another Mans Cause (FR) (Highest Honor (FR))
18[9] 302[7] 674[12]

Dahaam *Saeed Bin Suroor* a79 76
2 b c Red Ransom(USA) —Almansoora (USA) (Bahri (USA))
5528[2] *6162[2] (6772)*

Dahakaa *M A Jarvis* a79 78
2 ch c Bertolini(USA) —Dorrati (USA) (Dubai Millennium)
2295[3] *(4856)*

Dahama *C E Brittain* a40 64
3 b f Green Desert(USA) —Darling Flame (USA) (Capote (USA))
426[4] 3010[14]

Dahes (IRE) *B Smart* 58
2 b c Azamour(IRE) —Delphie Queen (IRE) (Desert Sun)
2813[5] 4888[10]

Dahindar (IRE) *John M Oxx* a67 89
4 b h Invincible Spirit(IRE) —Daftara (IRE) (Caerleon (USA))
2555a[6] 3435a[13]

Daily Double *D K Ivory* a63 60
3 gr g Needwood Blade—Coffee To Go (Environment Friend)
667[5] 753[5] (839) 1148[3] *1429[6]* 1462[17] 1811[8] *2489[9]* 3257[2]

Daily Planet (IRE) *B W Duke* a35 40
3 ch g Titus Livius(FR) —Flattering News (USA) (Pleasant Colony (USA))
4240[P]

Dainty Steps (IRE) *John Joseph Murphy* 82
2 b f Xaar—Lucky Achievement (USA) (St Jovite (USA))
6316a[10] 7258a[12]

Daisy Brown *N Tinkler* 52
2 b f Exceed And Excel(AUS) —Hazy Heights (Shirley Heights)
3152[5] 3686[7] 4138[2] 4398[4] 4889[6] 5976[6] 6589[12]

Daisy Moses (IRE) *D Nicholls* a51 74
3 br f Mull Of Kintyre(USA) —Starring (FR) (Ashkalani (IRE))
1505[8] 2198[12] *3225[8] 3953[6]*

Daisys Fantasy *S Parr*
4 br m Diktat—Double Fantasy (Mind Games)
488[6]

Dajen *D M Simcock* a66 40
3 b c Kyllachy—Eau Rouge (Grand Lodge (USA))
2862[10] 6551[7] *7067[6] 7479[4]*

Dakiyah (IRE) *Mrs L J Mongan* a93 89
5 b m Observatory(USA) —Darariyna (IRE) (Shirley Heights)
1753[4] 2212[8] *(3273)* 3797[3] 4212[6] *7589[5]*

Dakota Hills *J R Best* a69 71
3 ch g Danehill Dancer(IRE) —Karla June (Unfuwain (USA))
7327[12] 7518[9]

Dalarossie *E J Alston* a61 67
4 b g Kyllachy—Damalis (IRE) (Mukaddamah (USA))
1518[8] 1970[11] 2436[6] 3066[3] 4016[5] 4823[10] 5073[6] 5946[2] 6010[12] 6160[2] 6380[4]

Dalepak Flyer (IRE) *Paul Mason* a58 57
3 ch c Noverre(USA) —Hartstown House (IRE) (Primo Dominie)
831[5] 900[4] 1253[7] *1437[7] 3464[7]*

Dalesway *R A Fahey* 66
3 b g Muhtarram(USA) —Si Si Si (Lomitas)
4505[3] ◆ 5072[6]

Dalghar (FR) *A De Royer-Dupre* 106
3 b c Anabaa(USA) —Daltawa (IRE) (Miswaki (USA))
(7621a)

Dalnool *P M Phelan* a62 39
8 b g Unfuwain(USA) —Sardonic (Kris)
668[3]

Dalmunzie (IRE) *J J Quinn* 16
3 ch f Choisir(AUS) —Berenice (ITY) (Marouble)
2268[7] 2789[10]

Dalradian (IRE) *W J Knight* a92 78
3 b g Dansili—Aethra (USA) (Trempolino (USA))
(828) 1324[8] 1774[2] 2329[6] *(2399)* 2890[9] *3988[3]*

Dalrymple (IRE) *M Madgwick* a55 55
3 ch g Daylami(IRE) —Dallaah (Green Desert (USA))
776[6] 824[7] (1148) 1408[8] 1811[5] 2333[7] 2737[6] *3383[11]* 3741[10] 4734[6] 6788[8] *7549[12]*

Daltaban (FR) *P Salmon* a32 85
5 ch g Rainbow Quest(USA) —Daltaiyma (IRE) (Doyoun)
6676[11] 7084[12] *7423[11] 7712[6]*

Damaniyat Girl (USA) *W J Haggas* a79 106
3 ch f Elusive Quality(USA) —Dabaweyaa (Shareef Dancer (USA))
1293[2] 1873[5] 3016[9] 3320[2] 5064[4] 5588a[2] 6267[11] (6814)

Damascus Gold *Miss Z C Davison* 54
5 b h Thowra(FR) —Damasquiner (Casteddu)
5740[8] 6692[10]

Dame Anouska (IRE) *E J O'Neill* a60 78
3 b f Exceed And Excel(AUS) —True Joy (IRE) (Zilzal (USA))
1451[2] ◆ 3417a[4] 4130a[5] 4810a[2] 5783a[5] 6606a[2] *6980a[DSQ]* (7386a)

Dame Shanakill (USA) *H R A Cecil* a36
2 ch f Mr Greeley(USA) —Innovate (USA) (Relaunch (USA))
7050[10]

Dametime (IRE) *Daniel Mark Loughnane* a78 78
3 b f Danetime(IRE) —Fee Eria (FR) (Always Fair (USA))
(2321) *(2632)* 3096[2] 4044[6] *6167[4] 6459[9]*

Damiani *F & L Camici* 96
3 ch c Lomitas—Drifa (ITY) (Hamas (IRE))
1392a[4] 1904a[11]

Damien (IRE) *B W Hills* a98 108
3 gr c Namid—Miss Shaan (FR) (Darshaan)
912[4] 1602[6] 2485[3] 3747[15]

Damietta (USA) *Saeed Bin Suroor* a79 75
2 b f More Than Ready(USA) —Dixie Eyes Blazing (USA) (Gone West (USA))
4421[3] *(4980)* 5433[8] 5797[13]

Damika (IRE) *R M Whitaker* a97 111
6 ch g Namid—Emly Express (IRE) (High Estate)
2259[7] 2470[8] 3391[7] 4330[13] 5257[6] 5695[12] 6092[4] 6278[3]

Damini (USA) *Sir Michael Stoute* a57 75
3 b f Seeking The Gold(USA) —Dalisay (IRE) (Sadler's Wells (USA))
2607[8]

Dan Buoy (FR) *R C Guest* a17 78
6 b g Slip Anchor—Bramosia (Forzando)
7598[7]

Dancealot Lady (USA) *P Winkworth* a23 50
2 b f Theatrical(IRE) —Guadaira (IRE) (Grand Lodge (USA))
4265[7] 4869[8] 5153[6] 5715[15]

Dance And Dance (IRE) *E F Vaughan* a91 84
3 b c Royal Applause—Caldy Dancer (IRE) (Soviet Star (USA))
127[3] 227[2] 503[2] (663) 4841[6] 5154[2] 5418[7] 6111[5] (6776) 7027[2] 7356[12] 7523[3]

Dance Card *A G Foster* 77
4 b m Cape Cross(IRE) —Dance On (Caerleon (USA))
4354[4] (5394) 6015[7] 6764[11]

Dance Club (IRE) *W Jarvis* a63 70
3 b f Fasliyev(USA) —Two Clubs (First Trump)
4179[8] 4718[2] (5112) 5514[4] 6070[9]

Dance East *J Noseda* 45
2 b f Shamardal(USA) —Russian Dance (USA) (Nureyev (USA))
5317[9]

Dance For Julie (IRE) *P C Haslam* 76
2 b f Redback—Dancing Steps (Zafonic (USA))
2360[3] ◆ 3187[2] 4398[2] (5668) 6134[6]

Dance Gdansk (IRE) *M Blanshard* a55
3 b c Fasliyev(USA) --Tordasia (IRE) (Dr Devious (IRE))
5987[9] 6375[7] 7367[8] 7608[5] 7649[10]

Danceintothelight *K A Ryan* 72
2 gr g Dansili—Kali (Linamix (FR))
5466[5] 6136[6] 6763[4] 6982[2]

Dancelectic (IRE) *D R Lanigan* a17 15
3 b c Barathea(IRE) —Sheer Spirit (IRE) (Caerleon (USA))
1578[12]

Dance Pass (IRE) *D K Weld* 99
3 b f Sadler's Wells(USA) —Super Gift (IRE) (Darshaan)
1024a[4] 2304a[11] 2729a[3] 4609a[4] 5689a[21]

Dancer Cat (ITY) *B Grizzetti* 92
2 b c One Cool Cat(USA) —Mara Dancer (Shareef Dancer (USA))
6716a[8]

Dancer In Demand (IRE) *Sir Michael Stoute* a75 75
4 ch g Danehill Dancer(IRE) —Sought Out (IRE) (Rainbow Quest (USA))
1286[2]

Dancer's Legacy *J R Boyle* a67 80
4 ch g Nayef(USA) —Blond Moment (USA) (Affirmed (USA))
1633[8] 3766[7] 4150[10] 4714[6] 5190[9] 5569[4] 5723[5] 6208[3] 6565[4]

Dance Sauvage *B Storey* 50
6 ch g Groom Dancer(USA) —Peace Dance (Bikala)
2159[7] 2725[12] 3617[9] 5161[4]

Dance Society *T D Easterby* 49
3 b g Mull Of Kintyre(USA) —Gracious Imp (USA) (Imp Society (USA))
2343[5] 2719[8]

Dance The Star (USA) *D M Simcock* a95 92
4 b h Dynaformer(USA) —Dance The Slew (USA) (Slew City Slew (USA))
1216[6] 1696[14] 3273[4] ◆ 4644[2] 5909[4] 6816[10] 7465[2] ◆ 7720[3]

Dance With Chance (IRE) *W R Swinburn* a51 39
2 b f Kalanisi(IRE) —Persian Lass (IRE) (Grand Lodge (USA))
5752[10] 7183[16]

Dancing Again *E A Wheeler* a5 12
3 ch f Reel Buddy(USA) —Batchworth Breeze (Beveled (USA))
1752[12] 6551[11] 6856[13] 7254[9]

Dancing David (IRE) *B J Meehan* 109
2 b c Danehill Dancer(IRE) —Seek Easy (USA) (Seeking The Gold (USA))
5603[2] ◆ (6620) ◆ 7017[4] ◆

Dancing Deano (IRE) *R Hollinshead* a75 62
7 b g Second Empire(IRE) —Ultimate Beat (USA) (Go And Go)
133[5] 274[2] 452[2] 569[4] 793[6] 934[8]

Dancing Duo *D Shaw* a62 56
5 b m Groom Dancer(USA) —Affaire Royale (IRE) (Royal Academy (USA))
39[6] 210[2] 242[8] 513[7] 760[2] 1634[7]

Dancing Freddy (IRE) *J G Given* a77 83
2 b c Chineur(FR) —Majesty's Dancer (IRE) (Danehill Dancer (IRE))
1312[2] ◆ 1764[2] (2161) 2714[3] 2995[19] 3542[6] 4327[7] 6068[5] 6486[17] 6827[3] 7115[2] 7290[15]

Dancing Ghost (IRE) *Jane Chapple-Hyam* a16 18
3 gr f Verglas(IRE) —Ghost Dance (IRE) (Lure (USA))
4097[11] 7332[7]

Dancing In Silks (USA) *Carla Gaines* a121 92
4 b g Black Minnaloushe(USA) —Lemhi Love (USA) (Royal And Regal (USA))
(7306a)

Dancing Jest (IRE) *Rae Guest* a19 69
5 b m Averti(IRE) —Mezzanine (Sadler's Wells (USA))
1633[9] 1945[2] 2171[2] (2916) 3463[2] 3777[5] 5441[17] 6174[12]

Dancing Lyra *R A Fahey* a70 67
8 b g Alzao(USA) —Badaayer (USA) (Silver Hawk (USA))
171[7] 324[2] 603[6] 744[2] 2155[5] (2580) 3068[5] 3714[4] 3974[4]

Dancing Maite *S R Bowring* a78 89
4 ch g Ballet Master(USA) —Ace Maite (Komaite (USA))
297[4] 777[3] (1103) 1510[2] 1887[8] (2088) 2269[9] 2695[4] (2938) 4353[4] 4784[9] 5799[20] 6540[5] 6879[6] 7617[8]

Dancing Poppy *M R Channon* a56 58
2 b f Kyllachy—Broughtons Motto (Mtoto)
2765[5] 3106[3] 3716[8] 5543[8] 6722[6]

Dancing Queen (IRE) *M A Magnusson* 72
2 ch f Danehill Dancer(IRE) —Elauyun (IRE) (Muhtarram (USA))
4797[6] ◆ 5741[5] 6284[2] ◆

Dancing Red Devil (IRE) *Paul Green* 77
2 b f Desert Style(IRE) —Mannsara (IRE) (Royal Academy (USA))
(3370) 3805[5] 4357a[5] 4739[5] 5274a[9]

Dancing Rhythm *M S Saunders* a60 63
4 b g Piccolo—Will You Dance (Shareef Dancer (USA))
917[8] 1420[9] 1539[7] 1704[5] 1970[16] (Dead)

Dancing Storm *W S Kittow* a56 71
6 b m Trans Island—Stormswell (Persian Bold)
1194[11] 1773[6] 2352[5] 3217[7] 3581[4] 5063[10] 5179[6] 6968[9]

Dancing Wave *M C Chapman* a59 65
3 b f Baryshnikov(AUS) —Wavet (Pursuit Of Love)
(10) 366[2] 426[2] 492[2] 986[6] 1281[7] 1437[3] 1725[3] 1988[6] 2417[7] 2913[4] (3176) 3428[2] 3917[7] 4172[8] 6572[8] 6926[2] 7681[9] 7838[9]

Dancing Welcome *J M Bradley* a65 57
3 b f Kyllachy—Highland Gait (Most Welcome)
2073 ◆ 293[7] 736[9] 1424[4] 1772[6] 1985[7] 3225[2] 3926[3] 4155[5] 4643[2] 4937[2] 5155[4] 5634[4] 6175[8] 7176[2] (7240) 7424[2] (7521) ◆ 7591[3] 7715[7] 7860[9]

Dancing Wizard *Norma Twomey* a53
5 ch g Dancing Spree(USA) —Magic Legs (Reprimand)
969[12]

Dancourt (IRE) *Sir Michael Stoute* a75 98
3 b g Cadeaux Genereux—Stage Struck (IRE) (Sadler's Wells (USA))
2399[2] ◆ 2925[2] (3752) ◆ (4247) ◆ 4781[4]

Dandaad (NZ) *Bart Cummings* 108
6 ch g Istidaad(USA) —Lets Dance (NZ) (Dance Floor (USA))
6961a[2]

Dandarrell *Miss J A Camacho* a58 62
2 b g Makbul—Dress Design (IRE) (Brief Truce (USA))
7289[5] 7420[2]

Danderek *R A Fahey* a57
3 ch g Fantastic Light(USA) —Maureena (IRE) (Grand Lodge (USA))
7765[4]

Dandino *J G Given* 76
2 br c Dansili—Generous Diana (Generous (IRE))
6763[7] 7121[2]

Dandy Boy (ITY) *David Marnane* a96 84
3 b c Danetime(IRE) —Fleet Of Light (Spectrum (IRE))
5490a[15]

Dandy Man (IRE) *Saeed Bin Suroor* 118
6 b h Mozart(IRE) —Lady Alexander (IRE) (Night Shift (USA))
1676[9] 2481[9] 2991[7] 4456[5] 5233[7] (5546) 5765[4] 6427[4]

Dane Blue (IRE) *S J Treacy* 92
7 ch m Danehill Dancer(IRE) —Palace Blue (IRE) (Dara Monarch)
2285a[5] 2647a[7]

Dane Cottage *Miss Gay Kelleway* 4
2 ch f Beat Hollow—Lady Soleas (Be My Guest (USA))
6903[14]

Danehill Destiny *W J Haggas* 107
3 b f Danehill Dancer(IRE) —Comeraincomeshine (IRE) (Night Shift (USA))
1353[3] (2485) 3824[6] 5921a[6]

Danehill Intellect (IRE) *G A Butler* a60 69
2 ch f Danehill Dancer(IRE) —Intellectuelle (Caerleon (USA))
4980[6] 5547[4]

Danehill's Pearl (IRE) *Tom Dascombe* 103
3 b f Danehill Dancer(IRE) —Mother Of Pearl (IRE) (Sadler's Wells (USA))
(1327) 2036[5] 2846[6] (4334a)

Danehillsundance (IRE) *D H Brown* a91 94
5 b g Danehill Dancer(IRE) —Rosie's Guest (IRE) (Be My Guest (USA))
780[6] 2257[8] 2665[10] 2998[7] 3635[3] (3941) 4400[8] 5126[5] 6900[13]

Danesis (IRE) *A S Cruz* 99
5 b h Danehill(USA) —Sister Dot (USA) (Secretariat (USA))
1554a[9]

Danetime Lily (IRE) *Ms Joanna Morgan* a67 80
5 b m Danetime(IRE) —Millie's Lily (IRE) (Distinctly North (USA))
3784[5] 3898a[8]

Danetime Panther (IRE) *Ian Williams* a79 78
5 b g Danetime(IRE) —Annotate (Groom Dancer (USA))
1149[8] 1357[11] 2150[3] 2798[5]

Danger Mulally *A M Balding* a73 68
2 b g Governor Brown(USA) —Glittering Image (IRE) (Sadler's Wells (USA))
2328[7] 3344[5] (3785) 4565[12] 7434[9] 7604[7] (7685)

Dangerous Cat (IRE) *Mario Hofer* 79
2 b f Invincible Spirit(IRE) —Sweet Surrender (IRE) (Pennekamp (USA))
3648a[8]

Dangerous Midge (USA) *B J Meehan* 91
3 b c Lion Heart(USA) —Adored Slew (USA) (Seattle Slew (USA))
2930[12] (3425) 4481[3] (5828) ◆

Daniella De Bruijn (IRE) *A B Haynes* a72 74
2 b f Orpen(USA) —Ardent Lady (Alhaarth (IRE))
1782[4] 1939[4] (2196) 2875[2] 3424[4] 4017[5] (6431) 6586[4] 6721[3] 7139[8]

Daniel's Victory (FR) *G Botti* 63
2 ch c Vettori(IRE) —Meadowlark (FR) (Priolo (USA))
6322a[4]

Daniel Thomas (IRE) *Mrs A L M King* a79 75
7 b g Dansili—Last Look (Rainbow Quest (USA))
4211[7] 6365[8] 6778[7] 7048[7] 7229[2] 7362[4] 7481[3] 7575[8] 7752[5] (7858)

Danies Boy (IRE) *R Hannon* a69 70
3 b c Elusive City(USA) —Daniela Samuel (USA) (No Robbery)
951[4] 1071[3] 1250[3] (2009)

Dani's Girl (IRE) *P M Phelan* a80 93
6 bb m Second Empire(IRE) —Quench The Lamp (IRE) (Glow (USA))
5509[5] 5912[8] 6470[7] (7873)

Danish Art (IRE) *M W Easterby* a76 77
4 b g Danehill Dancer(IRE) —Lady Ounavarra (IRE) (Simply Great (FR))
934[9] 1477[6] 2133[13] 2576[12] 3174[11] 5842[6] ◆ 5982[5]

Dannios *L M Cumani* a63 57
3 b c Tobougg(IRE) —Fleuve D'Or (IRE) (Last Tycoon)
2320[16] 3863[13] 4734[11]

Danny's Choice *R M Beckett* 87
2 ch f Compton Place—Pie High (Salse (USA))
2919[2] (3634) 5057a[6] (5721) 6241[14]

Dansant *G A Butler* a117 113
5 b h Dansili—La Balagna (Kris)
484[2] 789a[6] (1004) 3139[3] 5023[5]

Danse Grecque (USA) *E Lellouche* 110
4 ch m Hold That Tiger(USA) —Distorted Blaze (USA) (Distorted Humor (USA))
1597a[5] 2428a[2] 4580a[9] 5300a[4] 6505a[2] 7208a[10]

Danse On Wood *J Noseda* a70 60
3 b c Dansili—Woodwin (IRE) (Woodman (USA))
2002[7] 2943[7] 4205[2] 5666[7] 6975[8]

Danseur Russe (FR) *J E Pease* 79
3 b c Fasliyev(USA) —Belle D'Argent (USA) (Silver Hawk (USA))
6222a[8]

Dansili Dancer *C G Cox* a105 105
7 b g Dansili—Magic Slipper (Habitat)
1117[3] 1696[4] (2471) 3142[6] 3620[8] ◆ 5173[17] 6302[4]

Dansilver *A W Carroll* a67 67
5 b g Dansili—Silver Gyre (IRE) (Silver Hawk (USA))
18[2] ◆ 59[3] ◆ (252) ◆

Dansimar *Miss Venetia Williams* a72 61
5 gr m Daylami(IRE) —Hylandra (USA) (Bering)
1665[5] 2127[3]

Dantari (IRE) *Evan Williams* a68 65
4 b h Alhaarth(IRE) —Daniysha (IRE) (Doyoun)
631[6] 3788[3] 4168[6]

Dante Deo (USA) *T D Barron* a55 59
3 b f Proud Citizen(USA) —Best Feature (USA) (El Gran Senor (USA))
144[6] 572[7] 1128[7] 1281[5] (1725) 1926[6] 2236[8]

Dan Tucker *Jim Best* a67 74
5 b g Dansili—Shapely (USA) (Alleged (USA))
877[4] (Dead)

Dan Tucket *B Olsen* a58 92
4 b h Dansili—Fanfare (Deploy)
2587a[7] 4585a[11] 5302a[13]

Danube (IRE) *H R A Cecil* 62
2 b f Montjeu(IRE) —Darabela (IRE) (Desert King (IRE))
5547[5]

Danum Dancer *N Bycroft* a68 62
5 ch g Allied Forces(USA) —Branston Dancer (Rudimentary (USA))
4225[11] 5675[3] 6877[5] 7269[9] 7418[4] (7680) 7762[8] 7870[9]

Danvilla *P R Webber*
2 b f Dansili—Newtown Villa (Spectrum (IRE))
6628[12]

Danzadil (IRE) *R A Teal* a56 60
3 b f Mujadil(USA) —Changari (USA) (Gulch (USA))
2776[8] 3272[9] 3917[8] 4452[3] 4791[10] 6337[10] 7069[4]

Danzatrice *C W Thornton* 76
7 b m Tamure(IRE) —Miss Petronella (Petoski)
1102[2] 1230[8] (1851) 2895[6] 3313[7] 3940[6] 4551[3] 4793[2] 5410[5] 5696[4] 6053[2] 6676[7] 7170[7]

Danzig Fox *M Mullineaux* a57 64
4 b g Foxhound(USA) —Via Dolorosa (Chaddleworth (IRE))
1081[0] 3851[5] 5364[11] 5729[13] 6674[9] 7085[12]

Danzili Bay *A W Carroll* a67 71
7 b h Dansili—Lady Bankes (IRE) (Alzao (USA))
1890[10]

Danzoe (IRE) *D Donovan* 77
2 b g Kheleyf(USA) —Fiaba (Precocious)
1939[2] 2358[2] 2721[6] (3064) 4017[4] 4327[11] 5033[10] 6366[5] 6693[12]

Dao Dao (AUS) *Michael, Wayne & John Hawkes* 119
6 br g Shinko Forest(IRE) —Casual Way (NZ) (Casual Lies (USA))
1553a[3]

Daphne Du Maurier (IRE) *I Semple* 35
2 b f Arakan(USA) —Butter Knife (IRE) (Sure Blade (USA))
3910[7] 4774[5] 5553[8] 5942[10]

Daraahem (IRE) *B W Hills* 106
4 ch g Act One—Shamah (Unfuwain (USA))
(1790)

Daraiym (IRE) *Paul Green* a57 65
4 b g Peintre Celebre(USA) —Dararita (IRE) (Halo (USA))
252[5] (1058) (1171) 1399[6]

Darbaza (FR) *A De Royer-Dupre* 82
3 gr f Verglas(IRE) —Darinska (IRE) (Zilzal (USA))
6222a[2]

Darcey *Miss Amy Weaver* a75 77
3 ch f Noverre(USA) —Firozi (Forzando)
2504[5] 2967[3] 4198[9] 4654[2] (4995) (5254) 5621[3] (5999) 6224[6] 6545[3] 7027[10] 7149[8]

Darcy's Pride (IRE) *P T Midgley* a43 69
5 bb m Danetime(IRE) —Cox's Ridge (IRE) (Indian Ridge)
1096[11] (1241) 1456[8] 1768[4] 2316[15] 2966[10] 3938[3] 4355[9] 4929[10] 5073[2] (5396) 5955[9] 6220[4] 6380[7] 6410[3] 7280[10]

Daredevil Dan *M H Tompkins* 65
3 b g Golden Snake(USA) —Tiempo (King Of Spain)
1260[3] 2170[3] 4319[9] 6789[3]

Dareh (IRE) *M Johnston* a66 62
3 b f Invincible Spirit(IRE) —Delage (Bellypha)
729[2] 1736[11]

Dar Es Salaam *James Moffatt* 84
5 ch g King's Best(USA) —Place De L'Opera (Sadler's Wells (USA))
2932[6] 3393[7] 3564[3] 4091[8] 4541[6] 6995[8]

Darfour *J S Goldie* 68
5 b g Inchinor—Gai Bulga (Kris)
2594[2] 3094[4] 3911[5] 4656[7] 4897[6] 5941[6]

Darielli (USA) *F Head* 45
2 b c War Chant(USA) —Dariela (USA) (Manila (USA))
6979a[0]

Daring Dream (GER) *J S Goldie* a65 70
4 ch h Big Shuffle(USA) —Daring Action (Arazi (USA))
1080[4] 1320[5] 1606[11] 2458[3] 3662[2] (5332) 6413[4] 6765[13] 6984[6]

Daring Man (IRE) *M J P O'Brien* a74 88
4 b g Talkin Man(CAN) —Emotions High (IRE) (Mujadil (USA))
1375a[12] 4360a[2]

Daring Racer (GER) *Mrs L J Mongan* a70 64
6 ch g Big Shuffle(USA) —Daring Action (Arazi (USA))
2221[4] 3215[3] 3525[5] 3949[6] 5186[5]

Daring Tiger (GER) *P Schiergen* 110
3 b c Tiger Hill(IRE) —Denial (Sadler's Wells (USA))
1395a[2]

Darjani (IRE) *Mlle S-V Tarrou* 101
3 b g Domedriver(IRE) —Darasa (FR) (Barathea (IRE))
7704a[0]

Dark Camellia *H J L Dunlop* a66 50
4 b m Olden Times—Miss Mirror (Magic Mirror)
162[5] 2921[5] 3946[12] 4748[8] 6255[5] 6587[8] 6999[6] (7228) 7481[9] 7591[8]

Dark Desert *A G Newcombe* a41 43
3 b c Best Of The Bests(IRE) —Dune Safari (IRE) (Key Of Luck (USA))
196[5]

Dark Echoes *Jedd O'Keeffe* a48 59
3 bl g Diktat—Calamanco (Clantime)
1595[5] 2091[17] 2236[5] 2865[5] 4004[12] 5306[5] 6880[4]

Dark Energy *M J Scudamore* a63 76
5 br g Observatory(USA) —Waterfowl Creek (IRE) (Be My Guest (USA))
4169[4] 4862[8] 6025[6] 7594[5] 7695[7]

Dark Eyes (IRE) *D J Coakley* a74 81
2 b f Camacho—Sherkova (USA) (State Dinner (USA))
(4219) ◆ 4706[3] 5580[5] 6481[3] ◆ 7187[7]

Dark Lane *R A Fahey* 86
3 b g Namid—Corps De Ballet (IRE) (Fasliyev (USA))
(1869) 2279[10] 3362[2] 3747[19] 4849[5] 5523[8] 5960[3] 6050[18]

Dark Mischief *H Candy* a91 102
3 b g Namid—Syrian Queen (Slip Anchor)
(1296) 1705[5] 2934[9] 3622[5] 4459[8] 5646[3] ◆ (5959)

Dark Moment *A Dickman* 76
3 gr g Spartacus(IRE) —Dim Ofan (Petong)
(3449) ◆ 3730[RR] 4013[4] (4879) (4998) (5158) 6309[8] 6847[6]

Dark Oasis *M C Chapman* a61 61
3 b g Dubai Destination(USA) —Silent Waters (Polish Precedent (USA))
479[2] 759[7] 1470[7] 1691[2] 1848[2] 3432[3] 3687[7] 4054[10] 4142[3] 4470[6] 5011[10] 5376[5]

Dark Planet *D W Thompson* a53 56
6 ch g Singspiel(IRE) —Warning Shadows (IRE) (Cadeaux Genereux)
7[12] 790[9] 1125[9] 1556[8] 1765[7]

Dark Prospect *M A Jarvis* a88 91
4 b g Nayef(USA) —Miss Mirasol (Sheikh Albadou)
1274[8] (2150) 2597[5] 3705[2] 4404[12] 5828[4] 6594[3] 6907[8]

Dark Quest *J L Dunlop* 71
3 b f Rainbow Quest(USA) —Pure Grain (Polish Precedent (USA))
1329[7] 2051[4] 2877[5] 3703[2] 4743[3]

Dark Ranger *T J Pitt* a64 64
3 bb g Where Or When(IRE) —Dark Raider (IRE) (Definite Article)
817[3] (1036) 1106[3] 1594[3] (1967) 3336[2] 3557[3] 4284[8] 4872[8] 7392[5] 7742[4]

Dark Tara *R A Fahey* a70 75
4 br m Diktat—Karisal (IRE) (Persian Bold)
76[8] (241) 305[5]

Dark Velvet (IRE) *E J Alston* a18 63
3 b f Statue Of Liberty(USA) —Lovingit (IRE) (Fasliyev (USA))
1973[7] 2786[15] 4105[14] 4528[5] 7082[10] 7678[12] 7787[12]

Darley Star *R A Harris* a57 62
4 gr m King's Best(USA) —Amellnaa (IRE) (Sadler's Wells (USA))
193[6] 541[8] 918[7]

Darley Sun (IRE) *D M Simcock* a61 111
3 b c Tiger Hill(IRE) —Sagamartha (Rainbow Quest (USA))
1464[6] (1842) 2208[4] ◆ (2838) ◆ 3276[2] (4260) 5824[2] (6851) ◆

Darli Girl (FR) *C Aubert*
2 gr f Slickly(FR) —Darlirad (FR) (Akarad (FR))
6960a[0]

Darling Buds *K A Ryan* a55
2 b f Reel Buddy(USA) —Its Another Gift (Primo Dominie)
7556[7] 7708[6] 7799[5]

Dar Re Mi *J H M Gosden* 119
4 b m Singspiel(IRE) —Darara (Top Ville)
2013^{2} (3412a) (5201) $5929a^{5}$ $6526a^{5}$ $7310a^{3}$

Darshonin *J Noseda* 61
2 ch g Pivotal—Incheni (IRE) (Nashwan (USA))
6054^{7} 6478^{22}

Dart *Mrs S Lamyman* a73 49
5 br m Diktat—Eilean Shona (Suave Dancer (USA))
3^{2} 325^{5} 2194^{7} 2766^{5} 6875^{4} 7336^{7} 7642^{2} ◆ (7842)

D'Artagnans Dream *G D Blake* a65 67
3 b g Cyrano De Bergerac—Kairine (IRE) (Kahyasi)
2763^{8} 4010^{8} 4275^{9} 5630^{6} 6073^{6} 6445^{2} 6917^{4} 7049^{8}

Darwind (FR) *J-L Pelletan* 65
2 b c Sinndar(IRE) —Miss Hernando (Hernando (FR))
$3935a^{6}$ $6751a^{10}$

Darwin's Dragon *P F I Cole* a66 66
3 ch g Royal Dragon(USA) —Darwinia (GER) (Acatenango (GER))
1752^{7} 2048^{13} 2578^{14} 2876^{11} 3302^{7}

Daryainur (IRE) *W De Best-Turner* a40 33
2 br f Auction House(USA) —Maylan (IRE) (Lashkari)
6109^{13} 6759^{13} 7064^{8}

Daryakana (FR) *A De Royer-Dupre* 115
3 ch f Selkirk(USA) —Daryaba (IRE) (Night Shift (USA))
(6504a) (7744a)

Daryal (IRE) *G L Moore* 33
8 b g Night Shift(USA) —Darata (IRE) (Vayrann)
3697^{7}

Dash Back (USA) *Adrian McGuinness* a83 80
4 b m Sahm(USA) —Nadwah (USA) (Shadeed (USA))
4134^{5} 7273^{2} 7496^{4} (7643) 7673^{4}

Dasheena *A J McCabe* a77 61
6 b m Magic Ring(IRE) —Sweet And Lucky (Lucky Wednesday)
108^{7} 133^{6} 242^{7}

Dasher Reilly (USA) *A Sadik* a50 5
8 b g Ghazi(USA) —Kutira (USA) (Dixieland Band (USA))
148^{8} 249^{8}

Dashing Daniel *N J Vaughan* a47 38
4 gr g Zamindar(USA) —Etienne Lady (IRE) (Imperial Frontier (USA))
1632^{7} 2366^{17} 3331^{11}

Dashing Doc (IRE) *D R C Elsworth* a45 77
2 ch g Dr Fong(USA) —Dashiba (Dashing Blade)
2631^{9} 3167^{3} 3522^{4} 4271^{4} 4758^{3} (5002) 5970^{4}

Database (IRE) *Saeed Bin Suroor* 77
2 ch c Singspiel(IRE) —Memory Green (USA) (Green Forest (USA))
6617^{3} (6931)

Dauntsey Park (IRE) *Miss Tor Sturgis* a55 49
2 ch c Refuse To Bend(IRE) —Shauna's Honey (IRE) (Danehill (USA))
4377^{11} 5785^{9} 6772^{9} 7389^{6}

Davana *W J H Ratcliffe* a49 42
3 b f Primo Valentino(IRE) —Bombay Sapphire (Be My Chief (USA))
1840^{11} 3221^{6} 4196^{3} 7004^{5} 7318^{6} 7581^{3} 7723^{3} 7814^{5}

Davaye *K R Burke* a41 67
5 b m Bold Edge—Last Impression (Imp Society (USA))
2032^{11}

Dave Diamond *P D Evans*
3 b g Deportivo—Blossoming (Vague Shot)
3862^{15}

Davenport (IRE) *B R Millman* a76 85
7 b g Bold Fact(USA) —Semence D'Or (FR) (Kaldoun (FR))
39^{3} 220^{9} 384^{5}

Daveron (GER) *A Trybuhl* 100
4 ch m Black Sam Bellamy(IRE) —Darwinia (GER) (Acatenango (GER))
$5296a^{4}$ $6152a^{6}$

David's Boy (FR) *C Baillet*
2 gr c Marchand De Sable(USA) —Oakdoun (FR) (Kaldoun (FR))
$7316a^{8}$

Davids City (IRE) *G A Harker* a53
5 b g Laveron—Irelands Own (IRE) (Commanche Run)
7137^{5} 7578^{9} 7670^{8}

Davids Mark *J R Jenkins* a63 55
9 b g Polar Prince(IRE) —Star Of Flanders (Puissance)
111^{5} ◆ (347) 460^{2} 646^{9} 853^{8} 1421^{4} 1846^{8} 3671^{6} 4748^{6} 6433^{10} 7774^{4} 7835^{8}

Davids Matador *Eve Johnson Houghton* a57 71
3 b g Dansili—Mousseline (USA) (Barathea (IRE))
2209^{6} 2432^{8} 3159^{6} 4691^{6} 5112^{6} 5582^{5} 5809^{5} 6339^{13} 7002^{5}

Davie's Story *B Grizzetti* 83
2 b c Observatory(USA) —Davie's Lure (USA) (Lure (USA))
$6716a^{11}$

Dawnbreak (USA) *Saeed Bin Suroor* a77 86
2 ch f Distorted Humor(USA) —Dawn Princess (USA) (Polish Numbers (USA))
(5752) 6055^{6} 6756^{2}

Dawn Dew (GER) *P Schiergen* 100
4 gr m Montjeu(IRE) —Dawn Dane (FR) (Danehill (USA))
$5296a^{9}$

Dawn Storm (IRE) *J L Spearing* a56
4 ch g City On A Hill(USA) —Flames (Blushing Flame (USA))
7195^{10} 7318^{5} 7649^{3} 7842^{3}

Dawn Wind *I A Wood* a50 45
4 b m Vettori(IRE) —Topper (IRE) (Priolo (USA))
567^{6} 670^{3} 902^{3} 1156^{8} 3617^{11} 4389^{13}

Dawson Creek (IRE) *B Gubby* a71 47
5 ch g Titus Livius(FR) —Particular Friend (Cadeaux Genereux)
155^{8} 4791^{9} 5019^{13} 5750^{6} 7180^{8} 7693^{7}

Dayanara (USA) *C G Cox* a49 53
3 bb f Action This Day(USA) —Dana Did It (USA) (Wagon Limit (USA))
3696^{12} 4648^{11} 5718^{8} 6445^{6} 6917^{6}

Day Care *R McGlinchey* a58 46
8 gr g Daylami(IRE) —Ancara (Dancing Brave (USA))
7214^{2}

Dayia (IRE) *J Pearce* a92 93
5 br m Act One—Masharik (IRE) (Caerleon (USA))
1426^{3} 1732^{2} 2486^{5} (6636) 6851^{4} 7117^{2}

Day In Dubai *J J Bridger* a18 53
3 b f Dubai Destination(USA) —Pazzazz (IRE) (Green Desert (USA))
1618^{6} 2010^{10} 2478^{8} 4304^{8} 4950^{9} 5965^{10} 6551^{9} 7198^{5}

Day Of The Eagle (IRE) *L M Cumani* 82
3 b g Danehill Dancer(IRE) —Puck's Castle (Shirley Heights)
4505^{14} 5215^{3} 5744^{5} 6621^{3} (7149)

Days Of Pleasure (IRE) *C Gordon* a67
4 b g Fraam—Altizaf (Zafonic (USA))
202^{12}

Days Of Thunder (IRE) *B R Summers* a26 21
4 b g Choisir(AUS) —Grazina (Mark Of Esteem (IRE))
1773^{13} 4372^{10} 4812^{9} 6172^{9} 7817^{10}

Dazakhee *P T Midgley* a46 47
2 ch f Sakhee(USA) —Ziya (IRE) (Lion Cavern (USA))
3528^{4} 4278^{9} 5253^{11} 5728^{9} 7335^{5}

Dazed And Amazed *R Hannon* a87 88
5 b g Averti(IRE) —Amazed (Clantime)
(1418) 1668^{4} 2012^{11} 2520^{4} 2946^{8} 4461^{22} 4567^{5} 5830^{4} 6631^{8}

Dazeen *P T Midgley* 72
2 b g Zafeen(FR) —Bond Finesse (IRE) (Danehill Dancer (IRE))
1866^{12} 2435^{2} 2940^{5} 5146^{2} 5392^{4}

Dazinski *M H Tompkins* 91
3 ch g Sulamani(IRE) —Shuheb (Nashwan (USA))
2371^{5} 3359^{3} 3962^{2} 4325^{3} (5252) 5481^{3} (6388) 7151^{15}

Dazzling Bay *T D Easterby* a85 80
9 b g Mind Games—Adorable Cherub (USA) (Halo (USA))
1309^{11} 1849^{6} 2438^{2} 2814^{3} 4134^{15} 5516^{9}

Dazzling Begum *J Pearce* a60 55
4 br m Okawango(USA) —Dream On Me (Prince Sabo)
107^{4} 147^{9} 368^{2} 493^{2} 623^{6} 790^{3} 972^{8} 1442^{9} 1537^{6} 2182^{8} 2785^{3} 3348^{3} (3714) 4388^{4} 4893^{5} 5359^{11} 5885^{3} (6188) 6457^{6} 6859^{11} 7642^{7} (7732) 7842^{5}

Dazzling Colours *T T Clement* a38 41
4 b h Oasis Dream—Dazzle (Gone West (USA))
1638^{10} 2149^{10} 3467^{10} 3673^{7} 4158^{9}

Dazzling Day *Kevin Prendergast* a78 89
2 b f Hernando(FR) —Dazzling Dancer (Nashwan (USA))
$6316a^{7}$

Dazzling Light (UAE) *J S Goldie* a69 82
4 bb m Halling(USA) —Crown Of Light (Mtoto)
1101^{3} 1231^{2} 1693^{3} 1990^{2} (2452) 3266^{5} 5034^{4} 5170^{10} 5696^{11} 6095^{3} 6280^{2} 6412^{4} 7117^{5}

Deacon Blues *J R Fanshawe* 79
2 b c Compton Place—Persario (Bishop Of Cashel)
6591^{5} (7058)

Dead Cat Bounce (IRE) *J Pearce* a60 54
3 b c Mujadil(USA) —Where's Charlotte (Sure Blade (USA))
280^{7} 548^{6} 759^{10} 943^{2} 1270^{10} 1520^{9} 2169^{4}

Deadline (UAE) *P T Midgley* a49 74
5 ch g Machiavellian(USA) —Time Changes (USA) (Danzig (USA))
618^{5} 857^{6}

Deadly Encounter (IRE) *R A Fahey* 86
3 br g Lend A Hand—Cautious Joe (First Trump)
2198^{5} (2841) 3375^{6} 3643^{4} 4459^{4}

Deadly Secret (USA) *R A Fahey* 96
3 b g Johannesburg(USA) —Lypink (USA) (Lyphard (USA))
1987^{11} 2273^{11} 2696^{2} ◆ 3049^{24} 4708^{5} 5070^{8}

Dead Womans Pass (IRE) *N Wilson* 39
2 b f High Chaparral(IRE) —Pedicure (Atticus (USA))
3310^{7} 4286^{9} 5693^{7} 6366^{7} 7114^{5}

Deal (IRE) *R Hannon* 86
2 b f Invincible Spirit(IRE) —Desert Order (IRE) (Desert King (IRE))
1749^{3} 1968^{3} (2972) 3583^{5} 4049^{3} 4295^{8} 4989^{11}

Deal Breaker *Edward Lynam* a92 96
4 ch g Night Shift(USA) —Photo Flash (IRE) (Bahamian Bounty)
$3435a^{8}$

Dealmaker Frank (USA) *Daniel Mark Loughnane* a53 69
4 b g Diesis—Armourette (USA) (Rahy (USA))
6224^{13}

Dean Iarracht (IRE) *Miss Tracy Waggott* a60 68
3 b g Danetime(IRE) —Sirdhana (Selkirk (USA))
1561^{3} 2578^{6} 2786^{3} 3062^{4} 3316^{7} 4079^{4} 4348^{3} 5331^{11} 5672^{10} 6052^{5} 7246^{4} 7632^{3}

Dean's Kitten (USA) *Michael J Maker* a36 111
2 ch c Kitten's Joy(USA) —Summer Theatre (USA) (Ide (USA))
$7304a^{6}$

Dear Boy (FR) *T Trapenard*
2 b c Priolo(USA) —Dear Queen (FR) (Always Fair (USA))
$7384a^{9}$

Dear Cat (FR) *R Martens* 30
2 gr f Android(USA) —Highest Spring (FR) (Hero's Honor (USA))
$6148a^{6}$

Dear Maurice *E A L Dunlop* a83 91
5 b g Indian Ridge—Shamaiel (IRE) (Lycius (USA))
1666^{4} 2103^{3} 2274^{7} 3008^{4} 3635^{4} 4149^{2} 4605^{6} 6004^{3} 6435^{3} 6973^{13}

Dear Mr Fantasy (IRE) *J W Hills* a61 47
2 b c Kingsalsa(USA) —Heart Ofthe Matter (Rainbow Quest (USA))
2383^{5} 2940^{8} 4080^{9} (5224) 5613^{11} 5985^{8} 6639^{9}

Deaufils (FR) *X Nakkachdji* a85 83
3 b f Divine Light(JPN) —Chanson Parfaite (FR) (Shining Steel)
$5462a^{2}$

Deauville Flyer *T D Easterby* 86
3 b g Dubai Destination(USA) —Reaf (In The Wings)
1015^{6} 1308^{9} 1562^{3} (2667) ◆ 3069^{3} 3827^{4} (4491) ◆ 5696^{2} 6995^{3}

Deauville Post (FR) *R Hannon* 86
2 b c American Post—Loyola (FR) (Sicyos (USA))
2889^{7} 4006^{4} 4439^{2} ◆ 5399^{3}

Deauville Royale *S Wattel* 56
3 b f Royal Applause—Mimalia (USA) (Silver Hawk (USA))
$4810a^{8}$

Deauville Vision (IRE) *M Halford* 105
6 b m Danehill Dancer(IRE) —Alexia Reveuse (IRE) (Dr Devious (IRE))
$2285a^{3}$ (2729a) $3882a^{5}$ $5076a^{4}$ $5487a^{6}$

Debbie Harri (IRE) *Michael Mulvany* a37 43
2 ch f Redback—Malthouse Mistress (IRE) (Peintre Celebre (USA))
$6401a^{9}$

Debdene Bank (IRE) *Mrs Mary Hambro* a67 69
6 b m Pivotal—Nedaarah (Reference Point)
60^{5} 253^{6} 1080^{7} 1254^{10} 2182^{2} 2580^{7} 4563^{2} 5229^{3} 6025^{2} 7440^{3} ◆ 7594^{6}

Debord (FR) *Jamie Poulton* a45 67
6 ch g Sendawar(IRE) —Partie De Dames (USA) (Bering)
3029^{12} 4703^{6}

Debussy (IRE) *J H M Gosden* a90 115
3 b c Diesis—Opera Comique (FR) (Singspiel (IRE))
(914) (1459) 1800^{3} 2705^{8} 3087^{10} (4367a) $5084a^{6}$

Decameron (USA) *R A Harris* a87 96
4 b g Theatrical(IRE) —Morning Pride (IRE) (Machiavellian (USA))
1527^{5} 2470^{12} 6357^{11} 6761^{5} 7229^{4} 7362^{7} 7845^{7}

December *Mrs C A Dunnett* a61 63
3 b g Oasis Dream—Winter Solstice (Unfuwain (USA))
1350^{12} 3117^{8} 7439^{3} ◆ 7665^{5} 7831^{6}

December Draw (IRE) *W J Knight* a86 87
3 br g Medecis—New York (IRE) (Danzero (AUS))
1751^{3} ◆ 2174^{5} 3220^{3} 7523^{9} 7684^{6}

Decency (IRE) *E A L Dunlop* a46 43
2 b f Celtic Swing—Siem Reap (USA) (El Gran Senor (USA))
4869^{7} 7145^{10} 7317^{8} ◆

Dechiper (IRE) *R Johnson* a35 75
7 bb g Almutawakel—Safiya (USA) (Riverman (USA))
1125^{5} 1556^{5} (1738) 2044^{9} 2315^{2} (2724) 3393^{2} 4345^{7} 4658^{6} 4941^{7} 5395^{4} 5698^{11} 6385^{4} 6767^{9} 6899^{4}

Decider (USA) *R A Harris* a69 50
6 ch g High Yield(USA) —Nikita Moon (USA) (Secret Hello (USA))
15^{7} 173^{3} 431^{6} 535^{3} 589^{6} 676^{3} 742^{4} 794^{2} 919^{4} 1564^{7} 2130^{11} 2682^{2} 3465^{7} 4372^{4} 5610^{5} 5629^{9} 5911^{3} (6119) 6251^{3} 7280^{4} (7397) 7483^{11} 7595^{2} 7689^{2} 7807^{4}

Decimus Meridius (IRE) *J Howard Johnson* 62
2 ch c Danehill Dancer(IRE) —Simaat (USA) (Mr Prospector (USA))
4618^{3} 5407^{8} 6136^{8}

Decision *C G Cox* 88
3 b g Royal Applause—Corinium (IRE) (Turtle Island (IRE))
1771^{2} 2077^{2} ◆ 2447^{4} 3117^{2} 4270^{3} 5209^{10} 5834^{10} (6907)

Deckchair *S Curran* a60 54
3 b f Monsieur Bond(IRE) —Silver Sun (Green Desert (USA))
140^{3} 229^{5} 316^{4} 348^{4} 542^{7} (736) 3118^{5} 3464^{11} 4155^{12} 5287^{4} 6170^{5} 6442^{7} 7535^{5}

Decorative (IRE) *M A Jarvis* 87
2 b f Danehill Dancer(IRE) —Source Of Life (IRE) (Fasliyev (USA))
(5478)

Decorum (USA) *J H M Gosden* a79 80
3 b c Dynaformer(USA) —Shy Greeting (ARG) (Shy Tom (USA))
1127^{3} 2038^{3} 3466^{2} 4319^{5} 6789^{2}

Decree Absolute (USA) *Miss J R Tooth* 74
2 bb g Orientate(USA) —Midriff (USA) (Naevus (USA))
(2793) 3452^{2} 4565^{14} 6367^{10}

Dedante *D K Ivory* a63 63
3 br f One Cool Cat(USA) —Cloridja (Indian Ridge)
34^{6} 316^{6} 2581^{10} 4155^{RR}

Dedo (IRE) *Kevin Prendergast* a90 94
4 b g Modigliani(USA) —Scant (FR) (Septieme Ciel (USA))
$2289a^{3}$ $3435a^{2}$ $4412a^{11}$

Dee Cee Elle *D Burchell* a53 50
5 b m Groom Dancer(USA) —Missouri (Charnwood Forest (IRE))
1154^{12} 2517^{5} 4862^{3}

Deely Plaza *R Hannon* a70 70
2 b g Compton Place—Anchorage (IRE) (Slip Anchor)
5317^{10} 5571^{4} 5852^{4} 6736^{5} 6895^{4}

Deem (IRE) *J Barton* 108
4 gr m Dalakhani(IRE) —Hijaz (IRE) (Sadler's Wells (USA))
(416a) ◆ $643a^{5}$ $1012a^{7}$

Deep Winter *R A Fahey* a64 91
4 ch m Pivotal—Russian Snows (IRE) (Sadler's Wells (USA))
1020^{2} $1268a^{3}$ 1673^{14} 3873^{11} 4328^{8}

Defector (IRE) *W R Muir* a79 73
3 b g Fasliyev(USA) —Rich Dancer (Halling (USA))
1196^{5} ◆ 1671^{8} 2761^{3} 3712^{2} 4154^{8} 4374^{4} 5370^{9} (5991) 6361^{5} 6725^{2} 6976^{3} 7111^{3} 7516^{7} 7627^{5} 7729^{3} (7876)

Defi (IRE) *D A Nolan* a75 55
7 b g Rainbow Quest(USA) —Danse Classique (IRE) (Night Shift (USA))
2155^{6} 2390^{12} 2532^{7} 3105^{9} 3656^{9} 5364^{13}

Definightly *R Charlton* 94
3 bb g Diktat—Perfect Night (Danzig Connection (USA))
1296^{11} 2270^{6} 2934^{11}

Deirdre *J H M Gosden* a71 78
2 b f Dubawi(IRE) —Dolores (Danehill (USA))
6163^{5} (6762)

Delegator *Saeed Bin Suroor* 123
3 b c Dansili—Indian Love Bird (Efisio)
(1300) 1675^{2} $2288a^{8}$ 2992^{2} 5426^{DSQ} ◆ 6271^{3} $7308a^{5}$

Deliberate *A Fabre* 86
3 b f King's Best(USA) —Dance Routine (Sadler's Wells (USA))
$7569a^{10}$

Dellaside (FR) *Rod Collet* a74 82
3 b g Della Francesca(USA) —Miss Fine (FR) (Kaldoun (FR))
$7386a^{5}$

Deloria *Eve Johnson Houghton* a72 74
2 ch f Mark Of Esteem(IRE) —Denica (IRE) (Night Shift (USA))
3534^{2} ◆ (4323) 5091^{5} 5433^{9} 6104^{6} 6906^{10}

Delta Sky (IRE) *Miss Amy Weaver* a52 62
2 ch f Refuse To Bend(IRE) —Delta Blues (IRE) (Digamist (USA))
3576^{9} 4226^{11} 4869^{5} 7884^{10}

Delta Storm (USA) *Mike Mitchell* a113 114
8 b g Storm Boot(USA) —Talkin To Delta (USA) (Diesis)
$7305a^{4}$

Delvita (FR) *J-V Toux* 106
5 gr m Pinmix(FR) —Very Very Nice (IRE) (Soviet Star (USA))
$2523a^{6}$ (3202a) $3908a^{2}$ $4837a^{12}$ $5928a^{5}$

Demeanour (USA) *E A L Dunlop* a75 74
3 ch f Giant's Causeway(USA) —Akuna Bay (USA) (Mr Prospector (USA))
1834^{2} 2982^{3} 3636^{4} 4206^{3} 4650^{4} 6031^{2} 6673^{3} 6975^{3}

Democrate *Saeed Bin Suroor* a86 113
4 rg h Dalakhani(IRE) —Aiglonne (USA) (Silver Hawk (USA))
3585^{7} 5004^{8}

Demolition *N Wilson* a72 96
5 ch g Starborough—Movie Star (IRE) (Barathea (IRE))
1347^{3} (1473) 1850^{5} 2815^{9} 3564^{5} (4288) 4597^{2} 4930^{3} 5671^{4} (6013) 6095^{2} 6644^{4}

Demonstrative (USA) *M Johnston* a51 71
2 b g Elusive Quality(USA) —Loving Pride (USA) (Quiet American (USA))
3546^{9} 4659^{3} 5251^{2} 5853^{3} 6874^{4} 7168^{6}

Dencolstina *Joss Saville* a9
2 b f Lujain(USA) —Buthaina (IRE) (Bahhare (USA))
2800^{11} 4856^{8} 4939^{5}

Denices Desert *M Botti* a26 45
3 b f Green Desert(USA) —Denice (Night Shift (USA))
5840^{8} 6332^{4} 6934^{9} 7438^{11}

Den Maschine *B N Pollock* a55 57
4 b g Sakhee(USA) —Flamingo Flower (USA) (Diesis)
970^{5} 1245^{7} 1520^{4} 2609^{2} 3303^{4} 3974^{2} 4944^{10} 5679^{10}

Denomination (USA) *Mme C Head-Maarek* 108
3 b f Smart Strike(CAN) —Dreamlike (USA) (Storm Cat (USA))
(1550a) $2952a^{9}$ $3668a^{3}$

Den's Boy *S Curran* a35 2
4 b g Josr Algarhoud(IRE) —Den's-Joy (Archway (IRE))
2378^{6} 3207^{13}

Den's Gift (IRE) *C G Cox* a92 89
5 rg g City On A Hill(USA) —Romanylei (IRE) (Blues Traveller (IRE))
(283) 1149^{7} 2434^{3} 2976^{2} 3523^{4} 4262^{5} 5746^{5} 7626^{2} 7883^{2}

Denton (NZ) *J R Gask* a73 74
6 b g Montjeu(IRE) —Melora (NZ) (Sir Tristram)
3710^{8} (4538) (4880) ◆ (6460) 6936^{9}

Denton Diva *M Dods* a66 63
3 b f Tobougg(IRE) —Seeking Utopia (Wolfhound (USA))
562^{4} 819^{2} 1098^{7} 1652^{4} 2234^{3} 5326^{6}

Denton Ryal *S W James* a41 58
2 b f Trade Fair—My Valentina (Royal Academy (USA))
6436^{10} 6920^{10}

Deora De *E A L Dunlop* 16
2 b f Night Shift(USA) —Photo Flash (IRE) (Bahamian Bounty)
6730^{16}

Deo Valente (IRE) *J M Bradley* a67 76
4 b g Dubai Destination(USA) —Pack Ice (USA) (Wekiva Springs (USA))
2495^{9} 3159^{13} 4648^{10} 5502^{10} 6252^{8} 7002^{3} 7241^{17} 7370^{11} 7703^{7}

Deportista *J A Pickering* a49 14
3 ch f Deportivo—Wadenhoe (IRE) (Persian Bold)
5882^{11} 7057^{11} 7278^{7} 7609^{9} 7753^{4} 7818^{7}

Deportment *J R Fanshawe* 88
3 b f Barathea(IRE) —Tina Heights (Shirley Heights)
4519^{3} ◆ 4991^{5} 6475^{2} (7101)

Deposer (IRE) *J R Best* a99 112
3 b g Kheleyf(USA) —Bezant (IRE) (Zamindar (USA))
863^{9} 1118^{2} 1822^{4} 2668^{3} 3011^{2}

Deputy Consort (USA) *Matthieu Palussiere* 88
6 b g Stravinsky(USA) —Possible Consort (USA) (Deputy Minister (CAN))
2305a[RR]

Deraaya (IRE) *K A Morgan* a76 82
4 b m Mujahid(USA) —Hawafiz (Nashwan (USA))
890[5] 1379[3] 3272[10]

Derbaas (USA) *E A L Dunlop* 106
3 b c Seeking The Gold(USA) —Sultana (USA) (Storm Cat (USA))
1294[5] 2273[3] 3783[4] 5655[3] 6732[10]

Derby Desire (IRE) *D G Duggan* a33 22
5 b m Swallow Flight(IRE) —Jaldi (IRE) (Nordico (USA))
7369[8]

Derek *H Blume* 92
3 b c Refuse To Bend(IRE) —Despoina (GER) (Aspros (GER))
6894a[6]

Derison (USA) *H De Waele* a70 104
7 b g Miesque's Son(USA) —Devolli (Saumarez)
3202a[7]

Derringbay (IRE) *Mme G Rarick* a63 27
3 b g Mull Of Kintyre(USA) —Rustle In The Wind (Barathea (IRE))
144[3] 506[8] 1361[14] 1811[14] 2169[10] 3193[10] 6980a[2]

Der Rosenkavalier (IRE) *A M Balding* a36 34
3 gr g Captain Rio—Brooks Masquerade (Absalom)
2151[6] 2496[14]

Derval (IRE) *K A Ryan* 37
2 b f One Cool Cat(USA) —Sagrada (GER) (Primo Dominie)
4427[7] 4889[12] 5553[10]

Dervis Aga (TUR) *S Mutlu* a111
4 b h Unaccounted For(USA) —Mesitas (GER) (Surumu (GER))
5587a[2]

Descargo *C R Dore* a11 23
5 ch m Delta Dancer—Secret Miss (Beveled (USA))
7815 [10]

Desdamona (IRE) *A Berry* 27
3 b f Desert Style(IRE) —Tattymulmona Queen (USA) (Royal Academy (USA))
1691[7] 1848[8] 2528[9] 3685[9] 4397[9]

Desert Aisling (IRE) *Edgar Byrne* a43 51
2 gr f Verglas(IRE) —Desert Sprite (IRE) (Tagula (IRE))
1742[7] 2889[9] 6617[11] 7139[6] 7335[9]

Desertar (FR) *P Demercastel* a89 95
3 b c Zamindar—Desert Melody (FR) (Green Desert (USA))
7621a[3]

Desert Auction (IRE) *R Hannon* a70 87
2 b c Desert Style(IRE) —Double Gamble (Ela-Mana-Mou)
1005[3] 1119[3] (1616) (1805) 2702[11] 2995[10] 3842[4] 4089[12] (4565) 5214[6] 5762[5] 6305[6] 7013[5]

Desert Ben (IRE) *C Grant* a62 68
6 b g Desert Prince(IRE) —Benefits Galore (IRE) (Brief Truce (USA))
2269[8] 2660[3] 3730[10] 4191[9] 4435[15] 4823[11] 5159[5]

Desert Bump *E F Vaughan* a70
3 b f Medicean—Greenfly (Green Desert (USA))
(251) 441[2]

Desert Code (USA) *David Hofmans* a112 120
5 ch h E Dubai(USA) —Chatta Code (USA) (Lost Code (USA))
7305a[13]

Desert Creek (IRE) *Sir Michael Stoute* 98
3 ch c Refuse To Bend(IRE) —Flagship (Rainbow Quest (USA))
(1751) ◆ (2273) ◆ 3049[21] 4296[5]

Desert Cry (IRE) *B Grizzetti* 98
3 b c Desert Prince(IRE) —Hataana (USA) (Robellino (USA))
1393a[7] 1904a[14] 2114a[10]

Desert Destiny *C Grant* a86 71
9 b g Desert Prince(IRE) —High Savannah (Rousillon (USA))
1690[8] 2043[4] 2362[11] (2656) 3059[2] 3544[5] 3679[5]

Desert Dreamer (IRE) *P D Evans* a85 88
8 b g Green Desert(USA) —Follow That Dream (Darshaan)
(70) 133[3] 266[3] (721) (868) 1169[3] 1248[2] 1403[2] 1723[10] (1894) 2269[2] 2883[5] 2976[4] (3335) 3523[2] 3801[7] 4293[15] 5206[5] 5349[4] 5746[5] 5884[8] 6212[8] (6278) 6702[6] 6944[8] 7133[9] 7252[10] 7437[8] 7662[2] 7801[2] 7845[6] 7891[3]

Desert Dust *H J Collingridge* a49 48
6 b g Vettori(IRE) —Dust (Green Desert (USA))
7519[5] 7680[7] 7709[7] 7839[6]

Desert Fairy *J W Unett* a50 46
3 b f Tobougg(IRE) —Regal Fairy (IRE) (Desert King (IRE))
2942[9] 3610[5] 6941[6] 7195[6] 7318[3] 7648[5] 7802[4]

Desert Falls *R M Whitaker* a86 84
3 b g Pyrus(USA) —Sally Traffic (River Falls)
1368[4] 1803[10] 2821[4] 3455[3] 3688[5] 4044[8] 4820[3] 5418[2] 5774[7] 7356[8]

Desert Fever *B W Hills* 72
3 b g Dubai Destination(USA) —Gaijin (Caerleon (USA))
1250[6] 3117[11] 3751[9] 4004[6]

Desert Forest (IRE) *J Howard Johnson* 70
2 b g Desert Style(IRE) —Minehostess (IRE) (Shernazar)
2467[11] 2788[2] 3494[2] 3971[2] 4651[4] 6821[10]

Desert Hawk *W M Brisbourne* a58 60
8 b g Cape Cross(IRE) —Milling (IRE) (In The Wings)
18[7] 107[5] 248[4] 469[11] 567[2] (578) 711[6] 775[5] 969[8] 1938[3] 2337[4] 2402[12] 3074[11] 3974[7] 4158[5] 5210[8] 5617[8] 6770[8] 7137[9] 7658[9] 7670[9]

Desert Hunter (IRE) *Micky Hammond* a54 57
6 b g Desert Story(IRE) —She-Wolff (IRE) (Pips Pride)
1243[9] 1276[7] (2532) 2804[7] 3457[2] 4070[5] 5289[8]

Desert Icon (IRE) *W J Knight* a69 86
3 b g Desert Style(IRE) —Gilded Vanity (IRE) (Indian Ridge)
2826[7] 3219[6] 3747[2] 4044[10] 5032[6] 5646[8] 6240[11]

Desert Kiss *W R Swinburn* a80 88
4 b m Cape Cross(IRE) —Kiss And Don'Tell (USA) (Rahy (USA))
1256[4] 2352[8] (2824) (3843) 4482[2] 5099[4] 5833[DSQ]

Desert Lark *K A Ryan* a48 44
4 b g Sakhee(USA) —Oyster Catcher (IRE) (Bluebird (USA))
210[9] 385[2] 537[4] 647[10]

Desert Leader (IRE) *W M Brisbourne* a53 39
8 b g Green Desert(USA) —Za Aamah (USA) (Mr Prospector (USA))
2684[10] 3721[10] 4857[4] 5210[10] 5680[10] 6342[7]

Desert Liaison *J Noseda* 62
2 b f Dansili—Toffee Nosed (Selkirk (USA))
4797[7]

Desert Light (IRE) *D Shaw* a63 43
8 b g Desert Sun—Nacote (IRE) (Mtoto)
27[7] 56[9] 153[6] 328[7] 474[5] 508[2]

Desert Links (SAF) *H J Brown* 101
6 b g Kahal—Selborne Park (SAF) (Home Guard (USA))
265a[15] 419a[13] 616a[9]

Desert Lord *K A Ryan* a101 111
9 b g Green Desert(USA) —Red Carnival (USA) (Mr Prospector (USA))
2094[8] 2704[17]

Desert Lover (IRE) *A M Hales* a51 50
7 b g Desert Prince(IRE) —Crystal Flute (Lycius (USA))
104[8] 221[7] 420[7] 537[3] 3322[6] 3851[13] 4640[13]

Desert Mile (IRE) *Ollie Pears* a80 76
6 b m Desert Style(IRE) —Maiskaya (IRE) (Mark Of Esteem (IRE))
7423[13] 7596[7] 7762[9]

Desert Nice (IRE) *G Angellotti* 88
3 b f Desert Style(IRE) —Annmary Girl (Zafonic (USA))
1659a[9]

Desert Nights (IRE) *D Windrif* a74 75
4 b m Desert Style(IRE) —Midnight Partner (IRE) (Marju (IRE))
5089a[0]

Desert Opal *C R Dore* a79 80
9 ch g Cadeaux Genereux—Nullarbor (Green Desert (USA))
83[6] 329[8] 431[4] 481[4]

Desert Party (USA) *Saeed Bin Suroor* a114
3 b c Street Cry(IRE) —Sage Cat (USA) (Tabasco Cat (USA))
(258a) (526a) ◆ 1009a[2] 1688a[14]

Desert Phantom (USA) *D M Simcock* 98
3 b c Arch(USA) —Junkinthetrunk (USA) (Top Account (USA))
7292[12]

Desert Poppy (IRE) *W R Swinburn* a76 73
2 b f Oasis Dream—Flanders (IRE) (Common Grounds)
5808[6] 6328[2] (6582) ◆ 7274[2] 7372[2]

Desert Pride *W S Kittow* a65 70
4 b g Desert Style(IRE) —Dalu (IRE) (Dancing Brave (USA))
1285[3] 1775[4] 2145[9] 2879[3] 3505[5] ◆ 4023[4] 6377[6] 6933[5] 7241[7]

Desert Rat (IRE) *Tim Vaughan* a43 67
5 b g Desert Sun—Virtue Rewarded (IRE) (Darshaan)
647[4]

Desert Realm (IRE) *A Al Raihe* a73 87
6 b g Desert Prince(IRE) —Fawaayid (USA) (Vaguely Noble)
433a[12]

Desert Recluse (IRE) *Pat Eddery* a41
2 ch c Redback—Desert Design (Desert King (IRE))
7024[10] 7376[9] 7885[8]

Desert Sage *R M Beckett* 73
2 ch f Selkirk(USA) —Prairie Flower (IRE) (Zieten (USA))
6592[2] ◆

Desert Sea (IRE) *D W P Arbuthnot* a103 103
6 b g Desert Sun—Sea Of Time (USA) (Gilded Time (USA))
(1007) 1790[4] (3642) 5173[18] 5823[11]

Desert Streak (FR) *C G Cox* a74 49
3 b c Green Desert(USA) —Niner's Home (USA) (Forty Niner (USA))
2640[10] (4749) 4859[2] 5584[4] 5991[7]

Desert Strike *P F I Cole* a79 77
3 b g Bertolini(USA) —Mary Jane (Tina's Pet)
(140) 1727[5] 2140[3] 2562[2] 3053[5] 6387[9] 6904[5] 7329[11]

Desert Vision *M W Easterby* a87 65
5 b g Alhaarth(IRE) —Fragrant Oasis (USA) (Rahy (USA))
4838[8] 5673[10] 6832[8] 7014[7] 7248[9] (7495) (7668) 7752[2] (7798) ◆ 7851[2]

Designated Decoy (USA) *D K Weld* a88 89
4 b g Danzig(USA) —Suitably Discreet (USA) (Mr Prospector (USA))
2290a[3]

Desire To Excel (IRE) *P F I Cole* a63 81
3 b g Desert Style(IRE) —Sanpala (Sanglamore (USA))
(1228) 2578[7] (2917) (3608) (4453)

De Soto *P R Webber* 70
8 b g Hernando(FR) —Vanessa Bell (IRE) (Lahib (USA))
3791[4] 4743[4]

Desperate Dan *A B Haynes* a83 83
8 b g Danzero(AUS) —Alzianah (Alzao (USA))
250[3] 518[9] (676) (756) 870[5] (1038) (1104) 1412[2] 1494[2] 1935[2] 1951[4] 2418[8] (2520) 2653[2] 2911[8] 3422[7] (3998) 4733[3] 4891[5] 5424[11] 5901[7] (6329) 6458[4] 6669[4] 6857[4] 7535[2]

Destination Aim *Saeed Bin Suroor* 77
2 b c Dubai Destination(USA) —Tessa Reef (IRE) (Mark Of Esteem (IRE))
4524[4] (5000)

Destination Finale *C Boutin* 63
2 b f Dubai Destination(USA) —Summer Sea (Bahhare (USA))
6148a[4]

Destination Place (IRE) *R Menichetti* 89
3 ch f Dubai Destination(USA) —Pleasure Place (IRE) (Compton Place)
1659a[11]

Destinationunknown (USA) *A J McCabe* a55
3 b f Arch(USA) —Private Funds (USA) (Private Terms (USA))
154[5] 564[5] 839[6] 1926[16]

Destiny Blue (IRE) *J A Osborne* a65
2 b c Danehill Dancer(IRE) —Arpege (IRE) (Sadler's Wells (USA))
7388[4]

Destiny Quest (USA) *A Selvaratnam* a51 72
3 b g Proud Citizen(USA) —Sunset Service (USA) (Deputy Minister (CAN))
524a[9]

Destiny Rules *John Berry*
2 br f Endoli(USA) —Up The Order (Forzando)
6542[7]

Destiny's Dancer *P C Haslam* 44
2 b f Dubai Destination(USA) —Cybinka (Selkirk (USA))
4187[5] 5036[6] 5253[5]

Destinys Dream (IRE) *Miss Tracy Waggott* 77
4 b m Mull Of Kintyre(USA) —Dream Of Jenny (Caerleon (USA))
1125[4] 1279[4] (1366) 1615[4] 2043[6] 3264[14] 3393[6] 3809[3] (4561) 5622[8] 6280[5] 6490[7]

Detonator (IRE) *M bin Shafya* a107 99
4 b g Fantastic Light(USA) —Narwala (Darshaan)
185a[11] 262a[9] 338a[8] 437a[14] 699a[12]

Deuce *Eve Johnson Houghton* a70 69
3 ch f Where Or When(IRE) —Justbetweenfriends (USA) (Diesis)
1407[12] 2540[2] 2881[7] 3454[8] 3923[2] 4867[2] (5131) ◆ 5579[2] 6121[3] 6432[5] 7005[7]

Deutschland (USA) *W P Mullins* a91 105
6 b g Red Ransom(USA) —Rhine Valley (USA) (Danzig (USA))
5173[8] 5824[5]

Devassa *C G Cox* a43 60
2 b f Reel Buddy(USA) —Signs And Wonders (Danehill (USA))
5060[6] 5380[3] 5714[2] 6185[4] 6494[7] 6970[7]

Develop U *W G M Turner* a39 37
2 b g Mutazayid(IRE) —Verdura (Green Desert (USA))
7120[10] 7474[10] 7616[5]

Dever Dream *W J Haggas* 68
2 b f Medicean—Sharplaw Venture (Polar Falcon (USA))
6061[5]

Deviant Ways *S Kirk*
3 b f Celtic Swing—Khwezi (Bering)
1585[11]

Devil May Care (USA) *Todd Pletcher* a110
2 b f Malibu Moon(USA) —Kelli's Ransom (USA) (Red Ransom (USA))
7283a[11]

Devil To Pay *J L Dunlop* 81
3 b g Red Ransom(USA) —My Way (IRE) (Marju (IRE))
1416[7] ◆ (1670) 2850[2] ◆ 4325[2] 4911[8] 6995[11]

Devil You Know (IRE) *D R C Elsworth* a83 86
3 b g Elusive City(USA) —Certainly Brave (Indian Ridge)
1592[4] (1840) 2148[4] (2826) 3219[2] 3688[4] 4849[8] 5001[8] 5974[4]

Devinius (IRE) *G A Swinbank* a17 66
4 ch m Choisir(AUS) —Vampress (IRE) (Marju (IRE))
2661[4] 4504[8] 4759[3] 5003[12] 5941[8] 6998[6]

De Viso (IRE) *R Gibson* 65
2 b c Sinndar(IRE) —Viva Maria (FR) (Kendor (FR))
5713a[5]

Devolution (IRE) *Miss C Dyson* a51
11 b g Distinctly North(USA) —Election Special (Chief Singer)
1568[14]

Devon Diva *J F Panvert* a49 4
3 b f Systematic—General Jane (Be My Chief (USA))
3228[11] 6934[12]

Devoted To You (IRE) *A P O'Brien* 101
2 b f Danehill Dancer(IRE) —Alleged Devotion (USA) (Alleged (USA))
4726a[2]

Devotee (USA) *Saeed Bin Suroor* a103 59
3 ch f Elusive Quality(USA) —Danuta (USA) (Sunday Silence (USA))
438a[10] (701a) 1698[13]

Devotion To Duty (IRE) *B W Hills* 83
3 b c Montjeu(IRE) —Charmante (USA) (Alydar (USA))
1289[4] 1822[7] (2447) 4518[6] 6681[11]

Deyas Dream *A M Balding* a66 75
3 b f Clodovil(IRE) —Dream On Deya (IRE) (Dolphin Street (FR))
1075[7] 1461[6] 1973[10] 2949[6]

D' Funnybone (USA) *Richard Dutrow Jr* a118
2 ch c D'Wildcat(USA) —Elbow (USA) (Woodman (USA))
7307a[13]

Dhaawiah (USA) *Saeed Bin Suroor* a89
3 b f Elusive Quality(USA) —Huja (IRE) (Alzao (USA))
4648[2] (5193) ◆ 5665[10]

Dhan Dhana (IRE) *W J Haggas* a50 48
2 b f Dubawi(IRE) —Kylemore (IRE) (Sadler's Wells (USA))
5752[11] 7050[8] 7183[11]

Dhania (IRE) *R A Teal* a70 73
3 b g Gulch(USA) —Novograd (USA) (Gentlemen (ARG))
1040[4] 1461[4] 1928[13] 2320[15] 3919[2] 4450[3] 4855[3] 5286[3] 6446[11] 6788[2]

Dhaular Dhar (IRE) *J S Goldie* a93 106
7 b h Indian Ridge—Pescara (IRE) (Common Grounds)
1861[3] 3091[26] 3818[10] 4297[18] 4796[6] ◆ 5249[7] 6270[20] 6482[8] 6675[4] 7294[14]

Dherghaam (IRE) *E A L Dunlop* 79
2 b c Exceed And Excel(AUS) —Alnasreya (IRE) (Machiavellian (USA))
5234[3] 6061[7] 6922[2]

Dhhamaan (IRE) *Mrs R A Carr* a61 70
4 b g Dilshaan—Safe Care (IRE) (Caerleon (USA))
576[7] 777[11] 886[11] 3227[4] ◆ 3720[10] 3929[3] 4859[7] 5225[10] 5842[12] 6221[9] 7678[10] 7754[10]

Dhushan *M A Jarvis* 88
3 b g Rainbow Quest(USA) —Abyaan (IRE) (Ela-Mana-Mou)
1328[4] (2323) 3090[12] 3778[7] 5419[12]

Diableside (FR) *Y Durepaire* 105
3 b c Diableneyev(USA) —Karnatika (FR) (Kendor (FR))
1207a[3] 1917a[8] 2096a[2]

Diabolical (USA) *Saeed Bin Suroor* a119 119
6 ch h Artax(USA) —Bonnie Byerly (USA) (Dayjur (USA))
770a[3] ◆ 1010a[3] 2116a[3] 3140[6]

Dialect *Mrs A J Perrett* a74 74
3 b f Diktat—Welsh Autumn (Tenby)
5449[12] 6621[11]

Dialogue *G A Harker* a89 84
3 b c Singspiel(IRE) —Zonda (Fabulous Dancer (USA))
2077[11] 2701[9] 3429[5] 4299[6] 6490[9]

Diamantino (FR) *B Goudot* 64
3 ch c Gold Away(IRE) —Good Blend (FR) (Darshaan)
6980a[F]

Diamond Affair (IRE) *M G Quinlan* a61 56
2 b f Namid—Subtle Affair (IRE) (Barathea (IRE))
1195[6] 1835[3] ◆ 2741[2] 3633[4] 4302[9] 4383[9] 5372[10] 6185[7] 6554[8]

Diamond Blade *T D Easterby* a71 59
3 ch g Needwood Blade—Branston Gem (So Factual (USA))
1563[2] 1852[3] 2265[3] 2574[2] 3175[10] 4514[4] 5041[5] 5145[6] 5599[4] (6221) (7418) (7681)

Diamond Daisy (IRE) *Mrs A Duffield* a62 76
3 b f Elnadim(USA) —Charlotte's Dancer (Kris)
1253[2] 1531[2] 2091[3] 2450[4] 3616[4] (3939) (4846) 4994[3] 5672[6] 6023[2] 6365[6]

Diamond Dee *M D I Usher* a46 48
3 ch f Deploy—Diamond Swan (Colonel Collins (USA))
1838[6] 2395[8]

Diamond Duchess (IRE) *D R Lanigan* a73 72
2 ch f Dubawi(IRE) —Tarakana (USA) (Shahrastani (USA))
3858[4] ◆ 4226[3] (4705) 5213[5] 5715[3] 6211[3] 6391[8]

Diamond Fire (IRE) *Adrian McGuinness* a59 56
5 b g King Charlemagne(USA) —Diamond Sun (Primo Dominie)
6414[5] (7462)

Diamondgeezer Luke (IRE) *F Costello* a46 68
2 b c War Chant(USA) —Banquise (IRE) (Last Tycoon)
1994a[6] 3895a[8] 6319a[18]

Diamond Jo (IRE) *Patrick Morris* 32
3 b f Johannesburg(USA) —Still As Sweet (IRE) (Fairy King (USA))
1825[10] 4347[11]

Diamond Johnny G (USA) *J R Best* a72 77
2 b c Omega Code(USA) —My Dancin Girl (USA) (Sun War Dancer (USA))
2631[2] ◆ 3046[6] 3779[10]

Diamond Lass (IRE) *R A Fahey* a48 68
4 b m Rock Of Gibraltar(IRE) —Keralba (USA) (Sheikh Albadou)
1333[3] ◆ 1778[7] 2263[10] 2569[5] 3653[2] 4822[8] 6023[9] 6900[9] 7403[5]

Diamond Laura *Mrs R A Carr* a78 85
2 gr f Lucky Story(USA) —Erracht (Emarati (USA))
1195[2] 1569[2] (1933) 2054[4] 2372[14] (3719) (4138) (4558) 4895[2] 5208[3] 5835[2] 6292[7]

Diamond Paula (IRE) *P D Evans* a26 26
3 b f Spartacus(IRE) —Balgren (IRE) (Ballad Rock)
4936[6] 5228[9]

Diamondrella *Angel Penna Jr* a99 118
5 b m Rock Of Gibraltar(IRE) —Tap Your Feet (USA) (Dixieland Band (USA))
7305a[11]

Diamond Surprise *R J Smith* a70 59
3 b f Mark Of Esteem(IRE) —Lucky Dip (Tirol)
149[2] 381[2] (421) 689[3] 6915[11] 7229[9]

Diamond Twister (USA) *J R Best* a78 72
3 b c Omega Code(USA) —King's Pact (USA) (Slewacide (USA))
69[3] 397[4] (529) 962[2] 1280[6] 1431[4] 1643[6] 1928[5] 2432[5] 2850[9] 3159[2] 3693[7] 4004[10] 4581a[2] 5575[4] 5723[6] 6257[7] 6719[2] 7048[8] 7364[8] 7524[5]

Diam Queen (GER) *L M Cumani* a85 69
2 b f Lando(GER) —Dance Solo (Sadler's Wells (USA))
(5722) 6805[2] (7434) ◆

Diana's Choice (SAF) *M F De Kock* a98 108
5 b m Windrush(USA) —Fly To The Stars (SAF) (Desert Team (USA))
264a[3] (433a) (637a) ◆ 770a[4] 2948[4] 3824[7] 4297[14]

Diane's Choice *Miss Gay Kelleway* a59 78
6 ch m Komaite(USA) —Ramajana (USA) (Shadeed (USA))
2124[5] 2349[7] 2460[6] 2712[7] 3465[3] 3720[3] 3947[7] 4222[2] (4692) 4929[7] 5374[7] 5678[9] 6038[3] 6335[4] 6933[4] 7239[4] 7438[4] 7679[10] 7880[5]

Dianeva (FR) *M Boutin* a78 87
3 b f Diableneyev(USA) —Grioun (FR) (Kaldoun (FR))
7385a[2]

Diapason (IRE) *Tom Dascombe* a72 72
3 b f Mull Of Kintyre(USA) —Suaad (IRE) (Fools Holme (USA))
2664^{3} (3630) 3921^{8} 4540^{10} 5940^{8} 6421^{7} 7715^{6} (7861) ◆

Dice (IRE) *L M Cumani* a79 80
3 b c Kalanisi(IRE) —Rain Dancer (IRE) (Sadler's Wells (USA))
1422^{2} 2126^{7} 2567^{6} (3674) 4911^{2} 5593^{6} 6027^{2} 6543^{2}

Dicey Affair *G L Moore* a65 58
3 b f Medicean—Lucky Dice (Perugino (USA))
2827^{14} 3299^{7} 3815^{4} 4240^{7} 5634^{11} 6005^{10} 6442^{6} 6787^{6} 6967^{10} 7774^{6} 7877^{4}

Dichoh *M Madgwick* a86 67
6 b g Diktat—Hoh Dancer (Indian Ridge)
(195) 536^{2} (765) (958) 1731^{9} 3211^{9} 3501^{2} 3977^{8} 4438^{7} 4731^{5} 5779^{2} (6399) (6783) 6967^{4} 7364^{3} 7575^{6} 7664^{4}

Dickie Deano *J M Bradley* a22
5 b g Sooty Tern—Chez Bonito (IRE) (Persian Bold)
6471^{11}

Dickie Le Davoir *R C Guest* a64 87
5 b g Kyllachy—Downeaster Alexa (USA) (Red Ryder (USA))
326^{7} 561^{5} 1169^{9} 1510^{13} 2130^{4} 2418^{3} 2769^{5} 3057^{4} 3224^{5} 3562^{2} (3706) 3855^{8} 4072^{8} 5225^{3} 5697^{8} 6233^{11} 7418^{5} 7503^{4} 7555^{6} 7681^{8}

Dick Turpin (IRE) *R Hannon* 112
2 b c Arakan(USA) —Merrily (Sharrood (USA))
(2771) (3865) (4487) ◆ (5274a) 6524a^{5} 6849^{6}

Dictation *Mrs Valerie Keatley* a36 44
7 bb m Diktat—Monaiya (Shareef Dancer (USA))
275^{8}

Diddums *P S McEntee* a84 77
3 b g Royal Applause—Sahara Shade (USA) (Shadeed (USA))
2336^{4} 2826^{9} 3341^{13} 3924^{10} 4707^{5} 5155^{3} (5477) 5805^{5} 6201^{8} 7028^{6} 7330^{6} 7394^{9} 7431^{7} 7519^{8} 7890^{10}

Diego Rivera *P J Makin* a69 72
4 b g Orpen(USA) —Manuka Too (IRE) (First Trump)
1576^{8} 959^{4} 1080^{8} (1413) 1833^{7} 3075^{7} 3722^{7} 6123^{3} 6437^{6} 6904^{7}

Die Haard *J R Gask* a59
3 ch g Haafhd—Decision Maid (USA) (Diesis)
6442^{10}

Dies Solis *I Semple* 56
2 ch c Exceed And Excel(AUS) —Rose Of America (Brief Truce (USA))
6047^{5} ◆ 6408^{5} 7167^{6}

Dig Deep (IRE) *J J Quinn* a79 86
7 b g Entrepreneur—Diamond Quest (Rainbow Quest (USA))
1685^{15} 2267^{9} 2770^{4} 3268^{4} 3787^{7} 4878^{7} (5182) 5418^{12} 6072^{8} 7191^{5} 7506^{2}

Diggeratt (USA) *R A Fahey* a71 77
3 rg f Maria's Mon(USA) —Miss Exhilaration (USA) (Gulch (USA))
2198^{7} 2821^{5} 3341^{2} 3843^{6} 4140^{6} (4589) (4821) 5016^{3} 5465^{5} 5779^{3} 6370^{8}

Digger Derek (IRE) *R A Fahey* a62 73
3 b g Key Of Luck(USA) —Carson Dancer (USA) (Carson City (USA))
1056^{4} 1280^{5} 1792^{9} 3808^{3} 4348^{6} 4892^{8} 5331^{4} 6052^{4} 6703^{7}

Digit *B Smart* a23 62
3 ch f Reel Buddy(USA) —Compact Disc (IRE) (Royal Academy (USA))
1924^{16} 2624^{3} 4196^{11} 5621^{10}

Digital *M R Channon* a80 85
12 ch g Safawan—Heavenly Goddess (Soviet Star (USA))
1150^{5} 1403^{4} 1668^{5} 2219^{4} 2359^{11} 2929^{9} 2980^{10} 3860^{3} 4268^{6} 4604^{10} 5073^{12}

Dijeerr (USA) *Saeed Bin Suroor* a110 113
5 b h Danzig(USA) —Sharp Minister (CAN) (Deputy Minister (CAN))
182a^{11} 265a^{16} (610a) ◆ 1008a^{9} 1929^{5} (5855)

Diktalina *W R Muir* a64 56
3 b f Diktat—Oiselina (FR) (Linamix (FR))
1570^{7} 2204^{11} 3157^{2} (3919) 4206^{4} 4917^{5} 5382^{7} 6097^{2} 6384^{7} 6917^{7}

Dikta Melody (FR) *P Demercastel* 80
2 br f Diktat—Desert Melody (FR) (Green Desert (USA))
5956a^{7}

Diktaram *J R Weymes* a45 46
3 b g Diktat—Aries (GER) (Big Shuffle (USA))
621^{5} 1231^{6} 1829^{8} 3157^{8} 3954^{7}

Diktatorship (IRE) *Jennie Candlish* a54 50
6 b g Diktat—Polka Dancer (Dancing Brave (USA))
449^{2} 567^{3} 1533^{3} 7649^{5} 7750^{6}

Diktat Queen *Rae Guest* 75
3 b f Diktat—Sakura Queen (IRE) (Woodman (USA))
2298^{6} (5789) 6621^{9} 6937^{8}

Dillenda *T D Easterby* 56
3 bb f Lend A Hand—Samadilla (IRE) (Mujadil (USA))
1725^{12} 2786^{13}

Dilli Dancer *G D Blake* a54 64
4 b m Dansili—Cup Of Kindness (USA) (Secretariat (USA))
2205^{5} 2820^{4} 4199^{6} 5429^{15} 6213^{4} 6456^{7} 6777^{5}

Dimaire *D Haydn Jones* a64 64
2 b f Kheleyf(USA) —Dim Ots (Alhijaz)
2825^{9} 3715^{7} 4688^{6} 5866^{2} 6354^{2} 6932^{4} 7331^{3} 7748^{2}

Diman Waters (IRE) *E J Alston* 65
2 br g Namid—Phantom Waters (Pharly (FR))
2195^{5} 2940^{4} 6796^{10} 7242^{6}

Dimashq *P T Midgley* a33 61
7 b m Mtoto—Agwaas (IRE) (Rainbow Quest (USA))
1000^{17} 1102^{6} 2159^{5} 2629^{6} (3068) 3499^{5} (3974) 4350^{8} 4462^{5} 4927^{3} 6845^{2} 7085^{9} 7336^{12}

Diminuto *M D I Usher* a80 78
5 b m Iron Mask(USA) —Thicket (Wolfhound (USA))
146^{8} 242^{9} 294^{12} 575^{6} 811^{12} 946^{9}

Dimoitoo (FR) *J Boisnard* 55
2 u f (USA) — (USA) (Bluebird (USA))
6576a^{4}

Diner En Ville (FR) *F Pardon* a65
5 ch m Barathea(IRE) —Singita (FR) (Highest Honor (FR))
6981a^{5}

Dingaan (IRE) *A M Balding* a93 88
6 b g Tagula(IRE) —Boughtbyphone (Warning)
2050^{10} 2434^{13} 2927^{3} 3335^{4} 3752^{2} (3996) 5243^{4} 5745^{6} 6429^{9}

Dinger Belle (IRE) *Andrew Oliver* a73 69
2 b f Captain Rio—Shoshana (IRE) (Perugino (USA))
6401a^{2}

Dinkie Short *W R Muir* a56 62
2 b g Reset(AUS) —Spring Sunrise (Robellino (USA))
4908^{11} 5428^{6} 5801^{6} 6431^{7} 6586^{10}

Dinky Deb *D K Ivory* a14
2 ch f Captain Rio—Debinnair (FR) (Wolfhound (USA))
1637^{7} 1934^{6} 2457^{7}

Dinkys Diamond (IRE) *B Ellison* 54
2 b g Modigliani(USA) —Along Came Molly (Dr Fong (USA))
3392^{9} 4308^{6} 4595^{5} 6046^{10}

Dinner Date *T Keddy* a76 64
7 ch g Groom Dancer(USA) —Misleading Lady (Warning)
157^{4} 318^{8} 878^{9} 1261^{8} 1945^{8} 5003^{13} 5266^{7} 5484^{3} 6017^{3} 6288^{2} (6720) 7054^{3} (7229) 7684^{7}

Dirar (IRE) *Gordon Elliott* a96 95
4 b g King's Best(USA) —Dibiya (IRE) (Caerleon (USA))
6851^{13} (7720) ◆

Directa's Digger (IRE) *M J Scudamore* 76
5 b h Daggers Drawn(USA) —Chita Rivera (Chief Singer)
2445^{10}

Direct Debit (IRE) *M Wellings* a84 66
6 b g Dansili—Dimple (Fairy King (USA))
17^{7} 218^{5} 392^{11} 1415^{10} 2245^{3} 2880^{7} 3112^{4} 3689^{11} (Dead)

Director's Chair *Miss J Feilden* a66 72
4 b g Catcher In The Rye(IRE) —Capegulch (USA) (Gulch (USA))
597^{7} (1014) 1945^{7} 2851^{4} 4054^{12} 4932^{13} 7440^{6}

Directorship *P R Chamings* 83
3 br c Diktat—Away To Me (Exit To Nowhere (USA))
2074^{14} (4246) 4902^{6} 5834^{6} 6740^{10}

Diriculous *T G Mills* a107 94
5 b g Diktat—Sheila's Secret (IRE) (Bluebird (USA))
1608^{3} 2059^{16} 2385^{6} 3318^{7} 4500^{3} 5001^{7} 5646^{5} 6631^{7} 6949^{9}

Discanti (IRE) *T D Easterby* a58 84
4 ch g Distant Music(USA) —Gertie Laurie (Lomond (USA))
1334^{3} 1565^{6} 2095^{7} 2363^{3} 2591^{6} 3236^{4} 4464^{5} (4891) 5436^{13} 6647^{7}

Dishdasha (IRE) *Mrs A M Thorpe* a81
7 b g Desert Prince(IRE) —Counterplot (IRE) (Last Tycoon)
(126) 202^{2} (497) ◆ 848^{4}

Dispol Antonio (IRE) *P T Midgley* 54
2 b g Antonius Pius(USA) —Brief Fairy (IRE) (Brief Truce (USA))
2099^{15} 2610^{9} 2997^{9} 3605^{5} 4190^{5} 4503^{6}

Dispol Diva *P T Midgley* a64 67
3 b f Deportivo—Kingston Rose (GER) (Robellino (USA))
520^{4} 620^{6} (883) 1063^{2} (1282) 1614^{5} 1829^{3} 2371^{6} 2667^{9} 3610^{2} 3976^{3} 4506^{5}

Dispol Fay (IRE) *P T Midgley* a32 32
2 b f Fayruz—Hever Rosina (Efisio)
6841^{7} 7079^{9} 7331^{9} 7637^{7}

Dispol Grand (IRE) *P T Midgley* a72 72
3 b g Raise A Grand(IRE) —Hever Rosina (Efisio)
685^{3} ◆ 966^{2} 1232^{6} 1469^{2} 1644^{4} 1720^{3} (2394) 2454^{2} (2726) 3704^{4} 4289^{5} 4653^{4} 4849^{7} 4999^{4} 5405^{11} 5517^{6}

Dispol Kabira *D W Thompson* 55
2 b f Kheleyf(USA) —Abir (Soviet Star (USA))
1277^{12} 1719^{6} (1827) 2100^{6} 2996^{6} 3542^{4} 4188^{7} 5303^{6} 5976^{12} 6554^{7} 6590^{8} 6819^{8} 7056^{9}

Dispol Keasha *T D Barron* 77
2 ch f Kheleyf(USA) —Easy Mover (IRE) (Bluebird (USA))
1344^{2} ◆ (1645) 2054^{6} 2714^{4}

Dispol Kylie (IRE) *P T Midgley* a46 84
3 b f Kheleyf(USA) —Professional Mom (USA) (Spinning World (USA))
685^{8} 1368^{9} 1627^{4} 2726^{3} 3173^{4} 3355^{4} 3973^{7} 4514^{5} 4942^{3} 5626^{5}

Distant Dreamer (USA) *Rae Guest* a9 12
3 ch f Rahy(USA) —Khazayin (USA) (Bahri (USA))
3764^{15} 5110^{5} 5965^{9} 7726^{9}

Distant Memories (IRE) *T P Tate* 108
3 b g Falbrav(IRE) —Amathia (IRE) (Darshaan)
2275^{2} 2935^{7} (4102) (5551)

Distant Pleasure *M Dods* 65
5 b m Diktat—Our Pleasure (IRE) (Lake Coniston (IRE))
2245^{6} 3077^{8} 4070^{7} 5332^{6} 6984^{9}

Distant Sun (USA) *Miss L A Perratt* a89 80
5 b g Distant View(USA) —The Great Flora (USA) (Unaccounted For (USA))
4134^{8} 4751^{8} 5343^{8} 5946^{7} 6159^{4} (6314) 6413^{16} 7119^{3}

Distant Vision (IRE) *H A McWilliams* a40 54
6 br m Distant Music(USA) —Najeyba (Indian Ridge)
1038^{8} 1689^{8} 1921^{2} 2158^{4} ◆ 2529^{3} 2625^{7} 2964^{8} 3111^{4} 3570^{2} 4823^{8} 6856^{5}

Di Stefano *M R Channon* 98
2 b g Bahamian Bounty—Marisa (GER) (Desert Sun)
1323^{4} 1669^{4} (2568) 2995^{3} 3583^{2} 5198^{11} 5521^{3} 5795^{11} 6398^{5}

Distinctive *B Smart* 101
2 b f Tobougg(IRE) —Blue Azure (USA) (American Chance (USA))
4331^{3} ◆ (5439) (6090) 6852^{7}

Distinctive Image (USA) *R Hollinshead* a101 84
4 b h Mineshaft(USA) —Dock Leaf (USA) (Woodman (USA))
(761) ◆ 915^{2} ◆ 1117^{2} ◆ 1696^{10} 2146^{4} 4197^{4} 4561^{2} (4840) ◆

Distinctly Game *K A Ryan* a90 86
7 b g Mind Games—Distinctly Blu (IRE) (Distinctly North (USA))
20^{5} 141^{4} (281) 533^{4} 600^{2} 780^{4} 892^{3} 1313^{10}

Ditzy Diva *B G Powell* 24
3 b f Imperial Dancer—Runs In The Family (Distant Relative)
5531^{15}

Diva Cattiva *B Grizzetti* 99
3 b f Lujain(USA) —Silver Cache (USA) (Silver Hawk (USA))
1659a^{12} 2310a^{6} 3186a^{11}

Diva Dolce (IRE) *Kevin Prendergast* a71 79
2 b f Domedriver(IRE) —Danzelline (Danzero (AUS))
1993a^{4}

Divertimenti (IRE) *S R Bowring* a74 55
5 b g Green Desert(USA) —Ballet Shoes (IRE) (Ela-Mana-Mou)
31^{4} 157^{7} (355) 387^{6} 573^{4} 2459^{8} 4202^{8} 5676^{6} 5750^{4} 6588^{10} 6918^{12} 7839^{3}

Divinatore *D Haydn Jones* a68 65
3 b g Sakhee(USA) —Divina Mia (Dowsing (USA))
201^{4} 659^{2} 1516^{2} 2038^{7} 2892^{10} 3922^{4} 7481^{5} 7699^{5}

Divine Comedy (FR) *D Smaga* 103
3 b f Daylami(IRE) —Lady Time (FR) (Orpen (USA))
1267a^{4} 2754a^{5} 4969a^{6} 5562a^{9}

Divine Design (IRE) *Seamus G O'Donnell* a18 48
5 b m Barathea(IRE) —Tortue (IRE) (Turtle Island (IRE))
4344^{8}

Divine Force *M Wigham* a68 56
3 b g Bertolini(USA) —Malcesine (IRE) (Auction Ring (USA))
160^{5} 298^{2} 394^{5} 673^{3} 797^{6} 3505^{15} 3989^{9} 6926^{5} 7521^{2} (7602) ◆

Divine Lady (FR) *Mme P Alexanian* 50
2 b f Divine Light(JPN) —Lonesome Dove (FR) (Petit Loup (USA))
4368a^{8}

Divine Spirit *M Dods* a63 84
8 b g Foxhound(USA) —Vocation (IRE) (Royal Academy (USA))
1685^{12} 2095^{2} 2228^{11} 2770^{5} 3607^{6} 3765^{7} 4141^{9} 4891^{11} 6010^{8} 6635^{8} 6857^{11} 7081^{10}

Divine Summer (FR) *C Boutin* 20
2 b f Polish Summer—Maldiviane (FR) (Hernando (FR))
6928a^{11}

Divine White *G P Enright* a62 45
6 ch m College Chapel—Snowy Mantle (Siberian Express (USA))
487^{3} 746^{7} 920^{2} 2134^{12} 2353^{8} 4533^{14} 4905^{8} 5971^{4} 6551^{12} 7869^{10}

Dixey *M A Jarvis* a93 96
4 br m Diktat—Hoh Dancer (Indian Ridge)
1210^{5} 1640^{7} 2927^{4} 3928^{7} 4560^{2} 5313^{4} 6092^{9} 6757^{5} 7032^{2} 7294^{10}

Dixie Bright (USA) *J G Given* a74 61
2 bb g Dixie Union(USA) —Tell Me Now (USA) (A.P. Indy (USA))
1610^{11} (3226) ◆ 4000^{5} 4858^{8} 5369^{11} 6227^{9} 6639^{10} 7056^{2}

Dixie Music (IRE) *A P O'Brien* 101
3 b c Montjeu(IRE) —Dixielake (IRE) (Lake Coniston (IRE))
1388a^{5}

Dixi Heights *J R Boyle* a18 59
2 b f Golan(IRE) —Ninfa Of Cisterna (Polish Patriot (USA))
2595^{6} 3692^{6} 4427^{3} 5526^{8} 6589^{14}

Diyakalanie (FR) *Y De Nicolay* a101 105
5 b m Ashkalani(IRE) —Diyawara (IRE) (Doyoun)
846a^{2} 1144a^{6} 1597a^{8} 2428a^{12}

Dizziness (USA) *R Charlton* 65
2 b f Stormy Atlantic(USA) —Danzante (USA) (Danzig (USA))
3356^{6}

Djalalabad (FR) *Mrs C A Dunnett* a64 53
5 b m King's Best(USA) —Daraydala (IRE) (Royal Academy (USA))
(984) 1194^{15} 1413^{5} 1535^{6} 1959^{7} 2223^{10} 2686^{4} 2924^{9} 3470^{5} 5998^{14} 6213^{6} 6719^{3} 6945^{4} 7051^{9} 7438^{3} 7652^{7} 7787^{6}

Django (SWE) *Jessica Long* a55 96
6 b g Acatenango(GER) —Praeriens Drottning (SWE) (Elmaamul (USA))
4585a^{4} 5933a^{9}

Django Reinhardt *J R Gask* a59
3 b g Tobougg(IRE) —Alexander Ballet (Mind Games)
3743^{9} 4199^{15} 5809^{12}

Do Be Brave (IRE) *Paul Mason* a58
3 ch g Kheleyf(USA) —Fear Not (IRE) (Alzao (USA))
951^{9} 1656^{9} 3302^{10} 3985^{8}

Dobravany (IRE) *K A Morgan* a52 60
5 b g Danehill Dancer(IRE) —Eadaoin (USA) (King Of Kings (IRE))
216^{7} 254^{10} 482^{5} 802^{2} 969^{3} 3552^{5}

Doc Jones (IRE) *P D Evans* a74 78
3 ch g Docksider(USA) —Quick Return (Polish Precedent (USA))
1491^{5} 1840^{4} 1972^{2} (2543) 3028^{10} 3804^{4} 4148^{5} 4494^{2} 5154^{5} 5183^{7} 5677^{3} 5719^{5} 5901^{5}

Docksil *B Grizzetti* a40 99
5 b m Docksider(USA) —Simil (USA) (Apalachee (USA))
1394a^{9} 1905a^{11}

Docofthebay (IRE) *J A Osborne* a103 112
5 ch g Docksider(USA) —Baize (Efisio)
278^{3} 527a^{12} 640a^{9} 913^{7} 997^{9} 2606^{3} 4486^{3} 4768^{5} 5200^{7} 6480^{30}

Docteur Carter (FR) *J De Chevigny* a73
2 b c Meshaheer(USA) —Urgence (FR) (Snurge)
6979a^{5}

Doctor Crane (USA) *J H M Gosden* a83 98
3 b g Doneraile Court(USA) —Sharons Song (USA) (Badger Land (USA))
1489^{4} (2296)

Doctor Delta *M Brittain* a48 46
4 b h Dr Fong(USA) —Delta Tempo (IRE) (Bluebird (USA))
174^{4} 221^{8} 275^{4} 368^{11} 2609^{9}

Doctor Dino (FR) *R Gibson* 121
7 ch h Muhtathir—Logica (IRE) (Priolo (USA))
1012a^{8}

Doctor Fremantle *Sir Michael Stoute* 120
4 b h Sadler's Wells(USA) —Summer Breeze (Rainbow Quest (USA))
(1799) 3139^{7} (3781) (6056) 6850^{11}

Doctor Hilary *A B Haynes* a83 62
7 b g Mujahid(USA) —Agony Aunt (Formidable (USA))
7518^{11} 7673^{10}

Doctor Of Music (IRE) *B Smart* 43
3 ch g Dr Fong(USA) —Sublime Beauty (USA) (Caerleon (USA))
4276^{12} 4505^{6} 5010^{8} 6184^{13}

Doctor Parkes *E J Alston* 89
3 b g Diktat—Lucky Parkes (Full Extent (USA))
(1824) 2443^{9} 2915^{4} (4601) 6283^{11}

Doctor Zhivago *M Johnston* a76
2 b c Shamardal(USA) —Balalaika (Sadler's Wells (USA))
(7638) ◆

Dodaa (USA) *N Wilson* a61 61
6 b g Dayjur(USA) —Ra'A (USA) (Diesis)
67^{7} 250^{5} 431^{7} 710^{6} 832^{5} ◆ 1182^{3} 1564^{8} 7839^{11}

Doggerbank (IRE) *H R A Cecil* 89
3 b f Oasis Dream—Discreet Brief (IRE) (Darshaan)
3214^{2} (3791) 4319^{2} (4948)

Dogubeyi (TUR) *B Akbulut* a87
4 b h Mountain Cat(USA) —Thunder Best (TUR) (The Best (TUR))
5587a^{10}

Dohasa (IRE) *G M Lyons* a113 110
4 b g Bold Fact(USA) —Zara's Birthday (IRE) (Waajib)
433a^{3} ◆ 638a^{3} 700a^{3} 1138a^{2} 1989^{10} 2870a^{2} 4297^{17} 6530a^{2} (7768)

Dollar Chick (IRE) *Noel Meade* a93 85
5 b m Dansili—Dollar Bird (IRE) (Kris)
1996a^{8} 4923a^{9} 5490a^{25}

Dollar Express (USA) *J Noseda* a62
3 ch g Broken Vow(USA) —Feminine (USA) (Tale Of The Cat (USA))
160^{6} ◆ 394^{6} 658^{4} 865^{4} 978^{4}

Dolled Up (IRE) *Robert Collet* 111
2 b f Whipper(USA) —Belle De Cadix (IRE) (Law Society (USA))
(3667a) 4366a^{3} 5299a^{4} 6044a^{2} 7231a^{3}

Dolly No Hair *N Wilson* a43 65
4 ch g Reel Buddy(USA) —Champagne Grandy (Vaigly Great)
2594^{6} 3124^{11} 4656^{8} 4845^{9} 6415^{8} 6880^{6} 7270^{9}

Dolly Penrose *M R Channon* 87
4 b m Hernando(FR) —Mistinguett (IRE) (Doyoun)
1519^{3} 1863^{5} 2486^{8} ◆ 2720^{2} 3146^{2} 3850^{4} (4078) 4458^{9} 4769^{6} 5410^{6} 5823^{6} 6536^{2} 7148^{7}

Dolly Will Do *N P Mulholland* 44
2 b f Bahamian Bounty—Desert Flower (Green Desert (USA))
1090^{10} 1782^{5} 2201^{8} 3987^{11} 4688^{8} 5498^{12}

Dolores Ortiz (IRE) *S C Williams* 56
3 b f High Chaparral(IRE) —Ma N'Ieme Biche (USA) (Key To The Kingdom (USA))
1297^{8} 2139^{2} 2640^{9} 4157^{9} 4719^{11}

Dolphin Rock *Mrs G S Rees* a67 68
2 b g Mark Of Esteem(IRE) —Lark In The Park (IRE) (Grand Lodge (USA))
1867^{9} 3226^{3} 3571^{5} 4371^{4} 4858^{2} 5207^{4} 5682^{6} 6793^{3} 6901^{2}

Domada *W J H Ratcliffe*
4 ch m Domedriver(IRE) —Estimada (Mark Of Esteem (IRE))
793^{14} 2229^{12}

Dome Rocket *W J Knight* a79 83
3 b g Domedriver(IRE) —Sea Ridge (Slip Anchor)
1464^{5} 2178^{4} (2681) 3321^{2} (4008) 4455^{9} 6209^{8} 6594^{9}

Domesday (UAE) *T T Clement* a51 43
8 b g Cape Cross(IRE) —Deceive (Machiavellian (USA))
4158^{4} 4667^{11} 6392^{7}

Domination *H Morrison* a37 70
2 b g Motivator—Soliza (IRE) (Intikhab (USA))
6697^{4} 7034^{10} 7266^{6}

Do More Business (IRE) *P M Phelan* a65 67
2 b g Dubai Destination(USA) —Tokyo Song (USA) (Stravinsky (USA))
(2325) 3522^{8} 4080^{8} 4868^{5} 5636^{4} 5967^{6}

Dom Polski *W R Swinburn* a66
3 b g Polish Precedent(USA) —Camerlata (Common Grounds)
2142^{4} ◆ 4981^{4} 5572^{5} ◆ 6124^{8} 6608^{3}

Dona Alba (IRE) *J L Dunlop* 98
4 b m Peintre Celebre(USA) —Fantastic Fantasy (IRE) (Lahib (USA))
1460^{3} 2003^{4} 2475^{11} 4404^{9} 5137^{5} ◆

Donair *P F I Cole* 43
2 ch c Nayef(USA) —Darwinia (GER) (Acatenango (GER))
6754^{10} ◆ 7121^{10}

Donard Lodge (IRE) *J Balding* a53 40
4 b m Elnadim(USA) —Knockatotaun (Spectrum (IRE))
198^{6} 480^{8}

Donativum *Saeed Bin Suroor* 114
3 rg g Cadeaux Genereux—Miss Universe (IRE) (Warning)
2278[4] 3011[5] (3649a) 4521[5] 5496a[5] 6448[4] 6848[3]

Don Carlos (GER) *A P O'Brien* 100
2 b c Galileo(IRE) —Dapprima (GER) (Shareef Dancer (USA))
7404a[4]

Doncaster Rover (USA) *D H Brown* a84 109
3 b g War Chant(USA) —Rebridled Dreams (USA) (Unbridled's Song (USA))
9121[2] 2485[2] (3621) 4087[3] (4559) ◆ 5079a[7]

Doncosaque (IRE) *P Howling* a87 83
3 b c Xaar—Darabela (IRE) (Desert King (IRE))
101[3] 209[3] 532[4] (595) 764[3] 1303[6] 1707[3] 2210[7] 2535[5] 3220[6]

Donegal (USA) *Robert Alan Hennessy* a92 113
4 b g Menifee(USA) —Vickey's Echo (CAN) (Clever Trick (USA))
2425a[7]

Don Fanucci (FR) *M Boutin*
2 b c Marchand De Sable(USA) —Easy To Go (FR) (Sillery (USA))
3935a[0]

Dongola (IRE) *P Winkworth* 13
2 b f Xaar—Laura Margaret (Persian Bold)
1569[12]

Donna Elvira *R Hannon* a15 72
2 b f Doyen(IRE) —Impatiente (USA) (Vaguely Noble)
6727[2] ◆ 7106[8]

Donny Bowl *I W McInnes* 26
4 b h Presidium—Perpetuo (Mtoto)
5971[6] 6755[17]

Don Pele (IRE) *R A Harris* a78 77
7 b g Monashee Mountain(USA) —Big Fandango (Bigstone (IRE))
(35) 89[2] 189[6] 314[3] 401[4] 589[4] (710) (762) 843[3] 882[2] 1072[5] 2137[5] 2980[3] 3252[7] 3691[9] 3956[9] 4167[4] 4428[4] 5065[8] 5576[5] 5836[6] 7815[3] 7839[9] 7890[4]

Don Picolo *R Curtis* a59 39
4 b g Bertolini(USA) —Baby Come Back (IRE) (Fayruz)
4891[2]

Don Pietro *R Curtis* a77 74
6 b g Bertolini(USA) —Silver Spell (Aragon)
244[4] 357[3] 489[6] 765[2] 872[4] 1314[5] (4220) 4563[4] (5243)

Don Renato (CHI) *J Barton* a109
6 ch h Edgy Diplomat(USA) —Tabla Redonda (CHI) (Braka (USA))
184a[3] ◆ 417a[6] 771a[5] 1008a[3]

Don Salsa (FR) *C Diard* a53 76
3 b c Kingsalsa(USA) —Midzan (FR) (Midyan (USA))
3417a[6] 6606a[8]

Don Stefano *W G M Turner*
2 b g Deportivo—Molly Music (Music Boy)
5371[11]

Dontbugthebunny (USA) *George Baker* a50 50
2 ch f Theatrical(IRE) —Stravinia (USA) (Stravinsky (USA))
3686[4] 5319[2] 6122[5] 7139[7] 7334[5] 7419[3]

Don't Panic (IRE) *P W Chapple-Hyam* 110
5 ch g Fath(USA) —Torrmana (IRE) (Ela-Mana-Mou)
997[RR] 1600[RR]

Dontpaytheferryman (USA) *B Ellison* a59 57
4 ch g Wiseman's Ferry(USA) —Expletive Deleted (USA) (Dr Blum (USA))
58[2] 107[3] 377[3] 4351[3] 4529[3] 5294[3] 6025[11] 6770[6]

Dontriskit *J L Spearing* a15
3 ch f Bertolini(USA) —Risky Valentine (Risk Me (FR))
154[9]

Don't Stop Me Now (IRE) *John Joseph Hanlon* a71 70
4 b m Catcher In The Rye(IRE) —Persian Flower (Persian Heights)
(1102) 5857[7] 6785[3]

Don't Tell Mary (IRE) *Tom Dascombe* 97
2 b f Starcraft(NZ) —Only In Dreams (Polar Falcon (USA))
(1981) ◆ (2372) ◆ 3015[10] 6660[14] 7033[6]

Dontuwishitwereso *P W D'Arcy* a69 43
3 b g Kyllachy—Prospering (Prince Sabo)
796[2] (881) 1068[7] 1656[7] 2137[7] 4275[12] 5326[5] 7703[5] 7787[5] 7869[4]

Doon Haymer (IRE) *I Semple* 85
4 b g Barathea(IRE) —Mutige (Warning)
3481[3] (4040) 4532[4] 5160[13] 5361[6]

Doonigan (IRE) *G Brown* a17 51
5 b g Val Royal(FR) —Music In My Life (IRE) (Law Society (USA))
1651[7] 2127[14]

Doorock (IRE) *S T Nolan* a52 60
5 b g Redback—Prime Time Girl (Primo Dominie)
6825[10]

Dorback *H Candy* 87
2 ch c Kyllachy—Pink Supreme (Night Shift (USA))
(3403) ◆ 4883[6] 6179[2] 6677[7] 7150[5]

Doriana (FR) *A De Royer-Dupre* 102
3 gr f Kendor(FR) —Urgence (FR) (Snurge)
1918a[8] 6579a[6]

Doric Echo *B Smart* a32 78
3 b g Bertolini(USA) —Latour (Sri Pekan (USA))
2841[5] 3341[12] 4333[13] 4878[5] 5333[4] 6014[3] 6361[10] 6824[8]

Doric Lady *J A R Toller* a86 85
4 b m Kyllachy—Tanasie (Cadeaux Genereux)
1572[4] (2334) 2886[4] (3565) 4096[9] 5263[9] 6171[7] 6964[7] (7395)

Dormer Fleet *J H M Gosden* a28 78
2 b c Kyllachy—Petong's Pet (Petong)
6372[12] (6797) ◆ 7097[7] 7290[18]

Dorn Dancer (IRE) *W M Brisbourne* a54 80
7 b m Danehill Dancer(IRE) —Appledorn (Doulab (USA))
606[7] 1060[9] 1885[8] 2071[7] 2312[13] 2590[7] 4281[6] 4504[10] 6495[8] 6637[11] 6846[9]

Dotada (IRE) *Peter Casey* a84 79
4 gr m Noverre(USA) —Nichodoula (Doulab (USA))
(7297a)

Do The Deal (IRE) *J J Quinn* a63 71
3 ch f Halling(USA) —Cairns (UAE) (Cadeaux Genereux)
1625[4] 2528[5] 3188[7]

Do The Strand (IRE) *B W Hills* 87
3 b c Galileo(IRE) —Aiming Upwards (Blushing Flame (USA))
1355[7] 3751[4] (4519)

Dot's Delight *M G Rimell* a51 49
5 b m Golden Snake(USA) —Hotel California (IRE) (Last Tycoon)
3158[13] (3927) 4170[8] 4735[4] 5246[4]

Douala *P Schiergen* 86
2 b f Dubawi(IRE) —Desca (GER) (Cadeaux Genereux)
6326a[8]

Double Act *Evan Williams* a82 59
3 br g Where Or When(IRE) —Secret Flame (Machiavellian (USA))
(136) (231) 547[3]

Double Banded (IRE) *K A Ryan* a73 94
5 b g Mark Of Esteem(IRE) —Bronzewing (Beldale Flutter (USA))
1790[9] 2486[12] 2931[6] 3146[6] 5857[2] 6115[4]

Double Bill (USA) *P F I Cole* a61 74
5 bb g Mr Greeley(USA) —Salty Perfume (USA) (Salt Lake (USA))
7861[3]

Double Carpet (IRE) *G Woodward* a71 58
6 b g Lahib(USA) —Cupid Miss (Anita's Prince)
1313[7] 2145[8] 2418[15] 3720[6] 4225[19]

Double Exposure *Jamie Poulton* a20 45
5 b g Double Trigger(IRE) —Last Night's Fun (IRE) (Law Society (USA))
670[8] 6417[3]

Double Fortune *Jamie Poulton* a48
2 b f Singspiel(IRE) —Four-Legged Friend (Aragon)
7764[7]

Double Handful (GER) *M Figge* 86
3 ro c Pentire—Durania (GER) (Surumu (GER))
3670a[16] 5783a[2] 6891a[7]

Double Moon *George Baker* 46
3 b g Makbul—Emoona (FR) (Linamix (FR))
2178[13] 3319[4] 3590[7] 4669[6]

Double Rollover *W R Muir* a43
2 b c Fantastic Light(USA) —Princess Miletrian (IRE) (Danehill (USA))
4194[10] 4534[14] 4973[7] 5224[5] 5811[10] 6034[11]

Double Spectre (IRE) *Jean-Rene Auvray* a65 74
7 b g Spectrum(IRE) —Phantom Ring (Magic Ring (IRE))
168[3] 1786[6] 1980[11] 2798[7] 4168[3] 6188[8] 7112[12]

Doublesvinsky (USA) *J-L Pelletan* 68
3 b c Stravinsky(USA) —Doubles Match (USA) (Danzig (USA))
5118a[0]

Double Valentine *R Ingram* a62 45
6 ch m Primo Valentino(IRE) —Charlottevalentina (IRE) (Perugino (USA))
803[3] 867[9] 1080[12] 1496[5] 1728[6] 5779[8] 6394[9] 6720[11] 7240[9] 7520[5]

Double Whammy *Jamie Poulton* 63
3 b g Systematic—Honor Rouge (IRE) (Highest Honor (FR))
2640[8] 4480[5] 5578[5]

Doubly Guest *Tim Vaughan* 76
5 b m Barathea Guest—Countess Guest (IRE) (Spectrum (IRE))
2760[3] 4301[2] 5857[6]

Doubnov (FR) *Ian Williams* a70 42
6 gr g Linamix(FR) —Karmitycia (FR) (Last Tycoon)
2055[14] 6290[10] 6665[12] (7549) 7811[9]

Doubtful Sound (USA) *R Hollinshead* a102 69
5 b g Diesis—Roam Free (USA) (Unbridled (USA))
(204) 359[4] 451[3] 785[6] 7090[8] 7414[6]

Douceur Nocturne (FR) *H-A Pantall* a69 74
4 b m Zieten(USA) —Dentelle (FR) (Apeldoorn (FR))
5013a[2]

Douchkette (FR) *John Berry* 42
3 b f Califet(FR) —Douchka (FR) (Fijar Tango (FR))
3696[10] 4057[15]

Doun Pearl (FR) *F Vermeulen* 61
2 gr f Blackdoun(FR) —Elite Super (USA) (Shadeed (USA))
3934a[7]

D'Outremer (FR) *D Smaga* a70 76
3 ch f Choisir(AUS) —Haskilclara (FR) (Green Tune (USA))
7385a[6]

Douze Points (IRE) *Joseph G Murphy* a78 86
3 b c Redback—Grade A Star (IRE) (Alzao (USA))
3898a[4]

Dove (IRE) *J H M Gosden* a70 75
4 b m Sadler's Wells(USA) —Golden Digger (USA) (Mr Prospector (USA))
(3703) 7131[10]

Dove Cottage (IRE) *W S Kittow* a65 83
7 b g Great Commotion(USA) —Pooka (Dominion)
1179[5] 4378[4] 5062[7] 5532[4] 5912[2] (6566) 6936[8]

Dovedon Angel *Miss Gay Kelleway* a56 37
3 b f Winged Love(IRE) —Alexander Star (IRE) (Inzar (USA))
3384[5] 7221[11] 7318[4] 7660[3] 7765[2]

Dovedon Diva *T Keddy* 52
2 b f Generous(IRE) —Alexander Star (IRE) (Inzar (USA))
6792[P] 7096[10] 7288[12]

Dovedon Earl *T Keddy* a56
3 b g Millkom—Syrian Flutist (Shaamit (IRE))
6287[11] 7590[4]

Dovedon Hero *P J McBride* a66 40
9 ch g Millkom—Hot Topic (IRE) (Desse Zenny (USA))
1014[13] 2129[7]

Dove Mews *M L W Bell* a57 81
3 b f Namid—Flying Fulmar (Bahamian Bounty)
1296[7] 2299[8] 3033[6] 4452[4] 5403[2] 5989[9]

Dovil Boy (IRE) *S Wattel* a86 101
3 b c Clodovil(IRE) —Lycius Girl (ITY) (Lycius (USA))
1858a[2] 3230a[4] 4113a[5]

Dovizioso (IRE) *P Caravati* 70
7 b h Sri Pekan(USA) —Piccola Barbara (ITY) (Scouting Miller)
1575a[7]

Dower Glen *I Semple* 65
2 b f Camacho—Aimee's Delight (Robellino (USA))
1504[5] 1827[2] 2372[8] 3058[3] 3478[5] 4463[3] 4773[4] 5292[6] 5976[11]

Dowlleh *G Brown* a71 36
5 b g Noverre(USA) —Al Persian (IRE) (Persian Bold)
5729[14]

Downhiller (IRE) *J L Dunlop* a99 105
4 ch g Alhaarth(IRE) —Ski For Gold (Shirley Heights)
1007[9] (1519) 1790[7]

Downhill Skier (IRE) *W M Brisbourne* a69 70
5 ch g Danehill Dancer(IRE) —Duchy Of Cornwall (USA) (The Minstrel (CAN))
(118) (242) 289[6] 309[4] 471[2] 573[2] 625[4] 683[3] 807[9] 932[4] (1132) 1413[8] (4508) 4772[6] 5332[8] 6596[7] 7023[4] 7321[4] 7480[5]

Downing Street (IRE) *Jennie Candlish* 82
8 b g Sadler's Wells(USA) —Photographie (USA) (Trempolino (USA))
3532[4] 5235[9]

Download (GER) *R Gross* 85
4 br g Indian Lodge(IRE) —Durania (GER) (Surumu (GER))
3201a[8] 3441a[11] 4128a[7]

Downstream *D M Simcock* a52 40
3 b f Marju(IRE) —Sister Moonshine (FR) (Piccolo)
135[8]

Downtoobusiness *Karen George* a50 43
2 b g Desert Sun—Mariette (Blushing Scribe (USA))
3785[9] 4201[7] 5312[8]

Doyenne Dream *J M P Eustace* 43
2 b f Doyen(IRE) —Cribella (USA) (Robellino (USA))
7095[9]

Draco Boy *Andrew Turnell* a20 46
2 gr g Silver Patriarch(IRE) —Miss Tehente (FR) (Tehente (FR))
4900[10] 5528[9] 6629[12]

Dragonessa (IRE) *B Palling* a42 57
2 b f Red Ransom(USA) —Principessa (Machiavellian (USA))
2533[7] 3226[12] 3979[9] (5967) 6343[8] 6589[2] 7242[8]

Dragon Flame (IRE) *M Quinn* a41 77
6 b g Tagula(IRE) —Noble Rocket (Reprimand)
1565[7] (2460) 2929[6] 4099[3] 4469[10] 5480[7]

Dragon Slayer (IRE) *John A Harris* a68 79
7 ch g Night Shift(USA) —Arandora Star (USA) (Sagace (FR))
1014[12] 1261[7] 1845[5] 2419[3] 2851[5] 3550[6] 3635[6] 3960[2] (4158) 4437[2] 5035[9] 5473[4] 6392[5] (7127)

Dramatic Jewel (USA) *J W Hills* a65 26
3 b g Diesis—Seeking The Jewel (USA) (Seeking The Gold (USA))
3207[10] 4084[6] 4867[7] 6287[4] 6497[3]

Dramatic Solo *A P Jarvis* a74 73
4 ch m Nayef(USA) —Just Dreams (Salse (USA))
(190) ◆ 219[6] 668[4] 894[3] 1171[4] 1851[3] 2294[4] (2448) 2720[3] 3544[3] 4325[5] (4873) 5185[3] 5943[3] 6822[3]

Dramatic Turn *Mme J Bidgood* 64
5 b m Pivotal—Eveningperformance (Night Shift (USA))
4637a[0]

Drawnfromthepast (IRE) *J A Osborne* a91 95
4 ch g Tagula(IRE) —Ball Cat (FR) (Cricket Ball (USA))
1608[4] 2078[8] 2474[6] 3091[20] 5826[9] 6282[12] 6723[4] 7026[4] 7155[4] 7395[4]

Drawn Gold *R Hollinshead* a68 72
5 b g Daggers Drawn(USA) —Gold Belt (IRE) (Bellypha)
194[8] 836[2] 1454[4] 2445[11] (2971) 3809[4] 4737[2] 5210[3] 6244[9] 7124[DSQ] 7461[6] 7594[3]

Dr Brass *B N Pollock* a73 81
4 b g Dr Fong(USA) —Tropical Heights (FR) (Shirley Heights)
392[12] 559[9] 1571[11]

Dream Catch Me (IRE) *J R Boyle* a48
3 b f Xaar—Dancerette (Groom Dancer (USA))
664[4] 722[3] 947[6] 1618[7]

Dreamcoat *J H M Gosden* 73
3 ch c Pivotal—Follow A Dream (USA) (Gone West (USA))
1350[4] 2081[3] 2857[8]

Dream Date (IRE) *W J Haggas* a80 44
3 b f Oasis Dream—Femme Fatale (Fairy King (USA))
(122) (276)

Dream Dealer (FR) *F Rohaut*
2 b f Marchand De Sable(USA) —Mandalay (USA) (Sovereign Dancer (USA))
7315a[4]

Dream Deer *P D Deegan* a98 92
2 b c Royal Applause—Tourmalet (Night Shift (USA))
2957a[4] 4357a[4] 5452a[3]

Dream Desert (IRE) *M R Channon* a93 93
4 ch h Elnadim(USA) —Bravo Dancer (Acatenango (GER))
801[3] 1458[6] 1798[8] 2671[8] 3443a[9]

Dream Eater (IRE) *A M Balding* a79 116
4 gr h Night Shift(USA) —Kapria (FR) (Simon Du Desert (FR))
1251[2] 1525[2] 2076[9] 2990[5] 3398[4] 3841[4] 4406[4] (5232) 5618a[2] 6304[8]

Dream Express (IRE) *P Howling* a73 78
4 b g Fasliyev(USA) —Lothlorien (USA) (Woodman (USA))
1132[9] 1333[9] 1737[3] 2235[11] 2998[9] 3488[9] (3558) (4133) 4312[4] 4775[3] 5107[5] 5612[4] 5836[7] 6112[6] 6738[6] 7180[7] 7330[5] 7587[10] 7716[11]

Dream Huntress *J W Hills* a67 64
3 ch f Dubai Destination(USA) —Dream Lady (Benny The Dip (USA))
205[8] 6124[7] 6787[2] 6968[5] 7417[8] 7693[3]

Dream Impact (USA) *L Riccardi* a13 108
8 b h Royal Academy(USA) —One Fit Cat (USA) (Storm Cat (USA))
336a[16]

Dream In Blue *J A Glover* a66 49
4 b g Oasis Dream—Blue Birds Fly (Rainbow Quest (USA))
310[2] 501[2] 779[2] 3191[8] 3997[6] 4617[8] 6840[8] 7504[4] 7670[6] (7761) 7851[3]

Dream In Waiting *B J Meehan* a80 84
3 b f Oasis Dream—Lady In Waiting (Kylian (USA))
6680[13] 7141[3]

Dream Lodge (IRE) *R A Fahey* a103 111
5 ch g Grand Lodge(USA) —Secret Dream (IRE) (Zafonic (USA))
997[14] 1346[3] 1673[8] 2015[14] (2787) 3089[8] (4002) 4352[4] 5137[4] 5231[2] 6093[5] 6485[4]

Dream Mountain *Ms J S Doyle* a41 62
6 b g Mozart(IRE) —Statua (IRE) (Statoblest)
809[7] 8771[0] 1069[9]

Dream Number (IRE) *W R Muir* a63 71
2 ch f Fath(USA) —Very Nice (Daylami (IRE))
5714[5] 5866[3] 6328[3] 6775[5] (7056) 7320[9]

Dream Of Fortune (IRE) *M G Quinlan* a86 78
5 b g Danehill Dancer(IRE) —Tootling (IRE) (Pennine Walk)
79[3] 271[3] (453) 766[2] ◆ 847[4] 3399[6] 5509[8] 6435[12] 6703[4] 6973[14] 7549[3] 7623[3] 7776[3] (7823)

Dream Of Gerontius (IRE) *R Hannon* a46 29
2 b f Oratorio(IRE) —Shades Of Rosegold (IRE) (Bluebird (USA))
1577[13] 1726[3] 2494[15] 5543[7]

Dream Of Olwyn (IRE) *J G Given* a65 75
4 b m Nayef(USA) —Jam (IRE) (Arazi (USA))
(1845) 2442[2] 7248[8]

Dreamonandon (IRE) *G A Swinbank* 61
3 b g Val Royal(FR) —Boley Lass (IRE) (Archway (IRE))
1470[6] 2091[9] 3018[8]

Dream On Connie *W J Knight* a60 66
3 b g Cape Cross(IRE) —Fantasize (Groom Dancer (USA))
1804[9] 2488[5] 3117[9] 3693[9] 4010[6] 4904[5] 5548[7] 6001[3] 6570[9] 7022[8]

Dream Quest (FR) *D Sicaud & Mme C Vergne* 70
3 b c Subliminal(FR) —Miss Rangoon (FR) (Rangoon (FR))
5118a[0]

Dream Rainbow *Joss Saville* a66 72
4 b g Oasis Dream—Bint Zamayem (IRE) (Rainbow Quest (USA))
3354[12] 4859[11] 4977[12]

Dreams Jewel *C Roberts* a62 56
9 b g Dreams End—Jewel Of The Nile (Glenstal (USA))
459[3] 604[7] 4332[11] 7594[8]

Dreamspeed (IRE) *A M Balding* 97
2 b c Barathea(IRE) —Kapria (FR) (Simon Du Desert (FR))
(3584) ◆ 4418[7] 5214[5] 6268[5]

Dream Spinner *J L Dunlop* a66 70
2 b g Royal Applause—Dream Quest (Rainbow Quest (USA))
2889[4] 3786[5] 4693[4] 5213[7] 6211[6] 6533[3]

Dream Street Rose (USA) *K R Burke*
4 bb m Yankee Victor(USA) —Dixie Fine (USA) (L'Emigrant (USA))
1530[13]

Dreamt *A Fabre* 106
3 b f Oasis Dream—Condition (Deploy)
4971a[5]

Dream Theme *D Nicholls* a61 91
6 b g Distant Music(USA) —Xaymara (USA) (Sanglamore (USA))
1016[20] 1438[3] 1689[2] 1921[12]

Dreamwalk (IRE) *R M Beckett* a84 85
3 b g Bahri(USA) —Celtic Silhouette (FR) (Celtic Swing)
1579[2] (2170) 2701[16] 3307[4] 4481[4] 5244[2] 5915[8] (6454)

Dream Win *Sir Michael Stoute* 75
3 b g Oasis Dream—Wince (Selkirk (USA))
1255[5]

Dreamy Eyed (IRE) *Mrs P N Dutfield* a54 10
2 b f Shamardal(USA) —Misty Eyed (IRE) (Paris House)
5212[9] 5604[16] 6582[7] 6938[7]

Dressed To Dance (IRE) *R A Harris* a78 93
5 b m Namid—Costume Drama (USA) (Alleged (USA))
70[4] 128[3] 351[6] 625[5] (1784) 3577[4] 4167[3] 4607[4] 4690[2] 5120[7] 5788[2] 6572[11] 6739[14]

Drews Lane *W G M Turner* 45
2 b f Forzando—Emerald Dream (IRE) (Vision (USA))
4080[6] 4503[10] 5319[6] 5543[14]

Dr Faustus (IRE) *Doug Watson* a66 98
4 gr g Sadler's Wells(USA) —Requesting (Rainbow Quest (USA))
263a[16] 415a[13]

Dr Finley (IRE) *M L W Bell* 71
2 ch g Dr Fong(USA) —Farrfesheena (USA) (Rahy (USA))
3957[4] 4534[2] 5119[4] 6786[3]

Drift And Dream *C F Wall* 71
2 b f Exceed And Excel(AUS) —Sea Drift (FR) (Warning)
(3006) 3865[5] 4208[2] 5992[2]

Drift Ice (SAF) *M F De Kock* a100 101
8 b g Western Winter(USA) —Donya (SAF) (Elliodor (FR))
259a[6] 418a[11]

Drifting Gold *C G Cox* a77 81
5 ch m Bold Edge—Driftholme (Safawan)
99[3] (243) 329[5] 539[5] 710[4] 1041[4] 1150[9] (1540) 2219[2] 2359[2] 3272[5] 4232[7] 5436[10] 6801[7]

Drill Sergeant *M Johnston* 111
4 br g Rock Of Gibraltar(IRE) —Dolydille (IRE) (Dolphin Street (FR))
263a^15 437a^12 699a^10 1017^2 1460^8 1674^3 2031^3 2471^3 2706^2 (3142) 3620^5 3874^6 4408^3 5171^2 5824^4 6303^8 6452^2 7031^5

Drinking Buddy *D W Thompson* 54
2 ch g Reel Buddy(USA) —Tancred Arms (Clantime)
4101^5 4503^5 4800^3 4973^4 5519^2 6096^6 6589^16 6895^7 7055^10

Driven (IRE) *Mrs A J Perrett* a80 79
4 b g Domedriver(IRE) —Wonderful World (GER) (Dashing Blade)
(1539) *1833^2* 2243^5 4641^3 5190^11 5565^3 *5991^10* 6337^8 6790^10

Drizzi (IRE) *Jim Best* a30 72
8 b g Night Shift(USA) —Woopi Gold (IRE) (Last Tycoon)
7842^7

Dr Jameson (IRE) *R A Fahey* a66 77
3 b g Orpen(USA) —Touraneena (Robellino (USA))
1474^3 (1950) 2406^5 5858^9 6250^5 *6640^6 7416^7 7782^3*

Dr Light (IRE) *M A Peill* a52 56
5 b g Medicean—Allumette (Rainbow Quest (USA))
378^5 567^7

Dr Livingstone (IRE) *C R Egerton* a90 95
4 b g Dr Fong(USA) —Radhwa (FR) (Shining Steel)
2407^2 2891^6 *5641^5* 7035^2

Dr Mathias *P D Evans* a62 70
2 b g Dubai Destination(USA) —Herminoe (Rainbow Quest (USA))
5428^11 (5868) *6491^7 7003^9*

Dr McFab *Miss Tor Sturgis* a36 52
5 ch g Dr Fong(USA) —Barbera (Barathea (IRE))
679^11 1974^3 2634^13 5367^12

Drogba (ARG) *M Botti* a69
4 b h Lucky Roberto(USA) —Gattara (ARG) (Potrillazo (ARG))
7810^6

Drombeg Pride (IRE) *G P Enright* a31 43
5 b g High Account(USA) —Proserpina (Most Welcome)
190^8

Dromore (IRE) *A M Balding* a58 75
2 ch g Traditionally(USA) —Try To Catch Me (USA) (Shareef Dancer (USA))
4200^7 ◆ (4945) 5864^9 6993^9

Drop The Hammer *T P Tate* a22 63
3 b f Lucky Story(USA) —Paperweight (In The Wings)
2042^6 2371^12 3233^3 (3575) *4175^5* 5131^3 5696^10 6384^8 6822^8

Dr Smart (IRE) *M Al Muhairi* a71 85
3 b c Dr Fong(USA) —All Glory (Alzao (USA))
258a^11 524a^3 769a^10

Drubinca *S C Williams* 43
2 b g Dubai Destination(USA) —Racina (Bluebird (USA))
4377^9 5512^7 6364^5

Drumadoon Bay (IRE) *G A Swinbank* 56
5 b g Marju(IRE) —Mythical Creek (USA) (Pleasant Tap (USA))
2532^8 3061^4 3350^P 3683^6

Drumbeat (IRE) *A P O'Brien* 108
3 b c Montjeu(IRE) —Maskaya (IRE) (Machiavellian (USA))
1294^2 1822^3 2288a^6 2756a^8 3438a^11

Drumbeats (AUS) *Peter Snowden* 110
4 b h Redoute's Choice(AUS) —Delicate Choice (AUS) (Last Tycoon)
7196a^8

Drum Dragon *M H Tompkins* a78 74
3 b f Beat Hollow—Qilin (IRE) (Second Set (IRE))
1174^9 *2685^2* (3485) 4143^6 4495^3 5594^4 6538^6 (6840) *7476^4 7539^6*

Drumfire (IRE) *M Johnston* 115
5 b h Danehill Dancer(IRE) —Witch Of Fife (USA) (Lear Fan (USA))
1875^3 2410^4 3190^2 3781^7 (4404) 4484^4 5447^7

Drumhallagh (IRE) *Tom Dascombe* a53 10
4 b g Barathea(IRE) —Nashua Song (IRE) (Kahyasi)
679^10 1254^15

Drum Major (IRE) *G L Moore* a74 73
4 b g Sadler's Wells(USA) —Phantom Gold (Machiavellian (USA))
103^4 319^8 2497^2 2983^5 *3737^10* 4744^5 5217^8

Drumpellier (IRE) *P T Midgley* a50 61
2 ch f Rakti—Early Memory (USA) (Devil's Bag (USA))
1126^4 1396^6 2311^6 2896^5 *3709^4* (4101) 4884^11 4975^4

Drunken Sailor (IRE) *Paul W Flynn* a77 104
4 b g Tendulkar(USA) —Ronni Pancake (Mujadil (USA))
(4510a) 6106^2

Drussell (IRE) *S Donohoe* a69 63
3 b g Orpen(USA) —Cahermee Queen (USA) (King Of Kings (IRE))
(902) 5857^8 6400^7 *6940^11 7048^9*

Dr Valentine (FR) *E J O'Neill* a66 73
3 ch g Dr Fong(USA) —Red Roses Story (FR) (Pink (FR))
2293a^3

Dr Wintringham (IRE) *Karen George* a70 66
3 b f Monsieur Bond(IRE) —Shirley Collins (Robellino (USA))
2137^11 2349^3 2651^3 3066^5 3345^3 4082^3 4536^2 (4938) 5449^4 5905^4 6399^3 *7591^2*

Dry Martini (USA) *Barclay Tagg* a117 104
6 rg g Slew Gin Fizz(USA) —Jon's Kimberly (USA) (Criminal Type (USA))
6512a^5

Dry Speedfit (IRE) *Micky Hammond* a72 57
4 b g Desert Style(IRE) —Annmary Girl (Zafonic (USA))
3862^8

Duaisbhanna (IRE) *J S Bolger* 91
3 ch f Rock Of Gibraltar(IRE) —Ovazione (Seeking The Gold (USA))
2304a^16

Dualagi *M R Bosley* a67 71
5 b m Royal Applause—Lady Melbourne (IRE) (Indian Ridge)
1468^7 1890^11 1985^2 (2202) 2920^7 *3272^3 3713^4* 3866^6 4428^5 4702^3 4950^3 6039^4 6933^9

Duar Mapel (USA) *Paul Mason* a73 65
3 b g Lemon Drop Kid(USA) —Pitchacurve (USA) (Defrere (USA))
939^3 1574^7 1928^9 2909^6

Dubai (IRE) *P Schiergen* 96
3 b f Galileo(IRE) —Dapprima (GER) (Shareef Dancer (USA))
2524a^8

Dubai Bounty *G A Butler* a66
2 ch f Dubai Destination(USA) —Mary Read (Bahamian Bounty)
(7844)

Dubai Creek (IRE) *M Johnston* a62 50
3 b g Cape Cross(IRE) —Humilis (IRE) (Sadler's Wells (USA))
6475^5 *6673^5*

Dubai Crest *Mrs A J Perrett* a69 91
3 b g Dubai Destination(USA) —On The Brink (Mind Games)
(1280) 1702^2 2701^8 3051^10 4520^14 (4827) 5419^6 5904^4 6239^6 6546^5 6907^13

Dubai Diva *C F Wall* a70 47
3 b f Dubai Destination(USA) —Marine City (JPN) (Carnegie (IRE))
1441^4 ◆ 7080^7 *(7255)* ◆ *7415^4 7760^7*

Dubai Dreamer (USA) *A Al Raihe* a79
7 gr g Stephen Got Even(USA) —Blacktie Bid (USA) (Black Tie Affair)
414a^16

Dubai Dynamo *P F I Cole* a97 99
4 b g Kyllachy—Miss Mercy (IRE) (Law Society (USA))
(1433) 1731^8 2083^11 2480^P 6732^15

Dubai Echo (USA) *Sir Michael Stoute* 85
3 bb g Mr Greeley(USA) —Entendu (USA) (Diesis)
1407^2 2030^4 (2613) 3526^4

Dubai Gem *Jamie Poulton* 66
3 b f Fantastic Light(USA) —Reflectance (Sadler's Wells (USA))
1804^6 2192^5 2679^5

Dubai Hills *B Smart* 81
3 b g Dubai Destination(USA) —Hill Welcome (Most Welcome)
1305^4 1869^11 5523^13

Dubai Legend *D M Simcock* a62 78
3 ch f Cadeaux Genereux—Royal Future (IRE) (Royal Academy (USA))
(2205) 2886^7 5007^5 5471^7 6798^16

Dubai Media (CAN) *D M Simcock* a68 66
2 b f Songandaprayer(USA) —Forty Gran (USA) (El Gran Senor (USA))
4792^7 *7135^4*

Dubai Meydan (IRE) *Miss Gay Kelleway* a90 85
4 b g High Chaparral(IRE) —Miss Golden Sands (Kris)
6614^8 6776^U 6944^3 (7111)

Dubai Miracle (USA) *D M Simcock* a79 98
2 ch c Consolidator(USA) —East Cape (USA) (Mr Prospector (USA))
2631^4 3270^3 (4200) 5214^2 ◆ 6268^10

Dubai Petal (IRE) *J S Moore* a64 77
4 b m Dubai Destination(USA) —Out Of Egypt (USA) (Red Ransom (USA))
103^8

Dubai Phantom (USA) *D M Simcock* a66 30
2 b g Arch(USA) —Sharp Apple (USA) (Diesis)
5787^11 *6291^5 6858^3*

Dubai Queen (IRE) *P Demercastel* a69 88
4 b m King Charlemagne(USA) —Dubai Victory (IRE) (Victory Note (USA))
7822a^6

Dubai Rose *H-A Pantall* 100
3 b f Dubai Destination(USA) —Russian Rose (IRE) (Soviet Lad (USA))
3968a^5 7347a^10

Dubai Set *R Hannon* 89
2 ch c Reset(AUS) —Bint Makbul (Makbul)
3218^4 3402^3 3692^2 4219^2 (5017) 5658^3 (7290)

Dubai Storming *E A L Dunlop* a81
3 b g Storming Home—Tropical Breeze (IRE) (Kris)
272^5 (455) (740) 840^4 1431^5 5667^10

Dubai's Touch *M Johnston* a109 109
5 b h Dr Fong(USA) —Noble Peregrine (Lomond (USA))
2606^4 2933^20 3312^11 (3796) 4486^15 4768^8

Dubai To Barnsley *D A Nolan* a56 61
4 b g Superior Premium—Oakwell Ace (Clantime)
87^8 327^8 2451^4 3109^2 3909^4 4036^4 4467^5 *6674^10 7460^9*

Dubai Tsunami *E A L Dunlop* a15 28
3 gr f Fantastic Light(USA) —Citrine Spirit (IRE) (Soviet Star (USA))
3228^12

Dubai Twilight *M bin Shafya* a96 97
5 b g Alhaarth(IRE) —Eve (Rainbow Quest (USA))
337a^13

Dubara Reef (IRE) *Paul Green* a24
2 ch g Dubawi(IRE) —Mamara Reef (Salse (USA))
5669^12 6285^8 *7463^8*

Dubawi Heights *S A Callaghan* 96
2 b f Dubawi(IRE) —Rosie's Posy (IRE) (Suave Dancer (USA))
3820^7 ◆ 4272^5 5199^3 6241^2 6477^2 6852^6

Dubawi Junior (IRE) *J-C Rouget* 89
2 b c Dubawi(IRE) —Lady Bex (IRE) (Sadler's Wells (USA))
4807a^7 5494a^2

Dubawi King *N Tinkler* 42
2 b g Dubawi(IRE) —Laughing Girl (USA) (Woodman (USA))
6592^12 7121^9

Dubawi Phantom *D M Simcock* 104
2 ch c Dubawi(IRE) —Anna Amalia (IRE) (In The Wings)
2218^5 2889^6 3395^2 (4006) 5261^3 6664^6 7030^7

Dubburg (USA) *W J Musson* a62 69
4 ch g Johannesburg(USA) —Plaisir Des Yeux (FR) (Funambule (USA))
1187^8 1514^6 2332^5 4759^7 *6074^6 6832^3* 7248^12

Ducal Daisey *A B Haynes* 29
3 b f Shahrastani(USA) —Jimgareen (IRE) (Lahib (USA))
5381^14

Ducal Destiny *J R Weymes* 43
2 b c Reset(AUS) —Lucky Thing (Green Desert (USA))
2449^5 2784^5

Ducal Regancy Duke *C J Teague* 56
5 gr g Bertolini(USA) —Fun Run (USA) (Skip Away (USA))
2361^13 2785^6 3171^13 3680^4 4347^9 4465^9 5147^7

Ducal Regancy Red *C J Teague* a57 44
5 ch m Bertolini(USA) —One For Jeannie (Clantime)
884^8 919^6

Duchess Dora (IRE) *J J Quinn* 90
2 b f Tagula(IRE) —Teodora (IRE) (Fairy King (USA))
1396^3 (1764) 4782^2 (5218) (5467) ◆ 6049^5 6677^6

Duchess Of Alba *G C Bravery* 2
4 b m Compton Place—Marie La Rose (FR) (Night Shift (USA))
4955^8 5435^9 *6166^9*

Duchess Of Doom (IRE) *C Gordon* a19 47
3 b f Exceed And Excel(AUS) —Tallahassee Spirit (THA) (Presidential (USA))
1940^8 *2143^9* 6001^8

Duchess Of Foxland (IRE) *Mark L Fagan* a70 80
2 br f Medecis—Itsanothergirl (Reprimand)
6401a^4

Duchess Ravel (IRE) *R Hannon* 59
2 br f Bachelor Duke(USA) —Bolero Again (IRE) (Sadler's Wells (USA))
3458^3 ◆

Dudley *J G Portman* 44
2 ch g Compton Place—Just A Glimmer (Bishop Of Cashel)
2793^9 3218^10 4478^7

Dudley Docker (IRE) *D C O'Brien* a80 75
7 b g Victory Note(USA) —Nordic Abu (IRE) (Nordico (USA))
113^6 218^4 576^8 807^10 2675^6 3322^4 4321^5 4916^4 *7668^5*

Duellant (IRE) *P Schiergen* 106
4 b h Dashing Blade—Dapprima (GER) (Shareef Dancer (USA))
415a^6 640a^6 1143a^9 1575a^3 3201a^6 5461a^8 6500a^6 7406a^10

Duellist *M Johnston* a60
2 b c Dubawi(IRE) —Satin Flower (USA) (Shadeed (USA))
7864^4

Duff (IRE) *Edward Lynam* a116 117
6 b g Spinning World(USA) —Shining Prospect (Lycius (USA))
633^2 1989^8 (2870a) 3140^8 3638^8 (5862) (6530a) 7746a^12

Dugatti *Mike Murphy*
3 b c Bertolini(USA) —Go Polar (Polar Falcon (USA))
1252^10 1592^11

Dukedom *T G McCourt* 73
6 gr g Highest Honor(FR) —Rose Noble (USA) (Vaguely Noble)
2290a^4

Duke Of Bothwell (USA) *R A Fahey* a1 44
3 ch g Hennessy(USA) —Crooked Wood (USA) (Woodman (USA))
4860^11 5163^5 5394^9 6414^12

Duke Of Burgundy (FR) *Jennie Candlish* 74
6 b g Danehill(USA) —Valley Of Gold (FR) (Shirley Heights)
4599^6 5531^2 5731^2 6595^6

Duke Of Milan (IRE) *Tom Dascombe* a71 61
6 ch g Desert Prince(IRE) —Abyat (USA) (Shadeed (USA))
22^2 118^2 309^2 387^9 2330^6 2806^3 3459^4 *3732^2* 3948^2 4479^5

Duke Of Normandy (IRE) *B P J Baugh* a68 52
3 gr g Refuse To Bend(IRE) —Marie De Bayeux (FR) (Turgeon (USA))
154^4 317^6 628^4 759^2 829^3 938^2 1470^13 2320^10 3336^4 4074^7 4562^9 4918^7 6124^10 7142^6 7369^9

Duke Of Rainford *M Herrington* a53 51
2 gr g Bahamian Bounty—Night Haven (Night Shift (USA))
1358^12 2335^7 *2595^3* (4076) 4195^8 4782^6 *5776^3* 5950^10 *7559^10 7778^7*

Duke Of Urbino *K A Ryan* a50 20
3 ch g Medicean—Nefeli (First Trump)
425^4 796^5 5010^9 5362^11

Dukes Art *J A R Toller* a85 83
3 b c Bachelor Duke(USA) —Creme Caramel (USA) (Septieme Ciel (USA))
1255^4 1632^4 *2399^10* (3566) (4386) *4984^2* 7027^7

Dulce Domum *A B Haynes* a46 44
3 b f Dansili—Enclave (USA) (Woodman (USA))
306^5 628^3 1811^10 *2742^9* 2802^5 *3157^6* 3474^5 4142^6

Dulcie *M H Tompkins* a78 83
3 b f Hernando(FR) —Dulcinea (Selkirk (USA))
2190^8 4045^3 4793^3 *5376^2* (5696) 7151^8

Dunaskin (IRE) *B Ellison* a98 101
9 b g Bahhare(USA) —Mirwara (IRE) (Darshaan)
1191^4 1790^13 2031^5 2499^6 2932^8 *4840^6 5837^6 6875^2 7640^2 7867^6*

Duncan *J H M Gosden* 120
4 b h Dalakhani(IRE) —Dolores (Danehill (USA))
(1460) (1859) 2670^4 3781^9 4780^3

Dundry *G L Moore* a81 86
8 b g Bin Ajwaad(IRE) —China's Pearl (Shirley Heights)
341^2 485^4

Duneen Dream (USA) *Mrs N S Evans* a52 54
4 ch g Hennessy(USA) —T N T Red (USA) (Explosive Red (CAN))
711^10 1496^13 6498^9 6770^5 7751^4

Dunelight (IRE) *C G Cox* a108 113
6 ch h Desert Sun—Badee'A (IRE) (Marju (IRE))
7588^6 7768^2

Dunes Queen (USA) *M R Channon* a81 82
3 b f Elusive Quality(USA) —Queen's Logic (IRE) (Grand Lodge (USA))
(862) 1293^5 1828^5 2373^4

Dunfishin (IRE) *M S Tuck*
2 ch c Chineur(FR) —Sisal (IRE) (Danehill (USA))
7859^12

Dungannon *A M Balding* 60
2 b g Monsieur Bond(IRE) —May Light (Midyan (USA))
3218^5 ◆

Dunkerque (FR) *Mme C Head-Maarek* 110
4 b h Highest Honor(FR) —Dissertation (FR) (Sillery (USA))
(2513a) 3231a^3 4837a^6 6503a^6 (7232a)

Dunkirk (USA) *Todd Pletcher* a119
3 gr c Unbridled's Song(USA) —Secret Status (USA) (A.P. Indy (USA))
1688a^11 2734a^2

Dunn'o (IRE) *C G Cox* 102
4 b g Cape Cross(IRE) —Indian Express (Indian Ridge)
1170^9 (1527) 1821^6 (2412) 3014^14 4768^6 5249^9 5874^3 6249^9

Dunwhinny *P W D'Arcy* a44
2 b g Tobougg(IRE) —Possibility (Robellino (USA))
2825^11 3715^10 3957^9

Duplicity *R Hannon* a68 95
2 b c Cadeaux Genereux—Artful (IRE) (Green Desert (USA))
3270^4 3786^2 (4049) 6752a^5

D'Urberville *J R Jenkins* a56 55
2 b g Auction House(USA) —Laser Crystal (IRE) (King's Theatre (IRE))
2218^7 2793^11 5722^5 6066^14 *6609^9 7389^4 7884^6*

Durgan *Mrs L C Jewell* a64 69
3 b c Dansili—Perryllys (Warning)
2080^4 ◆ 2638^10 *7833^6*

Durham Express (IRE) *M Dods* 72
2 b g Acclamation—Edwina (IRE) (Caerleon (USA))
4844^3 (5596) 6841^4

Durham Reflection (IRE) *J Howard Johnson* 75
2 b g Pastoral Pursuits—Opari (IRE) (Night Shift (USA))
2099^5 2623^6 3971^5 4738^2 5157^3 5595^5 (5942)

Durham Town (IRE) *D K Ivory* a34 62
2 b g Arakan(USA) —Southern Spectrum (IRE) (Spectrum (IRE))
1147^8 1404^4 *3270^9* 4377^6 4915^6

During The War (USA) *C A Dwyer* a39 65
2 b g Lion Heart(USA) —Carson's Star (USA) (Carson City (USA))
5807^11 6544^7 *7552^5*

Dushstorm (IRE) *R J Price* a75 52
8 b g Dushyantor(USA) —Between The Winds (USA) (Diesis)
78^7

Dusk *Mrs S J Humphrey* a71 71
4 b g Fantastic Light(USA) —Dark Veil (USA) (Gulch (USA))
279^3 476^5 2975^12 4158^7

Dusk And Dawn (IRE) *Mlle A Imaz-Ceca* a80 82
3 gr f Fasliyev(USA) —Splendida Idea (IRE) (Kenmare (FR))
7386a^10

Duster *H Morrison* a73 62
2 b g Pastoral Pursuits—Spring Clean (FR) (Danehill (USA))
4200^2 ◆ *4839^2 6638^5* 6905^9

Dustry (IRE) *R Hannon* a69 73
3 b c Chevalier(IRE) —Church Mice (IRE) (Petardia)
2600^11 3736^7 4149^5 4710^15 5384^14 5628^13

Dusty Spirit *W G M Turner* a60 76
2 b c Invincible Spirit(IRE) —Dusty Dazzler (IRE) (Titus Livius (FR))
4537^6 4844^8 5180^4 *5650^7* 5908^3 6185^2 *6700^4* (6932) 7290^7

Dutiful *M R Channon* a61 59
2 ch c Dubawi(IRE) —Pelagia (IRE) (Lycius (USA))
4986^10 5603^6 6054^10 *6609^10 7389^3 (7584) 7654^9*

Duty And Destiny (IRE) *B J Meehan* a77 73
2 b f Montjeu(IRE) —Swilly (USA) (Irish River (FR))
4055^4 4797^4 6331^2 *7359^2*

Duty Free (IRE) *C R Egerton* a71 87
5 b g Rock Of Gibraltar(IRE) —Photographie (USA) (Trempolino (USA))
1184^7 1581^7

Dvinsky (USA) *P Howling* a92 74
8 b g Stravinsky(USA) —Festive Season (USA) (Lypheor)
20^2 (128) 212^5 388^4 579^8 633^7 714^5 866^2 892^2 1169^2 1321^5 1607^6 1943^5 2396^8 2980^12 3030^9 3407^2 3738^6 4607^12 5167^4 5288^2 ◆ 5370^7 5753^5 6230^2 6434^8 (6726) 7026^6 7253^9 7613^5 7656^4 7702^6 7830^6

Dwilano (GER) *P Remmert* 102
6 ch h Silvano(GER) —Dwings (IRE) (In The Wings)
1143a^4 1549a^2 3441a^7 5461a^6 7039a^9

Dylanesque *M A Jarvis* 79
2 b f Royal Applause—Ventura Highway (Machiavellian (USA))
5021^7 (5969) 6471^6 7013^9

Dynaforce (USA) *William Mott* 115
6 b m Dynaformer(USA) —Aletta Maria (USA) (Diesis)
6510a[6] 7284a[8]

Dynamic Drive (IRE) *W R Swinburn* a63
2 b c Motivator—Biriyani (IRE) (Danehill (USA))
6772[6] ◆

Dynamic Idol (USA) *M A Magnusson* a57
2 bb c Dynaformer(USA) —El Nafis (USA) (Kingmambo (USA))
7638[4]

Dynamic Saint (USA) *Doug Watson* a106 78
6 b g Sweetsouthernsaint(USA) —Le Nat (USA) (Dynaformer (USA))
(337a) 523a[3] 773a[6]

Dynamo Dave (USA) *M D I Usher* a54 53
4 b g Distorted Humor(USA) —Nothing Special (CAN) (Tejabo (CAN))
43[3] 131[6] 192[7] 482[4] 587[8] 647[8] 1578[8] 1961[9] 2182[13] 2608[9] 2808[5] 3259[6] 3662[6] (4238) 4536[10] 4748[4] 5020[8] 5477[7] 6038[9] 6186[8] (7517) 7591[13] 7877[3]

Dynasty *A P O'Brien* a84 83
2 b c Danehill Dancer(IRE) —Dash To The Top (Montjeu (IRE))
6478[8]

Dyna Waltz *J H M Gosden* a82 103
2 b f Dynaformer(USA) —Valentine Waltz (IRE) (Be My Guest (USA))
4055[3] 4542[2] (5165) 6269[5]

Dzesmin (POL) *R A Fahey* a64 89
7 b g Professional(IRE) —Dzakarta (POL) (Aprizzo (IRE))
1051[5] 1990[6] 2452[6] 3313[5]

Eager To Bow (IRE) *P R Chamings* 50
3 b g Acclamation—Tullawadgeen (IRE) (Sinndar (IRE))
1746[13] 3672[6]

Eagle Mountain *M F De Kock* 124
5 b h Rock Of Gibraltar(IRE) —Masskana (IRE) (Darshaan)
7747a[5]

Eagle Nebula *B R Johnson* a67 62
5 ch g Observatory(USA) —Tarocchi (USA) (Affirmed (USA))
154[7] 309[9] 531[13] 2420[4] 2830[11] (5888) 6208[2] 7328[2] 7695[5]

Earl Of Fire (GER) *W Baltromei* 113
4 ch g Areion(GER) —Evry (GER) (Torgos)
2113a[4] (3416a) 5563a[3] 6323a[2] 6505a[12]

Earlsmedic *S C Williams* a97 90
4 ch g Dr Fong(USA) —Area Girl (Jareer (USA))
1309[5] (1943) 2474[12] 3347[9] 5767[4] 6050[8] 6279[13] 6540[4] 7026[3] (7454) (7478) 7862[5]

Early Dart *A Berry*
2 b f Auction House(USA) —Cozette (IRE) (Danehill Dancer (IRE))
7717[P]

Early Girl *P D Evans* a27
4 b m Compton Place—Reciprocal (IRE) (Night Shift (USA))
309[10] 488[4]

Early Morning Rain (IRE) *Rae Guest* 44
3 b f Rock Of Gibraltar(IRE) —Honorine (IRE) (Mark Of Esteem (IRE))
3278[7] 4786[8]

Earmark *Seamus Fahey* a58 43
6 b g Halling(USA) —Earlene (IRE) (In The Wings)
6860[2]

Earth Living (USA) *Michihiro Ogasa* a101
3 bb f Yonaguska(USA) —Etoufee (USA) (Tabasco Cat (USA))
438a[2] 701a[2]

Easterland (IRE) *A De Royer-Dupre* 92
3 b c Starborough—Aerdee (FR) (Highest Honor (FR))
(3417a)

Easterly Breeze (IRE) *Mrs L J Young* a72 77
5 b g Green Desert(USA) —Chiang Mai (IRE) (Sadler's Wells (USA))
5679[9] 6342[4] 6668[6] 7112[4] 7578[3]

Eastern Anthem (IRE) *Saeed Bin Suroor* 120
5 b h Singspiel(IRE) —Kazzia (GER) (Zinaad)
(419a) (613a) ◆ (1012a) 2670[6] 3048[5] 5082a[3] 5707a[2] 6324a[2]

Eastern Aria (UAE) *M Johnston* a87 105
3 br f Halling(USA) —Badraan (USA) (Danzig (USA))
440[2] (564) ◆ 763[3] (962) 2077[9] 2384[2] (2884) 3333[2] (3526) 3780[9] (4520) 5262[4] (5419) 5794[2] (6238a) 6872a[4]

Eastern Empire *J W Hills* a73 92
3 b g Dubai Destination(USA) —Possessive Artiste (Shareef Dancer (USA))
1185[3] (1804) (2329) 3049[22] 4409[6] 5070[4] 5419[3]

Eastern Gift *Miss Gay Kelleway* a79 84
4 ch g Cadeaux Genereux—Dahshah (Mujtahid (USA))
1283[5] 1603[13] 1821[11] 2086[10] 2351[8] 4060[7] 4788[4] 4992[2] 5190[2] ◆ 5511[3] 5780[8] 6496[12] 6726[6] 7192[10] 7423[10] 7643[6] ◆ 7803[2] 7860[5]

Eastern Hills *J S Wainwright* a69 80
4 b g Dubai Destination(USA) —Rainbow Mountain (Rainbow Quest (USA))
2073[13] 2402[11] 2938[3] 3612[3] 3825[14] 4796[12] 5404[6] 6015[8] 6596[2] 6847 [4] 6985[4] 7247[5]

Eastern Warrior *J W Hills* a62 79
3 ch g Barathea(IRE) —Shakalaka Baby (Nashwan (USA))
1509[2] 2198[2] 2856[2] (3690) 4211[5] 4741[6] 6474[5] 6937[3]

Eastfields Lad *S R Bowring* a33 29
7 b g Overbury(IRE) —Honey Day (Lucky Wednesday)
425[11] 619[12]

East Of Tara (IRE) *Desmond McDonogh* 42
2 b f Barathea(IRE) —Wildsplash (USA) (Deputy Minister (CAN))
6401a[7]

East Of The Sun (IRE) *T P Tate* 55
3 ch g Dr Fong(USA) —Arabis (Arazi (USA))
2199[5] 2943[11] 4599[9] 5554[10]

Eastwell Smiles *R T Phillips* a63 60
5 gr g Erhaab(USA) —Miss University (USA) (Beau Genius (CAN))
631[5] 1069[7] 1426[5] 2760[7]

Easy Sundae (IRE) *J E Pease* a90 93
3 b f Diableneyev(USA) —Sundae Girl (USA) (Green Dancer (USA))
5012a[5]

Easy Target (FR) *G L Moore* a90 102
4 ch h Danehill Dancer(IRE) —Aiming (Highest Honor (FR))
259a[11] 334a[10] 641a[8] 4983[6]

Easy Terms *B R Millman* 53
2 b f Trade Fair—Effie (Royal Academy (USA))
2175[7]

Easy Wonder (GER) *I A Wood* a51 60
4 b m Royal Dragon(USA) —Emy Coasting (USA) (El Gran Senor (USA))
575[8] 661[12] 812[6] 946[4] 1072[4] 1536[9] 1781[3] 2908[8] 3242[8] 7462[6] 7771[10] 7814 [11] 7880[4]

Eau Good *G J Smith* a86 89
5 ch g Cadeaux Genereux—Girl's Best Friend (Nicolotte)
9[7] (Dead)

Ebert *R A Fahey* a75 95
6 b g Polish Precedent(USA) —Fanfare (Deploy)
84[3] 187[3] 302[3] 423[4]

Ebiayn (FR) *M A Jarvis* a82 79
3 b g Monsun(GER) —Drei (USA) (Lyphard (USA))
1350[3] 2710[3] 4798[4] 6475[4]

Ebony Boom (IRE) *H R A Cecil* a74 74
2 b c Boreal(GER) —Elegant As Well (IRE) (Sadler's Wells (USA))
4811[9] 5192[4] 5770[2] 7199[3]

Ebony Eyes *W J Knight* a85 66
3 br f King's Best(USA) —Qui Liz (USA) (Benny The Dip (USA))
3100[6] 3984[3] 4234[5] 5195[6] (5782) 6376[3] (7476)

Ebony Rose (FR) *Mlle S-V Tarrou* a85 85
3 b f Polish Precedent(USA) —Highest Nobles (FR) (Highest Honor (FR))
5462a[4]

Eborbrav *T D Easterby* 47
3 b g Falbrav(IRE) —Eboracum (IRE) (Alzao (USA))
1739[5] 2090[8]

Ebraam (USA) *S Curran* a106 98
6 b g Red Ransom(USA) —Futuh (USA) (Diesis)
204[7] 359[5] 553[3] (714) 916[12] 1052[3] 1457[5] 1864[7] 2297[8] 3784[11] 4567[3] 4891[4] 6647[17] 6964[8] 7227[3] (7358) 7488[2] 7605[2] 7862[2]

Echo Dancer *T Wall* a74 62
3 br g Danehill Dancer(IRE) —Entail (USA) (Riverman (USA))
(306) 2048[9] 2685[11] 3026[6] 3955[2] 4275[7] 7093[9] 7615[9]

Echoes Rock (GER) *Ms C Erichsen* 108
6 ch g Tiger Hill(IRE) —Evening Breeze (GER) (Surumu (GER))
609a[2] 771a[15]

Echo Forest *J R Best* a41 42
3 b g Mark Of Esteem(IRE) —Engulfed (USA) (Gulch (USA))
3215[12] 3919[13]

Eclair De Lune (GER) *Y De Nicolay* 105
3 b f Marchand De Sable(USA) —Elegante (GER) (Acatenango (GER))
2952a[8] 4334a[4] 5298a[3]

Eclipsed (USA) *J R Best* 20
2 ch c Proud Citizen(USA) —Kamareyah (IRE) (Hamas (IRE))
6561[7] 6737[13]

Ecluso (FR) *S Guinoiseau* 2
2 b c Tonitruant(USA) —Magaloue (FR) (Round Sovereign (FR))
5378a[9]

Ecole D'Art (USA) *J J Lambe* a59 76
8 b g Theatrical(IRE) —Colour Chart (USA) (Mr Prospector (USA))
(6053)

Edas *T A K Cuthbert* a74 75
7 b g Celtic Swing—Eden (IRE) (Polish Precedent (USA))
(324) 406[3] 622[2] 1099[3] 2264[2] 2499[4] 2743[3] 3291[3] 4345[4] 5307[6] 5438[2] 6768[8] (7113)

Eddie Boy *M L W Bell* a59 68
3 b g Tobougg(IRE) —Maristax (Reprimand)
1440[3] 2548[12] 3099[10] 4004[16] 5127[4]

Eddie Jock (IRE) *M bin Shafya* a111 101
5 ch g Almutawakel—Al Euro (FR) (Mujtahid (USA))
644a[9] 703a[8]

Eden Park *M Dods* a56 31
3 ch f Tobougg(IRE) —Aegean Flame (Anshan)
1359[10] 2132[10]

Ede's *P M Phelan* a32
9 ch g Bijou D'Inde—Ballagarrow Girl (North Stoke)
7328[10]

Ede's Dot Com (IRE) *P M Phelan* a64 66
5 b g Trans Island—Kilkee Bay (IRE) (Case Law)
28[3] 545[3] 799[7] 959[11] 6226[8] 6967[2] (7105)

Edge Closer *R Hannon* a111 117
5 b h Bold Edge—Blue Goddess (IRE) (Blues Traveller (IRE))
1299[7] 1989[16] 2550[3] 4087[6]

Edge End *P D Evans* a61 61
5 ch g Bold Edge—Rag Time Belle (Raga Navarro (ITY))
7068[6] 7397[7] 7460[10]

Edgefour (IRE) *B I Case* a50 53
5 b m King's Best(USA) —Highshaan (Pistolet Bleu (IRE))
6225[6]

Edgewater (IRE) *J Akehurst* a84 78
2 b g Bahamian Bounty—Esteemed Lady (IRE) (Mark Of Esteem (IRE))
3920[10] 4323[4] 4646[3] 5369[2] 5787[4] (6534) 7611[4] (7878)

Edgeworth (IRE) *B G Powell* a66 79
3 b g Pyrus(USA) —Credibility (Komaite (USA))
394[4] 542[2] 1176[4] 1361[3] ◆ 1932[8] (2548) (3115) 4010[5] 4275[6] (5940) 6243[7] 6773[10] 7189[6]

Edinburgh Knight (IRE) *P W D'Arcy* 29
2 b c Selkirk(USA) —Pippas Song (Reference Point)
5029[11]

Edith's Boy (IRE) *S Dow* a75 70
3 ch g Trans Island—My Ramona (Alhijaz)
34[3] 208[4] 348[3] 592[2] 722[4] 4952[3] 5383[5] 5877[2] (6206) 6791[2] (7554) ◆ 7808 [8]

Ed's A Red *A Berry* 29
2 b f Auction House(USA) —Gracious Imp (USA) (Imp Society (USA))
4706[4] 5208[6] 5958[7]

Ed's Pride (IRE) *K A Ryan* a51 35
3 b c Catcher In The Rye(IRE) —Queenliness (Exit To Nowhere (USA))
196[4] 555[4] 620[5] 793[5]

Edward Lear *E F Vaughan* a32 1
2 b c Refuse To Bend(IRE) —Darrery (Darshaan)
5643[10] 6842[14]

Edward Longshanks (USA) *T P Tate* 49
2 b c More Than Ready(USA) —Amour Mio (USA) (Private Terms (USA))
4993[8] 5951[9] 6763[8]

Edward Whymper *M H Tompkins* a69 64
2 ch g Bahamian Bounty—Sosumi (Be My Chief (USA))
3113[9] 3546[7] 4176[7] 5166[13] 5595[2] 6736[3] 7363[5] ◆ 7513[2] 7604[2]

Eeny Mac (IRE) *N Bycroft* 39
2 ch g Redback—Sally Green (IRE) (Common Grounds)
2260[8] 4307[9] 4888[7]

Effervesce (IRE) *Sir Michael Stoute* a47
2 ch f Galileo(IRE) —Royal Fizz (IRE) (Royal Academy (USA))
7396[5]

Efficiency *M Blanshard* a81 73
3 b f Efisio—Trounce (Barathea (IRE))
1214[11] 2079[6] 2600[12] 3868[9] 4569[14] 5616[7] 7586[7]

Effigy *H Candy* a80 86
5 b g Efisio—Hymne D'Amour (USA) (Dixieland Band (USA))
1405[8] 1813[2] 2495[3] 3055[2] 3812[3] 4262[3] 4526[3] 5040[2] 5745[2] 6695[6]

Effort *M Johnston* a86 97
3 ch g Dr Fong(USA) —Party Doll (Be My Guest (USA))
1002[6] 1484[7]

Efidium *N Bycroft* a54 69
11 b g Presidium—Efipetite (Efisio)
1243[10] 1723[8] 2362[5] 2791[3] 3124[8] 3539[2] 3558[5] 4346[3] 4435[5] 4845[8] 5601[11] 6183[3] 6369[11] 6392[4] 6768[13] 7062[8]

Efisio Princess *J E Long* a73 72
6 br m Efisio—Hardiprincess (Keen)
(305) 806[4] 2864[8] 4082[4] 5008[15] (6738) 7337[4] 7738[10]

Efistorm *C R Dore* a83 93
8 b g Efisio—Abundance (Cadeaux Genereux)
518[4] ◆ 742[8] (1150) 2929[2] 3845[5] 4069[6] (4464) 4891[3] 5098[3] 5436[11] 5768[5] 5919[7] 6279[11]

Eforetta (GER) *A W Carroll* a67 65
7 ch m Dr Fong(USA) —Erminora (GER) (Highest Honor (FR))
8[9] ◆ 368[4] 623[5] 809[4] 967[3] (1439) (1732) 2429[4]

Egon (IRE) *W Hickst* 101
3 ch c Groom Dancer(USA) —Ernanda (GER) (Hernando (FR))
2954a[4] 3670a[9]

Egyptian Lord *Peter Grayson* a43 57
6 ch g Bold Edge—Calypso Lady (IRE) (Priolo (USA))
2130[10] 3678[U] 7710[11] 7838[12]

Egyptian Ra (NZ) *A S Cruz* 120
8 ch g Woodborough(USA) —Egyptian Queen (NZ) (Kariol Lad (AUS))
1553a[2] 7746a[4]

Egyptology (IRE) *M Johnston* a63 58
2 ch g Shamardal(USA) —Golden Digger (USA) (Mr Prospector (USA))
7099[9] 7276[6] 7430[5]

Eightdaysaweek *A J McCabe* a65 51
3 b f Montjeu(IRE) —Figlette (Darshaan)
1092[6] (1441) 2131[2] 2479[11] 4175[4] 4224[9] (5327) 5812[8] 6121[4] 6860[5] 7093[4] 7321[11] 7677[5] 7794[3]

Eighteenfifty *B W Hills* a77
5 ch g Hernando(FR) —Colleville (Pharly (FR))
(476) ◆ 787[3] 3793[8] 5094[2]

Eightfold Path (USA) *P Bary* 105
2 b c Giant's Causeway(USA) —Divine Proportions (USA) (Kingmambo (USA))
5708a[3] (6752a)

Eight Hours *R A Fahey* a60 64
2 b g Bahamian Bounty—Alchimie (IRE) (Sri Pekan (USA))
994[9] (1158) 4803[8] 5358[2] (5550) 6048[8]

Eijaaz (IRE) *G A Harker* 69
8 b g Green Desert(USA) —Kismah (Machiavellian (USA))
2068[14] 2569[6] 3121[2] 3350[8] 4619[6] 6218[3] 6490[8] 7222[7]

Eimear's Pride (IRE) *Daniel Mark Loughnane* 32
9 b g Sri Pekan(USA) —Elinor Dashwood (IRE) (Fools Holme (USA))
3444[9]

Einstein (BRZ) *Helen Pitts-Blasi* a121 119
7 b h Spend A Buck(USA) —Gay Charm (BRZ) (Ghadeer (FR))
(789a) 4809a[5] 7311a[11]

Eire *M Nigge* a98 92
5 ch m Medicean—Mavourneen (USA) (Dynaformer (USA))
7102a[8] 7704a[2]

Eireannach (IRE) *J S Bolger* 81
2 b c Rock Of Gibraltar(IRE) —Irish Question (IRE) (Giant's Causeway (USA))
3895a[7]

Eishin Deputy (JPN) *A Nomoto* 122
7 gr h French Deputy(USA) —Eishin McAllen (USA) (Woodman (USA))
7593a[6]

Eisteddfod *P F I Cole* a107 111
8 ch g Cadeaux Genereux—Ffestiniog (IRE) (Efisio)
(1006) 1608[2] 3405[10] 4516[2] 5196[4] 7837[4]

Eiswind *G Raveneau* 103
5 b h Monsun(GER) —Eiszeit (GER) (Java Gold (USA))
653a[5] 1555a[5]

Ei Tanniola (IRE) *G J Smith*
4 b m Dr Massini(IRE) —Academic Accuracy (Environment Friend)
1438[14] 2149[12]

Ejaab *W J Haggas* a79 76
2 bb g Kyllachy—Whittle Woods Girl (Emarati (USA))
1700[4] (4187) 5091[3] 5692[9]

Ejeed (USA) *Miss Z C Davison* a69 50
4 b g Rahy(USA) —Lahan (Unfuwain (USA))
2713[8] 2920[8] 3512[8] 7240[6] 7588[8] 7609[4] 7826[6]

Ekhtiaar *A Al Raihe* a94 76
5 b g Elmaamul(USA) —Divina Mia (Dowsing (USA))
264a[11] 335a[15] 641a[P]

Ekta *S Botti* 91
5 b m Danehill Dancer(IRE) —Switch Blade (IRE) (Robellino (USA))
7303a[3]

Ektimaal *E A L Dunlop* a86 78
6 ch g Bahamian Bounty—Secret Circle (Magic Ring (IRE))
4852[6] 5665[13] 6462[4] 6776[6] (7253) 7395[5] 7558[7] 7832[5]

Elaala (USA) *B D Leavy* a57 51
7 ch m Aljabr(USA) —Nufuth (USA) (Nureyev (USA))
2163[5]

Ela Gorrie Mou *T T Clement* 73
3 b f Mujahid(USA) —Real Flame (Cyrano De Bergerac)
1844[10] 4151[4] 4473[5] (5479) (5869)

El Ameen *M Johnston* a49 79
3 b c Haafhd—Gracious (Grand Lodge (USA))
4097[3] ◆ 5071[3] 5394[2] 5954[2] 6780[9]

Elation (IRE) *M Johnston* a80
2 b f Cape Cross(IRE) —Attraction (Efisio)
7585[4] ◆ (7772)

El Bravo *G L Moore* a80 82
3 ch g Falbrav(IRE) —Alessandra (Generous (IRE))
356[9] 529[4] 824[2] 957[3] (1156) 1408[2] 2038[6] 2208[5]

El Comodin (IRE) *J Hirschberger* 100
5 ch h Monsun(GER) —Elle Danzig (GER) (Roi Danzig (USA))
6521a[5]

Eldaafer (USA) *Diane Alvarado* a106
4 bb g A.P. Indy(USA) —Habibti (USA) (Tabasco Cat (USA))
7281a[7]

Eldalil *Sir Michael Stoute* a63
2 br f Singspiel(IRE) —White House (Pursuit Of Love)
5639[6]

El Dececy (USA) *J Balding* a85 93
5 b g Seeking The Gold(USA) —Ashraakat (USA) (Danzig (USA))
204[6] 533[5] 654[2] 910[3] 1016[15] 1170[3] (1243) 1343[6] (1536) 1660[8] 1798[10] 2267[7] (2361) 2665[12] (2876) 3234[7] 3623[8] 4040[5]

El Diego (IRE) *J R Gask* a87 70
5 b g Sadler's Wells(USA) —Goncharova (USA) (Gone West (USA))
(11) (139) 325[2] 1319[6] 6634[8]

El Dorado (JPN) *H Takaoka* 95
5 b g Stay Gold(JPN) —White Leap (JPN) (White Muzzle)
2117a[9]

Eleanora Duse (IRE) *Sir Michael Stoute* a78 38
2 b f Azamour(IRE) —Drama Class (IRE) (Caerleon (USA))
6164[6] 6567[9] (7451)

Eleanor Eloise (USA) *J R Gask* a58 49
5 b m Minardi(USA) —Javana (USA) (Sandpit (BRZ))
114[7] 2682[4] 3471[8] 4730[4] 5019[12]

Electioneer (USA) *M Johnston* 79
2 b g Elusive Quality(USA) —Secret Charm (IRE) (Green Desert (USA))
3256[4] (3606) 5033[9]

Electric City (IRE) *M G Quinlan* a63 73
2 b f Elusive City(USA) —Accell (IRE) (Magical Wonder (USA))
4200[8] 4497[3] 5360[4] 5841[6]

Electric Feel *M Botti* 100
2 b f Firebreak—Night Gypsy (Mind Games)
(2047) 2557a[6] 3396[3] 6447[2] (7033)

Electric Roi (GER) *H Hiller* 84
6 ch h Roi Danzig(USA) —Elle Plate (GER) (Platini (GER))
3045a[3]

Electric Warrior (IRE) *C R Dore* a92 92
6 b g Bold Fact(USA) —Dungeon Princess (IRE) (Danehill (USA))
70[2] (504) (650) 922[5] 1116[10] 1213[11] 6946[13] 7643[7] 7729[11] 7813 [6] 7858[8]

Electrolyser (IRE) *C G Cox* a90 102
4 gr h Daylami(IRE) —Iviza (IRE) (Sadler's Wells (USA))
2055[4] 3390[5] ◆ (6306) 6851[22]

Eledikris (FR) *A Couetil* 60
2 b c Diktat—Eglesia (GER) (Lavirco (GER))
5378a[5]

Elegant Beauty (GER) *H Blume* 91
4 b m Sholokhov(IRE) —Endless Love (GER) (Dashing Blade)
5013a[3]

Elegant Dancer (FR) *N Clement* 78
4 b g Anabaa(USA) —Sweet Story (IRE) (Green Tune (USA))
7387a[2]

Elegant Dancer (IRE) *Paul Green* 47
2 ch f Choisir(AUS) —Sofistication (IRE) (Dayjur (USA))
1396^4 1504^10 2161^3

Elements (IRE) *E J Alston* a46 49
3 b f Rock Of Gibraltar(IRE) —Ghita (IRE) (Zilzal (USA))
2229^6 4277^6 5306^9 5624^7 *5840^7* 6987^11

Elevate Bambina *A Berry* a1 37
3 b f Spartacus(IRE) —Miri (IRE) (Sillery (USA))
530^6

Elevate Bobbob *A Berry* a29
3 b g Observatory(USA) —Grandma Lily (IRE) (Bigstone (IRE))
855^9 5840^10 6880^10 7318^10 7796^9

El Gato Malo (USA) *Craig Dollase* a108 109
4 bb g El Corredor(USA) —One Bad Cat (USA) (Mountain Cat (USA))
7305a^8

Elhamri *S Kirk* a95 94
5 bb g Noverre(USA) —Seamstress (IRE) (Barathea (IRE))
1325^11 1672^4 1791^11 2704^16 *3212^7* 3694^9 4907^9

Elie Shore *P C Haslam* a54 47
2 b f Tobougg(IRE) —Mitsuki (Puissance)
5393^5 6136^9 *6431^8* 6895^13 *7616^8*

Elijah Pepper (USA) *T D Barron* a71 74
4 ch g Crafty Prospector(USA) —Dovie Dee (USA) (Housebuster (USA))
(1885) 3001^6 3164^5 3529^5 4783^3 5409^9 5955^11 6413^13 *7735^5*

Eliot (GER) *T Mundry* 116
3 b c Tiger Hill(IRE) —Esposita (GER) (Sternkoenig (IRE))
2954a^5 3670a^4 6324a^3

Elisheba (FR) *F Doumen* 90
2 b f Okawango(USA) —Art Fair (FR) (Fairy King (USA))
7230a^6

Elisiario (IRE) *J R Boyle* a81 38
4 b g Clodovil(IRE) —Kahla (Green Desert (USA))
230^2 (820) (1436) 2387^2 2828^6 4060^10

Elite Land *B Ellison* a69 72
6 b g Namaqualand(USA) —Petite Elite (Anfield)
1000^4 1692^5 2505^4 5698^3 (6102)

Elizabelle (IRE) *R Hannon* a55 65
2 b f Westerner—Jus'Chillin' (IRE) (Elbio)
3576^10 4194^3 *4980^10* 5589^8

Elizabeth's Quest *Miss N A Lloyd-Beavis* a22 60
4 b m Piccolo—Reina (Homeboy)
6880^12 7250^13

Eliza Doolittle *J R Fanshawe* a64 59
3 b f Royal Applause—Green Supreme (Primo Dominie)
2862^6 ◆ 4913^4 *5882^6* 6926^4 *(7051)*

El Jahid (FR) *P Monfort* 24
2 ch c Until Sundown(USA) —Particuliere (Spectrum (IRE))
6928a^9

Elkhart Lake (IRE) *Adrian McGuinness* a45 49
4 b g Fath(USA) —Danny's Joy (IRE) (Maelstrom Lake)
104^4 277^7

Elkhorn *Miss J A Camacho* a67 68
7 b g Indian Ridge—Rimba (USA) (Dayjur (USA))
352^3 540^10 2852^8 *3227^11* 3484^3 3852^4 4015^5 4823^2 4998^7 5443^2 5729^4 5955^6 6216^3 6926^3

Elk Trail (IRE) *Mrs P Sly* a71 81
4 ch g Captain Rio—Panpipes (USA) (Woodman (USA))
394 934 1478^3 7247^6

Ella *G A Swinbank* a73 96
5 b m Pivotal—Flossy (Efisio)
4840^8 5551^4 6795^3 7293^3

Ella Grace (USA) *R A Fahey* 65
2 bb f Broken Vow(USA) —Shy Swan (USA) (Nureyev (USA))
2914^4 4515^13 5036^9 6215^2 6391^4

Ella Woodcock (IRE) *E J Alston* a71 86
5 b g Daggers Drawn(USA) —Hollow Haze (USA) (Woodman (USA))
1557^3 5333^13 6023^14 6157^11 6280^6 6383^3 ◆ *6860^7 7153^5 7322^6 7615^2 (7752) 7798^5*

Ellbeedee (IRE) *M A Jarvis* 56
2 b f Dalakhani(IRE) —Tochar Ban (USA) (Assert)
6992^11

Ellemujie *D K Ivory* a91 96
4 b g Mujahid(USA) —Jennelle (Nomination)
1527^4 2083^5 (2639) 3014^12 3639^10 4409^10 5221^12 5437^4 6117^5 6429^10 6480^22 *6973^6*

Elleno (IRE) *F & L Camici* 98
5 b h Celtic Swing—El Gran Love (USA) (El Gran Senor (USA))
1903a^5

Ellen Vannin (IRE) *Eve Johnson Houghton* a54 55
2 ch f Tagula(IRE) —Felin Special (Lyphard's Special (USA))
4701^6 5528^7 *6436^9* 6905^10

Elle Shadow (IRE) *P Schiergen* 106
2 b f Shamardal(USA) —Elle Danzig (GER) (Roi Danzig (USA))
7045a^2

El Libertador (USA) *E A Wheeler* a73 73
3 bb g Giant's Causeway(USA) —Istikbal (USA) (Kingmambo (USA))
4246^4 *4648^4* 4854^3 5475^9 5833^4 6111^13 6908^4 7149^2 *7362^3 7456^5*

Ellies Image *B P J Baugh* a24 47
2 b f Lucky Story(USA) —Crown City (USA) (Coronado's Quest (USA))
2914^8 *3468^8* 4817^10 *5839^10*

Ellies Inspiration *M Mullineaux*
4 b m Puissance—Star View Lady (Precocious)
1400^13 2229^10 2446^15

Elliptical (USA) *G A Butler* a84 93
3 b g Arch(USA) —Citidance Missy (USA) (Citidancer (USA))
(2178) 2701^14 (3868) 5432^3 ◆ *6229^6* 6795^15

Elliwan *M W Easterby* a65 77
4 b g Nayef(USA) —Ashbilya (USA) (Nureyev (USA))
494^6 (790) 857^3 1568^4 2233^13 *7499^7*

Ellmau *E S McMahon* a89 91
4 ch g Dr Fong(USA) —Triple Sharp (Selkirk (USA))
2711^3 999^3 1347^4 2666^4 (6594) 7018^4 ◆

Ellmollell *S Kirk* a48 42
2 b f Piccolo—Runs In The Family (Distant Relative)
2135^10 2919^10 *3733^7* 4379^5 6241^26 *7210^9 7669^7 7706^7*

El Loco Uno (USA) *H R A Cecil* a86 76
3 ch c Fusaichi Pegasus(USA) —La Vida Loca (IRE) (Caerleon (USA))
1308^2 *1729^5 (2710)* 3431^7 4814^7

Elmfield Giant (USA) *R A Fahey* a68 78
2 ch g Giant's Causeway(USA) —Princess Atoosa (USA) (Gone West (USA))
3392^7 4396^6 4993^2 *5371^4*

El Miesquo (FR) *Robert Collet* a57 70
2 b c Miesque's Son(USA) —Angel Victory (IRE) (Exactly Sharp (USA))
6960a^0

El Milagro (SPA) *C Laffon-Parias*
2 ch g Leadership—Enti Alamal (Rainbow Quest (USA))
6751a^F

Elms School Story *Miss Venetia Williams* 37
3 b f Lucky Story(USA) —Elms Schoolgirl (Emarati (USA))
5531^8

Elmustanser *Doug Watson* a82 71
8 b h Machiavellian(USA) —Elfaslah (IRE) (Green Desert (USA))
337a^14

Elna Bright *B R Johnson* a99 93
4 b g Elnadim(USA) —Acicula (IRE) (Night Shift (USA))
815^3 (1093) 1149^6 1821^13 2606^5 (2794) 3174^4 3577^2 *4083^2* 4293^10 4438^3 4641^2 (6307) 6470^9 *7226^4 (7486) 7827^10*

Elnawin *R Hannon* a108 104
3 b c Elnadim(USA) —Acicula (IRE) (Night Shift (USA))
912^2 1602^5 2035^5

Eloise *Sir Mark Prescott* a56 39
3 ch f Hernando(FR) —Eternelle (Green Desert (USA))
4205^5 4838^10 4934^7 *(5328) 5812^6*

El Potro *J R Holt* a49 62
7 b g Forzando—Gaelic Air (Ballad Rock)
1248^5 1591^7 2852^14 7241^11 *7521^10 7819^5 7869^12*

El Presidente (IRE) *N B King* a88 86
4 gr g Daylami(IRE) —Todi (IRE) (Spinning World (USA))
6002^9

Elrond (IRE) *Unknown* 65
2 b c Catcher In The Rye(IRE) —Chia Laguna (IRE) (Ela-Mana-Mou)
4686a^5

El Segundo (NZ) *Colin Little* 120
8 b g Pins(AUS) —Palos Verdes (NZ) (Oak Ridge (FR))
7040a^4

Elsie Jo (IRE) *M Wigham* a56 42
3 b f Catcher In The Rye(IRE) —Joy St Clair (IRE) (Try My Best (USA))
594^2 ◆ *667^3 831^7*

Elsie's Orphan *P R Chamings* a59
2 br f Pastoral Pursuits—Elsie Plunkett (Mind Games)
5808^7 6582^6

Elspeth's Boy (USA) *J R Best* a80
2 bb c Tiznow(USA) —Miss Waki Club (USA) (Miswaki (USA))
(7209) ◆

Eltheeb *J L Dunlop* 66
2 gr c Red Ransom(USA) —Snowdrops (Gulch (USA))
5401^11 5966^8 6592^10 6965^3

Elusive Art (IRE) *David Marnane* a66 41
2 b f Elusive City(USA) —Ink Pot (USA) (Green Dancer (USA))
6401a^8

Elusive Award (USA) *Andrew Oliver* a99 81
2 b c Elusive Quality(USA) —Victoria Cross (IRE) (Mark Of Esteem (IRE))
7017^11

Elusive Dreams (USA) *P Howling* a67 70
5 ch g Elusive Quality(USA) —Bally Five (USA) (Miswaki (USA))
44^8 646^7 854^2 946^7 ◆

Elusive Fame (USA) *M Johnston* a81 68
3 b g Elusive Quality(USA) —Advancing Star (USA) (Soviet Star (USA))
1296^9 2072^13 2438^5 2786^9 3193^11 *(3713) 4374^6 (4841) 4984^6 5640^11 5884^11 6168^8* 6496^9 7000^10 (7423) 7575^10 7711^3 7759^6 7854^3

Elusive Galaxy (IRE) *B Cecil* a93 100
2 b f Elusive City(USA) —Lure Of The Moon (USA) (Lure (USA))
4726a^3 7282a^11

Elusive Gent (IRE) *J T Gorman* a63 61
2 b g Elusive City(USA) —Satin Cape (IRE) (Cape Cross (IRE))
2302a^6

Elusive Glen (IRE) *M Johnston* a49
3 b c Elusive City(USA) —Glenarff (USA) (Irish River (FR))
1054^5 1474^P

Elusive Hawk (IRE) *B J Curley* a83 73
5 b g Noverre(USA) —Two Clubs (First Trump)
141^2 1258^2 2168^6 *3713^3 (4374)* 6964^13 *7506^5 7758^12*

Elusive Moon (IRE) *J T Gorman* a59 66
3 b g Elusive City(USA) —Mrs Moonlight (Ajdal (USA))
4392a^14

Elusive Muse *M Dods* 56
3 ch g Exit To Nowhere(USA) —Dance A Dream (Sadler's Wells (USA))
1308^5 3155^6 4974^4 5442^10

Elusive Pimpernel (USA) *J L Dunlop* 115
2 bb c Elusive Quality(USA) —Cara Fantasy (IRE) (Sadler's Wells (USA))
(3750) ◆ (5133) 7017^2 ◆

Elusive Ronnie (IRE) *R A Teal* a65 57
3 b g One Cool Cat(USA) —Elusive Kitty (USA) (Elusive Quality (USA))
200^5 348^7 481^3 510^5 827^3 1046^4 3671^12 4643^15 *5644^11 (7427) 7484^2* 7572^2 7606^7 7890^9

Elusive Style (IRE) *S P Griffiths* 38
3 b f Elusive City(USA) —Brooklands Lodge (USA) (Grand Lodge (USA))
1683^11 2789^8 3975^3 5306^10 6219^10 7219^8

Elusive Sue (USA) *R A Fahey* 76
2 bb f Elusive Quality(USA) —Show Me The Stage (USA) (Slew The Surgeon (USA))
2893^7 3495^2 4430^2 5136^15 (5958)

Elusive Trader (USA) *R Hannon* a79 72
2 bb c Elusive Quality(USA) —Kumari Continent (USA) (Kris S (USA))
4746^2 5311^3 (5977)

Elusive Warrior (USA) *A J McCabe* a79 46
6 b g Elusive Quality(USA) —Love To Fight (CAN) (Fit To Fight (USA))
37^3 94^4 1438^4 2133^7 4843^4 5544^7 *6361^6 7349^2 7762^2*

Elusive Wave (IRE) *J-C Rouget* 118
3 b f Elusive City(USA) —Multicolour Wave (IRE) (Rainbow Quest (USA))
(1208a) (1918a) 3088^4 4580a^2 5710a^RR

Elvira Madigan *A M Balding* a73
2 b f Sakhee(USA) —Santa Isobel (Nashwan (USA))
7451^4 7622^3 7763^3

Elyaadi *John Queally* a76 86
5 b m Singspiel(IRE) —Abyaan (IRE) (Ela-Mana-Mou)
5689a^3

Email Exit (IRE) *C F Wall* 56
2 ch c Titus Livius(FR) —Christoph's Girl (Efisio)
3072^7 4176^9 4825^10 5596^7 6589^4

Embra (IRE) *T J Etherington* a64 68
4 b g Monashee Mountain(USA) —Ivory Turner (Efisio)
1518^13 2312^14 5978^15 *6377^3* 6989^13 *7224^3* ◆ *7483^9 7503^2*

Embsay Crag *Mrs K Walton* 85
3 b g Elmaamul(USA) —Wigman Lady (IRE) (Tenby)
1281^4 1626^6 2370^5 (2779) 3371^5 4074^2 4709^4 (5209) 6100^4 6680^3 6996^10

Emeebee *W J Musson* a80 79
3 b g Medicean—Broughtons Motto (Mtoto)
2600^7 7189^3 *7356^3*

Emeralda *Pat Eddery* 42
3 b f Desert Prince(IRE) —Edouna (FR) (Doyoun)
1362^6 1579^8

Emerald Commander (IRE) *Saeed Bin Suroor* 109
2 b c Pivotal—Brigitta (IRE) (Sadler's Wells (USA))
3750^4 ◆ (4048) 5133^2 (5659) 7207a^2

Emerald Girl (IRE) *R A Fahey* 73
2 b f Chineur(FR) —Faypool (IRE) (Fayruz)
2963^3 3263^2 (3937) 4327^3 4975^5 (6134) 6643^4

Emerald Glade (IRE) *T D Easterby* 54
2 b f Azamour(IRE) —Woodland Glade (Mark Of Esteem (IRE))
4331^6 4847^9 5439^10 5980^5

Emerald Hawk (IRE) *D H Brown* 36
3 bb c Hawk Wing(USA) —Fabulous Pet (Somethingfabulous (USA))
1168^7 3566^8 5465^10 6742^13 6899^5

Emerald Rock (CAN) *Tom Dascombe* a63 50
4 b g Johannesburg(USA) —Classic Jones (CAN) (Regal Classic (CAN))
217^4 386^6 571^4 6126^11 6818^5

Emeralds Spirit (IRE) *J R Weymes* 57
2 b f Rock Of Gibraltar(IRE) —Spiritual Air (Royal Applause)
1661^6 2388^9 4278^6 4875^6 6232^5

Emerald Wilderness (IRE) *A King* a106 97
5 b g Green Desert(USA) —Simla Bibi (Indian Ridge)
360^2 ◆ *(585)* 1301^6 3586^8 (4315)

Emergency *D Smaga* 110
3 ch f Dr Fong(USA) —Well Warned (Warning) (3892a) 4971a^2 5709a^3 6717a^4 7232a^10

Emily Blackwell *H-A Pantall* 84
3 ch f Dr Fong(USA) —Strike Hard (IRE) (Green Desert (USA))
3417a^3

Emily Blake (IRE) *J C Hayden* a89 106
5 b m Lend A Hand—Kirri (IRE) (Lycius (USA))
1374a^11 (1756a) (2285a)

Emily Harley (IRE) *W G M Turner* a37 50
3 b f Sulamani(IRE) —Princess Bankes (Vettori (IRE))
6935^5

Emirates Champion *Saeed Bin Suroor* a75 104
3 b c Haafhd—Janaat (Kris)
2029^5 (6986) ◆

Emiratesdotcom *M Johnston* 40
3 b g Pivotal—Teggiano (IRE) (Mujtahid (USA))
3984^8 4505^7 5520^10 6188^9

Emirates Dream (USA) *Saeed Bin Suroor* 105
2 b c Kingmambo(USA) —My Boston Gal (USA) (Boston Harbor (USA))
(3823) ◆ 5708a^4 6133a^3 6811^3

Emirates Gold (IRE) *E Charpy* a66 102
6 b h Royal Applause—Yara (IRE) (Sri Pekan (USA))
182a^5 439a^6 609a^4 697a^3

Emirates Hills *E F Vaughan* 73
2 b f Dubawi(IRE) —Starstone (Diktat)
4257^5 4797^8 (5096) 5797^7 6169^7

Emirates Line (USA) *M bin Shafya* a95 88
6 ch g Kingmambo(USA) —Style Setter (USA) (Manila (USA))
337a^10 435a^11

Emirates Roadshow (USA) *Saeed Bin Suroor* 92
3 ch g Distorted Humor(USA) —Just A Bird (USA) (Storm Bird (CAN))
1751^2 2696^3 3049^7 3780^8 5189^2 5475^11

Emirates Skyline (USA) *A bin Huzaim* a96 113
6 b g Sunday Silence(USA) —The Caretaker (Caerleon (USA))
182a^9 340a^4 439a^12 642a^8 *698a^15*

Emirates Sports *Saeed Bin Suroor* a91 88
3 b c King's Best(USA) —Time Saved (Green Desert (USA))
(3509) 4210^5 4801^3

Emirates World (IRE) *M Johnston* a73 71
3 b g Exceed And Excel(AUS) —Enrich (USA) (Dynaformer (USA))
(356) 672^5 924^5

Emitard (FR) *Mme M Verdu-Estrabol* 82
3 b c Tot Ou Tard(IRE) —Emitha (FR) (L'Emigrant (USA))
6150a^7

Emma Dora (IRE) *D R C Elsworth* a54 71
2 b f Medaglia D'Oro(USA) —My Girl Lisa (USA) (With Approval (CAN))
2494^13 2860^5 (3356) 3865^6 5399^7 *6211^8* 6735^5 7097^6 *7359^6*

Emma Jean Lass (IRE) *P D Evans* a67 59
2 b f Choisir(AUS) —Enlisted (IRE) (Sadler's Wells (USA))
1031^2 1706^6 4221^4 4478^2 4850^8 6563^9 *7799^3 7849^7*

Emmrooz *Saeed Bin Suroor* 107
4 b h Red Ransom(USA) —Nasmatt (Danehill (USA))
642a^2 2606^2

Emotional Rescue (FR) *Y Durepaire* 72
2 b f Diableneyev(USA) —Ampelopsis (FR) (Night Shift (USA))
6501a^8

Emotive *F P Murtagh* a59 32
6 b g Pursuit Of Love—Ruby Julie (Clantime)
5307^5

Emperor Claudius (USA) *A P O'Brien* 103
2 b c Giant's Causeway(USA) —Virginia Waters (USA) (Kingmambo (USA))
3138^2 ◆ 3817^6 5859^6

Emperor Court (IRE) *P J Makin* a89 89
5 ch h Singspiel(IRE) —Tarquina (USA) (Niniski (USA))
791^3 361^7 893^5 (2823) 3578^4 5321^3 5772^5 *6168^3 6830^5*

Emperor's Well *M W Easterby* a53 64
10 ch g First Trump—Catherines Well (Junius (USA))
1194^12 1612^12 1955^11 3490^10 4435^8 4588^2 4932^4 6184^5 *6800^5 7142^3*

Empire Seeker (USA) *Mrs H S Main* a53 60
4 br g Seeking The Gold(USA) —Lady From Shanghai (USA) (Storm Cat (USA))
1589^7 2830^7 3077^10 *4538^6*

Emporio (GER) *F Vermeulen* 99
5 ch h Kaldounevees(FR) —Eirehill (IRE) (Danehill (USA))
2118a^5

Empowered (IRE) *W J Haggas* a88 94
4 b h Fasliyev(USA) —Funsie (FR) (Saumarez)
1107^2 (1660) (1826)

Empress Leizu (IRE) *E A L Dunlop* a52 44
2 b f Chineur(FR) —Silk Point (IRE) (Barathea (IRE))
6921^10 *7199^7 7450^11 (7669)*

Empressofboogie *M Dods* a47 53
2 b f Tobougg(IRE) —Akhira (Emperor Jones (USA))
4652^4 5668^4 5942^5 *6431^9*

Empress of France (USA) *A P O'Brien* 90
3 ch f Storm Cat(USA) —Mr P's Princess (USA) (Mr Prospector (USA))
1024a^7

Enact *Sir Michael Stoute* 100
3 b f Kyllachy—Constitute (USA) (Gone West (USA))
1296^2 1987^8 2270^7 3747^9 4459^5 ◆ (5130) 5607^2 6240^2 6814^3

Enchanted Evening (IRE) *D K Weld* 93
3 b f High Chaparral(IRE) —Glen Kate (Glenstal (USA))
2306a^4

Enchanting Muse (USA) *Robert Collet* a46 99
3 b f Fusaichi Pegasus(USA) —Moon Flower (IRE) (Sadler's Wells (USA))
4394a^8

Encircled *J R Jenkins* a95 92
5 b m In The Wings—Ring Of Esteem (Mark Of Esteem (IRE))
549^6 1184^2 1348^3 *2597^11* 3406^5 *6724^9*

Encore Belle *Mouse Hamilton-Fairley* a26 59
4 b m Beat Hollow—Rada's Daughter (Robellino (USA))
948^6 1254^3 1538^6 1785^15 2517^6 3777^7 4220^6

Endeavoured (IRE) *D Carroll* a46 26
3 b g Peintre Celebre(USA) —Addaya (IRE) (Persian Bold)
6788^13

Enderby Spirit (GR) *B Smart* 108
3 gr c Invincible Spirit(IRE) —Arctic Ice (IRE) (Zafonic (USA))
1085^4 1602^2 2035^6 (3622) 3747^3 4523^10 5032^8 6661^17

End Of The Affair (IRE) *V C Ward* a71 87
5 ch m Indian Ridge—Blend Of Pace (IRE) (Sadler's Wells (USA))
5689a^10

En Fuego *P W Chapple-Hyam* 77
2 b c Firebreak—Yanomami (USA) (Slew O'Gold (USA))
6809^7 7096^3 ◆

England (IRE) *N P Littmoden* 55
2 b c Bertolini(USA) —Radha (Bishop Of Cashel)
2413^5 2887^5 3403^6

English Archer *A Kirtley* 11
6 b g Rock City—Fire Sprite (Mummy's Game)
4806^14 5162^8 5554^12 5734^15 6183^12

English City (IRE) *Mrs L B Normile* a45 56
6 ch h City On A Hill(USA) —Toledana (IRE) (Sure Blade (USA))
4873[3] 5359[5]
Engrupido (ARG) *M F De Kock* a87 111
6 gr g Potrillon(ARG) —Una Gata (ARG) (Equalize (USA))
185a[2]
Engulf (IRE) *W J Haggas* 56
2 b c Danehill Dancer(IRE) —All Embracing (IRE) (Night Shift (USA))
5029[5] ◆
Enhancing *J A Glover* a54 67
3 b f Hawk Wing(USA) —Enhance (Entrepreneur)
998[12] *1490[3]* 2236[6] 5601[18] *6070[11]* 6755[8] *6804[4]*
Enigma Code (UAE) *James McAuley* a76 73
4 b g Elusive Quality(USA) —Tempting Fate (IRE) (Persian Bold)
1376a[2]
Enjoyment *M L W Bell* 63
2 b f Dansili—Have Fun (Indian Ridge)
4226[4] ◆ 4666[7]
Enjoy The Moment *J A Osborne* 105
6 b g Generous(IRE) —Denial (Sadler's Wells (USA))
5903[6] 6851[30]
Enlightenment (IRE) *Evan Williams* a64 48
9 b g Presenting—Shaiybaniyda (He Loves Me)
(501) 4169[8]
Enlist *A J Lidderdale* a69
5 b g Beat Hollow—Dawna (Polish Precedent (USA))
970[3] *1133[6]*
Enrique Shaw (FR) *J Van Handenhove* a66 74
3 b c Enrique—Grenshaw (IRE) (Persian Heights)
5118a[0]
Enroller (IRE) *W R Muir* 112
4 b h Marju(IRE) —Walk On Quest (FR) (Rainbow Quest (USA))
(1351) 3139[4] 3781[6] 4457[5] 5171[5] 6324a[6] 7031[9]
Ensign's Trick *W M Brisbourne* a26 63
5 b m Cayman Kai(IRE) —River Ensign (River God (USA))
6924[15]
Ensnare *Ian Williams* a82 71
4 b g Pivotal—Entrap (USA) (Phone Trick (USA))
280[9] *468[4]* *570[6]* *(3470)* (3653) 4207[8] 5448[13] *(7236)* ◆ *7362[2]* *7633[6]*
Enthusius *G L Moore* a58 45
6 b g Generous(IRE) —Edouna (FR) (Doyoun)
168[5] 4855[7] 5579[10] 6692[14]
Enticement *Sir Michael Stoute* 102
3 b f Montjeu(IRE) —Ecoutila (USA) (Rahy (USA))
1988[3] 3442a[8] (6813) 7128a[7]
Entreat *Sir Michael Stoute* a76 84
3 ch f Pivotal—River Saint (USA) (Irish River (FR))
1488[3] 2006[3] 2738[5] *4085[3]* (5151) 5997[3] 6250[9]
Entre Deux Eaux (FR) *Robert Collet* a106 109
3 b f Ange Gabriel(FR) —Goutte D'Eau (FR) (Vacarme (USA))
1208a[2] 1918a[6] 2521a[6] 2757a[3] 4971a[9] 5709a[4] 7044a[12] *7697a[0]*
En Un Clin D'Oeil (IRE) *Ms Joanna Morgan* 100
2 b c Chineur(FR) —Sans Reserve (IRE) (Foxhound (USA))
3514a[2] 3895a[4]
Enzio (GER) *A Wohler* 100
3 ch g Next Desert(IRE) —Elle Diva (GER) (Big Shuffle (USA))
1718a[5] 2560a[7]
Eolith *W J Knight* a83 83
2 ch f Pastoral Pursuits—Evening Guest (FR) (Be My Guest (USA))
(4792) *(5639)*
Ephigenie (GER) *T Mundry* 97
3 b f Groom Dancer(USA) —Enrica (GER) (Niniski (USA))
6152a[5] 6715a[4]
Epic (IRE) *M Johnston* a76 76
2 b g Celtic Swing—Needwood Epic (Midyan (USA))
3522[6] *4646[5]* (5981) *6491[3]* *7003[7]* *7804[3]*
Epic Odyssey *Lee Smyth* a87 85
4 ch g Dubai Destination(USA) —Royal Gift (Cadeaux Genereux)
86[2] *(510)* *973[3]* 2389[11]
Epidaurian King (IRE) *D Shaw* a68 64
6 b g King's Best(USA) —Thurayya (Nashwan (USA))
21[5] *194[6]* *311[2]* *559[5]* 1279[11] 1475[13] 2264[6]
Epsom Salts *P M Phelan* a77 84
4 b g Josr Algarhoud(IRE) —Captive Heart (Conquistador Cielo (USA))
1426[8] 2177[7] 2760[4] 2983[8] (3521) 3814[5] 4696[4] (5185) 5509[3] (5802) 6115[3] 6473[7]
Equiano (FR) *B W Hills* 119
4 b h Acclamation—Entente Cordiale (IRE) (Ela-Mana-Mou)
1299[2] 1989[11] 2523a[9] 2991[8] 3819[8] 4456[8] ◆ 5233[8] 5657[5] 6522a[11]
Equinine (IRE) *Peter Grayson* a74 76
3 ch f Namid—Goldilocks (IRE) (Caerleon (USA))
2849[3] ◆ 4097[7] 4550[3] *4981[2]* (5599) 5916[2] *6294[8]* *7358[8]*
Equinity *J Pearce* a56 52
3 b f Ishiguru(USA) —Notable Lady (IRE) (Victory Note (USA))
2581[6] *3299[10]* 3663[4] 4596[7] (5155) 6038[11] *7069[9]* *7176[5]* *7572[9]* *7879[2]*
Equipe De Nuit *S C Williams* a70 83
3 ch c Sulamani(IRE) —Denica (IRE) (Night Shift (USA))
1185[6] 1992[13] 2701[17] 3644[6] 4242[3] 5108[2] 5127[3] 5482[4] *5574[4]* 5999[5] (6170) 6362[9] 6755[16]
Equuleus Pictor *J L Spearing* a93 94
5 br g Piccolo—Vax Rapide (Sharpo)
1685[9] 2095[4] (2228) (2897) 3582[5] 4099[6] 4461[17] 5654[12] 6647[3] 6843[4] 7015[14] *7676[2]* *7866[3]*
Ercolini (IRE) *F Rodriguez Puertas* 97
2 b f Pyrus(USA) —Bajan Belle (IRE) (Efisio)
7230a[3]

Erdiyna (IRE) *John M Oxx* a54 89
3 b f Selkirk(USA) —Ebareva (IRE) (Machiavellian (USA))
7263a[13]
Erebus (IRE) *S Kirk* a64 58
2 b c Fasliyev(USA) —Velvet Slipper (Muhtafal (USA))
6737[7] *7700[8]* *7859[6]*
Ereeford *M W Easterby*
3 b g Ishiguru(USA) —Miss Twiddles (IRE) (Desert King (IRE))
686[6] *1476[8]*
Erfaan (USA) *B W Hills* 65
2 bb c Forest Camp(USA) —Look For Good (USA) (Unbridled's Song (USA))
2844[11] 3750[8]
Ergo (FR) *James Moffatt* a71 76
5 b h Grand Lodge(USA) —Erhawah (Mark Of Esteem (IRE))
(657) *(898)* 1060[2] (1690) 2391[5] 2724[4] 4046[7] 5395[10] *5886[4]*
Erinjay (IRE) *M Wigham* a75
3 b g Bachelor Duke(USA) —Quinella (Generous (IRE))
7849 ◆ *(7826)* ◆
Ermine And Velvet *C E Brittain* a39 88
3 ch f Nayef(USA) —Ermine (IRE) (Cadeaux Genereux)
1327[4] *1605[9]* 2080[2] 2673[2] 3320[11] 3816[8] 4947[2] 6267[8]
Ermine Grey *S Gollings* a63 66
8 gr g Wolfhound(USA) —Impulsive Decision (IRE) (Nomination)
959[5] *1318[5]* 2261[5] *2746[10]* 5631[3] *6668[4]*
Ermine Sea *Miss H C Knight* a77 93
6 b g Rainbow Quest(USA) —Bint Pasha (USA) (Affirmed (USA))
1863[3] 2994[16] 4260[6] 5346[5]
Ermyn Express *P M Phelan* a63
2 b f Selkirk(USA) —Aymara (Darshaan)
6911[8] *7106[11]* *7655[3]* *7825[4]*
Ermyn Lodge *P M Phelan* a81 81
3 br g Singspiel(IRE) —Rosewood Belle (USA) (Woodman (USA))
(953) ◆ 1570[2] 1842[5] *3300[3]* 4442[2] (4911) *5666[2]* 6388[2]
Ermyntrude *P M Phelan* a56 41
2 bb f Rock Of Gibraltar(IRE) —Ruthie (Pursuit Of Love)
6441[5] 6727[9] *7106[4]* *7654[11]*
Ernies Keep *W Storey* 46
3 ch g Young Ern—Croeso Cynnes (Most Welcome)
1226[8] 1520[8] 2627[5] 2802[10] 4617[7] 5442[8] 5733[8]
Erra Go On *G T Lynch* a60 57
8 ch g Atraf—Pastelle (Tate Gallery (USA))
8441[3]
Errigal Lad *J Balding* a61 88
4 ch g Bertolini(USA) —La Belle Vie (Indian King (USA))
2405[2] 2695[5] 3097[7] 3377[2] 3706[6] 4387[5] 4507[6] 5516[8]
Errol Flynn (IRE) *B G Powell* a30 51
3 bb g Danehill Dancer(IRE) —Warusha (GER) (Shareef Dancer (USA))
1297[10] 3207[11] 4606[9] 5381[12] *6705[10]*
Ertiyaad *Sir Michael Stoute* a48
2 b f Sakhee(USA) —Asawer (IRE) (Darshaan)
7325[8]
Esaar (USA) *B W Hills* 85
2 b c Mr Greeley(USA) —Al Desima (Emperor Jones (USA))
4986[3] 6451[2]
Escape Artist *T D Easterby* 43
2 gr g Act One—Free At Last (Shirley Heights)
3823[9] 4396[9] 4888[6]
Escape Route (USA) *S Seemar* a98 101
5 b g Elusive Quality(USA) —Away (USA) (Dixieland Band (USA))
522a[7] ◆ *612a[7]*
Escape To Freedom (IRE) *E J O'Neill*
2 b c Red Ransom(USA) —Brief Escapade (IRE) (Brief Truce (USA))
6979a[0] 7264a[0]
Escape Wall *R J Hodges* a12
8 ch g Kirkwall—Island Escape (IRE) (Turtle Island (IRE))
6703[10]
Eseej (USA) *P W Hiatt* a82 78
4 ch g Aljabr(USA) —Jinaan (USA) (Mr Prospector (USA))
311[6] *406[4]* *497[2]* *(660)* *(745)* *952[7]* 4288[8] 4855[2] 5185[7] *6583[6]* *(6878)* 7151[14] 7279[4] 7373[9] 7851[4]
Eskendereya (USA) *Todd Pletcher* a102 86
2 ch c Giants Causeway—Aldebaran Light (USA) (Seattle Slew (USA))
7307a[9]
Esoterica (IRE) *J S Goldie* 97
6 b g Bluebird(USA) —Mysterious Plans (IRE) (Last Tycoon)
1229[6] 1649[8] 2073[5] (2391) (2589) 2780[5] 3872[13] 4297[19] 5206[8] 5249[5] 5363[6] 6050[4] 6278[8] (6815)
Espartaco (SPA) *C Laffon-Parias* 64
2 b c Leadership—Jarama (IRE) (Hector Protector (USA))
7315a[6]
Especially Special (IRE) *Peter Grayson* a75 72
3 b f Exceed And Excel(AUS) —Super Trouper (FR) (Nashwan (USA))
4712[6] *5370[11]* *6455[4]* *6701[7]* *7021[4]* *7397[10]* *7605[4]* *7808[9]*
Espero (IRE) *R A Farrant* a86 82
3 b g Celtic Swing—Zota (IRE) (Barathea (IRE))
3155[2] 4151[6] *4981[3]* *5677[2]* *(6073)* *(7141)*
Espiritu (FR) *J Noseda* 107
3 b g Dansili—Red Bravo (USA) (Red Ransom (USA))
1295[5] 2416[2] (2805) 3049[4] 3839[10] 4296[3] 5863[10] 6307[8] 6665[2]
Esposito *Frau E Mader* a68 77
7 ch g Inchinor—Celebrate (IRE) (Generous (IRE))
7822a[6]

Espresso Steps (USA) *P Howling* a25
3 bb f Medaglia D'Oro(USA) —Walk On Gold (USA) (Seeking The Gold (USA))
7411[9] *7576[6]* *7730[9]*
Esprit De Midas *K A Ryan* a83 93
3 b g Namid—Spritzeria (Bigstone (IRE))
(366) ◆ *(426)* *(492)* *1567[6]* (2148) *7639[6]*
Espy *I W McInnes* a73 82
4 b g Piccolo—Running Glimpse (IRE) (Runnett)
1094[7] *1321[7]* 1806[7] 2359[6] 3261[2] ◆ 3477[3] 3998[8] 4051[4] 4604[2] 5323[11] *5836[3]* *6028[4]* 6738[7] *7023[6]* *7673[2]*
Essex (IRE) *M J P O'Brien* 84
9 b g Sadler's Wells(USA) —Knight's Baroness (Rainbow Quest (USA))
2305a[4]
Essexbridge *R Hannon* a72 77
2 b c Avonbridge—Aonach Mor (Anabaa (USA))
6065[4] *6629[2]* (6962)
Esta Bailando (CHI) *J Barton* a83
4 rg m Dance Brightly(CAN) —Stangarella (ARG) (Equalize (USA))
181a[5] *438a[5]* *701a[6]*
Estate *D E Pipe* a74 80
7 b g Montjeu(IRE) —Fig Tree Drive (USA) (Miswaki (USA))
7701[7]
Esteem Dancer *J G Given* a49
3 ch g Mark Of Esteem(IRE) —Lake Diva (Docksider (USA))
230[4] *572[10]* *808[8]*
Esteem Lord *Jamie Poulton* a69 69
3 ch g Mark Of Esteem(IRE) —Milady Lillie (IRE) (Distinctly North (USA))
121[10] *599[2]* *800[2]* 1295[8] 2048[15] *3274[10]*
Esteem Machine (USA) *R A Teal* a83 91
5 b g Mark Of Esteem(IRE) —Theme (IRE) (Sadler's Wells (USA))
1212[10] *1467[5]* 2078[10] 2637[4] 2946[9] 3845[2] ◆ (4500) 4853[10] 5424[15] 6112[7] *6293[4]* 6904[4] *7516[5]* *7603[6]*
Estejo (GER) *R Rohne* 111
5 b h Johan Cruyff—Este (GER) (The Noble Player (USA))
2115a[6] 3013[8] 6506a[9] 7313a[10]
Estephe (IRE) *T Stack* 88
3 b f Sadler's Wells(USA) —Tarascon (IRE) (Tirol)
5689a[6]
Estihdaaf (USA) *A Al Raihe* a95 94
8 br g Distant View(USA) —Nadwah (USA) (Shadeed (USA))
610a[5]
Estimate (FR) *E Lellouche* 71
2 b c Westerner—Ela Merici (FR) (Beaudelaire (USA))
5561a[2]
Estonia *J H M Gosden* 36
2 b f Exceed And Excel(AUS) —Global Trend (Bluebird (USA))
5026[10]
Estrela Anki (BRZ) *G Duarte* 72
4 b m Thignon Lafre(BRZ) —Marne La Coquette (BRZ) (Effervescing (USA))
6506a[13]
Estrela Boa (BRZ) *P Bary* a71 79
4 b m Our Emblem(USA) —Notizia (BRZ) (Pallazzi (BRZ))
180a[6] *438a[8]*
Estrela Brage (USA) *Edward Lynam* a93 104
6 b g Silic(FR) —Devine Blade (USA) (Blade (USA))
3882a[RR]
Estrela Do Oriente (BRZ) *P Bary* 70
4 b h Redattore(BRZ) —Academia Real (USA) (Banker's Gold (USA))
183a[9]
Esuvia (IRE) *B Smart* a71 66
2 b f Whipper(USA) —Aoife (IRE) (Thatching)
7289[3] ◆ *7556[2]* *(7708)*
Etain (IRE) *Mrs Lawney Hill* a71 74
5 b m Alhaarth(IRE) —Brogan's Well (IRE) (Caerleon (USA))
7225[13]
Eternal Instinct *J S Goldie* 79
2 b f Exceed And Excel(AUS) —Glenhurich (IRE) (Sri Pekan (USA))
(1504) 2054[8] 2714[7] 3086[16] (3682) 4089[11] 4547[3] 5136[14] 5795[10] 6090[7] 7115[4]
Eternal Optimist (IRE) *Paul Green* a58 56
4 b m Bahri(USA) —Shore Lark (USA) (Storm Bird (CAN))
655[9]
Eternal Power *C Von Der Recke* 98
2 b c Tiger Hill(IRE) —Eternal Beauty (USA) (Zafonic (USA))
5652a[3] 7314a[5]
Ethics Girl (IRE) *John Berry* a81 82
3 b f Hernando(FR) —Palinisa (FR) (Night Shift (USA))
1671[6] 2528[2] 2790[8] (3803) ◆ 4481[5] (4957) 5419[11] 5725[4] 6473[2] *6855[3]* *7201[3]* *7583[3]*
Etihaad *R Bouresly* a87 87
7 b h Dubai Millennium—Elfaslah (IRE) (Green Desert (USA))
184a[10] *261a[5]*
Etoile D'Or (IRE) *M J Gingell* 61
5 ch m Soviet Star(USA) —Christeningpresent (IRE) (Cadeaux Genereux)
4931[0]
Etoile Du Ninian (FR) *D Windrif* 60
3 b f Little Rock—Crepuscule Indien (IRE) (Thatching)
7037a[6]
Etoile Nocturne (FR) *W Baltromei* a84 105
5 b m Medicean—Nachtigall (FR) (Night Shift (USA))
2097a[2] (3650a) 5493a[5] 7232a[11]
Eton Fable (IRE) *W J H Ratcliffe* a78 84
4 b g Val Royal(FR) —Lina Story (Linamix (FR))
648[2] *726[3]* (1175) 1274[5] 1665[3] 2283[7] 2766[9] 3564[7] (4696) 5067[2]

Eton Rifles (IRE) *J Howard Johnson* 96
4 b g Pivotal—Maritsa (IRE) (Danehill (USA))
2045[3] ◆ (2276) ◆ 3706[3] 4310[2] ◆ 5695[3] (6135)
Etruscan (IRE) *C Gordon* a35 79
4 b g Selkirk(USA) —Maddelina (IRE) (Sadler's Wells (USA))
6741[2] 7036[4] *7780[5]*
Ettrick Mill *M Johnston* a71 23
3 ch g Selkirk(USA) —Milly-M (Cadeaux Genereux)
3067 *440[5]* 5773[5] 6158[4]
Eureka Moment *E A L Dunlop* a68 70
4 b m Alhaarth(IRE) —Burn Baby Burn (IRE) (King's Theatre (IRE))
126[4] *299[2]* *393[4]*
Euroceleb (IRE) *H Morrison* a73 57
4 ch m Peintre Celebre(USA) —Eurobird (Ela-Mana-Mou)
11[3] *219[10]*
European Dream (IRE) *R C Guest* 90
6 br g Kalanisi(IRE) —Tereed Elhawa (Cadeaux Genereux)
1352[20] 5655[9] 7245[6]
Eurotanz (IRE) *H Morrison* a64 64
3 b f Danehill Dancer(IRE) —Eurostorm (USA) (Storm Bird (CAN))
2091[6] ◆ 4150[4] 4569[4] 4916[5] *6031[12]*
Euston Square *J H M Gosden* a83 86
3 b g Oasis Dream—Krisia (Kris)
1295[3] ◆ *1636[3]* 2298[3] (6573) *6944[6]*
Eva Kant *R Menichetti* 94
3 ch f Medicean—Quadri (Polish Precedent (USA))
1394a[10]
Evaluator (IRE) *M Ramadan* a68 62
8 b g Ela-Mana-Mou—Summerhill (Habitat)
697a[11]
Evaporation (FR) *C Laffon-Parias* a90 88
2 b f Red Ransom(USA) —Polygreen (FR) (Green Tune (USA))
4584a[3] *(5240a)*
Evasive *Saeed Bin Suroor* a84 115
3 ch c Elusive Quality(USA) —Canda (USA) (Storm Cat (USA))
1675[6] 2992[4] 5024[6]
Eva's Request (IRE) *M R Channon* a81 112
4 ch m Soviet Star(USA) —Ingabelle (Taufan (USA))
416a[3] 643a[7] 997[13] (1667) (2703) 3012[3] 3749[7] 4580a[5] (5588a) (7046a) 7498a[10]
Evelith Regent (IRE) *G A Swinbank* a31 72
6 b g Imperial Ballet(IRE) —No Avail (IRE) (Imperial Frontier (USA))
2264[5]
Evelyn May (IRE) *B W Hills* a81 79
3 b f Acclamation—Lady Eberspacher (IRE) (Royal Abjar (USA))
1078[4] 1486[8] 2148[3] 2562[3] 4148[8] 4483[6] 5471[6] *(5777)* 6118[7] *7253[4]* ◆
Even Bolder *E A Wheeler* a88 88
6 ch g Bold Edge—Level Pegging (IRE) (Common Grounds)
1494[3] 1836[9] 2637[8] 2911[7] 3386[7] 3845[3] 4567[6] ◆ 4907[11] 5219[6] 5724[7] 6205[6] (6422) (6666) 6791[12] *7395[2]* *7511[7]* *7656[9]*
Evening Glow *C E Brittain* a13 26
2 b f Fantastic Light(USA) —Kartuzy (JPN) (Polish Precedent (USA))
4980[14] 5969[11]
Evening Rushour (IRE) *A Kinsella* 86
5 b m Mull Of Kintyre(USA) —Tip Tap Toe (USA) (Pleasant Tap (USA))
2960a[6]
Evening Sunset (GER) *M G Quinlan* a62 69
3 b f Dansili—Evening Promise (Aragon)
1462[12] 1774[6] 2091[5] ◆ 2863[3] 3209[4] 3741[3] ◆ (4013) 4482[8] 4720[4] 5567[2] *6784[4]*
Evening Tale (IRE) *B J Meehan* a59
2 b f Rock Of Gibraltar(IRE) —Wondrous Story (USA) (Royal Academy (USA))
7135[12] *7396[3]*
Evens And Odds (IRE) *D Nicholls* a111 108
5 ch g Johannesburg(USA) —Coeur De La Mer (IRE) (Caerleon (USA))
1018[3] (1699) 1861[16] 3141[22] 4523[2] 6091[4]
Evenstorm (USA) *B Gubby* a50 61
4 ch m Stephen Got Even(USA) —Summer Wind Storm (USA) (Storm Cat (USA))
496[7]
Everaard (USA) *D R C Elsworth* a70 70
3 ch g Lion Heart(USA) —Via Gras (USA) (Montbrook (USA))
1036[5] 1253[3] 1574[3] (1746) 2370[3] 2863[9] 2982[4] 3279[3] 4759[10] 6116[2] 6549[4] *6784[2]* *6975[5]*
Ever A Gent *M W Easterby* a40
2 b g Gentleman's Deal(IRE) —Mill End Quest (King's Signet (USA))
7502[6] *7638[6]* *7705[6]*
Ever Cheerful *A B Haynes* a69 65
8 b g Atraf—Big Story (Cadeaux Genereux)
355[4] *708[3]* *844[2]* *961[3]* *1121[6]* *2598[10]* *4202[2]* *4791[11]* *7275[7]* 7520[4] 7662[12]
Evergreen Dancer (IRE) *J R Best* a25 57
2 b c Noverre(USA) —Persea (IRE) (Fasliyev (USA))
2376[4] 3218[8] 3692[7] *4647[9]* 5589[9] 5967[11]
Ever Loved (USA) *S Seemar* a83 58
3 ch f Gone West(USA) —Shawklit Delight (USA) (Pine Bluff (USA))
181a[6] *438a[4]* *701a[8]*
Ever So Bold *W R Muir* a68 64
2 b g Reset(AUS) —Bold Byzantium (Bold Arrangement)
1083[5] 1195[10] 2335[3] 3072[4] 4565[4] 5589[5] *6071[7]* *(6609)* *7320[4]* *7551[4]*
Everybody Knows *Miss Jo Crowley* a84 84
4 b g King's Best(USA) —Logic (Slip Anchor)
191[2] *1186[5]* (1813) 3378[9]
Everyday (FR) *F Wintz* 67
3 br g Rochesson(FR) —Lady Romaine (FR) (Roi De Rome (USA))
5783a[10]

Everyman *A W Carroll* a64 55
5 gr g Act One—Maid To Dance (Pyramus (USA))
427[5] 597[8] 885[5] 1463[4] 1785[5] 2601[4] 2830[6] 3717[5] 4220[3] 4382[6]

Everymanforhimself (IRE) *K A Ryan* a97 105
5 b g Fasliyev(USA) —Luisa Demon (IRE) (Barathea (IRE))
1018[19] 1278[3] 2012[2] 2297[2] 3236[2] 4485[14] (4784) 5039[11] 5860[2] 6091[16] 6282[6] 6675[2] 7486[3]

Everynight (IRE) *M Botti* a77 94
3 b g Rock Of Gibraltar(IRE) —Rasana (Royal Academy (USA))
(998) ◆ 1303[8] 2411[6] 2855[4] 5030[3] 5648[5] 6004[U]

Everything *P T Midgley* a61 73
4 bl m Namid—Flight Sequence (Polar Falcon (USA))
95[6]

Evette *H J Collingridge* a43 39
4 b m Loup Solitaire(USA) —La Scarlet (FR) (Highest Honor (FR))
343[6] 587[10]

Evianne *P W Hiatt* a23 42
5 b m Lugana Beach—Folk Dance (USA) (Bertrando (USA))
3501[8] 3949[10] 4731[6] 5569[8]

Evident Pride (USA) *B R Johnson* a93 73
6 b g Chester House(USA) —Proud Fact (USA) (Known Fact (USA))
(33) 360[7] 585[5] 801[8] 1621[6] 5190[14] 5649[3] 6566[6] 7066[4] 7573[3] 7811[6]

Evita Argentina (USA) *John W Sadler* a113
3 ch f Candy Ride(ARG) —Jealous Wildcat (USA) (Forest Wildcat (USA))
7285a[7]

Evna (USA) *R A Fahey* a72 65
3 ch f Grand Slam(USA) —Our Josephina (USA) (Tale Of The Cat (USA))
2446[7] 2937[12] (4174) ◆ 4530[3] 4707[9]

Exceed Elegance (IRE) *D Shaw* a59 62
3 b f Exceed And Excel(AUS) —Colleen (IRE) (Sadler's Wells (USA))
2151[8] 2700[5] 3229[5] 3704[2] 4131[3] 4343[5] 6492[8] 7129[9] 7371[2] 7595[6] 7835[10]

Exceedingly Bold *Miss Gay Kelleway* 88
2 b c Exceed And Excel(AUS) —Grey Pearl (Ali-Royal (IRE))
5256[2] 6154[3] (6615) 7030[9]

Exceedingly Good (IRE) *B Smart* 67
3 ch f Exceed And Excel(AUS) —Ikan (IRE) (Sri Pekan (USA))
2028[4] 2365[10] 4997[7] 5468[5]

Exceed Power *D M Simcock* a53 53
2 ch f Exceed And Excel(AUS) —Israar (Machiavellian (USA))
2563[8] 3101[9] 3370[5] 4208[8] 5310[4] 5776[9] 6938[4]

Exceedthewildman *J S Moore* a73 71
2 b c Exceed And Excel(AUS) —Naomi Wildman (USA) (Kingmambo (USA))
5867[3] ◆ 6199[3] 6616[7] 7434[6] (7551) 7654[4] 7806[3]

Excelerate (IRE) *Edward Lynam* a72 103
6 b g Mujadil(USA) —Perle D'Irlande (FR) (Top Ville)
5141a[4]

Excellent Day (IRE) *M R Channon* 75
2 b f Invincible Spirit(IRE) —Tosca (Be My Guest (USA))
3820[9] 4243[2] (4711)

Excellent Girl *Y De Nicolay* a78 103
3 b f Exceed And Excel(AUS) —Dame Blanche (IRE) (Be My Guest (USA))
1267a[5] 1657a[3] 2119a[4] 5562a[11] 7569a[9]

Excellent Guest *G G Margarson* 80
2 b c Exceed And Excel(AUS) —Princess Speedfit (FR) (Desert Prince (IRE))
2413[4] 3692[4] 4258[3] (4717) 5136[12]

Excellent Show *B Smart* a87 82
3 ch f Exceed And Excel(AUS) —Quiz Show (Primo Dominie)
1517[7] 2915[3] 3173[5] 4601[3] 5856[3] 6647[9] 7511[2] (7872)

Excellent Thought *W J Haggas* a74 70
2 b f Exceed And Excel(AUS) —Amiata (Pennekamp (USA))
2972[5] 3458[2] 6563[3] ◆ 6932[2] 7213[2] 7453[3]

Excellent Vision *B Smart* 70
2 b c Exceed And Excel(AUS) —Classic Vision (Classic Cliche (IRE))
6154[4] 6646[3]

Excellerator (IRE) *George Baker* a98 98
3 ch f Exceed And Excel(AUS) —Amsicora (Cadeaux Genereux)
3621[3] 5233[14] 6427[8] ◆ 7090[2]

Excelling (IRE) *P J Makin* a64 85
2 b f Exceed And Excel(AUS) —Nojoom (IRE) (Alhaarth (IRE))
3633[7] (4302) 4989[7] 5650[4] 6241[10]

Excelsior Academy *B J Meehan* a75 82
3 b g Montjeu(IRE) —Birthday Suit (IRE) (Daylami (IRE))
1416[5] 1747[3] 2208[9] (2866) ◆ 3300[4] 4319[4] (4709)

Exceptional Art *D Nicholls* a71 105
3 ch g Exceed And Excel(AUS) —Only In Dreams (Polar Falcon (USA))
1664[2] (2270) 3298[6] (5420) ◆

Excitable (IRE) *Mrs D J Sanderson* a52 54
3 b f Exceed And Excel(AUS) —Kalwada (USA) (Roberto (USA))
3176[3] 3611[4] 3938[8] 4204[4] 5341[11] 6553[13]

Exclamation *B J Meehan* a97 106
4 br g Acclamation—Summer Siren (FR) (Saint Cyrien (FR))
1299[4] 1699[3] 2078[9] 3141[24] 7090[3] 7394[6]

Excusez Moi (USA) *Mrs R A Carr* a114 101
7 b g Fusaichi Pegasus(USA) —Jiving (Generous (IRE))
2[5] 225[6] 266[2] 422[4] 579[11] 1016[9] (1229) 1560[5] (1849) ◆ 2059[8] (2259) 2570[4] ◆ 2941[11] 3389[4] 4037[5] 4330[3] 5039[13] 5695[U] 5826[8] 6678[9] 7015[2] 7294[6]

Exearti *A J McCabe* a69
2 b f Exceed And Excel(AUS) —Graffiti Girl (IRE) (Sadler's Wells (USA))
3987[8] 7556[5] 7708[3] 7836[3] (7864)

Execution (IRE) *E A L Dunlop* a59 64
2 b c Alhaarth(IRE) —Headrest (Habitat)
3715[8] 4201[4] 4385[6] 5573[10] 5985[6] 6639[3] 6736[9]

Exemplary *M Johnston* a70 79
2 b c Sulamani(IRE) —Epitome (IRE) (Nashwan (USA))
5324[4] 6125[3] (6331) ◆

Ex Gracia *K A Ryan* 25
3 ch f Efisio—Action De Grace (USA) (Riverman (USA))
3764[10] 4550[8]

Exgray (IRE) *B Smart* 82
2 ch f Exceed And Excel(AUS) —Mrs Gray (Red Sunset)
2449[2] ◆ (3478)

Exhibition (IRE) *F Castro* a97 101
4 b g Invincible Spirit(IRE) —Moonbi Ridge (IRE) (Definite Article)
6522a[12]

Exilissi (IRE) *P Meniconi* 68
3 b c Choisir(AUS) —Carolina My Love (IRE) (In The Wings)
2114a[9]

Existentialist *A E Price* a61 79
2 b f Exceed And Excel(AUS) —Owdbetts (IRE) (High Estate)
1569[3] (1810) 2372[16] 3430[3] 4089[16] 4989[13] 5241[5] (5835) 6541[8]

Existes Ons Nous (FR) *J-M Lefebvre* 61
2 ch c Le Fou(IRE) —Xistu (FR) (Lost World (IRE))
6507a[7] 6927a[9]

Exit Smiling *P T Midgley* a85 94
7 ch g Dr Fong(USA) —Away To Me (Exit To Nowhere (USA))
(490) 747[4] 995[16] 1306[4] 1722[4] 1952[6] 2101[2] 2612[9] 3067[2] 3560[3] 3941[2] (4663) 5040[5] 5522[5] 6014[4]

Exopuntia *R M Whitaker* 55
3 b f Sure Blade(USA) —Opuntia (Rousillon (USA))
3175[2] ◆ 3859[7] 4436[11] 5601[15] 6217[9]

Exotica (FR) *B Goudot* 75
2 ch f Tobougg(IRE) —Linda's Lady (FR) (Spectrum (IRE))
2694a[2] 7166a[9]

Exotic Beauty *M R Channon* 89
2 b f Barathea(IRE) —Lady Dominatrix (IRE) (Danehill Dancer (IRE))
2207[3] ◆ 2563[2] (2907) ◆ 4539[8] (5038) 5521[4] 6049[9] 6486[12]

Exotic Dream (FR) *A Trybuhl* 74
3 b f Fantastic Light(USA) —Elouallee (FR) (Anabaa (USA))
2524a[9]

Exotic Girl (IRE) *A Peraino* 82
2 b f Antonius Pius(USA) —Burn (Selkirk (USA))
2586a[5]

Expensive Dinner *E F Vaughan* a49 15
3 ch f Dr Fong(USA) —Reservation (IRE) (Common Grounds)
2455[6] 4981[7] (Dead)

Expensive Legacy *H J L Dunlop* a42 60
2 ch f Piccolo—American Rouge (IRE) (Grand Lodge (USA))
3576[8] 3979[10] 4945[11] 6366[6] 6930[10] 7474[6]

Expensive Problem *R J Smith* a63 76
6 b g Medicean—Dance Steppe (Rambo Dancer (CAN))
(3463) 3766[6] 5190[13] 6726[11]

Explorator (IRE) *George Baker* a55
2 b c Whipper(USA) —Certainly Brave (Indian Ridge)
7700[9] 7886[4]

Expressive *Sir Michael Stoute* a78
3 b f Falbrav(IRE) —Exclusive (Polar Falcon (USA))
2142[2] 4648[3] 5228[2] 6029[2] (6346)

Expresso Star (USA) *J H M Gosden* 113
4 b h War Chant(USA) —Caffe Latte (IRE) (Seattle Dancer (USA))
(997) ◆ 1799[3] 2670[7] 7208a[7]

Express Wish *J Noseda* a77 111
5 b h Danehill Dancer(IRE) —Waffle On (Chief Singer)
1138a[7] 3398[9] 4406[5] 5024[7] 5474[4] 5878[5]

Extracurricular (USA) *S Gollings* a62 48
3 ch f Thunder Gulch(USA) —Frans Lass (USA) (Shanekite (USA))
949[5] 1410[4] 2395[5] 4177[6] 4719[4] 5316[8]

Extraterrestrial *R A Fahey* a100 106
5 b g Mind Games—Expectation (IRE) (Night Shift (USA))
783[7] 995[2] 1209[3] (1352) 2015[8] 3639[7] 4486[8] 5200[13] (6094)

Extreme Green *A M Balding* 54
2 ch f Motivator—Ventura (IRE) (Spectrum (IRE))
6363[7] 6965[7]

Extremely So *P J McBride* a64 63
3 ch f Kyllachy—Antigua (Selkirk (USA))
1070[6] 1282[7] 2461[2] 2942[6] 3550[2] 4269[9] 5286[4] (6919) 7440[2] 7608[3]

Extreme Pleasure (IRE) *W J Knight* a63 64
4 b m High Chaparral(IRE) —Height Of Passion (Shirley Heights)
2944[9] 3739[10] 4935[9]

Extreme Warrior (IRE) *D R Lanigan* 82
2 ch g Dubawi(IRE) —Extreme Beauty (USA) (Rahy (USA))
2477[9] (3113) ◆ 3782[4] 4086[5]

Eye Candy (IRE) *Mrs Sandra McCarthy* a50 54
8 b g Princely Heir(IRE) —Timissa (IRE) (Kahyasi)
3654[7]

Eyeffess (IRE) *P J Rothwell* a63 57
8 ch g Pasternak—Ben Tack (Lucifer (USA))
7005[6]

Eye For The Girls *M R Channon* 58
3 ch g Bertolini(USA) —Aunt Ruby (USA) (Rubiano (USA))
1350[7] 1804[11] 2417[11] 3161[5] 3580[6] (4155) 4938[15] 5644[12] 5998[3] 6787[13]

Eye Of Eternity *Rae Guest* 23
2 b f Oratorio(IRE) —Eyeq (IRE) (Cadeaux Genereux)
7096[9]

Eyes Like A Hawk (IRE) *Tom Dascombe* 61
3 bb f Diktat—Mexican Hawk (USA) (Silver Hawk (USA))
2496[5] ◆ 4180[5] 5019[4] 5806[11]

Eyesore *S A Harris* a32
3 b f Reel Buddy(USA) —Segretezza (IRE) (Perugino (USA))
5442[11] 7796[8]

Eyshal (IRE) *J Moore* 110
5 b g Green Desert(USA) —Ebadiyla (IRE) (Sadler's Wells (USA))
7747a[9]

Eytarna (IRE) *John M Oxx* 99
3 ch f Dubai Destination(USA) —Ebaziya (IRE) (Darshaan)
5689a[13]

Ezdeyaad (USA) *G A Swinbank* 87
5 b g Lemon Drop Kid(USA) —August Storm (USA) (Storm Creek (USA))
1603[16] 2313[5] 2589[2] (2822) 3154[3] 3312[8] 3656[5] 6014[6] 6249[3] 6645[5]

Ezdiyaad (IRE) *M P Tregoning* a61 106
5 b g Galileo(IRE) —Wijdan (USA) (Mr Prospector (USA))
1351[6] 1673[10] 6665[5] 7059[3]

Faasel (IRE) *N G Richards* 79
8 b g Unfuwain(USA) —Waqood (USA) (Riverman (USA))
2486[9] 3146[7]

Fabiana *Andreas Lowe* 106
3 ch f Ashkalani(IRE) —Fox Croft (FR) (Bustino)
1914a[5] 2757a[2] 6717a[3]

Fabled Dancer (IRE) *E J Alston* 48
3 ch g Choisir(AUS) —Age Of Fable (IRE) (Entrepreneur)
4276[9] 5071[5] 5731[8]

Fabreze *P J Makin* a96 94
4 ch g Choisir(AUS) —Impulsive Decision (IRE) (Nomination)
3795[9]

Fabulous Strike (USA) *Todd M Beattie* a122 122
6 bb g Smart Strike(CAN) —Fabulous Find (USA) (Lost Code (USA))
6509a[2]

Fagutela *S Botti* 86
3 b f Dr Fong(USA) —Sumingasefa (Danehill (USA))
2310a[9] 3186a[9]

Faidibiri (IRE) *G Ligas* 85
3 b c Pyrus(USA) —Angelico (IRE) (Perugino (USA))
1392a[9] 1904a[15]

Faintly Hopeful *R A Teal* a51 45
4 b g Marju(IRE) —Twilight Patrol (Robellino (USA))
97[9] 189[7] 347[4] 472[8] 5018[11]

Fair Along (GER) *P J Hobbs* a67 90
7 b g Alkalde(GER) —Fairy Tango (FR) (Acatenango (GER))
6851[25]

Fair Bunny *A D Brown* a67 64
2 b f Trade Fair—Coney Hills (Beverley Boy)
5693[8] 5949[11] 6179[3] 6646[4] 6820[6] 7115[6] (7421) 7619[6] 7707[6]

Fairly Dancer (FR) *J-L Maroto-Abascal* 80
2 b c Fairly Ransom(USA) —Funambula Dancer (FR) (Funambule (USA))
7264a[3]

Fairly Honest *P W Hiatt* a56 57
5 b g Alhaarth(IRE) —Miller's Melody (Chief Singer)
186[6] 275[5] 452[6] 565[9] (598) 749[5] 1030[3] 1535[12] 2378[5] 3241[5] 3662[4]

Fairmile *George Baker* a101 107
7 b g Spectrum(IRE) —Juno Marlowe (IRE) (Danehill (USA))
1017[4] 1799[4] 2398[2] 3190[5] (3769) 4288[5] 7375[6] 7465[7]

Fair Nella *J G Portman* 65
2 b f Trade Fair—Zanella (IRE) (Nordico (USA))
4147[6] 4688[4] 5096[6]

Fair Passion *D Shaw* a65
2 b f Trade Fair—United Passion (Emarati (USA))
6971[6] ◆ 7213[3] ◆

Fairplaytomyself *P W Hiatt* a52 37
4 ch m Ballet Master(USA) —Over The Moon (Beveled (USA))
5531[9] 5840[6] 6332[5] 7374[7] 7581[4] 7653[9] 7814[2]

Fairson (TUR) *K Ozturk* a107
6 b h Royal Abjar(USA) —Fair Tail (TUR) (Cossack Guard (USA))
5587a[11]

Fair Trade *D R C Elsworth* 85
2 ch c Trade Fair—Ballet (Sharrood (USA))
6810[2] ◆

Fairy Flight (USA) *W J Knight* a76
2 bb f Fusaichi Pegasus(USA) —La Barberina (USA) (Nijinsky (CAN))
7491[5] (7622)

Fairy Flow (IRE) *Ms Joanna Morgan* a57 84
5 b m King Charlemagne(USA) —Fairy Express (IRE) (Fayruz)
1375a[10]

Fairy Promises (USA) *Pat Eddery* 77
2 ch f Broken Vow(USA) —Fairy Glade (USA) (Gone West (USA))
3858[10] (4468) 5994[4] 6447[7]

Fairys In A Storm (IRE) *P T Midgley* 41
2 gr f Choisir(AUS) —Fidra (IRE) (Vettori (IRE))
1275[9] 2099[12] 2414[5]

Fairywater Grey (IRE) *J J Bridger* a27 32
2 gr f Swift Gulliver(IRE) —Chilling (Chilibang)
3210[8] 3733[11] 4080[10]

Fait Accompli (GER) *J E Hammond* 72
3 ch f Bering—Fantastic Flame (IRE) (Generous (IRE))
4130a[2]

Fait Accompli (IRE) *Edward Lynam* a73 32
2 b g Whipper(USA) —Maritana (USA) (Rahy (USA))
5274a[14]

Faited To Pretend (IRE) *M L W Bell* a60
2 b f Kheleyf(USA) —Lady Moranbon (USA) (Trempolino (USA))
7135[7] 7326[9]

Faith And Reason (USA) *B J Curley* a72 73
6 b g Sunday Silence(USA) —Sheer Reason (USA) (Danzig (USA))
2172[6] 2760[9] 3550[7] 4207[6]

Faithful Duchess (IRE) *E A L Dunlop* a51 68
2 b f Bachelor Duke(USA) —Portelet (Night Shift (USA))
3820[12] 5478[4] 6069[8]

Faithful One (IRE) *D R Lanigan* a73 89
2 b f Dubawi(IRE) —Have Faith (IRE) (Machiavellian (USA))
5605[2] ◆ 6164[2] 6567[2] ◆ 7033[13]

Faithful Ruler (USA) *R A Fahey* a90 95
5 bb g Elusive Quality(USA) —Fancy Ruler (USA) (Half A Year (USA))
79[3] 163[4] 713[3] (834) ◆ 850[7] 4881[3] ◆ 5361[2] (6014) 6249[7] 6876[7] 7169[5] 7574[4] ◆ 7789[5]

Faith Jicaro (IRE) *Mrs L Williamson* 76
3 b f One Cool Cat(USA) —Wings To Soar (USA) (Woodman (USA))
2819[2] 3944[2]

Fajita *G L Moore* a51 74
3 b c Lahib(USA) —La Fija (USA) (Dixieland Band (USA))
1752[6] 2209[10] 2548[2] 3009[2] (3358) 3693[4] 4275[3] 5003[6] (5403) 5774[3] 5999[4] 6421[4]

Fajr (IRE) *Miss Gay Kelleway* a115 95
7 b g Green Desert(USA) —Ta Rib (USA) (Mr Prospector (USA))
206[9] 278[6] 388[6]

Falahill *R Hannon*
2 ch c Selkirk(USA) —Felucca (Green Desert (USA))
6620[14]

Falakee *P W Chapple-Hyam* 34
2 b c Sakhee(USA) —Sakhya (IRE) (Barathea (IRE))
6990[12]

Falasteen (IRE) *D Nicholls* 91
2 ch g Titus Livius(FR) —Law Review (IRE) (Case Law)
(2893) 4752[3] 5198[5] 5552[4] (6275)

Falcativ *M Botti* a102 101
4 b g Falbrav(IRE) —Frottola (Muhtarram (USA))
(1944) ◆ 2471[5] 3620[10] 4541[5] (7626) (7827) ◆

Falcharge *B Grizzetti* 84
3 b c Falbrav(IRE) —Polar Charge (Polar Falcon (USA))
1904a[20]

Falcolnry (IRE) *E F Vaughan* a39 84
4 b m Hawk Wing(USA) —Fear And Greed (IRE) (Brief Truce (USA))
128[7]

Falcon Rock (IRE) *S A Callaghan* a78 95
4 b g Hawk Wing(USA) —Champaka (IRE) (Caerleon (USA))
1972[3] ◆ 2775[2] 3024[2] (4378) 4602[2] 5437[2] 5865[2]

Falcon's Tribute (IRE) *P Salmon* 56
7 b m Beneficial—Early Storm (IRE) (Glacial Storm (USA))
6022[8] 6390[3]

Faldal *Tom Dascombe* a81 85
3 br f Falbrav(IRE) —Tidal (Bin Ajwaad (IRE))
(1613) 2190[7] 3968a[7]

Fallen Idol *J H M Gosden* a81
2 b c Pivotal—Fallen Star (Brief Truce (USA))
(5807)

Fallen In Love *J L Dunlop* 104
3 b f Galileo(IRE) —Fallen Star (Brief Truce (USA))
2190[2] 2846[3] 3619[2] 4566[2] 5202[6]

Falling Angel *P F I Cole* 75
2 b f Kylian(USA) —Belle Ile (USA) (Diesis)
2175[2] 2503[2] ◆ 3086[19]

Falpiase (IRE) *J Howard Johnson* a75 81
7 b g Montjeu(IRE) —Gift Of The Night (USA) (Slewpy (USA))
2932[10]

Falun (GER) *A Trybuhl* a97 100
3 ch c Pentire—Fortunata (GER) (Daun (GER))
5585a[3] 6327a[7]

Fame And Glory *A P O'Brien* 131
3 b c Montjeu(IRE) —Gryada (Shirley Heights)
(1388a) (1910a) ◆ 2705[2] (3438a) ◆ 5688a[2] 6526a[6] 6850[6]

Fame Is The Spur *J W Hills* 66
2 ch f Motivator—Subya (Night Shift (USA))
5605[7] 6241[16]

Familiar Territory *Saeed Bin Suroor* a110 104
6 br h Cape Cross(IRE) —Forever Fine (USA) (Sunshine Forever (USA))
339a[7] 523a[2] 698a[3]

Famous (IRE) *A P O'Brien* 104
2 ch f Danehill Dancer(IRE) —Starlight Dreams (USA) (Black Tie Affair)
4726a[5] 5488a[2] 6319a[4]

Famous Name *D K Weld* 122
4 b h Dansili—Fame At Last (USA) (Quest For Fame)
1758a[2] 2303a[2] (3882a) (5080a) 5710a[2] 6506a[3]

Famous Warrior (IRE) *Kevin Prendergast* a98 96
2 b c Alhaarth(IRE) —Oriental Fashion (IRE) (Marju (IRE))
5486a[5]

Fan Club *Mrs R A Carr* a53 41
5 ch g Zamindar(USA) —Starfan (USA) (Lear Fan (USA))
62[11] 177[9] 399[8] 2965[10] 3486[12] 3499[7] 3760[8] 4034[8]

Fancy Diamond (GER) *Frau E Mader* 92
3 b f Ransom O'War(USA) —Francais (Mark Of Esteem (IRE))
1240a[8]

Fancy Footsteps (IRE) *C G Cox* a81 72
4 gr m Noverre(USA) —Fancy Intense (Peintre Celebre (USA))
(157) ◆ 2125[7] 2775[11] 3381[3] 3980[3] (5095) 5663[4] 6168[12] 6614[6]
Fancy Set (IRE) *D J S Ffrench Davis* a19
3 b f Reset(AUS) —Crafty Fancy (IRE) (Intikhab (USA))
810[7] 1046[7] 1652[9]
Fancy Star *B W Hills* 54
2 b c Starcraft(NZ) —Lorien Hill (IRE) (Danehill (USA))
4048[13] 4524[12]
Fancy Starlett (FR) *O Auchere*
3 b f Martaline—Grey Starlett (FR) (Varxi (FR))
7166a[3]
Fandango Boy *J P Broderick* a76 68
8 b g Victory Note(USA) —Dancing Chimes (London Bells (CAN))
172[3] 2531[10] 478[8] 5711[10] 7672[5]
Fanditha (IRE) *R Hannon* a86 89
3 ch f Danehill Dancer(IRE) —Splendid (IRE) (Mujtahid (USA))
1381[2] 2209[4] 3165[6] 3870[4] 4422[13] 5475[7] 5996[3] (6203) 6618[3] 7148[3]
Fangfoss Girls *G L Moore* a69 57
3 ch f Monsieur Bond(IRE) —Bond Shakira (Daggers Drawn (USA))
34[2] 229[6] 509[6] 1095[5] 1424[6]
Fanjura (IRE) *B W Hills* 111
4 b g Marju(IRE) —Accelerating (USA) (Lear Fan (USA))
1093[2] 1352[5] 1798[7] 2933[16] (3586) (4261) (5262) 5794[3] 6202[3]
Fantasia *L M Cumani* 115
3 b f Sadler's Wells(USA) —Blue Symphony (Darshaan)
(1293) ◆ 1918a[3] 2952a[7] (5798) 6479[6]
Fantastical *C E Brittain* a60 45
3 b f Fantastic Light(USA) —First Musical (First Trump)
944[4] ◆ 1585[9] 2415[8]
Fantastic Cuix (FR) *L M Cumani* a71 64
2 gr f Fantastic Light(USA) —Cuixmala (FR) (Highest Honor (FR))
6992[9] 7450[4] ◆
Fantastic Dubai (USA) *M R Channon* a76 85
3 b c Storm Cat(USA) —Shy Lady (FR) (Kaldoun (FR))
(752) 1075[2] 2377[2] 2882[2]
Fantastic Fred (IRE) *J A Osborne* a61 16
3 br g Fantastic Light(USA) —Luxury Launch (USA) (Seeking The Gold (USA))
(196) (287) 450[6] 839[2] 1429[7] 1811[15]
Fantastic Morning *F Jordan* a58 38
5 ch g Fantastic Light(USA) —Gombay Girl (USA) (Woodman (USA))
2983[12] 3421[9] 6226[12] 6917[14]
Fantastic Owners (AUS) *B Dean* 103
6 b g Fantastic Light(USA) —Queen Of State (NZ) (Volksraad)
2116a[7]
Fantastic Pick *B J Meehan* 76
2 b g Fantastic Light(USA) —Umlilo (Mtoto)
2771[6] 2997[8] 3865[7] (5715) ◆ (6215) 6391[2] 6901[9]
Fantastic Prince *P F I Cole* 76
2 ch g Cadeaux Genereux—Fantaisiste (Nashwan (USA))
2033[7] 2280[2] 2588[3] 3792[9] 5801[5]
Fantastic Shift *B Grizzetti* 74
2 br c Fantastic Light(USA) —Rose Shift (IRE) (Night Shift (USA))
6716a[9]
Fantastic Strike (IRE) *M Johnston* 74
2 b c Noverre(USA) —Hariya (IRE) (Shernazar)
3292[5] 3613[8] 5439[2] 5715[4]
Fantasy Believer *J J Quinn* 73
11 b g Sure Blade(USA) —Delicious (Dominion)
1518[9] 2088[9] 2326[9] 2929[4] 3422[4] 3771[2]
Fantasy Explorer *J J Quinn* a96 91
6 b g Compton Place—Zinzi (Song)
1398[7] 1699[12] 6666[14] (7026) 7202[2] 7414[3] 7454[2]
Fantasy Fighter (IRE) *J J Quinn* a71 39
4 b g Danetime(IRE) —Lady Montekin (Montekin)
44[3] 292[9] 540[11] 4204[7] 4894[7] 6777[3] 7068[5] (7370) (7484) 7634[7] 7735[2]
Fantasy Gladiator *R M H Cowell* a81 73
3 b g Ishiguru(USA) —Fancier Bit (Lion Cavern (USA))
2888[5] 3362[3] 4668[2] (5373) (6230) ◆
Fantasy Land (IRE) *B J Meehan* a54 71
3 ch f Danehill Dancer(IRE) —Wondrous Story (USA) (Royal Academy (USA))
1327[14] 1683[3] 2179[3] 2845[15] 3272[6] 3630[8] 5112[7] 5972[10] 6252[10]
Fantasy Princess (USA) *G A Butler* a82 80
4 ch m Johannesburg(USA) —Fantasy (Cadeaux Genereux)
4422[14] 6346[9] 6634[11] 7092[4]
Fantasy Ride *J Pearce* a60 58
7 b g Bahhare(USA) —Grand Splendour (Shirley Heights)
443[2] 566[2] 816[10] 877[5] 1199[7] 2171[6] 3004[2] 4158[2] 5484[4] 5617[4] 6770[10] 6917[8] 7137[2] 7549[7] 7670[3] 7687[4] 7888[4]
Fantino *J Mackie* 70
3 b g Shinko Forest(IRE) —Illustre Inconnue (USA) (Septieme Ciel (USA))
2446[13] 2856[5] 3309[5] 4284[7] 5035[2] (5545) 5975[8] 6400[8] 6910[9]
Fanunalter *M Botti* a99 102
3 b g Falbrav(IRE) —Step Danzer (IRE) (Desert Prince (IRE))
1392a[11] (4648) 5832[2] ◆ 6307[9] 7375[3] ◆
Faraday (IRE) *N P Mulholland* a59 60
6 b g Montjeu(IRE) —Fureau (GER) (Ferdinand (USA))
469[12]
Faramir (IRE) *M Delcher-Sanchez* 103
4 b h Celtic Swing—Perfect Fun (Marju (IRE))
1552a[3]
Faraway Sound (IRE) *P C Haslam* a50 75
3 b g Distant Music(USA) —Queen Consort (Diesis)
5254[6] 5626[6]
Fardyieh *C E Brittain* a81 77
2 b f King's Best(USA) —Injaaz (Sheikh Albadou)
4497[8] 5026[2] (5571) 6241[9] 6619[9]
Fareeha *J Mackie* a50 61
4 b m King's Best(USA) —Shatarah (Gulch (USA))
7152[12]
Fareej (USA) *Saeed Bin Suroor* a92 85
2 b c Kingmambo(USA) —Adonesque (IRE) (Sadler's Wells (USA))
(6423) ◆ (6779) ◆
Fareer *E A L Dunlop* 103
3 ch c Bahamian Bounty—Songsheet (Dominion)
1324[3] (1801) 2273[5] (3049)
Fareham Town *S Kirk* a58
2 ch f Cape Town(IRE) —Fareham (Komaite (USA))
6069[12] 7630[3] 7799[12]
Fareion (GER) *S Smrczek* a90 85
6 ch h Areion(GER) —Fanfare (GER) (Surumu (GER))
6499a[7]
Fares (IRE) *Doug Watson* a98 88
5 b g Mark Of Esteem(IRE) —Iftitan (USA) (Southern Halo (USA))
261a[4] (334a) 522a[10] 639a[10] 771a[9]
Far From Old (IRE) *J E Hammond* a99 101
6 b h Vettori(IRE) —Jabali (FR) (Shirley Heights)
185a[4] ◆ 338a[4] 437a[10]
Farleigh *A M Balding* a63 74
3 b f Trans Island—Medway (IRE) (Shernazar)
(1752) 3870[3] 4956[6]
Farleigh House (USA) *Sir Mark Prescott* a89 88
5 b g Lear Fan(USA) —Verasina (USA) (Woodman (USA))
4852[5] 5262[14] 5437[6] 5667[9] 5887[2] ◆ 6190[3] ◆ (6435) 6830[2]
Farley Star *M G Quinlan* a88 98
5 b m Alzao(USA) —Girl Of My Dreams (IRE) (Marju (IRE))
6757[3] 7032[4]
Farmer Giles (IRE) *M L W Bell* a84 87
2 b c Danroad(AUS) —Demeter (USA) (Diesis)
1083[6] 1511[2] 1920[3] (3032) 3782[8] 4746[4] 5174[7] 5762[3] 6305[4] 6993[12]
Farmers Dream (IRE) *J L Spearing* a45 29
2 b f Antonius Pius(USA) —Beucaire (IRE) (Entrepreneur)
6615[12] 7061[11] 7234[6]
Farmers Wish (IRE) *J L Spearing* a78 81
2 b f Val Royal(FR) —Farmers Swing (IRE) (River Falls)
2793[4] 3686[2] (4265) (4706) 5022[6] 6134[2] 6619[5] 7108[4] 7290[14]
Farncombe (IRE) *R A Harris* a67 68
3 ch f Where Or When(IRE) —Promenade (Primo Dominie)
1327[8] 1671[3] 4913[3] 6611[6] 6804[3] (7198) 7426[5] 7665[8]
Farne Island *Micky Hammond* a62 59
6 ch g Arkadian Hero(USA) —Holy Island (Deploy)
1402[5] 1556[4] 3481[5]
Far 'n Wide *W J Haggas* 5
3 ch f Rainbow Quest(USA) —Raspberry Sauce (Niniski (USA))
2051[8]
Farrel (IRE) *B Grizzetti* 106
4 b h Fruits Of Love(USA) —Folcungi (IRE) (Mukaddamah (USA))
2525a[3] 7312a[6]
Farriers Gate *M E Rimmer* a19 26
3 ch f Lomitas—Mountain Stream (FR) (Vettori (IRE))
441[7] 722[7]
Farsighted *J M P Eustace* a42 72
4 b m Where Or When(IRE) —Classic Vision (Classic Cliche (IRE))
71[12] 186[9]
Far View (IRE) *J W Hills* a11
2 b c Oasis Dream—Night Mirage (USA) (Silver Hawk (USA))
7429[9]
Fascile *E J Creighton*
2 b g Forzando—Frankie Fair (IRE) (Red Sunset)
1404[15]
Fasette *M H Tompkins* 51
2 b f Fasliyev(USA) —Londonnet (IRE) (Catrail (USA))
2699[8]
Fashionable Gal (IRE) *Sir Mark Prescott* 52
2 b f Galileo(IRE) —Fashion (Bin Ajwaad (IRE))
5980[9]
Fashion Icon (USA) *T D Barron* a59 57
3 ch f Van Nistelrooy(USA) —Los Altos (USA) (Robin Des Pins (USA))
236[5] 379[5] 624[3] 736[4] 804[2] 1064[2] 1247[7] 1949[4] 2265[4] 2581[8]
Fashion Insider (USA) *B J Meehan* a74 70
2 bb f Indian Charlie(USA) —Shahalo (USA) (Halo (USA))
7182[4] ◆ 7624[2]
Fasilight *M Botti* a69 65
2 b f Fasliyev(USA) —Rajmata (IRE) (Prince Sabo)
1939[5] 2238[2] 3507[3] 4271[7] 4858[6] 5636[7] (6494)
Fasina (FR) *Mlle S-V Tarrou* 76
3 b f Pyramus(USA) —Fabulosa (GER) (Nebos (GER))
5462a[8]
Fasliyanne (IRE) *K A Ryan* a52 68
3 b f Fasliyev(USA) —Happy Memories (IRE) (Thatching)
273[7] 379[2] ◆ 686[4] 955[3] (1064) 1247[2] 1455[2] 1644[3] 2012[6] 2394[2] 4942[7] 5517[2] 6308[5] 6387[7] 6988[10] 7838[11]
Fastback (IRE) *S Wattel* 77
3 ch f Singspiel(IRE) —Glen Rosie (IRE) (Mujtahid (USA))
(6753a)
Fast Elaine (IRE) *Mrs L C Jewell* 34
2 ch f Bahamian Bounty—Miss A Note (USA) (Miswaki (USA))
4302[11] 5017[8] 5319[9] 6034[12]
Fast Freddie *Mrs A Malzard* a76 67
5 b g Agnes World(USA) —Bella Chica (IRE) (Bigstone (IRE))
329[9] 518[8] 632[6] 1456[6] 1540[8] 5541a[6]
Fast Living *A M Hales* a46
4 b g Fasliyev(USA) —Fairy Contessa (IRE) (Fairy King (USA))
3712[5] 6252[9]
Fastnet Storm (IRE) *T P Tate* 95
3 br g Rock Of Gibraltar(IRE) —Dreams (Rainbow Quest (USA))
1559[7] 1992[8] (2571) (3189) ◆ 4455[16] 5209[3] 6002[6] (6795) 7185[3]
Fastrac Boy *J R Best* a46 56
6 b g Bold Edge—Nesyred (IRE) (Paris House)
46[7]
Fatal Attraction *Rae Guest* a50 59
4 b m Oasis Dream—Millyant (Primo Dominie)
947[4] 2157[4] 2700[3] 5727[6] 6641[6] 6856[3]
Fatal Bullet (USA) *Reade Baker* a120 66
4 b g Red Bullet(USA) —Sararegal (CAN) (Regal Classic (CAN))
7306a[6]
Fatale Des Aigles (FR) *Mme C Barande-Barbe* a32 72
3 b f Enrique—Vervain (Vettori (IRE))
5118a[10]
Fatanah (IRE) *M P Tregoning* a71 65
2 b f Green Desert(USA) —Wijdan (USA) (Mr Prospector (USA))
6810[7] ◆ 7390[2]
Fat Boy (IRE) *P W Chapple-Hyam* a77 116
4 ch g Choisir(AUS) —Gold Shift (USA) (Night Shift (USA))
1676[15] 4456[12] 5434[9]
Fat Chance *Rae Guest* 54
3 gr f Linamix(FR) —Hymenee (USA) (Chief's Crown (USA))
1837[8] 3117[14] 3685[11]
Fateful Attraction *I A Wood* a73 47
6 b m Mujahid(USA) —Heavens Above (FR) (Pistolet Bleu (IRE))
190[6] 601[3] 669[11]
Fateh Field (USA) *Saeed Bin Suroor* a101 104
4 b h Distorted Humor(USA) —Too Cool To Fool (USA) (Foolish Pleasure (USA))
182a[2] 334a[3]
Fathayer (USA) *A Al Raihe* a107 101
4 ch h Volponi(USA) —Bright Generation (IRE) (Rainbow Quest (USA))
183a[10] 340a[15] 437a[5] 613a[10] 699a[11]
Father Figure (USA) *Heather Dalton* a47
3 rg g Mizzen Mast(USA) —Family (USA) (Danzig (USA))
6287[8] 6704[10]
Father Time *H R A Cecil* a89 114
3 b c Dansili—Clepsydra (Sadler's Wells (USA))
1326[3] 1872[3] 2277[2] (3087) ◆ 5134[3] 5861[4] 7281a[6]
Fathey (IRE) *R A Fahey* 73
3 ch g Fath(USA) —Christoph's Girl (Efisio)
1736[5] 2611[5] 2970[7] 3856[2] 4346[2] 4591[8] 5335[9] 5363[10] 5948[4] 6383[6] 6755[5]
Fathom Five (IRE) *C F Wall* 106
5 b g Fath(USA) —Ambria (ITY) (Final Straw)
(1457) 3351[11] 3844[6] 4341[13] 5654[5] 6843[3] 7015[13]
Fathsta (IRE) *D M Simcock* a96 101
4 b g Fath(USA) —Kilbride Lass (IRE) (Lahib (USA))
1018[6] 1212[5] 1821[3] 2266[2] 4560[11] 5206[12] 7252[6] 7486[4] 7613[2] ◆ (7702) ◆
Fathzo (IRE) *Gerard Keane* a49 57
5 b g Fath(USA) —Super Zoe (Bustino)
571[9] 6800[7]
Fauchizo (IRE) *R Avial Lopez*
2 b c Kingsalsa(USA) —Irish Spell (USA) (Irish River (FR))
7346a[8]
Fault *Stef Liddiard* a91 97
3 b g Bahamian Bounty—Trundley Wood (Wassl)
(1078) 1824[6] 2016[3] 2928[7] 4485[20] 5203[11] 5507[9] 5646[9] 5900[2] 6329[5] 6632[9] 6857[6] (7028) 7192[3] 7203[5] 7432[6]
Favorite Woods *W J Haggas* a67
2 b c Sakhee(USA) —South Club Hill (Danehill (USA))
5643[6]
Favouring (IRE) *M C Chapman* a32 32
7 ch g Fayruz—Peace Dividend (IRE) (Alzao (USA))
3558[10] 4372[9]
Favourite Girl (IRE) *T D Easterby* 103
3 b f Refuse To Bend(IRE) —Zuccini Wind (IRE) (Revoque (IRE))
1353[16] 1880[6] 2934[3] 3320[7] 3824[9] 4771[8] 5203[13] 5959[7] 6428[5] 6843[8] 7083[12]
Favours Brave *Mrs S Lamyman* a72 73
3 b g Galileo(IRE) —Tuning (Rainbow Quest (USA))
1087[4] 1286[3] 1842[9] 2881[4] 4838[4] 6498[11] 6951[7]
Fawley Green *W R Muir* 72
2 b g Shamardal(USA) —Wars (IRE) (Green Desert (USA))
2844[9] 3256[2] 5256[4] 5957[4] 6693[11]
Faylan (FR) *C Baillet* a86 97
3 b c Indian Rocket—Siran (FR) (R B Chesne)
2096a[3]
Fayre Bella *J Gallagher*
2 ch f Zafeen(FR) —Hollybell (Beveled (USA))
7182[19]
Fazbee (IRE) *P W D'Arcy* a86 85
3 b f Fasliyev(USA) —Kelpie (IRE) (Kahyasi)
1293[6] 1664[4] 2210[4] 2829[5] 3251[4] 3734[5] 5432[8] 5803[2] 6421[6] 7322[7] 7553[4] 7739[6]
Fazza *D W P Arbuthnot* a72 72
2 ch g Sulamani(IRE) —Markievicz (IRE) (Doyoun)
5934[11] 6386[2] 6700[5] 6896[9] 7824[2] (7886)
Feared In Flight (IRE) *Saeed Bin Suroor* 104
4 b g Hawk Wing(USA) —Solar Crystal (IRE) (Alzao (USA))
415a[11] 640a[5]
Fear Nothing *E S McMahon* a41 71
2 ch c Exceed And Excel(AUS) —Galatrix (Be My Guest (USA))
5611[6] 5957[3] 6556[5]
Feasible *J G Portman* a67 69
4 ch g Efisio—Zoena (Emarati (USA))
1785[9] 2330[4] 2924[2] 3735[2] 4645[2] 4824[7] 5905[8]
Feathered Crown (FR) *H R A Cecil* a55 80
3 ch c Indian Ridge—Attractive Crown (USA) (Chief's Crown (USA))
6022[2] (6475) 6875[5]
Featherweight (IRE) *B W Hills* a73 85
3 ch f Fantastic Light(USA) —Dancing Feather (Suave Dancer (USA))
(1931) 2356[6] 4050[8] 5101[3] (5915) 6733[4] 7148[2]
Federal Reserve *M Madgwick*
2 ch g Central Park(IRE) —Attlongglast (Groom Dancer (USA))
4646[11] 5119[7]
Feelin Foxy *J G Given* a87 85
5 b m Foxhound(USA) —Charlie Girl (Puissance)
1241[5] 1518[15] 1768[2] 2046[4] 2472[3] (2712) 3591[2] (3765) 4189[2] 4461[2] 5007[7] 5149[3] 5768[2] 6253[2] 6459[6] (6801) 7269[4] 7511[6]
Feeling (IRE) *D Burchell* a46 45
5 b g Sadler's Wells(USA) —La Pitie (USA) (Devil's Bag (USA))
5873[4] 7719[4]
Feeling Fab (FR) *M Johnston* a87 91
3 b f Refuse To Bend(IRE) —Les Planches (Tropular)
1484[4] 1860[4] 2504[9] 3293[3] 3839[7] 5092[3] 5206[4] 5665[5] (6311)
Feeling Fragile (IRE) *Pat Eddery* a72 53
2 b g Fasliyev(USA) —Boutique (Selkirk (USA))
4219[8] 7157[4] 7463[6] 7700[2]
Feeling Fresh (IRE) *Paul Green* a66 71
4 b h Xaar—Oh'Cecilia (IRE) (Scenic)
3657[3] ◆ (3852) 4496[3] 4772[3]
Feeling Peckish (USA) *M C Chapman* a43 42
5 ch g Point Given(USA) —Sunday Bazaar (USA) (Nureyev (USA))
3171[6] 3609[4] 4848[12]
Feeling Stylish (IRE) *N Tinkler* a34 48
3 b f Desert Style(IRE) —No Hard Feelings (IRE) (Alzao (USA))
1335[7] 1725[9] 2132[4] 2577[7] 2790[5] 3685[6] 4812[6]
Feels All Right (IRE) *E Libaud* 112
3 b c Danehill Dancer(IRE) —Zagreb Flyer (Old Vic)
2756a[17] 3669a[7]
Feel The Magic (IRE) *S Kirk* a48
2 b f Cadeaux Genereux—Triple Green (Green Desert (USA))
6069[11] 6607[12] 7024[8] 7514[6] 7616[6] 7749[5] 7757[9] 7884[7]
Feet Of Fury *W M Brisbourne* a56 62
3 b f Deportivo—Fury Dance (USA) (Cryptoclearance (USA))
1015[4] ◆ 1588[10] 1973[6] 2797[12] 3625[4] 4432[5] 5384[10] 6497[4]
Fei Fei (FR) *Mlle A Imaz-Ceca* a57
2 b f Sagacity(FR) —Garmeria (FR) (Kadrou (FR))
6960a[8]
Feisty's Brother *D M Simcock* 28
2 b c Dubawi(IRE) —Hawait Al Barr (Green Desert (USA))
2860[11] 3119[6]
Felday *H Morrison* a97 97
3 b g Bahamian Bounty—Monaiya (Shareef Dancer (USA))
1324[4] 1705[8] 5523[4] 6050[9] ◆ (6645) 6815[10] 7294[3] (7639) ◆
Felicia *J E Long* a56 43
4 b m Diktat—Gracia (Linamix (FR))
1728[7] 2221[12] 4084[4] 5987[3] 6612[8] 6941[7] 7549[10] 7660[2]
Felix (PER) *M bin Shafya* a85
4 gr g Farallon P(USA) —Shanti (PER) (Stallion (ARG))
258a[8] 336a[14]
Fellowship (NZ) *P O'Sullivan* 120
7 b g O'Reilly(NZ) —Mystical Flight (NZ) (Danzalion (USA))
1553a[10] 7746a[3]
Fell Pack *J J Quinn* 63
5 b g Lake Coniston(IRE) —All On (Dunbeath (USA))
1279[5] 1724[4] (2237) 2573[5] 3350[5] 4193[8] 4658[4] 4893[10] 5339[5] 6102[4]
Felsham *H Candy* a68 76
2 br c Kyllachy—Border Minstral (IRE) (Sri Pekan (USA))
4906[3] (6207) 6550[2] 7290[3]
Femme De Fer *C G Cox* a75 71
3 b f Hamas(IRE) —Ajeebah (IRE) (Mujtahid (USA))
2496[2] ◆ 3071[3] 5717[5] 6635[2] 7223[3] 7554[3] 7807[9]
Fencing Master *A P O'Brien* a86 117
2 b c Oratorio(IRE) —Moonlight Dance (USA) (Alysheba (USA))
6849[2] ◆
Fenella Rose *S C Williams* 73
2 b f Compton Place—Xtrasensory (Royal Applause)
1841[2] ◆ 2354[7] 3317[3] (5800) 6677[12]
Fenice (IRE) *S Seemar* a92 91
6 gr g Woodman(USA) —Venize (IRE) (Kaldoun (FR))
263a[8] ◆
Fenners (USA) *M W Easterby* a66 66
6 ch g Pleasant Tap(USA) —Legal Opinion (IRE) (Polish Precedent (USA))
18[4] 2629[2] 3023[2] 3654[5] 4350[5] 4893[4] 5339[3] 5600[3] 6097[4] 6457[9] 6558[10]
Fen Spirit (IRE) *J H M Gosden* a78 75
3 b f Invincible Spirit(IRE) —Irinatinvidio (Rudimentary (USA))
7516[9] 7656[5] 7832[9]

Fergus McIver (IRE) *J S Bolger* 107
3 b c Sadler's Wells(USA) —Danelissima (IRE) (Danehill (USA))
1388a^{2} 1910a^{3} 2288a^{5} 4033a^{4} 5141a^{7}

Fernando Torres *Matthew Salaman* a72 68
3 b g Giant's Causeway(USA) —Alstemeria (IRE) (Danehill (USA))
2446^{5} 2937^{10} 3485^{4} ◆ 5258^{6} 5672^{8} *(7432) 7587^{3} 7742^{3} 7876^{2}*

Ferneley (IRE) *B Cecil* a97 118
5 b h Ishiguru(USA) —Amber Tide (IRE) (Pursuit Of Love)
7308a^{7} 7746a^{5}

Fern House (IRE) *Bruce Hellier* a54 54
7 b g Xaar—Certain Impression (USA) (Forli (ARG))
574^{12} 1279^{16} 1723^{9} 2224^{8} 2532^{5} 3110^{4} 3683^{8} 4346^{8} 4778^{3} 5183^{8} 5504^{4} 6314^{8} 6410^{8} 7086^{7}

Ferris Wheel (IRE) *P F I Cole* a78 71
2 b f One Cool Cat(USA) —Saffron Crocus (Shareef Dancer (USA))
5212^{4} *(5638)* 6055^{8}

Fervent Prince *A bin Huzaim* a93 102
4 b g Averti(IRE) —Maria Theresa (Primo Dominie)
521a^{2} 639a^{9}

Fesko *M Johnston* a87 85
3 b f Shinko Forest(IRE) —Young Sue (Local Suitor (USA))
(562) 782^{3} 859^{2} 1744^{8} 2092^{4} 2607^{9} (2999) 3489^{3} 3872^{12} 4104^{8} 4549^{7} 4896^{5} 5409^{11} (5937) 6155^{3} 6540^{7} *6879^{2}*

Festival Dreams *Miss J S Davis* a51 54
4 ch g Largesse—Bright Spangle (IRE) (General Monash (USA))
116^{5}

Festival Princess (IRE) *Mrs John Harrington* 104
4 b m Barathea(IRE) —Uliana (USA) (Darshaan)
1996a^{2} 2647a^{4} 4923a^{4} 5487a^{3} 5890a^{5}

Festoso (IRE) *H J L Dunlop* a86 109
4 b m Diesis—Garah (Ajdal (USA))
1210^{6} (2271) 3516a^{6} 4087^{5} 6058^{3} 6661^{20} 7292^{8}

Fetching *B W Hills* a54
2 b f Zamindar(USA) —Esplanade (Danehill (USA))
7325^{6}

Feudal (IRE) *M Johnston* a64 57
3 b c Xaar—Noble Rose (IRE) (Caerleon (USA))
810^{8} 917^{7}

Feuille De Route (FR) *Mlle S-V Tarrou* 58
2 b f Sevres Rose(IRE) —Reaction Rapide (FR) (Bering)
6578a^{8}

Fever Tree *P J Makin* a52
2 b f Trade Fair—Spielbound (Singspiel (IRE))
7319^{8} 7663^{6}

Fiamma D'Oro (IRE) *David P Myerscough* a69 57
3 bb f Marju(IRE) —Gild (IRE) (Caerleon (USA))
5882^{5}

Fiancee (IRE) *R Charlton* 53
3 b f Pivotal—Name Of Love (IRE) (Petardia)
1327^{10} 4057^{14}

Fibs And Flannel *T D Easterby* 59
2 ch g Tobougg(IRE) —Queens Jubilee (Cayman Kai (IRE))
1735^{5} 2893^{6} 4492^{4} 5256^{8}

Ficogrande (FR) *C Boutin* a52 30
2 ch f Vangelis(USA) —Louisiana (IRE) (Bigstone (IRE))
6148a^{5}

Fiddlers Ford (IRE) *T Keddy* a61 61
8 b g Sadler's Wells(USA) —Old Domesday Book (High Top)
333^{5}

Fidler Bay *H Candy*
3 b g Falbrav(IRE) —Fiddle-Dee-Dee (IRE) (Mujtahid (USA))
2395^{12}

Fiefdom (IRE) *I W McInnes* a80 78
7 br g Singspiel(IRE) —Chiquita Linda (IRE) (Mujadil (USA))
1343^{9} 1723^{4} *1964^{2} 2387^{5} 3211^{5}* 3335^{3} 4019^{9} *4871^{7} 5107^{9} 5753^{6} 5780^{3}* 6178^{9} 6703^{5} 7153^{6} 7321^{6} 7481^{6} 7587^{8}

Field Day (IRE) *B J Meehan* 78
2 br f Cape Cross(IRE) —Naval Affair (IRE) (Last Tycoon)
(7183) ◆

Field Elect *Garry Moss*
2 b g Zafeen(FR) —Princess Carranita (IRE) (Desert Sun)
4062^{RR}

Fielder (IRE) *J G Portman* a67 18
4 b g Catcher In The Rye(IRE) —Miss Garuda (Persian Bold)
455^{3} 1073^{7}

Field Fantasy *Garry Moss* a43 37
3 ch f Bold Edge—Princess Carranita (IRE) (Desert Sun)
85^{6} 286^{4} 602^{8} 1335^{6} 2250^{11} 2355^{9} *2577^{12}*

Field Of Dream *L M Cumani* 96
2 b c Oasis Dream—Field Of Hope (IRE) (Selkirk (USA))
5743^{8}

Fierce Storm (IRE) *J Hirschberger* 78
2 b c Monsun(GER) —Fairy Queen (IRE) (Fairy King (USA))
6887a^{7}

Fiery Lad (IRE) *G M Lyons* a108 109
4 b g Mull Of Kintyre(USA) —Forget Paris (IRE) (Broken Hearted)
419a^{2} 640a^{3} 772a^{6} 5685a^{6} *6467a^{2}*

Fifer (IRE) *Patrick Morris* 33
3 b f Soviet Star(USA) —Fife (IRE) (Lomond (USA))
1950^{7} 3651^{11}

Fifth Amendment *A Berry* 73
3 ch g Presidium—Lady Magician (Lord Bud)
1335^{12} 2265^{7} 3093^{5} 3614^{8} 4131^{6} 5362^{12}

Fifth Petal (JPN) *Y Kato* 114
3 b c King Kamehameha(JPN) —Lilac Lane (USA) (Bahri (USA))
7498a^{8}

Fifth Zak *S R Bowring* a47 41
5 b g Best Of The Bests(IRE) —Zakuska (Zafonic (USA))
18 147^{10} 399^{6}

Fifty (IRE) *R Hannon* a60 78
4 b m Fasliyev(USA) —Amethyst (IRE) (Sadler's Wells (USA))
2011^{4} 2203^{7} *2598^{7}* 3581^{6} 4305^{3} *4645^{13}*

Fifty Cents *M F Harris* 86
5 ch g Diesis—Solaia (USA) (Miswaki (USA))
17^{P}

Fiftyfourth Street *P J Makin* a57 71
3 ch g Central Park(IRE) —Retaliator (Rudimentary (USA))
2496^{16} 3813^{4} *4174^{4}* 4990^{5}

Fifty Moore *Jedd O'Keeffe* 25
2 b g Selkirk(USA) —Franglais (GER) (Lion Cavern (USA))
2936^{7}

Figaro Flyer (IRE) *P Howling* a78 78
6 b g Mozart(IRE) —Ellway Star (IRE) (Night Shift (USA))
76^{7} 329^{3} 518^{3} 691^{5} 870^{4} 1103^{3} (1565) 2382^{5} 2929^{5} *3713^{6}* 4051^{10} 4842^{2} 5374^{2} 6635^{4} 7269^{6} 7519^{6} 7739^{11}

Fight Club (GER) *Evan Williams* 102
8 b h Lavirco(GER) —Flaming Song (IRE) (Darshaan)
6480^{29}

Fighting Talk (IRE) *M Johnston* 56
2 ch c Shamardal(USA) —Slap Shot (IRE) (Lycius (USA))
6214^{7}

Filemot *John Berry* a45 64
4 ch m Largesse—Hickleton Lady (IRE) (Kala Shikari)
2122^{7}

Filibuster *Mrs C A Dunnett*
2 b g Tobougg(IRE) —Blinding Mission (IRE) (Marju (IRE))
6423^{10}

Filligree (IRE) *Rae Guest* a90 93
4 b m Kyllachy—Clunie (Inchinor)
1510^{11} 2334^{6} (2653) 2911^{9} ◆ 3347^{2} 4485^{17} 5257^{4} (5901) 6282^{8} 6428^{7} *7227^{5}*

Film Festival (USA) *B Ellison* a72 82
6 ch g Diesis—To Act (USA) (Roberto (USA))
999^{13} 1230^{5} 2505^{7}

Film Maker (IRE) *G Raveneau* a96 92
4 b h Danetime(IRE) —Alexander Anapolis (IRE) (Spectrum (IRE))
464a^{10}

Film Set (USA) *F Vermeulen* a94 92
3 bb c Johar(USA) —Dippers (USA) (Polish Numbers (USA))
2270^{11} 3431^{3} *3988^{2}* 4954^{6} *7820a^{4}*

Fils D'Helene (FR) *J-P Delaporte* 60
3 b g Maximum Security(IRE) —Sparkbulle (FR) (Bulrush (FR))
7037a^{0}

Filun *A Middleton* a71 67
4 b g Montjeu(IRE) —Sispre (FR) (Master Willie)
704^{2} (848) 1081^{8} 2040^{8} 2983^{6} 3533^{8} 4263^{13} 4745^{3} *5227^{5}* 5545^{7} *6226^{13}*

Filwa (IRE) *B J Meehan* 72
2 b f Invincible Spirit(IRE) —Capessa (IRE) (Perugino (USA))
2906^{5} 5096^{2} 5379^{2} 5934^{12} 6896^{2}

Final Answer *E S McMahon* 80
2 b c Kyllachy—Valandraud (IRE) (College Chapel)
(4243) ◆

Final Bid (IRE) *A Berry* a17 56
6 b g Mujadil(USA) —Dusky Virgin (Missed Flight)
63^{8} 174^{10}

Final Drive (IRE) *E J Creighton* a72 41
3 b g Viking Ruler(AUS) —Forest Delight (IRE) (Shinko Forest (IRE))
1260^{11} 2737^{4} *4981^{5} 5582^{6} 6440^{8} (7200) (7239)*

Final Ovation (IRE) *J J Quinn* 71
2 b g Acclamation—Last Gasp (Barathea (IRE))
1661^{4} 2153^{2} 2896^{7} 3871^{8} 5292^{4} 5977^{2} 6556^{11}

Final Quest (IRE) *P J McKenna*
6 ch m King Charlemagne(USA) —Tuscaloosa (Robellino (USA))
7374^{12}

Final Rhapsody *J A Geake* a64 37
3 b f Royal Applause—Rivers Rhapsody (Dominion)
1985^{11} 2321^{16} *2632^{11}*

Final Salute *B Smart* a76 72
3 b g Royal Applause—Wildwood Flower (Distant Relative)
924^{2} 7082^{9} *7741^{11} 7870^{10}*

Final Son *A P Jarvis* a46 58
4 b g Fourstars Allstar(USA) —Dulzie (Safawan)
1752^{10} 2199^{4} *2922^{5} 3710^{10} 5775^{8}*

Final Tune (IRE) *Miss M E Rowland* a75 79
6 ch g Grand Lodge(USA) —Jackie's Opera (FR) (Indian Ridge)
618^{8}

Final Turn *H Candy* a50
2 b c Kyllachy—Eveningperformance (Night Shift (USA))
7436^{5} 7843^{6}

Final Verse *Matthew Salaman* a95 102
6 b g Mark Of Esteem(IRE) —Tamassos (Dance In Time (CAN))
2083^{2} 3014^{16} 3872^{16} 4091^{11} 6429^{8} 6733^{10} *7194^{11} 7350^{7} (7575)* ◆ *7775^{7} 7883^{7}*

Final Victory *A M Balding* a86 93
3 ch g Generous(IRE) —Persian Victory (IRE) (Persian Bold)
1427^{3} *(2232) (2829)* 3280^{3} 4248^{2} 4785^{3} 5230^{9} 6816^{3} *7373^{8}*

Finch Flyer (IRE) *G L Moore* a19 49
2 ch c Indian Ridge—Imelda (USA) (Manila (USA))
5829^{7} *6627^{13}* 6965^{6}

Fine Art Collector (IRE) *G L Moore* a55 45
3 ch g Choisir(AUS) —New Foundation (IRE) (College Chapel)
5747^{5} *6223^{11} 6430^{7}*

Fine Grain (JPN) *H Nagahama* 118
6 b h Fuji Kiseki(JPN) —Mill Grain (Polish Precedent (USA))
7498a^{15}

Fine Island (IRE) *A Cascio* 69
3 ch f Tagula(IRE) —Fine Project (IRE) (Project Manager)
1659a^{13}

Fine Lace (IRE) *D J S Ffrench Davis* a63 53
2 b f Barathea(IRE) —Fine Detail (IRE) (Shirley Heights)
4534^{13} *5165^{7}* 6284^{7} *(6639)* ◆ 6793^{5} *7235^{8} 7474^{3} 7804^{5}*

Fine Ruler (IRE) *M R Bosley* a70 70
5 b g King's Best(USA) —Bint Alajwaad (IRE) (Fairy King (USA))
25^{3} 512^{2} ◆ *725^{6} 959^{2} 1080^{6} 1495^{9} 5813^{7} 6224^{14} 6437^{8}* 6588^{7} (7109) 7417^{4} 7586^{4}

Fine Sight *R Hannon* a79 80
2 b c Cape Cross(IRE) —Daring Aim (Daylami (IRE))
2017^{6} 4041^{2} 4451^{2} 6548^{2} *(7130)*

Fine Silk (USA) *B Smart* 59
3 ch f Rahy(USA) —Meiosis (USA) (Danzig (USA))
3093^{7} 3876^{4} 5394^{5}

Finest Reserve (IRE) *M R Channon* 74
2 b c Royal Applause—Red Bandanna (IRE) (Montjeu (IRE))
4908^{8} 5542^{11} 5879^{2} 6235^{2}

Fine The World *G A Ham*
5 b m Agnes World(USA) —Fine Honor (FR) (Highest Honor (FR))
217^{9} 570^{13}

Fine Tolerance *Miss S L Davison* a56 57
3 b f Bertolini(USA) —Sashay (Bishop Of Cashel)
2679^{P} *3025^{7}* 4150^{2} 4382^{3} *5015^{4} 6289^{9}* 6788^{6} *7495^{7} 7658^{3}*

Finicius (USA) *Eoin Griffin* a108 106
5 b g Officer(USA) —Glorious Linda (FR) (Le Glorieux)
335a^{14} 642a^{3} 2647a^{5} 5141a^{11}

Finished Article (IRE) *Mrs D Thomas* a48 54
12 b g Indian Ridge—Summer Fashion (Moorestyle)
131^{11}

Finja (GER) *T Clout* 55
3 b f Paolini(GER) —Flamingo Pond (Sadler's Wells (USA))
5784a^{7}

Finjaan *M P Tregoning* 118
3 b c Royal Applause—Alhufoof (USA) (Dayjur (USA))
1675^{9} (4406) 5657^{8}

Finnegan McCool *R M Beckett* a77 89
3 b g Efisio—Royal Jade (Last Tycoon)
2140^{7} 2915^{8} 3592^{6} 4326^{6} 5065^{4} 6201^{10} *(6699) 6976^{7}*

Finnegans Rainbow *M C Chapman* a39 38
7 ch g Spectrum(IRE) —Fairy Story (IRE) (Persian Bold)
5936^{6} *7817^{7}*

Finney Hill *H Candy* 80
4 b m Mark Of Esteem(IRE) —Ringing Hill (Charnwood Forest (IRE))
2351^{2} 6733^{3} (6934) 7148^{9}

Finsbury *J S Goldie* a65 66
6 gr g Observatory(USA) —Carmela Owen (Owington)
2529^{2} 2812^{3} 4134^{6} 4466^{6} 5031^{14} 5601^{4} 5948^{10} (6414) 6765^{6} 7172^{12}

Fin Vin De Leu (GER) *M Johnston* a82 82
3 b g Dr Fong(USA) —Fairy Queen (IRE) (Fairy King (USA))
599^{3} (978) 1431^{2} 1643^{8} 2715^{7} 3051^{11} 3728^{3} 4420^{10} (4890) 5252^{4} 5696^{7} *6121^{2}* 6330^{2} *6636^{6}* 6875^{3}

Fire And Rain (FR) *Miss E C Lavelle* 63
6 b g Galileo(IRE) —Quatre Saisons (FR) (Homme De Loi (IRE))
2994^{14}

Fire And Stone (IRE) *Tom Dascombe* 66
2 b g Hawk Wing(USA) —Shinkoh Rose (FR) (Warning)
2328^{8} 3218^{3} 3420^{4} 4565^{13} 6735^{8}

Fireback *A M Balding* 66
2 b g Firebreak—So Discreet (Tragic Role (USA))
3792^{6} 4258^{8} 6108^{6}

Firebet (IRE) *R A Fahey* 112
3 b c Dubai Destination(USA) —Dancing Prize (IRE) (Sadler's Wells (USA))
1307^{2} ◆ 1677^{2} ◆ (2855) (3144) ◆ (3780) ◆ 4405^{2} (5508)

Fireflash (IRE) *Mrs A Duffield* 37
2 b c Noverre(USA) —Miss Langkawi (Daylami (IRE))
4430^{9} 4652^{7} 5674^{12} 6533^{9}

Firefly Mustique *George Baker* 39
2 b c Oasis Dream—My Ballerina (USA) (Sir Ivor (USA))
4717^{4} 5542^{13} 7095^{10}

Firehawk *J G Portman* a51 56
2 b g Firebreak—Distinctly Blu (IRE) (Distinctly North (USA))
4568^{5} 4946^{6} *6461^{6}*

Fire King *J A Geake* a61 65
3 b g Falbrav(IRE) —Dancing Fire (USA) (Dayjur (USA))
2763^{4} 3426^{4} (3985) 4378^{5} 4734^{8} 5121^{2} 5384^{4} *6224^{8}* 6394^{6} 6968^{7} *7392^{4} 7587^{11}*

Fire Me Gun *M Mullineaux* a44
3 b f Reel Buddy(USA) —Manderina (Mind Games)
138^{8} 570^{9} 3954^{6}

Firenza Bond *D Flood* a63 69
4 b g Captain Rio—Bond Stasia (IRE) (Mukaddamah (USA))
1412^{3} 1494^{6} 2219^{9}

Fire Raiser *A M Balding* a61 41
2 b g Firebreak—Mara River (Efisio)
6292^{5} 6903^{9}

Fire Sale (ARG) *A De Royer-Dupre* a81 91
4 ch m Not For Sale(ARG) —Flamme (ARG) (Pepenador (USA))
438a^{6} 701a^{5} 769a^{5} 7821a^{8}

Fireside *M A Jarvis* 74
4 b g Dr Fong(USA) —Al Hasnaa (Zafonic (USA))
995^{19} 2780^{9}

Firestorm (IRE) *C W Fairhurst* 40
5 b g Celtic Swing—National Ballet (Shareef Dancer (USA))
2592^{8} 6097^{8} 6558^{11} 6769^{9}

Firestreak *M bin Shafya* a82 105
4 b g Green Desert(USA) —Flash Of Gold (Darshaan)
334a^{6} 522a^{13}

Firetail *M L W Bell* a8
2 b f Selkirk(USA) —Snow Goose (Polar Falcon (USA))
7244^{16} *7451^{12}*

Firetrap *Mrs A Duffield* 61
2 b g Firebreak—Amber Mill (Doulab (USA))
2484^{7} 3613^{4} 4011^{4} 4342^{2} 4975^{3} 5358^{5}

Fire Up The Band *A Berry* a92 69
10 b g Prince Sabo—Green Supreme (Primo Dominie)
291^{6} 535^{9} 676^{8} 3020^{7} 4192^{10}

Firewalker *P T Dalton* a59 66
4 b m Bertolini(USA) —Crystal Canyon (Efisio)
286^{4} 328^{10} 884^{9} 1134^{11}

Firey Red (IRE) *D K Weld* 98
3 ch f Pivotal—Step With Style (USA) (Gulch (USA))
928a^{2} 1911a^{3} 4574a^{8}

Firsaan (IRE) *J R Norton* 53
3 b g Haafhd—Walayef (USA) (Danzig (USA))
1308^{8} *7504^{8}*

First Avenue *G L Moore* 96
4 b g Montjeu(IRE) —Marciala (IRE) (Machiavellian (USA))
6662^{13} 7293^{20}

First Bay (IRE) *J Howard Johnson* 83
3 b g Hawk Wing(USA) —Montmartre (IRE) (Grand Lodge (USA))
4347^{3} 5305^{3} 6137^{3}

First Blade *S R Bowring* a66 66
3 ch g Needwood Blade—Antonias Melody (Rambo Dancer (CAN))
804^{3} 1437^{6} 1595^{11} 3859^{2} *(4172) 4843^{5} (5105)* 6070^{4} 6387^{3} *6877^{6}* 7081^{3}

First Buddy *S Seemar* a72 103
5 ch g Rock Of Gibraltar(IRE) —Dance Treat (USA) (Nureyev (USA))
419a^{9} 644a^{8}

First Cat *R Hannon* a65 82
2 b g One Cool Cat(USA) —Zina La Belle (Mark Of Esteem (IRE))
2533^{13} *3270^{7} 4646^{6}* (5213) 5603^{3} 6067^{2}

First City *D M Simcock* 96
3 b f Diktat—City Maiden (USA) (Carson City (USA))
1293^{3} 2521a^{8} 3016^{5} 3746^{9} 4259^{7} 6272^{5} 6757^{4}

First Fandango *J W Hills* 67
2 b c Hernando(FR) —First Fantasy (Be My Chief (USA))
6620^{6} 7034^{5}

First Hand *M W Easterby* a33
3 b f Act One—Strong Hand (First Trump)
151^{5} 425^{10} 5328^{11} 6177^{7}

First In Command (IRE) *Daniel Mark Loughnane* a22 90
4 b g Captain Rio—Queen Sigi (IRE) (Fairy King (USA))
1375a^{9} (3377) 3787^{2} 4360a^{8} 4784^{3} 5183^{4} 5871^{4} ◆

First In Show *A M Balding* a49 42
4 b m Zamindar(USA) —Rose Show (Belmez (USA))
114^{4}

First Instance *M Johnston* a71 71
2 b c Cape Cross(IRE) —Court Lane (USA) (Machiavellian (USA))
3064^{10} 5993^{5} *6781^{4}*

First In The Queue (IRE) *S Kirk* a84 73
2 b c Azamour(IRE) —Irina (IRE) (Polar Falcon (USA))
5499^{9} 5787^{2} ◆ 6548^{8} 6930^{3} *(7277)*

First Lilly (GER) *Mario Hofer* 88
3 b f Tiger Hill(IRE) —First Smile (Surumu (GER))
1240a^{9}

First Maid *A B Haynes* a32 35
3 br f First Trump—Angel Maid (Forzando)
4205^{10} 4934^{8} 5381^{13} *7049^{9} 7137^{8}*

First Order *Miss A Stokell* a90 90
8 b g Primo Dominie—Unconditional Love (IRE) (Polish Patriot (USA))
67^{2} 128^{4} 424^{4} 1094^{5} *1494^{5}* 2053^{2} 2259^{9} 2591^{5} 2929^{3} *3212^{5}* 3422^{11} 3855^{7} 4516^{7} 4733^{9} 6159^{8} 6635^{11} 6877^{4} 7136^{4} 7398^{13} 7819^{2}

First Post (IRE) *D Haydn Jones* 20
2 b g Celtic Swing—Consignia (IRE) (Definite Article)
6930^{14} 7029^{12}

First Service (IRE) *R Charlton* a68 60
3 ch c Intikhab(USA) —Princess Sceptre (Cadeaux Genereux)
7067^{4} (7464)

First Spirit *J S Moore* a56 56
3 ch f First Trump—Flaming Spirt (Blushing Flame (USA))
630^{3} 824^{8} 1148^{5} 1408^{6} 1570^{8} 2204^{8} *(2487)* 2772^{3} *3157^{3} 3383^{10}* 3588^{3}

First Swallow *D H Brown* a68 64
4 ch g Bahamian Bounty—Promise Fulfilled (USA) (Bet Twice (USA))
1951^{6} ◆ 2316^{10} 2770^{10} 3765^{3} 4191^{10} 5150^{10} 5309^{6} 6989^{2} 7241^{5} *(7503)* ◆ *7680^{4} 7838^{2}* ◆

First Term *R Hannon* 62
2 b f Acclamation—School Days (Slip Anchor)
4421^{5} 5318^{4}

First Time (GER) *Karin Suter* 103
6 br m Silvano(GER) —First Wings (IRE) (In The Wings)
1555a^{2}

First To Call *P J Makin* a74 83
5 ch g First Trump—Scarlett Holly (Red Sunset)
7233^{11} 7539^{7} 7701^{4}

First Trim (IRE) *Seamus Fahey* a78 79
4 b g Acclamation—Spanker (Suave Dancer (USA))
250[6]

Fisadara *Jane Chapple-Hyam* 69
3 b f Nayef(USA) —Success Story (Sharrood (USA))
1329[12] 1874[2] 2858[8] (3260) 4722[6] 5035[4] 5726[7]

Fish Called Johnny *A Berry* a55 76
5 b g Kyllachy—Clare Celeste (Coquelin (USA))
378[8] 2779

Fishforcompliments *R A Fahey* a80 102
5 b g Royal Applause—Flyfisher (USA) (Riverman (USA))
1124[2] 1861[13] 2695[2] (2814) 3405[12] 4037[13] 4523[26] 5200[15] 5305[2] 5799[18] 6482[11] 7287[18] 7558[10] 7702[5] 7832[3]

Fistral *P D Niven* a43 55
5 b g Piccolo—Fayre Holly (IRE) (Fayruz)
1442[5] 1738[8] 2337[5] 2592[2] 2944[7] 3499[8] 4848[3] 5600[9] 5734[6]

Fitolini *Mrs G S Rees* a41 60
4 ch m Bertolini(USA) —Miss Fit (IRE) (Hamas (IRE))
15[13] 198[11] 474[12]

Fit The Cove (IRE) *H Rogers* a88 92
9 b g Balla Cove—Fit The Halo (Dance In Time (CAN))
4360a[10] (4574a)

Fitz *Matthew Salaman* a62 58
3 b g Mind Games—Timoko (Dancing Spree (USA))
4303[5] 5019[5] 5316[3] (5647) 6358[8] 6787[5]

Fitz Flyer (IRE) *D H Brown* a100 88
3 b c Acclamation—Starry Night (Sheikh Albadou) (7866)

Fitzolini *A D Brown* a58 70
3 b g Bertolini(USA) —Coney Hills (Beverley Boy)
1869[6] 2578[8] 2970[8] 3727[12] 4594[8] 5362[6] (7211) 7438[6] 7599[2] 7755[6]

Fitzwarren *A D Brown* a46 49
8 b g Presidium—Coney Hills (Beverley Boy)
472[5] 1766[8] 2257[10] 2529[11] 3234[10] 4436[15] 6184[2] 6818[7] 7113[8] 7666[5]

Fiulin *M Botti* a94 111
4 ch h Galileo(IRE) —Fafinta (IRE) (Indian Ridge)
(1191) 2056[5] 2409[5] 5023[6] 5823[10]

Fiumicino (NZ) *Michael, Wayne & John Hawkes* 120
6 b g Zabeel(NZ) —Latte (NZ) (Maroof (USA))
6871a[5] 7215a[22]

Fiuntas (IRE) *Shaun Harley* a53 55
6 b g Lil's Boy(USA) —Scarpetta (USA) (Seattle Dancer (USA))
602[4] 619[11]

Five A Side *Evan Williams* a28 63
5 b g Lomitas—Fifth Emerald (Formidable (USA))
139[11]

Five Cents *Saeed Bin Suroor* 75
2 b c Exceed And Excel(AUS) —Native Nickel (IRE) (Be My Native (USA))
5505[3] (5801) 6247[5] 6693[5]

Fivefold (USA) *J Akehurst* a77
2 bb c Hennessy(USA) —Calming (USA) (Wild Again (USA))
6629[8] 6911[2] ◆ 7209[8] 7551[2] ◆ 7654[3] 7685[4]

Fivefootnumberone (IRE) *J J Quinn* a72 84
3 b g Acclamation—Longueville Legend (IRE) (Cajun Cadet)
1345[7] 1517[5] 1803[4] (2443) 3173[6] 3623[6] 4043[6] 4877[2] 5293[4] 6051[12] 6857[3] 7219[6]

Five Gold Rings (IRE) *J A Osborne* a63
3 ch f Captain Rio—Metisse (IRE) (Indian Ridge)
429[2] (664) ◆ 986[9] 3281[11] 7021[9]

Fiveonthreeforjd *W J H Ratcliffe*
4 br g Compton Admiral—Patrician Fox (IRE) (Nicolotte)
7723[7]

Five Star Junior (USA) *Mrs L Stubbs* a101 96
3 b g Five Star Day(USA) —Sir Harriett (USA) (Sir Harry Lewis (USA))
(69) (203) (288) (396) 912[5] 1002[2] 1602[4] 2469[4] 3622[3] ◆ 4771[4] 5032[4] 5973[4] 7394[3] 7862[7]

Five Wishes *G A Harker* 67
5 b m Bahamian Bounty—Due West (Inchinor)
1690[13] 2264[9]

Fixation *Mrs L C Jewell* a66 45
5 ch g Observatory(USA) —Fetish (Dancing Brave (USA))
2983[13] 3986[5]

Fizzlephut (IRE) *Miss J R Tooth* a67 57
7 b g Indian Rocket—Cladantom (IRE) (High Estate)
243[6] 431[10] 596[2] (681) 818[5] 861[9] 956[4] 1038[10] 1182[10] 1591[6] 1890[3] 1970[4] 2349[9] 2596[10] 2682[6] 5345[11] 5900[10]

Flag Of Glory *C F Wall* 48
2 b g Trade Fair—Rainbow Sky (Rainbow Quest (USA))
4152[16] 6792[6] 7099[10]

Flagstone (USA) *Ian Williams* a46 57
5 ch g Distant View(USA) —Navarene (USA) (Known Fact (USA))
133[7] 353[12]

Flam *A M Hales* a68 75
4 b m Singspiel(IRE) —Delauncy (Machiavellian (USA))
103[11] 631[13]

Flambeau *H Candy* 71
2 b f Oasis Dream—Flavian (Catrail (USA))
6730[5]

Flamboyant Red (IRE) *Miss Gay Kelleway* a44 28
3 ch g Redback—Flamboyant (Danzero (AUS))
308[3] 390[7] 583[4] 1317[9] 3009[8]

Flame Creek (IRE) *E J Creighton* a81 70
13 b g Shardari—Sheila's Pet (IRE) (Welsh Term)
790[13] 2163[10] 2497[12] 3760[5] 3962[5]

Flame Of Gibraltar (IRE) *H R A Cecil* a93 103
3 b f Rock Of Gibraltar(IRE) —Spirit Of Tara (IRE) (Sadler's Wells (USA))
2002[2] (2633) 3047[2] ◆ 4094[4] 5202[3] 6003[5] 6853[10] 7131[5]

Flame Of Hestia (IRE) *J R Fanshawe* 67
3 ch f Giant's Causeway(USA) —Ellen (IRE) (Machiavellian (USA))
2282[3] 3531[2] ◆

Flamestone *A E Price* a56 52
5 b g Piccolo—Renee (Wolfhound (USA))
56[2] (153) 352[8] 472[4] 510[4] 674[4] 803[2] 853[3] 2518[8] 3269[9]

Flaming Blaze *P C Haslam* a38 34
3 b g Tobougg(IRE) —Catch The Flame (USA) (Storm Bird (CAN))
1476[6] 2104[11] 3541[6]

Flaming Cat (IRE) *F Watson* 49
6 bb g Orpen(USA) —Brave Cat (IRE) (Catrail (USA))
3539[7]

Flaming Miracle *A M Balding* a74 76
2 ch c Firebreak—Sukuma (IRE) (Highest Honor (FR))
3403[8] 3745[6] 4323[5] 5213[2] ◆ 5320[2] 6088[6] 6461[2] (6727)

Flamingo Fantasy (GER) *W Hickst* 117
4 ch h Fantastic Light(USA) —Flamingo Road (GER) (Acatenango (GER))
(2216a) (3441a) 4128a[2] 5082a[7]

Flamingo Hill *M Gasparini* 83
3 f Tiger Hill(IRE) —Flamingo Sea (USA) (Woodman (USA))
3186a[13]

Flaming Ruby *N Tinkler* a28 43
3 b f Hunting Lion(IRE) —Floral Spark (Forzando)
273[6] 379[9] 964[8]

Flamsteed (IRE) *M Quinn* a72 72
3 b c Clodovil(IRE) —Nautical Gem (IRE) (Alhaarth (IRE))
162[3] 315[3] (447) 709[2] 1032[3] 1180[2] 1414[5] 2005[7] 2377[4] 3676[4] 5581[4] 6914[9]

Flanders Fields *G L Moore*
4 b g Galileo(IRE) —Vimy Ridge (FR) (Indian Ridge)
279[8]

Flaneur *T D Easterby* 77
2 b g Chineur(FR) —Tatanka (IRE) (Lear Fan (USA))
1358[10] 2196[5] 2435[3] 3702[3] (4306) 4803[2] 5136[13] 5762[10] 6643[3] 7290[5]

Flannel (IRE) *J R Fanshawe* a58 68
3 gr g Clodovil(IRE) —La Captive (IRE) (Selkirk (USA))
1260[8] 1931[7] 2479[10] 4004[8] 4373[13] 5011[7]

Flapjack *R Hannon* a52 63
2 b f Trade Fair—Inya Lake (Whittingham (IRE))
1147[6] 1534[4] 1891[3] 2328[6] 4302[5] 4757[5] 5310[7] 5583[4] 6292[8] 6590[14]

Flapper (IRE) *J W Hills* a56 76
3 b f Selkirk(USA) —Pure Spin (USA) (Machiavellian (USA))
1804[4] 2431[4] 2942[7] (4284) (4799) 5175[11] 5996[2] 6311[7] 7149[5]

Flash Dance (IRE) *H-A Pantall* 101
3 ch f Zamindar(USA) —Resquilleuse (USA) (Dehere (USA))
4334a[2] 5562a[4]

Flash For Freedom (USA) *J R Best* a49
2 b c Essence Of Dubai(USA) —Isathriller (USA) (Buckaroo (USA))
3920[14] 6826[10] 7024[13] 7389[11] 7604[9]

Flashgun (USA) *M G Quinlan* a49 58
3 b c Lemon Drop Kid(USA) —Tolltally Light (USA) (Majestic Light (USA))
295[9] 1595[4] 3358[8]

Flash McGahon (IRE) *D Nicholls* a97 100
5 b g Namid—Astuti (IRE) (Waajib)
2502[14] 3122[6] 3784[14] 4311[6] 6051[6] 7758[9]

Flashy Lover (IRE) *M R Channon* 57
2 b f Trans Island—Irish Lover (USA) (Irish River (FR))
2494[7] 2792[6] 3240[5] 4101[3] (4757)

Flashy Max *Jedd O'Keeffe* a50 55
4 b g Primo Valentino(IRE) —Be Practical (Tragic Role (USA))
1475[15] 2473[15] 2804[11] 3331[7] 4944[12]

Flashy Photon *H Candy* a48 78
4 b g Compton Place—Showboat (USA) (Theatrical (IRE))
2828[12] 3347[12] 4428[10] 4905[4] 5429[11] 6596[10] 6926[11]

Flawed Genius *K A Ryan* a93 102
4 b g Fasliyev(USA) —Talented (Bustino)
783[6] 916[10] 995[6] 1365[6] (1684) 1821[7] 2342[14] 3014[20] (3568) 3872[3] 4549[9] 4801[4] 5522[6] 6024[9] 6217[RR] 6312[LFT] 7520[RR]

Flawless Diamond (IRE) *J S Moore* a57 57
3 ch f Indian Haven—Mystery Hill (USA) (Danehill (USA))
159[2] 214[5] 267[3]

Flaxen Lake *R Hollinshead* a70 68
2 b g Sampower Star—Cloudy Reef (Cragador)
2335[6] 6018[3] 6347[4] 7156[3] 7372[6] 7708[4]

Fleeting Echo *R Hannon* a82 85
2 b f Beat Hollow—Sempre Sorriso (Fleetwood (IRE))
2207[5] (2595) 3579[4] (4081) 4539[3] 5658[7] 6619[2] 7108[3]

Fleeting Shadow (IRE) *A Al Raihe* a91 99
5 b h Danehill(USA) —Rain Flower (IRE) (Indian Ridge)
340a[3] 697a[9]

Fleeting Spirit (IRE) *J Noseda* a109 123
4 b m Invincible Spirit(IRE) —Millennium Tale (FR) (Distant Relative)
2991[2] (3819) 5657[2] ◆ 6522a[2] 7306a[7]

Fleeting Star (USA) *J Noseda* a78 83
3 rg f Exchange Rate(USA) —Disperse A Star (USA) (Dispersal (USA))
3102[6] 3469[7] 4338[2] (4695) 6112[11]

Fleetwood Flame *W M Brisbourne* 35
4 ch m Fleetwood(IRE) —Barden Lady (Presidium)
1893[7] 3100[9] 4193[12]

Fleetwoodsands (IRE) *P C Haslam*
2 b g Footstepsinthesand—Litchfield Hills (USA) (Relaunch (USA))
3292[7]

Fleur De'Lion (IRE) *S Kirk* a65 57
3 ch f Lion Heart(USA) —Viburnum (USA) (El Gran Senor (USA))
196[6] 267[5] 594[7] 759[4] 953[9] 1070[8] 1441[7] 2380[3] 2709[6] 3257[11] 4065[4] 4224[4] (4640) 5123[7] 6172[5] 6497[2] 6742[12] 7250[6] 7455[2] (7737) 7831[4]

Fleur Enchantee (FR) *P Van De Poele* a97 98
5 br m Marchand De Sable(USA) —Mademoiselle Fleur (FR) (River Mist (USA))
7704a[3]

Fleurie *R Bouresly* a80 69
4 ch h Pivotal—Tipsy (Kris)
417a[8] 610a[8]

Fleurissimo *J L Dunlop* 80
3 ch f Dr Fong(USA) —Agnus (IRE) (In The Wings)
1329[2]

Fleuron *P Howling* a44
3 bb f Diktat—Forthwith (Midyan (USA))
160[9] 503[8]

Flexible Friend (IRE) *B J Llewellyn* 25
5 b h Danehill(USA) —Ripple Of Pride (IRE) (Sadler's Wells (USA))
3503[12] 4264[8]

Flight Tune (FR) *H-A Pantall*
2 ch c Green Tune(USA) —Flight Night (Night Shift (USA))
(7507a)

Flighty Fellow (IRE) *B G Powell* a55 85
9 ch g Flying Spur(AUS) —Al Theraab (USA) (Roberto (USA))
7581[5] 7803[6]

Flipacoin *S Dow* a38 28
4 b m Josr Algarhoud(IRE) —Eclectic (Emarati (USA))
674[8] 1177[5]

Flipando (IRE) *T D Barron* a106 105
8 b g Sri Pekan(USA) —Magic Touch (Fairy King (USA))
724[2] (783) 997[3] 1673[4] 2015[6] 2342[11] 2933[11] 3312[2] 3530[2] 4779[4] 5200[12] 5522[8] 6094[11] 6429[11] 6876[9]

Flip Flop (IRE) *B W Hills* a72 86
2 b f Footstepsinthesand—Dame Alicia (IRE) (Sadler's Wells (USA))
5318[2] 6164[4] (6563) 7187[5]

Flipping *W S Kittow* a77 79
2 br g Kheleyf(USA) —Felona (Caerleon (USA))
3500[7] (4075) 4883[4] 6173[4] 6805[5] 6993[8] 7434[7] 7669[2]

Flirty (IRE) *Rae Guest* a45 46
3 b f Lujain(USA) —Fifth Edition (Rock Hopper)
36[6] 1422[8] 2380[10] 3005[7] 5679[8] 6098[3] 6445[8] 6919[7] 7455[4] 7842[9]

Flodden Field *P W Chapple-Hyam* a50 61
3 ch g Selkirk(USA) —Sister Bluebird (Bluebird (USA))
4022[5] 6806[9]

Floodlit *J H M Gosden* a71 61
3 b f Fantastic Light(USA) —Westerly Air (USA) (Gone West (USA))
1871[9] 4948[10]

Floods Of Tears *I W McInnes* a36 58
3 br f Lucky Story(USA) —Lady Natilda (First Trump)
421[4] 492[6] 1036[8] 1281[11] 1573[14] 2820[7] 7126[11]

Floor Show *E S McMahon* 86
3 ch g Bahamian Bounty—Dancing Spirit (IRE) (Ahonoora)
(1561) 2072[2] 3643[8] 4326[11]

Flora's Pride *K G Reveley* 58
5 b m Alflora(IRE) —Pennys Pride (IRE) (Pips Pride)
1693[6] 2199[10] 2403[5] 2791[4] 3188[5] 3545[5] 4822[7] 5600[10] 5953[5] 6219[5] 6488[4] 6817[3] 7085[2]

Flora Trevelyan *W R Swinburn* a85 87
3 b f Cape Cross(IRE) —Why So Silent (Mill Reef (USA))
1605[2] (5222) 6618[2] ◆ 6813[13]

Florensky (IRE) *Saeed Bin Suroor* 67
2 br c Sinndar(IRE) —White Star (IRE) (Darshaan)
6235[4] 7116[6]

Florentia *Sir Mark Prescott* a72 71
3 ch f Medicean—Area Girl (Jareer (USA))
3982[10] 4174[3] 4374[7] 5582[3] 6070[3] (6333) (6565) 6861[3] 7428[8] 7668[3]

Florentiner (GER) *A Trybuhl* a82 98
6 ro g Waky Nao—Fatagiro (GER) (Mandelbaum (GER))
2097a[5] 4363a[10] 7822a[3]

Florentine Ruler (USA) *H R A Cecil* 67
2 b c Medicean—Follow That Dream (Darshaan)
7121[6] ◆

Flores Sea (USA) *T D Barron* a86 80
5 ch g Luhuk(USA) —Perceptive (USA) (Capote (USA))
404[2] 519[7] 807[2] (980) 1436[2] 1649[3] 1894[9] 2576[4] 2718[2] 7350[2] 7734[5] 7854[8]

Florio Vincitore (IRE) *E J Creighton* a80 81
2 b g High Chaparral(IRE) —Salome's Attack (Anabaa (USA))
2735[2] 3138[10] (3744) 4173[2] 4525[6] 5324[2] 5739a[6] 6063[6]

Flotate (USA) *Jane Chapple-Hyam* a57 4
2 bb f Orientate(USA) —Flo Jo (USA) (Graustark)
4980[8] 5368[8] 5722[10]

Flotation (USA) *B W Hills* 57
2 bb f Chapel Royal(USA) —Storm Dove (USA) (Storm Bird (CAN))
7183[7]

Flouncing (IRE) *W J Haggas* a77 77
2 b f Barathea(IRE) —Man Eater (Mark Of Esteem (IRE))
6163[3] ◆ 6728[2] ◆ 7177[2]

Flow Chart (IRE) *T D Barron* a70 67
2 b g Acclamation—Free Flow (Mujahid (USA))
1623[4] 3937[3] 4349[7] 4803[3] 4975[6] 5595[9] 6409[6] (7849)

Flower Belle (FR) *Y Barberot* a67 70
3 b f Bernebeau(FR) —Flower Spring (FR) (Poliglote)
5278a[5]

Flowerbud *G A Ham* a56 33
4 b m Fantastic Light(USA) —Maidment (Insan (USA))
310[5] 1430[5] 2971[10] 3275[9] 5246[11]

Flowers In Spring (FR) *David Marnane* 85
2 br f Country Reel(USA) —Wadayama (GER) (Surumu (GER))
5280a[5]

Flowing Cape (IRE) *R Hollinshead* a101 89
4 b g Cape Cross(IRE) —Jet Lock (USA) (Crafty Prospector (USA))
(538) ◆ (579) 783[5] 1212[3] ◆ 7375[7] 7486[8] 7639[5] 7837[6] 7862[4] ◆

Flure De Leise (IRE) *Eamon Tyrrell* a83 97
4 br m Viking Ruler(AUS) —Creme De Menthe (FR) (Green Tune (USA))
5490a[27]

Flute Magic *W S Kittow* a44 72
3 b g Piccolo—Overcome (Belmez (USA))
1491[8] 2010[15] 3075[11] 4199[5] 4730[8] 4937[12] 5584[6] 6497[8]

Fly Butterfly *M R Channon* a29 50
3 ch f Bahamian Bounty—Aconite (Primo Dominie)
1772[14] 2654[8] 2910[9]

Fly By Magic (IRE) *Patrick Carey* a81 85
5 b m Indian Rocket—Travel Tricks (IRE) (Presidium)
1375a[7] 3898a[11]

Fly By Nelly *H Morrison* a67 66
3 b f Compton Place—Dancing Nelly (Shareef Dancer (USA))
1620[2] 1839[3] 2797[2] 2949[7] 4305[10] 7180[2] 7716[10] 7829[4]

Flyinflyout *M R Channon* a55 72
2 b f Fath(USA) —Hana Dee (Cadeaux Genereux)
2175[4] 2360[5] (2514) 3086[12] 3396[9] 3993[5] 4488[16] 4901[8] 5369[8] 5715[12] 6345[10]

Flying Applause *S R Bowring* a70 80
4 b g Royal Applause—Mrs Gray (Red Sunset)
307[7] 577[4] 622[6] 841[11] (1194) 1514[7] 2149[6] 2769[8] (2852) 3860[2] 4225[6] 4469[5] 4783[7]

Flying Bantam (IRE) *J R Norton* a66 78
8 b g Fayruz—Natural Pearl (Petong)
1169[11] 1243[6] 1741[6] 3689[9] 4376[11] 4845[14]

Flying Blue (FR) *R Martin Sanchez* a101 85
4 b h Fly To The Stars—Viking's Cove (USA) (Miswaki (USA))
259a[9] 414a[13] 615a[10]

Flying Cloud (IRE) *Saeed Bin Suroor* 110
3 b f Storming Home—Criquette (Shirley Heights) (1657a) (3047) ◆ 7046a[6]

Flying Cloud (USA) *B J Meehan* a48 44
3 ch f Giant's Causeway(USA) —St Francis Wood (USA) (Irish River (FR))
1605[10] 2433[13] 3303[7]

Flying Destination *W J Knight* a72 74
2 ch g Dubai Destination(USA) —Fly For Fame (Shaadi (USA))
3920[8] 4439[4] 5220[7] 5742[2] 6373[5]

Flying Doctor *N G Richards* a36 37
6 b g Mark Of Esteem(IRE) —Vice Vixen (CAN) (Vice Regent (CAN))
252[7]

Flying Gazebo (IRE) *J S Moore* a30 55
3 b g Orpen(USA) —Grand Summit (IRE) (Grand Lodge (USA))
3207[8] 4322[6] 4731[4] 5503[5] 7687[8]

Flying Goose (IRE) *R A Harris* a86 83
5 ch g Danehill Dancer(IRE) —Top Of The Form (IRE) (Masterclass (USA))
187[8] 4264[9]

Flying Indian *J Balding* a61 65
4 ch m Hawk Wing(USA) —Poppadam (Salse (USA))
89[10] 146[6] 327[9] 508[5]

Flying Lady (IRE) *M R Channon* a70 80
3 b f Hawk Wing(USA) —Lady Nessa (USA) (Al Nasr (FR))
397[5] 586[9] 776[2] 839[3] (943) 1148[2] 1315[5] 1531[6]

Flying Phoebe *Mrs L Stubbs* 51
3 b f Sakhee(USA) —Altaweelah (IRE) (Fairy King (USA))
2403[9] 3379[5] 4270[10] 5470[4] 6177[3] 6310[7] 6919[9]

Flying Private (USA) *D Wayne Lukas* a115
3 b c Fusaichi Pegasus(USA) —Beautiful Treasure (USA) (Unbridled (USA))
1688a[19] 2098a[4] 2734a[6]

Flying River (IRE) *Tom Dascombe* a47
3 b f Bachelor Duke(USA) —Suzuran (Generous (IRE))
201[10] 556[5]

Flying Shadow (SWI) *H-A Pantall* a57
3 ch f Sinyar(IRE) —Formida (FR) (Highest Honor (FR))
5118a[8] 6980a[3]

Flying Silks (IRE) *J R Gask* a67 74
3 b g Barathea(IRE) —Future Flight (Polar Falcon (USA))
2151[4] 2797[8] 4079[3] (4660) 5169[5] 5602[6] 7246[13]

Flying Spur (USA) *William Mott* a100
3 ch f Giants Causeway—Lakeway (USA) (Seattle Slew (USA))
1763a[3]

Flying Squad (UAE) *M F Harris* a75 39
5 b g Jade Robbery(USA) —Sandova (IRE) (Green Desert (USA))
330[7] 490[7] 1067[6] 1213[10] 1479[5] 5227[10] 5532[11] 7354[4]

Flying Statesman (USA) *R A Fahey* 90
2 b g Johannesburg(USA) —Insomnie (USA) (Seattle Slew (USA))
2017[2] ◆ (2588) 2993[10]

Flying Valentino *Ian Williams* a77 83
5 b m Primo Valentino(IRE) —Flying Romance (IRE) (Flying Spur (AUS))
757[8] 974[3] 1405[6] 1860[13] 2916[3] (3408) 4482[3] 4641[15] 5099[10] 7158[8]

Flyingwithbebe (USA) *T Doumen* a81 89
3 b f Horse Chestnut(SAF) —Samut (IRE) (Danehill (USA))
1208a[7] 7696a[0]

Fly In Johnny (IRE) *J J Bridger* a51 58
4 b g Fasliyev(USA) —Goodness Gracious (IRE) (Green Desert (USA))
666[11] 891[3] 946[10] 2330[12] 2713[10] 3162[6] 3459[7] 4051[7] 4082[9] 4203[10]

Flynn's Island (IRE) *M Dods* 50
3 b g Trans Island—Cappuccino (IRE) (Mujadil (USA))
1015[9] 1683[7] 1888[9] 2236[11] 2790[10] 3108[9] 3614[5]

Fly Silca Fly (IRE) *M R Channon* 80
2 b f Hawk Wing(USA) —Nevis Peak (AUS) (Danehill (USA))
2034[5] 2401[2] 3138[14] 3658[2] (4100) 4306[6] (4850) 5208[2]

Fly With The Stars (USA) *A B Haynes* a60 34
4 ch g Fusaichi Pegasus(USA) —Forest Key (USA) (Green Forest (USA))
3960[9] 4935[10]

Focail Eile *J Ryan* a74 80
4 b g Noverre(USA) —Glittering Image (IRE) (Sadler's Wells (USA))
80[2] (255) 3112[9] 3637[4] (4473) (4816) ◆ 4881[4] 5673[13] 7229[7]

Fochabers *R Charlton* a65
2 b g Dr Fong(USA) —Celtic Cross (Selkirk (USA))
7390[12] 7663[4] 7865[5]

Fol Hollow (IRE) *D Nicholls* a72 103
4 b g Monashee Mountain(USA) —Constance Do (Risk Me (FR))
(1278) (1375a) 1647[6] 2704[8] 3122[4] (3236) 3898a[7] 4341[4] 4523[14] 4766[4] 5132[3] 5507[3] 6091[9] 6283[4]

Folie Express (FR) *Dominique Sepulchre* 59
3 ch f American Post—Eliza Orzeszkowa (IRE) (Polish Patriot (USA))
7037a[3]

Folio (IRE) *W J Musson* a85 85
9 b g Perugino(USA) —Bayleaf (Efisio)
(172) (361) 550[4] 847[3] 999[12] 1382[6] 1812[8] 2150[8] 2773[6]

Folk Tune (IRE) *J J Quinn* 75
6 b h Danehill(USA) —Musk Lime (USA) (Private Account (USA))
5067[6] 6095[9]

Folle Allure (FR) *J-C Rouget* 102
4 b m Poliglote—Irish Arms (FR) (Irish River (FR))
6438a[5] 7569a[8]

Folletta (IRE) *R Hannon* a64 69
2 b f Le Vie Dei Colori—Finnine (USA) (Zafonic (USA))
2430[4] 2792[4] 3101[8] 4195[2] 4850[11] 5935[5] 6211[7] 6441[2] 6963[9]

Fol Liam *A J McCabe* a69 81
3 b g Observatory(USA) —Tide Of Fortune (Soviet Star (USA))
1019[9] 1992[16] 2744[3] 3225[9] 4859[5] 5126[8] 5612[5] 5676[3]

Follow The Dream *Karen George* a67 57
6 b m Double Trigger(IRE) —Aquavita (Kalaglow)
779[6] 957[6] 1286[9] 2182[7] 3303[5] 3927[6] 4301[3] (4935) 5885[2] ◆ 7598[2] (7675) ◆

Follow The Flag (IRE) *A J McCabe* a85 79
5 ch g Traditionally(USA) —Iktidar (Green Desert (USA))
307[5] 558[3] (932) 1133[9] 1343[4] 1493[7] 1887[2] 2542[6] 2665[7] 3112[10] 4881[9] 5126[2] 5329[3] 5886[9] 6072[5] 6174[2] (6490) 6760[4] 7373[2] 7583[7] 7811[5]

Follow The Lead *F Head* 77
3 b c Rainbow Quest(USA) —Senkaya (FR) (Valanour (IRE))
2293a[2]

Follow The Sun (IRE) *Ronald O'Leary* a52 62
5 br g Tertullian(USA) —Sun Mate (IRE) (Miller's Mate)
2609[4] 5683[4] 6184[4] 6817[2] 7080[3] 7798[11]

Follow Your Spirit *B Palling* a53 51
4 b g Compton Place—Ymlaen (IRE) (Desert Prince (IRE))
4891[3] 1775[13]

Folly Bridge *R Charlton* 82
2 b f Avonbridge—Jalissa (Mister Baileys)
4900[3] (5749) 6397[3]

Folly Lodge *R M Beckett* a91 91
5 ch m Grand Lodge(USA) —Marika (Marju (IRE))
1566[2] 2188[7] 2434[9] (3763) 4088[8] 4259[8]

Folsomprisonblues (IRE) *E J O'Neill* 83
3 b c Mull Of Kintyre(USA) —Prosaic Star (IRE) (Common Grounds)
1354[7] 1677[6]

Fol Wizard *P C Haslam* 9
2 ch g Piccolo—Go Go Girl (Pivotal)
2788[10] 3119[9]

Fond *Ollie Pears* 39
2 br f Makbul—Favour (Gothenberg (IRE))
2996[5] 6819[15]

Fondant Fancy *H J L Dunlop* 69
3 b f Falbrav(IRE) —Foodbroker Fancy (IRE) (Halling (USA))
1092[3] 1579[5] 3693[14] 4303[7]

Fongoli *B G Powell* a52 55
3 b f Dr Fong(USA) —Darmagi (IRE) (Desert King (IRE))
1580[10] 2380[2] 2635[4] 4470[8]

Fong's Alibi *J S Moore* a74 68
3 b f Dr Fong(USA) —Alchemy (IRE) (Sadler's Wells (USA))
(397) 755[5] 1707[8] 2607[7] (3054) 3535[5] 3985[2] 4224[5] 4569[10] (5127) 5568[3]

Fontana (GER) *F Boccardelli* 78
3 br c Bahri(USA) —Firedance (GER) (Lomitas)
2114a[7]

Fonterutoli (IRE) *M Botti* 72
2 gr c Verglas(IRE) —Goldendale (IRE) (Ali-Royal (IRE))
2167[3] 2663[2] 3376[2]

Fontley *Eve Johnson Houghton* 81
2 b f Sadler's Wells(USA) —Horatia (IRE) (Machiavellian (USA))
5604[7] (5994) 7033[4]

Foolin Myself *M L W Bell* a105 98
4 b h Montjeu(IRE) —Friendlier (Zafonic (USA))
1357[4] ◆ 1673[12] 2671[P] 2933[18] 4262[2] (5375) 6030[6] 6815[16]

Foolish Ambition (GER) *David Wachman* 94
2 b f Danehill Dancer(IRE) —Foolish Act (IRE) (Sadler's Wells (USA))
2286a[2] ◆

Fools Gold *Paul Mason* a82 43
4 b g Ishiguru(USA) —Sally Green (IRE) (Common Grounds)
980[3] 1194[10] 1777[5] 1964[8] 4202[9]

Footsie (IRE) *J G Given* 64
2 b f Footstepsinthesand—Marlene-D (Selkirk (USA))
6477[9] 6992[13]

Footstepsofspring (FR) *R Hannon* a86 87
2 b c Footstepsinthesand—Moon West (USA) (Gone West (USA))
1700[6] 2187[2] 2547[2] (2979) 3782[7] 4272[4] 5250[3] 5580[4] 5763[6] 6398[6]

Forbidden (IRE) *Daniel Mark Loughnane* a76 74
6 ch g Singspiel(IRE) —Fragrant Oasis (USA) (Rahy (USA))
215[3] (569) 580[2] 841[6] (1883) 2352[7] 3094[2] 3448[2] 5780[4] 6168[5] 6190[7] 6496[5] 6861[6]

Forbidden Paradise (IRE) *K R Burke* a73 66
2 ch f Chineur(FR) —Villa Nova (IRE) (Petardia)
1521[2]

Forced Opinion (USA) *K A Morgan* a61 47
4 gr h Distant View(USA) —Kinetic Force (USA) (Holy Bull (USA))
944[6] 4721[10] 6998[8]

Force Freeze (USA) *Doug Watson* a109
4 bb g Forest Camp(USA) —Antifreeze (USA) (It's Freezing (USA))
264a[5] (525a) 1010a[5]

Force Group (IRE) *M H Tompkins* a75 84
5 b g Invincible Spirit(IRE) —Spicebird (IRE) (Ela-Mana-Mou)
2698[5] 2898[6] 3587[4] 3822[13] 4544[3] 5034[6] 5698[2] 5961[4] 6636[7] 6936[5] 7201[2] 7413[6] 7475[6]

Force Tradition (IRE) *M H Tompkins* a57 47
4 ch g Traditionally(USA) —Kind Of Loving (Diesis)
66[4] 346[13]

Foreign Investment (IRE) *P D Evans* a66 72
3 ch f Desert Prince(IRE) —Muneera (USA) (Green Dancer (USA))
236[4] (626) 817[8] (1106) 1452[2] 1937[8] 2841[6] 3209[3] 4266[4]

Foreign King (USA) *J W Mullins* a64 66
5 b g Kingmambo(USA) —Foreign Aid (USA) (Danzig (USA))
59[7]

Foreign Rhythm (IRE) *N Tinkler* 56
4 ch m Distant Music(USA) —Happy Talk (IRE) (Hamas (IRE))
1558[9] 1695[9] 3031[9] (3239) 3562[5] 3938[13] 4355[7] 4552[6] 4929[9] 5443[4] 5955[13] 6216[6] 6380[6] ◆ 7081[7]

Foresta (FR) *B De Montzey* 86
2 b f Forestier(FR) —Milanaise (FR) (Marignan (USA))
3967a[3] 4584a[7] 5279a[10]

Forest Crown *R M Beckett* a76 69
2 b f Royal Applause—Wiener Wald (USA) (Woodman (USA))
3277[3] 6582[4] (7234)

Forest Dane *Mrs N Smith* a78 74
9 b g Danetime(IRE) —Forest Maid (Thatching)
24[5] 281[3] 533[2] 2564[6] 3422[8] 3995[2] 4870[4] 5288[3] 6201[6] 6791[9] 7203[3] 7330[2] 7484[3] 7739[4] 7890[5]

Forest Runner *Saeed Bin Suroor* 75
2 b c Pivotal—Tiriana (Common Grounds)
5785[2]

Forest Storm *J S Bolger* 97
3 ch f Galileo(IRE) —Quiet Storm (IRE) (Desert Prince (IRE))
6298a[11]

Forethought *P Howling* 64
2 b f Lujain(USA) —Flourish (Selkirk (USA))
4792[8] 5741[9] 6062[10] 6821[8]

Forever Changes *L Montague Hall* a52
4 gr m Bertolini(USA) —Days Of Grace (Wolfhound (USA))
347[7] 646[12] 727[7] 7880[12]

Forever Nadine (GER) *Andreas Lowe* 87
3 ch f Kornado—Forever Nice (GER) (Greinton)
4583a[10]

Forever's Girl *G R Oldroyd* a76 48
3 b f Monsieur Bond(IRE) —Forever Bond (Danetime (IRE))
(135) 273[4] 379[3] ◆ 804[4] 4436[10] 4999[5] 5678[5] 6456[6] (7280) (7601)

Forever Together (USA) *Jonathan Sheppard* a110 119
5 rg m Belong To Me(USA) —Constant Companion (USA) (Relaunch (USA))
7284a[3]

Forget (IRE) *C E Brittain* a54 44
2 b f Tiger Hill(IRE) —Wajina (Rainbow Quest (USA))
1637[3] 1968[7]

Forget It *G L Moore* a71 65
4 b g Galileo(IRE) —Queens Way (FR) (Zafonic (USA))
6692[12]

Forgotten Army (IRE) *M H Tompkins* 70
2 b c Arakan(USA) —Brioney (IRE) (Barathea (IRE))
4385[10] 5527[8] (6065)

Forgotten Voice (IRE) *J Noseda* a108 115
4 b g Danehill Dancer(IRE) —Asnieres (USA) (Spend A Buck (USA))
(1213) ◆ (1731) ◆ (3014) 4002[4] 4419[4] ◆ 5231[5] 6448[3] 6850[12]

Foricherforpoorer *N Tinkler* 14
2 gr f Where Or When(IRE) —Bridal Path (Groom Dancer (USA))
2099[16] 2360[13] 4138[6] 4503[13] 4800[10]

For Joy *A De Royer-Dupre* 101
4 ch m Singspiel(IRE) —Fine And Mellow (FR) (Lando (GER))
7704a[0]

For Life (IRE) *J E Long* a80 73
7 b g Bachir(IRE) —Zest (USA) (Zilzal (USA))
1197[11] (2396) 3422[6] 4870[6] 7553[9] 7656[10]

Formation (USA) *J R Boyle* a99 91
4 ch g Van Nistelrooy(USA) —Miss Valedictorian (USA) (With Approval (CAN))
26[2] (284) (445) 563[3] 915[3] 1216[2] 1642[5]

Formax (FR) *M P Tregoning* 96
7 gr g Marathon(USA) —Fortuna (FR) (Kaldoun (FR))
1458[9] 1790[12]

Formidable Guest *J Pearce* a74 25
5 b m Dilshaan—Fizzy Treat (Efisio)
194[2] (253) (478) 597[2] 733[4] 897[3] 1133[4] 1604[3] 1834[5] 7752[7]

Formula (USA) *R Hannon* a82 74
3 bb g Stormin Fever(USA) —Misty Gallop (USA) (Victory Gallop (CAN))
1295[10] 1752[2] 1931[3] 4303[4] (5102) 5986[5] 6209[3] 6634[4] 6973[7]

Forrest Flyer (IRE) *I Semple* 71
5 b g Daylami(IRE) —Gerante (USA) (Private Account (USA))
1506[5] (2233) 2629[3] 2944[8] (3107) (3654) 4350[6] 4898[8] 5291[5] 6053[9] 7170[9]

Forrest Star *M Johnston* a41 61
4 ch m Fraam—Starfleet (Inchinor)
3021[8] 3296[7] 4466[11] 4772[9] 7680[11] 7855[11]

Forshour *E S McMahon* a64 67
2 ch g Forzando—Sharoura (Inchinor)
3715[2] 4847[3] 6461[8] 6901[10]

Fort Churchill (IRE) *B Ellison* a55 78
8 b g Barathea(IRE) —Brisighella (IRE) (Al Hareb (USA))
899[9] 1099[6] 1409[3] 1765[3]

Forte Dei Marmi *L M Cumani* a64 87
3 b g Selkirk(USA) —Frangy (Sadler's Wells (USA))
(2174) ◆ 2925[7]

Fortezza *C F Wall* 47
3 b f Efisio—Donna Anna (Be My Chief (USA))
3764[8] 4199[8] 4913[7]

Forthe Millionkiss (GER) *Uwe Ostmann* a24 113
5 bb h Dashing Blade—Forever Nice (GER) (Greinton)
1029a[10] 1525[5] 3416a[4] 4129a[8] 6713a[6] 7704a[0]

Fortina's Boy (USA) *W R Swinburn* a63 56
3 ch c Mr Greeley(USA) —Really Quick (USA) (In Reality (USA))
1257[9] 1730[9] 5242[5] 5813[11] 6492[10] 7484[8]

Fortuitous (IRE) *S Gollings* a43 13
5 ch g Tobougg(IRE) —Shallop (Salse (USA))
175[6] 2541[2]

Fortunate Bid (IRE) *Mrs L Stubbs* a51 74
3 ch g Modigliani(USA) —Mystery Bid (Auction Ring (USA))
1252[7] (3693) 4079[5] 4821[2] 5513[4] 6052[13] 6908[7] 7153[10]

Fortunate Flame *K A Ryan* a67 56
3 b g Key Of Luck(USA) —Candescent (Machiavellian (USA))
1054[2] 1451[4] 2142[3] 2578[5] 4657[9] 4816[6] 6123[11] 6804[12]

Fortunate Isle (USA) *R A Fahey* a91 68
7 ch g Swain(IRE) —Isla Del Rey (USA) (Nureyev (USA))
1100[5] 1279[14] 2965[14]

Fortunella *Miss Gay Kelleway* a61 48
4 b m Polish Precedent(USA) —Hazy Heights (Shirley Heights)
38[2] 1481[0] 1568[11] 1938[12]

Fortune Point (IRE) *A W Carroll* a51 23
11 ch g Cadeaux Genereux—Mountains Of Mist (IRE) (Shirley Heights)
483[5]

Fortunes Of Fire *G A Swinbank* 76
2 ch g Avonbridge—Lucky Arrow (Indian Ridge) (5728)

Fortuni (IRE) *Sir Mark Prescott* a96 57
3 b g Montjeu(IRE) —Desert Ease (IRE) (Green Desert (USA))
(1643) ◆ 4103[4]

Forty Thirty (IRE) *Miss Sheena West* a66 69
3 b g Poliglote—Ciena (FR) (Gold Away (IRE))
455[5] 670[6] 776[9] 2220[4] 4730[3]

Forum Magnum (USA) *A Fabre* 97
2 b c Elusive Quality(USA) —French Bid (AUS) (Anabaa (USA))
3667a[6] 6326a[2] 6752a[7]

Forward Feline (IRE) *B Palling* a74 74
3 b f One Cool Cat(USA) —Ymlaen (IRE) (Desert Prince (IRE))
1155[5] 1414[2] 2079[13] 2321[6] 2879[12] 6596[12] 7082[8] 7191[8] (7729)

Forward Planning (USA) *M Johnston* 47
3 ch f Orientate(USA) —Casa's Kids (USA) (Theatrical (IRE))
4277[8] 4947[4] 6390[15]

Forzarzi (IRE) *H A McWilliams* a63 63
5 b g Forzando—Zarzi (IRE) (Suave Dancer (USA))
580[9] 1244[6] 1475[12] 2531[7] 2626[4] 2968[5] 3615[11]

Fossgate *J D Bethell* a60 74
8 ch g Halling(USA) —Peryllys (Warning)
1851[7] 2573[8] 3561[6] 4403[3] (4600) 5162[5] 5469[3] 6183[6]

Foundation Room (IRE) *A M Balding* 95
3 ch f Saffron Walden(FR) —Bellagio Princess (Kris)
1801[3] ◆ 2273[14] 3320[5]

Four Dancers (GER) *Frau E Mader* 91
4 b h Seattle Dancer(USA) —Four Roses (IRE) (Darshaan)
4582a[6] 6323a[7] 7821a[9]

Four Kicks (IRE) *Muredach Kelly* 56
3 b f Pyrus(USA) —Dynamo Minsk (IRE) (Polish Precedent (USA))
5948[7]

Fourlanends *N Wilson* 32
2 ch c Dubawi(IRE) —Nova Cyngi (USA) (Kris S (USA))
5668[8]

Four Miracles *M H Tompkins* a64 88
5 b m Vettori(IRE) —North Kildare (USA) (Northjet)
1519[6] 1878[4]

Four Mirrors (CAN) *C R Dore* a29 44
3 b g Gulch(USA) —Solarity (CAN) (Ascot Knight (CAN))
6439[9] 6771[8]

Fourpenny Lane *Ms Joanna Morgan* a101 101
4 b m Efisio—Makara (Lion Cavern (USA))
1543a[9]

Four Tel *Tom Dascombe* a63 64
5 gr g Vettori(IRE) —Etienne Lady (IRE) (Imperial Frontier (USA))
1634[5] 3331[5] ◆ 6224[9] 6640[11]

Fourth Dimension (IRE) *Miss T Spearing* a53 76
10 b g Entrepreneur—Isle Of Spice (USA) (Diesis)
1786[10] 2172[7]

Fourth Generation (IRE) *G A Swinbank* 78
2 ch g Kris Kin(USA) —Merewood Lodge (IRE) (Grand Lodge (USA))
5674[7] 6821[2]

Fourtowns Flyer (IRE) *Lee Smyth* a76 57
5 b g Danetime(IRE) —Music Khan (Music Boy)
6135[7] (6856) 7398[3] ◆

Four Winds *M L W Bell* 107
3 b g Red Ransom(USA) —Fairy Godmother (Fairy King (USA))
1326[2] (2004) 3050[6] 4521[4] 5141a[2]

Foxhaven *P R Chamings* 110
7 ch g Unfuwain(USA) —Dancing Mirage (IRE) (Machiavellian (USA))
(5097) 6936[2]

Foxholes Lodge *J D Bethell*
4 b m Nasheyt—Duxford Lodge (Dara Monarch)
4174[12] 5071[8]

Foxtrot Alpha (IRE) *P Winkworth* a71 70
3 b f Desert Prince(IRE) —Imelda (USA) (Manila (USA))
1808[9] 2827[2] 3982[7] 4304[11] 5167[3] 6738[11] 7236[7]

Foxtrot Bravo (IRE) *Miss S L Davison* a62 59
3 b g Noverre(USA) —Standcorrected (Shareef Dancer (USA))
403[6] 662[6] 5574[2] 6399[6] 6720[8] 7110[12] 7492[11] 7652[5]

Foxtrot Charlie *P Winkworth* a73 69
3 b g Lucky Story(USA) —Holy Smoke (Statoblest)
1932[12] 2982[2] 4149[7] (5570) 6289[8]

Foxtrot Delta (IRE) *P Winkworth* a62
2 ch c Namid—Tarziyana (USA) (Danzig (USA))
5368[7] 6291[6] 6627[7]

Foxtrot Foxtrot *P Winkworth* a39
2 b g Royal Applause—Darmagi (IRE) (Desert King (IRE))
2187[12] 6162[8] 6629[10]

Foxy Music *E J Alston* a74 85
5 b g Foxhound(USA) —Primum Tempus (Primo Dominie)
985[6] 1052[8] 2228[4] 2481[11] 3268[2] 3372[7] 4043[7]

Fraamtaztiic *R J Hodges* a12 25
2 b f Fraam—Dahlawise (IRE) (Caerleon (USA))
5445[6] 6441[10] 6913[7]

Fraizer (IRE) *Adrian McGuinness* a53 51
5 b g City On A Hill(USA) —She's Our Lady (IRE) (Scenic)
242[3] 574[2]

Franali (IRE) *R F Fisher* 42
3 b f Kheleyf(USA) —Christeningpresent (IRE) (Cadeaux Genereux)
4617[11]

Francesca Conti (IRE) *K R Burke* 3
2 b f Atraf—Gentian Blue (IRE) (Tirol)
1884[7]

Francesco (FR) *Mrs L B Normile* 49
5 gr g Kaldounevees(FR) —Mount Gable (Head For Heights)
1102[5]

Franchesca's Gold *Jane Southcombe* a53 49
3 b f Monsieur Bond(IRE) —Anita Marie (IRE) (Anita's Prince)
6581[8] 7129[11] 7361[9] 7765[6]

Francis Albert *M Mullineaux* a19 53
3 b g Mind Games—Via Dolorosa (Chaddleworth (IRE))
2700[7] 3764[9] 4860[9] 5468[2] 6220[12]

Francis Walsingham (IRE) *H Morrison* a76 76
3 b g Invincible Spirit(IRE) —Web Of Intrigue (Machiavellian (USA))
1636[4] 2080[9] (2574) 3219[4] 4494[4] 4952[5] 6396[9]

Franco Is My Name *P R Hedger* a75 21
3 b g Namid—Veronica Franco (Darshaan)
5744[9] 5987[10] 6974[6] (7392)

Frankie Falco *G Fierro* a9
3 br g Bollin Eric—Marsh Marigold (Tina's Pet)
7725[5]

Franki J *D Donovan* a64
2 ch f Barathea(IRE) —Whassup (FR) (Midyan (USA))
6672[7] 7157[9] 7616[7] 7887[5]

Franklino (FR) *K Borgel*
2 ch g Gold Away(IRE) —Amour Fatal (IRE) (Rainbows For Life (CAN))
5850a[5]

Franksalot (IRE) *I W McInnes* a61 76
9 ch g Desert Story(IRE) —Rosie's Guest (IRE) (Be My Guest (USA))
23[10] 277[11]

Frank Street *Eve Johnson Houghton* 76
3 ch g Fraam—Pudding Lane (IRE) (College Chapel)
1419[3] 1744[9] 2336[8]

Frantic Storm (GER) *W Hickst* 102
3 b c Nayef(USA) —Flamingo Road (GER) (Acatenango (GER))
3670a[8]

Frantz De Galais (FR) *Y Fouin* 74
3 ch g Trempolino(USA) —Exceptionnel Lady (FR) (Vertical Speed (FR))
7037a[2]

Franziskaner (GER) *W Hefter*
6 bl g Medaaly—Famous Girl (GER) (Motley (USA))
466a[4]

Franz Quercus (FR) *Y De Nicolay* 57
2 b c Martaline—La Haie Blanche (FR) (Sanglamore (USA))
6322a^{6} 7384a^{7}

Fratellino *A J McCabe* 100
2 ch c Auction House(USA) —Vida (IRE) (Wolfhound (USA))
(1277) ◆ 1598^{4} 1788^{7} (1991) 2260^{4} 2408^{5} 2702^{4} 2995^{2} 6275^{4} 6660^{12}

Fravia *B J McMath* a27 12
3 b f Bertolini(USA) —Alizar (IRE) (Rahy (USA))
862^{5} 1045^{5}

Freda's Rose (IRE) *J Mackie* a29 54
5 b m Rossini(USA) —African Scene (IRE) (Scenic)
5072^{4} 5259^{5} 5730^{2} 6022^{4} 6488^{6} 7142^{9}

Freddie Bolt *F Watson* 19
3 b c Diktat—Birjand (Green Desert (USA))
5954^{10}

Freddie's Girl (USA) *Stef Liddiard* a66 59
2 bb f More Than Ready(USA) —Carib Gal (USA) (Awesome Again (CAN))
3744^{8} 4147^{8} 4688^{3} 5212^{7} 7772^{2}

Frederi (FR) *Unknown* 38
2 u u (USA) — (USA) (Fasliyev (USA))
4686a^{7}

Fred Kennet *M Salaman* a29
4 ch g Kadastrof(FR) —Evaporate (Insan (USA))
4838^{9}

Free Agent *R Hannon* 103
3 b g Dr Fong(USA) —Film Script (Unfuwain (USA))
2176^{4} 3087^{4} 3778^{4} 5609^{3} 6425^{4}

Freedom Fire (IRE) *J M P Eustace* a68 65
3 b g Alhaarth(IRE) —Feel Free (IRE) (Generous (IRE))
2857^{4} 3549^{4} 4178^{4} 6289^{4} 6720^{3}

Freedom Flying *Joss Saville* 31
6 b m Kalanisi(IRE) —Free Spirit (IRE) (Caerleon (USA))
1231^{9}

Freedom Light (FR) *C Boutin* 74
2 b f Divine Light(JPN) —Freedom Sweet (FR) (Sicyos (USA))
5713a^{9} 6927a^{6}

Freedom Pass (USA) *J A R Toller* a52
2 b f Gulch(USA) —Bold Desire (Cadeaux Genereux)
7429^{4}

Free Falling *A J Lidderdale* a55 50
3 ch f Selkirk(USA) —Free Flying (Groom Dancer (USA))
1531^{8} 2489^{12} 3302^{14} 5100^{5} 6189^{5} 7324^{8} 7660^{10} 7842^{6}

Free Flying Soul (USA) *Bruce Headley* a109
4 b m Quiet American(USA) —Ruby Surprise (USA) (Farma Way (USA))
7285a^{3}

Freeforaday (USA) *J R Best* a94 86
2 ch c Freefourinternet(USA) —All My Yesterdays (USA) (Wild Again (USA))
4906^{6} 5282^{2} 5749^{4} (6185) 6418^{4} (6619) ◆ (7108) ◆

Free For All (IRE) *S Kirk* 75
2 br c Statue Of Liberty(USA) —Allegorica (IRE) (Alzao (USA))
6061^{6} 6616^{3}

Free Grain *J L Dunlop* 67
2 b f Sakhee(USA) —All Grain (Polish Precedent (USA))
5604^{6} ◆ 7182^{20}

Freeing *J A R Toller* a52 54
3 b f Dansili—Sweeping (Indian King (USA))
4913^{6} 5971^{3} ◆ 7432^{10}

Free Judgement (USA) *J S Bolger* a96 108
2 b c Vindication(USA) —South Bay Cove (CAN) (Fusaichi Pegasus (USA))
6317a^{16} 6849^{8} (7072a)

Freemantle *A P O'Brien* 115
3 b c Galileo(IRE) —Patacake Patacake (USA) (Bahri (USA))
2014^{2} 3038^{4} (3055) ◆ 3970a^{4}

Freemusic (IRE) *L Riccardi* 113
5 b h Celtic Swing—Favignana (GER) (Grand Lodge (USA))
2115a^{3} 2955a^{7} 6718a^{7} 7313a^{6}

Freepressionist *R A Teal* a70 60
3 ch f Compton Place—Sophielu (Rudimentary (USA))
936^{9} 1618^{4} 2321^{5} 2712^{5} 2973^{9} 4172^{5} 4748^{7} 4982^{5} 6335^{9}

Free Tussy (ARG) *G L Moore* a84 77
5 b g Freelancer(USA) —Perlada (ARG) (Cipayo (ARG))
531^{4} 803^{12} 961^{6} (1589) 2923^{7} (3158) 4696^{8} 5594^{2} 5802^{3} 6392^{2} 6473^{4} (7134) (7475)

Freeze Style (FR) *B Dutruel* 67
3 b f Nuclear Freeze(USA) —Marishaan (IRE) (Darshaan)
4130a^{6}

Fregate Island (IRE) *A G Newcombe* a88 90
6 gr g Daylami(IRE) —Briery (IRE) (Salse (USA))
1863^{6}

Fremen (USA) *D Nicholls* a90 93
9 ch g Rahy(USA) —Northern Trick (USA) (Northern Dancer (CAN))
(910) 958^{2} 1079^{3} 1283^{4} (2816) 3525^{6} 4438^{2} (4750) (4897) 5944^{3}

Fremont (IRE) *R Hannon* 101
2 b c Marju(IRE) —Snow Peak (Arazi (USA))
(2477) ◆ 2993^{8} 5795^{4} (6397)

French Applause (IRE) *T P Tate* 80
3 b g Royal Applause—A Ma Guise (USA) (Silver Hawk (USA))
2104^{2} 2937^{2} 3566^{5}

French Art *N Tinkler* a71 88
4 ch g Peintre Celebre(USA) —Orange Sunset (IRE) (Roanoke (USA))
1603^{19} 2073^{11} 2939^{6} 3378^{8} 4046^{8} 4548^{13} 5395^{6} 6218^{4} 6411^{2} 6588^{2} 6908^{2} 7113^{4} (7587) ◆ 7693^{4}

French Connexion (IRE) *J S Moore* a54 59
2 b f Chineur(FR) —Hunzy (IRE) (Desert King (IRE))
1031^{6} 1577^{12} 2348^{3} 2906^{3} 3086^{17} 3424^{9} 4089^{20} 4693^{6} 5369^{9} 6292^{4}

French Fantasy *H Morrison* a41
2 ch f Cadeaux Genereux—Footlight Fantasy (USA) (Nureyev (USA))
6620^{16} 7135^{13} 7317^{10}

French Hollow *T J Fitzgerald* a71 59
4 b g Beat Hollow—Campaspe (Dominion)
7221^{3} 7367^{4} 7648^{2} ◆

French Seventyfive *T D Walford* 65
2 b g Pursuit Of Love—Miss Tun (Komaite (USA))
2663^{10} 3376^{4} 4652^{6}

French Wind *Pat Eddery* a43
2 b c Cadeaux Genereux—Blast (USA) (Roar (USA))
7800^{10}

Frequency *E A L Dunlop* a73 55
2 b c Starcraft(NZ) —Soundwave (Prince Sabo)
6591^{7} 6913^{2} ◆

Fresh Princess (FR) *R Gibson* a73 80
3 b f Dai Jin—Alpha City (Unfuwain (USA))
5278a^{4}

Freya's Flight (IRE) *K A Ryan* 55
3 ch f Viking Ruler(AUS) —Polish Saga (Polish Patriot (USA))
2250^{6} 2805^{5} 7853^{8}

Fricoteiro (ARG) *Niels Petersen* 91
6 ch h Lode(USA) —Fricote (USA) (Ogygian (USA))
2587a^{9}

Friends Hope *R Curtis* a80 83
8 ch m Docksider(USA) —Stygian (USA) (Irish River (FR))
176^{5} 330^{4} 456^{5} 688^{2} 805^{6} 1417^{5} 1566^{6} 7761^{7}

Friesan Fire (USA) *J Larry Jones* a121
3 b c A.P. Indy(USA) —Bollinger (AUS) (Dehere (USA))
1688a^{18} 2098a^{10}

Frightnight (IRE) *A B Haynes* a42
3 ch c Night Shift(USA) —Scared (Royal Academy (USA))
716^{6} 767^{7}

Frill A Minute *Miss L C Siddall* 30
5 b m Lake Coniston(IRE) —Superfrills (Superpower)
4346^{10} 4654^{12} 4977^{13} 7220^{12}

Fringe Success (IRE) *Sir Michael Stoute* a34 61
2 b f Selkirk(USA) —Stage Struck (IRE) (Sadler's Wells (USA))
5397^{8} 7140^{6}

Frisbee *D W Thompson* a64 78
5 b m Efisio—Flying Carpet (Barathea (IRE))
6764^{16} 7122^{2} ◆ 7273^{7}

Frisky Queen (IRE) *T G McCourt* a61 43
3 b f Val Royal(FR) —Frisky (IRE) (Hamas (IRE))
4754^{6} 4778^{6} 5336^{5} 6410^{11} 7714^{8}

Friston Forest (IRE) *Saeed Bin Suroor* 112
5 ch h Barathea(IRE) —Talented (Bustino)
(437a) 2501^{2} 3390^{3} 3874^{8} 4457^{6} 7293^{4}

Frognal (IRE) *B J Meehan* a81 91
3 b g Kheleyf(USA) —Shannon Dore (IRE) (Turtle Island (IRE))
5032^{16} 5646^{6} 6112^{4} 6476^{3} 6815^{3}

Fromsong (IRE) *D K Ivory* a88 77
11 b g Fayruz—Lindas Delight (Batshoof)
24^{4} 170^{3} 270^{6} 632^{3} 754^{3} 892^{8} 1152^{5} 1403^{5} 2124^{4} 2397^{3} 3422^{5} 3917^{6} 4604^{13} 5608^{7} 5989^{2} 6293^{8} 7329^{7} 7595^{5} 7682^{3} (7807)

Fromthebeginning *D R C Elsworth* a68 56
3 b g Lomitas—Zacchera (Zamindar (USA))
914^{7} 1932^{5}

Front House (IRE) *M F De Kock* 111
4 b m Sadler's Wells(USA) —Adjalisa (IRE) (Darshaan)
416a^{2} ◆ 643a^{2} (772a) ◆ 1012a^{9}

Frontline Boy (IRE) *A P Jarvis* 70
2 b c One Cool Cat(USA) —Diamant (IRE) (Bigstone (IRE))
4847^{11} 5234^{6} 5958^{3} 6534^{7}

Front Rank (IRE) *Mrs Dianne Sayer* a52 61
9 b g Sadler's Wells(USA) —Alignment (IRE) (Alzao (USA))
1938^{4} 3068^{7} 3291^{11} 4848^{2} 5307^{3} 5734^{3} 6768^{3}

Frosted *J H M Gosden* a60 60
3 ch f Dr Fong(USA) —Arctic Air (Polar Falcon (USA))
1532^{4}

Frosty Secret (USA) *M F De Kock* a105
5 bb h Put It Back(USA) —Secret From Above (USA) (Great Above (USA))
184a^{4} 641a^{5}

Frosty's Gift *J C Fox* a46 38
5 ch m Bold Edge—Coughlan's Gift (Alnasr Alwasheek)
61^{6} 254^{7} 2794^{13}

Frozen Fire (GER) *A P O'Brien* 122
4 b h Montjeu(IRE) —Flamingo Sea (USA) (Woodman (USA))
1823^{3} 2670^{5} 4298^{7}

Frozen Power (IRE) *Saeed Bin Suroor* 102
2 b c Oasis Dream—Musical Treat (IRE) (Royal Academy (USA))
3792^{4} (4233) (4901) (5416a) 6268^{7} 6898^{7}

Fuel Cell (IRE) *I W McInnes* a59 24
8 b g Desert Style(IRE) —Tappen Zee (Sandhurst Prince)
4887^{15}

Fuisse (FR) *Mme C Head-Maarek* 118
3 br c Green Tune(USA) —Funny Feerie (FR) (Sillery (USA))
(2096a) 2756a^{2}

Fujin Dancer (FR) *K A Ryan* a75 78
4 ch h Storming Home—Badaayer (USA) (Silver Hawk (USA))
1721^{4} 2392^{6} 7631^{2} 7776^{2}

Fulfilment (IRE) *W J Musson* a48 50
3 ch f Alhaarth(IRE) —Noble Dane (IRE) (Danehill (USA))
4057^{11} 6073^{7} 6673^{9}

Fulford *M Brittain* a49 59
4 ch g Elmaamul(USA) —Last Impression (Imp Society (USA))
13^{7} 303^{7} 1558^{12} 4225^{7} 4496^{9} 4998^{10} 7680^{9}

Fulham Broadway (IRE) *E F Vaughan* a91 70
3 ch c Exceed And Excel(AUS) —Lomalou (IRE) (Lightning Dealer)
3028^{2} ◆

Fullandby (IRE) *T J Etherington* a105 111
7 b g Monashee Mountain(USA) —Ivory Turner (Efisio)
1325^{3} 1699^{17} 2259^{2} 2481^{7} 3388^{7} 4135^{12} 5420^{9} 5860^{10} 6089^{5} 6675^{9} 7015^{4} (7227) (7292) 7488^{8}

Fullback (IRE) *J S Moore* a96 89
3 ch g Redback—Feet Of Flame (USA) (Theatrical (IRE))
258a^{7} 526a^{10} 1211^{9} 1641^{2} 4296^{4} 4760^{4} 5313^{7} 5648^{4}

Full Blue *S C Williams* 49
3 gb f Falbrav(IRE) —Miss University (USA) (Beau Genius (CAN))
2633^{8} 3976^{10} 5011^{16}

Full Mandate (IRE) *R Hannon* 98
2 b f Acclamation—Dani Ridge (IRE) (Indian Ridge)
3277^{4} (3534) 4295^{2} 5427^{2} 6317a^{2}

Full Of Gold (FR) *Mme C Head-Maarek* 107
4 ch h Gold Away(IRE) —Funny Feerie (FR) (Sillery (USA))
1029a^{6} 3443a^{8}

Full Of Honor (IRE) *J-Y Artu* 35
3 gr g Highest Honor(FR) —Delimara (IRE) (In The Wings)
7037a^{0}

Full Of Love (IRE) *B W Hills* a75 86
3 b f Hawk Wing(USA) —Charmingly (USA) (King Of Kings (IRE))
(1128) (1531) 2248^{2} 4088^{3} 4422^{2} ◆ 6618^{13}

Full Of Nature *S Kirk* a73 76
3 ch f Monsieur Bond(IRE) —Secret Circle (Magic Ring (IRE))
2008^{4} ◆ 4085^{9} 4569^{8} 4691^{3} 5099^{7} 5195^{4} 5285^{4} 5726^{5} 6460^{6}

Full Speed (GER) *G A Swinbank* 89
4 b g Sholokhov(IRE) —Flagny (FR) (Kaldoun (FR))
(2781) 3189^{8} 4261^{8} 5137^{8} 5828^{3} 6100^{5} 6681^{12}

Full Toss *P D Evans* a92 99
3 b g Nayef(USA) —Spinning Top (Alzao (USA))
3298^{7} 4517^{8} 4983^{7} 5832^{6} ◆ 6114^{3} (7623) 7789^{4} (7841) ◆ 7867^{4}

Full Victory (IRE) *R A Farrant* a83 75
7 b g Imperial Ballet(IRE) —Full Traceability (IRE) (Ron's Victory (USA))
1775^{5} (2125) 2352^{12} 3076^{4} 4064^{3} 4473^{4} 6861^{9} 6908^{3} 6937^{6}

Funatfuntasia *Ms Joanna Morgan* a95 92
5 b g Dansili—Guntakal (IRE) (Night Shift (USA))
3435a^{17} 4574a^{5} 7300a^{9}

Funday *G L Moore* 92
3 b f Daylami(IRE) —Morina (USA) (Lyphard (USA))
2640^{3} (3214) 4008^{3} 5028^{4} 5510^{2} (5771) 6452^{3}

Fun In The Sun *A B Haynes* a63 57
5 b g Piccolo—Caught In The Rain (Spectrum (IRE))
234^{2} 514^{7} (661) 803^{8} 1030^{5} 2630^{4} 2794^{11} 3948^{4} 5287^{7}

Funky Munky *G A Swinbank* a51 71
4 b g Talaash(IRE) —Chilibang Bang (Chilibang)
855^{5} 1228^{9} 1888^{5} 3448^{9} (4845) 6157^{6} 6349^{12}

Funky Town (IRE) *J Akehurst* 45
7 b g Anshan—Dance Rhythm (IRE) (Dancing Dissident (USA))
877^{12} 1030^{7} 1200^{13}

Furmagiatt *Mrs S Leech*
5 b g In The Wings—Sumingasefa (Danehill (USA))
978^{RR}

Furmigadelagiusta *K R Burke* a95 112
5 ch h Galileo(IRE) —Sispre (FR) (Master Willie)
1017^{3} (2055) (3190) 3874^{9}

Furnace (IRE) *Saeed Bin Suroor* a91 102
5 b g Green Desert(USA) —Lyrical Dance (USA) (Lear Fan (USA))
340a^{2} 615a^{7} (697a) 2015^{10}

Furthest Land (USA) *Michael J Maker* a120 101
4 bb g Smart Strike(CAN) —Flagrant (USA) (Rahy (USA))
(7309a)

Fusaichi Flyer (USA) *R Charlton* a70
2 bb g Fusaichi Pegasus(USA) —Songbook (Singspiel (IRE))
7644^{6} 7800^{2} ◆ 7859^{7}

Fusenam *Miss J A Camacho* a63 43
2 b g Refuse To Bend(IRE) —Namat (IRE) (Daylami (IRE))
5408^{6} 6763^{9} 7400^{7}

Future Gem *A Dickman* 67
3 b f Bertolini(USA) —Georgianna (IRE) (Petardia)
1335^{10} 1628^{12} (2265) 3176^{5} 3239^{8} 4016^{2} 4191^{2} 4942^{5} (5145) (5362) 5626^{2} 6140^{2} 6824^{12}

Future Regime (IRE) *Patrick Morris* a57 29
2 b f Xaar—Sadalsud (IRE) (Shaadi (USA))
6347^{9} 7079^{8} 7190^{3} 7559^{5} 7843^{5}

Futurist *Saeed Bin Suroor* 79
2 b c Halling(USA) —Crystal Gazing (USA) (El Gran Senor (USA))
5542^{14} 6331^{3} (6533)

Fuzzy Cat *T D Barron* a58 48
3 b g Nayef(USA) —Curfew (Marju (IRE))
1047^{8} 2723^{11} 3480^{5} 4172^{2} ◆ 5145^{10} (5326) 6926^{9} 7835^{3}

Fyelehk (IRE) *B R Millman* a64 74
3 b g Kheleyf(USA) —Opalescent (IRE) (Polish Precedent (USA))
817^{4} 986^{4} 1311^{4} (1465) 3580^{5} 3859^{3} (4237) (4454) 4788^{3} 5065^{11} 5836^{10} (6739)

Fylarchos (FR) *C Laffon-Parias* 72
2 ch c Muhtathir—Alfreda (Unfuwain (USA))
(6322a) 6927a^{3}

Fyodor (IRE) *P D Evans* a103 101
8 b g Fasliyev(USA) —Royale Figurine (IRE) (Dominion Royale)
204^{10} 1278^{13} 1564^{6} 1924^{12} 2184^{2} 2549^{8} 2782^{6} 3459^{8} 3994^{6} 5184^{13} 5678^{6} 6028^{8} 6670^{9}

Fyodorovich (USA) *J S Wainwright* 57
4 b g Stravinsky(USA) —Omnia (USA) (Green Dancer (USA))
1887^{10} 2362^{12} 2722^{9} 2964^{11} 3490^{4} 3558^{7} 4435^{10} 4654^{11} 4845^{6} 5730^{15}

Gabby's Golden Gal (USA) *Bob Baffert* a111
3 bb f Medaglia D'Oro(USA) —Gabriellina Giof (Ashkalani (IRE))
1763a^{6}

Gabriel's Spirit (IRE) *Miss Amy Weaver* 56
2 b c Invincible Spirit(IRE) —Over Rating (Desert King (IRE))
4497^{11} 5029^{4} 5527^{13}

Gaditana *Pat Eddery* 26
3 b f Rainbow Quest(USA) —Armeria (USA) (Northern Dancer (CAN))
6934^{7}

Gadobout Dancer *I W McInnes* 25
2 b f Tobougg(IRE) —Delta Tempo (IRE) (Bluebird (USA))
4888^{12} 5980^{11} 6389^{10}

Gaelic Rose (IRE) *S Kirk* a49 43
3 b f King Charlemagne(USA) —Harry's Irish Rose (USA) (Sir Harry Lewis (USA))
1579^{9} 1931^{11} 3157^{5}

Gaelic Silver (FR) *J-C Rouget* 94
3 b c Lando(GER) —Galatza (FR) (Johann Quatz (FR))
4685a^{8}

Gaia Prince (USA) *Mrs A J Perrett* 81
4 bb g Forestry(USA) —Castlebrook (USA) (Montbrook (USA))
1621^{3} 2052^{2} 2566^{3} 2931^{13}

Gaily Noble (IRE) *A B Haynes* a84 86
3 b c One Cool Cat(USA) —Dream Genie (Puissance)
(695) 840^{2} 1280^{2} 1679^{5} 1971^{2} 3543^{4} 4649^{5} 6137^{4} (6804) 7141^{4} 7322^{4} 7560^{6} 7759^{8}

Gainful (USA) *D Smaga* 97
3 b f Gone West(USA) —Fully Invested (USA) (Irish River (FR))
1550a^{4} 3968a^{9}

Gainshare *Mrs R A Carr* a72 68
4 b g Lend A Hand—Red Shareef (Marju (IRE))
76^{5} 606^{5} 691^{3}

Gala Casino Star (IRE) *R A Fahey* a89 93
4 ch g Dr Fong(USA) —Ahir (Soviet Star (USA))
1213^{7} 1798^{4} 2374^{5} 2822^{2} 3067^{3} 3872^{6} 4104^{4} 4549^{2} 5040^{3} 5137^{9} 6016^{2} 6795^{2} 7560^{3}

Galachiya *C E Brittain* 68
2 ch f Gulch(USA) —Empress Anna (IRE) (Imperial Ballet (IRE))
4257^{7}

Galactic Star *M bin Shafya* a105 115
6 ch h Galileo(IRE) —Balisada (Kris)
415a^{12} 527a^{14} 699a^{5}

Galactos (ARG) *M bin Shafya* 64
4 br h Bernstein(USA) —Refleja Toss (ARG) (Egg Toss (USA))
769a^{11}

Gala Evening *J A B Old* a99 96
7 b g Daylami(IRE) —Balleta (USA) (Lyphard (USA))
1007^{2} ◆ 1790^{8} 2994^{4}

Galana (GER) *P Schiergen* 102
3 b f Black Sam Bellamy(IRE) —Global World (GER) (Big Shuffle (USA))
2310a^{4}

Gala Sunday (USA) *M W Easterby* a52 67
9 b g Lear Fan(USA) —Sunday Bazaar (USA) (Nureyev (USA))
1192^{11} 1402^{10} 1881^{10} 2263^{11} (3450) 3943^{2} 4402^{7} 5438^{5} 6369^{6} 6817^{5}

Galatian *B R Millman* 72
2 ch g Traditionally(USA) —Easy To Imagine (USA) (Cozzene (USA))
6108^{9} 6615^{4} 7058^{5}

Galeota (IRE) *R Hannon* a80 102
7 b g Mujadil(USA) —Refined (IRE) (Statoblest)
3802^{8} 4059^{6} 4516^{8} 5900^{7}

Galidon (IRE) *R Brogi* 95
3 b c Galileo(IRE) —My Personal Space (USA) (Rahy (USA))
1392a^{10} 1904a^{13} 7313a^{9}

Galiego (RUS) *A Chuguevets*
5 b h Greben(RUS) —Flogera (UKR) (Goboj (RUS))
4369a^{3}

Galient (IRE) *N J Henderson* a97 90
6 b g Galileo(IRE) —Endorsement (Warning)
2994^{12}

Galilean Moon *Sir Michael Stoute* a60 77
3 b f Galileo(IRE) —Fascinating Rhythm (Slip Anchor)
1488^{6} 2877^{3} (4270) 4948^{5} 5837^{7}

Galiotto (IRE) *C F Wall* a55 58
3 b g Galileo(IRE) —Welsh Motto (USA) (Mtoto)
2240^{6} 2551^{8} 3056^{6} 4156^{2} ◆ 4722^{2} ◆ 5838^{5} 6457^{3}

Galix Du Val (FR) *P Duval*
4 u m (USA) — (USA) (Elusive Quality (USA))
5204a^{0}

Gallagher *B J Meehan* 115
3 ch c Bahamian Bounty—Roo (Rudimentary (USA))
3011^{4} (3536) 4521^{8} 5024^{5}

Gallant Eagle (IRE) *S Kirk* a79 78
2 ch c Hawk Wing(USA) —Generous Gesture (IRE) (Fasliyev (USA))
2844^{4} 4900^{6} 5317^{4} 5722^{3} (6071)

Gallant Gent (USA) *Craig A Lewis* a108 108
2 b g Yankee Gentleman(USA) —Bonne Nuite (USA) (Knights Choice (USA))
7304a^{7}

Gallantian (IRE) *David Anthony O'Brien* a50 29
7 gr g Turtle Island(IRE) —Galletina (IRE) (Persian Heights)
1533^{7} 1938^{8}

Gallantry *P Howling* a94 91
7 b g Green Desert(USA) —Gay Gallanta (USA) (Woodman (USA))
232^{6} 331^{6} (446) (694) 1116^{6} 1365^{8} 1942^{5} 2780^{8} 3335^{2} 3988^{7} 4954^{14} 5615^{5} 6024^{5} 6830^{9} 7252^{7} 7437^{4} 7617^{7} 7801^{8} 7883^{5}

Gallego *R J Price* a62 75
7 br g Danzero(AUS) —Shafir (IRE) (Shaadi (USA))
1581^{8} 1845^{6} 2244^{5} 2641^{10} 2851^{7} (3283) (4321) 4563^{15} 5602^{2} 5833^{6} 6392^{6}

Galley Slave (IRE) *M C Chapman* a62 29
4 b g Spartacus(IRE) —Cimeterre (IRE) (Arazi (USA))
132^{9} 516^{3} 4519^{12}

Gallic Star (IRE) *M R Channon* 99
2 b f Galileo(IRE) —Oman Sea (USA) (Rahy (USA))
2047^{7} (2914) 4245^{4} ◆ 4795^{5} 5825^{4} (6898)

Gallilei (FR) *A De Royer-Dupre* 98
3 ch c Ballingarry(IRE) —Spectacular Joke (USA) (Spectacular Bid (USA))
2951a^{4} 6198a^{5}

Gallions Reach (NZ) *Richard Yuill* 109
7 b g Victory Dance(IRE) —Dorinka (NZ) (Straight Strike (USA))
6961a^{13} 7215a^{13}

Galmalea (IRE) *A & G Botti* 100
3 b f Galileo(IRE) —Alma Alegre (IRE) (Lahib (USA))
2310a^{5}

Galpin Junior (USA) *B J Meehan* a52 102
3 ch g Hennessy(USA) —Reluctant Diva (Sadler's Wells (USA))
5878^{6} 6304^{14} 6949^{12}

Gambling Jack *A W Carroll* a56 61
4 b g First Trump—Star Of Flanders (Puissance)
869^{4} 1495^{12} 1890^{6} 2317^{11} 2534^{6}

Gambling Queen *Mrs P Sly* 28
2 b f Zafeen(FR) —Pure Speculation (Salse (USA))
3248^{9}

Gamedor (FR) *G L Moore* a42 68
4 ch g Kendor(FR) —Garmeria (FR) (Kadrou (FR))
6704^{7}

Game Face (USA) *Todd Pletcher* a122
4 ch m Menifee(USA) —Galleon Of Gold (USA) (Gone West (USA))
7285a^{9}

Gamegear *S R Bowring* a9
4 br m Tomba—Princess Of Hearts (Prince Sabo)
820^{7} 855^{8}

Game Lad *T D Easterby* a28 89
7 b g Mind Games—Catch Me (Rudimentary (USA))
1682^{11} 2045^{4} 3391^{8} 5697^{13} 6361^{13}

Game Roseanna *W M Brisbourne* a46 60
3 b f Mind Games—Rosy Sunset (IRE) (Red Sunset)
4042^{3} 4562^{6} 6098^{6} 6919^{6}

Games (IRE) *C N Kellett* 27
8 b g Lord Americo—Anns Run (Deep Run)
7842^{11}

Game Stalker (USA) *Saeed Bin Suroor* 79
3 bb c Elusive Quality(USA) —Windsharp (USA) (Lear Fan (USA))
1771^{4} (6189)

Gamesters Lady *W M Brisbourne* a66 70
6 br m Almushtarak(IRE) —Tycoon Tina (Tina's Pet)
299^{6} (688) 795^{4} 983^{6} 1454^{9} 1980^{12} 2493^{3} 2783^{9} 3247^{6} 3631^{6} 4710^{10} 4861^{10}

Gan Amhras (IRE) *J S Bolger* 119
3 b c Galileo(IRE) —All's Forgotten (USA) (Darshaan)
1675^{3} ◆ 2705^{11} 3438a^{6}

Gandalf *Miss Amy Weaver* a77 71
7 b g Sadler's Wells(USA) —Enchant (Lion Cavern (USA))
4951^{5} (5642) 6622^{7}

Gangbuster (USA) *J Keith Desormeaux* a99 96
4 ch h Langfuhr(CAN) —Foxcaller (USA) (Beau Genius (CAN))
7281a^{4}

Gap Princess (IRE) *G A Harker* a79 76
5 b m Noverre(USA) —Safe Care (IRE) (Caerleon (USA))
1241^{3} 1627^{3} 1894^{7} 1923^{2} 2589^{6} 3066^{2} (3479) 5406^{7} 7496^{5} (7673)

Gardening Leave *A M Balding* 91
2 b c Selkirk(USA) —Misty Waters (IRE) (Caerleon (USA))
6393^{7} (7034) 7404a^{6}

Garden Party *R A Harris* a79 72
5 b g Green Desert(USA) —Tempting Prospect (Shirley Heights)
215^{2} 307^{6} 536^{3} 706^{2}

Garlogs *R Hollinshead* a84 67
6 b g Hunting Lion(IRE) —Fading (Pharly (FR))
329^{10} 400^{8} 742^{7} 919^{7}

Garnera (IRE) *S Ibido* 93
3 b f Key Of Luck(USA) —Golden Honor (IRE) (Hero's Honor (USA))
3186a^{12}

Garnica (FR) *D Nicholls* 112
6 gr g Linamix(FR) —Gueridia (IRE) (Night Shift (USA))
1865^{4} 2483^{10} 6135^{9} 7019^{7} 7294^{12}

Garra Molly (IRE) *G A Swinbank* a70 70
4 b m Nayef(USA) —Aminata (Glenstal (USA))
678^{2} 897^{4} 5035^{13}

Garstang *J Balding* a86 70
6 ch g Atraf—Approved Quality (IRE) (Persian Heights)
975^{10} (1182) 1285^{11} (2596) 3765^{6} 4043^{3} 4978^{2} 5197^{2} 5518^{7} 6253^{4} 6459^{2} 6632^{3}

Garter Knight *Mrs P Sly* a60 73
3 b g Mark Of Esteem(IRE) —Granted (FR) (Cadeaux Genereux)
529^{8} 786^{6} ◆ 869^{7} 1361^{4} 3054^{2} 6910^{7} 7127^{2} 7246^{3}

Garter Star *H Morrison* a54 39
4 b m Mark Of Esteem(IRE) —Palace Affair (Pursuit Of Love)
1638^{6} 2205^{9}

Garynella (FR) *A Couetil*
2 b c Ballingarry(IRE) —Pimpinella (FR) (Highest Honor (FR))
5014a^{5}

Gasat (IRE) *A B Haynes* a73 62
8 b h Marju(IRE) —Pechenga (Nureyev (USA))
119^{2} 393^{8} 588^{2} 838^{3} (872) 1318^{2} 1578^{2} 2332^{8} 2537^{7} 5367^{4} 5750^{7} 6612^{9}

Gaselee (USA) *Rae Guest* a71 72
3 b f Toccet(USA) —Vingt Et Une (FR) (Sadler's Wells (USA))
1444^{4} 529^{7} 2710^{10} 3383^{4} (3680) 3942^{2} 5009^{4} 6698^{2} 6951^{2}

Gasparilla (IRE) *A J McCabe* a38 47
2 b f Fath(USA) —Tazmeera (IRE) (Priolo (USA))
1450^{3} 1624^{5} 2800^{3} 4884^{5} 5226^{6} 5519^{5} 5636^{10} 5976^{9} 6354^{9}

Gassin *M L W Bell* a83 69
3 b g Selkirk(USA) —Miss Riviera Golf (Hernando (FR))
(2857) 3624^{5} 4473^{9} 5003^{16} (6455) 6699^{3} (7000)

Gayanula (USA) *Miss J A Camacho* a63
4 b m Yonaguska(USA) —Betamillion Bock (USA) (Bet Twice (USA))
38^{3} 147^{2} 368^{8} 1654^{4} 2580^{6}

Gayego (USA) *Saeed Bin Suroor* a121
4 bb h Gilded Time(USA) —Devils Lake (USA) (Lost Code (USA))
(770a) ◆ 1008a^{2} 7306a^{4}

Gay Mirage (GER) *M A Jarvis* 53
2 b f Highest Honor(FR) —Geminiani (IRE) (King Of Kings (IRE))
7243^{6} ◆

Gazamali (IRE) *G A Harker* 36
2 b c Namid—Frond (Alzao (USA))
1126^{9} 1275^{6} 6842^{13}

Gazboolou *David Pinder* a79 71
5 b g Royal Applause—Warning Star (Warning)
950^{2} 1187^{4} 1493^{2} 2188^{12} 2713^{3} 3075^{6} 3463^{7} 5107^{2} 5780^{7} 6374^{3} 6725^{12}

Gearbox (IRE) *R Hannon* 41
3 br g Tillerman—Persian Empress (IRE) (Persian Bold)
5010^{6}

Gee Dee Nen *Jim Best* a95 98
6 b g Mister Baileys—Special Beat (Bustino)
1007^{5} 4769^{7} 5235^{7}

Gee Gina *P T Midgley* 57
3 b f Hunting Lion(IRE) —La Thuile (Statoblest)
3611^{8} 4596^{4} 4942^{4} 4999^{2} 5422^{5} (5468)

Gee Major *Tom Dascombe* 32
2 b g Reset(AUS) —Polly Golightly (Weldnaas (USA))
3571^{11} 6591^{14}

Geese A Laying (IRE) *J A Osborne* a31
3 b f Elusive City(USA) —King Of All (IRE) (King Of Clubs)
364^{8} 447^{5} 955^{8}

Geezers Colours *J R Weymes* a71 79
4 b g Fraam—Konica (Desert King (IRE))
388^{9} 2938^{16} 3488^{10} 4154^{6} 6703^{2} 7662^{9} 7845^{3}

Gelert (IRE) *A Berry* a46 51
4 b h Acclamation—Game Leader (IRE) (Mukaddamah (USA))
328^{6} 1921^{10} 2436^{10} 3125^{9} 3479^{7} 3853^{9} 4012^{5}

Gemma Dell'Olmo (USA) *R Menichetti* 83
2 ch f Stephen Got Even(USA) —Polly Alexander (IRE) (Foxhound (USA))
6892a^{10}

Gems Star *J J Quinn* 46
3 b g Elmaamul(USA) —Slipperose (Persepolis (FR))
3193^{9} 4552^{15} 4879^{4} 5145^{14}

Genari *Gordon Elliott* a59 79
6 b g Generous(IRE) —Sari (Faustus (USA))
7402^{7}

Gene Autry (USA) *R Hannon* 83
2 bb c Zavata(USA) —Total Acceptance (USA) (With Approval (CAN))
4048^{4} 4258^{4} (4851)

General Eliott (IRE) *P F I Cole* a73 113
4 b g Rock Of Gibraltar(IRE) —Marlene-D (Selkirk (USA))
1600^{DSQ} 2668^{8} 6110^{5} 6480^{25} 7245^{3} 7489^{8} 7810^{3}

General Feeling (IRE) *Ollie Pears* a75 58
8 b g General Monash(USA) —Kamadara (IRE) (Kahyasi)
125^{2} (192) (344) 873^{3} 1073^{6} 1194^{8} 1955^{5} 2186^{4} 2390^{7} 2965^{11} 7581^{10} 7776^{8}

General Quarters (USA) *Thomas R McCarthy* a117
3 gr c Sky Mesa(USA) —Ecology (USA) (Unbridled's Song (USA))
(1225a) 1688a^{10} 2098a^{9}

General Sam (USA) *R Hannon* a47
3 ch g Trippi(USA) —Milagro Blue (USA) (Cure The Blues (USA))
98^{7} 160^{7} 343^{7}

General Ting (IRE) *Sir Mark Prescott* a78 80
4 b h Daylami(IRE) —Luana (Shaadi (USA))
5649^{7} 6622^{8} 6822^{4}

General Tufto *C Smith* a73 72
4 b g Fantastic Light(USA) —Miss Pinkerton (Danehill (USA))
7^{4} 90^{6} 174^{3} 240^{3} (368) (514) (565) 608^{2} 683^{4} (885) 923^{5} 1051^{2} 1192^{9} 1306^{5} 1612^{14} 1845^{3} 1945^{3} 2068^{12} (2263) 2419^{7} 3557^{5} 3863^{6} 4054^{5} 4171^{6} 4402^{3} 4721^{2} 4880^{3} 7499^{3} ◆ 7677^{3} 5035^{10} 5548^{3} 5740^{7} 7127^{11}

General Zhukov *J M P Eustace* a51 70
3 b g Largesse—Hickleton Lady (IRE) (Kala Shikari)
1257^{7} 1585^{7} 1932^{7} (2357)

Generoso (USA) *S C Williams* 36
2 b c Gone West(USA) —Kentucky Rose (FR) (Hernando (FR))
4701^{7} 5512^{6} 7120^{11}

Generous Lad (IRE) *A B Haynes* a77 66
6 b g Generous(IRE) —Tudor Loom (Sallust)
751^{8} 816^{8} 1463^{2} 1537^{11} 1961^{5} 2182^{9} 2420^{5} 2762^{3} 3348^{6} 5484^{8} 5872^{7}

Generous Star *J Pearce* a63 55
6 ch g Generous(IRE) —Elegant Dance (Statoblest)
126^{3} 252^{4} 679^{2} 1426^{7}

Geneva Geyser (GER) *J M P Eustace* a75 88
3 b g One Cool Cat(USA) —Genevra (IRE) (Danehill (USA))
1033^{5} 1559^{8} 1971^{5} (2341) 2545^{3} (3543) 4455^{13} (5027) 5828^{11} 6855^{P}

Genghis Khan (TUR) *Y Simsek* 100
4 ch h Tobougg(IRE) —Folly Fox (Alhijaz)
5619a^{8}

Genki (IRE) *R Charlton* a53 109
5 ch g Shinko Forest(IRE) —Emma's Star (ITY) (Darshaan)
2550^{5} 3141^{26} 3405^{2} 4297^{4} (4523) 6091^{11} 6707a^{3}

Gentle Beat (IRE) *T D Easterby* 71
2 b g Whipper(USA) —Soft (USA) (Lear Fan (USA))
1330^{3} 1610^{10} 2610^{6} 3152^{3} 3542^{5} 4190^{7} 5467^{9} 5942^{4}

Gentle Guru *R T Phillips* a75 92
5 b m Ishiguru(USA) —Soft Touch (IRE) (Petorius)
1582^{7} 2271^{10} 3795^{7} 4096^{6} 4380^{7} 4907^{6} 5219^{4} 5592^{5} 6294^{10} 6915^{9} (7330) 7519^{7} 7739^{9} 7870^{3}

Geoffdaw *P D Evans* a78 67
4 b g Vettori(IRE) —Talighta (USA) (Barathea (IRE))
128^{6} 457^{8} 530^{3} 739^{5} 762^{5} 3691^{10} 3948^{5} 4732^{6}

Geojimali *J S Goldie* a82 89
7 ch g Compton Place—Harrken Heights (IRE) (Belmez (USA))
6050^{24} 6764^{9}

Geordie Dancer (IRE) *A Berry* a46 46
7 b g Dansili—Awtaar (USA) (Lyphard (USA))
574^{9}

Geordieland (FR) *J A Osborne* a96 121
8 gr h Johann Quatz(FR) —Aerdee (FR) (Highest Honor (FR))
(2409) 3048^{3} 5824^{3}

George Adamson (IRE) *G A Swinbank* 51
3 b g Where Or When(IRE) —Tactile (Groom Dancer (USA))
1950^{5} 2199^{8} 2789^{7} 3449^{5}

George Baker (IRE) *George Baker* a62 80
2 b g Camacho—Petite Maxine (Sharpo)
1511^{7} 2147^{3} 2995^{7} 3344^{8} 5109^{3} 5811^{5} 6292^{6} 6721^{12}

George Benjamin *D Nicholls* 72
2 b g Trade Fair—Unchain My Heart (Pursuit Of Love)
3032^{2} 3875^{3} 4410^{3} 4847^{2} 6046^{2} 6646^{2}

Georgebernardshaw (IRE) *A P O'Brien* a81 113
4 b h Danehill Dancer(IRE) —Khamseh (Thatching)
1138a^{8} 1374a^{12} 2287a^{9} 2870a^{3} 3435a^{14} 3881a^{2} 5135^{4}

George Rex (USA) *B J Meehan* 69
3 bb g Johannesburg(USA) —Royal Linkage (USA) (Linkage (USA))
2329^{11} 3009^{10}

George The Best (IRE) *Micky Hammond* a28 29
8 b g Imperial Ballet(IRE) —En Retard (IRE) (Petardia)
222^{12} 1310^{13} 5309^{9}

George Thisby *B R Millman* a70 78
3 b g Royal Applause—Warning Belle (Warning)
1015^{2} 1250^{4} 1703^{3} 3161^{2} (3712) 4990^{2} 6111^{6} 6798^{14}

Georgie Bee *T D Walford* a46 49
3 b f Ishiguru(USA) —Light Of Aragon (Aragon)
1173^{8} 1725^{6} 2143^{4} 3451^{4} 4656^{3} 4892^{4} 5470^{8} 6539^{8} 7422^{11}

Georgina Macrae *A M Balding* a46
3 b f Bahamian Bounty—Sadly Sober (IRE) (Roi Danzig (USA))
394^{8} 663^{9} 869^{11}

Gertmegalush (IRE) *J D Bethell* 83
2 b g One Cool Cat(USA) —Aiming Upwards (Blushing Flame (USA))
1450^{4} (1884) 2655^{4} 2896^{10} (3871) 4327^{9} 4782^{7} 5467^{2} 6048^{3} 6643^{11}

Gertrude Bell *J H M Gosden* a76 82
2 ch f Sinndar(IRE) —Sugar Mill (FR) (Polar Falcon (USA))
6062^{3} ◆ 6628^{3} 6992^{2}

Gessabelle *P S McEntee* a4 38
2 b f Largesse—Palmstead Belle (IRE) (Wolfhound (USA))
2354^{10} 4272^{7} 5029^{8} 6355^{11} 6591^{10}

Get A Grip (IRE) *J A R Toller* a81 70
2 b c Royal Applause—Landela (Alhaarth (IRE))
5000^{2} (6162)

Getaway (GER) *J Hirschberger* 125
6 b h Monsun(GER) —Guernica (Unfuwain (USA))
3441a^{2} (4128a) 5082a^{2} (5707a) 6526a^{13}

Getcarter *R Hannon* a83 84
3 b c Fasliyev(USA) —Pourquoi Pas (IRE) (Nordico (USA))
1932^{3} 2048^{5} 2849^{6} (4905) (4990) 5404^{10} 6112^{3} (6167) 7356^{9}

Get Funky (USA) *John W Sadler* a52 115
6 bb h Straight Man(USA) —Miss Popularity (USA) (Storm Bird (CAN))
7305a^{9}

Ghaayer *M P Tregoning* 27
3 ch c Nayef(USA) —Valthea (FR) (Antheus (USA))
1355^{12}

Ghaill Force *P Butler* a45 16
7 b g Piccolo—Coir 'A' Ghaill (Jalmood (USA))
2493^{15}

Ghanaati (USA) *B W Hills* a87 120
3 b f Giant's Causeway(USA) —Sarayir (USA) (Mr Prospector (USA))
(1698) ◆ (3088) ◆ 4419^{3} 6479^{2}

Ghaneema (USA) *M P Tregoning* 77
3 b f Forestry(USA) —Unify (USA) (Farma Way (USA))
4955^{2} ◆

Ghazwah *J H M Gosden* a70 75
2 b f Shamardal(USA) —Bahja (USA) (Seeking The Gold (USA))
3820^{4} ◆ 4460^{2} ◆ 4980^{3} 7145^{7}

Gheed (IRE) *K A Morgan* a42 53
4 b m Cape Cross(IRE) —Hareer (Anabaa (USA))
7648^{12} 7826^{10}

Ghent (IRE) *David P Myerscough* a62 63
3 b g Celtic Swing—Liege (IRE) (Night Shift (USA))
5782^{2} 6075^{5}

Ghimaar *D K Weld* a73 102
4 b g Dubai Destination(USA) —Charlecote (IRE) (Caerleon (USA))
2729a^{5} 3142^{8} 5539a^{4}

Ghost (IRE) *B W Hills* 79
2 b g Invincible Spirit(IRE) —Alexander Phantom (IRE) (Soviet Star (USA))
3402^{4} 4093^{2} 4377^{3} 6231^{5}

Ghost Dancer *J M Bradley* a71 80
5 ch g Danehill Dancer(IRE) —Reservation (IRE) (Common Grounds)
1493^{8} 1775^{7} 2491^{10} 2852^{3} 3208^{8} 3304^{6} 3866^{7} 4690^{4} 5020^{2} 5477^{4} (5525) 6216^{2} 6362^{2} 6596^{6} 7023^{3} 7203^{10}

Ghostwing *R A Fahey* 89
2 gr g Kheleyf(USA) —Someone's Angel (USA) (Runaway Groom (CAN))
1610^{3} (3147) ◆ 3779^{5} ◆ 4487^{5} 5198^{15} 5795^{15} 6677^{10}

Ghufa (IRE) *George Baker* a73 66
5 b g Sakhee(USA) —Hawriyah (USA) (Dayjur (USA))
(427) 493^{3} 733^{3} ◆ 841^{4} 885^{2} ◆ 1000^{8} 2851^{6} 4220^{12} (5679) 6210^{5} 6612^{3} 7137^{3} (7670) (7817) 7888^{2}

Giant Sequoia (USA) *Jane Chapple-Hyam* a82 49
5 ch g Giant's Causeway(USA) —Beware Of The Cat (USA) (Caveat (USA))
1771^{7} 2181^{7} 4373^{6} 4625^{9} (6371) ◆ (6918) ◆ 7112^{3} 7512^{9} (7699) ◆

Giant Slalom *T G McCourt* a63 71
5 b g Tomba—Fallara (FR) (Tropular)
6123^{6} 7417^{5}

Giants Play (USA) *Sir Michael Stoute* a77 76
2 b f Giant's Causeway(USA) —Playful Act (IRE) (Sadler's Wells (USA))
4980^{2} ◆ 6992^{4}

Giant Strides *P D Evans* a59
3 b f Xaar—Brandish (Warning)
19^{4} 144^{5}

Gibb River (IRE) *P W Chapple-Hyam* 87
3 ch g Mr Greeley(USA) —Laurentine (USA) (Private Account (USA))
1328^{6} 1809^{2} ◆ 2323^{2} 3090^{10} 3707^{2} 4743^{2} 5230^{5}

Gibraltar Blue (IRE) *T Stack* 94
2 ch f Rock Of Gibraltar(IRE) —Holly Blue (Bluebird (USA))
6317a^{7} 6852^{4}

Gibraltar Lass (USA) *H J Collingridge* a53
2 ch f Concerto(USA) —Mango Lassie (USA) (Montreal Red (USA))
6942^{7} 7582^{6}

Gibson Square (USA) *S C Williams* a47 32
3 b g Gilded Time(USA) —Beyond The Fence (USA) (Grand Slam (USA))
1130^{6} 2350^{17} 2635^{10} 3474^{7}

Giddywell *R Hollinshead* a62 58
5 b m Ishiguru(USA) —Understudy (In The Wings)
(81) 427^{3} 682^{3} 897^{9} 1153^{10} 1496^{9}

Gifted Apakay (USA) *E A L Dunlop* a75
2 ch f Leroidesanimaux(BRZ) —Sentimental Gift (USA) (Green Dancer (USA))
5643^{3} 6912^{7} (7624)

Gifted Heir (IRE) *A Bailey* a61 56
5 b g Princely Heir(IRE) —Inzar Lady (IRE) (Inzar (USA))
78^{10} 3092^{5} 4158^{12} 4389^{11} 4697^{2} 5111^{2} 5484^{6} 5888^{3} (6800) 6945^{7} 7250^{3} 7403^{10} 7581^{11} 7719^{13}

Gifted Icon (IRE) *N Clement* 81
3 ch f Peintre Celebre(USA) —Waldmark (GER) (Mark Of Esteem (IRE))
6150a^{5}

Gifted Leader (USA) *Ian Williams* 90
4 b g Diesis—Zaghruta (USA) (Gone West (USA))
1407^{5} 1990^{10} (2445) 2932^{2} 3797^{8} 6816^{8} 6995^{14}

Gift Horse *P D Evans* a85 96
9 ch g Cadeaux Genereux—Careful Dancer (Gorytus (USA))
1309^{12} 1510^{9} 2071^{2} (2389) 2782^{9} 3335^{9} 3995^{7} 4733^{7} 4914^{4} 5363^{9} 5565^{4} 5788^{7}

Gift Of Love (IRE) *D R C Elsworth* 49
2 b f Azamour(IRE) —Spot Prize (USA) (Seattle Dancer (USA))
4055^{12}

Giganticus (USA) *B W Hills* a99 106
6 ch g Giant's Causeway(USA) —Shy Princess (USA) (Irish River (FR))
916^{5} 1124^{8} 1861^{15} 2241^{4} (3091) 3818^{19} 4297^{7} 6270^{5} 6815^{8}

Gilded Age *A King* a75 79
3 b g Cape Cross(IRE) —Sweet Folly (IRE) (Singspiel (IRE))
1034^{5} ◆ 1245^{2} (1562) 2060^{11} 2829^{4} 3213^{5} 3635^{2} 5593^{5} 6203^{4}

Gile Na Greine (IRE) *J S Bolger* 84
2 b f Galileo(IRE) —Scribonia (IRE) (Danehill (USA))
5488a^{5}

Gillburg (USA) *K A Ryan* a73 76
2 ch g Johannesburg(USA) —Bourbon Ball (USA) (Peintre Celebre (USA))
1188^{3} 1358^{6} 3487^{5} 4017^{2} 4493^{2} 4884^{2} (5157) 5550^{2} 5853^{5} 6247^{9} 7410^{2} 7551^{9}

Gilt Edge Girl *C G Cox* a96 90
3 ch f Monsieur Bond(IRE) —Tahara (IRE) (Caerleon (USA))
1317[2] (1592) (1814) 2443[3] 6240[5] 6902[3] (7414)

Gimmy (IRE) *B Grizzetti* 112
5 b g Lomitas—Pursuit Of Life (Pursuit Of Love)
1903a[2] 2115a[4] 2955a[8]

Ginger Grey (IRE) *S A Callaghan* a66 67
2 gr g Bertolini(USA) —Just In Love (FR) (Highest Honor (FR))
2087[5] 2376[2] 2735[3] 3821[7] 4208[7] 4647[2] 4975[2] 5344[3] 5433[6] 5715[5] 6366[2] 6829[3] 6963[3]

Ginger Jack *Saeed Bin Suroor* a38 56
2 ch g Refuse To Bend(IRE) —Coretta (IRE) (Caerleon (USA))
5371[7] 6382[5]

Ginger Princess (IRE) *Oliver McKiernan* a74 74
7 b m Pistolet Bleu(IRE) —Palm Lake (IRE) (Spectrum (IRE))
557[5]

Ginger Ted (IRE) *R C Guest* a35 76
2 ch g Fath(USA) —Estertide (IRE) (Tagula (IRE))
1358[11] 1590[4] 1867[5] 2128[7] (4063) 4195[9] (4884) 5658[11]

Gingko Lady (USA) *J R Boyle* a52 56
4 ch m Mr Greeley(USA) —Highland Tide (USA) (Highland Blade (USA))
552[8] 749[8] 855[7] 1079[6]

Ginobili (IRE) *Andrew Reid* a65 96
3 b g Fasliyev(USA) —Imperial Graf (USA) (Blushing John (USA))
3802[5] 4490[6] 4766[9] 5263[13] 5507[6] 5902[7] (6293) 6476[11] 7028[9]

Gioacchino (IRE) *R A Harris* a61 60
4 b g Rossini(USA) —Gareyba (IRE) (Fairy King (USA))
2353[4] 2534[7] (2745) 2908[6] 3031[2] 3505[14] 4191[11] 5225[13] 5501[12]

Gioia (FR) *J-V Toux* 68
2 b f Okawango(USA) —Ascot One (FR) (Septieme Ciel (USA))
5057a[10]

Gio Ponti (USA) *Christophe Clement* a127 123
4 b h Tale Of The Cat(USA) —Chipeta Springs (USA) (Alydar (USA))
(4809a) 6511a[2] ◆ 7311a[2]

Giordana (IRE) *P Vovcenko* 76
3 b f Exceed And Excel(AUS) —Faraway Lady (Alzao (USA))
1394a[11]

Giptar (IRE) *E F Vaughan* a52 40
2 b g Kheleyf(USA) —Titania (Fairy King (USA))
6556[6] 7087[3]

Girl Of Star (FR) *F Pardon* 59
3 b f Fly To The Stars—Frise (FR) (Phantom Breeze)
(6149a)

Girolamo (USA) *Saeed Bin Suroor* a115
3 br c A.P. Indy(USA) —Get Lucky (USA) (Mr Prospector (USA))
7311a[12]

Girouette (IRE) *Tracey Collins* a90 107
4 br m Pivotal—Vassiana (FR) (Anabaa (USA))
1756a[3] 2285a[4] (5079a) 5921a[2]

Gist (IRE) *W J Martin* a95 95
6 b m Namid—Ali Dreamer (IRE) (Ali-Royal (IRE))
2647a[6] 2870a[9] 3435a[11]

Gitano Hernando *M Botti* a122 105
3 ch c Hernando(FR) —Gino's Spirits (Perugino (USA))
(1019) 1822[2] (6030) ◆ (6687a)

Giulietta Da Vinci *N Tinkler* a63 71
2 b f Mujahid(USA) —Gennie Bond (Pivotal)
3248[6] 3576[5] (4194) 4565[9] 6693[10] 6905[5] (7391) 7493[4] 7756[5]

Give (IRE) *R A Harris* a48 56
3 b f High Chaparral(IRE) —Generous Gesture (IRE) (Fasliyev (USA))
16[6] 272[8] 678[8]

Given A Choice (IRE) *J Pearce* a70 79
7 b g Trans Island—Miss Audimar (USA) (Mr. Leader (USA))
7475[11]

Give Us A Song (USA) *J S Moore* a67 29
3 bb g Songandaprayer(USA) —Mama G (USA) (Prospector's Bid (USA))
397[8] 672[6] 705[4] 3672[8] 4872[9] 7693[9] 7845[10]

Gizmondo *G L Moore* a61 65
6 ch g Lomitas—India Atlanta (Ahonoora)
132[6]

Gladiatorus (USA) *Saeed Bin Suroor* 129
4 b h Silic(FR) —Gmaasha (IRE) (Kris)
(260a) (614a) ◆ (1011a) 2990[6] 5086a[8] 5710a[5] (6718a) 7308a[9]

Glad Panther *Uwe Ostmann* 99
3 b g Seattle Dancer(USA) —Glady Beauty (GER) (Big Shuffle (USA))
(1718a) 2560a[5] 3670a[12] 5563a[6] 6152a[7]

Glad Sky *M Rulec* 100
3 b c Big Shuffle(USA) —Glady Sum (GER) (Surumu (GER))
3650a[3] 5493a[8]

Glad Tiger (GER) *Uwe Ostmann* 103
2 ch c Singspiel(IRE) —Glady Beauty (GER) (Big Shuffle (USA))
(6887a)

Gladyator (TUR) *R Tetik* 102
7 b h Mountain Cat(USA) —Cut Clear (Kris)
5618a[7]

Glamoroso (IRE) *A Kirtley* a47 35
4 b g Mull Of Kintyre(USA) —Tuneful (Pivotal)
61[3] 537[12] 4804[10] 4927[10] 5549[11] 6177[8]

Glamorous Spirit (IRE) *R A Harris* a91 91
3 b f Invincible Spirit(IRE) —Glamorous Air (IRE) (Air Express (IRE))
814[2] 1180[3] 1486[5] (1727) 2373[5] 3173[8] (3806) 4849[9] 5247[11] (7605)

Glamour Profession (IRE) *R Hannon* a49 55
2 ch f Captain Rio—Kriva (Reference Point)
3458[10] 3810[6] 5741[14] 6609[6]

Glamstar (FR) *J-C Rouget* 104
3 gr c Numerous(USA) —Dibenoise (FR) (Kendor (FR))
1858a[4] 2756a[10] 3649a[5]

Glan Lady (IRE) *G J Smith* a56 58
3 b f Court Cave(IRE) —Vanished (IRE) (Fayruz)
10[2] 365[3] 475[9] 605[5] 793[10] 1437[8] 2333[11] 3054[RR]

Glan Y Mor (IRE) *F J Brennan* 12
2 b f Mark Of Esteem(IRE) —Molly Mello (GER) (Big Shuffle (USA))
5605[16]

Glasclune (IRE) *Mme M Bollack-Badel* 56
2 b c Slickly(FR) —Guanhumara (Caerleon (USA))
4073a[6]

Glass Harmonium (IRE) *Sir Michael Stoute* 117
3 gr c Verglas(IRE) —Spring Symphony (IRE) (Darshaan)
1300[5] 2014[6] (3050) 6110[4] ◆ 6812[2] ◆

Glasshoughton *M Dods* a57 89
6 b g Dansili—Roseum (Lahib (USA))
1685[16] 2095[6] 3148[3] ◆ 4225[10] 5148[13] 5767[11] 6637[8] 6764[8]

Glass Of Red (IRE) *R M Beckett* a28 66
2 gr f Verglas(IRE) —Embassy Belle (IRE) (Marju (IRE))
2979[8] 3500[6] 4201[9] (7120)

Gleaming Spirit (IRE) *Peter Grayson* a49 73
5 b g Mujadil(USA) —Gleam (Green Desert (USA))
3570[10] 4283[10] 5341[7] 7100[11] 7136[10] 7605[6]

Glencairn Star *F Watson* a23 14
8 b g Selkirk(USA) —Bianca Nera (Salse (USA))
4192[9] 4436[P] 7503[12]

Glencalvie (IRE) *J Akehurst* a85 39
8 ch g Grand Lodge(USA) —Top Of The Form (IRE) (Masterclass (USA))
283[7] 446[5] 878[11] 1320[8] 1833[11] 2713[7] 3159[12]

Glen Lass *J Pearce* a71 59
2 ch f Zafeen(FR) —Welcome Aboard (Be My Guest (USA))
1323[6] 1569[8] 3605[6] 3958[3] 4757[2] 6034[3] 7235[9] 7474[9] 7616[2] (7731) (7788) (7874)

Glenlini *J S Goldie* 62
3 b f Bertolini(USA) —Glenhurich (IRE) (Sri Pekan (USA))
2157[2] 3678[5]

Glenluji *J S Goldie* 51
4 b g Lujain(USA) —Glenhurich (IRE) (Sri Pekan (USA))
4899[8] 5396[5] 5518[8] 5729[11] 6010[11] 6161[9] 6414[7] 6985[5] 7174[11]

Glen Molly (IRE) *B W Hills* 96
3 b f Danetime(IRE) —Sonorous (IRE) (Ashkalani (IRE))
1744[3] 2079[2] ◆ 3163[4] (4540) 5005[7] 7032[7] 7294[17]

Glenmuir (IRE) *J J Quinn* a46 75
6 b g Josr Algarhoud(IRE) —Beryl (Bering)
5598[4]

Glen Nevis (USA) *A Al Raihe* a105 105
5 bb h Gulch(USA) —Beating The Buzz (IRE) (Bluebird (USA))
183a[6] (261a) 417a[5] 523a[6] 698a[4] 773a[8]

Glenridding *J G Given* a76 83
5 b g Averti(IRE) —Appelone (Emperor Jones (USA))
1133[7] 1332[6] 2261[14] 3076[8] (3331) (3488) 3851[2] 4333[11] 4560[7] (5409) 5673[8] 6072[9] 6462[8] 7083[13] 7287[19]

Glen Shiel (USA) *M Johnston* 76
2 ch g Whywhywhy(USA) —Staffin (Salse (USA))
4424[6] 5337[2] (5867)

Glimmer *H-A Pantall* 68
3 b f Royal Applause—Mythic (Zafonic (USA))
3417a[7] 4810a[6] 6606a[9]

Glimpse Of Light (IRE) *A M Balding* a65
3 b f Passing Glance—Sankaty Light (USA) (Summer Squall (USA))
1317[8] 1563[9]

Glitter Baby (IRE) *Paul Cashman* 96
6 b m Danehill Dancer(IRE) —Gifts Galore (IRE) (Darshaan)
2305a[7]

Global *R Hannon* a77 88
3 ch g Bahamian Bounty—Tuppenny Blue (Pennekamp (USA))
1075[4] (2206) (2320) (2431) 2925[12] 3282[5] 3868[11] 4605[4] 5475[13] 6243[13] 6731[13]

Global City (IRE) *Saeed Bin Suroor* a102 107
3 b c Exceed And Excel(AUS) —Victory Peak (Shirley Heights)
1705[4] 2279[5] (2821) 3747[17] 4523[19] 5973[2] 6678[14] (7394)

Global Conquest (IRE) *Pat Eddery* a79 75
3 b f Captain Rio—Triphibious (Zafonic (USA))
2205[2] 3278[2] 3569[4] 4550[4] 6255[2] (6784) ◆

Global Strategy *O Sherwood* a47 67
6 b g Rainbow Quest(USA) —Pleasuring (Good Times (ITY))
459[9]

Global Traffic *R Ford* a70 68
5 br g Generous(IRE) —Eyes Wide Open (Fraam)
301[7] 627[P]

Global Village (IRE) *Miss D Mountain* a71 68
4 b g Dubai Destination(USA) —Zelding (IRE) (Warning)
552[4] 1422[6] 1592[5] 3007[2] 3227[3] (3732) (3983) 4665[5] 4824[3]

Globus (GER) *Uwe Ostmann* 111
3 ch c Areion(GER) —Globuli (GER) (Surako (GER))
1395a[4] 1915a[3] 3230a[5] 5585a[4] 6323a[6] 6713a[3]

Gloria De Campeao (BRZ) *P Bary* a117 120
6 b h Impression(ARG) —Audacity (BRZ) (Clackson (BRZ))
184a[5] 417a[4] (698a) 1013a[2] (2117a) 4809a[7]

Glorious Dreams (USA) *T J Pitt* a72 26
3 bb f Honour And Glory(USA) —Crissy Aya (USA) (Saros)
1414[9] 2058[13] 2973[10] 3625[8]

Gloucester *M J Scudamore* a71 80
6 b g Montjeu(IRE) —Birdlip (USA) (Sanglamore (USA))
597[4] (2552) (2818) 3697[3] 4007[6] 4988[4] 6244[8]

Glowing (IRE) *L M Cumani* a73 104
4 b m Dansili—Brightest (Rainbow Quest (USA))
(3516a) 6272[12]

Glowing Praise *E S McMahon* 88
3 ch g Fantastic Light(USA) —Beading (Polish Precedent (USA))
2925[6] (3309) 3868[4] 4433[4] 5432[7] 5832[4] (6243)

Glow Star (SAF) *G L Moore* a93 94
5 ch g Muhtafal(USA) —Arctic Glow (SAF) (Northern Guest (USA))
413a[7] 609a[5] 4768[7] 5476[9] 6270[18] 7133[3] 7626[3]

Gluteus Maximus (IRE) *A P O'Brien* a97 101
3 br c Statue Of Liberty(USA) —Skidmore Girl (USA) (Vaguely Noble)
5079a[9] 5490a[14] 6707a[12]

Go Alone (IRE) *G A Swinbank* a40 72
3 b g Elusive City(USA) —Ya Ya (IRE) (Royal Academy (USA))
1490[8] 2105[8] (2343) ◆ 3316[6] 3729[2] 4131[4] 4664[7]

Go Amwell *J R Jenkins* a61 64
6 b g Kayf Tara—Daarat Alayaam (IRE) (Reference Point)
1426[9] 2018[3] 2429[10] 3275[4] 3737[5]

Goathemala (GER) *P Schiergen* 108
4 b m Black Sam Bellamy(IRE) —Global World (GER) (Big Shuffle (USA))
5296a[6]

Gobama *J W Hills* a71 78
2 br f Dr Fong(USA) —Chine (Inchinor)
(3576) 5440[3] 5913[9] 6844[3] ◆ 7320[6]

Goblin *D E Cantillon* a50
8 b g Atraf—Forest Fantasy (Rambo Dancer (CAN))
8[4] 444[7]

Go Blue Chip *H Candy* a47 34
2 br g More Than Ready(USA) —Bon Vivant (USA) (Salt Lake (USA))
2533[9] 7736[10]

Go Country (FR) *P Schiergen* 99
2 b c Country Reel(USA) —Gerone (FR) (Saumarez)
(6151a)

Goddess Of Light (IRE) *Daniel Mark Loughnane* a73 45
2 b f Chineur(FR) —Blues Over (IRE) (Sri Pekan (USA))
5714[6] 6826[3] 7317[2] (7570) ◆

Godfrey Street *A G Newcombe* a81 80
6 ch g Compton Place—Tahara (IRE) (Caerleon (USA))
(83) 250[2] 424[6] 1104[5] 4222[4] 5183[2] 5374[6] 6857[12] 7219[3] 7758[10] 7852[4]

Go Forth North (USA) *M L W Bell* 66
2 ch f North Light(IRE) —Witch Tradition (USA) (Holy Bull (USA))
3160[3] 3576[4] 4385[4]

Go Free *J G M O'Shea* a56 43
8 gr g Easycall—Miss Traxdata (Absalom)
5217[11]

Go Go Green (IRE) *D H Brown* a82 96
3 b c Acclamation—Preponderance (IRE) (Cyrano De Bergerac)
2259[8] 4189[4] 4601[5] 5523[11] 5623[6] 5768[10] (6233) 6647[4] (6902) 7202[8]

Go Go Shoot (USA) *Bruce N Levine* a111
4 rg g Songandaprayer(USA) —Sailor Pluto (USA) ((USA))
6509a[4]

Going For Gold *R Charlton* a80 83
3 b f Barathea(IRE) —Flash Of Gold (Darshaan)
2847[3] ◆ (3527) 4709[3] 5876[4] 6613[5]

Going For Gold (ITY) *M Marcialis* 99
3 ch f Gold Away(IRE) —Stay Hernanda (Hernando (FR))
1659a[5] 3186a[4]

Going French (IRE) *R Curtis* a70 69
2 ch c Frenchmans Bay(FR) —Easy Going (Hamas (IRE))
2218[2] 2575[3] 2649[3] 3232[2] 4163[2] 4488[15] 7536[2] 7637[4]

Gojeri (IRE) *M A Jarvis* 68
2 ch g Choisir(AUS) —Lady Elysees (USA) (Royal Academy (USA))
6796[11] 7145[6]

Golan Knight (IRE) *K Schafflutzel* 88
4 bb h Golan(IRE) —Night Rhapsody (IRE) (Mujtahid (USA))
1555a[8]

Gold Again (USA) *W R Swinburn* a60 54
4 b m Touch Gold(USA) —Miss Insync (USA) (Miswaki (USA))
1285[6] 2598[8] 3224[12]

Gold And Song (FR) *A Couetil* 89
3 b c Gold Away(IRE) —Opera Song (In The Wings)
6150a[3]

Goldan Jess (IRE) *P A Kirby* a49 54
5 b g Golan(IRE) —Bendis (GER) (Danehill (USA))
3594[2] 4462[6] 4806[2] 5600[5] 6558[2]

Goldarover (IRE) *Noel Meade* 64
2 b c Fasliyev(USA) —Glamadour (IRE) (Sanglamore (USA))
2643a[4]

Gold Bubbles (USA) *J S Bolger* 99
2 b f Street Cry(IRE) —Well Revered (USA) (Red Ransom (USA))
1994a[2] 4726a[4] 5199[6] 5488a[6]

Gold Crusher (USA) *R M H Cowell* a63 57
2 b g Johannesburg(USA) —Compressed (USA) (Green Forest (USA))
2087[4] 4173[3] 5311[6]

Gold Diamond (USA) *M Johnston* a40 65
2 b g Seeking The Gold(USA) —Dubai Diamond (Octagonal (NZ))
3167[6] 3750[7] 4451[4] 5589[13] 6134[8] 6963[11] 7333[7]

Golden Acclamation (IRE) *A Renzoni* 93
2 b c Acclamation—Nelly Golden (USA) (Pentelicus (USA))
3185a[6]

Golden Aria (IRE) *R Hannon* 79
2 b f Rakti—Yellow Trumpet (Petong)
5021[4] 5605[3] (6062)

Golden Arrow (IRE) *E Charpy* a108 97
6 b h Danehill(USA) —Cheal Rose (IRE) (Dr Devious (IRE))
184a[9] 702a[12] 1008a[14]

Golden Bishop *R A Fahey* a73 72
4 ch g Medicean—Hen Harrier (Polar Falcon (USA))
105[13]

Golden Button (IRE) *Sir Mark Prescott* a77 69
4 ch m Trans Island—Velvet Appeal (IRE) (Petorius)
4303[2] (5228) 5511[6] 6346[3] 6648[6]

Golden Century (USA) *A Fabre* 106
3 b c El Prado(IRE) —Maple Syrple (CAN) (American Chance (USA))
(3230a) 5496a[6] 6505a[10]

Golden Chance (FR) *P Lefevre* 52
3 b f Gold Away(IRE) —Garamba (IRE) (Spectrum (IRE))
5784a[5]

Golden Clou (FR) *P Demercastel* a84 97
3 ch f Kendor(FR) —Glaoutchka (FR) (Glaieul (USA))
1657a[4] 2777a[8] 4394a[4]

Golden Desert (IRE) *T G Mills* a94 109
5 b g Desert Prince(IRE) —Jules (IRE) (Danehill (USA))
2241[3] 3091[6] 3628[10] 4293[2] 5025[2] (5424) ◆ (5874) 6270[10] 6661[7] 7019[11]

Golden Destiny (IRE) *P J Makin* a56 105
3 ch f Captain Rio—Dear Catch (IRE) (Bluebird (USA))
2079[17] 3787[3] (4244) (4712) (5245) (5902)

Golden Dixie (USA) *R A Harris* a66 89
10 ch g Dixieland Band(USA) —Beyrouth (USA) (Alleged (USA))
1418[7] 1565[4] 1836[4] 2203[2] 2326[10] 2680[8] 2911[3] (3208) 3691[4] 3866[5] 4167[10] 4907[5] 5608[5] 5719[15] 6362[4] 6738[12] 6825[8] 7138[11] 7483[10] 7503[6] 7680[5] 7709[6] 7834[3]

Golden Down (USA) *G Fratini* 90
2 b c City Place(USA) —Annie On Stage (USA) (Peteski (CAN))
7205a[9]

Golden Emperor (IRE) *G A Swinbank* a57 58
2 ro g Antonius Pius(USA) —Lily Shing Shang (Spectrum (IRE))
4652[8] 5290[3] 6461[4]

Golden Flight (IRE) *J W Hills* a55 64
3 ch g Hawk Wing(USA) —Cassilis (IRE) (Persian Bold)
1671[5] 2320[4] 2685[8] 3662[5]

Golden Future *P D Niven* a48 58
6 b g Muhtarram(USA) —Nazca (Zilzal (USA))
857[9] 1480[5] 2245[5] 2859[8] 4193[5] (4593) 5377[6] 5732[3] 6432[9] 6845[3]

Golden Games (IRE) *D C O'Brien* 67
3 b f Montjeu(IRE) —Ski For Gold (Shirley Heights)
1363[10] 1747[7] 2605[2] 3575[2] 5152[4]

Golden Gates (IRE) *Mrs A Duffield* 67
2 b g Key Of Luck(USA) —Golden Anthem (USA) (Lion Cavern (USA))
6533[4]

Golden Groom *P Beaumont* 61
6 b g Groom Dancer(USA) —Reine De Thebes (FR) (Darshaan)
(2573)

Golden Kiss *Paul Murphy* 9
3 b f Golden Snake(USA) —Kiss Me Again (IRE) (Cyrano De Bergerac)
1683[13] 2105[11]

Golden Penny *M Dods* a80 81
4 b g Xaar—Dog Rose (SAF) (Fort Wood (USA))
1229[11] 1646[6] (2235) 3265[15] 3656[7] 6016[10] 7172[7] 7711[8] 7782[7]

Golden Pippin *R Hannon* a42 56
2 b f Medicean—Surf The Net (Cape Cross (IRE))
3820[13] 4318[5] 4797[10] 5166[8] 5573[9] 7210[10]

Golden Pool (IRE) *S A Callaghan* a55 48
3 b f Danetime(IRE) —Miss Megs (IRE) (Croco Rouge (IRE))
1620[6] 2577[8] 2973[12]

Golden Prospect *Miss J R Tooth* a68 74
5 b g Lujain(USA) —Petonellajill (Petong)
878[4] 1080[10] 1413[9] 1748[5] 2202[10] (2736) 3283[5] 3659[3] 4305[12] 4697[6] 5429[12] (5569) 5842[3] 6339[5] 6828[5] 7403[7] 7480[8] 7591[9] 7650[2] 7813[8] 7861[6]

Golden Ramon (IRE) *B Grizzetti* 68
2 ch f Captain Rio—Solid Golden (USA) (Mountain Cat (USA))
4366a[6]

Golden Ring *P J O'Gorman* 42
3 b c Hawk Wing(USA) —Farhana (Fayruz)
1289[13] 2240[7] 3168[7]

Golden Riviera (SAF) *H J Brown* 87
5 b h Goldmark(SAF) —South Of France (SAF) (Elliodor (FR))
259a[12] 335a[11]

Golden Rock (IRE) *R Charlton* 77
3 ch g Rock Of Gibraltar(IRE) —Sister Golden Hair (IRE) (Glint Of Gold)
1289[5] 2002[6] 2981[2] 4518[10] 6907[10] 7248[7]

Golden Rosie (IRE) *B W Hills* 76
3 ch f Exceed And Excel(AUS) —Kelsey Rose (Most Welcome)
2917[5] 4700[3] 5937[6] 6739[7]

Golden Run *R Hollinshead* a24
6 b m Commanche Run—Goldengirlmichelle (IRE) (Project Manager)
1409[7]

Golden Shaheen (IRE) *Saeed Bin Suroor* a86 78
2 b g Invincible Spirit(IRE) —Cheeky Weeky (Cadeaux Genereux)
5330[2] 5807[2] 6478[10] (6943)

Golden Square *A W Carroll* a51 49
7 ch g Tomba—Cherish Me (Polar Falcon (USA))
43[10] 130[7] 469[3] 598[3] 647[7] 802[14] 7517[13]

Golden Stream (IRE) *Sir Michael Stoute* 106
3 b f Sadler's Wells(USA) —Phantom Gold (Machiavellian (USA))
1701[6] 3016[2] (3320) 4489[10] 5064[3] (6272) 6661[12]

Golden Sword *A P O'Brien* 120
3 b c High Chaparral(IRE) —Sitara (Salse (USA))
1145a[4] (1800) 2705[5] 3438a[2] 4298[5]

Golden Tiger *T P Tate* a69
2 br c Kyllachy—Roxy (Rock City)
7836[2]

Golden Waters *Eve Johnson Houghton* 65
2 b f Dubai Destination(USA) —Faraway Waters (Pharly (FR))
6393[5]

Gold Express *P J O'Gorman* a83 88
6 b g Observatory(USA) —Vanishing Point (USA) (Caller I.D. (USA))
1152[6] *1607[7]* 2086[7] *2396[3]* 3164[9] 3407[4] *(3736)* (4149) 5221[15]

Gold Fix (IRE) *M R Channon* a67 68
2 b f Fath(USA) —Gold Blended (IRE) (Goldmark (USA))
3534[7] 3810[9] 4047[7] 4565[2] 4651[3] (4973) *5224[6]* (5589) 6099[2] *6431[2]* 6844[6]

Goldikova (IRE) *F Head* 131
4 b m Anabaa(USA) —Born Gold (USA) (Blushing Groom (FR))
2120a[7] (3749) (4580a) (5086a) 6503a[3] (7308a)

Gold Maha *M E Sowersby* 57
3 b f Diktat—Westwood (FR) (Anabaa (USA))
1269[7] 1893[4] 2447[5] 2838[4] 4434[11] 6098[8]

Gold Music (FR) *J-L Pelletan* a63 88
3 b c Gold Away(IRE) —Sillery Music (FR) (Sillery (USA))
4581a[8]

Gold Party *K McAuliffe* a70 63
2 ch c Bahamian Bounty—West River (USA) (Gone West (USA))
5318[5] 5722[8] *7400[10]* *7773[3]* *7865[2]*

Gold Rock (FR) *A W Carroll* a59 90
4 b g Anabaa(USA) —Golden Sea (FR) (Saint Cyrien (FR))
730[5] *825[5]* *891[4]* *1042[9]*

Gold Rules *L M Cumani* 73
2 ch c Gold Away(IRE) —Raphaela (FR) (Octagonal (NZ))
3875[8] 4424[7] 5253[2] ◆

Gold Sovereign (IRE) *I Mohammed* a91 105
5 b g King's Best(USA) —Sassenach (IRE) (Night Shift (USA))
265a[14] 340a[14] 614a[7] *771a[14]*

Gold Story *B Ellison* 48
2 ch g Lucky Story(USA) —Incatinka (Inca Chief (USA))
2231[6] 2610[5] 3310[11] 5595[4]

Goldtrek (USA) *R Charlton* a64 25
2 b f Medallist(USA) —Traipse (USA) (Digression (USA))
6620[12] *7522[6]* *7622[6]*

Goliaths Boy (IRE) *R A Fahey* 91
3 ch g Medecis—Green Belt (FR) (Tirol)
1801[8] 2701[13] 2935[10] 4741[2] ◆ 5209[5] 6277[2] 6733[2]

Golos *A Couetil*
3 u f — (Diesis)
6753a[0]

Go Man Go (IRE) *B Storey*
7 b g Courtship—Rose Of Summer (IRE) (Taufan (USA))
4014[8]

Gomrath (IRE) *M R Channon* 68
2 b c Lomitas—Diner De Lune (IRE) (Be My Guest (USA))
4524[7]

Go Nani Go *B Smart* 82
3 b c Kyllachy—Go Between (Daggers Drawn (USA))
5203[8]

Gone Hunting *J Pearce* a85 81
3 b g Hunting Lion(IRE) —Arasong (Aragon)
159[3] *(293)* *819[6]* *912[13]* *1002[7]* 2934[20] *7875[8]*

Gone'N'Dunnett (IRE) *Mrs C A Dunnett* a58 50
10 b g Petardia—Skerries Bell (Taufan (USA))
56[10] *153[5]* *327[12]* 1634[11] 1957[7] 3677[9] 3959[6] 4182[2] 4668[7]

Good Again *G A Butler* a86 99
3 ch f Dubai Destination(USA) —Good Girl (IRE) (College Chapel)
(1381) 1679[4] (1860) 2273[4] 3016[6] 3746[13] (6535)

Good Ba Ba (USA) *D Cruz* 125
7 b g Lear Fan(USA) —Elle Meme (USA) (Zilzal (USA))
1553a[4] (7746a)

Good Buy Dubai (USA) *J R Best* a63 62
3 gr g Essence Of Dubai(USA) —Sofisticada (USA) (Northern Jove (CAN))
205[4] *506[2]* *953[4]* *(1070)* 1282[6] (1570) 1842[10] 2204[3] *2489[3]* *2709[3]* *3511[6]* *6446[5]* 6566[4] 6742[9] 6918[4]

Goodbye Cash (IRE) *P D Evans* a65 66
5 b m Danetime(IRE) —Jellybeen (IRE) (Petardia)
2202[8] 2456[7] 2812[10] (3948) 4694[3] 5120[3] (5287) 5364[5] 5502[7] 5569[5] 6339[4] 6568[4] *6828[6]* *7179[2]* ◆ *7432[7]* *7479[2]* 7716[5] 7729[5] 7845[9]

Goodbye Earl (IRE) *A Berry* 73
2 b f Bertolini(USA) —Begine (IRE) (Germany (USA))
1504[6] 1788[4] 2054[10] 2484[2] 2714[10] 3152[6] 3682[3] 3805[4] 4282[2] 4547[4] 4752[6] 5337[5] 5552[7] 5945[8]

Goodbye Mr Bond *E J Alston* a62 93
9 b g Elmaamul(USA) —Fifth Emerald (Formidable (USA))
1170[10] 1507[12] 2103[8] 2894[9] 3264[8] 3624[3] 4532[5] 4663[9]

Good Bye My Friend (FR) *N Clement* a98 98
3 b c Kendor(FR) —The Wise Lady (FR) (Ganges (USA))
1207a[5]

Good Cause (IRE) *Mrs S Lamyman* a48 51
8 b g Simply Great(FR) —Smashing Pet (Mummy's Pet)
4658[12]

Good Effect (USA) *Tim Vaughan* a65 73
5 ch g Woodman(USA) —River Dreams (USA) (Riverman (USA))
816[9] 1178[3] *1378[14]* 1537[10] 1980[10] 3348[4] *6025[13]*

Good For Her *J L Dunlop* a51 69
3 b f Rock Of Gibraltar(IRE) —Tyranny (Machiavellian (USA))
2947[6] ◆ 3630[3] 4642[4]

Good Gorsoon (USA) *B W Hills* a91 94
4 b h Stravinsky(USA) —Alwaysinbloom (USA) (Unbridled (USA))
1018[10] 1791[6] 2078[7] 2502[9] *3212[3]* 3582[8] 4273[4] 4461[10] 5098[8] 5257[12] (6112) *6631[10]* *6972[11]*

Good Humoured *Sir Mark Prescott* a63
3 b g Rock Of Gibraltar(IRE) —Humouresque (Pivotal)
1490[4] *1730[12]* *3989[5]* *4843[10]* *7022[3]*

Goodison Goal (IRE) *Patrick Morris* a53 52
2 b f Trade Fair—Chantilly (FR) (Sanglamore (USA))
5785[7] 6408[8] *6802[6]* *7421[6]* *7584[7]* *7884[3]*

Goodison Park *A G Foster* 58
2 ch f Big Shuffle(USA) —Perfect Dream (Emperor Jones (USA))
4993[9] 5440[4] 6762[8]

Good Karma (IRE) *P J Rothwell* a45
5 b g Shernazar—Kayrava (Irish River (FR))
7004[9]

Good Lord (FR) *F Doumen* 64
3 b g Lord Of Men—The Trollop (FR) (Double Bed (FR))
2293a[7]

Goodnitesleeptight (FR) *David Marnane*
3 b f Marchand De Sable(USA) —Montagne Bleue (Legend Of France (USA))
7385a[0]

Good Queen Best *B De Haan* 44
3 b f Best Of The Bests(IRE) —Spring Sunrise (Robellino (USA))
4533[15] 5384[13]

Good Star (FR) *B Dutruel* 78
3 ch f Bad As I Wanna Be(IRE) —Arctic Starry (FR) (Star Maite (FR))
7385a[0] *7696a[0]*

Goodwood Diva *J L Dunlop* a46 49
2 ch f Kyllachy—Donna Vita (Vettori (IRE))
3101[7] 4239[7] *6911[9]*

Goodwood Maestro *J L Dunlop* a71 84
2 b g Piccolo—Madurai (Chilibang)
(2187) *6585[5]* 7013[12]

Goodwood Starlight (IRE) *G L Moore* a94 97
4 br g Mtoto—Starring (FR) (Ashkalani (IRE))
1460[16] 2003[8] 2475[7] 3103[8] 3578[6] 5509[6] 5915[6] 6190[6] 6681[4] ◆ 6936[11]

Googoobarabajagal (IRE) *W S Kittow* 54
3 b g Almutawakel—Shamah (Unfuwain (USA))
1708[5] 2350[4] 3222[10] 5011[3] 5430[8] 6188[5]

Goolagong (IRE) *R M Beckett* 65
2 b f Giant's Causeway(USA) —Maroochydore (IRE) (Danehill (USA))
5220[4]

Goose Bay (GER) *F Head* 106
4 b m Groom Dancer(USA) —Golden Time (GER) (Surumu (GER))
1597a[6] 2428a[6] 3085a[8]

Gooseberry Bush *P J Makin* 65
2 b f Tobougg(IRE) —Away To Me (Exit To Nowhere (USA))
2207[7] 3218[7] 5060[2] 5714[8] 6241[8] 6903[6]

Goose Green (IRE) *R J Hodges* a67 69
5 b g Invincible Spirit(IRE) —Narbayda (IRE) (Kahyasi)
1974[8] (2221) 2739[4] (2912) (3675) ◆ 3949[5] 4300[7]

Gooseley Chope (FR) *C Boutin* 72
2 b f Indian Rocket—Gooseley Lane (Pyramus (USA))
5494a[6] 5713a[0]

Gordon Flash *R Hannon* 62
2 ch c Alhaarth(IRE) —Goslar (In The Wings)
4336[8] 4953[5] 5590[3] 6067[5]

Gordonsville *J S Goldie* a81 91
6 b g Generous(IRE) —Kimba (USA) (Kris S (USA))
(1230) 2055[13] 2815[5] (3146) 3822[4] 4260[3] 5235[5] 6138[3] 6281[4] 6851[6] (7117)

Gordy Bee (USA) *Pat Eddery* 71
3 b c More Than Ready(USA) —Honoria (USA) (Danzig (USA))
3472[2] 4057[8] 4846[9] 5429[3]

Gore Hill (IRE) *K R Burke* a18 51
3 ch g Exceed And Excel(AUS) —Eschasse (USA) (Zilzal (USA))
1061[3] 1455[9] 2970[11]

Gosforth Park *M Brittain* 61
3 ch c Generous(IRE) —Love And Kisses (Salse (USA))
1168[4] 1349[6] 1562[2] 2060[6] 2340[6] 2838[3] 3687[5] 4491[4] 6766[5]

Gospel Spirit *J R Jenkins* a22
4 b g Cool Jazz—Churchtown Spirit (Town And Country)
2981[U] *7826[14]*

Gosse De Sevres (FR) *Ron Caget*
2 b c Sevres Rose(IRE) —Sister Cayras (FR) (Agent Bleu (FR))
4807a[0]

Go Sunshine (IRE) *F Sheridan* a20
3 b g Tagula(IRE) —Taoveret (IRE) (Flash Of Steel)
1108[8] *1491[10]*

Goswick *Micky Hammond* 49
3 ch f Bertolini(USA) —Holy Island (Deploy)
1522[5] 2104[8] 2403[7] 2802[9] 4506[6] 5294[12] 5524[7] 5730[6]

Got Flash (FR) *E J O'Neill* a54
3 b g Xaar—Wild Flush (USA) (Pine Bluff (USA))
820[4] *968[6]* *1481[12]*

Gotlandia (FR) *Y De Nicolay* a76 87
2 b f Anabaa(USA) —Grenade (FR) (Bering)
5956a[4]

Go To Dubai *M W Easterby* a48 55
2 b f Dubai Destination(USA) —Black Belt Shopper (IRE) (Desert Prince (IRE))
2128[5] 2788[4] 3119[2] 3605[2] 4190[4]

Gotta Have Her (USA) *Jenine Sahadi* a97 114
5 b m Royal Academy(USA) —Winnowing (USA) (Rahy (USA))
7305a[2]

Gouray Girl (IRE) *W R Swinburn* a86 89
2 b f Redback—Brillano (FR) (Desert King (IRE))
(6069) 6418[2] *7108[2]* 7290[2]

Govenor Eliott (IRE) *A J Lockwood* a45 41
4 ch g Rock Of Gibraltar(IRE) —Lac Dessert (USA) (Lac Ouimet (USA))
5982[6] 6818[11] *7464[5]* *7681[10]*

Govern *H R A Cecil* a32 77
2 b c Empire Maker(USA) —Imroz (USA) (Nureyev (USA))
6000[2] ◆ 6561[3] *7130[7]*

Government (IRE) *M C Chapman* a53 53
8 b g Great Dane(IRE) —Hidden Agenda (FR) (Machiavellian (USA))
7[9] *37[5]* *63[10]* *222[11]* *405[5]* *514[5]* *607[12]* *748[13]*

Gower *R J Price* a51 60
5 b g Averti(IRE) —Alashaan (Darshaan)
235[10] *431[9]* *540[12]* *1528[5]* 1787[10] 1846[10] 6553[10] *7424[9]* *7460[3]* *7681[7]* *7839[5]*

Gower Sophia *M Brittain* a65 65
2 b f Captain Rio—Hollow Quaill (IRE) (Entrepreneur)
1277[2] 1521[3] 2069[3] ◆ 2339[7] 3263[4] *5372[12]* *6343[2]* 6555[2] *6827[5]* *7217[2]* *7331[8]* *7748[4]*

Gower Valentine *D Nicholls* 80
3 b f Primo Valentino(IRE) —Mania (IRE) (Danehill (USA))
1486[11] 2443[10] 2970[9] 5405[4] 6572[2] 6824[17]

Go Win Girl *P C Haslam*
2 gr f Mark Of Esteem(IRE) —Grey Again (Unfuwain (USA))
3487[10]

Gozome (IRE) *D G Bridgwater* a22
5 ch g Golan(IRE) —Schonbein (IRE) (Persian Heights)
786[10] *939[9]* 1087[9]

Gra Adhmhar (IRE) *D J Coakley* a40
2 b g Mull Of Kintyre(USA) —Enya (Orpen (USA))
7825[6]

Graceandgratitude *S C Williams* a52
2 b f Royal Applause—Shararah (Machiavellian (USA))
3772[9] *6970[6]* *7661[10]* *7698[6]*

Grace And Virtue (IRE) *Andrew Oliver* a60 77
2 b f Statue Of Liberty(USA) —One For Fun (Unfuwain (USA))
2302a[2]

Gracechurch (IRE) *R J Hodges* a54 67
6 b g Marju(IRE) —Saffron Crocus (Shareef Dancer (USA))
1318[10] 1773[7] 1980[8] 2516[4] 2650[2] 3259[3] 3946[5] 4150[7] *6208[10]* *6800[8]*

Graceful Descent (FR) *J S Goldie* a74 75
4 b m Hawk Wing(USA) —Itab (USA) (Dayjur (USA))
2916[2] 3557[2] 4139[2] 4740[2] (5161) 6310[2] 6987[2]

Grace Jicaro *Mrs L Williamson* 42
2 ch f Firebreak—Anita In Wales (IRE) (Anita's Prince)
994[14] 1249[5] 4018[7] 4463[5] 4639[5] 6185[5] 6932[9]

Gracelightening *Paul Green* a60 62
2 b f Reset(AUS) —Monica Geller (Komaite (USA))
4468[5] 5407[3] *5839[5]*

Grace O'Malley (IRE) *D K Weld* 98
3 b f Refuse To Bend(IRE) —Lionne (Darshaan)
1388a[6] (2960a) 3896a[4]

Gracie's Games *R J Price* a52 28
3 b f Mind Games—Little Kenny (Warning)
6251[8] *6777[4]* *7197[7]* *7411[7]* *7814[12]*

Gracie's Gift (IRE) *R C Guest* a63 65
7 b g Imperial Ballet(IRE) —Settle Petal (IRE) (Roi Danzig (USA))
(811) 1413[3] 1634[2] *(1655)* 2418[10] *7762[6]* *7815[2]*

Gracious Melange *M Botti* a76
2 b f Medicean—Goodness Gracious (IRE) (Green Desert (USA))
(7763)

Grail Knight *A G Foster* a37 33
4 ch g Carnival Dancer—Nashkova (Nashwan (USA))
1127[6] 1648[9] 2159[9]

Gramercy (IRE) *M L W Bell* a82
2 b c Whipper(USA) —Topiary (IRE) (Selkirk (USA))
6493[4] *7209[5]* *(7317)*

Grams And Ounces *Miss Amy Weaver* a68 4
2 b c Royal Applause—Ashdown Princess (IRE) (King's Theatre (IRE))
6990[14] *7616[3]* *7825[3]*

Granakey (IRE) *Ian Williams* a43
6 b m Key Of Luck(USA) —Grand Morning (IRE) (King Of Clubs)
6581[6] *7555[8]*

Granary Girl *J Pearce* a60 65
7 b m Kingsinger(IRE) —Highland Blue (Never So Bold)
(1881) 2419[2] 2859[3] 3864[5] 4193[7] 4498[9]

Grandad Bill (IRE) *J S Goldie* a47 73
6 ch g Intikhab(USA) —Matikanehanafubuki (IRE) (Caerleon (USA))
1506[9] 1692[6] 2159[3] 2898[2] 3107[3] 3679[3] 5294[2] (5698) 5947[2] 6768[6]

Grand Ami (FR) *Mme C Dufreche*
2 b c Nombre Premier—Vesolia (FR) (Solicitor (FR))
7316a[10]

Grand Art (IRE) *P T Midgley* a49 79
5 b g Raise A Grand(IRE) —Mulberry River (IRE) (Bluebird (USA))
1402[6] (1765) 2068[3] (2294) (2505) 2932[11] 3000[4] 3343[3] 3940[4] 4332[8] 4972[3] 5067[5] 5469[2] 5943[2]

Grandcamp (FR) *J-C Rouget* 104
3 gr c Platini(GER) —Gaudera (GER) (Big Shuffle (USA))
(1145a) 1761a[5]

Grand Court (IRE) *George Baker* a38 53
6 b m Grand Lodge(USA) —Nice One Clare (IRE) (Mukaddamah (USA))
215[11]

Grand Couturier *Robert Ribaudo* 123
6 b h Grand Lodge(USA) —Lady Elgar (IRE) (Sadler's Wells (USA))
6511a[3]

Grand Diamond (IRE) *J S Goldie* a68 71
5 b g Grand Lodge(USA) —Winona (IRE) (Alzao (USA))
1650[5] 2156[5] 2542[7] 3110[2] 3150[4] 3448[8] 3656[4] 4751[2] 4876[3] 5941[3] 7113[9]

Grand Duc (USA) *Mme C Head-Maarek* 86
2 b c Kingmambo(USA) —New Harmony (USA) (A.P. Indy (USA))
6507a[3]

Grand Ducal (IRE) *A P O'Brien* 108
3 b c Danehill Dancer(IRE) —Mood Swings (IRE) (Shirley Heights)
(2306a) 5688a[4] 6526a[17]

Grande Caiman (IRE) *R Hannon* a108 95
5 ch g Grand Lodge(USA) —Sweet Retreat (Indian Ridge)
33[2] ◆ *801[9]* *1117[8]* 1709[4]

Grande Fortune (FR) *Mme O Rouleau*
4 b m Grand Tresor(FR) —In Space (FR) (Epervier Bleu)
7038a[10]

Grande Haya (FR) *A Bonin* a65 73
10 b g Solid Illusion(USA) —Mlle Saumarez (FR) (Saumarez)
7038a[3]

Grande Saggio *M Botti* 73
2 gr c Cape Cross(IRE) —Success Story (Sharrood (USA))
7244[2]

Grand Exit *A J McCabe* a16
3 b f Exit To Nowhere(USA) —Little Feat (Terimon)
6375[10]

Grand Hombre (USA) *R Bouresly* a99 92
9 bb g Grand Slam(USA) —Santona (CHI) (Winning (USA))
263a[11] *334a[2]* *435a[8]* *612a[9]* *698a[8]* *771a[4]*

Grand Honour (IRE) *P Howling* a82 76
3 gr g Verglas(IRE) —Rosy Dudley (IRE) (Grand Lodge (USA))
276[5] *432[3]* *629[2]* *672[2]* *1033[8]* *1214[9]* 1895[7] 3115[10] *3512[5]* *3982[4]* 4304[6] *7742[8]* 7876[11]

Grand Mary (IRE) *P F I Cole* 43
2 ch f Kyllachy—Magic Sister (Cadeaux Genereux)
5380[7] 5966[10]

Grand Minstrel (IRE) *P J Lally* 48
5 ch m Ashkalani(IRE) —Blushing Minstrel (IRE) (Nicholas (USA))
4876[7] 4894[5]

Grand Opera (IRE) *Gordon Elliott* a90 85
6 b g City On A Hill(USA) —Victoria's Secret (IRE) (Law Society (USA))
7375[4] *7789[7]*

Grand Palace (IRE) *H J Evans* a76 39
6 b g Grand Lodge(USA) —Pocket Book (IRE) (Reference Point)
15[4] *95[7]* *(235)* *400[3]* *(499)* *665[3]* *780[9]* *843[6]* *5836[12]* 6120[9] 6825[12] 7023[5] 7484[7] 7602[5] 7774[2] ◆ *7889[2]*

Grand Passion (IRE) *C F Wall* a109 89
9 b g Grand Lodge(USA) —Lovers' Parlour (Beldale Flutter (USA))
360[5] *585[3]* *1003[14]* *1642[9]* *2597[9]* 3822[12] 5598[12]

Grand Pere *P D Evans* a43 52
3 b g Monsieur Bond(IRE) —Ejay (Emperor Jones (USA))
3718[5] 3984[7] 4381[7] 4606[8]

Grand Sefton *N R Mitchell* a16 52
6 br g Pivotal—Nahlin (Slip Anchor)
872[7]

Grand Stitch (USA) *D Carroll* 67
3 b g Grand Slam(USA) —Lil Sister Stich (USA) (Seattle Bound (USA))
2250[13]

Grand Value (USA) *R Ford* a52 63
4 b m Grand Slam(USA) —Privyet Nadya (USA) (Cure The Blues (USA))
567[12]

Grand Vista *G L Moore* a67 103
5 b g Danehill(USA) —Revealing (Halling (USA))
182a[10] 335a[12] 433a[7] *3988[8]* 4423[15]

Grand Vizier (IRE) *C F Wall* a93 78
5 b g Desert Style(IRE) —Distant Decree (USA) (Distant View (USA))
2775[13] *(3301)* 4060[9] *4983[5]* *7827[6]*

Grand Zafeen *M R Channon* 78
2 ch f Zafeen(FR) —Majestic Desert (Fraam)
(1396) 1805[2] 3015[11] 3559[2]

Grange Corner *Garry Moss* a26
4 ch m First Trump—Blennerville (IRE) (General View)
1[5] *1156[9]* *1778[5]*

Granite Girl *P J McBride* 69
2 b f Kyllachy—Native Ring (FR) (Bering)
5029[3] 6920[6]

Granny McPhee *A Bailey* a65 80
3 b f Bahri(USA) —Allumette (Rainbow Quest (USA))
1491[7] 3856[6] 4432[4] 4698[U] 5112[9] 6338[4] *(6497)*

Granski (IRE) *R Hannon* a56 68
3 b g Alhaarth(IRE) —Purple Haze (IRE) (Spectrum (IRE))
1928[4] 2206[11] 2850[8] 3358[7] 3629[4]

Granston (IRE) *J D Bethell* a99 93
8 gr g Revoque(IRE) —Gracious Gretclo (Common Grounds)
999[2] 1347[2] (1850) 2468[4] 2933[17] 4930[2] 5551[11] 6013[6] 6480[19]

Grantley Adams *E Charpy* a86 102
6 b g Dansili—Noble Peregrine (Lomond (USA))
257a[3] 413a[5] 638a[2] 696a[5]

Grant Me A Wish *S P Griffiths*
3 ch g Timeless Times(USA) —Baby Be (Bold Arrangement)
6823[18]

Grasp *P D Evans* a62 48
7 b g Kayf Tara—Circe (Main Reef)
3774[5] 4168[9]

Gratuitous (IRE) *L McHugh* a38 38
5 b g Rudimentary(USA) —Accell (IRE) (Magical Wonder (USA))
566[7]

Gravitas *M bin Shafya* a110 114
6 ch h Mark Of Esteem(IRE) —Bombazine (IRE) (Generous (IRE))
185a[10] (262a) 616a[5]

Gravitation *W Jarvis* 108
4 b m Galileo(IRE) —Guaranda (Acatenango (GER))
2482[9] 3642[5]

Graycliffe (IRE) *Patrick Morris* a64 60
3 gr g Val Royal(FR) —Popiplu (USA) (Cozzene (USA))
586[10] 759[6] (1183) 1363[7] *1431[3]* 2152[8] *3383[14]* 4874[5]

Graylyn Ruby (FR) *J Jay* a78 74
4 b g Limnos(JPN) —Nandi (IRE) (Mujadil (USA))
139[10] 1175[5] 1738[6] (2419) 3114[5] 4007[2] *5227[6]* 5975[7] 6385[8] 6758[3]

Graymalkin (IRE) *Saeed Bin Suroor* a82 83
2 b c Singspiel(IRE) —Pearl Grey (Gone West (USA))
5786[6] (6285) *6805[4]*

Graze On And On *J J Quinn* 38
4 ch m Elmaamul(USA) —Laena (Roman Warrior)
3486[8]

Grazeon Gold Blend *J J Quinn* 87
6 ch g Paris House—Thalya (Crofthall)
1849[13] 2267[8] (2570) 3001[2] 3377[4] 3877[13] 4549[5] 5465[2] 6645[6]

Greannmhar (USA) *J S Bolger* 87
3 ch f Distorted Humor(USA) —Copano Bay (USA) (Seattle Slew (USA))
5689a[15]

Great Art (IRE) *P W Chapple-Hyam* 83
3 b c One Cool Cat(USA) —Passe Passe (USA) (Lear Fan (USA))
4097[4] (6101) 6621[8] 6997[7]

Great Bounder (CAN) *A B Haynes* a64 43
3 bb g Mr Greeley(USA) —Jo Zak (USA) (Vilzak (USA))
4650[10] 5152[7] *6807[9]* 7153[7] *7369[2] 7500[2] 7614[11] 7860[6]*

Great Charm (IRE) *E J Alston* a81 95
4 b g Orpen(USA) —Briery (IRE) (Salse (USA))
1212[12] 1864[11] 2405[10] 4285[12] *6642[11] 6879[3] 7191[3] (7506)* ◆

Great Intrigue (IRE) *J S Moore* 67
2 b g Azamour(IRE) —Bakewell Tart (IRE) (Tagula (IRE))
2844[7] 3064[11] 6424[5]

Great Knight (IRE) *S Kirk* a67 67
4 b g Acclamation—Wild Vintage (USA) (Alysheba (USA))
352[4] (675) 811[6] 1846[11] *2686[5] (3227) 3720[5]* 3866[9] *4748[5]* 5018[12] *5225[9]*

Great Plains *E Charpy* a93 99
7 b h Halling(USA) —West Dakota (USA) (Gone West (USA))
263a[4]

Great Quest (IRE) *James Moffatt* 56
7 b m Montjeu(IRE) —Paparazzi (IRE) (Shernazar)
3927[13] 4462[7] 4742[4] 5068[12] 5734[10]

Great View (IRE) *Mrs A L M King* a65 74
10 b g Great Commotion(USA) —Tara View (IRE) (Wassl)
1786[5] 2294[7] 3798[4] 4625[11]

Great Western (USA) *P F I Cole* a49 21
3 bb c Gone West(USA) —Pleasant Temper (USA) (Storm Cat (USA))
1594[10]

Greek Envoy *T P Tate* 103
5 br g Diktat—South Shore (Caerleon (USA))
7018[P]

Greek Key (IRE) *M L W Bell* a64 62
2 ch c Selkirk(USA) —Doohulla (USA) (Stravinsky (USA))
4439[7] 4811[8] *5191[6]* 5748[8] 6367[5] 6906[9]

Greek Secret *J O'Reilly* a62 63
6 b g Josr Algarhoud(IRE) —Mazurkanova (Song)
234[6] 1558[10] 1889[9] (3938) 4436[14] 4998[5] 6799[16] *7370[6]* ◆ *7579[11] 7835[6] (7889)*

Greek Theatre (USA) *P S McEntee* a64 64
4 ch g Smoke Glacken(USA) —Theatre Flight (USA) (Theatrical (IRE))
7728[4]

Green Agenda *M Johnston* a80 81
3 b g Anabaa(USA) —Capistrano Day (USA) (Diesis)
(753) ◆ *(817) 968[2]* (1098) (1331) *1466[4]* 2248[4] 2787[3] 3144[7] 4262[10] 4846[2] 5189[7] *5663[14]* 6182[6] 7101[5]

Green Army *M R Channon* 41
2 b c Sulamani(IRE) —Dowhatjen (Desert Style (IRE))
6821[12]

Greenbelt *G M Moore* a62 56
8 b g Desert Prince(IRE) —Emerald (USA) (El Gran Senor (USA))
1442[3] 1654[2] 2233[11] *2580[4]* 6768[4] *7093[3]*

Green Beret (IRE) *J H M Gosden* 101
3 b g Fayruz—Grandel (Owington)
(1180) 1296[5] 1824[5] 3166[2] 3784[4] ◆ 4490[3] 5203[5]

Green Birdie (NZ) *C Fownes* 118
6 b g Catbird(AUS) —Mrs Squillionaire (AUS) (Last Tycoon)
7745a[4]

Green Coast (IRE) *Doug Watson* a105 95
6 b h Green Desert(USA) —Oriental Fashion (IRE) (Marju (IRE))
184a[2] 521a[3] ◆ *771a[3] 1008a[8]*

Green Community (USA) *E F Vaughan* a59 65
2 rg f El Prado(IRE) —Dreams (USA) (Silver Hawk (USA))
4427[4] *5106[4]* 5498[3] 5935[6]

Green Dandy (IRE) *E J O'Neill* a83 103
2 b f Green Desert(USA) —Hawas (Mujtahid (USA))
5956a[2] 6523a[5] 7103a[4]

Green Day Packer (IRE) *P C Haslam* a46 63
5 br g Daylami(IRE) —Durrah Green (Green Desert (USA))
169[6] 3499[13]

Green Dynasty (IRE) *M Johnston* a64 55
3 ch g Giant's Causeway(USA) —Rose Gypsy (Green Desert (USA))
280[6] 548[5] 716[4] 1595[13] 2357[14] 2779[11] 3480[4]

Green Earth (IRE) *Mrs A J Perrett* 74
2 b c Cape Cross(IRE) —Inchyre (Shirley Heights)
4945[8] 5220[10] 5564[3] 5938[6] (6366) 6735[9] 6963[10]

Green Endeavour (CAN) *Mrs A J Perrett* a44 20
3 b g Forestry(USA) —Zuri Ridge (USA) (Cox's Ridge (USA))
3303[10] 3675[9]

Green Energy *Mrs A J Perrett* 15
2 b g Rainbow Quest(USA) —Carambola (IRE) (Danehill (USA))
6615[13] 6930[15]

Green For Luck (IRE) *S Gollings* 63
2 b c Key Of Luck(USA) —Kasota (IRE) (Alzao (USA))
2444[7] 3376[6] 6033[3] 6533[8]

Greenisland (IRE) *H Morrison* a82 99
3 b f Fasliyev(USA) —Green Castle (IRE) (Indian Ridge)
1240a[3] 2057[7] 3016[17] (3746) 4259[3] 4489[8] 5069[7] 6272[3] *7132[11]*

Green Lagonda (AUS) *P D Evans* a61 75
7 gr g Crown Jester(AUS) —Fidelis (AUS) (John's Hope (AUS))
225 596[5] 645[5] 681[3] 832[2] 853[5] 1134[10] 1591[3] 1784[9] *1935[3]* 2137[9] 2349[2] 2564[8] 2758[3] 3204[3] (3775) 3860[4] 3998[9] 4736[2] (5125) 5184[6] 5576[12] (5900) 6329[2] 6669[10] 6791[3]

Green Lightning (IRE) *M Johnston* 78
2 b c Montjeu(IRE) —Angelic Song (CAN) (Halo (USA))
6046[6] 6759[6] (7244)

Green Manalishi *K A Ryan* a109 106
8 b g Green Desert(USA) —Silca-Cisa (Hallgate)
911[7] 1791[5] 3351[15] 3848[10] 4341[19] 5132[10] ◆ 5860[4] 6089[3] ◆ (6283) 6678[4] *7007a[5] (7202) 7341a[4] 7488[12]*

Green Moon (IRE) *H J L Dunlop* 79
2 b c Montjeu(IRE) —Green Noon (FR) (Green Tune (USA))
6620[8] 7029[4]

Green Onions *A J Lidderdale* a70 67
3 b g Royal Applause—Tremiere (FR) (Anabaa (USA))
(127) 229[7] 350[3] 685[4] 2005[6] 2443[2] 2774[6] 4051[9] *4374[11] 5836[11] 7418[11] 7652[11]* 7770[10]

Greenore Gordon *M S Saunders* 14
2 ch g Namid—Approaching Storm (IRE) (Entrepreneur)
1147[7] 4219[13]

Green Park (IRE) *D Carroll* a89 94
6 b g Shinko Forest(IRE) —Danccini (IRE) (Dancing Dissident (USA))
1684[16] 2095[8] 2405[9] 2897[3] 2938[4] 3149[6] 3607[9] 3877[17] 4141[3] 4285[5] 4399[3] 4469[6] *(6434) 6642[7]* 6897[8] *7155[9]* 7337[11] 7577[6] (7646)

Green Passion (USA) *M Johnston* a69 48
3 bb g Forestry(USA) —Date Stone (USA) (Forty Niner (USA))
1383[3] 272[6] 6490[10]

Green Poppy *B Smart* a34 63
3 b f Green Desert(USA) —Vimy Ridge (FR) (Indian Ridge)
1969[6] 2431[7] 3672[5] 6220[13] 6380[3] ◆ *6856[7]*

Green Ridge (FR) *J Van Handenhove* 81
2 b f Green Tune(USA) —Baino Ridge (FR) (Highest Honor (FR))
4577a[0]

Green Rock (FR) *F Doumen* a80 95
2 b c Green Tune(USA) —Pyramid Painter (IRE) (Peintre Celebre (USA))
(5739a)

Green Shoots *M E Sowersby* a7 2
2 b f Reset(AUS) —Cryptogam (Zamindar (USA))
3858[11] 4430[13] *6494[11]* 6821[17]

Greensleeves (FR) *J E Pease* 69
2 b f Green Tune(USA) —Princess Mix (FR) (Linamix (FR))
5956a[8]

Green Spirit (IRE) *Patrick Morris*
3 b g Invincible Spirit(IRE) —Randonneur (IRE) (Red Sunset)
1015[13] 1400[14]

Greensward *B J Meehan* 83
3 b g Green Desert(USA) —Frizzante (Efisio)
1870[6] 2926[2] 3801[4]

Green Tango (FR) *P Van De Poele* a95 106
6 ch h Majorien—Miss Bonfosse (FR) (Hard Leaf (FR))
5281a[5]

Green Velvet *P J Makin* a64 64
4 b m Iron Mask(USA) —Scarlett Ribbon (Most Welcome)
464 347[3] (895) (946) 1540[10] 2492[4] 4950[2] 6362[5] *7602[2]* ◆

Green Wadi *G L Moore* a81 76
4 b g Dansili—Peryllys (Warning)
7539[3] ◆ *7684[13]*

Greenwich Meantime *E J O'Neill* a92 94
9 b g Royal Academy(USA) —Shirley Valentine (Shirley Heights)
723 591[6] 5204a[2] *(5301a)*

Greenwich Village *W J Knight* a88 78
6 b g Mtoto—D'Azy (Persian Bold)
(233) 723[3] 3103[7]

Gremlin *I W McInnes* a66 72
5 b g Mujahid(USA) —Fairy Free (Rousillon (USA))
3223[2]

Grenane (IRE) *Mrs A Malzard* a63 62
6 b g Princely Heir(IRE) —Another Rainbow (IRE) (Rainbows For Life (CAN))
(5540a)

Grenso (ITY) *S Botti* 97
2 br c Martino Alonso(IRE) —Green Reew (IRE) (Sikeston (USA))
7206a[4]

Grethel (IRE) *A Berry* a35 65
5 b m Fruits Of Love(USA) —Stay Sharpe (USA) (Sharpen Up)
1306[6] 1472[7] 1690[15] 2246[6] 2442[6] 2590[5] 3019[2] 3060[4] 3451[5] 3943[10] 4495[6] 4588[5] 4932[8] 5294[6] 5423[10] 5733[7] 5947[11] 5962[11] 6219[6] 6310[6] 6840[7]

Grey Boy (GER) *A W Carroll* a84 76
8 gr g Medaaly—Grey Perri (Siberian Express (USA))
8417 1149[4] *(1320)* 1603[9] 2168[3] 2491[6] *2828[3]* 3154[4] 3812[7] 4501[10] 5031[12] 6596[9] *6725[6]* 6937[5] *7229[6] 7523[6]* ◆ 7741[7]

Grey Bunting *B W Hills* a57 63
2 gr c Oasis Dream—Ribbons And Bows (IRE) (Dr Devious (IRE))
6615[6] *7050[4]*

Grey Command (USA) *M Brittain* a58 74
4 gr h Daylami(IRE) —Shmoose (IRE) (Caerleon (USA))
1737[16] 2043[8] 2315[5] 2724[2] 2898[7] 3035[4] 3350[6] 5423[6] 6017[5] 6218[11] *7719[2]*

Greyfriarschorista *M Johnston* 61
2 ch c King's Best(USA) —Misty Heights (Fasliyev (USA))
4618[4]

Grey Garth (IRE) *J D Bethell* 21
2 gr g Verglas(IRE) —Again Royale (IRE) (Royal Academy (USA))
3392[6]

Grey Granite (IRE) *W Jarvis* 84
3 gr c Dalakhani(IRE) —Royal Ballerina (IRE) (Sadler's Wells (USA))
1681[5] (2199)

Grey Gurkha *I W McInnes* a31 42
8 gr h Kasakov—Royal Rebeka (Grey Desire)
2441[14] 3558[9] *4171[12]* 4313[7] 4887[9] 5983[9] *7586[11]*

Greylady (FR) *J-C Rouget* 96
3 gr f Poliglote—Lady Stella (FR) (Shining Steel)
7569a[4]

Greylami (IRE) *T G Mills* a95 98
4 gr g Daylami(IRE) —Silent Crystal (USA) (Diesis)
585[4] (1003) 1460[15] 2055[16] 3586[2] 4340[9] 5262[3] 5880[3] 6239[2] 6480[27]

Greystoke Prince *P S McEntee* a78 52
4 gr g Diktat—Grey Princess (IRE) (Common Grounds)
1186[9] 1493[9] 2168[5] *3211[11]* 5287[13] *5991[8] 6828[11] 7424[11] 7517[8] 7660[4] 7693[2]* 7774[5]

Grigorovitch (IRE) *Liam McAteer* a76 83
7 b g Fasliyev(USA) —Hasty Words (IRE) (Polish Patriot (USA))
7341a[14]

Grillonnie (FR) *X-L Le Stang*
4 gr m Visionary(FR) —La Grillonniere (FR) (Balleroy (USA))
7821a[0]

Grimes Faith *R C Guest* a78 69
6 b g Woodborough(USA) —Emma Grimes (IRE) (Nordico (USA))
894 146[2] 304[2] (380) (422) 582[6] 654[3] (742) (919) 4620[6] 4886[10] 5411[7] 6010[17] 6825[6] ◆ 6989[7] 7086[8] 7219[4] 7397[U] 7561[9] 7852[9]

Gripsholm Castle (USA) *H R A Cecil* 105
3 bb f Dynaformer(USA) —Randaroo (USA) (Gold Case (USA))
(2002) 3315[4] (6286) 6813[12]

Gris De Gris (IRE) *A De Royer-Dupre* a109 117
5 gr h Slickly(FR) —Deesse Grise (FR) (Lead On Time (USA))
(1029a) 1658a[2] 2120a[2] 5709a[5] 6506a[2] 7102a[3] 7746a[10]

Grissom (IRE) *A Berry* 85
3 b g Desert Prince(IRE) —Misty Peak (IRE) (Sri Pekan (USA))
1232[4] ◆ 1505[3] 2058[12] (3096) 3688[11] 4044[5] 4309[3] 4494[5] 4776[4] (5335) 6051[2] 6279[7] 7083[2] 7171[2] 7220[4]

Gris Tendre (FR) *J-C Rouget* a93 105
4 gr h Slickly(FR) —Tendre Pensee (FR) (Mujadil (USA))
3045a[7]

Gritstone *R A Fahey* 69
2 b g Dansili—Cape Trafalgar (IRE) (Cape Cross (IRE))
4888[2] 6046[4] 6478[12]

Grizedale (IRE) *M J Attwater* a64 61
10 ch g Lake Coniston(IRE) —Zabeta (Diesis)
1117 2341[0] 2921[6] *3732[6] 4202[5]* 5429[9]

Groove Master *A King* 57
2 b g Tobougg(IRE) —Magic Mistress (Magic Ring (IRE))
4811[7] 5499[13] 6331[5]

Gross Prophet *A J Lidderdale* a77 82
4 b g Lujain(USA) —Done And Dusted (IRE) (Up And At 'Em)
(1770) 2499[3] 3245[4] 3374[2] *3977[5]* 6204[8] 6761[2] *7204[7]*

Ground Patrol *N R Mitchell* a57 19
8 b g Ashkalani(IRE) —Good Grounds (USA) (Alleged (USA))
2516[7]

Group Captain *H J Collingridge* a92 96
7 b g Dr Fong(USA) —Alusha (Soviet Star (USA))
337 1458[5] 2706[6] 3510[3] 3822[8]

Group Leader (IRE) *J R Jenkins* a50 64
3 ch g Noverre(USA) —Stem The Tide (USA) (Proud Truth (USA))
4472[3] 5010[4] *6031[9]* 7101[7] 7246[14]

Group Therapy *N P Littmoden* a72 109
4 ch g Choisir(AUS) —Licence To Thrill (Wolfhound (USA))
1676[10] 2012[14] 2704[5] 3638[11] 3844[2] 4341[8] (4766) 5420[15] 5860[21] 6427[12]

Grove View Star *Patrick Morris* a65 64
4 ch g Auction House(USA) —Gracious Imp (USA) (Imp Society (USA))
7719[3] 7766[9]

Grudge *Ollie Pears* a74 74
4 b g Timeless Times(USA) —Envy (IRE) (Paris House)
3678[3] 4283[4] 4778[9] 5411[2] 6010[22] *6635[9] 6857[2]* 7086[5] *7397[2] (7595) 7852[2]*

Guantana (GER) *J Hirschberger* 103
4 b m Dynaformer(USA) —Guadalupe (GER) (Monsun (GER))
2428a[10] 5296a[2] 6324a[9]

Guarino (GER) *G L Moore* 93
5 b g Acatenango(GER) —Global World (GER) (Big Shuffle (USA))
3585[6]

Guendalina (FR) *J-M Beguigne* 57
3 ch f Highest Honor(FR) —Black Tulip (FR) (Fabulous Dancer (USA))
6753a[10]

Guerande (IRE) *A De Royer-Dupre* 92
3 b f Diesis—Gracefully (IRE) (Orpen (USA))
7697a[0]

Guertino (IRE) *C J Teague* a64 91
4 ch g Choisir(AUS) —Isana (JPN) (Sunday Silence (USA))
5959[8] 6180[5] *6434[12]* 6647[16] 7083[14]

Guesswork *W Jarvis* a29 60
2 ch f Rock Of Gibraltar(IRE) —Show Off (Efisio)
2034[4] 2853[4] *3210[7]* 5992[6]

Guest Book (IRE) *M Johnston* 82
2 b c Green Desert(USA) —Your Welcome (Darshaan)
5431[6] (5786) 6305[2] ◆

Guest Connections *D Nicholls* a91 77
6 b g Zafonic(USA) —Llyn Gwynant (Persian Bold)
1169[6] 1518[14] (1694) 1885[3] ◆ 5675[10] 6010[13] 6489[15]

Guestofthenation (USA) *M Johnston* a75 85
3 bb g Gulch(USA) —French Flag (Darshaan)
1702[4] 2189[7] *3466[3]* 4280[7] 4520[15]

Guest Ville (FR) *Mlle S-V Tarrou* a91 103
3 b c Highest Honor(FR) —Kadance Ville (FR) (Fabulous Dancer (USA))
1145a[2] 1761a[4] 2756a[11] 3230a[3] 6132a[8]

Guga (IRE) *George Baker* a69 58
3 b g Rock Of Gibraltar(IRE) —Attitre (FR) (Mtoto)
982[6] 1250[11] 3460[8] *(3710) 4373[2]* 4719[5]

Guidecca Ten *A M Balding* 76
2 b c Peintre Celebre(USA) —Silver Rhapsody (USA) (Silver Hawk (USA))
4713[4] ◆ 6548[3] (Dead)

Guilded Warrior *W S Kittow* a96 94
6 b g Mujahid(USA) —Pearly River (Elegant Air)
1467[3] 1861[23] 2780[6] 3431[4] 4236[2] 4954[2] 5476[7] 6278[7] 7060[10]

Guildenstern (IRE) *P Howling* a77 63
7 b g Danetime(IRE) —Lyphard Abu (IRE) (Lyphard's Special (USA))
71[6] (234) (277) 457[6] 576[2] 680[6] 799[2] 880[3] 1132[3] 1320[10] 1493[11] 3112[8] 3357[9] 3722[10] 4843[3] 5576[3] 6123[4] 6377[9] 7052[6] 7275[3] 7424[7] 7762[10] 7861[4]

Guilin (IRE) *P F I Cole* a46 52
3 b f Giant's Causeway(USA) —Chantress (Peintre Celebre (USA))
9531[1] 1148[7] *1967[7]* 2461[10] 3205[4] 5011[4] 5430[5]

Guiseppe Verdi (USA) *Miss Tor Sturgis* a65 57
5 ch g Sky Classic(CAN) —Lovington (USA) (Afleet (CAN))
(4084) 4987[5] *5750[3] 6210[8] 7857[2]*

Gulf Of Aqaba (USA) *M Johnston* 60
3 bb g Mr Greeley(USA) —Ocean Jewel (USA) (Alleged (USA))
2843[5] 3373[5] 3751[13] 4139[4]

Gulf President *M R Channon* a63 64
3 b c Polish Precedent(USA) —Gay Minette (IRE) (Peintre Celebre (USA))
833[3] 1034[4] 2038[8] 2320[7] 2982[5] *3718[3]* 4039[7] 4241[3]

Gulf Punch *M F Harris* a56 57
2 b f Dubawi(IRE) —Fruit Punch (IRE) (Barathea (IRE))
1968[5] 2238[5] *3027[4] 3719[3] 4371[6]* 4503[4] 4931[8] *5224[7]* 5589[7] 5715[7] 5938[11] 6215[7] 6367[8]

Gulnaz *C J Teague* a47 29
4 b m Tobougg(IRE) —Hymn Book (IRE) (Darshaan)
4170[4] 4593[9] 6766[7] 7085[11] *7504[6]*

Gumnd (IRE) *C E Brittain* a63 42
2 b c Selkirk(USA) —Surval (IRE) (Sadler's Wells (USA))
2889[12] *3270[6]*

Gundaroo *J L Dunlop* 70
2 b f Oasis Dream—Encore My Love (Royal Applause)
3356[5] 3858[2] 4468[3] 5344[6]

Gunfighter (IRE) *R A Farrant* a82 92
6 ch g Machiavellian(USA) —Reunion (IRE) (Be My Guest (USA))
680[RR]

Gun For Sale (USA) *P J Makin* a55 55
4 b g Quiet American(USA) —Do The Hustle (USA) (Known Fact (USA))
211[2] 1420[3] 1940[7] 4305[5] 5111[4] *6223[9]*

Gunga Din (IRE) *A Kinsella* 92
5 b h Green Desert(USA) —Caumshinaun (IRE) (Indian Ridge)
4360a[15] 5490a[21]

Gunnadoit (USA) *N B King* a66 62
4 bb g Almutawakel—Gharam (USA) (Green Dancer (USA))
448[8]

Gunner Be Lucky (IRE) *B Palling*
6 b g Key Of Luck(USA) —Iolanta (IRE) (Danehill (USA))
3501[10]

Gunner Lindley (IRE) *B W Hills* 87
2 ch c Medicean—Lasso (Indian Ridge)
3113[4] 3571[2] ◆ (4041) 4488[2] 5207[5] 5864[8]

Gunpowder (IRE) *Mme I T Oakes-Cottin* 45
5 b g Val Royal(FR) —Woodren (USA) (Woodman (USA))
7822a[0]
Gunslinger (FR) *M J Scudamore* a80 81
4 b g High Chaparral(IRE) —Gamine (IRE) (High Estate)
(6595) 7628[3] 7841[5]
Gurtavallig (IRE) *T J Pitt* 12
4 ch m Starborough—Alcadia (IRE) (Thatching)
1926[2] 2574[5]
Gurteen Diamond *P D Evans* a73 57
3 b f Kyllachy—Precious (Danehill (USA))
19[3] 236[2] 421[3] 655[12] (5882) 6028[3] 6216[5] 6725[7]
Guto *W J H Ratcliffe* a74 78
6 b g Foxhound(USA) —Mujadilly (Mujadil (USA))
326[10] 582[9] 742[3] 818[2] 884[4] ◆ 1360[13] (1564) 1776[6] 2225[6] 3713[2] 3959[2] 4183[4] (4886) (5374) 5675[6] (6051) 6359[8] 6791[14] 7355[8] 7577[10]
Guyno (NZ) *Lou Luciani* 107
6 br g O'Reilly(NZ) —River Century (NZ) (Centaine (AUS))
6961a[12]
Gwenllian (IRE) *J L Hassett* 48
2 b f Royal Dragon(USA) —Desiraka (Kris)
7288[13]
Gwerthybyd *B Palling* a53 44
3 b f Auction House(USA) —Minette (Bishop Of Cashel)
2143[6] 2681[7] 3257[3]
Gwilym (GER) *D Haydn Jones* a76 74
6 b g Agnes World(USA) —Glady Rose (GER) (Surumu (GER))
15[12] 99[2] 243[9] (329) 451[5] 539[4] 757[4] 1748[3] 1877[11] 3057[3] 3407[6] 3917[4] 4604[3] (5020) 5436[P] (6642) 7191[4] 7478[10]
Gwynedd (IRE) *E S McMahon* 70
2 br f Bertolini(USA) —Bethesda (Distant Relative)
2360[2] ◆ (2919) 3807[7] 4850[9]
Gwyre (IRE) *T D Easterby* 52
3 b f Mull Of Kintyre(USA) —Boadicea (Celtic Swing)
2042[8] 2364[3] 2723[4] 5442[9]
Gypsy Boy (USA) *R Curtis* a68
2 bb c Dixie Union(USA) —Think Fast (USA) (Crafty Prospector (USA))
5311[5] 5664[4]
Gypsy Jazz (IRE) *Jennie Candlish* a49 66
2 b f Antonius Pius(USA) —Dawn's Folly (IRE) (Bluebird (USA))
3262[3] 3858[12] 6069[9] (6589)
Haadeeth *M P Tregoning* a78 85
2 b g Oasis Dream—Musical Key (Key Of Luck (USA))
(5311) 6104[2] 7150[6]
Haafhds Delight (IRE) *W M Brisbourne* a25 34
3 b f Haafhd—Twitcher's Delight (Polar Falcon (USA))
555[6]
Haafhd Time (IRE) *Tom Dascombe* a64 53
3 b f Haafhd—Amusing Time (IRE) (Sadler's Wells (USA))
1329[13] 1708[3] 2802[6] (3303) 4325[7] (4650) 5168[4] 5570[6] 6376[11]
Haajes *J Balding* a96 100
5 ch g Indian Ridge—Imelda (USA) (Manila (USA))
225[7] 359[7] (451) 491[3] 553[6] 785[5] 1018[17] 1189[5] 2094[6] 2259[10] 2591[3] 2897[9] 3377[3] 4069[2] 4285[2] 5767[8] (5871) ◆ 6050[10] 6694[7]
Haakima (USA) *C E Brittain* a68 84
3 bb f Dixieland Band(USA) —Be Fair (BRZ) (Fast Gold (USA))
(949) 1353[10] 1860[8] 6614[12]
Haarth Sovereign (IRE) *W R Swinburn* a86 86
5 b g Alhaarth(IRE) —Summer Queen (Robellino (USA))
(1319) 2815[12] 4212[2] 5094[5] 5961[6] 6636[9]
Haasem (USA) *J R Jenkins* a69 74
6 b g Seeking The Gold(USA) —Thawakib (IRE) (Sadler's Wells (USA))
155[7] 344[4] 1539[12] 7860[4]
Haashed (USA) *M Johnston* a89
3 ch g Mr Greeley(USA) —Guerre Et Paix (USA) (Soviet Star (USA))
863[14]
Haatheq (USA) *J L Dunlop* 64
2 b c Seeking The Gold(USA) —Alshadiyah (USA) (Danzig (USA))
4048[9] 5400[7] 6199[5]
Habaayib *E A L Dunlop* 105
2 b f Royal Applause—Silver Kestrel (USA) (Silver Hawk (USA))
1298[3] (1841) (3086) ◆ 3748[2] 6449[8]
Habshan (USA) *C F Wall* a87 90
9 ch g Swain(IRE) —Cambara (Dancing Brave (USA))
2083[3] 2639[6] 3752[8] 4262[8]
Hachi *J L Spearing* a19 55
2 ch f Kyllachy—Milly-M (Cadeaux Genereux)
1404[9] 2201[5] 2978[2] 3626[3] 4384[9] 5636[11]
Hadaf (IRE) *M P Tregoning* a87 94
4 b h Fasliyev(USA) —Elhida (IRE) (Mujtahid (USA))
3844[9] 4753[9] 5263[12] 5436[12]
Hada Men (USA) *L M Cumani* a69 83
4 b g Dynaformer(USA) —Catchy (USA) (Storm Cat (USA))
(2566) 4197[3] 4882[2] 5235[11] 5961[7]
Hafawa (IRE) *M Johnston* 93
2 b f Intikhab(USA) —Banaadir (USA) (Diesis)
(3187) ◆ 5038[2] (6756)
Hail Bold Chief (USA) *G A Swinbank* a64 69
2 b c Dynaformer(USA) —Yanaseeni (USA) (Trempolino (USA))
6672[9] 7121[5]
Hail Caesar (IRE) *A P O'Brien* 103
3 gr c Montjeu(IRE) —Alabastrine (Green Desert (USA))
1022a[4] 1388a[4] 1910a[4] 2288a[7] 3087[11] 3970a[8]
Hail Promenader (IRE) *B W Hills* a81 89
3 b c Acclamation—Tribal Rite (Be My Native (USA))
1751[5] 2399[6] 2841[2] 3643[6] 4326[2] 4909[2] 6645[9]
Hairspray *M R Channon* 88
2 ch f Bahamian Bounty—Quickstyx (Night Shift (USA))
2218[4] (2490) 3396[5] 3748[9] (4272) 4989[6] 6090[13] 6660[10]
Hairs Vital (IRE) *E J O'Neill* a61 70
2 b g Pearl Of Love(IRE) —Blue Banner (IRE) (Grand Lodge (USA))
1805[4] 2231[4] 2694a[5] 4368a[9] 4370[5] 5371[5]
Hajar (USA) *M Johnston* 68
3 rg g Rahy(USA) —Laiyl (IRE) (Nureyev (USA))
2572[3] (3294)
Hajjaan (USA) *J L Dunlop* 79
2 b c Mr Greeley(USA) —Danzig Island (USA) (Danzig (USA))
7145[3] ◆
Hajmah (IRE) *Saeed Bin Suroor* a50 81
3 ch f Singspiel(IRE) —Midnight Line (USA) (Kris S (USA))
4991[3] (5718) 6552[5] 7066[8]
Hajoum (IRE) *Saeed Bin Suroor* a93 83
3 b c Exceed And Excel(AUS) —Blue Iris (Petong)
1704[2] (6551) 7026[2] 7227[4]
Halaak (USA) *D M Simcock* a66 66
3 br f Harlan's Holiday(USA) —Henderson Band (USA) (Chimes Band (USA))
41[2] (91) 229[4] 2654[6] 2882[5] 3118[3] 3663[2] 4237[2] 4454[3] 5164[4] 6028[7] 6341[2] 6877[3] ◆
Halam Bankes *W G M Turner* 42
2 b c Lucky Owners(NZ) —Grace Bankes (Efisio)
7410[8]
Halcyon Dancer *M Dods* a48 51
3 ch f Reset(AUS) —Volitant (Ashkalani (IRE))
3093[4] 3764[6] 4277[3] 4997[6] 5599[3] 6252[6]
Halcyon Princess (IRE) *D G Bridgwater* a30 61
3 b f Barathea(IRE) —Serene Princess (USA) (Louis Quatorze (USA))
5063[7] 5503[13] 6031[10] 6371[12]
Haldibari (IRE) *S Lycett* a45 57
5 b g Kahyasi—Haladiya (IRE) (Darshaan)
1156[6] 1399[2] 2766[3] 5068[7] 6021[8]
Half A Crown (IRE) *M Dods* a17 64
4 b h Compton Place—Penny Ha'Penny (Bishop Of Cashel)
2134[11] 2316[7] 2529[14] 3002[9] 3938[6] 4436[8] 4552[3] 5443[10] (5727) 6410[4] 6799[10] (6989)
Half Pint Bill *D Persson* a45 88
6 b g Green Horizon—Anywhichway (Bijou D'Inde)
5302a[10]
Half Sister (IRE) *R Hannon* 7
2 b f Oratorio(IRE) —Fifty Five (IRE) (Lake Coniston (IRE))
5021[10]
Halfway House *M L W Bell* a83 84
3 b g Dubai Destination(USA) —Zanzibar (IRE) (In The Wings)
1570[10] 2357[7] (3474) (4241) 4696[2] 5216[6] 5771[4] 6613[3]
Halfway There *J G Given*
2 b f Ishiguru(USA) —Hi Ho Silca (Atraf)
7816[10]
Halicarnassus (IRE) *M R Channon* a107 115
5 b h Cape Cross(IRE) —Launch Time (USA) (Relaunch (USA))
(415a) 613a[7] 703a[4] 913[4] 1004[6] (1306) 1526[6] 1799[8] 1875[2] 2327[2] 2677[2] 3089[9] 3585[5] 4329[8] 4484[3] 5023[2] (5619a) 6056[5] 6893a[4] 7031[11]
Haling Park (UAE) *G L Moore* a47 56
3 b f Halling(USA) —Friendly (USA) (Lear Fan (USA))
2433[10] 2795[15] 4180[8] 4704[4] 5775[10] 6338[6] 6787[9] 7765[5]
Haljaferia (UAE) *D R C Elsworth* a70 78
3 ch g Halling(USA) —Melisendra (FR) (Highest Honor (FR))
121[3] 272[3] 1349[4] (1681) 2060[9] 2850[5] 3090[13] 4319[11]
Halkin (USA) *F Nass* a97 78
7 br h Chester House(USA) —Estala (Be My Guest (USA))
340a[8] 414a[3] 521a[5] 770a[11]
Halla San *R A Fahey* a91 102
7 b g Halling(USA) —St Radegund (Green Desert (USA))
585[8] 1790[3] 2501[3] 3143[7]
Hallhoo (IRE) *D Selvaratnam* a60 86
7 gr g Indian Ridge—Nuit Chaud (USA) (Woodman (USA))
413a[12]
Hallie's Comet (IRE) *A Kinsella* a79 102
3 b f One Cool Cat(USA) —Secretariat's Tap (USA) (Pleasant Tap (USA))
1024a[8] 1911a[5] 2304a[6] 2777a[2]
Hallingdal (UAE) *J J Bridger* a85 77
4 b m Halling(USA) —Saik (USA) (Riverman (USA))
470[2] (557) 852[5] 866[7] 1067[8] 1405[10] 2434[8] 2775[3] 2977[3] 3408[6] 3812[5] 4150[8] 4441[7] 4714[3] 4899[4] (5285) 5602[7] 5915[5] 6346[2] 6583[4] 6973[9] 7323[6] 7539[8] 7775[4] 7823[2]
Hallingdal Blue (UAE) *H R A Cecil* a43 31
3 b f Halling(USA) —Blue Melody (USA) (Dayjur (USA))
2181[9] 3508[10]
Halling Gal *W R Muir* 76
3 b f Halling(USA) —Saik (USA) (Riverman (USA))
2433[5] (3100)
Hallstatt (IRE) *M Johnston* a77 83
3 ch c Halling(USA) —Last Resort (Lahib (USA))
(2395) 3026[5] 3573[3] 3808[2] 4008[2] 4247[6]
Hallucinating *H Candy* 10
2 b g Oasis Dream—Follow Flanders (Pursuit Of Love)
7145[14]
Halsion Challenge *J R Best* a50 31
4 b g King's Best(USA) —Zaynah (IRE) (Kahyasi)
43[4] 482[2] 587[3] 598[4]
Halsion Chancer *J R Best* a92 78
5 b g Atraf—Lucky Dip (Tirol)
163[3] 283[2] ◆ 2387[4] (2713) 3347[6] 3691[6] 4870[7] 5753[9]
Haltela (IRE) *K A Ryan* 84
2 b g Namid—Quivala (USA) (Thunder Gulch (USA))
2311[7] (2936) 4000[4] 4803[5] 6011[4] 6643[7] 7013[10]
Halyard (IRE) *W R Swinburn* 65
2 b c Halling(USA) —Brindisi (Dr Fong (USA))
3584[7] ◆ 5966[5]
Hamaasy *G A Ham* a68 53
8 b g Machiavellian(USA) —Sakha (Wolfhound (USA))
14[2] 95[2] 223[5] 489[2] 607[6] 619[10] 793[8] 921[3] 975[7] 1438[12] 4479[15] 5566[7] 6256[12]
Hambledon Hill *R Hannon* a64 75
3 ch g Selkirk(USA) —Dominica (Alhaarth (IRE))
2318[5] 2884[5] 3279[7] 3734[4] 4319[8] 4987[3]
Hambleton *B Smart* a46 26
2 b c Monsieur Bond(IRE) —Only Yours (Aragon)
1610[8] 6356[6]
Hamish McGonagall *T D Easterby* 106
4 b g Namid—Anatase (Danehill (USA))
1647[4] 2012[4] 2502[4] 2716[4] 3351[3] 4341[2] 5132[2] 5420[6] 5654[10] 6283[10] 6678[11] 7015[15]
Hamlool (AUS) *M F De Kock* a41
5 ch g Giant's Causeway(USA) —Sanctus (AUS) (Barathea (IRE))
521a[9] 639a[13]
Hamloola *W J Haggas* 72
2 b f Red Ransom(USA) —Dusty Answer (Zafonic (USA))
7288[3] ◆
Hammadi (IRE) *Doug Watson* a105 102
4 b h Red Ransom(USA) —Ruby Affair (IRE) (Night Shift (USA))
336a[8] 1010a[7]
Hammer *R T Phillips* a70 75
4 b g Beat Hollow—Tranquil Moon (Deploy)
102[2] 279[4] 660[6] 1571[8] 1892[6]
Hammer Of The Gods (IRE) *G C Bravery* a82 40
9 ch g Tagula(IRE) —Bhama (FR) (Habitat)
590[8]
Hamoody (USA) *P W Chapple-Hyam* 95
5 ch g Johannesburg(USA) —Northern Gulch (USA) (Gulch (USA))
1868[7] 4273[5] 5424[2] ◆ 5799[14]
Hanbelation (USA) *E F Vaughan* a51
2 bb f Malibu Moon(USA) —Baldellia (FR) (Grape Tree Road)
7585[10]
Hanbrin Bhoy (IRE) *R Dickin* a73 50
5 b g Cape Cross(IRE) —Sea Of Stone (USA) (Sanglamore (USA))
1604[10]
Handcuff *I Semple* a58 58
3 br g Lend A Hand—Peruvian Jade (Petong)
1095[4] 1583[9] 1969[11] 3672[7] 4196[5] 4425[5] 4937[9] 5629[14] 5946[11] 6010[8] 6380[10]
Hand Painted *P J Makin* a51 80
3 b g Lend A Hand—Scarlett Holly (Red Sunset)
229[9] 1969[3] (2377) (2810) 3592[2] 4148[2] (5154) 5937[5]
Handsinthemist (IRE) *P T Midgley* a67 57
4 b m Lend A Hand—Hollow Haze (USA) (Woodman (USA))
919[2] (976) (1055) 1241[6] 1564[5] 2130[5] 2625[5] 3002[10] 3657[5] 4192[6] 7709[3] ◆
Handsome Batchelor (IRE) *Andrew Oliver* 85
3 b c Trans Island—Batchelor's Button (FR) (Kenmare (FR))
2306a[8]
Handsome Cross (IRE) *W J Musson* a66 80
8 b g Cape Cross(IRE) —Snap Crackle Pop (IRE) (Statoblest)
4232[4] ◆ 4907[3] 5219[8] 6118[11] 6857[9] 7398[12] 7657[5] (7890)
Handsome Falcon *R A Fahey* a86 83
5 b g Kyllachy—Bonne Etoile (Diesis)
1123[5] 1722[2] 1952[2] 2891[4] 3353[6] 3560[4] 4400[2] 4881[2] 5333[8] 6250[2] ◆ (6496) 6645[7] 7194[5]
Handsome Maestro (IRE) *D Smaga* 109
3 b c Dansili—Graceful Bering (USA) (Bering)
1917a[5] 2755a[2] 3669a[6] 5496a[4] 6505a[4] 7208a[12]
Hannah Greeley (USA) *J R Boyle* a33 22
2 bb f Mr Greeley(USA) —Miss Hannah (USA) (Deputy Minister (CAN))
5807[12] 6592[11]
Hannicean *N B King* a73 78
5 ch g Medicean—Hannah's Music (Music Boy)
3024[4] 3635[8] 5035[7] 5698[10] 7416[11]
Hanoverian Baron *A G Newcombe* a85 92
4 b g Green Desert(USA) —Josh's Pearl (IRE) (Sadler's Wells (USA))
2470[14] 3091[28] 3467[4] 3956[11] (5997) (6733) ◆
Hansom (GER) *Frau E Mader* 102
3 b c Ransom O'War(USA) —Hosea (GER) (Lagunas)
2560a[3] 3670a[10]
Hansomis (IRE) *B Mactaggart* 72
5 b m Titus Livius(FR) —Handsome Anna (IRE) (Bigstone (IRE))
2366[2] (2529) (2964) 3148[2] 3484[2] 3612[8] 4657[3] 5069[10] 5514[7] 6221[4] 6413[8] 6765[16]
Hanson'D (IRE) *K A Ryan* 101
2 ch c Pivotal—Dinka Raja (USA) (Woodman (USA))
5234[4] ◆ (6046) 7017[7]
Hanta Yo (IRE) *J R Gask* a49 43
3 ch g Alhaarth(IRE) —Tekindia (FR) (Indian Ridge)
3161[7] 4860[8]
Happy And Glorious (IRE) *J W Hills* a48 39
3 ch f Refuse To Bend(IRE) —Wondrous Joy (Machiavellian (USA))
2516[6] 678[7] 3426[5] 3985[10] 5016[8]
Happy Anniversary (IRE) *Mrs D J Sanderson* a52 86
3 b f Intikhab(USA) —Happy Story (IRE) (Bigstone (IRE))
3341[3] 3825[2] ◆ 4228[2] 4708[4] 5175[5] 6695[10] 7287[5]
Happy Boy (BRZ) *M bin Shafya* a115 112
6 gr h Ski Champ(USA) —Ultra Maresca (BRZ) (Filago (USA))
184a[11] 417a[2] 773a[2] 1013a[9]
Happy Dubai (IRE) *B Smart* 73
2 ch c Indian Ridge—Gentle Wind (USA) (Gentlemen (ARG))
4774[2] 5360[3] 5669[3] 6214[3]
Happy Fellow (FR) *P Lefevre* a70 59
5 b m Astarabad(USA) —Helvetic Melody (FR) (Kendor (FR))
6981a[7]
Happy Forever (FR) *M Botti* a78 77
3 b f Dr Fong(USA) —Happyanunoit (NZ) (Yachtie (AUS))
1068[3] 1414[4] ◆ 1965[4] 2949[3]
Happy Light (FR) *G-E Martin* a39 25
10 ch m Officiel(FR) —On My Dress (FR) (Dress Parade)
5074a[6]
Happy Mood *G L Moore* 40
2 b f Piccolo—Love And Kisses (Salse (USA))
7182[15]
Happy Runner (BRZ) *E Martins* a103 88
6 b h Romarin(BRZ) —Miss Klairon (BRZ) (Turville (FR))
414a[10] 639a[12]
Happy Spirit (SAF) *H J Brown* 102
5 ch m Silvano(GER) —Happy Land (SAF) (Badger Land (USA))
180a[4] ◆ 416a[5] ◆ 643a[3] 772a[10]
Happy Wedding (IRE) *H-A Pantall* 85
3 b f Green Tune(USA) —Diamond White (Robellino (USA))
(5783a)
Happy Zero (AUS) *J Moore* 120
5 br g Danzero(AUS) —Have Love (AUS) (Canny Lad (AUS))
7746a[2]
Harald Bluetooth (IRE) *D M Simcock* a97 87
4 b h Danetime(IRE) —Goldthroat (IRE) (Zafonic (USA))
(17) ◆ (232)
Harbinger *Sir Michael Stoute* 116
3 b c Dansili—Penang Pearl (FR) (Bering)
1297[2] ◆ (1793) ◆ (4405) ◆ 5134[7] 7031[3]
Harbour Blues *A W Carroll* a83 89
4 ch h Best Of The Bests(IRE) —Lady Georgia (Arazi (USA))
1094[4] 1313[2] 1668[8]
Harcas (IRE) *M Todhunter* 65
7 b g Priolo(USA) —Genetta (Green Desert (USA))
1058[4] 1767[5] 2614[8] 3499[9] (4806) 5943[6] 6102[7]
Hardanger (IRE) *T J Fitzgerald* a36 64
4 b h Halling(USA) —Naughty Nell (Danehill Dancer (IRE))
3863[15] 4346[12] 5624[10] 6771[5]
Hard Ball *M Quinn* a57 74
3 b g Pivotal—Miss Pinkerton (Danehill (USA))
1034[10] 2048[16] 2863[14] 6742[15] 7094[8] 7246[7] (7727)
Hard Life (IRE) *A Candi* 100
2 ch f Peintre Celebre(USA) —Golden Fortune (Forzando)
6523a[10]
Hard Luck Story *I Semple* 68
3 br g Lucky Story(USA) —Howards Heroine (IRE) (Danehill Dancer (IRE))
1101[4] 1453[3] 1691[4] 5947[8]
Hard Rock City (USA) *M J Grassick* 93
9 b g Danzig(USA) —All The Moves (USA) (A.P. Indy (USA))
2289a[5] 4574a[6]
Harlech Castle *J R Boyle* a94 86
4 b g Royal Applause—Ffestiniog (IRE) (Efisio)
1227[12] 1510[7] 1806[3] 2276[14] 2980[2] 3347[5] 3956[12] 7026[12] 7437[10] 7478[3] 7613[8] ◆ (7870)
Harlequinn Danseur (IRE) *N B King* a45 57
4 b g Noverre(USA) —Nassma (IRE) (Sadler's Wells (USA))
(1960) 2222[5] 2294[6]
Harlestone Gold *J L Dunlop* 60
4 b g Golden Snake(USA) —Harlestone Lady (Shaamit (IRE))
1088[7]
Harlestone Snake *J L Dunlop* 79
3 b g Golden Snake(USA) —Harlestone Lady (Shaamit (IRE))
1670[10] ◆ 2479[3] (2881) 4442[6] 5666[P] (Dead)
Harlestone Times (IRE) *J L Dunlop* 73
2 b c Olden Times—Harlestone Lady (Shaamit (IRE))
4314[9] 5000[4] 5907[3] 6786[2]
Harley Fern *M E Rimmer* a25 5
3 b f Primo Valentino(IRE) —Its All Relative (Distant Relative)
7278[11]
Haroldini (IRE) *J Balding* a71 16
7 b g Orpen(USA) —Ciubanga (IRE) (Arazi (USA))
94[5] 224[5] 519[5] 607[2] ◆ 715[5] 823[6] 979[12] 1438[2] 1655[3] 2746[6] 3467[8] 3929[12]
Harquahala (IRE) *P Schiergen* a41 24
3 b f High Chaparral(IRE) —Distant Valley (Distant Relative)
5651a[11]
Harriet's Girl *A P Jarvis* 77
3 ch f Choisir(AUS) —Harriet (IRE) (Grand Lodge (USA))
1345[8] 1895[3] 2967[5] 3193[6] 4284[2] (4741) 5175[8] 5940[3] 7125[8] 7149[3]
Harrison George (IRE) *R A Fahey* a73 101
4 b g Danetime(IRE) —Dry Lightning (Shareef Dancer (USA))
1018[4] 2059[2] 3091[16] 3877[9] 4353[2] 4485[5] 5476[3] 5695[6] (6092) 6675[5]

Harrison's Flyer (IRE) *J M Bradley* a59 65
8 b g Imperial Ballet(IRE) —Smart Pet (Petong)
114[12] 242[11] 480[9] 2806[6] 2880[6] 3208[6] 5632[5] 5788[6]

Harris Tweed *Sir Mark Prescott* a65
2 b c Hernando(FR) —Frog (Akarad (FR))
6943[7] 7276[5]

Harris Tweed (NZ) *Murray & Bjorn Baker* 113
4 b g Montjeu(IRE) —Sally (NZ) (Prized (USA))
6871a[10] 7215a[5]

Harry Africa (IRE) *Mrs S Leech* 21
3 b g Catcher In The Rye(IRE) —Brave Dance (IRE) (Kris)
3740[7]

Harry Days (IRE) *P J Lally* a62 29
3 b c Alhaarth(IRE) —Blushing Minstrel (IRE) (Nicholas (USA))
7401[4]

Harry Hunt *Cecil Ross* a70 75
2 b g Bertolini(USA) —Qasirah (IRE) (Machiavellian (USA))
2302a[8] 7258a[8]

Harry Paget (IRE) *J R Best* 45
2 gr c Starcraft(NZ) —True Love (Robellino (USA))
4534[11] 6200[7] 6697[8]

Harry Patch *M A Jarvis* a87 89
3 b g Lujain(USA) —Hoh Dancer (Indian Ridge)
1639[3]

Harry The Hawk *T D Walford* 79
5 b g Pursuit Of Love—Elora Gorge (IRE) (High Estate)
2043[2] ◆ 2898[12] 4003[5] (4229) 4619[4] 5622[7]

Harry Up *M J Scudamore* a93 77
8 ch g Piccolo—Faraway Lass (Distant Relative)
2[4] (250) (349) 451[7] 553[5] (690) 756[4] 985[5] 1104[2] (1412) (1935) 2911[4] 3694[5] 7511[11] 7646[8]

Harting Hill *M P Tregoning* a62 48
4 b g Mujahid(USA) —Mossy Rose (King Of Spain)
1496[7] 1728[4] 4437[5] 5113[6] 6940[8] 7492[4] (7614)

Hartley *J D Bethell* 107
3 b g Lucky Story(USA) —Arctic Song (Charnwood Forest (IRE))
1987[2] 3846[3] 4521[2]

Hart Of Gold *R A Harris* a71 74
5 b g Foxhound(USA) —Bullion (Sabrehill (USA))
314[2] 475[2] 590[4] 739[3] 861[4] 1152[7] 1248[4] 1468[3] 1619[3] 1957[4] 2680[7] 2806[4] 3304[14] 3505[13] 7329[8] 7484[6] 7602[6] 7834[7] 7877[2]

Hartshead *W Storey* a84 86
10 b g Machiavellian(USA) —Zalitzine (USA) (Zilzal (USA))
4346[6] 4663[11] 4996[3] ◆ 5441[10] 5673[5] 6218[12]

Harty Boy (USA) *Jim Best* a67 48
3 ch g Stravinsky(USA) —Peanut Gallery (USA) (Mister Baileys)
386[4] 548[4] 649[4] 939[6] 1155[9] 1361[13] 1746[6] 7197[6] 7374[9] 7658[14]

Harvest Dancer (IRE) *B J Meehan* 79
2 ch c Danehill Dancer(IRE) —Autumnal (IRE) (Indian Ridge)
4986[4]

Harvest Song (IRE) *Sir Michael Stoute* 28
3 b g Sadler's Wells(USA) —La Mouline (IRE) (Nashwan (USA))
2090[10]

Hasanpour (IRE) *K J Burke* 65
9 b g Dr Devious(IRE) —Hasainiya (IRE) (Top Ville)
1399[8]

Hassadin *A B Haynes* a61 51
3 ch g Reset(AUS) —Crocolat (Croco Rouge (IRE))
662[7] 943[7] 1954[8] 2635[5] 4587a[3] 5123[4]

Hasty (IRE) *B W Hills* a72 90
2 b f Invincible Spirit(IRE) —Saramacca (IRE) (Kahyasi)
2017[5] 2711[2] 3270[2] (4239) 5797[5] 6447[3]

Hatch A Plan (IRE) *Mouse Hamilton-Fairley* a54 60
8 b g Vettori(IRE) —Fast Chick (Henbit (USA))
116[6] 443[5] 469[2] 601[7] 1409[6] 1578[5] 1980[5] 2516[2] (2650) 2912[3] (3533) 4150[9] 4563[14] 7767[8]

Hathaal (IRE) *Jim Best* a74 25
10 b g Alzao(USA) —Ballet Shoes (IRE) (Ela-Mana-Mou)
2634[11]

Hathaway (IRE) *W M Brisbourne* a47 51
2 ch f Redback—Finty (IRE) (Entrepreneur)
2089[5] 6245[6] 6544[10] 7799[9]

Hatheer (USA) *Kiaran McLaughlin* a100 86
2 b f Storm Cat(USA) —Golden Apples (IRE) (Pivotal)
7282a[4]

Hatman Jack (IRE) *B G Powell* a66 32
3 ch g Bahamian Bounty—Mary Hinge (Dowsing (USA))
315[4] 498[4] 826[8] 1095[7] 1580[13] 2515[13] 2630[3] (4748) 5584[5] 6699[11] 6914[7] 7890[6]

Hatta Diamond (IRE) *M Johnston* a68 76
3 ch c Pivotal—Moonshell (IRE) (Sadler's Wells (USA))
767[5] (939) ◆ 1428[6] 2356[4] 2571[6] 3543[3]

Hatta Fort *Saeed Bin Suroor* a109 112
4 b h Cape Cross(IRE) —Oshiponga (Barathea (IRE))
257a[6] (418a) 700a[2] 1299[8] 1989[6] 2668[7] 5618a[5]

Hattan (IRE) *M bin Shafya* a116 113
7 ch h Halling(USA) —Luana (Shaadi (USA))
527a[2] ◆ 772a[15]

Hatton Flight *A M Balding* a93 102
5 b g Kahyasi—Platonic (Zafonic (USA))
(1117) (1458) (1696) 3142[U] 3620[15] 5854[5]

Haulage Lady (IRE) *Karen McLintock* 64
3 b f Xaar—Blue Mantle (IRE) (Barathea (IRE))
1740[6] 2236[17] 2528[6] 3614[4] 4348[13]

Haunting *A G Foster* 16
3 b f Beat Hollow—Broken Spectre (Rainbow Quest (USA))
4599[12] 6766[9]

Hautevesne (FR) *Dominique Sepulchre*
2 ch f Okawango(USA) —Sizal (FR) (Sicyos (USA))
(7409a)

Have A Nice Day (GER) *S Smrczek* a55 63
4 b m Black Sam Bellamy(IRE) —Haraplata (GER) (Platini (GER))
5301a[4]

Havelock Flyer *C Grant* 32
2 b c Mujahid(USA) —Dragon Flyer (IRE) (Tagula (IRE))
2339[11] 2721[9] 3726[7]

Have More *B J Meehan* a44 32
2 ch f Haafhd—For More (FR) (Sanglamore (USA))
4603[15] 4980[11] 5284[12]

Having A Ball *P D Cundell* a71 51
5 b g Mark Of Esteem(IRE) —All Smiles (Halling (USA))
878[5] (1080) 1479[10] 6224[5] 6720[2] 6908[6] 7236[2] 7481[8]

Hawaana (IRE) *Miss Gay Kelleway* a85 78
4 b g Bahri(USA) —Congress (IRE) (Dancing Brave (USA))
(950) 1186[6] 1813[6] 3274[5] 3736[4] 4149[4] (6780) 7054[4] 7523[7] 7626[5] 7684[4]

Hawaass (USA) *M Johnston* 98
4 b g Seeking The Gold(USA) —Sheroog (USA) (Shareef Dancer (USA))
1172[2] 1460[12]

Hawkeyethenoo (IRE) *J S Goldie* a48 78
3 b g Hawk Wing(USA) —Stardance (USA) (Rahy (USA))
1740[4] 2143[3] 3018[5] 3684[2] (3942) 4171[8] 4594[6] 5158[3] (6308) ◆ 6489[2] ◆ (6988) ◆ 7119[4]

Hawkit (USA) *P Monteith* a72 78
8 b g Silver Hawk(USA) —Hey Ghaz (USA) (Ghazi (USA))
1690[11] 2718[7] 3098[2] 3911[8] 4529[4] 4898[3] 5334[6] 5732[2] 6156[5] 6769[4] 6987[5] 7174[2]

Hawkleaf Flier (IRE) *T D Easterby* 52
3 b f Hawk Wing(USA) —Flyleaf (FR) (Persian Bold)
1281[12] 1594[5] 1926[13] 2790[6] 4589[3] 4995[8]

Hawk Mountain (UAE) *J J Quinn* 90
4 b g Halling(USA) —Friendly (USA) (Lear Fan (USA))
(1665) 2283[4] 2895[2] (3380) 4332[2] 5235[4] 5823[5]

Hawksbury Heights *J J Lambe* a30 35
7 ch g Nashwan(USA) —Gentle Dame (Kris)
7751[12]

Hawk's Eye *M F De Kock* a41 86
3 br g Hawk Wing(USA) —Inchiri (Sadler's Wells (USA))
1928[2] 2206[9] 3115[3] 3357[3] (5101) (5366)

Hawks Home (USA) *M Al Muhairi* a82 94
6 b h Distant View(USA) —Altamura (USA) (El Gran Senor (USA))
262a[11] 415a[9]

Hawkspring (IRE) *S Parr* a70
3 b c Hawk Wing(USA) —Katavi (USA) (Stravinsky (USA))
4[4] (92) 205[7] 239[3] 363[2] 403[2] 530[2] 605[4] (649) 689[2] 776[8] 808[5] 924[6]

Hawkstar Express (IRE) *J R Boyle* a50 56
4 b g Hawk Wing(USA) —Band Of Angels (IRE) (Alzao (USA))
43[8] 169[4]

Hawridge King *W S Kittow* a65 85
7 b g Erhaab(USA) —Sadaka (USA) (Kingmambo (USA))
1571[6] 2194[6] 3073[5] (3532) 4212[4] 5252[2] 5917[5] 6368[4] 6734[4] 7151[2]

Hawridge Star (IRE) *W S Kittow* a42 73
7 b g Alzao(USA) —Serenity (Selkirk (USA))
6692[4] 6995[9]

Hayek *W Jarvis* a54 62
2 b c Royal Applause—Salagama (IRE) (Alzao (USA))
4756[10] 6061[12] 6781[12]

Hay Fever (IRE) *Eve Johnson Houghton* a60 76
3 b g Namid—Allergy (Alzao (USA))
4648[13] 5110[4] 6111[9] 6344[2] 6611[7] 7057[8]

Hayley's Girl *S W James* a45 38
3 b f Deportivo—Eurolink Artemis (Common Grounds)
4199[11] 5998[9] 6856[8] 7535[8] 7689[9]

Hayzoom *P W Chapple-Hyam* 65
2 b c Anabaa(USA) —Green Swallow (FR) (Green Tune (USA))
7099[5]

Hazelrigg (IRE) *T D Easterby* a78 81
4 b g Namid—Emma's Star (ITY) (Darshaan)
5148[9] 6159[3] 6434[3] 6846[10] 7171[9]

Hazelwood Ridge (IRE) *James Bernard McCabe* a71 57
6 b g Mozart(IRE) —Aguilas Perla (IRE) (Indian Ridge)
4360a[7] 7341a[13]

Hazy Dancer *M P Tregoning* a75 53
3 b f Oasis Dream—Shadow Dancing (Unfuwain (USA))
1789[6] 5876[7] 6634[5] 6975[4] 7238[7]

Hazytoo *P J Makin* a74 76
5 ch g Sakhee(USA) —Shukran (Hamas (IRE))
1121[3] ◆ 1320[11] (1890) 2549[10] 3057[7] 7627[8]

Headache *B W Duke* a60 53
4 b g Cape Cross(IRE) —Romantic Myth (Mind Games)
3735[9] 4376[4] 6256[5] 7152[5] 7239[2] 7462[4] 7517[3] 7591[7] (7726) 7796[7]

Head Down *Mrs L C Jewell* a80 81
3 b g Acclamation—Creese (USA) (Diesis)
98[3] 313[2] 548[3] 663[2] (869) 2638[2] 2926[3] 3341[7] 3801[3] 4322[4] (5016) 5574[7] 7883[9]

Head First *W Jarvis* a59 44
3 b f Dansili—Break Point (Reference Point)
4057[16] 4955[5] 5435[7] 6371[7] 6831[4] ◆ (7599) ◆ 7755[4] ◆ 7856[4]

Headford View (IRE) *James Halpin* a92 97
5 b m Bold Fact(USA) —Headfort Rose (IRE) (Desert Style (IRE))
3818[13] 5490a[26] 6267[3]

Head Hunted *E A L Dunlop* 63
2 b g Dubai Destination(USA) —Tropical Breeze (IRE) (Kris)
7243[4]

Heading East (IRE) *K A Ryan* a49 70
3 ch g Dubai Destination(USA) —Nausicaa (USA) (Diesis)
1040[5] 4074[6] 4660[8] 4822[10]

Heading To First *C E Brittain* 67
2 b c Sulamani(IRE) —Bahirah (Ashkalani (IRE))
3160[4] ◆ 3750[10]

Headline Act *J H M Gosden* a84 87
3 ch g Dalakhani(IRE) —Daring Miss (Sadler's Wells (USA))
1086[4] ◆ (1431) 1792[7] 2084[4] 4319[7]

Head To Head (IRE) *A D Brown* a58 56
5 gr g Mull Of Kintyre(USA) —Shoka (FR) (Kaldoun (FR))
62[3] (222) 327[5] 467[2] 619[9] 794[10] 895[10] 1781[2] 5729[9] 6433[11] 6581[3] 7176[6] 7427[2] 7572[4] 7709[2]

Head To Kerry (IRE) *D J S Ffrench Davis* a52 31
9 b g Eagle Eyed(USA) —The Poachers Lady (IRE) (Salmon Leap (USA))
65[6]

Heart Attack (FR) *G Martin* 88
3 b c Double Heart(FR) —Indefinite (FR) (Definite Article)
2755a[10]

Hearthstead Maison (IRE) *M Johnston* a107 117
5 b g Peintre Celebre(USA) —Pieds De Plume (FR) (Seattle Slew (USA))
183a[5] 703a[10]

Heart Of Dreams (AUS) *Mick Price* 121
4 b g Show A Heart(AUS) —Academy Of Dreams (AUS) (Royal Academy (USA))
7040a[7]

Heart Of Dubai (USA) *Micky Hammond* a69 50
4 b h Outofthebox(USA) —Diablo's Blend (USA) (Diablo (USA))
1366[8] 1520[5] 1955[10] 2237[16]

Heart Of Tuscany *W J Knight* a58 58
3 b f Falbrav(IRE) —Zarma (FR) (Machiavellian (USA))
1771[5] ◆ 2204[10] 3777[6] 4206[6] 4640[9]

Heartsease *J G Portman* a23 62
3 b f Pursuit Of Love—Balsamita (FR) (Midyan (USA))
1363[3] 1670[8] 2515[6] 3209[10] 3741[2] 4224[8] 4745[6]

Heart Shaped (USA) *A P O'Brien* 110
3 ch f Storm Cat(USA) —Twenty Eight Carat (USA) (Alydar (USA))
1024a[2] 1698[4] 3088[6] 3516a[5] 5079a[8] 5686a[7]

Hearts Of Fire *Pat Eddery* 117
2 b c Firebreak—Alexander Ballet (Mind Games)
(994) 1290[4] 2260[2] 2995[5] 4049[2] (5085a) (5652a) (6716a)

Heathyards Junior *R Hollinshead* a68
3 b g Beat All(USA) —Heathyards Lady (USA) (Mining (USA))
7004[6] 7278[5] (7671)

Heathyards Pride *R Hollinshead* a89 84
9 b g Polar Prince(IRE) —Heathyards Lady (USA) (Mining (USA))
82[2] 330[2]

Heaven *P J Makin* a73 79
4 ch m Reel Buddy(USA) —Wedgewood Star (Bishop Of Cashel)
2053[7] 3261[4] 3998[7] 4604[7] 5323[9] 5719[6]

Heavenly Encounter *K R Burke* a28
4 b m Lujain(USA) —Inchcoonan (Emperor Jones (USA))
561[1] 508[7]

Heavenly Saint *C Roberts* a32 51
4 b m Bertolini(USA) —Heavenly Glow (Shavian)
3800[10] 5063[8] 5179[8] 5790[11] 5872[5] 6674[6] 6945[13] 7152[9]

Heavenly Stella (USA) *G A Swinbank* 34
4 bb m Wild Wonder(USA) —Nijivision (USA) (Superoyale (USA))
5520[9]

Heaven Or Hell (IRE) *P D Evans* a21 62
3 b g Jammaal—Adjasalma (USA) (Lear Fan (USA))
5631[5] 5872[6]

Heaven Sent *Sir Michael Stoute* a103 115
6 ch m Pivotal—Heavenly Ray (USA) (Rahy (USA))
(1697) 3012[2] 3749[2] 4522[7] 5686a[2] 6479[5]

Heaven's Heart (IRE) *Y De Nicolay* 98
2 ch f Captain Rio—Heaven's Command (Priolo (USA))
5279a[4] 5927a[2] 7230a[5]

Heavens Peak *M J Grassick* a12 65
3 ch f Pivotal—Lurina (IRE) (Lure (USA))
6031[11]

Hebridean (IRE) *L M Cumani* a95 114
4 b g Bach(IRE) —Delphinium (IRE) (Dr Massini (IRE))
6812[12] 7188[4] 7589[6]

Hector's House *M Dods* 70
3 b g Tobougg(IRE) —Thrasher (Hector Protector (USA))
1629[5] 2230[6] 3942[6] 4280[8]

Hector Spectre (IRE) *P D Evans* a72 64
3 gr c Verglas(IRE) —Halicardia (Halling (USA))
663[8] 752[3] 1040[3] 1462[18] 1811[2] 2865[8] 3257[5] 3741[6] (3929) 5630[8] 6031[5] 6370[9] (6966) 7198[2] 7512[5] 7695[3] 7737[4] 7881[2]

Hedgerow (IRE) *A Dickman* 56
2 b f Azamour(IRE) —Miss Childrey (IRE) (Dr Fong (USA))
4278[5] 4817[7] 6378[4]

Hekaaya (IRE) *M P Tregoning* a52 34
3 b f Kheleyf(USA) —Victoria Regia (IRE) (Lomond (USA))
4749[9] 5479[11] 5882[9]

Helaku (IRE) *R Hannon* 53
2 b c Rakti—Saibhreas (IRE) (Last Tycoon)
6066[11] 6697[9]

Helieorbea *T D Easterby* a73 76
3 b g Reset(AUS) —Rendition (Polish Precedent (USA))
2805[3] 3237[2] 3680[3] 4805[2] (5163) 5677[6] 6019[11] 6357[6] 6537[4]

Heligoland *A G Newcombe* a50 31
2 b f Trade Fair—Fine Frenzy (IRE) (Great Commotion (USA))
5379[7] 6291[9] 7209[7] 7597[7]

Heliodor (USA) *R Hannon* a107 104
3 b c Scrimshaw(USA) —Playing Footsie (USA) (Valiant Nature (USA))
1294[3] 1678[6] 2277[5] 4090[6] 4405[6] 5662[6] (6290) 7031[4]

Helipad (FR) *F-X De Chevigny* a72 81
3 b g Green Tune(USA) —High Living (USA) (Diesis)
7696a[10]

Hellbender (IRE) *S Kirk* a86 61
3 ch g Exceed And Excel(AUS) —Desert Rose (Green Desert (USA))
4[2] (45) 203[2] 276[3] 4267[5] 4535[7] 5937[7] 6120[2] 6444[3] 6642[3] (7028) (7252) ◆ 7486[6] 7617[6]

Hellenio *S C Williams* a54 65
2 b c Cape Cross(IRE) —Llia (Shirley Heights)
4194[9] 4638[4] 5312[12] 5748[5] 5985[7] 6367[3] 7097[9]

Hello Morning (FR) *E Charpy* a89 112
4 gr h Poliglote—Hello Molly (FR) (Sillery (USA))
527a[7] 703a[12]

Hello My Lord (FR) *B Secly* a79 89
5 gr g Anabaa Blue—Hello Molly (FR) (Sillery (USA))
3045a[10]

Hello Sunshine *T J Pitt* a4 33
3 b g Deportivo—Full English (Perugino (USA))
1335[8] 1592[9] 1840[16] 4425[12] 5105[9]

Help From Heaven (IRE) *R Gibson* 97
2 b f Titus Livius(FR) —Heaven's Help (USA) (Royal Academy (USA))
6501a[6]

Helping Hand (IRE) *R Hollinshead* a65 69
4 b g Lend A Hand—Cardinal Press (Sharrood (USA))
108[9] 177[7] 1970[7] 3239[7] 3671[10] 3999[9] 5443[5] 5716[2] 6119[10]

Helpmeronda *W M Brisbourne* a49 61
3 b f Medicean—Lady Donatella (Last Tycoon)
137[3] 295[8] 403[5] 7857[12]

Hel's Angel (IRE) *Mrs A Duffield* 76
3 b f Pyrus(USA) —Any Dream (IRE) (Shernazar)
(2091) ◆ 2370[6] 2786[10] (3451) 3941[6] 4453[2] 4751[4] 4940[5] 5940[9] 6182[3]

Helvetio *Micky Hammond* a57 72
7 b g Theatrical(IRE) —Personal Love (USA) (Diesis)
735[8] 983[5]

Hendersyde (USA) *W R Swinburn* a88 96
4 ch g Giant's Causeway(USA) —Cimmaron Lady (USA) (Grand Slam (USA))
(1432) (2283) 3390[4] 4260[5] 6036[5] 6273[7]

Hennessy Island (USA) *T G Mills* a61 43
4 ch g Hennessy(USA) —Heavenly Dawn (USA) (Holy Bull (USA))
118[11] 6691[3] 2243[10] 2381[6]

Henry Havelock *C Grant* 37
2 ch c Noverre(USA) —Burmese Princess (USA) (King Of Kings (IRE))
6181[6] 6593[10] 7116[8]

Henry Holmes *Mrs L Richards* a53
6 b g Josr Algarhoud(IRE) —Henrietta Holmes (IRE) (Persian Bold)
3158[5]

Henry San (IRE) *A King* 74
2 ch c Exceed And Excel(AUS) —Esclava (USA) (Nureyev (USA))
4908[5] 5993[4] 6548[4]

Herawati *T D Easterby* 16
3 b g Celtic Swing—Lady Of Jakarta (USA) (Procida (USA))
1168[8]

Herbert Crescent *Ollie Pears* a64 75
4 b g Averti(IRE) —With Distinction (Zafonic (USA))
(321) 580[4] 959[12] 1276[13] 1734[14] 5229[9] 5883[4] 6674[2] 6800[2] 6999[2] 7599[8] 7782[6]

Herbier D'Ecajeul (FR) *X Betron* 69
2 b c Della Francesca(USA) —Bleuette D'Ecajeul (FR) (Epervier Bleu)
2694a[8]

Herecomesbella *P G Murphy* a51 50
3 b f Lujain(USA) —Blushing Belle (Local Suitor (USA))
296[4] 555[3] 678[4] 943[4] 1811[4] 2149[5] 2737[5] 3936[7] 4196[13]

Here Comes Danny *M Wigham* a75 60
3 b g Kyllachy—Clarice Orsini (Common Grounds)
208[6] (454) 797[5] 2300[11] 6455[6]

Herecomethegirls *M L W Bell* a53 38
3 b f Falbrav(IRE) —Always On My Mind (Distant Relative)
4472[6] 5348[4] 6029[6] 6608[6] 7211[7] 7374[5]

Hereford Boy *D K Ivory* a82 84
5 ch g Tomba—Grown At Rowan (Gabitat)
1150[11] 1425[2] 2053[5] 2397[7] 2929[8] 3860[10] 4203[3] 4791[7] 6588[6] 6738[2] (7052) 7479[9] (7586) 7830[4]

Here Now And Why (IRE) *K A Ryan* 87
2 br c Pastoral Pursuits—Why Now (Dansili)
1083[2] ◆ (1304) (1680) 3046[11] 4089[5] 4407[8] 5945[3] 6049[8] 6550[9]

Heritage Coast (USA) *H Morrison* a69 84
4 b m Dynaformer(USA) —Bristol Channel (Generous (IRE))
2796[4] 3250[3] 4828[2] (5205) 6733[7] 7048[12] 7413[9]

Hermione's Magic *P J McBride* a71 94
3 ch f Systematic—Eleonor Sympson (Cadeaux Genereux)
2001[3]

Hermoun (FR) *X Nakkachdji* 102
3 b c Septieme Ciel(USA) —Hermine (FR) (Kaldoun (FR))
7302a[2]

Hernando's Boy *K G Reveley* 69
8 b g Hernando(FR) —Leave At Dawn (Slip Anchor)
5625[11] 6097[7] 6558[5] 6845[4]

Heroes *Tim Vaughan* a84 85
5 b g Diktat—Wars (IRE) (Green Desert (USA))
(2378) 2773^{5} 4434^{5}

Heroi Do Bafra (BRZ) *Peter Miller* a90 106
7 br h Royal Academy(USA) —Brides Fantasy (BRZ) (Roi Normand (USA))
789a^{12}

Heron Bay *C F Wall* a103 101
5 b h Hernando(FR) —Wiener Wald (USA) (Woodman (USA))
1673^{13} 2342^{8} 3142^{13} 4091^{4} 4770^{3} *5641^{9}* 7018^{11}

Heronway (IRE) *W J Greatrex* a4
7 b g Heron Island(IRE) —French Willow (IRE) (Un Desperado (FR))
7557^{11}

Herrbee (IRE) *J L Spearing* a52 53
4 b g Mark Of Esteem(IRE) —Reematna (Sabrehill (USA))
215^{13}

Herrera (IRE) *R A Fahey* a64 76
4 b m High Chaparral(IRE) —Silk (IRE) (Machiavellian (USA))
(1125) 1366^{7} (2262) 2614^{6} 2895^{5} 3654^{6} 4332^{10} (5162) *5781^{4}* 6995^{10}

Herschel (IRE) *G L Moore* a78 75
3 br g Dr Fong(USA) —Rafting (IRE) (Darshaan)
1284^{9} 2174^{8} 2850^{4}

He's A Humbug (IRE) *J O'Reilly* a81 91
5 b g Tagula(IRE) —Acidanthera (Alzao (USA))
1885^{12} 1951^{11} 2059^{14} 2235^{8} 3339^{10} (3730) 4225^{18} 5073^{10} *7506^{7} 7643^{8}*

He's Cool (IRE) *Aidan Anthony Howard* a61 48
4 b g Viking Ruler(AUS) —Miss Progressive (IRE) (Common Grounds)
(7154) 7336^{10}

He's Got Rhythm (IRE) *David Marnane* a80 82
4 b g Invincible Spirit(IRE) —Kathy Jet (USA) (Singspiel (IRE))
6309^{6}

He's Invincible *B J Meehan* 59
2 b g Invincible Spirit(IRE) —Adamas (IRE) (Fairy King (USA))
2280^{6} 2853^{9} 3792^{5}

Heslington *M Brittain* a73 67
2 ch c Piccolo—Spice Island (Reprimand)
994^{11} 1188^{5} 1275^{2} *(6355)* ◆

Hettie Hubble *D W Thompson* 59
3 ch f Dr Fong(USA) —White Rabbit (Zilzal (USA))
1769^{7} 2593^{9} 3031^{7} 3614^{6} 3852^{3} 4528^{3} 4894^{2} 5306^{2} 5362^{4} 5621^{4}

Heureux (USA) *J Howard Johnson* 74
6 b g Stravinsky(USA) —Storm West (USA) (Gone West (USA))
1832^{5} 2156^{10} 2816^{3}

Hevelius *W R Swinburn* 97
4 b g Polish Precedent(USA) —Sharp Terms (Kris)
2468^{2} 3620^{6} ◆ 4340^{8} 6816^{2} 7293^{12}

Hey Presto *R Rowe* a51 19
9 b g Piccolo—Upping The Tempo (Dunbeath (USA))
2011^{9} *2824^{11}* 3421^{7}

Hey Up Dad *M Dods* 72
3 b g Fantastic Light(USA) —Spanish Quest (Rainbow Quest (USA))
1509^{5} 2230^{7} 2545^{5} 3156^{6} 3708^{4} 4004^{14} 5549^{5} 6052^{9}

H Harrison (IRE) *I W McInnes* a68 80
9 b g Eagle Eyed(USA) —Penrose (IRE) (Wolfhound (USA))
715^{6} 874^{3} 984^{8} 1060^{5} 1333^{10} 1766^{6} 2156^{11} 2381^{9} 2769^{13} 3331^{2} 3851^{7} 4977^{9} 5948^{8} 6103^{10} 6339^{9} 6587^{13} 7609^{8} 7787^{10}

Hibaayeb *C E Brittain* 110
2 b f Singspiel(IRE) —Lady Zonda (Lion Cavern (USA))
4792^{3} 5284^{2} 5825^{2} (6269)

Hibiki (IRE) *P J Hobbs* 85
5 b g Montjeu(IRE) —White Queen (IRE) (Spectrum (IRE))
(5509)

Hiccups *M Dods* 83
9 b g Polar Prince(IRE) —Simmie's Special (Precocious)
1016^{10} 1766^{4} 2269^{11} 2998^{2} 3488^{7} 4344^{4} 4592^{8} 4654^{5}

Hi Dancer *P C Haslam* a72 73
6 b g Medicean—Sea Music (Inchinor)
(8) 107^{8} (3291) 3450^{5}

Hidden Brief *M A Jarvis* 94
3 b f Barathea(IRE) —Hazaradjat (IRE) (Darshaan)
1488^{2} 1789^{4} (2847) 7291^{6} *7697a^{3}*

Hidden City (IRE) *J S Moore* 30
2 b c Elusive City(USA) —Lizanne (USA) (Theatrical (IRE))
2896^{13} 3547^{9} 4384^{12}

Hidden Door (IRE) *G Prodromou* a64 69
4 b m Montjeu(IRE) —Yaselda (Green Desert (USA))
1833^{9} 2332^{7} 5544^{11} *5886^{11}* 6001^{2} 6969^{10} 7094^{5}

Hidden Fire *D R C Elsworth* 54
2 b f Alhaarth(IRE) —Premier Prize (Selkirk (USA))
6730^{11}

Hidden Glory *Pat Eddery* a77 74
2 b g Mujahid(USA) —Leominda (Lion Cavern (USA))
6754^{4} *7326^{2} (7663)*

Hidden Horse *M R Channon*
5 b m Fasliyev(USA) —Hopping Higgins (IRE) (Brief Truce (USA))
230^{7}

Hierarch (IRE) *R Hannon* 60
2 b c Dansili—Danse Classique (IRE) (Night Shift (USA))
4336^{5}

Hi Fling *B J Meehan* a63 65
3 b c Oasis Dream—Crafty Buzz (USA) (Crafty Prospector (USA))
1730^{10} 2206^{8} 2865^{7} *(3383)* 4178^{12} 4917^{6} 5286^{12}

Higgy's Ragazzo (FR) *R Hannon* 77
2 b c Sinndar(IRE) —Super Crusty (IRE) (Namid)
5499^{5} (5787)

Higha (FR) *P Demercastel* a98 98
3 b f Vettori(IRE) —High Mecene (FR) (Highest Honor (FR))
5495a^{7} 6579a^{12}

High Achieved *P W Chapple-Hyam* 76
3 b f Dansili—Achieve (Rainbow Quest (USA))
(4324) 5007^{3}

High Ambition *R A Fahey* a37 84
6 b g High Estate—So Ambitious (Teenoso (USA))
2086^{14} 2665^{8} (3350) (4661) 5067^{3} *6878^{8}*

Highams Park (IRE) *J G Portman* 39
3 ch f Redback—Miss Caoimhe (IRE) (Barathea (IRE))
1440^{8} 2323^{12} 4470^{4} 4935^{8} 5430^{13}

Highcliffe Bridge (IRE) *N P Littmoden* a12 53
2 b f Avonbridge—Peig Sayers (IRE) (Royal Academy (USA))
1981^{6} 2319^{5} 2541^{3} 2861^{3} 3119^{3} (3958) 4271^{10} 4915^{9} *5573^{13}* 5935^{13}

High Comedy *Saeed Bin Suroor* 70
2 b c Exceed And Excel(AUS) —Ecstatic (Nashwan (USA))
6591^{4} 6922^{7}

High Constable *R Charlton* a78
2 b c Shamardal(USA) —Abbey Strand (USA) (Shadeed (USA))
7644^{3}

High Court (FR) *P Lefevre* a56 69
5 b g Trempolino(USA) —Linamox (FR) (Linamix (FR))
5204a^{5}

High Cross (IRE) *Sir Mark Prescott* a82 45
3 b f Cape Cross(IRE) —Overruled (IRE) (Last Tycoon)
306^{4} 488^{2} 621^{4} (759) 840^{3} 1105^{2} 1614^{7}

High Curragh *E J O'Neill* a70 91
6 b g Pursuit Of Love—Pretty Poppy (Song)
(1309) 1663^{4} 1849^{2} 2071^{12} 2570^{5} 3001^{11} 3828^{9} 4012^{3} *4372^{5}* 4621^{2} 4887^{3} 5409^{15} *5989^{8} 6458^{9}* 6924^{10} 7387a^{10} *7822a^{0}*

Highest Esteem *G L Moore* a74 55
5 b g Mark Of Esteem(IRE) —For More (FR) (Sanglamore (USA))
1154^{2}

High Five Society *S R Bowring* a59 62
5 b g Compton Admiral—Sarah Madeline (Pelder (IRE))
12^{6} 174^{8} (537) 578^{2} 792^{8} (2458) 4269^{12} *6074^{12}*

Highgate Cat *B R Millman* a54 56
3 b g One Cool Cat(USA) —Angry Bark (USA) (Woodman (USA))
503^{5} 869^{6} 2081^{9} 3075^{9}

High Heeled (IRE) *B W Hills* a81 117
3 b f High Chaparral(IRE) —Uncharted Haven (Turtle Island (IRE))
(1326) 1988^{4} 2672^{3} 3619^{3} (4287) 4522^{5} 6853^{4} (7031)

High Holborn (IRE) *B J Meehan* 67
2 b g Danehill Dancer(IRE) —Wedding Morn (IRE) (Sadler's Wells (USA))
3750^{12} 4258^{5} 4945^{7} 5742^{8}

High Importance (USA) *J Noseda* a69 71
2 b c Arch(USA) —Music Lane (USA) (Miswaki (USA))
6629^{4} ◆ 6962^{3}

Highkingofireland *A P Jarvis* 71
3 br g Danehill Dancer(IRE) —Lucky Date (IRE) (Halling (USA))
1015^{10} 1522^{4} (2105) 2925^{9} 3687^{6} 4074^{4} 7020^{7} 7247^{3}

Highland Bridge *D R C Elsworth* a59
2 b c Avonbridge—Reciprocal (IRE) (Night Shift (USA))
7199^{12} 7429^{3}

Highland Flight *J S O Arthur* 38
11 gr m Missed Flight—In The Highlands (Petong)
4586a^{6} 5541a^{8}

Highland Glen *Sir Michael Stoute* a101 102
3 b g Montjeu(IRE) —Daring Aim (Daylami (IRE))
(1874) 2275^{6} 3051^{6} ◆ *(6165)* (6571)

Highland Harvest *Jamie Poulton* a61 82
5 b g Averti(IRE) —Bee One (IRE) (Catrail (USA))
1603^{18} 2193^{8} 2434^{7} *3211^{8}* (3945) 4461^{7} 4733^{2} 5001^{10} 5916^{8} 6964^{15} *7327^{6}*

Highland Homestead *M R Hoad* a69 66
4 b g Makbul—Highland Rossie (Pablond)
6785^{12} 7328^{12}

Highland Jewel (IRE) *C G Cox* 59
2 b f Azamour(IRE) —Raysiza (IRE) (Alzao (USA))
5604^{12} 6730^{9}

Highland Knight (IRE) *A M Balding* 57
2 b c Night Shift(USA) —Highland Shot (Selkirk (USA))
6759^{8}

Highland Lassie (IRE) *B J Meehan* a26 64
3 b f Oasis Dream—Arlesiana (USA) (Woodman (USA))
2947^{12} 3696^{6} 4381^{2} 5063^{11} *5616^{8}*

Highland Legacy *M L W Bell* 95
5 ch g Selkirk(USA) —Generous Lady (Generous (IRE))
4260^{4} 5656^{7} 6851^{10} 7293^{8}

Highland Love *J T Stimpson* a67 72
4 b g Fruits Of Love(USA) —Diabaig (Precocious)
1845^{8} 4710^{16} *5227^{3}* 5622^{5} *6126^{7}*

Highland Quaich *D R C Elsworth* a75
2 ch c Compton Place—Bee One (IRE) (Catrail (USA))
6162^{6} (7024) 7363^{4} 7824^{6}

Highland River *A Sadik* a63 55
3 b g Indian Creek—Bee One (IRE) (Catrail (USA))
1193^{8} 1462^{9} 2982^{10} 5444^{7} *6720^{4} 7364^{9} 7752^{9} 7813^{9} 7855^{7}*

Highland Song (IRE) *R F Fisher* a53 52
6 ch g Fayruz—Rose 'n Reason (IRE) (Reasonable (FR))
327^{2} 480^{6}

Highland Starlight (USA) *C G Cox* a63 47
3 ch f Dixieland Band(USA) —Fran's Flash (USA) (Star De Naskra (USA))
3569^{6} 4240^{8} *5683^{6}* 6399^{9} *6771^{9}*

Highland Storm *B N Pollock* a58 78
3 b g Storming Home—Real Emotion (USA) (El Prado (IRE))
2126^{4} 2850^{7} 3222^{6} 3588^{2} 4740^{5} 5131^{9}

Highland Warrior *P T Midgley* a62 81
10 b g Makbul—Highland Rowena (Royben)
870^{6} 1227^{9} 1685^{14} 1951^{10} 2436^{7} 3065^{10} (3828) (3999) 4141^{11} 4311^{5} 4886^{12} 6010^{9} 6159^{5} 7081^{12}

Highly Acclaimed *Mrs A Duffield* a44 49
3 b f Acclamation—Ebba (Elmaamul (USA))
1174^{6} 1400^{9} 1725^{13} *2579^{5} 3955^{4}* 4279^{10} 4894^{8} 5145^{3} 5336^{4}

Highly Regal (IRE) *R A Teal* a86 77
4 b g High Chaparral(IRE) —Regal Portrait (IRE) (Royal Academy (USA))
(61) (210) (512) (807) 950^{3} (1187) 1603^{5} *3736^{3}* 4211^{9} 4501^{8} *(5663) 6944^{5} 7271^{5} 7523^{8}*

High Morning *D M Simcock* 43
3 br f Cape Cross(IRE) —Joharra (USA) (Kris S (USA))
1843^{8} 2318^{9} 3278^{8}

High 'n Dry (IRE) *M A Allen* a75 66
5 ch m Halling(USA) —Sisal (IRE) (Danehill (USA))
1122^{9}

High Office *R A Fahey* a69 79
3 b g High Chaparral(IRE) —White House (Pursuit Of Love)
1245^{3} 1953^{2} ◆ 2571^{4}

High On A Hill (IRE) *S Kirk* a52 74
2 b c Val Royal(FR) —Blue Kestrel (IRE) (Bluebird (USA))
5643^{9} 6162^{7} 6728^{3} *7267^{4}*

High Point (IRE) *G P Enright* a81 68
11 b g Ela-Mana-Mou—Top Lady (IRE) (Shirley Heights)
2429^{13}

High Profit (IRE) *James Moffatt* a61 58
5 ch g Selkirk(USA) —Spot Prize (USA) (Seattle Dancer (USA))
1062^{6} 1612^{5} 1955^{15} 2390^{9} *3223^{4}* 3499^{10}

High Ransom *M A Jarvis* 51
2 b f Red Ransom(USA) —Shortfall (Last Tycoon)
7034^{7}

High Resolution *Miss L A Perratt* a54 57
2 ch g Haafhd—Individual Talents (USA) (Distant View (USA))
3522^{7} 4209^{10} 4915^{11} *5224^{3} 5613^{3}* 6034^{2} *6491^{9}* 6983^{12}

High Ridge *J L Flint* a29 73
10 ch g Indian Ridge—Change For A Buck (USA) (Time For A Change (USA))
7176^{7} 7418^{12}

High Rolling *T D Easterby* 63
2 b g Fantastic Light(USA) —Roller Girl (Merdon Melody)
2721^{7} 3232^{6} 4138^{3} 4895^{4} 5595^{3} 6215^{5}

High Severa (IRE) *A P Jarvis* 78
3 b c High Chaparral(IRE) —Severa (GER) (Kendor (FR))
1328^{12} 2030^{3} (2229) 2855^{5} 3780^{10} 5333^{6}

High Spice (USA) *R M H Cowell* a80 83
2 b f Songandaprayer(USA) —Erin Moor (USA) (Holy Bull (USA))
(1700) ◆ 2408^{6} 3015^{9} 3762^{2} 4295^{9} 4752^{4} *6068^{3} 7108^{5}*

High Standing (USA) *W J Haggas* a87 118
4 bb g High Yield(USA) —Nena Maka (Selkirk (USA))
(1663) ◆ (2474) ◆ (3141) ◆ (4087) ◆ 5657^{3} ◆ 6304^{4}

High Tensile *J G Given* 24
3 b f Diktat—Shifty Mouse (Night Shift (USA))
4354^{11} 5010^{10}

Hightime Heroine (IRE) *J Noseda* a85 83
3 b f Danetime(IRE) —Esterlina (IRE) (Highest Honor (FR))
1704^{3} ◆ 2664^{2} ◆ 3764^{3} 4531^{2} (5110) 5937^{2} *6348^{2} 6630^{9} 7252^{3}*

High Trail (IRE) *Rae Guest* a29
2 b f Acclamation—Set Trail (IRE) (Second Set (IRE))
6228^{13}

High Twelve (IRE) *J H M Gosden* 103
2 b c Montjeu(IRE) —Much Faster (IRE) (Fasliyev (USA))
4209^{2} ◆ (4713) ◆ 6268^{4} 6849^{12}

High Ville (FR) *N Bertran De Balanda* a39
3 b f Highest Honor(FR) —Kadouville (FR) (Kaldoun (FR))
6980a^{8}

High Voltage *Mrs J L Le Brocq* 73
8 ch g Wolfhound(USA) —Real Emotion (USA) (El Prado (IRE))
(4586a)

Highway Code (USA) *M Johnston* 53
3 b g Street Cry(IRE) —Fairy Heights (IRE) (Fairy King (USA))
2930^{9} ◆ 3549^{7} 4347^{7}

Highway Magic (IRE) *A P Jarvis* a33 66
3 ch c Rainbow Quest(USA) —Adultress (IRE) (Ela-Mana-Mou)
2084^{6} 4389^{12}

Hikaru Ozora (JPN) *Y Ikee* 116
5 bl h Manhattan Cafe(JPN) —Cry With Joy (JPN) (Tony Bin)
7498a^{7}

Hilbre Court (USA) *B P J Baugh* a87 75
4 br g Doneraile Court(USA) —Glasgow's Gold (USA) (Seeking The Gold (USA))
125^{9} 224^{3} (362) 478^{10} 618^{2} 807^{7} (1479) 2274^{12} 3124^{9} 3811^{13} *6496^{11}* 6946^{3} 7271^{6} 7423^{3} 7711^{7} (7783) 7854^{2}

Hilbre Point (USA) *B J Meehan* 61
3 b g Giant's Causeway(USA) —Lady Carla (Caerleon (USA))
1295^{12} 1461^{12} 2038^{11} 2126^{12}

Hill Billy Rock (IRE) *Mrs S C Bradburne* a57 78
6 b g Halling(USA) —Polska (USA) (Danzig (USA))
3^{5} 2629^{5}

Hill Cross (IRE) *K G Reveley* 54
3 b g Barathea(IRE) —Darayna (IRE) (Shernazar)
1954^{9} 2340^{11}

Hill Of Clare (IRE) *G H Jones* a17 51
7 gr m Daylami(IRE) —Sarah-Clare (Reach)
1771^{12} 2318^{12} 4264^{2} 4935^{6} 6692^{13}

Hill Of Lujain *Ian Williams* a64 67
5 b g Lujain(USA) —Cinder Hills (Deploy)
292^{11} 473^{7} 682^{6} 1974^{12}

Hill Of Miller (IRE) *Rae Guest* a75 75
2 b g Indian Ridge—Roshani (IRE) (Kris)
2860^{3} ◆ 3613^{7} 4062^{4} *4647^{7}* 5274a^{6} 5769^{6} 6328^{6} *7477^{2} 7655^{4} 7786^{5} 7871^{7}*

Hillside Lad *R M Beckett* a71 66
3 b g Tobougg(IRE) —Cumbrian Concerto (Petong)
1414^{8} 2010^{6} 2478^{4} 2888^{3} *3299^{9}* (3866) 4223^{4} 4787^{9} 5628^{14}

Hilltop Alchemy *J R Jenkins* a27
3 ch g Zaha(CAN) —Saferjel (Elmaamul (USA))
3168^{11} 4151^{13} *6225^{10} 6375^{12} 7110^{14}*

Hilltop Artistry *S W James* a28 65
3 b c Polish Precedent(USA) —Hilltop (Absalom)
2317^{4} 2863^{11} 3207^{3} 3708^{3}

Hilltop Legacy *J R Jenkins* a35 53
6 b m Danzig Connection(USA) —Hilltop (Absalom)
552^{7} 661^{13} 3071^{4} 4183^{10} 4665^{6}

Hill Tribe *J R Best* 77
2 b f Tiger Hill(IRE) —Morning Queen (GER) (Konigsstuhl (GER))
4577a^{7} 5026^{5} 5284^{3}

Hillview Boy (IRE) *J S Goldie* 100
5 bb g Bishop Of Cashel—Arandora Star (USA) (Sagace (FR))
(2030) 2392^{2} 2932^{3} 3826^{7} (4517) ◆ 5262^{13} 6013^{3} 7018^{2} ◆ 7293^{2}

Himalya (IRE) *J Noseda* a106 108
3 b g Danehill Dancer(IRE) —Lady Miletrian (IRE) (Barathea (IRE))
5862^{6} 6427^{6} ◆ 7150^{3} *7488^{3} 7768^{4}*

Hindford Oak Sioux *Mrs L Williamson* 62
3 b f Green Card(USA) —Sharp Susy (Beveled (USA))
4066^{7} 4879^{8}

Hindu Kush (IRE) *D Nicholls* a47 110
4 b h Sadler's Wells(USA) —Tambora (Darshaan)
1017^{5} 1546a^{2} 1790^{11} (2425a) 3048^{6} 3700a^{5} 4408^{7} 5248^{10} 5656^{8} 6138^{9} 6681^{7} *6875^{6}*

Hint Of Honey *A G Newcombe* a57 21
3 ch f King Charlemagne(USA) —Jugendliebe (IRE) (Persian Bold)
874^{4} 425^{9} 667^{4} 1465^{8} 2132^{8} 3281^{9} *(7855)*

Hinton Admiral *R A Fahey* a88 103
5 b g Spectrum(IRE) —Shawanni (Shareef Dancer (USA))
1649^{9} 2045^{10} (2456)

Hip Hip Hooray *L A Dace* a68 72
3 ch f Monsieur Bond(IRE) —Birthday Belle (Lycius (USA))
1284^{5} 1751^{11} 1928^{3} 2212^{2} 2884^{7} (3427) 3695^{5} 4441^{5} 4714^{4} *5616^{5}* 5915^{11} *6289^{7}* 6549^{8} *6780^{10}*

Hiporoi (FR) *M Boutin* 69
2 b c Indian Rocket—Baronne (FR) (Beaudelaire (USA))
5117a^{5}

Hippodrome (IRE) *John A Harris* a66 74
7 b g Montjeu(IRE) —Moon Diamond (Unfuwain (USA))
743^{7} 918^{9}

Hippolytus *J J Quinn* 81
4 ch g Observatory(USA) —Pasithea (IRE) (Celtic Swing)
1737^{11} (3151) 3864^{4} 4532^{2} 5160^{6} 5551^{5}

Hisaronu (IRE) *H R A Cecil* a69 67
3 b f Stravinsky(USA) —Journey Of Hope (USA) (Slew O'Gold (USA))
1269^{5} ◆ *1532^{2}* ◆

Hi Shinko *B R Millman* 82
3 b g Shinko Forest(IRE) —Up Front (IRE) (Up And At 'Em)
(1045) 1305^{6} 2010^{13} (2562) 3118^{6} 3592^{4} 4223^{3} 4535^{2} 5154^{3} (5591) 5774^{2} 6476^{5} 6731^{14}

Hi Spec (IRE) *Miss M E Rowland* a52 38
6 b m Spectrum(IRE) —Queen Of Fibres (IRE) (Scenic)
78^{8} 210^{7} 3717^{8} 4376^{8} 4977^{8} 7110^{3} 7600^{3} 7719^{10}

Historical Giant (USA) *E F Vaughan* a49 57
4 ch g Giant's Causeway(USA) —Onima (USA) (Jade Hunter (USA))
193^{7} 444^{5}

Historic Occasion (IRE) *D K Weld* 75
2 b g Royal Applause—Intriguing (IRE) (Fasliyev (USA))
6317a^{14}

History Lesson *R Hannon* a82 91
3 ch c Golan(IRE) —Once Upon A Time (Teenoso (USA))
(1622) 2701^{4} 3280^{4} (3922) 4299^{8} 4827^{7} 6740^{2} 6996^{3}

Hitchens (IRE) *T D Barron* a104 111
4 b g Acclamation—Royal Fizz (IRE) (Royal Academy (USA))
(1367) 1989^{15} 2502^{6} 2716^{10} 3351^{8} 4523^{11} 5039^{6} 6091^{15} (6282) 6678^{3} 6994^{5}

Hitches Dubai (BRZ) *D Nicholls* 67
4 ch g A Good Reason(BRZ) —Orquidea Vermelha (BRZ) (Lucence (USA))
3175^{4} (3611) 4772^{8}

Hits Only Cash *J Pearce* a69 70
7 b g Inchinor—Persian Blue (Persian Bold)
1495^{3} 2458^{4} 3077^{2} *3470^{7} 3929^{7} (4645) 5103^{6}* 5364^{6} *5683^{7} (6074)* 6288^{10} 6860^{10}

Hits Only Jude (IRE) *D Carroll* a85 67
6 gr g Bold Fact(USA) —Grey Goddess (Godswalk (USA))
2576^{2} 2938^{19} *3956^{2} 4374^{2}* 4508^{4} 4662^{4} 5031^{9} 5675^{9} *6361^{2} 6495^{7} 7759^{4}*

Hits Only Time *D Carroll* a55 50
4 ch g Bertolini(USA) —South Wind (Tina's Pet)
2366^{14} 3561^{7} 3943^{14}

Hits Only Vic (USA) *D Carroll* a43 108
5 bb g Lemon Drop Kid(USA) —Royal Family (USA) (Private Terms (USA))
(2486) 3390^{8} (3874) 5173^{3} 5656^{10}

Hit The Switch *Patrick Morris* a65 69
3 b g Reset(AUS) —Scenic Venture (IRE) (Desert King (IRE))
797^{4} ◆ 1434^{10} 1740^{9} 2160^{10} 2227^{7} 2450^{6} 3099^{12} 3336^{9} 3976^{7} 4491^{7} 7418^{7} (7499) ◆ 7609^{5} 7678^{3} (7797) 7855^{6}

Hobby *R M Beckett* 100
4 b m Robellino(USA) —Wydah (Suave Dancer (USA))
1523^{2} 2974^{5} 3874^{10}

Hoboob (USA) *J L Dunlop* 58
3 ch f Seeking The Gold(USA) —Bint Salsabil (USA) (Nashwan (USA))
1488^{7}

Hobson *Eve Johnson Houghton* a76 76
4 b g Choisir(AUS) —Educating Rita (Emarati (USA))
(1634) 1773^{4} 2011^{3} 2459^{2} 2565^{2} 2799^{5} 3548^{5} 5429^{5} (6175) 6337^{5} 6562^{6}

Hogmaneigh (IRE) *J S Goldie* a106 111
6 b g Namid—Magical Peace (IRE) (Magical Wonder (USA))
1006^{2} 1676^{13} 2272^{6} 2704^{9} 3405^{8} 6091^{7} 6678^{12}

Hoh Hoh Hoh *R J Price* a68 111
7 ch g Piccolo—Nesting (Thatching)
785^{8} 996^{12} (1189) 1676^{2} 2481^{3} 2991^{13} 3848^{3} 4559^{6} 5765^{8} 6283^{14}

Hohrod *John A Harris* a13 37
3 ch g Tipsy Creek(USA) —Agara (Young Ern)
3712^{7} 4199^{12} 5010^{7} 7797^{8}

Holbeck Ghyll (IRE) *A M Balding* a97 99
7 ch g Titus Livius(FR) —Crimada (IRE) (Mukaddamah (USA))
1325^{12}

Holberg (UAE) *M Johnston* a82 108
3 b c Halling(USA) —Sweet Willa (USA) (Assert)
(1512) 2029^{3} (3090) ◆

Holden Eagle *A G Newcombe* a62 80
4 b h Catcher In The Rye(IRE) —Bird Of Prey (IRE) (Last Tycoon)
1357^{12} 2351^{3} 2932^{17} 5034^{7} 5532^{3} 6204^{5} 6941^{5}

Hold Fire *A W Carroll* a50 21
5 b m Lear Spear(USA) —Kahyasi Moll (IRE) (Brief Truce (USA))
2318^{11} 2851^{12} 3217^{12}

Hold Me *H R A Cecil* a57 37
2 ch f Hold That Tiger(USA) —Sultry Lass (USA) (Private Account (USA))
5839^{6} 6567^{11}

Hold Me Back (USA) *William Mott* a120 103
3 bb c Giant's Causeway(USA) —Restraint (USA) (Unbridled's Song (USA))
1225a^{2} 1688a^{12}

Hold On Tiger (IRE) *I Semple* 75
2 ch c Acclamation—Our Juliette (IRE) (Namid)
2623^{7} 2963^{2} (5360) 6048^{5} 6841^{6}

Hold The Bucks (USA) *J S Moore* a73 63
3 b g Hold That Tiger(USA) —Buck's Lady (USA) (Alleged (USA))
(16) 74^{3} 136^{4} 231^{2} 332^{2} 839^{4} 962^{9} 1148^{4} (1429) 1670^{5} 5574^{9} 6439^{3}

Hold The Star *Miss A Stokell* a65 51
3 b f Red Ransom(USA) —Sydney Star (Machiavellian (USA))
1198^{7} 1532^{8} 2141^{2} ◆ 4905^{9} 5121^{10} 6349^{6} 6807^{10} 7353^{10} 7459^{4} 7671^{7} 7730^{4} 7863^{6}

Hold Your Colour (IRE) *B J Meehan* 101
2 bg g Verglas(IRE) —Azia (IRE) (Desert Story (IRE))
2324^{6} (5256) (5521)

Holiday Cocktail *J J Quinn* a69 81
7 b g Mister Baileys—Bermuda Lily (Dunbeath (USA))
5671^{12} 6648^{12}

Holiday Maker *H-A Pantall* 27
3 b f Dubai Destination(USA) —Rawabi (Sadler's Wells (USA))
6150a^{9}

Holkham *N P Littmoden* a52 33
2 ch g Beat Hollow—Spring Sixpence (Dowsing (USA))
3944^{5} 5000^{13} 6026^{5}

Hollins *Micky Hammond* 79
5 b g Lost Soldier(USA) —Cutting Reef (IRE) (Kris)
(3705) 4541^{4} 5334^{8} 6681^{13}

Hollo Ladies (IRE) *James Coyle* 79
4 ch g Captain Rio—Lace Flower (Old Vic)
1546a^{5}

Hollow Green (IRE) *P D Evans* a41 88
3 b f Beat Hollow—Three Greens (Niniski (USA))
(1811) 2204^{9} 2350^{11} (2772) 3123^{6} (3462) 3922^{2} 4150^{5} (4166) (4382) 4827^{6} (5334) 6277^{3} 6419^{4} 6618^{12} 6996^{9} 7148^{8} 7291^{11}

Hollow Jo *J R Jenkins* a69 49
9 b g Most Welcome—Sir Hollow (USA) (Sir Ivor (USA))
(111) 234^{9} 461^{6} (467) 596^{3} (646) 861^{7} 1285^{7} 2920^{10} 5576^{4} 5989^{4} 7681^{5} 7839^{4} 7890^{2}

Holly Hawk (IRE) *Kevin F O'Donnell* 77
4 br m Dubai Destination(USA) —Kardashina (FR) (Darshaan)
5689a^{17}

Holly Hill (IRE) *Edward P Harty* a48 64
6 b m Indian Danehill(IRE) —Tidy Wager (IRE) (Catrail (USA))
2290a^{6}

Hollywood George *Miss M E Rowland* a57 55
5 b g Royal Applause—Aunt Tate (Tate Gallery (USA))
130^{8}

Holoko Heights *N J Vaughan* a61 65
4 br g Pivotal—Treble Heights (IRE) (Unfuwain (USA))
386^{10} 572^{9} 869^{10} 1254^{4} 1463^{3} 2233^{3} (2592)

Holyfield Warrior (IRE) *R J Smith* a65 28
5 b g Princely Heir(IRE) —Perugino Lady (IRE) (Perugino (USA))
(7438) 7718^{2} ◆ 7840^{3} ◆

Holyrood *Sir Michael Stoute* 87
3 b g Falbrav(IRE) —White Palace (Shirley Heights)
(1260) 2077^{3} 2715^{10} 4767^{8}

Home *C Gordon* a64 67
4 b g Domedriver(IRE) —Swahili (IRE) (Kendor (FR))
342^{7} 735^{2} 1378^{6} 3275^{5} 4951^{7} 7328^{9} 7751^{3}

Home Advantage *R Charlton* 28
2 b c Beat Hollow—Houseproud (USA) (Riverman (USA))
6792^{13}

Home Before Dark *R M Whitaker* a39 48
3 b g Bertolini(USA) —Compton Girl (Compton Place)
3449^{14} 4105^{12} 4995^{6} 6219^{9}

Homebound (USA) *J-C Rouget* 111
3 bb f Dixie Union(USA) —Black Speck (USA) (Arch (USA))
1237a^{4} (2521a) 4580a^{12}

Homebred Star *G P Enright* a47 40
8 ch g Safawan—Celtic Chimes (Celtic Cone)
2708^{8} 3158^{4} 5365^{10} 5975^{10}

Honest Broker (IRE) *M Johnston* a59 57
2 b c Trade Fair—Kashra (IRE) (Dancing Dissident (USA))
6381^{4} 6842^{7} 7167^{3} 7494^{4} 7722^{3}

Honest Quality (USA) *H R A Cecil* 97
3 b f Elusive Quality(USA) —Honest Lady (USA) (Seattle Slew (USA))
1599^{6} 3320^{10}

Honest Value (IRE) *Mrs L C Jewell* a57 56
4 b g Chevalier(IRE) —Sensimelia (IRE) (Inzar (USA))
(328)

Honey Berry (IRE) *Patrick Morris* a41 41
3 ch f Captain Rio—Daggers At Dawn (IRE) (Daggers Drawn (USA))
1120^{6} 1317^{10} 1400^{12} 2265^{6} 2593^{6} 3498^{6}

Honimiere (IRE) *G A Swinbank* 97
3 b f Fasliyev(USA) —Sugar (Hernando (FR))
2406^{4} 2786^{4} ◆ (3267) 3763^{3} (4139) (4401) 4896^{4} 5419^{2} (6114) 6813^{11}

Honkey Tonk Tony (IRE) *Luke Comer* a34 78
4 b h On The Ridge(IRE) —Lisa's Girl (IRE) (Distinctly North (USA))
6860^{9} 6918^{14} 7129^{12}

Honorable Endeavor *E F Vaughan* a63 61
3 b g Law Society(USA) —Lilac Dance (Fabulous Dancer (USA))
196^{2} 2489^{10} 2866^{4} 4703^{2} 5011^{13} 5990^{2} 6445^{4} 7415^{5} 7635^{7}

Honor In Peace (USA) *Wesley A Ward* a90
2 b c Peace Rules(USA) —Jeanne's Honor (USA) (Honour And Glory (USA))
3138^{16}

Honour Devil (ARG) *M F De Kock* a121
5 b h Honour And Glory(USA) —Diamond Fitz (ARG) (Fitzcarraldo (ARG))
610a^{3} 771a^{2} ◆

Honoured (IRE) *Sir Mark Prescott* a49
2 ch g Mark Of Esteem(IRE) —Traou Mad (IRE) (Barathea (IRE))
6638^{9} 7420^{7} 7522^{10}

Honours Stride (IRE) *Sir Michael Stoute* a47 82
3 b f Red Ransom(USA) —Dance Parade (USA) (Gone West (USA))
2192^{2} (2942)

Hoof It *M W Easterby* 66
2 b g Monsieur Bond(IRE) —Forever Bond (Danetime (IRE))
2663^{4} ◆ 4286^{4} (4652)

Hooligan Sean *H Candy* 73
2 ch g Ishiguru(USA) —Sheesha (USA) (Shadeed (USA))
4564^{6} 5722^{2}

Hoorang (NZ) *Ian Shaw* 106
7 b m Zerpour(IRE) —Kay Maree (NZ) (Rhythm (USA))
6961a^{5}

Hopeful Lady *I W McInnes* 27
3 b f Elmaamul(USA) —Tennessee Star (Teenoso (USA))
2789^{11} 3237^{4} 3975^{7} 5470^{12} 5972^{13}

Hope'N'Reason (USA) *D M Simcock* a32 30
2 bb f Stormy Atlantic(USA) —La Bataille (USA) (Out Of Place (USA))
3987^{10} 4711^{8}

Horatio Carter *K A Ryan* 99
4 b g Bahamian Bounty—Jitterbug (IRE) (Marju (IRE))
(1682) 2045^{2} 2266^{3} 3091^{9} (3391) ◆ 4297^{21} 4486^{13} 5695^{10} 6089^{24}

Horseford Hill *Miss J R Tooth* a85 90
5 b g In The Wings—Love Of Silver (USA) (Arctic Tern (USA))
6851^{23}

Horseradish *M L W Bell* a76 77
2 b g Kyllachy—Lihou Island (Beveled (USA))
6009^{2} 6356^{2} (6796)

Horseshoe Reef (AUS) *J R Gask* a81 70
6 b g Encosta De Lago(AUS) —Christies Beach (AUS) (Naturalism (NZ))
271^{2} ◆ 549^{7} 787^{5} 1051^{3} 1815^{9} 2923^{11} 3533^{3} 4169^{7}

Horsley Warrior *E S McMahon* a71 65
3 b c Alhaarth(IRE) —Polish Lake (Polish Precedent (USA))
1289^{8} 1780^{2} 2850^{11} 3466^{7}

Hosanna *J Barclay* a67 54
3 b f Oasis Dream—Rada's Daughter (Robellino (USA))
3656^{11} 4134^{14} 4531^{9} 4879^{6} 5396^{8} 5946^{9} 6410^{2}

Hoss Cartwright (IRE) *J Howard Johnson* 73
2 b g High Chaparral(IRE) —Her Grace (IRE) (Spectrum (IRE))
3823^{4} 4307^{2} (4811)

Hot Chilli *J R Fanshawe* a55
2 gr f Verglas(IRE) —Hot And Spicy (Grand Lodge (USA))
6372^{9}

Hot Diamond *P J Hobbs* a62 80
5 b g Desert Prince(IRE) —Panna (Polish Precedent (USA))
2706^{11}

Hotel Du Cap *Madeleine Smith* a92 95
6 br h Grand Lodge(USA) —Miss Riviera Golf (Hernando (FR))
2587a^{11}

Hot Form *M Botti* a45
2 b f Dr Fong(USA) —Hot Tin Roof (IRE) (Thatching)
6913^{6}

Hotgrove Boy *A G Foster* 44
2 b g Tobougg(IRE) —Tanwir (Unfuwain (USA))
5290^{6} 6011^{8} 6763^{10}

Hotham *N Wilson* a85 93
6 b g Komaite(USA) —Malcesine (IRE) (Auction Ring (USA))
1278^{16} 1849^{12} 2228^{8} 2363^{9} 2938^{10} 3354^{8} 3681^{3} 4134^{2} 4285^{4} (4355) 4899^{5} 5148^{2} 5343^{5} (5597) 5799^{2} 6050^{15} 6647^{2} (6897) 6994^{4}

Hot Prospect *M A Jarvis* 91
2 b c Motivator—Model Queen (USA) (Kingmambo (USA))
4286^{2} ◆ (5831) ◆ 6898^{6}

Hot Pursuits *H Morrison* a76 62
2 br f Pastoral Pursuits—Perfect Partner (Be My Chief (USA))
2175^{8} 3271^{3} 3745^{3} 6481^{14} (6903)

Hot Rod Mamma (IRE) *A Berry* a42 58
2 ch f Traditionally(USA) —Try The Air (IRE) (Foxhound (USA))
3571^{10} 3849^{5} 4349^{6} 5596^{4} 6169^{12} 7217^{3} 7331^{7}

Hot Six (BRZ) *G Duarte* 98
4 gr h Burooj—Babysix (USA) (With Approval (CAN))
6526a^{15}

Hot Spark *K A Ryan* a75 57
2 b c Firebreak—On The Brink (Mind Games)
5360^{6} 6493^{2}

Houda (IRE) *J G Portman* a35 49
2 ch f Trans Island—Islandagore (IRE) (Indian Ridge)
4603^{11} 4980^{12}

Houdella *B W Hills* 22
3 b f Josr Algarhoud(IRE) —Norbella (Nordico (USA))
1745^{9} 2151^{7}

Hounds Ditch *Eve Johnson Houghton* a30 58
2 b g Avonbridge—Pudding Lane (IRE) (College Chapel)
5866^{4} 6356^{9}

Houri (IRE) *J T Stimpson* a59 79
4 b m Alhaarth(IRE) —Witching Hour (IRE) (Alzao (USA))
1514^{9} 1785^{14} 2493^{12} 5469^{5} 6817^{10}

House Of Frills *T D Barron* 60
2 b f Paris House—Frilly Front (Aragon)
(1624) 3559^{3}

House Of Grace (USA) *Kenneth McPeek* a103 101
2 b f Limehouse(USA) —Gracility (USA) (Known Fact (USA))
7282a^{3}

House Of Rules *Miss J A Camacho* a24 60
2 b g Forzando—Bramble Bear (Beveled (USA))
5439^{6} 6356^{8} 6896^{6}

House Point *S C Williams* 56
2 b f Pivotal—Lighthouse (Warning)
6809^{8}

House Red (IRE) *B W Hills* a67 73
2 b g Antonius Pius(USA) —Cindy's Star (IRE) (Dancing Dissident (USA))
1404^{11} 2839^{5} 3792^{11} 5318^{6} (7055) 7359^{3}

Hovering Hawk (IRE) *B W Hills* a39
2 b f Hawk Wing(USA) —Cause Celebre (IRE) (Peintre Celebre (USA))
7396^{8} 7700^{12}

Howard *J L Dunlop* 72
3 ch c Haafhd—Dolores (Danehill (USA))
1489^{8} 1928^{8} 2548^{4} 3009^{5}

Howards Prince *D A Nolan* a6 48
6 gr g Bertolini(USA) —Grey Princess (IRE) (Common Grounds)
1096^{12} 1921^{11} 2436^{12} 3020^{8} 4036^{6} 5159^{9} 6161^{12}

Howards Tipple *I Semple* a66 67
5 b g Diktat—Grey Princess (IRE) (Common Grounds)
1558^{15} 2625^{2} 3020^{4} 3296^{5} 3484^{8} 4016^{8} 4778^{8} 5309^{4} 6160^{8}

Howards Way *D A Nolan* 62
4 b g Bertolini(USA) —Love Quest (Pursuit Of Love)
5727^{11}

Howdigo *J R Best* a92 94
4 b g Tobougg(IRE) —Woodrising (Nomination)
6106^{17} 6368^{3} 6440^{9} 6724^{2} 7018^{7}

Howdoyalikemenow (IRE) *K A Ryan* 31
2 ch f Captain Rio—Berenice (ITY) (Marouble)
2360^{11} 4001^{10} 4384^{13} 5942^{7}

How Many Times (IRE) *J R Gask* a37 72
4 b m Okawango(USA) —Blu Tu Miami (USA) (Robin Des Pins (USA))
849^{11}

How's She Cuttin' (IRE) *T D Barron* a99 93
6 ch m Shinko Forest(IRE) —Magic Annemarie (IRE) (Dancing Dissident (USA))
2^{3}

Huangdi (FR) *M Boutin* a69
3 b c Slickly(FR) —Lady Nora (FR) (Warrshan (USA))
(6980a)

Hubble Space *M Botti* a56
2 ch f Observatory(USA) —Double Stake (USA) (Kokand (USA))
7024^{6} 7450^{12} 7669^{4} 7788^{10}

Huck Finn (NZ) *M Madgwick* a53
9 b g Foxbay(NZ) —Reckless Spirit (NZ) (Straight Strike (USA))
193^{8} 346^{6} 443^{9}

Hucking Heat (IRE) *R Hollinshead* a84 70
5 b g Desert Sun—Vltava (IRE) (Sri Pekan (USA))
79^{6} 226^{3} 477^{4} 656^{8} 2442^{4} 2878^{6} 3721^{7} 4402^{5} 4710^{5} 6496^{6} 6806^{5} 7632^{4}

Hucking Hero (IRE) *J R Boyle* a76 73
4 b g Iron Mask(USA) —Selkirk Flyer (Selkirk (USA))
28^{2} 172^{4} 318^{7} 465a^{4} 653a^{6} 873^{4} 950^{4} 1073^{3} 1261^{6} 1382^{4} 1812^{3} 2039^{5} 5594^{5} 6758^{6} (7137) 7368^{6} 7490^{7} 7515^{5}

Hudoo *Saeed Bin Suroor* a70
2 ch f Halling(USA) —Zarara (USA) (Manila (USA))
(7157)

Huff And Puff *Mrs A J Perrett* 69
2 b c Azamour(IRE) —Coyote (Indian Ridge)
7146^{5}

Hugs Destiny (IRE) *M A Barnes* a64 64
8 b g Victory Note(USA) —Embracing (Reference Point)
1648^{10}

Hukba (IRE) *E A L Dunlop* a78 78
3 b f Anabaa(USA) —Banaadir (USA) (Diesis)
1329^{6} 2105^{2} 2942^{3}

Hulcote Rose (IRE) *S Kirk* a71 31
2 b f Rock Of Gibraltar(IRE) —Siksikawa (Mark Of Esteem (IRE))
3810^{12} 6722^{3} (6942)

Hum Again (IRE) *J S Moore* 19
2 b c Marju(IRE) —Kazatzka (Groom Dancer (USA))
4946^{12}

Humble Opinion *A King* a95 94
7 br g Singspiel(IRE) —For More (FR) (Sanglamore (USA))
761^{3} 1117^{4} 2597^{4} 2994^{20} 4274^{6} 4517^{7} 5321^{5} 5915^{3} 6059^{9}

Humidor (IRE) *R Charlton* 78
2 b g Camacho—Miss Indigo (Indian Ridge)
4377^{10} 6737^{2} 7058^{3}

Humourous (IRE) *B Storey* 46
7 b g Darshaan—Amusing Time (IRE) (Sadler's Wells (USA))
3059^{6} 3266^{P} 4873^{7}

Humungous (IRE) *C R Egerton* a87 104
6 ch g Giant's Causeway(USA) —Doula (USA) (Gone West (USA))
1798^{11} 2342^{12} 3067^{5}

Huntdown (USA) *Saeed Bin Suroor* 111
3 ch c Elusive Quality(USA) —Infinite Spirit (USA) (Maria's Mon (USA))
3398^{2} 5232^{5} 6058^{2} 6487^{7}

Hunterview *M A Jarvis* a96 98
3 ch g Reset(AUS) —Mount Elbrus (Barathea (IRE))
(1056) ◆ 1307^{4} 1801^{6} 4316^{6} 6229^{5} 6470^{2} (7018)

Hunting Country *M Johnston* a90 96
4 b g Cape Cross(IRE) —Steeple (Selkirk (USA))
1117^{6} 1593^{9}

Huntingfortreasure *M Dods* 75
2 b g Pastoral Pursuits—Treasure Trove (USA) (The Minstrel (CAN))
6047^{2} 6842^{2}

Hunting Haze *A Crook* a51 33
6 b g Foxhound(USA) —Second Affair (IRE) (Pursuit Of Love)
1767^{11} 2344^{12} 4193^{11} 4972^{11} 6817^{13} 7080^{11}

Hunting Tartan *J H M Gosden* 92
2 b c Oasis Dream—Delta (Zafonic (USA))
(5785) 6426^{8}

Hunting Tower *J J Lambe* a86 85
5 b g Sadler's Wells(USA) —Fictitious (Machiavellian (USA))
6095^{5} 6412^{2}

Hunting Tower (SAF) *M F De Kock* a86 112
7 ch g Fort Wood(USA) —Stirrup Cup (SAF) (Royal Chalice (SAF))
(257a) ◆ 339a^{9} 614a^{2} 770a^{7}

Hunt The Bottle (IRE) *M Mullineaux* a58 67
4 b h Bertolini(USA) —Zanoubia (USA) (Our Emblem (USA))
294^{9} 352^{6} 657^{5} 775^{3} 969^{6} 1496^{11} 1781^{13} 2245^{13}

Hurakan (IRE) *P D Evans* a79 78
3 gr g Daylami(IRE) —Gothic Dream (IRE) (Nashwan (USA))
6420^{9} 6740^{11} 6940^{2} (7362) 7607^{3} 7684^{5} 7811^{7} 7823^{4}

Hurforharmony (IRE) *Adrian McGuinness* a47 51
6 b m Orpen(USA) —Zolba (IRE) (Classic Secret (USA))
240^{5} 255^{6}

Hurlingham *M W Easterby* a77 84
5 b g Halling(USA) —Society (IRE) (Barathea (IRE))
999^{7} 1593^{4} 2249^{6} 3000^{2} 3266^{10} 4003^{7} 4471^{4} 4930^{6} 5671^{6} ◆ 6648^{11} 7271^{9}

Huroof (IRE) *Saeed Bin Suroor* a75 76
2 ch f Pivotal—Esloob (USA) (Diesis)
4797^{2} 5284^{4} (7396)

Hurricane Coast *D Flood* a64 36
10 b g Hurricane Sky(AUS) —Tread Carefully (Sharpo)
35^{3} 108^{3} (174) 216^{12} 682^{5} 832^{6} 921^{7} 1528^{8} 1938^{9} 2134^{6} 2441^{10}

Hurricane Hymnbook (USA) *Stef Liddiard* a82 104
4 b g Pulpit(USA) —April Squall (USA) (Summer Squall (USA))
2639^{10} 3431^{5}

Hurricane Spirit (IRE) *J R Best* a88 97
5 b h Invincible Spirit(IRE) —Gale Warning (IRE) (Last Tycoon)
3091^{22} 3795^{5} 4485^{21} 5104^{10} 5665^{7} (6168) 6633^{4}

Hurricane Thomas (IRE) *R A Fahey* a75 63
5 b g Celtic Swing—Viola Royale (IRE) (Royal Academy (USA))
2263[4] 2573[4] 3023[4] 3450[4] 4402[11] (4462) 4972[13] 5733[6] (6183) 6369[2] 6768[10] 7127[8]

Hurstpierpoint (IRE) *M G Rimell* a41 59
4 b m Night Shift(USA) —Double Gamble (Ela-Mana-Mou)
4538[10]

Hustle (IRE) *Miss Gay Kelleway* a89 91
4 ch g Choisir(AUS) —Granny Kelly (USA) (Irish River (FR))
766[5] 910[8] 1197[5] ◆ 1682[4] (2050) 2695[12] 3091[14] *3469[9]* 4064[6] 4641[5] *5167[5]* 6004[4] *6212[3]* ◆ *6630[8]* 7000[6] 7692[5] 7741[5]

Huygens *D J Coakley* a85 78
2 b c Zafeen(FR) —Lindfield Belle (IRE) (Fairy King (USA))
2649[5] (3344) *7685[3]*

Huzzah (IRE) *B W Hills* a89 105
4 b h Acclamation—Borders Belle (IRE) (Pursuit Of Love)
997[5] 1352[9] 3014[2] 3639[4] 4486[12] 5200[14] 6307[7] 6732[9]

Hyades (USA) *H R A Cecil* a96 95
3 bb c Aldebaran(USA) —Lingerie (Shirley Heights)
1328[5] (1632) 2296[2] 3049[6] 4455[6] *5313[6]*

Hyde Lea Flyer *E S McMahon* a84 71
4 b g Hernando(FR) —Sea Ridge (Slip Anchor)
199[2] ◆ 2495[10] 4881[10] 5441[14] *5887[11] 6496[7] 6861[5] 7672[4]*

Hydrant *P Salmon* a55 65
3 b g Haafhd—Spring (Sadler's Wells (USA))
7780[3]

Hymnsheet *Sir Michael Stoute* 83
2 b f Pivotal—Choir Mistress (Chief Singer)
(6920) ◆

Hyperbaric (USA) *Julio C Canani* a102 118
6 b g Sky Classic(CAN) —Teasing Charm (USA) (Skywalker (USA))
1011a[14]

Hyper Viper (IRE) *C Grant* a47 40
4 b g Atraf—Double Letter (IRE) (M Double M (USA))
3313[9]

Hypnosis *N Wilson* a40 90
6 b m Mind Games—Salacious (Sallust)
3236[5] 3565[3] 4753[2] 5436[14] 6051[3] *6359[12]* 6843[12]

Hypnotic *Jim Best* a19 69
7 ch g Lomitas—Hypnotize (Machiavellian (USA))
(3241) 3490[14] 3659[4] 5019[9] 5569[2] *6349[13] 7349[14]*

Hypnotic Gaze (IRE) *J Mackie* a63 72
3 b g Chevalier(IRE) —Red Trance (IRE) (Soviet Star (USA))
716[3] 939[4] 1193[4] 3156[5] 4070[3] 4348[2] 4562[5]

Hypnotist (UAE) *C E Brittain* a73 73
3 b g Halling(USA) —Poised (USA) (Rahy (USA))
786[3] ◆ *914[3] 1638[2]* 2329[5] 2535[6] 3321[7] 4918[5] 5475[6] 6174[4] 6997[4]

Hypnotized (USA) *M L W Bell* a82 69
2 b c Elusive Quality(USA) —Delighted (IRE) (Danehill (USA))
6754[5] ◆ *7130[5] (7430)*

Hysterical Lady *D Nicholls* a59 80
3 b f Choisir(AUS) —Royal Mistress (Fasliyev (USA))
(920) 1232[3] ◆ (1686) ◆ 3355[6] 4849[4] 5978[5] ◆ *6642[12]*

Iachimo *A P Jarvis* a54 54
3 ch g Sakhee(USA) —Latin Review (IRE) (Titus Livius (FR))
(889) 1157[9] 2162[13] 2454[3] 2726[5] 3176[10] 4343[3] 4942[6] 5345[9]

Ialysos (GR) *L M Cumani* 115
5 br h So Factual(USA) —Vallota (Polish Precedent (USA))
(2481) 3140[12] (3638) 4456[13] 5233[10]

I Am That (IRE) *S A Callaghan* a76 73
2 b c Statue Of Liberty(USA) —Victory Again (IRE) (Victory Note (USA))
(5146) 5445[4] *6585[3]*

I Am The Best *A Al Raihe* a92 92
3 ch c King's Best(USA) —Needles And Pins (IRE) (Fasliyev (USA))
526a[6] 768a[3] 1009a[11]

I Am The Man *B J McMath* a70
4 b g Auction House(USA) —Sally Gardens (Alzao (USA))
7694[2]

Iasia (GR) *Jane Chapple-Hyam* a73 97
3 b f One Cool Cat(USA) —Alanis (Warning)
1808[5] 3548[7] (3790) 4326[10] 5005[2] 5798[6] 6814[5] ◆ *7431[9]*

Ibbetson (USA) *W R Swinburn* a71 65
4 bb g Street Cry(IRE) —Object Of Virtue (USA) (Partners Hero (USA))
1401[5] 5869[9] 6547[6]

Ibmab *Mrs L Stubbs* a47 67
2 ch g Deportivo—Kilmovee (Inchinor)
2484[6] 2788[8] 4384[3] (4915) 5393[2] *5811[7]* 7098[12]

Ibn Hiyyan (USA) *M Johnston* a45 59
2 rg g El Prado(IRE) —Lovely Later (USA) (Green Dancer (USA))
3652[7] 5002[8] *6772[12]*

Ibrox (IRE) *A D Brown* a76 73
4 b g Mujahid(USA) —Ling Lane (Slip Anchor)
90[2] (178) 325[6] 493[9] (3098) 3654[8] 4710[3] 5308[4] 5962[9] *(7093) 7724[4]*

Ice And Fire *J T Stimpson* a53 44
10 b g Cadeaux Genereux—Tanz (IRE) (Sadler's Wells (USA))
967[5] 1273[7]

Ice Attack (IRE) *Patrick Morris* a38 44
3 gr f Verglas(IRE) —Little Whisper (IRE) (Be My Guest (USA))
881[5] 2530[4] 2740[5]

Ice Bellini *Miss Gay Kelleway* a68 58
4 ch m Erhaab(USA) —Peach Sorbet (IRE) (Spectrum (IRE))
168[2] 679[6] 1738[4] 1960[5]

Ice Cool Lady (IRE) *W R Swinburn* a62 72
2 gr f Verglas(IRE) —Cafe Creme (IRE) (Catrail (USA))
1569[6] *1933[6]* 2563[4] 3702[8] (5748) 6035[4] *7363[8]*

Ice Diva *P W D'Arcy* a70 70
2 gb f Verglas(IRE) —La Coqueta (GER) (Kris)
6567[7] 6992[5] *7277[2]*

Icelandic *F Sheridan* a107 112
7 b g Selkirk(USA) —Icicle (Polar Falcon (USA))
1384[4] 2287a[3] 2550[6] 4059[2] 5079a[3] 6661[14] 7292[6]

Iceman George *D Morris* a62 66
5 b g Beat Hollow—Diebiedale (Dominion)
792[3] ◆ *885[4]* 1014[4] *1463[10]* 1945[5] 2171[9] 2420[2] (2851) 3550[3] (4054) 4563[7] 5035[16]

Ice Planet *Mrs R A Carr* a78 87
8 b g Polar Falcon(USA) —Preference (Efisio)
401[5] 489[5] 2389[5] 4133[3] 4654[7] 6596[14]

I Certainly May *S Dow* a61 33
4 b g Royal Applause—Deep Ravine (USA) (Gulch (USA))
43[2] 186[8] 247[13] 482[9] 2675[13] 4450[7]

Icesolator (IRE) *R Hannon* a96 105
3 b g One Cool Cat(USA) —Zinnia (Zilzal (USA))
912[7] 1118[3] 1354[3] 1929[3]

Ice Viking (IRE) *J G Given* a68 68
2 b c Danehill Dancer(IRE) —Maddelina (IRE) (Sadler's Wells (USA))
4497[5] 5006[5] 5528[6] *6071[5]* 6478[18] 6793[6]

I Confess *P D Evans* a85 83
4 br g Fantastic Light(USA) —Vadsagreya (FR) (Linamix (FR))
1919 1248[6] 1682[5] 1876[3] *(2186)* 2491[5] 2976[5] *(3211)* 3628[8] 4409[14] 4560[5] 5206[2] 5243[5] *5753[3] 5887[3]* 6072[4] 6279[5] 6630[7] 6944[7] 7253[6] 7437[5] 7575[4] 7627[6] 7741[3] 7830[5]

Idealism *J H M Gosden* 35
2 b c Motivator—Fickle (Danehill (USA))
6792[10]

Ideal World (USA) *A Fabre* 116
4 b h Kingmambo(USA) —Banks Hill (Danehill (USA))
2522a[6] 3443a[6] 5497a[4]

Idefix De Cardam (FR) *J R Lotout*
13 b g Port Etienne(FR) —Seminole I (FR) (Faldor (FR))
5074a[0]

Ideology *A Fabre* 106
3 b c Oasis Dream—Kid Gloves (In The Wings)
4367a[5] 6657a[3]

Idle Power (IRE) *J R Boyle* a71 88
11 b g Common Grounds—Idle Fancy (Mujtahid (USA))
2188[11] *2396[5]* 2883[13] *3732[4]* 4009[8] *4791[3]* (5592) 6564[2] 6964[6] *7180[10]*

Idolino (GER) *J Hirschberger* 101
4 b h Tertullian(USA) —I Go Bye (GER) (Don't Forget Me)
2113a[7]

Idothea (IRE) *Dominique Sepulchre* 68
2 b f Sinndar(IRE) —Celestial Lagoon (JPN) (Sunday Silence (USA))
6576a[3]

Ifatfirst (IRE) *J S Goldie* a65 70
6 b g Grand Lodge(USA) —Gaily Grecian (IRE) (Ela-Mana-Mou)
(2817) 3095[4] 3654[2] 4345[5] 4755[6] 5291[6] (5943) 6313[3] 6822[7]

Iffy *A B Haynes* a55 48
8 b g Orpen(USA) —Hopesay (Warning)
5367[5] *6210[11] 6612[5] 7225[9]*

If I Were A Boy (IRE) *S Kirk* a77 76
2 b f Invincible Spirit(IRE) —Attymon Lill (IRE) (Marju (IRE))
5026[3] ◆ 5527[5] *5808[3]* 6693[6] *7003[2] 7359[5] 7434[3] 7604[5] 7622[5] (7816)*

If Only *J Jay* a63 60
3 ch g Monsieur Bond(IRE) —La Belle Dominique (Dominion)
394[3] 572[8] 1047[5] *1437[4] 2132[5] 4749[6]* ◆ *5809[2]* 6340[4]

If You Knew Suzy *R E Barr* a67 56
4 b m Efisio—Sioux (Kris)
178[2] 786[5] ◆ 1060[11] *1566[4] 1777[3]* 2246[12] *7728[8] 7853[6]*

Ignatieff (IRE) *Mrs L Stubbs* 83
2 b g Fasliyev(USA) —Genial Jenny (IRE) (Danehill (USA))
1126[5] 1358[5] 1623[2] 1920[4] 3006[2] 3446[3] 4327[8] (4546) (4875) 5945[5]

Igneous *D W Thompson* a30 48
3 ch g Lucky Story(USA) —Double Top (IRE) (Thatching)
3449[10] 4348[12] 5513[5] 5730[16]

Ignition *A Kirtley* a46 34
7 ch m Rock City—Fire Sprite (Mummy's Game)
564

Igor Protti *A bin Huzaim* a103 105
7 b h Opening Verse(USA) —La Busona (IRE) (Broken Hearted)
183a[7] *337a[9]*

Igotim *J Gallagher* a40 36
3 b g Umistim—Glistening Silver (Puissance)
2338[7] *2630[8]*

Igoyougo *G A Harker* 81
3 b g Millkom—Club Oasis (Forzando)
3063[2] ◆ (4777) (4942) 5517[4] 6387[2] (7119) ◆

Iguacu *George Baker* a58 58
5 b g Desert Prince(IRE) —Gay Gallanta (USA) (Woodman (USA))
1251[5] *1781[5]* 2223[3] 2353[6] 2879[10] 3215[2] (3631) *3929[13]* 6969[4] 7127[6] *7354[3] 7666[2] (7688) 7750[7]*

Iguazu Falls (USA) *Saeed Bin Suroor* a90 109
4 ch h Pivotal—Anna Palariva (IRE) (Caerleon (USA))
182a[12] *414a[15]*

Ike Quebec (FR) *J R Boyle* a77 69
4 ch g Dr Fong(USA) —Avezia (FR) (Night Shift (USA))
155[11] 309[3] 803[9] 898[7]

Iketi (GR) *Jane Chapple-Hyam* a62 31
3 b f Filandros(GR) —Eldora (FR) (Highest Honor (FR))
876[3] 1329[10] 5531[12] 6910[13]

Ildiko (USA) *Sir Mark Prescott* a63 36
2 b f Yes It's True(USA) —Eternity (Suave Dancer (USA))
6628[10] 6992[20] 7243[10]

Il Divo (GER) *A Wohler* 100
4 br h Dashing Blade—Independent Miss (GER) (Polar Falcon (USA))
1575a[6] 3201a[3] 5461a[3] *7704a[0]*

Ile De Re (FR) *F Head* 97
3 gr c Linamix(FR) —Ile Mamou (IRE) (Ela-Mana-Mou)
6198a[4]

Ile Royale *W S Kittow* a54 48
4 b m Royal Applause—Island Destiny (Kris)
2680[4] 3071[5] 3471[11]

Il Forno *D Nicholls* a59 72
2 b g Exceed And Excel(AUS) —Fred's Dream (Cadeaux Genereux)
2444[2] ◆ 3064[4] 3634[2] *3925[5]* 5853[7] 6556[2]

Il Grande Ardone *C Von Der Recke* a85
4 br h Dr Fong(USA) —Bombalarina (IRE) (Barathea (IRE))
226[8] 653a[14]

Ilie Nastase (FR) *E J O'Neill* a98 96
5 b g Royal Applause—Flying Diva (Chief Singer)
1684[9] 1821[10] 2197[4] 2612[5] *3509[5]* 3846[7] 4104[2] 4549[10] 4781[7] *6435[10] 7194[7] 7821a[0]*

Ilkley *M W Easterby* 44
2 b f Fantastic Light(USA) —Zakuska (Zafonic (USA))
5547[12] 5674[5] 6181[7]

I'Lldoit *G A Harker* 16
2 br g Tamayaz(CAN) —Club Oasis (Forzando)
4888[13]

Illicit *J R Holt* a65 33
4 b g Oasis Dream—Daring Miss (Sadler's Wells (USA))
4378[12] *7153[8] 7357[7] 7512[13]*

Illuminative (USA) *J H M Gosden* a74
3 b g Point Given(USA) —Pretty Clear (USA) (Mr Prospector (USA))
6073[2] 6608[2] (7004)

Illusive Spirit (IRE) *J H M Gosden* a68 70
3 b g Clodovil(IRE) —Poker Dice (Primo Dominie)
1297[7] *1963[5]* 2415[6] 2845[11] (4472) 6621[10]

Illustrious Blue *W J Knight* a113 114
6 bb h Dansili—Gipsy Moth (Efisio)
2327[4] 2677[3] 3139[6] (4484) 5619a[5] 6303[7] 7031[10]

Illustrious Prince (IRE) *J Noseda* a62 81
2 b c Acclamation—Sacred Love (IRE) (Barathea (IRE))
6627[5] 7145[2]

Il Portico *M R Channon* 47
2 b g Zafeen(FR) —Diddymu (IRE) (Revoque (IRE))
4048[11] 4933[6] 5907[10]

Ilston Lord (IRE) *M P Tregoning* 66
2 b c One Cool Cat(USA) —Canouan (IRE) (Sadler's Wells (USA))
4410[6] ◆ 5428[9] 5907[5]

Imaam *J L Dunlop* 87
3 ch c Pivotal—Khulood (USA) (Storm Cat (USA))
(1047) 2890[5] 3868[5] 4540[2] (4814)

I'm Agenius *D Burchell* a35 43
6 br m Killer Instinct—I'm Sophie (IRE) (Shalford (IRE))
12[9] 793[12]

Imaginary Diva *G G Margarson* a67 66
3 b f Lend A Hand—Distant Diva (Distant Relative)
34[7] 804[11] 1271[4] 1359[2] 2460[3] 2740[3] 3428[3] 4514[3] 4829[5] *5881[4]* 6186[4] 7100[6]

I'Malwaysright (IRE) *D R C Elsworth* a72 65
2 b g Namid—Tashyra (IRE) (Tagula (IRE))
1835[2] *2383[7] 2595[2] 2825[4]* 3006[8] *5776[2] (6802) 7156[8]*

Imbongi (SAF) *M F De Kock* 120
5 ch h Russian Revival(USA) —Garden Verse (SAF) (Foveros)
418a[2] 614a[4] 774a[4] ◆ 1553a[6] (3398) 3841[3]

Imco Spirit (IRE) *G M Lyons* a83 85
3 b g Invincible Spirit(IRE) —Treasure Hope (IRE) (Treasure Kay)
1801[5]

I'm In The Pink (FR) *P D Evans* 80
5 b g Garuda(IRE) —Ahwaki (FR) (River Mist (USA))
1407[13] 1681[4] 1771[3] 2351[6] (2442) 2781[2] 3206[4] 3847[8] 4561[3] 5028[7] (7248)

Imjin River (IRE) *M H Tompkins* a79 59
2 b c Namid—Lady Nasrana (FR) (Al Nasr (FR))
5431[9] 5693[6] 6754[8] *(7088) (7453)* ◆ *7536[3]*

Immaculate Red *C Roberts* a35 54
6 ch g Woodborough(USA) —Primula Bairn (Bairn (USA))
7766[10]

I'mneverwrong (IRE) *D R C Elsworth* 63
2 ch f Compton Place—Anthyllis (IRE) (Night Shift (USA))
2238[3] ◆

Im Ova Ere Dad (IRE) *D E Cantillon* a90 87
6 b g Second Empire(IRE) —Eurolink Profile (Prince Sabo)
1405[2] *2144[5]*

Impeccable Guest (IRE) *J Mackie* a30 59
6 b m Orpen(USA) —Perfect Guest (What A Guest)
1654[7]

Imperial Angel (IRE) *D Carroll* 54
3 gr f Tagula(IRE) —New Deal (Rainbow Quest (USA))
1954[10] 2340[12] 3018[12]

Imperial Delight *H Candy* 77
2 b g Royal Applause—Playgirl (IRE) (Caerleon (USA))
4568[4] 6737[3] 7145[8] ◆

Imperial Djay (IRE) *J R Holt* a64 67
4 b g Dilshaan—Slayjay (IRE) (Mujtahid (USA))
242[10] 381[5] 540[3] 675[2] 811[10] 844[7] 984[5] 1039[6] 2686[3] 2921[4] 3470[9] 3730[9] 4105[6] 4787[6] 5633[9]

Imperial Echo (USA) *T D Barron* a77 79
8 b g Labeeb—Regal Baby (USA) (Northern Baby (CAN))
2453[6] 2531[4] 5443[3] 5729[5] 6005[9] 6415[4]

Imperial Guest *G G Margarson* 98
3 ch g Imperial Dancer—Princess Speedfit (FR) (Desert Prince (IRE))
1300[7] 1675[15] 2035[8] 2469[5] 2934[17] 3747[6] 4148[3]

Imperial Harry *Jean-Rene Auvray* a77 36
6 b g Alhaarth(IRE) —Serpentara (Kris)
202[7] (311) 559[8] 848[3] 952[8] 4169[9] 4378[11] *6210[10]*

Imperial House *R A Harris* a65 67
3 b c Imperial Dancer—Cotton House (IRE) (Mujadil (USA))
2795[6] (3175) 4494[8] 5672[13] 6824[3] *7027[9] 7645[6]* ◆

Imperial Skylight *M R Channon* a68 64
3 gr g Imperial Dancer—Sky Light Dreams (Dreams To Reality (USA))
214[3] 267[2] 366[4] (542) 705[2] 826[2] 960[6] 1839[10] 2300[8] 2719[6] 3010[7] 4237[6] 4791[13] 5287[10] 5576[6] 6005[4] 6339[7] 6701[4] 7052[10] 7480[7] 7653[4] 7845[5] 7880[6]

Imperial Sword *T D Barron* a56 73
6 b g Danehill Dancer(IRE) —Hajat (Mujtahid (USA))
1039[10] (1310) 1694[2] 1832[4] (2225) 2436[11] 2966[8] 3065[6] 3612[7] 4015[6] 4508[2] (4772) 5516[10] 6989[9]

Imperial Warrior *H Morrison* a58 71
2 ch g Imperial Dancer—Tribal Lady (Absalom)
2187[6] ◆ 2792[3] 3920[7] 4488[11] 6619[8] *6948[3]*

Imperium *Jean-Rene Auvray* a66 65
8 b g Imperial Ballet(IRE) —Partenza (USA) (Red Ransom (USA))
(59) 311[3] 485[8] 597[3] 816[3] 1741[5] 2331[4] 2739[6] 5429[13] 5790[14] *6226[10] 7052[7] 7110[4]* 7417[9] 7688[11]

Implication *E A L Dunlop* a82 77
3 b f Pivotal—Insinuation (IRE) (Danehill (USA))
1128[2] ◆ 1406[7] *1937[2] 2600[2]* 2845[13] 4275[2] *5102[2]* (5731) *6168[6]* 6621[6] *7092[3]*

Imply *James Leavy* a73 86
3 b g Beat Hollow—Insinuate (USA) (Mr Prospector (USA))
2289a[4]

Imposing *Sir Michael Stoute* 96
3 b c Danehill Dancer(IRE) —On Fair Stage (IRE) (Sadler's Wells (USA))
1303[2] ◆

Impossible Dream (IRE) *A Kinsella* a63 97
5 b g Indian Danehill(IRE) —Recoleta (USA) (Wild Again (USA))
3898a[15] 4574a[14] 5141a[10]

Impressible *E J Alston* a52 96
3 b f Oasis Dream—Imperial Bailiwick (IRE) (Imperial Frontier (USA))
1190[2] (1505) 2058[3] (2530) 3173[2] (3372) 3806[7] (4530) ◆ 5203[10] 5871[5] 6283[2]

Impressionist Art (USA) *Patrick J Flynn* a65 59
3 ch f Giant's Causeway(USA) —Chalamont (IRE) (Kris)
7632[9]

Impressioniste (IRE) *E J O'Neill* 81
2 ch c Peintre Celebre(USA) —Al Amlah (USA) (Riverman (USA))
(5014a) 5494a[4] 5739a[7] 6927a[8]

Impression Sunrise (FR) *F Vermeulen* 68
3 ch c Peintre Celebre(USA) —Nimble Lady (AUS) (Fairy King (USA))
6149a[11]

Imprimis Tagula (IRE) *A Bailey* a104 71
5 b g Tagula(IRE) —Strelitzia (IRE) (Bluebird (USA))
1334 (606) 739[2] 934[2] (965) (1477) 1663[6] 1943[6] *2185[2] (2576)* 3097[4] 3469[5] 3497[3] 3956[8] 5370[2] 6010[20] 6359[10] 6434[6] 6879[4] (7337) (7656) 7741[2] (7837) ◆ (7862)

Impromptu *P G Murphy* a73 83
5 b g Mujadil(USA) —Pie In The Sky (Bishop Of Cashel)
799[3] 1121[7]

Improper (USA) *Mouse Hamilton-Fairley* a23 42
3 b g Northern Afleet(USA) —Bare It Properly (USA) (Proper Reality (USA))
2317[12] 2551[10] 4735[7] 5217[12] *6611[10]*

Impure Thoughts *D W Thompson* a42
4 br g Averti(IRE) —Blooming Lucky (IRE) (Lucky Guest)
7466[13]

I'm Super Too (IRE) *G A Swinbank* 71
2 b g Fasliyev(USA) —Congress (IRE) (Dancing Brave (USA))
4590[8] 5668[2] ◆ 5981[5]

Inca Noble (ARG) *M F De Kock* 90
5 ch m Ride The Rails(USA) —Inca (ARG) (Interprete (ARG))
180a[7] 416a[10]

Incanto Dream *C Lerner* 115
5 ch h Galileo(IRE) —Atlantic Blue (USA) (Nureyev (USA))
5932a[3] 6527a[8]

Inca Slew (IRE) *P C Haslam* a51 51
3 ch g City On A Hill(USA) —Con Dancer (Shareef Dancer (USA))
77[6] 134[8] 2802[8]

Inca Soldier (FR) *S A Harris* a66 62
6 br g Intikhab(USA) —Chrysalu (Distant Relative)
198[2] 292[8] 1258[8] *1606[6]* 4977[10] 5443[7]

Incendo *J R Fanshawe* a86 77
3 ch g King's Best(USA) —Kindle (Selkirk (USA))
1595[6] 2048[6] *3511[2]* ◆ 4545[4] 5035[5] 5975[2] *(6613)*

Inchando (FR) *A W Carroll* a21 57
5 ch h Hernando(FR) —Nordican Inch (Inchinor)
2150[11] 2851[11] *3710[11]* 4263[5] 4625[2] 4935[2]

Inch Lodge *Miss D Mountain* a70 66
7 ch h Grand Lodge(USA) —Legaya (Shirley Heights)
285[7] (507) 813[2] 3734[3] 3977[9] 4721[9] *5015[7] (5577) 6210[9]* 6303[12] *6584[4]* 7112[9] 7425[4] 7628[4] 7767[3]

Inchnadamph *T J Fitzgerald* a60 93
9 b g Inchinor—Pelf (USA) (Al Nasr (FR))
1383[9] 1790[6] 2895[7] 3793[5] 4332[3] 5235[8] 6115[10] 7117[4]

Inchpast *M H Tompkins* a76 80
8 ch g Inchinor—Victor Ludorum (Rainbow Quest (USA))
1635[6] 2018[4] (2429) (2614) 3191[6] 5410[8] 5642[4] 5917[3] 6115[6]

Incline (IRE) *R McGlinchey* a102 92
10 b g Danehill(USA) —Shalwar Kameez (IRE) (Sadler's Wells (USA))
1376a[13]

Incomparable *J A Glover* a84 87
4 ch g Compton Place—Indian Silk (IRE) (Dolphin Street (FR))
76[6] 243[2] 329[2] 400[2] (539) 632[4] 901[3] 4461[23] 5516[2] 5597[6] (5768) ◆ 6171[4] 6647[15]

Inconspicuous Miss (USA) *George Baker* a69 41
3 bb f War Chant(USA) —Orissa (USA) (Devil's Bag (USA))
1937[9] 2539[8] 3548[9] (6031) 6376[8] 6804[8] 6940[3] 7332[8] 7524[12]

Incy Wincy *J M Bradley* a39 31
3 b g Zahran(IRE) —Miss Money Spider (IRE) (Statoblest)
555[5] 598[5] 964[6] 1046[5] 7520[7] 7653[8] 7719[9]

Independent James (IRE) *S C Williams* a52 31
3 b g Singspiel(IRE) —Massomah (USA) (Seeking The Gold (USA))
599[5] 1047[12] 1255[9] 2340[13] 4065[5]

Indiana Fox *B G Powell* a15 55
6 b m Foxhound(USA) —Ridgewood Ruby (IRE) (Indian Ridge)
100[12] 187[7]

Indiana Gal (IRE) *Patrick Martin* a99 101
4 b m Intikhab(USA) —Genial Jenny (IRE) (Danehill (USA))
928a[7] 2647a[3] 6867a[6] (7300a)

Indian Art (IRE) *R Hannon* a81 89
3 b c Choisir(AUS) —Eastern Ember (Indian King (USA))
1324[10] 1677[5] 2826[2] 3116[7] 3455[2] (3577) 5182[2] 5575[9] 6630[5] 6731[9]

Indian Blessing (USA) *Bob Baffert* a117
4 bb m Indian Charlie(USA) —Shameful (USA) (Flying Chevron (USA))
1010a[2]

Indian Daffodil (IRE) *S Wattel* 109
4 b h Hernando(FR) —Danseuse Indienne (IRE) (Danehill (USA))
846a[9] 7704a[0]

Indian Days *J G Given* a105 108
4 ch h Daylami(IRE) —Cap Coz (IRE) (Indian Ridge)
1526[8] 1799[5] 2410[9] 3089[6] 3781[4] 4484[8] 5662[3] 5854[3] 6303[10]

Indian Diva (IRE) *P T Midgley* a86 83
4 b m Indian Danehill(IRE) —Katherine Gorge (USA) (Hansel (USA))
(179) ◆ 278[5] 538[7] 793[4] 922[7] 1020[9] 1436[7] 1832[8] 5254[11]

Indian Haze (IRE) *Daniel Mark Loughnane* a37 44
3 bb f Indian Haven—Hollow Haze (USA) (Woodman (USA))
5873[9]

Indian Pipe Dream (IRE) *S Gollings* 20
7 br g Indian Danehill(IRE) —Build A Dream (USA) (Runaway Groom (CAN))
6281[8]

Indian Saphir (FR) *R Lecomte*
4 b g Artan(IRE) —Indian Joy (GER) (Kings Lake (USA))
7821a[10]

Indian Skipper (IRE) *R C Guest* a89 81
4 b g Indian Danehill(IRE) —Rosy Lydgate (Last Tycoon)
1812[2] ◆ 2243[2] 2894[16] 4322[5] 4761[4] (5288) 5916[6] 6112[9] 6755[2] 7639[3] 7711[4] 7837[5]

Indian Story (IRE) *G C Bravery* a16
3 b f Indian Ridge—Law Tudor (IRE) (Law Society (USA))
503[9]

Indian Tonic (IRE) *W Jarvis* a63 73
3 b f Tiger Hill(IRE) —Wellspring (IRE) (Caerleon (USA))
4057[13] 5544[5] 5940[6] 6588[5] 6924[11]

Indian Trail *D Nicholls* a74 104
9 ch g Indian Ridge—Take Heart (Electric)
1053[4] 1457[3] 1849[8] 2363[4] (2704) 2897[6] 3351[5] 3784[7] 4341[5] 4461[4] 4485[10] 5132[13] 5507[4]

Indian Valley (USA) *Rae Guest* a73 70
2 b f Cherokee Run(USA) —Shade Dance (USA) (Nureyev (USA))
5981[2] 6372[2] 7033[8]

Indian Violet (IRE) *P F I Cole* a20 73
3 b g Indian Ridge—Violet Spring (IRE) (Exactly Sharp (USA))
1295[9] 1729[11] 2795[10] 3427[2] 4275[4] 4655[4] 5503[7] 6333[5]

India Tiberina (CHI) *M F De Kock* a97 33
4 ch m Indy Dancer(USA) —Isola Tiberina (CHI) (Rich Man's Gold (USA))
181a[2] 438a[9] 524a[12]

Indicible (FR) *A King* a89 83
5 ch g Dyhim Diamond(IRE) —Caslon (FR) (Deep Roots)
82[7] 4696[9]

Indigo Belle (IRE) *Mrs A Duffield* 29
3 b f Mull Of Kintyre(USA) —Frances Canty (USA) (Lear Fan (USA))
1440[6] 2042[11] 3123[9] 3614[7] 4617[6]

Indigo Ink *Miss Amy Weaver* a31 55
2 b f Rock Of Gibraltar(IRE) —Blue Indigo (FR) (Pistolet Bleu (IRE))
6451[8] 7120[3] 7482[8] 7690[6]

Indiscutible (CHI) *M F De Kock* a71 83
4 ch g Indy Dancer(USA) —Noche De Mayo (CHI) (Dancing Groom (USA))
258a[10] 435a[10] 524a[7]

Indochina *M Johnston* 73
2 b g Sulamani(IRE) —Lane County (USA) (Rahy (USA))
5590[5] 5951[4] 6533[2]

Indomito (GER) *P Vovcenko* 97
3 br c Areion(GER) —Insola (GER) (Royal Solo (IRE))
3669a[9]

Indonesia *T D Walford* a68 82
7 ch g Lomitas—Idraak (Kris)
1506[8] 2766[7] 3313[8]

Indy Driver *Matthew Salaman* a84 82
4 ch g Domedriver(IRE) —Condoleezza (USA) (Cozzene (USA))
932[5] 1192[2] 2052[4] 2684[6] 2916[4] 3637[7] (4305) (5511) 6004[5] 6476[6] 6695[9] 7054[2] 7684[3] 7848[7]

Inestimable *A Fabre* 106
4 b g Mark Of Esteem(IRE) —Tiyi (FR) (Fairy King (USA))
5497a[5]

Infamous Angel *R Hannon* 103
3 b f Exceed And Excel(AUS) —Evangeline (Sadler's Wells (USA))
1353[11] 1667[4] 1873[6] 2703[6] 3824[8] 4489[11]

Infanta (IRE) *Saeed Bin Suroor* 57
2 b f Cape Cross(IRE) —Maria Isabella (USA) (Kris)
7114[3]

Infinite Patience *T D McCarthy* a29 65
4 bb m High Chaparral(IRE) —Idma (Midyan (USA))
4084[8]

Infinity Bond *G R Oldroyd* a56 68
4 b g Forzando—Bond Girl (Magic Ring (IRE))
1737[10] 2156[4] 2453[2] 3105[6]

Infinity World *G R Oldroyd* a56 51
2 b f Lucky Story(USA) —Musical Refrain (IRE) (Dancing Dissident (USA))
4817[13] 5439[7] 7463[3] 7799[6]

Infiraad *B W Hills* 104
3 ch c Haafhd—Razzle (IRE) (Green Desert (USA))
(1295) ◆ (1677) ◆ 3011[16] 7185[9]

Inflammable *Sir Mark Prescott* a70 73
3 b f Montjeu(IRE) —Flame Valley (USA) (Gulch (USA))
6951[4] 7178[4] 7504[3] 7557[2] (7648)

In Footlights (USA) *Saeed Bin Suroor* 83
3 b c Elusive Quality(USA) —Triple Act (USA) (Theatrical (IRE))
(3168) ◆ 4020[5]

Informal Affair *J D Bethell* 49
3 b g Makbul—Fontaine Lady (Millfontaine)
3690[8] 4599[8] 4974[5]

Informed (USA) *Doug O'Neill* a113
5 b h Tiznow(USA) —Cajun Two Step (USA) (Tabasco Cat (USA))
1008a[7] 6687a[8]

Informed Decision (USA) *Jonathan Sheppard* a121
4 rg m Monarchos(USA) —Palangana (USA) (His Majesty (USA))
(7285a)

Ingenue *P Howling* a55 59
3 b f Hernando(FR) —I Do (Selkirk (USA))
4145[13] 5093[7] 5381[15] 6102[10] 6188[7] (6558) ◆ 6785[2] 7415[6]

Ingleby Arch (USA) *T D Barron* a99 93
6 b g Arch(USA) —Inca Dove (USA) (Mr Prospector (USA))
(382) 491[4] 1309[13] 1663[11] 2071[5] 2276[2] 2438[6] 2938[11] 3354[3] 3956[7] 4285[9] 6495[5] 6765[3] (6879) (6949) 7639[2] 7837[2]

Ingleby Lady *T D Barron* 96
3 ch f Captain Rio—Petra Nova (First Trump)
(1174) 2299[6] 2393[4] (3173) 3973[3] (4820) 5799[12] 6050[2]

Ingleby Princess *T D Barron* a64 74
5 br m Bold Edge—Bob's Princess (Bob's Return (IRE))
1169[12] 1369[5] 1890[8] 2529[4] 2964[9] 3296[3] 3484[6] 3972[2] 4375[5] 4552[5] 4876[5] 5730[4] 5953[4] 6414[6] 6987[6] (7050) 7422[4] 7678[4]

Ingleby Spirit *R A Fahey* a79 83
2 b g Avonbridge—Encore Du Cristal (USA) (Quiet American (USA))
1847[7] ◆ (2195) 3311[3] 4488[10] 5324[3] 6088[4]

Ingleby Star (IRE) *N Wilson* a67 79
4 b g Fath(USA) —Rosy Scintilla (IRE) (Thatching)
2225[8] 3002[7] 3445[4] (3657) 3909[2] (4136) 4283[2] (4467) 4877[4] 6233[9] 6489[6] 6902[9] 7119[7] 7758[6]

Inheritor (IRE) *B Smart* a91 87
3 b g Kheleyf(USA) —Miss Devious (IRE) (Dr Devious (IRE))
1971[4] 2504[3] 3062[3] 3643[5] (4591) 5432[6] 5766[7] 7189[13] 7558[2] (7734)

Inhibition *A M Balding* a84 86
3 br f Nayef(USA) —Spurned (USA) (Robellino (USA))
(1430) 1871[6] 2989a[4] 3778[6]

Inis Boffin *S Kirk* a74 78
3 b f Danehill Dancer(IRE) —Windmill (Ezzoud (IRE))
1491[3] (1937) ◆ 2858[9] 3209[2] 3462[7] 4050[11] 5063[2] 5366[5]

Inittowinit *W R Muir* a16 37
2 ch f Trade Fair—Moly (FR) (Anabaa (USA))
3160[8] 3716[10] 5543[12]

Inka Dancer (IRE) *B Palling* a64 56
7 ch m Intikhab(USA) —Grannys Reluctance (IRE) (Anita's Prince)
347[6] 473[2] 575[4] 661[8] 937[3] 1039[7] 1741[15]

Inler (IRE) *J R Best* 93
2 br c Red Ransom(USA) —Wedding Gift (FR) (Always Fair (USA))
(6809) ◆

Inlovingmemory (IRE) *R A Fahey* 62
2 b f Dubai Destination(USA) —Oiselina (FR) (Linamix (FR))
2541[2]

Innactualfact *L A Dace* a66 57
3 b f Lujain(USA) —Alzianah (Alzao (USA))
101[5] (205) 389[6] 595[6] 1193[11] 1834[13] 6705[11] 6917[10] 7250[14] 7687[10]

Inner Angel *M Botti* a72
2 ch f Motivator—Sea Angel (Nashwan (USA))
7106[3] 7451[2]

Inner Voice (USA) *J J Lambe* a22 57
6 gr g Cozzene(USA) —Miss Henderson Co (USA) (Silver Hawk (USA))
627[7]

Inn For The Dancer *J C Fox* a53 20
7 b g Groom Dancer(USA) —Lady Joyce (FR) (Galetto (FR))
213[5] 566[5] 734[6] 4263[14]

Inn Swinger (IRE) *W G M Turner* a42 26
3 b f Makbul—Sheik'n Swing (Celtic Swing)
75[9] 200[8]

Inpursuitoffreedom *P J McBride* a49 63
2 bb f Pastoral Pursuits—Quilt (Terimon)
5000[3] 6858[5]

Inquest *Mrs A J Perrett* a62 72
4 b g Rainbow Quest(USA) —Katy Nowaitee (Komaite (USA))
244[3] 500[2] 588[6]

Inquisitress *J J Bridger* a66 53
5 b m Hernando(FR) —Caribbean Star (Soviet Star (USA))
25[9] 100[4] 210[5] 443[7] 674[5] 813[6] 948[5] 4538[5] (5015) 5365[6] 5577[12] 5602[4] 6565[5] 6968[6] (7110) 7200[4] 7433[6] 7512[4] 7586[6] 7666[3] 7880[10]

In Secret *J L Dunlop* a67 75
3 b f Dalakhani(IRE) —Conspiracy (Rudimentary (USA))
1804[10] 3876[3] 4337[3] 5035[14] 5910[2] 6740[9] 6934[2] 7428[10] 7550[2] 7725[2]

Inshaallah *J G Given* a49 43
2 ch g Doyen(IRE) —Lake Diva (Docksider (USA))
6792[11] 7121[8] 7420[5]

Inside Knowledge (USA) *G Woodward* a48 57
3 rg g Mizzen Mast(USA) —Kithira (Danehill (USA))
686[8] 1882[10] 3955[7] 4230[3] 4491[6] 7080[10]

Inside Story (IRE) *C R Dore* a70 75
7 b g Rossini(USA) —Sliding (Formidable (USA))
155[4] 241[4] 289[7] 362[2] 512[4] 571[5] (622) 795[5] 1279[12] 2166[3] (2330) 2532[3] 3457[4] 4046[6] 4333[7] 4548[5] 5126[7] 5631[6] 6349[8] 6720[6] 7225[10] 7856[7]

Inside Track (IRE) *P T Midgley* a77 80
2 b g Bertolini(USA) —True Crystal (IRE) (Sadler's Wells (USA))
5220[9] 5627[2] 6291[2] 6727[5] 7177[6] 7435[6] 7669[3] 7690[3] (7781)

Inside Trade (IRE) *N P Mulholland* a47 53
3 b g Xaar—Azolia (IRE) (Alzao (USA))
1350[9] 2082[6] 2795[9] 5016[6] 5367[11] 6720[10] 7105[9] 7239[12]

Insignia (IRE) *Mrs A M Thorpe* a38 53
7 b g Royal Applause—Amathea (FR) (Exit To Nowhere (USA))
443[10]

Insolence (USA) *Sir Michael Stoute* a76 72
3 b f Mr Greeley(USA) —Brianda (IRE) (Alzao (USA))
2947[5] 3696[3] 4234[4] 5128[3] 6257[2] 6934[4] 7195[3] (7399)

In Some Respect (IRE) *Andrew Oliver* a102 104
2 b c Indian Haven—Burnin' Memories (USA) (Lit De Justice (USA))
3436a[2] 4359a[4] 5274a[2] 5661[4]

Insomnitas *Seamus Fahey* a54 54
4 b g Lomitas—Sleepless (Night Shift (USA))
5283[2] 6800[3] 7369[12]

Insouciance (FR) *D Prod'Homme* 64
2 b f Diktat—Zizoune (FR) (Kadrou (FR))
5956a[9]

Inspainagain (USA) *Paul Mason* a30 79
5 ch g Miswaki(USA) —Counter Cat (USA) (Hennessy (USA))
1776[8] 3407[7]

Inspector (TUR) *U Bekmezci* 117
5 b h Bin Ajwaad(IRE) —Pandora (GER) (Platini (GER))
5619a[6]

Inspector Clouseau (IRE) *T P Tate* a60 81
4 gr g Daylami(IRE) —Claustra (FR) (Green Desert (USA))
1886[4] 2392[9] 2783[2] 3380[5] 3809[8] (4972) 6280[7]

Inspiration (AUS) *J Moore* 119
6 ch g Flying Spur(AUS) —La Bamba (AUS) (Last Tycoon)
2116a[9] 7745a[9]

Inspirina (IRE) *R Ford* a75 79
5 b g Invincible Spirit(IRE) —La Stellina (IRE) (Marju (IRE))
2783[4] 3450[6] (3809) 3847[5] (4235) 4449[RR] 4561[4] 5802[4] 6560[4] 7020[2]

Instalment *R Hannon* 103
3 b g Cape Cross(IRE) —New Assembly (IRE) (Machiavellian (USA))
(1705) 3011[13] 3621[4]

Instant Recall (IRE) *M Al Muhairi* a48 103
8 ch g Indian Ridge—Happy Memories (IRE) (Thatching)
257a[2] 433a[2] 611a[2] 700a[5]

In Step *W J Haggas* a51 57
3 b f Montjeu(IRE) —Heart's Harmony (Blushing Groom (FR))
134[4] 205[9]

Instructor *C A Mulhall* a88 69
8 ch g Groom Dancer(USA) —Doctor's Glory (USA) (Elmaamul (USA))
4431[11]

Intabih (USA) *C E Brittain* a93 86
4 bb h More Than Ready(USA) —Lookaway Dixieland (USA) (Dixieland Band (USA))
(747) ◆ 1170[12] 1642[8] 2669[5] 3213[6]

Intapeace (IRE) *Francis Ennis* a87 90
2 b f Intikhab(USA) —Magical Peace (IRE) (Magical Wonder (USA))
1993a[10] 5452a[7] 5895a[8] 7258a[3]

Intavac Boy *S P Griffiths* a13 36
8 ch g Emperor Fountain—Altaia (FR) (Sicyos (USA))
3233[8] 4402[14] 6818[8] 7085[8] 7733[7]

Integral (GER) *R Rohne* 106
5 b h Lando(GER) —Incenza (GER) (Local Suitor (USA))
2525a[4] 4364a[4] 5059a[6]

Integration *Miss M E Rowland* a44 44
9 b g Piccolo—Discrimination (Efisio)
377[8]

Integria *J M P Eustace* a74 69
3 b g Intikhab(USA) —Alegria (Night Shift (USA))
2160[7] 2849[7] 3512[3] 4181[5] (6224) 6455[7] 6977[11]

Intense *B W Hills* a89 95
3 b f Dansili—Modesta (IRE) (Sadler's Wells (USA))
(6117) 6482[7] 7132[8]

Intense Focus (USA) *J S Bolger* 118
3 b c Giant's Causeway(USA) —Daneleta (IRE) (Danehill (USA))
1022a[2] 2992[5]

Interactif (USA) *Todd Pletcher* a77 115
2 b c Broken Vow(USA) —Broad Pennant (USA) (Broad Brush (USA))
7304a[3]

Interactive (IRE) *D Burchell* a71 68
6 b g King's Best(USA) —Forentia (Formidable (USA))
189[5] (245) 495[2] 721[2] 868[6] 1710[8] 5788[3] 6335[6] 6670[6] 7273[9] 7412[7] 7496[12]

Interakt *M R Channon* 69
2 b f Rakti—Amelie Pouliche (FR) (Desert Prince (IRE))
3249[5] ◆ 3522[2] 4638[3] 5505[4] 5787[3] 5970[5]

Interchoice Star *R Hollinshead* a59 52
4 b g Josr Algarhoud(IRE) —Blakeshall Girl (Piccolo)
480[3] 575[2] 746[5] 937[8] 1535[3] 1741[7] 6940[7] 7195[9] 7361[3] 7579[4] 7754[4] 7858[6]

Interdiamonds *M Johnston* a81 79
3 b f Montjeu(IRE) —Interpose (Indian Ridge)
2613[2] 2943[2] (3379) 3761[2] 4299[7] 4785[2] 5291[2] 5660[6] 6360[2]

Interest Free *T D Easterby* 54
2 b f Kyllachy—Holly Hayes (IRE) (Alzao (USA))
5949[8]

Interlace *Sir Mark Prescott* a78 61
2 ch f Pivotal—Splice (Sharpo)
5478[11] (5808) 6844[8] 7536[5]

Inter Mondo (GER) *Frau M Weber* 105
6 ch g Hondo Mondo(IRE) —In Natura (GER) (Monsun (GER))
5059a[11]

Internationaldebut (IRE) *J Balding* a102 98
4 b g High Chaparral(IRE) —Whisper Light (IRE) (Caerleon (USA))
204[9] 225[5] 284[4] 445[7] 551[3] 636[3] 724[8] 778[6] 913[12] 996[10] 1791[9] 1821[5] (2012) 2259[5] 2502[5] 2707[10] 2941[3] 3142[15] 3621[5] 4037[14] 5799[15] 6702[11]

Interpatation (USA) *Robert Barbara* 114
7 b g Langfuhr(CAN) —Idealistic Cause (USA) (Habitony)
(6511a) 7593a[14]

Intersky Charm (USA) *R M Whitaker* a73 80
5 ch g Lure(USA) —Catala (USA) (Northern Park (USA))
1192[10] 1478[6] (2968) 3264[5] 3615[3] 4941[3] 5441[11] 6019[9] (6640)

Intersky Music (USA) *Jonjo O'Neill* 48
6 b g Victory Gallop(CAN) —Resounding Grace (USA) (Thunder Gulch (USA))
4263[6]

Inter Vision (USA) *A Dickman* a96 102
9 b g Cryptoclearance(USA) —Fateful (USA) (Topsider (USA))
2094[7] 2570[7] 2941[8] 3389[10] 3877[6] 4507[7] 4802[6] 4996[6] 5597[4] 5623[4] 6178[2] 6902[5] 7083[5] 7220[9]

Inthawain *N Wilson* a62 63
3 b f Bertolini(USA) —Ambassadress (USA) (Alleged (USA))
137[4] 365[2] 797[2] 1098[5] 1437[2] 4707[6] 5158[8] 6308[6] 7270[7] 7418[9] 7679[11]

In The Mist *F Head* 81
3 gr f Pivotal—Kenmist (Kenmare (FR))
(4810a)

In The Mood (IRE) *W Jarvis* a58 70
3 ch f Hawk Wing(USA) —Grecian Glory (IRE) (Zafonic (USA))
5965[4] 6399[2] 6778[8] 7149[11]

In The Slips (USA) *P F I Cole* a46 92
2 b f More Than Ready(USA) —Tjinouska (USA) (Cozzene (USA))
3979[7] 4603[9] 5096[3] (5797) (6232)

Intikama (IRE) *M H Tompkins* a23 71
3 ch f Intikhab(USA) —Really Gifted (IRE) (Cadeaux Genereux)
2857[6] 3960[4] 4320[5] 5108[3] 5327[5] 6919[8] 7094[7]

Intimar (IRE) *R J Smith* a26 37
3 b f Intikhab(USA) —Genetta (Green Desert (USA))
5222[4] 7324[11] 7765[7]

Inti Raimi (JPN) *S Sasaki* 121
7 b h Special Week(JPN) —Andes Lady (JPN) (Northern Taste (CAN))
7593a[14]

Intolerable (IRE) *R M Beckett* a62 75
3 b g Intikhab(USA) —Institutrice (IRE) (College Chapel)
2122[4] ◆ 2603[3] (3161) 3982[12] 6630[12]

Into Mac *N Bycroft*
3 b g Shinko Forest(IRE) —Efipetite (Efisio)
3338[11]

Intomeisee (IRE) *Daniel Miley* a52 49
2 b f Tagula(IRE) —Thank One's Stars (Alzao (USA))
6401a[13]

Into My Arms *M S Saunders* a22 43
3 gr f Kyllachy—True Love (Robellino (USA))
1420[8]

Into The Light *E S McMahon* a69 71
4 b g Fantastic Light(USA) —Boadicea's Chariot (Commanche Run)
1815[4] 2684[5] 3308[2] 4021[6]

Intrepid Jack *H Morrison* a102 115
7 b h Compton Place—Maria Theresa (Primo Dominie)
418a[4] 700a[7] 1989[7] 2550[2] 3140[14] 3536[4] 3819[11] 4330[6] 5132[4] 5860[18] 6091[12]

Invasian (IRE) *P W D'Arcy* a96 92
8 ch g Desert Prince(IRE) —Jarrayan (Machiavellian (USA))
(1357) *1779[7] 2597[13]* (3961) (4021) 4288[3]

Invention (USA) *Miss E C Lavelle* a65 75
6 b g Lear Fan(USA) —Carya (USA) (Northern Dancer (CAN))
1581[2] *1966[6]* 2429[5]

Inventor (IRE) *B J Meehan* a103 102
4 b g Alzao(USA) —Magnificent Bell (IRE) (Octagonal (NZ))
5662[5] 6662[18]

Investissement *A Fabre* 100
3 b c Singspiel(IRE) —Underwater (USA) (Theatrical (IRE))
5711a[3]

Invincible Ash (IRE) *M Halford* a98 99
4 b m Invincible Spirit(IRE) —Fully Fashioned (IRE) (Brief Truce (USA))
1543a[5] 2555a[3] *7007a[8] 7297a[2]*

Invincible Force (IRE) *Paul Green* a100 100
5 b g Invincible Spirit(IRE) —Highly Respected (IRE) (High Estate)
856[4] 995[15] 1398[9] 1791[12] 1821[14] (4360a) (4560) ◆ 6089[17] 6278[6] 6675[15]

Invincible Heart (GR) *Jane Chapple-Hyam* a85 95
3 b c Invincible Spirit(IRE) —Flamingo Bay (IRE) (Catrail (USA))
1295[2] (1803) 2049[6]

Invincible Hero (IRE) *J Noseda* a43 68
2 b c Invincible Spirit(IRE) —Bridelina (FR) (Linamix (FR))
5807[10] 6065[3]

Invincible Isle (IRE) *H R A Cecil* a85 85
3 b f Invincible Spirit(IRE) —Ile De France (ITY) (Danehill (USA))
1198[2] ◆ *1605[6]* (2664) 4056[2] 4540[5] 5130[3] 5523[7] (6020) *6348[4] 6879[5]*

Invincible Joe (IRE) *John Joseph Hanlon* a66 88
4 b g Invincible Spirit(IRE) —Abbey Park (USA) (Known Fact (USA))
2290a[10] *6780[7]*

Invincible Lad (IRE) *E J Alston* a98 93
5 b g Invincible Spirit(IRE) —Lady Ellen (Horage)
1685[10] (2359) ◆ 2637[3] 3149[7] 4461[3] 5247[6] 5420[13] 5768[6] *(6359)* ◆ *6949[3]* 7015[9]

Invincible Miss (IRE) *M Wigham* a60
3 b f Invincible Spirit(IRE) —Saramacca (IRE) (Kahyasi)
572[2] 741[3] (1492)

Invincible Prince (IRE) *R M Beckett* a78 64
2 b g Invincible Spirit(IRE) —Forest Prize (Charnwood Forest (IRE))
(3270) 4294[7] 5603[5] 6811[5]

Invincible Son (IRE) *A Ikier* 98
3 b c Orpen(USA) —Safe Exit (FR) (Exit To Nowhere (USA))
5618a[8]

Invincible Soul (IRE) *R Hannon* 85
2 b c Invincible Spirit(IRE) —Licorne (Sadler's Wells (USA))
4524[8] 4985[8] 6451[3] ◆ (6810)

Invincible Vibes (IRE) *G M Lyons* a84
2 b c Invincible Spirit(IRE) —Miss Sandy Claws (IRE) (Catrail (USA))
5452a[10]

Invisible Man *J H M Gosden* a83 99
3 ch c Elusive Quality(USA) —Eternal Reve (USA) (Diesis)
1295[4] *1729[4]* (2082) 3049[13] 3839[4] (4316) (5070) ◆ 5880[9]

Inwood (IRE) *Paul Magnier* a81 82
6 b g Bluebird(USA) —Hardshan (IRE) (Warrshan (USA))
1376a[15]

Inxile (IRE) *D Nicholls* 111
4 b g Fayruz—Grandel (Owington)
996[3] (1374a) 1919a[3] (2555a) 3434a[3] 4456[3] 5765[5] 6427[5]

Iolith (GER) *J Hirschberger* 105
4 b h Monsun(GER) —Indian Jewel (GER) (Local Suitor (USA))
3416a[5] 4129a[4] 6713a[2]

Ionisphere *W McCreery* a45 38
4 b g Vettori(IRE) —Liska's Dance (USA) (Riverman (USA))
7336[5]

Ipswich Lad *A M Balding* a72 69
2 ch c Halling(USA) —Poised (USA) (Rahy (USA))
5787[5] 6066[4] *6607[3] 7683[3]*

Iptkaar (USA) *C E Brittain* 72
2 br f Dixie Union(USA) —Low Tolerance (USA) (Proud Truth (USA))
4424[3] 4817[4] 6064[7] 6477[12]

Ireland Dancer (IRE) *John Berry* a29 9
5 ch g Trans Island—Come Dancing (Suave Dancer (USA))
7492[12]

Irian (GER) *J Hirschberger* 117
3 b c Tertullian(USA) —Iberi (GER) (Rainbow Quest (USA))
(1395a) (1915a) 3669a[3] 5086a[4]

Irika (GER) *H J Groschel* 56
4 b m Areion(GER) —Ingrid (GER) (Nebos (GER))
6605a[6]

Irini (GER) *H J Groschel* 97
3 ch f Areion(GER) —Ircanda (GER) (Nebos (GER))
6886a[6]

Irish Ballad *S Dow* a64 56
7 b g Singspiel(IRE) —Auenlust (GER) (Surumu (GER))
112[6] 190[4] 502[2] (732) 1069[4] 1378[13]

Irish Bay (IRE) *Luke Comer* a32 52
6 b g Brief Passing(IRE) —Echo Bay (IRE) (Barry's Run (IRE))
7411[8]

Irish Cat (IRE) *Robert Collet* a83 101
2 b f One Cool Cat(USA) —Babacora (IRE) (Indian Ridge)
(1482a) 5057a[5] *5240a[5]* 5927a[3] 6044a[4] 6752a[2] 7230a[7]

Irish Eyes *Jedd O'Keeffe*
2 b g Mark Of Esteem(IRE) —Diabaig (Precocious)
4308[10] 5669[13]

Irish Heartbeat (IRE) *David P Myerscough* 92
4 b g Celtic Swing—She's All Class (USA) (Rahy (USA))
3435a[3] 4360a[4] 6678[8]

Irish Jugger (USA) *A P Jarvis* 68
2 ch g Johannesburg(USA) —Jinny's Gold (USA) (Gold Fever (USA))
2813[3] 3395[5] 5038[5]

Irish Mayhem (USA) *Saeed Bin Suroor* a108 87
4 bb h Woodman(USA) —Adventurous Di (USA) (Private Account (USA))
183a[11] *337a[5] 612a[2] 698a[5]*

Irish Music (IRE) *A P Jarvis* a67 62
4 b g Namid—Kelly's Tune (Alhaarth (IRE))
3459[5] 7100[4] *7223[2] 7533[2] 7819[8]*

Irish Pearl (IRE) *K R Burke* a104 89
4 b m Statue Of Liberty(USA) —Helen Wells (IRE) (Sadler's Wells (USA))
2[6] 86[7]

Irish Queen (FR) *H-A Pantall* 93
3 b f Speedmaster(GER) —Intention (GER) (Nebos (GER))
2989a[2] 3968a[4] 4969a[7] 6714a[7]

Irish Saint (IRE) *T J Pitt* a56 39
3 ch g Kheleyf(USA) —Tarifana (IRE) (Dr Devious (IRE))
677[10] 938[7] 1725[8] 1926[12] 4664[10]

Irish Stream (USA) *B G Powell* a56 39
11 ch g Irish River(FR) —Euphonic (USA) (The Minstrel (CAN))
813[4] 1770[9] 1974[7]

Iron Condor *J M P Eustace* a60 63
2 b g Tobougg(IRE) —Coh Sho No (Old Vic)
4152[4] 4666[4] *5192[3]* 6993[17]

Iron Duke *John Joseph Murphy* a47 44
3 gr c Refuse To Bend(IRE) —Arinaga (Warning)
5544[13]

Iron Hague (IRE) *O Brennan* 5
8 b g Among Men(USA) —Conditional Sale (IRE) (Petorius)
2337[7]

Iron Man Of Mersey (FR) *A W Carroll* a28 54
3 b g Poliglote—Miss Echo (Chief Singer)
1579[7] 2496[10] 2982[7] 4079[7] *5644[10]* 5905[12] 6399[10]

Iron Master *J J Bridger* 42
3 gr g High Chaparral(IRE) —Blushing Queen (IRE) (Desert King (IRE))
2211[7] 2885[8] 3432[5] *7576[9]*

Iron Max (IRE) *Tom Dascombe* a21 46
3 b g Iron Mask(USA) —Starisa (IRE) (College Chapel)
1662[5] 2070[10] 2593[10] *7727[11]*

Iron Out (USA) *R Hollinshead* a89 76
3 b g Straight Man(USA) —Fit Fighter (USA) (Fit To Fight (USA))
364[2] 572[4] 782[4] 2357[12] *2744[2]* 2918[8] (3305) *3711[2] 3955[3]* 4284[6] *4841[2] 4984[4]* 5544[2] *5806[4]* 6997[2] 7062[2] 7246[2] 7423[2] (7620) (7667) 7775[9] 7848[3]

Iron Prince *Mlle A Imaz-Ceca*
2 c Antonius Pius(USA) —Open Your Heart (IRE) (Soviet Star (USA))
6325a[0]

Iron Velvet (USA) *M Johnston* 78
2 b g Dubawi(IRE) —Not For Turning (USA) (Deputy Minister (CAN))
3500[10] 3875[2] ◆ 4286[10] (4975) ◆ 5550[9] 6099[6]

Isabella Grey *K A Ryan* 91
3 gr f Choisir(AUS) —Karsiyaka (IRE) (Kahyasi)
2057[4] 2273[12] 2673[8]

Isabella Romee (IRE) *Jane Chapple-Hyam* a50 60
3 gr f Bahri(USA) —Silver Clasp (IRE) (Linamix (FR))
3711[6] 4097[8] 5031[8]

Isabella's Fancy *A G Newcombe* a57 45
4 br m Captain Rio—Princess Of Spain (King Of Spain)
14[7] 150[3] 420[6] 792[10] 1710[15] 3241[9] 5634[6]

Isabelonabicycle *A M Balding* a75 75
4 b m Helissio(FR) —Santa Isobel (Nashwan (USA))
1156[2] (1426) 1892[3] 2177[6] 2944[2] *(3737)* 4092[8] 4951[8]

Isabel's Pet *Karen George* a20
3 b f Lucky Story(USA) —Perle D'Azur (Mind Games)
7411[11]

Isaman *C Laffon-Parias* 74
2 b c Sulamani(IRE) —Isabena (Star Appeal)
(5378a)

Isanous (FR) *M Roussel* a97 97
4 gr m Zamindar(USA) —Douceur Creole (FR) (Highest Honor (FR))
2513a[13] 5495a[9]

Isaonor (FR) *Y Fouin* 96
3 gr f Highest Honor(FR) —Illusive Grey (Nikos)
2777a[9] 6657a[0] *7697a[9]*

Isdaar (IRE) *J H M Gosden* 66
2 b g Invincible Spirit(IRE) —Kildare Lady (IRE) (Indian Ridge)
1866[10] 6285[4] 6759[5] 6965[11]

I See Nice Sea *Ollie Pears* 59
3 b f Miesque's Son(USA) —North Sea (IRE) (Selkirk (USA))
1843[5] 2415[11] 4818[6] 5342[8] 5982[11]

Is Feidir Linn (IRE) *J T Gorman* 97
2 b c Footstepsinthesand—Jolie Clara (FR) (Kahyasi)
6319a[5]

Ishe A Lord *W G M Turner* a48 58
2 b g Ishiguru(USA) —Lady Killer (IRE) (Daggers Drawn (USA))
4018[2] *7175[5] 7410[7] 7661[11]*

Ishe Mac *N Bycroft* 81
3 b f Ishiguru(USA) —Zacinta (USA) (Hawkster (USA))
(1683) 1987[6] 2504[7] (5405) ◆ 5523[10]

Ishetoo *A Dickman* 103
5 b g Ishiguru(USA) —Ticcatoo (IRE) (Dolphin Street (FR))
1398[5] 2059[11] (2502) 2716[6] 3351[9] 3877[10] 4341[3] 5039[5] 5257[8] 5420[7] 5695[9] 5860[5] 6180[3] 6843[7]

Ishiadancer *E J Alston* a80 80
4 b m Ishiguru(USA) —Abaklea (IRE) (Doyoun)
(4432) 5332[2] *6361[3]* 6846[2] (6984) 7171[6] *7558[4] 7801[7]*

Ishibee (IRE) *J J Bridger* a54 54
5 b m Ishiguru(USA) —Beauty (IRE) (Alzao (USA))
27[3] 56[7] 111[6] 727[2] 895[7] 1876[10] 2011[5] 2223[6] 2680[5] 2712[6] 3283[3] 3671[4] 4533[5] (4702) 4950[8] 5287[8] 6422[9] 7051[12] 7176[4] 7239[9]

Ishipink *R J Hodges* 15
2 ch f Ishiguru(USA) —Christmas Rose (Absalom)
2121[4] 2514[5] 5380[8]

Ishismart *R Hollinshead* a52 49
5 ch m Ishiguru(USA) —Smartie Lee (Dominion)
6558[3] *7318[2] 7490[10]*

Ishtar Gate (USA) *P F I Cole* 87
2 bb c Gone West(USA) —Sometime (IRE) (Royal Academy (USA))
(3052) 4418[9] 6472[5]

Isi Going (IRE) *C Von Der Recke* 72
3 b f King Charlemagne(USA) —Indian Goddess (IRE) (Indian Ridge)
7385a[4]

Isintshelovely (IRE) *B G Powell* 39
6 ch m Broken Hearted—Sarah Blue (IRE) (Bob Back (USA))
5939[9]

Isitcozimcool (IRE) *D E Cantillon* a52 42
4 b g Shinko Forest(IRE) —Hazarama (IRE) (Kahyasi)
2185[10] 2862[8] 3175[8]

Is It Time (IRE) *Mrs P N Dutfield* a66 54
5 b m Danetime(IRE) —Ishaam (Selkirk (USA))
309[10] 3252[12]

Isla Canela (USA) *A De Royer-Dupre* 61
3 b f Gone West(USA) —Islington (IRE) (Sadler's Wells (USA))
7569a[0]

Island Chief *K A Ryan* a54 74
3 b g Reel Buddy(USA) —Fisher Island (IRE) (Sri Pekan (USA))
1740[8] 2154[2] 2236[12] (2450) 2719[3] 3234[3] 3616[2] (3684) 5670[9] 6014[10] 6846[4] 7057[10]

Island Express (IRE) *Miss A Stokell* 58
2 b c Chineur(FR) —Cayman Expresso (IRE) (Fayruz)
1044[10] 1249[2] 1610[6] 1891[7] 2260[6] 2467[7] 2588[5]

Island Legend (IRE) *J M Bradley* a73
3 b g Trans Island—Legend Of Tara (USA) (Gold Legend (USA))
1317[3] 1840[17] *(4860)* ◆ 5405[13] *5777[4] 6120[11] 6635[6]*

Island Music (IRE) *J J Quinn* a64 70
4 b m Mujahid(USA) —Ischia (Lion Cavern (USA))
1737[7] 2362[9] 2724[3] 3098[7] 3150[6] 3857[5] 4144[2] 5037[6] 6218[8] *6862[4]* 7113[6] *7403[9]*

Island Sunset (IRE) *W R Muir* a70 77
3 ch f Trans Island—Islandagore (IRE) (Indian Ridge)
(3574)

Island Vista *M A Jarvis* a6 87
4 b m Montjeu(IRE) —Colorvista (Shirley Heights)
2249[8] *3273[11]*

Isle De Maurice *G L Moore* a64 52
7 b g Sinndar(IRE) —Circe's Isle (Be My Guest (USA))
6785[6] ◆ *7608[2]*

Isle Of Ellis (IRE) *A J McCabe* a32 6
2 b g Statue Of Liberty(USA) —Fable (Absalom)
994[16] *1312[7]*

Isma'First (FR) *Mme C Dufreche* 62
2 b c Coroner(IRE) —Ismalia (FR) (Johann Quatz (FR))
7264a[9]

Isphahan *A M Balding* a77 93
6 b g Diktat—Waltzing Star (IRE) (Danehill (USA))
1527[6] 2083[12] 2480[10] 3796[5] 4262[4] 5221[2] 5874[5] 6117[9] *7575[7]*

Issabella Gem (IRE) *C G Cox* 64
2 b f Marju(IRE) —Robin (Slip Anchor)
6729[8]

Issacar (IRE) *A De Watrigant* 71
2 ch c Traditionally(USA) —Indolente (IRE) (Diesis)
6501a[7] 7316a[2]

Isshe A Lady *W G M Turner* a22
3 b f Ishiguru(USA) —Lady Killer (IRE) (Daggers Drawn (USA))
664[8]

Ista Kareem (NZ) *Colin Little* 110
9 ch g Germano—Princesses Touch (NZ) (Touching Wood (USA))
7215a[15]

Istidlaal *Sir Michael Stoute* 60
2 ch c Singspiel(IRE) —On A Soapbox (USA) (Mi Cielo (USA))
6423[9]

Istiqdaam *M W Easterby* a80 77
4 b g Pivotal—Auspicious (Shirley Heights)
2142[6] 2439[5] ◆ 3021[4] 4285[10] 4620[11] 5624[5] ◆ 7173[6] *(7480) 7643[2] (7715)* ◆

Itainteasybeingme *J R Boyle* a57 61
3 ch g Lucky Story(USA) —Concubine (IRE) (Danehill (USA))
1271[5] 1462[15] 2417[2] 2863[5] 3693[11]

Italian Dame *J R Turner* 35
3 b f Bertolini(USA) —Soyalang (FR) (Alydeed (CAN))
4505[15] 5254[9] 5599[5]

Italiano *Mrs Marjorie Fife* 39
10 b g Emperor Jones(USA) —Elka (USA) (Val De L'Orne (FR))
2965[13] 3233[6] 3974[13]

Italian Tom (IRE) *R A Harris* a80 80
2 b c Le Vie Dei Colori—Brave Cat (IRE) (Catrail (USA))
1511[5] (3203) *3742[6]* 4912[2] *(5776)* (5992) 6398[8] *6827[9] 7274[6] 7453[4]* ◆ *(7674) 7793[4]*

Italica (FR) *T Callejo-Solana* 74
3 b f Slickly(FR) —Belle Bleue (Blazing Saddles (AUS))
7385a[7]

Itcanbedone Again (IRE) *J W Unett* a53 47
10 b g Sri Pekan(USA) —Maradata (IRE) (Shardari)
4861[11]

Ithbaat (USA) *J H M Gosden* 90
3 bb c Arch(USA) —Annul (USA) (Conquistador Cielo (USA))
1632[2] (1941) 2406[7] 2925[4] 3535[2]

Ithinkbest *Sir Michael Stoute* a91 75
3 b g King's Best(USA) —Monturani (IRE) (Indian Ridge)
1461[5] 2165[2] 3120[3] 4246[3] (6539) *(6830)*

Itlaaq *J L Dunlop* a89 85
3 b c Alhaarth(IRE) —Hathrah (IRE) (Linamix (FR))
2048[12] (2432) 4520[5] *6613[2]*

It Must Be Love *D Flood*
3 b f Piccolo—True Bird (IRE) (In The Wings)
1664[5] 2199[12]

Itri (FR) *M Boutin* a73 68
2 b f Agnes Kamikaze(JPN) —Nera Zilzal (IRE) (Zilzal (USA))
7103a[2] 7346a[6]

It's A Date *A King* a28 89
4 b g Kyllachy—By Arrangement (IRE) (Bold Arrangement)
2505[2] (2945) 3587[6] (4197) 4988[10]

It's A Deal (IRE) *P Winkworth* a43 41
2 b f Indian Haven—Gold And Blue (IRE) (Bluebird (USA))
2175[11] *3507[8] 3979[8]* 5748[6]

Itsagroom (SWE) *Karola Larsson* 83
4 b h Itsabrahma—Saucy Girl (FR) (Taufan (USA))
4585a[9]

Its Alright (IRE) *A Bailey* 83
2 b f King's Best(USA) —Lightwood Lady (IRE) (Anabaa (USA))
(1298) ◆

It's A Mans World *K M Prendergast* a67 68
3 b g Kyllachy—Exhibitor (USA) (Royal Academy (USA))
74[4] 200[2] 356[6] 530[5] 1490[5] 2126[13] 2863[6] *3299[2]* 3505[12] 4552[2] (4594) 5391[3] ◆

Itsawindup *Miss Sheena West* a53 21
3 b g Elnadim(USA) —Topwinder (USA) (Topsider (USA))
169[7] 443[3] (469) 546[6] 647[5] 1200[11]

Its Beyond Me *F P Murtagh*
5 ch g And Beyond(IRE) —Hand On Heart (IRE) (Taufan (USA))
2527[9]

It's Dubai Dolly *A J Lidderdale* a71 79
3 ch f Dubai Destination(USA) —Betrothal (IRE) (Groom Dancer (USA))
(1286) 1643[9] 3047[9] (4569) *5168[10]* 6113[7] 7291[12]

Itsher *S C Williams* a61 75
3 br f Diktat—Shararah (Machiavellian (USA))
135[5] 542[3] 2417[6] 2776[4] 2973[2] 3281[2] (3471) (3625) ◆ (3663)

Itshim *S C Williams* a71 7
3 b g Ishiguru(USA) —Sumitra (Tragic Role (USA))
(508) (624) ◆ *(705)*

It's Josr *I A Wood* a58 61
4 b g Josr Algarhoud(IRE) —It's So Easy (Shaadi (USA))
4149[12] 4563[5] 4938[13] 5503[10] 5790[10] *6770[2] 6918[2]*

Its Moon (IRE) *T D Walford* 69
5 b m Tobougg(IRE) —Shallat (IRE) (Pennekamp (USA))
1767[6]

It's My Day (IRE) *C Gordon* a69 72
4 ch g Soviet Star(USA) —Ezana (Ela-Mana-Mou)
125[5] 392[9] 507[3] 813[11] 3244[7] 3919[12] 4698[5] 5122[6]

Itsthursdayalready *J G Given* a75 77
2 b g Exceed And Excel(AUS) —Succinct (Hector Protector (USA))
2339[2] (2778) 2995[16] 4089[15] 4803[10] 5526[5] *7846[2]*

Itsy Bitsy *W J Musson* a47 51
7 b m Danzig Connection(USA) —Cos I Do (IRE) (Double Schwartz)
377[9] 3450[7] 4158[10] 4498[6] 4927[11]

Itwasonlyakiss (IRE) *J W Hills* 80
2 b f Exceed And Excel(AUS) —Reem One (IRE) (Rainbow Quest (USA))
1810[5] 2207[2] 3015[12] 4147[2]

Iver Bridge Lad *J Ryan* a104 108
2 b c Avonbridge—Fittonia (FR) (Ashkalani (IRE))
1147[2] 1290[3] *(2825)* (3583) 4407[10] *5661[2]* 6275[6] 6660[3] 7030[4]

Ivor Novello (IRE) *G A Swinbank* a14 47
3 b g Noverre(USA) —Pearly Brooks (Efisio)
1061[4] *1465[10]* 1926[5]

Ivory Jazz *D K Ivory* a39 67
2 b c Dubai Destination(USA) —Slow Jazz (USA) (Chief's Crown (USA))
3715[11] 4176[3]

Ivory Lace *S Woodman* a79 88
8 b m Atraf—Miriam (Forzando)
1149[10] 1539[9] 2188[3] 2491[7] 2736[3] 2883[3] ◆ 3104[3] 3523[5] 4694[4] (5124) 5918[4] 6187[7] *6726[8] 7364[4] 7575[11]*

Ivory Land (FR) *R Martin Sanchez* 93
2 ch c Lando(GER) —Ivory Coast (FR) (Peintre Celebre (USA))
(4686a)

Ivory Silk *J R Gask* a93 84
4 b m Diktat—Ivory's Joy (Tina's Pet)
170[2] 2946[2] ◆ 3845[10] 4567[7] 5830[5] ◆ *6253[3]* 6897[5] *7414[2] 7613[6]*

Ivy The Terrible *Dr J D Scargill* 1
3 b f Bahamian Bounty—Emerald Fire (Pivotal)
2455[9] 3319[7]
Izaaj (USA) *Saeed Bin Suroor* 78
2 ch c Giant's Causeway(USA) —Miss Coronado (USA) (Coronado's Quest (USA))
1700[3] (2167) 3138[15]
Izuizorizuain't (IRE) *K A Ryan* a44 57
2 ch f Johannesburg(USA) —Justly Royal (USA) (Royal Academy (USA))
3726[2] 4018[3] 4817[6] 6099[4] 6590[4] 6819[3] 7055[11] 7501[4] 7616[9]
Izzibizzi *E A L Dunlop* a81 86
4 b m Medicean—Sleave Silk (IRE) (Unfuwain (USA))
1860[12] 4088[9] 4799[4] 6015[5] 6725[5] 7065[10]
Izzi Mill (USA) *D R C Elsworth* a70 73
3 rg f Lemon Drop Kid(USA) —Lets Get Cozzy (USA) (Cozzene (USA))
1252[2] 1814[4] 2375[7] 2661[2] 2949[8] 5789[3] 6444[5] 6738[8]
Izzy Lou (IRE) *K A Ryan* 71
3 ch f Spinning World(USA) —High Spot (Shirley Heights)
3228[13] 4013[7]
Jabal Tariq *B W Hills* a91 90
4 ch h Rock Of Gibraltar(IRE) —Sueboog (IRE) (Darshaan)
1172[5] 1666[3] 3273[2] 3822[10] 4661[4] 5641[6] 5909[5] 6239[11]
Jabroot (IRE) *M A Jarvis* a67 57
3 ch f Alhaarth(IRE) —Walesiana (GER) (Star Appeal)
2395[4] 2943[5] 3951[3] 4498[10]
Jacdan (FR) *J Rossi* a79 83
3 b c Septieme Ciel(USA) —Meehania (FR) (Homme De Loi (IRE))
(7820a)
Jachol (IRE) *W J Haggas* a59 62
3 b g Bachelor Duke(USA) —Restiv Star (FR) (Soviet Star (USA))
2950[2] ◆ 3099[8] 4157[2] 4545[3] 5331[3] 5838[2]
Jack Cool (IRE) *P W Chapple-Hyam* a82 89
3 b c One Cool Cat(USA) —Rachrush (IRE) (Sadler's Wells (USA))
1289[9] 2664[10] (3009) 3341[4] 4064[2] 4540[11] 6946[8]
Jack Dawkins (USA) *H R A Cecil* a100 103
4 b g Fantastic Light(USA) —Do The Mambo (USA) (Kingmambo (USA))
1527[9] (2468) 3586[7] 4543[5] 5137[13]
Jackday (IRE) *T D Easterby* 70
4 b g Daylami(IRE) —Magic Lady (IRE) (Bigstone (IRE))
2262[3] ◆ 2614[2] ◆ 3313[4] 3486[2] 4551[4] 4890[2] 5554[2] 6021[4] (6559) 7084[4]
Jack Galvin (IRE) *J R Gask* a28 44
3 b g Danetime(IRE) —Tumbleweed Pearl (Aragon)
6551[6] 6856[10]
Jackie Danny *C A Dwyer* 52
2 b f Mujahid(USA) —Baileys Applause (Royal Applause)
1569[13] 1835[5] 2457[4]
Jackie Kiely *R Brotherton* a69 68
8 ch g Vettori(IRE) —Fudge (Polar Falcon (USA))
493[8] 745[4] 1254[5] 1568[3] 1974[5] 2182[10] 2580[2] 2971[2] 3503[9] 4264[7] 4857[7] 7354[2] 7425[3] 7635[3] 7840[2]
Jack Junior (USA) *D Nicholls* a102 102
5 bb g Songandaprayer(USA) —Ra Hydee (USA) (Rahy (USA))
260a[8] 435a[4] 612a[8] 916[13] 1209[6] 3014[23] 3928[8] 4486[16] 5694[9] 6137[5] 6495[4]
Jack Kane *J A McShane* 8
2 ch c Ishiguru(USA) —Armada Grove (Fleetwood (IRE))
4993[11]
Jack Luey *L A Mullaney* a59 66
2 b c Danbird(AUS) —Icenaslice (IRE) (Fayruz)
2311[4] 2568[6] 5146[3] 5620[5] 6409[5] 6796[5] 7079[3] 7242[4] (7352)
Jack My Boy (IRE) *P D Evans* 84
2 b c Tagula(IRE) —Bobanlyn (IRE) (Dance Of Life (USA))
1083[3] (1275) (2041) 2702[12] (3452) 4294[6] 5136[6] 5658[13] 6486[18] 6619[3] 7290[4]
Jack O'Lantern *J H M Gosden* 73
2 b g Shamardal(USA) —Bush Cat (USA) (Kingmambo (USA))
6991[3] ◆
Jackpot Delight (NZ) *C Fownes* 109
6 gr g Danasinga(AUS) —Principation (NZ) (Prince Echo (IRE))
7744a[12]
Jack Rackham *B Smart* a78 75
5 ch g Kyllachy—Hill Welcome (Most Welcome)
13[2] 68[5] 1885[10] 4783[2] 6413[15] 7739[3]
Jack Rio (IRE) *Niall Moran* a53 71
4 gr m Captain Rio—Order Of Success (USA) (With Approval (CAN))
7817[8]
Jack's House (IRE) *Miss J A Camacho* a50 53
3 b g Danetime(IRE) —Groupetime (USA) (Gilded Time (USA))
92[3] 366[5] 2456[4] 3010[10] 3449[13] 5158[7] 5972[5]
Jacobite Prince (IRE) *M H Tompkins* a6 65
3 b g Chevalier(IRE) —Kind Gesture (IRE) (Alzao (USA))
1462[7] 3009[13] 3708[9] 3961[6] 5482[7] 5750[9]
Jaconet (USA) *T D Barron* a110 95
4 ch m Hussonet(USA) —Radiant Rocket (USA) (Peteski (CAN))
(738) (1227) ◆ (1627) 2716[15] 3122[3] 3582[10] 4485[3] (5104) (5646) 5860[7] 6283[7] (7488)
Jacopin (FR) *T Larriviere* 25
3 b g Sagacity(FR) —Beauty Queen (FR) (Exit To Nowhere (USA))
6149a[8]
Jacqueline Quest (IRE) *H R A Cecil* 90
2 b f Rock Of Gibraltar(IRE) —Coquette Rouge (IRE) (Croco Rouge (IRE))
5021[2] ◆ (6274) ◆ 7033[7]
Jadalee (IRE) *G A Butler* a82 80
6 b g Desert Prince(IRE) —Lionne (Darshaan)
1966[5] 2194[9] 3510[4] 3977[6] (4098) 4840[5] 5642[2] (5837) 6258[6] 6704[2] 7201[4]
Jafaru *G L Moore* a69 70
5 b g Silver Hawk(USA) —Rafha (Kris)
1378[3] (2222) 2634[2] 3029[2] 3244[3] 3950[3] 4170[5]
Jaffal (USA) *A Al Raihe* a55
7 ch h Conquistador Cielo(USA) —Savina (USA) (Nijinsky (CAN))
435a[12] 610a[6]
Jafir (USA) *B J Meehan* 57
3 ch c Speightstown(USA) —Day Mate (USA) (Dayjur (USA))
6741[7]
Jagger *G A Butler* a94 94
9 gr g Linamix(FR) —Sweetness Herself (Unfuwain (USA))
1383[6] 1709[5] 2146[5]
Jago (SWI) *A M Hales* a72 52
6 b g Brief Truce(USA) —Jariyah (USA) (It's The One (USA))
392[13] 631[8] 836[9] 1042[4] 2039[7]
Jaguar Mail (JPN) *N Hori* 118
5 gr h Jungle Pocket(JPN) —Haya Beni Komachi (JPN) (Sunday Silence (USA))
7744a[4]
Jairzihno *J R Best* a82 82
2 b c Royal Applause—Polish Belle (Polish Precedent (USA))
(3306) 4000[3] 4488[6] 5320[4] 6373[2] 6693[3]
Jakarta Jazz (IRE) *Kevin Prendergast* 94
3 b f Marju(IRE) —Jakarta Jade (IRE) (Royal Abjar (USA))
1996a[4] 2960a[3] 3412a[7]
Jake The Snake (IRE) *A W Carroll* a85 85
8 ch g Intikhab(USA) —Tilbrook (IRE) (Don't Forget Me)
(26) (495) 650[3] 671[3] (730) 878[3] (1079) 1283[2] 1607[3] 2794[5] 3211[3] 3509[4] 4502[3]
Jakkalberry (IRE) *E Botti* 106
3 b c Storming Home—Claba Di San Jore (IRE) (Barathea (IRE))
1904a[3] 6893a[6]
Jakonda (USA) *A De Royer-Dupre* a77 98
3 b f Kingmambo(USA) —Mystery Trip (USA) (Belong To Me (USA))
3668a[7] 3968a[2] 4969a[5] 5562a[3]
Jakor (ITY) *M Marcialis* 98
3 b c Orpen(USA) —Jackie (ITY) (Horage)
7206a[8]
Jalamid (IRE) *M A Barnes* a47 46
7 b g Danehill(USA) —Vignelaure (IRE) (Royal Academy (USA))
735[11] 1226[7]
Jalil (USA) *M bin Shafya* a120 87
5 bb h Storm Cat(USA) —Tranquility Lake (USA) (Rahy (USA))
698a[12] 771a[7]
Jalmira (IRE) *E Charpy* a105 109
8 b m Danehill Dancer(IRE) —Jaldini (IRE) (Darshaan)
180a[5] 416a[7] 643a[8] 698a[16]
Jamaahir (USA) *George Baker* 66
6 b g Bahri(USA) —Elrehaan (Sadler's Wells (USA))
107[11]
Jamaayel *Kevin Prendergast* a77 86
2 b f Shamardal(USA) —Walayef (USA) (Danzig (USA))
(7258a)
Jamarjo (IRE) *S Gollings* a51 62
2 b g Marju(IRE) —Athlumney Lady (Lycius (USA))
4062[2] 5674[10] 7491[6]
Jamary (IRE) *C E Brittain* 48
2 bb f Grand Reward(USA) —Datsdawayitis (USA) (Known Fact (USA))
3027[7]
Jambalaya (GER) *A Wohler* 97
3 b f Samum(GER) —Jumble (Desert Prince (IRE))
1914a[7] 2874a[5] 3604a[9]
James Barrymore *R Hannon* a69 68
2 b c Fraam—Nine Red (Royal Applause)
4790[6] 5106[3] 5312[4] 5748[3] 6334[2] 7644[5] 7788[7]
Jamesina (AUS) *D Ferraris* 112
6 b g Orpen(USA) —Double Platinum (AUS) (Metal Precieux (IRE))
7744a[8]
James Pollard (IRE) *B J Llewellyn* a64 61
4 ch g Indian Ridge—Manuetti (IRE) (Sadler's Wells (USA))
1194[6] 1606[7] 1890[15] 6208[12]
James Street (IRE) *Peter Grayson* a46 14
6 b g Fruits Of Love(USA) —Humble Mission (Shack (USA))
1438[13] 3655[8] 4894[10]
Jamieson Gold (IRE) *Miss L A Perratt* a59 80
6 b g Desert Style(IRE) —Princess Of Zurich (IRE) (Law Society (USA))
3150[7] 3481[10] 3653[13] 4465[6] 4750[2] 4876[2] ◆ 5289[5] 5364[7] 5941[10] 6411[5]
Jane Blue (FR) *L Larrigade* 104
4 b g Indian Rocket—Rastella (FR) (Funambule (USA))
1043a[3]
Janeiro (IRE) *Tom Dascombe* a81 87
2 b g Captain Rio—Aspired (IRE) (Mark Of Esteem (IRE))
2128[4] 2260[3] ◆ 2599[2] 3579[2] 3745[8] (4385) 4901[5]
Jane Of Arc (FR) *J S Goldie* 57
5 ch m Trempolino(USA) —Aerleon Jane (Caerleon (USA))
1226[4] 1648[8] 2448[4] 3107[4] 3291[5]
Jane's Payoff (IRE) *Mrs L C Jewell* a69 61
4 b m Danetime(IRE) —Alimony (IRE) (Groom Dancer (USA))
83[8] 4204[8]
Janshe Gold *J G Portman* a43 57
4 ch m Bertolini(USA) —Rekindled Flame (IRE) (Kings Lake (USA))
1420[5] 1974[11]
January *T M Walsh* a84 70
6 gr g Daylami(IRE) —Noushkey (Polish Precedent (USA))
17[6] 653a[15]
Jan Vermeer (IRE) *A P O'Brien* 117
2 b c Montjeu(IRE) —Shadow Song (IRE) (Pennekamp (USA))
(7207a)
Ja One (IRE) *B W Hills* a68 67
3 b f Acclamation—Special Dancer (Shareef Dancer (USA))
2206[3] 2567[8] 3222[4] 3575[4] 4168[5] (6785) 7025[2]
Japan (GER) *D Smaga* a89 98
4 gr m Key Royal(GER) —Jeanine (GER) (Neshad (USA))
1029a[7]
Japura (USA) *T J Pitt* a56 69
5 ch g Giant's Causeway(USA) —Exchange Place (USA) (Affirmed (USA))
217[5] 448[6] 546[9]
Jaq's Sister *M Blanshard* a49
3 b f Bertolini(USA) —Polly Golightly (Weldnaas (USA))
251[3] 658[6] 900[7] 2950[12] 7609[13]
Jargelle (IRE) *K A Ryan* a81 103
3 b f Kheleyf(USA) —Winter Tern (USA) (Arctic Tern (USA))
181a[4] 524a[5] 2928[2] 3145[6] 4456[16] 5203[3] 5507[2]
Jaroslaw (SAF) *D M Simcock* a80
6 b g Jallad(USA) —Dacha (SAF) (Russian Fox (USA))
7431[4] (7810)
Jarrah Bay *J G M O'Shea* a44 47
3 b f Mark Of Esteem(IRE) —Wannaplantatree (Niniski (USA))
3803[9]
Jarrow (IRE) *M Johnston* a81 77
2 ch c Shamardal(USA) —Wolf Cleugh (IRE) (Last Tycoon)
7288[2] (7436) 7552[3]
Jarvo *I W McInnes* a58 58
8 b g Pursuit Of Love—Pinkie Rose (FR) (Kenmare (FR))
81[6] 275[10] 3450[12] 3943[P] 4402[15] 4932[14]
Jaser *P W Chapple-Hyam* a76 97
4 ch h Alhaarth(IRE) —Waafiah (Anabaa (USA))
1352[15] 4091[6] 4517[9] 6168[9]
Jaslyn (IRE) *J R Weymes* a46 46
3 bb f Pyrus(USA) —Ruby Julie (Clantime)
10[6]
Jasmeno *H Morrison* 61
2 b f Catcher In The Rye(IRE) —Jasmick (IRE) (Definite Article)
5906[7] 6727[4]
Jasmine Scent (IRE) *J A Osborne* 1
2 ch f Namid—Sky Galaxy (USA) (Sky Classic (CAN))
1810[11] 2978[14]
Jasmin Noir (USA) *R Menichetti* 78
2 b f Leroidesanimaux(BRZ) —Lover Come Back (USA) (Dynaformer (USA))
2586a[6]
Jasper Cliff *Mark Gillard* 39
3 b g Lucky Owners(NZ) —Catmint (Piccolo)
1573[13] 1708[7] 2318[8] 3215[10]
J'Assume (FR) *K Borgel* 68
2 b c Bachelor Duke(USA) —Fay Wray (FR) (Primo Dominie)
6148a[2]
Jawaab (IRE) *Mark Buckley* a82 83
5 ch g King's Best(USA) —Canis Star (Wolfhound (USA))
3378[4] 3840[3] 4340[10] 5266[6] (5532) 7020[5]
Jawaaher (USA) *M Johnston* a57 24
3 b f Empire Maker(USA) —Winsome (Kris)
572[3] 752[7] 1128[11]
Jay Ell The Trier (IRE) *Tim Vaughan* a36
5 br g Talkin Man(CAN) —Killoughey Pride (IRE) (Top Of The World)
501[8]
Jay Gee Wigmo *A W Carroll* a35 53
4 b g First Trump—Queen Of Shannon (IRE) (Nordico (USA))
1741[9] 2473[8] 2824[9] 3432[4] 3800[12] 5242[7]
Jay Peg (SAF) *H J Brown* 123
6 b h Camden Park(USA) —Laptop Lady (SAF) (Al Mufti (USA))
260a[4] ◆ 774a[2] ◆ 1011a[11] 2117a[12]
Jayyid (IRE) *C E Brittain* a53
4 b g Daylami(IRE) —Mellow Jazz (Lycius (USA))
500[8]
Jazacosta (USA) *Mrs A J Perrett* a64 81
3 ch g Dixieland Band(USA) —Dance With Del (USA) (Sword Dance)
1284[8] 1707[7] 2845[10] 4642[2] 5003[7] 5940[12] 6333[8] 6784[8]
Jazrawy *A J McCabe* a60 59
7 b g Dansili—Dalila Di Mare (IRE) (Bob Back (USA))
7761[2] 7840[11]
Jazz Age (IRE) *J A Glover* a57 68
2 b c Shamardal(USA) —Tender Is Thenight (IRE) (Barathea (IRE))
6931[4] 7491[9] 7764[5]
Jealous Again (USA) *Wesley A Ward* a96 115
2 b f Trippi(USA) —Chi Sa (CAN) (Bold Ruckus (USA))
(3015)
Jeanie Johnston (IRE) *A P Jarvis* 92
2 b f One Cool Cat(USA) —Bahamamia (Vettori (IRE))
2226[2] (2819) 3396[2] 4295[5] 6090[8] 7147[8]
Jean Jeannie *W J Haggas* 59
2 b f Giant's Causeway(USA) —Moon Dazzle (USA) (Kingmambo (USA))
3187[10] 4542[7]
Jeannie (IRE) *A Bailey* a44 28
3 b f Acclamation—Saraluna (IRE) (Mark Of Esteem (IRE))
1825[9] 5882[10] 6857[10]
Jeannie Galloway (IRE) *R A Fahey* 78
2 b f Bahamian Bounty—Housekeeper (IRE) (Common Grounds)
3147[6] 4001[2] 4993[3] (6009) (6643)
Jebel Ali (IRE) *B Gubby* a78 64
6 b g Fruits Of Love(USA) —Assertive Lass (USA) (Assert)
1962[5]
Jebel Tara *A D Brown* a71 83
4 b g Diktat—Chantilly (FR) (Sanglamore (USA))
607[4] ◆ 807[5] 1194[4] (1332) 1612[3] 1952[4] 2313[8] 2722[10] 3689[5] 4431[9]
Jeczmien (POL) *N J Gifford* a39
6 b g Fourth Of June(USA) —Jetka (POL) (Five Star Camp (USA))
233[7]
Jedi *Sir Michael Stoute* 89
3 ch g Pivotal—Threefold (USA) (Gulch (USA))
1489[5] ◆ 1792[3] ◆ 4520[10]
Jeer (IRE) *M W Easterby* a86 96
5 ch g Selkirk(USA) —Purring (USA) (Mountain Cat (USA))
99[14] 1593[10] 2666[5] 3189[4] ◆ 3705[6] 5551[3] 6236[3] 7475[3] 7667[6] 7777[3]
Jehu *M R Channon* a74 81
2 b c Antonius Pius(USA) —Chalosse (Doyoun)
2033[5] 2430[2] (2997) 3821[9] (4190) 4565[5] 5265[4] 5515[5] 5868[3] 6099[3] 6228[2] 6557[6] 6819[4]
Jelly Bean *K A Ryan* 52
2 ch f Observatory(USA) —Grandma Lily (IRE) (Bigstone (IRE))
3187[12] 4001[7]
Jelly Mo *W M Brisbourne* a70 57
4 b m Royal Applause—Flawless (Warning)
2912[5] 3594[5] 4158[6] 4944[14]
Jellytot (USA) *I W McInnes* a41 48
6 b m Minardi(USA) —Dounine (Kaldoun (FR))
1259[11] 4887[12]
Jemimaville (IRE) *G C Bravery* 44
2 b f Fasliyev(USA) —Sparkling Isle (Inchinor)
5096[11] 7183[13]
Jeninsky (USA) *Rae Guest* a83 95
4 ch m Stravinsky(USA) —Don't Ruffle Me (USA) (Pine Bluff (USA))
2927[6] (4228) (4796) 6886a[9]
Jennerous Blue *D K Ivory* a54
2 b f Generous(IRE) —Jennelle (Nomination)
6163[10] 6772[11] 7390[6] 7597[4]
Jennie Jerome (IRE) *C F Wall* a79 81
4 br m Pivotal—Colourfast (IRE) (Spectrum (IRE))
7247[2] 7475[4]
Jenny Potts *L Lungo* 74
5 b m Robellino(USA) —Fleeting Vision (IRE) (Vision (USA))
1128[5] 1474[4] 2090[6] (3019)
Jenny Soba *Lucinda Featherstone* a52 68
6 b m Observatory(USA) —Majalis (Mujadil (USA))
2971[4] 3864[7] 4193[6] 4498[2] 5733[5] 7085[5] 7291[18] 7461[12] 7658[7] 7751[5]
Jenny's Pride (IRE) *John A Harris* a53 53
3 ch f Fath(USA) —Softly (IRE) (Grand Lodge (USA))
3228[5] 3862[5] (4425) 5306[6] 6170[11] 6570[12] 7796[4]
J'En Sais Rien (FR) *P Demercastel* 54
2 b c Divine Light(JPN) —Dis Nous Tout (FR) (Exit To Nowhere (USA))
7384a[6]
Jeremiah (IRE) *J G Portman* a70 73
3 ch g Captain Rio—Miss Garuda (Persian Bold)
963[4] 1196[2] 1563[11] 1814[11] 2010[8] 3009[7] 3743[6] (4730) 5429[4] 6370[6] 7057[9] 7479[10]
Jeronimo Joe *A B Haynes* a48 61
3 ch g Primo Valentino(IRE) —Yanomami (USA) (Slew O'Gold (USA))
2333[8] (3588) 3923[7] 4177[5] 4818[2] 6570[6]
Jerusalem (IRE) *A Bailey* a50
3 ch g Indian Haven—Wilrock (IRE) (Dockside (USA))
381[3] 386[8]
Jesse James (IRE) *J H M Gosden* a80 92
3 b g King's Best(USA) —Julie Jalouse (USA) (Kris S (USA))
917[2] 1804[2] (5100) 5914[4]
Jessica Hayllar (USA) *G L Moore* 62
2 b f Arch(USA) —Pearl Pride (USA) (Theatrical (IRE))
2771[9] 3101[4] 3458[5] 4153[2] 6418[10] 6906[3]
Jessica Wigmo *A W Carroll* a63 50
6 b m Bahamian Bounty—Queen Of Shannon (IRE) (Nordico (USA))
25[8] 114[9] (472) 513[4] 661[5] 728[3] 803[5] 2686[7] 3269[10] 4533[13]
Je Suis La (FR) *D Guillemin* a76
2 br g Panis(USA) —Halix (FR) (Tropular)
6960a[3]
Jet (BRZ) *H J Brown* a68
6 ch h Yagli(USA) —Inflacionaria (BRZ) (Clackson (BRZ))
771a[12]
Jet D'Eau (FR) *G L Moore* a42 98
3 b f Numerous(USA) —La Fontainiere (IRE) (Kaldoun (FR))
5032[5] ◆ 5474[5] 5874[10] 6267[12] 7032[10] 7486[9]
Jet Express (SAF) *A Al Raihe* a102 107
7 b g Jet Master(SAF) —Outback Romance (SAF) (Sharp Romance (USA))
184a[7] 522a[U] 639a[6] 773a[11]
Jethro Bodine (IRE) *W J H Ratcliffe* 56
3 b g Fath(USA) —John's Ballad (IRE) (Ballad Rock)
1064[5] (1247) 1455[4] ◆
Jeu D'Esprit (IRE) *Mrs L J Mongan* a71 72
6 b m Montjeu(IRE) —Cielo Vodkamartini (USA) (Conquistador Cielo (USA))
3737[P]
Jeunopse (IRE) *B Smart* 68
3 b f Hawk Wing(USA) —Innocence (Unfuwain (USA))
2375[5] 3485[2] 4014[5]

Jewelled *J W Hills* a42 75
3 b f Fantastic Light(USA) —Danemere (IRE) (Danehill (USA))
2178[5] 2763[5] 3425[5] 4071[4] 4704[5] 5384[2] ◆ 5869[5] 6333[2] 6909[3] 7356[10]

Jewelled Dagger (IRE) *I Semple* a82 98
5 b g Daggers Drawn(USA) —Cappadoce (IRE) (General Monash (USA))
70[5] 1649[2] 2101[5] 2589[4] 3097[6] 4592[7] 5522[12]

Jewelled Reef (IRE) *Eve Johnson Houghton* 63
3 b f Marju(IRE) —Aqaba (Lake Coniston (IRE))
1361[12] 1670[9] 2515[2] 2910[5] 3387[7] 3803[3] 4642[7] 4937[5] 5502[14] 5789[4] 5905[3] 6333[3] 6787[10] 6910[14]

Jezza *Karen George* a52
3 b g Pentire—Lara (GER) (Sharpo)
4789[9] 5228[6] 5751[10] 6918[7] 7461[5] 7687[3]

Jhinga Palak (IRE) *Mrs K Waldron* a43 68
3 b f Fath(USA) —Livius Lady (IRE) (Titus Livius (FR))
19[7] 1746[15] 3502[9]

Jibrrya *M R Channon* 78
2 b c Motivator—Takarna (IRE) (Mark Of Esteem (IRE))
4713[5] (5407)

Jigajig *N Wilson* 26
2 ch g Compton Place—Eau Rouge (Grand Lodge (USA))
3446[8] 3910[6] 5337[10] 5950[12] 6555[7]

Jiggalong *Jim Best* a55 62
3 ch f Mark Of Esteem(IRE) —Kalamansi (IRE) (Sadler's Wells (USA))
3071[2] 3591[8] 3859[6] ◆ 4279[3] 4819[2] 5574[3] 5782[7] 5988[13] 7109[9] 7438[12] (7740) 7840[4]

Jill Le Brocq *M Dods* 61
3 b f Reset(AUS) —Our Krissie (Kris)
2343[4] 3036[9] 3764[5] 4589[2]

Jillolini *T D Easterby* 38
3 gr f Bertolini(USA) —Someone's Angel (USA) (Runaway Groom (CAN))
1335[5] 2250[10] 3125[5]

Jilly Why (IRE) *Paul Green* a63 84
8 b m Mujadil(USA) —Ruwy (Soviet Star (USA))
1528[13] 2840[9] 3002[4] 3331[3] 3570[6] 3999[4] 4281[2] (4469) 4783[6] 5149[4] 5411[8] 6175[10] 6799[5] 7123[4] 7371[13]

Jiminor Mack *W J H Ratcliffe* a49 51
6 bl m Little Jim—Copper Trader (Faustus (USA))
145[6] 469[6] 537[5] 601[6] 1651[3] 2601[10] 3004[9] 4158[3] 4880[3]

Jim Martin *Miss L A Perratt* a72 72
4 b g Auction House(USA) —Folly Finnesse (Joligeneration)
3481[9] 5305[4] 6012[9] 7173[7]

Jimmy Dean *M Wellings* a46 49
4 b g Ishiguru(USA) —Sister Sal (Bairn (USA))
133[9]

Jimmy Ryan (IRE) *T D McCarthy* 65
8 b g Orpen(USA) —Kaysama (FR) (Kenmare (FR))
5263[14] 5919[9] 6904[3] 7122[10]

Jimmy Styles *C G Cox* 110
5 ch g Inchinor—Inya Lake (Whittingham (IRE))
1864[2] (2297) ◆ 3141[12] 3405[5] 4523[22] 5039[4] 5434[3] 5826[3] (6091) 6661[5]

Jimmy The Poacher (IRE) *T D Easterby* a57 69
2 gr g Verglas(IRE) —Danish Gem (Danehill (USA))
3823[6] ◆ 4557[4] 5251[3] 5692[12] 6829[7]

Jimwil (IRE) *M Dods* a35 77
3 b g One Cool Cat(USA) —Vulnerable (Hector Protector (USA))
1400[3] 2070[9] 2602[7] (2786) 2970[5] 3790[4] 4433[7] 5340[10] 5677[12] 5955[8] 6170[6] 6824[2]

Jinksy Minx *Miss Suzy Smith* a44 18
2 b f Piccolo—Medway (IRE) (Shernazar)
3160[11] 7624[8]

Jinto *R M H Cowell* a62
2 ch g Halling(USA) —Sweet Willa (USA) (Assert)
6607[8] 7199[10] 7266[4]

Jira *C E Brittain* 96
2 b f Medicean—Time Saved (Green Desert (USA))
1862[4] (2533) 3086[7] (3396) 4295[4] 4795[8] 5606[4] 6064[3] 6477[5]

J J The Jet Plane (SAF) *R Hannon* a80 121
5 b g Jet Master(SAF) —Majestic Guest (SAF) (Northern Guest (USA))
525a[6] (700a) (2550) 3140[4] 3819[3] 4406[7] 5657[14] 5878[4] 6107[3] 6304[9]

Joanna (IRE) *B Grizzetti* 107
2 b f High Chaparral(IRE) —Secrete Marina (IRE) (Mujadil (USA))
2586a[2] (5279a) 6523a[3]

Joannadarc (USA) *S A Callaghan* a69
3 ch f Johannesburg(USA) —Game Player (USA) (Drumalis)
122[4] 503[3] 826[6] 1183[6]

Joan's Legacy *J C Fox* a16 53
2 b f Piccolo—CC Canova (Millkom)
4047[12] 4323[7] 4906[5] 7050[12]

Jobe (USA) *K A Ryan* a69 104
3 b g Johannesburg(USA) —Bello Cielo (USA) (Conquistador Cielo (USA))
1118[7] 1602[3] (1828) 2485[6] 3011[10] 4459[12] 5032[13]

Jobekani (IRE) *Mrs L Williamson* a61 64
3 b g Tagula(IRE) —Lyca Ballerina (Marju (IRE))
1193[7] 1746[3] 2515[8] 2779[6] 3336[8] 3680[5] 7004[3] 7369[7] 7818[8]

Jo'Burg (USA) *Lady Herries* a75 85
5 b g Johannesburg(USA) —La Martina (Atraf)
959[7] 1785[4] (2244) 2678[2] 2764[2] (3811) 4207[2] 4930[5] 6470[5]

Jocheski (IRE) *A G Newcombe* a64 63
5 b g Mull Of Kintyre(USA) —Ludovica (Bustino)
147[12]

Jodawes (USA) *J R Best*
2 bb c
7885[4]

Joe Caster *J M P Eustace* a89 87
3 b c Makbul—Oedipus Regina (Fraam)
912[10] 1002[11] 1639[7] 2140[6] 3469[10]

Joe Jo Star *R A Fahey* a58 81
7 b g Piccolo—Zagreb Flyer (Old Vic)
(78) 145[2] (2594) 2803[2] (2898) 3266[8] 5067[7]

Joe Louis (ARG) *J Barton* a93 94
6 br h Lode(USA) —Jolie Caresse (USA) (Septieme Ciel (USA))
1013a[13]

Joel The Mole *D Nicholls* 31
2 ch g Reel Buddy(USA) —Fly South (Polar Falcon (USA))
2788[6] 2996[11] 5519[18]

Joe Packet *J G Portman* 76
2 ch c Joe Bear(IRE) —Costa Packet (IRE) (Hussonet (USA))
2324[5] 3920[2] 4534[4] 4945[2] 6104[5]

Joe Rua (USA) *J Ryan* a36 53
2 bb c Johannesburg(USA) —Red Tulle (USA) (A.P. Indy (USA))
6424[8] 6696[6] 7121[13] 7513[7] 7685[7]

Johanan (FR) *F-X De Chevigny* a88 102
3 b c Canyon Creek(IRE) —Josapha (FR) (Tropular)
7216a[3] 7458a[6]

Johannes (IRE) *R A Fahey* a72 101
6 b g Mozart(IRE) —Blue Sirocco (Bluebird (USA))
(2267) 2658[2] (3122) 3825[8] (4485) (5257) 5860[11] ◆ 6089[19] 6678[10] ◆ 6994[3] ◆

Johannesgray (IRE) *D Nicholls* 70
2 gr g Verglas(IRE) —Prepare For War (IRE) (Marju (IRE))
6096[2]

Johannes Mozart (IRE) *Elisabetta Bernadini* 96
3 ch c Spinning World(USA) —Nicolitta (IRE) (Nicolotte)
7312a[7]

Johann Zoffany *A P O'Brien* 106
3 b c Galileo(IRE) —Belle Allemande (CAN) (Royal Academy (USA))
3051[15] 5685a[4]

John Charles (IRE) *B De Haan* a66 56
7 b g Fraam—Norwegian Queen (IRE) (Affirmed (USA))
4053[7]

John Dillon (IRE) *P C Haslam* a60 58
5 ch g Traditionally(USA) —Matikanehanafubuki (IRE) (Caerleon (USA))
126[5] 623[10] 4403[9]

John Forbes *B Ellison* a79 75
7 b g High Estate—Mavourneen (USA) (Dynaformer (USA))
3350[9] 3940[8] 4288[2] 4742[5] 5307[2] (5359) 5625[3] (6432) 6803[2] 7170[4]

John Keats *J S Goldie* a53 86
6 b g Bertolini(USA) —Nightingale (Night Shift (USA))
2276[13] 3001[3] 3377[5] 3529[2] 4134[9] 4507[4] 5001[4] 5406[8] 5516[3] 5955[3] 6309[3] 6413[3] 6764[13] 6984[10]

Johnmanderville *A P Jarvis* a76 82
3 b g Kheleyf(USA) —Lady's Walk (IRE) (Charnwood Forest (IRE))
1307[7] (1559) 1987[7] 2696[9] 3489[2] 4296[7] 5189[6] 6250[6] 6804[2]

Johnnycometomamie (FR) *Robert Collet* a88 89
2 b c One Cool Cat(USA) —Alfa (Johann Quatz (FR))
(4368a)

Johnny Friendly *K R Burke* a65 68
4 b g Auction House(USA) —Quantum Lady (Mujadil (USA))
344[5] 715[9] 1057[13] 1520[6] 1889[12] 2404[4]

Johnnyleary (IRE) *D Nicholls* 1
2 ch g Fayruz—Forgren (IRE) (Thatching)
1802[9] 2195[10]

Johnny Rocket (IRE) *K A Ryan* 58
4 ch g Viking Ruler(AUS) —Karen Blixen (Kris)
1739[3] 2090[9] 2232[6]

John Potts *B P J Baugh* a57 27
4 b g Josr Algarhoud(IRE) —Crown City (USA) (Coronado's Quest (USA))
275[3] 581[2] 711[5] 775[7] 969[9] 1556[15] 7718[6] 7818[3] 7857[10]

Johnston's Baby (IRE) *E J Alston* a65 68
7 b m Bob Back(USA) —Mirror Of Flowers (Artaius (USA))
452[4] 476[3] 564[6] 744[8] 1131[2] 1881[2] 2155[3] 2314[4] 2859[4] 3267[3] 3847[6] 4658[8] 5103[10]

Johnston's Glory (IRE) *E J Alston* a66 69
5 b m Desert Sun—Clos De Tart (IRE) (Indian Ridge)
1369[3] 1694[4] 2088[11] 2312[RR] 4436[RR]

Johnstown Lad (IRE) *Daniel Mark Loughnane* a89 89
5 b g Invincible Spirit(IRE) —Pretext (Polish Precedent (USA))
1375a[11] 2911[5] (5719) 6201[3] 7395[2] 7553[5] 7646[4]

John Terry (IRE) *Mrs A J Perrett* a100 97
6 b g Grand Lodge(USA) —Kardashina (FR) (Darshaan)
124[5] 360[6] 445[8] 585[2] 801[6] 2242[2] 2475[8]

Joinedupwriting *R M Whitaker* a46 70
4 b g Desert Style(IRE) —Ink Pot (USA) (Green Dancer (USA))
(1848) 2314[2] (2569) 3121[7] 4597[8]

Join In The Dance (USA) *Todd Pletcher* a108
3 bb c Sky Mesa(USA) —Dance Darling (USA) (Devil's Bag (USA))
1225a[5] 1688a[7] 7306a[9]

Join Up *W M Brisbourne* a59 53
3 b g Green Desert(USA) —Rise (Polar Falcon (USA))
2141[10] 2417[14] 2918[13] 3449[4] 4279[6] 4734[3] ◆ 4944[4] 5470[10] 6439[5] 6705[9] 7142[8] 7211[3] 7609[2] (7652) 7818[2] 7856[2]

Jojesse *W Storey* a56 48
5 ch g Compton Place—Jodeeka (Fraam)
14[10] 1924[10] 2155[9] 2404[9] 2532[9] 7052[11] 7631[7] 7732[9]

Jokers Wild *A M Balding* a20
2 b c Compton Place—Lady Hibernia (Anabaa (USA))
7430[10] 7571[12]

Jolies Dee *J R Jenkins* a36
4 br m Diktat—Jolies Eaux (Shirley Heights)
102[7]

Jolly Ranch *A G Newcombe* a59 44
3 gr f Compton Place—How Do I Know (Petong)
(286) 568[4] 2478[6] 3229[7] 4223[7] 5105[3] 5881[2] 6939[3] ◆ 7651[2]

Jonnie Skull (IRE) *P S McEntee* a71 74
3 b g Pyrus(USA) —Sovereign Touch (IRE) (Pennine Walk)
231[3] 332[5] 808[2] 820[2] 902[2] 968[3] 1156[3] 1440[4] 2417[8] 2807[4] 2863[12] 3710[3] 3783[6] 4697[5] (5316) 5644[3] 6005[2] 6070[8] 6339[12] 7480[10] 7589[8] (7678) 7723[4] 7797[2]

Jonny Ebeneezer *D Flood* a46 66
10 b g Hurricane Sky(AUS) —Leap Of Faith (IRE) (Northiam (USA))
2224[4] 2436[5]

Jonny Lesters Hair (IRE) *T D Easterby* a71 79
4 b g Danetime(IRE) —Jupiter Inlet (IRE) (Jupiter Island)
1333[6] 1649[6] 2257[6] 3496[3] 4657[4] 5107[6] 6361[7] 6765[10] 6984[2] 7172[5]

Jonny Mudball *Tom Dascombe* a98 66
3 b c Oasis Dream—Waypoint (Cadeaux Genereux)
6551[4] (7067) 7486[2]

Jonny No Eyebrows *I A Wood* a48
2 b g Auction House(USA) —She's Expensive (IRE) (Spectrum (IRE))
7661[8] 7749[LFT]

Jonquil (IRE) *F Nass* a109
7 ch h Machiavellian(USA) —Jumilla (USA) (El Gran Senor (USA))
435a[3] 522a[2] 639a[5] 773a[7]

Jonquille (IRE) *T J Pitt* a49 42
4 ch m Rock Of Gibraltar(IRE) —Moonlight Wish (IRE) (Peintre Celebre (USA))
275[9] 300[11] 972[5] 1786[13] 2344[10]

Jord (IRE) *J A Glover* a73 53
5 b m Trans Island—Arcevia (IRE) (Archway (IRE))
489[8] 617[3] 715[3] ◆ 934[3] (1039) 1132[2] (1411) 1566[3] 2473[5] 3924[8] 4191[4] 4435[4] 6801[8] 7179[11] 7275[2] 7423[8] 7561[3] 7596[6] 7795[6]

Jordan's Light (USA) *T J Pitt* a11 65
6 rg g Aljabr(USA) —Western Friend (USA) (Gone West (USA))
1690[9] (4898) 5162[3] 5733[10] 6558[9] 7425[12]

Jordan Strada (ITY) *S Santella* 77
5 br h Glen Jordan—Strada Facendo (Final Straw)
1905a[10]

Jordaura *W R Swinburn* a79 86
3 br c Primo Valentino(IRE) —Christina's Dream (Spectrum (IRE))
(1322) ◆ 1639[8] 5167[10] 5719[2] 5937[4] 6642[4] ◆ 6798[4] 7189[2] (7287)

Jordi Roper (IRE) *S Parr* a61 54
4 ch g Traditionally(USA) —Xema (Danehill (USA))
1[3] (95) 174[2] 222[2] 303[4] 514[6] 607[10] 791[6]

Jose Adan (USA) *Saeed Bin Suroor* a95 80
3 bb g Crypto Star(USA) —Markofclass (USA) (Benchmark (USA))
524a[6] 768a[2] 1009a[8]

Joseph Henry *D Nicholls* a81 100
7 b g Mujadil(USA) —Iris May (Brief Truce (USA))
1018[9] 1212[9] ◆ (1376a) 2015[12] 2470[11] 3141[8] 3435a[6] 3818[4] ◆ 4486[19] 5039[9] 6089[16] 6675[19]

Josephine Malines *Mrs A Duffield* a33 56
5 b m Inchinor—Alrisha (IRE) (Persian Bold)
1496[12] 3070[6] 4313[2] 4932[5] 5364[3]

Jose Thomas (IRE) *Mlle V Voute*
12 gr g Tirol—Marie D'Orsini (Zeddaan)
5074a[P]

Joshua Tree (IRE) *A P O'Brien* 112
2 b c Montjeu(IRE) —Madeira Mist (IRE) (Grand Lodge (USA))
(6268)

Josh You Are *Ian Williams* a76 58
6 b g Josr Algarhoud(IRE) —Cibenze (Owington)
139[7] 324[9] 511[7] 679[13] 1767[12] 2419[11]

Josiah Bartlett (IRE) *Ian Williams* a62 58
3 b g Invincible Spirit(IRE) —Princess Caraboo (IRE) (Alzao (USA))
134[11] 287[5] (594) 707[2] 826[4] 900[11] 1311[10] 1839[15] 2005[9] 2810[5] 4237[5] 6456[10] 7110[7] 7240[7] 7561[2] 7591[6] ◆ 7680[8] 7814[7] 7877[7]

Josphiel (IRE) *A Berry* 59
4 b m Okawango(USA) —Indian Honey (Indian King (USA))
1627[8] 1922[4] 2268[3] 2820[3] 3175[12] 3498[7]

Josr's Magic (IRE) *T E Powell* a70 52
5 b g Josr Algarhoud(IRE) —Just The Trick (USA) (Phone Trick (USA))
6288[12] 6719[8] 7197[2] 7517[4] 7693[8]

Joss Stick *J J Bridger* a69 65
4 b g Josr Algarhoud(IRE) —Queen's College (IRE) (College Chapel)
27[6] (166) 269[3] 326[6] 590[7] 762[6] 937[5] 1072[2] 1182[9] 1536[2] 1787[4] 2349[5] 2811[9] 3242[3] (3947) 4736[10] 4978[6] 5125[7] 5323[13] 5477[2] 5989[11] 6205[11] 6904[14] 7023[8] 7240[10]

Joukov (FR) *F Seguin*
2 b c Panis(USA) —Voliere (USA) (Arctic Tern (USA))
(6325a)

Jounce (USA) *J H M Gosden* a60
2 ch f Gone West(USA) —Shoogle (USA) (A.P. Indy (USA))
7396[2] ◆

Joury *S A Callaghan*
2 b f Oratorio(IRE) —Contradictive (USA) (Kingmambo (USA))
6254[11]

Joy And Fun (NZ) *D Cruz* 115
6 b g Cullen(AUS) —Gin Player (NZ) (Defensive Play (USA))
7745a[3]

Joyeaux *Ollie Pears* a67 73
7 b m Mark Of Esteem(IRE) —Divine Secret (Hernando (FR))
1768[10] 2032[4] 2436[8] 3164[10] 3483[3] 3855[5] 4281[8] 4530[5] 4929[2] 5518[4] 6010[7] 6159[6] 6572[5] ◆ 6799[2] 7081[4] 7273[4] 7555[5]

Jozafeen *R Bastiman* 61
2 ch f Zafeen(FR) —Faithful Beauty (IRE) (Last Tycoon)
3686[8] 4590[2] 5290[2] 6241[23] 6797[2]

Jubail (IRE) *A King* 51
2 ch c Redback—Daneville (IRE) (Danetime (IRE))
4945[10]

Jubilant Note (IRE) *Michael David Murphy* a68 69
7 b g Sadler's Wells(USA) —Hint Of Humour (USA) (Woodman (USA))
2351[10]

Jubilee Juggins (IRE) *N P Littmoden* a64 70
3 b c Clodovil(IRE) —Alleged Touch (USA) (Alleged (USA))
804[5]

Judd Street *Eve Johnson Houghton* a107 109
7 b g Compton Place—Pudding Lane (IRE) (College Chapel)
434a[3] (611a) 700a[6] 911[2] 1189[3] 2259[4] (2948) 3405[13] 3638[5] 4523[18] 5196[2] 5657[10]

Judge 'n Jury *R A Harris* a106 111
5 ch g Pivotal—Cyclone Connie (Dr Devious (IRE))
911[3] ◆ 1043a[6] 1374a[5] 1676[11] 2191[7] 3434a[6] 3844[4] (4341) 4766[3] 5039[14] 5491a[2] 5860[14] 7015[7]

Judgethemoment (USA) *Jane Chapple-Hyam* a92 102
4 br h Judge T C(USA) —Rachael Tennessee (USA) (Matsadoon (USA))
(1435) (1863) (2994) 3642[4] 4457[9] 5235[14] 6851[11] 7151[10]

Judiciary (IRE) *Saeed Bin Suroor* a76 74
2 b c Invincible Spirit(IRE) —Theory Of Law (Generous (IRE))
6382[2] ◆ 6810[8] (7266)

Juicy Pear (IRE) *M L W Bell* a75
2 b g Pyrus(USA) —Cappadoce (IRE) (General Monash (USA))
6638[3] ◆ 7157[8] 7325[2]

Jukebox Jury (IRE) *M Johnston* 120
3 gr c Montjeu(IRE) —Mare Aux Fees (Kenmare (FR))
3230a[7] 3640[6] (4780) 5134[4] (5497a) (6324a) 6873a[2]

Julie Mill (IRE) *R A Teal* a38 23
3 b f Apprehension—Ann's Mill (Pelder (IRE))
4867[9] 6223[10] 7250[11] 7452[8]

Julienas (IRE) *W R Swinburn* a77
2 b c Cape Cross(IRE) —Dora Carrington (IRE) (Sri Pekan (USA))
6943[4]

Jul's Lad (IRE) *D Carroll* a68 67
3 b g Modigliani(USA) —Woodenitbenice (USA) (Nasty And Bold (USA))
741[2] 1108[3] 1470[12] 3336[13] 3718[9] 7650[10] 7784[8]

July Days (IRE) *David Marnane* a79 78
3 b f Exceed And Excel(AUS) —Tocade (IRE) (Kenmare (FR))
6311[6]

July Jasmine (USA) *Sir Michael Stoute* 101
3 b f Empire Maker(USA) —Camanoe (USA) (Gone West (USA))
1871[2] ◆ 3047[5] 3619[7] 5472[3]

Jumaana (IRE) *J L Dunlop* 64
3 b f Selkirk(USA) —Weqaar (USA) (Red Ransom (USA))
2006[8] 2865[4] 3661[3]

Jumbajukiba *Mrs John Harrington* 115
6 b g Barathea(IRE) —Danseuse Du Soir (IRE) (Thatching)
1138a[6] (1543a) 2287a[2] 3881a[5] 6867a[2]

Jumeirah Queen (FR) *B Dutruel* a78 78
3 gr f Bernebeau(FR) —Reine Du Desert (FR) (Simon Du Desert (FR))
7037a[0]

Jung (USA) *J R Gask*
3 bb g Stroll(USA) —Witching Well (IRE) (Night Shift (USA))
2070[13] 6670[10]

Jungle Bay *A Fabre* 97
2 b c Oasis Dream—Dominica (Alhaarth (IRE))
4073a[4]

Jungle Tale (USA) *Steven Asmussen* a99 102
2 ch f Lion Heart(USA) —Mary Kies (USA) (Opening Verse (USA))
7282a[5]

Junia Tepzia (IRE) *P Schiergen* a85 104
2 b f Rock Of Gibraltar(IRE) —Marie Laurencin (Peintre Celebre (USA))
7282a[12]

Jupiter Fidius *Mrs K Walton* 75
2 b c Haafhd—Kyda (USA) (Gulch (USA))
1920[5] 6842[6] (7116)

Just A Monkey *R Curtis* 38
2 ch c Auction House(USA) —Wedgewood Star (Bishop Of Cashel)
3920[13] 5319[10]

Justaroundmidnight (IRE) *David Wachman* a75 72
2 b f Danehill Dancer(IRE) —Strategy (Machiavellian (USA))
2557a[7]

Just As Well (USA) *Jonathan Sheppard* 119
6 bb h A.P. Indy(USA) —No Matter What (USA) (Nureyev (USA))
4809a[2] 6873a[5] 7593a[7]

Just Bond (IRE) *G R Oldroyd* a91 89
7 b g Namid—Give Warning (IRE) (Warning)
6[5] 17[3] 199[3] 283[8] 430[2] 453[5] 834[4] 974[4] (1100) 1229[5] 1507[2] 1684[11] (4801) 5598[7] 5887[5] ◆ 6249[10] 6485[12] 7194[6] 7360[5] (7583) 7633[3] 7734[4] 7848[8]

Just Call Me Dave (USA) *Paul Green* a19 45
3 b g Gneiss(USA) —Proud Future (USA) (Proud Birdie (USA))
4974[8] 5531[10] 5939[8] 6432[12] 7500[13]

Justcallmehandsome *D J S Ffrench Davis* a81 67
7 ch g Handsome Ridge—Pearl Dawn (IRE) (Jareer (USA))
1316[4] 1964[7] 2144[2] 3024[10] 3322[3] ◆ 3863[4] 4321[6] 4714[5] 5190[5] 6072[7] 7054[6] 7322[5] 7575[9] (7615) 7812[3]

Just Crystal *B P J Baugh* a47 22
5 b m Polar Prince(IRE) —Grandads Dream (Never So Bold)
1734[5] 2361[7]

Just Dan *R Hollinshead* a53 43
3 b g Best Of The Bests(IRE) —Scapavia (FR) (Alzao (USA))
2605[7] 3588[4] 3954[4] 4397[7] 5328[7] 6098[9]

Just Dennis *D G Bridgwater* a16
5 b g Superior Premium—Sweets (IRE) (Persian Heights)
779[10] 902[7]

Justenuffhumor (USA) *Kiaran McLaughlin* 120
4 b h Distorted Humor(USA) —Justenuffheart (USA) (Broad Brush (USA))
7308a[3]

Just Five (IRE) *M Dods* a69 77
3 b g Olmodavor(USA) —Wildsplash (USA) (Deputy Minister (CAN))
(520) 620[4] (968) 1656[2] ◆ (2236) 3316[8] (3936) (6182) 7141[7]

Just For Mary *Daniel Mark Loughnane* a73 88
5 b g Groom Dancer(USA) —Summer Dance (Sadler's Wells (USA))
3148[4] (3898a) 4135[2] 4574a[13]

Just Jimmy (IRE) *P D Evans* a67 64
4 b g Ashkalani(IRE) —Berkeley Hall (Saddlers' Hall (IRE))
61[2] 211[3] 387[4] (473) 657[6] 874[5] 984[9] 1535[7] 1741[11] 2352[9] 2880[4] 3208[2] 3505[8] 5634[10] 6945[2] 6968[8] 7240[4] (7417) 7492[5] (7650) (7860)

Just Joey *J R Weymes* a52 70
5 b m Averti(IRE) —Fly South (Polar Falcon (USA))
198[7] 738[6] 1091[2] 1241[14] 2316[16] 2801[13] 2966[12] 3477[4] 3677[4] 3947[6] 4778[12] 4929[6] 5341[8]

Just Like Silk (USA) *G A Butler* a77 93
3 b g Elusive Quality(USA) —Ocean Silk (USA) (Dynaformer (USA))
917[5] ◆ 1643[4] 2432[2] 2884[2] 4058[5] (5028)

Just Lille (IRE) *Mrs A Duffield* 96
6 b m Mull Of Kintyre(USA) —Tamasriya (IRE) (Doyoun)
1306[3] 1613[6] 1850[2] 2103[4] 2768[2] 2815[2] (3293) 3620[7] 4339[3] 4896[2] (5346) 5823[7] 6138[4] 6536[3]

Just Mandy (IRE) *R A Fahey* 66
2 ch f Noverre(USA) —Unicamp (Royal Academy (USA))
3849[3]

Just Mossie *W G M Turner* a63 34
4 ch g Ishiguru(USA) —Marinsky (USA) (Diesis)
1496[8]

Just Mustard (USA) *G A Butler* a65 65
3 rg g Johannesburg(USA) —After All (IRE) (Desert Story (IRE))
917[6] 1295[11] 1831[4] 3630[7]

Just Nu (SWE) *H I Larsen* 74
4 br h Inchrory—Just In Time (SWE) (Opening Verse (USA))
5933a[10]

Just Observing *P T Midgley* a74 59
6 ch g Observatory(USA) —Just Speculation (IRE) (Ahonoora)
172[2] 477[6] 713[10] 848[6] 923[3] 1014[11] 1099[5] 1881[5] 2803[5] 3121[4]

Justonefortheroad *R A Fahey* a73 75
3 b g Domedriver(IRE) —Lavinia's Grace (USA) (Green Desert (USA))
1508[3] ◆ 1925[3] 2845[5] (5954) 6374[7] 6731[11]

Just Oscar (GER) *W M Brisbourne* a42 58
5 b g Surako(GER) —Jade Chequer (Green Desert (USA))
963[5] 1972[5] 2223[2] 2921[12] 3322[9] 3331[14] 3851[10] 4617[5]

Just Pegasus (USA) *S Wattel* 82
3 b f Fusaichi Pegasus(USA) —Just Too Too (USA) (In Excess)
2119a[6]

Just Pickles *G A Swinbank* 30
4 b g Piccolo—Tenderetta (Tender King)
1057[10] 1226[9]

Just Sam (IRE) *R E Barr* a61 73
4 b m Mull Of Kintyre(USA) —Strawberry Sands (Lugana Beach)
1243[2] 1734[3] 1955[7] (2366) 2812[13] 3558[4] 4191[8] (4436) (4823) 5391[10] 5597[9] 5955[2] (6216) 6765[14]

Just Serenade *Mrs Lawney Hill* a39
10 ch m Factual(USA) —Thimbalina (Salmon Leap (USA))
301[8] 443[8]

Just Spike *B P J Baugh* a48 63
6 ch g Cayman Kai(IRE) —Grandads Dream (Never So Bold)
4016[7] 4823[13] 5179[7] 7152[4]

Just The Lady *D Nicholls* a62 72
3 b f Ishiguru(USA) —Just Run (IRE) (Runnett)
(207) 268[3] 379[4] 560[2] 673[7] 804[6] 955[6] 1157[5]

Just The Tonic *Mrs Marjorie Fife* a32 73
2 ch f Medicean—Goodwood Blizzard (Inchinor)
2328[3] 2494[5] 3576[2] 3971[4] 4226[12] 4565[10] 4800[2] 5166[12] 5519[3] 5976[4] 6215[6]

Just Timmy Marcus *B P J Baugh* a69 59
3 ch g Ishiguru(USA) —Grandads Dream (Never So Bold)
(655) ◆ (986) 1736[10] 2365[6] 4914[9] 5612[10] 6070[6] 6437[4] 6637[2] 7715[3] 7813[4] 7860[3]

Jutland *M Johnston* 78
2 b g Halling(USA) —Dramatique (Darshaan)
3494[4] 4209[6] (4638) 5265[6]

Juwireya *M P Tregoning* 48
2 b f Nayef(USA) —Katayeb (IRE) (Machiavellian (USA))
5741[13]

Kaabari (USA) *C E Brittain* a77 92
3 bb f Seeking The Gold(USA) —Cloud Castle (In The Wings)
(890) ◆ 1293[8] 1870[3] 2174[10] 4052[5] 4566[9] 5064[7] 6187[2] 6487[5]

Kaage (IRE) *F Head* 96
2 b c Monsun(GER) —Koed (USA) (Royal Academy (USA))
6507a[6] 7404a[5]

Kabeer *A J McCabe* a98 47
11 ch g Unfuwain(USA) —Ta Rib (USA) (Mr Prospector (USA))
9[6] 404[6] 490[6] 777[5] 841[12] 932[8]

Kabira (FR) *A Couetil*
3 b f Equerry(USA) —Braya (FR) (Simon Du Desert (FR))
6150a[10]

Kabis Amigos *Ollie Pears* a67 76
7 ch g Nashwan(USA) —River Saint (USA) (Irish River (FR))
97[7] 133[2] 277[10] 289[3] 868[5] (934) 1039[3] 1132[5] 1413[7] 2156[2] 2453[5] (2804) 3110[3] 3496[6] 4887[6]

Kabougg *A J McCabe* a30
3 b f Tobougg(IRE) —Karameg (IRE) (Danehill (USA))
7126[9] 7332[11] 7557[10]

Kachgai (IRE) *Y De Nicolay* a88 108
6 b g Kaldounevees(FR) —Toujours Juste (FR) (Always Fair (USA))
265a[11] (439a) 697a[2] 5496a[3] 6505a[8] 7621a[4]

Kadabra (IRE) *F & L Camici* 77
2 b f Dubawi(IRE) —Windy Britain (Mark Of Esteem (IRE))
2586a[4]

Kahail (USA) *Miss D Mountain* a56 61
2 b c Rahy(USA) —Al Ihsas (IRE) (Danehill (USA))
3113[10] 3546[5] 4430[5] 4856[5]

Kahfre *E A L Dunlop* a63 53
2 ch g Peintre Celebre(USA) —Minerva (IRE) (Caerleon (USA))
6066[12] 6593[8] 7064[5]

Kai Broon (IRE) *Miss Lucinda V Russell* 56
2 b c Marju(IRE) —Restiv Star (FR) (Soviet Star (USA))
4307[7] 4774[3] 5360[5]

Kaijai (IRE) *Mrs L C Jewell* 41
3 b f Trans Island—Consultant Stylist (IRE) (Desert Style (IRE))
2981[9] 3508[11] 3919[15] 5367[9]

Kaikoura *G Woodward* a34 40
3 br f High Chaparral(IRE) —Landowska (USA) (Langfuhr (CAN))
1451[7] 2090[11] 3569[5]

Kai Mer (IRE) *Miss J A Camacho* a23 28
4 b m Captain Rio—No Shame (Formidable I (USA))
399[7] 537[11]

Kai Mook *R Ingram* a75 65
2 gb f Littletown Boy(USA) —Beenaboutabit (Komaite (USA))
6207[7] 6730[8] 7630[2] ◆ (7806) 7824[5]

Kaiser Willie (IRE) *B W Duke* a20 47
3 b g Xaar—Miss Bellbird (IRE) (Danehill (USA))
1036[11] 1416[13] 4351[8]

Kaitlins Joy (IRE) *Patrick Martin* a89 91
4 b m Mark Of Esteem(IRE) —Cieladeed (USA) (Shadeed (USA))
4412a[6]

Kajima *R Hannon* 71
2 b g Oasis Dream—Mambo Mistress (USA) (Kingmambo (USA))
3420[5] ◆ 5786[5] 7146[7]

Kakapuka *Mrs A L M King* a52 69
2 br c Shinko Forest(IRE) —No Rehearsal (FR) (Baillamont (USA))
1920[7] 3634[3] 4219[5] 4647[8] 6018[4] 6534[6]

Kakatosi *A M Balding* 62
2 br c Pastoral Pursuits—Ladywell Blaise (IRE) (Turtle Island (IRE))
7146[9] ◆

Kalahari Desert (IRE) *R M Whitaker* a57 64
2 b c Captain Rio—Sally Traffic (River Falls)
4546[4] 5146[4] 5693[4] 5977[7] 6355[5] 6796[3] 7088[4]

Kalahari Gold (IRE) *Doug Watson* a88 117
4 ch g Trans Island—Neat Shilling (IRE) (Bob Back (USA))
702a[3] ◆ 1008a[11]

Kalam Daleel (IRE) *M R Channon* 90
2 gr c Clodovil(IRE) —Three Days In May (Cadeaux Genereux)
2007[3] (2376) 5347[6]

Kalasam *M W Easterby* a82 71
5 ch g Noverre(USA) —Spring Sixpence (Dowsing (USA))
1014[8] 1615[8] 2200[3] 2440[3] 3124[3] 3689[6] 3943[3] 4548[4] 4658[7] 5548[4] 5698[6] 5962[P]

Kalasi (FR) *Mme J Hendriks* 62
3 u f —(Diesis)
6753a[5]

Kal Barg *M bin Shafya* a82 101
4 b g Medicean—Persian Air (Persian Bold)
265a[2] 439a[13]

Kaldougold (BEL) *Andre Hermans* 31
3 b f Kaldounevees(FR) —Lions Gold (GER) (Java Gold (USA))
3934a[5]

Kaldoun Kingdom (IRE) *R A Fahey* a47 106
4 b g King's Best(USA) —Bint Kaldoun (IRE) (Kaldoun (FR))
2012[8] 2502[7] 3877[7] 4330[4] 5695[2] (6089) (6678)

Kaleo *S Dow* a71 86
5 ch g Lomitas—Kazoo (Shareef Dancer (USA))
636[6] 1460[11] 2003[6] 2706[9] 3769[2] 4526[5] (5186) 5772[3] (5963) (6470)

Kalhan Sands (IRE) *J J Quinn* a6 74
4 b g Okawango(USA) —Night Spirit (IRE) (Night Shift (USA))
1766[10] 2235[6] 2722[11] 3354[10] 4136[3] 4436[5] 4778[5] 5184[15] 5518[13] 6999[11]

Kalidaha (IRE) *John M Oxx* a94 100
4 ch m Cadeaux Genereux—Kalimanta (IRE) (Lake Coniston (IRE))
1756a[4] 2644a[5] 3516a[3]

Kalimanka (FR) *M Halford* a69 66
3 b f Daylami(IRE) —Kalimanta (IRE) (Lake Coniston (IRE))
7790[5]

Kalimutxo (FR) *R Avial Lopez* 65
2 b c Equerry(USA) —Keiko (FR) (Always Fair (USA))
7264a[8]

Kalla *A Fabre* 107
3 b f Monsun(GER) —Kittiwake (Barathea (IRE))
3442a[3] (4969a) 5929a[11]

Kalligal *R Ingram* a54 68
4 br m Kyllachy—Anytime Baby (Bairn (USA))
447[4] 2492[6] 2811[2] 3677[10] 4082[10] 5008[11] 5323[10] 5566[4]

Kaloni (IRE) *Mrs P Sly* a75 95
3 b f Kalanisi(IRE) —Santarene (IRE) (Scenic)
2232[4] 2858[3] (3636) 4050[4] (5037) 6003[7] 6813[5]

Kalypso (IRE) *David P Myerscough* a69 65
3 ch f Barathea(IRE) —Russian Waltz (IRE) (Spectrum (IRE))
6123[5]

Kalypso King (USA) *R Hannon* 98
2 ch c Giant's Causeway(USA) —Kalypso Katie (IRE) (Fairy King (USA))
5317[3] 6054[3] (6617) 6811[2]

Kamanja (UAE) *M J Attwater* a59 40
3 b f Red Ransom(USA) —Nasmatt (Danehill (USA))
98[4] 364[3] 705[3] 817[9] 1036[10] 1620[8] 1958[13] 7411[6] 7521[5] 7614[6] 7814[10] 7881[4]

Kames Park (IRE) *R C Guest* a66 72
7 b g Desert Sun—Persian Sally (IRE) (Persian Bold)
40[7] 3561[4] 4593[10] 5294[10] 6917[3] ◆ 7490[3] (7687) (7847)

Kammaan *M A Jarvis* a59 81
3 b f Diktat—Qasirah (IRE) (Machiavellian (USA))
1379[2] 2142[5] 2789[3] (3352) 3804[6] 4591[3]

Kamsin (GER) *P Schiergen* 119
4 b h Samum(GER) —Kapitol (GER) (Winged Love (IRE))
(1549a) 2309a[5] 3441a[4] 4128a[4] 5707a[5]

Kanace *Ian Williams* a46
2 ch c Pastoral Pursuits—Pendulum (Pursuit Of Love)
5611[12] 6026[8] 6347[10]

Kanaf (IRE) *E A L Dunlop* 74
2 b c Elnadim(USA) —Catcher Applause (Royal Applause)
2853[3]

Kandalek *Rod Collet* 83
3 b f Hawk Wing(USA) —Reveuse De Jour (IRE) (Sadler's Wells (USA))
2777a[10]

Kandidate *C E Brittain* a113 108
7 b h Kabool—Valleyrose (IRE) (Royal Academy (USA))
284[6] (563) 634[4] 913[10] 1004[2] 1525[7] 3089[14] 4781[12] 5137[10] 5662[8] 6106[18]

Kangrina *George Baker* a65 67
7 b m Acatenango(GER) —Kirona (Robellino (USA))
148[5] 252[8]

Kankan Prince (IRE) *M G Quinlan* 11
2 b c Arakan(USA) —Risanda (Kris)
4912[8]

Kannon *A J McCabe* a62 69
4 b m Kyllachy—Violet (IRE) (Mukaddamah (USA))
256[5] 395[12] 867[10] 5883[7] 6339[11] 6755[9] 6800[6] 7080[9] 7795[8]

Kanpai (IRE) *J G M O'Shea* 68
7 br g Trans Island—David's Star (Welsh Saint)
6021[7]

Kansai Spirit (IRE) *J H M Gosden* a80 82
3 ch c Sinndar(IRE) —Daanat Nawal (Machiavellian (USA))
3751[3] 4606[3] 5649[8]

Kansas Gold *J Mackie* a72 65
6 b g Alhaarth(IRE) —Star Tulip (Night Shift (USA))
81[13]

Kaolak (USA) *J Ryan* a78 100
3 bb c Action This Day(USA) —Cerita (USA) (Magesterial (USA))
1001[7] 1082[4] 1882[4] 2048[4] 3050[10] 3359[5] 4010[4] 4320[2] (5003) 5070[2] (5475) (5914) 6277[5] 6480[24]

Kapelad Junior (IRE) *Pat Eddery* a55 59
2 gr g Clodovil(IRE) —Prosaic Star (IRE) (Common Grounds)
4219[10] (4800) 5636[5] 5967[7] 6589[13] 7210[6] 7419[6]

Kappalyn (IRE) *J R Boyle* a24 46
4 b m Marju(IRE) —Miss Tardy (JPN) (Lammtarra (USA))
1636[10] 2184[7]

Kaprun (IRE) *Brian Nolan* 80
4 b g Montjeu(IRE) —Marefonic (Zafonic (USA))
2305a[3]

Kapsiliat (IRE) *J Noseda* a73 69
3 b f Cape Cross(IRE) —Kootenay (IRE) (Selkirk (USA))
2082[3] 3100[4] 4085[4] 4822[11]

Kaptain Kirkup (IRE) *M Dods* 96
2 ch c Captain Rio—Aquatint (Dansili)
(2231) (3311) (4493) ◆ 5658[6] 6486[2]

Karaburan (GER) *P Monteith* 37
5 ch g Samum(GER) —Kimora (GER) (Dashing Blade)
5359[14]

Karaka Jack *M Johnston* a90 76
2 ch c Pivotal—Mauri Moon (Green Desert (USA))
6231[4] 6478[14] (6679) (6948)

Karamojo Bell *T P Tate* 72
2 b c Selkirk(USA) —Shabby Chic (USA) (Red Ransom (USA))
5002[5] 5793[6] 6533[P] (Dead)

Karanga (FR) *A Lyon* 74
3 b c Slickly(FR) —Oopsie Daisy (Singspiel (IRE))
4581a[0]

Karashar (IRE) *Evan Williams* a71 67
4 b g Kalanisi(IRE) —Karaliyfa (IRE) (Kahyasi)
7067[9] 7368[4] 7461[10]

Karate Queen *R E Barr* a57 35
4 b m King's Best(USA) —Black Belt Shopper (IRE) (Desert Prince (IRE))
1456[7] 1628[11] 3541[10]

Karelian (USA) *George R Arnold II* 117
7 b g Bertrando(USA) —Leaning Tower (USA) (Theatrical (IRE))
7308a[6]

Kargali (IRE) *John M Oxx* 110
4 gr h Invincible Spirit(IRE) —Karliyka (IRE) (Last Tycoon)
1138a[3] 1758a[7] 2729a[4]

Kargan (IRE) *R A Farrant* a62 75
4 b g Intikhab(USA) —Karkiyla (IRE) (Darshaan)
256[3] 657[2] ◆ 1650[2] 2269[3] 2453[4] 3105[4] (3655) 4466[3] 5190[3] (5630) 5997[5]

Karky Schultz (GER) *J M P Eustace* a66 64
4 gr g Diktat—Kazoo (Shareef Dancer (USA))
213[12] (2830) 3074[2] 3737[9] 4156[3]

Karlisse (IRE) *H-A Pantall* 92
3 gr f Celtic Swing—Karlinaxa (Linamix (FR))
7347a[5] 7697a[6]

Karmei *R Curtis* a51 59
4 b g Royal Applause—Lafite (Robellino (USA))
581[3] 711[11] 760[7] 2182[12] 2608[5] 2975[6] 3348[8]

Karmest *A D Brown* a78 73
5 ch m Best Of The Bests(IRE) —Karmafair (IRE) (Always Fair (USA))
139[8] 299[3] 384[3] 2505[8] 3019[8] 3974[8] 4373[11]

Karoush (USA) *Sir Michael Stoute* 82
4 b h Gone West(USA) —Victorica (USA) (Exbourne (USA))
5100[4]

Karta (IRE) *H-A Pantall* a64 75
3 br f Diktat—Echo River (USA) (Irish River (FR))
425[6] 855[2] ◆ 1423[4] 4810a[9] 7386a[0]

Kartica *P Demercastel* 97
2 b f Rainbow Quest(USA) —Cayman Sunset (IRE) (Night Shift (USA))
6889a[4]

Kasaa Ed *M Johnston* 66
3 b f Marju(IRE) —Muwajaha (Night Shift (USA))
1173[9] 1400[7] 2528[8]

Kasbah Bliss (FR) *F Doumen* a78 117
7 b g Kahyasi—Marital Bliss (FR) (Double Bed (FR))
1552a[8] 5497a[3] (5932a) 6527a[2] 7744a[3]

Kasban *Ian Williams* 81
5 b g Kingmambo(USA) —Ebaraya (IRE) (Sadler's Wells (USA))
1506[7] 2497[9] (3346) 3793[4] 4417[10]

Kashimin (IRE) *G A Swinbank* a82 85
4 b g Kyllachy—Oh So Misty (Teenoso (USA))
2267[3] 2658[3] 2814[5] 4784[7] 5404[5] 6645[15] 7000[2] 7220[8] 7617[9]

Kashmina *Miss Sheena West* a67 70
4 ch m Dr Fong(USA) —Lady Melbourne (IRE) (Indian Ridge)
1786[7] (3217) 5365[9] 7524[7] 7777[5] 7873[7]

Kashubian Quest *D R Lanigan* 11
3 b g Rainbow Quest(USA) —Kartuzy (JPN) (Polish Precedent (USA))
6794[13]

Kaspirit (IRE) *M Wigham* 83
2 b f Invincible Spirit(IRE) —Kathy Kab (IRE) (Intikhab (USA))
1616[2] (1939) 2586a[3]

Kassuta *R M H Cowell* a37 55
5 b m Kyllachy—Happy Omen (Warning)
3451[2] 4179[3] 5111[3] 5888[10] 6968[3]

Katapulpe (FR) *J Boisnard*
2 b c Ballingarry(IRE) —Double Line (FR) (What A Guest)
7409a[9]

Katchmore (IRE) *Jean-Rene Auvray* a62 40
2 br g Catcher In The Rye(IRE) —One For Me (Tragic Role (USA))
5787[9] 7400[8] 7885[2]

Katehari (IRE) *A M Balding* 71
2 b f Noverre(USA) —Katariya (IRE) (Barathea (IRE))
4792[9] (5318) 5899[6] 6418[3]

Kate Skate *Miss Gay Kelleway* a55 63
2 ch f Mark Of Esteem(IRE) —Saristar (Starborough)
1090[6] 1504[9] 1783[2] 2325[DSQ] 3086[18] 3719[6] 6034[6] 6228[5] 6775[7]

Kate The Great *C G Cox* a75 75
3 b f Xaar—Ros The Boss (IRE) (Danehill (USA))
2148[11] 2915[7]

Kathanikki Girl (IRE) *Mrs L Williamson* a30 12
3 b f Tagula(IRE) —Tenalist (IRE) (Tenby)
1530[9] 2404[10] 3305[8]

Kathindi (IRE) *J S Moore* a69 41
2 ch c Pearl Of Love(IRE) —Turfcare Flight (IRE) (Mujadil (USA))
3744[3] 4200[3] 4825[9] 7604[3] 7886[3]

Kathleen Cox (IRE) *Daniel Mark Loughnane* a28 47
4 ch m Alhaarth(IRE) —Gintilgalla (IRE) (Grand Lodge (USA))
7369[13]

Kathleen Frances *M H Tompkins* 55
2 b f Sakhee(USA) —Trew Class (Inchinor)
7099[7]

Kathy Ridge (IRE) *A Peraino* 76
3 b f Indian Ridge—Katy Guest (IRE) (Be My Guest (USA))
1394a[6]

Katie Girl *Mrs G S Rees* a39 43
3 b f Makbul—Katie Komaite (Komaite (USA))
1410[5] 2105[6] 3019[7] 3336[6] 3976[9] 4506[4] 4892[7] 5328[6] 5738[2] 6559[10] 7361[4] 7753[10]

Katie Kingfisher *T T Clement* a46 42
5 b m Fraam—Sonic Sapphire (Royal Academy (USA))
377[7] 588[7]

Katie The Hatter (IRE) *Mike Murphy* a48
3 b f Celtic Swing—Kathleen's Dream (USA) (Last Tycoon)
7067[10] 7826[8]

Katiyra (IRE) *John M Oxx* 117
4 b m Peintre Celebre(USA) —Katiykha (IRE) (Darshaan)
3412a[5] 4522[6]

Kattar D M Simcock a62 56
3 ch c Singspiel(IRE) —Lady Zonda (Lion Cavern (USA))
1629[6] 3349[4] 4453[4]

Katya Kabanova J R Fanshawe a4 7
3 b f Sadler's Wells(USA) —Kiftsgate Rose (FR) (Nashwan (USA))
4519[15] 5093[6] 5939[10]

Katy's Secret W Jarvis a66
2 b f Mind Games—Katy O'Hara (Komaite (USA))
7618[2] 7799[8]

Kavachi (IRE) G L Moore a67 95
6 b g Cadeaux Genereux—Answered Prayer (Green Desert (USA))
1170[4] 1460[9] 2003[2] 2412[3] (2933) 3014[8] 4486[9] 6106[19] 6665[9]

Kavak M Botti a83 70
2 ch c Dubawi(IRE) —Kelang (Kris)
3167[4] 3957[6] (4790)

Kavaloti (IRE) G L Moore a84 83
5 b g Kahyasi—Just As Good (FR) (Kaldounevees (FR))
72[4] 233[2] 459[2] (1069) (1215) 3510[8]

Kayak (SAF) D M Simcock a99 87
7 b g Western Winter(USA) —Donya (SAF) (Elliodor (FR))
206[7]

Kayceebee R M Beckett a46 55
3 b g Cyrano De Bergerac—Twice Upon A Time (Primo Dominie)
2162[10] 2651[6]

Kayf Aramis Miss Venetia Williams a66 94
7 b g Kayf Tara—Ara (Birthright)
(2018) 2177[5] 2994[6]

Kayfiar (USA) P F I Cole a60 65
3 ch c Lion Heart(USA) —Ivor Jewel (USA) (Sir Ivor (USA))
3099[6] 3535[6] 3985[7] 4745[10]

Kayfour (IRE) M J Grassick a35 55
4 b m Raise A Grand(IRE) —Sunrise (IRE) (Sri Pekan (USA))
902[5]

Kay Gee Be (IRE) W Jarvis a98 99
5 b g Fasliyev(USA) —Pursuit Of Truth (USA) (Irish River (FR))
1673[3] 2342[13] 3312[3] 3872[5] 4543[2] 5200[8] 5863[6] 6480[14]

Kaystar Ridge D K Ivory a65 46
4 b g Tumbleweed Ridge—Kayartis (Kaytu)
27[2] 235[11] 461[7] 2579[12] 3227[7] 4082[11] 4916[3] 5617[13] 6001[6]

Kay Two (IRE) R J Price a87 94
7 ch g Monashee Mountain(USA) —Tricky (Song)
2094[5] 2897[2] 3582[9] 4069[4] 5183[3] 5871[9] 6666[P]

Kazbow (IRE) L M Cumani a79 63
3 b g Rainbow Quest(USA) —Kasota (IRE) (Alzao (USA))
5744[7] 6807[2] 7212[2] ◆ 7476[2] (7590)

Kazzene (USA) F Chappet 52
2 b c Cozzene(USA) —Coconut Willamina (USA) (Pleasant Colony (USA))
7507a[3]

Keelung (USA) R Ford 83
8 b g Lear Fan(USA) —Miss Universal (IRE) (Lycius (USA))
1692[9] 2766[10]

Keen As Mustard M D I Usher a56 41
4 ch g Keen—Dark Dolores (Inchinor)
570[10] 800[5] 939[8] 1037[5] 1420[11] 1961[6] 2608[12]

Keen Bidder D M Simcock 72
2 ch c Auction House(USA) —Lady-Love (Pursuit Of Love)
2196[7] 2860[8] 3344[4] (4271) 4758[4] 5589[4] 5938[4] 6305[3] 6993[3]

Keenes Day (FR) M Johnston a99 100
4 gr g Daylami(IRE) —Key Academy (Royal Academy (USA))
(1383) 2994[9] 3390[10] 4769[4] ◆ 5248[5] 5903[4] 6306[4] 6851[29]

Keenes Royale P C Haslam 51
2 b f Red Ransom(USA) —Kinnaird (IRE) (Dr Devious (IRE))
4001[8] 4817[12] 7244[6]

Keen Warrior Mrs S Lamyman a12
9 gr g Keen—Briden (Minster Son)
621[9]

Keep Cool Andreas Lowe 95
2 bb c Starcraft(NZ) —Kirov (Darshaan)
7314a[3]

Keep Dancing (IRE) A M Balding a63 73
3 ch f Distant Music(USA) —Miss Indigo (Indian Ridge)
1077[3] 1359[6] 2122[3] 2321[7] 3118[4] (3591) 4380[5] 4829[6] 5584[8] 6904[12]

Keep Discovering (IRE) E Charpy a57 101
4 b g Oasis Dream—Side Of Paradise (IRE) (Sadler's Wells (USA))
335a[10] 637a[6]

Keepholdin (IRE) N P Mulholland a47
4 b g King's Best(USA) —Dafariyna (IRE) (Nashwan (USA))
6375[8] 6974[12]

Keep Icy Calm (IRE) W J Haggas a64
3 br f One Cool Cat(USA) —Alazima (USA) (Riverman (USA))
19[6] 188[4]

Keep Ringing (USA) W J Haggas a77
3 bb f More Than Ready(USA) —No Knocks (USA) (A.P. Indy (USA))
664[6] 890[3] ◆ (1040) 1284[4]

Keepsgettingbetter (IRE) J R Gask a64
4 b g Modigliani(USA) —Adua (IRE) (Kenmare (FR))
255[5] 478[12]

Keep Silent W J H Ratcliffe 28
2 gr f Largesse—Not A Word (Batshoof)
5431[11] 7061[10]

Keeptheboatafloat (USA) A P Jarvis a90 90
3 b g Fusaichi Pegasus(USA) —The Perfect Life (IRE) (Try My Best (USA))
258a[13] 769a[7] 863[13] 1453[2] 5186[4]

Kefalonia (USA) B W Hills a71 58
3 rg f Mizzen Mast(USA) —Zante (Zafonic (USA))
949[2] ◆ 1245[5] 3228[4] (4789)

Keibla Spirit R Ingram a54 36
3 b f Auction House(USA) —Rave On (ITY) (Barathea (IRE))
4786[11] 5193[4] 5747[6] 6377[12] 7592[10] 7691[8]

Keisha Kayleigh (IRE) B Ellison a47 80
6 b m Almutawakel—Awtaar (USA) (Lyphard (USA))
897[7] 1020[4] 1226[3] 2129[5] 2263[5] (3314) 3350[3] 4465[4] 4815[3] (5361)

Keithshazel (IRE) R C Guest a17 3
2 b f Fasliyev(USA) —La Poterie (FR) (Bering)
3032[15] 3634[7] 3709[12] 6819[17]

Kelamon S C Williams a75 81
5 b g Keltos(FR) —Faraway Moon (Distant Relative)
901[4] 1403[11] 2088[14] 3694[10] 4787[11] 6377[7] 7424[12]

Keleyf Byon Belief (IRE) Edgar Byrne a39 34
2 ch f Kheleyf(USA) —Carrozzina (Vettori (IRE))
5312[7] 5741[16]

Kellys Eye (IRE) B Smart 76
2 b g Noverre(USA) —Limit (IRE) (Barathea (IRE))
5728[4] 6408[2] 6896[5]

Keltina (FR) M Roussel
2 b f Keltos(FR) —Chic Marie (FR) (In Fijar (USA))
6325a[5]

Kelty In Love (FR) T Larriviere 100
2 b f Keltos(FR) —Ever In Love (FR) (Nevermeyev (USA))
6044a[3] 6752a[4]

Kenaaya (FR) J H M Gosden 58
3 bb f Monsun(GER) —Jindy's Dream (USA) (A.P. Indy (USA))
2847[7]

Kenai W K Goldsworthy a52 61
4 ch g Arkadian Hero(USA) —Hicklam Millie (Absalom)
217[7] 973[5]

Kenchop (FR) Mme C Vergne & D Sicaud a79 87
5 b g Nombre Premier—Ducie (Distant Relative)
2513a[8]

Kendalewood T D Walford 26
3 b g Viking Ruler(AUS) —Wilsonic (Damister (USA))
1362[7] 1611[11] 2042[9]

Kensei (IRE) R M Beckett a69 73
2 ch g Peintre Celebre(USA) —Journey Of Hope (USA) (Slew O'Gold (USA))
3420[3] 4534[5] 5192[2] 7003[6] ◆

Ken's Girl W S Kittow a64 76
5 ch m Ishiguru(USA) —There's Two (IRE) (Ashkalani (IRE))
1743[8] 2498[5] 2949[2] 3537[2] 4266[2] 5182[7] 5804[6] 6739[11]

Kensington (IRE) A J McCabe a79 80
8 b g Cape Cross(IRE) —March Star (IRE) (Mac's Imp (USA))
143[5] 218[3] 297[U] 398[8] 404[3] 576[3] 625[2] 806[5] 1152[8] 7000[5] 7337[13] 7643[5] 7830[3] 7876[9]

Kensington Oval Sir Michael Stoute a92 89
4 b g Sadler's Wells(USA) —Request (Rainbow Quest (USA))
2407[3] 4274[3] 4840[2]

Kenswick Pat Eddery a44 62
2 b f Avonbridge—The Jotter (Night Shift (USA))
6797[4] 7061[6] 7317[9]

Kentavr's Dream P Howling a47 23
6 b m Robellino(USA) —Very Good (Noalto)
145[P]

Kenton Street Michael J Browne a69 69
4 ch g Compton Place—Western Applause (Royal Applause)
7587[5]

Kentucky Boy (IRE) Jedd O'Keeffe a10 60
5 b g Distant Music(USA) —Delta Town (USA) (Sanglamore (USA))
604[9] 1171[6]

Kentucky Lakes Jedd O'Keeffe 48
3 b g Generous(IRE) —Inya Lake (Whittingham (IRE))
1625[7] 1950[6] 2723[9] 3708[8]

Kentucky Ray (IRE) Gianluca Bietolini 59
3 b c Noverre(USA) —Siwaayib (Green Desert (USA))
1392a[3]

Kenyan Cat George Baker 64
2 br f One Cool Cat(USA) —Nairobi (FR) (Anabaa (USA))
5934[3] 6544[4] 7061[3]

Kerchak (USA) W Jarvis 77
2 b c Royal Academy(USA) —Traude (USA) (River Special (USA))
4908[6] 5550[6] 6061[3] ◆ 6809[6]

Keredari (IRE) John M Oxx 103
2 b c Oasis Dream—Kerataka (IRE) (Doyoun)
7072a[3]

Kermiyan (FR) J-C Rouget a85 94
2 b c Green Desert(USA) —Kerasha (FR) (Daylami (IRE))
5739a[2]

Kerolad (IRE) N Wilson 30
2 ch g Kyllachy—Absolute Precision (USA) (Irish River (FR))
2017[10] 2997[13] 3310[9] 4286[11] 4527[2]

Kerrys Requiem (IRE) M R Channon 96
3 b f King's Best(USA) —Moonlight Wish (IRE) (Peintre Celebre (USA))
1602[7] 2049[5] 2474[2] 2915[6] 3688[3] 4309[2] 4598[3] 4771[9] 5263[8] 5507[5] 5902[6] 6155[2] 6694[13]

Kersimon (FR) Mlle B Joly a77 98
6 ch h Simon Du Desert(FR) —Blue Mary (FR) (Fabulous Dancer (USA))
7821a[6]

Kersivay Ollie Pears a79 72
3 b g Royal Applause—Lochmaddy (Selkirk (USA))
1228[3] (1451) 1803[6] 3455[4] 4591[6] 5677[10] 6455[2] 7057[5] 7356[5] 7577[3]

Kessraa (IRE) M R Channon a32 70
3 b g Kheleyf(USA) —Safe Care (IRE) (Caerleon (USA))
3773[2] 4180[4] 4655[5] 5072[2] 5773[3]

Kestrel Cross (IRE) A W Carroll a77 73
7 b g Cape Cross(IRE) —Lady Rachel (IRE) (Priolo (USA))
163[5] 361[3] 453[P] (Dead)

Ketter (BRZ) R Bouresly a78
8 ch g Much Better(BRZ) —Diana-Bela (BRZ) (Empire Day (BRZ))
435a[7] 522a[12]

Kevkat (IRE) D E Pipe a95 75
8 br g Dushyantor(USA) —Diamond Display (IRE) (Shardari)
2597[12] 4091[10] 5244[3]

Keyala (IRE) David P Myerscough a79 78
4 b m Key Of Luck(USA) —Alwiyda (USA) (Trempolino (USA))
6667[12] 7297a[6] 7634[13]

Key Art (IRE) J Noseda a68 73
2 b c Kheleyf(USA) —Gift Of Spring (USA) (Gilded Time (USA))
1862[4] 2161[2] 4331[5] 4906[2] 6018[2] 6443[4] 6971[4]

Key Breeze J H M Gosden a60 64
2 b c Exceed And Excel(AUS) —Cayman Sound (Turtle Island (IRE))
2467[5] 4233[5] 4537[4]

Key Decision (IRE) Shaun Harley a75 80
5 br g Key Of Luck(USA) —Adalya (IRE) (Darshaan)
(621)

Key Light (IRE) J W Hills a74
2 b f Acclamation—Eva Luna (IRE) (Double Schwartz)
7234[4] ◆ (7585)

Key Of Fortune (IRE) Jennie Candlish a57 52
3 b f Key Of Luck(USA) —Alaynia (IRE) (Hamas (IRE))
138[5] 677[6] 740[5] 1363[9] 1724[5] 2350[10] 4593[5]

Key Regard (IRE) P F I Cole a75
3 br g Key Of Luck(USA) —Disregard That (IRE) (Don't Forget Me)
343[2] (704) 865[3] 6975[9] 7238[3] 7476[5] (7578)

Key Signature Pat Eddery a76 85
3 b f Dansili—Musical Key (Key Of Luck (USA))
1324[7] 2079[8] 2638[5] 2926[9] 3628[3] 4228[11] 4909[8] 6695[2]

Keys Of Cyprus D Nicholls a26 86
7 ch g Deploy—Krisia (Kris)
2266[5] 3265[14] (4104) 4549[11] 5409[7] 6016[4] 6946[12] (7171)

Keyta Bonita (IRE) M G Quinlan 71
2 b f Denon(USA) —Miss Corinne (Mark Of Esteem (IRE))
3356[4] 4385[7] 4666[2] 5392[2] 5981[4] 6481[15]

Key To Love (IRE) A J Chamberlain a64 69
3 b f Key Of Luck(USA) —Ski For Me (IRE) (Barathea (IRE))
900[6] 1190[10] 1772[15] 7069[8]

Key To Pleasure (GER) Mario Hofer 105
9 b h Sharp Prod(USA) —Key To Love (FR) (Alzao (USA))
2097a[3] 3650a[5] 4363a[7] 7044a[11]

Key To The Stars (IRE) S Wattel a80 80
3 b g Key Of Luck(USA) —Baratheastar (Barathea (IRE))
(4581a)

Kfar Yona (FR) A Bonin 89
6 ch g Marchand De Sable(USA) —Gilboa (FR) (Antheus (USA))
7621a[10]

K'Gari (USA) B Ellison a57 40
3 ch g Fusaichi Pegasus(USA) —To Act (USA) (Roberto (USA))
4354[9] 4943[9] 7137[6] (7415) 7649[8]

Khadar (GER) W Baltromei a63
4 ch g Sholokhov(IRE) —Kiew (GER) (Alzao (USA))
5089a[10]

Khajaaly (IRE) E A L Dunlop a69
2 b c Kheleyf(USA) —Joyfullness (USA) (Dixieland Band (USA))
6607[5]

Khanivorous J R Boyle a76 59
2 b g Dubai Destination(USA) —Bright Edge (Danehill Dancer (IRE))
1835[4] 2595[4] (7429) 7685[5]

Khanjar (USA) J Pearce a81 47
9 ch g Kris S(USA) —Alyssum (USA) (Storm Cat (USA))
3247[7]

Khan Tengri (IRE) M P Tregoning a66 78
3 gr g Sadler's Wells(USA) —Ela Athena (Ezzoud (IRE))
970[2] 1286[6] 1489[10]

Khateeb (IRE) M A Jarvis a92 112
4 b h King's Best(USA) —Choc Ice (IRE) (Kahyasi)
1875[4] (2606) 3089[12] (4352) 4949[4] 6448[9]

Khattaab (USA) B W Hills 94
2 bb c Dixie Union(USA) —Jemima (Owington)
(4738) ◆ 6426[6]

Khayar (IRE) M H Tompkins 67
3 b c Refuse To Bend(IRE) —Khatela (IRE) (Shernazar)
1151[6] 2943[4] 4178[11] 4917[3] 5442[2] 5952[7] 6384[3] (6543)

Khazara A King 32
2 ch f Starcraft(NZ) —Mystery Lot (IRE) (Revoque (IRE))
5984[13] 6792[12] 6930[11]

Khazina (FR) R Gibson 69
3 b f Alhaarth(IRE) —Khalisa (IRE) (Persian Bold)
6753a[3]

Kheley (IRE) W M Brisbourne a67 72
3 b f Kheleyf(USA) —Namesake (Nashwan (USA))
(75) 135[2] (246) (273) 498[P] (5626) 6028[10] 7021[3] 7273[11] 7738[4]

Kheskianto (IRE) M C Chapman a63 83
3 b f Kheleyf(USA) —Gently (IRE) (Darshaan)
(403) 1281[6] 1437[5] 1725[2] 1973[3] 2370[7] 2918[4] 3193[7] 3608[2] 4056[5] 5007[11] 5258[3] 5940[5] 6358[13] 6568[2] 7062[7] 7348[7] 7767[8] 7797[5]

Kheylide (IRE) Mrs D J Sanderson a76 72
3 ch g Kheleyf(USA) —Jayzdoll (IRE) (Stravinsky (USA))
1505[6] 1720[2] (2005) 2227[9] 2460[5] 3304[4] 3483[5] 3607[3] 3765[8] 4399[9] 4662[9] 5391[7] 6160[5] 6220[6] 6379[5] 6857[7]

Khor Dubai (IRE) Saeed Bin Suroor a109 103
3 b c Kheleyf(USA) —Dievotchkina (IRE) (Bluebird (USA))
2114a[6] 2673[6] 3536[3] 3839[3] 4459[9] (5092) 5529[2] 6030[3] (7431)

Khun John (IRE) W J Musson a82 66
6 b g Marju(IRE) —Kathy Caerleon (IRE) (Caerleon (USA))
428[5] 798[2] 2552[7] 3273[13] 3961[3] 4378[7] 6640[9]

Kiai D Camuffo 80
3 ch c Zamindar(USA) —Special Society (IRE) (Imp Society (USA))
2114a[5]

Kiama Bay (IRE) J J Quinn 67
3 b g Fraam—La Panthere (USA) (Pine Bluff (USA))
1725[7] (3018)

Kibbutz (NZ) Jarrod McLean 111
5 b g Golan(IRE) —Misskap (NZ) (Kaapstad (NZ))
7215a[9]

Kickahead (USA) Ian Williams a55 65
7 b g Danzig(USA) —Krissante (USA) (Kris)
1606[4] 2518[9] 3735[10] 7688[4]

Kidlat B G Powell a85 83
4 b g Cape Cross(IRE) —Arruhan (IRE) (Mujtahid (USA))
271[6] 392[2] 847[2] ◆ 1088[5] 1357[7] 1812[9] (2351) 2641[3] 4716[5] 5266[5] 5802[7] 6059[6] 6973[12]

Kidnap (IRE) M G Quinlan a31
2 b c Desert Style(IRE) —Rosalia (USA) (Red Ransom (USA))
7001[9] 7749[11]

Kidnapping (IRE) S Botti 98
2 b c Intikhab(USA) —Claba Di San Jore (IRE) (Barathea (IRE))
7205a[3]

Kidogo (FR) E Drai a35
3 gr c Enrique—Gaelique (FR) (Gay Mecene (USA))
6980a[9]

Kidson (USA) George Baker a27 54
3 bb g Lemon Drop Kid(USA) —Solo (USA) (Halo (USA))
2479[8] 2866[2] 4142[2] 4470[3]

Kielty's Folly B P J Baugh a59 48
5 gr g Weet-A-Minute(IRE) —Three Sweeties (Cruise Missile)
537[2] 674[2] 867[6] 1773[5] 2390[5] 3637[9] 7600[2] 7755[5] (7814)

Kiho Eve Johnson Houghton a53 66
4 b g Dashing Blade—Krim (GER) (Lagunas)
1000[6] 1287[9] 1892[5] 2040[11] 2519[3] 3216[3] 3788[4]

Kilburn A J Lidderdale a76 74
5 b g Grand Lodge(USA) —Lady Lahar (Fraam)
25[2] (959) 1288[3] 1813[8] 2495[6]

Kildangan Girl W R Muir a31 43
2 b f Refuse To Bend(IRE) —Paola Maria (Daylami (IRE))
2914[5] 4427[6] 5368[9] 5613[10]

Kildare Sun (IRE) J Mackie a79 73
7 b g Desert Sun—Megan's Dream (IRE) (Fayruz)
79[12] 737[3] 981[3] 1192[5] 1332[3] ◆ 1887[3] 2166[2] 2542[2] 2665[3] 3331[12] 4548[12] 6174[9] 6462[5] (6806)

Kilkenny Bay W Jarvis a57 21
3 b f Tobougg(IRE) —Miss Arizona (IRE) (Sure Blade (USA))
2082[8]

Killeeter (IRE) Kevin Prendergast a66 55
2 ch f Kheleyf(USA) —Moet (IRE) (Mac's Imp (USA))
6401a[5]

Killer Class J S Goldie 70
4 ch m Kyllachy—Class Wan (Safawan)
4464[7] 4530[7] 5148[8] 6010[5] 6159[9] 6314[3] 7081[13]

Killusty Fancy (IRE) D J S Ffrench Davis a28 65
2 b c Refuse To Bend(IRE) —Crafty Fancy (IRE) (Intikhab (USA))
2771[12] 4006[8] 4811[3] 6071[10]

Kilmanseck Eve Johnson Houghton 65
2 b g Royal Applause—Corndavon (USA) (Sheikh Albadou)
2844[12] 5527[9] 5867[7] 6364[2] 6590[13]

Kilmeena Dream J C Fox a31
5 b m Foxhound(USA) —Kilmeena Glen (Beveled (USA))
2184[8] 2794[14] 3071[9]

Kilmeena Magic J C Fox a20 47
7 b m Fumo Di Londra(IRE) —Kilmeena Lady (Inca Chief (USA))
6612[7]

Kilmun K A Ryan a18 35
3 b g Zamindar(USA) —Didicoy (USA) (Danzig (USA))
5599[10] 6390[10] 6823[14] 7592[7] 7796[12]

Kilo Alpha Mme C Head-Maarek 97
2 b f King's Best(USA) —Anasazi (IRE) (Sadler's Wells (USA))
6523a[9]

Kilsyth (IRE) S Parr a16 56
3 b f Marju(IRE) —Easter Song (USA) (Rubiano (USA))
564[7]

Kilt Rock (IRE) T G Mills a71 60
2 ch g Giant's Causeway(USA) —Eliza (USA) (Mt. Livermore (USA))
4336[8] 4985[9] 5317[7] 6345[2] (6610) 6829[5]

Kimberlais (FR) Rod Collet
2 gr f Equerry(USA) —Reine Du Desert (FR) (Simon Du Desert (FR))
5956a[0]

Kimberley Downs (USA) M Johnston a90 89
3 gr g Giant's Causeway(USA) —Fountain Lake (USA) (Vigors (USA))
(1105) 1792[6] 3051[12] 5870[7] (6273) 6734[8]

Kimberley Rocks (IRE) *R M Beckett* a46 58
3 b f Intikhab(USA) —Kalimar (IRE) (Bigstone (IRE))
2082[P] 3696[5] 4381[3] 4648[12] 5384[11] 6031[8]
Kina Jazz *J Ryan* a47 10
3 b f Kyllachy—Tapas En Bal (FR) (Mille Balles (FR))
135[4] 390[9] 664[5] 758[6] 6968[11] 7462[8]
Kindest *C F Wall* 80
3 b f Cadeaux Genereux—Star Profile (IRE) (Sadler's Wells (USA))
1406[11] 2139[5] 2856[4] 3408[5] (4079) 4473[2] 4799[2]
Kind Heart *P Howling* a77 77
3 b f Red Ransom(USA) —Portorosa (USA) (Irish River (FR))
4280[4] 4740[3] 5327[4] (5953) 6570[2]
Kindlelight Blue (IRE) *N P Littmoden* a80 71
5 gr g Golan(IRE) —Kalimar (IRE) (Bigstone (IRE))
873[5]
Kinetic Art (IRE) *R M Whitaker* 7
4 b g Mull Of Kintyre(USA) —Sylviani (Ashkalani (IRE))
3731[6] 6248[7]
Kinetix *J H M Gosden* a59 74
3 gr f Linamix(FR) —Kalambara (IRE) (Bluebird (USA))
1844[2] ◆ 2848[2] 4234[2] 5718[2] 6166[3] 7367[3]
Kingaroo (IRE) *G Woodward* a67 57
3 b g King Charlemagne(USA) —Lady Naomi (USA) (Distant View (USA))
228[2] 287[4] 520[3] 620[2] 1155[7] 1361[8] 2357[11] 4171[11] 4375[8] 4669[3] 7127[13]
King Bathwick (IRE) *A B Haynes* a60 67
4 b g Golan(IRE) —Princess Sabaah (IRE) (Desert King (IRE))
42[8]
King Charles *E A L Dunlop* a88 105
5 b g King's Best(USA) —Charlecote (IRE) (Caerleon (USA))
1673[6] ◆ 2055[6] 2342[7] 2891[4] (4091) 4315[5] 4770[7] 5437[7] 6013[10] 6470[4] 6816[5] 7035[8]
King Columbo (IRE) *Miss J Feilden* a86 79
4 ch g King Charlemagne(USA) —Columbian Sand (IRE) (Salmon Leap (USA))
1633[5] 2052[3] 2244[4] 3112[6] (3357) 4060[4] 4502[5] 5003[8] 6004[2] 6476[8] 7189[12]
King De Lune (FR) *C E Longsdon* a63
7 ch g Muhtathir—Eclipse De Lune (USA) (Shahrastani (USA))
679[3] 835[6]
Kingdom Of Fife *Sir Michael Stoute* 113
4 b g Kingmambo(USA) —Fairy Godmother (Fairy King (USA))
1798[2] (2342) 3873[2] ◆ 5447[3] 6303[3]
Kingdom Of Light *J Howard Johnson* 94
2 gr c Exceed And Excel(AUS) —Silver Chime (Robellino (USA))
1610[2] ◆ (1866) 3046[10] 3871[2] 4547[6] 5198[7] 6486[4]
Kingdom Of Munster (IRE) *A P O'Brien* 93
2 b c Danehill Dancer(IRE) —Kitty O'Shea (Sadler's Wells (USA))
4250a[4] 5275a[5]
King Fernando *P Beaumont* 44
6 gr g Silver Patriarch(IRE) —Kastelruth (Midyan (USA))
3068[10]
King Fingal (IRE) *J J Quinn* 85
4 b g King's Best(USA) —Llia (Shirley Heights)
1990[4] 2698[2] ◆ 3266[9] 3826[8] 4561[5] 5671[5] 6681[14]
King Gabriel (IRE) *Andrew Turnell* a50 43
7 b g Desert King(IRE) —Broken Spirit (IRE) (Slip Anchor)
248[5] 669[5]
King Goldenfort (IRE) *J Van Handenhove* a50
3 b g King Charlemagne(USA) —Goldenfort Queen (IRE) (Distinctly North (USA))
5784a[0]
King In Waiting (IRE) *J Hetherton* a63 68
6 b g Sadler's Wells(USA) —Ballerina (IRE) (Dancing Brave (USA))
3154[6] 3393[5] 3705[7] 4350[10] 4551[9] 4972[8] 5734[5] 6432[2] 6676[5]
King Jock (USA) *R J Osborne* a82 112
8 b g Ghazi(USA) —Glen Kate (Glenstal (USA))
182a[4] 265a[7] 413a[3] 697a[6] 5249[11] 5924a[8] 6530a[6]
King Kenny *Mrs A Malzard* a78 79
4 ch g Lomitas—Salanka (IRE) (Persian Heights)
558[7] 6541[3] 1132[4] 1244[14] 1343[11] 1694[14] 5540a[4]
King Ledley (USA) *Darrin Miller* 104
2 b c Stormin Fever(USA) —Mt Kobla (USA) (Mt. Livermore (USA))
1994a[4] 2957a[2] 3436a[3] 3895a[2] 4359a[6] 5275a[3] 6317a[3] 7304a[10]
King Of Axum (IRE) *M Johnston* 79
2 b c Soviet Star(USA) —Ezana (Ela-Mana-Mou) (1661) 1991[4] 2413[3] 3702[7]
King Of Cadeaux (IRE) *M A Magnusson* a54 40
4 br g Cadeaux Genereux—Purple Haze (IRE) (Spectrum (IRE))
781[1] 746[8]
King Of Charm (IRE) *M Hill* a53 42
6 ch g King Charlemagne(USA) —Pumpona (USA) (Sharpen Up)
22[9]
King Of Connacht *M Wellings* a64 64
6 b g Polish Precedent(USA) —Lady Melbourne (IRE) (Indian Ridge)
1254[12] 1496[4] (1785) 2171[3] 2878[4] 3247[9] 4054[9] 4721[4] 4861[2] (5103) 5479[10] 6668[9] 6806[4] 6998[4] 7599[7] (7719) 7798[6] 7856[6]
King Of Dalyan (IRE) *Miss Tracy Waggott* 26
4 ch g Desert Prince(IRE) —Fawaayid (USA) (Vaguely Noble)
4051[1]
King Of Defence *M A Jarvis* a74 63
3 ch g Kyllachy—Duena (Grand Lodge (USA))
1620[3] 2797[10] 6699[2] ◆ (7180) 7432[8] 7692[2] 7876[10]

King Of Dixie (USA) *W J Knight* a111 115
5 ch g Kingmambo(USA) —Dixie Accent (USA) (Dixieland Band (USA))
(815) 1346[5] (1641) 2476[5]
King Of Eden (IRE) *E J Alston* 49
3 b g Royal Applause—Moonlight Paradise (USA) (Irish River (FR))
2820[5] 3764[4] 4505[12] 5158[9] 6823[5] 7082[11]
King Of Legend (IRE) *D Morris* a70 59
5 b g King Charlemagne(USA) —Last Quarry (Handsome Sailor)
(216) 5543 ◆ 823[2] 898[8] 2441[12] (3092) 3448[4] 4034[6] 4465[7] 6349[11] 7109[2] 7236[9] 7475[12]
King Of Reason *D M Simcock* a68 76
2 b c King's Best(USA) —Sheer Reason (USA) (Danzig (USA))
2825[3] 3310[4] 4233[3]
King Of Rhythm (IRE) *D Carroll* a62 81
6 b g Imperial Ballet(IRE) —Sharadja (IRE) (Doyoun)
2166[8] 2531[3] 2769[6] 3002[13] 3234[8] 3264[12] 3653[10] 7599[4] 7755[3] ◆ (7796)
King Of Rome (IRE) *M F De Kock* a102 114
4 b h Montjeu(IRE) —Amizette (USA) (Forty Niner (USA))
702a[9] ◆ 772a[3] 1012a[13] 5662[7] 6056[6] 6290[8] 7185[10]
King Of Sparta (USA) *T J Fitzgerald* a45 38
4 b h Van Nistelrooy(USA) —Selling Sunshine (USA) (Danzig (USA))
3098[11] 3561[11]
King Of Swords (IRE) *N Tinkler* a54 78
5 b g Desert Prince(IRE) —Okey Dorey (IRE) (Lake Coniston (IRE))
1685[13] 1877[2] 2225[7] 2472[7] 2770[6] 2897[11] 3065[8] 3445[10] 3860[12] 4191[7] (4662) (5073) 5518[2] (5978) 6233[2] 6666[6] 6897[7]
King Of Sydney (USA) *Mario Hofer* 111
3 b c Diesis—Padmore (USA) (French Deputy (USA))
1395a[3] 1915a[7] (4582a) 5585a[7] 6718a[4] 7208a[9]
King Of The Beers (USA) *R A Harris* a68 54
5 rg g Silver Deputy(CAN) —Pracer (USA) (Lyphard (USA))
186[3] 514[2] 669[3] 737[7] 791[4] (918) 1122[8] 1442[2] 1568[6] 2878[8] 2912[11] 3503[10] 3929[9] 4170[3] 4373[5] 5377[4] 6584[12]
King Of The Moors (USA) *R C Guest* a56 77
6 b g King Of Kings(IRE) —Araza (USA) (Arazi (USA))
1279[3] 1514[5] 1830[3] 2166[6] 3401[3] 3457[7] 3863[9] 4435[16] 4845[10] 5289[3] (5944) 6012[3] (6312) 6547[3] 6760[12] 7247[9] 7615[7] 7783[5]
King Of Wands *J L Dunlop* 103
3 b c Galileo(IRE) —Maid To Treasure (IRE) (Rainbow Quest (USA))
(1427) 2208[2] (3276) (4248) ◆ 5425[5]
King Of Windsor (IRE) *R M Beckett* a66 80
2 b g Intikhab(USA) —Kismah (Machiavellian (USA))
4900[4] 5212[2] 6802[5]
King Olav (UAE) *A W Carroll* a94 88
4 ch g Halling(USA) —Karamzin (USA) (Nureyev (USA))
(550) 801[2] 1003[12] 1666[2] 2242[8] 5437[11] 6648[5] 7018[9] 7233[2]
King O'The Gypsies (IRE) *J Howard Johnson* 96
4 b h Sadler's Wells(USA) —Love For Ever (IRE) (Darshaan)
2471[7]
King Pin *Miss Tracy Waggott* 66
4 b g Pivotal—Danehurst (Danehill (USA))
1243[7] 1734[8] 2361[2] 2722[2] (3124) ◆ 3857[3] 4435[7] 5601[12]
King Red *Tom Dascombe* a80
5 ch h King's Best(USA) —Pearl Barley (IRE) (Polish Precedent (USA))
1286[4] (7557) (7785)
King Royal (IRE) *Patrick J Flynn* a53 77
4 br g Val Royal(FR) —Hadawah (USA) (Riverman (USA))
4510a[8]
Kings Ace (IRE) *A P Jarvis* a60 62
3 b g King's Best(USA) —Full Cream (USA) (Hennessy (USA))
(1437) 1839[9] 2132[7] 2417[3] 3010[9] 5362[2] 6140[8] 6914[8] 7180[4] 7416[4] 7479[6] 7817[11]
King's Alchemist *M D I Usher* a24 59
4 b g Slickly(FR) —Pure Gold (Dilum (USA))
1001[0]
Kings Aphrodite *Miss Gay Kelleway* 42
2 gr g Reset(AUS) —Arctic Queen (Linamix (FR))
1358[7] 1534[7] 2187[11]
King's Apostle (IRE) *W J Haggas* a89 119
5 b h King's Best(USA) —Politesse (USA) (Barathea (IRE))
1676[7] ◆ 1989[2] ◆ 3140[10] 3819[5] (4837a)
King's Approach (IRE) *R Hannon* a57 73
2 gr c Fasliyev(USA) —Lady Georgina (Linamix (FR))
1358[3] (1511) 2087[3] 2702[8] 3424[5] 4488[17] 5344[8] 5908[6] 6585[6]
King's Bastion (IRE) *Luke Comer* a79 90
5 b g Royal Applause—Aunty Mary (Common Grounds)
1376a[11]
Kings Bayonet *H R A Cecil* a76 73
2 ch g Needwood Blade—Retaliator (Rudimentary (USA))
4176[2] 5198[14] (6254)
King's Caprice *J A Geake* a98 89
8 ch g Pursuit Of Love—Palace Street (USA) (Secreto (USA))
1288[9] 2434[12] 2883[12]
King's Chorister *Miss Gay Kelleway* a61 61
3 ch g King's Best(USA) —Chorist (Pivotal)
77[8] 2281[0] 296[7] 1363[6] 1594[6] 2220[3] 2487[3] 2802[7] 3685[3] (4177) 4279[2] 4397[6]

King's Colour *B R Johnson* a90 85
4 b g King's Best(USA) —Red Garland (Selkirk (USA))
155[3] 398[6] 726[4] 4293[4] (5429) ◆ (5804) 6614[5] 7111[2] (7437) ◆ 7516[2]
King's Counsel (IRE) *J Hetherton* a41 63
3 ch g Refuse To Bend(IRE) —Nesaah's Princess (Sinndar (IRE))
3294[3] 3703[5] 4230[4] 4431[2] 4822[12] 4846[6] 5733[11] 6342[6]
Kingsdale Ocean (IRE) *D K Weld* a97 96
6 b g Blue Ocean(USA) —Madmosel John (IRE) (Martin John)
1376a[4] 3435a[9] 4360a[13]
Kingsdale Orion (IRE) *B Ellison* a82 91
5 bb g Intikhab(USA) —Jinsiyah (USA) (Housebuster (USA))
766[6] 999[3] 1170[11] 1990[12] 2055[8] 2932[13] 3266[3] (3393) 3977[3] 4102[5] 4840[3] 5334[4] 5671[3]
Kings Destiny *M A Jarvis* a86 106
3 b g Dubai Destination(USA) —Jalousie (IRE) (Barathea (IRE))
(1086) ◆ 1792[4] 2715[2] (4103) 5656[4] 6662[2] 7293[10]
Kingsdine (IRE) *M S Saunders* 61
2 b c King's Best(USA) —Lunadine (FR) (Bering)
4424[9] 4946[5] 5499[15]
King's Fable (USA) *Karen George* a68 65
6 b g Lear Fan(USA) —Fairy Fable (IRE) (Fairy King (USA))
3927[9] 4538[9] 5444[2] 5680[5] 6226[6]
Kingsfort (USA) *Kevin Prendergast* 117
2 bb c War Chant(USA) —Princess Kris (Kris) (5892a) ◆
Kings Gambit (SAF) *T P Tate* 112
5 ch g Silvano(GER) —Lady Brompton (SAF) (Al Mufti (USA))
436a[5] 642a[4] 772a[5] 1012a[15] 4329[3] ◆ 5023[7] 5764[4] 6644[5]
Kingsgate Castle *Miss Gay Kelleway* a71 65
4 b g Kyllachy—Ella Lamees (Statoblest)
499[5] 2088[7] 2418[9] 3732[8] 3983[6] 4536[7] 4748[9] 5254[4] 5729[2] 5842[4] 6216[8] 6252[2] 6783[2] 6967[9] (7770) 7834[2]
Kingsgate Choice (IRE) *J R Best* a76
2 b c Choisir(AUS) —Kenema (IRE) (Petardia)
7317[3] ◆ (7556)
Kingsgate Native (IRE) *Sir Michael Stoute* 123
4 b g Mujadil(USA) —Native Force (IRE) (Indian Ridge)
3140[13] (4456) ◆ 5233[6]
Kingsgate Storm (IRE) *J R Best* a61 80
3 gr g Mujadil(USA) —In The Highlands (Petong)
85[4] 4535[9] 5031[13] 5506[5] 6205[9] 6340[9] 7002[9] 7052[3]
King's Head (IRE) *Miss L A Perratt* a96 98
6 b g King's Best(USA) —Ustka (Lomond (USA))
(456) 584[5] 5551[10] 6095[10] 6313[7] 6412[3] 6986[6]
Kingshill Prince *W J Musson* a23 62
3 b g Mark Of Esteem(IRE) —Trefoil (FR) (Blakeney)
1255[7] 2320[14] 3302[12]
Kingsholm *N Wilson* a71 67
7 ch g Selkirk(USA) —Putuna (Generous (IRE))
238[9] 1011[5] 3689[8] 3943[12] 4139[6] 6012[14] 6987[9]
King's Icon (IRE) *M Wigham* a74 70
4 b g King's Best(USA) —Pink Sovietstaia (FR) (Soviet Star (USA))
1475[6] 3401[4] 3637[2] ◆ 4938[3] (5111) 5479[2] 5617[2] 5683[2] 5842[2]
King's Jester (IRE) *Lee Smyth* a54 51
7 b g King's Best(USA) —Scent Of Success (USA) (Quiet American (USA))
6415[5] 7579[7] 7755[10] 7818 [4]
King's Kazeem *G L Moore* a56 64
4 b m King's Best(USA) —Kazeem (Darshaan)
2384[5] 3462[10]
King's La Mont (IRE) *Mrs A J Perrett* a66 77
3 b c King's Best(USA) —La Leuze (IRE) (Caerleon (USA))
1407[3] 1809[5] 2126[11] 4714[8] 5101[5] 5726[6] 6338[7]
Kings Maiden (IRE) *James Moffatt* a65 68
6 b m King's Theatre(IRE) —Maidenhair (IRE) (Darshaan)
1556[2] (1936) ◆ 2233[2] 2969[4] 4068[2]
Kingsmaite *S R Bowring* a74 58
8 b g Komaite(USA) —Antonias Melody (Rambo Dancer (CAN))
223[3] (292) 489[7] 619[4] 882[3] 975[3] 1438[10] 1558[3] 1889[6] 2133[8] (2579) 2745[7] 3722[9] 3924[4] 4375[11] 5612[8] 7728[7]
King's Majesty (IRE) *A M Hales* a69 61
7 b g King's Best(USA) —Tiavanita (USA) (J O Tobin (USA))
319[3] 485[2] 534[2] 1178[4] 7888[8]
King's Masque *W R Muir* a74 59
3 b g Noverre(USA) —Top Flight Queen (Mark Of Esteem (IRE))
1380[4] 1730[7] 2710[5] 3321[6] 4177[4] 4719[9] (6370) 6968[4]
King's Miracle (IRE) *J R Gask* a41
3 ch f King's Best(USA) —Pretty Sharp (Interrex (CAN))
1379[8] 7464[4] 7826[11]
Kings 'n Dreams *D K Ivory* a61 74
2 b g Royal Applause—Last Dream (IRE) (Alzao (USA))
6616[9] 7288[4] 7537[4]
Kings Of Leo *J R Boyle* a69 83
2 b f Compton Place—Mrs Brown (Royal Applause)
1569[5] (1742) 1788[8] 2907[3] 3430[2] 3742[7] 3993[2] 6550[10] 7108[9] 7536[6] 7698[4] 7871[3]
Kings On The Roof *G C Bravery* a55 49
3 b c King Charlemagne(USA) —Stylish Clare (IRE) (Desert Style (IRE))
592[8] 752[4] 1465[4] 1940[4] 2577[9] 4155[9] 4648[14]
King's Parade *Sir Michael Stoute* a72 72
2 b c Dynaformer(USA) —Bay Tree (IRE) (Daylami (IRE))
4811[2] ◆ 5528[3] 6672[5]
Kingspark Boy (IRE) *W K Goldsworthy* 11
2 b g Tillerman—Malacca (USA) (Danzig (USA))
5907[13]

Kings Point (IRE) *D Nicholls* a89 98
8 b h Fasliyev(USA) —Rahika Rose (Unfuwain (USA))
995[10] 1124[7] 1684[6] 1821[4] 2612[8] 3014[7] 3391[9] 4293[16] 5206[7] 5944[4] 6217[4]
King's Ransom *S Gollings* a78 70
6 b g Daylami(IRE) —Luana (Shaadi (USA))
398[5] 798[6] 910[7] 1014[3] 3112[13] 3450[13] 4721[6] 5577[14]
King's Realm (IRE) *Sir Mark Prescott* a34 52
2 ch g King's Best(USA) —Sweet Home Alabama (IRE) (Desert Prince (IRE))
6162[9] 6285[6] 6592[8]
King's Revenge *S Lycett* a59 65
6 br g Wizard King—Retaliator (Rudimentary (USA))
1192[6] 1815[6] 2040[10] 6342[5]
King's Sabre *R C Guest* a66 81
3 ch g King's Best(USA) —Lightsabre (Polar Falcon (USA))
1638[4] 2674[13] 3341[11] 3982[2] 4700[7] 5403[4] 5676[10] 6170[2] 6442[2] 6914[10] 7057[12] 7219[5] 7280[13] 7424[6] 7595[7] 7709[11] 7796[2]
King's Salute (USA) *M Johnston* a97 68
3 b c Kingmambo(USA) —Imperial Gesture (USA) (Langfuhr (CAN))
(6974) ◆ (7573) ◆
King's Siren (IRE) *A M Balding* a71 64
3 b f King's Best(USA) —Blue Siren (Bluebird (USA))
1808[7] 2498[9]
King's Song (IRE) *Sir Michael Stoute* a76 74
3 ch c Indian Ridge—Alleluia (Caerleon (USA))
4519[6] ◆ (5616) 6059[4]
King's Starlet *H Morrison* a87 95
3 b f King's Best(USA) —Brightest Star (Unfuwain (USA))
(1605) 2036[6] 3016[11] 3641[4] 4489[7] 5260[6] 5798[7] 6814[9]
Kingston Acacia *A M Balding* a63 46
2 b f King Of Roses(AUS) —Derartu (AUS) (Last Tycoon)
5580[7] 5807[6] 6617[9] 7389[2]
Kingston Folly *A B Haynes* a60
2 gr g Septieme Ciel(USA) —Napapijri (FR) (Highest Honor (FR))
7663[5]
Kings Topic (USA) *A B Haynes* a77 53
9 ch g Kingmambo(USA) —Topicount (USA) (Private Account (USA))
47[2] 2531[1] 8131[0] (948) 1122[10] 6640[12] 7250[5] 7524[11] 7623[6]
Kings Troop *A King* a70 85
3 ch g Bertolini(USA) —Glorious Colours (Spectrum (IRE))
4814[5] 5221[14] 5670[6] 5986[7] 7428[5]
King Supreme (IRE) *R Hannon* a82 88
4 b h King's Best(USA) —Oregon Trail (USA) (Gone West (USA))
726[2] 798[4] (1179) 1666[6] 1753[2] 2475[13] 2566[2] 2945[3] 3406[3] (4042) 4450[5] 4644[8] 5667[6] 6936[4] (7201)
King's Warrior (FR) *G L Moore* 69
2 b c King's Best(USA) —Save Me The Waltz (FR) (Halling (USA))
7146[4] ◆
Kingswinford (IRE) *P D Evans* a80 85
3 b g Noverre(USA) —Berenica (IRE) (College Chapel)
1869[12] 2934[12] 3341[6] 3806[6] 4227[4] 4567[2] 4788[2] 5335[2] 5363[2] 6279[3] ◆ 6434[5] 6731[3] (6904) 7220[3] 7287[11]
King's Wonder *W R Muir* a93 97
4 ch g King's Best(USA) —Signs And Wonders (Danehill (USA))
(2434) 4423[13] 5196[7] 5476[5] 5874[6] 6702[5]
King Tune (FR) *Mme I Pacault* 75
8 ch g Green Tune(USA) —Kingram Palace (IRE) (Crystal Glitters (USA))
(5074a)
Kinian (USA) *J R Best*
2 ch c Langfuhr(CAN) —Back It Up (USA) (Mt. Livermore (USA))
5722[11]
Kinigi (IRE) *R A Harris* a60 53
3 gr f Verglas(IRE) —Kamalame (USA) (Souvenir Copy (USA))
403[3] 620[8] 2744[5] 3426[7] (3953) 4172[10] 4425[7] 5326[8] 5716[4] 6170[4] 6252[3] 7370[3] 7503[5] 7681[3] 7726[3] 7835[4]
Kinky Afro (IRE) *J S Moore* a70 61
2 b f Modigliani(USA) —Feet Of Flame (USA) (Theatrical (IRE))
2494[10] 4790[4] 5428[5] 6071[2] 6481[12]
Kinout (IRE) *K A Ryan* a63 74
4 b g Invincible Spirit(IRE) —Kinn (FR) (Suave Dancer (USA))
35[4] 95[9] 619[7] 921[6]
Kinouzeme (FR) *P Costes* 65
3 b f Ski Chief(USA) —Epiploom (FR) (Nicolotte)
6222a[6]
Kinsman (IRE) *T D McCarthy* a51 34
12 b g Distant Relative—Besito (Wassl)
43[6] (131) 247[6] 513[5] 674[9] 7197[10]
Kinsya *M H Tompkins* a86 95
6 ch g Mister Baileys—Kimono (IRE) (Machiavellian (USA))
1813[4] 2412[10] 3008[2] 3752[10] 5375[7] 6014[9] 6695[4]
Kintyre Bay *T D Barron* 31
2 gr g Mull Of Kintyre(USA) —Dim Ofan (Petong)
5668[10] 6896[10]
Kipchak (IRE) *C R Dore* a79 82
4 bb g Soviet Star(USA) —Khawafi (Kris)
274[4] (357) (505) 618[3] 777[4] (1030) 1169[5] (1244) 1510[3] 1766[7] 2071[14] (2185) 2828[4] 2998[8] 3243[3] 3457[8] 4181[8] 4787[10] 5124[3] 5349[5] 5601[10] 6120[8] 6739[6] 7506[3] 7561[6] (7716) 7762[3] 7876[6]
Kip Deville (USA) *Richard Dutrow Jr* a107 122
6 rg h Kipling(USA) —Klondike Kaytie (USA) (Encino (USA))
1011a[10]

Kiribati King (IRE) *M R Channon* a62 84
4 b g Kalanisi(IRE) —Everlasting (Desert King (IRE))
1356[6] 2018[7] 2766[6] 4332[4]

Kirkby's Gem *A Berry* 48
2 b f Firebreak—Just A Gem (Superlative)
2963[8] 3613[10] 4011[5] 4844[6] 5146[6] 5553[3] 5950[8] 6555[9]

Kirkie (USA) *T J Pitt* a68 27
4 bb g Gulch(USA) —Saleela (USA) (Nureyev (USA))
554[11] 675[RR] 918[11] 7802[5]

Kirklees (IRE) *Saeed Bin Suroor* a121 119
5 b h Jade Robbery(USA) —Moyesii (USA) (Diesis)
339a[3] (527a) ◆ 773a[4] 1012a[10] (3585) (4329) (5662) 6871a[7]

Kirk Michael *H Candy* a89 89
5 b g Selkirk(USA) —Pervenche (Latest Model)
1288[6] 2188[2] 2883[2]

Kirkson *P W Chapple-Hyam* 60
3 ch g Selkirk(USA) —Viva Maria (Hernando (FR))
1250[10] 1407[15] 2169[2] 3005[5] 3588[5]

Kirsty's Boy (IRE) *J S Moore* a73 78
2 ch g Tagula(IRE) —Mayfair (Green Desert (USA))
1005[8] (1669) 2136[3] 2995[22] 3424[6] 4089[7] 5198[18] 6104[10] 7435[2] (7690) 7874[2]

Kirstys Lad *M Mullineaux* a65 59
7 b g Lake Coniston(IRE) —Killick (Slip Anchor)
427[6] 554[10] 1153[3] 1495[8] 1938[6] 2263[2] 2783[10] 2971[12] 6256[7] 6818[10] 7152[8] 7416[8] 7599[6] 7718[3] 7798[7] 7814[3]

Kiss A Prince *D K Ivory* a75 70
3 b g Fraam—Prancing (Prince Sabo)
160[3] 394[2] (826) 1839[14] 2578[13] 3982[3] (4872) 5575[10] 7149[4]

Kissing The Camera *R Pritchard-Gordon* 103
3 b f Galileo(IRE) —Hoh Dear (IRE) (Sri Pekan (USA))
7208a[8]

Kiss 'n Tell *G L Moore* 2
3 ch f Sakhee(USA) —Time For Tea (IRE) (Imperial Frontier (USA))
4955[9]

Kite Hunter (IRE) *Mario Hofer* 99
2 ch c Muhtathir—Miss Chryss (IRE) (Indian Ridge)
6151a[5] 6887a[3] 7314a[4]

Kite Wood (IRE) *Saeed Bin Suroor* 121
3 b c Galileo(IRE) —Kite Mark (Mark Of Esteem (IRE))
2014[5] 2705[9] (3778) (5023) ◆ 5861[2] ◆

Kithonia (FR) *H R A Cecil* 73
2 b f Sadler's Wells(USA) —Ratukidul (FR) (Danehill (USA))
(5604) ◆

Kit Kat *George Baker* a7
2 b g One Cool Cat(USA) —Tanda Tula (IRE) (Alhaarth (IRE))
3786[11] 4152[12] 5106[9]

Kitty Allen *C N Kellett* a54 44
3 br f One Cool Cat(USA) —Aly McBe (USA) (Alydeed (CAN))
214[10] 583[5] 812[9]

Kitty Kiernan *J S Bolger* 96
2 b f Pivotal—Alstemeria (IRE) (Danehill (USA))
(1993a) 2557a[2] 3436a[4] 4028a[3]

Kiwi Bay *M Dods* a88 93
4 b g Mujahid(USA) —Bay Of Plenty (FR) (Octagonal (NZ))
1309[14] 1663[7] 2093[5] ◆ 2695[3] 3097[2] 3265[8] 3567[5] 3825[11] 4802[2] 5441[4] (6019) 6645[3] 7125[2] 7287[2]

Kiyari *M Botti* a63 36
3 b f Key Of Luck(USA) —Ashford Castle (USA) (Bates Motel (USA))
(332) 662[2] 938[4] 1183[5]

Kladester (USA) *B Smart* a62 47
3 ch g Van Nistelrooy(USA) —Longing To Dance (USA) (Nureyev (USA))
1452[6] 2091[16]

Kleio *H R A Cecil* a35
2 b f Sadler's Wells(USA) —Colza (USA) (Alleged (USA))
7624[10]

Kloof *K A Ryan* a77 74
3 b c Cape Cross(IRE) —Ravine (Indian Ridge)
917[4] ◆ 1257[4] 1490[7] 2795[2] 5598[6] 5884[3] ◆ 6348[7] 6539[4] 6823[9]

Klynch *B J Meehan* a92 87
3 b g Kyllachy—Inchcoonan (Emperor Jones (USA))
3028[7] 3219[3] 3592[10] 3747[14] (4044) 4227[8] 4761[3] 5523[14] 6167[10] 6458[7]

Knavesmire (IRE) *M Brittain* 91
3 b f One Cool Cat(USA) —Caribbean Escape (Pivotal)
1987[P] 3622[11] 3877[14] 4228[8] 6645[10]

Kneesy Earsy Nosey *Miss A Stokell* a51 51
3 ch f Compton Place—Evie Hone (IRE) (Royal Academy (USA))
228[6] 363[9] 450[3] 677[11] 759[8] 1982[9] 2809[8] 3426[3] 3852[5] 4397[8] 4994[6] 5254[10]

Knight Eagle (IRE) *Kevin Prendergast* a43 81
2 b g Night Shift(USA) —Heart's Desire (IRE) (Royal Applause)
3514a[4] 7258a[7]

Knightfire (IRE) *W R Swinburn* a58 35
2 b g Invincible Spirit(IRE) —The Castles (IRE) (Imperial Ballet (IRE))
1726[6] 2147[5] 2649[8] 7584[2] 7791[2]

Knight's Victory (IRE) *M Johnston* a53 74
3 b g Cape Cross(IRE) —Diminuendo (USA) (Diesis)
4838[6] (5259) 5551[7]

Knockback (IRE) *P R Chamings* a45 42
2 b g Redback—Knockanure (USA) (Nureyev (USA))
4219[11] 4646[7] 5017[6] 6736[10] 7482[7] 7513[8]

Knockdolian (IRE) *R Charlton* 67
2 b c Montjeu(IRE) —Doula (USA) (Gone West (USA))
6423[8] 7034[3]

Knockenduff *M R Channon* a59 63
2 b f Oratorio(IRE) —Sewards Folly (Rudimentary (USA))
3187[4] ◆ 3534[6] 4278[3] 4758[6] 5213[4] 5573[7] 5985[3] 6215[13]

Knock Three Times (IRE) *W Storey* a36 51
3 b f Hernando(FR) —Tawoos (FR) (Rainbow Quest (USA))
1128[6] 1691[5] 2104[7] 2627[8] 3541[9] 4506[7] 4806[4] 5442[6] 5734[8]

Knotgarden (IRE) *J R Fanshawe* 55
3 b f Dr Fong(USA) —Eilean Shona (Suave Dancer (USA))
3379[4]

Knot In Wood (IRE) *R A Fahey* a113 115
7 b g Shinko Forest(IRE) —Notley Park (Wolfhound (USA))
996[3] ◆ 1299[3] 1367[2] 1989[9] 2287a[7] 3141[10] (3388) 4037[4] (4330) 4523[3] 6091[3] 6304[10] 6661[9] 7232a[7]

Know By Now *T P Tate* a72 51
3 b g Piccolo—Addicted To Love (Touching Wood (USA))
154[3] 386[2] 2142[7] 3120[4] 4588[11] 5258[7] 6023[12]

Knowledgeable *B Palling* 45
2 b g Reset(AUS) —Belle's Edge (Danehill Dancer (IRE))
4933[11] 5542[12] 5786[7] 7055[4]

Know No Fear *A J Lidderdale* a79 80
4 b g Primo Valentino(IRE) —Alustar (Emarati (USA))
170[4] 270[9] 539[6] 654[5] 757[9] 3031[8] 3465[8] 3562[13] 7280[9] 7591[10] 7768[10]

Kochanski (IRE) *J R Weymes* a58 59
3 ch f King's Best(USA) —Ascot Cyclone (USA) (Rahy (USA))
151[4] 343[4] (677) 1070[12] 1282[2] 1397[3] 1829[5] 2131[11] 2540[4] 2838[5] 3454[13] (4397) 4640[8] 4927[2] ◆ 5342[5] 5838[12]

Kodiak Kowboy (USA) *Steven Asmussen* a123
4 b h Posse(USA) —Kokadrie (USA) (Coronado's Quest (USA))
(6509a) ◆

Kokkokila *Lady Herries* a60 70
5 b m Robellino(USA) —Meant To Be (Morston (FR))
1273[4] 1807[5] 3029[9] 4625[6] (6692) 7124[4]

Kolokol (IRE) *D Prod'Homme* 104
2 b c Statue Of Liberty(USA) —Hecterine (IRE) (Hector Protector (USA))
3667a[5] 5057a[4]

Komreyev Star *R E Peacock* a55 49
7 b g Komaite(USA) —L'Ancressaan (Dalsaan)
7[10] 224[10] 405[2] 578[6] 823[5] 979[8] 5631[4] 6909[12] 7500[10] 7728[6] 7784[6]

Kona Coast *J H M Gosden* 94
2 b c Oasis Dream—Macadamia (IRE) (Classic Cliche (IRE))
4497[6] 4986[5] (5564) 6064[11] 6478[2]

Konig Bernard (FR) *W Baltromei* 106
3 br c Touch Down(GER) —Kween (GER) (Surumu (GER))
6657a[9] 6891a[2] 7302a[8]

Konig Concorde (GER) *C Sprengel* 106
4 b h Big Shuffle(USA) —Kaiserin (GER) (Ile De Bourbon (USA))
3416a[9] 4129a[3] 5563a[2] 6323a[3]

Konig Turf (GER) *C Sprengel* 113
7 b h Big Shuffle(USA) —Kaiserin (GER) (Ile De Bourbon (USA))
2113a[2]

Konka (USA) *E F Vaughan* a20 15
3 ch f Johannesburg(USA) —Defining Style (USA) (Out Of Place (USA))
920[6] 1176[6]

Koo And The Gang (IRE) *B Ellison* a69 61
2 b g Le Vie Dei Colori—Entertain (Royal Applause)
994[15] 1653[2] (2128) 2714[9] 6354[8] 7156[10]

Kookie *R E Barr* 48
2 b f Makbul—Breakfast Creek (Hallgate)
4100[7] 4430[6] 4817[9] 5440[5] 5595[12]

Kool Katie *Mrs G S Rees* a57 61
4 b m Millkom—Katie Komaite (Komaite (USA))
4496[11] 4710[8] 5205[2] 5423[7] 6157[12] 6760[9] 6900[4] ◆ 7174[8] 7361[2] 7599[9]

Koraleva Tectona (IRE) *Pat Eddery* a61 79
4 b m Fasliyev(USA) —Miss Teak (USA) (Woodman (USA))
1016[16] 2188[4] 2498[7] 2883[4] 3787[6] (4452) 5005[5] 5697[7] 6476[9] 7189[9]

Kostar *C G Cox* a96 86
8 ch g Komaite(USA) —Black And Amber (Weldnaas (USA))
3405[7] 5039[15] 5424[12]

Kotmaille (FR) *F Leralle* 33
4 ch g Maille Pistol(FR) —Kotine (FR) (Phantom Breeze)
7038a[9]

Kougouar (FR) *J-M Beguigne* 97
4 gr h Verglas(IRE) —Kouraya (FR) (Solid Illusion (USA))
3045a[2]

Krestena (FR) *Dominique Sepulchre*
3 b f Kendor(FR) —Arikaria (IRE) (Sri Pekan (USA))
5118a[0]

Kris Kin Line (IRE) *Sir Michael Stoute* a76 76
3 ch c Kris Kin(USA) —Shell Garland (USA) (Sadler's Wells (USA))
2178[3] ◆ (2922) 3827[7]

Kristallo (GER) *P R Webber* 65
4 ch g Lando(GER) —Key West (GER) (In The Wings)
2983[4] 3593[3] 3788[7]

Kristen Jane (USA) *Miss L A Perratt* 53
2 ch f Forest Wildcat(USA) —British Columbia (Selkirk (USA))
4342[4] 4752[7] 5360[9] 5945[6] 6134[4] 6409[7] 6983[15]

Kristopher James (IRE) *W M Brisbourne* a58 61
3 ch g Spartacus(IRE) —Ela Alethia (Kris)
1481[9] 2131[5] 3336[3] 3741[8] 4074[5] 4562[8] 4943[4] 5331[10] 6705[8] 7022[4] (7143)

Kronful *M A Jarvis* 62
2 b f Singspiel(IRE) —Albahja (Sinndar (IRE))
5417[3]

Krugerrand (USA) *W J Musson* a77 75
10 ch g Gulch(USA) —Nasers Pride (USA) (Al Nasr (FR))
285[12] 584[6] 877[2] 1081[2] 1314[3] 1815[2]

Krymian *Sir Michael Stoute* a81 53
2 gr g Bahamian Bounty—Kryena (Kris)
4908[10] 6125[2] 6592[7]

Krysanthe *J A Geake* a32
2 b f Kyllachy—Aegean Magic (Wolfhound (USA))
6942[8] 7326[13]

Kuanyao (IRE) *P J Makin* a76 66
3 b g American Post—Nullarbor (Green Desert (USA))
2496[8] (3580) 4304[3] 5112[3] 5581[2] (6701) (7479) (7729)

Kudu Country (IRE) *T P Tate* 77
3 gr g Captain Rio—Nirvavita (FR) (Highest Honor (FR))
2060[4] 3069[6] 3827[8] 4882[3] 5660[4]

Kumbeshwar *P D Evans* 81
2 b g Doyen(IRE) —Camp Fire (IRE) (Lahib (USA))
3692[16] 5251[6] (5852) 6397[5] 6557[3] (7218)

Kummel Excess (IRE) *George Baker* a65
2 ch f Exceed And Excel(AUS) —Ipanema Beach (Lion Cavern (USA))
6582[11] 6942[4] 7331[2] ◆ 7570[4] (7748)

Kunte Kinteh *D Nicholls* a69 69
5 b g Indian Lodge(IRE) —Summer Siren (FR) (Saint Cyrien (FR))
6216[12] 7173[11]

Kurtanella *R Hannon* a83 85
2 bb f Pastoral Pursuits—Aconite (Primo Dominie)
1706[2] ◆ (2034) 3086[U] 3396[10] (4647) 5187[3] ◆ 5913[4] 6471[5]

Kurtiniadis (IRE) *S Kulak* 112
6 b h Mujahid(USA) —Fiddler's Moll (IRE) (Dr Devious (IRE))
5618a[4]

Kwami Biscuit *G A Harker* 46
2 ch g Clerkenwell(USA) —Singer On The Roof (Chief Singer)
4188[5] 4503[12] 5519[9]

Kyber *J S Goldie* a27 66
8 ch g First Trump—Mahbob Dancer (FR) (Groom Dancer (USA))
2592[5] 3095[5] 3444[4] 4873[4]

Kyle (IRE) *C R Dore* a77 86
5 ch g Kyllachy—Staylily (IRE) (Grand Lodge (USA))
1150[3] 1565[5] 2276[8] 3030[8] 3738[5] 4072[11] (4154) 4607[6] 4787[4] 5167[9] 5436[8] 5767[7] 6220[5] 6635[12] 6916[4] 7203[4] 7807[3] 7870[7]

Kyleene *J Noseda* a78 74
3 b f Kyllachy—Mrs Nash (Night Shift (USA))
4164[2] (4859)

Kyle Of Bute *B P J Baugh* a50 67
3 ch g Kyllachy—Blinding Mission (IRE) (Marju (IRE))
1620[7] 2602[9] 3241[3] 3672[4] 4240[4] 4734[4] 5482[5] 5568[2] 5963[2] 6338[5] (6570) ◆ 6910[5] 7127[5]

Kyllachy King *Mrs A J Perrett* 34
3 b g Kyllachy—Baileys Dancer (Groom Dancer (USA))
2551[9] 2930[14]

Kyllachy Star *R A Fahey* a98 95
3 b g Kyllachy—Jaljuli (Jalmood (USA))
1002[5] 1214[4] 1869[10] (2504) (2926) ◆ 3816[6] 4459[6] 4814[3] 5490a[17] 6092[5] (6702) 7294[18]

Kyllachy Storm *R J Hodges* a65 79
5 b g Kyllachy—Social Storm (USA) (Future Storm (USA))
1403[3] (1787) ◆ (2124) 2520[5] 2911[2] 3691[8] 3995[5] 4907[7] 5065[2] 5719[10] 5901[6] 6915[7]

Kylladdie *S Gollings* a72 76
2 ch g Kyllachy—Chance For Romance (Entrepreneur)
1866[4] (2099) 3452[4] 4493[3] 5550[5] 7320[5] 7494[3] 7786[4]

Kyoatee Kilt *P F I Cole* a54
2 ch c Kyllachy—Oatey (Master Willie)
2631[7] 7213[7] 7429[5] 7597[5] 7683[5] 7887[10]

Kyzer Chief *R E Barr* 74
4 b g Rouvres(FR) —Payvashooz (Ballacashtal (CAN))
1310[5] (1518) 2717[8] 3002[6] 3491[7] 3828[2] 4189[5] 4311[4] 4753[10] 5341[6] 5518[10] 5978[4] 6220[8] 6489[5]

La Adelita (IRE) *M L W Bell* 93
3 b f Anabaa(USA) —Aiming (Highest Honor (FR))
7032[11]

Laafet *K A Morgan* a76 76
4 b g Royal Applause—Golden Way (IRE) (Cadeaux Genereux)
(4180) 4881[5] 6973[10] 7734[3] ◆

Laaheb *M A Jarvis* 116
3 b g Cape Cross(IRE) —Maskunah (IRE) (Sadler's Wells (USA))
3117[10] (3549) (4058) 4541[2] (6234) ◆ (7188)

Laa Rayb (USA) *M Johnston* a87 117
5 b g Storm Cat(USA) —Society Lady (USA) (Mr Prospector (USA))
1600[2] 1929[6] 2483[9] 3404[3] 3818[14] (4486) 4949[3] 5496a[7] 5995[4]

Laazim (USA) *M Johnston* a57 83
3 b g Seeking The Gold(USA) —Lindy Wells (USA) (A.P. Indy (USA))
4599[3] 5070[6] 6539[2] 6773[8]

La Badia (IRE) *L Riccardi* 90
3 b f Stravinsky(USA) —Goldendale (IRE) (Ali-Royal (IRE))
1394a[4]

La Bamba (GER) *A Wohler* 99
5 b m Samum(GER) —Loja (GER) (Spectrum (IRE))
5296a[3] 6714a[4]

La Belle Dane *J Noseda* 6
3 b f Danetime(IRE) —Lindfield Belle (IRE) (Fairy King (USA))
1837[9]

La Belle Joannie *S Curran* a56 60
4 b m Lujain(USA) —Sea Clover (IRE) (Ela-Mana-Mou)
3207[9] 3473[3] 3862[3] 4084[7] 4812[2] 5501[10] 5628[2] 6208[7] 7350[5] 7422[10]

Labisa (IRE) *H Morrison* a77 76
3 b f High Chaparral(IRE) —Damiana (IRE) (Thatching)
1193[2] 1281[2] (1973) 3102[4] 4072[7] 7158[6] 7356[2] 7627[4] 7828[5]

La Boum (GER) *Robert Collet* a92 117
6 br m Monsun(GER) —La Bouche (GER) (In The Wings)
1144a[9] 1552a[2] 2118a[4] 2428a[3] 3969a[5] 5300a[3] 6526a[7] 7128a[4]

Labretella (IRE) *D W Thompson* a52 50
2 b f Bahamian Bounty—Known Class (USA) (Known Fact (USA))
4383[6] 4595[9] 5397[10] 6819[7] 7334[3] 7501[3] 7638[3] 7792[8]

La Brigitte *J A Glover* a75 89
3 ch f Tobougg(IRE) —Bardot (Efisio)
2373[6] 4601[2] 7155[10]

La Capriosa *J A Glover* a75 73
3 ch f Kyllachy—La Caprice (USA) (Housebuster (USA))
(41) 91[3] 149[5] 421[2] (560) 605[3] 784[5] (819) 936[8] 1311[2] (1469) 1628[2] 1720[6] 3229[2] 3765[5] 4355[2] (4514) 4929[3] 5405[3] 5978[3] 6798[13] 7123[5] 7223[10]

La Columbina *H J Evans* a70 80
4 ch m Carnival Dancer—Darshay (FR) (Darshaan)
999[15] 4434[6] 4804[9] 5549[8] 6758[12] 7779[6]

La Cortezana *A P Jarvis* a36
5 ch m Piccolo—Blushing Belle (Local Suitor (USA))
4828[P]

La Coveta (IRE) *B J Meehan* a77 84
4 b m Marju(IRE) —Colourful Cast (IRE) (Nashwan (USA))
1405[9] 1964[6] 2495[4] 3008[3] (3627) 4328[7] 5062[10] 7092[6]

La Creme (IRE) *M R Channon* 65
3 b f Clodovil(IRE) —Dawiyda (IRE) (Ashkalani (IRE))
1327[7] 1745[5]

Lacrosse *M A Jarvis* a68 66
3 b g Cape Cross(IRE) —La Sky (IRE) (Law Society (USA))
272[4] 391[3] 4145[6] ◆ 4270[7]

Lacy Sunday (USA) *A Trybuhl* 78
3 b f King's Best(USA) —Lungta (USA) (Storm Cat (USA))
6605a[8]

La De Two (IRE) *Saeed Bin Suroor* a83 93
3 ch c Galileo(IRE) —Firecrest (IRE) (Darshaan)
(7278)

La Di Da *I Semple* 57
2 b f Oratorio(IRE) —So Admirable (Suave Dancer (USA))
6982[4] ◆

Ladiesandgentlemen (ITY) *R Feligioni* 98
2 b c Celtic Swing—Flying Flag (IRE) (Entrepreneur (USA))
6716a[4]

Ladies Best *B Ellison* a81 104
5 b g King's Best(USA) —Lady Of The Lake (Caerleon (USA))
(1172) 1460[4] 2031[4] 3873[5] ◆ 5173[15] 6013[7] 7293[11] 7720[9]

Ladies Dancing *J A Osborne* a77 41
3 b g Royal Applause—Queen Of Dance (IRE) (Sadler's Wells (USA))
(391) 755[3] 5876[8] 7413[8] 7620[4] 7794[5]

La Diosa (IRE) *Mrs S Lamyman* a60 70
3 b f Dansili—El Divino (IRE) (Halling (USA))
(296) (555) 677[5] 883[5] 5095[9] 5975[9] 6497[10]

Ladoga *R Gibson* 88
2 ch f Exceed And Excel(AUS) —Lamballe (USA) (Woodman (USA))
3967a[5] 5057a[7] 6326a[6]

Ladouce (FR) *Robert Collet* 89
3 b f Ski Chief(USA) —Veliana (FR) (Vettori (IRE))
7385a[5] 7696a[0]

Lady Alida *W Figge* 102
3 b f Tobougg(IRE) —Lady Annina (FR) (Dashing Blade)
(3186a) 4364a[5] 5585a[5] 6715a[3]

Lady Amberlini *C R Dore* a62 42
4 ch m Bertolini(USA) —Deco Lady (Wolfhound (USA))
1413[4] 1883[8] 2686[6] 3272[8] 5842[11] 7176[9]

Lady Anne Nevill *C W Fairhurst* 50
5 b m Nomadic Way(USA) —Prudent Pet (Distant Relative)
2090[7] 2403[10] 3120[9] 3486[9] 4403[6] 4593[8] 5554[8]

Lady Artemisia (IRE) *M L W Bell* 94
3 b f Montjeu(IRE) —Crimson Glory (Lycius (USA))
1573[8] 2006[2] 2403[2] (3250) 4103[2] 4458[5] 5828[2] 6594[6]

Lady Asheena *J Jay* a59
4 gr m Daylami(IRE) —Star Profile (IRE) (Sadler's Wells (USA))
378[6] (601)

Lady Aspen (IRE) *Ian Williams* a59 56
6 b m Elnadim(USA) —Misty Peak (IRE) (Sri Pekan (USA))
60[2] 114[8] (290) 569[6] 1037[6] 1254[9] 1538[4] 1983[7]

Lady Avon *W G M Turner*
2 ch f Avonbridge—Lady Filly (Atraf)
4689[7]

Lady Bahia (IRE) *Peter Grayson* a61 57
8 b m Orpen(USA) —Do The Right Thing (Busted)
46[6] 177[8] 467[3]

Lady Bluesky *A C Whillans* 50
6 gr m Cloudings(IRE) —M N L Lady (Polar Falcon (USA))
3093[6] 3352[6] 4347[6]

Lady Brickhouse *M D Squance* a45
2 b f Choisir(AUS) —Music Maid (IRE) (Inzar (USA))
6032[7] 6567[14] 7001[7] 7331[5] 7849[4]
Lady Brora *A M Balding* a80 79
4 b m Dashing Blade—Tweed Mill (Selkirk (USA))
1417[3] 1778[2] 2212[9] 4085[8] 4441[4] 5321[4] 6907[9]
Lady Bucket *Paul Green* a22 29
2 b f Avonbridge—Heart Of India (IRE) (Try My Best (USA))
1504[12] 2161[4] 4001[11] 5337[7] 6018[9] 7352[9]
Lady Calido (USA) *Sir Mark Prescott* a65 51
4 bb m El Prado(IRE) —Hydro Calido (USA) (Nureyev (USA))
1834[14] 4403[10] (4861)
Lady Cavendish (IRE) *A Bailey* a61 50
2 ch f Indian Haven—Madame Marjou (IRE) (Marju (IRE))
6441[6] 6672[8] 7064[9] 7120[5] 7334[8] 7474[12]
Lady Champagne *Miss J Feilden* a52
3 b f Zaha(CAN) —Slavonic Dance (Muhtarram (USA))
7671[10]
Lady Charlemagne *N P Littmoden* a50 11
4 b m King Charlemagne(USA) —Prospering (Prince Sabo)
61[7] 247[11]
Lady Christie *M Blanshard* a35 35
2 b f Tobougg(IRE) —Atnab (USA) (Riverman (USA))
5605[14] 6912[9]
Lady Compton *R Bastiman* 46
2 ch f Compton Place—Bright Spells (Salse (USA))
4889[8] 5553[7] 6245[12] 6555[8]
Lady Darshaan (IRE) *J S Moore* 108
2 b f High Chaparral(IRE) —Diary (IRE) (Green Desert (USA))
3101[3] (3430) ◆ 3748[3] 6269[2]
Lady Deauville (FR) *R Curtis* 113
4 gr m Fasliyev(USA) —Mercalle (FR) (Kaldoun (FR))
846a[10] 1758a[6] 2974[4] 3894a[6]
Lady Dinsdale (IRE) *T Keddy* a32 41
3 b f Refuse To Bend(IRE) —Lady Digby (IRE) (Petorius)
2862[9] 3859[12] 4155[10] 4819[9] 5470[9] 6390[11] 7517[10] 7591[12] 7686[6]
Lady Drac (IRE) *B W Hills* a62 73
3 gr f Hawk Wing(USA) —Cause Celebre (IRE) (Peintre Celebre (USA))
2640[5] 3427[10]
Lady Dunhill (IRE) *E W Tuer* a54 46
3 br f High Chaparral(IRE) —Ribbon Glade (UAE) (Zafonic (USA))
36[3] 228[3] 383[3] 621[13] 4819[16]
Lady Fas (IRE) *A W Carroll* a50 50
6 b m Fasliyev(USA) —Lady Sheriff (Taufan (USA))
56[8] 115[P]
Lady Florence *A B Coogan* a60 71
4 gr m Bollin Eric—Silver Fan (Lear Fan (USA))
1065[3] 2221[9] 2806[2] 3241[2] (3473) (3662) 3735[5] 4140[2] 4435[13] (4694) 5063[4] 5124[7] 5565[6] 6178[7] 6790[3] 6968[2] 7057[4] 7632[8] 7840[7]
Lady Francesca *W R Muir* a80 99
3 b f Montjeu(IRE) —Purring (USA) (Mountain Cat (USA))
1461[2] 1667[2] 4259[6] 4991[2] 5562a[7] (6029) 6267[7] 6891a[3]
Lady Gem *D H Brown* a46 50
3 b f Captain Rio—Cosmic Song (Cosmonaut)
246[6]
Lady Hestia (USA) *M P Tregoning* a49 73
4 b m Belong To Me(USA) —Awtaan (USA) (Arazi (USA))
1200[2] (1537) (5483) 5642[6] (6330) 6822[9]
Lady Hetherington *Jamie Poulton* a59
2 b f Kyllachy—Silver Top Hat (USA) (Silver Hawk (USA))
5752[8] 6781[10] 7451[6]
Lady Hopeful (IRE) *Peter Grayson* a49 28
7 b m Lend A Hand—Treble Term (Lion Cavern (USA))
153[9] 328[8] 474[6] 812[2] 2158[13] 2758[10]
Lady Jane Digby *M Johnston* a101 103
4 b m Oasis Dream—Scandalette (Niniski (USA))
6[3] (124) ◆ 284[2] 445[5] (1642) 2031[2] 2697[2] 2974[3] (3315) (5296a)
Lady Jinks *R J Hodges* a50 64
4 ch m Kirkwall—Art Deco Lady (Master Willie)
1786[12] 2222[8] 2517[2] 2762[5] 3503[2] 3997[5] 4146[5] 5246[10]
Lady Kingston *K R Burke* 11
3 ch f Kyllachy—Ash Moon (IRE) (General Monash (USA))
982[9]
Lady Lam *George Baker* a40 44
3 b f Slip Anchor—Tamara (Marju (IRE))
2710[9] 3590[5] 4246[11]
Lady Laurem *D A Nolan* 33
2 b f Avonbridge—Majestic Diva (IRE) (Royal Applause)
4463[7] 5292[9] 6049[10]
Lady Lefroy (IRE) *R A Fahey* a47 60
2 b f Oratorio(IRE) —Dos Talas (USA) (You And I (USA))
2940[6] ◆ 3487[7] 4100[3] 5207[9] 5543[5] 6034[4] 6721[5] 7168[7]
Lady Lion *W G M Turner* a21 51
2 b f Hunting Lion(IRE) —Miss Brookie (The West (USA))
1195[7] (1364) 1706[5] 1934[5] 2325[5]
Lady Llanover *P D Evans* a24 45
9 ch m Halling(USA) —Francia (Legend Of France (USA))
248[11] 385[8]
Lady Longcroft *J Pearce* a61 61
4 ch m Tobougg(IRE) —Top Of The Morning (Keen)
217[2] 323[2] (516) 688[3] 857[8] 7857[11]
Lady Lu *P F I Cole* a46 44
3 b f Lujain(USA) —Noble Story (Last Tycoon)
1465[9]
Lady Luachmhar (IRE) *R A Fahey* 87
3 b f Galileo(IRE) —Radhwa (FR) (Shining Steel)
1611[4] (2104) (4074) 4520[3] 6681[6]
Lady Lube Rye (IRE) *N Wilson* 65
2 b f Catcher In The Rye(IRE) —Lady Lucia (IRE) (Royal Applause)
1126[8] 1344[4] (1623) 2372[13] 3702[6] 4076[3] 4327[4] 4875[4] 5199[10] 5358[6]
Lady Lupus (IRE) *A P O'Brien* 98
2 b f High Chaparral(IRE) —Lady Icarus (Rainbow Quest (USA))
6316a[5] (6708a)
Lady Marian (GER) *Saeed Bin Suroor* 123
4 b m Nayef(USA) —La Felicita (Shareef Dancer (USA))
1011a[16] 4580a[7] 5300a[2] 5890a[4] 6525a[6] 7046a[5]
Lady Marmelade (ITY) *D Ducci* a82 93
6 b m Diktat—Ridge Reef (IRE) (Indian Ridge)
1394a[14] 1905a[12]
Lady Maya *Paul Henderson* a36 47
4 br m Prince Sabo—Monte Mayor Lady (IRE) (Brief Truce (USA))
3811[11] 4382[7] 5217[7]
Lady Meagan (IRE) *Patrick Carey* a73 45
4 b m Val Royal(FR) —Born To Glamour (Ajdal (USA))
1375a[13]
Lady Meg (IRE) *B Palling* 20
3 b f Spartacus(IRE) —Carna (IRE) (Anita's Prince)
5348[5] 5789[7] 6170[12]
Lady Mickataine (USA) *M J Grassick* a66 65
3 b f Speightstown(USA) —Ivy Leaf (IRE) (Nureyev (USA))
7719[7]
Lady Micklegate (USA) *J R Best* a73 63
3 b f Johar(USA) —Crimson Native (USA) (The Name's Jimmy (USA))
890[4] 1423[5] 1839[8] 2206[13] 6783[RR]
Lady Navara (IRE) *M Brittain* 8
2 b f Trans Island—Changari (USA) (Gulch (USA))
1735[7] 2663[11] 4226[14]
Lady Norlela *T J Fitzgerald* a33 44
3 b f Reset(AUS) —Lady Netbetsports (IRE) (In The Wings)
135[6] 3942[8] 4876[8] 5306[3]
Lady Oaksey *W S Kittow* a55 47
3 b f Tobougg(IRE) —Silk Law (IRE) (Barathea (IRE))
1573[10] 2323[9] 3951[5] 4625[13] 4904[10]
Lady Of Akita (USA) *J H M Gosden* a76
2 ch f Fantastic Light(USA) —Chancey Squaw (USA) (Chief's Crown (USA))
7522[5] (7630)
Lady Of Diktat (FR) *Mme C Vergne & D Sicaud* 55
2 b f Diktat—Ladygoon (FR) (Rangoon (FR))
1482a[8]
Lady Of Garmoran (USA) *P F I Cole* 43
2 bb f Mr Greeley(USA) —Poetically (CAN) (Silver Deputy (CAN))
6730[15]
Lady Of La Garenne (FR) *Mlle C Azzoulai*
4 br m Dark Moondancer—Alexa Dela Garenne (FR) (Lute Antique (FR))
5089a[0]
Lady Of Namid (IRE) *R Curtis*
2 ch f Namid—Princess Killeen (IRE) (Sinndar (IRE))
5284[11]
Lady Of The Desert (USA) *B J Meehan* 112
2 ch f Rahy(USA) —Queen's Logic (IRE) (Grand Lodge (USA))
(2354) 3015[6] (4295) ◆ (5199) 6449[3]
Lady Pacha *T J Pitt* 44
2 b f Dubai Destination(USA) —St Radegund (Green Desert (USA))
4618[8] 5466[6] 6274[7]
Lady Pattern (IRE) *P W D'Arcy* a67 79
2 gr f Verglas(IRE) —Patteness (FR) (General Holme (USA))
1569[7] 2563[3] (3248) 3782[9] 4539[6] 5265[5] 5835[3] 6292[3] 6774[5]
Lady Picola *Tom Dascombe* a4
3 b f Piccolo—Sukuma (IRE) (Highest Honor (FR))
6255[10]
Lady Pilot *Jim Best* a74 62
7 b m Dansili—Mighty Flyer (IRE) (Mujtahid (USA))
1767[4] 2172[2] 2519[4] 6188[10]
Lady Rangali (IRE) *Mrs A Duffield* 90
4 b m Danehill Dancer(IRE) —Promising Lady (Thunder Gulch (USA))
2266[7] 2768[3] 2999[3] 3312[6] 3560[2] 4102[6]
Lady Rockfield (IRE) *M J Grassick* a54 63
3 b f Rock Of Gibraltar(IRE) —Quiet Mouse (USA) (Quiet American (USA))
7715[9]
Lady Romanov (IRE) *P Butler* a30 57
6 br m Xaar—Mixremember (FR) (Linamix (FR))
4263[8] 4563[10] 5028[10] 7549[13] 7608[10]
Lady Rose Anne (IRE) *T D Barron* 66
4 b m Red Ransom(USA) —Surval (IRE) (Sadler's Wells (USA))
4350[9] 4822[14]
Lady Roulard (FR) *P Lenogue* 55
2 b f Voix Du Nord(FR) —Lise Des Bois (FR) (Dear Doctor (FR))
7166a[8]
Lady Royal Oak (IRE) *M Botti* a70 66
2 b f Exceed And Excel(AUS) —Enclave (USA) (Woodman (USA))
2604[3] ◆ 3015[13] ◆ 4746[3]
Lady Rusty (IRE) *P Winkworth* a73 73
3 gr f Verglas(IRE) —Patteness (FR) (General Holme (USA))
2174[7] 4050[7] 4650[2] 5168[5] 5666[6] 6698[3]
Lady Sadowa *B Grizzetti* 93
3 ch f Nayef(USA) —Sadowa (GER) (Lomitas)
3186a[4]
Lady Salama *K R Burke* a58 64
3 b f Fasliyev(USA) —Change Of Heart (IRE) (Revoque (IRE))
322[4] 689[5] 1253[9] 1531[11] 2169[7]
Lady's Art (FR) *E F Vaughan* a64 46
3 gr f Verglas(IRE) —Calithea (IRE) (Marju (IRE))
121[4] 1269[12] 5215[5] 6439[8] (6771)
Lady Slippers (IRE) *H J L Dunlop* 67
2 ch f Royal Academy(USA) —Woodland Orchid (IRE) (Woodman (USA))
5604[2] ◆ 6363[4] 7058[9]
Lady Songbird (IRE) *C F Swan* a72 77
6 b m Selkirk(USA) —Firecrest (IRE) (Darshaan)
5689a[22]
Lady Sorcerer *A P Jarvis* a70 74
4 b m Diktat—Silk Law (IRE) (Barathea (IRE))
1000[13] 1081[6] 1609[9] 2419[4] 2830[4] 4388[6] 5359[4] 6102[9] 7094[2]
Lady Splodge *George Baker* a35 56
5 b m Mark Of Esteem(IRE) —La Victoria (GER) (Rousillon (USA))
767[8]
Lady Springbank (IRE) *P D Deegan* 99
2 gr f Choisir(AUS) —Severa (GER) (Kendor (FR))
2401[3] (2940) 3528[3] 4245[6] (6316a)
Lady's Purse *Saeed Bin Suroor* 38
2 b f Doyen(IRE) —Jetbeeah (IRE) (Lomond (USA))
5605[13]
Lady Sugar (FR) *Mlle M-L Mortier* 51
4 b m Limnos(JPN) —Lady Suki (FR) (Caerwent (IRE))
5074a[3]
Lady Trish *C A Dwyer* a47
3 b f Red Ransom(USA) —Artifice (Green Desert (USA))
7464[9] 7610[9] 7771[11]
Lady Valentino *B D Leavy* a52 58
5 b m Primo Valentino(IRE) —Mystery Night (FR) (Fairy King (USA))
2149[7] 2333[2] 2608[8] 4021[4] 4818[3] 5679[5] 5888[8]
Lady Valiant *R M Beckett* a64
2 ch f Dr Fong(USA) —Protectorate (Hector Protector (USA))
3027[3] 3507[5]
Lady Vivien *D H Brown* a69 55
3 b f Kyllachy—Elsie Plunkett (Mind Games)
(140) (350) ◆ 1359[11] 2888[6] 3704[7] 4997[5] 5374[9] 5881[5] ◆ 6456[9]
Lady Willa (IRE) *B W Hills* a67 63
2 b f Footstepsinthesand—Change Partners (IRE) (Hernando (FR))
5604[8] 6163[6]
Lady Zena *M W Easterby* a31 36
3 b f Mind Games—Alustar (Emarati (USA))
2132[3] 2581[5] 3651[7]
Lady Zoe (IRE) *D Donovan*
2 b f Chineur(FR) —Petarga (Petong)
5553[9] 6207[11] 6494[12]
La Estrella (USA) *D E Cantillon* a95 92
6 b g Theatrical(IRE) —Princess Ellen (Tirol)
(66) (84) 456[2] 761[4]
La Fee Merchante (FR) *P Khozian* 42
3 ch f Ultimately Lucky(IRE) —Trilogie (FR) (Kendor (FR))
4130a[9]
La Fortunata *J R Jenkins* a72 69
2 b f Lucky Story(USA) —Phantasmagoria (Fraam)
1841[3] 2354[3] 2919[3] 3993[4] 4711[5] 5282[3] 6582[2] 6971[2]
Lagan Handout *C Gordon* a47 55
3 gr g Lend A Hand—Due To Me (Compton Place)
1322[5] 1746[8] 2141[12]
La Gifted *M R Channon* a72 64
3 b f Fraam—Aileen's Gift (IRE) (Rainbow Quest (USA))
869[3] 1128[4] 1253[5] 1746[4] 2141[9] 2515[4] 2797[9] 3018[10] 4105[7] 4643[10] 4937[10] (5581) (5883) (6103) 6699[5] 6720[5] 7051[7] (7129) (7158) (7275) 7321[5] 7643[11]
Lago Indiano (IRE) *Mrs A J Perrett* a71
2 b c Namid—My Potters (USA) (Irish River (FR))
6913[3] ◆ 7234[3]
Laguna Salada (IRE) *R Feligioni* 95
3 b f Invincible Spirit(IRE) —Flying Flag (IRE) (Entrepreneur (USA))
2310a[14] 6715a[5]
Lahaleeb (IRE) *M R Channon* 115
3 b f Redback—Flames (Blushing Flame (USA))
(1353) 1698[10] 2304a[2] 3088[5] 4580a[8] 5924a[5] (6872a)
Laid Bare *Mrs P N Dutfield* a28
2 b f Barathea(IRE) —Lady Eberspacher (IRE) (Royal Abjar (USA))
6931[12] 7177[8]
Lairy (IRE) *M F Harris* a46 56
2 ch g Fath(USA) —Akebia (USA) (Trempolino (USA))
1884[4] 2100[3] 2376[3] 3958[6] 4063[3] 4884[10] 5526[10] 5635[10] 5967[2] 6366[10] 7242[11] 7698[5] 7757[5]
Laish Ya Hajar (IRE) *P R Webber* a64 79
5 ch g Grand Lodge(USA) —Ya Hajar (Lycius (USA))
2351[4] 2675[4] (2878)
Lajidaal (USA) *M P Tregoning* 38
2 b c Dynaformer(USA) —Tayibah (IRE) (Sadler's Wells (USA))
5831[8]
La Joie (FR) *J-C Rouget* 90
2 b f Montjeu(IRE) —Last Trip (FR) (Anabaa (USA))
3934a[4] 7346a[4]
Lake Chini (IRE) *M W Easterby* a34 72
7 b g Raise A Grand(IRE) —Where's The Money (Lochnager)
1951[12] 2436[4] 3065[7] 3999[3] 4141[6] 4886[2] ◆ 5309[3] 6410[5] 6877[8]
Lake Kalamalka (IRE) *J L Dunlop* a69 73
3 b f Dr Fong(USA) —Lady Of The Lake (Caerleon (USA))
1050[2] (1580) 1930[8] 2829[6] 3300[6] 3776[3] 4948[6] 6376[9]
Lakeman (IRE) *B Ellison* a72 81
3 b g Tillerman—Bishop's Lake (Lake Coniston (IRE))
1471[5] 2248[8] 2578[4] 3316[5] 4309[5] 4591[7] 4841[5] (5295) 5598[11]
Lake Nakuru *H S Howe* a19
2 ch f Bahamian Bounty—Social Storm (USA) (Future Storm (USA))
2914[10] 4747[6] 5096[12]
Lake Palace *N Clement* 98
3 ch f Nayef(USA) —Lia (IRE) (Desert King (IRE))
7697a[2]
Lake Poet (IRE) *C E Brittain* a71 104
6 ch h Galileo(IRE) —Lyric (Lycius (USA))
847[5] 1172[4] 1460[2] 2671[2]
Lake Sabina *M R Hoad* a72 69
4 b m Diktat—Telori (Muhtarram (USA))
96[8] 269[9] 460[5] 661[9] 854[7] 1076[7] 1536[7] 1959[10]
Lake Wakatipu *R Ford* a65 27
7 b m Lake Coniston(IRE) —Lady Broker (Petorius)
972[11]
Lakuta (IRE) *F Rohaut* 87
4 ch m Pivotal—Ventura (IRE) (Spectrum (IRE))
7347a[8]
La Marea (FR) *F Danloux* a73 65
4 b m Green Tune(USA) —Ballade Viennoise (FR) (Cricket Ball (USA))
7822a[0]
La Marseillaise (IRE) *B W Hills* a68 69
3 ch f Medicean—Saturnalia (Cadeaux Genereux)
1327[11] 1825[3] 5572[2] 6348[10] 7067[2]
Lambency (IRE) *J S Goldie* a49 61
6 b m Daylami(IRE) —Triomphale (USA) (Nureyev (USA))
5443[12] 5729[8] ◆ 6160[10] 6216[10]
Lambourn Genie (UAE) *Tom Dascombe* a52 45
3 b g Halling(USA) —Mystery Play (IRE) (Sadler's Wells (USA))
2350[7] 2909[8] 3942[4] 4157[6]
Lambrini Lace (IRE) *Mrs L Williamson* a33 65
4 b m Namid—Feather 'n Lace (IRE) (Green Desert (USA))
5332[4] 5729[6] 6989[8] 7370[8] 7802[9] 7869[13]
La Mere Germaine (IRE) *Kevin Prendergast* a62 81
3 b f Indian Ridge—Champs Elysees (USA) (Distant Relative)
7297a[10]
Lamh Albasser (USA) *Saeed Bin Suroor* 96
2 ch g Mr Greeley(USA) —Madame Boulangere (Royal Applause)
2358[4] (3170) (3821) 4294[4] 5347[3] 5795[6] 6663[4]
Laminka *G C Bravery* a44 20
3 b f Intikhab(USA) —Lamees (USA) (Lomond (USA))
716[5] 849[8] 2082[9]
Lana's Charm *P J Makin* a53 42
3 b f Lend A Hand—Eljariha (Unfuwain (USA))
188[5] ◆ 348[6] 3625[5] 5647[13] 7002[13]
Lancaster Lad (IRE) *A B Haynes* a58 60
4 b h Piccolo—Ruby Julie (Clantime)
514[4] 749[10] 1741[10] 2737[3] 3241[11] 3473[8] 5905[13] 6336[5]
Lancetto (FR) *K R Burke* a55 102
4 b g Dubai Destination(USA) —Lanciana (IRE) (Acatenango (GER))
1458[15] 2031[7] 2305a[9]
Land Hawk (IRE) *J Pearce* a75 70
3 br c Trans Island—Heike (Glenstal (USA))
1214[5] 1466[5] 2300[5] 5524[5] 6124[3] 6365[3]
Landikhaya (IRE) *D K Ivory* a58 72
4 ch g Kris Kin(USA) —Montana Lady (IRE) (Be My Guest (USA))
114[11] 213[7]
Land 'n Stars *Jamie Poulton* a83 100
9 b g Mtoto—Uncharted Waters (Celestial Storm (USA))
1007[10] 1435[10]
Land Of Plenty (IRE) *E A L Dunlop* a43 33
2 b f Azamour(IRE) —Bring Plenty (USA) (Southern Halo (USA))
4705[7] 5330[7] 5942[8] 7493[2] 7731[5]
Landofthefourones (USA) *D R Lanigan* a57 68
3 b c Aldebaran(USA) —Cuanto Es (USA) (Exbourne (USA))
4057[5] 4472[4] 5071[2] 5840[4]
Lando Junior (FR) *X Nakkachdji* 91
3 b c Lando(GER) —Alcidiana (FR) (Linamix (FR))
1858a[9]
Landolino (FR) *J-M Lefebvre* 44
4 b g Trempolino(USA) —Champagne Sorbet (FR) (Kaldounevees (FR))
5204a[9]
Landora (FR) *A De Royer-Dupre* 87
3 b f Lando(GER) —Saquiace (USA) (Sagace (FR))
7302a[7] 7569a[0]
Landowner *Saeed Bin Suroor* 89
2 b c Shamardal(USA) —Rentless (Zafonic (USA))
5564[4] (6364) (6895) ◆ 7097[2]
Landskia (FR) *A Fabre* 101
3 b f Lando(GER) —Plissetskaia (FR) (Caerleon (USA))
2754a[7] 3968a[6] 5562a[12]
Landucci *S Curran* a83 69
8 b g Averti(IRE) —Divina Luna (Dowsing (USA))
97[6] 504[2] 725[9] 868[4] 1065[4] (1606) 1883[6] 2185[5] 2378[4] (2737) 3242[4] 3948[3] 4697[4] (5179)
La Nez (USA) *J Eric Kruljac* a99
2 bb f Storm Creek(USA) —Iza Bay (USA) (Iz A Saros (USA))
7282a[6]
Langford Decoit (IRE) *M R Channon* 60
3 b c Peintre Celebre(USA) —Litchfield Hills (USA) (Relaunch (USA))
1611[12] 1809[6] 2323[4] 2865[11] 3222[13]
Langham House *J R Jenkins* a63 32
4 ch g Best Of The Bests(IRE) —Dafne (Nashwan (USA))
118[3]
Langland Bay *W R Muir* a45 58
3 b f Diktat—Dodo (IRE) (Alzao (USA))
1379[6] 2795[7] 3876[5] 4375[9] 7158[7] 7236[14]

Lang Shining (IRE) *Sir Michael Stoute* 110
5 ch g Dr Fong(USA) —Dragnet (IRE) (Rainbow Quest (USA))
2015[9] 3640[9] 3872[4] 4404[6] 5262[8] 6094[7]

Lanizza *E A L Dunlop* a37 16
2 ch g Alhaarth(IRE) —Cerulean Sky (IRE) (Darshaan)
3167[11] 5192[7]

Lansdowne Princess *G A Ham* 42
7 b m Cloudings(IRE) —Premier Princess (Hard Fought)
4264[6]

Laokoon (GER) *Mario Hofer* a81 91
4 b h Areion(GER) —Little Movie Star (Risk Me (FR))
1043a[5] 6499a[6]

La Pantera *R Hannon* a79 82
2 b f Captain Rio—Pantita (Polish Precedent (USA))
1810[3] (2175) 6104[8] 6619[7] 7320[3]

Lapina (IRE) *A Middleton* a70 69
5 ch m Fath(USA) —Alpina (USA) (El Prado (IRE))
126[2] 330[6] 751[5] 1049[6] 3073[4] 3593[5]

La Poesie (GER) *W Baltromei* 94
3 b f Pentire—L'Heure Bleue (IRE) (Kendor (FR))
2874a[3] 3604a[6]

La Polka *H Morrison* a38 66
3 ch f Carnival Dancer—Indubitable (Sharpo)
1931[8] 2395[10] 4480[6] 5131[4] 5430[9]

La Preciosa *I W McInnes*
4 b m Arrasas(USA) —Morning Star (Statoblest)
7671[13] 7780[8]

L'Arcobaleno (FR) *J Rossi* a12
3 ro c Zieten(USA) —Nuvola (Highest Honor (FR))
4581a[10]

L'Arco Baleno (IRE) *S A Callaghan* a53 39
3 b f Catcher In The Rye(IRE) —Rainbow Java (IRE) (Fairy King (USA))
664[3] ◆ 820[3] 951[8] 1361[15] 2417[9] 2709[8]

Larehaan (USA) *B W Hills* 54
2 bb f Smarty Jones(USA) —Wendy Vaala (USA) (Dayjur (USA))
3820[10]

Largem *J R Jenkins* a60 25
3 b g Largesse—Jem's Law (Contract Law (USA))
4472[7] 5314[5] (5838) 6446[4]

Laristan (FR) *J-C Rouget*
2 gr c Sinndar(IRE) —Laxlova (FR) (Linamix (FR))
(5850a)

Larkham (USA) *R M Beckett* a79 92
3 bb g Action This Day(USA) —La Sarto (USA) (Cormorant (USA))
(1410) (2356) 3578[3] 5027[DSQ] 6234[4]

Larkrise Star *D K Ivory* a67 55
2 b f Where Or When(IRE) —Katy Ivory (IRE) (Night Shift (USA))
2771[5] 3507[4] 3979[4]

Larmont (FR) *E Libaud*
3 b g Kendor(FR) —Freedom Herself (FR) (Freedom Cry)
2293a[0]

La Rosa Nostra *W R Swinburn* a75 78
4 ch m Dr Fong(USA) —Rose Quantas (IRE) (Danehill (USA))
1348[2] 2150[5] 2641[6] 3114[2] 3721[3] 4495[7] 5243[6] 5910[6] 6640[4]

La Somome *B De Montzey* a55 71
2 b f Hernando(FR) —Far Across (Common Grounds)
3648a[10]

Lassarina (IRE) *B W Hills* 98
3 b f Sakhee(USA) —Kalanda (Desert King (IRE))
1353[5] 4317[3]

Lasse (GER) *P Vovcenko* 52
6 b g Hamond(GER) —Liberia (GER) (Pentathlon)
7821a[7]

Lasso The Moon *M R Channon* 83
3 b g Sadler's Wells(USA) —Hotelgenie Dot Com (Selkirk (USA))
1328[7] 1681[2] 2077[4] 2701[3] 3051[17] 3780[13]

Last Flight (IRE) *P Bowen* 64
5 b m In The Wings—Fantastic Fantasy (IRE) (Lahib (USA))
4417[12]

Lasting Applause (IRE) *F Doumen* 93
3 b f Royal Applause—Everlasting Love (Pursuit Of Love)
3968a[3] 4969a[9]

Lastkingofscotland (IRE) *G C Bravery* a62 92
3 b g Danehill Dancer(IRE) —Arcade (Rousillon (USA))
1755a[6] 7759[10]

Last Of The Line *B N Pollock* a78 56
4 b g Efisio—Dance By Night (Northfields (USA))
489[11] 545[6]

Lastofthemohicans (FR) *A P O'Brien* 86
2 b c Galileo(IRE) —Peace Time (GER) (Surumu (GER))
6318a[6]

Last Of The Ravens *J F Coupland* a21
2 b f Zaha(CAN) —Eccentric Dancer (Rambo Dancer (CAN))
7836[5] 7864[7]

Last Orders (IRE) *M G Quinlan* 48
2 gr c Bertolini(USA) —Sassania (IRE) (Persian Bold)
1616[5] 1939[9] 4153[8]

Lastroarofdtiger (USA) *J R Weymes* a78 54
3 b g Cherokee Run(USA) —Innocent Affair (IRE) (Night Shift (USA))
(1040) 1561[7] 2399[5] 3156[7] 3928[6] 4870[9] 7891[8]

Lastroseofsummer (IRE) *Rae Guest* a38 49
3 ch f Haafhd—Broken Romance (IRE) (Ela-Mana-Mou)
7126[6] 7648[8]

Last Sovereign *Jane Chapple-Hyam* a88 86
5 b g Pivotal—Zayala (Royal Applause)
(457) 1016[2] 1405[7] 2073[3] 2434[6] 4501[4] 5001[3] 5697[4] 6212[11] 6564[4]

Last Three Minutes (IRE) *E A L Dunlop* a89 98
4 b g Val Royal(FR) —Circe's Isle (Be My Guest (USA))
1603[4] ◆ 2073[10] (2387) 2933[3] ◆ 3752[6] ◆ 4261[6]

La Sylvia (IRE) *E J O'Neill* a76 98
4 b m Oasis Dream—Hawas (Mujtahid (USA))
1582[8] 1880[9] (5651a) 7458a[4]

Latansaa *M P Tregoning* 80
2 b c Indian Ridge—Sahool (Unfuwain (USA))
7029[3]

Laterly (IRE) *S Gollings* a96 102
4 b g Tiger Hill(IRE) —La Candela (GER) (Alzao (USA))
2055[12] 3620[9] 3873[14] 4781[3] 5137[7] 6106[9] 7465[3] 7720[5] 7789[10]

Late Romance (USA) *A Fabre* 89
2 b f Storm Cat(USA) —Illustrious Miss (USA) (Kingmambo (USA))
(5956a)

Lathaat *J L Dunlop* 46
2 bb f Dubai Destination(USA) —Khulood (USA) (Storm Cat (USA))
2490[9]

Latin Connection (IRE) *Lee Smyth* a33
3 b g Soviet Star(USA) —Via Verbano (IRE) (Caerleon (USA))
7361[10] 7401[8] 7863[8]

Latin Love (IRE) *David Wachman* 102
3 ch f Danehill Dancer(IRE) —Ho Hi The Moon (IRE) (Be My Guest (USA))
2960a[7] 3894a[2] 5487a[2]

Latin Scholar (IRE) *A King* a78 80
4 ch g Titus Livius(FR) —Crimada (IRE) (Mukaddamah (USA))
(3206) 3977[4] 4957[5] 5532[7]

Latin Tinge (USA) *P F I Cole* a84 87
3 rg f King Cugat(USA) —Southern Tradition (USA) (Family Doctor (USA))
1381[5] 1613[7] 2189[6] 6209[9] 6618[10] 6804[10]

La Tournesol (GER) *P Schiergen* 92
4 ch m Samum(GER) —La Bouche (GER) (In The Wings)
4365a[6] 6521a[6] 7569a[5]

La Toya J (IRE) *R Curtis* a60
2 b f Noverre(USA) —Bevel (USA) (Mr Prospector (USA))
7326[7] 7700[3] 7885[5]

La Tride (FR) *S Labate* 45
3 b f Le Triton(USA) —Envergure (Kenmare (FR))
6149a[4]

Lauberhorn *Eve Johnson Houghton* 48
2 b g Dubai Destination(USA) —Ski Run (Petoski)
4385[13] 5787[7]

Laudatory *W R Swinburn* a92 89
3 b g Royal Applause—Copy-Cat (Lion Cavern (USA))
(1214) ◆ 1870[4] ◆ 2329[3] 2890[8] 4540[4] 4983[4] 5640[4] 5986[2] 6535[6]

Laughing Boy (IRE) *L M Cumani* a43 81
3 b g Montjeu(IRE) —Mala Mala (IRE) (Brief Truce (USA))
2930[4] ◆ 3703[4] 4606[2] 5322[3] 6243[15] 6878[7]

Laughter (IRE) *Sir Michael Stoute* 87
4 b m Sadler's Wells(USA) —Smashing Review (USA) (Pleasant Tap (USA))
2697[5] 3315[7]

Laura Land *W M Brisbourne* a38 48
3 b f Lujain(USA) —Perdicula (IRE) (Persian Heights)
2943[12] 5205[6] 5531[7] 6705[7]

Laura's Lady (IRE) *G A Swinbank* 57
3 b f Namid—Catapila (USA) (Tactical Cat (USA))
(1922) 2365[5] ◆ 3381[4] 3614[3]

Laurel Creek (IRE) *M J Grassick* a93 82
4 b g Sakura Laurel(JPN) —Eastern Sky (AUS) (Danehill (USA))
(559) ◆ (899)

Laureldean Desert *R A Fahey* a40 58
2 b f Green Desert(USA) —Heady (Rousillon (USA))
4928[6] 5949[10] 6922[5] 7389[7]

Laureldeans Best (IRE) *R A Fahey* a59 67
3 b f King's Best(USA) —Vanishing River (USA) (Southern Halo (USA))
4354[3] 7401[3] 7648[3]

Laureldean Spirit (IRE) *R A Fahey* 73
2 br f Whipper(USA) —Mise (IRE) (Indian Ridge)
3823[2] ◆ 4460[4] 5852[3]

Laurel Guerreiro (JPN) *Mitsugi Kon* 118
5 b h King Halo(JPN) —Big Tenby (JPN) (Tenby)
7745a[13]

Lauren's Kitty (IRE) *J C Fox*
2 b f One Cool Cat(USA) —Home Comforts (Most Welcome)
6729[15]

Laurie Grove (IRE) *T G Mills* a86 83
3 b g Danehill Dancer(IRE) —Fragrant (Cadeaux Genereux)
763[2] 1001[4] 1291[14] 6243[4] 6731[16] 7141[2] 7583[8] 7833[7] 7881[3]

Lautenspielerin (GER) *Frau Marion Rotering* 81
3 br f Areion(GER) —Lutte Marie (GER) (Frontal)
1914a[9]

L'Auvergnat (IRE) *Mlle C Cardenne* a71 65
7 gr g Saddlers' Hall(IRE) —L'Authie (FR) (Linamix (FR))
7387a[9]

Lava Lamp (GER) *G A Harker* 74
2 b c Shamardal(USA) —La Felicita (Shareef Dancer (USA))
4595[6] 5129[2] 5785[4] 6247[3] ◆ 6534[5] 7290[12]

Lava Steps (USA) *P T Midgley* a77 59
3 b c Giant's Causeway(USA) —Miznah (IRE) (Sadler's Wells (USA))
3674[4] 6338[8] 7504[2] (7725)

L'Aventurier (FR) *J De Roualle* a73 78
3 gr g One Cool Cat(USA) —White Quartz (IRE) (Sadler's Wells (USA))
(5278a) (7037a)

La Verte Rue (USA) *Mrs A Malzard* a64 65
3 b f Johannesburg(USA) —Settling In (USA) (Green Desert (USA))
826[5] 5540a[6]

La Ville Lumiere (USA) *Saeed Bin Suroor* a50 70
2 b f Rahy(USA) —La Sylphide (SWI) (Barathea (IRE))
4869[6] 5547[3] 5906[5] 6921[9]

Lavirca Nath (FR) *D Barone*
0 b f Lavirco(GER) —Etoile De Pelmer (FR) (En Calcat (FR))
6325a[0]

La Voile Rouge *R M Beckett* a73 63
4 ch g Daggers Drawn(USA) —At Amal (IRE) (Astronef)
3469[8] 4500[8]

Law And Order *Miss J R Tooth* a46 60
3 b g Lear Spear(USA) —Sarcita (Primo Dominie)
1895[6] 2797[11] 3741[13] 5775[11]

Law Of Attraction (IRE) *J R Gask* 47
2 b g Invincible Spirit(IRE) —Karatisa (IRE) (Nishapour (FR))
3692[11] 4062[3]

Law Of The Jungle (IRE) *Tom Dascombe* a64 74
3 b f Catcher In The Rye(IRE) —Haut Volee (Top Ville)
7693[5] 7857[3]

Lawyer To World *Mrs C A Dunnett* a48 39
5 gr g Marju(IRE) —Legal Steps (IRE) (Law Society (USA))
302[5] 423[5] 1273[8] 2420[14] 3631[10]

Layali Al Andalus *M Johnston* 105
2 b c Halling(USA) —Lafite (Robellino (USA))
2588[2] ◆ (3376) (5515) ◆ 5859[5] 6318a[2] 7404a[9]

Lay Claim (USA) *Sir Michael Stoute* a75 85
2 bb c Seeking The Gold(USA) —Promptly (IRE) (Lead On Time (USA))
6109[2] ◆ 6679[4] ◆ 7130[4]

Layer Cake *J W Hills* a73 66
3 b c Monsieur Bond(IRE) —Blue Indigo (FR) (Pistolet Bleu (IRE))
1585[6] 2602[8] 3228[2] 3718[2] 4789[7] 5228[5] 5348[3] 5806[2] 6223[3] 6421[5] 6977[6]

Layla's Boy *R A Fahey* a75 79
2 ch g Sakhee(USA) —Gay Romance (Singspiel (IRE))
3017[4] 3652[2] ◆ 4194[2] 5251[8] 5682[4] 6136[4] 6727[3]

Layla's Dancer *R A Fahey* 81
2 b c Danehill Dancer(IRE) —Crumpetsfortea (IRE) (Henbit (USA))
(5674) ◆ 6993[4] ◆

Layla's Hero (IRE) *D Nicholls* 105
2 b g One Cool Cat(USA) —Capua (USA) (Private Terms (USA))
3487[4] ◆ (4011) 4525[2] (4739) 5198[10] (5658) (6677) ◆ (7016)

Layla's Lad (USA) *R A Fahey* a61
2 b c Dixieland Band(USA) —Requesting More (USA) (Norquestor (CAN))
7001[6] ◆ 7276[7] 7582[4] 7791[5]

Layla's Lexi *D Nicholls* 53
2 b f Reset(AUS) —Tricoteuse (Kris)
5620[3] 5977[12]

Layla's Prince (IRE) *D Nicholls* 50
2 b g Statue Of Liberty(USA) —Nihonpillow Mirai (IRE) (Zamindar (USA))
5253[6] 6646[9]

Layline (IRE) *R M Beckett* 92
2 b g King's Best(USA) —Belle Reine (King Of Kings (IRE))
(5627) 6472[3] 6993[13]

La Zamora *T D Barron* 85
3 b f Lujain(USA) —Love Quest (Pursuit Of Love)
1173[3] 1662[2] (2157) 2546[5] ◆ (3166) ◆ 4490[5] 5203[15] 5293[3] 6051[14]

Lazarus (FR) *J Parize* 74
2 b c Numerous(USA) —Loretta Gianni (FR) (Classic Account (USA))
3935a[5]

Lazy Darren *C Grant* a79 70
5 b g Largesse—Palmstead Belle (IRE) (Wolfhound (USA))
2666[7]

Leadenhall Lass (IRE) *P M Phelan* a70 76
3 ch f Monsieur Bond(IRE) —Zest (USA) (Zilzal (USA))
1814[5] 2632[9] 3281[3] 4231[4] 4952[4] 5506[3] (5805) 6476[2] 6731[12]

Leader Of The Land (IRE) *D R Lanigan* a59 48
2 ch c Halling(USA) —Cheerleader (Singspiel (IRE))
7244[10] 7522[8] 7721[4]

Leading Edge (IRE) *M R Channon* a76 78
4 gr m Clodovil(IRE) —Ja Ganhou (Midyan (USA))
167[2] 281[5] 557[3] 738[2] 1091[5] 5675[11] 6230[8] 6572[7] ◆ 6738[3] 6989[4] 7138[3] 7273[5] (7555) 7828[11]

Leaf Hollow *M Madgwick* 25
3 ch f Beat Hollow—Lauren (GER) (Lightning (FR))
5963[5]

League Champion (USA) *R Bouresly* a101 96
6 b g Rahy(USA) —Meiosis (USA) (Danzig (USA))
264a[4] 336a[5] 414a[5] 521a[6] 638a[5] 696a[8]

Leahurst (IRE) *J Noseda* a109 92
3 gr g Verglas(IRE) —Badee'A (IRE) (Marju (IRE))
(1491) 2270[2] (5615)

Leamington (USA) *H Graham Motion* a87 91
4 b m Pleasant Tap(USA) —Muneefa (USA) (Storm Cat (USA))
6510a[5]

Lean Burn (USA) *A G Newcombe* a40 56
3 b g Johannesburg(USA) —Anthelion (USA) (Stop The Music (USA))
5628[5] 6741[8] 7278[9]

Leandros (FR) *G M Lyons* a102 109
4 br g Invincible Spirit(IRE) —Logjam (IRE) (Royal Academy (USA))
259a[2] 418a[6] 615a[4] 696a[9] 1821[9] 4297[20]

Lean Machine *R Hannon* 77
2 b c Exceed And Excel(AUS) —Al Corniche (IRE) (Bluebird (USA))
3167[2] 3867[2] 5431[2] 5867[4]

Leap Ahead (IRE) *F Rohaut* a84 90
4 ch g Desert Prince(IRE) —Lady Vettori (Vettori (IRE))
2513a[9] 3231a[7] 5464a[8]

Leap The Liffey (IRE) *Mrs Valerie Keatley* a61 57
6 ch g Carrowkeel(IRE) —Golden Leap (Salmon Leap (USA))
6999[12]

Learo Dochais (USA) *M A Jarvis* a74 76
3 b g Mutakddim(USA) —Brush With The Law (USA) (Broad Brush (USA))
1636[6] 2336[5] (4303) 4535[3] 5448[12] 7516[6] 7891[7]

Leaving Alone (USA) *R Hannon* a75 66
2 ch f Mr Greeley(USA) —Spankin' (USA) (A.P. Indy (USA))
6729[6] ◆ 7451[3] 7622[2] 7772[5]

Le Big (GER) *U Stoltefuss* 108
5 b h Big Shuffle(USA) —La Luganese (IRE) (Surumu (GER))
5493a[3] 6499a[3] 7044a[2] (7303a)

Le Cadre Noir (IRE) *D K Weld* 110
5 b h Danetime(IRE) —Rinass (IRE) (Indian Ridge)
1374a[3] 1543a[3] 6707a[11]

Le Castellanais (FR) *B Dutruel* 47
2 b c Alberto Giacometti(IRE) —Zarina (FR) (Johann Quatz (FR))
1482a[10]

Leceile (USA) *W J Haggas* a64 91
3 b f Forest Camp(USA) —Summerwood (USA) (Boston Harbor (USA))
(2042) (5009) ◆ 5472[2]

Le Chiffre (IRE) *Miss Sheena West* a76 67
7 br g Celtic Swing—Implicit View (Persian Bold)
7481[10] 7664[11]

Le Citadel (USA) *P D Deegan* a76 89
4 b g Stravinsky(USA) —Halholah (USA) (Secreto (USA))
2289a[13]

Le Corvee (IRE) *A W Carroll* a73 57
7 b g Rossini(USA) —Elupa (IRE) (Mtoto)
1192[8] 1415[9] 2171[8] 2634[6] 3074[4] 3503[5] 3594[3] 5246[6]

Ledgerwood *A J Chamberlain* a64 54
4 b g Royal Applause—Skies Are Blue (Unfuwain (USA))
2745[13] 3215[8]

Led Zeppelin (TUR) *G Subasi* a99
4 ch h Always A Classic(CAN) —Luce (TUR) (Bachelor Party (USA))
5587a[7]

Leelu *D W P Arbuthnot* a66 13
3 b f Largesse—Strat's Quest (Nicholas (USA))
1937[10] 2498[11] 3279[11] 3710[5] 4085[7] 4872[2] 5326[10] 5751[3] (6611) 7051[3] 7432[3] 7591[4]

Lees Anthem *C J Teague* a53 73
2 b g Mujahid(USA) —Lady Rock (Mistertopogigo (IRE))
1126[0] 1661[3] 2260[7] 2408[8] 5957[7] 6354[4] 6841[11] 7088[7]

Leftontheshelf (IRE) *Miss T Spearing* a85 80
3 ch f Namid—Corryvreckan (IRE) (Night Shift (USA))
1923[4] 2456[2] 3592[3] 3945[5] 5719[13] 6572[9] 7136[3]

Legal Eagle (IRE) *Paul Green* a82 86
4 b g Invincible Spirit(IRE) —Lupulina (CAN) (Saratoga Six (USA))
973[2] 1685[2] 2093[2] 2276[10] (2624) 2941[5] 3001[12] 3372[3] 3623[3] 4043[2] 4341[17] 4784[8] 5148[7] 6171[3] 6279[12] 6642[2] 6843[6] 7269[5]

Legal Legacy *M Dods* 84
3 ch g Beat Hollow—Dans Delight (Machiavellian (USA))
1686[4] ◆ (2154) (2719) ◆ (3341) ◆ 4591[2] 5432[4] 6645[18]

Legal Lover (IRE) *R Hollinshead* a29 59
7 b g Woodborough(USA) —Victoria's Secret (IRE) (Law Society (USA))
1655[10] 2746[12] 3322[7] 3675[8] 4376[12]

Legendary Guest *D W Barker* a17 73
4 b g Bahamian Bounty—Legend Of Aragon (Aragon)
561[6] 1057[7] 1243[8]

Legendary Lad (IRE) *D K Weld* 82
2 b c Dubawi(IRE) —Lishaway (FR) (Polish Precedent (USA))
6319a[17]

Legend Of Greece (IRE) *Mrs N Smith* 43
3 b g Danetime(IRE) —Lodema (IRE) (Lycius (USA))
4854[9] 5531[11] 6189[4] 6789[6]

Legion D'Honneur (UAE) *L Lungo* 79
4 b g Halling(USA) —Renowned (IRE) (Darshaan)
1692[3] 2018[5]

Legislate *B W Hills* a80 91
3 b c Dansili—Shining Water (Kalaglow)
(917) 1303[3] ◆ 2077[7] 3429[3] 5551[6] 6429[2]

Legnani *George Baker* a77 14
3 b f Fasliyev(USA) —Top Sauce (Hector Protector (USA))
3685[8] 4812[10]

Le Grenelle (FR) *F Doumen* 62
2 b g Green Tune(USA) —L'Annee Folle (FR) (Double Bed (FR))
6501a[15] 6927a[7]

Le Havre (IRE) *J-C Rouget* 121
3 b c Noverre(USA) —Marie Rheinberg (GER) (Surako (GER))
(1207a) 1917a[2] (2756a)

Leica Ding (AUS) *Darren Weir* 109
5 ch m Redding(NZ) —Leica Mine (AUS) (Belong To Me (USA))
(6961a) 7215a[14]

Leiloken (FR) *F-X De Chevigny* 72
2 ch c Lando(GER) —Leila (FR) (Lahint (USA))
3935a[8]

Leitmotiv (IRE) *M Al Muhairi* 94
6 b h Sadler's Wells(USA) —Moselle (Mtoto)
262a[10] 437a[8]

Leitzu (IRE) *M R Channon* a64 69
2 b f Barathea(IRE) —Ann's Annie (IRE) (Alzao (USA))
4460[9] 5165[6] (5498) 6067[4] 6391[5]

Lekita *W R Swinburn* a76 77
4 b m Kyllachy—Tender Moment (IRE) (Caerleon (USA))
2188[5] 3030[7]

Lelah Dorak (KSA) *B Resaque* a68
3 ch c Frequent—Bint Garaah (KSA) (Vanlandingham (USA))
1009a[5]

Leleyf (IRE) *M R Channon* a78 77
2 b f Kheleyf(USA) —Titchwell Lass (Lead On Time (USA))
(1031) (1706) 2054[12] 2372[3] 3086[11] 3430[5] 3807[5] 4089[10] 4525[7] 5207[6] (5526) 5550[6] 5908[4] 6068[2] 6275[7] 6550[4] 6827[6]

Le Miracle (GER) *W Baltromei* 108
8 bb g Monsun(GER) —L'Heure Bleue (IRE) (Kendor (FR))
1552a[7]

Lemon N Sugar (USA) *J Noseda* a92 88
4 b m Lemon Drop Kid(USA) —Altos De Chavon (USA) (Polish Numbers (USA))
(36) 1965[3] ◆ (2382) (2886) ◆ 3795[4] ◆ (6631)

L'Enchanteresse (IRE) *M L W Bell* 72
2 ch f Kyllachy—Enchant (Lion Cavern (USA))
3356[3] 4331[2] 4626[3] 5800[2] 6481[13] 6820[3]

Lend A Grand (IRE) *Miss Jo Crowley* a79 64
5 br g Lend A Hand—Grand Madam (Grand Lodge (USA))
31[2] 457[4] 708[7] 844[8] 1080[2] 1495[5] 2330[13]

Lend A Light *I W McInnes* a46 55
3 b c Lend A Hand—No Candles Tonight (Star Appeal)
667[7]

Lenkiewicz *B R Millman* 76
2 gr f Oratorio(IRE) —Philadelphie (IRE) (Anabaa (USA))
3277[6] 4945[5] 5605[5] 6241[3] 6727[8]

Lennie Briscoe (IRE) *S Kirk* a52 67
3 b g Rock Of Gibraltar(IRE) —Tammany Hall (IRE) (Petorius)
1034[7] 1416[6] 1670[13] 4642[8] 5121[6] 5287[3] 5905[6] 6358[12]

Lenny Bee *D H Brown* a81 89
3 rg g Kyllachy—Smart Hostess (Most Welcome)
947[2] ◆ (1317) 1727[2] ◆ 2393[2] 2915[2] 3166[6] 3806[3] 4289[4] (5436) 5919[3] 6283[6]

Leoballero *K M Prendergast* a83 82
9 ch g Lion Cavern(USA) —Ball Gown (Jalmood (USA))
2378[7] 2876[12]

Leocorno (IRE) *Sir Michael Stoute* 108
3 br f Pivotal—Highland Gift (IRE) (Generous (IRE))
(2212) 3047[4] 5202[2] 6813[8]

Leonaldo (USA) *J R Gask* a83 74
4 b g Silver Deputy(CAN) —Electric Talent (USA) (Capote (USA))
318[3] 694[2] ◆ 866[4] 974[5] 5884[10]

Leonid Glow *M Dods* a70 82
4 b m Hunting Lion(IRE) —On Till Morning (IRE) (Never So Bold)
1309[10] 1682[14] 2071[3] 2938[14] 4015[3] 4657[5] 4996[4] 5514[2] 6015[2] 6667[6] 6764[2] 7171[7] 7287[10]

Leopard Hills (IRE) *J Howard Johnson* 63
2 b g Acclamation—Sadler's Park (USA) (Sadler's Wells (USA))
2041[4] 3170[6] 4187[6]

Leo The Lion (IRE) *M Johnston* a64
3 b g Sulamani(IRE) —Sail Away (GER) (Platini (GER))
310[3] 455[4] (630) 1614[8]

Le Petit Vigier *P Beaumont* a49 47
3 b f Groom Dancer(USA) —Fallujah (Dr Fong (USA))
228[4] 520[2] 620[3] 963[6] 1054[6]

Le Pitalugue (FR) *A Bonin* a65 67
2 b c Panis(USA) —Belle Tranquille (FR) (Reste Tranquille (FR))
4368a[5]

Leptis Magna *R H York* a59 68
5 ch g Danehill Dancer(IRE) —Dark Eyed Lady (IRE) (Exhibitioner)
3980[8] 4645[7] 6968[12]

Le Reve Royal *G R Oldroyd* a44 58
3 ch f Monsieur Bond(IRE) —Bond Royale (Piccolo)
1736[7] 2091[14] 3352[3] 3710[9] 4004[15] 7460[8] 7814[9]

Le Ribot (GER) *Carmen Bocskai* 76
5 br h Starborough—La Prima (GER) (Surumu (GER))
465a[6] 4335a[9]

Le Roc (FR) *C Boutin* 94
3 b c Montjeu(IRE) —Lady Vettori (Vettori (IRE))
7820a[5]

Les Fazzani (IRE) *K A Ryan* a107 109
5 b m Intikhab(USA) —Massada (Most Welcome)
1996a[6] 2482[2] 2960a[8] (5689a) 7046a[3] 7291[4] (7589)

Lesley's Choice *R Curtis* a97 76
3 b g Lucky Story(USA) —Wathbat Mtoto (Mtoto)
109[5] 509[2] 685[2] (814) 859[3] 1078[6] 3166[9] 3582[12] 3973[6] 4733[12] 5724[6] 6359[2] 6879[7] (7269) (7511) (7676)

Leslingtaylor (IRE) *J J Quinn* a73 76
7 b g Orpen(USA) —Rite Of Spring (Niniski (USA))
139[5] 428[4] 5698[4]

Lesoto Diamond (IRE) *P A Fahy* a79 79
7 b m Darnay—Fallon (IRE) (Arcane (USA))
5689a[20] 7701[6]

Lessing (FR) *X-Thomas Demeaulte* a99 106
4 b m Orpen(USA) —Lady Morgane (IRE) (Medaaly)
180a[2] 335a[7] 637a[7] 4489[5]

Less Moi Rire (FR) *Y Fouin* 75
3 b c Enrique—Joy Of Life (FR) (Exit To Nowhere (USA))
6682a[7]

Lesson In Humility (IRE) *A P Jarvis* 115
4 b m Mujadil(USA) —Vanity (IRE) (Thatching)
(1880) (2644a) 3140[3] 3824[2] 4837a[3] 5493a[4]

Les Yeux Bleus (IRE) *N Clement*
2 gr f Verglas(IRE) —Sanpala (Sanglamore (USA))
7103a[7]

Les Yeux Noirs (FR) *F Rossi*
2 b c Diktat—Les Yeux Mauves (FR) (Tot Ou Tard (IRE))
5850a[8]

Letcho (FR) *D Leblond* 63
2 br c Sagacity(FR) —Silver Singing (USA) (Topsider (USA))
5378a[8] 6576a[5]

Lethal *M J Scudamore* a71 78
6 ch g Nashwan(USA) —Ipanema Beach (Lion Cavern (USA))
68[3] (223) 304[6] 739[6] (921) (1259) 1480[6] 1734[7] 2576[6] 2908[5] 2980[11] 3512[2] 3738[2] 3983[5] 4978[4] 7053[3] 7329[2] (7535) 7738[6]

Lethal Combination (USA) *W J Haggas* a76 84
2 b g Broken Vow(USA) —Yard (USA) (Boundary (USA))
4093[9] 4451[3] (5191) 5515[6] (6067)

Lethal Glaze (IRE) *R Hannon* a100 96
3 gr g Verglas(IRE) —Sticky Green (Lion Cavern (USA))
(2138) 3090[8] 3618[5] (4045) (5315) 5870[8] 6662[10] 7151[5]

Lethal Heat (USA) *Barry Abrams* a111 107
4 b m Unusual Heat(USA) —Lethal Leta (USA) (Synastry (USA))
7286a[7]

Letham Island (IRE) *R M Stronge* a44 77
5 b m Trans Island—Common Cause (Polish Patriot (USA))
4301[10]

Let It Rock (IRE) *K R Burke* 52
2 b f Noverre(USA) —Green Life (Green Desert (USA))
1841[7]

Letizia Relco (IRE) *B Grizzetti* 91
2 br f Lucky Story(USA) —Speedybird (IRE) (Danehill (USA))
6892a[8]

Le Toreador *K A Ryan* a99 97
4 ch g Piccolo—Peggy Spencer (Formidable (USA))
1227[5] ◆ 1685[3] 2363[2] 2897[12] (3149) (3491) 4461[5] ◆ 4753[8] 5247[2] 5767[3] 5856[6] (6171) (6459) 6678[18] 6843[15]

Lets Get Cracking (FR) *A E Jones* a51 70
5 b h Anabaa Blue—Queenhood (FR) (Linamix (FR))
17[8]

Let's Go Outside (FR) *J Helouy* a43 48
3 b g Lando(GER) —Regal Green (USA) (Lear Fan (USA))
6980a[F]

Lets Move It *D Shaw* a46
2 b c Piccolo—Park Star (Gothenberg (IRE))
7317[12] 7485[7] 7582[7] 7778[3] 7871[10]

Lets Roll *C W Thornton* 83
8 b g Tamure(IRE) —Miss Petronella (Petoski)
1230[7] 1506[8] 3059[5] 3609[2] 3940[5] 4873[5] 5554[6] 6053[5] 6767[10] 7124[5]

Let Them Eat Cake *R A Fahey* a52 29
2 b f Danehill Dancer(IRE) —Lady Adnil (IRE) (Stravinsky (USA))
6274[6] 6672[11] 6874[3]

Lettori (FR) *F Bossert* a59 72
8 b g Vettori(IRE) —Laodicee (FR) (Dancehall (USA))
5301a[7]

Leulahleulahlay *Evan Williams* a75 75
3 ch g Dr Fong(USA) —Fidelio's Miracle (USA) (Mountain Cat (USA))
1464[4] 4599[2] 7737[3] 7873[5]

Leverage (IRE) *L M Cumani* a81 89
3 b c Xaar—She Looks On High (USA) (Secreto (USA))
3338[2] (3813) 6540[2] 6776[9] 7027[4]

Leviathan *T P Tate* 90
2 b c Dubawi(IRE) —Gipsy Moth (Efisio)
(2813) 3311[5] 4271[3] 5692[7] (7013) ◆

Levitation (IRE) *W S Kittow* a71 73
3 b f Vettori(IRE) —Uplifting (Magic Ring (IRE))
2317[6] 2947[2] 4050[10] 4902[7] 7428[6] 7671[4] (7863)

Lewyn *K A Ryan* a72 65
2 b f Exceed And Excel(AUS) —Panoramic View (Polar Falcon (USA))
1504[11] 2089[3] 2435[4] 5950[2] 6355[3] (6827) 7115[9] 7274[7] 7372[10]

Lexi's Layla (IRE) *D M Simcock* a64 68
2 ch f Kheleyf(USA) —Woodstamp (IRE) (Woodborough (USA))
4427[2] 4626[2] 5379[9] 6971[3]

Lexlenos (IRE) *D R C Elsworth* a80 105
3 ch f Intikhab(USA) —Blazing Glory (IRE) (Glow (USA))
158[2]

Leyte Gulf (USA) *C C Bealby* a70 61
6 b g Cozzene(USA) —Gabacha (USA) (Woodman (USA))
3714[10] 4388[5] (4742) 5554[9] (6025) 6457[2] 6636[5] (7214) 7461[2] 7675[3]

Lhashan *M A Jarvis* a39
3 b f Green Desert(USA) —Society Lady (USA) (Mr Prospector (USA))
4097[12] 5882[7]

L'Hirondelle (IRE) *M J Attwater* a89 89
5 b g Anabaa(USA) —Auratum (USA) (Carson City (USA))
232[3] (318) 1433[8] 1861[9] 3282[4] 6168[11] 7523[5] 7626[4] (7833)

L'Homme De Nuit (GER) *G L Moore* a75 60
5 b g Samum(GER) —La Bouche (GER) (In The Wings)
7255[3]

Liang Kay (GER) *Uwe Ostmann* 113
4 b h Dai Jin—Linton Bay (GER) (Funambule (USA))
2113a[3] 3416a[3] 4364a[8] 5461a[4] 6500a[2] (7039a) 7406a[2]

Libano (IRE) *D K Weld* 112
3 b c Indian Ridge—Daniela Grassi (Bound For Honour (USA))
(1393a) 5924a[6] 6867a[5]

Libel Law *M A Jarvis* 111
3 ch c Kingmambo(USA) —Innuendo (IRE) (Caerleon (USA))
(1407) 1822[6] 4020[2] (4781)

Liberally (IRE) *B J Meehan* a53 87
4 b m Statue Of Liberty(USA) —Specifically (USA) (Sky Classic (CAN))
1357[6] 3034[4] (3635) 4365a[0] 6618[6]

Liberate *P J Hobbs* a88 93
6 ch g Lomitas—Eversince (USA) (Foolish Pleasure (USA))
2994[18]

Liberation (IRE) *Saeed Bin Suroor* 108
3 b c Refuse To Bend(IRE) —Mosaique Bleue (Shirley Heights)
769a[2] ◆ 1291[13] 7185[6]

Libertino (IRE) *B J Meehan* a67 69
2 ch c Bertolini(USA) —Villafranca (IRE) (In The Wings)
2328[5] 6542[2] 7430[4]

Liberty Beau (IRE) *D R C Elsworth* a59
3 b g Statue Of Liberty(USA) —La Shalak (IRE) (Shalford (IRE))
205[3]

Liberty Chery *J E Hammond* a81 97
3 b f Statue Of Liberty(USA) —Marion (IRE) (Doyoun)
2989a[3] 3442a[6] 7697a[0]

Liberty Diamond *K R Burke* 72
3 br f Needwood Blade—Take Liberties (Warning)
1686[9] 2028[8]

Liberty Estelle (IRE) *P D Evans* a19 17
3 gr f Statue Of Liberty(USA) —Bella Estella (GER) (Sternkoenig (IRE))
1490[10] 1793[11]

Liberty Island (IRE) *W McCreery* a80 63
4 b g Statue Of Liberty(USA) —Birthday (IRE) (Singspiel (IRE))
(6635)

Liberty Lady (IRE) *D Donovan* a62
2 b f Statue Of Liberty(USA) —Crossed Wire (Lycius (USA))
6207[2] ◆ 7582[2] 7736[6]

Liberty Lodge (IRE) *G A Swinbank* 19
3 b g Statue Of Liberty(USA) —Lady Justice (Compton Place)
1440[5] 1950[P]

Liberty Power (IRE) *Garry Moss* 12
2 b g Statue Of Liberty(USA) —Shaydeylaydeh (IRE) (Shaddad (USA))
3634[6]

Liberty Seeker (FR) *John A Harris* a36 42
10 ch g Machiavellian(USA) —Samara (IRE) (Polish Patriot (USA))
2971[9] 3486[10]

Liberty Ship *J D Bethell* a66 77
4 b g Statue Of Liberty(USA) —Flag (Selkirk (USA))
15[3] 884[6] 1360[2] (1768) 2095[5] 2657[2] 3065[2] 3607[2]

Liberty Square (USA) *Saeed Bin Suroor* 67
2 ch c Street Cry(IRE) —Gracious Hope (USA) (Rahy (USA))
6000[7] 6593[4] 6930[4]

Liberty Trail (IRE) *I Semple* a70 74
3 b g Statue Of Liberty(USA) —Karinski (USA) (Palace Music (USA))
2450[2] 2719[7] 3093[2] 3480[3] 4466[7] 4772[2] (5304) 6140[6] 6413[5] (6824) 7172[10] 7356[11] 7496[6]

Liberty Valance (IRE) *P M Phelan* a71 67
4 b g Statue Of Liberty(USA) —Tabdea (USA) (Topsider (USA))
118[5] 155[2] 234[3] 531[10] 590[5] 3269[12]

Libia (IRE) *C Laffon-Parias* 72
3 b f Singspiel(IRE) —Omara (USA) (Storm Cat (USA))
4130a[3]

Libre *F Jordan* a56 67
9 b g Bahamian Bounty—Premier Blues (FR) (Law Society (USA))
1199[9] 1773[9] 2458[5] 3007[3] 3490[5] 3800[7] 4389[8] 4938[6] 5631[2] 5888[5] 6208[13] 7142[11] 7466[3] 7600[10] 7802[2] 7857[6]

Licence To Till (USA) *M Johnston* a85 68
2 b c War Chant(USA) —With A Wink (USA) (Clever Trick (USA))
3446[7] 4187[3] 5066[2] 5467[3] (7773) ◆ 7846[3]

Liebelei (USA) *H J L Dunlop* a35 46
2 bb f Royal Academy(USA) —Part With Pride (USA) (Executive Pride)
4226[10] 6254[8] 6931[8]

Liebermann (GER) *D K Weld* a82 99
3 bb c Big Shuffle(USA) —La Ola (GER) (Dashing Blade)
1022a[5]

Lieu Day Louie (IRE) *N Wilson* 64
2 b g Bahamian Bounty—Nebraska Lady (IRE) (Lujain (USA))
4282[8] 4889[2] 5596[10] 6983[4] 7115[5]

Lieutenant Pigeon *Paul Mason* a80 73
4 ch g Captain Rio—Blue Velvet (Formidable (USA))
843[7] 975[6] 2145[12] 4203[6]

Life And Soul (IRE) *Mrs A J Perrett* a72 75
2 b c Azamour(IRE) —Way For Life (GER) (Platini (GER))
6199[9] 6593[2] 7064[2]

Life Is Sweet (USA) *John Shirreffs* a119 97
4 b m Storm Cat(USA) —Sweet Life (USA) (Kris S (USA))
(7286a)

Life's Challenge (USA) *M Johnston* a72 82
3 ch f Mr Greeley(USA) —Danse Du Diable (IRE) (Sadler's Wells (USA))
(5071) 5834[3] 6946[11] 7769[7]

Lifetime Endeavour *R E Barr* 33
5 b g Aragon—Musical Star (Music Boy)
1061[7] 1689[9] 1924[9] 2361[10] 3123[10]

Lift The Gloom *Andrew Oliver* a70 69
3 gr g Verglas(IRE) —Leinster Mills (IRE) (Doyoun)
4392a[11]

Light Dubai (IRE) *M R Channon* a68 77
3 b f Fantastic Light(USA) —Seeking A Way (USA) (Seeking The Gold (USA))
914[2] 1329[3] 1622[2] 2008[8] 2715[5] 3022[4] 4166[4]

Lighterman *E J Alston* 25
2 ch g Firebreak—Manuka Too (IRE) (First Trump)
3571[9] 4307[8] 4557[10] ◆

Light From Mars *B R Millman* 106
4 gr g Fantastic Light(USA) —Hylandra (USA) (Bering)
(1149) 1527[2] 2412[7] 3014[21] 3567[3] 5221[3] 6249[2] (6675) 7019[6]

Lighthearted (FR) *C G Cox* a68 68
3 ch f Fantastic Light(USA) —My Heart's Deelite (USA) (Afternoon Deelites (USA))
862[2] 1322[4] (1839) 2431[6] 2827[9] 3387[8]

Light Nights (IRE) *T D Easterby* 38
2 b f Acclamation—Grecian Grail (IRE) (Rainbow Quest (USA))
5417[7] 7217[6] 7419[10]

Light Silver (FR) *P Bary* 77
3 b c Divine Light(JPN) —Millora (FR) (Exit To Nowhere (USA))
7386a[4]

Light Sleeper *P W Chapple-Hyam* a71 75
3 b c Kyllachy—Snoozy (Cadeaux Genereux)
3155[4] 7459[3] 7610[5]

Light The City (IRE) *C E Brittain* 29
2 b g Fantastic Light(USA) —Marine City (JPN) (Carnegie (IRE))
6033[6]

Light The Light (IRE) *M D Squance* a55
4 ch m King Charlemagne(USA) —Saana (IRE) (Erins Isle)
98[6] 309[8] 2806[8]

Light The Way *P J Makin* a54 54
2 b c Fantastic Light(USA) —Monteleone (IRE) (Montjeu (IRE))
4946[8] 5564[5] 6334[9] 6911[6] 7477[3] 7698[9]

Light Vision (NZ) *Robert Smerdon* 112
6 b g Zerpour(IRE) —Switched (AUS) (Naturalism (NZ))
6871a[17]

Light Years Ahead *P D Deegan* 65
2 b g Aldebaran(USA) —Dragonada (USA) (Nureyev (USA))
3514a[5]

Ligne Claire (FR) *Y De Nicolay* a46 60
3 b f Lando(GER) —Vandalixa (FR) (Linamix (FR))
6980a[5]

Like For Like (IRE) *R J Hodges* a66 72
3 ch f Kheleyf(USA) —Just Like Annie (IRE) (Mujadil (USA))
2349[12] 2654[5] 2973[4] 3257[8] 3502[2] 4222[6] 5384[12] 5716[10] 7427[9]

Like Magic (IRE) *Patrick Martin* a87 95
3 b c Invincible Spirit(IRE) —Magic Annemarie (IRE) (Dancing Dissident (USA))
1375a[14]

Lilac Moon (GER) *Tom Dascombe* a67 71
5 b m Dr Fong(USA) —Luna De Miel (Shareef Dancer (USA))
873[8] 3151[4] 6490[5] 7212[3] 7699[13]

Lilac Wine *D J S Ffrench Davis* a54 45
6 ch m Dancing Spree(USA) —Stay With Me Baby (Nicholas Bill)
1286[11] 1586[5] 2127[10] 4862[4] 5217[6] 5579[6]

Lil Ella (IRE) *C Roche* 75
2 b f Pearl Of Love(IRE) —Royal Jubilee (IRE) (King's Theatre (IRE))
7258a[10]

Lileo (IRE) *L M Cumani* 64
2 b g Galileo(IRE) —Jabali (FR) (Shirley Heights)
7096[4] ◆

Lilia (GER) *W Hickst* 99
5 gr m Dashing Blade—Lindia (GER) (Konigsstuhl (GER))
6714a[9]

Lilleput *E A Wheeler* a19 47
4 b m High Estate—A Little Hot (Petong)
69[7] 386[13] 2981[6] 3260[4] 3533[6] 4146[7] 7200[10]

Lillie Langtry (IRE) *A P O'Brien* a96 107
2 bb f Danehill Dancer(IRE) —Hoity Toity (Darshaan)
1993a[2] (2557a) ◆ 3086[2] (4726a) 5488a[3] (6477) 7282a[8]

Lillie Le Quesne *Jane Southcombe* a57 38
6 b m Desert Prince(IRE) —Bathe In Light (USA) (Sunshine Forever (USA))
2322[7]

Lilly Be (IRE) *Paul Magnier* a81 74
6 ch m Titus Livius(FR) —Mystery Hill (USA) (Danehill (USA))
7646[7]

Lilly Blue (IRE) *R Brotherton* a60 86
3 b f Hawk Wing(USA) —Holly Blue (Bluebird (USA))
865[6] 1050[5] 1397[5] 1670[12] 2431[8] 2681[2] 3383[12] 4304[5] 5384[5] 7211[8]

Lilly Gold (FR) *Mlle S-V Tarrou* a58 61
3 ch f Gold Away(IRE) —Elite Super (USA) (Shadeed (USA))
5784a[4] 6980a[4]

Lilly Grove *G A Swinbank* a56 45
4 b m Mtoto—Armada Grove (Fleetwood (IRE))
6673[6] 7004[2]

Lilly Royal (IRE) *B Palling* 69
3 b f Tillerman—Ervedya (IRE) (Doyoun)
4246[12] 4472[2] 5181[6] 6595[4] 6789[5] 7246[10]

Lilyannabanana *P D Evans* 68
2 ch f Avonbridge—Bundle (Cadeaux Genereux)
2919[12] 4900[12] 5360[2] 5852[6]

Lily De Vauville (FR) *Jack Barbe*
2 b f Ski Chief(USA) —Clockwork (FR) (Octagonal (NZ))
5014a[7]

Lily Eva *D Donovan* a34
3 ch f Definite Article—Avanindra (Zamindar (USA))
7671[12] 7882[9]

Lily In The Pond *Miss Gay Kelleway* a60
2 br f Kyllachy—Tidal (Bin Ajwaad (IRE))
7177[4] 7622[9] 7886[8]

Lily Jicaro (IRE) *Mrs L Williamson* a21 60
3 ch f Choisir(AUS) —Mourir D'Aimer (USA) (Trempolino (USA))
1228[7] *2141[11]* 2343[3] 3036[7] 3449[12] 3947[2] 4643[11] 4736[7] 5145[15] 6340[10] *6581[7]* 6824[14]

Lily Lenor (IRE) *B Ellison* 51
2 b f Bertolini(USA) —Mosaique Beauty (IRE) (Sadler's Wells (USA))
1126[7] 1277[11] 1719[4] 2936[10]

Lily Lily *K McAuliffe* a62
2 b f Efisio—Bel Tempo (Petong)
7277[6] *7400[12]* *7706[2]* *(7792)*

Lilymay *B P J Baugh* 33
9 b m Sovereign Water(FR) —Maysimp (IRE) (Mac's Imp (USA))
3527[5] 4742[9]

Lily Of Laguna (IRE) *Tracey Collins*
2 b f Zafeen(FR) —Schust Madame (IRE) (Second Set (IRE))
6401a[12]

Lily Of The Nile (UAE) *J G Portman* 38
3 ch f Halling(USA) —Covet (Polish Precedent (USA))
2323[11] 4828[9] 6172[8]

Lily Rio (IRE) *W R Muir* 29
2 bb f Marju(IRE) —Jinsiyah (USA) (Housebuster (USA))
6284[10] 6729[13]

Lily Wood *J W Unett* a48
3 ch f Central Park(IRE) —Lady Castanea (Superlative)
7126[12] *7671[8]* *7753[6]*

Limatus (GER) *P Vovcenko* 104
8 br g Law Society(USA) —Limaga (Lagunas)
2216a[7] 3493a[2]

Limelight (USA) *Sir Mark Prescott* a53 58
4 gr m Dalakhani(IRE) —Last Second (IRE) (Alzao (USA))
169[2] *444[3]* *732[6]* *918[2]*

Lime Tree Valley (IRE) *David Marnane* a85 85
4 b g Val Royal(FR) —Khayrat (IRE) (Polar Falcon (USA))
2289a[15]

L'Impetueux (FR) *U Suter* a69 79
3 ch g Muhtathir—Red Sea (FR) (Marignan (USA))
5278a[6] 6682a[9]

Lim's Fighter (AUS) *J Meagher* 107
7 b g Flying Spur(AUS) —Sky Watch (AUS) (Star Watch (AUS))
2116a[12]

Limurn (IRE) *Dominique Sepulchre* a69 70
3 b f Peintre Celebre(USA) —Lexington Belle (FR) (Danehill (USA))
5783a[6]

Linby (IRE) *Miss Tor Sturgis* a31 57
4 b g Dr Fong(USA) —Dubious (Darshaan)
3348[9] 3561[8]

L'Inconscient (FR) *K Borgel* 56
2 b c Numerous(USA) —Ombre Folle (Celtic Swing)
6148a[3]

L'Indiscreta *B Grizzetti* 103
4 b m Desert Prince(IRE) —I Remember (IRE) (Dominion)
(1394a) 1905a[8] 6717a[10] 6894a[3] 7206a[6]

Lindoro *M G Quinlan* a93 93
4 b g Marju(IRE) —Floppie (FR) (Law Society (USA))
2470[6] 3391[6] *3928[4]* 4954[9] *5665[6]* (6476) *7350[P]* *7645[12]*

Lindy Hop (IRE) *K A Ryan* a64 65
3 b f Danehill Dancer(IRE) —Healing Music (FR) (Bering)
1173[6] 1743[5] ◆ *6701[6]* ◆ *7180[6]* *7481[7]* *7797[6]* *7863[5]*

Lion Mountain *Saeed Bin Suroor* 77
2 b c Tiger Hill(IRE) —Cal Norma's Lady (IRE) (Lyphard's Special (USA))
7099[2] ◆

Lion Road (USA) *A B Haynes* 5
3 ch g Lion Heart(USA) —Elusive Road (USA) (Elusive Quality (USA))
6158[7] 6789[7]

Lion Sands *A bin Huzaim* a111 115
5 b g Montjeu(IRE) —Puce (Darshaan)
185a[8] 437a[4] 527a[10] 699a[9] 772a[14]

Lion's Blood (SAF) *H J Brown* 91
5 ch h Dominion Royale—Corn Lily (SAF) (Dancing Champ (USA))
257a[7] 413a[8] 703a[7]

Lipocco *H J Brown* a80 109
5 br g Piccolo—Magical Dancer (IRE) (Magical Wonder (USA))
434a[2] 638a[8] 696a[2]

Lips Arrow (GER) *Andreas Lowe* 102
4 b m Big Shuffle(USA) —Lips Plane (IRE) (Ashkalani (IRE))
1394a[2] 2097a[9] 3650a[2] 4363a[4]

Lips Motion (GER) *Andreas Lowe* 66
3 b f Zinaad—Lips Plane (IRE) (Ashkalani (IRE))
6682a[2]

Liquid Asset (FR) *A M Balding* 73
2 ch g Refuse To Bend(IRE) —Lilyfoot (IRE) (Sanglamore (USA))
2889[2] 3750[9]

Lisahane Bog *P R Hedger* a69 55
2 b c Royal Applause—Veronica Franco (Darshaan)
5527[7] *5807[9]* 6393[11] 6697[13] *(7389)* *(7513)* ◆ *(7654)*

Lisa's Kitten (USA) *Michael J Maker* a96 101
2 ch f Kitten's Joy(USA) —Chianti Red (USA) (Woodman (USA))
7282a[10]

Lisbon Lion (IRE) *James Moffatt* a62 62
4 bg g Mull Of Kintyre(USA) —Ludovica (Bustino)
623[3] 6766[4] 7085[6]

L'Isle Joyeuse *P Winkworth* a33 38
2 b f Compton Place—Sabalara (IRE) (Mujadil (USA))
4688[9] 5282[5] 5714[9] *6700[7]*

Lis Pendens *W R Muir* a57 63
2 b g Tobougg(IRE) —In Good Faith (USA) (Dynaformer (USA))
5993[7] 6697[11] *7400[9]*

Lisselan Castle (USA) *Mme J Bidgood* 103
4 ch g Weekend Cruise(USA) —Dinner Speaker (USA) (Formal Dinner (USA))
4637a[7]

Lisselan Catcher (IRE) *Mme J Bidgood* 61
4 b g Catcher In The Rye(IRE) —The Midnight Blues (USA) (Cure The Blues (USA))
5204a[8]

Lisselan Queen (IRE) *Mme J Bidgood* a41 11
3 b f King Charlemagne(USA) —Laura Beth (Danehill Dancer (IRE))
5118a[6]

Listen Carefully (IRE) *Patrick Morris* a42 23
5 ch m Lil's Boy(USA) —Join The Party (Be My Guest (USA))
240[7] 2660[8] 2806[7]

Listillo (USA) *H J L Dunlop* a72 72
2 ch c More Than Ready(USA) —Dowry (USA) (Belong To Me (USA))
2033[6] 2636[4] *3226[2]* *3925[2]* 4165[2] 4379[2] *4537[8]* 5526[13] *5611[2]*

Liszt (IRE) *A P O'Brien* 96
3 gr c Galileo(IRE) —Corrine (IRE) (Spectrum (IRE))
1388a[10] 1910a[6]

Litenup (IRE) *A J Lidderdale* a58 39
3 b f Trans Island—Common Cause (Polish Patriot (USA))
383[2] *817[10]* *2709[2]* *7392[13]* *7688[9]* *7826[9]* *7882[4]*

Liteup My World (USA) *B Ellison* a61 58
3 ch g Hennessy(USA) —Liteup My Life (USA) (Green Dancer (USA))
3939[5] 4436[13]

Lithaam (IRE) *J M Bradley* a77 73
5 ch g Elnadim(USA) —Elhida (IRE) (Mujtahid (USA))
177[6] *535[5]* *596[4]* *794[9]* *2682[9]* 3239[3] 3477[8] 3947[3] 4182[6] 4736[6] (5008) 5184[4] (5504) *5610[4]* (5792) 6205[3] 6422[10] 6635[7] 6791[5] (7136) 7355[5] 7398[6] 7554[5] ◆ 7682[2] 7807[2]

Little Arrows (IRE) *W McCreery* a84 83
3 b c Danehill Dancer(IRE) —Lovers Walk (USA) (Diesis)
1755a[7] *6642[8]* *7192[2]*

Little Billie *Mike Murphy*
3 b f Efisio—Kembla (Known Fact (USA))
6794[15]

Little Blacknumber *R Hannon* a51
3 b f Superior Premium—The Synergist (Botanic (USA))
583[6] *707[6]*

Little Bones *J F Coupland* a53 54
4 ch m Tobougg(IRE) —City Gambler (Rock City)
5254[14]

Little Brazilien *P F I Cole* a58 60
2 ch f Kyllachy—Girl From Ipanema (Salse (USA))
1569[4] 4478[4] 4688[13] *5310[3]* 5714[3] 6366[9]

Little Buddy *R J Price*
2 ch g Reel Buddy(USA) —Little Kenny (Warning)
3500[13] 3786[10] 6386[7]

Little Calla (IRE) *E A L Dunlop* a55 59
3 ch f Indian Ridge—Queen Of Palms (IRE) (Desert Prince (IRE))
1838[2] 2776[13] *4174[11]*

Little Carmela *S C Williams* a69 65
5 gr m Beat Hollow—Carmela Owen (Owington)
(168) *299[4]* *692[5]* *1069[6]* 2123[6] 5483[2] *6025[8]* *6704[4]* *7255[5]* *7608[9]* *7695[9]* 7750[2]

Littledodayno (IRE) *M Wigham* a70 63
6 b m Mujadil(USA) —Perfect Welcome (Taufan (USA))
235[7] *461[4]* *861[12]*

Little Dreams (FR) *F Rossi* a100 104
3 b c Della Francesca(USA) —Little Anchor (FR) (Kendor (FR))
2755a[4]

Little Eden (IRE) *T D Barron* a67 59
4 b g Piccolo—Paradise Eve (Bahamian Bounty)
976[8] 1360[11] 1846[14]

Little Edward *R J Hodges* a98 96
11 gr g King's Signet(USA) —Cedar Lady (Telsmoss)
204[2] *359[3]* *553[2]* *714[8]* *(985)* 1321[10] 2191[5] 2474[13]

Little Fighter (GER) *J-P Carvalho* 98
4 b h Montjeu(IRE) —Lohsa (IRE) (Aragon)
5461a[11] 7406a[13]

Little Finch (IRE) *S Curran* a32 54
4 b m Acclamation—Hard To Lay (IRE) (Dolphin Street (FR))
6940[10]

Little Firecracker *Miss M E Rowland* a61 62
4 b m Cadeaux Genereux—El Hakma (Shareef Dancer (USA))
537[7]

Little Garcon (USA) *M Botti* a82 64
2 b g Bernstein(USA) —Demure (Machiavellian (USA))
6061[8] *6493[7]* *(7001)*

Little Knickers *E J Creighton* a71 66
4 b m Prince Sabo—Pants (Pivotal)
830[8] *945[5]* *1074[11]*

Little Lost (IRE) *Karen George* a41
3 b f Tagula(IRE) —Prima Marta (Primo Dominie)
655[8] *758[7]* *955[5]* *6645[7]* *6641[10]*

Little Meadow (IRE) *Miss J Feilden* a48 15
2 b f Antonius Pius(USA) —Cresalin (Coquelin (USA))
3344[11] *4790[9]* *7792[5]*

Little Miss Ginger *P S McEntee* a3
5 ch m Whittingham(IRE) —Miss Tress (IRE) (Salse (USA))
286[8]

Littlemisssunshine (IRE) *J S Moore* a74 73
4 b m Oasis Dream—Sharp Catch (IRE) (Common Grounds)
2712[8] 4692[4] 5125[3] (5184) 5421[5] *7554[4]* *7808[3]* *7872[4]*

Little Opera (IRE) *Aidan Anthony Howard* 59
3 b f Fasliyev(USA) —El Opera (IRE) (Sadler's Wells (USA))
7143[12]

Little Oz (IRE) *E A L Dunlop* 68
2 br f Red Ransom(USA) —Australie (IRE) (Sadler's Wells (USA))
6062[6] 6992[12] 7244[4]

Little Pandora *L R James* a32 39
5 b m Komaite(USA) —Little Talitha (Lugana Beach)
1480[11] 3352[8] 3972[8] 4281[12] 5309[11]

Little Perc (IRE) *G L Moore*
2 ch c Pearl Of Love(IRE) —Bitter Sweet (Deploy)
1195[13] 1783[10]

Little Perisher *A P Jarvis* a75 88
2 b c Desert Sun—Sasperella (Observatory (USA))
1323[9] 1534[2] 1598[3] (1862) 2702[6] 2995[11] 3583[6] 3805[6] 4826[4] 5136[17] 6048[11] 6134[5] 6534[9] 6906[8] *(7175)* *7320[10]* *7410[5]*

Little Pete (IRE) *I W McInnes* a89 97
4 ch g City On A Hill(USA) —Full Traceability (IRE) (Ron's Victory (USA))
1457[7] ◆ 1672[2] 2191[3] 2704[13] 3405[9] 3784[5] 4461[18] 4485[18] *6253[5]* *6723[2]* *7395[10]* *7613[3]* *7702[7]*

Little Prudence *R M Beckett* 68
3 ch f Generous(IRE) —Redgrave Devil (Tug Of War)
1874[3] 2877[4] 3791[5] 4855[5] 5430[9]

Little Richard (IRE) *M Wellings* a66 59
10 b g Alhaarth(IRE) —Intricacy (Formidable (USA))
103[3] *202[4]* *836[7]* *972[3]* *7495[6]* *7594[7]* *7732[4]* *7847[2]*

Little Rococoa *R J Price* a39 8
4 b g Killer Instinct—Little Kenny (Warning)
658[7] *857[10]*

Little Roxy (IRE) *Miss A M Newton-Smith* a43
4 b m Dilshaan—Brunswick (Warning)
310[7] *455[9]*

Little Rufus *K A Morgan* 62
2 b c Lujain(USA) —Compendium (Puissance)
4349[4]

Little Sark (IRE) *P D Evans* a60 55
4 b g Singspiel(IRE) —Notenqueen (GER) (Turfkonig (GER))
1771[8] 2181[8] 3121[6] 3503[3] 3986[7] 4625[10] *6210[7]* *6612[4]* *(6770)* *7112[2]* *7336[8]*

Little Scotland *T D Easterby* 90
2 b f Acclamation—Belladera (IRE) (Alzao (USA))
1661[2] ◆ 2054[3] 2372[5] 2995[4] 3748[8] 5199[8]

Little Weed (IRE) *B Palling*
2 bb g Statue Of Liberty(USA) —Carna (IRE) (Anita's Prince)
7190[4]

Little White Lie (IRE) *A bin Huzaim* a103 111
5 b g Orpen(USA) —Miss Informed (IRE) (Danehill (USA))
413a[4] ◆ *522a[3]* ◆ *610a[4]* ◆

Live Concert (IRE) *T Shirai* 118
5 b g Singspiel(IRE) —Dance Lively (USA) (Kingmambo (USA))
7498a[9]

Lively Blade *E S McMahon* a46
3 ch g Needwood Blade—Breezy Day (Day Is Done)
227[5] *425[7]*

Lively Fling (USA) *J H M Gosden* 91
3 b g Dynaformer(USA) —Creaking Board (Night Shift (USA))
(1088) 1512[2] 2208[8] 4518[9] 5771[3] (6552)

Living It Large (FR) *R F Fisher* a89 78
2 ch c Bertolini(USA) —Dilag (IRE) (Almutawakel)
3292[2] (4463) 6557[6] (6983) ◆ *(7156)* *(7274)* *7536[4]*

Living The Dream *Karen George* a46
7 b g Double Trigger(IRE) —Aquavita (Kalaglow)
779[9] *957[7]* *1286[8]* 2221[13]

Lixirova (FR) *D Smaga* 103
2 gr f Slickly(FR) —Linorova (USA) (Trempolino (USA))
4579a[3] 5279a[6] 6045a[6] (7230a)

Lizard Island (USA) *P F I Cole* a94 81
4 b h Danehill Dancer(IRE) —Add (USA) (Spectacular Bid (USA))
2015[11]

Lizzero (GER) *R Rohne* 96
3 b c Paolini(GER) —Lizzy (GER) (Big Shuffle (USA))
5585a[8]

Llandovery *P J McBride* a68 65
2 b c Auction House(USA) —Sweet Coincidence (Mujahid (USA))
3167[7] *3715[3]* 4666[3] 5320[6] *(5682)* *6491[4]* 6993[18]

Loaded *P Winkworth* a61
2 b c Tobougg(IRE) —Missed Again (High Top)
5191[7]

Local Hero (GER) *T P Tate* 65
2 b c Lomitas—Lolli Pop (GER) (Cagliostro (GER))
2997[5] ◆

Localiser (IRE) *D Nicholls* 68
3 b g Iron Mask(USA) —Becada (GER) (Cadeaux Genereux)
1625[3] 6539[3] 6823[11]

Location *P D Evans* a61 63
3 b f Dansili—Well Away (IRE) (Sadler's Wells (USA))
655[6] *786[9]* ◆ *(900)* 1253[4] *1531[4]* 2246[2] 2357[6] 2892[11] 3462[4] 3685[2] 5381[5] 5936[4] 6333[4] 6369[4] 6570[10] 6705[3] 6969[3] (7022) 7142[4] 7250[9]

Lochan Mor *M L W Bell* a86 86
3 b g Kyllachy—Bright Moll (Mind Games)
2070[2] ◆ (2455) *2826[2]* 4044[4] *6434[2]* 6964[2] *7155[3]*

Lochbroom Sunset *S C Williams* a64 53
2 b c Firebreak—Woore Lass (IRE) (Persian Bold)
2383[9] 2853[12] 4152[15] 4384[7] *5583[2]* *5811[9]* *6122[4]* *6292[10]* *6586[9]*

Loch Dubh (USA) *Jeff Talley* a105
3 b c Friends Lake(USA) —Star Landing (USA) (Caller I.D. (USA))
1225a[6]

Lochiel *G A Swinbank* a91 96
5 b g Mind Games—Summerhill Special (IRE) (Roi Danzig (USA))
360[4] 2242[5] 2815[3] 3826[2] 4274[U] *4840[7]* (6281) (6483) ◆ 7018[10]

Loch Jipp (USA) *J S Wainwright* 84
4 b m Belong To Me(USA) —Miss Keyonna (USA) (Septieme Ciel (USA))
4285[14] 4891[12] 5978[16]

Loch Linnhe (USA) *J H M Gosden* 104
3 b g Elusive Quality(USA) —Firth Of Lorne (IRE) (Danehill (USA))
(2282) 3011[7] 3783[3] ◆ 4296[9]

Loch Long (IRE) *Tracey Collins* 97
3 b c Galileo(IRE) —Spinney (Unfuwain (USA))
3438a[8] 5688a[6] 6502a[5] 7263a[9]

Lochstar *A M Balding* a92 78
5 b g Anabaa(USA) —Lochsong (Song)
1836[6] *(2397)* 2897[7] *3212[4]* 3694[6] 3844[8] *6972[6]*

Lockland (FR) *C Morineau*
2 ch c Martaline—Hiracina (FR) (Dom Racine (FR))
7507a[9]

Lock 'N' Load (IRE) *B Smart* 69
3 b f Johannesburg(USA) —Margay (IRE) (Marju (IRE))
6311[8]

Locksley Hall (USA) *E F Vaughan* a78 91
2 ch g Songandaprayer(USA) —Wonderously (USA) (Awesome Again (CAN))
5778[2] 6054[2]

Locmaria Ker (FR) *Y Fouin* a51 56
3 ch f Sendawar(IRE) —Star Du Rhuis (FR) (Star Maite (FR))
5278a[0]

Locum *M H Tompkins* a73 72
4 ch g Dr Fong(USA) —Exhibitor (USA) (Royal Academy (USA))
(1945) 2332[3] *2684[7]* 3550[4] 4150[6] 4658[2] 5210[4] 5509[4] 6244[4] 6473[8]

Loden *L M Cumani* a48 66
2 b c Barathea(IRE) —Tentpole (USA) (Rainbow Quest (USA))
5401[9] 5907[4] *6291[11]*

Lodi (IRE) *J Akehurst* a85 91
4 ch g Bertolini(USA) —Lady Of Leisure (USA) (Diesis)
1116[8] 1572[12] 2086[8] (2491) 2883[9] 3523[8] 4019[7] 4852[8] 5404[3] 5804[3] 6187[4] 6562[2] *6726[4]*

Lofthouse *M R Channon* a59 56
2 b g Hunting Lion(IRE) —Noble Destiny (Dancing Brave (USA))
1323[8] 1610[7] 2037[3] 3579[8] 5344[7] *5583[5]* 5942[6] *6586[6]* *7363[12]*

Logic Way (USA) *Miss D Mountain* 108
5 b g Freud(USA) —Just A Ginny (USA) (Go For Gin (USA))
1301[5] 1799[9] 2055[18] 6106[16]

Logos Astra (USA) *D R Lanigan* a73 72
2 b c Elusive Quality(USA) —Wild Planet (USA) (Nureyev (USA))
3584[4] ◆ 4209[3] *5106[2]* ◆ *5682[5]*

Lois Darlin (IRE) *R A Harris* a54 43
3 ch f Indian Haven—Miriana (IRE) (Bluebird (USA))
41[4] *214[7]* *268[2]* *602[5]* *736[7]* 1956[7]

Lombok *M L W Bell* 77
3 b c Hernando(FR) —Miss Rinjani (Shirley Heights)
1349[5] 1611[6] 2152[5] 2605[4] (3861)

Lombrici (IRE) *M J Grassick* a31 22
2 b f Medecis—Placate (Rainbow Quest (USA))
6708a[8]

Lomica *Miss J A Camacho* a32 56
3 ch f Lomitas—Ecstatic (Nashwan (USA))
228[8] *2131[9]* 2528[4] 3629[3] 4397[4] 4818[7]

London Bridge *J H M Gosden* 82
3 br g Beat Hollow—Cantanta (Top Ville)
998[4] (2240) 2701[7] 3051[19] 4910[7]

London Girl (IRE) *A J McCabe* a42 36
2 b f Trans Island—Sweet As A Nut (IRE) (Pips Pride)
1764[10] *2128[8]* *2741[6]* 4973[6] *5226[9]* *5835[8]*

London Gold *H Candy* 78
2 b c Fraam—Princess Londis (Interrex (CAN))
6054[4] 6696[2] (7289)

London Stripe (IRE) *Sir Michael Stoute* 79
2 ch c Rock Of Gibraltar(IRE) —Agenda (IRE) (Sadler's Wells (USA))
6620[5] (7096)

Lonely Star (IRE) *D R Lanigan* a49 78
3 b f Bachelor Duke(USA) —Soviet Belle (IRE) (Soviet Star (USA))
1269[3] 2164[2] 3100[5]

Lonesome Maverick (IRE) *Donal Kinsella* a86 86
5 gr g Celtic Swing—Abyat (USA) (Shadeed (USA))
2289a[8]

Lone Wolfe *Jane Chapple-Hyam* a97 100
5 b g Foxhound(USA) —Fleet Hill (IRE) (Warrshan (USA))
123[6] (Dead)

Longboat Key *M Johnston* a64 77
3 b g Dr Fong(USA) —You Are The One (Unfuwain (USA))
201[5] *468[2]* *621[7]* 1231[3] 1842[3] 3192[5] 3788[2] 3940[2] 4442[5] 4793[9]

Long Distance (FR) *Miss Lucinda V Russell* a79 52
4 bb g Storming Home—Lovers Luck (IRE) (Anabaa (USA))
139[2] 6681[18]

Long Lashes (USA) *Saeed Bin Suroor* 107
2 b f Rock Hard Ten(USA) —Border Dispute (USA) (Boundary (USA))
(4795) ◆ 5488a[4] 6269[8]

Longliner *Sir Michael Stoute* 77
2 gr c Dalakhani(IRE) —Ive Gota Bad Liver (USA) (Mt. Livermore (USA))
6393[3] 7095[2]

Longoria (GER) *Helga Dewald*
5 b m Desert Prince(IRE) —La Donna (Shirley Heights)
3493a[10]

Longspur *M W Easterby* a75 79
5 br g Singspiel(IRE) —Bunting (Shaadi (USA))
4288[P] 6219[11] 7247[12]

Lonsdale Lad *R C Guest* a27 14
3 b g Elusive City(USA) —Winchcombe (Danehill (USA))
37[10]

Looby Loo *P W Chapple-Hyam* a56
3 b f Kyllachy—Halland Park Lass (IRE) (Spectrum (IRE))
6206[2] 7107[6]

Look Busy (IRE) *A Berry* 111
4 b m Danetime(IRE) —Unfortunate (Komaite (USA))
(1582) 1880[3] (2272) 3824[3] 4135[6] 5233[11] 5491a[7] 6107[5] 6499a[2]

Look Here *R M Beckett* 121
4 b m Hernando(FR) —Last Look (Rainbow Quest (USA))
2670[3] 3412a[3] 4298[6] 6056[2] 6872a[7]

Lookin At Lucky (USA) *Bob Baffert* a119
2 b c Smart Strike(CAN) —Private Feeling (USA) (Belong To Me (USA))
7307a[2]

Look Officer (USA) *Tom Dascombe* a63 66
3 b f Officer(USA) —Inn Between (USA) (Quiet American (USA))
7694[3]

Looks Like Slim *P F I Cole* a35 55
2 b c Passing Glance—Slims Lady (Theatrical Charmer)
2328[9] 2792[11] 4379[4] *5166[10]* 5935[2]

Looks The Business (IRE) *A B Haynes* a64 61
8 b g Marju(IRE) —Business Centre (IRE) (Digamist (USA))
2634[8] 3216[4] (3594) 4806[13] (5246) *5885[10] 7214[9]*

Look To This Day *R Charlton* a46 79
4 ch m In The Wings—Yanka (USA) (Blushing John (USA))
1753[3] 2177[9] 3423[3] 4098[6]

Look Whos Next *E S McMahon* a75 71
2 ch c Compton Place—Look Here's Carol (IRE) (Safawan)
2484[3] 3072[3] 3918[4] 4884[3] ◆ 5526[2] *(6347)*

Looping The Loop (USA) *J G Portman* a49 56
4 rg g Alphabet Soup(USA) —Citidance Missy (USA) (Citidancer (USA))
2601[6] 3275[11]

Loose Caboose (IRE) *A J McCabe* a76 71
4 b m Tagula(IRE) —Tama (IRE) (Indian Ridge)
13[10] 89[7] 937[2] 1103[9] 1412[6] 1558[2] 1846[12] *(2130)* 2316[5] (2472) 2657[5] 2801[10] 3268[7] 6877[2] 7090[7] 7273[10] 7355[13] 7577[4] 7679[4] 7758[8] 7852[5]

Looter (FR) *P Butler* a56 55
4 b g Red Ransom(USA) —Water Echo (USA) (Mr Prospector (USA))
42[7] 393[9] 443[11] 598[10] 1177[6] 2675[14]

Lope De Vega (IRE) *A Fabre* 112
2 ch c Shamardal(USA) —Lady Vettori (Vettori (IRE))
(5927a) 6524a[4]

Lopinot (IRE) *M R Bosley* a73 77
6 br g Pursuit Of Love—La Suquet (Puissance)
(25) 512[3] (725) 841[5] 1035[6] 1187[5] 1833[4] 2387[8] 2824[12] 6720[9] 7110[9] 7236[8] 7587[6]

Lord Admiral (USA) *Charles O'Brien* a103 113
8 b h El Prado(IRE) —Lady Ilsley (USA) (Trempolino (USA))
1913a[7] 2870a[5] 4253a[2] 5231[6] 5688a[5] *6467a[5]*

Lord Aeryn (IRE) *R A Fahey* 72
2 b g Antonius Pius(USA) —White Paper (IRE) (Marignan (USA))
3310[5] (3910) 5136[7] (6471)

Lord Chancellor (IRE) *M Johnston* a93 79
3 b c King's Best(USA) —Summer Serenade (Sadler's Wells (USA))
(32) 595[3] (755) ◆

Lord Chaparral (IRE) *R Brogi* 94
2 b c High Chaparral(IRE) —Freccia D'Oro (GER) (Acatenango (GER))
7205a[5]

Lord Deevert *W G M Turner* a68 66
4 br g Averti(IRE) —Dee-Lady (Deploy)
297[5] 961[2] 1152[13] *1285[5]* 2381[3] 2806[5] *7203[8] 7483[5] 7606[2]*

Lord Des Evees (FR) *J Boisnard* 86
3 b c Lord Of Men—Freedream (FR) (Freedom Cry)
6150a[6]

Lord Fidelio (IRE) *A M Balding* a71 70
3 b g Xaar—Rekindled Affair (IRE) (Rainbow Quest (USA))
1297[9] *1729[7]* 2496[3] 2879[9] *7432[4] (7610)*

Lord High Admiral (IRE) *A P O'Brien* 103
2 b c Galileo(IRE) —Splendid (IRE) (Mujtahid (USA))
6319a[8] 6849[14] 7072a[2]

Lord Hill (GER) *C Zeitz* 114
5 b h Tiger Hill(IRE) —Lady Fox (GER) (Monsun (GER))
2309a[8] 3201a[4]

Lord Laing (USA) *H J Collingridge* a53 46
6 bb g Chester House(USA) —Johanna Keene (USA) (Raise A Cup (USA))
59[10]

Lord Of The Dance (IRE) *J M P Eustace* a66 59
3 ch c Indian Haven—Maine Lobster (USA) (Woodman (USA))
6255[3] 6611[3] 6910[6] *7403[3] 7481[2] 7499[6]* ◆ *7610[2]*

Lord Of The Flame *W De Best-Turner* 13
3 br g Largesse—Maylan (IRE) (Lashkari)
3090[14]

Lord Of The Reins (IRE) *J G Given* a80 91
5 b g Imperial Ballet(IRE) —Waroonga (IRE) (Brief Truce (USA))
1278[8] 1672[9] 2228[9] 2717[6] 3001[8] 3828[12] 4355[4] 4662[10] 5421[3] 6799[12] 7123[7] ◆ *(7223) 7398[10] (7682) 7872[7]*

Lord Oroko *J G M O'Shea* a58 65
5 ch g Lord Of Men—Wannaplantatree (Niniski (USA))
848[7] 1171[7] 1786[4] (2519) 3544[7] 3997[7]

Lord Orpen (IRE) *Patrick Morris* a41 36
5 b g Orpen(USA) —Kenyane (IRE) (Kahyasi)
5788[9] *6612[10]*

Lord Raglan (IRE) *A P Jarvis* a48 62
2 b g Noverre(USA) —Raglan Rose (USA) (Giant's Causeway (USA))
3572[3] 4132[3] 6009[18] *7210[7]*

Lords A Leaping (IRE) *J A Osborne* a72 69
3 b c Bahamian Bounty—Joonayh (Warning)
659[3] 2395[3] 2659[2]

Lord Shanakill (USA) *Richard E Mandella* 119
3 bb c Speightstown(USA) —Green Room (USA) (Theatrical (IRE))
1675[12] 2992[3] (3669a) 4419[5] 7305a[12]

Lordship (IRE) *A W Carroll* a63 76
5 b g King's Best(USA) —Rahika Rose (Unfuwain (USA))
2352[14] 2880[14] 3077[4] 3504[5] 4140[9] 4181[6] 4938[9] 5332[3] (5364) (5634) 6545[8] 6937[9] (7172) 7220[5] *7350[8]*

Lord Silvano (GER) *M Lisek* 96
5 b h Silvano(GER) —Lorica (IRE) (Bluebird (USA))
4335a[2]

Lord's Seat *A Berry* a33 51
2 b g Trade Fair—Clashfern (Smackover)
1645[6] 2027[4] 2435[8] 3058[6] 4342[3] 4590[9] 5303[7] 7168[5] 7218[5] *7335[8]*

Lord Theo *N P Littmoden* a81 86
5 b g Averti(IRE) —Love You Too (Be My Chief (USA))
362[4] 597[6] 724[10] 807[3] 959[3] 1194[5] *2400[9]* 2975[10] 3112[5] 3357[2] 3811[5] 3960[6] (4759) (5035) ◆ 5185[2] (5437) 5656[12] 6002[7] 6483[5] 6795[12]

Lord Victor *A J McCabe* a66 34
2 ch c Needwood Blade—La Victoria (GER) (Rousillon (USA))
5637[6] 6125[7] 6591[12] *7210[3] 7319[9] 7352[2] 7501[7] 7713[4] (7756) 7849[3]* (7868)

Lord Wheathill *Mrs L Williamson* 49
2 b g Tobougg(IRE) —Classic Quartet (Classic Cliche (IRE))
4041[8] 4557[9] 7121[12]

Lord Zenith *A M Balding* 98
2 b c Zamindar(USA) —Lady Donatella (Last Tycoon)
2844[6] ◆ (3420) ◆ 3817[5]

Lorroy (FR) *Mlle M-L Mortier*
3 gr g Kouroun(FR) —Landevennec (FR) (Gairloch)
6682a[0]

Los Cristianos (FR) *A Couetil* 113
3 ch c Gold Away(IRE) —Perspective (FR) (Funambule (USA))
6502a[2]

Los Nadis (GER) *P Monteith* 78
5 ch g Hernando(FR) —La Estrella (GER) (Desert King (IRE))
1102[4] 1230[6] 1648[7] 2044[5]

Loss Leader (IRE) *T D Easterby* 30
2 ch g Captain Rio—Nenagh (IRE) (Barathea (IRE))
1623[7] 6018[8]

Lost Cause *R Charlton* a60 59
2 b c Dubawi(IRE) —Crystal (IRE) (Danehill (USA))
4314[8] 4811[6] 5317[6] *6609[4]* 6793[10]

Lost Horizon (IRE) *R Hannon* 82
2 b f Elusive City(USA) —Souvenir Souvenir (Highest Honor (FR))
5604[10] 6055[2] 6730[12]

Lost In France (IRE) *T G McCourt* a48 37
4 ch m Atraf—Sharply's Gift (IRE) (Nicolotte)
6558[8]

Lost In Paris (IRE) *T D Easterby* a70 71
3 b g Elusive City(USA) —Brazilia (Forzando)
1193[5] 1626[7] 3108[3] 3316[3] 3727[8] 4105[5] 5624[3] 6140[3] 6308[2] (6410) *7398[4]*

Lost In The Desert (IRE) *M Botti* 64
3 b g Nayef(USA) —Desert Harmony (Green Desert (USA))
2856[9] 3531[4] 4284[12]

Lost In The Forest *A P Jarvis* 43
2 ch f Trade Fair—Fallujah (Dr Fong (USA))
4817[11] 5669[5]

Lost In The Moment (IRE) *J Noseda* 55
2 b c Danehill Dancer(IRE) —Streetcar (IRE) (In The Wings)
6679[6]

Lost Soldier Three (IRE) *D Nicholls* a79 98
8 b g Barathea(IRE) —Donya (Mill Reef (USA))
1017[9] *1383[8]* 4288[4] 5067[4] 5252[8] 6100[3] 6281[5] 6681[10] 6840[2] 7118[2] *7332[2] 7505[2] 7760[2]*

Lou Bear (IRE) *J Akehurst* a63
2 b c Lujain(USA) —Dream Of Dubai (IRE) (Vettori (IRE))
7700[4] 7886[7]

Loudeacien (FR) *Unknown* 36
2 u u (USA) — (USA) (Fasliyev (USA))
4686a[8]

Lough Beg (IRE) *Miss Tor Sturgis* a65 49
6 b g Close Conflict(USA) —Mia Gigi (Hard Fought)
816[6] 1154[8] 1463[7]

Louidor *M R Bosley* a56 70
3 b g Lujain(USA) —Simonida (IRE) (Royal Academy (USA))
1574[8] 2320[17] *2683[11]*

Louie's Lad *J J Bridger* a20 54
3 gr g Compton Place—Silver Louie (IRE) (Titus Livius (FR))
1617[7] 1982[10] *2386[7]* 2478[3] 2740[2] 2810[2] 3252[4] 3477[2] 3676[5] 4231[6] 4643[9] 4736[4] 5125[12] 5477[11] 5877[10]

Louisa (GER) *P Monteith* 56
5 b m Seattle Dancer(USA) —La Ola (GER) (Dashing Blade)
4034[4] 4345[6] 4593[6] 4898[6] 5162[7] 5359[10] 5734[12]

Louise Aron (IRE) *Sante Zanardino* 103
3 b f Intikhab(USA) —Liszewska (IRE) (Desert King (IRE))
1659a[3] 2310a[8] 7046a[7]

Louise Bonne (USA) *C G Cox* 79
3 bb f Yes It's True(USA) —Blushing Issue (USA) (Blushing John (USA))
(2433) 2925[10]

Louise Sauvage *M D I Usher* a49 53
3 b f Loup Sauvage(USA) —Breezy Louise (Dilum (USA))
4324[U] 4786[5] *5193[5]* 5789[DSQ] 6551[8]

Louisiade (IRE) *R C Guest* a59 64
8 b g Tagula(IRE) —Titchwell Lass (Lead On Time (USA))
7[11] 63[5] 224[7] 399[3] 480[2] 514[9] 748[7] 984[11] 1243[11] *1438[6]* 1655[5] 4621[4] 6038[8] 7652[2] 7727[5] 7855[10]

Louisiana Gift (IRE) *J W Hills* a67
2 b g Cadeaux Genereux—Southern Queen (Anabaa (USA))
5807[5] 6254[6] 6911[7]

Loulou (USA) *S A Callaghan* a59 62
3 ch f El Prado(IRE) —Hatoof (USA) (Irish River (FR))
(1594) 1954[3] 2380[7]

Loup Breton (IRE) *E Lellouche* 119
5 b h Anabaa(USA) —Louve (USA) (Irish River (FR))
846a[4] 1144a[4] 1551a[2] 2120a[8] 5059a[7]

Louphole *J R Jenkins* a84 75
7 ch g Loup Sauvage(USA) —Goodwood Lass (IRE) (Alzao (USA))
665[2] 728[2] 799[8] 1152[12] 1619[5] (2224) 2680[9] 3243[6] 3345[4] 3673[3] *4203[2] 5196[6]* 5805[2] *7203[6]*

Loustone (FR) *Mlle S Morosi* 64
4 b m Loup Solitaire(USA) —Clarstone (FR) (Bigstone (IRE))
7387a[7]

Love Action (IRE) *R Hannon* a68 72
2 b f Motivator—Speciale (USA) (War Chant (USA))
3249[4] ◆ 3810[8] *7450[6]*

Love Allowed *Jamie Poulton* a47 55
3 br f Diktat—Love Song (Kris)
592[10] 752[9] 1047[3] 1422[3] 2498[12] 3693[13] 3946[8] 5429[18] *5647[9] 6442[8] 6783[10]*

Love And Devotion *Saeed Bin Suroor* 62
2 b f Shamardal(USA) —Romantic Myth (Mind Games)
4603[5] 5021[8] 5380[6] 6378[5]

Love Angel (USA) *J J Bridger* a51 51
7 bb g Woodman(USA) —Omnia (USA) (Green Dancer (USA))
825[RR]

Love Bird (IRE) *David Wachman* 94
3 ch f Pivotal—My Emma (Marju (IRE))
2304a[7]

Love Call (IRE) *W R Muir* a39 62
3 ch f Indian Haven—Cap And Gown (IRE) (Royal Academy (USA))
4337[6] *4867[6]* (5348)

Love Delta (USA) *M Johnston* a79 76
2 bb c Seeking The Gold(USA) —Delta Princess (USA) (A.P. Indy (USA))
4524[5] 4888[3] 5728[6] *7763[7]*

Love Galore (IRE) *M Johnston* a60 106
4 b g Galileo(IRE) —Lobmille (Mill Reef (USA))
262a[8] 338a[3] 419a[7] 613a[6] *864[5]* 2706[10] 3620[13] 3873[12]

Love In The Park *R Brotherton* a51 75
4 b m Pivotal—Naughty Crown (USA) (Chief's Crown (USA))
881[3] 1066[9] 1972[8] 2352[11] 2921[2] (3215) 3811[3] (4300) (4745) 5532[6] 5964[6]

Loveinthesand (IRE) *M Johnston* 76
2 b c Footstepsinthesand—Love Emerald (USA) (Mister Baileys)
2813[2] 4331[4] 5763[7]

Love In The West (IRE) *G A Swinbank* 60
3 b f Fruits Of Love(USA) —Sandhill (IRE) (Danehill (USA))
2937[9] 3373[4] (3685) 3936[2] 4898[5] 5342[3] 5947[9]

Love Intrigue (IRE) *T Stack* a92 102
4 b m Marju(IRE) —Love Contest (IRE) (Love The Groom (USA))
2644a[8]

Lovelace *M Johnston* a112 118
5 b h Royal Applause—Loveleaves (Polar Falcon (USA))
1138a[4] 1525[6] 2015[4] 2668[6] 3014[9] ◆ 4486[5] 5200[9]

Love Lockdown (IRE) *G M Lyons* a109 99
2 gr g Verglas(IRE) —Out Of Thanks (IRE) (Sadler's Wells (USA))
(2957a) 3436a[6] 5174[3] *(5661)*

Lovely Doyoun (TUR) *A Atci* 57
6 b m Doyoun—Castle Blaze (USA) (Lac Ouimet (USA))
5588a[12]

Lovely Eyes (IRE) *D M Simcock* 67
2 b f Red Ransom(USA) —Polygueza (FR) (Be My Guest (USA))
5906[4] 6331[4]

Lovely Samantha *Mario Hofer* 58
2 ch f Doyen(IRE) —Shining Vale (USA) (Twilight Agenda (USA))
6927a[5]

Lovely Steps (USA) *D M Simcock* a53
3 bb f Gone West(USA) —Magicalmysterycat (USA) (Storm Cat (USA))
2011[1] 583[2] 673[6]

Lovely Thought *W J Haggas* 94
3 b f Dubai Destination(USA) —Fairy Flight (IRE) (Fairy King (USA))
(1271) ◆ 2079[3] 3033[7] 3746[15] 4148[7] 6731[7] (7082) 7292[3]

Love Match *R Charlton* a64 69
2 b f Danehill Dancer(IRE) —Name Of Love (IRE) (Petardia)
2699[5] 4047[5] 4701[3] *6227[8]* 6554[2] *6775[4]*

Love Pegasus (USA) *M Johnston* a96 71
3 b c Fusaichi Pegasus(USA) —Take Charge Lady (USA) (Dehere (USA))
(386) (2600) 2855[9]

Lovers Causeway (USA) *M Johnston* a74 32
2 b c Giant's Causeway(USA) —Heeremandi (IRE) (Royal Academy (USA))
5907[11] *7844[2]* ◆

Love You Louis *J R Jenkins* a76 75
3 b g Mark Of Esteem(IRE) —Maddie's A Jem (Emperor Jones (USA))
203[6] 288[7] (509) 685[5] 2140[8] 4829[7] *5777[3] 6916[8] 7634[12]* 7738[5]

Lowdown (IRE) *M Johnston* 90
2 ch c Shamardal(USA) —Mood Swings (IRE) (Shirley Heights)
3392[5] 3957[2] (4410) ◆ 5795[14] 6064[9] 6478[4]

Lower Dicker (FR) *Mlle M-L Mortier* a49
6 ch g Limnos(JPN) —Garde Toi (FR) (Garde Royale)
5301a[8]

Lowther *A Bailey* a89 101
4 b h Beat All(USA) —Ever So Lonely (Headin' Up)
(2415) (2780) 3116[6] 4779[9] 5249[2] 5826[10] 6089[2] 6278[5] *6876[8]* 6994[11]

Loyaliste (FR) *R Hannon* 66
2 ch c Green Tune(USA) —Whitby (FR) (Gold Away (IRE))
6200[3] 6533[6]

Loyal Royal (IRE) *J M Bradley* a69 68
6 b g King Charlemagne(USA) —Supportive (IRE) (Nashamaa)
166[4] 242[4] 294[3] 395[2] 531[5] 715[2] 803[6] 961[9] 2880[12] 3075[8] 3224[6] 4202[3] 5019[10] 5225[2] 5678[7] 6492[5] 6828[2] 7051[8] (7138) 7329[4] 7432[12] 7716[6] 7876[3]

Luberon *M Johnston* a88 101
6 b g Fantastic Light(USA) —Luxurious (USA) (Lyphard (USA))
864[4] 7640[5]

Luca Brasi (FR) *F Castro* a105 97
5 b g Singspiel(IRE) —Diamond Field (USA) (Mr Prospector (USA))
2587a[3] 4585a[3] 5302a[11] 5933a[5]

Lucayan Dancer *D Nicholls* a77 77
9 b g Zieten(USA) —Tittle Tattle (IRE) (Soviet Lad (USA))
981[6] 1226[2] 1402[7] 1765[2] (2155) 2527[2] 2718[4] (3123) 3854[3] 4434[2] 4804[2] 5438[6] 6012[11]

Luciole (FR) *Mme G Matter* a67 65
3 b f Panis(USA) —Halix (FR) (Tropular)
5783a[8]

Luc Jordan *L M Cumani* a84 92
3 b c Intikhab(USA) —Saphila (IRE) (Sadler's Wells (USA))
1941[2] ◆ 2318[2] 2789[2] 3549[6] 4180[3] 5181[2] *(5614) (6209)* (6996)

Luckette *M Brittain* 32
3 b f Lucky Story(USA) —Thea (USA) (Marju (IRE))
1683[10] 1953[6] 2802[11] 3338[6] 3498[8]

Luckier (IRE) *S Kirk* a75 51
3 gr f Key Of Luck(USA) —Ibiza (GER) (Linamix (FR))
137[2] 1381[4] 2001[10] 2498[10] *6361[8] 6667[2] 7027[11]*

Luck Of The Draw (IRE) *Sir Mark Prescott* a52
2 b g Key Of Luck(USA) —Sarifa (IRE) (Kahyasi)
5807[7] 6026[6] 6627[9]

Luck Will Come (IRE) *H J Collingridge* a77 79
5 b m Desert Style(IRE) —Petite Maxine (Sharpo)
1633[4] *(2144)* 2665[2] 3188[2] 3627[9] *4085[2]* 4441[2] 5511[7] *6496[3]*

Lucky Art (USA) *Mrs R A Carr* a59 85
3 b g Johannesburg(USA) —Syrian Summer (USA) (Damascus (USA))
1368[8] 2717[5] 3173[9] 3623[9] 4192[2] 4601[4] 4653[3] (4849) 5517[5] 6387[8] 6798[3] 7082[3] *7269[7] 7506[12]*

Lucky Bid *J M Bradley* a34 19
3 b g Josr Algarhoud(IRE) —Double Fault (IRE) (Zieten (USA))
1465[5] 1982[12]

Lucky Breeze (IRE) *W J Knight* a46
2 b f Key Of Luck(USA) —Lasting Chance (USA) (American Chance (USA))
7663[8]

Lucky Buddha *Jedd O'Keeffe* 59
3 gr g Kyllachy—Heaven-Liegh-Grey (Grey Desire)
1190[5] 1736[3] 1969[8] 3651[6] 3729[8] 4594[3] 6161[8]

Lucky Character *N J Vaughan* a47 42
4 br g Key Of Luck(USA) —Gay Heroine (Caerleon (USA))
530[4] 587[9]

Lucky Dan (IRE) *Paul Green* a77 72
3 b g Danetime(IRE) —Katherine Gorge (USA) (Hansel (USA))
313[6] 572[6] 3003[5] 3304[8] 3804[7] (3856) 4343[8] 4494[9] 4707[8] 5073[4] 5405[2] *5836[2]* 5937[3] 6798[11]

Lucky Dance (BRZ) *A G Foster* a80 98
7 b h Mutakddim(USA) —Linda Francesa (ARG) (Equalize (USA))
783[12] 995[5] 1352[17] 2470[3] 3014[19] 3312[10] 3872[15] 4310[6] 6429[6] ◆ *6876[6]* ◆ 7185[4] *7489[7] 7810[4]*

Lucky Dancer *D R C Elsworth* a62 57
4 ch g Selkirk(USA) —Spot Prize (USA) (Seattle Dancer (USA))
279[6] 1122[6] 1273[5] *1609[2]* 1851[5] *3029[7]*

Lucky Diva *Rae Guest* 41
2 ch f Lucky Story(USA) —Cosmic Countess (IRE) (Lahib (USA))
5714[7]

Luckydolly (IRE) *F Costello* a66 57
3 ch f Daggers Drawn(USA) —Dolly Dimpler (IRE) (Nordico (USA))
432[4] 7715[8] 7730[5]

Lucky Find (SAF) *M F De Kock* a116 113
6 ch g Rich Man's Gold(USA) —Little Erna (SAF) (Ernani)
641a[3] ◆ 771a[6] 1008a[15]

Lucky Flyer *Rae Guest* 17
2 br f Lucky Story(USA) —Fly Like The Wind (Cyrano De Bergerac)
2636[8]

Lucky Forteen *P W Hiatt* a31
6 b m Forzando—Grey Blade (Dashing Blade)
706[10] 1465[7] 1743[12]

Lucky Fortune (IRE) *Miss Amy Weaver* a58
3 ch g Lucky Story(USA) —Majborah (IRE) (Entrepreneur)
158[3] 317[7] 707[3] 1036[6] 1746[12]

Lucky General (IRE) *R Hannon* 108
2 b c Hawk Wing(USA) —Dress Code (IRE) (Barathea (IRE))
2844[5] (3402) ◆ 3817[4] 4418[10] (4826) 5022[4] 5795[3] (6317a)

Lucky Leigh *M R Channon* a81 95
3 b f Piccolo—Solmorin (Fraam)
1582[11] 2928[10] 3389[12] 4712[2] 4990[7] 5203[9] 5777[8] 5974[5] (6632) 6902[8] 7553[6] 7634[5]

Lucky Like (FR) *E J O'Neill* 104
2 bb c Lucky Story(USA) —Land Bound (USA) (Boundary (USA))
3648a[5] 4073a[2] 4487[4] (5117a) 5416a[5] (6486) ◆

Lucky Mellor *D K Ivory* a84 71
2 b c Lucky Story(USA) —Lady Natilda (First Trump)
1083[9] (1653) 1927[4] 2599[5] 3952[2] 4639[7] 4868[3] 5650[2] 6068[4] 6905[3] 7372[3] 7636[2] (7793)

Lucky Numbers (IRE) *Paul Green* 90
3 b c Key Of Luck(USA) —Pure Folly (IRE) (Machiavellian (USA))
1305[5] 1345[2] 1803[2] 1824[8] 2934[6] 3375[7] 3622[6] 4044[2] 4338[7] 4776[2] 5203[6] 5523[3] 5959[5]

Lucky Punt *B G Powell* a99 58
3 ch g Auction House(USA) —Sweet Coincidence (Mujahid (USA))
1580[4] (2131) (2742) 3069[7] (6360) 6878[2] (7091) (7640)

Lucky Quality (AUS) *Y S Tsui* a81 106
5 br h Elusive Quality(USA) —Wishing Stone (USA) (Dayjur (USA))
1010a[9]

Lucky Quay (IRE) *W R Swinburn* a44
2 b g Key Of Luck(USA) —Lakatoi (Saddlers' Hall (IRE))
7522[9]

Lucky Rave *D H Brown* a93 94
2 b c Lucky Story(USA) —Rave On (ITY) (Barathea (IRE))
1867[3] 2839[4] 3613[2] (3925) (5369)

Lucky Ray (ARG) *Doug Watson* a97
6 b h Halo Sunshine(USA) —Rubia Blonde (ARG) (Candy Stripes (USA))
773a[13]

Lucky Score (IRE) *Mouse Hamilton-Fairley* a66 68
3 b f Lucky Story(USA) —Musical Score (Blushing Flame (USA))
1670[3] 2206[5] 7228[2] 7416[3] 7632[5] 7742[5] 7829[6]

Lucky Traveller *T D Easterby* 44
2 b g Lucky Story(USA) —Bollin Sophie (Efisio)
3262[5] 4652[5] 5253[14]

Lucky Windmill *G A Swinbank* 54
2 b g Lucky Story(USA) —Windmill Princess (Gorytus (USA))
3392[4] 6646[7]

Lucullus *M Blanshard* a73 51
4 b g Bertolini(USA) —Calcavella (Pursuit Of Love)
1186[4]

Lucy Brown *R Hannon* a67 77
3 br f Compton Place—Harambee (IRE) (Robellino (USA))
3278[4] 3815[2] ◆ 4380[8] (4950) 5506[4] 6112[2] 7111[6] 7327[7]

Lucy Gliters *T P Tate* 45
2 ch f Observatory(USA) —Bombay Sapphire (Be My Chief (USA))
3032[6] 5337[6] 5668[12] 5976[3]

Lucy's Perfect *B R Millman* 59
3 ch f Systematic—Water Flower (Environment Friend)
1092[9] 1708[4] 2323[10] 2909[3] 4687[4] 5720[6] (6549) 6910[8]

Ludwigshafen (IRE) *John Geoghegan* a74 72
5 b m Cape Cross(IRE) —Cape Clear (Slip Anchor)
290[2] 558[4]

Lugato (GER) *Lee Smyth* a42 54
7 br g Winged Love(IRE) —Lugano (GER) (Orofino (GER))
6126[9]

Lui Rei (ITY) *A Renzoni* 111
3 b c Reinaldo(FR) —My Luigia (IRE) (High Estate)
1393a[5] 1905a[5]

Luisant *J A Nash* a105 106
6 ch g Pivotal—La Legere (USA) (Lit De Justice (USA))
3014a[22] 4360a[3] 6707a[2] 7007a[6]

Luisa Tetrazzini (IRE) *John A Harris* a55
3 b f Hawk Wing(USA) —Break Of Day (USA) (Favorite Trick (USA))
4199[14] 5840[5] 7067[5] 7353[3] 7464[3] 7629[3] 7797[4]

Lui Seul (IRE) *J-C Rouget* a78
2 b c Dubawi(IRE) —Lia (IRE) (Desert King (IRE))
(6979a)

Lujano *Ollie Pears* a71 74
4 b g Lujain(USA) —Latch Key Lady (USA) (Tejano (USA))
2133[11] 2531[12] 3070[16] 4435[3] 5289[10] (5886) ◆ (6383) 6861[11] 7322[9]

Lujeanie *D K Ivory* a88 80
3 br g Lujain(USA) —Ivory's Joy (Tina's Pet)
2849[5] (3299) 3738[4] 4540[9] (4787) 7828[8] (7875)

Lujiana *M Brittain* a41 66
4 b m Lujain(USA) —Compact Disc (IRE) (Royal Academy (USA))
4508[8] 4998[9] 5396[10] 7561[10]

Lukatara (USA) *Miss Sheena West* a21
4 b g Kayrawan(USA) —Hey Winnie (USA) (Hey Big Spender (USA))
279[7] 663[10]

Lukes Desire (IRE) *F Costello* a73 69
2 gr f Royal Applause—Splendida Idea (IRE) (Kenmare (FR))
1993a[12]

Lukian (GER) *Werner Glanz* 31
4 b h Orpen(USA) —Ladywell Blaise (IRE) (Turtle Island (IRE))
7303a[11]

Lukrecia (IRE) *P Schiergen* 98
3 b f Exceed And Excel(AUS) —Quecha (IRE) (Indian Ridge)
1914a[2] 2757a[5] 4363a[8]

Luluti (IRE) *S A Callaghan* a58
2 b f Kheleyf(USA) —Amsicora (Cadeaux Genereux)
3987[6]

Lumiere Astrale (FR) *A De Royer-Dupre* 97
4 ch m Trempolino(USA) —Lumiere Rouge (FR) (Indian Ridge)
4365a[0]

Luminosa *D Donovan* a27
2 ch f Zaha(CAN) —Lightning Blaze (Cosmonaut)
7580[10]

Luminous Eyes (IRE) *D K Weld* 103
3 ch f Bachelor Duke(USA) —Mood Indigo (IRE) (Indian Ridge)
2304a[9] 3516a[2] 3894a[7]

Luminous Gold *C F Wall* a72 79
4 b m Fantastic Light(USA) —Nasaieb (IRE) (Fairy King (USA))
1748[8] (2418) 3347[4] 4154[4] 4787[3] 5597[3] 6118[3] 6666[11]

Luminous Star (USA) *R M Beckett* a77 76
2 bb g Aldebaran(USA) —Best Of Memories (USA) (Halo (USA))
3692[5] 4323[6] 4638[2] (5119) 5682[3] 6491[5]

Luna Landing *Jedd O'Keeffe* a74 82
6 ch g Allied Forces(USA) —Macca Luna (IRE) (Kahyasi)
1519[7] 2452[4] 3191[3] 3728[6] 4332[6] 5252[10]

Lunar Limelight *P J Makin* a67 53
4 b g Royal Applause—Moon Magic (Polish Precedent (USA))
186[4] 2039[14] 7152[3] 7466[12] (7666) (7754) ◆

Lunar River (FR) *David Pinder* a73 67
6 b m Muhtathir—Moon Gorge (Pursuit Of Love)
1318[6] (1834) 2039[10] 2923[3] 3217[2] 3777[4] 4300[6] 5195[2] 5886[8] 6346[6] 6806[2] 7134[4] 7399[8]

Lunar Romance *T J Pitt* a31 50
3 b f Royal Applause—Witness (Efisio)
6831[9] 7353[11]

Lunar Storm (IRE) *Mrs R A Carr* a44 15
5 b g Machiavellian(USA) —Moonshell (IRE) (Sadler's Wells (USA))
779[11] 855[6] 1101[7] 1556[12] 2785[7] 4656[9]

Lunar Victory (USA) *J H M Gosden* 80
2 b c Speightstown(USA) —Lunar Colony (USA) (A.P. Indy (USA))
6057[3] ◆ 6620[4]

Lunaticus *M J Attwater* a10
3 b f Lujain(USA) —Steppin Out (First Trump)
7533[7] 7829[10]

Lunces Lad (IRE) *G Brown* a86 81
5 gr g Xaar—Bridelina (FR) (Linamix (FR))
1748[6] 1970[9] 2224[10] 7179[12]

Lunduv (IRE) *C Von Der Recke* a92 92
4 b m Pivotal—Another Dancer (FR) (Groom Dancer (USA))
4365a[7] 5296a[11] 7569a[2]

Lungwa (IRE) *E Lellouche* a94 103
3 b f One Cool Cat(USA) —Louve Sacree (USA) (Seeking The Gold (USA))
(6891a) 7347a[7]

Lupita (IRE) *B G Powell* 63
5 ch m Intikhab(USA) —Sarah (IRE) (Hernando (FR))
1426[10] 2519[11]

Luscivious *J A Glover* a93 89
5 ch g Kyllachy—Lloc (Absalom)
68[7] 901[11] 971[3] 1313[8] 2228[2] 2770[15] (3956) 4311[2] 4461[8] (4842) 5104[6] 5623[9] 6051[9] 6359[7]

Lush (IRE) *R Hannon* a69 75
4 b m Fasliyev(USA) —Our Hope (Dancing Brave (USA))
2322[4] 2675[7] 3217[10] 5365[2] 6074[8]

Lush Lashes *J S Bolger* 121
4 b m Galileo(IRE) —Dance For Fun (Anabaa (USA))
2303a[3] 3012[6] 3412a[4]

Lutece Eria (FR) *C Diard* a93 95
3 ch f Gold Away(IRE) —Dark Mile (USA) (Woodman (USA))
7216a[4]

Luthien (IRE) *A M Hales* a66 56
3 b f Polish Precedent(USA) —Triplemoon (USA) (Trempolino (USA))
1532[5] 2006[10] 3222[7] 3776[6] 5011[14] 6371[10] 6497[6] 6967[11] 7369[11]

Lutine Bell *Sir Mark Prescott* a61 52
2 ch g Starcraft(NZ) —Satin Bell (Midyan (USA))
3106[5] 3715[4] 4200[5]

Lutine Charlie (IRE) *P Winkworth* a84 77
2 b g Kheleyf(USA) —Silvery Halo (USA) (Silver Ghost (USA))
4515[2] 5571[2] ◆ 5778[4] 6619[14] 7243[5]

Lutine Lady *P Winkworth* 41
2 b f Exceed And Excel(AUS) —Hillside Girl (IRE) (Tagula (IRE))
1706[7] 2135[8]

Luv Gov (USA) *D Wayne Lukas* a107
3 b c Ten Most Wanted(USA) —City Of Silver (USA) (Nepal (USA))
2098a[8] 2734a[5]

Luv U Noo *A P Jarvis* a44 60
2 b f Needwood Blade—Lady Suesanne (IRE) (Cape Cross (IRE))
4398[5] 4773[3] 5553[5] 7089[5]

Lyceana *M A Jarvis* a85 79
4 ch m Medicean—Wax Lyrical (Safawan)
3165[5] 3921[5] 4948[2] 5532[8] 5997[8]

Lydia's Legacy *T J Etherington* 34
4 b m Bahamian Bounty—Lydia's Look (IRE) (Distant View (USA))
1241[9] 1628[13] 2603[8]

Lyra's Daemon *W R Muir* a79 74
3 b f Singspiel(IRE) —Seven Of Nine (IRE) (Alzao (USA))
(1416) 2212[6] 6760[8] 7048[6] (7413) 7539[5] 7811[8]

Lyrical Intent *P Howling* a57
3 ch g Imperial Dancer—Magical Flute (Piccolo)
230[5] 440[8] 599[4] 1075[9] 6349[10] 6860[11] 7022[7] 7658[8] 7767[6] 7814[4]

Lyric Art (USA) *B Smart* a61 61
3 b f Red Ransom(USA) —String Quartet (IRE) (Sadler's Wells (USA))
425[2] ◆ 564[3] 1098[4] 3381[9] 4819[6] (5624) 6358[4]

Lyric Poet (USA) *Saeed Bin Suroor* 51
2 bb c Distorted Humor(USA) —Baltic Nations (USA) (Seattle Slew (USA))
5401[10] 5831[6]

Lytham (IRE) *A W Carroll* a67 66
8 b g Spectrum(IRE) —Nousaiyra (IRE) (Be My Guest (USA))
(116) (494) (669) 711[9] 877[3] 1000[3] 1318[8] 1604[2] 2149[8] 3740[3] 3923[5] 4563[9] 4861[4] ◆ 5377[10] 5888[9]

Lytton *R Ford* a76 86
4 b g Royal Applause—Dora Carrington (IRE) (Sri Pekan (USA))
676[7] 811[11] 921[9] 1057[2] (1475) 5813[13] 6103[12]

Maadraa (IRE) *B J Llewellyn* a81 79
4 br g Josr Algarhoud(IRE) —Del Deya (IRE) (Caerleon (USA))
1356[12] (1815) 3406[6] 4042[4]

Maany (USA) *M A Jarvis* 51
2 ch f Mr Greeley(USA) —Dixie Card (USA) (Dixieland Band (USA))
4797[11]

Maashooq *M P Tregoning* a55 74
2 ch g Observatory(USA) —Chatifa (IRE) (Titus Livius (FR))
5311[9] 6809[3]

Mabait *L M Cumani* a91 97
3 b c Kyllachy—Czarna Roza (Polish Precedent (USA))
(2611) 3347[7] 4540[7] 5523[12] (6072) (6348) (7060)

Mabuya (UAE) *P J Makin* 91
3 b g Halling(USA) —City Of Gold (IRE) (Sadler's Wells (USA))
1671[2] 2126[2] 2432[3] (3279) 3840[2] 4767[7] 5475[8] 6203[3]

Macademy Royal (USA) *Miss N A Lloyd-Beavis* a14 34
6 b g Royal Academy(USA) —Garden Folly (USA) (Pine Bluff (USA))
7521[9]

Macarthur *M F De Kock* 122
5 b g Montjeu(IRE) —Out West (USA) (Gone West (USA))
642a[7] 772a[8] 1012a[14] 6303[11]

Macassar *A Fabre* 90
2 b c Tertullian(USA) —Minaccia (GER) (Platini (GER))
6080a[4]

Mac Dalia *A J McCabe* a68 70
4 b m Namid—Maugwenna (Danehill (USA))
146[7]

Macdillon *W S Kittow* a89 96
3 b g Acclamation—Dilys (Efisio)
2049[2] 2934[10] 5263[4] 6240[10] 6631[6] 7202[5]

Mac Don (IRE) *G J Smith* a64 74
5 b g Soviet Star(USA) —Sharena (IRE) (Kahyasi)
805[8]

Mac Gille Eoin *J Gallagher* a93 112
5 b h Bertolini(USA) —Peruvian Jade (Petong)
1299[10] 1699[6] 2297[7] 2707[2] 3405[4] (3524) 4523[5] 5878[2] 6091[22]

Machinate (USA) *W M Brisbourne* a72 29
7 bb g Machiavellian(USA) —Dancing Sea (USA) (Storm Cat (USA))
221[5] 256[4] 554[6] 657[10] 682[8] 984[10] 1131[5] 1530[10] 5465[11]

Machine Gun Kelly (IRE) *G L Moore* 66
2 b g Johannesburg(USA) —West Brooklyn (USA) (Gone West (USA))
4410[8] 5017[3] 5829[4] 6305[7] 6736[6] 6963[7]

Machinist (IRE) *D Nicholls* a95 106
9 br g Machiavellian(USA) —Athene (IRE) (Rousillon (USA))
1018[11] 1560[8] (2093)

Machismo (USA) *John W Sadler* a107 70
5 b g Trippi(USA) —Le Nat (USA) (Dynaformer (USA))
1010a[8]

Macho Again (USA) *Dallas Stewart* a127
4 rg h Macho Uno(USA) —Go Donna Go (USA) (Wild Again (USA))
6512a[4]

Mackintosh (IRE) *Patrick Morris* a55 55
3 ch g Kyllachy—Louhossoa (USA) (Trempolino (USA))
7740[6] 7817[3] 7857[4]

Mackten *W J Knight* a72 70
3 b g Makbul—Tender (IRE) (Zieten (USA))
1423[3] ◆ (1838) 2399[9]

Mac Love *Stef Liddiard* a109 116
8 b g Cape Cross(IRE) —My Lass (Elmaamul (USA))
2476[4] (2668) 2990[9] (4949) 5426[4] (5875)

Macnas (USA) *J S Bolger* 76
2 ch f Orientate(USA) —All My Lovin' (USA) (Cat's Career (USA))
2302a[3]

Macorville (USA) *G M Moore* 90
6 b g Diesis—Desert Jewel (USA) (Caerleon (USA))
4329[9] 4769[9] 5656[14]

Macroy *B R Millman* 62
2 b g Makbul—Royal Orchid (IRE) (Shalford (IRE))
3072[6] 5180[7] 6386[4]

Mac's Power (IRE) *P J O'Gorman* a93 14
3 b g Exceed And Excel(AUS) —Easter Girl (Efisio)
1077[4] 1592[10] 2596[4] 2826[5] (3028) 3738[3] 4984[3] 5092[6] 5665[2] ◆ (5986) ◆ 6229[4]

Mac Tiernan (IRE) *P J Lally* a57
2 b g Minashki(IRE) —Softly Softly (IRE) (Lucky Guest)
6401a[11]

Mactrac *R Hannon* a48 32
2 b g Marju(IRE) —Zanna (FR) (Soviet Star (USA))
2201[9] 2599[6] 5212[11] 7474[8] 7884[9]

Mac Wolf *M G Quinlan* a48 55
2 b c Polish Precedent(USA) —Herminoe (Rainbow Quest (USA))
1289[11] 1622[4] 1941[8] 4320[6] 5988[9]

Mad About You (IRE) *D K Weld* 114
4 b m Indian Ridge—Irresistible Jewel (IRE) (Danehill (USA))
928a[3] (1138a) 1756a[2] 1913a[4] 3881a[3]

Madame Boot (FR) *P J Makin* 53
2 b f Diktat—Esprit Libre (Daylami (IRE))
4603[10] 5604[13]

Madame Excelerate *W M Brisbourne* a70 43
2 b f Pursuit Of Love—Skovshoved (IRE) (Danetime (IRE))
6274[5] 6842[12] 7157[2]

Madame Guillotine (USA) *R M Beckett* a45 62
3 rg f Proud Citizen(USA) —Paris Gem (USA) (Rubiano (USA))
2947[7] ◆ 3297[8] 6611[5]

Madame Jourdain (IRE) *S A Harris* 64
3 b f Beckett(IRE) —Cladantom (IRE) (High Estate)
1469[7] 1949[10] 5145[13] 5336[6] 5362[5] 6988[9] 7246[15]

Madame McManus *P D Evans* a4
3 ch f Needwood Blade—Madame Jones (IRE) (Lycius (USA))
7576[7] 7596[11] 7753[13]

Madame Rio (IRE) *E J Cooper* a26 42
4 b m Captain Rio—Glenviews Purchase (IRE) (Desert Story (IRE))
3296[8]

Madame Roulin (IRE) *M L W Bell* a68 57
2 b f Xaar—Cradle Rock (IRE) (Desert Sun)
6441[4] 6727[7] 7277[5]

Madame Trop Vite (IRE) *K A Ryan* a82 104
3 b f Invincible Spirit(IRE) —Gladstone Street (IRE) (Waajib)
2116a[11] 3202a[6] 3638[7] 4087[7] 6091[23] 6814[7] 7007a[11]

Madam Isshe *M S Saunders* 56
2 b f Ishiguru(USA) —Lucky Dip (Tirol)
4265[8] 4478[5] 4688[10] 5379[3] 5714[4]

Madamlily (IRE) *J J Quinn* a71 74
3 b f Refuse To Bend(IRE) —Rainbow Dream (Rainbow Quest (USA))
1019[8] 2060[8] 3069[4] 3687[4] 4068[7] 4506[2] 6075[2] 6313[6]

Madam Macie (IRE) *J Hetherton* 77
2 ch f Bertolini(USA) —Dictatrice (FR) (Anabaa (USA))
(6842) ◆ 7033[5]

Madam President *W R Swinburn* a74 71
4 b m Royal Applause—White House (Pursuit Of Love)
(1318) 2052[9] 5195[8] 5975[5] 6566[9]

Madam Ruby (IRE) *A King* 59
2 ch f Observatory(USA) —Azur (IRE) (Brief Truce (USA))
5498[6] 6729[10] 6931[6]

Madam'X *Mrs A Duffield* a50 46
3 b f Xaar—Bonne Etoile (Diesis)
5524[4] 6177[4] 6384[6]

Ma Dauphine (FR) *Y Barberot* 71
2 b f Martillo(GER) —Notre Dauphine (FR) (Dauphin Du Bourg (FR))
6927a[4]

Madda's Force (ITY) *R Betti* 100
3 b f Blu Air Force(IRE) —Madda'sblueyes (Selkirk (USA))
1394a[13]

Maddy *George Baker* a62 60
4 b m Daggers Drawn(USA) —Summer Lightning (IRE) (Tamure (IRE))
78[9] 443[6] 500[4] 1520[3] 1651[9] 2149[3] 2333[3] 2537[3] 2808[6] 3473[7] 3961[4] 4667[7]

Made To Ransom *J H M Gosden* 94
4 b g Red Ransom(USA) —Maid For The Hills (Indian Ridge)
(1771) ◆ 2327[7]

Mad Existence (IRE) *Mrs Valerie Keatley* a58 57
5 b m Val Royal(FR) —Hanzala (FR) (Akarad (FR))
7732[2]

Madhaaq (IRE) *J L Dunlop* 66
2 b f Medicean—Winsa (USA) (Riverman (USA))
7183[5]

Madhal *Matthew Salaman* a56 55
3 b g First Trump—Jane Grey (Tragic Role (USA))
1956[3] 2317[13] 2652[8] 6587[5] 7002[6] 7614[10] 7787[11]

Madiba (GER) *J E Pease* 89
2 b c Bertolini(USA) —Moonlight Melody (GER) (Law Society (USA))
5280a[4]

Madison Belle *J R Weymes* a72 53
3 ch f Bahamian Bounty—Indian Flag (IRE) (Indian Ridge)
16[3] (64) (365) 605[2] (684) 819[3] 1652[2] 7870[8]

Madison Park (IRE) *H R A Cecil* a68 65
3 b c Montjeu(IRE) —Crystal Gaze (IRE) (Rainbow Quest (USA))
2240[8] 3117[7] 4205[4] 4650[7]

Madj's Baby *H S Howe* 56
2 b f Footstepsinthesand—Madamoiselle Jones (Emperor Jones (USA))
2792[8] ◆ 3810[11] 5212[8]

Madman (FR) *C N Kellett*
5 br g Kaldou Star—Shirlauges (FR) (Port Lyautey (FR))
6673[12]
Mad Millie (IRE) *J Hetherton* a47 69
2 b f Pyrus(USA) —Tipsy Lady (Intikhab (USA))
3487[6] 4278[2] 4595[2] 5199[11] 5620[U] 5980[8] 6354[7]
Madonna Incognito (USA) *F Rohaut* 92
3 b f El Prado(IRE) —Fiscal Year (IRE) (Half A Year (IRE))
(4130a) 5012a[4]
Mad Rush (USA) *L M Cumani* 117
5 b g Lemon Drop Kid(USA) —Revonda (IRE) (Sadler's Wells (USA))
(2677) 3413a[5]
Mae Cigan (FR) *M Blanshard* a55 73
6 gr g Medaaly—Concert (Polar Falcon (USA))
3029[8] 4169[2] 4737[5] 6457[10] 6936[7]
Maestro Of Murano (AUS) *Roslyn Day* 34
4 ch g Bianconi(USA) —Talent Lover (NZ) (Lucky Ring)
6961a[16]
Mafaaz *J H M Gosden* a102 99
3 ch c Medicean—Complimentary Pass (Danehill (USA))
(863) 1225a[8]
Mafaheem *A B Haynes* a76 77
7 b g Mujahid(USA) —Legend Of Aragon (Aragon)
(87) 245[6] 304[8] 762[4] 937[4] 2864[7] 3227[9] 4183[8] 5225[8]
Mafasina (USA) *B Smart* a70 24
4 b m Orientate(USA) —Money Madam (USA) (A.P. Indy (USA))
1778[3] 2133[3]
Mafeking (UAE) *M R Hoad* a92 84
5 b g Jade Robbery(USA) —Melisendra (FR) (Highest Honor (FR))
156[6] 2407[8] 2891[10] 3734[2] 4716[2] 6973[2] 7226[P] 7684[2] 7775[2]
Mafra (IRE) *Y Fouin* 80
3 b f Kalanisi(IRE) —Sovana (IRE) (Desert King (IRE))
6682a[4]
Magadan (IRE) *E Lellouche* 119
4 b h High Chaparral(IRE) —Molasses (FR) (Machiavellian (USA))
(1762a) 2522a[3] 3443a[5] 6526a[9]
Magaling (IRE) *L M Cumani* 92
3 ch c Medicean—Fling (Pursuit Of Love)
(2072) 2696[8] 3049[25]
Magdala (FR) *F Rohaut* 81
3 ch f Hawk Wing(USA) —Miss Chryss (IRE) (Indian Ridge)
4334a[0]
Magen's Star (IRE) *T Stack* 95
4 b m Galileo(IRE) —Bluffing (IRE) (Darshaan)
4609a[6]
Magenta Strait *R Hollinshead* a60
2 b f Sampower Star—Vermilion Creek (Makbul)
5835[7] (7749)
Mageska (FR) *J-P Gauvin* a72
4 ch m Smadoun(FR) —Magesq (FR) (Fabulous Dancer (USA))
6981a[4]
Maggie Kate *R Ingram* a66 69
4 b m Auction House(USA) —Perecapa (IRE) (Archway (IRE))
590[9] 799[10] 1360[9] 1787[8] 2180[12] 2381[8] 3671[9] 3947[5] (4736) (5629)
Maggie Lou (IRE) *K A Ryan* a50 86
3 b f Red Ransom(USA) —Triomphale (USA) (Nureyev (USA))
1078[8] 1869[4] 2198[4] 2926[5] 4198[7] 5335[8]
Maggie Maggie May (IRE) *P C Haslam* 5
7 b m Spectrum(IRE) —Liberty Song (IRE) (Last Tycoon)
2366[15]
Maggi Fong *H-A Pantall* a85 85
3 ch f Dr Fong(USA) —Maggi For Margaret (Shavian)
3892a[8] 5651a[5]
Magical Destiny (IRE) *B Smart* a69
3 b g Exceed And Excel(AUS) —Magic Lady (IRE) (Bigstone (IRE))
855[4]
Magical Fantasy (USA) *Patrick Gallagher* a109 116
4 ch m Diesis—Kissing Gate (USA) (Easy Goer (USA))
7284a[5]
Magical Macey (USA) *T D Barron* 80
2 ch g Rossini(USA) —Spring's Glory (USA) (Honour And Glory (USA))
2153[10] 5620[2] (5957) 7115[7]
Magical Mimi *K G Wingrove* a30
8 b m Magic Ring(IRE) —Naval Dispatch (Slip Anchor)
198[13] 4751[0] 581[7] 682[10]
Magical Molecule *G D Blake*
2 b g Whittingham(IRE) —Fontaine House (Pyramus (USA))
2887[6]
Magicalmysterytour (IRE) *W J Musson* 106
6 b g Sadler's Wells(USA) —Jude (Darshaan)
2075[5] 3406[2] 3874[3] 5173[9] 5656[11] 6662[16] 7018[6] 7293[13]
Magical Song *J Balding* a59 58
4 ch g Forzando—Classical Song (IRE) (Fayruz)
14[8] 150[2] 223[4] 791[3] 979[3] 1438[8] 1655[6] 1889[4] 3296[2] 3852[2]
Magical Speedfit (IRE) *G G Margarson* a77 78
4 ch g Bold Fact(USA) —Magical Peace (IRE) (Magical Wonder (USA))
(1181) 1418[8] 2219[7] 3386[4] 3694[7] 3784[13] 3945[3] 4607[8] 5156[2] 5480[4] 5724[2] 5974[6] 6666[3] (6791) 7123[3]
Magic Amigo *J R Jenkins* a54 18
8 ch g Zilzal(USA) —Emaline (FR) (Empery (USA))
117[3] 469[9] 775[6] 4158[11]
Magic Cat *A P Jarvis* 101
3 b g One Cool Cat(USA) —Magic Music (IRE) (Magic Ring (IRE))
1602[8] 2485[7] 6091[24] 6678[20]
Magic Cloud *John Joseph Hanlon* a61 66
4 b g Cloudings(IRE) —Magic Orb (Primo Dominie)
6783[7]
Magic Doll (USA) *Saeed Bin Suroor* a78 72
2 ch f Elusive Quality(USA) —Meniatarra (USA) (Zilzal (USA))
5398[3] (6164)
Magic Echo *M Dods* a88 92
5 b m Wizard King—Sunday News'N'Echo (USA) (Trempolino (USA))
1347[7] 1850[8] 2073[2] 4003[4] 4328[11] 4815[6] 5363[5] 6016[5] 6986[7]
Magic Eye (IRE) *Andreas Lowe* a100 105
4 b m Nayef(USA) —Much Commended (Most Welcome)
1268a[4] 5588a[5] 6323a[5] 7704a[4]
Magic Footsteps *Jedd O'Keeffe* 70
2 b c Footstepsinthesand—Dayville (USA) (Dayjur (USA))
1866[7] 2623[2]
Magic Glade *Peter Grayson* a74 72
10 b g Magic Ring(IRE) —Ash Glade (Nashwan (USA))
44[6] 165[6] 645[7] 832[11] 895[6] 1055[10] 3386[8]
Magic Haze *Miss S E Hall* 58
3 b g Makbul—Turn Back (Pivotal)
4432[6] 4892[9] 6217[10]
Magician's Cape (IRE) *Sir Michael Stoute* a85 79
2 b c Montjeu(IRE) —Seven Magicians (USA) (Silver Hawk (USA))
(5966) ◆ 6779[3]
Magic Kahyasi (IRE) *G L Moore* a53 68
6 b g Kahyasi—Magic Play (IRE) (Deploy)
346[7] 502[10]
Magic Lantern *R Hannon* a76 75
2 ch f Halling(USA) —Papabile (USA) (Chief's Crown (USA))
2494[8] ◆ 3979[2] 4946[2] 5428[7] 6241[17] 6722[5]
Magic Millie (IRE) *J Hetherton* 52
2 bb f Marju(IRE) —Fille De La Terre (IRE) (Namaqualand (USA))
4226[8] 4430[7] 4817[14] 5981[9]
Magic Mornings (IRE) *M Halford* a77 86
3 b f Bahri(USA) —Yaselda (Green Desert (USA))
7297a[9]
Magic Place *R Hannon*
2 b c Compton Place—Michelle Shift (Night Shift (USA))
7289[14]
Magic Prospect (FR) *E J O'Neill* 82
2 b c Miesque's Son(USA) —Clarissa Dalloway (FR) (Sillery (USA))
7384a[3]
Magic Queen (IRE) *A P Jarvis* a52 39
3 b f Aptitude(USA) —Second Wind (USA) (Hennessy (USA))
6101[5] 6430[6] 6611[11] 7004[12] 7240[14]
Magic Rush *Norma Twomey* a78 71
7 b g Almaty(IRE) —Magic Legs (Reprimand)
950[6] 1320[2] 1538[2] 2518[5] 5095[3]
Magic Spirit *J S Moore* a62
2 ch f Kirkwall—Flaming Spirt (Blushing Flame (USA))
7622[8]
Magic Warrior *J C Fox* a69 53
9 b g Magic Ring(IRE) —Clarista (USA) (Riva Ridge (USA))
47[3] 157[5] 253[7] 1080[11] 1496[2] 1728[12] 1974[P] 2221[6] 2675[5] 5211[8]
Magistrate (IRE) *Andrew Turnell* a60
4 b g Nayef(USA) —Alabastrine (Green Desert (USA))
6673[7] 7367[5]
Magners Hill (IRE) *Gerard Keane* a69 53
5 b g Desert Sun—Tropicana (IRE) (Imperial Frontier (USA))
255[3] 7718[11] 7733[9]
Magnetic Force (IRE) *Sir Michael Stoute* a73 73
2 gr g Verglas(IRE) —Upperville (IRE) (Selkirk (USA))
5220[6] 5879[3] 6607[2]
Magneto (IRE) *E J Creighton* a60 53
2 b g Fasliyev(USA) —Shashana (IRE) (King's Best (USA))
1653[7] 2128[10] 2533[6] 2906[7] 3547[4] 5583[9] 5811[4] 6461[3] 6829[11] 7120[6] 7235[12]
Magnificence *Sir Michael Stoute* a55 60
2 gr f Sadler's Wells(USA) —Doctor's Glory (USA) (Elmaamul (USA))
4055[6] 5604[11] 6032[5] 6609[5] 6923[5]
Magnifico (FR) *Mrs K Waldron* a28
8 b g Solid Illusion(USA) —Born For Run (FR) (Pharly (FR))
970[9] 1439[10]
Magnitude *M E Rimmer* a71 84
4 ch g Pivotal—Miswaki Belle (USA) (Miswaki (USA))
357[5] 544[7] 958[4] 1578[10] 2052[7] 2459[3] 3008[5] 3357[4] 3960[8] 4824[9] 5124[4] 7695[13]
Magnum (ARG) *Darrell Vienna* a117
8 bb h El Compinche(ARG) —Merrymaker (ARG) (Rainbow Corner)
789a[5]
Magnus Thrax (USA) *R Hannon* a81 81
2 b c Roman Ruler(USA) —Wild Catseye (USA) (Forest Wildcat (USA))
2844[10] (4933) 6064[10] 6478[6] 7063[4]
Magritte (ITY) *R Menichetti* 104
4 b m Modigliani(USA) —Star Of Siligo (USA) (Saratoga Six (USA))
1394a[12] 6717a[11] 7303a[4]
Magroom *R J Hodges* a72 75
5 b g Compton Place—Fudge (Polar Falcon (USA))
1539[11] 2352[6] 2518[2] 2977[6] 3283[6] 3996[2] (4992) 5062[8] 5630[2] (5791) 6337[2] 6547[4] 6937[4] 7153[4]
Ma Gypsy Dancer (FR) *F Cohen*
2 ch f Noverre(USA) —Vagabond Chanteuse (Sanglamore (USA))
5956a[0]
Mahaatheer (IRE) *F Head* 101
4 b m Daylami(IRE) —Al Ihtithar (IRE) (Barathea (IRE))
5058a[6] 6438a[2]
Mahadee (IRE) *C E Brittain* a105 86
4 br g Cape Cross(IRE) —Rafiya (Halling (USA))
(278) 458[4] 635[7] 783[4] 913[8] (1209) 1641[3] 3014[10] 4768[9] 5863[12]
Mahie (FR) *Mme O Rouleau* 26
8 b m Garuda(IRE) —Danezia (FR) (Zayyani)
5013a[8]
Mahiki *S A Callaghan* a71 56
2 ch f Compton Place—Sound Of Sleat (Primo Dominie)
1700[5] 1939[6] 3072[5] (3709) (3952) 4868[7] 5033[8] 6494[6]
Mahjong Girl *R M Beckett* 62
2 ch f Kirkwall—Gulchina (USA) (Gulch (USA))
3810[10] 4908[7] 5498[4]
Mahlak (IRE) *C E Brittain* 50
2 ch f Pastoral Pursuits—Bint Al Hammour (IRE) (Grand Lodge (USA))
5397[11]
Maidanni (USA) *J R Gask* a64
7 bb g Private Terms(USA) —Carley's Birthday (USA) (Marfa (USA))
253[12] 631[14] 823[14]
Maid In Heaven (IRE) *W R Swinburn* a58
2 b f Clodovil(IRE) —Serious Delight (Lomond (USA))
7326[5] ◆
Maidin Maith (IRE) *J S Bolger* a77 88
3 b f Montjeu(IRE) —Majinskaya (FR) (Marignan (USA))
1911a[6]
Maid Of Stone (IRE) *D R C Elsworth* a54 50
3 ch f Rock Of Gibraltar(IRE) —Gold Flair (Tap On Wood)
2633[4] 3508[7] 4057[12] 4498[12] 5403[10]
Maidstone Marble (FR) *H-A Pantall* 59
3 gr c Take Risks(FR) —Shelton Sea (FR) (Desert Style (IRE))
2293a[6]
Maidtorun (IRE) *R A Fahey* 66
2 ch f Rakti—Bayletta (IRE) (Woodborough (USA))
1277[5] (1719) 2244[7] 2800[9]
Maigh Eo (IRE) *Patrick Morris* a51 20
3 b g Elusive City(USA) —Princess Magdalena (Pennekamp (USA))
1317[4] 1662[9] 2562[8] 3464[10] 4777[6]
Maille Tartare (FR) *Mme A Charbonnier* 29
3 b f Maille Pistol(FR) —Magic Tartare (FR) (Lesotho (USA))
4130a[11]
Main Aim *Sir Michael Stoute* 123
4 b h Oasis Dream—Orford Ness (Selkirk (USA))
(2078) ◆ (2483) 2990[4] 3819[2] 4406[8] 5657[13] 6848[4]
Main Spring *Sir Michael Stoute* a41
2 b f Pivotal—Fairy Godmother (Fairy King (USA))
7388[8]
Mainstay *J H M Gosden* a66
3 b f Elmaamul(USA) —Felucca (Green Desert (USA))
7452[2]
Maison Brillet (IRE) *J Howard Johnson* 74
2 b g Pyrus(USA) —Stormchaser (IRE) (Titus Livius (FR))
2153[3] ◆ (2388) 4035[3] 4739[4] 5515[9] 6048[6]
Maison Dieu *E J Alston* a58 66
6 bb g King Charlemagne(USA) —Shining Desert (IRE) (Green Desert (USA))
921[10] 1244[2] 1650[3] 2312[3] 2628[3] 2660[4] (3148) 3497[4] 3851[4] 4504[12] 5941[5] 6221[2] 6413[6] 6825[13]
Maison D'Or *R Ingram* a57 38
3 b g Auction House(USA) —Figura (Rudimentary (USA))
121[12] 506[6] 817[7] 1036[9] 1461[10] 3215[13] 4934[9]
Maitre Pierre (FR) *C Diard* 55
2 b c Konig Shuffle(GER) —Table Race (GER) (Sir Felix (FR))
6322a[7]
Maiwand *Mrs R A Carr* a30 38
2 b f Reset(AUS) —Iris May (Brief Truce (USA))
3733[10] 4188[8] 4503[9] 4931[12] 5393[6] 5980[12] 6983[16] 7088[9]
Majaji *P Salmon*
5 b m Bal Harbour—Petaz (Petong)
1769[8]
Majd Aljazeera *D M Simcock* a61 45
3 b g King's Best(USA) —Tegwen (USA) (Nijinsky (CAN))
391[4] 3475[6] 4206[8] 4872[7] 5775[9]
Majehar *A G Newcombe* a76 62
7 b g Marju(IRE) —Joonayh (Warning)
(47) 392[7] (1051) 2351[9] 3869[6] 4644[6] 6210[2] ◆ (7332)
Majestical (IRE) *J S O Arthur* a63 65
7 b g Fayruz—Haraabah (USA) (Topsider (USA))
4586a[4] 5541a[4]
Majestic Cheer *John A Harris* a67 60
5 b g Royal Applause—Muwasim (USA) (Meadowlake (USA))
35[5] 150[6] 327[6] 2534[5] 3401[7]
Majestic Chief *Miss Lucinda V Russell* a61 44
5 b g Xaar—Grand Splendour (Shirley Heights)
1738[7] 2233[16]
Majestic Lady (IRE) *Mlle C Comte* a55 59
3 b f Royal Applause—Kiris World (Distant Relative)
2151[5] 2973[5] 3611[2] 4164[6] 4860[4] 5326[3] 6641[4] 7385a[0]
Majestic Times (IRE) *Liam McAteer* a100 93
9 b g Bluebird(USA) —Simply Times (USA) (Dodge (USA))
3435a[10] 3898a[3] 4360a[5] 4574a[7]
Majoran (FR) *T Larriviere* 50
3 b c Majorien—Ancre Marine (FR) (Tropular)
6149a[3]
Major Cadeaux *R A Fahey* 119
5 ch h Cadeaux Genereux—Maine Lobster (USA) (Woodman (USA))
2076[5] 6135[3] 6718a[5]
Major Eazy (IRE) *B J Meehan* a35 99
4 b g Fasliyev(USA) —Castilian Queen (USA) (Diesis)
2474[5]
Major Lawrence (IRE) *J Noseda* a67 77
3 b c Fasliyev(USA) —Ziffany (Taufan (USA))
3813[2] ◆ 4786[3] 5572[4] 7067[7] 7686[4] 7863[3]
Major Magpie (IRE) *M Dods* 89
7 b g Rossini(USA) —Picnic Basket (Pharly (FR))
1507[13] 1722[10] 2073[9] 3265[9] 3615[10] 4346[11] 4663[12] 5333[7]
Major Maximus *George Baker* a73
2 br c Domedriver(IRE) —Madame Maxine (USA) (Dayjur (USA))
6254[3] ◆ 6638[4] 6826[4] 7708[5] 7874[3]
Major Monty (IRE) *Tom Dascombe* a52
2 b g Orpen(USA) —Mari-Ela (IRE) (River Falls)
7556[8] 7637[5]
Major Phil (IRE) *L M Cumani* a81 77
3 b c Captain Rio—Choral Sundown (Night Shift (USA))
1639[5] ◆ 2198[8] 2638[7] (3469) 3996[5]
Major Promise *Jane Chapple-Hyam* a59 63
4 b g Lomitas—Distant Diva (Distant Relative)
7214[5] 7642[9] 7733[2]
Major Value *C G Cox* a30 54
3 b c Tobougg(IRE) —Surrealist (ITY) (Night Shift (USA))
3221[5] 4246[10] 4813[3] 5790[16] 6910[11]
Majura (GER) *A Fabre* 96
4 b m Samum(GER) —Majorata (GER) (Acatenango (GER))
7569a[6]
Majuro (IRE) *K A Ryan* a106 100
5 b g Danetime(IRE) —First Fling (IRE) (Last Tycoon)
6[2] ◆ 225[2] 551[2] 635[2] 785[3] 995[3] ◆ 1352[14] 1684[4] 1861[10]
Makaam (USA) *M P Tregoning* a82 62
3 ch c Giant's Causeway(USA) —Elaflaak (USA) (Gulch (USA))
1185[2] 1636[2] 2862[11] 3590[4] 4648[8] 6374[10]
Makaamen *B W Hills* 100
3 ch g Selkirk(USA) —Bird Key (Cadeaux Genereux)
(1015) (1324) 2270[8] 6675[12]
Makani (GER) *J E Pease* a64 87
2 b c A.P. Indy(USA) —Moonlight's Box (USA) (Nureyev (USA))
6979a[9]
Makarthy *H A McWilliams*
2 b c Makbul—Royal Shepley (Royal Applause)
7749[12]
Makayla *E J Alston* 58
3 b f Makbul—Primum Tempus (Primo Dominie)
2918[12] 4137[5]
Makbullet *J Howard Johnson* 79
2 gr g Makbul—Gold Belt (IRE) (Bellypha)
1920[6] 2449[3] 2936[3] 3540[4] 4187[2] (4595) 5198[17]
Make Amends (IRE) *R J Hodges* a65 69
4 b m Indian Ridge—Chill Seeking (USA) (Theatrical (IRE))
311[10] 478[9] 682[3] 871[9] 1589[2] ◆ 1785[6] 2123[4] 2331[5] 2912[2] 3074[6] (3777) 5063[5] 5211[3] 5740[9] 7632[7] (7856)
Make My Dream *J Gallagher* a77 80
6 b g My Best Valentine—Sandkatoon (IRE) (Archway (IRE))
1181[4] 1418[4] 1970[2] 2359[8] 2637[11] 3407[3] 4225[8] 4787[5] (5830) 6171[6] 6632[3] 7123[2] 7519[2] 7554[6] 7739[8]
Makhaaleb (IRE) *B W Hills* a73 73
3 b g Haafhd—Summerhill Parkes (Zafonic (USA))
914[4] 2092[3] 2845[4] 3531[3]
Making Music *T D Easterby* 58
6 b m Makbul—Crofters Ceilidh (Scottish Reel)
2966[9] 3239[6] 3445[8]
Makoto *B Grizzetti* 87
4 b m Efisio—Spirit Of Peace (Singspiel (IRE))
6715a[7]
Makshoof (IRE) *I W McInnes* a85 87
5 b g Kyllachy—Tres Sage (Reprimand)
1689[3] 1924[5] 2276[17] 3021[5] 3713[7] 4023[7] 4225[12] 4887[14] 7348[10] 7484[4] 7606[3] 7774[8]
Makt (FR) *T Doumen* 104
3 gr c Chichicastenango(FR) —Molene (FR) (Legend Of France (USA))
6198a[2] 6890a[2]
Malakhan (FR) *G Henrot*
2 b c Monsun(GER) —Miliana (IRE) (Polar Falcon (USA))
7507a[5]
Mal And Dave (IRE) *D Nicholls* 69
2 b g Redback—Louvolite (IRE) (Fayruz)
1645[4] 1866[6] 2311[5] 2800[2] 3152[2] (3446)
Malapropism *M R Channon* a60 86
9 ch g Compton Place—Mrs Malaprop (Night Shift (USA))
3002[16] 3246[8] 3422[12] 3677[3] 4051[12] 5125[13] 5156[4] 5323[7] 5724[8] 5792[11] 6433[3] 6777[2] (7069) 7483[12] 7561[11] 7657[8] 7835[11] 7889[8]
Malavita *H-A Pantall* 85
3 b f Singspiel(IRE) —Crime (USA) (Gulch (USA))
6150a[4]
Malayeen (AUS) *A Selvaratnam* a93
7 br h Anabaa(USA) —Wily Trick (USA) (Clever Trick (USA))
336a[9] 525a[9]
Malcheek (IRE) *T D Easterby* a75 87
7 br g Lend A Hand—Russland (GER) (Surumu (GER))
(1060) 1365[4] 1849[7] 2266[11] 3001[7] 4333[10] 4598[9] 5409[2] 5884[4] (6309) 6645[17] 7083[9] 7558[9]
Maldon Prom (IRE) *C A Dwyer* a73 66
2 br g Kheleyf(USA) —Misty Peak (IRE) (Sri Pekan (USA))
4272[6] 4497[7] 4856[3] 7156[9] 7290[9] 7637[2] (7786)
Malegria (FR) *J-P Delaporte* a74 81
3 b f Johann Quatz(FR) —Manu (FR) (Green Tune (USA))
7386a[7]
Malguru *J A McShane* 59
5 b g Ishiguru(USA) —Vento Del Oreno (FR) (Lando (GER))
4876[10]

Malibu Bay (USA) *A P O'Brien* 99
3 b c El Prado(IRE) —Favorite Funtime (USA) (Seeking The Gold (USA))
1485[3] 2756a[16] 3640[8] 4253a[7] 4419[8]

Malindi (FR) *J Van Handenhove* 58
3 ch c Anabaa Blue—Museum Piece (Rainbow Quest (USA))
7037a[10]

Malinsa Blue (IRE) *B Ellison* a63 63
7 b m Desert Style(IRE) —Talina's Law (IRE) (Law Society (USA))
1279[10] 1475[5] 2314[7] 2441[5] 2968[6]

Mallorey *A M Hales* a54 64
3 ch g Medicean—In Luck (In The Wings)
5782[12] 7831[7]

Malt Empress (IRE) *B W Duke* a52
4 b m Second Empire(IRE) —Sunset Malt (IRE) (Red Sunset)
248[13]

Malt Or Mash (USA) *R Hannon* a68 108
5 gr h Black Minnaloushe(USA) —Southern Tradition (USA) (Family Doctor (USA))
3620[14] 4261[9] (4987) 5694[5] 6116[4] 6734[6] 6995[13] 7332[6]

Mambo Light (USA) *A Wohler* 101
3 ch f Kingmambo(USA) —Piquetnol (USA) (Private Account (USA))
2757a[9] 3520a[3] 6605a[2]

Mambo Meister (USA) *Philip A Gleaves* a114 114
4 b g King Cugat(USA) —Bleu'slittlesecret (USA) (Desert Secret (IRE))
7309a[5]

Mambo Spirit (IRE) *Stef Liddiard* a86 86
5 b g Invincible Spirit(IRE) —Mambodorga (USA) (Kingmambo (USA))
1334[5] 1685[5] 1951[5] 2359[4] 2460[4] 3065[9] 7518[4] 7682[10]

Mambo Sun *R Curtis* a72 70
6 ro g Superior Premium—The Manx Touch (IRE) (Petardia)
(63) 224[4] 253[3] 622[3]

Mamlakati (IRE) *R Hannon* 81
3 b f Invincible Spirit(IRE) —Elba (IRE) (Ela-Mana-Mou)
2536[4] 3219[8] 3789[5] 4452[8] 4607[13] 4952[6] 5345[4] (5500) 5877[9] (6335) 6798[12]

Mamlook (IRE) *D E Pipe* 100
5 br g Key Of Luck(USA) —Cradle Brief (IRE) (Brief Truce (USA))
6851[2]

Mana Kourou (FR) *D Windrif* 69
2 b c Kouroun(FR) —Mana Margaeux (IRE) (Ela-Mana-Mou)
3935a[10] 6751a[3]

Manana Manana *J Balding* a65 63
3 b g Tobougg(IRE) —Midnight Allure (Aragon)
917[9] 1662[3] 2154[11] 7853[5]

Manarah (USA) *J H M Gosden* 51
3 ch f Giant's Causeway(USA) —Ishtak (Nashwan (USA))
1488[12] 2051[7]

Manassas (IRE) *B J Meehan* 104
4 b g Cape Cross(IRE) —Monnavanna (IRE) (Machiavellian (USA))
(995) 1352[16] 1929[7] 3014[11] (5863)

Manchestermaverick (USA) *Dr J R J Naylor* a65 63
4 ch g Van Nistelrooy(USA) —Lydia Louise (USA) (Southern Halo (USA))
194[7] 531[3] 715[4] 1710[2] 2202[7] 2794[7] (5120) 5569[9] 7861[8]

Mandalay King (IRE) *Mrs Marjorie Fife* a49 76
4 b g King's Best(USA) —Mahamuni (IRE) (Sadler's Wells (USA))
1244[5] (1456) 1650[8] 2312[12] 2531[5] 2966[6] 3483[7] 4015[2] ◆ (4285) ◆ 4620[2] 5148[6] 5623[8]

Mandarin Express *B J Meehan* a39 53
2 ch g Dubai Destination(USA) —Hsi Wang Mu (IRE) (Dr Fong (USA))
4048[10] 4377[7] 5017[5] 5573[8] 6034[10]

Mandarin Spirit (IRE) *Miss L A Perratt* a75 76
9 b g Primo Dominie—Lithe Spirit (IRE) (Dancing Dissident (USA))
5395[12] 5886[10] (6159) 6309[10] 6489[7] 6635[5] 6985[9] 7119[2] 7735[8]

Mandela (NZ) *Richard Yuill* 109
8 br g Ebony Grosve(NZ) —Wairongoa Belle (NZ) (Sea Anchor)
7196a[10]

Mandelieu (IRE) *Ollie Pears* a59 73
4 b g Acclamation—Notley Park (Wolfhound (USA))
518[10] 832[13] 1169[13] 1591[12] 1921[4] 2316[6] 2529[7] 3471[4] 3972[4] 4192[7]

Mandhooma *P W Hiatt* a54 63
3 b f Oasis Dream—Shatarah (Gulch (USA))
45[2] 4183[16] (4643) 5065[12] 7561[8] 7795[9]

Mandobi (IRE) *D Selvaratnam* a95 95
8 ch h Mark Of Esteem(IRE) —Miss Queen (USA) (Miswaki (USA))
257a[10] 611a[6]

Mandrake (IRE) *M Johnston* 1
2 b c Bertolini(USA) —Aquaba (USA) (Damascus (USA))
2311[11]

Mandurah (IRE) *B P J Baugh* a70 94
5 b g Tagula(IRE) —Fearfully Grand (Grand Lodge (USA))
971[4] 1310[9] (1685) 2716[8] 2782[8] (2840) (3845) 4341[9] 4461[16] 4766[8] 6283[5] 6647[7] 6902[4]

Manere Bay *J L Dunlop* 73
4 b m Olden Times—Madurai (Chilibang)
1048[5] 2880[3] 4060[3] 4936[2] 6909[7]

Mangano *A Berry* a41 42
5 b g Mujadil(USA) —Secret Dance (Sadler's Wells (USA))
3105[11] 3655[7] 4750[5]

Mangham (IRE) *D H Brown* a41 101
4 b g Montjeu(IRE) —Lovisa (USA) (Gone West (USA))
995[20] 1684[7] 2101[6] 5040[9] 5375[12] 6168[13]

Mango Music *M Quinn* a62 91
6 ch m Distant Music(USA) —Eurolink Sundance (Night Shift (USA))
1411[3] 1627[6] 2088[6] 2334[2] ◆ (3153) 3453[7] 4096[8] 5436[9] 6118[9] 6904[2] 7679[7]

Manhattan Fox (USA) *B J Meehan* 92
2 ch c Elusive Quality(USA) —Safeen (USA) (Storm Cat (USA))
4985[7] 5407[2] (5879) 6426[7] 6849[15]

Manhattan Rain (AUS) *Mrs Gai Waterhouse* 116
3 b c Encosta De Lago(AUS) —Shantha's Choice (AUS) (Canny Lad (AUS))
7040a[2]

Manhattan Sunrise (USA) *Paul Mason* a53
3 ch f Hold That Tiger(USA) —Sellsey (USA) (Pulpit (USA))
2577[13]

Manifest *H R A Cecil* 107
3 b c Rainbow Quest(USA) —Modena (USA) (Roberto (USA))
3751[2] ◆ (4798) ◆ 6425[3]

Manighar (FR) *A De Royer-Dupre* 119
3 gr g Linamix(FR) —Mintly Fresh (USA) (Rubiano (USA))
5711a[2] (6502a) 7047a[3]

Man In Black (IRE) *David P Myerscough* 46
2 b g Trans Island—Go Indigo (IRE) (Cyrano De Bergerac)
5274a[16]

Man In The Mirror (IRE) *P L Gilligan* a31 49
2 b g Captain Rio—Shyshiyra (IRE) (Kahyasi)
4201[10] 5371[10] 5627[8] 7098[5] 7722[6]

Manipura (GER) *H Steguweit* 99
4 b m Dansili—Macara (GER) (Acatenango (GER))
3520a[5] 6886a[8]

Manita (IRE) *C Boutin* a74 80
4 ch m Peintre Celebre(USA) —Mosquera (GER) (Acatenango (GER))
1268a[7] 6981a[3]

Mannello *S W Hall* a61 59
6 b m Mamalik(USA) —Isle Of Sodor (Cyrano De Bergerac)
1072[3] 1259[10] 1536[6] 1958[10]

Mannlichen *M Johnston* a86 77
3 ch g Selkirk(USA) —Robe Chinoise (Robellino (USA))
1992[11] ◆ 2767[4] 6435[4] 6878[4] (7238) ◆ 7539[2] 7628[2]

Man Of Action (USA) *J H M Gosden* 74
2 ch c Elusive Quality(USA) —Dixie Melody I (USA) (Dixieland Band (USA))
7146[3] ◆

Man Of Gwent (UAE) *P D Evans* a87 79
5 b g In The Wings—Welsh Valley (USA) (Irish River (FR))
139[9] 172[5] 392[5] 550[3] 660[7] 2374[4] 2878[2] 3450[11] 3578[7] 3847[10]

Man Of Iron (USA) *A P O'Brien* a119 91
3 ch c Giant's Causeway(USA) —Better Than Honour (USA) (Deputy Minister (CAN))
5080a[5] 6467a[4] (7281a)

Manolito Montoya (IRE) *J W Hills* a65 66
3 b g High Chaparral(IRE) —Queens Wharf (IRE) (Ela-Mana-Mou)
1429[5] 1928[11] 2357[8] 2892[8] 3383[9] 3629[5]

Manresa (IRE) *F Belmont* 60
3 b f Domedriver(IRE) —Moneypenny (GER) (Neshad (USA))
6753a[6]

Manshoor (IRE) *Mrs L Wadham* a85 83
4 gr g Linamix(FR) —Lady Wells (IRE) (Sadler's Wells (USA))
(1073) (1382) 1966[4] 2671[7] 3361[2]

Mansii *P J McBride* a65 63
4 b g Dr Fong(USA) —Enclave (USA) (Woodman (USA))
166[6] 460[6] 867[8] 2921[13] 4182[4] 4668[3] 5391[8] 5883[2] 6674[3]

Mantadia (FR) *B De Montzey*
2 b f Muhtathir—Mystery Night (FR) (Fairy King (USA))
6325a[0]

Mantoro (GER) *A De Royer-Dupre* 102
3 b c Dashing Blade—Mistic World (Monsun (GER))
1915a[4] 3649a[3] 4685a[2]

Manx Miss (USA) *David P Myerscough* a78 56
2 bb f El Corredor(USA) —Final Legacy (USA) (Boston Harbor (USA))
7147[10]

Many A Slip *J L Dunlop* 76
2 gr g Verglas(IRE) —Tri Pac (IRE) (Fairy King (USA))
2792[12] 3218[2] ◆ 3785[4] (4946) 5399[5]

Manyriverstocross (IRE) *A King* 104
4 b g Cape Cross(IRE) —Alexandra S (IRE) (Sadler's Wells (USA))
2475[3] 2932[7] 3822[2] (4408) 5173[6] 5823[2]

Many Welcomes *B P J Baugh* a57 62
4 ch m Young Ern—Croeso Cynnes (Most Welcome)
(575) 675[3] 1846[3] 2353[5] 3331[U] (3851) 4665[2] 5019[11] 5998[2] 6925[2]

Manzila (FR) *Mme C Barande-Barbe* 107
6 ch m Cadeaux Genereux—Mannsara (IRE) (Royal Academy (USA))
1278[9] 1582[9] 5495a[10] 5928a[6]

Maoi Chinn Tire (IRE) *J S Moore* a68 63
2 b g Mull Of Kintyre(USA) —Primrose And Rose (Primo Dominie)
1044[6] 1404[6] 3572[2] 4565[3] 4884[4] 5369[4] 6609[2] 7625[6]

Maoineach (USA) *J S Bolger* 105
3 ch f Congaree(USA) —Trepidation (USA) (Seeking The Gold (USA))
(1024a) 1353[8] 1756a[9] 2644a[3] 3516a[8]

Mapale (FR) *X-Thomas Demeaulte*
2 gr f Kendor(FR) —Miss Bedouine (FR) (Bering)
7315a[8]

Ma Patrice *T D McCarthy* a46 38
3 ch f Tumbleweed Ridge—Ma Barnicle (IRE) (Al Hareb (USA))
1464[8] 3100[8] 4704[9] 5751[9] 6289[12]

Maqaam *M Johnston* 74
3 b g Dubai Destination(USA) —Desert Lynx (IRE) (Green Desert (USA))
(2364)

Maraased *S Gollings* a64 91
4 b g Alhaarth(IRE) —Fleeting Rainbow (Rainbow Quest (USA))
7221[12] 7790[2]

Marafong *Miss J Feilden* a60 83
2 ch g Dr Fong(USA) —Marakabei (Hernando (FR))
2825[5] 3716[5] 4385[5] 4883[2] 5166[11]

Maragna (IRE) *Paul Green* a39 51
2 b c Invincible Spirit(IRE) —Bradwell (IRE) (Taufan (USA))
5668[6] 5958[5] 6246[4] 7333[5] 7619[5]

Marajaa (IRE) *W J Musson* a83 94
7 b g Green Desert(USA) —Ghyraan (IRE) (Cadeaux Genereux)
878[6] (1067) 1316[3] 1603[6] 2193[2] (3008) 3752[5] (4409) 5221[8] 6480[16]

Maram (USA) *Chad C Brown* 112
3 bb f Sahm(USA) —American Dreamer (USA) (Quest For Fame (USA))
7284a[6]

Maranda (IRE) *Liam P Cusack* a59 46
5 b m Spectrum(IRE) —Mariyba (IRE) (Be My Guest (USA))
3092[8]

Marbled Cat (USA) *M Johnston* a66 69
3 b c Cherokee Run(USA) —Catstar (USA) (Storm Cat (USA))
313[5]

Marbush (IRE) *D Selvaratnam* a104 89
8 ro h Linamix(FR) —Fig Tree Drive (USA) (Miswaki (USA))
414a[8]

Marceti (IRE) *E Leenders* 90
2 gr g Verglas(IRE) —Darasa (FR) (Barathea (IRE))
6507a[2] (7103a)

Marchand D'Or (FR) *F Head* a56 126
6 gr g Marchand De Sable(USA) —Fedora (FR) (Kendor (FR))
1010a[12] 1919a[4] 2523a[8]

Marching Time *Sir Michael Stoute* 101
3 b g Sadler's Wells(USA) —Marching West (USA) (Gone West (USA))
1992[6] ◆ 2701[5] 2935[4] (4902) (5476) ◆ 6270[28] 6732[4]

Marchin Star (IRE) *M Brittain* 50
2 ch c Chineur(FR) —March Star (IRE) (Mac's Imp (USA))
1330[4] 2041[6] 2568[9] 5036[7] 5595[16]

March Mate *B Ellison* a66 61
5 b g Warningford—Daira (Daring March)
(554) ◆

Marcus Cicero (IRE) *P Winkworth* 86
2 b g Le Vie Dei Colori—Stroke Of Six (IRE) (Woodborough (USA))
3500[4] (4825) 5658[14] (6104) 6398[4]

Marcus Galerius (IRE) *T Stack* 73
2 b c Antonius Pius(USA) —Surprise Me (IRE) (Imperial Frontier (USA))
2286a[10]

Marechale (FR) *Mme C Head-Maarek* a79 77
3 b f Anabaa(USA) —Malaisie (USA) (Bering)
7385a[9]

Mared (USA) *J Noseda* a85 87
3 ch c Speightstown(USA) —Unbridled Lady (USA) (Unbridled (USA))
1729[6] ◆ 2002[3] 2710[2]

Marek (GER) *W Sonntag Jr* a97 100
6 br g Kallisto(GER) —Marquesa Island (GER) (Hondo Mondo (IRE))
(3045a) (4335a)

Mareva *Ollie Pears*
3 ch f Reel Buddy(USA) —Margarets First (Puissance)
3975[11] 4654[13]

Marfach (USA) *J S Bolger* 99
2 b c Leroidesanimaux(BRZ) —Rhondaling (Welsh Pageant)
4250a[2] 5275a[4] 6319a[2]

Margarets John (IRE) *G A Swinbank* 4
2 b g Kalanisi(IRE) —Tarrara (UAE) (Lammtarra (USA))
7167[8]

Margarita (IRE) *J R Fanshawe* a63 69
3 b f Marju(IRE) —Kalinka (IRE) (Soviet Star (USA))
2179[5] 2664[9] 5449[3] 5886[6] 6547[10] 6925[9]

Margie's World (GER) *S Wegner* 82
5 ch m Spinning World(USA) —Margie's Darling (USA) (Alydar (USA))
6605a[3]

Maria Antonia (IRE) *D G Bridgwater* a61 60
6 ch m King's Best(USA) —Annieirwin (IRE) (Perugino (USA))
744[4] 918[6]

Maria Di Scozia *P W Chapple-Hyam* a74 83
4 ch m Selkirk(USA) —Viva Maria (Hernando (FR))
2796[7] 7020[6] 7475[7] 7841[4]

Maria Nunziata *J Noseda* a73 75
3 b f Green Desert(USA) —Napoleon's Sister (IRE) (Alzao (USA))
1804[3] 2551[3] 3214[3] (7401)

Marias Dream (IRE) *J G Coogan* a80 91
7 bb m Desert Sun—Clifton Lass (IRE) (Up And At 'Em)
4412a[5] 5490a[16]

Maricath (FR) *C Lotoux* 60
3 ch f Septieme Ciel(USA) —Lush Life (FR) (Dolphin Street (FR))
4810a[7]

Ma Ridge *T D McCarthy* a57 48
5 ch g Tumbleweed Ridge—Ma Barnicle (IRE) (Al Hareb (USA))
43[5] 131[9] 247[8] 482[6] 647[2] 872[6] 3074[8] 3215[6] 3525[7]

Marie Cuddy (IRE) *M R Channon* 63
2 b f Galileo(IRE) —Corrine (IRE) (Spectrum (IRE))
6274[3]

Marie De Medici (USA) *M Johnston* 104
2 ch f Medicean—Mare Nostrum (Caerleon (USA))
2819[3] 3823[3] (6567) ◆ 6929a[2] 7187[4]

Marie Louise *L A Dace* a57 59
4 b m Helissio(FR) —Self Esteem (Suave Dancer (USA))
2040[12] 2331[6] 3029[14]

Marieschi (USA) *R F Fisher* a51 68
5 b g Maria's Mon(USA) —Pennygown (Rainbow Quest (USA))
476[8] 1442[6]

Marie Tempest *M R Bosley* a55 48
4 b m Act One—Hakkaniyah (Machiavellian (USA))
290[6] 469[10] 2221[8] 3215[5]

Marillos Proterras *Mrs A Duffield* a7 61
3 b f Fraam—Legend Of Aragon (Aragon)
1168[6] 1724[12] 2236[10] 3731[2] 3976[8] 4142[5]

Marina (GER) *C Von Der Recke* 78
2 b f Paolini(GER) —Maria Magdalene (GER) (Alkalde (GER))
(6751a)

Marina Of Venice (IRE) *J S Bolger* 87
3 ch f Galileo(IRE) —Dame's Violet (IRE) (Groom Dancer (USA))
1996a[7]

Marina's Ocean *S R Bowring* a46 47
5 b m Beat All(USA) —Ocean Song (Savahra Sound)
5614[7] 6073[8] 6390[6] 7080[8] 7374[8] 7726[11]

Marina Walk *H Morrison* a53 39
3 ch f Compton Place—Raindrop (Primo Dominie)
315[6] 592[5] 920[7] 3281[7] 3580[9] 4479[11]

Marine Boy (IRE) *Tom Dascombe* 104
3 b g One Cool Cat(USA) —Bahamamia (Vettori (IRE))
1292[5] 1602[9] 2035[4] 2500[9] 6815[5] 7150[2]

Marine Officer (USA) *J-C Rouget* 71
2 b c Kingmambo(USA) —Asti (IRE) (Sadler's Wells (USA))
4807a[6] 5561a[3]

Marine Spirit (GER) *Saeed Bin Suroor* a71 84
2 b c Big Shuffle(USA) —Molly Dancer (GER) (Shareef Dancer (USA))
2477[4] ◆ 4093[3] (4701) 5344[2] 6643[6] 7108[8]

Marino Prince (FR) *T Wall* a54 47
4 b g Dr Fong(USA) —Hula Queen (USA) (Irish River (FR))
3074[10] 3501[6] 4861[8]

Marinous (FR) *F Head* a90 100
3 br c Numerous(USA) —Marende (FR) (Panoramic)
6198a[3] (7302a)

Mariol (FR) *Robert Collet* 116
6 b g Munir—La Bastoche (IRE) (Kaldoun (FR))
2513a[3] 3231a[6] 3908a[4] 4837a[2] (5495a) 6304[7] 6503a[10]

Maristar (USA) *G A Butler* a77 77
2 b f Giant's Causeway(USA) —Jewel Princess (USA) (Key To The Mint (USA))
6055[3] ◆ 6628[5] (6947)

Mariston (GER) *W Baltromei* 69
3 ch c Banyumanik(IRE) —Mavirca (GER) (Lavirco (GER))
7820a[6]

Marius Maximus (IRE) *M Johnston* 41
2 b c Kheleyf(USA) —Marju Guest (IRE) (Marju (IRE))
5693[10] 6246[3]

Mariyca (IRE) *John M Oxx* a90 88
3 gr f Daylami(IRE) —Masakala (IRE) (Cadeaux Genereux)
5141a[6]

Marjolly (IRE) *M Botti* a54 40
2 b c Marju(IRE) —Lost Icon (IRE) (Intikhab (USA))
6032[6] 6356[3] 7087[5] 7389[5] 7757[3]

Marju King (IRE) *W S Kittow* 70
3 b c Marju(IRE) —Blue Reema (IRE) (Bluebird (USA))
2930[5] 4481[7] 5223[3]

Marjury Daw (IRE) *J G Given* a59 56
3 b f Marju(IRE) —The Stick (Singspiel (IRE))
5775[7] 7022[11] 7143[2] 7438[7] 7600[13]

Markab *H Candy* a107 108
6 b g Green Desert(USA) —Hawafiz (Nashwan (USA))
1861[6] 3141[4] ◆ 4523[4] ◆ (5039) 5860[16] 6661[5]

Markadam *Miss S E Hall* a43 60
3 b g Mark Of Esteem(IRE) —Elucidate (Elmaamul (USA))
2370[9] 3561[9] 4822[6] 5442[4] 6559[8] 7670[7] 7751[9]

Mark Anthony (IRE) *K A Ryan* 78
2 b g Antonius Pius(USA) —Zuniga's Date (USA) (Diesis)
4286[5] 4705[3] (5036)

Markazzi *Sir Michael Stoute* 88
2 b c Dansili—Bandanna (Bandmaster (USA))
4985[2] ◆ (5542) 6478[11]

Mark Carmers *T D Barron* 38
2 b g Mark Of Esteem(IRE) —Queen Lea (FR) (Alzao (USA))
2388[10] 5728[12]

Market Watcher (USA) *Seamus Fahey* a60 56
8 b g Boundary(USA) —Trading (USA) (A.P. Indy (USA))
(249) 6859[6] 7578[7]

Markhesa *J R Boyle* a60 64
3 b f Sakhee(USA) —Marciala (IRE) (Machiavellian (USA))
1269[9] 1632[3] ◆ 4275[10] 5806[3] 6455[5] (6755) 7149[10]

Markington *P Bowen* a74 76
6 b g Medicean—Nemesia (Mill Reef (USA))
(2944) (3191) (3313) 4417[11] 6899[2] 7151[9]

Mark Of Brazil (IRE) *F Chappet* 78
2 b f Mark Of Esteem(IRE) —Exeter (FR) (Kabool)
5279a[9] 5956a[5]

Mark Of Meydan *M Dods* a81 79
4 ch g Mark Of Esteem(IRE) —Rose Bounty (Polar Falcon (USA))
1563[3] 2235[5] 2769[10] (3354) 3706[10] 4285[11] *5107*[3] *5884*[2] ◆ *6630*[13]
Mark Twain (IRE) *D M Simcock* 82
2 b g Rock Of Gibraltar(IRE) —Lady Windermere (IRE) (Lake Coniston (IRE))
2643a[2] 7258a[5]
Markyg (USA) *K R Burke* a95 90
3 bb c Fusaichi Pegasus(USA) —Spring Pitch (USA) (Storm Cat (USA))
(672) ◆ *863*[10] ◆ *1211*[4] 2273[6] 3049[30]
Marlow (GER) *Mario Hofer* 88
3 b c Lomitas—Manon (Alzao (USA))
3670a[15]
Marly Gomont (FR) *S Jesus*
2 ch g Sabiango(GER) —Minervitta (Warrshan (USA))
6751a[0]
Marmooq *M J Attwater* a73 62
6 ch g Cadeaux Genereux—Portelet (Night Shift (USA))
71[5] *(155)* *289*[4] *387*[3] *505*[2] *708*[2] *841*[9] *(878)* *1035*[5] 1320[13] 5095[7] 5429[16] 5745[8] 6224[12] 6719[12] 7065[5] ◆ 7236[3] 7416[5] (7524) ◆ 7699[3]
Marning Star *Ian Williams* a67 83
4 b g Diktat—Mustique Dream (Don't Forget Me)
199[5] *430*[3] 1750[7] 2243[8] 4262[9] 4473[3] (4881) 5448[9] *6357*[10]
Maroon Machine (IRE) *E J O'Neill* 98
2 ch c Muhtathir—Mediaeval (FR) (Medaaly)
(3935a) 5088a[3] 5280a[2] (6507a) 6849[11] 7346a[2]
Marosh (FR) *R M H Cowell* a46 59
2 b c American Post—Madragoa (FR) (Kaldoun (FR))
1482a[4] 2000[4] *2599*[4] *3925*[7]
Marquesa (USA) *David Wachman* a80 103
3 b f Kingmambo(USA) —Dietrich (USA) (Storm Cat (USA))
5141a[12]
Marrayah *M A Jarvis* 80
2 b f Fraam—Mania (IRE) (Danehill (USA))
(5109) ◆
Marron (DEN) *S Jensen* 92
5 b g Be My Chief(USA) —Relate (Distant Relative)
4585a[7]
Marsam (IRE) *M G Quinlan* a33 95
6 gr g Daylami(IRE) —Dancing Prize (IRE) (Sadler's Wells (USA))
7761[9]
Marshade (ITY) *S Botti* 104
2 b c Martino Alonso(IRE) —Universal Shade (ITY) (Pursuit Of Love)
3185a[2] 6716a[5]
Marshal Plat Club *G R Oldroyd* a44
2 b f Monsieur Bond(IRE) —Bond May Day (Among Men (USA))
7331[6]
Marsh Side (USA) *Neil Drysdale* a103 117
6 br h Gone West(USA) —Colonial Play (USA) (Pleasant Colony (USA))
1012a[5] 6873a[4] 7593a[17]
Marsh Warbler *M Johnston* 82
2 ch g Barathea(IRE) —Echo River (USA) (Irish River (FR))
(2784) ◆ 2993[13] 4488[9]
Marsool *M P Tregoning* 60
3 br g Key Of Luck(USA) —Chatifa (IRE) (Titus Livius (FR))
3472[4]
Martalina (FR) *S Wattel*
3 b f Martaline—Sandsea (FR) (River Sand (FR))
6606a[0]
Martha's Girl (USA) *D Carroll* a27 56
3 ch f E Dubai(USA) —Blue Stream (USA) (King Of Kings (IRE))
998[11] 1397[7] *7504*[5] *7642*[10] *7782*[10]
Martilzo *S Botti* 97
2 b c Martino Alonso(IRE) —Sfilza (Indian Ridge)
7205a[4]
Martingrange Boy (IRE) *J Balding* a64 23
4 b g Danetime(IRE) —Coloma (JPN) (Forty Niner (USA))
884[5] ◆ *956*[9] 1360[15] *1587*[7]
Martingrange Lass (IRE) *S Parr* a46 49
4 b m Chevalier(IRE) —Jellybeen (IRE) (Petardia)
1[7] *175*[12] *305*[4] *508*[8] *920*[4]
Martin's Friend (USA) *Mrs L Wadham* a43
4 b g Grand Slam(USA) —Dans La Ville (CHI) (Winning (USA))
3024[13] 4054[13]
Martyr *R Hannon* a91 96
4 b g Cape Cross(IRE) —Sudeley (Dancing Brave (USA))
1357[13] (1750) (2242) 2706[3] 3142[3] 3826[11]
Maruka Shenck (JPN) *H Kawachi* 116
6 b h Sunday Silence(USA) —Shenck (Zafonic (USA))
7498a[18]
Marvin Gardens *P S McEntee* a56 47
6 b g Largesse—En Grisaille (Mystiko (USA))
198[8] *347*[8] *467*[4] *646*[11]
Marvo *M H Tompkins* a62 89
5 b g Bahamian Bounty—Mega (IRE) (Petardia)
1690[10] *2133*[6] (2245) (2939) 4211[4] 4641[7] (5160) 6013[12] 6795[5] 7185[7]
Mary Celest (IRE) *K A Ryan* a41 52
2 b f Barathea(IRE) —Rack And Ruin (IRE) (King's Best (USA))
1866[9] 2360[9] 3232[3] *5985*[13] 6391[7] *7139*[9] *7210*[12]
Marygate (IRE) *M Brittain* 54
3 b f Spartacus(IRE) —Thorn Tree (Zafonic (USA))
1455[7] 1949[11]
Mary Goodnight *J Noseda* a63 84
3 b f King's Best(USA) —Disco Volante (Sadler's Wells (USA))
(4145) 4827[3] *6634*[9]
Mary Helen *W M Brisbourne* a64 54
2 b f Dandoun—Hotel California (IRE) (Last Tycoon)
1504[7] 2100[4] 2414[3] (2861) 4188[6] 4503[2] 4931[4] *5573*[4] *(7139)* *(7474)* *7731*[2]
Mary Josephine (IRE) *H Rogers* a89 88
4 b m Monashee Mountain(USA) —Chance It Again (IRE) (Sri Pekan (USA))
7007a[9] *7297a*[11]
Mary Mason *M Hill* a34 71
3 b f Hunting Lion(IRE) —Kalarram (Muhtarram (USA))
1068[8] 2321[11]
Maryolini *Tom Dascombe* a73 76
4 b m Bertolini(USA) —Mary Jane (Tina's Pet)
329[6] *582*[8] *738*[3] 6216[9] *6456*[8] *6939*[10]
Mary's Precedent (FR) *C Lerner* a74 101
3 ch f Storming Home—Suvretta Queen (IRE) (Polish Precedent (USA))
3668a[6] (4394a) 4971a[6]
Mary West (IRE) *Patrick Morris* a18 52
3 b f Pyrus(USA) —Pivot D'Amour (Pivotal)
1157[11] 4137[8]
Marzy *M Botti* a44
3 br f Kyllachy—Amarella (FR) (Balleroy (USA))
1077[6] *1379*[10] *2683*[13] (Dead)
Masaalek *Doug Watson* a105 110
4 b h Green Desert(USA) —Hammiya (IRE) (Darshaan)
182a[7] 340a[12]
Masafi (IRE) *E J Cooper*
8 b g Desert King(IRE) —Mrs Fisher (IRE) (Salmon Leap (USA))
3223[12]
Masai Moon *B R Millman* a101 101
5 b g Lujain(USA) —Easy To Imagine (USA) (Cozzene (USA))
1321[2] ◆ 1864[6] 2470[9] 3116[4] 3628[6] 4796[14] 5025[3] *5615*[4] 5959[3] *6949*[5]
Masamah (IRE) *E A L Dunlop* a97 87
3 gr g Exceed And Excel(AUS) —Bethesda (Distant Relative)
1296[10] 1824[10] *6631*[2]
Mascarpone (GER) *M Weiss* 83
5 b h Monsun(GER) —Mamourina (IRE) (Barathea (IRE))
1555a[3]
Mascotte Du Maine (FR) *L Godard*
2 b f Maresca Sorrento(FR) —Kallie Du Bournez (FR) (Acteur Francais (USA))
7409a[8]
Mashaahed *E Charpy* a88 111
6 b h In The Wings—Patacake Patacake (USA) (Bahri (USA))
339a[4] 642a[6] 774a[14]
Maskan *W J Haggas* 61
2 ch g Starcraft(NZ) —Silence Is Golden (Danehill Dancer (IRE))
6786[5]
Maskateer (IRE) *Mrs A M Thorpe* 46
3 b g Iron Mask(USA) —Indescent Blue (Bluebird (USA))
2323[7] 3205[6]
Masked Dance (IRE) *K A Ryan* a48 77
2 gr g Captain Rio—Brooks Masquerade (Absalom)
1277[4] *1653*[5] 2069[5] 4063[4] 4912[3] 5292[3] 5303[2] (5519) 6906[5] 7168[2]
Masking Baldini (IRE) *J Hetherton* a47 12
5 b g Iron Mask(USA) —Royal Baldini (USA) (Green Dancer (USA))
3123[12] 3707[6] 4600[9]
Maslak (IRE) *P W Hiatt* a88 92
5 b g In The Wings—Jeed (IRE) (Mujtahid (USA))
360[9] *761*[5] *915*[4] *1779*[6] 2898[3] 3423[4] 3521[7] 4350[2] (4602) 5028[8] 5308[2] *5649*[2] *5837*[4] 6204[7] 6560[9] *7272*[6] 7724[2] 7777[2]
Mason Hindmarsh *Karen McLintock* 70
2 ch g Dr Fong(USA) —Sierra Virgen (USA) (Stack (USA))
2721[8] 3478[6] 4993[7] 6215[4] 6895[2] ◆ 7116[5]
Masquenada (FR) *W Baltromei* 93
4 b m Muhtathir—Macarena (GER) (Platini (GER))
3520a[8] 6886a[2]
Massilah *B W Hills* a57 69
3 b f Namid—Loveleaves (Polar Falcon (USA))
1327[6] 1825[4] *7067*[3]
Massone (USA) *Ronald McAnally* a112 105
3 ch c Menifee(USA) —Stoneleigh's Hope (Damascus (USA))
1225a[3]
Mass Rally (IRE) *J H M Gosden* a89 78
2 b c Kheleyf(USA) —Reunion (IRE) (Be My Guest (USA))
2889[10] 6423[5] *6781*[2] 7096[2] *(7325)* *(7494)* ◆
Masstorm (ITY) *F Saggiomo* 98
3 b c Storming Home—La Maschera (FR) (Belmez (USA))
1392a[7] 1904a[9]
Masta Plasta (IRE) *D Nicholls* a111 114
6 b g Mujadil(USA) —Silver Arrow (USA) (Shadeed (USA))
1384[2] 1543a[7] 2272[8] 2716[3] 3202a[2] 3638[3] 3848[8] 4637a[4] 4885[4] 5420[12]
Master At Arms *Daniel Mark Loughnane* a85 78
6 ch g Grand Lodge(USA) —L'Ideale (USA) (Alysheba (USA))
3146[3]
Mastercraftsman (IRE) *A P O'Brien* a121 129
3 gr c Danehill Dancer(IRE) —Starlight Dreams (USA) (Black Tie Affair)
1675[5] (2288a) (2992) 5135[2] 5688a[3] *(6467a)* *7309a*[4]
Master Fong (IRE) *B W Hills* a80 77
3 b g Dr Fong(USA) —Last Cry (FR) (Peintre Celebre (USA))
2638[9] *3509*[8] 4058[4] 4481[6] (5223) 5725[5] 6552[4] *7048*[2]
Masterful Act (USA) *J R Best* a71 9
2 ch g Pleasantly Perfect(USA) —Catnip (USA) (Flying Paster (USA))
4534[9] *5192*[6] *5839*[3] *6211*[9]
Master Leon *B Smart* a70 71
2 b c Monsieur Bond(IRE) —Bollin Rita (Rambo Dancer (CAN))
4308[7] 5981[7] 6821[3] 7116[4] *7351*[3] *7638*[2] *7721*[2]
Master Lightfoot *W R Swinburn* a80 65
3 b c Kyllachy—Two Step (Mujtahid (USA))
6632[7] *6916*[7] *(7254)* *7634*[4] *7828*[9]
Master Mahogany *R J Hodges* a63 69
8 b g Bandmaster(USA) —Impropriety (Law Society (USA))
28[6] *194*[11] 1415[5] 1785[11] 2125[4] 2330[10] 2518[4] 3258[4] 4938[7] 5179[9]
Master Marvel (IRE) *T J O'Mara* 83
8 ch g Selkirk(USA) —Insijaam (USA) (Secretariat (USA))
2290a[2]
Master Mylo (IRE) *D K Ivory* 58
2 ch c Bertolini(USA) —Sheboygan (IRE) (Grand Lodge (USA))
1147[4] 1404[5] 2187[5] 3842[8] 4699[8] 6903[4]
Master Nimbus *J J Quinn* a53 69
9 b g Cloudings(IRE) —Miss Charlie (Pharly (FR))
2159[2] 2344[4] (3171) (3544) 4350[3] 4873[6] 5600[8]
Masterofceremonies *W M Brisbourne* a68 70
6 ch g Definite Article—Darakah (Doulab (USA))
558[5] *660*[5] (1226) 1615[9] 1886[3] 2392[5] 2818[4] 3481[6] *3923*[6] (4465) 5438[9]
Master Of Dance (IRE) *R Hannon* a83 78
2 ch c Noverre(USA) —Shambodia (IRE) (Petardia)
1862[6] ◆ 2324[4] 2887[3] (3256) 3821[5] 4271[8] 5769[4] 6104[4] 6693[4] *7320*[7] *7552*[2] *7611*[2] *7685*[6]
Master Of Disguise *C G Cox* 101
3 b c Kyllachy—St James's Antigua (IRE) (Law Society (USA))
(1486) 2934[7] 4490[4] 6089[9]
Master Of Song *S R Bowring* a29 44
2 ch g Ballet Master(USA) —Ocean Song (Savahra Sound)
6792[15] 7058[8] *7616*[10] *7757*[8]
Masterofthehorse (IRE) *Miss D Mountain* 120
3 b c Sadler's Wells(USA) —Shouk (Shirley Heights)
1800[2] 2705[3] 3438a[4] 4405[8] 6303[9]
Master O'Reilly (NZ) *Danny O'Brien* 120
7 bb g O'Reilly(NZ) —Without Remorse (NZ) (Bakharoff (USA))
6871a[6] 7196a[5] 7215a[4]
Master Pegasus *J R Boyle* a86 89
6 b g Lujain(USA) —Seeking Utopia (Wolfhound (USA))
47[5]
Master Rooney (IRE) *B Smart* 93
3 bb c Cape Cross(IRE) —Wimple (USA) (Kingmambo (USA))
5695[16] 6897[3] ◆
Mastership (IRE) *J J Quinn* a101 102
5 ch g Best Of The Bests(IRE) —Shady Point (IRE) (Unfuwain (USA))
1018[13] *1640*[4] 2933[6] 3172[4] 3752[4] (4310) 4560[6] 4796[13] *5375*[9] 6089[4] 6675[10]
Masters House (IRE) *Mrs J C McGregor* 16
6 b g Indian Lodge(IRE) —Aster Aweke (IRE) (Alzao (USA))
2965[12]
Mastery *Saeed Bin Suroor* a116 119
3 b c Sulamani(IRE) —Moyesii (USA) (Diesis)
863[4] (1904a) 3090[3] 3970a[3] 5134[2] (5861) *7281a*[3]
Mastoora (IRE) *W J Haggas* 83
3 b f Acclamation—Sacred Love (IRE) (Barathea (IRE))
(1423) ◆ 2673[7] 3163[6] 3746[11]
Maswerte (IRE) *L M Cumani* a76 85
3 b c Fraam—Rose Chime (IRE) (Tirol)
(2849) ◆ 3643[2] 4095[4] 4909[7] 6187[3] *6773*[7]
Mataaleb *M A Jarvis* 51
2 b c Dalakhani(IRE) —Elfaslah (IRE) (Green Desert (USA))
6759[11]
Mata Hari Blue *J R Holt* a46 64
3 ch f Monsieur Bond(IRE) —Feeling Blue (Missed Flight)
3926[6] 4199[2] 4786[4] 5477[3]
Mata Keranjang (USA) *P F I Cole* 106
2 bb c More Than Ready(USA) —Love Sick (USA) (Salt Lake (USA))
3648a[3] 4418[2] 5133[6] 5743[2] 6426[3] 6716a[3]
Mataram (USA) *W Jarvis* a89 71
6 b g Matty G(USA) —Kalinka (USA) (Mr Prospector (USA))
195[2] *550*[7]
Mater Mater *M J Scudamore* a64
2 gr f Silver Patriarch(IRE) —Emily-Mou (IRE) (Cadeaux Genereux)
2825[12] *7450*[7] *7624*[7]
Mathaaq *M A Jarvis* a82 75
3 b c Nayef(USA) —Mouwadh (USA) (Nureyev (USA))
4519[13] *4979*[2] (5531)
Matilda Poliport *W R Swinburn* a52 59
3 b f Mind Games—Poppy Carew (IRE) (Danehill (USA))
1380[7] 4057[7] 4569[9]
Matinee Idol *Mrs S Lamyman* a45 49
6 ch m In The Wings—Bibliotheque (USA) (Woodman (USA))
38[8] *148*[12] *603*[7]
Matjar (IRE) *Joseph Quinn* a68 55
6 ch g Grand Lodge(USA) —Tajawuz (Kris)
7798[2]
Matraash (USA) *M Johnston* 92
3 b c Elusive Quality(USA) —Min Alhawa (USA) (Riverman (USA))
1508[2] 2030[2] (2723) (3307) 4420[9] 5137[16] 5865[6]
Matsunosuke *A B Coogan* a117 109
7 b g Magic Ring(IRE) —Lon Isa (Grey Desire)
2[9] *(86)* *204*[3] *(359)* *(553)* *(633)* *785*[7] *911*[8] 1299[9] 1676[12] 2385[7] 3405[3] 3638[4] 3844[7] 4456[14] 5039[10] 5196[8] 6180[4] 6427[7] 7015[20] 7862[3]
Mattamia (IRE) *B R Millman* 99
3 b g Makbul—Lady Dominatrix (IRE) (Danehill Dancer (IRE))
(1190) 2058[7] 2774[2] (3053) (3362) 4099[2] 4490[2] 5203[4] 5654[9]
Matterofact (IRE) *M S Saunders* a67 75
6 b m Bold Fact(USA) —Willow Dale (IRE) (Danehill (USA))
1540[4] 1985[5] 2492[2] 2712[2] (3386) 3917[2] 3998[2] 4268[7] 4604[6] 4692[3] 5323[2] 5608[6] 6329[3]
Matto Mondo (CHI) *Richard E Mandella* a113 107
5 bb h Sir Cat(USA) —Muy Euforica (CHI) (Sadlers Congress)
789a[3]
Matuza (IRE) *P R Chamings* a92 70
6 ch h Cadeaux Genereux—Aoife (IRE) (Thatching)
(3459) 4607[7] 6904[6]
Maundy Money *David Marnane* a82 97
6 b g King's Best(USA) —Royal Gift (Cadeaux Genereux)
4412a[2] 4574a[3] 6530a[7]
Mausin (IRE) *H Morrison* 51
2 b f Monsun(GER) —Cote Quest (USA) (Green Desert (USA))
6389[4]
Mavalenta (IRE) *J W Hills* 38
2 b f Montjeu(IRE) —Velouette (Darshaan)
6055[11]
Maverick's Magic *W G M Turner* a42
3 ch g Karinga Bay—Magical Day (Halling (USA))
7888[7]
Maverin (IRE) *Tom Dascombe* a77 77
3 b c King's Best(USA) —Minerva (IRE) (Caerleon (USA))
1257[3] *1730*[4] 2415[3] 2862[2] 3036[3] (3460) 6396[8]
Mawaddah (IRE) *R Hannon* a75 75
2 b c Intikhab(USA) —Handsome Anna (IRE) (Bigstone (IRE))
4323[9] 5993[6] 6592[3] 6792[3] *7326*[3]
Mawatheeq (USA) *M P Tregoning* a83 122
4 b h Danzig(USA) —Sarayir (USA) (Mr Prospector (USA))
1352[11] (5794) (6303) ◆ 6850[2] ◆
Mawzoon (IRE) *M A Jarvis* 75
2 ch c Pivotal—Two Clubs (First Trump)
7145[4] ◆
Maxijack (IRE) *G Brown* a53
2 b g Governor Brown(USA) —Aster Fields (IRE) (Common Grounds)
7773[10] *7885*[9]
Maximix *G L Moore* a57 57
6 gr g Linamix(FR) —Time Will Show (FR) (Exit To Nowhere (USA))
1287[7] *1609*[5]
Maximus Aurelius (IRE) *J Jay* a76 73
4 b g Night Shift(USA) —Dame's Violet (IRE) (Groom Dancer (USA))
3960[10] *6640*[8]
Max One Two Three (IRE) *Tom Dascombe* 99
4 b m Princely Heir(IRE) —Dakota Sioux (IRE) (College Chapel)
996[6] 1325[7] 1880[4] 2271[6] 2536[3]
Maxwell Hawke (IRE) *P W Chapple-Hyam* 79
3 br g Rock Of Gibraltar(IRE) —Twice The Ease (Green Desert (USA))
(1252) 2072[9] 4333[12] 5404[13] 5799[11] 6111[8]
Maxwil *P M Phelan* a78 90
4 b g Storming Home—Lady Donatella (Last Tycoon)
585[10] 4954[12] 5508[4] 6059[7] *6634*[10]
Mayadeen (IRE) *R A Fahey* a57 61
7 b g King's Best(USA) —Inaaq (Lammtarra (USA))
161[4] *300*[10] 2264[8] 2969[3] 3444[6]
Maybach *Lars Bexell* a99 87
8 gr h Machiavellian(USA) —Capote Line (USA) (Capote (USA))
2587a[10]
Maybe Grace (IRE) *Mrs John Harrington* a83 82
3 b f Hawk Wing(USA) —Close Regards (IRE) (Danehill (USA))
7297a[4]
Maybe I Will (IRE) *S Dow* a70 73
4 b m Hawk Wing(USA) —Canterbury Lace (USA) (Danehill (USA))
1812[10] 2212[3] 2518[6]
Maybe I Wont *Lucinda Featherstone* a72 70
4 b g Kyllachy—Surprise Surprise (Robellino (USA))
76[4] *167*[8] *344*[7] *898*[5] 1402[3] 2171[10] 2261[7] (2859) (3074) *3734*[9] 4139[3] 4449[7] 4880[2] 5532[9]
Maybeme *N Bycroft* 71
3 b f Lujain(USA) —Malvadilla (IRE) (Doyoun)
2105[4] 2937[5] 4401[2] 5419[4] 5979[4] 6900[5] 7014[6]
May Chorus (IRE) *J R Boyle* a67 38
2 b f Night Shift(USA) —Chorus (USA) (Darshaan)
5808[9] *6942*[3] 7145[12] *7824*[7]
Mayfair's Future *J R Jenkins* a64 59
4 b h High Estate—Riva La Belle (Ron's Victory (USA))
813[12] *1318*[9] 1538[3] 1881[7] 2221[7] *3303*[2] *3929*[6] 4745[11]
May Martin *Rae Guest* a59 44
3 b f Monsieur Bond(IRE) —Calcavella (Pursuit Of Love)
(686) *804*[7] 1271[3] 2776[14] *7068*[10]
May Need A Spell *J G M O'Shea* a55 51
3 b g Needwood Blade—Under My Spell (Wizard King)
1746[17] 2918[15] *3743*[11]
Mayolynn (USA) *H R A Cecil* a73 64
3 ch f Johannesburg(USA) —Civilynn (USA) (Lost Code (USA))
2416[10] *3508*[3] 3984[4] 4813[2] 5151[3] *5570*[11]
Mayoman (IRE) *D Carroll* a64 70
4 b g Namid—America Lontana (FR) (King's Theatre (IRE))
654[10] *2145*[6] 3331[4] 3943[6] 4977[4] 5341[3] (5729) 6103[6] *(6492)* *7138*[9]
Mayorstone (IRE) *B Smart* 10
3 ch f Exceed And Excel(AUS) —Coolrain Lady (IRE) (Common Grounds)
5599[11]
Mayouta (FR) *B Goudot* a50
3 b f Highest Honor(FR) —Mia's Baby (USA) (Rahy (USA))
6980a[7]

May Parkin (IRE) *M Wigham* a48 1
4 b m Acclamation—Pretext (Polish Precedent (USA))
7152^{11} 7240^{5}

Mays Louise *B P J Baugh* a64 15
5 ch m Sir Harry Lewis(USA) —Maysimp (IRE) (Mac's Imp (USA))
12^{11} 290^{9} 556^{4} 760^{11} 2473^{14} 2843^{7}

Mayta Capac (USA) *D M Simcock* a57
3 ch c Thunder Gulch(USA) —Yvecrique (FR) (Epervier Bleu)
7401^{6} 7694^{5}

Mayuska (TUR) *A Atci* 41
4 b m Mountain Cat(USA) —Licola (USA) (Crafty Prospector (USA))
5588a^{13}

Mazamorra (USA) *M Botti* a44
2 bb f Orientate(USA) —Mumbo Jumbo (USA) (Kingmambo (USA))
7199^{6}

Maze (IRE) *B Smart* a72 95
4 ch g Dr Fong(USA) —Aryadne (Rainbow Quest (USA))
1398^{4} 1861^{19} 2405^{4} 2814^{7} 3706^{8} 4549^{8} 6830^{8}

Mazel Baby (FR) *Mlle C Azzoulai* a74 41
6 gr m Medaaly—Rain Follow (FR) (Baillamont (USA))
5074a^{10}

Mazzola *M R Channon* a80 82
3 b g Bertolini(USA) —Elegant Dance (Statoblest)
396^{4} 814^{4} 1078^{3} 1272^{3} 1517^{2} 1869^{3} 2058^{11} 2840^{8} 3570^{7} 3998^{5} 4231^{2} 4454^{6} 4483^{7} 5164^{3} 5264^{6} 5517^{DSQ} 5877^{8} 6205^{4} 6341^{5} 6669^{3} 6799^{3} 6988^{2} 7122^{3}

McCartney (GER) *Saeed Bin Suroor* 104
4 bb h In The Wings—Messina (GER) (Dashing Blade)
2500^{7} 2953a^{5}

Mcconnell (USA) *G L Moore* a89 82
4 ch g Petionville(USA) —Warsaw Girl (IRE) (Polish Precedent (USA))
163^{7} (307) 490^{4} 5640^{10} 5997^{7} (6357) ◆ 6614^{4} 6946^{5} 7271^{2} (7782)

Mccormack (IRE) *Miss T Jackson* a7 54
7 b g Desert Story(IRE) —La Loba (IRE) (Treasure Kay)
(1556) 1883^{11} 2233^{10} 3121^{3} 3499^{4} 5423^{12} 5548^{9} 5983^{6} 6184^{14}

Mceldowney *M C Chapman* a44 50
7 b g Zafonic(USA) —Ayodhya (IRE) (Astronef)
1851^{4} 2018^{13} 2656^{5} 7332^{9}

Mcqueen (IRE) *B D Leavy* a53 65
9 ch g Barathea(IRE) —Bibliotheque (USA) (Woodman (USA))
2445^{7} 4806^{12}

Mdawee (IRE) *Tom Dascombe* 86
2 b c Choisir(AUS) —Its All Eurs (IRE) (Barathea (IRE))
(3317) 3583^{7} 3805^{2} 4407^{9} 6541^{5}

Mean Machine (IRE) *J W Unett* a49 36
7 b g Idris(IRE) —Date Mate (USA) (Thorn Dance (USA))
4170^{6} 4862^{9}

Mean Mr Mustard (IRE) *J A Osborne* a56 44
3 b g Invincible Spirit(IRE) —White Lavender (USA) (Mt. Livermore (USA))
135^{3} 246^{3} 348^{5}

Mecox Bay (IRE) *A M Balding* 65
2 b c Noverre(USA) —Birdsong (IRE) (Dolphin Street (FR))
4209^{7} 4953^{3}

Media Jury *J S Wainwright* 42
2 b g Lucky Owners(NZ) —Landofheartsdesire (IRE) (Up And At 'Em)
5977^{11} 6646^{10}

Media Stars *R Johnson* a65 55
4 gr g Green Desert(USA) —Starine (FR) (Mendocino (USA))
256^{6} 320^{8} (393) 1125^{6} 1556^{14} 6383^{12} 6769^{13} 7080^{12}

Medicean Man *J R Gask* 87
3 ch g Medicean—Kalindi (Efisio)
2496^{11} 3036^{4} (3338) 4044^{3} (4494) 5130^{4} (5523) 6665^{4}

Medicea Sidera *E F Vaughan* a96 99
5 br m Medicean—Broughtons Motto (Mtoto)
123^{5} 1873^{7} 2500^{6} 6272^{11}

Medici (CHI) *J Barton*
4 br h Sir Cat(USA) —Dhion (CHI) (Royal Danzig (USA))
768a^{6}

Medicinal Compound *K A Ryan* 78
2 b g Dr Fong(USA) —Liska's Dance (USA) (Riverman (USA))
5408^{3} 5852^{2} (6821)

Medici Pearl *T D Easterby* a39 97
5 b m Medicean—In Love Again (IRE) (Prince Rupert (FR))
995^{8} 1352^{3} 1684^{12} 2015^{7} 2933^{8} 3315^{3} 3873^{8} 4287^{6} (4896) 5522^{11} 6675^{17}

Medici Time *T D Easterby* 77
4 gr g Medicean—Pendulum (Pursuit Of Love)
1369^{2} 1885^{6} 2312^{9} 2769^{11} 3002^{3} 3491^{2} (4783) 5031^{10} (6010) 6647^{18}

Medieval Maiden *Mrs L J Mongan* a62 56
6 gr m Zaha(CAN) —Brillante (FR) (Green Dancer (USA))
1378^{12} 1537^{2} 2222^{2} (2708) 5152^{5} 5577^{6} 5812^{7} 6226^{9} 6770^{7}

Mediterranean Sea (IRE) *J R Jenkins* a53 61
3 b f Medecis—High Glider (High Top)
2139^{10} 2433^{12} 4828^{4} 5782^{8} 5988^{7} 6371^{8} 7324^{3}

Meer Royal (FR) *P Demercastel* 80
2 b c Meshaheer(USA) —Royal Lights (FR) (Royal Academy (USA))
6131a^{2}

Meer Und Wind (GER) *P R Webber* a62 52
2 b f Xaar—Moneypenny (GER) (Neshad (USA))
3101^{6} 3786^{9} 5527^{10} 6441^{7}

Meethaaq (USA) *Sir Michael Stoute* 93
4 b g Kingmambo(USA) —New Harmony (USA) (A.P. Indy (USA))
1986^{6} 2471^{2} 3390^{11} 6816^{7}

Meetings Man (IRE) *Micky Hammond* 55
2 br c Footstepsinthesand—Missella (IRE) (Danehill (USA))
2610^{8} 4067^{6} 5728^{7} 6235^{6} 6679^{8}

Meezaan (IRE) *J H M Gosden* a84 62
2 b c Medicean—Varenka (IRE) (Fasliyev (USA))
6478^{15} (6781) ◆

Meeznah (USA) *D R Lanigan* 76
2 b f Dynaformer(USA) —String Quartet (IRE) (Sadler's Wells (USA))
4797^{3} 6921^{3}

Mefraas (IRE) *E A L Dunlop* a79 79
3 b g King's Best(USA) —Khaizarana (Alhaarth (IRE))
2567^{2} 3309^{2} 4957^{3} 5570^{3} 6190^{2} 6475^{3}

Mega Dame (IRE) *D Haydn Jones* a12
5 b m Iron Mask(USA) —Easter Girl (Efisio)
1410^{9} 2859^{16}

Megalala (IRE) *J J Bridger* a64 68
8 b g Petardia—Avionne (Derrylin)
1178^{7} (1728) 2039^{3} (2379) 2678^{7} 3811^{8} (3949) 4382^{5} 6584^{11} 6967^{6} 7036^{11} 7225^{6}

Megalo Maniac *R A Fahey* a63 62
6 b g Efisio—Sharanella (Shareef Dancer (USA))
5374^{12} 5678^{10} 7068^{3} 7371^{5} 7424^{4} 7579^{10} 7834^{10}

Megasecret *R Hannon* a64 70
3 b c Falbrav(IRE) —Silver Quest (Rainbow Quest (USA))
1419^{4} 1839^{4} 2849^{8} 4304^{7} 4947^{6}

Mega Steps (IRE) *Jennie Candlish* a36 43
5 b g Groom Dancer(USA) —Marmaga (IRE) (Shernazar)
448^{7} 566^{11}

Megavista (USA) *Paul Mason* a30 53
3 rg f Medaglia D'Oro(USA) —Bodhavista (USA) (Pass The Tab (USA))
2848^{7} 4205^{9}

Mega Watt (IRE) *W Jarvis* 81
4 b g Acclamation—Kilshanny (Groom Dancer (USA))
2003^{3} 2823^{3} 3273^{12} 4207^{5}

Meg Jicaro *Mrs L Williamson* a41 62
3 b f Reel Buddy(USA) —Anita In Wales (IRE) (Anita's Prince)
273^{8} 356^{10} 583^{3} 722^{6} 1064^{7} 1652^{8} 1848^{12}

Meglio Ancora *J G Portman* 81
2 ch g Best Of The Bests(IRE) —May Fox (Zilzal (USA))
(2037) 3138^{11} 4565^{11}

Mehendi (IRE) *B Ellison* a67 73
3 b g Indian Danehill(IRE) —Wedding Cake (IRE) (Groom Dancer (USA))
1461^{9} 2356^{10} 3636^{7} 5672^{7} 6342^{3} 6769^{5}

Meikle Barfil *J M Bradley* a54 51
7 b g Compton Place—Oare Sparrow (Night Shift (USA))
467^{5} 596^{6} 727^{4} (812) 895^{3} 1055^{9} 1134^{8} 1787^{7} 2811^{6} 3239^{11} 4222^{5} 5125^{6} 5345^{6} 5504^{7} 5629^{12} 5792^{6} 6119^{9} 7689^{6}

Meiner Falke (JPN) *K Kayano* 119
4 b h Mutafaweq(USA) —Bingo Hanako (JPN) (Park Regent (CAN))
7498a^{2}

Meiner Kitz (JPN) *S Kunieda* 120
6 b h Chief Bearhart(CAN) —Takara Kanna (JPN) (Soccer Boy (JPN))
7593a^{8}

Meirig's Dream (IRE) *Miss N A Lloyd-Beavis* a66 54
3 b g Golan(IRE) —Women In Love (IRE) (Danehill (USA))
6742^{11} 7392^{8} 7688^{3} 7873^{2}

Mejala (IRE) *J L Dunlop* 74
3 b f Red Ransom(USA) —Wissal (USA) (Woodman (USA))
1804^{7} 2206^{6} (3099) 3627^{8} 4569^{5} 5128^{2}

Mejd (IRE) *M R Channon* 22
2 b c Desert Style(IRE) —Rainstone (Rainbow Quest (USA))
6810^{12}

Mekong Miss *J Jay* a61 58
3 ch f Mark Of Esteem(IRE) —Missouri (Charnwood Forest (IRE))
953^{2} 1070^{11} 2131^{4} 2742^{2} 7840^{14}

Melange (USA) *P F I Cole* a69 62
3 b g Alphabet Soup(USA) —Garendare (Vacarme (USA))
1185^{9} (1440) 1747^{8} 2204^{5} 2605^{9} 2772^{8}

Melkatant *N Bycroft* 53
3 b f Rock City—Change Of Image (Spectrum (IRE))
3939^{7} 4819^{3} 5259^{9} 5549^{6} 5953^{3} 6219^{4} 6766^{3}

Mellifera *W R Swinburn* a68 73
2 b f Leporello(IRE) —Christina's Dream (Spectrum (IRE))
3271^{4} 3987^{4} ◆ 5284^{5} 6071^{6} 7453^{8}

Mellifluous (IRE) *W S Kittow* a33 43
4 b m Noverre(USA) —Danestar (Danehill (USA))
5367^{6}

Mellow Mixture *S Kirk* a78 72
3 b c Marju(IRE) —Night Owl (Night Shift (USA))
32^{2} 391^{2} 630^{7} 2126^{6} 2567^{3} 2892^{7} 3630^{6} 4650^{12} 5101^{7} 5988^{5} (6705)

Melody In The Mist (FR) *T D Barron* 72
2 b f Intikhab(USA) —She's All Class (USA) (Rahy (USA))
2339^{6} 3478^{2} 4011^{3} (4773) (5292)

Melodyman (FR) *N Clement* 107
2 b c Green Tune(USA) —The Wise Lady (FR) (Ganges (USA))
(4073a) 7231a^{4}

Melt (IRE) *R Hannon* a65 61
4 b m Intikhab(USA) —Kindle (Selkirk (USA))
344^{11} 395^{5} 661^{2} (830) 945^{2} 1074^{3} ◆ 1417^{4} 1710^{6}

Melting Bob (USA) *Dr J D Scargill* a51
3 rg f Johannesburg(USA) —Dancingonice (USA) (Robyn Dancer (USA))
7826^{7} ◆

Melundy *Mrs L Stubbs* 69
2 b f Best Of The Bests(IRE) —Nova Zembla (Young Ern)
5439^{2} 5949^{5}

Meml *J D Bethell* a47 47
3 b f Mark Of Esteem(IRE) —Matisse (Shareef Dancer (USA))
3690^{6} 4505^{11} 5259^{6} 7004^{4} 7318^{8}

Memorandum *R Charlton* a75 65
2 b f Oasis Dream—Marani (Ashkalani (IRE))
6328^{5} 6932^{3} (7365) ◆ 7570^{5} 7878^{3}

Memory And Magic (USA) *C G Cox* a66 63
2 b f Sahm(USA) —Aljawza (USA) (Riverman (USA))
3772^{2} ◆ 4711^{7} 5808^{4} 6366^{4} 7363^{11}

Memphis Man *P D Evans* a81 86
6 b g Bertolini(USA) —Something Blue (Petong)
141^{5} 780^{5} 1150^{12} 1572^{6} 2045^{6} 2276^{5} 2549^{4} (2980) 3694^{2} 3787^{5} 3917^{3} 4154^{5} 4387^{3} 4607^{5} 4787^{2} 5363^{3} 6279^{10} 6540^{9} 6964^{9} 7083^{8}

Memphis Marie *P J McBride* a60 39
5 b m Desert Sun—Spirito Libro (USA) (Lear Fan (USA))
4179^{12} 5111^{6} 5998^{12}

Mena Rl *Karen George*
2 b f Sulamani(IRE) —Natalie (Dushyantor (USA))
7451^{13}

Mendip (USA) *Saeed Bin Suroor* a84
2 bb c Harlan's Holiday(USA) —Well Spring (USA) (Coronado's Quest (USA))
(5637) ◆

Menediva *L A Mullaney* 42
2 b f Danbird(AUS) —Princess Ismene (Sri Pekan (USA))
2800^{7} 3187^{13} 3726^{4} 4138^{4} 4800^{8}

Menelas *P Bary* 88
2 b c Refuse To Bend(IRE) —Blanche (FR) (Loup Solitaire (USA))
5927a^{4}

Menelaus *K A Morgan* a39 50
8 b g Machiavellian(USA) —Mezzogiorno (Unfuwain (USA))
4264^{4} 6859^{8}

Menhir Bay *D K Ivory* a52
3 b g Sure Blade(USA) —Turkish Delight (Prince Sabo)
188^{6}

Menkaura *John R Upson* a37 79
6 b g Pivotal—Nekhbet (Artaius (USA))
147^{11}

Meohmy *M R Channon* a49 48
6 b m Marju(IRE) —Meshhed (USA) (Gulch (USA))
443^{12} 484^{3}

Mercers Row *A Dickman* 69
2 b g Bahamian Bounty—Invincible (Slip Anchor)
2526^{4} 3446^{2} ◆ 4282^{7} 4875^{3} 5620^{6} 5977^{3} 6408^{4}

Merchant Man *J D Bethell* a46 60
3 b g Mark Of Esteem(IRE) —Birsay (Bustino)
2104^{4} 3531^{5} 4347^{10} 4892^{3} ◆ 5442^{5} 6027^{5}

Merchant Marine (USA) *Doug Watson* a114
5 b g Tiznow(USA) —Head East (USA) (Gone West (USA))
773a^{12}

Merchant Of Dubai *G A Swinbank* a103 102
4 b g Dubai Destination(USA) —Chameleon (Green Desert (USA))
5004^{3} (5402) 6138^{2} ◆ 7031^{8} 7293^{6} (7465)

Merchant Of Medici *W R Muir* a73 68
2 b g Medicean—Regal Rose (Danehill (USA))
2430^{3} 5934^{2} 6591^{9} 6911^{4} 7193^{3} 7359^{7}

Mercoliano *M Botti* a68
2 b g Medicean—Mega (IRE) (Petardia)
7193^{4} ◆ 7400^{5}

Merdaam *J L Dunlop* 81
3 ch g Dubai Destination(USA) —Faydah (USA) (Bahri (USA))
1355^{3} 2082^{2} 2613^{3} 4354^{6} 6595^{8}

Merlin's Dancer *S Dow* a91 95
9 b g Magic Ring(IRE) —La Piaf (FR) (Fabulous Dancer (USA))
754^{4} 1181^{3} 1457^{6} 1836^{3} 2704^{15} 3347^{8} 3524^{4} 4232^{8}

Merrion Tiger (IRE) *A G Foster* a74 69
4 ch g Choisir(AUS) —Akita (IRE) (Foxhound (USA))
(147) ◆ (402) 899^{7} 1648^{2} 2044^{12} 3059^{3} 3654^{4} 4350^{12} 4462^{8} 6053^{14} 6767^{15} (7635) 7842^{2}

Merry Diva *C F Wall* a66 76
3 b f Bahamian Bounty—Merry Rous (Rousillon (USA))
1814^{9} 2632^{8} 3193^{2} 4227^{3} 4664^{3} 5506^{2} 5968^{3}

Merrymadcap (IRE) *Matthew Salaman* a79 74
7 b g Lujain(USA) —Carina Clare (Slip Anchor)
3104^{2} ◆ (3421) 3811^{9} 4262^{7} 4992^{5} (5244) 5802^{6} 5964^{4} 6460^{3} 6634^{3} 7204^{4} 7475^{2}

Merry May *S Kirk* a33 34
3 b f Compton Place—Swift Dame (IRE) (Montjeu (IRE))
4172^{11} 4950^{10} 5632^{10}

Merseyside Star (IRE) *A P Jarvis* 71
2 ch c Kheleyf(USA) —The Oldladysays No (IRE) (Perugino (USA))
2195^{6} 2610^{4} (3262) 3702^{4} 3842^{3} 4327^{6} 5187^{4}

Merton Lad *T G Mills* a67 38
3 ch g Fantastic Light(USA) —Artistic Blue (USA) (Diesis)
740^{3} 865^{5} 1408^{15}

Merton Matriarch *P Winkworth* a67
2 ch f Cadeaux Genereux—Tesary (Danehill (USA))
6942^{2}

Merveilles *Mrs John Harrington* a67 101
6 b g Vettori(IRE) —Finlaggan (Be My Chief (USA))
2425a^{6}

Mesbaah (IRE) *R A Fahey* a87 91
5 b g Noverre(USA) —Deyaajeer (USA) (Dayjur (USA))
1990^{11} 2257^{9} 4333^{15} 4941^{8} 5423^{9} 7085^{7}

Meshtri (IRE) *M A Jarvis* a106 100
4 ch g Dalakhani(IRE) —Arctic Hunt (IRE) (Bering)
1007^{3} 3390^{11}

Mesmerize Me *R McGlinchey* a48 92
4 b g Mind Games—Exotic Forest (Dominion)
1376a^{16}

Messiah Noire (FR) *T Lerner*
2 b f Diktat—Listen Daddy (FR) (Piccolo)
7316a^{0}

Metal Guru *R Hollinshead* a69 70
5 ch m Ishiguru(USA) —Gemtastic (Tagula (IRE))
15^{10} 3677^{5} 4929^{12} (5610) (6456) 7280^{12} 7601^{3} 7839^{2} 7852^{6}

Metal Madness (IRE) *M G Quinlan* a67 74
4 b g Acclamation—Dosha (Touching Wood (USA))
172^{6} 285^{9}

Metal Princess *K Borgel* 38
3 b f Royal Applause—Speechless (Desert King (IRE))
6149a^{5}

Metal Soldier (IRE) *J J Quinn* 74
2 b g Antonius Pius(USA) —Shenkara (IRE) (Night Shift (USA))
(1802)

Methaaly (IRE) *M Mullineaux* a92 89
6 b g Red Ransom(USA) —Santorini (USA) (Spinning World (USA))
351^{2} ◆ 538^{5} 579^{2} 714^{4} 985^{9} 1016^{14} 1309^{8} 1510^{6} 1682^{8} (2071) 2782^{4} 2938^{5} 3335^{6} 3529^{8} 4461^{11} 4485^{19} 5799^{8} 5960^{5} 6279^{14} (6540) 6949^{10} 7155^{7} 7702^{3} 7875^{5}

Metroland *D Nicholls* 76
3 b f Royal Applause—Chetwynd (IRE) (Exit To Nowhere (USA))
1368^{7} 1505^{2} ◆ 1869^{2} 2299^{4} 2546^{6} 3479^{5}

Metropolitan Chief *P Burgoyne* a47 41
5 b g Compton Place—Miss Up N Go (Gorytus (USA))
234^{11} 347^{10} 472^{6} 575^{10} 812^{8} 946^{6} 3252^{8} 3732^{11} 4023^{6} 4203^{7} 4736^{8} 5020^{9} 7517^{11} 7592^{3} 7770^{8}

Metropolitan Man *D M Simcock* a91 113
6 ch g Dr Fong(USA) —Preceder (Polish Precedent (USA))
6030^{7}

Mexican Bob *C E Longsdon* a67 70
6 b g Atraf—Eskimo Nel (IRE) (Shy Groom (USA))
3811^{7} (4893) 5530^{9} 7847^{3}

Mexican Jay (USA) *B Smart* 56
3 b f Elusive Quality(USA) —Mistle Song (Nashwan (USA))
2403^{3}

Mexican Milly (IRE) *B W Hills* a47 56
2 ch f Noverre(USA) —Forest Bride (USA) (Woodman (USA))
1298^{10} 4515^{3} 5036^{3} 6343^{6}

Mexican Pete *A King* a79 83
9 b g Atraf—Eskimo Nel (IRE) (Shy Groom (USA))
835^{2} 1069^{5}

Mey Blossom *R M Whitaker* a78 92
4 ch m Captain Rio—Petra Nova (First Trump)
1333^{5} 1766^{5} 2312^{4} 2998^{5} 3453^{2} 3825^{12} 4072^{2} 4929^{8} 6434^{13} 6764^{10} 7191^{7}

Meydan City (USA) *M bin Shafya* a87 106
4 b h Kingmambo(USA) —Crown Of Crimson (USA) (Seattle Slew (USA))
263a^{6} ◆ 436a^{7}

Meydan Dubai (IRE) *J R Best* a72 91
4 b h Alzao(USA) —Rorkes Drift (IRE) (Royal Abjar (USA))
7523^{10} 7699^{10}

Meydan Groove *R Johnson* a66 67
3 b f Reset(AUS) —In The Groove (Night Shift (USA))
741^{6} 1098^{6} 2234^{7} 2593^{8} 2967^{8} 3108^{8} 4016^{3} 4594^{9}

Meydan Style (USA) *J Balding* a52 37
3 b g Essence Of Dubai(USA) —Polish Ruby (USA) (Polish Pro (USA))
966^{6} 1157^{6} 1481^{7} 4879^{7} 5373^{5} 6880^{11} 6950^{6}

Meyyal (USA) *B W Hills* a72 78
3 b c War Chant(USA) —Tamgeed (USA) (Woodman (USA))
4979^{3} 6287^{3} 6595^{5}

Mezenah *Saeed Bin Suroor* 86
3 b f Cape Cross(IRE) —Saytarra (USA) (Seeking The Gold (USA))
4337^{2} (4955)

Mezuzah *Miss J E Foster* a57 89
9 b g Barathea(IRE) —Mezzogiorno (Unfuwain (USA))
7711^{9}

Mezzanisi (IRE) *M L W Bell* a94 96
4 b g Kalanisi(IRE) —Mezzanine (Sadler's Wells (USA))
1458^{2} (2146) 3620^{3} ◆

Mezzo Forte (USA) *J-C Rouget* a78 78
5 ch h Stravinsky(USA) —Calming (USA) (Wild Again (USA))
5464a^{7}

Mharadono (GER) *P Hirschberger* 103
6 b h Sharp Prod(USA) —Monalind (GER) (Park Romeo)
1029a^{9} 3416a^{11} 4582a^{5}

Miacarla *H A McWilliams* a33 61
6 b m Forzando—Zarzi (IRE) (Suave Dancer (USA))
1041^{7} 1241^{12} 1591^{9} 1695^{13} 3570^{9} 3909^{9} 5309^{7} 6410^{13} 7136^{9}

Miami Gator (IRE) *J R Weymes* a64 59
2 ch g Titus Livius(FR) —Lovere (St Jovite (USA))
2339^{9} (2788) 2896^{4} 3572^{5} 4895^{6} 7168^{10} 7661^{5} (7884)

Miami Mix *B N Pollock* a42
3 gr c Fair Mix(IRE) —Granma (Little Wolf)
391^{7} 659^{5} 914^{8} 1363^{15}

Mia's Boy *C A Dwyer* a110 113
5 b h Pivotal—Bint Zamayem (IRE) (Rainbow Quest (USA))
997^{4} ◆ 1352^{6} 1631^{2} 2015^{3} 2500^{2} 3014^{3} 4419^{7} 5200^{10} 6030^{2} (7019) 7294^{2}

Mibar (USA) *Gianluca Bietolini* 56
3 ch c Refuse To Bend(IRE) —Bow River Gold (Rainbow Quest (USA))
1393a[13]

Miccolo *P T Midgley* 59
2 b c Piccolo—Ashkernazy (IRE) (Salt Dome (USA))
1097[6] 1847[8] 2153[8] 2893[5] 4282[9]

Michael Collins (IRE) *G J Smith* a66 57
3 b g Oasis Dream—West Virginia (IRE) (Gone West (USA))
298[4] 306[2] 6358[11] 7349[13]

Michael Laskey *B R Millman* a50 49
3 b g Lujain(USA) —Enchanted Ocean (USA) (Royal Academy (USA))
828[5] 1151[7] 1771[9] 7687[7] 7818[9]

Michaelmas Daisy *P Howling* a54 67
2 b f Camacho—Desert Daisy (IRE) (Desert Prince (IRE))
1031[5] 1090[7] 2457[3] (3579) 3807[2] 4558[6] 5166[7] 6586[8] 7089[6] 7410[6]

Michaels Dream (IRE) *N Wilson* a39 35
10 b g Spectrum(IRE) —Stormswept (USA) (Storm Bird (CAN))
249[9]

Michelle (IRE) *P Butler* a48
3 b f Marju(IRE) —Bel Sole (ITY) (Spectrum (IRE))
441[3] 547[5] 662[9] 1036[12]

Michevious Spirit (IRE) *K A Ryan* 70
2 ch f Dalakhani(IRE) —Roseanna (FR) (Anabaa (USA))
5417[5] 6389[2] 6762[6] ◆

Mick Is Back *G G Margarson* a53 65
5 b g Diktat—Classy Cleo (IRE) (Mujadil (USA))
1199[8] 2171[5] 2378[2] 2739[2] 2807[3] (3946) 4262[13] 4389[10] 4721[5] 5888[6] 6208[8] 6790[9] 6966[9] 7127[7]

Mick's Dancer *W R Muir* a79 89
4 b g Pivotal—La Piaf (FR) (Fabulous Dancer (USA))
1415[2] 1812[6] 2183[7] (3349) (3847) 4541[3] (5062) 5725[2] 6546[4]

Micky Mac (IRE) *C J Teague* a66 70
5 b g Lend A Hand—Gazette It Tonight (Merdon Melody)
4504[11] 4823[3] 5391[2] 5601[19] 6596[3] 6846[13] 7280[2] 7555[10]

Micky P *S C Williams* 57
2 gr c Dr Fong(USA) —Carmela Owen (Owington)
6737[9] 7146[15]

Micky's Bird *R C Guest* a28 52
2 ch f Needwood Blade—Silver Peak (FR) (Sillery (USA))
1841[9] 2128[12] 2414[2] 5290[8] 6241[24] 7352[8] 7501[8] 7706[8]

Micky's Knock Off (IRE) *R C Guest* a66 78
2 b g Camacho—La Grace (Lahib (USA))
4067[10] 4282[10] 5292[2] 5559[6] (5945) 6550[6] 6827[8] 7115[3] 7274[5] 7410[4] 7636[7]

Mickys Mate *A Crook* a13 39
4 b g Choisir(AUS) —Adept (Efisio)
215[12] 933[8] 1061[6] 1243[19] 1628[9]

Midas Touch *A P O'Brien* 105
2 b c Galileo(IRE) —Approach (Darshaan)
7207a[4]

Midas Way *P R Chamings* a81 84
9 ch g Halling(USA) —Arietta's Way (IRE) (Darshaan)
2994[10]

Midday *H R A Cecil* 120
3 b f Oasis Dream—Midsummer (Kingmambo (USA))
1459[2] (1871) 2672[2] 3896a[3] (4522) 6525a[3] (7284a)

Middle Club *R Hannon* 103
2 b f Fantastic Light(USA) —Anna Oleanda (IRE) (Old Vic)
3249[3] (3810) ◆ 4245[2] (6045a)

Middlemarch (IRE) *J S Goldie* a64 79
9 ch g Grand Lodge(USA) —Blanche Dubois (Nashwan (USA))
1343[5] 2402[3] 2665[11] 3353[4] 3615[9] 4293[7] 4897[5] 5441[7] (5694) 6012[7] 7014[9]

Middle Of Nowhere (USA) *M A Magnusson* a79 11
4 b h Carson City(USA) —Ivy Leaf (IRE) (Nureyev (USA))
120[2] ◆ 320[2] (493) ◆

Midfielder (USA) *J H M Gosden* a54
2 ch c Smart Strike(CAN) —Quiet Weekend (USA) (Quiet American (USA))
6772[8]

Midget *M A Magnusson* 59
2 b f Invincible Spirit(IRE) —Sharp Mode (USA) (Diesis)
(2800)

Mid Mon Lady (IRE) *H Rogers* a96 96
4 br m Danetime(IRE) —Shining Desert (IRE) (Green Desert (USA))
7300a[8]

Midnight Bay *P D Evans* a65 66
3 br g Domedriver(IRE) —Serriera (FR) (Highest Honor (FR))
479[4] 740[6] 2487[8] 3257[7] 3502[7] 3862[7] 4279[15] 7647[3] 7767[5] 7888[9]

Midnight Cruiser (IRE) *R Hannon* a69 99
3 ch c Captain Rio—Kriva (Reference Point)
1118[8] 1484[3] 2855[3] (3429) 3840[8] 4455[14] 5508[2]

Midnight Dreamer *J E Hammond* 93
4 b m Fantastic Light(USA) —Zuleika Dobson (Cadeaux Genereux)
4365a[5]

Midnight Fantasy *Rae Guest* a76 79
3 b f Oasis Dream—Midnight Shift (IRE) (Night Shift (USA))
(1852) 2160[5] 2776[5] (3272) 3688[9] (4997) 5591[2] 6765[8]

Midnight In May (IRE) *W R Muir* 78
3 b g Mull Of Kintyre(USA) —Birthday (IRE) (Singspiel (IRE))
1462[3]

Midnight Martini *T D Easterby* 90
2 b f Night Shift(USA) —Shaken And Stirred (Cadeaux Genereux)
2258[4] ◆ 2765[4] (3263) (4547) (5198) 6090[2]

Midnight Strider (IRE) *Tom Dascombe* a71
3 br c Golan(IRE) —Danish Gem (Danehill (USA))
7730[2] ◆ 7863[2]

Midnight Uno *W G M Turner* a52 54
2 b g Desert Style(IRE) —Carati (Selkirk (USA))
1653[4] 1827[3] 2218[3] 3160[10] 3925[11]

Midnite Blews (IRE) *M A Barnes* a29 61
4 gr g Trans Island—Felicita (IRE) (Catrail (USA))
3068[6] 3291[8]

Midshipman (USA) *Saeed Bin Suroor* a118
3 ch c Unbridled's Song(USA) —Fleet Lady (USA) (Avenue Of Flags (USA))
7309a[3]

Midsummer Madness (IRE) *David Pinder* a49 7
3 b f Alhaarth(IRE) —Robalana (USA) (Wild Again (USA))
1148[8]

Mid Valley *J R Jenkins* a52 58
6 ch g Zilzal(USA) —Isabella D'Este (IRE) (Irish River (FR))
443[4] 745[7] 1378[9] 1728[9] 2222[9] 2634[5] 3962[4] 4388[9] 7666[7] 7888[10]

Midwestern (USA) *M L W Bell* 71
2 bb g Tiznow(USA) —She's Enough (USA) (Exploit (USA))
6054[6] 6591[11] 6922[4] ◆

Mid Wicket (USA) *Mouse Hamilton-Fairley* a52 50
3 b g Strong Hope(USA) —Sunday Bazaar (USA) (Nureyev (USA))
2551[6] 4606[12] 7755[12]

Miesko (USA) *M G Quinlan* a55 42
4 b g Quiet American(USA) —Polish Style (USA) (Danzig (USA))
7605[5]

Mighty Aphrodite *Rae Guest* 46
2 b f Observatory(USA) —Sahara Rose (Green Desert (USA))
6797[7]

Mighty Clarets (IRE) *R A Fahey* 65
2 br g Whipper(USA) —Collected (IRE) (Taufan (USA))
2099[9] 2663[7] 3487[3] 5935[4] 6895[3]

Mighty Kitchener (USA) *P Howling* a54 55
6 br g Mighty(USA) —Libeccio (NZ) (Danzatore (CAN))
743[5] 877[8]

Mighty Mambo *Jane Chapple-Hyam* a66
2 b c Fantastic Light(USA) —Mambo's Melody (Kingmambo (USA))
7502[2]

Mighty Moon *R A Fahey* a78 85
6 gr g Daylami(IRE) —Moon Magic (Polish Precedent (USA))
1215[9] (1356) 2085[6]

Mighty Mover (IRE) *B Palling* a59 57
7 ch g Bahhare(USA) —Ericeira (IRE) (Anita's Prince)
5630[3] 6394[3] (7152) 7416[6] 7600[12]

Migliori *Rae Guest* a14 55
3 b g Royal Applause—Millyant (Primo Dominie)
686[5] 3764[7] 4199[4] 4718[5] 4937[8] 5716[6] 6755[14]

Mijas Playa *C A Dwyer* 78
2 b f Avonbridge—Rainbow Spectrum (FR) (Spectrum (IRE))
1298[2] ◆ 1788[5] 2034[2] 2295[2] 2408[7] (4165) 4547[7] 5033[7] 5908[5] 6841[8]

Mik *Dr J R J Naylor*
3 b g Baryshnikov(AUS) —Daphne's Doll (IRE) (Polish Patriot (USA))
3425[11]

Mikado *Jonjo O'Neill* a44 74
8 b g Sadler's Wells(USA) —Free At Last (Shirley Heights)
3[6]

Mikhail Glinka (IRE) *A P O'Brien* 106
2 b c Galileo(IRE) —Lady Karr (Mark Of Esteem (IRE))
6268[6] 7404a[2]

Mikos (FR) *Robert Collet* 73
9 b g Sicyos(USA) —Sex Pistol (FR) (Pistolet Bleu (IRE))
5464a[4]

Milanais (FR) *A Chaille-Chaille* 118
3 ch c Dyhim Diamond(IRE) —Milanaise (FR) (Marignan (USA))
1238a[6] 2755a[9] 3230a[6] 3669a[8]

Mildoura (FR) *Mrs L J Mongan* a91 88
4 b m Sendawar(IRE) —Miliana (IRE) (Polar Falcon (USA))
299[5] (1049) 1357[2] 6618[9] 7131[9] (7539) (7811)

Mile High Lad (USA) *George Baker* a74 53
3 bb g Sky Mesa(USA) —Thunder Warmth (USA) (Thunder Gulch (USA))
32[3] 389[3] 4320[4] 6951[8] 7094[4] 7361[5] 7455[7] 7576[8]

Milemilia (IRE) *H Morrison* a63 49
3 b f Milan—Emilia Romagna (GER) (Acatenango (GER))
386[12] 529[9] 824[3] 1063[7] 1842[11] 2742[8] 3511[11] 3739[6] 4142[8]

Miles Gloriosus (USA) *R Menichetti* a108 111
6 b h Repriced(USA) —Treasure Coast (CAN) (Foolish Pleasure (USA))
2525a[2] 6718a[10]

Milford Sound *A Fabre* 94
3 bb f Barathea(IRE) —Docklands (USA) (Theatrical (IRE))
3668a[8]

Militarist (USA) *J H M Gosden* a63 92
3 b g War Chant(USA) —Season's Greetings (IRE) (Ezzoud (IRE))
(1297) 1487[2] 2281[6] 4316[5] 4909[4] 5986[12]

Military Call *E S McMahon* 74
2 b c Royal Applause—Trump Street (First Trump)
1358[4] 1590[2] 2153[5] (3542) 4195[5] 4739[6]

Military Power *Saeed Bin Suroor* a104 100
4 b h Dubai Destination(USA) —Susun Kelapa (USA) (St Jovite (USA))
263a[5] 417a[7] 522a[9] 2342[4]

Millagros (IRE) *I Semple* a26 47
9 b m Pennekamp(USA) —Grey Galava (Generous (IRE))
679[12] 897[8] 1738[9] 2592[3]

Mill Beattie *J Mackie* a45 54
4 b m Beat All(USA) —Step On Degas (Superpower)
147[13] 678[5] 857[7]

Millden *H Candy* a55
2 b g Compton Place—Pretty Poppy (Song)
7736[8]

Milldown Story *B R Millman* a71 71
3 b f Lucky Story(USA) —Barnacla (IRE) (Bluebird (USA))
2205[6] 3813[3] 4164[3] 4936[3] 5373[2] 5717[3] (6344) 7138[12]

Millefeuille (FR) *Carmen Bocskai*
7 gr g Medaaly—Ma Priorite (GER) (Great Lakes)
465a[7]

Millers Crossing *W J H Ratcliffe* 61
3 b g Tobougg(IRE) —Tweed Mill (Selkirk (USA))
2298[4] 2862[5] ◆ 3175[9]

Millfield (IRE) *P R Chamings* a81 79
6 br g Elnadim(USA) —Eschasse (USA) (Zilzal (USA))
143[6] 457[2] 544[6] 878[10] 950[5] 2186[9] 2675[9] 2977[8] 3322[8] 4645[3] 5124[5] (5779) 6294[2] (6725) 7111[4] 7327[3] 7575[5]

Millfields Dreams *G C Bravery* a72 76
10 b g Dreams End—Millfields Lady (Sayf El Arab (USA))
1775[2] 2088[4] 2352[3] 2713[5] 2880[2] 3206[2] 3389[6] 3639[16] 3802[4] 4167[6] 5003[14] 5182[8]

Millharbour (IRE) *B W Hills* a56 69
3 b g Nayef(USA) —My Funny Valentine (IRE) (Mukaddamah (USA))
1151[4] 2850[10] 3538[4] 5322[4] 6124[6] 6475[6]

Millie's Rock (IRE) *K A Ryan* a78 71
4 b m Rock Of Gibraltar(IRE) —Miletrian (IRE) (Marju (IRE))
(125) ◆ 361[2] 559[10] 651[4] 1020[7] 2150[12] 2389[8] 4876[9] 7399[12]

Million Dollars (USA) *Saeed Bin Suroor* a63 56
2 ch f Pleasant Tap(USA) —Six Zeroes (USA) (Hold For Gold (USA))
5284[8] 5984[4]

Million Kiss (IRE) *C Von Der Recke* 74
2 gr f Clodovil(IRE) —Masakira (IRE) (Royal Academy (USA))
6501a[18]

Milloaks (IRE) *Paul W Flynn*
4 b m Tamayaz(CAN) —Jaldini (IRE) (Darshaan)
304[9]

Millville *M A Jarvis* a115 91
9 ch g Millkom—Miss Top Ville (FR) (Top Ville)
33[3] 1458[14]

Millway Beach (IRE) *Pat Eddery* a69 72
3 b g Diktat—Cape Cod (IRE) (Unfuwain (USA))
(317) 586[4] 829[4] 1839[13] 2567[4] 3222[11] 4300[11] 5570[7] 6376[7]

Milly Rose *George Baker* a44 56
3 br f Diktat—Milly Fleur (Primo Dominie)
2973[13] 3474[9]

Milnagavie *R Hannon* a77 67
2 ch f Tobougg(IRE) —Abyaan (IRE) (Ela-Mana-Mou)
5165[3] ◆ 5627[4] 6607[6]

Milne Bay (IRE) *D M Simcock* a79 78
4 b g Tagula(IRE) —Fiction (Dominion)
(141) 241[6] 954[5] 1313[3] 2088[2] 5991[2] 6120[6] 6642[10]

Milouk (FR) *T Cambefort* 15
4 b m Until Sundown(USA) —Relative Fly (FR) (Distant Relative)
5074a[9]

Milton Of Campsie *J Balding* a60 79
4 ch m Medicean—La Caprice (USA) (Housebuster (USA))
179[5] 281[7] 2590[8] 3227[8] 3381[5] 5518[3] (5911) (6160) (6413) 6764[15]

Miltons Choice *J M Bradley* a57 64
6 b g Diktat—Starosta (Soviet Star (USA))
1248[12] 1421[10] 1528[3]

Mina Alsalaam *S Peto* a22 13
7 b m Lujain(USA) —Rain And Shine (FR) (Rainbow Quest (USA))
464a[9] 652a[8]

Mind Alert *D Shaw* a68 41
8 b g Mind Games—Bombay Sapphire (Be My Chief (USA))
27[4] 71[9] 222[8] 461[5]

Minder *J G Portman* a57 63
3 b g Mind Games—Exotic Forest (Dominion)
1361[5] 2320[6]

Mind Of Her Own *P D Evans* a56 55
2 b f Pastoral Pursuits—Mindfulness (Primo Dominie)
1277[6] 1364[2] 2358[7] 7319[4] 7482[11] 7514[10] 7619[8] 7707[4] 7749[9] 7757[7]

Mind The Monarch *R A Teal* a56 60
2 b f Mind Games—Enford Princess (Pivotal)
1726[4] 2074[4] 2563[10] 3210[5] 3952[6] 4747[3] 5583[6] 7482[9] 7698[2] 7805[5] 7884[4]

Mine Behind *J R Best* a71 49
9 b g Sheikh Albadou—Arapi (IRE) (Arazi (USA))
1152[14] 1421[11]

Miner's Escape (USA) *Nicholas Zito* a40
3 b c Mineshaft(USA) —Spy Novel (USA) (Broad Brush (USA))
2734a[10]

Mine That Bird (USA) *Bennie L Woolley Jr* a121
3 b g Birdstone(USA) —Mining My Own (USA) (Smart Strike (CAN))
(1688a) 2098a[2] 2734a[3] 6687a[6] ◆ 7311a[9]

Ming Master (FR) *W J Haggas* a73
2 b g Tobougg(IRE) —Sakura Queen (IRE) (Woodman (USA))
7571[9] 7644[4] 7763[4]

Mingun Bell (USA) *H R A Cecil* a92 79
2 b c Mingun(USA) —Miss Tippins (USA) (Squadron Leader (USA))
2663[3] 3052[3] (3786) (5324) ◆ 6472[4] 7184[6]

Ming Vase *P T Midgley* a55 54
7 b g Vettori(IRE) —Minstrel's Dance (CAN) (Pleasant Colony (USA))
515[4] 608[6] 744[3] 918[13] 1276[5] 1883[7] 2263[9] 2965[6] 3123[2] 3450[8] 4351[5] 4434[4] 4710[11] 5730[7]

Minibuzz *Mrs G S Rees* a35
3 b g Superior Premium—Amy Leigh (IRE) (Imperial Frontier (USA))
236[12] 881[4] 1451[9]

Minimalist *Mme C Head-Maarek* 79
2 ch f Observatory(USA) —Minority (Generous (IRE))
4577a[6]

Mini Max *B W Duke* a63 58
2 b f Tobougg(IRE) —Maxilla (IRE) (Lahib (USA))
4985[11] 5639[5] 6729[12] 7056[4]

Minimum Fuss (IRE) *M C Chapman* a28 50
5 b m Second Empire(IRE) —Jamis (IRE) (Be My Guest (USA))
401[8] 1477[5] 1970[6] 2534[12]

Minimusic *B Palling* a32
2 b f Distant Music(USA) —Minette (Bishop Of Cashel)
7491[10]

Ministerofinterior *G L Moore* a60 65
4 b g Nayef(USA) —Maureen's Hope (USA) (Northern Baby (CAN))
59[4] 2808[4] 3382[5]

Miniyamba (IRE) *J L Dunlop* 69
2 b f Sadler's Wells(USA) —Atlantide (USA) (Southern Halo (USA))
4797[9] 5605[6] ◆ 6062[9] 6993[11]

Minnie Rocket *R C Guest* 8
2 ch f Monsieur Bond(IRE) —Real Popcorn (IRE) (Jareer (USA))
1939[8] 2128[14] 2414[8] 5292[7] 5950[18]

Minnola *Rae Guest* a52 58
4 b m Royal Applause—Miss Anabaa (Anabaa (USA))
1077[5] 4105[3] 4552[9] 5316[7] 5501[4] 5624[8] 6213[7] 6433[6] 6674[4] 7877[10]

Minority Report *K A Ryan* a57 88
9 b g Rainbow Quest(USA) —Queen Sceptre (IRE) (Fairy King (USA))
1016[3] 1123[7] 1365[5] 1507[8] 2612[10] 2787[4] 3124[6] 3353[8] 4400[10] 5780[10]

Minortransgression (USA) *G L Moore* a66
2 ch g Yes It's True(USA) —Casting Pearls (USA) (Fusaichi Pegasus (USA))
7806[4]

Minotaurious (IRE) *K R Burke* a66 79
3 b f Acclamation—Bella Vie (IRE) (Sadler's Wells (USA))
19[2] 85[3] 350[2] 1062[9]

Minstalad *G R Oldroyd* 44
5 ch g Minster Son—Denby Wood (Lord Bud)
4974[3]

Minted (FR) *E Charpy* a91 91
4 gr g Clodovil(IRE) —Mintly Fresh (USA) (Rubiano (USA))
414a[9] 639a[11]

Mintoe *K A Ryan* a58 63
3 b g Noverre(USA) —West One (Gone West (USA))
2660[10] 3727[6] 4279[7]

Minturno (USA) *Mrs A Duffield* 74
3 b g Ten Most Wanted(USA) —Panama Jane (USA) (Perrault)
1062[4] 1335[4] 1625[2] 1969[7] (2365) 3108[2] ◆ 3316[4] 3729[3] (4131) 4707[7] 5340[5] 5955[4] 6178[10]

Mint Whip (IRE) *R Hannon* a59 64
2 b f Whipper(USA) —Aminata (Glenstal (USA))
7058[6] 7317[6]

Minwir (IRE) *W M Brisbourne* a59 68
4 b g Green Desert(USA) —Elshamms (Zafonic (USA))
192[8] 540[6] 5883[10] 6800[9]

Mirabella (IRE) *R Hannon* a83
2 b f Motivator—Anayid (A.P. Indy (USA))
6163[4] 6628[8] 7135[2] (7363) ◆

Miracle Baby *J A Geake* a56 50
7 b m Atraf—Musica (Primo Dominie)
308[6] 868[8] 2794[9] 6782[6]

Miracle Match (IRE) *Mrs John Harrington* a96 88
2 b c Oratorio(IRE) —Miss Demure (Shy Groom (USA))
4250a[5]

Miracle Seeker *C G Cox* 103
4 br m Rainbow Quest(USA) —Miracle (Ezzoud (IRE))
3619[8]

Miracle Wish (IRE) *R M Beckett* 17
2 b f One Cool Cat(USA) —Bentley's Bush (IRE) (Barathea (IRE))
2494[12]

Miranda's Girl (IRE) *Thomas Cleary* a89 96
4 b m Titus Livius(FR) —Ela Tina (IRE) (Ela-Mana-Mou)
4412a[9] 7297a[8] 7801[9]

Mirjan (IRE) *L Lungo* 79
13 b g Tenby—Mirana (IRE) (Ela-Mana-Mou)
2044[10]

Miroslav (IRE) *L Camici* 79
3 b c Fasliyev(USA) —Magiustrina (IRE) (Indian Ridge)
1393a[11]

Mirrored *Sir Michael Stoute* a86 105
3 b g Dansili—Reflections (Sadler's Wells (USA))
(1466) (2209) ◆ 3049[3] ◆ 3639[3] ◆ 4455[3] 5200[17] 6277[4]

Mirror Lake *Mrs A J Perrett* a65
2 b f Dubai Destination(USA) —Reflections (Sadler's Wells (USA))
7135[5]

Misaro (GER) *R A Harris* a86 96
8 b g Acambaro(GER) —Misniniski (Niniski (USA))
1457[11] 1672[8] 2203[4] 2520[3] 2911[6] (3422) ◆ 3623[5] 4232[5] 4341[15] 5098[6] 5247[4] 5623[7] 5900[3] 6329[6] (6669) 6972[10] (7534) 7646[3] 7656[7] 7832[4]

Misbehaviour *P Butler* a32 10
10 b g Tragic Role(USA) —Exotic Forest (Dominion)
5028[11]

Mischief Making (USA) *E A L Dunlop* a99 102
4 bb m Lemon Drop Kid(USA) —Fraulein (Acatenango (GER))
1601[2] 2216a[9] 3390[13] 6242[3] 6854[7]

Misdaqeya *B W Hills* a84 94
3 br f Red Ransom(USA) —Crystal Power (USA) (Pleasant Colony (USA))
1293[9] 3016[10] 4020[3] 7291[10]

Misheer *C E Brittain* 109
2 b f Oasis Dream—All For Laura (Cadeaux Genereux)
(1630) ◆ (2054) 3015[2] (3748) 5822[9] 6449[2]

Mishrif (USA) *J R Jenkins* a98 94
3 bb g Arch(USA) —Peppy Priscilla (USA) (Latin American (USA))
1211[3] 1485[6] 2673[5] 3049[20] 4708[6] 5092[7] 5375[10] 5986[9] 6695[11] 6996[12]

Miskin Flyer *B Palling* a58 40
3 b f Lend A Hand—Sipsi Fach (Prince Sabo)
4381[9] 5179[11] 5617[12]

Miskin Nights *B Palling* 68
2 b f Zafeen(FR) —Risalah (Marju (IRE))
2771[14] 3500[3] 4163[5]

Miskin Spirit *B Palling* a40 43
3 b f Bertolini(USA) —Risalah (Marju (IRE))
6741[9] 7067[11] 7278[10] 7459[8]

Misphire *M Dods* 85
6 b m Mister Baileys—Bombay Sapphire (Be My Chief (USA))
2102[10] 2938[12] 3339[5] 4228[5] 5363[8] 6847 [10] 7172[14]

Misplaced Fortune *N Tinkler* a46 84
4 b m Compton Place—Tide Of Fortune (Soviet Star (USA))
1244[10] (1846) (2312) 3057[2] 3706[4] 4285[3] 5007[4] 5697[6] 6020[2] (6764) 7189[5] 7287[3]

Miss Antonia (IRE) *H R A Cecil* a69 75
2 b f Antonius Pius(USA) —Masharik (IRE) (Caerleon (USA))
5752[3] ◆ 6284[4] 6920[4]

Miss Beat (IRE) *B J Meehan* a73 89
3 b f Beat Hollow—Bolas (Unfuwain (USA))
1315[3] 2001[7] 2190[5] 2846[9] 3870[6]

Miss Blueandblack (IRE) *Jean-Rene Auvray*
3 ch f Hawkeye(IRE) —Don't Tell Trigger (IRE) (Mujadil (USA))
6941[10]

Miss Bootylishes *A B Haynes* a74 76
4 b m Mujahid(USA) —Moxby (Efisio)
1256[6] (4266) 5723[7] 6790[8] 7172[2] 7337[6] 7762[4]

Miss California *Miss Tor Sturgis* 31
2 b f Mtoto—Lightning Princess (Puissance)
6567[12]

Miss Cameo (USA) *R M Whitaker* a50 56
3 b f Mizzen Mast(USA) —Angela Niner (USA) (Forty Niner (USA))
134[3] ◆ 1281[3] 1481[2] 1725[P]

Miss Chamanda (IRE) *P D Evans* a78 89
3 ch f Choisir(AUS) —Smandar (USA) (Sahm (USA))
852[3] 1305[7] 1870[8] (3219) 4167[9] 4380[3] (5098) 5436[5] 5856[5]

Miss Chaumiere *M L W Bell*
2 b f Selkirk(USA) —Miss Corniche (Hernando (FR))
4460[13]

Miss Christophene (IRE) *Mrs S Lamyman* a73 67
3 bl f Christophene(USA) —Lotus Flower (IRE) (Grand Lodge (USA))
151[2] (488) (689) 2356[9] 4799[5] 5034[10] 5329[8]

Miss Clarice (USA) *J R Jenkins* a49 56
4 bb m Mr Greeley(USA) —Mutton Maniac (USA) (Wolf Power (SAF))
760[3] 867[11]

Miss Cracklinrosie *J R Weymes* a54 60
3 b f Tobougg(IRE) —Anatase (Danehill (USA))
450[5] 677[12] 968[4] 1281[13] 2528[7]

Miss Cueta (IRE) *M Halford* a58 66
2 b f Rock Of Gibraltar(IRE) —Miss Serendipity (IRE) (Key Of Luck (USA))
6317a[12]

Miss Daawe *B Ellison* a58 74
5 b m Daawe(USA) —Feiticeira (USA) (Deposit Ticket (USA))
1310[11] 1411[4] 2046[5] 2436[3] 3153[3] 3354[5] 3938[5] 4283[7] 4355[6] 4464[2] 4754[5] 5836[9] 6010[23] 6489[10] 6799[15]

Miss Dee Lady (IRE) *Patrick Morris* 19
3 ch f Captain Rio—Windomen (IRE) (Forest Wind (USA))
1228[11] 3614[10]

Miss Doodle *Eve Johnson Houghton* a39 62
3 ch f Dubai Destination(USA) —Running Flame (IND) (Steinbeck (USA))
3025[8] 3538[3] 4270[6] 4911[6] 5430[12]

Miss Dreamy *P C Haslam*
2 b f Whipper(USA) —Highest Dream (IRE) (Highest Honor (FR))
1623[10]

Missed Mondays *Patrick Morris* a53 42
3 ch f Distant Music(USA) —Lilting Prose (IRE) (Indian Ridge)
626[5] 831[11] 1465[11] 2132[6] 2593[5] 7069[7]

Miss Europa (GER) *P Schiergen* 107
3 b f Monsun(GER) —Miss Hoeny (USA) (Rahy (USA))
(2524a) 3604a[2]

Miss Eze *M L W Bell* a78 81
3 b f Danehill Dancer(IRE) —Miss Corniche (Hernando (FR))
2079[10] ◆ 2270[10] 3981[6] 6731[8] 7158[2] 7362[5]

Miss Fancy Pants *Noel Meade* a62 83
5 gr m Act One—Sweetness Herself (Unfuwain (USA))
7263a[11]

Miss Ferney *A Kirtley* 62
5 ch m Cayman Kai(IRE) —Jendorcet (Grey Ghost)
3350[10] 3490[15] 4068[6] (4818) (4944) 5423[3] 5732[6] 6218[2]

Miss Firefly *R J Hodges* a66 65
4 b m Compton Place—Popocatepetl (FR) (Nashwan (USA))
1787[12] 2180[2] ◆ 2758[6] 3505[6] 3671[7] 3926[2] 3994[3] 4736[3] 5065[6] 5632[3] 5792[7] 6251[2] 6587[10] 7371[4] 7771[8]

Miss Frangipane (IRE) *J Noseda* a67 70
3 b f Acclamation—Snap Crackle Pop (IRE) (Statoblest)
3338[4] ◆ 4324[3] 4913[2] 5599[2] (5971) 6701[3]

Miss Fritton (IRE) *M Botti* a67 66
3 b f Refuse To Bend(IRE) —Golly Gosh (IRE) (Danehill (USA))
(322) 450[8]

Miss Gibboa (IRE) *P C Haslam* 50
3 ch f Spartacus(IRE) —Ludovica (Bustino)
1281[9] 1724[7] 2790[7] 4142[7]

Miss Gibbs *P D Evans* 34
2 b f Needwood Blade—Katy-Q (IRE) (Taufan (USA))
1577[10]

Miss Glitters (IRE) *H Morrison* a90 78
4 b m Chevalier(IRE) —Geht Schnell (Fairy King (USA))
1185[4] ◆ (1476) 2011[2] (2133) 2639[8] 3509[6] 4592[6] 5375[8] (7092) 7759[2]

Miss Gorica (IRE) *Ms Joanna Morgan* a101 105
5 b m Mull Of Kintyre(USA) —Allegorica (IRE) (Alzao (USA))
(180a) 259a[3] 433a[5] 611a[7] 700a[10] 2555a[2] 3434a[7] 3516a[4] 7007a[7]

Miss Hollybell *J Gallagher* a53 74
3 b f Umistim—Hollybell (Beveled (USA))
1814[8] 2227[6] (2776) 3592[5] 4148[12] 6997[9] 7327[10] 7518[10]

Missionaire (USA) *W J Knight* 82
2 bb c El Corredor(USA) —Fapindy (USA) (A.P. Indy (USA))
2771[2] (3395) 4294[5] 5399[4]

Mission Control (IRE) *Tim Vaughan* a83 73
4 ch g Dubai Destination(USA) —Stage Manner (In The Wings)
139[6] (319) 511[2] 591[3] 899[5] 7515[4]

Mission Impossible *Miss Tracy Waggott* a70 80
4 gr g Kyllachy—Eastern Lyric (Petong)
329[7] 606[9] 1060[14] 3999[10] 4894[9] 6221[10] 6985[8] (7241)

Mission Lodge *B J Meehan* 22
3 b f Selkirk(USA) —Hiddendale (IRE) (Indian Ridge)
2139[13] 2847[9]

Miss Isle Control *A J McCabe* a32
2 ch f Monsieur Bond(IRE) —Sea Isle (Selkirk (USA))
5638[8] 6181[8] 6567[P] 6874[9]

Mississippian (IRE) *C J Mann* a63 54
5 b g Montjeu(IRE) —Swilly (USA) (Irish River (FR))
4378[13] 5779[7] 6288[7] 6909[9]

Miss Jabba (IRE) *Miss J Feilden* a40 43
3 b f Bertolini(USA) —Najaaba (USA) (Bahhare (USA))
6005[7] 6611[9] 6787[3] 7499[8] 7653[10]

Miss Jodarah (USA) *J R Best* a47 16
3 b f Action This Day(USA) —Suzie Diamond (USA) (Secreto (USA))
4789[10] 5193[10] 5614[8] 5744[10] 6166[7] 6417[5]

Miss Kadee *J S Moore* a44 55
3 ch f Needwood Blade—Deco Lady (Wolfhound (USA))
1772[9] 2009[9] 2630[6]

Miss Kamikaze (FR) *M Boutin* a54 46
2 b f Agnes Kamikaze(JPN) —Myliane (FR) (Nombre Premier)
6751a[8]

Miss Keck *G A Swinbank* a63 73
5 b m Inchinor—En Vacances (IRE) (Old Vic)
621[3] 779[4] 978[3] 1242[5] 1648[6] 2344[7] (2725) 3191[4] 3940[3] (4551) 4890[4] 5625[5]

Miss Keller (IRE) *John M Oxx* 94
3 b f Montjeu(IRE) —Ingozi (Warning)
3894a[4]

Miss Kitty Grey (IRE) *J R Boyle* 50
2 gr f One Cool Cat(USA) —Nortolixa (FR) (Linamix (FR))
4302[6] 4688[11]

Miss Kittyhawk (IRE) *Rae Guest* 66
3 b f Hawk Wing(USA) —Canterbury Lace (USA) (Danehill (USA))
3168[3] 3660[4] 4097[9] 6101[4] 6787[12]

Miss Lady Kiang (FR) *A Rudelin* 35
4 br m Sin Kiang(FR) —Mystery Lady (FR) (Le Pommier D'Or)
5013a[7]

Miss Lauz *R Hannon* 34
2 b f Whipper(USA) —Absolve (USA) (Diesis)
2161[5] 2604[8] 3626[5]

Miss Leona *J M Bradley* 28
3 b f Kyllachy—Feather Circle (IRE) (Indian Ridge)
5500[7]

Miss Lesley *D K Ivory* a75 78
2 b f Needwood Blade—You Found Me (Robellino (USA))
1147[5] 2135[3] 2575[2] 3733[2] (4147) 4539[5] 6619[13] 7290[16] 7435[7] 7661[4] ◆ (7805) 7871[5]

Miss Marani (IRE) *W G M Turner* a13 20
2 b f Statue Of Liberty(USA) —Countess Bankes (Son Pardo)
1653[8] 1783[8]

Miss Maren (NZ) *Mick Price* 112
5 ch m Stravinsky(USA) —Deebee Lady (NZ) (Brilliant Invader (AUS))
7196a[2]

Miss Medusa *Mrs C A Dunnett* a16
4 b m Medicean—College Night (IRE) (Night Shift (USA))
626[8]

Miss Minnies (IRE) *David P Myerscough* a84 76
3 bb f Fraam—Gold Majesty (Josr Algarhoud (IRE))
(5780) 5884[5]

Miss Miracle *C G Cox* 68
2 gr f Motivator—Miracle (Ezzoud (IRE))
5397[4] ◆ 6062[5]

Miss Mittagong (USA) *R M Beckett* a54 75
2 b f Pleasantly Perfect(USA) —Go Go (USA) (Falstaff (USA))
6163[11] 7182[3]

Miss Mojito (IRE) *J W Hills* a66 73
3 ch f Lucky Story(USA) —Lamanka Lass (USA) (Woodman (USA))
214[2] 667[6] 817[2] 1253[12] 2515[5] (2950) 3302[2] 3843[4] 5169[9] (5602) 6243[9]

Miss Moloney (IRE) *Mrs S Lamyman* a45 46
3 b f Sesaro(USA) —Mickey Towbar (IRE) (Mujadil (USA))
620[11] 3305[11]

Miss Mujanna *J Akehurst* a77 73
4 b m Mujahid(USA) —Robanna (Robellino (USA))
191[4] 1288[8] (2949) 3581[5] 4060[5] 4714[6] 5810[10]

Miss Naline (FR) *Andreas Lowe* 92
4 b m Trempolino(USA) —Miss Naelle (FR) (Al Nasr (FR))
3493a[5] 7387a[5]

Missoula (IRE) *Miss Suzy Smith* 92
6 b m Kalanisi(IRE) —Medway (IRE) (Shernazar)
2486[14] 2994[17]

Miss Pelling (IRE) *B J Meehan* a69 73
4 b m Danehill Dancer(IRE) —Morningsurprice (USA) (Future Storm (USA))
1845[2] 2332[2] (3076)

Miss Perfectionist *P Howling* a67 43
3 b f Invincible Spirit(IRE) —To The Woods (IRE) (Woodborough (USA))
3299[11] 3955[6] 4375[13] 5775[6] 7195[4] 7599[10] 7818 [12]

Miss Polly Plum *C A Dwyer* a43
2 b f Doyen(IRE) —Mrs Plum (Emarati (USA))
7772[8]

Miss Porky *R Hollinshead* 61
3 b f Deportivo—Carati (Selkirk (USA))
1173[5] 1451[5] 1840[8] 2950[5]

Missprint *B P J Baugh*
2 b f Ishiguru(USA) —Miss Up N Go (Gorytus (USA))
7556[13]

Miss Pusey Street *P D Evans* a43 51
3 ch f Compton Place—Pusey Street Girl (Gildoran)
1045[4] 1840[13] 4643[8] 4732[2] 5155[4] 5336[3] 5362[10] 5629[13] 7645[8] 7770[5] 7838[10]

Miss Reel (FR) *F Rohaut*
2 b f Country Reel(USA) —Dame Carcas (FR) (Shining Steel)
6325a[4]

Missrepresentation *J C Fox* 55
3 b f Intikhab(USA) —Fairy Story (IRE) (Persian Bold)
2081[6] 2947[13] 3278[6] 4266[10] 5602[P]

Miss Roma (IRE) *R A Harris* a34 35
2 b f Le Vie Dei Colori—Saffa Garden (IRE) (King's Best (USA))
1534[8] 4100[6] 4370[7] 4689[4] 6328[8]

Miss Sampower (IRE) *D Carroll*
3 b f Sampower Star—Miss Mimosa (IRE) (Salmon Leap (USA))
251[11]

Miss Scarlet *K A Ryan* 64
3 b f Red Ransom(USA) —Give Warning (IRE) (Warning)
2091[18] 3305[12]

Miss Serena *Mrs P Sly* a75 76
4 gr m Singspiel(IRE) —Valnerina (IRE) (Caerleon (USA))
723[5] 899[4] 1215[5] 2163[11]

Miss Smilla *K A Ryan* a74 77
2 b f Red Ransom(USA) —Snowing (Tate Gallery (USA))
1097[4] (3858) 4306[5] 5762[4] 6232[4] 7003[3]

Miss Sophisticat *W J Knight* a76 77
3 b f Alhaarth(IRE) —She's Classy (USA) (Boundary (USA))
1430[7] 2138[6] 2942[5] 3708[2] 4151[5] 4720[2] 5449[7] 6223[4] (6909) (7204) 7248[10] 7399[10]

Miss Starlight *P J McBride* a78 66
2 b f Trade Fair—Redeem (IRE) (Doyoun)
5398[6] (6125) 7434[8]

Miss Taken (IRE) *D Carroll* a55 67
2 b f Dubai Destination(USA) —Miss Takeortwo (IRE) (Danehill Dancer (IRE))
4067[2] 4398[3] 4659[5] 5515[8] 6232[6] 6431[12] 7088[5] 7333[4] 7421[4] 7501[2] 7584[8] 7756[3] 7791[3] 7868[5]

Miss Tango Hotel *J H M Gosden* 73
3 b f Green Desert(USA) —Inchyre (Shirley Heights)
1825[2] 2179[6]

Miss Tara (FR) *W Baltromei* 83
2 b f Country Reel(USA) —Miss Maybach (FR) (Monsun (GER))
4577a[3]

Miss Thippawan (USA) *P T Midgley* a43 43
3 bb f Street Cry(IRE) —Sheathanna (USA) (Mr. Leader (USA))
889[9] 1064[9] 2454[6]

Miss Tikitiboo (IRE) *E F Vaughan* a59 60
3 b f Elusive City(USA) —Sabindra (Magic Ring (IRE))
586[6] 753[3] 2918[5] 4749[P]

Miss Tonic (FR) *K Borgel* a73 67
5 b m Priolo(USA) —Tonic Stream (FR) (Bering)
5301a[2]

Miss Totnes *M Hill* 29
5 b m Bandmaster(USA) —Kingston Black (Shaab)
4828[10]

Miss Understanding *J R Weymes* a47 44
4 br m Dansili—Crossed Wire (Lycius (USA))
145[3] 368[9] 578[4] 647[6] 791[7] 1520[10] 1848[11]

Miss Wendy *M H Tompkins* a58 36
2 b f Where Or When(IRE) —Grove Dancer (Reprimand)
4427[8] 5637[3]

Miss Whippy *M L W Bell* 58
2 b f Whipper(USA) —Glorious (Nashwan (USA))
4757[4] (5319) 6232[3]

Miss Xu Xia *G R Oldroyd* a45 41
3 b f Monsieur Bond(IRE) —Bond Girl (Magic Ring (IRE))
5[3]

Miss Zooter (IRE) *R M Beckett* 80
2 b f Intikhab(USA) —Laraissa (Machiavellian (USA))
4688[5] 6544[6] (7061)

Mistaken Identity (FR) *P Bary* 100
3 b c Vettori(IRE) —Misplace (IRE) (Green Desert (USA))
1239a[4] 6891a[5] 7820a[3]

Mista Rossa *H Morrison* a75 75
4 br g Red Ransom(USA) —Cloud Hill (Danehill (USA))
(1287) 1807[2] 2283[5] 2497[7] 3273[7] 4644[3] 5642[5] (6210) 6758[7] 7036[2]

Mister Angry (IRE) *M Johnston* a84 87
2 b c Cape Cross(IRE) —Yaya (USA) (Rahy (USA))
3106[2] (3715) ◆ (3971) (4527) 5864[7] 6993[15] (7717)

Mister Arjay (USA) *B Ellison* a60 81
9 b g Mister Baileys—Crystal Stepper (USA) (Fred Astaire (USA))
1557[4] 1886[8] 2262[8]

Mister Benedictine *B W Duke* a58 81
6 b g Mister Baileys—Cultural Role (Night Shift (USA))
3734[8]

Mister Benji *B P J Baugh* a54 31
10 b g Catrail(USA) —Katy-Q (IRE) (Taufan (USA))
14[3] 150[7] 405[4] 608[3] 748[10] 867[4] 1131[7]

Mister Biscuit (USA) *Miss L A Perratt* 24
3 b g Proud Citizen(USA) —Nouvelle (USA) (Hazaam (USA))
4277[13] 4531[8] 5163[8] 6158[6] 6414[8]

Mister Bombastic (IRE) *N J Vaughan* 61
3 ch c Monsieur Bond(IRE) —Sheen Falls (IRE) (Prince Rupert (FR))
2779[8]

Mister Camilau (FR) *Mlle A Imaz-Ceca* 66
2 b c Sagacity(FR) —Land Bridge (FR) (Bering)
7264a[6]

Mister Charm (FR) *J-C Rouget* a79 16
9 gr g Linamix(FR) —Miss Sacha (IRE) (Last Tycoon)
7216a[5]

Mister Completely (IRE) *Ms J S Doyle* a73 62
8 b g Princely Heir(IRE) —Blue Goose (Belmez (USA))
2429[15] 3029[5]

Mister Dee Bee (IRE) *B W Hills* a53 96
3 b g Orpen(USA) —Acidanthera (Alzao (USA))
(1308) (1971) (2535) 3780[4] 4409[2]

Mister Fantastic *M Dods* 69
3 ch g Green Tune(USA) —Lomapamar (Nashwan (USA))
1252[3] 2845[14] 5335[7] 5672[11]

Mister Fasliyev (IRE) *E Charpy* a97 87
7 b g Fasliyev(USA) —Carisheba (USA) (Alysheba (USA))
337a[6] 419a[11] 640a[10]

Mister Fizzbomb (IRE) *T D Walford* a62 73
6 b g Lend A Hand—Crocus (IRE) (Mister Baileys)
(4755) 4893[2] 5210[6] 5469[7] 6236[5]

Mister Frosty (IRE) *G Prodromou* a55 57
3 gr g Verglas(IRE) —La Chinampina (FR) (Darshaan)
1584[7] 2416[8] 2863[7] 3551[8] 3923[9] 7666[8] 7766[3] 7794[2] 7851[5]

Mister Green (FR) *K McAuliffe* a81 88
3 b g Green Desert(USA) —Summertime Legacy (Darshaan)
1803[9] 3028[9] 7664[2]

Mister Hardy *R A Fahey* a93 103
4 b g Kyllachy—Balladonia (Primo Dominie)
(1016) (1124) (1821) 3091[18] 3818[17] 4423[6] 6089[13] 6270[6] 6815[4] 7294[11]

Mister Hughie (IRE) *M R Channon* 92
2 b c Elusive City(USA) —Bonne Mere (FR) (Stepneyev (IRE))
3256[6] 3606[3] 3918[3] 4282[5] (4689) (5033) 5945[2] 6048[2] (6247) 6486[5]

Mister Humphrey (FR) *J-P Carvalho* a70 70
3 b c Kendor(FR) —Princess Victoria (Deploy)
6682a[10]

Mister Incredible *J M Bradley* a56 3
6 b g Wizard King—Judiam (Primo Dominie)
62[6] 108[4] 198[5] 292[3] 474[8] 746[2] 1055[3] 1421[12] 1781[7]

Misterisland (IRE) *M Mullineaux* a29 46
4 b h Spectrum(IRE) —Carranita (IRE) (Anita's Prince)
7417[10] 7614[13] 7714[7] 7819 [9] 7858[7]

Mister Jingles *R M Whitaker* a61 66
6 ch g Desert Story(IRE) —Fairy Free (Rousillon (USA))
1475[3] 1723[3] 2531[6] 2804[5] 3448[5] 3689[3] 4140[11] 6023[10] 6415[3] (6674) 7240[2] 7348[9]

Mister Laurel *R A Fahey* 88
3 b g Diktat—Balladonia (Primo Dominie)
(1305) 1517[8] 2227[10] 2915[5] 3828[6] 4289[3] (4309) 4598[10]

Mister Lux (FR) *C Boutin* a48 62
3 b g Diableneyev(USA) —Luxukarada (FR) (Akarad (FR))
5012a[7]

Mister Manannan (IRE) *D Nicholls* 110
2 b c Desert Style(IRE) —Cover Girl (IRE) (Common Grounds)
1304[3] ◆ (1610) ◆ 2995[9] 4407[2] ◆ 5174[2] 5822[3] (6049)

Mister Maq *A Crook* a27 48
6 b g Namaqualand(USA) —Nordico Princess (Nordico (USA))
237^6 1276^4 1556^7 2261^{12} 2965^5

Mister Minister (GER) *C Von Der Recke* a67 70
4 ch h Artan(IRE) —Misniniski (Niniski (USA))
465a^2 652a^7

Mister New York (USA) *Noel T Chance* a89 68
4 b h Forest Wildcat(USA) —Shebane (USA) (Alysheba (USA))
17^4 225^4 283^3 538^4 2775^{10} 3509^{11} 4060^{12} 5649^5 6724^3 (7066) 7233^9 7720^2 7811 ^{4}

Mister Pete (IRE) *W Storey* 66
6 b g Piccolo—Whistfilly (First Trump)
1058^6 1242^6 2044^3 2614^5 3068^9

Mister Ross *G L Moore* a84 89
4 b g Medicean—Aqualina (IRE) (King's Theatre (IRE))
1603^8 ◆ 2188^{16}

Mister Standfast *J M P Eustace* a50 58
3 b g Haafhd—Off The Blocks (Salse (USA))
1594^P

Mister Tee *G M Lyons* a100 105
2 b g Danehill Dancer(IRE) —Clipper (Salse (USA))
5275a^2 5895a^3

Mister Tinktastic (IRE) *M Dods* 84
3 ch g Noverre(USA) —Psychic (IRE) (Alhaarth (IRE))
1062^2 1736^8 2786^6 (2970) (3193) 3727^3 (4664) 4776^3 5148^{11}

Mister Trickster (IRE) *R Dickin* a61 61
8 b g Woodborough(USA) —Tinos Island (IRE) (Alzao (USA))
496^2 657^8 1199^2 1606^3 2332^6 2830^3 3735^7 6588^6 6909^{10}

Mister Wilberforce *M Mullineaux*
3 b g Paris House—She's A Breeze (Crofthall)
3498^9 5987^{13}

Mistic Academy (IRE) *Miss J E Foster* 26
4 ch m Royal Academy(USA) —Mistic Sun (Dashing Blade)
4599^{11} 4974^6 6022^7 6390^{12}

Mistic Magic (IRE) *P F I Cole* 87
2 b f Orpen(USA) —Mistic Sun (Dashing Blade)
2919^4 (3249) 4245^8 6481^4 7033^{10}

Mistoffelees *L M Cumani* a64 29
3 b c Tiger Hill(IRE) —Auenlust (GER) (Surumu (GER))
5322^8 5987^6 6287^5

Mistress Cooper *W J Musson* a65 68
4 bb m Kyllachy—Litewska (IRE) (Mujadil (USA))
118^9 461^3

Mistress Eva *L Corcoran* a62 76
4 br m Diktat—Foreign Mistress (Darshaan)
142^7

Mistress Greeley (USA) *M Botti* a64 85
4 ch m Mr Greeley(USA) —My Reem (USA) (Chief's Crown (USA))
694^7

Misty Dancer *Miss Venetia Williams* 87
10 gr g Vettori(IRE) —Light Fantastic (Deploy)
6302^8 6734^{11}

Misty Kit *W M Brisbourne* a18
4 b m Umistim—River Ensign (River God (USA))
7648^{11} 7670^{10}

Misyaar (IRE) *M A Jarvis* a65
3 b f Dubai Destination(USA) —Saafeya (IRE) (Sadler's Wells (USA))
138^6 280^5 356^4

Mith Hill *Ian Williams* 83
8 b g Daylami(IRE) —Delirious Moment (IRE) (Kris)
(5857) 6273^3 6676^2

Mito *B R Millman* 47
8 b m Mtoto—Shibui (Shirley Heights)
2877^8 3503^6 3798^P

Mitra Jaan (IRE) *W R Swinburn* a71 67
3 b f Diktat—Persian Lass (IRE) (Grand Lodge (USA))
1574^6 2892^6 3693^5 5806^9

Mixfeeling (IRE) *C Laffon-Parias* 70
2 b f Red Ransom(USA) —Goldamix (IRE) (Linamix (FR))
4577a^8

Mixing *M J Attwater* a65 57
7 gr g Linamix(FR) —Tuning (Rainbow Quest (USA))
848^8 1081^7 1200^4 1287^8 2182^5 (2601) 3247^2 3521^6 4235^{10} 5577^7 6226^P 6704^{11} 7368^7 7688^{10} 7766^8

Mix N Match *R M Stronge* a59 35
5 b g Royal Applause—South Wind (Tina's Pet)
100^3 (186) 494^3 2830^5 4300^{12}

Miyasaki (CHI) *Rune Haugen* a91 90
7 b g Memo(CHI) —Cantame Al Oido (CHI) (Yendaka (USA))
7185^8

Mizair Nouvair (IRE) *J R Weymes* a14 18
2 b g Noverre(USA) —Arzachena (FR) (Grand Lodge (USA))
4503^{14} 4993^{10} 5224^9

M'Lady Rousseur (IRE) *D R C Elsworth* a61 59
3 ch f Selkirk(USA) —Millay (Polish Precedent (USA))
1729^8 2488^3 3025^5 4054^8 5782^6 6446^2 6807^4 (7025)

Mlle Lando (GER) *M Rulec* 71
2 b f Lando(GER) —Mlle Angelique (GER) (Law Society (USA))
6151a^7

Mme De Stael *Sir Mark Prescott* 53
2 ch f Selkirk(USA) —Scandalette (Niniski (USA))
6389^9 6759^9 6920^{12} 7244^3

Mnarani (IRE) *J S Moore* a61 66
2 b g Oasis Dream—Finity (USA) (Diesis)
2430^7 2793^8 2875^4 4901^9 5274a^{13} 7604^8

Mnasikia (USA) *L M Cumani* a66
2 b f Rahy(USA) —Entendu (USA) (Diesis)
7001^{10} 7772^3 7859^2

Moandei *R Ingram* a53 54
5 b m Silver Wizard(USA) —Its All Too Much (Chaddleworth (IRE))
455^7

Moayed *N P Littmoden* a70 67
10 b g Selkirk(USA) —Song Of Years (IRE) (Shareef Dancer (USA))
554^4 725^5 867^4 959^{10} 1153^2

Mocha Java *Matthew Salaman* a69 46
6 b g Bertolini(USA) —Coffee Cream (Common Grounds)
23^5 78^3 210^4 (327) 496^5 (607) 1710^9 2137^{10} 2876^8 (3467) 3983^9 4375^7 5634^8 6458^3 7129^4 7348^6 7521^4 7679^2 ◆ 7845^8

Mochua (IRE) *Adrian Sexton* 33
5 ch g Moscow Society(USA) —Devilabit (IRE) (Buckskin (FR))
621^{11}

Modeyra *Saeed Bin Suroor* 83
2 br f Shamardal(USA) —Zahrat Dubai (Unfuwain (USA))
(6992) ◆

Mogadishio (FR) *A Couetil* 78
2 br c American Post—Nebraska I (FR) (Octagonal (NZ))
(6928a)

Moggy (IRE) *G A Harker* a50 54
3 br f One Cool Cat(USA) —Termania (IRE) (Shirley Heights)
2942^{12} 3629^2 4065^2 4943^8 6098^4 6219^3 6840^6 7324^{12}

Mogok Ruby *L Montague Hall* a86 82
5 gr g Bertolini(USA) —Days Of Grace (Wolfhound (USA))
128^5 (212) ◆ 533^3 (600) 780^3 892^6 1668^3 1864^{12} 2980^{14} 5031^{15} 6201^7 6723^8 7026^8 7702^9

Mohanad (IRE) *M R Channon* a71 76
3 b g Invincible Spirit(IRE) —Irish Design (IRE) (Alhaarth (IRE))
440^4 824^4 1614^6 2567^7 3575^6

Mohathab (IRE) *Tim Vaughan* a83 86
4 b g Cadeaux Genereux—Zeiting (IRE) (Zieten (USA))
(1380) 1673^{15} 4526^7 5095^2 5772^6 7574^7 7734^6

Mohawk Ridge *M Dods* a53 68
3 b g Storming Home—Ipsa Loquitur (Unfuwain (USA))
1470^8 2091^2 3018^3 3684^4 (5306) 5672^5 6052^3 6860^8

Mohawk Star (IRE) *I A Wood* a75 69
8 ch g Indian Ridge—Searching Star (Rainbow Quest (USA))
1215^{10} 1435^6 3986^2 4301^4 4951^9

Moheebb (IRE) *Mrs R A Carr* a63 98
5 b g Machiavellian(USA) —Rockerlong (Deploy)
1100^4 1722^5 2073^6 (2274) 2440^2 2894^3 3265^4 3872^{17} 4102^3 (4549) (4597) 4930^8 5137^3 5437^8 6013^{11}

Mohtashem (IRE) *Sir Michael Stoute* a87 85
3 b c Haafhd—Showering (Danehill (USA))
1729^3 ◆ 2165^3 (2885) ◆ 3816^9 4549^{13} 5070^3 5665^9

Moi Mel *L A Mullaney*
2 b f Danbird(AUS) —Lady Double U (Sheikh Albadou)
4396^{14}

Moiqen (IRE) *Kevin Prendergast* 108
4 b g Red Ransom(USA) —Za Aamah (USA) (Mr Prospector (USA))
1758a^3 2303a^4 3700a^4

Mojave Moon *A Fabre* 100
3 br c Singspiel(IRE) —Moon Cactus (Kris)
5297a^2 5711a^6

Mojeerr *A J McCabe* a55 54
3 b g Royal Applause—Princess Miletrian (IRE) (Danehill (USA))
5982^{10} 6184^3 6371^6 7143^3 7374^3 7499^9 7796^3

Mojito Royale (IRE) *Eoin Doyle* a99 99
5 b g Val Royal(FR) —Beseeching (IRE) (Hamas (IRE))
335a^3 439a^{10} 609a^9 697a^5

Molitor (FR) *A Spanu* 72
7 ch g Almutawakel—Missanticia (FR) (Sicyos (USA))
(7387a)

Molly Max (GER) *M Rulec* 100
5 ch h Big Shuffle(USA) —Molly Dancer (GER) (Shareef Dancer (USA))
2113a^8

Molly The Witch (IRE) *W J Musson* a59 59
3 b f Rock Of Gibraltar(IRE) —Tree Peony (Woodman (USA))
4145^9 ◆ (4719) 6124^9 6705^{12}

Molly Two *L A Mullaney* a53 71
4 ch m Muhtarram(USA) —Rum Lass (Distant Relative)
(1591) 2046^9 2472^6 4662^7 4929^{11} 5149^7 5341^{12} 6314^7 6553^9 6877^{10}

Molnaya (IRE) *A Manuel* a49 33
3 b c Statue Of Liberty(USA) —Minerwa (GER) (Protektor (GER))
258a^{12}

Molon Labe (IRE) *T P Tate* 73
2 ch g Footstepsinthesand—Pillars Of Society (IRE) (Caerleon (USA))
5000^{10} 6763^6 7243^2

Moment Of Clarity *R C Guest* a71 66
7 b g Lujain(USA) —Kicka (Shirley Heights)
194^5 285^{13} 420^2 554^{13}

Mo Mhuirnin (IRE) *R A Fahey* a63 84
3 b f Danetime(IRE) —Cotton Grace (IRE) (Case Law)
1592^3 1831^3 2157^3 2786^2 (2967) (3381) ◆ 3746^2 5175^9 5607^9

Momtaz *C E Brittain* a44 70
2 b f Motivator—Sahra Alsalam (USA) (Gone West (USA))
5741^4 ◆ 6164^{11} 6628^{11}

Monaadema (IRE) *W J Haggas* 81
4 b m Elnadim(USA) —Suhaad (Unfuwain (USA))
(2565)

Monaadi (IRE) *R Hollinshead* a68 56
4 b g Singspiel(IRE) —Bint Albaadiya (USA) (Woodman (USA))
178^4 (448) 692^3 835^3 899^6 1171^5 2337^2 2445^8 2783^{12} 3594^8

Monaco (GER) *L M Cumani* a76
3 b c Monsun(GER) —Miss Holsten (USA) (Diesis)
5840^2

Monaco Dream (IRE) *W Jarvis* a71 74
3 b f Hawk Wing(USA) —Parvenue (FR) (Ezzoud (IRE))
440^3 1804^8 2633^2 3056^4

Monaco Mistress (IRE) *N Tinkler* 55
3 b f Acclamation—Bendis (GER) (Danehill (USA))
1725^{10} 3727^{10} 7173^{12} 7425^{13}

Monagasque (IRE) *S Kirk* a34 37
3 ch f King Charlemagne(USA) —Amiela (FR) (Mujtahid (USA))
2318^7 2652^6 3228^6 4991^8 5328^{12}

Monahullan Prince *Gerard Keane* a76 68
8 b g Pyramus(USA) —Classic Artiste (USA) (Arctic Tern (USA))
(6803)

Monalini (IRE) *B Smart* 76
2 b g Bertolini(USA) —Mona Em (IRE) (Catrail (USA))
(1097) 4752^5 5198^{19} 5467^{10} 6534^8

Monashee Rock (IRE) *Matthew Salaman* a71 76
4 b m Monashee Mountain(USA) —Polar Rock (Polar Falcon (USA))
3258^2 3662^3 3996^3 5063^6 5544^3 6370^4 6782^4 7110^8 (7412) 7520^2 7662^4 7716^4

Monba (USA) *Todd Pletcher* a114 102
4 gr h Maria's Mon(USA) —Hamba (USA) (Easy Goer (USA))
789a^4

Mon Brav *D Carroll* 76
2 b c Sampower Star—Danehill Princess (IRE) (Danehill (USA))
(2258) ◆ 2702^7 3871^4

Mon Cadeaux *A M Balding* 99
2 b c Cadeaux Genereux—Ushindi (IRE) (Montjeu (IRE))
4318^2 (4900) 5743^7 (6398) ◆

Mondego (GER) *George Baker* a69
7 b g Big Shuffle(USA) —Molto In Forma (GER) (Surumu (GER))
(6831) (6917)

Mondovi *Tom Dascombe* a96 95
5 b m Kyllachy—Branston Fizz (Efisio)
(6253) 6843^9 7202^9 7676^8

Mondovino (FR) *Rod Collet* a88 104
6 b h Black Minnaloushe(USA) —Divinite (USA) (Alleged (USA))
1762a^8

Monetaire (FR) *C Laffon-Parias* 77
3 b c Anabaa(USA) —Monitrice (FR) (Groom Dancer (USA))
2293a^5

Monetary Fund (USA) *G A Butler* a88 83
3 b g Montjeu(IRE) —Maddie G (USA) (Blush Rambler (USA))
1289^6 1888^2 2317^5 4045^5 4838^3 5259^2 (5773) 6360^3 6613^7

Monet's Gold *Mme C Jung* a61 70
4 b g Peintre Celebre(USA) —Golden Wings (USA) (Devil's Bag (USA))
5074a^7

Moneycantbuymelove (IRE) *M L W Bell* 115
3 b f Pivotal—Sabreon (Caerleon (USA))
1291^5 ◆ 1701^3 (2190) (3016) 4522^3 6510a^4

Money For Nothing (FR) *R Pritchard-Gordon*
2 ch c Dubai Destination(USA) —Carmel (FR) (Highest Honor (FR))
3935a^0 6751a^0

Money Lender *N J Vaughan* 45
3 b c Lend A Hand—Ellen Mooney (Efisio)
1611^5

Money Money Money *P Winkworth* a64 62
3 b f Generous(IRE) —Shi Shi (Alnasr Alwasheek)
1580^6 2204^6

Moneysupermarket (IRE) *Patrick Morris* a43 51
3 b f Acclamation—Almaviva (IRE) (Grand Lodge (USA))
1120^5 1825^{12} 2700^4 3651^5 4343^6 4777^4 5158^6 5881^7 7051^{13}

Money Trader (IRE) *J T Gorman* 82
2 br c Trade Fair—Honey For Money (IRE) (Alzao (USA))
7258a^6

Monfils Monfils (USA) *R E Barr* a74 83
7 b g Sahm(USA) —Sorpresa (USA) (Pleasant Tap (USA))
477^3 656^3 932^6 (1000) 1125^7 1175^2 1366^5 1665^7 2068^7 2505^6 3068^8 3350^7 4345^8 (4402) 4972^6 5438^{11} 6769^8 7851^8

Monitor Closely (IRE) *P W Chapple-Hyam* 117
3 b c Oasis Dream—Independence (Selkirk (USA))
1291^2 1675^8 2014^4 3050^3 4329^5 (5134) 5861^3 ◆

Monivea (IRE) *Brian Nolan* 95
3 b f Fasliyev(USA) —Night Rhapsody (IRE) (Mujtahid (USA))
1024a^{10} 1911a^4 2304a^{10} 3516a^7 5686a^6

Monkey Glas (IRE) *J R Gask* a97 76
5 b h Mull Of Kintyre(USA) —Maura's Pet (IRE) (Prince Of Birds (USA))
113^7 452^8

Monkton Vale (IRE) *N Wilson* 65
2 b g Catcher In The Rye(IRE) —Byproxy (IRE) (Mujtahid (USA))
6046^3 ◆ 6982^6

Mon Mon (IRE) *G A Swinbank* a30
2 b f Refuse To Bend(IRE) —Adaja (Cadeaux Genereux)
7638^8

Monmouthshire *R J Price* a49 64
6 b g Singspiel(IRE) —Croeso Cariad (Most Welcome)
2912^{12} 3631^9

Mon Nono (IRE) *Mlle A Imaz-Ceca* 91
2 b c Statue Of Liberty(USA) —Alsu (IRE) (Fasliyev (USA))
4584a^6

Monograph *J W Hills* a61 51
2 b g Kyllachy—Beading (Polish Precedent (USA))
6054^{12} 6616^{10} 7859^8

Monomakh (USA) *A Chuguevets*
4 b h Mineshaft(USA) —Everhope (USA) (Danzig (USA))
(4369a)

Monopole (IRE) *P R Webber* 55
5 b g Montjeu(IRE) —Pretty (IRE) (Darshaan)
2981^5 3374^7

Mono's Only *Paul Mason* a55 18
3 br f Red Ransom(USA) —Mono Lady (IRE) (Polish Patriot (USA))
914^5 1198^{13}

Monreale (GER) *G Brown* 74
5 b g Silvano(GER) —Maratea (USA) (Fast Play (USA))
4091^7 7248^4

Monroe Gold *Jennie Candlish* a42 20
9 ch g Pivotal—Golden Daring (IRE) (Night Shift (USA))
712^5 3233^{11}

Mons Calpe (IRE) *P F I Cole* a65 74
3 b g Rock Of Gibraltar(IRE) —Taking Liberties (IRE) (Royal Academy (USA))
1416^8 1614^4 (1953) (2567) 2982^8 3321^5

Monsieur Bob (FR) *R Laplanche*
3 b g Anabaa(USA) —Dynella (FR) (Sillery (USA))
7820a^7

Monsieur Chevalier (IRE) *R Hannon* a106 108
2 b c Chevalier(IRE) —Blue Holly (IRE) (Blues Traveller (IRE))
(1195) ◆ (1290) ◆ (2136) (2408) 3046^5 (4089) (4407) 5172^3 5661^3 6522a^8

Monsieur Fillioux (USA) *J R Fanshawe* a79
3 ch g Hennessy(USA) —Eventually (USA) (Affirmed (USA))
4871^8 7830^2

Monsieur Harvey *B Smart* 37
3 ch g Monsieur Bond(IRE) —Annie Harvey (Fleetwood (IRE))
1852^5 2070^{11} 2343^7

Monsieur Joe (IRE) *W R Swinburn* a83 85
2 b c Choisir(AUS) —Pascali (Compton Place)
1404^2 ◆ 1862^3 (5282) (6068) 6550^5 6660^9

Monsieur Jourdain (IRE) *T D Easterby* 50
3 b g Royal Applause—Palwina (FR) (Unfuwain (USA))
4105^{13}

Monsieur Kiss Kiss *R J Osborne* 59
3 b c Monsieur Bond(IRE) —Known Class (USA) (Known Fact (USA))
5019^{15}

Monsieur Pontaven *R Bastiman* 28
2 b c Avonbridge—Take Heart (Electric)
5596^{12} 6896^8

Monsieur Reynard *J M Bradley* a72 82
4 ch g Compton Place—Tell Tale Fox (Tel Quel (FR))
1970^8 2124^9 2596^5 2801^9 3860^8 4736^9 5184^2 5345^8 5504^5 5792^3 6119^2 6456^2 6553^7 6939^9 7397^3 7601^2 7651^5

Montaff *M R Channon* 107
3 b c Montjeu(IRE) —Meshhed (USA) (Gulch (USA))
1872^2 2705^{12} 3087^9 4405^5 4760^2 6106^{13} 6202^4

Mont Agel *M L W Bell* 89
2 b c Danehill Dancer(IRE) —Miss Riviera Golf (Hernando (FR))
6000^3 ◆ (6548)

Montagne Lointaine (IRE) *N Clement* a71 102
4 b m Numerous(USA) —Memoire (FR) (Sadler's Wells (USA))
5089a^8

Montbretia *H R A Cecil* a92 98
4 b m Montjeu(IRE) —Bayswater (Caerleon (USA))
1642^4 2482^6

Mont Cervin *Mrs R A Carr* a58 74
4 b g Sakhee(USA) —Daylight Dreams (Indian Ridge)
224^{12} 420^4 580^{10} 607^{13} 760^{12} 2722^{12}

Montchara (IRE) *M Todhunter* a75 47
6 b g Montjeu(IRE) —Mochara (Last Fandango)
2159^6 3023^9

Monte Alto (IRE) *A Al Raihe* a96 98
5 b g Danehill Dancer(IRE) —Peruvian Witch (IRE) (Perugino (USA))
610a^7

Monte Cassino (IRE) *J O'Reilly* a64 64
4 ch g Choisir(AUS) —Saucy Maid (IRE) (Sure Blade (USA))
1951^{13} 2366^5 3125^4 3227^2 3720^7 4355^3 5073^8 6902^{10} 7503^{11} 7601^8 7834^9

Montecchio (IRE) *Kevin Prendergast* 101
2 gr c Acclamation—Fritta Mista (IRE) (Linamix (FR))
6318a^4

Montego Breeze *John A Harris* a46 51
3 b f Tipsy Creek(USA) —Mofeyda (IRE) (Mtoto)
6573^3 7126^7 7853^4

Montelissima (IRE) *E A L Dunlop* 62
2 b f Montjeu(IRE) —Issa (Pursuit Of Love)
4239^8 7183^6

Monte Major (IRE) *D Shaw* a67 42
8 b g Docksider(USA) —Danalia (IRE) (Danehill (USA))
89^3 146^3 431^2 (535) 596^9 681^5 832^8 1134^5 6456^3 7100^9 7280^6 7484^{10}

Monte Mayor Eagle *D Haydn Jones* a56 39
3 ch f Captain Rio—Ink Pot (USA) (Green Dancer (USA))
831^8 986^5 3862^{10} 4172^7 4812^7 4982^2 5326^2 5632^8 7002^8 7350^9

Monte Mayor One *D Haydn Jones* a38 65
2 b f Lujain(USA) —Alvarinho Lady (Royal Applause)
1841^5 2135^6 2972^7 3733^9 (4626) 5218^6 6619^{12} 7156^{11}

Monte Pattino (USA) *C J Teague* a51 64
5 ch g Rahy(USA) —Jood (USA) (Nijinsky (CAN))
1568^5 1780^4 (2159) 2344^2 2854^3 (3444) 3940^9

Monterey (IRE) *T G Mills* a68 40
2 b c Montjeu(IRE) —Magnificient Style (USA) (Silver Hawk (USA))
5831[7] *6772[4]*

Monteriggioni (IRE) *John Geoghegan* a102 103
7 b g Blue Ocean(USA) —Jibabit (IRE) (Waajib)
4412a[13]

Monterosso *M Johnston* a59
2 b c Dubawi(IRE) —Porto Roca (AUS) (Barathea (IRE))
7376[5]

Montiboli (IRE) *K A Ryan* a76 76
4 ch m Bahamian Bounty—Aunt Sadie (Pursuit Of Love)
94[7] 297[6] 557[4] 683[6] 1332[14] *2133[4]* 2542[4] (3070) (3689) 4346[4] 4496[2]

Montiyra (IRE) *Miss L C Siddall* 68
5 b g Montjeu(IRE) —Shiyra (Darshaan)
7336[11] 7495[11]

Montmartre (USA) *David Pinder* a36 62
3 b g Awesome Again(CAN) —Sacre Coeur (USA) (Saint Ballado (CAN))
2165[5] ◆ 2662[6] 2876[4] (3257) 5019[14] 5384[9] 5905[9] *6440[7]* 6787[7]

Montmorency (IRE) *S Seemar* a22 84
3 ch c Pivotal—Clear Spring (USA) (Irish River (FR))
524a[4] 769a[9]

Montpellier (IRE) *A Al Raihe* a86 99
6 br g Montjeu(IRE) —Ring Of Esteem (Mark Of Esteem (IRE))
260a[5] 335a[13] 696a[10]

Monyati *D M Simcock* a42
2 ch c Kyllachy—Mustique Dream (Don't Forget Me)
7663[11]

Monzante (USA) *Mike Mitchell* a112 116
5 gr g Maria's Mon(USA) —Danzante (USA) (Danzig (USA))
6687a[7] 7310a[6]

Mooakada (IRE) *J H M Gosden* a105 100
3 gr f Montjeu(IRE) —Sulaalah (IRE) (Darshaan)
2036[4] 3047[8] 4094[8] 6003[2] 6813[9] 7291[2] *7589[2]*

Moobeyn *M P Tregoning* a71 19
2 ch g Selkirk(USA) —Key Academy (Royal Academy (USA))
6627[11] 6965[9] *7276[3]*

Mood Music *Mario Hofer* a100 109
5 b g Kyllachy—Something Blue (Petong)
911[9] (1919a) 2523a[5] 3908a[10]

Moody Tunes *A P Jarvis* a58 86
6 b g Merdon Melody—Lady-Love (Pursuit Of Love)
2816[2] 2939[4] 3264[10] 4312[2] (4344) (4588) 4897[4] 6016[8] 7169[3]

Mooinooi *T D Walford* 64
2 b f Kyllachy—Amused (Prince Sabo)
3337[7] 4427[9] 5949[2] 6245[7]

Moojeh (IRE) *M Botti* a79
3 ch f King's Best(USA) —Bahareeya (USA) (Riverman (USA))
2710[7] 3025[4] (5572) 6667[8] 7456[7] (7830)

Moonage Daydream (IRE) *T D Easterby* a61 73
4 b g Captain Rio—Thelma (Blakeney)
1169[8] 1737[14] 1924[13] 2804[6] 3124[7] (4140) 4504[13] 5418[4] 6157[4] 6411[3] 6761[7]

Moonbalej *M Johnston* 57
2 ch g Motivator—Glam Rock (Nashwan (USA))
5401[12] 6136[7] 6930[13]

Moonbeam Dancer (USA) *D M Simcock* a80 65
3 bb f Singspiel(IRE) —Shepherd's Moon (USA) (Silver Hawk (USA))
1430[2] 5093[4] 5939[3] 6332[3] *(7368) 7461[7] (7515) 7701[2]*

Moon Crystal *E A L Dunlop* a76
4 b m Fasliyev(USA) —Sabreon (Caerleon (USA))
60[4] 176[3] (470) 651[2] 738[4] 830[2] 945[3]

Moondarra Blade *J R Weymes* 10
2 b g Needwood Blade—Beechy Bank (IRE) (Shareef Dancer (USA))
3119[8] 4188[11]

Moon Indigo *A P O'Brien* 95
3 b g Sadler's Wells(USA) —Solo De Lune (IRE) (Law Society (USA))
5891a[6]

Moonlife (IRE) *Saeed Bin Suroor* a107 104
3 b f Invincible Spirit(IRE) —Marania (IRE) (Marju (IRE))
2057[2] 3016[19] (6757) ◆ *(7132)* ◆

Moonlight Affair (IRE) *E S McMahon* 75
3 b f Distant Music(USA) —Petite Maxine (Sharpo)
1686[6] 2227[2] 3341[10] 4198[4]

Moonlight Babe (USA) *I W McInnes* 32
2 b f Thunder Gulch(USA) —Autumn Moon (USA) (Mr Prospector (USA))
2604[10] 3495[7] 4928[7] 5417[8]

Moonlight Blaze *C W Fairhurst* 59
2 b g Barathea(IRE) —Moonlight (IRE) (Night Shift (USA))
3310[8] 3823[10] 4888[5] 5515[11] 6901[8]

Moonlight Cass (IRE) *David P Myerscough* 69
2 b f Danehill Dancer(IRE) —Moon Drop (Dominion)
6317a[11]

Moonlight Man *C R Dore* a86 86
8 ch g Night Shift(USA) —Fleeting Rainbow (Rainbow Quest (USA))
1777[2] 1962[4] 7854[6]

Moon Lightning (IRE) *M H Tompkins* a76 73
3 b g Desert Prince(IRE) —Moon Tango (IRE) (Last Tycoon)
2209[8] 2504[8] 3551[5] 4284[3] 4562[4] 6052[7] 6157[13] 7149[6] 7246[12]

Moonlight Rock (IRE) *P D Deegan* 77
2 b f Rock Of Gibraltar(IRE) —Moonlight Dream (USA) (Banker's Gold (USA))
6708a[7]

Moonlight Serenade *W G M Turner* a54 54
2 b f Mind Games—Rasseem (IRE) (Fasliyev (USA))
1742[8] 1981[4] 2319[8] *7661[6] 7749[4] 7868[4] 7887[3]*

Moonline Dancer (FR) *R Hannon* 78
2 b f Royal Academy(USA) —Tulipe Noire (USA) (Alleged (USA))
4542[3] (5026) 6055[5] 6619[6]

Moon Mix (FR) *J R Jenkins* a88 76
6 gr g Linamix(FR) —Cherry Moon (USA) (Quiet American (USA))
311[9] 507[5] 1199[6] 1537[7] 3960[7] 4156[7] 4388[11]

Moon Money (IRE) *K A Ryan* a51 60
3 b g King's Theatre(IRE) —Last Drama (IRE) (Last Tycoon)
2943[6] 3680[2] 4014[6] 4432[9] 6184[8] 6559[5] *7025[4] 7425[9]*

Moonquake (USA) *Saeed Bin Suroor* a104 109
4 bb h Mr Greeley(USA) —Beaming Meteor (USA) (Pleasant Colony (USA))
337a[2] 612a[6] (1986) 3089[2] 3873[15]

Moonraker's Choice (IRE) *R Hannon* 61
2 ch f Choisir(AUS) —Staploy (Deploy)
3576[12] 4478[8]

Moonreach (IRE) *P D Deegan* a90 94
2 b c Chineur(FR) —Ribbon Glade (UAE) (Zafonic (USA))
5452a[5] 7072a[8]

Moonshine Beach *P W Hiatt* a66 64
11 b g Lugana Beach—Monongelia (Welsh Pageant)
2262[9]

Moonshine Creek *P W Hiatt* a70 70
7 b g Pyramus(USA) —Monongelia (Welsh Pageant)
871[10] (1178) (1581) 1786[8] 2497[6] 2983[2] *6832[6] 7212[4] (7440) 7695[2] 7779[2]*

Moon Sister (IRE) *W Jarvis* 103
4 b m Cadeaux Genereux—Tanz (IRE) (Sadler's Wells (USA))
1697[4] 2933[10] 3315[8] 4287[4] 5004[6]

Moonstreaker *R M Whitaker* a73 70
6 b g Foxhound(USA) —Ling Lane (Slip Anchor)
1279[6] 1615[10] 2237[12] 2527[5] 3314[4]

Moonwalking *Jedd O'Keeffe* a34 63
5 b g Danehill Dancer(IRE) —Macca Luna (IRE) (Kahyasi)
1000[5] 2445[9] 4600[5]

Moon Warrior *C Smith* a28 16
3 b g Yoshka—Lunalux (Emarati (USA))
2104[12]

Mooretown Lady (IRE) *H Rogers* a75 94
6 b m Montjeu(IRE) —Chaturanga (Night Shift (USA))
2870a[8] 3516a[12]

Moorhouse Girl *D H Brown* 70
2 b f Makbul—Record Time (Clantime)
4928[2] 5693[3]

Moorhouse Lad *B Smart* a91 116
6 b g Bertolini(USA) —Record Time (Clantime)
1676[14] 4456[11] 5233[9] 5765[7]

Moorside Diamond *A D Brown* a53 53
5 b m Elmaamul(USA) —Dispol Diamond (Sharpo)
78[12] 211[9] 469[14] 587[2] 792[9]

Moose Moran (USA) *H R A Cecil* a66
2 rg c Lemon Drop Kid(USA) —After All (IRE) (Desert Story (IRE))
6629[5]

Mooted (UAE) *Miss J A Camacho* a71 75
4 b g Mtoto—Assraar (Cadeaux Genereux)
2362[8] 3035[2] (3447)

Mooteeah (IRE) *M A Jarvis* a68 71
3 b f Sakhee(USA) —Cerulean Sky (IRE) (Darshaan)
(2488) 4068[3]

Mootriba *W J Haggas* a72 67
3 ch f Nayef(USA) —Tarbiyah (Singspiel (IRE))
2375[3] 3358[3]

Moral Duty (USA) *J S Moore* 69
4 ch h Silver Deputy(CAN) —Shoogle (USA) (A.P. Indy (USA))
4023[3] 4428[13] 5502[15]

Morana (IRE) *P W Chapple-Hyam* 108
2 b c Alhaarth(IRE) —Blushing Barada (USA) (Blushing Groom (FR))
5831[2] ◆ 6416[2] (6664) 7017[5]

Moran Gra (USA) *Ms Joanna Morgan* 93
2 ch g Rahy(USA) —Super Supreme (IND) (Zafonic (USA))
(2643a) 2993[4] 4487[7] 5275a[7] 6317a[9]

Morbick *W M Brisbourne* a78 55
5 ch g Kyllachy—Direcvil (Top Ville)
220[8] 428[3] 559[3] 660[2] 734[4]

More Bountiful (NZ) *J Size* 116
5 br g Van Nistelrooy(USA) —Centaine Gu Li (NZ) (Centaine (AUS))
1553a[8]

More For Less *T D Barron* 49
2 b g Danbird(AUS) —Patricia Philomena (IRE) (Prince Of Birds (USA))
1450[5] 1719[5] 2788[9]

More Lashes (USA) *M G Quinlan* a55 74
2 ch f More Than Ready(USA) —Red Piano (USA) (Red Ransom (USA))
2034[7] 3762[5] 3875[10] 4349[3] 4711[2] 4989[12] 5769[5] *6068[8]*

Moresco *W R Swinburn* a71 76
3 gr g Dalakhani(IRE) —Majoune (FR) (Take Risks (FR))
1151[5] *1431[6]* 4319[3] 4911[7]

Morestead (IRE) *B G Powell* a14 54
4 ch g Traditionally(USA) —Itsy Bitsy Betsy (USA) (Beau Genius (CAN))
4935[7]

Mores Wells *R Gibson* 118
5 b h Sadler's Wells(USA) —Endorsement (Warning)
2118a[6] 3089[5]

More Tea Vicar (IRE) *Patrick Morris* a63 45
3 b f Bahhare(USA) —Grand Splendour (Shirley Heights)
628[6] 1050[8] 3485[6] 4879[5] 5306[7] *5647[10]*

More Than Many (USA) *R A Fahey* 76
3 bb c More Than Ready(USA) —Slewnami (AUS) (Seattle Slew (USA))
(1281) ◆

More Time Tim (IRE) *J R Boyle* a93 78
4 b g Namid—Lady Nasrana (FR) (Al Nasr (FR))
115[3] 255[2] (323) (618) ◆ *(683) 747[9] (1964)* 2669[6] *(3928) 5615[3]* 6876[12]

Morgan Drive (IRE) *M Gasparini* 105
4 b h Namid—Morning Prancer (Caerleon (USA))
1905a[3] 6894a[2] (7206a)

Morgans Choice *J L Spearing* a37 73
2 b g Namid—Polar Dawn (Polar Falcon (USA))
3218[12] 4302[2] 5060[3] (5866) *6827[11]*

Moriwood (ITY) *S Botti* a78 96
5 b h Morigi—Black Wood (USA) (Woodman (USA))
7303a[10]

Mormeatmic *M W Easterby* a51 58
6 b g Orpen(USA) —Mimining (Tower Walk)
2389[4] 3002[17] 4552[10]

Morning Calm *R Charlton* 65
3 b f Montjeu(IRE) —Tempting Prospect (Shirley Heights)
2006[7] 2881[6] 3575[8] 4241[5]

Morning Dress (USA) *M Johnston* a28 40
3 rg g Smart Strike(CAN) —Black Tie Kiss (USA) (Danzig (USA))
4276[7] *4979[7]* 5322[10]

Morning Drive *W R Swinburn* a54
2 ch f Motivator—Bright Hope (IRE) (Danehill (USA))
6163[11]

Morning Queen (IRE) *C G Cox* a47 60
3 b f Night Shift(USA) —Woodland Glade (Mark Of Esteem (IRE))
2122[5] 2913[2] 3281[5] 4164[5]

Morning Sir Alan *S A Callaghan* a72 78
3 b c Diktat—Menhoubah (USA) (Dixieland Band (USA))
786[4] 939[2] 1130[3] 1428[2] 1707[9] *2488[2]* (2763) 3222[5]

Morning Spring *D Shaw*
4 b m Montjoy(USA) —Dino's Girl (Sabrehill (USA))
7863[9]

Morning View (USA) *J H M Gosden* a12
2 b f North Light(IRE) —Vignette (USA) (Diesis)
7451[11]

Morocchius (USA) *Miss J A Camacho* a65 70
4 b g Black Minnaloushe(USA) —Shakespearean (USA) (Theatrical (IRE))
1734[15] 3007[8] 3683[3] (4466) 4845[2] (5289) (5395) 5869[3] 6908[5]

Morristown Music (IRE) *J S Wainwright* 51
5 b m Distant Music(USA) —Tongabezi (IRE) (Shernazar)
1734[11] 2046[7]

Morse (IRE) *J A Osborne* a65 62
8 b g Shinko Forest(IRE) —Auriga (Belmez (USA))
166[5] 292[6] 854[5] 984[6]

Mosa Mine *D H Brown* a58 54
2 b f Exceed And Excel(AUS) —Baldemosa (FR) (Lead On Time (USA))
3762[4] *7213[4] 7365[5]*

Moscow Ali (IRE) *J A McShane*
9 ch g Moscow Society(USA) —Down The Bog (IRE) (Down The Hatch)
2030[11]

Moscow Eight (IRE) *E J O'Neill* a80 92
3 b c Elusive City(USA) —Hurricane Lily (IRE) (Ali-Royal (IRE))
1803[8] *6167[9] 6459[7] 6857[5]* 7216a[2] 7265a[2] 7385a[3] *7696a[3] 7820a[2]*

Moscow Oznick *D Donovan* a66 63
4 bb g Auction House(USA) —Cozette (IRE) (Danehill Dancer (IRE))
2237[8] 2859[7] 6172[4] 6488[5] 6758[2] *7677[10] 7790[3]*

Mosqueras Romance *M Botti* a86 33
3 gr f Rock Of Gibraltar(IRE) —Mosquera (GER) (Acatenango (GER))
626[3] 849[2] 1128[10] *(3981)*

Mosqueta *P D Evans* a56 16
2 b f Doyen(IRE) —Arantxa (Sharpo)
6493[12] 6903[11] *7213[5]*

Mossmann Gorge *A Middleton* a46 56
7 b g Lujain(USA) —North Pine (Import)
1533[8] (2182) 3074[7] 4235[5] 4625[4] 5246[7]

Mostashaar (FR) *Doug Watson* a17 68
7 b h Intikhab(USA) —Nasanice (IRE) (Nashwan (USA))
340a[11]

Most Definitely (IRE) *R M Stronge* a71 63
9 b g Definite Article—Unbidden Melody (USA) (Chieftain)
497[7]

Mostofitleft (IRE) *A Berry* 12
2 ch f Pastoral Pursuits—Gold Majesty (Josr Algarhoud (IRE))
1450[7] 1624[6] 1884[6] 2996[9]

Motafaany (USA) *Kevin Prendergast* 85
4 b g Sahm(USA) —Hamasah (USA) (Irish River (FR))
1376a[14]

Motafarred (IRE) *Micky Hammond* a72 86
7 ch g Machiavellian(USA) —Thurayya (Nashwan (USA))
3265[2] 3796[8] 4663[2] 4801[8] 6019[8] 6234[3] 6648[9]

Motarjm (USA) *J Pearce* a76 84
5 br g Elusive Quality(USA) —Agama (USA) (Nureyev (USA))
6973[11] 7233[12] 7539[9]

Motivated Choice *Miss Amy Weaver* a69 67
4 b m Compton Place—Makhsusah (IRE) (Darshaan)
31[8] 289[5] 470[3] 495[3] 607[5] 737[6]

Motivational (IRE) *D R Lanigan* a69 68
2 ch c Motivator—Park Romance (IRE) (Dr Fong (USA))
2358[3] 2853[7] *3468[3] 4371[3]* 4975[10] *6071[8]*

Motor Home *A M Balding* a37 77
3 b g Tobougg(IRE) —Desert Dawn (Belfort (FR))
1462[11] 1774[8] 2300[14] 3476[2] 3946[6] *4749[11]* 5124[9] *5316[10]* 6333[9]

Motrice *Sir Mark Prescott* a63 40
2 gr f Motivator—Entente Cordiale (USA) (Affirmed (USA))
5752[9] ◆ *6163[13] 6436[7]* 6921[11]

Motto Bello (IRE) *Andrew Oliver* a80 62
2 ch f Titus Livius(FR) —Sea Of Stone (USA) (Sanglamore (USA))
5895a[9]

Motty's Gift *W R Swinburn* a48 42
2 ch g Lucky Story(USA) —Oatcake (Selkirk (USA))
2358[6] 3218[14] *5311[10] 7513[10]*

M'Oubliez Pas (USA) *J-C Rouget* 83
2 b f El Corredor(USA) —Manureva (USA) (Nureyev (USA))
4584a[8]

Mountain Cat (IRE) *G A Swinbank* a91 91
5 b g Red Ransom(USA) —Timewee (USA) (Romanov (IRE))
2269[6] 2531[2] (2626) (2806) (3110) 4801[5] 5160[2] *(5887)* ◆ 6117[3] 6485[9]

Mountain Coral (IRE) *F Oakes* a98 89
5 b g Jammaal—Coral Windsor (IRE) (Woods Of Windsor (USA))
(3435a) 3898a[12] *7341a[10]*

Mountain Fairy *M W Easterby* a8 71
6 gr m Daylami(IRE) —Mountain Spirit (IRE) (Royal Academy (USA))
743[6]

Mountain Forest (GER) *H Morrison* a49 52
3 b g Tiger Hill(IRE) —Moricana (GER) (Konigsstuhl (GER))
1441[11] 2605[6] 3661[6] *6771[4] 7197[4] 7499[5] 7666[6] 7740[3]*

Mountain Pass (USA) *B J Llewellyn* a66 65
7 b g Stravinsky(USA) —Ribbony (USA) (Dayjur (USA))
97[8] 216[4] 344[3] 505[7] 1039[2] 1153[9] 1775[6] 2352[10] 2737[2] 2807[6] 3501[7]

Mountain Pride (IRE) *J L Dunlop* 97
4 b g High Chaparral(IRE) —Lioness (Lion Cavern (USA))
1405[5] 2050[11] (2407) 3586[4] 4261[3] 4526[2] 6665[6]

Mountain Quest *M L W Bell* 68
2 b c Hernando(FR) —Miss Katmandu (IRE) (Rainbow Quest (USA))
6821[5] 7121[7]

Mount Athos (IRE) *J W Hills* 59
2 b c Montjeu(IRE) —Ionian Sea (Slip Anchor)
6617[8] 7029[11]

Mount Ella *J R Boyle* a34 55
3 b f Royal Applause—Hiraeth (Petong)
1620[4] *2141[7]* 2776[9] 4533[11] 4702[6] 5188[9]

Mount Hadley (USA) *G A Butler* a83 93
5 b g Elusive Quality(USA) —Fly To The Moon (USA) (Blushing Groom (FR))
1603[2] *2387[6]* (3615) 4409[15] 4852[9] (5418) 6002[5] 6429[12] *7271[4]*

Mount Hermon (IRE) *H Morrison* a85 79
5 b g Golan(IRE) —Machudi (Bluebird (USA))
1524[10] 3055[6] 3811[2] 4759[4] 5062[9] 6488[2]

Mount Juliet (IRE) *S A Callaghan* a65 62
2 b f Danehill Dancer(IRE) —Stylist (IRE) (Sadler's Wells (USA))
5311[11] 5605[8] *6347[2]*

Mountrath *B R Johnson* a31 76
2 b g Dubai Destination(USA) —Eurolink Sundance (Night Shift (USA))
3270[10] 3522[5] 4564[5] 5589[3] 6066[2] 6735[2]

Mount Usher *Miss Diana Weeden* a61 77
7 br g Polar Falcon(USA) —Division Bell (Warning)
489[9] 515[5] 7433[5] ◆ *7524[9] 7754[6]*

Mourayan (IRE) *John M Oxx* 118
3 b c Alhaarth(IRE) —Mouramara (IRE) (Kahyasi)
1388a[3] 1910a[2] 3438a[3] 4962a[2] 5861[5]

Mourilyan (IRE) *H J Brown* a107 119
5 b h Desert Prince(IRE) —Mouramara (IRE) (Kahyasi)
437a[3] 699a[2] 772a[7] 4457[2] 5023[4] (5425) 7215a[3]

Mourinho (IRE) *Edward Lynam* a87 91
4 bb g Cape Cross(IRE) —Shining Prospect (Lycius (USA))
1913a[8]

Moves Goodenough *A G Foster* a70 87
6 ch g Woodborough(USA) —Rekindled Flame (IRE) (Kings Lake (USA))
1357[3] 2407[11] 4003[12] 4597[11] 5441[19] 6014[11]

Moyenne Corniche *M L W Bell* 107
4 ch g Selkirk(USA) —Miss Corniche (Hernando (FR))
2953a[6] 4002[3] 4404[11] 5655[4] 6658a[2] 7208a[11]

Moynahan (USA) *P F I Cole* a103 103
4 ch g Johannesburg(USA) —Lakab (USA) (Manila (USA))
2015[15] 4423[2] 4768[2] ◆ 5522[4] 6480[15] *6876[10]* 7185[5] *7375[8]*

Moyoko (IRE) *M Salaman* a61 57
6 b m Mozart(IRE) —Kayoko (IRE) (Shalford (IRE))
81[4] 216[2] 353[4] 494[7] 608[4] 969[5] 1199[3] 1537[9] 1959[9]

Mozayada (USA) *M Brittain* a85 71
5 ch m Street Cry(IRE) —Fatina (Nashwan (USA))
6[4] (176) 225[3] 354[4] 747[5] 1020[8] *1778[4]* 2999[7] 3488[6] 3763[7] (4548) 5673[12] 6178[8] *6357[8]* 6985[10] 7092[5] 7506[4] 7711[2] ◆ 7783[3]

Mr Aitch (IRE) *R T Phillips* a82 63
7 b g Soviet Star(USA) —Welsh Mist (Damister (USA))
139[4] 384[4] (591) 723[2] 899[3] 1215[2] 3346[7]

Mr Brock (SAF) *Mme C Head-Maarek* 111
6 b g Fort Wood(USA) —Cape Badger (SAF) (Badger Land (USA))
527a[4] ◆ 613a[4] *698a[11]* 3085a[6] 4113a[2] 5059a[9] 6327a[4] 6658a[3]

Mr Burton *M Mullineaux* a55 61
5 gr g Thethingaboutitis(USA) —Quay Four (IRE) (Barathea (IRE))
567[9]

Mr Chocolate Drop (IRE) *Miss M E Rowland* a62 34
5 b g Danetime(IRE) —Forest Blade (IRE) (Charnwood Forest (IRE))
71[2] 256[7] 531[8] 657[4] 711[4] 792[2] 874[2] 979[5]

Mr Corby (IRE) *M R Channon* a69 71
2 b c Camacho—Clochette (IRE) (Namaqualand (USA))
4564[3] 5251[4] 5512[3] 6227[2] 6619[15] 6905[12]

Mr Crystal (FR) *Micky Hammond* a41 84
5 ch g Trempolino(USA) —Iyrbila (FR) (Lashkari)
(1399) 2766[2] 3191[2] 3793[7] 6536[4] 6676[3]

Mr David (USA) *B J Meehan* 103
2 b c Sky Mesa(USA) —Dancewiththebride (USA) (Belong To Me (USA))
3403[4] (4093) 5172[4]

Mr Deal *Eve Johnson Houghton* a55 51
3 b g King's Best(USA) —One Of The Family (Alzao (USA))
4206[7] 4450[6] 4744[12] 7426[4] 7660[5]

Mr Emirati (USA) *B Smart* 66
2 ch c Mr Greeley(USA) —Kathy K D (USA) (Saint Ballado (CAN))
6982[3] ◆

Mr Fantozzi (IRE) *D Donovan* a66 67
4 br g Statue Of Liberty(USA) —Indian Sand (Indian King (USA))
1589[10] (1959) 2381[2] 2458[9] 3070[9] 3662[10] 4060[11] 7667[7] 7855[8]

Mr Flannegan *H Candy* 65
3 ch g Forzando—Star Of Flanders (Puissance)
1196[12] 1516[6] 2009[2] 2797[13] 3257[13] 3577[5] 4425[10] 5120[9]

Mr Forthright *J M Bradley* a24 51
5 b g Fraam—Form At Last (Formidable (USA))
1787[3] ◆ 2124[10] 3204[8] 3994[5] 4479[6] 4690[6] 4982[8]

Mr Freddy (IRE) *R A Fahey* 77
3 b g Intikhab(USA) —Bubble N Squeak (IRE) (Catrail (USA))
1462[6] 1740[2] (2370) 3156[3] 4102[2] 4518[3]

Mr Funshine *D Shaw* a62 51
4 b g Namid—Sunrise Girl (King's Signet (USA))
1775[14] 1970[10] 2382[6] 2682[8] 7358[6] 7535[6] 7710[3] (7838) ◆

Mr Garston *J R Boyle* a79 91
6 b g Mull Of Kintyre(USA) —Ninfa Of Cisterna (Polish Patriot (USA))
155[9]

Mr Grinch (IRE) *M Dods* 88
2 b g Green Tune(USA) —Flyamore (FR) (Sanglamore (USA))
(4590) (5392) 5762[8]

Mr Harmoosh (IRE) *E F Vaughan* 62
2 b g Noverre(USA) —Polish Affair (IRE) (Polish Patriot (USA))
5400[8] 5787[6] 6334[4] 7056[7]

Mr Hichens *Karen George* a84 91
4 b g Makbul—Lake Melody (Sizzling Melody)
1731[5] 2197[6] 2891[12] 4815[7] 5448[11] 6909[8] 7236[12] ◆ (7481) 7664[10]

Mr. Hot Stuff (USA) *Eoin Harty* a110
3 bb c Tiznow(USA) —Sweet Damsel (USA) (Turkoman (USA))
1688a[15] 2734a[8]

Mr Irons (USA) *Sir Michael Stoute* 80
2 ch c Mr Greeley(USA) —Jive Talk (USA) (Kingmambo (USA))
5542[10] (6484)

Mr Kartoffel (IRE) *H Candy* 33
4 b g Night Shift(USA) —Diamant (IRE) (Bigstone (IRE))
2318[10] 2981[13] 3205[8]

Mr Kintyre (ITY) *S Cannavo* 101
3 b c Mull Of Kintyre(USA) —Achorde (FR) (Slip Anchor)
4367a[9]

Mr Lambros *Miss Gay Kelleway* a99 78
8 ch g Pivotal—Magical Veil (Majestic Light (USA))
86[6] 204[8] 282[2]

Mr Loire *A J Chamberlain* a55 44
5 b g Bertolini(USA) —Miss Sancerre (Last Tycoon)
111[9] 198[12] 308[2] 475[5] 574[3] 676[5] 762[7] 2758[7] 2908[9] 3208[11] 3673[5] 3947[9]

Mr Lu *J S Goldie* a64 69
4 b g Lujain(USA) —Libretta (Highest Honor (FR))
1123[13] 1650[7] 2235[7] 2628[4] 3148[6] 3683[10] 4312[11] 5289[9] 5601[6] (6415) 6984[U]

Mr Macattack *N J Vaughan* a91 85
4 b h Machiavellian(USA) —Aunty Rose (IRE) (Caerleon (USA))
573[5] (680) (777) 1861[7] ◆ 2470[4] ◆ 3091[12]

Mr Mahoganeigh *M L W Bell* a85
2 b c Mark Of Esteem(IRE) —Sweet Cando (IRE) (Royal Applause)
(5643) ◆

Mr Maximas *B Palling* 50
2 ch g Auction House(USA) —Cashiki (IRE) (Case Law)
5499[12] 5785[11] 6331[6]

Mr Medici (IRE) *L Ho* a101 111
4 b h Medicean—Way For Life (GER) (Platini (GER))
7747a[8]

Mr Mischief *C Gordon* a72 44
9 b g Millkom—Snow Huntress (Shirley Heights)
877[7] 1081[9] 1609[8] 2127[7]

Mr Mohican (IRE) *Mrs A Duffield* 47
2 b g Barathea(IRE) —Tipi Squaw (King's Best (USA))
5669[8] 6382[8] 6842[8]

Mr Money Maker *Tom Dascombe* 57
2 ch c Ishiguru(USA) —Ellopassoff (Librate)
6903[5]

Mr Napoleon (IRE) *G L Moore* a74 69
7 gr g Daylami(IRE) —Dathuil (IRE) (Royal Academy (USA))
21[6] 726[5]

Mr Plod *M J Scudamore* a65 53
4 ch g Silver Patriarch(IRE) —Emily-Mou (IRE) (Cadeaux Genereux)
5314[8] 5873[3] 6371[4] 6770[4] (7658) 7767[7]

Mr Prize Fighter *I W McInnes* 45
2 b g Piccolo—Lv Girl (IRE) (Mukaddamah (USA))
5006[6] 5669[10] 6246[5]

Mr Prolific *B W Hills* 54
3 b g Haafhd—Rumpipumpy (Shirley Heights)
1363[2] ◆ 1580[11] 2350[9]

Mr Rainbow *G A Swinbank* a79 90
3 ch g Efisio—Blossom (Warning)
(6430) 6731[2] ◆

Mr Rev *J M Bradley* a55 53
6 b g Foxhound(USA) —Branston Berry (IRE) (Mukaddamah (USA))
23[13] 153[2] 247[3] 473[6] 674[6] 748[8] 802[5] 1047[4] 1536[4] 1784[3] 2223[4] 2366[3] 2759[5] 2879[6] 4730[6] 5120[5] 5283[8]

Mr Rio (IRE) *A P Jarvis* a58 58
4 b g Captain Rio—Amoras (IRE) (Hamas (IRE))
3712[3] 4082[16] 5150[13] 5406[9] 6777[6] 6904[8] 7105[4] 7239[5] 7534[5] 7834[11]

Mr Rooney (IRE) *A Berry* a59 65
6 b g Mujadil(USA) —Desert Bride (USA) (Key To The Kingdom (USA))
89[5] 173[4] (367) 681[7] 1310[10] 1695[10] 2451[8] 2657[7] 2717[10] 3111[6] 4467[8] 5159[7] 6161[10] 7219[7]

Mrs Beeton (IRE) *W R Swinburn* a66 74
3 b f Dansili—Eliza Acton (Shirley Heights)
(2947) ◆ 3627[7]

Mrs Boss *B R Millman* a71 78
2 b f Makbul—Chorus (Bandmaster (USA))
1504[8] 1706[3] 2054[7] 2711[3] 3210[3] 3918[8] 5899[4] 6241[7]

Mrs Bun *K A Ryan* a75 52
4 b m Efisio—Card Games (First Trump)
(7) (152) ◆ 307[2] 519[4] 934[10]

Mrs E *M W Easterby* 55
2 b f Doyen(IRE) —Fille De Bucheron (USA) (Woodman (USA))
6284[8] 6982[5]

Mr. Sidney (USA) *William Mott* a101 119
5 b h Storm Cat(USA) —Tomisue's Delight (USA) (A.P. Indy (USA))
4809a[6] 7309a[7]

Mr Sir (USA) *X Nakkachdji* 72
3 b c Mr Greeley(USA) —She's The General (USA) (General Meeting (USA))
6682a[0]

Mrs Jones And Me (IRE) *P T Midgley* a56 58
2 b f Namid—Meadow (Green Desert (USA))
1044[5] 1344[7] 2503[5] 2896[6] 3495[4] 4138[8] 4370[4] 5226[8] 5372[11]

Mr Skipiton (IRE) *B J McMath* a65 73
4 b g Statue Of Liberty(USA) —Salty Air (IRE) (Singspiel (IRE))
71[8] 198[10] 675[4] (854) (1076) 1360[5] 2920[6] 3505[2] (4183) 4536[4] 5576[8]

Mrs Medley *D Shaw* a27
3 b f Rambling Bear—Animal Cracker (Primo Dominie)
2250[14] 5882[13] 6344[11] 6641[9] 7510[7] 7710[10] 7829[9]

Mr Smithson (IRE) *B Ellison* a65 67
2 br g Xaar—Amanda Louise (IRE) (Perugino (USA))
1097[2] 1277[8] 1764[3] 2311[2] 2714[8] 3871[9] 3952[3] 4839[5] 5467[8] 6345[12]

Mrs Mogg *N J Vaughan* 52
2 b f Green Desert(USA) —Maybe Forever (Zafonic (USA))
3633[6]

Mr Snowballs *R A Farrant* a43 58
3 gr g Monsieur Bond(IRE) —Swissmatic (Petong)
1322[8]

Mrs Penny (AUS) *J R Gask* a91 92
5 br m Planchet(AUS) —Respective (AUS) (Noalcoholic (FR))
(197) ◆ 579[10] 785[4] 7646[5] 7862[8]

Mrs Puff (IRE) *P D Evans* a48 46
2 gr f Trans Island—Canosa (IRE) (Catrail (USA))
1090[11] 4439[8] 4825[8] 5284[9] 5967[9] 6169[5] 6721[7] 7098[4] 7319[5] 7334[6]

Mrs Slocombe (IRE) *Mrs N S Evans* a51 78
3 b f Masterful(USA) —Mrs Beatty (Cadeaux Genereux)
158[4] 2797[3] 3159[11] 3209[15] 3740[4] 4687[5] 5063[14]

Mr Toshiwonka *D Nicholls* a14 69
5 b g Compton Place—Victoria (Old Vic)
980[7] 2156[12] 2842[4]

Mr Udagawa *R M Beckett* a70 76
3 b g Bahamian Bounty—Untold Riches (USA) (Red Ransom (USA))
2048[3] 2320[13] 4321[2] 4691[2] 6073[3] (6390) 6907[14]

Mr Willis *J R Best* a96 51
3 b g Desert Sun—Santiburi Girl (Casteddu)
(960) ◆ (1075) 1214[3] (7523) ◆ (7603) 7789[2]

Mr Wolf *J J Quinn* a77 81
8 b g Wolfhound(USA) —Madam Millie (Milford)
1518[6] 1885[11] 2267[6] (2770) 3372[6] 3706[12] 4662[8] 5343[2] 5768[12] 6233[3] 6847[8]

Ms Sophie Eleanor (USA) *T D Barron* 68
3 bb f Grand Slam(USA) —Population (IRE) (General Assembly (USA))
3175[7] (4276) 4879[2] 5941[9]

Ms Vanenzza (USA) *Juan C Vazquez* a100
2 b f Successful Appeal(USA) —Speaking Of Time (USA) (Gilded Time (USA))
7283a[9]

Mt Desert *E W Tuer* a24 70
7 b g Rainbow Quest(USA) —Chief Bee (Chief's Crown (USA))
7505[11]

Mt Kintyre (IRE) *M H Tompkins* a39 76
3 b g Mull Of Kintyre(USA) —Nihonpillow Mirai (IRE) (Zamindar (USA))
1168[2] 1362[2] 1693[4] 2855[7] 4151[3] 4867[8] 6680[7] 7101[6]

Mtoto Girl *J J Bridger* a53 36
5 b m Mtoto—Shalati (FR) (High Line)
598[9]

Mubrook (USA) *L M Cumani* a82 90
4 b g Alhaarth(IRE) —Zomaradah (Deploy)
2891[9] 3564[4] 4544[4] 6375[2] 6995[2]

Much Acclaimed (IRE) *T P Tate* 75
2 b g Sulamani(IRE) —Much Commended (Most Welcome)
6214[2] 6991[6]

Mucho Loco (IRE) *R Curtis* a48 64
6 ch g Tagula(IRE) —Mousseux (IRE) (Jareer (USA))
385[6]

Mudaaraah *J L Dunlop* 103
2 b f Cape Cross(IRE) —Wissal (USA) (Woodman (USA))
(2563) 3396[8] (4245) ◆ 5427[2] ◆ 6269[9]

Mudawin (IRE) *James Moffatt* a99 93
8 b g Intikhab(USA) —Fida (IRE) (Persian Heights)
2486[10] 3146[5] 3532[3] 4078[2] (4332)

Mudhish (IRE) *C E Brittain* a73 75
4 b g Lujain(USA) —Silver Satire (Dr Fong (USA))
(420) 576[4] 706[5] 793[7] 956[10] 1285[2] 1587[2] 2168[2] 2459[7] 3469[3] 3548[4] 4914[2] 6175[4]

Mufarrh (IRE) *J L Dunlop* 89
2 b c Marju(IRE) —What A Picture (FR) (Peintre Celebre (USA))
5220[3] ◆ 6108[2] (6754)

Muffett's Dream *J J Bridger* a45 52
5 b m Fraam—Loveless Carla (Pursuit Of Love)
1980[9] 2222[7] 3247[10] 3533[4] 3739[4]

Muftarres (IRE) *G A Butler* a81 89
4 b h Green Desert(USA) —Ghazal (USA) (Gone West (USA))
4273[8] 4761[6] 5370[6] 6294[3] (6545) 6760[2] 7233[6]

Mufti (IRE) *B J Meehan* 75
2 b c Noverre(USA) —Dark Indian (IRE) (Indian Ridge)
5002[4] 5527[6]

Mugeba *C A Dwyer* a49 49
8 b m Primo Dominie—Ella Lamees (Statoblest)
4665[9] 5883[12] 6739[12] 7100[7]

Muhannak (IRE) *R M Beckett* a112 113
5 b g Chester House(USA) —Opera (Forzando)
773a[5] 1013a[10] 4484[7] 5662[P] 6030[8] 6303[5] 7281a[5]

Mujaadel (USA) *D Nicholls* a88 83
4 ch g Street Cry(IRE) —Quiet Rumour (USA) (Alleged (USA))
1649[5] ◆ 2101[9] 3172[7] 3530[3] 3847[7] 4548[7] (4802) 5409[6] 6015[9] (6847)

Mujada *M Brittain* a52 39
4 b m Mujahid(USA) —Catriona (Bustino)
748[9] 1781[11] 4995[7]

Mujamead *A W Carroll* a68 28
5 b g Mujahid(USA) —Island Mead (Pharly (FR))
112[9]

Mujdeya *J H M Gosden* 79
2 gr f Linamix(FR) —Majhud (IRE) (Machiavellian (USA))
6921[5] ◆

Mujma *S Parr* a60 49
5 gb g Indian Ridge—Farfala (FR) (Linamix (FR))
565[6] 802[6] (896) 976[2] 1134[3] 1591[13] 1695[12]

Mujood *Eve Johnson Houghton* a79 98
6 b g Mujahid(USA) —Waqood (USA) (Riverman (USA))
1187[7] 1631[5] 1864[9] (2193) 2480[2] 2639[2] 2822[7] 3282[2] 3752[3] 4409[9] 4423[10] 4954[8] 5424[6] (5746) (5918) 6278[10] 6694[8]

Muktasb (USA) *D Shaw* a68 52
8 b g Bahri(USA) —Maghaarb (Machiavellian (USA))
22[4] 177[5] (294) 460[3] 499[3] 681[4] 832[3] 1134[4] 1528[4] 2145[3] 2579[8] 3227[12]

Mulaazem *A M Hales* a62 69
6 b g King's Best(USA) —Harayir (USA) (Gulch (USA))
346[4] 502[5] 668[7]

Mulaqat *D Selvaratnam* a97 104
6 b g Singspiel(IRE) —Atamana (IRE) (Lahib (USA))
616a[7] 699a[8]

Mulazem (USA) *W J Haggas* 16
3 rg c El Prado(IRE) —Muwakleh (Machiavellian (USA))
1941[9]

Mullein *R M Beckett* a102 108
4 b m Oasis Dream—Gipsy Moth (Efisio)
(1321) ◆ 2271[11] 3360[3] 4330[7] (5069) 5878[3] 6304[3] 6661[10]

Muller (ARG) *N L Bruss* a96
6 br g El Compinche(ARG) —Martina Girl (ARG) (Mat-Boy (ARG))
1013a[4]

Mullglen *T D Easterby* 83
3 b g Mull Of Kintyre(USA) —However (IRE) (Hector Protector (USA))
1517[6] 2058[10] 3607[8] (3973) 4309[6] 4601[7] 4849[3] 5523[6] 6902[6]

Mullitovermaurice *J G Given* a65
3 ch g Pursuit Of Love—Ellovamul (Elmaamul (USA))
136[2] 295[2] 479[3] 689[6] 7798[9]

Mull Of Dubai *T P Tate* a49 102
6 b g Mull Of Kintyre(USA) —Enlisted (IRE) (Sadler's Wells (USA))
1593[5] 1798[9] (2932) 4517[4]

Mull Of Killough (IRE) *J L Spearing* 102
3 b g Mull Of Kintyre(USA) —Sun Shower (IRE) (Indian Ridge)
(1250) (2092) 2855[2] 4708[3] 5419[8] (6249)

Multahab *M Wigham* a62 69
10 bb g Zafonic(USA) —Alumisiyah (USA) (Danzig (USA))
431[3] 1540[7] 1957[3] 2596[9] 3246[2] (3677) 5125[4] 6118[4] 6314[4] 7280[11]

Multakka (IRE) *M P Tregoning* a96 54
6 b g Alhaarth(IRE) —Elfaslah (IRE) (Green Desert (USA))
1731[2] 5663[11] 6633[8]

Multames (IRE) *Saeed Bin Suroor* 93
2 b c Cape Cross(IRE) —Elutrah (Darshaan)
3167[8] (7029) ◆

Multichope (FR) *C Boutin* a54 73
2 b f Indian Rocket—Alhena (FR) (Kaldoun (FR))
4368a[3] 5057a[9]

Multiplication *W J Knight* 82
3 b f Marju(IRE) —Lunda (IRE) (Soviet Star (USA))
(1893) 2535[4] 6242[8] 6757[6]

Multi Tasker *Miss J R Tooth* a52 49
3 b c Lear Spear(USA) —Lola Lola (IRE) (Piccolo)
135[7]

Mumaathel (IRE) *W R Muir* a58 86
6 b g Alhaarth(IRE) —Alhufoof (USA) (Dayjur (USA))
87[9]

Mumtaz Begum *J E Long* 32
4 ch m Kyllachy—Indian Gift (Cadeaux Genereux)
4180[11] 5193[9] 5747[15]

Munaddam (USA) *E Charpy* a22 113
7 ch g Aljabr(USA) —Etizaaz (USA) (Diesis)
(259a) 418a[9] 637a[2] 700a[9]

Muncaster Castle (IRE) *R F Fisher* a57 58
5 b g Johannesburg(USA) —Eubee (FR) (Common Grounds)
(405) 6080[10]

Munching Mike (IRE) *K M Prendergast* a34 60
6 br g Orpen(USA) —Stargard (Polish Precedent (USA))
2580[12] 3275[8] 3927[11]

Mundo's Magic *N Wilson* a38 58
5 b g Foxhound(USA) —Amber's Bluff (Mind Games)
4435[12] 4818[4]

Mundybash *N Clement* 111
4 b h Diktat—Cootamundra (FR) (Double Bed (FR))
5059a[8] 6506a[6] 7102a[6]

Munich (IRE) *Mrs S Leech* a78 78
5 b g Noverre(USA) —Mayara (IRE) (Ashkalani (IRE))
342[9] 708[11] 1606[2] 2598[4] 3732[5] 3983[7] 4389[4]

Munlochy Bay *W S Kittow* a57 75
5 b m Karinga Bay—Meghdoot (Celestial Storm (USA))
1049[2] 1435[9] 2127[6] 2429[2] 2931[11]

Munnings (USA) *Todd Pletcher* a117
3 ch c Speightstown(USA) —La Comete (USA) (Holy Bull (USA))
6509a[3]

Munsarim (IRE) *J L Dunlop* 80
2 b c Shamardal(USA) —Etizaaz (USA) (Diesis)
4756[3] 5793[4] 6810[3]

Munsef *Ian Williams* 111
7 b g Zafonic(USA) —Mazaya (IRE) (Sadler's Wells (USA))
263a[12] 527a[8] 616a[8] (3374) 3620[2] (4340) (5248) 5933a[2] 7215a[12]

Muntami (IRE) *John A Harris* a41 59
8 gr g Daylami(IRE) —Bashashah (IRE) (Kris)
38[9] 3760[6] 5483[7] 7124[6] 7642[4]

Muraco *A M Hales* a58 74
5 b g Bertolini(USA) —Miss Honeypenny (IRE) (Old Vic)
320[12]

Muraweg (IRE) *J H M Gosden* a80 88
3 b c Kheleyf(USA) —Lady Moranbon (USA) (Trempolino (USA))
(944) ◆ 1303[4] ◆ 1992[5] ◆ 5828[5] 6203[5] 6594[12]

Murcar *C G Cox* a82 79
4 ch g Medicean—In Luck (In The Wings)
1287[5] 2194[5] (2497) ◆ 2854[6] 4951[4] 5837[2] 6281[3] 6676[4] (7005)

Murcielago (FR) *T Castanheira* a99 109
4 ch h Spinning World(USA) —So Long Girl (Selkirk (USA))
6505a[3] 7208a[6]

Mureb (USA) *Saeed Bin Suroor* a71
2 b c Elusive Quality(USA) —Sumoto (Mtoto)
7209[3] ◆

Murfreesboro *D Shaw* a98 90
6 b g Bahamian Bounty—Merry Rous (Rousillon (USA))
26[3] 171[3]

Murhee (USA) *D R Lanigan* a62 62
3 b c Rahy(USA) —Grand Ogygia (USA) (Ogygian (USA))
1380[5] ◆ 2548[6] 5035[17]

Muriel (IRE) *Andreas Lowe* 97
3 b f Fath(USA) —Hoodwink (IRE) (Selkirk (USA))
2757a[11] 4363a[3]

Murrays Magic (IRE) *D Nicholls* 43
3 b f Bahri(USA) —Fiina (Most Welcome)
1098[10] 1481[11]

Murrin (IRE) *T G Mills* a81 74
5 bb g Trans Island—Flimmering (Dancing Brave (USA))
(143) 505[3] 841[2] 1035[3] 1539[4] 2824[4] 5190[8] 5745[5] 6337[4] 6780[2] 7054[9] 7362[6]

Murrumbidgee (IRE) *Mike Murphy* a61 60
6 gr g Bluebird(USA) —Blanche Neige (USA) (Lit De Justice (USA))
1199[4] 2171[4] (2608)

Musaafer (IRE) *M A Jarvis* a76 98
2 b c Marju(IRE) —Alexander Icequeen (IRE) (Soviet Star (USA))
5637[2] ◆ (6235) ◆ 7017[9] ◆

Musaalem (USA) *W J Haggas* 110
5 gr g Aljabr(USA) —Atyab (USA) (Mr Prospector (USA))
2297[5] 3091[24] (3567) 4796[15] 5826[4] (6487)

Musashi (IRE) *Mrs L J Mongan* a75 56
4 ch g Hawk Wing(USA) —Soubrette (USA) (Opening Verse (USA))
90[5] 1848[4] 2129[6] 2923[8] 3158[7] 3919[5] 7549[8]

Musca (IRE) *J Wade* 78
5 b g Tendulkar(USA) —Canary Bird (IRE) (Catrail (USA))
1694[10] 2235[13]

Mushagak (IRE) *E A L Dunlop* a58
2 b f Oratorio(IRE) —Tetou (IRE) (Peintre Celebre (USA))
7622[11]

Mushka (USA) *William Mott* a114 103
4 bb m Empire Maker(USA) —Sluice (USA) (Seeking The Gold (USA))
7286a[2]

Mushreq (USA) *Sir Michael Stoute* 69
2 b c Distorted Humor(USA) —Casual Look (USA) (Red Ransom (USA))
5400[4] 6451[5]

Musiara *M R Channon* 49
2 b f Hunting Lion(IRE) —Search Party (Rainbow Quest (USA))
11954 13446 16243 16802 21007 40184 491513 571513 621510

Musical Bridge *Mrs L Williamson* a62 78
3 b g Night Shift(USA) —Carrie Pooter (Tragic Role (USA))
21222 (2603) 30965 37043 42313 46537 69883 73557

Musical Delight *A P Jarvis* 23
2 b g Oratorio(IRE) —Living Daylights (IRE) (Night Shift (USA))
25997 45688 60478

Musical Maze *W M Brisbourne* a57 66
3 b f Distant Music(USA) —Maze Garden (USA) (Riverman (USA))
153110 20917 25283 27792 30194 33365 33716 40743 45068 4562P

Musical Script (USA) *Mouse Hamilton-Fairley* a80 55
6 b g Stravinsky(USA) —Cyrillic (USA) (Irish River (FR))
243 2122 3519 6003 51678 55927 59916 62125 64447 672610 69158 70535 73293 ◆ 74322 75194 773910 78286

Music Box Express *George Baker* a70 76
5 b g Tale Of The Cat(USA) —Aly McBe (USA) (Alydeed (CAN))
4994 6914 8843 99613 12487 169412 21243 25644 27582 32463 33188 402310 768012 7819 7

Music Maestro (IRE) *B W Hills* a77 74
2 b g Oratorio(IRE) —Adjalisa (IRE) (Darshaan)
45246 56742 66724 72092

Music Note (USA) *Saeed Bin Suroor* a123
4 b m A.P. Indy(USA) —Note Musicale (Sadler's Wells (USA))
(6508a) 7286a3

Music Of The Moor (IRE) *T P Tate* 76
2 ch g Rock Of Gibraltar(IRE) —A La Longue (GER) (Mtoto)
22474 ◆ 31704 47052 54077 62855 689512 72183

Music Show (IRE) *M R Channon* 110
2 b f Noverre(USA) —Dreamboat (USA) (Mr Prospector (USA))
(4688) (5241) ◆ 609010 (6852)

Musigny (USA) *W Jarvis* a62 65
3 bb g Forest Wildcat(USA) —Water Rights (USA) (Kris S (USA))
286315 40838 528310 59722 69242

Musketier (GER) *Roger L Attfield* 115
7 rg h Acatenango(GER) —Myth And Reality (Linamix (FR))
6511a6

Musket Man (USA) *Derek S Ryan* a120
3 bb c Yonaguska(USA) —Fortuesque (USA) (Fortunate Prospect (USA))
1688a3 2098a3

Musleh (USA) *Saeed Bin Suroor* a98
3 b c Forestry(USA) —Lucifer's Stone (USA) (Horse Chestnut (SAF))
(4649) (4983) ◆ 56639 62293

Mustajed *B R Millman* a79 86
8 b g Alhaarth(IRE) —Jasarah (IRE) (Green Desert (USA))
2026 (341) (406) 22006 25055 28519 35633 38692 41693 46023 48558 77614

Mustakhlas (USA) *B P J Baugh* a9 46
8 ch g Diesis—Katiba (USA) (Gulch (USA))
78428

Mustakmil (IRE) *S Dow* a83 76
3 b c Haafhd—Elfaslah (IRE) (Green Desert (USA))
36903 45197 50102 55203 58584 (7576) (7769)

Mustalainen (FR) *Mme R-W Allen* a48 46
5 gr m Medaaly—Frundin (Anshan)
5204a6

Mustaqer (IRE) *B W Hills* 90
3 b g Dalakhani(IRE) —Al Ihtithar (IRE) (Barathea (IRE))
14597 29358

Mut'Ab (USA) *C E Brittain* a90 93
4 b g Alhaarth(IRE) —Mistle Song (Nashwan (USA))
11169 152711 19432 240214

Mutadarek *Ms Joanna Morgan* a57 80
8 b g Machiavellian(USA) —Nasheed (USA) (Riverman (USA))
7263a12

Mutafajer *Saeed Bin Suroor* a78 64
2 bb c Oasis Dream—Shahaamah (IRE) (Red Ransom (USA))
66165 70503 ◆ 72342

Mutajaaser (USA) *K A Morgan* a63 11
4 b g War Chant(USA) —Hazimah (USA) (Gone West (USA))
427611 76715

Mutajarred *W J Haggas* a113 108
5 ch g Alhaarth(IRE) —Bedara (Barathea (IRE))
40907 45437

Mutamaashi *W J Haggas* a94 99
3 b g Sakhee(USA) —Almahab (USA) (Danzig (USA))
(440) 13072 ◆ 22963 304919 40583 56482 ◆ (6277) 66653

Mutamared (USA) *M J Scudamore* a94 99
9 ch g Nureyev(USA) —Alydariel (USA) (Alydar (USA))
(57) (189) (266) (442) 7142 7785 11164 13213 16997 27075 306612 47752 51048 54066 56764 (5916) 62936 66319 702611 72537 76568

Mutamayez *M A Jarvis* a77
3 b c Dalakhani(IRE) —Blue Oasis (IRE) (Sadler's Wells (USA))
(6287)

Mutasallil (USA) *Doug Watson* a99 72
9 bb h Gone West(USA) —Min Alhawa (USA) (Riverman (USA))
523a3 612a5

Mutawarath (IRE) *W J Haggas* a72 87
3 b c Marju(IRE) —Castlerahan (IRE) (Thatching)
180412 24164 (2937) 53634 598611 64744

Mutayam *D A Nolan* 46
9 b g Compton Place—Final Shot (Dalsaan)
245111 31096 344513

Mutheeb (USA) *Saeed Bin Suroor* a105 109
4 b h Danzig(USA) —Magicalmysterykate (USA) (Woodman (USA))
(1631) ◆ 23853 30914 38183

Mutually Mine (USA) *Mrs P Sly* a69 68
3 ch f Golden Missile(USA) —Gal Of Mine (USA) (Mining (USA))
9626 13312 15163 31156 35483 51128 54495 60236 73993 751212 76679

Muwakaba (USA) *Sir Michael Stoute* a82
2 ch f Elusive Quality(USA) —Saleela (USA) (Nureyev (USA))
(6163)

Muwalla *C E Brittain* 80
2 b c Bahri(USA) —Easy Sunshine (IRE) (Sadler's Wells (USA))
48884 53477 57933 61732

Muy Ponderado (ARG) *M bin Shafya* a76
4 ch h Mutakddim(USA) —Ponderosa Noche (USA) (Royal Roberto (USA))
768a5 1009a12

Muzmin (USA) *E A L Dunlop* 60
4 bb g Seeking The Gold(USA) —In On The Secret (CAN) (Secretariat (USA))
14225 241510 31505

Muzo (USA) *J Noseda* a70
3 b c Gone West(USA) —Bowl Of Emeralds (USA) (A.P. Indy (USA))
66734 69743

My Arch *Ollie Pears* 74
7 b g Silver Patriarch(IRE) —My Desire (Grey Desire)
66819

Myasun (FR) *C Baillet* 72
2 ch c Panis(USA) —Spain (FR) (Bering)
7316a5

My Aunt Fanny *A M Balding* a71 92
4 b m Nayef(USA) —Putuna (Generous (IRE))
44225 ◆ 54726 610615

My Best Bet *Stef Liddiard* a87 78
3 ch f Best Of The Bests(IRE) —Cibenze (Owington)
453 2293 (313) 20797 25446 29677 33872 35372 ◆ 38155 42673 (4700) 51544 58102 59685 63486 66675 69973 (7487) 77693

My Best Man *B R Millman* a67 68
3 b g Forzando—Victoria Sioux (Ron's Victory (USA))
195 1493 3223 4263 17744 23203 27976 34266 42685 49376 518414

My Bodyguard (FR) *H J L Dunlop* a33 36
3 b c Alhaarth(IRE) —Hollow Dynasty (USA) (Deputy Commander (USA))
157312 209012 27437

My Boy Davis (IRE) *N Clement*
2 b c Whipper(USA) —Aldovea (Nashwan (USA))
6979a0

My Boy Nick *D L Williams*
7 b g Bold Fort—Suelizelle (Carnival Dancer)
153012

Mycana (IRE) *Lee Smyth* a1
3 b g Tikkanen(USA) —Amme Enaek (IRE) (Wolverlife)
664111

Mycenean Prince (USA) *S A Harris* a47 41
6 b g Swain(IRE) —Nijinsky's Beauty (USA) (Nijinsky (CAN))
11319 49729 618410

My Central (ITY) *H J Brown* 103
5 b m Central Park(IRE) —My Luigia (IRE) (High Estate)
416a6 (643a) 702a6

My Chestnut Girl (USA) *H R A Cecil* 81
3 ch f Horse Chestnut(SAF) —Mien (USA) (Nureyev (USA))
14888 21924 27633 32144 36742 (4599)

My Choice *A P Jarvis* a34 27
3 b g Groom Dancer(USA) —Beleza (IRE) (Revoque (IRE))
14409

My Condor (IRE) *D McCain Jnr*
8 b g Beneficial—Margellen's Castle (IRE) (Castle Keep)
48579

Mydy Easy (USA) *P W Chapple-Hyam* 60
3 bb g Speightstown(USA) —Eze (USA) (Williamstown (USA))
48545 65735

My Flame *J R Jenkins* a59 62
4 b g Cool Jazz—Suselja (IRE) (Mon Tresor)
10472 14236 (1535) 19595 22239 46657 528712 65874 71057 743310 76145

My Friend Fritz *P W Hiatt* a74
9 ch g Safawan—Little Scarlett (Mazilier (USA))
(3) 654 3258 6034 (977) 17327 21298

My Gacho (IRE) *M Johnston* a96 96
7 b g Shinko Forest(IRE) —Floralia (Auction Ring (USA))
735 11165 136510 169914 25897 34976 (4019) (4641) (4996) (5206) 608914 627812 667816 78377

My Girl Jode *M H Tompkins* a66 68
3 ch f Haafhd—Brush Strokes (Cadeaux Genereux)
24169 28585 (4157) 42302 61395 691015 72043 752414

My Grand Duke (USA) *J A Osborne* a52
2 b c Johannesburg(USA) —Hit It Here Cafe (USA) (Grand Slam (USA))
75807 77216 78659

My Immortal *J J Quinn* 79
7 b g Monsun(GER) —Dame Kiri (FR) (Old Vic)
123010 27204 31915 37287

My Indy (ARG) *Saeed Bin Suroor* a117
5 br h Indygo Shiner(USA) —My Light (ARG) (Southern Halo (USA))
(184a) (417a) 1013a5

My Jeanie (IRE) *J C Fox* a36 49
5 ch m King Charlemagne(USA) —Home Comforts (Most Welcome)
307711 58839 63945 76609

My Kaiser Chief *W J H Ratcliffe* a58 72
4 bl g Paris House—So Tempted (So Factual (USA))
4608 803 11

My Kingdom (IRE) *H Morrison* a82 90
3 b g King's Best(USA) —Nebraas (Green Desert (USA))
17444 23994 31637 37714 44542 (4733) 55923 59167 62794 ◆ 67236

Mykingdomforahorse *M R Channon* 81
3 b c Fantastic Light(USA) —Charlecote (IRE) (Caerleon (USA))
193211 30994 35512 40044 (4918) 50273 58762 (6400) 66769

My Learned Friend (IRE) *A M Balding* a72 83
5 b g Marju(IRE) —Stately Princess (Robellino (USA))
18764 ◆ 24919 32432 (3659) 42939 51826 64767

My Legal Eagle (IRE) *E G Bevan* a40 49
15 b g Law Society(USA) —Majestic Nurse (On Your Mark)
222213

My Les *Jim Best* a60 65
3 b f Josr Algarhoud(IRE) —Ashantiana (Ashkalani (IRE))
48675 513110 (6788) 69183

My Mandy (IRE) *Ian Williams* a61 69
2 b f Xaar—Ikan (IRE) (Sri Pekan (USA))
10314 ◆ 13443 15042 17886 33704 39372 49283 53374 60185 63543 67003 69134

Mymateeric *J Pearce* a55 69
3 b g Reset(AUS) —Ewenny (Warrshan (USA))
14288 235713 330213 36855 41782 47227 49174 59903 64324 67859 70257

My Mate Granite (USA) *H J Collingridge* a45
5 ch g High Yield(USA) —Fellwaati (USA) (Alydar (USA))
5162 9786 3275P

My Mate Mal *B Ellison* a67 68
5 b g Daawe(USA) —Kandymal (IRE) (Prince Of Birds (USA))
89811 12766 15302 23616 (2404) 307018 33532 39806 431210 53613 601212 63422 76315 77528 77613

My Mate Max *R Hollinshead* a79 79
4 b g Fraam—Victory Flip (IRE) (Victory Note (USA))
11179 15062 30732 37886 52529 55303 (6368) 71514

My Mentor (IRE) *Sir Mark Prescott* a83
5 b g Golan(IRE) —Vanille (IRE) (Selkirk (USA))
3074 3842 6224 7336 8869 397710 43739

My Mirasol *D E Cantillon* a68 65
5 ch m Primo Valentino(IRE) —Distinctly Blu (IRE) (Distinctly North (USA))
663 3246 62312

Mymumsaysimthebest *G L Moore* a64 86
4 b g Reel Buddy(USA) —Night Gypsy (Mind Games)
16368 23262 29806

My One Weakness (IRE) *B Ellison* a69 75
2 ch g Bertolini(USA) —Lucina (Machiavellian (USA))
30643 33923 39377 (4371) 51364 ◆ 55157 (6048)

My Paris *Ollie Pears* a38 94
8 b g Paris House—My Desire (Grey Desire)
14799

Myraid *Ollie Pears* 33
2 b g Danbird(AUS) —My Desire (Grey Desire)
682115

My Red Kite *G D Blake* a53 60
2 ch g Avonbridge—Cup Of Love (USA) (Behrens (USA))
25335 28898 40067 72356

Myriola *D Shaw* a40 49
4 ch m Captain Rio—Spaniola (IRE) (Desert King (IRE))
76298 77145 783910

My Shadow *S Dow* a83 75
4 b g Zamindar(USA) —Reflections (Sadler's Wells (USA))
(597) 79811 10352 13822 19835 (3104) 35263 42118 578013

Myshkin *I Semple* a53 51
3 b g Refuse To Bend(IRE) —Marmaga (IRE) (Shernazar)
3435 12314

My Sister *M D I Usher* a52 63
2 b f Royal Applause—Mysistra (FR) (Machiavellian (USA))
32487 48254 52125 579712 63435 67356

Mystery Star (IRE) *M H Tompkins* a83 104
4 ch g Kris Kin(USA) —Mystery Hill (USA) (Danehill (USA))
11493 12742 ◆ (1666) 23425 26712 33995 362011 43402 47706 52482 60363 666214

Mystical Ayr (IRE) *Miss L A Perratt* a17 61
7 br m Namid—Scanno's Choice (IRE) (Pennine Walk)
30199 30946 40349

Mystical Spirit (IRE) *J R Weymes* a37 46
3 b f Xaar—Samsung Spirit (Statoblest)
1789P

Mystic Art (IRE) *C R Egerton* a71 68
4 b g Peintre Celebre(USA) —Mystic Lure (Green Desert (USA))
(588) 8253 8722 15787 19614 24207 270810

Mystickhill (IRE) *J Balding* a65 60
4 ch m Raise A Grand(IRE) —Lady Eberspacher (IRE) (Royal Abjar (USA))
1735

Mystic Millie (IRE) *C G Cox* 46
2 ch f Bertolini(USA) —Present Imperfect (Cadeaux Genereux)
44218 57498 64165

Mystic Prince *Miss Tor Sturgis* 65
3 b g Dubai Destination(USA) —Hazy Heights (Shirley Heights)
207412 295010 35889

Mystic Roll *Jane Chapple-Hyam* a59 48
6 br g Medicean—Pain Perdu (IRE) (Waajib)
241814 40056

Mystic Touch *A B Haynes* a60 49
3 b g Systematic—Lycius Touch (Lycius (USA))
3567 ◆ 8283 11307 167011 29504 36629 45339 58736 (7142) 73927 751712

Mystic Ways (IRE) *Traugott Stauffer*
5 b g Testa Rossa(AUS) —Metal Chimes (USA) (Chimes Band (USA))
652a9

Mystified (IRE) *R F Fisher* a37 61
6 b g Raise A Grand(IRE) —Sunrise (IRE) (Sri Pekan (USA))
(2785) 29692 31712 34442 44622 48067 55544 60213 65587

My Sweet Baby (USA) *R Menichetti* 103
3 b f Minardi(USA) —Gmaasha (IRE) (Kris)
(1659a) 2310a17 6717a5

My Sweet Georgia (IRE) *Stef Liddiard* a73 76
3 b f Royal Applause—Harda Arda (USA) (Nureyev (USA))
(149) 2395 3452 (605) 6842 8194 623012 637013 67838 (7348) 757711 76439 77973

Mythical Blue (IRE) *J M Bradley* a64 83
3 b g Acclamation—Proud Myth (IRE) (Mark Of Esteem (IRE))
14243 19822 (2349) (2651) 32293 (4223) 44835 (5345) (5877) 664710

Mythical Border (USA) *J Noseda* 102
3 ch f Johannesburg(USA) —Border Dispute (USA) (Boundary (USA))
523316

Mythical Charm *J J Bridger* a59 64
10 b m Charnwood Forest(IRE) —Triple Tricks (IRE) (Royal Academy (USA))
439

Mythical Flight (SAF) *S g Tarry* 112
6 ch g Jet Master(SAF) —Mythical Bird (SAF) (Harry Hotspur (SAF))
2116a6 299111 523312

Mythical Thrill *J G Given*
3 b g Alhaarth(IRE) —Mythical Girl (USA) (Gone West (USA))
44728 501011

Mythicism *B Smart* 71
3 b f Oasis Dream—Romantic Myth (Mind Games)
12328 173614

Mythie *E J O'Neill* 60
2 b f Orpen(USA) —Mythical Creek (USA) (Pleasant Tap (USA))
5713a10 (6148a)

Mytivil (IRE) *M Salaman* a64 69
3 gr f Clodovil(IRE) —Mytilene (IRE) (Soviet Star (USA))
1366 19322 232012 26859 285810

Myttons Maid *A Bailey* a21 49
3 b f Bertolini(USA) —The In-Laws (IRE) (Be My Guest (USA))
194012 41772

My Verse *M A Jarvis* a72 83
3 b f Exceed And Excel(AUS) —Reematna (Sabrehill (USA))
(5520) (5996) 65354

Naaqoos *F Head* 119
3 b c Oasis Dream—Straight Lass (IRE) (Machiavellian (USA))
1207a2 1917a6 4837a10

Nabeeda *M Brittain* a63 59
4 b g Namid—Lovellian (Machiavellian (USA))
144 953 2223 2775 18895 76814 77104

Nabra *M Brittain* a50 56
5 b m Kyllachy—Muja Farewell (Mujtahid (USA))
17510 45087 (5041) 53919 616011 622111

Nabrina (IRE) *M Brittain* a45 53
2 ch f Namid—My Cadeaux (Cadeaux Genereux)
36335 37626 48899 55536 59503 65898 70886 77574

Nacho Libre *M W Easterby* a76 77
4 b g Kyllachy—Expectation (IRE) (Night Shift (USA))
127817 16896 207116 257611 30664 419112 69844 (7371) 74243 77353

Nadal (IRE) *Frau Doris Smith* 81
6 ch g Shinko Forest(IRE) —Carpet Lady (IRE) (Night Shift (USA))
6499a10

Naddwah *M A Jarvis* 68
2 ch f Pivotal—My Dubai (IRE) (Dubai Millennium)
67306

Nadeen (IRE) *M R Channon* 85
2 b c Bahamian Bounty—Janayen (USA) (Zafonic (USA))
(1534) 25473

Nafaath (IRE) *Kevin Prendergast* a82 100
3 ch g Nayef(USA) —Alshakr (Bahri (USA))
1388a9 2306a5 4962a4

Nafura *Saeed Bin Suroor* a86 62
2 b f Dubawi(IRE) —Mysterial (USA) (Alleged (USA))
49805 53977 59807 (7003) ◆ (7359)

Naheell *G Prodromou* a71 68
3 ch c Lomitas—Seyooll (IRE) (Danehill (USA))
34666 536611 61892 (6668) 71018 74758 76648

Naias (IRE) *R A Fahey* a7 45
4 ch m Namid—Sovereign Grace (IRE) (Standaan (FR))
15312

Naipe Marcado (URU) *E Charpy* a61 91
6 ch h Timber'o(URU) —Nadinka Foss (URU) (Full Toss (ARG))
263a10 439a8

Nairana *J G Given* a34
3 b f Lend A Hand—Flukes (Distant Relative)
2986

Naizak *J L Dunlop* a56 72
3 ch f Medicean—Sunny Davis (USA) (Alydar (USA))
119313 174310

Najd (USA) *Saeed Bin Suroor* 83
2 ch c Storm Cat(USA) —Miss Halory (USA) (Mr Prospector (USA))
(4986) (Dead)

Nakoma (IRE) *B Ellison* a66 64
7 b m Bahhare(USA) —Indian Imp (Indian Ridge)
4347[4] 4599[4] 5291[7] (6768) (7357) 7490[6] 7785[7]

Naledi *J R Norton* a47 40
5 b g Indian Ridge—Red Carnation (IRE) (Polar Falcon (USA))
175[11] 581[5] 1974[10] 3322[10]

Nalin Isyani (TUR) *H H Basi* 73
5 b h Dilum(USA) —Truthful (Shareef Dancer (USA))
5618a[9]

Namaskar *J H M Gosden* 80
2 b f Dansili—Namaste (Alzao (USA))
(5741)

Namastee (GER) *F Kurz* 1
3 b f Areion(GER) —Never Say Never (IRE) (Scenic)
6605a[10]

Namecheck (GER) *Saeed Bin Suroor* 98
2 ch c Shamardal(USA) —Nadia (Nashwan (USA))
5728[3] (6181) 6898[3]

Named At Dinner *Miss Lucinda V Russell* 48
8 ch g Halling(USA) —Salanka (IRE) (Persian Heights)
3444[8]

Namibian Orator (IRE) *Sir Michael Stoute* 92
3 br c Cape Cross(IRE) —Drama Class (IRE) (Caerleon (USA))
(1573) ◆ 2296[6] 6429[3] 7035[4]

Namir (IRE) *H J Evans* a69 83
7 b g Namid—Danalia (IRE) (Danehill (USA))
1776[9] 1943[7] 2472[2] 2770[12] 2840[4] 3236[6] 3784[12] 4069[7] 4399[6] 4662[2] 4886[8] 5719[12] 6118[6] 6422[2] 7122[6] 7329[6]

Nampour (FR) *P J Hobbs* a78 87
4 gr g Daylami(IRE) —Nadira (FR) (Green Desert (USA))
5912[4]

Namu *Miss T Spearing* a70 64
6 b m Mujahid(USA) —Sheraton Heights (Deploy)
(22) 155[6] 167[7] 289[9] 387[8] 2852[13] 3471[2] (3671) 4702[2] 5125[5] 5288[6] 5576[9] 5911[8] 6340[3] 6377[5] 6933[8]

Nan (USA) *Craig Dollase* a107 107
3 bb f High Yield(USA) —Trip Around Heaven (USA) (Halo (USA))
1763a[5]

Nannarella (IRE) *P Giannotti* 93
3 b f Kheleyf(USA) —Nuzhaat (IRE) (Diesis)
1659a[6]

Nanny Doe (IRE) *Lee Smyth* a23
3 b f Mujadil(USA) —Prima (Primo Dominie)
7401[7] 7730[8]

Nanotech (IRE) *Jarlath P Fahey* a93 98
5 ch g Fath(USA) —Wing And A Prayer (IRE) (Shalford (IRE))
1374a[10] 2289a[10] 3435a[12] 3898a[14]

Nantha (IRE) *S Botti* 101
2 ch f King's Best(USA) —Nashatara (USA) (Nashwan (USA))
6892a[2]

Nanton (USA) *J S Goldie* a94 109
7 rg g Spinning World(USA) —Grab The Green (USA) (Cozzene (USA))
995[12] 2342[2] 3014[3] 3873[13] 4297[9] 4781[2] 5173[4] (5823) ◆ 6093[4] 6480[3] 6851[9] 7720[4]

Naomh Geileis (USA) *M Johnston* a69 57
4 ch m Grand Slam(USA) —St Aye (USA) (Nureyev (USA))
124[8] 278[7] 490[5] 4532[7] 5128[4] 6156[8] 6926[6] (7349) 7506[6] 7728[3] 7762[5] 7870[12]

Napa Starr (FR) *C Byrnes* a78 71
5 b g Marchand De Sable(USA) —Jade D'Eau (IRE) (Lion Cavern (USA))
6780[4]

Naples (AUS) *M F De Kock* a84
6 b g Xaar—Lyphard Street (USA) (Lyphard (USA))
435a[9] 522a[6] 612a[3]

Napoleons Mistress (IRE) *P F I Cole* 44
2 ch f Peintre Celebre(USA) —State Crystal (IRE) (High Estate)
6389[6]

Napoletano (GER) *S Dow* a75 76
8 b g Soviet Star(USA) —Noble House (GER) (Siberian Express (USA))
31[6] 318[9] 708[8] 1539[2] 2491[4] 2736[5] 3159[7] 3243[7] 4009[2] 5188[3] 6337[6] 6783[5]

Napoletano (ITY) *R Johnson* 47
3 b g Kyllachy—Nationality (Nashwan (USA))
820[8] 1562[7] 1739[7] 5342[7]

Naramix (FR) *L A Urbano-Grajales* a82 86
5 gr g Linamix(FR) —Narasimha (USA) (Nureyev (USA))
5281a[9]

Naranja (GER) *J-P Gauvin* a74 91
6 b m Lando(GER) —Narissa (GER) (Platini (GER))
(6981a)

Narc (SAF) *H J Brown* a92 85
7 ch g National Assembly(CAN) —She's No Secret (SAF) (Our Casey's Boy (USA))
418a[12] 525a[11]

Nareion (GER) *W Baltromei* 101
3 b c Areion(GER) —Ninigretta (GER) (Dashing Blade)
7044a[5]

Narjan *D Prod'Homme* 74
3 b c Efisio—Nadira (FR) (Green Desert (USA))
(2293a) 6682a[0]

Naseby (USA) *Miss S L Davison* a58
2 ch c Maria's Mon(USA) —Branchbury (USA) (Mt. Livermore (USA))
4201[8] 6228[14] 6774[9]

Naseehah (USA) *Saeed Bin Suroor* a90
3 ch c Rahy(USA) —Helwa (USA) (Silver Hawk (USA))
(7195) 7360[2]

Nashmiah (IRE) *C E Brittain* a105 110
3 b f Elusive City(USA) —Frond (Alzao (USA))
(912) 1698[9] (2057) 3088[8] 3846[5] 4522[10] 5260[3] (5472) (6003) 6479[8] 7046a[4]

Nasri *B J Meehan* 104
3 b c Kyllachy—Triple Sharp (Selkirk (USA))
1354[6] 2278[2] 2673[3] 3011[12]

Nassar (IRE) *G Prodromou* a66 67
6 b h Danehill(USA) —Regent Gold (USA) (Seeking The Gold (USA))
1122[5] (1496) 1589[3] 1960[3] 2332[4] 3361[5] 3552[4] 5365[3] 6565[7] 6860[4] 7204[6]

Nassau Beach (IRE) *T D Easterby* 44
3 b g Bahamian Bounty—Oh'Cecilia (IRE) (Scenic)
1061[5] 1452[9] 2572[5] 3125[10]

Natalie N G *J R Jenkins*
2 b f Zamindar(USA) —Tango Teaser (Shareef Dancer (USA))
7289[11]

Nathan Dee *M R Bosley* a41 55
4 ch g Guys And Dolls—Blu Air Flow (ITY) (Entrepreneur)
1568[9]

National Face (HUN) *S Szabolcs* a25
4 u g Satin Stone(USA) —National Art (IRE) (Petardia)
464a[8]

National Monument (IRE) *J A Osborne* a69
3 b g Statue Of Liberty(USA) —Panpipes (USA) (Woodman (USA))
386[3] 658[3] 767[4] 5123[8] 6288[13] 7703[11]

Native Dame (IRE) *Edgar Byrne* a61 52
3 b f Spartacus(IRE) —Wisecrack (IRE) (Lucky Guest)
2350[14] 2709[9] 3449[2] 4155[6] 4240[5] 7572[8] 7703[11]

Native Ruler *H R A Cecil* 105
3 b c Cape Cross(IRE) —Love Divine (Diesis)
1289[2] ◆ (1611) ◆ 2014[7] 3087[7] 4760[3]

Nativity *J L Spearing* a57 63
3 ch f Kyllachy—Mistral's Dancer (Shareef Dancer (USA))
2654[7] 3053[6] 5747[7] 5971[2] 6362[7] 7107[2] 7592[5] 7610[6] 7770[2] 7835[5]

Natural Flair (USA) *P W Chapple-Hyam* 85
3 ch f Giant's Causeway(USA) —Forest Lady (USA) (Woodman (USA))
(1329) 1701[7] 4520[6] 5027[4] (6618) 7302a[10]

Natural Law (IRE) *Saeed Bin Suroor* a80 80
2 b g Lomitas—Flying Squaw (Be My Chief (USA))
5499[8] 5770[3] (6291) 7184[5]

Natural Leader *H-A Pantall* a85 82
4 b h Dansili—Flamenco Red (Warning)
5089a[2]

Natural Rhythm (IRE) *Mrs R A Carr* a50 64
4 ch g Distant Music(USA) —Nationalartgallery (IRE) (Tate Gallery (USA))
1194[14] 2245[15] 3070[14] 3689[10] 4040[6] (4144) 4496[5] 5289[13] 6023[11] 6999[7] 7173[4]

Naughty Girl (IRE) *John A Harris* a28 50
9 b m Dr Devious(IRE) —Mary Magdalene (Night Shift (USA))
63[7] 399[9]

Naughty Norris *R Bastiman* 27
2 ch g Needwood Blade—Leave It To Lib (Tender King)
5668[13] 6214[8] 7244[14]

Nautical *J R Holt* a64 86
11 gr g Lion Cavern(USA) —Russian Royal (USA) (Nureyev (USA))
62[2] 150[4] 327[7] 399[2] 513[10] (581) 823[12]

Navajo Chief *A P Jarvis* 82
2 b c King's Best(USA) —Navajo Rainbow (Rainbow Quest (USA))
(2547) 3782[5] 4294[3] 7030[14]

Navajo Joe (IRE) *R Johnson* a85 86
4 ch g Indian Ridge—Maid Of Killeen (IRE) (Darshaan)
822[5] 1436[6] 1737[15] 2235[3] 2402[12] 4592[9] 5343[6] 6221[8] 6383[10]

Navajo Nation (IRE) *B J Meehan* a68 70
3 b g Indian Haven—Kathy Desert (Green Desert (USA))
3566[3] 4520[8] 4918[2] 5570[10] 5975[4] 6257[6] 6549[3]

Naval Officer (USA) *J Barton* a65 108
3 b c Tale Of The Cat(USA) —Wandering Star (USA) (Red Ransom (USA))
769a[3] 1009a[6]

Nave (USA) *M Johnston* a73 63
2 b c Pulpit(USA) —Lakabi (USA) (Nureyev (USA))
2195[8] 2610[3] 4067[9] 4647[6] 6829[4] (7235) ◆ 7434[2] 7685[2]

Navene (IRE) *C F Wall* a44 70
5 b m Desert Style(IRE) —Majudel (IRE) (Revoque (IRE))
2166[13]

Navy List (FR) *Saeed Bin Suroor* a80 90
2 b c Nayef(USA) —Fasliyeva (FR) (Fasliyev (USA))
4314[11] 4790[2] 5312[2] (5951) 6993[5]

Nawaadi (USA) *J H M Gosden* a78 76
3 ch g El Corredor(USA) —Louise's Time (USA) (Gilded Time (USA))
1001[6] 1303[7] ◆ 1707[4] 2060[10] 5223[2] 5834[5] 6613[6]

Nawaaff *M Quinn* a57 65
4 ch g Compton Place—Amazed (Clantime)
347[4] (474) 575[12] 896[10] 1535[8] 1784[11] 2660[7] 3031[13] 3242[5] 3671[3] 6581[5] 7771[9]

Nawamees (IRE) *P D Evans* a79 80
11 b g Darshaan—Truly Generous (IRE) (Generous (IRE))
237[4] (302) (517) 935[5] 977[4] 1586[2] 1786[9] 2129[4] (2264) 2499[7] 2743[5] 4021[3] 4146[2] 4263[4] 4857[6] 4987[2] 5097[4] 5185[4] 5857[4] 6560[7] 6704[9] 7036[6] 7137[7] 7272[4] 7549[6]

Nawojka (IRE) *J G Given* 53
3 gr f Daylami(IRE) —Panna (Polish Precedent (USA))
2856[7] 4066[6]

Naxox (FR) *George Baker* a68
8 ch g Cupidon(FR) —Frou Frou Lou (FR) (Groom Dancer (USA))
7578[2] 7724[6]

Nayef Star *J Noseda* 64
4 b g Nayef(USA) —Satin Bell (Midyan (USA))
2199[3]

Nayessence *M W Easterby* 56
3 ch g Nayef(USA) —Fragrant Oasis (USA) (Rahy (USA))
6818[4] 7080[6]

Naywye *M W Easterby* a5
3 b f Nayef(USA) —Mount Hillaby (IRE) (Mujadil (USA))
819[7] 1652[7]

Nazreef *H Morrison* a75
2 b c Zafeen(FR) —Roofer (IRE) (Barathea (IRE))
(7502)

Nbhan (USA) *L M Cumani* a80 81
3 b c With Approval(CAN) —Crisp And Cool (USA) (Ogygian (USA))
2892[3] 3644[2] 4426[2] 5102[3] 5834[7]

Nchike *R C Guest* a44 67
3 b g Zaha(CAN) —Tinkerbird (Music Boy)
924[7] 1057[12] 2154[4] 2234[2] 3541[7] 3955[5] 5362[9] 5621[6] 6001[7]

Ndola *P Butler* a46 42
10 b g Emperor Jones(USA) —Lykoa (Shirley Heights)
601[4] 734[11]

Near Galante (GER) *A Wohler* 97
3 b f Galileo(IRE) —Night Year (IRE) (Jareer (USA))
2524a[5] 3604a[7] 4583a[5] 6715a[6]

Near The Front *Miss Gay Kelleway* a56 57
4 b g Compton Place—Once In My Life (IRE) (Lomond (USA))
541[2]

Neatico (GER) *P Schiergen* 104
2 bb c Medicean—Nicola Bella (IRE) (Sadler's Wells (USA))
(7314a)

Neat 'n Tidy *A E Jones* a23 25
5 b m Josr Algarhoud(IRE) —Raspberry Sauce (Niniski (USA))
4266[8] 7462[12]

Neboisha *M Wigham* a53 44
5 ch m Ishiguru(USA) —Mariette (Blushing Scribe (USA))
2244[12] 2441[7] 2806[P]

Ned Ludd (IRE) *J G Portman* 77
6 b g Montjeu(IRE) —Zanella (IRE) (Nordico (USA))
1356[8] 2177[3] 2429[6] 6692[7]

Neduardo *P W Chapple-Hyam* a49
2 ch c Monsieur Bond(IRE) —Bond Shakira (Daggers Drawn (USA))
7477[5]

Needleleaf (USA) *A Fabre* a87 83
2 b c Kingmambo(USA) —Forest Heiress (USA) (Forest Wildcat (USA))
5085a[5]

Needsamaite *D J S Ffrench Davis* 47
2 b c Needwood Blade—Dekelsmary (Komaite (USA))
1249[4]

Needs A Treat *N Tinkler* 32
2 b f Needwood Blade—Goes A Treat (IRE) (Common Grounds)
1364[5] 1624[7]

Needwood Dancer *Peter Grayson* a26 29
2 br f Needwood Blade—Waterline Dancer (IRE) (Danehill Dancer (IRE))
1005[10] 1450[6] 1802[10] 1934[4] 2457[5]

Needy McCredie *J R Turner* 41
3 ch f Needwood Blade—Vocation (IRE) (Royal Academy (USA))
4276[8] 4550[5] 5071[7] 5948[9]

Nefyn *W R Muir* a31 60
2 b f Tiger Hill(IRE) —Bread Of Heaven (Machiavellian (USA))
5906[6] 6920[9] 7140[7]

Negligee (USA) *John Terranova II* a112
2 b f Northern Afleet(USA) —Naughty Notions (USA) (Relaunch (USA))
7283a[6]

Negotiation (IRE) *J H M Gosden* a70 90
3 b g Refuse To Bend(IRE) —Dona Royale (IRE) (Darshaan)
951[3] (1255) 4440[2] (5030) 5475[10]

Nehaam *J H M Gosden* 108
3 b g Nayef(USA) —Charm The Stars (Roi Danzig (USA))
(1291) ◆ 2014[10] 3087[8] 6425[2] 6854[2]

Neko Bay (USA) *John Shirreffs* a110
6 bb h Giant's Causeway(USA) —Brulay (USA) (Rubiano (USA))
7309a[6]

Nelson (GER) *M Trybuhl* a85 78
4 ch h Kornado—Nostalgia (GER) (Monsun (GER))
(5089a)

Nelsons Prospect (IRE) *R A Teal* a2
4 b g Fayruz—Kiva (Indian Ridge)
3384[7]

Nemo Spirit (IRE) *W R Muir* a97 98
4 gr g Daylami(IRE) —La Bayadere (Sadler's Wells (USA))
1383[4] 2486[11] (2895) 4332[7] 5656[2] 6851[28]

Neon Blue *R M Whitaker* a54 63
8 bb g Atraf—Desert Lynx (IRE) (Green Desert (USA))
1402[4] 1615[13] 2362[10] 2965[9] 3557[4] 3911[S] 4431[8] 4927[6] 5694[10] 6818[12]

Neon Light (GER) *A Wohler* 108
2 b f Refuse To Bend(IRE) —No Merci (GER) (General Assembly (USA))
(7045a)

Neo's Mate (IRE) *Paul Green* a53 60
3 br f Modigliani(USA) —Gute (IRE) (Petardia)
308[11] 1921[13] (3498) 4079[6] (4191) 4977[5] 5145[5] 6862[7] 7417[7] 7555[7] 7787[2]

Nepotism *M S Saunders* a35 74
2 b c Piccolo—Craic Sa Ceili (IRE) (Danehill Dancer (IRE))
1981[5] 2649[7] 2979[2] (3385) 5650[6]

Nero West (FR) *I Semple* a41 78
8 ch g Pelder(IRE) —West River (USA) (Gone West (USA))
219[7]

Nesayem (IRE) *D M Simcock* a67 71
3 b f Diktat—Zibet (Kris)
1752[4] 2375[4] 3384[3] 5910[5] 6276[2] 6789[4]

Nesno (USA) *J D Bethell* a72 71
6 ch g Royal Academy(USA) —Cognac Lady (USA) (Olympio (USA))
5395[7] 6074[9] 6862[10]

Netta (IRE) *P J Makin* 85
3 b f Barathea(IRE) —Nishan (Nashwan (USA))
4057[4] (4947) 5996[8]

Networker *P J McBride* a76 71
6 ch g Danzig Connection(USA) —Trevorsninepoints (Jester)
143[7] 868[3] 1258[9] 1495[4] 2261[2] 2459[4] 7798[3]

Neuchatel (GER) *M Johnston* a80 79
3 b g Rahy(USA) —Nalani (IRE) (Sadler's Wells (USA))
101[4]

Neva A Mull Moment (IRE) *D Nicholls* 65
3 b g Mull Of Kintyre(USA) —Serious Contender (IRE) (Tenby)
2543[3] 4276[3] 5041[3] 5338[2] 5599[12]

Nevada Desert (IRE) *R M Whitaker* a84 84
9 b g Desert King(IRE) —Kayanga (Green Desert (USA))
1952[10] 2274[9] 3067[7] 4104[6] 4400[6] 4549[6] 4663[8] 6250[7] 6460[7] 6640[2] (6860) (7014) 7194[13]

Neve Lieve (IRE) *M Botti* a56 90
4 bb m Dubai Destination(USA) —Love Of Silver (USA) (Arctic Tern (USA))
2085[5]

Never Bouchon (JPN) *M Ito* 117
6 b h Marvelous Sunday(JPN) —Pearl Necklace (Mill Reef (USA))
7593a[10]

Never Ending Tale *E F Vaughan* a87 89
4 ch g Singspiel(IRE) —Bright Finish (USA) (Zilzal (USA))
1316[2] (2666) 3154[7]

Never Lose *C E Brittain* a81 93
3 br f Diktat—Enchanted Princess (Royal Applause)
(796) 1002[9] 1214[10] 1639[4] (2079) 2271[3] 2928[4] 3746[8] 4088[7] 4771[5] 6814[11]

Never On Sunday (FR) *J-C Rouget* 123
4 gr h Sunday Break(JPN) —Hexane (FR) (Kendor (FR))
1144a[5] (2120a) 3013[3] 5086a[7] 6850[10]

Never Sold Out (IRE) *J G M O'Shea* a48 58
4 ch g Captain Rio—Vicious Rosie (Dancing Spree (USA))
666[10] 1535[4] ◆ 1741[12] 2518[3] 2912[8] 3473[9] 5211[7]

Never The Waiter *B J Meehan* a86 95
2 b c Kyllachy—Talighta (USA) (Barathea (IRE))
4986[6] ◆ (6493) 6677[3] ◆

New Adventure *P F I Cole* 44
3 b g Generous(IRE) —Sari (Faustus (USA))
2350[15]

New Beginning (FR) *H J L Dunlop* a66 47
3 b f Nayef(USA) —Chrysalu (Distant Relative)
1416[12] 2685[13] 4196[10]

New Beginning (IRE) *Mrs S Lamyman* a73 84
5 b g Keltos(FR) —Goldthroat (IRE) (Zafonic (USA))
6[7] 39[5] 220[5] 478[4] 1192[3] 1279[2] 1615[12]

Newbury Street *R A Fahey* a65 67
2 b g Namid—Cautious Joe (First Trump)
1590[3] 4187[4] 5066[3] 6035[2] (6345) 6983[3]

Newby Abbey (IRE) *D Flood* a12
8 b g Lord Of Appeal—Turramurra Girl (IRE) (Magical Wonder (USA))
1530[11] 2129[12]

Newcastle Sam *J J Bridger* a6 35
4 b g Atraf—Ballyewry (Prince Tenderfoot (USA))
5963[6]

New Christmas (USA) *B J Meehan* a84 69
2 rg c Smoke Glacken(USA) —Occhi Verdi (IRE) (Mujtahid (USA))
4497[4] 5109[U] 5528[10] 7157[5] (7604) (7804) ◆

New Couture (IRE) *P W Chapple-Hyam* a54
3 b f Montjeu(IRE) —New Design (IRE) (Bluebird (USA))
7439[7] 7648[4] 7882[6]

New Den *J R Boyle* a56 55
2 ch c Piccolo—Den's-Joy (Archway (IRE))
2631[11] 2844[13] 7764[6] 7865[7]

New England *F Sheridan* a65 65
7 ch g Bachir(IRE) —West Escape (Gone West (USA))
571[3] 805[3] (935) 1533[2] 2068[9] 2419[8] 2493[2] 2783[6] 3374[5] 3923[3] (4857) 5227[8] 6612[6] 6998[10]

New Fan *D Baltromei* 97
5 b g Dashing Blade—Nicara (GER) (Nebos (GER))
2097a[7] 2513a[14] 6499a[9]

New Freedom (BRZ) *M Al Muhairi* a101 105
8 b g Burooj—Beautiful Maria (BRZ) (Ghadeer (FR))
336a[6] 525a[7] 770a[12]

Newgate (UAE) *Mrs R A Carr* a60 33
5 b g Jade Robbery(USA) —Patruel (Rainbow Quest (USA))
823[8]

New Guinea *E Charpy* a93 107
6 b g Fantastic Light(USA) —Isle Of Spice (USA) (Diesis)
437a[9]

New Innocence *G A Butler* a72 74
2 ch c Where Or When(IRE) —Scottendale (Zilzal (USA))
3750[6] 4396[4] 7199[4]

New Leyf (IRE) *J R Gask* a83 77
3 bb g Kheleyf(USA) —Society Fair (FR) (Always Fair (USA))
2070[6] 2496[9] (3036) 3592[9] 4056[3] 4338[5] *7828[2]* ◆

Newmarket Story (IRE) *W J Austin* a38 56
7 b m Desert Story(IRE) —Faramisa (IRE) (Doyoun)
(2634)

Newpark Rio (IRE) *Emmanuel Hughes* a60 73
2 b c Captain Rio—Newpark Lady (IRE) (Foxhound (USA))
5274a[11]

Newport (AUS) *Paul Perry* 112
7 gr g Encosta De Lago(AUS) —Sibelienne (Nishapour (FR))
7196a[6] 7215a[10]

New Star (UAE) *W M Brisbourne* a85 77
5 b g Green Desert(USA) —Princess Haifa (USA) (Mr Prospector (USA))
220[4] (477) 577[2] (737) 910[2] 1107[6] 1133[2]

Newton Circus *Ollie Pears* a67 69
2 gr c Verglas(IRE) —Flying Finish (FR) (Priolo (USA))
2793[3] *3715[9]* 4515[7] *5369[5] (5811) 6586[3]* 6819[2]

Newtons Cradle (IRE) *J Howard Johnson* 40
2 b g Noverre(USA) —Lady Of Kildare (IRE) (Mujadil (USA))
3823[11] 4595[10]

New Tricks *I Semple* 71
3 b g Falbrav(IRE) —Numberonedance (USA) (Trempolino (USA))
1829[2] 2340[9] (2627) 3809[7] 4898[9]

New World Order (IRE) *Edgar Byrne* a68 53
5 b g Night Shift(USA) —Kama Tashoof (Mtoto)
3024[9] 3734[7] 4437[6] *(6208) 6256[9] 6918[8] 7403[2]*

New World Symphony (IRE) *J Howard Johnson* a5 60
2 b c War Chant(USA) —Bold Classic (USA) (Pembroke (USA))
2997[6] *5324[6]*

New York Lights (IRE) *M D I Usher* a54 43
2 b f Statue Of Liberty(USA) —Nautical Light (Slip Anchor)
1249[U] 1404[12] 1783[9] *4201[5] 4747[2] 5583[10] 5636[8]* 6034[7] 6736[11] *7690[7] 7887[9]*

Nexcity (FR) *Mlle V Dissaux* a71 78
3 b c Sagacity(FR) —Nexia (FR) (Linamix (FR))
7696a[7]

Next Move (IRE) *Saeed Bin Suroor* a79
2 b c Tiger Hill(IRE) —Cinnamon Rose (USA) (Trempolino (USA))
(7326)

Next Vision (IRE) *J Hirschberger* 97
3 ch c Rock Of Gibraltar(IRE) —Night Petticoat (GER) (Petoski)
1915a[8]

Nezami (IRE) *J Akehurst* a94 96
4 b g Elnadim(USA) —Stands To Reason (USA) (Gulch (USA))
73[3] 1467[4] 1861[2] *7827[7]*

Nianga (GER) *P Schiergen* 91
2 b f Lomitas—Nobilissima (GER) (Bluebird (USA))
7045a[3]

Nibani (IRE) *Sir Michael Stoute* 74
2 ch c Dalakhani(IRE) —Dance Of The Sea (IRE) (Sinndar (IRE))
6810[4] ◆

Nicaldani *M Blanshard*
2 ch f Compton Place—Thamud (IRE) (Lahib (USA))
3576[13] *4839[7]*

Nicea (GER) *P Schiergen* 101
2 b f Lando(GER) —Nicolaia (GER) (Alkalde (GER))
5652a[5] 6892a[5]

Nice Girl (FR) *F Cohen* 54
2 b f Gold Away(IRE) —Josephine (Emperor Jones (USA))
6751a[6]

Nice Time (IRE) *M H Tompkins* a64 75
3 ch f Tagula(IRE) —Nicea (IRE) (Dominion)
1670[6] 2432[6] 2942[2] 3822[7] *5168[9]* 6236[4] 6742[4]

Nice To Know (FR) *G L Moore* a89 79
5 ch m Machiavellian(USA) —Entice (FR) (Selkirk (USA))
2768[7] 3102[8] *3509[2] 3736[2]* 4259[9]

Nicholas Pocock (IRE) *Sir Michael Stoute* 76
3 b g King's Best(USA) —Sea Picture (IRE) (Royal Academy (USA))
1295[6]

Nickel Silver *B Smart* a94 85
4 gr g Choisir(AUS) —Negligee (Night Shift (USA))
(15) (96) (165) 270[3] 1227[10] 2716[7] 3149[3] 3372[5] 4753[3] 5031[4] 6171[5] *6459[4]* (7123) *7646[2] (7758)*

Nicky Nutjob (GER) *J Pearce* a62 60
3 b c Fasliyev(USA) —Natalie Too (USA) (Irish River (FR))
295[5] 506[7] 677[8] 865[7] 1050[4] 1363[12] 1594[8] 2790[9] 4156[11]

Niconero (AUS) *David Hayes* 117
8 b g Danzero(AUS) —Nicola Lass (AUS) (Scenic)
1011a[4] 1554a[8]

Nicosia *M R Channon* 8
2 b f Imperial Dancer—Stride Home (Absalom)
2978[11] 4101[6]

Nidamar *Mrs R A Carr*
2 b f Redoubtable(USA) —Marabar (Sri Pekan (USA))
1344[10] 1450[8] 2541[8] *5226[11] 6354[11] 7674[5] 7707[7]*

Nideeb *C E Brittain* 104
2 ch c Exceed And Excel(AUS) —Mantesera (IRE) (In The Wings)
3395[4] (3957) (4294) ◆ 5659[2] 6426[5]

Night Affair *D W P Arbuthnot* a79 79
3 b f Bold Edge—Twilight Mistress (Bin Ajwaad (IRE))
2632[4] 3506[2] 4952[2] 5264[7] 5877[4]

Nightboat To Cairo (IRE) *P A Kirby* 25
5 b m Turtle Island(IRE) —Garryduff Breeze (IRE) (Strong Gale)
2785[4]

Night Crescendo (USA) *Mrs A J Perrett* a94 102
6 bb g Diesis—Night Fax (USA) (Known Fact (USA))
1696[5] ◆ 2085[7] 3142[7] 4340[11] 4661[6] 4770[2] 5262[15] 5865[3] 6302[10]

Nightdance Paolo (GER) *P Schiergen* 95
2 b c Paolini(GER) —Nightdance (GER) (Shareef Dancer (USA))
6887a[4] 7314a[7]

Nightjar (USA) *K A Ryan* a103 87
4 b h Smoke Glacken(USA) —Night Risk (USA) (Wild Again (USA))
(9) 106[5] (225) 579[9] 783[8] (856) 995[13] 1124[9] 1398[8] 1864[3] 2078[3] 2814[8] *5615[9]* 6429[7] 6876[4] 6949[2] 7837[3]

Night Knight (IRE) *M L W Bell* a64 69
3 b g Bachelor Duke(USA) —Dark Albatross (USA) (Sheikh Albadou)
1470[9] (1926) 3115[15] 3637[8] 4916[8] (6001) *6439[4]*

Night Lily (IRE) *J Jay* a68 74
3 b f Night Shift(USA) —Kedross (IRE) (King Of Kings (IRE))
317[3] 1839[7] 2001[4] 2667[5] 3334[2] 4054[11] 4910[5] *5582[2] (6223)*

Night Magic (GER) *W Figge* 111
3 br f Sholokhov(IRE) —Night Woman (GER) (Monsun (GER))
1718a[3] 2524a[3] (3604a) (4583a) 6525a[9] 7046a[2]

Night Of Idaho (FR) *M Houdoin*
2 b f Idaho Quest—Night Symphony (GER) (Big Shuffle (USA))
5956a[0]

Night Of Magic (IRE) *H Steinmetz* 107
3 b f Peintre Celebre(USA) —Night Teeny (Platini (GER))
(2310a) 4367a[8] 6521a[2] 7046a[12]

Night Orbit *Miss J Feilden* a71 72
5 b g Observatory(USA) —Dansara (Dancing Brave (USA))
(103) 342[4] 485[6] 735[4] 7124[2]

Night Premiere (IRE) *R Hannon* a59 61
4 b m Night Shift(USA) —Star Studded (Cadeaux Genereux)
99[4] 596[8] 710[8]

Night Prospector *R A Harris* a62 68
9 b g Night Shift(USA) —Pride Of My Heart (Lion Cavern (USA))
27[11]

Nights Cross (IRE) *B Al Abed* a73 96
8 b g Cape Cross(IRE) —Cathy Garcia (IRE) (Be My Guest (USA))
433a[4] 611a[9] 696a[7]

Night Sky *P J Makin* 50
2 b f Starcraft(NZ) —War Shanty (Warrshan (USA))
6730[13]

Nightstrike (IRE) *Luke Comer* a45 67
6 b m Night Shift(USA) —Come Together (Mtoto)
7129[8] 7609[11]

Night Trade (IRE) *Mrs D J Sanderson* a72 75
2 b f Trade Fair—Compton Girl (Compton Place)
5006[7] *5611[3]* 6207[3] (6554) 6841[3] *7156[4]*

Nihalim (TUR) *Y Simsek* 95
4 b m Royal Abjar(USA) —Concordia (HUN) (Law Society (USA))
5588a[9]

Nikki Bea (IRE) *Jamie Poulton* a66 64
6 ch m Titus Livius(FR) —Strong Feeling (USA) (Devil's Bag (USA))
97[4] 192[2] 321[2] 505[6] 706[9]

Nimbelle (IRE) *J C Tuck* a56 50
4 bb m Namid—Bellissi (IRE) (Bluebird (USA))
347[9]

Nimmy's Special *M Mullineaux* a57 60
3 ch f Monsieur Bond(IRE) —Mammas F-C (IRE) (Case Law)
450[7] 1106[4] 2141[6] 2357[15] *3955[8]* 5145[2] 5362[3]

Nimue (USA) *P F I Cole* a51 84
2 bb f Speightstown(USA) —Flag Support (USA) (Personal Flag (USA))
4421[2] 5199[12] *6582[8]*

Nina Celebre (IRE) *P Schiergen* 97
3 b f Peintre Celebre(USA) —Next Gina (GER) (Perugino (USA))
4583a[6]

Nina Rose *C G Cox* 70
2 ro f Pastoral Pursuits—Magnolia (Petong)
2514[2] 2771[3] 3858[3] 4901[4] 5938[9] 6793[4]

Nino Zachetti (IRE) *E J Alston* 49
3 ch g Daggers Drawn(USA) —Paganina (FR) (Galetto (FR))
2786[8] 3018[6] 4105[4] 4594[10] 4995[9] 5599[9] 6415[6]

Ninth House (USA) *Mrs R A Carr* a79 79
7 b h Chester House(USA) —Ninette (USA) (Alleged (USA))
238[7] 932[9] 1316[7] 2441[3] 2722[7] 2804[3] 3110[5] *(3224) 3470[2] 3722[4] 3924[2]* (4435) 4548[2] 4751[5] 4941[2] (5107) 5441[9] (5673) 6016[9] 7000[8] 7125[7] 7172[8] 7633[7]

Niqaab *W J Musson* a63 70
5 ch m Alhaarth(IRE) —Shanty (Selkirk (USA))
38[6] 169[10]

Niran (IRE) *C E Brittain* 80
2 b c Captain Rio—Valley Lights (IRE) (Dance Of Life (USA))
(2087) (2413) 3779[11]

Nisaal (IRE) *J J Quinn* a67 80
4 b g Indian Ridge—Kahalah (IRE) (Darshaan)
1016[4] 1524[9] 2274[8] 2842[2] 4046[4] 4655[6] 5438[7] 6157[2] *6640[5]*

Nite Light (USA) *Todd Pletcher* a113
5 b h Thunder Gulch(USA) —Lite Light (USA) (Majestic Light (USA))
7281a[8]

Nizaa (USA) *B W Hills* a69 66
2 bb c Dixieland Band(USA) —Star Queen (USA) (Kingmambo (USA))
4659[4] 5401[3] *6943[5]*

Nizhoni (USA) *B Smart* a54 36
4 ch m Mineshaft(USA) —Carinae (USA) (Nureyev (USA))
36[9] 758[3]

Nizhoni Dancer *C F Wall* a58 78
3 b f Bahamian Bounty—Hagwah (USA) (Dancing Brave (USA))
2890[7]

Noafal (IRE) *M A Jarvis* 82
2 ch c Bahamian Bounty—Miss Party Line (USA) (Phone Trick (USA))
5431[3] ◆ (6616)

Noah Jameel *A G Newcombe* a61 61
7 ch g Mark Of Esteem(IRE) —Subtle One (IRE) (Polish Patriot (USA))
494[2] ◆ *669[2] 969[4]* 1254[2] 1983[6] 2608[11] *5377[2]* ◆ *6288[5] 7687[5] 7857[5]*

Nobelix (IRE) *J R Gask* a86 86
7 gr g Linamix(FR) —Nataliana (Surumu (GER))
(142) 3343[2]

Nobilissima (IRE) *Miss Tor Sturgis* a65 88
5 b m Orpen(USA) —Shadow Smile (IRE) (Slip Anchor)
3272[7]

Noble Alpha (IRE) *Mario Hofer* 106
2 b c Shamardal(USA) —Nouvelle Noblesse (GER) (Singspiel (IRE))
5652a[2] 6887a[2] 7231a[5]

Noble Attitude *N Tinkler* 59
3 b f Best Of The Bests(IRE) —Charming Lotte (Nicolotte)
3175[11] 4066[3] 4531[5]

Noble Bedouin (IRE) *J Barton* 92
5 b g Hernando(FR) —Hijaz (IRE) (Sadler's Wells (USA))
262a[14]

Noble Citizen (USA) *D M Simcock* a102 97
4 b h Proud Citizen(USA) —Serene Nobility (USA) (His Majesty (USA))
265a[8] *414a[2] 639a[2]* ◆ 1821[12] 3116[10] 3524[2] 4796[10] 5874[2] 6270[22]

Noble Court (USA) *John W Sadler* a111 109
5 b h Doneraile Court(USA) —Grey Dawn Grey (USA) (Grindstone (USA))
7305a[7]

Noble Dictator *E F Vaughan* a67 65
3 b g Diktat—Noble Desert (FR) (Green Desert (USA))
1361[7] 2300[10] 2548[8] 5366[10] *6289[2] 6784[3]*

Noble Galileo (IRE) *John M Oxx* 91
3 b f Galileo(IRE) —Almarai (USA) (Vaguely Noble)
7263a[6]

Noble Greek (USA) *J R Best* a79 79
2 bb c Omega Code(USA) —Regal Beauty (USA) (Explosive Red (CAN))
2825[2] 3779[9] 5234[2] *6443[3]*

Noble's Promise (USA) *Kenneth McPeek* a115 93
2 b c Cuvee(USA) —The Devil's Trick (USA) (Clever Trick (USA))
7307a[3]

Noble Storm (USA) *E S McMahon* 110
3 b c Yankee Gentleman(USA) —Changed Tune (USA) (Tunerup (USA))
1486[2] 1824[2] (2373) 2928[5] 3806[2] (4490) (5203) 5420[4] ◆ 6427[2]

Nobunaga *Richard Brabazon* 74
4 ch g Beat Hollow—Absolute Precision (USA) (Irish River (FR))
2290a[5]

Noche De Reyes *E J Alston* a55 60
4 b g Foxhound(USA) —Ashleigh Baker (IRE) (Don't Forget Me)
2789[5] 4351[6] 4710[6] *5617[11] 6950[4]* 7173[5] *7599[3]*

No Complaining (IRE) *B J Curley* 38
2 b f Alhaarth(IRE) —Rambler (Selkirk (USA))
5029[7] 5431[12] 7096[11]

No Explaining (IRE) *B J Curley* 76
2 b f Azamour(IRE) —Claustra (FR) (Green Desert (USA))
5096[10] 5397[9] (6591)

No Greater Love (FR) *C E Longsdon* a68 81
7 b g Take Risks(FR) —Desperate Virgin (BEL) (Chief Singer)
1051[4]

No Grouse *E J Alston* a62 74
9 b g Pursuit Of Love—Lady Joyce (FR) (Galetto (FR))
1060[4] 1333[7] 1885[5] 2531[9] 2852[2] 3529[7] 3851[6] 4312[9] 5948[2] 6103[9] 6989[12] *7179[5]*

No Hubris (USA) *P F I Cole* 92
2 b c Proud Citizen(USA) —Innateness (USA) (Flying Paster (USA))
(2017) ◆ 2993[6]

Nolecce *R C Guest* 36
2 ch g Reset(AUS) —Ghassanah (Pas De Seul)
2467[9] 5674[11] 6091[17]

Nolhac (FR) *P Khozian* 89
5 b h Smadoun(FR) —One Way (FR) (Exit To Nowhere (USA))
4335a[4]

Nomadic Warrior *J R Holt* a52 40
4 b g Nomadic Way(USA) —Jesmund (Bishop Of Cashel)
476[9] 779[7]

Nom De La Rosa (IRE) *G L Moore* 66
2 b f Oratorio(IRE) —Cheal Rose (IRE) (Dr Devious (IRE))
4460[12] 5096[4] 5564[7] 6305[8]

Nom Du Jeu (NZ) *Murray & Bjorn Baker* 118
5 br h Montjeu(IRE) —Prized Gem (NZ) (Prized (USA))
7040a[13]

No Mean Trick (USA) *C G Cox* a68
3 b c Grand Slam(USA) —Ruby's Reception (USA) (Rubiano (USA))
7401[2] 7826[3]

Nomoreblondes *P T Midgley* a66 76
5 ch m Ishiguru(USA) —Statuette (Statoblest)
1041[5] (1096) 1334[8] 1518[3] 1627[5] 2657[4] 3304[U] 4399[10] 4976[5] 5345[2] (5518) 5830[7] 6489[13] *7224[6] 7398[7]*

Nomoretaxes (BRZ) *Miss D Mountain* a49 32
7 b g First American(USA) —Raghida (BRZ) (Roi Normand (USA))
1301[7] *3736[13]*

Non Dom (IRE) *H Morrison* a60 85
3 br g Hawk Wing(USA) —Kafayef (USA) (Secreto (USA))
(1930) 2152[2] 2715[3] 3276[4] 4299[3] ◆ 5216[2] 5870[4] 6552[3]

No Nightmare (USA) *A P Jarvis* a39 51
3 b f Lion Heart(USA) —Attasliyah (IRE) (Marju (IRE))
4860[7] 5338[5] 6414[10]

Non Sucre (USA) *J Gallagher* a47 76
4 bb g Minardi(USA) —Vieille Rose (IRE) (Dancing Spree (USA))
866[8] 1072[7] 1248[13]

Noodles Blue Boy *Ollie Pears* a76 80
3 b g Makbul—Dee Dee Girl (IRE) (Primo Dominie)
859[4] 1155[6] 1736[12] (1949) 2530[3] 2726[2] (3355) 3704[5] 4653[2] (5517) 5978[10] 6279[9] ◆ 6765[2] 7082[4]

No One Likes Us *S Curran* a49
2 b g Lucky Owners(NZ) —Habibi (Alhijaz)
6721[6] 7120[17] *7482[10]*

Noor Al Bahar (IRE) *M R Channon* 4
3 b f Bahri(USA) —Barbaresque (IRE) (Green Desert (USA))
2042[10] 2738[6]

Noordhoek Kid *C R Egerton* a71 63
3 b g Dansili—Anqood (IRE) (Elmaamul (USA))
2126[15] 4918[4] 5381[6]

No Quarter (IRE) *A Dickman* 62
2 b g Refuse To Bend(IRE) —Moonlight Wish (IRE) (Peintre Celebre (USA))
2997[7] 4307[10] 4847[4] 5290[7] 6096[7]

Nora Chrissie (IRE) *Niall Moran* a74 52
7 b m Bahhare(USA) —Vino Veritas (USA) (Chief's Crown (USA))
319[9]

Nora Mae (IRE) *S Kirk* a80 88
3 ch f Peintre Celebre(USA) —Wurfklinge (GER) (Acatenango (GER))
1353[15] 5607[7] ◆ 5996[6] 6618[14] *7356[7] 7487[2] 7540[5] 7741[9]*

Norcroft *Mrs C A Dunnett* a73 56
7 b g Fasliyev(USA) —Norcroft Joy (Rock Hopper)
(14) 155[5] 289[8] 519[6] 3722[11] 3983[10] 4202[10] 4375[3] 4665[8] 5287[2] 5544[6] 5998[8] 6123[9] 6336[4] 6828[10] 7180[9] 7348[8]

Norderney (GER) *P Schiergen* 102
3 ch f Dai Jin—Nouvelle Princesse (GER) (Bluebird (USA))
(1240a) 2757a[4] 3604a[3] 4578a[7] 6152a[3] (6714a)

Nordic Light (USA) *J M Bradley* a51 54
5 bb g Belong To Me(USA) —Midriff (USA) (Naevus (USA))
23[9] 104[9] 153[4] 308[12] 328[3] 474[2] 508[6] 574[10] 746[13] 1038[4] 1536[8] 1784[10] 2811[5] 4222[7] 5345[14] 5788[10] 7689[8]

Norman Beckett *R T Phillips* a64 74
6 b g Beckett(IRE) —Classic Coral (USA) (Seattle Dancer (USA))
1568[13]

Norman The Great *A King* a74 82
5 b g Night Shift(USA) —Encore Du Cristal (USA) (Quiet American (USA))
(2493) (3169) (3768) 5028[6] *5649[6]*

Norse Warrior (USA) *Peter Grayson* a68 66
3 ch g Newfoundland(USA) —Spicy Red (USA) (Tactical Advantage (USA))
(7629) 7872[8]

Northburn *G M Lyons* a82 86
5 b g Tobougg(IRE) —Duxyana (IRE) (Cyrano De Bergerac)
3435a[7]

North Cape (USA) *H Candy* a76 79
3 b g Action This Day(USA) —Cape (USA) (Mr Prospector (USA))
1252[5] 1595[3] 2206[2] (2892) 4827[4] *5315[3]*

North Central (USA) *J Howard Johnson* 65
2 bb c Forest Camp(USA) —Brittan Lee (USA) (Forty Niner (USA))
2714[6] 3310[6] 5253[4]

North East Corner (USA) *B W Hills* 79
3 b g Giant's Causeway(USA) —Saree (Barathea (IRE))
1987[12]

Northern Acres *D Nicholls* 70
3 b g Mtoto—Bunting (Shaadi (USA))
1508[4] 1793[10] 6052[14]

Northern Bolt *D Nicholls* a68 86
4 b g Cadeaux Genereux—Shafir (IRE) (Shaadi (USA))
985[8] 3828[10] *3956[6]* 4461[6] 4753[6] 5148[4] 5623[3] 6050[5] 6647[12] (7219)

Northern Champ (IRE) *Patrick G Kelly* a49 41
3 b g Mull Of Kintyre(USA) —Comprehension (USA) (Diesis)
214[8] 839[7]

Northern Dare (IRE) *D Nicholls* a92 100
5 b g Fath(USA) —Farmers Swing (IRE) (River Falls)
(901) 1791[10] 2707[4] 3582[4] (4069) 4485[2] 5263[3] 5654[13] 5860[8] 6843[13] 7015[16]

Northern Desert (IRE) *S Curran* a75 56
10 b g Desert Style(IRE) —Rosie's Guest (IRE) (Be My Guest (USA))
(97) 357[2] 495[4] (530) 706[6] 2630[2] 3007[7] *3717[2]* 4731[2] 5179[5] 5634[7] *6703[3]*

Northern Dune (IRE) *B J Curley* a56 60
5 b g Dilshaan—Zoudie (Ezzoud (IRE))
(1242)

Northern Empire (IRE) *F Jordan* a83 100
6 ch g Namid—Bumble (Rainbow Quest (USA))
67[5] 212[3] 270[2] 351[7] 539[7] 589[2] (891) 1477[7] *1564[4]* (1921) 2359[5] 2451[2] 3020[2] 3465[2] 3945[6] 4469[7] 4886[4] 5156[3] 5341[10] 7601[11] 7682[7] 7838[13] 7890[12]

Northerner (IRE) *J O'Reilly* a53 63
6 b g Mark Of Esteem(IRE) —Ensorceleuse (FR) (Fabulous Dancer (USA))
4350[13] *7504[11]*

Northern Fling *J S Goldie* a17 104
5 b g Mujadil(USA) —Donna Anna (Be My Chief (USA))
264a^{10} 638a^{4} ◆ 1018^{16} 1278^{10} 2012^{10} 2470^{10} 3351^{7} 4353^{12} 4461^{13} 6051^{11} 6897^{6} ◆ 7171^{4}

Northern Flyer (GER) *J J Quinn* a35 71
3 b g Hawk Wing(USA) —Nachtigall (GER) (Danehill (USA))
810^{5} 1481^{6} 2236^{3} 2719^{2} (3108) ◆ 3727^{2} 3939^{2} ◆ 4664^{3} 5295^{2} 5672^{4} 6182^{5}

Northern Genes (AUS) *M R Bosley* a44
3 b g Refuse To Bend(IRE) —Cotswold Dancer (AUS) (Carnegie (IRE))
6287^{7} 7439^{9} 7550^{4}

Northern Glory *W Figge* 101
6 b g Rainbow Quest(USA) —Northern Goddess (Night Shift (USA))
4364a^{6}

Northern Jem *Jane Chapple-Hyam* 82
5 b g Mark Of Esteem(IRE) —Top Jem (Damister (USA))
2052^{6} (4060) 4502^{9} 6648^{13} 7014^{3}

Northern Shore (IRE) *K A Ryan* a50
3 br g Clodovil(IRE) —Distant Shore (IRE) (Jareer (USA))
92^{7} 363^{4} 594^{8} 684^{5}

Northern Spy (USA) *S Dow* a78 78
5 b g War Chant(USA) —Sunray Superstar (Nashwan (USA))
1815^{5} 2641^{7} 3024^{7} (3770) 4852^{4} 5190^{4} 5511^{5} 6168^{2} 6695^{13} 7475^{10} 7662^{8}

Northern Tour *P F I Cole* a79 80
3 b g Tobougg(IRE) —Swift Spring (FR) (Bluebird (USA))
1001^{5} 1489^{9} 7575^{12} 7817^{4}

Northgate (IRE) *Joseph G Murphy* a97 85
4 b g Mujadil(USA) —Arcevia (IRE) (Archway (IRE))
2729a^{7} 6467a^{10}

Northgate Lodge (USA) *M Brittain* a45 23
4 ch g Hold That Tiger(USA) —Sabaah Elfull (Kris)
5599^{8} 7718^{10}

North Parade *A W Carroll* a78 85
4 b g Nayef(USA) —Queen Sceptre (IRE) (Fairy King (USA))
483^{3} (617) 737^{5} 805^{2} 1524^{5} 1812^{4} 2200^{8}

North Shadow *A D Brown* a60 62
2 ch g Motivator—Matoaka (USA) (A.P. Indy (USA))
4993^{6} 5669^{6} 5951^{7} (6590) 6948^{5} 7453^{6} 7597^{12}

Northside Prince (IRE) *G A Swinbank* 70
3 b g Desert Prince(IRE) —Spartan Girl (IRE) (Ela-Mana-Mou)
1611^{3} 2371^{4} 2667^{4} 3911^{8} 4822^{2} 5331^{2} 5731^{3}

North South Divide (IRE) *K A Ryan* a69 85
5 b g Namid—Bush Rose (Rainbow Quest (USA))
208^{7} 896^{7} 1055^{8} 1831^{5} 3020^{6} 7068^{4} 7462^{11} 7877^{11}

North Walk (IRE) *B N Pollock* a57 84
6 b g Monashee Mountain(USA) —Celtic Link (IRE) (Toca Madera)
3029^{11}

Northwester (FR) *L Viel* 33
4 b g Slickly(FR) —Northern Riga (FR) (Bering)
7038a^{8}

No Rules *M H Tompkins* a60 75
4 b g Fraam—Golden Daring (IRE) (Night Shift (USA))
790^{5} (1273) 2725^{6} 3029^{3} (3760) 4388^{2} 6053^{7} 6692^{5} (7084)

Norwegian *Ian Williams* a55 57
3 b g Halling(USA) —Chicarica (USA) (The Minstrel (CAN))
1176^{6} 2543^{3} 368^{5}

Norwegian Dancer (UAE) *E S McMahon* a80 92
3 b c Halling(USA) —Time Changes (USA) (Danzig (USA))
1793^{5} 2356^{11} (3373) (3808) 4420^{14} 5209^{4} 5648^{7} 5904^{5} 6239^{10} 6740^{8} 6996^{5} 7373^{4}

Nosedive *W J Haggas* 98
2 ch c Observatory(USA) —Resistance Heroine (Dr Fong (USA))
(2887) 3046^{4} ◆ 3779^{8} 4487^{6} 5174^{5} 6044a^{5} 6486^{3}

Nosferatu (IRE) *J Howard Johnson* 84
6 b g In The Wings—Gothic Dream (IRE) (Nashwan (USA))
(2499) 3191^{7}

Nostaltir (FR) *D Prod'Homme* a57 84
7 b m Muhtathir—Nostalchia (FR) (Genereux Genie)
5300a^{6}

No Sting *W S Kittow* a42 49
3 b f Exit To Nowhere(USA) —Beacon Silver (Belmez (USA))
1464^{7} 2323^{5} 2881^{9} 3205^{3}

No Supper (IRE) *Tim Vaughan* a55 32
5 ch g Inchinor—Be Thankfull (IRE) (Linamix (FR))
4021^{9} 5790^{13}

Nota Bene *D R C Elsworth* a111 106
7 b g Zafonic(USA) —Dodo (IRE) (Alzao (USA))
434a^{8} 611a^{3} 696a^{3} 2385^{4} 3141^{16} 3818^{8} (4059)

Nota Liberata *Ollie Pears* a10 69
5 b g Spinning World(USA) —Kyda (USA) (Gulch (USA))
571^{11}

Note Perfect *M W Easterby* a54 55
4 b m Diktat—Better Still (IRE) (Glenstal (USA))
1241^{13} 1781^{14}

Nothing Is Forever (IRE) *L Corcoran* a56 64
5 b g Daylami(IRE) —Bequeath (USA) (Lyphard (USA))
112^{4} 449^{P}

Notice Given *H R A Cecil* 70
2 b c Oasis Dream—Well Warned (Warning)
3957^{8} 5401^{7} 6032^{4} 7096^{6}

Not In The Clock (USA) *J R Best* a58
2 b c Chapel Royal(USA) —Bavarian Girl (USA) (Unbridled (USA))
7477^{9} 7655^{5} 7886^{9}

Not Just Swing (IRE) *J-M Beguigne* a111 115
5 b h King's Best(USA) —Misbegotten (IRE) (Baillamont (USA))
6890a^{5}

Not My Choice (IRE) *J Balding* a88 89
4 ch g Choisir(AUS) —Northgate Raver (Absalom)
539^{8} 654^{12} 2472^{11} 5421^{9} 5768^{4} 6642^{9} 7192^{11} 7555^{4}

Not Now Lewis (IRE) *F P Murtagh* a59 61
5 b g Shinko Forest(IRE) —Pearl Egg (IRE) (Mukaddamah (USA))
1558^{5} 2404^{3} 2964^{6} (3490) 4313^{6} 4588^{8} 4977^{6} 5730^{9} 6256^{11}

Notorize *R M Beckett* 88
2 ch c Hernando(FR) —Hypnotize (Machiavellian (USA))
(5428) ◆ 6011^{2}

No Trimmings (IRE) *Gerard Keane* a39 65
3 ch f Medecis—Cheviot Indian (IRE) (Indian Ridge)
4392a^{6}

Notte Di Note (IRE) *L M Cumani* a59 53
2 b f Le Vie Dei Colori—Effetto Ottico (IRE) (Foxhound (USA))
6334^{5} 6826^{5} 7317^{5}

Nouailhas *R Hollinshead* a20 53
3 b g Mark Of Esteem(IRE) —Barachois Princess (USA) (Barachois (CAN))
1410^{8} 1972^{10} 2447^{8} 3054^{3} 3629^{6} 6098^{5} 6570^{7} 6788^{9}

Noubian (USA) *C R Dore* a72 74
7 ch g Diesis—Beraysim (Lion Cavern (USA))
79^{11} 428^{6} 559^{7} 679^{9}

Nounou *Miss J E Foster* a63 60
8 b g Starborough—Watheeqah (USA) (Topsider (USA))
449^{11}

Nouriya *Sir Michael Stoute* a76
2 b f Danehill Dancer(IRE) —Majestic Sakeena (IRE) (King's Best (USA))
6628^{4} ◆

Nova Med (IRE) *Y Durepaire* 84
2 b c Whipper(USA) —Prima Volta (Primo Dominie)
7264a^{2}

Nova San (IRE) *F Sanchez*
2 b c Whipper(USA) —Bodeguita (FR) (Cape Cross (IRE))
6325a^{6}

Novastasia (IRE) *W R Swinburn* a62 39
3 b f Noverre(USA) —Pink Sovietstaia (FR) (Soviet Star (USA))
1066^{6} 1588^{4} 2001^{11} 3427^{11} 4179^{13} 5229^{7} 6497^{11}

Novay Essjay (IRE) *P C Haslam* a54 71
2 ch g Noverre(USA) —Arabian Hideway (IRE) (Desert Prince (IRE))
(1847) 2041^{5} 5550^{3} 5595^{6} 6099^{5} 6354^{6}

Novellen Lad (IRE) *E J Alston* a69 93
4 b g Noverre(USA) —Lady Ellen (Horage)
1682^{3} 2086^{3} (2658) (3172) 3706^{7} 4784^{5} 5206^{5} 5960^{2} 6050^{14} 6282^{4}

Noverre Over There (IRE) *M E Rimmer* a58 58
2 b g Noverre(USA) —Shirley Moon (IRE) (Montjeu (IRE))
4385^{11} 4915^{8} 5400^{11} 6034^{5} 6858^{4} 7139^{5}

Noverre To Go (IRE) *Tom Dascombe* a89 98
3 ch c Noverre(USA) —Ukraine Venture (Slip Anchor)
1002^{4} ◆ 1324^{13} 3622^{3} (4771) 5032^{12} 6240^{8}

Noverre To Hide (USA) *J R Best* a64 54
3 b g Noverre(USA) —Zanoubia (USA) (Our Emblem (USA))
1772^{4} 2548^{9} 3010^{8} 3334^{5} 3946^{10} 4083^{9} 5018^{8} 6206^{6}

Novikov *G L Moore* a87 93
5 ch g Danehill Dancer(IRE) —Ardisia (USA) (Affirmed (USA))
1527^{12} 6633^{12}

Novillero *J C Fox* a41 42
2 b c Noverre(USA) —Fairy Story (IRE) (Persian Bold)
5212^{10} 6108^{14} 6616^{11} 7513^{5}

Novita (FR) *P Schiergen* 98
3 b f American Post—Nouvelle Reine (GER) (Konigsstuhl (GER))
1240a^{2} 1914a^{3} 2777a^{3} 3892a^{9} 6886a^{4}

Novlime (FR) *J-V Toux* 66
2 b f Noverre(USA) —Dolce Vita Yug (Emperor Jones (USA))
1482a^{5} 5014a^{9}

Novy Nick (FR) *C Diard* 50
2 b c Okawango(USA) —Apparemment (IRE) (Anabaa (USA))
6322a^{9} 7507a^{0}

Now *P Winkworth* 58
3 br f Where Or When(IRE) —Tup Tim (Emperor Jones (USA))
1772^{8} 3209^{13}

Nowhere To Hide (USA) *Nicholas Zito* a102
3 b c Vindication(USA) —Stirring (USA) (Seeking The Gold (USA))
1688a^{17}

Now Look Who'Shere *E S McMahon*
2 b g Kyllachy—Where's Carol (Anfield)
4384^{15}

No Wonga *P D Evans* a58 68
4 b g Where Or When(IRE) —Fizzy Fiona (Efisio)
5359^{3} (5962) 6258^{7} 7080^{2} 7222^{4}

Now You See Me *D Flood* a67 27
5 b m Anabaa(USA) —Bright Vision (Indian Ridge)
269^{2} 326^{8} 654^{9} 794^{11}

Nufoudh (IRE) *Miss Tracy Waggott* 63
5 b g Key Of Luck(USA) —Limpopo (Green Desert (USA))
2361^{9} 3105^{3} 3488^{3} (3683) 4466^{4} 4823^{9} (4977) 5941^{2} 6103^{2}

Nuit D'Ete (GER) *H-A Pantall* 42
2 b f Dashing Blade—Nachtigall (GER) (Danehill (USA))
6928a^{7}

Nuit Sombre (IRE) *G A Harker* a25 78
9 b g Night Shift(USA) —Belair Princess (USA) (Mr Prospector (USA))
3496^{7} 4140^{12} 4504^{9} 5418^{3} 6178^{14} 6846^{6} 7581^{8} 7754^{11}

Number One Guy *M H Tompkins* 72
2 br c Rock Of Gibraltar(IRE) —Dubious (Darshaan)
2936^{6} 3584^{5} 4557^{6} ◆ 6067^{6} (6923)

Numide (FR) *G L Moore* a99 105
6 b g Highest Honor(FR) —Numidie (FR) (Baillamont (USA))
7237^{4}

Nun Today (USA) *Karen George* a59 54
3 b f Chapel Royal(USA) —Oldupai (USA) (Gulch (USA))
214^{9} 267^{4} 1492^{5} 1973^{8} 2141^{3} 3463^{8} 4083^{5} 4202^{7} 4905^{7} 5503^{11} 5647^{8} 7051^{14}

Nurai *P W D'Arcy* a8
2 b f Danehill Dancer(IRE) —Lady High Havens (IRE) (Bluebird (USA))
5637^{7} 6254^{10}

Nurture (IRE) *R Hannon* a72 101
2 ch f Bachelor Duke(USA) —Silesian (IRE) (Singspiel (IRE))
5808^{5} 6069^{2} 6319a^{3} 7187^{2}

Nusoor (IRE) *Peter Grayson* a62 76
6 b g Fasliyev(USA) —Zulfaa (USA) (Bahri (USA))
1150^{10} 1768^{11} 2158^{12} 2682^{7}

Nusrat (TUR) *I E Dizdar* a54
3 b f Mujtahid(USA) —Pigeon Pea (USA) (Topsider (USA))
5587a^{12}

Nut Hand (IRE) *T D Easterby* a16 57
3 b g Noverre(USA) —Walnut Lady (Forzando)
1281^{8} 1926^{7} 2802^{3} 3454^{5} 3954^{5} 4822^{5}

Nuts About You (IRE) *A Berry*
2 b f Rakti—La Noisette (Rock Hopper)
1504^{13} 1933^{8} 3119^{10} 3572^{12}

Nyetimber (USA) *J A Osborne* a55
3 ch c Forest Wildcat(USA) —Once Around (CAN) (You And I (USA))
7278^{6} 7455^{5} 7557^{4} 7712^{5}

Oakbridge (IRE) *R Brotherton* a40 55
7 b g Indian Ridge—Chauncy Lane (IRE) (Sadler's Wells (USA))
117^{8}

Oak Leaves *J G Portman* 56
2 b f Mark Of Esteem(IRE) —Exotic Forest (Dominion)
4603^{12} 5026^{7} 7029^{15}

Oasis Dancer *R M Beckett* 95
2 bg c Oasis Dream—Good Enough (FR) (Mukaddamah (USA))
5220^{8} 6199^{2} (6478)

Oasis Jade *G L Moore* a64 68
2 b f Oasis Dream—Royal Jade (Last Tycoon)
3277^{5} 3772^{3} 4147^{5} 4639^{6} 5748^{7} 6227^{4} 6905^{13}

Oasis Knight (IRE) *M P Tregoning* 104
3 b c Oasis Dream—Generous Lady (Generous (IRE))
1303^{9} ◆ (4988) 5425^{3} 6306^{2} 6854^{5}

Obara D'Avril (FR) *S G West* 57
7 gr m April Night(FR) —Baraka De Thaix II (FR) (Olmeto)
1765^{5} 5694^{8} 6022^{3} 6558^{6} 6769^{3}

Obe Brave *Lee Smyth* a65 86
6 b g Agnes World(USA) —Pass The Rose (IRE) (Thatching)
2391^{8} 4878^{8} 5287^{5} (5842) ◆ 6120^{3} 6413^{9} 6637^{7} 7403^{12} 7735^{6} 7813^{7} 7860^{8}

Obe Gold *P Howling* a93 98
7 b g Namaqualand(USA) —Gagajulu (Al Hareb (USA))
821^{2} (892) 1278^{5} 1398^{3} 1864^{10} 2658^{6} 3268^{3} (4012) (4192) 4690^{3} 4976^{3} 5018^{5} 5406^{4} 7026^{9} 7327^{11} 7535^{3} 7596^{2} 7691^{4} 7813^{3} (7879)

Obelisk (USA) *J Hirschberger* 67
7 b h Chester House(USA) —Classy Tipper (USA) (Vice Regent (CAN))
3201a^{7}

Obe One *A Berry* a48 57
9 b g Puissance—Plum Bold (Be My Guest (USA))
575^{9} 1456^{9} 1832^{6} 2316^{13} 2529^{8} 2628^{7} 2812^{9} 3148^{5} 3852^{7} 4552^{11} 5150^{3} 5332^{7} 6414^{11}

Oberlin (USA) *T Keddy* a74 63
4 ch g Gone West(USA) —Balanchine (USA) (Storm Bird (CAN))
38^{11} 148^{11} 627^{9} 877^{11}

Obe Royal *P D Evans* a81 76
5 b g Wizard King—Gagajulu (Al Hareb (USA))
57^{3} 167^{5} 235^{6} 245^{5} 303^{2} 401^{3} 460^{4} (489) (519) 671^{2} (793) 868^{2} 933^{2} 980^{2} 1132^{10} (1186) 1436^{4} 2266^{9} 2576^{5} 3030^{4} 3301^{8} 3717^{7} 3851^{8} 4202^{6} 4859^{3} 5332^{9} 5676^{7} 5991^{11} 6024^{7}

Obezyana (USA) *A Bailey* a79 85
7 ch g Rahy(USA) —Polish Treaty (USA) (Danzig (USA))
680^{5} 932^{2} 1067^{4} 1887^{5} 2186^{6} 2527^{6} 3076^{9}

Observatory Star (IRE) *T D Easterby* 88
6 br g Observatory(USA) —Pink Sovietstaia (FR) (Soviet Star (USA))
1952^{5} 2787^{2} 3265^{4} 4549^{3} 4801^{2} 5441^{6} 5697^{3} 7125^{3} 7287^{7}

Obvious *Miss J Feilden* a57 26
3 b f Falbrav(IRE) —Bright And Clear (Danehill (USA))
5531^{13} 5774^{8} 7796^{10}

Ocarito (GER) *G F Bridgwater* a4
8 b g Auenadler(GER) —Okkasion (Konigsstuhl (GER))
125^{10} 256^{11}

Occasion *G M Moore* 32
4 b m Zamindar(USA) —Set Fair (USA) (Alleged (USA))
4277^{9}

Occhio Della Mente (IRE) *R Brogi* 98
2 b c Le Vie Dei Colori—Croanda (IRE) (Grand Lodge (USA))
7205a^{2}

Oceana Blue *A M Balding* a81 88
4 b m Reel Buddy(USA) —Silken Dalliance (Rambo Dancer (CAN))
1288^{5} 1733^{4} (2086) (2695) 3102^{9} 3628^{9} 4317^{7} 6482^{13}

Ocean Blaze *B R Millman* a83 88
5 b m Polar Prince(IRE) —La Belle Vie (Indian King (USA))
1425^{6} 1836^{2} 2472^{5} 3998^{10} 5098^{5} 5436^{3} ◆ 5767^{5} (5919) (6118) 6359^{6} ◆ 6647^{6} 6972^{2}

Ocean Club *B W Hills* a36
2 ch g Storming Home—Strictly Cool (USA) (Bering)
6943^{9}

Ocean Countess (IRE) *Miss J Feilden* a61 72
3 b f Storming Home—Pennycairn (Last Tycoon)
849^{7} 1269^{10} (1940) 2143^{11} 3551^{7} 4694^{2} 5479^{6} 5998^{7} (6339) (6787) (6968) 7487^{5} 7742^{6}

Ocean Glory (IRE) *Patrick Morris* a46 16
4 b g Redback—Finty (IRE) (Entrepreneur)
2801^{12}

Oceanic Dancer (IRE) *Patrick Morris* a2 47
3 b f Danetime(IRE) —Almasa (Faustus (USA))
862^{P} 982^{8} 1359^{8} 4942^{10} 5336^{7}

Ocean Legend (IRE) *Miss J Feilden* a84 78
4 b g Night Shift(USA) —Rose Of Mooncoin (IRE) (Brief Truce (USA))
232^{2} 318^{5} 544^{3} 850^{8} 1524^{4} 2186^{5} 2775^{8} 3274^{6} 3980^{9} 4386^{3} 5329^{7} 5665^{8} 6361^{11} (6703) 7062^{6} 7422^{5} 7631^{6}

Ocean Of Peace (FR) *M R Bosley* a54 53
6 b g Volochine(IRE) —Sumatra (IRE) (Mukaddamah (USA))
4053^{6} 4640^{4} 5577^{3} 6226^{7} 6966^{6}

Ocean Pride (IRE) *L Wells* a52 82
6 b g Lend A Hand—Irish Understudy (ITY) (In The Wings)
346^{12}

Ocean Rosie (IRE) *Miss J Feilden* a40
2 b f One Cool Cat(USA) —Rose Of Mooncoin (IRE) (Brief Truce (USA))
6164^{13}

Ocean's Minstrel *J Ryan* a98 101
3 b c Pivotal—Minstrel's Dance (CAN) (Pleasant Colony (USA))
(1118) 1675^{10} (2673) 3011^{15} 3846^{4} 4521^{7}

Ocean's Song (FR) *A De Watrigant* 49
2 b f Sagacity(FR) —Summer Rain (Cadeaux Genereux)
7316a^{7}

Ocean Terminal (FR) *J Boisnard*
3 b c Fasliyev(USA) —Ocean Reef (Lugana Beach)
2293a^{0}

Ocean Transit (IRE) *R J Price* a74 87
4 b m Trans Island—Wings Awarded (Shareef Dancer (USA))
1894^{2} 2334^{5} 2639^{11} (2976) 3801^{2} 4088^{2} 4422^{10} 6016^{P} 6618^{11} 7032^{3} 7125^{4} ◆ 7287^{8}

Ochilview Warrior (IRE) *R Bastiman* 52
2 b c Trans Island—Lonely Brook (USA) (El Gran Senor (USA))
4011^{7} 4847^{P} 5330^{5} 5981^{8} 6796^{7} 6983^{2} 7168^{9}

Oddshoes (IRE) *K M Prendergast* a62 71
7 b g Mujadil(USA) —Another Baileys (Deploy)
194^{3}

Oddsmaker (IRE) *M A Barnes* a42 71
8 b g Barathea(IRE) —Archipova (IRE) (Ela-Mana-Mou)
1123^{9} 1230^{11} 1692^{7} 1886^{7} 2499^{11} 4588^{9} (5294) 5698^{5} (5947) 6156^{3} 6832^{7} 6986^{5} (7118)

Off Chance *T D Easterby* 89
3 b f Olden Times—La Notte (Factual (USA))
1128^{3} (1522) 2060^{7} (2528) 3267^{4} 4328^{6} (4994) (5258) 5670^{3}

Offert (FR) *J Van Handenhove*
2 b f Loup Solitaire(USA) —Histoire (SWI) (Sicyos (USA))
3934a^{8}

Off Hand *T D Easterby* a23 42
3 b f Lend A Hand—Off Camera (Efisio)
1174^{8} 1335^{9} 1725^{14} 2234^{4} 3711^{7} 3936^{3} 4819^{11}

Officer In Command (USA) *J S Moore* a79 77
3 bb c Officer(USA) —Luv To Stay N Chat (USA) (Candi's Gold (USA))
1751^{8} 4649^{10} 5169^{6} 5366^{4}

Officer Mor (USA) *A Berry* a63 68
3 ch g Officer(USA) —Hot August Nights (USA) (Summer Squall (USA))
10^{4} 2683^{2} 3031^{12} 5809^{10} 6988^{11} 7082^{7}

Official Style *Sir Michael Stoute* 78
2 b c Dansili—Reel Style (Rainbow Quest (USA))
5542^{8} 6108^{3} ◆ 6754^{2} ◆

Oglumemre (TUR) *Sab Arslan* a76 90
4 ch h Royal Abjar(USA) —Sketch (TUR) (Ezy Koter)
5619a^{10}

Ogre (USA) *P D Evans* a78 84
4 bb m Tale Of The Cat(USA) —Soverign Lady (USA) (Aloha Prospector (USA))
2144^{4} 2665^{9} 3245^{3} (3525) (4005) 5190^{7} (5594) 5804^{2} 6657a^{6}

Oh Goodness Me *J S Bolger* 105
3 b f Galileo(IRE) —Coyote (Indian Ridge)
(928a) 1918a^{9} 2304a^{3} 2672^{7} 3896a^{5} 5487a^{7}

Ohiyesa (IRE) *G M Lyons* a93 93
3 b f Noverre(USA) —Crohal Di San Jore (Saddlers' Hall (IRE))
1755a^{4} 2644a^{6} 6707a^{9}

Oh Landino (GER) *P Monteith* 46
4 b g Lando(GER) —Oh La Belle (GER) (Dashing Blade)
1692^{10} 2594^{4} 3098^{10} 3654^{9} 4529^{9}

Oh Mambo Girl (USA) *S Botti* 94
3 b f Arch(USA) —Second Pres (USA) (Kingmambo (USA))
3186a^{3}

Oh So Saucy *C F Wall* a60 85
5 b m Imperial Ballet(IRE) —Almasi (IRE) (Petorius)
2188^{9} 3339^{6} 4386^{6} 5697^{11}

Oil Strike *P Winkworth* a79 76
2 b g Lucky Story(USA) —Willisa (Polar Falcon (USA))
1669^2 *(6913)* 7290^8

Oiseau De Feu (USA) *J-C Rouget* a97 118
3 b c Stravinsky(USA) —Slewadora (USA) (Seattle Slew (USA))
$1238a^3$ $1917a^4$ (2755a) $3669a^2$ $5710a^4$ $6503a^{DSQ}$

Oisin's Boy *J R Boyle* a59 60
3 b g Catcher In The Rye(IRE) —Red Storm (Dancing Spree (USA))
1271^6 1462^{16}

Okadoun (FR) *C Lotoux* 73
2 gr f Okawango(USA) —Kiridoun (FR) (Kaldounevees (FR))
$6928a^3$

Okafranca (IRE) *J A B Old* a63 75
4 b g Okawango(USA) —Villafranca (IRE) (In The Wings)
6734^{13}

Oke Bay *R M Beckett* a58 55
3 b f Tobougg(IRE) —Barakat (Bustino)
1579^{11} 2447^3 2881^5 *3954^2 7840^{13}*

Oken Bruce Lee (JPN) *H Otonashi* 122
4 b h Jungle Pocket(JPN) —Silver Joy (CAN) (Silver Deputy (CAN))
$7593a^2$

Ok Katie *R M Beckett* a6
6 b m Slip Anchor—Darling Splodge (Elegant Air)
957^8 1286^{13}

Old Devil Moon (IRE) *T G Mills* a52 42
2 br g Johannesburg(USA) —Tencarola (IRE) (Night Shift (USA))
4243^{11} 6199^{10} *6627^8 7089^4*

Old Firm *D A Nolan* a51
3 ch g Compton Place—Miriam (Forzando)
4531^{11} 5727^{10} *7459^5*

Oldjoesaid *H Candy* a108 113
5 b g Royal Applause—Border Minstral (IRE) (Sri Pekan (USA))
1325^6 1699^8 2704^4 ◆ 3405^{11} 5263^6 5860^6 ◆ 6283^{12}

Old Money *H J L Dunlop* 77
2 ch f Medicean—Nouveau Riche (IRE) (Entrepreneur)
5096^7 5786^3 6561^2

Old Romney *P Howling* a78 76
5 br g Halling(USA) —Zaeema (Zafonic (USA))
(320) 427^2 733^2 873^2 893^2 1615^4 2052^8 3864^{11} 4150^{11} 4759^9 *7524^{13}*

Old Sarum (IRE) *D R C Elsworth* a59 28
3 b g Elusive City(USA) —Quintellina (Robellino (USA))
229^{10}

Olga D'Or (USA) *R Gibson* a87 82
3 b f Medaglia D'Oro(USA) —Fasateen (USA) (Alysheba (USA))
$4130a^7$ $6606a^3$ *$7696a^0$*

Olive Green (USA) *Pat Eddery* 73
3 b f Diesis—Zaghruta (USA) (Gone West (USA))
1843^4 2433^4 2885^5 4473^{10} 6390^2

Olivino (GER) *B J Llewellyn* a20 51
8 ch g Second Set(IRE) —Osdemona (GER) (Solarstern (FR))
342^{10}

Olney Lass *W J H Ratcliffe* a45 72
2 b f Lucky Story(USA) —Zalebe (Bahamian Bounty)
6163^{14} 6591^3 7289^2

Olvia (IRE) *C Laffon-Parias* 98
2 b f Giant's Causeway(USA) —Mill Guineas (USA) (Salse (USA))
$6523a^7$

Olympic Ceremony *R A Fahey* a63 66
2 br g Kyllachy—Opening Ceremony (USA) (Quest For Fame)
1827^7 2311^3 3875^{12} 4306^3 4782^4 5256^7 5957^5 6408^3 7079^2 *7636^4*

Olympic Dream *R A Fahey* 79
3 b g Kyllachy—Opening Ceremony (USA) (Quest For Fame)
1015^5 1228^4 2248^6 (3316) 4433^6 4802^3 5409^{13}

Olympic Glory (BRZ) *A Al Raihe* a84 51
5 b m Choctaw Ridge(USA) —Glorious Glory (BRZ) (Minstrel Glory (USA))
$416a^{11}$

Olynard (IRE) *R M Beckett* a86 97
3 b g Exceed And Excel(AUS) —Reddening (Blushing Flame (USA))
1879^5 2946^4 ◆ 3694^3 (4148) ◆ (4853) 5263^{10}

Omnium Duke (IRE) *J W Hills* a73 68
3 ch c Indian Haven—Please Be Good (IRE) (Prince Of Birds (USA))
3228^3 (3718) 4275^{13} *5095^5 5575^{13} 6124^2 6496^{10} 6861^7*

Omokoroa (IRE) *M H Tompkins* a62 90
3 b g Hawkeye(IRE) —Alycus (USA) (Atticus (USA))
2341^3 3069^2 (3976) 4229^2 5660^2 6734^2

Onceaponatime (IRE) *M D Squance* a77 84
4 b g Invincible Spirit(IRE) —Lake Nyasa (IRE) (Lake Coniston (IRE))
600^6 880^4 1132^7 1259^3 *1468^2* 1572^3 2088^3 *5370^8* 5974^7 *6230^6 6458^2 6915^6* 7053^4 (7191) 7355^3 ◆ 7496^8 7577^5 7673^3 ◆ 7735^4 7870^2

Once More Dubai (USA) *Saeed Bin Suroor* a109 111
4 bb h E Dubai(USA) —Go Again Girl (USA) (Broad Brush (USA))
$527a^5$ ◆ $703a^3$ 2327^5 6644^6 (7059) *(7237)*

On Cue (IRE) *J M P Eustace* a54 49
3 ch f Indian Haven—On Time Arrival (USA) (Devil's Bag (USA))
1481^4 1967^2 2143^8 2461^8 *3383^2*

Onebidkintymill (IRE) *R Hollinshead* a30 71
4 b g Mull Of Kintyre(USA) —More Risk (IRE) (Fayruz)
(3505) 4783^5

One Cat Diesel (IRE) *N Wilson*
2 b g One Cool Cat(USA) —Awaaser (USA) (Diesis)
6982^9

One Clever Cat (IRE) *T Clout* a87 106
3 b f One Cool Cat(USA) —Burn Baby Burn (IRE) (King's Theatre (IRE))
$3668a^2$ $4578a^4$ $7128a^6$ $7569a^0$

One Cool Buck (IRE) *R Hannon* 65
2 b g One Cool Cat(USA) —Simply Katie (Most Welcome)
1323^{13} 2430^5

One Cool Deal (IRE) *T D Easterby* a50 52
2 b g One Cool Cat(USA) —Acciacatura (USA) (Stravinsky (USA))
2963^6 3487^9 *3719^5* 4188^9 5358^9

One Cool Dream *W R Swinburn* a61 60
3 b f One Cool Cat(USA) —Swift Baba (USA) (Deerhound (USA))
3297^7 ◆ 4854^4 5747^4 6572^3 6824^{10}

One Cool Kitty *M G Quinlan* a62 70
3 b f One Cool Cat(USA) —Exultate Jubilate (USA) (With Approval (CAN))
1155^4 1618^5 *2827^6* 4179^{10} *5809^3 6492^{12} 7432^{11}*

One Cool Mission (IRE) *Tom Dascombe* a53 24
3 b f One Cool Cat(USA) —San Luis Rey (Zieten (USA))
236^3 4267^6 *4749^{13}*

One Cool Poppy (IRE) *H J L Dunlop* a45 57
2 b f One Cool Cat(USA) —Elusive Kitty (USA) (Elusive Quality (USA))
4946^4 6241^{21} *6858^6*

One Cool Slash (IRE) *M J McGrath* a40
2 b f One Cool Cat(USA) —Sun Slash (IRE) (Entrepreneur)
7436^7 7806^6

One For Joules (IRE) *John Joseph Hanlon* a53 65
2 b f Choisir(AUS) —Stuttgart (Groom Dancer (USA))
7391^9

Onega Lake (IRE) *E Lellouche* 88
3 ch f Peintre Celebre(USA) —Odessa (IRE) (Sadler's Wells (USA))
$2952a^{12}$

One Good Emperor (IRE) *J R Best* a77 58
2 b c Antonius Pius(USA) —Break Of Day (USA) (Favorite Trick (USA))
4410^5 ◆ *5368^3 6372^3 6826^8*

One Hit Wonder *Mouse Hamilton-Fairley* a56
2 b g Whipper(USA) —Swiftly (Cadeaux Genereux)
2595^5 ◆ *2825^6*

One Little David (GER) *Y Fertillet* 100
9 b g Camp David(GER) —Open Heart (GER) (Sure Blade (USA))
$5074a^0$

Onemix *B W Hills* a76 78
3 gr f Fair Mix(IRE) —One For Philip (Blushing Flame (USA))
731^2 ◆ *876^2* (1092) 2164^4 3251^3 3697^2 4166^5 *6671^3*

Onemoreandstay *M D Squance* a71 73
4 ch m Dr Fong(USA) —Subito (Darshaan)
(90) 406^5 813^9 1049^3 1261^5 *(1478) 7641^2 7779^3*

One More Round (USA) *P D Evans* a79 76
11 b g Ghazi(USA) —Life Of The Party (USA) (Pleasant Colony (USA))
87^2 189^2 245^4 (314) 475^4 1313^9 2184^4 3994^4 4238^2 4621^8 *7129^7* 7358^5 7370^{13} 7521^{13} 7606^9 7645^{11}

Onenightinlisbon (IRE) *J R Boyle* a76 75
5 br m Bold Fact(USA) —Mickey Towbar (IRE) (Mujadil (USA))
60^7 344^8 2598^9 4305^7 4704^3 4916^2 *5195^9* 5449^{10} *6208^6* 6547^7

Oneofapear (IRE) *G A Swinbank* a57 80
3 b g Pyrus(USA) —Whitegate Way (Greensmith)
3485^5 *4838^5* 5520^2 (6158)

Oneofthesedayz (IRE) *Mrs D J Sanderson* 44
3 b f Acclamation—Thornby Park (Unfuwain (USA))
1725^{15} 1926^9 3305^7

One Oi *D W P Arbuthnot* a63
4 b g Bertolini(USA) —Bogus Penny (IRE) (Pennekamp (USA))
2400^2 ◆ *2924^7 4645^4*

One Scoop Or Two *F Sheridan* a55 56
3 b g Needwood Blade—Rebel County (IRE) (Maelstrom Lake)
833^6 1108^5 1410^3 2779^7 3575^9 *5838^8 6497^5 7105^8*

One Set (IRE) *G M Lyons* a83 49
2 ch c Footstepsinthesand—Impassion (FR) (In The Wings)
$2643a^5$

One Slick Chick (IRE) *M Botti* a70
3 b f One Cool Cat(USA) —Ms Mary C (IRE) (Dolphin Street (FR))
(556)

On Est Bien (IRE) *E Lellouche* 114
3 b c Enrique—Doucelisa (FR) (Cardoun (FR))
(1239a)

One Tou Many *C W Fairhurst* 52
4 b m Tobougg(IRE) —Reine De Thebes (FR) (Darshaan)
2232^3 2725^7 3171^7 *3714^{12}* 4617^{10}

One Upmanship *M Salaman* a35
8 ch g Bahamian Bounty—Magnolia (Petong)
569^9 775^{11}

One Way Or Another (AUS) *J R Gask* a88 99
6 b g Carnegie(IRE) —True Blonde (AUS) (Naturalism (NZ))
2695^7 ◆ (3154) 3796^2 4779^6 5522^{10} 6482^2 7294^{13} *7560^4*

One Way Ticket *J M Bradley* a54 65
9 ch g Pursuit Of Love—Prima Cominna (Unfuwain (USA))
166^8 308^7 508^3 896^3 1540^9 1787^{16} 2811^4 3204^4 3677^6 5504^6 5629^6 5792^{13}

One World (AUS) *J Moore* 116
5 bb h Danehill Dancer(IRE) —River Serenade (AUS) (Hurricane Sky (AUS))
$7745a^2$

One Zero (USA) *M G Quinlan* a61 62
4 ch m Theatrical(IRE) —Binary (Rainbow Quest (USA))
279^5 476^4

Ongoodform (IRE) *P W D'Arcy* a92 90
2 b c Invincible Spirit(IRE) —Elfin Queen (IRE) (Fairy King (USA))
4093^7 *5778^3* (6032) 6541^2 *7063^2 7251^2*

On Her Way *H R A Cecil* 20
2 ch f Medicean—Singed (Zamindar (USA))
7183^{19}

On Holiday *M W Easterby* 29
2 b f Dubai Destination(USA) —Mount Hillaby (IRE) (Mujadil (USA))
4844^{12} 5157^5 5417^9

Oniz Tiptoes (IRE) *J S Wainwright* 47
8 ch g Russian Revival(USA) —Edionda (IRE) (Magical Strike (USA))
4806^6

On Khee *H Morrison* a58 34
2 b f Sakhee(USA) —Star Precision (Shavian)
6617^{13} ◆ *7135^8 7325^4*

Only A Game (IRE) *I W McInnes* a61 67
4 b g Foxhound(USA) —Compendium (Puissance)
106^7 218^9 561^7 793^{11} 2145^7 2529^5 (2801) 3562^4 3938^{12} 3999^8 4355^{11} 6103^8 6339^3 ◆ *6587^7* 6755^{12} 7370^4 7680^2 (7771)

Only A Grand *R Bastiman* a58 53
5 b m Cloudings(IRE) —Magic Orb (Primo Dominie)
71^3 150^9 405^8 608^8

Only A Splash *Mrs R A Carr* a32 56
5 b g Primo Valentino(IRE) —Water Well (Sadler's Wells (USA))
2660^6 2966^{11} 3125^8 3683^2 (4105) 4466^9 4620^9 *4843^8* 5332^5

Only Green (IRE) *F Head* a104 104
3 b f Green Desert(USA) —Only Seule (USA) (Lyphard (USA))
$1208a^3$ $2521a^5$ $3231a^4$ $3908a^{11}$ $4580a^{11}$ $5086a^9$ *$7285a^5$*

Only Hope *P S McEntee* a53 27
5 b m Marju(IRE) —Sellette (IRE) (Selkirk (USA))
227^4 315^8 381^4 447^3 602^7

On Offer (IRE) *T D Easterby* 74
3 b f Clodovil(IRE) —Camassina (IRE) (Taufan (USA))
1307^6 1561^9 2227^3 3033^5 3453^5 4309^7 5335^5 5597^8

On Our Way *H R A Cecil* 107
3 b g Oasis Dream—Singed (Zamindar (USA))
1294^4 3050^9

On Terms (USA) *S Dow* a54
3 b f Aptitude(USA) —Silver Yen (USA) (Silver Hawk (USA))
7694^4

On The Bounty *R A Fahey* 70
2 b c Bahamian Bounty—Dark Eyed Lady (IRE) (Exhibitioner)
(2069) 3559^5 4195^3 4884^6 5795^{18}

On The Cusp (IRE) *M A Jarvis* a67 57
2 b g Footstepsinthesand—Roman Love (IRE) (Perugino (USA))
5664^5 $6319a^{16}$ 6990^9

On The Loose (IRE) *T G McCourt* a8 63
5 gr g Great Palm(USA) —Marys Rival (IRE) (Soughaan (USA))
(7173)

On The Piste (IRE) *L A Mullaney* a50 64
2 b f Distant Music(USA) —Lady Piste (IRE) (Ali-Royal (IRE))
1884^3 (2457) 2800^5 (3726) *5372^{13}* (5950) 6555^5 *7372^5*

On Verra (IRE) *F Doumen* a89 107
2 b f Smart Strike(CAN) —Karmifira (FR) (Always Fair (USA))
$4577a^5$ $6045a^3$ $6523a^2$

Onyx Of Arabia (IRE) *B J Meehan* 75
2 b c Avonbridge—Fiamma Royale (IRE) (Fumo Di Londra (IRE))
4377^5 4699^2 5786^4 6842^{11}

Oondiri (IRE) *T D Easterby* 68
2 b f Trans Island—Nullarbor (Green Desert (USA))
1277^6 1623^3 (2339) 2655^3 3540^3 4327^5 4803^7 5467^5 5950^4 6554^5

Oops Another Act *W R Swinburn* a59 42
4 rg m Act One—Oops Pettie (Machiavellian (USA))
1589^{11} 2171^{11}

Oor Wee Miracle (GER) *M Dods*
3 b f Tiger Hill(IRE) —Old Tradition (IRE) (Royal Academy (USA))
3022^7

Open Glory (FR) *Tom Dascombe* a57 62
2 b f Lando(GER) —Lovigna (GER) (Komtur (USA))
3249^8 3576^{11} 4047^{10} *5369^7 5985^{11}*

Openide *B W Duke* a42 37
8 b g Key Of Luck(USA) —Eyelet (IRE) (Satco (FR))
627^5 2127^9

Opening Hand *G J Smith* a38 58
4 b g Observatory(USA) —Belle Ile (USA) (Diesis)
1037^8 1442^{14}

Open Intent (IRE) *M Gasparini* 91
3 b c Nayef(USA) —Carol Alt (IRE) (Celestial Storm (USA))
$1904a^{10}$

Open Sesame (IRE) *P W Chapple-Hyam* a73 92
3 b g Key Of Luck(USA) —Chiquita Linda (IRE) (Mujadil (USA))
(144) (2048) (2230)

Opera Comica (BRZ) *G Duarte* 61
3 b f Giant Gentleman(USA) —Cientifica (ARG) (Cipayo (ARG))
$6503a^{13}$

Opera Gal (IRE) *A M Balding* 74
2 b f Galileo(IRE) —Opera Glass (Barathea (IRE))
4985^5 5603^4 6729^2

Opera Music *J P Cahill* a78 78
5 b g Kirkwall—Optaria (Song)
$1376a^7$

Opera Prince *S Kirk* a89 93
4 b g Kyllachy—Optaria (Song)
1003^7 1460^{18} 2891^7 3639^{11} 4262^{14} 6695^7 6907^6

Opera Wings *Sir Michael Stoute* a60 65
3 ch f Medicean—Wings Of Love (Groom Dancer (USA))
4606^4 *5093^5*

Opera Writer (IRE) *R Hollinshead* a71 74
6 b g Rossini(USA) —Miss Flite (IRE) (Law Society (USA))
324^7

Ophistrolie (IRE) *H J Manners* 22
7 b g Foxhound(USA) —Thoughtful Kate (Rock Hopper)
3533^7

Opinion Poll (IRE) *M A Jarvis* 109
3 b c Halling(USA) —Ahead (Shirley Heights)
1702^3 (2275) ◆ 3051^7 (6662) ◆

Optical Illusion (USA) *R A Fahey* a61 67
5 b g Theatrical(IRE) —Paradise River (USA) (Irish River (FR))
1650^4 2453^3 2964^{10} (3484) 4015^7 4878^3 5941^4 *6492^9* 6925^5

Optical Seclusion (IRE) *K W Hogg* a56 16
6 b g Second Empire(IRE) —Theda (Mummy's Pet)
574^{13} 2155^{11}

Optimistic Duke (IRE) *W R Muir* a19 53
2 ch g Bachelor Duke(USA) —Gronchi Rosa (IRE) (Nashwan (USA))
6627^{12} 7034^{11} *7325^{14}*

Optimum (IRE) *J T Stimpson* a50 56
7 br g King's Best(USA) —Colour Dance (Rainbow Quest (USA))
8^7 148^6

Opus Dei *J A Glover* a72 69
2 b g Oasis Dream—Grail (USA) (Quest For Fame)
2721^3 3113^6 5668^9 *7320^2 7494^7*

Opus Maximus (IRE) *M Johnston* a87 96
4 ch g Titus Livius(FR) —Law Review (IRE) (Case Law)
388^5 551^6 724^5 995^7 *1209^8* (1649) 1821^2 1861^{26} 2933^8 3391^5 3706^{11} 4037^{12} 4560^4 ◆ 4779^3 5249^3 5522^{14} 6217^2 6485^5

Oracle West (SAF) *H J Brown* 103
8 b g Western Winter(USA) —Noble Prophet (SAF) (Noble Ambition (USA))
$339a^8$ $527a^6$ $703a^{11}$

Orangeleg *S C Williams* a64 55
3 b g Intikhab(USA) —Red Shareef (Marju (IRE))
(3672) 5121^3 *(7877)*

Orange Pip *R Hannon* a84 86
4 ch m Bold Edge—Opopmil (IRE) (Pips Pride)
1572^7 *1733^2* 2326^5 2637^5 4761^7 5719^{11}

Orange Square (IRE) *D W Barker* a65 48
4 br g King Charlemagne(USA) —Unaria (Prince Tenderfoot (USA))
327^4 487^8 746^3 812^4 1055^7

Oranor (FR) *H-A Pantall* 79
2 ch f Starborough—Panthesilea (FR) (Kendor (FR))
$7103a^6$

Oratory (IRE) *R Hannon* a82 90
3 b g Danehill Dancer(IRE) —Gentle Night (Zafonic (USA))
5695^8 ◆ *6702^{12}*

Orbitor *M L W Bell* a74 78
3 b g Galileo(IRE) —Peacock Alley (IRE) (Salse (USA))
1019^3 1512^3

Orchard House (FR) *Evan Williams* a54 43
6 b g Medaaly—Louisa May (IRE) (Royal Abjar (USA))
502^3 1399^9

Orchard Supreme *R Hannon* a106 96
6 ch g Titus Livius(FR) —Bogus Penny (IRE) (Pennekamp (USA))
(291) 458^7 551^4 635^5 1016^{12} 1149^{11} 5448^7 5745^4 *6633^{10} 7486^7 7626^6*

Orchestration (IRE) *Garry Moss* a49 58
8 ch g Stravinsky(USA) —Mora (IRE) (Second Set (IRE))
475^3

Orchestrion *Miss T Jackson* 63
4 ch m Piccolo—Mindomica (Dominion)
4139^8

Orchid Wing *R A Fahey* a68 68
2 ch c Avonbridge—First Ace (First Trump)
6646^5 7058^7 7288^9 *7674^2* ◆

Ordensfrau (GER) *Mario Hofer* 67
2 gr f Refuse To Bend(IRE) —Dramraire Mist (Darshaan)
$7045a^7$

Ordenstreuer (IRE) *R Dzubasz* 105
3 b c Nayef(USA) —Dramraire Mist (Darshaan)
$3670a^6$ $6521a^7$ $7039a^5$

Order Me (USA) *F Head* 76
3 b f Elusive Quality(USA) —Top Order (USA) (Dayjur (USA))
$6606a^6$

Order Order *H J L Dunlop* a64 62
3 br f Diktat—Brocheta (Hector Protector (USA))
900^3 1361^9 *1937^4* 2797^{16} *4749^{10} 6439^6 (7318) 7413^7*

Ordnance Row *R Hannon* 117
6 b g Mark Of Esteem(IRE) —Language Of Love (Rock City)
1600^3 1865^2 (1929) 2327^6 3404^4 3841^7 5249^6 5426^2 (5474) 5655^8 6448^8

Ordoney (IRE) *L M Cumani* a90 88
4 b h Intikhab(USA) —Mitawa (IRE) (Alhaarth (IRE))
4276^2 ◆ (4805) 5266^3 ◆ (5725) *6435^2* 6907^4 *7233^8*

Oriental Cat *J H M Gosden* 57
2 b c Tiger Hill(IRE) —Sentimental Value (USA) (Diesis)
6990^6

Oriental Cavalier *R Hollinshead* a76 73
3 ch g Ishiguru(USA) —Gurleigh (IRE) (Pivotal)
1470^2 ◆ 2230^5 2779^3 5858^3 6248^4 6538^7 *7195^2 (7361) 7620^2 7752^4 7847^4*

Oriental Girl *J A Geake* a62 68
4 b m Dr Fong(USA) —Zacchera (Zamindar (USA))
1834[6] 2352[4] 2910[4] 3581[8] 4904[2] 5503[9] 5915[2] 6733[8]

Orientalist Art *P W Chapple-Hyam* a93 90
4 b g Green Desert(USA) —Pink Cristal (Dilum (USA))
5025[8]

Oriental Lion *Uwe Ostmann* 98
3 b c Seattle Dancer(USA) —Oriental Flower (GER) (Big Shuffle (USA))
2954a[2] 3670a[11]

Oriental Rose *G M Moore* 76
3 b f Dr Fong(USA) —Sahara Rose (Green Desert (USA))
2102[8] 2602[2] 2967[6] 3729[4] 4664[2] 4820[4] 4997[4] 6233[12]

Oriental Scot *W Jarvis* a69 64
2 ch c Selkirk(USA) —Robe Chinoise (Robellino (USA))
6991[5] 7491[2] ◆ 7721[5]

Original Dancer (IRE) *M Johnston* 44
2 b c Danehill Dancer(IRE) —Courtier (Saddlers' Hall (IRE))
2017[8] ◆ 6047[7]

Orion Star (FR) *H-A Pantall* 115
7 gr g Sternkoenig(IRE) —Okocha (GER) (Platini (GER))
6527a[6]

Orizaba (IRE) *Saeed Bin Suroor* 112
3 b c Orpen(USA) —Jus'Chillin' (IRE) (Elbio)
2755a[3] 2992[7] 4352[2] 4949[5]

Orkney (IRE) *Miss J A Camacho* a72 58
4 b g Trans Island—Bitty Mary (Be My Chief (USA))
923[7] 3095[6] 4737[7]

Orlando's Tale (USA) *J R Fanshawe* a45 83
4 ch g Tale Of The Cat(USA) —Tell Seattle (USA) (A.P. Indy (USA))
2416[7] 3319[2] 4019[2] 4501[11] (5747)

Oronsay *B R Millman* a38 54
4 ch m Elmaamul(USA) —Glenfinlass (Lomond (USA))
1538[8] 1974[6] 2322[2] 3259[7] 3739[9] 4625[5] 5567[5] 6565[3] 6966[7]

Oroveso (BRZ) *G Duarte* 75
3 gr c Fahim—Voile D'Or (BRZ) (Effervescing (USA))
6505a[14]

Orpailleur *Ms Joanna Morgan* a92 91
8 gr g Mon Tresor—African Light (Kalaglow)
2289a[18]

Orpen All Hours (IRE) *P C Haslam* a18 26
2 b f Orpen(USA) —Devious Miss (IRE) (Dr Devious (IRE))
3392[8] 3572[9] 3925[9] 5620[F] 6034[9] 6355[10]

Orpen Arms (IRE) *R A Fahey* 61
2 b f Orpen(USA) —Lindas Delight (Batshoof)
1920[2] 2258[3] 2896[2] 3292[4] 4889[5] 5595[7] 5942[2] 7055[6]

Orpen Bid (IRE) *A M Crow* 51
4 b m Orpen(USA) —Glorious Bid (IRE) (Horage)
2233[15] 2816[7]

Orpenella *K A Ryan* a68 32
4 b m Orpen(USA) —M N L Lady (Polar Falcon (USA))
1[2] 58[3] 323[3] (Dead)

Orpen Grey (IRE) *Tom Dascombe* 112
2 gr g Orpen(USA) —Sky Red (Night Shift (USA))
2477[5] (3072) (3424) ◆ 3779[2] 5172[5]

Orpenindeed (IRE) *M Botti* a96 99
6 bb g Orpen(USA) —Indian Goddess (IRE) (Indian Ridge)
579[4] 778[3] 1116[2] 1467[6] 2297[3] 3795[8] 6024[2] 6495[3] (7155) 7414[4]

Orpen Lady *J M Bradley*
3 b f Orpen(USA) —Gargren (IRE) (Mujtahid (USA))
3813[10] 4860[13]

Orpen's Art (IRE) *S A Callaghan* a77 75
4 b h Invincible Spirit(IRE) —Bells Of Ireland (UAE) (Machiavellian (USA))
241[8] 937[6] 1038[3] 1360[10] (1957) 2130[3] 2219[5] 2596[6] 3002[11] 3246[7] (3477) 3677[2]

Orpen Shadow (IRE) *B Grizzetti* 109
2 b c Orpen(USA) —Mujadil Shadow (IRE) (Mujadil (USA))
(3185a) 4366a[4]

Orpen Wide (IRE) *M C Chapman* a89 89
7 b g Orpen(USA) —Melba (IRE) (Namaqualand (USA))
490[3] 680[7] 1053[5] (1089) 1405[12] 1722[7] 2822[4] 3116[9] 3353[3] 4501[9] 6645[12]

Orpen Winger (IRE) *A J Martin* a54 58
4 b g Orpen(USA) —Tahdid (Mtoto)
6399[5]

Orphan Boy *H J Collingridge* a14
4 b g Tipsy Creek(USA) —Miss Jingles (Muhtarram (USA))
166[9]

Orphaned Annie *B Ellison* a56 57
3 b f Lend A Hand—Great Exception (Grundy)
1063[4] 1397[6]

Orpsie Boy (IRE) *N P Littmoden* a107 104
6 b g Orpen(USA) —Nordicolini (IRE) (Nordico (USA))
579[6] 633[3] 785[2] 1006[4] 1299[5] 1699[4] 3141[9] 3818[9] 4297[10] 4523[23] 4776[7] 5263[7] 5860[20] 6279[8] 6540[3]

Orse Gul (TUR) *M B Oktar* 86
3 b f Sri Pekan(USA) —Ghyraan (IRE) (Cadeaux Genereux)
5588a[10]

Orsett Lad (USA) *J R Best* a68 65
2 b g Essence Of Dubai(USA) —Sofisticada (USA) (Northern Jove (CAN))
3160[6] 3745[4] 4200[4] 4699[3] 5913[8] 6211[12] 7363[6] 7513[9] 7887[6]

Orsippus (USA) *Michael Smith* a78 74
3 bb g Sunday Break(JPN) —Mirror Dancing (USA) (Caveat (USA))
595[5] 755[6] 840[6] 1063[3] 1643[7] 1930[4] 2371[8] 3005[14] 6384[2] 6767[7]

Orthology (IRE) *M H Tompkins* a56 79
3 b g Kalanisi(IRE) —Al Shakoor (Barathea (IRE))
2084[5] 2232[5] 5151[4] 5751[5] 6549[5] 6758[5] (7094)

Oscar Wild *I Semple* 53
7 b g Tragic Role(USA) —Minster Lascar (Scallywag)
1769[4] 2314[9] 5332[10] 7173[9]

Osiris Way *P R Chamings* a89 100
7 ch g Indian Ridge—Heady (Rousillon (USA))
2474[4] 3141[15] 3802[9] 4523[25] 4853[5] 5424[7] 6694[12]

Oskari *P T Midgley* a70 54
4 b g Lear Spear(USA) —Cedar Jeneva (Muhtarram (USA))
963[2] 1476[2] 2261[13] 3339[11] 4171[3] 4822[4] 5329[5]

Osorios Trial *M Johnston* 25
2 ch c Osorio(GER) —Skytrial (USA) (Sky Classic (CAN))
3750[14]

Osservatorio (ITY) *R Menichetti* 98
3 br c Colossus(IRE) —Oropa (IRE) (Indian Ridge)
1393a[3]

Ostaadi *M A Jarvis* a83 66
3 b c Nayef(USA) —Blodwen (USA) (Mister Baileys)
1289[7] (1780) 2829[2] 3300[2]

Ostella (GER) *Katja Gernreich* 50
8 b m In A Tiff(IRE) —Ordessa (GER) (Perrault)
7038a[7]

Ostentation *M Johnston* a53 60
2 ch g Dubawi(IRE) —Oshiponga (Barathea (IRE))
6181[5] 6591[8] 7390[8] 7551[6] ◆

Osteopathic Care (IRE) *Miss Tracy Waggott* 57
5 b g Montjeu(IRE) —Super Gift (IRE) (Darshaan)
1655[12]

Osteopathic Remedy (IRE) *M Dods* a89 100
5 ch g Inchinor—Dolce Vita (IRE) (Ela-Mana-Mou)
995[17] 1124[6] 1365[9] 1684[15] 2093[3] 2405[6] 3172[2] 3391[2] 3872[10] 4310[5] 5522[3] 6092[2] 6633[5] 7169[4]

Osterhase (IRE) *J E Mulhern* a78 99
10 b g Flying Spur(AUS) —Ostrusa (AUT) (Rustan (HUN))
1375a[3] 2012[5] 3435a[15]

Ostland (GER) *P Schiergen* 110
4 b g Lando(GER) —Ost Tycoon (GER) (Last Tycoon)
(1143a) 1549a[6] 2216a[8]

Otello Azzy (ITY) *A Cascio* 100
3 ch c Dane Friendly—Aileen Elliott (ITY) (Elmaamul (USA))
1392a[3]

Othello (IRE) *E F Vaughan* a53 40
2 b g Azamour(IRE) —Bonheur (IRE) (Royal Academy (USA))
7244[12] 7325[9] 7430[7]

Otou (GER) *S Smrczek* a71
2 b c Big Shuffle(USA) —Old Tradition (IRE) (Royal Academy (USA))
4970a[3]

Otterton *R Hollinshead* 39
2 b f Sampower Star—Parkside Prospect (Piccolo)
3572[6] 4503[11]

Ottoman Empire (FR) *D R Lanigan* a99 87
3 ch g Pivotal—Chesnut Bird (IRE) (Storm Bird (CAN))
1297[5] ◆ 1611[2] ◆ 2002[5] (4838) (5781) 6165[2] 6795[9]

Ottomax (GER) *Andreas Lowe* 98
4 ch h Banyumanik(IRE) —Omicenta (IRE) (Platini (GER))
2513a[7] 6713a[5]

Oui Non (IRE) *Y De Nicolay* a71 76
2 ch c Footstepsinthesand—Slinky (Ashkalani (IRE))
6979a[6]

Ouqba *B W Hills* 116
3 b c Red Ransom(USA) —Dancing Mirage (IRE) (Machiavellian (USA))
(1292) 1675[11] (3011) 4406[6] 5862[4] 6848[2]

Our Acquaintance *W R Muir* a62 73
4 ch g Bahamian Bounty—Lady Of Limerick (IRE) (Thatching)
1412[7] 1564[9] 2349[13] 2908[7]

Our Apolonia (IRE) *A Berry* 49
3 b f Intikhab(USA) —Algaira (USA) (Irish River (FR))
2250[8] 3108[10] 4105[8] 4589[4] 5306[8] 5549[13]

Ourbelle *Miss Tracy Waggott* 10
4 b m Bertolini(USA) —Guardienne (Hector Protector (USA))
5946[12]

Our Blessing (IRE) *A P Jarvis* a75 68
5 b g Lujain(USA) —Berenice (ITY) (Marouble)
1285[4] 1748[2] 2088[8]

Our Boy Barrington (IRE) *R Hannon* 62
2 b c Catcher In The Rye(IRE) —Daily Double (FR) (Unfuwain (USA))
2853[11] 3395[7] 4908[9]

Our Day Will Come *R Hannon* a71 71
3 b f Red Ransom(USA) —Dawnus (IRE) (Night Shift (USA))
1176[5] 1973[9] 2321[9]

Our Dream Queen *B W Hills* 70
2 b f Oasis Dream—Our Queen Of Kings (Arazi (USA))
1323[3] ◆ 1866[5] (4163) 4739[3] 6619[11] 7290[20]

Our Fugitive (IRE) *C Gordon* a68 71
7 gr g Titus Livius(FR) —Mystical Jumbo (Mystiko (USA))
294[13] 727[5] 1055[6]

Our Georgie Girl *G G Margarson* 34
2 ch f Zafeen(FR) —Rosina May (IRE) (Danehill Dancer (IRE))
1195[11] 1630[6] 2414[7] 2861[6] 2978[8]

Our Girl Ally (IRE) *A Berry* 2
3 b f Captain Rio—Glenviews Big Bird (USA) (Danehill (USA))
1828[6] 2265[8] 5163[6] 5304[4]

Our Glenard *J E Long* a40 28
10 b g Royal Applause—Loucoum (FR) (Iron Duke (FR))
838[6]

Our Joe Mac (IRE) *R A Fahey* 88
2 b g Celtic Swing—Vade Retro (IRE) (Desert Sun)
4286[3] ◆ (4847) 6088[5]

Our Jonathan *K A Ryan* a103 114
2 b c Invincible Spirit(IRE) —Sheik'n Swing (Celtic Swing)
3571[3] ◆ (5066) (5452a) 5822[8] ◆ (6660) (7231a)

Our Kes (IRE) *P Howling* a68 67
7 gr m Revoque(IRE) —Gracious Gretclo (Common Grounds)
320[3] 478[13] 733[9] 871[12] 2859[13] 3929[8] 4269[11] 4538[2] 5103[4] (5680) 6126[3] 6668[10] 6917[2] 7403[6] 7512[6] 7766[5]

Our Last Call (IRE) *Sir Mark Prescott* a39
3 gr f Hernando(FR) —On Call (Alleged (USA))
3025[9] 3297[11] 3508[12] 7154[12]

Our Nations *D Carroll* a70 44
4 gr g Highest Honor(FR) —Lines Of Beauty (USA) (Line In The Sand (USA))
11[2] 249[P] (Dead)

Our Piccadilly (IRE) *W S Kittow* a83 84
4 b m Piccolo—Dilys (Efisio)
1150[2] 1425[3] (1836) 3845[7] 4232[3] ◆ 4461[14] 5183[6] 5919[4] 6632[2] 6972[7]

Ours (IRE) *John A Harris* a85 78
6 b g Mark Of Esteem(IRE) —Ellebanna (Tina's Pet)
220[3] 558[2] 747[2] 1170[7] 1479[7] 2576[3] 3378[5] 4070[2] 4663[4] 4816[4] 5329[2] 6174[3] 6357[2] 6878[5] 7125[6] 7759[3] (7854)

Our Serendipity *R C Guest* 1
6 ch m Presidium—Berl's Gift (Prince Sabo)
1127[8]

Our Teddy (IRE) *R Curtis* a46 83
9 ch g Grand Lodge(USA) —Lady Windley (Baillamont (USA))
7393[7]

Our Wee Girl (IRE) *Miss Tor Sturgis* a58 77
3 bb f Choisir(AUS) —Zwadi (IRE) (Docksider (USA))
4479[13] 6119[8] 6433[8]

Ouste (FR) *Mrs S Leech* a44 46
7 ch g Ragmar(FR) —Elbe (FR) (Royal Charter (FR))
541[6]

Ouster (GER) *D R C Elsworth* 93
3 b c Lomitas—Odabella's Charm (Cadeaux Genereux)
1459[4]

Outdroad *P M Phelan* a28
3 ch c Desert Sun—Loch Fyne (Ardkinglass)
441[6]

Outer Hebrides *J M Bradley* a62 63
8 b g Efisio—Reuval (Sharpen Up)
234[4] 473[4] 803[10] 984[4] 1039[8] (1781) 2223[8] 2745[2] 2876[2] 3459[2] 4183[5] 4479[4] 4938[14] 5283[6] (5501) 5632[4] 5788[5] 6790[7] 6933[6] 7239[3] 7349[3] 7418[3] 7517[7] 7602[3]

Outland (IRE) *M H Tompkins* a34 63
3 br g Indian Haven—Sensuality (IRE) (Idris (IRE))
2131[8] (2865) 3482[2] 4156[5] 5600[2] 6767[2] 7124[10]

Outlandish *Miss E C Lavelle* a84 81
6 b g Dr Fong(USA) —Velvet Lady (Nashwan (USA))
2945[2] 3343[4] 4696[5] 5321[7]

Out Of Control (TUR) *Y Simsek* 113
6 b h Cape Cross(IRE) —Committal (USA) (Chief's Crown (USA))
5619a[12]

Out Of Eden *H R A Cecil* 55
2 b c Monsun(GER) —Eden (USA) (Holy Bull (USA))
7034[8]

Out Of Honour (IRE) *John Geoghegan* a67 71
3 ch f Highest Honor(FR) —Out Of Thanks (IRE) (Sadler's Wells (USA))
4392a[2]

Out Of India *P T Dalton* a51 56
7 b m Marju(IRE) —Tide Of Fortune (Soviet Star (USA))
1103[8] 1655[9]

Out Of Nothing *K M Prendergast* a58 66
6 br m Perryston View—Loves To Dare (IRE) (Desert King (IRE))
1775[10]

Outofoil (IRE) *R M Beckett* 79
3 b g King's Best(USA) —Simplicity (Polish Precedent (USA))
2329[8]

Outrageous Request *Pat Eddery* a82 85
3 ch g Rainbow Quest(USA) —La Sorrela (IRE) (Cadeaux Genereux)
998[6] 1407[6] ◆ 1573[2] 4519[4] 7221[2] 7780[2] 7867[2]

Outshine *J H M Gosden* 71
2 ch f Exceed And Excel(AUS) —Sunny Davis (USA) (Alydar (USA))
3820[3] 4147[3] 5478[7]

Out The Ring (IRE) *Miss Gay Kelleway* a66 59
2 b g Acclamation—Residual (IRE) (Trempolino (USA))
1005[2] 1126[3] 1624[2] 1934[2] 2325[2] 2800[4] 6343[9] 6775[6] 7421[9] 7559[2] 7661[7] 7748[5]

Overrule (USA) *B Ellison* 95
5 b g Diesis—Her Own Way (USA) (Danzig (USA))
(1059) 1665[4] 1990[9] 2666[3] ◆ (3266) 4340[14] 4769[10]

Oversighted (GER) *Mrs Y Dunleavy* a72 54
8 b g Selkirk(USA) —Obvious Appeal (IRE) (Danehill (USA))
6862[8]

Over To You Bert *R J Hodges* a66 38
10 b g Overbury(IRE) —Silvers Era (Balidar)
234[8] (480) 666[12] 874[8] 984[7] 1413[12] 1535[9]

Overturn (IRE) *W R Swinburn* a94 101
5 b g Barathea(IRE) —Kristal Bridge (Kris)
2480[7] 3213[3] 3797[7] 5667[2] 6281[2] ◆ (6734)

Ovthenight (IRE) *Mrs P Sly* a57 74
4 b h Noverre(USA) —Night Beauty (King Of Kings (IRE))
1454[6] 2294[3] 2854[2] 3169[7] 5028[5]

Owain James *M Salaman* a36 39
4 ch g Dancing Spree(USA) —Jane Grey (Tragic Role (USA))
2519[9] 3675[6]

Owed *R Bastiman* a66 28
7 b g Lujain(USA) —Nightingale (Night Shift (USA))
811[13] 975[9] 2134[8] 2579[3] 2745[8] 4016[9] 4372[8]

Owen Jones (USA) *P W Hiatt* 61
3 b g Rahy(USA) —Batique (USA) (Storm Cat (USA))
6741[4]

Owls FC (IRE) *M C Chapman* 28
3 b f King's Best(USA) —Sadinga (IRE) (Sadler's Wells (USA))
6425[5] 7221[10] 7780[7]

Owner Occupier *Miss Susan A Finn* a51 54
4 ch g Foxhound(USA) —Miss Beverley (Beveled (USA))
7753[12]

Oxbridge *J M Bradley* a47 53
4 ch g Tomba—Royal Passion (Ahonoora)
5501[13] 5633[7] 7350[10] 7427[7] 7533[4]

Oxford City (IRE) *P M Phelan* a58 68
5 ch g City On A Hill(USA) —Bold Nora (IRE) (Persian Bold)
7823[7]

Oxus (IRE) *B R Johnson* a52
4 ch g Sinndar(IRE) —River Dancer (Irish River (FR))
120[3] 310[8] 578[5]

Ozone Trustee (NZ) *G A Swinbank* a36 82
5 b g Montjeu(IRE) —Bold Faith (Warning)
2437[3] 2743[8] 3123[7] 4312[6] 4344[6]

Pab Special (IRE) *B R Johnson* a72 64
6 b g City On A Hill(USA) —Tinos Island (IRE) (Alzao (USA))
256[2] (580) 725[2] 1539[8] 2183[8] 2807[8]

Pachakutek (USA) *L M Cumani* a62 71
3 ch g Giant's Causeway(USA) —Charlotte Corday (Kris)
1350[10] 1573[11] 7803[4]

Pachattack (USA) *G A Butler* a103 100
3 ch f Pulpit(USA) —El Laoob (USA) (Red Ransom (USA))
1701[5] 1988[5] 6114[2] 6813[2] 7323[2] 7589[4]

Pacific Bay (IRE) *R A Fahey* a63 64
3 b f Diktat—Wild Clover (Lomitas)
4131[5] 4432[3] 5158[5] 5624[9] (5983) 6333[6] 6701[5]

Pacific Pride *J J Quinn* 79
6 b g Compton Place—Only Yours (Aragon)
1309[9] 1518[12] (1951) 2363[8] 3021[7] 3607[5] 3828[11] 4504[6] 4941[6] 5406[10] 5675[8] 6233[6] 6489[8]

Packing Winner (NZ) *L Ho* 117
7 b g Zabeel(NZ) —Musical Note (AUS) (Marscay (AUS))
1554a[5] 7744a[11]

Paco Boy (IRE) *R Hannon* a101 127
4 b h Desert Style(IRE) —Tappen Zee (Sandhurst Prince)
1011a[8] (1525) 2076[4] (2990) 3819[4] 4419[2]

Paddy Bear *R A Fahey* 71
3 b c Piccolo—Lily Of The Guild (IRE) (Lycius (USA))
(1335) 1686[7] 2611[6] 3065[13] (3972) 4133[7]

Paddy Jack *J R Weymes* a2 61
4 ch g Rambling Bear—Bayrami (Emarati (USA))
1591[5] 2316[12] 2657[6] 3002[15] 3498[5] 3853[3] 5041[7] 5159[6] 7086[U] 7629[9]

Paddy Partridge *N J Vaughan* 58
3 b c Pivotal—Treble Heights (IRE) (Unfuwain (USA))
1087[8] 1793[8] 2199[7] 3336[7]

Paddy Rielly (IRE) *P D Evans* a68 68
4 b g Catcher In The Rye(IRE) —The Veil (IRE) (Barathea (IRE))
745[2] 816[5] (1442) 1654[3] 2798[2] 3544[6] 4169[6]

Padlocked (IRE) *D M Simcock* a76 95
5 b g Key Of Luck(USA) —Accelerating (USA) (Lear Fan (USA))
910[9]

Padmini *Saeed Bin Suroor* a75
2 b f Tiger Hill(IRE) —Petrushka (IRE) (Unfuwain (USA))
(7135) ◆

Pagan Flight (IRE) *Mrs A J Perrett* 51
3 b g Hawk Wing(USA) —Regal Darcey (IRE) (Darshaan)
2282[7] 2881[10] 3919[3] 4177[8]

Pagan Force (IRE) *Mrs A J Perrett* a39 64
3 b c Green Desert(USA) —Brigitta (IRE) (Sadler's Wells (USA))
5572[10] 5965[6] 6399[8] 6701[10]

Pagan Starprincess *G M Moore* a57 61
5 b m Robertico—Pagan Star (Carlitin)
1439[4] 2262[2] 6053[6] 6767[12]

Pagan Sword *D G Bridgwater* a62 92
7 ch g Selkirk(USA) —Vanessa Bell (IRE) (Lahib (USA))
7005[9]

Painswick (USA) *J L Dunlop* 63
2 ch c Elusive Quality(USA) —Pleine Lune (IRE) (Alzao (USA))
5401[8] 6109[12] 6754[7]

Paintball (IRE) *W R Muir* a64
2 b c Le Vie Dei Colori—Camassina (IRE) (Taufan (USA))
7864[3]

Paint By Numbers *J A Glover* a38
2 b g Haafhd—Attention Seeker (USA) (Exbourne (USA))
7618[7] 7825[8]

Painted Sky *R A Fahey* a66 66
6 ch g Rainbow Quest(USA) —Emplane (USA) (Irish River (FR))
7623[4] 7817[6]

Paint Splash *T D Barron* a57 51
3 ch f Beat Hollow—Questa Nova (Rainbow Quest (USA))
322[6] 492[3] 1057[3] 1437[9] 1691[3] 1926[3] 3614[2] 4013[3] 4279[4] 4819[5] 5983[10] 6497[7]

Paint Stripper *W Storey* 41
4 b g Prince Sabo—Passing Fancy (Grand Lodge (USA))
1276[12] 1734[4] 2404[5] 2722[8] 3066[8] 4621[5] 5150[11] 5254[7]

Paint The Town (IRE) *J G Given* a66 42
4 b m Sadler's Wells(USA) —Minnie Habit (Habitat)
2200[9] 3188[8]

Paint The Town Red *H J Collingridge* a79 79
4 b g Mujahid(USA) —Onefortheditch (USA) (With Approval (CAN))
(1514) 2052[10] 3343[5] 4207[7] 5003[10] 5594[7] *6498[6]* 6761[10] *7214[7]* *7461[4]*

Pairumani Pat (IRE) *J Pearce* a48 53
4 ch g Pairumani Star(IRE) —Golden Skiis (IRE) (Hector Protector (USA))
1439[8]

Paisley *L M Cumani* 77
3 ch f Pivotal—Pongee (Barathea (IRE))
4097[5] ◆ (5215) 5910[4]

Pajada *M D I Usher* a48 49
5 b m Bertolini(USA) —Last Ambition (IRE) (Cadeaux Genereux)
193[9] *482[8]*

Paktolos (FR) *John A Harris* a100 95
6 b g Dansili—Pithara (GR) (Never So Bold)
33[6] 1458[12] *2597[8]* 3797[9] *7465[8]* *7640[4]* *7811[2]*

Palacefield (IRE) *P W Chapple-Hyam* a74 81
3 b g Green Desert(USA) —Multaka (USA) (Gone West (USA))
1255[2] 1683[2] (2318) 3489[5] 5448[4] 5833[5] *6773[5]*

Palace Moon *H Morrison* 114
4 b g Fantastic Light(USA) —Palace Street (USA) (Secreto (USA))
(1018) ◆ 2948[2] 5024[4] (5434) 6304[12] 6661[8]

Palais Polaire *J A Geake* a62 60
7 ch m Polar Falcon(USA) —Palace Street (USA) (Secreto (USA))
711[1] *234[12]* *874[13]* 4266[7]

Palavicini (USA) *J L Dunlop* 112
3 b c Giant's Causeway(USA) —Cara Fantasy (IRE) (Sadler's Wells (USA))
1326[4] 1678[2] (2277) 3050[8] (5231) 5875[4] 6303[6] 6812[3]

Palawi (IRE) *J J Quinn* 72
2 ch c Dubawi(IRE) —Palwina (FR) (Unfuwain (USA))
6763[3] 7116[3]

Paleo (IRE) *R Hannon* 82
2 ch f Indian Ridge—Crossbreeze (USA) (Red Ransom (USA))
4047[8] 4460[8] (5398) 5797[3] 6481[10] 6852[9]

Palermo (GER) *C Zschache* 101
3 br c Kalatos(GER) —Palma (GER) (Goofalik (USA))
5585a[2] 6500a[4]

Palio Square (USA) *H R A Cecil* 82
2 bb c Harlan's Holiday(USA) —Teewee's Hope (CAN) (Defrere (USA))
4286[7] ◆ 5347[4] ◆ 7121[4]

Palisades Park *R Hannon* 78
2 b c Compton Place—Brooklyn's Sky (Septieme Ciel (USA))
2007[6] 2636[2] (3218) 3799[5] 4089[13] 4525[11] 5218[5]

Pallantes Cross *M Johnston* a95 95
2 b c Cape Cross(IRE) —Palinisa (FR) (Night Shift (USA))
2196[10] (3106) 4499[2] 5433[3] *(5681)* 6151a[4]

Pallaton *R M Beckett* a43 59
3 ch g Bertolini(USA) —Miss Honeypenny (IRE) (Old Vic)
1771[6] 2178[8] *2922[6]*

Pallodio (IRE) *J E Hammond* a93 103
4 br h Medecis—Bent Al Fala (IRE) (Green Desert (USA))
527a[9] 774a[12] *7704a[9]*

Palmeral (IRE) *Mlle L Beccaert* a68 89
3 b c Kendor(FR) —Acola (FR) (Acatenango (GER))
4581a[3] 7385a[0]

Palme Royale (IRE) *E Lellouche* 94
3 b f Red Ransom(USA) —Palmeraie (USA) (Lear Fan (USA))
3968a[8]

Panadin (IRE) *Mrs L C Jewell* 43
7 b g Desert King(IRE) —Strident Note (The Minstrel (CAN))
3774[8]

Pan American *P J Makin* a74 73
2 b g American Post—Pan Galactic (USA) (Lear Fan (USA))
3925[4] 6544[2] ◆ *6912[3]* *7317[4]* *(7655)*

Panceltica *Karen George* a31
4 b g Makbul—Lady Kate (Bay Express)
2142[12] *3223[11]*

Panpiper *G L Moore* 66
2 ch c Piccolo—Phi Beta Kappa (USA) (Diesis)
3403[7] 3658[3]

Pan River (TUR) *R Tetik* 113
4 b h Red Bishop(USA) —Wanganui River (Unfuwain (USA))
5619a[2]

Pansy Potter *B J Meehan* a59 56
3 b f Auction House(USA) —Ellway Queen (USA) (Bahri (USA))
2160[14] 2498[8] 3010[11] *3299[8]*

Pantherii (USA) *P F I Cole* a60 64
4 ch m Forest Wildcat(USA) —Saraa Ree (USA) (Caro)
2590[2]

Panto Princess *H Candy* 74
3 b f Act One—Bob's Princess (Bob's Return (IRE))
2981[3] 5744[2] 6794[5] 7101[4]

Panyu (GER) *P Schiergen* 98
3 b c Monsun(GER) —Prairie Darling (Stanford)
2954a[3] 3670a[17] 5585a[6] 6500a[9]

Papa Clem (USA) *Gary Stute* a116 98
3 b c Smart Strike(CAN) —Miss Houdini (USA) (Belong To Me (USA))
1688a[4] ◆ *2098a[6]*

Papageno *J R Jenkins* a62 62
2 b c Piccolo—Fresh Fruit Daily (Reprimand)
1195[9] 2295[5] 3385[4] 4208[9] *5310[2]* *5776[4]* 6903[13] *7365[9]*

Papa Power (IRE) *K M Prendergast* 9
6 b g Polish Precedent(USA) —Guignol (IRE) (Anita's Prince)
5911[10]

Paparaazi (IRE) *I W McInnes* a62 62
7 b g Victory Note(USA) —Raazi (My Generation)
3450[9] 3943[8]

Papa's Princess *J S Goldie* a17 62
5 b m Mujadil(USA) —Desert Flower (Green Desert (USA))
1690[4] 2314[6] 2590[6] 3098[6] 3447[5] 3911[4] 4465[3] 4751[3] 4876[11] 5364[9] 5730[13] 5944[5]

Papetti (ITY) *B Grizzetti* 111
4 b h Shantou(USA) —Pasionaria (IRE) (Celtic Swing)
1575a[2] 1903a[6] 6893a[5]

Papillio (IRE) *J R Fanshawe* a77 68
4 b g Marju(IRE) —Danish Gem (Danehill (USA))
866[6] *1186[7]* *1493[3]* 2086[15] 2759[2] 3338[3] *3713[12]*

Pappoose *H Candy* 49
4 b m Namid—Bryn (Saddlers' Hall (IRE))
2353[7] *3743[10]* 4479[12]

Papradon *N A Twiston-Davies* a70 70
5 b g Tobougg(IRE) —Salvezza (IRE) (Superpower)
342[8]

Papyrian *W Jarvis* a77 82
3 b g Oasis Dream—La Papagena (Habitat)
1941[3] 2415[5] 2849[2] ◆ 3590[2] 5242[4] 6390[4] *6977[3]*

Paquerettza (FR) *D H Brown* 87
3 ch f Dr Fong(USA) —Cover Look (SAF) (Fort Wood (USA))
(1626) (4275) 5030[4] 5175[2] 5670[7] 6243[8] 6680[2]

Parading (USA) *Claude McGaughey III* a118 111
6 ch h Pulpit(USA) —On Parade (USA) (Storm Cat (USA))
6687a[4]

Paradise Dancer (IRE) *J A R Toller* a80 68
5 b m Danehill Dancer(IRE) —Pintada De Fresco (FR) (Marignan (USA))
125[7] *318[10]*

Paradise Dream *J Noseda* a64 59
2 b c Kyllachy—Wunders Dream (IRE) (Averti (IRE))
1726[2] 1991[3] 2853[10] 3682[4]

Paradise Rain *Mario Hofer* 97
2 b f Compton Place—Goldenrain (USA) (Nureyev (USA))
3667a[4] 5652a[7]

Paradise Spectre *K R Burke* 79
2 b c Firebreak—Amber's Bluff (Mind Games)
2588[4] 3017[2] 3875[11] 4306[2]

Paraguay (USA) *Mrs D J Sanderson* a78 86
6 b g Pivotal—Grisonnante (FR) (Kaldoun (FR))
1479[6] 1876[2] (2257) 2665[6] 3265[6] *3736[10]* 4400[4] 4663[10] (Dead)

Parallel (IRE) *J H M Gosden* 57
3 b f Refuse To Bend(IRE) —Iktidar (Green Desert (USA))
5222[3] 6741[6]

Parallel Blossom (FR) *P Demercastel* 92
3 gr f Slickly(FR) —Parallel Universe (Hector Protector (USA))
2989a[7]

Par Avion *Paul Murphy* 56
4 b m Efisio—Blow Me A Kiss (Kris)
2030[5]

Parbold Hill *T D Barron* 68
2 br f Exceed And Excel(AUS) —Let Alone (Warning)
1610[5] ◆ 2089[2] 2372[7] 2893[3] 3540[6]

Parc Aux Boules *Paul Stafford* a67 71
8 gr g Royal Applause—Aristocratique (Cadeaux Genereux)
1375a[4] *7634[11]*

Parc Des Princes (USA) *A M Balding* a76 66
3 bb g Ten Most Wanted(USA) —Miss Orah (Unfuwain (USA))
1580[5] 1930[7] 2357[4] 3222[3] (3321) 3535[3] *(4206)*

Parcelle Perdue (FR) *Mme C Dufreche* 93
3 b f Coroner(IRE) —Nada Es Amor (IRE) (Zafonic (USA))
4334a[10]

Pareia (GER) *Uwe Ostmann* 91
5 b m Areion(GER) —Party Bloom (FR) (Baillamont (USA))
5651a[3] 6499a[4]

Parfum Des Dieux *J-C Rouget* a88 100
4 b h Cape Cross(IRE) —Moonbaby (FR) (Le Balafre (FR))
2513a[5] 6579a[13]

Pariala (GER) *P Schiergen* 92
3 b f Lando(GER) —Pariana (USA) (Bering)
2757a[7]

Parisella (IRE) *Mario Hofer* 96
2 b f Key Of Luck(USA) —O'Keefe (IRE) (Be My Guest (USA))
5085a[7] 6892a[4]

Parisian Art (IRE) *J Noseda* a80 86
3 b g Clodovil(IRE) —Cafe Creme (IRE) (Catrail (USA))
2821[7]

Parisian Dream *T J Pitt* a46 68
5 b g Sakhee(USA) —Boojum (Mujtahid (USA))
3335[8] 3628[11] 4658[15] 5548[10] *6498[12]* *6998[7]*

Parisian Gift (IRE) *J R Gask* a75 84
4 b g Statue Of Liberty(USA) —My Micheline (Lion Cavern (USA))
189[3] *721[3]* 1628[3]

Parisian Pyramid (IRE) *D Nicholls* 98
3 gr g Verglas(IRE) —Sharadja (IRE) (Doyoun)
1517[3] ◆ 1803[11] 1824[7] 2279[3] 2674[4] 2934[2] 3747[5] 4485[15] 5206[11] 5654[7] 6678[19] 7015[5]

Paris In Mind *C N Kellett*
3 b f Mind Games—Paris Babe (Teenoso (USA))
3071[10]

Parisis (FR) *J-M Capitte*
2 b c Le Fou(IRE) —Dissidente (FR) (Double Bed (FR))
5850a[9] 7166a[6]

Paris Perfect (SAF) *N L Bruss* a96
5 ch h Muhtafal(USA) —Candle Princess (NZ) (Honor Grades (USA))
1013a[3]

Paris Vegas (USA) *F Chappet* a75
2 gr c Maria's Mon(USA) —Tell Seattle (USA) (A.P. Indy (USA))
6979a[4]

Park Lane *B W Hills* a72 81
3 b g Royal Applause—Kazeem (Darshaan)
828[2] *1380[2]* 2318[3] 4057[2] (5072) 5437[5] *5986[10]*

Park Melody (IRE) *B J Meehan* a34 59
3 b f Refuse To Bend(IRE) —Park Charger (Tirol)
2848[4] ◆ 3250[4] 4606[10] *5988[14]* *6860[13]*

Park's Prodigy *G A Harker* a14 63
5 b g Desert Prince(IRE) —Up And About (Barathea (IRE))
2366[4] 3486[7] 4944[11] 5733[4] 6102[2] 6559[2] (7080) *7154[11]*

Park View *B W Hills* 53
2 ch f With Approval(CAN) —Bayswater (Caerleon (USA))
7183[10]

Parkview Love (USA) *A G Newcombe* a61 70
8 bb g Mister Baileys—Jerre Jo Glanville (USA) (Skywalker (USA))
5617[5] *5888[7]* *7653[7]* *7784[9]*

Parnassian *J A Geake* a60 60
9 ch g Sabrehill(USA) —Delphic Way (Warning)
103[5] 4263[12]

Parson's Punch *P D Cundell* a72 70
4 b g Beat Hollow—Ordained (Mtoto)
392[10]

Parthenon *Saeed Bin Suroor* 105
3 b g Dubai Destination(USA) —Grecian Slipper (Sadler's Wells (USA))
(1487) (2029) 2756a[14]

Partner (IRE) *David Marnane* a76 61
3 b g Indian Ridge—Oregon Trail (USA) (Gone West (USA))
(7518) ◆

Partner Shift (IRE) *H-A Pantall* a78 103
3 b g Night Shift(USA) —What A Picture (FR) (Peintre Celebre (USA))
3649a[7] 6657a[0]

Party Doctor *Tom Dascombe* 104
2 ch c Dr Fong(USA) —Wedding Party (Groom Dancer (USA))
2533[2] ◆ 2844[3] 3138[3] 4294[2] 5133[4]

Party In The Park *J R Boyle* a62 68
4 b g Royal Applause—Halland Park Girl (IRE) (Primo Dominie)
2891[10] *580[8]* 1846[7] 2361[12] 2459[5] 3234[2] 3730[5] 4977[11] 5544[9] 6339[6] *6945[6]* *7110[2]* *7200[2]* 7438[8] 7653[2] 7754[2]

Party Palace *H S Howe* a52 60
5 b m Auction House(USA) —Lady-Love (Pursuit Of Love)
1786[3] 1980[3] (2322) 2517[7] 2798[4] 3814[4] 3997[3]

Parvaaz (IRE) *M A Jarvis* 69
2 ch c Rahy(USA) —Saabga (USA) (Woodman (USA))
7099[3]

Pascal (USA) *E Charpy* a99 53
4 b h Menifee(USA) —La Pascua (SWI) (Caerleon (USA))
771a[8]

Paschendale *Saeed Bin Suroor* 72
2 b c Refuse To Bend(IRE) —Fading Light (King's Best (USA))
6548[5] 6821[9]

Pas De Refus (FR) *D Bressou* 63
3 gr f Refuse To Bend(IRE) —Silver Singing (USA) (Topsider (USA))
5118a[0]

Pas Mure (IRE) *F Head* 78
3 b f Green Tune(USA) —Special Green (FR) (Sadler's Wells (USA))
4578a[8]

Paso De Gloria (ARG) *M bin Shafya* a83
4 br h Honour And Glory(USA) —Morning Pleasure (ARG) (Morning Bob (USA))
768a[4]

Passage To India (IRE) *Miss J R Tooth* a72
3 ch f Indian Ridge—Kathy College (IRE) (College Chapel)
2578[3] ◆ *3274[9]*

Passavanti (IRE) *F & L Camici* 92
3 ch f Desert Prince(IRE) —Poulkovo (IRE) (Sadler's Wells (USA))
1659a[14]

Passionate Cry (USA) *W J Knight* a52 25
2 bb c Street Cry(IRE) —Virtus (USA) (Silver Charm (USA))
5807[8] 6617[16] *7050[5]*

Passion For Gold (USA) *Saeed Bin Suroor* 117
2 b c Medaglia D'Oro(USA) —C'Est L' Amour (USA) (Thunder Gulch (USA))
(5408) ◆ 6318a[3] (7404a)

Passion Overflow (USA) *J Noseda* a72
2 b f Hennessy(USA) —Polar Bird (Thatching)
7571[2] ◆ *(7736)*

Passkey *Sir Mark Prescott* a80 76
3 b f Medicean—Revival (Sadler's Wells (USA))
4955[3] ◆ *5193[2]* 6158[2] *7576[3]* *7730[7]*

Pass The Port *D Haydn Jones* a88 87
8 ch g Docksider(USA) —One Of The Family (Alzao (USA))
787[2]

Pasta Prayer *D E Cantillon* a60 55
4 br g Bertolini(USA) —Benedicite (Lomond (USA))
1465[12] 1889[P]

Pastel Blue (IRE) *M L W Bell* a68 64
2 b f Shamardal(USA) —Painted Moon (USA) (Gone West (USA))
2711[4] *3271[5]* *3987[5]* ◆ *5369[3]*

Pastello *R Hannon* a59 72
2 ch f Exceed And Excel(AUS) —Pastel (Lion Cavern (USA))
4055[8] 4693[2] 5547[2] 6066[5] 6481[6] 6793[13] *7359[8]* *7551[7]*

Pastoral Player *H Morrison* 92
2 b g Pastoral Pursuits—Copy-Cat (Lion Cavern (USA))
(6054) 7030[10] 7150[7]

Patachou *R J Smith* a43 49
2 b f Domedriver(IRE) —Pat Or Else (Alzao (USA))
4101[4] 4503[3] *7064[7]*

Patavian (IRE) *B Storey* 42
5 b g Titus Livius(FR) —Five Of Wands (Caerleon (USA))
2817[4] 3233[10]

Patavium (IRE) *E W Tuer* a55 66
6 b g Titus Livius(FR) —Arcevia (IRE) (Archway (IRE))
2159[P] 3486[4] (4193) 4806[5] (5423) 5947[4] 6560[3] 6769[2]

Patavium Prince (IRE) *Miss Jo Crowley* a64 81
6 ch g Titus Livius(FR) —Hoyland Common (IRE) (Common Grounds)
114[3] *646[4]* *853[2]* 1152[9] 2736[2] (3243) 4607[2] 4733[4] 5565[5] 6964[11]

Patch Patch *M Dods* 71
2 b g Avonbridge—Sandgate Cygnet (Fleetwood (IRE))
3058[2] (4342) 4875[7]

Patena (USA) *Richard Dutrow Jr* a99
3 b c Seeking The Gold(USA) —Handpainted (USA) (A.P. Indy (USA))
1225a[10]

Path Of Peace *J D Bethell* 44
2 b f Rock Of Gibraltar(IRE) —Persian Song (Persian Bold)
6378[6] 6990[7]

Path To Glory *Miss Z C Davison* a50 33
5 b g Makbul—Just Glory (Glory Of Dancer)
3104[RR]

Pathway To Heaven (IRE) *J J Quinn* 47
2 ch f Indian Haven—Beckerson (IRE) (Alzao (USA))
6762[9]

Patience Rewarded *J S Moore* a23
3 ch f Dr Fong(USA) —Breathing Space (USA) (Expelled (USA))
154[8] *345[8]*

Patio *David Marnane* a93 93
4 b m Beat Hollow—Maze Garden (USA) (Riverman (USA))
1756a[7] 4574a[RR]

Patkai (IRE) *Sir Michael Stoute* 121
4 ch h Indian Ridge—Olympienne (IRE) (Sadler's Wells (USA))
(1601) 2409[2] 3048[2]

Patriarchal *A Fabre* 73
2 b c Dubai Destination(USA) —Polska (USA) (Danzig (USA))
5561a[4]

Patrician's Glory (USA) *T P Tate* 103
3 b c Proud Citizen(USA) —Landholder (USA) (Dixieland Band (USA))
2004[2] 3011[6] 3536[5] 5200[19]

Patricks Lodge *J D Bethell* 39
2 ch g Redoubtable(USA) —Duxford Lodge (Dara Monarch)
4430[12] 5466[7]

Patriot Jack (IRE) *T G McCourt* a50 56
4 b g Desert Prince(IRE) —Summer Crush (USA) (Summer Squall (USA))
7732[11]

Patronne *Miss A Stokell* a56
3 b f Domedriver(IRE) —Pat Or Else (Alzao (USA))
296[6] ◆ *(363)* *620[10]*

Pat Seamur *E A L Dunlop* a67 63
2 b g Compton Place—Superlove (IRE) (Hector Protector (USA))
2663[8] 2853[6] 3064[8] *6071[4]* *6829[2]* ◆

Patteresa Girl *Mrs L Stubbs* a45 69
2 b f Auction House(USA) —Ellway Queen (USA) (Bahri (USA))
1031[7] (1344) 2372[9] 3086[21]

Pattern Mark *Ollie Pears* 54
3 b g Mark Of Esteem(IRE) —Latch Key Lady (USA) (Tejano (USA))
1926[11] 2790[3] ◆ 3454[6] 5011[6] 5442[7]

Pat Will (IRE) *M R Hoad* a9 51
5 b m Danetime(IRE) —Northern Tara (IRE) (Fayruz)
946[12]

Paul's Pet *Karen George* a44 58
4 b g Tobougg(IRE) —Cape Siren (Warning)
1638[8] 1972[7] 2317[7] 2975[7] 3463[3] *3735[8]* 4904[11] *5888[11]* *6255[7]*

Pavement Games *R C Guest* 47
2 b f Mind Games—Pavement Gates (Bishop Of Cashel)
4590[5] 5360[8] 5668[5] 6241[25] 6797[9] 7242[5]

Pavershooz *N Wilson* 101
4 b g Bahamian Bounty—Stormswept (USA) (Storm Bird (CAN))
1309[2] ◆ 2059[9] 2405[8] (2716) (3351) 3877[2] (4135) 5860[22] 6843[10]

Pawan (IRE) *Miss A Stokell* a99 97
9 ch g Cadeaux Genereux—Born To Glamour (Ajdal (USA))
(2) *451[6]* *579[7]* *821[4]* *1052[7]* 1189[2] 1647[7] 3318[6] 4485[13] *4842[4]* 4885[5] 6135[5] 6180[2] *6359[5]* 6879[9] 7019[10] 7090[5] 7245[7] 7553[7] 7676[7] 7758[3] 7866[5]

Pax Soprana (IRE) *Edward P Harty* a72 85
3 b f Namid—Sportsticketing (IRE) (Spectrum (IRE))
4360a[6]

Paydaar *B J Meehan* 72
2 ch c Sulamani(IRE) —Eternal Reve (USA) (Diesis)
6930[7]

Paymaster In Chief *M D I Usher* a46 62
3 b g Minardi(USA) —Allegedly (IRE) (Alhaarth (IRE))
149[6] 594[6] 817[5] 1046[3] 1811[6] *2744[4]* 3257[9] 3693[10] 3919[4] 4065[3]

Pazko (FR) *L A Urbano-Grajales*
2 br g Indian Rocket—Kim My Love (FR) (Courtroom (FR))
6325a[8]

Peace And Glory (IRE) *J W Unett*
2 b f Antonius Pius(USA) —Rosy Lydgate (Last Tycoon)
5852[7]

Peace And Liberty (FR) *M Pimbonnet*
2 b c Statue Of Liberty(USA) —Peace Fonic (FR) (Zafonic (USA))
5850a[7]

Peace Camp (USA) *A Fabre* 103
3 b f Storm Cat(USA) —Loving Kindness (USA) (Seattle Slew (USA))
3892a[6] 4637a[2] 5651a[6] (6579a) 7232a[12]

Peace Concluded *B R Millman* a65 68
3 b f Bertolini(USA) —Effie (Royal Academy (USA))
1315[7] 2567[10] 2794[4] *3711[5]* 4322[8] 5602[9]

Peace Corps *J R Fanshawe* a59 74
3 ch g Medicean—Tromond (Lomond (USA))
1730[11] 2165[6] ◆ 2446[4] 2892[12] 3279[2]

Peaceful Rule (USA) *D Nicholls* 75
3 b g Peace Rules(USA) —La Cat (USA) (Mr Greeley (USA))
1461[7] 2364[2] 2715[11] 4143[2] 4432[2] 4846[8] 5520[11]

Peaceful Soul (USA) *D R Lanigan* 61
2 b f Dynaformer(USA) —Serenity Jane (USA) (Affirmed (USA))
7182[8]

Peace In Paradise (IRE) *J A R Toller* a39 21
3 b f Dubai Destination(USA) —Paola Maria (Daylami (IRE))
1605[11] 2487[6] 3233[7]

Peace Of Cake (FR) *Mme M-C Naim* a56 68
5 b m Victory Note(USA) —Wondernight (FR) (Shining Steel)
5301a[10]

Peace Offering (IRE) *D Nicholls* a107 113
9 b g Victory Note(USA) —Amnesty Bay (Thatching)
1384[3] 2259[11] 2481[5] 4059[3] 4516[6] 5546[2]

Peace Royale (GER) *Mario Hofer* 103
4 b m Sholokhov(IRE) —Peace Time (GER) (Surumu (GER))
416a[4] 643a[4] 3231a[9]

Peachey Moment (USA) *H J Collingridge* a20
4 bb g Stormin Fever(USA) —Given Moment (USA) (Diesis)
6880[9]

Peachmelba (USA) *J-C Rouget* 97
4 b m Theatrical(IRE) —Peachtree City (USA) (Carson City (USA))
4365a[3] 6438a[4]

Peach Pearl *Y De Nicolay* a104 98
3 b f Invincible Spirit(IRE) —Paix Royale (Royal Academy (USA))
1208a[4] 6579a[7]

Peak (IRE) *H Morrison* a41 56
3 b c Exceed And Excel(AUS) —Glympse (IRE) (Spectrum (IRE))
1638[9] 1838[5] 2320[8] 2809[5] *3383[13]*

Peak District (IRE) *K A Ryan* a97 100
5 b g Danehill(USA) —Coralita (IRE) (Night Shift (USA))
1564[3] 2397[2] 2502[2] *(3212)* 4135[15] 4341[10] 5132[9] 5420[14] 5860[13] *7866[8]*

Peal Park *Karen George* a60 38
3 b f Sulamani(IRE) —Cape Siren (Warning)
2652[5] 3803[8] 3984[5] *5016[11]* 5381[8] *5750[8]*

Peanut Girl (IRE) *B Palling* a57 56
3 b f Tillerman—Phintia (IRE) (Tagula (IRE))
664[9] 736[5] 1084[3] *1492[2]* 1772[3] 2321[14]

Pearl Dealer (IRE) *N J Vaughan* a75 69
4 b g Marju(IRE) —Anyaas (IRE) (Green Desert (USA))
1941[3] 420[5]

Pearlescence (USA) *J-C Rouget* 100
3 gr f Pleasantly Perfect(USA) —Grisonnante (FR) (Kaldoun (FR))
4969a[3] 7347a[14]

Pearl Of Charm (FR) *Y De Nicolay* a89 95
3 b f Poliglote—Severina (Darshaan)
1267a[6]

Pearl Of Kent (IRE) *P D Evans* 50
2 ch f Pearl Of Love(IRE) —Kentmere (FR) (Galetto (FR))
4564[7] 5868[4] 7098[10]

Pearl Of Manacor (IRE) *M R Channon* a79 76
3 b g Danehill Dancer(IRE) —Mountain Law (USA) (Mountain Cat (USA))
(236) ◆ *8513* *1082[5]* 6004[7] 6695[14]

Pearly King (USA) *M Al Muhairi* a92 89
6 br g Kingmambo(USA) —Mother Of Pearl (IRE) (Sadler's Wells (USA))
262a[13] 415a[5] *773a[15]*

Pearly Wey *I W McInnes* a91 104
6 b g Lujain(USA) —Dunkellin (USA) (Irish River (FR))
3141[20] 3802[7] 4853[9] 5039[12] 5424[5] 5826[6] 6282[5] ◆ 6482[9] *7613[12] 7702[10]*

Peas And Carrots (DEN) *L Reuterskiold Jr* a99 105
6 b g Final Appearance(IRE) —Dominet Hope (Primo Dominie)
2587a[2] (4585a) 5302a[12]

Peas 'n Beans (IRE) *T Keddy* a49 48
6 br g Medicean—No Sugar Baby (FR) (Crystal Glitters (USA))
112[7] 168[6] 3851[0]

Pebblesonthebeach *J W Hills* 67
2 b g Footstepsinthesand—Peep Show (In The Wings)
3867[6] 4439[5] 4945[4] 5715[9]

Peckforton Castle *Patrick Morris* a50
2 b g Celtic Swing—Fleuve D'Or (IRE) (Last Tycoon)
7463[5]

Pedasus (USA) *T Keddy* a75 51
3 b c Fusaichi Pegasus(USA) —Butterfly Cove (USA) (Storm Cat (USA))
951[11] 1295[13] 4930[10]

Pedra Pompas *M Gasparini* a86 105
5 ch h Mark Of Esteem(IRE) —Edwardian Era (Bering)
1575a[4] 6153a[8]

Pedregal *J S Goldie* a41 51
3 b g Diktat—Bella Chica (IRE) (Bigstone (IRE))
236[10] 366[3] 753[6] 817[11] 1247[5] 1455[3] 1644[6] 2593[4] 3063[3] 3651[8] 4137[7]

Pegasus Again (USA) *T G Mills* a93 86
4 b g Fusaichi Pegasus(USA) —Chit Chatter (USA) (Lost Soldier (USA))
(31) 113[5] 318[2] 850[2] 1067[2] 1405[3] (5448) 5746[4] 7189[11] *7603[2] (7883)*

Pegasus Dancer (FR) *R H York* a67 40
5 b g Danehill Dancer(IRE) —Maruru (IRE) (Fairy King (USA))
99[6] 269[7] 1787[13] 2180[15]

Pegasus Gold (USA) *W R Swinburn* a64 59
4 ch g Fusaichi Pegasus(USA) —Little Treasure (FR) (Night Shift (USA))
1638[5] ◆ 2856[6]

Pegasus Lad (USA) *M Johnston* a87 84
3 bb g Fusaichi Pegasus(USA) —Leo Girl (USA) (Seattle Slew (USA))
851[2] 1082[3] 2073[8] 2674[11] 2925[11] 3457[6] 4040[8] 4714[2] 4956[3] 5295[6] 5803[6] *6614[11]*

Pegasus Prince (USA) *J Wade* a72 67
5 b g Fusaichi Pegasus(USA) —Avian Eden (USA) (Storm Bird (CAN))
7505[6]

Peintre D'Argent (IRE) *W J Knight* a59 60
3 ch f Peintre Celebre(USA) —Petite-D-Argent (Noalto)
506[3] 2350[5] 3482[5] *6446[8] 7143[9] 7688[5]*

Peinture Rare (IRE) *E Lellouche* 110
3 b f Sadler's Wells(USA) —Peinture Bleue (USA) (Alydar (USA))
3442a[7] 4969a[2] 6504a[2]

Pekan One *John G Carr* a31 47
7 ch g Grand Lodge(USA) —Ballet (Sharrood (USA))
5885[8]

Pekan Star *M A Jarvis* 63
2 b c Montjeu(IRE) —Delicieuse Lady (Trempolino (USA))
5401[4] ◆

Pekan Three (IRE) *P F I Cole* 71
2 b c Sadler's Wells(USA) —Frappe (IRE) (Inchinor)
6810[6] ◆

Peking Prince *A M Balding* a59 89
3 b g Passing Glance—Brandon Princess (Waajib)
1155[8] 1895[4] 2209[5] ◆ (2845) ◆ 3144[3] 4296[2] 4909[6]

Pelham Crescent (IRE) *B Palling* a70 85
6 ch g Giant's Causeway(USA) —Sweet Times (Riverman (USA))
253[4] 478[5] 571[2] 836[4] 871[2] 1042[2] (1415) (1786) (1983) 2407[9] 3461[3] 3635[5] *5837[5]* (6204) 6733[9] 6936[10]

Peligroso (FR) *Saeed Bin Suroor* 107
3 ch c Trempolino(USA) —Pitpit (IRE) (Rudimentary (USA))
2560a[2] 2954a[6] 6110[3] (6644)

Pellinore (USA) *E F Vaughan* a41 41
3 bb f Giant's Causeway(USA) —Glatisant (Rainbow Quest (USA))
2710[8] 4955[6] 5773[4]

Pembo *R A Harris* a52 52
4 b g Choisir(AUS) —Focosa (ITY) (In The Wings)
124 302[8] 399[5] 5371[3] 608[5]

Pena Dorada (IRE) *A P Jarvis* 72
2 b c Key Of Luck(USA) —Uluwatu (IRE) (Unfuwain (USA))
5408[5] 6136[2] 6533[5]

Penang Cinta *P D Evans* a68 72
6 b g Halling(USA) —Penang Pearl (FR) (Bering)
311[5] 571[6] 871[3] 1042[5] 1514[4] 2182[3] 2294[5] 2783[8] (3244) 3475[2] 3766[4] (3950) (4735) 5509[7] 5594[6]

Penangdouble O One *R M Beckett* a72
2 ch c Starcraft(NZ) —Penang Pearl (FR) (Bering)
7064[3] ◆ *7390[5]*

Penang Princess *R M Beckett* a85 88
3 gr f Act One—Pulau Pinang (IRE) (Dolphin Street (FR))
949[4] ◆ 1408[4] 1842[2] (2208) *(3300)* 5230[7] *6803[3]*

Penchesco (IRE) *Pat Eddery* a76 75
4 b g Orpen(USA) —Francesca (IRE) (Perugino (USA))
807[4] 5780[5] *6435[9]* 6594[4]

Penderyn *C Smith* a42 48
2 b f Sakhee(USA) —Brecon (Unfuwain (USA))
6730[14] 6962[6] *7391[6] 7792[6]*

Pendragon (USA) *B Ellison* a56 53
6 ch g Rahy(USA) —Turning Wheel (USA) (Seeking The Gold (USA))
7855[3]

Penel (IRE) *P T Midgley* a50 61
8 b g Orpen(USA) —Jayess Elle (Sabrehill (USA))
75 ◆ *150[5] 223[9]*

Peninsula Girl (IRE) *M R Channon* a49 69
3 b f Cape Cross(IRE) —Rio De Jumeirah (Seeking The Gold (USA))
1379[4] 1618[8] 2321[8] 2797[14] 2973[6] 3625[6] 3859[14]

Peninsular War *R A Fahey* a62 80
3 b g Deportivo—Queens Jubilee (Cayman Kai (IRE))
862[4] 1272[5] 2058[4] 2443[6] 4399[2] 5978[13] ◆ 6233[4] *6669[8]* 7119[8] *7829[5]*

Penitent *W J Haggas* a107 87
3 b g Kyllachy—Pious (Bishop Of Cashel)
3764[2] ◆ (4097) *5092[2] (6229)* ◆ *6876[2]* ◆

Pennine Rose *A Berry* 41
3 b f Reel Buddy(USA) —Adorable Cherub (USA) (Halo (USA))
1455[10] 1852[8] 2450[8]

Pennybid (IRE) *C R Wilson* 40
7 b g Benny The Dip(USA) —Stamatina (Warning)
1243[17] 2656[8] 3123[11]

Pennyprince (GER) *Uwe Ostmann* 71
3 c Samum(GER) —Pepperjuice (GER) (Big Shuffle (USA))
2954a[7]

Penny's Gift *R Hannon* 108
3 b f Tobougg(IRE) —Happy Lady (FR) (Cadeaux Genereux)
1292[3] 1698[6] (2757a) 3749[5] 4489[9] 6272[8]

Penolva (IRE) *P D Deegan* a58 64
3 b f Galileo(IRE) —Jabali (FR) (Shirley Heights)
1893[5] 3056[5] 3538[2] 4039[4] 5113[3] *7336[4]*

Penperth *J M P Eustace* a65 37
3 b f Xaar—Penelewey (Groom Dancer (USA))
1269[13] *2827[5] 3274[12]* 4157[10]

Penrod Ballantyne (IRE) *B J Meehan* 58
2 ch c Indian Ridge—Silvia Diletta (Mark Of Esteem (IRE))
6754[9] ◆

Pension Policy (USA) *J M P Eustace* a75 68
4 bb m Danzig(USA) —Domain (USA) (Kris S (USA))
143[3] 1613[10] *1833[8]* 2168[4]

Pentominium *M Johnston* 71
2 b c Dubai Destination(USA) —Mouriyana (IRE) (Akarad (FR))
6382[3] ◆

Penton Hook *P Winkworth* a82 71
3 gr g Lucky Owners(NZ) —Cosmic Star (Siberian Express (USA))
(6778) ◆ *7134[2]*

Penzena *A M Balding* a75 70
3 ch f Tobougg(IRE) —Penmayne (Inchinor)
1844[4] 2433[9] 3165[2] 3921[4] *(7452) 7664[5]*

Peopleton Brook *B G Powell* a67 67
7 b h Compton Place—Merch Rhyd-Y-Grug (Sabrehill (USA))
861[2] 1152[10] *1285[9]* 1619[6] 1957[6] (2180) 2472[4] 2637[7] 3162[4] 3570[3] 3775[4] 4604[9] 5020[3] 5525[4] 5919[5] 6205[7] *6377[2]* 7179[6] 7330[11] 7534[4] 7808[7] 7879[3]

Peper Harow (IRE) *M D I Usher* a74 79
3 b f Compton Place—Faraway Moon (Distant Relative)
1840[9] 2162[5] 2478[7] 3428[7] (3815) ◆ 4535[6] (5007) 5404[11] *6070[2] (6437) 6667[7] 7000[9]*

Pepin (IRE) *D Haydn Jones* a58 21
3 ch g King Charlemagne(USA) —Consignia (IRE) (Definite Article)
246[7] 390[6] 542[6] 1084[6] *1412[4] 1652[3] 1935[4] (2132)* 3580[10] *3953[3] 4172[6]* 5326[4] 7002[10]

Pepi Royal (IRE) *Pat Eddery* a68 63
2 b f Royal Applause—Alenushka (Soviet Star (USA))
1742[4] 2494[6] 4147[9] ◆ 4884[7] 5938[10] *6494[3] (6775)*

Peponi *P J Makin* a68
3 ch c Kris Kin(USA) —Polmara (IRE) (Polish Precedent (USA))
7576[2] 7829[2]

Pepper Lane *J Hetherton* a58 67
2 ch f Exceed And Excel(AUS) —Maid To Matter (Pivotal)
1847[2] ◆ 2449[4] 3152[7] 5439[5] 5553[4] *6345[3]* 6557[5] 6819[5]

Peppertree Lane (IRE) *A P Boxhall* 114
6 ch g Peintre Celebre(USA) —Salonrolle (IRE) (Tirol)
6306[6]

Perception (IRE) *R Charlton* a69 69
3 b f Hawk Wing(USA) —Princesse Darsha (GER) (Darshaan)
2126[9] 2850[6] 4319[6] 4703[4] *(5990)*

Perceptive *J R Fanshawe* a69 18
2 b f Carnival Dancer—Discerning (Darshaan)
5000[16] *5839[4] 7199[2]*

Percolator *P F I Cole* a70 106
3 b f Kheleyf(USA) —Coffee Cream (Common Grounds)
2481[8] 3145[8] 6180[7]

Percussionist (IRE) *J Howard Johnson* 53
8 b g Sadler's Wells(USA) —Magnificient Style (USA) (Silver Hawk (USA))
2056[7]

Percys Corismatic *J Gallagher* 62
3 b f Systematic—Corisa (IRE) (Be My Guest (USA))
3257[15] 3946[11] 4640[14]

Perdiccas (FR) *J-C Bertin* 64
4 b h Kapgarde(FR) —Horcyllia Tuxon (FR) (Cyborg (FR))
2118a[8]

Perequito (FR) *Peter Scotton*
2 ch c American Post—Pantelleria (IRE) (Barathea (IRE))
1482a[11]

Perez Prado (USA) *W Jarvis* 63
4 b g Kingmambo(USA) —Marisa (USA) (Swain (IRE))
3155[5] 3863[12] 4730[9]

Perfect Act *C G Cox* a86 69
4 b m Act One—Markova's Dance (Mark Of Esteem (IRE))
354[6] 470[4] 4871[6] 5429[8] *5989[3] 6230[3] (6915) 7478[6] 7741[8] (7828)*

Perfect Affair (USA) *R M Beckett* a59 72
3 b g Perfect Soul(IRE) —Caribbean Affair (USA) (Red Ransom (USA))
951[7] 1185[11] 1882[3] 2206[7]

Perfect Blossom *I W McInnes* 62
2 b f One Cool Cat(USA) —Perfect Peach (Lycius (USA))
2503[4] 3337[5] 4546[5] 4928[9]

Perfect Ch'l (IRE) *I A Wood* a73 81
2 b f Choisir(AUS) —Agouti (Pennekamp (USA))
1569[10] 1891[5] (2860) 3865[2] (4883) 5392[3] 5795[7] 6241[15] *6585[4]* 6844[5] *7320[8]*

Perfect Citizen (USA) *W R Swinburn* a80 85
3 ch g Proud Citizen(USA) —Near Mint (USA) (Dehere (USA))
1751[10] *2399[8]* 2926[6] *4841[3]* 5475[5] *6462[6]*

Perfect Class *C G Cox* a72 73
3 b f Cape Cross(IRE) —Liberty (Singspiel (IRE))
(229) 673[2] 960[5] 1196[8] 1973[3] 2300[2] 2917[3] 3476[5] *3981[2]* (4482) 5099[8]

Perfect Flight *M Blanshard* 98
4 b m Hawk Wing(USA) —Pretty Girl (IRE) (Polish Precedent (USA))
2078[4] 4423[14] 5607[6] 6694[11]

Perfect Friend *S Kirk* a70 83
3 b f Reel Buddy(USA) —Four Legs Good (IRE) (Be My Guest (USA))
1315[9] 1588[2] (1743) 2321[2] 2539[2] 3102[3] 3387[4] (3537) 3870[2] 4326[8] 4422[12] *5810[8]* 6621[5]

Perfect Honour (IRE) *D Shaw* a58
3 ch f Exceed And Excel(AUS) —Porcelana (IRE) (Highest Honor (FR))
364[4] 626[4] 831[6] 889[2] (1157) 1529[5]

Perfect Note *Saeed Bin Suroor* 68
2 b f Shamardal(USA) —Mezzo Soprano (USA) (Darshaan)
7183[4] ◆

Perfect Polly *James M Ryan* a99 103
4 b m Efisio—Nashira (Prince Sabo)
5079a[2] 5491a[6] 6707a[4] *7007a[3]*

Perfect Portrait *Mrs A Malzard* 52
9 ch g Selkirk(USA) —Flawless Image (USA) (The Minstrel (CAN))
4586a[5]

Perfect Pride (USA) *C G Cox* 89
3 b f Forest Wildcat(USA) —Kisses To Yall (USA) (Copelan (USA))
(2882) 4148[10] 5471[4] 5918[5]

Perfect Season (SAF) *H J Brown* a78 98
5 b g Jallad(USA) —T-Model (SAF) (Model Man (SAF))
265a[6] ◆ 340a[U] 615a[5]

Perfect Secret *A M Balding* a55 61
3 b f Spinning World(USA) —Sharp Secret (IRE) (College Chapel)
1671[4] *7829[3]*

Perfect Shot (IRE) *J L Dunlop* 89
3 b g High Chaparral(IRE) —Zoom Lens (IRE) (Caerleon (USA))
1489[7] 2138[2] (3205) 3861[2] (4793) 5481[4] 6273[6] 6676[6] 7151[7]

Perfect Silence *C G Cox* a83 83
4 b m Dansili—Perfect Echo (Lycius (USA))
2334[3] 2886[3] (3789) 5005[8] *(5810) 6374[4] 6776[7]* 7189[4] ◆

Perfect Star *C G Cox* a101 105
5 b m Act One—Granted (FR) (Cadeaux Genereux)
1210[2] ◆ 1667[5] 2285a[6] 4259[4] 6757[2] 7291[9] *7560[5]*

Perfect Stride *Sir Michael Stoute* 115
4 b h Oasis Dream—First (Highest Honor (FR))
(1600) 2476[6] (3089) 5231[3] 5875[3] 6202[2]

Perfect Symmetry (IRE) *G M Lyons* a69 95
2 b c Le Vie Dei Colori—Wide Range (IRE) (Spectrum (IRE))
(3514a) 4250a[3]

Perfect Truth (IRE) *A P O'Brien* a97 103
3 ch f Galileo(IRE) —Charroux (IRE) (Darshaan)
(1789) 2672[10] 4609a[2] 5796[9]

Perfect Vision *C G Cox* a72 57
2 b f Starcraft(NZ) —Auspicious (Shirley Heights)
4946[9] 5741[10] *(7106)*

Pergamon (IRE) *J H M Gosden* a39 80
3 b g Dalakhani(IRE) —Pinaflore (FR) (Formidable (USA))
1291[10] *1780[6]*

Perino (IRE) *W McCreery* 64
2 b f Speightstown(USA) —Alshoowg (USA) (Riverman (USA))
1993a[6]

Perks (IRE) *J L Dunlop* a72 112
4 b g Selkirk(USA) —Green Charter (Green Desert (USA))
1758a[5] 2410[10] 3089[7] 4002[2] 4352[3] *6290[9]* 7188[5]

Perky (FR) *J Morin* a53 70
3 b f Poliglote—For Ever Hopefull (Halling (USA))
7386a[2]

Perlachy *J R Holt* a73 50
5 b g Kyllachy—Perfect Dream (Emperor Jones (USA))
352[2] (461) (654) ◆ *880[6] 971[7] 7138[7] 7398[2] (7496) 7577[2]* 7634[3]

Perle D'Amour (IRE) *R Hannon* 7
2 b f Pearl Of Love(IRE) —Bella Vie (IRE) (Sadler's Wells (USA))
2514[4]

Permalosa *L Riccardi* 83
3 b f Nayef(USA) —Persian Filly (IRE) (Persian Bold)
2310a[11]

Permesso *F & L Camici* 112
4 b h Sakhee(USA) —Persian Filly (IRE) (Persian Bold)
2115a[8] 2955a[6]

Perpetually (IRE) *M Johnston* 95
3 b c Singspiel(IRE) —Set In Motion (USA) (Mr Prospector (USA))
(1303) ◆

Perse *W Jarvis* 42
2 br f Rock Of Gibraltar(IRE) —La Persiana (Daylami (IRE))
7183[15]

Persian Buddy *Jamie Poulton* a67 46
3 b g Reel Buddy(USA) —Breeze Again (USA) (Favorite Trick (USA))
397[6]

Persian Heroine (IRE) *J L Dunlop* 38
2 b f Intikhab(USA) —Persian Fantasy (Persian Bold)
4701[5] 6567[13]

Persian Memories (IRE) *J L Dunlop* a67 72
3 br f Indian Ridge—Persian Fantasy (Persian Bold)
1408[11] *1834[9]* 2540[3] 3462[2] 4241[2] 4744[3] 5382[5] *5990[7]* 6538[5] *7049[6]*

Persian Peril *G A Swinbank* a87 92
5 br g Erhaab(USA) —Brush Away (Ahonoora)
226[7] (1779) 4315[3] ◆ 4471[3] 5334[10] 5671[10] 6648[2] *6878[3] 7375[11]*

Persian Poet *M Johnston* 44
2 b g Dubai Destination(USA) —Salim Toto (Mtoto)
5787^{10} 6593^{9} 6821^{11}

Persian Storm (GER) *G L Moore* a62 103
5 b g Monsun(GER) —Private Life (FR) (Bering)
634^{5} 4438^{4} 4731^{3}

Persian Tomcat (IRE) *Miss J Feilden* a51 51
3 gr g One Cool Cat(USA) —Persian Mistress (IRE) (Persian Bold)
817^{6} 1036^{3} 1183^{3} 2635^{2} 2865^{9} 3383^{3} 3776^{4} 4241^{6} 5328^{5} 6183^{14} 6440^{3} 6705^{5} 7142^{5} 7426^{6} 7737^{5}

Persistent (IRE) *D G Bridgwater* a58 36
4 b g Cape Cross(IRE) —Insistent (USA) (Diesis)
5381^{11}

Persona Non Grata (IRE) *R Charlton* a65 71
2 b g Azamour(IRE) —Private Life (FR) (Bering)
6162^{4} 6548^{6} 6721^{11}

Personify *J L Flint* a57 54
7 ch g Zafonic(USA) —Dignify (IRE) (Rainbow Quest (USA))
1770^{4} 3503^{7} 3949^{11}

Pertemps Power *B G Powell* a58 55
5 b g Zaha(CAN) —Peristyle (Tolomeo)
735^{3} 935^{2} 1936^{11} 2762^{4} 2971^{5} 3223^{3} 6457^{4} 7154^{5}

Petella *C W Thornton* 63
3 b f Tamure(IRE) —Miss Petronella (Petoski)
1509^{4} 2164^{5} 4039^{5} 4506^{9} 4755^{9} 5131^{2} 7124^{9}

Peter Grimes (IRE) *H J L Dunlop* a63 71
3 ch g Alhaarth(IRE) —Aldburgh (Bluebird (USA))
(1050) 1428^{4} 2038^{9} 2909^{5} 4054^{3} 4563^{3} 5570^{9}

Peter Island (FR) *J Gallagher* a83 94
6 b g Dansili—Catania (USA) (Aloma's Ruler (USA))
954^{3} (1510) 1668^{6} 2474^{10} 3318^{4} 4232^{6} 4485^{8} 4853^{6} 5424^{10} 5805^{3} 6964^{14}

Peter's Follie *Tom Dascombe* 57
2 gr f Highest Honor(FR) —Fabulous Speed (USA) (Silver Hawk (USA))
4383^{4} 4889^{3} 5714^{11} 6590^{11}

Peter's Gift (IRE) *K A Ryan* a75 74
3 b f Catcher In The Rye(IRE) —Eastern Blue (IRE) (Be My Guest (USA))
1098^{2} 1561^{5} (1656) ◆ 3062^{5} 3574^{3} 3982^{5} 4284^{9} 6348^{9}

Peters Pride *M W Easterby*
7 b g Silver Patriarch(IRE) —Manzanilla (Mango Express)
1780^{7}

Peter's Storm (USA) *K A Ryan* a78 75
4 ch g Van Nistelrooy(USA) —Fairy Land Flyer (USA) (Lyphard's Wish (FR))
76^{3} 197^{3} 400^{9} 576^{6} 606^{8} 739^{8} 882^{4} 937^{7}

Peter Tchaikovsky *A P O'Brien* 94
3 b c Dansili—Abbatiale (FR) (Kaldoun (FR))
5685a^{7} 6867a^{13}

Pete's Passion *R A Fahey* 2
3 b f Rock Of Gibraltar(IRE) —Three Days In May (Cadeaux Genereux)
3876^{7}

Pethers Dancer (IRE) *W R Muir* a5
3 b g Kyllachy—La Piaf (FR) (Fabulous Dancer (USA))
1729^{12} 3305^{10}

Petidium *N Bycroft* 40
4 b m Presidium—Efipetite (Efisio)
6880^{13}

Petit Belle *N P Littmoden* a18
2 b f Piccolo—Tallulah Belle (Crowning Honors (CAN))
6903^{15} 7317^{11} 7556^{11}

Petit Ecuyer (FR) *A Couetil* 71
3 b c Equerry(USA) —Petite Majeste (FR) (Riverquest (FR))
2293a^{4}

Petite Mambo *W De Best-Turner* a51 62
2 b g Miesque's Son(USA) —Chalet (Singspiel (IRE))
3402^{7} 3785^{8} 4086^{6} 6735^{11} 6930^{12} 7391^{7}

Petite Rocket (IRE) *J A McShane*
3 b f Fayruz—Courtisane (Persepolis (FR))
2157^{13}

Petomic (IRE) *M Hill* a66 68
4 ch g Dubai Destination(USA) —Petomi (Presidium)
2185^{8} 3504^{3} 4824^{6} 5179^{3} (5503) 5630^{5} 6288^{4} 6862^{5} 7236^{13}

Petougg *W Jarvis* 76
2 b g Tobougg(IRE) —Piroshka (Soviet Star (USA))
(4492) 4883^{5} 6247^{6}

Petrafied (FR) *P J Prendergast* a23 66
3 ch f Gold Away(IRE) —Thai Rose (USA) (Gulch (USA))
5016^{9}

Petrenko *R A Fahey* a23
3 b g Efisio—Lambast (Relkino)
85^{7} 227^{6} 716^{8}

Petrocelli *A J McCabe* a28 72
2 b g Piccolo—Sarcita (Primo Dominie)
1511^{4} 1719^{3} 2358^{5} 2467^{3} 4858^{7}

Petroglyph *M G Quinlan* a32 64
5 ch g Indian Ridge—Madame Dubois (Legend Of France (USA))
2241^{3} 6770^{13}

Petrograd (IRE) *E Lellouche* 97
8 b h Peintre Celebre(USA) —Palmeraie (USA) (Lear Fan (USA))
1762a^{10} 2522a^{7} 3443a^{10}

Petrovsky *M Johnston* a87 101
3 gr c Daylami(IRE) —Russian Society (Darshaan)
(137) ◆ (389) 2084^{2} (5909) 6138^{5}

Petsas Pleasure *Ollie Pears* a66 70
3 b g Observatory(USA) —Swynford Pleasure (Reprimand)
1953^{9} 2578^{12} 3115^{4} 3480^{2} (3857) 5160^{10} 5940^{10} 6383^{9} 6861^{11} 7212^{8}

Pevensey (IRE) *J J Quinn* a94 100
7 b g Danehill(USA) —Champaka (IRE) (Caerleon (USA))
33^{4} 766^{8} 1172^{6} 1696^{13} 2706^{15} (6100) 6662^{4} 7293^{16}

Pezula *R T Phillips* a44 49
3 b f Diktat—Mashmoum (Lycius (USA))
4606^{6} 4955^{7} 6371^{9} 7025^{8}

Pha Mai Blue *J R Boyle* a73 66
4 b g Acclamation—Queen Of Silk (IRE) (Brief Truce (USA))
157^{8} 725^{3} 1634^{3} (1833) 2186^{3} 2387^{7} 4378^{6} (4871) 5886^{7} 6909^{4} 7065^{4} 7364^{5} 7479^{8} 7664^{9} 7876^{8}

Phantasy Rock (IRE) *W P Mullins* a63 55
3 b f Rock Of Gibraltar(IRE) —Phariseek (IRE) (Rainbow Quest (USA))
7794^{6}

Phantom Ridge (IRE) *R Hannon* a62 71
3 b f Indian Ridge—Phantom Waters (Pharly (FR))
2433^{14} 3297^{6} 4145^{3} 4828^{6}

Phantom Serenade (IRE) *M Dods* 65
4 b g Orpen(USA) —Phantom Rain (Rainbow Quest (USA))
3092^{6} (4034) 4313^{8} 5601^{16} 5953^{6} (6219) 6769^{10} 6817^{12}

Phantom Whisper *B R Millman* a66 99
6 br g Makbul—La Belle Vie (Indian King (USA))
1325^{8} 1864^{8} 2078^{5} 2474^{9} 3318^{3} 3802^{6} 4485^{7} 4853^{7} 5349^{12} 6396^{6} 6694^{5} 7026^{10}

Pharaohs Justice (USA) *N P Littmoden* a60 38
4 br g Kafwain(USA) —Mary Linoa (USA) (L'Emigrant (USA))
94^{6} 457^{9} 725^{11} 867^{7} 961^{8} 2473^{9} 2921^{15}

Pherousa *M Blanshard* 66
2 b f Dubawi(IRE) —Sea Nymph (IRE) (Spectrum (IRE))
2793^{2} 3248^{12} 3865^{9} 4302^{4} 4688^{7} 5060^{5} 5526^{4} (5714) 6185^{6} 6418^{9}

Philander *E J O'Neill* 80
2 b c Red Ransom(USA) —Fidelio's Miracle (USA) (Mountain Cat (USA))
4807a^{4} 5561a^{5} 5831^{3} 6578a^{2} 7315a^{5}

Philario (IRE) *K R Burke* a104 108
4 ch h Captain Rio—Salva (Grand Lodge (USA))
458^{2} 781^{5} 997^{6} 1346^{7} 2015^{2} (2289a) 2669^{3} 3014^{24}

Philatelist (USA) *M A Jarvis* a112 108
5 b h Rahy(USA) —Polent (Polish Precedent (USA))
124^{4} 445^{4} (801) 4780^{8} 5262^{16} 5587a^{8} 6290^{5} 6816^{11} 7323^{3} 7704a^{6}

Philippa Jane *P Winkworth* a45
2 ch f Muhtathir—Ante Futura (FR) (Suave Dancer (USA))
5984^{12} 7106^{7} 7700^{10}

Phillipina *Sir Michael Stoute* 103
3 b f Medicean—Discerning (Darshaan)
1329^{5} 1789^{2} 2672^{6} (4066) 4566^{8} 6242^{7}

Philmack Dot Com *D Donovan* a63
3 b g Traditionally(USA) —Lilli Marlane (Sri Pekan (USA))
201^{6} 6492^{11} 7129^{10} (7579) 7719^{12}

Phinerine *A Berry* a50 30
6 ch g Bahamian Bounty—Golden Panda (Music Boy)
62^{4} 95^{5} 177^{4}

Phluke *Eve Johnson Houghton* a82 88
8 b g Most Welcome—Phlirty (Pharly (FR))
1213^{6} 1524^{8} 1894^{3} 2257^{2} 2824^{6} 2883^{8} 3770^{5} 4211^{10} 5511^{9} 6224^{4} 6790^{6} 7110^{9} 7250^{7}

Phoenix Enforcer *George Baker* a30 72
3 b f Bahamian Bounty—Kythia (IRE) (Kahyasi)
2192^{8} 3217^{4} (4065) (4196) 5128^{5}

Phoenix Flight (IRE) *H J Evans* a90 88
4 b g Hawk Wing(USA) —Firecrest (IRE) (Darshaan)
163^{6} 271^{9} 687^{2} (750) 899^{2} (952) 1230^{2} 1435^{4} 4038^{3} 4619^{3} 5097^{3} 5781^{2} 6855^{5} 7151^{11}

Phoenix Hill (IRE) *D R Gandolfo* a54 49
7 b g Montjeu(IRE) —Cielo Vodkamartini (USA) (Conquistador Cielo (USA))
601^{2} 816^{12} 3348^{2} 3774^{4}

Phoenix King (FR) *E Lellouche* a56 80
3 b g Enrique—Almadina (FR) (Pistolet Bleu (IRE))
6682a^{5}

Phoenix Nights (IRE) *A Berry* 26
9 b g General Monash(USA) —Beauty Appeal (USA) (Shadeed (USA))
2592^{6} 2656^{9}

Phoenix Rising *H Morrison* a2 34
3 b f Dr Fong(USA) —Dead Certain (Absalom)
503^{10} 1704^{11} 2947^{11}

Phoenix Rose (IRE) *J R Best* a54
2 ch f Rakti—Fez (Mujtahid (USA))
3744^{4} 5778^{7} 6356^{5} 6938^{11} 7389^{10} 7514^{9}

Phonic (IRE) *J L Dunlop* 73
2 ch c Green Tune(USA) —Superfonic (FR) (Zafonic (USA))
4209^{9} 6066^{3} 6697^{7}

Photographic *B W Hills* a85 99
3 b f Oasis Dream—Prophecy (IRE) (Warning)
(849) ◆ (1679) ◆ 1987^{2} 3016^{14} 3746^{5} 6815^{6}

Pianoforte (USA) *E J Alston* a60 68
7 b g Grand Slam(USA) —Far Too Loud (CAN) (No Louder (CAN))
2626^{7} 2965^{4} 3070^{4} 3264^{3} 3490^{8} 4344^{7} 4804^{4} 5513^{6} 5730^{5} 5888^{2} 6217^{8} (6256) 6862^{9} 7581^{7} 7600^{5}

Piazza San Pietro *A B Haynes* a59 84
3 ch g Compton Place—Rainbow Spectrum (FR) (Spectrum (IRE))
286^{2} 394^{9} 2908^{2} 3305^{2} (3502) (3994) 4203^{9} 5124^{8} 5480^{3} 5719^{3} 6422^{7} 7057^{2} 7534^{6}

Piccadilly Filly (IRE) *E J Creighton* a93 96
2 ch f Exceed And Excel(AUS) —Tortue (IRE) (Turtle Island (IRE))
3271^{2} 3733^{8} 3987^{2} (4537) (5057a) 5822^{6} 6660^{13}

Piccaso's Sky *A B Haynes* a49 38
3 b c Piccolo—Skylark (Polar Falcon (USA))
316^{5} 955^{4} 1247^{10} 1982^{11} 2651^{5} 3926^{11}

Piccola Stella (IRE) *R M H Cowell* 23
2 b f Antonius Pius(USA) —Beeper's Lodge (IRE) (Grand Lodge (USA))
4546^{8}

Piccolinda *W R Muir* a64 47
3 b f Piccolo—Belinda (Mizoram (USA))
1588^{12} 3464^{5} 4202^{13} 4535^{10} 5316^{4}

Piccolo Diamante (USA) *S Parr* a62 46
5 bb g Three Wonders(USA) —Bafooz (USA) (Clever Trick (USA))
173^{6} 292^{7} 565^{8} 608^{12} 675^{6} 748^{11}

Piccolo Express *B P J Baugh* a50 54
3 b g Piccolo—Ashfield (Zilzal (USA))
716^{7} 833^{5} 1108^{4} 2652^{3} 3334^{4} 4079^{8} 4819^{15}

Piccolo Mondo *P Winkworth* a73 75
3 b g Piccolo—Oriel Girl (Beveled (USA))
1585^{3} 2048^{18} 3159^{8} 3630^{2} 6621^{2} 6977^{5} 7452^{3}

Piccolo Pete *R Johnson* 61
4 b g Piccolo—Goes A Treat (IRE) (Common Grounds)
1127^{7} 1242^{13} 1558^{7} 1734^{13} 3031^{11} 4016^{11}

Piccolo Pride *M A Barnes* a12
4 ch g Piccolo—Jaycat (IRE) (Catrail (USA))
3294^{6}

Pickering *E J Alston* a65 77
5 br g Prince Sabo—On The Wagon (Then Again)
(1169) 1309^{3} 2438^{3} 3488^{8} 5421^{6} 6413^{7}

Pick Of The Day (IRE) *J G Given* a52 40
4 ch g Choisir(AUS) —Reveuse De Jour (IRE) (Sadler's Wells (USA))
38^{4} 147^{6} 790^{12}

Picky *C C Bealby* a62 29
5 b g Piccolo—Passerella (FR) (Brustolon)
3308^{4}

Picnic Party *J Noseda* a63 62
2 ch f Indian Ridge—Antediluvian (Air Express (IRE))
6591^{6} 7436^{2}

Picobella (GER) *A Wohler* 91
4 ch m Big Shuffle(USA) —Palanda (GER) (Lando (GER))
5651a^{4} 6886a^{12}

Picot De Say *C Roberts* a13 58
7 b g Largesse—Facsimile (Superlative)
3798^{3} (4625) 5790^{9}

Pictorial (USA) *Sir Michael Stoute* a17 83
3 b g Pivotal—Red Tulle (USA) (A.P. Indy (USA))
2074^{6} (2551) 3822^{14} 5315^{7}

Picture Frame *J T Stimpson* a43 59
5 ch g Fraam—Floral Spark (Forzando)
1413^{11} 2876^{5} 3174^{8} 3501^{4} 4434^{9} 4845^{13}

Picture Hat (USA) *H-A Pantall* a81 98
3 b f El Prado(IRE) —Maiden Tower (Groom Dancer (USA))
4394a^{2}

Picture Perfect (IRE) *David Wachman* 93
2 b f Danehill Dancer(IRE) —Makarova (IRE) (Sadler's Wells (USA))
6316a^{6}

Pictures (IRE) *L M Cumani* a73 73
2 b f Le Vie Dei Colori—So Glam So Hip (IRE) (Spectrum (IRE))
5119^{2} 6069^{3} 6436^{2} 7097^{3} 7363^{7}

Picturethatmoment (USA) *K R Burke* 43
3 bb f Mr Greeley(USA) —I'Maknightschoice (USA) (Knights Choice (USA))
2165^{11}

Pic Up Sticks *B G Powell* a55 70
10 gr g Piccolo—Between The Sticks (Pharly (FR))
2180^{6} (2758) 3252^{3} 3477^{5} 3677^{7} 3845^{9} 5608^{4} 5792^{8} 6186^{5} 6799^{11} 7180^{11}

Pie Poudre *R Brotherton* a57 49
2 ch g Zafeen(FR) —Eglantine (IRE) (Royal Academy (USA))
5749^{10} 6386^{6} 6737^{10} 7700^{11} 7788^{2}

Piermarini *P T Midgley* a68 76
4 b g Singspiel(IRE) —Allespagne (USA) (Trempolino (USA))
105^{11} 171^{9} 480^{4} 578^{8}

Pilannski *R A Teal* a16 37
2 b f Pilsudski(IRE) —Honey Mill (Milford)
5741^{15} 7522^{12}

Pilgrim Dancer (IRE) *Emmanuel Hughes* 80
2 b c Danehill Dancer(IRE) —Pilgrim's Way (USA) (Gone West (USA))
2286a^{6}

Pilot Light *T D Easterby* 54
3 b g Falbrav(IRE) —Bollin Jeannie (Royal Applause)
1470^{11} 1724^{10} 2370^{13}

Pinball (IRE) *Mrs L Williamson* a58 63
3 b f Namid—Luceball (IRE) (Bluebird (USA))
784^{2} ◆ 1157^{4} 1247^{3} 1359^{4} 1529^{6} (1985) 2162^{3} 2454^{U} 5719^{7} 5877^{6} 6377^{10} 6739^{5} 6933^{10} 7241^{4} 7483^{6} 7651^{4} 7834^{8}

Pinch Of Salt (IRE) *A M Balding* a99 96
6 b g Hussonet(USA) —Granita (CHI) (Roy (USA))
4261^{7} 5262^{10} 5641^{7} 6724^{10}

Pin Cushion *B J Meehan* 73
2 ch f Pivotal—Frizzante (Efisio)
4603^{7} 5021^{3} 6737^{4}

Pinewood Legend (IRE) *P D Niven* a47 21
7 br g Idris(IRE) —Blue Infanta (Chief Singer)
1439^{3} 4848^{11}

Pinewood Lulu *S A Harris* a7 54
4 br m Lujain(USA) —Lucy Glitters (USA) (Cryptoclearance (USA))
2166^{12} 2366^{16} 5283^{9} 5983^{12} 6029^{9}

Pinewood Polly *S A Harris* a5
2 b f Lujain(USA) —Polmara (IRE) (Polish Precedent (USA))
7396^{11}

Pink Candie (FR) *Y De Nicolay* a76 89
3 b f Fath(USA) —Lyphard's Dream (IRE) (Lyphard (USA))
7696a^{4}

Pink Flames (IRE) *T P Tate* 40
2 ch f Redback—Flames (Blushing Flame (USA))
5674^{6}

Pink Flower (IRE) *J-L Pelletan*
2 br f Hawk Wing(USA) —Sail Storm (USA) (Topsider (USA))
6960a^{0}

Pinkiskass (FR) *J-P Gallorini* 36
2 b f Rakti—Dancing Rose (FR) (Dancing Spree (USA))
6751a^{0}

Pink Lemonade (IRE) *John Joseph Murphy* 62
2 b f Shinko Forest(IRE) —Popular Tune (IRE) (Grand Lodge (USA))
1993a^{8} 4463^{2} 4590^{7}

Pink Please (IRE) *Tom Dascombe* 12
2 ch f Camacho—Inonder (Belfort (FR))
6591^{15}

Pink Symphony *P F I Cole* 84
2 b f Montjeu(IRE) —Blue Symphony (Darshaan)
4460^{5} ◆ 5398^{2} 6477^{4} ◆

Pinnacle Lad (IRE) *J L Spearing* a43 67
2 b g Titus Livius(FR) —Alyska (IRE) (Owington)
1577^{6} 1847^{3} 2258^{2} 2906^{4} 6347^{8} 6796^{4} 6903^{10} 7242^{9}

Pinnacle Point *G L Moore* a52 64
4 ch g Best Of The Bests(IRE) —Alessandra (Generous (IRE))
2708^{4} 3348^{5} 3675^{5}

Pinpoint (IRE) *W R Swinburn* a96 114
7 b g Pivotal—Alessia (GER) (Warning)
1929^{2} 2327^{9} 3089^{13}

Pintano *J M Bradley* a23 63
4 ch g Dr Fong(USA) —Heckle (In The Wings)
1528^{10} 1710^{14} 2534^{10} 2879^{13} (3632) 4238^{4} 4732^{8} 5018^{6} 5501^{15} 5628^{11}

Pintura *M R Channon* 74
2 ch g Efisio—Picolette (Piccolo)
1404^{3} ◆ 1590^{6} 3792^{7} 4525^{3} (4803) 5136^{5} ◆ 5433^{4} ◆ 5658^{5} 5913^{5} (6367) 6693^{14}

Pioneerof The Nile (USA) *Bob Baffert* a115
3 bb c Empire Maker(USA) —Star Of Goshen (USA) (Lord At War (ARG))
1688a^{2} ◆ 2098a^{11}

Pipedreamer *J H M Gosden* 121
5 b h Selkirk(USA) —Follow A Dream (USA) (Gone West (USA))
1526^{2} 2410^{5} (6506a) 6850^{4}

Piperita *F & L Camici* 100
3 ch f Observatory(USA) —Pursuit Of Charge (Pursuit Of Love)
1659a^{7}

Pipers Piping (IRE) *J A Osborne* a68 58
3 b g Noverre(USA) —Monarchy (IRE) (Common Grounds)
356^{8} 454^{3} (1129) 1567^{2} 1969^{12} 2810^{3} 3225^{10} 5678^{3} 5989^{5} 6587^{6}

Piper's Song (IRE) *Patrick Morris* a67 84
6 gr g Distant Music(USA) —Dane's Lane (IRE) (Danehill (USA))
1107^{5} 1318^{4} 1533^{6} 1738^{2} 1980^{2} 2163^{8} 2783^{11} 3447^{4} 3679^{2} ◆ 4169^{5} 4670^{4} 5577^{2} 5947^{10} 7490^{8}

Pipette *A M Balding* 97
2 b f Pivotal—Amaryllis (IRE) (Sadler's Wells (USA))
(5605) ◆ 7033^{3} ◆

Pippbrook Gold *J R Boyle* a78 78
4 ch g Golden Snake(USA) —Chiaro (Safawan)
708^{6} 1048^{4} 2086^{4} 2775^{12} 4236^{4} 4714^{11} 5188^{5} 5365^{11} 6967^{5} 7225^{3}

Piquante *M L W Bell* a64 73
3 b f Selkirk(USA) —China (Royal Academy (USA))
1329^{4} 2139^{6} 2858^{4} 4948^{4} 5524^{6} 6289^{5} (6967)

Piquetera *A Fabre*
2 b f Oratorio(IRE) —Pot Pourri (Sadler's Wells (USA))
7166a^{7}

Pirate's Song *J A R Toller* a63 63
2 b c Bahamian Bounty—Soviet Terms (Soviet Star (USA))
5431^{7} 6032^{3} 6443^{5}

Pires *A J Martin* a92 92
5 br g Generous(IRE) —Kaydee Queen (IRE) (Bob's Return (IRE))
3142^{5} 4412a^{12} 5490a^{10}

Piscean (USA) *T Keddy* a93 97
4 bb g Stravinsky(USA) —Navasha (USA) (Woodman (USA))
(2191) 2707^{9} 2941^{9} 3351^{12} 4341^{18} 4461^{12} 5132^{12} 5263^{5} ◆ 5507^{8} 5799^{19} 6283^{13}

Piscitelli (USA) *Gregory D Sacco* a114
2 bb c Victory Gallop(CAN) —Rayelle (USA) (Relaunch (USA))
7307a^{4}

Piste *Miss T Jackson* a68 72
3 b f Falbrav(IRE) —Arctic Char (Polar Falcon (USA))
1359^{3} 1583^{4} 2386^{4} 2478^{2} 3003^{4} (3428) 4289^{6} 4653^{9} 5411^{11} 5517^{3} 5978^{12} 6413^{12}

Piste Perdue *Robert Collet* a82 80
3 b g Exceed And Excel(AUS) —Portella (GER) (Protektor (GER))
4581a^{9}

Pitbull *Mrs G S Rees* a63 68
6 b g Makbul—Piccolo Cativo (Komaite (USA))
1042^{12} 3615^{7} 4046^{3} 4351^{2} 4499^{6} 4710^{7} 6761^{11}

Piteur (FR) *E Leenders* a51 63
3 ch g Polish Summer—Noce Bleue (FR) (Saint Andrews (FR))
5278a^{10} 6682a^{0}

Pittodrie Star (IRE) *A M Balding* a76 59
2 ch c Choisir(AUS) —Jupiter Inlet (IRE) (Jupiter Island)
7146^{12} (7477) 7611^{5}

Pitton Justice *Dr J R J Naylor* a20
7 ch g Compton Place—Blind Justice (Mystiko (USA))
3204^{12} 3577^{9}

Piuside (IRE) *F Sanchez*
2 b c Antonius Pius(USA) —Shining White (Zafonic (USA))
6325a^{2}

Piverina (IRE) *Miss J A Camacho* a55 56
4 b m Pivotal—Alassio (USA) (Gulch (USA))
2233^{7} (3023) 3714^{9} 4403^{5} 4893^{7} 5732^{4}

Pivotal Express (IRE) *J F Panvert* 24
3 ch g Pivotal—Forest Express (AUS) (Kaaptive Edition (NZ))
6741^{11}

Pixel Power (IRE) *Liam McAteer* a48 48
2 gr c Elusive City(USA) —Silver Fizz (IRE) (Desert Story (IRE))
2302a^{7}

Place The Duchess *A J Lidderdale* a52 50
3 b f Compton Place—Barrantes (Distant Relative)
3242^{9} *6344^{6} 6856^{11} 7703^{2} 7853^{3} 7869^{9}*

Placidity *A J McCabe* a25
3 ch f Compton Place—Wittily (Whittingham (IRE))
920^{8} 982^{7}

Plaisterer *C F Wall* a58 101
4 b m Best Of The Bests(IRE) —Lumiere D'Espoir (FR) (Saumarez)
1571^{3} 2052^{5} (2773) 2977^{2} (4003) 6013^{2} 6813^{6} 7291^{16}

Plaka (FR) *W M Brisbourne* a56 38
4 gr m Verglas(IRE) —Top Speed (IRE) (Wolfhound (USA))
711^{12} 939^{7} 984^{3} 1741^{13} 1972^{9} 2539^{9}

Plane Painter (IRE) *B G Powell* a77 83
5 b g Orpen(USA) —Flight Sequence (Polar Falcon (USA))
3143^{10}

Planetary Motion (USA) *M Johnston* a85 60
4 gr h Gone West(USA) —Gaviola (USA) (Cozzene (USA))
(648) 999^{8} *1432^{4}*

Planet Five (USA) *P Bary* 104
3 bb c Storm Cat(USA) —Six Perfections (FR) (Celtic Swing)
3908a^{8} 6579a^{5}

Planet Red (IRE) *R Hannon* 83
2 ch c Bahamian Bounty—Aries (GER) (Big Shuffle (USA))
1323^{2} ◆ (4377) 5133^{7}

Planteur (IRE) *E Lellouche* 89
2 b c Danehill Dancer(IRE) —Plante Rare (IRE) (Giant's Causeway (USA))
(4807a)

Platinum Bounty *J A Geake* 33
3 ch f Bahamian Bounty—Maxizone (FR) (Linamix (FR))
2433^{11}

Plato (JPN) *H R A Cecil* a79
2 ch c Bago(FR) —Taygete (USA) (Miswaki (USA))
5637^{5} 6672^{2} ◆

Platoche (IRE) *G A Butler* a60 60
4 b h Galileo(IRE) —Political Parody (USA) (Doonesbury (USA))
1378^{7} 2182^{15} *2830^{9}* 4084^{3} *4538^{7}*

Plavius (USA) *A bin Huzaim* a94 74
4 br h Danzig(USA) —Sharp Minister (CAN) (Deputy Minister (CAN))
435a^{13} 522a^{5}

Playboy Blues (IRE) *P W Chapple-Hyam* a73
2 b c Bertolini(USA) —Ingeburg (Hector Protector (USA))
7463^{4} (7800)

Playful Asset (IRE) *P Howling* a56 62
3 ch f Johannesburg(USA) —Twickin (USA) (Two Punch (USA))
1252^{4} 2246^{8} 2808^{2} (3629) 4918^{3} 5286^{8} *5679^{6} 7586^{13} 7740^{4} 7888^{3}*

Play It Sam *W R Swinburn* a76 78
3 b g Bahamian Bounty—Bombalarina (IRE) (Barathea (IRE))
1837^{5} 2548^{5} 3427^{4} (4070) 4660^{2} 4956^{2} *5575^{5}* 6421^{2} ◆

Play Master (IRE) *B J Llewellyn* a62 61
8 b g Second Empire(IRE) —Madam Waajib (IRE) (Waajib)
346^{9} 502^{8}

Play To Win (IRE) *D R C Elsworth* a61 61
3 b c Singspiel(IRE) —Spot Prize (USA) (Seattle Dancer (USA))
1747^{9} 1930^{10} 2635^{11}

Play Up Pompey *J J Bridger* a59 32
7 b g Dansili—Search For Love (FR) (Groom Dancer (USA))
47^{4} 193^{2} 494^{5} 669^{8} 1589^{5} 2331^{7} *2923^{5} 3158^{10}* 3769^{3} *4538^{8}* 5211^{6} 5473^{8}

Pleasant Day (IRE) *B J Meehan* a79 102
2 b g Noverre(USA) —Sunblush (UAE) (Timber Country (USA))
4314^{12} 4618^{7} *(5192)* 5762^{2} (6305) 7030^{2}

Pleasant Way (IRE) *D R Lanigan* a34 61
2 ch f Barathea(IRE) —Eman's Joy (Lion Cavern (USA))
6920^{8} *7199^{9}*

Please Sing *M R Channon* 100
3 b f Royal Applause—Persian Song (Persian Bold)
1353^{6} 1873^{3} 3016^{3} 4489^{3} 5064^{2} 5260^{7} 5798^{9} 6272^{7}

Plenilune (IRE) *M Brittain* a53 67
4 b g Fantastic Light(USA) —Kathleen's Dream (USA) (Last Tycoon)
1000^{18} 1123^{11} 2569^{7} 2894^{8} 4313^{5} 4710^{13} *7093^{7} 7600^{6} 7678^{5} 7754^{9} 7784^{4}*

Plenty O'Toole *Mrs D J Sanderson* a69
2 ch g Monsieur Bond(IRE) —Marie La Rose (FR) (Night Shift (USA))
7087^{7} 7326^{4} 7538^{2}

Pluie D'Or (IRE) *E Lellouche* 81
4 b m Bering—Prairie Runner (IRE) (Arazi (USA))
(7038a)

Plumage *M Salaman* a64 67
4 b m Royal Applause—Cask (Be My Chief (USA))
2145^{2} 2418^{2} 2852^{5} 2879^{8} 3505^{4} (4023) ◆ 4051^{5}

Plumania *A Fabre* 113
3 b f Anabaa(USA) —Featherquest (Rainbow Quest (USA))
1267a^{2} 2119a^{5} 2952a^{3} 4578a^{3} 5929a^{2} 6504a^{3}

Plume *R Hannon* 77
2 b f Pastoral Pursuits—Polar Storm (IRE) (Law Society (USA))
5605^{11} (6245) ◆

Plume Du Peintre (FR) *N Leenders* 68
2 b f Equerry(USA) —Green Gem (BEL) (Pharly (FR))
6576a^{2} 6928a^{10}

Plum Pudding (IRE) *R Hannon* a101 113
6 b g Elnadim(USA) —Karayb (IRE) (Last Tycoon)
(1251) 2669^{2} 3536^{2} (3818) 5024^{3} 7186^{5} 7245^{2} *7489^{5} 7588^{7} 7809^{5}*

Plush *Tom Dascombe* a87 36
6 ch g Medicean—Glorious (Nashwan (USA))
(238) ◆ *694^{4} (7633) 7848^{5}*

Plus Ultra (IRE) *H R A Cecil* 50
2 b g Rock Of Gibraltar(IRE) —Tafseer (IRE) (Grand Lodge (USA))
4314^{14}

Plutocraft *J R Fanshawe* a68 38
2 ch g Starcraft(NZ) —Angry Bark (USA) (Woodman (USA))
3306^{4} *7024^{3}*

Plymouth Rock (IRE) *J Noseda* 86
3 b c Sadler's Wells(USA) —Zarawa (IRE) (Kahyasi)
(2981) ◆ 3922^{3} 6203^{2}

Poaka Beck (IRE) *R F Fisher* a29 33
3 b c Fath(USA) —Star Of The Future (USA) (El Gran Senor (USA))
429^{6}

Pobs Trophy *R C Guest* a15
2 bb g Umistim—Admonish (Warning)
7420^{8}

Poca A Poca (IRE) *G C Bravery* a40 48
5 b m Namid—Cliveden Gail (IRE) (Law Society (USA))
1423^{8} 1745^{6} *1963^{11}* 2381^{10} *2579^{7}* 3207^{5} 4070^{6} 4164^{8} *5015^{13}* 5719^{15}

Pocket's Pick (IRE) *G L Moore* a73 83
3 ch g Exceed And Excel(AUS) —Swizzle (Efisio)
1486^{9} 1814^{12} *2386^{2}* 2882^{7} *3506^{5} 3989^{11} 5197^{4} 5584^{9}* 5968^{8} *7270^{5} 7483^{2} 7606^{4}* (7839) 7890^{7}

Pocket Too *Matthew Salaman* a52 76
6 b g Fleetwood(IRE) —Pocket Venus (IRE) (King's Theatre (IRE))
7785^{10}

Poet *A P O'Brien* 118
4 b h Pivotal—Hyabella (Shirley Heights)
5080a^{3} (5141a) (5490a) (5685a) 5924a^{2}

Poet's Place (USA) *T D Barron* a76
4 b g Mutakddim(USA) —Legion Of Merit (USA) (Danzig (USA))
(7853) ◆

Poet's Voice *Saeed Bin Suroor* 114
2 b c Dubawi(IRE) —Bright Tiara (USA) (Chief's Crown (USA))
3750^{3} ◆ (4499) 5133^{3} ◆ (5859) ◆ 6450^{4}

Point Calimere (IRE) *Miss Maura McGuinness* a80 82
8 b g Fasliyev(USA) —Mountain Ash (Dominion)
1375a^{16}

Pointillist (IRE) *R M Beckett* 63
3 b f Peintre Celebre(USA) —For Example (USA) (Northern Baby (CAN))
2551^{5} 3425^{10} 4704^{10} 5121^{9}

Pointilliste (USA) *E Lellouche* a104 111
6 ch h Giant's Causeway(USA) —Peinture Bleue (USA) (Alydar (USA))
(1552a) 2118a^{2} 3969a^{4} 5932a^{2} 6527a^{10}

Pointing North (SAF) *B Smart* 104
5 b g Joshua Dancer(USA) —Compass Point (SAF) (Model Man (SAF))
335a^{8} 609a^{7} 5232^{7} 5434^{8}

Point Of Light *Sir Mark Prescott* a45 90
3 b g Pivotal—Lighthouse (Warning)
(4320) (4481) (4687) (4855) (4917) (5979) 6204^{6}

Point Out (USA) *J H M Gosden* a75
2 ch c Point Given(USA) —Dock Leaf (USA) (Woodman (USA))
7024^{2} ◆

Point To Prove *Miss Amy Weaver* a69 69
2 b c Refuse To Bend(IRE) —On Point (Kris)
1630^{5} 2335^{5} 3385^{2} 4208^{6} 4639^{7} *5091^{2} 5635^{11} 6227^{6} 6970^{4}* 7242^{12} *7268^{3} 7559^{4} (7636)*

Poisson Pilote (FR) *R Litt* 47
2 b c Numerous(USA) —Comme Ci (IRE) (Fasliyev (USA))
4686a^{6} 7316a^{0}

Pokfulham (IRE) *J S Goldie* a51 67
3 b g Mull Of Kintyre(USA) —Marjinal (Marju (IRE))
1462^{13} 2652^{4} 3305^{4} 3659^{5} 5295^{4} ◆ 5335^{3} 5362^{8} (6052) 6411^{9} 6997^{11}

Polan (FR) *R Martin Sanchez* 97
4 ch h Golan(IRE) —Slinky (Ashkalani (IRE))
262a^{15}

Polar Annie *M S Saunders* a73 83
4 b m Fraam—Willisa (Polar Falcon (USA))
852^{6} 2520^{8} 2980^{7} 4167^{8} 4428^{7} 4950^{4} 5502^{12}

Polar Gold *A J Chamberlain*
7 b m Lujain(USA) —Polar Fair (Polar Falcon (USA))
6175^{11} *6800^{10}*

Polarix *H-A Pantall* a91 103
3 gr c Linamix(FR) —Freezing (USA) (Bering)
1858a^{5} 3649a^{2} 4685a^{5} 6657a^{7} *7621a^{5}*

Polar Wind (ITY) *R Menichetti* a72 99
5 ch h Rob's Spirit(USA) —Miss Buffy (Polar Falcon (USA))
1905a^{13}

Polebrook *J R Jenkins* 38
2 ch g Lomitas—Fifth Emerald (Formidable (USA))
1749^{6} 2940^{10} 4152^{14} 6200^{9} 6754^{13}

Polemica (IRE) *E A L Dunlop* a50 62
3 b f Rock Of Gibraltar(IRE) —Lady Scarlett (Woodman (USA))
1605^{7} 2139^{7} 2679^{6} 3381^{12} 4179^{4} 4452^{7}

Pole Star *Ms V S Lucas* 63
11 bb g Polar Falcon(USA) —Ellie Ardensky (Slip Anchor)
(5074a)

Poletto *Mario Hofer* a76
2 ch g Monsieur Bond(IRE) —Prince's Feather (IRE) (Cadeaux Genereux)
6960a^{4}

Polidalite (FR) *C Lotoux* 55
3 b c Poliglote—Sodalite (IRE) (Arnaqueur (USA))
2293a^{10}

Polish Power (GER) *J S Moore* a84 96
9 br h Halling(USA) —Polish Queen (Polish Precedent (USA))
271^{14} 1382^{7} (1586) 1660^{5} *(1962)* 2129^{9} 3961^{5} *4084^{2} 4644^{7}* 4987^{6} *6498^{7}*

Polish Pride *M Brittain* 89
3 b f Polish Precedent(USA) —Purple Tiger (IRE) (Rainbow Quest (USA))
1345^{9} 1987^{13} 2270^{9}

Polish Red *Jane Chapple-Hyam* a30 67
5 b g Polish Precedent(USA) —Norcroft Joy (Rock Hopper)
2068^{11} 2983^{10} *3714^{8}* 4156^{13}

Polish Steps (IRE) *J A Osborne* a32 47
2 b f Footstepsinthesand—Polish Spring (IRE) (Polish Precedent (USA))
3458^{9} 4688^{12} *6207^{8} 7089^{8}*

Polish World (USA) *T J Etherington* a65 26
5 b g Danzig(USA) —Welcometotheworld (USA) (Woodman (USA))
794^{7} 1924^{11}

Pollan Bay (IRE) *S Kirk* a53 54
2 b g High Chaparral(IRE) —Rossa Di Rugiada (IRE) (College Chapel)
4945^{12} 5319^{8} 5868^{5} *6431^{6} 6639^{8}*

Pollen (IRE) *T Stack* 99
4 br m Orpen(USA) —On Air (FR) (Chief Singer)
1756a^{5}

Pollenator (IRE) *R Hannon* 107
2 ch f Motivator—Ceanothus (IRE) (Bluebird (USA))
3249^{6} 4239^{2} 4792^{2} (5397) (5825)

Pollish *A Berry* a39 39
3 b f Polish Precedent(USA) —Fizzy Fiona (Efisio)
2250^{12} 2454^{5} 3063^{8} 3936^{5}

Polly Macho (IRE) *P D Evans* 62
2 b g Camacho—Polly Mills (Lugana Beach)
1511^{6} 1867^{7} 2099^{8} 3626^{4} 4384^{11}

Polly's Mark (IRE) *C G Cox* 104
3 b f Mark Of Esteem(IRE) —Kotdiji (Mtoto)
1198^{3} 1489^{2} (2164) 3051^{16} 4166^{3} (4566) (4767) 6242^{2}

Polmaily *J Akehurst* a51 75
4 b g Hawk Wing(USA) —Hampton Lucy (IRE) (Anabaa (USA))
1748^{9} 1958^{7} *2630^{5}*

Polo Springs *W G M Turner* 31
2 gb f Baryshnikov(AUS) —Cristal Springs (Dance Of Life (USA))
5319^{11}

Poltergeist (IRE) *R Hannon* 83
2 b c Invincible Spirit(IRE) —Bayalika (IRE) (Selkirk (USA))
4048^{8} 4986^{2}

Polyegos (IRE) *C Laffon-Parias* 81
3 b f Hawk Wing(USA) —Kresna (FR) (Distant Relative)
5462a^{3} 6222a^{5}

Polyfonico (FR) *Y Barberot*
2 b g Poliglote—Green Melody (FR) (Green Tune (USA))
7507a^{8}

Pomander (IRE) *C Gordon* a20 46
6 b m Bob's Return(IRE) —Pheisty (Faustus (USA))
116^{11}

Pomeroy *Tom Dascombe* a65 46
2 b c Green Desert(USA) —Ela Paparouna (Vettori (IRE))
6108^{12} *7580^{4} 7800^{6}*

Pompeii Ruler (AUS) *Mick Price* 121
7 ch g Genuine(JPN) —West With Night (NZ) (Pompeii Court (USA))
2117a^{4}

Pompeyano (IRE) *S Seemar* 102
4 b g Rainbow Quest(USA) —Lady Lodger (Be My Guest (USA))
(640a) 772a^{9}

Pong Ping *T D Easterby* a1 26
2 ch f Dr Fong(USA) —Hoh Chi Min (Efisio)
1653^{10} 1884^{5} 3119^{5}

Pontardawe *T D Easterby* 35
3 ch f Noverre(USA) —Blaina (Compton Place)
1062^{8}

Pont D'Avignon *F J Brennan* a60
2 ch f Avonbridge—Ambonnay (Ashkalani (IRE))
5808^{8} 6228^{4} 6586^{2} 7210^{8}

Pont De Nuit *R Hannon* a70 70
2 b g Avonbridge—Belle De Nuit (IRE) (Statoblest)
5571^{5} 6108^{11} 6620^{11} 6797^{3} *7333^{10}*

Pont Des Arts (FR) *A Scharer* 104
5 b h Kingsalsa(USA) —Magic Arts (IRE) (Fairy King (USA))
(1555a) 7039a^{2} 7406a^{8}

Ponte Di Legno (FR) *Y De Nicolay* a86 87
3 ch f Sinndar(IRE) —Porlezza (FR) (Sicyos (USA))
5012a^{6}

Ponticello (GER) *Manfred Turk* 31
6 b g Law Society(USA) —Pretty Su (IRE) (Surumu (GER))
3201a^{9}

Ponting (IRE) *P T Midgley* a67 72
3 gr g Clodovil(IRE) —Polar Lady (Polar Falcon (USA))
869^{5} 1595^{8} 2048^{7} 3580^{3} *4172^{4}* 6551^{2} *(7270) 7555^{9} (7795)*

Ponty Rossa (IRE) *T D Easterby* a78 92
5 ch m Distant Music(USA) —Danish Gem (Danehill (USA))
1309^{6} 1682^{6} (2102) 2780^{4} 3389^{7}

Poor Prince *C G Cox* 78
2 b g Royal Applause—Kahira (IRE) (King's Best (USA))
3584^{2} ◆ 4524^{3} 6754^{6}

Popcorn Rosie *C J Down* a52
6 b m Diktat—Real Popcorn (IRE) (Jareer (USA))
501^{7}

Popmurphy *K R Burke* 101
3 b c Montjeu(IRE) —Lady Lahar (Fraam)
(1151) ◆ 1459^{3} 2029^{4} 3090^{5} 3778^{8}

Poppanan (USA) *S Dow* a75 75
3 b g Mr Greeley(USA) —Tiny Decision (USA) (Ogygian (USA))
4786^{7} (5717) ◆ *6444^{2} 6916^{5} 7656^{3} 7891^{5}*

Poppet's Lovein *A B Haynes* 83
3 b f Lomitas—Our Poppet (IRE) (Warning)
3696^{2} 4337^{7} (4936) ◆ (5514) 6311^{5} 6731^{15}

Poppet's Treasure *R Pritchard-Gordon* a84 98
2 b f Dansili—Our Poppet (IRE) (Warning)
6045a^{5}

Poppy Dean (IRE) *J G Portman* a58 48
4 ch m Night Shift(USA) —Miss Devious (IRE) (Dr Devious (IRE))
469^{7} 802^{12} 945^{6} 4824^{5} 4938^{10}

Poppy Morris (IRE) *A B Haynes* a30
4 b m Namid—Coco Palm (Selkirk (USA))
5716^{14} 6329^{10} *6458^{8}*

Poppy N'Penny (IRE) *W J Haggas* a69 80
2 b f Redback—Lulu Island (Zafonic (USA))
3006^{3} ◆ 3633^{3} 4176^{4} *5166^{2} 5369^{6}* 6241^{11} (6906)

Poppy Red *C J Gray* a53 42
4 ch m Lear Spear(USA) —Pooka's Daughter (IRE) (Eagle Eyed (USA))
187^{2} 248^{12} 528^{4} 1586^{4} 1770^{11}

Poppy Seed *R Hannon* 72
2 br f Bold Edge—Opopmil (IRE) (Pips Pride)
4047^{4}

Poppy's Rose *I W McInnes* a66 72
5 b m Diktat—Perfect Peach (Lycius (USA))
1258^{11} 1650^{10} 2769^{7} *3224^{2} 3722^{3}* 4072^{3} 4281^{4} *5225^{4}*

Poquelino (IRE) *Gabriel Mosse* 46
11 b h King's Theatre(IRE) —Queenemara (IRE) (King Of Clubs)
4335a^{10}

Por Chablis (IRE) *P J Lally* 22
10 b g Key Of Luck(USA) —State Princess (IRE) (Flash Of Steel)
4874^{7} 4897^{9}

Porgy *Mme C Head-Maarek* 98
4 b g Dansili—Light Ballet (Sadler's Wells (USA))
6658a^{8}

Porta Westfalica (IRE) *W Hickst* 99
4 ch m Noverre(USA) —Silk Point (IRE) (Barathea (IRE))
1268a^{5}

Port Cros (GER) *J Hirschberger* 88
2 ch c Monsun(GER) —Page Dans Ma Vie (FR) (Generous (IRE))
6151a^{6}

Port Hill *W M Brisbourne* a32 51
2 ch g Deportivo—Hill Farm Dancer (Gunner B)
3468^{6} 4041^{7} 4557^{11}

Port Ronan (USA) *J S Wainwright* a18 57
3 rg c Cozzene(USA) —Amber Token (USA) (Hennessy (USA))
986^{8} 1736^{13} 2365^{7} 2918^{14} 3176^{7} 3611^{5} 3938^{7} 4594^{5} 5422^{6} 5468^{3} 5954^{5} 6101^{6}

Portrush Storm *D Carroll* a8 70
4 ch m Observatory(USA) —Overcast (IRE) (Caerleon (USA))
2314^{3} 2894^{15} 3188^{6} 3264^{13} 3864^{10} 4344^{5} 4845^{12} 4887^{13}

Portugese Caddy *P Winkworth* a47 80
3 b g Great Palm(USA) —Paintbrush (IRE) (Groom Dancer (USA))
2926^{8} *3509^{13}* 4378^{9} *5574^{6}* 5972^{4} 6170^{13}

Portus Blendium (USA) *C Laffon-Parias* 104
3 gr c Highest Honor(FR) —Kalpita (USA) (Spinning World (USA))
4685a^{3}

Porzapone (FR) *N Clement* a73 79
2 b c Vespone(IRE) —Porza (FR) (Septieme Ciel (USA))
3935a^{4}

Pose (IRE) *R Hannon* 82
2 b f Acclamation—Lyca Ballerina (Marju (IRE))
3918^{7} 4603^{4} 5180^{2} 5992^{4} 6241^{5} 6418^{5}

Poseidon Adventure (IRE) *W Figge* 116
6 b h Sadler's Wells(USA) —Fanny Cerrito (USA) (Gulch (USA))
1549a^{5} 3441a^{3} 5082a^{6} 6324a^{4}

Positivity *B Smart* a54 67
3 ch f Monsieur Bond(IRE) —Pretty Pollyanna (General Assembly (USA))
2046^{10} 2265^{5} 2530^{5} 3449^{11} *4172^{3} 5373^{3}* 6415^{9} *6880^{2} 7353^{7} 7727^{3} 7869^{8}*

Possibly A Ten (USA) *J H M Gosden* 56
3 b f Seeking The Gold(USA) —Possibly Perfect (USA) (Northern Baby (CAN))
1488^{9} 2051^{6}

Postage (USA) *K A Morgan* a62 48
6 bb g Chester House(USA) —Nimble Mind (USA) (Lyphard (USA))
(647) 816^{7} 1314^{2} 1785^{13} *2400^{11}*

Postman *B Smart* a75 75
3 b g Dr Fong(USA) —Mail The Desert (IRE) (Desert Prince (IRE))
(1481) (1595) 1925^{4} 3394^{4} 4143^{3} 4741^{5}

Posy Fossil (USA) *S C Williams* a60 63
2 bb f Malibu Moon(USA) —Fire And Shade (USA) (Shadeed (USA))
5284^{13} 6245^{2} *6582^{5} 7363^{9}*

Potemkin (USA) *A King* a6 59
4 bb g Van Nistelrooy(USA) —Bolshoia (USA) (Moscow Ballet (USA))
3074^{12} *3303^{13}*

Potentiale (IRE) *J W Hills* a80 87
5 ch g Singspiel(IRE) —No Frills (IRE) (Darshaan)
1287^{2} 1807^{3} 2379^{3} 2678^{3} 4992^{3} (5473) (5772) 6470^{10}

Potosina (USA) *Mark Shuman* a98 94
2 bb f Cactus Ridge(USA) —Cristalline (CHI) (Northair (USA))
7282a^{7}

Pounced (USA) *J H M Gosden* 117
2 ch c Rahy(USA) —Golden Cat (USA) (Storm Cat (USA))
4258^{2} ◆ (4985) 6524a^{2} (7304a)

Pouvoir Absolu *E Lellouche* 114
4 b h Sadler's Wells(USA) —Pine Chip (USA) (Nureyev (USA))
5497a[2] 6527a[4] 7047a[5]

Powerful Melody (USA) *Saeed Bin Suroor* a74
2 b c Dynaformer(USA) —Song Track (USA) (Dixieland Band (USA))
(7400) ◆

Powerful Pierre *Jedd O'Keeffe* 68
2 ch g Compton Place—Alzianah (Alzao (USA))
2099[13] 3310[3] 3606[7] 4306[9] 5256[6] 5595[13] 5976[2] 6409[2] 6905[4]

Power Of Dreams (IRE) *M H Tompkins* a56 72
2 b c Pearl Of Love(IRE) —Pussie Willow (IRE) (Catrail (USA))
5109[5] 5400[12] 6548[9] 7055[2] 7335[7]

Power Of Speech *J Gallagher*
4 b g Advise(FR) —Marsara (Never So Bold)
902[8]

Power Series (USA) *J H M Gosden* 45
2 rg c Mizzen Mast(USA) —Diese (USA) (Diesis)
4534[12] 5000[9]

Power Shared (IRE) *P G Murphy* a7 71
5 gr g Kendor(FR) —Striking Pose (IRE) (Darshaan)
7154[13]

Poyle Meg *R M Beckett* a89 80
3 b f Dansili—Lost In Lucca (Inchinor)
2795[4] 3278[3] 4246[2] (5010) 5833[2] (6973) 7366[3] (7684)

Practitioner *H J L Dunlop* 88
2 b g Dr Fong(USA) —Macina (IRE) (Platini (GER))
(2792) 3424[3] 4086[2] 5022[2] 5827[3]

Praesepe *W J Haggas* a69
2 b f Pivotal—Superstar Leo (IRE) (College Chapel)
7843[2] ◆

Pragmatist *P Winkworth* a68 68
5 b m Piccolo—Shi Shi (Alnasr Alwasheek)
2381[7]

Prairie Hawk (USA) *Tim Vaughan* a68 72
4 bb g Hawk Wing(USA) —Lady Carla (Caerleon (USA))
(449) (502) 3346[3]

Prairie Spirit (FR) *C E Longsdon* a67 93
5 ch g Grape Tree Road—Prairie Runner (IRE) (Arazi (USA))
445[9] 585[11]

Prairie Storm *A M Balding* a83 85
4 b g Storming Home—Last Dream (IRE) (Alzao (USA))
1593[8] 2150[6] 3024[3]

Praise Of Folly *A G Newcombe* a50 53
3 b f Selkirk(USA) —Song Of Hope (Chief Singer)
572[5] 900[9] 1183[11]

Prakasa (FR) *W Hickst* 94
2 b f Areion(GER) —Pepples Beach (GER) (Lomitas)
6151a[3] 7045a[4]

Prankster *A Fabre* 102
3 b g Rock Of Gibraltar(IRE) —Coraline (Sadler's Wells (USA))
5711a[5]

Pravda Street *P F I Cole* a74 94
4 ch g Soviet Star(USA) —Sari (Faustus (USA))
1089[4] ◆ 1212[11] 1510[4] (2050) 2927[8] 3116[3] 4293[11] 6482[15]

Prayer Boat (IRE) *John Joseph Murphy* a82 82
3 b c Oasis Dream—Reasonably Devout (CAN) (St Jovite (USA))
5665[12]

Precious Boy (GER) *W Hickst* 116
4 br h Big Shuffle(USA) —Pretty Su (IRE) (Surumu (GER))
1658a[3] 2953a[3] 4364a[2] 5059a[3] 6718a[8]

Precious Citizen (USA) *J R Gask* a49 55
4 ch m Proud Citizen(USA) —Fasateen (USA) (Alysheba (USA))
3929[10] 4300[3] 5246[5] 5790[4]

Precious Coral (IRE) *S A Callaghan* a68 68
2 gr f Elusive City(USA) —Somaggia (IRE) (Desert King (IRE))
3820[14] 4093[11] 4542[8] 5310[6] ◆ 5635[2] ◆ 5935[3] 6819[9]

Precious Secret (IRE) *C F Wall* a55 62
3 b f Fusaichi Pegasus(USA) —Gharam (USA) (Green Dancer (USA))
1422[4] 3427[9] 4157[5]

Precipitate *D Smaga* 82
2 b f Barathea(IRE) —Love The Rain (Rainbow Quest (USA))
6578a[3]

Precision Break (USA) *P F I Cole* a93 103
4 b g Silver Deputy(CAN) —Miss Kitty Cat (USA) (Tabasco Cat (USA))
1696[7] 4408[2] 5173[16] (5865)

Precocious Air (IRE) *J A Osborne* a61
3 b f Redback—Wee Merkin (IRE) (Thatching)
134[2] 231[6] 296[3] 441[4]

Predatory Pricer (AUS) *Paul Murray* 120
4 ch h Street Cry(IRE) —Shady Stream (AUS) (Archregent (CAN))
6871a[12]

Prelude *W M Brisbourne* 77
8 b m Danzero(AUS) —Dancing Debut (Polar Falcon (USA))
2783[5] 3527[3] 3809[9] 4561[7] 5359[13]

Prema (GER) *W Hickst* 99
3 ch f Big Shuffle(USA) —Pretty Su (IRE) (Surumu (GER))
6886a[11]

Premier Angel (USA) *Ollie Pears* a61 18
3 b f Arch(USA) —Angel Song (USA) (Reign Road (USA))
121[9] 391[5] 4846[10]

Premier Demon (IRE) *P D Evans* a22 53
3 b f Tagula(IRE) —Luisa Demon (IRE) (Barathea (IRE))
293[8] 1584[9] 3257[12] 3502[5]

Premier Krug (IRE) *P D Evans* a55 62
3 b f Xaar—Perugia (IRE) (Perugino (USA))
1243[14] 1520[7] 2876[3] 3241[4] 3451[6] 3541[4]

Premier Lad *T D Barron* a80 65
3 b g Tobougg(IRE) —Al Joudha (FR) (Green Desert (USA))
(364) 562[2] 1567[4] 7337[8] 7506[8] 7828[10]

Premier Superstar *M H Tompkins* 53
3 ch f Bertolini(USA) —Absolve (USA) (Diesis)
1931[12] 2635[12]

Premio Loco (USA) *C F Wall* a114 113
5 ch g Prized(USA) —Crazee Mental (Magic Ring (IRE))
(30) (458) 913[2] (2476) 3404[2] (5563a) (6323a)

Premium Charge *C A Dwyer* a47 41
2 ch g Footstepsinthesand—Kallavesi (USA) (Woodman (USA))
6756[4] 7731[7]

Presbyterian Nun (IRE) *J L Dunlop* 99
4 b m Daylami(IRE) —Conspiracy (Rudimentary (USA))
1191[3] 3103[6] 4458[7] 5170[4] 5828[6] 6286[2] 6618[8] 7148[4]

Prescription *Sir Mark Prescott* a102 93
4 gr m Pivotal—Doctor's Glory (USA) (Elmaamul (USA))
4228[6] ◆ (4870) 5104[2] 6702[3] 7292[4] 7488[6]

Present *Miss Diana Weeden* a39 45
5 ch m Generous(IRE) —Miss Picol (Exit To Nowhere (USA))
378[7] 5975[11] 6037[4] 7124[7]

Present Alchemy *H Morrison* 89
3 ch c Cadeaux Genereux—Desert Alchemy (IRE) (Green Desert (USA))
1355[6] ◆ 2229[5] 4324[2] 4786[2] (5422)

Present Of Heaven (GER) *W Baltromei* 75
3 ch c Areion(GER) —Party Bloom (FR) (Baillamont (USA))
7386a[3]

Presious Passion (USA) *Mary Hartmann* 122
6 ch g Royal Anthem(USA) —Princesa's Passion (USA) (Marquetry (USA))
4809a[8] 7310a[2]

Presque Perdre *G M Moore* 53
5 ch g Desert Prince(IRE) —Kindle (Selkirk (USA))
2044[4]

Pressed For Time (IRE) *E J Creighton* a62 52
3 b f Traditionally(USA) —Desert Palace (Green Desert (USA))
1311[11] 1469[3] 1982[6] 2162[16] 3465[6] 3663[7] 4596[12]

Pressing (IRE) *M A Jarvis* 118
6 bb h Soviet Star(USA) —Rafif (USA) (Riverman (USA))
2076[8] (2525a) (4364a) (5618a) 7312a[3] 7746a[14]

Pressing Matters (IRE) *M Botti* a72 74
3 br c Oasis Dream—Pasithea (IRE) (Celtic Swing)
1466[8] 3159[4] (3548) 3982[9] 4914[7] 5403[3] 5779[11] 6924[7]

Press The Button (GER) *J R Boyle* a102 98
6 b g Dansili—Play Around (IRE) (Niniski (USA))
(1216) 1460[10] 1798[5] 2706[16] 4247[2] (4770) 5248[8] 6106[7]

Press To Reset *W G M Turner* a18 53
2 b g Reset(AUS) —Lady De Londres (Mtoto)
4080[11] 5319[3] 5543[11] 7139[10]

Presvis *L M Cumani* a108 122
5 b g Sakhee(USA) —Forest Fire (SWE) (Never So Bold)
(263a) ◆ (703a) 1011a[2] (1554a) 2117a[2] 7489[2] 7747a[3]

Prettiest Star (IRE) *K A Ryan* a48 57
2 ch f Footstepsinthesand—Alyousufeya (IRE) (Kingmambo (USA))
1521[6] 2335[4] 2914[6] 3540[5] 4190[9] 4503[7] 4800[5] 5226[2] 5976[8] 6555[4] 6819[14] 7352[7]

Pretty Bonnie *A E Price* a90 93
4 b m Kyllachy—Joonayh (Warning)
1582[12] (1733) ◆ 2102[3] 3360[2] 4096[5] 4516[5] 5069[3] 5607[5] 6282[9]

Pretty Officer (USA) *Rae Guest* a38 59
4 b m Deputy Commander(USA) —La Samanna (USA) (Trempolino (USA))
1651[6] 2420[6] 2608[2] 3004[3] 4824[4] (5484) 5602[8] 6184[6]

Pretty Orchid *P T Midgley* a43 51
4 b m Forzando—Dunloe (IRE) (Shaadi (USA))
3338[10] 4105[9] 5338[3]

Pride Du Clos (FR) *L Godard*
2 ch c Bad As I Wanna Be(IRE) —Solena De Pirey (FR) (Solon (GER))
7507a[0]

Pride Of Kings *M Johnston* 89
3 b c King's Best(USA) —Aunty Mary (Common Grounds)
1462[4] (1882) 2535[2] 2890[3] (3530) 4296[8] 4801[6] 5522[7]

Pride Of Nation (IRE) *A J McCabe* a92 81
7 b h Danehill Dancer(IRE) —Anita Via (IRE) (Anita's Prince)
1731[7] 3301[9] 6732[13] 7350[11] 7412[3] 7492[9] 7581[2] 7631[4] 7810[5] 7858[3]

Pride Of Northcare (IRE) *D Shaw* a77 62
5 gr g Namid—Pride Of Pendle (Grey Desire)
742[9]

Priestley (IRE) *J G Given* a28 26
2 b g Bahri(USA) —Siskin (IRE) (Royal Academy (USA))
6990[15] 7243[12] 7376[11]

Primaeval *J R Fanshawe* 82
3 ch c Pivotal—Langoustine (AUS) (Danehill (USA))
3566[2] 4947[3] (6823)

Prima Fonteyn *Miss Sheena West* a51 34
3 ch f Imperial Dancer—Flying Wind (Forzando)
32[6] 455[8] 647[9]

Prima Luce (IRE) *J S Bolger* 109
4 b m Galileo(IRE) —Ramona (Desert King (IRE))
928a[6]

Primary Colors *C G Cox* 65
2 ch c Nayef(USA) —Red Yellow Blue (USA) (Sky Classic (CAN))
5400[5] 6617[6]

Prime Arrival (IRE) *Y Fouin* 70
3 b c Montjeu(IRE) —Freedom Flame (Darshaan)
5278a[0]

Prime Aspiration (USA) *B Smart* a77 60
4 bb h Tale Of The Cat(USA) —Bank On Her (USA) (Rahy (USA))
4346[7]

Prime Circle *M Johnston* 70
3 b g Green Desert(USA) —First Of Many (Darshaan)
3036[8] 3590[3]

Prime Classique (USA) *B Smart* 45
3 b f Elusive Quality(USA) —Via Borghese (USA) (Seattle Dancer (USA))
3703[6]

Prime Defender *B W Hills* a105 115
5 ch h Bertolini(USA) —Arian Da (Superlative)
(996) 2116a[13] 3819[9] 4087[2] 5024[8] 6058[5] 6304[5] ◆ 6661[15]

Prime Exhibit *R Charlton* 96
4 b g Selkirk(USA) —First Exhibit (Machiavellian (USA))
4064[4] (4954) ◆ 6092[3] 6732[2]

Prime Mood (IRE) *B Smart* 92
3 ch c Choisir(AUS) —There With Me (USA) (Distant View (USA))
2469[6] 2934[18]

Primera Rossa *J S Moore* a46 52
3 ch f Needwood Blade—Meandering Rose (USA) (Irish River (FR))
752[10] 839[8] 2876[9] 3257[10] 3919[6] 4084[5] 4397[5] (4934) 5382[2] 5579[5] 6446[9]

Primera Vista *L M Cumani* a72 67
3 b c Haafhd—Colorvista (Shirley Heights)
3168[10] 4057[6] 4519[5] 5616[4]

Prime Spirit (IRE) *X-Thomas Demeaulte* 95
3 b c Invincible Spirit(IRE) —Turtulla (IRE) (Night Shift (USA))
4077[2] ◆ 4459[10] 6222a[4]

Primo De Vida (IRE) *R M Beckett* a65 60
2 b g Trade Fair—Rampage (Pivotal)
4219[12] 4478[3] 6874[2]

Primo Dilettante *W J Knight* a66 65
3 b g Primo Valentino(IRE) —Jezadil (IRE) (Mujadil (USA))
1811[3] 1967[9] (2380) 2489[7] 2809[3] 3511[5] 3949[4] 4734[5] (5750) 5873[10] 6440[5] 6966[2]

Primo Way *D A Nolan* a76 65
8 b g Primo Dominie—Waypoint (Cadeaux Genereux)
1690[16] 2235[9] 2391[7] 3098[4] 3653[3] 4040[4] 4532[3] 5160[8] 6093[8] 6157[9]

Primrose Bankes *W G M Turner* a68
2 b f Mark Of Esteem(IRE) —Lady Bankes (IRE) (Alzao (USA))
5371[6] 5643[5] 5984[7]

Princability (IRE) *M R Channon* a72 76
3 b g King's Best(USA) —Harmonic Sound (IRE) (Grand Lodge (USA))
917[3] 1280[3] 1707[6] 2189[8] 4520[11] 4910[4] 6698[6] 6975[11]

Prince Andjo (USA) *I W McInnes* a58 34
3 b g Van Nistelrooy(USA) —Magic Flare (USA) (Danzatore (CAN))
1108[2] 1281[10] 6705[14]

Prince Charlemagne (IRE) *G L Moore* a74 79
6 br g King Charlemagne(USA) —Ciubanga (IRE) (Arazi (USA))
353[5] ◆ (444) (546) ◆ (816) 948[4] 1081[3] 1378[2] 1609[3] 6288[14] 6917[5] 7495[2] (7594) 7695[4] 7785[8]

Prince De Fortune *Mrs C A Dunnett* a49 51
3 b g Lend A Hand—Fortuitious (IRE) (Polish Patriot (USA))
3718[11] 4180[9] 5747[12] 6587[12] 7179[9]

Prince Evelith (GER) *J J Quinn* 87
6 b g Dashing Blade—Peace Time (GER) (Surumu (GER))
1507[4] ◆ 1830[4] 2313[3] (2894) 3034[P]

Prince Fasliyev *Niels Petersen* a99 104
5 b h Fasliyev(USA) —Malaisienne (FR) (Saumarez)
(3419a) 5302a[6]

Prince Flori (GER) *S Smrczek* 111
6 br h Lando(GER) —Princess Liberte (GER) (Nebos (GER))
2115a[5] 3201a[2]

Prince Fortune *Mrs L Stubbs* 66
2 b g Namid—Plumeria (Revoque (IRE))
2167[5] 4342[6] (4912)

Prince Golan (IRE) *R J Price* a71 74
5 b g Golan(IRE) —Mohican Princess (Shirley Heights)
65[5] 220[10] 713[4] 885[8] 2166[10] 2442[5] 3224[8] 6358[3] 6668[5] (7500) 7668[7]

Princely Hero (IRE) *C Gordon* a89 82
5 b g Royal Applause—Dalu (IRE) (Dancing Brave (USA))
747[3] ◆ 850[3] 1288[2] 1894[6] 6059[8]

Princelywallywogan *John A Harris* a25 73
7 b g Princely Heir(IRE) —Dublivia (Midyan (USA))
1192[7] 1514[8] 2537[2] 3864[2] 4054[P]

Prince Maggio *Pat Eddery* 10
3 b c Prince Sabo—Pieta (IRE) (Perugino (USA))
3975[10] 4303[10]

Prince Namid *D Nicholls* a80 79
7 b g Namid—Fen Princess (IRE) (Trojan Fen)
2276[12] 4072[10] (4141) 4399[8] 5421[12] 7119[10]

Prince Noel *N Wilson* a80 70
5 b g Dr Fong(USA) —Baileys On Line (Shareef Dancer (USA))
94[9] 215[4] 569[3] 737[2] 932[7] 1131[3] 1276[8] 1530[6]

Prince Of Dance *Tom Dascombe* 112
3 b c Danehill Dancer(IRE) —Princess Ellen (Tirol)
(2080) (6732) (7186)

Prince Of Delphi *Mrs A L M King* a78 77
6 b g Royal Applause—Princess Athena (Ahonoora)
460[9] 590[3] 728[4] 861[6] 1787[11] 2366[10] 3246[10]

Prince Of Dreams *W J Knight* 72
2 b c Sadler's Wells(USA) —Questina (FR) (Rainbow Quest (USA))
7034[2]

Prince Of Johanne (IRE) *J Noseda* a42 90
3 gr c Johannesburg(USA) —Paiute Princess (FR) (Darshaan)
1638[7] 1941[4] (2081) (4605) (5266) 5828[7] 6114[5]

Prince Of Medina *J R Best* a53 57
6 ch g Fraam—Medina De Rioseco (Puissance)
117[2] 169[3] 213[9] 385[5] 444[2] 502[6] 541[4] 601[8] 732[4]

Prince Of Sorrento *J Akehurst* a73
2 ch c Doyen(IRE) —Princess Galadriel (Magic Ring (IRE))
7436[3] (7700)

Prince Of Thebes (IRE) *M J Attwater* a89 89
8 b g Desert Prince(IRE) —Persian Walk (FR) (Persian Bold)
1213[3] 1607[4] 1813[7] 2480[9] 2639[9] 3274[3] 3523[6] 3770[6] 4293[14] 5095[8] 5511[11] 5663[7] 5914[8] 6394[7] 6778[4] 7054[10] 7664[3] 7823[8]

Princeofthedesert *G Woodward*
3 b g Nayef(USA) —Twilight Sonnet (Exit To Nowhere (USA))
4519[16]

Prince Of Vasa (IRE) *Saeed Bin Suroor* a68
2 b c Kheleyf(USA) —Suzy Street (IRE) (Dancing Dissident (USA))
5325[3]

Prince Picasso *R A Fahey* a81 82
6 b g Lomitas—Auspicious (Shirley Heights)
5772[2] 6250[3] 7640[3] 7775[6]

Prince Pippin (IRE) *S Curran* a17
3 b g King Charlemagne(USA) —Staploy (Deploy)
5987[11]

Prince Rhyddarch *I Semple* a18 73
4 b g Josr Algarhoud(IRE) —Nova Zembla (Young Em)
4038[5] 4898[7] 5359[7] 5734[13] 6053[10] 7354[11]

Prince Rodrigue (FR) *Y Rougegrez* 31
5 b g (FR) — (FR) (Kaldounevees (FR))
5204a[10]

Prince Rossi (IRE) *A E Price* a57 67
5 b g Royal Applause—Miss Rossi (Artaius (USA))
(247) (513) 1199[5] (1773) (2352) 3357[7] 3800[11]

Prince Samos (IRE) *C A Mulhall* a85 76
7 b g Mujadil(USA) —Sabaniya (FR) (Lashkari)
2791[6] 3499[6] 3974[11] 4434[10]

Prince Shaun (IRE) *Doug Watson* a105 107
4 b g Acclamation—Style Parade (USA) (Diesis)
265a[3] 413a[13] 697a[8]

Prince Siegfried (FR) *Saeed Bin Suroor* a89 118
3 b g Royal Applause—Intrum Morshaan (IRE) (Darshaan)
3298[3] 4367a[3] (4760) (6093) 7188[2]

Princess Aliuska *Mrs S Lamyman* 53
4 b m Domedriver(IRE) —Aliuska (IRE) (Fijar Tango (FR))
2613[5] 3120[2] 4798[U] 5093[8]

Princess Cagliari *R Hannon* a74
3 b f Efisio—Queenie (Indian Ridge)
69[2] 162[2] 229[2] 498[2] (797) 1068[6]

Princess Charlmane (IRE) *C J Teague* a56 61
6 b m King Charlemagne(USA) —Bint Alreeys (Polish Precedent (USA))
811[2] 881[2] 975[12] 1781[12] 2157[7] 3002[14] (3678) 3909[8] 4192[4] 4467[3] (4754) 5008[12] 5729[12] 6379[7] 6553[12]

Princess Cocoa (IRE) *R A Fahey* a82 78
6 b m Desert Sun—Daily Double (FR) (Unfuwain (USA))
271[8] 453[6] 477[5]

Princess Emma *R A Fahey* a44 55
2 b f Fantastic Light(USA) —Rosablanca (IRE) (Sinndar (IRE))
6181[3] 6638[8]

Princess Flame (GER) *B G Powell* a64 76
7 br m Tannenkonig(IRE) —Pacora (GER) (Lagunas)
485[7] 1049[5] 1357[10] 1615[6] 2040[6] 2493[13] 4449[2] 5244[4] 5545[2] 6236[6] 7036[5]

Princess Gee *B J McMath* a63 49
4 b m Reel Buddy(USA) —Queen G (USA) (Matty G (USA))
1495[10] 1728[8] 2741[13]

Princess Haya (USA) *Michael Matz* 108
4 b m Street Cry(IRE) —Sally Slew (USA) (Slew City Slew (USA))
6872a[3]

Princess Janet *A B Coogan* a18 16
3 ch f Deportivo—Idolize (Polish Precedent (USA))
1108[7] 1270[9]

Princess Lala (GER) *Mario Hofer*
3 ch f Royal Dragon(USA) —Princess Li (GER) (Monsun (GER))
7037a[0]

Princess Lexi (IRE) *K A Ryan* 54
2 ch f Rock Of Gibraltar(IRE) —Etaaq (IRE) (Sadler's Wells (USA))
6245[5] 6556[10]

Princess Lomi (IRE) *Andrew Heffernan* a75 75
4 b m Lomitas—Athlumney Lady (Lycius (USA))
7684[8] 7724[5]

Princess Mandy (IRE) *K A Ryan* a52 48
2 gr f Desert Style(IRE) —Lady Fabiola (USA) (Open Forum (USA))
6802[7] 7079[4] 7396[6] 7584[3]

Princess Neenee (IRE) *Paul Green* 12
2 b f King's Best(USA) —Precedence (IRE) (Polish Precedent (USA))
4847[10] 5408[8] 6245[13]

Princess Of Aeneas (IRE) *A G Foster* a48 38
6 b m Beckett(IRE) —Romangoddess (IRE) (Rhoman Rule (USA))
3098[9] 3499[12]

Princess Pivotal *G A Butler* a47
4 gr m Pivotal—Santa Sophia (IRE) (Linamix (FR))
7067[8]

Princess Podge *M D I Usher* 41
2 b f Desert Sun—Medici Princess (Medicean)
2175[9]

Princess Rainbow (FR) *Jennie Candlish* a68 76
4 b m Raintrap—Chausseneige (FR) (Mad Captain)
1615[11] (2200) 3151[3] 3527[2] 4078[3] 4890[6] 5625[2]

Princess Rebecca *H J Collingridge* a47 36
3 ch f Compton Place—Sunley Stars (Sallust)
1620[10] *2132[11]*

Princess Rose Anne (IRE) *J R Best* a74 81
4 ch m Danehill Dancer(IRE) —Hawksleys Jill (Mujtahid (USA))
31[5] 191[12] 464a[3] (652a) *799[4]* (1091) (1425) 1672[7] 1836[10] 3162[3] 3261[5] 3386[6]

Princess Seren *B R Millman* 2
2 b f King's Best(USA) —Gold Field (IRE) (Unfuwain (USA))
3101[10]

Princess Shamal *J R Jenkins* a56 55
2 b f Kheleyf(USA) —Gentle Dame (Kris)
2207[8] 2860[7] *3210[6]* 3772[5] 4383[5] *5372[7] 6354[5]* 6905[14] *7421[5] 7772[6]*

Princess Shirl *A D Brown*
5 b m Shahrastani(USA) —Shirl (Shirley Heights)
7504[10]

Princess Soraya *R Dickin* 43
3 ch f Compton Place—Eurolink Cafe (Grand Lodge (USA))
1355[11] 1840[15] 2178[10]

Princess Taylor *M Botti* a94 103
5 ch m Singspiel(IRE) —Tapas En Bal (FR) (Mille Balles (FR))
1347[5] 1613[2] 2013[3] 2482[5] 2974[2] 4094[2] 4458[4] 5202[5] 5796[5] 6242[4] *7131[4] 7589[7]*

Princess Teddy (IRE) *Edgar Byrne* a51 51
6 b m Sayarshan(FR) —Bajan Girl (IRE) (Pips Pride)
395[10] 513[9]

Princess Valerina *D Haydn Jones* a89 87
5 ch m Beat Hollow—Heart So Blue (Dilum (USA))
(20) 197[4] 600[5] 780[2] 901[5] (1313) 1880[7] 2271[9] 4853[8] *5104[11]* 6050[16] 6396[4] *7155[6]* 7454[7] 7613[7] ◆ 7875[6]

Princess Zhukova (IRE) *M Wellings* a41
4 b m Terroir(IRE) —Miss Bussell (Sabrehill (USA))
80[5] 290[10] 381[6] 574[8] 7782[8]

Princess Zohra *E A L Dunlop* a62
3 b f Royal Applause—Desert Royalty (IRE) (Alhaarth (IRE))
(572) 829[6] 2632[10]

Prince Tamino *A Al Raihe* a78 110
6 b g Mozart(IRE) —Premiere Dance (IRE) (Loup Solitaire (USA))
257a[5] 418a[8] 638a[7] 700a[8]

Prince Valentine *G L Moore* a50 58
8 b g My Best Valentine—Affaire De Coeur (Imperial Fling (USA))
3241[7] 3671[11] 4697[3] 5569[6] 6966[4] *7653[3] 7880[9]*

Prince Yarraman (IRE) *J A Osborne* a68
2 b c Chineur(FR) —Church Mice (IRE) (Petardia)
7537[5] 7705[2] 7825[2] 7865[3]

Prince Zafonic *C A Dwyer* a76 67
6 ch g Zafonic(USA) —Kite Mark (Mark Of Esteem (IRE))
5113[5] 5545[5]

Principal Role (USA) *H R A Cecil* 80
2 b f Empire Maker(USA) —Interim (Sadler's Wells (USA))
(6921) ◆

Principe Uromonte (IRE) *Mario Hofer* 89
3 ch c Talkin Man(CAN) —Pichola Lake (USA) (Quest For Fame)
2096a[4]

Print (IRE) *M R Channon* 68
3 b c Exceed And Excel(AUS) —Hariya (IRE) (Shernazar)
1704[9] 2160[8]

Prise De Risque (FR) *T Clout* a88 92
3 b f Take Risks(FR) —Palissandre (FR) (Phantom Breeze)
2777a[7] 4394a[7]

Priti Fabulous (IRE) *A J McCabe* a87 84
4 b m Invincible Spirit(IRE) —Flying Diva (Chief Singer)
1603[15] 2083[4] *2828[14] 7269[8] 7511[8] 7682[6] 7872[6]*

Private Equity (IRE) *W Jarvis* a63 46
3 b f Haafhd—Profit Alert (IRE) (Alzao (USA))
5999[6] 6570[4] (7324) ◆ *(7461) 7740[5]*

Private Olley *J Akehurst* a51 44
2 ch c Exceed And Excel(AUS) —My Daisychain (Hector Protector (USA))
2636[7] *3745[7]* 4568[7]

Private Passion (IRE) *Pat Eddery* a57 55
3 b g Captain Rio—Victoria's Secret (IRE) (Law Society (USA))
(390) 594[3] 753[4] 831[3] 900[8] 1253[11] *2577[10]* 2918[2] 3671[13] 5155[6] 5287[9]

Private Soldier *Tom Dascombe* a47 40
6 gr g Dansili—Etienne Lady (IRE) (Imperial Frontier (USA))
2473[6] 3077[14] *6800[4]*

Private Story (USA) *R Hannon* 92
2 b c Yes It's True(USA) —Said Privately (USA) (Private Account (USA))
(5220) 6057[2] 6319a[10] 7184[4]

Privy Speech (IRE) *Rae Guest* a57
2 ch f El Corredor(USA) —Privileged Speech (USA) (General Assembly (USA))
7792[3]

Prix Masque (IRE) *Christian Wroe* a51 33
5 b g Iron Mask(USA) —Prima Marta (Primo Dominie)
23[7] 280[11] 357[9] 588[P]

Prize Fighter (IRE) *A Berry* a74 72
7 b g Desert Sun—Papal (Selkirk (USA))
1343[10]

Prizefighting (USA) *J H M Gosden* a80 102
2 ch c Smart Strike(CAN) —Allencat (USA) (Storm Cat (USA))
(7050) ◆ 7207a[5]

Prize Point *K A Ryan* 76
3 ch g Bahamian Bounty—Golden Symbol (Wolfhound (USA))
1559[3] 2355[4]

Proclaim *M Johnston* a82 99
3 b c Noverre(USA) —Pescara (IRE) (Common Grounds)
1214[6] (1345) (1517) 2279[4] (2469) 2934[13] 3622[8] 3747[10] 4423[3] 4771[7] 5032[15] 5424[3] 6270[3]

Professor Bollini (IRE) *H J L Dunlop* a52
2 b c Bertolini(USA) —Nofa's Magic (IRE) (Rainbow Quest (USA))
5571[11] 6781[13]

Professor John (IRE) *M L W Bell* a77 81
2 b g Haafhd—Dancing Flower (IRE) (Compton Place)
3546[6] (3944) 4758[10] 5207[3] *5580[6]* 5970[6] 6693[13] 7218[7]

Professor Malone *M S Tuck* a48 29
4 ch g Ishiguru(USA) —Molly Malone (Formidable (USA))
3994[9] *6344[8] 6719[13]*

Professor Twinkle *I W McInnes* a61 70
5 ch h Dr Fong(USA) —Shining High (Shirley Heights)
289[11]

Proficiency *T D Walford* 64
4 gr m El Prado(IRE) —Talent Quest (IRE) (Rainbow Quest (USA))
2263[7] 2859[6] 3864[3] (4071) 4498[11]

Profit's Reality (IRE) *M J Attwater* a91 96
7 br g Key Of Luck(USA) —Teacher Preacher (IRE) (Taufan (USA))
156[3] 330[8] 456[6] 584[3] (687) 1007[11] 1458[7] *1779[4]* 2566[4] 2932[5] 3587[5] 3797[6] (7724) 7841[2]

Profligate (IRE) *W Jarvis* 28
2 b f Soviet Star(USA) —Profit Alert (IRE) (Alzao (USA))
7182[18]

Profound Beauty (IRE) *D K Weld* 112
5 b m Danehill(USA) —Diamond Trim (IRE) (Highest Honor (FR))
(3413a) (4033a) (4962a) 5891a[4]

Progress (IRE) *J Noseda* 65
2 br f Green Desert(USA) —Mille (Dubai Millennium)
6809[5]

Prohibit *J H M Gosden* a108 107
4 b g Oasis Dream—Well Warned (Warning)
1299[6] 1699[11] 3141[5] 4523[12] 6282[2]

Prohibition (IRE) *W J Haggas* a66 82
3 b c Danehill Dancer(IRE) —Crumpetsfortea (IRE) (Henbit (USA))
7620[7]

Project Dane (IRE) *L Polito* 104
5 ch h Dane Friendly—Sweet College (IRE) (College Chapel)
7312a[8]

Prom *M Brittain* 40
3 b f Lujain(USA) —Ball Gown (Jalmood (USA))
3685[10]

Promesse De L'Aube (FR) *P Schiergen* 98
4 b m Galileo(IRE) —White Rose (GER) (Platini (GER))
5461a[12] 6714a[8]

Promised Gold *J A Geake* a31 36
4 ch g Bahamian Bounty—Delphic Way (Warning)
2127[13]

Promise Maker (USA) *T D Walford* a48 71
4 b g Empire Maker(USA) —Sunday Bazaar (USA) (Nureyev (USA))
(2609) 2971[8] 3499[2] 4193[2] 4600[7] 5339[2] (5625) 6021[5]

Prompter *M L W Bell* 108
2 b c Motivator—Penny Cross (Efisio)
3794[2] ◆ (4557) 5261[6] 6664[2]

Proper Littlemadam *M Botti* a58 68
2 b f Statue Of Liberty(USA) —Aly McBe (USA) (Alydeed (CAN))
2699[4] 3337[4] 4226[13] *5573[U] 5811[6] 6721[8]*

Proponent (IRE) *R Charlton* 104
5 b g Peintre Celebre(USA) —Pont Audemer (USA) (Chief's Crown (USA))
1352[18] 1673[9] 2412[4] 3399[3] 4339[2] 5262[7] 5880[6] (6429)

Proportional *Mme C Head-Maarek* 112
3 b f Beat Hollow—Minority (Generous (IRE))
1237a[3] 1918a[4] 4578a[2] 5298a[4]

Prospect Court *A C Whillans* a37 69
7 ch g Pivotal—Scierpan (USA) (Sharpen Up)
3148[8] 3655[9] 4043[8] 4346[9] 5309[8] 5729[15]

Prospect Wells (FR) *A Fabre* 118
4 b h Sadler's Wells(USA) —Brooklyn's Dance (FR) (Shirley Heights)
1144a[7] 1762a[7]

Protaras (USA) *H R A Cecil* 74
2 bb c Lemon Drop Kid(USA) —Seven Moons (JPN) (Sunday Silence (USA))
6423[7] 6759[2]

Protector (SAF) *A G Foster* a94 98
8 b g Kilconnel(USA) —Mufski (SAF) (Al Mufti (USA))
4037[9] 4310[8] 6089[11] ◆ 7019[8] 7292[7]

Protiva *Karen George* a62 62
3 ch f Deportivo—Prowse (USA) (King Of Kings (IRE))
1075[5] 1429[3] 1834[10] 3005[13] 4535[5] 5063[12]

Proud Boris (GER) *J Hanacek* 88
5 b h Silvano(GER) —Parista (Armistice Day)
6153a[7]

Proud Junior (USA) *S A Callaghan* 45
3 b c Proud Citizen(USA) —Endless Reward (USA) (End Sweep (USA))
1257[10] 2664[11] 3161[6] 3473[4] 3985[9]

Proud Killer *J R Jenkins* a69 67
6 b g Killer Instinct—Thewaari (USA) (Eskimo (USA))
4183[13]

Proud Linus (USA) *J Ryan* a37 92
4 b g Proud Citizen(USA) —Radcliffe Yard (USA) (Boston Harbor (USA))
7459[10] 7595[11]

Proud Times (USA) *G A Swinbank* 77
3 b g Proud Citizen(USA) —Laura's Pistolette (USA) (Big Pistol (USA))
1769[2] 2229[2] 2789[6] 4014[2] 4280[5]

Providanza (FR) *N Clement* 107
3 b f Okawango(USA) —Hill Tigress (IRE) (Robellino (USA))
1918a[7] (2777a) 3668a[4] 4971a[7]

Proviso *Robert Frankel* a114 112
4 b m Dansili—Binche (USA) (Woodman (USA))
2120a[5] 3012[8] 4580a[3] (5709a) *7286a[4]*

Provost *M W Easterby* a74 85
5 ch g Danehill Dancer(IRE) —Dixielake (IRE) (Lake Coniston (IRE))
(823) ◆ *885[3] 5329[14] 5886[12] 6361[14] 7855[5]*

Prowl *E A L Dunlop* 55
3 b f One Cool Cat(USA) —Go Supersonic (Zafonic (USA))
4913[5] 5717[6]

Psalmson (IRE) *Emmanuel Hughes* 17
2 b g Pyrus(USA) —Casaveha (IRE) (Persian Bold)
5274a[15]

Pseudonym (IRE) *M F Harris* a73 72
7 ch g Daylami(IRE) —Stage Struck (IRE) (Sadler's Wells (USA))
190[2] 252[3] 3346[6] (3593) (3940) 4793[6] 4890[5] 5252[6] 5346[4] 5530[2] 5903[P]

Psychic Ability (USA) *Saeed Bin Suroor* a70 85
2 b c Kingmambo(USA) —Speed Of Thought (USA) (Broad Brush (USA))
6672[6] (7121)

Psychopathicsandra (IRE) *A Berry* 35
2 ch f Reel Buddy(USA) —Waltzing Star (IRE) (Danehill (USA))
1802[8] 3332[5] 3805[7] 5066[4] 7079[11]

Ptolomeos *Thomas McLaughlin* a57 65
6 b g Kayf Tara—Lucy Tufty (Vin St Benet)
3447[6]

Public Image *Jamie Poulton* 29
3 b f Bahamian Bounty—Shouting The Odds (IRE) (Victory Note (USA))
2795[16] 4786[9]

Public Service (IRE) *B J Meehan* a74 72
2 ch g Danehill Dancer(IRE) —Sintra (IRE) (Kris)
2467[8] 3113[8] 4075[7] 5748[2] *6071[9] 6774[6]*

Puchet (ARG) *J-M Beguigne* 96
5 b h Potrillon(ARG) —Palmtin (ARG) (Cautin (ARG))
6890a[7]

Puerto De Baune (FR) *C Plisson*
2 b g April Night(FR) —Mickaela De Baune (FR) (Le Coureur (FR))
7507a[7]

Puff (IRE) *R M Beckett* a80 106
2 b f Camacho—Kelsey Rose (Most Welcome)
(3987) 5199[4] 6049[2] 6449[4] 7147[2]

Puitin *M Madgwick* a37
4 b g Red Ransom(USA) —Pagoda (FR) (Sadler's Wells (USA))
7826[12]

Pullyourfingerout (IRE) *B G Powell* 76
2 b c Indian Haven—Sandomierz (IRE) (Nordico (USA))
994[8] 1323[7] 1616[4] 2328[2] 2735[4] 3579[5] 4271[6] 4901[7] (5938) 6793[2]

Pulsion (USA) *Patrick L Biancone* a109
2 b c Include(USA) —Spring (USA) (Stravinsky (USA))
7307a[11]

Pumpkin *Sir Michael Stoute* a88 90
3 ch f Pivotal—Gallivant (Danehill (USA))
2298[2] (2862) *(3738)* ◆ 4273[2] 4500[9]

Punch Drunk *J G Given* a71 76
3 b f Beat Hollow—Bebe De Cham (Tragic Role (USA))
1470[10] *1937[3] 2685[7]* 2942[4] 4004[2] 4495[2] 5009[2] 5622[6] 5858[5] 6538[8] 7014[5]

Puncher Clynch (IRE) *J S Bolger* 86
2 b c Azamour(IRE) —Dance Troupe (Rainbow Quest (USA))
7258a[9]

Punching *C R Dore* a79 74
5 b g Kyllachy—Candescent (Machiavellian (USA))
15[8] 96[4] 235[5] (303) 326[4] 561[3] 818[3] 1060[10] *(1480)* 1775[3] 2381[5] 2852[11] 4787[8] 5073[11] 5612[7] 6028[13] 6669[5] 7223[7] (7424) 7483[3]

Punta Galera (IRE) *Paul Green* a71 66
6 br g Zafonic(USA) —Kobalt Sea (FR) (Akarad (FR))
311[11] 554[12] 1001[6] 4193[10] 5150[14]

Pure Clan (USA) *Robert E Holthus* a109 117
4 ch m Pure Prize(USA) —Gather The Clan (IRE) (General Assembly (USA))
(6510a) 7284a[2]

Pure Crystal *M G Quinlan* a53 57
3 ch f Dubai Destination(USA) —Crystal Flute (Lycius (USA))
876[8] 1724[2] 2340[5] 2866[5] 4470[10] *7049[3] 7557[5]*

Pure Heir (USA) *T D Barron* 51
3 b f Perfect Soul(IRE) —Regal Baby (USA) (Northern Baby (CAN))
3352[4] 4550[7] 5394[6] 5972[12]

Pure Land (FR) *Mme E Augonnet* a66
3 b g Rainbow Quest(USA) —Visions On Space (IRE) (Lure (USA))
4581a[6]

Purely By Chance *J Pearce* a55 64
4 b m Galileo(IRE) —Sioux Chef (Be My Chief (USA))
(7328) 7649[6] 7750[10]

Pure Nostalgia (IRE) *J Howard Johnson* 63
2 ch f Choisir(AUS) —Montmartre (IRE) (Grand Lodge (USA))
2360[4] 2784[2] 3187[9] (4101) 5303[4] 6557[4]

Pure Poetry (IRE) *R Hannon* a102 110
3 b g Tagula(IRE) —Express Logic (Air Express (IRE))
(1211) 1300[3] 1675[7] 2476[2] 2992[6] 4521[3] 5084a[7] 5447[5]

Pure Rhythm *S C Williams* a48 59
3 b f Oasis Dream—Degree (Warning)
2602[3] (2918)

Purissima (USA) *Sir Michael Stoute* 88
3 b f Fusaichi Pegasus(USA) —Willstar (USA) (Nureyev (USA))
4423[9]

Purple Gallery (IRE) *J S Moore* a57
2 b c Whipper(USA) —Daftara (IRE) (Caerleon (USA))
7571[8] 7773[7]

Purple Moon (IRE) *L M Cumani* 120
6 ch g Galileo(IRE) —Vanishing Prairie (USA) (Alysheba (USA))
772a[4] 1012a[3]

Purple Sage (IRE) *E Martins* a90 91
3 b f Danehill Dancer(IRE) —Kylemore (IRE) (Sadler's Wells (USA))
181a[3] 438a[3] 701a[7]

Pursestrings *R Charlton* a57
2 b f Red Ransom(USA) —New Assembly (IRE) (Machiavellian (USA))
7450[9] 7624[4]

Pursuit Of Glory (IRE) *David Wachman* a93 106
3 b f Fusaichi Pegasus(USA) —Sophisticat (USA) (Storm Cat (USA))
1698[8] 2644a[10]

Pursuit Of Gold *J R Best* a51 60
2 b f Pastoral Pursuits—Sheer Gold (USA) (Cutlass (USA))
1511[8] 1841[6] 2135[5] *6610[6] 6775[10]* 6905[6] *7513[11]*

Pursuit Of Purpose *G L Moore* a43 39
3 b f Dansili—Sinead (USA) (Irish River (FR))
828[7] 1198[12] *2489[11]* 3661[4] *6445[5]*

Purus (IRE) *R A Teal* a81 88
7 b g Night Shift(USA) —Pariana (USA) (Bering)
1186[2] 1288[4] 2086[2] ◆ 2565[3] 2976[10] 3523[7] 4641[8] 5188[6] 5804[8] 6790[11] *7179[7] 7586[10]*

Pusey Street Lady *J Gallagher* a81 105
5 b m Averti(IRE) —Pusey Street Girl (Gildoran)
996[2] 1582[6] 2271[2] 3388[3] 3824[5] 4330[9] 5069[5] 6089[15] 6814[10]

Push Me (IRE) *A J McCabe* a64 45
2 gr f Verglas(IRE) —Gilda Lilly (USA) (War Chant (USA))
(6122) 7056[6] *7210[2] 7722[5] 7791[4]*

Puteri (IRE) *M A Jarvis* a64 61
2 b f One Cool Cat(USA) —London Pride (USA) (Lear Fan (USA))
4055[7] 4534[3] *5165[5] 7792[4]*

Putney Bridge (USA) *Mme C Head-Maarek* 108
4 b g Mizzen Mast(USA) —Valentine Band (USA) (Dixieland Band (USA))
1658a[7] 4113a[3] 6327a[2]

Putra Laju (IRE) *J W Hills* a73 51
5 b h Trans Island—El Corazon (IRE) (Mujadil (USA))
42[3] 216[6]

Putra One (IRE) *M A Jarvis* a85 83
3 b g Danehill Dancer(IRE) —Veronica Cooper (IRE) (Kahyasi)
1257[2] 1573[3] (3538) *5649[4] 6583[3]*

Puy D'Arnac (FR) *G A Swinbank* a76 83
6 b g Acteur Francais(USA) —Chaumeil (FR) (Mad Captain)
226[4] 325[9] 1692[4] 2194[4] 2766[4] 3728[4] 4078[5] 4742[6] (5291) (5622) 6767[3] ◆ 6995[6] 7170[3]

Puzzlemaster *Jane Chapple-Hyam* a74 89
3 ch g Lomitas—Norcroft Joy (Rock Hopper)
(1130) 1992[7] ◆ 2341[6] (4471) *5315[6]* 6681[5] 6996[7]

Pycian *Mrs L Stubbs* 78
2 b g Mark Of Esteem(IRE) —Beejay (Piccolo)
(1867) 3340[3] 4086[7]

Pyro (USA) *Saeed Bin Suroor* a120
4 bb h Pulpit(USA) —Wild Vision (USA) (Wild Again (USA))
7309a[10]

Pyrrha *C F Wall* 107
3 b f Pyrus(USA) —Demeter (USA) (Diesis)
2882[3] 3746[4] (4317) (5005)

Pyrus Time (IRE) *J S Moore* a76 72
3 b g Pyrus(USA) —Spot In Time (Mtoto)
121[5] 280[3] 731[3] 1585[2] *2395[2] 2922[2] 3384[2]* 3674[3] *4789[3] 5314[4]* 5366[6] 6248[2] 6537[5] (7694)

Pytheas (USA) *M Johnston* a80 79
2 b g Seeking The Gold(USA) —Neptune's Bride (USA) (Bering)
3170[2] ◆ 3584[8] 4396[3] *5682[2]* 6763[2] 7121[3]

Qadar (IRE) *N P Littmoden* a79 75
7 b g Xaar—Iktidar (Green Desert (USA))
197[5] 442[2] 754[2] ◆ *843[5] 973[4] 1104[4]*

Qalahari (IRE) *D J Coakley* a87 92
3 b f Bahri(USA) —Daqtora (Dr Devious (IRE))
912[8] ◆ 2536[2] 3016[12] 4422[11]

Qaraaba *J L Dunlop* 82
2 b f Shamardal(USA) —Mokaraba (Unfuwain (USA))
4055[2] ◆ 5397[3] (6730)

Qaraqum (USA) *D J Coakley* a53
2 bb f Vindication(USA) —Code Of Ethics (USA) (Honour And Glory (USA))
7106[5] 7624[5]

Qedaam (IRE) *Patrick Morris* a21
3 b f Daylami(IRE) —Zafzala (IRE) (Kahyasi)
1286[10]

Qeethaara (USA) *P A Fahy* a85 86
5 gr m Aljabr(USA) —Aghsaan (USA) (Wild Again (USA))
5689a[16]

Qelaan (USA) *M P Tregoning* a68 92
3 b f Dynaformer(USA) —Irtahal (USA) (Swain (IRE))
1198[4] 1515[2] *4650[6]* (5726) (5964) 6419[2] 7148[5]

Qertaas (IRE) *F Head* 101
3 gr f Linamix(FR) —Qurrah (IRE) (Zafonic (USA))
4969a[7] 5562a[5] 7128a[11]

Qeyaada (USA) *James M Ryan* a89 82
4 b m Elusive Quality(USA) —Al Desima (Emperor Jones (USA))
7297a[13]

Quadrifolio *Paul Green* 31
3 b g Key Of Luck(USA) —Berkeley Note (IRE) (Victory Note (USA))
7126[8]

Quadrille *R Hannon* a95 102
2 b c Danehill Dancer(IRE) —Fictitious (Machiavellian (USA))
(4564) ◆ *(5664)* 6663[2]

Quaestor (IRE) *Tom Dascombe* a78 80
2 b c Antonius Pius(USA) —Lucky Oakwood (USA) (Elmaamul (USA))
2383[6] 2663[5] 3744[2] 4176[6] 5274a[10] 5749[2] 6104[7]

Quai D'Orsay *M Johnston* 102
3 ch c Sulamani(IRE) —Entente Cordiale (USA) (Affirmed (USA))
1792[2] 2275[8] (2715) ◆ 3051[8] (3618) 3874[5] ◆ 4408[9] 4767[5] 5865[5] (6412) 6662[9]

Quaker Parrot *Tom Dascombe* a80 83
2 ch f Compton Place—Little Greenbird (Ardkinglass)
1577[11] (1968) 2372[10] 3430[6] 3762[3] (3993) 4539[10] 5899[2] 6169[2] 7274[4] 7494[2] 7846[7]

Qualitas *M W Easterby* a41 57
3 b g Orpen(USA) —Kiss Me Kate (Aragon)
2070[5] 3036[13] 4174[8] 4552[12] 6831[5]

Quality Mover (USA) *D M Simcock* a57 63
2 bb f Elusive Quality(USA) —Katherine Seymour (Green Desert (USA))
4542[6] 5165[8]

Quality Road (USA) *Todd Pletcher* a125
3 b c Elusive Quality(USA) —Kobla (USA) (Strawberry Road (AUS))
6512a[2]

Quality Street *P Butler* a72 67
7 ch m Fraam—Pusey Street Girl (Gildoran)
321[9] 531[12]

Quam Celerrime *R Curtis* a76 95
4 b g Xaar—Divine Secret (Hernando (FR))
330[9]

Quanah Parker (IRE) *R M Whitaker* 94
3 b c Namid—Uncertain Affair (IRE) (Darshaan)
2270[3] 2504[2] 2934[5] 3622[9]

Quanita Pierji (FR) *E Leenders* a60 70
5 b m Lucky Dream(FR) —Yerville (FR) (Luthier)
5281a[10]

Quaroma *Jane Chapple-Hyam* a69 97
4 ch m Pivotal—Quiz Time (Efisio)
1367[4] 1880[10]

Quarrel (USA) *W J Haggas* 103
2 rg c Maria's Mon(USA) —Gender Dance (USA) (Miesque's Son (USA))
(4336) (5250) 6105[3]

Quartz Jem (IRE) *Mme Pia Brandt* 101
5 b g Sakhee(USA) —Erinys (FR) (Kendor (FR))
1552a[5] 5932a[9]

Quasi Congaree (GER) *I A Wood* a73 73
3 ch g Congaree(USA) —Queens Wild (USA) (Spectacular Bid (USA))
1837[6] 2455[2] 3036[2] 6230[4] 6635[13] 6915[3] 7028[8] 7223[5] 7254[6]

Quatz Seanium (FR) *Mme C Herisson*
2 ch c Johann Quatz(FR) —Sea Music (FR) (Bering)
7507a[0]

Que Beauty (IRE) *R C Guest* a46 26
4 b m Val Royal(FR) —Ardbess (Balla Cove)
8[3] 252[6] 301[9] 402[5]

Que Belle (IRE) *Tom Dascombe* a34
2 b f Hawk Wing(USA) —Enaya (Caerleon (USA))
7792[7]

Que Calor La Vida (FR) *N Wilson*
5 b m Lavirco(GER) —Hasta Manana (FR) (Useful (FR))
1231[8] 1681[9]

Queen America (FR) *Robert Collet* a87 100
3 b f American Post—Gandelia (FR) (Ganges (USA))
1208a[5] 1918a[10]

Queen Eleanor *J H M Gosden* a81 75
3 b f Cape Cross(IRE) —Rainbow Queen (Rainbow Quest (USA))
1605[3] 3100[2] 3456[3] (4085) 5009[9]

Queen Excalibur *B J Llewellyn* a21 61
10 ch m Sabrehill(USA) —Blue Room (Gorytus (USA))
4263[10]

Queen Margot (FR) *X Puleo* 59
5 b m Muhtathir—Tora Tune (FR) (Green Tune (USA))
5464a[6]

Queen Martha (USA) *M A Magnusson* a64 84
3 b f Rahy(USA) —Cryptoqueen (USA) (Cryptoclearance (USA))
890[6] 1406[8] (1844) (2662) 3315[6]

Queen Of Dobbin (IRE) *Lee Smyth* a52 28
3 b f King Charlemagne(USA) —Tajikistan (IRE) (Among Men (USA))
7397[8] 7555[11]

Queen Of Hearts (USA) *James Jerkens* 104
4 ch m Thunder Gulch(USA) —Betrayer (ARG) (Fain (ARG))
6510a[3]

Queen Of Pentacles (IRE) *J Noseda* a81 103
3 b f Selkirk(USA) —Maid To Perfection (Sadler's Wells (USA))
2074[4] (3025) 4566[4] 6003[4] ◆ 6813[4] (7291)

Queen Of Thebes (IRE) *G L Moore* a63 79
3 b f Bahri(USA) —Sopran Marida (IRE) (Darshaan)
2209[11] 2562[7] 3387[5] 3803[6] 5581[6] 5813[9] 6439[7]

Queen Of Troy (IRE) *A P O'Brien* a86 93
2 b f Storm Cat(USA) —Warrior Queen (USA) (Quiet American (USA))
5895a[6] 6316a[4]

Queen Of Wands *J L Dunlop* 54
2 b f Sakhee(USA) —Maid To Treasure (IRE) (Rainbow Quest (USA))
4542[10] 5498[9]

Queen Sally (IRE) *Tom Dascombe* a56 72
3 b f Key Of Luck(USA) —Crystal Blue (IRE) (Bluebird (USA))
4266[3] 5007[6] 5991[9] 6799[13]

Queen Sensazione (IRE) *B Grizzetti* 94
3 b f King Charlemagne(USA) —Sensazione (Cadeaux Genereux)
2310a[12] 3186a[6]

Queen's Envoy *L M Cumani* a69 55
2 b f King's Best(USA) —Allied Cause (Giant's Causeway (USA))
6567[6] 7135[3]

Queens Flight *Tom Dascombe* a57 44
3 b f King's Best(USA) —Birdie (Alhaarth (IRE))
4505[5] 5316[11] 6340[8]

Queens Forester *P F I Cole* 35
3 b f Needwood Blade—Bonsai (IRE) (Woodman (USA))
2652[7]

Queen's Grace *H Morrison* 102
2 ch f Bahamian Bounty—Palace Affair (Pursuit Of Love)
4564[8] (5021) ◆ 5606[3] (7147)

Queen's Hawk *D J Coakley* 72
2 ch c Hawk Wing(USA) —Queen Of Africa (USA) (Peintre Celebre (USA))
1577[8] (2324) 3138[8] 3794[5] 4195[7] 4758[8] 5715[6] 6367[6] 6963[6]

Queen Spumante (JPN) *S Kojima* 115
5 b m Jungle Pocket(JPN) —Sembon Zakura (JPN) (Sakura Yutaka O (JPN))
7747a[10]

Que Je T'Aime *C Ferland* 87
2 b f Dr Fong(USA) —Queen Of Fairies (IRE) (Fairy King (USA))
5739a[4]

Quella *J H M Gosden* a33 39
3 ch f Falbrav(IRE) —Qirmazi (USA) (Riverman (USA))
849[10] 1092[8]

Quentindemontargis (FR) *Mme C Madamet*
2 b c Enrique—Samarcande (FR) (Thatching)
5014a[0]

Querari (GER) *A Wohler* 109
3 b c Oasis Dream—Quetena (GER) (Acatenango (GER))
1395a[6] 3416a[6] 4129a[2] 4582a[2] (6152a)

Querido (GER) *M Bradstock* 57
5 b g Acatenango(GER) —Quest Of Fire (FR) (Rainbow Quest (USA))
6005[13] 7174[9]

Quest For Success (IRE) *R A Fahey* a85 104
4 b g Noverre(USA) —Divine Pursuit (Kris)
1124[5] (1365) 1861[20] 2405[7] 2927[2] (4037) 6089[6] 6678[6] 6949[4] (7015)

Quetsche (USA) *J-C Rouget* a91 101
3 b f Gone West(USA) —Que Belle (CAN) (Seattle Dancer (USA))
(2754a) 5058a[7]

Quick Gourmet *G A Swinbank* 61
3 b f Lend A Hand—Rhiann (Anshan)
2030[6] 2719[5] 3108[6] 4531[3] 4894[3] 5158[4] 6766[8]

Quick Off The Mark *J G Given* a71 53
4 b m Dr Fong(USA) —Equity Princess (Warning)
176[2] 354[2] 688[4] 897[6] 2237[7] 2859[9] 3717[3] 3862[4] 4667[13] 4861[3] 5103[8]

Quick Reaction *R Hannon* 77
2 b g Elusive Quality(USA) —Arutua (USA) (Riverman (USA))
5542[7] 5793[5] 6393[8]

Quick Release (IRE) *D M Simcock* a79 78
4 b h Red Ransom(USA) —Set The Mood (USA) (Dixie Brass (USA))
3301[5] 3736[14] 5095[4] 5640[6] 6460[2] 6973[5] 7523[4] 7603[4] (7812)

Quicksand (SAF) *M F De Kock* a80
5 ch h Announce(SAF) —Secret Sands (SAF) (Secret Prospector (USA))
261a[3] 414a[6] 639a[3]

Quick Single (USA) *P S McEntee* a69 66
3 bb g Doneraile Court(USA) —Summer Strike (USA) (Smart Strike (CAN))
127[5] 200[3] 268[4] 498[3] (552) (593) 709[6] 1180[5] 1839[16] 2004[6] 2300[7] 2761[4] 3299[4] 3783[7] 3989[10] 4059[9] 4237[4] 5581[10] 6701[9] 7022[12] 7198[4] 7588[10]

Quicks The Word *T A K Cuthbert* a28 65
9 b g Sri Pekan(USA) —Fast Tempo (IRE) (Statoblest)
2316[8] 2529[16] 3852[9] 5443[14]

Quick Way (FR) *Mme N Madamet*
3 ch c Gold Away(IRE) —Tabletiere (FR) (Kaldounevees (FR))
2293a[0]

Quick Wit *Saeed Bin Suroor* a70 80
2 b c Oasis Dream—Roo (Rudimentary (USA))
6781[5] 6990[2] ◆ (7146) ◆

Quiet *R Charlton* 94
2 ch f Observatory(USA) —Quandary (USA) (Blushing Groom (FR))
(5547) 5825[7]

Quiet Elegance *E J Alston* 92
4 b m Fantastic Light(USA) —Imperial Bailiwick (IRE) (Imperial Frontier (USA))
996[11] 1880[8] 2197[9] 2941[10] 4096[3] 4353[10] 6050[19]

Quiet Mountain (IRE) *Ollie Pears* a58
4 ch g Monashee Mountain(USA) —Shalstayholy (IRE) (Shalford (IRE))
1476[7] 7459[6] 7753[5] ◆

Quijano (GER) *P Schiergen* 119
7 ch g Acatenango(GER) —Quila (IRE) (Unfuwain (USA))
772a[2] 1012a[6] (2955a) 6873a[P]

Quilboquet (BRZ) *L Reuterskiold Jr* a86 99
6 br h Jules(USA) —Greystoke (BRZ) (Tokatee (USA))
2587a[6] 5302a[5] 5933a[8]

Quillaja (GER) *W Hickst* 95
3 b f Tiger Hill(IRE) —Qelle Amie (CAN) (Beau Genius (CAN))
3604a[4] 4583a[11]

Quillin *E J O'Neill* 69
2 b c Orpen(USA) —Gaily Grecian (IRE) (Ela-Mana-Mou)
5850a[4] 6322a[3] 6751a[7]

Quince (IRE) *J Pearce* a86 84
6 b g Fruits Of Love(USA) —Where's Charlotte (Sure Blade (USA))
237[2] 393[2] 456[4] 584[2] (712) 1175[6] 1615[3] 2150[7] 3461[7] 5186[3] 5694[7] 5936[2] 6218[10] 6612[2] 7357[2] 7578[5] 7777[8]

Quinmaster (USA) *M Halford* a103 99
7 gr g Linamix(FR) —Sherkiya (IRE) (Goldneyev (USA))
2289a[12] 2647a[2] 3014[15] 5080a[4]

Quinner (IRE) *P D Evans* a17 62
2 ch c Arakan(USA) —Quintellina (Robellino (USA))
4265[6] 4568[3] 4825[12] 5358[10] 6343[11]

Quinsman *J S Moore* a72 69
3 b c Singspiel(IRE) —Penny Cross (Efisio)
1355[9] 2496[4] 2795[5] 3309[6] 3868[6] 4691[5] 6248[3] (6440) 7665[3] (7831)

Quintalina (FR) *C Boutin* 85
2 b f Okawango(USA) —Ti Francaise (FR) (Marignan (USA))
3967a[6]

Quiquillo (USA) *P D Evans* a62 70
3 ch f Cape Canaveral(USA) —Only Seventeen (USA) (Exploit (USA))
2789[4] 3456[4] 4004[5] (4937) 6455[10] 6798[5]

Quirina *R M Beckett* a89 92
4 b m Red Ransom(USA) —Qirmazi (USA) (Riverman (USA))
2384[3] 2891[5] 3509[7]

Quiron (IRE) *Carmen Bocskai* a67 107
8 b g Desert King(IRE) —Quebra (GER) (Surumu (GER))
653a[8]

Quite A Fella (USA) *Andrew Turnell* a69
4 b g Swain(IRE) —Magnificent Star (USA) (Silver Hawk (USA))
(279) 726[P]

Quite Something *A M Balding* 64
2 b f Footstepsinthesand—Quite Elusive (USA) (Elusive Quality (USA))
6616[4]

Quite Sparky *T P Tate* 72
2 b g Lucky Story(USA) —Imperialistic (IRE) (Imperial Ballet (IRE))
4847[6] 5669[2]

Quitit (IRE) *Mrs S A Watt* a61 73
4 b g Kalanisi(IRE) —Wattrey (Royal Academy (USA))
3609[5]

Quiza Quiza Quiza *L Riccardi* 102
3 b f Golden Snake(USA) —Quiz Chow (ITY) (Pelder (IRE))
2310a[3] 3668a[9] 7046a[8]

Quo Dubai (GER) *Mario Hofer* 105
3 b c Dubai Destination(USA) —Quest Of Fire (FR) (Rainbow Quest (USA))
1718a[6] 2560a[4] 3670a[5]

Raaeidd (IRE) *M A Jarvis* a78 86
3 b c King's Best(USA) —Bahr (Generous (IRE))
1992[3] ◆ 3644[5] 4102[4] 4502[4] 5511[8]

Rabbit Fighter (IRE) *D Shaw* a71 78
5 ch g Observatory(USA) —Furnish (Green Desert (USA))
14[14] 1468[5] (1528) 1737[12] 6123[12] 6437[12] 6764[12] 6825[5]

Rabeera *A M Balding* 59
4 b m Beat Hollow—Gai Bulga (Kris)
1415[8]

Raccoon (IRE) *Mrs R A Carr* 81
9 b g Raphane(USA) —Kunucu (IRE) (Bluebird (USA))
(1360) 1768[3] 2451[3] (2657) 2840[3] ◆ 3109[3] 3483[2] 3681[4] 4012[2] 4036[2] (4753) (4877) 5293[7] 5767[9]

Racecar Rhapsody (USA) *H J Brown* a102
4 b h Tale Of The Cat(USA) —Reflect The Music (USA) (A.P. Indy (USA))
771a[11]

Racer Forever (USA) *J H M Gosden* a111 112
6 b g Rahy(USA) —Ras Shaikh (USA) (Sheikh Albadou)
1513[5] 3091[5] 3818[5] 4297[8] 5249[10]

Rachel Alexandra (USA) *Steven Asmussen* a129
3 b f Medaglia D'Oro(USA) —Lotta Kim (USA) (Roar (USA))
(1763a) (2098a)

Rachmaninov (FR) *F Doumen* 91
3 gr c Verglas(IRE) —Restless Rixa (FR) (Linamix (FR))
1207a[7]

Racing Along (FR) *C Boillot*
3 b g Oliviero(FR) —Racing Pearl (Dancing Spree (USA))
6682a[0]

Racinger (FR) *F Head* 115
6 b h Spectrum(IRE) —Dibenoise (FR) (Kendor (FR))
1029a[3] 1658a[4] (5496a) 6505a[9] 7208a[3]

Racing Hero (IRE) *J Noseda* a69 91
3 b g Montjeu(IRE) —Aim For The Top (USA) (Irish River (FR))
2211[3] ◆ (2943) 3461[5] 6583[7] (7020) 7101[2]

Racing To Win (AUS) *John O'Shea* 122
7 gr g Encosta De Lago(AUS) —Surrealist (AUS) (Kenny's Best Pal (AUS))
7196a[4] 7746a[13]

Racketeer (IRE) *J H M Gosden* a86 102
3 b c Cape Cross(IRE) —Flirtation (Pursuit Of Love)
(1484) 2411[5]

Racy *Sir Michael Stoute* a85 86
2 b c Medicean—Soar (Danzero (AUS))
5829[2] ◆ (6231) ◆ 7063[3]

Raddy 'Ell Pauline (IRE) *K A Ryan* a81 85
2 ch f Dubawi(IRE) —Run For Me (IRE) (Danehill (USA))
2699[7] (3271) 3748[7] 4752[2] 5199[9] 5658[10]

Radhakunda *C Laffon-Parias* 99
4 b m Galileo(IRE) —Nawasib (IRE) (Warning)
6715a[8]

Radiator Rooney (IRE) *Patrick Morris* a68 60
6 br g Elnadim(USA) —Queen Of The May (IRE) (Nicolotte)
590[6] 1310[7] 1695[8] 1890[4] 2145[5] 2224[3] 2564[9] 7023[U] 7224[10] 7484[9] 7595[3] ◆ 7657[3] 7774[3] 7835[7] 7889[5]

Radio City *R M Beckett* a72 78
2 b g Intikhab(USA) —Red Shareef (Marju (IRE))
1726[4] 2201[3] 3767[6] 4208[3] (4639) 5033[6] (5769) 6068[6] 6541[3]

Radiohead *B J Meehan* a107 117
2 ch c Johannesburg(USA) —Security Interest (USA) (Belong To Me (USA))
1700[2] ◆ (2121) (3046) ◆ 5233[3] ◆ 6105[4] 6450[2] 7307a[7]

Radio Wave *J H M Gosden* 78
2 ch f Dalakhani(IRE) —Tuning (Rainbow Quest (USA))
6920[3] ◆

Radsky *J G Portman* 43
2 ch c Where Or When(IRE) —Radiant Sky (IRE) (Spectrum (IRE))
4986[11] 5319[7] 6331[7]

Rafaan (USA) *M Johnston* 84
3 bb g Gulch(USA) —Reem Al Barari (USA) (Storm Cat (USA))
(1127) ◆ 1489[11] 2935[11]

Rafale Bere (FR) *D Prod'Homme* a80 79
4 gr m Verglas(IRE) —Fitness Queen (USA) (Gilded Time (USA))
7821a[5]

Raffanetti (IRE) *T D Barron* 16
3 b g Raphane(USA) —Proud Boast (Komaite (USA))
2439[6] 3003[8]

Rafiki (IRE) *W R Swinburn* a17
2 b g Kheleyf(USA) —Jemalina (USA) (Trempolino (USA))
6802[9]

Rafiqa (IRE) *C F Wall* 96
3 b f Mujahid(USA) —Shamara (IRE) (Spectrum (IRE))
3163[3] 3868[2] ◆ 5070[5] 6239[4]

Rafta (IRE) *T T Clement* 81
3 b f Atraf—First Kiss (GER) (Night Shift (USA))
2298[7] (3281) (4061) (4198) (4281) 4814[2] 5090[RR] 5471[RR]

Ragamuffin Man (IRE) *W J Knight* a80 83
4 gr g Dalakhani(IRE) —Chamela Bay (IRE) (Sadler's Wells (USA))
4793[4] 5410[2] 6115[5] (6899)

Ragdollianna *Norma Twomey* a58 87
5 b m Kayf Tara—Jupiters Princess (Jupiter Island)
2931[15] 3532[5] 7201[5]

Ragetti (IRE) *J Howard Johnson* 64
2 b f Hawk Wing(USA) —Renada (Sinndar (IRE))
5674[4]

Raggle Taggle (IRE) *R M Beckett* a64 97
3 b f Tagula(IRE) —Jesting (Muhtarram (USA))
1582[15] (3360) 4096[10] 5902[9] 6949[11]

Ragheed (USA) *E Charpy* a46 112
5 ch h Rahy(USA) —Highbury (USA) (Seattle Slew (USA))
265a[9] (335a) 615a[2] 702a[11]

Ragsta (IRE) *C A Dwyer* a61 67
2 b f Key Of Luck(USA) —Rag Top (IRE) (Barathea (IRE))
2121[2] 2490[4] (2978) 3978[7] 5543[2] 5938[8] 6228[6] 6491[8] 6609[11] 6923[4] 7098[7]

Ragtimeband (IRE) *S Onofrio* 72
3 b c Danetime(IRE) —True Freedom (FR) (Freedom Cry)
2114a[8]

Rahaala (IRE) *Sir Michael Stoute* a65
2 b f Indian Ridge—Mythie (FR) (Octagonal (NZ))
5752[5]

Rahya Cass (IRE) *T Stack* a90 93
2 b f Rahy(USA) —Its On The Air (IRE) (King's Theatre (IRE))
5452a[4] 5895a[4]

Raimond Ridge (IRE) *J Jay* a76 78
3 bb g Namid—Jinsiyah (USA) (Housebuster (USA))
75[4] (200) 348[2] (498) 593[2] (1032) 1414[3] 1686[2] 1814[6] 2336[6] 2970[4] 3193[4] 3676[3] 3989[4] 4695[2] 4990[3] 5245[3] 5383[2] 5506[7] 5877[3] 5968[6] 6387[6] 6791[6] 7028[4] 7808 [6]

Rain And Shade *E W Tuer* a76 52
5 ch g Rainbow Quest(USA) —Coretta (IRE) (Caerleon (USA))
1279[13] 1454[8] 2068[16]

Rainbow Above You (IRE) *Noel Lawlor* a51
3 b f Mujadil(USA) —Kibarague (Barathea (IRE))
7358[4] 7371[11]

Rainbow Bay *Miss Tracy Waggott* a70 59
6 b g Komaite(USA) —Bollin Victoria (Jalmood (USA))
367[8] 1558[14] 1924[8] 2628[8] 3972[5] 4191[5] 6160[9] 6216[4] 6379[6]

Rainbow Dancing *Mlle H Van Zuylen* 109
4 b m Rainbow Quest(USA) —Danceabout (Shareef Dancer (USA))
1597a[7] 2428a[5] 4113a[6] 6658a[4] 7128a[3] 7347a[6]

Rainbow Desert (USA) *Saeed Bin Suroor* 90
3 bb f Dynaformer(USA) —Tuscoga (USA) (Theatrical (IRE))
(6741) 7291[8]

Rainbow Mirage (IRE) *E S McMahon* a92 92
5 b g Spectrum(IRE) —Embers Of Fame (IRE) (Sadler's Wells (USA))
834[2] 5221[4] 5375[3]

Rainbow Muhtatir (FR) *M Rolland* 87
4 b m Muhtathir—Village Rainbow (FR) (Village Star (FR))
7569a[0]

Rainbow Peak (IRE) *M A Jarvis* a92 110
3 b g Hernando(FR) —Celtic Fling (Lion Cavern (USA))
(1729) ◆ (6239) (7035)

Rainbow Six *M Botti* a54
2 b g Tiger Hill(IRE) —Birthday Suit (IRE) (Daylami (IRE))
7277[8] 7491[4]

Rainbow View (USA) *J H M Gosden* a105 117
3 b f Dynaformer(USA) —No Matter What (USA) (Nureyev (USA))
1698[5] 2672[4] 3088[3] 3749[4] 4522[2] (5686a) 6872a[2] 7286a[5]

Rainbow Zest *W Storey* 67
6 b g Rainbow Quest(USA) —Original (Caerleon (USA))
1125^{11} 1332^{12} 4351^{9} 4588^{13} 5441^{18} 6817^{9}

Rain Delayed (IRE) *G M Lyons* a99 108
3 b g Oasis Dream—Forever Phoenix (Shareef Dancer (USA))
2928^{3} 5203^{2} 7007a^{2}

Raine's Cross *P Winkworth* 95
2 b c Cape Cross(IRE) —Branston Jewel (IRE) (Prince Sabo)
(1577) ◆ 2408^{3} ◆ 2993^{12} 3865^{4} 4488^{3} 5214^{4} (5603) 6472^{2}

Raine Supreme *E S McMahon* a42 52
2 b f Mind Games—Supreme Angel (Beveled (USA))
2604^{6} 3263^{7} 4973^{3} 5543^{6} 7749^{7}

Rainfall Shadow (IRE) *J-C Rouget* 59
2 b c Night Shift(USA) —Marie Rheinberg (GER) (Surako (GER))
7346a^{7}

Rainiers Girl *R A Teal* a46
3 b f Tobougg(IRE) —Premier Night (Old Vic)
4789^{8} 5314^{7} 7228^{5} 7653^{5}

Rain In The Course *M R Channon* 13
2 b f Royal Applause—Numanthia (IRE) (Barathea (IRE))
5498^{14} 5980^{13}

Rain Is Luck (FR) *F Cohen* 56
3 ch g Rifapour(IRE) —Sainte Margaux (FR) (Saint Estephe (FR))
2293a^{0}

Rain On The Wind (IRE) *S C Williams* a63
2 b g Bahamian Bounty—Mix Me Up (FR) (Linamix (FR))
5311^{8} 5571^{7} 6207^{4}

Rainsborough *S Curran* a66 58
2 b g Trans Island—Greeba (Fairy King (USA))
2676^{5} 3420^{7} (3626) 4271^{9} 5515^{10} 5811^{2} 6173^{3} 6228^{12} 6721^{10} 7055^{8} 7334^{2} 7482^{2} 7706^{5} 7824^{10}

Rain Stops Play (IRE) *N G Richards* a57 58
7 b g Desert Prince(IRE) —Pinta (IRE) (Ahonoora)
254^{5} 2390^{2} 3092^{4} 4588^{4} 5438^{4} 6184^{11} 6818^{9}

Rainy Night *R Hollinshead* a66 70
3 b g Kyllachy—Rainy Day Song (Persian Bold)
1840^{6} 2160^{2} ◆ 2602^{4} 3338^{5} 5130^{7} 5422^{2} 5717^{4} (5881) ◆ 6825^{4}

Raise All In (IRE) *N Wilson* a64 65
3 b f Exceed And Excel(AUS) —Inforapenny (Deploy)
1628^{10} 2361^{11}

Raise A Mind (IRE) *H-A Pantall* 78
3 gr f Zamindar(USA) —Vickarita (USA) (Lyphard (USA))
3417a^{5}

Raise Your Heart (IRE) *Ms Joanna Morgan* 109
6 b g Raise A Grand(IRE) —Gobolino (Don)
5490a^{2}

Rajamand (FR) *Miss E C Lavelle* a84 82
3 gr g Linamix(FR) —Ridafa (IRE) (Darshaan)
7323^{5} 7612^{4}

Rajeh (IRE) *J L Spearing* 97
6 b g Key Of Luck(USA) —Saramacca (IRE) (Kahyasi)
1458^{3} 1709^{3} 2994^{11} 3826^{5} 4408^{6}

Rajik (IRE) *C F Swan* 92
4 b g Kalanisi(IRE) —Ridaiyma (IRE) (Kahyasi)
4510a^{2}

Rajsaman (FR) *A De Royer-Dupre* a81 99
2 gr c Linamix(FR) —Rose Quartz (Lammtarra (USA))
(6080a) 6656a^{4}

Ra Junior (USA) *B J Meehan* a61 99
3 b g Rahy(USA) —Fantasia Girl (IRE) (Caerleon (USA))
1009a^{9} 3873^{17} 4455^{7} 5137^{15} 6795^{10}

Rakaan (IRE) *B J Meehan* a78 98
2 ch g Bahamian Bounty—Petite Spectre (Spectrum (IRE))
2033^{2} 2477^{2} 2993^{3} 4487^{8} 5029^{2} 5368^{2} 5795^{17} (6328)

Rakhapura (IRE) *P R Webber* a64 50
2 b c Arakan(USA) —Indistinto (Groom Dancer (USA))
5934^{10} 6772^{5} 7064^{6}

Rakhine (IRE) *P F I Cole* a40 60
2 b g Arakan(USA) —Amorous Pursuits (Pursuit Of Love)
2037^{5} 2649^{4} 2896^{8} 3547^{6} (6034) 6721^{13}

Raleigh Quay (IRE) *Micky Hammond* 70
2 b c Bachelor Duke(USA) —Speedbird (USA) (Sky Classic (CAN))
3292^{6} 3613^{6} 4659^{2} (5290) 6895^{10}

Ramamara (IRE) *P D Evans* a80 80
2 ch f Trans Island—Kaskazi (Dancing Brave (USA))
1802^{6} ◆ (4747) 5241^{2} (5445) 5580^{3} 5797^{14} 6275^{3} 6841^{9} 7063^{6} 7410^{3} 7435^{3} 7552^{4} 7625^{3} 7713^{2} 7805^{4} 7824^{9}

Ramayana (IRE) *M R Channon* a44 38
2 b f Arakan(USA) —Dance Land (IRE) (Nordance (USA))
6055^{10} 6245^{8} 6582^{9} 7391^{11}

Ramblin Bob *W J Musson* a54 41
4 b g Piccolo—Bijan (IRE) (Mukaddamah (USA))
587^{12} (727) 854^{9} 1076^{10} 2180^{10} 3269^{6} 3401^{10}

Rambling Dancer (IRE) *Mrs Valerie Keatley* a65 53
5 b g Imperial Ballet(IRE) —Wayfarer's Inn (IRE) (Lucky Guest)
194^{4} 7803^{3}

Rambling Light *A M Balding* a84 79
5 b g Fantastic Light(USA) —Rambler (Selkirk (USA))
2193^{4} 2883^{7}

Rambling Rosie (IRE) *C Drew* a1 35
3 b f Rambling Bear—La Noisette (Rock Hopper)
1327^{15} 1729^{13} 2683^{12} 3632^{4}

Ramona Chase *M J Attwater* a98 102
4 b g High Chaparral(IRE) —Audacieuse (Rainbow Quest (USA))
1216^{4} 1460^{14} 1673^{7} 2671^{6} 3586^{5} 3840^{10} 5510^{3} 5915^{7}

Ramora (USA) *H R A Cecil* a71 77
3 br f Monsun(GER) —Madame Cerito (USA) (Diesis)
2051^{3} 3250^{2} 5061^{3} 6287^{2} 6671^{2} 6975^{13}

Rampant Ronnie (USA) *Mrs A M Thorpe* a53 60
4 b g Honor Glide(USA) —Jalfrezi (Jalmood (USA))
186^{10} 353^{11} 565^{4} 5179^{14}

Ramvaswani (IRE) *N B King* a56 41
6 b g Spectrum(IRE) —Caesarea (GER) (Generous (IRE))
377^{2} 567^{10} 627^{4}

Randama Bay (IRE) *I A Wood* a81 70
4 bb g Frenchmans Bay(FR) —Randama (Akarad (FR))
17^{2} 195^{4} 282^{3} 3301^{6} 3736^{9} 4321^{8} 4563^{6} 4740^{4} 5962^{2} 6288^{6}

Randonneur (USA) *E Lellouche* a96 96
3 b c Tale Of The Cat(USA) —Rolly Polly (IRE) (Mukaddamah (USA))
4685a^{7}

Rangefinder *Jane Chapple-Hyam* 95
5 gr h Linamix(FR) —Risen Raven (USA) (Risen Star (USA))
1850^{3} ◆ 2242^{7} 4003^{3} 4815^{2} (5671) 6662^{11} 7293^{15}

Rangirangdoo (NZ) *Chris Waller* 114
5 b g Pentire—She Wishes (NZ) (Kenfair (NZ))
7196a^{7}

Rank Bajin *E J Alston* 32
2 b f Red Ransom(USA) —Sharp As A Tack (IRE) (Zafonic (USA))
2819^{7}

Rann Na Cille (IRE) *P T Midgley* a67 66
5 br m Agnes World(USA) —Omanah (USA) (Kayrawan (USA))
896^{4} 1038^{9}

Rannoch Rose (IRE) *J L Spearing* a47 44
3 b f Court Cave(IRE) —Lady Semillon (IRE) (Semillon)
570^{8} 670^{2} 779^{8} 1848^{5} 2635^{9}

Ransom Demand *P Chevillard* 66
3 b g Red Ransom(USA) —Fine And Mellow (FR) (Lando (GER))
6682a^{0}

Ransomed Bride *D K Weld* a92 77
4 b m Cape Cross(IRE) —Rapid Ransom (USA) (Red Ransom (USA))
7300a^{2}

Ransom Hope *P Bary* 95
4 b h Red Ransom(USA) —Field Of Hope (IRE) (Selkirk (USA))
3045a^{4}

Ransom Note *B W Hills* 77
2 b c Red Ransom(USA) —Zacheta (Polish Precedent (USA))
3750^{11} (5251) 5762^{7} (6693)

Rapanui Belle *G L Moore* a51 47
3 b f Compton Place—Belle Ile (USA) (Diesis)
827^{5} 889^{7} 1157^{2} 1529^{8} 1985^{10} 2740^{4} 3246^{9} 4155^{3} 5125^{9} 5633^{10} 5881^{3} 6206^{4} 6581^{P}

Raphaelus (FR) *C Laffon-Parias* 88
2 b c Whipper(USA) —Eximius (Atticus (USA))
6080a^{5}

Rapid City *G L Moore* a72 76
6 b g Dansili—West Dakota (USA) (Gone West (USA))
29^{6} (187) 302^{6} 500^{3} 588^{3} 712^{4} (825) 981^{2} (1538) 1785^{12} 7776^{5}

Rapid Desire (IRE) *J R Weymes* 53
3 b f Statue Of Liberty(USA) —Whistfilly (First Trump)
2723^{3} 4519^{10} 4838^{11} 5554^{5} 6767^{11} 7084^{13}

Rapid Flow *J W Unett* a48 22
7 b g Fasliyev(USA) —Fleet River (USA) (Riverman (USA))
62^{8} 1935^{5} 3304^{10}

Rapid Light *E A L Dunlop* a66
3 ch f Tobougg(IRE) —La Coqueta (GER) (Kris)
2710^{12}

Rapid Water *A M Balding* 86
3 b g Anabaa(USA) —Lochsong (Song)
(1704) ◆ 2148^{5} 3219^{5} (4338) ◆ 4990^{4}

Raptor (GER) *A P Jarvis* a90 106
6 b g Auenadler(GER) —Royal Cat (Royal Academy (USA))
783^{11} 995^{14} 2197^{3} 2939^{3} 3312^{7} 5363^{11}

Raqeeb (USA) *Sir Michael Stoute* a38
2 b c Seeking The Gold(USA) —Sayedah (IRE) (Darshaan)
7390^{7}

Raquel White *J L Flint* a70 64
5 b m Robellino(USA) —Spinella (Teenoso (USA))
(40) 368^{6} ◆

Rare Art *S A Callaghan* a69 74
3 b c Kyllachy—Succumb (Pursuit Of Love)
1196^{3} ◆ 1567^{5} 3738^{8}

Rare Bet *W G M Turner* 40
3 b f Bertolini(USA) —Rare Old Times (IRE) (Inzar (USA))
1956^{8} 5181^{5} 5716^{13}

Rare Coincidence *R F Fisher* a68 68
8 ch g Atraf—Green Seed (IRE) (Lead On Time (USA))
(1154) 1242^{3} 1439^{9} 3291^{6} 4862^{7} 6767^{13} 7490^{5} 7594^{9} 7751^{11}

Rare Malt (IRE) *Miss Amy Weaver* a78 69
2 b f Intikhab(USA) —A'Bunadh (USA) (Diesis)
4542^{4} 5165^{2} 5643^{2}

Rare Ransom *D K Weld* 96
3 b f Oasis Dream—Rapid Ransom (USA) (Red Ransom (USA))
2304a^{4} 6298a^{8}

Rare Ruby (IRE) *Jennie Candlish* 73
5 b m Dilshaan—Ruby Setting (Gorytus (USA))
2163^{2} (2854) (3788) 5068^{5} 5530^{6} 5961^{3} 7084^{7}

Rare Virtue (USA) *H R A Cecil* 30
3 b f Empire Maker(USA) —Heat Haze (Green Desert (USA))
1329^{11}

Rasaman (IRE) *J S Goldie* a86 91
5 b g Namid—Rasana (Royal Academy (USA))
1334^{2} (2095) 2363^{6} 2814^{4} 3001^{10} 3372^{4} 3877^{11} 4192^{3} (4621) 5247^{10} 5767^{2} 5799^{6} 6050^{12} (6279) 6647^{13}

Rascal In The Mix (USA) *R M Whitaker* a56 50
3 rg f Tapit(USA) —Ready Cat (USA) (Storm Cat (USA))
2574^{3} 3175^{6} 4354^{7} 5982^{12} 6831^{2} 7197^{11}

Rascasse *Bruce Hellier* 46
4 b g Where Or When(IRE) —Sure Flyer (IRE) (Sure Blade (USA))
1057^{11} 1693^{7} 2527^{8} 2969^{7}

Rashaad (USA) *B W Hills* 81
2 b c Smart Strike(CAN) —Martinique (USA) (Pleasant Colony (USA))
(6991) ◆

Rash Judgement *W S Kittow* 94
4 b g Mark Of Esteem(IRE) —Let Alone (Warning)
(1197) 1668^{2} 2474^{3} 5424^{9} 6050^{17} 6694^{9}

Raslan *D E Pipe* 87
6 b g Lomitas—Rosia (IRE) (Mr Prospector (USA))
5903^{3} ◆ 6851^{27}

Rasmy *M P Tregoning* 85
2 b c Red Ransom(USA) —Shadow Dancing (Unfuwain (USA))
6109^{5} (6930)

Rasselas (IRE) *B W Hills* 75
2 b g Danehill Dancer(IRE) —Regal Darcey (IRE) (Darshaan)
3750^{5} 4314^{4} 6478^{9} 6810^{9}

Rathbawn Girl (IRE) *Miss J Feilden* a58 43
2 br f Alamshar(IRE) —Rathbawn Realm (Doulab (USA))
6563^{8} 7736^{4} 7864^{5}

Rathlin Light (USA) *W R Swinburn* a65 70
3 bb f Grand Slam(USA) —Baltic Sea (CAN) (Danzig (USA))
1077^{2} 1617^{2} (2492) 3145^{7}

Rathmolyon *D Haydn Jones* a58 62
4 ch m Bahamian Bounty—Feather Circle (IRE) (Indian Ridge)
1787^{15} 3677^{11} 5345^{13} 5629^{7} 6329^{9}

Rattan (USA) *Rae Guest* a96 93
4 ch h Royal Anthem(USA) —Rouwaki (USA) (Miswaki (USA))
1170^{8} 2197^{2} ◆ 2597^{2} 5522^{13}

Raucous (GER) *Mrs R A Carr* a73 75
6 b g Zinaad—Roseola (GER) (Acatenango (GER))
822^{4} (1099) 1230^{9} (1557) 1765^{4}

Ravenel (GER) *R Rohne* a80 99
3 b f Touch Down(GER) —Resafe (FR) (Poliglote)
1240a^{6} (6717a)

Ravenfield (IRE) *D H Brown* 59
2 b c Xaar—Rubyanne (IRE) (Fasliyev (USA))
5977^{6}

Ravens Rose *J G Portman* a62
2 b f Bold Edge—Marjeune (Marju (IRE))
3248^{13} (6441)

Ravi River (IRE) *P D Evans* a85 58
5 ch g Barathea(IRE) —Echo River (USA) (Irish River (FR))
106^{2} (576) (671) 834^{7} 1065^{2} 4870^{5} 6072^{6} (6630) 7252^{5} 7437^{7} 7596^{3} 7801^{6} 7883^{4}

Rawaabet (IRE) *R Hollinshead* a48 52
7 b g Bahhare(USA) —Haddeyah (USA) (Dayjur (USA))
3233^{4} 3974^{9} 4021^{7}

Rawaaj *Sir Michael Stoute* a61 62
3 ro g Linamix(FR) —Inaaq (Lammtarra (USA))
6975^{10}

Rawdon (IRE) *Miss Gay Kelleway* a81 74
8 b g Singspiel(IRE) —Rebecca Sharp (Machiavellian (USA))
172^{7} 302^{2} (423) 517^{2} 660^{9} 795^{2} 894^{2} 1175^{7} 1478^{2} 1815^{8} 2129^{3} 2379^{4} 2708^{5} 3244^{5}

Rawnaq (IRE) *M Johnston* 61
2 b c Azamour(IRE) —Sharemata (IRE) (Doyoun)
5801^{4}

Ray Diamond *M Madgwick* a52 52
4 ch g Medicean—Musical Twist (USA) (Woodman (USA))
120^{4}

Rayeni (IRE) *John M Oxx* 114
3 ch c Indian Ridge—Rayyana (IRE) (Rainbow Quest (USA))
2288a^{2} 5924a^{4} (6707a)

Rayhani (USA) *D Nicholls* a96 99
6 b g Theatrical(IRE) —Bahr Alsalaam (USA) (Riverman (USA))
4247^{7} 4510a^{11} 5671^{11} 6095^{11} (6560)

Ray Of Joy *J R Jenkins* a88 82
3 b f Tobougg(IRE) —Once Removed (Distant Relative)
(1068) 1345^{11} 3028^{3} 4148^{6} 4870^{8} 6167^{2} 7027^{3} 7454^{4} 7702^{8} 7875^{7}

Razkalla (USA) *R Bouresly* a80 90
11 b g Caerleon(USA) —Larrocha (IRE) (Sadler's Wells (USA))
644a^{6} 772a^{16}

Reach For The Sky (IRE) *R Hannon* a61 68
2 b f Elusive City(USA) —Zara Whetei (IRE) (Lomond (USA))
(2328) 4089^{17} 4539^{14} 4850^{4} 5636^{6} 6227^{10} 6906^{4}

Reach The Crown (JPN) *K Hashiguchi* 114
3 b c Special Week(JPN) —Crownpiece (JPN) (Seattle Slew (USA))
7593a^{9}

Reaction *M R Channon* a69 79
3 ch g Alhaarth(IRE) —Hawas (Mujtahid (USA))
6621^{4} 6977^{9}

Readily *J G Portman* a58 67
3 ch f Captain Rio—Presently (Cadeaux Genereux)
91^{4} 200^{7} 390^{4} 955^{7}

Read The Script (IRE) *Tom Dascombe* a55 46
4 b g King's Best(USA) —Grizel (Lion Cavern (USA))
5883^{3} ◆ 6674^{11}

Ready For Battle (IRE) *D W Thompson* 57
3 b g Namid—Enamoured (Groom Dancer (USA))
3689^{12} 4105^{15} 4348^{11} 5342^{9} 5621^{12}

Readymade (IRE) *Sir Michael Stoute* 72
2 b g Dubai Destination(USA) —Onda Nova (USA) (Keos (USA))
6000^{6} 6792^{2}

Ready's Echo (USA) *Todd Pletcher* a118 97
4 bb h More Than Ready(USA) —Menekineko (USA) (Kingmambo (USA))
7309a^{2}

Ready To Crown (USA) *J Mackie* a60 58
5 b m More Than Ready(USA) —Dili (USA) (Chief's Crown (USA))
18^{8} 100^{2} 494^{4} 3927^{8} 4156^{8} 5015^{3}

Ready To Lift (AUS) *Gerald Ryan* 106
6 ch m More Than Ready(USA) —On The Rise (NZ) (Crested Wave (USA))
6871a^{11}

Ready To Prime *Mike Murphy* a35 24
3 ch f Primo Valentino(IRE) —Blue Topaz (IRE) (Bluebird (USA))
7105^{12} 7426^{7}

Ready To Rocknroll (IRE) *J T Gorman* a79 89
4 b g Statue Of Liberty(USA) —Stream (Unfuwain (USA))
2289a^{14}

Real Desire *I Semple* 58
3 ch g Haafhd—Stop Press (USA) (Sharpen Up)
2723^{7} 2943^{10} 3294^{2} 4039^{8} 5524^{8} 6139^{8} 6385^{9}

Real Diamond *A Dickman* 72
3 b f Bertolini(USA) —Miss Fit (IRE) (Hamas (IRE))
2365^{12} (3729) 3973^{5} 4620^{8} 4940^{7} 5405^{8} 7082^{2}

Realisation (USA) *M Johnston* 82
2 b g Alhaarth(IRE) —Live Your Dreams (USA) (Mt. Livermore (USA))
4041^{3} 4557^{3} (5770) 6569^{2}

Realism (FR) *M W Easterby* a84 66
9 b g Machiavellian(USA) —Kissing Cousin (IRE) (Danehill (USA))
2129^{2} 2499^{8} (2743) 2898^{11} 4288^{6} 5694^{6} 6769^{7} 6878^{6} 7776^{7}

Reallymissgreeley (USA) *K A Ryan* a62 60
2 bb f Mr Greeley(USA) —Holiday Gold (USA) (Touch Gold (USA))
2819^{4} 3262^{7} 4430^{11} 5611^{8} 7140^{2}

Realt Na Mara (IRE) *H Morrison* a81 77
6 bb g Tagula(IRE) —Dwingeloo (IRE) (Dancing Dissident (USA))
(13) 382^{4} 625^{7} 1169^{10} 1477^{3} 1846^{13} 3304^{7} 3691^{2} 4536^{5} (4843) (5150) 5343^{9} 5719^{9} 6739^{13} (7062) 7287^{20}

Re Barolo (IRE) *M Botti* a112 107
6 b h Cape Cross(IRE) —Dalaiya (USA) (Irish River (FR))
(634) 913^{6} 1004^{4} 2342^{3} 3089^{4} 3873^{9} 4781^{6} 7300a^{3} 7588^{2}

Rebecca De Winter *David Pinder* a75 83
3 b f Kyllachy—Miss Adelaide (IRE) (Alzao (USA))
1727^{6} 2397^{6} 2888^{9} 3926^{5} 5164^{2} 5576^{7} 7021^{6}

Rebecca Romero *D J Coakley* a46 49
2 b f Exceed And Excel(AUS) —Cloud Dancer (Bishop Of Cashel)
2494^{9} 3402^{10} 3925^{6} 5166^{9} 5589^{14}

Rebel Chieftain (IRE) *Saeed Bin Suroor* 19
2 b c Dansili—Desert Royalty (IRE) (Alhaarth (IRE))
6484^{7}

Rebel City *S A Callaghan* a73 58
3 b c Elusive City(USA) —Seguro (IRE) (Indian Ridge)
98^{2} 160^{2} 2998^{11} 3243^{5} 3712^{9}

Rebel Duke (IRE) *Ollie Pears* a99 94
5 ch g Namid—Edwina (IRE) (Caerleon (USA))
2^{2} (67) 821^{3} 1052^{2} 1457^{4} 6359^{3} 7414^{9} 7676^{5} 7866^{2}

Rebellious Spirit *S Curran* a85 81
6 b g Mark Of Esteem(IRE) —Robellino Miss (USA) (Robellino (USA))
79^{9}

Rebel Prince (IRE) *M G Quinlan* a45 56
3 b g Barathea(IRE) —Rebel Clan (IRE) (Tagula (IRE))
272^{9} 970^{8} 1594^{2} 1954^{6} 2350^{8} 2742^{4} 4491^{5} 5328^{13} 6919^{10}

Rebel Raider (IRE) *B N Pollock* a38
10 b g Mujadil(USA) —Emily's Pride (Shirley Heights)
449^{5}

Rebel Swing *W R Muir* a36 63
3 b g Robellino(USA) —Ninia (USA) (Affirmed (USA))
1570^{5} 2350^{6}

Rebelwithoutacause (IRE) *George Baker* a45 45
3 b g Redback—Christmas Kiss (Taufan (USA))
134^{7}

Rebel Woman *J A Osborne* a58 52
3 b f Royal Applause—Wild Woman (Polar Falcon (USA))
951^{12} 4164^{7} 5789^{6} 6771^{2} 7110^{6} 7369^{5} 7517^{6}

Recalcitrant *S Dow* a59 64
6 b g Josr Algarhoud(IRE) —Lady Isabell (Rambo Dancer (CAN))
3675^{3} 4449^{6} (4697) 5122^{2} (5365) (5790) 6565^{2}

Recession Proof (FR) *S A Callaghan* a80 97
3 ch g Rock Of Gibraltar(IRE) —Elevate (Ela-Mana-Mou)
2138^{5} 2845^{12} 3463^{4} 4269^{2} (4563) (4658) 4794^{2} (5402) ◆ 5870^{5}

Recette *R Ingram* a16 49
2 b f Reset(AUS) —Sunny Times (IRE) (Raise A Grand (IRE))
4243^{9} 5282^{4} 5800^{6} 7389^{12}

Recharge (IRE) *Kevin Prendergast* 111
3 b c Cape Cross(IRE) —Rebelline (IRE) (Robellino (USA))
(1022a) 2288a^{4} 3438a^{5}

Recoil (IRE) *R Johnson* 39
4 b g Red Ransom(USA) —Dazilyn Lady (USA) (Zilzal (USA))
2723[8] 3314[8] 4344[9] 4654[10] 4995[5]

Record Breaker (IRE) *M Johnston* 107
5 b g In The Wings—Overruled (IRE) (Last Tycoon)
1458[8] 1696[8] 2085[2] 2486[4] (2815) 3142[2] 3390[15] 4340[5] 5173[13] 5823[4] (6302) 6662[5]

Recurring Dream *P J Hobbs* 32
3 b f Beat All(USA) —Rewbell (Andy Rew)
4480[9]

Red *Mrs S J Humphrey* a24 66
5 ch m Fraam—Great Tern (Simply Great (FR))
2580[8]

Red Amaryllis *H J L Dunlop* a61 63
4 ch m Piccolo—Passiflora (Night Shift (USA))
1248[9] 1587[11] 2680[10] 2879[14]

Red Amy *M L W Bell* a48 54
2 b f Hawk Wing(USA) —Ballet Ballon (USA) (Rahy (USA))
4055[9] 4699[5] 5192[5]

Red Army Commander (IRE) *J A Geake* a49 50
4 b g Soviet Star(USA) —Penny Fan (Nomination)
4867[4] 5215[6] 5322[5] 5579[9] 6969[13]

Redarsene *S Wynne* a71 71
4 ch h Sakhee(USA) —Triple Zee (USA) (Zilzal (USA))
215[6]

Red Avalanche (IRE) *P F I Cole* a99 96
2 gr c Verglas(IRE) —Maura's Guest (IRE) (Be My Guest (USA))
1005[9] 1188[2] ◆ (1590) 1927[2] 2702[3] 2995[21] 3799[4] 4089[4] 5057a[3] 5661[5] 6660[11]

Red Badge (IRE) *R Hannon* 92
2 ch c Captain Rio—Red Fuschia (Polish Precedent (USA))
3500[2] 3920[3] 4410[2] ◆ 5198[6] (5433) ◆ 7030[12]

Red Ballerina (IRE) *Dominique Sepulchre* 75
3 ch f Hawk Wing(USA) —Red Star (IRE) (Lure (USA))
6753a[0]

Red Barcelona (IRE) *M H Tompkins* 60
2 ch c Indian Haven—Purepleasureseeker (IRE) (Grand Lodge (USA))
4176[8] 5428[8] 6235[7]

Red Birr (IRE) *P R Webber* a76 82
8 b g Bahhare(USA) —Cappella (IRE) (College Chapel)
2775[9] 3206[3] 3635[10]

Red Cadeaux *E A L Dunlop* a87 94
3 ch g Cadeaux Genereux—Artisia (IRE) (Peintre Celebre (USA))
1255[6] 1730[8] 2104[3] (3466) ◆ 3721[2] (4518) 5660[5]

Red Cape (FR) *Mrs R A Carr* a86 95
6 b g Cape Cross(IRE) —Muirfield (FR) (Crystal Glitters (USA))
68[4] 218[2] 573[3] 757[3] 1060[12] 1169[15] 1313[4] 2156[3] (2660) 2769[9] (3001) 3354[4] ◆ (3497) 3706[2] 3825[3] 4353[9] 4507[2] (4598) 4784[2] 5257[2] 5799[10] 6089[22] 6282[3] 6994[17]

Red Cell (IRE) *I W McInnes* a68 59
3 b g Kheleyf(USA) —Montana Lady (IRE) (Be My Guest (USA))
(268) 568[6] 1469[5] 1644[9] 3176[9] 4596[2] 5396[7] 5626[3] 5881[8] 6341[9] 6553[11]

Red Century *Paul Mason* a12
4 ch m Captain Rio—Red Millennium (IRE) (Tagula (IRE))
1131[12]

Red Chieftain (FR) *Mrs H S Main* a50 34
4 b g Red Ransom(USA) —Delimara (IRE) (In The Wings)
1636[9] 2229[7]

Red China Blues (USA) *R E Barr* 64
3 ch g Royal Academy(USA) —Viewy (USA) (Majestic Light (USA))
1611[8] 2042[4] 2450[3] 3316[12] 4344[2] 5255[5] 5672[12]

Red Courtier *P F I Cole* a80 58
2 b c Red Ransom(USA) —Lady In Waiting (Kylian (USA))
3794[6] 7277[3] (7683)

Red Current *R A Harris* a58 68
5 b m Soviet Star(USA) —Fleet Amour (USA) (Afleet (CAN))
42[2] 192[4] 221[3] 321[5] 480[7] 706[7] 1030[2] 1254[7] 1417[6] 1578[6] 1770[5] 1959[6] 2333[6] 2675[11] 2912[9] (3501) 3929[4] 4376[10] 4938[5] 5179[4] 7200[6] 7433[3] 7609[6] 7660[7] 7787[8]

Red Dagger (IRE) *R J Price* a44 52
3 b g Daggers Drawn(USA) —Dash Of Red (Red Sunset)
828[8] 1461[11] 1967[8] 2220[5] 2635[8] 3215[11] 5633[3] 5998[10]

Redden *W J Haggas* 65
2 b g Pivotal—Coy (IRE) (Danehill (USA))
5958[6] 6991[7] 7289[4]

Red Desire (JPN) *Mikio Matsunaga* 117
3 ch f Manhattan Cafe(JPN) —Great Sunrise (Caerleon (USA))
7593a[3]

Redding Colliery (USA) *H J Brown* a97
3 rg c Mineshaft(USA) —Joop (USA) (Zilzal (USA))
258a[3] 526a[3] 1009a[7]

Red Dune (IRE) *M A Jarvis* 103
4 b m Red Ransom(USA) —Desert Beauty (IRE) (Green Desert (USA))
2703[8] 3846[6] 4489[4] 5069[11] 5798[4] 6272[2] 6886a[3] 7621a[6]

Reddy Ronnie (IRE) *D W Thompson* a41 55
5 b g Redback—Daffodil Dale (IRE) (Cyrano De Bergerac)
2404[7] 2965[15] 3448[12] 3730[13] 4750[4] 5513[8] 5983[11]

Reddy To Star (IRE) *C G Cox* a63 76
2 b g Redback—Grade A Star (IRE) (Alzao (USA))
1669[7] 1891[2] 2335[2] 2778[2] 3317[2] 4089[14] 4868[8] 6328[4] 6693[7] 6911[3]

Red Eddie *B J Meehan* 60
2 b c Red Ransom(USA) —Sister Bluebird (Bluebird (USA))
4756[14] 5220[11] 5785[6] 6367[9] 6895[11]

Redeemed *M Brittain* a44 72
4 b m Red Ransom(USA) —Pastel (Lion Cavern (USA))
12[8] 216[10]

Red Eric *W M Brisbourne* a14 40
3 ch g Reset(AUS) —Lady Soleas (Be My Guest (USA))
134[10]

Redesignation (IRE) *R Pritchard-Gordon* a80 103
4 b g Key Of Luck(USA) —Disregard That (IRE) (Don't Forget Me)
(1347) 1696[2] 2055[15] 5281a[4]

Red Expresso (IRE) *Ollie Pears* a68 78
4 ch g Intikhab(USA) —Cafe Creme (IRE) (Catrail (USA))
(6342) 7093[6] 7647[6]

Red Eye Express (IRE) *John M Oxx* a102 94
4 b h Giant's Causeway(USA) —Snowfire (Machiavellian (USA))
419a[6] 642a[10]

Red Fama *N Bycroft* a65 84
5 ch g Fraam—Carol Again (Kind Of Hush)
226[6] 4003[9] 4332[9]

Red Fantasy (IRE) *B W Hills* 77
2 b f High Chaparral(IRE) —Petite Fantasy (Mansooj)
6055[4] 6363[5]

Red Farasi (IRE) *B W Duke* a27
2 ch g Redback—Boristova (IRE) (Royal Academy (USA))
4945[13] 5583[11] 7334[9]

Redford (IRE) *M L W Bell* 108
4 b g Bahri(USA) —Ida Lupino (IRE) (Statoblest)
1868[4] 3091[3] ◆ 3818[6] ◆ 4297[3] 6091[10] 6270[21]

Red Gulch *E A L Dunlop* a65
2 b c Kyllachy—Enrapture (USA) (Lear Fan (USA))
7537[3] ◆

Red Horse (IRE) *M L W Bell* a44 52
3 ch g Bachelor Duke(USA) —Miss Childrey (IRE) (Dr Fong (USA))
5121[7] 5644[9] 6570[5] 7022[9]

Red Hot Desert *W R Swinburn* a67
3 b g Green Desert(USA) —Red Carnation (IRE) (Polar Falcon (USA))
6673[11] 6974[9] (7367) 7665[6] 7823[9]

Red Humour (IRE) *M McDonagh* a74 60
3 b g Elusive City(USA) —Arctic Flight (Polar Falcon (USA))
4392a[10]

Red Intrigue (IRE) *Mrs A J Perrett* a71 62
2 b f Selkirk(USA) —Red Affair (IRE) (Generous (IRE))
5605[9] 6363[8] 6772[3]

Red Jade *R A Fahey* 89
4 ch g Dubai Destination(USA) —Red Slippers (USA) (Nureyev (USA))
1593[2] 2290a[7] 2933[12] 3705[4] 4517[6] 5334[3] 6002[3] 6470[6] 6648[3]

Red Jazz (USA) *B W Hills* 103
2 b c Johannesburg(USA) —Now That's Jazz (USA) (Sword Dance)
(1147) ◆ (1598) 2993[7] 3779[3]

Red Kestrel (USA) *K A Ryan* a93 89
4 ch g Swain(IRE) —The Caretaker (Caerleon (USA))
1986[7] 2706[14] 3826[6] 4882[4] 6281[6]

Red Kimi (IRE) *R Santini* 88
3 b c Denon(USA) —Happy Flight (IRE) (Titus Livius (FR))
1392a[8]

Red Kyte *K A Ryan* a73 82
3 br f Hawk Wing(USA) —Ruby Affair (IRE) (Night Shift (USA))
912[14] 1345[10] 1639[9] 2028[3] 2544[5] 3096[8] (3704) 4530[4] 4664[5] 5405[6] 5937[9]

Red Lord (AUS) *Anthony Cummings* 109
6 b g Redoute's Choice(AUS) —Dame Cath (NZ) (Zabeel (NZ))
6871a[14]

Redlynch *S Parr*
4 b g Sinndar(IRE) —Red Azalea (Shirley Heights)
90[9] 178[7] 791[10] 3460[12]

Red Margarita (IRE) *D R C Elsworth* a37 53
3 ch f Dalakhani(IRE) —Red Bartsia (Barathea (IRE))
1034[9] 1257[8] 1570[6] 2461[7] 3303[9] 4142[9]

Red Max (IRE) *T D Easterby* 57
3 b g Kheleyf(USA) —Set Trail (IRE) (Second Set (IRE))
1736[9] 2162[12]

Red Merlin (IRE) *C G Cox* a83 107
4 ch g Soviet Star(USA) —Truly Bewitched (USA) (Affirmed (USA))
1319[3] ◆ 1571[2] (1826) (2475) (3620) 5173[12]

Red Oriental *N P Littmoden* 80
3 ch f Zamindar(USA) —Pan Galactic (USA) (Lear Fan (USA))
4151[11]

Redoubtable Grace *Mrs R A Carr* a7 44
2 b g Redoubtable(USA) —Full Of Grace (Lucky Wednesday)
5620[9] 5977[10] 7582[8] 7674[6]

Red Parisi (IRE) *A & G Botti* 68
3 b f Red Ransom(USA) —Rebecca Parisi (IRE) (Persian Heights)
2310a[16]

Red Red Rascal *A M Balding* 25
3 b f Red Ransom(USA) —Normandy (CHI) (Great Regent (CAN))
2848[8] 3297[12]

Red Reef *D J Coakley* a55 68
3 ch f King's Best(USA) —Rafiya (Halling (USA))
2008[9] 2909[4] 4224[6] 4745[2] 5122[7] 5366[8] 5782[9] 6226[11] 6804[13]

Red River Boy *C W Fairhurst* 53
4 ch g Bahamian Bounty—Riviere Rouge (Forzando)
1628[5] 2158[5] 2801[6] 3239[9] 3612[5] 3999[5]

Red River Rebel *J R Norton* a50 59
11 b g Inchinor—Bidweaya (USA) (Lear Fan (USA))
1442[13] 1938[10]

Red Rock Canyon (IRE) *A P O'Brien* 112
5 b h Rock Of Gibraltar(IRE) —Imagine (IRE) (Sadler's Wells (USA))
1551a[7] 1913a[6] 3882a[3] 4253a[5] 5076a[3] 5539a[5]

Red Rocks (IRE) *B J Meehan* 118
6 bb h Galileo(IRE) —Pharmacist (IRE) (Machiavellian (USA))
1012a[12] 6303[4] 7310a[5]

Red Rosanna *R Hollinshead* 82
3 b f Bertolini(USA) —Lamarita (Emarati (USA))
1505[4] 1720[7] 2546[4] 3053[2] (3118) ◆ 3570[8] (3623) 3806[5] 4043[5]

Red Rossini (IRE) *R Hannon* a73 77
3 b g Rossini(USA) —La Scala (USA) (Theatrical (IRE))
1196[6] 2010[3] 2160[6] 2602[5] 4454[7] 4695[5] 5155[9] 5345[5] 5716[5]

Red Rudy *A W Carroll* a75 67
7 ch g Pivotal—Piroshka (Soviet Star (USA))
24[7] 57[4] 245[7] (471) 875[3] 1037[2] 1187[3] 1530[8] 1748[7]

Red Ruler (NZ) *John Sargent* 118
5 b g Viking Ruler(AUS) —Ransom Bay (USA) (Red Ransom (USA))
6871a[18]

Red Scintilla *N Tinkler* 55
2 b f Doyen(IRE) —Red To Violet (Spectrum (IRE))
7288[10]

Red Skipper (IRE) *N Wilson* 66
4 ch g Captain Rio—Speed To Lead (IRE) (Darshaan)
1650[11] 2718[5] 3150[2] 3653[5] 4465[2] 4710[4] 5289[7] 5364[4] 6012[4] 6411[8] 7174[4]

Red Somerset (USA) *R J Hodges* a103 93
6 b g Red Ransom(USA) —Bielska (USA) (Deposit Ticket (USA))
30[2] (206) 331[2] 551[5] 724[6] 916[2] 1093[3] 1212[6] 1641[4] 1861[21] 6633[11] 7133[8] 7375[10] 7492[2] 7626[9] 7789[9] (7845)

Red Stiletto *Rae Guest* a34 36
3 b f Red Ransom(USA) —The Blade (GER) (Sure Blade (USA))
1423[9]

Red Suede Shoes *B R Millman* a82 70
3 ch g Storming Home—Dipple (Komaite (USA))
121[8] 272[2] 630[2] 2884[6] 3309[4] 3800[4] 4440[4] ◆ 4872[3] 5223[4] 6370[5] (6719) 6977[2] 7153[3] (7456) 7603[3] 7769[4]

Red Tarn *B Smart* a64 72
4 gr g Fraam—Cumbrian Melody (Petong)
(1) 147[8]

Red Twist *M Hill* a63 57
4 b g Red Ransom(USA) —Spinning The Yarn (Barathea (IRE))
310[4] 604[8] 2497[11] 2859[15]

Red Valerian Two (IRE) *P T Midgley*
2 ch c Hawk Wing(USA) —La Turque (IRE) (Diesis)
6874[8] 7266[10]

Redwater River *Mrs R A Carr* a65 68
5 b g Kyllachy—Red Tulle (USA) (A.P. Indy (USA))
93[5] 515[6] 571[12] 1413[10] 2235[10] 2312[16] 2579[6] 4072[6] 4191[3] 4436[3] 4508[5] (4620) 5150[8] 5391[5] 5601[14]

Red Willow *J E Long* 32
3 ch f Noverre(USA) —Chelsea Blue (ITY) (Barathea (IRE))
4324[11] 4936[5] 5747[8]

Red Wine *J A Glover* a68 85
10 b g Hamas(IRE) —Red Bouquet (Reference Point)
3[8] 202[8] 319[5] 631[11] 1000[2] 1175[4] 1665[2] (2068) 2283[8] 3761[4] 4737[6] 5410[3] 5625[6] 6767[5] 7084[3] 7222[5] 7505[4] 7642[8]

Redwood *B W Hills* 108
3 b c High Chaparral(IRE) —Arum Lily (USA) (Woodman (USA))
(1294) 2014[9]

Red Yarn *G L Moore* a57
2 b f Lucky Story(USA) —Aunt Ruby (USA) (Rubiano (USA))
7700[6] 7885[3]

Red Zoe (USA) *M L W Bell* 57
3 b f Danehill Dancer(IRE) —Starbourne (IRE) (Sadler's Wells (USA))
2139[8] 2446[8]

Reeds Bay (IRE) *E S McMahon* 79
2 br c Monsieur Bond(IRE) —Paradise Blue (IRE) (Bluebird (USA))
1866[3] 2231[5] (2839) 3340[4] 5265[10] 5692[4] 6134[3] 6534[3]

Reel Bluff *N Wilson* 53
3 b g Reel Buddy(USA) —Amber's Bluff (Mind Games)
2667[10] 3108[7] 3541[8] 6488[9]

Reel Buddy Star *G M Moore* 86
4 ch g Reel Buddy(USA) —So Discreet (Tragic Role (USA))
2043[9] 2822[5] 3067[6] 3378[2] 4801[6] (4941) 5221[7] 5598[3] 6249[4] 6485[7]

Reel Credit Crunch *I W McInnes* a64 65
2 ch f Reel Buddy(USA) —Four Legs Good (IRE) (Be My Guest (USA))
1312[3] 1521[5] 1802[2] 1884[2] 2604[4] 2800[6] 5226[5] 5950[14] 5976[14] 6586[13]

Reel Easy *J R Holt* a27 9
2 b c Reel Buddy(USA) —Easy Feeling (IRE) (Night Shift (USA))
994[19] 1249[7] 3709[11]

Reel Hope *J R Best* a41 46
3 b f Reel Buddy(USA) —Compton Amber (Puissance)
5647[12] 6166[8]

Reel Love *J R Holt* a31
2 b c Reel Buddy(USA) —Love Affair (IRE) (Tagula (IRE))
2099[14] 3468[7]

Reel Man *D K Ivory* a49 49
4 ch g Reel Buddy(USA) —Yanomami (USA) (Slew O'Gold (USA))
5577[11] 5987[7] 6941[8]

Reflective Glory (IRE) *J S Wainwright* a27 40
5 ch m City On A Hill(USA) —Sheznice (IRE) (Try My Best (USA))
4804[7]

Refuse To Decline *D M Simcock* a32 50
3 ch f Refuse To Bend(IRE) —Oulianovsk (IRE) (Peintre Celebre (USA))
196[9]

Refuse To Sell (IRE) *F Costello* a67 69
4 b g Brahms(USA) —Ruby Cairo (IRE) (Nashwan (USA))
7729[12]

Refuse To Tell *C E Brittain* a42 40
2 b g Refuse To Bend(IRE) —Zibet (Kris)
3546[10] 4646[8] 5590[6] 6067[8]

Refuse Toulouse (IRE) *C G Cox* a46 53
3 b c Refuse To Bend(IRE) —Continuous (IRE) (Darshaan)
998[8] 1350[8] 2211[6] 5782[11] 6289[11] 6758[9]

Refuse To Wait (IRE) *T D Easterby* 68
2 b f Refuse To Bend(IRE) —I'Ll Be Waiting (Vettori (IRE))
1847[4] ◆ 2226[3] (2721) 4539[18] 5207[7] 5550[4]

Regal Angel *Jean-Rene Auvray* a62 55
6 ch m Roi De Rome(USA) —Dominion's Dream (Dominion)
102[3] 279[2] 501[3] 5074a[4] 5217[10] 5720[4]

Regal Blush *A M Balding* 65
3 b f Bachelor Duke(USA) —Royale Rose (FR) (Bering)
2080[7] 2947[8] 3751[11] 4569[2] 4904[7] 5720[3] 5990[13] 6788[3]

Regal Dream (IRE) *J W Unett* a64 44
7 b g Namid—Lovely Me (IRE) (Vision (USA))
2964[13]

Regal Guest *M R Channon* 75
2 b c King's Best(USA) —Zuleika Dobson (Cadeaux Genereux)
5499[10] 6200[2] 6697[2]

Regal Holiday (USA) *F-X De Chevigny*
2 b c Harlan's Holiday(USA) —Regal Heir (CAN) (Regal Intention (CAN))
7166a[5]

Regal Lyric (IRE) *T P Tate* 71
3 b g Royal Applause—Alignment (IRE) (Alzao (USA))
1561[4] 2544[10] 3124[10] 3689[7] 4600[2] 5469[4] 6139[2] 6538[3]

Regal Parade *D Nicholls* a97 121
5 ch g Pivotal—Model Queen (USA) (Kingmambo (USA))
1006[6] 1513[2] (2500) 3140[9] (3846) 4406[3] 5024[2] (5657)

Regal Park (IRE) *J Noseda* 60
2 b c Montjeu(IRE) —Classic Park (Robellino (USA))
6617[5] ◆

Regal Ransom (USA) *Saeed Bin Suroor* a118
3 bb c Distorted Humor(USA) —Kelli's Ransom (USA) (Red Ransom (USA))
258a[2] 526a[2] (1009a) 1688a[8] 7311a[8]

Regal Rave (USA) *J R Best* 60
2 b c Wild Event(USA) —Golden Crown (USA) (Defensive Play (USA))
3402[9] 4323[8] 5129[6] 7056[11]

Regal Royale *Peter Grayson* a70 74
6 b g Medicean—Regal Rose (Danehill (USA))
1053[3] 1197[9] 1565[3] 1776[3] 2032[8] 2472[12] 4134[13] 4203[4] (4536) 4870[3]

Regal Tradition (IRE) *G J Smith* a29 73
4 b g Traditionally(USA) —Dathuil (IRE) (Royal Academy (USA))
1314[8] 1523[4] 1848[9] 2129[11]

Regardless *Mrs G S Rees* a60 68
2 ch f Reset(AUS) —Princess Of Garda (Komaite (USA))
1764[7] 2339[3] 2741[3] 3807[4] 4492[2] 4739[2] 5658[15]

Regency Art (IRE) *D R C Elsworth* 72
2 b c Titus Livius(FR) —Honey Storm (IRE) (Mujadil (USA))
1590[7] (6542)

Regeneration (IRE) *M L W Bell* a80 77
3 b g Chevalier(IRE) —Cappuchino (IRE) (Roi Danzig (USA))
2862[4] (3743) ◆ 4375[2] (4791) 5112[2] (5677) 6243[6] 7189[8]

Regent's Secret (USA) *J S Goldie* a85 67
9 br g Cryptoclearance(USA) —Misty Regent (CAN) (Vice Regent (CAN))
3023[6] 3481[4] 3854[4] 4040[3] 4874[2] 5162[4] 5947[7]

Reggae Dancer (IRE) *A P O'Brien* a76 75
2 b c Rock Of Gibraltar(IRE) —Don't Care (IRE) (Nordico (USA))
4359a[8] 6317a[15]

Reggane *A De Royer-Dupre* 115
3 b f Red Ransom(USA) —Reine Zao (FR) (Alzao (USA))
2521a[2] 3088[2] ◆ 4580a[6] 6505a[6]

Regional Counsel *A M Hales* a88 64
5 b g Medicean—Regency Rose (Danehill (USA))
2239[6] 2773[7] 3055[7] 5780[6]

Regionalista (BRZ) *P Bary* a76 65
4 b g Roi Normand(USA) —Repeat Rafaela (BRZ) (Ghadeer (FR))
526a[7]

Registrar *Mrs C A Dunnett* a60 68
7 ch g Machiavellian(USA) —Confidante (USA) (Dayjur (USA))
1258[7] 1634[6] 2166[11] 3548[2] 4183[11] (4914) 5544[10] 6005[3] 6925[8]

Rehabilitation *W R Swinburn* a76 67
4 ch g Dr Fong(USA) —Lamees (USA) (Lomond (USA))
2773[8] 4150[12] 4745[4] 5365[4] 6369[9] 7212[7]

Reignier *K R Burke* 98
2 b c Kheleyf(USA) —Komena (Komaite (USA))
1590[5] (2153) 2714[2] 3046[2] 3779[4] 4407[6]

Reigning In Rio (IRE) *P C Haslam* a51 44
3 br f Captain Rio—Saibhreas (IRE) (Last Tycoon)
(383) 620[7] 1481[3]

Reigning Monarch (USA) *Miss Z C Davison* a56 53
6 b g Fusaichi Pegasus(USA) —Torros Straits (USA) (Boundary (USA))
27[10] 472[3] 2564[7] 2713[9] 4051[3] 4536[12] 5219[5] 7176[3] 7535[4] 7703[4]

Reiteration (USA) *J S Bolger* 89
2 b c Vindication(USA) —For Dixie (USA) (Dixieland Band (USA))
6318a[8]

Reject *W J Haggas* 78
3 b g Green Desert(USA) —Wardat Allayl (IRE) (Mtoto)
1400[6] 1852[2] (2439) ◆ 2917[4] 4338[8] 5154[6] 5968[2] ◆ 6201[4] 6798[8]

Relative Strength (IRE) *A M Balding* a82 84
4 ch g Kris Kin(USA) —Monalee Lass (IRE) (Mujtahid (USA))
1571[10] 2242[3] 3103[3] 3797[2] 4417[8] 5094[6] 5857[3] 6273[5]

Relco Italy (IRE) *B Grizzetti* 101
3 b c Dansili—Lietta (IRE) (Grand Lodge (USA))
1393a[6] 1904a[17]

Remaadd (USA) *D Selvaratnam* a86 103
8 gr g Daylami(IRE) —Bint Albaadiya (USA) (Woodman (USA))
337a[12]

Remark (IRE) *M W Easterby* a54 31
5 b g Machiavellian(USA) —Remuria (USA) (Theatrical (IRE))
6758[10] 7492[6] 7500[8]

Remarque (IRE) *L Riccardi* 104
4 b h Marju(IRE) —Run For Me (IRE) (Danehill (USA))
259a[5] 433a[9] (1905a) 7206a[4] 7303a[6]

Remember Dougie (IRE) *A Berry*
2 b f Namid—Proud Myth (IRE) (Mark Of Esteem (IRE))
4398[8] 5292[8] 5977[13]

Remember Ramon (USA) *J R Gask* a86 88
6 ch g Diesis—Future Act (USA) (Known Fact (USA))
156[4] (692) 1184[4] (4274) 4770[8] 6258[8]

Reminiscent (IRE) *B P J Baugh* a50 48
10 b g Kahyasi—Eliza Orzeszkowa (IRE) (Polish Patriot (USA))
8[8] 300[5] 378[4] 735[5]

Rendezvous (IRE) *Sir Michael Stoute* 90
3 b c Sadler's Wells(USA) —Gwynn (IRE) (Darshaan)
4020[4] 5004[9] 6816[9]

Renege The Joker *S Regan* a35
6 b g Alflora(IRE) —Bunty (Presidium)
1273[9] 5483[10]

Renowing (UAE) *B Grizzetti* 101
3 ch c Halling(USA) —Renowned (IRE) (Darshaan)
(1392a) 1904a[21]

Repealed *H Morrison* a68 65
3 b c Reset(AUS) —Great Verdict (AUS) (Christmas Tree (AUS))
1440[2] ◆

Repetischa (IRE) *E J O'Neill* a68 71
3 ch f Peintre Celebre(USA) —Brief Escapade (IRE) (Brief Truce (USA))
1297[6] 2192[3] 3297[3] 4799[7] 6753a[0]

Replicator *Pat Eddery* a73 65
4 b g Mujahid(USA) —Valldemosa (Music Boy)
13[4] 167[11] 518[7] 818[8] 1846[5] 2686[F]

Reportage (USA) *J H M Gosden* 73
3 b g Elusive Quality(USA) —Journalist (IRE) (Night Shift (USA))
1350[6] 2317[3] 3751[10] 4354[2]

Reprieved *Miss J A Camacho* a58 11
4 ch g Bertolini(USA) —Crystal Seas (Zamindar (USA))
377[5] 972[9]

Requisite *I A Wood* a73 86
4 ch m Pivotal—Chicarica (USA) (The Minstrel (CAN))
1965[5] 2397[8] 2864[3] (3065) 3252[10] 4399[5] 4464[3] 4530[2] 4907[8] 5149[4] 5919[8] 6791[8] 6915[10] 7203[7] 7337[14]

Rescent *Mrs R A Carr* a54 55
2 ch f Reset(AUS) —Bukhoor (IRE) (Danehill (USA))
4384[2] 4747[4] (5393) 6901[6] 7168[11] 7335[10] 7791[9]

Resentful Angel *Pat Eddery* a74 68
4 b m Danehill Dancer(IRE) —Leaping Flame (USA) (Trempolino (USA))
1332[8] 1743[2] 2166[4] 3983[3] 4533[3] 5195[5] 5698[9] (7250) ◆ 7524[3] ◆ (7632) 7699[2]

Reset City *A B Haynes* 67
3 ch f Reset(AUS) —City Of Angels (Woodman (USA))
4022[6] 4480[2] 5718[5] 6698[7]

Residency (IRE) *B Smart* a68 67
3 b g Danetime(IRE) —Muckross Park (Nomination)
3611[6] 4174[2] 4653[8] 5336[2] 5727[8] 7337[5] 7815[4]

Resolute Defender (IRE) *R Johnson* 49
4 b g Namid—Snowspin (Carwhite)
4312[12] 4656[10]

Resort *Sir Michael Stoute* 94
3 b f Oasis Dream—Gay Gallanta (USA) (Woodman (USA))
(1302) 1801[7] 3746[7] 4316[3] (5099) 5880[2] 6267[9]

Resounding Glory (USA) *R A Fahey* 80
4 b g Honour And Glory(USA) —Resounding Grace (USA) (Thunder Gulch (USA))
4532[9]

Respite *W J Haggas* a79 72
3 ch f Pivotal—Truce (Nashwan (USA))
(1066) 2072[5] 3921[7] 5090[2] 5575[6] 6667[10]

Resplendent Ace (IRE) *P Howling* a79 70
5 b g Trans Island—Persian Polly (Persian Bold)
202[11] 311[7] 1533[4] 2923[6] (3923) 6070[4] 6288[9] 6584[2] 6860[6] 7048[3] (7272) 7368[3] 7475[5] 7668[2] 7760[3] 7851[6]

Resplendent Alpha *P Howling* a85 79
5 ch g Best Of The Bests(IRE) —Sunley Scent (Wolfhound (USA))
24[6] (533) 600[4] 665[4] 892[7] 954[2] 1197[6] 1572[11] 1806[5] 2549[7] 3164[8] 3529[4] 5753[11] 6112[8] 7191[6] 7337[12] 7738[2] ◆ 7828[4]

Resplendent Light *W R Muir* a69 96
4 b g Fantastic Light(USA) —Bright Halo (IRE) (Bigstone (IRE))
1696[6] 1875[5] 2706[8] 3406[4] 3826[3] 4661[2] 5170[8] 5909[3] 6483[2]

Resplendent Nova *P Howling* a90 74
7 b g Pivotal—Santiburi Girl (Casteddu)
9[3] (113) 232[5] 4005[7] 4181[10] 5188[8] 5676[8] 6614[9] 6976[9] 7327[8] 7516[3] 7741[4] 7876[4]

Restart (IRE) *Lucinda Featherstone* a50 58
8 b g Revoque(IRE) —Stargard (Polish Precedent (USA))
8[6] 190[7]

Rest By The River *A G Newcombe* 52
3 ch f Reset(AUS) —Palace Green (IRE) (Rudimentary (USA))
2205[10] 3281[10]

Restless Genius (IRE) *B Ellison* a73 78
4 b g Captain Rio—Mainmise (USA) (Septieme Ciel (USA))
24[2] 1096[6] 1768[6] (2145) 2438[4] 2717[4] 3268[5] 6361[4] 6776[11] 7355[2] 7561[5] 7673[8] 7870[6]

Restless Swallow *R A Harris* 20
4 gr g Bandmaster(USA) —Pink Petal (Northern Game)
2981[11] 3205[7] 5720[7]

Restyle *D K Ivory* 23
2 b f Reset(AUS) —Surrealist (ITY) (Night Shift (USA))
1569[15] 4147[12] 4915[10] 5749[9] 5811[13]

Resurge (IRE) *W S Kittow* a92 94
4 b g Danehill Dancer(IRE) —Resurgence (Polar Falcon (USA))
1527[8] 2083[10] 2480[5] 3055[4] (3461) 3695[2] 4261[5] 5221[10] 5880[8] 6733[5] 7066[6]

Resuscitator (USA) *Mrs H S Main* a75
2 b c Bernstein(USA) —Lac Du Printemps (USA) (Meadowlake (USA))
5191[2] 5807[4]

Retrato (USA) *Rae Guest* 65
2 bb f Fusaichi Pegasus(USA) —Painted Lady (USA) (Broad Brush (USA))
6593[3]

Retro (IRE) *R Hannon* a75 73
3 b c Tagula(IRE) —Cabcharge Princess (IRE) (Rambo Dancer (CAN))
2174[9] 2849[12] 6230[11] 6725[8] 6904[9]

Rettorical Lad *Jamie Poulton* a59 48
4 rg g Vettori(IRE) —Reciprocal (IRE) (Night Shift (USA))
501[5] 732[7] 816[11]

Reve D'Ailleur (FR) *J-V Toux* a71 81
5 b m Panis(USA) —O'Tango (FR) (Fijar Tango (FR))
6981a[6]

Reve De Mardi *George Baker* a22 27
2 b g Cyrano De Bergerac—Dreams Forgotten (IRE) (Victory Note (USA))
5839[9] 6727[11]

Revelator (IRE) *A P Jarvis* 74
2 b c One Cool Cat(USA) —Capades Band (FR) (Chimes Band (USA))
4738[4] (7079)

Revered *Sir Michael Stoute* 79
2 b f Oasis Dream—Arrive (Kahyasi)
6729[3] ◆ (7182)

Reverence *E J Alston* a103 108
8 ch g Mark Of Esteem(IRE) —Imperial Bailiwick (IRE) (Imperial Frontier (USA))
1374a[2] 2272[9] 2481[4] 4135[4] 4456[9] (5491a) 6522a[13]

Reve Vert (FR) *Tim Vaughan* a56 49
4 b h Oasis Dream—Comme D'Habitude (USA) (Caro)
1741[8] 2441[8] 2746[14]

Revoltinthedesert *E S McMahon* 53
2 b f Dubai Destination(USA) —Cloud Hill (Danehill (USA))
2819[6] 4194[4]

Revolving World (IRE) *L R James* a39 40
6 b g Spinning World(USA) —Mannakea (USA) (Fairy King (USA))
1851[8] 6818[14]

Revue Princess (IRE) *T D Easterby* a61 72
4 b m Mull Of Kintyre(USA) —Blues Queen (Lahib (USA))
1241[11] (2046) 2546[7] 3065[11] 3565[6] 4141[12] 6161[3] (6380) 6764[5] 6801[5] 7086[9] 7269[11]

Rex Regina (IRE) *J-C Rouget* 104
3 b f King's Best(USA) —Mrs Ting (USA) (Lyphard (USA))
4578a[6]

Rezwaan *M J McGrath* a58 75
2 b g Alhaarth(IRE) —Nasij (USA) (Elusive Quality (USA))
3270[8] 3957[5] 4638[6] 5399[2] 6067[3] (6793) 7654[8]

Rhapsilian *J R Jenkins* a66 63
5 br m Dansili—Rivers Rhapsody (Dominion)
2202[5] 2564[2] 2920[4] 3407[9] 4702[5] 5008[4] 5480[9] 6039[8] 6581[4]

Rhonaldino (GER) *T Doumen* 69
2 b c Sholokhov(IRE) —Rote Rose (GER) (Zinaad)
5494a[7]

Rhythmic Star *W J Haggas* 38
2 ch c Starcraft(NZ) —Markova's Dance (Mark Of Esteem (IRE))
5000[11]

Ricci De Mare *G J Smith* a58 58
4 b m Cadeaux Genereux—Procession (Zafonic (USA))
66[5] 254[11]

Riccoche (IRE) *J H M Gosden*
2 b f Oasis Dream—Ammo (IRE) (Sadler's Wells (USA))
7491[11]

Richardlionheart (USA) *M Madgwick* a24 39
3 ch g Lion Heart(USA) —Cleito (USA) (Unbridled's Song (USA))
1838[9] 3459[6] 6771[10] 6966[8]

Richard's Kid (USA) *Bob Baffert* a122 106
4 bb h Lemon Drop Kid(USA) —Tough Broad (USA) (Broad Brush (USA))
6687a[3] 7311a[6]

Richardthesecond (IRE) *W M Brisbourne* a57 48
4 b g Acclamation—Tahlil (Cadeaux Genereux)
832[7] 1134[9] 1360[12]

Richboy *Mrs L J Mongan* a65 34
2 ch c Bahamian Bounty—West Humble (Pharly (FR))
4851[6] 7436[4] 7538[4]

Richelieu *J J Lambe* a79 74
7 b g Machiavellian(USA) —Darling Flame (USA) (Capote (USA))
3435a[16] 6072[10] 7341a[3]

Richo *S A Harris* a78 79
3 ch g Bertolini(USA) —Noble Water (FR) (Noblequest (FR))
1561[2] 2544[8] 2841[3] 3163[9] 3804[8] 4312[8] 4995[4] 5544[8] 5869[4] 6016[6] 7246[11]

Rich Red (IRE) *R Hannon* a28 61
3 ch g Redback—Pink N Prosperous (IRE) (Grand Lodge (USA))
162[7]

Ricoco (BRZ) *P Shaw* 61
5 gr g Put It Back(USA) —Giggi Fazi (BRZ) (Bright Again (USA))
2117a[11]

Ride A White Swan *D Shaw* a63 64
4 gr g Baryshnikov(AUS) —The Manx Touch (IRE) (Petardia)
1132[8] 1320[14] 1606[10] 1890[9] 2404[6] 2628[5] 2879[5] 7460[4] 7533[3] 7727[10]

Ridge City (IRE) *P Khozian*
2 gr c Elusive City(USA) —Absolutely Cool (IRE) (Indian Ridge)
5850a[2]

Ridgetime Anna (IRE) *Daniel Mark Loughnane* a43 43
4 b m Chevalier(IRE) —Annaduff (IRE) (Indian Ridge)
2634[9]

Ridgeway Jazz *M D I Usher* a69
4 b m Kalanisi(IRE) —Billie Holiday (Fairy King (USA))
78[4] 216[5] (275) 353[3] 497[4] (711) 775[2] (897) 981[8]

Ridgeway Sapphire *M D I Usher* a26 54
2 b f Zafeen(FR) —Barefooted Flyer (USA) (Fly So Free (USA))
4047[9] 4933[5] 5811[11] 6355[9]

Ridgeway Silver *M D I Usher* a65 65
3 b f Lujain(USA) —Barefooted Flyer (USA) (Fly So Free (USA))
4[5] 293[4] 1492[4] 1772[7] 2141[4] 2683[7] 4238[7] 4749[12] 4982[4] 5644[5] 6442[9]

Ridley Didley (IRE) *N Wilson* a60 60
4 b g Tagula(IRE) —Dioscorea (IRE) (Pharly (FR))
96[2] 177[2] 367[9] 1096[5] 2158[2] 2657[8] 3111[6]

Rievaulx World *K A Ryan* 102
3 b g Compton Place—Adhaaba (USA) (Dayjur (USA))
1189[6] 1676[5] 2016[2] 2991[15] 3848[6] 4456[17]

Riffelalp (IRE) *Eve Johnson Houghton* a33 52
2 ch f Bachelor Duke(USA) —Alpenrot (IRE) (Barathea (IRE))
1669[6] 2135[9] 3027[5] 4699[6] 5543[9]

Riflessione *R A Harris* a74 76
3 ch c Captain Rio—Hilites (IRE) (Desert King (IRE))
313[4] 568[3] 797[3] 936[2] 1196[10] (1583) 2010[4] 2336[3] 3193[3] 3341[8] 3989[3] 4483[4] 5383[4] 5968[7] 7861[9]

Rigat *J S Goldie* a68 72
6 b g Dansili—Fudge (Polar Falcon (USA))
571[7] 898[3]

Rigged *J A Osborne* a49 42
3 b g Desert Sun—Emma Peel (Emarati (USA))
196[3] 239[6] 383[4]

Riggins (IRE) *L M Cumani* a92 104
5 b g Cape Cross(IRE) —Rentless (Zafonic (USA))
2083[8] (2480) 3873[16]

Riggs (IRE) *Peter Grayson*
3 b c Daggers Drawn(USA) —Jay And-A (IRE) (Elbio)
5645[8] 7254[8]

Rightcar *Peter Grayson* a54 51
2 b c Bertolini(USA) —Loblolly Bay (Halling (USA))
2153[6] 2435[6] 3106[8] 3742[4] 3952[4] 5310[8] 5372[8] 6345[11] 6700[6] 7156[5] 7242[13] 7559[6] 7619[4] 7757[10] 7849[5] 7884[2]

Rightcar Dominic *Peter Grayson* a49
4 b h Kyllachy—Vallauris (Faustus (USA))
1661[0] 6641[8] 7254[7] 7592[9] 7629[6] 7869[11]

Rightcar Lewis *Peter Grayson* a53 49
4 ch m Noverre(USA) —Abeyr (Unfuwain (USA))
46[3] 177[10] 812[5] 895[8] 1617[5] 2070[12] 2366[6] 2758[8] 3125[11] 3479[4] 3853[7] 5159[3] 5422[4] 5629[4]

Rightcar Marian *Peter Grayson* a30
2 b f Oasis Dream—Top Flight Queen (Mark Of Esteem (IRE))
5611[13] 6207[10] 6582[10] 7778[9] 7843[7]

Rightful Ruler *N Wilson* a59 53
7 b g Montjoy(USA) —Lady Of The Realm (Prince Daniel (USA))
1938[11]

Right Grand *W J Haggas* a77
2 b c Exceed And Excel(AUS) —Baileys Dancer (Groom Dancer (USA))
7580[9] (7705) ◆

Right Of Veto *P J Rothwell* a11 39
3 b c Lucky Owners(NZ) —Lana Turrel (USA) (Trempolino (USA))
7002[12]

Right Option (IRE) *J L Flint* a83 79
5 b g Daylami(IRE) —Option (IRE) (Red Ransom (USA))
(459) 591[4] 1356[7] 5903[5]

Right Rave (IRE) *P J McBride* a69 68
2 b f Soviet Star(USA) —Genuinely (IRE) (Entrepreneur)
3113[7] (4383) 4850[6] 5433[5] 5985[2] 6215[3]

Right Step *A P Jarvis* 84
2 b c Xaar—Maid To Dance (Pyramus (USA))
4336[3] (4993) 6011[5]

Right Stuff (FR) *G L Moore* a85 90
6 bb g Dansili—Specificity (USA) (Alleged (USA))
952[2] (1184) 4988[2]

Right You Are (IRE) *Paul Green* a52 52
9 ch g Right Win(IRE) —Ancadia (Henbit (USA))
3450[15]

Rigid *J G Given* a52 67
2 ch g Refuse To Bend(IRE) —Supersonic (Shirley Heights)
2467[4] ◆ 3138[13] 4308[4] 6829[8]

Rigidity *H R A Cecil* 81
2 b c Indian Ridge—Alakananda (Hernando (FR))
5002[2] (6033)

Rigid Rock (IRE) *J T Gorman* a84 84
2 b c Refuse To Bend(IRE) —Delia (IRE) (Darshaan)
2286a[8] 4357a[6] 5452a[6] 6317a[13]

Riguez Dancer *P C Haslam* a97 78
5 b g Dansili—Tricoteuse (Kris)
(219) (333) (384) 2932[18]

Riley Boys (IRE) *J G Given* a70 81
8 ch g Most Welcome—Scarlett Holly (Red Sunset)
1952[12] 2374[7] 3035[5]

Riley Queen Bee (USA) *K R Burke* 57
3 b f Mr Greeley(USA) —Quarrel Over Halo (USA) (Halo (USA))
1825[7] 3093[10] 3352[9]

Rimsky Korsakov (IRE) *Micky Hammond* 53
5 b g Sadler's Wells(USA) —Tedarshana (Darshaan)
1399[3]

Rindless *J F Panvert* a35 26
4 b m Bertolini(USA) —Streaky (IRE) (Danetime (IRE))
592[9] 1958[9] 5963[7]

Ring Of Fire *J L Spearing* a49
2 b c Firebreak—Sweet Patoopie (Indian Ridge)
7538[7] 7764[9]

Ringo Zaar *A B Haynes* a55 16
3 b g Xaar—Tomanivi (Caerleon (USA))
205[10] 520[8]

Ringsider (IRE) *R J Osborne* a51 2
8 ch g Docksider(USA) —Red Comes Up (USA) (Blushing Groom (FR))
5015[8]

Rinky Dink Lady (IRE) *W R Swinburn* 40
3 b f Tiger Hill(IRE) —Glady Starlet (GER) (Big Shuffle (USA))
4381[5]

Rio Caribe (IRE) *T D Walford* 68
2 b g Captain Rio—Kadja Chenee (Spectrum (IRE))
1623[5] 2069[2] 2258[5] 4515[8]

Rio Carnival (USA) *J H M Gosden* a47 20
3 b f Storm Cat(USA) —Zenda (Zamindar (USA))
1128[12]

Rio Cobolo (IRE) *Paul Green* a78 79
3 b c Captain Rio—Sofistication (IRE) (Dayjur (USA))
859[5] 1505[11] 2160[13] 2530[2] 2918[3] 3053[3] (3334) 3616[3] 3804[2] 4392a[9] 4707[2] 5340[3] (5623) 5856[9] 5960[4] (6178) 6434[11] 6798[10] 7141[5] 7337[2] 7506[10]

Rio Command (IRE) *Daniel Mark Loughnane* 79
2 b g Captain Rio—Happy To Chat (IRE) (Alzao (USA))
5499[3]

Rio De La Plata (USA) *Saeed Bin Suroor* 118
4 ch h Rahy(USA) —Express Way (ARG) (Ahmad (ARG))
5655[10] 6448[2] 6812[5]

Rio Guru (IRE) *M R Channon* a83 83
4 b m Spartacus(IRE) —Montessori (Akarad (FR))
1348[4] 1613[9] 2013[5] 2678[4] 2768[5] 3461[2] 3627[10] 4328[4] 4495[5] 5910[3] 6286[5] 7248[2] 7684[10]

Rioja Ruby (IRE) *S G West* 43
3 b f Redback—Bacchanalia (IRE) (Blues Traveller (IRE))
1926[14] 2790[13]

Rioliina (IRE) *J G Portman* a65 82
3 b f Captain Rio—Anneliina (Cadeaux Genereux)
1965[6] 2079[14] 2794[12] (7057) 7520[3] 7662[11]

Rio L'Oren (IRE) *N J Vaughan* a62 39
4 ch m Captain Rio—Princess Sofie (Efisio)
309[7] 531[11] 666[2] 803[13] 1039[11] 2529[13] 2686[9] 3479[6]

Rio Mist *R Hannon* a59 54
2 b f Captain Rio—Welsh Mist (Damister (USA))
2919[6] 3271[7]

Rio Pomba (IRE) *D Carroll* 55
3 b f Captain Rio—Lyrebird (USA) (Storm Bird (CAN))
2162[11] 3125[12] 3239[14]

Rio Royale (IRE) *Mrs A J Perrett* a76 78
3 b g Captain Rio—Lady Nasrana (FR) (Al Nasr (FR))
532[3] 672[7] 829[5] (2010) 2227[8] 2761[2] 2882[4] 3347[11] 4695[4] 5403[5] 5968[9] 6916[9] 7329[12]

Rio Sands *R M Whitaker* a34 76
4 b g Captain Rio—Sally Traffic (River Falls)
1169[14] 1310[6] 1768[8] 2316[3] 2801[7] 3497[5] 3713[9] 4355[5] 5254[3] 6220[9] (6379) 6670[8] 6765[11]

Rio's Girl *R M Whitaker* 7
2 b f Captain Rio—African Breeze (Atraf)
3032[13]

Riotista (IRE) *E J O'Neill* a76 88
3 b f Captain Rio—Elitista (FR) (Linamix (FR))
4394a[10] 5462a[5] 6150a[8] 6981a[8]

Riptide *C F Wall* 63
3 b g Val Royal(FR) —Glittering Image (IRE) (Sadler's Wells (USA))
2199[9] 3192[4] 4178[7]

Rip Van Winkle (IRE) *A P O'Brien* a95 132
3 b c Galileo(IRE) —Looking Back (IRE) (Stravinsky (USA))
1675^{4} 2705^{4} 3640^{2} (4419) (6271) 7311a^{10}

Riqaab (IRE) *E A L Dunlop* a70 77
4 b g Peintre Celebre(USA) —Jeed (IRE) (Mujtahid (USA))
1179^{2} 1581^{6}

Rising Force (IRE) *J L Spearing* a67 71
6 b g Selkirk(USA) —Singing Diva (IRE) (Royal Academy (USA))
2419^{6} 5577^{8} 7670^{12}

Rising Kheleyf (IRE) *G A Swinbank* 77
3 ch g Kheleyf(USA) —Rising Spirits (Cure The Blues (USA))
(1452) ◆ 1626^{2} 2072^{4} 2450^{5} (3616) 4140^{4} 4591^{5} 6015^{12}

Rising Prospect *L M Cumani* a76 82
3 ch c Traditionally(USA) —La Sylphide (Rudimentary (USA))
6830^{7} 7141^{P}

Rising Shadow (IRE) *A D Brown* a81 101
8 b g Efisio—Jouet (Reprimand)
2059^{15} 2707^{14} 2941^{12} 3941^{7} 6015^{3} 6765^{5} ◆ 6847 ^{11} 7287^{17}

Risk Runner (IRE) *James Moffatt* 71
6 b g Mull Of Kintyre(USA) —Fizzygig (Efisio)
2725^{10}

Risky Lady (IRE) *J Ryan* a28 35
3 b f Tamarisk(IRE) —My Croft (Crofter (USA))
1490^{11} 1838^{7} 2132^{9} 2338^{8} 2633^{9}

Risque Belle *E J Creighton*
3 b f Fantastic Light(USA) —Risque Lady (Kenmare (FR))
272^{10}

Risque Heights *J R Boyle* a83 74
5 b g Mark Of Esteem(IRE) —Risque Lady (Kenmare (FR))
550^{6} 798^{7} 3024^{11} 4007^{4} 4235^{8} 5035^{15}

Risquillo (FR) *A Sanchez* a98
3 b c Ballingarry(IRE) —Alexia Fedorovna (USA) (Steinlen)
7704a^{7}

River Ardeche *P C Haslam* a84 85
4 b g Elnadim(USA) —Overcome (Belmez (USA))
139^{3} (226) 1059^{2} 1184^{3} 3000^{3} 7640^{6}

River Captain (IRE) *S Kirk* a82 101
3 ch c Captain Rio—Pardoned (IRE) (Mujadil (USA))
1105^{3} (1462) 2077^{6} (2701) ◆ 3049^{5} 4455^{4}

River Danube *T J Fitzgerald* a65 68
6 b g Dansili—Campaspe (Dominion)
1439^{11} 2044^{13} 4551^{10} 5625^{7} 7084^{5} 7222^{6} 7635^{6}

River Dee (IRE) *D Donovan* a6 76
3 b g Almutawakel—Fiaba (Precocious)
2048^{10} 2377^{3} 3193^{5} ◆ 3624^{4} 3939^{3} 4428^{8} 5326^{12}

River Falcon *J S Goldie* a93 102
9 b g Pivotal—Pearly River (Elegant Air)
1018^{8} 1647^{5} 2059^{5} 2502^{3} 2716^{2} 3351^{13} 4135^{3} 4330^{11} 5132^{11} 5860^{19} 6089^{7} 6283^{9} 6994^{7} 7015^{8}

River Kirov (IRE) *M Wigham* a86 85
6 b g Soviet Star(USA) —Night Shifter (IRE) (Night Shift (USA))
(24) (76) 212^{7} 2938^{17} (3164) 4273^{3} 4387^{2} 4500^{5} 5167^{7} 5404^{14} (6458) 7253^{2} 7454^{8} 7478^{8} 7553^{8} 7662^{10}

River Landing *R M Beckett* 34
2 b c Lucky Story(USA) —Beechnut (IRE) (Mujadil (USA))
6199^{11} 6727^{12}

River Of Glory (ITY) *J Heloury* 26
3 b c Prospects Of Glory(USA) —Celtic River (IRE) (Caerleon (USA))
6149a^{7}

River Rye (IRE) *J S Moore* a71 76
3 b f Acclamation—Rye (IRE) (Charnwood Forest (IRE))
75^{6} 159^{4} 200^{4} 667^{2} 1046^{2} 1492^{10} 2321^{13}

Riverside *M Brittain* a16 27
4 b m Kyllachy—My Cadeaux (Cadeaux Genereux)
5982^{9} 7678^{13}

River Thames *K A Ryan* a73 85
6 b g Efisio—Dashing Water (Dashing Blade)
13^{8}

River Tiber *Saeed Bin Suroor* 106
6 b g Danehill(USA) —Heavenly Whisper (IRE) (Halling (USA))
340a^{7} 439a^{9}

River Till (IRE) *W Jarvis* 65
3 b f Bachelor Duke(USA) —The Poachers Lady (IRE) (Salmon Leap (USA))
2862^{3} ◆ 3338^{8}

Riviera Chic (USA) *R M Beckett* a63
2 b f Medaglia D'Oro(USA) —Hurricane Warning (USA) (Thunder Gulch (USA))
7580^{3} ◆ 7816 ^{3}

Riviera Red (IRE) *L Montague Hall* a51
9 b g Rainbow Quest(USA) —Banquise (IRE) (Last Tycoon)
131^{7} 321^{4} (482) 7197^{12}

Rivitivo *W M Brisbourne* a31
2 b f Deportivo—River Ensign (River God (USA))
1504^{14} 3719^{7} 4188^{10}

Rjeef (IRE) *C E Brittain* 69
2 b c Red Ransom(USA) —Sun Chaser (IRE) (King's Best (USA))
2195^{2} 2610^{2} 5542^{5}

Road To Love (IRE) *M Johnston* a94 88
6 ch g Fruits Of Love(USA) —Alpine Flair (IRE) (Tirol)
1673^{11} 1986^{8} 3142^{14} 3586^{9} 3840^{9} 4716^{4}

Road To Rock (AUS) *Anthony Cummings* 119
5 b h Encosta De Lago(AUS) —Trewornan (Midyan (USA))
7040a^{10}

Roan Inish (CAN) *J S Bolger* a92 89
2 b f Elusive Quality(USA) —Inish Glora (CAN) (Regal Classic (CAN))
6316a^{8}

Roaring Forte (IRE) *W J Haggas* a108 111
4 b h Cape Cross(IRE) —Descant (USA) (Nureyev (USA))
(2241) 4297^{11} (5200)

Roar Of Applause *B J Meehan* a85 91
3 b g Royal Applause—Les Hurlants (IRE) (Barathea (IRE))
(1774) ◆ 1882^{5} (1932) 2209^{3} 2890^{4} 3868^{7} 4296^{6} 4649^{2} 5189^{3} 5575^{7} 5999^{3} 6243^{3} (6474) 6537^{2}

Roar Of The King (USA) *J Noseda* a60 58
3 b c Lion Heart(USA) —V V S Flawless (USA) (Deputy Minister (CAN))
1636^{7} 2282^{6} (Dead)

Roar Talent (USA) *J R Best* a19
2 ch c Roar Of The Tiger(USA) —Laurie's Folly (USA) (Kris S (USA))
6291^{13} 6913^{P}

Roatan *P Bary* a87 102
4 gr g Daylami(IRE) —Celestial Lagoon (JPN) (Sunday Silence (USA))
5281a^{2}

Robbmaa (FR) *A W Carroll* a30 49
4 bl g Cape Cross(IRE) —Native Twine (Be My Native (USA))
1960^{4} 2878^{7} 3259^{5}

Robby Bobby *M Johnston* a102 90
4 ch g Selkirk(USA) —Dancing Mirage (IRE) (Machiavellian (USA))
(360) 563^{2} 585^{9} 801^{4} 1003^{15} 1458^{18} 1798^{3} ◆ 2055^{10} 2891^{8} 3797^{5} 4340^{12} 4561^{6} 4840^{4}

Robens Rock (IRE) *A B Haynes* a67 61
2 b g Rock Of Gibraltar(IRE) —Qhazeenah (Marju (IRE))
4888^{8} 5867^{6} 6700^{2} 6932^{5}

Robert Burns (IRE) *Miss D Mountain* a1 71
4 b g Invincible Spirit(IRE) —Double Red (IRE) (Thatching)
1606^{14}

Robert The Brave *P R Webber* a82 68
5 b g Primo Valentino(IRE) —Sandicliffe (USA) (Imp Society (USA))
4053^{4}

Robinson Cruso *M A Jarvis* 82
2 b c Footstepsinthesand—Miss Hawai (FR) (Peintre Celebre (USA))
5317^{2} 6064^{6} 6991^{2}

Robin The Till *R Hannon* a67 62
3 ch g Bold Edge—My Dancer (IRE) (Alhaarth (IRE))
842^{3} 1032^{2} 3580^{11} 3859^{4} 4567^{9} 4712^{5} 4937^{7} 5323^{14} 5500^{5}

Robust Wish (USA) *B J Meehan* a78
2 b g Strong Hope(USA) —Copper Rose (USA) (Unbridled (USA))
5807^{13} 6254^{2} 6772^{2} (7580)

Rockabilly Rebel *B W Hills* 64
2 b c Kyllachy—Its All Relative (Distant Relative)
3218^{9} 3920^{5} 4243^{3} 5033^{5} 5526^{6}

Rockabout (IRE) *B J Meehan* a50 61
3 b f Rock Of Gibraltar(IRE) —Capades Dancer (USA) (Gate Dancer (USA))
1844^{6} 2433^{15} 3221^{4} 3803^{7} 4872^{10} 5384^{8} 5790^{7} 6440^{4} 7143^{11}

Rock A Doodle Doo (IRE) *W Jarvis* 51
2 b c Oratorio(IRE) —Nousaiyra (IRE) (Be My Guest (USA))
2533^{8} 6424^{7} 6737^{12}

Rock And Roll Kid (IRE) *Anthony Mullins* 105
4 b g Danehill Dancer(IRE) —Milly's Song (Millfontaine)
2289a^{2} (4412a) 5655^{5}

Rock Anthem (IRE) *Mike Murphy* a75 81
5 ch g Rock Of Gibraltar(IRE) —Regal Portrait (IRE) (Royal Academy (USA))
39^{2} 157^{2} 362^{6} 683^{5} 2125^{2} 2493^{4} 2824^{8} 3770^{3} 3996^{4} 4389^{5} (5019) (5211) 5640^{8} (5833) 7060^{3} 7229^{5}

Rock Art (IRE) *Karen George* a51 59
3 ch f Rock Of Gibraltar(IRE) —Lindesberg (Doyoun)
2947^{9} ◆ 3569^{2} 4179^{6} 4704^{8} 5367^{8} 5628^{7} 7586^{9} 7677^{11}

Rock Ascot (URU) *G L Moore* a100 87
5 gr h Mantle Rock(USA) —Maria Fumadora (URU) (Sportin' Gold (USA))
261a^{9} 4090^{8} 4408^{13} 6290^{7} (6633) 7226^{6}

Rocker *G L Moore* a74 85
5 b g Rock Of Gibraltar(IRE) —Jessica's Dream (IRE) (Desert Style (IRE))
1672^{3} 2228^{3} 2637^{9} 3386^{2} 3694^{4} (4232) 4461^{21} 5098^{4} 5592^{4} 6667^{2} 6964^{5}

Rocket (IRE) *H J Manners* a12 27
8 ch g Cadeaux Genereux—Prends Ca (IRE) (Reprimand)
5028^{13}

Rocketball (IRE) *Mrs L Williamson* a62 69
4 b g Namid—Luceball (IRE) (Bluebird (USA))
596^{7} 794^{4} 976^{6} 1591^{2} (1695) 2032^{9} 2625^{4} (3111) (3445) 3570^{4} 4467^{4} 5411^{10} 5518^{6} 5919^{6} 6314^{4}

Rocket Man (AUS) *P Shaw* 121
4 b g Viscount(AUS) —Macrosa (NZ) (Mcginty (NZ))
2116a^{2}

Rocket Rob (IRE) *S A Callaghan* a69 88
3 b g Danetime(IRE) —Queen Of Fibres (IRE) (Scenic)
936^{5} 1720^{5} 2148^{7} (3010) 3476^{3} (4231) 4454^{4} (4952) 5098^{2} (5264) 5436^{4} 5871^{8}

Rocket Ruby *D Shaw* a61 58
3 br f Piccolo—Kitty Kitty Cancan (Warrshan (USA))
273^{5} 390^{2} 831^{4} 986^{DSQ} 2162^{2} 2581^{7} 3999^{2} 4137^{2} 7601^{10} 7629^{2} 7714^{3} 7889^{7}

Rockette (FR) *Y De Nicolay* a89 94
4 ch m Ange Gabriel(FR) —Racoon (FR) (Be My Guest (USA))
3419a^{5} 7621a^{2}

Rock Exhibition *B W Duke* a30 70
4 ch m Rock Of Gibraltar(IRE) —Finity (USA) (Diesis)
1405^{11} 1778^{6} 7225^{11}

Rockfella *D J Coakley* a59 82
3 ch g Rock Of Gibraltar(IRE) —Afreeta (USA) (Afleet (CAN))
2126^{3} 2892^{5} 3472^{5} (4150) (5876) 6420^{5} (6936) 7373^{6}

Rockfield Lodge (IRE) *Ian Williams* a75 81
4 b g Stravinsky(USA) —La Belle Simone (IRE) (Grand Lodge (USA))
1468^{6} 1784^{6} 2349^{6} 3242^{6} 4268^{4} 4479^{3} 7051^{6} 7348^{3} 7726^{5}

Rockhampton (IRE) *A P O'Brien* a95 99
3 b c Galileo(IRE) —Green Rosy (USA) (Green Dancer (USA))
1291^{3} 3049^{28} 3438a^{9} 3882a^{4} 4298^{8} 5688a^{8}

Rockhorse (IRE) *B Grizzetti* 104
4 ch g Rock Of Gibraltar(IRE) —Maelalong (IRE) (Maelstrom Lake)
2525a^{5} 6718a^{3} 7303a^{2}

Rockinit (IRE) *R A Harris* a32 67
3 b f Rock Of Gibraltar(IRE) —Tidal Reach (USA) (Kris S (USA))
306^{9} 741^{7}

Rockin N Reelin (USA) *J T Gorman* 70
2 b c Forest Camp(USA) —Dusti's Tune (USA) (Unbridled's Song (USA))
1994a^{5} 6319a^{15}

Rock Jock (IRE) *Tracey Collins* a96 99
2 b c Rock Of Gibraltar(IRE) —Perfect Touch (USA) (Miswaki (USA))
3436a^{5} 4359a^{7} 5452a^{2} 5895a^{10}

Rockjumper *Mrs Lawney Hill* a54 57
4 br g Cape Cross(IRE) —Bronzewing (Beldale Flutter (USA))
116^{4} 1442^{11}

Rock Kingdom (AUS) *Mrs Gai Waterhouse* 112
4 ch g Rock Of Gibraltar(IRE) —Happy Empress (AUS) (St Covet (AUS))
7040a^{8}

Rock Me (IRE) *Mrs Lawney Hill* a48 41
4 ch g Rock Of Gibraltar(IRE) —Final Farewell (USA) (Proud Truth (USA))
7881^{5}

Rock My Soul (IRE) *Uwe Ostmann* 100
3 b f Clodovil(IRE) —Rondinay (FR) (Cadeaux Genereux)
3520a^{9} (6886a)

Rock My World (IRE) *M A Jarvis* a70
2 b f Rock Of Gibraltar(IRE) —Arctic Hunt (IRE) (Bering)
7522^{2} ◆

Rocknest Island (IRE) *P D Niven* a59 58
6 b m Bahhare(USA) —Margin Call (IRE) (Tirol)
2344^{9} 2969^{6} 3444^{7} 4848^{9}

Rock'N'Roll Dream (FR) *A Spanu* 85
3 ch c Lomitas—Vignola (Machiavellian (USA))
1207a^{6}

Rock 'N' Royal *R A Fahey* 79
2 b c Royal Applause—Grande Terre (IRE) (Grand Lodge (USA))
(6896) ◆

Rock Of Behistun (IRE) *P L Gilligan* a8 11
2 b g Antonius Pius(USA) —Persian Flower (Persian Heights)
4200^{11} 5224^{P} 5811^{12} 7120^{14}

Rock Of Eire *E J Creighton* a49 55
2 b g Rock Of Gibraltar(IRE) —Graceful Lass (Sadler's Wells (USA))
4717^{3} 5312^{10} 6065^{6} 7502^{5}

Rock Of Love (IRE) *M Johnston* 89
2 b c Rock Of Gibraltar(IRE) —Ridotto (Salse (USA))
1610^{4} ◆ 1827^{4} 2167^{2} 2623^{3} (3232) 3821^{4} 4488^{14}

Rock Of Nassau (FR) *F Head* 96
3 ch c Rock Of Gibraltar(IRE) —Solosole (USA) (Gulch (USA))
3649a^{6}

Rock Of Rochelle (USA) *A Kinsella* a89 111
4 br h Rock Of Gibraltar(IRE) —Recoleta (USA) (Wild Again (USA))
1989^{5} 2870a^{7} 3141^{3} 3881a^{6} 5618a^{6} 7044a^{3}

Rock Peak (IRE) *B J Llewellyn* a67 76
4 b g Dalakhani(IRE) —Convenience (IRE) (Ela-Mana-Mou)
102^{6} 341^{8} 502^{4}

Rock Relief (IRE) *Sir Mark Prescott* a59 66
3 gr g Daylami(IRE) —Sheer Bliss (IRE) (Sadler's Wells (USA))
4206^{5} 4650^{11}

Rocks Off (ARG) *M F De Kock* a92 97
4 br h Orpen(USA) —Lava Gold (USA) (Java Gold (USA))
258a^{5} 526a^{9} 615a^{9} 769a^{8}

Rockson (IRE) *Ian Williams* a53 53
3 bb f Rock Of Gibraltar(IRE) —Opera Star (IRE) (Sadler's Wells (USA))
876^{7} 1532^{9} 3302^{6} 3710^{12} 4196^{2} 5316^{12} 6175^{12} 7109^{8} 7349^{7} 7500^{12} 7818 ^{6}

Rocksy *D J Coakley* a38 62
3 b f Kyllachy—Sea Music (Inchinor)
1253^{13}

Rock Tech *J R Jenkins* a52 34
4 b h High Estate—Mrs Fire Cracker (Rock City)
1185^{12} 3319^{6} 3460^{11} 4667^{8} 7609^{10} 7767^{4}

Rock The Stars (IRE) *M G Quinlan* a53 47
2 ch g Rock Of Gibraltar(IRE) —Crimphill (IRE) (Sadler's Wells (USA))
7243^{9} 7773^{9}

Rockweiller *C R Egerton* a26 69
2 b c Rock Of Gibraltar(IRE) —Ballerina Suprema (IRE) (Sadler's Wells (USA))
5017^{7} 5318^{3} 5611^{10} 6829^{12}

Rocky Heights (IRE) *J L Dunlop* 57
3 b f Rock Of Gibraltar(IRE) —Height Of Fantasy (IRE) (Shirley Heights)
1407^{8} 2006^{9} 2635^{3} ◆ 3454^{2}

Rockymountainhigh (IRE) *David Wachman* 80
2 b c Danehill Dancer(IRE) —Gentle Night (Zafonic (USA))
1994a^{3}

Rocky's Pride (IRE) *G L Moore* a81 78
3 b g Rock Of Gibraltar(IRE) —L'Animee (Green Tune (USA))
2885^{2} 3221^{2} (3472) 6907^{12} 7612^{3} (7881)

Rocoppelia (USA) *Mrs A J Perrett* a63 59
3 ch c Hennessy(USA) —Eternally (USA) (Timeless Moment (USA))
74^{6} (348) 593^{3}

Rodarte *B Grizzetti* 84
2 b f Kyllachy—Infiel (Luge)
5279a^{11}

Rodios (FR) *Dominique Sepulchre* 51
3 b c Loxias(FR) —Messini (IRE) (Ballad Rock)
2293a^{8}

Rodrigo De Freitas (IRE) *J R Boyle* a60 60
2 b g Captain Rio—Brazilian Sun (IRE) (Barathea (IRE))
2631^{10} 4006^{9} 4534^{6} 5573^{2} 5985^{5} 6736^{4} 6793^{14}

Rodrigo De Torres *H R A Cecil* 89
2 ch c Bahamian Bounty—Leonica (Lion Cavern (USA))
(4331) ◆ 5198^{U} 6486^{16} 6811^{4}

Rogalt (IRE) *B Smart* 67
3 b c Rock Of Gibraltar(IRE) —Rills (USA) (Clever Trick (USA))
1739^{8} 2250^{3} 2439^{2} 3355^{5} 3856^{5}

Rohaani (USA) *Doug Watson* a95 100
7 ch h High Yield(USA) —Strawberry's Charm (USA) (Strawberry Road (AUS))
185a^{6} 338a^{12}

Roi De Slic (FR) *J-P Roman*
3 gr g Slickly(FR) —Reine Cotiere (FR) (Roi De Rome (USA))
6980a^{0}

Roi Des Sables (FR) *B De Montzey* 103
3 b c Marchand De Sable(USA) —Guirlande (USA) (Rahy (USA))
1917a^{9}

Roi De Vitesse (IRE) *B R Millman* 102
2 ch c Chineur(FR) —Face The Storm (IRE) (Barathea (IRE))
1044^{7} (1358) (2247) 2957a^{3} 3817^{2} 4418^{5} 5416a^{4} 5859^{4} 6524a^{7}

Roisin's Prince (IRE) *M Sheppard* a56 28
7 br g Bold Fact(USA) —Rosie Jaques (Doyoun)
148^{2} 2519^{8} 3617^{10}

Roker Park (IRE) *K A Ryan* 103
4 b g Choisir(AUS) —Joyful (IRE) (Green Desert (USA))
2059^{13} 2716^{14} (2941) (3389) 4037^{3} 4330^{10} 5420^{3} 6089^{19} 6270^{9}

Rokoko (TUR) *A Basyigit* 96
3 gr f Distant Relative—Cihanyandi Lutfiye (TUR) (Kilicaslan (TUR))
5588a^{8}

Roleplay (IRE) *J M P Eustace* a61 50
4 b m Singspiel(IRE) —In Your Dreams (IRE) (Suave Dancer (USA))
3007^{9} 3720^{2} 4202^{12} 5111^{7} 5680^{3} 6126^{8} 7374^{6}

Rolling Bag (FR) *M Roussel* 103
3 ro c Rashbag—Kiritsou (FR) (Great Palm (USA))
1979a^{6}

Rolling Hills (IRE) *H Candy* 75
2 b g Celtic Swing—Silk Suivante (IRE) (Danehill (USA))
6696^{8} 7058^{2}

Roly Boy *R Hannon* a83 89
3 b g Dansili—Night At Sea (Night Shift (USA))
851^{4} 1751^{9} 1971^{6} 2432^{12} 3461^{6} 3525^{4} 4005^{4} 5403^{7}

Romancea (USA) *E F Vaughan* 51
2 ch f Mr Greeley(USA) —Two Halos (USA) (Saint Ballado (CAN))
4055^{10}

Roman Emperor (NZ) *Bart Cummings* 114
4 b h Montjeu(IRE) —Gussy Godiva (NZ) (Last Tycoon)
6871a^{2} 7215a^{21}

Roman Empress (IRE) *A P O'Brien* 115
3 b f Sadler's Wells(USA) —Ionian Sea (Slip Anchor)
3412a^{6} 3896a^{6} 4609a^{5} 4923a^{2} 5201^{3} 5890a^{2} 6298a^{10}

Roman Glory (IRE) *B J Meehan* 94
3 b g Soviet Star(USA) —Putout (Dowsing (USA))
1972^{4} 2273^{15} 2674^{15}

Roman History (IRE) *Miss Tracy Waggott* a58 59
6 b g Titus Livius(FR) —Tetradonna (IRE) (Teenoso (USA))
3314^{6} 4804^{3} 4944^{7}

Roman Maze *W M Brisbourne* a59 95
9 ch g Lycius(USA) —Maze Garden (USA) (Riverman (USA))
4859^{9} 6123^{10} 6999^{10} 7240^{11} 7462^{10}

Roman Republic (FR) *M Johnston* 105
3 b c Cape Cross(IRE) —Mare Nostrum (Caerleon (USA))
(2696) 3049^{11} 3639^{6} 3780^{2} ◆ (4455)

Roman Sioux (IRE) *R Bastiman*
2 b c Antonius Pius(USA) —Blue Sioux (Indian Ridge)
6679^{11}

Roman's Run (USA) *Doug Watson* a100
5 br h Tiznow(USA) —Ensnare (USA) (Seeking The Gold (USA))
(435a) 698a^{13}

Roman The Emperor (IRE) *S W Hall* 35
3 ch g Spartacus(IRE) —Honey Bee (Alnasr Alwasheek)
1260^{10} 1622^{5} 2181^{10}

Romantic Bond *T D Easterby* 18
3 ch f Monsieur Bond(IRE) —Romantic Drama (IRE) (Primo Dominie)
4277^{12} 5422^{8}

Romantic Interlude (IRE) *A P Jarvis* a56 48
3 b f Hawk Wing(USA) —Kissin A Lot (USA) (Kissin Kris (USA))
1070^{9} 1363^{8} 2131^{13} 2461^{14} 4084^{9} 4995^{10}

Romanticize *Dr J D Scargill* 77
3 b f Kyllachy—Romancing (Dr Devious (IRE))
(1703) 2299^{2} ◆ 3163^{8}

Romantic Man (GER) *M Rulec* 68
6 b h Big Shuffle(USA) —Romanze (GER) (Surumu (GER))
466a[3] 653a[12]
Romantic Queen *George Baker* a69 52
3 b f Medicean—Bandit Queen (Desert Prince (IRE))
(19) 45[4] 593[4] 826[3] 936[6] 4604[F] *(6252)* 6572[10] *6782[8] 6914[3] 7138[8] 7273[6]* 7484[5] 7602[10]
Romantic Retreat *G L Moore* a54 62
4 ch m Rainbow Quest(USA) —Magical Retreat (USA) (Sir Ivor (USA))
102[5] 501[6] 972[10]
Romantic Verse *S Curran* a71 62
4 b m Kyllachy—Romancing (Dr Devious (IRE))
241[7] 557[2] 777[9] (937) ◆ *4374[12] 4859[10]* 5449[11] *5813[12] 6588[13] 7579[5]* 7774[7] 7815 [11]
Romany Princess (IRE) *R Hannon* a88 95
4 b m Viking Ruler(AUS) —Fag End (IRE) (Treasure Kay)
1733[3] 2050[8] *2828[5] 3301[7]* (3921) (4211) 4422[6] ◆ 5221[5] 5607[4] 6307[6]
Romeos Girl *Jennie Candlish* 55
2 b f Statue Of Liberty(USA) —Fadaki Hawaki (USA) (Vice Regent (CAN))
4075[4] 5547[7] 5934[5]
Romeo's On Fire (IRE) *G M Lyons* a93 77
5 b g Danehill(USA) —Fighting Countess (USA) (Ringside (USA))
3435a[19] *7341a[7]*
Rondeau (GR) *P R Chamings* a82 76
4 ch g Harmonic Way—Areti (GR) (Wadood (USA))
3208[5] 3691[5] *(4203)* 4604[12] *5167[6]* 5719[8] *6230[9]* (6790) *7327[4] 7627[2] 7830[10]*
Ronnie Howe *S R Bowring* a59 72
5 b g Hunting Lion(IRE) —Arasong (Aragon)
149 146[4] 303[3] 367[7] 575[5] 746[9] 1360[3] 1591[4] 1877[10] 2801[8] 3304[12] 3765[9] 3999[11] 6221[7] 7838[7]
Ronnies Girl *C J Teague*
5 b m Tobougg(IRE) —Tryptonic (FR) (Baryshnikov (AUS))
7931[3] 963[8]
Ron The Don *A Berry* 21
2 ch g Paris House—Hillside Heather (IRE) (Tagula (IRE))
1735[8] 2260[9] 3478[8] 4101[8] 6557[11] 6819[16] *7419[11]*
Rony Dony (IRE) *M E Rimmer* a27 39
5 b g Revoque(IRE) —Farrans Guest (IRE) (Tagula (IRE))
2185[12] 2415[12] *4083[10]* 4703[7] 4916[9] 5124[11]
Roodee King *Patrick Morris* a40 55
3 b g Auction House(USA) —Antithesis (IRE) (Fairy King (USA))
2700[6] 3498[2] *5645[4] 6206[5] 7052[12]*
Roodle *Eve Johnson Houghton* 89
2 b f Xaar—Roodeye (Inchinor)
3277 [2] (3799) ◆ 4295[6] 4989[5] 5763[2] 6486[9] 7147[6]
Rookwith (IRE) *T G McCourt* a65 63
9 b g Revoque(IRE) —Resume (IRE) (Lahib (USA))
(4751) (Dead)
Rope Bridge (IRE) *Mrs J L Le Brocq* a40 60
4 b g Orpen(USA) —Carhue Journey (IRE) (Barathea (IRE))
4586a[7] 5541a[7]
Rory Anna (IRE) *John J Walsh* 79
3 b f Viking Ruler(AUS) —Montana Miss (IRE) (Earl Of Barking (IRE))
2960a[9] 3896a[7]
Rosabee (IRE) *Mrs D J Sanderson* 97
3 ch f No Excuse Needed—Tilbrook (IRE) (Don't Forget Me)
3622[7] 3746[14] 4352[8]
Rosa Del Dubai (IRE) *B Grizzetti* 103
4 b m Dubai Destination(USA) —Rosa Di Brema (ITY) (Lomitas)
6715a[10] 7046a[15]
Rosa Gurney (IRE) *J R Best* 56
2 b f Antonius Pius(USA) —Nonsense (IRE) (Soviet Star (USA))
2563[9] 4460[11] 6563[5]
Rosaleen (IRE) *B J Meehan* a96 99
4 b m Cadeaux Genereux—Dark Rosaleen (IRE) (Darshaan)
(2768) 3017[2] 4259[5] 4566[3] 5260[8] *7132[5]*
Rosa Muscosa (USA) *J S Bolger* 77
2 b f Dixie Union(USA) —Sun Princessa (USA) (Pleasant Colony (USA))
6316a[12]
Rosanara (FR) *A De Royer-Dupre* 114
2 gr f Sinndar(IRE) —Rosawa (FR) (Linamix (FR))
(6523a) ◆ 7207a[3]
Rosa Rosa (FR) *X Betron* 52
3 b f Oumnaz(FR) —Belle Lyse (FR) (Baylis)
4130a[8]
Rosas A Sandra (IRE) *C Laffon-Parias* 76
2 b f Refuse To Bend(IRE) —Petite Rose (IRE) (Turtle Island (IRE))
3648a[9]
Rosbay (IRE) *T D Easterby* 92
5 b g Desert Prince(IRE) —Dark Rosaleen (IRE) (Darshaan)
1557[2] 1990[14] 2374[3] 2781[4] 3034[2] 3826[10] 4471[5] 4597[5] 4930[4] 5334[7] 5671[9] 6648[4]
Rosco Flyer (IRE) *J R Boyle* a71 57
3 b g Val Royal(FR) —Palace Soy (IRE) (Tagula (IRE))
4872[6] 6224[2] 6440[6] 6698[5]
Ros Cuire (IRE) *W A Murphy* a60 51
4 br h Expelled(USA) —Haven Island (IRE) (Revoque (IRE))
4375[14] 5869[10] 6414[3] *6828[8]* 6984[7]
Rose Alba (IRE) *J L Dunlop* 66
2 gr f Verglas(IRE) —Green Rosy (USA) (Green Dancer (USA))
3810[7] 4534[7] 5498[2] 6067[9]
Rose Aurora *M P Tregoning* a27 39
2 gr f Pastoral Pursuits—Khaladja (IRE) (Akarad (FR))
5749[5] *7234[9]*
Rose Avelina *I W McInnes* 25
3 b f Xaar—B'Elanna Torres (Entrepreneur)
3237[5] 3690[7] 4354[10] 4994[7] 5470[11] 6098[10]
Rose Bed (IRE) *M G Quinlan* a52 40
2 ch f Namid—Daqtora (Dr Devious (IRE))
1719[7] *6228[11]*
Rose Bien *P J McBride* a61 67
7 bb m Bien Bien(USA) —Madame Bovary (Ile De Bourbon (USA))
1069[3] 1273[6] *1609[7]* 2018[2] 2944[5] 4388[3] (5068)
Rose Blossom *R A Fahey* 97
2 b f Pastoral Pursuits—Lamarita (Emarati (USA))
(2435) ◆ 3015[7] (3528) 5199[7] 5822[4]
Rose Catherine (USA) *Todd Pletcher* a74 96
2 bb f Speightstown(USA) —Great Plains Lady (USA) (Peaks And Valleys (USA))
7282a[2]
Rose Cheval (USA) *M R Channon* a60 72
3 ro f Johannesburg(USA) —La Samanna (USA) (Trempolino (USA))
556[3] 970[7] 1774[7] 4079[9] 4719[3] 5367[3] 5905[2] 6219[7]
Rosedale *J A R Toller* a54 57
2 b f Pastoral Pursuits—Wyoming (Inchinor)
1569[11] 2000[5] *2383[4]* (4195) 4884[8] *5635[6]* 6169[3] 7097[4]
Rose De Rita *L P Grassick* a26 36
4 br m Superior Premium—Rita's Rock Ape (Mon Tresor)
3204[11]
Rose Diamond (IRE) *R Charlton* a102 101
3 gr f Daylami(IRE) —Tante Rose (IRE) (Barathea (IRE))
1292[4] 1599[3] 3016[13]
Rose Hip (IRE) *Joseph G Murphy* a74 99
5 b m Rossini(USA) —Rose Tint (IRE) (Salse (USA))
4412a[7] 5490a[13] 6298a[3]
Rosemarkie *J M Bradley* a1 25
5 br m Diktat—Sparkling Isle (Inchinor)
3717[11] 4220[11] 5120[10]
Rosendhal (IRE) *A Renzoni* 91
2 ch c Indian Ridge—Kathy College (IRE) (College Chapel)
3185a[4]
Rose Of Coma (IRE) *A G Juckes* a47 59
3 br f Kheleyf(USA) —Rosalia (USA) (Red Ransom (USA))
1270[11] 1620[9] 1848[3] (2333) *2709[5]* 2808[3] 3005[4] 3314[2] 3661[2] 4734[7] 5123[5] 5470[6] 6919[4] 7094[6]
Rose Row *Mrs Mary Hambro* a85 72
5 gr m Act One—D'Azy (Persian Bold)
1287[4] 2552[4] 4378[8] 4498[13] *(5227) (5812) 6258[2]* ◆ *6636[4]*
Roses *G A Swinbank* 47
4 b m Muhtarram(USA) —Sublime (Conquering Hero (USA))
3731[5]
Roses For The Lady (IRE) *John M Oxx* 112
3 b f Sadler's Wells(USA) —Head In The Clouds (IRE) (Rainbow Quest (USA))
1789[3] 2960a[5] 3896a[2]
Roses 'N' Wine (CAN) *David R Bell* a89 95
4 ch m Broken Vow(USA) —Regent's Fancy (CAN) (Vice Regent (CAN))
6872a[8]
Rose Street (IRE) *M A Jarvis* a94 101
5 b m Noverre(USA) —Archipova (IRE) (Ela-Mana-Mou)
1986[5] ◆
Rosetta Hill *J R Jenkins* 48
2 ch f Compton Place—Fruit Of Glory (Glory Of Dancer)
3458[8] 5969[9] 6903[12]
Rosewin (IRE) *A Dickman* a20 72
3 b f Hawkeye(IRE) —African Scene (IRE) (Scenic)
1276[9] 1611[7] 1893[3] (2802) 3233[5] 3974[3] 4806[8] (5342) (5732) 5979[2] 6560[6]
Rosey De Megeve *F Rohaut* 110
3 ch f Efisio—Lady Golconda (FR) (Kendor (FR))
1237a[5] 3892a[3] 4971a[4]
Rosie Cross (IRE) *Eve Johnson Houghton* a61 64
5 b m Cape Cross(IRE) —Professional Mom (USA) (Spinning World (USA))
231[1] 56[5] 587[4] 802[10]
Rosie Says No *A J McCabe* a70 68
4 b m Catcher In The Rye(IRE) —Curlew Calling (IRE) (Pennine Walk)
2145[4] 2579[13] 4154[3] *5576[2]* ◆ *6377[4]* 6799[14] (7100) *7280[5] 7596[8] 7645[4] 7838[3] 7852[8]*
Rosie's Magic *W De Best-Turner* 36
2 b f Auction House(USA) —Sachiko (Celtic Swing)
6055[12] 6756[5]
Rosie Two *W S Kittow* a50 37
3 b f Acclamation—Just A Glimmer (Bishop Of Cashel)
2205[11] 3017[7] 3460[5] 4223[6] 4937[13] *5316[6]* 6170[7]
Rosika *Sir Michael Stoute* a100 99
3 b f Sakhee(USA) —Blush Rambler (IRE) (Blushing Groom (FR))
(1579) (2008) 3618[7] 5904[2] (6419) *7131[2]* ◆
Rosiliant (IRE) *C G Cox* a48 59
2 ch f Refuse To Bend(IRE) —Rosy Dudley (IRE) (Grand Lodge (USA))
4603[14] *5571[9]* 5934[7] 6367[7] *6829[9]* 7056[5]
Rosko *B Ellison* a66 76
5 b g Selkirk(USA) —Desert Alchemy (IRE) (Green Desert (USA))
476[7] 570[3] 767[3] 1245[6] 1402[5] 1690[2] 2362[6] 3124[4] (3353) 4548[3] 4941[4] 5160[11]
Rossatron *T T Clement* a48 53
3 b c Primo Valentino(IRE) —Sunday Night (GER) (Bakharoff (USA))
670[4] 902[6] 1362[4] 2004[7]
Rossett Rose (IRE) *M Brittain* a37 66
3 ch f Rossini(USA) —Sabaah Elfull (Kris)
2726[4] 3176[6] 3729[7] 4105[10] 4279[14] 5254[5]
Rossini's Dancer *R A Fahey* a63 73
4 b g Rossini(USA) —Bint Alhabib (Nashwan (USA))
(1153) 1475[4] 1955[6] 2261[8] 3070[12] 4034[2] 4402[9] 4876[6] (5549) 6012[5] (6769)
Ross Moor *Mike Murphy* a64 70
7 b g Dansili—Snipe Hall (Crofthall)
894[5] 1192[12] *1604[7]* 2183[2] 2442[3] 3563[8] (4207) 4437[3] 5532[10] *7695[12] 7776[P]*
Rosy Alexander *G G Margarson* a56 72
4 ch m Spartacus(IRE) —Sweet Angeline (Deploy)
2052[11]
Rosy Dawn *J J Bridger* a55 56
4 ch m Bertolini(USA) —Blushing Sunrise (USA) (Cox's Ridge (USA))
877[9] 1122[7] 1728[10] 1961[2] 2222[12] *2601[2] 2923[4]* 3074[P] 3533[5] 3777[2] 4235[7] 4300[4] (4704) 5122[8] 5365[7] 5577[9] 6565[6] 6770[12] 7250[10]
Rotative *W R Swinburn* a82 96
4 ch m Spinning World(USA) —Kristal Bridge (Kris)
(2684) 3273[9] 4197[2] (4882) (5917)
Rothesay Dancer *J S Goldie* a77 88
6 b m Lujain(USA) —Rhinefield Beauty (IRE) (Shalford (IRE))
901[2] 1227[4] 1627[2] 2032[3] 2228[6] (2591) 2716[12] 3145[3] (3295) 3784[8] 4135[9] 4530[6] 4753[7] (5149) 5293[8] 5768[9] 6051[7] 6155[5] 6902[7]
Rouge Emery (FR) *A Couetil* 69
3 b f Bonnet Rouge(FR) —Natashwan (Shining Steel)
6753a[2]
Rougham *A M Balding* a63 75
3 b g Red Ransom(USA) —Louella (USA) (El Gran Senor (USA))
4270[4] 5061[2] *6225[4]*
Rough Rock (IRE) *C A Dwyer* a35 67
4 ch g Rock Of Gibraltar(IRE) —Amitie Fatale (IRE) (Night Shift (USA))
1074[12] 2137[4] 2456[8] 2864[4] 3075[5] 3401[9] (4182) 4469[9] 4668[5] 5008[10] 5998[4] 6738[4] 7100[2]
Rough Sketch (USA) *Sir Mark Prescott* a64 61
4 b g Peintre Celebre(USA) —Drama Club (IRE) (Sadler's Wells (USA))
132[5] 494[8] (679) 751[4] 967[4] 2725[11] 3348[7] (3475) 5483[5] 5975[12] 6566[7]
Roundthetwist (IRE) *K R Burke* a71 63
4 b g Okawango(USA) —Delta Town (USA) (Sanglamore (USA))
187[5] 872[5]
Round Won (USA) *W J Knight* a71 61
2 ch c Two Punch(USA) —Indy Go Go (USA) (A.P. Indy (USA))
5000[15] 5907[7] *6629[3]*
Rousseau (FR) *Frau C Bocskai* 55
3 b c Where Or When(IRE) —Illumination (Saddlers' Hall (IRE))
5784a[9]
Rowaad *A E Price* a69 72
4 ch g Compton Place—Level Pegging (IRE) (Common Grounds)
1889[8] 2880[11] 3208[7] 3541[3] 3863[3] 4435[17] 5549[12]
Rowan Light *J R Boyle* 54
3 b f Fantastic Light(USA) —Filippa (GER) (Dashing Blade)
1269[8]
Rowan Lodge (IRE) *Ollie Pears* a65 69
7 ch g Indian Lodge(IRE) —Tirol Hope (IRE) (Tirol)
129[3] 194[12] (1276) 2155[2] (2527) (2965) 3123[5] 4344[3] *4861[7]* 5513[3] *6256[4]* 6987[7] *7600[9] 7755[7]*
Rowan Rio *W J Haggas* a71 90
4 ch g Lomitas—Lemon Tree (USA) (Zilzal (USA))
2475[9] 2931[9] *3273[8]* 3635[7] 3840[11] 4269[7] 4544[7]
Rowan River *A Middleton* a64 74
5 b m Invincible Spirit(IRE) —Lemon Tree (USA) (Zilzal (USA))
2808[7]
Rowan Tiger *J R Boyle* a79 59
3 b g Tiger Hill(IRE) —Lemon Tree (USA) (Zilzal (USA))
1461[8] *2489[5]* 2865[6] *(5988) (6376) (6634)*
Rowayton *J D Bethell* a86 85
3 bg f Lujain(USA) —Bandanna (Bandmaster (USA))
2279[8] 2934[4] 3166[5] 3747[4] 4601[6]
Rowe Park *Mrs L C Jewell* a109 109
6 b g Dancing Spree(USA) —Magic Legs (Reprimand)
911[6] (1384) 1676[6] 4341[6] 4456[6] 5878[7] 6661[11] *(7090) 7488[9]*
Roxy Flyer (IRE) *Mrs A J Perrett* a62 67
2 b f Rock Of Gibraltar(IRE) —Dyna Flyer (USA) (Marquetry (USA))
6729[4] *7135[6]*
Royaaty (IRE) *Saeed Bin Suroor* a84
3 b c Singspiel(IRE) —Whisper To Dream (USA) (Gone West (USA))
(7439) ◆
Royal Acclamation (IRE) *G A Harker* a48 71
4 b g Acclamation—Lady Abigail (IRE) (Royal Academy (USA))
108[8] 1456[10] 1694[9] 2660[2] 2964[4] 3296[4]
Royal Adelaide (IRE) *J A Osborne* a37 40
3 ch f Redback—Ball Cat (FR) (Cricket Ball (USA))
1250[9] *1563[8]* 1837[7] 6175[5] 6787[14] *7105[11]*
Royal Amnesty *I Semple* a84 88
6 br g Desert Prince(IRE) —Regal Peace (Known Fact (USA))
79[8] 713[5] (893) 1646[2] 1986[11] 2815[8] 3847[3] 5915[4]
Royal And Regal (IRE) *M A Jarvis* 119
5 b g Sadler's Wells(USA) —Smart 'n Noble (USA) (Smarten (USA))
1351[4] 2056[8] 5171[3]
Royal Applord *P T Midgley* a74 67
4 b g Royal Applause—Known Class (USA) (Known Fact (USA))
1612[7] 1955[14] 2404[8] 3174[6]
Royal Arthur *L A Dace* a28 35
3 ch g Imperial Dancer—Scenic Lady (IRE) (Scenic)
1380[10] 1670[14] 2380[9] 3697[6] 4241[8] 4640[11] 5131[7] 5579[11]
Royal Bench (IRE) *Robert Collet* 99
2 b c Whipper(USA) —Hit The Sky (IRE) (Cozzene (USA))
6131a[3] 7207a[6]
Royal Bet (IRE) *M L W Bell* a57 61
3 b g Montjeu(IRE) —Queen Of Norway (USA) (Woodman (USA))
1515[7] 2105[7] 4917[2] 5113[4] *6371[5]*
Royal Blade (IRE) *A P Jarvis* a22 71
2 ch g Needwood Blade—Royal Dream (Ardkinglass)
2196[9] 2636[6] (4379) 5033[11] *5650[9]*
Royal Bloom (IRE) *J R Fanshawe* 48
4 b m Royal Applause—Bethesda (Distant Relative)
2139[11] 2857[7] 3215[9] 3632[2] 4238[6]
Royal Box *A J McCabe* a72 74
2 b c Royal Applause—Diamond Lodge (Grand Lodge (USA))
3692[12] (4424) *5091[4]* 5853[6] *7435[5] 7669[8]*
Royal Challenge *I W McInnes* a79 72
8 b g Royal Applause—Anotheranniversary (Emarati (USA))
606[8] 777[2] 886[6] 1103[6] 1480[10] 2156[9] 2769[12] 4072[9] *4859[8]* 5465[7] *(5676) 6123[8]* 6336[2] 6782[9] 7275[10]
Royal Cheer *Mrs A Duffield* 6
2 b f Royal Applause—Rise 'n Shine (Night Shift (USA))
4430[14] 5957[6]
Royal Choir *H E Haynes* a56 39
5 ch m King's Best(USA) —Harmonic Sound (IRE) (Grand Lodge (USA))
100[9] 253[9] 1254[14] *1589[12]*
Royal Collection (IRE) *J Pearce* a82 72
3 b c Val Royal(FR) —Rachel Green (IRE) (Case Law)
(160) (312)
Royal Composer (IRE) *T D Easterby* 67
6 b g Mozart(IRE) —Susun Kelapa (USA) (St Jovite (USA))
1369[4] 1951[8] 2529[12] 3488[4] 4140[10] 4977[3] 5443[11] 6174[11]
Royal Confidence *B W Hills* 107
4 b m Royal Applause—Never A Doubt (Night Shift (USA))
1873[4] 2483[6] 3012[9] 4489[12] 5232[3] 5798[5] 6272[6] 6487[4]
Royal Crest *J A Osborne* a63 59
3 b g Royal Applause—Noble Lady (Primo Dominie)
425[3] (810) 1839[11] 2797[7] 4304[9] *5683[5] 6804[11]*
Royal Defence (IRE) *D Nicholls* 85
3 b g Refuse To Bend(IRE) —Alessia (GER) (Warning)
1683[4] 2165[4] 2571[8] (4505) (5255) 5670[4]
Royal Desert *M R Channon* 83
2 b c Pastoral Pursuits—Overcome (Belmez (USA))
1188[6] 1511[3] (1782) 2702[10] 3424[2] 4049[5]
Royal Destination (IRE) *J Noseda* 105
4 b g Dubai Destination(USA) —Royale (IRE) (Royal Academy (USA))
(3155) (3656) ◆ 4404[3] ◆ (5137) ◆ 6106[14] 6480[28]
Royal Diamond (IRE) *Sir Mark Prescott* a101 90
3 b g King's Best(USA) —Irresistible Jewel (IRE) (Danehill (USA))
1829[9] 4045[2] (4442) (4670) (5870) ◆ *(6671)*
Royal Dignitary (USA) *D Nicholls* a90 85
9 br g Saint Ballado(CAN) —Star Actress (USA) (Star De Naskra (USA))
(922) 1213[8] (1777) 3174[2] 3568[5] (5465) *5779[4]* 6217[7]
Royale Again (FR) *P Monfort* a83 81
4 b m Fasliyev(USA) —Royale Figurine (IRE) (Dominion Royale)
6981a[2]
Royal Encore *J R Fanshawe* a65 58
5 b m Royal Applause—Footlight Fantasy (USA) (Nureyev (USA))
217[3]
Royal Entourage *C A Mulhall* a82 86
4 b g Royal Applause—Trempkate (USA) (Trempolino (USA))
6100[6] 6676[12]
Royal Envoy (IRE) *P Howling* a78 86
6 b g Royal Applause—Seven Notes (Zafonic (USA))
191[8] ◆ *(460) 618[4] 841[3]* 1152[4] 2276[16] *2824[5] 3512[6] 3924[6] 5612[2]* 6024[8] 6783[6] 7053[7] 7321[8] 7506[9]
Royal Etiquette (IRE) *H J L Dunlop* a72 75
2 b g Royal Applause—Alpine Gold (IRE) (Montjeu (IRE))
3867[3] 4424[5] 5907[2] *7400[3]*
Royal Executioner (USA) *D M Simcock* a84 89
3 b c Royal Academy(USA) —Guillotine (USA) (Proud Truth (USA))
(548) 1001[2] 2399[3] (3156)
Royal Fantasy (IRE) *N Tinkler* a84 85
6 bb m King's Best(USA) —Dreams (Rainbow Quest (USA))
2894[17] 3151[6] 3545[8] 4351[4] 4804[5] 5438[8] 6017[6] 6184[7]
Royal Flynn *Mrs K Walton* 64
7 b g Royal Applause—Shamriyna (IRE) (Darshaan)
999[11] 1660[7] 2898[5] 3563[4] 4350[4] 5307[8] 6768[7] 6822[10]
Royal Force (ITY) *A Renzoni* 94
3 ch c Blu Air Force(IRE) —Royal Revue (FR) (Octagonal (NZ))
2114a[3]
Royal God (USA) *Saeed Bin Suroor* 104
4 b g Royal Academy(USA) —Gold Splash (USA) (Blushing Groom (FR))
2606[6]
Royal Holiday (IRE) *B Ellison* a69 50
2 ch g Captain Rio—Sunny Slope (Mujtahid (USA))
4595[7] *(4839) 6829[10]*
Royaline (IRE) *A Spanu* a69 71
4 b m Royal Applause—Lina Bella (FR) (Linamix (FR))
6981a[10]
Royal Infidelity (IRE) *T Stack* a82 83
2 b c Royal Applause—Aweless (USA) (Seattle Slew (USA))
2286a[4]

Royal Intruder *S Donohoe* a92 98
4 b g Royal Applause—Surprise Visitor (IRE) (Be My Guest (USA))
1375a[15] 2799[4] (2929) (4907) 5001[5] 5830[3] (6396) (6972) ◆

Royal Island (IRE) *M G Quinlan* a82 86
7 b g Trans Island—Royal House (FR) (Royal Academy (USA))
1911[3] 2851[1] 886[10] 1042[11] 3811[15] 4305[15] 4645[10] 5443[9] 6256[2] ◆

Royal Jasra *Mrs S Leech* a66 77
5 b g Royal Applause—Lake Pleasant (IRE) (Elegant Air)
497[8]

Royal Jet *Mrs S Leech* a98 92
7 b g Royal Applause—Red Bouquet (Reference Point)
1586[3] 1863[7] 3382[7]

Royal Keva (IRE) *A D Brown* a65 46
3 b g Medecis—Karmafair (IRE) (Always Fair (USA))
2236[15] 2723[5] 3018[7] 3449[6] 4348[8] 6102[6] 6498[10] 6807[7] 7143[4] 7369[4] 7500[3] 7727[2]

Royal Manor *Tom Dascombe* a70 57
4 b m King's Best(USA) —She's Classy (USA) (Boundary (USA))
15[6] 6362[6] 7275[6] 7586[2] 7650[6]

Royal Max (IRE) *C G Cox* a54 54
3 b g Hawkeye(IRE) —Baccara (IRE) (Sri Pekan (USA))
3099[5] 3511[3]

Royal Menantie (FR) *J Boisnard*
2 b c Kendor(FR) —Heleniade (FR) (Entrepreneur)
(7315a)

Royal Merit (FR) *R Lecomte*
2 ch f Russian Blue(IRE) —Transe Lucide (FR) (Marignan (USA))
5014a[3]

Royal Mischief (IRE) *P D Evans* a34 32
3 b f Val Royal(FR) —Anearlybird (USA) (Sheikh Albadou)
69[5] 135[9] 196[8] 403[7]

Royal Orissa *D Haydn Jones* a48 69
7 b g Royal Applause—Ling Lane (Slip Anchor)
327[13] 387[10] 598[11]

Royal Patriot (IRE) *W J Haggas* 43
2 b c King's Best(USA) —Lady Ragazza (IRE) (Bering)
5401[14]

Royal Power (IRE) *D Nicholls* a107 103
6 b g Xaar—Magic Touch (Fairy King (USA))
265a[13] 439a[14] 521a[4] 639a[14] 997[19] 2669[4] 3014[17] 4412a[14] 5522[16] 6094[6] 6312[3]

Royal Premier (IRE) *H J Collingridge* a63 65
6 b g King's Theatre(IRE) —Mystic Shadow (IRE) (Mtoto)
1807[6] 2445[6] 2854[4] 3760[4] 4388[12] 4670[2] 5483[11] 5975[6] 7354[12] 7767[10]

Royal Premium *Mrs G S Rees* a14 62
3 b c Superior Premium—Royal Shepley (Royal Applause)
1652[6] 1926[2] 3018[2] 3334[3] 3616[5] (4496) 4819[4] 5295[5] 6103[7] 6411[10]

Royal Prince *Doug Watson* a64 94
8 gr h Royal Applause—Onefortheditch (USA) (With Approval (CAN))
263a[7] 419a[8]

Royal Prodigy (USA) *R J Hodges* 48
10 ch g Royal Academy(USA) —Prospector's Queen (USA) (Mr Prospector (USA))
2519[6]

Royal Rainbow *P W Hiatt* a52 45
5 ch g Rainbow Quest(USA) —Royal Future (IRE) (Royal Academy (USA))
5548[8] 5939[6] 7214[10] 7354[6] 7750[3]

Royal Ranger (FR) *F-X De Chevigny*
3 b g Marchand De Sable(USA) —Noble Note (FR) (Noblequest (FR))
4581a[0]

Royal Rationale (IRE) *D E Pipe* a76 92
5 b g Desert Prince(IRE) —Logic (Slip Anchor)
2994[3] 6851[17]

Royal Record *M Brittain* 67
2 b f Royal Applause—First Musical (First Trump)
3686[6] 4226[6] 4515[4] 5036[2] 5668[3] 6241[19] 6820[7]

Royal Revival *A Fabre* 85
2 gr c King's Best(USA) —Holy Nola (USA) (Silver Deputy (CAN))
(6131a)

Royal Rock *C F Wall* a89 115
5 b g Sakhee(USA) —Vanishing Point (USA) (Caller I.D. (USA))
(1868) ◆ 2481[6] 5921a[4] (6661) 7232a[9]

Royal Salsa (IRE) *R A Fahey* a46 52
3 b f Royal Applause—Lady Salsa (IRE) (Gone West (USA))
77[3] 196[7] 383[8]

Royal Society *R A Farrant* a63 54
3 b g King's Best(USA) —Nawaiet (USA) (Zilzal (USA))
695[3] 865[2] 2340[14] 3018[13] 5331[12] 6987[12] (7600) 7688[8] 7856[11]

Royal Spider (GER) *M Trybuhl*
3 ch f Paolini(GER) —Rudolfina (CAN) (Pleasant Colony (USA))
5118a[0]

Royal Straight *B N Pollock* a74 63
4 ch g Halling(USA) —High Straits (Bering)
119[4] 357[6] 500[7]

Royal Superlative *R M Beckett* a56 79
3 b f King's Best(USA) —Supereva (IRE) (Sadler's Wells (USA))
2318[4] (3207) 3803[2] ◆ 4569[12] 5803[4] 6346[8]

Royal Torbo (ISR) *George Baker* a51
2 b c Tabari(GER) —Royal Dutch (GER) (Monsun (GER))
7800[8]

Royal Treasure (IRE) *J A Osborne* a44
2 b c Arakan(USA) —Isticanna (USA) (Far North (CAN))
7277[7] 7391[8]

Royal Trooper (IRE) *J G Given* a75 78
3 b g Hawk Wing(USA) —Strawberry Roan (IRE) (Sadler's Wells (USA))
1953[3] 2943[3] 3359[4] 3687[3] (4280) 4709[5] 5230[11] 5402[7] 6075[4] 6360[4] 6995[5] (7222)

Royal Victory (TUR) *H Yildiz* a101
5 b m Royal Abjar(USA) —Victory Demo (IRE) (Danehill Dancer (IRE))
5587a[5]

Royal Vintage (SAF) *M F De Kock* a115 97
5 ch g Rich Man's Gold(USA) —Derry Wood (SAF) (Fort Wood (USA))
184a[6] 339a[10]

Royal Wedding *N J Gifford* a62
7 b g King's Best(USA) —Liaison (USA) (Blushing Groom (FR))
361[8] 485[5] 631[12]

Royal Willy (IRE) *W Jarvis* a74 71
3 b g Val Royal(FR) —Neat Dish (CAN) (Stalwart (USA))
2048[19] 2685[3] 3551[4] 5593[7] 6400[9] 6784[6] 7211[9]

Roybuoy *H J L Dunlop* a58 48
2 b c Royal Applause—Wavy Up (IRE) (Brustolon)
6199[12] 6727[10] 7050[13] 7604[6] 7773[6] 7887[7]

Rubacuori (FR) *J Rossi* a69
2 b c Vettori(IRE) —Signorinella (FR) (Kendor (FR))
6979a[7]

Rubbinghousedotcom (IRE) *P M Phelan* a48 51
3 b g Desert Style(IRE) —Marain (IRE) (Marju (IRE))
752[8] 1420[4] 1811[11] 1967[12]

Rubenstar (IRE) *Patrick Morris* a71 72
6 b g Soviet Star(USA) —Ansariya (USA) (Shahrastani (USA))
777[7] 933[3] 1048[3] (1121) ◆ 1320[7] 7860[2]

Rubicon Bay (IRE) *C J Teague* 38
2 b f One Cool Cat(USA) —Mrs Moonlight (Ajdal (USA))
2936[8] 7114[6]

Rubirosa (IRE) *C Alonso Pena* a92 90
4 b g Acclamation—Bendis (GER) (Danehill (USA))
7265a[4]

Rublevka Star (USA) *J Noseda* a67 63
3 b f Elusive Quality(USA) —Al Desima (Emperor Jones (USA))
1505[7] 2386[5]

Rub Of The Relic (IRE) *P T Midgley* a63 75
4 b g Chevalier(IRE) —Bayletta (IRE) (Woodborough (USA))
634 224[11] 514[3] 623[7] 711[7] 791[2] 979[10]

Ruby Best *D K Ivory* a43 43
3 b f Best Of The Bests(IRE) —Ice Bird (Polar Falcon (USA))
159[8]

Ruby Dancer (IRE) *Alessandro Turco* 93
4 b m King's Best(USA) —Beauty Dancer (IRE) (Alzao (USA))
1394a[3]

Ruby Delta *A G Juckes* a56 45
4 b g Delta Dancer—Picolette (Piccolo)
448[9]

Ruby Tallulah *C R Dore* a73 75
3 b f Piccolo—Tallulah Belle (Crowning Honors (CAN))
140[4] 350[4] 509[5] 568[5] 673[5] 736[6] 889[6] 955[9]

Rudolph Schmidt (IRE) *David P Myerscough* a79 81
3 br f Catcher In The Rye(IRE) —Enaya (Caerleon (USA))
(6442)

Rudry World (IRE) *M Mullineaux* a53 68
6 ch g Spinning World(USA) —Fancy Boots (IRE) (Salt Dome (USA))
3068[2] 4263[15] 5307[4] 6768[2] 7036[13] 7440[8]

Rue De Cabestan (IRE) *T G McCourt* a21 57
4 b m Orpen(USA) —Beaufort Lady (IRE) (Alhaarth (IRE))
5294[9] 7174[3]

Rue Soleil *J R Weymes* a29 53
5 ch m Zaha(CAN) —Maria Cappuccini (Siberian Express (USA))
5159[8] 5309[10]

Ruff Diamond (USA) *J S Moore* a82 81
4 bb g Stormin Fever(USA) —Whalah (USA) (Dixieland Band (USA))
648[3] 893[3] 1319[4] 1635[4] 1966[9] 3143[8]

Rufus Roughcut *S C Williams* 34
2 b c Auction House(USA) —Shining Oasis (IRE) (Mujtahid (USA))
1195[8] 3344[12] 3957[10] 6922[10] 7098[9]

Rugell (ARG) *H R A Cecil* 89
4 b h Interprete(ARG) —Realize (ARG) (Confidental Talk (USA))
3769[4] 5004[5] 5402[3] 6036[6]

Rule Of Nature *Sir Michael Stoute* 77
2 b f Oasis Dream—Jolie Etoile (USA) (Diesis)
6363[2] (6922)

Ruler Of All (IRE) *H Candy* 79
3 b g Sadler's Wells(USA) —Shabby Chic (USA) (Red Ransom (USA))
1127[2] 1328[8] 6734[7] 6936[12]

Ruler Of My Heart (IRE) *Tom Dascombe* 101
2 br f Green Tune(USA) —Dirigeante (FR) (Lead On Time (USA))
4797[5] (5280a) 6045a[8]

Ruler's Honour (IRE) *T J Etherington* a33
2 b g Antonius Pius(USA) —Naughty Reputation (IRE) (Shalford (IRE))
7485[6]

Rulesn'regulations *Matthew Salaman* a91 96
3 b c Forzando—Al Awaalah (Mukaddamah (USA))
(6240) 7015[18] 7227[8]

Ruling Reef *M R Bosley* a54 51
7 b m Diktat—Horseshoe Reef (Mill Reef (USA))
566[10]

Rumble Of Thunder (IRE) *D W P Arbuthnot* a77 89
3 b g Fath(USA) —Honey Storm (IRE) (Mujadil (USA))
1464[3] 1792[8] (2126) 2432[13] 4481[2] 5266[2] 6453[2]

Rum Jungle *H Candy* a73 87
5 b g Robellino(USA) —Anna Karietta (Precocious)
2434[15] 3116[12] 4501[6]

Rum King (USA) *R Hannon* 92
2 bb c Montbrook(USA) —Cut Class Leanne (USA) (Cutlass (USA))
4756[13] 5749[3] (6424) (7150)

Rumool *C E Brittain* a85 67
2 b c Exceed And Excel(AUS) —Silent Heir (AUS) (Sunday Silence (USA))
2280[5] (2599)

Rumoush (USA) *M P Tregoning* a76
2 b f Rahy(USA) —Sarayir (USA) (Mr Prospector (USA))
(7388) ◆

Rum Raisin *John Joseph Murphy* a63 65
3 b f Invincible Spirit(IRE) —Femme Femme (USA) (Lyphard (USA))
6847 [2]

Rumramah (USA) *D M Simcock* a32 56
3 b f Mr Greeley(USA) —She's Vested (USA) (Boundary (USA))
5193[8] 5789[5] 6497[13]

Runaway *R Pritchard-Gordon* 111
7 b h King's Best(USA) —Anasazi (IRE) (Sadler's Wells (USA))
846a[6] 2120a[3] 3085a[5] 5086a[5] 6323a[4] 7102a[7]

Runaway Pegasus (USA) *H R A Cecil* 48
4 b m Fusaichi Pegasus(USA) —Runaway Venus (USA) (Runaway Groom (CAN))
1427[5]

Run For Ede's *P M Phelan* a71 84
5 b m Peintre Celebre(USA) —Raincloud (Rainbow Quest (USA))
(1571) 2183[4] 3766[3] (3797) (4007) 4340[4] ◆ 4544[2] 6936[13]

Run For The Hills *J H M Gosden* 105
3 b c Oasis Dream—Maid For The Hills (Indian Ridge)
2035[7] 3747[11] 4771[6] 6427[3]

Run Free *N Wilson* a63 53
5 b g Agnes World(USA) —Ellie Ardensky (Slip Anchor)
63[6] 223[8] 519[3] 607[8] 823[7] 3314[7] 3943[13] 4375[6] 4874[3] 5294[11] 5953[9]

Running Buck (USA) *A Bailey* a49 54
4 b h Running Stag(USA) —Dinghy (USA) (Fortunate Prospect (USA))
87[7] 666[4] 775[12]

Running Flush (USA) *J R Gask* a59 50
3 ch g Grand Slam(USA) —Holiday Gold (USA) (Touch Gold (USA))
3338[7] 3813[8] 4860[3] 5632[6] 6492[6] 6914[6] 7240[8] 7614[3] 7796[11]

Running Home (GER) *A Wohler* 93
3 b c Storming Home—Roma Libera (GER) (Pharly (FR))
1915a[6]

Running Mate (IRE) *J H M Gosden* 75
2 b c Acclamation—It Takes Two (IRE) (Alzao (USA))
1867[4] 2280[4] 3046[8] (4062) 4525[9]

Runswick Bay *G M Moore* 27
4 b g Intikhab(USA) —Upend (Main Reef)
2101[10] 2898[13] 3705[8] 3974[12]

Run To Win (FR) *H Billot* a64 56
2 br f Bedawin(FR) —Coureuse (FR) (Jeune Homme (USA))
6960a[0]

Rupestrian *M Johnston* a70 73
3 b g Fantastic Light(USA) —Upper Strata (Shirley Heights)
(824) 1019[6]

Rusee Des Ongrais (FR) *P Chemin*
4 gr m Saint Preuil(FR) —Cecile Des Ongrais (FR) (Valanjou (FR))
5074a[0]

Rushing Dasher (GER) *Natalie Friberg* a75 60
7 ch g Dashing Blade—Roma Libera (GER) (Pharly (FR))
(464a) 652a[5]

Russiana (IRE) *A Fabre* a91 101
3 b f Red Ransom(USA) —Trumbaka (IRE) (In The Wings)
5562a[2] 7697a[0]

Russian Angel *Jean-Rene Auvray* a54 54
5 gr m Baryshnikov(AUS) —Eventuality (Petoski)
58[4] 3074[9] 3800[3] 4321[3] 5013a[4] 5791[5] 7051[5] 7200[3] 7466[2] 7802[8]

Russian Brigadier *M Brittain* 38
2 b g Xaar—Brigadiers Bird (IRE) (Mujadil (USA))
6990[11]

Russian Davis (IRE) *R M H Cowell* a68 62
2 b c Mull Of Kintyre(USA) —Sunny Isles Beauty (USA) (Tale Of The Cat (USA))
3032[8] 3634[4] 4370[6] (5166) 5841[3] 6829[6] 6983[5]

Russian Empress (IRE) *David P Myerscough* a95 95
5 b m Trans Island—Russian Countess (USA) (Nureyev (USA))
928a[4] 1756a[8] 2285a[8] 5141a[8] 6707a[5] 7132[6]

Russian Epic *Andrew Turnell* a58 84
5 b g Diktat—Russian Rhapsody (Cosmonaut)
1753[5]

Russian George (IRE) *S Gollings* a76 81
3 ch g Sendawar(IRE) —Mannsara (IRE) (Royal Academy (USA))
(1888) 2281[3] 3264[15] 3608[4] 5255[2] 5834[9] 6680[14]

Russian Invader (IRE) *R C Guest* a66 68
5 ch g Acatenango(GER) —Ukraine Venture (Slip Anchor)
923[4] 977[2] 1154[7] 1273[3] 1439[5] 2163[7] 7635[8] 7840[5]

Russian Jar (IRE) *M A Jarvis* 90
3 b g Xaar—Lady Windermere (IRE) (Lake Coniston (IRE))
(2338) ◆ 5030[2] ◆ 5432[2] ◆ 5766[5] 6732[11]

Russian Music (USA) *Ian Williams* a60 51
4 b g Stravinsky(USA) —Private Seductress (USA) (Private Account (USA))
1062[10] 1400[10] 1592[8] 3710[2] 5332[12] 5983[5] 7658[2] ◆ (7751)

Russian Rave *J G Portman* a76 68
3 ch f Danehill Dancer(IRE) —Russian Ruby (FR) (Vettori (IRE))
1588[3] 1973[5] 2498[6] (2827) 3981[4] 5090[5] 5449[8] 6699[7]

Russian River (FR) *Mlle V Dissaux* a69 61
2 b f Russian Blue(IRE) —My First Love (FR) (Northern Crystal)
4970a[5]

Russian Rock (IRE) *R A Teal* 78
2 b c Rock Of Gibraltar(IRE) —Mala Mala (IRE) (Brief Truce (USA))
1669[5] (2007) 2995[12]

Russian Rocket (IRE) *Mrs C A Dunnett* a72 74
7 b g Indian Rocket—Soviet Girl (IRE) (Soviet Star (USA))
818[4] 1259[6] 1776[4] 3465[5] (3860) 4204[3] 4886[6] 5374[13] 5974[8] 6799[9] 7100[3]

Russian Sage (SAF) *M F De Kock* a94 122
5 b h Jallad(USA) —Sage Blue (SAF) (Badger Land (USA))
439a[2] 774a[2] 1012a[11] 5231[7] 6812[7] 7323[4]

Russian Saint *D Shaw* 32
3 b f Red Ransom(USA) —Tessara (GER) (Big Shuffle (USA))
1605[13]

Russian Spirit *M A Jarvis* 91
3 b f Falbrav(IRE) —Russian Rhapsody (Cosmonaut)
3460[2] (3764) 4227[2] 6020[3] (6647) 6994[9]

Russian Symphony (USA) *C R Egerton* a82 81
8 ch g Stravinsky(USA) —Backwoods Teacher (USA) (Woodman (USA))
654[4] 757[6] 891[2]

Rusty Pelican *P J Makin*
2 ch g Tobougg(IRE) —Opalite (Opening Verse (USA))
7024[14]

Rutba *M P Tregoning* a70 63
4 b m Act One—Elhilmeya (IRE) (Unfuwain (USA))
1426[11] 1732[6]

Ruten (USA) *Andreas Lowe* 105
4 gr h El Prado(IRE) —Rash (USA) (Miswaki (USA))
2216a[2] 3441a[8] 6521a[9]

Rutherienne (USA) *Christophe Clement* 113
5 bb m Pulpit(USA) —Ruthian (USA) (Rahy (USA))
7284a[7]

Ruthie Babe *W J Haggas* a66 67
2 b f Exceed And Excel(AUS) —Lady Oriande (Makbul)
4711[6] 5256[5] 5611[4] (5908) 6185[3] 6827[4]

Ruud Revenge (USA) *Mrs D J Sanderson* 76
3 b g Van Nistelrooy(USA) —Savannah's Revenge (USA) (West By West (USA))
1681[3] ◆ 2090[2] 2545[4] 2932[19]

Ruwain *P J McBride* a56 48
5 b g Lujain(USA) —Ruwaya (USA) (Red Ransom (USA))
(145) 248[7] 427[9] 1122[4] 1496[6] 2608[4] 2924[6] 3215[7] 7466[8]

R Woody *Mrs L C Jewell* a74 23
2 ch g Ishiguru(USA) —Yarrita (Tragic Role (USA))
3920[12] 5368[11] 6026[7] (7637) 7871[4]

Ryan (IRE) *J Hanacek* 107
6 b h Generous(IRE) —Raysiza (IRE) (Alzao (USA))
2216a[5]

Ryan's Rock *R J Price* a48 33
4 b g Lujain(USA) —Diamond Jayne (IRE) (Royal Abjar (USA))
1741[14]

Rydal (USA) *Miss Jo Crowley* a61 52
8 ch g Gilded Time(USA) —Tennis Partner (USA) (Northern Dancer (CAN))
309[5] 531[6] 1065[5] 2921[9] 6251[10]

Ryedale Ovation (IRE) *G L Moore* a76 73
6 b g Royal Applause—Passe Passe (USA) (Lear Fan (USA))
21[7] 311[4] 726[8] 921[8] (1065) 1187[2] 1539[5] 1876[6]

Ryedane (IRE) *T D Easterby* a71 66
7 b g Danetime(IRE) —Miss Valediction (IRE) (Petardia)
15[5] 1591[8] 1877[6] (2316) 2801[3] 2966[3] 3497[7] 4620[5] 4998[3] 5411[5] 5678[8] 5978[9] 6216[11]

Ryedon Bye *T D Easterby* 48
3 ch g Distant Music(USA) —Payphone (Anabaa (USA))
1335[11] 1625[8] 1926[17]

Rye Rhythm (IRE) *P Cluskey* 41
2 b f Fasliyev(USA) —Ridiya (IRE) (Last Tycoon)
6401a[6]

Ryker (IRE) *J W Hills* a62 57
3 ch g Halling(USA) —Charlock (IRE) (Nureyev (USA))
2081[8] 2664[8] 5751[7] 7110[13] 7718[4] 7765[3]

Ryland (SWI) *H-A Pantall* a48
3 b c King Of Kings(IRE) —Ryme Intrinseca (Hector Protector (USA))
5278a[9]

Saachi's Vision (IRE) *D K Ivory* a38 41
2 ch f Compton Place—Ash Moon (IRE) (General Monash (USA))
1195[12] 1637[6] 1933[7] 2414[6] 2978[7] 3709[8] 4018[P] 6610[8]

Saafia (USA) *M Johnston* 77
2 b f Swain(IRE) —Reem Al Barari (USA) (Storm Cat (USA))
4001[5] 4460[6] (5417)

Saa'Ida (IRE) *C E Brittain* 81
3 ch f Diesis—Westernize (USA) (Gone West (USA))
1198[8] 1291[9] (2192) 2701[15] 4050[9] 4881[8] 5940[4] 6420[6]

Saalewuste (GER) *J-P Gallorini* a59 62
4 b m Next Desert(IRE) —Salondame (Godswalk (USA))
7387a[8]

Saameq (IRE) *D W Thompson* a61 52
8 b g Bahhare(USA) —Tajawuz (Kris)
3223[7]

Sabancaya *Mrs P Sly* a73 65
4 b m Nayef(USA) —Serra Negra (Kris)
(38) 148[4] (300) 402[3] 604[6] 734[3]

Sabander Bleue (IRE) *M R Channon* 73
2 b c Peintre Celebre(USA) —Sabander Bay (USA) (Lear Fan (USA))
4756[6] 5022[5] 5466[2] 5770[3] 6136[3] 6382[6]

Sabantuy *C Von Der Recke* 102
3 bb c Mujahid(USA) —Sabanila (GER) (In The Wings)
1395a[7] 2755a[5]

Sabatini (IRE) *J Pearce* a79 65
2 b f One Cool Cat(USA) —Two Sets To Love (IRE) (Cadeaux Genereux)
3248[8] 6728[4] 6896[4] (7410) ◆ (7625) 7786[2]

Sabelotodo (FR) *M Boutin* a48 66
3 b g Enrique—Lorraine Melody (FR) (Port Lyautey (FR))
6980a[10]

Sabii Sands (IRE) *R Hannon* 80
2 b c Invincible Spirit(IRE) —Miriana (IRE) (Bluebird (USA))
(2676) ◆ 3782[3] 4086[4]

Sabirli (TUR) *C Kurt* 109
8 b h Strike The Gold(USA) —Free Trade (TUR) (Shareef Dancer (USA))
5618a[3]

Sabi Star *J H M Gosden* 76
3 b c Green Desert(USA) —Balisada (Kris)
2416[5] 2856[3] 4057[3] 4381[6]

Sabolienne (FR) *Dominique Sepulchre* a84 86
6 b m Marchand De Sable(USA) —Ecole De Guerre (FR) (Comrade In Arms)
5281a[0]

Saborido (USA) *Mrs A J Perrett* a33 72
3 gr g Dixie Union(USA) —Alexine (ARG) (Runaway Groom (CAN))
1416[3] 1747[2] 2152[4] 2881[11] 4071[3] 4241[4] (4951) (5530) 6037[2] (6935)

Sabotage (UAE) *M Johnston* 103
3 b g Halling(USA) —Cunas (USA) (Irish River (FR))
2178[2] ◆ (2538) 3090[9] 3827[2] ◆ 4340[3] 4420[8] 4767[3] 5248[3]

Saboteur *Saeed Bin Suroor* a79 89
2 b c Shamardal(USA) —Croeso Cariad (Most Welcome)
5431[4] ◆ 5807[3] 6064[4] 6478[13] (6792) 6993[7]

Sabre Light *J Pearce* a85 69
4 b g Fantastic Light(USA) —Good Grounds (USA) (Alleged (USA))
(119) (244) 577[3] 825[2]

Sacco D'Oro *M Mullineaux* a12
3 b f Rainbow High—Speedy Native (IRE) (Be My Native (USA))
7882[8]

Sacho (GER) *W Kujath* 102
11 br g Dashing Blade—She's His Guest (IRE) (Be My Guest (USA))
3202a[8] 4637a[8] 6499a[8]

Sacred Kingdom (AUS) *P F Yiu* 125
6 b g Encosta De Lago(AUS) —Courtroom Sweetie (AUS) (Zeditave (AUS))
(2116a) 3140[5] (7745a)

Sacred Star (IRE) *M Brittain* 39
2 b f Xaar—Mono Star (IRE) (Soviet Star (USA))
1847[5] 2089[7] 3032[11] 3726[6]

Sadaska *S C Williams* a52 47
3 ch f Fantastic Light(USA) —Sadaka (USA) (Kingmambo (USA))
298[3] ◆ 951[14] 2633[6] 3454[10] 3962[3] 5131[8] 6375[11]

Saddlers Lodge *G A Swinbank* 75
2 b g Motivator—Grandalea (Grand Lodge (USA))
4349[2] 5006[2]

Sadeek *B Smart* a67 83
5 ch g Kyllachy—Miss Mercy (IRE) (Law Society (USA))
2086[16] 5409[16] 5697[9] 6846[11] 7643[4] 7830[8]

Sadiri (FR) *A De Royer-Dupre* 91
3 gr c Dr Fong(USA) —Sage Et Jolie (Linamix (FR))
1858a[6]

Sadler's Kingdom (IRE) *R A Fahey* a54 81
5 b g Sadler's Wells(USA) —Artful Pleasure (USA) (Nasty And Bold (USA))
2249[7]

Sadler's Mark *T P Tate* 55
2 b c Sadler's Wells(USA) —Waldmark (GER) (Mark Of Esteem (IRE))
6792[7] 7244[5]

Sadler's Star (GER) *A King* a64 56
6 b g Alwuhush(USA) —Sadlerella (IRE) (King's Theatre (IRE))
4815[5]

Safari *S Curran* a25 35
6 b m Namaqualand(USA) —Breakfast Creek (Hallgate)
3207[7] 3740[5] 4146[6]

Safari Camp (IRE) *A Berry* a28 54
2 b c Camacho—Consensus (IRE) (Common Grounds)
1195[5] 1534[6] 1783[6] 2325[3] 3203[3] 4639[9] 5620[8] 6409[9] 6556[3] 7115[8] 7213[8] 7637[6]

Safari Guide *P Winkworth* a57 74
3 b g Primo Valentino(IRE) —Sabalara (IRE) (Mujadil (USA))
1423[2] 1839[2] 2377[6] 3743[8] 4303[3] 4700[4] 6699[6] 7246[16]

Safari Journey (USA) *P J Hobbs* a64 72
5 ch h Johannesburg(USA) —Alvernia (USA) (Alydar (USA))
2781[5] 3247[4]

Safari Mischief *P Winkworth* a96 97
6 b g Primo Valentino(IRE) —Night Gypsy (Mind Games)
2191[4] 2704[11] 3582[7] 4341[16]

Safari Song (IRE) *B Smart* 72
3 b c War Chant(USA) —Leopard Hunt (USA) (Diesis)
4277[2] 4846[7] 5954[6]

Safari Special *P Winkworth* a67 67
2 ch g Pastoral Pursuits—Quiz Time (Efisio)
1616[3] 2348[5] 3745[5] (6774)

Safari Sunup (IRE) *P Winkworth* a100 103
4 b g Catcher In The Rye(IRE) —Nuit Des Temps (Sadler's Wells (USA))
1460[17] 1642[2] 4091[3] 4517[3] 5641[2] 6662[3] 7293[18]

Safaseef (IRE) *K A Morgan* a51 55
4 b m Cadeaux Genereux—Asaafeer (USA) (Dayjur (USA))
4718[11] 7200[9] 7726[10] 7770[7]

Safebreaker *K A Ryan* a74 76
4 b g Key Of Luck(USA) —Insijaam (USA) (Secretariat (USA))
(130) (399) 513[2] 823[3] (1402) 1568[2] 2068[2] 2237[3] 4658[3] 5028[2] (5210) 6244[2] 6900[3]

Safe Investment (USA) *B N Pollock* a63 89
5 b g Gone West(USA) —Fully Invested (USA) (Irish River (FR))
749[9]

Saffron's Son (IRE) *R Ducasteele* a49 56
3 b c Saffron Walden(FR) —Try My Rosie (Try My Best (USA))
677[9] 1282[8] 1562[6] 1954[11] 2340[3] 2605[3] 4142[4] 4397[3] 4927[4] 5342[4] (6098) 7302a[11]

Safin (GER) *R Curtis* a64
9 b g Pennekamp(USA) —Sankt Johanna (GER) (High Game)
(107) 213[2] 252[10] 301[2] 502[9] (623) ◆ 679[7] 795[3] 972[4] 1568[7]

Safina *Sir Michael Stoute* 70
2 ch f Pivotal—Russian Rhythm (USA) (Kingmambo (USA))
7183[3] ◆

Safranine (IRE) *Miss A Stokell* a40 61
12 b m Dolphin Street(FR) —Webbiana (African Sky)
3671[0]

Saga De Tercey (FR) *G A Swinbank* 92
4 b g Sagacity(FR) —Fanciulla Del West (USA) (Manila (USA))
(1231) 4345[2] (4619) 5235[2] ◆ (5410) ◆ 6115[8]

Saga Hill (FR) *W Menuet* 62
2 b c Sagacity(FR) —Cootehill (FR) (Compton Place)
6322a[5]

Sagara (USA) *Saeed Bin Suroor* 113
5 b g Sadler's Wells(USA) —Rangoon Ruby (USA) (Kingmambo (USA))
2677[5] 3048[4]

Sagarian (FR) *J-C Rouget* 92
3 b c Cape Cross(IRE) —Saga D'Ouilly (FR) (Linamix (FR))
6150a[2]

Sagarich (FR) *M G Quinlan* 68
5 gr m Sagamix(FR) —Baranciaga (USA) (Bering)
1261[9] 4269[3] 4893[9] 6244[10]

Sagawest (FR) *Ecurie Saint Simeon* 37
3 b c Man O West(FR) —Sagarom (FR) (Legend Of France (USA))
5783a[0]

Saggiatore *E A L Dunlop* 53
2 b f Galileo(IRE) —Madame Dubois (Legend Of France (USA))
6062[12]

Sagredo (USA) *Jonjo O'Neill* a76 70
5 b g Diesis—Eternity (Suave Dancer (USA))
6273[9] 6734[12] 7091[5] 7413[4]

Sagunt (GER) *S Curran* a59 72
6 ch g Tertullian(USA) —Suva (GER) (Arazi (USA))
18[10] (1254) (2762) 3950[2] (4263) 6566[5]

Sahaal (USA) *M P Tregoning* a74 80
3 b c Rahy(USA) —Thaminah (USA) (Danzig (USA))
2165[7] 2885[3] 3425[7] 4097[6] 4914[3] (5242) 5803[5] 6973[8]

Sahabah (USA) *J E Hammond* a76 92
3 ch f Swain(IRE) —Siyadah (USA) (Mr Prospector (USA))
5562a[6] 7697a[4]

Sahara Boy (GER) *G Raveneau* 89
4 br h Big Shuffle(USA) —Script Girl (GER) (Lavirco (GER))
652a[2]

Sahara Kingdom (IRE) *Saeed Bin Suroor* a93
2 gr c Cozzene(USA) —Rose Indien (FR) (Crystal Glitters (USA))
(6629) ◆ (7251) ◆

Saharan Royal *Matthew Salaman* a48 65
3 b f Val Royal(FR) —Saharan Song (IRE) (Singspiel (IRE))
3581[10] 7428[11] 7776[10]

Sahara Prince (IRE) *K A Morgan* a44 49
9 b g Desert King(IRE) —Chehana (Posse (USA))
131[10]

Sahara Sunshine *Mrs L J Mongan* a39 75
4 b m Hernando(FR) —Sahara Sunrise (USA) (Houston (USA))
233[8] 2983[14] 3790[3] 4207[9] 4744[7]

Saharia (IRE) *J Noseda* a80
2 b c Oratorio(IRE) —Inchiri (Sadler's Wells (USA))
7571[7] (7644)

Sahpresa (USA) *Rod Collet* 119
4 b m Sahm(USA) —Sorpresa (USA) (Pleasant Tap (USA))
2953a[2] 4580a[4] 5496a[2] (6479) ◆ 7498a[3]

Sahrati *D R C Elsworth* a83 98
5 ch g In The Wings—Shimna (Mr Prospector (USA))
1319[2] 2055[2] 3273[6] 3822[5] 4517[5] 5170[11]

Saif Al Fahad (IRE) *E J O'Neill* a77 70
3 ch c Shinko Forest(IRE) —Golden Ciel (USA) (Septieme Ciel (USA))
1824[4] 2148[8]

Sailor Moon (IRE) *H-A Pantall*
2 b f Tiger Hill(IRE) —Seralia (Royal Academy (USA))
5014a[4]

Sailors Warn (IRE) *Timothy Doyle* a64 61
2 b g Redback—Coral Dawn (IRE) (Trempolino (USA))
6401a[3]

Sainglend *S Curran* a40 76
4 b g Galileo(IRE) —Verbal Intrigue (USA) (Dahar (USA))
2552[5]

Saint Arch (CAN) *M Johnston* a101 91
3 b g Arch(USA) —Halo Silver (USA) (Silver Buck (USA))
(1001) 1211[6] 1459[5]

Saint Chapelle (IRE) *Mrs A J Perrett* a11 51
3 b f Noverre(USA) —Chartres (IRE) (Danehill (USA))
5987[12] 6332[6]

Saints Bay (IRE) *R Hannon* a56 2
3 b f Redback—Alexander Eliott (IRE) (Night Shift (USA))
230[3] 552[2] 592[3] 753[8] 1536[10]

Saint Sebastian (IRE) *E S McMahon* a31 66
2 ch c Captain Rio—Paris Song (IRE) (Peintre Celebre (USA))
2721[4] 3306[2] 3937[6] 4590[4] 5303[3] 5613[7] 5976[5] 6590[2]

Saint Thomas (IRE) *J A Osborne* a59 74
2 b g Alhaarth(IRE) —Aguilas Perla (IRE) (Indian Ridge)
4693[3] 5786[8] 6125[4] 6736[13] 7391[2] 7474[2]

Sairaam (IRE) *C Smith* a55 63
3 b f Marju(IRE) —Sayedati Eljamilah (USA) (Mr Prospector (USA))
1462[10] 2357[5] 3451[7] 4142[12] 4719[7] 5108[7] (5972) 6568[3] 6824[4] 7062[3] 7246[9] 7348[4] 7600[4] ◆ 7727[7] 7856[9]

Sakami (ITY) *A Prasciolu* 93
3 b f Kalanisi(IRE) —Sa Miniera (IRE) (Perugino (USA))
2310a[7]

Sakhee's Pearl *Miss Gay Kelleway* a82 86
3 gr f Sakhee(USA) —Grey Pearl (Ali-Royal (IRE))
(3569) 4228[4] 6155[6] 6667[4] 7032[9]

Sakhr (FR) *F Doumen*
3 b c Statue Of Liberty(USA) —Dalaika (CAN) (Rhythm (USA))
2293a[0]

Sakile *P W Chapple-Hyam* a77 57
2 ch f Johannesburg(USA) —Crooked Wood (USA) (Woodman (USA))
3187[5] 3772[6] 7365[3] ◆ (7485)

Sakza (IRE) *M Delzangles* 96
4 b m Sakhee(USA) —Miss Sazanica (FR) (Zafonic (USA))
4365a[9] 6714a[5]

Salaam Dubai (AUS) *A Selvaratnam* a104 88
8 b g Secret Savings(USA) —Gulistan (AUS) (Rubiton (AUS))
264a[7] 770a[10]

Saladin's Vow (USA) *G A Butler* a54 36
2 ch c Broken Vow(USA) —Morena Park (Pivotal)
5029[9] 6372[10]

Salamon *P F I Cole* a42 56
3 gr f Montjeu(IRE) —Farfala (FR) (Linamix (FR))
3696[9] 4066[4] 4730[5] 5470[5]

Salattus (GER) *G Raveneau* 94
8 b g Acatenango(GER) —Saas Fee (Top Ville)
653a[9]

Salden Licht *J M P Eustace* a78 102
5 b g Fantastic Light(USA) —Salde (GER) (Alkalde (GER))
6030[9] 6732[7] 7035[3] 7293[5]

Saldenzar (GER) *Sandor Kovacs* 86
5 ch h Zinaad—Saldengeste (IRE) (Be My Guest (USA))
653a[10]

Salerosa (IRE) *Mrs A Duffield* a86 69
4 b m Monashee Mountain(USA) —Sainte Gig (FR) (Saint Cyrien (FR))
1472[6] 1723[2] (2261) 2473[4] (2590) 3019[3] 4104[7] 4333[3] ◆ 4932[9] 6178[3] (6361) 6847 [5] 7092[2] (7271) (7711)

Salgrev (IRE) *Irene J Monaghan* a25 55
3 gr f Verglas(IRE) —Leverick Bay (Octagonal (NZ))
900[10] 2593[2]

Salient *M J Attwater* a87 92
5 b g Fasliyev(USA) —Savannah Belle (Green Desert (USA))
1405[4] 1894[4] 2188[10] 2387[3] 2976[9] 3736[12] 4211[6] 4409[4] 4871[4] 5221[6] 5476[4] 5918[3] 6307[10] 6695[8] 7133[7] 7271[7]

Saliyna (FR) *J-C Rouget* 95
3 gr f Linamix(FR) —Slipstream Queen (USA) (Conquistador Cielo (USA))
5012a[3]

Sally Bawn (IRE) *Gordon Elliott* a65 54
4 b m Rossini(USA) —Finnegans Dilemma (IRE) (Marktingo)
7399[5] 7785[4]

Sally Forth *R Charlton* a83 71
3 b f Dubai Destination(USA) —Daralbayda (IRE) (Doyoun)
3250[6] 3791[3] 4798[3] (5376) 6388[5]

Sally O'Riley *F Watson*
3 ch f Vettori(IRE) —Swallow Breeze (Salse (USA))
3120[13] 4347[13]

Sally's Dilemma *W G M Turner* a55 79
3 b f Primo Valentino(IRE) —Lake Mistassiu (Tina's Pet)
10[5] 64[4]

Sally's Swansong *M Wellings* a33 34
3 b f Mind Games—Sister Sal (Bairn (USA))
1174[11] 1491[9] 2744[7] 3031[16] 3632[5] 4281[14]

Salontiger (GER) *P J Hobbs* 91
7 b g Tiger Hill(IRE) —She's His Guest (IRE) (Be My Guest (USA))
2351[11]

Saloon (USA) *Jane Chapple-Hyam* a79 80
5 b g Sadler's Wells(USA) —Fire The Groom (USA) (Blushing Groom (FR))
(1463) 1936[2] (2331) 2818[2] 3114[3] 3380[2] 4098[4] 5034[8] 6560[2] 6995[7] 7539[4] 7675[2]

Salpado (FR) *R Martin Sanchez* 103
3 b c Royal Applause—Moonbaby (FR) (Le Balafre (FR))
(7265a)

Salsavana (FR) *Rod Collet* a49 76
3 br g Kingsalsa(USA) —Conciliante (FR) (Highest Honor (FR))
6980a[6]

Saltagioo (ITY) *I A Wood* a92 91
5 b g Dr Devious(IRE) —Sces (Kris)
199[4] 544[2] (879) 1209[9] 1942[3] 2666[10] 3008[8] (4438) 5725[8]

Salt Lake (GER) *John Joseph Murphy* 62
7 b g Monsun(GER) —Shine (GER) (Sanglamore (USA))
5642[9]

Salt Of The Earth (IRE) *T G Mills* a73 62
4 b g Invincible Spirit(IRE) —Get The Accountant (Vettori (IRE))
28[5] 241[3] 512[8] 844[4] 1080[3] 2011[10] 2330[14] 2598[12]

Salt River (FR) *J Bertran De Balanda* 70
3 gr f Take Risks(FR) —Sagienne (FR) (Galetto (FR))
(6682a)

Saluscraggie *R E Barr* 64
7 b m Most Welcome—Upper Caen (High Top)
1454[2] 1692[P]

Salut Adrien (FR) *Robert Collet* a63 85
3 b g Miesque's Son(USA) —Salut Bebs (FR) (Kendor (FR))
7385a[8]

Salute (IRE) *P G Murphy* a83 89
10 b g Muhtarram(USA) —Alasib (Siberian Express (USA))
72[2] 233[6] (787) 1215[4] 1435[8] 2743[9] 3510[5] 3737[6] 5837[9]

Salute Him (IRE) *A J Martin* 106
6 b g Mull Of Kintyre(USA) —Living Legend (ITY) (Archway (IRE))
3089[3] ◆ 6480[23]

Salut L'Africain (FR) *Robert Collet* a96 104
4 b h Ski Chief(USA) —Mamana (IRE) (Highest Honor (FR))
2513a[10] 7232a[2] 7458a[2] 7621a[12]

Salut Royale (FR) *S Jesus* 66
2 b f Ski Chief(USA) —Salut Simone (FR) (Simon Du Desert (FR))
2694a[7]

Salut Saint Cloud *G L Moore* a58 58
8 b g Primo Dominie—Tiriana (Common Grounds)
1378[10] 1609[13] 2429[8]

Salvation *M L W Bell* 4
2 b f Montjeu(IRE) —Birdie (Alhaarth (IRE))
7243[14]

Salve Germania (IRE) *Todd Pletcher* 110
4 ch m Peintre Celebre(USA) —Salve Regina (GER) (Monsun (GER))
1597a[4] 2428a[9] 6872a[5]

Salybia Bay *R Hannon* a67 70
3 b f Fraam—Down The Valley (Kampala)
1193[9] 1416[10] 1580[2] 1930[2] 2204[2] 2850[3] 3222[8] 3511[4] 4569[7] 5286[2] 5988[4] 6226[2] 6395[3] 6910[3] 7392[3]

Salza Du Moulin (FR) *F Meckes*
3 ch f Adieu(GER) —Crysta Du Moulin (FR) (Northern Crystal)
5783a[0]

Samaaha *Saeed Bin Suroor* a82 76
3 b f Singspiel(IRE) —Genovefa (USA) (Woodman (USA))
4066[2] 4828[3] 5578[2] (6166) 7178[2] 7402[5]

Samarinda (USA) *Mrs P Sly* a101 77
6 ch g Rahy(USA) —Munnaya (USA) (Nijinsky (CAN))
206[3] 458[6] 783[9] 1209[4] 1433[6] 1603[14] 6019[7] 7626[8]

Samba Mirander *C Drew* a53
3 b f Zaha(CAN) —Silent Scream (IRE) (Lahib (USA))
3025[3] 3508[9]

Samba School (IRE) *Kevin Prendergast* a79 91
3 b f Sahm(USA) —Lulua (USA) (Bahri (USA))
7341a[9]

Sambulando (FR) *T R George* a71 79
6 gr g Kouroun(FR) —Somnambula (IRE) (Petoski)
621[2]

Samizdat (FR) *Mrs Dianne Sayer* 59
6 b g Soviet Star(USA) —Secret Account (FR) (Bering)
1454[5] 1738[5] 3314[5] 6769[11]

Sam Jicaro *Mrs L Williamson* 42
2 b g Mind Games—Claradotnet (Sri Pekan (USA))
3064[12] 4557[7]

Sam Lord *A King* a86 90
5 ch g Observatory(USA) —My Mariam (Salse (USA))
549[9] 2475[5] 2931[7] (3423) 4098[5]

Sammy The Snake (IRE) *B W Duke* a86 58
4 b g Diktat—Love Emerald (USA) (Mister Baileys)
1608[5] 1865[9] 2941[13] 3509[12] 5676[9] 6909[11]

Sampi *Mrs A J Perrett* a66 82
3 ch f Beat Hollow—Delta (Zafonic (USA))
2796[11] 5475[12]

Sampower Quin (IRE) *D Carroll* a61 66
3 b g Sampower Star—Quinolina (Shareef Dancer (USA))
2371[11] 2779[10] 3474[8] 5838[11] 6919[11]

Sampower Rose (IRE) *D Carroll* a10 65
3 b f Sampower Star—Rosebank (USA) (El Prado (IRE))
2091[13] 2370[8] 3574[2] 5331[7] 5672[2] 6182[7] 6637[10] 6924[16]

Sampower Sarge (IRE) *D Carroll* a4
3 b f Sampower Star—Desert Skimmer (USA) (Shadeed (USA))
251[9]

Sampower Shamrock (IRE) *D Carroll* a35
3 b f Sampower Star—Sans Escale (USA) (Diesis)
251[10] 364[6]

Sam's Cross (IRE) *J J Bridger* a78 74
4 b g Cape Cross(IRE) —Fancy Lady (Cadeaux Genereux)
398[9] 671[4] 2326[4] ◆ 2680[3] 2769[4] 3407[8] (3673) 4236[8] 4733[11] 5020[5] 5429[17] 5477[6] 5813[8] 5918[7] (6377) 7023[7] 7535[7] 7879[6]

Sam Sharp (USA) *H R A Cecil* a80 83
3 bb g Johannesburg(USA) —Caffe (USA) (Mr Prospector (USA))
1730[2] ◆ (2074) 2701[11] 4058[6] 4649[7] 5209[6] 5876[5] 6420[2] 6680[4]

Sams Lass *D Nicholls* 79
3 b f Refuse To Bend(IRE) —Dina Line (USA) (Diesis)
3175[U] 3566[7] (4164)

Samson Quest *B Smart* a53
7 b g Cyrano De Bergerac—Zenita (IRE) (Zieten (USA))
(43) 131[4]

Sam's Secret *G A Swinbank* a69 87
7 b m Josr Algarhoud(IRE) —Twilight Time (Aragon)
1682[13] 1923[3] 2402[7] 2999[4] 3174[5]

Sams Spirit *P J McBride* a59 13
3 br g Diktat—Winning Girl (Green Desert (USA))
800[6] 1047[7] 1281[14]

Samurai Warrior *Jamie Snowden* a68 73
4 br g Beat All(USA) —Ma Vie (Salse (USA))
(132) 186[2] 478[3] 554[2] ◆ 1131[6] 1773[10] (2183) (2516) 2923[12] 2983[7] 3258[3] 3374[3] 3864[9] 3961[2] 4220[2] 4951[10]

Sam Winner (FR) *G Cherel* 74
2 b c Okawango(USA) —Noche (IRE) (Night Shift (USA))
5378a[4]

Sana Abel (IRE) *M A Jarvis* a79 73
3 b f Alhaarth(IRE) —Midway Lady (USA) (Alleged (USA))
1269[4] ◆ 2042[6] 3214[5] 4480[4] 5093[2] 5718[7] (6417)

San Antonio *Mrs P Sly* a96 81
9 b g Efisio—Winnebago (Kris)
3076[2]

Sa Nau *T Keddy* a46 62
6 b g Generous(IRE) —Trellis Bay (Sadler's Wells (USA))
6432[10] 6785[13]

Sanbuch *M bin Shafya* a86 115
5 b g Tobougg(IRE) —Monte Calvo (Shirley Heights)
262a[4] 338a[9] 616a[3] 699a[4]

San Carlo (JPN) *Y Okubo* 112
3 b c Symboli Kris S(USA) —Diva (JPN) (Crafty Prospector (USA))
7498a[12]

San Cassiano (IRE) *R M Beckett* a75 88
2 b g Bertolini(USA) —Celtic Silhouette (FR) (Celtic Swing)
(5778) 6398[3]

Sancho Panza *Miss J Feilden* a43 38
2 b g Zafeen(FR) —Malvadilla (IRE) (Doyoun)
2825[7] 3750[13] 4839[8]

Sanctuary *B Smart* 87
3 ch g Dr Fong(USA) —Wondrous Maid (GER) (Mondrian I (GER))
2042[3] 2447[2] (2843) 4401[4] 5671[2] 6138[8]

Sanctum *Dr J D Scargill* a37 58
3 b f Medicean—Auspicious (Shirley Heights)
2488[9] 3025[10] 4828[5]

Sandalphon (JPN) *Masahiro Matsunaga* 110
6 b h Sakura Bakushin O(JPN) —Koyu Love (JPN) (Jade Robbery (USA))
7498a[17]

Sand Du Lys (FR) *J-L Guillochon* 50
4 b m Marchand De Sable(USA) —Sikay (FR) (Le Balafre (FR))
5013a[5]

San Deng *Micky Hammond* a68 59
7 gr g Averti(IRE) —Miss Mirror (Magic Mirror)
1058[5] 1242[4]

Sandfairyann *B R Johnson* a24
2 b f Dubai Destination(USA) —Alhufoof (USA) (Dayjur (USA))
4980[13] 6942[9] 7106[12]

San Diego Prince *Muredach Kelly* 55
5 bb g Primo Valentino(IRE) —Lalique (IRE) (Lahib (USA))
5946[4] 6410[10]

Sandor *P J Makin* a90 95
3 ch g Fantastic Light(USA) —Crystal Star (Mark Of Esteem (IRE))
(1585) 2174[2] 3026[3] (3644) 4455[5] 5209[11]

Sand Repeal (IRE) *Miss J Feilden* a58 68
7 b g Revoque(IRE) —Columbian Sand (IRE) (Salmon Leap (USA))
324[5] 534[9] 734[10] 1200[3] 2127[4] 2971[3] (3348) 3774[2] 5210[9] 5444[3] 5740[2] 6188[6] 6244[6] 6969[9]

Sand River (IRE) *E Lellouche* 92
3 b f High Chaparral(IRE) —Special Delivery (IRE) (Danehill (USA))
5562a[10]

Sands Crooner (IRE) *J G Given* a84 85
6 b g Imperial Ballet(IRE) —Kurfuffle (Bluebird (USA))
2[7] (1970) 2180[RR] 2840[2] (3162) 3607[4] 3784[10] 4891[6] 5247[9] 5436[6] 6666[9] 6897[10] 7122[5] ◆ 7398[9]

Sand Skier *M Johnston* 87
2 b c Shamardal(USA) —Dubai Surprise (IRE) (King's Best (USA))
5006[4] 5542[2] ◆ (6154) 7013[3] ◆

Sands Of Barra (IRE) *I W McInnes* a61 73
6 gr g Marju(IRE) —Purple Risks (FR) (Take Risks (FR))
666[6] 874[9] 1258[13] 1475[9] 3105[3] 3683[4] 3851[11] 4466[5] 4552[17] 4845[3]

Sands Of Dee (USA) *J A Glover* 66
2 b g Dixieland Band(USA) —Diamond Bracelet (USA) (Metfield (USA))
2339[8] 2623[4] 2788[7] 4773[2] (5303) 6071[11]

Sand Tiger (IRE) *A Fabre* 97
3 ch c Indian Ridge—Anayid (A.P. Indy (USA))
1238a[8]

Sand Vixen *Saeed Bin Suroor* a83 108
2 b f Dubawi(IRE) —Fur Will Fly (Petong)
2819[5] (3733) 4295[3] (4989) (5822) ◆ 6449[7]

Sandwith *A G Foster* a70 81
6 ch g Perryston View—Bodfari Times (Clantime)
654[8] 1096[2] 1227[2] 1685[11] 2032[2] 2717[7] 3681[2] 4311[7] 4464[9] 6051[10] 6765[9] 7119[5]

Sandy Par *J M Bradley* a53 55
4 ch g No Excuse Needed—Nesting (Thatching)
1038[7] 1317[7] 1617[4] 2122[6] 2603[4] 2758[11] 3947[8] 5008[7] 5345[3] 5501[7] 5629[10] 5792[9] 6553[4] 7107[8] 7462[7] 7510[5] 7714[4]

Sandy Shaw *J W Hills* a58 69
2 ch f Footstepsinthesand—Susi Wong (IRE) (Selkirk (USA))
4980[7] 5428[10] 5906[3]

Sandy Toes *J A Glover* 34
2 b g Footstepsinthesand—Scrooby Baby (Mind Games)
2147[8] 2467[10] 4738[5]

Sangh Blue (FR) *D Allard*
2 b f Anabaa Blue—Sangeh (IRE) (Turtle Island (IRE))
7166a[4]

San Giustino (IRE) *B P Galvin* a8 63
7 b g Night Shift(USA) —Nambucca (Shirley Heights)
7754[12]

Sanjay's Choice (IRE) *T G McCourt* a74 17
3 br g Trans Island—Livy Park (IRE) (Titus Livius (FR))
5335[10] 6072[3] 7273[3] 7411[3]

San Jemeniano (IRE) *P W Chapple-Hyam* a75 80
2 b c Bertolini(USA) —Kafayef (USA) (Secreto (USA))
3403[3] 4318[3] 6493[3] 6809[4]

San Marco (GER) *P Butler* a58
7 b g Military(USA) —Stormin' Sun (USA) (Buddy (USA))
7524[10]

Sans Chichi (FR) *Y Barberot* a85 100
5 b m Chichicastenango(FR) —Titine (FR) (Adieu Au Roi (IRE))
3085a[4] 6327a[3] 7102a[9]

Sans Frontieres (IRE) *J Noseda* 111
3 ch c Galileo(IRE) —Llia (Shirley Heights)
1300[2] 2014[3]

San Sicharia (IRE) *Ms Joanna Morgan* a105 105
4 ch m Daggers Drawn(USA) —Spinamix (Spinning World (USA))
(1873) 2644a[2] 2870a[6] 3749[6] 4489[6] 5686a[5]

Sansili *Pat Eddery* a62 24
2 gr c Dansili—Salinova (FR) (Linamix (FR))
7121[11] 7388[6]

San Silvestro (IRE) *Mrs A Duffield* a59 68
4 b g Fayruz—Skehana (IRE) (Mukaddamah (USA))
1194[13] 2245[11] 2404[2] (2718) 3098[8] (3448) 4144[4] 4528[2] 4876[4]

Santa Margherita *H J L Dunlop* 64
2 b f Titus Livius(FR) —A Simple Path (IRE) (Imperial Ballet (IRE))
5966[4] ◆ 6416[4] 6786[4]

Sant'Antonio (ITY) *S Botti* 114
4 b h Shantou(USA) —Nonna Rina (IRE) (Bluebird (USA))
6893a[2] 7313a[3]

Santas Pal *C J Teague* a30 14
2 b f Chineur(FR) —Khafayif (USA) (Swain (IRE))
1521[7] 2089[10] 2575[9] 3709[9]

Santefisio *P J Makin* a86 85
3 b g Efisio—Impulsive Decision (IRE) (Nomination)
1703[12] (2496) 3163[2] ◆ 3643[3] ◆ 4326[3] (5753) ◆ (6111)

Santero (GER) *N Sauer* 90
4 b h Black Sam Bellamy(IRE) —Strofa (POL) (Winds Of Light (USA))
3493a[9]

Santiago Atitlan *P Monteith* a95 81
7 b g Stravinsky(USA) —Sylvette (USA) (Silver Hawk (USA))
257a[11] 434a[9] 4037[15] 4310[10] 4941[9] 5333[14] 5943[7] 7171[8]

Santino (GER) *J-P Carvalho* 92
2 b c Rock Of Gibraltar(IRE) —Selana (GER) (Lomitas)
6887a[6]

Santo Padre (IRE) *David Marnane* a98 107
5 b g Elnadim(USA) —Tshusick (Dancing Brave (USA))
3898a[5] (5860) 7007a[4]

Sanvean (IRE) *M R Channon* a67 91
3 b f Danehill Dancer(IRE) —Russian Muse (FR) (Machiavellian (USA))
(800) 1599[7] 1871[7] 2275[9] 3608[6] 3870[7] 4198[5] 4940[2] 5514[3]

Saorocain (IRE) *Mrs John Harrington* a43 39
3 b f Kheleyf(USA) —Compradore (Mujtahid (USA))
4819[17]

Saphir (GER) *P Schiergen* 111
3 b c Black Sam Bellamy(IRE) —Salontasche (GER) (Dashing Blade)
1718a[2] (2560a) 3670a[7] 5082a[5] 7039a[8]

Saphira's Fire (IRE) *W R Muir* a105 111
4 b m Cape Cross(IRE) —All Our Hope (USA) (Gulch (USA))
3619[5] 4522[8] 5201[6] 6853[3] 7188[3] 7589[3] 7809[4]

Saphir Du Vallon (FR) *C Lotoux* 57
3 b g Victorieux(FR) —Glamour Du Vallon (FR) (Bojador (FR))
7037a[7]

Saphir River (FR) *C Lerner* 107
3 gr c Slickly(FR) —Miss Bio (FR) (River Mist (USA))
4685a[4] 6657a[10]

Sapphire Prince (USA) *J R Best* a72 74
3 b c Read The Footnotes(USA) —Anna Jackson (USA) (Houston (USA))
2329[7] 2600[8] 3115[5] 3868[12] 4181[9] 4791[12] (6547) 6908[10] 7048[4] 7238[6] 7456[8] 7742[7]

Sapphire Rose *J G Portman* a54 63
3 b f Tobougg(IRE) —Pearly River (Elegant Air)
1594[9] (2515) 2910[3] 3581[9] 4224[10] 6370[11]

Sapphire Spirit (USA) *J R Best* a5 43
2 rg g Unbridled Time(USA) —Mimi's Tizzy (USA) (Cee's Tizzy (USA))
2595[9] 6696[7] 6903[16]

Saptapadi (IRE) *Sir Michael Stoute* a70 108
3 ch g Indian Ridge—Olympienne (IRE) (Sadler's Wells (USA))
1485[4] ◆ 1800[5]

Saraab (GER) *P Vovcenko* 71
7 bb g Alwuhush(USA) —Sohaila (GER) (Owington)
466a[5] 653a[7]

Sarabia (GER) *A Wohler* 98
3 b f One Cool Cat(USA) —Siberienne (USA) (Kingmambo (USA))
4363a[5]

Sarah Park (IRE) *B J Meehan* a98 90
4 ch m Redback—Brillano (FR) (Desert King (IRE))
2186[7] (2775) 3301[3] 3796[3] 4262[6] (5190) (5745) 6267[4] 6633[2] 7132[10] 7588[5]

Sarah's Art (IRE) *Stef Liddiard* a85 77
6 gr g City On A Hill(USA) —Treasure Bleue (IRE) (Treasure Kay)
71[3] (108) (198) 235[4] 329[4] 499[6] 1103[5] 1152[2] (1248) 4607[9] (5031) 5404[9] (7735)

Sarahthecarer (IRE) *P M Mooney* a59 61
2 b f Littletown Boy(USA) —Peaceful Sarah (Sharpo)
2401[6] 3249[U] 3332[3]

Sarakan (FR) *C Goudrain*
2 b c Diktat—Sarekat (IRE) (Cadeaux Genereux)
7316a[6]

Sara Louise (USA) *Saeed Bin Suroor* a109
3 b f Malibu Moon(USA) —Kings Lynn (USA) (Mt. Livermore (USA))
7285a[4]

Sarando *R Charlton* a65 62
4 b g Hernando(FR) —Dansara (Dancing Brave (USA))
126[6]

Sarasota Sunshine *N P Littmoden* a80 75
3 b f Oasis Dream—Never Explain (IRE) (Fairy King (USA))
(667) ◆ 960[3] 2776[2] (2973) (3464) 4061[3] (4707) (5090) 5432[12]

Saratoga Black (IRE) *Gianluca Bietolini* 87
2 br c Pyrus(USA) —Mary Martins (IRE) (Orpen (USA))
7205a[10]

Sard *M A Jarvis* 51
2 b f Bahamian Bounty—Clincher Club (Polish Patriot (USA))
5431[8] ◆ 6563[10]

Sardan Dansar (IRE) *Mrs A Duffield* a28 53
3 b f Alhaarth(IRE) —Peruvian Witch (IRE) (Perugino (USA))
1725[5] 2143[7] 3449[9] 3729[5] 3972[6] 4281[3] 4823[12] 5621[7]

Sariska *M L W Bell* 123
3 b f Pivotal—Maycocks Bay (Muhtarram (USA))
1353[4] ◆ (1988) (2672) (3896a) 5201[2] 6850[3]

Sarissa (BRZ) *P Bary* a100 100
6 b m Music Prospector(USA) —Sylicon Purple (BRZ) (Purple Mountain (USA))
336a[4]

Saristan (FR) *A De Royer-Dupre* 68
2 b c Azamour(IRE) —Sarkala (IRE) (Caerleon (USA))
6131a[6]

Sarmad (USA) *C E Brittain* 55
2 bb f Dynaformer(USA) —Performing Arts (IRE) (The Minstrel (CAN))
2047[9] 4396[11] 5547[10]

Saronsla Belle (FR) *L Edon*
2 b f Cardoun(FR) —Northern Honor (FR) (Northern Crystal)
7103a[3]

Sarraaf (IRE) *I Semple* a60 59
13 ch g Perugino(USA) —Blue Vista (IRE) (Pennine Walk)
216[9] 1556[6] 2440[4]

Sarrera (AUS) *Michael Moroney* 118
9 b g Quest For Fame—Zamsong (NZ) (Zabeel (NZ))
2117a[6] 6871a[16]

Sarrsar *M A Jarvis* 74
2 b g Shamardal(USA) —Bahr (Generous (IRE))
7095[3]

Sarwin (USA) *G A Swinbank* a67 71
6 rg g Holy Bull(USA) —Olive The Twist (USA) (Theatrical (IRE))
152[7] 777[10] (1495) (1955) 2362[3] (2440) 2532[6] 5395[9] 5673[6] 6019[5] 6900[10]

Sasheen *J R Boyle* a72
2 b f Zafeen(FR) —Sashay (Bishop Of Cashel)
7522[7] 7624[3] ◆ 7763[5]

Sassanian (IRE) *Jane Chapple-Hyam* a55 62
2 b g Clodovil(IRE) —Persian Sally (IRE) (Persian Bold)
2388[7] 4188[4] 6065[5] 6424[9] 7335[4] 7731[4]

Sassoaloro (GER) *H Blume* 110
5 ch h Acatenango(GER) —Spartina (USA) (Northern Baby (CAN))
2309a[4] 3441a[5] 5619a[3] (6521a) 7047a[7]

Sassy Gal (IRE) *Peter Maher* a70 86
4 ch m King's Best(USA) —Dancing Prize (IRE) (Sadler's Wells (USA))
2290a[9]

Satchmo Bay (FR) *C Boutin* a82 90
8 b g Alamo Bay(USA) —Royale Aube (FR) (Garde Royale)
3419a[8]

Satier (FR) *Mario Hofer* 108
4 b g Lord Of Men—Stiletta (GER) (Primo Dominie)
3493a[6]

Satindra (IRE) *C R Dore* a65 53
5 b g Lil's Boy(USA) —Voronova (IRE) (Sadler's Wells (USA))
117[4] 147[7] 385[4]

Satin Princess (IRE) *A M Hales* a26 48
2 b f Royal Applause—College Of Arms (Lujain (USA))
2972[8] 4302[7] 5829[8] 6554[4] 7372[9] 7453[10]

Satisfaction Life (IRE) *M Botti* a72 69
3 b f Acclamation—Etica (IRE) (Barathea (IRE))
2310a[15] 5168[8] 5616[6]

Saturn Girl (IRE) *S A Callaghan* 71
3 ch f Danehill Dancer(IRE) —Lilissa (IRE) (Doyoun)
1406[4] (3221) 5670[8] 6174[8]

Saturnine (IRE) *N Clement* 98
4 gr m Galileo(IRE) —Katchina Quest (FR) (Highest Honor (FR))
(6438a) 7347a[11]

Saturn Way (GR) *P R Chamings* a53 72
3 b g Bachelor Duke(USA) —Senseansensibility (USA) (Capote (USA))
1839[6] 2431[2] 2548[14] 4010[9] 4956[4]

Satwa Crown *E A L Dunlop* a29 24
2 b c Dubai Destination(USA) —Crown Of Spring (USA) (Chief's Crown (USA))
3226[9] 3692[14] 4200[9]

Satwa Excel *E A L Dunlop* 24
2 b f Exceed And Excel(AUS) —Pericardia (Petong)
4542[12]

Satwa Gold (USA) *E A L Dunlop* a88 57
3 ch c Rahy(USA) —No More Ironing (USA) (Slew O'Gold (USA))
(786) 1082[2] 4649[11] 5648[8] 6594[10] (6940) 7198[3] (7455) 7612[5]

Satwa Lady (FR) *J De Roualle* a74 70
4 b m Okawango(USA) —Still The One (Muhtarram (USA))
5089a[3]

Satwa Laird *E A L Dunlop* a86 92
3 b c Johannesburg(USA) —Policy Setter (USA) (Deputy Minister (CAN))
1987[4] 2674[10] 3049[8] 3839[8] 4326[4] 5746[2] 6243[2] 6702[7]

Satwa Moon (USA) *E A L Dunlop* a77
3 ch c Horse Chestnut(SAF) —Double Schott (USA) (Demons Begone (USA))
4789[6] 5228[3] 5614[6]

Satwa Prince (FR) *J De Roualle* a102 103
6 b h Munir—Toryka (Vettori (IRE))
6658a[5]

Satwa Ruby (FR) *J De Roualle* a73 95
3 gr f Verglas(IRE) —Vezina (FR) (Bering)
2989a[5] 3050[12] 4334a[7]

Satwa Son (IRE) *E A L Dunlop* a58 31
2 gr c Oasis Dream—Cozy Maria (USA) (Cozzene (USA))
3792[8] 5191[9]

Satwa Star (IRE) *E A L Dunlop* a70 56
3 b g King's Best(USA) —Sheppard's Watch (Night Shift (USA))
1636[5] 2857[5] 4199[7] 4791[5] 5677[4] 6294[7] 6701[8]

Satwa Street (IRE) *D M Simcock* a89 86
3 br c Elusive City(USA) —Black Tribal (IRE) (Mukaddamah (USA))
109[4] 203[3] 396[2] 1002[3] 1824[9] 2140[5] 2653[5] 3028[5] (3676) 3945[2] 4338[3] 5032[14]

Saucy *Tom Dascombe* a71 52
8 b m Muhtarram(USA) —So Saucy (Teenoso (USA))
125[3] 651[5]

Saucy Brown (IRE) *R Hannon* 95
3 b g Fasliyev(USA) —Danseuse Du Bois (USA) (Woodman (USA))
1085[3] 1324[12] (1664) 2469[3] 3011[11] 3628[5] 4423[7] 5025[5]

Saucy Girl (IRE) *T D Easterby* a42 67
2 b f Footstepsinthesand—Leenane (IRE) (Grand Lodge (USA))
1304[2] 1645[3] 3064[9] 5253[7] 5620[7] 6345[7]

Saunton Sands *A G Newcombe* 33
3 ch g Best Of The Bests(IRE) —Victoriet (Hamas (IRE))
2950[13]

Saute *W R Swinburn* a72 38
3 br g Hawk Wing(USA) —Lifting (IRE) (Nordance (USA))
1308[12] 1729[9] 4171[9] 5838[3] 6446[7] (7049) 7336[2] (7642)

Savaronola (USA) *B J Curley* a73 79
4 ch g Pulpit(USA) —Running Debate (USA) (Open Forum (USA))
40[5] 1568[8]

Saveiro (FR) *G A Swinbank* 13
5 b g Raintrap—Branceilles (FR) (Satin Wood)
1681[8]

Savile's Delight (IRE) *Tom Dascombe* a78 83
10 b g Cadeaux Genereux—Across The Ice (USA) (General Holme (USA))
89[9] 165[5] ◆ 304[7] 606[10] 739[7]

Saving Grace *E J Alston* a47 42
3 br f Lend A Hand—Damalis (IRE) (Mukaddamah (USA))
7678[11] 7754[8]

Saviour Sand (IRE) *T Keddy* a77 76
5 b g Desert Sun—Teacher Preacher (IRE) (Taufan (USA))
505[5] 656[4] 1833[12]

Savoie (FR) *Y Barberot* 92
3 b f Anabaa(USA) —Seacleef (FR) (A.P. Indy (USA))
7302a[4] (7697a)

Sawab *C E Brittain* a68 69
3 b f Tobougg(IRE) —Skew (Niniski (USA))
1130[2] 1380[3] 1667[8] 2356[8] 3188[4] 3550[5]

Sawpit Sunshine (IRE) *J L Spearing* a19 60
4 b m Mujadil(USA) —Curie Express (IRE) (Fayruz)
1775[12] 2598[13] 2880[10] 6596[11]

Saxby (IRE) *G A Harker* a70 70
2 ch c Pastoral Pursuits—Madam Waajib (IRE) (Waajib)
2348[6] 2793[6] (2996) 3542[3] 3842[6] 4195[6] 4858[5] 5187[2] 5841[2] (6292) 6557[9]

Saxford *Mrs L Stubbs* 104
3 b g Reset(AUS) —Bint Makbul (Makbul)
1292[10] 2035[9]

Saxona (IRE) *Ian Williams* 61
5 b m Jade Robbery(USA) —Saxon Maid (Sadler's Wells (USA))
2447^{9} 2877^{9} 3205^{2} (3617) 4703^{5} 5068^{8}

Say Anything (IRE) *Patrick Allen* a53 48
8 b m Perugino(USA) —Dama De Noche (Rusticaro (FR))
934^{4}

Sayif (IRE) *P W Chapple-Hyam* 119
3 b c Kheleyf(USA) —Sewards Folly (Rudimentary (USA))
(1085) 2485^{4} 4837a^{5} 5657^{4} (6304)

Say No Now (IRE) *D R Lanigan* a84 104
3 b f Refuse To Bend(IRE) —Star Studded (Cadeaux Genereux)
(1843) 2190^{3} 3016^{8} 3641^{2} 5260^{5} 5798^{3} 6605a^{4}

Say You Say Me *N J Vaughan* 63
3 b f Acclamation—Mindfulness (Primo Dominie)
2070^{7} 2820^{2}

Scalded Cat (IRE) *Sean P Hennessy* 45
6 b m Raise A Grand(IRE) —Piccolo Rose (Piccolo)
4360a^{12}

Scamperdale *B P J Baugh* a98 62
7 br g Compton Place—Miss Up N Go (Gorytus (USA))
79^{5} 271^{7} 477^{2} 694^{5} 1107^{3} 2392^{8} 3374^{8} (3977) 7465^{9} 7684^{9} (7848)

Scandal *Andrew Turnell* a65
4 b g Reel Buddy(USA) —Milliscent (Primo Dominie)
501^{4} 704^{3}

Scandola (USA) *G Botti* a73 85
2 b f Afleet Alex(USA) —Look Of The Lynx (USA) (Forest Wildcat (USA))
6751a^{2} (6960a)

Scarab (IRE) *T D Walford* a87 83
4 br g Machiavellian(USA) —Russian Society (Darshaan)
(156) 549^{5} 5961^{8} 6681^{17}

Scarboro Warning (IRE) *J G Given* a30 74
2 ch g Footstepsinthesand—Spring Easy (IRE) (Alzao (USA))
5674^{3} 6254^{9} 7146^{18}

Scarcity (IRE) *E A L Dunlop* 55
2 b f Invincible Spirit(IRE) —Sanpa Fan (ITY) (Sikeston (USA))
5969^{10} 6729^{9}

Scarlet Oak *A M Hales* a63 70
5 b m Zamindar(USA) —Flamenco Red (Warning)
96^{5} 314^{5} 481^{2} 645^{8} 1134^{2}

Scarlet O'Hara (IRE) *D K Weld* a79 92
4 b m Sadler's Wells(USA) —Agnetha (GER) (Big Shuffle (USA))
928a^{5} 5141a^{5} 6867a^{4}

Scarlet Ridge *D K Ivory* a38
2 ch f Tumbleweed Ridge—Kayartis (Kaytu)
5984^{14} 7663^{10}

Scarlett Angel (IRE) *W J Knight* 34
3 b f Xaar—Mildred (IRE) (Peintre Celebre (USA))
1752^{11} 2178^{12} 2487^{7}

Scarth Hill (IRE) *G M Moore* a22 53
3 ch g Selkirk(USA) —Louve Sereine (FR) (Sadler's Wells (USA))
1308^{11} 1926^{15}

Scar Tissue *E J Creighton* a53 31
5 ch m Medicean—Possessive Lady (Dara Monarch)
2220^{6} 2519^{10}

Scartozz *M Botti* a92 99
7 b g Barathea(IRE) —Amazing Bay (Mazilier (USA))
834^{8} (1283) 6030^{11}

Sceilin (IRE) *J Mackie* a52 66
5 b m Lil's Boy(USA) —Sharifa (IRE) (Cryptoclearance (USA))
107^{10} 2333^{5} (3259) 4300^{2} (5122) (6369) 6760^{6}

Scene Two *L M Cumani* a75 78
3 gr g Act One—Gleaming Water (Kalaglow)
1643^{5} 4229^{6} 4650^{9} (6698)

Scenic Blast (AUS) *Daniel Morton* 127
5 bb g Scenic—Daughter's Charm (AUS) (Delgado (USA))
(2991) ◆ 3819^{10} 7745a^{14}

Scenic Shot (AUS) *Daniel Morton* 121
7 b g Scenic—Sweepshot (AUS) (Dr Grace (NZ))
7040a^{5} (7196a)

Schachspieler (GER) *W Figge* 77
3 ch c Samum(GER) —English Rose (FR) (Caerleon (USA))
2560a^{8}

Scheibenhard (FR) *J-L Guillochon* 78
2 gr c Okawango(USA) —Shan State (USA) (Aljabr (USA))
6576a^{DSQ} 6960a^{0}

Schiaparelli (GER) *Saeed Bin Suroor* 121
6 ch h Monsun(GER) —Sacarina (Old Vic)
3781^{3} (4457) (5297a) 5891a^{3} (6893a) 7047a^{2}

Schiller Danon (GER) *W Hickst* 115
3 ch c Samum(GER) —Soljanka (GER) (Halling (USA))
5082a^{4} 6324a^{5} 7039a^{4} 7406a^{3}

Schinken Otto (IRE) *J M Jefferson* a55 36
8 ch g Shinko Forest(IRE) —Athassel Rose (IRE) (Reasonable (FR))
213^{10} 567^{4} 734^{5}

Scholars Lass (IRE) *J Balding* a47 26
4 b m Spartacus(IRE) —Blanche Neige (USA) (Lit De Justice (USA))
666^{8} 746^{4} 946^{8} 1563^{10}

Schoolboy Champ *Patrick Morris* a69 74
2 ch g Trade Fair—Aswhatilldois (IRE) (Blues Traveller (IRE))
(3152) 4746^{5} 5198^{16} 6486^{20} 6906^{2} 6983^{9}

Schutzenjunker (GER) *Uwe Ostmann* 108
4 b h Lord Of Men—Schutzenliebe (GER) (Alkalde (GER))
5461a^{9} (6713a) 7208a^{4}

Sciatin (IRE) *David P Myerscough* a84 89
6 b g Alhaarth(IRE) —Robalana (USA) (Wild Again (USA))
2289a^{16}

Scilly Breeze *A M Hales* 58
2 gr g Linamix(FR) —Mitraillette (USA) (Miswaki (USA))
2414^{4} 2861^{2} 3232^{4} 3958^{2}

Scintillating (IRE) *R Hollinshead* a47 33
2 b f Cape Cross(IRE) —Announcing Peace (Danehill (USA))
2914^{9} 3306^{P} 5613^{P} 6436^{12} 6992^{21} 7120^{9} 7319^{7} 7419^{4} 7706^{6}

Scintillo *R Hannon* a114 115
4 ch h Fantastic Light(USA) —Danseuse Du Soir (IRE) (Thatching)
634^{3} (864) (913) 1351^{7} 1823^{2} (2522a) 3443a^{7} 4298^{9} 6890a^{6} 7593a^{11}

Scipion L'Africain (FR) *B De Montzey* a66 65
2 b c Nombre Premier—Mitsou (FR) (The Quiet Bidder)
4368a^{4}

Scooby Dee *R M Whitaker* 49
2 b f Captain Rio—Scooby Dooby Do (Atraf)
4659^{7} 4928^{5} 5949^{12} 6895^{8}

Scopey *Gerard Keane* a65 72
4 b g Bertolini(USA) —Red Symphony (Merdon Melody)
7275^{4} 7716^{9}

Scorn (USA) *J H M Gosden* 74
2 b f Seeking The Gold(USA) —Sulk (IRE) (Selkirk (USA))
6730^{4} ◆ 7183^{2}

Scotch And Soda (IRE) *Jedd O'Keeffe* a17 50
3 b f Mull Of Kintyre(USA) —Buddy And Soda (IRE) (Imperial Frontier (USA))
1174^{5} 1625^{6} 1922^{5} 4070^{8} 4594^{7} 5621^{11} 6880^{8}

Scottish Affair *E A L Dunlop* a66 52
3 b g Selkirk(USA) —Southern Queen (Anabaa (USA))
707^{5} (938) 1580^{9} 2152^{6} 3511^{10}

Scottish Boogie (IRE) *S Kirk* 77
2 b c Tobougg(IRE) —Scottish Spice (Selkirk (USA))
6054^{8} 6334^{7} 6615^{3} (7097) ◆

Scottish Glen *P R Chamings* 40
3 ch g Kyllachy—Dance For Fun (Anabaa (USA))
3319^{5}

Scotty's Future (IRE) *A Berry* a39 58
11 b g Namaqualand(USA) —Persian Empress (IRE) (Persian Bold)
2263^{12} 4402^{16} 4588^{14} 6817^{15}

Scrapper Smith (IRE) *A C Whillans* a65 68
3 b g Choisir(AUS) —Lady Ounavarra (IRE) (Simply Great (FR))
2394^{3} 3096^{6} 3651^{4} (4343) 4894^{6} (5336) 6988^{6} 7172^{3}

Screaming Brave *M R Channon* a55 65
3 br g Hunting Lion(IRE) —Hana Dee (Cadeaux Genereux)
121^{11} 239^{4} 677^{7} 953^{5} 1070^{4} 1282^{3} 2340^{2} (2461) (2635) 3454^{3} 3869^{5} 4178^{6} 4722^{4} 5123^{6} 5470^{2} 5838^{6} 5872^{2}

Screen Hero (JPN) *Y Shikato* 123
5 ch h Grass Wonder(USA) —Running Heroine (JPN) (Sunday Silence (USA))
7593a^{13}

Scruffy Skip (IRE) *Mrs C A Dunnett* a58 56
4 b g Diktat—Capoeira (USA) (Nureyev (USA))
746^{6} 946^{11} 1536^{5} 1634^{10} 2920^{9} 3007^{10} 3471^{5} 3671^{2} 4082^{12} 4183^{6} 4732^{7} (5566) 6038^{7} 6340^{7} 6433^{9} 6777^{7} 6926^{13}

Scrupulous *Tom Dascombe* a60 65
3 gr f Dansili—Mrs Gray (Red Sunset)
7620^{6}

Scuffle *R Charlton* a100 103
4 gr m Daylami(IRE) —Tantina (USA) (Distant View (USA))
1210^{3} 1667^{6} 4794^{4} 5200^{5} 6094^{5}

Scutch Mill (IRE) *P C Haslam* a63 65
7 ch g Alhaarth(IRE) —Bumble (Rainbow Quest (USA))
81^{2} 145^{4}

Seachantach (USA) *J S Bolger* a77 104
3 b g Elusive Quality(USA) —Subtle Breeze (USA) (Storm Cat (USA))
4574a^{11}

Sea Cliff (IRE) *Jonjo O'Neill* a67 36
5 b g Golan(IRE) —Prosaic Star (IRE) (Common Grounds)
(148) 190^{5} 300^{2} 449^{3} 604^{3} 1609^{4}

Sea Country (FR) *J Rossi* a39 18
2 b f Country Reel(USA) —Sea Of Luck (Ezzoud (IRE))
6148a^{7}

Sea Cove *Mrs Dianne Sayer* a33 40
9 b m Terimon—Regal Pursuit (IRE) (Roi Danzig (USA))
3617^{5} 4462^{10} 4848^{8}

Sea Crest *M Brittain* a30 65
3 b f Xaar—Talah (Danehill (USA))
3611^{11} 4514^{2} 4707^{3} 5041^{2} 5373^{6} 5422^{7} 6988^{7}

Seader (USA) *Tim Vaughan* a66 56
4 b g Mr Greeley(USA) —Evangel (USA) (Danzig (USA))
4625^{8} 5103^{5} ◆

Sea Dubai *R Hannon* a72 65
2 b c Mark Of Esteem(IRE) —Royal Flame (IRE) (Royal Academy (USA))
3420^{6} 4646^{2} 5528^{11}

Seafield Towers *D A Nolan* 57
9 ch g Compton Place—Midnight Spell (Night Shift (USA))
1227^{13} 1647^{8} 1924^{14} 2389^{6} 2451^{9} 3148^{7}

Sea Fight (USA) *N Clement* 92
3 ch c Smart Strike(CAN) —Incredulous (FR) (Indian Ridge)
3649a^{9}

Sea Hunter *A Al Raihe* a95 98
7 b h Lend A Hand—Ocean Grove (IRE) (Fairy King (USA))
264a^{6} 525a^{4} 641a^{4}

Sea Land (FR) *B Ellison* a67 48
5 ch g King's Best(USA) —Green Bonnet (IRE) (Green Desert (USA))
(3720) 3983^{8} 4552^{4} 5150^{9} 5676^{5} 6024^{10} 6123^{2} 6437^{7} 6861^{10}

Sea Lavender *R Charlton* a29 75
3 b f Diktat—Satin Bell (Midyan (USA))
1327^{9} 3297^{9} 4606^{5} 5548^{2} 6742^{10} 6975^{12}

Sea Lord (IRE) *M Johnston* 87
2 b c Cape Cross(IRE) —First Fleet (USA) (Woodman (USA))
4006^{2} (4258) 5133^{9} 5658^{12} 6063^{2} ◆ 7013^{13}

Seamster *M Johnston* a66 46
2 ch g Pivotal—Needles And Pins (IRE) (Fasliyev (USA))
3546^{8} 3957^{7} 7580^{2}

Seamus Shindig *H Candy* a59 94
7 b g Aragon—Sheesha (USA) (Shadeed (USA))
1864^{5} 2474^{11} 2941^{7} 4500^{4} (5001) 5799^{16} 6694^{4} 6994^{10}

Sea Of Heartbreak (IRE) *R Charlton* a69 37
2 b f Rock Of Gibraltar(IRE) —Top Forty (Rainbow Quest (USA))
7029^{10} (7276)

Sea Of Leaves (USA) *J S Goldie* 99
3 b f Stormy Atlantic(USA) —Dock Leaf (USA) (Woodman (USA))
3746^{10} 4135^{5} 5032^{2} ◆ 5695^{13} 6089^{10} (6428) 6814^{4}

Seaquel *A B Haynes* a54 58
3 b f Kyllachy—Broughton Singer (IRE) (Common Grounds)
6787^{4} 7174^{6} 7660^{8} 7740^{2}

Search For The Key (USA) *P F I Cole* a66 64
2 bb c El Corredor(USA) —Lo Cal Bread (USA) (Native Prospector (USA))
4492^{3} 5778^{6}

Sea Rover (IRE) *M Brittain* a73 76
5 b h Jade Robbery(USA) —Talah (Danehill (USA))
1885^{2} 2312^{5} 2472^{10} 2770^{8} 2998^{12} (3529) 3828^{7} 3877^{15} 4285^{16} 4783^{10} 5955^{10} 6765^{7} 7555^{2} 7595^{8}

Sea Salt *R E Barr* a59 87
6 b g Titus Livius(FR) —Carati (Selkirk (USA))
1924^{15} 3972^{3} 4312^{5} 4504^{4} (4654) 4977^{2} 5343^{7} 5516^{7} (5675) 6135^{4} 6309^{2} 6764^{7} 7083^{6}

Seasider *Sir Michael Stoute* a90 79
4 b g Zamindar(USA) —Esplanade (Danehill (USA))
3091^{21}

Seaside Sizzler *R M Beckett* 73
2 ch g Rahy(USA) —Via Borghese (USA) (Seattle Dancer (USA))
5400^{10} 5785^{5} 6393^{4}

Seasonal Cross *S Dow* a60 74
4 b m Cape Cross(IRE) —Seasonal Blossom (IRE) (Fairy King (USA))
1074^{9} 1741^{3} 2330^{2} 2977^{4} 3581^{3} ◆ 4441^{3} 5003^{2} 5429^{7} (5905) (6394) 6790^{5}

Seasons Estates *F J Brennan* 9
7 b m Mark Of Esteem(IRE) —La Fazenda (Warning)
3322^{11}

Sea Storm (IRE) *James Moffatt* a67 52
11 b g Dolphin Street(FR) —Prime Interest (IRE) (Kings Lake (USA))
6769^{6}

Sea The Stars (IRE) *John M Oxx* 138
3 b c Cape Cross(IRE) —Urban Sea (USA) (Miswaki (USA))
(1675) ◆ (2705) ◆ (3640) (5135) (5688a) (6526a)

Seattle Speight (USA) *W J Knight* a12 23
2 b f Speightstown(USA) —Gal From Seattle (USA) (A.P. Indy (USA))
5604^{15} 5752^{13}

Seaway *Saeed Bin Suroor* 94
3 b c Dr Fong(USA) —Atlantic Destiny (IRE) (Royal Academy (USA))
2282^{2} 2937^{3} (4022)

Sebastian Flyte *Francis Ennis* 103
2 ch c Observatory(USA) —Aravonian (Night Shift (USA))
5486a^{3} 6426^{2}

Second Brook (IRE) *R Hollinshead* a52 52
2 b g Celtic Swing—Mur Taasha (USA) (Riverman (USA))
3052^{4} 6991^{9} 7317^{7} 7597^{9} 7722^{4}

Second Reef *T A K Cuthbert* a64 42
7 b g Second Empire(IRE) —Vax Lady (Millfontaine)
3852^{8} 4588^{6} 5150^{7} 5513^{9} 6817^{14}

Second To Nun (IRE) *Jean-Rene Auvray* a48 62
3 b f Bishop Of Cashel—One For Me (Tragic Role (USA))
(1420) 2515^{3} 2950^{9} ◆ 3803^{5} 4734^{9} 5384^{7} 5905^{5} 7587^{12}

Secrecy *Saeed Bin Suroor* 116
3 b g King's Best(USA) —Wink (Salse (USA))
5863^{3} ◆ 6732^{3} ◆ (7185) ◆

Secret Assassin (IRE) *Mrs J L Le Brocq* a77 77
6 b g Daggers Drawn(USA) —Lypharden (IRE) (Lyphard's Special (USA))
5540a^{2}

Secret City (IRE) *R Bastiman* 59
3 b g City On A Hill(USA) —Secret Combe (IRE) (Mujadil (USA))
1452^{10} 2786^{5} (3651) 5405^{12} 6103^{5} 6926^{7}

Secret Desert *D M Simcock* a50 60
3 b g Dubai Destination(USA) —Lady Bankes (IRE) (Alzao (USA))
4381^{8} 4979^{6} 5578^{4} 6549^{7} 6788^{4} 6919^{2}

Secret De Vie *B Grizzetti* 90
3 gr f Fantastic Light(USA) —Grey Way (USA) (Cozzene (USA))
3186a^{8}

Secret Dubai (IRE) *Mrs L Stubbs* a75 79
4 b h Dubai Destination(USA) —Secret Pride (Green Desert (USA))
218^{6} 457^{5} 980^{4} 1259^{2} 1689^{5} 1885^{7} 2312^{11} 2624^{4} 3227^{6} 4183^{9} 4654^{9} 5443^{13}

Secret Hero *Lee Smyth* a48 76
3 b c Cadeaux Genereux—Valiantly (Anabaa (USA))
951^{10} 1355^{10} 2080^{6} (2797) ◆ 3790^{5} 4267^{2} (4535) 6111^{12} 6909^{6} 7672^{7}

Secretive *M Johnston* a77
2 b c Shamardal(USA) —Samsung Spirit (Statoblest)
(7836)

Secret Life *J Noseda* a81 76
3 b c Montjeu(IRE) —Bright Halo (IRE) (Bigstone (IRE))
2082^{11} 2488^{4} 2930^{3} 4979^{4} 6855^{2}

Secret Millionaire (IRE) *Patrick Morris* a84 86
2 b g Kyllachy—Mithl Al Hawa (Salse (USA))
1358^{2} ◆ 4282^{3} (5180) 5467^{4} (5650) 5908^{2} 6486^{8}

Secret Night *C G Cox* a90 88
6 gr m Dansili—Night Haven (Night Shift (USA))
(1116) 1343^{3} 1860^{2} 2780^{3} 4293^{5}

Secret Ploy *H Morrison* 71
9 b g Deploy—By Line (High Line)
3788^{3} 4551^{5} 5068^{9} 6021^{6}

Secret Queen *B J Meehan* a66 85
2 b f Zafeen(FR) —Gold Queen (Grand Lodge (USA))
2514^{3} 3249^{2} 3810^{2} ◆ 5165^{4} (5949) 6486^{6}

Secret Rose *W G M Turner* a10
2 b f Deportivo—Kingston Rose (GER) (Robellino (USA))
1031^{8} 1249^{8}

Secret Society *M L W Bell* a85 109
3 b c Exceed And Excel(AUS) —Shady Point (IRE) (Unfuwain (USA))
(1071) 2281^{4} (2544) 3049^{2} (3839) ◆ 4297^{2} ◆ 5232^{4} 5709a^{6}

Secret Venue *Jedd O'Keeffe* 77
3 ch g Where Or When(IRE) —Sheila's Secret (IRE) (Bluebird (USA))
1505^{10} (2454) (3063) (3681) 4289^{2} 4464^{8} 5768^{8} 5856^{8} (6387)

Secret Witness *R A Harris* a81 52
3 ch g Pivotal—It's A Secret (Polish Precedent (USA))
(1638) ◆ 2198^{11} 4540^{14} 5753^{2} 6212^{10} 6776^{10} 7662^{6} 7795^{5}

Secundus (GER) *M Nigge* a83 78
4 b g Daliapour(IRE) —Sly (GER) (Monsun (GER))
5281a^{3}

Securitisation (IRE) *B J Curley* 26
2 ch c Rock Of Gibraltar(IRE) —Maria Delfina (IRE) (Giant's Causeway (USA))
3546^{11} 4243^{10} 6593^{11} 6991^{10}

Sedge (USA) *P T Midgley* a59 70
9 b g Lure(USA) —First Flyer (USA) (Riverman (USA))
1153^{11}

Seductive Witch *J Balding* a61 45
4 ch m Zamindar(USA) —Thicket (Wolfhound (USA))
946^{5} 1182^{8}

Seedless *A M Balding* a58 64
4 br m Mtoto—Unseeded (Unfuwain (USA))
2123^{5} 2497^{13}

See Elsie Play *Miss Z C Davison* 48
3 b f King O' The Mana(IRE) —Liebside Lass (IRE) (Be My Guest (USA))
2862^{7} ◆ 3161^{8}

Seeker Rainbow *Mrs L C Jewell* a8 40
2 ch f Mark Of Esteem(IRE) —Seeker (Rainbow Quest (USA))
3160^{7} 4200^{10}

Seeking Dubai *E F Vaughan* a82 91
2 b f Dubawi(IRE) —Placement (Kris)
3337^{3} 4257^{2} (4603) (5091) 6326a^{4} 7147^{9}

Seeking Faith (USA) *C G Cox* a42 50
3 bb f Chapel Royal(USA) —Padrao Global (USA) (Storm Bird (CAN))
3696^{8} 4145^{14}

Seeking Rio *R J Hodges* a39
2 b f Captain Rio—True Seeker (Lujain (USA))
7630^{7} 7749^{8} 7859^{11}

Seeking Rose *E A L Dunlop* a36 35
2 b f Where Or When(IRE) —Selkirk Rose (IRE) (Pips Pride)
5547^{9} 5984^{9} 6728^{7}

Seeking Stardom *P M Phelan* 58
2 ch g Starcraft(NZ) —Lunar Goddess (Royal Applause)
4825^{13} 5749^{7} 6054^{9}

Seeking The Buck (USA) *R M Beckett* 97
5 b g Seeking The Gold(USA) —Cuanto Es (USA) (Exbourne (USA))
(2003) (2671) 3213^{2} 3873^{4} 5170^{5}

Seek N' Destroy (IRE) *B W Hills* a84 96
3 b c Exceed And Excel(AUS) —Very Nice (Daylami (IRE))
(951) 1214^{2} (1870) 2504^{4} 3375^{3} (5432) 6270^{23}

Seek The Cash (USA) *M Quinn* a53
2 ch c Mr Greeley(USA) —Cash Deal (USA) (Danzig (USA))
7773^{8}

Seek The Fair Land *J R Boyle* a91 76
3 b g Noverre(USA) —Duchcov (Caerleon (USA))
(1108) (1434) 1870^{5} 2826^{4} 3028^{11} 6776^{4} 7189^{10} 7356^{4} 7456^{4} ◆ (7627) (7741) 7833^{2} ◆

See That Girl *B Smart* a3 44
3 b f Hawk Wing(USA) —Hampton Lucy (IRE) (Anabaa (USA))
3352^{7} 5954^{4} 7176^{8}

Seeu Central (IRE) *P J Rothwell* a61 38
5 br g Lahib(USA) —Mottaret (IRE) (Forest Wind (USA))
255^{4}

Sefton Park *C R Egerton* a51 51
2 b g Dansili—Optimistic (Reprimand)
5528^{8} 5966^{11} 6772^{10}

Segal (IRE) *A M Hales* a82 76
4 b g Cadeaux Genereux—Camcorder (Nashwan (USA))
2566^{6}

Sehoy (USA) *J H M Gosden* a91 90
3 bb c Menifee(USA) —Another Storm (USA) (Gone West (USA))
(957) 1643^{2} ◆ 2077^{10} 4715^{4} 5216^{4} 5909^{2} 6724^{8}

Sehrezad (IRE) *Andreas Lowe* 114
4 b h Titus Livius(FR) —Trebles (IRE) (Kenmare (FR))
3416a^{2} (4129a) 6713a^{7} 7312a^{2}

Seihali (IRE) D Selvaratnam a98 107
10 b h Alzao(USA) —Edwina (IRE) (Caerleon (USA))
182[3] 335a[5] 615a[8] 702a[5] 774a[11]
Sejanus K A Ryan a81 67
2 b g Dubai Destination(USA) —Agrippina (Timeless Times (USA))
2196[6] 3147[5] 4067[4] 4371[2] 4931[9] (5839) 6491[2] 6805[8]
Seldom (IRE) M Brittain a68 70
3 b g Sesaro(USA) —Daisy Dancer (IRE) (Distinctly North (USA))
1335[2] ◆ (1625) 2058[9] 2365[3] 2544[9] 2786[7] 3316[10] 5601[17] 6824[F] 7716[2]
Seldom Seen Kid (IRE) T D Easterby a41 45
2 ch c Captain Rio—North Cider Rose (IRE) (Goldmark (USA))
3064[7] 3716[7] 4067[8] 4503[8] 4800[7]
Select (IRE) P W Chapple-Hyam 101
3 ch f Choisir(AUS) —Intercession (Bluebird (USA))
(1173) 1873[8] 3320[3] 3892a[4] 4489[2]
Select Committee J J Quinn 75
4 b g Fayruz—Demolition Jo (Petong)
2032[5] 3065[4] 3562[3] 3765[2] 4141[2] 4355[12] (4399) 4886[9] 5341[5] (5421) 5978[7] 6159[2] 6233[7] (6489)
Select Reason (BRZ) E Martins a90
5 b g A Good Reason(BRZ) —Place D'Armes (BRZ) (Fast Gold (USA))
336a[7] 521a[10]
Selina Rio L A Mullaney a29 21
2 ch f Captain Rio—Encanto (IRE) (Bahhare (USA))
3937[9] 4398[6] 4889[11] 6554[6] 7217[7] 7352[6] 7501[12]
Selmis V Caruso 115
5 ch h Selkirk(USA) —Nokomis (Caerleon (USA))
(1575a) (2115a)
Semah Harold E S McMahon a68 63
4 b g Beat All(USA) —Semah's Dream (Gunner B)
81[5] 277[6]
Semi Detached (IRE) J W Unett a59 63
6 b g Distant Music(USA) —Relankina (IRE) (Broken Hearted)
107[6]
Seminal Moment J G Given a60 49
3 b f Sakhee(USA) —Thracian (Green Desert (USA))
2857[9] 3731[4] (4175) 4470[5] 5011[15] 7025[6] 7354[13] 7642[11]
Seminole Shield (ITY) G Fois 76
3 b c Philomatheia(USA) —Sasparella (ITY) (Be My Master (USA))
1904a[19]
Senate J H M Gosden a42
2 ch c Pivotal—Sauterne (Rainbow Quest (USA))
7491[8]
Senate Majority T D Easterby a53 59
2 ch g Avonbridge—Benjarong (Sharpo)
1304[6] 2484[4] 3032[4] 4547[5] 4884[9] 6068[7]
Senatore (TUR) S Aydemir 90
4 b h Lear White(USA) —Rose Gem (IRE) (Taufan (USA))
5619a[11]
Senators Alibi T J O'Mara a52 80
11 b g Caerleon(USA) —Salul (Soviet Star (USA))
4574a[12]
Sendali (FR) J D Bethell 57
5 b g Daliapour(IRE) —Lady Senk (FR) (Pink (FR))
(5734)
Sendreni (FR) M Wigham a79 76
5 b g Night Shift(USA) —Sendana (FR) (Darshaan)
31[7] 141[3] (1048) 1734[10] 2185[9] 6294[9] 7192[12] 7412[9] 7596[9]
Seneca Village (FR) M Weiss a73 50
5 b g Silvano(GER) —Espridoma (Primo Dominie)
464a[2] 652a[4]
Seneschal A B Haynes a74 81
8 b g Polar Falcon(USA) —Broughton Singer (IRE) (Common Grounds)
959[6] 1074[2] (1258) 1539[10] (1958) (2011) 2434[4] 2883[6] 3539[3] 4009[9] 4181[2] 5120[6] 5182[9] 5566[6]
Senior Edward Lynam 108
2 ch c Medicean—Muschana (Deploy)
5892a[5] 6318a[9]
Senlis (IRE) E Botti 110
4 b h High Chaparral(IRE) —Senebrova (Warning)
2525a[6] 7303a[7]
Senora Verde P T Midgley a35 37
3 ch f Bahamian Bounty—Spain (Polar Falcon (USA))
41[7] 379[8] 1084[7]
Senor Benny (USA) M McDonagh a85 102
10 br h Benny The Dip(USA) —Senora Tippy (USA) (El Gran Senor (USA))
1374a[9] 2287a[8] 2555a[7] 3898a[2] 7341a[12]
Senor Berti B Smart 73
3 b g Bertolini(USA) —Pewter Lass (Dowsing (USA))
2917[6] (Dead)
Sensacion Sensual J G Given a43 58
3 b f Josr Algarhoud(IRE) —Charlie Girl (Puissance)
1173[11]
Sensazione World (IRE) B Grizzetti 99
4 b m Spinning World(USA) —Sensazione (Cadeaux Genereux)
7303a[8]
Senses (USA) J Noseda a73 82
3 ch c Rahy(USA) —Sweet And Steady (USA) (Steady Growth (CAN))
1730[6] ◆ 2240[2] (2640) 3644[4] 4299[5] (5834) 6483[3]
Sent From Heaven (IRE) B W Hills a80 105
2 b f Footstepsinthesand—Crystal Valkyrie (IRE) (Danehill (USA))
(3979) ◆ 4795[3] ◆ (5427) 6269[4]
Separate Ways (IRE) David Marnane a74 91
4 b g Chevalier(IRE) —Choralli (Inchinor)
5490a[7]
Septemberintherain T G Mills a72 52
2 gr c Verglas(IRE) —Gwyneth (Zafonic (USA))
2889[11] 7390[4] ◆
Sequillo R Hannon a85 85
3 b g Lucky Story(USA) —Tranquillity (Night Shift (USA))
1466[11] 2432[4] (2982) (4242) 4715[2] 4910[2] 5663[3] 5834[4] 6546[3] 6996[14]
Seradim P F I Cole a97 95
3 ch f Elnadim(USA) —Seren Devious (Dr Devious (IRE))
1698[12] 2057[3] 2777a[5] 3320[4] 3641[6] 5175[4]
Serafina's Flight W R Muir a72 67
2 b f Fantastic Light(USA) —Seven Of Nine (IRE) (Alzao (USA))
5604[4] ◆ 5984[3] 6638[2]
Serasana A De Royer-Dupre 87
3 gr f Red Ransom(USA) —Serasia (FR) (Linamix (FR))
6238a[5]
Seren Arian B Palling a8 2
3 ro f Dreams End—Westfield Mist (Scallywag)
6934[13] 7278[13] 7596[12]
Sereth (IRE) B J Curley 103
6 b g Monsun(GER) —Saderlina (IRE) (Sadler's Wells (USA))
1351[9] 1696[12] 2085[8] 3822[11] 4274[5] 6851[3]
Sergeant Pink (IRE) S Gollings a57 70
3 b c Fasliyev(USA) —Ring Pink (USA) (Bering)
2230[3] 3976[4] 7084[6]
Sergeant Sharpe H J Evans a64 65
4 ch g Cadeaux Genereux—Halcyon Daze (Halling (USA))
745[5] 918[10]
Serhaal (IRE) Sir Michael Stoute a65 68
2 b c Green Desert(USA) —Lucky For Me (USA) (King Of Kings (IRE))
4717[2] 6781[7]
Serienhoehe (IRE) P Schiergen 99
3 b f High Chaparral(IRE) —Saldenehre (GER) (Highest Honor (FR))
4583a[4] 5296a[7]
Serious Attitude (IRE) Rae Guest 113
3 b f Mtoto—Zameyla (IRE) (Cape Cross (IRE))
1698[7] (3824) 4837a[8]
Serious Choice (IRE) J R Boyle a59 83
4 b g Choisir(AUS) —Printaniere (USA) (Sovereign Dancer (USA))
(1274) 2003[7] 2931[12] 3734[11]
Serious Drinking (USA) W R Swinburn a62 66
3 b f Successful Appeal(USA) —Cup Match (USA) (Kingmambo (USA))
6430[4] 6741[3]
Serious Impact (USA) J H M Gosden 89
4 b g Empire Maker(USA) —Diese (USA) (Diesis)
(1515) 1990[3] 5321[6]
Serious Spirit Rae Guest
2 b f Pastoral Pursuits—Motto (FR) (Mtoto)
6620[15]
Sermons Mount (USA) Mouse Hamilton-Fairley a66 56
3 b g Vicar(USA) —Ginny Auxier (USA) (Racing Star (USA))
800[4] 1580[7] 1839[12] 2143[10] 3672[2] 4082[5] 4240[2] 4730[7] 4905[5] 5644[2] 6213[2] 6611[2] 7052[2]
Serva Jugum (USA) P F I Cole a86 110
3 bb c Fusaichi Pegasus(USA) —Shake The Yoke (Caerleon (USA))
5447[4] 5764[2] 6198a[8]
Serva Padrona (IRE) H-A Pantall
2 b f Statue Of Liberty(USA) —Semiramide (IRE) (Persian Bold)
7409a[4]
Servetius (USA) G A Butler a52
2 b c Eurosilver(USA) —Golden Envoy (USA) (Dayjur (USA))
6026[4] 6493[13]
Servoca (CAN) Mike Murphy a99 98
3 gr c El Prado(IRE) —Cinderellaslipper (USA) (Touch Gold (USA))
(982) 1296[3] 1879[2] 2443[7] 3622[2] 4459[11] 5424[8] 5799[5] 6240[6] 6666[2] (6994) 7227[2]
Sesenta (IRE) W P Mullins 102
5 b m King's Theatre(IRE) —Cincuenta (IRE) (Bob Back (USA))
(2305a) 2994[2] 4510a[7] (5173) 5796[6]
Sesimbra (IRE) Robert Collet a55 81
2 b f Key Of Luck(USA) —Campiglia (IRE) (Fairy King (USA))
4970a[6]
Sestet S Dow a54 46
4 b m Golden Snake(USA) —Sestina (FR) (Bering)
58[5] 494[11] 5775[3] 6208[5] 7666[4]
Seta L M Cumani 104
2 ch f Pivotal—Bombazine (IRE) (Generous (IRE))
(4542) ◆ 5825[3]
Setareh (GER) P Olsanik 105
4 b h Areion(GER) —Sety's Spirit (USA) (Seattle Song (USA))
2953a[9] 4129a[7] 7044a[9]
Set Back D Nicholls 53
2 b g Reset(AUS) —No Comebacks (Last Tycoon)
6556[4] 6896[12] 7289[8]
Set Em Up Mo M J Attwater a54
3 b f Reset(AUS) —Mo Stopher (Sharpo)
394[7] 594[9] 5316[13] 6223[12] 6941[9] 7439[5] 7882[7]
Set In Ice Mark Gillard a37 41
2 b g Reset(AUS) —Masrora (USA) (Woodman (USA))
4219[14] 4713[6] 5319[12] 6931[7] 7391[10] 7644[7]
Set Sail (IRE) A P O'Brien 108
3 ch c Danehill Dancer(IRE) —Ahdaab (USA) (Rahy (USA))
1238a[4] 2756a[15] 2992[10] 3640[10] 5135[3] 5688a[9] 6526a[18] 6850[14]
Sette E Mezzo (USA) William Mott a74 106
4 b h Dynaformer(USA) —Lovely Lyric (USA) (Alydar (USA))
6512a[6]
Set The Trend A M Balding a100 96
3 bb c Reset(AUS) —Masrora (USA) (Woodman (USA))
(503) ◆ 1033[3] (1284) ◆ 2273[2] ◆ 3298[2] ◆ 4455[8] 5663[8]
Settigano (IRE) Michael Joseph Fitzgerald a104 104
6 b g Sadler's Wells(USA) —Bonita Francita (CAN) (Devil's Bag (USA))
4412a[17] 7809[3]
Set To Go H J L Dunlop a59 36
2 b g Reset(AUS) —Golubitsa (IRE) (Bluebird (USA))
6291[12] 6728[8] 7024[7] 7235[11]
Set To Rock J G Portman a32 14
2 ch g Reset(AUS) —Crocolat (Croco Rouge (IRE))
5371[9] 6792[16] 7120[16]
Seul Blue (ITY) R Menichetti 95
3 b c Tout Seul(IRE) —Bluebold (IRE) (Bluebird (USA))
1392a[6]
Seven Gifts Lee Smyth 28
2 b f Avonbridge—Julia Domna (Dominion)
1993a[13]
Sevenna (FR) H R A Cecil a93 102
4 b m Galileo(IRE) —Silvassa (IRE) (Darshaan)
1383[5] 2471[6] 3103[2] (4458) 7047a[9]
Seven Of Diamonds (IRE) T D Easterby 62
2 gr f Clodovil(IRE) —Tres Sage (Reprimand)
2401[4] 3875[4] 4278[4] 6820[4]
Seven Royals (IRE) Miss A M Newton-Smith a29 62
4 b g Val Royal(FR) —Seven Notes (Zafonic (USA))
7105[10]
Seven Sky (FR) P F I Cole
6 b g Septieme Ciel(USA) —Nuit De Crystal (FR) (Crystal Glitters (USA))
1471[4] 872[9]
Seventh Cavalry (IRE) A King a67 79
4 gr g No Excuse Needed—Mixwayda (FR) (Linamix (FR))
2039[6] 2851[10] 3421[2] 3869[3] 4759[2] 5266[4] 5802[2]
Seventh Hill M Blanshard a69 70
4 ch g Compton Place—Dream Baby (Master Willie)
1318[3] 1581[3] 2039[11] 2497[5] 2878[3] 3421[6] 5790[8] 6126[2] 6498[8] 7112[8] 7225[2] 7524[4]
Seventh Street (USA) Saeed Bin Suroor a119
4 ch m Street Cry(IRE) —Holiday Runner (USA) (Meadowlake (USA))
7285a[8]
Severio (IRE) A P Jarvis 59
3 b f Captain Rio—Good Forecast (Unfuwain (USA))
4277[7] 4805[5] 5731[5] 6950[8] 7173[10]
Sew'N'So Character (IRE) M Blanshard a75 93
8 b g Imperial Ballet(IRE) —Hope And Glory (USA) (Well Decorated (USA))
558[6] 841[8] 1121[2] 1320[3] 1493[5] 1833[5] 2400[6] 3983[14] 4645[12] 5377[11] 5577[5] 6208[11]
Sgt Roberts (IRE) J S Moore a73 73
3 b g Diktat—Ann's Annie (IRE) (Alzao (USA))
755[4] ◆ 824[6] 962[5] 1408[9] 2126[8]
Sgt Schultz (IRE) J S Moore a102 85
6 b g In The Wings—Ann's Annie (IRE) (Alzao (USA))
124[3] 337a[11] 522a[11] (915) 1117[7] 1571[7] 1944[2] 2242[4] 2566[5] 2932[14] 7574[5] 7720[7]
Shaaridh (USA) M Johnston 73
3 bb f Dixieland Band(USA) —Boston Lady (USA) (Boston Harbor (USA))
1168[3] 4955[4]
Shaayeq (IRE) M P Tregoning a72 82
2 bb c Dubawi(IRE) —Shohrah (IRE) (Giant's Causeway (USA))
5191[3] (5590) 6057[4] 6569[3]
Shabak Hom (IRE) D M Simcock a60 70
2 b c Exceed And Excel(AUS) —Shbakni (USA) (Mr Prospector (USA))
5191[8] 5590[2] 6125[5]
Shabib (USA) B W Hills a84 94
3 b c Intidab(USA) —Muklah (IRE) (Singspiel (IRE))
1071[2] (1422) (4056) 4954[10]
Shaded Edge D W P Arbuthnot a77 76
5 b g Bold Edge—Twilight Mistress (Bin Ajwaad (IRE))
71[7] 531[2] 844[3] (961) 1121[4] (1710) (1876) 2086[5] 4293[13] 4871[2] 5349[11] 5753[10] 6726[2] 6976[6] 7364[2] 7627[9] 7891[2]
Shade Of Pale (GER) Yvonne Durant 93
4 ch g Funambule(USA) —See Me (SWE) (Spectrum (IRE))
5933a[7]
Shadow Bay (IRE) Miss Z C Davison a68 75
3 b g Deportivo—Champion Tipster (Pursuit Of Love)
1196[11] (1424) 1839[5] 2562[6] 3299[12] 6293[5] 6699[8] 7053[8]
Shadow Jumper (IRE) J T Stimpson a36 47
8 b g Dayjur(USA) —Specifically (USA) (Sky Classic (CAN))
12[7] 215[8] 489[10] 603[5] 744[7]
Shadows Lengthen M W Easterby a86 56
3 b g Dansili—Bay Shade (USA) (Sharpen Up)
1441[5] 2131[7] 4943[3] 5331[6] 5838[7] 6768[9] (7425) ◆ (7490) (7641) (7677) ◆ (7712)
Shadowtime Miss Tracy Waggott a73 73
4 b g Singspiel(IRE) —Massomah (USA) (Seeking The Gold (USA))
1244[13] 1332[4] 1612[10] 1955[2] 2261[3] 2968[2] 3264[11] 3857[2] 4333[6] 4400[3] 5160[7] 5395[5] 6019[4] 6157[7] 6383[4]
Shady Gloom (IRE) K A Ryan a71 85
4 b g Traditionally(USA) —Last Drama (IRE) (Last Tycoon)
999[10] 1319[9] 2666[2] 2932[4] 3235[5] 3573[5] 4426[7] 5308[3] 5962[10] 6832[2]
Shady Lady (IRE) M Johnston a36 78
3 b f Celtic Swing—Viola Royale (IRE) (Royal Academy (USA))
7066[9]
Shafrons Canyon (IRE) P J Lally a47 74
6 b m Lend A Hand—Carroll's Canyon (IRE) (Hatim (USA))
1496[10]
Shahwardi (FR) A De Royer-Dupre 103
3 b c Lando(GER) —Shamdara (IRE) (Dr Devious (IRE))
(6198a) 6890a[3]
Shakalaka (IRE) G L Moore a81 81
3 b g Montjeu(IRE) —Sweet Times (Riverman (USA))
2551[2] 3984[2] 5986[4] 6209[4] 7550[3] 7737[2] (7882)
Shake On It M R Hoad a72 88
5 b g Lomitas—Decision Maid (USA) (Diesis)
321[3] ◆ 398[2] 458[8] 505[4] 725[8] 910[10] 961[10] 2739[7] 3112[7] 3662[7] 4083[4] 4305[14] 5779[6] 6213[3] 6587[9] 6945[3] 7109[4] 7200[7] 7480[11] 7652[4] (7802)
Shaker Style (USA) J D Bethell a64 64
3 ch g Gulch(USA) —Carr Shaker (USA) (Carr De Naskra (USA))
295[4] (628) 740[4] 1063[5]
Shakespearean (IRE) M Johnston 107
2 b c Shamardal(USA) —Paimpolaise (IRE) (Priolo (USA))
(2444) ◆ 3138[5] 3817[3] (5261) (6319a) 7017[6]
Shakespeare's Son H J Evans a75 74
4 b g Mind Games—Eastern Blue (IRE) (Be My Guest (USA))
191[11] 2359[10] 2880[9] 3407[5] 3691[3] 4023[2] 4183[7] 5374[8] 5792[4] 6038[5] 6492[2] 7275[11] 7330[8] 7503[13] 7601[6] 7770[3] 7889[3]
Shakin John E J O'Neill 52
3 b g Refuse To Bend(IRE) —Qudrah (IRE) (Darshaan)
1441[12] 1594[11]
Shalanaya (IRE) M Delzangles 115
3 ch f Lomitas—Shalamantika (IRE) (Nashwan (USA))
4578a[5] (5562a) (6525a)
Shallal P W Chapple-Hyam 101
4 b h Cape Cross(IRE) —First Waltz (FR) (Green Dancer (USA))
1865[5] 3388[4] 4087[8] 6815[13]
Shaloo Diamond R M Whitaker 91
4 b g Captain Rio—Alacrity (Alzao (USA))
1850[7] 2197[8] 2823[4] 3266[4] (3761) 4003[2] 4517[2] 4661[5] 5334[2] 5671[7] 6681[8]
Shaluca E S McMahon a47 69
2 bb f Shamardal(USA) —Noushkey (Polish Precedent (USA))
6389[3] 7140[4]
Shamakiya (IRE) A De Royer-Dupre 103
3 b f Intikhab(USA) —Shamadara (IRE) (Kahyasi)
2754a[2] 3442a[3] (3968a)
Shamalgan (FR) A Savujev 101
2 ch c Footstepsinthesand—Genevale (FR) (Unfuwain (USA))
5652a[6] 6889a[3]
Shamali W J Haggas a92 107
4 ch h Selkirk(USA) —Shamaiel (IRE) (Lycius (USA))
2412[8] 2891[3] (3840) ◆ (4339) ◆
Shamandar (FR) W J Haggas 100
2 ch f Exceed And Excel(AUS) —Sensational Mover (USA) (Theatrical (IRE))
(3686) ◆ 4089[2] ◆ 4989[2] (5606) (6241) 6449[5]
Shame The Devil (IRE) Jonjo O'Neill 23
4 b g Danehill Dancer(IRE) —Iles Piece (Shirley Heights)
2229[8]
Shamir Miss Jo Crowley a78 66
2 b c Dubai Destination(USA) —Lake Nyasa (IRE) (Lake Coniston (IRE))
6109[7] 6627[2] 7130[2] 7388[3]
Shampagne P F I Cole a101 106
3 b c Orpen(USA) —Arndilly (Robellino (USA))
863[6] 1211[2] 1679[2] 2004[3] 3049[14] 3783[5] 5012a[2] 6222a[3] 7588[4]
Shamrock Lady (IRE) J Gallagher a81 76
4 b m Orpen(USA) —Shashi (IRE) (Shaadi (USA))
4009[6] 4733[10] 5099[6] 5746[9] 6630[10]
Sham Sheer L M Cumani a82 76
3 br g Cape Cross(IRE) —Viola Da Braccio (IRE) (Vettori (IRE))
1491[4] 2048[11] 2667[6] 4230[6] (5723) (6124) 6545[2] (6977)
Shamwari Lodge (IRE) R Hannon 107
3 b f Hawk Wing(USA) —Ripalong (IRE) (Revoque (IRE))
(2049) 2674[2] 3747[8] ◆ 4459[2] (5175) ◆ 5798[2] 6267[5] ◆ 6505a[7]
Shanaco (FR) Robert Collet a43 84
2 b c Ski Chief(USA) —Hollyhead (FR) (Green Tune (USA))
4073a[5]
Shanafarahan (IRE) K A Morgan a68 64
4 b g Marju(IRE) —Sedna (FR) (Bering)
126[8] (751) (877) (1081) 1200[8] 1319[8] 7461[13] 7732[5]
Shanavaz C J Teague a58 63
3 gr f Golden Snake(USA) —Safinaz (Environment Friend)
1595[12] 2230[9] 2779[5] 3321[4] 3721[4] 3976[5] 4710[9] 5470[7] 5732[10] 6097[5] 6384[4] 6558[4] 7084[8] 7425[7] 7557[6]
Shandelight (IRE) Miss J A Camacho a55 63
5 b m Dilshaan—By Candlelight (IRE) (Roi Danzig (USA))
7670[2] ◆
Shangani H Candy a70 85
3 b f Ishiguro(USA) —Sheesha (USA) (Shadeed (USA))
(2795) 3537[5] (4380) 5130[6] 5916[3] 6731[4] 7032[5]
Shanghai Star (IRE) Patrick Allen a41 76
5 b g Soviet Star(IRE) —Sweet Surrender (IRE) (Pennekamp (USA))
4818[5] 5679[11]
Shannersburg (IRE) D E Pipe a69 70
4 bb g Johannesburg(USA) —Shahoune (USA) (Blushing Groom (FR))
5725[6] 6778[10] 6937[7] 7699[7] (7888)
Shannon Golden S R Bowring a61 44
3 b g Tumbleweed Ridge—Cledeschamps (Doc Marten)
1476[4] 3764[14] 4174[5] 5008[9] 5326[14] (7002) 7241[10] 7615[5]

Shannon Weir (IRE) *E J Creighton*
7 b g Norwich—Go Meekly (IRE) (Bulldozer)
2738[7]
Shanzu *G L Moore* a65 81
4 b m Kyllachy—Limuru (Salse (USA))
1149[9] 1524[12] 2796[10] 3980[11] 4262[15]
Shape Shifter (USA) *J R Best* 40
3 ch g Performing Magic(USA) —Shot Gun Frances (USA) (Commemorate (USA))
4698[8] 5483[8] 6188[11] 6758[13]
Sharaayeen *B W Hills* a67 77
2 br c Singspiel(IRE) —Corinium (IRE) (Turtle Island (IRE))
5312[5] (5907) 6993[14]
Sharakti (IRE) *A J McCabe* a16
2 b g Rakti—Easter Parade (Entrepreneur)
6125[8]
Shared Moment (IRE) *J Gallagher* 65
3 ch f Tagula(IRE) —Good Thought (IRE) (Mukaddamah (USA))
1270[3] 3005[2] (3862) 4279[5] 4642[3] 5101[6] 5503[4] 5940[2] 6174[10] 6394[8]
Share Option *A W Carroll* a45 55
7 b g Polish Precedent(USA) —Quota (Rainbow Quest (USA))
1609[10]
Shark Man (IRE) *P J McBride* a78 78
2 b g Arakan(USA) —Sharkiyah (IRE) (Polish Precedent (USA))
9945 1119[2] (1312) 2087[2] 2247[8] 3424[8] 3978[5] 5265[8] 5970[7] (6586) 6774[2] (7319)
Sharp And Chic *M L W Bell* a47 16
2 b f Needwood Blade—Moreover (IRE) (Caerleon (USA))
6441[9] 6728[12]
Sharpazmax (IRE) *P J Makin* a84 79
5 b g Daggers Drawn(USA) —Amour Toujours (IRE) (Law Society (USA))
2715 2407[6] 2945[4] 5667[3] 6060[6] 6583[2] 7775[11]
Sharp Bullet (IRE) *W R Swinburn* a74 76
3 b g Royal Applause—Anna Frid (GER) (Big Shuffle (USA))
2140[4] 5098[9] 5777[5] 6434[7]
Sharp Discovery *J M Bradley* 26
3 b f Needwood Blade—You Found Me (Robellino (USA))
1772[13] 1843[9] 2744[9]
Sharp Eclipse *K A Ryan* 65
2 ch g Exceed And Excel(AUS) —Helen Sharp (Pivotal)
1275[5] ◆ 1735[3] 2099[10]
Sharpened Edge *B Palling* 87
3 b f Exceed And Excel(AUS) —Beveled Edge (Beveled (USA))
1353[14] 2205[3] (2888) ◆ 3582[3] ◆ 3845[6] 4244[3] 5264[4] 5871[3] 6666[16]
Sharpener (IRE) *R Hannon* a69 71
3 b f Invincible Spirit(IRE) —Daily Double (FR) (Unfuwain (USA))
2035
Sharpour (IRE) *Z Koplik* 91
5 b h Desert Sun—Sharamana (IRE) (Darshaan)
6505a[15]
Sharps Gold *D Morris* a56 40
4 ch m Twice As Sharp—Toking N' Joken (IRE) (Mukaddamah (USA))
71[13] 405[7] (587) 749[6] 868[9] 2924[10]
Sharp Shoes *Mrs A Duffield* 57
2 br g Needwood Blade—Mary Jane (Tina's Pet)
4546[7] 5066[5] 6246[2] 6542[3]
Sharp Sovereign (USA) *Miss L A Perratt* 67
3 b g Cactus Ridge(USA) —Queen Of Humor (USA) (Distorted Humor (USA))
1509[6] 1829[4] 2371[10] 3069[5] 3482[8] 4348[7] 4529[7] 4943[5] 5294[14] 5733[9] 6156[4] 6987[10]
Shava *H J Evans* a56 48
9 b g Atraf—Anita Marie (IRE) (Anita's Prince)
141[1] 587[6] 661[6]
Shavansky *B R Millman* a88 90
5 b g Rock Of Gibraltar(IRE) —Limelighting (USA) (Alleged (USA))
(2641) (3213) 3840[4] ◆ 4526[8] 6234[5] 6480[5] 7194[8]
Shavoulin (USA) *P W Hiatt* a31 58
5 bb g Johannesburg(USA) —Hello Josephine (USA) (Take Me Out (USA))
2221[2] ◆ 2675[3] 2830[10] 3675[4] 4071[5] 4697[7] 4916[10]
Shaweel *Saeed Bin Suroor* 117
3 b c Dansili—Cooden Beach (IRE) (Peintre Celebre (USA))
1354[5] 1917a[7] 7186[2]
Shawnee Saga (FR) *W Baltromei* 102
4 b h Sagacity(FR) —Shawnee (GER) (Dashing Blade)
1549a[3] 2216a[3] 3441a[9]
Shaws Diamond (USA) *D Shaw* a81 81
3 ch f Ecton Park(USA) —Dear Abigail (USA) (Dehere (USA))
276[2] 556[2] 782[2] 2279[6] 2674[7] 3360[4] (3876) 4317[8] 5005[4]
Shayera *B R Johnson* a56 66
4 b m Hawk Wing(USA) —Trick (IRE) (Shirley Heights)
102[4] 346[14]
Shayla *G A Swinbank* 59
2 ch f Pastoral Pursuits—Honours Even (Highest Honor (FR))
6154[5] 6762[7]
Shaylee *T D Walford* 61
4 b m Muhtarram(USA) —Fairywings (Kris)
2237[6] 2527[3] 2803[4] (3561)
Shayrazan (IRE) *James Leavy* 89
8 ch g Zilzal(USA) —Shayraz (Darshaan)
2289a[17]
She Be Wild (USA) *Wayne Catalano* a115
2 bb f Offlee Wild(USA) —Trappings (USA) (Seeking The Gold (USA))
(7283a)
Shediyama (FR) *A De Royer-Dupre* 109
3 b f Red Ransom(USA) —Shemaka (IRE) (Nishapour (FR))
2952a[6]
Sheer Fantastic *P C Haslam* a72 70
4 b g Fantastic Light(USA) —Sheer Bliss (USA) (Relaunch (USA))
171[4] 219[5] (428)
Sheer Force (IRE) *W J Knight* a74 70
2 b g Invincible Spirit(IRE) —Imperial Graf (USA) (Blushing John (USA))
2844[8] 3792[3] 4410[9] 5191[4] 5913[3] 6627[3]
Shegarrdi *K A Ryan* 16
2 b c Efisio—Elleray (IRE) (Docksider (USA))
4844[11] 5360[10]
She Goes Nowhere (IRE) *M S Tuck* a46
3 br f Pyrus(USA) —Peking Dancer (USA) (King Of Kings (IRE))
5572[11] 6344[6]
Sheik'N'Knotsterd *J F Coupland* a42 57
4 ch g Zaha(CAN) —Royal Ivy (Mujtahid (USA))
1276[15] 1477[4] 1924[6] 2366[9] 2745[12] 3031[4] 3175[3] 3539[4] 4436[6] 4823[16] 5254[12]
Sheila's Castle *S Regan* a63 71
5 b m Karinga Bay—Candarela (Damister (USA))
(4867) 5545[3] 6704[6] 7461[8] 7785[11]
Sheila Toss (IRE) *R Hannon* a68
2 b f Galileo(IRE) —Palacoona (FR) (Last Tycoon)
6164[5]
Sheka *I W McInnes* 72
2 b f Ishiguru(USA) —Maid For Running (Namaqualand (USA))
1304[4] (1521) 2372[6] 3559[4]
Shekan Star *K G Reveley* a53 59
7 b m Sri Pekan(USA) —Celestial Welcome (Most Welcome)
(1472) 2246[3] 2629[4] 3123[8] 3233[2] 3561[5] 3943[4] 4593[2] 4893[3] ◆ 5469[6] 5733[2] 6310[5]
She Knows It All (IRE) *G A Swinbank* 57
2 gr f Verglas(IRE) —Tatamagouche (IRE) (Sadler's Wells (USA))
3058[7] (3605)
Shela House *J H Culloty* a80 94
5 ch g Selkirk(USA) —Villa Carlotta (Rainbow Quest (USA))
4510a[9]
Shelfah (IRE) *M A Jarvis* 58
2 b f Selkirk(USA) —Pass The Peace (Alzao (USA))
5605[15] 6245[4] 6792[5]
Shemima *A De Royer-Dupre* 110
4 gr m Dalakhani(IRE) —Shemaka (IRE) (Nishapour (FR))
(1597a) 2428a[4] 3969a[3] 5058a[2] 5796[4]
Shemiyla (FR) *A De Royer-Dupre* 111
3 b f Dalakhani(IRE) —Shemala (IRE) (Danehill (USA))
7128a[2]
Shemoli *M A Jarvis* 81
3 ch g Singspiel(IRE) —Felawnah (USA) (Mr Prospector (USA))
1088[2] 1349[2] 2090[3] (3192) 3861[4] 5216[8]
Shenandoah Girl *Miss Gay Kelleway* a57 62
6 b m Almushtarak(IRE) —Thundering Papoose (Be My Chief (USA))
377[10] (443) 601[5]
Shercon (IRE) *N Tinkler* 30
2 ch g Redback—Snow Eagle (IRE) (Polar Falcon (USA))
3376[7] 4515[10] 6819[12]
Sheriff's Silk *B N Pollock* a70 46
5 b g Forzando—Sylhall (Sharpo)
823[10] 4668[6] 5479[13]
Sherjawy (IRE) *Miss Z C Davison* a62 62
5 b g Diktat—Arruhan (IRE) (Mujtahid (USA))
22[6] (56) 111[4] 153[3] 467[8] (853) 884[7] 1055[2] 1182[5] 1748[4] 1970[5] 2224[7] (2680) 2864[10] 3162[7] 5020[12] 5219[7] 5477[8] 6422[8] 7503[3] 7710[2] (7835)
Sherman McCoy *B R Millman* 86
3 ch g Reset(AUS) —Naomi Wildman (USA) (Kingmambo (USA))
1416[2] 1930[3] (2479) 3222[2] (4319) 4911[4] 5660[3] 6388[4]
Shernando *M Johnston* 67
2 b c Hernando(FR) —Shimmering Sea (Slip Anchor)
6592[5]
She's A Character *R A Fahey* 94
2 b f Invincible Spirit(IRE) —Cavernista (Lion Cavern (USA))
(2699) ◆ 3086[4] 4418[6] 5606[7] 6090[9]
She's A Model *R Ingram* a26 17
3 b f Erhaab(USA) —Bedtime Model (Double Bed (FR))
2633[10] 3382[8]
She Say'S *J-C Rouget*
2 b f Oasis Dream—Cas Royaux (USA) (Woodman (USA))
4577a[0]
Shesha Bear *W R Muir* a65 76
4 b m Tobougg(IRE) —Sunny Davis (USA) (Alydar (USA))
2764[5] 3217[11] 3766[2] 4207[3] (4744)
Sheshali (IRE) *Evan Williams* 74
5 b g Kalanisi(IRE) —Sheshara (IRE) (Kahyasi) (4480)
She's In The Money *R A Fahey* 84
3 b f High Chaparral(IRE) —Luminda (IRE) (Danehill (USA))
1174[2] 1302[9] 2700[2] 3342[6] 4284[5] (4940) 5340[2] 5514[5] (6015) 6311[2]
She's My Rock (IRE) *S Kirk* a56
2 b f Rock Of Gibraltar(IRE) —Love And Affection (USA) (Exclusive Era (USA))
4980[9] 7234[8] 7436[6] 7597[3] 7722[7] 7887[4]
She's Ok (IRE) *C E Brittain* 79
2 b f Xaar—Silvertine (IRE) (Alzao (USA))
2207[6] 3101[2] ◆ 3849[2] 4385[2] (4539) 5136[9] 5658[9] 6241[4]
She's Our Beauty (IRE) *S T Mason* a51 56
6 b m Imperial Ballet(IRE) —Eleonora D'Arborea (Prince Sabo)
89[6] 380[4] 727[9] 919[5]
She's Our Dream *R C Guest* a39 20
4 b m Statue Of Liberty(USA) —Mainly Sunset (Red Sunset)
794[12] 945[7] 1243[16] 1628[8] 1689[10]
She's Our Mark *Patrick J Flynn* a101 109
5 ch m Ishiguru(USA) —Markskeepingfaith (IRE) (Ajraas (USA))
2729a[2] 3012[5] (3894a) (4253a) 4923a[3] 5890a[3] 6298a[7]
She's Pivotal (IRE) *J A Osborne* a28 40
3 ch f Pivotal—Born Beautiful (USA) (Silver Deputy (CAN))
2139[12] 6430[9] 6573[6] 7374[11]
She's So Pretty (IRE) *G L Moore* a75 68
5 ch m Grand Lodge(USA) —Plymsole (USA) (Diesis)
341[5]
She Who Dares Wins *L R James* a41 48
9 b m Atraf—Mirani (IRE) (Danehill (USA))
1055[4]
Shianda *G L Moore* 47
2 b f Kyllachy—Limuru (Salse (USA))
7183[12]
Shibhan *C E Brittain* 73
2 ch f Compton Place—Untold Riches (USA) (Red Ransom (USA))
1939[3] 2765[3] 3248[5] 3576[7] 4383[7] 4782[3] (5207) 5748[4] 6534[2]
Shifting Gold (IRE) *K A Ryan* a67 72
3 b g Night Shift(USA) —Gold Bust (Nashwan (USA))
(228) 689[7] 1063[8] 2152[3] 2742[7] (4529) 4898[4] 5162[2] (5733)
Shifting Star (IRE) *W R Swinburn* a103 103
4 ch g Night Shift(USA) —Ahshado (Bin Ajwaad (IRE))
1699[9] 2474[8] 3091[8] 3818[12] 7454[3]
Shimah (USA) *Kevin Prendergast* 109
3 ch f Storm Cat(USA) —Sayedat Alhadh (USA) (Mr Prospector (USA))
1698[11]
Shimmering Moment (USA) *H R A Cecil* a66 64
2 ch f Afleet Alex(USA) —Vassar (USA) (Royal Academy (USA))
4869[3] 6729[7]
Shimmering Surf (IRE) *P Winkworth* a76
2 b f Danehill Dancer(IRE) —Sun On The Sea (IRE) (Bering)
5752[4] ◆ 6628[2]
Shimoni *G L Moore* a85 88
5 b m Mark Of Esteem(IRE) —Limuru (Salse (USA))
(1753)
Shine A Line (FR) *U Suter* a82 78
2 ch f Tertullian(USA) —Sparkling Star (FR) (Art Sebal (USA))
1482a[6] 4970a[2]
Shingara (IRE) *W Hefter* 59
3 b f Milan—Silver Swan (USA) (Silver Hawk (USA))
5784a[2]
Shining Sun (FR) *J Bertran De Balanda* 45
2 b c Bernebeau(FR) —Shining Light (FR) (Shining Steel)
6751a[9]
Shining Times (IRE) *P T Midgley* a25 48
3 br f Danetime(IRE) —Shining Desert (IRE) (Green Desert (USA))
5145[12] 5341[9] 5396[11] 6308[8] 7270[6]
Shinko's Best (IRE) *A Kleinkorres* 106
8 ch g Shinko Forest(IRE) —Sail Away (GER) (Platini (GER))
3650a[6]
Ship's Biscuit *Sir Michael Stoute* a70
2 b f Tiger Hill(IRE) —Threefold (USA) (Gulch (USA))
7450[5] ◆
Shirley High *P Howling* a51
3 b f Forzando—Ripple Effect (Elmaamul (USA))
390[8] 2455[8] 5105[5] 6641[2] 7411[13] 7510[4] 7629[5] 7714[9]
Shi Shan *T D Barron* 65
2 b c Sampower Star—Nanna (IRE) (Danetime (IRE))
4282[6] ◆ 5439[4]
Shmookh (USA) *Doug Watson* a46 51
5 b h Green Desert(USA) —Elrafa Ah (USA) (Storm Cat (USA))
434a[11]
Shocking (AUS) *Mark Kavanagh* 115
4 b h Street Cry(IRE) —Maria Di Castiglia (Danehill (USA))
(7215a)
Shooting Party (IRE) *R Hannon* a76 77
3 b g Noverre(USA) —L-Way First (IRE) (Vision (USA))
2890[6] 4649[9] 5997[9] 6733[11]
Shoot The Pot (IRE) *R M Beckett* a69 33
2 b g Intikhab(USA) —Kerasana (IRE) (Kahyasi)
6728[9] (7825)
Shopton Lane (USA) *Doug Watson* a89
5 b h Quiet American(USA) —Lightfoot Lane (USA) (Phone Trick (USA))
334a[7] 698a[9]
Shore Thing (IRE) *C R Egerton* 73
6 b g Docksider(USA) —Spicebird (IRE) (Ela-Mana-Mou)
4417[9] 5530[4]
Short Affair *L M Cumani* 99
4 b m Singspiel(IRE) —L'Affaire Monique (Machiavellian (USA))
(2697) ◆ 4287[5] 5472[8] 7291[13]
Short Cut *Ian Williams* a52 55
3 b g Compton Place—Rush Hour (IRE) (Night Shift (USA))
2918[9] 4643[3] 4730[2] 4937[4] 5644[4] 6039[3] 7787[4]
Short Sharp Shock *J Mackie* a59 39
3 b c Mujahid(USA) —Possibility (Robellino (USA))
2230[8] 3710[13] 4845[15]
Short Supply (USA) *T D Walford* a22 48
3 b f Point Given(USA) —Introducing (USA) (Deputy Minister (CAN))
5520[6] 5731[7] 7353[9]
Shortwall Lady (IRE) *J L Spearing* a29
4 b m Court Cave(IRE) —Vanished (IRE) (Fayruz)
12[5] 210[10] (Dead)
Shoshiba (IRE) *Alessandro Turco* 72
6 b m Plumbird—Magic Surprise (Bluebird (USA))
1394a[5]
Shosolosa (IRE) *S A Harris* a55 60
7 b m Dansili—Hajat (Mujtahid (USA))
1955[16] 2246[7] 2441[11] 5037[8] 5438[13] 5872[8]
Shotley Mac *N Bycroft* 88
5 ch g Abou Zouz(USA) —Julie's Gift (Presidium)
1016[13] 2938[7] (3339) 3825[4] 4310[9]
Shouldntbethere (IRE) *Mrs P N Dutfield* a68 56
5 ch g Soviet Star(USA) —Octomone (USA) (Hennessy (USA))
187[6] 528[6]
Showcasing *J H M Gosden* 116
2 b c Oasis Dream—Arabesque (Zafonic (USA))
2844[2] ◆ (3546) (5172) ◆ 6450[3]
Show Willing (IRE) *A P Jarvis* a60 25
2 b f Elusive City(USA) —Showboat (USA) (Theatrical (IRE))
6009[16] 6292[9] 6556[7] 6912[5] 7177[5]
Shreyas (IRE) *J S Bolger* 108
4 gr m Dalakhani(IRE) —Sadima (IRE) (Sadler's Wells (USA))
1758a[4] (2647a) 4962a[3] 5685a[3] 6298a[5]
Shubbaan (USA) *M P Tregoning* a72
4 bb h Kingmambo(USA) —Sayedah (IRE) (Darshaan)
6974[2] ◆
Shunkawakhan (IRE) *Miss L A Perratt* a70 65
6 b g Indian Danehill(IRE) —Special Park (USA) (Trempolino (USA))
3110[7] 3448[13] 3655[10] 4466[10] 4878[6] 5289[12] 5948[3] 6415[2] 6637[9]
Shy *P Winkworth* a75 80
4 ch m Erhaab(USA) —Shi Shi (Alnasr Alwasheek)
2123[2] 2854[7] 4301[9]
Shybutwilling (IRE) *Mrs P N Dutfield* a28 49
4 ch m Best Of The Bests(IRE) —Reticent Bride (IRE) (Shy Groom (USA))
1703[9] 2205[8] 2603[5] 3577[6] 3994[7]
Shy Glance (USA) *P Monteith* a76 77
7 b g Red Ransom(USA) —Royal Shyness (Royal Academy (USA))
1690[5] 2043[3] 2392[3] (3150) 4532[8] 5160[12] 5334[9] (6157) 6648[10]
Si Belle (IRE) *Rae Guest* a78 91
4 gr m Dalakhani(IRE) —Stunning (USA) (Nureyev (USA))
2501[6] 3493a[7] 4566[7] 5248[7]
Siberian Tiger (IRE) *A J Martin* a87 107
4 b g Xaar—Flying Millie (IRE) (Flying Spur (AUS))
3142[10] 5173[11] 6662[6] 7293[17]
Sicilian Warrior (USA) *P F I Cole* a66
3 b c War Chant(USA) —Gravina (CAN) (Sir Ivor (USA))
16[4] (134)
Side Glance *A M Balding* 90
2 br g Passing Glance—Averami (Averti (IRE))
(6061) 6397[2]
Sidney Melbourne (USA) *J R Best* a67 65
2 ch c Lemon Drop Kid(USA) —Tolltally Light (USA) (Majestic Light (USA))
5934[5] 6544[8] (7463)
Siegfrieds Night (IRE) *M C Chapman* a24 54
8 ch g Night Shift(USA) —Shelbiana (USA) (Chieftain)
66[6] 148[9] 252[9]
Siena *Mrs C A Dunnett* a56 30
4 b m Lomitas—Sea Lane (Zafonic (USA))
5651[0] 661[14] 748[6] 813[13]
Siena Star (IRE) *Stef Liddiard* a69 69
11 b g Brief Truce(USA) —Gooseberry Pie (Green Desert (USA))
125[6] 320[7] (1199) 1785[2] 1983[3] 2516[6] 7524[8] 7699[6]
Sienna Lake (IRE) *T D McCarthy* a60 63
3 b f Fasliyev(USA) —Lolita's Gold (USA) (Royal Academy (USA))
6699[10]
Sierra Alpha *Mrs A J Perrett* 78
2 b c Dansili—Sound Asleep (USA) (Woodman (USA))
(5528)
Sierra Femina (FR) *J Boisnard*
2 b f Sagacity(FR) —Fanissa (GER) (Exit To Nowhere (USA))
7316a[3]
Sight Unseen *H R A Cecil* 105
3 b c Sadler's Wells(USA) —High Praise (USA) (Quest For Fame)
(1328) 1800[4] 2176[3] ◆
Sight Winner (NZ) *J Size* 119
6 b g Faltaat(USA) —Kinjinette (NZ) (Kinjite (NZ))
(1553a) 7746a[11]
Signal (FR) *F Head* 76
2 b c Numerous(USA) —Seduisante (FR) (Anabaa (USA))
3935a[3]
Signaller (USA) *M Johnston* 75
3 ch g Rahy(USA) —Tango Charlie (USA) (Cure The Blues (USA))
1308[3] ◆ 1522[2] 1874[6]
Signalman *P Monteith* 61
5 gr g Silver Patriarch(IRE) —Kairine (IRE) (Kahyasi)
1692[8]
Signella *P W Chapple-Hyam* a66 62
3 ch f Selkirk(USA) —Sarah Georgina (Persian Bold)
(272) 1050[6]
Sign Of Approval *K R Burke* a79 81
3 b c Refuse To Bend(IRE) —Scarlet Plume (Warning)
122[3] 389[5] (659) 1291[12] 2571[2] 3026[2] 3543[2]
Sign Of Life *W R Swinburn* a62 63
2 b f Haafhd—Three Piece (Jaazeiro (USA))
5752[7] ◆ 6567[4]
Sign Of Oasics (IRE) *F Rohaut*
2 b c Oasis Dream—Sign Of The Vine (FR) (Kendor (FR))
7264a[0]

Sign Of The Cross *C R Dore* a78 80
5 b g Mark Of Esteem(IRE) —Thea (USA) (Marju (IRE))
392[6] 798[9] (1530) (2149) 2775[7] 3331[9] 3736[8] 4144[5] 4645[9] 5329[13] 6123[7] 6349[9] 6588[9] 7129[3] 7239[13]

Signora Frasi (IRE) *A G Newcombe* a62 74
4 b m Indian Ridge—Sheba (IRE) (Lycius (USA))
762[3] 3208[10] 4667[3] (6945)

Signor Peltro *H Candy* a86 108
6 b g Bertolini(USA) —Pewter Lass (Dowsing (USA))
1861[4] (2470) 3818[7] 4297[5] 4796[2] ◆ 5476[2] ◆ 6091[14] 6270[15] 6732[6]

Signor Verdi *B J Meehan* 45
2 b c Green Tune(USA) —Calling Card (Bering)
6990[10]

Silaah *D Nicholls* a91 99
5 b g Mind Games—Ocean Grove (IRE) (Fairy King (USA))
1186[3] 1663[5] 2050[6] 2396[2] (2828) 5001[2] 5959[2] 6050[6]

Silca Meydan *R J Price* a65 44
3 b g Diktat—Golden Silca (Inchinor)
121[6] 503[4] 592[4] 758[2] 4718[10] 4860[5] 5791[11] 7579[8] 7755[9]

Silenceofthewind (USA) *K R Burke* 95
2 b c Eddington(USA) —Betty's Solutions (USA) (Eltish (USA))
2247[6] (3310) 3817[8]

Silent Act (USA) *Mrs A J Perrett* a73 66
3 b f Theatrical(IRE) —Vinista (USA) (Jade Hunter (USA))
1488[5] 1893[2] 4156[14] 4904[4] 5988[3] 6538[2] (7112) 7238[2]

Silent Applause *Dr J D Scargill* a53 71
6 b g Royal Applause—Billie Blue (Ballad Rock)
(3114)

Silent Dancer (IRE) *S Donohoe* a46 64
2 b g Danehill Dancer(IRE) —Silent Crystal (USA) (Diesis)
6965[12] 7050[7]

Silent Decision (USA) *J S Bolger* 83
3 ch f Mr Greeley(USA) —Aly Sangue (USA) (Alydar (USA))
7263a[4]

Silent Hero *M A Jarvis* a86 78
3 b g Oasis Dream—Royal Passion (Ahonoora)
1434[5] 1870[7] (2578) 3220[5] 3956[10] 5591[3] 6348[3] 6946[6]

Silent Lucidity (IRE) *P D Niven* a51 40
5 ch g Ashkalani(IRE) —Mimansa (USA) (El Gran Senor (USA))
4972[7] 6457[8] 6845[9] 7733[6]

Silent Majority (IRE) *E A L Dunlop* a42 58
2 b c Refuse To Bend(IRE) —Queen Shy (Marju (IRE))
6990[5] ◆ 7376[7]

Silent Oasis *B J Meehan* 72
3 b f Oasis Dream—Silence Is Golden (Danehill Dancer (IRE))
2139[4] 2679[2] 3100[3] 3574[4] 6621[7]

Silent Secret (IRE) *R Hannon* 77
2 ch f Dubai Destination(USA) —Charita (IRE) (Lycius (USA))
3820[11] 5026[4] 5212[3] 5741[2] (5980) 7033[14]

Silent Sunday (IRE) *H-A Pantall* a95 98
4 b m Testa Rossa(AUS) —Snow Lady (SWI) (Vision (USA))
3520a[7] 6717a[6]

Silent Treatment (IRE) *Miss Gay Kelleway* a58 62
3 ch f Captain Rio—Without Words (Lion Cavern (USA))
2417[12] 3302[4] 3711[8] 4279[13]

Silidan *Miss M E Rowland* a57 55
6 b g Dansili—In Love Again (IRE) (Prince Rupert (FR))
97[12] (666) 874[12] 1074[5] 7349[12]

Silk Affair (IRE) *M G Quinlan* 94
4 b m Barathea(IRE) —Uncertain Affair (IRE) (Darshaan)
6851[18]

Silk And Satin (USA) *H R A Cecil* 55
3 bb f Storm Cat(USA) —Rafina (USA) (Mr Prospector (USA))
4828[7] 5205[4] 5718[9] 6189[3]

Silk Cotton (USA) *E A L Dunlop* a70 64
3 b f Giant's Causeway(USA) —Calico Moon (USA) (Seeking The Gold (USA))
1928[12] 2685[12]

Silken Aunt *J A R Toller* a56
2 b f Barathea(IRE) —Aunt Susan (Distant Relative)
7376[4] 7630[4]

Silken Promise (USA) *W R Swinburn* a66 68
3 bb f Pulpit(USA) —Banksia (Marju (IRE))
1488[4] ◆ 2006[5] 3462[6] 6584[5] 7112[13] 7392[10] 7688[2] 7766[2]

Silken Sands (IRE) *C G Cox* a54 55
3 b f Green Desert(USA) —Arctic Silk (Selkirk (USA))
6741[5] 7826[5]

Silkenveil (IRE) *R A Fahey* a38
2 b f Indian Ridge—Line Ahead (IRE) (Sadler's Wells (USA))
7816[7]

Silk Gallery (USA) *E J Alston* a60 64
4 b m Kingmambo(USA) —Moon Flower (IRE) (Sadler's Wells (USA))
36[2] ◆ 305[2] 454[4] 655[3] 920[5] 1241[10] 4046[5] 4550[2] 5163[2] 5624[4] 5882[8] (7081) 7241[3] 7355[10] 7503[9]

Silk Hall (UAE) *A King* a87 90
4 b g Halling(USA) —Velour (Mtoto)
1878[2] 2283[6]

Silk Mascara (IRE) *David Wachman* 85
3 b f Barathea(IRE) —Subito (Darshaan)
2960a[10]

Silk Runner (IRE) *J W Hills* a35 51
2 ch f Barathea(IRE) —Sao Gabriel (IRE) (Persian Bold)
4542[11] 5984[10]

Silk Slippers *John Joseph Murphy* a61 31
2 b f Oasis Dream—Interpose (Indian Ridge)
5638[4] 6317a[20]

Silk Star (IRE) *Patrick Morris* a36 34
3 b f Pyrus(USA) —Silk Feather (USA) (Silver Hawk (USA))
2415[9] 3228[9] 7500[6]

Silk Street (USA) *R A Fahey* a78 76
2 b c Street Cry(IRE) —High Potential (USA) (Pleasant Colony (USA))
6796[2] ◆ 7050[2]

Silk Trail *Saeed Bin Suroor* a70 72
3 b f Dubai Destination(USA) —Satin Flower (USA) (Shadeed (USA))
2139[3] 2947[3] 3352[2] (3773)

Silky Steps (IRE) *H-A Pantall* a66 81
4 gr m Nayef(USA) —Legal Steps (IRE) (Law Society (USA))
3419a[6]

Silky Way (GR) *P R Chamings* a60 70
3 b f Harmonic Way—Flourishing Way (Sadler's Wells (USA))
(2478) 3229[6] 4223[5] 5877[7]

Sills Vincero *D Shaw* a61 68
3 b f Piccolo—Aegean Magic (Wolfhound (USA))
34[5] 91[5] 246[4] 390[3] (568) 624[2] 784[3] 889[8] 1041[3] 1190[7] 1311[6] 1529[10]

Silly Gilly (IRE) *R E Barr* a40 65
5 b m Mull Of Kintyre(USA) —Richly Deserved (IRE) (Kings Lake (USA))
1332[7] (1889) 2473[3] 3188[3] 3730[2] 4140[7] 4588[3] 4932[7] 5289[4] 5395[3] 5601[3] 6183[10] 7500[11]

Silvador *W R Muir* 70
3 gr g Selkirk(USA) —Dali's Grey (Linamix (FR))
2181[2]

Silvanus (IRE) *P T Midgley* a81 80
4 b g Danehill Dancer(IRE) —Mala Mala (IRE) (Brief Truce (USA))
83[2] 351[3] 901[7] 1227[6] 1518[5] ◆ 1689[4] 2032[7] 2451[6] 2717[3] ◆ (3109) 3295[4] 3479[3] 4036[5] (4976) 5421[11] 5678[4] 6314[5] 6877[12]

Silvee *J J Bridger* a23 52
2 gr f Avonbridge—Silver Louie (IRE) (Titus Livius (FR))
1669[9] 1810[10] 2477[6] 2919[11] 3458[7] 4147[10] 4639[10] 5213[12] 5636[9] 5967[5]

Silver Arrow (ITY) *R Menichetti* 109
4 b h Silver Wizard(USA) —Eros Love (ITY) (Love The Groom (USA))
(7312a)

Silver Blue (IRE) *W K Goldsworthy* a64 74
6 ch g Indian Lodge(IRE) —Silver Echo (Caerleon (USA))
2379[5] 3504[6] 4698[10] 5444[6]

Silver Cat *J Boisnard*
2 b c One Cool Cat(USA) —She Is Zen (FR) (Zieten (USA))
5014a[0]

Silver Deal *J A Pickering* a42 42
4 b m Lujain(USA) —Deal In Facts (So Factual (USA))
328[9]

Silver Frost (IRE) *Y De Nicolay* 119
3 gr c Verglas(IRE) —Hidden Silver (Anabaa (USA))
(1238a) (1917a) 2756a[6] 5086a[6]

Silver Games (IRE) *M R Channon* a81 91
3 gr f Verglas(IRE) —Mise (IRE) (Indian Ridge)
912[11] 1324[14] 1808[4] 2174[3] (2406) 3016[4] 3293[2] 3843[3] 4088[5] 5175[3] 5607[3] 6267[16]

Silverglas (IRE) *M P Tregoning* a70 79
3 gr g Verglas(IRE) —Yellow Trumpet (Petong)
1638[3] 4648[5] 5475[2] (6190) 6740[7]

Silver Grecian *J Ryan* 114
2 gr c Haafhd—Regrette Rien (USA) (Unbridled's Song (USA))
(3167) ◆ (3589) (3817) 5859[3] ◆ 6849[7]

Silver Grey (IRE) *R Ingram* 98
2 gr f Chineur(FR) —Operissimo (Singspiel (IRE))
2348[2] ◆ (3767) 4539[7] 4850[2] 5265[3] 5743[5] 6656a[2]

Silver Guest *M R Channon* a84 73
4 br g Lujain(USA) —Ajig Dancer (Niniski (USA))
2191[8] 3091[29] 3877[16] 5025[7] 5424[13] 5805[4] 6201[9] (6637) (6825) 7000[4] 7575[3] 7627[3]

Silver Hotspur *C R Dore* a88 75
5 b g Royal Applause—Noble View (USA) (Distant View (USA))
79[7] 195[5] 331[5] 490[2] 747[6] 893[6] 3928[10] 4333[16] 4548[9] 4881[7] 5479[5] 5569[7] 6374[11] 6725[9] 7229[8] 7643[10] 7711[6] 7854[10]

Silver In The Sand *J D Bethell* 61
2 b f Fasliyev(USA) —Dances With Dreams (Be My Chief (USA))
2089[6] 2526[3] 4282[4] 4975[9] 5550[7] 6215[15]

Silver Lady (FR) *J-P Carvalho* 80
3 b f Sagamix(FR) —Secret Of Salome (IRE) (Vision (USA))
5783a[3]

Silver Linnet (IRE) *M G Quinlan* a35 68
2 gr f Acclamation—Nadeema (FR) (Linamix (FR))
2089[8] 2568[3] 3058[5] 5553[2] 5797[10] 6409[3] (6555) 7849[6]

Silvermine Bay (IRE) *A P Jarvis* a48 37
2 br f Act One—Quittance (USA) (Riverman (USA))
5668[7] 6009[11] 6441[8]

Silver Mist (SAF) *M F De Kock* 115
7 gr g Western Winter(USA) —Palace Bride (AUS) (Palace Music (USA))
(182a) (339a)

Silver Prelude *S C Williams* a73 68
8 gr g Prince Sabo—Silver Blessings (Statoblest)
170[6] 600[7] 880[5] 1421[5] 1877[8] 2596[2] (3959) 4182[8] (4978) 5480[2] 6118[8] 6635[3] 7224[4] 7554[9] 7682[4]

Silver Print (USA) *W R Swinburn* a76 76
3 rg g Maria's Mon(USA) —Shutterbug (USA) (Deputy Minister (CAN))
3736[5] ◆ 4275[11] 4910[6] 5616[3] 6376[5]

Silver Rime (FR) *Miss L A Perratt* 91
4 gr h Verglas(IRE) —Severina (Darshaan)
4779[12] 5363[7] 6016[3] 6645[13] 7169[6]

Silver Rock (IRE) *M A Magnusson* 84
2 ch f Rock Of Gibraltar(IRE) —Ribblesdale (Northern Park (USA))
(6055) 6852[8]

Silver Salsa *J R Jenkins* a49 50
3 b f Lujain(USA) —Tango Teaser (Shareef Dancer (USA))
246[5] 1271[7] 2431[11] 2810[6] 3459[9]

Silver Sceptre (IRE) *W J Musson* a35 39
3 b g Intikhab(USA) —Silver Pursuit (Rainbow Quest (USA))
5328[4]

Silverside (USA) *M Delcher-Sanchez* 97
3 b c Pleasantly Perfect(USA) —Lyrical Ghost (USA) (Silver Ghost (USA))
2755a[8] 3649a[8]

Silver Silence (JPN) *J S O Arthur* a40 40
8 bb g Sunday Silence(USA) —Island Of Silver (USA) (Forty Niner (USA))
4587a[4]

Silver Socks *Miss L A Perratt* 58
2 br c Captain Rio—Silver Blessings (Statoblest)
5728[5] 6046[5] 6408[9] 6983[13]

Silver Spruce *D Flood* a47 65
4 gr g First Trump—Red Typhoon (Belfort (FR))
100[11] 132[8] 145[5] 247[7]

Silver Surprise *J J Bridger* a57 52
5 gr m Orpen(USA) —Dim Ofan (Petong)
3462[9] 3774[3] 4301[6] 4735[8] 4948[8] 5217[9] 5579[12]

Silver Swallow (USA) *Bruce Headley* a106 79
5 gr m Alphabet Soup(USA) —Topsum (USA) (Red Ransom (USA))
7285a[6]

Silver Symphony (IRE) *P F I Cole* a82 79
2 bb f Pastoral Pursuits—Streak Of Silver (USA) (Dynaformer (USA))
1298[8] 2047[4] 2494[2] (3027) 4858[3] 5797[15]

Silver Timber (USA) *Chad C Brown* 120
6 gr g Prime Timber(USA) —River Princess (CAN) (Alwuhush (USA))
7305a[6]

Silvertown Boy *H A McWilliams* a35
3 gr g Cape Town(IRE) —Optimistic Dreamer (IRE) (Topanoora)
2364[5] 5228[10] 5731[12] 7361[7] 7464[8]

Silver Valny (FR) *Mlle M-L Mortier* 68
3 ch g Vertical Speed(FR) —Mendoreva (FR) (Mendocino (USA))
6682a[6]

Silver Waters *Tim Vaughan* a68 65
4 gr g Fantastic Light(USA) —Silent Waters (Polish Precedent (USA))
2983[11] 3308[5]

Silver Wind *P D Evans* a83 89
4 b g Ishiguru(USA) —My Bonus (Cyrano De Bergerac)
106[4] (133) 291[5] 2297[6] 2938[2] 3377[7] 3877[5] 4333[8] 4500[2] (4761) 5257[9] 5404[4] 5695[5] (5799) 6050[20] 6282[10] 6994[14]

Silvester *R M H Cowell* a40 21
3 gr g Silver Patriarch(IRE) —Raintree Venture (Good Times (ITY))
5751[11] 6608[8] 6794[10] 7318[7] 7694[7]

Simenon (IRE) *A M Balding* 99
2 b c Marju(IRE) —Epistoliere (IRE) (Alzao (USA))
3395[3] (4314) 5261[5] (6011) 6664[3]

Simla Sunset (IRE) *J R Gask* a72 72
3 b f One Cool Cat(USA) —Simla Bibi (Indian Ridge)
6111[14] 7321[2] (7459) 7830[7]

Simola *R A Fahey* 42
3 ch f Bold Edge—Amused (Prince Sabo)
3003[6] 4276[5]

Simonas (IRE) *A Wohler* 99
10 gr g Sternkoenig(IRE) —Sistadari (Shardari)
1143a[6] 1555a[9]

Simon De Montfort (IRE) *A Fabre* 88
2 b c King's Best(USA) —Noble Rose (IRE) (Caerleon (USA))
(6578a) 7404a[8]

Simon Gray *R Hannon* a89 87
3 b c Act One—Shardette (IRE) (Darshaan)
(1509) (2038) (3026)

Simonside *B Ellison* a75 78
6 b g Shahrastani(USA) —Only So Far (Teenoso (USA))
570[12] (779) 983[4] 1175[3] 1863[10] 2315[9] 3068[3] 3313[3] (4345) 5185[6] 5696[3] 6053[3] 6767[4]

Simple Jim (FR) *J Hetherton* a66 59
5 b g Jimble(FR) —Stop The Wedding (USA) (Stop The Music (USA))
3291[7] 3486[5] 4403[4] 4848[6] (5600) (6097) 6559[4] (6845) 7080[4]

Simple Rhythm *J Ryan* a68 87
3 b f Piccolo—Easy Beat (IRE) (Orpen (USA))
293[3] 673[8] 1129[2] 1247[9] 1949[2] 2162[4] (2581) 3063[4] 3506[4] 4596[3] 5254[2] 5724[4] (5968) 5989[10] (6341) (6596) 6791[4] 6877[7]

Simple Solution (USA) *B W Hills* a81 83
3 b f Dynaformer(USA) —Super Staff (USA) (Secretariat (USA))
1789[5] 2275[10] 3280[5] 6165[5]

Simplification *R Hannon* a78 78
3 gr f Daylami(IRE) —Bella Cantata (Singspiel (IRE))
890[2] 1284[3] 3333[3] 3627[6] 3751[5]

Simplified *M C Chapman* a47 43
6 b m Lend A Hand—Houston Heiress (USA) (Houston (USA))
129[6]

Simply Sensational (IRE) *Patrick Morris* 16
3 ch g Tendulkar(USA) —Grange Clare (IRE) (Bijou D'Inde)
2543[7] 3936[6]

Simpsons Gamble (IRE) *R A Teal* a66 61
6 b g Tagula(IRE) —Kiva (Indian Ridge)
44[4] 166[3] 294[10] 1076[3] 1587[7] 1959[4] 2400[8] 2924[4] 3732[10] 3980[10] (5367) 5963[4] 7109[12]

Simulate *Sir Michael Stoute* 41
3 b c Dansili—Orford Ness (Selkirk (USA))
6794[9]

Sina (GER) *S Smrczek* 82
4 b m Trans Island—Soiree De Vienne (IRE) (Marju (IRE))
7821a[4]

Sinbad The Sailor *J W Hills* a58 75
4 b g Cape Cross(IRE) —Sinead (USA) (Irish River (FR))
1660[6] 2039[9] 2493[7] (2739) 3247[5] 3521[4] 4325[4] 4951[6] 5740[3] 6208[4] 6226[3] 6969[2]

Sinchiroka (FR) *R J Smith* a30 58
3 b c Della Francesca(USA) —Great Care (USA) (El Gran Senor (USA))
7694[8]

Sindjil Mountain *Mlle C Nicot* a77 46
6 b g Monashee Mountain(USA) —Sylflore (FR) (Marignan (USA))
7265a[7]

Singapore Fun (FR) *C Laffon-Parias* 60
2 b c Green Tune(USA) —Brilliante (Sillery (USA))
6928a[6]

Singapore Gift (FR) *Unknown* 19
2 u u (USA) — (USA) (Fasliyev (USA))
4686a[9]

Singapore Girl *G R Oldroyd* a48 24
3 b f Danehill Dancer(IRE) —Musical Refrain (IRE) (Dancing Dissident (USA))
36[4] 251[5] 381[7] 2157[9] 2726[6] 3334[6] 3611[7] 4174[10] 7709[12]

Singbella *C G Cox* 63
3 b f Singspiel(IRE) —B Beautiful (IRE) (Be My Guest (USA))
1406[9] 2165[10] 2947[10]

Singeur (IRE) *R Bastiman* a72 101
2 b c Chineur(FR) —Singitta (Singspiel (IRE))
2128[2] (2575) (3540) (4327) (4752) 5174[4] 6486[11] 6677[4] 7016[2]

Singinginthe rain (IRE) *T G Mills* a63
2 ch f Kyllachy—Comeraincomeshine (IRE) (Night Shift (USA))
7585[7] 7772[4]

Singing Machine (USA) *M Delzangles* 90
3 b f Rossini(USA) —Circuit City (IRE) (Exit To Nowhere (USA))
7697a[0]

Singing Poet (IRE) *E Charpy* a94 78
8 b g Singspiel(IRE) —Bright Finish (USA) (Zilzal (USA))
337a[8] 523a[5] 698a[10]

Singing Scott (IRE) *R Bastiman* 34
2 b g Royal Applause—Ciel Bleu (Septieme Ciel (USA))
6896[7] 7288[15]

Singin' The Blues *J M P Eustace* a54 63
2 b g Superior Premium—Not So Generous (IRE) (Fayruz)
6493[11] 6797[5] 7288[8]

Singleb (IRE) *Miss Gay Kelleway* a79 75
5 b g Intikhab(USA) —Bubble N Squeak (IRE) (Catrail (USA))
(129) (215) (573) 708[4] 806[6] 2775[6] 3211[10] 3568[3] 3980[13]

Sing Of Run *J F Panvert*
2 bl c Singspiel(IRE) —Crimson Rosella (Polar Falcon (USA))
5499[16]

Singora Lady (IRE) *P T Midgley* a53 64
4 ch m Intikhab(USA) —Unicamp (Royal Academy (USA))
307[8] 565[5] 823[4] 969[11] 2245[4] 2441[2] 2626[3] ◆ (3188) 3451[3] (4431) 4721[3] ◆ 5035[11]

Sing Sweetly *G A Butler* a77 62
2 b f Singspiel(IRE) —Sweetness Herself (Unfuwain (USA))
6163[2] 6477[11]

Sioduil (IRE) *J S Bolger* a91 98
3 gr f Oasis Dream—Indian Belle (IRE) (Indian Ridge)
1375a[2] 7341a[5]

Sion Hill (IRE) *John A Harris* a61 70
8 b g Desert Prince(IRE) —Mobilia (Last Tycoon)
37[6] 216[2] 554[8] 1846[9] 2473[10] 3112[3] 3269[2] 3490[2] 3863[2] 4389[3] 4667[6] 5479[9] 6175[6] 6999[5] 7755[11]

Sioux City Sue *J R Boyle* 12
3 b f Noverre(USA) —Sartigila (Efisio)
5322[9]

Sioux Rising (IRE) *R A Fahey* 84
3 b f Danetime(IRE) —Arvika (FR) (Baillamont (USA))
(2250) (3453) 3839[6] 5032[11]

Siraj *J Ryan* a58 59
10 b g Piccolo—Masuri Kabisa (USA) (Ascot Knight (CAN))
496[10] 646[10] 854[8]

Sir Billy Nick *S Wynne* a67 70
4 b h Bertolini(USA) —Follow Flanders (Pursuit Of Love)
63[9] 6342[9] 6999[9]

Sir Boss (IRE) *D E Cantillon* a75 86
4 b g Tagula(IRE) —Good Thought (IRE) (Mukaddamah (USA))
2244[3] 2493[6] 3450[2] (3798) (4169) 4544[6] 5034[9] 5667[8] 6059[10] 6473[6]

Sir Bruno (FR) *B Palling* 73
2 ch g Hernando(FR) —Moon Tree (FR) (Groom Dancer (USA))
3052[8] 3785[2] 5119[3] 5499[4] 6366[3]

Sir Christie *N Tinkler* 60
2 b g Auction House(USA) —Dazzling Quintet (Superlative)
1847[9] 2258[6] 2788[11] 3058[4] 3446[6] (Dead)

Sircozy (IRE) *S C Williams* a72 50
3 b g Celtic Swing—Furnish (Green Desert (USA))
1617[8] 3693[8] 4545[10] 5775[2] ◆ 6371[2] 7049[7] (7374) (7665) ◆ (7777) ◆ 7831[2]

Sir Dave (USA) *Jack Carava* a91 109
4 ch g Untuttable(USA) —Queen Kaboom (USA) (Sword Dance (USA))
7281a[P]

Sir Des Brousses (FR) *F Chappet* a67 75
2 b c Equerry(USA) —Baby Risks (FR) (Take Risks (FR))
3935a[2] 6960a[9]

Sir Don (IRE) *E S McMahon* a45 25
10 b g Lake Coniston(IRE) —New Sensitive (Wattlefield)
99[7] 2801[11] 5610[9]
Sir Ector (USA) *J E Pease* 85
2 b c Dynaformer(USA) —Beyond The Waves (USA) (Ocean Crest (USA))
6131a[4]
Sir Edwin Landseer (USA) *G L Moore* a93 83
9 gr g Lit De Justice(USA) —Wildcat Blue (USA) (Cure The Blues (USA))
3212[2] 5031[16] 5646[12] 6972[5] 7689[3] 7879[5]
Sirena (IRE) *H-A Pantall*
2 b f One Cool Cat(USA) —Sylflore (FR) (Marignan (USA))
7409a[6]
Siren's Gift *A M Balding* a100 102
5 ch m Cadeaux Genereux—Blue Siren (Bluebird (USA))
1582[3] 2502[8] 2704[6] 3145[4] 4456[15] (5507) 5765[9] 6427[9]
Sirenuse (IRE) *B Smart* a62 85
3 b f Exceed And Excel(AUS) —Cefira (USA) (Distant View (USA))
4849[2] 5149[2] 6253[10]
Sir Frank Wappat *M Johnston* 62
2 b c Oasis Dream—Trevillari (USA) (Riverman (USA))
6032[4] 6386[5]
Sir Freddie *Lady Herries* a57 72
3 b g Fraam—Height Of Folly (Shirley Heights)
1579[4] ◆ 2126[14] 4442[4]
Sirgarfieldsobers (IRE) *A P O'Brien* a83 95
3 b c Montjeu(IRE) —Funsie (FR) (Saumarez)
2306a[7]
Sir Geoffrey (IRE) *J A Glover* a83 79
3 b g Captain Rio—Disarm (IRE) (Bahamian Bounty)
109[6] 203[7] 396[5] 1078[7] 1368[3] 2058[6] 2373[3] 2826[8] 5856[10] 6253[8] 6765[15]
Sir George (IRE) *P D Evans* a69 51
4 b g Mujadil(USA) —Torrmana (IRE) (Ela-Mana-Mou)
6755[6] 7412[5] (7596) 7729[4] 7861[2]
Sir Gerry (USA) *J R Best* a97 116
4 ch h Carson City(USA) —Incredulous (FR) (Indian Ridge)
1989[12] 7292[10] 7488[7] 7768[7]
Sir Haydn *J R Jenkins* a59 49
9 ch g Definite Article—Snowscape (Niniski (USA))
59[8] 385[3] 541[3] 647[3] 816[2] 1200[6] (1651) 2420[10] 2830[8] 5377[5] 5577[10] 7250[4] ◆ 7354[5] 7658[11] 7766[4]
Sir Ike (IRE) *W S Kittow* a67 71
4 b g Xaar—Iktidar (Green Desert (USA))
266[6] 344[2] 512[5] 706[3] (3800) 4321[4] (5283) 5676[11] 6755[13]
Sir Isaac *W J Haggas* 87
3 b g Key Of Luck(USA) —Rainbow Queen (FR) (Spectrum (IRE))
(1671) 2638[4] 2890[2] 3062[2] 4540[3] (4909)
Sir Jake *T T Clement* a53 34
5 b h Killer Instinct—Waikiki Dancer (IRE) (General Monash (USA))
4670[6] 5642[11] 7336[14]
Sir Joey *B D Leavy* a51 51
4 ch g Forzando—Estabella (IRE) (Mujtahid (USA))
169[13] 302[12]
Sirjosh *D Donovan* a55 60
3 b g Josr Algarhoud(IRE) —Special Gesture (IRE) (Brief Truce (USA))
1941[5] 2488[7] 3192[P] 3718[6] 4202[11] 4425[3] 5316[5] 5479[8] 5549[9]
Sir Kyffin's Folly *J A Geake* a37 71
4 b m Dansili—Persia (IRE) (Persian Bold)
5503[12] 7505[7] 7840[12]
Sir Liam (USA) *Tom Dascombe* a70 69
5 b g Monarchos(USA) —Tears (USA) (Red Ransom (USA))
18[11] 248[3] (346) 668[2] 751[3] 871[5]
Sir Loin *P Burgoyne* a43 2
8 ch g Compton Place—Charnwood Queen (Cadeaux Genereux)
467[9] 727[8] 896[5] 5323[16] 6119[6] 7460[5]
Sir Louis *R A Fahey* 62
2 b g Compton Place—Heuston Station (IRE) (Fairy King (USA))
4067[5] 5256[11] 6646[8]
Sir Nod *Miss J A Camacho* a80 80
7 b g Tagula(IRE) —Nordan Raider (Domynsky)
(351) ◆ 1313[6] 2071[15] 2418[7] (3268) 3483[4] 4141[4] 4662[6] 5421[4] 5768[7]
Sirocco Breeze *Saeed Bin Suroor* a111 94
4 b h Green Desert(USA) —Baldemosa (FR) (Lead On Time (USA))
(7133) ◆
Sir Orpen (IRE) *J F Panvert* a36 50
6 gr g Orpen(USA) —Yalciyna (Nishapour (FR))
5869[7] 6568[6] 7197[8]
Sir Parky (IRE) *R Hannon* 104
2 b c Choisir(AUS) —Jorghinia (FR) (Seattle Slew (USA))
1867[8] (2201) (2875) 3821[3] (4086) 5198[8] 5743[6] (6426)
Sir Pitt *J H M Gosden* 75
2 b c Tiger Hill(IRE) —Rebecca Sharp (Machiavellian (USA))
6763[5] ◆ 7029[8]
Sirri *C E Brittain* a40 40
2 b f Ishiguru(USA) —Sumitra (Tragic Role (USA))
2383[10] 5005[12]
Sir Royal (USA) *G A Swinbank* 80
4 b g Diesis—Only Royale (IRE) (Caerleon (USA))
1473[5] 1886[6] 2391[2] 2791[2] 3265[7]
Sir Sandicliffe (IRE) *W M Brisbourne* a70 69
5 b g Distant Music(USA) —Desert Rose (Green Desert (USA))
1892[2] 2194[3] 2944[6] 3073[7] 3444[3] 3850[5] 4551[7] 4862[2] 5339[4] 5625[4] 6097[3] 6432[8] 6859[9] 7154[7] 7751[7]
Sir Slick (NZ) *Graeme Nicholson* 116
8 b g Volksraad—Miss Opera (NZ) (Paris Opera (AUS))
7196a[11]
Sir Tom *J J Bridger* a44
4 b g Medicean—Shasta (Shareef Dancer (USA))
7610[7] 7826[13]
Sirvino *T D Barron* 105
4 b g Vettori(IRE) —Zenita (IRE) (Zieten (USA))
(1279) (1646) (2103) (2392) (3873) ◆ 6480[26]
Sir Walter Raleigh *Sir Michael Stoute* 53
2 b g Galileo(IRE) —Elizabethan Age (FR) (King's Best (USA))
7244[7]
Sir William Orpen *P M Phelan* a63 66
2 b g Orpen(USA) —Ashover Amber (Green Desert (USA))
5571[8] 5801[3] 6372[6]
Sir Xaar (IRE) *B Smart* a58 94
6 bb g Xaar—Cradle Brief (IRE) (Brief Truce (USA))
1124[4] 1649[12] 2045[8] 3312[12] 5697[15]
Siryena *B I Case* a57 55
4 b m Oasis Dream—Ard Na Sighe (IRE) (Kenmare (FR))
192[6] 494[9] 577[6] 1538[9]
Sister Clement (IRE) *R Hannon* a85 75
3 b f Oasis Dream—Miss Party Line (USA) (Phone Trick (USA))
2417[10] 3580[2] (4051) 4380[2] 4604[5] 5007[9] 6915[2] (7203)
Sister Earth (IRE) *J H M Gosden* a49
2 ch f Galileo(IRE) —Time Ahead (Spectrum (IRE))
7140[3]
Sister Moonshine *W R Muir* a46 61
4 b m Averti(IRE) —Cal Norma's Lady (IRE) (Lyphard's Special (USA))
1465[3] 1890[14]
Sisters Warning *J Ryan* a23 31
2 b f Bishop Of Cashel—Slite (Mind Games)
2741[7] 3356[8] 7106[10] 7463[7] 7683[7]
Sitwell *J R Fanshawe* a64 67
3 b g Dr Fong(USA) —First Fantasy (Be My Chief (USA))
2178[7] 2551[7] 4054[6] 4721[7] (5152) 5545[6] 6457[5] (6758)
Sivola Gambler (FR) *T Trapenard*
2 b c Discover D'Auteuil(FR) —Neva De Sivola (FR) (Blushing Flame (USA))
7384a[8]
Sixbox *D Shaw*
2 br f Kyllachy—Lady's Walk (IRE) (Charnwood Forest (IRE))
2401[8] 4856[11] 5611[11]
Six Diamonds *H Morrison* a81 75
2 b f Exceed And Excel(AUS) —Daltak (Night Shift (USA))
1569[14] 2649[2] (2906) 4539[11] 5033[2] (5194) 5650[3] 5945[4]
Six O'Clock News (NZ) *P & T Busuttin* 101
5 b g Zabeel(NZ) —Maurine (NZ) (Harbor Prince (USA))
6961a[9]
Six Of Clubs *W G M Turner* a33
3 ch g Bertolini(USA) —Windmill Princess (Gorytus (USA))
5987[8]
Six Of Hearts *Cecil Ross* a93 98
5 b g Pivotal—Additive (USA) (Devil's Bag (USA))
3091[15] 4412a[18] 6089[18] 6707a[6] 6867a[3] 7341a[6]
Sixpenny Moon (USA) *R Hannon* a60 60
2 b f Johannesburg(USA) —Shirazi (USA) (Stephen Got Even (USA))
1569[9] 2047[8] 3249[9] 3978[3] 5213[6] 5573[11] 6391[11] 6586[5] 6721[9]
Sixth Zak *M W Easterby* a53
4 br g Fantastic Light(USA) —Zakuska (Zafonic (USA))
425[5] 898[10] 1154[9] 1938[5] 3068[14]
Sixties Gift (UAE) *Rae Guest* a56 37
3 bb f Singspiel(IRE) —Sicily (USA) (Kris S (USA))
2142[11] 3117[12] 6788[5]
Sixties Rock *J A Glover* a53 51
2 ch g Rock Of Gibraltar(IRE) —Scene (IRE) (Scenic)
6046[8] 6381[2] 6754[15] 7619[7] 7791[6]
Sixties Swinger (USA) *M A Jarvis* a71 74
3 b g Refuse To Bend(IRE) —Kardashina (FR) (Darshaan)
1431[7] 2038[10] 2738[2] 3674[5] 4904[8] 5482[2] 6395[2] 6940[9]
Six Wives *J A Glover* a78 68
2 b f Kingsalsa(USA) —Regina (Green Desert (USA))
1298[6] ◆ 1742[3] (1934) 2372[11] 2599[3] 3742[3] 3871[6] 4327[10] (4868) 5194[2] 5467[6] 5650[5] 6774[3] 6827[2] 7274[3] 7536[7] 7636[3] 7793[2] 7871[8]
Siyaadah *Saeed Bin Suroor* 82
2 b f Shamardal(USA) —River Belle (Lahib (USA))
(4817) 5427[8] 6477[6]
Siyouni (FR) *A De Royer-Dupre* 119
2 b c Pivotal—Sichilla (IRE) (Danehill (USA))
4366a[2] 5708a[2] (6524a)
Skhilling Spirit *T D Barron* 103
6 b g Most Welcome—Calcavella (Pursuit Of Love)
2059[6]
Skimi (FR) *Y Fertillet* 57
2 b c Ski Chief(USA) —Kimi Nouche (FR) (Bahamian Bounty)
5014a[8]
Skins Game *J-C Rouget* 97
3 b c Diktat—Mouriyana (IRE) (Akarad (FR))
6657a[2]
Skybob *D W Thompson* 14
3 b g Tobougg(IRE) —Heavens Above (FR) (Pistolet Bleu (IRE))
3975[9] 4354[13] 4974[7] 5554[13] 6098[P]
Sky Crusader *M Nigge* a105 91
7 b g Mujahid(USA) —Red Cloud (IRE) (Taufan (USA))
5662[4] (7704a) 7809[6]
Skyflight *Eve Johnson Houghton* a63 68
2 ch f Observatory(USA) —Flight Soundly (IRE) (Caerleon (USA))
4900[9] 5580[8] (6386)
Sky Gate (USA) *B J Meehan* a79 63
3 b c Arch(USA) —Mista Mayberry (USA) (Touch Gold (USA))
2767[6] 3051[18]
Sky High Kid (IRE) *M R Channon* a64 57
3 b g One Cool Cat(USA) —Market Hill (IRE) (Danehill (USA))
3868[10] 4223[9] 4479[10] 5155[2] 5468[8] 5716[11] 5809[11] 6442[12]
Skylarker (USA) *T A K Cuthbert* 19
11 b g Sky Classic(CAN) —O My Darling (USA) (Mr Prospector (USA))
2442[8] 6769[12]
Skylla *J R Holt* 93
2 b f Kyllachy—Day Star (Dayjur (USA))
(3633) 4000[2] (4782) 5521[2] 6049[6] 7147[11]
Sky Quest (IRE) *J R Boyle* a69 71
11 b g Spectrum(IRE) —Rose Vibert (Caerleon (USA))
(21) 1318[13] 1604[8] 2601[7] (4053) 4269[4] 5185[5] (5444) 5740[4] 6244[5]
Skyrider (IRE) *R Charlton* 75
2 gr f Dalakhani(IRE) —Future Flight (Polar Falcon (USA))
6591[2]
Skysurfers *Saeed Bin Suroor* a92
3 b c E Dubai(USA) —Fortune (IRE) (Night Shift (USA))
(6880)
Skyteam (FR) *Mme C Head-Maarek* a88 100
5 b g Anabaa(USA) —Spenderella (FR) (Common Grounds)
3202a[4] 4637a[10]
Skywards *E Charpy* a100 92
7 b g Machiavellian(USA) —Nawaiet (USA) (Zilzal (USA))
414a[7] 639a[7]
Slam *B W Hills* a100 91
4 b g Beat Hollow—House Hunting (Zafonic (USA))
1306[2] 1986[12]
Slam Warrior (USA) *J-C Rouget* a46
3 b c Grand Slam(USA) —Wilderness Area (USA) (Deputy Minister (CAN))
5118a[4]
Slant (IRE) *Eve Johnson Houghton* a52 78
3 bb f Spinning World(USA) —Sweet Honesty (IRE) (Charnwood Forest (IRE))
1185[7] 2001[P]
Slap Shade (IRE) *P Bary* a80 96
3 b f Invincible Spirit(IRE) —Hiragana (Arazi (USA))
2777a[6]
Slasl *C E Brittain* a54 32
2 b f Dubawi(IRE) —Mazuna (IRE) (Cape Cross (IRE))
3271[8] 3987[9] 5637[4] 6590[10]
Sleepy Blue Ocean *J Balding* a18 68
3 b c Oasis Dream—Esteemed Lady (IRE) (Mark Of Esteem (IRE))
1255[8] (2820) 6140[9] 6824[15] 7418[10]
Sleepy Dove *M E Sowersby* a1 13
4 b m Muhtarram(USA) —Robins Meg (Skyliner)
5072[5] 7361[12]
Sleepy Hollow *H Morrison* a69 93
4 b g Beat Hollow—Crackling (Electric)
5509[2] 5781[7] 6734[3]
Sleepy Mountain *A Middleton* a61 63
5 ch g Beat Hollow—La Sorrela (IRE) (Cadeaux Genereux)
7425[10] 7549[15]
Sleepy Silver *J Mackie*
4 gr m Silver Patriarch(IRE) —Hustle An Bustle (USA) (Lomond (USA))
2447[10]
Sleepy Valley (IRE) *A Dickman* 57
3 b f Clodovil(IRE) —Kilkee Bay (IRE) (Case Law)
1174[10] 1662[7] 2268[2] 3355[7] 5626[8] 6308[7] 6823[7]
Slew Charm (FR) *Noel T Chance* a62
7 b g Marathon(USA) —Slew Bay (FR) (Beaudelaire (USA))
107[2] 493[4]
Sley (FR) *B J Meehan* a54 65
3 ch f Lomitas—Samara (IRE) (Polish Patriot (USA))
1937[11] 2515[7] 3387[9]
Slice (IRE) *Eve Johnson Houghton* a56 75
2 b c Daggers Drawn(USA) —Windomen (IRE) (Forest Wind (USA))
1577[5] (3500) 4525[12] 5274a[12] 5769[7] 6211[10]
Slickdalay (IRE) *Mrs A Malzard*
5 gr m Slickly(FR) —Mandalay (USA) (Sovereign Dancer (USA))
4587a[6]
Slicker (IRE) *David P Myerscough* a39 49
3 b g Marju(IRE) —Farthingale (IRE) (Nashwan (USA))
6445[7]
Slickly Royal (FR) *P Demercastel* a93 95
5 bl h Slickly(FR) —Royal Bride (FR) (Garde Royale)
3419a[2] 7621a[13]
Slick Mover (IRE) *B G Powell* a57 33
4 gr m Slickly(FR) —Agnessa (FR) (Niniski (USA))
6166[6] 6417[4] 6741[10] 7112[5]
Slieve Mish (IRE) *J S Bolger* a72 97
3 b f Cape Cross(IRE) —Aspiration (IRE) (Sadler's Wells (USA))
5490a[11]
Sligo *A J McCabe* a75 59
4 b h Sadler's Wells(USA) —Arabesque (Zafonic (USA))
7221[9] 7293[19]
Slip *Tim Vaughan* a89 90
4 b g Fraam—Niggle (Night Shift (USA))
(29) ◆ 244[5] (3740) 4450[4] 7628[5]
Slip Silver *R C Guest* a20 41
5 gr m Slip Anchor—New Wind (GER) (Windwurf (GER))
1242[14] 1478[9] 1533[11]
Slip Sliding Away (IRE) *J R Best* a66
2 b c Whipper(USA) —Sandy Lady (IRE) (Desert King (IRE))
7251[3] ◆ 7325[13] 7485[4] 7619[3] 7625[4] 7846[4]
Slip Star *T J Etherington* a18 56
6 b m Slip Anchor—Shiny Kay (Star Appeal)
1244[11] 1887[6] 2473[7] 3019[5] 3381[11] 4281[10] 4977[7] 5948[6] 6218[13]
Sloop Johnb *R A Fahey* 89
3 b g Bahamian Bounty—Soundwave (Prince Sabo)
1232[2] (1720) (2058) 2934[19] 3747[13] 3973[4] 4490[9]
Slugger O'Toole *S C Williams* a89 100
4 br g Intikhab(USA) —Haddeyah (USA) (Dayjur (USA))
995[18] 1352[21] 1861[17] 3091[23] 7287[15]
Slumdog (IRE) *Garry Moss*
4 b h Alzao(USA) —Chardania (IRE) (Rainbows For Life (CAN))
4354[14] 4812[11]
Smalkie (FR) *G Cherel*
2 b f Smadoun(FR) —Selkie (Danehill (USA))
5014a[6]
Smalljohn *B Smart* a73 76
3 ch g Needwood Blade—My Bonus (Cyrano De Bergerac)
64[3] 2998[13] 4504[7] 5601[13] 6455[11] 7596[4] 7691[2]
Smart Coco (USA) *T Stack* 97
3 b f Smarty Jones(USA) —Djebel Amour (USA) (Mt. Livermore (USA))
1024a[3] 1911a[7] 5141a[9]
Smart Diplomacy (USA) *A De Royer-Dupre* 85
3 b c Hennessy(USA) —Peacock Alley (USA) (Fast Play (USA))
(6606a)
Smart Endeavour (USA) *W R Swinburn* a88 83
3 ch g Smart Strike(CAN) —Luminance (USA) (Deputy Minister (CAN))
(1490) 2504[6] 3220[4] 4715[7]
Smarten Die (IRE) *Frau E Mader* a101 89
6 ch h Diesis—Highest Dream (IRE) (Highest Honor (FR))
633[6]
Smart Enough *F Reuterskiold* a107 96
6 gr g Cadeaux Genereux—Good Enough (FR) (Mukaddamah (USA))
2587a[5] 3416a[12] 5302a[3]
Smarterthanuthink (USA) *R A Fahey* a73 71
4 b g Smart Strike(CAN) —Dance Gaily (USA) (Nureyev (USA))
2505[9] 3235[6]
Smarties Party *C W Thornton* a55 53
6 b m Tamure(IRE) —Maries Party (The Parson)
2403[4] 7221[6] 7557[3]
Smart John *S T Lewis* 13
9 b g Bin Ajwaad(IRE) —Katy-Q (IRE) (Taufan (USA))
5530[11]
Smart Pick *Mrs L Williamson* a48 47
6 ch m Piccolo—Nevita (Never So Bold)
4465[10] 6183[15]
Smart Seattle (USA) *H Graham Motion* a100 98
2 b f Smart Strike(CAN) —Seattle Bay (USA) (Opening Verse (USA))
7282a[9]
Smart Tazz *S T Lewis* a36 26
4 b g Mujahid(USA) —Katy-Q (IRE) (Taufan (USA))
1771[10] 2221[11] 2684[11] 5102[4] 5614[12]
Smarty Socks (IRE) *P T Midgley* a80 90
5 ch g Elnadim(USA) —Unicamp (Royal Academy (USA))
(404) 922[4] 1016[17] (1343) 2086[6] 2939[5] 3172[9] (3825) 4310[4] 4592[3] 5375[11]
Smayal (USA) *C E Brittain* 34
2 b f Kingmambo(USA) —Cloud Castle (In The Wings)
6484[6]
Smelly Cat *D W Thompson* 47
3 b f One Cool Cat(USA) —Grecian Halo (USA) (Southern Halo (USA))
1062[5] 1644[5] 2624[6] 3614[9] 3852[10]
Smetana *E J Creighton* a57 56
4 b g Kylian(USA) —Shimmer (Bustino)
161[6] 744[6] 2580[11]
Smicker Smacker *George Baker* a56 56
2 gr f Verglas(IRE) —Vallee Blanche (IRE) (Zafonic (USA))
2187[7] 2765[7] 3507[6] 5498[15]
Smile Jack (JPN) *S Kobiyama* 119
4 b h Tanino Gimlet(JPN) —She C'Est Moi (JPN) (Sunday Silence (USA))
7498a[6]
Smirfys Copper (IRE) *D Nicholls*
2 ch f Choisir(AUS) —Fer De Lance (IRE) (Diesis)
4187[8]
Smirfy's Silver *E S McMahon* a31 71
5 b g Desert Prince(IRE) —Goodwood Blizzard (Inchinor)
5438[15]
Smirfys Systems *E S McMahon* a71 53
10 b g Safawan—Saint Systems (Uncle Pokey)
294[2] (540) ◆ 757[5] 961[5] 1103[4] 7860[7]
Smitain *Mrs S Lamyman* 32
3 b g Lujain(USA) —Mitsuki (Puissance)
1683[12] 3238[6]
Smog (IRE) *B J Meehan* a25 41
2 gr c Verglas(IRE) —Dollysister (FR) (Alydar (USA))
3571[7] 4265[4] 4705[8] 5613[8]
Smokey Oakey (IRE) *M H Tompkins* a76 113
5 b g Tendulkar(USA) —Veronica (Persian Bold)
2410[12] 3639[8] 4090[5] 4329[7] 5426[6] 5655[7] 6480[32] 7245[5]
Smokey Ryder *R A Harris* a96 91
3 ch f Bertolini(USA) —Another Secret (Efisio)
(109) 203[4] (685) (709) 912[3] 1002[10] 1293[11] 1705[6] 1879[4] 3033[8] 4771[10] 7862[10]

Smokey Rye *George Baker* a83 78
4 b m Bertolini(USA) —Another Secret (Efisio)
26^{4} (706) 830^{7} (945) 958^{3} (1037) 1210^{7} 1256^{3}

Smokin Beau *N P Littmoden* a72 46
12 b g Cigar—Beau Dada (IRE) (Pine Circle (USA))
956^{8}

Smokin Joe *J R Best* a82 6
8 b g Cigar—Beau Dada (IRE) (Pine Circle (USA))
708^{10} 1589^{13}

Smoky Cloud (IRE) *W McCreery* a75 71
2 ch c Refuse To Bend(IRE) —Pirie (USA) (Green Dancer (USA))
7258a^{4}

Smooth As Silk (IRE) *C R Egerton* a70 70
4 b m Danehill Dancer(IRE) —Doula (USA) (Gone West (USA))
2601^{3} 3247^{8} 3927^{4} 4373^{8} 5227^{4} 6126^{4} 6584^{3} 7440^{10}

Smoothly Does It *Jim Best* a43 58
8 b g Efisio—Exotic Forest (Dominion)
1463^{13}

Smooth Operator (GER) *Mario Hofer* 112
3 b g Big Shuffle(USA) —Salzgitter (Salse (USA))
2097a^{4} (3231a) 5493a^{2} 6503a^{7} 7044a^{4}

Smooth Sovereign (IRE) *M Johnston* a60 67
4 ch g King's Best(USA) —Mellow Park (IRE) (In The Wings)
570^{5} 786^{8} 979^{7} 1125^{2}

Smugglers Bay (IRE) *T D Easterby* 77
5 b g Celtic Swing—Princess Mood (GER) (Muhtarram (USA))
1721^{5} 2044^{7} 2315^{8}

Snaafy (USA) *M Al Muhairi* a117 92
5 b h Kingmambo(USA) —Nafisah (IRE) (Lahib (USA))
(414a) (639a) ◆ (771a) 1013a^{7}

Snaefell (IRE) *M Halford* 115
5 gr g Danehill Dancer(IRE) —Sovereign Grace (IRE) (Standaan (FR))
1374a^{6} 2287a^{5} 3434a^{2} 3881a^{7} 5079a^{6} 5491a^{4} (5921a) 6707a^{8}

Snake Skin *J Gallagher* a44 66
6 ch m Golden Snake(USA) —Silken Dalliance (Rambo Dancer (CAN))
494^{10} 623^{9}

Sneak Preview *E S McMahon* 98
3 ch f Monsieur Bond(IRE) —Harryana (Efisio)
1085^{2}

Sneem's Rock *P R Hedger* a10
8 b g Daylami(IRE) —Urchin (IRE) (Fairy King (USA))
5015^{11}

Snoozing *Mrs L C Jewell* a18
3 b f Where Or When(IRE) —Tenpence (Bob Back (USA))
92^{5} 231^{7} 363^{10} 1046^{8}

Snoqualmie Boy *T P Tate* a97 99
6 b g Montjeu(IRE) —Seattle Ribbon (USA) (Seattle Dancer (USA))
1850^{4} 2342^{10} 3840^{6} 4274^{2} 5235^{10} 5865^{4} 6681^{2} 6878^{9} 7018^{12}

Snoqualmie Girl (IRE) *D R C Elsworth* a68 103
3 b f Montjeu(IRE) —Seattle Ribbon (USA) (Seattle Dancer (USA))
1292^{6} 1701^{8} 2846^{5} 5202^{4} (5854) 6242^{6} 6853^{7} 7131^{12}

Snoqualmie Star *D R C Elsworth* 67
2 ch f Galileo(IRE) —Seattle Ribbon (USA) (Seattle Dancer (USA))
4756^{5} 5398^{5} 7099^{8}

Snow Bay *B Smart* a87 82
3 ch c Bahamian Bounty—Goodwood Blizzard (Inchinor)
2544^{4} (3727) 4316^{8} 5340^{6} 6348^{5} 7181^{3} 7516^{8} (7759) 7837^{8}

Snowberry Hill (USA) *Lucinda Featherstone* a64 63
6 b g Woodman(USA) —Class Skipper (USA) (Skip Trial (USA))
112^{2} 301^{12} 972^{6} 1171^{2} 2262^{7} 2766^{8} 3760^{9} 4862^{6} 5339^{6} 5579^{3} (5885) 6025^{4}

Snowbound (FR) *J-C Rouget*
2 gr c Verglas(IRE) —Serena (IRE) (Rainbow Quest (USA))
(7316a)

Snow Dancer (IRE) *H A McWilliams* a78 72
5 b m Desert Style(IRE) —Bella Vie (IRE) (Sadler's Wells (USA))
18^{6} (353) 478^{2} 897^{2} 1279^{7} 1472^{3} 2043^{7} 2362^{7} 2823^{2} 3060^{2} 3267^{2} 3573^{2} 4930^{7} 5441^{3} 6250^{8} 6668^{2} 6860^{3} (7360) 7583^{5} 7848^{6}

Snowed Under *J D Bethell* a79 86
8 gr g Most Welcome—Snowy Mantle (Siberian Express (USA))
(1721) 2150^{10} 3235^{3} 4426^{9}

Snow Fairy (IRE) *E A L Dunlop* a84 103
2 b f Intikhab(USA) —Woodland Dream (IRE) (Charnwood Forest (IRE))
3248^{3} (3745) 4539^{2} ◆ 4795^{4} 5427^{3} 7033^{9}

Snow Lark *Ms V S Lucas* 17
11 br m Weld—Snow Child (Mandrake Major)
4587a^{2}

Snowy Indian *M Botti* a65 74
4 b m Indian Ridge—Snow Princess (IRE) (Ela-Mana-Mou)
290^{7} 512^{6}

Soap Wars *M Halford* a95 80
4 b g Acclamation—Gooseberry Pie (Green Desert (USA))
3141^{18} 7341a^{11}

Soba Jones *J Balding* a64 41
12 b g Emperor Jones(USA) —Soba (Most Secret)
35^{6} 222^{10} 487^{9} 619^{6} 746^{12}

So Bazaar (IRE) *G A Swinbank* 65
2 b g Xaar—Nature Girl (USA) (Green Dancer (USA))
3910^{3} 4307^{5} 4844^{5} 6096^{5}

Soberania (GER) *A Wohler* 111
3 b f Monsun(GER) —Sasuela (GER) (Dashing Blade)
2524a^{4} 3201a^{5} 4583a^{2} 5929a^{4}

So Blissful (IRE) *Mrs L Wadham* a60 78
3 b f Cape Cross(IRE) —Royal Devotion (IRE) (Sadler's Wells (USA))
440^{6} (2179) 3320^{9} 4482^{7} 4799^{6} 6761^{4}

Soccer (USA) *Tom Dascombe* a92 87
2 ch c Van Nistelrooy(USA) —Bonita Gail (USA) (Geiger Counter (USA))
(1119) 1290^{2} 2408^{4} 3742^{2} ◆ 4407^{7} 5241^{3} 6550^{7}

Soccerjackpot (USA) *C G Cox* a100 82
5 b g Mizzen Mast(USA) —Rahbaby (USA) (Rahy (USA))
(850) (974) 3014^{13} 3567^{4} 4983^{3} 7431^{5}

Social Grace *D H Brown* 73
2 gr f Pastoral Pursuits—Zilkha (Petong)
2000^{2} 2339^{4} 3633^{2} (3849) 4089^{18} 4547^{8} 4975^{8} 5467^{11} 5950^{9} 6555^{6} 6819^{11}

Social Rhythm *A C Whillans* a71 65
5 b m Beat All(USA) —Highly Sociable (Puissance)
(4876) 5289^{6} 6157^{5} (6411) 7173^{3}

Society Music (IRE) *M Dods* 74
7 b m Almutawakel—Society Fair (FR) (Always Fair (USA))
1332^{2} ◆ 1887^{7} 2261^{9} 2590^{3} 5730^{14} 6383^{11}

Society Rock (IRE) *J R Fanshawe* 94
2 b c Rock Of Gibraltar(IRE) —High Society (IRE) (Key Of Luck (USA))
4314^{5} ◆ (5006) (6064) 6478^{7}

Society Venue *Jedd O'Keeffe* 80
4 b g Where Or When(IRE) —Society Rose (Saddlers' Hall (IRE))
1401^{3} 1721^{3} 2237^{2} (2314) 3350^{2} 3563^{6} 4597^{6} 5551^{9} 6157^{3} 6760^{3}

Sofia's Star *S Dow* a81 75
4 bb g Lend A Hand—Charolles (Ajdal (USA))
70^{3} 283^{5} 950^{7} 1813^{5} 2193^{7} 2807^{2}

Sofinella (IRE) *A W Carroll* a59 63
6 gr m Titus Livius(FR) —Mystical Jumbo (Mystiko (USA))
896^{2} 1182^{4} 1787^{6} 2180^{8} 2225^{12} 3204^{5} 3999^{13} 4886^{5} 5504^{10} 5629^{8} 7100^{5}

Sofonisba *M L W Bell* a31 54
3 b f Rock Of Gibraltar(IRE) —Lothlorien (USA) (Woodman (USA))
1481^{10} 2143^{12}

Softly Killing Me *B Forsey* a52 56
4 b m Umistim—Slims Lady (Theatrical Charmer)
749^{11} 874^{10}

Softly Spoken *A W Carroll* 49
2 b f Forzando—Star Of Flanders (Puissance)
3306^{5} 3918^{6} 4302^{10} 5992^{7}

So Glamorous *C F Wall* 53
4 b m Diktat—Gena Ivor (USA) (Sir Ivor (USA))
4180^{7} 4786^{6} 6005^{11} 6926^{12}

Sohcahtoa (IRE) *R Hannon* a100 96
3 b g Val Royal(FR) —Stroke Of Six (IRE) (Woodborough (USA))
863^{3} 1211^{8} 1484^{5} 2004^{5} 4210^{4} 4409^{5} ◆ 6732^{8} 7035^{12} 7226^{5}

Soho Secrets *M Johnston* a24 62
3 b f Lucky Owners(NZ) —Meritxell (IRE) (Thatching)
160^{10} 1844^{5} 3061^{5}

Soho Theatre *D R C Elsworth* a72 69
2 b c Indian Ridge—Costa Brava (IRE) (Sadler's Wells (USA))
5400^{13} 6544^{5} 6781^{3} 7095^{7}

Sohraab *H Morrison* a77 108
5 b g Erhaab(USA) —Riverine (Risk Me (FR))
1325^{2} ◆ (1791) 2550^{4} 3141^{21} 3848^{4} ◆ 4559^{2} 5420^{2} 6107^{8} 6522a^{14}

Sokar (FR) *J Boisnard* 108
3 gr c Slickly(FR) —Mia Stella (FR) (Courtroom (FR))
1239a^{5} 1979a^{8} 6891a^{6} 7621a^{9}

Sokoke *D A Nolan* a2 25
8 ch g Compton Place—Sally Green (IRE) (Common Grounds)
2451^{10} 3853^{10}

Solapur (GER) *A Wohler* 99
4 ch h Ekraar(USA) —Shina (GER) (Lomitas)
1143a^{7}

Solarea (FR) *T Clout* a69 78
2 b f Prince Kirk(FR) —Elessar (FR) (Kendor (FR))
6501a^{11}

Solar Graphite (IRE) *J L Dunlop* 81
3 b g Rock Of Gibraltar(IRE) —Solar Crystal (IRE) (Alzao (USA))
(1428) 2189^{3} 3359^{2} 4299^{4} ◆ 5216^{5} 6936^{6}

Solar Spirit (IRE) *J J Quinn* a76 90
4 b g Invincible Spirit(IRE) —Misaayef (USA) (Swain (IRE))
1663^{2} ◆ 1849^{3} 2405^{3} 2897^{8} 3706^{5} 4069^{3} 4507^{5} 6050^{23} 6279^{6} 6776^{5}

Solas Alainn (IRE) *M Johnston* 77
4 b g Fantastic Light(USA) —Littlepacepaddocks (IRE) (Accordion)
1366^{3} 1506^{3} 2040^{9} 2262^{4} 2815^{6} 3447^{3} 3731^{3} 4098^{3} 4742^{7}

Soldier Soldier *J R Jenkins* 5
3 ch g Tobougg(IRE) —Bijan (IRE) (Mukaddamah (USA))
1422^{10} 1941^{11} 3773^{5} 5972^{11}

Solemn *J M Bradley* a81 76
4 b g Pivotal—Pious (Bishop Of Cashel)
2180^{7} (3204) (3562) 3938^{2} (4268) (4604) 5219^{3} 5719^{4} 6201^{5} 6739^{2} (6799) 7269^{2}

Solent Ridge (IRE) *J S Moore* a80 80
4 b g Namid—Carrozzina (Vettori (IRE))
283^{4} 694^{3} 910^{4} (1035) 1633^{7} 2186^{10} 4322^{9} 4698^{6} 5211^{10} 6370^{12}

Sole Power *Edward Lynam* a92 92
2 b g Kyllachy—Demerger (USA) (Distant View (USA))
4357a^{2} 5198^{3} 6660^{8}

Solicitor *M Johnston* a83 72
2 ch c Halling(USA) —Tolzey (USA) (Rahy (USA))
7095^{4} ◆ (7420)

Solicitude *D Haydn Jones* a65 9
6 ch m Bertolini(USA) —Sibilant (Selkirk (USA))
14^{6} 97^{3} 155^{12}

Solis *J J Quinn* a40 68
3 b g Josr Algarhoud(IRE) —Passiflora (Night Shift (USA))
796^{6} (1253) 1736^{2} 2154^{3}

Solis (GER) *P Monteith* 71
6 ch g In The Wings—Seringa (GER) (Acatenango (GER))
5732^{11} 6012^{13} 6156^{7}

Solitary *H Candy* a51 72
3 b f Lahib(USA) —Bond Solitaire (Atraf)
4198^{6} 5007^{10} 6120^{10}

Solo Attempt *M Botti* a87 82
3 b f Anabaa(USA) —Sonja's Faith (IRE) (Sharp Victor (USA))
3509^{3}

Solo Choice *I W McInnes* a65 68
3 b g Needwood Blade—Top Of The Class (IRE) (Rudimentary (USA))
144^{2} 322^{2} 455^{2} 1034^{8} 1570^{4} 1800^{8} 2742^{6} 2982^{11} 6440^{9} 6817^{11} 7142^{7} 7425^{11}

Solo River *P J Makin* a68 72
4 b m Averti(IRE) —Surakarta (Bin Ajwaad (IRE))
285^{4} 1122^{2} 1538^{10} 1834^{4} 2220^{2} (2537) 3259^{4} 5108^{4} 5569^{3} 6394^{2} 7524^{6}

Some Sunny Day *H Morrison* a79 79
3 ch f Where Or When(IRE) —Palace Street (USA) (Secreto (USA))
1585^{5} 1963^{6} 2338^{2} 3581^{2} ◆ 3803^{4} ◆ 4789^{2} (5195) (5910) ◆ 6680^{5} 7134^{3}

Something (IRE) *D Nicholls* a99 103
7 b g Trans Island—Persian Polly (Persian Bold)
(1212) 2707^{3} 3091^{10} 3435a^{5} 4330^{19} 4423^{5} 5104^{7} 6092^{7} 6270^{3} 6482^{5} 6675^{6}

Something Perfect (USA) *H R A Cecil* a81 85
3 b f Perfect Soul(IRE) —Lady Angharad (IRE) (Tenby)
1381^{3} 2281^{3} 3165^{3} 3429^{2} 5996^{7} 6773^{9}

Some Time Good (IRE) *M R Channon* a69 69
3 bg g Clodovil(IRE) —El Alma (IRE) (Goldmark (USA))
957^{4} ◆ 1408^{12} 1829^{6} 2380^{8}

Sometsuke *P J Makin* a68 74
3 br g Efisio—Peyto Princess (Bold Arrangement)
5572^{8} 5717^{2} ◆ 6430^{3} 6798^{15}

Somewhere Else *A Berry* a4 16
2 b f Firebreak—Royal Future (IRE) (Royal Academy (USA))
3606^{11} 4308^{8} 4773^{5} 6355^{12}

Sommersturm (GER) *B J Curley* a77 103
5 b g Tiger Hill(IRE) —Sommernacht (GER) (Monsun (GER))
226^{10} 660^{8} 848^{5} 1478^{8} 4373^{12}

Som Tala *M R Channon* a94 101
6 ch g Fantastic Light(USA) —One Of The Family (Alzao (USA))
1790^{10} 2994^{5} (3390) 4417^{14} 5173^{14} 5656^{13} 6851^{15} 7117^{6}

Sonara (IRE) *J Howard Johnson* 74
5 b g Peintre Celebre(USA) —Fay (IRE) (Polish Precedent (USA))
1058^{2} 2452^{5} 3313^{2}

Sonate De La Tour (FR) *J L Flint* 39
4 b m Timboroa—Damanka (IRE) (Slip Anchor)
4263^{11}

Soneva (USA) *Y De Nicolay* 110
3 bb f Cherokee Run(USA) —Lakabi (USA) (Nureyev (USA))
1237a^{2} 1918a^{5} 3892a^{2} (4971a) 6503a^{11}

Songful (IRE) *Pat Eddery* a57 45
3 bb f Captain Rio—Trillie (Never So Bold)
849^{5} 949^{6} 1066^{12} 1420^{6} 4155^{11} 4812^{8} 5018^{10} 5574^{11}

Song Of My Heart (IRE) *David Wachman* 102
2 ch f Footstepsinthesand—Catch The Moon (IRE) (Peintre Celebre (USA))
(5895a) ◆ 6449^{6}

Song Of Parkes *E J Alston* 35
2 b f Fantastic Light(USA) —My Melody Parkes (Teenoso (USA))
7167^{4}

Song Of Praise *M Blanshard* a78 63
3 b f Compton Place—Greensand (Green Desert (USA))
317^{4} (673) (936) 1322^{2} 2010^{9} 2632^{2} 2888^{7} 3625^{7} 3989^{6} 5810^{9} 6230^{5} 6915^{12}

Song Of Victory (GER) *M Weiss* 64
5 b g Silvano(GER) —Song Of Hope (GER) (Monsun (GER))
465a^{3} (653a) 1555a^{10}

Song To The Moon (IRE) *A M Balding* 65
2 b f Oratorio(IRE) —Jojeema (Barathea (IRE))
6477^{13} 6992^{7}

Sonhador *G Prodromou* a68 68
3 b g Compton Place—Fayre Holly (IRE) (Fayruz)
2219^{6} 2456^{11} 2683^{9} 3926^{9} 4718^{8} 6581^{2} (7176) 7460^{7} 7770^{6} 7889^{6}

Sonic Anthem (USA) *B D Leavy* a39 46
7 b g Royal Anthem(USA) —Whisperifyoudare (USA) (Red Ransom (USA))
4893^{8} 7354^{9}

Sonnengold (GER) *B J Llewellyn* 59
8 bb m Java Gold(USA) —Standing Ovation (ITY) (Law Society (USA))
4264^{5}

Sonning Gate *D R C Elsworth* a87 92
3 b g Desert Sun—Sunley Scent (Wolfhound (USA))
1487^{3} 1751^{4} 2273^{9}

Sonny G (IRE) *J R Best* a50 40
2 ch c Desert Sun—Broughton Zest (Colonel Collins (USA))
6416^{8} 6542^{6} 6629^{9} 7884^{5}

Sonny Parkin *J Pearce* a56 81
7 b g Spinning World(USA) —No Miss Kris (USA) (Capote (USA))
2243^{6} (3112) 3357^{P} 4502^{6} 4759^{11} 5003^{11} 6004^{6} 7065^{9} 7512^{11}

Sonny Red (IRE) *D Nicholls* 106
5 b g Redback—Magic Melody (Petong)
1325^{4} 2012^{7} (3844) 4523^{24} 5132^{6} 5654^{8} 6091^{5} 6270^{24}

Sonny Sam (IRE) *R A Fahey* a58 64
4 b g Black Sam Bellamy(IRE) —Purple Risks (FR) (Take Risks (FR))
1242^{2} 1648^{3} 2018^{9}

Sonofdon *C W Moore* 10
2 ch g Stage Pass—Moore Appeal (Homo Sapien)
5253^{12}

Son Of Monsieur *G R Oldroyd* a49 46
3 ch g Monsieur Bond(IRE) —Triple Tricks (IRE) (Royal Academy (USA))
1888^{6} 2543^{4} 3120^{8} ◆ 3974^{10} 4434^{8} 7464^{7} 7615^{4} 7818^{10}

Son Of My Heart (USA) *P F I Cole* a65 63
4 bb g Dynaformer(USA) —Sophie My Love (USA) (Danzig (USA))
1407^{7} 1780^{8} 2221^{3} 3158^{3}

Son Of The Cat (USA) *B Gubby* a101 100
3 b g Tale Of The Cat(USA) —Dixieland Gal (USA) (Dixieland Band (USA))
912^{9} 1085^{5} 1639^{6} 3028^{4} (4788) 5092^{5} 6240^{3} 6694^{2} 7394^{2} ◆ 7488^{4}

Soopacal (IRE) *B Smart* a92 82
4 b g Captain Rio—Fiddes (IRE) (Alzao (USA))
86^{3} 351^{8} 714^{6} 901^{10} 965^{4}

Sophie's Beau (USA) *B J Meehan* a64 79
2 b g Stormy Atlantic(USA) —Lady Buttercup (USA) (Meadowlake (USA))
5000^{5} 6061^{2} 7001^{4}

Sophist (IRE) *Evan Williams* a60 59
6 b g Montjeu(IRE) —Cordon Bleu (USA) (D'Accord (USA))
603^{3}

Sopranist *J H M Gosden* 108
3 b c Singspiel(IRE) —Trefoil (Kris)
(1289) ◆ 1678^{7} 4058^{2} 4455^{2}

So Pretty (GER) *T Mundry* 86
3 f Ransom O'War(USA) —Silvetta (Lando (GER))
5296a^{10}

Sorciere (IRE) *C Lerner* 106
2 b f Orpen(USA) —Serandine (IRE) (Hernando (FR))
(3648a) 4579a^{2} (6044a)

Sordino (GER) *W Hickst* 109
3 ch c Samum(GER) —Serenata (GER) (Lomitas)
3670a^{2}

Soriniere Du Lac (FR) *J-L Mace* 61
5 gr m Verglas(IRE) —Rivonia (USA) (Irish River (FR))
(5013a)

Sorrel Point *H J Collingridge* a58 44
6 b h Bertolini(USA) —Lightning Princess (Puissance)
3077^{12} 3548^{8} 4552^{8} 4718^{6} 5971^{5} 6641^{3} 7100^{8} 7371^{3}

Sorrel Ridge (IRE) *M G Quinlan* a57 43
3 ch g Namid—She Legged It (IRE) (Cape Cross (IRE))
75^{5} 246^{2} 273^{2} 316^{7} 736^{8} 1084^{4} 1424^{5} 1958^{12}

Sorrento Moon (IRE) *G A Harker* a28 52
5 b m Tagula(IRE) —Honey For Money (IRE) (Alzao (USA))
2233^{8} 2609^{7} 3171^{11}

Sory *L M Cumani* 20
2 b g Sakhee(USA) —Rule Britannia (Night Shift (USA))
7099^{11}

Sos Brillante (CHI) *Saeed Bin Suroor* a102 23
4 b m Dance Brightly(CAN) —Strike Out (CHI) (Mashaallah (USA))
(181a) 438a^{7} 701a^{3}

So Shiny (ARG) *J Barton* a103
4 ch m Indygo Shiner(USA) —Sorpresiva (ARG) (Southern Halo (USA))
(438a) 701a^{4} 1009a^{4}

Sostenuto *T H Caldwell* 26
2 ch f Compton Place—Hufflepuff (IRE) (Desert King (IRE))
7061^{12}

Sosua (IRE) *A De Royer-Dupre* 66
3 b f Exceed And Excel(AUS) —Scandisk (IRE) (Kenmare (FR))
5462a^{9}

So Sublime *M C Chapman* a69 45
4 b g Bertolini(USA) —Petalite (Petong)
104^{10} 175^{8} 223^{7} 250^{4} 328^{2} 487^{7} 574^{11} 981^{9} 1438^{9} 1848^{10} 2456^{13}

So Surreal (IRE) *G L Moore* a73 68
2 b f Avonbridge—Secret Circle (Magic Ring (IRE))
3458^{6} 3987^{3} 4421^{7} 4850^{12} 6241^{13} (6826) 7108^{7} 7551^{5}

Sotelo *S Gollings* a66 10
7 ch h Monsun(GER) —Seringa (GER) (Acatenango (GER))
4197^{5} 6668^{7}

Sotik Star (IRE) *K A Morgan* a75 79
6 b g Elnadim(USA) —Crystal Springs (IRE) (Kahyasi)
129^{2} 357^{7} 841^{10} 3717^{4} 4667^{2} (5229)

Soto *M W Easterby* a34 70
6 b g Averti(IRE) —Belle Of The Blues (IRE) (Blues Traveller (IRE))
975^{11} 1369^{6} 1924^{3} 2389^{2} 2801^{2} 3354^{2} 3612^{4} 4436^{4} 4654^{3} 5150^{5} 6103^{4} 6414^{2} 6847^{12}

Sottone *B Grizzetti* 103
3 b c Observatory(USA) —Scundes (IRE) (Barathea (IRE))
1393a^{2} 1904a^{5} 7313a^{8}

Soul City (IRE) *R Hannon* 112
3 b c Elusive City(USA) —Savage (IRE) (Polish Patriot (USA))
2288a^{3} 2992^{8}

Soul Heaven *M L W Bell* a76 77
2 b g Oratorio(IRE) —Pilgrim Spirit (USA) (Saint Ballado (CAN))
1891^{4} ◆ (2383) (3842) ◆

Soul Murmur (IRE) *F Sheridan* a61 79
4 br g Indian Ridge—My Potters (USA) (Irish River (FR))
1493^{12} 6755^{15}

Soul Singer *J G Portman* a53 52
3 br f Where Or When(IRE) —Tancholo (So Factual (USA))
455[6] (670) 953[7] 3303[14] 3739[8] 4146[3] 4934[3] 5381[3] 5990[4] 7137[10] 7324[7]

Soul Sista (IRE) *J L Spearing* a49 77
3 b f City On A Hill(USA) —Fraamtastic (Fraam)
1345[12] 2227[5] 4044[9] 5405[10] 6925[4] 7246[6] 7587[9]

Soul Station (FR) *R Charlton* a65 84
2 b g Starcraft(NZ) —Allumette (Rainbow Quest (USA))
6372[5] (6728)

Soum (GER) *C Sprengel* a74 97
4 b h Monsun(GER) —Suivi (GER) (Darshaan)
3441a[12] 5281a[8]

Soundbyte *J Gallagher* a79 79
4 b g Beat All(USA) —Gloaming (Celtic Swing)
952[3] 1230[3] 1635[3] 2018[12] 2854[5] 4007[5] 4696[10] (5740) 5962[5] 6634[6] 6995[4] 7222[2]

Sounds Of Jupiter (IRE) *D M Simcock* a71 82
3 ch g Galileo(IRE) —Sena Desert (Green Desert (USA))
(310) 740[2] 1397[4] 1842[7] 2371[9] 4687[3] (5123) (5286) 5641[8]

Sounds Of Thunder *H J L Dunlop* a70 66
2 b f Tobougg(IRE) —Distant Music (Darshaan)
3576[6] 4239[5] 5528[4] 5938[5] 6793[11] 7359[4] (7597)

Sound The Drum (USA) *A Al Raihe* a85 94
7 b g Stravinsky(USA) —Uhavethebeat (USA) (Unbridled (USA))
336a[12]

Sour Mash (IRE) *L M Cumani* 48
2 b c Danehill Dancer(IRE) —Landmark (USA) (Arch (USA))
6810[10]

Souter Point (USA) *R Charlton* a72 89
3 bb g Giant's Causeway(USA) —Wires Crossed (USA) (Caller I.D. (USA))
1151[2] ◆ 1407[4] 3425[3] 3791[2] (4205) 5062[3] 5532[2] 5904[3] 6552[2] 6571[2]

South African (USA) *M A Magnusson* a65
3 rg f Johannesburg(USA) —River Cache (USA) (Unbridled (USA))
4860[2] 5882[2]

South African Gold (USA) *J M P Eustace* a69 24
2 ch c Johannesburg(USA) —Coesse Gold (USA) (Seeking The Gold (USA))
3920[11] 7571[10] 7859[4]

Southandwest (IRE) *J S Moore* a94 91
5 ch g Titus Livius(FR) —Cheviot Indian (IRE) (Indian Ridge)
(106) 113[3] 388[7] 538[2] 635[3] 724[7] 916[9] 1116[7] 1433[11] 1607[8] 4796[7] 5221[9] 5448[6] 7437[2] 7558[3] 7633[5] 7883[3]

South Cape *G L Moore* a94 95
6 b g Cape Cross(IRE) —Aunt Ruby (USA) (Rubiano (USA))
2669[8] 3091[17] 4293[6] 4409[U] 4954[7] 5746[3] 5914[7] 6645[10] (7125)

South Easter (IRE) *W J Haggas* 105
3 ch c Galileo(IRE) —Dance Treat (USA) (Nureyev (USA))
1350[2] ◆ (1822) 3087[6]

Southern Breeze *S Kirk* a14
2 b c Dansili—Michelle Ma Belle (IRE) (Shareef Dancer (USA))
7537[10]

Southern Goddess (IRE) *P D Evans* 38
2 b f Avonbridge—Northern Secret (Sinndar (IRE))
1783[7] 2319[7]

Southern Mistral *Miss Gay Kelleway* a62 61
4 b g Desert Prince(IRE) —Hyperspectra (Rainbow Quest (USA))
1199[10] (1520) 1728[5] 1881[9]

Southern Waters (FR) *G A Swinbank* 46
5 br g Sinndar(IRE) —Due South (Darshaan)
1099[7]

Southoffrance (IRE) *W G M Turner* a42 26
3 b f Dr Fong(USA) —Mystery Solved (USA) (Royal Academy (USA))
6788[12] 7369[10]

Southwark Newshawk *Mrs C A Dunnett* a52 55
2 ch f Piccolo—Be Bop Aloha (Most Welcome)
1630[7] 1939[7] 2128[3] 2383[8] 3006[7] 3709[3] 4173[4] 4383[3] 4912[7] 5372[5] 5950[16] 7331[4]

South Wing (IRE) *Eoin Griffin* a86 86
5 ch g In The Wings—Desert Grouse (USA) (Gulch (USA))
4510a[5] 5909[9]

Sovento (GER) *Shaun Harley* a59 63
5 ch g Kornado—Second Game (GER) (Second Set (IRE))
6845[5] 7687[2]

Sovereign Remedy (USA) *Saeed Bin Suroor* a111 97
3 ch c Elusive Quality(USA) —Lailani (Unfuwain (USA))
1729[2] ◆ (2165) 2935[6] 3816[3] 4316[2] 6474[2] (6876) ◆ 7060[6]

Sovereign Secure (IRE) *Lee Smyth* a62 68
2 ch f Kyllachy—Affaire Royale (IRE) (Royal Academy (USA))
4286[12] 4856[7] 5256[3] 6048[9] 7156[6] 7372[4]

Sovereign Spirit (IRE) *C Gordon* a25 30
7 b g Desert Prince(IRE) —Sheer Spirit (IRE) (Caerleon (USA))
7608[11]

Sovereignty (JPN) *D K Ivory* a73 73
7 b g King's Best(USA) —Calando (USA) (Storm Cat (USA))
1403[7] 1710[16] 2682[5] 2745[9] (3269) (3735) 4645[5] 5329[9] 5813[5] 6224[3] 6588[12] 6904[10] 7109[6] 7592[4] 7691[7] 7834[6]

Soviet Rhythm *M Dods* 65
3 b f Soviet Star(USA) —Aldevonie (Green Desert (USA))
1888[10] 2786[14] 4942[8] 5145[4]

Soviet Sceptre (IRE) *Tim Vaughan* a54 62
8 ch g Soviet Star(USA) —Princess Sceptre (Cadeaux Genereux)
2337[6]

Sovietta (IRE) *Ian Williams* a56 60
8 b m Soviet Star(USA) —La Riveraine (USA) (Riverman (USA))
8[11] 385[7] 734[8] 2601[13]

Sowaylm *Saeed Bin Suroor* a82
2 b c Tobougg(IRE) —Ameerat (Mark Of Esteem (IRE))
(7199)

So Will I *Doug Watson* a61 109
8 ch g Inchinor—Fur Will Fly (Petong)
257a[4] 433a[8] 611a[4]

Soy Libriano (ARG) *M bin Shafya* a99
4 br h Ride The Rails(USA) —Soy Ariana (ARG) (Equalize (USA))
(768a) 1009a[3]

So You Think (NZ) *Bart Cummings* 121
3 b c High Chaparral(IRE) —Triassic (NZ) (Tights (USA))
(7040a)

Space Pirate *J Pearce* a52 58
4 b g Bahamian Bounty—Science Fiction (Starborough)
100[8] 132[10] 2221[10] 3158[12] 3949[9] 4667[9]

Space Station *S Dow* a76 74
3 b g Anabaa(USA) —Spacecraft (USA) (Distant View (USA))
5572[9] 5965[2] 6476[4] 6915[5] 7516[4] 7739[2] 7876[5]

Space Tune (FR) *M Pimbonnet* a66
3 b f Green Tune(USA) —Domniga (IRE) (Be My Guest (USA))
6981a[9]

Spacious *J R Fanshawe* 115
4 b m Nayef(USA) —Palatial (Green Desert (USA))
2703[3] (3012) 3749[3] 4522[9] 6479[3]

Spain Blues (FR) *X-Thomas Demeaulte* a76 66
3 b f Anabaa Blue—Strike Alight (USA) (Gulch (USA))
5462a[10]

Spanish Acclaim *J G Portman* 76
2 b g Acclamation—Spanish Gold (Vettori (IRE))
1323[11] 2007[2] 2649[U] 5318[8]

Spanish Ace *J M Bradley* a47 55
8 b g First Trump—Spanish Heart (King Of Spain)
104[6] 308[9] 328[4] 508[4] 574[5] 676[6] 812[3] 1038[6] 1784[8] 3204[9]

Spanish Bounty *J G Portman* a87 98
4 b g Bahamian Bounty—Spanish Gold (Vettori (IRE))
1321[6] 1699[10] 2078[6] 2948[3] 3818[15] 4423[4] 5476[8] 5826[11] 6482[10]

Spanish Conquest *P J Hobbs* a75 76
5 b g Hernando(FR) —Sirena (GER) (Tejano (USA))
6368[2]

Spanish Cross (IRE) *G Prodromou* a51 64
4 gr m Cape Cross(IRE) —Espana (Hernando (FR))
1533[10] 2458[8] 6966[5] 7094[3] 7466[4]

Spanish Cygnet (USA) *Mrs A J Perrett* a90 84
3 b f El Corredor(USA) —Dixie Dos (USA) (Dixieland Band (USA))
4540[12] 5005[9]

Spanish Duke (IRE) *J L Dunlop* a82 77
2 b g Big Bad Bob(IRE) —Spanish Lady (IRE) (Bering)
3344[7] 4080[5] 4699[4] 5715[2] (6334) (6805)

Spanish Hidalgo (IRE) *J L Dunlop* 107
5 b g Night Shift(USA) —Spanish Lady (IRE) (Bering)
1523[3] 2075[P]

Spanish Moon (USA) *Sir Michael Stoute* a117 121
5 b h El Prado(IRE) —Shining Bright (Rainbow Quest (USA))
1012a[2] (3443a) (5931a) 7310a[4] 7744a[2]

Spanish Moss (IRE) *A Dupont* a70 83
8 b g Fasliyev(USA) —Valses Pour Moi (USA) (Gate Dancer (USA))
3419a[7]

Spares And Repairs *Mrs S Lamyman* a67 51
6 b g Robellino(USA) —Lady Blackfoot (Prince Tenderfoot (USA))
217[6] 857[2] 978[5] 1402[9] 1881[8] 2171[7] 2458[11] 2746[11]

Sparkaway *W J Musson* a49 65
3 ch g Gold Away(IRE) —West River (USA) (Gone West (USA))
1070[5] (3454) (3962) 6027[6] 6742[2] 7214[11]

Sparkbridge (IRE) *S C Burrough* a42 56
6 b g Mull Of Kintyre(USA) —Persian Velvet (IRE) (Distinctly North (USA))
3275[6]

Sparking *Mrs G S Rees* a56 8
2 ch f Exceed And Excel(AUS) —Twilight Time (Aragon)
3152[8] 7618[3]

Sparkle Park *B J Meehan*
2 b f Kyllachy—Petonellajill (Petong)
7886[10]

Sparkling Crown *J Ryan* a50 49
2 br f Xaar—Crown Water (USA) (Chief's Crown (USA))
4385[8] 4542[14] 7451[9] 7683[8]

Sparkling Crystal (IRE) *B W Hills* a71 78
3 ch f Danehill Dancer(IRE) —Crystal Curling (IRE) (Peintre Celebre (USA))
1837[3] 2662[2] (3220) 3870[5] 4482[5] 5037[3] 5910[8] 6975[7]

Sparkling Smile (IRE) *D R Lanigan* a63 60
2 bb f Cape Cross(IRE) —Starlight Smile (USA) (Green Dancer (USA))
5969[8] 6274[4] 6628[9]

Sparkling Suzie *J S Moore* a61 35
3 b f Deportivo—Sparkling Jewel (Bijou D'Inde)
4324[10] 4694[5] 5316[9] 5644[13] 6445[11]

Sparky Vixen *C J Teague* a51 56
5 b m Mujahid(USA) —Lucy Glitters (USA) (Cryptoclearance (USA))
792[4] 1226[5] 1777[7] 2155[8] 7500[7]

Spartan Dance *J A Geake* a65 33
5 ch g Groom Dancer(USA) —Delphic Way (Warning)
2634[10] 4735[6] 5122[5]

Spartan Prince (USA) *T D Barron* a67 69
3 b c Mr Greeley(USA) —Yalta (USA) (Private Terms (USA))
138[4] (570) 1280[8] 1629[2] 2667[8] 4431[4]

Spartan Princess (IRE) *M Brittain* 15
3 ch f Spartacus(IRE) —Stormchaser (IRE) (Titus Livius (FR))
4550[11]

Spartan Storm (IRE) *M Brittain* 18
3 b c Spartacus(IRE) —Sylvan Princess (Sylvan Express)
3764[11] 4805[8]

Sparton Duke (IRE) *K A Ryan* a83 84
4 b g Xaar—Blueberry Walk (Green Desert (USA))
1510[5] 2071[13] 2402[6] 3274[4] 3509[9] 3615[8]

Spa's Dancer (IRE) *J W Hills* 85
2 b c Danehill Dancer(IRE) —Spa (Sadler's Wells (USA))
4209[4] 4986[7] 5994[2] 6931[3]

Spate River *C F Wall* a93 85
4 b g Zaha(CAN) —Rion River (IRE) (Taufan (USA))
4954[5] 5640[7] (6462)

Spavento (IRE) *William Durkan* a61 73
3 gr f Verglas(IRE) —Lanasara (Generous (IRE))
4392a[3]

Speagle (IRE) *A J Chamberlain* a37 53
7 ch g Desert Sun—Pohutakawa (FR) (Affirmed (USA))
3681[3] 6231[3] 682[9] 1568[10] 1786[11] 1980[4] 2182[4] 2580[9] 2762[6] 3244[6] 3594[7] 3997[8]

Speak Freely *C Smith* 17
3 b f Domedriver(IRE) —Miss Tolerance (USA) (Mt. Livermore (USA))
920[9] 1362[8]

Speak The Truth (IRE) *J R Boyle* a74 73
3 br g Statue Of Liberty(USA) —Brave Truth (IRE) (Brief Truce (USA))
316[2] (429) 568[2] 784[8] (955) (1072) 1311[3] (1583) 2005[5] 3506[6] (4483) 4829[2] 5164[8] 6444[4] 6798[6] 7203[9] (7329) 7577[8] 7739[5]

Spear Thistle *C J Mann* a87 68
7 ch g Selkirk(USA) —Ardisia (USA) (Affirmed (USA))
7248[3]

Special Adviser *T J Etherington* a52 19
3 b g Dr Fong(USA) —Dimakya (USA) (Dayjur (USA))
2543[6] 3120[12]

Special Betty *D Haydn Jones* a52
2 b f Tamayaz(CAN) —Natural Key (Safawan)
7001[11] 7556[10] 7618[4] 7799[10] 7871[9]

Special Bond *J A Osborne* a66 57
3 b f Monsieur Bond(IRE) —Fizzy Treat (Efisio)
164[3] 231[8] 363[3] 441[5]

Special Chapter (IRE) *A B Haynes* a39 47
4 b m Acclamation—Literary (Woodman (USA))
42[6] 240[4] 838[5] 2333[10] 4021[5] 4640[3] 5381[7] 7336[9] 7761[8]

Special Cuvee *A B Haynes* a78 67
3 b g Diktat—Iris May (Brief Truce (USA))
685[7] 819[5] 924[4] (1046) (1270) 1595[10] 3790[6] 4279[16] 4719[6] 7173[8] 7727[4] 7784[3] 7818[13]

Special Days (NZ) *J Size* 113
6 br g Keeper(AUS) —Eva's Belle (NZ) (Grosvenor (NZ))
7747a[7]

Special Duty *Mme C Head-Maarek* 117
2 ch f Hennessy(USA) —Quest To Peak (USA) (Distant View (USA))
3648a[2] (4366a) 5299a[2] (6449) ◆

Specialising *M R Channon* 57
2 ch f Nayef(USA) —Spry (Suave Dancer (USA))
4421[6] 6930[8]

Special Reserve (IRE) *R Hannon* a74 89
4 b h Sadler's Wells(USA) —Ionian Sea (Slip Anchor)
1621[2] (1812) 2239[3] 2475[6] 3695[6] 4315[4] (5321) 6594[7] 6907[3]

Spectacle Du Mars (FR) *C Martens* a72 72
2 b g Martillo(GER) —Spectacular Groove (USA) (Trempolino (USA))
3935a[7] 5713a[3] 6322a[2]

Spectaculaire *J-J Boutin* 81
6 ch g Spectrum(IRE) —Gold Round (IRE) (Caerleon (USA))
7038a[4]

Spectait *Jonjo O'Neill* a100 100
7 b g Spectrum(IRE) —Shanghai Girl (Distant Relative)
(79) (199) (766) 995[LFT] 1352[4] ◆ 3628[7] 4486[2]

Spectral (FR) *J Merienne* a52 59
7 b g Spectrum(IRE) —Poli Knight (Polish Precedent (USA))
5301a[0]

Speed Dating *Sir Mark Prescott* a53 72
3 ch g Pivotal—Courting (Pursuit Of Love)
1740[3] 4079[2] (4348) 5101[4] 5524[2]

Speed Gifted *Lee Freedman* 116
5 b g Montjeu(IRE) —Good Standing (USA) (Distant View (USA))
7040a[12]

Speed Pearl (FR) *L Viel* a64 73
3 gr f Kadence(FR) —Coral Pearl (FR) (Iron Duke (FR))
6606a[10]

Speed Song *W J Haggas* 90
4 b m Fasliyev(USA) —Superstar Leo (IRE) (College Chapel)
1582[13] 2093[7] 2653[3]

Speed Ticket *Mrs John Harrington* a67 94
5 b g Galileo(IRE) —Kassiyra (IRE) (Kendor (FR))
2305a[2]

Speedyfix *Mrs C A Dunnett* a47 43
2 b g Chineur(FR) —Zonnebeke (Orpen (USA))
3006[9] 3744[6] 4176[12] 5776[11] 5950[7] 6345[4] 6610[2] 7088[8] 7333[11] 7453[7]

Speedy Guru *H Candy* a70 75
3 b f Ishiguru(USA) —Gowon (Aragon)
3387[10] 4061[5] (6572) 6997[13] 7496[7] 7738[8]

Speedy Senorita (IRE) *J J Quinn* a64 79
4 b m Fayruz—Sinora Wood (IRE) (Shinko Forest (IRE))
1518[4] 2046[3] 2546[3] 2840[10] 3295[2] 3565[5] 4753[5] (4929) 5421[8] 5767[10] 6489[11] 7122[7]

Spell Caster *R M Beckett* a82 91
4 ch m Bertolini(USA) —Princess Claudia (IRE) (Kahyasi)
2239[4] 2796[2] 3840[5] 7035[10]

Spensley (IRE) *J R Fanshawe* a50 79
3 ch g Dr Fong(USA) —Genoa (Zafonic (USA))
1729[10] 2930[8] 3117[5] 3761[8] 4759[6] (6760)

Spent *Mouse Hamilton-Fairley* a58 64
4 b g Averti(IRE) —Top (Shirley Heights)
803[7] 1030[6] 2807[7]

Sphere (IRE) *J Mackie* a56 76
4 b m Daylami(IRE) —Apple Town (Warning)
1049[4] 2172[4] 2760[6] 3073[6] 4498[4] 5015[9] 5679[4] 5947[3] (6177) 6845[7] 7357[6]

Sphinx (FR) *E W Tuer* a59 86
11 b g Snurge—Egyptale (Crystal Glitters (USA))
5410[7] 6053[12] 6676[10] (7170)

Spice Fair *M D I Usher* a67
2 ch g Trade Fair—Focosa (ITY) (In The Wings)
7663[2] 7885[6]

Spice Route *Roger L Attfield* a109 114
5 ch g King's Best(USA) —Zanzibar (IRE) (In The Wings)
6873a[6]

Spice Run *Stef Liddiard* a74 29
6 b g Zafonic(USA) —Palatial (Green Desert (USA))
5572[6] (7411)

Spic 'n Span *R A Harris* a72 66
4 b g Piccolo—Sally Slade (Dowsing (USA))
(177) 269[6] 326[9] 518[5] 742[5] (884) 965[2] 1564[2] 1776[2] 2180[11] 3204[10] 3465[4] (3926) 5184[3] 5374[4] 5504[3] 6329[7] 6669[11]

Spiders Star *S G West* 69
6 br m Cayman Kai(IRE) —Kiss In The Dark (Starry Night (USA))
2614[4] (3486) (3609) 4890[3] 5068[2] (5339) 5696[9]

Spiders Tern *J M Bradley* a19
4 b g Sooty Tern—Miss Money Spider (IRE) (Statoblest)
6172[10] 7278[12] 7596[10]

Spiekeroog *H R A Cecil* a22 84
3 ch c Lomitas—Special (Polar Falcon (USA))
2211[2] ◆ 3192[2] (3731) 4785[4] 6803[4]

Spin Again (IRE) *D Nicholls* a73 78
4 b g Intikhab(USA) —Queen Of The May (IRE) (Nicolotte)
980[6] 1060[7] 1246[5] 1887[12] 1952[7] 2269[10] 3354[14] 3558[2] 3924[5] ◆ 4845[5]

Spin Around (AUS) *Steven Cooper* 112
9 ch g Spinning World(USA) —Be Yourself (USA) (Noalcoholic (FR))
6961a[10] 7215a[20]

Spin Cycle (IRE) *B Smart* 111
3 b c Exceed And Excel(AUS) —Spinamix (Spinning World (USA))
(1647) 2991[12] 4456[7] 5420[5] 5765[2] 6107[6] (6427)

Spinight (IRE) *M Botti* a64 60
3 b c Spinning World(USA) —Adjtiya (IRE) (Green Desert (USA))
345[3] 426[5] 827[2] 960[4] 3305[3] 3632[9]

Spinners End (IRE) *A P Jarvis* 88
3 b c Royal Applause—Needwood Epic (Midyan (USA))
1193[3] (2248) 2845[3] (3062) 3144[9] 3816[7] (4326) 4591[4]

Spinning *T D Barron* a103 87
6 ch g Pivotal—Starring (FR) (Ashkalani (IRE))
6[6] (430) 3172[5] 3872[8] 4104[5] 4549[12] 5040[7] 5441[8] 5887[10] 6462[2] 6830[4] 7194[4] (7322) (7560) 7827[3]

Spinning Bailiwick *G L Moore* a81
3 b f Spinning World(USA) —Zietunzeen (IRE) (Zieten (USA))
5541a[5] 7254[4] (7510) (7572) (7651) 7828[3]

Spinning Crystal (IRE) *S Szuna* a53 60
5 b m Spinning World(USA) —Crystal Valkyrie (IRE) (Danehill (USA))
464a[4] 652a[3]

Spinning Joy *J R Boyle* a54 28
3 b f Josr Algarhoud(IRE) —Den's-Joy (Archway (IRE))
949[7] 1183[13] 2431[10]

Spinning Ridge (IRE) *R A Harris* a64 61
4 ch g Spinning World(USA) —Summer Style (IRE) (Indian Ridge)
25[7] 478[11] 6588[11] 6999[8] (7197) 7438[2] 7579[2] 7716[3] 7784[11] 7856[5]

Spinning Spirit (IRE) *J G Given* a63 66
2 b g Invincible Spirit(IRE) —Vencera (FR) (Green Tune (USA))
5129[7] 5527[3] 5852[5] 6793[8] 7088[3] 7514[8]

Spinning Waters *Eve Johnson Houghton* a57 67
3 b g Vettori(IRE) —Secret Waters (Pharly (FR))
(1397) 1747[6] 2479[7] 2909[2] 3475[3] 3776[5] 5990[6] 6330[4]

Spinning Well (IRE) *R M Beckett* a64 75
3 ch f Pivotal—Kiltubber (IRE) (Sadler's Wells (USA))
7439[4]

Spinning Wings (IRE) *T Hogan* 82
3 ch f Spinning World(USA) —Wings To Soar (USA) (Woodman (USA))
5689a[12]

Spin Sister *J Gallagher* a36 6
3 b f Umistim—Gloaming (Celtic Swing)
4084[10] 5628[9] 6029[8] 6788[11]

Spiosra (USA) *C J Teague* 29
3 ch f Mr Greeley(USA) —Laptop (USA) (Phone Trick (USA))
5731[10] 5954[9] 6823[16]

Spirit Child (USA) *J A Osborne* 7
3 bb f Hennessy(USA) —Babeinthewoods (USA) (Woodman (USA))
6430[10] 6573[9]

Spirit Is Needed (IRE) *M Johnston* 88
3 b g No Excuse Needed—The Spirit Of Pace (IRE) (In The Wings)
2538[P] (5939) 6313[2]

Spirit Land (IRE) *M H Tompkins* a50 52
2 ch c Indian Haven—Reborn (IRE) (Idris (IRE))
6000[8] 6235[5] 6544[9] 7334[4] 7482[6]

Spirit Of Adjisa (IRE) *Pat Eddery* a84 90
5 br g Invincible Spirit(IRE) —Adjisa (IRE) (Doyoun)
156[2] 693[4] 2194[11] 2552[2] 2898[4] 3564[6] 4229[4] (5593) (6280) 7151[6]

Spirit Of A Nation (IRE) *D H Brown* a89 92
4 b h Invincible Spirit(IRE) —Fabulous Pet (Somethingfabulous (USA))
5640[3] ◆ 6014[2]

Spirit Of Coniston *P T Midgley* a59 73
6 b g Lake Coniston(IRE) —Kigema (IRE) (Case Law)
294[5] 535[8] 794[3] 976[3] 1310[3] 1528[7] 2158[7] 2801[4] 3111[3] 3445[5] 4355[10] (5341) 5629[5] 5946[6] ◆ (7086) 7398[11]

Spirit Of Dubai (IRE) *D M Simcock* 101
3 b f Cape Cross(IRE) —Questina (FR) (Rainbow Quest (USA))
1871[4] 2310a[13] 3373[2] 4991[4] (5578) (6242)

Spirit Of France (IRE) *D Carroll* 74
7 b g Anabaa(USA) —Les Planches (Tropular)
1309[15] 1682[10] 2245[9] 2362[2] ◆ 2569[3] 2804[4] 2894[5] 3121[5]

Spirit Of Love (IRE) *M Wigham* a66
2 b g Pearl Of Love(IRE) —Sesleria (IRE) (Mark Of Esteem (IRE))
7556[4] ◆

Spirit Of Normandy *R Ingram* a22
2 ch f Auction House(USA) —Charlottevalentina (IRE) (Perugino (USA))
7430[9]

Spirit Of Sharjah (IRE) *Miss J Feilden* a95 100
4 b g Invincible Spirit(IRE) —Rathbawn Realm (Doulab (USA))
1299[11] 1672[6] 2259[6] 2941[4] 3347[3] 3825[6] (4236) 4485[11] 4954[3] 5221[11] 6117[4] 6482[6] 6702[2] 7133[4]

Spirit Of Sport (IRE) *A Candi* 101
3 b c Marju(IRE) —Be Crafty (USA) (Crafty Prospector (USA))
(1392a)

Spirit Of The Glen *Jamie Poulton* a50 28
3 b f Catcher In The Rye(IRE) —Sentiment (Dancing Brave (USA))
32[5] 630[4] 2847[8] 4569[15]

Spiritofthewest (IRE) *D H Brown* a74 82
3 b g Invincible Spirit(IRE) —Rosie's Guest (IRE) (Be My Guest (USA))
1345[6] 2443[4] 2821[3] 2840[7] 3173[7] 4227[7] 5978[14] 6233[5] 6642[5] 6798[7] 7481[4] 7759[7]

Spiritonthemount (USA) *P W Hiatt* a70 77
4 bb g Pulpit(USA) —Stirling Bridge (USA) (Prized (USA))
8[10] 126[11] 751[7] 809[5] 860[4] 967[6] 1439[2] 1767[13] 7336[13] 7873[3]

Spiritual Art *L A Dace* a79 69
3 b f Invincible Spirit(IRE) —Oatey (Master Willie)
3455[6] 4984[7] 5477[5] 6111[11] 6630[6] 6701[2] 7065[2] (7364) 7487[4] 7883[6]

Spiritual Bond *R A Harris* a48 18
3 b f Monsieur Bond(IRE) —Country Spirit (Sayf El Arab (USA))
267[7]

Spiritual Healing (IRE) *J A Osborne* a65
3 b f Invincible Spirit(IRE) —Tarbela (IRE) (Grand Lodge (USA))
315[5] (381)

Spiritual Treasure (USA) *M A Magnusson* a74 14
3 bb g Perfect Soul(IRE) —Storm Runner (USA) (Miswaki (USA))
3026[7] 3466[5] 4481[8] 6832[10]

Spit And Polish *C A Dwyer* a63 67
3 b g Polish Precedent(USA) —Brooklyn's Sky (Septieme Ciel (USA))
1075[6] 1584[2] 1958[2] 2148[10] 2386[6] 2683[10] 2918[10] 3225[6]

Spitfire *J R Jenkins* a97 101
4 b g Mujahid(USA) —Fresh Fruit Daily (Reprimand)
1212[4] 1861[27] 2470[13] 3795[3] 4353[6] 5025[6] 6633[3] 7252[4] 7393[4] 7626[10]

Splashdown *L M Cumani* a75 105
3 ch f Falbrav(IRE) —Space Time (FR) (Bering)
2190[4] ◆ (2846) ◆ 4094[5] 4903[2] 6003[3] 6813[3]

Splash The Cash *K A Ryan* a65 78
4 b g Lomitas—Bandit Queen (Desert Prince (IRE))
167[10] 355[5] 540[5] 715[8] (1057) 1694[7] 2156[7] (2269) 2658[4] 2998[P]

Splendorinthegrass (IRE) *R Charlton* 99
3 ch c Selkirk(USA) —Portelet (Night Shift (USA))
2543[2] (4057) 4796[3] 6675[20]

Splinter Cell (USA) *M Botti* a99 96
3 bb c Johannesburg(USA) —Rock Salt (Selkirk (USA))
764[2] ◆ 1086[7] ◆ 2275[5] 2767[3] (4143) 5670[5] (6740) 6996[4] 7574[9] (7789)

Split The Pot (IRE) *P R Chamings* a21 57
2 ch g Chevalier(IRE) —Autumn Fall (USA) (Sanglamore (USA))
2218[6] 2979[5] 3658[4] 5573[12] 6610[9]

Spoken *R Charlton* 76
2 ch c Medicean—Spout (Salse (USA))
5831[4] ◆ (6393)

Sponge *P R Chamings* a38 53
4 b g Zaha(CAN) —Glensara (Petoski)
3158[11] 3919[7] 4263[16]

Spoof Master (IRE) *C R Dore* a73 81
5 b g Invincible Spirit(IRE) —Talbiya (IRE) (Mujtahid (USA))
99[5] 177[3] 1587[6] 2579[4] 2745[5] 2924[5] 3735[6] (6939) 7651[6] 7839[7]

Sporting Gesture *M W Easterby* a32 77
12 ch g Safawan—Polly Packer (Reform)
1366[6] 1654[8] 2068[10] 2573[7] 3563[5] (4350) 4755[5] 5698[8] 5962[4]

Spotty Muldoon (IRE) *R M Beckett* a41 77
4 b g Mull Of Kintyre(USA) —Fashion Guide (IRE) (Bluebird (USA))
1524[11] 2387[9] 2977[10]

Spouk *L M Cumani* a79 85
4 b m Pivotal—Souk (IRE) (Ahonoora)
4328[2]

Spring Adventure *E A L Dunlop* a77 78
3 b f Dr Fong(USA) —Yavari (IRE) (Alzao (USA))
1302[3] (1963) ◆ 2399[7] 3400[4] 3921[3] 4440[3] 5745[7] 6977[7]

Spring Breeze *J J Quinn* a59 62
8 ch g Dr Fong(USA) —Trading Aces (Be My Chief (USA))
3760[3]

Spring Bridge (IRE) *Mrs L C Jewell* a43 33
3 b g Tagula(IRE) —Miss Lainey (IRE) (Woodborough (USA))
3773[4] 4303[11] 4786[10] 5283[11] 5645[3] 6119[11] 6206[7]

Spring Fashion (IRE) *M Botti* a51 48
3 b f Galileo(IRE) —Darina (IRE) (Danehill (USA))
6934[6] 7278[4] 7557[7] 7687[9]

Spring Goddess (IRE) *A P Jarvis* a83 83
8 b m Daggers Drawn(USA) —Easter Girl (Efisio)
(1020) 1348[8] 3008[6] 3796[6] 5671[13] 6012[6] (6924) 7475[9]

Spring Green *H Morrison* a81 81
3 b f Bahamian Bounty—Star Tulip (Night Shift (USA))
1703[7] (2122) 2632[3] ◆ (3506) 3747[7] 4380[6] 5370[4] 6051[4] 6647[11]

Spring Hawk (IRE) *T G McCourt* a58 58
3 ch f Hawk Wing(USA) —Spring Easy (IRE) (Alzao (USA))
7798[4]

Spring Heather (IRE) *J L Dunlop* 48
2 b f Montjeu(IRE) —Spotlight (Dr Fong (USA))
5966[9] 6363[10]

Spring Jim *J R Fanshawe* 94
8 b g First Trump—Spring Sixpence (Dowsing (USA))
(999) 1347[6] (1990) 3620[4] 4340[7] 5656[6] 6036[2] 7018[8]

Spring Of Fame (USA) *Saeed Bin Suroor* a102 111
3 b c Grand Slam(USA) —Bloomy (USA) (Polish Numbers (USA))
(763) ◆ 863[2] ◆ 1678[3] 2411[3] 3050[7] (3783) (4685a) 5231[4] 6505a[11]

Spring Quartet *Pat Eddery* a56 57
3 b g Captain Rio—Alice Blackthorn (Forzando)
77[10] 506[5] 677[3] 953[3] 1070[7] 2131[3] 2350[12] 4640[7] 5328[2]

Spring Secret *B Palling* 72
3 b g Reset(AUS) —Miss Brooks (Bishop Of Cashel)
1746[7] 2350[16] 3054[7] 3502[4] 3946[3] 4425[4] 5121[5] (5384) 5503[2] (5631) 5791[2] 7247[8]

Springwell Giant (IRE) *A J McCabe* a65 49
2 ch g Choisir(AUS) —Glasnas Giant (Giant's Causeway (USA))
5543[3] 6122[3] 6431[4] 7003[8]

Sprinkler *C W Thornton* 21
6 b m Emperor Fountain—Ryewater Dream (Touching Wood (USA))
2785[5]

Spruzzo *C W Thornton* a46 36
3 b g Emperor Fountain—Ryewater Dream (Touching Wood (USA))
138[7] 621[8] 1363[13] 7750[11]

Spume (IRE) *S Parr* a60 67
5 b g Alhaarth(IRE) —Sea Spray (IRE) (Royal Academy (USA))
126[9] 237[3] 301[4] 346[5] 449[7] 534[6] 554[7] 790[8]

Sputnik One (IRE) *J S Moore* 54
2 b c Soviet Star(USA) —Walnut Lady (Forzando)
4478[10] 4915[15] 5543[13]

Spy Gun (USA) *T Wall* a53 51
9 ch g Mt. Livermore(USA) —Takeover Target (USA) (Nodouble (USA))
150[11] 175[7] 254[2] 427[8] 537[10] 578[10]

Spying *Mrs A Duffield* 91
2 ch g Observatory(USA) —Mint Royale (IRE) (Cadeaux Genereux)
(4396) (4939) 5795[12]

Squad *S Dow* a70 74
3 ch g Choisir(AUS) —Widescreen (USA) (Distant View (USA))
280[8] 506[4] 962[4] 1580[3] 2204[7] 2809[6] 3427[3] 3741[5] 4010[3] (4734) 5366[2] 5964[2] (6338) 6566[3] 7699[9] ◆

Squadron *A King* a64 70
5 b g Sakhee(USA) —Machaera (Machiavellian (USA))
1356[5]

Squander *Sir Michael Stoute* 36
3 b f Dr Fong(USA) —Ghariba (Final Straw)
4180[10]

Square Eddie (CAN) *Doug O'Neill* a116 105
3 ch c Smart Strike(CAN) —Forty Gran (USA) (El Gran Senor (USA))
7305a[10]

Square Of Gold (FR) *A W Carroll* 37
3 ch g Gold Away(IRE) —All Square (FR) (Holst (USA))
3207[6] 3590[9] 4199[10] 5632[11]

Square Pants (IRE) *J A Osborne* a46
2 b g Kheleyf(USA) —Bron Hilda (IRE) (Namaqualand (USA))
6431[10]

Squirtle (IRE) *W M Brisbourne* a69 69
6 ch m In The Wings—Manilia (FR) (Kris)
112[5] 249[5] (3073) 4388[8] 4551[6] 4848[13] 5885[4] 6859[4] 7154[3] 7214[3] 7415[3] 7649[4] (7750)

Sri Kandi *P F I Cole* a73 74
3 ch f Pivotal—Aunt Pearl (USA) (Seattle Slew (USA))
2008[7] 2384[6]

Sri Kuantan (IRE) *R C Guest* a80 82
5 ch g Spinning World(USA) —Miss Asia Quest (Rainbow Quest (USA))
683[7] 805[4] 948[2] 1261[2] 1274[4] (1635) 1878[6] 1944[3] 2374[2] 3399[7] 5185[8] 5802[10] 6002[8] 6648[15]

Sri Putra *M A Jarvis* 113
3 b c Oasis Dream—Wendylina (IRE) (In The Wings)
1354[4] 1915a[5] (4296) (5084a) 6132a[5] 7313a[7]

Stacelita (FR) *J-C Rouget* 122
3 b f Monsun(GER) —Soignee (GER) (Dashing Blade)
(2119a) (2952a) (5929a) 6526a[7]

Stadium Of Light (IRE) *H Morrison* 36
2 b g Fantastic Light(USA) —Treble Seven (USA) (Fusaichi Pegasus (USA))
3160[9] 6617[15] 6965[8]

Stafford Charlie *J G M O'Shea* a29 28
3 ch g Silver Patriarch(IRE) —Miss Roberto (IRE) (Don Roberto (USA))
659[6] 1580[12]

Staff Sergeant *M Johnston* a51
2 b c Dubawi(IRE) —Miss Particular (IRE) (Sadler's Wells (USA))
7429[7]

Stage Acclaim (IRE) *C J Down* a46 72
4 b g Acclamation—Open Stage (IRE) (Sadler's Wells (USA))
7212[6]

Stagecoach Emerald *R W Price* a62 46
7 ch g Spectrum(IRE) —Musician (Shirley Heights)
1936[9] 2419[10] 3714[7] 6785[10] (7336) 7635[4]

Stagecoach Jade (IRE) *M Johnston* a73 76
3 ch f Peintre Celebre(USA) —Starring Role (IRE) (Glenstal (USA))
(970) (1315) ◆ 2341[2] 3393[4]

Stage Dream (IRE) *Lee Smyth* a44 66
4 b m Golan(IRE) —Bernhardt (IRE) (Alzao (USA))
7142[12] 7719[11]

Stage Performance (IRE) *J H M Gosden* 31
3 ch f Danehill Dancer(IRE) —Stage Presence (IRE) (Selkirk (USA))
4991[7] 6934[8]

Stags Leap (IRE) *R Hannon* 87
2 b c Refuse To Bend(IRE) —Swingsky (IRE) (Indian Ridge)
4209[5] (4524) ◆ (5347) 6664[7]

Stalingrad (IRE) *Thomas Cleary* a68 63
4 ch g King's Best(USA) —Bold Bold (IRE) (Sadler's Wells (USA))
7785[12]

Stalking Shadow (USA) *Saeed Bin Suroor* a92 98
4 b h Storm Cat(USA) —Strategic Maneuver (USA) (Cryptoclearance (USA))
1942[4] 3116[8]

Stamford Blue *R A Harris* a46 86
8 b g Bluegrass Prince(IRE) —Fayre Holly (IRE) (Fayruz)
1403[6] 1540[6] 2202[9] 2353[10] 3283[7] 3505[3] 3866[4] (4082) 4268[3] 4536[6] 5184[8] 5502[8] 5719[14]

Stand And Fight (IRE) *Kevin Prendergast* a83 89
2 b g Invincible Spirit(IRE) —Up On Points (Royal Academy (USA))
2995[14]

Stand Guard *P Howling* a96 70
5 b g Danehill(USA) —Protectress (Hector Protector (USA))
79[2] 271[4] 453[4] (713) (847) 1003[8] 1460[19] 1990[16] 4644[4] 5640[2] 6435[11] 7194[3] (7375) 7574[8] 7827[9]

Stand In Flames *George Baker* a42 84
4 b m Celtic Swing—Maid Of Arc (USA) (Patton (USA))
1806[8] 2491[11] 3789[7] 4473[7] (4812) 5502[9] 5628[3] 6755[3] 6966[11] 7057[6] 7348[12] 7416[9]

Standpoint *Sir Michael Stoute* a75 79
3 b g Oasis Dream—Waki Music (USA) (Miswaki (USA))
1400[2] (1972) 2696[6] 3643[7]

Stanley Bridge *A Berry* 25
2 b g Avonbridge—Antonia's Folly (Music Boy)
2153[11] 2526[7] 3263[9] 4492[6] 6982[8] 7168[8]

Stanley Goodspeed *J W Hills* a83 76
6 ch g Inchinor—Flying Carpet (Barathea (IRE))
954[4] 1186[8] 2071[6] 2276[6] 2927[7] 3469[6] 4009[4] 4236[5] 4816[5] 5502[2] 5813[3] 6437[2] 6637[6] 7321[7] 7480[3] 7716[7] 7870[11]

Stanley Rigby *C F Wall* 41
3 b g Dr Fong(USA) —Crystal (IRE) (Danehill (USA))
2199[11] 5322[6]

Stan's Cool Cat (IRE) *P F I Cole* a81 89
3 b f One Cool Cat(USA) —Beautiful France (IRE) (Sadler's Wells (USA))
2544[7] 3400[3] (4050) 5009[3] 5648[9] 6286[4] 7366[4] 7540[6]

Stanstill (IRE) *G A Swinbank* 94
3 b g Statue Of Liberty(USA) —Fervent Wish (Rainbow Quest (USA))
1693[2] 2042[2] 2767[2] (3371) (4299) (4785) 6095[6]

Star Acclaim *E V Stanford* a48 67
4 b m Acclamation—Tropical Lass (IRE) (Ballad Rock)
2852[16] 3713[13] 4171[7] 4376[9] 5883[5]

Star Addition *E J Alston* 61
3 ch g Medicean—Star Cast (IRE) (In The Wings)
2820[6] 3611[14] 4531[10] 5041[8] 6379[3] ◆ 6410[7] 6823[2] 6988[5]

Starbougg *K G Reveley* 27
5 b m Tobougg(IRE) —Celestial Welcome (Most Welcome)
7084[11]

Starburst *A M Balding* a67 61
4 b m Fantastic Light(USA) —Rasmalai (Sadler's Wells (USA))
1287[12] 6760[5] 7367[2] 7590[2] (7790)

Starburst Excel *M G Quinlan* a46 69
2 b f Exceed And Excel(AUS) —Homeward (IRE) (Kris)
1298[4] 1991[5] 3772[8] 6494[8] 6970[8]

Star Choice *J Pearce* a72 72
4 ch g Choisir(AUS) —Bay Queen (Damister (USA))
103[2] ◆ 319[4] 559[2] 732[5] (836) 1081[4] 1178[2] 1319[5] 1960[2] 2294[10] 2975[4] 3950[7] 4449[5] 7695[11]

Starclass *W R Swinburn* 68
2 b f Starcraft(NZ) —Classic Millennium (Midyan (USA))
6730[7] ◆

Starcross Maid *A G Juckes* a59 61
7 ch m Zaha(CAN) —Maculatus (USA) (Sharpen Up)
790[6] 918[3] 1651[2]

Star Crowned (USA) *R Bouresly* a110 110
6 b h Kingmambo(USA) —Fashion Star (USA) (Chief's Crown (USA))
264a[2] 418a[5] 525a[2] 641a[2]

Star Cruiser (USA) *T D Easterby* 49
2 b g Golden Missile(USA) —Beautiful Star (USA) (War Chant (USA))
2997[12] 4430[8]

Stardust Memories (UAE) *John Berry* a35
3 b f Halling(USA) —Clarinda (IRE) (Lomond (USA))
5751[12] 6794[12] 7367[10]

Starfala *P F I Cole* a89 106
4 gr m Galileo(IRE) —Farfala (FR) (Linamix (FR))
1859[2] 2482[4] 3619[3] 4458[8] 5202[7] 5796[2] 6854[6]

Stargaze (IRE) *A Bailey* a88 98
2 b c Oasis Dream—Dafariyna (IRE) (Nashwan (USA))
1323[14] 1577[4] (1835) ◆ (4221) ◆ 4487[3] 6105[5] 7806[2]

Stargazing (IRE) *B J Meehan* 37
3 b f Galileo(IRE) —Autumnal (IRE) (Indian Ridge)
6390[9]

Stargazy *A J Lidderdale* a56 51
5 b g Observatory(USA) —Romantic Myth (Mind Games)
23[12] (104) 242[6] 277[3] 473[10] 7609[14] 7768[11]

Star Godess (FR) *J De Roualle* 80
5 b m Testa Rossa(AUS) —Aglaya (FR) (Tropular)
7822a[2]

Starkat *Jane Chapple-Hyam* a36 74
3 b f Diktat—Star Of Normandie (USA) (Gulch (USA))
2710[11] 4151[2] 6794[4]

Stark Contrast (USA) *M D I Usher* a68 49
5 ch g Gulch(USA) —A Stark Is Born (USA) (Graustark)
125[8] 238[6] 580[5] 657[7] 898[4] 1042[8] 1133[8] 1495[6] 2011[8] 2650[3] 2808[8] 3258[6] 7586[3] 7653[6] 7856[12]

Starla Dancer (GER) *R A Fahey* a74 84
3 b f Danehill Dancer(IRE) —Starla (GER) (Lando (GER))
1888[3] 2375[2] 3238[4] 4347[2] 4655[2] 5259[4] 6257[4] (6680) 7014[2]

Starlight (FR) *E Libaud* a58 67
3 b f Xaar—Sakura Moon (IRE) (Cadeaux Genereux)
(5118a)

Starlight Boy *S Wynne*
2 b c Firebreak—Dispol Verity (Averti (IRE))
5958[8]

Starlight Gazer *J A Geake* a62 87
6 b g Observatory(USA) —Dancing Fire (USA) (Dayjur (USA))
7321[12] 7728[5]

Star Links (USA) *R Hannon* a85 87
3 b c Bernstein(USA) —Startarette (USA) (Dixieland Band (USA))
2174[4] 2329[2] 3030[3] 3868[3] 4210[2] 4540[6] 5189[4] 5832[7] 6243[11] 6537[6]

Starlish (IRE) *E Lellouche* a103 115
4 b h Rock Of Gibraltar(IRE) —Stylish (Anshan)
3085a[2] 6506a[5] (7102a) 7747a[6]

Starlit Sands *Sir Mark Prescott* a103 105
4 b m Oasis Dream—Shimmering Sea (Slip Anchor)
1582[10] 5507[7]

Starmaamul *K A Ryan*
2 b g Elmaamul(USA) —Catwalk Girl (Skyliner)
5407[10]

Starmaria (FR) *N Leenders* a84 86
5 b m Starborough—Fair Pay (FR) (Bluebird (USA))
4365a[10]

Starmendi (FR) *P Lhoste* 75
4 b m Starborough—Anna Maria (IRE) (Turtle Island (IRE))
7265a[5]

Star Of Kalani (IRE) *G M Moore* 38
2 b g Ashkalani(IRE) —La Bekkah (FR) (Nononito (FR))
5466[8] 6792[14] 7120[12]

Star Of Memory (FR) *D G Bridgwater* 36
5 b g Starborough—Desert Memory (FR) (Desert King (IRE))
5061[7] 6392[8]

Star Of Pompey *A B Haynes* a62 63
5 b m Hernando(FR) —Discerning (Darshaan)
2601[11] (3275) 3997[2] 4301[5] 5425[7] 6622[6] 6785[7]

Star Of Soho (IRE) *E J Creighton* 36
2 b f Starcraft(NZ) —Trois Graces (USA) (Alysheba (USA))
7182[16]

Star Of Sophia (IRE) *Mrs A Duffield* a39 7
3 b f Hawk Wing(USA) —Sofia Aurora (USA) (Chief Honcho (USA))
1183[12]

Star Pattern (USA) *M Weiss* 63
4 ch h Seeking The Gold(USA) —Starlore (USA) (Spectacular Bid (USA))
(465a)

Star Promise *T D Barron* a76 76
2 b f Mujahid(USA) —Diamond Promise (IRE) (Fayruz)
3032[7] (4370) 4875[2] 6827[10] 7850[2]

Star Rover (IRE) *P D Evans* a82 102
2 ch c Camacho—Charlene Lacy (IRE) (Pips Pride)
(1005) (1188) (1330) (1788) 1805[3] 2408[2] 2995[6] 3046[7] 4089[6] 4407[4] (5174) 5822[7] 6486[13] 6660[7]

Star Ruby (IRE) *P W Chapple-Hyam* 109
3 b f Rock Of Gibraltar(IRE) —Purple Spirit (IRE) (Sadler's Wells (USA))
(1488) 1988[2] ◆

Starry Mount *A B Haynes* 73
2 ch c Observatory(USA) —Lady Lindsay (IRE) (Danehill Dancer (IRE))
4933^7 5512^4 6136^5 (7168)

Starstreamer (IRE) *M P Tregoning* 31
2 ch f Captain Rio—Petra Nova (First Trump)
5026^{11}

Star Strider *T Keddy* a80 67
5 gr g Royal Applause—Onefortheditch (USA) (With Approval (CAN))
238^2 398^4 544^5 1179^6 1401^7 2330^9 2713^4 3007^5 4305^9 4732^3 5031^{11} 6926^{15} 7236^5 7412^6 (7592) 7798^{10} 7861^7

Starstruck Peter (IRE) *Jim Best* a58 64
5 b g Iron Mask(USA) —Daraliya (IRE) (Kahyasi)
346^8 528^8 (3503) (3774) 3927^{10}

Start Right *L M Cumani* a82 83
2 b c Footstepsinthesand—Time Crystal (IRE) (Sadler's Wells (USA))
3692^{10} 4286^6 ◆ 5527^2 5864^3 6285^2 (6672)

Star Twilight *D R Lanigan* a45 58
2 b f King's Best(USA) —Star Express (Sadler's Wells (USA))
3820^8 4239^4 7325^{11} 7619^{12}

Starwatch *J J Bridger* a59 82
2 b g Observatory(USA) —Trinity Reef (Bustino)
4336^7 4826^2 5994^6 6057^6 6737^8 7235^4 7513^4 7824^4

Stash *R Hollinshead* a81 42
3 b g Bold Edge—Gemtastic (Tagula (IRE))
288^3 560^3 784^6 6791^{13} 7122^9 7398^5 7673^7

State Banquet (USA) *H Morrison* a82 90
3 br g Fusaichi Pegasus(USA) —Gracie Lady (IRE) (Generous (IRE))
2210^2 ◆ 3695^3 4420^2 5315^5 6203^6

State Fair *P F I Cole* a31 79
2 b g Marju(IRE) —Baralinka (IRE) (Barathea (IRE))
1323^5 ◆ 2147^2 2477^3 6754^3 7029^7 7209^9

State Function (IRE) *G Prodromou* a20 60
4 b g Grand Slam(USA) —Well Designed (IRE) (Sadler's Wells (USA))
1956^6 6256^{10}

State Gathering *H Candy* 55
2 b c Royal Applause—Flag (Selkirk (USA))
6615^9 7145^9 ◆

State General (IRE) *Miss J Feilden* a81 64
3 b g Statue Of Liberty(USA) —Nisibis (In The Wings)
(101) 1303^{10} 2829^7 4602^8 6680^P

Stately Home (IRE) *A P O'Brien* 100
3 b c Montjeu(IRE) —Pescia (IRE) (Darshaan)
2029^2 3090^6 4962a^6 (Dead)

Stateside (CAN) *R A Fahey* a12 68
4 b m El Corredor(USA) —Double Trick (USA) (Phone Trick (USA))
1974^2 (2390) (3481) 3545^2 4068^5 5160^3 5698^{14}

State Visit *W R Muir* a64 59
2 b c Dr Fong(USA) —Saint Ann (USA) (Geiger Counter (USA))
5907^8 6285^7 7024^5

Station Place *A B Haynes* a39 55
4 b m Bahamian Bounty—Twin Time (Syrtos)
1940^9 4305^{13} 5283^5 7068^9

Statute Book (IRE) *S Kirk* a76 72
3 br c Statue Of Liberty(USA) —Velvet Slipper (Muhtafal (USA))
(620) (707) (851) 1056^3 2600^9 3358^4 3644^7 4083^3 4322^3 5169^3 5574^{10} 6024^6 6370^7

Stay Cool (FR) *D Smaga* a54 67
3 b c One Cool Cat(USA) —A La Longue (GER) (Mtoto)
7386a^6

Staying On (IRE) *W R Swinburn* a84 110
4 b g Invincible Spirit(IRE) —Lakatoi (Saddlers' Hall (IRE))
(1346) 1799^2 2410^6 3882a^2 4780^5 5447^6

Stay On Track (IRE) *E F Vaughan* 9
2 b c Refuse To Bend(IRE) —Blue Lightning (Machiavellian (USA))
2771^{13}

Steady As A Rock (FR) *S Peto* 81
5 ch h Rock Of Gibraltar(IRE) —Metisse (USA) (Kingmambo (USA))
7303a^5

Steady Gaze *M A Allen* a40 28
4 b g Zamindar(USA) —Krisia (Kris)
444^8 578^7 1081^{10}

Steamer (IRE) *P Winkworth* 32
3 b g Xaar—Antigone (IRE) (Cape Cross (IRE))
2009^8 2355^7 3501^9

Steel Blue *R M Whitaker* a52 75
9 b g Atraf—Something Blue (Petong)
1849^{10} 2276^{11} 3066^7 3354^{13} 3852^6 4285^7 4399^7 4654^6 (5159) 5406^2 5675^4 5804^5 6413^{11} 7358^7 7418^8

Steel City Boy (IRE) *D Shaw* a76 75
6 b g Bold Fact(USA) —Balgren (IRE) (Ballad Rock)
83^4 243^4 400^5 (582) 971^5 6028^{12} 6635^{10} 6877^9 7122^8 7330^7 7601^9 7807^7

Steelcut *M J Scudamore* a74 85
5 b g Iron Mask(USA) —Apple Sauce (Prince Sabo)
1227^3 ◆ (1334) ◆ 1672^5 2095^3 2716^{13} 2897^5 3149^4 3268^8 4043^4 4461^{19} 4899^4 5147^2 5436^7 5946^3 (5989) 6396^3 6632^8 7758^{11}

Steele Tango (USA) *R A Teal* a78 113
4 ch h Okawango(USA) —Waltzing Around (IRE) (Ela-Mana-Mou)
1301^2 1526^4 1859^3 2410^7 3139^8 3640^5 6526a^{19} (6812)

Steeley Flyer *P D Evans* a18 42
2 b f Needwood Blade—Gymcrak Flyer (Aragon)
2311^8 2996^7 3547^2 3958^5 4747^7

Steel Free (IRE) *M L W Bell* a67 76
3 b f Danehill Dancer(IRE) —Candelabra (Grand Lodge (USA))
1327^2 2151^3 (3590) 4228^7 5090^6 5591^6 6015^4 6997^5

Steel Giant (USA) *J J Lambe* 44
4 b g Giant's Causeway(USA) —Ride The Wind (USA) (Meadowlake (USA))
4599^{10}

Steel Mask (IRE) *M Brittain* a37 47
4 b h Iron Mask(USA) —Thorn Tree (Zafonic (USA))
7709^9

Steel My Heart (IRE) *Miss D Mountain* a44 45
2 b f Clodovil(IRE) —Antigonel (IRE) (Fairy King (USA))
3547^{10} 4153^4 4757^6 4973^5 5583^8

Steel Stockholder *M Brittain* a52 70
3 b c Mark Of Esteem(IRE) —Pompey Blue (Abou Zouz (USA))
1335^3 1561^6 1736^6 2091^4 2662^7 3342^5 3727^4 4284^4 4548^8 4846^4 5258^2 5624^2 6101^2 (6997) 7729^{10}

Steel Trade *M Brittain* 75
3 b g Sakhee(USA) —Hammiya (IRE) (Darshaan)
1308^6 1683^5 1950^2 2937^7 3238^3 3690^4 4230^7 4655^3 4892^6 5259^3 6182^4

Steely Bird *Miss Jo Crowley* 60
2 gr g Needwood Blade—La Cygne Blanche (IRE) (Saddlers' Hall (IRE))
6393^{10} 6931^{10}

Steeple Caster *J M Bradley*
3 ch g Compton Place—Antonia's Double (Primo Dominie)
1419^8 2122^{11}

Stef And Stelio *G A Butler* a74 42
2 ch g Bertolini(USA) —Cashmere (Barathea (IRE))
2187^{10} 3613^9 4839^3 5256^9 (5613) 6948^2 7320^{11}

Stefanki (IRE) *R Curtis* a54 75
2 b g Danehill Dancer(IRE) —Ghana (IRE) (Lahib (USA))
5867^2 ◆ 6991^8 7580^8

Stefer (USA) *D Smaga* 104
3 ch f Johannesburg(USA) —Ardere (USA) (El Prado (IRE))
1208a^6 2521a^9

Steig (IRE) *C Moore* a74 88
6 b g Xaar—Ring Of Kerry (IRE) (Kenmare (FR))
1495^2 1690^6 2243^3 2378^3 (2807) 3245^2 5490a^{18}

Steinbeck (IRE) *A P O'Brien* 116
2 b c Footstepsinthesand—Castara Beach (IRE) (Danehill (USA))
(1994a) 6849^4 ◆

Stella Di Quattro *Uwe Ostmann* 104
5 b m Best Of The Bests(IRE) —Search For Love (FR) (Groom Dancer (USA))
1143a^8 1597a^9 2428a^{11} 4365a^4 5296a^8

Stella Francesca (FR) *C Boutin* a50 59
3 b f Della Francesca(USA) —Rince Deas (IRE) (Alzao (USA))
7386a^0

Stellar Cause (USA) *P F I Cole* 71
3 ch g Giant's Causeway(USA) —Stellar (USA) (Grand Slam (USA))
2074^5 2981^{14} 3207^4 5940^7 6248^6

Stellarina (IRE) *G A Swinbank* a68 65
3 b f Night Shift(USA) —Accelerating (USA) (Lear Fan (USA))
1173^{10} 1743^3 2769^{14}

Stellino (GER) *James Moffatt* 79
6 b g Monashee Mountain(USA) —Sweet Tern (GER) (Arctic Tern (USA))
6100^8

Stellite *J S Goldie* a71 77
9 ch g Pivotal—Donation (Generous (IRE))
1734^8 (2156) 2453^7 (3097) 3656^6 4133^2 4775^4 4878^2 5333^2 6015^{13} 6309^4 6985^2 7171^3

Stelrock (FR) *P Bary* 77
2 b c Kingsalsa(USA) —Hill Tiger (IRE) (Indian Ridge)
(5561a)

Step At A Time (IRE) *M Johnston* 4
3 ch f Danehill Dancer(IRE) —Zing Ping (IRE) (Thatching)
3703^8

Step Fast (USA) *M Johnston* a37 44
3 ch f Giant's Causeway(USA) —Nannerl (USA) (Valid Appeal (USA))
1724^{11} 2627^4 3482^{10}

Step In Time (IRE) *M Johnston* 83
2 b c Giant's Causeway(USA) —Cash Run (USA) (Seeking The Gold (USA))
1866^2 (2280) 3138^7 3842^2 5136^{16} 5795^{13} 6317a^{19}

Step Into Sunshine (USA) *M Johnston* 34
3 b f The Cliff's Edge(USA) —Iridescence (USA) (Mt. Livermore (USA))
4505^8 5072^7 5348^6

Step It Up (IRE) *J R Boyle* a83 77
5 ch g Daggers Drawn(USA) —Leitrim Lodge (IRE) (Classic Music (USA))
167^4 461^2 582^2 645^2 710^3 2180^3 2680^6 3775^3 3998^6 4604^8 4907^2 (5156) (5219) 5477^9 6118^2 6666^4 (6916) 6972^3

Stepping Up (IRE) *E Charpy* a81 91
6 ch g Soviet Star(USA) —Rise And Fall (Mill Reef (USA))
265a^5 340a^{13} 521a^7 609a^6

Step This Way (USA) *M Johnston* a83 92
4 ch m Giant's Causeway(USA) —Lady In Waiting (USA) (Woodman (USA))
1059^4 1230^4 1473^3 1878^5 2283^2 2452^2 2895^{10} 4696^3 4948^9 5235^{13}

Step To It (IRE) *K A Ryan* 23
3 b g Footstepsinthesand—Lilly Gee (IRE) (Ashkalani (IRE))
2896^{12} 5519^8 5942^9

Sterling Moll *W De Best-Turner* a37 46
6 gr m Lord Of Men—Princess Maud (USA) (Irish River (FR))
3143^9

Sterling Prince (NZ) *Wayne Hillis* 112
6 b g Colombia(NZ) —Sterling Princess (NZ) (One Pound Sterling)
6961a^3

Sterling Sound (USA) *M P Tregoning* a66 94
3 b f Street Cry(IRE) —Lady In Silver (USA) (Silver Hawk (USA))
1808^3 3408^3 (4337) 4903^3 5472^9

Sternian *M E Rimmer* a26
2 ch f Where Or When(IRE) —Fly In Style (Hernando (FR))
7865^6

Sternlight (IRE) *E S McMahon* 70
2 b c Kheleyf(USA) —Sail By Night (USA) (Nureyev (USA))
5317^8 6000^4 6364^3

Stern Opinion (USA) *P Bary* 112
4 rg h Mizzen Mast(USA) —Helstra (USA) (Nureyev (USA))
(4637a) 5928a^2 6522a^9

Steuben (GER) *J Hirschberger* 92
3 ch c Monsun(GER) —Schwarzach (GER) (Grand Lodge (USA))
7039a^3

Stevie Gee (IRE) *Ian Williams* a77 96
5 b g Invincible Spirit(IRE) —Margaree Mary (CAN) (Seeking The Gold (USA))
1467^7 1849^9 2266^8 2780^2 3001^9 (3265) 3615^5 4310^7 4597^9 6732^{14} 7060^7 7252^9

Stevie Thunder *Ian Williams* a64 94
4 ch g Storming Home—Social Storm (USA) (Future Storm (USA))
1527^3 2101^4 3796^4 4560^9 5137^2 6013^5 6480^6 6665^8

St Ignatius *R M Beckett* a65
2 b g Ishiguru(USA) —Branston Berry (IRE) (Mukaddamah (USA))
6372^8 7024^4 7700^5 ◆

Still Dreaming *R J Price* a61 54
5 ch m Singspiel(IRE) —Three Green Leaves (IRE) (Environment Friend)
237^7 5097^6 5444^5 5962^{12}

Stimulation (IRE) *H Morrison* 118
4 b h Choisir(AUS) —Damiana (IRE) (Thatching)
5862^5 ◆ 6058^4

St Jean Cap Ferrat *S Jensen* a76 93
4 bb g Domedriver(IRE) —Miss Cap Ferrat (Darshaan)
1593^{13} 2468^7 (3578) 4585a^6

St Moritz (IRE) *M Johnston* a95 97
3 b g Medicean—Statua (IRE) (Statoblest)
(98) (432) ◆ 1395a^5

St Nicholas Abbey (IRE) *A P O'Brien* 123
2 b c Montjeu(IRE) —Leaping Water (Sure Blade (USA))
(6318a) ◆ (7017) ◆

Stockman *H Morrison* a44
5 b g Kylian(USA) —Fabriana (Northern State (USA))
11^8 744^5 918^8 1586^8

Stoic (IRE) *J Noseda* a103 99
3 b g Green Desert(USA) —Silver Bracelet (Machiavellian (USA))
5100^2 (5435) ◆ (5832) ◆ (6229) ◆

Stoic Leader (IRE) *R F Fisher* a65 78
9 b g Danehill Dancer(IRE) —Starlust (Sallust)
427^4 531^7 682^2 1153^7 1246^4 1401^8 1887^9 2968^4 3448^6 3655^4 4861^6 7600^7 7718^9 7754^7

Stolen Affection *J R Weymes*
2 b g Pursuit Of Love—Thieves Welcome (Most Welcome)
5942^{11}

Stolt (IRE) *N Wilson* a84 93
5 b g Tagula(IRE) —Cabcharge Princess (IRE) (Rambo Dancer (CAN))
2012^{15} 2363^7 2716^{11} 3149^5 4891^8 5293^6 5767^6 (5856) 6051^{13} 6843^{14} 7202^6 7414^8 7758^4

Stoneacre Baby (USA) *Peter Grayson* a36 35
4 ch m Stravinsky(USA) —Katiba (USA) (Gulch (USA))
46^8 681^8 884^{10} 2157^8 2625^{10}

Stoneacre Donny (IRE) *Peter Grayson* a54 22
5 br h Lend A Hand—Election Special (Chief Singer)
57^5 153^{10} 2032^{10} 2473^{16}

Stoneacre Joe (IRE) *Peter Grayson*
2 b c Iron Mask(USA) —Jarmar Moon (Unfuwain (USA))
6443^7 7485^8 7850^4

Stoneacre Lad (IRE) *Peter Grayson* a106 82
6 b h Bluebird(USA) —Jay And-A (IRE) (Elbio)
359^8 911^{10} 1052^6 1384^5 2012^9 2094^4 2502^{11} 2897^4 3212^9 4135^{14} 4842^6 5293^5

Stoneacre Pat (IRE) *Peter Grayson* a56 51
4 b h Iron Mask(USA) —Sans Ceriph (IRE) (Thatching)
449 165^8 681^{10} 896^8 1134^6 7223^{11} 7657^9

Stonecrabstomorrow (IRE) *R A Fahey* a80 78
6 b g Fasliyev(USA) —Tordasia (IRE) (Dr Devious (IRE))
87^3 245^2 (475) (757) 843^2 1103^2 1229^3 (1689) (1924) 2402^{13}

Stonehaugh (IRE) *J Howard Johnson* 81
6 b g King Charlemagne(USA) —Canary Bird (IRE) (Catrail (USA))
1060^8 1723^5 (2531) 4621^7

Stone Legacy (USA) *D Wayne Lukas* a86
3 b f Birdstone(USA) —Gulch Legacy (USA) (Gulch (USA))
1763a^2

Stone Of Scone *E A L Dunlop* a89 103
4 b g Pivotal—Independence (Selkirk (USA))
(1593) 1986^3 ◆ 3089^{15}

Stoop To Conquer *A W Carroll* a77 72
9 b g Polar Falcon(USA) —Princess Genista (Ile De Bourbon (USA))
751^6 3593^4 7124^8

Stop Making Sense *R Pritchard-Gordon* a90 104
7 b g Lujain(USA) —Freeway (FR) (Exit To Nowhere (USA))
(7216a) 7621a^7

Storey Hill (USA) *D Shaw* a81 53
4 bb g Richter Scale(USA) —Crafty Nan (USA) (Crafty Prospector (USA))
170^7 442^4 582^7 757^{10}

Stormbeam (USA) *G A Butler* a59 64
4 b g Tale Of The Cat(USA) —Broad Smile (USA) (Broad Brush (USA))
2601^8

Stormburst (IRE) *A J Chamberlain* a51 49
5 b m Mujadil(USA) —Isca (Caerleon (USA))
104^7 153^7 314^6 666^9 746^{10} 2534^4 6028^{11} 7068^8 7771^3 7869^6

Storm Command (IRE) *B Smart* 59
2 ch g Halling(USA) —Clarinda (IRE) (Lomond (USA))
4396^{13} 4705^5 5466^4 5951^2 6391^9

Stormglass *W R Muir* 50
2 ch c Galileo(IRE) —Aberdovey (Mister Baileys)
6200^6 6478^{21} (Dead)

Storm Hawk (IRE) *Pat Eddery* 70
2 b g Hawk Wing(USA) —Stormy Larissa (IRE) (Royal Applause)
2636^5 3064^5 3306^3 4190^2 4931^{11} 5935^8 6736^{12} 6901^4

Stormhill (AUS) *Clinton McDonald* 112
8 b h Danehill(USA) —Torrential Storm (NZ) (Sir Tristram)
6961a^4

Storming Sioux *W J Haggas* a64 68
3 b f Storming Home—Sueboog (IRE) (Darshaan)
1745^2 3061^2 4655^7 6375^3 6941^4

Storm Mountain (IRE) *B Grizzetti* 110
6 b h Montjeu(IRE) —Lady Storm (IRE) (Mujadil (USA))
2115a^7 6153a^6

Stormy Blues (FR) *P Munsch* 48
3 b g Green Tune(USA) —Matin De Tempete (FR) (Cardoun (FR))
5784a^0

Stormy Morning *W R Swinburn* a63 65
3 ch g Nayef(USA) —Sokoa (USA) (Peintre Celebre (USA))
1407^{10} 1573^9 4022^4 4545^8 (5382) 5990^8 6457^7

Stormy's Prelude *P Winkworth* a60 61
3 ch f Alhaarth(IRE) —Far Reaching (USA) (Distant View (USA))
529^3 1198^5 2051^P

Stormy Summer *R W Price* a69 61
4 b g Observatory(USA) —Khambani (IRE) (Royal Academy (USA))
1260^7 2244^7 3158^8 3714^6 5004^7 7272^2 7505^8 7712^2 7842^{10}

Stormy Weather (FR) *J Howard Johnson* 102
3 gr g Highest Honor(FR) —Stormy Moud (USA) (Storm Bird (CAN))
2275^3 7293^{22}

Storyland (USA) *W J Haggas* a96 95
4 b m Menifee(USA) —Auspice (USA) (Robellino (USA))
1696^{11} 2706^4 ◆ 3103^5 4340^6 5202^9 6113^2 6302^5 7131^3

Stotsfold *W R Swinburn* a95 119
6 b g Barathea(IRE) —Eliza Acton (Shirley Heights)
1525^4 2410^3 (3085a) 4809a^3 5875^2 6506a^4 6812^6

Strabinios King *A Berry* a84 73
5 b g King's Best(USA) —Strawberry Morn (CAN) (Travelling Victor (CAN))
191^3 (218) 297^2 ◆ 446^3 1649^{11} 2045^9 2389^9 2658^9 3467^9 4133^6 5147^8

Straboe (USA) *S C Williams* a53 53
3 b g Green Desert(USA) —Staff Nurse (USA) (Arch (USA))
1047^{11} 1423^{10} 3637^{10} (4718) 7834^5

Straight And Level (CAN) *Miss Jo Crowley* a72 63
4 gr g Buddha(USA) —Azusa (USA) (Flying Paster (USA))
398^{10} 737^7 7364^7 7586^8

Straight Face (IRE) *Miss Gay Kelleway* a61 61
5 b g Princely Heir(IRE) —Dakota Sioux (IRE) (College Chapel)
114^{13} 222^5 327^3 472^2 (748) 792^6 1558^6 (1734) 1889^{11} 2921^7 3717^6 3948^7 4312^3 4665^3 5602^5 5730^8 (6213) 6587^{11} (6782) 7349^9 7726^4

Straight Laced *W J Knight* 55
3 b f Refuse To Bend(IRE) —Gaelic Swan (IRE) (Nashwan (USA))
1893^6 2181^6 2877^{11}

Straitjacket *Miss J R Tooth* a57 70
3 b f Refuse To Bend(IRE) —Thara'A (IRE) (Desert Prince (IRE))
1322^3 2321^{15} (2630) 2683^6 3302^{11} 3948^8 4202^{14}

Straits Of Hormuz (USA) *M Johnston* a66 84
3 rg f War Chant(USA) —Tjinouska (USA) (Cozzene (USA))
(3456) 4050^3 4274^3 5771^6 6671^5

Strait Street (IRE) *P Winkworth* a29
2 gr f Verglas(IRE) —Savoy Street (Vettori (IRE))
7135^{14}

Strandhill (IRE) *Brian Nolan* 65
2 bb f Footstepsinthesand—Cosabawn (IRE) (Barathea (IRE))
4028a^5

Strange Fiction *R A Fahey*
2 ch c Avonbridge—Science Fiction (Starborough)
1275^{12} 1624^9 (Dead)

Strataciella (USA) *G Henrot*
3 u f Aldebaran(USA) — (Diesis)
6753a^0

Strategic Knight (USA) *R C Guest* a62 61
4 b g Johannesburg(USA) —Western Friend (USA) (Gone West (USA))
280^{10} 362^8 478^7 715^7 1258^{12} 1401^4 1538^{11} 2149^{11} 2332^{10} 2420^{13} 3490^{13} 3717^{10}

Strategic Mount *P F I Cole* a63 106
6 b g Montjeu(IRE) —Danlu (USA) (Danzig (USA))
3142^{16} 4340^{15} 5170^7 ◆

Strategic Mover (USA) *P Butler* a71 77
4 ch g Grand Slam(USA) —Efficient Frontier (USA) (Mt. Livermore (USA))
1185^5 6856^6 7057^3 7323^8 7440^{12} 7586^{12} 7668^8 7834^4

Strategic News (AUS) *H J Brown* 111
6 ch h Strategic(AUS) —Sensuous (AUS) (Grand Lodge (USA))
(340a) 640a^2 774a^7

Strategic Princess (IRE) *P F I Cole* a57 57
3 b f Hawk Wing(USA) —Puteri Wentworth (Sadler's Wells (USA))
2877^7 3250^5 *3951^4* 4935^5 5430^4 *5990^{11}*

Strategos (FR) *Mlle A Imaz-Ceca*
2 ch c Ballingarry(IRE) —Parallel Universe (Hector Protector (USA))
7316a^9

Stratford Bridge *J L Spearing* 12
6 b g Fraam—Moorland Stroll (IRE) (Inzar (USA))
6551^{10}

Strathcal *H Morrison* a79 82
3 b g Beat Hollow—Shall We Run (Hotfoot)
1747^4 (2204) (2850) ◆ 3587^2 4442^3 4988^6 *7178^3 7476^3*

Strathmore (IRE) *R A Fahey* a73 68
5 gr g Fath(USA) —In The Highlands (Petong)
235^3 380^3 691^7 762^2 1310^2 1518^7 2032^6 2534^2 2812^4 3562^9 3938^4 4141^7 4894^4 5159^4 5396^4 5729^{10} 6220^{14}

Stratton Banker (IRE) *S C Williams* 51
2 b g One Cool Cat(USA) —Birthday (IRE) (Singspiel (IRE))
4699^7 5722^7

Stravella (IRE) *R M Beckett* 80
4 b m Stravinsky(USA) —Princess Ellen (Tirol)
1804^5 (2317) 2775^5 3627^3 ◆ 4526^{10}

Straversjoy *R Hollinshead* a25 44
2 b f Kayf Tara—Stravsea (Handsome Sailor)
6992^{18} 7243^8 *7638^{10}*

Stravita *R Hollinshead* a68 63
5 b m Weet-A-Minute(IRE) —Stravsea (Handsome Sailor)
8^5 301^3 7425^8 7642^5 7751^6 7840^6

Stravonian *D A Nolan* 47
9 b g Luso—In The Evening (IRE) (Distinctly North (USA))
1102^7

Strawberrydaiquiri *Sir Michael Stoute* 116
3 gr f Dansili—Strawberry Morn (CAN) (Travelling Victor (CAN))
1406^2 ◆ (2139) (3641) ◆ (4259) (5260) ◆ 6479^4 ◆

Strawberry Moon (IRE) *B Smart* 79
4 b m Alhaarth(IRE) —Dancing Drop (Green Desert (USA))
(1923) 2313^4

Stream Cat (USA) *Patrick L Biancone* a108 117
6 br h Black Minnaloushe(USA) —Water Course (USA) (Irish River (FR))
789a^{10}

Street Crime *R Lee* a66 65
4 b g Tagula(IRE) —Brandon Princess (Waajib)
3223^9

Street Devil (USA) *R Curtis* a80 73
4 gr g Street Cry(IRE) —Math (USA) (Devil's Bag (USA))
(1054) 1415^4 *1479^3* 2263^6

Street Diva (USA) *A B Haynes* a64 42
4 ch m Street Cry(IRE) —Arctic Valley (USA) (Arctic Tern (USA))
1417^7 4697^9 5184^{11} 5501^5 5632^9

Street Entertainer (IRE) *Mrs A J Perrett* a80 50
2 br c Danehill Dancer(IRE) —Opera Ridge (FR) (Indian Ridge)
6620^9 *7388^2* ◆ *7522^4*

Street Power (USA) *J R Gask* a96 84
4 bb g Street Cry(IRE) —Javana (USA) (Sandpit (BRZ))
(71) (309) 387^7 (590) ◆ *757^2* 1943^3 2276^4 *(3030)* ◆ (3795) *(5167)* 5646^2 *7558^8*

Street Romance (USA) *D Smaga* a91 94
3 b f Street Cry(IRE) —Walewskaia (IRE) (Slip Anchor)
2777a^4 4334a^8

Streets Apart (USA) *W R Swinburn* a75 68
4 b m Street Cry(IRE) —Saintly Speaking (USA) (Dahar (USA))
1945^4 2331^3 3068^{13} 4054^2 4904^3 *6074^4*

Streets Of War (USA) *P W Chapple-Hyam* 57
2 bb c Street Cry(IRE) —Saint Boom (USA) (Saint Ballado (CAN))
7034^6

Street Spirit (USA) *T D Easterby* a53 51
3 bb f Street Cry(IRE) —Be Good Or Be Gone (USA) (Gulch (USA))
1061^2 1400^{11} 1592^7 *2577^3* 3018^{11} 3449^7

Street Warrior (IRE) *H J Evans* a83 55
6 b g Royal Applause—Anne Bonny (Ajdal (USA))
1014^{10}

Strensall *R E Barr* a32 56
12 b g Beveled(USA) —Payvashooz (Ballacashtal (CAN))
1921^7 2158^3 2657^{10} 3657^6 4754^4 4976^2 6314^6 6553^2 7081^8

Strevelyn *Mrs A Duffield* 47
3 br g Namid—Kali (Linamix (FR))
2236^{14} 2627^7 *3711^{10}*

Stricke (FR) *Mme C Head-Maarek* a88 98
3 b c Della Francesca(USA) —Salvia (FR) (Septieme Ciel (USA))
1207a^4 *4581a^7*

Strictly *Sir Michael Stoute* a68 87
3 b f Falbrav(IRE) —Dance On (Caerleon (USA))
1592^2 (2070) 3166^3 4244^2 4490^8 5264^2 5902^3 *6167^7*

Strictly Dancing (IRE) *A M Balding* 70
2 b f Danehill Dancer(IRE) —Lochangel (Night Shift (USA))
6054^5 6615^2

Strictly Lambada *J H M Gosden* 71
2 b f Red Ransom(USA) —Bella Lambada (Lammtarra (USA))
6920^5

Strictly Royal *M R Channon* a27 21
3 ch g Imperial Dancer—Royal Logic (Royal Applause)
1070^{10} 1270^8

Strident (USA) *N P Moore* a40 57
8 ch g Deputy Commander(USA) —Regrets Only (USA) (Black Tie Affair)
1691^{1}

Striding Edge (IRE) *W R Muir* a82 72
3 bb g Rock Of Gibraltar(IRE) —For Criquette (IRE) (Barathea (IRE))
1434^8 3115^7 3693^2 4149^3 4605^5 *(5169) 5575^2 5986^6 6496^4*

Strike A Deal (IRE) *C F Wall* 62
2 b f Chineur(FR) —Bishop's Lake (Lake Coniston (IRE))
4176^{11} 6727^6 7095^5

Strike Ballot (USA) *Mme C Head-Maarek* 87
3 b c Smart Strike(CAN) —Call Account (USA) (Private Account (USA))
1858a^8 6198a^7

Strike Force *Miss J Feilden* a70 67
5 b g Dansili—Miswaki Belle (USA) (Miswaki (USA))
341^7 478^6 571^8 1881^6 2294^2 2493^8 3244^2 3450^3 3950^5 4698^3 4972^5 *5617^3 6126^5* 6369^7 6832^4 6998^3 7143^7 7495^9

Strikemaster (IRE) *B Ellison* a54 73
3 b g Xaar—Mas A Fuera (IRE) (Alzao (USA))
295^3 677^2 953^8 1842^4 2350^3 ◆ (4142) 4470^2

Striker Torres (IRE) *B Smart* a73 80
3 ch g Danehill Dancer(IRE) —Silver Skates (IRE) (Slip Anchor)
1228^5 2072^6 2406^8 4433^5 6680^{15} 6997^{10} *7715^2 (7813)*

Strike Shot *W R Muir* a56 73
2 b g Avonbridge—Final Shot (Dalsaan)
1835^6 (2484) 2875^5 4089^{19} 4493^5 *5194^6*

Strike The Deal (USA) *J Noseda* a110 116
4 ch h Van Nistelrooy(USA) —Countess Gold (USA) (Mt. Livermore (USA))
1676^4 1989^4 *(2385)* 3140^7 3908a^5 5434^6 (5765) (6107) 7305a^{14}

Strike The Tiger (USA) *Wesley A Ward* 101
2 bb g Tiger Ridge(USA) —R Lucky Strike (USA) (In Excess)
(2995)

Strike Up The Band *D Nicholls* a103 110
6 b g Cyrano De Bergerac—Green Supreme (Primo Dominie)
264a^8 336a^{15} 525a^{10} 911^4 1189^4 1791^2 2012^6 2704^3 3848^9 5654^3 6522a^{10} *7090^4*

Striking Spirit *D Nicholls* 106
4 b g Oasis Dream—Aspiring Diva (USA) (Distant View (USA))
(1864) 2297^{10} 2707^7 3141^7 (3877) 4330^{15} 4523^8 ◆ 5039^7 5860^9 6091^{17}

Stringsofmyheart *J J Quinn* a81 82
5 b m Halling(USA) —Heart's Harmony (Blushing Groom (FR))
1478^7 2322^3

Strongarm *A Bailey* 49
3 b g Refuse To Bend(IRE) —Surf The Net (Cape Cross (IRE))
3222^{12} 3588^6 *3923^{12}*

Strong Garuda (JPN) *T Kubota* 108
3 br c Dance In The Dark(JPN) —Phoenix Bird (JPN) (Kingmambo (USA))
7498a^{14}

Strong Storm (USA) *H J Collingridge* a71 74
3 ch g Giant's Causeway(USA) —Sweeping Story (USA) (End Sweep (USA))
(201) ◆ 1408^5 1928^7 4431^3 5122^3 (5482) *7428^9*

Strong Vigilance (IRE) *P W Chapple-Hyam* 65
2 ch c Mr Greeley(USA) —Zabadani (Zafonic (USA))
6991^4

Stroppi Poppi *Norma Twomey* a37 7
5 b m Mtoto—Capricious Lass (Corvaro (USA))
5281^0 6471^2

St Savarin (FR) *M S Tuck* a64 101
8 ch g Highest Honor(FR) —Sacara (GER) (Monsagem (USA))
66^2 302^{10} 584^8 7677^9

Stubbs Art (IRE) *M F De Kock* a84 113
4 ch h Hawk Wing(USA) —Rich Dancer (Halling (USA))
609a^3 *771a^{10}* 4297^{16} 4543^6

Stunning View (IRE) *D K Weld* 93
2 ch c Shamardal(USA) —Sabaah (USA) (Nureyev (USA))
6319a^{11}

Style Award *W J H Ratcliffe* a71 87
4 b m Acclamation—Elegant (IRE) (Marju (IRE))
632^5 799^5 870^7 1241^7 (1748) 1890^{13} 2460^7 3763^6 4281^{13} 6341^3 ◆ 6739^8 *7280^3*

Style De Lois (FR) *Robert Collet* 78
2 b c Blackdoun(FR) —Ziama (FR) (Jeune Homme (USA))
5713a^8 6507a^5

Style Icon *Rae Guest* a62 62
4 ch g Mark Of Esteem(IRE) —Break Point (Reference Point)
1258^6 1787^9 ◆ 2864^5 3261^6

Style Queen (IRE) *J S Bolger* 80
2 b f Galileo(IRE) —Carson Dancer (USA) (Carson City (USA))
6319a^{13}

Stylish Mover *R Ingram* a44 45
4 b g Auction House(USA) —Dam Certain (IRE) (Damister (USA))
1626 869^9 4303^8 6038^4 *6255^{12}*

Suailce (IRE) *D K Weld* a78 102
4 gr m Singspiel(IRE) —Katch Me Katie (Danehill (USA))
2425a^4 3413a^4 4458^6 *6467a^{11}*

Suakin Dancer (IRE) *H Morrison* a58 59
3 ch f Danehill Dancer(IRE) —Wedding Morn (IRE) (Sadler's Wells (USA))
1416^{11} 2950^8 3580^8 4240^6

Suas An Staire (IRE) *Adrian Sexton* a54 54
2 b f Atraf—Visitation (Bishop Of Cashel)
1993a^{11}

Suba (USA) *L M Cumani* a83 86
3 b f Seeking The Gold(USA) —Zomaradah (Deploy)
(2607) 5030^5 5475^4 *6346^4*

Subasta *M Brittain*
4 b m Auction House(USA) —Travel Mystery (Godswalk (USA))
6766^{11}

Sublimity (FR) *Robert Alan Hennessy* 106
9 b g Selkirk(USA) —Fig Tree Drive (USA) (Miswaki (USA))
2425a^3

Subtefuge *H R A Cecil* 80
2 b f Observatory(USA) —Artifice (Green Desert (USA))
4701^2 5478^5 (6363) 7013^7

Suburbia (USA) *M A Jarvis* 50
3 b g Street Cry(IRE) —Green Lady (IRE) (Green Desert (USA))
5747^9 6390^8

Suchita Devious (ITY) *G Cassanelli* 98
3 b f Dr Devious(IRE) —Suchita (IRE) (Alzao (USA))
7046a^{13}

Such Optimism *R M Beckett* a70 87
3 b f Sakhee(USA) —Optimistic (Reprimand)
3870^8 4422^7 5009^6 *7841^3*

Sudden Impact (IRE) *Paul Green* a59 96
4 bb m Modigliani(USA) —Suddenly (Puissance)
858^3 1089^9 3491^3 3855^2 (4043) (4507) 5069^4 5529^6 5654^{15} 6089^{23}

Sudden Impulse *A D Brown* a76 78
8 b m Silver Patriarch(IRE) —Sanshang (FR) (Astronef)
1615^2 2068^5 2237^5 2724^8 2975^5

Sue And Sue *G Woodward*
2 b f Needwood Blade—Bahamian Belle (Bahamian Bounty)
5934^{13}

Sue Princesse (IRE) *Ruaidhri Joseph Tierney* a49 49
6 ch m Alhaarth(IRE) —Princesse Sharpo (USA) (Trempolino (USA))
213^6 248^9

Suerte Loca (IRE) *Mario Hofer* 84
2 ch f Peintre Celebre(USA) —Omara (USA) (Storm Cat (USA))
6501a^{19}

Suestado (GER) *J Hirschberger* 103
3 b c Monsun(GER) —Suivi (GER) (Darshaan)
3670a^{14}

Sufad *T D McCarthy* a53 81
4 b g Alhaarth(IRE) —Alshakr (Bahri (USA))
271^{11} 4417^{15} *5094^8* 5802^5 6400^6 6566^8

Sufficient Warning *R J Smith* a48
5 b g Warningford—Efficacious (IRE) (Efisio)
3735^{11} 7109^{10} 7200^8 7433^{12}

Suffolk Punch (IRE) *A M Balding* a63 82
2 ch c Barathea(IRE) —Lamanka Lass (USA) (Woodman (USA))
2875^3 *3226^4* (3522) 4488^8 5347^5

Sugarbaby Princess (IRE) *S W James* a23 1
3 gr f Verglas(IRE) —Alkifaf (USA) (Mtoto)
3205^9

Sugar Free (IRE) *T Stack* 99
3 b f Oasis Dream—Much Faster (IRE) (Fasliyev (USA))
2644a^4 (3145) 4456^{10} 5491a^3 6427^{10}

Sugar Ray (IRE) *Saeed Bin Suroor* 107
5 b g Danehill(USA) —Akuna Bay (USA) (Mr Prospector (USA))
185a^5 613a^3 3190^4 3874^4 4408^{12}

Sugar State *J L Spearing* a38
4 gr g M'Bebe—Sweet Patoopie (Indian Ridge)
217^8 476^{10} 970^{10} 4388^{13}

Suhailah *M J Attwater* a63
3 ch f Sulamani(IRE) —Vrennan (Suave Dancer (USA))
391^8 630^5 704^6 824^5 957^5 3739^{11} 4234^6 *5988^{12} 6705^{13} 6918^9* 7324^9 7590^6

Suhayl Star (IRE) *P Burgoyne* a70 64
5 b g Trans Island—Miss Odlum (IRE) (Mtoto)
292^2 472^7 749^2 (844) 874^4 (1074) 1320^6 (1587) 1890^2 *2382^2* 2799^9 7518^5 7627^7

Suitably Accoutred (IRE) *Mrs A Duffield* 54
3 b f Acclamation—Cliveden Gail (IRE) (Law Society (USA))
1128^8 *1441^{13}* 1724^8 2605^5 (3482) 3561^{10}

Suited And Booted (IRE) *R Hannon* 81
2 ch c Tagula(IRE) —Carpet Lady (IRE) (Night Shift (USA))
3395^8 3794^4 5401^2 ◆ 6061^4

Suits Me *T P Tate* a112 103
6 ch g Bertolini(USA) —Fancier Bit (Lion Cavern (USA))
(484) 634^2 913^{11} 5863^{13} 6110^6 6506a^8 7188^6 *7489^3 7809 ^{2}*

Sula Dream *J Pearce* 45
3 ch g Sulamani(IRE) —Bonella (IRE) (Eagle Eyed (USA))
4151^{10} 4606^{11} 5939^7 *6445^{10}*

Sularno *J Pearce* a78 63
5 ch g Medicean—Star Precision (Shavian)
224^8 885^7 1442^{12} 2149^2 *2746^3 3269^{14}* 3946^{13} *6862^{13}*

Sullenberger (IRE) *J A Osborne* a70 61
3 ch g Namid—Bint Alhaarth (IRE) (Alhaarth (IRE))
695^2 (833) 2548^7 3099^7 *3511^8* 6031^4 *6668^3 6862^2 7065^7*

Sultana (GER) *Mrs L C Jewell* a8 20
7 b m Law Society(USA) —Sweet Second (IRE) (Second Set (IRE))
3291^9

Sultan's Choice *P D Evans* a58 60
2 b f Sulamani(IRE) —Royal Wish (Royal Applause)
2861^4 (4188) *4858^4 5573^5*

Sultans Way (IRE) *P F I Cole* a61 67
3 b g Indian Ridge—Roses From Ridey (IRE) (Petorius)
3115^{13} 4010^{10} *4749^4* 5287^6 *5582^4* 6339^8

Sulution *M Botti* a74
3 b c Sulamani(IRE) —Streccia (Old Vic)
548^2

Sulwaan (IRE) *M Johnston* 85
2 b g King's Best(USA) —Iktidar (Green Desert (USA))
4993^4 (5466) (5970)

Sumani (FR) *S Dow* a71 66
3 b g Della Francesca(USA) —Sumatra (IRE) (Mukaddamah (USA))
663^4 944^5 1670^7 *(2489)* 3099^3 3776^2 *4206^2* 4910^8 5726^2 *6376^4*

Sumay Buoy (IRE) *Mrs J C McGregor* 48
2 b c Fasliyev(USA) —Mourir D'Aimer (USA) (Trempolino (USA))
5360^7 6009^{10} 6408^{11}

Sumbe (USA) *M P Tregoning* 73
3 bb g Giant's Causeway(USA) —Sumoto (Mtoto)
1291^{15} 1872^5

Summa Cum Laude *Mrs A Duffield* a3 48
2 gr f With Approval(CAN) —Sulitelma (USA) (The Minstrel (CAN))
3606^8 4100^5 *4856^9* 5439^9 5976^7 *6343^{12}*

Summer Affair (IRE) *B I Case* a59
4 b g Alhaarth(IRE) —Late Summer (USA) (Gone West (USA))
6375^4 6974^{10} 7278^3 7495^4 ◆

Summer Bird (USA) *Tim Ice* a127
3 ch c Birdstone(USA) —Hong Kong Squall (USA) (Summer Squall (USA))
1688a^6 (2734a) (6512a) 7311a^4

Summer Bounty *F Jordan* a51 52
13 b g Lugana Beach—Tender Moment (IRE) (Caerleon (USA))
169^9 254^4 775^4 1200^5 2127^{12} 2762^7 *6918^{15}*

Summer Capers (USA) *J Gallagher* a62 61
4 b m Mt. Livermore(USA) —Crown Capers (USA) (Chief's Crown (USA))
1743^{11} *2184^6*

Summercove (IRE) *John Joseph Murphy* a67 67
4 b m Cape Cross(IRE) —Reasonably Devout (CAN) (St Jovite (USA))
4593^3 6822^6

Summer Dancer (IRE) *P T Midgley* a83 89
5 br g Fasliyev(USA) —Summer Style (IRE) (Indian Ridge)
1332^{10} 1612^6 2156^6 2722^5 (3105) ◆ (3234) 3496^4 4333^4 4802^5 (4878) 5188^2 5349^3 5799^{17} 6278^9

Summer Doldrums (USA) *Doug Watson* a109 103
5 bb h Street Cry(IRE) —Dance For Dixie (USA) (Unaccounted For (USA))
436a^6 644a^3 *1008a^4*

Summer Fete (IRE) *B Smart* 104
3 gr f Pivotal—Tamarillo (Daylami (IRE))
1293^{10} 4052^3 (4489) 5710a^8

Summer Gold (IRE) *E J Alston* 87
5 b m Barathea(IRE) —Eman's Joy (Lion Cavern (USA))
2392^4 2787^7 2842^3 3530^4 3763^2 (4328) 4781^{10} 5828^9 6286^3 6485^8

Summerinthecity (IRE) *J Noseda* 85
2 ch c Indian Ridge—Miss Assertive (Zafonic (USA))
2936^2 (4000)

Summer Lodge *J A Glover* a75 79
6 b g Indian Lodge(IRE) —Summer Siren (FR) (Saint Cyrien (FR))
836^{10} 972^2 1154^4 2573^2 *2830^2* (3035) 3814^2 ◆ (4403) 5210^5 5622^4 6385^2 *6724^5 7357^3*

Summer Rose *R M H Cowell* a56 22
4 gr m Kyllachy—Roses Of Spring (Shareef Dancer (USA))
4204^5 7100^{14} *7427^{10} 7703^9*

Summer's Lease *M L W Bell* 86
4 b m Pivotal—Finlaggan (Be My Chief (USA))
1613^8 1860^9

Summer Soul (IRE) *Miss Lucinda V Russell* 77
7 b g Danehill(USA) —Blend Of Pace (IRE) (Sadler's Wells (USA))
(2044) 3095^3 5291^3 6053^4 6767^6 7170^6

Summers Target (USA) *R M H Cowell* a36 86
3 ch g Mr Greeley(USA) —She's Enough (USA) (Exploit (USA))
2298^5 3161^3 3460^3 4338^{10} 5112^5 5403^{11} 5591^7

Summer Winds *T G Mills* a82 88
4 ch g Where Or When(IRE) —Jetbeeah (IRE) (Lomond (USA))
163^2 361^4 (2052) 2641^{11} (3361) 4247^3 4957^4 5725^7

Summit Surge (IRE) *G M Lyons* a109 112
5 b g Noverre(USA) —Lady Peculiar (CAN) (Sunshine Forever (USA))
(413a) 614a^5 702a^{10} 1138a^5 (1913a)

Summon Up Theblood (IRE) *M R Channon* a65 97
4 b g Red Ransom(USA) —Diddymu (IRE) (Revoque (IRE))
1684^{14}

Sunarise (IRE) *R Hannon* a80 63
2 b f Galileo(IRE) —Sun Silk (USA) (Gone West (USA))
6477^{10} *(6912)* 7187^{13}

Sun Catcher (IRE) *P G Murphy* a74 57
6 b g Cape Cross(IRE) —Taaluf (USA) (Hansel (USA))
1535^5 2137^8 2921^{11} *3467^2 3983^{13}*

Sunceleb (IRE) *H Morrison* 73
3 ch f Peintre Celebre(USA) —Suntory (IRE) (Royal Applause)
1406^5 1843^3 2947^4 (3660) 4482^9 5567^6 6742^6

Sundae *C F Wall* a35 96
5 b g Bahamian Bounty—Merry Rous (Rousillon (USA))
2078^{11} 3377^6 (4387) 6994^{18} *7454^9*

Sunday Symphony *S Seemar* a77 96
7 br g Sunday Silence(USA) —Darrery (Darshaan)
262a^5

Sundown (FR) *T Clout* a80 87
3 ch f Singspiel(IRE) —Gerone (FR) (Saumarez)
7302a^6

Sundream *Tom Dascombe* 64
2 b f Desert Sun—I Have A Dream (SWE) (Mango Express)
4946^7 5528^5 6728^{10}

Sunley Smiles *P Howling* a50
4 ch m Arkadian Hero(USA) —Sunley Scent (Wolfhound (USA))
1940[13]

Sunley Sovereign *Mrs R A Carr* a61 64
5 b g Josr Algarhoud(IRE) —Pharsical (Pharly (FR))
1695[5] (2436) 2625[8] 2812[12] 3484[4] 3730[8] 4016[6] 4225[4] 4436[7] 4657[7] 4899[2] 5147[4] 5309[2] 5396[2] 6010[6] 6161[2]

Sunley Spinalonga *D R C Elsworth* a44
2 ch f With Approval(CAN) —Sunley Scent (Wolfhound (USA))
7772[7]

Sunnandaeg *I Semple* 85
2 ch c Haafhd—Come Away With Me (IRE) (Machiavellian (USA))
4307[3] (4774) 6677[5] 7013[4]

Sunny Future (IRE) *M S Saunders* a76 78
3 b g Masterful(USA) —Be Magic (Persian Bold)
2795[13] 3207[2] 3996[9] 4267[4] 4691[4] 5384[3] 7065[11]

Sunny King (FR) *T Lerner*
2 b c Della Francesca(USA) —Queen Elodie (FR) (Cardoun (FR))
7264a[0]

Sunnyside Tom (IRE) *R A Fahey* a84 92
5 b g Danetime(IRE) —So Kind (Kind Of Hush)
1737[6] (2313) 2391[3] (3264) 3615[2] 4409[12] (5305) 6137[2] 6312[2] 6946[4]

Sunny Spells *S C Williams* a73 52
4 b g Zamindar(USA) —Bright Spells (Salse (USA))
6719[9] 7048[10] 7733[5] (7840) ◆ 7867[3]

Sunny Sprite *J M P Eustace* a70 69
4 b g Lujain(USA) —Dragon Star (Rudimentary (USA))
495[5]

Sunraider (IRE) *B W Hills* 83
2 b c Namid—Doctrine (Barathea (IRE))
4825[3] (5317) 5795[8]

Sunrise (FR) *Mme R-W Allen* 65
2 gr f Diktat—Risque De Verglas (FR) (Verglas (IRE))
4577a[10]

Sunrise Lyric (IRE) *P F I Cole* a63
2 b f Rock Of Gibraltar(IRE) —Dawn Air (USA) (Diesis)
5752[6] ◆

Sunrise Safari (IRE) *R A Fahey* a73 94
6 b g Mozart(IRE) —Lady Scarlett (Woodman (USA))
1278[15] 1560[2] ◆ 1849[4] 2266[6] 2707[13] 3389[3] ◆ 3825[5] (4353) 4485[16] 5257[5] 5799[4] 6050[7] 6994[6] 7395[8]

Sunrise Shuffle *B W Hills* 59
2 b f Danehill Dancer(IRE) —Silky Dawn (IRE) (Night Shift (USA))
7182[9]

Sunrise Spirit (FR) *F Doumen* a80 86
8 b g Double Bed(FR) —Belle Chaumiere (Gildoran)
7038a[6]

Sunset Boulevard (IRE) *Miss Tor Sturgis* a68 46
6 b g Montjeu(IRE) —Lucy In The Sky (IRE) (Lycius (USA))
103[6] (202) 341[9] 750[2] (838) 1073[2] 2708[2] 2851[8] 3382[2] 3923[11]

Sunshine Always (IRE) *T D McCarthy* a87 89
3 gr g Verglas(IRE) —Easy Sunshine (IRE) (Sadler's Wells (USA))
(2142) ◆ 2841[4] ◆ 3394[2] 4095[2] 4814[4] (5574) 5986[3] 6374[2] 6773[6] 7181[4] 7540[4] 7741[6] 7891[4]

Sunshine Buddy *J R Holt* a6
2 b f Reel Buddy(USA) —Bullion (Sabrehill (USA))
3979[11]

Sunshine Ellie *D Shaw* a44 51
3 ch f Desert Sun—Lindoras Glory (USA) (Gone West (USA))
41[6] 753[7] 1157[7] 7714[6]

Sunshine Lemon (USA) *A H Derov*
5 b h Lemon Drop Kid(USA) —Awesome Strike (USA) (Theatrical (IRE))
4369a[2]

Suntil (FR) *Mme C Barande-Barbe* a74 77
3 b c Until Sundown(USA) —My Secret Life (FR) (Zieten (USA))
5278a[3]

Suntrap *W J Knight* 61
2 ch g Desert Sun—Regal Gallery (IRE) (Royal Academy (USA))
5401[5] 6199[6]

Supaseus *H Morrison* 112
6 b g Spinning World(USA) —Supamova (USA) (Seattle Slew (USA))
417a[9] 4352[7] 4780[6] 5262[5] (6480) 6812[10]

Supaverdi (USA) *H Morrison* a73 89
4 br m Green Desert(USA) —Supamova (USA) (Seattle Slew (USA))
(1417) ◆ 1860[6] 2495[8] 4085[6] (4495) (5128)

Supera (IRE) *M H Tompkins* a43 43
3 ch f Spartacus(IRE) —Lauretta Blue (IRE) (Bluebird (USA))
2082[10] 3936[4] 4177[9]

Super Academy (USA) *J A Osborne* a69 75
3 ch f Royal Academy(USA) —Super Supreme (IND) (Zafonic (USA))
626[2] ◆ 752[2] (3278) 5090[7] 5902[8]

Supercast (IRE) *N J Vaughan* a83 82
6 b g Alhaarth(IRE) —Al Euro (FR) (Mujtahid (USA))
220[11] 656[2] 798[3] 1133[5] 1660[4] 2200[4] (2678) 3635[9] 5915[10] 6460[4] 6760[11] 7048[5] 7848[4]

Super Collider *M A Jarvis* 77
2 b g Montjeu(IRE) —Astorg (USA) (Lear Fan (USA))
4314[6] ◆ 5408[2] 6285[3]

Superduper *R Hannon* a46 88
4 b m Erhaab(USA) —I'm Magic (First Trump)
1572[2] 1806[6] 3377[9] 3694[8] 4982[3]

Super Duplex *P M Phelan* a63 65
2 b c Footstepsinthesand—Penelope Tree (IRE) (Desert Prince (IRE))
1119[4] 2324[3] 3767[3] 4081[6] 5650[8] 5967[10] 6906[7]

Super Fourteen *R Hannon* a60 65
3 b c Lucky Story(USA) —Beechnut (IRE) (Mujadil (USA))
2548[11] 3302[3] 3693[3] 5179[16] 5581[7] 6370[3]

Super Frank (IRE) *J Akehurst* a86 73
6 b g Cape Cross(IRE) —Lady Joshua (IRE) (Royal Academy (USA))
191[5] 457[3] (708) (843) 954[8] (1421) (1619) 2011[6] 3691[7] 5020[11] 5477[10] 6562[8]

Superhoops *H S Howe* 31
2 b g Hunting Lion(IRE) —Colonial Lady (Dansili)
4790[10] 5319[13] 5868[9]

Superior Duchess *Jane Chapple-Hyam* a44 57
4 b m Superior Premium—Downclose Duchess (King's Signet (USA))
2458[6] 3007[6] 3568[4] 6375[9] 7652[9]

Superior Edge *B Palling* 54
2 b f Exceed And Excel(AUS) —Beveled Edge (Beveled (USA))
5021[9] 5380[5]

Superior Officer (FR) *A Gilibert* 65
7 b h Anabaa(USA) —Supergirl (USA) (Woodman (USA))
7038a[5]

Superior Service *C C Bealby*
2 b f Superior Premium—Dolly Bevan (Another Realm)
4100[8]

Super Kenny (IRE) *N Clement* a79 98
3 b g Kendor(FR) —Zalida (IRE) (Machiavellian (USA))
7302a[3]

Super King *A D Brown* a41 37
8 b g Kingsinger(IRE) —Super Sisters (AUS) (Call Report (USA))
174[9] 378[8] 468[5] 603[8] 4434[7] 5423[8]

Supermassive Muse (IRE) *E S McMahon* a90 93
4 br g Captain Rio—Cautionary (IRE) (Warning)
1278[6] 1457[9] 2012[13] 2782[7] 4784[10] 5247[5] 5856[4] 6459[10]

Supernoverre (IRE) *P Howling* a73 78
3 b g Noverre(USA) —Caviare (Cadeaux Genereux)
164[4] 209[5] 389[4] (662) 776[3] (865) (1063) 3359[6] 4008[5] 4911[10] 5570[5] 6075[7] 6376[6] 6807[3] 7025[5] 7214[6]

Super Sensation (GER) *G L Moore* a53
8 ch g Platini(GER) —Studford Girl (Midyan (USA))
566[4] 732[3]

Super Sleuth (IRE) *B J Meehan* 110
3 ch f Selkirk(USA) —Enemy Action (USA) (Forty Niner (USA))
1353[2] ◆ 1698[3] ◆ 2304a[13]

Superstition (FR) *W Hefter* 98
3 b f Kutub(IRE) —Secada (GER) (Saint Andrews (FR))
4334a[5] 6238a[2]

Superstitious Me (IRE) *B Palling* a57 57
3 b f Desert Prince(IRE) —Royal Rival (IRE) (Marju (IRE))
1594[7] 2143[2] 2539[4] 2910[8] 6787[8] 7153[11] 7417[11]

Super Yellow *J A Osborne* a59
2 b c Exceed And Excel(AUS) —Almost Amber (USA) (Mt. Livermore (USA))
7001[5] ◆ 7376[10]

Supplementary (IRE) *M J Coombe* a52
7 b m Rudimentary(USA) —Will She What (IRE) (Lafontaine (USA))
6673[10] 6974[13] 7367[7] 7666[10]

Support Fund (IRE) *Eve Johnson Houghton* a73 81
5 ch m Intikhab(USA) —Almost A Lady (IRE) (Entitled)
2188[8] 2498[3] 2775[4] 2949[4] 3789[2] (4009) 4452[6] 4641[13] 5991[3] 6294[5] 6937[2] 7229[3] 7487[6] 7664[6]

Supreme Glimpse *Mrs N Smith*
3 b f Piccolo—Running Glimpse (IRE) (Runnett)
1419[9] 1838[10]

Supreme Speedster *A G Newcombe* a62 59
5 br g Superior Premium—Effervescent (Efisio)
794[8] 975[5] 1558[16] 2223[7] 3242[2] 3471[10] 4479[9] 5184[9] 5633[6] 5788[8]

Supsonic *R Le Gal* a79 70
6 br g Marju(IRE) —Nicely (IRE) (Bustino)
423[2] (743) ◆ 822[3] (967) 2895[9] 3587[7] 5301a[9]

Suranam *W J Haggas* a77 66
2 ch g Tobougg(IRE) —Miss Grimm (USA) (Irish River (FR))
6018[6] 6826[2] 7157[7] 7582[3]

Sure Fire (GER) *B J Curley* a68
4 b g Monsun(GER) —Suivez (FR) (Fioravanti (USA))
7367[6] 7725[3]

Surpressa (FR) *Y De Nicolay* 82
3 gr f Take Risks(FR) —Shining Express (FR) (Shining Steel)
7621a[15]

Surprise Party *C F Wall* 85
3 b f Red Ransom(USA) —Surprise Visitor (IRE) (Be My Guest (USA))
1516[5] 2001[5] 2863[2] (4179) (4720) ◆ (4956)

Surprise Pension (IRE) *J J Quinn* a56 66
5 b g Fruits Of Love(USA) —Sheryl Lynn (Miller's Mate)
656[6] 1000[10] 1254[8] (2332) 3421[3]

Suruor (IRE) *D M Simcock* a79 101
3 b g Intikhab(USA) —Kismah (Machiavellian (USA))
1155[2] (1744) (2281) 3049[17] 3839[2] (4459) 5874[8]

Surwaki (USA) *R M H Cowell* a67 79
7 b g Miswaki(USA) —Quinella (Generous (IRE))
(42) 471[3]

Sushitan (GER) *G L Moore* a72 66
4 ch g Lomitas—Subia (GER) (Konigsstuhl (GER))
3425[6] 4205[3] 5270[5] 6258[5]

Sussex Dancer (IRE) *J A Osborne* a70 52
3 ch f Danehill Dancer(IRE) —Wadud (Nashwan (USA))
1937[7] 2827[12] 3661[5]

Susurrayshaan *Mrs G S Rees* a49 52
3 b g Dilshaan—Magic Mistral (Thowra (FR))
1363[4] 1953[5] 2340[8] 2843[4] 3454[14] 4710[14] 4943[10] 5614[5] 5885[11]

Sutton Veny (IRE) *J R Gask* a75 70
3 b f Acclamation—Carabine (USA) (Dehere (USA))
3460[9] 4164[4] (4786) 5264[8] 5937[8] 7191[2] 7496[9] (7739)

Suzhou *Tom Dascombe* 53
2 b f Tiger Hill(IRE) —Tora Bora (Grand Lodge (USA))
7288[11]

Suzie Quw *A P Jarvis* a46 80
3 ch f Bahamian Bounty—Bonkers (Efisio)
1869[7] (2227) 3706[9] 4228[10] 5523[15] 6879[8]

Suzi's A Smartlady (IRE) *M Johnston* a57 63
2 b f Rakti—Shesasmartlady (IRE) (Dolphin Street (FR))
3987[7] 4430[3] 5036[4] 5595[11] 6844[9]

Suzi's Challenger *H J Collingridge* 39
2 b f Tobougg(IRE) —La Tiziana (Rudimentary (USA))
5547[11] 6389[7] 7061[8]

Suzi's Dancer *H J Collingridge* a57
3 b f Groom Dancer(USA) —La Tiziana (Rudimentary (USA))
5572[7] 6073[5] 6611[4] 7686[3]

Suzi's Decision *P W D'Arcy* 107
4 gr m Act One—Funny Girl (IRE) (Darshaan)
(2482)

Suzi Spends (IRE) *H J Collingridge* a86 86
4 b m Royal Applause—Clever Clogs (Nashwan (USA))
2193[5] ◆ 2697[3] 4328[10] 4815[4] 6346[5] 6614[3] 7233[10] 7775[5]

Suzuka Causeway (JPN) *M Hashida* 112
5 b h Giant's Causeway(USA) —French Riviera (USA) (French Deputy (USA))
7498a[16]

Suzy Alexander *G G Margarson*
2 b f Red Ransom(USA) —Fivefive (IRE) (Fairy King (USA))
5478[12]

Suzybee *M R Hoad* a29
2 b f Bahamian Bounty—Greenfly (Green Desert (USA))
7450[13] 7825[7]

Suzys Dream (IRE) *P T Midgley* 4
2 gr f Arakan(USA) —Blue Velvet (Formidable (USA))
2099[11] 2741[8] 2800[10]

Svindal (IRE) *K A Ryan* a67 60
3 ch g Tomba—Princess Sadie (Shavian)
205[2] (295) 1740[7] 3274[11]

Swain's Quest (USA) *Eve Johnson Houghton*
2 b f Swain(IRE) —Questonia (Rainbow Quest (USA))
7816[9]

Swallow Senora (IRE) *M C Chapman* a34 37
7 b m Entrepreneur—Sangra (USA) (El Gran Senor (USA))
37[7] 981[10]

Swanee River (FR) *M Pimbonnet* 16
2 b c King Charlemagne(USA) —Swanson (USA) (Diesis)
6148a[8]

Swans A Swimming (IRE) *J A Osborne* a58 60
3 b c Mujadil(USA) —Danestar (Danehill (USA))
722[2] 982[4] 2009[3]

Swansea Jack *S C Williams* 48
2 ch g Singspiel(IRE) —Welsh Diva (Selkirk (USA))
6737[14] 6922[8]

Swan Wings *A M Balding* 89
2 b f Bahamian Bounty—Star Tulip (Night Shift (USA))
2887[2] ◆ (3277) 3748[10] 4295[7] 4989[4] 5822[10]

Sweet Applause (IRE) *A P Jarvis* a76 82
3 b f Acclamation—Nice Spice (IRE) (Common Grounds)
1078[5] 1727[3] 2058[8] 2456[5] 2651[2] 6010[14] 6801[4] 7411[4]

Sweet Avon *Matthew Salaman* a56
2 gr f Avonbridge—Sweet Whisper (Petong)
7585[8]

Sweet Baby Jane (IRE) *R A Fahey* 48
2 b f Royal Applause—Nebulae (IRE) (Unfuwain (USA))
1891[6] 2153[9] 3487[8] 6923[12]

Sweet Caroline (IRE) *B W Hills* a22
2 b f Motivator—Figlette (Darshaan)
7396[10]

Sweet Child O'Mine *R C Guest* a74
2 b f Singspiel(IRE) —Vendors Mistake (IRE) (Danehill (USA))
(7721) 7844[3]

Sweet Clementine (IRE) *W J Knight* a52 55
2 b f Shamardal(USA) —Heavenly Whisper (IRE) (Halling (USA))
6730[10] 7135[10]

Sweet Day (GER) *A Trybuhl* 84
4 b m Dai Jin—Silvetta (Lando (GER))
3493a[8]

Sweet Gale (IRE) *Mike Murphy* a82 79
5 b m Soviet Star(USA) —Lady Moranbon (USA) (Trempolino (USA))
179[3] 708[9] 886[7] 1413[2] ◆ (2598) (2913) 3030[2] 3453[4] 4019[5] 4607[3] 5001[6] 5404[2] 5810[5] 5916[4] 6374[5] 6726[9]

Sweetheart *Jamie Poulton* a73 83
5 b m Sinndar(IRE) —Love And Adventure (USA) (Halling (USA))
(2177) (2760) 3346[4] 3793[2] (4417) 6273[4] 6851[12]

Sweet Hearth (USA) *A De Royer-Dupre* 116
3 ch f Touch Gold(USA) —Sweet Gold (USA) (Gilded Time (USA))
4394a[3] 4971a[10] 6503a[2] 7746a[9]

Sweet Hollow *C G Cox* a79 83
3 b f Beat Hollow—Three Piece (Jaazeiro (USA))
2051[2] 2877[2] 4229[7] 4709[8] (5168) 5667[5] (6060) 6419[6] 6936[3]

Sweet Kiss (USA) *M J Attwater* a66 71
4 gr m Yes It's True(USA) —Always Freezing (USA) (Robyn Dancer (USA))
2598[11] 3112[12] 5020[10] 6293[3] 6904[11] 7270[4] 7484[11] 7703[8] 7770[9]

Sweet Lightning *W R Muir* a93 97
4 b g Fantastic Light(USA) —Sweetness Herself (Unfuwain (USA))
1003[2] 1460[6] 3873[6] 4404[2] 4781[11] 6106[3]

Sweet Lilly *M R Channon* a74 106
5 b m Tobougg(IRE) —Maristax (Reprimand)
4287[3] 4903[6] 5764[5] 6003[8]

Sweet Mirasol (IRE) *K A Ryan* a17 64
2 b f Celtic Swing—Sallwa (IRE) (Entrepreneur)
2226[6] 3292[3] 4492[5] 5325[6] 6245[14] 6554[10] 6901[12]

Sweetner (FR) *C Rouget* 63
3 b f Stravinsky(USA) —Sachet (USA) (Royal Academy (USA))
4810a[5]

Sweet Pilgrim *M D I Usher* a40 49
2 b f Talkin Man(CAN) —Faraway Moon (Distant Relative)
6615[8] 7365[7]

Sweet Possession (USA) *A P Jarvis* a62 72
3 b f Belong To Me(USA) —Bingo Meeting (USA) (General Meeting (USA))
1066[4] 1509[9] 2455[3] 3815[3] 4338[6] 4940[4]

Sweet Request *Dr J R J Naylor* a55 53
5 ch m Best Of The Bests(IRE) —Sweet Revival (Claude Monet (USA))
877[6] 1156[7] 3798[8]

Sweet Secret *R Hannon* 68
2 ch f Singspiel(IRE) —Ballymore Celebre (IRE) (Peintre Celebre (USA))
6615[11] 7029[5]

Sweet Sixteen (IRE) *J R Jenkins* a61 89
4 b m Sadler's Wells(USA) —User Friendly (Slip Anchor)
876[5]

Sweet Sonnet (USA) *Saeed Bin Suroor* 97
2 ch f Seeking The Gold(USA) —Minister's Melody (USA) (Deputy Minister (CAN))
(2503) 3086[8] 5606[2]

Sweet Virginia (USA) *K R Burke* a50 27
3 bb f Arch(USA) —Hey Hey Sunny (USA) (Known Fact (USA))
287[8] 649[3] 943[6] 1106[5]

Sweet Wake (GER) *Noel Meade* 68
8 ch g Waky Nao—Sweet Royale (GER) (Garde Royale)
2305a[8]

Sweet World *B J Llewellyn* a64 69
5 b g Agnes World(USA) —Douce Maison (IRE) (Fools Holme (USA))
500[9]

Swift Chap *B R Millman* a76 92
3 b g Diktat—Regent's Folly (IRE) (Touching Wood (USA))
1001[8] 3868[8] 4440[5] 4910[3] 5366[7] 5834[8] (6421) (6621) 7060[2] 7189[7]

Swift Gift *B J Meehan* a89 103
4 b g Cadeaux Genereux—Got To Go (Shareef Dancer (USA))
(1861) 3091[11] (5025) 6270[7]

Swift Return *S C Williams* a75 73
2 b g Fantastic Light(USA) —Swift Dispersal (Shareef Dancer (USA))
5317[5] 5966[2] ◆ 6291[3] 7096[8]

Swift Sailing (USA) *Patrick Allen* a48 64
8 b g Storm Cat(USA) —Saytarra (USA) (Seeking The Gold (USA))
4874[4]

Swilly Ferry (USA) *B W Hills* a81 96
2 b c Wiseman's Ferry(USA) —Keepers Hill (IRE) (Danehill (USA))
994[3] ◆ 1802[3] (2631) 3782[10] 4081[3] 5136[3] ◆ 5198[4] (5795) 6426[9] 6677[9]

Swinbrook (USA) *R A Harris* a82 82
8 ch g Stravinsky(USA) —Dance Diane (USA) (Affirmed (USA))
35[7] (882) (1053) 1169[7] 1477[2] 1921[3] (2184) 2389[3] (2769) 3354[6] (4372) (4690) 5065[3] 5421[7] 5900[5] 6670[2] 6857[8] 7337[9] 7519[9] 7679[8]

Swindler (IRE) *A M Balding* 92
3 b g Sinndar(IRE) —Imitation (Darshaan)
4405[9]

Swing It Ruby (IRE) *Mrs D J Sanderson* a48 48
3 br f Celtic Swing—Golconda (IRE) (Lahib (USA))
1724[9] 2742[10] 3450[14]

Swingkeel (IRE) *J L Dunlop* a96 104
4 ch g Singspiel(IRE) —Anniversary (Salse (USA))
1356[2] 1863[2] (3510) ◆ 4417[3] ◆ (5235) 6306[3] 6851[24]

Swirl Tango *F Jordan*
3 b f Lujain(USA) —Tangolania (FR) (Ashkalani (IRE))
6223[14] 6794[14]

Swish Dish (CAN) *R Hannon* 55
2 bb f El Corredor(USA) —Amelia Saratoga (JPN) (Dehere (USA))
6616[12] 7183[9]

Swiss Act *M Johnston* a95 89
5 ch g Act One—Dancing Mirage (IRE) (Machiavellian (USA))
30[5] 206[8] 466a[6] 653a[13] 761[2] (822) 1003[6] 1555a[6]

Swiss Art (IRE) *R Hollinshead* a78 61
3 b g One Cool Cat(USA) —Alpine Park (IRE) (Barathea (IRE))
10[3] 159[5] 684[3] (808) (964) 1492[6] 1811[9] 2009[5] (2744) 3225[5] (3711) 3953[2] (4171) 4284[10] 4841[4] 5672[3] 6357[4] 6946[10] 7271[8] (7422) 7631[8] 7782[5] 7858[5]

Swiss Cross *G A Butler* 86
2 b c Cape Cross(IRE) —Swiss Lake (USA) (Indian Ridge)
2853[5] 5829[3] (6451) ◆ 7013[6]

Swiss Diva *D R C Elsworth* a94 106
3 br f Pivotal—Swiss Lake (USA) (Indian Ridge)
1345[3] ◆ (1639) ◆ 2049[3] (2934) 3824[4] ◆ 5434[2]

Swiss Franc *D R C Elsworth* a105 107
4 br g Mr Greeley(USA) —Swiss Lake (USA) (Indian Ridge)
359[2] 633[4]

Swiss Lake Sweetie (USA) *George Baker* a49 62
3 ch f Action This Day(USA) —Almost Blue (USA) (Mr Greeley (USA))
19[8]

Swop (IRE) *L M Cumani* a91 108
6 b g Shinko Forest(IRE) —Changing Partners (Rainbow Quest (USA))
265a[10] 439a[4] (615a) ◆ 997[15] 5476[6] 5863[8] ◆ 6480[7]

Swords *R E Peacock* a71 56
7 b g Vettori(IRE) —Pomorie (IRE) (Be My Guest (USA))
3[4] 219[9] 2971[13] 3714[3] 3927[5] ◆ 4373[7] 4862[5] 5680[4] 6025[12] (7354) 7425[2] 7635[5]

Swordsman (GER) *C Gordon* a81 76
7 b g Acatenango(GER) —Saiga (Windwurf (GER))
2760[5] 3346[2] (3986) 4092[3] 4417[13] 4793[8] 6692[11]

Sworn Pro (GER) *Mario Hofer* 101
3 br f Protektor(GER) —Sweet Tern (GER) (Arctic Tern (USA))
2524a[6] 3604a[5] 4583a[8] 6714a[2] 7128a[12]

Sybelio (FR) *W Hefter* 99
5 b h Lord Of Men—Trueville (GER) (Top Ville)
465a[5] 653a[P]

Sybil's Surprise *J Mackie* 19
4 b m Puissance—Fervent Fan (IRE) (Soviet Lad (USA))
3862[9] 5549[14]

Sydney Bridge *I Semple* 60
2 b g Danbird(AUS) —Miss Prim (Case Law)
3263[6] 4132[5] 6009[7] 6819[10] 6983[10]

Sydney Cove (IRE) *R Allan* a35 47
3 b g Cape Cross(IRE) —First Fleet (USA) (Woodman (USA))
2030[10] 2236[13] 2627[3] 3482[6] 4039[6] 4348[10] 4943[11] 5331[9]

Sydneysider *Eve Johnson Houghton* a63 67
4 b g Averti(IRE) —Cajole (IRE) (Barathea (IRE))
5525[7] 6223[5] 7479[5] 7610[8]

Sylber Harbor (FR) *F Cohen* 50
2 b c Zieten(USA) —Sylberlev (USA) (Boston Harbor (USA))
4368a[6]

Symba's Dream (USA) *J-C Rouget* a88 90
3 gr f Vindication(USA) —Lyphard Gal (USA) (Lyphard (USA))
4334a[9] 7697a[0]

Synergy (FR) *Y Durepaire* 110
4 b m Victory Note(USA) —Kuddam (IRE) (Doyoun)
(4365a) 5300a[5] (7347a)

Synonymy *M Blanshard* a66 62
6 b g Sinndar(IRE) —Peony (Lion Cavern (USA))
2760[8]

Syrian *M L W Bell* 94
2 b g Hawk Wing(USA) —Lady Lahar (Fraam)
(4152) ◆ 5659[5] 6011[3]

Syrinx (IRE) *J Noseda* a70 73
3 b f One Cool Cat(USA) —Latest Chapter (IRE) (Ahonoora)
(154)

Syvilla *Rae Guest* 95
4 b m Nayef(USA) —Dance Steppe (Rambo Dancer (CAN))
1613[4] ◆ 2482[7] 2974[7] 3315[2] 4094[6] 4903[4] 5472[11] 7291[5]

Szaba *J Akehurst* a51 28
4 ch m Tipsy Creek(USA) —Compton Alice (Compton Place)
44[7] 192[10] 308[8] 598[6]

Taajub (IRE) *W J Haggas* 109
2 b c Exceed And Excel(AUS) —Purple Tiger (IRE) (Rainbow Quest (USA))
3792[2] ◆ (4497) 5172[2] ◆ 5795[2] 6660[2]

Ta Aleem *M P Tregoning*
3 ch f Galileo(IRE) —Tadris (USA) (Red Ransom (USA))
5151[5]

Taameer *M P Tregoning* 108
3 b c Beat Hollow—Vayavaig (Damister (USA))
1485[5]

Taarab *Saeed Bin Suroor* 84
3 ch g Refuse To Bend(IRE) —Tanzania (USA) (Darshaan)
1739[2] 2090[5]

Taaresh (IRE) *K A Morgan* a40 80
4 b h Sakhee(USA) —Tanaghum (Darshaan)
7201[6] 7823[11]

Tabaahi (IRE) *Gordon Elliott* a52 62
4 ch g Alhaarth(IRE) —Lovelyst (IRE) (Machiavellian (USA))
7369[6] 7719[5] 7732[8]

Tabadul (IRE) *M Al Muhairi* a61 61
8 b g Cadeaux Genereux—Amaniy (USA) (Dayjur (USA))
419a[14]

Tabaran (FR) *L A Dace* a58 19
6 ch g Polish Precedent(USA) —Tabariya (IRE) (Doyoun)
1286[5] 1609[11] 2429[14]

Tabaret *R M Whitaker* a99 100
6 ch g Bertolini(USA) —Luanshya (First Trump)
3122[8] 3351[6] 3784[2] 3877[3] 4598[7] 5132[7] 5654[4] 6359[9] 6897[4] 7202[7] 7414[10]

Tabassum (IRE) *Sir Michael Stoute* 108
2 b f Nayef(USA) —Tomoohat (USA) (Danzig (USA))
(4797) (6447) ◆ 6852[3]

Taboor (IRE) *R M H Cowell* a61 58
11 b g Mujadil(USA) —Christoph's Girl (Efisio)
46[2] 294[4] 474[3] 727[6] 3959[3] 4182[9] 7100[10]

Taborcillo *T D Barron* 66
2 b g Lucky Story(USA) —Trust In Paula (USA) (Arazi (USA))
4546[2] 5693[9] 5977[9]

Tabulate *P Howling* a66 43
6 b m Dansili—Let Alone (Warning)
100[6] 193[5] 469[4] 541[5] 760[4] 4146[4] 4667[12]

Tactful (IRE) *R M Beckett* a93 89
4 b m Intikhab(USA) —Crozon (Peintre Celebre (USA))
1210[4] 2697[4] 3894a[8] 6876[11]

Tactic *J L Dunlop* 106
3 b c Sadler's Wells(USA) —Tanaghum (Darshaan)
1328[2] (1809) ◆ 2275[4] 3090[4] 3778[2] 4405[4] 5609[5] 7059[4]

Tactician *M L W Bell* 82
2 b c Motivator—Tempting Prospect (Shirley Heights)
5793[2] 6617[4]

Tadalavil *Miss L A Perratt* a76 81
4 gr g Clodovil(IRE) —Blandish (USA) (Wild Again (USA))
3149[8] 3483[8] 3855[9] 4134[11] 4311[3]

Tadhkeer *W J Haggas* 45
2 ch g Refuse To Bend(IRE) —Shuruk (Cadeaux Genereux)
6542[5] 6842[10]

Tadjinne (FR) *J Van Handenhove*
2 b f Okawango(USA) —Adjinne (FR) (Octagonal (NZ))
5713a[0]

Tadlil *J M Bradley* a58 58
7 b g Pivotal—Pretty Poppy (Song)
62[7] 111[2] 198[3] 292[5] 480[5] 3261[3] 3505[9] 3860[9] 4183[14] 5633[4] 6293[7] 7534[7] 7681[2] 7869[3]

Tae Kwon Do (USA) *Miss J A Camacho* a61 60
3 b g Thunder Gulch(USA) —Judy's Magic (USA) (Wavering Monarch (USA))
322[5] 759[3] 938[3] 1441[3] 1954[2] 2340[4] 3482[7] 4806[10] 5342[6] 5952[8]

Taeping (IRE) *R Hollinshead* a52 56
2 b c Invincible Spirit(IRE) —Simil (USA) (Apalachee (USA))
5234[9] 6542[4] 6809[9] 7421[3] 7584[6] 7619[10] 7778[10] 7793[6]

Tafaool (IRE) *M P Tregoning* a64 83
3 b f Green Desert(USA) —Sundus (USA) (Sadler's Wells (USA))
5435[3] 7126[3]

Tafawut *B W Hills* 44
2 b f Nayef(USA) —Rohita (IRE) (Waajib)
5398[8]

Tagalura (IRE) *P T Midgley*
3 b g Tagula(IRE) —Allurah (IRE) (Goldmark (USA))
621[12]

Tagar Bere (FR) *M Pimbonnet* 92
2 ch c High Yield(USA) —Arrondie (FR) (Inchinor)
2694a[3] 6080a[3]

Tag's Book (IRE) *U Suter*
2 ch c Tagula(IRE) —First Book (Ashkalani (IRE))
6979a[0]

Tagseed (IRE) *W J Haggas* 72
3 b c Elusive City(USA) —Allegorica (IRE) (Alzao (USA))
1840[3]

Tag Team (IRE) *John A Harris* a59 43
8 ch g Tagula(IRE) —Okay Baby (IRE) (Treasure Kay)
13[9] 146[5] 303[6] 487[10] 575[3] 746[11] 1781[4] 2812[15] 3465[10] 7460[2] 7681[6] 7795[4] 7869[2]

Tagula Breeze (IRE) *I W McInnes* 82
3 b g Tagula(IRE) —Pearl Egg (IRE) (Mukaddamah (USA))
1345[5] 2049[4] 2611[3] 3053[4] 3688[10] 4227[6] 4601[8] 4891[13] (5411) 5421[10]

Tagula Minx (IRE) *J Pearce* a51 20
3 b f Tagula(IRE) —Persian Fantasia (Alzao (USA))
7004[11] 7614[12] 7818[11]

Tagula Night (IRE) *W R Swinburn* a90 84
3 ch g Tagula(IRE) —Carpet Lady (IRE) (Night Shift (USA))
(4607) (5370) ◆ 5799[9] 6631[5]

Tagula Pearl (IRE) *I W McInnes* 43
2 b f Tagula(IRE) —Pearl Egg (IRE) (Mukaddamah (USA))
1344[9] 1504[4] 2017[7] 2435[9] 3686[11] 7463[9] 7713[7]

Tagula Sands (IRE) *J C Fox* a42
5 b g Tagula(IRE) —Pomme Pomme (USA) (Dayjur (USA))
43[11] 153[11] 245[9]

Taguna (IRE) *M Brittain* 14
3 ch f Tagula(IRE) —Tahlil (Cadeaux Genereux)
5254[13] 5621[9]

Tahayab (ITY) *M Johnston* 57
3 b f Nayef(USA) —Zaffrani (IRE) (Danehill (USA))
2375[6] 3093[9]

Tahfeez (IRE) *I Semple* a59 50
3 b f Alhaarth(IRE) —Ghazal (USA) (Gone West (USA))
1508[10] 4013[5]

Tahkeem *M P Tregoning* a16 72
3 b f Green Desert(USA) —Katayeb (IRE) (Machiavellian (USA))
(5744) 6420[7]

Tahseen *M P Tregoning* 67
2 b c Haafhd—Merayaat (IRE) (Darshaan)
6057[5] 6962[4]

Tai Hang (IRE) *A P Jarvis* 17
2 br f Celtic Swing—Victoria Peek (IRE) (Cape Cross (IRE))
4257[9] 6096[9]

Taikoo *H Morrison* a92 88
4 b g Dr Fong(USA) —So True (So Blessed)
142[4] 1779[2] 2249[2] 2932[16]

Taine (IRE) *J R Gask* a70 44
4 b h Invincible Spirit(IRE) —Farjah (IRE) (Charnwood Forest (IRE))
5717[7]

Tajaaweed (USA) *Sir Michael Stoute* 115
4 br h Dynaformer(USA) —Uforia (USA) (Zilzal (USA))
1551a[8] 3139[9]

Tajneed (IRE) *D Nicholls* a94 103
6 b g Alhaarth(IRE) —Indian Express (Indian Ridge)
1052[5] 3389[8] 4037[7] 4330[5] ◆ 4574a[9] 5695[7] 6089[8] 6282[7]

Takaamul *K A Morgan* a59 62
6 ch g Almutawakel—Mafaatin (IRE) (Royal Academy (USA))
130[4] 355[7] 646[2] 844[5] 1773[2] 2400[7] (3007) 3548[6] (4665)

Takaatuf (IRE) *M Johnston* 91
3 b g Dubai Destination(USA) —Karlaka (IRE) (Barathea (IRE))
1086[3] ◆ (1702) 2296[4] 3051[13] 3780[7] 4455[15] 5209[7] 6100[9]

Takafu (USA) *W S Kittow* a68 79
7 b g Lemon Drop Kid(USA) —Proper Protocol (USA) (Deputy Minister (CAN))
2177[4] 2931[8] 4988[7]

Take D'Or (FR) *J Boisnard* a90 103
3 gr c Take Risks(FR) —Fedora (FR) (Kendor (FR))
1238a[7] 1858a[7] 7621a[14]

Take It Easee (IRE) *Mrs Prunella Dobbs* a33 80
4 b m Noverre(USA) —Fairy Lore (IRE) (Fairy King (USA))
(7247)

Take It There *A J Lidderdale* a47 47
7 ch m Cadeaux Genereux—Feel Free (IRE) (Generous (IRE))
6208[9]

Take It To The Max *G M Moore* 95
2 b c Bahamian Bounty—Up And About (Barathea (IRE))
994[13] 1304[8] 2196[3] 2940[2] (3702) 5133[10] 5659[4] (7184)

Take Me There *John Berry* a82
6 b g Cape Cross(IRE) —Mill Path (Mill Reef (USA))
226[2] 325[3]

Take My Hand *M R Channon* a56 56
2 ch f Imperial Dancer—Royal Logic (Royal Applause)
2919[7] 3344[6] 6109[8] 6343[3] 6590[6]

Takeover Bid (USA) *M Johnston* a84 70
3 b g Empire Maker(USA) —Seba (Alzao (USA))
(4) 288[6] (859) 1033[2]

Takeover Target (AUS) *Joe Janiak* 121
10 b g Celtic Swing—Shady Stream (AUS) (Archregent (CAN))
2116a[8] 3819[7]

Take Ten *M Johnston* 94
2 b c Bahamian Bounty—See You Later (Emarati (USA))
2484[5] 2907[2] ◆ (4844) (5344) ◆ 5795[5] 6064[2] ◆ 6478[3]

Take That *S P Griffiths* 25
4 b g Kasakov—Baby Be (Bold Arrangement)
1061[8] 5309[12] 6379[10] 7219[10]

Take The Hint *Mme C Head-Maarek* 107
3 b f Montjeu(IRE) —Insinuate (USA) (Mr Prospector (USA))
(1701) 3047[6] 3619[6] 7128a[5] 7347a[4]

Take The Micky *C F Wall* a69 69
3 b g Beat Hollow—Ailincala (IRE) (Pursuit Of Love)
1466[7] 2329[9] 2600[13] 7769[8]

Take The Points (USA) *Todd Pletcher* a109 110
3 gr c Even The Score(USA) —Ginger Ginger (USA) (Fred Astaire (USA))
2098a[3]

Take The Race (FR) *W J Cargeeg* 12
3 b g Take Risks(FR) —Mesquery (FR) (Nikos)
6149a[9]

Takhir (IRE) *P Schiergen* 88
3 b c Lando(GER) —Tocopilla (FR) (Medaaly)
7406a[12]

Takitwo *P D Cundell* a65 65
6 b g Delta Dancer—Tiama (IRE) (Last Tycoon)
(114) 309[6] 471[5] 545[2] 1080[5] 1606[5] 2598[6] 2794[3] 4645[11] 5779[9] 6213[8] 6719[11]

Takizada (IRE) *J R Gask* a38 80
4 b m Sendawar(IRE) —Takarouna (USA) (Green Dancer (USA))
3718[7] 4495[4] 5227[11]

Takounba (FR) *J Schiestel Fils*
3 gr g Dounba(FR) —Take Freedom (FR) (Take Risks (FR))
5784a[U]

Talamahana *A B Haynes* a49 48
4 b m Kyllachy—Bahawir Pour (USA) (Green Dancer (USA))
1784[4] 2456[9] 2794[10] 3204[6] 3994[8] 4222[3] 4586a[P] 4690[5] 5541a[3] 5716[3] 6329[8] 7069[10] 7521[8] 7592[2]

Talayeb *M P Tregoning* a44 76
4 bb g Nayef(USA) —Paper Chase (FR) (Machiavellian (USA))
1603[3] 4822[9]

Talenti (IRE) *Miss E C Lavelle* a75 96
6 b g Sadler's Wells(USA) —Sumoto (Mtoto)
1007[12]

Tale Of Two Cities (IRE) *Luke Comer* a71 78
4 b h Sadler's Wells(USA) —Kasora (IRE) (Darshaan)
1546a[8]

Taliesin *Mrs A M Thorpe* 14
2 br g Passing Glance—Silver Bird (IRE) (Vision (USA))
5180[8] 5907[12] 6331[8]

Talimos (IRE) *R M Beckett* 80
3 b g Lomitas—Silvertone (FR) (Highest Honor (FR))
1708[2] ◆ 2181[4] (2738) 3090[11] 3827[6]

Talka (FR) *J-L Guillochon* a54 50
2 b f Vettori(IRE) —Romanche (FR) (Galetto (FR))
6960a[10]

Talking Hands *S Kirk* a90 100
3 b g Mujahid(USA) —With Distinction (Zafonic (USA))
863[11] 5476[10] 6106[20]

Talk Of Saafend (IRE) *P Monteith* a78 83
4 b m Barathea(IRE) —Sopran Marida (IRE) (Darshaan)
1100[7] 1229[7] 1507[14] 1830[6] 2391[6] 3019[6] 3267[5] 3481[2] 3911[8] 4532[6] 4896[3]

Tallawalla (IRE) *M R Channon* 67
2 b f Oratorio(IRE) —Edetana (USA) (Diesis)
4792[10] 5284[6] 5741[11]

Tall Chief (IRE) *R Pritchard-Gordon* 85
2 b c Observatory(USA) —Ballerina Rosa (FR) (Anabaa (USA))
(3934a) 5927a[6]

Tallest Peak (USA) *M G Quinlan* a63
4 b g Giant's Causeway(USA) —Hum Along (USA) (Fappiano (USA))
7438[9] 7599[13] (7787) 7802[6]

Tallulah Mai *Matthew Salaman* a59
2 b f Kayf Tara—Al Awaalah (Mukaddamah (USA))
7622[10]

Tallulah's Secret *J Gallagher* 23
3 b f Bertolini(USA) —Ascend (IRE) (Glint Of Gold)
1046[6]

Tallulah Sunrise *M D I Usher* a58 24
4 b m Auction House(USA) —Tallulah Belle (Crowning Honors (CAN))
842[7] 945[8] 1589[6] 1834[12] 2400[10] 3735[12] 3811[14] 4533[16] 5063[13]

Talon (IRE) *G A Swinbank* a48 59
4 ch g Indian Ridge—Brief Lullaby (IRE) (Brief Truce (USA))
2389[10]

Talsarnau (IRE) *W M Brisbourne* a53 35
3 b g Kheleyf(USA) —Ezilana (IRE) (Shardari)
16[5] 134[9] 196[10]

Talulah Bells *A W Carroll* a14 42
3 br f Superior Premium—Hullo Mary Doll (Lidhame)
5[5]

Tamaathul *B W Hills* 84
2 gr c Tiger Hill(IRE) —Tahrir (IRE) (Linamix (FR))
6620[2] (6990)

Tamada *N Clement* a77 85
3 b f Lucky Story(USA) —Play Around (IRE) (Niniski (USA))
(5462a)

Tamagin (USA) *J Pearce* a109 114
6 b g Stravinsky(USA) —Luia (USA) (Forty Niner (USA))
204[5] 388[2] 579[3] 996[8] (1560) 1868[5] 2385[2] 3141[13] (3405) 4037[2] 4523[15] 5039[2] 5434[4] (5878) 6304[2] 6661[16]

Tamanaco (IRE) *T D Walford* 74
2 b g Catcher In The Rye(IRE) —Right After Moyne (IRE) (Imperial Ballet (IRE))
2444[3] 2940[9] (4067)

Tamarah *Miss D Mountain* 73
3 b f Beat Hollow—Valagalore (Generous (IRE))
4151[9] 4720[8]

Tamara Who (IRE) *John E Kiely* 49
2 b f Invincible Spirit(IRE) —Miss Tardy (JPN) (Lammtarra (USA))
5895a[11] 6317a[18]

Tamarind (IRE) *A P O'Brien* 105
3 b f Sadler's Wells(USA) —Sharata (IRE) (Darshaan)
1996a[5] (4609a) 5201[5]

Tamarind Hill (IRE) *A J McCabe* a68 42
2 b g Shamardal(USA) —Amandian (IRE) (Indian Ridge)
6054[14] 6629[6] 6943[6] 7319[10] 7435[4] 7661[2] 7749[3] 7805[7] 7850[3]

Tamasou (IRE) *A J McCabe* a83 83
4 b g Tamarisk(IRE) —Soubresaut (IRE) (Danehill (USA))
2245[2] 3104[4] 3911[3] 4496[7] (5813) 6212[2] 6496[2] 6630[14] (7220) 7287[14] 7633[2] 7759[5]

Tamazirte (IRE) *J-C Rouget* a104 116
3 b f Danehill Dancer(IRE) —Tanami Desert (Lycius (USA))
(1237a) 1918a[2] 2952a[2] 5298a[6] (6505a)

Tamimi's History *P D Evans* a89 92
5 b g Kalanisi(IRE) —Polish Pink (IRE) (Polish Precedent (USA))
766[7] 1003[13] 1519[4]

Taminas Desert *M Botti* a54
4 b m Green Desert(USA) —Tamise (USA) (Time For A Change (USA))
678[P]

Tamino (IRE) *P Howling* a62 67
6 b g Mozart(IRE) —Stop Out (Rudimentary (USA))
27[9] 111[3] 496[6] 675[7] 1710[12] 2921[14] 5883[11] 7609[3] (7774) 7814[6] 7880[2]

Tam Lin *Saeed Bin Suroor* 117
6 b g Selkirk(USA) —La Nuit Rose (FR) (Rainbow Quest (USA))
702a[7] 774a[13]

Tammela *A P Jarvis* a56
2 b f Beat Hollow—On The Wing (Pivotal)
6291[8] 6607[9]

Tampa Boy (IRE) *M F Harris* a70
7 b g Montjeu(IRE) —Tirolean Dance (IRE) (Tirol)
11[4] 249[4] 333[6]

Tamtara *Mrs A J Perrett* a61 64
2 b f Red Ransom(USA) —Tamalain (USA) (Royal Academy (USA))
5397[12] 5741[6] 6781[6]

Tan Bonita (USA) *R J Smith* a40 34
4 bb m More Than Ready(USA) —Time For Hennessy (USA) (Hennessy (USA))
5125[11] 5323[15] 6777[9] 7689[7]

Tanfidh *M P Tregoning* 94
3 b f Marju(IRE) —Wijdan (USA) (Mr Prospector (USA))
5520[7] 5939[2] (6332) (6761) ◆ 6996[6]

Tanforan *B P J Baugh* a70 71
7 b g Mujahid(USA) —Florentynna Bay (Aragon)
1042[10] 1612[13] 2166[7] 2352[2] 2626[6] 3070[17] (3322) (3637) 3863[5] 4046[2] 4496[4] 4824[2] 5160[5] 5869[6] 6217[6]

Tangaspeed (FR) *R Laplanche* 114
4 b m Vertical Speed(FR) —Fitanga (FR) (Fijar Tango (FR))
1762a[9] 5929a[9] 6526a[11] 7569a[7]

Tangerine Trees *B Smart* a73 79
4 b g Mind Games—Easy To Imagine (USA) (Cozzene (USA))
1951[3] 2312[2] (2628) (3296) (4015) 5597[7] 6233[10] 6846[3] 7321[3] 7506[11]

Tango Step (IRE) *D Carroll* a40 45
9 b g Sesaro(USA) —Leitrim Lodge (IRE) (Classic Music (USA))
6783^{9} 7081^{11} 7136^{8} 7723^{5}

Tanley *J F Coupland* a60 59
4 gr g Compton Admiral—Secret Pursuit (Chilibang)
6380^{2} 6877^{11} 7086^{13} 7241^{13} 7427^{3} 7645^{7} 7710^{7} 7815^{6}

Tanoura (IRE) *John M Oxx* 109
3 b f Dalakhani(IRE) —Takarouna (USA) (Green Dancer (USA))
2960a^{2} (5202) 5796^{3} 6504a^{3}

Tantawangelo *R Pritchard-Gordon* 74
2 b g Action House(USA) —Kyle Akin (Vettori (IRE))
5378a^{3}

Tanto Faz (IRE) *W J Haggas* a88 91
4 b g Rock Of Gibraltar(IRE) —Sharakawa (IRE) (Darshaan)
2101^{DSQ} 2822^{3} 3639^{12} 5887^{9} 6116^{3} 6724^{7}

Tanto Quanto (IRE) *W R Muir* a75 70
2 b c Le Vie Dei Colori—Fear Not (IRE) (Alzao (USA))
4163^{6} 4915^{2} (5371) 6088^{9} 6491^{6}

Tantris (IRE) *J A Osborne* a68 65
4 b g High Chaparral(IRE) —Emerald Cut (Rainbow Quest (USA))
1081^{5} 1314^{9}

Tantsor (FR) *P T Midgley*
2 ch g Brier Creek(USA) —Norova (FR) (Hawker's News (IRE))
5466^{9} 6763^{11} 7266^{9}

Tapas Lad (IRE) *G J Smith* a62 57
4 b h Modigliani(USA) —Missish (Mummy's Pet)
81^{8} 578^{9} 792^{7} 1409^{8} 2333^{12}

Tap Dance Way (IRE) *P R Chamings* a50
2 b f Azamour(IRE) —Dance Lively (USA) (Kingmambo (USA))
6164^{10}

Taper Jean Girl (IRE) *Mrs R A Carr* a65
2 b f Elusive City(USA) —Ruacana Falls (USA) (Storm Bird (CAN))
4980^{4} 5643^{8} 6228^{7} 7210^{4} (7419) 7501^{9} 7706^{4} 7756^{6}

Tapioka Express (IRE) *F & L Camici* 90
3 b f Bahri(USA) —Tapioka City (USA) (Danehill (USA))
3186a^{7} 7046a^{11}

Tapis Wizard *M W Easterby* 76
3 b g Alhaarth(IRE) —Just Call Me (NZ) (Blues Traveller (IRE))
1595^{7} 1740^{5} 2060^{3} 3069^{9} 4004^{3} 4280^{2}

Tapitsfly (USA) *Dale Romans* a112 101
2 gr f Tapit(USA) —Flying Marlin (USA) (Marlin (USA))
(7282a)

Tappanappa (IRE) *A M Balding* 14
2 b c High Chaparral(IRE) —Itsibitsi (IRE) (Brief Truce (USA))
7029^{13}

Tap Tip (USA) *F Danloux* a53 64
3 b f Pleasant Tap(USA) —Noblissima (IRE) (Sadler's Wells (USA))
6682a^{0}

Taqdeyr *M A Jarvis* a105 106
4 ch g Dubai Destination(USA) —Pastorale (Nureyev (USA))
(1288) ◆ (1467) 2500^{5} 3621^{2} 4297^{6} ◆ 4796^{11} (5529) 6487^{3}

Taqleed (IRE) *J H M Gosden* 42
2 bb c Shamardal(USA) —Thakafaat (IRE) (Unfuwain (USA))
6617^{12} ◆

Taqseem (IRE) *M Al Muhairi* a84 96
6 b g Fantastic Light(USA) —Elshamms (Zafonic (USA))
525a^{5}

Tar (IRE) *John A Harris* a55 79
5 b g Danzig(USA) —Royal Show (IRE) (Sadler's Wells (USA))
4071^{8} 5377^{3} 6358^{7} 7142^{10} 7354^{8} 7499^{10}

Taralga (IRE) *S J Treacy* 83
4 b m Sinndar(IRE) —Tarabaya (IRE) (Warning)
4510a^{3} 5689a^{5}

Tarankali (IRE) *John M Oxx* 105
3 ch g Selkirk(USA) —Tarakala (IRE) (Dr Fong (USA))
1388a^{8} 1910a^{5}

Taran Tregarth *W M Brisbourne* a42 34
5 b m Tobougg(IRE) —Little Change (Grundy)
240^{6}

Tara's Garden *M Blanshard* a41 61
4 b m Dr Fong(USA) —Tremiere (FR) (Anabaa (USA))
1773^{12} 2859^{11} 3798^{7} 4149^{10} 4376^{7}

Tarawa Atoll *M R Channon* a57 48
3 b f Imperial Dancer—Musical Capers (Piccolo)
287^{3} 594^{5} 707^{7} 2515^{11}

Tardrou (FR) *J-L Dubord* a96 101
6 b g Tot Ou Tard(IRE) —Tadrou (FR) (Kadrou (FR))
846a^{7}

Targs (IRE) *Peter Grayson* 17
3 b c Elusive City(USA) —Cannikin (IRE) (Lahib (USA))
3975^{8} 4425^{11}

Tariq *P W Chapple-Hyam* 119
5 ch h Kyllachy—Tatora (Selkirk (USA))
2076^{6} 2483^{7} 6058^{6} 6848^{8}

Tarita (IRE) *R Hannon* 74
2 ch f Bahamian Bounty—Zonic (Zafonic (USA))
2238^{4} 4243^{4} (4928) 5797^{16}

Tarkamara (IRE) *P F I Cole* a58 61
5 ch m Medicean—Tarakana (USA) (Shahrastani (USA))
81^{3} 130^{2} 211^{4}

Tarkari (IRE) *W P Mullins* a81 81
4 ch g Fantastic Light(USA) —Taraza (IRE) (Darshaan)
7263a^{2}

Tarkheena Prince (USA) *C Von Der Recke* a103 103
4 b g Aldebaran(USA) —Tarkheena (USA) (Alleged (USA))
(3493a) 6521a^{3}

Tarqua (IRE) *R Hannon* 44
3 b f King Charlemagne(USA) —Shining Creek (CAN) (Bering)
2496^{13} 2795^{12} 2947^{14} 3741^{11} 4223^{8}

Tarraad *M Botti*
3 b g Selkirk(USA) —Mingora (USA) (Mtoto)
998^{13} 1286^{12}

Tarrants Way *Jennie Candlish* a53 51
2 b c Auction House(USA) —Thicket (Wolfhound (USA))
2195^{7} 2575^{4} 3263^{3} 4076^{7} ◆ 4844^{9} 5526^{11} 5935^{10}

Tarruji (IRE) *Mme G Rarick* a70 60
3 gr g Verglas(IRE) —Polish Affair (IRE) (Polish Patriot (USA))
1311^{8} 2377^{5} 3464^{9} 5118a^{5}

Tartan Bearer (IRE) *Sir Michael Stoute* 125
4 ch h Spectrum(IRE) —Highland Gift (IRE) (Generous (IRE))
(1526) 3013^{2} 4298^{2}

Tartan Gigha (IRE) *M Johnston* a96 99
4 b g Green Desert(USA) —High Standard (Kris)
(866) 974^{2} 1089^{6} 1433^{2} 1527^{7} (1722) 1942^{2} 2101^{8} (2669) 3091^{25} 3872^{9} 4486^{11} 4768^{4} 5249^{12} 5663^{2} 5863^{11} 6480^{2}

Tartan Gunna *M Johnston* a84 96
3 b g Anabaa(USA) —Embraced (Pursuit Of Love)
(298) (532) 629^{3} (1471) 1801^{2} 1987^{5} 2674^{5} 3049^{29} 5375^{5} (5880) 6307^{5} 6665^{4}

Tartan Trip *A M Balding* a77 80
2 b g Selkirk(USA) —Marajuana (Robellino (USA))
2936^{4} 6451^{4} 6943^{3}

Tartan Turban (IRE) *R Hannon* a51 65
3 b c Invincible Spirit(IRE) —Tappen Zee (Sandhurst Prince)
75^{7} 231^{9}

Tartatartufata *J G Given* a70 72
7 b m Tagula(IRE) —It's So Easy (Shaadi (USA))
2^{8} 2225^{3} 2546^{2} 3565^{2} 3860^{5} 4469^{8} 4842^{5} 5675^{2} 6799^{7} 7086^{3} 7269^{12} 7355^{12} 7577^{7} 7852^{3}

Tartesos *P Chatelain* 78
4 b h In The Wings—Bimbola (FR) (Bikala)
7387a^{6}

Tartufo Dolce (IRE) *J G Given* a71 57
2 b f Key Of Luck(USA) —Corn Futures (Nomination)
1841^{4} 6069^{4} 6493^{5} (7213) 7636^{5}

Tarus (IRE) *A Berry* a12 52
5 ch m Tagula(IRE) —Wasaif (IRE) (Lomond (USA))
2439^{7} 3125^{7} 3484^{7} 3853^{8} 4775^{5} 5041^{4} 5338^{6} 5422^{9} 5727^{9} 6410^{14}

Tarzan (IRE) *M Johnston* 86
3 ch g Spinning World(USA) —Run To Jane (IRE) (Doyoun)
1280^{4} 1626^{2} (1925) 2406^{2} 2701^{10} 3049^{26} 3770^{4} 4400^{5} 5258^{4} 6019^{6} 6680^{18}

Tarzane (FR) *F Foresi*
2 b f Sulamani(IRE) —Tashkiyla (FR) (Alzao (USA))
6751a^{F}

Tascata Sorte (JPN) *H Fujiwara* 118
5 b h Jungle Pocket(JPN) —Brilliant Cut (JPN) (Northern Taste (CAN))
2117a^{5}

Tasdeer (USA) *Doug Watson* a103 103
4 b g Rahy(USA) —Mehthaaf (USA) (Nureyev (USA))
260a^{6} 638a^{10}

Tasheba *N J Henderson* a91 91
4 ch g Dubai Destination(USA) —Tatanka (IRE) (Lear Fan (USA))
3143^{4}

Tashkandi (IRE) *Mrs S J Humphrey* a69 84
9 gr g Polish Precedent(USA) —Tashiriya (IRE) (Kenmare (FR))
423^{7} 528^{9}

Tashzara (IRE) *Christopher Phillips* 85
2 ch f Intikhab(USA) —Sun Shower (IRE) (Indian Ridge)
5980^{3} 7187^{6}

Tasmeem (IRE) *B W Hills* 83
2 gr c Acclamation—Park Approach (IRE) (Indian Ridge)
4062^{5} 4568^{2} (5253) 5658^{8}

Tassara (FR) *Y De Nicolay* a88 100
3 br f Sendawar(IRE) —Trice (FR) (Highest Honor (FR))
1550a^{3}

Tastahil (IRE) *B W Hills* a94 114
5 ch g Singspiel(IRE) —Luana (Shaadi (USA))
(1017) 1351^{3} (2075) 2409^{3} 7031^{2} 7293^{9}

Taste Of Honey (IRE) *D W P Arbuthnot* a60 39
3 b f Deportivo—Long Tall Sally (IRE) (Danehill Dancer (IRE))
1066^{5} (1584) 2009^{7} 2355^{8} 2827^{10} 3302^{8} 3741^{12}

Taste The Victory (USA) *G A Swinbank* 76
2 b g Victory Gallop(CAN) —Tastetheteardrops (USA) (What Luck (USA))
6679^{2} ◆ 7116^{2}

Taste The Wine (IRE) *J S Moore* a67 74
3 gr g Verglas(IRE) —Azia (IRE) (Desert Story (IRE))
1193^{10} 1594^{4} 2131^{12} (2350) (2605) 2866^{7} 3861^{5} 4545^{7} 4911^{5} 5382^{6} 6473^{9} 6543^{4} 7665^{2} 7777^{4} 7831^{2}

Tasteyville (USA) *E Charpy* a113
6 rg r With Approval(CAN) —Rahfee (USA) (Rahy (USA))
334a^{8} 435a^{6} 639a^{4} 698a^{7}

Tatawor (IRE) *M P Tregoning* a71 25
2 b g Kheleyf(USA) —Romea (Muhtarram (USA))
3792^{10} 4537^{3}

Tatiana Romanova (USA) *R A Fahey* a61 74
2 ch f Mr Greeley(USA) —Bank On Her (USA) (Rahy (USA))
6154^{2} 6722^{4} (7114)

Tattercoats (FR) *M Botti* a44 24
3 b f Whywhywhy(USA) —Driscilla (USA) (Stately Don (USA))
5905^{10}

Tau *J E Pease* a65 94
4 ch h Lemon Drop Kid(USA) —Tobiano (USA) (Mt. Livermore (USA))
6658a^{7}

Tauman (IRE) *V Caruso* 101
2 b c Blu Air Force(IRE) —Time Of Gold (USA) (Banker's Gold (USA))
(7205a)

Taurakina *E Borromeo* 83
3 b f Selkirk(USA) —Asmita (Efisio)
1659a^{15} 2310a^{10}

Taurus Twins *R J Price* a64 82
3 b g Deportivo—Intellibet One (Compton Place)
379^{6} 583^{7} 686^{2} (804) 966^{7} 1190^{6} (1644) 2010^{2} (2160) 2774^{5} 3355^{2} 3592^{7} 6010^{2} 6647^{5} 6902^{2} (7122) 7395^{7}

Tawaabb *M R Channon* 99
2 ch c Kyllachy—Penmayne (Inchinor)
1749^{2} ◆ (2147) ◆ 3046^{3} ◆ 3779^{7} 5552^{5} 6660^{5}

Tawaash (USA) *E Charpy* a94 101
4 bb h Storm Cat(USA) —Victory Ride (USA) (Seeking The Gold (USA))
413a^{14} 522a^{4}

Tawaassol (USA) *E Charpy* a100 105
6 br h War Chant(USA) —Montecito (USA) (Seeking The Gold (USA))
336a^{2} 641a^{7}

Tax Dodger (IRE) *Liam McAteer* a26 55
3 b g Catcher In The Rye(IRE) —Stonor Lady (USA) (French Deputy (USA))
7416^{10}

Tax Free (IRE) *D Nicholls* a89 117
7 b g Tagula(IRE) —Grandel (Owington)
(1299) ◆ 1989^{3} (2523a) 2991^{14} 5233^{4} 6522a^{7}

Taxman (IRE) *A G Newcombe* a60 77
7 ch g Singspiel(IRE) —Love Of Silver (USA) (Arctic Tern (USA))
252^{2} 449^{4}

Tayacoba (CAN) *J H M Gosden* 57
2 bb g Smart Strike(CAN) —Bienandanza (USA) (Bien Bien (USA))
6930^{6}

Tayman (IRE) *N A Twiston-Davies* a43 66
7 bb g Sinndar(IRE) —Sweet Emotion (IRE) (Bering)
7005^{8}

Tayseer *J E Hammond* a103 106
4 ch g Medicean—Rohita (IRE) (Waajib)
1919a^{5} 2523a^{7} 5495a^{3} 6579a^{2}

Tazbar (IRE) *K G Reveley* 73
7 b g Tiraaz(USA) —Candy Bar (IRE) (Montelimar (USA))
7221^{8}

Tazeez (USA) *J H M Gosden* 117
5 bb g Silver Hawk(USA) —Soiree Russe (USA) (Nureyev (USA))
(1301) 2120a^{9} 3013^{5} 4329^{6}

T-Bird (SAF) *Doug Watson* a77 96
8 ch h Special Preview(SAF) —Lady Greystoke (SAF) (Lords (SAF))
265a^{12} 439a^{11}

Teachers Choice (IRE) *Adrian McGuinness* a65 76
6 b g Fruits Of Love(USA) —Son Chou (Cyrano De Bergerac)
4133^{4}

Tealing *R C Guest* a68
2 ch g Ishiguru(USA) —Renaissance Lady (IRE) (Imp Society (USA))
6896^{11} 7351^{4} (7501) 7722^{2} (7791)

Team Victory (BRZ) *S Seemar* a25
5 ch h Public Purse(USA) —Incitante (BRZ) (Minstrel Glory (USA))
612a^{10} 773a^{14}

Teasing *J Pearce* a82 73
5 b m Lujain(USA) —Movieland (USA) (Nureyev (USA))
29^{2} 125^{4} 195^{3} (274) (354) 504^{4} 713^{7} 730^{4} 1020^{3} 1179^{4} 1348^{5} 1815^{3} 2146^{3} 2499^{F}

Tech Exceed (GER) *A Wohler* 83
2 b f Exceed And Excel(AUS) —Technik (GER) (Nebos (GER))
7045a^{6}

Tecktal (FR) *P M Phelan* a58 57
6 ch m Pivotal—Wenge (USA) (Housebuster (USA))
595^{5} ◆ (541) 669^{4} 816^{4} 1463^{6} 3766^{5} 4235^{2} 4449^{3}

Teddy West (IRE) *Patrick Morris* a45 55
3 b g Trans Island—Duckmore Bay (IRE) (Titus Livius (FR))
621^{10} 938^{5} 1226^{6} 1691^{6}

Ted Spread *M H Tompkins* 93
2 b c Beat Hollow—Highbrook (USA) (Alphabatim (USA))
4314^{7} (6697) 7184^{3}

Teeky *J H M Gosden* a82 85
3 b f Daylami(IRE) —Las Flores (IRE) (Sadler's Wells (USA))
1092^{2} 2858^{7} (4498) 5168^{2} 5666^{5} (7148) 7569a^{0}

Teen Ager (FR) *P Burgoyne* a69 65
5 b g Invincible Spirit(IRE) —Tarwiya (IRE) (Dominion)
189^{8} 269^{4} 535^{7} (645) 832^{10} 956^{5} 1182^{6} 1468^{9} 1587^{3} 1890^{5} 2185^{4} (2400) 2824^{2} 3104^{6}

Teenie Girl (FR) *W J Cargeeg*
3 b f Ski Chief(USA) —Teenie Band (FR) (Exit To Nowhere (USA))
6149a^{10}

Teeraha (IRE) *D Shaw* a40 12
2 b f Arakan(USA) —Lovely Me (IRE) (Vision (USA))
5109^{8} 5337^{9} 5613^{9} 5835^{6} 6169^{13} 6590^{15}

Teia Tephi *P W Chapple-Hyam* a11 43
3 ch f Elnadim(USA) —Tatora (Selkirk (USA))
4913^{8} 5373^{7}

Tejime *J H M Gosden* a75
3 b g Royal Applause—Pizzicato (Statoblest)
7459^{2} ◆ 7730^{3} 7853^{7}

Tellelle (IRE) *Liam McAteer* a83 80
3 bb f Trans Island—Lomond Heights (IRE) (Lomond (USA))
(4392a) 7297a^{3}

Tell Halaf *M L W Bell* 64
2 b c Oasis Dream—Topkamp (Pennekamp (USA))
7145^{15} 7288^{6}

Telling (USA) *Steve Hobby* a90 114
5 b h A.P. Indy(USA) —Well Chosen (USA) (Deputy Minister (CAN))
6511a^{4} ◆ 7310a^{7}

Telling Stories (IRE) *B D Leavy* a55 35
3 b f Lucky Story(USA) —Yes Virginia (USA) (Roanoke (USA))
1156^{4} 1441^{6}

Tell Me A Story *M Brittain* 69
2 ch f Lucky Story(USA) —Cantina (Tina's Pet)
4100^{2} (4398) 6983^{14}

Telluride *J E Hammond* a89 109
3 b c Montjeu(IRE) —Bayourida (USA) (Slew O'Gold (USA))
1761a^{2}

Temecula (IRE) *M Halford* a73 78
4 b m High Chaparral(IRE) —Gujarat (USA) (Distant View (USA))
5689a^{18}

Tempelstern (GER) *M Delzangles* a94 115
5 gr h Sternkoenig(IRE) —Temple Esprit (Esprit Du Nord (USA))
1762a^{5} 6500a^{3}

Temperence Hall (USA) *J R Best* a69 66
3 ch g Graeme Hall(USA) —Sue's Temper (USA) (Temperence Hill (USA))
2300^{13} 2567^{11} 3009^{11} 3427^{7} 3743^{3} 3989^{2} 4082^{13} 5118a^{2} 5581^{3}

Templar Knight *Sir Michael Stoute* a55 70
3 b g Montjeu(IRE) —Vas Y Carla (USA) (Gone West (USA))
3425^{9} 4145^{4}

Temple Fair (USA) *M Johnston* a48 55
2 b g Tiger Hill(IRE) —Forty Marchanta (ARG) (Roar (USA))
5106^{7} 6033^{4} 6931^{11}

Temple Queen *S Kirk* a65 49
2 ch f Sulamani(IRE) —Indiana Blues (Indian Ridge)
5984^{5} ◆ 6291^{4} 6638^{6} 6905^{11}

Templet (USA) *T T Clement* a31 44
9 b g Souvenir Copy(USA) —Two Step Trudy (USA) (Capote (USA))
2601^{12} 3004^{7} 3552^{7}

Templetuohy Max (IRE) *J D Bethell* a72 79
4 b g Orpen(USA) —Eladawn (IRE) (Ela-Mana-Mou)
(194) 453^{2} 713^{11} 1845^{4} (2362) 2665^{4} 3189^{7} 3847^{9} 4597^{4} 5441^{4} 6490^{4}

Tenacestream (CAN) *J R Best* a79
2 b c Grand Slam(USA) —Heart Lake (CAN) (Unbridled (USA))
(7571) ◆ 7878^{4}

Tenacious *F Sheridan* a13
5 b m Pivotal—Invincible (Slip Anchor)
976^{9}

Tenancy (IRE) *S A Harris* a61 57
5 b g Rock Of Gibraltar(IRE) —Brush Strokes (Cadeaux Genereux)
1528^{9} 1695^{14} 2130^{7} 2225^{2} 5008^{17} 6161^{5} 7086^{10} 7424^{8} 7709^{4} 7869^{5}

Ten Day Wonder *R W Price* 52
4 gr m Daylami(IRE) —Tenable (Polish Precedent (USA))
4145^{8}

Tender Charm (USA) *R M Beckett* a58 61
3 bb g Malibu Moon(USA) —Tender Years (CAN) (Regal Classic (CAN))
1120^{3} 1703^{6} 2496^{15} 3302^{9} 4322^{10}

Tender Moments *B Smart* a40 60
5 br m Tomba—Cherish Me (Polar Falcon (USA))
2237^{11} 2746^{8} 4034^{3} 4403^{2} 4893^{6} 5359^{8} 6845^{8}

Tender Process (IRE) *J R Boyle* a74 65
6 b g Monashee Mountain(USA) —Appledorn (Doulab (USA))
37^{4} 186^{3} (289) (401) 619^{8} 1438^{7}

Ten Down *M Quinn* a77 73
4 b g Royal Applause—Upstream (Prince Sabo)
15^{11} (99) 243^{11} 589^{5} 710^{2} (870) 1150^{4} 1970^{17} 2359^{9} 4978^{7} 5323^{12} 5724^{3} 6186^{7} 6916^{10} 7223^{8} 7807^{6}

Tenement (IRE) *Jamie Poulton* a56 53
5 b g Mull Of Kintyre(USA) —Afifah (Nashwan (USA))
29^{5} 119^{5} 186^{7}

Tenessee *C G Cox* 76
2 b c Nayef(USA) —Shukran (Hamas (IRE))
6620^{3}

Tenga Venga *P S McEntee* a54 34
2 ch g Beat Hollow—Fanny's Fancy (Groom Dancer (USA))
5029^{10} 5371^{8} 7477^{7} 7705^{4} 7781^{4} 7865^{8}

Tenjack King *Joss Saville* a80 61
4 b g Kyllachy—Rash (Pursuit Of Love)
2894^{19} 3941^{8} 7867^{10}

Ten Pole Tudor *R A Harris* a66 78
4 b g Royal Applause—Amaniy (USA) (Dayjur (USA))
105^{6} 242^{2} 309^{11} 536^{4} 765^{6} 844^{14} 979^{2} 1177^{4} 1409^{2} 1530^{7} 1710^{7} 2746^{4} 2876^{6} 3467^{6} 6862^{11} 7499^{12} (7581) 7599^{11} 7718^{12} (7723) 7782^{4} 7817^{2} 7858^{2}

Ten Spot (IRE) *Stef Liddiard* a64 21
4 b m Intikhab(USA) —Allergy (Alzao (USA))
105^{3} 275^{6} 346^{10} 517^{3}

Tentears *H R A Cecil* a78 22
3 b f Cadeaux Genereux—Garmoucheh (USA) (Silver Hawk (USA))
2679^{8} 3168^{12} 5193^{3}

Ten To The Dozen *S T Mason* a55 66
6 b g Royal Applause—Almost Amber (USA) (Mt. Livermore (USA))
210^{3}

Tepmokea (IRE) *R A Fahey* a71 84
3 ch c Noverre(USA) —Eroica (GER) (Highest Honor (FR))
1019[2] 2060[2] 2701[2] 2935[9] 5419[5]
Terenzium (IRE) *Micky Hammond* a52 59
7 br g Cape Cross(IRE) —Tatanka (ITY) (Luge)
2344[6] 2614[3] 3486[6] 3760[2] 4806[9] (5307) 6899[7]
Termagant (IRE) *Kevin Prendergast* 110
2 b f Powerscourt—Rock Salt (Selkirk (USA))
(5488a)
Terminate (GER) *A Berry* a63 66
7 ch g Acatenango(GER) —Taghareed (USA) (Shadeed (USA))
59[2] ◆ 448[2] 631[7] 1786[2] (1980) 2264[3] 2656[2] (3382) 4220[5] 4857[2] 5161[3] 5943[4] 6102[8] 6818[6] 7113[10]
Terracotta Warrior *J Jay* a47 47
3 ch g Dubai Destination(USA) —Tamesis (IRE) (Fasliyev (USA))
1441[14] 1481[8] 3005[6] 4196[12]
Terradelice (FR) *Mme L Audon* 67
2 b f Marchand De Sable(USA) —Premonitary Dream (FR) (Exit To Nowhere (USA))
5713a[4] 6501a[16]
Terrain (USA) *Albert Stall Jr* a113
3 ch g Sky Mesa(USA) —Minery (USA) (Forty Niner (USA))
1225a[4] 2098a[7]
Terra Nova (FR) *Robert Collet* a88 88
2 b f American Post—Las Americas (FR) (Linamix (FR))
5494a[3]
Terrasini (FR) *J Howard Johnson* 59
4 gr g Linamix(FR) —Trazando (Forzando)
1399[4]
Terre Du Vent (FR) *Y De Nicolay* 104
3 b f Kutub(IRE) —Phlizz (FR) (Kaldoun (FR))
3442a[2] 6238a[6] 7128a[8] 7569a[0]
Terrific Challenge (USA) *S Seemar* a103 105
7 ch h Royal Academy(USA) —Clever Empress (Crafty Prospector (USA))
264a[12] 525a[8]
Terrymene Prince *L A Mullaney* a11 31
3 b g Bollin Terry—Princess Ismene (Sri Pekan (USA))
1681[7] 2104[6] 2723[12] 3233[9] 3685[7] 3711[9]
Tertiary (USA) *Saeed Bin Suroor* a48 71
2 b c Singspiel(IRE) —Allez Les Trois (USA) (Riverman (USA))
(6965) 7267[5]
Tertio Bloom (SWE) *F Reuterskiold* a107 95
4 ch g Tertullian(USA) —Yankee Bloom (USA) (El Gran Senor (USA))
3231a[5] 4363a[6]
Tertullus (FR) *Rune Haugen* 105
6 br g Monsun(GER) —Tryphosa (IRE) (Be My Guest (USA))
4582a[4] 5302a[7]
Tesserae *A B Haynes* a46 57
3 b f Reset(AUS) —Moxby (Efisio)
2181[5] 2447[6] 2738[3] 3260[3] 4934[2] 6310[4] 6788[7] 7324[5] 7670[4]
Tessie Bear *E J Creighton* a47
4 b m Red Ransom(USA) —Macaerleon (IRE) (Caerleon (USA))
1442[10]
Tesslam *M A Jarvis* a70 80
2 ch g Singspiel(IRE) —Rowaasi (Green Desert (USA))
4756[8] 6484[2] ◆ 7209[4]
Testama (FR) *J De Roualle* a88 104
5 gr m Testa Rossa(AUS) —Maid Of Honor (FR) (Highest Honor (FR))
2953a[4] 4580a[10]
Tevez *D Donovan* a63 67
4 b g Sakhee(USA) —Sosumi (Be My Chief (USA))
224[6] 2739[3] 2975[9] 3382[4] 3943[11] 4333[2] 5003[15] 5035[3] 5329[6]
Tewin Wood *A Bailey* a74 72
2 ch g Zaha(CAN) —Green Run (USA) (Green Dancer (USA))
5000[14] 6679[4] 6922[3] (7320) 7494[6] 7654[10]
Texan Star (IRE) *J H M Gosden* 80
2 b c Galileo(IRE) —Guignol (IRE) (Anita's Prince)
4048[2] 4524[10]
Texas Queen *M R Channon* a76 69
2 b f Shamardal(USA) —Min Asl Wafi (IRE) (Octagonal (NZ))
5021[6] 5398[4] 5752[2] 6096[3] 6481[8] 7001[3] 7843[3]
Thaahira (USA) *M A Jarvis* 67
2 b f Dynaformer(USA) —Mehthaaf (USA) (Nureyev (USA))
6729[5]
Thabaat *J M Bradley* a62 87
5 ch g Pivotal—Maraatib (IRE) (Green Desert (USA))
71[4] 118[6] 234[5] 496[9] 793[9]
Thabit (USA) *M A Jarvis* a74
3 ch c Mr Greeley(USA) —Matsue (USA) (Lure (USA))
1730[5] ◆
Thalamon (FR) *P Schiergen* 84
5 br h Monsun(GER) —Tryphosa (IRE) (Be My Guest (USA))
653a[4]
Thaliwarru *J R Gask* a46 61
2 b g Barathea(IRE) —Autumn Pearl (Orpen (USA))
2979[7] 3218[6] 4152[11] 4973[2] 6609[7]
Thanatos *P Schiergen* 95
4 ch h Fantastic Light(USA) —Tryphosa (IRE) (Be My Guest (USA))
6658a[6]
That Boy Ronaldo *A Berry* a47 55
3 b f Pyrus(USA) —Red Millennium (IRE) (Tagula (IRE))
92[4] 363[8]
Thatlittlecolt *D H Brown* a35
2 ch g Ishiguru(USA) —Bhima (Polar Falcon (USA))
7331[10] 7477[11] 7868[6]

That'll Do Nicely (IRE) *N G Richards* a70 73
6 b g Bahhare(USA) —Return Again (IRE) (Top Ville)
256[8] 711[3] (857) 1125[3] (1648) 2452[3] 3059[4] 3679[4] 4619[8] 5294[7] 6385[7]
That'Lldonowthen (IRE) *J S Moore* a33 54
2 ch c Chineur(FR) —Credit Crunch (IRE) (Caerleon (USA))
2771[15] 3572[8] 4018[5] 4384[6] 4689[6] 4912[5] 5613[6]
That's My Style *J H M Gosden* 52
2 gr f Dalakhani(IRE) —Pearl Dance (USA) (Nureyev (USA))
6992[14]
That's Showbiz *W J Knight* a56
2 sk g I Was Framed(USA) —Angelic Dancer (Komaite (USA))
7663[7]
Thaumatology (USA) *S Parr* a57
3 ch f Distorted Humor(USA) —Crystal Ballet (USA) (Royal Academy (USA))
560[6] 684[4] 736[10] 808[7]
Theatre Street (IRE) *S Dow* a73 80
3 b f Invincible Spirit(IRE) —Markova (IRE) (Marju (IRE))
188[2] (358) 709[3] 1272[7] (5506) 5805[6]
Theatrical Award (NOR) *Marianne Tveter* a91 77
4 br m Academy Award(IRE) —Theatre Antique (USA) (Theatrical (IRE))
(5302a)
The Bear *Miss L A Perratt* a56 78
6 ch g Rambling Bear—Precious Girl (Precious Metal)
818[7] 1096[9] 1694[13] 2389[7] 4036[3] 4136[6] (4899) (5309) 6010[24] 6161[4] 6413[10] 7171[10]
The Beat Is On *A W Carroll* a26 11
3 b f Beat All(USA) —Lady Ezzabella (Ezzoud (IRE))
6225[9] 6918[11]
Thebes *M Johnston* a97 101
4 ch g Cadeaux Genereux—See You Later (Emarati (USA))
(785) 916[4] 1018[18] 1212[8] 1398[2] 1560[3] 1699[2] 2297[4] 3389[5] (3802) 4037[8] 4297[13] 4523[16] 5257[10] 5695[15] 6089[12] 6482[4] 6815[12] 7227[6]
The Betchworth Kid *M L W Bell* a83 107
4 b g Tobougg(IRE) —Runelia (Runnett)
1191[2] 1546a[3] 2075[3] 2425a[5] 3390[9] 4457[3] 5173[7] ◆ (5609) 6306[5]
The Blue Dog (IRE) *George Baker* a42 32
2 b f High Chaparral(IRE) —Jules (IRE) (Danehill (USA))
6759[14] 6947[4] 7396[7] 7630[6] 7816[6]
The Blue God (IRE) *R Brogi* 96
3 b f Elnadim(USA) —Blue Inlet (IRE) (Bluebird (USA))
1659a[8]
The Boat Shed (IRE) *B W Duke* a50 38
3 b g Barathea(IRE) —Silver Hut (USA) (Silver Hawk (USA))
1328[11] 1780[5] 2074[13]
The Bogberry (USA) *A De Royer-Dupre* 116
4 ch h Hawk Wing(USA) —Lahinch (IRE) (Danehill Dancer (IRE))
1144a[2] 1551a[5] 5059a[5] 6526a[14] 6890a[10]
The Buck (IRE) *John Joseph Murphy* 52
6 ch g Quws—Erin Anam Cara (IRE) (Exit To Nowhere (USA))
4462[9]
The Bull Hayes (IRE) *Mrs John Harrington* 102
3 b c Sadler's Wells(USA) —No Review (USA) (Nodouble (USA))
2306a[3] 3438a[7] 4962a[5] 5539a[2]
The Bully Wee *J Jay* a62 62
3 b c Bishop Of Cashel—Red Barons Lady (IRE) (Electric)
855[3] 1289[10] 1440[7] 2048[17] 2567[9] 3741[9]
The Canny Dove (USA) *T D Barron* a33 34
3 b g Monashee Mountain(USA) —Who's Sorry Now (USA) (Ogygian (USA))
363[7] 383[7] 520[6] 1129[6] 3031[15]
The Caped Crusader (IRE) *T P Tate* 60
2 b g Cape Cross(IRE) —Phariseek (IRE) (Rainbow Quest (USA))
2467[14] 3052[6] 3823[5] 4396[8]
The Cardinal's Hat (FR) *P Winkworth* a57 62
2 b c High Yield(USA) —Rince Deas (IRE) (Alzao (USA))
1981[3] 4933[8] 5643[7] 6211[13]
The Carlton Cannes *M L W Bell* a98 90
5 b h Grand Lodge(USA) —Miss Riviera Golf (Hernando (FR))
1117[5]
The Cayterers *A W Carroll* a96 96
7 b g Cayman Kai(IRE) —Silky Smooth (IRE) (Thatching)
113[4] 191[6] ◆ 1813[3] 2495[5] (2977) (3431) (3695) 4339[4] 6249[6] 6480[8] 7574[2]
The Cheka (IRE) *Eve Johnson Houghton* 106
3 b c Xaar—Veiled Beauty (USA) (Royal Academy (USA))
(4052)
The Chip Chopman (IRE) *R A Harris* a25 53
7 b g Sri Pekan(USA) —Firstrusseofsummer (USA) (Summer Squall (USA))
7578[10]
The City Kid (IRE) *G D Blake* a68 25
6 b m Danetime(IRE) —Unfortunate (Komaite (USA))
14[5] 5225[6] 5634[9] 6828[7] 7348[5] 7579[3] 7678[6] 7877[6]
The Coach *T Wall* a37
3 ch g Central Park(IRE) —E Minor (IRE) (Blushing Flame (USA))
3718[P] 5228[8] 6073[9] 7557[12]
The Composer *M Blanshard* a60 61
7 b g Royal Applause—Superspring (Superlative)
1609[14] 2182[14] 4168[4] 5217[4] 5579[8] 6330[3] 6692[8]
The Confessor *H Candy* 72
2 b c Piccolo—Twilight Mistress (Bin Ajwaad (IRE))
3500[12] 6696[3] 6896[3]

The Countess *J Clais* a67 84
4 b m Numerous(USA) —Nachtigall (FR) (Night Shift (USA))
5301a[6]
The Cuckoo *M Quinn* a73 38
3 b g Invincible Spirit(IRE) —Aravonian (Night Shift (USA))
140[5] 560[4] 955[2] 1190[9] 5584[11] 6118[12] 7241[16]
The Desert Saint *A M Balding* a71 69
3 b g Dubai Destination(USA) —Maria Theresa (Primo Dominie)
1703[4] 2198[9] 2849[10] 3982[8]
The Dial House *J A Osborne* a77 75
3 b g Tagula(IRE) —Marliana (IRE) (Mtoto)
1105[5] 2890[10] 5101[8] 6289[3] 6940[5] 7455[3] 7699[12] 7776[4]
The Ducking Stool *H J Collingridge* a18 43
2 ch f Where Or When(IRE) —Dance Sequel (Selkirk (USA))
3167[10] 4497[10] 6874[7]
The Fifth Member (IRE) *J R Boyle* a96 96
5 b g Bishop Of Cashel—Palace Soy (IRE) (Tagula (IRE))
995[4] ◆ 1731[4] 2412[13] 2933[19] 6695[3] 6907[2] 7035[9] 7375[2] 7560[7]
Thefillyfromepsom *P M Phelan* a55 19
3 b f Royal Academy(USA) —For Love (USA) (Sultry Song (USA))
890[8] 1183[8] 1839[17] 3815[8] 4643[12]
Theflyingscottie *D Shaw* a55 57
7 gr g Paris House—Miss Flossa (FR) (Big John (FR))
2294[11]
The Fonz *Sir Michael Stoute* a74 83
3 b g Oasis Dream—Crystal Cavern (USA) (Be My Guest (USA))
(1474) 2210[3] 3429[4] 4299[2]
The Frying Pan (IRE) *Dr J D Scargill* a30 27
2 ch f Barathea(IRE) —Hello Mary (IRE) (Dolphin Street (FR))
3027[6] 4152[8] 4666[8] 6735[14] 7501[11] 7706[9]
The Galloping Shoe *A C Whillans* a83 84
4 b g Observatory(USA) —My Way (IRE) (Marju (IRE))
1149[2] 1964[4] 2274[11] 2980[9] 3339[4] 4273[10] 4853[3] 6187[6] 6564[3] 6964[4] 7287[4]
The Game *Tom Dascombe* a98 86
4 b g Compton Place—Emanant (Emarati (USA))
204[4] (Dead)
The Geester *Stef Liddiard* a67 51
5 b g Rambling Bear—Cledeschamps (Doc Marten)
173[2] (326) 535[2] 2130[6] 7807[8]
The Gillie *R A Fahey* 56
2 b g Pivotal—Red Tiara (USA) (Mr Prospector (USA))
7289[6] ◆
Thegirlsgonewild (USA) *H J L Dunlop* a52 47
3 bb f Gone West(USA) —Coconut Girl (USA) (Cryptoclearance (USA))
1605[8] 2199[6] 2709[12]
The Graig *J R Holt* a60 58
5 b g Josr Algarhoud(IRE) —Souadah (USA) (General Holme (USA))
78[2] (211) 494[13] 657[3] 791[5] (969) 1254[6] 1514[10] 3470[10] 7433[7] 7755[8]
The Great Husk (IRE) *J S Moore* a26 49
2 b g Alamshar(IRE) —Stardance (USA) (Rahy (USA))
3160[12] 4757[7] 5543[4] 7683[6]
The Grey One (IRE) *J M Bradley* a74 66
6 gr g Dansili—Marie Dora (FR) (Kendor (FR))
1318[7] 1539[6] 1710[13] 2166[9] 2330[8] 2859[14] 3077[7] 3470[6] 3929[2] 4645[14] 4938[11] 5103[2] 5229[4] 5683[3] 5886[5] 6074[5] 6588[3] 6719[5] (6998) 7109[3] 7423[5] 7512[3] 7632[2] 7699[4] ◆ 7823[5]
The Hague *J H M Gosden* a68 69
3 b c Xaar—Cox Orange (USA) (Trempolino (USA))
862[3] ◆ 1054[4] 2320[5] 3099[2]
The Happy Hammer (IRE) *E V Stanford* a64 64
3 b g Acclamation—Emma's Star (ITY) (Darshaan)
1490[6] 2600[4] 4056[9] (4440) 5030[7] 5663[15] 6124[5] 6637[3] 7179[3] 7479[7]
The Hermitage (IRE) *M Johnston* 82
2 b f Kheleyf(USA) —Russian Countess (USA) (Nureyev (USA))
1719[2] (2000) 2372[2] 2995[13] 6486[21]
The History Man (IRE) *B D Leavy* a63 72
6 b g Titus Livius(FR) —Handsome Anna (IRE) (Bigstone (IRE))
1528[2] 1877[3] 2625[3] 2812[11] 3304[9] 3999[7] 5008[3] 5374[11] 5501[2] 6119[3] 6251[5] 6596[4] (6933) 7086[4]
The Hornet (AUS) *D Dragon* 96
5 b g High Yield(USA) —Millennium Miss (AUS) (Flying Spur (AUS))
2117a[8]
The Human League *M R Channon* 84
2 b g Tobougg(IRE) —Noble Desert (FR) (Green Desert (USA))
3113[3] (3392) ◆ 3782[6] 4488[7]
The Jailer *J G M O'Shea* a64 67
6 b m Mujahid(USA) —Once Removed (Distant Relative)
661[11] 853[9] 1535[10] 2876[7] 3948[6]
The Jobber (IRE) *M Blanshard* a93 92
8 b g Foxhound(USA) —Clairification (IRE) (Shernazar)
985[7] 1457[12] 2228[5] 2397[4] (2946) 3582[2] 3784[3] 4341[11] 4567[4] 5098[7] 5871[2] 6171[8] 6459[5] 6647[14] 6972[9]
The Jostler *Mrs L Wadham* a84 91
4 b m Dansili—The Jotter (Night Shift (USA))
232[7] 3102[7] 3537[9]
The Kyllachy Kid *S Gollings* a93 89
3 b g Kyllachy—All Business (Entrepreneur)
1803[3] 2934[16] 3033[2] 3688[6] 6949[8] 7287[12] (7356) 7558[5]
Theladyinquestion *A M Balding* 78
2 b f Dubawi(IRE) —Whazzat (Daylami (IRE))
3534[5] (5212) ◆ 6241[12]

Theladyisatramp *M L W Bell* a57 40
2 b f Bahamian Bounty—Affair Of State (IRE) (Tate Gallery (USA))
5096[8] 6228[9] 6774[10]
The Last Alzao (IRE) *R A Fahey* a70 76
3 b f Alzao(USA) —Balakera (FR) (Lashkari)
758[8] 810[6] 1400[8] 2236[9] (2790) ◆ (3721) ◆ (3943) ◆ 5009[8]
The Last Bottle (IRE) *W M Brisbourne* a64 65
4 ch g Hawk Wing(USA) —Mesmerist (USA) (Green Desert (USA))
7648[7]
The Last Don (IRE) *D R Lanigan* a95 81
3 b c Redback—Banco Solo (Distant Relative)
1257[6] 1585[10] 1963[7] (3511) 4175[2] (4545) (5666) (6121) ◆
The Last Hurrah (IRE) *Mrs John Harrington* 82
9 b g In The Wings—Last Exit (Dominion)
4510a[10]
The Little Master (IRE) *D R C Elsworth* a59 53
5 bb g Tendulkar(USA) —Minatina (IRE) (Ela-Mana-Mou)
193[10]
The London Gang *S Wynne* a60 43
6 b g Mind Games—Nom Francais (First Trump)
195[7] 215[7] 254[6] 748[12] (933) 1037[7] 3224[11] 3467[11]
The Lord *W G M Turner* a63 74
9 b g Averti(IRE) —Lady Longmead (Crimson Beau)
742[6] 956[3] 1150[6] 1468[11] 2130[9]
The Love Guru *J R Boyle* a62 40
2 b g Ishiguru(USA) —Beauty (IRE) (Alzao (USA))
6162[10] 6792[8] 7419[8] 7654[5] (7757) 7849[2]
The Magic Blanket (IRE) *Stef Liddiard* a71 44
4 b g Bahamian Bounty—Zietunzeen (IRE) (Zieten (USA))
(46) ◆ (956) ◆ 1970[12] 2596[11] 3252[11] 7689[5]
The Magic Of Rio *Peter Grayson* a86 88
3 b f Captain Rio—Good Health (Magic Ring (IRE))
207[P] 4776[5] 5197[5] 5777[7] 6444[8] 6669[12] 7136[7]
Themanforacrisis (IRE) *R M Beckett* 61
2 b c Oratorio(IRE) —Sister Golden Hair (IRE) (Glint Of Gold)
3867[5] 4945[9] 5527[12] 6391[6]
Theme Catcher (IRE) *G Brown* 63
4 b g Red Ransom(USA) —Canouan (IRE) (Sadler's Wells (USA))
5152[6] 5683[11]
Themelie Island (IRE) *A Trybuhl* 102
4 b m Montjeu(IRE) —Thelema (IRE) (Caerleon (USA))
5296a[5] 6153a[3] 6714a[3] 7406a[7]
The Midshipmaid *Lucinda Featherstone* a6 51
2 b f Zafeen(FR) —Ebba (Elmaamul (USA))
1867[11] 2604[5] 3337[6] 5310[10] 5526[12]
The Mighty Atom (USA) *P J Prendergast* a76 54
2 ch f Sky Mesa(USA) —Nurse Cleo (USA) (Rahy (USA))
5452a[8] 5866[5]
The Mighty Mod (USA) *M Johnston* 54
2 b g Gone West(USA) —Michelle's Monarch (USA) (Wavering Monarch (USA))
3052[7] 5907[9] 6620[13] 6901[11]
The Miniver Rose (IRE) *R Hannon* 106
3 b f High Chaparral(IRE) —Bloemfontain (IRE) (Cape Cross (IRE))
1291[4] 1701[4] 2036[2] 2672[5] (5796) 7047a[8]
The Miss McArdle (GER) *Dr A Bolte* 63
2 b f Tannenkonig(IRE) —The Bastienne (FR) (Baylis)
6751a[5]
The Mouse Carroll (IRE) *B R Johnson* a64 70
5 b g Barathea(IRE) —Grecian Glory (IRE) (Zafonic (USA))
7830[11]
The Mumbo *W Jarvis* a66 49
3 b f Bahamian Bounty—Mandolin (IRE) (Sabrehill (USA))
(121) 2548[10] 6782[5] 7236[4] 7456[6]
The Name Is Frank *Mark Gillard* a59 64
4 b g Lujain(USA) —Zaragossa (Paris House)
3204[7] 3505[10] 3994[2] 4222[8] 5008[2] 5396[3] 5443[8] 5729[3] 6186[2] 6340[2] (6553) 6933[2] 7330[3] 7418[6] 7657[6] 7771[2] 7835[9]
The Nifty Fox *T D Easterby* a80 93
5 b g Foxhound(USA) —Nifty Alice (First Trump)
2897[10] 3268[6] 3855[3] (4189) 4753[4] 5148[5] (5293) 5623[2] 6051[5] 6359[4] (6843) 7015[17]
Theocritus (USA) *D M Simcock* a89 90
4 b g Theatrical(IRE) —Candace In Aspen (USA) (Woodman (USA))
1460[20] 1753[6] (2220) (2808) 3525[2] 3847[4] 4437[8] (4698) (5108) 5473[2] 5963[3]
Theola (IRE) *M H Tompkins* a51 85
3 bl f Kalanisi(IRE) —Third Dimension (FR) (Suave Dancer (USA))
2877[6] 3192[3] 4491[3] 5113[2] 5430[2] (6021) (6676) ◆
Theologist (IRE) *Mrs A J Perrett* 76
3 b c Galileo(IRE) —Medina (IRE) (Pennekamp (USA))
1838[3] ◆ 2206[4] 2479[6] 4545[5] 5217[2] 5430[3] 6400[2] 6543[3] 6935[3]
Theology *J Noseda* 77
2 b c Galileo(IRE) —Biographie (Mtoto)
6423[3] ◆ 6810[13]
Theonebox (USA) *N P Moore* a84 80
4 ch g Johannesburg(USA) —Khalifa Of Kushog (USA) (Air Forbes Won (USA))
199[6] 713[6] 2313[11] 3076[3] 3481[8] 7607[7] 7759[11]
The Only Boss (IRE) *W J Haggas* 90
2 ch c Exceed And Excel(AUS) —Aljafliyah (Halling (USA))
6000[5] (6381) ◆ (6841)
The Only Key *P Schiergen* 86
3 b f Key Of Luck(USA) —Sierra Virgen (USA) (Stack (USA))
7697a[7]

The Osteopath (IRE) *M Dods* 98
6 ch g Danehill Dancer(IRE) —Miss Margate (IRE) (Don't Forget Me)
995[9] 1684[13] (2045) (3312) 4779[11] 6094[10] 6675[8] 7294[15]

The Pirate (DEN) *Eva Sundbye* a68 95
6 b h Primatico(USA) —Medinova (Mas Media)
5302a[14]

The Power Of Phil *Tom Dascombe* a47
5 b g Komaite(USA) —Starboard Tack (FR) (Saddlers' Hall (IRE))
131[5] 247[5] 323[4]

The Quiet Genius *Jedd O'Keeffe* a36 63
3 b g Daylami(IRE) —Shallat (IRE) (Pennekamp (USA))
1335[14] 1522[6] 2042[5] 3454[12] 4230[5] 5011[11] 5733[3] 6432[11]

Thereafter (USA) *R Charlton* a71
2 ch f Lion Heart(USA) —Alvernia (USA) (Alydar (USA))
5638[3] 6164[8]

The Rectifier (USA) *Stef Liddiard* 79
2 bb c Langfuhr(CAN) —Western Vision (USA) (Gone West (USA))
5542[9] 6108[4] 6616[2]

Theregoesjojo (USA) *Kenneth McPeek* a108
3 b c Brahms(USA) —Slewie Blues (USA) (Seattle Slew (USA))
1225a[9]

There We Go (IRE) *G A Swinbank* 34
3 b g Pyrus(USA) —Ghayaat (USA) (Lyphard (USA))
3975[6] 4347[8] 4531[4]

The Rising (TUR) *C Kurt* 102
5 b m Strike The Gold(USA) —Free Trade (TUR) (Shareef Dancer (USA))
5588a[7]

The Salwick Flyer (IRE) *I Semple* a64 64
6 b g Tagula(IRE) —Shimla (IRE) (Rudimentary (USA))
3021[9]

The Saucy Snipe *P Winkworth* a64 59
3 b f Josr Algarhoud(IRE) —The Dark Eider (Superlative)
1428[7] 2357[9] 3739[5] (4146) 5097[5] 5812[4] 5990[5] 6446[10]

The Scorching Wind (IRE) *S C Williams* a97 78
3 b c Fasliyev(USA) —Rose Of Mooncoin (IRE) (Brief Truce (USA))
1422[7] 2160[9] 3010[2] (3342) ◆ 4056[6] 4304[2] (5575) ◆ (5665) 5780[2] 6243[14] 7827[8] ◆

Thescottishsoldier *A G Foster* 25
2 ch g Observatory(USA) —Twenty Seven (IRE) (Efisio)
4308[9] 6408[10] 7116[9]

The Shuffler *G L Moore* a66 58
2 b g Reset(AUS) —Lucky Dice (Perugino (USA))
1404[14] 2201[4] 2631[5] 3579[6] 4208[5] 4525[4] 4868[9] 6589[15]

The Slider *Mrs L C Jewell* a48 15
5 b m Erhaab(USA) —Cottage Maid (Inchinor)
171[10] 2708[11]

The Snatcher (IRE) *R Hannon* a96 96
6 b h Indian Danehill(IRE) —Saninka (IRE) (Doyoun)
1433[9] 1731[3] 4409[16] 4954[13] 5663[12] 6212[6] 7054[7]

The Spicer *F Sheridan* a58
4 b g Lujain(USA) —Spicey (Mizoram (USA))
1185[10] 1410[7] 1662[10] 2924[11] 3632[10]

The Staffy (IRE) *Tom Dascombe* a62 35
4 b g Redback—Lady Charlotte (Night Shift (USA))
570[2] 767[6] 2352[13] 2975[11] 6495[9] 6831[P] (Dead)

The Starboard Bow *S Kirk* a86 86
2 b c Observatory(USA) —Overboard (IRE) (Rainbow Quest (USA))
(4666) 5214[7] 5681[2] 6305[9] 6805[7]

The Strig *S C Williams* a69 47
2 b g Mujahid(USA) —Pretty Kool (Inchinor)
4243[8] 6971[5] ◆ 7571[3]

The Tatling (IRE) *J M Bradley* a92 88
12 bb g Perugino(USA) —Aunty Eileen (Ahonoora)
67[4] (424) 714[9] 821[5] 965[3] 1334[6] 1418[3] 1806[2] 1943[4] 2326[3] 2520[2] 2653[4] 3204[2] 3623[4] 3995[3] (4222) (4567) 5183[5] 5436[2] 5768[3] 5901[3] 6171[9] 6666[5] 7155[8] 7511[5] 7605[3] 7758[13] 7872[2]

Theta Wave (USA) *J R Gask* a62 68
3 ch g Buckhar(USA) —Let's Dance (USA) (Thorn Dance (USA))
1274 358[3] 986[7] 3859[8] (4596) 5155[7] 5716[7] 6252[7]

Thetearsthaticry (IRE) *A E Jones* a39 44
3 b g King Charlemagne(USA) —Zeddaana (FR) (Arctic Tern (USA))
216[11] 2912[6]

The Thrifty Bear *C W Fairhurst* a17 16
6 ch g Rambling Bear—Prudent Pet (Distant Relative)
5351[0]

The Tooth Fairy (IRE) *Michael Mulvany* a76 91
3 b c Statue Of Liberty(USA) —Fairy Lore (IRE) (Fairy King (USA))
4574a[10]

The Two G'S *P D Evans* a56 30
2 b f Mark Of Esteem(IRE) —Intellibet One (Compton Place)
1968[8] 2533[12] 6207[5] 6610[10] 7268[5] 7559[11] 7707[5] 7757[6]

Thewaytosanjose (IRE) *Patrick J Flynn* a57 38
3 b f Fasliyev(USA) —Soltura (IRE) (Sadler's Wells (USA))
(77) 628[5] 741[5] 817[12] 6867a[15]

Thewayyouare (USA) *A P O'Brien* 117
4 b h Kingmambo(USA) —Maryinsky (IRE) (Sadler's Wells (USA))
1551a[4] 2303a[5]

The Wee Chief (IRE) *J C Fox* a69 64
3 ch g King Charlemagne(USA) —La Belle Clare (IRE) (Paris House)
4324[4] (7533) 7738[11]

The Which Doctor *J Noseda* a91 93
4 b g Medicean—Oomph (Shareef Dancer (USA))
3431[8] 3988[4] 4409[3] 4781[5] 5262[9] 5510[6] (6059) 6480[18] 7035[5]

The Wily Woodcock *T Wall* a64 36
5 b g Mark Of Esteem(IRE) —Lonely Shore (Blakeney)
344[6] 1883[12] 2686[11] 5617[10] 5842[10] 7500[14]

The Winged Assasin (USA) *J Akehurst* a68 74
3 b g Fusaichi Pegasus(USA) —Gran Dama (USA) (Rahy (USA))
315[2] 851[5] (1196) 1462[5] 4956[7] 5448[8] 5774[6] 6190[9] 6547[RR]

Thewinnatakesitall *H J Evans* a58 58
2 ch f King's Best(USA) —Powder Puff (IRE) (Sadler's Wells (USA))
3226[11] 3858[8] 4811[4] 5985[10] 6589[9] 7056[10] 7268[2] 7559[8] 7778[5]

They All Laughed *Mrs Marjorie Fife* a79 78
6 ch g Zafonic(USA) —Royal Future (IRE) (Royal Academy (USA))
37 219[2] 341[4] 485[3] 511[3] 604[2] 743[3] (795) 1059[3] 1478[5] 1635[5] 2194[12] 2783[3] (3233) 5308[5] 5698[13] 6102[5] 6559[3] 7336[3] 7425[5] 7842[4]

Theymistim *Mrs L Stubbs* 80
2 b g Kyllachy—Dance Sequence (USA) (Mr Prospector (USA))
(4889)

Thief *L M Cumani* 64
3 b c Falbrav(IRE) —Eurolink Raindance (IRE) (Alzao (USA))
2338[5]

Thief Of Time (IRE) *P W Chapple-Hyam* a92 90
3 b g Clodovil(IRE) —Cape Flattery (IRE) (Cape Cross (IRE))
154[2] (280) 1086[2] 1484[2] 2273[7] 2925[5] 4954[4] 6117[7] 6944[2]

Thinking *T D Easterby* a47 62
2 b g Makbul—Concentration (IRE) (Mind Games)
2467[12] 5668[14] 5977[5] 6355[8] 6983[11] 7242[3]

Thinking Robins (IRE) *Alessandro Turco* 105
6 b h Plumbird—Rose Jasmine (ITY) (Sikeston (USA))
1905a[6] (7206a)

Think Its All Over (USA) *T P Tate* 75
2 b c Tiznow(USA) —A P Petal (USA) (A.P. Indy (USA))
4939[4] (6136)

Thin Red Line (IRE) *E A L Dunlop* a92 93
3 b c Red Ransom(USA) —Albaiyda (IRE) (Brief Truce (USA))
1105[4] 2209[7] (2767) 3618[2] ◆ 4520[7] 5828[8] (6724) ◆

Third Set (IRE) *M bin Shafya* a100 114
6 b g Royal Applause—Khamseh (Thatching) (183a) 339a[2] 774a[16]

Thirtyfourthstreet (IRE) *W R Muir* a51 36
4 gr m Beat Hollow—Peacock Alley (IRE) (Salse (USA))
678[6] 779[3] 978[8] 1200[9] 1430[6]

This Is Real (IRE) *Brian Nolan* a71 62
2 b f Bertolini(USA) —Banba (IRE) (Docksider (USA))
2286a[5]

This Ones For Eddy *J Balding* a77 76
4 b g Kyllachy—Skirt Around (Deploy)
518[2] 561[4] 606[3] 799[6] (886) 1000[14] 1194[3] (1401) 1612[2] 1690[3] 2269[4] 2313[9] 2626[2] 2880[8] 3403[9] 3624[7] 4040[7] 5418[6] 5884[7] ◆ 6411[4] 6847[3] 6989[2] 7192[8]

This Ones For Pat (USA) *S Parr* a68 41
4 bb g Proud Citizen(USA) —Lace Curtain Irish (USA) (Cryptoclearance (USA))
884[2] 1169[16] 1480[12] 1591[10]

Thistimesforgood (IRE) *Paul Stafford* a48 56
6 ch g Rossini(USA) —Midsummer Night (IRE) (Fairy King (USA))
7632[10]

Thistle *George Baker* a49 55
8 ch g Selkirk(USA) —Ardisia (USA) (Affirmed (USA))
4376[6] 5377[8]

Thistlestar (USA) *R A Fahey* a65 60
2 bb f Lion Heart(USA) —Katiba (USA) (Gulch (USA))
6047[3] 7585[5] 7800[5]

Thomaraz (FR) *J-L Dubord*
2 ch c Nombre Premier—Niraz (FR) (Nikos)
7315a[7]

Thomas Baines (USA) *M L W Bell* a74 76
2 b g Johannesburg(USA) —Foofaraw (USA) (Cherokee Run (USA))
1147[3] ◆ 1404[7] 1630[3] 4243[5] 4901[6] (5841) 6071[3]

Thompsons Walls (IRE) *D Nicholls* a59 74
4 b g Trans Island—Nordic Living (IRE) (Nordico (USA))
981[7] 1276[11] 1628[6] 1955[13]

Thoosa *P S McEntee* a42 14
3 ch f Best Of The Bests(IRE) —Natural Grace (Zamindar (USA))
286[9] 358[4] 552[3] 602[6] 1045[7] 2455[7] 2862[12]

Thornaby Green *T D Barron* a59 67
8 b g Whittingham(IRE) —Dona Filipa (Precocious)
7[3] 2211[2] 324[8] 3681[0]

Thornton George *T J Fitzgerald* 40
4 b g Piccolo—Princess Emily (IRE) (Dolphin Street (FR))
2232[7] 3120[7]

Thorny Mandate *W M Brisbourne* a64 63
7 b g Diktat—Rosa Canina (Bustino)
660[4] 871[6] (972) 1154[6] 1506[4] 1936[4] 2497[3] 2783[7] 3169[5] 3447[2] 3809[6] 5210[7] 5530[10] 5680[8] 6025[9] 6280[8]

Thoughtful (IRE) *J W Hills* a56 42
2 b f Acclamation—Truly Generous (IRE) (Generous (IRE))
5638[5] 6241[20]

Thoughtsofstardom *P S McEntee* a81 71
6 b g Mind Games—Alustar (Emarati (USA))
270[5] 359[6] 382[6] 442[5] 486[4] 870[9] 901[9] 1094[6] 1181[6] 1877[9] 1957[5] 2053[6] 2418[12] 2758[12] 2811[3] 3239[5] 3304[3] 3386[5] 3677[8] 4059[8] 5008[13] 5610[3] 6119[4] (6186) 6341[10] 7606[5] 7657[2] (7709) 7771[6] (7808) 7838[4]

Thousandkissesdeep (IRE) *J H M Gosden* 77
2 b f Night Shift(USA) —Interim Payment (USA) (Red Ransom (USA))
5498[8] 6920[2]

Thousand Miles (IRE) *P W Chapple-Hyam* 88
3 br c Danehill Dancer(IRE) —Mille Miglia (IRE) (Caerleon (USA))
(1257) 2096a[5] 3816[5] 4210[3] 4909[5] 6014[7] 6731[10]

Three Boars *S Gollings* a67 17
7 ch g Most Welcome—Precious Poppy (Polish Precedent (USA))
168[7] 967[2] 7124[12] 7760[6]

Three Bodies (IRE) *P Bary* 111
3 gr c Domedriver(IRE) —Three Mysteries (IRE) (Linamix (FR))
5084a[2]

Three Ducks *L M Cumani* a74 74
3 b f Diktat—Three Terns (USA) (Arctic Tern (USA))
1882[7] 2432[9] 3551[2]

Three Gold Leaves *D W Thompson* a52 29
4 ch g Zaha(CAN) —Tab's Gift (Bijou D'Inde)
1127[5] 2237[15] 2532[10]

Three Good Friends (IRE) *P T Midgley* a68 29
2 b f Orpen(USA) —Eastern Blue (IRE) (Be My Guest (USA))
1044[9] (2741)

Three Moons (IRE) *H J L Dunlop* a73 103
3 b f Montjeu(IRE) —Three Owls (IRE) (Warning)
(1198) 1701[2]

Three Rocks (IRE) *J S Bolger* a83 111
4 b h Rock Of Gibraltar(IRE) —Top Crystal (IRE) (Sadler's Wells (USA))
1913a[2] 2287a[6] 2870a[4] 3434a[5] (3881a) 5080a[2] 6530a[3]

Three's A Crowd *D R C Elsworth* a55 52
2 b f Royal Applause—Thracian (Green Desert (USA))
2490[6] 3210[4] 3810[14] 6775[9]

Three Sons *I W McInnes* a16 30
2 b g Reset(AUS) —Zuloago (USA) (Stravinsky (USA))
2800[8] 3719[9] 4101[7] 4138[7]

Threestepstoheaven *B W Hills* 74
3 b g Haafhd—Bella Bianca (IRE) (Barathea (IRE))
1573[5] 2126[10] 3695[7]

Three Strings (USA) *P D Niven* a70 63
6 b g Stravinsky(USA) —Just Cause (Law Society (USA))
40[6] (1568) 4373[3]

Three Thieves (UAE) *Jim Best* a47 55
6 ch g Jade Robbery(USA) —Melisendra (FR) (Highest Honor (FR))
7658[6] 7688[6]

Three Times *D R Lanigan* a24 32
2 ch f Bahamian Bounty—Triple Joy (Most Welcome)
6947[6] 7183[18]

Three Way Stretch (IRE) *J T Gorman* 89
3 b g Intikhab(USA) —Chapka (IRE) (Green Desert (USA))
1755a[8] 6707a[7] 6867a[14]

Thrill *J H M Gosden* a72 81
2 ch f Pivotal—Irresistible (Cadeaux Genereux)
6164[3] ◆ (6729) ◆ 7187[8]

Through The Forest (USA) *W R Swinburn* a58 52
3 bb f Forestry(USA) —Lakefront (USA) (Deputy Minister (CAN))
3696[7] 4246[9] 4828[8] 5775[4] 6371[3] (7794)

Throw The Dice *A Berry* a29 24
7 b g Lujain(USA) —Euridice (IRE) (Woodman (USA))
3109[7] 3657[8]

Thrust Control (IRE) *M R Channon* 74
2 ch g Fath(USA) —Anazah (USA) (Diesis)
(6544)

Thumberlina *Mrs C A Dunnett* a40 48
3 b f Choisir(AUS) —Capstick (JPN) (Machiavellian (USA))
552[9] 664[7] 812[10] 947[8] 1190[4] 1359[7] 1455[5] 2162[8] 3663[5] 3959[7] 4155[7] 4736[11] 5105[7] 5480[8] 5974[9] 6335[11]

Thumbs Up (NZ) *C S Shum* 118
5 b g Shinko King(IRE) —Regelle (NZ) (Exploding Prospect (USA))
1554a[3] 7744a[7]

Thunderball *J A Glover* a86 84
3 ch g Haafhd—Trustthunder (Selkirk (USA))
1019[7] 1471[3] 1744[2] 2072[10] 2544[3] 3116[2] 6019[12] 6773[2] 6973[4] 7360[4]

Thunder Bay *R A Fahey* a64 76
4 b g Hunting Lion(IRE) —Floral Spark (Forzando)
1096[10] 1694[11] (2158) 2717[9] 2966[7] 3445[3] 3562[12] 4136[7] 4772[5] 5518[12] 5955[7] 6220[3] 6379[9] 7053[2] 7358[2] 7397[5] 7503[7] 7645[9]

Thunder Bridge (USA) *D K Weld* 105
2 b c Bernstein(USA) —Hasardeuse (USA) (Distant View (USA))
(6401a) 7072a[5]

Thunder Gorge (USA) *Mouse Hamilton-Fairley* a74 78
4 b g Thunder Gulch(USA) —Renaissance Fair (USA) (Theatrical (IRE))
1067[5] 1603[11] (2243) 2894[18] 4211[3] 4526[6] 5243[8] 5745[9] 6568[7]

Thundering Home *E A L Dunlop* a72
2 gr c Storming Home—Citrine Spirit (IRE) (Soviet Star (USA))
7388[7] 7663[3] (7865)

Thunderonthemount *M J Attwater*
4 ch g Zaha(CAN) —Vrennan (Suave Dancer (USA))
3791[7]

Thunderous Mood (USA) *P F I Cole* a81 102
3 bb c Storm Cat(USA) —Warm Mood (USA) (Alydar (USA))
2016[7] 2278[7] 2934[14] 5902[4] 6240[9] 6815[15] 7026[5] 7613[4]

Thunder Rock (IRE) *Jonjo O'Neill* 75
7 b g King's Best(USA) —Park Express (Ahonoora)
4793[5]

Thunderstruck *J A Glover* a83 74
4 b g Bertolini(USA) —Trustthunder (Selkirk (USA))
2150[9] 2261[10] 2569[8] 5962[13] 6183[4] 6818[2] 6998[2] (7225) (7403) 7512[2] 7667[4] 7823[3] ◆

Thunderwing (IRE) *James Moffatt* a39 65
7 bb g Indian Danehill(IRE) —Scandisk (IRE) (Kenmare (FR))
448[10] 1767[3] 2044[8]

Thurston (IRE) *D J S Ffrench Davis* a66
3 ch g Barathea(IRE) —Campiglia (IRE) (Fairy King (USA))
1656[6] 2578[9] 4375[12] 6070[12] 6442[11]

Thyan (FR) *C Baillet* 65
2 b c Indian Rocket—Slyders (IRE) (Hector Protector (USA))
7264a[7]

Tiago (USA) *John Shirreffs* a123 94
5 b h Pleasant Tap(USA) —Set Them Free (USA) (Stop The Music (USA))
6687a[10]

Tia Juana (IRE) *Saeed Bin Suroor* a65 60
2 b f Shamardal(USA) —Tiavanita (USA) (J O Tobin (USA))
4869[4] 5380[4] 5969[4]

Tian Shan (IRE) *D K Weld* 94
5 b h Barathea(IRE) —Most Charming (FR) (Darshaan)
1138a[9]

Ticket To Freedom (NZ) *J J Quinn* 65
7 bl g Cape Cross(IRE) —Macrowave (NZ) (Crested Wave (USA))
2944[3]

Ticket To Paradise *D R Lanigan* 16
2 b c Singspiel(IRE) —Dream Ticket (USA) (Danzig (USA))
7243[13]

Tidal Force (USA) *A J McCabe* a61 76
3 ch g High Yield(USA) —Shady Waters (CAN) (Rahy (USA))
1284[7] 2300[3] 2849[14] 3358[5] 3577[7] 4425[8] 7627[10]

Tiddliwinks *K A Ryan* a93 57
3 b g Piccolo—Card Games (First Trump)
5228[4] 5394[4] (6255) 6997[12] 7172[13] 7575[2] (7692) ◆

Tiegs (IRE) *P W Hiatt* a52 47
7 ch m Desert Prince(IRE) —Helianthus (Groom Dancer (USA))
1161[0] 3001[3]

Tierra Luna (IRE) *Y De Nicolay* 89
2 b f Giant's Causeway(USA) —Luna Wells (IRE) (Sadler's Wells (USA))
4577a[4]

Tifernati *G L Moore* a86 94
5 b g Dansili—Pain Perdu (IRE) (Waajib)
1458[17]

Tiffany Lady *M D I Usher* a44
3 ch f Generous(IRE) —Art Deco Lady (Master Willie)
138[9] 298[5] 520[7] 938[6] 6446[12] 6917[9] 7666[9]

Tiger Breeze (USA) *Miss Jo Crowley* 55
3 b g Roar Of The Tiger(USA) —M. S. Gripsholm (USA) (Goldwater (USA))
2795[8] 4303[6]

Tigerbythetale (IRE) *D R C Elsworth* a55
4 b g Tiger Hill(IRE) —Goldkatze (GER) (Czaravich (USA))
171[5]

Tiger Court *E A L Dunlop* 41
2 b f Tiger Hill(IRE) —Cruinn A Bhord (Inchinor)
7182[14]

Tiger Dream *K A Ryan* a79 88
4 b g Oasis Dream—Grey Way (USA) (Cozzene (USA))
1016[7] 1123[10] 1480[2] 1737[2] 2274[2] 2724[5] 2939[2] 3339[9] 3825[7] 4400[7] 4548[10] 4897[3] 5395[2] 6178[5] (6250) 6460[5] 6986[8] 7523[2]

Tiger Flash *W J Haggas* a69 77
3 b c Dansili—Miss Penton (Primo Dominie)
1255[3] 1515[3] 3644[8] 4669[2] 5482[3] 6075[3] 6549[2] 6758[4]

Tiger Girl *R Charlton* 27
2 b f Tiger Hill(IRE) —Girl Of My Dreams (IRE) (Marju (IRE))
4792[12]

Tiger Hawk (USA) *P D Evans* a63 45
2 b c Tale Of The Cat(USA) —Aura Of Glory (CAN) (Halo (USA))
3750[15] 4451[6] 4915[3] 5786[10] 7319[11] (7334) 7474[11] 7597[8] 7616[4] (7706) 7791[7]

Tiger Reigns *M Dods* 97
3 b g Tiger Hill(IRE) —Showery (Rainbow Quest (USA))
(1061) (1740) 2341[4] 3144[2] (3394) (4708) (5670) 6094[4]

Tiger's Eye (FR) *Miss A Casotti* a32 78
6 ch g Majorien—Peche De Nuit (FR) (Sicyos (USA))
464a[6]

Tiger's Rocket (IRE) *S Gollings* a71 66
4 b h Monashee Mountain(USA) —Brown Foam (Horage)
93[3] 224[14] 302[9] 514[8]

Tiger Star *J M P Eustace* a76
2 b g Tiger Hill(IRE) —Rosy Outlook (USA) (Trempolino (USA))
7537[9] 7763[2]

Tiger Tee (IRE) *John A Quinn* a53 51
4 b g Spectrum(IRE) —Frill (Henbit (USA))
(4862)

Tiger Trail (GER) *Mrs N Smith* a51 65
5 b g Tagula(IRE) —Tweed Mill (Selkirk (USA))
1419[7] 1704[7] 2202[4] 3252[9] 6205[2] 6422[4]

Tightrope (IRE) *T D McCarthy* a58 47
3 b g Refuse To Bend(IRE) —Sisal (IRE) (Danehill (USA))
731[5] 869[8] 1120[4] 1322[6] 1536[3] 1617[9] 1956[5] 2162[7] 3161[10] 3471[12] 3775[5] 5566[5] 6335[5] *7254[5]* 7774[11]

Tignello (IRE) *G L Moore* a68 63
4 b g Kendor(FR) —La Genereuse (Generous (IRE))
1538[7] 2125[3] 2330[3] *2924[3]* 3463[5] 3800[6] 4533[8] 5905[11]

Tikka Masala (IRE) *Tom Dascombe* a65 73
3 b f One Cool Cat(USA) —Raysiza (IRE) (Alzao (USA))
1066[2] ◆ *1588[7]* (2539) 2910[6] 3408[7] 6476[10] *7028[7]*

Tilapia (IRE) *Miss Gay Kelleway* a69 77
5 ch g Daggers Drawn(USA) —Mrs Fisher (IRE) (Salmon Leap (USA))
3721[11]

Tilerium's Dream (IRE) *K A Ryan* 54
3 b g Tillerman—Thai Princess (IRE) (Hamas (IRE))
1308[13] 1625[5] 1926[4] 4552[18] 4819[10] 5972[7]

Tillerdan (IRE) *A Peraino* 86
3 ch f Tillerman—Daneville (IRE) (Danetime (IRE))
1659a[10]

Tillers Satisfied (IRE) *R Hollinshead* a63 62
3 b f Tillerman—Lady Of Pleasure (IRE) (Marju (IRE))
2144 293[2] 1772[10] *2683[8]* 2973[11] *3225[3]*

Tillietudlem (FR) *J S Goldie* a35 49
3 gr g Kutub(IRE) —Queenhood (FR) (Linamix (FR))
570[11] 2627[6] 3482[3] 4039[3] 4529[6] 5442[3]

Tilly Shilling (IRE) *Norma Twomey* a50 47
5 b m Montjeu(IRE) —Antiguan Jane (Shirley Heights)
704[4] 1938[7] 2127[8]

Tillys Tale *P T Midgley* 81
2 ch f Lucky Story(USA) —Otylia (Wolfhound (USA))
1304[5] 1764[4] (2089) 2372[12] 2655[2] 3370[3] 3871[7] 4547[2] 4875[5] 5552[2]

Tilos Gem (IRE) *M Johnston* a82 81
3 ch c Trans Island—Alpine Flair (IRE) (Tirol)
1410[2] (2652) 3008[7] 4453[3] 4957[8] 6060[3] 6473[3] *6975[2] 7373[7]*

Tilsworth Glenboy *J R Jenkins* a62
2 b c Doyen(IRE) —Chara (Deploy)
7325[12] 7538[5]

Tilt *B Ellison* a94 99
7 b g Daylami(IRE) —Tromond (Lomond (USA))
1458[16] 1790[14] 2055[3] 2486[3] 3390[6] 6851[26] *7091[RR]* 7293[RR] *7465[5]*

Timabiyra (IRE) *John M Oxx* a94 94
3 gr f Linamix(FR) —Timarida (IRE) (Kalaglow)
1996a[9] 2960a[4] 3894a[3] 4923a[6] 6298a[6]

Timbaa (USA) *Rae Guest* a50 51
3 b g Anabaa(USA) —Timber Ice (USA) (Woodman (USA))
3157[4] 3382[9] 3474[3] 3740[6]

Timber Treasure (USA) *Paul Green* a64 85
5 bb g Forest Wildcat(USA) —Lady Ilsley (USA) (Trempolino (USA))
1089[8] 1278[14] 1510[12] 1885[9] 3529[6] (4346) 4592[4] 5343[3] 5409[10] 5673[3] 6017[7] 6250[10] *7138[6] 7275[5]*

Time Book (IRE) *J H M Gosden* a77 79
3 b c Galileo(IRE) —Pocket Book (IRE) (Reference Point)
1328[9] 6794[3] ◆ 7221[5] *(7504)*

Time For Gold (FR) *Mme M Bollack-Badel* a82 85
4 ch g Gold Away(IRE) —Time For Romance (Cure The Blues (USA))
7704a[0]

Time For Old Time *I A Wood* a59 59
3 b f Olden Times—Pink Supreme (Night Shift (USA))
5018[9] 5500[8] 6039[9] *7052[13] 7592[11]*

Timeless Dream *P W Chapple-Hyam* a74 71
3 b f Oasis Dream—Simply Times (USA) (Dodge (USA))
2827[11] 5110[2] *(5584) 6120[7]* 6572[6] 6824[6]

Timeless Elegance (IRE) *J Howard Johnson* 52
2 b f Invincible Spirit(IRE) —Tidy Wager (IRE) (Catrail (USA))
4278[10] 5620[4] 6378[3]

Timeless Whisper (IRE) *J G Burns* 72
2 b f Footstepsinthesand—Manuscript (Machiavellian (USA))
7072a[10]

Timelord (IRE) *S Kirk* a59 67
2 ch g Chineur(FR) —My Gray (FR) (Danehill (USA))
1577[9] 2187[3] 2328[4] 3424[7] 3579[3] 3842[9] 5589[2] 5715[10] *6228[8] 6586[7]* 6963[5]

Time Loup *S R Bowring* a43 56
3 b g Loup Sauvage(USA) —Bird Of Time (IRE) (Persian Bold)
365[5] 1084[5] 1949[6] *2581[9]*

Timely Jazz (IRE) *B J Meehan* a84 97
2 b c Noverre(USA) —Ricadonna (Kris)
3395[9] 3750[2] 4314[2] *(5106)* 5794[3] 6268[8] 6849[13]

Time Machine (UAE) *J H M Gosden* a67 80
3 ch g Halling(USA) —Tempting Fate (IRE) (Persian Bold)
1260[2] 1809[4] 2763[2] (3117)

Time Medicean *M R Channon* a62 85
3 gr g Medicean—Ribbons And Bows (IRE) (Dr Devious (IRE))
951[6] (1400) ◆ 2148[2] ◆ 2674[3] 3033[4] 4326[7] 5523[5]

Time 'N' Talent *James Leavy* a85 81
3 b c Act One—Turn Of A Century (Halling (USA))
5880[7]

Timepiece *H R A Cecil* a80 101
2 b f Zamindar(USA) —Clepsydra (Sadler's Wells (USA))
6062[2] ◆ *(6628)* (7187) ◆

Times Ahead (USA) *P W Chapple-Hyam* 62
2 b c Proud Citizen(USA) —Nanas Cozy Account (USA) (Langfuhr (CAN))
4756[9]

Times Up *J L Dunlop* 98
3 b g Olden Times—Princess Genista (Ile De Bourbon (USA))
1931[2] 2538[3] 3117[3] (3707) 4518[5] (5034) 5870[3] 6734[10]

Times Vital (IRE) *E J O'Neill* a79 93
4 b g Danetime(IRE) —Flying Freedom (IRE) (Archway (IRE))
5089a[5] 5281a[6]

Timeteam (IRE) *A Bailey* a87 88
3 b g Danetime(IRE) —Ceannanas (IRE) (Magical Wonder (USA))
1324[15] 1705[2] 2279[11] 2674[12] 3219[7] 3747[16] *7692[4]*

Time To Play *T T Clement* a62 65
4 b g Best Of The Bests(IRE) —Primavera (Anshan)
618[7] 6925[10] *7687[6]*

Time To Regret *I W McInnes* a69 63
9 b g Presidium—Scoffera (Scottish Reel)
256[9] 1153[5] 1194[9] *1496[3]* 2441[4] 3092[2] *3470[4] 3735[4]* 4313[9]

Timetowynagain *C W Fairhurst*
2 ch g Reset(AUS) —Ideal Figure (Zafonic (USA))
5439[13] 6763[13]

Timoca (IRE) *Edward Lynam* a87 83
4 br m Marju(IRE) —Tara Gold (IRE) (Royal Academy (USA))
7300a[7]

Timocracy *T D Walford* 81
4 br g Cape Cross(IRE) —Tithcar (Cadeaux Genereux)
(1615) 2505[3] 3761[7] 4426[3] 5334[14]

Timos (GER) *T Doumen* 113
4 ch h Sholokhov(IRE) —Triclaria (GER) (Surumu (GER))
1762a[6] 2522a[5]

Timpanist (USA) *Mme C Head-Maarek* 52
2 b f Roman Ruler(USA) —Jazz Drummer (USA) (Dixieland Band (USA))
5956a[10]

Tinaar (USA) *G A Butler* a95 78
3 b f Giant's Causeway(USA) —Seattle Tac (USA) (Seattle Slew (USA))
3751[6] 4337[4] (4828) *(5667)* ◆ *6165[3] 7066[2]*

Tina's Best (IRE) *E J Alston* a64 79
4 b m King's Best(USA) —Phantom Waters (Pharly (FR))
3496[8] 4821[3] 5514[8] 6755[11]

Tin Cha Woody (USA) *Daniel Mark Loughnane* a81 63
4 bb g Johannesburg(USA) —I'm Beguiled Again (USA) (Wild Again (USA))
7394[10] 7643[3] 7752[10]

Tinder Ball (FR) *J Van Handenhove* 70
2 gr c Johann Quatz(FR) —Habemus (FR) (Bluebird (USA))
3935a[9] 6751a[4]

Ting Ting (USA) *T P Tate* a37 53
2 b f Empire Maker(USA) —My Sweet Heart (USA) (You And I (USA))
5466[3] 5951[3] *6672[12]*

Tinkerbelle (IRE) *J L Dunlop* a64 56
3 br f Marju(IRE) —Pershaan (IRE) (Darshaan)
1183[4] 2350[2] 2866[3] *3303[3]* 5286[10] *5838[4] (6446) 6807[5]*

Tinshu (IRE) *D Haydn Jones* a90 83
3 ch f Fantastic Light(USA) —Ring Of Esteem (Mark Of Esteem (IRE))
(138) 595[2] 840[5] 1019[4] *1431[8]* (1928) 2356[2] 2796[9] 3921[2] 4605[2] 5996[5] 6740[5] *(7233) (7366) 7489[6]*

Tin Town Boy (IRE) *H Rogers* a75 84
8 b g Danehill Dancer(IRE) —Sushari (IRE) (Shardari)
4510a[6] 7263a[7]

Tipperary Boutique (IRE) *B W Hills* 75
2 b f Danehill Dancer(IRE) —Moselle (Mtoto)
4542[5] (7167)

Tip Toe (FR) *F Doumen* 92
2 b c Footstepsinthesand—Midnight Queen (GER) (Platini (GER))
5088a[4] (5494a)

Tip Top Style *A Crook* a54 29
6 b g Tipsy Creek(USA) —Eliza Jane (Mistertopogigo (IRE))
2264[10]

Tiradito (USA) *M Botti* a72 73
2 bb c Tale Of The Cat(USA) —Saratoga Sugar (USA) (Gone West (USA))
1630[2] 2007[5] 2280[3] *7824[8]*

Tirovia (FR) *J-M Plasschaert*
3 u f— (Shining Steel)
6753a[0]

Tishtar *Doug Watson* a82 82
3 br c Kyllachy—Xtrasensory (Royal Applause)
524a[10]

Tisifone *C G Cox* a11 59
3 b f American Post—Mary Rose (ITY) (Royal Academy (USA))
1745[4] 2633[7] 3100[7] *5103[11]*

Tislaam (IRE) *M R Channon* 77
2 gr c With Approval(CAN) —Lady Angola (USA) (Lord At War (ARG))
1867[10] 3017[3] 3875[5] 4323[2] 5036[5] 6009[15]

Tislimeen *M R Channon* 66
2 b f Alhaarth(IRE) —Torgau (IRE) (Zieten (USA))
5604[5] ◆ 7033[12]

Tis Mighty (IRE) *P J Prendergast* a96 97
6 bb m Fruits Of Love(USA) —Floating Agenda (USA) (Twilight Agenda (USA))
2289a[11] 5490a[12]

Titan Triumph *W J Knight* a101 72
5 b g Zamindar(USA) —Triple Green (Green Desert (USA))
206[2] (551) 997[18] *1209[10] 1640[6]*

Titfer (IRE) *A W Carroll* a57 65
4 ch g Fath(USA) —Fur Hat (Habitat)
116[9]

Titinius (IRE) *Micky Hammond* 68
9 ch g Titus Livius(FR) —Maiyria (IRE) (Shernazar)
1099[4] 1279[8] 1454[3] 2264[4] 2569[4] 3450[16]

Tito (IRE) *B N Pollock* a41 69
4 b g Diktat—T G's Girl (Selkirk (USA))
2145[11] 5465[12] (Dead)

Titoli Di Coda (IRE) *L M Cumani* a27 43
2 ch f Bertolini(USA) —Mystic Tempo (USA) (El Gran Senor (USA))
3772[7] 4302[8] 6245[10] *6938[8]*

Titurel (GER) *J Hirschberger* 100
4 ch h Dr Fong(USA) —Tucana (GER) (Acatenango (GER))
6500a[5]

Titus Andronicus (IRE) *K A Ryan* 92
3 b g Danetime(IRE) —Scarlet Empress (Second Empire (IRE))
(1232) ◆ 2058[5] 2717[2] ◆ 2782[2] 3173[3] 3806[8] 3973[2] 4490[7] 5203[14]

Titus Awarded (IRE) *G Ligas* 78
2 b c Titus Livius(FR) —Wings Awarded (Shareef Dancer (USA))
7205a[12]

Titus Gent *R A Harris* a75 69
4 ch g Tumbleweed Ridge—Genteel (IRE) (Titus Livius (FR))
192[9] 473[5] 608[11] 803[4] 895[5] 1076[9] 1259[7] 1958[8] *3743[2]* (4552) 4823[5] 6039[6] 6492[3] (6670) 6825[3] 7203[2] 7273[8] 7518[2] 7673[6]

Titus Shadow (IRE) *B Grizzetti* 109
5 ch h Titus Livius(FR) —Mujadil Shadow (IRE) (Mujadil (USA))
1905a[7] (6894a) 7206a[3]

Tivers Song (USA) *John A Harris* a57 53
5 gr g Buddha(USA) —Rousing (USA) (Alydar (USA))
11[9] 2129[10] 2608[3] 4402[2] 4944[2] 5423[5] 6183[2] 6369[3] *6770[3] 7214[4] 7594[11]*

Tiza (SAF) *A De Royer-Dupre* a91 115
7 b g Goldkeeper(USA) —Mamushka (SAF) (Elliodor (FR))
(1043a) (3908a) 4837a[7] 7232a[4] 7458a[5]

Tiz Now Tiz Then (USA) *S Seemar* a109
4 br h Tiznow(USA) —Trepidation (USA) (Seeking The Gold (USA))
610a[2] 773a[9] 1008a[6]

Tizway (USA) *Harold James Bond* a115
4 br h Tiznow(USA) —Bethany (USA) (Dayjur (USA))
6512a[3]

Tj's Joy (IRE) *Patrick Martin* 31
2 b c Fasliyev(USA) —Night Lodge (IRE) (Grand Lodge (USA))
6401a[10]

Toasted Special (USA) *W McCreery* a52 80
4 ch m Johannesburg(USA) —Sajjaya (USA) (Blushing Groom (FR))
1376a[6] 4360a[14]

Tobago Bay *Miss Sheena West* a49 66
4 b g Tobougg(IRE) —Perfect Dream (Emperor Jones (USA))
1426[2] 2519[5] 4703[3]

Tobago Reef *C W Moore* a56 46
5 b g Tobougg(IRE) —Silly Mid-On (Midyan (USA))
760[6] 3331[10] 3851[9] 4710[12]

Toballa *P Leech* a47 51
4 b m Tobougg(IRE) —Ball Gown (Jalmood (USA))
1515[6] 2415[7] 3004[6] 5035[12] 5435[8] *7200[5] 7521[11] 7727[9]*

Tobanjaro (HUN) *Z Nagy* a48
6 ch h Bakharoff(USA) —Tubarozsa (HUN) (Gilmore (FR))
464a[5]

Tobar Suil Lady (IRE) *J L Spearing* a69 61
4 b m Statue Of Liberty(USA) —Stellarette (IRE) (Lycius (USA))
157[9]

To Be Or Not To Be *John Berry* a73 81
4 b m Tobougg(IRE) —Lady Mayor (Kris)
179[2] 1493[4] (2168) 2883[11] 5007[8] 5409[4] *5810[7]* 6311[4] 7032[6]

Toberogan (IRE) *W A Murphy* a17 58
8 b g Docksider(USA) —Beltisaal (FR) (Belmez (USA))
4376[13] 5872[9] 6411[13]

Toboggan Lady *Mrs A Duffield* a46 70
5 b m Tobougg(IRE) —Northbend (Shirley Heights)
1851[6] 2262[6]

Tobond (IRE) *M Botti* a96 86
3 b g Tobougg(IRE) —Rajmata (IRE) (Prince Sabo)
912[6] 1296[6] 1987[10] 2855[6]

Tobouggie On Down *J A Glover* 55
2 ch f Tobougg(IRE) —Park Ave Princess (IRE) (Titus Livius (FR))
5949[6]

Tobrata *M Brittain* a64 64
3 ch g Tobougg(IRE) —Sabrata (IRE) (Zino)
4277[5] ◆ 5520[5] *6950[2] 7353[2] 7671[3] 7753[3]*

To Bubbles *A G Newcombe* a68 39
4 b m Tobougg(IRE) —Effervescent (Efisio)
14[12] 152[6] 420[3] 657[12] 979[11]

Toby Tyler *P T Midgley* a74 70
3 b g Best Of The Bests(IRE) —Pain Perdu (IRE) (Waajib)
(924) 1509[8] *1656[5]* 2300[4] 3341[9] 4660[6]

Toc (FR) *C Boutin* a59 67
2 b c Chineur(FR) —Tocade (IRE) (Kenmare (FR))
5088a[5] 5378a[7]

Today's The Day *M A Jarvis* a73 69
3 b f Alhaarth(IRE) —Dayville (USA) (Dayjur (USA))
1173[4] 1359[5] 1618[2]

Todber *M P Tregoning* a78 71
4 b m Cape Cross(IRE) —Dominica (Alhaarth (IRE))
1360[4] *6632[5]* ◆ *(7023)* ◆ *7138[4] 7518[8]*

Toga Tiger (IRE) *M R Channon* a87 82
2 b g Antonius Pius(USA) —Minerwa (GER) (Protektor (GER))
1577[3] 1981[2] 2324[2] 2721[5] (3160) 3589[3] *(3978)* 5214[8] 5864[5] 6693[8] 6993[6]

Toggle *Ms V S Lucas* a51 66
5 b g Tobougg(IRE) —Niggle (Night Shift (USA))
4586a[3] 5541a[2]

Togiak (IRE) *E A L Dunlop* a81 98
2 b c Azamour(IRE) —Hawksbill Special (IRE) (Taufan (USA))
4756[4] *(5312)* 5970[2] 6664[5]

Toledo Gold (IRE) *E J Alston* 79
3 ch g Needwood Blade—Eman's Joy (Lion Cavern (USA))
3316[2] 3804[3] ◆ 4227[11] 4708[7] 4801[9] 6485[13]

Toll Road *E A L Dunlop* a51
3 b f Dubai Destination(USA) —Endorsement (Warning)
115[6]

Tomatin *P W Chapple-Hyam* a70 80
2 b c Kyllachy—Lowrianna (IRE) (Cyrano De Bergerac)
6802[4] 7016[8]

Tombi (USA) *J Howard Johnson* 112
5 b g Johannesburg(USA) —Tune In To The Cat (USA) (Tunerup (USA))
2500[4] 3621[6] 4037[6] 5232[8] 6091[6] 6487[8]

Tombov (FR) *A King* 74
3 bb g Laveron—Zamsara (FR) (Zino)
3636[9] 4687[6]

Tom Folan *H J Collingridge* a54 70
2 b f Namid—My Golly (Mozart (IRE))
1044[2] ◆ 1277[3] 1788[3] 3871[5] (4076) 4539[13] *4868[6]*

Tominator *R Hollinshead* 98
2 gr g Generous(IRE) —Jucinda (Midyan (USA))
4041[5] 4557[2] (4888) 5692[6] (6099) ◆ 6898[2]

Tomintoul Singer (IRE) *H R A Cecil* 98
2 ch f Johannesburg(USA) —Shivaree (Rahy (USA))
2354[2] ◆ 2860[2] (3772) 7147[3]

Tomintoul Star *H R A Cecil* 61
3 gr f Dansili—Lixian (Linamix (FR))
1488[11] 4545[6] 5286[6]

Tommy Tobougg *Miss Lucinda V Russell* a43 52
5 ch g Tobougg(IRE) —Celebrate (IRE) (Generous (IRE))
1556[3] 2390[11] 2817[5] 3105[10]

Tomodachi (IRE) *M Botti* 78
2 b f Arakan(USA) —Ivory Bride (Domynsky)
6921[2] ◆

Toms Laughter *R A Harris* a92 102
5 ch g Mamalik(USA) —Time Clash (Timeless Times (USA))
5420[11] 5871[6] ◆ 6107[9] 6843[5] *7202[3] 7227[7] 7414[7]* ◆ *7676[10]* ◆ *7862[9]*

Tom Tower (IRE) *A C Whillans* 77
5 b g Cape Cross(IRE) —La Belle Katherine (USA) (Lyphard (USA))
(3094) 3655[3] (4046) 4496[8] 5333[3] 5673[2]

Tom Wade (IRE) *M A Jarvis* a64
2 b g Rakti—Plutonia (Sadler's Wells (USA))
6162[5] 6607[10] 7199[8]

Tone It Down (USA) *William Komlo* a62
3 b c Medaglia D'Oro(USA) —Chattin (USA) (Rollicking (USA))
2098a[12]

Tongalooma *James Moffatt* a56 36
3 ch f Shinko Forest(IRE) —Schatzi (Chilibang)
5394[8] *5882[4] (6641) 7595[10]*

Tony The Tap *W R Muir* a95 95
8 b g Most Welcome—Laleston (Junius (USA))
3582[6] 3844[5] 4341[7] (5183) 5263[2] 5860[17]

Too Grand *J J Bridger* a62 53
4 ch m Zaha(CAN) —Gold Linnet (Nashwan (USA))
(23) 61[5] 192[11] 395[9] 830[4] 945[4]

Toolentidhaar (USA) *Andrew Turnell* a72 72
5 b m Swain(IRE) —Rababah (USA) (Woodman (USA))
2679[3] *3297[2]* 4234[3] 5099[9] 5449[13] *5780[12]*

Too Much Trouble *M R Channon* 102
3 b g Barathea(IRE) —Tentpole (USA) (Rainbow Quest (USA))
(1453) 1800[6] 3050[4] ◆ 3778[5] 4420[6] 5230[12] 6114[4]

Too Nice Name (FR) *Robert Collet* a68 97
2 br c Kingsalsa(USA) —Namona (IRE) (Halling (USA))
1482a[2] 5085a[6] 6326a[3] 6752a[8] 7103a[5]

Too Putra (IRE) *R Charlton* a73
2 b c Oratorio(IRE) —Urgent Liaison (IRE) (High Estate)
(7538) ◆

Too Tall *J R Boyle* a73 72
3 b c Medicean—Embark (Soviet Star (USA))
2845[7] 3341[5] 4733[5] 5124[2] *6257[3] 6498[3]* 7101[3] *7426[2]*

Top Act (FR) *P Schiergen* 54
2 b f Fantastic Light(USA) —Topline (GER) (Acatenango (GER))
7045a[8]

Top Bid *T D Easterby* a59 69
5 b g Auction House(USA) —Trump Street (First Trump)
1360[6] 2436[2] 2770[7] (3570) 3828[4] 4225[2] 4469[4] 5518[9] 5675[7] 6413[U] 6764[6] 6989[10] 7122[4]

Topclas (FR) *P Demercastel* 109
3 b c Kutub(IRE) —Noble Presence (FR) (Fasliyev (USA))
1239a[2] 1979a[4] 2756a[9] 5930a[5]

Topcroft *D Shaw* a75 49
3 b g Mujahid(USA) —Starminda (Zamindar (USA))
(770) 1632[5] *2143[5]* 3009[9] *5574[5] (7609)* ◆ *(7703)* ◆ *(7784)*

Topflightrebellion *Mrs G S Rees* a52 43
4 b m Mark Of Esteem(IRE) —Jamarj (Tyrnavos)
833[4] 1568[12]

Top Flight Splash *Mrs G S Rees* a54 49
3 b f Bertolini(USA) —Making Waves (IRE) (Danehill (USA))
1452[4] *2132[2]* 2577[2] 2973[7] 3727[9] *7105[3] 7349[6] 7561[7] 7727[8]*

Topix (FR) *Mlle M-L Mortier*
3 gr g Linamix(FR) —Esneh (IRE) (Sadler's Wells (USA))
6682a[0]

Top Jaro (FR) *Mrs R A Carr* a52 77
6 b g Marathon(USA) —Shahmy (USA) (Lear Fan (USA))
174^6 221^6 300^7 377^{12} 567^8

Topkapi Diamond (IRE) *E Kurdu* 99
4 b m Acclamation—Anthyllis (IRE) (Night Shift (USA))
5651a^8

Top Level (IRE) *Ms V S Lucas* a55 51
6 b m Fasliyev(USA) —Aiming Upwards (Blushing Flame (USA))
(5541a)

Top Man Dan (IRE) *T D Walford* 59
4 b g Danetime(IRE) —Aphra Benn (IRE) (In The Wings)
2233^6 2975^{13}

Topolski (IRE) *M Johnston* 91
3 b g Peintre Celebre(USA) —Witching Hour (IRE) (Alzao (USA))
(1470) ◆ (1629) 1992^{12} 2545^2 3051^5 ◆ 4420^{11} 5170^9

Top Pursuit *Ms V S Lucas* 23
7 b g Pursuit Of Love—Top Of The Parkes (Mistertopogigo (IRE))
4586a^2 5074a^8

Top Rocker *E W Tuer* 25
5 b g Rock City—Top Hand (First Trump)
4848^{10}

Top Seed (IRE) *M S Tuck* a68 72
8 b g Cadeaux Genereux—Midnight Heights (Persian Heights)
220^6 428^7 1014^2 4745^{12} 5631^8 6126^{12} 6806^6

Top Spin (AUS) *L Laxon* 100
6 ch g Arena(AUS) —Gas (AUS) (Strategic (AUS))
2117a^{10}

Top Spin (IRE) *John Joseph Murphy* 85
2 bb c Cape Cross(IRE) —Beguine (USA) (Green Dancer (USA))
5542^3 6318a^7 6898^8

Top Ticket (IRE) *D E Pipe* a69 82
4 ch g Alhaarth(IRE) —Tathkara (USA) (Alydar (USA))
4563^{12} 5217^5

Top Tiger *D W Barker* a67 65
5 b g Mtoto—Topatori (IRE) (Topanoora)
311^8 623^2 745^6 809^6 1058^{11}

Top Tigress *Sir Michael Stoute* a63
2 b f Tiger Hill(IRE) —Top Romance (IRE) (Entrepreneur)
7276^4 ◆

Top Tinker *M H Tompkins* a51 41
3 b g Vettori(IRE) —Topatori (IRE) (Topanoora)
1183^{10} 2340^{10} 2743^6 3157^7

Top Town Girl *R M Beckett* a73 85
3 b f Efisio—Halland Park Girl (IRE) (Primo Dominie)
1002^8 1869^9 2774^4 3272^4 4380^4 4788^4 6230^7 6739^4

Top Tribute *T P Tate* 66
4 b g Acclamation—Mary Hinge (Dowsing (USA))
1244^7 1480^{13} 5513^2 6217^5

Toraidhe (IRE) *J S Bolger* a81 96
3 br g High Chaparral(IRE) —Ramona (Desert King (IRE))
5490a^6

Tora Petcha (IRE) *B D Leavy* a44 48
6 b g Bahhare(USA) —Magdalene (FR) (College Chapel)
4742^8

Torch Of Freedom (IRE) *Sir Mark Prescott* a80 76
4 b g Statue Of Liberty(USA) —Danse Royale (IRE) (Caerleon (USA))
318^4 490^8 694^6 798^{10} (875) 981^5 4658^{14} 5108^5

Toreno Jubilee (JPN) *H Fujiwara* 113
6 b h Sakura Bakushin O(JPN) —Tenzan Kirari (JPN) (Golden Pheasant (USA))
7498a^{13}

Torina (IRE) *M J Grassick* a61 63
4 ch m Golan(IRE) —Tordasia (IRE) (Dr Devious (IRE))
7732^3

Tori Parry (FR) *Y Fouin* 83
6 ro g Simon Du Desert(FR) —L'Eternite (FR) (Cariellor (FR))
5204a^7 7387a^3

Tornadodancer (IRE) *T G McCourt* a86 92
6 b g Princely Heir(IRE) —Purty Dancer (IRE) (Foxhound (USA))
1543a^8 3435a^4 3898a^9 5293^2 7341a^8

Torquemada (IRE) *M J Attwater* a60 61
8 ch g Desert Sun—Gaelic's Fantasy (IRE) (Statoblest)
114^5 355^3 395^3 531^9 646^8 5287^{11} 6568^8 7129^5 7517^{14}

Torran Sound *J M P Eustace* a45
2 b g Tobougg(IRE) —Velvet Waters (Unfuwain (USA))
7477^8 7571^{11}

Torrens (IRE) *P D Evans* a64 66
7 b g Royal Anthem(USA) —Azure Lake (USA) (Lac Ouimet (USA))
1578^3 1770^7 1936^8

Torres (GER) *Frau E Mader* 91
3 b c Gold Away(IRE) —Tizia (IRE) (Linamix (FR))
1718a^4 6713a^4

Torres Del Paine *J C Fox* a66
2 b c Compton Place—Noble Story (Last Tycoon)
7436^8 7571^4 7736^2

Torrid Hell (FR) *S Wattel* a94 101
4 b h Vettori(IRE) —Heleniade (FR) (Entrepreneur)
3085a^9

Toshi (USA) *J S Goldie* a57 60
7 b g Kingmambo(USA) —Majestic Role (FR) (Theatrical (IRE))
1000^{11} 2440^5 (2783) 4462^3

Total Command *Sir Michael Stoute* 85
2 b c Sadler's Wells(USA) —Wince (Selkirk (USA))
6451^6 ◆ 7029^2

Total Gallery (IRE) *J S Moore* 121
3 br c Namid—Diary (IRE) (Green Desert (USA))
(1602) 2272^5 3011^{14} 3638^9 (3747) 4456^2 ◆ 6107^2 (6522a) 7745a^6

Total Impact *R A Fahey* a82 95
6 ch g Pivotal—Rise 'n Shine (Night Shift (USA))
(2363) 2716^9 3351^4 4069^9 4461^9 5247^7 (5767) 5974^3 6171^2 6329^4 7534^2 7795^3 (7852)

Totalitarian *S A Callaghan* a68 69
3 ch g Pivotal—Shalimar (IRE) (Indian Ridge)
5572^3 5954^3 6430^5

Totally Devoted (USA) *A P O'Brien* 98
3 bb f Seeking The Gold(USA) —Crystal Crossing (IRE) (Royal Academy (USA))
1911a^8 2304a^{14} 3047^7 5686a^4 6272^{10} 6530a^5

Totally Focussed (IRE) *S Dow* a86 55
4 rg g Trans Island—Premier Place (USA) (Out Of Place (USA))
113^2 232^4 635^6 850^5 7692^3 7883^8

Totally Invincible (IRE) *E S McMahon* 84
2 b f Invincible Spirit(IRE) —Sebastene (IRE) (Machiavellian (USA))
2354^8 2972^4 (3495) (3805) 4407^{11}

Totally Ours *W R Muir* a76
2 bb f Singspiel(IRE) —Totally Yours (IRE) (Desert Sun)
6722^8 (7177)

Tot Hill *C N Kellett* 29
6 b m Syrtos—Galava (CAN) (Graustark)
3631^8

Toto Skyllachy *S Gollings* a84 89
4 b g Kyllachy—Little Tramp (Trempolino (USA))
1722^9 (2101) 2933^{15} 4064^5 6776^3 7083^4 7287^9 7617^5

Tottie *Mrs A J Perrett* a55 95
3 b f Fantastic Light(USA) —Katy Nowaitee (Komaite (USA))
1871^3 2672^8 3315^5 4328^5 4422^4 4715^6

Touching (IRE) *R Hannon* a78 92
3 b f Kheleyf(USA) —Feminine Touch (IRE) (Sadler's Wells (USA))
1353^9 4983^9 5260^9 7181^6

Touch Of Hawk (FR) *Wido Neuroth* 108
3 br c Hawk Wing(USA) —Touch Of Class (GER) (Be My Guest (USA))
(5933a)

Touch Of Style (IRE) *T D McCarthy* a63 70
5 b g Desert Style(IRE) —No Hard Feelings (IRE) (Alzao (USA))
186^5 248^6 669^{12} 4538^3 5015^5 5790^{15} 6369^{13} 6770^{14}

Touch Tone *B W Hills* 67
2 b f Selkirk(USA) —Payphone (Anabaa (USA))
4001^6 5397^5

Toufan Express *Adrian McGuinness* a75 87
7 ch g Fraam—Clan Scotia (Clantime)
6678^{13}

Toughness Danon *A Wohler* 109
3 b c Tiger Hill(IRE) —Templerin (GER) (Acatenango (GER))
3670a^3 (5585a) 6324a^{10}

Tough Regime (IRE) *Niall Moran* a63 21
2 ch f Trans Island—Lady Naryana (IRE) (Val Royal (FR))
7731^8 7816^4

Toujours Souriante *M Johnston* 76
3 b f Lucky Story(USA) —Tous Les Jours (USA) (Dayjur (USA))
1228^{10} 1508^8 1745^3 2357^3 ◆ 2715^{12} (4038) 4988^9

Tour D'Amour (IRE) *R Craggs* a54 55
6 b m Fruits Of Love(USA) —Touraneena (Robellino (USA))
399^4 2237^4 2362^{13} (3545)

Tourist *D Shaw* a88 80
4 b g Oasis Dream—West Devon (USA) (Gone West (USA))
278^4 331^3 713^2 ◆ 766^3 834^5 999^{16} 1213^2 1731^6 2144^3 5107^{11} 5418^5 5663^{13} 6174^5 6460^9 6861^2 (7192) 7327^9 (7577) 7617^3 7801^3 7866^4

Tournedos (IRE) *D Nicholls* a75 105
7 b g Rossini(USA) —Don't Care (IRE) (Nordico (USA))
1052^9 1791^4 2012^{12} 2704^{14} 3351^{16} 3848^7 4341^{12} 4559^8 4976^4 6670^7

Tous Les Deux *G L Moore* a87 70
6 b g Efisio—Caerosa (Caerleon (USA))
191^7 (398) (544) 778^2 834^3 1079^2 1283^6

Tout Chocolat (FR) *Robert Collet*
2 b c Daliapour(IRE) —Charming Quest (USA) (Quest For Fame)
6751a^0

Tovaria *Edward P Harty* 83
5 b m Muhtarram(USA) —Budoor (IRE) (Darshaan)
5689a^8

Towanda (USA) *J H M Gosden* a53 60
3 b f Dynaformer(USA) —Desert Gold (USA) (Seeking The Gold (USA))
1198^6 1430^4

Towbaat *M A Jarvis* 69
2 b f Halling(USA) —Nasmatt (Danehill (USA))
6920^7

Town And Gown *J S Goldie* a73 56
4 br m Oasis Dream—Degree (Warning)
3909^7 4136^8 4467^9 4778^{11} 5599^7 5727^2 5946^5 6010^4 6160^4

Towneley Arms (IRE) *G A Harker* 46
2 b c Pyrus(USA) —Grangeclare Lily (UAE) (Green Desert (USA))
4396^7

Town House *B P J Baugh* a53 57
7 gr m Paris House—Avondale Girl (IRE) (Case Law)
4741^1 681^9 2225^{11} 3304^{16} 3570^5 3999^6 4182^3 5504^9 6220^{10} 6380^5 7100^{15}

Towthorpe *M Brittain* 65
3 ch g Tobougg(IRE) —Snow Shoes (Sri Pekan (USA))
4805^3 5071^4 5259^8 5672^9 5954^7

Towy Boy (IRE) *I A Wood* a71 70
4 b g King Charlemagne(USA) —Solar Flare (IRE) (Danehill (USA))
799^9 1076^8 1421^8 1528^6 2124^7 2418^{11} 2879^4 3283^2 3743^4 4428^U 4748^2 5323^3 5792^5 6251^4 6553^6 6880^3

Towy Valley *C G Cox* a75 67
4 b m Bertolini(USA) —Ulysses Daughter (IRE) (College Chapel)
69^4 (208) 582^3 756^2 1091^4 1412^5

Toxeas (FR) *C Laffon-Parias* a77 83
2 b c One Cool Cat(USA) —Arikaria (IRE) (Sri Pekan (USA))
1482a^7 4368a^2 6501a^3

Toy Razor (IRE) *H Candy* 41
2 b c Refuse To Bend(IRE) —Child Prodigy (IRE) (Ballad Rock)
6451^7

Toy Top (USA) *M Dods* a14 69
6 rg m Tactical Cat(USA) —I'll Flutter By (USA) (Concorde's Tune (USA))
1241^8 2046^8 (2546) 3002^2 3657^2 4283^6 4778^{10} 5411^4 5518^{11} 6220^{11}

Trachonitis (IRE) *J R Jenkins* a76 86
5 b g Dansili—Hasina (IRE) (King's Theatre (IRE))
1571^9 3169^3 3814^8 4235^6 4670^5 (5912) 6204^4 6704^5 7212^9 (7851) ◆

Trade Centre *George Baker* a77 79
4 b g Dubai Destination(USA) —Khubza (Green Desert (USA))
655^2 (729) 892^4 1152^3 ◆ 1861^{25} 2976^8 3924^9 5753^7 (6294) 6630^3 7054^8 7662^3 (7691) 7845^4

Trade Fairle *P R Webber* a4
2 ch c Trade Fair—Lady Le Quesne (IRE) (Alhaarth (IRE))
3385^6 3745^9 4219^{15}

Trade Name (IRE) *H Candy* a44 62
2 b f Trade Fair—Red Rabbit (Suave Dancer (USA))
5752^{12} ◆ 6563^4 7061^5

Trade Price (GR) *I Semple* a30 50
3 b g Kyllachy—Snowdrift (Desert Prince (IRE))
947^5 1617^{10} 2439^4 3063^7 3449^3 4531^7 4777^5 5295^{11} 6158^5 6415^{10}

Trade Secret *M Brittain* 71
2 b c Trade Fair—Kastaway (Distant Relative)
994^4 1126^2 2017^4 2893^2 3606^5 6646^6

Tradewinds *Mrs Prunella Dobbs* a69 66
3 b g Bertolini(USA) —Fleeting Vision (IRE) (Vision (USA))
4392a^5

Trading Nation (USA) *P W Hiatt* 74
3 b g Tiznow(USA) —Nidd (USA) (Known Fact (USA))
1840^2 ◆ 2496^7 2849^{15} 7627^{11}

Trafalgar Bay (IRE) *K R Burke* 98
6 b g Fruits Of Love(USA) —Chatsworth Bay (IRE) (Fairy King (USA))
1016^5 (1603) 1861^5 2927^P (Dead)

Trafalgar Square *M J Attwater* a89 73
7 b g King's Best(USA) —Pat Or Else (Alzao (USA))
(191) ◆ (282) 388^3 2193^9 2434^{11} 2828^{11} 3509^{10} 4262^{12} 5473^7 5663^{10} 6212^{12} 6630^2 6908^8 7252^8 7437^6 7603^5

Traffic Guard (USA) *P F I Cole* a89 121
5 b h More Than Ready(USA) —Street Scene (IRE) (Zafonic (USA))
339a^6 614a^6 698a^6 4090^3 4780^4 (5446) 5854^2 6890a^8

Trailblazing *M Johnston* 86
2 b c Green Desert(USA) —Pioneer Bride (USA) (Gone West (USA))
2839^6 3262^2 (3792) 5795^{19} 6471^3

Train Deal (IRE) *F Jovine* 91
2 ch f Camacho—Fanciful (IRE) (Mujtahid (USA))
6892a^9

Trajano (USA) *T Callejo-Solana* 103
4 b h Elusive Quality(USA) —Fly To The Moon (USA) (Blushing Groom (FR))
2513a^6 4363a^9

Trajectory *D Smaga* 71
2 b c Dubai Destination(USA) —Prove (Danehill (USA))
4807a^5 5561a^6

Tramp Stamp (IRE) *Matthieu Palussiere* 52
5 b m King's Theatre(IRE) —Return Again (IRE) (Top Ville)
1546a^7

Tranos (USA) *Micky Hammond* a65 10
6 b g Bahri(USA) —Balancoire (USA) (Diesis)
3035^6

Tranquil Tiger *H R A Cecil* a112 117
5 ch h Selkirk(USA) —Serene View (USA) (Distant View (USA))
(2327) 3585^3 4780^7 5508^3 (7489) (7809)

Transacoustic (TUR) *S Kulak* a100
3 b f Sri Pekan(USA) —Number Ten (Polish Precedent (USA))
5587a^6

Transcend *J H M Gosden* a100 103
5 ch g Beat Hollow—Pleasuring (Good Times (ITY))
3116^{14}

Transcentral *T Wall* a54 69
3 ch f Kheleyf(USA) —Khafayif (USA) (Swain (IRE))
1529^7 1969^{10} 2581^4 2683^4 3225^7 3926^{10} 5326^{11}

Transfer *A M Balding* a89 76
4 br g Trans Island—Sankaty Light (USA) (Summer Squall (USA))
5753^4 6212^{13} 6547^5

Transfered (IRE) *Lucinda Featherstone* a47 55
3 b f Trans Island—Second Omen (Rainbow Quest (USA))
5011^2 ◆ 5530^8 5734^{14} 7324^6 7461^9 7557^8

Transfixed (IRE) *P D Evans* a79 79
2 b f Trans Island—Rectify (IRE) (Mujadil (USA))
(1249) 1450^2 1783^3 (2100) 2319^3 3542^2 (3807) 4017^3 4081^2 4165^3 4558^3 4850^{10} (5187) 5207^2 5762^9 5853^2 6048^{10} 6275^5 6619^{10} (6844) 6963^2 7218^4 7494^5 (7552) 7625^5 7786^3 7846^6 7878^2

Transformer (IRE) *W J Knight* a64 57
3 b g Trans Island—Lady At War (Warning)
1585^4 ◆ 1932^9 2809^4 3551^6 4320^3 5015^2 5577^4 5988^{10} (6439) 6705^2

Transmission (IRE) *B Smart* a73 70
4 b g Galileo(IRE) —Individual (USA) (Gulch (USA))
(12) 63^2 93^2 747^7 1192^{13} 4431^{10} 4932^2 6157^{14} 6862^{12} 7631^9 7782^2 7855^4

Transmit (IRE) *T D Easterby* 44
2 ch g Trans Island—Apple Brandy (USA) (Cox's Ridge (USA))
4659^6 5408^7

Transporter (IRE) *T D Easterby* 39
3 b g Trans Island—Ascoli (Skyliner)
3707^4 4142^{10}

Trans Siberian *P F I Cole* a92 92
5 b g Soviet Star(USA) —Dina Line (USA) (Diesis)
1149^5 1357^5 1750^2 2597^7 3461^4 6795^{13}

Trans Sonic *J Hetherton* a73 67
6 ch g Trans Island—Sankaty Light (USA) (Summer Squall (USA))
40^2 324^3 493^5 622^5 1475^{14} 2746^7 7855^2

Transvaal Sky *Tom Dascombe* a81 87
2 bb f Avonbridge—Glider (IRE) (Silver Kite (USA))
4047^6 (4869) 5763^4 6481^5

Transvestite (IRE) *Miss Tor Sturgis* a79 84
7 b g Trans Island—Christoph's Girl (Efisio)
(330)

Traphalgar (IRE) *P D Evans* a83 88
4 br g Cape Cross(IRE) —Conquestadora (Hernando (FR))
1952^8 2480^6 2773^2 (3235) 3695^8 5694^{11} 5936^3 (6172) (6488) 7413^2 7623^2 7775^3 7848^9

Travellers Kingdom (IRE) *P D Evans* 45
2 b f Xaar—Mermaid Melody (Machiavellian (USA))
1404^8

Tray My Force (ITY) *V Caruso* 98
3 b c Blu Air Force(IRE) —Try Sympathy (IRE) (Habitat)
(2114a)

Treadingtheboards *Mouse Hamilton-Fairley*
2 b f Haafhd—Rada's Daughter (Robellino (USA))
6372^{13}

Treadwell (IRE) *J A Osborne* a90 93
2 b c Footstepsinthesand—Lady Wells (IRE) (Sadler's Wells (USA))
(2636) 2993^5 5827^2 5994^5 (6585) 7063^5

Treasure (FR) *Mme C Head-Maarek* a88 101
3 b f Anabaa(USA) —Treasure Queen (USA) (Kingmambo (USA))
4637a^6 5495a^8

Treasure Islands (IRE) *S W Hall* a56 52
4 b m Trans Island—Gold Prospector (IRE) (Spectrum (IRE))
670^7

Treasure Town *Saeed Bin Suroor* a79 73
2 b c King's Best(USA) —Shinko Hermes (IRE) (Sadler's Wells (USA))
6759^3 (7064) ◆

Treasure Way *P R Chamings* 62
2 ch f Galileo(IRE) —Gold Mark (Mark Of Esteem (IRE))
5741^8

Treasury Bond *P T Midgley* 42
2 ch g Monsieur Bond(IRE) —Rainbow Treasure (IRE) (Rainbow Quest (USA))
1867^{13} 2231^{10} 3119^4 3958^4

Treat Gently *Robert Frankel* 116
4 b m Cape Cross(IRE) —Kid Gloves (In The Wings)
6872a^6

Treble Jig (USA) *Sir Michael Stoute* 85
2 b c Gone West(USA) —Light Jig (Danehill (USA))
4756^7 (5401) ◆

Treeko (IRE) *P A Kirby* a50 35
4 b g Alhaarth(IRE) —Allegheny River (USA) (Lear Fan (USA))
5438^{10}

Trees Of Green (USA) *M Wigham* a49 26
5 bb g Elusive Quality(USA) —Grazia (Sharpo)
7601^0

Treetops Hotel (IRE) *L R James* a7 52
10 ch g Grand Lodge(USA) —Rousinette (Rousillon (USA))
169^{14} 1000^{15} 1454^7 1556^{13} 2608^{10} 3171^{10} 5339^8 6017^8 6817^7 7733^8

Tregony Bridge *M Blanshard* a47 21
2 b g Avonbridge—Serotina (IRE) (Mtoto)
5627^{10} 6911^{10} 7177^9

Treize Heureux (FR) *C Boutin* a73 75
4 b g Nombre Premier—Saraganes (FR) (Ganges (USA))
5464a^5

Trelawny Wells *M R Channon* 26
2 b g Pastoral Pursuits—Kythia (IRE) (Kahyasi)
2121^3 2477^8 3500^{11}

Tremoto *F & L Camici* 100
4 b m Generous(IRE) —Therese Chenu (IRE) (Local Suitor (USA))
1903a^4 2955a^9

Trempari *Mike Murphy* a37 54
6 ch g Trempolino(USA) —Ariadne (GER) (Kings Lake (USA))
704^7 1427^4 3056^7 3617^6 4301^7 4935^4 (5579) 6021^{10} 6692^9 7608^7

Tres Amigos *D Nicholls* a75 59
2 ch g Exceed And Excel(AUS) —Canterloupe (IRE) (Wolfhound (USA))
6047^6 6484^5 (6874)

Tres Borrachos (USA) *C Beau Greely* a117 84
4 b g Ecton Park(USA) —Pete's Fancy (CAN) (Peteski (CAN))
6687a^9

Tres Chic (FR) *S Curran* 57
3 gr f Kaldounevees(FR) —Chic Emilie (FR) (Policeman (FR))
1329^9 1752^9

Tresco (FR) *M Figge* a76
4 b g Kaldounevees(FR) —Dream Of Prairie (IRE) (Platini (GER))
5089a^6

Tres Coronas (IRE) *T D Barron* a83 77
2 b g Key Of Luck(USA) —Almansa (IRE) (Dr Devious (IRE))
1275[3] ◆ (1735) 2041[2] 3821[2] 4488[13] 5515[4] 6088[7] 6901[3] *(7267)*

Tres Froide (FR) *N Tinkler* a73 67
4 ch m Bering—Charmgoer (USA) (Nureyev (USA))
1990[15] 2724[9] 3378[6] 4496[10] *5329[10]* 5698[15] (6818) 7127[10]

Tres Rapide (IRE) *H-A Pantall* 113
4 b m Anabaa Blue—Tres Ravi (GER) (Monsun (GER))
1597a[2] 2309a[2] 4128a[6] 5058a[3] 5929a[8]

Trevian *Tim Vaughan* a60 54
8 ch g Atraf—Ascend (IRE) (Glint Of Gold)
5246[P]

Trewarthenick *A M Balding* a59 55
2 br g Cape Cross(IRE) —Play With Fire (FR) (Priolo (USA))
4568[6] *5312[6]*

Tribal Myth (IRE) *K A Ryan* 57
2 b g Johannesburg(USA) —Shadow Play (USA) (Theatrical (IRE))
3875[13] 4194[6] 4618[6] 5595[8]

Tribal Rule *Mrs A J Perrett* a38 70
3 gr c Daylami(IRE) —Native Justice (USA) (Alleged (USA))
1931[6] 2763[6] *6287[10]*

Tribe *P R Webber* a73 72
7 b g Danehill(USA) —Leo Girl (USA) (Seattle Slew (USA))
2760[2] 3313[6] 3986[3]

Tri Chara (IRE) *R Hollinshead* a73 48
5 ch g Grand Slam(USA) —Lamzena (IRE) (Fairy King (USA))
(94) 152[4] 404[5] 777[6] 886[4] 975[4] 3401[11] *3722[5]* 4225[15] *4843[6] 5678[2] 6437[9]* 7349[4] 7680[10]

Tricien (FR) *L A Urbano-Grajales* a92 95
5 b h Lomitas—Cherry Moons (FR) (Alysheba (USA))
262a[16]

Trick Or Two *Mrs R A Carr* a68
3 gr g Desert Style(IRE) —Vax Star (Petong)
34[4] 149[4] 350[5] 1232[9]

Tricky Situation *J G Given* 76
3 b f Mark Of Esteem(IRE) —Trick Of Ace (USA) (Clever Trick (USA))
2446[3] 2843[3]

Tricky Trev (USA) *S Curran* a62 52
3 ch g Toccet(USA) —Lady Houston (USA) (Houston (USA))
214[6] 2515[14] 3239[12] 3471[3] 3947[3] 4643[14] *7572[7]*

Tried And True (FR) *H R A Cecil* a62 66
4 b m Marju(IRE) —Test The Rest (USA) (Take Me Out (USA))
1515[4] *1962[7]* 2537[5]

Trifti *Miss Jo Crowley* a79 51
8 b g Vettori(IRE) —Time For Tea (IRE) (Imperial Frontier (USA))
392[3] (873) 1382[5] 2221[P] *7204[5] 7823[6]*

Trimlestown (IRE) *P D Evans* a76 83
6 b g Orpen(USA) —Courtier (Saddlers' Hall (IRE))
20[6] 654[11] ◆ *934[6]* 7321[10] *7358[3] 7691[5] 7762[12]*

Trincot (FR) *Saeed Bin Suroor* 119
4 b h Peintre Celebre(USA) —Royal Lights (FR) (Royal Academy (USA))
846a[8] (1144a) 2115a[2] 3013[7] 4364a[3]

Trinculo (IRE) *R A Harris* a67 71
12 b g Anita's Prince—Fandangerina (USA) (Grey Dawn II)
235[8] 303[8] 681[6] 739[4] 854[4] 976[7] 2134[10]

Trinder *R A Fahey* 75
2 b c Pastoral Pursuits—Quiz Show (Primo Dominie)
2027[2] 2388[6] 3606[2] 4132[4] 5256[10] 6556[8]

Trinity College (USA) *M F De Kock* a82 108
5 ch h Giant's Causeway(USA) —City College (USA) (Carson City (USA))
184a[12]

Tripbiyah (USA) *G A Swinbank* a61 64
3 b g Trippi(USA) —Jathibiyah (USA) (Nureyev (USA))
4354[5] 5072[3] 5727[4] *6637[5]*

Tripitaka *M A Jarvis* a94
3 b g Sulamani(IRE) —Memo (Groom Dancer (USA))
(1464) 6613[9] (7612)

Triple Aspect (IRE) *W J Haggas* 116
3 b c Danetime(IRE) —Wicken Wonder (IRE) (Distant Relative)
2035[2] ◆ (2928) 3638[2] 6107[4] 6661[2]

Triple Axel (IRE) *J Noseda* a65 54
5 b m Danehill Dancer(IRE) —Across The Ice (USA) (General Holme (USA))
152[3] 297[3]

Triple Cee (IRE) *M R Channon* a62 71
3 b f Cape Cross(IRE) —Karri Valley (USA) (Storm Bird (CAN))
876[4] 2858[6] 3209[11] 3610[6] 4224[3] 4569[6] 5382[8] 6276[3] 6338[2] *6705[4] 7022[5] 7392[6] 7857[9]*

Triple Dream *J M Bradley* a68 86
4 ch g Vision Of Night—Triple Joy (Most Welcome)
1048[6] *1320[12]* 1710[5] 1787[2] 2366[7] 2758[5] 3252[2] 3959[5] 4604[4] (5065) 5525[2] (5608) (6220) ◆ 6396[2] 6422[3] 6666[12]

Trip Switch *G Prodromou* a69 58
3 b g Reset(AUS) —Caribbean Star (Soviet Star (USA))
664[2] (722) 936[4] 1744[6] *2826[10]* 3502[8] *5989[12] 6252[11] 7890[8]*

Trip The Light *R A Fahey* a92 89
4 b g Fantastic Light(USA) —Jumaireyah (Fairy King (USA))
1000[7] (1454) 1665[6] 2499[5] (3000) 3532[2] (4737) 4972[2] 5402[4] *5837[3]* 5961[5] (6681) *7091[2] 7465[4]*

Trireme (IRE) *K A Morgan* 53
5 b g Fantastic Light(USA) —Dreamboat (USA) (Mr Prospector (USA))
1967[14] 4220[10]

Triskaidekaphobia *Miss J R Tooth* a55 44
6 b g Bertolini(USA) —Seren Teg (Timeless Times (USA))
431[8] 645[9] 681[DSQ] 896[9] 1134[12] 5345[7] 5900[9] *6119[7] (7657)*

Triton Des Places (FR) *F Nicolle*
2 b g Le Triton(USA) —Amiraute (FR) (Septieme Ciel (USA))
7316a[0]

Triumphant Welcome *H J Evans* a63 68
4 b g Piccolo—Shoof (USA) (Dayjur (USA))
1528[12] 2349[8] *2745[3] 3227[10]* 6933[11] *7606[8] 7869[7]*

Trivia (IRE) *J J Bridger* a81 44
5 br m Marju(IRE) —Lehua (IRE) (Linamix (FR))
846[6] 853[6] 1248[10] 2011[7] 2330[16] 2713[6] 3252[5] 4051[8]

Trofee Dore (FR) *Mme R-W Allen* 63
2 b f Country Reel(USA) —Frundin (Anshan)
5956a[0] 6578a[7]

Trois Rois (FR) *F Head* 111
4 b h Hernando(FR) —Trevise (FR) (Anabaa (USA))
6327a[5]

Troom Girl (FR) *N Leenders*
4 gr m With The Flow(USA) —Troom (FR) (Courtroom (FR))
7822a[10]

Troopingthecolour *J H M Gosden* a86 86
3 b c Nayef(USA) —Hyperspectra (Rainbow Quest (USA))
2930[2] ◆ 4519[2] 6794[2] *7439[2] (7550)*

Tropical Bachelor (IRE) *T J Pitt* a52 72
3 b g Bachelor Duke(USA) —Tropical Coral (IRE) (Pennekamp (USA))
1362[5] 1451[3] 2060[5] 2371[3] 2715[8] 2838[2] 3575[5] 5068[11] 6098[2] 6177[2] 6845[11]

Tropical Blue *Jennie Candlish* a79 77
3 b g Fath(USA) —Tropical Zone (Machiavellian (USA))
2230[2] 3373[3] 3861[6] 4426[4] 4822[13] *7785[3]*

Tropical Duke (IRE) *R E Barr* a62 65
3 ch g Bachelor Duke(USA) —Tropical Dance (USA) (Thorn Dance (USA))
324[2] 272[7] 1408[13] 1842[8] 4348[9] (4819) 5983[3] (6184) 6818[3]

Tropical Paradise (IRE) *P Winkworth* a92 104
3 gr f Verglas(IRE) —Ladylishandra (IRE) (Mujadil (USA))
4052[4] 4771[2] ◆ (5607) 6272[9]

Tropical Strait (IRE) *D W P Arbuthnot* a102 106
6 b g Intikhab(USA) —Tropical Dance (USA) (Thorn Dance (USA))
2075[4]

Tropical Tradition (IRE) *D W P Arbuthnot* a67
4 ch g Traditionally(USA) —Tropical Coral (IRE) (Pennekamp (USA))
213[3] 202[9]

Tropical Treat *R M Beckett* 85
2 b f Bahamian Bounty—Notjustaprettyface (USA) (Red Ransom (USA))
(3918) 7016[7]

Tropico (FR) *S Wattel* 72
2 b g Xaar—Tropical Mark (Mark Of Esteem (IRE))
6501a[9]

Trouble Mountain (USA) *M W Easterby* a24 68
12 br g Mt. Livermore(USA) —Trouble Free (USA) (Nodouble (USA))
1279[15] 2237[9] 2724[6] (3121) 3350[4] 3864[8] 4431[6] 4710[2] 6817[6] *7093[8]*

Troubletimestwo (FR) *H J L Dunlop* a60 58
3 gr g Linamix(FR) —Time Of Trouble (FR) (Warning)
970[4] 1282[5] 1811[12]

Trovare (USA) *Mrs A J Perrett* 61
2 b c Smart Strike(CAN) —Abita (USA) (Dynaformer (USA))
6108[7] 6617[10] ◆ 7146[10] ◆

Truckers Delight (IRE) *John Joseph Hanlon* a64 84
8 b g Darazari(IRE) —Windmill Star (IRE) (Orchestra)
6851[20]

Trueblue Wizard (IRE) *W R Muir* a74
3 ch g Bachelor Duke(USA) —Truly Bewitched (USA) (Affirmed (USA))
276[4] 689[4] 6209[6] 6778[6] 6977[10]

True Britannia *A M Hales* a64 55
3 b f Lujain(USA) —Surf Bird (Shareef Dancer (USA))
(164) 205[6] (506) 662[3] 962[7] 1148[6] 1958[3] 2169[3]

True Decision *S Kirk* a69 62
3 b g Reset(AUS) —True Precision (Presidium)
842[2] (963) 1322[7] 1583[8] 2010[5] *5016[7] 5581[8] 6349[5] 6914[5] 7052[4]* 7225[5] 7422[9] 7426[3]

True Loves Kiss *J A Glover* 63
2 ch f Tobougg(IRE) —Bob's Princess (Bob's Return (IRE))
2069[6] 2360[DSQ] 5669[11]

True Red (IRE) *Mrs N S Evans* a57 64
2 ch f Redback—Red Trance (IRE) (Soviet Star (USA))
1005[7] 1090[2] 1534[5] 1783[5] 2319[4] 3203[2] *3709[2]* 4165[5] 4689[2] 5218[3] 5908[7] *6345[5] 6938[2] 7372[12]* 7559[12] 7778[6]

True To Form (IRE) *Sir Mark Prescott* a44
2 b g Rock Of Gibraltar(IRE) —Truly Yours (IRE) (Barathea (IRE))
6356[7] 6802[8] 7001[8] 7177[7]

Truism *Mrs A J Perrett* 93
3 b g Daylami(IRE) —Real Trust (USA) (Danzig (USA))
1324[5] 5448[2] 5914[2] 6535[2]

Truly Asia (IRE) *R Charlton* 82
3 b g Acclamation—Tasha's Dream (USA) (Woodman (USA))
2081[4] 3221[3] 4097[2] 4505[2] 5151[2] 5833[3] (6937)

Truly Divine *C A Dwyer* a62 64
4 b g Invincible Spirit(IRE) —Shabarana (FR) (Nishapour (FR))
1076[4] 1258[16] *1587[10]* 1777[8] *7606[10] 7880[11]*

Truly Magic *H J L Dunlop* a5 60
2 ch f Traditionally(USA) —Truly Bewitched (USA) (Affirmed (USA))
2825[10] 3786[7] 4688[14] 5379[6] (5935) 6367[4] ◆ 6895[9]

Trumpet Lily *J G Portman* a66 91
4 b m Acclamation—Periwinkle (FR) (Perrault)
(1405) 1860[3] 2412[9] 2768[6] 3400[5] 4422[9] 5099[3] 6618[4] *7132[12]*

Trumpstoo (USA) *R A Fahey* 72
3 b g Perfect Soul(IRE) —Cozzy Love (USA) (Cozzene (USA))
1307[8] 1992[15] 4143[5] 4660[3] 5295[8] 5858[6] 6384[5]

Trusted Venture (USA) *J R Best* a59 14
3 b g Trust N Luck(USA) —Afleet Canadian (CAN) (Bucksplasher (USA))
267[6] 542[4] 586[11] 6720[12] 6998[9]

Trust N Dustan (USA) *Doug Watson* a91
4 ch g Trust N Luck(USA) —Lorraine (USA) (Western Playboy (USA))
337a[3] 435a[5]

Tryanon (FR) *C Boutin* 69
2 b g Le Triton(USA) —Juan Gris (FR) (Subotica (FR))
6751a[0]

Tryst *Sir Michael Stoute* a87 98
4 gr g Highest Honor(FR) —Courting (Pursuit Of Love)
(1636) ◆ *2241[2]* ◆ 6239[3] 6480[20]

Tsar Bomba (USA) *T D Barron* 65
2 bb g Red Bullet(USA) —Larry's Blackhoney (USA) (Hennessy (USA))
2339[5]

Tsar De Russie (IRE) *E Lellouche* 102
4 b h Montjeu(IRE) —Tamariyya (IRE) (Alzao (USA))
5281a[0]

Tuaoi (USA) *J Morin* a78 88
4 ch h Rahy(USA) —Turning Wheel (USA) (Seeking The Gold (USA))
7822a[5]

Tubby Littlejohns (IRE) *B J Llewellyn* 57
5 ch h Desert Sun—Brookhouse Lady (IRE) (Polish Patriot (USA))
4617[2] 5061[5]

Tubular Bells (USA) *H-A Pantall* 98
4 gr m Kingmambo(USA) —Summer Symphony (IRE) (Caerleon (USA))
1597a[10] 2428a[8] 4365a[0]

Tucker's Law *B R Millman* a67 68
2 b g Country Reel(USA) —Silvereine (FR) (Bering)
1577[14] 2201[2] 2792[5] 3317[6] 4063[5] *4647[4] 5091[6] 5776[6] 6494[5] 6775[2] (7210)*

Tudor Key (IRE) *Mrs A J Perrett* a94 91
3 br g Key Of Luck(USA) —Anne Boleyn (Rainbow Quest (USA))
1303[5] ◆ 2296[5] 3049[12] *(3988)* 4296[10] *4983[8]* 5221[13] 6117[6] 6474[3]

Tudor Prince (IRE) *A W Carroll* a76 82
5 bb g Cape Cross(IRE) —Savona (IRE) (Cyrano De Bergerac)
(1468) 2276[9] 2799[3] 3164[4] *3512[4]* 4387[7] 5001[11] *6028[2]* 6738[10] *(7179) 7496[11]*

Tudor Princess *W R Muir* 52
2 b f King's Best(USA) —Santorini (USA) (Spinning World (USA))
5969[7] 6563[7]

Tuesday Joy (NZ) *Mrs Gai Waterhouse* 111
6 b m Carnegie(IRE) —Joie Denise (AUS) (Danehill (USA))
1011a[9]

Tufton *R A Fahey* a83 82
6 b g King's Best(USA) —Mythical Magic (Green Desert (USA))
1660[2] 2043[5] 3123[3] (3854) (4434) 4930[9] 6012[8] 7118[4]

Tukitinyasok (IRE) *R F Fisher* a63 84
2 b g Fath(USA) —Mevlana (IRE) (Red Sunset)
3170[3] (3652) 4086[3] 4558[4] 5433[7] *7717[3]*

Tulip Explosion *D Shaw* a45 42
2 b f Exceed And Excel(AUS) —Comme Ca (Cyrano De Bergerac)
3634[8] *4370[9]* 4889[10] *5226[3] 5776[8]*

Tullamore (USA) *Z Koplik* 102
4 b h Theatrical(IRE) —Bungalow (USA) (Lord Avie (USA))
2309a[7] 6526a[16]

Tumblecloud (IRE) *W A Murphy* a45 43
4 b m Mujadil(USA) —Sudden Interest (FR) (Highest Honor (FR))
6831[10]

Tumbled Again *M E Rimmer* a24
2 br g Tumbleweed Ridge—Amber Brown (Thowra (FR))
4318[7] *7199[11]*

Tumbleweed Di *John A Harris* a47 47
5 ro m Tumbleweed Ridge—Peggotty (Capricorn Line)
5982[13]

Tumeritespius (IRE) *F Sanchez*
2 b f Antonius Pius(USA) —Imperial Conquest (IRE) (Imperial Ballet (IRE))
6325a[0]

Tump Mac *N Bycroft* 61
5 ch g Compton Admiral—Petite Elite (Anfield)
2366[11] 3174[12] 4071[7] 5465[8] 5954[11] 6488[8]

Tunder Bool (IRE) *F Sheridan* a22
4 b g Intikhab(USA) —Tirolean Dance (IRE) (Tirol)
537[8]

Tune Up The Band *R J Hodges* a22 60
5 b g Bandmaster(USA) —Name That Tune (Fayruz)
475[8]

Tungsten Strike (USA) *Mrs A J Perrett* 113
8 ch g Smart Strike(CAN) —Bathilde (IRE) (Generous (IRE))
1601[5] 2409[4] 4457[10] 4769[8] 5402[6] 6273[8]

Tuning Fork *M J Attwater* a53 4
9 b g Alzao(USA) —Tuning (Rainbow Quest (USA))
231[4] 117[9] 3269[13]

Tuning Mozart *S Wattel* a77 80
6 b g Mozart(IRE) —Tuneful Nine (USA) (Dixieland Band (USA))
(7822a)

Tuppenny Piece *W R Swinburn* a59 16
3 ch f Sakhee(USA) —Tuppenny (Salse (USA))
3508[4] 4722[9] 5782[4] 6226[4] 7214[8]

Turati *G Pucciatti* 120
3 b c Lomitas—Torrigiana (Celtic Swing)
1393a[4] 1904a[2] 7313a[2]

Turbo Shandy *D Burchell* a43 47
6 b g Piccolo—Carn Maire (Northern Prospect (USA))
4324[7] 4885[6] 5242[6] *7495[8]*

Turfliebe (GER) *M Rulec* 82
3 b f Dashing Blade—Turfaue (GER) (Big Shuffle (USA))
1914a[8]

Turf Time *J A Glover* a48
2 b g Zafeen(FR) —Next Time (IRE) (Danetime (IRE))
2575[5] ◆ 3032[14] *5611[7]* 5950[17] 6554[9] *7778[2]*

Turf Trivia *G M Moore* 64
2 gr g Alhaarth(IRE) —Exclusive Approval (USA) (With Approval (CAN))
2195[4] 3376[5] 4308[3] 6793[12]

Turfwolke (GER) *Mrs H S Main* a51 65
4 b m Medicean—Turfaue (GER) (Big Shuffle (USA))
1743[4] *2133[12]* 2330[11] 4533[6] *5195[7] 7614[8]*

Turjuman (USA) *W J Musson* a10 73
4 ch g Swain(IRE) —Hachiyah (IRE) (Generous (IRE))
2039[4] (2983) (3697) 5034[3] 5912[5] 6473[5]

Turkish Lokum *J M P Eustace* a63 64
3 b f Bertolini(USA) —Malabarista (FR) (Assert)
1588[8] 2148[9] 3075[3] 4179[5] *6344[3] 6828[3] 7052[9]*

Turkish Sultan (IRE) *J M Bradley* a57 55
6 b g Anabaa(USA) —Odalisque (IRE) (Machiavellian (USA))
81[7] 100[7] 211[6] 469[5] 578[3] 669[10] 802[4] 1037[3] 1770[8] *7152[7]* 7422[12] 7466[5] 7652[3] 7718[7]

Turner's Touch *G L Moore* a60 73
7 ch g Compton Place—Chairmans Daughter (Unfuwain (USA))
342[3] 528[3] 750[4] 838[2] 1586[7] 2708[7] 3223[6] 3950[4] 4640[5] 6969[7] *7549[9]* 7658[5]

Turning Circle *M Brittain* a49
3 b c Spinning World(USA) —Willow Dale (IRE) (Danehill (USA))
7671[9]

Turning For Home (FR) *H-A Pantall* 107
4 ch m Spinning World(USA) —Nanty (IRE) (Nashwan (USA))
3520a[6]

Turning Top (IRE) *S A Callaghan* a59 86
3 b f Pivotal—Pietra Dura (Cadeaux Genereux)
2416[3] *2710[6]* (3319) 3752[11] 4452[2] 4695[3] (5449) 5607[8]

Turnkey *D Nicholls* 100
7 br g Pivotal—Persian Air (Persian Bold)
1018[12] 2814[6] (3066) 4069[5] 4621[3] (4775) (5147) 6050[13]

Turn Me On (IRE) *T D Walford* a85 88
6 b g Tagula(IRE) —Jacobina (Magic Ring (IRE))
(1333) (1766) 2266[10] 3496[2] 3825[10] 5409[5] 5697[10] 6019[2] *6435[6]* 6645[8] 7083[7]

Turn On The Style *J Balding* a109 107
7 ch g Pivotal—Elegant Rose (Noalto)
123[2] 553[4] 7090[6] 7488[11]

Turn To Dreams *P D Evans* a58 51
3 b f Auction House(USA) —Seren Teg (Timeless Times (USA))
16[2] 77[4] 136[5] 231[4] 287[2] 332[3] 450[4] 479[6] 555[2] 586[5] 628[2] 759[5] 776[10] 808[6] 7127[12] 7200[11] 7818[5]

Tuscan Gold *Sir Mark Prescott* a63 49
2 ch c Medicean—Louella (USA) (El Gran Senor (USA))
6061[11] *6372[7]* 6912[6]

Tuscan King *P Howling* a68 35
2 ch g Medicean—Castaway Queen (IRE) (Selkirk (USA))
6561[5] *7130[6] 7391[3] (7493) 7731[3] 7788[3]*

Tusculum (IRE) *B J Curley* a53 38
6 b g Sadler's Wells(USA) —Turbaine (USA) (Trempolino (USA))
(385) ◆ 1767[8]

Tussian Bere (FR) *E J O'Neill* 82
2 ch g Russian Blue(IRE) —Fitness Queen (USA) (Gilded Time (USA))
3934a[3] 4686a[4] 5378a[2]

Tut (IRE) *A P Jarvis* 73
2 b f Intikhab(USA) —Radiant Energy (IRE) (Spectrum (IRE))
3495[3] (5330) 6088[8]

Tutor (IRE) *Mrs A M Thorpe* a72 66
5 ch g Dr Fong(USA) —Glandore (IRE) (Persian Bold)
112[3] 631[10]

Tuxedo *P W Hiatt* a77 75
4 ch g Cadeaux Genereux—Serengeti Bride (USA) (Lion Cavern (USA))
251[0] (387) 625[3] 708[5] 1876[9] 2565[6] 3075[2] 3504[4] (4181) 4504[3] 5746[11] *6725[4] 6976[4]* 7327[2]

Tuxsumdoin *J R Weymes* a7
5 ch m Zaha(CAN) —Roisin Clover (Faustus (USA))
1[6]

Tweeter (USA) *D Wayne Lukas* a72
3 ch f Unbridled's Song(USA) —Dear Birdie (USA) (Storm Bird (CAN))
1763a[7]

Twenty Score *Miss J R Tooth* a65 34
3 ch f Lear Spear(USA) —Milladella (FR) (Nureyev (USA))
251[8] 842[5] 1985[9] 2417[13] *2681[6]*

Twice Over *H R A Cecil* a125 123
4 b h Observatory(USA) —Double Crossed (Caerleon (USA))
1301[3] 2076[3] 3013[4] 3640[7] (5764) (6202) (6850) *7311a[3]*

Twilight Dawn *L Lungo* 72
5 ch m Muhtarram(USA) —Indigo Dawn (Rainbow Quest (USA))
1472[4] 2445[3]

Twilight Memory (USA) *B J Meehan* 48
2 ch f Smart Strike(CAN) —Southern Swing (USA) (Dixieland Band (USA))
5604[14] 6389[5]

Twilight Star (IRE) *R A Teal* a84 89
5 b g Green Desert(USA) —Heavenly Whisper (IRE) (Halling (USA))
(1524) 2083[6] *2828[13]* 3770[2] 4236[3] 4641[6] 5511[10] 6336[3]

Twilight Tear *M L W Bell* 45
2 ch f Rock Of Gibraltar(IRE) —Clara Bow (IRE) (Sadler's Wells (USA))
6920[13]

Twill (IRE) *D Burchell* a67 83
6 ch g Barathea(IRE) —Khafaya (Unfuwain (USA))
2684[4] 3721[9]

Twin Deficit *R Litt*
2 gr c Oratorio(IRE) —Seldom Found (IRE) (Unfuwain (USA))
6325a[0]

Twinlight (FR) *G Cherel* 75
2 b g Muhtathir—Fairlight (GER) (Big Shuffle (USA))
4807a[3]

Twinned (IRE) *Mike Murphy* a59 45
6 ch g Soviet Star(USA) —Identical (IRE) (Machiavellian (USA))
173[8]

Twist Again (IRE) *P Howling* a56 77
3 b f Sakhee(USA) —Dance Clear (IRE) (Marju (IRE))
1963[8] 2240[5] 2640[7] *3383[7]* 4178[3] 4722[3] (5011) (5442) 5952[6] (6384)

Twist Bookie (IRE) *S Lycett* a64 63
9 br g Perugino(USA) —Twist Scarlett (GER) (Lagunas)
1153[8]

Twisted *J H M Gosden* 76
3 ch c Selkirk(USA) —Winding (USA) (Irish River (FR))
2074[3] 2640[4] 2943[9]

Twoellies *Ollie Pears* a39 14
2 ch f Trade Fair—Fancier Bit (Lion Cavern (USA))
2568[10] 3310[10] *7788[9]*

Two Kisses (IRE) *B G Powell* a64 66
2 b f Spartacus(IRE) —Flight Sequence (Polar Falcon (USA))
1742[5] 2047[6] 2563[5] 3256[3] 4565[8] 5379[5] *7451[7] 7654[6] (7799)*

Two Minds (FR) *T Cambefort*
2 ch c Choisir(AUS) —Dynamic Dream (USA) (Dynaformer (USA))
7507a[10]

Twos And Eights (IRE) *Paul Mason* a53 19
3 bb g Kyllachy—Docklands Grace (USA) (Honour And Glory (USA))
831[12]

Twosheetstothewind *M Dods* a68 76
5 ch m Bahamian Bounty—Flag (Selkirk (USA))
1096[4] 2046[2] 2316[11] (3002) 3445[6] 3565[4] (3909) 4136[2]

Two Step Salsa (USA) *Saeed Bin Suroor* a122 99
4 bb h Petionville(USA) —Two To Waltz (USA) (Seattle Slew (USA))
(641a) ◆ *(1008a)*

Two Together (USA) *D R Lanigan* a52 48
3 b c Theatrical(IRE) —Miasma (USA) (Lear Fan (USA))
6794[7] *6974[11]*

Two Tone *G Woodward* 28
3 bb g Diktat—Fireburst (Spectrum (IRE))
3168[8] 3531[6] 4354[12]

Two Turtle Doves (IRE) *M Mullineaux* a38 60
3 b f Night Shift(USA) —Purple Rain (IRE) (Celtic Swing)
1683[9] 2250[7] 2937[6] *3464[6]* 3939[6] 4594[2] 4937[11] 5158[2] 6140[4] 6824[5] 7082[5]

Tycoon's Buddy *S Wynne* a29
4 ch g Reel Buddy(USA) —Tycoon's Last (Nalchik (USA))
150[12] 255[7]

Tyfos *W M Brisbourne* a74 83
4 b g Bertolini(USA) —Warminghamsharpish (Nalchik (USA))
2418[4] (2864) 3164[6] (3771) 4134[3] 4387[4] 5247[3]

Typical Female *A B Haynes* a22
2 b f Pursuit Of Love—Angel Maid (Forzando)
4646[10] 5786[9] *7139[U] 7669[9]*

Tyrana (GER) *Ian Williams* a64 57
6 ch m Acatenango(GER) —Tascalina (GER) (Big Shuffle (USA))
623[4] 1785[10] 3074[5] *6945[10] (7766)*

Tyrannosaurus Rex (IRE) *D Shaw* a73 86
5 b g Bold Fact(USA) —Dungeon Princess (IRE) (Danehill (USA))
22[8] (431) 535[6] ◆ *654[6] (832) 971[2]* (1877) (2782) 3623[2] 4135[11] 4891[9] 5247[8]

Tyrrells Wood (IRE) *T G Mills* a88 98
4 b g Sindar(IRE) —Diner De Lune (IRE) (Be My Guest (USA))
631[2] (2766) 3143[2] ◆ 4417[2]

Tyzack (IRE) *Stef Liddiard* a75 58
8 b g Fasliyev(USA) —Rabea (USA) (Devil's Bag (USA))
519[2] ◆ *618[6]*

Uace Mac *N Bycroft* 70
5 b m Compton Place—Umbrian Gold (IRE) (Perugino (USA))
3066[9] 3381[10] 4281[7] 4508[3] 4823[14] 5150[12]

Ubenkor (IRE) *B Smart* a31 73
4 b g Diktat—Lucky Dancer (FR) (Groom Dancer (USA))
1737[13] 2257[4]

Ubiquitous *S Dow* 56
4 b m Erhaab(USA) —Lady Isabell (Rambo Dancer (CAN))
1961[8] 2739[5] 3739[2] 4382[2] 5152[2]

Ucanchoose (IRE) *Andrew Slattery* a60 67
3 b g Choisir(AUS) —Ruacana Falls (USA) (Storm Bird (CAN))
4392a[8]

Ucandri (IRE) *C Ferland* 86
2 ch c Refuse To Bend(IRE) —Original (Caerleon (USA))
(6927a)

Udabaa (IRE) *M P Tregoning* a71
2 b c Alhaarth(IRE) —Addaya (IRE) (Persian Bold)
5312[3] ◆

Uddy Mac *N Bycroft* 61
2 ch f Reel Buddy(USA) —Befriend (USA) (Allied Forces (USA))
3032[5] 3875[7] 4226[9] 4803[4] 5136[10] 5692[5] 5980[4]

Ugenius *Mrs C A Dunnett* a74 56
5 b g Killer Instinct—I'm Sophie (IRE) (Shalford (IRE))
607[9] 725[4] 844[10] 979[9] 1258[4] *1606[9]* 2458[10] 3007[11] *3269[3] 3735[3] 3980[2]* (4375) 4859[6] 5329[4] 5813[2] (6123) 6361[9] (7065)

Ugly Betty *Bruce Hellier* a16 25
4 b m Where Or When(IRE) —Dancing Steps (Zafonic (USA))
581[8] 3379[8] 6766[12]

Uhuru Peak *M W Easterby* a51 61
8 ch g Bal Harbour—Catherines Well (Junius (USA))
3490[7] 3863[10] 4588[12] 4932[10]

Uig *H S Howe* a68 72
8 ch m Bien Bien(USA) —Madam Zando (Forzando)
1983[4] 2212[5] 2351[5] 2678[8] 2878[5] 3206[5] 3462[3] 4169[10] 4744[8] 5790[3] *6770[9]*

Ullalujah *L Wells* 39
7 b m Josr Algarhoud(IRE) —Ulla Laing (Mummy's Pet)
1427[6]

Ultimate *H Morrison* a94 80
3 b c Anabaa(USA) —Nirvana (Marju (IRE))
(151) ◆ 1707[5] 2038[4] 5068[10] *(6946)*

Ultimate Respect (USA) *M Johnston* a72 59
3 b c Elusive Quality(USA) —Zelanda (IRE) (Night Shift (USA))
4246[8] *4648[6]* 5163[4] 5506[6] *5886[3]* 6178[11] *6462[7]*

Ultravox (USA) *B J Meehan* 77
2 b c Lemon Drop Kid(USA) —Lynnwood Chase (USA) (Horse Chestnut (SAF))
4048[5] 4908[3]

Ulysees (IRE) *I Semple* a52 56
10 b g Turtle Island(IRE) —Tamasriya (IRE) (Doyoun)
4529[5] 5364[2] 5730[11] 6156[2] 7113[11] 7174[7]

Ulzana (IRE) *Sir Mark Prescott* a69
3 b g High Chaparral(IRE) —Maritsa (IRE) (Danehill (USA))
5840[3] ◆

Umirage *H Blume* 102
4 b m Monsun(GER) —Ungarin (GER) (Goofalik (USA))
5058a[4] 5929a[12]

Umpa Loompa (IRE) *B J McMath* a32 14
5 ch g Indian Lodge(IRE) —Bold Fashion (FR) (Nashwan (USA))
4982[6]

Umverti *N Bycroft* 77
4 b m Averti(IRE) —Umbrian Gold (IRE) (Perugino (USA))
1472[5] 1955[3] (2246) 2803[6] 3235[2] (3557) (4068) 4658[13] 5671[8]

Una Pelota (IRE) *N J Vaughan* 80
3 b c Refuse To Bend(IRE) —Sombreffe (Polish Precedent (USA))
1508[5] 1793[3] 2229[4]

Unavita (GER) *H Blume* a56 75
3 b f Vettori(IRE) —Ungarin (GER) (Goofalik (USA))
5783a[7]

Unawatuna *Mrs K Walton* 64
4 b m Golden Snake(USA) —Laylee (Deploy)
1851[2] ◆ 3617[4] 4551[8] 5068[10] (5554) (6767)

Unbelievable Jeff *J Balding* a37 51
3 b g Oasis Dream—Sunshine N'Showers (Spectrum (IRE))
227[7] 306[10] 655[10] 3176[2] ◆ 3239[2] 3342[4] 6140[5]

Unbreak My Heart (IRE) *R A Fahey* 98
4 ch g Bahamian Bounty—Golden Heart (Salse (USA))
(1170) 1460[5] 2342[6] 3873[7] 4404[13] 6013[9] 6093[7]

Unbridled Belle (USA) *Todd Pletcher* a117
6 b m Broken Vow(USA) —Little Bold Belle (USA) (Silver Buck (USA))
6508a[2]

Uncle Bertie *Tom Dascombe* a69 72
4 b g Bertolini(USA) —Resourceful (IRE) (Entrepreneur)
570[7] (767) 1615[7] 2200[11] 2362[4] *6460[10]*

Uncle Brit *Sir Mark Prescott* a71 12
3 b c Efisio—Tarneem (USA) (Zilzal (USA))
162[8] 315[7] 381[9] 572[11] 1656[4] (3955) 4171[4] 4562[10] *4872[4] 5806[8]*

Uncle Eric (IRE) *Mrs John Harrington* a70 76
4 b g Alhaarth(IRE) —Kirk Wynd (Selkirk (USA))
2290a[11]

Uncle Fred *P R Chamings* a91 86
4 b g Royal Applause—Karla June (Unfuwain (USA))
2186[2] (2495) *3274[2]* 4641[12] *(6583)* ◆ *7233[7]*

Uncle Keef (IRE) *M P Tregoning* a60 44
3 b g Sadler's Wells(USA) —Love For Ever (IRE) (Darshaan)
6475[7] 6794[8] *6974[8]*

Uncle Tom (BRZ) *G Duarte* 80
3 b c First American(USA) —Just Lucky (BRZ) (Spend A Buck (USA))
6505a[13]

Unconsoled *J Hetherton* a48 63
3 b f Ishiguru(USA) —Chantilly (FR) (Sanglamore (USA))
3975[4] 4432[8] 4550[6] 4823[18] 5468[6] 5983[7] *7353[4] 7678[7]*

Undaunted Affair (IRE) *K A Ryan* a79 92
3 ch f Spartacus(IRE) —Party Bag (Cadeaux Genereux)
1024a[5] 1918a[11] 5921a[7] 6814[8] 7032[8] *7297a[7]*

Under Fire (IRE) *A W Carroll* a66 66
6 b g Lear Spear(USA) —Kahyasi Moll (IRE) (Brief Truce (USA))
6224[10] 6719[7] 6968[10] *7240[12] 7767[2]*

Under Review (IRE) *T D Barron* a73 70
3 b g Danetime(IRE) —Coloma (JPN) (Forty Niner (USA))
358[2] ◆ *(602) 1032[5]* 1505[9] 5877[5] 6220[7] 6489[4] ◆ 6988[4] ◆ *7355[6]*

Under Warranty (ITY) *F Sheridan* a75
5 ch g Della Scala(IRE) —Serengate (GER) (Highest Honor (FR))
235[2] 292[4] (352)

Underworld *M Al Muhairi* a93 107
4 ch g Cadeaux Genereux—Mythic (Zafonic (USA))
335a[6] *414a[12]*

Underworld Dandy *P D Evans* a65 63
2 gr g Fraam—Eastern Lyric (Petong)
1749[5] (2319) 2875[6] 4190[8] 4901[10] *5613[4] (5985) 6431[5] 6639[5]* 6963[8] *7139[3] 7235[5] 7474[4]* 7669[5]

Une Autre Aventure (FR) *C Boutin* 77
2 ch f Diableneyev(USA) —Zelenski (USA) (Woodman (USA))
5494a[5] 5713a[2] 6501a[17]

Union Island (IRE) *K A Ryan* a68 89
3 b g Rock Of Gibraltar(IRE) —Daftiyna (IRE) (Darshaan)
(1101) 1992[2] 2701[12] 2935[2] 3780[14] 4401[5] 5209[9] *6209[11]*

Union Jack Jackson (IRE) *John A Harris* a43 52
7 b g Daggers Drawn(USA) —Beechwood Quest (IRE) (River Falls)
3066[11] 3304[13] 4023[8] 4667[5] (4887) 5111[8] *6674[8]*

Unique Jewellery (NZ) *J Size* 111
5 b g O'Reilly(NZ) —Aulide (AUS) (Snippets (AUS))
1553a[11]

Uniquely Poised (USA) *J H M Gosden* a92 84
3 bb g More Than Ready(USA) —No Other Like You (USA) (Cozzene (USA))
1289[12] *(1730)* ◆ 2696[7] 3049[15] *6633[9]*

United Nations *N Wilson* a81 80
8 ch g Halling(USA) —Congress (IRE) (Dancing Brave (USA))
(39) (93) 274[3] 515[3] 693[6] 858[2] 7723[6]

Universal Circus *M R Channon* a74 80
2 b f Imperial Dancer—Wansdyke Lass (Josr Algarhoud (IRE))
3249[11] 3810[4] 4152[3] (4451) 5659[6] 6063[3] 6471[4] *6805[6]*

Universal Pride *J Gallagher* 33
2 b f Danbird(AUS) —Frisson (Slip Anchor)
5800[8] 6544[12]

Unleashed (IRE) *H R A Cecil* a94 107
4 br g Storming Home—Uriah (GER) (Acatenango (GER))
1351[8] 2075[7] 2677[4] 3190[3] 4484[5] 5248[9] 6302[3] 6662[15]

Unnefer (FR) *H R A Cecil* 114
4 b h Danehill Dancer(IRE) —Mimalia (USA) (Silver Hawk (USA))
1346[2] (1875) 2476[8] 5059a[10]

Unquenchable Fire (IRE) *C Ferland* 88
4 b g Invincible Spirit(IRE) —Tasha's Dream (USA) (Woodman (USA))
3419a[3]

Unshakable (IRE) *Bob Jones* a96 99
10 b g Eagle Eyed(USA) —Pepper And Salt (IRE) (Double Schwartz)
2412[12] 2927[9] 5262[12] 6594[11]

Unshakable Will (IRE) *B Smart* 79
2 b g Refuse To Bend(IRE) —Miss Devious (IRE) (Dr Devious (IRE))
2623[5] 5512[2] (6047) 6557[2] ◆ 7013[11]

Until The Man (IRE) *R Ingram* a68 61
2 b c Tillerman—Canoe Cove (IRE) (Grand Lodge (USA))
5017[9] 5505[9] 6199[7] 6589[5] 6923[2] *7235[3] 7886[2]*

Until When (USA) *B Smart* a70 73
5 b g Grand Slam(USA) —Chez Cherie (Wolfhound (USA))
1096[3]

Up And Coming (IRE) *J E Pease* a93 96
5 b g Compton Place—Uplifting (Magic Ring (IRE))
2513a[11]

Up At Last *W J Haggas* 54
2 b f Cape Cross(IRE) —Upend (Main Reef)
6920[11]

Uphold *B W Hills* 58
2 b c Oasis Dream—Allegro Viva (USA) (Distant View (USA))
7146[13] ◆

Up In Arms (IRE) *P Winkworth* a73 66
5 b g Daggers Drawn(USA) —Queenliness (Exit To Nowhere (USA))
103[10] 402[4] 668[6] 1200[U] 1426[4] 1980[6]

Upper Key *K A Ryan* 30
3 b g Exceed And Excel(AUS) —Ard Na Sighe (IRE) (Kenmare (FR))
1888[11] 2234[8]

Upstairs *Paul Henderson* a67 59
5 ch g Sugarfoot—Laena (Roman Warrior)
192[5] 281[4] 1187[6] 2011[11] 2202[11] 3421[8]

Upton Seas *M W Easterby* a60 78
3 b f Josr Algarhoud(IRE) —Crystal Seas (Zamindar (USA))
(3610) ◆ (4506) 4892[5] ◆ (5524) 5771[5] 6680[11] *6951[6]* 7020[4]

Uptown Lad (IRE) *R Johnson* 46
10 b g Definite Article—Shoka (FR) (Kaldoun (FR))
2725[8] 3313[10] 3617[3] 5734[7] 6767[14] 6899[6]

Urban Bounty *M J McGrath*
4 ch m Bahamian Bounty—Bathe In Light (USA) (Sunshine Forever (USA))
2633[11]

Urban Clubber *J Howard Johnson* 70
2 b g Dubai Destination(USA) —Surprise Visitor (IRE) (Be My Guest (USA))
1867[6] 2247[5] 2963[4] 4190[6]

Urban Dream (FR) *A Bonin* a63 62
3 b c Urban Ocean(FR) —Kalanna (FR) (Homme De Loi (IRE))
5278a[8]

Urban Poet (USA) *Saeed Bin Suroor* 109
3 bb c Dynaformer(USA) —Preach (USA) (Mr Prospector (USA))
(4014) ◆ 4405[3] ◆ 5425[6] 5854[6] (6536) 6854[8]

Urban Space *D Burchell* a53 71
3 ch g Sulamani(IRE) —Rasmalai (Sadler's Wells (USA))
630[6] 883[6] (1363) 1614[3] 1930[5] 2540[7] 2772[2] (3222) 3535[4] 4319[10] 5097[2] 6116[5]

Urban Tiger (GER) *Tim Vaughan* a23 87
6 b g Marju(IRE) —Ukraine Venture (Slip Anchor)
6724[12]

Urban Warrior *Ian Williams* a74 75
5 b g Zilzal(USA) —Perfect Poppy (Shareef Dancer (USA))
656[7] 836[6]

Ursis (FR) *S Gollings* a62 80
8 b g Trempolino(USA) —Bold Virgin (USA) (Sadler's Wells (USA))
2194[2] 2445[2] *3510[9]*

Ursula (IRE) *R M Beckett* a86 85
3 b f Namid—Fritta Mista (IRE) (Linamix (FR))
2198[3] ◆ 3727[5] (4227) ◆ 4309[4] *6667[3] 7111[5] 7478[7]*

Ursus *C R Wilson* a52 63
4 ch g Rambling Bear—Adar Jane (Ardar)
3065[3] 3483[6] 3765[4] 4436[9] 5396[6] 5729[7] 6379[2] ◆ 7081[9] *7503[8] 7709[10]*

Usbeke (GER) *J-P Carvalho* 101
3 b g Big Shuffle(USA) —Ustimona (GER) (Mondrian I (GER))
(6657a) 7208a[5]

Usetheforce (IRE) *M Quinn* a53 35
4 ch g Black Minnaloushe(USA) —Polynesian Goddess (IRE) (Salmon Leap (USA))
97[10] 446[6] 2420[15]

Usquaebach *S Curran* a53
2 b f Trade Fair—Mashmoum (Lycius (USA))
994[18] 1298[11] *1653[3]* 2167[6] 2444[9] *5372[3] 6356[11] 6970[9]*

Ustilago (GER) *W Baltromei* 60
2 ch c Lando(GER) —Ungarin (GER) (Goofalik (USA))
4807a[10]

Usual Suspects *Peter Grayson* a38 46
3 b f Royal Applause—Soft Breeze (Zafonic (USA))
273[10]

Utmost Respect *R A Fahey* 121
5 b g Danetime(IRE) —Utmost (IRE) (Most Welcome)
(1989) ◆ (2287a)

Utrillo (IRE) *A P O'Brien* a94 94
2 b c Encosta De Lago(AUS) —Mary McGlinchy (USA) (Pleasant Colony (USA))
5275a[6] 6319a[9] 7072a[7]

Uvinza *W J Knight* a83 101
3 ch f Bertolini(USA) —Baddi Heights (FR) (Shirley Heights)
1599[4] 2036[3] 3047[3] 4094[3] 5202[8] 6242[5] *7131[7]*

Vadaspeed (FR) *C Boutin* 39
2 b c Vadasin(IRE) —Speeding (FR) (Great Palm (USA))
4073a[9]

Vadition (IRE) *J J Bridger* a13 43
2 b f Halling(USA) —Retail Therapy (IRE) (Bahhare (USA))
2007[7] *2595[8]* 3249[13] 5213[11] 6200[8] 6736[8] *7390[11]*

Vadiya (FR) *A De Royer-Dupre* 85
3 b f Peintre Celebre(USA) —Vadaza (FR) (Zafonic (USA))
4334a[0]

Vaduz *M R Channon* a20 53
2 b f Imperial Dancer—Summer Shades (Green Desert (USA))
1090[8] 1249[3] 1364[4] 3547[7] *3719[8]*

Vain Boteli (GER) *R Ford* 3
3 b g Bertolini(USA) —Vanity Fair (Nashwan (USA))
5940[13] *7272[8]*

Vainglory (USA) *D M Simcock* a94 96
5 ch h Swain(IRE) —Infinite Spirit (USA) (Maria's Mon (USA))
1433[4] 1798[6] 2480[3] (3055) 3431[2] 4261[3] 4794[5] *5663[6]* 6429[4] *6876[5]* ◆

Valantino Oyster (IRE) *J Howard Johnson* 40
2 bb g Pearl Of Love(IRE) —Mishor (Slip Anchor)
1827[5] 2231[7] 2940[11]

Valatrix (IRE) *C F Wall* a85 83
4 b m Acclamation—Dramatic Entry (IRE) (Persian Bold)
1411[2] 1733[5] 2980[5] 3789[4] 4500[7] 5349[7] *6630[11]*

Val C *N P Littmoden* a55 67
2 b f Dubawi(IRE) —Valjarv (IRE) (Bluebird (USA))
2604[7] 2972[3] 3385[3] 4208[4] *4537[5]* 5033[3] 5550[8] 5950[5]

Valdan (IRE) *M A Barnes* a71 81
5 b g Val Royal(FR) —Danedrop (IRE) (Danehill (USA))
(1886) 2315[6] 2815[4] 3000[5] 3809[2] 4417[16] 4696[11] *6855[6]*

Valdemar *A D Brown* a54 50
3 ch g Tobougg(IRE) —Stealthy Times (Timeless Times (USA))
91[7] 207[2] 293[6] 379[7] (583) 831[9] 1057[4] 1452[5] *2577[5]* 2964[3]

Val d'Espoir (IRE) *H-A Pantall* 84
5 b h In The Wings—Vert Val (USA) (Septieme Ciel (USA))
3045a[6] 4335a[3]

Valdino (GER) *Uwe Ostmann* 114
4 b g Black Sam Bellamy(IRE) —Valdina (GER) (Lomitas)
2216a[6] 3493a[4] 6521a[8]

Valedictum (AUS) *Danny O'Brien* 112
9 ch g Umatilla(NZ) —Wunderschoen (AUS) (Twig Moss (FR))
413a[6] (609a) 774a[6]

Valentine Bay *M Mullineaux* a18 42
3 b f Reel Buddy(USA) —Bullion (Sabrehill (USA))
6221[13] 6344[10] 6950[7] 7270[8]
Valentine Blue *A B Haynes* a50 50
4 ch g Tobougg(IRE) —Blue Topaz (IRE) (Bluebird (USA))
240[2] 790[4] 918[5]
Valentino Rossi (BRZ) *A G Foster* 82
7 b g New Colony(USA) —Great Sola (BRZ) (Duke Of Marmalade (USA))
2501[7] 2994[19] 3390[17]
Valentino Swing (IRE) *Miss T Spearing* a69 73
6 ch g Titus Livius(FR) —Farmers Swing (IRE) (River Falls)
118[4] 540[4] 7151[0] 933[5] 1259[8] 7239[11] 7534[3] 7715[10] (7834) 7890[2]
Vale Of York (IRE) *Saeed Bin Suroor* a116 116
2 b c Invincible Spirit(IRE) —Red Vale (IRE) (Halling (USA))
(4286) ◆ 5133[5] (5743) 6268[3] 6716a[2] (7307a)
Valery Borzov (IRE) *D Nicholls* a94 111
5 b g Iron Mask(USA) —Fay's Song (IRE) (Fayruz)
257a[12] 434a[10] 1560[4] (2059) 2385[5] 4330[16] 4523[6] 5039[8] 6091[20]
Valfurva (IRE) *L M Cumani* a64 55
3 b f Celtic Swing—Kiriyaki (USA) (Secretariat (USA))
3297[5] ◆ 4151[8] 4981[6] 6224[11] 6437[5]
Valiant Knight (FR) *R Hannon* 79
2 ch c Night Shift(USA) —Pilgrim Of Grace (FR) (Bering)
4258[7] 4713[3] 5220[2] 5505[8] 6199[8]
Valiant Romeo *R Bastiman* a15 56
9 b g Primo Dominie—Desert Lynx (IRE) (Green Desert (USA))
1243[20] 1921[5] 2758[4] 3239[13] 3445[9]
Validor (FR) *H-A Pantall* a91 110
3 ch c American Post—Panthesilea (FR) (Kendor (FR))
1145a[5] 1979a[5] 2951a[6]
Valid Point (IRE) *Sir Mark Prescott* a75 87
3 b g Val Royal(FR) —Ricadonna (Kris)
69[6] 230[6] 5121[4] (5331) (5470) (5617) (6139) ◆ (6236) 6360[5]
Valid Reason *Mrs A J Perrett* a78
2 b c Observatory(USA) —Real Trust (USA) (Danzig (USA))
7522[3] (7764)
Valkov *Tom Dascombe* a64 60
2 b f Val Royal(FR) —Petrikov (IRE) (In The Wings)
3925[10] 4945[6] 5527[4] 5935[11] 7513[3]
Valkyrie (IRE) *N P Littmoden* a57 53
3 b f Danehill Dancer(IRE) —Ridotto (Salse (USA))
752[6] 1183[9] 1481[5] 2131[6] 2461[3] 3383[8] 4669[4] 5328[3] 6446[3] 7025[3] 7324[4]
Valletta *H-A Pantall* a54 101
3 b f Cape Cross(IRE) —Vituisa (Bering)
6504a[7] 7347a[12]
Vallodiadriano (IRE) *S Onofrio* 73
3 b c Elusive City(USA) —Pink Cashmere (IRE) (Polar Falcon (USA))
7206a[11]
Valmari (IRE) *C E Brittain* a80 91
6 b m Kalanisi(IRE) —Penza (Soviet Star (USA))
1017[7] 1383[7] 1944[4] (3343) 5235[12] 6036[4] 6113[5]
Valmina *Tom Dascombe* a74 42
2 b c Val Royal(FR) —Minnina (IRE) (In The Wings)
3344[10] 6737[11] 7190[2] (7372) 7625[2] 7707[2]
Valmont Du Pecos (FR) *S Morineau*
3 ch c Execute(FR) —Valana (FR) (Valanour (IRE))
7820a[8]
Valse De La Tour (FR) *Mme A-C Trouve* 68
4 b m Anabaa Blue—Boukala (FR) (Sadler's Wells (USA))
5013a[6]
Val's Princess *J R Jenkins*
2 b f Trade Fair—Eleonora D'Arborea (Prince Sabo)
1653[11] 2414[9]
Valvignenres (IRE) *E A L Dunlop* a76 71
4 gr g Dalakhani(IRE) —Albacora (IRE) (Fairy King (USA))
1287[3] 1966[3] 4670[3]
Vamos (IRE) *J R Gask* a65 61
3 b g Royal Applause—Feather Boa (IRE) (Sri Pekan (USA))
947[3] 1120[2] 1583[3] 1969[9] 3299[5] ◆ 3580[4] 4061[2] 4749[3] 5581[5] 6442[5] (6862) 7211[4] 7417[2]
Vanadium *A J Lidderdale* a66 71
7 b g Dansili—Musianica (Music Boy)
2686[2] 3104[5] 3283[4] 3722[6] 4082[6] 4305[2] 4536[8] 5019[8] 5842[5] 6256[3] 6587[2] 6933[7] 7051[4] 7292[11] 7438[5] 7592[8]
Vanatina (IRE) *W M Brisbourne* a53 46
5 b m Tagula(IRE) —Final Trick (Primo Dominie)
62[5] 104[5] (175) 327[11] 473[8] 1480[7] 1781[8]
Van Bossed (CAN) *D Nicholls* a88 101
4 ch g Van Nistelrooy(USA) —Embossed (CAN) (Silver Deputy (CAN))
1457[10] 2570[8] 2707[15] 3141[11] 3389[11] 4341[14] 4485[12] 4891[10] 5697[17]
Vanilla Bally (ISR) *George Baker* a3 40
4 ch m Supreme Commander(FR) —Rozalyn Bally (ISR) (Verardi)
256[12] 4158[8] 4938[16]
Vanilla Loan (IRE) *M Botti* a62
2 b f Invincible Spirit(IRE) —Alexander Anapolis (IRE) (Spectrum (IRE))
5639[7] 6436[8] 6947[3]
Vanilla Rum *H Candy* 74
2 b g Reset(AUS) —Snoozy (Cadeaux Genereux)
6797[6] 7058[4]
Vanishing Grey (IRE) *B J Meehan* 85
2 gr f Verglas(IRE) —Native Force (IRE) (Indian Ridge)
2354[4] ◆ 3396[6] 4933[3] (5380) 6049[7] 6486[10] 6660[15]
Vanquisher (IRE) *Ian Williams* a56 71
5 br g Xaar—Naziriya (FR) (Darshaan)
116[2] 249[2] 346[2] 449[8]

Vantage Point (FR) *Mlle C Cardenne* 82
6 ch h Zafonic(USA) —Victory Cry (IRE) (Caerleon (USA))
3045a[0]
Vaporetto (IRE) *P J Rothwell* a55 51
7 gr m Soviet Star(USA) —Tarikhana (Mouktar)
6998[5]
Varachi *E A L Dunlop* 66
2 b g Kyllachy—Miss Rimex (IRE) (Ezzoud (IRE))
6066[9] 6592[6] 6962[5]
Varah *R A Harris*
3 b g Tobougg(IRE) —Relativity (IRE) (Distant Relative)
6673[13]
Varenar (FR) *A De Royer-Dupre* 120
3 ch c Rock Of Gibraltar(IRE) —Visor (USA) (Mr Prospector (USA))
3231a[2] 4837a[4] 5709a[2] (6503a)
Varsity *C F Swan* a102 101
6 b m Lomitas—Renowned (IRE) (Darshaan)
185a[7] 263a[14] 415a[14] 643a[6] 773a[16]
Vattene (IRE) *M Gasparini* 103
4 br m Kendor(FR) —Voglia Matta (IRE) (Second Set (IRE))
6717a[7] 7312a[4]
Vaultage (USA) *E A L Dunlop* a68 57
2 ch f El Corredor(USA) —Ten Carats (USA) (Capote (USA))
7182[10] 7430[2]
Vegano (FR) *C Von Der Recke*
8 br g Waky Nao—Vega Sicilia (Environment Friend)
466a[7] 653a[11]
Vegas Baby (IRE) *J A Osborne* a81 81
3 ch f Kheleyf(USA) —Gift Of Spring (USA) (Gilded Time (USA))
396[3] 709[5] 1584[5] 1982[4] (2137) 2355[10] 2759[6]
Vegas Palace (IRE) *Tom Dascombe* a83 73
2 ch f Captain Rio—Verify (IRE) (Polish Precedent (USA))
6730[3] ◆ 6947[2] (7351)
Veiled *Sir Mark Prescott* a85 89
3 b f Sadler's Wells(USA) —Evasive Quality (FR) (Highest Honor (FR))
4175[3] ◆ (5113) ◆ 5376[3] (5952) (6037) ◆ 6258[4]
Veiled Applause *J J Quinn* a75 92
6 b g Royal Applause—Scarlet Veil (Tyrnavos)
490[9] 787[6] 999[4] 1170[6] 1660[3] 1850[6] 2103[5] 4663[6] 5441[13] 6014[5] (6648) 6761[3] 7014[4]
Vella *H J L Dunlop* a43 50
2 b f Mtoto—Villella (Sadler's Wells (USA))
1579[6] 2006[11] 2350[13] 3303[12]
Velle Est Valere *C J Teague*
2 b f Reset(AUS) —Bond Solitaire (Atraf)
7289[13]
Velvet Band *P F I Cole* a72 75
2 gr f Verglas(IRE) —Applaud (USA) (Rahy (USA))
2175[3] ◆ 2604[2] 2972[6] (3658) 4539[17] 5526[9] 6481[9] 6774[4]
Velvet Flicker (IRE) *Kevin Prendergast* a87 92
3 b f Fasliyev(USA) —Velvet Appeal (IRE) (Petorius)
4028a[4] 4357a[3] 6317a[8]
Velvet Nayef *J Pearce* 28
3 b f Nayef(USA) —Laughing Girl (USA) (Woodman (USA))
4270[9]
Venetian Lady *Mrs A Duffield* a58 41
3 b f Tobougg(IRE) —Perfect Partner (Be My Chief (USA))
1725[11] 2141[5] 2365[11] 4105[11] 4281[11] 6255[8]
Venir Rouge *Matthew Salaman* a72 76
5 ch g Dancing Spree(USA) —Al Awaalah (Mukaddamah (USA))
2493[5] ◆ (3247) 3814[6] 7440[5] 7677[4] ◆ 7847[6]
Veni Vedi Veci (IRE) *A M Balding* a26 57
2 b f Antonius Pius(USA) —Consultant Stylist (IRE) (Desert Style (IRE))
5312[9] 6620[7]
Ventura (USA) *Robert Frankel* a123 122
5 bb m Chester House(USA) —Estala (Be My Guest (USA))
7285a[2]
Ventura Cove (IRE) *R A Fahey* 77
2 ch g Bahamian Bounty—Baby Bunting (Wolfhound (USA))
1645[2] ◆ 1991[2] 2260[5]
Venture Capitalist *B Ellison* a63 69
3 b c Diktat—Ventura Highway (Machiavellian (USA))
1595[9] 2357[2] 2865[10] 3675[2] 4178[8] 5123[3] 7790[7] 7863[11]
Venture Girl (IRE) *T D Easterby* a54 52
2 ch f Footstepsinthesand—Bold Assumption (Observatory (USA))
2099[6] 2503[6] 4515[5] 5372[4] 6169[9]
Venutius *E S McMahon* a78 74
2 b g Doyen(IRE) —Boadicea's Chariot (Commanche Run)
4385[3] 5627[3] 5839[2] (6461) 7003[4]
Veracity *Saeed Bin Suroor* a73 116
5 ch h Lomitas—Vituisa (Bering)
437a[2] ◆ (699a) ◆ 2056[3] 3048[P] (Dead)
Vera's Moscou (IRE) *N Clement* a69 79
3 b g Kheleyf(USA) —Inching (Inchinor)
4581a[4]
Verba (FR) *R Gibson* 105
4 gr m Anabaa(USA) —Tambura (FR) (Kaldoun (FR))
1029a[4]
Verdant *Sir Michael Stoute* a80 70
2 b c Singspiel(IRE) —Orford Ness (Selkirk (USA))
6065[2] (6627)
Verenitsa (FR) *E Lellouche* 91
3 b f Peintre Celebre(USA) —Veleni (IRE) (Doyoun)
6238a[4] 7302a[5]
Verglacial (IRE) *C Lerner* 76
2 gr c Verglas(IRE) —Apostrophe (IRE) (Barathea (IRE))
6501a[4]

Verinco *B Smart* a67 78
3 b g Bahamian Bounty—Dark Eyed Lady (IRE) (Exhibitioner)
4199[3] 5338[4] 6221[3] 6764[4] 6988[8] 7270[3] 7762[13]
Verity Lane (USA) *R M H Cowell* a79
2 b f Yes It's True(USA) —Easy Pass (USA) (Easy Goer (USA))
5681[3] 6628[7] 7277[4]
Vermentino (FR) *M Roussel* 79
2 ch c Anabaa Blue—Moon Gorge (Pursuit Of Love)
7264a[4]
Verona Lad *Jennie Candlish* 55
2 gr c Needwood Blade—Silver Spell (Aragon)
4041[6] 4424[8] 4847[12] 5938[12]
Veronicas Boy *G M Moore* 70
3 br c Diktat—Thamud (IRE) (Lahib (USA))
1629[4] 1953[4] 3689[4] 4070[4] 4348[4] 4600[4] 5011[12]
Veronicas Way *G J Smith* a38 40
4 b m High Estate—Mimining (Tower Walk)
1318[8] 4051[0] 536[5]
Veroon (IRE) *J G Given* a82 78
3 b g Noverre(USA) —Waroonga (IRE) (Brief Truce (USA))
1882[2] (2572) 3156[4] 3636[6] 3976[6] 4562[2] (4892) 5255[4] 5616[2] (5858) 6209[2] 6680[9] 7233[5]
Versaki (IRE) *Ian Williams* a61 93
3 gr g Verglas(IRE) —Mythie (FR) (Octagonal (NZ))
258a[14] 524a[8] 1002[12] 1744[10] 5349[10] 5677[8] 5972[3] 6170[3] 6358[6] 7105[6]
Vertana (IRE) *H-A Pantall*
2 b f Sinndar(IRE) —Verzasca (IRE) (Sadler's Wells (USA))
5956a[0]
Vert Chapeau *E F Vaughan* a60
2 ch c Sakhee(USA) —Green Bonnet (IRE) (Green Desert (USA))
6163[7] 6722[9]
Vertigineux (FR) *Mme C Dufreche* a111 116
5 bb h Nombre Premier—Very Gold (FR) (Goldneyev (USA))
439a[3] 702a[2] 774a[10] (1658a)
Vertigo On Course (IRE) *R A Fahey* a56 68
4 b m Anabaa(USA) —Due South (Darshaan)
(6005) ◆ 6349[3] 7113[3]
Vertueux (FR) *A W Carroll* a36 60
4 gr g Verglas(IRE) —Shahrazad (FR) (Bering)
3593[7] 4862[10] 7124[11]
Very Distinguished *S Kirk* a62 67
3 b f Diktat—Dignify (IRE) (Rainbow Quest (USA))
1193[12] 1428[9] 2635[7] 3099[9] 4178[10] 6223[6] 7004[7] 7228[3] 7324[2] 7740[7] 7856[10]
Very Good Day (FR) *M R Channon* 73
2 b c Sinndar(IRE) —Picture Princess (Sadler's Wells (USA))
4953[2] ◆
Very Well Red *P W Hiatt* a63 75
6 b m First Trump—Little Scarlett (Mazilier (USA))
7[7] 130[3] 211[5] 565[2] 608[7] (791) (867) 979[4] 1612[9] 2261[11] (2910) 3408[4] 3996[6] 4816[2] 5063[3] 5449[9] 5673[9] 6174[6] 6545[7] 7693[U] 7784[10]
Vested Interest *George Baker* a19 76
2 ch g Footstepsinthesand—Ingozi (Warning)
2128[9] (3547)
Vestris (IRE) *J-M Beguigne*
4 ch g Vettori(IRE) —Parting Gift (Cadeaux Genereux)
7822a[4]
Vesuve (IRE) *E Lellouche* 110
3 b c Green Tune(USA) —Verveine (USA) (Lear Fan (USA))
1858a[3] 2756a[7] 4367a[7] 5084a[5] 6132a[6]
Vhujon (IRE) *P D Evans* a90 94
4 b g Mujadil(USA) —Livius Lady (IRE) (Titus Livius (FR))
212[4] 1197[4] ◆ 1309[4] 1510[10] (2203) 2267[5] 2570[2] 2814[2] 3122[7] 4461[15] 4485[4] 4853[4] 5257[11] 5424[14] 5799[7] 6050[22] 6187[5] 6396[7] 6723[9] 7832[2] 7875[2]
Via Aurelia (IRE) *J R Fanshawe* 60
2 b f Antonius Pius(USA) —Goldthroat (IRE) (Zafonic (USA))
5109[4] 5958[4] 7061[9]
Viable *Mrs P Sly* a63 49
7 b g Vettori(IRE) —Danseuse Davis (FR) (Glow (USA))
2420[9]
Via Galilei (IRE) *J S Bolger* a87 103
4 b h Galileo(IRE) —Manger Square (IRE) (Danehill (USA))
263a[9] 415a[8] 644a[7] 3700a[3] 5076a[5] 6467a[8] 6867a[9]
Via Mia *George Baker* a73 62
3 b f Namid—Coming Home (Vettori (IRE))
1232[7] 1414[6] 1584[3] 7153[2] 7428[3] 7615[6]
Viceroy Of India (USA) *A P O'Brien* a81 80
3 ch c Galileo(IRE) —Hishi Lover (USA) (Pleasant Colony (USA))
2288a[9]
Vicious Warrior *R M Whitaker* a72 80
10 b g Elmaamul(USA) —Ling Lane (Slip Anchor)
2200[10] 2499[10] 3034[3]
Victoire De Lyphar (IRE) *P C Haslam* 82
2 b g Bertolini(USA) —Victory Peak (Shirley Heights)
2444[6] (2663) ◆ 3340[2] 5433[11] 5692[2] 6035[6]
Victoria Montoya *A M Balding* a78 101
4 br m High Chaparral(IRE) —Spurned (USA) (Robellino (USA))
(2085) 2931[2] ◆ 3642[2] 4458[3] 5425[2] 5796[7]
Victorian Art (IRE) *M A Magnusson* a59 72
2 b f Chineur(FR) —Alexander Nitelady (IRE) (Night Shift (USA))
1031[3] 1933[5] 2360[10] 2906[2] 3006[5]
Victorian Bounty *Stef Liddiard* a71 97
4 b g Bahamian Bounty—Baby Bunting (Wolfhound (USA))
1321[9] 1663[9] 2637[6] 2946[7]

Victorian Tycoon (IRE) *E J O'Neill* a66 68
3 b c Choisir(AUS) —New Tycoon (IRE) (Last Tycoon)
1361[2] ◆ 1470[4] 2091[12] 2685[4] 5118a[7] 5278a[2] 5784a[6] 6149a[2] 6682a[3] 7037a[9]
Victoria Sponge (IRE) *R Hannon* a86 94
3 b f Marju(IRE) —Trill (Highest Honor (FR))
1466[3] 1744[7] 2001[2] (3102) (3523) 3787[4] 4317[6] 6167[3] 6396[5] (6731)
Victory Ide Say (IRE) *P W Chapple-Hyam* a67
2 ch g Fath(USA) —Ide Say (IRE) (Grand Lodge (USA))
7736[3]
Victory Kid (FR) *J-V Toux* 36
2 b c Victory Note(USA) —Sherala (USA) (Shahrastani (USA))
5378a[6]
Victory Quest (IRE) *Mrs S Lamyman* a79 70
9 b g Victory Note(USA) —Marade (USA) (Dahar (USA))
3[3] 325[7] (604) 809[3] 860[5] 1399[5] 7675[5] 7760[5] 7867[11]
Victory Spirit *D A Nolan* a55 45
5 b g Invincible Spirit(IRE) —Tanouma (USA) (Miswaki (USA))
81[10] 221[11] 277[12] 1558[4] 2155[10] 3105[7] 3657[7]
Vien (IRE) *R Hannon* a49 50
3 br c Captain Rio—Fairy Free (Rousillon (USA))
77[9] 134[6] 296[11]
Viewed (AUS) *Bart Cummings* 124
6 b h Scenic—Lovers Knot (NZ) (Khozaam (USA))
(6871a) ◆ 7196a[3] 7215a[7]
Viewforth *S T Mason* a41 35
11 b g Emarati(USA) —Miriam (Forzando)
308[5] 1259[13]
View From The Top *Patrick Allen* a60 50
5 b g Mujahid(USA) —Aethra (USA) (Trempolino (USA))
5617[9] 5683[12]
Vigor (NZ) *Danny O'Brien* 117
5 br g O'Reilly(NZ) —Rationable (NZ) (Housebuster (USA))
6871a[3]
Vigorosa (IRE) *P Howling* a46 28
3 b f Red Ransom(USA) —Hejraan Two (IRE) (Green Desert (USA))
849[9] 1838[8] 2664[12] 3303[11] 6831[11] 7195[5] 7439[6] 7666[11]
Viking Awake (IRE) *J W Unett* a46 68
3 b g Almutawakel—Norwegian Queen (IRE) (Affirmed (USA))
1744[11] 2338[6] 2970[6] 4707[4] 5502[11] 6175[9]
Viking Dancer *A M Balding* 80
2 b c Danehill Dancer(IRE) —Blue Siren (Bluebird (USA))
4410[7] ◆ 5220[5] 5786[2] 6364[4]
Viking Spirit *W R Swinburn* a107 105
7 b g Mind Games—Dane Dancing (IRE) (Danehill (USA))
3405[6] 3802[3] 4330[18] 4598[2] ◆ 4853[11] 5646[4] 6694[6] 7227[9]
Villa Molitor (FR) *F Rohaut* a99 105
3 b f Muhtathir—Sizal (FR) (Sicyos (USA))
1267a[3] 2119a[7] 3442a[5] 4969a[10]
Villaruz (IRE) *J W Unett* a65 54
3 b g Fayruz—Villaminta (IRE) (Grand Lodge (USA))
75[3] 655[7] 831[2] 900[2] 1075[8] 1247[4] (1529) 3464[12] 7815[9]
Vilnius *M R Channon* a59 61
2 b f Imperial Dancer—Aces Dancing (GER) (Big Shuffle (USA))
1090[4] (1450) 3540[2] 3682[2] 3871[3] 4076[5] 4165[6] 4639[2] 5194[4] 5218[4] 5467[7] 5776[5] 5976[10] 6554[3] 7156[2] (7242) (7559) 7570[7] 7884[8]
Vimiero (USA) *W R Swinburn* 85
2 bb c Dynaformer(USA) —Merrymaker (ARG) (Rainbow Corner)
6109[4] ◆ 6663[3] ◆
Vinces *T D McCarthy* a71 71
5 gr g Lomitas—Vadinaxa (FR) (Linamix (FR))
319[6] 534[7] (733) 873[6] (1122) 2678[5] 3349[3] 3811[4] 4300[5] 4745[7] 5365[5] 6566[2] 7250[2] 7512[8] 7777[7]
Vin De Rose *John A Harris* a37 35
3 b g Tipsy Creek(USA) —Rosewings (In The Wings)
2416[14] 3228[8] 4157[7] 4722[8] 5482[8] 5840[9] 6170[14]
Vineyard Haven (USA) *Saeed Bin Suroor* a123
3 gr c Lido Palace(CHI) —Princess Aloha (USA) (Aloha Prospector (USA))
526a[4]
Vinorine (FR) *R P Burns* a49 34
5 b m Majorien—Vin Sur Vin (FR) (Saint Estephe (FR))
1949
Vin Royal (FR) *E Lellouche* a67 72
4 b h Sadler's Wells(USA) —Verveine (USA) (Lear Fan (USA))
5089a[9]
Vintage (IRE) *J Akehurst* a87 66
5 b g Danetime(IRE) —Katherine Gorge (USA) (Hansel (USA))
2396[4] 7832[8]
Viola Rosa (IRE) *J G Given* a42 32
4 b m Fraam—Bleu Cerise (Sadler's Wells (USA))
2723[10] 3379[7] 4550[10]
Violent Velocity (IRE) *J J Quinn* a71 85
6 b g Namid—Lear's Crown (USA) (Lear Fan (USA))
1060[13] 1332[11] 1887[11] (3401) 3488[5] 3851[3] 4140[3] 4504[2] (4657) (5188) 5409[8] 5697[2] 6309[7] 7220[10]
Violon Sacre (USA) *J-C Rouget* 106
4 b h Stravinsky(USA) —Histoire Sainte (FR) (Kendor (FR))
7621a[8]
Viper *R Hollinshead* a89 95
7 b g Polar Prince(IRE) —Maradata (IRE) (Shardari)
2409[7] 6851[32] 7515[2] 7701[5]

Virginia Hall *Sir Mark Prescott* a75 104
2 b f Medicean—Odette (Pursuit Of Love)
2972^{9} 3210^{2} (3458) 3799^{2} (4173) 4584a^{2} 5279a^{2} 5825^{6}

Virtual *J H M Gosden* 119
4 b h Pivotal—Virtuous (Exit To Nowhere (USA))
1525^{3} (2076) 3013^{6} 5086a^{3} 5710a^{3} 6850^{8}

Virtuality (USA) *B Smart* a16 60
4 bb m Elusive Quality(USA) —Hold To Ransom (USA) (Red Ransom (USA))
1400^{5} 1694^{8} 2579^{11} 4432^{7}

Viscaya (IRE) *N J Vaughan* a26 57
4 b m Xaar—Fearfully Grand (Grand Lodge (USA))
215^{9}

Viscount Nelson (USA) *A P O'Brien* 112
2 b c Giant's Causeway(USA) —Imagine (IRE) (Sadler's Wells (USA))
5859^{2} 7304a^{8}

Viscount Rossini *S Gollings* a50 50
7 bb g Rossini(USA) —Spain (Polar Falcon (USA))
169^{5}

Vision And Power (NZ) *Joseph Pride* 115
7 b g Carnegie(IRE) —Escada (NZ) (Centaine (AUS))
7040a^{11}

Vision D'Etat (FR) *E Libaud* 124
4 b h Chichicastenango(FR) —Uberaba (FR) (Garde Royale)
1144a^{3} (1551a) (3013) 5931a^{2} 6526a^{10} (7747a)

Visions Of Johanna (USA) *R A Fahey* a88 87
4 b g Johannesburg(USA) —Belle Turquoise (FR) (Tel Quel (FR))
2197^{5} 2437^{2} 4042^{2} 4526^{9} 5040^{8} 5409^{14}

Visit *Robert Frankel* a88 114
4 b m Oasis Dream—Arrive (Kahyasi)
7284a^{4}

Visite Royale (USA) *Sir Michael Stoute* a66 79
3 b f Danehill Dancer(IRE) —Fantasy Royale (USA) (Pleasant Colony (USA))
2179^{2} ◆ 2679^{4} 3627^{2} ◆ (4347)

Visterre (IRE) *B Smart* 83
3 ch f Noverre(USA) —Twiggy's Sister (IRE) (Flying Spur (AUS))
2443^{8} 3096^{7}

Vita Mia *P D Evans* a52 68
3 b f Central Park(IRE) —Ma Vie (Salse (USA))
1198^{11} 1245^{4} 1441^{8} 1746^{9} 2370^{4} 2461^{5} (2540) 2866^{6} 3474^{2} (3776) (4562) 4855^{6} 5382^{4} 5858^{7} 6280^{3} 6338^{3} 6784^{5}

Vitoria (IRE) *B Smart* a79 102
3 b f Exceed And Excel(AUS) —Karayb (IRE) (Last Tycoon)
1291^{11} 1599^{8} 4317^{2} 5175^{6} 5766^{2} (6155) ◆ 6428^{3} 6814^{2}

Vito Volterra (IRE) *A B Haynes* a69 73
2 b c Antonius Pius(USA) —River Abouali (Bluebird (USA))
4825^{11} 6627^{6} (6819) (7098) 7319^{3} (7661)

Vitruvian Man *John M Oxx* 104
3 b c Montjeu(IRE) —Portrait Of A Lady (IRE) (Peintre Celebre (USA))
1388a^{7}

Vittachi *J D Bethell* a50 46
2 b g Bertolini(USA) —Miss Lorilaw (FR) (Homme De Loi (IRE))
4847^{13} 5512^{5} 5981^{6} 6901^{5} 7722^{8} 7788^{4}

Vitznau (IRE) *R Hannon* a109 105
5 b h Val Royal(FR) —Neat Dish (CAN) (Stalwart (USA))
781^{2} 996^{4} 1865^{7} 2668^{5} 3398^{8} 3536^{6} 4486^{18} 5313^{5} 5874^{4} 6270^{19} 6732^{5} ◆

Viva Agrippina (USA) *J Bertran De Balanda* 53
3 ch f Swain(IRE) —Nasaayem (USA) (Gulch (USA))
7037a^{0}

Viva Averti *R M Beckett* 35
4 b g Averti(IRE) —Julia Domna (Dominion)
1704^{8} 3460^{P} (Dead)

Vivachi (IRE) *R M Beckett* a70 78
3 b f Red Ransom(USA) —Charita (IRE) (Lycius (USA))
2488^{8} 3425^{4} 4145^{2} (4813) 5168^{6} 6740^{6}

Viva La Vida *J Ryan* a36 66
3 ch f Medicean—Moonlight (IRE) (Night Shift (USA))
503^{7} 1302^{6} 1825^{5} 2432^{10} 4720^{9} 5295^{10} 5806^{10}

Viva Macau (FR) *J Moore* 113
6 bb h Sendawar(IRE) —Diyawara (IRE) (Doyoun)
1554a^{7}

Viva Pataca *J Moore* a84 126
7 b g Marju(IRE) —Comic (IRE) (Be My Chief (USA))
1554a^{2} 7744a^{6}

Viva Ronaldo (IRE) *R A Fahey* a92 99
3 b g Xaar—Papaha (FR) (Green Desert (USA))
1211^{5} 1801^{4} 2273^{13} 3049^{23} 4814^{6} 5432^{11}

Viva Vettori *D R C Elsworth* a95 93
5 ch h Vettori(IRE) —Cruinn A Bhord (Inchinor)
879^{2} 1216^{5} 1673^{2} 2083^{7} 3282^{3}

Viva Volta *A C Whillans* a83 79
6 b g Superior Premium—La Volta (Komaite (USA))
3105^{2} 5601^{2} (6765)

Viviani (IRE) *Mrs A J Perrett* 67
2 ch g Galileo(IRE) —Bintalreef (USA) (Diesis)
6109^{11} 6393^{6} 6697^{12} 6965^{5}

Vivre Libre *E Lellouche* 76
2 b c Sadler's Wells(USA) —Vallee Enchantee (IRE) (Peintre Celebre (USA))
6131a^{8}

Vlavianus (CZE) *M Weiss* 61
8 b g Rainbows For Life(CAN) —Vlnka (CZE) (Amyndas)
(466a) 653a^{3}

Vocabulary *B W Hills* a31
2 br f Observatory(USA) —Zathonia (Zafonic (USA))
7326^{8}

Vocalised (USA) *J S Bolger* 109
3 b c Vindication(USA) —Serena's Tune (USA) (Mr Prospector (USA))
(1354) (1755a) 1917a^{10} 5079a^{5} 5921a^{5}

Vodka (JPN) *Katsuhiko Sumii* 122
5 b m Tanino Gimlet(JPN) —Tanino Sister (JPN) (Rousillon (USA))
774a^{5} ◆ 1011a^{7} (7593a)

Vodka Shot (USA) *M L W Bell* a50
3 bb f Holy Bull(USA) —Absoluta (IRE) (Royal Academy (USA))
77^{11} 296^{9}

Vogarth *M C Chapman* a69 57
5 ch g Arkadian Hero(USA) —Skara Brae (Inchinor)
(37) 129^{4} 224^{2} 6925^{6} 7813^{10}

Voila Ici (IRE) *V Caruso* 119
4 gr h Daylami(IRE) —Far Hope (Barathea (IRE))
(1903a) 2955a^{3} (3969a) (6153a) 6893a^{3} (7313a)

Volatilis (IRE) *J W Hills* a56 63
2 b c Antonius Pius(USA) —Fire Flower (Sri Pekan (USA))
2037^{7} 2430^{6} 2793^{5} 3944^{3} 5166^{5} 5589^{11}

Vol De Nuit *G Pucciatti* 109
8 gr h Linamix(FR) —Bedside Story (Mtoto)
1903a^{3} 2955a^{4}

Volito *Jonjo O'Neill* a67 70
3 ch c Bertolini(USA) —Vax Rapide (Sharpo)
663^{3} 842^{4} 982^{5} 1583^{7} 1969^{4} (2602) 2852^{7} 3342^{7} 4783^{9}

Volo Cat (FR) *B Olsen* a70 101
5 ch h Volochine(IRE) —The Cat Eater (FR) (Tagel (USA))
2587a^{8} 4585a^{10} 5302a^{8} 5933a^{4}

Volochkova (USA) *J R Fanshawe* a79 80
3 b f War Chant(USA) —Ballerina Princess (USA) (Mr Prospector (USA))
1269^{6} (1588) 2079^{9} 2949^{5} (3924) 4317^{4} 4799^{8}

Volomist (FR) *Mlle I Desagnat*
4 b m Volochine(IRE) —Preaux Mist (FR) (River Mist (USA))
3045a^{0}

Volver (IRE) *J-C Rouget* 96
3 ch f Danehill Dancer(IRE) —Chanteleau (USA) (A.P. Indy (USA))
(5012a) 5929a^{10} 7697a^{8}

Von Jawlensky (IRE) *A P O'Brien* 106
3 b c Montjeu(IRE) —Zivania (IRE) (Shernazar)
3700a^{2} 4033a^{6} 5861^{8}

Voodoo's Son (FR) *Dominique Sepulchre* a84 98
3 b g Homme De Loi(IRE) —Black Voodoo (FR) (Tel Quel (FR))
(6150a)

Voortrekker *D J Coakley* a71 73
3 b g Imperial Dancer—Sweet Wilhelmina (Indian Ridge)
1752^{3} ◆ 2652^{2} (3228) 4481^{9} 5915^{9} 6908^{11}

Voxna (FR) *Robert Collet* 92
5 br m Take Risks(FR) —Vouivre (FR) (Matahawk)
7821a^{3}

Vumbura (IRE) *W J Knight* 47
2 b g Alhaarth(IRE) —Mathaayl (USA) (Shadeed (USA))
6990^{13} 7146^{16}

Waabel *M A Jarvis* 58
2 bb c Green Desert(USA) —Najah (IRE) (Nashwan (USA))
4093^{6}

Waahej *P W Hiatt* a67 66
3 b g Haafhd—Madam Ninette (Mark Of Esteem (IRE))
3115^{12} 3357^{5} 4642^{10} 5126^{3} 5806^{6} (6257) ◆ 6439^{2} 6951^{3} 7423^{7} 7667^{3} 7752^{6}

Waajida *D K Weld* 67
2 b f Dubawi(IRE) —Ruby Affair (IRE) (Night Shift (USA))
2643a^{3}

Waarid *G L Moore* a50 66
4 b g Alhaarth(IRE) —Nibbs Point (IRE) (Sure Blade (USA))
300^{6}

Wabbraan (USA) *M Hill* a78 59
4 b g Aldebaran(USA) —Madame Modjeska (USA) (Danzig (USA))
(603) 723^{6} (923) 1215^{3} 1356^{9} 2040^{13} 2854^{8} 7272^{5} 7402^{4} 7785^{6}

Wabi Sabi (IRE) *N Tinkler* a63 60
3 b f Xaar—Taroudannt (IRE) (Danehill (USA))
1015^{7} 1270^{5} 2091^{10} 2361^{5} 3054^{5}

Wacato King (IRE) *R A Farrant* a48
3 br g King Charlemagne(USA) —Daralaka (IRE) (The Minstrel (CAN))
7067^{13} 7459^{7} 7755^{13}

Wadaat *C E Brittain* a73 107
3 b f Diktat—Shining Vale (USA) (Twilight Agenda (USA))
849^{3} ◆ 1034^{2} (1269) 1871^{8} 2310a^{2} 2672^{9} 3641^{3} 4094^{7}

Wadjeka (USA) *Y De Nicolay* a95 96
3 b f Oasis Dream—Woman Secret (IRE) (Sadler's Wells (USA))
2777a^{11}

Wadnaan *M Johnston* a73
2 ch c Shamardal(USA) —Australian Dreams (Magic Ring (IRE))
5371^{3} ◆

Wadowice (FR) *Mme Pia Brandt* 82
2 b f High Yield(USA) —Zita Blues (IRE) (Zieten (USA))
5956a^{3}

Waffle (IRE) *J Noseda* 107
3 ch g Kheleyf(USA) —Saphire (College Chapel)
2016^{5} 2373^{2} 6661^{18} 7015^{3} ◆

Wahan (USA) *C E Brittain* a58 44
3 b g Theatrical(IRE) —Abrade (USA) (Mr Prospector (USA))
425^{8} 620^{9} 953^{6} 1070^{2} 2131^{14} 2461^{9} 2709^{4} 3005^{11} 3985^{5}

Wahoo Sam (USA) *P D Evans* a68 73
9 ch g Sandpit(BRZ) —Good Reputation (USA) (Gran Zar (MEX))
244^{2} 452^{7} 577^{7} 1883^{9}

Waikato (NZ) *L Laxon* 111
6 b g Pins(AUS) —Skywalker Wilkes (USA) (Skywalker (USA))
2116a^{4}

Wait For The Light *Mrs S Leech* a76 32
5 b g Fantastic Light(USA) —Lady In Waiting (Kylian (USA))
848^{2} 952^{6} 1732^{5} 4988^{12}

Wajaha (IRE) *J H M Gosden* a99 71
3 ch f Haafhd—Amanah (USA) (Mr Prospector (USA))
(1082) ◆ 1293^{7} 3016^{18} 6229^{7}

Wajanaat *M P Tregoning* a70
2 b f Sakhee(USA) —Tadris (USA) (Red Ransom (USA))
5643^{4}

Wajir (FR) *E Lellouche* 115
3 b c Danehill Dancer(IRE) —War Game (FR) (Caerleon (USA))
1145a^{3} (1761a) 2756a^{12} 3970a^{5} (5711a)

Wake Me Now (IRE) *R M Beckett* a69 77
3 b f Almutawakel—Shiyra (Darshaan)
2126^{5} (2858)

Wake Up Call *C F Wall* a78 73
3 b f Noverre(USA) —Up And About (Barathea (IRE))
3168^{2} 5747^{2} (7107) 7519^{3} ◆

Wakita (IRE) *Aidan Anthony Howard* a62 49
6 b m Bold Fact(USA) —Pleasant Outlook (USA) (El Gran Senor (USA))
6862^{6}

Waky Love (GER) *P Schiergen* 100
5 b m Royal Dragon(USA) —Waky Su (IRE) (Konigsstuhl (GER))
(1268a) 3520a^{4} 4129a^{5}

Walcot Square (IRE) *R Charlton* 71
2 b g Marju(IRE) —Lyrical Dance (USA) (Lear Fan (USA))
4048^{6} 4985^{6} 5564^{2}

Waldorf (IRE) *W R Muir* a66 60
4 b h Sadler's Wells(USA) —Durrah Green (Green Desert (USA))
80^{4} 476^{6} (682) 898^{2} 1318^{14} 2684^{8} 3077^{5} 3224^{10} 3768^{4}

Waldvogel (IRE) *L M Cumani* a102 106
5 ch g Polish Precedent(USA) —Wurftaube (GER) (Acatenango (GER))
616a^{6} 4408^{14} 5173^{10} 5823^{9} 6302^{6} ◆ 7226^{2} 7789^{3}

Walero (GER) *Uwe Ostmann* 109
3 br c Big Shuffle(USA) —Waterbor (GER) (Lagunas)
(7044a)

Walistol (FR) *S Jesus* 74
2 b c Maille Pistol(FR) —Waldouma (FR) (Ajdayt (USA))
2694a^{6}

Walkingonthemoon *Tom Dascombe* 95
2 ch c Footstepsinthesand—Bendis (GER) (Danehill (USA))
(1323) ◆ 1598^{5} 2247^{2} 2702^{2} 4049^{4} 5085a^{3} 6486^{19} 7016^{9}

Walking Talking *H R A Cecil* a99 101
5 b g Rainbow Quest(USA) —Wooden Doll (USA) (Woodman (USA))
1351^{5} 2055^{7}

Walk On Bye (IRE) *T Stack* 106
2 b f Danehill Dancer(IRE) —Pipalong (IRE) (Pips Pride)
(3895a) 4359a^{3} 6317a^{6}

Walk On Water *H R A Cecil* 94
2 ch f Exceed And Excel(AUS) —The Cat's Whiskers (NZ) (Tale Of The Cat (USA))
(4257) (5208) 5606^{6}

Wallgate *Miss J A Camacho* 28
2 b f Namid—Lay A Whisper (Night Shift (USA))
1735^{6} 2360^{12} 4800^{9}

Wall Street Runner *Mrs J L Le Brocq* 47
8 ch m Kirkwall—Running Tycoon (IRE) (Last Tycoon)
5540a^{7}

Walls Way *A W Carroll* a33 31
5 ch g Karinga Bay—Wilming (Komaite (USA))
5322^{7} 6225^{7}

Walnut Rise *M H Tompkins* 34
2 b f Mujahid(USA) —Seasonal Blossom (IRE) (Fairy King (USA))
3187^{11} 4152^{10} 4757^{8} 4915^{12} 7098^{8}

Walragnek *J G M O'Shea* a59 54
5 gr g Mind Games—Eastern Lyric (Petong)
2349^{11} 2758^{9} 2879^{11} 3947^{10} 5345^{12}

Waltzalong (IRE) *T D Easterby* 54
3 b f Carnival Dancer—Flawless (Warning)
2105^{9} 2403^{8} 2659^{4} 3545^{7} 4142^{11} 4819^{12}

Waltz Around (IRE) *C E Brittain* 73
2 b f Bertolini(USA) —Mellow Jazz (Lycius (USA))
(4427) 4883^{3} 5433^{10} 5992^{5}

Waltzing Buddy *P T Midgley* a21 46
3 ch f Reel Buddy(USA) —Waltzing Star (IRE) (Danehill (USA))
1015^{8} 1174^{7} 1437^{10} 1949^{7} 2624^{5}

Walvis Bay (IRE) *T P Tate* 82
2 gr g Footstepsinthesand—Limpopo (Green Desert (USA))
5693^{2} ◆ 6009^{5} (6646) 7290^{6}

Walzertraum (USA) *J Hirschberger* 102
4 b h Rahy(USA) —Walzerkoenigin (USA) (Kingmambo (USA))
3416a^{7} 5461a^{2} 6152a^{4} 6500a^{8}

Wanchai Whisper *P D Evans* a70 57
2 b f Bahamian Bounty—Tiger Waltz (Pivotal)
4176^{5} 4666^{6} (5226) 5899^{8} 6068^{9} 6494^{9} (6970) 7156^{7} 7175^{3} 7372^{7} 7570^{2} (7698) (7871)

Wandering Minstral *H J L Dunlop* 45
6 br g Accordion—Vagrancy (Dancing Brave (USA))
2843^{6} 3531^{7}

Wanna (IRE) *T Stack* 84
3 b f Danehill Dancer(IRE) —Wannabe (Shirley Heights)
2306a^{6} 3700a^{6} 4923a^{8}

Wanna Be (GER) *W Hickst* 85
3 ch f Nayef(USA) —Wakytara (GER) (Danehill (USA))
2874a^{4}

Wannabee (IRE) *J J Bridger* a41 15
2 ch f Bahamian Bounty—Lyric Dances (FR) (Sendawar (IRE))
5808^{11} 6696^{10} 7585^{11}

Wannabe King *D R Lanigan* 108
3 b c King's Best(USA) —Wannabe Grand (IRE) (Danehill (USA))
1324^{2} 1751^{6} 2270^{4} 4056^{4} ◆ 4433^{2} (4852) (5189) ◆ (5522) 6480^{12}

Wannarock (IRE) *M C Chapman* a17 65
4 bb g Rock Of Gibraltar(IRE) —Propensity (Habitat)
1088^{6} 1407^{9} 1724^{6} 2018^{6} 2419^{5} 3068^{4} 3609^{3} 4402^{13} 4848^{5} 5554^{7} 6037^{3}

War And Peace (IRE) *Jane Chapple-Hyam* a79 77
5 b g Danehill(USA) —Pipalong (IRE) (Pips Pride)
76^{2} 208^{2} 982^{2} 1248^{3} 2088^{5} 2980^{8} 7321^{9} 7645^{5} 7679^{6}

War Artist (AUS) *J M P Eustace* a116 120
6 b g Orpen(USA) —Royal Solitaire (AUS) (Brocco (USA))
4087^{4} 4516^{4} (5493a) (5928a) 6522a^{3} 7745a^{12}

Waringham (GER) *F-X De Chevigny* 71
3 b g Royal Dragon(USA) —Wild Melody (GER) (Big Shuffle (USA))
7385a^{10}

Warling (IRE) *J Noseda* 56
2 gr f Montjeu(IRE) —Walkamia (FR) (Linamix (FR))
7183^{8}

War Native (IRE) *J Noseda* a96 94
3 b c Cape Cross(IRE) —Walkamia (FR) (Linamix (FR))
1354^{8} 1664^{3}

Warners Bay (IRE) *R Bastiman* a38 49
4 b g Iron Mask(USA) —Romangoddess (IRE) (Rhoman Rule (USA))
2366^{12} 2812^{7} 3683^{7} 4552^{16} 5254^{8} 6005^{14}

Warne's Way (IRE) *B G Powell* 71
6 ch g Spinning World(USA) —Kafayef (USA) (Secreto (USA))
(7036)

Warning Song (USA) *Mrs A J Perrett* a77 77
2 bb c Successful Appeal(USA) —Tia Lea (USA) (Songandaprayer (USA))
2007^{4} 2533^{3} 2636^{3} 6696^{5} 6943^{2} 7325^{3}

War Of The Roses (IRE) *R Brotherton* a91 54
6 b g Singspiel(IRE) —Calvia Rose (Sharpo)
360^{8} (549) 915^{6} 1215^{8}

War Party *Dr R D P Newland* 87
5 b g Fantastic Light(USA) —War Game (FR) (Caerleon (USA))
2242^{6} ◆ 2706^{5} 2932^{12} 3587^{8}

Warpedsenseofhumor (FR) *H R A Cecil* 79
3 ch c Distorted Humor(USA) —Eden (USA) (Holy Bull (USA))
(1245) 4827^{5}

War Power (USA) *J-C Rouget* a95 99
3 b c Pulpit(USA) —Tempo West (USA) (Rahy (USA))
1239a^{6}

Warrants Attention (IRE) *A M Balding* a27 58
3 b g Fruits Of Love(USA) —Irish Lover (USA) (Irish River (FR))
2930^{13} 3205^{5} 3791^{6} 4442^{7} 4934^{6} 5775^{13}

Warren Bank *Mrs Mary Hambro* a57
4 b g Nayef(USA) —Neptunalia (Slip Anchor)
7278^{2} 7504^{9} 7766^{7}

Warringah *Chris Waller* a62 114
4 b g Galileo(IRE) —Threefold (USA) (Gulch (USA))
2055^{11} (3406) 3874^{2} 4484^{2} 5173^{5} 5446^{2} 7215a^{23}

Warrior Conquest *W J Knight* a73 65
4 b g Alhaarth(IRE) —Eilean Shona (Suave Dancer (USA))
1809^{7} 2181^{3} 2798^{6} 3737^{2} 4301^{8} 5094^{3} 5642^{7} 6400^{4}

Warrior Nation (FR) *A J Chamberlain* a73 73
3 br g Statue Of Liberty(USA) —Tadawul (USA) (Diesis)
5964^{8} 6977^{12} 7065^{12} 7732^{10}

Warrior One *J Howard Johnson* 83
3 gr g Act One—River Cara (USA) (Irish River (FR))
1992^{14} 2767^{5}

Warsaw (IRE) *M F De Kock* a109 101
4 ch h Danehill Dancer(IRE) —For Evva Silca (Piccolo)
434a^{4} (521a) 641a^{6}

Warsaw Pact (IRE) *P J Hobbs* a93 47
6 b g Polish Precedent(USA) —Always Friendly (High Line)
1790^{16}

War Wolf *T D Easterby* 36
2 br g Lucky Story(USA) —Bollin Janet (Sheikh Albadou)
2041^{7} 2784^{4} 3032^{12} 5036^{10} 6821^{14}

Wasan *E A L Dunlop* a111 104
4 ch h Pivotal—Solaia (USA) (Miswaki (USA))
2015^{13} (2398) 3397^{2} 6290^{2} 6644^{2}

Waseet *J L Dunlop* 109
2 ch c Selkirk(USA) —Najayeb (USA) (Silver Hawk (USA))
4314^{3} ◆ (4953) ◆ 6268^{2}

Washington Irving (IRE) *J Howard Johnson* 114
4 b g Montjeu(IRE) —Shouk (Shirley Heights)
2056^{4} 3048^{P}

Wasmi (IRE) *C E Brittain* a79 48
2 b f Exceed And Excel(AUS) —Trim (IRE) (Ela-Mana-Mou)
2494^{11} 3006^{4} (3716) 4081^{4} 5166^{4} (5635) (6227) ◆ 6643^{10}

Wasp (AUS) *W Jarvis* a94 86
7 bb g Octagonal(NZ) —Establishment (AUS) (Star Watch (AUS))
(331) 636^{5} 724^{4} 1684^{10} 2239^{5} 2927^{5} 3525^{8}

Wassiljew (IRE) *K Schafflutzel* 101
5 b h Zinaad—Wassiliki (IRE) (Night Shift (USA))
1555a^{4}

Watch Amigo (IRE) *W R Swinburn* a74
3 b g Royal Applause—Miss Red Ink (USA) (Red Ransom (USA))
7464^2 ◆ (7730)

Watch Chain (IRE) *M H Tompkins* a54 70
2 b c Traditionally(USA) —Dangle (IRE) (Desert Style (IRE))
2568^5 3064^6 4318^6 4639^4 (5372) 5721^3 5950^6 6418^8 7268^6

Watchmaker *Miss Tor Sturgis* a73 62
6 b g Bering—Watchkeeper (IRE) (Rudimentary (USA))
253^2 (1409) 1604^4 2039^13

Watch Out *D Burchell* a46 45
5 b g Observatory(USA) —Ballet Fame (USA) (Quest For Fame)
7154^6

Watchoverme *J R Fanshawe* a30 58
3 ch f Haafhd—Bryony Brind (IRE) (Kris)
2981^8 3707^5 4205^8 5108^6 5483^6

Watch The Master *B I Case* a60 4
3 b g Passing Glance—Fine Arts (Cadeaux Genereux)
4270^11 5015^12 5328^10

Water Biscuit *B J Meehan* 83
2 b f Bertolini(USA) —Waterfall One (Nashwan (USA))
3356^2 3820^2 (4460) 5427^6 5797^9 6844^7

Watergate (IRE) *Sir Mark Prescott* a79 89
3 gr g Verglas(IRE) —Moy Water (IRE) (Tirol)
4316^4 5209^8 5419^7 5725^3 5986^13 6594^2

Water Gipsy *G L Moore* 55
2 bb f Piccolo—Creek Dancer (Josr Algarhoud (IRE))
6061^9

Water Hen (IRE) *R Charlton* a60 65
3 b f Diktat—Waterfall One (Nashwan (USA))
2540^5 3279^8

Waterloo Corner *R Craggs* a65 58
7 b g Cayman Kai(IRE) —Rasin Luck (Primitive Rising (USA))
2859^5 3171^4 3486^3 4431^7 4944^15

Waterloo Dock *M Quinn* a68 50
4 b g Hunting Lion(IRE) —Scenic Air (Hadeer)
61^4 (592) 1076^2 7602^8 7691^9

Waterside (IRE) *S Curran* a91 69
10 ch g Lake Coniston(IRE) —Classic Ring (IRE) (Auction Ring (USA))
357^11 588^8 805^5 (1131) 1314^7 1530^5 2493^11 3223^5 3740^2 4861^5 5179^2

Watson's Bay *P Howling* a73 74
4 b h Royal Applause—Multaka (USA) (Gone West (USA))
(80) 238^5 737^4 1042^3 1318^11 1728^3 2333^4 2552^3 2684^3 2983^3 3169^4 3521^2 3768^3 4007^3 4235^3 4449^4 4696^6 5035^8 5227^2 5975^3 6244^7

Waveband *M Johnston* a73 86
2 ch f Exceed And Excel(AUS) —Licence To Thrill (Wolfhound (USA))
3478^4 ◆ 3799^3 4233^2 4711^3 5253^3 (5611) 6064^8 6477^3

Wavertree Bounty *C F Wall* 53
2 b f Pastoral Pursuits—Grecian Halo (USA) (Southern Halo (USA))
5785^10 6728^6 7095^8

Wavertree Princess (IRE) *C F Wall* a72 67
4 gr m Invincible Spirit(IRE) —Blushing Queen (IRE) (Desert King (IRE))
4886^11 ◆ 5792^12 7100^12 7241^15

Wavertree Warrior (IRE) *N P Littmoden* a79 60
7 br g Indian Lodge(IRE) —Karamana (Habitat)
28^4 143^2 398^3 544^4 873^7 1035^7 1741^4 2125^9 3076^6 4533^7 5791^7

Waziri (IRE) *M Hill* 35
8 b g Mtoto—Euphorie (GER) (Feenpark (GER))
3798^5 4992^8

Weald *Doug Watson* a98 98
4 b g Bering—New Abbey (Sadler's Wells (USA))
613a^9 699a^6

Weald Park (USA) *R Hannon* a97 101
3 ch g Cozzene(USA) —Promptly (IRE) (Lead On Time (USA))
863^5 1291^7 2077^12 4296^11 4794^8 6695^12 7393^6

Wealthy (IRE) *A Fabre* 82
2 b c Refuse To Bend(IRE) —Enrich (USA) (Dynaformer (USA))
4807a^2

Webbow (IRE) *N Tinkler* a69 101
7 b g Dr Devious(IRE) —Ower (IRE) (Lomond (USA))
1684^2 2101^3 3091^7 3872^2 ◆ 4486^4 5200^4 5863^9 6675^3 7294^5

Wedding Dream *K A Ryan* a56
2 b f Oasis Dream—Gretna (Groom Dancer (USA))
3937^10 4370^10 5949^13 6874^5 7419^5 (7722)

Wedding List *W J Haggas* a83 58
3 ch f Pivotal—Confetti (Groom Dancer (USA))
2821^8

Wedding March (IRE) *A Fabre* 107
2 br f Dalakhani(IRE) —Elopa (GER) (Tiger Hill (IRE))
6523a^4

Wednesdays Boy (IRE) *P D Niven* a54 61
6 b g Alhaarth(IRE) —Sheen Falls (IRE) (Prince Rupert (FR))
2245^14 3070^13 4144^7 4588^10 5888^4 7174^5

Wee Bizzom *A Berry* a50 44
3 b f Makbul—Lone Pine (Sesaro (USA))
41^5 91^2 429^4 624^7 1064^6 1644^8 2154^6 2450^7 3651^9

Wee Bobbie *Mrs P N Dutfield* a33 36
2 b f Acclamation—Bobbie Dee (Blakeney)
5714^10 6911^11

Wee Buns *P Burgoyne* a69 59
4 b g Piccolo—Gigetta (IRE) (Brief Truce (USA))
799^11 961^11 1103^10 1152^15

Wee Charlie Castle (IRE) *I Semple* a71 82
6 b g Sinndar(IRE) —Seasonal Blossom (IRE) (Fairy King (USA))
2817^2 3150^3 (3679) 4078^4 (5469) 5912^7 6313^5 6986^3

Wee Giant (USA) *K A Ryan* a77 60
3 ch g Giant's Causeway(USA) —Christmas In Aiken (USA) (Affirmed (USA))
2341^7 6680^10 6996^15 7141^6

Weekend Away (IRE) *S Kirk* a63 55
3 b g Invincible Spirit(IRE) —March Star (IRE) (Mac's Imp (USA))
2317^9 3813^5 4648^7 5503^8 6825^9 7138^10 7275^9

Weekend Millionair (IRE) *P D Evans* 68
2 ch g Arakan(USA) —Almi Ad (USA) (Silver Hawk (USA))
4265^3 5330^3 6214^4

Weeping Willow (IRE) *J H M Gosden* 41
3 b f Kheleyf(USA) —Bezant (IRE) (Zamindar (USA))
4603^13

Wee Sonny (IRE) *Tom Dascombe* a78 75
3 b g Refuse To Bend(IRE) —Coup De Coeur (IRE) (Kahyasi)
1328^10 2535^3 3279^4 3697^4 4562^3

Weet A Surprise *J W Unett* a79 69
4 b m Bertolini(USA) —Ticcatoo (IRE) (Dolphin Street (FR))
818^6 882^5 2225^4 (2682) 2966^5 3591^3 4283^3 4469^3 5504^2 (5678) 5836^5 6572^4 6801^6 7158^3 (7273)

Weetentherty *J S Goldie* 51
2 b c Bertolini(USA) —Binaa (IRE) (Marju (IRE))
1645^7 2153^7 2388^8 4035^5

Weetfromthechaff *M A Barnes* a62 3
4 gr g Weet-A-Minute(IRE) —Weet Ees Girl (IRE) (Common Grounds)
108^12 242^5 353^8 535^4 655^4 1562^9

Weet In Nerja *J W Unett* a55 26
3 b g Captain Rio—Persian Fortune (Forzando)
75^2 293^5 624^5 736^3 831^10 900^5 1129^4 1492^8 4279^12 7609^12

Wee Ziggy *M Mullineaux* a31 45
6 b g Ziggy's Dancer(USA) —Midnight Arrow (Robellino (USA))
7608^6

We Have A Dream *W R Muir* a78 92
4 bb g Oasis Dream—Final Shot (Dalsaan)
1197^10 1403^8 1619^2 2549^5 3057^8 3771^3 (4134) 5167^2 5592^2 (6201) (6564) 6694^10 6994^2

Weimarland (IRE) *J A Osborne* a55
2 b c Elusive City(USA) —Night Spirit (IRE) (Night Shift (USA))
7087^6 7477^6 7582^5 7698^7

Welcome Applause (IRE) *M G Quinlan* a57 57
3 b f Acclamation—Waseyla (IRE) (Sri Pekan (USA))
2461^13 3054^4 3862^12

Welcome Approach *J R Weymes* a64 54
6 b g Most Welcome—Lucky Thing (Green Desert (USA))
352^5 540^9 2529^15 3562^10 3678^6 4750^3 5610^6 6433^2 7371^6 (7561) (7815)

Welcome Bounty *D R Lanigan*
2 ch c Bahamian Bounty—Welcome Home (Most Welcome)
7243^15

Welcome Cat (USA) *A D Brown* a67 73
5 b g Tale Of The Cat(USA) —Mangano (USA) (Quiet American (USA))
300^8 805^7

Welcome Releaf *P Leech* a63 64
6 ch g Most Welcome—Mint Leaf (IRE) (Sri Pekan (USA))
175^9 377^6 601^9

Weliketobouggie *J S Moore* a54 36
2 ch c Tobougg(IRE) —Country Spirit (Sayf El Arab (USA))
3865^8 4201^6 ◆

Well Armed (USA) *Eoin Harty* a128 97
6 b g Tiznow(USA) —Well Dressed (USA) (Notebook (USA))
(1013a)

We'll Come *M A Jarvis* 113
5 b g Elnadim(USA) —Off The Blocks (Salse (USA))
1861^8 (3282) 3639^15 (4768) 5863^7 6448^7

We'll Deal Again *M W Easterby* a64 68
2 b c Gentleman's Deal(IRE) —Emma Amour (Emarati (USA))
2099^2 ◆ 3823^7 4595^3 ◆ 5253^9 5692^3 6895^5 7088^2 7168^3

Wellesley *W R Swinburn* a63 58
3 b g Bertolini(USA) —Markova's Dance (Mark Of Esteem (IRE))
1252^9 1932^4 2863^4 3985^6 5103^9 6183^7

Wellington Fair *C G Cox* 80
2 br g Trade Fair—Milly's Lass (Mind Games)
3402^5 4906^U 5180^5 (5829) 6550^3

Wellington Square *H Morrison* a89 89
4 b g Millkom—Tempestosa (Northern Tempest (USA))
1990^13 (2883) 3523^3 4409^7 4954^11 6695^5 6830^3

Wellmarked (IRE) *John A Quinn* a87
3 b g Choisir(AUS) —Radiance (IRE) (Thatching)
4856^2 (7618) (7846)

Wellmond (GER) *H Blume* 90
2 ch c Hamond(GER) —Wellista (GER) (Sternkonig (GER))
7314a^6

Well Of Echoes *A J McCabe* a53 59
3 b f Diktat—Seeker (Rainbow Quest (USA))
2662^3 2942^8 5229^11 5647^DSQ 5982^7 6251^7 6755^4 6939^8 7353^5 7422^8 7787^3 7880^7

Wells Lyrical (IRE) *B Smart* 100
4 b h Sadler's Wells(USA) —Lyrical (Shirley Heights)
1519^2 ◆ 3390^2 3642^3 6412^6 6851^19

Welsh Anthem *W R Muir* a61 71
3 b f Singspiel(IRE) —Khubza (Green Desert (USA))
1406^3 2433^6 2845^9 3981^5 4224^2 ◆ 4498^7

Welsh Artist *Mrs A J Perrett* a67
2 b g Sakhee(USA) —Gwen John (USA) (Peintre Celebre (USA))
7234^7 7430^6 7538^3

Welsh Emperor (IRE) *T P Tate* a89 111
10 b g Emperor Jones(USA) —Simply Times (USA) (Dodge (USA))
1865^6 2483^8 (4077) 6503a^12 7019^P

Welsh Legacy (IRE) *B W Duke* a43 41
2 b c Saffron Walden(FR) —Silver Harbour (USA) (Silver Hawk (USA))
2033^8 2187^9 3218^11 4371^5 7055^12

Welsh Opera *S C Williams* a70 64
4 b m Noverre(USA) —Welsh Diva (Selkirk (USA))
22^3 108^6 454^2 (596) 710^7 832^4 (1041) 4051^11 4380^9 5008^5 (6039) 6186^3 6335^3 6801^3 6926^10

Welsh Passion *D Haydn Jones* 10
3 b f Marju(IRE) —Focosa (ITY) (In The Wings)
4854^10 5789^11

We'Re Delighted *T D Walford* a55 75
4 b g Tobougg(IRE) —Samadilla (IRE) (Mujadil (USA))
1123^3 1737^5 2269^7 2916^6 3235^4 4658^9 4941^5

Wessex (USA) *R Curtis* a93 88
9 ch g Gone West(USA) —Satin Velvet (USA) (El Gran Senor (USA))
331^7 491^6 2576^13

West End Lad *S R Bowring* a74 79
6 b g Tomba—Cliburnel News (IRE) (Horage)
(224) 362^7 617^4 807^8 1479^11 (2166) 3637^6 (3863) 4473^6 5126^6 5418^9 6178^6 6545^6 7062^9 7783^4 ◆

Wester Lodge (IRE) *J M P Eustace* a62 58
7 ch g Fraam—Reamzafonic (Grand Lodge (USA))
341^3 554^5 ◆ 734^2 1014^6 1153^6 1936^5 2244^8 2971^7 5740^6 6432^3 6859^3 7154^2

Western Art (USA) *Miss Gay Kelleway* a24 55
4 bb g Hennessy(USA) —Madam West (USA) (Gone West (USA))
933^9 1477^9 2133^14 2576^9 3066^10 5982^3 7220^11 7802^10

Western Isle (USA) *H-A Pantall* a95 85
3 b f Gone West(USA) —Miss Linda (ARG) (Southern Halo (USA))
6222a^7

Western Pearl *W J Knight* a64
2 b f High Chaparral(IRE) —Pulau Pinang (IRE) (Dolphin Street (FR))
7451^5 ◆

Western Roots *P Butler* a72 73
8 ch g Dr Fong(USA) —Chrysalis (Soviet Star (USA))
875^2 (1177) 1770^3 2493^10 2675^12 4698^9 5211^9 7667^8 7776^9

Wester Ross (IRE) *J M P Eustace* 71
5 b g Fruits Of Love(USA) —Diabaig (Precocious)
5122^4 6400^5 6622^4

West Kirk *W Jarvis* a62 70
3 b g Alhaarth(IRE) —Naughty Crown (USA) (Chief's Crown (USA))
356^5 ◆ 6924^5 7452^4 7803^7

West Leake (IRE) *B W Hills* a68 66
3 b g Acclamation—Kilshanny (Groom Dancer (USA))
1361^6 (1567) 2160^3 2852^15 3859^13 4061^8

West Leake Star (IRE) *B W Hills* a63 73
2 b c Antonius Pius(USA) —Red Beach (IRE) (Turtle Island (IRE))
2853^8 4219^9 4424^2 4856^4 5325^7 6737^5

Westlin' Winds (IRE) *C R Egerton* a71 69
3 b c Montjeu(IRE) —Uliana (USA) (Darshaan)
828^6 4145^5 5061^4 6027^4

Westphalia (IRE) *A P O'Brien* 115
3 b c Danehill Dancer(IRE) —Pharapache (USA) (Lyphard (USA))
1238a^2 1917a^3 2756a^3 3669a^5

Westport *R Bastiman* a81 81
6 b g Xaar—Connemara (IRE) (Mujadil (USA))
3304^11 3678^7 5150^4 5998^6 7113^12 7499^11

West Side Bernie (USA) *Kelly Breen* a111
3 bb c Bernstein(USA) —Time Honored (USA) (Gilded Time (USA))
1688a^9

Weststern (GER) *G L Moore* a75 66
6 b g Dashing Blade—Westafrika (GER) (Aspros (GER))
549^12 6204^9

West With The Wind *T P Tate* a81 88
4 b g Fasliyev(USA) —Midnight Angel (GER) (Acatenango (GER))
3266^11 3761^6 5438^12 6218^9

West With The Wind (USA) *P W Chapple-Hyam* a69 74
3 b f Gone West(USA) —Opera Aida (IRE) (Sadler's Wells (USA))
1588^5 2320^2 3630^4 (4655) 5449^2 6257^8

Westwood *D Haydn Jones* a77 77
4 ch g Captain Rio—Consignia (IRE) (Definite Article)
(1572) 2276^7 2929^12 4787^7 5612^13 7828^7

Westwood Dawn *D Shaw* a61
4 gr g Clodovil(IRE) —Ivory Dawn (Batshoof)
108^5 540^2 6856^2 7002^2 7179^4 7411^5 7510^2

Wet Feet *P R Chamings* 49
2 br g Footstepsinthesand—Swoon (Night Shift (USA))
4900^8

Weybridge Light *Eoin Griffin* a76 67
4 b g Fantastic Light(USA) —Nuryana (Nureyev (USA))
7255^6 7461^3 7701^8

Whaston (IRE) *J D Bethell* a58 58
4 b g Hawk Wing(USA) —Sharafanya (IRE) (Zafonic (USA))
898^9 1332^15 1520^2 1848^6 2314^5 3490^6 (3911) 4431^5 5513^7

What About Me (IRE) *Brian Nolan* 87
2 bb f Bertolini(USA) —Marefonic (Zafonic (USA))
2557a^4 2957a^6

What A Day *J J Quinn* 67
3 b g Daylami(IRE) —Sensation (Soviet Star (USA))
1331^5 1882^9 2370^12 3454^11 4004^11 4892^2 5470^13

What A Fella *Mrs A Duffield* 60
3 b g Lujain(USA) —Fred's Dream (Cadeaux Genereux)
1628^4 2154^5 2593^3 3125^3 3562^11 (3853) 4137^3 4596^9 4778^2 5105^10 5468^4 6161^7

Whatagoodcatch (IRE) *R Hannon* a47 72
3 b f Bachelor Duke(USA) —Truly Generous (IRE) (Generous (IRE))
4648^9

Whatami *E A L Dunlop* a68 56
3 bg f Daylami(IRE) —Wosaita (Generous (IRE))
2395^6 2922^3

What Do You Know *A M Hales* a76 87
6 b g Compton Place—How Do I Know (Petong)
1425^5 1833^10 2224^2

What Katie Did (IRE) *J M Bradley* a78 74
4 b g Invincible Spirit(IRE) —Chatterberry (Aragon)
(27) 243^3 460^7 (799) (861) (1152) 1425^4 1970^15 2911^10

Whatsthescript (IRE) *John W Sadler* a97 117
5 b h Royal Applause—Grizel (Lion Cavern (USA))
7308a^8

What's Up Doc (IRE) *Mrs Lawney Hill* a79 79
8 b g Dr Massini(IRE) —Surprise Treat (IRE) (Shalford (IRE))
172^8 307^3 650^4 (1314) (3245) (4450)

What's Up Pussycat (IRE) *David Wachman* 97
3 b f Danehill Dancer(IRE) —Sangita (Royal Academy (USA))
1024a^6 1755a^5

Whatyouwoodwishfor (USA) *R A Fahey* a76 76
3 ch g Forestry(USA) —Wishful Splendor (USA) (Smart Strike (CAN))
1345^4 2072^12 3455^5 4227^10 4664^9 7813^11

Whaxaar (IRE) *R Ingram* a63 68
5 b g Xaar—Sheriyna (FR) (Darshaan)
7255^2 7873^9

Whelkeen Rock (IRE) *K A Ryan* 18
2 b c Xaar—Mizillablack (IRE) (Eagle Eyed (USA))
2195^9 ◆ 2449^P (Dead)

When Doves Cry *B W Hills* a49 63
3 b f Grandera(IRE) —Deeply (IRE) (Darshaan)
1570^9 2548^3 3209^7 3693^6

Whenever *R T Phillips* 89
5 ch g Medicean—Alessandra (Generous (IRE))
2931^14 3793^6 5696^8 6400^3

Where's Charlie *P Leech* 47
3 br g Where Or When(IRE) —Kennedys Prima (Primo Dominie)
5435^6

Where's Dids *P D Evans* a22 42
4 b m Piccolo—Who Goes There (Wolfhound (USA))
56^12 104^11

Where's Killoran *E J Alston* a46 27
4 b m Iron Mask(USA) —Calypso Lady (IRE) (Priolo (USA))
748^4 1131^4 1243^12 1476^5

Wheresmeneckstrap (IRE) *T G McCourt* a3 37
4 b g Tel Quel(FR) —St Clair (Distant Relative)
7790^8

Where's Reiley (USA) *T D Barron* a66 68
3 bb g Doneraile Court(USA) —Plateau (USA) (Seeking The Gold (USA))
429^3 966^3 1232^5 (1736) 2028^5 2365^2 2719^4 3096^3 4061^4 4436^12 7815^7

Where's Susie *M Madgwick* a65 68
4 ch m Where Or When(IRE) —Linda's Schoolgirl (IRE) (Grand Lodge (USA))
(2123) 2574^7 3216^2 (3739) 4948^3 5642^3 7695^6

Where's The Soap (FR) *Tom Dascombe* a85 86
2 bb f Country Reel(USA) —Sister Celestine (Bishop Of Cashel)
3385^5 4233^4 (4970a) 5240a^4 5927a^5 6326a^7

Where To Now *Mrs C A Dunnett* a28 29
4 b m Where Or When(IRE) —Starminda (Zamindar (USA))
674^10 765^7

Where You Will *S W Hall* a42 55
3 ch f Where Or When(IRE) —Red Duchess (Halling (USA))
296^8 520^5

Whiepa Snappa (IRE) *P M Phelan* a61 65
2 b g Whipper(USA) —Boudica (IRE) (Alhaarth (IRE))
3160^5 4006^6 4451^5 5213^3 5573^3 6391^3 6735^3

Whinhill House *T T Clement* a49 72
9 ch g Paris House—Darussalam (Tina's Pet)
1104^6 1360^14 1587^9 2130^8 2456^10 2736^6 3283^11

Whipitydooda (IRE) *Tracey Collins* 68
2 b f One Cool Cat(USA) —Little Glasgow (IRE) (King's Theatre (IRE))
1993a^5

Whipma Whopma Gate (IRE) *D Carroll* a59 57
4 b m Rossini(USA) —The Gibson Girl (IRE) (Norwich)
3092^7 3689^2 3911^8 4071^2 4402^8 4944^6 5294^4 5549^7 (5730) 5953^7 6999^3

Whipper's Delight (IRE) *D Donovan* a55 33
2 b f Whipper(USA) —Darling Smile (IRE) (Darshaan)
5478^10 6493^8 7130^8

Whippers Love (IRE) *M Johnston* a67 83
2 b c Whipper(USA) —Danadoo (FR) (Septieme Ciel (USA))
994^17 1304^7 1867^12 3147^4 3978^2 4190^3 (4931) (5399) ◆ 5864^4 6993^16

Whipperway (IRE) *M R Channon* a56 72
2 b f Whipper(USA) —Prince's Passion (Brief Truce (USA))
4147^7 4460^3 5722^12 6199^4 6735^10 7098^2 7210^5 7319^6 (7482)

Whip Up (IRE) *J G Portman*
2 b g Whipper(USA) —Fizz Up (Alzao (USA))
1577^15 1782^7 2319^9

Whirlijig (IRE) *G A Swinbank* 68
4 ch m Spinning World(USA) —Dariyba (IRE) (Kahyasi)
3022^3 3379^2 3703^3 4229^8 5549^3

Whirly Dancer *H R A Cecil* a72 75
2 b f Danehill Dancer(IRE) —Whirly Bird (Nashwan (USA))
3858[9] 5417[2] 5980[2] 6436[3] 6844[2]

Whiskey Creek *C A Dwyer* a89 83
4 ch g Tipsy Creek(USA) —Judiam (Primo Dominie)
27[5] (44) (173) (269) (400) 424[2] 539[2] 632[2] 1052[4] 1278[7] 1457[13] 1836[8] 2053[4] 2397[5] 2938[18]

Whiskey Junction *M Quinn* a94 88
5 b g Bold Edge—Victoria Mill (Free State)
1006[9] 1181[5] 1418[5] 2203[6] 2396[6] 3212[8] (3995) (4982) 5370[5] 5974[2] 6666[13]

Whisky Galore *C G Cox* 74
3 ch c Kyllachy—Owdbetts (IRE) (High Estate)
2048[14] 2356[5] 2892[9] 4744[2] 5430[7] 6742[5]

Whisky Jack *W R Muir* a70 70
3 b g Bahamian Bounty—Dress Design (IRE) (Brief Truce (USA))
1414[7] 3718[4] 4304[10] (5582) 6455[12] 7000[11]

Whispered Dreams (GER) *Mario Hofer* a75 99
4 ch m Platini(GER) —Waconda (GER) (Pursuit Of Love)
3520a[2] 5064[5]

Whispered Lands (IRE) *J R Boyle* a38 43
3 b f Elusive City(USA) —Happy Talk (IRE) (Hamas (IRE))
1638[11] 2981[10] 4145[10] 5779[10] 6289[P]

Whispered Times (USA) *P C Haslam* a41 75
2 bb g More Than Ready(USA) —Lightning Show (USA) (Storm Cat (USA))
2069[4] (2623) 3542[7] 4895[5] 5393[7] 7242[10] 7419[7]

Whispered Wish *W J Haggas* 41
3 b f Rainbow Quest(USA) —Cyclone Connie (Dr Devious (IRE))
1269[11]

Whispering Gallery *M Johnston* 114
3 b g Daylami(IRE) —Echoes In Eternity (IRE) (Spinning World (USA))
(3022) 3826[4] (4794) (5170) ◆

Whispering Spirit (IRE) *Mrs A Duffield* a58 64
3 b f Catcher In The Rye(IRE) —Celtic Guest (IRE) (Be My Guest (USA))
2236[4] (3975) 4375[10] 4845[11] (5621)

Whispering Wind (IRE) *Ms Joanna Morgan* a36 84
6 b m Sunshine Street(USA) —Soul Fire (IRE) (Exactly Sharp (USA))
5689a[11]

Whisper Softly (IRE) *T D Walford* 41
3 b f Tagula(IRE) —Whisper Dawn (IRE) (Fasliyev (USA))
2070[8] 2700[8] 3338[9] 3853[5] 3938[14]

Whistle Blower *J H M Gosden* a69 67
2 b c Exceed And Excel(AUS) —Song Of Hope (Chief Singer)
4756[12] 5590[4] 6066[7] (6963) 7363[3]

Whistledownwind *J Noseda* a106 106
4 b g Danehill Dancer(IRE) —Mountain Ash (Dominion)
30[4] 636[2] 997[16] 1352[8]

Whistleinthewind (IRE) *G L Moore* a81 75
2 b g Oratorio(IRE) —Lady Scarlett (Woodman (USA))
6931[2] 7390[3] (7522) ◆

Whistleupthewind *J M P Eustace* a53 60
6 b m Piccolo—The Frog Queen (Bin Ajwaad (IRE))
87[6]

Whistling Wind *Paul Green*
2 b g Needwood Blade—Empire Of The Sun (Second Empire (IRE))
1802[11] 3572[11]

Whiston Pat *S R Bowring* a45
4 ch g Lomitas—Fille De Bucheron (USA) (Woodman (USA))
11[6] 178[5]

Whitbarrow (IRE) *B R Millman* a78 90
10 b g Royal Abjar(USA) —Danccini (IRE) (Dancing Dissident (USA))
13[3] 94[3] 241[5] 561[2] 886[3] 980[5] 6782[2] 7192[9] 7412[4] 7645[3] (7762)

Whitby (IRE) *M W Easterby* a51
2 br f Dubawi(IRE) —Hymenee (USA) (Chief's Crown (USA))
7502[4] 7638[5] 7705[3]

Whitcombe Minister (USA) *M Botti* a98 98
4 b h Deputy Minister(CAN) —Pronghorn (USA) (Gulch (USA))
783[3] ◆ 1003[16] 1642[7]

Whitcombe Spirit *Jamie Poulton* a65 62
4 b g Diktat—L'Evangile (Danehill (USA))
1426[6] 2163[4] 2725[3] 3986[4] 5734[2] 6622[3] 6692[6]

Whiteball Wonder (IRE) *M Halford* a62 85
3 b g Tagula(IRE) —Notanother (Inchinor)
4360a[9]

Whitechapel *W R Muir* 34
2 b g Oasis Dream—Barathiki (Barathea (IRE))
4323[10]

White Daffodil (IRE) *R Hannon* 68
2 b f Footstepsinthesand—Sparky's Song (Electric)
1706[4] 2135[2] (2604) 3430[7] 5033[4] 5344[4] 6169[8]

White Dart *M R Channon* a79 73
2 b c Rakti—Feather Boa (IRE) (Sri Pekan (USA))
3867[7] 4258[10] 5400[6] 5938[2] 6211[2] ◆ (6373)

White Deer (USA) *G A Harker* a83 86
5 b g Stravinsky(USA) —Brookshield Baby (IRE) (Sadler's Wells (USA))
922[6] 1333[2] ◆ 1479[4] 1660[9] (2998) 3656[3] 3825[15] 4996[7] 5746[8] (6217) 6485[11] 6645[16] 7492[10]

White Devil *A M Balding* 75
2 ch g Zafeen(FR) —Costa Balena (CHI) (Great Regent (CAN))
3584[9] 4439[3] ◆ 4908[4] 5801[2]

White Ledger (IRE) *R E Peacock* a47 50
10 ch g Ali-Royal(IRE) —Boranwood (IRE) (Exhibitioner)
3331[8] 4824[10] 5629[2] 7424[10] 7815[8]

White Lightning (GER) *U Stech* 100
7 gr h Sternkoenig(IRE) —Whispering Grass (GER) (Konigsstuhl (GER))
6500a[7] 7039a[6] 7406a[9]

White Moss (IRE) *Jim Best* a50 67
5 b m Peintre Celebre(USA) —Saint Ann (USA) (Geiger Counter (USA))
311[12] 1178[5] 1318[12]

Whiteoak Lady (IRE) *J L Spearing* a50 76
4 ch m Medecis—French Toast (IRE) (Last Tycoon)
1152[11] 1403[9] 3713[8] 4428[9] (5406) ◆ 6596[15]

Whiterocks *M R Channon* a34 51
3 ch g Imperial Dancer—Thailand (Lycius (USA))
3660[5] 4145[11] 4480[8] 4934[5] 5430[11] 5775[12]

White Rose (ITY) *Luigi Rosa* a95 62
5 ch m Handsome Ridge—Pursuit Of Rose (FR) (Pursuit Of Love)
1394a[7] 7206a[10]

White Shift (IRE) *P Howling* a87 88
3 b f Night Shift(USA) —Ivy Queen (IRE) (Green Desert (USA))
690[4] 784[4] 1196[7] 1368[5] 1505[5] (1982) (2299) 2611[2] 2821[2] (3033) 3166[8] 3360[6] 3688[8] 4338[4] 5245[2] 5902[5] 6564[6] 7253[10] 7478[12] 7673[9] 7738[9]

White Spire (FR) *F Rohaut* a90 90
4 b m Septieme Ciel(USA) —White Love (FR) (Northern Crystal)
7265a[3]

Whitley Bay (USA) *J R Best*
2 b c Lion Heart(USA) —Sea Witch (USA) (Sea Hero (USA))
7376[12]

Who Art Thou (USA) *D R Gandolfo* 51
3 bb g More Than Ready(USA) —Silk Sails (USA) (Ocean Crest (USA))
5872[11]

Whobegotyou (AUS) *Mark Kavanagh* 120
4 ch g Street Cry(IRE) —Temple Of Peace (JPN) (Carnegie (IRE))
7040a[6]

Whodunit (UAE) *P W Hiatt* a63 47
5 b g Mark Of Esteem(IRE) —Mystery Play (IRE) (Sadler's Wells (USA))
81[9] (674) 760[9] 7876[12]

Whooshka (USA) *P W Chapple-Hyam* 80
3 b f Smart Strike(CAN) —Bushra (USA) (Danzig (USA))
(2848) 3627[4] 4709[9] 6996[13]

Who's Shirl *C W Fairhurst* 74
3 b f Shinko Forest(IRE) —Shirl (Shirley Heights)
1922[2] 2343[2] 2970[3] 3381[8] 4436[2] 4997[2] (5391) 5955[6] 6309[9]

Who's Winning (IRE) *B G Powell* a63 64
8 ch g Docksider(USA) —Quintellina (Robellino (USA))
1421[6] 1787[5] ◆ 2124[6] 2564[3] 3208[4] 3471[6] 3671[5] 5120[4] 5566[3] (5788) 6293[2] 6335[2] 6587[3]

Whotsit (IRE) *Miss Amy Weaver* a57 66
3 ch g Choisir(AUS) —Charming Victoria (IRE) (Mujadil (USA))
159[7] 296[12] (441) 547[2] 776[5] 839[5] 1746[11] 2169[6] 2950[6] ◆ 3426[2] 4389[2] (4533) 5019[2] 5473[9] 6052[6]

Whozart (IRE) *A Dickman* a62 62
6 b g Mozart(IRE) —Hertford Castle (Reference Point)
367[2] 487[6] 794[6] 921[5] 976[5] 1695[4] 2316[9] 2812[5] 3002[8]

Whozthecat (IRE) *D Carroll* 80
2 b c One Cool Cat(USA) —Intaglia (GER) (Lomitas)
1661[5] (1920) 5038[6]

Why Nee Amy *T Keddy* a65 59
3 ch f Tipsy Creek(USA) —Ashleen (Chilibang)
160[4] 312[3] 492[5] 649[2] 943[3] 1270[2] (2169) 2461[11] 2863[8] 3005[9] 4279[9] (5982) 6804[5] 6924[3] 7211[2] (7426)

Wibbadune (IRE) *D Shaw* a82 80
5 ch m Daggers Drawn(USA) —Becada (GER) (Cadeaux Genereux)
754[5] 870[8] 1041[6] 1627[7] 2492[5] 3145[9] 3565[7] 3860[7] 4530[8] 4692[2] 4886[13]

Wicked Daze (IRE) *K A Ryan* a92 96
6 ch g Generous(IRE) —Thrilling Day (Groom Dancer (USA))
1007[6] 1863[9] 3380[4] 5252[5] 5917[2] 6100[2] 7151[13] 7402[2] 7573[4] 7701[3]

Wickedly Fast (USA) *George Baker* a49
3 b f Gulch(USA) —Need More Business (IRE) (Alzao (USA))
345[7] 594[10]

Wicked Wilma (IRE) *A Berry* a44 67
5 b m Tagula(IRE) —Wicked (Common Grounds)
2966[2] 3445[2] ◆ 3828[3] 3909[5] 4283[5] 4464[6] 4929[5] 5149[6] 5411[3] (5946) 6010[21] 6314[2] 7119[9]

Wicklewood *Mrs C A Dunnett* a49 45
3 b g Mujahid(USA) —Pinini (Pivotal)
722[5] 842[8] 1452[7] 1940[6] 2918[11] 3711[4] 3953[5] 4155[8] 4718[7] 5112[4] 5326[7] 5972[6] 6919[12] 7452[7] 7610[4] 7787[7]

Wicksy Creek *G C Bravery* a55 41
4 b g Tipsy Creek(USA) —Bridal White (Robellino (USA))
447[2] 602[9] 1617[11] 1935[7] 2180[13] 3283[9] 3743[5] 3999[15] 4269[5] 4602[7] 5018[7] 5509[9]

Wide Ranging *R Charlton* a57
2 gr c With Approval(CAN) —Widescreen (USA) (Distant View (USA))
6607[11]

Widezain (IRE) *M R Channon* 64
2 b c Chineur(FR) —Silk Fan (IRE) (Unfuwain (USA))
6066[6]

Wi Dud *K A Ryan* 109
5 b g Elnadim(USA) —Hopesay (Warning)
1367[3] 1543a[4] 2094[3] 2272[3] 2704[7] 2991[9] 4885[2] 5132[8] 6091[21] 6678[5] 7015[11]

Wiener Walzer (GER) *J Hirschberger* 122
3 b c Dynaformer(USA) —Walzerkoenigin (USA) (Kingmambo (USA))
(2954a) (3670a) (5082a) 5707a[4]

Wiesenpfad (FR) *W Hickst* 116
6 ch h Waky Nao—Waldbeere (Mark Of Esteem (IRE))
2113a[5] (5461a)

Wigan Lane *P Howling* a63 68
2 b f Kheleyf(USA) —Nesting (Thatching)
2360[6] 2778[3] (3337) 3842[7] 4739[7] 5226[4] 5636[3] 6343[7] 6610[5] 7389[9]

Wiggy Smith *H Candy* a84 86
10 ch g Master Willie—Monsoon (Royal Palace)
1593[3] 2407[7] 3361[3] 4247[4] 5028[3]

Wightgold *H J L Dunlop* a47 52
3 ch f Golden Snake(USA) —Main Brand (Main Reef)
1045[6] 1420[10] 1967[4] 2489[8] 5726[3] 6188[4] 6935[2]

Wigmore Hall (IRE) *M L W Bell* 90
2 b g High Chaparral(IRE) —Love And Laughter (IRE) (Theatrical (IRE))
5000[8] (6066) 6663[5]

Wigram's Turn (USA) *A M Balding* a96 87
4 ch g Hussonet(USA) —Stacey's Relic (USA) (Houston (USA))
1467[2] 1607[5] 3091[13] 5665[3] (6374) 7431[8]

Wigwam Willie (IRE) *K A Ryan* 96
7 b g Indian Rocket—Sweet Nature (IRE) (Classic Secret (USA))
1507[10] 1722[6] 2103[2] (3034) 4412a[4] 5490a[23] 6094[9]

Wijikura (IRE) *J J Quinn* 62
2 ch c Zafeen(FR) —Azolia (IRE) (Alzao (USA))
3937[5] ◆ 4349[5] 4800[6] 4889[4] 5519[6] 6215[8]

Wikaala (USA) *Gordon Elliott* a79 80
4 ch g Diesis—Roseate Tern (Blakeney)
7360[6] 7373[3]

Wilbury Star (IRE) *R Hannon* a78 80
3 br g Trans Island—Gold Blended (IRE) (Goldmark (USA))
840[7] 1086[6] 1462[2] 1774[5] 2600[3] 3349[2] 3736[6] 4149[9] (4904) 5366[3] 5858[2] 6421[3]

Wild Adventure (IRE) *John Joseph Murphy* a47
2 b f Oasis Dream—Knight's Place (IRE) (Hamas (IRE))
5486a[6]

Wild By Nature *P Leech* 40
4 b m Tipsy Creek(USA) —Kinraddie (Wuzo (USA))
670[9] 1941[7] 2416[13] 3241[10]

Wild Cat Card (USA) *D M Simcock* a56
3 bb f Mr Greeley(USA) —Wildcat Victory (USA) (Forest Wildcat (USA))
729[4]

Wildcat Wizard (USA) *P F I Cole* 99
3 b g Forest Wildcat(USA) —Tip the Scale (USA) (Valiant Nature (USA))
1292[9] 1677[3] 5766[6] 6482[14]

Wild Demon (FR) *C Boutin* 62
3 br f Della Francesca(USA) —Brave Tune (FR) (Green Tune (USA))
6149a[6]

Wild Desert (FR) *Ian Williams* a85 92
4 bb g Desert Prince(IRE) —Sallivera (IRE) (Sillery (USA))
330[5] 549[3]

Wildfahrte (GER) *T Mundry* 96
3 ch f Mark Of Esteem(IRE) —Wurfspiel (GER) (Lomitas)
2524a[7] 6886a[5]

Wild Fell Hall (IRE) *J Hetherton* a80 77
6 ch g Grand Lodge(USA) —Genoa (Zafonic (USA))
4229[10] 4600[8] 4972[10]

Wild Heather *J R Holt* a42
2 b f Bertolini(USA) —Heather Mix (Linamix (FR))
5638[9] 7485[5] 7698[8] 7749[6] 7843[8]

Wild Lyph *N P Mulholland* a17
3 b g Loup Sauvage(USA) —A Lyph (USA) (Lypheor)
824[9] 1176[7]

Wild Rhubarb *C G Cox* 86
4 ch m Hernando(FR) —Diamant Noir (Sir Harry Lewis (USA))
1427[2] (1892) 2486[6] 2931[3] 3380[3]

Wild Rockette *B J Meehan* a72 72
2 b f Rock Of Gibraltar(IRE) —Wild Floridian (IRE) (Indian Ridge)
5026[9] 5605[4] 6164[7] 6736[2] 7434[4]

Wild Rose *M L W Bell* a82 60
2 gr f Doyen(IRE) —Makhsusah (IRE) (Darshaan)
5498[5] (5984) (6491) 7187[11]

Wilfred Pickles (IRE) *Mrs A J Perrett* 79
3 ch g Cadeaux Genereux—Living Daylights (IRE) (Night Shift (USA))
1474[2] 2210[6] 4902[2] 5242[3] 5435[4] 6111[2] 6823[4]

Willent *Miss J A Camacho* 35
3 b g Lend A Hand—Lapu-Lapu (Prince Sabo)
2104[9] 2446[12] 3036[12] 5145[8]

Will Exell (IRE) *M J Scudamore* a10
6 b m Exit To Nowhere(USA) —Woodhouse Bay (IRE) (Zaffaran (USA))
678[9]

Will He Wish *S Gollings* a89 82
13 b g Winning Gallery—More To Life (Northern Tempest (USA))
21[2] 220[2] 1633[2] 2916[5] 3624[8] 4144[6] 4502[2] 5003[5]

William Arnold *C W Fairhurst* 63
2 ch g Rambling Bear—Dancing Shirl (Dancing Spree (USA))
2568[8] 3032[10] 3494[5] 4618[2] 4931[3] 5595[14] 6099[7] 6557[10]

William Blake *M Johnston* a93 93
4 b g Rainbow Quest(USA) —Land Of Dreams (Cadeaux Genereux)
2671[4] 3189[3] 3822[6] 4261[2] 4404[4] 4770[4] 5137[11] 5437[3] 5641[3] 6234[2] 6816[6] 7035[7]

William Hogarth *W K Goldsworthy* a75 85
4 b g High Chaparral(IRE) —Mountain Holly (Shirley Heights)
5909[8]

William Morgan (IRE) *R A Fahey* 76
2 ch g Arakan(USA) —Dry Lightning (Shareef Dancer (USA))
3262[4] 3613[3] 3875[6] ◆ 4651[2] (5595) (5692) 5795[16]

William's Kitten (USA) *Michael J Maker* a106 82
2 bb c Kitten's Joy(USA) —Blush (USA) (Menifee (USA))
7307a[8]

William's Way *I A Wood* a79 82
7 b g Fraam—Silk Daisy (Barathea (IRE))
103[9] 285[5] (342) 534[4] (734) 860[2] 1014[5] 1571[5] 1966[7]

Williamtown Lad (IRE) *J R Boyle*
8 b g Anshan—Hazy River (Over The River (FR))
4205[12]

William Van Gogh *J H M Gosden* 80
2 b c Dansili—Flower Girl (Pharly (FR))
6423[2] ◆ 6810[5]

Willie Ever *I W McInnes* a76 56
5 b g Agnes World(USA) —Miss Meltemi (IRE) (Miswaki Tern (USA))
218[7] 238[8] 569[10] 868[RR]

Willing Foe (USA) *Saeed Bin Suroor* a63
2 bb c Dynaformer(USA) —Thunder Kitten (USA) (Storm Cat (USA))
7400[6]

Willkandoo (USA) *D M Simcock* a86 78
4 bb g Unbridled's Song(USA) —Shannkara (IRE) (Akarad (FR))
106[6] 388[8] 650[2] 730[3]

Willow Dancer (IRE) *W R Swinburn* a88 95
5 ch g Danehill Dancer(IRE) —Willowbridge (IRE) (Entrepreneur)
2639[7] 3639[9] 4409[13] 6633[6]

Willow Mist *M W Easterby*
2 b f Gentleman's Deal(IRE) —Baymist (Mind Games)
2896[10]

Willridge *J M Bradley* a38 72
4 ch g Tumbleweed Ridge—Minnina (IRE) (In The Wings)
2326[11] 2880[15] 3722[12] 5019[16]

Willyn (IRE) *J S Goldie* a48 60
4 b m Lujain(USA) —Lamasat (USA) (Silver Hawk (USA))
2390[3] 2590[4] 3098[3] 3653[7] 3911[2] 4751[7] 5438[14] 5944[7]

Willywell (FR) *J-P Gauvin* a101 105
7 br h Jimble(FR) —Basilissa (FR) (Gay Minstrel (FR))
3085a[7] 7704a[5]

Wilmington *Mrs J C McGregor* a69 59
5 ch g Compton Place—Bahawir Pour (USA) (Green Dancer (USA))
823[13] 1101[6] 2390[10] 2968[7] 3092[3] 3448[10] 3653[9] 5947[12]

Wilside (IRE) *M Delzangles* 105
3 b f Verglas(IRE) —Sigonella (IRE) (Priolo (USA))
(3668a) 4971a[3] 5588a[3] 6718a[11]

Wiltshire (IRE) *P T Midgley* a65 62
7 br g Spectrum(IRE) —Mary Magdalene (Night Shift (USA))
22[7] 108[2] 245[3] 352[7] 540[7] 619[3] 811[4] 921[2] 1243[5] 1924[4] 2134[2] 2628[6] 2964[2] 4372[2]

Wind Flow *C A Dwyer* a81 58
5 b g Dr Fong(USA) —Spring (Sadler's Wells (USA))
(161) 319[2] 393[3] 631[9] (693) 787[4] 1073[5] 1432[2] 2146[2] 2743[4] 3273[10] 3977[7] 4644[9] 5227[7] 5679[3] 6498[2] 6634[2] 6832[9] 7066[7]

Windjammer *L A Mullaney* a63 73
5 b g Kyllachy—Absolve (USA) (Diesis)
2657[9] 3999[14] 5341[2] 6314[10] 7241[9]

Wind Of Victory (FR) *J E Hammond* a83 92
3 b c Marchand De Sable(USA) —Fifty Niner (FR) (Fijar Tango (FR))
1979a[7]

Windpfeil (IRE) *J H M Gosden* a57 64
3 bl g Indian Ridge—Flying Kiss (IRE) (Sadler's Wells (USA))
2865[3] 3511[9] 4178[5] 5011[8] 5990[14] (6742)

Wind Shuffle (GER) *J S Goldie* 85
6 b g Big Shuffle(USA) —Wiesensturmerin (GER) (Lagunas)
1100[3] 1646[3] 1830[2] 3265[12] 4102[7]

Windsor Palace (IRE) *A P O'Brien* a87 101
4 b h Danehill Dancer(IRE) —Simaat (USA) (Mr Prospector (USA))
1913a[5] 5141a[3] 5490a[8] 6527a[P] 6867a[7] 7300a[11]

Wind Star *G A Swinbank* 91
6 ch g Piccolo—Starfleet (Inchinor)
1646[4] ◆ (2043) (2374) 2468[6] 3374[4]

Wine 'n Dine *G L Moore* a96 76
4 b g Rainbow Quest(USA) —Seasonal Splendour (IRE) (Prince Rupert (FR))
(72) 360[3] 693[2] 1007[7] 1383[2] 2085[9] 2475[12]

Win For Sure (GER) *A Wohler* 104
4 b g Stravinsky(USA) —Win For Us (GER) (Surumu (GER))
6718a[2]

Wingbeat (USA) *I Mohammed* a52 100
4 b h Elusive Quality(USA) —Infinite Spirit (USA) (Maria's Mon (USA))
336a[13] 610a[9]

Wing Collar *T D Easterby* 101
8 b g In The Wings—Riyoom (USA) (Vaguely Noble)
1519[9]

Wing Diva (IRE) *B Smart* a61 55
4 b m Hawk Wing(USA) —Sasimoto (USA) (Saratoga Six (USA))
90[4] 4071[6] 7093[2] 7272[3] 7728[2]

Winged (IRE) *B W Hills* a61 48
2 b f Hawk Wing(USA) —Aurelia (Rainbow Quest (USA))
4055[13] 4646[4]

Winged Arrow (IRE) *Jonjo O'Neill* a68 78
7 b g In The Wings—Lightstorm (IRE) (Darshaan)
249[3] ◆ 459[8]

Winged D'Argent (IRE) *B J Llewellyn* 87
8 bb g In The Wings—Petite-D-Argent (Noalto)
1356[4] 2018[10] 4092[9]

Winged Farasi *Miss J E Foster* a58 37
5 b h Desert Style(IRE) —Clara Vale (IRE) (In The Wings)
221[4] 569[7] 791[8] 1276[10]

Winged Harriet (IRE) *W J Haggas* 80
3 bb f Hawk Wing(USA) —Hawala (IRE) (Warning)
1837[4] (2268)
Wing Express (IRE) *J E Hammond* 117
5 b h Montjeu(IRE) —Eurobird (Ela-Mana-Mou)
5497a[6]
Wing Forward (IRE) *A Berry* 26
2 b f Hawk Wing(USA) —Stroppy (IRE) (Xaar)
4546[6] 4774[6] 5512[9]
Wing N Prayer (IRE) *A Berry* 43
2 b f Xaar—Jazmeer (Sabrehill (USA))
3106[4] 5290[9] 6408[7]
Wing Of Faith *S Kirk* a58 60
2 ch c Kirkwall—Angel Wing (Barathea (IRE))
2477[7] 2979[6] 3785[6] 4195[4] 5213[10] 5636[2] 5967[8] 6610[4] 6970[5]
Wing Play (IRE) *H Morrison* a94 87
4 b g Hawk Wing(USA) —Toy Show (IRE) (Danehill (USA))
1493[6] 1876[7] 2518[7] (2923) 3847[2] 4378[2] (4716) 5551[8] 6059[3] 6594[5] (7194) 7574[3]
Wings Of Kintyre (IRE) *A Berry*
5 b m Mull Of Kintyre(USA) —Tiger Wings (IRE) (Thatching)
5731[11]
Wingstar (IRE) *Robert Collet* 98
5 b m In The Wings—Thirtysomething (USA) (Thirty Six Red (USA))
846a[5]
Wing Stealth (IRE) *M G Quinlan* a64 70
4 br m Hawk Wing(USA) —Starlight Smile (USA) (Green Dancer (USA))
11[7]
Winifred Jo *J R Gask* a46
2 ch f Bahamian Bounty—Coming Home (Vettori (IRE))
6207[6] 6722[10]
Winker Watson *P W Chapple-Hyam* 116
4 ch h Piccolo—Bonica (Rousillon (USA))
1251[4] 2076[11] 3398[7]
Winkle (IRE) *M Delzangles* 107
4 b m High Chaparral(IRE) —Bernique (USA) (Affirmed (USA))
1762a[3] 2955a[5] 3969a[2] 5058a[8] 5932a[4]
Winning Show *C Gordon* a62 70
5 b g Muhtarram(USA) —Rose Show (Belmez (USA))
546[3] 1463[12] (7767)
Winrob *Patrick Morris* a37 57
3 b g Exceed And Excel(AUS) —High Standard (Kris)
1015[11] 1228[6] 1490[9] 2779[9] 3474[4] 4013[2] (4279) 4588[7]
Winston's Lad *P Howling* a43 31
2 gr g Act One—Hernani (FR) (Ezzoud (IRE))
2860[9] 3218[13] 5839[8]
Winterbourne *M Blanshard* a44 44
3 rg f Cadeaux Genereux—Snowing (Tate Gallery (USA))
1529[4] 3071[8] 6641[7] 7651[8]
Winterbrook King *J R Best* a59 64
3 br g Gleaming(IRE) —Alice Holt (Free State)
2206[12] 2709[7] 2909[7] 3383[6] 4397[2] (4470) (4703)
Wintercast *W R Swinburn* a93 97
4 ch g Spinning World(USA) —Bright Hope (IRE) (Danehill (USA))
1433[3] 2412[5] ◆ 2891[2] 3399[2] 6665[10] 7035[11] 7375[5]
Winterfell *C F Wall* a56 57
3 b f Haafhd—It Girl (Robellino (USA))
1406[12] 2104[10] 3010[4] 4389[6] 5647[3] 6771[3]
Winter Fever (SAF) *J M P Eustace* a87 82
5 ch g Western Winter(USA) —Fashion Fever (SAF) (Model Man (SAF))
7827[11]
Winterwind (IRE) *Frau Carmen Bocksai*
4 b h Orpen(USA) —Brickey Beech (IRE) (Precocious)
(7821a)
Wisdom's Kiss *J D Bethell* a82 69
5 b g Ocean Of Wisdom(USA) —April Magic (Magic Ring (IRE))
17[5]
Wisecraic *Tom Dascombe* 84
2 ch c Kheleyf(USA) —Belle Genius (USA) (Beau Genius (CAN))
(4478) ◆ 5274a[4] 6105[7]
Wise Dennis *A P Jarvis* a15 101
7 b g Polar Falcon(USA) —Bowden Rose (Dashing Blade)
340a[5] ◆ 439a[5] 644a[4] 697a[7] 4261[10] 5200[18] 6013[13] 6876[13]
Wiseman's Diamond (USA) *P T Midgley* a68 73
4 b m Wiseman's Ferry(USA) —Aswhatilldois (IRE) (Blues Traveller (IRE))
607[11] 1475[9] 1650[9] 1889[10] 2361[3] 3174[3] 3541[2] 3862[2] 4435[2] (4656) (4932) 5395[8] (6023)
Wise Melody *W J Haggas* a90 97
4 b m Zamindar(USA) —Swellegant (Midyan (USA))
1699[5] 2102[2]
Wise Princess *W G M Turner*
3 ch f Riverwise(USA) —Princess Penny (King's Signet (USA))
2488[11] 2808[9]
Wishbone (IRE) *M G Quinlan* 78
2 b f Danehill Dancer(IRE) —Intricate Design (Zafonic (USA))
5026[6] ◆ 5478[3] (6378) ◆
Wishformore (IRE) *J S Moore* a58
2 b f Chevalier(IRE) —Terra Nova (Polar Falcon (USA))
7463[2]
Wishlad (FR) *J De Roualle* 63
3 ch g Ocean Of Wisdom(USA) —Lady Valerie (FR) (Sillery (USA))
7037a[4]
Witch Of The Wave (IRE) *Miss J S Davis* a57
3 ch f Dr Fong(USA) —Clipper (Salse (USA))
115[5] 677[4] 1747[11]
Witchry *A G Newcombe* a50 71
7 gr g Green Desert(USA) —Indian Skimmer (USA) (Storm Bird (CAN))
4428[2] 5031[7] 6175[3] ◆ 6825[7] 7275[8]
With Flying Colors (USA) *Todd Pletcher* a81
4 b m A.P. Indy(USA) —My Flag (USA) (Easy Goer (USA))
6508a[5]
With Interest *M bin Shafya* 113
6 b h Selkirk(USA) —With Fascination (USA) (Dayjur (USA))
183a[4] 339a[5] 436a[4] 527a[11]
Without A Prayer (IRE) *R M Beckett* a116 114
4 ch h Intikhab(USA) —Prayer (IRE) (Rainbow Quest (USA))
261a[8] 415a[3] 644a[2] 913[5] 2668[4] (3404) 3841[6] 4949[6] (7588)
Without Prejudice (USA) *J Noseda* a87 94
4 ch g Johannesburg(USA) —Awesome Strike (USA) (Theatrical (IRE))
2086[11] 2695[9] 3339[3] 3825[9] (4501) 4802[4] (5697) 6270[11] 6702[9] 6815[6]
Wivny (USA) *H J Evans* a7 41
4 b m Yonaguska(USA) —Mostly Sassy (USA) (Green Dancer (USA))
2317[10] 3269[11] 3590[8] 4182[10] 5717[10]
Wiwurgh (USA) *C Boutin* a74 46
3 b c Touch Gold(USA) —Grooms Derby (USA) (Groomstick (USA))
6222a[9]
Wizard Looking *P T Midgley* a69 59
8 b g Wizard King—High Stepping (IRE) (Taufan (USA))
871[13] 1654[6] 1938[2] ◆ 2182[6] 2233[4] 3223[8]
Wizard Of Us *M Mullineaux* a53 43
9 b g Wizard King—Sian's Girl (Mystiko (USA))
4588[15] 5359[6] 5732[12]
Wizzy Izzy (IRE) *N Wilson* 30
4 rg m Shinko Forest(IRE) —Strelitzia (IRE) (Bluebird (USA))
80[8] 227[8]
Wo Ay Ni (BEL) *Mlle M Dere* 80
2 gr f Fabulous White(FR) —Veuve Lechat (FR) (Aragon)
1482a[9] 6326a[9]
Wogan's Sister *D R C Elsworth* a65 72
4 b m Lahib(USA) —Dublivia (Midyan (USA))
1812[5] 2246[9]
Woldgate *G R Oldroyd* a58 53
2 b g Monsieur Bond(IRE) —Chicago Bond (USA) (Real Quiet (USA))
5977[8] 6493[9] 6679[9]
Wolumla (IRE) *R Pritchard-Gordon* a46
2 b f Royal Applause—Audacieuse (Rainbow Quest (USA))
4970a[7]
Wolverine (FR) *Mme C Head-Maarek* 87
2 b c Take Risks(FR) —Sevres (USA) (Lyphard's Wish (FR))
6080a[6] 6501a[2]
Wolverton (IRE) *N P Littmoden* a38 24
3 ch g Alhaarth(IRE) —Debbie's Next (USA) (Arctic Tern (USA))
2395[11] 3117[13] 4175[6]
Womaniser (IRE) *T Keddy* a58 58
5 br g Rock Of Gibraltar(IRE) —Top Table (Shirley Heights)
4438[5] 6349[4] 6860[12] 7143[10] 7521[6] 7609[7] 7662[7]
Wonderfilly (FR) *P Demercastel* 98
2 b f Invincible Spirit(IRE) —Wicken Wonder (IRE) (Distant Relative)
4366a[5] 4579a[5] (6326a) 6752a[6] 7230a[4]
Woodcote (IRE) *Peter Grayson* a86 83
7 b g Monashee Mountain(USA) —Tootle (Main Reef)
83[7] 380[2] (481) 589[3] 676[2] 756[6] 1494[4] 2095[9] 2460[8] 4204[10] 4978[8] 5610[10] 6939[11] 7427[11] 7709[8]
Woodcote Place *P R Chamings* a92 95
6 b g Lujain(USA) —Giant Nipper (Nashwan (USA))
1288[7] 1607[2] (2188) 2828[2] 3628[2] 4409[11]
Woodenitbenice *D Shaw* a34
2 gr f Needwood Blade—Nightingale (Night Shift (USA))
3226[13] 3468[10] 4856[10] 5224[8] 7722[9]
Wooden King (IRE) *M S Saunders* a59 58
4 b g Danetime(IRE) —Olympic Rock (IRE) (Ballad Rock)
321[7] 395[8] 2353[2] 2458[12] 4536[9] 4905[6] 5065[7]
Woodface *B J Meehan* 37
2 ch c Avonbridge—Amazed (Clantime)
3402[11] 3920[9] 4331[7] 4915[14]
Wood Fair *A P Jarvis* 60
2 b f Trade Fair—To The Woods (IRE) (Woodborough (USA))
2360[7] 2765[6] 3187[7] 6215[9]
Wood Fairy *R A Fahey* a61 69
3 b f Haafhd—Woodbeck (Terimon)
(4277) 4896[7] 5395[11] 6218[5] 7149[7] 7428[4] 7665[4]
Woodford Belle (USA) *B J Meehan* 72
2 bb f Arch(USA) —Tis Me (USA) (Notebook (USA))
6062[4] 6762[4]
Woodhouse Mill (IRE) *N Tinkler* 35
2 b f Oratorio(IRE) —Wurfklinge (GER) (Acatenango (GER))
2936[9] 3337[9] 4515[11] 5036[8] 5595[17] 5981[10]
Woodland Violet *I A Wood* a44
3 b f Reset(AUS) —Be My Tinker (Be My Chief (USA))
7228[7] 7452[5] 7652[10] 7660[6]
Woodlark (IRE) *R Tugusev* 62
3 ch c Danehill Dancer(IRE) —Greenvera (USA) (Riverman (USA))
5585a[9]
Woodlark Island (IRE) *M P Tregoning* a81 76
3 b g Tagula(IRE) —Be My Lover (Pursuit Of Love)
951[2] ◆ 1130[4] 5027[2] (5751) 6243[5] 6583[5]
Woodsley House (IRE) *A G Foster* a61 76
7 b g Orpen(USA) —Flame And Shadow (IRE) (Turtle Island (IRE))
1369[7] 1694[6] 1832[7] (2453) 3097[3] 3496[9] 4134[7] 4504[5] 4657[6] 5333[5] 5673[4] 6157[15] 6411[6] 6984[5] 7113[7]
Wood White (USA) *R Menichetti* 94
3 b c Aljabr(USA) —Off You Go (USA) (Seattle Slew (USA))
1392a[5]
Woody Valentine (USA) *Mrs Dianne Sayer* 44
8 ch g Woodman(USA) —Mudslinger (USA) (El Gran Senor (USA))
1058[9]
Woody Waller *J Howard Johnson* 75
4 ch g Lomitas—Reamzafonic (Grand Lodge (USA))
1886[5] 6053[11]
Woolfall Sovereign (IRE) *G G Margarson* a63
3 b c Noverre(USA) —Mandragore (USA) (Slew O'Gold (USA))
(7753)
Woolfall Treasure *G L Moore* 94
4 gr g Daylami(IRE) —Treasure Trove (USA) (The Minstrel (CAN))
(1709) 2994[6] 4417[4] 5903[2] 6273[2] 6851[14]
Woolston Ferry (IRE) *David Pinder* a80 77
3 b g Fath(USA) —Cathy Garcia (IRE) (Be My Guest (USA))
288[4] (345) (827) 1466[6] 2399[11] 3159[10] 3982[6] 4872[5] 6726[7] 7192[5] 7432[9]
Woqoodd *D Shaw* a54 63
5 b g Royal Applause—Intervene (Zafonic (USA))
2682[11] 3066[6] 3239[10] 3465[9]
Workforce *Sir Michael Stoute* 93
2 b c King's Best(USA) —Soviet Moon (IRE) (Sadler's Wells (USA))
(6199)
World Heritage *P Bary* 114
3 b c Kahyasi—Imbabala (Zafonic (USA))
2951a[2] 4367a[2] 6132a[2]
Worldly Wise *Patrick J Flynn* a94 100
6 b g Namid—Tina Heights (Shirley Heights)
1376a[9] 5490a[3] 6867a[8]
World Of Choice (USA) *M W Easterby* a66 57
4 b g Distorted Humor(USA) —Palace Weekend (USA) (Seattle Dancer (USA))
152[5] (378) (1654) 2580[5] 3923[8] 4593[7] 5732[5]
World Ruler *Doug Watson* a72 105
4 b g Dansili—Revealing (Halling (USA))
703a[6] 774a[15]
World Time *Tim Vaughan* a57 76
4 ch g Dalakhani(IRE) —Time Ahead (Spectrum (IRE))
5936[5]
Worth A King'S *Sir Michael Stoute* a93 91
3 b g Red Ransom(USA) —Top Romance (IRE) (Entrepreneur)
2892[4] 3535[7] 4518[4] 5216[3] 5667[4] (6027) (6473) 6636[2]
Wotashirtfull (IRE) *J R Boyle* a89 89
4 ch g Namid—Madrina (Waajib)
(170) ◆ 424[3] 491[2] (665) 856[3] 1053[2] 1181[2] 1457[2] 2704[12] 4567[10] (5197) 5592[6]
Wotasparkler *W S Kittow* 66
3 b f Pyrus(USA) —Colourflash (IRE) (College Chapel)
1327[13] 1704[6] 2151[2] 2776[11] (3071) 3625[3] 4167[5] 4950[7] 5211[5] 5582[10]
Wotatomboy *R M Whitaker* a63 68
3 ch f Captain Rio—Keen Melody (USA) (Sharpen Up)
1452[8] 1720[4] 4664[6] 5836[8] 6182[8] 6824[16] 7239[8] 7417[6]
Wotavadun (IRE) *D Flood* a33 22
6 ch g King Of Kings(IRE) —Blush With Love (USA) (Mt. Livermore (USA))
2041[1] 2917
Wotchalike (IRE) *Miss S Johnstone* a65 60
7 ch g Spectrum(IRE) —Juno Madonna (IRE) (Sadler's Wells (USA))
2725[5] 3444[5] 4848[7]
Woteva *T P Tate* a67 71
3 b f Kyllachy—Happy Omen (Warning)
1282[9] 1531[9] 2091[8] 2236[16] 6997[8] 7246[5] 7428[7] 7650[8]
Would I Lie To You *J R Jenkins* a10 16
5 b g Bahamian Bounty—Pallas Athene (Jupiter Island)
115[8] 356[11] 1941[10]
Wovoka (IRE) *K A Ryan* a81 86
6 b g Mujadil(USA) —Common Cause (Polish Patriot (USA))
(1123) ◆ (1246) 1507[7] (2073) 2612[6] 2787[5] 3312[4] 3872[11] 4312[7] 4804[6] 5333[9] (5513) 6312[5] 6490[6] 6924[8]
Woy Woy (IRE) *L Reuterskiold Snr* 96
5 ch g City On A Hill(USA) —Best Niece (Vaigly Great)
7406a[11]
Wray Castle (IRE) *Ian Williams* a71
4 b g Desert Prince(IRE) —Blushing Gleam (Caerleon (USA))
476[2] 704[5]
Wrecker's Moon (IRE) *T J Etherington* a12
4 b m Shinko Forest(IRE) —Coast Is Clear (IRE) (Rainbow Quest (USA))
2789[12]
Wreningham *P Leech* a69 61
4 br g Diktat—Slave To The Rythm (IRE) (Hamas (IRE))
3860[11] 4182[5] 5184[7] 5989[6] 6456[5] 7021[7] 7397[6]
Wrens Hope *N Bycroft* 44
3 ch f Shinko Forest(IRE) —Star Dancer (Groom Dancer (USA))
1247[6] 3036[11] 3498[4] 4596[13]
Wriggle (IRE) *W J Haggas* a62 75
2 b g Refuse To Bend(IRE) —Isana (JPN) (Sunday Silence (USA))
3786[3] 4200[6] 6493[6]
Wrighty Almighty (IRE) *P R Chamings* a76 76
7 b g Danehill Dancer(IRE) —Persian Empress (IRE) (Persian Bold)
545[4] 813[8] 959[8] 1959[3] 2223[DSQ] 2381[4] 2807[5]
Writ (IRE) *I Semple* a52 60
7 ch g Indian Lodge(IRE) —Carnelly (IRE) (Priolo (USA))
289[12]
Wrong Answer *Kevin Prendergast* a86 101
2 gr f Verglas(IRE) —Wrong Key (IRE) (Key Of Luck (USA))
(2286a) 2557a[5] 5488a[7] 5895a[2] 7072a[6]
Wulfrida (IRE) *J R Fanshawe* 76
2 b f King's Best(USA) —Panna (Polish Precedent (USA))
6066[3] 6921[4] ◆
Wulimaster (USA) *D W Barker* a59 59
6 br g Silver Hawk(USA) —Kamaina (USA) (Mr Prospector (USA))
1767[9] 2159[4] 2448[5] 2656[4] 3291[4] 3974[6]
Wunder Strike (USA) *J R Boyle* a71 64
3 b g Smart Strike(CAN) —Bishop's Mate (USA) (Lyphard (USA))
(802) 1036[4] ◆ 1420[2] (1516) 1595[2] 1932[6] 2548[13] 4149[11] 4714[9] 5506[8] 6787[11] 7197[3] (7433) (7693) (7742)
Wusuul *R A Harris* a60 68
4 br m Kyllachy—Cartuccia (IRE) (Doyoun)
105[7] 678[3] 765[5] 849[4] 1074[10] 1535[11]
Wyatt Earp (IRE) *P Salmon* a91 93
8 b g Piccolo—Tribal Lady (Absalom)
1663[3] 2093[6] 2267[2] 2658[5] 3122[5] 3877[8] 4353[8] 4784[6] 5516[5]
Wyeth *G L Moore* a75 67
5 ch g Grand Lodge(USA) —Bordighera (USA) (Alysheba (USA))
(668)
Wymering File (IRE) *M J Grassick* a90 83
4 b m Medecis—Ensenada (IRE) (Sri Pekan (USA))
4903[7] 6030[10] 6467a[6] 7300a[4]
Wynberg (IRE) *Stef Liddiard* a73 66
4 b g Danetime(IRE) —Jayzdoll (IRE) (Stravinsky (USA))
467[6] 540[8] 661[10]
Wyn Dixie (IRE) *B Storey* 18
10 b g Great Commotion(USA) —Duchess Affair (IRE) (Digamist (USA))
4874[6]
Wysiwyg Lucky (FR) *J-L Gay* a72 93
6 b m Ultimately Lucky(IRE) —Les Estelles (FR) (Dress Parade)
(7569a)
Xaara Star (IRE) *Eve Johnson Houghton* 55
2 b f Xaar—Bint Kaldoun (IRE) (Kaldoun (FR))
1810[8] 2563[6] 2792[8] 3240[4] 3726[3] 4384[8] 4689[8]
Xaarienne *H-A Pantall* 91
2 b f Xaar—Saharienne (USA) (A.P. Indy (USA))
5739a[3] 6929a[6] 7346a[3]
Xandra (IRE) *W M Brisbourne* a52 44
4 b m Xaar—Talah (Danehill (USA))
581[10] 934[7] 1745[10]
Xenes *R Menichetti* a102 102
5 b h Xaar—Lucia Tarditi (FR) (Crystal Glitters (USA))
1905a[9] 6894a[4] 7206a[9]
Xilerator (IRE) *D Nicholls* 73
2 b g Arakan(USA) —Grandel (Owington)
7167[2]
Xpres Maite *S R Bowring* a93 84
6 b g Komaite(USA) —Antonias Melody (Rambo Dancer (CAN))
9[5] (68) 382[2] (491) 714[7] 778[4] 856[2] 1089[7] 1612[8] 2086[9] (2459) 2791[5] 3339[7] 3928[5] 4428[6] 4842[3] 5104[5] 5375[2] 5615[6] 6946[7] 7322[2] 7759[6]
Xtension (IRE) *C G Cox* 117
2 br c Xaar—Great Joy (IRE) (Grand Lodge (USA))
(2430) 2993[2] (4418) 6849[3]
Xtra Special *Sir Michael Stoute* a46 70
3 b f Xaar—Misleading Lady (Warning)
2002[4] 5987[5]
Xtra Torrential (USA) *D M Simcock* a77 100
7 b g Torrential(USA) —Offering (USA) (Majestic Light (USA))
974[6] 1132[6] 1316[6]
Xtravaganza (IRE) *Jamie Snowden* a59 68
4 b m Xaar—Royal Jubilee (IRE) (King's Theatre (IRE))
5631[7]
Xtraxtra (IRE) *M J Grassick* 80
2 ch g Titus Livius(FR) —Extra Time (Shadeed (USA))
6401a[14]
Xtreme (IRE) *A Bailey* a54 51
2 b g Xaar—Emerald Storm (USA) (Diesis)
6461[7] 7120[7]
Yaa Wayl (IRE) *M A Jarvis* 90
2 b g Whipper(USA) —Lidanna (Nicholas (USA))
3920[4] (4282) 5658[2] ◆ 6534[4] 7013[2]
Yab Adee *M P Tregoning* a67 58
5 b g Mark Of Esteem(IRE) —Kotdiji (Mtoto)
6342[10]
Ya Boy Sir (IRE) *N Wilson* a51 59
2 ch c Alhaarth(IRE) —Champs Elysees (USA) (Distant Relative)
2813[4] 3262[6] 5290[5] 5942[3] 6983[6] 7372[8] 7757[2]
Yabtree (IRE) *R Charlton* a33 64
2 b c Clodovil(IRE) —Lorientaise (IRE) (Xaar)
5785[3] 6930[5] 7326[10]
Yaddree *M bin Shafya* a89 110
4 ch h Singspiel(IRE) —Jathaabeh (Nashwan (USA))
182a[6] 263a[2] ◆
Yahrab (IRE) *Saeed Bin Suroor* a114 109
4 gr g Dalakhani(IRE) —Loire Valley (IRE) (Sadler's Wells (USA))
419a[12] 642a[9] 703a[2] 772a[11] 1799[7] 2327[8]
Yahwudhee (FR) *M W Easterby* a34 79
4 b g Zamindar(USA) —Lady Marshall (FR) (Octagonal (NZ))
965[6] 1477[8] 2389[12] 4192[8] 5883[8]

Yakama (IRE) *Mrs C A Dunnett* a62 61
4 b g Indian Danehill(IRE) —Working Progress (IRE) (Marju (IRE))
706^{8} 1260^{9} 1475^{8} 1632^{6} 1959^{2} 2166^{5} 7716^{12}

Yaldas Girl (USA) *J R Best* a39 48
3 rg f Unbridled's Song(USA) —Marina De Chavon (USA) (Exploit (USA))
4872^{11} 5644^{8} 6831^{6} 7255^{8} 7324^{13}

Yamal (IRE) *Saeed Bin Suroor* a108 115
4 b g Green Desert(USA) —Pioneer Bride (USA) (Gone West (USA))
335a^{2} (522a) ◆ 615a^{2} (2015) 2476^{3}

Yamam *A Fabre* a87 89
2 b f Elusive City(USA) —Elle S'Voyait Deja (USA) (Carson City (USA))
(4577a) 5240a^{2}

Yamanin Kingly (JPN) *H Kawachi* 116
4 b h Agnes Digital(USA) —Yamanin Arena (JPN) (Sunday Silence (USA))
7593a^{18}

Yanbu (USA) *R W Price* 45
4 b m Swain(IRE) —Dufoof (USA) (Kingmambo (USA))
2416^{12} 3951^{7}

Yankee Bright (USA) *J G Given* 69
2 b f Elusive Quality(USA) —Sharp Minister (CAN) (Deputy Minister (CAN))
6284^{5} ◆ 6762^{3} 7187^{10}

Yankee Doodle *A P O'Brien* 115
3 gr c Dalakhani(IRE) —Bella Lambada (Lammtarra (USA))
3090^{2} 3413a^{3} 4033a^{2} ◆

Yankee Storm *H J Collingridge* a78 62
4 b g Yankee Gentleman(USA) —Yes Virginia (USA) (Roanoke (USA))
3211^{7} 3713^{5} 4374^{3} 4843^{2} 5374^{3} 5612^{6} 6776^{2} 6976^{8} 7518^{3} 7738^{7}

Yanza *J R Gask* a68 70
3 b f Bahamian Bounty—Locharia (Wolfhound (USA))
(1077) 1505^{12} 2160^{11} 2632^{12} 5584^{7} 6252^{4} 6825^{2} 7138^{2} 7330^{3} 7601^{7} 7819 ^{10} 7852^{7}

Yard-Arm (SAF) *R Bouresly* 51
10 b g Western Winter(USA) —Fashing (SAF) (Dancing Champ (USA))
413a^{11}

Yarra River *A M Balding* 79
2 bb g Dr Fong(USA) —River Cara (USA) (Irish River (FR))
3402^{2} 4006^{3} 4524^{2} 5153^{2} 6478^{19}

Yashkur *C E Brittain* a31 51
3 ch f Needwood Blade—Silent Tribute (IRE) (Lion Cavern (USA))
2403^{6} 3813^{6} 4151^{12} 4819^{14} 5751^{8} 6223^{13}

Yashtrack (FR) *M Rolland*
3 b f Milford Track(IRE) —Miss Onyx (FR) (Bluebird (USA))
7037a^{0}

Yasoodd *D Selvaratnam* a87 100
6 br g Inchinor—Needwood Epic (Midyan (USA))
183a^{3} 340a^{6} 642a^{5}

Yawary *C E Brittain* a57 64
2 b f Medicean—Sociable (Danehill (USA))
2324^{8} 2860^{4} 3240^{2} 3686^{9} 4271^{5} 4868^{4} 5573^{6} 5934^{6}

Yeadon *R A Fahey* a71 71
2 b c Fraam—Harryana (Efisio)
2099^{3} 2526^{2} 4370^{2} 4774^{4} 5835^{4} 6096^{4} 6494^{4} 7268^{4} 7333^{2} 7805^{6}

Yeah *Patrick Morris* a43 54
2 b g Gentleman's Deal(IRE) —Snugfit Dubarry (Ali-Royal (IRE))
2147^{4} 3017^{6} 4163^{4} 5372^{9} 6610^{7}

Yeats (IRE) *A P O'Brien* 126
8 b h Sadler's Wells(USA) —Lyndonville (IRE) (Top Ville)
1546a^{6} (3048) 5891a^{8} 6527a^{3}

Yellow Printer *F J Brennan* a76 77
3 b g Royal Applause—Robsart (IRE) (Robellino (USA))
1466^{9} 1774^{3} 1971^{3} 2329^{4} 2794^{2} 3309^{3} 6621^{12} 6780^{6} 7065^{8} 7456^{3}

Yellow Ridge (IRE) *Luke Comer* a32 48
6 ch g On The Ridge(IRE) —Jonathan's Rose (IRE) (Law Society (USA))
6859^{12} 6917^{12}

Yellow River (USA) *E J Creighton* a44 68
3 ch f Johannesburg(USA) —Ascension (IRE) (Night Shift (USA))
92^{2} 200^{9} 667^{8} 964^{5} 2737^{7} 4425^{14} 4596^{10} 4937^{16} 6340^{11}

Yellowstone (IRE) *P F I Cole* 116
5 b h Rock Of Gibraltar(IRE) —Love And Affection (USA) (Exclusive Era (USA))
2075^{6} 2501^{4} 3142^{12} 3397^{4} 6662^{19} 7038a^{2}

Yeoman Of England (IRE) *C F Wall* a64 64
3 b g Pyrus(USA) —Regal Lustre (Averti (IRE))
2300^{17} 3075^{10} 4183^{15} 4719^{8} 6001^{4} 6570^{8} 6919^{5}

Yer Woman (IRE) *R Hannon* a89 81
2 b f Kyllachy—Genny Lim (IRE) (Barathea (IRE))
1782^{2} (2135) 3424^{10} (4208) 5797^{8} 6541^{4} (7536)

Yes Chef *J Gallagher* 62
2 ch c Best Of The Bests(IRE) —Lady Chef (Double Trigger (IRE))
6759^{12} 6990^{4}

Yes Maggie (IRE) *M R Channon* 42
2 b f Vindication(USA) —Westerly Gale (USA) (Gone West (USA))
6108^{10}

Yes Mr President (IRE) *M Johnston* a82 106
4 b g Montjeu(IRE) —Royals Special (IRE) (Caerleon (USA))
2698^{4} (3103) 3266^{2} 3620^{12} 4408^{4} 4769^{2} 5170^{3} (5656) 6851^{31}

Yesnabay (USA) *G A Swinbank* 86
2 bb g Grand Slam(USA) —Speedy Sonata (USA) (Stravinsky (USA))
3478^{3} ◆ (4132)

Yes One (IRE) *K A Ryan* a78 87
5 ch g Peintre Celebre(USA) —Copious (IRE) (Generous (IRE))
9^{8} 195^{6} 671^{5} 1079^{5} 1409^{4}

Yes Please *K A Ryan* a42 56
4 b g Efisio—Shall We Dance (Rambo Dancer (CAN))
381^{10} 3093^{8} 5163^{3} 5624^{13} 5842^{8}

Yes She Can Can *Peter Grayson* a34
3 ch f Monsieur Bond(IRE) —Antonia's Folly (Music Boy)
75^{8} 207^{4} 804^{10} 955^{10} 1064^{10}

Yirga *Saeed Bin Suroor* a76 87
3 b c Cape Cross(IRE) —Auratum (USA) (Carson City (USA))
2229^{3} (2890) (3489) 4242^{2} 4794^{7}

Ykikamoocow *G A Harker* 68
3 b f Cape Town(IRE) —Pigeon (Casteddu)
(2661) 3727^{7} 4846^{5} 6824^{7} 6984^{3}

Ymir *M J Attwater* a65 58
3 b c Zaha(CAN) —Anastasia Venture (Lion Cavern (USA))
74^{7} 1462^{14} 1671^{9} 2431^{3} 3790^{3} 4275^{8} 5169^{8} 5647^{2} 6720^{7} 7239^{10} 7433^{2} 7587^{4} 7693^{6}

Yogaroo (USA) *Wesley A Ward* a90 59
2 ch g Bring The Heat(USA) —Harper N Abbey (USA) (Outflanker (USA))
3046^{9}

Yonder *H Morrison* a45 72
5 br m And Beyond(IRE) —Dominance (Dominion)
902^{4} 1171^{3} 1399^{7} (2798) (3216) 3940^{7} 4948^{7} 5802^{8}

Yorgunnabelucky (USA) *M Johnston* 89
3 b c Giant's Causeway(USA) —Helsinki (Machiavellian (USA))
(3120) 4058^{7} 5137^{14} 5419^{9} 5832^{5} 6249^{5} 6535^{5}

York Cliff *W M Brisbourne* a62 61
11 b g Marju(IRE) —Azm (Unfuwain (USA))
81^{3} 213^{4} 377^{11} 566^{6} 4264^{3} 4927^{9} 5210^{11} 7670^{11}

Yorke's Folly (USA) *C W Fairhurst* a38 54
8 b m Stravinsky(USA) —Tommelise (USA) (Dayjur (USA))
4754^{2} 5041^{6}

York Key Bar *B Ellison* a53 70
3 b g Presidium—Onemoretime (Timeless Times (USA))
1015^{12} 1129^{3} 1469^{4} 2234^{6} 2683^{5} 3355^{3} 3999^{12}

Yorkshire Blue *J S Goldie* a43 73
10 b g Atraf—Something Blue (Petong)
4775^{7} 5391^{6} 5601^{5} (5955) 6221^{6} 6413^{2} 6989^{6}

Yorksters Girl (IRE) *M G Quinlan* 93
3 ch f Bachelor Duke(USA) —Isadora Duncan (IRE) (Sadler's Wells (USA))
1353^{7} 3641^{7}

Yorksters Prince (IRE) *M G Quinlan* a59 44
2 b g Beat Hollow—Odalisque (IRE) (Machiavellian (USA))
6810^{11} 7844^{4}

Yosolito (FR) *L A Urbano-Grajales* a58 57
2 b c Keltos(FR) —Fusee Francaise (FR) (Anabaa (USA))
6979a^{10}

Yossi (IRE) *Jim Best* 83
5 b g Montjeu(IRE) —Raindancing (IRE) (Tirol)
3768^{2} 4007^{8} 5802^{9}

You Avin A Laugh *C A Dwyer* a61 33
3 ch g Bertolini(USA) —High Stepping (IRE) (Taufan (USA))
592^{6} 784^{7} 889^{3} 966^{4} 1129^{5} 1529^{2} 1949^{8} 2683^{3} 2888^{8} 3225^{4} 3464^{8}

Youcanalwaysdream (IRE) *K A Ryan* a80 27
2 b f Exceed And Excel(AUS) —Al Shadeedah (USA) (Nureyev (USA))
6932^{8} 7213^{9} 7365^{2} ◆ 7485^{2} (7582)

You'll Be Mine (USA) *A P O'Brien* 105
2 b f Kingmambo(USA) —Quarter Moon (IRE) (Sadler's Wells (USA))
6269^{3} ◆

Youm Jamil (USA) *B J Meehan* 76
2 rg c Mizzen Mast(USA) —Millie's Choice (IRE) (Taufan (USA))
6393^{2} ◆ 7146^{2}

Youmzain (IRE) *M R Channon* 128
6 b h Sinndar(IRE) —Sadima (IRE) (Sadler's Wells (USA))
1012a^{4} 2670^{2} 3443a^{3} 5707a^{3} 6526a^{2} 7744a^{10}

Young Americans (IRE) *M Botti* a65 64
3 b f Nayef(USA) —Life At Night (IRE) (Night Shift (USA))
3641^{8} 4287^{7} 5168^{7}

Young Bertie *H Morrison* a70 77
6 ch g Bertolini(USA) —Urania (Most Welcome)
398^{7} 505^{8}

Young Centaur (AUS) *John Sargent* 99
7 br g Jeune—Centafit (NZ) (Centaine (AUS))
6961a^{11}

Young Dottie *P M Phelan* a79 70
3 b f Desert Sun—Auntie Dot Com (Tagula (IRE))
1462^{8} 2498^{4} 3387^{3} 4236^{6} 5099^{5} 5570^{8} 6421^{8} 6910^{4} (7664)

Young Firth *J R Norton* a23 52
2 b g Lucky Story(USA) —Le Petit Diable (IRE) (Trans Island)
3716^{9} 4307^{6} 4705^{6} 6639^{12}

Young George *C W Fairhurst* a38 10
2 b g Danroad(AUS) —Bo' Babbity (Strong Gale)
6556^{9} 7556^{9}

Young Gladiator (IRE) *Miss J A Camacho* a69 65
4 b g Spartacus(IRE) —Savona (IRE) (Cyrano De Bergerac)
1655^{11} (2722) 3224^{7} 3612^{6} (4312) 5601^{7} 6985^{6} 7348^{2}

Young Ivanhoe *C A Dwyer* a54 50
4 b g Oasis Dream—Cybinka (Selkirk (USA))
574^{4} 812^{7} 921^{4} 1072^{6} 1781^{9} 1958^{4} 2224^{6} 2456^{12}

Young Mick *G G Margarson* a91 111
7 br g King's Theatre(IRE) —Just Warning (Warning)
33^{8} 338a^{2} 437a^{6} (616a) 772a^{12} 1017^{8} 1601^{4} 2085^{3} 3142^{4} 6662^{7} 7237^{5}

Young Ollie *E A Wheeler* 14
4 ch m Piccolo—Miss Michelle (Jalmood (USA))
1420^{12}

Young Pretender (FR) *Saeed Bin Suroor* 112
4 b h Oasis Dream—Silent Heir (AUS) (Sunday Silence (USA))
6448^{5} 7019^{2} 7245^{4}

Young Simon *G G Margarson* a55 77
2 ch c Piccolo—Fragrant Cloud (Zilzal (USA))
4851^{8} 5109^{2} 6903^{7} 7234^{5}

Young Star Gazer *H R A Cecil* 68
3 ch g Observatory(USA) —Ash Glade (Nashwan (USA))
1752^{8} 2338^{3} 3120^{6} 3960^{3}

You Or No One (IRE) *Mme B Valenti* 84
3 b f Falbrav(IRE) —Desperate Virgin (BEL) (Chief Singer)
5562a^{8}

You'relikemefrank *J Balding* a50
3 ch g Bahamian Bounty—Proudfoot (IRE) (Shareef Dancer (USA))
91^{6} 273^{3} 316^{3} 3229^{4} 4514^{6} 5105^{2} 5881^{6} 6206^{3}

Your Gifted (IRE) *P J Prendergast* 72
2 b f Trans Island—Dame Laura (IRE) (Royal Academy (USA))
5274a^{5}

Your Golf Travel *M Wigham* a48 40
4 b m Bertolini(USA) —Scottish Spice (Selkirk (USA))
247^{2} 1959^{8} 2420^{16} 3004^{8}

Yourgolftravel Com *M Wigham* 13
4 b g Fasliyev(USA) —Hiddnah (USA) (Affirmed (USA))
2862^{13}

Your Lad *C F Wall* a52
2 b c Dubawi(IRE) —Krisalya (Kris)
7764^{8}

Your Old Pal *J Noseda* 107
3 ch c Rock Of Gibraltar(IRE) —Questabelle (Rainbow Quest (USA))
1326^{5} (1678) 2277^{4} 3087^{2}

Your True Love (IRE) *A Berry* 36
3 b f Pyrus(USA) —Columbine (IRE) (Pivotal)
1062^{7} 1831^{6} 2157^{12}

You Say I Say (USA) *Sir Michael Stoute* 66
3 bb f Unbridled's Song(USA) —Insight (FR) (Sadler's Wells (USA))
2006^{6}

You've Been Mowed *R J Price* a68 68
3 ch f Ishiguru(USA) —Sandblaster (Most Welcome)
982^{3} 1311^{9} 1583^{6} 1982^{7} 2355^{3} (2577) 2910^{2} (3209) 3637^{5} 4482^{6} 4841^{7} 5403^{6} 6070^{10} (6337) 6778^{9}

Ytartfawn (IRE) *P T Midgley* 36
2 ch c Chineur(FR) —Lady Montekin (Montekin)
1126^{6} 1330^{5} 2258^{9} 2788^{5} 3626^{6}

Yughanni *C E Brittain* a45 53
3 b f Oasis Dream—Bedazzling (IRE) (Darshaan)
1066^{10} 1379^{9} 1940^{10} 2539^{3} 3176^{8} 3476^{6}

Yungaburra (IRE) *J Balding* a92 71
5 b g Fath(USA) —Nordic Living (IRE) (Nordico (USA))
351^{3} 676^{4} 1935^{6} 3002^{5} 3562^{6} 4355^{13}

Yurituni *Eve Johnson Houghton* 83
2 b f Bahamian Bounty—Vax Star (Petong)
3458^{4} ◆ 3772^{4} 4603^{8} (5136) 5797^{2} (5899) 6275^{2} 6660^{16}

Yushka (FR) *P Bary* 91
2 b f Kingsalsa(USA) —Yacht Club (USA) (Sea Hero (USA))
3967a^{4} 5279a^{7}

Yvonne Evelyn (USA) *J R Gask* a67 60
4 rg m Cozzene(USA) —One Great Lady (USA) (Fappiano (USA))
3217^{6} 3869^{7} 5195^{3} 5964^{5} 6584^{13}

Zaahid (IRE) *B W Hills* 107
5 ch h Sakhee(USA) —Murjana (IRE) (Pleasant Colony (USA))
997^{2} 1352^{19} 1861^{18}

Zaahy (USA) *P W Chapple-Hyam* a90 69
2 ch c More Than Ready(USA) —Sangam (USA) (Majestic Light (USA))
4499^{4} (5580) ◆

Zaaqya *J L Dunlop* 91
3 b f Nayef(USA) —Classical Dancer (Dr Fong (USA))
1303^{11} 2008^{6} 2796^{3} (3535) 4103^{3} 4988^{3} 5771^{7} 6681^{3} 7148^{6}

Zabeel House *John A Harris* a69 19
6 b g Anabaa(USA) —Divine Quest (Kris)
81^{2} 405^{6} 598^{2} 813^{7} 1030^{4} 1276^{17}

Zabeel Tower *R Allan* a10 79
6 b g Anabaa(USA) —Bint Kaldoun (IRE) (Kaldoun (FR))
2313^{10} 2589^{3} 3097^{5} 3331^{6} 3857^{4} 4346^{5} 4466^{2} 4751^{6} 4878^{4} 5160^{9} 6309^{5} 6847 ^{9} 7403^{11}

Zabellah *J Balding*
4 ch m Zaha(CAN) —Polar Refrain (Polar Falcon (USA))
323^{5}

Zabougg *D W Barker* 52
4 b g Tobougg(IRE) —Double Fault (IRE) (Zieten (USA))
1058^{10} 1242^{10} 1556^{9}

Zachary Boy (IRE) *B G Powell* a63 46
2 b c Orpen(USA) —Shun (Selkirk (USA))
2324^{9} 2533^{10} 4194^{8} 7319^{2}

Zach's Harmoney (USA) *Miss M E Rowland* a63 69
5 ch g Diesis—Cool Ashlee (USA) (Mister Baileys)
1051^{2}

Zacinto *Sir Michael Stoute* 125
3 b c Dansili—Ithaca (USA) (Distant View (USA))
(4521) ◆ (5426) ◆ 6271^{2} 7308a^{11}

Zacroona (NZ) *Lee Freedman* 82
5 b g Zabeel(NZ) —Singalong (NZ) (Danasinga (AUS))
6961a^{15}

Zaffaan *E A L Dunlop* a88 84
3 ch g Efisio—Danceabout (Shareef Dancer (USA))
1484^{8} 2270^{12}

Zaffature *M Botti* a59 58
2 b f Zafeen(FR) —Alice Blackthorn (Forzando)
3716^{4} 3979^{5} 4915^{4} 5224^{2} 5613^{2} 7120^{2}

Zaffeu *A G Juckes* a66 65
8 ch g Zafonic(USA) —Leaping Flame (USA) (Trempolino (USA))
8^{2} 300^{4} 743^{2} 1439^{7} 1936^{10}

Zafisio (IRE) *R Curtis* 114
3 b c Efisio—Goldthroat (IRE) (Zafonic (USA))
1915a^{2} 2756a^{13} 5924a^{3} (7208a) (7406a)

Zafranagar (IRE) *A W Carroll* 74
4 b g Cape Cross(IRE) —Zafaraniya (IRE) (Doyoun)
7221^{7}

Zaftil (IRE) *H S Howe* a2 35
3 br f Tillerman—Zafine (Zafonic (USA))
1429^{8} 1772^{5} 1985^{8} 2794^{8} 3209^{14}

Zagarock *B Palling* 52
2 b f Rock Of Gibraltar(IRE) —Zagaleta (Sri Pekan (USA))
5547^{8} 6617^{7} 6931^{5}

Zagora (FR) *Y De Nicolay* 102
2 ch f Green Tune(USA) —Zaneton (FR) (Mtoto)
6929a^{4}

Zaham (USA) *M Johnston* a98 116
5 ch g Silver Hawk(USA) —Guerre Et Paix (USA) (Soviet Star (USA))
1859^{6} 2398^{4} 3190^{6}

Zahoo (IRE) *J L Dunlop* 75
2 b f Nayef(USA) —Tanaghum (Darshaan)
4792^{5} 5741^{3} ◆ (6284)

Zaif (IRE) *D J S Ffrench Davis* a68 82
6 b g Almutawakel—Colourful (FR) (Gay Mecene (USA))
1750^{8} 4437^{7} 4644^{5} 5028^{12} 6204^{12} 6288^{8} 6584^{10} (6969) 7490^{9}

Zain (IRE) *J G Given* a22 48
5 b g Alhaarth(IRE) —Karenaragon (Aragon)
2420^{11} 3077^{13} 5730^{12} 7581^{9}

Zalka (FR) *Jean-Francois Clais* a19 62
4 ch m Indian Rocket—Zaleema (IRE) (Bluebird (USA))
6579a^{10}

Zalkani (IRE) *J Pearce* a66 47
9 ch g Cadeaux Genereux—Zallaka (IRE) (Shardari)
202^{5} 320^{4} 534^{5} 631^{4} 751^{2} 871^{4} 1378^{8} (1533) 2601^{5} 3927^{3} 5680^{6} 6226^{5} 6342^{8} 6704^{8} 6918^{6}

Zambezi Sun *Robert Frankel* a104 121
5 b h Dansili—Imbabala (Zafonic (USA))
789a^{9}

Zambuka (FR) *R Curtis* 44
2 gr f Zieten(USA) —Mercalle (FR) (Kaldoun (FR))
1298^{9} 1866^{8}

Zando's Pearl *C J Price*
2 b f Forzando—Siouxtabul (Makbul)
7556^{12}

Zanzibari (USA) *A Fabre* 113
2 b c Smart Strike(CAN) —Zinziberine (USA) (Zieten (USA))
(4579a) 5299a^{5}

Zaplamation (IRE) *J J Quinn* a40 63
4 b g Acclamation—Zapatista (Rainbow Quest (USA))
3123^{4} 3450^{10} (4313) 4656^{2} 5289^{2} 5982^{2} (6817)

Zarah Top (GER) *Dr A Bolte* 9
3 b f Big Shuffle(USA) —Zorina (Shirley Heights)
6605a^{9}

Zarema (JPN) *H Otonashi* 108
5 b m Dance In The Dark(JPN) —Shenck (Zafonic (USA))
7498a^{11}

Zarilan (IRE) *Evan Williams* a51 67
4 b g Namid—Zarlana (IRE) (Darshaan)
488^{3}

Zarinski (IRE) *Jim Best* a79 90
3 b g Dalakhani(IRE) —Zarafsha (IRE) (Alzao (USA))
3051^{4} 4520^{13}

Zariyan (FR) *Mlle C Nicot* a92 79
6 b g Anabaa(USA) —Zarkana (IRE) (Doyoun)
5464a^{2} 7822a^{8}

Zarly (FR) *F Rohaut* 78
2 gr c Fairly Ransom(USA) —Besca Nueva (FR) (Lesotho (USA))
4686a^{2}

Zars Gold (IRE) *J Gallagher* a67 67
4 b m Xaar—Affirmed Crown (USA) (Affirmed (USA))
861^{5} ◆ 1066^{7} 1634^{4} 1890^{7} 2185^{7}

Zaskia (IRE) *K A Ryan* a46 44
2 ch f Tomba—Flamenco Dancer (Mark Of Esteem (IRE))
1158^{5} 1344^{8} 2541^{4} 3572^{10} 3709^{5} 6345^{8} 6555^{3} 7089^{7}

Zaungast (IRE) *W Hickst* 108
5 b h Alkalde(GER) —Zauberwelt (Polar Falcon (USA))
1143a^{3} 1575a^{5} 2309a^{6} (3201a)

Zavite (NZ) *Anthony Cummings* 113
7 b g Zabeel(NZ) —Miss Vita (USA) (Alleged (USA))
6871a^{9} 7215a^{19}

Zaya (GER) *A Wohler* 98
4 b m Diktat—Zayala (Royal Applause)
1268a^{2} 4363a^{2} 6717a^{9}

Za Za *H R A Cecil* 57
3 br f Barathea(IRE) —Madiyla (Darshaan)
3379^{3} 4270^{8}

Za Za Zoom (IRE) *B W Hills* 97
2 b f Le Vie Dei Colori—Emma's Star (ITY) (Darshaan)
5021^{5} (6737) 7033^{2}

Zazou (GER) *Mario Hofer* 105
2 b c Shamardal(USA) —Zaza Top (GER) (Lomitas)
5652a^{4} 7404a^{3}

Zazous *J J Bridger* a64 51
8 b g Zafonic(USA) —Confidentiality (USA) (Lyphard (USA))
1710^{11}

Zazy's Gift *George Baker* 7
2 b f Pastoral Pursuits—Tintac (Intikhab (USA))
6363[12] 6965[13]

Zebrano *Miss E C Lavelle* a77 83
3 br g Storming Home—Ambience Lady (Batshoof)
1931[10] *2600[5]* 2849[13] 3659[2] (4267) 5154[7] 6964[3] *7395[12]*

Zeffirelli *M Quinn* a62 59
4 ch g Tomba—Risky Valentine (Risk Me (FR))
1074[4] 1258[5] 2458[13] 2921[6] 4812[5] *7678[2]* *7796[6]*

Ze Finale *T D Easterby*
2 b f Zafeen(FR) —Dominelle (Domynsky)
1396[8] 1624[8]

Zefooha (FR) *T D Walford* a68 68
5 ch m Lomitas—Bezzaaf (Machiavellian (USA))
1000[9] 1242[8] 1648[5] (2344) (2969) 3544[2] 4873[2] 5600[4] 5962[8] 6385[5]

Zegna (IRE) *B Smart* a78 78
3 gr g Clodovil(IRE) —Vade Retro (IRE) (Desert Sun)
7411[2] *(7686)* *7875[9]*

Zeitoper *Saeed Bin Suroor* 102
2 b c Singspiel(IRE) —Kazzia (GER) (Zinaad)
(5993) (6472) (6889a)

Zeloca (IRE) *Mrs L C Jewell*
2 ch f Refuse To Bend(IRE) —Lily's Girl (IRE) (Hamas (IRE))
4825[14] *5643[11]* *6122[7]*

Zelos Diktator *Rae Guest* a38 63
3 br g Diktat—Chanterelle (IRE) (Indian Ridge)
1410[6] 3336[10] 3708[6] 4519[14] 6116[6] (6766)

Zelos Dream (IRE) *R A Harris* a60 64
2 ch f Redback—Endless Peace (IRE) (Russian Revival (USA))
2741[4] 3686[5] 4383[2] 4688[2] 5060[4] (5976) *6774[7]* *6970[3]* *7352[3]* *7661[3]* *7713[6]*

Zelos Girl (IRE) *J G Given* a50 72
3 ch f Exceed And Excel(AUS) —Sedna (FR) (Bering)
2005[8] 2740[6] 3428[4] 4596[6] 5155[8] 5626[4] *5881[10]* 6308[3]

Zelos Spirit *Rae Guest* 23
2 b f Tiger Hill(IRE) —Good Mood (USA) (Devil's Bag (USA))
6796[8]

Zemario (IRE) *M A Jarvis* 75
3 b g Dalakhani(IRE) —Noushkey (Polish Precedent (USA))
(5322)

Zenarinda *M H Tompkins* 64
2 b f Zamindar(USA) —Tenpence (Bob Back (USA))
4318[4] 7099[4]

Zennerman (IRE) *W M Brisbourne* a50 72
6 b g Observatory(USA) —Precocious Miss (USA) (Diesis)
3851[12] 4465[8] 4845[7] (5126) *5229[6]* *5683[8]* *6024[11]*

Zenone (IRE) *Laura Grizzetti* 104
5 b h Orpen(USA) —Luna D'Estate (Alzao (USA))
7312a[9]

Zensational (USA) *Bob Baffert* a124
3 rg c Unbridled's Song(USA) —Joke (USA) (Phone Trick (USA))
7306a[5]

Zenyatta (USA) *John Shirreffs* a128
5 bb m Street Cry(IRE) —Vertigineux (USA) (Kris S (USA))
(7311a)

Zepnove (IRE) *M Wigham* a62 47
3 b f Noverre(USA) —Royal Zephyr (USA) (Royal Academy (USA))
1574[10] 1953[7] 2169[8] *2487[4]*

Zerkeriya (IRE) *A De Royer-Dupre* 99
3 b f Soviet Star(USA) —Zarkasha (IRE) (Kahyasi)
4969a[4]

Zero Cool (USA) *G L Moore* a83 82
5 br g Forestry(USA) —Fabulous (USA) (Seeking The Gold (USA))
29[4] *483[2]* *706[4]* *872[3]* *1604[6]*

Zero Money (IRE) *R Charlton* a75 79
3 ch g Bachelor Duke(USA) —Dawn Chorus (IRE) (Mukaddamah (USA))
(2151) 6111[3] ◆ 6562[5] *6976[5]*

Zero Seven *C E Brittain* 35
2 b c Halling(USA) —Tempting Fate (IRE) (Persian Bold)
1290[7] 2358[8]

Zerzura *H R A Cecil* a51
3 b g Oasis Dream—River Fantasy (USA) (Irish River (FR))
7882[5]

Zeyadah (IRE) *M A Jarvis* a67 42
3 b f Red Ransom(USA) —Beraysim (Lion Cavern (USA))
1605[5] *3025[2]* *4085[10]*

Zeydnaa (IRE) *C R Wilson* a40 56
9 b g Bahhare(USA) —Hadawah (USA) (Riverman (USA))
2344[13]

Zhukhov (IRE) *T G McCourt* a81 81
6 ch g Allied Forces(USA) —Karameg (IRE) (Danehill (USA))
1375a[8] 7171[5]

Zidane *J R Fanshawe* a94 113
7 b g Danzero(AUS) —Juliet Bravo (Glow (USA))
1299[12] 1868[3] 3141[25] (4516) 5434[5] 6091[19] 6994[13] 7294[16]

Zifron (IRE) *F Caenepeel* a33
2 b c Kheleyf(USA) —Fife (IRE) (Lomond (USA))
3934a[9] 7409a[5]

Ziggy Lee *S C Williams* a80 82
3 b g Lujain(USA) —Mary O'Grady (USA) (Swain (IRE))
154[6] *425[12]* *(1311)* ◆ 2005[2] (2219)

Zilva (USA) *H Graham Motion* a109 87
2 b f Successful Appeal(USA) —Spellmaker (USA) (Storm Cat (USA))
7283a[7]

Zim Ho *J Akehurst* a67
3 b c Zilzal(USA) —Robanna (Robellino (USA))
2300[16] *3982[11]* 4304[12] *4749[8]* *5644[7]* *6777[10]*

Zinjbar (USA) *C E Brittain* a62 72
2 b f Dynaformer(USA) —Renowned Cat (USA) (Storm Cat (USA))
1810[9] 2914[3] 3534[3] *3978[4]* *4647[5]* 6063[4]

Zinzoline (FR) *C Diard*
2 b f Charming Groom(FR) —Trempolinissime (FR) (Trempolino (USA))
7409a[7]

Zip Lock (IRE) *J Noseda* 31
3 b g Invincible Spirit(IRE) —Buckle (IRE) (Common Grounds)
1703[10]

Zipping (AUS) *John D Sadler* 120
8 b g Danehill(USA) —Social Scene (IRE) (Grand Lodge (USA))
7040a[3]

Zip Quik (USA) *Patrick L Biancone* a94 100
2 b c City Zip(USA) —Senita Lane (CAN) (Ascot Knight (CAN))
7304a[11]

Zircjorien (FR) *D Guillemin*
2 b c Majorien—Zircon Lady (FR) (Kings Lake (USA))
7315a[2]

Zizou (IRE) *S Curran* a27 56
6 b g Fantastic Light(USA) —Search Committee (USA) (Roberto (USA))
7766[11]

Zizou Des Fosses (FR) *P Larbodiere* 36
7 b g Pinmix(FR) —Bella Morena (FR) (Port Lyautey (FR))
5074a[5]

Zomerlust *J J Quinn* 98
7 b g Josr Algarhoud(IRE) —Passiflora (Night Shift (USA))
1016[11] 1682[9] 2266[4] 3335[5] (4333) 4996[5] (5363) 6092[6] 6815[11] 7060[8]

Zomorroda (IRE) *R Gibson* 82
2 b f Chineur(FR) —Esterlina (IRE) (Highest Honor (FR))
3934a[2]

Zonic Boom (FR) *Heather Dalton* a56 2
9 bb g Zafonic(USA) —Rosi Zambotti (IRE) (Law Society (USA))
5483[9]

Zouk *W R Swinburn* 70
3 ch g Zilzal(USA) —Annette Vallon (IRE) (Efisio)
1308[4] 1752[5] 2885[7] 3708[5] 5503[3]

Zowington *S C Williams* a29 91
7 gr g Zafonic(USA) —Carmela Owen (Owington)
1150[7] 1572[9] 2053[3] 2549[2] (3057) (3347) 3845[8] 4273[6] 4761[2] 5031[2] 5746[10] 6482[12] 6666[8] 7189[15]

Zubova *M J Attwater* a73 75
2 b f Dubawi(IRE) —Jalousie (IRE) (Barathea (IRE))
4047[2] 4257[4] 4603[3] *7485[3]* *7585[2]* *7690[2]* *7805[2]* *7864[2]*

Zulu Chief (USA) *M F De Kock* a95 106
4 b g Fusaichi Pegasus(USA) —La Lorgnette (CAN) (Val De L'Orne (FR))
5995[5]

Zulu Moon *A M Balding* a71 56
3 b g Passing Glance—Mory Kante (USA) (Icecapade (USA))
1963[4]

Zuwaar *Ian Williams* a78 77
4 b g Nayef(USA) —Raheefa (USA) (Riverman (USA))
(112) *233[5]* *899[8]* (1506) 1878[3] 2194[10] 3593[2] 3850[2] 4332[5] 5252[3] 5530[5] 6021[2] 6280[4] *7578[3]* *7598[3]* *7760[4]*

Zuzu (IRE) *M A Jarvis* 93
3 b f Acclamation—Green Life (Green Desert (USA))
2271[4] 3622[10] 4059[7] 5654[16]

Leading Turf Flat Trainers 2009

(28th March - 7th November 2009)

NAME	WINS-RUNS	2nd	3rd	4th	WIN £	TOTAL £	£1 STAKE
Sir Michael Stoute	99 429 23%	81	57	42	£2,077,609	£3,421,892	-64.76
A P O'Brien	12 78 15%	14	10	6	£1,593,835	£2,984,713	+32.53
M Johnston	214 1214 18%	163	137	128	£1,740,023	£2,833,484	-130.50
R Hannon	188 1365 14%	162	156	152	£1,751,642	£2,812,241	-187.61
Saeed Bin Suroor	148 530 28%	82	72	44	£1,743,062	£2,758,262	+17.67
J H M Gosden	88 514 17%	79	65	55	£1,447,841	£2,308,709	-95.55
B W Hills	87 565 15%	73	70	53	£1,357,837	£1,949,046	-52.61
R A Fahey	164 108415%	137	142	123	£1,121,010	£1,651,517	+44.22
John M Oxx	5 12 42%	0	2	1	£1,599,639	£1,634,280	+7.57
H R A Cecil	62 322 19%	54	47	36	£930,851	£1,388,360	+8.00
W J Haggas	69 345 20%	50	49	39	£793,312	£1,319,411	-52.39
M R Channon	108 1110 10%	134	144	123	£655,057	£1,258,045	-418.19
B J Meehan	61 503 12%	59	58	60	£623,844	£1,227,797	-33.91
M L W Bell	47 369 13%	43	42	49	£793,607	£1,180,870	-97.13
D Nicholls	84 685 12%	74	65	68	£742,938	£1,167,733	-10.59
J Noseda	61 332 18%	47	53	46	£710,380	£1,157,282	-63.89
R M Beckett	56 389 14%	43	46	46	£839,644	£1,054,241	+73.94
K A Ryan	96 858 11%	121	78	80	£603,356	£1,022,124	-304.68
M A Jarvis	71 376 19%	60	37	44	£634,768	£939,952	-42.84
C E Brittain	44 361 12%	36	33	44	£592,748	£888,175	+14.96
C G Cox	51 350 15%	45	44	33	£568,679	£863,588	+68.95
A M Balding	67 496 14%	61	54	51	£458,009	£780,823	-40.77
J L Dunlop	50 366 14%	57	51	32	£445,644	£766,705	-107.86
L M Cumani	48 317 15%	50	30	34	£484,661	£704,993	-79.46
T D Easterby	54 628 9%	50	80	74	£423,562	£691,719	-229.88
P D Evans	109 920 12%	97	94	107	£427,832	£647,218	-32.39
P Chapple-Hyam	35 245 14%	29	21	24	£298,228	£591,693	+16.26
H Morrison	56 431 13%	49	42	55	£391,741	£571,221	+71.13
B Smart	49 470 10%	57	66	51	£287,974	£542,754	-154.73
D M Simcock	42 346 12%	53	35	48	£347,667	£537,980	-79.77
M P Tregoning	30 180 17%	18	23	16	£375,329	£522,133	-38.03
E A L Dunlop	40 408 10%	51	53	41	£289,490	£499,781	-115.08
J R Fanshawe	24 192 13%	21	17	23	£306,666	£490,942	+0.25
P F I Cole	37 404 9%	43	38	47	£204,133	£486,673	-147.07
T D Barron	50 346 14%	39	32	35	£373,503	£481,279	+18.57
K R Burke	38 292 13%	35	39	31	£222,029	£468,431	-28.16
J S Goldie	35 400 9%	38	47	43	£219,096	£423,529	-82.00
Tom Dascombe	56 419 13%	53	42	46	£255,262	£419,056	-109.08
G L Moore	49 532 9%	56	53	63	£248,164	£414,782	-265.63
S A Callaghan	34 217 16%	36	30	16	£109,675	£409,591	-66.29
M Botti	35 282 12%	35	43	33	£216,948	£393,375	-20.52
M Dods	49 424 12%	48	37	46	198,291	£377,052	-96.56
W R Muir	45 356 13%	38	36	31	£210,577	£373,325	+56.49
D R C Elsworth	18 214 8%	20	30	33	£231,641	£367,965	-91.75
R Charlton	35 236 15%	27	42	28	£240,250	£364,855	-38.83
G A Swinbank	49 365 13%	39	42	37	£246,796	£363,784	-57.83
C F Wall	31 234 13%	25	25	19	£252,954	£354,742	-45.75
W R Swinburn	40 394 10%	46	28	51	£182,717	£353,691	-133.38
J S Moore	24 324 7%	33	43	37	£157,412	£316,286	-144.73
J R Boyle	58 423 14%	48	36	36	£230,735	£313,555	+18.34

Leading Turf Flat Jockeys 2009

(28th March - 7th November 2009)

NAME	WIN-RIDES	2nd	3rd	4th	WIN £	TOTAL £	£1 STAKE
Ryan Moore	179 874 20%	140	112	90	£3,097,314	£4,871,255	-157.64
Richard Hughes	144 768 19%	98	92	70	£1,375,507	£2,245,151	+35.38
Jamie Spencer	130 695 19%	110	82	65	£1,070,055	£1,755,946	-111.48
Chris Catlin	121 1261 10%	134	110	125	£507,409	£821,303	-338.29
N Callan	119 881 14%	124	84	91	£1,004,765	£1,539,774	-176.33
Paul Hanagan	119 999 12%	115	128	120	£720,817	£1,188,089	-115.10
Robert Winston	119 906 13%	104	111	93	£495,995	£827,668	-181.58
Jim Crowley	117 1042 11%	109	121	84	£562,128	£1,023,547	-119.00
T P Queally	108 821 13%	93	99	94	£1,472,779	£2,080,319	-35.99
Joe Fanning	108 696 16%	91	72	71	£641,856	£1,111,537	+8.64
Seb Sanders	106 790 13%	77	91	95	£1,063,529	£1,387,967	-69.28
Phillip Makin	106 737 14%	70	78	82	£513,047	£713,545	-143.64
L Dettori	103 429 24%	57	47	45	£1,401,355	£2,267,057	-21.22
R Hills	98 424 23%	70	49	33	£1,986,100	£2,814,792	+26.29
Eddie Ahern	98 689 14%	92	80	79	£872,254	£1,278,942	-77.68
Ted Durcan	94 617 15%	73	73	53	£927,636	£1,321,893	-75.90
Steve Drowne	91 875 10%	82	91	90	£541,011	£877,853	-56.53
Tom Eaves	85 983 9%	91	106	89	£341,264	£696,122	-396.20
Greg Fairley	85 575 15%	67	65	54	£483,192	£685,553	-122.00
Dane O'Neill	83 802 10%	83	88	88	£417,627	£701,953	-134.78
Martin Dwyer	82 764 11%	87	78	83	£561,933	£1,158,276	-117.03
Adam Kirby	82 718 11%	89	82	88	£371,428	£720,863	-105.10
Jimmy Quinn	81 1016 8%	116	121	107	£296,181	£550,356	-298.20
Grah'm Gibbons	80 701 11%	83	65	77	£314,968	£550,506	-10.59
Shane Kelly	77 761 10%	69	101	88	£364,058	£595,998	-260.44
David Probert	77 672 11%	60	71	77	£291,608	£476,633	-0.83
Darryll Holland	74 553 13%	60	52	62	£351,571	£613,672	-91.41
Jimmy Fortune	73 586 12%	70	73	63	£1,336,859	£2,380,045	-106.35
L P Keniry	73 788 9%	69	72	84	£344,042	£507,149	-158.46
Frederik Tylicki	71 495 14%	84	53	44	£392,346	£582,499	-24.85
S De Sousa	68 507 13%	58	45	49	£328,739	£475,209	+70.60
Luke Morris	68 788 9%	61	105	78	£244,199	£387,045	-210.27
William Buick	66 543 12%	57	60	50	£669,705	£977,813	-55.48
Rich. Kingscote	66 536 12%	58	60	56	£287,443	£469,522	-97.04
Fergus Sweeney	64 703 9%	71	71	100	£253,874	£410,392	-269.27
George Baker	63 609 10%	72	66	84	£460,338	£676,008	-211.26
Tony Hamilton	63 613 10%	59	67	56	£280,516	£428,464	-134.78
Pat Cosgrave	61 577 11%	57	44	58	£273,190	£424,271	-95.90
S Donohoe	59 642 9%	64	60	60	£224,005	£427,503	-190.12
Hayley Turner	57 527 11%	71	62	62	£246,499	£472,356	-107.23
Michael Hills	56 386 15%	51	40	39	£628,816	£1,025,908	-110.63
Francis Norton	55 523 11%	54	51	57	£356,600	£555,567	+111.36
Tony Culhane	53 608 9%	70	68	59	£295,885	£501,465	-157.50
Alan Munro	51 592 9%	71	51	61	£307,807	£753,497	-198.61
K Fallon	50 292 17%	37	36	24	£343,696	£556,827	-10.34
T P O'Shea	49 454 11%	38	53	35	£377,915	£568,213	-149.44
Liam Jones	48 588 8%	47	61	67	£262,108	£448,428	-196.12
Paul Mulrennan	48 625 8%	71	58	63	£215,419	£378,691	-259.40
Cath. Gannon	48 508 9%	59	37	65	£169,877	£304,737	+109.45
Micky Fenton	47 538 9%	56	50	49	£378,724	£541,929	-114.61

Leading Flat Owners 2009

(28th March - 7th November 2009)

NAME	WINS-RUNS	2nd	3rd	4th	WIN £	TOTAL £
Hamdan Al Maktoum	134 678 20%	96	86	57	£2,218,058	£3,149,091
Godolphin	148 530 28%	82	72	44	£1,743,062	£2,758,262
K Abdulla	73 310 24%	42	41	29	£1,440,729	£2,074,047
Christopher Tsui	4 4 100%	0	0	0	£1,575,935	£1,575,935
Sh. Hamdan Bin Mohammed	101 500 20%	71	62	46	£750,128	£1,368,028
Ballymacoll Stud	10 47 21%	10	2	7	£703,377	£1,210,417
D Smith, Mrs J Magnier, M Tabor	4 30 13%	7	4	0	£346,834	£989,064
M Tabor, D Smith & Mrs J Magnier	3 19 16%	3	2	2	£653,259	£924,981
Cheveley Park Stud	48 251 19%	50	41	20	£482,764	£896,333
Saeed Manana	35 307 11%	27	32	36	£436,989	£681,782
Mrs J Magnier, M Tabor & D Smith	2 22 9%	3	3	3	£312,235	£632,697
H R H Princess Haya Of Jordan	32 181 18%	29	21	23	£299,297	£619,026
Mrs M E Slade	5 21 24%	6	4	1	£573,985	£597,453
Dr Marwan Koukash	44 336 13%	51	38	37	£333,619	£554,850
Sheikh Ahmed Al Maktoum	20 155 13%	20	22	22	£366,751	£476,933
The Searchers	6 15 40%	3	1	1	£254,167	£384,242
Findlay & Bloom	26 197 13%	19	29	26	£247,369	£376,217
Jaber Abdullah	23 132 17%	25	17	15	£215,799	£371,240
Lady Bamford	5 15 33%	1	3	2	£249,028	£361,080
Patrick J Fahey	4 14 29%	0	3	1	£225,163	£334,307
Mrs J Wood	16 109 15%	9	8	15	£157,510	£328,914
J C Smith	19 169 11%	11	15	29	£197,485	£327,151
Dab Hand Racing	10 38 26%	9	5	2	£246,272	£325,637
The Calvera Partnership No 2	2 13 15%	1	0	5	£224,242	£324,298
R A Green	7 57 12%	6	11	3	£305,615	£319,144
The Queen	20 100 20%	10	15	16	£199,612	£318,949
Mrs P Good	6 37 16%	5	4	2	£113,866	£304,804
Saeed Suhail	12 62 19%	9	13	6	£201,752	£284,464
Jacques Detre	1 1 100%	0	0	0	£255,465	£255,465
Mrs Fitri Hay	10 129 8%	15	8	19	£100,697	£254,148
Lawrie Inman	2 10 20%	1	2	2	£89,764	£253,034
A D Spence	18 164 11%	26	22	15	£133,164	£247,329
Golding, Kirtland & N A Callaghan	0 6	2	1	0	£0	£238,380
George Strawbridge	10 42 24%	7	5	4	£97,777	£235,734
Windflower Overseas Holdings Inc	9 71 13%	13	8	9	£148,271	£235,336
Mr & Mrs R Scott	6 44 14%	9	5	7	£159,224	£234,347
John C Grant	4 23 17%	1	6	2	£197,702	£221,966
James Edgar & William Donaldson	2 6 33%	1	1	1	£158,956	£199,306
Valerie Hubbard & Ian Higginson	6 9 67%	0	2	0	£173,026	£196,512
Normandie Stud Ltd	12 61 20%	8	9	8	£109,924	£196,229
D A West	7 34 21%	6	3	4	£167,474	£190,534
Lord Lloyd-Webber	1 2 50%	1	0	0	£175,987	£189,975
Coleman Bloodstock Limited	3 21 14%	3	5	0	£97,480	£187,202
Elio Anthony Galante & Partners	1 2 50%	0	0	0	£170,310	£170,310
Saleh Al Homaizi & Imad Al Sagar	7 56 13%	8	7	6	£96,189	£167,294
Mrs H Steel	14 45 31%	6	4	1	£120,824	£159,410
Mrs Susan Roy	9 66 14%	9	9	16	£97,210	£157,888
M Barber	10 48 21%	11	5	5	£91,485	£157,820
Sh. Sultan Bin Khalifa Al Nahyan	9 74 12%	11	4	9	£90,321	£156,222

Leading All-Weather Flat Jockeys

(9th Nov 2008 - 27th March 2009)

NAME	WIN-RIDES	2nd	3rd	4th	WIN £	TOTAL £	£1 STAKE
Chris Catlin	67 568 12%	68	73	61	£193,157	£326,134	-183.75
Jamie Spencer	64 249 26%	37	25	27	£293,177	£365,020	-24.34
Luke Morris	47 323 15%	27	50	37	£179,917	£234,422	+7.08
Jim Crowley	42 301 14%	30	50	36	£144,319	£213,505	-17.20
Robert Winston	40 249 16%	28	32	29	£142,368	£185,698	-0.65
Jimmy Quinn	38 354 11%	50	45	37	£108,736	£180,344	-36.33
Greg Fairley	36 167 22%	22	11	15	£147,628	£183,802	+48.33
George Baker	35 224 16%	30	36	34	£128,990	£214,645	-86.75
N Callan	34 184 18%	25	27	20	£134,303	£198,899	-38.38
Adam Kirby	34 276 12%	38	37	29	£106,565	£159,354	-26.01
Joe Fanning	33 145 23%	17	16	15	£102,919	£134,736	+107.06
Dane O'Neill	32 247 13%	34	23	39	£99,400	£156,298	-64.67
Shane Kelly	31 228 14%	32	43	30	£92,651	£151,813	-64.96
Tom Eaves	27 205 13%	16	25	19	£95,892	£125,961	-43.49
Rich. Kingscote	27 137 20%	19	17	11	£88,835	£116,512	-25.10
Grah'm Gibbons	27 193 14%	27	17	25	£71,875	£107,781	+126.71
Hayley Turner	26 275 9%	38	39	34	£97,117	£163,083	-100.62
S Donohoe	26 203 13%	22	19	15	£77,060	£104,604	-20.19
L P Keniry	25 236 11%	18	24	31	£80,575	£112,537	-35.04
Martin Dwyer	25 205 12%	19	23	22	£65,272	£106,216	-59.23
Fergus Sweeney	23 223 10%	22	26	34	£69,320	£124,331	-88.37
Paul Hanagan	21 146 14%	19	16	14	£70,840	£109,769	+108.67
Pat Cosgrave	21 189 11%	24	21	17	£63,794	£104,928	-2.29
T P Queally	21 165 13%	15	15	21	£67,723	£93,605	-7.33
Tony Culhane	18 132 14%	18	13	18	£48,925	£78,747	-20.89
Paul Mulrennan	16 200 8%	30	19	25	£67,280	£103,863	-42.67
Andrea Atzeni	16 129 12%	21	14	13	£63,593	£94,954	-25.84
Micky Fenton	15 175 9%	21	19	18	£125,885	£175,754	-90.92
Darryll Holland	15 84 18%	9	9	11	£43,103	£63,048	-0.57
Eddie Ahern	14 112 13%	16	14	15	£86,527	£133,317	-50.13
Ian Mongan	14 159 9%	20	16	21	£50,918	£86,285	-41.50
Steve Drowne	14 188 7%	20	16	23	£41,520	£68,492	-70.69
Jerry O'Dwyer	13 113 12%	14	8	11	£30,135	£43,785	+12.25
Liam Jones	12 195 6%	18	14	29	£40,451	£66,529	-132.48
Paul Doe	12 119 10%	14	12	9	£33,474	£54,715	-45.38
Amy Baker	12 102 12%	10	10	14	£25,504	£36,089	+5.63
James Doyle	11 147 7%	15	17	14	£28,571	£60,964	-78.50
Francis Norton	11 114 10%	13	11	9	£37,486	£56,261	-49.58
T G McLaughlin	11 143 8%	12	19	15	£25,242	£46,181	-24.00
Nicky Mackay	11 99 11%	12	8	8	£27,883	£41,580	+16.13
M C Geran	10 107 9%	19	11	9	£39,878	£75,893	-40.40
Tolley Dean	10 102 10%	3	7	11	£41,530	£52,268	-17.17
Patrick Donaghy	10 76 13%	10	9	5	£27,404	£39,904	+15.09
Darren Williams	9 121 7%	15	12	14	£23,686	£40,986	-74.68
F McDonald	9 164 5%	10	13	12	£22,291	£34,019	-49.75
Ross Atkinson	9 45 20%	5	4	5	£21,576	£32,474	+5.66
Richard Hughes	8 46 17%	10	5	3	£96,190	£121,197	-6.47

Leading All-Weather Trainers

(9th Nov 2008 - 27th March 2009)

NAME	WINS-RUNS	2nd	3rd	4th	WIN £	TOTAL £	£1 STAKE
M Johnston	51 187 27%	27	14	23	£224,912	£284,585	+38.67
R Hannon	20 170 12%	32	18	19	£174,211	£258,606	-60.25
K A Ryan	34 189 18%	31	26	24	£118,939	£189,815	-68.53
C E Brittain	15 64 23%	2	9	10	£125,948	£142,919	+36.99
M Botti	14 80 18%	15	12	12	£89,992	£131,479	-3.50
P Howling	19 158 12%	16	23	19	£81,661	£126,832	-13.17
J R Boyle	23 146 16%	25	18	13	£82,846	£124,505	-10.69
R Hollinshead	22 143 15%	18	18	18	£92,785	£121,538	+27.96
G L Moore	28 198 14%	21	21	30	£76,465	£117,888	-80.31
P D Evans	26 257 10%	31	29	34	£72,788	£111,753	-63.40
T D Barron	15 69 22%	9	8	7	£90,977	£109,612	+22.88
Tom Dascombe	25 94 27%	16	10	5	£83,487	£104,643	-1.71
M R Channon	21 128 16%	20	17	21	£55,442	£94,661	-19.41
A J McCabe	19 161 12%	16	24	10	£64,656	£91,584	-38.75
R A Harris	19 198 10%	25	26	20	£50,697	£87,627	-87.33
J H M Gosden	7 37 19%	5	4	5	£68,687	£87,539	-14.07
S Parr	16 205 8%	21	23	19	£53,142	£83,301	-81.25
G A Butler	2 21 10%	5	5	2	£45,416	£80,721	-11.75
K R Burke	15 117 13%	12	17	10	£39,738	£75,272	-46.27
S A Callaghan	13 68 19%	13	11	9	£49,374	£75,168	-17.39
R A Fahey	14 112 13%	12	18	11	£50,045	£74,618	+36.54
A B Coogan	5 14 36%	2	3	1	£60,722	£72,246	+6.75
C F Wall	3 17 18%	4	2	1	£33,209	£70,780	-8.76
M A Jarvis	13 49 27%	4	11	9	£55,543	£70,136	-4.95
T P Tate	5 11 45%	4	1	0	£50,595	£70,123	+10.25
J Pearce	18 118 15%	25	10	20	£45,471	£68,338	-20.38
Stef Liddiard	7 57 12%	6	8	8	£50,737	£65,092	-5.50
R J Hodges	7 47 15%	10	3	3	£38,150	£63,859	-5.62
J R Gask	14 78 18%	9	11	9	£44,199	£61,661	-10.91
J A Osborne	13 110 12%	17	29	10	£31,592	£58,472	-18.17
D Shaw	13 165 8%	22	21	18	£29,073	£58,343	-80.54
A W Carroll	17 126 13%	10	21	14	£39,834	£58,153	-6.13
J S Moore	9 73 12%	5	14	15	£40,352	£56,577	+1.65
S Kirk	14 84 17%	16	9	5	£36,693	£56,297	+36.25
Edward Lynam	2 4 50%	1	0	0	£45,416	£54,024	+4.63
D M Simcock	11 63 17%	7	6	6	£40,738	£53,357	+0.49
C R Dore	11 105 10%	5	7	22	£38,426	£52,235	-35.79
W J Knight	9 17 53%	2	2	0	£45,085	£51,133	+13.15
D R C Elsworth	10 62 16%	8	9	6	£29,480	£51,108	-16.93
Miss G Kelleway	12 147 8%	18	15	14	£26,323	£49,194	-73.13
M J Attwater	11 84 13%	5	14	6	£34,433	£47,562	-7.15
W M Brisbourne	12 129 9%	12	16	16	£29,494	£46,938	-61.75
P W Hiatt	16 100 16%	7	8	14	£35,017	£44,835	+36.46
I Semple	4 35 11%	5	2	3	£34,647	£44,605	+2.00
M Bradley	9 166 5%	18	25	23	£22,882	£42,976	-104.25
M Wigham	9 66 14%	14	9	3	£27,878	£42,046	-6.54
J Noseda	11 32 34%	5	5	4	£30,169	£41,890	+19.83
D Nicholls	8 34 24%	8	3	3	£30,479	£41,050	+7.71

Racing Post top rated 2009

(Best performance figures recorded between 1st January and 31st December 2009)

Sea The Stars (IRE)	138
Rip Van Winkle (IRE)	132
Goldikova (IRE)	131
Fame And Glory	131
Gladiatorus (USA)	129
Mastercraftsman (IRE)	129
Rachel Alexandra (USA)	129
Well Armed (USA)	128
Zenyatta (USA)	128
Company (JPN)	127
Conduit (IRE)	127
Gio Ponti (USA)	127
Scenic Blast (AUS)	127
Macho Again (USA)	127
Summer Bird (USA)	127
Paco Boy (IRE)	126
Yeats (IRE)	125
Youmzain (IRE)	125
Racing To Win (AUS)	125
Sacred Kingdom (AUS)	125
Aqlaam	125
Twice Over	125
Tartan Bearer (IRE)	125
Zacinto	125
Cavalryman	125
Quality Road (USA)	125
Rail Trip (USA)	125
Ask	124
Getaway (GER)	124
Viewed (AUS)	124
Big City Man (USA)	124
Vision D Etat (FR)	124
Deep Sky (JPN)	124
Bullsbay (USA)	124
California Flag (USA)	124
Zensational (USA)	124
Commentator (USA)	123
Grand Couturier	123
Monterey Jazz (USA)	123
Kingsgate Native (IRE)	123
Fleeting Spirit (IRE)	123
Kodiak Kowboy (USA)	123
Casual Conquest (IRE)	123
Main Aim	123
Never On Sunday (FR)	123
Screen Hero (JPN)	123
Music Note (USA)	123
Delegator	123
Vineyard Haven (USA)	123
Capt. Candyman Can (USA)	123
Sariska	123
St Nicholas Abbey (IRE)	123
Vermilion (JPN)	122
Super Hornet (JPN)	122
Fabulous Strike (USA)	122
Presious Passion (USA)	122
Ventura (USA)	122
Vodka (JPN)	122
Dream Journey (JPN)	122
Presvis	122
Matsurida Gogh (JPN)	122
Famous Name	122
Icon Project (USA)	122
Bronze Cannon (USA)	122
Mawatheeq (USA)	122
Jay Peg (SAF)	122
Game Face (USA)	122
Two Step Salsa (USA)	122
Gitano Hernando	122
Russian Sage (SAF)	122
Oken Bruce Lee (JPN)	122
Richard s Kid (USA)	122
Stacelita (FR)	122
Wiener Walzer (GER)	122
Courageous Cat (USA)	122
Geordieland (FR)	121
Viva Pataca	121
Cesare	121
Borderlescott	121
Takeover Target (AUS)	121
Apache Cat (AUS)	121
Champs Elysees	121
Scenic Shot (AUS)	121
Spanish Moon (USA)	121
Einstein (BRZ)	121
Kirklees (IRE)	121
Schiaparelli (GER)	121
Utmost Respect	121
Regal Parade	121
Collection (IRE)	121
Asakusa Kings (JPN)	121
Albertus Maximus (USA)	121
Patkai (IRE)	121
Cannonball (USA)	121
Colonel John (USA)	121
Gayego (USA)	121
Total Gallery (IRE)	121
Kite Wood (IRE)	121

Raceform median times 2009

ASCOT

5f 1m 0.5
5f 110y..........1m 07.5
6f 1m 14.4
6f 110y..........1m 21.8
7f 1m 28.0
1m Str..........1m 40.6
1m Rnd..........1m 40.7
1m 2f 2m 7.0
1m 4f 2m 32.5
2m 3m 29.0
2m 4f 4m 21.0
2m 5f 194y..........4m 56.5

AYR

5f 1m 0.1
6f 1m 13.6
7f 50y..........1m 33.4
1m 1m 43.8
1m 1f 20y..........1m 58.4
1m 2f 2m 12.0
1m 5f 13y..........2m 54.0
1m 7f 3m 20.4
2m 1f 105y..........4m 0.5

BATH

5f 11y..........1m 2.5
5f 161y..........1m 11.2
1m 5y..........1m 40.8
1m 2f 46y..........2m 11.0
1m 3f 144y..........2m 30.6
1m 5f 22y..........2m 52.0
2m 1f 34y..........3m 51.9

BEVERLEY

5f 1m 3.5
7f 100y..........1m 33.8
1m 100y..........1m 47.6
1m 1f 207y..........2m 7.0
1m 4f 16y..........2m 40.9
2m 35y..........3m 39.8

BRIGHTON

5f 59y..........1m 2.3
5f 213y..........1m 10.2
6f 209y..........1m 23.1
7f 214y..........1m 36.0
1m 1f 209y..........2m 3.6
1m 3f 196y..........2m 32.7

CARLISLE

5f 1m 0.8
5f 193y..........1m 13.7
6f 192y..........1m 27.1
7f 200y..........1m 40.0
1m 1f 61y..........1m 57.6
1m 3f 107y..........2m 23.1
1m 6f 32y..........3m 7.5
2m 1f 52y..........3m 53.0

CATTERICK

5f 59.8s
5f 212y..........1m 13.6
7f 1m 27.0
1m 3f 214y..........2m 38.9
1m 5f 175y..........3m 3.6
1m 7f 177y..........3m 32.0

CHEPSTOW

5f 16y..........59.3s
6f 16y..........1m 12.0
7f 16y..........1m 23.2
1m 14y..........1m 36.2
1m 2f 36y..........2m 10.6
1m 4f 23y..........2m 39.0
2m 49y..........3m 38.9
2m 2f 4m 3.6

CHESTER

5f 16y..........1m 1.0
6f 18y..........1m 13.8
7f 2y..........1m 26.5
7f 122y..........1m 33.8
1m 2f 75y..........2m 12.2
1m 3f 79y..........2m 26.6
1m 4f 66y..........2m 39.9
1m 5f 89y..........2m 53.2
1m 7f 195y..........3m 28.0
2m 2f 147y..........4m 4.8

DONCASTER

5f 1m 0.5
5f 140y..........1m 8.5
6f 1m 13.6
6f 110y..........1m 19.9
7f 1m 26.3
1m Str..........1m 39.3
1m Rnd..........1m 39.7
1m 2f 60y..........2m 11.2
1m 4f 2m 35.1
1m 6f 132y..........3m 6.7
2m 110y..........3m 40.4
2m 2f 3m 58.2

EPSOM

5f 55.7s
6f 1m 9.4
7f 1m 23.3
1m 114y..........1m 46.1
1m 2f 18y..........2m 9.7
1m 4f 10y..........2m 38.9

FOLKESTONE

5f 1m
6f 1m 12.7
7f 1m 27.3
1m 1f 149y..........2m 4.9
1m 4f 2m 40.9
1m 7f 92y..........3m 29.7
2m 93y..........3m 37.2

GOODWOOD

5f 58.4s
6f 1m 12.2
7f 1m 27.4
1m 1m 39.9
1m 1f 1m 56.3
1m 1f 192y..........2m 8.0
1m 3f 2m 28.3
1m 4f 2m 38.4
1m 6f 3m 3.6
2m 3m 29.0
2m 5f 4m 33.1

HAMILTON

5f 4y..........1m
6f 5y..........1m 12.2
1m 65y..........1m 48.4
1m 1f 36y..........1m 59.7
1m 3f 16y..........2m 25.6
1m 4f 17y..........2m 38.6
1m 5f 9y..........2m 53.9

HAYDOCK

5f (inner)..........1m 1.1
5f (outer)..........1m 0.5
6f (inner)..........1m 14.5
6f (outer)..........1m 14.0
7f 30y..........1m 30.2
1m 30y..........1m 43.8
1m 2f 95y..........2m 13.0
1m 3f 200y..........2m 33.2
1m 6f 3m 4.3
2m 45y..........3m 36.0

KEMPTON AW

5f 1m 0.5
6f 1m 13.1
7f 1m 26.0
1m 1m 39.8
1m 1f 1m 55.8
1m 2f 2m 8.0
1m 3f 2m 21.9
1m 4f 2m 34.5
2m 3m 30.1

LEICESTER

5f 2y..........1m
5f 218y..........1m 13.0
7f 9y..........1m 26.2
1m 60y..........1m 45.1
1m 1f 218y..........2m 7.9
1m 3f 183y..........2m 33.9

LINGFIELD TURF

5f 58.2s
6f 1m 11.2
7f 1m 23.3
7f 140y..........1m 32.3
1m 1f 1m 56.6
1m 2f 2m 10.5
1m 3f 106y..........2m 31.5
1m 6f 3m 10.0
2m 3m 34.8

LINGFIELD AW

5f 58.8s
6f 1m 11.9
7f 1m 24.8
1m 1m 38.2
1m 2f 2m 6.6
1m 4f 2m 33.0
1m 5f 2m 46.0
2m 3m 25.7

MUSSELBURGH

5f 1m 0.4
7f 30y..........1m 30.3
1m 1m 41.2
1m 1f 1m 54.7
1m 4f 2m 39.7
1m 4f 100y..........2m 42.0
1m 5f 2m 52.0
1m 6f 3m 5.3
2m 3m 36.1

NEWBURY

5f 34y..........1m 1.4
6f 8y..........1m 13.0
6f 110y..........1m 19.3
7f 1m 25.7
1m 1m 39.7
1m 1f 1m 55.5
1m 2f 6y..........2m 8.8
1m 3f 5y..........2m 21.2
1m 4f 5y..........2m 35.5
1m 5f 61y..........2m 52.0
2m 3m 32.0

NEWCASTLE

5f 1m 0.7
6f 1m 15.2
7f 1m 28.7
1m Rnd..........1m 45.3
1m 3y Str..........1m 43.2
1m 1f 9y..........1m 58.1
1m 2f 32y..........2m 11.9
1m 4f 93y..........2m 45.6
1m 6f 97y..........3m 11.3
2m 19y..........3m 36.2

NEWMARKET ROWLEY

5f 59.1s
6f 1m 12.2
7f 1m 25.4
1m 1m 38.6
1m 1f 1m 51.7
1m 2f 2m 5.8
1m 4f 2m 33.5

1m 6f 2m 58.5
2m 3m 30.8
2m 2f 3m 54.8

NEWMARKET JULY

5f 59.1s
6f 1m 12.5
7f 1m 25.7
1m 1m 40.0
1m 2f 2m 5.5
1m 4f 2m 32.9
1m5f 2m 44.0
1m 6f 175y...............3m 11.3
2m 24y......................3m 27.0

NOTTINGHAM

Due to reconfiguration of the track there is currently insufficient data to calculate median times.

PONTEFRACT

5f 1m 3.3
6f 1m 16.9
1m 4y........................1m 45.9
1m 2f 6y....................2m 13.7
1m 4f 8y....................2m 40.8
2m 1f 22y..................3m 50.0
2m 1f 216y................4m 3.9
2m 5f 122y................5m 8.8

REDCAR

5f 58.6s
6f 1m 11.8
7f 1m 24.5
1m 1m 38.0
1m 1f 1m 53.0
1m 2f 2m 7.1
1m 3f 2m 21.7
1m 6f 19y..................3m 4.7
2m 4y........................3m 31.4

RIPON

5f 1m 0.7
6f 1m 13.0
1m 1m 41.4
1m 1f 1m 54.7
1m 1f 170y................2m 5.4
1m 4f 10y..................2m 36.7
2m 3m 31.8

SALISBURY

5f 1m 0.8
6f 1m 14.8
6f 212y......................1m 29.0
1m 1m 43.5
1m 1f 198y................2m 9.9
1m 4f 2m 38.0
1m 6f 21y..................3m 7.4

SANDOWN

5f 6y..........................1m 1.6
7f 16y........................1m 29.5
1m 14y......................1m 43.3
1m 1f 1m 56.3
1m 2f 7y....................2m 10.5
1m 6f 3m 6.6
2m 78y......................3m 38.7

SOUTHWELL TURF

6f 1m 15.8
7f 1m 29.4
1m 2f 2m 13.1
1m 3f 2m 27.8
1m 4f 2m 41.7
2m 3m 38.6

SOUTHWELL AW

5f 59.7s
6f 1m 16.5
7f 1m 30.3
1m 1m 43.7
1m 3f 2m 28.0
1m 4f 2m 41.0
1m 6f 3m 8.3
2m 3m 45.5

THIRSK

5f 59.6s
6f 1m 12.7
7f 1m 27.2
1m 1m 40.1
1m 4f 2m 36.2
2m 3m 32.8

WARWICK

5f 59.6s
5f 110y......................1m 5.9
6f 1m 11.8
7f 26y........................1m 24.6
1m 22y......................1m 41.0
1m 2f 188y................2m 21.1
1m 4f 134y................2m 44.6
1m 6f 213y................3m 19.0
2m 39y......................3m 33.8

WINDSOR

5f 10y........................1m 0.3
6f 1m 13.0
1m 67y......................1m 44.7
1m 2f 7y....................2m 8.7
1m 3f 135y................2m 29.5

WOLVERHAMPTON AW

5f 20y........................1m 2.3
5f 216y......................1m 15.0
7f 32y........................1m 29.6
1m 141y....................1m 50.5
1m 1f 103y................2m 1.7
1m 4f 50y..................2m 41.1
1m 5f 194y................3m 6.0
2m 119y....................3m 41.8

YARMOUTH

5f 43y........................1m 2.2
6f 3y..........................1m 14.4
7f 3y..........................1m 26.6
1m 3y........................1m 40.6
1m 2f 21y..................2m 10.5
1m 3f 101y................2m 28.7
1m 6f 17y..................3m 7.6
2m 3m 34.6

YORK

5f 59.3s
5f 89y........................1m 4.3
6f 1m 11.9
7f 1m 25.3
1m 1m 38.8
1m 208y....................1m 52.0
1m 2f 88y..................2m 12.5
1m 4f 2m 33.2
1m 6f 3m 0.2
2m 88y......................3m 34.5
2m 2f 3m 58.4

Raceform Flat record times

ASCOT

Distance	Time	Age	Weight	Going	Horse	Date
5f	59.77 sec	2	9-3	Gd To Firm	Drawnfromthepast(IRE)	Jun 19 2007
5f	57.44 sec	6	9-1	Gd To Firm	Miss Andretti (AUS)	Jun 19 2007
6f	1m 12.46	2	9-1	Gd To Firm	Henrythenavigator(USA)	Jun 19 2007
6f	1m 12.46	2	9-1	Gd To Firm	Henrythenavigator(USA)	Jun 19 2007
7f	1m 26.76	2	7-12	Gd To Firm	Relative Order	Aug 11 2007
7f	1m 25.89	4	8-9	Gd To Firm	Dabbers Ridge (IRE)	Jly 29 2006
7f	1m 25.89	6	8-12	Good	Advanced	Sept 26 2009
1m (R)	1m 39.55	2	8-12	Good	Joshua Tree (IRE)	Sep 26 2009
1m (R)	1m 38.32	3	9-0	Gd To Firm	Ghanaati (USA)	Jun 19 2009
1m (S)	1m 37.21	5	9-0	Gd To Firm	Ramonti (FR)	Jun 19 2007
1m 2f	2m 3.24	4	9-5	Gd To Firm	Perfect Stride	Jun 19 2009
1m 4f	2m 27.24	3	8-9	Gd To Firm	Linas Selection	Jun 23 2006
2m	3m 24.13	3	9-1	Gd To Firm	Holberg (UAE)	Sept 16 2009
2m 4f	4m 18.29	8	9-1	Gd To Firm	Full House (IRE)	Jun 19 2007
2m 5f 159y	4m 49.07	4	9-5	Gd To Firm	Honolulu (IRE)	Jun 21 2008

AYR

Distance	Time	Age	Weight	Going	Horse	Date
5f	56.9 secs	2	8-11	Good	Boogie Street	Sep 18 2003
5f	55.68 secs	3	8-11	Gd to Firm	Look Busy (IRE)	Jun 21 2008
6f	69.7 secs	2	7-10	Good	Sir Bert	Sep 17 1969
6f	68.37 secs	5	8-6	Gd to Firm	Maison Dieu	Jun 21 2008
7f	1m 25.7	2	9-0	Gd to Firm	Jazeel	Sep 16 1993
7f	1m 24.9	5	7-11	Firm	Sir Arthur Hobbs	Jun 19 1992
7f 50y	1m 28.9	2	9-0	Good	Tafaahum (USA)	Sep 19 2003
7f 50y	1m 28.2	4	9-2	Gd to Firm	Flur Na H Alba	Jun 21 2003
1m	1m 39.2	2	9-0	Gd to Firm	Kribensis	Sep 17 1986
1m	1m 36.0	4	7-13	Firm	Sufi	Sep 16 1959
1m 1f 20y	1m 50.3	4	9-3	Good	Retirement	Sep 19 2003
1m 2f	2m 4.0	4	9-9	Gd to Firm	Endless Hall	Jly 17 2000
1m 2f192y	2m 13.3	4	9-0	Gd to Firm	Azzaam	Sep 18 1991
1m 5f 13y	2m 45.8	4	9-7	Gd to Firm	Eden s Close	Sep 18 1993
1m 7f	3m 13.1	3	9-4	Good	Romany Rye	Sep 19 1991
2m 1f105y	3m 45.0	4	6-13	Good	Curry	Sep 16 1955

BATH

Distance	Time	Age	Weight	Going	Horse	Date
5f 11y	59.50 secs	2	9-2	Firm	Amour Propre	Jly 24 2008
5f 11y	58.75 secs	3	8-12	Firm	Enticing (IRE)	May 1 2007
5f 161y	68.70 secs	2	8-12	Firm	Qalahari (IRE)	Jly 24 2008
5f 161y	68.1 secs	6	9-0	Firm	Madraco	May 22 1989
1m 5y	1m 39.7	2	8-9	Firm	Casual Look	Sep 16 2002
1m 5y	1m 37.2	5	8-12	Gd to Firm	Adobe	Jun 17 2000
1m 5y	1m 37.2	3	8-7	Firm	Alasha (IRE)	Aug 18 2002
1m 2f 46y	2m 5.8	3	9-0	Gd to Firm	Connoisseur Bay(USA)	May 29 1998
1m 3f144y	2m 25.74	3	9-0	Hard	Top Of The Charts	Sep 8 2005
1m 5f 22y	2m 47.2	4	10-0	Firm	Flown	Aug 13 1991
2m 1f 34y	3m 43.4	6	7-9	Firm	Yaheska (IRE)	Jun 14 2003

BEVERLEY

Distance	Time	Age	Weight	Going	Horse	Date
5f	61.0 secs	2	8-2	Gd to Firm	Addo (IRE)	Jly 17 2001
5f	60.1 secs	4	9-5	Firm	Pic Up Sticks	Apr 16 2003
7f 100y	1m 31.1	2	9-7	Gd to Firm	Champagne Prince	Aug 10 1995
7f 100y	1m 31.1	2	9-0	Firm	Majal (IRE)	Jly 30 1991
7f 100y	1m 29.5	3	7-8	Firm	Who s Tef	Jly 30 1991
1m 100y	1m 43.3	2	9-0	Firm	Arden	Sep 24 1986
1m 100y	1m 42.2	3	8-4	Firm	Legal Case	Jun 14 1989
1m 1f 207y	2m 1.00	3	9-7	Gd to Firm	Eastern Aria (UAE)	Aug 29 2009
1m 3f 216y	2m 30.8	3	8-1	Hard	Coinage	Jun 18 1986
1m 4f 16y	2m 34.88	6	10-0	Firm	WeeCharlieCastle(IRE)	Aug 30 2009
2m 35y	3m 29.5	4	9-2	Gd to Firm	Rushen Raider	Aug 14 1996

BRIGHTON

Distance	Time	Age	Weight	Going	Horse	Date
5f 59y	60.1 secs	2	9-0	Firm	Bid for Blue	May 6 1993
5f 59y	59.3 secs	3	8-9	Firm	Play Hever Golf	May 26 1993
5f 213y	68.1 secs	2	8-9	Firm	Song Mist (IRE)	Jly 16 1996
5f 213y	67.3 secs	3	8-9	Firm	Third Party	Jun 3 1997
5f 213y	67.3 secs	5	9-1	Gd to Firm	Blundell Lane	May 4 2000
6f 209y	1m 19.9	2	8-11	Hard	Rain Burst	Sep 15 1988
6f 209y	1m 19.4	4	9-3	Gd to Firm	Sawaki	Sep 3 1991
7f 214y	1m 32.8	2	9-7	Firm	Asian Pete	Oct 3 1989
7f 214y	1m 30.5	5	8-11	Firm	Mystic Ridge	May 27 1999
1m 1f 209y	2m 4.7	2	9-0	Gd to Soft	Esteemed Master	Nov 2 2001
1m 1f 209y	1m 57.2	3	9-0	Firm	Get The Message	Apr 30 1984
1m 3f 196y	2m 25.8	4	8-2	Firm	New Zealand	Jly 4 1985

CARLISLE

Distance	Time	Age	Weight	Going	Horse	Date
5f	60.1 secs	2	8-5	Firm	La Tortuga	Aug 2 1999
5f	58.8 secs	3	9-8	Gd to Firm	Esatto	Aug 21 2002
5f 193y	1m 12.45	2	9-6	Gd to Firm	Musical Guest (IRE)	Sep 11 2005
5f 193y	1m 10.83	4	9-0	Gd to Firm	Bo McGinty (IRE)	Sep 11 2005
6f 192y	1m 24.3	3	8-9	Gd to Firm	Marjurita (IRE)	Aug 21 2002
6f 206y	1m 26.5	2	9-4	Hard	Sense of Priority	Sep 10 1991
6f 206y	1m 25.3	4	9-1	Firm	Move With Edes	Jly 6 1996
7f 200y	1m 37.34	5	9-7	Gd to Firm	Hula Ballew	Aug 17 2005
7f 214y	1m 44.6	2	8-8	Firm	Blue Garter	Sep 9 1980
7f 214y	1m 37.3	5	7-12	Hard	Thatched (IRE)	Aug 21 1995
1m 1f 61y	1m 53.8	3	9-0	Firm	Little Jimbob	Jun 14 2004
1m 3f 107y	2m 22.25	5	9-6	Gd to Firm	Overrule (USA)	Jun 24 2009
1m 4f	2m 28.8	3	8-5	Firm	Desert Frolic (IRE)	Jun 27 1996
1m 6f 32y	3m 2.2	6	8-10	Firm	Explosive Speed	May 26 1994
2m 1f 52y	3m 46.2	3	7-10	Gd to Firm	Warring Kingdom	Aug 25 1999

CATTERICK

Distance	Time	Age	Weight	Going	Horse	Date
5f	57.6 secs	2	9-0	Firm	H Harrison	Oct 8 2002
5f	57.1 secs	4	8-7	Fast	Kabcast	Jly 7 1989
5f 212y	1m 11.4	2	9-4	Firm	Captain Nick	Jly 11 1978
5f 212y	69.8 secs	9	8-13	Gd to Firm	Sharp Hat	May 30 2003
7f	1m 24.1	2	8-11	Firm	Lindas Fantasy	Sep 18 1982
7f	1m 22.5	6	8-7	Firm	Differential (USA)	May 31 2003
1m 3f 214y	2m 30.5	3	8-8	Gd to Firm	Rahaf	May 30 2003
1m 5f 175y	2m 54.8	3	8-5	Firm	Geryon	May 31 1984
1m 7f 177y	3m 20.8	4	7-11	Firm	Bean Boy	Jly 8 1982

CHEPSTOW

Distance	Time	Age	Weight	Going	Horse	Date
5f 16y	57.6 secs	2	8-11	Firm	Micro Love	Jly 8 1986
5f 16y	56.8 secs	3	8-4	Firm	Torbay Express	Sep 15 1979
6f 16y	69.4 secs	2	9-0	Fast	Royal Fifi	Sep 9 1989
6f 16y	68.1 secs	3	9-7	Firm	America Calling (USA)	Sep 18 2001
7f 16y	1m 20.8	2	9-0	Gd to Firm	Royal Amaretto (IRE)	Sep 12 1996
7f 16y	1m 19.3	3	9-0	Firm	Taranaki	Sep 18 2001
1m 14y	1m 33.1	2	8-11	Gd to Firm	Ski Academy (IRE)	Aug 28 1995
1m 14y	1m 31.6	3	8-13	Firm	Stoli (IRE)	Sep 18 2001
1m 2f 36y	2m 4.1	5	8-9	Hard	Leonidas	Jly 5 1983
1m 2f 36y	2m 4.1	5	7-8	Gd to Firm	It s Varadan	Sep 9 1989
1m 2f 36y	2m 4.1	3	8-5	Gd to Firm	Ela Athena	Jly 23 1999
1m 4f 23y	2m 31.0	3	8-9	Gd to Firm	Spritsail	Jly 13 1989
1m 4f 23y	2m 31.0	7	9-6	Hard	Maintop	Aug 27 1984
2m 49y	3m 27.7	4	9-0	Gd to Firm	Wizzard Artist	Jly 1 1989
2m 2f	3m 56.4	5	8-7	Gd to Firm	Laffah	Jly 8 2000

CHESTER

Distance	Time	Age	Weight	Going	Horse	Date
5f 16y	60.06 secs	2	8-9	Gd to Firm	Not For Me (IRE)	Jly 14 2006
5f 16y	59.2 secs	3	10-0	Firm	Althrey Don	Jly 10 1964
6f 18y	1m 12.8	2	8-10	Gd to Firm	Flying Express	Aug 31 2002
6f 18y	1m 12.7	3	8-3	Gd to Firm	Play Hever Golf	May 4 1993
6f 18y	1m 12.7	6	9-2	Good	Stack Rock	Jun 23 1993
7f 2y	1m 25.2	2	9-0	Gd to Firm	Due Respect (IRE)	Sep 25 2002
7f 2y	1m 23.75	5	8-13	Gd to Firm	Three Graces (GER)	Jly 9 2005
7f 122y	1m 32.2	2	9-0	Gd to Firm	Big Bad Bob (IRE)	Sep 25 2002
7f 122y	1m 30.91	3	8-12	Gd to Firm	Cupid's Glory	Aug 18 2005
1m 2f 75y	2m 7.15	3	8-8	Gd to Firm	Stotsfold	May 7 2002
1m 3f 79y	2m 22.17	3	8-12	Gd to Firm	Perfect Truth (IRE)	May 6 2009
1m 4f 66y	2m 33.7	3	8-10	Gd to Firm	Fight Your Corner	May 7 2002
1m 5f 89y	2m 45.4	5	8-11	Firm	Rakaposhi King	May 7 1987
1m 7f 195y	3m 20.3	4	9-0	Gd to Firm	Grand Fromage (IRE)	Jly 13 2002
2m 2f 147y	3m 58.89	7	9-2	Gd to Firm	Greenwich Meantime	May 9 2007

DONCASTER

Distance	Time	Age	Weight	Going	Horse	Date
5f	58.1 secs	2	8-11	Gd to Firm	Sand Vixen	Sep 11 2009
5f	57.2 secs	6	9-12	Gd to Firm	Celtic Mill	Sep 9 2004
5f 140y	67.2 secs	2	9-0	Gd to Firm	Cartography (IRE)	Jun 29 2003
5f 140y	65.6 secs	9	9-10	Good	Halmahera (IRE)	Sep 8 2004
6f	69.6 secs	2	8-11	Good	Caesar Beware (IRE)	Sep 8 2004
6f	69.56 secs	3	8-10	Gd to Firm	Proclaim	May 30 2009
6f 110y	1m 17.22	2	8-3	Gd to Firm	Swilly Ferry (USA)	Sep 10 2009
7f	1m 22.6	2	9-1	Good	Librettist (USA)	Sep 8 2004
7f	1m 21.6	3	8-10	Gd to Firm	Pastoral Pursuits	Sep 9 2004
1m	1m 36.5	2	8-6	Gd to Firm	Singhalese	Sep 9 2004
1m (R)	1m 35.4	2	8-10	Good	Playful Act (IRE)	Sep 9 2004
1m	1m 35.52	4	8-9	Gd to Firm	Dream Lodge	Jly 24 2008
1m (R)	1m 34.46	4	8-12	Gd to Firm	Staying On (IRE)	Apr 18 2009
1m 2f 60y	2m 13.4	2	8-8	Good	Yard Bird	Nov 6 1981
1m 2f 60y	2m 4.81	4	8-13	Gd to Firm	Red Gala	Sep 12 2007
1m 4f	2m 27.7	3	8-12	Gd to Firm	Takwin (IRE)	Sep 9 2000

1m 6f 132y	3m 1.07	3	8-7	Gd to Firm	Hi Calypso (IRE)	Sep 13 2007
2m 2f	3m 48.41	4	9-4	Gd to Firm	Septimus (IRE)	Sep 14 2007

EPSOM

Distance	Time	Age	Weight	Going	Horse	Date
5f	55.0 secs	2	8-9	Gd to Firm	Prince Aslia	Jun 9 1995
5f	53.6 secs	4	9-5	Firm	Indigenous	Jun 2 1960
6f	67.8 secs	2	8-11	Gd to Firm	Showbrook	Jun 5 1991
6f	67.21 secs	5	9-13	Gd to Firm	Mac Gille Eoin	Jul 2 2009
7f	1m 21.3	2	8-9	Gd to Firm	Red Peony	Jly 29 2004
7f	1m 20.1	4	8-7	Firm	Capistrano	Jun 7 1972
1m 114y	1m 42.8	2	8-5	Gd to Firm	Nightstalker	Aug 30 1988
1m 114y	1m 40.7	3	8-6	Gd to Firm	Sylva Honda	Jun 5 1991
1m 2f 18y	2m 3.5	5	7-13	Good	Crossbow	Jun 7 1967
1m 4f 10y	2m 32.3	3	9-0	Gd to Firm	Lammtarra	Jun 10 1995

FOLKESTONE

Distance	Time	Age	Weight	Going	Horse	Date
5f	58.4 secs	2	9-2	Gd to Firm	Pivotal	Nov 6 1995
5f	58.22 secs	7	8-11	Gd to Firm	Green Lagonda(AUS)	Jul 9 2009
6f	1m 10.8	2	8-9	Good	Boomerang Blade	Jly 16 1998
6f	69.38 secs	4	9-8	Gd to Firm	Munaddam (USA)	Sep 18 2006
6f 189y	1m 23.7	2	8-11	Good	Hen Harrier	Jly 3 1996
6f 189y	1m 21.4	3	8-9	Firm	Cielamour (USA)	Aug 9 1988
7f	1m 25.01	2	9-0	Gd to Firm	Dona Alba (IRE)	Sep 2 2007
7f	1m 23.76	3	8-11	Gd to Firm	Welsh Cake	Sep 18 2006
1m 1f 149y	1m 59.7	3	8-6	Gd to Firm	Dizzy	Jly 23 1991
1m 4f	2m 33.2	4	8-8	Hard	Snow Blizzard	Jun 30 1992
1m 7f 92y	3m 23.1	3	9-11	Firm	Mata Askari	Sep 12 1991
2m 93y	3m 34.9	3	8-12	Gd to Firm	Candle Smoke (USA)	Aug 20 1996

GOODWOOD

Distance	Time	Age	Weight	Going	Horse	Date
5f	57.5 secs	2	8-12	Gd to Firm	Poets Cove	Aug 3 1990
5f	56.0 secs	5	9-0	Gd to Firm	Rudi s Pet	Jly 27 1999
6f	69.8 secs	2	8-11	Gd to Firm	Bachir (IRE)	Jly 28 1999
6f	69.10 secs	6	9-10	Gd to Firm	Tamagin (USA)	Sep 12 2009
7f	1m 24.9	2	8-11	Gd to Firm	Ekraar	Jly 29 1999
7f	1m 23.8	3	8-7	Firm	Brief Glimpse (IRE)	Jly 25 1995
1m	1m 37.21	2	9-0	Good	Caldra (IRE)	Sep 9 2006
1m	1m 35.6	3	8-13	Gd to Firm	Aljabr (USA)	Jly 28 1999
1m 1f	1m 52.8	3	9-6	Good	Vena (IRE)	Jly 27 1995
1m 1f 192y	2m 2.81	3	9-3	Gd to Firm	Road To Love (IRE)	Aug 3 2006
1m 3f	2m 23.0	3	8-8	Gd to Firm	Asian Heights	May 22 2001
1m 4f	2m 31.5	3	8-10	Firm	Presenting	Jly 25 1995
1m 6f	2m 58.5	4	9-2	Gd to Firm	Mowbray	Jly 27 1999
2m	3m 21.55	5	9-10	Gd to Firm	Yeats (IRE)	Aug 3 2006
2m 4f	4m 11.7	3	7-10	Firm	Lucky Moon	Aug 2 1990

GREAT LEIGHS (A.W)

Distance	Time	Age	Weight	Going	Horse	Date
5f	60.36	2	8-12	Standard	Rublevka Star (USA)	Oct 23 2008
5f	59.34	6	9-0	Standard	Almaty Express	May 28 2008
6f	1m 13.13	2	8-9	Standard	Calahonda	Nov 15 2008
6f	1m 11.52	6	9-1	Standard	Nota Bene	May 29 2008
1m	1m 39.24	2	9-0	Standard	Shampagne	Sep 27 2008
1m	1m 37.16	3	8-8	Standard	Roaring Forte (IRE)	Sep 27 2008
1m 2f	2m 5.02	4	8-12	Standard	Mutajarred	May 28 2008
1m 5f 66y	2m 48.87	5	9-7	Standard	Red Gala	Sep 27 2008
1m 6f	3m 0.73	3	9-7	Standard	Detonator	Sep 14 2008
2m	3m 28.69	4	9-1	Standard	Whaxaar (IRE)	Apr 30 2008

HAMILTON

Distance	Time	Age	Weight	Going	Horse	Date
5f 4y	57.95 secs	2	8-8	Gd to Firm	Rose Blossom	May 29 2009
5f 4y	57.95 secs	2	8-8	Gd to Firm	Rose Blossom	May 29 2009
6f 5y	1m 10.0	2	8-12	Gd to Firm	Break The Code	Aug 24 1999
6f 5y	69.3 secs	4	8-7	Firm	Marcus Game	Jly 11 1974
1m 65y	1m 45.8	2	8-11	Firm	Hopeful Subject	Sep 24 1973
1m 65y	1m 42.7	6	7-7	Firm	Cranley	Sep 25 1972
1m 1f 36y	1m 53.6	5	9-6	Gd to Firm	Regent's Secret	Aug 10 2005
1m 3f 16y	2m 19.32	3	9-0	Gd to Firm	Captain Webb	May 16 2008
1m 4f 17y	2m 30.52	5	9-10	Gd to Firm	Record Breaker (IRE)	Jun 10 2009
1m 5f 9y	2m 45.1	6	9-6	Firm	Mentalasanythin	Jun 14 1995

HAYDOCK

Distance	Time	Age	Weight	Going	Horse	Date
5f	59.2 secs	2	9-4	Firm	Money For Nothing	Aug 21 1964
5f	57.15 secs	3	8-11	Gd to firm	Fleeting Spirit (IRE)	May 24 2008
6f	1m 10.9	4	9-9	Gd to Firm	Wolfhound (USA)	Sep 4 1993
6f	69.9 secs	4	9-0	Gd to Firm	Iktamal (USA)	Sep 7 1996
7f 30y	1m 29.4	2	9-0	Gd to Firm	Apprehension	Sep 7
7f 30y	1m 26.8	3	8-7	Gd to Firm	Lady Zonda	Sep 28
1m 30y	1m 40.6	2	8-12	Gd to Firm	Besiege	Sep 7 1996
1m 30y	1m 40.1	3	9-2	Firm	Untold Riches (USA)	Jly 11 1999
1m2f 95y	2m 9.95	3	8-8	Good	Jukebox Jury (IRE)	Aug 8 2009
1m 2f 120y	2m 22.2	2	8-11	Soft	Persian Haze	Oct 9 1994
1m 2f 120y	2m 8.5	3	8-7	Gd to Firm	Fahal (USA)	Aug 5 1995
1m 3f 200y	2m 26.4	5	8-2	Firm	New Member	Jly 4 1970
1m 6f	2m 58.46	3	8-10	Gd to Firm	Meshtri (IRE)	Sep 27 2008
2m 45y	3m 27.0	4	8-13	Firm	Prince of Peace	May 26 1984
2m 1f 130y	3m 55.0	3	8-12	Good	Crystal Spirit	Sep 8 1990

KEMPTON (A.W)

Distance	Time	Age	Weight	Going	Horse	Date
5f	60.29 sec	2	9-1	Standard	Inflight (IRE)	Aug 23 2006
5f	59.77 sec	5	8-7	Standard	Harry Up	Dec 10 2006
6f	1m 11.91	2	9-0	Standard	Elnawin	Sep 6 2008
6f	1m 11.11	4	9-4	Standard	Edge Closer	May 29 2008
7f	1m 25.93	2	9-0	Standard	Boscobel	Nov 22 2006
7f	1m 23.65	3	8-10	Standard	Seek The Fair Land	Dec 13 2009
1m	1m 37.47	3	9-1	Standard	Evident Pride (USA)	Nov 29 2006
1m 2f	2m 3.77	6	8-13	Standard	Kandidate	Mar 29 2008
1m 3f	2m 17.74	4	9-9	Standard	Ajhar (USA)	Sep 5 2008
1m 4f	2m 30.48	3	8-11	Standard	Dansant	Nov 3 2007
2m	3m 27.49	4	9-2	Standard	Velvet Heights (IRE)	Apr 26 2006

LEICESTER

Distance	Time	Age	Weight	Going	Horse	Date
5f 2y	58.4 secs	2	9-0	Firm	Cutting Blade	Jun 9 1986
5f 2y	59.85 secs	5	9-5	Gd to Firm	The Jobber (IRE)	Sep 18 2006
5f 218y	1m 10.1	2	9-0	Firm	Thordis (IRE)	Oct 24 1995
5f 218y	69.12 secs	6	8-12	Gd to Firm	Peter Island (FR)	Apr 25 2009
7f 9y	1m 22.60	2	9-0	Gd to Firm	Marie De Medici (USA)	Oct 6 2009
7f 9y	1m 20.8	3	8-7	Firm	Flower Bowl	Jun 9 1986
1m 60y	1m 44.05	2	8-11	Gd to Firm	Congressional (IRE)	Sep 6 2005
1m 60y	1m 41.89	5	9-7	Gd to Firm	Vainglory	Jun 18 2009
1m 1f 218y	2m 5.3	2	9-1	Gd to Firm	Windsor Castle	Oct 14 1996
1m 1f 218y	2m 2.4	3	8-11	Firm	Effigy	Nov 4 1985
1m 1f 218y	2m 2.4	4	9-6	Gd to Firm	Lady Angharad (IRE)	Jun 18 2000
1m 3f 183y	2m 27.1	5	8-12	Gd to Firm	Murghem (IRE)	Jun 18 2000

LINGFIELD (TURF)

Distance	Time	Age	Weight	Going	Horse	Date
5f	57.1 secs	2	8-9	Good	Emerald Peace	Aug 6 1999
5f	56.2 secs	3	9-1	Gd to Firm	Eveningperformance	Jly 25 1994
6f	68.36 secs	2	8-12	Gd to Firm	Folly Bridge	Sept 8 2009
6f	68.2 secs	6	9-10	Firm	Al Amead	Jly 2 1986
7f	1m 21.3	2	7-6	Firm	Mandav	Oct 3 1980
7f	1m 20.1	3	8-7	Gd to Firm	Zelah (IRE)	May 13 1998
7f 140y	1m 28.7	2	9-3	Gd to Firm	Al Muheer	Aug 4 2007
7f 140y	1m 26.7	3	8-6	Fast	Hiaam	Nov 7 1978
1m 1f	1m 52.4	4	9-2	Gd to Firm	Quandary (USA)	Jly 15 1995
1m 2f	2m 4.6	3	9-3	Firm	Usran	Jly 15 1989
1m 3f 106y	2m 23.9	3	8-5	Firm	Night-Shirt	Jly 14 1990
1m 6f	2m 59.1	5	9-5	Firm	Ibn Bey	Jly 1 1989
2m	3m 23.7	3	9-5	Gd to Firm	Lauries Crusader	Aug 13 1988

LINGFIELD (A.W)

Distance	Time	Age	Weight	Going	Horse	Date
5f	58.46 secs	2	8-2	Standard	Ruby Tallulah	Aug 12 2008
5f	57.26 secs	8	8-12	Standard	Magic Glade	Feb 24 2007
6f	1m 10.75	2	9-4	Standard	Global City (IRE)	Oct 15 2008
6f	69.61	6	9-0	Standard	Excusez Moi (USA)	Feb 23 2008
6f	69.61	4	9-5	Standard	Jaconet (USA)	Sept 4 2009
7f	1m 23.68	2	8-4	Standard	Young Dottie	Oct 21 2008
7f	1m 22.19	4	8-7	Standard	Red Spell	Nov 19 2005
1m	1m 36.5	2	9-5	Standard	San Pier Niceto	Nov 30 1989
1m	1m 34.77	4	9-3	Standard	Baharah (USA)	Oct 30 2008
1m 2f	2m 1.79	5	9-0	Standard	Cusoon	Feb 24 2007
1m 4f	2m 28.10	3	8-10	Standard	Falcativ	Oct 27 2008
1m 5f	2m 42.47	3	9-2	Standard	Raffaas	July 3 2007
2m	3m 20.0	3	9-0	Standard	Yenoora	Aug 8 1992

MUSSELBURGH

Distance	Time	Age	Weight	Going	Horse	Date
5f	57.7 secs	2	8-2	Firm	Arasong	May 16 1994
5f	57.3 secs	3	8-12	Firm	Corunna	Jun 3 2000
7f 30y	1m 27.46	2	8-8	Good	DurhamReflection(IRE)	Sept 14 2009
7f 30y	1m 26.3	3	9-5	Firm	Waltzing Wizard	Aug 22 2002
1m	1m 40.3	2	8-12	Gd to Firm	Succession	Sep 26 2004
1m	1m 38.64	7	8-13	Gd to Firm	Just Bond (IRE)	Apr 3 2009
1m 1f	1m 50.6	6	8-8	Gd to Firm	KingOfTheMoors(USA)	Sept 27 2009
1m 4f	2m 33.7	3	9-11	Firm	Alexandrine	Jun 26 2000
1m4f 100y	2m 40.93	8	9-2	Good	Oddsmaker (IRE)	Sept 14 2009
1m 5f	2m 47.51	6	9-11	Gd to Firm	Dimashq	Jly 31 2008
1m 6f	2m 59.2	3	9-7	Firm	Forum Chris	Jly 3 2000
2m	3m 26.6	5	9-6	Gd to Firm	Jack Dawson (IRE)	Jun 1 2002

NEWBURY

Distance	Time	Age	Weight	Going	Horse	Date
5f 34y	59.1 secs	2	8-6	Gd to Firm	Superstar Leo	Jly 22 2000
5f 34y	59.2 secs	3	9-5	Gd to Firm	The Trader (IRE)	Aug 18 2001
6f 8y	1m 11.07	2	8-4	Gd to Firm	Bahati (IRE)	May 30 2009
6f 8y	69.42 secs	3	8-11	Gd to Firm	Nota Bene	May 13 2005
7f	1m 23.0	2	8-11	Gd to Firm	Haafhd	Aug 15 2003
7f	1m 21.5	3	8-4	Gd to Firm	Three Points	Jly 21 2000
1m	1m 37.5	2	9-1	Gd to firm	Winged Cupid (IRE)	Sep 16 2005
1m	1m 33.59	6	9-0	Firm	Rakti	May 14 2005
1m 1f	1m 49.6	3	8-0	Gd to Firm	Holtye	May 21 1995
1m 2f 6y	2m 1.2	3	8-7	Gd to Firm	Wall Street (USA)	Jly 20 1996
1m 3f 5y	2m 16.5	3	8-9	Gd to Firm	Grandera (IRE)	Sep 22 2001
1m 4f 5y	2m 28.26	4	9-7	Gd to Firm	Azamour (IRE)	Jul 23 2005
1m 5f 61y	2m 44.9	5	10-0	Gd to Firm	Mystic Hill	Jly 20 1996
2m	3m 25.4	8	9-12	Gd to Firm	Moonlight Quest	Jly 19 1996

NEWCASTLE

Distance	Time	Age	Weight	Going	Horse	Date
5f	58.8 secs	2	9-0	Firm	Atlantic Viking (IRE)	Jun 4 1997
5f	58.0 secs	4	9-2	Firm	Princess Oberon	Jly 23 1994
6f	1m 12.18	2	9-0	Gd to Firm	Stepping Up (IRE)	Sep 5 2005
6f	1m 10.6	8	9-5	Firm	Tedburrow	Jly 1 2000
7f	1m 24.2	2	9-0	Gd to Firm	Iscan (IRE)	Aug 31 1998
7f	1m 23.3	4	9-2	Gd to Firm	Quiet Venture	Aug 31 1998
1m	1m 38.9	2	9-0	Gd to Firm	Stowaway	Oct 2 1996
1m	1m 38.9	3	8-12	Firm	Jacamar	Jly 22 1989
1m 3y	1m 37.1	2	8-3	Gd to Firm	Hoh Steamer (IRE)	Aug 31 1998
1m 3y	1m 37.3	3	8-8	Gd to Firm	Its Magic	May 27 1999
1m 1f 9y	2m 3.2	2	8-13	Soft	Response	Oct 30 1993
1m 1f 9y	1m 52.3	3	6-3	Good	Ferniehurst	Jun 23 1936
1m 2f 32y	2m 6.5	4	8-9	Fast	Missionary Ridge	Jly 29 1990
1m 4f 93y	2m 37.3	5	8-12	Firm	Retender	Jun 25 1994
1m 6f 97y	3m 6.4	3	9-6	Gd to Firm	One Off	Aug 6 2003
2m 19y	3m 24.3	4	8-10	Good	Far Cry (IRE)	Jun 26 1999

NEWMARKET (ROWLEY)

Distance	Time	Age	Weight	Going	Horse	Date
5f	58.7 secs	2	8-5	Gd to Firm	Valiant Romeo	Oct 3 2002
5f	56.8 secs	6	9-2	Gd to Firm	Lochsong	Apr 30 1994
6f	69.56 secs	2	8-12	Gd to Firm	Bushranger (IRE)	Oct 3 2008
6f	69.56 secs	2	8-12	Gd to Firm	Bushranger (IRE)	Oct 3 2008
7f	1m 22.39	2	8-12	Gd to Firm	Ashram (IRE)	Sep 21 2004
7f	1m 22.2	4	9-5	Gd to Firm	Perfolia	Oct 17 1991
1m	1m 35.7	2	9-0	Gd to Firm	Forward Move (IRE)	Sep 21 2004
1m	1m 34.07	4	9-0	Gd to Firm	Eagle Mountain	Oct 3 2008
1m 1f	1m 47.2	4	9-5	Firm	Beauchamp Pilot	Oct 5 2002
1m 2f	2m 4.6	2	9-4	Good	Highland Chieftain	Nov 2 1985
1m 2f	2m 0.13	3	8-12	Good	New Approach (IRE)	Oct 18 2008
1m 4f	2m 27.1	5	8-12	Gd to Firm	Eastern Breeze	Oct 3 2003
1m 6f	2m 51.59	3	8-7	Good	Art Eyes (USA)	Sep 29 2005
2m	3m 19.5	5	9-5	Gd to Firm	Grey Shot	Oct 4 1997
2m 2f	3m 47.5	3	7-12	Hard	Whiteway	Oct 15 1947

NEWMARKET (JULY)

Distance	Time	Age	Weight	Going	Horse	Date
5f	58.5 secs	2	8-10	Good	Seductress	Jly 10 1990
5f	56.09 secs	6	9-11	Good	Borderlescott	Aug 22 2008
6f	1m 10.35	2	8-11	Good	Elnawin	Aug 22 2008
6f	69.5 secs	3	8-13	Gd to Firm	Stravinsky (USA)	Jly 8 1999
7f	1m 24.01	2	9-0	Good	Golden Stream (IRE)	Aug 22 2008
7f	1m 22.5	3	9-7	Firm	Ho Leng (IRE)	Jly 9 1998
1m	1m 37.47	2	8-13	Good	Whippers Love (IRE)	Aug 28 2009
1m	1m 35.5	3	8-6	Gd to Firm	Lovers Knot	Jly 8 1998
1m 110y	1m 44.1	3	8-11	Good	Golden Snake	Apr 15 1999
1m 2f	2m 0.9	4	9-3	Gd to Firm	Elhayq (IRE)	May 1 1999
1m 4f	2m 25.11	3	8-11	Good	Lush Lashes	Aug 22 2008
1m 6f 175y	3m 4.2	3	8-5	Good	Arrive	Jly 11 2001
2m 24y	3m 20.2	7	9-10	Good	Yorkshire	Jly 11 2001

NOTTINGHAM

Distance	Time	Age	Weight	Going	Horse	Date
5f 13y	57.9 secs	2	8-9	Firm	Hoh Magic	May 13 1994
5f 13y	57.6 secs	6	9-2	Gd to firm	Catch The Cat (IRE)	May 14 2005
6f 15y	1m 11.4	2	811	Firm	Jameelapi	Aug 8 1983
6f 15y	1m 10.0	4	9-2	Firm	Ajanac	Aug 8 1988
1m75y	1m 46.93	2	9-0	Gd to Firm	Psychic Ability	Oct 28 2009
1m 75y	1m 43.35	3	9-1	Gd To Firm	Scuffle	Jun 11 2008
1m 1f 213y	2m 5.6	2	9-0	Firm	Al Salite	Oct 28 1985
1m 1f 213y	2m 2.3	2	9-0	Firm	Ayaabi	Jly 21 1984
1m 2f 50y	2m 10.27	3	9-0	Gd To Firm	Hunting Country	Jly 5 2008
1m 6f 15y	2m 57.8	3	8-10	Firm	Buster Jo	Oct 1 1985
2m 9y	3m 24.0	5	7-7	Firm	Fet	2036
2m 2f 18y	3m 55.1	9	9-10	Gd to Firm	Pearl Run	1 1990

PONTEFRACT

Distance	Time	Age	Weight	Going	Horse	Date
5f	61.1 secs	2	9-0	Firm	Golden Bounty	Sep 20 2001
5f	60.8 secs	4	8-9	Firm	Blue Maeve	Sep 29 2004
6f	1m 14.0	2	9-3	Firm	Fawzi	Sep 6 1983
6f	1m 12.6	3	7-13	Firm	Merry One	Aug 29 1970
1m 4y	1m 42.8	2	9-13	Firm	Star Spray	Sep 6 1983
1m 4y	1m 42.8	2	9-0	Firm	Alasil (USA)	Sep 26 2002
1m 4y	1m 40.6	4	9-10	Gd to Firm	Island Light	Apr 13 2002
1m 2f 6y	2m 10.1	2	9-0	Firm	Shanty Star	Oct 7 2002
1m 2f 6y	2m 8.2	4	7-8	Hard	Happy Hector	Jly 9 1979
1m 2f 6y	2m 8.2	3	7-13	Hard	Tom Noddy	Aug 21 1972
1m 4f 8y	2m 33.72	3	8-7	Firm	Ajaan	Aug 8 2007
2m 1f 22y	3m 40.67	4	8-7	Gd to Firm	Paradise Flight	June 6 2005
2m 1f 216y	3m 51.1	3	8-8	Firm	Kudz	Sep 9 1986
2m 5f 122y	4m 47.8	4	8-4	Firm	Physical	May 14 1984

REDCAR

Distance	Time	Age	Weight	Going	Horse	Date
5f	56.9 secs	2	9-0	Firm	Mister Joel	Oct 24 1995
5f	56.01 secs	10	9-3	Firm	Henry Hall	Sep 20 2006
6f	68.8 secs	2	8-3	Gd to Firm	Obe Gold	Oct 2 2004
6f	68.6 secs	3	9-2	Gd to Firm	Sizzling Saga	Jun 21 1991
7f	1m 21.28	2	9-3	Firm	Karoo Blue	Sep 20 2006
7f	1m 21.0	3	9-1	Firm	Empty Quarter	Oct 3 1995
1m	1m 34.37	2	9-0	Firm	Mastership	Sep 20 2006
1m	1m 32.42	4	10-0	Firm	Nanton	Sep 20 2006
1m 1f	1m 52.4	2	9-0	Firm	Spear (IRE)	Sep 13 2004
1m 1f	1m 48.5	5	8-12	Firm	Mellottie	Jly 25 1990
1m 2f	2m 10.1	2	8-11	Good	Adding	Nov 10 1989
1m 2f	2m 1.4	5	9-2	Firm	Eradicate	May 28 1990
1m 3f	2m 17.2	3	8-9	Firm	Photo Call	Aug 7 1990
1m 5f 135y	2m 54.7	6	9-10	Firm	Brodessa	Jun 20 1992
1m 6f 19y	2m 59.81	4	9-1	Gd to Firm	Esprit De Corps	Sep 11 2006
2m 4y	3m 24.9	3	9-3	Gd to Firm	Subsonic	Oct 8 1991
2m 3f	4m 10.1	5	7-4	Gd to Firm	Seldom In	Aug 9 1991

RIPON

Distance	Time	Age	Weight	Going	Horse	Date
5f	57.8 secs	2	8-8	Firm	Super Rocky	Jly 5 1991
5f	57.6 secs	5	8-5	Good	Broadstairs Beauty	May 21 1995
6f	1m 10.4	2	9-2	Good	Cumbrian Venture	Aug 17 2002
6f	69.8 secs	4	9-8	Gd to Firm	Tadeo	Aug 16 1997
6f	69.8 secs	5	7-10	Firm	Quoit	Jly 23 1966
1m	1m 39.79	2	8-6	Good	Top Jaro (FR)	Sep 24 2005
1m	1m 36.62	4	8-11	Gd to Firm	Granston (IRE)	Aug 29 2005
1m 1f 170y	1m 59.12	5	8-9	Gd to Firm	Wahoo Sam (USA)	Aug 30 2005
1m 2f	2m 2.6	3	9-4	Firm	Swift Sword	Jly 20 1990
1m 4f 10y	2m 32.06	4	8-8	Good	Hearthstead Wings	Apr 29 2006
2m	3m 27.07	5	9-12	Gd to Firm	Greenwich Meantime	Aug 30 2005

SALISBURY

Distance	Time	Age	Weight	Going	Horse	Date
5f	59.3 secs	2	9-0	Gd to Firm	Ajigolo	May 12 2005
5f	59.3 secs	2	9-0	Gd to Firm	Ajigolo	May 12 2005
6f	1m 12.1	2	8-0	Gd to Firm	Parisian Lady (IRE)	Jun 10 1997
6f	1m 11.3	3	8-1	Firm	Bentong (IRE)	May 7 2006
6f 212y	1m 25.9	2	9-0	Firm	More Royal (USA)	Jun 29 1995
6f 212y	1m 24.9	3	9-7	Firm	High Summer (USA)	Sep 5 1996
1m	1m 40.4	2	8-13	Firm	Choir Master (USA)	Sep 17 2002
1m	1m 38.29	3	8-7	Gd to Firm	Layman (USA)	Aug 11 2005
1m 1f 198y	2m 4.9	3	8-6	Gd to Firm	Zante	Aug 12 1998
1m 4f	2m 31.6	3	9-5	Gd to Firm	Arrive	Jun 27 2001
1m 6f 15y	2m 59.4	3	8-6	Gd to Firm	Tabareeh	Sep 2 1999

SANDOWN

Distance	Time	Age	Weight	Going	Horse	Date
5f 6y	59.4 secs	2	9-3	Firm	Times Time	Jly 22 1982
5f 6y	58.8 secs	6	8-9	Gd to Firm	Palacegate Touch	Sep 17 1996
7f 16y	1m 26.56	2	9-0	Gd to Firm	Raven's Pass (USA)	Sep 1 2007
7f 16y	1m 26.3	3	9-0	Firm	Mawsuff	Jun 14 1983
1m 14y	1m 41.1	2	8-11	Fast	Reference Point	Sep 23 1986
1m 14y	1m 39.0	3	8-8	Firm	Linda s Fantasy	Aug 19 1983
1m 1f	1m 54.6	2	8-8	Gd to Firm	French Pretender	Sep 20 1988
1m 1f	1m 52.4	7	9-3	Gd to Firm	Bourgainville	Aug 11 2005
1m 2f 7y	2m 2.1	4	8-11	Firm	Kalaglow	May 31 1982
1m 3f 91y	2m 21.6	4	8-3	Fast	Aylesfield	Jly 7 1984
1m 6f	2m 56.9	4	8-7	Gd to Firm	Lady Rosanna	Jly 19 1989
2m 78y	3m 29.9	6	9-2	Firm	Sadeem	May 29 1989

SOUTHWELL (TURF)

Distance	Time	Age	Weight	Going	Horse	Date
6f	1m 15.03	2	9-3	Good	Trepa	Sep 6 2006
6f	1m 13.48	4	8-10	Good	Paris Bell	Sep 6 2006
7f	1m 27.56	2	9-7	Good	Hart Of Gold	Sep 6 2006

7f	1m 25.95	3	9-0	Good	Aeroplane	Sep 6 2006
1m 2f	2m 7.470	3	8-11	Good	Desert Authority(USA)	Sep 6 2006
1m 3f	2m 20.13	4	9-12	Good	Sanchi	Sep 6 2006
1m 4f	2m 34.4	5	9-3	Gd to Firm	Corn Lily	Aug 10 1991
2m	3m 34.1	5	9-1	Gd to Firm	Triplicate	Sep 20 1991

SOUTHWELL (A.W)

Distance	Time	Age	Weight	Going	Horse	Date
5f	58.89 secs	2	8-6	Standard	Egyptian Lord	Dec 15 2005
5f	57.14 secs	5	9-5	Standard	Godfrey Street	Jan 24 2008
6f	1m 14.00	2	8-5	Standard	Panalo	Nov 8 1989
6f	1m 13.50	4	10-02	Standard	Saladan Knight	Dec 30 1989
7f	1m 27.10	2	8-2	Standard	Mystic Crystal	Nov 20 1990
7f	1m 26.80	5	8-4	Standard	Amenable	Dec 13 1990
1m	1m 38.00	2	8-9	Standard	Alpha Rascal	Nov 13 1990
1m	1m 38.00	2	8-10	Standard	Andrew s First	Dec 30 1989
1m	1m 37.25	3	8-6	Standard	Valira	Nov 3 1990
1m 3f	2m 21.50	4	9-7	Standard	Tempering	Dec 5 1990
1m 4f	2m 33.90	4	9-12	Standard	Fast Chick	Nov 8 1989
1m 6f	3m 1.60	3	7-8	Standard	Erevnon	Dec 29 1990
2m	3m 37.60	9	8-12	Standard	Old Hubert	Dec 5 1990

THIRSK

Distance	Time	Age	Weight	Going	Horse	Date
5f	57.2 secs	2	9-7	Gd to Firm	Proud Boast	Aug 5 2000
5f	56.9 secs	5	9-6	Firm	Charlie Parkes	April 11 2003
6f	69.2 secs	2	9-6	Gd to Firm	Westcourt Magic	Aug 25 1995
6f	68.8 secs	6	9-4	Firm	Johayro	Jly 23 1999
7f	1m 23.7	2	8-9	Firm	Courting	Jly 23 1999
7f	1m 22.8	4	8-5	Firm	Silver Haze	May 21 1988
1m	1m 37.9	2	9-0	Firm	Sunday Symphony	Sep 4 2004
1m	1m 34.8	4	8-13	Firm	Yearsley	May 5 1990
1m 4f	2m 29.9	5	9-12	Firm	Gallery God	Jun 4 2001
2m	3m 22.3	3	8-11	Firm	Tomaschek	Jly 17 1981

WARWICK

Distance	Time	Age	Weight	Going	Horse	Date
5f	57.95 secs	2	8-9	Gd to Firm	Amour Propre	Jun 26 2008
5f	57.7 secs	4	9-6	Gd to Firm	Little Edward	Jly 7 2002
5f 110y	63.6 secs	5	8-6	Gd to Firm	Dizzy In The Head	Jun 27 2004
6f	1m 11.22	2	9-3	Gd to Firm	Hurricane Hymnbook	Sep 15 2007
6f	69.44	5	8-12	Gd to Firm	Peter Island	Jun 26 2008
7f 26y	1m 22.9	2	9-0	Firm	Country Rambler(USA)	Jun 20 2004
7f 26y	1m 20.7	4	8-8	Good	Etlaala	Apr 17 2006
1m 22y	1m 37.1	3	8-11	Firm	Orinocovsky (IRE)	Jun 26 2002
1m 2f 188y	2m 14.98	4	8-12	Gd to Firm	Ronaldsay	Jun 16 2008
1m 4f 134y	2m 39.5	3	8-13	Gd to Firm	Maimana (IRE)	Jun 22 2002
1m 6f 135y	3m 7.5	3	9-7	Gd to Firm	Burma Baby (USA)	Jly 2 1999
2m 39y	3m 27.9	3	8-1	Firm	Decoy	Jun 26 2002

WINDSOR

Distance	Time	Age	Weight	Going	Horse	Date
5f 10y	58.75 secs	2	8-12	Gd to Firm	Hoh Mike (IRE)	May 15 2006
5f 10y	58.3 secs	5	7-10	Gd to Firm	Beyond The Clouds	Jun 2 2001
6f	1m 10.5	2	9-5	Gd to Firm	Cubism (USA)	Aug 17 1998
6f	1m 10.06	6	8-11	Gd to Firm	Presto Shinko	Aug 4 2007
1m 67y	1m 42.78	2	8-11	Gd to Firm	Sequillo	Sep 29 2008
1m 67y	1m 40.27	4	9-3	Gd to Firm	Librettist (USA)	Jul 1 2006
1m 2f 7y	2m 3.0	3	9-1	Firm	Moomba Masquerade	May 19 1990
1m2f 7y	2m 2.44	4	9-0	Gd to Firm	Campanologist (USA)	Aug 29 2009
1m 3f 135y	2m 21.5	3	9-2	Firm	Double Florin	May 19 1980

WOLVERHAMPTON (A.W.)

Distance	Time	Age	Weight	Going	Horse	Date
5f 20y	61.13 sec	2	8-8	Std to Fast	Yungaburra (IRE)	Nov 8 2006
5f 20y	60.35 sec	11	8-13	Standard	Little Edward	Mar 29 2009
5f 216y	1m 12.61	2	9-0	Std to Fast	Prime Defender	Nov 8 2006
5f 216y	1m 13.32	5	8-12	Standard	Desert Opal	Sep 17 2005
7f 32y	1m 27.70	2	9-5	Standard	Billy Dane	Aug 14 2006
7f 32y	1m 26.65	4	8-12	Std to Fast	Capucci	Sept 30 2009
1m 141y	1m 48.08	2	8-9	Std to Fast	Worldly	Aug 30 2006
1m 141y	1m 46.48	3	8-9	Standard	Gitano Hernando	Sept 17 2009
1m 1f 103y	2m 0.76	2	9-0	Standard	Mr Excel (IRE)	Nov 14 2005
1m 1f 103y	1m 57.34	4	8-13	Standard	Bahar Shumaal (IRE)	Aug 31 2006
1m 4f 50y	2m 35.71	3	9-2	Std to Fast	Steppe Dancer (IRE)	Aug 30 2006
1m 5f 194y	2m 59.85	6	9-12	Std to Fast	Valance (IRE)	Aug 30 2006
2m 119y	3m 35.85	5	8-11	Std to Fast	Market Watcher (USA)	Nov 21 2006

YARMOUTH

Distance	Time	Age	Weight	Going	Horse	Date
5f 43y	60.4 secs	2	8-6	Gd to Firm	Ebba	Jly 26 1999
5f 43y	59.8 secs	4	8-13	Gd to Firm	Roxanne Mill	Aug 25 2002
6f 3y	1m 10.4	2	9-0	Fast	Lanchester	Aug 15 1988
6f 3y	69.9 secs	4	8-9	Firm	Malhub (USA)	Jun 13 2002
7f 3y	1m 22.2	2	9-0	Gd to Firm	Warrshan	Sep 14 1988
7f 3y	1m 22.12	4	9-4	Gd to Firm	Glenbuck (IRE)	Apr 26 2007
1m 3y	1m 36.3	2	8-2	Gd to Firm	Outrun	Sep 15 1988
1m 3y	1m 33.9	3	8-8	Firm	Bonne Etoile	Jun 27 1995
1m 1f	1m 53.70	3	9-2	Good	Crystal Feather	Aug 6 2009
1m 2f 21y	2m 2.83	3	8-8	Firm	Reunite (IRE)	Jul 18 2006
1m 3f 101y	2m 23.1	3	8-9	Firm	Rahil	Jly 1 1993
1m 6f 17y	2m 57.8	3	8-2	Gd to Firm	Barakat	Jly 24 1990
2m	3m 26.7	4	8-2	Gd to Firm	Alhesn (USA)	Jly 26 1999
2m 2f 51y	3m 56.8	4	9-10	Firm	Provence	Sep 19 1991

YORK

Distance	Time	Age	Weight	Going	Horse	Date
5f	57.3 secs	2	7-8	Gd to Firm	Lyric Fantasy	Aug 20 1992
5f	56.1 secs	3	9-3	Gd to Firm	Dayjur	Aug 23 1990
5f 89y	62.31 secs	6	9-5	Gd to Firm	Barney McGrew (IRE)	Aug 18 2009
6f	69.28 secs	2	8-12	Gd to Firm	Showcasing	Aug 19 2009
6f	68.58 secs	7	9-4	Firm	Cape Of Good Hope	Jun 16 2005
7f	1m 22.45	2	9-0	Gd to Firm	ElusivePimpernel(USA)	Aug 18 2009
7f	1m 21.98	5	9-6	Good	Iffraaj	Sep 9 2006
1m	1m 39.20	2	8-1	Gd to Firm	Missoula (IRE)	Aug 31 2005
1m	1m 36.35	3	9-1	Gd to Firm	Mostashaar (FR)	Jun 16 2005
1m 208y	1m 46.76	5	9-8	Gd to Firm	Echo Of Light	Sep 5 2007
1m 2f 88y	2m 5.29	3	8-11	Gd to Firm	Sea The Stars (IRE)	Aug 18 2009
1m 4f	2m 26.28	6	8-9	Firm	Bandari (IRE)	Jun 18 2005
1m 5f 194y	2m 51.8	3	8-7	Gd to Firm	Tuning	Aug 19 1998
1m 7f 195y	3m 18.4	3	8-0	Gd to Firm	Dam Busters	Aug 16 1988
2m 88y	3m 30.63	4	9-1	Gd to Firm	Askar Tau (FR)	Aug 19 2009

Raceform Flat speed figures 2009

(Best time performances achieved 1st January - 31st December 2009 (min rating 110, 2-y-o 105)

THREE YEAR-OLDS AND UPWARDS - Turf

Acquisition 113 (14f,Hay,S,Sep 5)
Acrostic 114 (8f,Yor,GF,Aug 20)
Adjaliya 110 (12f,Leo,GY,Sep 5)
Adlerflug 116 (10½f,Lon,G,Apr 26)
Advanced 111 (6f,Rip,GF,Aug 15)
African Rose 111 (5f,Cha,G,May 31)
Again 110 (8f,Cur,HY,May 24)
Age Of Aquarius 115 (12f,Lon,GS,Jly 14)
Aizavoski 116 (15f,Lon,GS,Oct 3)
Akbabend 110 (12f,Cat,GF,Aug 14)
Akmal 112 (14f,Nmk,GF,Oct 1)
Al Muheer 112 (7f,Asc,G,Jly 25)
Alanbrooke 111 (18f,Nmk,GF,Sep 19)
Alandi 116 (20f,Lon,G,Oct 4)
Alazeyab 115 (8f,Yor,GF,Aug 20)
Albaqaa 110 (10½f,Yor,GF,Jly 11)
Alexandros 112 (9f,Nad,G,Mar 28)
All The Aces 111 (13f,Nby,S,May 16)
Allied Powers 110 (12f,Ham,G,May 15)
Allybar 111 (10f,Dea,G,Aug 16)
Almiqdaad 115 (10f,Nby,GF,Sep 19)
Alpen Glen 111 (10½f,Chs,GF,Jun 26)
Alpine Rose 116 (12f,Sai,S,Jun 28)
Alwaary 115 (12f,Asc,G,Jly 25)
Amico Mio 111 (15f,Lon,GS,Sep 6)
Amour Propre 114 (5f,Yor,GF,Aug 21)
Antinori 110 (10f,Nby,GF,Sep 19)
Aqlaam 119 (8f,Dea,G,Aug 16)
Arabian Gleam 111 (7f,Nmk,G,Oct 17)
Arch Rebel 113 (10f,Ayr,G,Sep 19)
Armure 112 (20f,Lon,G,Oct 4)
Aromatic 110 (10f,Sal,F,May 14)
Art Connoisseur 110 (6f,Asc,GF,Jun 20)
Arthur s Edge 110 (6f,Don,S,Nov 7)
As De Trebol 113 (7f,Lon,G,May 30)
Ashram 112 (7f,Nby,GF,Sep 18)
Ask 116 (12f,Asc,G,Jly 25)
Askar Tau 113 (20f,Lon,G,Oct 4)
Aspectoflove 111 (8f,Leo,G,Aug 13)
Asset 114 (6f,Asc,GF,Jun 20)
Axiom 110 (7f,Asc,G,Sep 26)

Baila Me 114 (10f,Ayr,G,Sep 19)
Balcarce Nov 112 (7f,Yor,GF,Aug 21)
Balius 115 (9f,Nad,GF,Mar 5)
Balthazaar s Gift 110 (7f,Chs,GF,Jly 11)
Bankable 112 (10f,Wdr,GF,Aug 29)
Barney McGrew 110 (5½f,Yor,GF,Aug 18)
Barshiba 115 (10f,Nmk,G,Oct 17)
Bassel 110 (15½f,Lon,G,Sep 13)
Beach Bunny 113 (8f,Cur,HY,May 23)
Beacon Lodge 113 (8f,Cha,GS,Jun 14)
Becqu Adoree 112 (12f,Lon,G,Sep 13)
Beheshtam 114 (12f,Lon,G,Oct 4)
Benbaun 116 (5f,Yor,GF,Aug 21)
Bernie The Bolt 113 (18f,Nmk,GF,Sep 19)
Biarritz 112 (7½f,Nad,G,Jan 22)
Black Bear Island 113 (10½f,Yor,G,May 14)
Black Mambazo 114 (5f,Cha,G,May 31)
Blek 111 (15½f,Sai,HY,Nov 14)
Blue Cayenne 111 (6f,Msn,HO,Nov 3)
Blue Ksar 110 (9f,Nad,GF,Mar 5)
Bluefields 110 (15½f,Lon,G,Sep 13)
Board Meeting 112 (12f,Lon,G,Sep 13)
Bon Grain 112 (10f,Lon,GS,Oct 3)
Bonnie Charlie 110 (6f,Asc,GS,Oct 10)
Borderlescott 117 (5f,Yor,GF,Aug 21)
Boulavogue 111 (16f,Leo,HY,Nov 5)
Brave Prospector 111 (6f,Asc,GS,Oct 10)
Brett Vale 110 (10f,San,G,Aug 12)
Bronze Cannon 116 (12f,Asc,GF,Jun 20)
Buccellati 112 (12f,Lon,G,Sep 13)
Byword 111 (10f,Dea,G,Aug 16)

Callow Lake 112 (16f,Leo,GY,Aug 6)
Calming Influence 116 (7½f,Nad,G,Jan 22)
Calvados Blues 110 (8f,Cha,G,Jly 5)
Campanologist 115 (12f,Asc,GF,Jun 20)
Candy Gift 117 (15f,Dea,G,Aug 23)
Caracciola 110 (16f,Goo,G,Jly 30)
Cassique Lady 110 (11f,War,GS,Jun 15)
Casual Conquest 115 (10f,Cur,SH,Aug 16)
Cat Junior 110 (7f,Goo,GF,Aug 30)
Cavalryman 117 (12f,Lon,G,Oct 4)
Celebrissime 118 (9f,Lon,S,May 17)
Cesare 112 (8f,Asc,GF,Jun 16)
Changing The Guard 110 (10½f,Yor,G,Jun 13)
Charm School 113 (10f,Nby,GF,Sep 19)
Chasing Stars 112 (7f,Lon,G,May 30)
Checklow 110 (10½f,Yor,GF,May 13)
Chiberta King 112 (12f,Nmk,GF,May 16)
Chief Editor 111 (5f,Nby,GS,Apr 17)
Chinchon 110 (10f,Lon,GS,Sep 6)
Chinese White 112 (10f,Cur,S,Sep 12)
Chock A Block 110 (12f,Nmk,GF,Oct 2)
Cill Rialaig 112 (10f,Nby,GF,Sep 19)
Cima De Triomphe 114 (10½f,Lon,G,Apr 26)
Cirrus Des Aigles 115 (12f,Lon,GS,Oct 18)
City Leader 116 (10f,Nmk,G,Oct 17)
Claremont 113 (11f,Lon,G,May 4)
Class Is Class 113 (10f,Nby,GF,Sep 19)
Classic Vintage 111 (12f,Goo,G,Jly 29)
Clerk s Choice 112 (10½f,Chs,GF,Aug 21)
Clowance 114 (14f,Cur,S,Sep 12)
Clowance House 110 (12f,Nmk,GF,May 16)
Colleoni 111 (16f,Leo,HY,Nov 5)
Conduit 118 (12f,Asc,G,Jly 25)
Confront 115 (7f,Yor,GF,Aug 21)
Cool Strike 112 (12f,Nmk,GF,Jly 10)
Court Canibal 110 (10f,Lon,G,Apr 5)
Croisultan 110 (6f,Cur,SH,Aug 16)
Crossharbour 114 (12f,Lon,G,Sep 13)
Cruel Sea 112 (12f,Leo,GY,Sep 5)
Crystal Capella 110 (10f,Lon,G,Oct 4)
Cuis Ghaire 113 (8f,Nmk,GF,May 3)
Curtain Call 114 (9f,Lon,S,May 17)
Cutlass Bay 111 (10f,Sai,HY,May 12)

Dandy Man 110 (5f,Yor,GF,Aug 21)
Dane Blue 110 (8f,Cur,HY,May 23)
Dansant 113 (12f,Asc,GF,Jun 20)
Danse Grecque 111 (10f,Dea,G,Aug 23)
Dar Re Mi 116 (12f,Lon,G,Oct 4)
Daring Man 118 (6f,Cur,HY,Jly 26)
Darley Sun 112 (18f,Nmk,G,Oct 17)
Dazinski 111 (16f,Chs,GF,Aug 22)
Deauville Vision 111 (8f,Cur,HY,May 23)
Debussy 111 (12f,Chs,GF,May 7)
Deem 110 (8f,Nad,G,Feb 5)
Delegator 114 (8f,Nmk,GF,May 2)
Demolition 110 (10f,Ayr,GS,Sep 17)
Deposer 110 (8½f,Eps,G,Jun 5)
Desert Sea 111 (16½f,San,G,Jly 4)
Designated Decoy 110 (8f,Cur,S,Mar 22)
Diana s Choice 112 (6f,Nad,GF,Feb 6)
Diyakalanie 111 (10f,Lon,G,Apr 5)
Dohasa 111 (6f,Nad,GF,Feb 26)
Donnas Palm 112 (16f,Leo,HY,Nov 5)
Dream Eater 115 (7f,Yor,GF,Aug 21)
Dream Lodge 112 (10f,Ayr,G,Sep 19)
Drill Sergeant 111 (12f,Don,G,Mar 29)
Drumfire 111 (10f,San,G,May 28)
Drunken Sailor 114 (10f,Nby,GF,Sep 19)
Duncan 111 (12f,Asc,GF,May 9)
Dunkerque 113 (6½f,Dea,GS,Aug 9)

Ebadiyan 111 (16f,Cur,Y,Apr 5)
Edge Closer 110 (6f,Wdr,GF,Jun 1)
Elusive Wave 112 (8f,Dea,S,Aug 2)
Elyaadi 110 (12f,Leo,GY,Sep 5)
Embsay Crag 113 (10½f,Chs,GF,Aug 21)
Emily Blake 114 (8f,Cur,HY,May 23)
Enroller 111 (12f,Asc,GF,Jun 20)
Equiano 110 (6f,Nmk,GF,Apr 15)
Estrela Brage 111 (8f,Cur,S,Mar 22)
Ethics Girl 110 (9f,San,G,Aug 13)
Eva s Request 111 (8f,Goo,G,May 2)
Evasive 111 (8f,Nmk,GF,May 2)
Exceptional Art 112 (5f,Bev,GF,Aug 29)

Falcon Rock 113 (12f,Don,GF,Sep 12)
Fame And Glory 123 (10f,Leo,GY,Sep 5)
Famous Name 116 (8f,Cur,GY,Jun 28)
Fastnet Storm 112 (10½f,Chs,GF,Aug 21)
Fateh Field 117 (7½f,Nad,GF,Jan 15)
Father Time 113 (12f,Asc,GF,Jun 19)
Fergus McIver 111 (10f,Leo,GY,Apr 19)
Fiery Lad 110 (9f,Leo,G,Jun 18)
Final Approach 110 (16f,Leo,HY,Nov 5)
Finjaan 110 (7f,Goo,G,Jly 28)
Firebet 110 (8f,Ayr,GF,Jun 20)
Fiulin 111 (14f,Not,GF,Apr 8)
Fleeting Spirit 116 (6f,Nmk,GF,Jly 10)
Forgotten Voice 110 (8f,Goo,G,Jly 29)
Freemantle 113 (12f,Lon,GS,Jly 14)
Fuisse 111 (10½f,Cha,G,Jun 7)
Fullandby 111 (6f,Don,S,Nov 7)
Fully Funded 110 (12f,Lon,GS,Apr 12)
Furmigadelagiusta 111 (12f,Pon,GF,Jun 21)
Furnace 111 (8f,Nad,GF,Feb 26)

Gan Amhras 113 (8f,Nmk,GF,May 2)
Geordieland 119 (16½f,San,G,May 28)
Georgebernardshaw 111 (7f,Cur,S,Jly 11)
Getaway 112 (12f,Lon,G,Oct 4)
Ghanaati 115 (8f,Nmk,GF,May 3)
Girouette 113 (6f,Cur,SH,Aug 16)
Gitano Hernando 110 (10f,Don,G,Mar 29)
Gladiatorus 119 (7½f,Nad,G,Jan 22)
Glass Harmonium 111 (10½f,Yor,G,May 14)
Glow Star 110 (7½f,Nad,G,Feb 5)
Golden Sword 114 (12f,Chs,GF,May 7)
Goldikova 125 (8f,Dea,G,Aug 16)
Goliaths Boy 112 (10½f,Chs,GF,Aug 21)
Good Again 110 (8f,Pon,GF,Oct 5)
Grand Ducal 113 (10f,Leo,GY,Sep 5)
Grantley Adams 111 (7½f,Nad,G,Feb 5)
Grey Soldier 111 (8f,Dea,G,Aug 16)
Gris De Gris 121 (9f,Lon,S,May 17)
Guest Ville 112 (11f,Lon,G,May 4)

Halicarnassus 110 (10f,Goo,GF,May 25)
Hallie s Comet 112 (7f,Cur,Y,Jun 27)
Handsome Maestro 110 (8f,Dea,G,Aug 30)
Harrison George 110 (6f,Yor,S,May 15)
Hatta Fort 111 (6f,Nad,GF,Feb 26)
Hattan 110 (10f,Nad,G,Feb 12)
Hawridge King 110 (16f,Chs,GF,Aug 22)
Headford View 113 (7f,Cur,Y,Jun 27)
Heart Shaped 112 (8f,Nmk,GF,May 3)
Heaven Sent 112 (8f,Leo,GY,Sep 5)
Hidden Brief 110 (11½f,Chs,GF,May 6)
High Heeled 111 (12f,Eps,G,Jun 5)
High Standing 115 (6f,Asc,GF,Jun 20)
Holberg 115 (16f,Asc,GF,Jun 19)
Hollo Ladies 110 (16f,Cur,Y,Apr 5)
Huntdown 112 (7f,Yor,GF,Aug 21)
Hunting Tower 110 (8f,Nad,G,Feb 19)

Ialysos 113 (5f,San,G,Jly 4)
Icelandic 111 (6f,Cur,SH,Aug 16)
Ideal World 114 (12f,Sai,S,Jun 28)
Illustrious Blue 111 (12f,Asc,GF,Jun 20)
Imbongi 113 (9f,Nad,GF,Mar 5)
Imposing 110 (10f,Nmk,GF,Apr 16)
Incanto Dream 113 (15½f,Lon,G,Sep 13)
Indian Days 110 (10f,San,G,May 28)
Indiana Gal 110 (8f,Cur,GY,Jun 28)
Inestimable 111 (12½f,Dea,G,Aug 30)
Instant Recall 111 (6f,Nad,GF,Feb 6)
Intrepid Jack 110 (6f,Wdr,GF,Jun 1)
Investissement 112 (15f,Lon,GS,Sep 6)
Invincible Force 121 (6f,Cur,HY,Jly 26)
Inxile 113 (5f,Lon,G,May 10)
Irian 113 (8f,Cha,G,Jly 5)
Irish Heartbeat 113 (6f,Cur,HY,Jly 26)

J J The Jet Plane 116 (6f,Wdr,GF,Jun 1)
Jay Peg 113 (9f,Nad,GF,Mar 5)
Jimmy Styles 110 (6f,Asc,GF,May 9)
Judd Street 111 (6f,Sal,GF,Jun 14)
Judge n Jury 110 (5f,Cur,HY,Aug 30)
Jukebox Jury 115 (12½f,Dea,G,Aug 30)
Jumbajukiba 111 (6f,Cur,HY,May 23)

Kachgai 111 (8f,Dea,G,Aug 30)
Kaolak 110 (9f,Goo,GF,Aug 30)
Kargali 111 (8f,Leo,GY,Apr 19)
Kasbah Bliss 115 (20f,Lon,G,Oct 4)
Kayf Aramis 110 (18f,Yor,G,May 14)
Kenchop 110 (7f,Lon,G,May 30)
Khateeb 111 (8f,Pon,G,Jly 26)
King Jock 115 (7½f,Nad,G,Feb 5)
King s Apostle 117 (6½f,Dea,GS,Aug 9)
Kingdom Of Fife 112 (10½f,Yor,GF,Jly 11)
Kingsgate Native 113 (5f,Goo,G,Jly 30)
Kirklees 113 (10f,Nad,G,Feb 12)
Kite Wood 111 (10½f,Yor,G,May 14)
Knot In Wood 111 (6f,Don,GF,Mar 28)
Kudu Country 110 (14f,Hay,S,Sep 5)

La Boum 115 (12f,Lon,G,Oct 4)
Laa Rayb 111 (8f,Goo,G,Jly 31)
Lady Marian 113 (10f,Dea,G,Aug 23)
Le Havre 113 (10½f,Cha,G,Jun 7)
Les Fazzani 113 (12f,Leo,GY,Sep 5)
Lesson In Humility 116 (6½f,Dea,GS,Aug 9)
Libano 111 (7f,Leo,HY,Nov 5)
Libel Law 111 (10½f,Hay,G,Aug 8)
Little White Lie 112 (7½f,Nad,G,Feb 5)
Loch Long 110 (15f,Lon,GS,Oct 3)
Look Busy 110 (5f,Hay,HY,May 23)
Look Here 110 (12f,Asc,G,Jly 25)
Lord Admiral 113 (10f,Leo,YS,Jly 23)
Lord Shanakill 114 (8f,Cha,G,Jly 5)
Los Cristianos 117 (15f,Lon,GS,Oct 3)
Loup Breton 116 (10½f,Lon,G,Apr 26)
Luisant 114 (6f,Cur,HY,Jly 26)

Mac Gille Eoin 112 (6f,Goo,GF,Sep 12)
Mac Love 112 (8½f,Eps,G,Jun 5)
Mad About You 113 (7f,Cur,Y,Apr 5)
Mad Rush 111 (12f,Goo,GF,Jun 5)
Magadan 115 (12f,Lon,G,Oct 4)
Main Aim 114 (6f,Nmk,GF,Jly 10)
Makt 111 (12f,Lon,GS,Oct 18)
Manifest 110 (14f,Nmk,GF,Oct 1)
Manighar 118 (15f,Lon,GS,Oct 3)
Manyriverstocross 111 (14f,Goo,G,Jly 28)
Mariol 116 (6½f,Dea,GS,Aug 9)
Markab 112 (6f,Rip,GF,Aug 15)
Masta Plasta 111 (5f,San,G,Jly 4)
Mastercraftsman 122 (10½f,Yor,GF,Aug 18)
Masterofthehorse 112 (12f,Chs,GF,May 7)
Mastery 113 (12f,Lon,GS,Jly 14)
Matsunosuke 110 (5f,San,G,Jly 4)
Mawatheeq 118 (10f,Nmk,G,Oct 17)
Mick s Dancer 112 (10½f,Chs,GF,Jly 11)
Midday 112 (12f,Eps,G,Jun 5)
Mischief Making 110 (16f,Asc,GF,Apr 29)
Mojave Moon 118 (15f,Dea,G,Aug 23)
Monitor Closely 112 (10f,Nmk,GF,Apr 15)
Mood Music 111 (5f,Lon,G,May 10)
Moonquake 111 (10½f,Yor,GF,May 13)
Mountain Coral 110 (6f,Cur,GY,Jun 28)
Mourayan 113 (12f,Cur,GY,Jun 28)
Mourilyan 118 (16f,Goo,G,Jly 30)
Mujood 110 (8f,Goo,G,May 30)
Mullein 111 (6f,Asc,GF,Sep 27)
Mundybash 112 (10f,Lon,GS,Oct 3)
Munsef 111 (12f,Hay,GF,Jly 4)

Naaqoos 110 (8f,Lon,G,May 10)
Nanton 112 (10f,Ayr,G,Sep 19)
Nehaam 113 (10f,Nmk,GF,Apr 15)
Never On Sunday 122 (9f,Lon,S,May 17)
Night Crescendo 111 (12f,Don,GF,Sep 12)
Noble Storm 110 (5f,Bev,GF,Aug 29)
Norwegian Dancer 112 (10½f,Chs,GF,Aug 21)

Oiseau De Feu 113 (8f,Cha,G,Jly 5)
Omokoroa 111 (14f,Hay,S,Sep 5)
Only Green 111 (7f,Lon,G,Jun 22)
Opinion Poll 111 (12f,Asc,GS,Oct 10)
Ordnance Row 112 (7f,Goo,GF,Aug 30)
Orion Star 112 (20f,Lon,G,Oct 4)
Otterstown Lady 113 (16f,Leo,GY,Aug 6)
Ottomax 111 (7f,Lon,G,May 30)
Ouqba 110 (7f,Asc,GF,Jun 17)

Paco Boy 115 (8f,Goo,G,Jly 29)
Palace Moon 111 (6f,Nmk,GF,Aug 29)
Parfum Des Dieux 112 (7f,Lon,G,May 30)
Patkai 116 (16½f,San,G,May 28)
Penny s Gift 111 (8f,Nmk,GF,May 3)
Perfect Polly 112 (6f,Cur,SH,Aug 16)
Perfect Stride 111 (10f,Asc,GF,Jun 19)
Perfect Truth 114 (11½f,Chs,GF,May 6)
Perpetually 111 (10f,Nmk,GF,Apr 16)
Petrovsky 111 (12f,Nmk,GF,May 16)
Phillipina 113 (11½f,Chs,GF,May 6)
Pipedreamer 117 (10f,Nmk,G,Oct 17)
Plum Pudding 110 (7f,War,GF,Apr 13)
Plumania 112 (12f,Lon,G,Sep 13)
Poet 112 (10f,Leo,GY,Sep 5)
Pointilliste 113 (15½f,Lon,G,Sep 13)
Pointing North 111 (7f,Yor,GF,Aug 21)
Pollen 112 (8f,Cur,S,Mar 22)
Popmurphy 110 (16f,Asc,GF,Jun 19)
Pouvoir Absolu 114 (12½f,Dea,G,Aug 30)
Precision Break 114 (12f,Don,GF,Sep 12)
Premio Loco 111 (8f,Goo,G,May 30)
Present Alchemy 111 (5f,Bev,GF,Aug 29)
Press The Button 111 (10f,Nby,GF,Sep 19)
Presvis 114 (9f,Nad,G,Mar 28)
Prime Defender 115 (6f,Don,GF,Mar 28)
Prince Siegfried 117 (10f,Ayr,G,Sep 19)
Princess Taylor 110 (12f,Nmk,G,Jly 18)
Profound Beauty 113 (14f,Cur,Y,Jun 27)
Prospect Wells 110 (10f,Lon,G,Apr 5)
Proviso 116 (9f,Lon,S,May 17)
Pure Poetry 110 (8f,Goo,G,May 30)
Pusey Street Lady 114 (6f,Don,GF,Mar 28)

Quinmaster 110 (8f,Leo,GF,Jun 4)

Racinger 113 (8f,Dea,G,Aug 30)
Ragheed 111 (7½f,Nad,GF,Jan 29)
Rainbow View 114 (8f,Leo,GY,Sep 5)
Raise Your Heart 111 (10f,Leo,Y,Oct 26)
Rayeni 111 (6f,Cur,S,Oct 11)
Red Merlin 112 (12f,Hay,GF,Jly 4)
Red Rock Canyon 113 (10½f,Lon,G,Apr 26)
Regal Parade 115 (6f,Hay,GS,Sep 5)
Rekaab 110 (16f,Leo,GY,Aug 6)
Reverence 112 (5f,Cur,HY,Aug 30)
Riggins 111 (8f,Goo,G,May 30)
Rip Van Winkle 121 (10f,San,G,Jly 4)
Rite Of Passage 116 (16f,Leo,HY,Nov 5)

River Captain 110 (10f,Eps,G,Jun 6)
Roaring Forte 117 (8f,Yor,GF,Aug 20)
Rock And Roll Kid 110 (8f,Cur,S,Mar 22)
Rock Of Rochelle 110 (6f,Asc,GF,Jun 20)
Rockhampton 111 (10f,Nmk,GF,Apr 15)
Roker Park 111 (5f,Bev,GF,Aug 29)
Roman Empress 112 (12f,Yor,GF,Aug 20)
Rose Hip 110 (8f,Leo,G,Aug 13)
Roses For The Lady 113 (12f,Cur,HY,Jly 12)
Royal Confidence 114 (7f,Yor,GF,Aug 21)
Royal Executioner 110 (8f,Hay,G,Jun 20)
Royal Rock 113 (6f,Asc,GS,Oct 10)
Runaway 118 (9f,Lon,S,May 17)
Russian Sage 113 (9f,Nad,GF,Mar 5)

Sahpresa 114 (8f,Nmk,GF,Oct 3)
Salut L Africain 112 (6f,Msn,HO,Nov 3)
Salute Him 110 (10f,Asc,GF,Jun 19)
Sam Sharp 111 (10½f,Chs,GF,Aug 21)
San Sicharia 110 (7f,Lin,GF,May 9)
Sans Frontieres 112 (10½f,Yor,G,May 14)
Saptapadi 110 (12f,Chs,GF,May 7)
Sariska 117 (10f,Nmk,G,Oct 17)
Sayif 115 (6½f,Dea,GS,Aug 9)
Scenic Blast 115 (5f,Asc,GF,Jun 16)
Schiaparelli 120 (15f,Dea,G,Aug 23)
Scuffle 110 (8f,Yor,GF,Aug 20)
Sea The Stars 125 (10f,Leo,GY,Sep 5)
Secret Society 114 (7f,Yor,GF,Aug 21)
Seeking The Buck 110 (10½f,Yor,GF,Jly 11)
Seihali 112 (7½f,Nad,GS,Jan 15)
Serious Attitude 113 (6f,Yor,G,Jly 10)
Serva Jugum 111 (10f,Wdr,GF,Aug 29)
Set Sail 110 (8f,Lon,GS,Apr 12)
Sevenna 110 (14f,Goo,G,Jly 30)
Shahwardi 110 (12f,Lon,GS,Oct 18)
Shalanaya 114 (10f,Lon,G,Oct 4)
Shamwari Lodge 111 (8f,Yor,GF,Aug 19)
She s Our Mark 114 (10f,Leo,YS,Jly 23)
Sherman McCoy 111 (14f,Hay,S,Sep 5)
Shreyas 113 (8f,Leo,GF,Jun 4)
Sight Unseen 110 (12f,Chs,GF,May 7)
Silver Frost 113 (8f,Lon,GS,Apr 12)
Silver Mist 119 (7½f,Nad,GS,Jan 15)
Sirvino 115 (10½f,Yor,GF,Jly 11)
Smooth Operator 113 (7f,Lon,G,Jun 22)
Snaefell 113 (6f,Cur,S,Sep 13)
Snoqualmie Girl 111 (12f,Chs,GF,Sep 12)
Soberania 112 (12f,Lon,G,Sep 13)
Sohraab 111 (5f,Bev,GF,Aug 29)
Spacious 111 (8f,Nmk,G,Jly 8)
Spanish Moon 117 (12f,Sai,S,Jun 28)
Sporting Gesture 110 (12f,Pon,G,Jly 26)
Sri Putra 112 (10f,Dea,G,Aug 16)
Stacelita 115 (12f,Lon,G,Oct 4)
Starla Dancer 111 (10½f,Yor,G,Oct 10)
Starlish 114 (10f,Lon,GS,Oct 3)
Stately Home 110 (16f,Asc,GF,Jun 19)
Staying On 113 (8f,Don,GF,Apr 18)
Steele Tango 112 (9f,Nmk,GF,Apr 16)
Stern Opinion 112 (5f,Lon,G,Sep 13)
Stoic 111 (8f,Nmk,GF,Aug 29)
Stotsfold 114 (10f,Lon,GS,Oct 3)
Strategic News 110 (9f,Nad,GF,Mar 5)
Strawberrydaiquiri 110 (8f,Asc,G,Jly 24)
Strike The Deal 111 (5f,Don,GF,Sep 9)
Striking Spirit 112 (6f,Asc,GF,May 9)
Suailce 110 (14f,Cur,Y,Jun 27)
Sudden Impact 111 (6f,Thi,G,Jly 31)
Suits Me 110 (10f,Lon,GS,Oct 3)
Summit Surge 117 (7½f,Nad,G,Feb 5)
Sundae 110 (6f,Yar,G,Jly 27)
Supaseus 111 (9f,Nmk,GF,Oct 3)
Super Sleuth 112 (8f,Nmk,GF,May 3)
Suruor 110 (7f,Asc,GF,Jly 11)
Sweet Hearth 112 (7f,Lon,GS,Oct 3)
Sweet Lightning 113 (10f,Nby,GF,Sep 19)
Sweetheart 113 (21f,Goo,G,Jly 29)
Swingkeel 110 (21f,Goo,G,Jly 29)
Swiss Diva 110 (6f,Yor,G,Jun 13)

Tactic 112 (16f,Asc,GF,Jun 19)
Tajaaweed 112 (10½f,Lon,G,Apr 26)
Takeover Target 110 (6f,Nmk,GF,Jly 10)
Tamagin 113 (6f,Goo,GF,Sep 12)
Tangaspeed 114 (12f,Lon,G,Oct 4)
Taralga 110 (12f,Leo,GY,Sep 5)
Tartan Bearer 116 (12f,Asc,G,Jly 25)
Tartan Gigha 110 (8½f,Eps,G,Jun 5)
Tastahil 114 (16½f,San,G,May 28)
Tax Free 115 (5f,Cha,G,May 31)
Tazeez 116 (9f,Nmk,GF,Apr 16)
Telluride 113 (11f,Lon,G,May 4)
The Betchworth Kid 112 (16f,Goo,G,Jly 30)
The Bogberry 114 (10½f,Lon,G,Apr 26)
The Miniver Rose 111 (10f,Nmk,GF,Apr 15)
Thewayyouare 115 (10½f,Lon,G,Apr 26)
Third Set 111 (9f,Nad,GS,Jan 15)
Three Bodies 111 (10f,Dea,G,Aug 16)
Three Rocks 113 (7f,Cur,S,Jly 11)
Tis Mighty 110 (7f,Cur,Y,Jun 27)
Tiza 113 (6½f,Dea,GS,Aug 9)
Tombi 110 (7f,Yor,GF,Aug 21)
Total Gallery 115 (5f,Lon,G,Oct 4)
Traffic Guard 110 (10½f,Hay,G,Aug 8)
Trajano 111 (7f,Lon,G,May 30)
Tranquil Tiger 111 (10f,Goo,GF,May 25)
Tres Rapide 110 (12f,Lon,G,Sep 13)
Tres Rock Danon 110 (15½f,Sai,HY,Nov 14)
Trincot 115 (10f,Lon,G,Apr 5)
Triple Aspect 112 (5f,San,G,Jly 4)
Trois Rois 110 (10f,Lon,GS,Sep 6)
Twice Over 119 (10f,Nmk,G,Oct 17)
Tyrrells Wood 111 (21f,Goo,G,Jly 29)

Unnefer 112 (8f,Don,GF,Apr 18)
Utmost Respect 115 (6f,Cur,HY,May 23)

Valedictum 111 (9f,Nad,GF,Mar 5)
Valery Borzov 114 (6f,Yor,S,May 15)
Varenar 115 (6½f,Dea,GS,Aug 9)
Vesuve 111 (10f,Dea,G,Aug 16)
Victoria Montoya 110 (16½f,San,G,Jly 4)
Virtual 114 (8f,Dea,G,Aug 16)
Vision D Etat 117 (10½f,Lon,G,Apr 26)
Vitznau 111 (6f,Don,GF,Mar 28)
Vodka 113 (9f,Nad,GF,Mar 5)

Wajir 115 (15f,Lon,GS,Sep 6)
War Artist 113 (5f,Lon,G,Sep 13)
Webbow 110 (8f,Yor,GF,Aug 20)
Wells Lyrical 110 (16½f,San,G,Jly 4)
Westphalia 112 (8f,Lon,GS,Apr 12)
Wing Express 111 (12½f,Dea,G,Aug 30)
Wing Play 111 (10½f,Chs,GF,Jly 11)
Winkle 111 (15½f,Lon,G,Sep 13)
Woolfall Treasure 110 (21f,Goo,G,Jly 29)
World Heritage 110 (10f,Lon,G,Sep 19)
Worldly Wise 111 (8f,Cur,S,Sep 13)

Yahrab 110 (10f,Nad,GF,Feb 26)
Yamal 110 (8f,Goo,G,May 30)
Yankee Doodle 113 (16f,Asc,GF,Jun 19)
Yeats 115 (20f,Lon,G,Oct 4)
Youmzain 117 (12f,Lon,G,Oct 4)
Your Old Pal 110 (12f,Asc,GF,Jun 19)

Zacinto 111 (8f,Asc,GF,Sep 26)
Zarinava 112 (16f,Cur,Y,Apr 5)
Zorija Rose 110 (7f,Cur,Y,Jun 27)

THREE YEAR-OLDS AND UPWARDS - Sand

Abbondanza 118 (8f,Lin,SD,Mar 1)
Ace Of Hearts 116 (10f,Lin,SD,Feb 7)
Aeroplane 110 (7f,Lin,SD,Mar 21)
Agilete 112 (9½f,Wol,SD,Feb 16)
Ahlawy 110 (9½f,Wol,SD,Jan 19)
Al Gillani 113 (6f,Kem,SD,Mar 25)
Al Muheer 113 (10f,Lin,SD,Feb 7)
All The Aces 111 (12f,Kem,SD,Sep 5)
Almaty Express 112 (5f,Wol,SD,Mar 26)
Ancien Regime 110 (6f,Lin,SD,Aug 20)
Ancient Lights 112 (10f,Lin,SD,May 1)
Arganil 111 (5f,Lin,SD,Mar 21)
Art Man 112 (10f,Lin,SD,Jan 10)
Artistic License 110 (6f,Wol,SD,Feb 27)
Asiatic Boy 115 (10f,Nad,FT,Mar 5)
Autumn Blades 112 (7f,Sth,SD,Mar 11)

Baila Me 116 (13f,Lin,SD,Oct 29)
Bassinet 110 (12f,Lin,SD,Mar 1)
Baylini 116 (10f,Lin,SD,Feb 7)
Bazergan 114 (8f,Lin,SD,Mar 1)
Bell Island 111 (13f,Lin,SD,Feb 21)
Big City Man 117 (6f,Nad,FT,Mar 28)
Billy Red 112 (6f,Grl,SD,Jan 15)
Bonus 110 (8f,Kem,SD,Feb 8)
Born Tobouggie 111 (8f,Kem,SD,Apr 11)
Brave Tin Soldier 110 (8f,Nad,FT,Mar 28)
Brief Look 110 (11f,Sth,SD,Aug 10)
Bronze Cannon 110 (10f,Lin,SD,Mar 21)
Broomielaw 111 (12f,Wol,SD,Nov 20)
Bugaku 110 (11f,Kem,SD,Sep 4)

Calzaghe 111 (13f,Lin,SD,Apr 19)
Cape Express 111 (12f,Wol,SD,Jan 7)
Capricorn Run 112 (7f,Lin,SD,May 1)
Caprio 111 (7f,Sth,SD,Mar 11)
Carte Diamond 113 (16f,Lin,SD,Apr 19)
Ceremonial Jade 111 (6f,Lin,SD,Feb 21)
Charm School 112 (11f,Kem,SD,Sep 4)
Chjimes 117 (5f,Lin,SD,Mar 4)
Cloudy Start 114 (8f,Kem,SD,Jun 25)
Colonel Sherman 110 (10f,Lin,SD,Jan 9)
Contest 111 (6f,Lin,SD,Jan 10)
Copperbeech 110 (10f,Kem,SD,Sep 26)

Daddy s Gift 113 (6f,Kem,SD,Dec 2)
Dance The Star 113 (12f,Wol,SD,Nov 20)
Davids Mark 111 (6f,Kem,SD,Feb 8)
Dayia 111 (14f,Wol,SD,Oct 9)
Desert Party 116 (7f,Nad,FT,Jan 22)
Dijeerr 110 (8f,Nad,FT,Feb 19)
Dirar 116 (12f,Wol,SD,Dec 11)
Dishdasha 112 (12f,Kem,SD,Feb 11)
Distinctive Image 110 (12f,Sth,SD,Aug 10)
Don Renato 111 (8f,Nad,FT,Mar 28)
Doric Lady 110 (6f,Lin,SD,Nov 14)
Doubtful Sound 113 (6f,Lin,SD,Jan 17)
Dubai Dynamo 110 (8f,Kem,SD,Apr 21)
Duff 115 (6f,Lin,SD,Feb 21)
Dvinsky 110 (6f,Kem,SD,Dec 2)

Ebraam 113 (6f,Wol,SD,Feb 27)
Elna Bright 110 (7f,Lin,SD,Nov 21)
Emerald Wilderness 112 (11f,Kem,SD,Feb 18)
Eseej 111 (11f,Sth,SD,Oct 18)
Evident Pride 110 (12f,Lin,SD,Jan 3)

Fairmile 110 (12f,Wol,SD,Nov 20)
Fathsta 112 (6f,Kem,SD,Dec 2)
Flame Of Gibraltar 110 (13f,Lin,SD,Oct 29)
Flipando 117 (8f,Lin,SD,Mar 1)
Flowing Cape 111 (6f,Wol,SD,Feb 17)
Formation 117 (10f,Lin,SD,Feb 7)
Fortuni 113 (12f,Lin,SD,May 1)
Fromsong 113 (5f,Lin,SD,Mar 4)
Fullandby 110 (6f,Kem,SD,Nov 3)

Gandalf 112 (16f,Kem,SD,Sep 4)
Gayego 113 (6f,Nad,FT,Mar 5)
Giganticus 110 (7f,Lin,SD,Mar 21)
Gilt Edge Girl 110 (5f,Wol,SD,Nov 16)
Gitano Hernando 112 (9f,Wol,SD,Sep 17)
Global City 111 (6f,Lin,SD,Nov 14)
Gloria De Campeao 111 (9f,Nad,FT,Feb 26)
Grand Passion 111 (11f,Kem,SD,Feb 18)
Green Manalishi 110 (5f,Lin,SD,Nov 1)
Greylami 110 (11f,Kem,SD,Feb 18)

Happy Boy 113 (10f,Nad,FT,Mar 5)
Harry Up 112 (5f,Wol,SD,Jan 22)
Heliodor 112 (10f,Kem,SD,Sep 26)
Highland Glen 112 (12f,Kem,SD,Sep 21)
Himalya 110 (6f,Lin,SD,Nov 21)
Honour Devil 113 (8f,Nad,FT,Mar 5)

Imprimis Tagula 110 (7f,Sth,SS,Dec 22)
Indian Blessing 115 (6f,Nad,FT,Mar 28)
Internationaldebut 113 (8f,Lin,SD,Feb 14)
Ivory Silk 110 (6f,Kem,SD,Dec 2)

Jaconet 114 (6f,Lin,SD,Nov 21)
Jadalee 111 (16f,Kem,SD,Sep 4)
Jessica Wigmo 111 (6f,Kem,SD,Feb 9)
John Terry 113 (10f,Lin,SD,Jan 10)

Keenes Day 115 (16f,Lin,SD,Apr 19)
Kings Maiden 111 (14f,Wol,SD,May 11)
Kirklees 112 (12f,Kem,SD,Sep 5)

Lady Jane Digby 116 (10f,Lin,SD,Jan 10)
Laterly 113 (12f,Wol,SD,Nov 20)
Laurel Creek 113 (12f,Wol,SD,Feb 14)
Les Fazzani 112 (12f,Kem,SD,Nov 29)
Little Edward 110 (6f,Lin,SD,Jan 17)
Little Pete 111 (6f,Kem,SD,Dec 2)
Luscivious 111 (6f,Sth,SD,Jly 14)

Majuro 113 (8f,Lin,SD,Feb 14)
Matsunosuke 116 (6f,Lin,SD,Feb 21)
Merchant Of Dubai 114 (12f,Wol,SD,Nov 20)
Merlin s Dancer 112 (5f,Lin,SD,Mar 4)
Methaaly 110 (6f,Wol,SD,Feb 17)
Mia s Boy 110 (9f,Wol,SD,Sep 17)
Middle Of Nowhere 111 (12f,Sth,SD,Feb 10)
Mister New York 114 (12f,Wol,SD,Dec 11)
Monetary Fund 110 (11f,Sth,SD,Aug 10)
Mooakada 111 (12f,Kem,SD,Nov 29)
Morbick 110 (12f,Wol,SD,Feb 14)
Muktasb 110 (6f,Kem,SD,Feb 8)
Murcar 110 (14f,Wol,SD,Sep 11)
Mutamared 111 (6f,Wol,SD,Feb 27)
Mutheeb 111 (6f,Lin,SD,May 27)
My Indy 113 (8f,Nad,SD,Jan 15)

Nemo Spirit 112 (16f,Lin,SD,Apr 19)
Nightjar 111 (7f,Sth,SD,Jan 20)
Nota Bene 111 (6f,Lin,SD,May 27)

Obe Royal 111 (7f,Sth,SD,Feb 12)
Old Romney 110 (10f,Lin,SD,Jan 28)
Opus Maximus 113 (8f,Lin,SD,Mar 1)
Orchard Supreme 111 (8f,Lin,SD,Feb 14)
Orpsie Boy 112 (6f,Lin,SD,Feb 21)
Ottoman Empire 112 (11f,Sth,SD,Aug 10)

Pachattack 110 (12f,Kem,SD,Nov 29)
Paktolos 110 (12f,Wol,SD,Nov 20)
Pelham Crescent 110 (9½f,Wol,SD,Feb 16)
Philario 111 (8f,Kem,SD,Feb 8)
Philatelist 115 (10f,Lin,SD,Feb 7)
Premio Loco 113 (8f,Kem,SD,Feb 8)
Prince Charlemagne 110 (13f,Lin,SD,Apr 19)
Princess Taylor 111 (13f,Lin,SD,Oct 29)

Qadar 114 (5f,Lin,SD,Mar 4)

Ray Of Joy 111 (6f,Kem,SD,Apr 1)
Re Barolo 111 (8f,Kem,SD,Nov 29)
Red Somerset 113 (8f,Lin,SD,Mar 1)
Redding Colliery 111 (7f,Nad,FT,Jan 22)
Regal Ransom 115 (7f,Nad,FT,Jan 22)
Riguez Dancer 111 (14f,Wol,SD,Jan 19)
River Kirov 112 (6f,Kem,SD,Jan 3)
Rosika 113 (13f,Lin,SD,Oct 29)
Royal Envoy 112 (6f,Kem,SD,Feb 8)

Safari Sunup 113 (10f,Lin,SD,May 1)
Saloon 110 (14f,Wol,SD,May 11)
Saphira s Fire 111 (12f,Kem,SD,Nov 29)
Scintillo 112 (10f,Lin,SD,Mar 21)
Seek The Fair Land 112 (7f,Kem,SD,Dec 13)
Sehoy 110 (12f,Lin,SD,May 1)
Set The Trend 110 (8f,Kem,SD,Jun 25)
Settigano 110 (10f,Lin,SD,Dec 19)
Sevenna 112 (16f,Lin,SD,Apr 19)
Sgt Schultz 114 (10f,Lin,SD,Jan 10)
Shakalaka 110 (10f,Lin,SD,Dec 30)
Smarten Die 110 (6f,Lin,SD,Feb 21)
Snaafy 116 (8f,Nad,FT,Mar 5)
Son Of The Cat 110 (6f,Lin,SD,Nov 14)
Southandwest 112 (8f,Lin,SD,Mar 1)
Spectait 111 (9½f,Wol,SD,Jan 7)
Stand Guard 110 (9f,Wol,SD,Nov 13)
Star Choice 111 (12f,Wol,SD,Feb 14)
Star Crowned 112 (6f,Nad,FT,Jan 22)
Storyland 111 (13f,Lin,SD,Oct 29)
Strike The Deal 114 (6f,Lin,SD,May 27)
Suits Me 112 (10f,Lin,SD,Dec 19)
Summer Doldrums 110 (8f,Nad,FT,Mar 28)
Swiss Franc 112 (6f,Lin,SD,Feb 21)

Tamagin 113 (6f,Lin,SD,May 27)
Thebes 111 (7f,Lin,SD,Mar 21)
They All Laughed 110 (14f,Wol,SD,Jan 19)
Thunderous Mood 111 (6f,Kem,SD,Dec 2)
Tilt 112 (12f,Wol,SD,Nov 20)
Tinaar 111 (12f,Kem,SD,Sep 21)
Titan Triumph 115 (8f,Lin,SD,Feb 14)
Tiz Now Tiz Then 110 (8f,Nad,FT,Mar 28)
Trafalgar Square 110 (7f,Lin,SD,Jan 16)
Tranquil Tiger 113 (10f,Lin,SD,Dec 19)
Trip The Light 113 (12f,Wol,SD,Nov 20)
Two Step Salsa 115 (8f,Nad,FT,Mar 28)
Tyrannosaurus Rex 111 (5f,Wol,SD,Feb 6)
Tyrrells Wood 110 (13f,Lin,SD,Feb 21)
Tyzack 110 (7f,Sth,SD,Feb 12)

Wasan 111 (10f,Kem,SD,Sep 26)
Wasp 113 (8f,Lin,SD,Mar 1)
Well Armed 121 (10f,Nad,FT,Mar 28)
Wibbadune 110 (5f,Lin,SD,Mar 4)
William Blake 111 (11f,Kem,SD,Sep 4)
Wine n Dine 113 (16f,Lin,SD,Apr 19)
Without A Prayer 114 (8f,Kem,SD,Nov 29)
Woodcote 111 (5f,Lin,SD,Feb 10)
Worth A King S 110 (14f,Wol,SD,Oct 9)

Xpres Maite 112 (6f,Sth,SS,Jan 6)

TWO YEAR-OLDS - Turf

Above Limits 109 (5f,Don,GF,Sep 9)
Absolute Music 106 (7f,Msn,HO,Nov 3)
Admire The View 105 (7f,Thi,G,Jly 24)
Alfred Nobel 105 (7f,Leo,G,May 28)
Ameer 106 (8f,Nby,GF,Sep 18)
American Nizzy 106 (8f,Lon,G,Oct 4)
Arasin 105 (8f,Lon,G,Sep 19)
Arcano 112 (6f,Nmk,G,Jly 9)
Atasari 109 (7f,Nmk,G,Oct 17)
Awzaan 109 (6f,Nmk,GF,Oct 2)
Azizi 105 (8f,Don,GF,Sep 12)
Azmeel 105 (7f,Nby,GF,Aug 15)

Baahama 105 (8f,Lon,G,Oct 4)
Beethoven 112 (7f,Nmk,G,Oct 17)
Behkabad 106 (8f,Lon,G,Sep 19)
Blue Maiden 105 (7f,Nmk,G,Aug 8)
Bossy Kitty 106 (6f,Yor,G,Oct 9)
Bould Mover 108 (5f,Don,GF,Sep 11)
Buzzword 109 (7f,Lon,G,Oct 4)

Cabaret 108 (7f,Leo,Y,Jly 16)
Canford Cliffs 113 (6f,Asc,GF,Jun 16)
Carnaby Street 105 (7f,Nby,S,Oct 24)

Dick Turpin 107 (7f,Lon,G,Oct 4)
Dolled Up 107 (6f,Dea,G,Aug 23)

Elusive Pimpernel 111 (7f,Yor,GF,Aug 18)
Emerald Commander 110(7f,Yor,GF,Aug 18)
Ercolini 106 (7f,Msn,HO,Nov 3)
Exotic Beauty 105 (6f,Rip,GF,Aug 15)

Fencing Master 111 (7f,Nmk,G,Oct 17)
Free Judgement 106 (7f,Leo,Y,Oct 26)

Green Dandy 108 (8f,Lon,G,Oct 4)

Hibaayeb 108 (8f,Asc,G,Sep 26)
Hot Prospect 107 (8f,San,GF,Sep 11)

Iver Bridge Lad 109 (5f,Asc,GS,Oct 10)

Jealous Again 107 (5f,Asc,GF,Jun 17)
Jeannie Galloway 106 (6f,Yor,G,Oct 9)
Joanna 109 (8f,Lon,G,Oct 4)
Joshua Tree 109 (8f,Asc,G,Sep 26)

Lady Darshaan 107 (8f,Asc,G,Sep 26)
Lady Of The Desert 108 (6f,Yor,GF,Aug 20)
Lady Springbank 105 (7f,Cur,G,Sep 27)
Layali Al Andalus 105 (8f,Ncs,GF,Aug 31)
Layla s Hero 110 (6f,Hay,GS,Sep 5)
Lillie Langtry 105 (7f,Nmk,GF,Oct 3)
Lixirova 109 (7f,Msn,HO,Nov 3)
Long Lashes 107 (7f,Nmk,G,Aug 8)
Lope De Vega 108 (7f,Lon,G,Oct 4)
Lucky Like 109 (6f,Red,GF,Oct 3)

Marie De Medici 107 (7f,Lei,GF,Oct 6)
Mikhail Glinka 107 (10f,Sai,HY,Nov 14)
Misheer 105 (6f,Nmk,G,Jly 8)
Mister Manannan 108 (5f,Don,GF,Sep 11)
Monsieur Chevalier 110 (5f,Lon,G,Oct 4)
Morana 105 (8f,San,GF,Sep 11)
Multames 105 (8f,Nby,S,Oct 24)
Music Show 110 (7f,Nmk,G,Oct 17)

Nebula Storm 106 (7f,Leo,HY,Nov 5)

Olvia 106 (8f,Lon,G,Oct 4)
On Verra 110 (8f,Lon,G,Oct 4)
Orpen Grey 111 (6f,Nmk,G,Jly 9)
Our Jonathan 110 (5f,Asc,GS,Oct 10)

Party Doctor 108 (7f,Yor,GF,Aug 18)
Passion For Gold 112 (10f,Sai,HY,Nov 14)
Pleasant Day 106 (7f,Asc,GF,Sep 27)
Poet s Voice 110 (7f,Yor,GF,Aug 18)
Pounced 110 (7f,Lon,G,Oct 4)
Private Story 105 (8f,Nby,GF,Sep 18)

Radiohead 114 (5f,Yor,GF,Aug 21)
Red Jazz 107 (6f,Nmk,G,Jly 9)
Rezwaan 105 (8f,Nmk,G,Aug 28)
Rosanara 112 (8f,Lon,G,Oct 4)
Rose Blossom 106 (5f,Don,GF,Sep 11)

Sand Vixen 110 (5f,Don,GF,Sep 11)
Sent From Heaven 105 (8f,Asc,G,Sep 26)
Shamandar 105 (5f,Nby,GS,Jly 18)
Showcasing 107 (6f,Nmk,GF,Oct 2)
Silver Grecian 105 (7f,Nmk,G,Oct 17)
Sir Parky 105 (7f,Nmk,GF,Oct 1)
Siyouni 112 (7f,Lon,G,Oct 4)
Special Duty 108 (6f,Nmk,GF,Oct 2)
Steinbeck 111 (7f,Nmk,G,Oct 17)
Summerinthecity 105 (6f,Don,GS,Jly 16)

Taajub 109 (5f,Asc,GS,Oct 10)
Tabassum 108 (7f,Nmk,G,Oct 17)
Tawaabb 105 (5f,Asc,GS,Oct 10)

Vale Of York 107 (8f,Asc,G,Sep 26)

Waseet 107 (8f,Asc,G,Sep 26)
Wedding March 109 (8f,Lon,G,Oct 4)
Whippers Love 106 (8f,Nmk,G,Aug 28)
Wonderfilly 105 (7f,Msn,HO,Nov 3)

Xtension 111 (7f,Nmk,G,Oct 17)

TWO YEAR-OLDS - Sand

Avonvalley 105 (5f,Wol,SD,May 11)

Diamond Laura 106 (5f,Wol,SD,May 11)

Elspeth s Boy 107 (7f,Wol,SD,Nov 2)

Memorandum 108 (5f,Lin,SD,Nov 13)
Mirabella 105 (7f,Lin,SD,Nov 13)
Music Maestro 105 (7f,Wol,SD,Nov 2)

Nafura 106 (9f,Wol,SD,Nov 12)

Sakile 107 (5f,Lin,SD,Nov 13)

Wanchai Whisper 106 (5f,Kem,SD,Dec 30)

Youcanalwaysdream 107 (5f,Lin,SD,Nov 13)